WHO KNOWS —AND WHAT

The
A.N. Marquis Company
Founded 1897

★

STANDARD
AMERICAN SELECTIVE
BIOGRAPHICAL
REFERENCE

★

WHO KNOWS — AND WHAT
among Authorities-Experts-and the Specially Informed

STANDARD AMERICAN SELECTIVE BIOGRAPHICAL REFERENCE

THE A. N. MARQUIS COMPANY

FOUNDED 1897

●

The yellow-paper section of this book was set
directly on film with the Intertype Fotosetter
and lithographed by the Advance Lithograph-
ing Co., Chicago

The main body of this book was type set, printed and bound
by the Von Hoffmann Press, St. Louis

WHO KNOWS – AND WHAT
among Authorities-Experts-and the Specially Informed

With a Roster of Selected General Authorities and
a Locator Index "keying" 12,000 selected knowers
to 35,000 subjects chosen for entry in it

THE REVISED EDITION

Compiled under the supervision of the Editors
of "Who's Who in America"

MARQUIS-WHO'S WHO
INCORPORATED — A NON-PROFIT FOUNDATION

Publishers of "Who's Who in America"   Marquis Publications Building

CHICAGO-11 USA

> *Knowledge is of two kinds: we know a subject ourselves, or we know where we can find information upon it.*
>
> Boswell's Life of Dr. Johnson

HOW THIS BOOK CAME TO BE—ITS PURPOSE—HOW TO USE IT.

This book is an idea.

This idea is that an everyday need exists for a new reference tool making possible reference from subject to <u>knower</u> (instead of the traditional from subject to <u>writings</u>).

It is this, The Idea, you have here as a book, on paper and between two covers—a unique, daily-useful, reference tool that both provides pertinent career data of over 12,000 selected knowers, listed alphabetically, and "keys" these knowers to 35,000 selected subjects with which they have reported conversance.

Although The Idea has come through extensive in-use testing handsomely—for typical comment, and a definite statement of exactly what is, and what is not, to be expected of this revision, see the leaflet placed under the front cover of this copy at the bindery—trial and test through several successive editions will be required for the rounded realization of it. Accordingly, if The Idea interests you, your opinions for developing it, your nominations to listing, and your suggested delenda, will be heartily welcomed.

No more than passing consideration of The Idea is required to make evident what several years of work on actualizing it have clearly demonstrated—that its inherent catholicity creates the principal problem encountered in reducing it to practical reference usefulness. Each lawyer, each medical man, each engineer, knows more about his profession than those among the laity in respect to that calling. Each writer of a Ph.D. thesis—there are tens of thousands—presumably knows more than the majority about his theme subject. Each successful business man is versed in his trade.

Mere lists of groups of knowers are, in short, simply directories—whether frankly so designated, or cloaked, perhaps to capitalize on vanity, beneath ostentatious titles.

The selection of knowers under The Idea is, then, the essential task.

The task obviously hinges principally on the following:

The knowers' subjects should not be exceedingly minute. An everyday reference tool will not be turned to— at least logically—for knowers in connection with, for example, the shrikes of New Jersey or instances of social aggregation among tadpoles.

On the other hand, those widely accepted as ranking general authorities in respect to certain fields may be assumed to be generally known, and therefore—and on occasion—be properly merely designated, for these widely-recognized figures are comprehensively treated in many readily available reference works. On the other hand, it would be logical to note their special interests not likely known to many, yet considered to be in the line of everyday enquiry.

As our objective is to materialize The Idea around such a framework, we decided, after testing under our original plans, not to extend the book to medical practice, as such, among the laity—an earnest effort to observe this delimitation followed.

Many directories, selective listings and professionally qualified sources, provide professional data and other information in connection with practising members of the medical professions. A fundamental of our conception of The Idea is avoidance of duplication of available reference tools.

For reasons in the main corresponding, the general practice of law as such was placed beyond the scope finally fixed for the book. Broadly similar classifications have also been excluded including certain literary, journalistic, industrial and commercial vocations as such.

The above cited content limitations reflecting experience gained during compilation, and those initially established before compilation began, shaped a screening procedure which practically automatically excluded thousands of the 105,000 on the overall roll of prospective listees. These rejections were largely and solely caused by the scope arbitrarily fixed for the book. Therefore each and every knower who cooperated by supplying data, rates, and is here tendered, our thanks for assisting the idea toward realization—totally irrespective of whether or not his or her name happened to place within the book's scope as finally arbitrarily delimited. In many borderline situations, requests for additional information were written.

The searching out of prospective listees was, as a matter of fact, purposely definitely overexpanded, rather than otherwise, by intentionally assaying in a number of general directions—the memberships of several organizations of high repute; those noted as speaking or writing on specialized subjects; and similar groupings—despite the obvious prospect that very few selections actually within the book's scope would thereby be uncovered. The considerable additional expense, and the increased screening load involved, were felt to be justified by the possibility that some information would be reached that might otherwise be overlooked, and a wider overall understanding of the broad compilative problem obtained.

"Who's Who in America" was similarly intentionally canvassed in an exploratory, rather than a definitive, way. Although the results—again as anticipated—increased the screening load and created several particularly complex listing and indexing difficulties, exceedingly useful information was obtained that otherwise undoubtedly might have been passed over.

When appropriate additional data had come to hand, substitutes for the "Who's Who in America" sketches were written in the exact format established for this book, or in a variation of it in exceptional instances. Although in each instance the specific practice followed was carefully selected as most effectively fitting the listing into the book's scope, we recognize the decisions to have been arbitrary, and that for other reasons they are subject to reconsideration.

We anticipated the scope arbitrarily fixed for the compilation would be far from self-apparent, but we did not foresee the large number of listings—sought and suggested, and naturally in the main clearly outside that scope—we were actually to receive. For use in processing them, to facilitate answering the continuous flow of general enquiry stimulated by word getting around that the revision was in compilation, and to provide definitive information for our office associates, a four-page question-and-answer memorandum was prepared. Enquiries caused it to be sent throughout this continent, and to many overseas addresses— as being of possible interest, the first page of it is reproduced (page 10).

Since these and other techniques for most effectively realizing The Idea necessarily developed from trial and test during revision, it was not possible to apply them with the thoroughness that should be feasible eventually. Scrutiny will encounter resulting instances of both inclusion and omission.

Singularly, those singled out above, and other irregularities perhaps to be more or less expected, do not react upon the book's serviceability to consultants. The unique Locator Index is responsible for this exceptional advantage, which was availed of whenever necessary. The unusual flexibility of this distinctive index format, and the fact that the "locators" of course could not be assembled until the listee content was complete and actually in numbered pages, combined to afford ample opportunity to forestall content irregularities from affecting the unique usefulness of the book.

Although important, this specific contribution of the Locator Index to compilation under The Idea, is but incidental. For this novel indexing procedure provides an essential which is vital to making The Idea practical. By it literally tens of thousands of subjects may be so "keyed" to thousands of knowers that linking a selected conversancy to specific knowers is both rapid and convenient.

Familiarity with the Locator Index therefore means understanding how to use this book most advantageously. Accordingly, page 870 has been given over to a somewhat detailed discussion of it.

Where and how The Idea originated, and the like, probably should be made of record here. The Idea was suggested by an item in "The Saturday Review of Literature" which proposed as needed several then non-existent reference works, including "a book of authorities."

The title under which this Revised Edition issues is naturally a final selection from among several experimented with more or less thoroughly. It was suggested by M. Lincoln Schuster.

Obviously used in a "'coined" sense, one factor influencing its selection was our desire, if possible, to signal by the title what we consider falls under The Idea, and what we consider does not. Some discussion of this conception will be found in the intra-office memorandum (page 10) issued to our associates during compilation, and mentioned above.

We consider as within our conception of The Idea those everyday subjects we arbitrarily assume may naturally be subject to normal enquiry; men and women our file information indicates to us are conversant with these subjects, either as authorities and/or experts, or as the result of being specially informed about them; and sources which may provide, or show a way to, information about such subjects (see page 851).

We do not consider The Idea extends to grading knowers; to signifying more than suggestively who may or may not be ranked as general authorities; to indicating either comparative ability or individual ability (in respect to consultations under compensation, or otherwise); or to cataloging all who know about all subjects.

The original planning included listing men and women resident in, and natives of, countries other than the United States and its territories. Experience has indicated that this undertaking should be deferred, despite the interest it immediately attracted. Listings in hand and affected by this decision have been added to the material already rapidly accumulating for future consideration.

"Articles in field" has been used to signal discussion participations and papers, or similar writings related to subjects "keyed" to listees' entries in the locator index. The listee's own wording and description has in so far as practicable been rather closely followed for listing summaries and index entries, instead of arbitrarily enforcing uniform phraseology or style. Addresses have been omitted, and the symbol indicating availability for consultation appended, at the listees' requests. The symbols shown on page viii have been used to indicate the meanings there detailed.

In the nineteenth century its Editor wrote this paragraph into the preface of a book just completed:
"Whatever may be thought of it in other respects,
'   ' can with confidence claim for itself the distinction of being something new in American book-making . . . The need of such a volume has long been apparent."

He is gone. The book continues, grows, improves.

"Who's Who in America" filled the blank in that paragraph. We now ask you to reread, putting "Who Knows—And What" there—for its every word most exactly fits our book—which, too, will continue, grow, improve—beyond our days.

The Publishers.

CONTENTS

TABLE OF ABBREVIATIONS AND SYMBOLS

The Symbols

©Following an entry signifies inclusion of the listee in the Roster of Selected General Authorities (page 831).

†Following his career data signifies the listee has indicated availability for consultation.

The Abbreviations

AAA—Agricultural Adjustment Administration; Anti-Aircraft Artillery
AAAS—American Association for the Advancement of Science
AAC—Army Air Corps
A and M—Agricultural and Mechanical
AAF—Army Air Forces
AAUP—American Association of University Professors
AB (also BA)—Bachelor of Arts
ABC—American Broadcasting Company
AC—Air Corps
acad—academy; academic
adj—adjutant
adj gen—adjutant general
adm—admiral
adminstr—administrator
adminstrn—administration
adv—advocate; advisory
advt—advertising
AE—Agricultural Engineer
AEF—American Expeditionary Forces
AFD—Doctor of Fine Arts
AF of L—American Federation of Labor
agr—agriculture
agrl—agricultural
agron—agronomy; agronomist
agt—agent
AHA—American Historical Association
AIA—American Institute of Architects
Ala—Alabama
ALA—American Library Association
Am—American; America
AM (also MA)—Master of Arts
AMA—American Medical Association
Am Inst EE—American Institute of Electrical Engineers
Am Soc CE—American Society of Civil Engineers
Am Soc ME—American Society of Mechanical Engineers
ANA—Associate National Academician
anthrop—anthropology; anthropological
apptd—appointed
ARC—American Red Cross
archeol—archeological
archtl—architectural
Ariz—Arizona
Ark—Arkansas
Arts D—Doctor of Arts
arty—artillery
AS—Air Service
ASCAP—American Society of Composers, Authors and Publishers
assn—association
asso—associate; associated
asst—assistant
astron—astronomical
astrophys—astrophysical
atty—attorney
AUS—Army of the United States
av—avenue

b—born
B—Bachelor
BA (also AB)—Bachelor of Arts
bact—bacteriology; bacteriologist
B Agr—Bachelor of Agriculture
B Arch—Bachelor of Architecture
BAS—Bachelor of Agricultural Science
BBA—Bachelor of Business Administration
batn, or bn—battalion

BC—British Columbia
BCE—Bachelor of Civil Engineering
BCS—Bachelor of Commercial Science
bd—board
BD—Bachelor of Divinity
B Di—Bachelor of Didactics
BE—Bachelor of Education
BFA—Bachelor of Fine Arts
bibl—biblical
bibliog—bibliographical
biog—biographical
biol—biological
BJ—Bachelor of Journalism
BL (or Litt B)—Bachelor of Letters
bldg—building
BLS—Bachelor of Library Science
blvd—boulevard
BO—Bachelor of Oratory
bot—botanical
BP—Bachelor of Painting
BPE—Bachelor of Physical Education
BPd (or Pd B)—Bachelor of Pedagogy
br—branch
brig—brigadier
brig gen—brigadier general
Brit—British; Britannica
BS (also SB or Sc B)—Bachelor of Science
BS in Ry ME—Bachelor in Railway Mechanical Engineering
BSA—Bachelor of Agricultural Science
BSD—Bachelor of Didactic Science
BTh—Bachelor of Theology
bull—bulletin
bur—bureau
bus—business
BWI—British West Indies

CA—Central America
CAC—Coast Artillery Corps
Calif—California
Can—Canada
capt—captain
Cath—Catholic
cav—cavalry
CBS—Columbia Broadcasting System
CE—Civil Engineer
Ch D—Doctor of Chemistry
chem—chemical
Chem E—Chemical Engineer
chmn—chairman
CIO—Congress of Industrial Organizations
climatol—climatological
clin—clinical
clk—clerk
co—company; county
C of C—Chamber of Commerce
col—colonel
coll—college
Colo—Colorado
com—committee
comd—commanded
comdg—commanding
comdr—commander
comdt—commandant
commd—commissioned
comml—commercial
commn—commission
commr—commissioner
condr—conductor

conf—conference
Confed—Confederate
Congl—Congregational; Congressional
Conn—Connecticut
cons—consulting; consultant
consol—consolidated
constl—constitutional
constn—constitution
constrn—construction
contbd—contributed
contbg—contributing
contbns—contributions
contbr—contributor
conv—convention
coop (or co-op)—cooperative
corp—corporation
corr—correspondent; corresponding; correspondence
cos—companies; counties
CPA—Certified Public Accountant
CPH—Certificate of Public Health
CSB—Bachelor of Christian Science
CSD—Doctor of Christian Science
ct—court
CT—Candidate in Theology
CWS—Chemical War Service
cyclo—cyclopedia

D Agr—Doctor of Agriculture
DC—District of Columbia
DCL—Doctor of Civil Law
DCS—Doctor of Commercial Science
DD—Doctor of Divinity
DDS—Doctor of Dental Surgery
deg—degree
Del—Delaware; delegate
Dem—Democratic
D Eng (also Dr Engring, or ED)—Doctor of Engineering
dep—deputy
dept—department
dermatol—dermatological
DHL—Doctor of Hebrew Literature
dir—director
dist—district
div—division; divinity
D Litt (also LHD)—Doctor of Literature
DPH (also Dr PH)—Diploma in Public Health or Doctor of Public Health or Doctor of Public Hygiene
Dr—Doctor
DRE—Doctor of Religious Education
DSc (also Sc D)—Doctor of Science
DSC—Dinstinguished Service Cross
DSM—Distinguished Service Medal
DST—Doctor of Sacred Theology
DTM—Doctor of Tropical Medicine

E—East
eccles—ecclesiastical
ecol—ecological
econ—economic
ed—editor; educated
ED (also D Eng or Dr Engring)—Doctor of Engineering
Ed B—Bachelor of Education
Ed D—Doctor of Education
edit—edition
Ed M—Master of Education
edn—education

ednl—educational
EE—Electrical Engineer
Egyptol—Egyptological
elec—electrical
electrochem—electrochemical
electrophys—electrophysical
EM—Engineer of Mines
ency—encyclopedia
Eng—England
engr—engineer
engring—engineering
engrs—engineers
entomol—entomological
ethnol—ethnological
exam—examination; examining
exec—executive
exhbn—exhibition
expdn—expedition
expt—experiment
exptl—experimental
ext—extension

F—Fellow
FA—Field Artillery
FAO—Food and Agriculture Organization (United Nations)
FBI—Federal Bureau of Investigation
FCC—Federal Communications Commission
FE—Forest Enginneer
fed—federal
Fedn—Federation
Fgn—Foreign
Fla—Florida
FM—Frequency Modulation
Found—Foundation
FSA—Federal Security Administration
Ft—Fort

Ga—Georgia
GD—Graduate in Divinity
gen—general
geod—geodetic
geog—geographical; geographic
geol—geological
geophys—geophysical
GHQ—General Headquarters
govt—government
grad—graduate; graduated
Gt—Great

Hdqrs—Headquarters
HI—Hawaiian Islands
HM—Master of Humanies
H Ty (or HT)—Hawaiian Territory
hist—historical
hon—honorary; honorable; honorably
Ho of Reps—House of Representatives
hort—horticultural
hosp—hospital
hydrog—hydrographic

Ia—Iowa
Ida—Idaho
Ill—Illinois
illus—illustrated
inc—incorporated
Ind—Indiana; Independent

See pages 11, 801 and 831 for knowers; page 851 for information sources; and page 871 for the Locator Index of selected subjects to which they are "keyed."

indsl—industrial
inf—infantry
ins—insurance
insp—inspector
insp gen—inspector general
inst—institute
instn—institution
instr—instructor
internat—international
intro—introduction

JD—Doctor of Jurisprudence
journ—journal
jr—junior
jud—judicial

Kan—Kansas
Ky—Kentucky

La—Louisiana
lab—laboratory
lang—language
laryngol—laryngological
LHD—Doctor of Letters of Humanity
LI—Long Island
lieut (or lt)—lieutenant
limnol—limnology; limnologist
lit—literary; literature
Litt B (or BL)—Bachelor of Letters
Litt D—Doctor of Letters
LL B—Bachelor of Laws
LL D—Doctor of Laws
LL M (or ML)—Master of Laws
lt col—lieutenant colonel
lt gen—lieutenant general
ltd—limited

MA (or AM)—Master of Arts
M Agr—Master of Agriculture
maj—major
maj gen—major general
M Arch—Master in Architecture
Mass—Massachusetts
math—mathematical
MBA—Master of Business Administration
MBS—Mutual Broadcasting System
MCS—Master of Commercial Science
Md—Maryland
MD—Doctor of Medicine
MDi—Master of Didactics
Me—Maine
ME—Mechanical Engineer
mech—mechanical
med—medical
MEE—Master of Electrical Engineering
mem—member
metall—metallurgical
Met E—Metallurgical Engineer
meteorol—meteorological
metrol—metrological
MF—Master of Forestry
MFA—Master of Fine Arts
mfg—manufacturing
mfr—manufacture; manufacturer
mfrs—manufacturers
mgr—manager
MI—Military Intelligence
Mich—Michigan
micros—microscopical
mil—military
mineral—mineralogical
Minn—Minnesota
Miss—Mississippi

MIT—Massachusetts Institute of Technology
ML (or LLM)—Master of Laws
MLitt—Master of Literature
MME—Master of Mechanical Engineering
mng—managing
Mo—Missouri
Mont—Montana
MPd—Master of Pedagogy
MPE—Master of Physical Education
MRE—Master of Religious Education
MS (or MSc)—Master of Science
MSF—Master of Science of Forestry
MST—Master of Sacred Theology
Mt—Mount
mus—museum; musical
Mus B—Bachelor of Music
Mus D (or Mus Doc)—Doctor of Music
Mus M—Master of Music
mycol—mycological

N—North
NA—National Academician; North America; National Army
NAACP—National Association for the Advancement of Colored People
NAM—National Association of Manufacturers
nat—national
nav—navigation
NB—New Brunswick
NBC—National Broadcasting Company
NC—North Carolina
ND—North Dakota
NE—Northeast; New England
NEA—National Education Association
Neb—Nebraska
Nev—Nevada
NH—New Hampshire
NJ—New Jersey
NM—New Mexico
NRA—National Recovery Administration
NS—Nova Scotia
NT—New Testament
numis—numismatic
NW—Northwest
NY—New York
NYC—New York city

O—Ohio
obs—observatory
oceanog—oceanography; oceanographer
ofcl—official
Okla—Oklahoma
Ont—Ontario
OPA—Office of Price Administration
ophthal—ophthalmological
OPM—Office of Production Management
OQMG—Office of Quartermaster General
ORC—Officers' Reserve Corps
Ore—Oregon
orgn—organization
ornithol—ornithological
OSRD—Office of Scientific Research and Development
OSS—Office of Strategic Services
OT—Old Testament
OUAM—Order United American Mechanics
OWI—Office of War Information

Pa—Pennsylvania
parasitol—parasitology; parasitologist
path—pathological
Pd B (or B Pd)—Bachelor of Pedagogy

Pd D—Dotcor of Pedagogy
Pd M—Master of Pedagogy
PEN—Poets, Playwrights, Editors, Essayists and Novelists
penol—penological
pharm—pharmaceutical
Pharm D—Doctor of Pharmacy
Pharm M—Master of Pharmacy
Ph B—Bachelor of Philosophy
Ph C—Pharmaceutical Chemist
Ph D—Doctor of Philosophy
Ph G—Graduate in Pharmacy
Phila—Philadelphia
philol—philological
philos—philosophical
photog—photographic
phys—physical
physiol—physiological
PI—Philippine Islands
Pl—Place
polit—political
poly—polytechnic
pomol—pomological
PQ—Province of Quebec
PR—Puerto Rico
prep—preparatory
pres—president
prin—principal
proc—proceedings
prodn—production
prof—professor
prog—progressive
pro tem—pro tempore (for the time being)
psychiat—psychiatrical; psychiatric
psychol—psychological
pub—public; publisher; publishing; published
pvt—private
Py B—Bachelor of Pedagogy

qm—quartermaster
QMC—Quartermaster Corps
qm gen—quartermaster general
Que—Quebec

RC—Reserve Corps
rd—road
Rep—Republican; representative
Res—Reserve
ret—retired
rev—review; revised
RFC—Reconstruction Finance Corp
rhinol—rhinological
RI—Rhode Island
röntgenol—röntgenological
ROSC—Reserve Officers' Sanitary Corps
ROTC—Reserve Officers' Training Corps
rr—railroad
ry—railway

S—South
SA—South America
san—sanitary
SB (also BS or Sc B)—Bachelor of Science
SC—South Carolina
SCAP—Supreme Commander for Allied Powers
ScD (or D Sc)—Doctor of Science
SCD—Doctor of Commercial Science
sch—school
sci—science; scientific
SD—South Dakota
SE—Southeast

SEC—Securities and Exchange Commission
sec—secretary
sect—section
seismol—seismological
sem—seminary
SJD—Doctor Juristic Science
SLA—Special Libraries Association
SM—Master of Science
So—Southern
soc—society
sociol—sociological
spl—special
splty—specialty
sq—square
sr—senior
St—Saint; street
sta—station
statis—statistical
STB—Bachelor of Sacred Theology
STD—Doctor of Sacred Theology
STL—Licentiate in Sacred Theology; Lector of Sacred Theology
supt—superintendent
SW—Southwest

tech—technical; technology
technol—technological
temp—temporary
Tenn—Tennessee
Ter (or Ty)—Territory
Tex—Texas
TH (or HT)—Territory of Hawaii
Th D—Doctor of Theology
Th M—Master of Theology
theol—theological
topog—topographical
trans—transactions; transferred
transl—translation; translations
treas—treasurer
TVA—Tennessee Valley Authority
typog—typographical

U—University
UAW—United Automobile Workers
UN—United Nations
UNESCO—United Nations Educational, Social and Cultural Organization
UNRRA—United Nations Relief and Rehabilitation Administration
US—United States
USN—United States Navy
USO—United Service Organizations
USPHS—United States Public Health Service
USSR—Union of Soviet Socialist Republics

v—vice
Va—Virginia
vp—vice president
vis—visiting
vol—volume
Vt—Vermont

W—West
Wash—Washington (state)
WI—West Indies
Wis—Wisconsin
WPB—War Production Board
W Va—West Virginia
Wyo—Wyoming

zoöl—zoölogical

See pages 11, 801 and 831 for knowers; page 851 for information sources; and page 871 for the Locator Index of selected subjects to which they are "keyed."

Subject: WHO KNOWS — AND WHAT
(Questions and Answers Indicative of Scope)

Question: Is the title Who Knows — And What to be taken literally?

Answer: No. It is of course used in a "coined" sense to suggest a purpose — an endeavor to supply a new reference source to those who know about subjects likely to be asked about, but who in many instances cannot be easily traced through existent reference sources The book would have to list practically everybody if its title applied literally, for almost everyone is especially informed about something.

Question: Is the title Who Knows — And What intended to indicate the book will list all who are versed in general subjects or especially trained for professions?

Answer: No. The title, being figuratively used to suggest the especial editorial objective just mentioned, is not intended to represent that, for example, lawyers will be listed simply because they know more about law than laymen, men of medicine because they are qualified members of the medical profession, business men because they usually know more about business (or a general line of business) than those not engaged in commerce and/or industry, and so on. There are standard directories available which list those with such qualifications.

Question: Will Who Knows — And What endeavor, then, to list all specialists?

Answer: No. The book's title, used in the "coined" sense mentioned, means that the Editors endeavor to search out those who, frequently not easily traced through readily available reference channels, know about subjects the Editors felt likely to be generally asked about, and which they therefore have entered in the Locator Index. A dermatologist, for instance, is a specialist, but there are medical directories of the specialists, and Who Knows - And What would be of an unusual size, in addition to being duplicative instead of distinctive, if it attempted to supply what these directories supply. However, an outstanding dermatologist recognized as an authority on poison ivy, for example, might be appropriately listed in Who Knows - And What on that score, instead of on account of his exceptional standing as a specialist in dermatology, since his conversance with poison ivy might not be readily available to the reference consultant, while poison ivy is frequently enquired about. Similarly, a practising member of a medical profession who is an outstanding cancer authority would not be listed as such in Who Knows - And What - there are many reference sources available to lay enquirers about cancer, while those professionally interested can turn to many special sources.

Question: Will Who Knows — And What, then, list no outstanding general authorities?

Answer: Selected general authorities will be either name-listed or sketched when incumbencies, writings or other indicators suggest to the Editors that doing so is appropriate.

Question: Will Who Knows — And What carry overseas listings?

Answer: Not for the present. Many have expressed the hope that such listings would be possible at once, but the compilative task involved has been found to be so formidable that current plans call for scheduling it for a later date.

The Knowers

The significance of the circle (⊚), and the dagger (†) is explained on page 8. All listings are "subject keyed" to the Locator Index (beginning on page 871) in the manner detailed in "About the 'Keying Locator Index'" (opposite page 871).

See pages 801 and 831 for additional knowers; page 851 for information sources; and page 871 for selected subjects "keyed" to knowers and information sources.

10 AALL, Christian Hiorth. Electric smelting furnaces; Calcium carbide; phosphorus. b'13. Ingenieur Electrochimiste '34—Ingenieur Docteur '38 (Institut d'Electrochimie et d'Electrometallurgie de Grenoble France); Licencié ès Sciences '38—Docteur ès Sciences Physiques d'Etat '39 (Université de Grenoble). Author: Contribution à l'Etude du Carbure de Calcium Industriel '39. Plant mgr Odda Smelteverk (Norway) '39-'42; tech advisor Norwegian Govt and Norwegian High Command London '43-'45; cons Imperial Chem Industries Runcorn (Eng) '44-'45; cons Monsanto Chem Co Anniston (Ala) '46, asst to chief engr phosphate div '47-'49, asst research dir Anniston and Columbia (Tenn) since '50. Den Norske Ingeniorforening—Assn des Ingenieurs Electrochimistes et Electrometallurgistes — ACS — Am Inst Mining Engrs—Soc Chem Industry. Monsanto Chemical Co., Anniston, Ala.

11 AALTO, Johan August. Water supply. b'08. BS (civil engring) '33 (NY U); MCE '36 (Brooklyn Poly Inst). Supervisor on maintenance and operation of Catskill watersheds and aqueduct of New York City water supply system, maintenance and improvement of forest plantations for ground cover and lumber supply, supervision of operation of aqueduct structures, shops, sewage treatment plants and chlorinators, development and use of silver iodide smoke generating apparatus in connection with cloud seeding experiments in producing rainfall. Asst engr Borough of Bronx '29-39; engr NYC Office Comptroller '39-49; dist engr Dept of Water Supply, Gas and Elec NYC since '49. Iota Alpha—NY State Soc Prof Engrs—Am Water Works Assn—NY Sewage and Indsl Wastes Assn. New York City Department of Water Supply, Box 908, Kingston, N.Y.

12 AAMODT, Olaf Sverre. Alaskan and grassland agriculture; Range and pastures; Plant breeding and genetics. b'92. BS '17—PhD '27 (U Minn). Exploratory investigations of agricultural problems, Alaska '46. Author articles in field. Survey agrl prodn Iceland Uruguay PR. Plant path US Dept Agr '20-28; prof genetics and plant breeding U Alberta Edmonton Can '28-35, head dept field crops '30-35; prof agron, chmn dept U Wis '35-39; head Div Forage Crops and Diseases US Dept Agr Washington since '39. AAAS(F)—Am Soc Agron (F, pres '48)—Am Phytopath Soc—Am Naturalists—Genetics Society America—Sigma Xi—Gamma Sigma Delta. U.S. Department of Agriculture, Plant Industry Station, Beltsville, Md.⊚

13 AARON, Isador Morris. Morphology; Meristems; Precision machining in layout. b'04. BS '26—MS '34 (Pa State Coll). Author articles in field. Technician feed analysis livestock rations free lance writer and cons in ind. AAAS—Torrey Bot Club—Bot Soc Am—Internat Soc Plant Morphology. R.D. No. 1, Butler, Pa.

14 AASE, Hannah Caroline. Allium cytology (North American species); Cereal cytology. b'83. BA '06 (U SD); PhD '14 (U Chicago). Author: Cytology of Cereals '46; also articles in field. Instr bot State Coll Wash '14-19, asst prof '19-36, asso prof '36-46, prof '46-49. professor emeritus since '49. Botanical Soc Am—Am Genetic Assn—Soc Study Evolution—AAAS. Department of Botany, State College of Washington, Pullman, Wash.

15 ABARBANEL, Albert (pen name Albert A Brandt). International affairs; Medieval philosophy. b'99. BA (Johanneum Lueneburg); Student (U Berlin) (Marburg U) (Heidelburg U) (U Munich); LL B U Wuerzburg). Author article: An Assault on Civilization '34, and others. Lecturer and writer philos and social sci; asst prof U Newark NJ '33-39; commentator radio sta WMCA and WEVD since '41. Kent Gesellschaft—Nat Acad Social and Polit Soc—Am Philos Assn. 319 W. 108th St., NYC.

16 ABBETT, Robert William. Harbor facilities; Shore protection; Bridges; Highways; Railroads; Beach erosion. b'02. BS '27—CE '33 (U Mo Sch of Mines); MS '32 (Yale). Supervised surveys of the ports of Camden Philadelphia Miami and Baltimore. Author: Engineering Contracts and Specifications '48. Editor in Chief American Civil Engineer's Handbook (in press). Partner Knappen Tippetts Abbett & McCarthy NYC since '45. Lt, later commander Civil Engineers Corps US Naval Reserve '41-45. ASCE—AICE—Am Concrete Inst—Sigma Xi. 62 W. 47th St., NYC 19.

17 ABBOTT, Charles David. Howard Pyle. b'00. AB '22 (Haverford Coll); MA '24 (Columbia); BLitt, Rhodes Scholar '27 (Oxford U England). Founder, director of collection of materials in contemporary poetry, librarian of Lockwood Memorial Library. Author: Howard Pyle—A Chronicle. Editor: Poets at Work '48. Dir of libraries, prof Eng U Buffalo since '34. ALA—NY State Library Assn—Modern Lang Assn—Am Bibliog Soc—Oxford Bibliog Soc—Phi Beta Kappa. Lockwood Memorial Library, University of Buffalo, Buffalo.

18 ABBOTT, Ernest James. Measurement of polished surface irregularities. b'00 BSE(EE) '24—MS '25—PhD '35 (U Mich). Measurement of machined and ground surfaces; manufacturer of instruments for measurement of surface roughness, waviness, and profiles; developed tehnique for calibration of minute irregularities. Holds patents on tracer method for measurement of surfaces. Founder Physicists Research Co '35, now pres and mgr. Acoustical Soc Am (F)—Am Soc ME. Micrometical Mfg Co., 345 S. Main St., Ann Arbor.

19 ABBOTT, Harald Wallace. Carbon products. b'90. BS '14 (Middlebury Coll); grad (Alexander Hamilton Inst). Research in industrial application of graphite and carbon and development of special grades of materials for new applications, production of extremely pure graphites used for various purposes. Inventor electrical brush connection, silver impregnated filters for liquid sterilization; co-inventor: impregnated electrical brush. Chem, asst chief chem, tech supervisor, Aluminum Co of Am Massena Plant '15-21; research engr supt carbon plant dir research Stackpole Carbon Co '21-27; research engr Combustion Utilities Corp '27; pres Carbon Inc '27; chief chem Republic Carbon Co '27-29; research engr Speer Carbon Co '29-36, dir labs '30-39, dir research '39-51, manager research since '51; dir research Intern Graphite and Electrode Corp '39-51. Inst Radio Engrs (asso mem)—Am Welding Soc (asso mem). Speer Carbon Co., St. Mary's Pa.

20 ABBOTT, Howard Maxwell. Plasticizers; Fatty acids; Chemical esters. b'00. Educated Churchman Inst. Member United States Mint Assay Commission '48. Pres and dir Twentieth Century Chemicals Ltd Toronto; vp, dir Century Stearic Acid Candle Works Inc, W C Hardesty Co Inc, Hardesty Chem Co Inc, NYC. Am Oil Chem Soc—AAAS—Synthetic Organic Chem Mfrs Assn US—Soc Chem Industry—Am Numismatic Soc. 41 E. 42d St., NYC 17.

21 ABBOTT, Kenneth Morgan. Arts and science (Terence, Cicero, Seneca). b'06. AB '28 (Harvard); PhD '34 (U Ill). Co-author: Index Apuleianus '34; Index Verborum Ciceronis Epistularum '38; also articles in field. With Ohio

State U since '34, now prof. Am Philol Assn—Classical Assn Midwest and South—Am Classical League. 214 Derby Hall, Ohio State University, Columbus 10, O. H: 159 W. Jeffrey Pl., Columbus 2.

10 ABBOTT, Nabia. Arabic paleography, epigraphy and papyri; Islamic history and institutions; Historic women in Islam. b'97. AB '19 (U Allahabad); AM '25 (Boston U); PhD '33 (U Chicago). Author: The Kurrah Papyri '38; The Rise of the North Arabic Script '39; Aishah, the Beloved of Mohammed '42; Two Queens of Baghdad '46; also articles in field. Teacher hist and math in Eng schs India '19-21; dir govt girls' schs Ministry Edn Baghdad Iraq '22-23; asso prof edn Asbury Coll '25-27, prof hist, head dept '27-33; travelling fellow and research asso Oriental Inst U Chicago '33-37, asst prof Islamic studies '38-43, asso prof '43-49; prof since '49. AAUP—AHA—Am Oriental Soc. 212 James Breasted Hall, U of Chicago, Chicago 37.†◎

11 ABBOTT, Robert R(owell). Steel and heat treatment. b'79. BS '02—EM '12 (Case Inst Tech); Met E '06 (Harvard). Research on heat treatment and use of plain and alloy steels, development of mathematical formulae connecting chemical with all physical properties of iron and steel; one of first discoveries of practical chemical substitute for carburizing materials to replace bone in steel treatment. Holds patent in field. Author articles in field. Exptl chem Dow Chem Co '02-03; metall engr Timken Roller Bearing Co and Timken-Detroit Axle Co '09-10; metall engr charge research Peerless Motor Car Co '10-25; dir metall White Motor Co since '25. Lt Col US Army metal br engring div ordnance dept since '25. Edward Longstreth medal Franklin Inst State of Pa '16. White Motor Company, Cleveland.

12 ABBOTT, Robert Tucker. Conchology; Medically important mollusks; Disease carriers; Venomous seashells. b'19. BS '46 (Harvard Coll); grad Sch Arts and Science '46 (Harvard University); MS '47 (Columbian College, George Washington University). Mem Archbold expedn to Melanesia '40-41. Author: articles in field. Asst cur div mollusks US Nat Mus Wash '46-50; asso cur div mollusks since '50; malacologist US Naval Med Research Unit '44-46. Am Malacological Union—Boston Malacological Soc. Division of Mollusks, U.S. National Museum, Washington 25.†

13 ABEL, Charles. Professional photography; Photographic literature. b'91. Educated public schools and De-Witt Clinton High School New York City. Gen referred to as the "key man" of the professional photographic industry; owner large private collection of photographic books including many of the rarest items. Author or co-author of numerous books and of booklets and articles in field. Trustee (life) Winona Sch Photography Winona Lake Ind. Member advisory com photog department Rochester (NY) Inst Tech. Pres Charles Abel Inc; editor and publisher The Professional Photographer (Mo) since '14, The Commercial Photographer (Mo) '25-50. Photographers Assn Am (exec mgr '33-49)—O-M-I. Internat Photog Assn (secretary '27-32)—Photog Soc America—Prof Photog Soc of Ohio(hon life)—Ky Prof Photog Assn(hon life)—Royal Photog Soc Gt Brit(asso)—Conn Prof Photog Assn(hon life)—Southeastern Mass Prof Photog Assn (hon life). Awarded degree Hon Master of Photography by The Photographers Assn of

Am '39; Distinguished Service Medal '45. Caxton Bldg., Cleveland 15.

14 ABEL, Donald F. Allergy tests. b'98. BPh (U Chicago). Medical laboratory testing, particularly of allergies. With Abel Laboratories Inc Chicago since '21, dir since '48 of reading of allergy tests. Ill Assn Clin Labs (pres '51)—Nat Assn Clin Labs (dir '51). 7 W. Madison St., Chicago.

15 ABELL, Theodore Curtis. Theology; Social welfare. b'91. AB'16 O Wesleyan U) BD'20 (Garrett Bibl Inst Evanston Ill) grad study 1 yr (Northwestern U). Minister Unitarian Soc Hollywood, Cal., '21-28; founder '29 dir Hollywood Humanist Soc; editor The Humanist '29-34; field worker Cal State Relief Administration '34-41; field dir ARC overseas services '42-44; social welfare agent Cal State Dept Pub Welfare '44-46; minister First Unitarian Soc Sacramento since '46. 1415 27 St., Sacramento 16, Cal.

16 ABELS, Robert. Firearms (Antique); Weapons (Sharp edged). b'03. Ed pub schs. Research on shot and long arms antique weapons dating from 16th to 19th century in both Europe and America, and edged weapons such as swords and daggers. Author: Early American Firearms '50. In antique bus since '28, specializing in weapons from '39. Nat Rifle Assn—Nat Muzzle Loading Rifle Assn—Co Mil Hist and Collectors. 860 Lexington Av., NYC 21.

17 ABERLE, David Friend. Navajo Indian society; Mongol society. b'18. AB '40 (Harvard); Ph D '50 (Columbia). Research on nativistic religion among the Navaho and contemporary Mongol society. Instr Dept Soc Relations Harvard '47-50; vis asso prof Johns Hopkins U '50-52; asso prof U Mich since 52; research Window Rock Area Office, Office Indian Affairs, US Dept Interior '49-50. Research Navajo Indians (Soc Sci Research Council and Nat Inst Mental Health) '51-52. Am Anthrop Assn—Am Ethnol Soc—Soc Applied Anthrop—Am Sociol Soc—Soc Projective Tehniques—Phi Beta Kappa. Research F mental health Harvard '48-50. Received Soc Sci Research Council demobilization award '46-47. University of Michigan, Ann Arbor.

18 ABERLE, Sophie D. Medical administration; Pueblo Indians. AB '23—AM '25—PhD '27 (Stanford U); Alexander Cox Brown fellow '29-30—MD '30—Sterling fellow '30-31 (Yale U Sch Med). Engaged in part time field work among Pueblo Indians under grant from Committee for Research in Problems of Sex of National Research Council and from Carnegie Corporation of NY '27-35. Gen supt United Pueblos Indian Agency for US Dept Interior '35-44; sec Southwest Supt Council US Indian Service, '35-44; with Div Med Sci Nat Research Council '33-49; University of New Mexico since '49; chmn board dirs Southwest Field Training Sch for Fed Service '37-41. Soc Res Child Development (F)—Am Assn Anatomists—Am Anthrop Assn (F)—AAAS—AMA—Sigma Xi—Alpha Omega Alpha—Iota Sigma Pi. U of NM, Albuquerque, N Mex.

19 ABRAHAMSON, John Deinhart. Cartography; Economic geography; Reclamation economics. b'09. AB '35—SM '36 (U Chicago); PhD prep '40-41 (U Mich). Engaged geological studies clay and coal deposits LaSalle and Vermillion Counties Ill; research on geographical problems, preparation and publication maps, relative to war effort, international trade; conducting investigations and preparing economic reports Missouri Basin Project de-

velopment program. Geol Ogden Engring Co Chicago '39-40; unit chief map design, construction OSS Washington '42-43; chief div maps and graphics, geog to adminstrn Fgn Econ Adminstrn '43-45; chief div maps and graphics Office Internat Trade US Dept Commerce Wash '45-46; chief economic resources branch Reclamation Reg VI US Dept Interior Billings Mont since '46. Assn Am Geographers—Am Geog Soc—West Farm Econ Assn—Sigma Xi (asso)—Phi Beta Kappa. Bureau of Reclamation, Region VI, Billings, Mont.

20 ABRAMS, Allen. Paper chemistry and technology; Pulp lignin. b'89. BA '10—MS (hon) '15—DSc (hon) '37 (Washington & Jefferson Coll); BS '15 (MIT). Research on lime and electrolytic bleaching, viscosity and sticking strength of binders, vapor transmission through papers, protective wrapping, lignin. Author articles: Effect of Chemical Reagents On the Microstructure of Woods '21; The Disk Colormeter for Matching Colors '24; The Penescope—A New Penetration Tester '27; Factors Affecting the Determination of Water Vapor Permeability '36; New Packaging Materials for the Food Industry '27; Pulp and Paper 1918-1939 '39; Pulp and Paper in World War II '42, '43, and others. Vice-pres in charge research and chem div Marathon Corp since '26. AAAS—Am Chem Soc—Am Soc Testing Materials—Am Oil Chem Soc—Tech Assn Pulp and Paper Industry (past pres). Marathon Corporation, Rothschild, Wis. H: 815 Tenth St., Wausau, Wis.

21 ABRAMS, Ernest Russell. Public utilities economics (gas and electric); Communication utilities. b'89. LL B '07 (U Iowa . Consulting economist on public utilities and related industries; publicizing utilities rate and control contests. Author numerous reports and summaries of surveys of public utilities; articles in journals and magazines. Pamphlet: Statutory Renegotiation of Electric Utility War Contracts '45. Pres Boise (Ida) Water Co to '34; Standard Statistics '30-40; cons since '42. 310 E. 44 St., NYC 17.

22 ABRAMS, Talbert. Photogrammetry; Aerial Surveys. b'95. Student (USN Aeronautical Sch). Aerial photographic surveys and mapping. Author: Essential of Aerial Surveys and Photo Interpretation 1942. With Abrams Aerial Survey Crop since '23, Abrams Instrument Corp since '39. Am Soc Photogrammetry (pres '51)—Am Geog Soc F)—Mich Soc Engrs—Detroit Soc Engrs—Am Mil Engrs. Abrams Aerial Survey Corp., 606 E. Shiawassee St., Lansing, Mich.

23 ACHELIS, Elisabeth. Calendar revision. Student (Bklyn Heights Sem) (Ogontz Sch Pa). Author: The World Calendar '37; The Calendar for Everybody '43; many pamphlets. Contbr to Jour of Calendar Reform. Pres The World Calendar Assn Inc since '30. Ofcl Am observer League of Nations Calendar Reform Conf '31; Am guest Universal Christian Council confs '32-36, asso del conf Oxford Eng '37; del Internat C of C Vienna '33. 630 Fifth Av., NYC 20.

24 ACKERLY, Ernest. Caves. b'24. Student '42-44 (Emory U Atlanta); '44 (Columbia); BS (Chem) '47 (U Ga). Discovery new species subterranian amphipod; expedition to study Mexican caves; exploration and discovery of many unrecorded caves; television shows of caving. Bd govs Nat Speleological Soc since '45, organizer and exec vp Metropolitan Grotto since '48. Nat Speleological Soc—Gamma Sigma Epsilon. Dibble Realty Co., Sunrise

Highway and Rockaway Av., Valley Stream, L.I., N.Y. H: 12 Sheridan St., L.I NY

10 ACKERMAN, Carl William. Journalism education (foreign affairs; public opinion). b'90. AB '11–AM '17 (Earlham Coll Richmond; B Litt '13 (Columbia U Sch Journalism); LLD '35 (U Richmond, Northwestern U, Earlham Coll); Dr Honoris Causa '44 (U San Marcos Lima Peru; U Havana). Co-founder with Dr. Hollington K Tong first grad sch of journalism in Chungking, China; sec adv bd on Pulitzer prizes since '32; adminstr Maria Moors Cabot prizes in Latin American journalism since '37. Author: Germany: The Next Republic? '17; Mexico's Dilemma '18; Trailing the Bolshevik '19; Dawes, the Doer '24; Biography of George Eastman '30. Dean Columbia University Graduate School Journalism since '31; ed pub (with Sevellon Brown) Providence Journal Bulletin; est Am Press Inst '46. Union Nacional de Periodistas de Ecuador—Am Soc Newspaper Editors (World Free Press Com '45). Awarded gold medal by Inter-Am U Panama '44; Columbia U Alumni Federation Medal '45; Comdr Order Southern Cross Brazil '52. Pulitzer Bldg., Columbia University, NYC 27.

11 ACKERMAN, Edward A(ugustus). Japan (Natural resources). b'11. AB '34—Am '36—PhD '39 (Harvard). Technical advisor natural resources section general headquarters allied powers Tokyo '46-48, visiting expert consultant '48-49; staff, Natural Resources Task Force, Hoover Commission, '48; staff, President's Water Resources Policy Commission, '50. Author: New England Fishing Industry '41; Japanese Natural Resources '49; American Resources '52. Chief geog reports section and chief topographer Europe-Africa division OSS '41-43; prof geog U Chicago since '48; chief Natural Resources pub wks section Bur of Budget '51-52; asst gen mgr TVA since '52. Association American Geog—Phi Beta Kappa—Sigma Xi. New Sprankle Bldg, TVA, Knoxville, Tenn.⊙

12 ACKERMAN, Walter Tod. Rural electrification. b'94. BS '15 (U Conn); BSAE '22—AE '40 (Ia State Coll). Executive committee New England Rural Electrification Committee, Governor's committee '35; supervisor Farm Housing Design and Electrification Projects ERA. Author articles in field. Asst prof agrl engring Va Polytech Inst '23-24; project dir and engr NE rural electrification project UNH '25-28, asst prof charge agrl engring '28-41; dist engr US Dept Agr '41-45; farm service dir Conn Light and Power Co; farm utilization com Edison Elec Inst since '45. Am Soc Agrl Engrs. Connecticut Light and Power Co., P.O. Box 2010, Hartford, Conn.

13 ACKERSON, Clifton Walter. Poultry; Hen metabolism (Nitrogen, mineral); Chicks (Vitamin requirements, growth rate). b'96. BSc '21—MSc '22 (U Minn); PhD '26 (U Neb). Author articles in field. Prof agrl chem, chem expt sta and chmn dept agrl chem U Neb since '46. Neb Acad Sci—Am Chem Soc—AAAS. College of Agriculture, Lincoln, Neb.†⊙

14 ACKLEY, Parker Otto. Gun theory; Rifles (Cartridges). b'03. BS '27 (Syracuse U). Designed improved rifle cartridges; developed bullet for use on big game. Holds patents in field. Gun smith since '36; organized training course for gun smiths Trinidad State Jr Coll Colo since '47. Head ordnance service dept Ogden Arsenal

World War II. Phi Kappa Phi. Jansen, Colo.

15 ADAMEC, Charles Joseph. Comparative philology; Herodotus; Tacitus. b'95. BA '17—PhD '21 (Yale). Prof classics Knox Coll since '29, chmn dept classics '29-36 and since '46. Am Philol Assn—Linguistic Soc Am—Classical Assn Middle West and So—Phi Beta Kappa. 202 W Brooks St., Galesburg, Ill.

16 ADAMS, Arthur. Historic sites (New Jersey). b'81. AB '02 (Rutgers); AM '03—PhD '05 (Yale); BD '10 (Berkeley Div Sch); STM '16 (Phila Div Sch). Director New Jersey State Commission on Historic Sites '31-32. Editor: Index of Ancestors and Honor Roll Soc Colonial Wars '22, 1st supplement '41; General Register of the Order of Founders and Patriots '26; Cheshire Visitation Pedigrees, 1663 '41. Asst prof Eng '06-08, asso prof '08-11 Trinity Coll, prof since '11, librarian '14-51 emeritus '51; librarian New England Historic Geneal Soc '51. Editor: New England Historical and Genealogical Register '49. American Antiquarian Society—AHA—Soc Colonial Wars (registrar gen)—Order Founders and Patriots (registrar gen and former gov general)—Conn Historical Soc—Soc Geneal(F, London) —Soc Antiquaries of London(F)—Am Soc Geneal (pres)—Phi Beta Kappa. 9 Ashburton Place Boston 8.

17 ADAMS, Arthur Frank. Electrical manufacturing; Telephone business administration; Telephone manufacturing. b'81. Ed public schools. Telephone engineering in Mid-West; member General Operating Board in charge federal operation telegraph and telephone systems by appointment of Postmaster General Burleson '18-19. Pres Theodore Gary & Co Kansas City; chm Anglo Canadian Telephone Co Montreal Automatic Electric Co Chicago; Asso Tel & Tel Co Telephone Bond & Share Co Wilmington Automatic Electric Co Wilmington and others. 1100 King St., Wilmington, Del.

18 ADAMS, Clarence Delmer. Water purification. b'00. Student '22-24 (Willamette U ; BS '29 (Ore State Coll). Research on stream pollution, water treatment and purification, corrosion study. San engr Ind State Bd Health '30-31; supt water purification plant Ind Gas and Water Co. '31-47; chem engr Colgate-Palmolive-Peet Co since '47; cons chem engr. ACS—Am Water Works Assn (chmn Ind sect '45)—Central States Sewage Works Assn. Research F Ore State Coll '29-30. Postoffice Box 307, New Albany, Ind.

19 ADAMS, Clifford R(ose). Marriage and family relations; Personality (Tests). b'02. AB '28—AM '36—teach fellow '31, 36 (U NC); PhD '40 (Pa State Coll). Senior author: How to Pick a Mate; Proceedings of the 1944 and 1946 Marriage Institutes; 14 personality tests; Looking Ahead to Marriage; The Marriage Happiness Prediction Inventory; also articles in field. Professor psychol Pa State Coll since '37, dir marriage counseling service since '40, founder annual inst marriage and home adjustment '44; cons psychol marriage problems since '40. Am Psychol Assn (F, diplomate in clinical psychol)—Am Conf Personnel Assn—AAAS—Nat Conf Family Relations—Am Assn Marriage Counselors—Sigma Xi(F)—Phi Kappa Phi. Burrowes Building, State College, Pa.⊙

20 ADAMS, Comfort Avery. Welding; Electrical machinery; Induction heating; Underground cables; Gas explosions. b'68. BS '90—EE '05—DE '25 (Case Applied Sci); '91-93 (Har-

vard); DE (hon) '38 (Lehigh U). Author: Dynamo Design Schedules '10; also articles in field. Chmn Gen Engring Com Council National Defense World War I, welding com Emergency Fleet Corp; mem internat jury awards department electricity St Louis Expn '04. Instr phys Case Sch Applied Sci, asst prof '96-05, prof elec engring '06-16; Lawrence prof engring Harvard '14-36, Gordon McKay prof elec engring '35-36, prof emeritus since '36, dean '19; cons engr, The Okonite Co since '15, and others. AIEE (pres '18-19)—Am Acad Arts Sci—Nat Research Council (chmn div engring '19-21)—ASME—AAAS—Nat Acad Sci—Inst Elec Engrs—Verein Deutscher Elek—Soc Francaise Elec—ASCE—Am Soc Engring Edn—Am Phys Soc—Am Welding Soc (pres '19-20)—Am Bur Welding (dir '19-36)—Engring Found (chmn welding research council since '36)—Am Engring Council—Am Engring Standards Com (chmn '18-20). Awarded 1st Miller medal '29, Lamme medal AIEE '40. 417 W. Price St., Phila. 44.⊙

21 ADAMS, Elmer Wade. Petroleum lubricants; oils; greases; insecticides. b'97. AB '18 (West Ill Coll); BS '19—MS '20 (U Ill); PhD '24 (U Wis); '21-22 (Ia State Coll). Research and Development of Products. Author: Pinacol Hydrate '25; Catalysis in Acetal Formation '25; Relation of Structure, Affinity and Reactivity in Acetal Formation '25. Head dept chem Mo Mil Acad '20-21; prof dept chem Kan State Teachers Coll '24-25; prof West Ill State Coll summers '22, '24; research chemist Standard Oil Co '25-40, asst dir research since '40. ACS—Sigma Xi. Research Department, Standard Oil Company (Indiana), P.O Box 431, Whiting, Ind.

22 ADAMS, Frederick Johnstone. City and regional planning. b'01. Student '17-20 (Royal Naval Coll Can); '20-21 (McGill U); '21-25 (Arch Assn Sch London); BArch '28 (Columbia). Special consultant Regional Plan Association New York '43-44, United Nations Committee on Permanent Headquarters '46; US delegate to Conference on Planning Housing Committee League of Nations Geneva '39, International Congress on Housing and Town Planning England '46. Head dept planning MIT since '32, prof since '44; cons on planning and zoning since '34. Am Inst Planners (bd govs '37, '38, '39, sec treas '44-45, vp '46-47, pres '48)—Am Soc Planning Officials (bd dir '47-50)—Am Pub Health Assn (com hygiene housing). 19 Coolidge Hill Rd., Cambridge, Mass.⊙

23 ADAMS, Frederick Wildes. Sewing threads. b'01. BS '21—MS '22—DSc '28 (MIT); Senior industrial fellow—plate glass fellowship '36-42 (Mellon Inst). Holds US patents. Author articles in field. Dir research Clark Thread Co Newark. Am Inst Chem Engrs—Am Chem Soc—Soc Chem Industry—Textile Research Inst—Textile Inst (Brit)—Assn Research Directors —Am Assn Textile Chem and Colorists. Spool Cotton Co., 745 Fifth Av., NYC 22.

24 ADAMS, Gail Dayton, Jr. Betatron. b'18. BS '40 (Case Sch Applied Sci); MS '42—PhD '43 (U Ill). Connected with technical developments on betatron under contract OEM-241 '42-45, with design construction and testing of two betatrons one rated at 80 MEV and one at 300 MEV since '45; research in absorption of quanta up to 20 MEV. Holds patent in field. Author articles in field. Research physicist U Ill '43-45, research asst prof physics since '45. Am Phys Soc(F)—Tau Beta Phi—Sigma Xi.

Physics Research Laboratory, Champaign, Ill.

10 ADAMS, George Worthington. American Civil War; Medical history; Military medicine; American social history. b'05. AB '27(Ill Coll Jacksonville) AM '28 PhD '46 (Harvard). Author: Doctors in Blue: the Medical History of the Union Army in the Civil War '52. Asso prof history MacMurray Coll for Women Jacksonville Ill '33-37; asso prof head dept history Lake Forest Coll Ill '37-42; asst counsellor for vets Harvard '45-46 sec Grad Sch Arts & Scis '46-49 dean special students dir U Extension '46-49; dean Coll prof history Colorado Coll since '49; mem exec com State Fullbright Scholarship Com since '50. Am Hist Assn-Miss Valley Hist Assn. 1019 N. Nevada Ave., Colorado Springs, Colo.†◎

11 ADAMS, James Edward. Cotton culture; Plant bio-chemistry; Soil chemistry and fertility. b'98. AB '20 (William Jewell Coll); MS '22 (Purdue); PhD '36 (Ia State Coll). Author: Mechanization of Cotton '45; Mechanization of Cotton Production '46; also articles in field. Head dept agron Tex A&M Coll and Tex Agrl Expt Sta since '46. Am Chem Soc—Am Soc Agron—Soil Sci Soc Am—AAAS—Phi Kappa Phi—Gamma Sigma Delta—Sigma Xi—Phi Lambda Upsilon. Department of Agronomy, Texas A&M College, College Station, Tex.

12 ADAMS, James Jewett. Radio (Design of small and portable receiving equipment, gang condenser tracking, intermediate frequency amplifiers). b'12. BS (EE) '34—MS '35 (U Colo). Design and production engineering of portable AC/DC and battery radios, also shortwave and midget portables; calculated new standardized gang curves for industry '45; research and design of intermediate frequency amplifier for portable radios and frequency modulation receivers. Holds patent on radio receiving apparatus. Radio engr Philco Radio Corp Phila '36-38; radio engr in charge portable design Zenith Radio Corp since '39. Inst Radio Engrs—AAAS—Soc Am Mil Engrs. 6001 Dickens Av., Chicago 39. H: 447 Cottage Hill, Elmhurst, Ill.

13 ADAMS, John Emery. Reefs (Fossil); Reef sedimentation. b'99. BA—MS '22 (U Ia); '23-24 (U Chicago); '25 (U Wis); '26-27 (U Tex). Faculty Tex A&M Coll '25-26; asso Tex Bur Econ Geol '26-27; problem geol Calif Co Standard Oil Co Tex since '27. W Tex Geol Soc (v-pres '35, pres '40)—Am Assn Petroleum Geol (v-pres '50)—Geol Soc Am (councilor '45-47 —Am Geophys Union. Postoffice Box 1660, Midland, Tex.◎

14 ADAMS, Kenneth Tress. Hydrographic and photogrammetric Surveying; Radio ranging. b'91. BS '12 (Kenyon Coll). Research on soundings and radio acoustic ranging; member Federal Board Surveys and Maps '38-42. Author: Hydrographic Manual '44; also articles in field. With Coast and Geodetic Survey since '12, chief Div Photogrammetry Coast and Geodetic Survey '45-49 asst dir of bureau '49-51; retired May '51. Am Soc Photogrammetry (dir and exec com)—US Bd Geog Names (chmn since Oct '52; chmn domestic names committee)—Am Congress Surveying and Mapping(dir) —Sigma Xi—Phi Beta Kappa—Research and Development Board (panel cartography and geodesy of com geophys sci). H: 4103 N. Chesterbrook Rd., Falls Church, Va.†◎

15 ADAMS, Ludwig. Wind tunnels; Liquefaction and storage of natural gas; Mollier diagrams. b'16. BS (CE) '36 (NY U); MS (CE) '37 (Rensselaer Poly Inst); '38-40 (Carnegie Inst Tech); '41-42 (Pa State Coll); '42-47 (U Pittsburgh). Research and development on equipment design, performance data, and thermodynamics of supersonic wind tunnels; study metallurgy, welding, paint, and other corrosion protection for wind tunnels; tests on thermodynamics of liquefaction cycles, refrigeration, dehumidification, heat exchange, insulation, compression, and expansion; design, construction and welding of alloy steel containers, piping, and control equipment for liquefaction and storage of natural gas; construction Mollier diagrams for dry air at pressures 100 psia to O.1 psia, for use in design of wind tunnels and liquefaction of air. Holds copyright on Mollier diagram for dry air. Steel fabrication and welding wind tunnels Pittsburgh-Des Moines Co '37-42, research coordinator since '46; refrigeration engr Cleveland wind tunnels Nat Adv Com Aeronautics '42; Mellon Inst Indsl Research '42-46. AAAS—Am Soc CE—Am Welding Soc—Am Soc Refrigerating Engrs—Sigma Xi—Tau Beta Pi—Sigma Pi Sigma. Professional Engr, Pa. O. Pittsburgh-Des Moines Companies, Pittsburgh 25. H: 205 Thompson Drive, Pittsburgh 29.

16 ADAMS, Martin Ray. English literature (French Revolution influences, Wordsworth's early radicalism, Joel Barlow, Samuel Parr, George Dyer, William Godwin). b'92. AB '12—AM '12 (Roanoke Coll); AM '23—PhD '27—fellow in Eng '26-27 (Princeton). Author: Studies in the Literary Backgrounds of English Radicalism with Special Reference to the French Revolution; also articles in field. Prof Eng Franklin and Marshall Coll Lancaster Pa since '27, head Eng dept since '44. Coll Eng Assn—Modern Lang Assn—Phi Beta Kappa. Franklin and Marshall College, Lancaster, Pa.

17 ADAMS, Quincy. Economics; Statistics of economics; Small businesses. b'01. AB (NYU) AM(Am U). Investment analysis, sales research; organization and operation small businesses. Editor: The Commodity Chart Book '41-43; Author: The Retail Survey '34-35. Investment analyst '24-31; editor Dun's Review '31-37; mgr sales Dun & Bradstreet, Inc., '37-41; dep chief gen statistics staff WPB '41-43; chief div small bus bur fgn and domestic commerce Dept Commerce '44-45; cons since '45. Am Marketing Assn—Am Statist Assn—Am Econ Assn—Phi Delta Theta. Cosmos Club, Washington, D.C.◎

18 ADDICOTT, Fredrick T. Guayule (Physiological anatomy); Abscission; Plant hormones. b'12. AB '34 (Stanford U); PhD '39 (Calif Inst Tech). Discovered niacin as root growth hormone; research on growth factor requirements of pollen germination and pollen tube growth, physiological anatomy of guayule, and anatomy of abscission of its leaves, physiology and anatomy of abscission in horticultural plants. Author: articles in field. Asst prof bot U Calif '46-48, asso prof since '48. Am Soc Plant Physiol—Bot Soc Am—Western Soc Naturalists—AAAS (F)—Sigma Xi. Division of Botany, University of California, Los Angeles 24.†

19 ADEL, Arthur. Infrared spectroscopy; Atmospheres of the solar system; Molecular structure. b'08. AB '31 —PhD '33 (U Mich); research fellow physics '35-36 (Johns Hopkins). Analyzed spectrum of Venus and determined temperature and amount of carbon dioxide in Venus' atmosphere '33-37; made analyses of spectra of Jupiter, Saturn, Uranus and Neptune to determine constitution of their atmospheres '33-35; mapped infrared spectra of solar and terrestrial atmospheres in great detail with prisms and gratings '35-41; determined infrared temperature of sun '39; determined infrared transmission of earth's atmosphere '35-41; discovered new gas N_2O in earth's atmosphere '39-41; identified heavy water vapor HDO in earth's atmosphere '41; determined which heat radiations from Venus penetrate earth's atmosphere '41; extended infrared limit of solar spectrum '42. Developed '47, applied '48, method for measuring temperature of upper atmosphere (ozonosphere). Author articles in field. Now prof physics Ariz State Coll since '48. Am Phys Soc(F) — AAAS(F) — Am Astron Soc—Phi Beta Kappa—Sigma Xi. Arizona State College, Flagstaff, Ariz.◎

20 ADKINS, Dorothy Christina. Theory of mental tests; Public personnel tests. b'12. BSc '31—PhD '36 (O State U). Consultant on examinations American Public Health Association '43; asso ed Educational and Psychological Measurement since '41; asst mng ed Psychometrika '38-49; mng ed since '50. Co-author: Construction and Analysis of Achievement Tests '47; also articles in field. Chief Test Development Unit US Civil Service '48; prof dept psychol UNC since '48; chmn dept since '50. Psychometric Soc (pres '49-'50)—Am Psychological Assn (recording sec '49-52; secretary-treas division evaluation and measurement '48-51, pres '52-53)—NC Psychological Assn(pres '51-52)—Sigma Xi. Department of Psychology, University of North Carolina, Chapel Hill, N.C.†

21 ADKINS, Walter Scott. Geology (Stratigraphy, paleontology, Mesozoic, Jurassic, Cretaceous; Mexican). b'90. BS '10 (U Tenn); grad study (Columbia, U Paris, British Museum). Author: Handbook of Texas Cretaceous Fossils '28; also articles in field. Stratigrapher exploration and production research div Shell Oil Co Houston since '45. Geol Soc Am—Société géologique de France—Sociedad Geológica Mexicana. Shell Oil Company, Houston, Tex. H: Niles Rd., Austin, Tex.

22 ADKINS, William Misener. Captain Robert Falcon Scott. b'98. Research and writing on the life and works of Robert Falcon Scott; Antarctic explorer and hero. Asst editor U publications Ind U. Indiana University, Bloomington, Ind. H: 405 S. Jordan Av., Bloomington, Ind.

23 ADKINSON, Burton Wilbur. Geographical nomenclature; cartography. b'09. BA '36—MA '39 (U Wash); PhD '42 (Clark U). Asst chief maps div Library Congress '45-46, chief '47—49; director reference dept since '49. Am Geog Soc NY(F)—Assn Am Geog —Am Soc Profl Geog—Am Congress Surveying and Mapping—Am Soc Photogrammetry—Special Libraries Assn—ALA—AAAS. Library of Congress, Washington 25. H: 5006 Baltimore Av., Washington 16.

24 ADLER, Charles, Jr. Airplane, automotive and railroad safety engineering (Electric lights and signals). b'99. Student (The Park School, Johns Hopkins). Invented rotating disc, highway railroad crossing signal, Adler flashing relay, traffic sound detector, double filament incandescent airplane lamps, railroad and traffic signals, color-design signal lenses, highway speed control signal systems, alternately flashing airplane position lights, airplane proximity indicator. Holds over 40 patents. Author articles in field. SAE—Nat Aeronaut Assn—Assn Am RR—Inst

Traffic Engrs (affiliated mem, signal sect). Mount Royal Station, Baltimore.

10 ADLER, Robert. Electronics (Beam tubes, frequency modulation, magnetostriction at high frequencies). b'13. PhD '37 (U Vienna). Engaged research electron beam tubes, electromechanical transducers (high frequency magnetostriction), theory synchronized oscillators. Invented phasitron tube system frequency modulation, gated beam tube for FM reception, high frequency magnetostrictive oscillator (electromechanical vibrator) and electro-mechanical band-pass filter. Author articles: Study of Locking Phenomena in Oscillators '46; A New System of Frequency Modulation '47; Compact Electro-Mechanical Filter '47; Piezoelectric Effect in Polycrystalline Barium Titanate '47. Engr develop lab Sci Acoustics Ltd London '39-40; engr lab Asso Research Inc Chicago '40-41; engr research group Zenith Radio Corp Chicago since '41. Inst Radio Engrs (sr)—AAAS. Zenith Radio Corp, 6001 Dickens Av, Chicago 39.

11 ADLERBLUM, Nima H. (Mrs.) Jewish philosophy and culture; American philosophy. b'86. PhD '26 (Columbia). Research studies in philosophy, philosophy of history, Jewish literature, and foreign affairs; founded cultural work of Hadassah, Jewish Women's organization, national cultural chairman; study of problems and conflicts of minority nationalities in Central Europe, Soviet Russia. Author: A Study of Gersonides in His Proper Perspective '26; A Perspective of Jewish Life Through Its Festivals '31; also articles in field. Lecturer on Am philos. Am Philos Assn. P.O. Box 303, Long Branch, N.J. H: 220 Ocean av.

12 ADRIANCE, Guy Webb. Horticulture; Plant propagation; Sub-tropical fruit. b'95. BS '15 (Tex A&M Coll); MS '17 (U Calif); PhD '29 (Mich State Coll); Nat Res fellowship '31-32 (Cornell U). Research on fruit setting in pecan '25-29, root formation in cuttings '30-31, root distribution in citrus since '45. Co-author: Propagation of Horticultural Plants '39; also articles in field. Hort Arlington Heights Fruit Co Riverside Calif '15-16, United Fruit Co Tela Honduras '20; asst prof, later prof hort and head dept program Tex A&M College since '21. Fulbright research grant, citrus and deciduous fruits, Italy, '49-50. AAAS—Am Soc Hort Sci—Am Pomol Soc—Am Assn U Profs—Sigma Xi. Department of Horticulture, College Station, Tex.†

13 AFRICANO, Alfred. Rockets (Propulsion, fuel, flight). b'08. ME '29—grad study '38-39—MS '14 (Stevens Inst Tech); grad study '36-38 (NYU). Author articles in field. Asst dir Jet Propulsion Research Lab Indian Head Maryland '42-43; asst to dir Allegany Ballistics Lab Cumberland Md '44-45; sr project engr Curtiss-Wright Corp Caldwell NJ since '46. Adjunct asst prof aeronautical engring department New York U since '52. AAAS—Am Rocket Soc (past pres)—Inst Aeronaut Sci—ASME. Awarded Internat REP—Hirsch rocket prize ex aequo Am Rocket Soc '36; OSRD certificate for war work on rockets '46. Curtiss-Wright Corp., Caldwell, N.J. H: 25 Forest Av.†

14 AGAR, Herbert Sebastian. United States Federal government (History); History of Platonism; John Milton. b'97. AB '19 (Columbia U); AM '20—PhD '22 (Princeton U); Litt D '36 (Southwestern U); LLD '41 (Boston U). Author: Milton and Plato '28; Bread and Circuses '30; The People's Choice '33; Land of the Free '35; What

is America? '36; Pursuit of Happiness '38; A Time for Greatness '42. Spl asst Am ambassador at London Eng. Phi Beta Kappa. La Osa Ranch, Susabe, Ariz.

15 AGATHA, Mother Mary. Indian and Negro Catholic education. AB '21 (Catholic U Am); MA '23 (Villanova) LLD Cath U of Am, '48. Author: Catholic Education and the Negro '42; Catholic Education and the Indian '42; also articles in field. Pres Xavier U since '32. Xavier University, Palmetto and Pine Sts., New Orleans.

16 AGERSBORG, H(elmer) P(areli de Wold) K(jerschow). Histology; Embryology; Fish culture; Cell study Parasitism; Conservation biology; Hay fever abatement. b'81. AB '17 (Osolo); BS '16—MS '16 (U Wash); MA '20 (Columbia); PhD '23—fellow '22 (U Ill). Author: Laboratory Manual in Animal Biology '26; Plant Record for High Schools, Normal Schools and Colleges '30; Nature Lore '34, vols 2-5 '41-42; also articles in field. Traveling lecturer on conservation of land, water and wildlife resources since '37; prof histology and embryology and air research Des Moines Still Coll of Osteopathy and Surgery '47-49; founder and owner Agersborg Biol Laboratory Centralia since '49. AAAS(F)—Nat Assn Biol Teachers (Ill membership chmn '44-45, nat membership chmn '45-46)—Am Acad Polit Social Sci—Nat Wildlife Fed—Am Soc Zool—Am Fisheries Soc—Ia Acad Sci—Ill State Acad Sci—Tenn Acad Sci—Sigma Xi.—Sigma Zeta. 4021-2 Johnston St., Centralia, Ill.

17 AGHA, Mehemed Fehmy. Graphic arts; Photography; Pictorial journalism. b'96. Grad '13 (Emperor Alexander Tech Sch, Nicolaieff)—'18 (Poly Inst Emperor Peter the Great, Petrograd)—'23 (École Nat des Langues Orientales Vivantes, Paris). Pioneer in candid camera photography and pictorial journalism. Studio chief Conde Nast Paris div France '24-27, NYC '29-43; art director German edition Vogue magazine Berlin '27-29. Cons art dir since '43. Art Directors Club (pres '34-35). 140 W. 57th St., NYC.

18 AGNEW, John Thomas. Spectroscopy (Infrared, visible); Thermodynamics; Heat transfer. b'18. BS (Chem engring) '40—MS (Metall Engring) '42—PhD '44 (Purdue U). Design and construction of infrared instrumentation, particularly a 10-channel infrared spectrograph; collaboration in design image orthicon spectrograph for fast scanning in range 4000-10000A; studies of oxidation of hydrocarbons and carbon disulfide, especially the development of instrumentation to study the development of intermediate products. Staff Purdue U '42-'46; research engr Franklin Inst '46-'48, chief thermodynamics and radiation sect '48-'51; prof mech engr Purdue U since '51; on leave Oak Ridge Nat Lab '51-'52. Am Soc ME—Optical Soc Am—Tau Beta Pi—Sigma Xi—Sigma Pi Sigma. Mechanical Engineering Dept., Purdue University, Lafayette, Ind.

19 AGNEW, Peter Lawrence. Business education (Office equipment and procedures). b'01. B Bus Adminstrn '23 (Boston U); MA '28—PhD '40 (NYU); MEd '31 (Harvard). Author: Office machines course '43; Secretarial office practice '43; series of instruction books on adding machines and calculating machines '39-43. Prof sch edn NYU since '48, asst dean since '48. Eastern Business Teachers Assn (exec bd '35-39, pres '39-40, ed Yearbook '39—Nat Assn Teacher Training Instns (vp '46-47, pres '48-49)—Nat Bus Teachers

Assn—Comml Edn Assn NYC and Vicinity—United Bus Edn Assn—Internat Bus Edn Soc—Nat Office Management Assn (dir edn activities '46—49)—Phi Delta Kappa. School of Education, New York University, Washington Square, NYC.

20 AGTHE, Frederick Thomas. Minerals (Crushing, grinding, concentration). b'86. EM '09 (Lehigh U). Deleterious coatings of the media in dry ball mill; mine concentrating processes; cement plant design and development. Patents on packing and air swept ball mill system. Supt mine and concentrating mill Carolina Barytes Co Stackhouse NC '09-11; mine engr Harold Mine Oliver Mining Co Hibbing Minn '11-12; mine and quarry supt Atlas Portland Cement Co Hannibal Mo '12-18 plant engr '18-20; chief engr Hardinge Co York Pa '20-22; appliction engr Worthington Pump and Machinery Corp Pittsburgh '22-24 Allis Chalmers Mfg Co Milwaukee '24-42 cement plant designer since '42 process engr. Am Interprofessional Inst—Nat Soc Prof Engrs—A.A.A.S.—AIMME—Am Soc Engring Edn. PO Box 512 Milwaukee 1.

21 AHERN, John Joseph. Fires and explosions (Prevention, protection); Industrial safety. b'13. BS '35 (Ill Inst Tech). Author: How Fire-Safe Is a Fire-Proof Building '47; Fire Causes and Lessons They Teach '46 Gas Explosions '48. Compiled industrial safety manual for Army Ordnance Department. Dir Dept Fire Protection and Safety Engring Ill Inst Tech; cons engr, chief training unit, head indsl safety unit, Safety and Security Div Office of Chief Ordnance Army Ordnance Dept '42-45. Am Soc Engring Ed (chmn Comm Industrial Hygiene)—Western Soc Engrs—Nat Fire Protection Assn (chmn Comm Fire Protection Engring)—Internat Assn Fire Chiefs. Illinois Institute of Technology, Chicago 16.†

22 AHLGREN, Gilbert Harold. Forage crops (Management, cultural phases, origin and distribution, breeding). b'13. BS '36 (U Wis); MS '38—PhD '41 (Rutgers U). Author: Forage Crops '49. Co-author: (with R S Snell, J C Anderson, M A Sprague) Practical Field Crop Production for the Northeast '47; (with G Klingman, D Wolf) Principles of Weed Control '51. Also articles in field. Agent United States Dept Agr '38-39; instr agron Rutgers U '39-42, asst prof and asst research specialist '42-43, asso prof and asso research specialist '43-44, chmn dept farm crops, prof and research specialist since '44. Am Soc Agron—Soil Conservation Soc Am—Am Soc Genetics—Sigma Xi. Farm Crops Department, College of Agriculture, New Brunswick, N.J.◎

23 AITCHISON, Beatrice. Transportation economics and statistics. b'08. AB '28 (Goucher Coll); AM '31—PhD '33 (Johns Hopkins); MA '37—graduate study '39-42 (University Oregon). Work in development elasticity of demand for rail passenger travel, passenger traffic revenues and expenses, rationalization of distance rate scales, relation of weight and value to classification ratings, sampling and forecasting procedure used in short term forecasting rail freight waybill studies, index of freight rates, rail traffic estimates for use in revenue cases, relation of rail freight revenue to value of commodities transported, and other aspects of transportation. Author: Preliminary Examination of Factors Affecting the Demand for Rail Passenger Travel '41; A Description of the Principal Class Rate Scales

Prescribed by the Interstate Commerce Commission '43; Weight-Density and Value as Factors in Freight Classification '46; also articles in field. In charge traffic analysis and forecasting ODT '42-44; mem spl com on freight commodity classification Assn Am RR accounting div since '46. Am Econ Assn—Am Statis Assn—Econometric Soc—Inst Math Statis—Phi Beta Kappa—Sigma Xi. Interstate Commerce Commission, Washington 25.

10 AITON, Arthur Scott. Latin American history (Sixteenth century Mexico); Inter-American diplomatic relations (Eighteenth century); History of Spain. b'94. AB '16—Am '18—traveling fellow in Spain '20-21—PhD '23 (U Calif); fellow Nat Social Sci Research France and Spain '28-29. Author: Antonio de Mendoza, First Viceroy of New Spain '27; also articles in field. Prof Hispanic-Am hist U Mich since '29; mem bd editors Hispanic Am Hist Review since '26. AHA (mem council '41-45)—Soc Am Historians—Mich Acad Arts Sci Letters—Miss Valley Hist Assn—Quivira Soc (founder)—Inter Am Bibliog Assn—Hispanic Soc Am (corr mem)—Phi Kappa Phi. 2020 Seneca St., Ann Arbor.☉

11 AKAMINE, Ernest Kisei. Seed germination; Weed control; Sugarcane growth; Flower shipment. b'12. BS '35—MS '41 (U Hawaii). Research on methods of increasing germination of koa haole seed '42, germination of Asystasia gangetica '47, root stimulation in sugarcane '40, effect of temperature and humidity on viability of stored seeds in Hawaii '43, germination of Hawaiian range grass seeds '44, plant growth regulators as selective herbicides '48. Author articles in field. Asst in agr U Hawaii Agr Expt Sta '35-36, asst in agron '36-38, asst in plant physiol '38-42, asso '42-44, jr plant physiol asst plant physiol since '52; cons agrl chemist Pacific science board National Research Council '52. American Society Plant Physiologists—AAAS—Hawaiian Academy Science—Hawaiian Bot Soc—Sigma Xi. University of Hawaii Agricultural Experiment Station, Honolulu 14, T.H. H: 2255 Hulali Pl., Honolulu 17.

12 AKHILANANDA, Swami. Indian and Hindu philosophy; Hindu psychology, religious and mystic practices. b'94. Grad (Calcutta U). Author: Hindu Psychology '46; Sri Ramakrishna and Modern Psychology '36; Hindu View of Christ '49; Mental Health and Hindu Psychology '51; also articles in field. Founded and head of Vedanta Soc Providence RI '28, Ramakrishna Vedanta Society Boston '41; taught Hindu phil and rel Annanala U India '23-24; Am Philos Assn—Am Association Advancement Sci—Institute Pastoral Care—Oriental Society Am—Nat Assn Biblical Instructors—Philos Soc RI—RI Council Churches—RI Minister Union—World Affairs Council of RI—Nat Fgn Policy Assn—Conference on Sci Philos, Religion—Fellowship of Reconciliation — Ramakrishna Mission India. 58 Deerfield St., Boston 15.

13 ALBAUGH, Gaylord Pierce. Journalism (Religious). b'10. AB '32 (O State U); BD '36 (Colgate-Rochester Div Sch); '36-39 (U Chicago Div Sch). Research on US religious newspapers and periodicals 1730-1830 and compilation of 700-page bibliography of material. Contributor: An Encyclopedia of Religion '45. Pastor U Baptist Church '39-42; with McMaster U Div Sch since '42, now asso prof. Phi Beta Kappa—Am Soc Church Hist. McMaster University, Hamilton, Ont., Can.

14 ALBEN, Arthur O(tto). Pecans (Fertilizers, culture); Soil technology. b'95. BS '26 (OSC); MS '27—PhD '29 (Ia State Coll). Author: Fertilizing the Pecan '31; Pecan Rosette '46; Analyses of Pecan Leaves as an Aid in Fertility Studies '47. Co-author: Reactions of Some Pecan Soils and the Effects of Fertilizers on Soil Reaction '33; The Zinc Content of Soils, Soil Reaction and Rosette of Pecans '35; Pecan Soils of the Gulf and Southeastern States and Maintenance of Their Fertility '38; Fertilizing the Pecan '39. Asst soil tech US Bur Chem and Soils '28-36; asso soil tech US Bur Plant Ind '36-46, soil tech since '46. Am Soc Agron—ACS—Soil Sci Soc Am—Am Hort Soc—Phi Kappa Phi—Sigma Xi—Gamma Sigma Delta. 606 Court House, Shreveport, La.

15 ALBERS, Carl Clarence. Medicinal plants; History of pharmacy. b'98. PhG '23—BS—BA '30 (U Tex); PhD '36 (U Wis). Research in pharmacognosy of the Castilian malva, pharmacognosy and chemurgic aspects of native Texas Plantago species, phytochemical aspects of podophyllin, studies of Verbesina species, Texas Monarda oils; research on the botany course as a foundation for pharmacognosy of stem and bark drugs, history of castor oil as revealed by scientific literature, the herbal in pharmacy and medicine '45. Author articles in field. Instr pharmacy U Tex '23-27, asst prof pharmacy '28-37, asso prof '38-47, prof since '47. AAAS—Tex Acad Sci—Am Pharm Assn—Am Inst of Hist of Pharmacy—Tex Pharm Assn—Sigma Xi—Phi Beta Kappa. University of Texas, Austin 12, Tex.

16 ALBERS, Vernon M(artin). Development of medical instruments; Chlorophyll and synthetic porphyrins; Naval torpedoes; Administration of research. b'02. AB '23 (Carleton Coll); MA '25—PhD '28 (U Ill); Nat Research Council fellow '29-30 (Princeton U). Developed instruments for heartbeat and respiration measurements; conducted research in photosynthesis, chlorophyll preparation, and spectoroscopic properties of the chlorophylls, synthetic porphyrins and carotene. Co-inventor recording microphotometer. Author articles in field. Head phys dept Eastern Ky State Teachers Coll '28-29; research physicist C F Kettering Found for Study of Chlorophyll and Photosynthesis '30-43; research asso Harvard Underwater Sound Lab '43-45; asso prof engring research Ordnance Research Lab Pa State Coll '45-46, prof since '46, asst dir since '48. Am Phys Soc—Acoustical Soc Am—Sigma Xi. Received US Navy Bur of Ordnance Development award. Ordnance Research Laboratory, P.O. Box 30, State College, Pa.

17 ALBERT, Alphaeus Homer. American uniform and historical buttons. b'91. BSc '13 (Albright Coll); '13-14 (Lehigh U); MEd '38 (Rutgers U). Author: Washington Historical Buttons '49; Record of American Uniform and Historical Buttons '50; also articles in field. Sci teacher Hightstown High Sch NJ '18-29 and since '31, vice-prin since '39. Sons of the Revolution—Phi Delta Kappa. Hightstown, N.J.

18 ALBERT, Jerry David. Non-alcoholic beverages (Flavor solvents); Hydroponics (Soilless gardening). b'15. BS '41 (Northwestern U). Author articles in field. Research in hydroponics with Chemical Gardening Co Evanston Ill '38-40; dir research Mason & Mason Inc flavor mfgrs. Am Chem Soc. Mason & Mason, Inc., 213 N. Desplaines, Chicago, Ill.†

19 ALBERT, Lillian Smith. Historical and costume buttons. b'95. Author: A Button Collector's Journal '41; A Button Collector's Second Journal '41. Co-author: (with Kathryn Kent) The Complete Button Book '49. Co-author: (with Jane Ford Adams) The Button Sampler '51. Associated editor American Antiques Journal button dept since '47. NJ State Button Soc (pres '41-44, ed publ '41-47)—Nat Button Soc (nat ed Button Bulletin since '42). Hightstown, N.J.

20 ALBIG, John William. Sociology of public opinion. b'99. AB '21—AM '23 (Gettysburg Coll); fellow '23-24 (U Wash); PhD '29 (U Mich). Theory of public opinion; content studies of radio, cartoons, comics and advertising. Author: Public Opinion '39; also articles in field. Prof and chmn dept sociol U Ill since '40. Am Sociol Soc—Am Polit Sci Assn. University of Illinois, Urbana, Ill.☉

21 ALBION, Robert Greenhalgh. History (Maritime, shipping, naval). b'96. AB '18—LittD '48 (Bowdoin); AM '20—PhD '24 (Harvard). Author: Forests and Sea Power. The Timber Problem of the Royal Navy '26; Introduction to Military History '29; Square Riggers on Schedule '38; Rise of New York Port '39. Co-author: History of England and the Brit Empire '37; Sea Lanes in Wartime '42; also articles in field. Expert cons War Dept '43; historian naval administration Office Sec of Navy '43-50; cons historian Maritime Adminstrn since '52; with Princeton University '22-49, professor history '39-49; Gardiner professor oceanic history affairs Harvard University since '49. Soc Nautical Research (Eng hon)—Am Mil Inst (pres '41-45)—Econ Hist Assn (vp '45-47)—Am Naval Found (vp '47-50)—Phi Beta Kappa. Study 181, Widener Library, Cambridge 38, Mass. H: 15 E St., S. Portland 7, Me.

22 ALBJERG, Victor Lincoln. American neutrality; History of Europe since 1870. b'92. BA '18 (U Minn); MA '24—PhD '26 (U Wis). Author articles: Foundations of American Neutrality '26; From Sedan to Stress, Europe Since 1870 (with M H Albjerg) '37; Richard Owen, a Biography '46; Europe From 1914 to the Present '50. Asst prof hist Purdue U '26-28, prof since '37. AHA—Modern Hist Assn—Ind State Hist Assn—AAUP—Phi Delta Kappa. Department of History, Purdue University, West LaFayette, Ind. H: 618 Northridge Dr.

23 ALBRIGHT, Horace Marden. Potash. b'90. BL '12 (U Cal); LLB '14 (Georgetown U). Mem National Minerals Advisory Council; national resources committee Hoover Commission to Reorganize the Executive Branch of the Government. Vice pres and gen mgr US Potash Co '33-46, now pres and gen mgr. Am Potash Inst(dir)—Potash Export Assn—Resources for the Future(pres)—Phi Delta Phi—Beta Gamma Sigma—Cosmos Club—Explorers Club. 30 Rockefeller Plaza, NYC.

24 ALBRIGHT, Penrose Strong. Non-electrolytes (Dielectric Constants); Electro-plating; Salting-out effect. b'96. BS '22 (Rensselaer Poly Inst); MS 29—Ph D '36 (U Wis). Research on measurements of dielectric constants of aueruqous solutions of nonelectrolytes and their application to the salting-out effect and to theory and practice of addition agents to electro-plating baths. From instr chem to chmn div natural sci Southwestern Coll '25-43; head phys dept U Wichita since '43. Kan Acad Sci (past pres —ACS—Am Inst Chem—APS—Am Inst Phys—Inst Aeronautical Sci—Am Soc

Engring Edn. University of Wichita, Wichita 14, Kan.

10 ALBRIZIO, Conrad Alfred. Fresco painting. b'94. Student '14-18 (Beaux Art Inst NYC). Executed 850 square foot fresco in Louisiana State Capitol Building '31, 14 tempera panels for Church of St Cecilla Detroit '34, and others; executed during '48-49 seven panels and ceiling in Waterman Office Bldg Mobile; measured and photographed the important Romanico Pugliese architectural monuments in Puglia, Italy '28-29. Author articles in field. Prof fine arts dept La State U since '36. Am Fed Arts—Am Artists' Equity. Awarded Rosenwald fellowship for creative painting '45-47. Louisiana State University, Baton Rouge, La. H: 814 Dumain St. New Orleans.

11 ALDEN, Harold L(ee). Astronomy; Stellar parallaxes; Invisible companions of stars; Orbits and mass ratios. b'90. AB '12 (Wheaton (Ill) Coll); MS '13 (U Chicago); PhD '17 (U Va). Author articles in field. Asst and asso prof astron, astronomer in charge, Southern Station Yale U Observatory Johannesburg S Africa '25-45; prof astron, dir Leander McCormick Observatory U Va since '45. Royal Astron Soc(F)—AAAS(F)—Am Astron Soc—Am Assn Variable Star Observers—Internat Astron Union—Societe Astronomique de France—Astron Soc S Africa (pres '32)—S African Assn for Advancement of Sci—Phi Beta Kappa—Sigma Xi. Leander McCormick Observatory, University of Virginia, Charlottesville, Va.◎

12 ALDEN, John Douglas. Propane gas. b'77. ME '03 (Stevens Inst Tech). United Gas Improvement Co '03-14; Supt prodn and distribution gas and elec Bronx Gas & Elec Co NYC '14-20, Consol Gas Co NYC '20-24; gas engr Nat Pub Service Corp NYC '24-28, Midwest Utilities System '28-32; head gas operations Jersey Central Power & Light Co Asbury Park NJ '32-44; now cons gas engr. Am Soc ME—NJ Gas Assn (pres '33)—Am Gas Assn —New Eng Gas Assn. 40 Lexington St., Newark 5, N.J.

13 ALDEN, Philip E. Shade trees. b'96. BS '18 (U Mich). Editor: The Shade Tree (monthly bull of NJ Fed of Shade Tree Commns). Forester shade dept Kearny NJ since '19; sectreas NJ Fed of Shade Tree Commns since '25. Nat Shade Tree Conf—Soc NJ Certified Tree Experts. Municipal Building, Kearny, N.J.

14 ALDEN, Richard Champney. Petroleum engineering. b'96. BS (electrometall) '18 (Lehigh U). Developed seasonal volatility of motor fuels; pioneered in work on liquefied petroleum gases; research on fractional distillation of light petroleum hydrocarbons; development of isopentane for high octane gasoline; hydrocarbon gas conversion processes, thermal and catalytic alkylation and polymerization, dehydrogenation, hydrogenation, isomerization; research on cumene for high octane gasoline; catalytic desulfurization of petroleum naphthas. Chem Phillips Petroleum Co '25-31, asst dir research '31-'33, dir research '33-'50, chmn research planning bd since '50. ACS—AAAS—ASTM—Natural Gas Assn Am—Soc Automotive Engrs. Received Hanlon Award of Natural Gas Assn Am '37. Phillips Petroleum Co., Bartlesville, Okla.†

15 ALDERFER, Harold Freed. Pennsylvania and local government; Public administration. b'03. AB '22 (Bluffton O Coll); AM '26—PhD '28 (Syracuse U). Editor Pennsylvania Township

Commissioners Magazine; editor-in-chief Commonwealth the Magazine for Pennsylvania. Co-author: (with J Tanger) Pennsylvania Government, State and Local '33; (with F P Weaver) County Government Costs in Pennsylvania '33; (with A Sukel) American Citizenship for Pennsylvanians '35; (with L Young) Know Pennsylvania—Your State and Local Government '46. Asst prof polit sci Pa State Coll '28-31, asso prof '31-35, prof since '36; dir Bur Municipal Affairs of Dept Internal Affairs, Commonwealth of Pa since '44; planning cons Am Municipal Assn '43. Local govt specialist Mutual Aid Administration, Greece '50-52. Pennsylvania State Assn of Boroughs (sec)—League of Cities of the 3d Class in Pa (dir publs)—Pa Chiefs of Police Assn (ed)—Am Polit Sci Assn—Am Municipal Assn (vp '47-48)—Nat Municipal League—Am Soc Pub Administrn—Internat City Mgrs Assn—Tax Inst—Pub Service Inst Bd Commonwealth of Pennsylvania (chmn). 733 Holmes St., State College, Pa.◎

16 ALDERSON, Wroe. Prices; Price policies; Marketing costs; Urban land use; Theory of competition. b'98. AB'27 (George Washington U). Management and marketing counselling; marketing studies and theory; theories of competition. With Dept Commerce '25-34; Curtis Pub Co '36-43; pres Alderson & Session, Inc since '44; chm bd gov Perlin Meml lectures. Am Marketing Assn (pres '48)—Am Econ Assn—Am Statis Assn—Nat Indsl Advt Assn. 1401 Walnut St., Phila 2.†◎

17 ALDRICH, Benjamin M. Heat transfer; Machine design. b'99. BS (mech engring) '27 (U Neb); MS '34 (SD State Coll); certificate in metallography '29 (Sauveur and Boylston). Research on domestic heating and ventilating systems, design and testing of gas ranges, pressure gages, heat treatment of ferrous metals in magnetic field. Granted patent in field. Asst prof machine design SD State Coll '30-41; asso prof mech engring Okla A&M Coll since '41. Sigma Xi—Am Soc ME—Am Soc Engring Edn—Okla Soc Prof Engrs—Nat Soc Prof Engrs. College Station, Stillwater, Okla.

18 ALDRICH, Willard W(alker). Fruit production; Fertilization; Fruit quality; Irrigation. b'01. BS '23 (Johns Hopkins); MS '26—PhD '30 (U Md). Research on pear irrigation; sub-tropical fruit production. Author articles in field. Asst hort Bur Plant Industry '29-34; Asso, sr, prin hort US Dept Agr '35-45; hort, dir tech activities Am Fruit Growers Hagerstown Md since '46. Am Soc Hort Sci—Am Soc Plant Physiol—Soil Sci Am. American Fruit Growers, Inc., Hagerstown, Md.

19 ALDRIN, Edwin Eugene. Aviation (All weather flying, airplanes as flying showrooms). b'96. BA '15 (Clark U); grad '16 (Worcester Poly Inst); MS '17—DSc '28 (MIT); grad '20 (US Air Corps Engring Sch McCook Field Dayton O). Flew first American airplane making business tour Europe '29; created first flying showroom with motion picture lecture facilities, making world-wide tour '46-48, established first communication ground telephone system from DC4 airplane on same tour. Author articles in field. Tech adv Guggenheim Safe Aircraft Competition; mem adv com aeronautical course and visiting com dept mech engring MIT; aviation mgr and cmdr Atlas Sky Merchant since '46. US Army '17-28, founder and sec Air Service Engring Sch '19-21, resigned as

capt '28; commd col US Air Corps '42, assigned as chief all weather flying center Wright Field '45. Mem adv com Harmon Trophy award. Inst Aeronautical Sci Inc (Charter mem, F, mem council, treas '34, vp '35)—Royal Aeronautical Soc (asso F)—ASME—SAE—Am Soc Testing Materials (mem tech com gasoline, com motor oils)—Nat Aeronautic Assn (vp '38)—Aero Club France—Sigma Xi. Decorated Commendatore Order Crown of Italy '33. Atlas Supply Co., 744 Broad St., Newark, N.J. H: 180 Walnut St., Montclair, N.J.◎

20 ALEXANDER, Allen Leander. Chemistry; Protective coatings (Anticorrosive; antifouling, camouflage). b'10. BS '31—MS '32—PhD '36 (UNC). Author articles in field. Research chem Sherwin Williams Co '36-38; organizer and head protective coatings sect Naval Research Lab Washington since '38. Am Chem Soc—Nat Assn Corrosion Engrs—Am Inst Chem—Sigma Xi. Naval Research Laboratory, Washington 25.†

21 ALEXANDER, Charles P(aul). Entomology; Taxonomy, biology and phylogeny of living and fossil craneflies of the world. b'89. BS '13—PhD '18 (Cornell U). Author The Craneflies of New York, part 1 '19, part 2 '20; Craneflies of the Baltic Amber '31; also six hundred articles in field. Prof entomol Mass State Coll since 30, head dept entomol and zool since '38, dean sch sci since '46. Entomol Soc Am (F, pres '42-43)—Entomol Soc, London(F)—Entomol Soc, France(F)—Sigma Xi—Phi Kappa Phi. 39 Old Town Rd., Amherst, Mass.

22 ALEXANDER, Collin Herbert. Films (Evaporated). b'16. BSc (Alma Coll); student (MIT) (U Chicago). Development products and processes, including permanent anti-reflection films, photo-engraved and photo evaporated reticules, interference filters, selective interference filters; design of manufacturing equipment for production of vacuum evaporated film. Holds patents in field. Cons on thin films Bausch & Lomb Optical Co Rochester NY '41-41; project engr vapor metalizing new products div Minn Mining & Mfg Co since '51. ACS—AP S—Am Optical Soc. Minnesota Mining & Manufacturing Co., 900 Fauquier Av., St. Paul.

23 ALEXANDER, Edward Johnston. Cacti and succulent plants; Flora of southeastern United States. b'01. BS '38 (U NC). Southern Appalachian expedition '33, Rocky Mountain expedition '36; Mexican expedition '44-45; Puerto Rico collecting trip '47 from which many new species were discovered and many new subjects introduced to horticulture. Author articles in field. Museum aide, later asso curator NY Bot Garden since '26. Bot Soc Am—Am Soc Plant Taxonomists—So Appalachian Bot Club—Cactus and Succulent Soc Am. New York Botanical Garden, NYC 58.

24 ALEXANDER, Edwin Petri. Railroad and industrial scale models; American railroad history. b'05. Student (Columbia). Author: Model Railroads '39; Iron Horses '41; The Pennsylvania Railroad '47, Steel Steeds '49. After several years building scale model railroad equipment as a hobby started first business in this line '27 which has developed into a specialized custom-built scale model enterprise including all types of miniatures. Authors League—Phila Art Alliance—Eugene Field Soc (hon)—Hist Soc Pa. Box 528 Yardley, Pa.

25 ALEXANDER, John Aleck. Greek archeology (Potidaea); Greece (Ancient coins). b'12. AB '34—MA '35 (Emory U); '35-36 (Washington U); Ph D '39 (Johns Hopkins U). Research on history, archeology and coins of Potidaea and Cassandreia in northern Greece. Author: Potidaea, Its History and Archaeological Remains '52; also articles in field. Archeol field work with Johns Hopkins U expdn to Olynthus, Greece '38; asst prof classics and ancient hist St Bonaventure Coll '41-42; asso prof hist Atlanta Div U Ga since '47. AHA—Archeol Inst Am—Classical Assn Middle W and S—Am Acad Polit Sci. Atlanta Division, University of Georgia, Atlanta.

10 ALEXANDER, John Lacy. Irrigation development; Metal mining (Mexico and Arizona). b'02. Student '19-22 (Ga Tech) (La State U). Consultant on Management and Mining Production problems. Mgr dir owner various properties Ariz and Mexico; registered professional mining engr Ariz. Am Assn Engrs—AIMME. Box 1745, Miami, Ariz.

11 ALEXIS, Algert Daniel. Engineering administration of design; Public works (Construction and maintenance). b'97. CE '19 (Lafayette Coll Easton Pa). Charge public works and public utilities in naval shore establishments. Apptd lt (jg) CEC US Navy '21 to rear adm '50; staff comdr service force Pacific staging invasion Japan '45; public works officer Norfolk Naval Shipyard '45-48, dist pub works officer 5th Naval Dist '48-50; dir Atlantic div Bur Yards and Docks NYC since '50. Am Soc CE—Tau Beta Pi. Navy Commendation medal with ribbon, Am Defense, Am campaign, Asiatic-Pacific and Victory World War II medals US, Medal of Honor and Merit (Rep Haiti). Director, Atlantic Division, Bureau of Yards and Docks, Dept of Navy, 90 Church St., NYC. H: Morattico, Va.©

12 ALEXIS, Joseph Emanuel Alexander. Philology German Spanish). b'85. AB '05 (Augustana Coll); AM '06 (U Mich); PhD '18 (U Chicago); '11 (U Lund Sweden); '21 (U Madrid U Paris); Dr d'université '30 (U Paris). Author: German Relatives in 18th Century Prose; La littérature suédoise d'Amérique; First Course in Spanish; En Espana; En France; I Sverige. Coauthor First Course in German; In der deutschen Republik. Editor: Strindberg's Stories and Poems, Easter, and Master Olof; Ludwig Thoma's Geschichten aus Bayern. Prof mod langs University Neb since '40. Mod Lang Assn—Linguistic Soc Am—Soc Advancement Scandinavian Study—Phi Beta Kappa. Recipient Knight Order of Vasa conferred by Gustaf V of Sweden '44. University of Nebraska, Lincoln, Neb.©

13 ALFANGE, Dean. Constitutional law; Government; Israel (Non-governmental American assistance to). b'99. AB '22 (Hamilton Coll) LLB '25 (Columbia). Author: The Supreme Court and the National Will '37. Advisor various governmental and welfare agencies and committees. Chm Enemy Alien Hearing Bd Southern Dist NY; dir Better Understanding Found Religious & Racial Tolerance; nat chm com to Save Jewish People of Europe; chmn Am Christian Palestine Com; trustee NY Fashion Inst of Tech; mem NY State Bd of Inquiry into Longshore Industry. Am Acad Polit Soc Sci—UN Assn—NAACD—Nat Inst Soc Sci—Phi Beta Kappa. 9 East 40 St., NYC†◉

14 ALI, Asaf. India; Urdu Language. b'88. Student (St Stephens Coll Delhi India). General secretary '37-45, deputy leader Congress Party in Central Legislature when Pandit Jawaharlal Nehru assumed office; held portfolio of transport in Nehru cabinet in Interim Government; became first ambassador from India to US '46; Author political and literary books in Urdu; also articles in field. Govr orissa since '48. 2107 Massachusetts Av., N.W., Washington.

15 ALICATA, Joseph Everett. Parasitology. b'04. AB '28 (Grand Island Coll)—MA '28 (Northwestern U); PhD '34 (George Washington U). Author articles in field. Parasitol and prof parasitol U Hawaii Agrl Expt Sta since '35. Washington Acad Sci (hon)—Am Soc Parasitol—Am Soc Tropical Med—Helminthol Soc Wash—Hawaiian Acad Sci—Sigma Xi—Phi Kappa Phi. University of Hawaii, Honolulu 14, T.H.

16 ALIKONIS, Justin John. Food chemistry; Confectionery. b'12. BSc '35 (Ill Wesleyan U); MS '36 (U Ill). Research on effect of particle size on "bloom" in chocolate; effect of uniform air cell structure in foam confections; stabilization of plastic confections. Holds patents on foam and chocolate confectionery. Author articles in field. Dir Al-Chem Lab Bloomington Ill '36-43; chem Bloomington and Normal San Dist '43; dir research Paul F Beich Co Bloomington since '43. Am Inst Chem(F)—Am Chem Soc—Am Assn Candy Tech —Central States Sewage Assn. Paul F. Beich Company, Bloomington, Ill.

17 ALLAN, Sherman A(lbern). World War II (Logistics). b'22. Student '39-41 (Concordia Collegiate Inst); BS '43 (NYU). Collaborator: (with Eudora Ramsay Richardson) Quartermaster Supply in the European Theater of Operations in World War II; Quartermaster Supply in the Fifth Army in World War II. Asst to hist Office Chief Quartermaster European Theater of Operations '43-46, hist The Quartermaster Tech Training Service The Quartermaster Center Camp Lee Va since '46. Quartermaster Technical Training Service, The Quartermaster Center, Camp Lee, Va. H: 226 Battery Place, Colonial Heights.

18 ALLEMAN, G(ellert) S(pencer). English literature; Restoration comedy (1660-1714); Marriage and divorce laws to 1754. b'13. BA '34 (Lehigh U); AM '37—PhD '42 (U Pa). Author: Matrimonial Law and the Materials of Restoration Comedy 1660-1714 '42. Asst prof Eng Newark Colleges Rutgers U since '47. Mod Lang Assn Am—Mod Humanities Research Assn. Newark Colleges, Rutgers University, 40 Rector St., Newark 2, N.J. H: Route 3, Media, Pa.

19 ALLEN, Charles Laurel. Advertising; Publishing; Marketing research; Rural newspapers. b'02. AB '24 (U ND) AM '27(U Ill) PhD '48(Northwestern . Author: Country Journalism '27; Journalists' Manuel of Printing '29; Publication Laws of New Jersey '39; Free Circulation Newspapers '40; Editor Chicago Daily News Almanac, National Almanac, Denver Post Almanac, Rocky Mountain Empire Yearbook. Asst to prof journalism '25-37 U Ill; dir dept journalism '37-40 Rutgers; asst dean dir research Medill Sch Journalism Northwestern since '40; chief rural press sect news bur OWI '42 chief '43. Am Assn Schs and Depts Journalism—Am Assn Teachers Journalism—Nat Editorial Assn—Am Press Inst—Phi Beta Kappa—Sigma Delta Chi. Northwestern University, Evanston, Ill.◉

20 ALLEN, Clyve Charles. Asphalt; Bitumens; Naphthas. b'00. PhD '30 U Calif). Research on bituminous composition, formulation, manufacture and application, and naphtha super-refining. Sr staff research chem Shell Development Co '30-38; asst dir and dir research and development lab Anderson-Prichard Oil Corp Cyril Okla since '40. ACS—AICE—Nat Assn Corrosion Engrs. Anderson-Prichard Oil Corp., Research and Development Laboratory, Cyril, Okla.

21 ALLEN, Denver I(rving). Human nutrition (Military). b'13. BS '38—PhD '42 (U Mo); '48-49 (George Washington U). Co-author: (with H L Swain and others) Three Nutrition Surveys at Fort Churchill Manitoba Canada in 1947-48, '49. Nutritionist US Army Zone of Interior '43-44, nutritionist and hosp mess supervisor US Army SW Pacific Area '44-45, chief Nutrition Br Office of The Surg Gen since '46. Am Bd Nutrition (diplomate '49). Medical Division, Hdqrs USAR EUR, APO 403, c/o PM NYC.

22 ALLEN, Durward L. Wildlife management; mammalian ecology. b'10. AB '32 (Mich U); PhD '37 (Mich State Coll). Made ecological study of vertebrate populations of 500-acre farm '35-37; supervised research on fox squirrel, cottontail rabbit, raccoon pheasant, other farm wildlife; investigates and manages wildlife on agricultural lands; determines wildlife effects of soil conservation measures and modern agricultural methods. Developed new census techniques for cottontail rabbit, skunk, ringnecked pheasant; worked out breeding potential and population mechanisms in fox squirrels; demonstrated effects of heavy hunting on small game populations in southern Michigan. Author: Michigan Fox Squirrel Management '43. Biologist Div Wildlife Research US Fish and Wildlife Serv Md since '46. Wildlife Soc—Am Soc Mammalogists—Wilson Ornithol Club—Soil Conservation Soc of Am—Friends of the Land—Ecol Soc of Am—Wilderness Soc. Annual literary award The Wildlife Soc for book Mich Fox Squirrel Management. Patuxent Research Refuge, Laurel, Md.

23 ALLEN, E. Ross. Herpetology. b'08. Student '26 (Stetson U). Began milking snakes '27; began furnishing venom to drug industry and medical profession '31; provided 90% all venoms used by Army and Navy doctors during World War II, handled personally more than 37,000 poisonous snakes in this work '43 and total of over 73,000 during war years. Author articles in field. Organized Ross Allen's Reptile Inst Silver Springs Fla '31. Soc Herpetol and Icthyol—Herpetologists League—Fla Acad Sci—So Assn Sci and Ind—AAAS—Fla Anthrop Soc—Fla Audubon Soc. Silver Springs, Fla.

24 ALLEN, Edward Weber. Fisheries (International law). b'85. Student '92-03 (Oshkosh State Normal Sch); '03-05 (U Chicago); LLB '09—Alumnus Summa Laude Dignatus '47 (U Wash). Member US commission to review Japanese fishery situation '49; Member US delegation Food and Agriculture meeting Baguio '48, annual meetings Washington '48 and '49. Author: North Pacific '36; Laperouse, A Check List '41; also articles in field. Mem firm Allen Hilen Froude DeGarmo & Leedy; US commr, chmn or sec Internat Fisheries Commn since '32; US commr Internat Salmon Fisheries Commn '37-51. Adviser to US delegation to Tokyo to negotiate the North Pacific Fisheries Treaty with Japan and Canada '51. American Bar Association (exchairman Internat Law Sect)—Internat Bar Assn—Am Judicature Soc—Am Law Inst—Am Soc International Law—Inst World Polity—Bibliog Soc Am. Northern Life Tower, Seattle.

10 ALLEN, Edwin Brown. Mathematics (Analysis, applied); History of mathematics and astronomy (India, Near East); Oriental languages (Arabic, Coptic, Sanskrit, Pali). b'98. EE '20—MS '30—PhD '34 (Rensselaer Poly Inst); AM '34 (Harvard). Co-author: Vital Mathematics '44; also articles in field. Head dept math Rensselaer Poly Inst since '37. Am Math Soc—Am Astron Soc—Soc Symbolic Logic—Math Assn Am—Am Oriental Soc—Hist Sci Soc—Sigma Xi. 4 Sheldon Av., Troy, NY.

11 ALLEN, Frank W. Pomology; Deciduous fruits (Ripening, shipping, storage). b'87. BSA '10 (U Missouri); MS '13 (Ia State Coll). Investigational studies on fruit maturity, handling, packing, shipping and storage of California deciduous fruits since '20 in close cooperation with state and nation-wide organizations. Author over 100 articles in field. Asst horticulturist U S Bureau Markets '17-20; asst prof pomology U Calif at Davis '20-29, asst pomologist '39-43; pomologist since '43; prof pomology since '46. Am Soc for Horticultural Science—Phi Kappa Phi—Sigma Xi. Department of Pomology, University of California, Davis, Calif.†

12 ALLEN, Gay Wilson. Walt Whitman; Versification. b'03. AB '26—MA '28 (Duke U); PhD '34 (U Wis). Trustee, Walt Whitman Foundation. Author: American Prosody '35; Literary criticism: Pope to Croce '41; Walt Whitman Handbook '46. Editor Handbooks of American Authors Series. Asso prof NYU '46-48, prof since '48. Modern Lang Assn Am—Phi Beta Kappa. New York University, University Heights, NYC 53. 454 Grove St., Oradell, N.J.

13 ALLEN, Harry W. Oriental fruit moth (Biological control). b'92. BS '13 (U Mass); MS '22 (Miss State Coll); PhD'26 (O State U). Supervisor of search for Oriental fruit moth parasites in Japan. Australia, and southern Europe; development of methods for propagation of oriental fruit moth parasites in US; discovery of technique for control of fruit moth by mass liberations of parasite (hymenopterous) Macrocentrus ancylivorus; determination economical breeding methods for parasites of fruit moth. Co-author articles: (with Holloway, Haeussler) Importation, Rearing, and Colonization of Parasites of the Oriental Fruit Moth '40; (with Brunson) Control of Nosema Disease of Potato Tuber Worm—a Host used in the Mass Production of Macrocentrus ancylivorus '47, and others. With USDA '13-17 and since '26, now entomol Bur Entomol and Plant Quarantine; instr advancing to asso prof entomol and zool Miss A&M Coll '20-26. Am Assn Econ Entomol—Entomol Soc Am—Phi Kappa Phi—Sigma Xi—Gamma Alpha. U.S. Bureau of Entomology and Plant Quarantine, Box 150, Moorestown, N.J.

14 ALLEN, Hope Emily. Medieval English literature (Margery Kempe Ancrene Riwle Richard Rolle). b'83. AB '05—AM '06 (Bryn Mawr Coll); grad student (Radcliffe Coll); research student '10-11 (Newnham Coll). Spent many years hunting and studying medieval MSS English and Continental Libraries. Author: Writings and Ascribed to Richard Rolle '27; The English Writings of Richard Rolle '31; The Book of Margery Kempe Vol 1 '40 (in part) (preparing general introduction as Vol II); also articles in field. Free lance scholar. Medieval Academy Am(F), Essay prize Bryn Mawr Coll '05; Crawshay prize of British Acad '29; fellow in Europe of Assn U Women '10; grants from Am Council Learned

Socs. LHD Smith Coll '46. Kenwood Station. Oneida, N.Y.

15 ALLEN, Ida Cogswell Bailey. Home economics; Food dietetics and nutrition. Educated Oread Inst Domestic Sci Worcester Mass; grad dietitian Metropolitan Hosp NYC. Founder Mrs. Allen's School of Good Cookery '20; director domestic science Wcman's World '21; contributor or editor home economics sections Good Housekeeping, Ladies' Home Journal, Medical Review of Reviews and others; lecturer US Food Administration, Bakers and Cooks Schools US Army '42; founder and president National Home Makers' Club and conductor of network broadcast, television programs; food columnist King Features Syndicate; consultant for national food firms. Author Mrs. Allen's Cook Book '16; Cooking Around the World '32; The Budget Cook Book '34; Cooking Within Your Income '36; Kitchenette Cooking for Two '38; The Everyday Cook Book '39; Successful Entertaining; Double Quick Cooking '43; Pressure Cooking '47; Food for Two '47; and others; The Money Saving Cook Book '48; The Picture Cook Book '49. Hotel Iroquois, 49 W. 4th St., NYC 18.

16 ALLEN, J. Edward. Freemasonry (History). b'87. AB '07—AM '08 (Wake Forest Coll NC). Mason, grand master North Carolina '39-40, chief presiding officer all other Masonic bodies and Shrine North Carolina, initiate member Masonic Societies Great Britain, Ireland, France, Switzerland; reviewer, statistician since '22. Author volumes of Masonic Reviews; Grand Lodge, Grand R. A. Chapter, Grand Commandery K.T., annually since '23. Editor (with Melvin M Johnson) of Am edition Gould History Freemasonry '36. Supt pub instrn Warren Co since '19. Philalethes Soc(F). 1 Academy Av., Warrenton, N.C.

17 ALLEN, Jay. History of steamboats. b'05. AB '27—AM '29 (Harvard); BLS '39 (Columbia U Sch Library Sci); diploma '28 (Longy Sch of Music). Special studies on steamboats north and east of New York City, especially in Maine; founder, editor: Steamboat Bill of Facts '40-43, associate editor since '43. Author: The Steamer J T Morse, Her History and Adventures '37. Conductor U Ill A Cappella Choir '46-48, Choristers '48-49; asst conductor University Chorus '46-49 conductor '50-51. Steamship Historical Society America. 220 Smith Music Hall, Urbana, Ill. H: Saffer Court 2.

18 ALLEN, John Eldridge. International relations; History of Washington, DC. b'11. BBA '34 (U Miami); MA '37 (Nat U Washington); '37 (Am U, Washington). Spl hist research asst to Doctor John Barrett, '31-33; spl asst to Doctor Arthur F Sheldon, '31-34. Author: The Situation in Manchuria and China '32; World Economic Conference Needed '32; Certain Aspects of Far Eastern History, 1842-1937, '37; Russian History, 1917-37, '37. AHA—Columbia Hist Soc—Archaeological Soc. US Dept of the Army, Washington 25; H: 2262 Cathedral Ave., N.W., Washington 8, D.C.

19 ALLEN, John Eliot. Geology and physiography (Crater Lake National Park, California, Oregon); Paleontology; Mineralogy, (Oregon); Economic geology. b'08. BA '31—MA '32 (U Ore); PhD '45 (U Calif). Engaged research and writing structures in dacitic flows Crater Lake National Park Ore, chromite deposits of California, Oregon, Washington; field work geological investigations Columbia

River Gorge, Oregon, Monterey Bay area Calif, Virginia City, Nev, Wallowa Mountains, Ore., perlite in central Oregon, clay limestone and coal in western Oregon, Central Pa. coal. Author: Contributions to the Structure, Stratigraphy, and Petrology of the Lower Columbia River Gorge (thesis) '31; Caves Within Crater Lake National Park (unpub mss park files) '35; bulletins: Chromite Deposits in Oregon '38; Chromite Deposits of California '41; Geology of the San Juan Bautista Quadrangle, California '46; Reconnaissance Geology of Limestone Deposits in the Willamette Valley Oregon '46; Bibliography of Geology and Mineral Resources of Oregon, 1936-1945 '46; and others. Ranger naturalist Crater Lake Nat Park Ore '35; field geologist Rustless Iron & Steel Corp Baltimore '35-38; field geologist Ore Dept Geology & Mineral Industries '38-39, chief geologist '39-47; asso prof geology Pa State Coll '47 to 49; prof geol dept chmn NM Sch of Mines, Socorro, '49-52; econ geologist NM Bur Mines. Geol Soc Am(F)—Am Assn Petroleum Geologists(F)—Am Inst Mining & Metall Engrs—Seismolog Soc Am—AAAS—Geophys Union—Ore Country Geol Soc—Phi Beta Kappa—Sigma Xi. NM School of Mines, Box 27, Campus Station, Socorro, New Mexico.†

20 ALLEN, Merlin W(alters). Plant parasitic nemotodes; Systematics of free-living nematodes. b'12. BS '35—MS '37 (Utah State Agrl Coll); PhD '47 (U Calif). Author articles in field. Asst nematologist US Dept Agr Forest Service '43; asso expt sta U Calif '44-47; asst prof entomol and asst nematologist since '47. Helminthol Soc Washington—Am Assn Econ Entomol—Am Phytopath Soc—AAAS—Sigma Xi. 112 Agricultural Hall, University of California, Berkeley.†

21 ALLEN, Rhesa M(cCoy), Jr. Economic and structural geology; Petrology. b'16. BS '38 (VPI); MS '40 (U Idaho); PhD '47 (Cornell U). Author articles in field. Asso prof geol Va Poly Inst '48-49; mining engr French Coal Bluefield, WVa since '49. Geol Soc Am—Am Inst Mining Metall Engrs—Phi Beta Kappa—Sigma Xi—Phi Kappa Phi—Tau Beta Pi. 2409 Bland Rd., Bluefield, W.Va.

22 ALLEN, Richard Sanders. Covered Wooden Bridges. b'17. Research on location, dates of construction and builder, date first used and present condition of covered bridges throughout United States; collector historical items on covered bridges since '37. Author articles: Theodore Burr, Bridge Builder '44; Covered Bridges of the Farmington River '48; Covered Bridges for Fun and Profit '48. Co-editor Covered Bridge Topics (quarterly) since '43. U.S. Post Office, Round Lake, N.Y.†

23 ALLEN, Robert M(orris). Brain injury and diseases (Effects on personality); Psychometrics; Projective techniques; Encephalopathy; Criminal psychology (Parole risk). b'09. BS '32—PhD '40 (NY U); MA '33 (U Tex); '39 (Rorschach Inst Columbia U). Devised method of pattern analysis of Wechsler-Bellevue Intelligence scale for discovering true organic damage of patients. Author articles in field. Prof psychol U Miami Fla since '47; Lt US Army Adjutant General's office as chief psychologist of neuropsychiatric service of army hosps '42-45. American Psychological Assn(F)—Fla Psychol Assn—Soc. Proj. Tech. & Rorsch. Inst. Department of Psychology, University of Miami, Coral Gables, Fla.†

10 ALLEN, T(homas) Warren. Highway design and construction; Civil engineering. b'64. CE '86 (Union Coll). Mixing asphalt and stone at place of deposition on road; self dumping garbage scows; railroad construction Iowa and Ohio; river and harbor works New York; highway engineering, design and construction. Civil engr US and possessions to '09; state highway commnr New York '09-11; supt pub works Puerto Rico '11-13; Bur Pub Rds USDA '13-37; cons highway engr Hawaii '37-40; cons highway engr Conn '40-42. 9615 Glencrest Lane, Kensington, Md.

11 ALLEN, Victor Thomas. Clay petrography; China, refractory, ceramic and diaspore clay; Kaolin; Bauxite; Bentonite; Fullers earth; Foundary and concrete sands. b'98. AB '21—MS '22 (U Minn); PhD '28 (U Calif). Served as member of geological survey of Minn, Ill, Mo, US, pertaining to clay. Author articles in field. Dir geol dept St Louis U since '46. Geol Soc Am(F)—Mineral Soc Am(F)—AAAS(F)—Geol Soc Wash(F)—Am Soc Engring Edn—Sigma Xi. Department of Geology, St. Louis University, St. Louis 8.†☉

12 ALLER, Lawrence. Astrophysics; Spectroscopy; Atomic structure. b'13. AB '36 (U Calif); MA '38—PhD '43 (Harvard). Research on rotation of triangulum spiral nebula M33 (with N U Mayall), theory gaseous nebulae, stellar atmospheres, atomic structure, kinetic theory, statis mechanics, spectrophotometry stars and gaseous nebulae; experimental work in optics, spectroscopy, discharge electricity through gases, photographic photometry. Co-author: (with L Goldberg) Atoms, Stars and Nebulae '43. Physicist U Calif '43-45; asst prof astron Ind U '45-48; research asso McDonald Observatory U Tex '45-48; asso prof U Mich since '48. Astron Soc Pacific—Am Astron Soc—Internat Astron Union—Sigma Xi. The Observatory, University of Michigan, Ann Arbor.†

13 ALLIN, Benjamin Casey. Harbor, wharf, airport design; Port operation. b'86. Student '08 U Chicago). Designed overall physical and operational plans and policies including railroad network (with legal structure), waterfront utilization, construction and operation, wharves, grain elevator, fire-boat, etc., developed commerce from start to position of 4th US port at Houston, Stockton, and other places; prepared overall plan for marine terminal Leslie Salt Co; airport and harbor development plan for Miami; port for Bhavnigar India; designed improved system railroad-wharf connections; prepared master plans various California airports. Author "Allin amendment" to shipping acts. Dir port and chief engr Houston Tex '19-31, Stockton Calif '31-42; cons engr and tech appraiser since '45, also western asso Airways Engring Corp. Am Soc CE—Am Soc Tech Appraisers. 582 Market St., San Francisco 4.

14 ALLISON, Fred. Magneto-optics. b'82. AB '04—LLD '33 (Emory and Henry Coll); '07-08, '10-11 (Johns Hopkins); AM '21—PhD '22 (U Va); DSc '31 (Ala Poly Inst). Developed magneto-optic method of analysis from which with co-workers announced evidence for discovery of Element 87 '30, Element 85 '31. Author: College Physics Laboratory Instructions. Head prof physics Ala Poly Inst since '22, dean grad sch since '49, dir Auburn Rsrch Found '49-51. Am Phys Society (F, chmn SE sect '41)—AAAS—Ala

Acad Sci (pres '29)—Phi Beta Kappa—Phi Kappa Phi—Sigma Xi. Awarded President and Visitors' Research Prize U Va '25; Herty Research medal '33. Alabama Polytechnic Institute, Auburn, Ala.☉

15 ALLISON, Irl. Music education. b '96. AB '15 (Baylor U) AM'22 DrMus '47(Southwestern Cons Dallas) piano study Hoffman, Evans, Grainger, Hutcheson, von Mickwitz, Gilewicz. Instr piano Baylor Coll for Women '21-23; dean music Hardin Simmons U '27-34; pres Nat Guild Piano Teachers '34-45; Am Coll Musicians since '45. Editor The Guild Yearbook '36-45; Nat Directory Piano Teachers '36-45. 1500 Murray Lane, Austin 6, Tex.

16 ALLISON, J(oseph) Lewis. Plant pathology; Forage crop diseases. b'11. BS '34 (Mont State Coll); MS '36 (Wash State Coll); PhD '40 (U Minn). Research in, breeding for, disease resistance in forage legumes and grasses. Author articles in field. Charge disease investigations div forage crops and diseases Bur Plant Ind Soils and Agrl Engring US Dept Agr Beltsville, Md., '46-49; research prof plant path and senior plant path NC Agrl Expt Sta, Raleigh, NC. Am Phytopath Soc—Am Soc Agron—AAAS. 409 Yarmouth Rd., Raleigh, N.C.

17 ALLISON, Lowell Edward. Soils (Saline and alkaline); Soil microbiology. b'04. BS '30 (Purdue U); MS '33—PhD '42 (U Ill). Research on organic matter accumulation as affected by soil treatment, bacteriological analysis of soil, effect of chemical seed treatment on nodulation of legumes; isolation and testing of economic species of rhizobia for nitrogen-fixing efficiency; research on effect of potassium salts on ammonification and nitrification '36, phosphate fixation by soils and clays, microbial reduction, and seed and soil sterilization by gaseous treatment '37-42, water-repellant and toxic water-repellant preservative treatments for wood and fabrics '42-44; investigation of leaching and drainage to reclaim saline and alkali soils in Coachella Valley Calif and Delta area Utah. Author: Effect of Microorganisms on the Permeability of Soils Under Prolonged Submergence '47; (with R C Reeve and D F Peterson Jr) Reclamation of Saline-Alkali Soils by Leaching '48; (with others). Diagnosis and Improvement of Saline and Alkali Soils '47; also articles in field. Research asst soil chem and microbiol U Ill Agrl Expt Sta '30-36; asst prof soils Purdue U '37-42; research chem I F Laucks Inc Seattle '42-44; soil scientist US Salinity Laboratory Bur Plant Ind US Dept Agr Riverside, Calif since '44. Western Soc Soil Sci—Soil Sci Soc Am—AAAS—Sigma Xi. U.S. Salinity Laboratory, Riverside, Cal.

18 ALLMAN, H. B. Teacher training. b'90. BS '10 (Tri State Coll); '13-14 (Purdue U); AM '31—grad study (Ind U). Member Commission on Teacher Training and Licensing of Indiana State Board of Education '45-49; member staff State Survey of Education in Indiana '48-49. Co-author: Handbook on Teacher Education; also articles in field. Dir supervised teaching Ind U '30-36, dir summer sessions since '46. NEA (chmn com on tenure and academic freedom '42-48). Administration Building, Indiana University, Bloomington, Ind.

19 ALLPORT, Floyd Henry. Social psychology (Attitudes, psychology of morale, propaganda, rumor, personality); Public opinion; Behavior. b'90. AB '13—PhD '19 (Harvard).

Author: Social Psychology '24; Institutional Behavior '33, and others; also articles in field. Prof social and polit psychol Syracuse U since '24; acting ed Jour Abnormal and Social Psychol '21-24; mem Rumor Clinic and dir Morale Seminar of Syracuse U World War II, Social Sci Research Council '25-27 and 29-31, research sub-com President Hoover's Conf on Home Bldg and Home Ownership '31. AAAS(F)—Am Psychol Assn—Am Sociol Soc—Upper NY Psychol—Eastern Psychol Assn—Nat Inst Psychol—Soc Psychol Study Social Issues (council of dirs '38-40, chmn program com '38, chmn '40-41)—Sigma Xi—Phi Beta Kappa (hon). 164 Edgehill Rd., Syracuse 3, N.Y.☉

20 ALLPORT, Gordon Willard. Psycnology (Radio, personality, rumor). b'97. AB '19—AM '21—PhD '22 (Harvard); '22-23 (U Berlin, U Hamburg); '23-24 (Cambridge U). Author: Personality—A Psychological Interpretation '37; The Psychology of Radio '35; Psychology of Rumor '47. Prof psychol Harvard since '42. Am Psychol Assn (pres '39)—Eastern Psychol Assn (pres '43)—Sigma Xi—Phi Beta Kappa. 4 Arlington St., Cambridge 40.☉

21 ALMEN, John Otto. Fatigue of metals; Strength of materials; Residual stresses; Gear design and lubrication. b.'86. Student '08-10 (Wash State Coll). Designed, patented and developed numerous testing machines, tools and instruments in extensive use such as Neon engine spark timing protractor, Almen lubricants testing machines, tools and instruments for shot peening, hammer peening and pressure rolling, automatic transmissions and Hydramatic control system, resonance engine intake silencers, automatic valve adjusters, practical formulas for determining the scoring tendencies of aircraft gears. Author article: Durability of Automobile Gears '35; also articles on fatigue strength of materials. Research cons Research Labs Gen Motors Corp since '47. AAAS—Engring Soc Detroit—SAE—Am Soc Metals—Am Ordnance Assn—Am Gear Mfg Assn. Received Modern Pioneer award '40, Manly Memorial Medal '44, materials and methods achievement award '46, Edward P Connell award '45. Research Laboratory Division, General Motors Corporation, Detroit.†

22 ALMQUIST, Herman James. Animal nutrition. b'03. BS '25 (Mont State Coll); PhD '32 (U Cal); DSc(hon) '52 (Mont State Coll). Research in mechanism of auto-oxidation; nutritional role and requirements of amino acids and proteins, interrelation of choline, betaine and methionine carotene conversion and vitamin A requirements; preparation and use of protein hydrolysates; manufacture of shark liver oils; co-discoverer isolation identification of pure forms and synthesis of vitamin K. Author articles in field. Instr, asst prof, asso prof U Cal Coll Agr '32-44; dir research FE Booth Co '44-48; dir research and nutrition, also vice pres The Grange Company since '48. American Chemical Society—American Society Biological Chemists—AAAS(F)—Soc Exptl Biol and Med—Am Inst Nutrition—Poultry Sci Assn—Inst Food Tech. Received Borden award in poultry nutrition '39. The Grange Co. Modesto, Cal.

23 ALPERT, Carl. Jewish history (Modern). b'13. '29-30 (Hebrew Teachers Coll Boston); '31-34 (Boston U); '42 (George Washington U). Editor The New Palestine '40-46. Author: Oracle, Jewish Reference Book '35; To the Land of Their Fathers '37; Jewish Contributions to Civilization

'38; The Truth About the Jews '39; Palestine Between Two Wars '45; also articles in field. Asso ed Jewish Advocate Boston '35-40, Universal Jewish Encyclopedia since '39; nat pres Young Judaea '40-41; nat dir edn dept Zionist Organization of Am since '46; asso ed World-Scope Encyclopedia since '47. 41 East 42nd St., NYC 17. H: 200 Tompkins Av., Staten Island 4, N. Y.

10 ALPERT, Harry. Social statistics (Population, vital statistics, criminal statistics, public health); French sociology. b'12. AB '32 (Coll City NY ; Certificate '32 (U Paris); Certificat de Sociologie '33 (U Bordeaux); AM '35—PhD '38 (Columbia). Research in public opinion and tension area; social and political structure of enemy and occupied countries; local community problems. Author: Emile Durkheim and His Sociology '39. Instr and asst prof sociol Coll City NY '33-47; pub opinion analyst OWI '43-44; pub opinion and rationing statis analyst OPA '44-45; social statis analyst Bur the Budget '45-48; asso prof sociol and chmn dept anthrop and sociol Queens Coll '48-50; Social Statis Analyst Bur the Budget since '50. Am Sociol Soc—Eastern Sociol Soc—Am Assn for Pub Opinion Research—Am Statis Assn—Am Anthrop Assn—DC Sociol Soc—Population Assn Am—Phi Beta Kappa. Inst Internat Edn Franco-American Exchange Fellow; Columbia U University Fellow in Sociology; Social Sci Research Council Postdoctoral Research Fellow. Bureau of the Budget, Washington 25.

11 ALPERT, Leo. Climatology; Military geography; Meteorology; Artificial precipitation; Artificial modification of clouds. b'15. BS Ed '37 (Massachusetts State Teachers Coll); MA '39—PhD '46 (Clark U). Research in tropical meteorology Caribbean and Eastern Pacific Ocean area, forecast verification, aircraft weather accidents, applied meteorology and climatology, military geography of Latin America and Antarctic, geographic factors in military operations. Author articles: The Intertropical Convergence Zone of the Eastern Pacific Region '45, 46; Weather Over the Tropical Eastern Pacific Ocean '46; Atmospheric Cross-Sections of the Stratus Zone of the Tropical Eastern Pacific Ocean '46; and others. Chief applied meteorol sect research and development branch Hq Air Weather Service Oct-Nov '46; research geog and specialist climatology Terrain Sect Topographic Branch Intelligence Div Office Chief Staff US War Dept '46-47; spl analyst and cons climatology Topographic Branch Intelligence Div Dept Army since '47. Weather officer US Air Forces '40-46, asst tech advisor research and development branch HQ Air Weather Service '43-46. Am Meteorol Soc—Am Soc Profl Geog. Department of the Army, Washington 25.†

12 ALT, Franz Leopold. High-speed electronic automatic digital computing machines. b'10. PhD '32 (U Vienna). Research in point set geometry, foundations of geometry, numerical methods; studies high-speed electronic automatic digital computing machines, mathematical economics, economic forecasting, time series analysis. Author: On the Measurability of Utility '36; Distributed Labs '42; A Bell Telephone Laboratories Computing Machine '48; Steady State Solution of the Equation of Burning '48; Boundary Value Problems from Multiply Connected Domains '52. Successively research prin., chief analyst, asst dir research Econometric Inst NY '38-43, '45-46; dep chief computation lab Nat Bur Standards since '48, asst chief

'48-52, asst chief applied math div since '52. Washington Acad Sci—Am Math Soc—Am Statis Assn—Econometric Soc—Inst Math Statis—Assn Computing Machinery. National Bureau of Standards, Washington.†

13 ALTER, Amos Joseph. Arctic sanitary engineering. b'16. BS '38—CE '49 (Purdue U); M Pub Health '48 (U Mich). Investigations water supply practice, waste disposal practice and housing in Arctic Alaska; developed policies for sanitary engineering practice; provided consultation through official agency to builders and operators sanitary engineering facilities in Alaska; investigation water and sewage treatment methods under low temperature conditions; cold weather protection of sanitary facilities; sources water supply in regions where ground is permanently frozen; impounding reservoir design for water systems located in subarctic; occurrence filthborne diseases in Arctic and subarctic. Author: Arctic Sanitary Engineering '49. Contributor: Encyclopedia Arctica '49. San engr Alaska Dept Health since '46. Am Soc CE—Am Water Works Assn—Am Pub Health Assn—Pacific NW Sewage Works Assn—Conf State San Engrs—Tech Assn Pulp and Paper Industry—NRC (subcom on waste disposal of san engring com)—Alaska Water Pollution Control Bd (adminstr.) Box 1931, Juneau, Alaska.†

14 ALTER, Chester M. Education administration; Social services administration; Chemistry (Atomic energy). b'06. BS '27(Ball State Teacher's Coll) AM '28 (Ind U) PhD'36 (Harvard). Prof chemistry Boston U since '40 acting dean Grad Sch '44-45 tech cons since '38 dean since '45; tech cons mem research com Sec commn research and atomic energy New England Council; pres New England Conf on Grad Edn '48-49; pres Newton Community Chest. Am Chem Soc—Alpha Chi Sigma—Sigma Xi—Phi Lambda Upsilon. 725 Commonwealth Ave., Boston.†⊙

15 ALTHAUSEN, Darrell. Flavors (Manufacture, composition, evaluation); Essential oils (Production, constitution, evaluation). b'01. BSc '25 (U Okla); PhD '32 (U Ill). Co-author: Chemistry of Essential Oils '49; also articles in field. Mgr Clifton Factory Fritzsche Bros Inc Clifton NJ '46-51; tech dir Ungerer & Co since '51. Major AUS assigned QM subsistence research and development Lab Chicago '44-45. Am Chem Soc—QM Food and Container Inst (liaison and sci adv bd). Ungerer & Co 650 Union Blvd., Totowa, N.J.

16 ALTLAND, Paul Daniel. Reproductive cycles of turtles and lizards; High altitude exposure effect on reproductive potential (mammals). b'13. BS '34 (Gettysburg Coll); AM '36—PhD '37 (Duke U); '39 (U Ia). Research in aviation medicine, investigation of the effect of short daily exposures to high altitude on growth development behavior and longevity of animals, cytology of hypophysis of fence lizard. Author articles in field. Asst prof biol Gettysburg Coll '40-44; asst physiol Nat Inst Health Bethesda Md '44-46, asso physiol '46-47, physiol since '47. Pa Acad Sci—Am Soc Zool—AAAS—Soc Exptl Biol and Med—Am Physiol Soc—Sigma Xi. Nat Inst of Arthritis and Metabolic Diseases, National Institutes of Health, Bethesda, Md.

17 ALVAREZ, Daniel Armando, Jr. Mosquito control. b'24. BS '43 AB '43—MS '44 (Camaguey Coll); MD '50 (Haven U Med Coll); PhD '51 (Cornell

U). Research on use of female love call of mosquito to exterminate male mosquitoes. Lecturer Havana U Med Sch '49; faculty mem Cornell U Med Coll since '51. Am Soc Parasitol—Am Soc Tropical Med and Hygiene—Cuban Soc Natural Hist—AAAS—Cuban Med Soc. Cornell University Medical College, 1300 York Av., NYC 21.

18 ALVAREZ, Luis W. Nuclear physics; Radar; Air navigation. b'11. Engaged in radar research and development MIT '40-43; atomic bomb research and development Los Alamos NM '43-45. Prof physics U Calif since '45. Am Phys Soc(F)—Nat Acad Sci—Phi Beta Kappa—Sigma Xi. Awarded Collier Aviation Trophy '47. University of California, Berkeley.⊙

19 ALY, Bower. Rhetoric; Public address; American public address (History); Alexander Hamilton (Life and speeches); forensic speaking. b'03. BS '25 (S E Mo State Coll); AM '26 (U Mo); PhD '41 (Columbia); '29 (U Calif). Author: A Course Book in Public Speaking '34, '39; The Rhetoric of Alexander Hamilton '41; Editor: Radio Control and Operation '33; Equalizing Educational Opportunity '34 World Organization '42; Youth Suffrage '44; Medical Care '46; American Labor '47. Prof speech and dir forensics U Mo since '44. Speech Assn Am (exec council; 1st vp '43, pres '44)—Am Acad Polit and Social Sci—Foreign Policy Assn—AHA—Kappa Delta Pi. 321 Switzler Hall, Columbia, Mo.⊙

20 AMACKER, David Muir. International relations; History Political Theory; Agricultural legislation; Political science. b'97. AB '17 (Princeton) BA '22 MA '27 (Oxford). Farm operator; cotton raiser; international political organizations; international relations; cotton farmer organizations; agricultural legislation. Co-editor: La. Dept. Public Works Bull., '51 Asst prof polit sci Dartmouth '30-36; asso prof history La Poly Inst '27-28; prof polit sci Southwestern U since '36. Mem. Memphis Atlantic Union Com., Beltwide Cotton Acreage Conf., '49. Southwestern University, Memphis 12, Tenn.⊙

21 AMBERG, Charles Rhodimer. Ceramic engineering (Refractories, Whitewares, Vitreous enamels, Glass, Heavy clay products, Raw materials, Optical mineralogy, X-ray diffraction, crystal chemistry). b'05. BS '27 (Alfred U); MS '29 (U Ill); PhD '48 (Penn State Coll). Holder with others patents on vitreous coating refractory material and antiseptic cement. Author articles in field. Head dept ceramic research NY State Coll Ceramics '43—51; dir Alfred U Research Lab since '49. Am Ceramic Soc(F)—AAAS(F)—Am Soc Engring Edn—Inst Ceramic Engrs—Ceramic Ednl Council—Sigma Xi. Alfred U Research Lab., R.R. 1, Box 212B, Kingston, N.Y.

22 AMBERG, Hans George. Theatre arts, history and aesthetics; Stage design and directing; The dance. b'01. Student (Us Kiel, Munich, Cologne); PhD '29 (U Cologne). Founder progressive theatre Cassette Cologne '23. Author: Art in Modern Ballet '46; Ballet in America '49; also articles in field. Theatre arts consultant, The Mus Modern Art NYC since '43, lecturer in arts NYU. Am Soc Aesthetics—Am Nat Theatre and Acad—Theatre Library Assn—Coll Art Assn. Museum of Modern Art, 11 W. 53rd St., NYC 19.

23 AMBERG, Raymond Michael. Hospital surveys. b'95. PhC '20 (U Minn). Chmn Minn State Hospital Survey) dir University of Minnesota Hospitals. 1575 Northrop St., St. Paul 8.

10 AMBLER, Charles Henry. History & Politics of Virginia and West Virginia. b'76. AB '04—Am '05 (W Va U); PhD '08 (U Wis). Sectionalism in Virginia; Ohio Valley transportation. Author: Sectionalism in Virginia from 1777 to 1861 '10; Thomas Ritchie—A Study in Virginia Politics '12; Life of John Floyd '18; A History of Transportation in the Ohio Valley with Special Reference to Waterways '32; A History of West Virginia '33; George Washington and the West '36; Francis H. Pierpont, Union War Governor of Virginia and Father of West Virginia '37; West Virginia Stories and Biographies '37; West Virginia, The Mountain State '40; also pamphlets and articles; editor: John P. Branch Hist Papers '08-17; also many other papers, letters etc. Prof History and Polit Sci Randolph-Macon Coll Ashland Va '08-17; prof History W Va U since '17, also head dept History '29-46; prof summers sessions U Tex '18-20 and '24; vis prof O State U '28-29; pres Sch Bd Monongalia County W Va '33-39. AHA—So Hist Assn—Miss Valley Hist Assn (pres '42-43)—Phi Beta Kappa—Tau Kappa Alpha. 128 Simpson Morgantown, W. Va.⊚

11 AMBLER, Charles Melville. Centrifuges (Industrial application). b'07. BS '27 (U Pa). Holder US patents on oil purification, methods of purifying lubrication oils, extracting tar acids from crude tar, purifying used oils, recovering tar acid, purifying extracting solvent. Author articles in field. Chem Texas Co, '27-28; process engr, chief chem Sharples Corp predecessor Sharples Specialty Co since '28. Am Inst Chem Engrs—Assn Iron Steel Engrs. The Sharples Corporation, 2300 Westmoreland St., Phila. 40.†

12 AMEEL, Donald Jules. Parasitology; Helminthology. b'07. BA '28 (Wayne U); MA '30—ScD '33 (Mich U). Research on life history, distribution in North America and taxonomy of Paragonimus, life history of Crepidostomum cornutum and Nudacotyle novicia, cercariae infecting Pomatiopsis lapidaria. Author articles in field. Prof and head dept zool Kan State Coll since '45. Kan Acad Sci—Am Microscopical Soc—AAAS—Am Soc Parasitol. Department of Zoology, Kansas State College, Manhattan, Kan.†

13 AMERINE, Maynard Andrew. Enology; Plant physiology. b'11. BS '32—PhD '36 (U Calif). Author articles in field. Instr enology and jr enologist Expt Sta U Calif '36, asso prof enology and asso enologist '47-52, prof enology and enologist since '52. Inst Food Tech—AAAS—Am Assn Hort Sci—Am Chem Soc—Sigma Xi. Division of Viticulture, University of California, Davis, Cal.

14 AMES, Lawrence Marion. Dermatology; Fungi (Coprophilous, dermatophytes, cellulose destroying); Berberis and Mahonia. b' 00. MS '37 (Mich State Coll); PhD '33 (Harvard). Author: articles in field. Patent pending on an ointment registered as AFO for treatment of fungal skin diseases; more than 2000 cases of army and civilian personnel have been successfully treated. Research Mycologist Engr Research and Development Labs Ft Belvoir Va since '45. Mycol Soc Am—Torrey Bot Club—New Eng Bot Club—Washington Bot Soc. Sigma Xi. Materials Branch, Engineering Research and Development Laboratories, Fort Belvoir, Va.

15 AMIRIKIAN, Arsham. Structures (framed and welded, precast concrete, cellular framing and floating); Bomb-proof design and construction. b'99. Grad '17 (Coll Bezazian Constantinople); '19 (Ecole Superieure des Ponts et Chaussees (Constantinople); CE '23 (Cornell U). Developed newer methods analysis and applied to design shore structures and auxiliary floating craft for Navy; originated and developed new construction technique utilizing thin-wall cells and hollow-section precast reinforced concrete segments and applied to framings various structures; developed system wedge-beam framing. Author: Analysis of Rigid Frames '42; also articles in field. Assistant engineer design, supervision public works structures steel, concrete, timber Bur Yards and Docks US Navy Dept Washington '28-29, head designing engr since '45; lecturer nat defense engring training courses George Washington U '41-42; passive defense courses US Navy '42-43, grad sch US Dept Agr, Rensselaer Poly Inst '46-48, and others. Member ASCE—Soc Am Mil Engrs—Naval Architects and Marine Engrs—Am Concrete Inst (chmn com precast concrete structures)—Am Welding Soc—Washington Acad Sciences—Sigma Xi—Internat Assn Nav Congresses. Received (with Capt C A Trexel) first grand award '42 and first divisional award '47 James F. Lincoln Arc Welding Found; Fuertes Graduate Metal Cornell U '43; meritorious service award US Navy '46 Bureau of Yards and Docks, Navy Department, Washington. H: 6526 Western Av., Chevy Chase 15, Md.†⊚

16 AMIS, Edward Stephen. Electrochemistry. b'05. BS '30—MS '33 (U Ky); PhD '38 (Columbia). Research on comparison of glass, hydrogen, and quinhydrone electrodes; conductivity of electrolytes at infinite dilution as function of dielectric constant; dielectric constant and ionic strength effects on rates of chemical reaction. Author: Kinetics of Chemical Change in Solution '49 Instr, asst prof and asso prof chem La State U '39-46; research chem and sr research chem Carbide and Carbon Chem Corp '46-47; prof chem U Ark since '47; research participant Oak Ridge Nat Lab '51. ACS—Sigma Xi—Sigma Pi Sigma—Pi Mu Epsilon—Phi Lambda Upsilon—Alpha Chi Sigma. Chemistry Department, University of Arkansas, Fayetteville, Ark.†

17 AMNER, Floyd Dewey. Spanish-American magazines. b'00 AB '23 (Colgate U); MA '27 (Denison U) PhD '38 (O State U). Initiation and operation of service agency to procure Spanish-American magazines for libraries and schools. Author: Hispano-American Culture Studied Through Hispano-American Literature in Translation '42; Revista de America (2 vols) '43, '46. Instr advancing to asso prof modern langs Denison U '25-45; prof fgn langs Kent State U '45-50; prof Hispanic Studies since '50. Kent State University, Kent, O.

18 AMSTUZ, John O. Abrasives (Coated). b'93 EE '18 (Switzerland). Research on mechanical coating processes and electrocoating, using electrostatic field forces for grain and fiber orientations, electrocoated textile fabrics, floor coverings, design and building of equipment. Granted patents on coating, electrostatic coating process, abrasive disks, pile fabrics and methods for making them. Designer NY Edison Co '21-22; in charge radio div Maxim Mfg Co '22-24; designer, constr and field engr Thomas E Murray and D P Robinson Cons Engrs '25-28; with Behr-Manning Corp since '29, dir and vp in charg engring and mfg since 1946. Am Inst EE—Am Soc ME—Nat Soc Prof Engrs Soc Am Mil Engrs—Tau Beta Pi—Pi Tau Sigma—Sigma Xi. Behr-Manning Corp., Troy, N.Y.

19 AMYX, D(arrell) A(rlynn). Classical archaeology; History of ancient art; Greek vases. b'11. AB '30 (Stanford); MA '32—PhD '37 (U Calif); fellow '35-36 (Am Sch Classical Studies Athens). Commissioned to prepare emergency catalogue of Greek vases in Portland Art Museum Ore '43. Author: An Amphora with a Price Inscription in the Hearst College at San Simeon '41; Corinthian Vases in the Hearst Collection at San Simeon '43. Instr Latin U Calif '46, asst prof art '46-52, asso prof since '52, asst curator ancient Mediterranean art '48-52, asso cur since '52 asso ed publications in classical archaeol since '47. Am Philol Assn—Philol Assn Pacific Coast—Archaeol Inst Am (sec-treas San Francisco Soc since '48, nominating com '49)—Classical Assn Pacific States—Phi Beta Kappa. Travelaid grant Am Council of Learned Socs '41. Spreckels Art Building, University of California, Berkeley 4.

20 ANDER, O(scar) Fritiof. History of immigration; Sweden (history). b '03. BA '26 (Augustana Coll); MA'27—PhD '30 (U Ill). Grant for research Swedish-American press Am Council Learned Soc '34, '35; Guggenheim Memorial fellowship research history Sweden since 1815 '38-40; mem editorial com American Heritage '47. Author: T N Hasselquist, The Career and Influence of a Swedish-American Clergyman, Journalist, and Educator '31; Swedish-American Political Newspapers; A Guide '36. Co-author: (with O L Nordstrom) The American Origin of the Augustana Synod '42; Guide to Material on Swedish History in the Augustana College Library '34. Editor: Industrial Rock Island '47; The Indians in the History of the United States, Illinois, and Rock Island County '47; also articles in field. Asst prof hist Augustana Coll Rock Island Ill '30-31, asso prof '31-33, prof since '33, head hist dept since '35, chmn div social studies since '43. AHA (mem Com Teaching Am Hist in Schools and Coll)—Miss Valley Hist Assn (mem Com Teaching Am Hist in Schs and Coll)—Nat Council Social Studies (mem Com Teach Am Hist in Schs and Coll)—Ill State Hist Soc (chmn Com Teaching State and Local Hist in pub schs, vp '43, dir '40). Ill Council for Social Studies (chmn Com Teaching State and Local Hist in pub schs) —Am - Scandinavian Foundation — Augustana Inst Swedish Culture (dir '41). Augustana Coll., Rock Island, Ill.†⊚

21 ANDERS, John Olson. Swedish-American history; Rural sociology. b'92. BA '15—MA '18 (U SD); fellowship '21-22 (U Chicago); PhD '30 (U Minn). Research, historical and sociological, in American immigration, especially Swedish, and cultural role of immigrant in American rural life. Author: Origin and History of Swedish Religious Organizations in Minnesota '32; The Swedes on the American Church Frontier '38; Educational Beginnings in a Typical Prairie County '42; also articles in field. Prof social science Northern Teachers Coll., Aberdeen, S.D., since '48. AHA—Rural Sociological Soc—Norwegian-American Historical Assn—Minn Hist Soc. Northern State Teachers College, Aberdeen, S. D.†

22 ANDERSEN, Arthur Olaf. Music education; Orchestrations; musical theory. b'80. Dr Mus '34 (Am Conservatory Music). Teacher musical theory '04 head theory dept Am Conservatory Mus '29-34; dir Sch Music and dean Coll Fine Arts U Ariz since

'34. Author: Harmony, First Forty Lessons, '23 Second Forty Lessons, '23; Musical Theory Books I and II, '26; Strict and Free Counterpoint, '31; Practical Orchestration, '29; Harmony, Modern Resources, '38. Nat Music Teachers Assn—ASCAP—Nat Collegiate Players. Catalina Foothills, Tucson, Ariz.☉

10 ANDERSEN, Axel Langvad. Agricultural plant pathology (Celery, onion, peppermint, ornamentals, beans). b'14. BS '37 (U Minn); MS '41—PhD '47 (Mich State Coll); '32-34 (Grand View Coll). Research in control of plant diseases of celery, onions, peppermint and ornamentals by hybridization and application of fungicides; experimented in relation of soil temperature and moisture to infection of onions and in methods of increasing effectiveness of plant inoculation. Author articles: The Pink Root Disease of Onions '42; The Relation of Hydrogen-ion Concentration to Growth and Sporulation of Gibberella Zeae Headblight of Wheat '48; and others. Research asst in plant path Mich Agr Expt Sta '39-42; 1st lt CWS US Army, conductor research plant path '43-45; plant path Chem Corps Camp Detrick Md '46-48; asso plant path div fruit and vegetable crops and diseases US Dept Agr since '48. Am Phytopath Soc—Bot Soc Am—AAAS—Sigma Xi. Department of Botany and Plant Pathology, Michigan State College, East Lansing, Mich. H: 1028 Snyder Road.

11 ANDERSON, Agnes Graves Donalson. Children (Under foster care, state supported institutional care). b'06. AB '48 (Wesleyan Coll Ga); MA '41 (U Chicago); '34-35 (Sch Social Work Tulane U). Special studies in field made of San Antonio, Atlanta, Dayton and San Diego. Author articles in field. Cons and supervisor children's instns Ga State Dept Pub Welfare '36-40; regional supervisor USO Traveler's Aid '41-44; field rep Nat Traveler's Aid Assn '44-45; asst prof social work div social service Ind U since '45. Am Acad Polit Social Sci—Am Assn Social Workers—Am Assn Schs Social Work (on preprofessional com '48, '49, '50). Division of Social Service, Indiana University, Bloomington, Ind.

12 ANDERSON, Alfred L(eonard). Mining geology and ore genesis; Geology and ore deposits of Idaho. b'00. BS '22—MS '23 (U Idaho); PhD '31 (U Chicago). Extensive research in genesis of ore deposits, structural control of ore deposition and petrology; genetic and structural aspects of mineralization, nature and origin of igneous rocks and significance and origin of various land features. Co-author: Influence of Structure in Localizing Ore '40; also articles in field. Asst geol Idaho Bur Mines and Geol '26-27, geol '28-31, '42-52; asst geol US Geol Survey; geol '49; asst prof geol U Idaho Sch Mines '28-31, prof '31-39; asst prof geol Cornell U '39-40 associate professor '40-52, professor since '52; geologist WAE US Geological Survey since '49. Soc Econ Geol—Geol Soc Am(F)—AAAS (F)—Mineral Soc Am(F)—Am Inst Mining Metal Engrs—Am Geophys Union—Sigma Xi. Department of Geology, McGraw Hall, Cornell University, Ithaca, N.Y.

13 ANDERSON, Bruce E. Propellants; Ballistics; Ignition; Explosives. b'97. AB '24 (Colo Coll). Assistant editor Chemical Abstracts, charge section 24 (explosives and explosions) since '47. Author: Courses of Instruction on Ballistics; also articles in field. Ordnance engr chief of propellant and primer sect Research and Development Div

US Army Ordnance Office since '29. Am Ordnance Assn—Philos Soc Washington—Am Chem Soc. Office, Chief of Ordnance, U.S. Army, Washington 25.

14 ANDERSON, Carl David. Gamma and cosmic rays; Positron. b'05. BS '27 —PhD '30—Coffin research fellow '27-28 —teach fellow '28-30—research fellow '30-33 (Calif Inst Tech); hon ScD '37 (Colgate U). Research on X-Ray photoelectrons '27-30; research on gamma rays and cosmic-rays since '30; discoverer of positron '32. Prof physics Calif Inst Tech since '39. Am Phys Soc—Am Philos Soc—Nat Acad Sci— Tau Beta Pi—Sigma Xi. Awarded gold medal Am Inst City NY '35; Nobel prize physics '36; Elliott Cresson medal of the Franklin Inst '37. California Institute of Technology, Pasadena, Calif.☉

15 ANDERSON, Charles A(lfred). Volcanic rocks (United States); Ariz copper deposits. b'02. AB '24 (Pomona Coll); PhD '28 (U Calif). Research on volcanoes in northern California '28-38, volcanic rocks in central Nevada '38-40, geology of islands in Gulf of California '40, molybdenum deposits in western U. S. '42-43, copper deposits Arizona since '43. Author: Volcanic History of Glass Mountain, Northern California '33; Tuscan Formation of Northern California '33; Volcanoes of Medicine Lake Highland California '41. Co-author: (with R H Finch) The Quartz Basalt Eruptions of Cinder Cone, Lassen Volcanic National Park, California '30. Instr geol U Calif '28-30, asst prof geol '30-38, asso prof '38-42; geol US Geol Survey since '42. Geol Soc Am(F)—Mineral Soc Am(F)—Am Geophys Union—Soc Econ Geol—Am Inst Mining Metall Engrs. US Geological Survey Washington 25.†

16 ANDERSON, C(harles) Arnold. Social mobility (Role of education and mate selection). b'07. BA '27—MA '28—PhD '32 (U Minn); '29-30 (Harvard). Comparative selectivity of educational opportunity, comparative social class systems. Author articles in field. Sociol prof Ia State Coll and Ia Agrl Expt Sta '36-44; sociol prof U Ky since '45. Am Sociol Soc—Rural Sociol Soc—Population Assn Am—Sigma Xi—Phi Beta Kappa. Department of Sociology, University of Kentucky, Lexington, Ky.

17 ANDERSON, Charles Roberts. American Literature (Herman Melville; Sidney Lanier; Cultural History of Charleston, S.C.). b'02. AB '24—AM '28 (U Ga); PhD '39 (Columbia); Rosenwald fellow '38-39. Author: Melville in the South Seas '39; editor Journal of a Cruise in the Frigate United States with notes on Melville '37; gen editor Centennial Edition of Sidney Lanier (10 vols) '45; contbr professional jours. Instr English U Ga '27-30; instr English Duke U '30-35 asst prof '35-39 asso prof '39-41; asso prof Am Lit Johns Hopkins U '41-45 prof since '46 chmn Eng Dept since '50; managing editor Am Lit '32-33; asso editor Modern Language Notes since '42; guest prof Heidelberg U '49; Modern Lang Assn Am—Phi Beta Kappa—Middle Atlantic Soc for Am Studies—Soc Am Historians. Add: Johns Hopkins University, Baltimore 18, Md.; H: Rockland, Brooklandville, Md.☉

18 ANDERSON, Chester Reed. Business English; Correspondence; Business report writing; Direct mail. b'98. AB '18 (Hedding Coll); AM '20 (U Ill). Author: Articles in field. Prof and head div business Eng U Ill. Am Business Writing Assn (sec and editor since '36) —Am Marketing Assn—College Eng

Assn. 101 David Kinley Hall, Urbana, Ill.

19 ANDERSON, Curtis E(dwin). Trade relations (Intra-European). b'10. AB '33 (Oberlin Coll); '41 (U Chicago Bus Sch); '45 (Am U); '48 (Northeastern U). Author: Automatic Merchandising Sales Goal Three Billion '47; An Expanded Outline of a Study in Geo-Economics of the City of Lorain '32; also articles in field. Tech recruitment specialist Personnel Div WPB Washington '41, sr indsl specialist rubber sect '42; asst to vp Rubber Development Corp RFC Washington '42-43; indsl specialist service trades div WPB Washington '43-45; marketing analyst War Assets Administrn Washington '46; spl asst U S Dept Commerce '46-48; asst exec sec Econ Coop Adminstrn Washington since '48, sec Fiscal and Trade Problems Adv Com since '48. Am Marketing Assn (treas Wash chap '49-50)— Am Econ Assn—Royal Econ Soc(F). 800 Connecticut Av., Washington 25. H: Laurel Ridge Farm, R.F.D. 3, Box 132, Herndon, Va.

20 ANDERSON, Dewey. Economics (Taxation, American labor, small business problems, economic power concentration, monopoly practices). b'97. AB '27—MA '28—PhD '32 (Stanford). Author: Our California State Taxes, Facts and Problems '37; Taxation, Recovery and Defense '40; Report of the Executive Secretary on the Concentration of Economic Power in the United States '41; California State Government '42; Recent Trends in American Labor '45, and others; also articles in field. Co-dir Inst Occupational Research Stanford U since '36; exec dir Pub Affairs Inst since '47. Phi Beta Kappa. 312 Penna Av., Washington.☉

21 ANDERSON, Earl Jennings. Root diseases. b'08. BS '32—MS '34 (Wash State Coll); PhD '37 (U Md). Emergency Production Committee Honolulu '41-43, exec committee Washington State Postwar Planning Committee '43. Research path Pineapple Research Inst U Hawaii Honolulu TH since '45; head pathology department since '50. AAAS —Am Phytopath Soc—Phi Kappa Phi— Sigma Xi. Awarded fellowship Nat Research Council '37. Pineapple Research Institute, University of Hawaii, Honolulu, T.H.

22 ANDERSON, Earl William. Teacher supply and demand; Personnel. b'97. Diploma '16 (Eastern Ill State Normal Sch); BA '18 (U Ill); MA '24 —PhD '26—post doctorate fellow '35-36 (Columbia U). Author: Articles in field. Prof edn in teacher edn and higher edn Ohio State U since '37. Am Edn Research Assn (com to prepare three-year Reviews in Teacher Personnel '31, chmn '34, '37, '43, '46). Arps Hall, Ohio State University, Columbus 10, O.

23 ANDERSON, Edgar. Plant genetics; Maize; Hybridization. b'97. BS '18 (Mich State Coll); MS ScD '22 (Harvard). Co-author: Corn and Corn Growing. Prof bot Washington U since '35. Soc Am Naturalists—Herb Soc Am— Bot Soc Am—Sigma Xi. Guggenheim fellow '43-44, '50-51. Missouri Botanical Garden, St. Louis.☉

24 ANDERSON, Edwin Joseph Arthur. Beekeeping. b'00. BS '24 (Pa State Coll); MS '25 (Cornell U). Research on equipment for extracting, heating, and bottling honey, uses and properties of honey, apiary management, rearing of queen bees; editor of Pennsylvania Beekeeper since '27. Author: Diseases and Enemies of the Honeybee. Faculty Pa State Coll '21-24; apiary insp Pa State Dept Agr '20-24; faculty Clemson Coll '25-26;

24 *For selected subjects "keyed" to information sources, turn to Locator Index (page 871).*

with Pa State Coll since '26, asso prof apiculture since '47. Am Assn Econ Entomol—Am Beekeeping Fedn. Dairy Building, State College, Pa.

10 ANDERSON, John Merrick. Wildlife management (Waterfowl, muskrat). b'17. BSc '40 (O State U). Research on study waterfowl species nesting Pennsylvania '38, trapping and banding waterfowl to study migration, kill-rate, longevity and sex-age ratios Illinois River '39-40, census and life history Trumpeter Swan Montana '39, survival and growth rate game fish Illinois lakes '40-41; research waterfowl migration, local nesting, food habits, hunting pressure and muskrat ecology southwestern Lake Erie marshes to develop practical management program for region for Winous Point Shooting Club since '46;Elected Chairman of Mississippi Flyway Waterfowl Committee '48. Author articles: Sex Ratio and Weights of Southwestern Lake Erie Muskrats '47; Lake Erie Waterfowl Populations and Kill '47. Wildlife Soc—Am Soc Mammalogists—Am Ornithol Union—Wilson Ornithol Club—Am Audubon Soc—AFA. Winous Point Shooting Club, Port Clinton, O.

11 ANDERSON, Lawrence B. Heating (Solar). b'06. BS (Architecture) '27 (U Minn); M Arch '30 (MIT); '30-33 (Ecole des Beaux Arts). Member of committee on design, construction, and operation of 600 square foot dwelling heated almost entirely by sun during winters '48-49 and '49-50. Staff sch architecture and planning MIT since '33. Massachusetts Institute of Technology, Cambridge 38, Mass.†☉

12 ANDERSON, Marjorie. Old English; Chaucer; Middle English. b'92. AB '13 (Smith Coll); AM '16 (Columbia); '22-23 (Johns Hopkins); PhD '26—fellow '24-26 (U Chicago). Research on Alice Chaucer and her husbands, Blanche, Duchess of Lancaster. Author: (with Blanche Colton Williams) An Old English Handbook '35. Asst prof Eng Hunter Coll '32-42, asso prof since '42, chmn dept since '47. Modern Lang Assn Am—Mediaeval Acad—Nat Council Teachers Eng—Phi Beta Kappa. Hunter College, 695 Park Av., NYC 21.

13 ANDERSON, Martin. Church (Planning, financing). '82. BA '06 (St Olaf Coll Northfield Minn); CT '09 (Luther Theol Sem St Paul Minn); DD '15 (Fargo Coll ND). Consultant church building and financing projects, church architecture. Author: Planning and Financing the New Church (3rd edit) '49. Assisted in planning and financing new church, First Lutheran Church Albert Lea Minn '20-27, United Lutheran Church Oak Park Ill '27-37; church bldg cons since '37. H: 644 N. Oak Park Av., Oak Park, Ill.

14 ANDERSON, Nelson Jay. Physical chemistry (Plastics); Quartermaster Corps (history). b'94. BS '20 (Kan State Coll); MS '22 (U Ill); PhD '34 (U Chicago). Developed method of soldering aluminum '39-40; research '36-39 on solubility of sulfides in polysulfides; research in chemical thermodynamics, chemical inspection, research and development plastic armor; research on cooling curves for aqueous solutions of alkilis halides; wrote histories of development of QM items. Author articles in field. Prof chem Billings Polytechnic Inst '39-40; prof chem Evansville '46-48; prof and dir dept chemistry and mathematics Suffolk U since '48. Major, Lieutenant colonel US Army '40-46. Am Chem Soc—Ind Acad Sci—Phi Kappa Phi—Sigma Xi. Suffolk University, Boston.†

15 ANDERSON, Norval Eugene. Sewage and waste treatment. b'97. Student '16-18 (Colo Coll); BS (CE) '20—CE '34 (U Ill). Design plants for treatment of sewage and industrial wastes; development of activated sludge process. Author articles: The Economical Depth of Aeration Tanks of the Diffused Air Type for the Activated Sludge Process of Sewage Treatment '34; Design of Final Settling Tanks for Activated Sludge '45; Tests and Studies on Air Diffusers for Activated Sludge '50. Engr Sanitary Dist Chicago since '20, now engr treatment plant design, in charge design dept since '35; cons engr since '26. Asociacion Interamericana de Ingenieria Sanitaria—Am Soc CE—Fedn Sewage and Indsl Wastes Assns—Am Water Works Assn—Sigma Tau. 910 S. Michigan Av., Chicago 5

16 ANDERSON, Paul A(lexander). Electronic work functions (metals); Surface physics; Thermodynamics. b'97. BA '20 (U Ill); PhD '25 (Harvard U); Nat research fellow in physics '29-31 (Harvard U, U Berlin). Author articles in field. Prof physics, head dept State Coll Wash since '31. Am Phys Soc—Sigma Xi. 1911 Indiana St., Pullman, Wash.

17 ANDERSON, Paul Russell. Philosophy in America. b'07. BA '28 (O Wesleyan U); PhD '33 (Columbia); '30 (Union Theol Sem); '32 (New Sch Social Research). Honorary member, Ninth International Congress of Philosophy, Paris '37. Author: Science in Defense of Liberal Religion, A Study of Henry More's Attempt to Link Seventeenth Century Religion with Science '33. Co-author: Philosophy in America from the Puritans to James '39. Editor: Universal Military Training and National Security '45. Asso prof philos Lawrence Coll '40-41, prof and dean of coll '41-45; on leave cons Am Council on Edn '44-45; pres Pa Coll for Women since '45; mem Com Measurement and Guidance Am Council on Edn. Pa Assn Colls and U—Am Philos Assn—AAAS—AAUP—Phi Beta Kappa—Pennsylvania College for Women, Woodland Rd., Pittsburgh 32.

18 ANDERSON, Raymond E. Pollution control. b'14. BS '36 (Wheaton Coll); '43-45 (Ill Inst Tech). Research on Lake Michigan water as affected by sewage treatment plant effluents industrial discharges storm water overflows from combined sewerage systems, ravines creeks etc., tracing of pollution sources. Analytical chem Abbott Lab '36-44; chem engr North Shore San Dist since '44. Nat Soc Profl Engrs—Ill Soc Profl Engrs—Central States Sewage Works Assn—ACS—Water and Sewage Works Assn. Received Sanitation Award from Izaak Walton League '50. North Shore Sanitary District, Dahringer Rd., Waukegan, Ill.

19 ANDERSON, Robert B. Catalysis; Kinetics. b'15. AB '38 (Augustana Coll); MS '40—PhD '42 (State U Ia). Studied surface properties of carbon blacks and gas mask charcoals; engaged research on Fischer-Tropsch synthesis, properties of catalysts, catalyst development and kinetics of synthesis; research and writing on role of carbide in cobalt catalysts, surface properties of unreduced cobalt catalysts and reduced cobalt catalysts, tests of cobalt catalysts at atmospheric pressure, studies of iron catalysts, comparison of surface areas of carbon blacks from electron micrographs with those from BET, modifications of BET equation I and II. Co-author: (with Henry Harrington Storch and N Columbic) The Fischer-Tropsch and Related Syntheses '51. Author articles: Kinetics of the Thermal Decomposition of n-Propyl and Isopropyl Formates '43; Etherates of Magnesium Bromides '40; Magnetic Stirrer '39; others in field. NDRC Project Johns Hopkins '43-44; physical chemist Bur Mines Pittsburg since '44; now assistant chief synthetic fuels research branch. Am Chem Soc—Sigma Xi. Post doctoral fellowship in chem engring dept. Johns Hopkins '42-43. 1953 Ipatieff Prize for research in catalytic chemistry, '52. Bureau of Mines, 4800 Forbes Street, Pittsburgh.

20 ANDERSON, Robert John. Light metals metallurgy (aluminum; magnesium). b'92. BSc '14—MetE '17 (Case Sch Applied Sci); DSc '25 (Mass Inst Tech). Author: Metallurgy of Aluminum Alloys '25; Secondary Aluminum '31; also articles in field. Cons engr since '24; cons on light metals to US Govt and to Soviet Govt. Chmn Conservation Com OGMG US Army and contact officer to WPB and OUSW Washington World War II. British Inst Metals—Am Foundrymen's Assn (McFadden Medallist). Tau Beta Pi—Sigma Xi. 3932 Illinois Ave., N.W. Washington 11, D.C.

21 ANDERSON, Russell Howard. History of agricultural technology; The Shakers. b'96. Diploma '16 (Eastern Ill State Teachers Coll); BS ED '23—AM '25—PhD '29 (U Ill). Research on agriculture in Illinois during Civil War Period 1850-70, history of technology particularly relating to agriculture and principles of milling and textiles; local consulant on sericulture; has available collection of manuscript sources concerning Shakers. Editor, Historical Society News. Author: New York Agriculture Meets the West '32; Grain Drills Through Thirty-nine Centuries '36; The Technical Ancestry of Grain Milling Devices '35; The White Man Begins to Farm in Illinois '36; Advancing Across the Mississippi Valley '43; A National Agricultural Center as a Focal Point '39; Carding and Spinning Wool; also articles in field. Prof hist, head dept State Teachers Coll Peru Neb '27-28; tech staff Museum Sci and Industry Chicago '29-46; dir Western Reserve Hist Soc Cleveland since '47; regional dir Ill Survey Fed Archives '36-37.—AHA—Agrl Hist Soc (pres '38-39)—Miss Valley Hist Assn—Soc Am Archivists—Am Assn State Local Hist Spec Libraries Assn —Econ Hist Assn—Newcomen Soc of Eng. Western Reserve Historical Society, 10825 East Boulevard, Cleveland 6.†

22 ANDERSON, Scott. Structure and properties of glass. b'13. BS '35 (Ill Wesleyan U); PhD '40 (U Ill). Research on mechanism of oxidation of metals, luminescence of metals, bubble formation of liquids, infrared, visible, and ultraviolet spectroscopy, optical properties of glass, adhesion of metals to glass, surface, thermal properties and structure of glass. Author articles in field. With Aluminum Research Labs New Kensington Pa '40-43; cons U Chicago Metall Lab '44-45; with Anderson Physical Lab Champaign Ill since '45. 609 S. Sixth St., Champaign, Ill.

23 ANDERSON, William Stacy. Cucumber breeding; Sweet potato starch. b'97. BS '22 (Miss A&M Coll); MS '37 (Mich State Coll). Pioneered research with production of sweet potatoes for starch making. Author articles in field. Asst hort Tex Ext Service '22-23; hort So Miss Expt Sta '23-34, asso hort Miss Expt Sta '34-41, head dept hort Miss State Coll and Miss Expt Sta since '41. Am Soc Hort

Sci (chmn so region '42-45, exec com). State College, Miss.ⓒ

10 ANDERSON, William Strachan. Boiler design; Heating; Heat transfer; Combustion. b'93. Student (Stevens Sch Stevens Inst Tech, Columbia). Developed forced circulation radiant heat absorbing equipment; designed Axeman-Anderson Anthratube, device for greatly improved method of burning anthracite coal. Partner with J E Axeman in Axeman-Anderson Co since '45. Am Soc Heat and Ventilating Engrs. 233 West St., Williamsport, Pa.

11 ANDERSON, (Earl) Wing. Sleep suggestion. b'90. BA '15 (U Ill). Research for twenty years in reactions to suggestion given during sleep; president National Psychological Institute. Author: The Next Nine Years '38; Seven Years That Change The World '40; Prophetic Years '47; Health, Wealth and Happiness While You Sleep '48; also articles in field. Owner Kosmon Industries, mfg clock-controlled record players mechanized suggestion during sleep, suggestion records for correction psychosomatic ills; pres Essenes of Kosmon, Calif Assn Counselors, Psychotherapists. Kosmon Industries, 2208 W. 11th St., Los Angeles 6.

12 ANDES, Ralph Verne. Physical chemistry (Inks, organic coatings, plastics, Portland cement, chlorinated hydrocarbons, electrolytic caustic soda). b'07. BS '30 (Mont State Coll); PhD '35 (Ia State College); '37-39 (U Chicago. Author articles in field. Research chem Universal Atlas Cement Co '37-40; Westvaco Chlorine Products Corp '40-44; assistant supt of laboratory Brown and Bigelow St Paul since '44; lecturer physical chemistry Hamline U since '47. Am Chem Soc—Phi Lambda Upsilon. Brown and Bigelow, St. Paul.†

13 ANDRAE, William Cook. Power plant measurements; Dimensional analysis. b'94. ME '15—MME '24 (Cornell U) Design of precision mechanical instruments; instrumentation and testing of power plant equipment. Author: Experimental Mechanical Engineering. Co-author: (with Diederichs) Experimental Engineering. Chief draftsman div weights and measures Nat Bur Standards '17-20; faculty dept mech engring Cornell U since '20, now asso prof. Am Soc ME (com on instruments and apparatus since '37). Sibley School of Mechanical Engineering, Cornell University, Ithaca, N.Y.

14 ANDREASSEN, John Christian Ludvig. Library and relief administration. b'09. PhB '31 (U Wis); '29 (Tulane U); MA '35 (La State U). Displaced persons specialist UNRRA London '44-45; UNRRA representative Sweden and Austria '45-46, acted as chief of mission part of period. Author: Internal Improvements in Louisiana '47; also articles in field. State supervisor WPA hist records survey New Orleans '37-41, regional supervisor '41-42, field supervisor service projects Ft Worth '42-43; administrative officer War Pub Services Div Fed Works Agency Washington '43-44; cons adminstrn Library of Congress '46, dir since '46. AHA—Soc Am Archivists—So Hist Assn—Am Assn State and Local Hist—La Hist Soc—Miss Hist Soc—Okla Hist Soc—Phi Kappa Phi. Library of Congress, Washington 25.

15 ANDREW, Warren. Age in man (Change of tissue cells). b'10. BA '32 (Carleton Coll); MS '33—Arnold fellow '32-33 (Brown U); PhD '36 (Yale U, U Ill); MD '43 (Baylor U Sch Med. Research with animals and man on cellular changes with age in the nervous system, pancreas and salivary glands, spleen, lymph nodes and thyroid, neuronophagia, intracellular position of lymphocytes in normal intestinal epithelium, similarity of neuroglia fibers to those of other connective tissues, relation of old age to development of cancer. Author articles in field. Asst prof anat Baylor U Sch Med '39-43; asso prof histol Southwestern Med Coll '43-45, prof '46-47; prof anat and chmn dept George Washington U since '47. Am Assn Anat—Am Soc Zool—AAAS—Soc Exptl Biol and Med—Am Gerontol Soc—Sigma Xi—Phi Beta Kappa. Department of Anatomy, The George Washington University School of Medicine, 1335 H St. N.W., Washington.

16 ANDREWS, Alfred Carleton. Ancient foods (Mediterranean region). b'04. AB '26 (Bowdoin Coll); MA '31—PhD (U Pa). Author articles in field. Asso prof Classics U Miami since '47. Am Philol Assn—Classical Soc Am Acad Rome—Classical Assn Middle West and South—Fla Acad Scis. P.O. Box 72, University of Miami, Miami, Fla.

17 ANDREWS, Donald Hatch. Physical chemistry; Thermodynamics; Solution theory; Cryogeny; Molecular structure; Infra-red spectroscopy. b'98. BA '20—PhD '23 (Yale). Research asst in chemistry Yale '23; nat research fellow U Calif '24-25; internat research fellow U Leiden '25-26; research fellow Bartol Research Found '26-27; with Johns Hopkins U since '27 prof since '30, chmn dept dir chemn laboratory '36-44; dir of Cryogeny Laboratory '43-48. First Sci Commission—L'Inst Internat de Froid—Am Phys Soc(F)—Am Inst Chem—Royal Chem Soc (Eng)—AAAS—Soc of Chem Industry—Am Philos Soc—Phi Beta Kappa—Sigma Xi. Johns Hopkins University, Baltimore.ⓒ

18 ANDREWS, Dorothy Craighead. Child psychology; Education of the exceptional child. b'07. BS '28—MA '31 (U Pa). MS '36 (U Maine). Dir and owner Brewster Hall Tutorial Sch Bradenton Fla since '48. AAAS—Am Assn Mental Deficiency(F)—Am Psychol Assn—Am Hearing Soc—Fla Acad Scis—Internat Council Edn Exceptional Children—Nat Vocational Rehabilitation Assn—Pa Psychol Assn. Brewster Hall, Bradenton, Fla.

19 ANDREWS, Edward Deming. Shakers. b'94. BA '16 (Amherst Coll); PhD '30 (Yale). Collector of Shaker literature and art, furniture, industrial products, tools. utensils, costumes, and textiles; expert consultant National Committee on Folk Arts. Author: Community Industries of the Shakers '32; The Gift to be Simple—Songs, Dances and Rituals of the American Shakers '40; The Dance in Shaker Ritual '42; Fifteen Shaker Songs '44. Co-author: (with Faith Andrews) Shaker Furniture—The Craftsmanship of an American Communal Sect (2nd edit) '50. Curator hist NY State Mus '32-33; Guggenheim Fellow, 1937-38; dean and head hist dept Scarborough Sch Scarborough-on-Hudson NY since '42. Scarborough Sch, Scarborough-on-Hudson, N.Y. H: Glenwood Gardens, Yonkers 2, N.Y.

20 ANDREWS, F(rank) Emerson. Publishing; Philanthropy; Duodecimal system. b'02. BS '23—LHD '52 (Franklin and Marshall Coll). Conducted brief surveys of publishing programs of numerous organizations including International Labour Office, Social Science Research Council, Welfare Council of New York City; conducted extensive surveys of philanthropic foundations, philanthropy, and corporation giving; studies in field family allowances. Made first popular presentation in US of advantages of counting by duodecimal system, helped found Duodecimal Society of America. Author: New Numbers '35; Philanthropic Giving '50; Corporation Giving '52. Co-author: American Foundations for Social Welfare '46; Russell Sage Foundation, 1907-1946 '47; also articles in field. With Macmillan Co '23-28; dir publications Russell Sage Foundation since '28; cons on publications Twentieth Century Fund since '41. Am Inst Graphic Arts (ed '40-41, treas '44-45, dir '45-48)—Nat Conf Social Work—The Duodecimal Soc Am (pres '44-50, chmn of board since '50, winner first annual award '44). 34 Oak St., Tenafly, N.J.

21 ANDREWS, James Clarence. Nutrition; Biochemistry (Sulfur). b'92. BS in chem '15 (U Ia); PhD '18 (Columbia). Chemistry and metabolism of the biologically important compounds of sulfur and phosphorus. Author articles in field. Prof biol chem and nutrition medical sch UNC since '37; exchange prof in biol chemistry, University of San Carlos, Guatemala, CA, '44 and 48. Honorary member faculty of the Univ of San Carlos. Am Chem Soc—Am Soc Biol Chem—NC Acad Sci—Elisha Mitchell Sci Soc—Sigma Xi. School of Medicine, University of North Carolina, Chapel Hill, N.C.

22 ANDREWS, John S(cott). Internal parasites of cattle, sheep, swine and goats. b'05. BS '27—MS '29—P F Williams fellow (Purdue U); '33-34 (George Washington U); DSc '38 (Johns Hopkins U). Author articles in field. Junior and asst zool US Dept Agric '30-38; parasitol Insular Expt sta, Rio Piedras, Puerto Rico '38-41; assoc and parasitol Zool Div BAI Tifton Ga since '41. Helminthol Soc Washington—Am Soc Parasitol—Washington Acad Sci—Am Microscopical Soc—Sigma Xi. Coastal Plain Experiment Station, Tifton, Ga.†

23 ANDREWS, Justin M(eredith). Parasitic protozoology (Epidemiology); Public health. b'02. PhB cum laude '23 (Brown U); ScD '26 (Johns Hopkins); certificate '49 (AUS Chem Corps Sch); LLD '51 (Johns Hopkins). Research on epidemiology, control, and laboratory methodology of general parasitic protozoology; control and eradication of malaria; development of practical health programs for control and eradication of malaria and other diseases spread by insects; consultant on amebiasis Fresnillo Mexico, on malaria to Government US of Venezuela, Imperial Government of Iran. Author numerous articles in field. From instr to asso prof protozool Johns Hopkins '26-'38; spl mem Rockefeller Found '29; vis prof parasitology U Philippines '30-'31; dir div malaria and hookworm service Georgia Dept Pub Health '38-'42, also ed Ga Malaria Bulletin; asso prof pub health Emory U since '40; Major Lt. Col & Col. Army of US, Theater Malariologist Mediterranean Theater '42-'45, Pacific Theater '45; dir profl functions Malaria Control in War Areas USPHS Atlanta '46; dep officer in charge PHS Communicable Disease Center Atlanta '46-'51; officer in charge Communicable Disease Center '52. AAAS (F)—Am Pub Health Assn (F)—Am Acad Tropical Med—Am Soc Tropical Med—Nat Malaria Soc (pres '51)—Am Soc Parasitologists—NRC (insect and rodent control com '48-'51)—World Health Organization (expert adv panel malaria '48-55 insecticides '50-'55)—Sigma Xi—Sci Research Soc Am—Phi Sigma. Federal Security Agency, Public Health Service, Communicable Disease Center, 50 Seventh St., N.E., Atlanta 5.

10 ANDREWS, Lale Clark. Stress analysis (High temperature). b'00. Student '17-22 (Kan U). Development of methods and apparatus for model test analysis of reactions, stresses, and deflections in high temperature piping due to thermal expansion, weight, wind, and vibratory loading. Author articles: Electrical Robot Determines Stress in Piping Systems '46; Model Test Analysis of Steam Piping Systems '49; Piping Flexibility Analysis by Model Test '51, and others. Engring design '25-34; piping design and stress analysis M W Kellogg Co NYC since '35, now stress analyst and cons high temperature and high pressure piping. Soc Exptl Stress Analysis—A AAS—Nat Farm Chemurgic Council. 225 Broadway, NYC 7.

11 ANDREWS, Mildred Gwin Barnwell. Textile technology; Cotton technology and economics. b'03. Grad '21 (Nat Cathedral Sch Wash); spl work '37 (Ark Agrl Coll); '32 (NC State Coll). Com on indsl salvage War Production Board '43-46. Author: Faces We See '38; Cotton Magic '43; also articles in field. Exec asst So Combed Yarn Spinners Assn '30-36, exec sec '36-46; com rep Textile Com Pub Relations. Expert cons and textile tech textile sect office of Qm Gen '41-46. Awarded Am Trade Assn Execs award for War Prodn achievements '44. Rt 4, Vienna, Va.

12 ANDREWS, Robert Edmund. Violins (History). b'80. AB '03—BS '05 (U Mich). Research regarding life Gasparo Bertolotti, known as Gasparo da Salo, reputed inventor modern violin, and existing instruments made by him; assembled unpublished facts of interest; compiling list of instruments made by or attributed to Gasparo and grouped according to their authenticity. H: 1030 Shattuck Av., Berkeley 7, Calif.

13 ANDREWS, Roy Chapman. Paleontology, zoology and geology of the Gobi desert; Water mammals. b'84. BA '06—ScD (hon) '28 (Beloit Coll); MA '13 (Columbia); ScD (hon) '26 (Brown U). Series of expeditions '22-30 mapped much new area in the Gobi Desert, discovered many geological strata previously unknown, discovered some of richest fossil fields in world, also first dinosaur eggs, skulls and parts of skeleton of Baluchitherium—largest known mammal and many other fossil mammals and reptiles previously unknown to science. Author: On the Trail of Ancient Man; Meet Your Ancestors; This Business of Exploring '35; also articles in field. Dir Am Mus Natural Hist, retired '42; appointed hon dir, fellow Nat Geog Soc—AAAS—Am Geog Soc—NY Zool Soc—Phi Beta Kappa. Elisha Kent Kane gold medal Phila Geog Soc '29; Hubbard gold medal Nat Geog Soc '31; Explorers Club medal '32; Charles P. Daly gold medal '36; Vega gold medal Royal Swedish Anthrop and Geog Soc '37; Loczy medal Hungarian Geog Soc '37. American Museum of Natural History, NYC.⊚

14 ANDREWS, Thomas Gayleon. Japan (Iron ores, cobalt ores, nickel ores). b'03. AB '25—AM '27 (Vanderbilt U); PhD '32 (U Minn). Scientific consultant natural resources section Supreme Command Allied Powers Tokyo '46; Collected Statistics on production, imports and exports of iron, cobalt and nickel ores of Japan; examined representative mines produc-

ing these commodities in Japan. Instr to prof geol U Ala since '32, head dept since '40; rodman and recorder US Geol Survey '35-37, asst geol '37-45, geol parttime since '46. Geol Soc Am (F)—AAAS (F)—Am Geog Soc (F)—Soc Econ Geol—Am Assn Mining and Metall Engrs—Am Assn Petroleum Geol—Am Mineral Soc—Am Geophys Union—Seismol Soc Am—Soc Econ Paleontologists and Mineral—Ala Acad Sci—Sigma Xi. Department of Geology, University of Alabama, University, Ala.

15 ANDRUS, Elwin A. Patent lawyer. b'04. LLB '27 (U Wis). Private practice patent, trade mark and copyright law since '39. Am Patent Law Assn. 735 Water St., Milwaukee 2.⊚

16 ANDRUS, J(ames) Russell. Economics of Burma, India, Ceylon, Siam and Indo-China. b'02. BA '25 (U Redlands); MA '26—PhD '34 (U Calif). Secretary agricultural debtors protection committee appointed by government of Burma '31-32; economic analyst Far Eastern Unit Bureau of Foreign and Domestic Commerce '42, senior economic analyst '43-44; director intelligence Office War Information New Delhi India '44-45; Burma-Ceylon specialist Division of the South Asian Affairs Department of State '45-47. Author: Rural Reconstruction in Burma '36; Burmese Economic Life '48; also articles in field. Second sec, consul American Embassy Rangoon Burma '47-49; first sec and consul Am Embassy Karachi Pakistan '49-50; ednl adviser to Far East, Mutual Security Agency '51-52. American Economic Association—Inst Pacific Relations—Middle West Inst. Mutual Security Agency, Washington 25.

17 ANGELL, Robert Cooley. Sociological theory; Urban sociology; Am soc. b'99. AB '21—AM '22—PhD '24 (University Mich). Author: The Campus '28; A Study in Undergraduate Adjustment '30; The Family Encounters the Depression '36; The Integration of American Society '41; The Moral Disintegration of American Cities '51; co-author: A Research in Family Law '30; Introductory Sociology '33; Editor Am Sociol Rev '46-48; also articles in field. With dept Sociology U Mich since '22, chmn dept '40-52; acting director social science dept UNESCO Paris '49-50 vice chmn US nat com for UNESCO '52. American Sociology Society (pres '51)—Mich Sociol Soc—Sociol Research Assn—Mich Acad Sciences Arts and Letters—Phi Beta Kappa. 1007 Berkshire Road, Ann Arbor.

18 ANGELLO, Stephen James. Semiconductors; Rectifiers. b'18. BS (elec engring) '39—MS (elec engring) '40—PhD (phys) '42 (U Pa). Research on electrical properties of semiconductors, role of Hall effect in determination of fundamental electrical data for semiconductors, developed silicon crystal rectifier, developed process for reducing electrical noise of unit to low values, noise generation at semiconductor contacts. Research engr Westinghous Elec Corp Research Lab since '42. APS (mem div solid state and electron phys)—Am Inst EE. Westinghouse Research Laboratories, East Pittsburgh, Pa.

19 ANGIER, James Franklin. Aerodromes. b'06. BS '33—'33-36 (Geo Wash U). Development of national and international standards; recommendations and specifications for facilities and equipment aerodromes to meet requirements of aircraft operators; research on photometric methods; testing aeronautical lighting equipment and accessories; represented US

for Airways Systems at International Civil Aviation Conference Chicago '44, for Aerodromes, air routes and ground aides at subsequent conferences and meetings in Montreal, London, Paris, Melbourne, New Delhi, Lima, Cairo, Istanbul, other foreign areas; US Technical representative on Provisional International Civil Aviation Organization's Technical Mission to Greece '46. Research Nat Bur Standards '26-38; Eng Civil Aeronautics Adminstrn '38-44, cons to adminstr, chief fgn sect, International Aerodromes, Air Routes and Ground Aids Specialist since '44. AAAS—Am Inst EE—Optical Soc Am—Soc Automotive Engrs—Am Instr Physics—Illuminating Engring Soc—ACS—Instrument Soc Am. Civil Aeronautics Administration, Washington 25. H: 239 Maple Av., Washington 12.

20 ANGLE, Glenn D(ale). Aircraft and internal combustion engines. b'91. '11-13 (U Mich); ME(hon) '36 (Lawrence Inst Tech). Introduced numerous engine design practices and methods for analysis. Approximately 90 patents granted. Author: Airplane Engine Encyclopedia '21; Engine Dynamics and Crankshaft Design '25; Aerosphere '39, '41, '42, '43; also articles in field. In charge engine design US Army Air Corps '18-24; vp, chief engr LeBlond Aircraft Engine Corp Cincinnati '28-31; prof mech engring Lawrence Inst Tech '34-39; cons engr since '39; pres Angle Engineering-Sales Corp Brooklyn Mich. Inst Aeronautical Sci (asso F). Brooklyn, Mich.

21 ANIGSTEIN, Ludwik. Preventive and tropical medicine; Public health; Rickettsial diseases; Malaria. b'91. PhD magna cum laude '13 (U Heidelberg); med diploma '15 (U Dorpat); MD '23 (U Poznan); certificate '23 (London Sch Tropical Medicine). Specialist in research in rickettsial diseases typhus and spotted fevers and in medical field surveys. Contr many articles on protozoology bacteriology epidemiology immunology tropical diseases. Prof preventive medicine and public health since '46. Cons medical division Oak Ridge Institute of Nuclear Studies. Served as UNRRA (lectr on communicable diseases med teaching mission to Poland '46)—Royal Society Tropical Medicine and Hygiene, London(F)—Malaria Society—Am Soc Tropical Medicine—American Public Health Assn(F)—Tex Pub Health Association—Soc Am Bacteriologists—Soc Exptl Biology and Medicine—AAAS(F) —Tex Acad Sci(F)—NY Acad Sci(F)—Sigma Xi. University of Texas Medical Branch, 927 Strand St., Galveston, Tex.⊚

22 ANSON, Edward Hiram. Electric power (Generation, transmission, distribution, and utilization). b'02. BS (EE) (NY U). Design of thermal-electric plants with turbine generator capacities from 5000 to 100,000 kilowatts, and design electrical transmission systems on wood poles, and on steel structures, with capacities up to 100,000 kilowatts; design and supervision of construction overhead and underground electric distribution systems; utilization of electricity for municipalities, and industrial processes and manufacturing. Vp and engr Gibbs & Hill Inc (cons engrs, designers, and constructors) since '40. Am Inst Cons Engrs—Am Soc CE—Soc Am Mil Engrs—Am Ry Engring Assn—Assn Am Rrs. Gibbs & Hill, Inc., Pennsylvania Station, NYC 1.

23 APFEL, Earl T(aylor). Glacial geology; Sedimentation. b'92. AB '23 Cornell Coll) MS '25 PhD '26 (U Iowa). Geologist Syracuse Andean Venezuela expedition; Antarctic regions; paleontological studies of sediment areas. Author numerous articles and reports on glacial geology. Prof geology dir John Wesley Powell Museum '26-28 Ill Wesleyan U; asso prof geol '28-35 Syracuse U prof since '35, chmn dept since '45; asso geologist Ill Geol Survey '29-30; temporary geol NY State Mus '35-40; US Geol Survey since '42; geol Syracuse-Andean Expdn Venezuela '30-31 Second Antarctic Development project US Navy '47-48. Geol Soc Am(F)—AAAS—AIMME—Sigma Xi. Geology Dept., Syracuse University, Syracuse 10, N.Y.†☉

10 APP, Frank. Farm production; farm economics; agricultural economics. b'86. BS '11 (Penn State Coll) PhD '19 (Cornell U). Investigations of farm economics; agronomy and agricultural economics; farm management; distribution of perishable foods. Author: Farm Economics '24; The Farmer and his Farm. Chief div agronomy and agricultural economics NJ State U Agrl Expt Station '18-23; cons agrl econ NJ State Dept Agr '20-23; mem exec com Am Farm Bur Fedn; agrl rep Rep Nat Com '24; dir orgn Fed Fruit & Vegetable Growers ' 24-25; agrl ed Camden Post '27. Pres NJ Farm Bur '24-42; cons USDA '34; mem bd vis NJ Coll Agr; mem bd mgrs NJ Agrl Expt Sta '35-44. Mem Am Farm Econ Assn—Am Farm Bur—Sigma Xi. H: Bridgeton, N.J.†☉

11 APPEL, Theodore Burton, Jr. Structural engineering. b'04. BS '26 (Franklin and Marshall Coll); SB (civil engring) '29 (MIT). Arrangement and design of plants for dam construction, water front installations, design for manufacturing of equipment concrete batching plants, manufacture of interlocked and automatic scales. Asso structural engr TVA Construction Plant Div '36-41; office engr TVA Fontana Project '42; construction engr Arundel Consol Hardaway Contractors '42-43; chief engr C S Johnson Co since '44. Am Soc CE—Am Welding Soc—Phi Beta Kappa—Tau Beta Pi—Chi Epsilon. C. S Johnson Co., Champaign, Ill. H: 905 W. Hill St.†

12 APPLEBY, Walter Goode. Catalysis; Kinetics; Thermodynamics; Petroleum separation and analysis. b'13. BS Ch E '36—MA '37 (Rice Inst). Research in improved meter for measurement of gas flow rates, vapor phase dehydration of 1-Heptanol over activated alumina, kinetics and mechanism of thermal decomposition of n-Heptane, alkylation of thiophene with olefins. Author: Analytical Chemistry '48; also articles in field. With Shell Oil Co Inc since '41, research lab tech adviser since '45. Am Chem Soc. Shell Oil Co., Inc., Box 2527, Houston, Tex. H: 4707 Winnetka, Houston 4.†

13 APPLEGARTH, Alexander Rufus, Jr. Aircraft communication. b'13. BS '36—MS '36 (MIT). Development aircraft radio receivers including Navy ARB; radar type radio altimeters for USAF; lightweight aircraft navigation and communication sets; lightweight radar. Development of TV receivers and sync gen Philco '36-39. Aircraft receiver and radar design engr Radio Corp Am '39-42; radar development officer aircraft radio lab USAF Wright Field '42-46; vp and chief engr Nat Aeronautical Corp since '46. Inst Radio Engrs—Franklin Inst. National Aeronautical Corp., Ambler, Pa.

14 APPLEGATE, Homer E. Air navigation radio; Radio communications facilities. b'01. Student (Defiance Coll O) (Carnegie Inst Tech). Chief transmitter test and insp Westinghouse Elec & Mfg Co '28-32; with Civil Aeronautics Adminstrn since '34, now dep chief facilities div fourth region. Inst Radio Engrs. Civil Aeronautics Administration, Box 1689, Fort Worth 1, Tex. H: 2125 Yucca, Fort Worth 11.

15 APPLEMAN, Milo Don. Food bacteriology; Food technology. b'09. BA '31—MS '35—PhD '40 (U Ill). Engaged research studying quick-freezing and vacuum-drying bacteria, soil microbiology, azotobacter flora of morrow plots, morphological characteristics nodule bacteria as shown by electron microscope, effect DDT on nodulation legumes, lyophiled cultures, lyophile storage Rhizobium leguminosarum cultures. Author: Artificial Manures '43; Report of Commercial Legume Inoculants '44; Inoculation of Legumes '44; The Place of Soybeans on Soil Productivity '44; 1945 Report of Commercial Legume Inoculants '46; also articles in field. Asso prof dept bact parasitol U So Calif since '47; chmn dept bacteriology since '49. Soc de Diplomes Univ Nantes (France)—Inst Food Tech—Electron Microscope Soc—Soc Am Bact—Soil Soc Am—Am Soc Agron—Sigma Xi. 1939 W. 79th St., Los Angeles 47.†

16 ARANT, Frank Selman. Peanut, corn, and cotton insects; Insect toxicology. b'04. BS '26—MS '29 (Ala Poly Inst); PhD '37 (Ia State Coll); '43 (U Mich). Author articles in field. Asst prof zool entomol Ala Poly Inst '31-38, asso prof '38-42; entomol Ala Agrl Expt Sta since '46; head dept zool—entomol since '49. Am Assn Econ Entomol (pub bd official jour of Assn)—Am Soc Parasitol—Sigma Xi—Phi Kappa Phi—Gamma Sigma Delta. Department of Zoology and Entomology, Alabama Polytechnic Institute, Auburn, Ala.†

17 ARBINGAST, Stanley Alan. Geography of Texas; Industrialization of Texas; Water economics. b'10. BS '34 (Winona State Teachers Coll); MA '49 (U Wash). Research on industrial and municipal water needs for next 50 years in Texas, based on analysis of resources in each area in relation to trends of population, water use, industrial output, and income on national and state basis. With Bur Bus Research U Tex since '49, asst dir since '51. Am Geog Soc (F)—Assn Am Geog—Assn Pacific Coast Geog—AAU P—SW Soc Sci Assn—Asso U Bur Bus Research—Delta Sigma Pi—Nu Alpha Chi Pi. Bureau of Business Research, University of Texas, Austin 12, Tex.

18 ARCENEAUX, Thomas Joseph. Agronomy (Corn breeding); Rural life. b'08. BS '29 (Southwest La Inst); MS '31 (Tex A&M); research fellow '32-34—PhD '34 (Ia State Coll). Author articles in field. Instr agron Southwest La Inst '34-35, dean Coll Agr, prof agron since '41. Am Soc Agron—Am Genetic Assn—La Acad Sci—La Teachers Assn—Nat Cath Rural Life Conf (vp, chmn laity)—So Rural Life Council (mem church com)—Phi Kappa Phi. Southwestern Louisiana Institute, Lafayette, La.

19 ARCHER, Allan Frost. Entomology (Mollusks, spiders, ticks); Medical entomology; Ecology. b'08. BA '31 (Harvard); '35 (U Ala); MA '33—PhD '36 (U Mich). Field work Cuba '30, Harvard southeastern US expeditions '31-32, Ala and Ark '35; Field work, habits and habitats of spiders and snails; ecological distribution of spiders and snails; nests, egg-sacs, and brooding practices of spiders; morphology of spiders; species and geography of termites in Alabama; demonstration of relation between lone-star tick and tulanemia. Author articles in field. Asst dept mullusca Univ Mus U Mich '36-37, Horace H Rackham postdoctoral fellow '37-38; curator mollusks and arachnids Ala Mus Natural Hist since '38; state ecol Ala Dept Conservation '39-47; state ecol Geol Survey Ala '47-52; head of biology department Union University, Jackson, Tenn. In Sanitary Corps Medical Department US Army '42-46. Am Entomol Society—Am Malacological Union—Ecol Soc Am—Ala Acad Sci—Sigma Xi.

20 ARCHER, Robert Samuel. Steel and aluminum alloys. b'95. BChE '15—MS '17 (U Mich). Granted patents on aluminum alloys and methods of treatment, a heat-resisting alloy used for electric furnace resistors, a method of coating molds to improve the surface of steel ingots. Co-author: (with Jeffries) Science of Metals '24; (with Briggs and Loeb) Molybdenum Steels, Irons, Alloys '48; also articles in field. Research labs Aluminum Co Am '19-30; dir metall AO Smith Corp Milwaukee '30-34; chief metall Chicago dist Republic Steel Corp '34-44; metall engr Climax Molybdenum Co since '44. AIME—Iron and Steel Inst (Brit)—ASM (pres '34-35). Climax Molybdenum Co., 500 5th Av., NYC 18. H: 45 Forest Av., Rye, N.Y.

21 ARCHIBALD, Francis Magoun. Chemistry of petroleum white oil, sulphonates, and alcohols. b'99. BS '19 (Acadia U, NS); BS (chem engring) '23 (McGill U); MS '26—PhD '28 (U Toronto). Work on development of processes for above-mentioned products, holder 31 patents in field. Author articles in field. Contributor: Science of Petroleum. Chem Imperial Oil Ltd '23; Standard Oil Development Co '28; lab head Chem Products Lab '29-49; head of laboratories Esso Standard Oil Refinery since '49. ACS. Esso Standard Oil Refinery, Linden, N.J.

22 ARENSBERG, Walter Conrad. Shakespeare; Bacon. b'78. AB '00 (Harvard). Research in the Shakespeare-Bacon problem. Author: The Cryptography of Dante '21; The Cryptography of Shakespeare '22; The Secret Grave of Francis Bacon at Lichfield '23; The Burial of Francis Bacon and His Mother in Lichfield Chapter House '25; Baconian Keys '27; The Shakespearean Mystery '28; Francis Bacon William Butts and the Pagets of Beaudesert '29; The Magic Ring of Francis Bacon '30. Pres Francis Bacon Foundation, Ind. Trustee Southwest Mus Modern Art. H: 7065 Hillside Ave., Hollywood 28, Cal.☉

23 ARENTS, Chester Abbo. Machine Design; Heat Power Engineering; Vibration Engineering; Electric Power Engineering. b'10. BS '32—MS '46 (Ore State Coll). Prof Ill Inst Tech Chicago since '47; cons engr in mech and elect engring licensed in the States of Ore and Ill since '43. Am Soc Mech Engrs—Am Inst Electrical Engrs (asso)—Am Soc Engring Edn—Sigma Xi—Tau Beta Pi—Pi Tau Sigma—Eta Kappa Nu. Illinois Institute of Technology, 3300 Federal St., Chicago 16.☉

24 ARIES, Robert S(ancier). Chemical engineering; Economic and market surveys. b'19. Grad '37 (Am Coll Sofia); '37-39 (U Lyon); '41 (Columbia); '42-44—MSc '48 (Yale); BChE '41—MChE '43—DChE '47 (Poly Inst); AM '42 (U Minn); PhD '50 (Paris). Cons chem engr on chem manufacturing and product development, economic and market surveys, wood utilization, pulp, molasses and plastics products. Holder of 12 patents. Co-author: The Marketing of Chemical Products '48. Also articles in field. Tech dir Northeastern Wood Utilization Council since

'43; lecturer Polytechnic Institute Grad Sch since '45, prof chem engring since '47; pres R S Aries and Asso, cons engr, econ since '48. Am Chem Soc—Soc Advancement Management—Am Econ Soc—Am Marketing Assn—Am Statis Assn—Nat Soc Profl Engrs—Am Inst CE—Am Management Assn—Chem Market Research Assn—Pa Soc Profl Engrs—Nat Farm Chemurgic Council—Forest Products Research Soc—ASME—Am Inst Chem—TAPPI. 400 Madison Ave., N.Y. City 17.†☉

10 ARKLEY, Rodney John. California soils (Structure and origin of sedimentary); Hardpan (Origin). b'15. AB '40 (U Calif) Survey soil formation in Merced County California; field study Pleistocene sediments of San Joaquin Valley and Merced County, and probable relation to Sierra Nevada orogeny and glaciers; research on formation of red hardpan, relation to moist layers in soil and extreme dessication of soil in summer. Author article: Soil Survey of Merced Area California '50, and others. Soil sci US Soil Conservation Service Wis and Ill '41-45; asst specialist in soils Agrl Expt Sta Berkeley Calif since '45. Western Soil Sci Soc. 120 Hilgard Hall, University of California, Berkeley 4, Calif.

11 ARLITT, Ada Hart. Infant, child and adolescent development and psychology. b'90. BA '13 (Tulane U); PhD '17 (U Chicago). Associate editor: National Parent Teacher '27-43. Author: Psychology of Infancy and Early Childhood '28, '46; The Child from One to Twelve '31; Adolescent Psychology '33; Family Relationships '42; editor: Parent Education Yearbook '30-32, '34. Prof and head dept child care and training since '25 and prof psychol Grad Sch Arts and Sci U Cincinnati '47-51 professor emeritus since '51. AAAS(F)—Society Research Child Development—Am Psychol Association—Phi Beta Kappa—Sigma Xi. Omicron Nu National Honorary. 3420 Manor Hill Dr., Cincinnati.☉

12 ARMITAGE, Merle. Book integration. b'93. Ed private tutors. Writer or editor and designer of 55 books, specializing in motivation of design through integration of text, pictures and typography. Art director Look Magazine. 230 E. 58th St., NYC.

13 ARMOUR, Alexander William. Philanthropy; American history. b'87. Student (McGill, Montreal, Columbia). Author: A Manual of Financial Policies and Accounting Procedure for Non-Profit Corporations '26; Have Common Stocks a Place in the Investment Portfolios of Non-Profit Corporations '27; Notables and Autographs '39; also articles in field. Aide, Hon Raymond B Fosdick; spl responsibility philanthropic interests J D Rockefeller Jr; wound up affairs Interchurch World Movement Inc ($12,900,000 liabilities) on collapse summer '20; dir study administrative, financial affairs North Baptist organs; administrative duties various Rockefeller philanthropic corps, especially Gen Edn Bd '20-38; retired '38; preparation checklist personal collection Am hist manuscripts (1680-1865) since '38. AHA—Hist Soc Pa—Friends Hist Soc—Princeton Hist Soc. Nassau Club, Princeton, N.J.

14 ARMS, John Taylor. Etching; Prints (Historical development); American graphic art. Design in flower arrangement. b'87. BS '11—MS '12 (MIT); MA (hon) '39 (Wesleyan U)—'47 (Princeton); Litt D(hon) '40 (Hobart Coll). Engaged research black and white prints, lithographs,

engravings, etchings, historical development art; lecturer prints, design of flower arrangement before many groups; represented in over 45 permanent collections; founded National Committee Engraving '39, directed program international exchange of prints. Author: Handbook of Print Making and Print Makers '34; Design in Flower Arrangement (with D N Arms) '37; art editor: Bicentennial Pageant of George Washington '33. Contbg ed Print since '40, Print Collector's Quart. Nat Acad (1st v-p)—Soc Am Etchers, Gravers, Lithograph Woodcutters (pres emeritus)—Am Nat Com Engraving (pres)—Nat Inst Arts Letters—Am Color Print Soc (vp)—Am Fedn Arts—Am Artists Profl League—Soc Independent Artists—Soc Medalists—Woodcut Soc—Soc Print Connoisseurs—Artists Equity Assn (vp)—Artists Guild, Inc—Nat Commn Advance Art—Fine Arts Found (mem bd control). Awarded Chevalier of Legion of Honor France '33, gold medal Am Inst Architects '45, gold medal Dealer's Assn NY, gold medal Paris Internat Exposition '37. Mill Stones Studio, Fairfield, Conn.☉

15 ARMSTRONG, A. Joseph. English literature (Browning); American poetry. b'73. BA '02—MA '04—Litt D '32 (Wabash Coll); PhD '08 (U Pa); '09-10 (Brit Mus); LittD '25 (Georgetown Ky Coll). Lecturer Browning and other literature subjects; presented largest collection Browningiana in world to Baylor U. Author: Operatic Performances in England before Handel '18; Browning Through French Eyes '32. Editor: Letters of Robert Browning to Isa Blagden '23; Baylor Browning Interests (1st to 5th series); Browning the World Over '33; Browning's Testament of Hope '35; Browning's Roman Murder Story as Recorded in a Hitherto Unknown Italian Contemporary Manuscript (property Baylor Collection) '39; also articles in field. Prof Eng ad interim Baylor U '08-09, prof and head dept since '12; Poetry's Lovers' Soc Am—Poetry Soc Tex—Nat Council Teach Eng—Dante Soc Am (nat com)—Modern Lang Assn Am—Shakespeare Assn Am—Am Research Soc—Linguistic Soc Am—Poetry Soc Am (asso)—Eng-Speaking Union—Tex Inst Letters—Internat di Lettere e Sci Naples (corr academician)—Internat Longfellow Soc (hon)—NY Browning Soc—Boston Browning Soc—Los Angeles Browning Soc—Kansas City Browning Soc (hon). Baylor University, Waco, Tex.

16 ARMSTRONG, George Miller. Fusarium wilt diseases. b'93. BS '14 (Clemson A&M Coll); MA '17 (U Wis); PhD '21 (Washington U); Lackland fellow '19-21 (Mo Bot Garden). Author articles in field. Head dept bot and bact Clemson Coll since '28. AAAS(F)—Am Phytopath Soc—Bot Soc Am—Am Soc Plant Physiol—SC Acad Sci. Department of Botany and Bacteriology, Clemson College, Clemson, S.C.

17 ARMSTRONG, George Simpson. Industrial engineering. b'86. BS '08—CE '09—ME '13 (NY U). Author: Essentials of Industrial Costing; an Engineering Interpretation of the Economic and Financial Aspects of American Industry. Pres indsl engrs and mgmt cons George S Armstrong & Co NYC since '32. Am Inst Cons Engrs (pres '45-46)—Assn Cons Mgmt Engrs (pres '41-42)—ASME—Am Inst Mining Metall Engrs—SAE—Royal Soc Encouragement Arts Mfr Commerce (London)—Inst Aeronautical Sci (indsl mem)—Newcomen Soc—Tau Beta Pi—Pi Tau Sigma. 52 Wall St., NYC 5.†☉

18 ARMSTRONG, John C(harles). Marine biology (Carcinology, oceanography). b'13. AB '36 (Yale); '37-39 (Harvard). Santo Domingo expedition '32-33, Askoy expedition '41, Thetis expedition '41. Author: New Species of Caridea from the Bermudas '40; The Caridea and Stomatopoda of the Second Templeton Crocker-American Museum Expedition to the Pacific Ocean '41; The Maintenance of Instability in the Surface Waters of the Ocean '47; New Caridea from the Dominican Republic. Asst curator dept living invertebrates Am Mus Nat Hist since '42. US Army '42-46, asso oceanog '42. Am Geog Soc—Geophys Union—NY Acad Sci (sec sect oceanog meteorol '41)—Limnol Soc Am—AAAS. American Museum of Natural History, 77th St at Central Park West, NYC 24.†

19 ARMSTRONG, Richard H. Public and criminal law; Legal psychology; Pleading; Criminology. b'03. LL B '24 (Mercer U); BS '25 (Portland U); LLM, PhD '30 (McKinley-Roosevelt U). Author: Florida Chancery Jurisprudence '27; Index to Maine Statutes '44; Nursing Jurisprudence '45. Lawyer and law writer since '24; mem Armstrong, Wheeler & Pomeroy, Portland Me since '47; dean and prof public law Portland U. Am, Maine and York bar assn. 193 Middle St., Portland, Me.

20 ARMSTRONG, Walter, Jr. Latin American exploration and development; Chemical processes and products. b'17. BA (asso) '37 (Blackburn Coll); BS ChE '39 (Mich Coll Mining & Tech); MS '41 (State U Ia). Engaged research metal finishing, textile coatings, instrumentation, high vacuum systems, ozone, pilot plant design, plant design and installation, utilization waste products Henequen Industry, economic and engineering studies for creation new industries Mexico. Discovered new wax with properties similar to carnauba wax. Author articles: Influence of Ozone on Diesel Engine Performance '44; Apparatus for Evaluating Surface Roughness on Coated Fabrics '45; The Future of Henequen Fiber '46; and others. Research chem engr Armour Research Found Chicago '41-45, in charge field lab Merida Yucatan Mex '45-47, in charge chem eng research of internat div Mexico City since '47; asst dir internat div '50. Am Chem Soc—Am Inst Chem Engring—Sigma Xi. Armour Research Foundation, 35 W 33 St., Chicago 16, Ill.

21 ARMSTRONG, Zella. Tennessee History and Genealogy. b'82. Privately educated. Originator and executive director Chattanooga Cotton Ball produced annually since '32; vice president committee in charge Chattanooga Centennial Celebration. Author: Southern Families '22; Tennessee Heroes of the Revolution '30-39; Twenty-Four Hundred Tennessee Pensioners, Revolution and War of 1812 '37; The Crockett Family '38; Who Discovered America? The Amazing Story of Madoc '49. Editor and pub "The Lookout" Chattanooga Tenn since '08; historian for Hamilton Co Tenn since '30. Tenn State Hist Commn. 869 McCallie Av., Chattanooga.

22 ARNASON, H(jorvardur) Harvard. Art historian; Art curator. b'09. BS '31 AM '37 (Northwestern U) MFA '39 (Princeton). Instr Northwestern U '36-38; research asst lectr Frick Collection NY City '38-42; lectr Hunter Coll '39-42; field rep OWI Iceland '42-44 asst dep dir for Europe in Washington '44-45; chief program planning and evaluation Office Internat Info and Cultural Affairs Dept State '45-

46; vis asso prof art U Chicago '47; prof chm dept U Minn since '47 dir Walker Art Center Minneapolis since '47. Coll Art Assn—Archaeol Inst Am. University of Minnesota, Minneapolis. H: 1719 Bryant Avenue South, Minneapolis.◎

10 ARNDT, Charles H(omer). Photopathology; Seedling diseases (Fungicides). b'92. AB '14 (Lebanon Valley Coll); MS '16 (Purdue U); PhD '21 (U Pa). Author articles: The Growth of Field Corn as Affected by Iron and Aluminum Salts '22; Infection of Cotton Seedlings by C gossypii as affected by Temperature '44. Dir Coffee Expt Sta Haiti '25-30; botanist SC Agrl Expt Sta since '30. Am Bot—Am Soc Plant Physiol—Am Phytopath Soc. Clemson, S.C.

11 ARNDT, William John. Highways (Engineering). b'07. BS '31—CE '34 (Kan State Coll). Developed tri-axial compression method for positive design of flexible pavements of all types, developed tests to determine quality of asphaltic products for road use, constructed experimental concrete pavements, developed concrete saw for use in concrete pavement joint formings, developed soil stablized with bituminous materials, developed concrete pavement joint sealing compound. With State Highway Commn of Kan since '31, engr in charge of research since '50. Sigma Tau—Kan Engring Soc. Masonic Temple Building, Topeka, Kan.

12 ARNOLD, Earl Lee. Farms (Waters, plumbing and sewage disposal systems, refrigeration). b'07. BS '30—MS '35—PhD '40 (Cornell). Member of joint committee on rural sanitation, making recommendations on farm water, farm wastes, and farm sewage, engineering and economic phases of those items. Ext agrl engr Cornell '30-35; faculty Cornell '35-37; ext agrl engr U Ark '37-41; water system and plumbing spl Rural Elec Adminstrn USDA since '41. Am Soc Agrl Engrs (chmn rural water supplies com). Rural Electrification Administration, US Department of Agriculture, Washington 25.

13 ARNOLD, John G., Jr. Parasites of North American rabbits. b'09. AB '30 (Ohio State U); AM '32 (Wesleyan U); PhD '34 (NYU). Author: Laboratory Manual of General Biology '40; also articles in field. Prof biol and chmn dept Loyola U since '34, chmn dept med tech since '35. AAAS—Am Soc Parasitol—Am Microscopic Soc—New Orleans Acad Sci—New Orleans Bot Soc—Sigma Xi. Loyola University, New Orleans.◎

14 ARNOLD, Lionel Kenneth. Vegetable oil extraction; Agricultural by-product utilization. b'95. AB '20 (Ellsworth Coll); BS in chem engring '21—MSc '26—PhD '30 (Ia State Coll). Designed several solvent extraction plants for soybeans. Author articles in field. Cons engr Crown Iron Works Co since '47; cons agrl by-product and oil extraction plants; research prof chemical engring Ia Engring Expt Sta since '48. Am Chem Soc—Am Inst Chem Engrs—Am Oil Chem Soc—Am Soybean Assn—Ia Acad Sci—Phi Kappa Phi—Sigma Xi. West Chemical Engineering Building, Iowa State College, Ames, Ia.†

15 ARNOLD, Melvin R(oy). Gases (Production, purification); Military explosives; Smokeless powder. b'15. BS '38 (Jamestown Coll); '38-39 (U SD); MS '40 (ND State Agrl Coll). Holds two US patents on extraction thimble for smokeless powder '45, preferential absorption of hydrocarbons '46. Author

articles in field. Became supervisor research and development labs Gas Processes Division The Girdler Corp '43 now with The Miner Labs. Am Chem Soc. The Miner Laboratories, 9 S. Clinton St., Chgo 6.

16 ARNOLD, Samuel Tomlinson. Education administration. b'92. AB '13 ScM '14 PhD '16 (Brown U). Administration of higher education; college administration within universities. Prof chemistry Brown U since '30 dean undergraduates '30-37 dean coll '37-46 dean university '46-49 provost since '49; cons War Dept '43-46. Mem Nat Selection Com Fulbright Awards '50. Mem exec com Coll Entrance Exam Bd '46. Assn Academic Deans (vp '48-49)—Am Chem Soc—Eastern Assn Deans and Adv Men(pres '36-37)—Arts Program Assn Am Colls—Am Council Edn—Nat Assn Deans and Adv Men—Eastern Coll Personnel Officers—Phi Beta Kappa—Sigma Xi. Brown University, Providence, R.I. H: 10 Euclid Ave., Providence 6, R.I.†◎

17 ARNSPIGER, Varney Clyde. Instructional films; Public school curriculum. b'96. AB '17 (Tex Christian U); PhD '33 (Columbia U). Author: Measuring the Effectiveness of Sound Pictures as Teaching Aids '33. Co-author: The Educational Talking Picture '33. Spl cons Signal Corps Photographic Center, US Army '42-44, vp Encyclopedia Britannica Films Inc since '43, exec vp and mem bd dirs since '45, lecturer U Wis. '43-45. Am Acad Polit Social Sci—Am Ednl Research Assn—NEA. 1150 Wilmette Av., Wilmette, Ill.

18 ARNSTEIN, Karl. Aeronautical engineering and designing; Airship design and construction; Structural engineering (Research, development and production engineering). b'87. Dr Tech Sci '12 (U Prague); Dr Engring (hon) '27 (U Aix-La-Chapelle). Designed reconstruction foundation Cathedral of Strassburg; designed about 70 military and commercial airships including American ship Los Angeles, supervised construction, participated major trial flights of most of ships; developed designs two military rigid airships of 6,500,000 cubic feet capacity for US Navy, directed design and constrn USS Akron, USS Macon, large airship dock, pressure type airships, stratosphere balloons, lightweight streamline train, heavier-than-air craft. Author: Einflusslinien '12; Co-author: Aerodynamic Theory (vol 6) '36; also articles in field. Vice-pres and chief engr Goodyear Aircraft Corp since '40. ASME(F)—Inst Aeronautical Sci(F)—SAE—Soc Exptl Stress Analysis. Goodyear Aircraft Corp, Akron, O. H: 817 Delaware Av.◎

19 ARONSON, Lester Ralph. Animal behavior (Reproduction); Neurology; Endocrinology; Ichthyology; Herpetology. b'11. BA '32—MA '33 (Cornell U); PhD '45 (NYU). Research in reproductive behavior of vertebrates—fish, African mouthbreeding cichlids, tilapia macrocephala and poeciliid fishes; amphibia—leopard frog, bull frog, mink frog, green frog, American toad, Fowler's toad, South African claw toad, Anderson's tree frog; mammals—cats; physiological (endocrinological neurological and phsychological) mechanisms controlling reproductive behavior; effect of mammalian gonadal hormones on fish; neuroanatomy of forebrain and diencephalon of fish, amphibia and mammals. Author articles in field. Asst Am Mus Natural Hist '38, staff asst '42, asst curator '43, acting chmn and asso curator '46-48; chmn '49. Am Soc Ichthyologists and Herpetologists —Am Soc Naturalists—Am Assn Zool

—NY Zool Soc—NY Acad Sci—AAAS. The American Museum of Natural History, Central Park West at 79th St., NYC 24.◎

20 ARONSTAM, Milton Sheldon. Safety engineering. b'06. BS civil engineering '32 (Tri-State Coll); BS (mech engring) '39—BS (indsl engring) '40 Northwestern Inst). Research on accident prevention, industrial ventilation, industrial hygiene and fire protection in atomic energy and chemical industries; traffic control. With Ill Dept Pub Works and Bldgs '32-39; US Army Engrs '39-45; Sherwin-Williams Co '45-47; with Atomic Energy Commn since '47. Am Soc CE—W Soc Engrs—Soc Am Mil Engrs—Am Soc Safety Engrs. Postoffice Box 6140A, Chicago 80. H: 309 S. West Av., Elmhurst, Ill.

21 ARRANDALE, Roy Samuelson. Glass technology. b'11. BS '33 (U Ill); MS '34 (Carnegie Inst Tech); D Eng '39 (Yale U). Raw materials preparation and specification; plant and furnace design; analysis composition of glass; decoration of glassware. Process engr Standard Oil Development Co Elizabeth NJ '38-41; tech adv Thatcher Glass Mfg Co since '41. AC S—Am Ceramic Soc—AICE—Soc Glass Tech Brit—Am Soc Rheology—Sigma Xi—Phi Lambda Upsilon—Sigma Tau. 628 Water St., Elmira, N.Y.

22 ARTHUR, John Morris. Plants (Climate effects). b'93. BS '19—PhD '26 (U Chicago). Study plant growth in artificial climates, effect of radiant energy on plants, effect of day-length on flowering, effect of various temperatures on growth; devised method for heating and lighting greenhouses with intermittent light; experiment with effect of ultra violet on red pigment production in apples, and carbohydrate-nitrogen ratios in relation to radiant energy. Author articles: Some Effects of Artificial Climates on the Growth and Chemical Composition of Plants '30; Heating and Lighting Greenhouses with Intermittent Light '38. Contributor: Biological Effects of Radiation '36; Encyclopedia Britannica (Vol 5). Asst plant physiol Ia State Coll '16, Md Agrl Coll '17; biochem Boyce Thompson Inst Plant Research Inc since '21, dep dir since '49. AAAS—Bot Soc Am—NY Acad Sci—ACS—Optical Soc Am—Hort Soc Am—Sigma Xi. Boyce Thompson Institute for Plant Research, Inc., Yonkers 3, N.Y

23 ARTHUR, Marion Abrahams. Plastics (Casting); Protective coatings (Testing); Quantitative spectroscopy (Emission). b'11. BS '31 (Haverford Coll); MS '32 (Harvard). Reduced to practice protective embedding large objects in acrylic, phenolic, and polyester resins; Developed accurate electrical method evaluation moisture barrier any non-conducting protective coating. Granted patents of method and apparatus for taking spectrograph measurements, and others in field. Author articles in field. Geophysicist, Humble Oil Refining Co. Houston since '33; project supervisor proximity fuze safety sect Johns Hopkins Applied Physics Lab Silver Spring Md '43-45. Soc Exploration Geophysicists—Am Inst Physics—Soc Plastics Engrs. Humble Bldg., Houston 1.

24 ARVIDSON, Robert Benjamin, Jr. Poultry breeding. b'20. BSA '42—MS '50 (Purdue U). Development of inbred lines of poultry by use of related individuals in matings; expansion of lines used in most superior combinations and thus duplicate original mating for commercial sale. Co-author article: (with A W Nordskog) Experimental Design for Testing Performance of Hybrids '48. Poultry geneticist and head breeding dept HyLine Poultry Farms since '47. Poultry Sci Assn.

10 **ASAKAWA, Kwan-Ichi.** Feudalism; Institutional history of Japan; Medieval institutions of western Europe. b'73. Student '92-95 (Waseda U Tokio Japan); B Litt '99 (Dartmouth Coll); PhD '02 (Yale). Author: The Early Institutional Life of Japan '03; Ni-hon no kwa-ki Tokyo, '09 Translator and editor: The Documents of Iriki, Illustrative of the Development of Japanese Feudal Institutions '29; contbr chapters in Japan '04; History of Nations '07; Pacific Ocean in History '17; also articles in field. Prof emeritus hist Yale U since '42; curator of Japanese and Chinese collections since '09. Instit Historique et Heraldique de France (corr hon)—AHA—Asiatic Soc Japan—Japanese Hist Assn (Shigakkwai)—Phi Beta Kappa. Yale University, New Haven.

11 **ASBURY, Samuel Erson.** American folklore; Texas history; Climbing roses. b'72. BS '93—MS '96 (NC State Coll); '08-09 (Harvard). Research Colonial (1820-35), Revolutionary (1835-36) and Ante-bellum (1846-61) Texas history various state archives historical documents for past fifty years; interested over 200 historical projects; consultant breaking historical mysteries Texas, Southern and American history and folklore; research "Texians" active in Texas Revolution, previous and after lives of famous, infamous and unfamous "Texians" of colonial revolutionary; Texas, Reconstruction in counties of Texas and other slave states experimented climbing roses, maximum plant growth and yield as limited by soil, water and climate; origin of the elements, origin of life. Analytical chem state control labs NC, Va, Tenn '94-04, Tex '04-45; retired. AHA—South Hist Assn—Tex State Hist Assn(F). Box 208, College Station, Tex.

12 **ASDELL, Sydney Arthur.** Mammalian reproduction lactation, growth (Farm animals). b'97. BA '22—PhD '25—MA '26 (Cambridge U); '26 (Rochester U, Calif U). Consultant on selenium problems in livestock; engaged research on effect of inbreeding on mental ability in man, reproduction in mammals, sterility in farm animals; studies in field at Animal Nutrition Institute, Cambridge, England '37. Chairman North Eastern States Technical Advisory Committee on Sterility in Dairy Cattle. Author: Patterns of Mammalian Reproduction '46. Author articles: Hormones and Sterility in Dairy Cattle; Nutrition and Sterility in Dairy Cattle; and others. Research asst Animal Nutrition Inst Cambridge Eng '22-23; lecturer nutrition and physiol farm animals New Zealand U '28-30; with Cornell U since '30, now prof animal physiol. AAAS(F)—Am Assn Anatomists—Soc Exptl Biol and Med—Am Soc Animal Production—Sigma Xi. Fellow Internat Edn Bd Rochester U '26. Laboratory of Animal Nutrition, Cornell University, Ithaca, N.Y.†

13 **ASHBROOK, Frank Getz.** Fur animals (trade, production, conservation, utilization, rabbits). b'92. BS '14 (Pa State Coll). Engaged research all aspects fur animal production and utilization; also swine production; Supt cattle shipments, French high cmm '19-21; investigated methods dressing dog, lamb and kid skins imported to US from Japan and China for US government '37; expert witness proceedings between Federal Government and fur importers Court Customs and Patent Appeals '38; consultant and advisor matters pertaining to fur Quartermaster General's Office '42; Commissioner general US Fur Trade Expedition and Congress Leipzig '30. Author: Fur Farming for Profit '47; Rabbits for Food and Fur '30; '31; Birds '31; The Blue, Red and Green Books '31; How to Raise Rabbits for Food and Fur '43; Cooking Wild Game '45; also articles in field. In charge wild fur animal investigations, Fish and Wild Life Service US Dept Interior since '21. Wildlife Soc—Soc Animal Production. Fish and Wildlife Service, U. S. Department of Interior, Washington 25.

14 **ASHBY, Wallace.** Farm buildings; Rural housing; Agricultural engineering. b'90. BS '13—profl degree agrl eng '24 (Ia State Coll). Studies in land drainage, development, and farming operations in connection with reclaiming railroad grant lands; testing plows and similar equipment used in corn borer control; assisted in carrying out hemp program in US Department of Agriculture, including construction of 42 hemp mills; planning and supervision of research to develop better and more economical farm houses and related facilities. Author articles in field. With US Dept Agr since '28, head div farm bldgs and rural housing Bur Plant Industry Soils and Agrl Engring since '43. Am Soc Agrl Engrs—Gamma Sigma Delta—Phi Kappa Phi. Agricultural Research Center, U.S. Department of Agriculture, Beltsville, Md.†

15 **ASHE, Bowman Foster.** Education administration; Manpower administration. b'85. BS '12 LLD '27 (U Pittsburgh) LLD (John B Stetson U) LittD (Fla Southern Coll). Asso prof econ U Pittsburgh '20 student counselor U examiner '21-26; exec sec U Miami '26 pres since '26; regional dir Social Security Bd southeastern states '36-38; regional dir War Manpower Com southeastern states '42 Sigma Alpha Epsilon—Omicron Delta Kappa—Beta Gamma Sigma. University of Miami, Coral Gables, Fla.©

16 **ASHLEY, Carlyle Martin.** Air conditioning and refrigeration engineering. b'99. ME '24 (Cornell U). Humidity measurement, heat transfer, refrigerant properties, fluid flow including ejectors, outlets and free jets and duct losses, control of noise in buildings by air conditioning; patents include several air conditioning units, steam ejector equipment for railway cars, evaporative condensers, nonfreeze-non-stratifying heater, special types of heat transfer surface, refrigeration equipment associated with centrifugal and absorption refrigeration, air conditioning systems for multi-room air conditioning. With Carrier Corp since '24, chief development engr. Am Soc Refrigeration Engrs—Am Soc Heating and Ventilating Engrs—Tau Beta Pi. Carrier Corp., 300 S. Geddes St., Syracuse 1, N.Y.

17 **ASHTON, Edward (Ned) Lowell.** Bridges (Design). b'03. BS '25—MS (hydraulic and structural engring) '26 (State U Ia). Structural design bridges and structures as Navy's new 600-inch radar telescope; 480-foot all welded deck girder highway bridge Iowa City; 1540-foot continuous Tied Arch Bridge, Dubuque; Oklahoma Aircraft Assembly Plant structures; Kansas City Southern Lift Bridge, Beaumont; Harry S Truman Lift Span, Kansas City; research on behavior of pre-stretched and pre-compressed steel. Author: Studies in Structural Arc Welding. Asso engr James A Hooke St Louis '29-'32; asst engr div dams US Bur Reclamation Denver '33-'35;

asso engr Howard Needles Tammen and Bergerdoff Kansas City '35-'42; chief structural engr Okla Aircraft Assembly Plant Austin Co Okla City '42-43; asso prof civil engring State U Ia '43-'51; also cons engr. Am Soc CE—Am Welding Soc—Am Chem Inst—Am Soc EE—AAUP—Ia Engring Soc—Sigma Xi—Tau Beta Pi—Chi Epsilon—Theta Tau—Dolphin. 820 Park Rd., Iowa City, Ia.

18 **ASKER, Gunnar Carl Fred.** Air conditioning (Moisture control). b'13. MA (nav archt and marine engring) '36 (Royal Inst Tech Stockholm); '46-47 (George Washington U). Research and design of adsorbent dehumidifiers and automatic moisture control units. Chief engr Dry Air Products Corp '47; v-pres Daly Merritt and Sullivan Inc since '49. Am Soc Heating and Ventilating Engrs—Soc Nav Archt and Marine Engrs—Am Soc Swedish Engrs—Am Soc Nav Engrs—Wash Soc Engrs. Desomatic Products Division, Daly, Merritt and Sullivan Inc., 1109 W. Broad St, Falls Church, Va.

19 **ASMUNDSON, Vigfus Samundur.** Genetics and breeding of Poultry. (Domestic and turkey). b'95. BSA '18 (U Saskatchewan); MSA '20 (Cornell U); PhD '30 (U Wis). Engaged research in formation of the hen's egg; inheritance of egg production, weight, conformation, lethals, and plumage color in turkeys and domestic fowl; artificial light and reproduction in turkeys; effect of pre-incubation care of eggs on hatchability. Author articles in field. Asst prof poultry husbandry U Calif Davis '33-38, asso prof '38-46, prof since '46. AAAS—Poultry Sci Assn—Genetics Soc Am—Soc Exptl Biol and Med—Soc Study Evolution—Sigma Xi. Poultry Sci research prize '31; Borden award and gold medal '42; Nat Turkey Fed award and plaque '47. Poultry Husbandry Division, University of California, Davis, Calif.

20 **ASPLUND, Arne Johan Arthur.** Wallboard; Fibre board; Roofing felt; Flooring felt; Pulp (Semichemical); Wood sugar; Alcohol methyl. b'03. BS '27 (U Wis). Invented defibrator for defibration of fibrous ligno-cellulosic materials, invented refiner for use with wallboard, paper and paper board stock. Sulphate pulp mill engr Mo and Domsjo Aktiebolag '27-28; with Nordmalings Angsags AB '28-31; vice gen mgr and mem bd dir AB Defibrator '32-51 chairman bd dir AB Defibrator since '51. Alpha Chi Sigma—Swedish Assn Engrs and Archts. Received gold medal '47 from Royal Swedish Acad Engring Sci. AB Defibrator, Stockholm 40, Sweden

21 **ASSEL, Walter John.** Furnaces (Electric melting); Seamless tube mills; Furnaces (Heat treating); Heating (Inductive); Gas furnaces. b'89. BS (mech engring) '12 (O State U). Research and design of electric melting furnaces, application of fume elimination equipment to electric melting furnaces; originated method and mill for producing seamless tubing and adapted it for rolling shell forgings. Granted US and foreign patents in field. Chief engr Timken Steel and Tube Div since '25. Assn Iron and Steel Engrs—Am Ordnance Assn—Nat Soc Prof Engrs. Timken Roller Bearing Co., 1835 Dueber Av., S.W., Canton 6, O H: 3723 Darlington Rd., N.W., Canton 8.

22 **ASTON, Royden Newton.** Water treatment. b'17. BS '38 (Middlebury Coll). Research on use of chlorine dioxide in water treatment and industrial waste treatment, chemistry, uses, and production of sodium chlorite. Granted patents in field. With

Mathieson Chem Corp since '38, tech rep from '50 ACS—Am Water Works Assn—Am Assn Textile Chem and Colorists. Mathieson Chemical Corp., Dixie Terminal Building, Cincinnati 2. H: 7003 Rowan Hill Dr., Cincinnati 27.

10 **ATCHISON, Joseph Edward.** Pulp and paper. b'14. BS (Chem E) '38 (La State U); MS '40—PhD '42 (Inst Paper Chem Appleton Wis). Review and analysis pulp and paper mill investment projects foreign mills; study and promotion possibilities of development pulp and paper industries in dependent overseas territories; promotion use of waste paper, straw, esparto grass, poplar, eucalyptus and other fast growing raw materials in European countries; survey world flow of pulp and paper, production possibilities in various countries, and consumption requirements; research on pulp and paper production from agricultural residues; supervision installation of equipment and coordination mill modernization programs. Author articles: Suggestions for Technical Assistance Projects for the European Pulp and Paper Industry '49; The Use of Straw and other Agricultural Residues for Pulp, Paper and Board in the United States '49; The Use of Hardwoods for Pulp and Paper in the United States '49, and others. Tech dir John Strange Paper Co Menasha Wis '46-48; chief pulp and paper br Econ Cooperation Adminstrn Washington since '48. 800 Connecticut Av., N.W., Washington 25.

11 **ATHERTON, Lewis Elden.** Business history; Mercantilism. b'05. Student '23-25 (U Okla); BA '27—MA '30—PhD '37 (U Mo). Guggenheim memorial foundation fellowship for study country and small town store in slavery days. Author articles: Disorganizing Effects of the Mexican War on the Santa Fe Trade '37; The Services of the Frontier Merchant '37; Auctions as a Threat to American Business in the Eighteen Twenties and Thirties '37; The Merchant Sutler in the Pre-Civil War Period '38; The Pioneer Merchant in Mid-America, '39; Western Mercantile Participation in the Indian Trade '40; Itinerant Merchandising in the Ante-Bellum South '45; The Southern Country Store 1800-1860, '49. Instructor hist '36-39, asst prof '39-42, asso prof '42-45, prof since '45, chmn hist dept '44-50, dir Western historical manuscripts collection U Mo since '51. AHA (mem sub-committee business records) —Mississippi Valley Historical Assn (teachers com)—Agrl Hist (ed bd)— Phi Beta Kappa. 318 Jesse Hall, University of Missouri, Columbia, Mo.†

12 **ATKINS, Cyril Fitzgerald.** Agricultural byproducts in paper chemistry. b'99. BS '24 (Tufts Coll); MS '25 —PhD '35 (U Ia). Research on cotton stalks as pulp extender in paper and paper products; prepared serviceable paper from cotton stalks. Author articles in field. Prof chem Morgan State Coll since '47. AAAS—Am Chem Soc. Morgan State College, Baltimore 12.

13 **ATKINS, John Gilmer, Jr.** Rice, oat and truck crop diseases. b'16. BS '38 (Central Mo State Coll); MS '40 (La State U); PhD '47 (Cornell U). Author articles in field. Asst plant path La Agrl Expt Sta since '47. Am Phytopath Soc—La Acad Sci—Sigma Xi— Phi Kappa Phi. Louisiana Agricultural Experiment Station, Baton Rouge, La.†

14 **ATKINS, Paul Moody.** International economic affairs. b'92. AB '14 AM '15 (Yale) Docteur de l'Universite de Paris '25. Investment counselling; market analysis; banking and foreign exchange specialist; Iran finances. Author: Economic Briefs of Europe '27;

Secondary Reserves of Banks, '28; Economic Briefs of Latin America '28; Bank Secondary Reserves and Investments '29; The Investment of Corporation Reserves '29; Bank Secondary Reserves and Investment Policies, '30; Bank Bond Investment and Secondary Reserve Management '40. Chief Argentina-U r u g u a y-Paraguay unit Am Hemisphere Div Bd Econ Warfare '42; econ adviser Ministry of Finance Iran '43; bus and foreign exchange specialist since '42; banking and foreign exchange specialist Am Mission for Aid to Greece '47; temporary banking adviser for Japan to Sec Army '48. Am Econ Assn—Phi Beta Kappa—Pi Gamma Mu H: 199 Inwood Ave., Upper Montclair, N.J.†⊙

15 **ATKINSON, Carroll Holloway.** Radio education. b'96. AB '20 (Lawrence Coll); MA '20 (U Southern Calif); PhD '38 (George Peabody Coll for Teachers). Conference leader on radio education, school administration and youth movements. Author: American Universities and Colleges That Have Held Broadcast License '41; Radio Extension Courses Broadcast for Credit '41; Public School Broadcasting to the Classroom '42; Broadcasting to the Classroom by Universities and Colleges '42; Radio Programs Intended for Classroom Use '42; Radio in State and Territorial Educational Departments '42, and others. Asso prof and dir radio Jersey City and Newark State Teachers Colls, '39-41; columnist Honolulu Star-Bulletin and radio producer '46-47; dean of men Southwestern U '47-49; dir teacher training Dak Wesleyan '49-51; supervising prin Pojoaque Valley (N.M.) pub schools since '51. NEA —Am Assn School Adminstrs—Society Advancement Learning—Calif Elementary Sch Prins Assn (p pres)—Tex Acad Sci—AAAS. Rte 1, Box 251, Santa Fe, N. Mex.

16 **ATKINSON, Clinton Edwin.** Anadromous fish; Marine fish. b'13. BS '37—'40, '43-45 (U Wash). Author: The Problem of Enumerating Spawning Populations of Sockeye Salmon '44; also articles in field. Apprentice fish culturist US Bur Fisheries '37; research asst Internat Fisheries Commn '37; sci asst Internat Pacific Salmon Fisheries Commn '38-41, asst sci '42-44, sr sci '45-48; chief middle and S Atlantic fishery investigations Fish and Wildlife Service US Dept Interior '48-52, charge Beaufort Fishery Lab '49-52; Chief Pacific Coast Salmon Investigations since '52. Am Soc Limnol Oceanog—Atlantic Estuarine Soc —Pacific Fishery Biol (secretary-treas '46)—Sigma Xi. U.S. Fish and Wildlife Service, 2725 Montlake Blvd., Seattle.

17 **ATKINSON, Francis Edward.** Food processing. b'05. BS '29 (Ore State Coll). Research on processing cherries and berries in sulphur dioxide solution, candying process of glace fruits, natural apple juice. Head Fruit and Vegetable Products Lab Dominion Expt Sta since '29. Inst Food Tech— Agrl Inst Can—Prof Inst Can—Alpha Zeta—Phi Kappa Phi. Dominion Experiment Station, Summerland, B.C.

18 **ATKINSON, Ralph Hall.** Platinum metals (Refining); Platinum metals (Alloys); Platinum metals (Catalysts). b'90 BA '12—MA '16 (Cambridge U). Refining of platinum metals, gold and silver recovered as by-products in refining of nickel and copper, preparation of platinum and palladium catalysts used in manufacture of synthetic organics, discovery and development of new uses for platinum metals. Contributor: Metals Handbook '48. Asst mgr precious metals refinery Mond Nickel Co '23-40; chief research chem

Internat Nickel Co Can Ltd '41; research chem Merck and Co '42; research metall Internat Nickel Co Inc since '43, head platinum metals sect research lab from '44. AIMME—Soc Chem Industry—Chem Soc—Royal Inst Chem—Electrodepositors Tech Soc. International Nickel Co., Research Laboratory, Oak St., Bayonne, N.J.

19 **ATWATER, Gordon A(lbert).** Celestial navigation. b'04. EE '26 (Purdue U). Initiated Newport navy conference on LTA applications in Polar regions '46, Lakehurst and Washington navy conference on proposed LTA eclipse expedition '47; designer navigation training building Ft Schuyler '44, originator new navigation training organization, methods and teaching techniques. Invented devices for presenting astronomical phenomena in Planetarium. Author articles in field. Chmn and curator Hayden Planetarium since '45; council sci staff AMNH since '45. Head Navigation Dept USNRMS Ft Schuyler '44-45, head navigation dept NTS Boston '42-43. Sci Mus and Planetaria — USNR — ION—AAAS. Hayden Planetarium, 81st St. and Central Park West, NYC 24.

20 **ATWATER, Harry Arthur.** Combustion (Oil, gas). b'89. ME '12 (Cornell U). Patentee of inventions relating to oil burners, gas burners, firing methods for oil refinery stills, boilers, locomotives, air heaters, recirculation systems, safety pilot, related devices. Fuel engr Central Coal and Coke Co Kansas City '17-18; chief engr Lientz Oil Furnace Co '19-22, Combustion Equipment Co since '22. Am Soc ME—Am Soc Heating and Ventilating Engrs—Nat Soc Profl Engrs—Am Gas Assn—Oil Heat Inst—Eta Kappa Nu. Combustion Equipment Co., 1820 Cherry St., Kansas City 8, Mo. H: 641 West 67th St., Kansas City 5, Mo.

21 **ATWATER, Mary M(eigs).** Hand weaving; Textile design. b'78. Student (Chicago Art Inst Sch Design, Chicago Art Academy, Ecole Colarossi Paris). Made special trip to Guatemala to study native weaving of that country; extensive studies of native weaves of North and South America; pioneered in modern revival of hand weaving; prepared course of instruction by correspondence through which many skilled weavers learned art. Author: The Shuttle-Craft Book of American Hand Weaving; Shuttle-Craft Guild Recipe Book; Guatemala Visited; also articles in field. Organized Shuttle-Craft Guild and prepared and published a monthly bulletin for members issued since '24. 6120 S. 23rd East, Salt Lake City.†

22 **ATWATER, Montgomery Meigs.** Forest management; Forestry (Avalanche control, fire control). b'04. BS '26 (Harvard). Author: Government Hunter '40; Flaming Forest '42; Ski Patrol '43; Hank Winton, Smokechaser '47; Second-Year Man '49. Co-author: The Alta Snow and Avalanche Studies '48; also articles in field. Forest fire control foreman '39-42; gen dist asst US Forest Service Alta Utah since '45. Served US Army '42-45 as instr mountain and winter warfare. 6150 S. 23rd East, Salt Lake City 7.†

23 **ATWOOD, John Murray.** Theology; Education administration. b'69. BA '89 MA '00 (St Lawrence U) BD '93 (Canton Theol Seminary) DD '06 (Lombard Coll) '39 (St Lawrence U). Prof sociol and ethics '05-13 (Canton Theol Sch); prof philosophy '13-14 St Lawrence U dean theol dept since '14 mem bd administration since '19. Pres. mem bd trustees Universalist Gen Conf '23-27. Phi Beta Kappa. 25 College St., Canton, NY.⊙

10 AUDRIETH, Ludwig Frederick. Nitrogen and phosphorus chemistry. b'01. BS '22 (Colgate U); PhD '26 (Cornell U); research fellow '31-32 (U Rostock, Germany). Also research on rare metals, non-aqueous solvents, explosives (military), electrochemistry. Holds 15 patents. Author articles in field. Dept chem U Ill since '28, now prof; chem cons indsl concerns official investigator Nat Defense Research Com '40-42; capt maj Ordnance Dept US Army '42-46, chief research div Picatinny Arsenal, and head phys sci U Training Com MTOUSA Florence Italy. Noyes Laboratory, University of Illinois, Urbana, Ill.

11 AUERBACH, Frank L. Immigration U.S., nationality U.S., naturalization U.S., Admission of displaced persons to U.S. b'10. JUD '33 (U Heidelberg); MS '42 (Columbia). Author: The Admission and Resettlement of Displaced Persons in the U.S. '50 The Immigration and Nationality Act '53. Contrib: Social Work Year Book Cons US Dept of Interior '44; asst case cons Internat Social Service '44-46; ed Interpreter Release, and chief individual services Common Council for Am Unity since '46; lecturer Columbia since '47; cons to chief visa div Dept of State since '48. Am Assn of Social Workers—Nat Council on Naturalization and Citizenship (mem exec bd). 1383 Congress St., SE, Washington 20.

12 AUERBACH, Richard C. Wine (Chemistry, production) Champagne (production). b'98. Student (Sch Viticulture Geisenheim Germany), (U Grenoble France). Champagne-maker, Eltville, Germany. Co-author article: (with W E Kite) Champagne Production '49. Tech dir winery and champagne factory T Langenbach & Sons Worms Germany; gen mgr brandies, vermouths, cordials, Metzger & Boehm Nueremberg Germany; at present chief chem, supt quality-control Roma Wine Co & wine dir Schenley Industries Fresno Calif. ACS—Soc Wine Chem San Yoaquin Valley. Roma Wine Co., Fresno, Calif. H: 3119 Balch Ave., Fresno, Calif.

13 AUFRICHT, Hans. International law and relations (League of Nations, bibliography). b'02. Dr rer pol '26—Dr Jur Sc '37 (U Vienna). Research assistant Commission to Study the Organization of Peace '41-43. Author: War, Peace and Reconstruction: A Classified Bibliography '43; World Organization: An Annotated Bibliography '46; Guide to League of Nations Publications: A Bibliographical Survey of the Work of the League, 1920-1947 '51; also articles in field. Asst on Internat Organization Affairs Dept State '46-47; legal dept Internat Monetary Fund Washington since '47; lectr graduate school American Univ Washington DC '49-52. Am Society International Law—Am Polit Sci Assn. Carnegie fellow '35 '40-41; grants-in-aid Carnegie Corp and Rockefeller Found. International Monetary Fund, Washington.

14 AULT, E(ugene) Stanley. Machine design; Bearings; Gears. b'98. BE 20 (Johns Hopkins); ME '21—MME '24 (Cornell U). Co-author: (with Norman and Zarobsky) Fundamentals of Machine Design '38; also articles in field. Engr Western Elec Co '21, '30; test engr Pa Power and Light Co '22; statis Adirondack Power and Light Co Schenectady '23; asst bridge engr City Houston '25-27; asst prof machine design Lehigh U '27-30; asso prof machine design Case Inst Tech '30-37; prof machine design, charge of machine design Purdue U since '37; tool engr Kingsbury Ordnance Plant '41;

engr cons since '27; ed cons since '30. ASME (past chmn Cleveland sect, past chmn nat machine design com)—Am Gear Mfg Assn—Sigma Xi. Purdue University, Lafayette, Ind.⊙

15 AULTMAN, William Whitescarver. Water treatment plant operation and design. b'05. Student '22-24 (U Calif); BS '27 (Calif Inst Tech). Research on carbon black production; preliminary investigations and design of $200,000,000 Colorado River Aqueduct; charge special research projects pertaining to water treatment. Author articles in field. Field engr geophys investigations '27-29; research engr '29-30; became engr and water purification engr Met Water Dist So Cal '30; now asst dir dept water and sewers City of Miami. Am Water Works Assn—ASCE—Sigma Xi—Tau Beta Pi. P.O. Box 316, Coconut Grove Station, Miami 33, Fla.

16 AUSEMUS, Elmer Rex. Genetics and breeding of spring and winter wheat. b'95. BS '23 (Kansas State Coll); MS '24 (State Coll Washington); PhD '32 (U Minn). Research in wheat improvement with particular reference to breeding for disease resistance. Produced several improved wheat varieties. Author articles in field. Junior and asst agron US Dept Agr Mandan ND '25-29; asst agron, asso agron, and agron US Dept Agr St Paul since '29; prof U Minn since '47. AAAS—Am Soc Agron—Am Genetics Soc. Division of Agronomy and Plant Genetics, University Farm, St. Paul 1.†⊙

17 AUTREY, Kenneth Maxwell. Dairy husbandry. b'17. BS '38 (La State U); MS '39—PhD '41 (Ia State Coll) Research on dairy feeding, grass and legume silage. Studies on physiologic and economic efficiency in milk production of various rations. Co-author articles: (with C Y Cannon, D L Espe) Efficiency of Dairy Rations Containing Various Quantities of Grains '42; (with C B Knodt, P S Williams) Grass and Legume Silage Studies Using Two Quart Glass Jars as Miniature Silos '47. Asst prof dairying U Ga 1941 to 1944; asso prof dairy husbandry Pa State Coll 1946; now head prof dairy husbandry Ala Poly Inst. Am Dairy Sci Assn—Sigma Xi. Alabama Polytechnic Institute, Department of Dairy Husbandry, Auburn, Ala.

18 AVERITT, Paul. Coal resources of the United States; Geology of coal and asphalt deposits. b'08. BS '30—MS '31 (U Ky); '31-33 (Northwestern U); '33-34 (Johns Hopkins). Chief coal resources section fuels branch US Geological Survey since 49. Author: Map of the Coal Fields of the United States '42; Coal resources of the U.S. '50; Coking Coal Deposits of the Western U.S. '51. Junior geologist US Geol Survey '38-40, assistant geologist '40-42, associate geol '42-44, geologist '44-47, sr geol since '47. Geol Soc Am—Am Assn Petroleum Geol—Soc Econ Geol (coal resource com)—Geol Soc Wash—Am Soc Testing Materials (com on coal and coke). U.S. Geological Survey, Washington 25.

19 AVRAM, M(ois) H. Industrial engineering (Industrial processes, machinery, plants, rayon industry). BSc '04—ME '05 (NYU). Author: The Rayon Industry '31; Patenting and Promoting Inventions '19. General engr pvt practice since '12. Cons engr. Pres The Slide Fastener Assn Inc. ASME—Am Ordnance Assn—Natl Aeronautical Assn. 25 5th Av., NYC.

20 AVRETT, William Robert. Spanish grammar; Spanish drama (Mod-

ern); Spanish American literature; Comparative literature; American poetry (Contemporary). b'01. AB '27—AM '28 (U Tex); Harrison F Romanics '36-37, '38 (U Pa). Authorized translator of Spanish poetry of Mexican poet Enrique González Martínez, editorial consultant for PMLA on Spanish American literary articles, editor Entre Nosotros since '51, assistant editor in charge Spanish book reviews for Modern Language Journal since '51. Author: Outline Spanish Review Grammar '40; The Dream Comes First '49. Instr to asst prof modern lang Tex W Coll '28-45; dir Inst Cultural Argentino-Norteamericano (Buenos Aires) US Dept State '45-46; with U Tenn since '47, asso prof Romance lang and lit form '51. Sigma Delta Pi (acting nat exec sec since '51)—Pi Delta Phi—Phi Delta Kappa—Omicron Delta Kappa—Poetry Soc Am (asso mem)⊙University of Tennessee, Knoxville 16, Tenn.

21 AXELROD, Daniel I(ssac). Tertiary paleobotany; Floristic evolution; Miocene and Pliocene floras of western North America; Vegetation history. b'10. PhD '38 (U Calif). Studies of origins of modern units of vegetation; recognized Madro-Tertiary flora, a semiarid major continental Tertiary flora which spread northward over southwestern North America during the middle and later Tertiary; ecotypes in the fossil record; development of criteria for correlation of dissimilar types of vegetation; Middle Pliocene climate as a factor in evolution of species and vegetation; origin of desert environments; theory of angiosperm evolution. Author articles in field. Professor geol U California since '46. Geol Soc Am—Soc Study Evolution—Calif Bot Soc. Nat Research Council fellow '39-40, '40-41; Guggenheim fellow '52-53. Department of Geology, University of California, Los Angeles 24.†

22 AXILROD, Benjamin M. Mechanical properties of plastics. b'12. BS EE '33—MS '34—'34-35 (U Minn); '37-42, '46-'49 PhD (George Wash U). Author articles in field. With Nat Bur Standards, organic plastics sect, jr physicist, transparent and reinforced plastics for aircraft '35-39, asst physicist laminated plastics for aircraft applications '40-43, asso physicist properties of laminated plastics at various temperatures '43-45, physicist adhesives, laminates, aircraft glazing '45-51, polymer physics since '51. National Bureau of Standards, Connecticut Av. at Upton N.W., Washington.

23 AYARS, William Stewart. Mechanical, marine and industrial engineering (Design estimation); Steam locomotives; Pumping machinery; Manufacturing processes. b'73. ME '96 (Lehigh U). Engaged in supervising trial trips new ships; consultant and technical witness in public utilities and patents cases; prepared home study course practical mechanical design Columbia University. Author articles in field. Prof elec and mech engring Nova Scotia Tech Coll Halifax '11-16; sr performance engr emergency fleet corp US Shipping Bd Phila '17-19; chief estimator and marine engr Pusey & Jones Corp Wilmington Del '19-22; asso prof indsl engring Columbia U '22-40; cons Am Locomotive Co '41-45. ASME—Nova Scotia Soc Engrs (past pres)—AIEE—Am Mgmt Assn—Sigma Xi—Tau Beta Pi. 269 Leonia Av., Leonia, N.J.

24 AYDELOTTE, Frank. Rhodes scholarships and Guggenheim fellowships; English literature (Elizabethan). b'80. AB '00 (Indiana); AM

03 (Harvard); BLitt 08; eleven honorary degrees Am and fgn univs. Author: Elizabethan Rogues and Vagabonds '13; College English '13; The Oxford Stamp '17; *Breaking the Academic Lock Step, '44; The American Rhodes Scholarships '46, published in England as The Vision of Cecil Rhodes '46; also articles in field. Dir Instn for Advanced Study '39-47; Am sec to Rhodes trustees since '18; pres Assn of Am Rhodes Scholars since '30; chmn edn advisory bd John Simon Guggenheim Mem Found since '25. Modern Lang Assn Am—Am Philos Soc—AHA—Phi Beta Kappa (mem senate since '31). Inst. for Advanced Study, Princeton, N.J.⊚

10 AYDELOTTE, William Osgood. History of modern England and Europe. b'10. BA '31 (Harvard); PhD '34 (Cambridge U). Research on British and German imperialism and foreign policy; also English economic, social, religious and intellectual history in 19th century. Author: Bismarck and British Colonial Policy; The Problem of South West Africa, 1883-1885 '37; also articles in field. Prof history, chmn hist dept State U Ia. Phi Beta Kappa—AHA. Visiting fellow in hist Yale '41-42; Hodder fellow Princeton U '45-46. Department of History, State University of Iowa, Iowa City, Ia.

11 AYERS, Alvin Dearing. Soil chemistry; Plant physiology. b'09. BS '32—MS '34 (U Ariz); PhD '38 (U Calif. Research on use of anhydrous ammonia in irrigation water as a fertilizer '35; developed the use of sodium hexametaphosphate for inhibiting precipitation of $CaCO_3$ when NH_3 was added to irrigation water; intake of potassium by excised barley roots from solutions and colloidal clay suspensions '36-38; soil and plant chemistry in relation to salt tolerance of plants; clay membrane electrodes for determination of cation activities. Author articles: The Influence of the Degree of Saturation of Soil Colloids on the Nutrient Intake by Roots '39. Co-author articles: (with C H Wadleigh and O C Magistad) The Interrelationships of Salt Concentration and Soil Moisture Content with the Growth of Beans '43; (with J S Hoskins) Comparative Behavior of Ammonia and Ammonium Salts in Soils '45. Asst agrl chem '32-33; chem Salt River Valley Water User' Assn Phoenix Ariz '34, Assn lab Anaheim Calif '35; chem US Regional Salinity Labs Riverside Cal '38-51; agriculturist USDA Field Com Arkansas-White-Red Basins Office, Tulsa. Soil Science Soc Am—Am Soc Agron—Western Soc Soil Science—Am Soc Plant Physiol—Sigma Xi—Phi Kappa Phi—Gamma Sigma Delta. H: 4413 E 26th St., Tulsa.

12 AYERS, Archie Raymond. Educational administration. b'10. BS'35 (U SC) AM '37 (Duke) PhD '44 (George Peabody Coll for Teachers). Administrative asst dir audio-visual edn New Hanover Schs Wilmington NC '37-41; head physics Peabody Coll '41-46; asso prof edn prin lab sch Eastern Ill State Coll Charleston '46-49; academic dean Lycoming Coll Williamsport Pa '49-50; dean univ Kan Wesleyan U Salina Kan '50-51; pres Detroit Inst Tech since '51. NEA—Am Phys Soc—Am Assn Sch Adminstrs—AAAS-Pi Mu Epsilon—Sigma Pi Sigma. 2020 Witherell St., Detroit 26.⊚

13 AYERS, John Carr. Marine hydrography and ecology; Antifouling paint; Shell-fish biology. b'12. AB '34 (Kalamazoo Coll); MS '36 (Kan State Coll); PhD '39—teaching fellow '36-39 (Duke U). Research in develop-

ment and testing of antifouling ship-bottom paints, chemistry and hydrography of ocean waters, hydrography and ecology of estuaries and shellfish biology. Author articles in field. Research asso Woods Hole Oceanog Instn '44-49; asso prof oceanog Cornell U since '50. Am Soc Limnol Oceano—Sigma Xi. Department of Conservation, Cornell University, Ithaca, N.Y.†

14 AYERS, Joseph Williams. Colors; Pigments; Carbon black; Flour Chromium Oxides; Cuprous Oxide. b'04. AB (Chem) '27—'27-28 (Cornell U) Research in chemistry, physics and processing of inorganic colors and non-opaque inorganic pigments; industrial vegetable shell; manufacture carbon black. Issued patents in field. Contributor: Protective and Decorative Coatings '42. With C K Williams and Co since '28, dir research '30-48, dir since '35, vp since '45; vp, dir, tech adv Agrashell Inc Los Angeles '39-45, pres and dir since '45; pres Productos Oleaginosos Mexico since 1944; cons US Engrs on camouflage problems '42-43. Am Inst Chem (F)—AICE (F)—ACS—Intercolor Council —ASTM—AAAS—Soc Rheology. CK Williams and Co, 640 North 13th St., Easton, Pa.

15 AYRES, Arthur U(nderwood). Centrifuges (Design); Vegetable oils (Refining process). b'93. AB '13 (Swarthmore Coll). Research on centrifuge design and application; co-developer continuous vegetable oil refining process. Holds patents on mechanical design of centrifuges, applications centrifuges to special processes and technique continuous vegetable oil refining. Author articles: Automatic Controls '40; Air Driven Ultra Centrifuge '40; Separation by Centrifugal Force '44. Transmission engr Chester Valley Electric Co '13; elec engr Valdosta Lighting Co '14; motor application engr Westinghouse Elec & Mfg Co '16; power engr Atlantic City Electric Co; chief engr Sharples Corp Phila '18-50; cons since '50. Am Oil Chem Soc—Phi Beta Kappa. 2300 Westmoreland Sts., Phila 40.

16 AYRES, Eugene. Petroleum by-products (Alcohols, lanolin, chlorinated hydrocarbons). b'91. AB '12 (Swarthmore Coll). Established first American manufacture of diphenylamine, wool grease, lanolin, amorphous petroleum wax and synthetic alcohols from petroleum; developed presently used methods of large scale direct chlorination of hydrocarbons. Holder of patents in field. Co-author: Energy Sources, the Wealth of the World '52. Organization and management of research concerned with manufacture and sale petroleum products Gulf Research and Development Company since '34. AAAS—ACS—ASTM—SAE. Gulf Research and Development Co., P.O. Box 2038, Pittsburgh 30.

17 AYRES, John C(lifton). Microbiology of meat and poultry products. b'13. BE '36 (Ill State Normal U); MS '38—PhD '42—Scholastic fellow '41-42 (U Ill); '44-45 (U Minn). Researches on synthetic detergents, quarternary ammonium compounds and other germicides, water sanitation studies, preparation of cultured soy cheeses, controlled egg white fermentations, methods for destruction of pathogens in dried egg products, studies of changes in stored poultry and cured meats, effects of gases on keeping qualities of meats, development of methods for determining anaerobes in meats, packing plant studies in cooperation with USQMC. Author articles in field. Research bact Wm S Merrell Co Cincinnati '42-43; project leader food microbiol research Gen Mills Inc Minneap-

olis '43-46; asst prof bact and food tech Agr Expt Sta Ia State Coll '46-48, asso prof since '48, research asst prof bact '46-48, research asso prof since '48. Ia Acad Sci—Inst Food Technol—Soc Am Bact—Associates Food and Container Inst (inst mem)—Sigma Xi. Department of Bacteriology, Iowa State College, Ames, Ia. H: 1412 Harding St.

18 AYRES, Quincy Claude. Drainage and flood control. b'91. BE '12—BS '12—CE '20 (U Miss). Appointed part time patent manager for Iowa State College to develop patent policies and organize and administer a patent-holding agency '35. Author: Soil Erosion and Its Control '36. Co-author: Land Drainage and Reclamation '39; also articles in field. Prof agrl engring, exec officer research foundation Ia State Coll since '20. ASCE (pres Ia sect '30)—Am Soc Agrl Engrs—Am Soc Engring Edn—Ia Engring Soc (vp '34-36, pres '36). Award for outstanding service by Ia Engring Soc '44. 117 Beardshear Hall, Iowa State College, Ames, Ia.†⊚

B

19 BABCOCK, Ernest Brown. Genetics; Plant taxonomy; Plant breeding; Plant evolution. b'77. BS '06—MS '11—LLD '50 (U Cal). Author: The American Species of Crepis '38; The Genus Crepis '47. Co-author: (with Dr Roy E Clausen) Genetics Laboratory Manual '18, Genetics in Relation to Agriculture '18; (with Dr G Ledyard Stebbins Jr) The Genus Youngia '37. With U Cal since '07 asst prof plant path '07-10, asst prof agrl edn '10-13 prof genetics '13-47 prof emeritus since '47. Pres sect exptl taxonomy VII Internat Botany Congress Stockholm '50. AAAS—Am (vp '34) and Western socs naturalists—Genetics Soc Am—Am Genetics Assn—Bot Soc Am—Nat Acad Scis—Phi Beta Kappa—Sigma Xi—Alpha Zeta—Phi Sigma. University of California, Berkeley 4, Cal.⊚

20 BABCOCK, Horace W. Astrophysics; Electronics; Diffraction gratings; Magnetic field of sun; Microphotometer. b'12. BS '34 (California Institute Tech); PhD '38 (U Calif). Research stellar spectroscopy; study of Andromeda Nebula and magnetic fields of stars. Measured rotation of the Andromeda Nebula '39; discovered and measured general magnetic fields of stars '46; spectrum of night sky; photoelectric guider for astronomical telescopes, electronic code translator, direct-intensity microphotometer. With OSRD '41-45, Mount Wilson Observatory Carnegie Inst Washington since '46. Am Astron Soc—Internat Astron Union—Astron Soc Pacific—Sigma Xi—Tau Beta Pi. Mount Wilson Observatory, 813 Santa Barbara St., Pasadena, Calif.

21 BABEL, Fred John. Dairy bacteriology; Cheese manufacturing. b'11. BS '35 (Mich State Coll); MS '36 (Purdue U); PhD '39 (Ia State Coll). Engaged research on bacteriology and chemistry of cheese ripening, enzymes important in dairy products, bacteriophage, quality tests for dairy products. Co-author: (with B. W. Hammer). Bacteriology of Cheese. IV. Factors Affecting the Ripening of Swiss-Type Cheese Made from Pasteurized Milk '39; also articles in field. Research professor Purdue U since '51. Phi Kappa Phi—Sigma Xi—Am Dairy Sci Assn. Fellowship, Dairy and Ice Cream Machinery and Supplies Assn '35-36. Dairy Department, Smith Hall, Purdue University, W. Lafayette, Ind.†

10 BABER, Clinton W(iley). Chemistry of tobacco processing; Nicotine insecticides. b'09. BS '35 (Va Poly Inst). Lab asst Tobacco By-Products & Chem Corp '27-31, plant control and research chem '35-39; research chem engr Larus & Bro Co Inc '39-40, mgr chem research dept since '45. Am Chem Soc—Va Acad. Sci. Larus & Brother Company, Incorporated, P.O. Box 6-S, Richmond, Va. H: RFD 9, Box 155.

11 BABER, Ray Erwin. Family; Marriage; Divorce (Mixed, husband-wife relations); Parent-child relationship; Differential fertility. b'91. BA '13 (Campbell Coll); MA '20—PhD '23 (U Wis). Research on problems of marriage and the family, study of shrinkage of family size as correlated with various factors, mate selection standards of college students and their parents, interfaith and interracial marriages, counseling students on premarital and marital problems. Author: Marriage and the Family '39. Co-author (with E A Ross) Changes in the Size of American Families in One Generation '24. Faculty U Wis, U Ill '20-25; prof sociol NY U '29-39; prof social, chmn dept sociol Pomona Coll since '39. Nat Council on Family Relations (bd dir)—Family Relations Council S Calif (exec com)—Am Family Relations Inst (trustee)—Am Sociol Soc—Pacific Sociol Soc (past pres)—Population Assn Am. Pomona College, Claremont, Cal.

12 BABSON, Roger Ward. Economic statistics and forecasting; Investments. b'75. BS '98 (MIT); LLD '27 (U Fla); LLD '37 (Elon Coll); LLD '38 (Hendrix Coll); LLD '39 (Am Theol Sem); LLD '40 (Lebanon Valley Coll); LLD '40 (Stetson U). Author: Business Barometers '09; Selected Investments '11; Bonds and Stocks '12; Business Fundamentals; Enduring Investments; Storing Up Triple Reserves; The Fundamentals of Success; Fighting Business Depressions; If Inflation Comes; Consumer Protection; The Folly of Installment Buying; Better Living for Less Money, and others. Founder Bus Statis Orgn Babson Park Mass, Babson Inst); chmn bd Babson's Reports Inc; now engaged study gravity; organized and endowed Gravity Research Found New Boston NH. Royal Statis Soc London (F). 370 Washington St., Wellesley Hills, Mass.†⊚

13 BACH, Richard F(ranz). History of architecture, art and industrial design; Decorative arts; Theory and history of design. b'87. AB '08 (Columbia). Made special study on industrial art in survey on Recent Social Changes for President Hoover's Research committee on Social Trends, Carnegie Corporation and Social Science Research Council '31; research abroad on economic aspects of design in industrial arts, General Education Board and Metropolitan Museum of Art '29; delegate and adviser to numerous American and international art exhibitions. Author articles in field. Cons indsl art Met Mus since '49; dean education and ext Met Museum Art '41-49; chmn John Wesley Hyatt award in plastics since '42; trustee Am Fed Arts since '37, School Art League '41-50; Am Craftsmen's Cooperative Council since '42; adv council Cooper Union Art Sch since '43, chmn since '45; Trustee New York-Phoenix Sch of Design since '44, vp since '44; mem adv bd Am Council Style and Design since '46. Am Assn Museums—AIA (hon) Amer Inst. Decorators (hon)—Amer. Designers Inst (hon)—Nat Soc Mural Painters (hon)—Municipal Art Soc NY—Archtl League NY (hon, vp '46-47). Recipient Friedsam medal in indsl art, Archtl League NY '30. Grosvenor Av., Riverdale, NYC 71.⊚

14 BACHARACH, Eric William. Water purification. b'83. Student '02-03 (engring coll U Cincinnati); BSc '06 (U Mich). Pioneer in introduction modern methods water purification; designed and installed plants for more than 500 towns, cities and industrial concerns, and with others for 250 towns and cities; built plants for US government in connection war projects. Inventor chemical feeding machines, other water purification devices installed throughout world. Pittsburgh Filter and Engring Co '05, western mgr, 1st vp '22; owner, propr E W Bacharach Co (water purification plants) Kansas City since '22; pres E W Bacharach Inc since '48. Am Pub Health Assn—Asociacion Interamericana De Ingenieria Sanitaria—ASCE—Am Soc Mil Engrs—Am Water Works Assn-Southwest Water Works Assn—Nat Assn Mfrs. Rialto Building, KC 6, Mo.†⊚

15 BACHMAN, Charles Herbert. Electron physics (Optics, microscopy, diffraction, vacuum); Discharge in gases; Television. b'08. BS '32—MS '33—PhD '35 (Ia State Coll). Holder numerous patents. Author: Techniques in Experimental Electronics '48; also articles in field. Asso prof physics Syracuse U since '46. Am Inst Physics—Electron Microscope Soc of America—Inst Radio Engrs—Sigma Xi—Tau Beta Pi. Steele Hall, Physics Department, Syracuse University, Syracuse, N.Y.†

16 BACHMAN, Gustave Bryant. Organic chemistry; Synthetic polymers and medicinals. b'05. BA '26 (U Colo); PhD '30 (Yale); '29-30 (U Munich). Author articles in field. Prof chem Purdue U since '41. Am Chem Soc (past chmn Purdue sect)—AAAS—Ind Acad Sci—Ind Chem Soc—Sigma Xi—Phi Beta Kappa. Purdue University, Lafayette, Ind.†

17 BACHMANN, Jean George. Physiology (Mammalian); Cardiology. b'77. MD '07 Jefferson Med Coll) MS '22 (Emory U). Research venous pulse, heart-block, interauricular conduction, heart innervation, metabolism of glucose and fructose, calcium, phosphorus, caffeine. Co-author: The Essentials of Physiology and Pharmacodynamics (with A Richard Bliss Jr) '24 revised edit '26 '40. Prof physiology Emory U Sch Med '15-47; cons cardiology since '47. Cardiovascular examiner US Army '17-18. Fellow AA AS—Am Coll Phys(F)—Am Physiol Soc—NY and Ga acads sci—Alpha Omega Alpha—Phi Beta Kappa—Sigma Xi—Phi Rho Sigma.⊚

18 BACHNER, Martin. Plastics (Vinyl). b'10. BS '32 (Capitol U Columbus O); MA '40 (U Pittsburgh). Development of cold temperature resistant materials for US Army; development of polyethylene monofilament for use in aerial tow targets with superior cold and tear resistance for Army and Navy Air Corps; research and product application of vinyl chloride polymer and co-polymer plastic film and sheeting, also poly-vinylidine chloride monofilament. Development project group leader of bullet sealing fuel cells Firestone Tire & Rubber Co '41-43; mgr engring and development of bullet sealing fuel cells Firestone Aircraft Co Conshocton O '43-45; processing and construction of plastic non-metallic materials for use on gasoline and oil tanks of combat aircraft and land vehicles. Dist mgr and sales engr vinyl plastics Firestone Plastics Co '46-48, mgr comml development since '48. Soc Plastics Industry—Plastic Film and Coatings Assn. Firestone Plastics Co., Pottstown, Pa.

19 BACHRACH, Alice (Mrs. Alfred R. Bachrach). Volunteer social welfare. b'02. Grad NY Sch Fine and Applied Arts '21. Service to men and women of armed forces, hospitalized veterans. Volunteer social work since '20; mem bd Nat USO since '43, vp since '51; mem women's adv council Dept of Def since '43; mem nat adv com VA Voluntary Service; former mem nat civilian adv com WAC. Frank L Weil award for contribution to service for men and women in the armed forces '52. H: 911 Park Av., NYC 21.⊚

20 BACHRACH, Arthur Julian. Clinical psychology (Rorschach, Thermatic apperception test); Group psychotherapy. b'23. BS '47 (Coll City NY) MA '50 (Western Reserve U) PhD '50 (U Va). Clinical use of diagnostic psychological techniques; projective techniques such as Rorschach and Thematic Apperception test; group psychotherapy. Psychol Cleveland State Receiving Hosp '48-49; clin psychol '49 research psychol '49-50 Cleveland Soc Crippled Children. Author several technical articles. AAAS—Am Psychol Assn—Soc Projective Techniques and Rorschach Inst—Soc Psychol Study Social Issues—Am Soc Group Psychotherapy and Psychodrama—Phi Delta Kappa. Div. Clin. and Med. Psychology, Univ. of Va. Hosp., Charlottesville, Va.

21 BACK, George Irving. Communications (World wide). b'94. AB '21 (Morningside Coll); grad work '20-21 (Yale). Chief wire communications engring sect Office Chief Signal Officer, Washington '24-29, Signal Corps Labs '29-33; chief Army Communications Service '34-38; sec Signal Corps Bd '39-41; chief communications div signal sect GHQ '41-42; exec officer engring and supply service Office Chief Signal Officer '42-43; dir distbn div '43-44; chief signal officer Mediterranean Theatre Operations since '44; chief Army Communications Service '45-46; signal officer GHQ, FEC and chief civil communications sect SCAP since '47; apptd maj gen, chief signal officer US Army '51. Legion of Merit (US). H: 327 Junioper Lane, Ravenwood, Falls Church, Va.⊚

22 BACK, Frank Gerard. Optics (Photographic, television). b'02. ME '25—ScD '31 (Tech U Vienna Austria). Inventor of light-weight catadioptric camera objectives of very long focal length, high speed lenses, and varifocal lens for motion pictures and television; an instrument for measuring and classifying image othicon cameras and for accurate lighting and adjusting of television cameras, a varifocal viewfinder for Signal Corps combat cameras, and an instrument to photograph inside the human stomach. Holds US, French, and Austrian patents in field. Now VP Television Zoomar Corp, Tr F. G. Back Video Corp, pres Zoomar Corp NYC. Soc Am Mil Engrs—Optical Soc Am—Soc Motion Picture and Television Engrs—Royal Photog Soc (F)—Photog Soc Am (F). 381 Fourth Ave., NYC 16.

23 BACKHAUS, Albert Paul. Structural engineering; Building code; Tunnel designs; Stadium designs. b'15. BS (civil engring) '38 (U Md) '47 (Baltimore Coll Commerce). Research on approval of methods and materials and writing of building codes, building codes for Maryland, construction codes for one and two-family dwellings and regulations applicable to multiple dwellings in New York; member Upper Potomac River Flood Control Survey Commission. Engr Consol Gas Elec Light and Power Co of Baltimore '41; structural engr and prin bldg engr Md Dept Pub Improvements '47-49; tech dir NY State Bldg Code Commn since '51; cons. Md Soc Prof Engrs—Constrn Specifications Inst—Bldg Ofcls Conf Am—Soc Am Mil Engrs. State Building Code Commission NY 1740 Broadway, NYC 19. H: 843 Glen Allen Dr., Hunting Ridge, Balt 29.

10 BACKMAN, Jules. Subsidies; Prices; Wages; Economics of American industry. b'10. BCS '31—AM '32—MBA '33—DSC '35 (NYU). Author: Adventures in Price Fixing '36; Government Price Fixing '38; Price Flexibility and Inflexibility '40; Wartime Price Control and the Retail Trade '40; Wartime Subsidies '45; Wages and Prices '47; Economics of Armament Inflation '51; Multi Employer Bargaining '51; War and Defense Economics '52; Economics of Annual Improvement Factor Wage Increases '52. Co-author: War Economics '42; Wages During the Transition '45; Economics of the Potash Industry '46; Economics of the Cotton Textile Industry '46; Who Gets the Railroad Dollar? '47; Behavior of Wages '48; Surety Rate Making '49; Economics of Fourth Round Wage Increases, '49. Prof sch commerce NYU since '50. Am Econ Assn—Am Statis Assn—NYU Men in Finance—Beta Gamma Sigma. New York University, Washington Sq., NYC 3.†

11 BACKUS, Edythe N. Music history (English, American) Music bibliography; Music Printing. b'97. AB '19 (Pomona Coll); AM '29 (Columbia). Research in restoration stage music and English song in general; history of early 15th to 19th century music printing techniques; English psalter tunes and harmony; American 18th century secular songs, hymn tunes and harmony. Author Catalogue of Music in the Huntington Library Printed before 1801. Contributor: Grove's Dictionary of Music and Musicians '40 et seq. Cataloguing and research Huntington Library '28-'42. Music Library Assn—MLA. H: 523 W. Foothill Blvd., Monrovia, Cal.†

12 BACKSTROM, Rudolph John L. Coats-of-arms; Trade marks: Heraldic engraving; Genealogy. b'94. Student West Phila High Sch. Heraldic and genealogical research in this country, Great Britain, and continental Europe. In heraldic business since '28; asst chief heraldic section OQMG '42-43. Dir Internat Heraldic Inst Ltd Washington. 6034 Broad St., Washington 16.†

13 BACKUS, Myron Port. Mycology; Ascomycetes (Spermatia). b'08. BA '28—MA '29—PhD '31 (U Wis). Research in spontaneous and induced mutation in penicillin-producing molds. Advisory editor in mycology to The Botanical Review since '48; editorial board: Mycologia since '49. Author articles in field. With U Wis since '34, prof bot since '47. Mycol Soc Am—Am Phytopath Soc—Phi Beta Kappa—Sigma Xi. Botany Department, University of Wisconsin, Madison 6, Wis.

14 BACON, Osborne Coster. Evaluation of detergents. b'04. Student '25 (Rothesay Can Collegiate Sch); BS '29 (Colby Coll); ScB '31 (Brown U). Research on preparation for finishing and finishing of textiles; evaluation and application of detergents. Holder of patents on water repellent treatment for textile fibers; flameproof organic fibrous material and composition. Author articles: The Heats of Adsorption of Oxygen on Nickel and Copper Catalysts, '32; A Practical Laboratory Test for Evaluating Scouring Agents for Cotton, '45; Detergent Action '48.

In charge plant development US Finishing Co '34-38; head research div Fine Chemicals Div Tech Lab E I du Pont de Nemours & Co since '46. Am Chem Soc—Am Assn Textile Chem and Colorists—ASTM. E. I. du Pont de Nemours & Co Inc, Box 386, Wilmington, Del.

15 BACON, Raymond Foss. Industrial research; Chemical engineering (Sulphur, sulphur ores). b'80. BS '99—MA '00—'19 (DePauw U); PhD '04 (U Chicago); DSc '18 (U Pittsburgh). Invented processes for manufacture gasoline, recovery cuprous sulphide from ores, hydrogenating vegetable oils, manufacturing sulphur from sulphide ores. Co-author: (with W A Hamor) American Petroleum Industry (2 vols) '16; (with Hamor) American Fuels (2 vols) '22; also articles in field. Chem US Bur Sci Manila PI '05-10; sr fellow petroleum fellowship dept indsl research U Pittsburgh '11-12, asso dir Mellon Inst Indsl Research '12-14, dir '14-21; cons engr NY since '21; sci adviser Philippine Govt '39. Col chem warfare service US Army '17-18. Am Inst Chem Engrs—AAAS—Soc de Chimie Industrielle—Chem Soc Lond. 500 Fifth Av., NYC.

16 BACON, Selden Daskam. Alcohol, alcoholism and crime (Sociological implications). b'09. BA '31—MA '35—PhD '39—fellow (Yale). Author: Drunkenness in Wartime Connecticut '43; Sociology and the Problems of Alcohol '44; Inebriety, Social Integration and Marriage '45; also articles in field. Bd dirs Conn Prison Assn since '40; chmn Conn Commn on Alcoholism since '46; professor sociology Yale U since '52; alcohol studies Laboratory Applied Physiol Yale since '43, dir Yale Center of Alcoholic Studies since '48; Sec-treas Nat Comm for Education on Alcoholism '45-50; Eastern Sociol Society—Am Sociol Soc—New Haven Hist Soc—Conn Acad Arts Scis—Phi Gamma Mu. 52 Hillhouse Avenue, New Haven, Conn.†

17 BACOTE, Clarence Albert. Negro in Southern politics; History and political science (Southern states). b'06. AB '26 (U Kan); AM '29—grad study '33-34, '37-38 (U Chicago). Author articles: The Morrill Act of 1862 and Its Influence on Education in the South '36; The Truth from the Point of View of the Investigator '40; Some Aspects of the Voting System in the South '42; and others. Visiting prof hist Wiley Coll Marshall Tex '34; lecturer Am Inst on Race Relations Fisk U '46; asst prof hist Atlanta U '30-39 prof since '39. NAACP Citizenship Schs—Assn Study Negro Life and Hist—AHA. Atlanta University, Atlanta. H: 1029 Simpson St., NW.

18 BADGER, Walter Lucius. Theory of evaporation and design of evaporators; Crystallization; Solar evaporation; Production of salt and caustic soda by evaporation. b'86. BA '07—BS (Chem) '08—SM '09 (U Minn). Design of plant for solar evaporation, and advisor to government of New Zealand on processes; design of large salt evaporators; consultant on salt projects to governments of New Zealand and Colombia, and commercial firms in US; design of caustic soda evaporators and in charge of engineering on caustic soda plant for England. Author: Heat Transfer and Evaporation '26, also articles in field. Contributor: Encyclopedia of Chemical Technology. Dir research Swenson Evaporator Co Harvey Ill '17-37, cons engr since '17; prof chem engring U Mich '18-37; cons engr Dow Chem Co Midland Mich since '34; cons to govt of Colombia since '46, New Zealand '47.

ACS—AICE. William H Walker award '40. 309 S. State St., Ann Arbor.◉

19 BAERG, Gerhard. Germany (Language and literature). b'87. AB '16 (U Kan); AM '18—PhD '20 (Cornell). German language and literature since 1800. Author: The Supernatural in Modern German Drama '20; German Grammar Review with Composition '30; Alternate German Grammar Review '33; Deutschland, ein Kulturlesebuch '38. Prof German and head German dept De Pauw U since '31; guest prof Gottingen U Germany summer '49; interpreter 89th Div, US Army 18-19. DePauw U., Greencastle, Ind.◉

20 BAEZ, Albert Vinicio. X-Ray optics (Image formation). b'12. BA '33 (Drew U); MA '36 (Syracuse U); '37-44 (Columbia, NYU, Brown U); Ph D '50 (Stanford). Research in image formation by focusing X-rays; assisted Prof Paul Kirkpatrick in discovery of methods of producing magnified images of small objects by specular (not Bragg) reflection of X-rays from curved mirrors; studies on absolute energies of K-radiation from thick targets of silver; apparent depth and virtual caustic; (Fermat's) principle and minimum problems. Author articles: X-Ray Optical Images '47; Geometrical Optics of Grazing Incidence Reflectors (with Kirkpatrick and Newell) '48; and others. Prof Wagner Coll '40-44; instr physics Stanford '44-46, acting instr math '46-47, research asst '47-49; applied physics and operations research Cornell Lab '49-50; prof physics U of Redlands '50-51 and '52-53; head UNESCO tech mission to Baghdad (to set up physics dept at Univ Coll) '51-52. Am Phys Soc—Math Assn Am—Sigma Xi (asso). University of Redlands, Redlands, Cal.

21 BAHNER, Carl Tabb. Aliphatic nitro and fluoro compounds; Salts of heterocyclic nitrogen compounds; Chemotherapy. b'08. BA '27 (Hendrix Coll); MS '28 (U Chicago); ThM '31 (So Baptist Theol Sem); PhD '36 (Columbia U); '31-32 (Yale). Holder US patents on ethers of primary nitroalkanes and method of preparing them; aliphatic nitro derivatives of ketoesters and method for preparing them; beta-diketones and process for preparing them, and others. Author articles in field. Prof chem Carson-Newman Coll since '37; cons Carbide and Carbon Chemicals Corp Oak Ridge Tenn since '48; cons Med Div Oak Ridge Inst Nuclear studies. Am Soc Cancer Resch—Am Chem Society—AAAS—So Assn Sci Industry—Tenn Acad Sci—Sigma Xi. Carson-Newman College, Jefferson City, Tenn.†

22 BAILAR, John Christian, Jr. Complex inorganic compounds; Inorganic stereochemistry. b'04. BA '24—MA '25 (U Colo); PhD '28 (U Mich). Studies on valence stabilization; dye lakes; and new methods of resolving optically active compounds. Co-author: (with B S Hopkins) Essentials of General Chemistry '46; General Chemistry for Colleges '51; also articles in field. With University Ill since '28, prof chem since '43, sec dept since '37; Ed-in-chief Inorganic Syntheses. Electrochem Soc—Am Chem Soc (chmn div chem edn '46-47, sec div phys and inorganic chem '47-48)—Phi Beta Kappa—Sigma Xi. University of Illinois, Urbana, Ill.†◉

23 BAILEY, Allen C. Water purification. b'09. CE '33 ,(Rensselaer Poly Inst). Design, installation, and operation water purification plants, pumping stations, intakes, and transmission mains; devised slime removal systems for cooling water systems in cooling towers and condensers, high and low pressure water softening systems for boiler plants; development methods for solution specialized problems in water treatment for industrial uses. Author article: New Intake Installation at Kodak Park '48. Water development engr Eastman Kodak Co since '36; expert cons Lake Ontario Water Purification Plant City of Rochester since '50. Am Waterworks Assn—NY State Soc Professional Engrs—Nat Soc Professional Engrs. Eastman Kodak Co., Rochester 4, N.Y.

10 BAILEY, Clyde H. Cereal technology (flour, wheat products). b'87. BS '13 (ND Coll Agr); MS '16 (U Minn); PhD '21 (U Md). Author: Chemistry of Wheat Flour '25; Physical Tests of Flour Quality '40; Constituents of Wheat and Wheat Flour '44; also articles in field. Prof biochem U Minn since '20, biochem Minn Agrl Expt Sta since '11, dean and dir dept agr since '42. AAAS(F)—Am Chem Soc (chmn agr and food div '23-25)—Inst Food Technol—Am Assn Cereal Chemistry—Alpha Chi Sigma—Phi Lambda Upsilon—Sigma Xi (pres Minn chap '27-28)—Gamma Sigma Delta (nat sec '21-23, 40-42, pres Minn chap '22-23). Thomas Burr Osborne medalist '32; Nicolas Appert medalist '46. 2304 Doswell Av., St. Paul 8.

11 BAILEY, Edgar Herbert. Geology of quicksilver deposits; Rocks and structure of Franciscan group; Origin of Glaucophane schists; Optical mineralogy. b'14. AB '34 (U Redlands); PhD '41 (Stanford). Author articles in field. With US Geol Survey since '38, now geol. Geol Soc Am(F)—Mineral Soc Am—Soc Econ Geologists —Sigma Xi. U.S. Geological Survey, Mineral Dept. Branch, Old Mint Bldg., San Francisco.†

12 BAILEY, Edward Thomas Walter. Fuels (Steel plant); Furances. b'01. BASc '26—Chem E '32 (U Toronto Ont Can). Introduction of commercially pure oxygen adjacent to point of fuel entry in open hearth furnaces for increase of burning capacity. Holds patent in field. Contributor: Iron Steel Engineer Yearbook '37-48. With Steel Co of Can Ltd since '28, now chief combustion engr. Engring Inst Can—Assn Iron and Steel Engrs—Professional Engrs Ont. Plummer medal Invention Oxygen Accelerated Combustion Process '47; Kelly award '48. The Steel Company of Canada, Ltd., Hamilton, Can.

13 BAILEY, Ervin George. Combustion of fuels; Meters for fluids; Automatic controls; Steam boilers and furnaces; Pulverized coal. b'80. ME '03—DEng '41 (O State U); DEng '37 (Lehigh U); ScD '42 (Lafayette Coll). Engaged research fuels, combustion, power development; coal processing, gasification of coal. Holds patents in field. Author articles in field. Founder, pres '16-44, Bailey Meter Co Cleveland, chmn since '44; vp and dir Babcock & Wilcox Co NYC since '30. ASME(F, pres '48, medal '42)—Am Inst Mining Metall Engrs—Soc Naval Architects Marine Engrs—Cleveland Engring Soc —Inst ME London (hon)—Clayton Lecture '49—Tau Beta Pi—Pi Tau Sigma—Sigma Xi. Awarded Longstreth medal Franklin Inst '30, Lamme medal O State U '36, Percy Nicholls award by fuels div ASME and coal div Am Inst Mining Metall Engrs '42. 85 Liberty St., NYC.⊚

14 BAILEY, George William. Radio engineering; Amateur radio. b'87. AB '07 (Harvard). Executive Secretary Institute Radio Engineering, chief scien-

tific personnel office Office Scientific Research and Development; chairman committee 1, member committees 12 and 13, War Communications Board; Secretary Radio Technical Planning Board; chief radio aide War Emergency Radio Service of DC; United Nations Amateur Radio Aide; owner amateur radio station W2KH. Am Radio Relay League (pres)—Veteran Wireless Operators Assn (hon)—Inst Radio Engrs—Armed Forces Communications Assn (dir Post No 1)—Internat Amateur Radio Union (pres)—Radio Club Am. Received Marconi Medal of Service '42. 1 East 79 St., NYC 21.

15 BAILEY, Harold Leslie. Seed potato certification; Economic entomology. b'86. AB '08 (Tufts Coll). Inspector in Vermont seed potato certification service at outset of its establishment by Commissioner of Agriculture '15, closely identified with work in Vermont to date; Vermont representative on Eastern Plant Board; participant in many interstate conferences of certification officials. Author articles in field. Charge insect control Vt Dept Agr since '13, deputy commr agr since '47. Potato Assn Am. Vermont Department of Agriculture, State Office Building, Montpelier, Vt.

16 BAILEY, John Hays. Plant antibiotics; Bacteriology. b'00. BS '24—PhD '28 (U Chicago); DPH '38 (U Mich); Resch fellow '28-29 (Nelson Morris Inst Chgo). Resch bact '42-46, Chief div bact Sterling-Winthrop Research Inst since '46. Soc Am Bact—Inst Med Chicago—NY Acad Sci—AAAS—Soc General microbiol—Sigma Xi. Rt 1, Castleton-on-Hudson, N.Y.

17 BAILEY, John S(earls). Fruit growing. b'99. BS '22 (Mich State Coll); MS '23 (Ia State Coll); '26-27 (Cornell U). Research in blueberry, peach growing, peach breeding, winter hardiness of peaches and raspberries. Author: Blueberry Culture in Massachusetts '41; Peach Growing in Massachusetts '43; Beach Plum in Massachusetts '44. Asso research prof pomol Mass Agrl Expt Sta since '26. Am Soc Hort Sci—Sigma Xi. French Hall, University of Massachusetts, Amherst, Mass.

18 BAILEY, John Wendell. Mammals and reptiles of Virginia; Stream improvement; Industrial waste utilization. b'95. BS '15—MS '17 (Miss State Coll); AB '16—AM '25 (Cornell U); MA '27—PhD '28 (Harvard). Author: The Mammals of Virginia '46; also articles in field. Dir biol research Chesapeake Corp '37-41; cons biol since '38. AAAS(F)—Am Ornithol—Biol Soc Washington—Va Acad Sci—Am Soc Ichthyologists and Herpetologists—Am Soc Mammalogists—Am Soc Zool—Sigma Xi. Awarded Bowdoin prize '27. 27 Willway Road, Richmond, Va.

19 BAILEY, Margaret Lee. History of Tudor England; Colonial American history. b'07. AB '30 (Wilson Coll); MA '31—PhD '46 (U Pennsylvania). With Historical Society Pa, '36-46 asst ed Pennsylvania Magazine of History and Biography; Inst of Early Am History and Culture '46-49; asso editor William and Mary Quarterly. AHA—Soc Am Historians. 6604 Blakemore St., Phila. 19.

20 BAILEY, Margery. Shakespeare, Restoration and eighteenth century plays. b'91. AB '14—AM '16 (Stanford); PhD '22—fellow '21-22 (Yale); study European theaters '27-28. Collector library of early editions, restoration and 18th century drama, actors' and modern directors' cuts of Shakespeare and restoration plays for pro-

duction. Editor: Boswell's Hypochondriack Essays '28; also articles in field. With Stanford U since '18, now asso prof Eng lit. Mod Lang Assn—Authors' League—Phi Beta Kappa—Dramatists' Alliance. Stanford University, Cal.†

21 BAILEY, Neil Phillips. Thermodynamics (Research, analysis). b'00. BS '24 (U Colo); MS '27 (U Ida). Specializes in Gas turbines, jet propulsion, heat transfer, combustion. Author: Principles of Heat Engineering '42; also articles in field. Head mech engring Rensselaer Poly Inst since '44. ASME—Soc Promotion Engring Edn—Sigma Xi. 33 Center View Dr., Troy, N.Y.⊚

22 BAILEY, Reeve M(aclaren). Systematics, ecology and zoogeography of fresh-water fishes of North America. b'11. AB '33—PhD '38 (U Mich). Author articles in field. Asso prof zool U Mich since '50, asso curator fishes U Mich Museum of Zool '44-'48, curator since '48. Am Fisheries Soc (asso ed since '46)—Am Soc Ichthyol and Herpetol (ed bd Copeia '45-49)—Ecol Soc Am—Mich Acad Sci—AAAS—Evol Soc—Biol Soc Washington. Museum of Zoology, University of Michigan, Ann Arbor.

23 BAILEY, Rex Raines. Farm management; Rural appraising. b'93. BS '22 (U Mo). Author articles in field. Staff Doane Agrl Service Inc since '24, now vp charge field div. Past pres Am Soc Farm Managers and Rural Appraisers (accrediting com several yrs, instr sch com 2 yrs). Secured title of accredited rural appraiser '37, accredited Farm Mgr '39 from Am Soc Farm Mgrs and Rural Appraisers. Chamber of Commerce Building, Quincy, Ill.†

24 BAILEY, Stanley F. Entomology; Economic insect pest control; Thrips. b'06. BSc '29 (Mass State Coll); PhD '31 (U Calif). Author articles in field. With U Cal since '29, now professor entomol. Lt comdr malaria and epidemic disease control Pacific Area US Navy '42-46. Am Assn Econ Entomol —Pacific Coast Entomol Soc—Sigma Xi. Division Entomology and Parasitology, University of California, Davis, Calif.

25 BAILEY, T(homas) L(afayette) W(alker), Jr. Textile microscopy. b'05. BS '26 (Clemson Coll). Member subcommittee on abrasion resistance committee on quartermaster problems National Research Council '46; subcommittee on raw cotton fiber maturity fineness and microscopy American Society for Testing Materials; member annual Spinner-Breeder Conference. Author articles in field. Field asst SC Expt Sta '26-27, research asst '28-29; asst cotton tech US Dept Agr '29-36, asso '36-41, cotton tech So Regional Research Lab '41-46; research microscopist Inst Textile Tech Charlottesville Va since '46. AAAS—Fiber Soc—Sigma Xi. Institute of Textile Technology, Charlottesville, Va.

26 BAILEY, Thomas Laval. Geology (Oil and water). b'97. BA '17 (USC); MA '21—PhD '26 (U Calif). Located adequate deep underground water supply for City of Ventura, California when reservoir was nearly empty '48. Co-inventor oriented punch core barrel, and method of obtaining numerous oriented cores for working out geological structure where no surface outcrops are present. Cons geol Ventura Calif since '45. Geol Soc Am(F)—Am Assn Petroleum Geol—Am Geophys Union—AAAS. 223 Chrisman Av., Ventura, Calif.

10 BAILEY, Worth. Washingtoniana; Americana (Cultural history). b'08. Student '28-29 (William and Mary Coll); AB '32 (U Pa). Co-author: Christmas with the Washingtons '48; series of Documentary Christmas Greetings; also articles in field. Research asso and curator Mt Vernon Mansion and Museum Mt Vernon Ladies' Assn Mt Vernon Va '48-51; curator Woodlawn Plantation Mt Vernon Va Nat Trust for Historic Preservation. American Assn Mus—Assn Preservation Virginia Antiquities—Society Architectural Historians—Alexandria Association Hist (vp)—Nat Soc Autograph collectors. Woodlawn Plantation, Mt. Vernon, Va.

11 BAILKEY, Nels Martin. History of culture (Babylonian). b'11. MA '35 —PhD '38 (U Wis). Asso prof and head dept hist and polit sci U Tulsa '39-46; asst prof ancient and medieval hist U Okla '46-47; asso prof ancient and medieval hist Tulane U since '47. AHA —Miss Valley Hist Assn. Department of History, Tulane University, New Orleans 15.†

12 BAIN, Edgar Collins. Metallurgical engineering (Steel treating, management of research). b'91. BSc '12—MSc '16 —Chem E '23—Dr Sci (hon) '47; (O State U); Dr Engring (hon) '36 (Lehigh U). Research in Metallography of tungsten and molybdenum; crystal structure by x-rays; nature of solid solutions; mechanism of hardening steel; cause of secondary hardness in high speed steel; metallography of stainless steel; nature and remedy of intergranular deterioration of stainless steel; transformation rates in steel; fundamental factors of heat-treatment. Author: Functions of the Alloying Elements in Steel '39. Co-author: (with M. A. Grassman) High Speed Steel '31; also articles in field. Research metall US Steel Corp '28-35, asst vp '35-43 vp research and tech since '51; vp in charge research and tech Carnegie Ill Steel Corp since '43; Howe memorial lecturer, AIME NY '32; E. De M. Campbell memorial lecturer, ASM, Buffalo NY '32. Am Phys Soc(F)—Am Inst Mining Metall Engrs—Am Soc Metals (pres '37, dir '34-38, chmn NY sect '29) —Am Soc Testing Materials. Awarded Robert W. Hunt medal work on non-rusting steels '29, Henry Marion Howe medal work on hardening steel '31, Am Iron and Steel Inst medal work on alloy steel '35, Benjamin Lamme medal eminence in engring U Ohio '37. Albert Sauveur Achievement Award '46. H: 513 Maple Lane, Edgeworth, Sewickley, Pa.

13 BAIN, George William. Geology of New England; Building stone; Mining geology. b'01. BSc '21—MSc '23 (McGill U); PhD '27 (Columbia); MA (hon) '41 (Amherst Coll). Author: Marble Deposits of Newfoundland '37; Flow of Time Through the Connecticut Valley '43. Instr geol Amherst Coll '26, prof since '41; geol US War Dept '44-46; dir Pratt Mus of Geol '48. Geol Soc Am—Mineral Soc Am—Soc Econ Geol—Am Inst Mining Metall Engrs— Can Inst Mining and Metall—Geol Soc South Africa—Sigma Xi. Awarded British assn medal McGill U '21, pres's gold medal Can Inst Mining and Metall '26, medal and commendation US War Dept '46. 22 Hitchcock Rd., Amherst, Mass.

14 BAIN, Henry F(ranklin). Cranberry production and diseases; Strawberry diseases. b'93. BA '16 (U Tenn); MS '17 (Brown U). Author articles in field. Cranberry specialist Wis Dept Agr '26-29; Sr path cranberry and strawberry diseases US Dept Agr '29-44; tech cons cranberry production numerous companies Wis since '44. AAAS—Am Phytopath Soc. Box 362, Wisconsin Rapids, Wis.

15 BAINTON, Roland Herbert. Reformation (Religious history). b'94. BA '14 (Whitman Coll Walla Walla Wash); BD '17—PhD '21 (Yale). Author: Castellio Concerning Heretics '35; Life of George Lincoln Burr '43; The Martin Luther Christmas Book '48; Here I Stand—A Life of Martin Luther '50, The Travail of Religious Liberty '51; The Reformation of the Sixteenth Century '52; Hunted Heretic: the life and death of Michael Servetus '53; also articles in field. Faculty Yale Division Sch since '20, prof eccles hist since '36. Am Church Hist Soc. 409 Prospect St., New Haven.

16 BAIR, George Joshua. Glass (Optical); Ceramics; Whiteware; Non-Metallic processing. b'05. BS '27— MS '30 (Pa State Coll); ScD '36 (Mass Inst Tech); sr fellow '36-42 (Mellon Inst). Author articles in field. Mgr optical plant Corning Glass Works since '46. Am Ceramic Soc(F)—Inst Ceramic Engrs—Am Chem Soc—Soc Glass Tech, Eng. Corning Glass Works, Corning, N.Y.

17 BAIRD, Alexander. Russia (Foreign policy, economics). b'12. BA '31— LLM '35 (U Warsaw); PhD '40—student Statis Inst (U Paris); '38-40 (Ecole Libre d'Arts ed Metiers) (Acad Commerce); '42-44—Pan Europ research fellow (NY U). Research on Russian foreign policy in Eastern Europe, and Near and Far East; studies on comparative international finance; especially cartels and their relation to the state; economics of statism in Russia; government intervention in national economy; executive secretary Pan-European Conference '44; econometric analysis and forecast of business trends. Co-author: Pan-European Federation '43, author, Statism (France, Italy, Germany), '51. Asso ed to fgn corr Eastern Commercial Daily '34-36; vice dir br of Eastern Econ Agency '34-36; research dir inquiry in Russian fgn policy in Far East Alfred Kohlberg Inc (Chinese textiles) '45; sr analyst Econometric Inst NYC '45-46; prof govt and bus relations Babson Inst Bus Adminstrn Boston '46-47; head dept econ Bradley U since '47, also founder and dir Sch Internat Studies. AAUP—Am Acad Polit and Sociol Sci. Amer. Econ. Assn.; Amer. China Policy Assn. (bd. dirs.) Bradley University, Peoria 5, Ill.

18 BAIRD, Ralph Waldo. Water runoff (Effects of agricultural practices, sediment); Texas (Blackland soils). b'03. BS '24 (Kan State Coll); MS '25 (Ia State Coll). Study of effect of conservation methods on rate and amount of runoff small and large agricultural areas, amount of suspended material in small streams draining such areas; examination of infiltration, soil moisture changes, and crop yields, especially black clay soil of Texas. Author articles: The Effects of Conservation Practices on Peak Rates of Runoff '46; Rates and Amounts of Runoff for the Blacklands of Texas '50, and others. Asso prof agrl engring Okla A&M Coll '25-30; asso agrl engr Soil Conservation Expt Sta USDA Tyler Tex '30-35, hydraulic engr and soil conservationist Blacklands Exptl Watershed Waco Tex '35-42 and since '45. Am Geophys Union—Am Soc CE—Am Soc AE—Sigma Tau—Gamma Sigma Delta. P.O. Box 1583, Waco, Tex.

19 BAIRSTOW, Mildred Wright. Cultures, costumes and customs of Latin America and the West Indies. b'93. Many years of study of Latin American culture and customs; exhibits of Latin American handicrafts. Natl League Am Pen Women—Nat Geog Soc—Pan Am Council. 325 Cory Av., Waukegan, Ill.

20 BAITSELL, George Alfred. Human biology; Protozoa; Tissue culture; Connective tissue. b'85. BS '08—LLD '45 (Central Coll Ia); AM '09—PhD '14 (Yale); fellow since '47 (Calhoun Coll). Author: Manual of Biology Forms '23; Manual of Biology '41; Manual of Animal Biology '32; Human Biology '40; Editor: The Evolution of Man '22; Science in Progress '39; American Scientist '40, and others. Colgate prof biol Yale since '47. Asst physiol Army-Navy Gas investigation '17-18, capt chem Warfare Service '18. AAAS (F, council since '35, sec sect F '35-40, nat exec com since '47)— Am Soc Zool—Am Soc Naturalists— Am Soc Anatomists—Am Physiol Soc— Soc Exptl Biol and Med—Genetics Soc—Sigma Xi (nat pres '38; nat exec sec since '40). 234 Lawrence St., New Haven.

21 BAITY, Herman Glenn. Sanitary and public health engineering; Public works administration. b'95. BA '17— BS '22 (U NC); '19 (U Sorbonne Paris); MS '26—ScD '28 (Harvard); fellow research sanitary engineering Rockefeller Found '24-26, research in water purification, sewage and industrial waste treatment, stream pollution. Designed sewage treatment works Chapel Hill. Chmn com indsl and agrl research North Carolina Plan, Inc '30-'32; mem NC State Bd Examiners plumbing and heating contractors since '31, NC State Bd of Health '31-43; prof sanitary engring Sch Pub Health U NC since '36, acting dean '46-47; cons practice engring since '30; spl cons USPHS since '41; chief sanitary engr for Brazil Office Coordinator Inter-Am Affairs Rio de Janeiro '43-44, cons since '44. ASCE—Am Pub Health Assn—Am Water Works Assn—Fedn Sewage Works Assn—Assn Mgrs Sewage Disposal Works (Eng)—NC Water and Sewage Works Assn (pres '36-37)— Sigma Xi—Phi Beta Kappa. H: Mason Farm Rd., Chapel Hill, N.C.

22 BAKENHUS, Reuben Edwin. Civil engineering. b'73. BS '96 (MIT); grad '24 (Naval War Coll). Co-author: The Panama Canal '14; Manual of the Bureau of Yards and Docks. Commd jr lt US Navy '01, advanced thru grades to rear adm CE Corps '32, retired '37; cons engr NYC since '37. AAAS(F)— ASCE (past dir)—Soc Am Mil Engrs (p pres)—Permanent Internat Assn Navigation Congresses (Am sect)—Am Inst Cons Engrs (past pres)—NY Soc Mil and Naval Officers—Am Inst Cons Engineers (sec '47). 75 West Street, NYC 6.

23 BAKER, Charles P(arker). Nuclear physics; Chain reactors. b'10. AB '33 (Dennison U); AM '35—PhD '40—Research '40-42 (Cornell U); research OSRD and Manhattan Project '42-43 (Purdue U). Research worker on atomic bomb Los Alamos NM '43-46, went to Tinian for final assembly and delivery '45. Author articles in field. Asst prof Lab Nuclear Studies Cornell U since '46; cons for several govt and indsl labs; Brookhaven National Laboratory. Am Phys Soc—Sigma Xi—Phi Kappa Phi. Brookhaven National Lab., Upton, L.I., N.Y.

24 BAKER, Charles Chaney. History of California. b'87. Author articles: Mexican Land Grants '14; The Rise and Fall of The City of Gladstone '14; Don Enrique Dalton of The Azusa '17; Don Enrique Dalton of The Azusa, The Grizzly Bear '16; The Zamorano Family of California and Its Spanish Ancestry '25; The Dispensing of Justice under The Mexican Regieme '17; A List of Newspapers in The Los Angeles City Library '15-16. Dir Hist Soc So Calif since '15. AHA—Am Acad Polit Social Sci. 3539 Linwood Pl., Riverside, Calif.

10 BAKER, Donald McCord. Hydrology; Traffic engineering; Engineering economics. b'90. BS in CE hon '13 (U Calif). Made studies, reports, investigations, surveys, valuations and appraisals, financial analyses, on matters involving hydrology, surface and underground water supplies, water systems, city and regional planning, street and highway traffic, urban and suburban transit, population growth and distribution. Co-author: (with H. Conkling) Water Supply and Utilization '30; also articles in field. Hydraulic engr '17-24; construction engrs '24-42; partner Ruscardon Engrs Los Angeles since '42; cons National Resources Planning, Los Angeles Board City Planning Commissioners, other Los Angeles municipal commissions. ASCE (chmn com meteorol data '31-40, com nat water policy '35-38, com hydrology since '41, chmn Alfred Noble Joint Prize com since '47)—Am Assn Engrs—Am Acad Polit Social Sci—Am Geophys Union—Am Geog Soc(F)—Officier Ordre Alouite Ouissam (Morocco)—Tau Beta Pi—Sigma Xi. 448 S. Hill St., L.A. 13.

11 BAKER, Dwight Lynds. Industrial enzymes Enzyme and surface chemistry. b'10. AB '33 (Amherst Coll); AM '34—PhD '40 (Columbia U). Research in purification of potato tyrosinase, tyrosinase in potato respiration, purification and elucidation of kidney laccase; developed chillproofing assay methods, stable and highly active preparation of the enzyme catalase for industrial use, enzyme system for removal molecular oxygen and reducing sugar from food and beverages. Author articles in field. Became tech dir Vita-Zyme Lab Chicago '43; now dir research Froma Research Co Div Froedtert Corporation American Soc Brewing Chem—Masters Brewers Assn Am—AAAS—Am Chem Soc. P.O Box 712, Milwaukee.

12 BAKER, Edward William. Mites. b'14. BS '36—PhD '38 (U Calif). Author articles in field. Div fruit fly investigation in Mexico City, Mexico studying biol of fruit flies '39-44; acarologist US Dept Agr bur entomol and plant quarantine, div insect identification since '44. U.S. National Museum, Washington.†

13 BAKER, Edwin R. Warfare (Chemical). b'08. BS '29 (Sheffield Sci Sch of Yale); LLD '39 (Suffolk U Law Sch). Research and development of flame throwers, flame fuels, and incendiaries. Chem Plymouth Co '32-40; with Quaker Chem Products Co '40-41; in charge research and development CWS US Army '41-46; with Emery Industries '46-48; with Continental Oil Co since '48. Sigma Xi—ACS—Armed Forces Chem Assn (dir). Received Legion of Merit '45. Continental Oil Co., Ponca City, Okla.

14 BAKER, Elizabeth Hoyt. Social Service administration; Social service case work. b'12. BA '33 (Mich State Coll) AM '42 (U Chicago). Dir girl's work Abraham Lincoln Center Chicago '33-36 dir social service and camp '36-42; child care cons Va Dept Pub Welfare '42-44; exec sec Neighborhood Center and Neighborhood Council Montclair NJ '44-48; school social service administration E Orange

NJ since '48. Am Assn Social Workers—Am Assn Psychiatric Social Workers—Nat Assn Sch Social Workers—Nat Conf Social Work—Internat Conf Social Work. 48 N. Walnut St., E. Orange, NJ.

15 BAKER, Gladys Elizabeth. Mycology; Cyto-genetics (Fungi). b'08. Jessie R Barr fellow '33-35—PhD '35 (Washington U); BA '30—MS '32 (State U Ia). Author articles in field. Prof plant sci dept Vassar Coll since '51, chmn since '48. Mycol Soc Am—Am Genetic Assn—AAAS(F)—Bot Soc America—Sigma Xi. Plant Science Department, Vassar College, Poughkeepsie, N.Y.†

16 BAKER, H(enry) Dean. Temperature measurement; Calorimetry. b'04. BA '32—PhD '38 (U Wis). Author: Temperature Measurement in Engineering; also articles in field. Cons temperature measurement expert Pratt & Whitney Aircraft Corp since '42; dir research dept mech engring Columbia since '42; now asso prof mech engring. ASME (com testing technique since '47)—Am Phys Soc—Soc Exptl Stress Analysis—Sigma Xi—Phi Beta Kappa. Columbia University, NYC 27.

17 BAKER, James Seldon. Economics of metal and mineral mining industries of Latin America and Far East. b'06. BS '29—'31 (U Ariz). Research on improvement of mining operation techniques and study of various prospects to determine feasibility of exploration; special negotiator in Brazil, deputy director of US Commercial Company mission to Philippines. Author articles in field. Engr Calumet and Ariz Mining Co '29-30; engr, purchasing agt Nat Tank & Mfg Co '31-32; engr Philippines '33-34; engr foreman Benguet Consol Mining Co '34-35; cons engr '36-41; with War Prod Bd & Fgn Econ Admn '42-45; pres and mgr James S Baker Co, San Francisco and Thomco Mfg Co Inc Redwood City, Calif. Am Inst Mining Engrs. 311 California, San Francisco 4. H: 1711 Encinal, Atherton, Calif.

18 BAKER, James Stannard. Automobile accidents (Interpretation of physical evidence); Licensing of automobile drivers; Registration systems for automobiles. b'99. BS '22 (U Wis). Serves extensively as expert in interpretation physical evidence in automobile accidents, including such aspects as speed, position, and behavior of vehicles in accidents as indicated by skidmarks, damage to vehicles and photographic evidence; consultant and training specialist to 30 states in driver licensing and training; designed and installed Delaware system motor vehicle registration and inspection, now prototype for modern methods. Author: Traffic Work of Police Departments '29; Traffic Courts and Violations Bureaus '30; Driver Improvement Through Licensing Procedures '50; Driver-Asleep Accidents '35; also articles in field. Tech ed Fairbanks, Morse & Co, A C Nielsen Co Chicago '26-28; traffic engr, cons driver licensing Nat Safety Council '28-45; dir safety Detroit Street Rys '45-46; dir research Traffic Inst Northwestern U since '46. Inst Traffic Engrs. 1704 Judson Av., Evanston, Ill.

19 BAKER, (Sarah) Janet Bassett Johnson. Maryland history. b'99. State Teachers Coll; BS '23—AM '27—PhD '28 (Johns Hopkins); AM '38 (Columbia U); '32 (Oxford U). Spent 14 years in American libraries and British museums doing research work on Marylanders, especially the loyalists, visited and made pictures of places

mentioned in manuscripts; collector of material from original documents; writer, director, coach of historical plays and pageants. Author: Retention of History '28; Robert Alexander: Maryland Loyalist '42; also articles in field. Instr ednl psychology Baltimore Christian Training Sch. Phi Beta Kappa—Md Hist Soc. 804 Hatherleigh Rd., Stoneleigh 12, Baltimore 12.

20 BAKER, John Francis. Weight engineering (Helicopter); Stress analysis (Anti-aircraft guns). b'11. Certificate '44 (Central Inst Tech); certificate '45 (Pa State Ext). Research on calculated gun cycle diagrams, analysis of breech mechanisms of anti-aircraft guns, special weights and balance analysis, firing loads analysis; weight and balance of helicopters. With Platt Le Page Aircraft Co '44-46; Rheem Mfg Co '46-47; Delaval Steam Turbine Co '47-49; project engr H L Yoh Co since '49. Soc Exptl Stress Analysis—Am Ordnance Assn. H: 2845 Gillingham St., Phila. 37.

21 BAKER, June Marshall. Chemistry; Purification of substance through ion exchange. b'22. BA '44 (Mo Valley Coll) MA '50 (Ohio State U). Zion exchange as used for quantitive removal of various liquids in the presence of ions for which the exchanger is more selective. Instr chem Mo Valley Coll '47-49; grad asst agrl biochem Ohio State U '50; Mo Agrl Experiment Station since '50. Am Chem Soc—Phi Lambda Upsilon—AAUP. Rte. 2, Napton, Mo.

22 BAKER, Kenneth Frank. Diseases of ornamental plants; Seedborne pathogens; Mycology. b'08. BS '30—PhD '34—research fellow '30-34 (Wash State Coll); Nat Research fellow bot '34-35 (U Wisconsin); '47-48 (Cornell). Botanical exploration eastern South America '38-39. Author articles in field. Asso path Pineapple Research Inst Honolulu TH '36-39; asst prof plant path, asst plant path exp sta U Calif '39-42, asso prof, asso plant path '42-48, prof, plant path since '48. Am Phytopath. Soc—AAAS(F)—Bot Soc Am—Mycol. Soc Am—Brit Mycol Soc—Sigma Xi—Phi Kappa Phi. Department of Plant Pathology, University of California, 405 Hilgard Av., Los Angeles 24.

23 BAKER, Marjorie Osborne. Literature of the platinum metals (Chemical, physical and technological). b '00. Spl courses (NYU), (Columbia), (Newark State Tchrs Coll); bus courses personnel counselling (Newark U). Librarian, research library Baker & Co Inc, in charge collection literature relating to the platinum metals; gives reference service to Engelhard Industries. Asst inspector engineering material USN, specializing in compressed gases and metallurgical problems. Spl Libraries Assn. Baker & Co., Inc., 113 Astor St., Newark 5.

24 BAKER, William Jennings. Wood waste utilization; Wood seasoning; Forest products fabrication and utilization; Wood preservation; Wood properties. b'00. BS (forestry) '27—MS '28 (Ore State Coll). Research on anatomy, identification, properties, seasoning and inspection of wood, sources, production, and utilization of forest products, aircraft wood inspection, aircraft veneer and plywood production, repair of wood aircraft, fabrication of laminated wood ship and truck body parts, wood ship inspection, overseas packaging of war materiel, utilization of forest materials that are now unused or used at low economic levels. Co-author: Forest Products (Their Sources, Production, and Utilization) '50. Head wood products dept Ore State Coll '30-36; asso prof forestry Mich State Coll '36-42; tech, chief tech training div US Forest Products Lab '42-47; chief indsl service sect, chief tech, adminstrn Ore Forest Products Lab 47-50, chief research from '50. Xi Sigma Pi—Kappa Delta Pi—Forest Products Research Soc. Oregon Forest Products Laboratory, Corvallis, Ore.

10 BAKEWELL, Charles Montague. Plato; History of philosophy. b'67. AB '89 (U Calif); AM '92—PhD '94 (Harvard); '94-96 (U Berlin, U Strassburg and Paris); AM(hon) '05 (Yale); LLD (hon) '43 (U Calif). Author: Source Book in Ancient Philosophy '39. Co-author: George Herbert Palmer. Editor: William James' Selected Papers on Philosophy; Emerson's Poems; also articles in field. Prof philos Yale U '05-33, emeritus. Am Philos Assn (pres '10)—AAAS—Brit Inst Philos—Nat Inst Social Sci—Phi Beta Kappa. 437 Humphrey St., New Haven.

11 BAKKEN, Henry H. Marketing and Cooperation. b'96. AB '22—AM '24 (U Wis); (Social Sci F) '29-'30 (Harvard). Studies in market theory and in the basic philosophy, decisive principles, practical methodology of cooperatives. Author: Economics of Co-operative Marketing '37; Cooperation to the Finnish '39; Theory of Markets and Marketing '51. With U Wis since '23, prof agrl econ since '24; prin econ OPA '43-44; price chief Allied Control Commn Fgn Econ Adminstrn Rome '44-45; attache State Dept London and Oslo Embassies '45-46; econ cons GHQ SCAP Tokyo '46-47. Am Econ Assn—Royal Econ Soc—Am Farm Econ Assn—Western Farm Econ Assn—Canadian Agrl Econ Soc. 309 Agriculture Hall, University of Wisconsin, Madison 6, Wis.

12 BALASSA, Leslie L. Textiles (Finishing); Paint; Pigment; Cellulose; Starch. b'03. PhD '26 (U Vienna). Research and development on paints, pigments, synthetic resins, varnishes, automotive finishes, industrial finishes, corrosion protective finishes, textile finishing processes and materials, chemical modification of cellulose and starch, dyeing and printing of fabrics, fabric coating processes and compositions, pigment printing processes and compositions. Holds 12 patents. Author articles in field. Mexican dept Am Smelting & Refining Co '28-30; Fabrics and Finishes dept EI duPont de Nemours '30-44; research and development US Finishing Co '44-49; now chem cons. Am Inst Chem (F)—Am Chem Soc—AAAS—NY Acad Sci—Textile Research Inst—Soc Dyers and Colourists—Am Assn Textile Chem and Colorists. 110 W 40th St., NYC. H: 47 Laurel Way, Madison, N.J.

13 BALCHEN, Bernt. Aviation (Arctic). b'99. Student '19 (Army Field Artillery Sch Norway); '21 (Mil Flying Sch Norway); '23 (Härnoesand Technicum Sweden). Member Amundsen Ellsworth expeditions to Spitsbergen '25, '26, Hudson Bay expedition '26-27, Greenly Island '28; chief pilot Byrd Antarctic expedition '28-30, across South Pole '29; Ellsworth Antarctic Expedition '33-35. Co-author: (with Ford, La Farge) War Below Zero. Test and engring pilot Fokker, Gen Motors, Douglas Aircraft, and Northrop '26-33; operations mgr Norwegian Airlines '35-40, pres '45-48. Lt Norwegian Naval Air Force '20-41; transferred from Royal Norwegian Air Force to U.S. Air Force '41; with Task Force building airbases in Greenland AUS '41-43, comdr Tenth Rescue Squadron Alaska '48-50. Explorers Club NY — Quiet Birdmen — Wings Club.

Holder numerous aviation awards and decorations. Headquarters, U.S. Air Force, Washington 25. H: Hunting Towers West, No 730, Alexandria, Va.

14 BALD, Frederick Clever. History of Michigan, Detroit, and the Old Northwest. b'97. BA '20—PhD '43 (U Mich); MA '37 (Wayne U); '14-18 (Franklin & Marshall Coll); '19 (U Aix-Marseille France). Engaged research Michigan and old northwest in public and private libraries and collections since '33. Author: The French Seigniory at Sault Ste Marie '37; Patrick McNiff's Plan of the Settlements at Detroit, 1796 '46; Detroit's First American Decade, 1796-1805 '48; A Portrait of General Anthony Wayne '48; also articles in field. Teacher hist Hudson Sch Detroit '22-29, headmaster '29-32; prof hist and govt Detroit Inst Tech '32-43; asst dir Mich Hist Collections since '47, lecturer hist since '47. AHA—Mich Acad—Hist Soc Mich—Washtenaw Historical Society (historian)—Algonquin Club (vp). Michigan Historical Collections, Rackham Building, Ann Arbor.

15 BALD, Robert Cecil. Elizabethan and seventeenth century English literature (Bibliography, Shakespeare, Donne, Coleridge). b'01. BA '22 (U Melbourne); PhD '29 (U Cambridge); LLB '30—D Litt '47 (U Adelaide). Editor: Thomas Middleton's A Game at Chesse '29; Hengist, King of Kent '38; Literary Friendships in the Age of Wordsworth '33; Donne's Influence in English Literature '33 and others; also articles in field. Prof Eng Cornell U since '37. Mod Lang Assn Am—Bibliog Soc (London, America). Research fellow Folger Shakespeare Library Washington '36-37; Guggenheim fellow '46-47. English Department, Cornell University, Ithaca, N.Y.†

16 BALDRIDGE, Harry Alexander. Naval history and art; Ship models since 1649. b'80. BS '02 (US Naval Acad); grad '21 (US Naval War Coll). Editor: US Naval Inst Proceedings '25-28; revisor: Knight's Seamanship '30. Commd ensign US Navy '02, advanced through grades to capt '24, developed E for efficiency '05, head dept seamanship and flight tactics and dir aviation US Naval Acad '24-27, comdr USS Rochester during revolution in Nicarauga '28-30, dir naval intelligence Navy Dept '30-31, retired '32, recalled to active duty '37, curator US Naval Acad Mus '37-49, dir since '47. Newcomen Soc Eng—Am Biographical Soc—Assn Am Mus. U.S. Naval Academy Museum. Annapolis, Md.

17 BALDWIN, Armand-Jean. Russia (Revolution); Russia (Institutions). b'17. AB '40—MA '44 (St Vincent Coll); '43 (U Pittsburgh); MA '46—PhD '48 (Georgetown U). Research on revolutionary movements in Russia in 19th century as background for revolution of November '17, Russian institutions of Soviet government. Author: Russia from the Decembrists to the Bolsheviks (1825-1917) '51. Head econ dept St Vincent Coll since '50. Am Learned Soc—Econometric Soc—Am Econ Assn—Cath Econ Assn—Nat Acad Econ and Polit Sci—Am Soc Internat Law—Acad Polit and Soc Sci—Am Benedictine Acad—Am Econ Found. St. Vincent College, Latrobe, Pa. H: St. Vincent Archabbey.

18 BALDWIN, Arthur Richard. Nutrition (Vitamin C); Milk fats. b'18. BS '40 (John B Steson U); PhD '43 (U Pittsburgh). Research on nutritional aspects vitamin C, composition and digestibility of shortenings, composition of human milk fats, and preparation of synthetic glycerides. Author

articles in field. Sect leader Corn Products Refining Co since '44; ed Jour Am Oil Chem Soc since '49. Am Oil Chem Soc—Am Chem Soc—Inst Food Technol—Am Assn Cereal Chem—Sigma Xi. Corn Products Refining Co., Argo, Ill.

19 BALDWIN, George Jesse. Cosmic rays; Optical contents of metals. b'01. AB '24 (U Notre Dame); MA '29 (Catholic U Am); '34-37 (U Chicago). Constructed a table of optical constants of metals in single crystal form for wave lengths from far infra-red through ultra-violet; work in comparison with data obtained from thermionic and photoelectric measurements on same metals. Author articles in field. Research and teaching U Notre Dame since '39. Am Phys Soc—Am Assn Physics Teachers. University of Notre Dame, Notre Dame, Ind.†

20 BALDWIN, Henry Ives. Forest tree seed physiology and origin; New England forests and forestry. b'96. BA '19—MF '22—PhD '31 (Yale). Author: Forest Tree Seed '42; Forestry in New Eng '42; Wooden Dollars '49. Editor: Important Tree Pests of the Northeast '40; also articles in field. Research forester NH Forestry and Recreation Committee since '33. AAAS(F)—NH Acad Sci (pres '38)—Ecol Soc Am (ed bd)—Soc Am Foresters — Internat Union Forest Research Orgns (comm forest tree seeds and tree races)—Sigma Xi. Fellow Am Scandinavian Found '23-24. New Hampshire Forestry and Recreation Commission, Concord, N.H.†

21 BALDWIN, John Thomas Jr. Cytogeography of plants; Hevea; Tropical agriculture; Flora of Liberia. b'10. AB '32 (Coll William & Mary); PhD '37 (U Va); Gen Edn Bd fellow '37-38 (Cornell U). Traveled throughout Amazon Valley, built up comprehensive assemblage of living Hevea and accumulated data for monographic treatment of genus '42-44; walked throughout Liberia to estimate agricultural problems and possibilities of Republic, collected specimens of approximately two-thirds its species of plants '47-48. Author articles in field. Prof biol William and Mary Coll since '46. Bot Soc Am—Am Genetic Assn—New Eng Bot Soc—Calif Bot Soc—Soc Study Evolution—Am Geog Soc—Phi Beta Kappa—Sigma Xi—Phi Kappa Phi. College of William and Mary, Williamsburg, Va.†⊚

22 BALDWIN, Paul Herbert. Ornithology (Hawaiian, ecology). b'13. AB '36—grad study '46 (U Calif); MS '39 (U Hawaii); '39 (Harvard); PhD '50 (Univ Calif). Comparative ecology of Hawaiian Honey Creepers, research in population and foods of Hawaiian goose, life histories of Laysan rail and leiothrix, effects of war on birds of Midway Islands, temperature resistance of some Hawaiian decapoda, littoral ecology of a Hawaiian shore. Author articles in field. Asst zool U Calif '46-48. Ecol Soc Am—Am Soc Mammalogists—Cooper Ornith Club—Hawaiian Acad Scis—Sigma Xi. Colorado A&M College, Fort Collins, Colo.

23 BALDWIN, William Marsh, Jr. Physical metallurg (Metal forming, wire and tube drawing, press work). b'15. ChE '36 (Rensselaer Polytech Inst); PhD '45 (Case Inst Tech); '36-37 (U Munich, Eidgenossische Tecnische Hochschule Zurich). Author article: Dimensional Changes Encountered in Tube Sinking '44, and others. Research prof Case Inst Tech since '48. Am Inst Mining Metall Engrs—Am Soc Metals—Sigma Xi. Annual award Inst

Metals Div Am Inst Mining Metall Engrs for most notable contribution to metall lit published by div within three years preceding date of award '45. Case Institute of Technology, Cleveland.†

10 BALINSKY, Benjamin. Psychology (Tests). b'13. BA '35 (Brooklyn Coll); MA '37 (Columbia); PhD '40 (NY U). Research on Rorschach tests with application to business and industrial situations and on Wechsler-Bellevue intelligence tests; consultant to United Service for New Americans and Vocational Advisory Service. Co-author: Counseling and Psychology '51. Author articles in field. Psychol Bellevue Hosp '35-39; asst prof psychol City Coll NY since '50. Diplomate in Clinical Psychology—Am Psychol Assn (F div clin psychol, counseling and guidance)—professional member, Nat Vocational Guidance Assn. City College, 17 Lexington Av., NYC 10.

11 BALKE, Harry Albert. Bridges (Steel); Railroad turntables. b'03. BS (civil engring) '26—CE '51 (U Ky). Research and design, reinforcing and erecting schemes of steel bridges, including continuous girders, main cantilever spans, and falsework; granted patent on disc center for railroad turntables. With Am Bridge Co '26-46, civil engr '35-46; cons engr from '46. Am Soc CE—Am Ry Engring Assn—Am Soc Mil Engrs. Honorable mention Lincoln Award Programs '38, '42. 800 Broadway, Cincinnati 2.

12 BALL, Charles Olin. Food technology; Containers for heat processed foods; Milk processing and packaging. b'93. '12 (Kan State Coll); '13-17 (Washburn Coll); '19 (Cambridge); BA '20—MS '22—PhD '26 (Geo Washington U). Research on cause of spoilage and deterioration of food products; improvement of processing technic and development of advanced technique for sterilization, flaw detection in sterilization technique; sanitation in food production, packing, distribution; containers and container parts particularly metal, coating materials and baking operations. Holds patents on processing milk, design of paper milk containers, methods and apparatus for sterilizing canned foods US, Canada and England. Author: Thermal Process Time for Canned Foods '23; Mathematical Solution of Problems on Thermal Processing of Canned Foods; Advancement in Sterilization Methods for Canned Foods; Short Time Pasteurization of Milk; Containers for Heat Processed Foods; Public Health Legal Control of Paper Milk Containers; also articles in field. Tech dir '42-44, dir process and product research '44-47, Owens-Ill Can Co; editor of Food Technology '47-50; ed emer since '50; research specialist food tech Rutgers University since 50. Cons food tech since '47. NY Acad Sci(F)—AAAS(F)—Am Pub Health Assn(F)—Am Chem Soc—Inst Food Tech—Internat Assn Milk Sanitarians. Awarded Nicholas Appert Medal '47. 6 Liberty St., New Brunswick, N.J.

13 BALL, John Sigler. Sulfur compounds of petroleum; Petroleum and shale oil chemistry. b'14. BS—MS '36 (Texas Tech Coll); '36-38 (U Colo). Developed methods for analysis types of sulfur compounds and petroleum; study of properties of sulfur compounds of petroleum; research on composition of shale oil. Author articles in field. Chem engr petroleum expt sta US Bur Mines Laramie Wyo '38-42, chem '42-46, refinery engr since '46. Am Chem Soc—Am Soc Testing Materials. Petroleum and Oil-Shale Experiment Station, Bureau of Mines, Laramie, Wyo.†

14 BALL, John Waldron. Daniel Defoe; American negro folk music. b'20. AB '41—AM '42 (Miami U); PhD '47 (U Cincinnati). Built extensive reference collection of negro primitive and folk music for Archive of Ohio Folklore. Taught pioneer course in American Jazz Music, U of Cincinnati Eve Coll. Author: A Commentary on Daniel Defoe's Essay on Projects '47. Asso prof dept English Miami U '41-50 prof since '50; lectr U Cincinnati Evening Coll since '46; dir Archive of Ohio Folklore since '49. MLA—Coll English Assn—Nat Council Teachers English—Am Folklore Soc—O Folklore Soc. 228 Upham Hall, Miami University, Oxford, O. H: Silvoor Lane, Oxford, O.

15 BALL, Max Waite. Reservoir engineering; Gas storage (Underground); Oil Storage (Underground); Petroleum (Economics). b'85. EM '06 (Colo Sch Mines); LLB '14—LLM '14 (Nat U). Author: This Fascinating Oil Business '40; also articles in field. Pres W Pipe Line Co '21-26; pres Argo Oil Co '21-28; cons '28-44, since '48; pres Abasand Oils Ltd (Can) '30-43; pres Royal Royalties Ltd '31-44; spl asst dept petroleum adminstr Petroleum Adminstrn for War '44-45; dir Oil and Gas Div US Dept Interior '46-48. Geol Soc Am (F)—Am Geog Soc—Am Assn Petroleum Geol (pres '23-24)—AIMME—Can Inst Mining and Metall—AAAS—Acad Polit Sci—Am Petroleum Inst—Nat Petroleum Council. Medal of Merit for distinguished achievement Colo Sch Mines '47, Gold Medal for distinguished service U.S. Dept Interior '49, Freedoms Found gold medal award '50. 1025 Vermont Av., Washington 5.†☉

16 BALL, Robert Cragin. Pond fish culture; Fertilization of lakes and ponds. b'12. '32-34 (Otterbein Coll); AB—MSc '37 (O State U); PhD '43 (U Mich). Research on pond fish culture, fertilization of lakes and ponds, food fish production. Author articles: An Experiment in the Use of Derris Root on the Fish and Fish Food '42; A Tagging Experiment on the Fish Population of Third Sister Lake '44. Fisheries biol stream surveys and management O Div Conservation '37-38; fisheries biol Inst for Fisheries Research Mich '38-42; teaching asst U Mich '42-43; professor research and zool Mich State Coll since '51. Officer USPHS '43-46. Limnol Soc—Am Fisheries Soc—Wildlife Soc. Zoology Department, Michigan State College, East Lansing, Mich.

17 BALLARD, James Francis. Medical bibliography and classification; Medical Americana and incunabula; Medical books before 1800. b'78. Student (Dwight Sch Boston). Author: Boston Medical Library Classification '44; William Norton Bullard Collection of Medical Incunabula '29; Catalogue of Medieval and Renaissance Manuscripts and Incunabula in the Boston Medical Library '44; also articles in field. With Boston Med Library since '92, now dir, mem hon cons Army Med Library since '44. Med Library Assn (pres '37-39). 8 Fenway, Boston.

18 BALLARD, Stanley Sumner. Optics; Optical and Infrared Instruments; Spectroscopy; Spectrochemical analysis; Volcanic gas collection and analysis. b'08. AB '28 (Pomona Coll); MA '32—PhD '34 (U Calif). US delegate to first formal meeting of International Commission of Optics in Delft Holland '48, and London England '50, elected vice-pres '48, re-elected '50; chairman US National Committee, International Commission of Optics since '48. Author articles in field. Prof physics and dept chmn Tufts Coll since '46; cons physicist Polaroid Corp and Baird Asso Inc since '46. Served as lt, lt comdr and comdr US Naval Res active duty '41-46, officer in charge research and development optics and infrared instruments Bur Ordnance Navy Dept and radiometry sect tech staff Joint Task Force One, atom bomb tests; research asso in geophysics Hawaiian Volcano Observatory '35-41. Am Phys Soc(F)—AAAS—Optical Soc Am (sec local sects since '47)—Am Assn Physics Teachers—Am Soc Engring Edn—Hawaiian Acad Sci—Physical Soc London (optical group)—Phi Beta Kappa—Sigma Xi. Tufts College, Medford 55, Mass.

19 BALLARD, William Norval. Subsurface geology (Dakota basin); Stratigraphy. b'06. BS '29—MS '30 (Okla U); '25 (Okla City U). Author articles in field. Geol Phillips Petroleum Co '30-33, research geol eastern half US '34-35, chief research geol '36-37; cons geol '37-47; mgr exploration Northern Ordnance Inc since '48. Am Assn Petroleum Geol—Okla City Geol Soc—Independent Petroleum Assn Am—Nat Oil Scouts and Landmen's Assn—Phi Beta Kappa. 932 Commerce Exchange Building, Oklahoma City 2, Okla.

20 BALLENGER, Howard C. Otolaryngology; Medical instruction; Effects of smoke on the Throat. b'86. MD '11 (U Indiana). Cons surg otolaryngology USPHS '18-22; asst surg Otolaryngology Ill Charitable Eye & Ear Infirmary '17-20; asso surgeon Evanston Hosp '18-36 surgeon since '36; asso Northwestern U Med Sch '30-36 asst prof '36-40 asso prof '49-47 prof chmn dept otolaryngology since '47. Co-author: Ballenger's Diseases of the Nose, Throat and Ear (ninth edition) '47; Eye, Ear, Nose and Throat (with A. G. Wippern) '17; Otology, Rhinology and Laryngology '47. Am Laryngol Assn—Am Otol Soc—Am Laryngol Rhinol Otol Soc—Am Acad Ophthal Otol—Am Coll Surg. 303 E. Chicago Av., Chicago.

21 BALLOCH, John Carroll. Rorschach technique. b'22. BS '45—Am '45 (Boston U); PhD '50 (Mich State Coll). Study effects of Rorschach test administration on blood pressure, pulse rate, and respiratory rate and amplitude; research on differential responses to Rorschach of Negro and white children. Vocational adv Vets Adminstrn '45-47; research psychol child life and development program US Children's Bur Fisk U since '50. Am Psychol Assn—Soc Projective Techniques—Sigma Xi. Fisk University, Nashville, Tenn.

22 BALLS, Arnold Kent. Enzyme chemistry. b'91. PhD '17 (Columbia); PhD '29 (Prague U). Research on proteolytic and amylolytic enzymes, enzyme problems related to growth and preservation of agricultural products; crystallization and study of amylases, work on miscellaneous reactions relating to mode of action of hydrolytic enzymes. Author articles in field. Sr chem enzyme research lab Bur Agrl and Indsl Chem '31-37, prin chem '37-40, head chem since '40; adjunct prof biochem George Washington U since '34. Am Soc Biol Chem (sec '40-45, councillor '45-48)—Soc Exptl Biol and Med—Inst Food Tech—Sigma Xi. Enzyme Research Lab, 800 Buchanan St., Albany 6, Cal.

10 BALSAM, Charles P. Heating; Ventilation: Air Conditioning. b'02. Student (Johns Hopkins U). Author Emergency Substitutes for Metals; Opportunity in Summer Ventilating and Cooling; The Story of Winter Air Conditioning; Servicing Gas Boilers. Combustion engr '26-28; mfrs rep Washington '28-31; dir sales Washington Gas Light Co '31-33 Peoples Gas Light & Coke Co Chicago '33-36; organizer and mgr Nat Home Equipment Co since '38. Am Gas Assn—So Gas Assn—Am Soc Heating and Ventilating Engrs (house heating com). 50 Church St., N.Y.C. 7.

11 BALSEIRO, Jose A(gustin). Spanish literature (Modern novelists). b'00. LLB, DLitt (U PR); grad study (Madrid). Delegate US government to First International Congress on Teaching of Hispanic American Literature Mexico City '38; speaker at First Inter-American Congress on Libraries and Publications Washington '39; first foreign author to be invited to deliver the yearly oration in honor of Cuban writer Hernandez-Cata at the Colon Cemetery Havana '47. Author: La Copa de Anacreonte '24; La Ruta Eterna '24; El Vigia, vol 1-3, '25, '28, '42; Novelistas Espanoles Modernos '33; La Pureza Cautiva '46; Blasco Ibanez Unamuno, Valle Inclan y Baroja; Cuatro Individualistas de Espana '49; also articles in field. Prof Hispanic Am and Spanish Studies U Miami Fla since '46. Spanish Acad (Madrid)—Academia Hispanoamericana de Ciencias y Artes—Mod Lang Assn Am (chmn mod Spanish com '37)—Sigma Delta Pi. Winner of the Hispanic-American Literary prize awarded by Spanish Acad Lit Madrid '25; Puerto Rican Inst Lit prize San Juan '42. The University of Miami Branch, Miami, Fla.

12 BALTZER, Otto John. Guided missiles; Electronics. b'16. AB '38—MS '39—PhD '41 (Wash U). Research physicist Defense Research Lab U Tex since '46. Am Phys Soc—Inst Radio Engrs (sr mem)—Sigma Xi—Phi Beta Kappa. University Station, Box 1, Austin, Tex.

13 BALYS, Jonas. Lithuanian folklore. b'09. PhD '33 (U Vienna). Author: Motif-Index of Lithuanian Narrative Folk-Lore '36; Lithuanian Folk Legends '40; Litauische Hochzeitsbrauche '46; Handbook of Lithuanian Folklore '48. Editor: Tautosakos Darbai '35-40. Dir Lithuanian Folklore Archives Kaunas and Vilnius '33-44; docent for folklore and ethnol U Vilnius '42-44; asst German folksongs archives Freiburg Germany '44-45; asso prof folklore and ethnol Baltic U Hamburg Germany '46-47; instr East European Area program, research asst to dean grad sch Ind U since '48. Lithuanian Acad Sci—Internat Commn Folk Art and Folklore. Indiana University, Bloomington, Ind.

14 BALZER, Robert Lawrence. California wines; History of California wines and vineyards. b'12. AB '35 (Stanford). Semi-annual vintage tours through California since '35; study grape growing, vinification processes and personal histories California wineries; judge state wines Los Angeles County Fairs '48-50. Author: California's Best Wines '48. Author article California Wines Come of Age '49. Gen mgr Balzer's (retail wine, food) since '35; contributor of column Concerning Wines and Foods Beverly Hills Citizen Calif '39-41. Wine and Food Soc of Los Angeles Cordon Bleu award. 133 N. Larchmont Blvd., Los Angeles 4.

15 BANCROFT, Caroline. Colorado history and folklore (Central City);

Cornish folklore. b'02. AB '23 (Smith Coll); MA '43 (Denver U). Author: Guide to Central City '46; Lost Mine Legends of Colorado '43. Lit ed and columnist Denver Post '23-33. Colo Folklore Soc (vp)—Colo Authors League (pub chmn)—Colo Hist Soc (life). 1081 Downing St., Denver.

16 BANCROFT, Margaret. Ethnic distribution and social organization of western Europe in the Old Stone Age; Spread of Roman citizenship in Greece. b'91. AB '12 (Wellesley Coll); AM '13 (Columbia U). Research in museums and ancient remains in Europe and at Columbia University and Cambridge University Library relative to specialism. Teacher medieval hist Wellesley Coll '18-22; teacher ancient hist Columbia U since '23. AHA—Hist Sci Soc. Columbia University NYC 27.†

17 BANCROFT, Theodore Alfonso. Statistics (Design and analysis of experiments and sampling surveys); Mathematical statistics. b'07. AB '27 (U Fla); MA '34 (U Mich); PhD '43 (Ia State Coll). Author articles: On Biases in Estimation Due to the Use of Preliminary Tests of Significance '44; Note on an Identity in the Incomplete Beta Function '45; Statistical Centers in America '46; Recent Developments in the United States in Large Scale Sampling '47. Head math dept Mercer U '38-41; asst prof statis math Ia State Coll '41-46; asso prof statis math U Ga '46-47; dir statis lab Ala Polytech Inst '47-49; dir statis lab Ia State Coll since '50. Institute Math Statis—Am Statis Assn—Econometric Soc—Am Math Assn—Am Math Soc—Sigma Xi—Phi Kappa Phi. Statistical Lab, Iowa State College, Ames, Ia.†

18 BANDELIN, Fred John. Chemistry of germicides, local anesthetics, pyrogens, and vitamins. b'13. BS '36—'36-39 (U Cincinnati); '39-42 (Antioch Coll Yellow Springs O); '42-43 (Stevens Inst Tech); '46-47 (U Ill). Synthesis and testing of sulfonamides, quaternary ammonium salts, local anesthetics, fever producing substances; development analytical methods for therapeutic substances in vitamin field. Research chem William S Merrell Co Cincinnati '36-39; asst prof pharm U Cincinnati '39-41; tech dir Fidelity Med Supply Co Dayton O '41-43, Flint, Eaton & Co Decatur since '44. ACS—Am Pharm Assn—AAAS—Am Inst Chem (F)—Assn Vitamin Chem. 300 E. Main St., Decatur, Ill.

19 BANDY, William Thomas. Baudelaire. b'03. AB '23—AM '25 (Vanderbilt U); PhD '31 (Peabody Coll for Teachers); grad study (U Ill, U Grenoble, Paris, Strasbourg). Owner of one of largest collections of Baudelairiana in existence; compiler of an unpublished bibliography of Baudelaire comprising more than 5000 references grouped under first editions of Baudelaire's works, reprints, anthologies and collections, translations of Baudelaire's works, works set to music, iconography, references to Baudelaire in books and periodicals. Asso prof French U Wis since '46. Mod Lang Assn Am—Am Assn Teachers French. Bascom Hall, University of Wisconsin, Madison 6, Wis.†

20 BANE, Frank. Government; Public administration; Public Welfare administration; State and local co-operation; Federal state co-operation. b'93. AB '14 (Randolph-Macon Coll) student '14-14 (Columbia). Sec Va State Bd Charities and Corrections '20-23; dir Pub Welfare Knoxville '23-26; asso prof sociology U Va '26-28; commnr Pub Welfare Va '26-32; mem Pres Emergency Employment Com '30-31;

dir Am Pub Welfare Assn '32-35; lectr pub welfare administration U Chicago since '32; exec dir Fed Social Security Bd '35-38; dir div state and local co-operation adv commn council Nat Defense '40-41; mem civilian protection office Office Civil Defense '41; dir field operations OPA '41-42; homes utilization div Nat Housing Authority '42; sec treas Gov's Conf since '38; exec dir Council State Govts since '38. Am Polit Sci Assn—Nat Inst Social Scis—Nat Municipal League. 1313 E. 60th St., Chicago 37.⊚

21 BANGHAM, Walter N. Breeding and culture of rubber producing plants; Tropical agriculture. b'03. BS in Agr '26 (O State U); SM '29—Sheldon travelling fellow '29 (Harvard). Author articles in field. Dir plant research dept Goodyear Rubber Plantations Co '33-46; ed La Hacienda and A Fazenda since '47; mem survey party Intercontinental Rubber Co to investigate war damage to their properties in Sumatra in '48. La Hacienda, 20 Vesey St., NYC 7.†

22 BANGO, Henry Leonard. Timber estimating and appraising. b'12. BS (Forestry) (La State U). Forester land holding firm La '42-45; cons forester since '46. Soc Am Foresters—Forest Products Research Soc—La Forestry Assn. P.O. Box 4072, Shreveport, La.

23 BANK, Arnold. Calligraphy; Lettering; Typography. b'08. Author articles in field. Free lance book and advt designer, instr lettering and layout at Art Students League and Brooklyn Mus Art Sch NYC, taught at Columbia University and Reed College, lectr on hist and techniques of writing and lettering; specs in hist and techniques of Latin scripts. Typophiles—American Institute Graphic Arts—Type Directors Club NYC. 10 Monroe St., NYC 2.

24 BANKS, C(larence) Kenneth. Organometallic compounds; Heterocyclic organic compounds; Chemotherapy. b'14. AB '36 (U Kan City Mo); MSc '38—PhD '39 (U Nebr). Research on organic compounds of arsenic, antimony, bismuth, selenium; heterocyclic compounds pyridines, thiazoles, quinolines, pyrimidines, triazines; sulfon drugs, determination of arsenic in organic compounds, analytical methods for drugs. Author: Organometallic Compounds as Chemotherapeutic Agents in Advancing Fronts in Chemistry (vol II Chemotherapy) '46; also articles in field. Research chem Parke Davis and Co '40, '42, div head chemotherapy '42-49; research chem NDRC War Gases '41; dir research and development Metal and Thermit Corp since '49. Am Chem Soc—Am Pharm Assn—AAAS—Mich Acad Pharmacy—Sigma Xi. Metal and Thermit Corp., Box 471, Rahway, N.J. H: 280 Chestnut St., Bound Brook, N.J.

25 BANKS, James Filson. Yeast cultures; Industrial waste disposal. b'13. BEd '34 (Ill State Coll). In charge all research and development work of Schenley Distilleries Inc on stream pollution since '46, all pure culture yeast propagation since '35. Patent pending on method of producing monosodium glutamate from wheat gluten. Chief chem Geo T Stagg Co Frankfort Ky '34-44, research chem since '44. ACS—Fed Sewage Works Assn—Kappa Delta Pi. George T. Stagg Co., Leestown Pike, Frankfort, Ky.

26 BANKS, Theodore Howard. Milton; Denham; Jacobean and Caroline poets. b'95. BA '17—PhD '23 (Yale); MA '20 (Harvard). Author: The Poetical Works of Sir John Denham '28; Sir

Gawain and the Green Knight '29; Milton's Imagery '50. With Wesleyan U since '28, now professor. AAUP—Mod Lang Assn Am. Wesleyan University, Middletown, Conn.†

10 BANNER, Albert Henry. Distribution and classification of Crustacea; Biology of marine plankton, oysters, and Pribilof fur seal. b'14. Student '31-32 (Bellingham State Normal); BS '35—PhD '43 (U Washington); MS '39 (U Hawaii). Research taxonomy Hawaiian shrimp, taxonomy and distribution Crustacea, biology of Pribilof fur seal, biology of and effects of pollution upon oysters, marine plankton production. Author articles in field. Asso prof zool U Hawaii Honolulu. AAAS—Am Microscopic Soc—Am Soc Limnol Oceanog—Am Soc Systematic Zool—Hawaiian Acad Sci—Sigma Xi. University of Hawaii, Honolulu 14, T.H.†

11 BANNERMAN, Harold MacColl. Precambrian and mining geology; Mineral resource appraisal. b'97. BS '24 (Acadia U); PhD '27 (Princeton U); AM hon '34 (Dartmouth). Author articles in field. With Dartmouth College '27-42, prof geol '34-42; geol US Geol Survey Washington, since '42, chief division economic geol '44-'48, assistant chief geologist since '48. Geol Soc Am—Am Mineral Soc—Soc Econ Geol—Am Inst Mining Metall Engrs. U.S. Geological Survey, Federal Works Building, Washington 25.

12 BANNON, John Francis. History of Latin America. b'05. BA '28—MA '29—STL '36 (St Louis U); PhD '39 (U Calif); traveling fellowship Europe '26-28 (Mo Province Ed Inst). Lecturer Latin American history, inter-American affairs; missionary enterprise in colonial Latin America; church and state in Latin America; expulsion of Jesuits from colonial Latin America. Dir Inst Foreign Trade (Export Managers' Club and Saint Louis U) since '43; member committee conf Latin Am hist, Am Hist Assn '49. Author: Epitome of Western Civilization '48; Latin America; An Historical Survey '47, and others. Asst hist dept St Louis U '32-36, instr hist '39-41, asst prof '41-44, asso prof since '44, dir dept hist since '43, ed The Hist Bull since '43. Am Hist Assn—Miss Valley Hist Assn. St. Louis University, St. Louis 3.

13 BARBER, Donald McArthur. Photography (Portrait, pictorial, lighting, composition). b'18. Grad (Winona Sch Photog Winona Lake Ind). Study and experiment portrait and pictorial photography since '23; photographic exhibits US and abroad. Southeastern Photog Assn—Photog Assn Am—Royal Photog Soc Great Brit. NC Photog Assn grand award cups; Southeastern Photog Assn grand commercial award. Barber Studio, Hendersonville, N.C.

14 BARBER, Joseph, Jr. History of Hawaii. b'09. AB '31 (Harvard); '31-32 (U Munich, Germany); BS '33 (Columbia U); Pulitzer traveling scholarship '33. Author: Hawaii: Restless Rampart '41; also articles in field. Public relations counsel Honolulu T H '38-40; dir Com on Fgn Relations affiliated with Council on Fgn Relations Inc NYC since '46. 58 East 68th St., NYC.

15 BARBERIS, Fortunato Felice. Automotive engineering. b'95. Dr Mech Engring '22—Dr Aircraft Engring '23 (Royal Politecnic Turin Italy). Engine design and stress analysis of parts trucks busses engine and chassis design and stresses analysis of parts. Automotive body design and development. Aircraft engine design and calculation relating to in line engine and radial engine development and calculations of special aircraft & automotive accessory. Issued Italian patents on variable pitch propeller and on electromagnetic block control system and grade crossing control for railroad. Corp since 33. Soc Exptl Stress Analysis. General Motor Corp., AC Division, Flint 2, Mich.

16 BARBOUR, Philip Lemont. Broadcasting (International). b'98. Student '14-17 (Columbia U); '17-19 (Cornell). Rockefeller Foundation Fellow for study educational aspects of international broadcasting; inauguration Inter-American foreign language broadcasts '37; study of propaganda foreign language broadcasting, and devised techniques for short wave broadcasting; investigation foreign countries' broadcasting techniques. Author articles: Beamed Programs over Short-Wave '40; International Radio in the Three Americas '40; Commercial and Cultural Broadcasting in Mexico '40; Open Questions in Inter-American Broadcasting '41, and others. Dir inter-American broadcasts World Wide Broadcasting Found Boston '37-38; in charge fgn press and sta relations internat div NBC NYC '38-41; prin radio program officer Coordinator Inter-Am Affairs NYC '41-42; chief intelligence sect Berlin Sector US Mil Govt '46-48, asst to dir Radio in Am Sector Berlin '48; with Radio Free Europe since '49, dir spl events since '50. Am Oriental Soc—Medieval Acad Am. Radio Free Europe, 110 West 57th St., N.Y.C. 19. H: Silvermine, Norwalk, Conn.

17 BARCLAY, Hartley Wade. Industrial engineering, (Management and distribution); Public, industrial, trade and government relations. b'03. Arbitrator, American Arbitration Association; secretary American Conference National Defense; has specialized in developing basic customer and public relations, research, and operating systems with leading American industrial corporations, since '43. Author: Survey of Industrial Distribution '31; Ford Production Methods '36; The American Economy, '38; Labor's Stake in the American Way '38; Executive sec Management Research Inst, cons research dir Taft-Pierce Mfg Co, Marine Products Co, Henry G Thompson and Son Co, cons Gen Motors Corp, ed Mill and Factory mag, dir, sec Conover Mast Pub Corp '31-42. Newcomen Soc—Am Soc Tool Engrs—Army Ordnance Assn. 250 Park Av., NYC.

18 BARD, Philip. Zoology; Physiology; Biology; Neurophysiology. b'98. AB '23 ScD (hon) '47 (Princeton) AM '25 PhD '27 (Harvard). Mem. editorial bd Am. Jour. Physiology; editor and contbr. Macleod's Physiology in Modern Medicine '41. Asst prof biology Harvard Med Sch '31-33; prof physiology and dir dept Johns Hopkins U Sch Med since '33. AAAS(F)—Am Acad Arts & Scis—Nat Acad Scis—Am Physiol Soc—Am Neur Assn—Harvey Soc—Soc Exptl Biol and Med—Nat Research Council—Assn Research Nervous and Mental Dis—Phi Beta Kappa—Sigma Xi. Johns Hopkins Medical School, Baltimore 5.⊙

19 BARDEEN, John. Theory of solid state (Metals, matter, semi-conductors). b'08. BS '28—MS '29 (U Wis); PhD '36 (Princeton U); jr fellow '35-38 (Harvard). Co-inventor with W H Brattain of the transistor, a semiconductor triode. Research in theory of matter at high pressure, of metals including electrical conductivity, of semi-conductors and crystal rectifiers. Author articles in field. Geophysicist Gulf Research and Development Corp '30-33; physicist Naval Ordnance Lab Washington '41-45; research physicist Bell Telephone Labs '45-51; with dept physics U Ill since '51. Am Phys Soc. Dept of Physics, Univ. of Ill., Urbana, Ill.

20 BARGER, Edgar Lee. Agricultural engineering (Power and machinery). b'05. BS Agrl Engring '29—MS '34 (Kan State Coll). Research in tractor fuels, cost and service of farm machinery, rice and grain driers, forage handling machinery and equipment for chemical weed control. Invented rice drier, developed combination packer-seeder, sumac leaf harvester, weed sprayer for row crops. Author bulletin: Tractor Fuels '39; and others. Prof, research prof, mgr Farm Service Dept Ia State Coll since '44. Am Soc Agrl Engrs—Am Soc Engring Edn—Sigma Xi—Sigma Tau—Gamma Sigma Delta. Paper award, Am Soc Agrl Engrs, for Power Alcohol in Tractors and Farm Engines '41. Iowa State College, Ames, Ia. H: 433 N. Franklin.

21 BARGER, William Ross. Transportation and storage of fruits and vegetables. b'96. BS '21 (Mich State Coll). Development of new handling methods to obtain optimum transit temperature in refrigerator cars; improvement of stowing and refrigerating methods for perishable produce in ships' holds; study of proper temperature and humidity for storage of dried fruit; design of light weight air shipment case with self-contained refrigeration for small lots of fruit, and light weight insulating blanket for large lots of precooled fruit; research on produce shipments by air. Research citrus fruit handling Orlando Fla '21-23, Pasadena Calif '24-29; research date handling and storage Indo Calif '30-37; research fruit, vegetable, and cut flower handling and storage Fresno Calif since '38. U.S. Department of Agriculture, Route 3, Box 307, Fresno, Calif.†

22 BARGHOORN, Elso Sterrenberg. Paleobotany; Plant anatomy; tissue deterioration. b'15. AB '37 (Miami U); MA '38—PhD '41 (Harvard). Author articles in field. Assoc prof bot Harvard since '49. Field service cons OSRD Washington '44-46, research in prevention of deterioration of military equipment for OQMG. AAAS—Bot Soc Am—Geol Soc Am(F)—Soc Economic Geol—Society Study Evolution—Sigma Xi. Biological Laboratories, Harvard University, Cambridge, Mass.

23 BARGMEYER, Ernest G(erard) H(enry). Latex chemistry; Foam rubber; Special adhesives; Latex dipping and coating compositions. b'08. BS '30 (U Wash); '42-45 (Notre Dame U). Development, analysis, physical testing, textiles, miscellaneous phases of rubber compounding factory control; development work on foam rubber, special adhesives, latex dipping and coating compositions from laboratory to factory installation. Holds three patents in field. Analytical chem US Rubber Co '30-42, latex chem since '34, exec research chem since '42. Am Chem Soc. U.S. Rubber Co., Mishawaka, Ind.†

24 BARHAM, Harold Nathan. Starch (Chemistry); Sorghum Grains. b'97. Certificate '19 (U Caen France); AB '21 (Bethany Coll Lindsborg Kan); MS '22 (O State U); PhD '28 (U Kan). Research on physico-organic chemistry '21-22, physical chemistry '26-28, oxidation products of paraffin hydrocarbon '28-29, industrial utilization sorghum grains and other crops, dry milling of sorghum grains, chemistry and characterization of starches, starch choloride, properties starch pastes, structure starch granules. Process developed for dry milling sorghum grain, holds patent on chlorination of starch and starch products. Author article Starch—Am Industrial Raw Material '46. Prof chem Mont Wesleyan Coll Helena '22-23, Bethany Coll Lindsborg Kan '24-26; faculty chem dept Kan State Coll since '29, prof chem since '43; indsl chem Kan Agrl Expt Sta since '38. ACS—Kan Acad Sci—Sigma Xi—Gamma Sigma Delta. Dept. Chemistry, Kansas State Coll., Manhattan, Kan.

10 BARINGER, William Eldon. Civil War (Political aspects, campaign songs); Abraham Lincoln. b'09. BS '31 —AM '32—PhD '40 (U Ill). Author: Lincoln's Rise to Power '37; A House Dividing '45; also articles in field. Asst prof Tulane U New Orleans '42-43; exec sec Abraham Lincoln Assn Springfield Ill '43-47; ed Abraham Lincoln Quar '45-47; asso prof social sci U Fla since '47. Soc Am Hist—Abraham Lincoln Assn—Ill State Hist Soc—So Hist Assn—Kappa Delta Pi. University of Florida, Gainesville, Fla.†

11 BARISH, Thomas. Ball and roller bearings; Gearing; Theoretical machine design. b'97. AB '17—ME '20 (Columbia). Holder of seventeen patents on items including universal joints, controllable propellers, ball bearings, aircraft wheels and brakes. Author articles in field. Cons engr Aero Products Div GMC Dayton O, Lear Inc Grand Rapids Mich, Watson-Flagg Machine Co Paterson NJ, Fredric Flader Inc, Bell Aircraft Corp Niagara Falls NY and Cleveland Hobbing Machine Co Cleveland. SAE—Inst Aeronautical Engrs—Am Soc Metals—Soc for Exptl Stress Analysis. ASME. 132 Sheridan N.E., Washington 11.

12 BARKALOW, Frederick Schenck, Jr. Wild life management. b'14. BS '36 (Ga Sch Tech); MS '39—PhD '48 (U Mich). Prof zool, in charge wildlife conservation and management curriculum NC State Coll Agr and Engring since '47; prin biol NC Wildlife Resources Commn. Research on mammals of southeastern US; made game inventory of Alabama. In charge Pittman-Robertson wildlife research program Ala '39-41; head zool div biol sci NC State College Agr and Engineering since '50. Am Society Mammalogists — Ornithol Union — Wilson Ornithol Club—Wildlife Soc—Soc Syst Zool—Ga Ornithol Soc—NC Acad Sci—Phi Kappa Phi—Phi Sigma—Phi Beta Kappa—Sigma Xi. Julius Rosenwald fellowship U Mich '47. Department of Zoology, North Carolina College of Agriculture and Engineering, Raleigh, N.C. H: 2607 Barmettler St.

13 BARKER, George Carpenter. Bilingualism; Pachuco argot. b'12. AB '35 (UCLA); MS '36 (Columbia); MA '43—PhD '47—fellow '41-42 (U Chicago). Travel and study in Mexico '48-49. Author: Pachuco; An American-Spanish Argot and its Social Functions in Tucson, Arizona '49; also articles in field. Am Anthrop Assn(F). 535 Alma Real Dr., Pacific Palisades, Calif.

14 BARKER, Harry. Electrical engineering (Economics). b'81. BS '04 U Vt. Valuation of public utility properties; Economics of public utility operations. Author: Public Utility Rates '17. Author articles booklets and brochures in field. Mem Barker & Wheel-

er engrs NY City and Albany; cons engr to Vt Pub Service Commn '25-39; adv engr Municipal Electric Utility Assn NY since '35; cons engr TVA '36-39; lectr on practice engring U Vt. Capt Engr Corps US Army 17-18. Am Inst EE—ASME—Phi Beta Kappa. 11 Park Pl NYC 7.†ⓒ

15 BARKER, Joseph Warren. Electrical engineering; Industrial and office illumination; Electrical precipitation. b'91. BS '16—MS '25 (MIT); and six honorary degrees Am Colls and Univs. Prof elec engring MIT '25-29; prof and head dept elec engring Lehigh U '29-30; dean of faculty engring Columbia '30-46; special asst to Sec Navy '41-45; chmn bd dirs and pres Research Corp since '45. AIEE (F, vp '40)—AAAS (exec com '41)—ASME—ASCE—Am Inst Mining Metall Engrs—Illuminating Engrs Soc (pres '32-33)—Am Soc Engring Edn—NY Elec Soc—Tau Beta Pi—Sigma Xi. 405 Lexington Av., NYC 17.ⓒ

16 BARKER, Maurice Eugene. Chemical warfare; Biological warfare; Activated charcoal; Clothing (Testing). b'94. BS—Pd B '15 (Valparaiso U); AM '24 (U SC); ScD '30 (MIT). Granted 15 US patents on chemical and biological warfare, four US patents on manufacture of activated charcoal; research, testing, design and actual wear of clothing in field. Author 58 articles in field. With US Army '17-48, tech dir Edgewood Arsenal '24-27, chief research div Chem Warfare Service '30-31, instr Chem Warfare Sch '31-35 and comdg officer '44-48; head dept chem engring U Ark since '48. ACS—Armed Forces Chem Assn—Am Soc Engring Edn—Soc Am Mil Engrs—AICE. Department of Chemical Engineering, University of Arkansas, Fayetteville, Ark.ⓒ

17 BARKLEY, John E(lbert). Surface chemistry; Photoconductivity; Phosphors. b'16. AB '39 (Ft Hays Kans State Coll); MSc '40—PhD '42 (Ohio State U). Author articles in field. Asso phys chem '44, now supervisor phys chem research, Armour Research Found Chicago. Am Chem Soc—AAAS—Sigma Xi. Armour Research Foundation, 35 W. 33 St., Chicago 16.

18 BARKLEY, John Ferdinand. Fuels and fuel utilization; Smoke and fly-ash abatement; Boiler water conditioning. b'88. BS '10—EM '10 (Mich Coll Mines). Author articles in field. Chief Fuels Utilization Div US Bur Mines Washington since '46; cons on design, operation and fuel use, fed fuel-burning plants. ASME—Am Inst Mining Metall Engrs—Air Pollution Control Assn (hon). Bureau of Mines, U.S. Department of Interior, Washington.

19 BARLOW, Wallace Dudley. Mineral economics; Mining geology; Traffic engineering. b'09. BS '26-30—MS '34-36 (Va Polytech Inst); '39-40 (Harvard); registered professional engineer since '52. Field geologist Northern Rhodesia '30-32, Ariz '32-34, California '34-35. Invented non-stop (continuous control) automotive traffic signal, airport runway deicing equipment '46, slave driven radio transmitter '47; developed five-cent coin containing no nickel for US Govt World War II. Author: Regional Estimates of Future Mineral Production '40; Soviet Resources Reconsidered '40; Mineral Position of the United States '48. Chief metals and minerals sect Commodities Div Planning Br Office Asst Sec War Washington '40-41; chief tin, lead nickel sect Civilian Supply Div WPB Washington '41-42;

mineral econ east region US Bur Mines Interior Dept '42-43; purchasing officer General Purchasing Agency US Army Rio de Janeiro '43-44; prof staff mem for minerals and petroleum, Interior & Insular Affairs Com, US Senate since '48. Royal Econ Soc—Am Econ Assn—Econometric Soc—Am Acad Pol Sci—Am Inst Mining Metallurgical Engrs—Inst Traffic Engr—Pan Am Inst Mining Engring and Geol—AAAS. Ager Rd. at 19th Pl., Hyattsville, Md.†

20 BARNER, John Lemuel. Radiology; Oncology. b'07; AB '29 (Grinnell Coll); '39 (Cincinnati U); MD '33 (Jefferson Med Coll). Designed interchangeable treatment cones X-ray therapy machine '40, radium applicator with interchangeable filters '39, biopsy tissue forceps '37. Author articles in field. Dir Athens (Ga) Tumor Clinic since '46; radiologist Athens Gen Hosp, St Marys Hosp since '46. X-ray therapist US Army Lawson Gen Hosp Ga '41-46. Am Coll Radiology—Am Radium Soc—Radiology Soc No Am—Ptolomy Soc—AMA—Ga Radiolog Soc —Assn Mil Surgeons. Fellow Nat Cancer Inst, Cincinnati Gen Hosp '38-39. Athens General Hospital, Athens, Ga.

21 BARNES, Bentley Tiffany. Light sources; Spectral intensities. b'01. BA '21 (Park Coll); MA '23—fellow '21-23 (Rice Inst); '23 (U Chicago); PhD '25 —Loomis fellow '24-25 (Yale). Research on electron emission from thoriated tungsten, carbonized tungsten, spectral intensities, design of monochromators, characteristics of mercury vapor lamps, efficiency of fluorescent lamps, colorimeter design, techniques for measuring transient phenomena in gaseous discharges, starting characteristics of fluorescent lamps, dynamic and static characteristics of low-pressure mercury vapor discharges. Author articles in field. Research physicist Lamp Development Lab Gen Elec Co since '25. Am Phys Soc—Optical Soc Am (asso). Lamp Development Laboratory, General Electric Company, Nela Park, Cleveland 12.

22 BARNES, Clifford Adrian. Sea ice. b'05. BS '30—PhD '36 (U Wash). Oceanographer First Aleutian Island Survey expedition US Navy 33, Bering Sea cruise Coast Guard Cutter Chelan '34, International Ice Patrol '40-'42, Hydrographic Office '46. Author articles in field. Asso prof oceanog U Washington since '47. Officer US Coast Guard '42-46, headed war-time ice information and ice patrol service North Atlantic area. Am Chem Soc—Am Geophys Union—Oceanog Soc Pacific—Am Soc Limnol Oceanog. University of Washington, Oceanographic Laboratories, Seattle 5.†

23 BARNES, Edgar Charles. Industrial dusts. b'09. BS '30 (Pa State Coll); '30-31 (U Pittsburgh). Co-holder patent on electrostatic dust weight sampler '43. Author articles in field. Indsl hygiene engr hdqtrs med dept Westinghouse Elec Corp '33-49, mgr indsl hygiene Atomic Power Div since '49; indsl hygiene engr Dept Indsl Hygiene Sch Med U Pittsburgh since '37. Am Indsl Hygiene Assn (pres '49-50, past sec and bd dirs)—AAAS—Am Soc Safety Engrs. Westinghouse Electric Corporation, P.O. Box 1468, Pittsburgh 30.

24 BARNES, James Anderson. American history since 1865; Free silver; Microphotography. b'98. AB '24 (Bowling Green Ky Teachers Coll); MA '25—PhD '28—fellow Am hist '27-28 (U Wis); Pioneer in use of miniature camera as copying instrument for historians. Prof hist Temple U

Phila since '47; historian QMC Army Service Forces US War Dept '42-45. Soc Am Historians—Am, Miss Valley, So, Pa Hist Assns—Am Econ Hist Assn —Am Acad Polit Social Sci—Phi Alpha Theta. Fellow Brookings Instn '29-30; fellow Social Sci Research Council '32-33, awarded grant-in-aid '38; Hayes Memorial Foundation '40. Temple University, Phila.☺

10 BARNES, Nathanial Waring. Commercial correspondence; Business management council. b'84. AB '03—AM '05 (Columbia U). Executive sec and treasurer 7th International Management Congress '37-39. Author: How to Teach Business Correspondence '16; Manual of Business Communications '18; Business Writing Manual '35; Management Engineering—A Vocational Monograph '41. Dir Bur of Research and Edn of Internat Advt Assn '27-30; exec sec Assn of Cons Management Engrs since '32; professorial lecturer on bus corr, Northwestern U Sch of Commerce '21-27; lecturer, bus writing, Sch Bus and U Ext Columbia since '30. Am Marketing Soc (ex-nat sec)—Nat Assn Teachers of Marketing and Advt (p pres)—Am Management Assn —Am Bus Writing Assn—Soc Advancement Management—Phi Beta Kappa. 347 Madison Av., NYC 17.

11 BARNES, Virgil E(verett). Geology (Tektites). b'03. BS '25—MS '27 (State Coll Wash); PhD '30 (U Wis). Only expert on tektites in western hemisphere. Author articles in field. Geol Bur Econ Geol Austin Tex since '35. Geol Soc Am—Mineral Soc Am—Geophys Union—Am Assn Petroleum Geol—Sigma Xi. Bureau of Economic Geology, Austin 12, Tex.

12 BARNES, William B. Wildlife management. b'08. '26-29 (Pa State Forest Sch); BS '30 (NC State Coll); '42 (Ind U). Wildlife Technician, Pittman-Robertson Wildlife Research Project 2-R and leader in charge statewide investigations of wildlife. Author articles: The Sportsman's Questionnaire Method of Estimating the Game Kill in Indiana; The Snowy Owl Invasion; The Distribution of Indiana's Bobwhite Quail. With Resettlement Adminstrn and Soil Conservation Service US Dept Agr '35-40; chief forester land use project in so Ind in charge forestry and wildlife development since '40. Wildlife Soc Am—Am Soc Mammalogist — Am Ornithol Union — Ind Acad Sci. 311 W. Washington St., Ind Dept of Conservation, Indpls.

13 BARNETT, Homer Garner. Cultural dynamics; Language and culture of the Palau Islands; Applied anthropology. b'06. AB '27 (Stanford U); PhD '38 (U Calif). Executive secretary Pacific Science Survey Ethnogeographic Board '44; Pacific Science Conference, National Academy of Sciences '46; West Coast Advisory Committee Pacific Science Board; coordinated investigation of micronesian anthropology. Author articles: Cultural Growth by Substitution '42; Culture Processes '40; Invention and Cultural Change '42; Personal Conflicts and Cultural Change '41. Professor anthrop U Ore since '50; anthrop Smithsonian Institution '44, '46. University of Oregon, Eugene, Ore.

14 BARNETT, Horace Leslie. Mycology; Physiology of fungi. b'09. AB '31 (DePauw U); MS '33 (N D Agrl Coll); PhD '37 (Mich State Coll). Research on edible mushrooms of North Dakota '33, development and structure of Longia texensis '43; notes on sexuality of Heterobasidiae '37. Author articles in field. Instr, asst prof biol NM State Coll '38-43; asst prof bot

Mich State Coll '39-40; emergency plant disease prevention project US Dept Agr '43-44; asso prof, now prof mycol W Va U since '45. W Va Acad Sci—Bot Soc Am—Mycol Soc Am—Am Phytopath Soc—Sigma Xi. Department of Plant Pathology, West Virginia University, Morgantown, W. Va.

15 BARNEY, Winfield S(upply). Romance languages (French); Evolution of French literature; 17th Century salons and literature. b'83. BA '05 (Dartmouth Coll); '05-06 (Harvard); MA '11 (Hobart Coll); certificate '11 (U Grenoble); PhD '16 (Syracuse U). Special fields are interrelation of salons and literature and more human aspect of the salon groups, Corneilles comedies as a mirror of contemporary events and of theories of French polite society in first half of seventeenth century, and evolution and classification of various types of novel. Chairman Southern States Modern Foreign Language investigation '24-27. Author: Practical French Review Grammar '40; Premier Livre de Lecture '28. Editor: Merimee's Colomba '18; Loti's Pecheur d'Islande '22; Daudet's Le Petit Chose '25; also articles in field. Instr physics Hobart Coll '07-11, instr Romance lang '11-14, prof French '14-15; head dept Romance langs Gettysburg (Pa) Coll '16-18; head dept Spanish Ohio U '18-19; head dept Romance langs Woman's Coll U NC since '19. Am Assn Teachers Span (life)—Modern Lang Assn Am—Am Assn Teachers French (pres NC chapter '45-46)—South Atlantic Modern Lang Assn (founder, pres '29-31)—NC Modern Lang Assn (co-founder, pres '21-23)—Phi Beta Kappa. 127 McIver St., Greensboro, N.C.☺

16 BARNHART, Clarence Lewis. Lexicography; Encyclopedia editor; American speech. b'00. PhB '30—grad work '34-37 (U Chicago). Editor: Thorndike Century Jr Dictionary '35, '42; Thorndike Century St Dictionary '41; Dictionary of US Army Terms '43; Thorndike Century Beginning Dictionary '45; American College Dictionary '48. Founder and pres C L Barnhart Inc '47; asso ed Am Speech since '48; ed War Dept '43. Am Acad Polit Social Sci—AAAS—Am Dialect Soc—Am Folklore Soc—Linguistic Soc —Mod Lang Assn—Nat Council Teachers Eng—Phi Beta Kappa. Hon research asso Inst Psychol Research Columbia '45, '46. 141 Parkway Rd., Bronxville 8, N.Y. H: 9 Lookout Ave., Bronxville 8.†☺

17 BARNHART, John Donald. American, Middle Western and Indiana history. b'95. BA '16 (Ill Wesleyan); BD '19 (Garrett Bibl Inst); MA '19 (Northwestern); PhD '30 (Harvard). Editor Indiana Magazine of History since '41; research on Ohio Valley frontier, Southern migration north of the Ohio River, and Henry Hamilton's expedition to Vincennes in '78-'79. Author articles in field. Temp asso prof hist Ind U '25-26, asso prof '41-46, prof since '46, acting head hist dept '47-48, instr hist W Va U '26-28, asst prof '28-32, asso prof '32-34; head dept social studies West Lib W Va State Teach Coll '34-36; asso prof hist La State U '36-41; dir Ind War Hist Commn '43-47. AHA—So Hist Assn (mem ed bd '36-39)—AAUP—Ind Hist Soc—Miss Valley Hist Assn (chmn program com '47-48, mem program com '46-47, exec council '42-46)—Ind Hist Teach Assn (vp '46-47, pres '47-48). History Department, Indiana University, Bloomington, Ind.

18 BARNITZ, Wirt Whitcomb. History (Lapland, Scandinavia, Gotland

Island, radio); World War I and II (Backgrounds). b'87. Special study Harvard. Lecturer on travel since '12; special correspondent New York World in Central Europe; Scandinavia '15-16; Founder The Nomad, editor '24-30; founder Nomad organization for world peace through human contacts in travel; assisted in organization War Camp Community Service; traveled twice to Lapland for survey purposes preparatory exploration outer reaches Lapp tundra; pioneer radiolog broadcasting; pioneer radio commentator. Author articles in field. Free lance writer. 453 W. 47th St., NYC.

19 BARON, Hans. Medieval, Renaissance and Reformation history; History of humanism and political thought; Political theories of the Reformation; History of German Free Cities. b'00. '18-23 (Univs Berlin and Leipzig); PhD '22 (U Berlin). Travelling fellow Italian humanism studies Florence and Rome '25-27 (Notgemeinschaft der deutschen Wissenschaft); associate archival research pre-Reformation German Diets '28-33 (Bavarian Acad of Sciences); research on humanism and Florentine Commonwealth in Italian Renaissance; editor Ernst Troeltsch's collected works on intellectual history and politics '24-25. Author: Calvins Staatsanschauung und das Konfessionelle Zeitalter '24; Leonardo Bruni Aretino, Humanistisch - Philosophische Schriften, mit einer Chronologie '28; Humanism and Political Literature in Florence About 1400 '51; also articles in field. Mem sch humanistic studies Inst Advanced Study Princeton NJ '44-48; fellow and bibliographer Newberry libry since '49; lecturer Berlin '29-33; Johns Hopkins '46-47; Guggenheim fellow '42-43. AHA—Medieval Acad Am—Am Soc Church Hist—Research grants Am Philos Soc, Rockefeller Found. Newberry Library, Chicago 10.

20 BARON, Salo W. Jewish history and sociology; Near Eastern Affairs; Modern nationalism; History; Sociology; Theology and religion. b'95. PhD '17 (U Vienna) ScD '22 JurD '23 (U Vienna) MHL '20 (Jewish Theol Seminary Vienna) DHL '44 (Hebrew Union Coll Cincinnati). Author: Die Judenfrage auf dem Wiener Congress '20; Die Politische Theorie Ferdinand Lassalle's '23; The Isrealitish Population under the Kings (Hebrew) '33; A Social and Religious History of the Jews '37; The Jewish Community '42; Modern Nationalism and Religion '47; several essays and articles. Prof Religion acting librarian Jewish Inst Religion '27-30 dir dept advanced studies '28-30; prof Jewish history literature and instns Columbia since '30; dir Center of Israel Studies since '50. Pres Conf on Jewish Relations; pres academic council The Hebrew U. Mem Am Jewish Hist Soc—Am Hist Assn—Soc Bibl Lit. H: Canaan, Conn.☺

21 BAROODY, Bahij Joseph. Medical parasitology. b'09. BA ' 32—'32-33 (Duke U); '33 (W Reserve U Med Sch); grad '45 (US Army Med Field Service Sch). Registered Technologist and Specialist Certificate Parasitology '48 (Can Soc Lab Tech). Developed diagnostic method for schistosomiasis Japonica '46, developed improved method for diagnosis of parasitic infections in fecal specimens. Research med parasitol '33-43; research parasitol, tropical med since '46. Am Soc Tropical Med—Am Soc Parasitol—Am Soc Systematic Zool—Can Soc Med Tech (asso mem)—Royal Soc Tropical Med and Hygiene (London) (F). Timmonsville, S. C.

10 BARR, Alvin Haley. Firearms and ammunition (Hunting, target). b'07. Student pub schs Va. Author articles: Making Your Own Bullets; Rebedding Single-Shot Rifles; Varmint Rifle Mounts; Introduction To Handloading; Mounts For Hunting Scopes; Stith's Master Mounts; Selecting A Reloading Tool. Tech div staff Nat Rifle Assn Am, ed staff The American Rifleman since '35; cons on firearms. Bench Rest Shooter's Assn. National Rifle Association, 1600 Rhode Island Av., Washington 6.

11 BARR, Claude Arno. Great Plains (Plants). b'87. BA '14 (Drake U). Collector data on plants of garden interest and compilation list of 635 plants; growth and sale indigenous species of flowering plants, ferns, and shrubs. Author articles: Garden Adventure on the High Prairies; The Life Span of Penstemons; Dwarf Western Asters; Jewels of the Great Plains; Cushion Astragali, and others. Operator of nursery since '34. Am Soc Plant Taxonomists—Am Rock Garden Soc—Am Penstemon Soc—SD Hort Soc—Am Hort Soc. Prairie Gem Ranch, Smithwick, S.D.

12 BARR, E(rnest) Scott. Infrared spectroscopy (Aqueous solutions, sugars, vegetable oils); Proximity fuze; Ram jet. b'05. AB '26—MA '33—PhD '36 (UNC). Author articles in field. Instr physics Tulane U '36-37, asst prof '37-39, asso prof '40-47; sr physicist applied physics lab Johns Hopkins '45-46; prof phys U Ala since '47. Am Phys Soc(F)—Am Optical Soc—Sigma Xi. Box 714, University, Ala.

13 BARR, Glenn Ross. Latin American affairs; Nineteenth century Spanish literature. b'97. AB '19 (Allegheny Coll); MA '27 (O State U); PhD '37 (Wis U); '27 (Centro de Estudios Históricos, Madrid). Co-author: (with W K Jones), Un Verano in Mexico '42; (with Jones) (Resumen Gramatical '42; (with Jones); Our South American Friends '49; also articles in field. Asst cultural relations officer in US Embassy, Buenos Aires '41-42, Montevideo '42-44; prof Romantic languages Miami U since '46. Phi Beta Kappa—Modern Language Assn. Miami University, Oxford, O.

14 BARR, William Elliott. Scientific glass blowing; Glass apparatus (For research in petroleum chemistry and electronics). b'06. Ed pub schls. Coauthor: (with V J Anhorn) Scientific and Industrial Glass Blowing '49. Author articles in field. With Westinghouse Research Corp '24-36; supt Gulf Research and Development Co since '36, Instrument Soc Am. Gulf Research and Development Co., Post Office Drawer 2038, Pittsburgh 30. H: 425 Eleventh St., Oakmont, Pa.

15 BARR, William Milton. Railway chemistry and metallurgy; Lubrication; Water treatment. b'78. BSc '02 (U Ia); MA '04 (Grinnell Coll); PhD '08—Harrison fellow chem '07-08 (U Pa). Research on boiler-feed water treatment for locomotives; alloy steels in locomotives, wheels; pitting and corrosion locomotive boilers; railway forgings and castings; lubrication and fuels for diesel locomotives. Author articles in field. Chem and metall engr Union Pacific RR '16-'44, research and standards cons since '44; asso prof metall Ia State Coll '09-11. Am Soc Metals—Am Welding Soc—Am Chem Soc—Am Inst Chem Engrs—Am Ry Engring Assn—Am Soc Test Materials (pres '40-41)—Sigma Xi. Awarded $1000 prize for article Pitting and Corrosion in Locomotive Boilers by Railway Review '26. 1416 Dodge St., Omaha, Neb.

16 BARRATT, Roswell Forman. Meteorology (Aeronautical aerology); Architecture. b'92. BS '14 (Mass Inst Tech). Architect for Little America antarctic houses '29-32, first to design insulated structural wall moistureproofed on warm side. Independent archtl practice NYC since '28; pres Audubon Holding Corp; dir Forman Ford & Co. Served as lt USNR '17-19, organized and directed European Weather Service of US Naval Aviation and Transatlantic Flight of NC4 '19; aerol officer Naval Air Transport Service '42-43 and Naval Air Bases 5ND '44-46. AIA—Royal Meteorol Soc (London)—Inst Aeronautical Sci—Am Meteorol Soc (profl mem). 10 W. 33d St., NYC 1.

17 BARRETT, Charles S(anborn). Physical metallurgy (X-ray and electrons application); Crystallography; Age hardening; Transformations of metals; Deformation of metals. b'02. BS '25 (U SD); PhD '28 (U Chicago). Author: Structure of Metals '43; also articles in field. Prof Inst Study Metals U Chicago since '46; ed metals sect Structure Reports '48-50. Am Inst Mining Metall Engineers—Am Society Metals—Am Phys Soc—Sigma Xi—Phi Beta Kappa. Received Howe Medal Am Soc Metals; annual award twice Inst Metals Div AIMME. Institute for the Study of Metals, University of Chicago, Chicago 37.

18 BARRETT, Clifford Leslie. Legal philosophy; Political philosophy; Ethics; Value theory; Symbolism. b'94. AB '17 (Occidental Coll); MA '20 (Princeton); PhD '26 (Syracuse). Research England and France '39; Harvard '50. Author: Ethics '33; Philosophy '35; articles in field. Editor: Contemporary Idealism in America '32. Prof philosophy Associated Colls of Claremont Cal. Am Philos Assn—Mind Assn (Eng). Claremont Graduate School, Claremont, Cal.ⓒ

19 BARRETT, Elliott P(ierce). Bone char; Sugar refining; Adsorbents. b'02. AB '24—MA '26—PhD '33 (Columbia); sr fellow '35 (Mellon Inst). Member advisory committee US Cane Sugar Refiners' Bone Char Research Project '39, American committee International Commission for Uniform Methods of Sugar Analysis '48; research bone black pigments. Author articles in field. Holds nine patents in field. Dir research and development The Baugh Co since '44. Am Chem Soc—AAAS(F)—Pa Chem Soc (sec treas)—Sigma Xi. Mellon Institute, Pittsburgh 13.

20 BARRETT, Leslie Park. Geology of iron and uranium ore deposits. b'87. BS '13 (U Mich). Asst state geol, state mine appraiser '19-27; with Jones & Laughlin Steel Corp since '27, chief geol and v-pres iron ore mining subsidiaries from '34. Geol Soc Am (F)—AAAS (F)—Sigma Xi—Soc Econ Geol—AIMME. Jones & Laughlin Building, Pittsburgh.

21 BARRINGER, Edwin C. Iron and steel scrap. b'92. Student '10-12 (Case Sch Applied Sci, Western Reserve U). War Department Overseas Scrap Advisory Committee '45. Author articles in field. Mng editor weekly mag Steel and editor Daily Metal Trade Cleveland '26-38, dir pub co '36-42; exec sec Inst Scrap Iron and Steel Inc Washington '42-46, pres and bd dirs '42-46, exec vp since '46. Washington Bd Trade. 1346 Connecticut Av., Washington 6.

22 BARROW, William James. Preservation and restoration of paper and documents; Paper acidity; Papermaking iron-gall writing inks (Seventeenth and Eighteenth centuries). b'04

Grad '23 (Randolph-Macon Acad); '23-25 (Randolph-Macon Coll). Invented calendar roll type laminator for strengthening and protecting deteriorated documents by impregnating them with a homogeneous thermoplastic cellulose acetate foil '37; developed procedures for processing documents previous to and after lamination to give maximum strength and best appearance to finished product; developed methods and equipment for neutralizing acidity in paper which has been the primary cause of deterioration in early manuscripts '39; equipment for above two processes has been installed in Library of Congress and elsewhere. Author articles in field. Self employed since '32, operates lab for making specialized test on early inks and papers; cons to institutions preserving valuable documents. Soc Am Archivists. State Library Building, Richmond 19, Va.

23 BARRY, Arthur J(ohn). Synthesis of organosilicon compounds. b'09. BS '32—PhD '36—fellow '32-36 (Syracuse U). Research in the preparation of cellulose derivatives, plastics, reactions in liquid ammonia, synthesis of organosilicon compounds, investigations of polysiloxane resins and fluids of high termal stability. Holds many patents in field. Author articles in field. Research chem Dow Chem Co '37-47; research group supervisor Dow Corning Corp Midland Mich since '47. Am Chem Soc (councilor '46-49)—Sigma Xi. Dow Corning Corporation, Midland, Mich.

24 BARTELL, Floyd Earl. Colloid and surface chemistry. b'83. AB '05 (Albion (Mich) Coll); AM '08—PhD '10 (U Mich). Adsorption, adhesion and wetting of solids by liquids; petroleum recovery. With U Mich since '10, prof chemistry since '24; cons War Dept '38-42; gen cons OSRD '43-45. Capt nitrate div ordnance Dept US Army '17-18. AAAS(F)—ACS—Phi Beta Kappa—Sigma Xi—Phi Kappa Phi—Phi Lambda Upsilon—Gamma Alpha—Alpha Chi Sigma. Chemical Laboratory, University of Mich, Ann Arbor.ⓒ

25 BARTENBACH, Angela. Medical illustration. b'09. AB '31 (Trinity Coll); '28 (Chicago Acad Fine Arts); '33 (Johns Hopkins U Sch Med). Illustrations in The Surgical Technic of Abdominal Operations '35; Office Gynecology '39; Obstetrics in General Practice '40; Operations of General Surgery '44; Office Treatment of the Eye '47; Psychology and Life '48; also articles in field. Free lance med illus—St Luke's Hosp Chicago '33-35; Cook Co Hosp '35-40; staff artist U Kan Sch Med '40-44; staff artist Cook Co Grad Sch Med and Cook Co Hosp since '44. Assn Med Illus (charter mem). Cook County Graduate School of Medicine, 427 S. Honore St., Chicago 12. H: 820 Judson Av., Evanston.

26 BARTH, Theodore H. Norden bombsight; Catapult and arresting gear for launching and landing naval aircraft. b'91. Co-inventor US Norden bombsight '23, US Navy catapult and arresting gear for launching and landing aircraft on the USS Saratoga and USS Lexington '28. Carl L. Norden Inc., 285 Madison Ave., NYC.

27 BARTHEL, Christopher Ernest Jr. Photographic sensitometry; Electronic computers; Scientific research administration. b'11. BS '32—fellow '30-33 —MS '33 (La State U); fellow '38-40—PhD '40 (Ia State U). Instr physics Wash and Lee U Lexington Va '33-38, Ia State Coll '40-41; mem tech staff Naval Ordnance Lab Washington '41-47, chief magnetic model sect '41-44, dir personnel '44-46, chief electronic computing and control div '46-47; asst chmn physics research Armour Research Foundation Ill Inst Tech '47-48, chmn '48. AAAS—Am Phys Soc—Optical Soc Am—Am Soc Engring Edn—Sigma Xi—Phi Kappa Phi—Tau Beta Pi. Awarded US Navy Distinguished Civilian Service Award '46. 35 W. 33rd St., Chicago 16. H: 1545 Spruce St., Northbrook, Ill.

10 BARTHELEMY, Roger Eugene Jean. Minerals and mineral economics of Indo-China, French Guiana, and Belgian Congo. b'02. Student '25 (Ecole Nationale Superieure des Mines Paris France). Mining research expedition Indo-China '33-36; survey economic possibilities and mining conditions Inini French Guiana '40 and '49-50. Holds patent on differential flotation process for complex copper and zinc-iron ores. Author articles in field. Cons engr Bank of Indo-China since '40; chief metall and asst dir research copper ores and uranium deposits Union Miniere du Haut Katanga Belgian Congo '30-33; cos engr and gen mgr Soc d'Etudes and Exploitations Minieres de l'Indochine French Indo-China '33-36; mem bd sci research Indo-China '33-36; mining cons engr Lima Peru '37-38, Latin Am since '38; dir and gen mgr Compagne Miniere et Metallurgique de l'Indochine Hanoi-French Indo-China '46-47. AIMME. 1329 Polk St., Hollywood, Fla.

11 BARTHOLOMEW, Earl. Automotive fuels; Internal combustion engines; Management of research laboratories. b'01. BA '21—BS '22—MS '23 (U Okla). Developed antiknock fluids for gasolines, equipment for fuel antiknock rating, and information concerning processes within internal combustion engines. Author articles: Potentialities of the New Fuels in the Design of Passenger Car Engines '46; Critical Speeds of Loaded Shafts '24; Power-Plant Equipment and Operation '25, and others. Dir engring research Ethyl Corp '27-45, gen mgr research labs since '45. SAE—ASME—Engring Soc Detroit—Am Petroleum Inst—Am Soc Testing Materials. 1600 W Eight Mile Rd., Det 20.

12 BARTHOLOMEW, Howard W. Die casting and moulding. b'97. Educated Sheffield Scientific School. Holds US patents on machines, die designs, and processes used in die casting, moulding, die making, machine tool, and related fields. Doehler Jarvis Corporation, Pottstown, Pa.

13 BARTLETT, Charles Elmer. Ores (Beneficiation). b'06. BS '27 (U Utah). Laboratory research on ores to plant design construction and operation; in charge starting operating five plants (gold, silver, lead, zinc, copper) using flotation, cyanidation, amalgamation and jigging; modernized crushing and grinding plants handling non-metallic minerals. Testing engr Internat Smelting Co Tooele Utah '27-29; asst mill supt US Smelting Co Midvale Utah '29-35; mill supt Ill Zinc Co Deming NM '35-36, West Dip Mine, Ophir Utah '36, Snyder Mines Mercur Utah '37-42; metall mgr Combined Metals Reduction Co Salt Lake City '46-48; dir milling operations Combined Metals Reduction Co Salt Lake City. Am Inst Mining Engrs—Tau Beta Pi—Sigma Gamma Epsilon. 218 Felt Bldg., Salt Lake City.

14 BARTLETT, Harley Harris. Plant genetics (mutation); Rubber-bearing plants (hevea, guayule); Palms, Aroids; Oenothera; Ethnobotany, languages (Philippines, Indonesia); Indonesian languages (Sumatran, Philippines). b'86. AB '08 (Harvard). Member scientific expeditions to Formosa and Sumatra '26-27, Mexico '30, Guatemela and British Honduras '31. With U Mich since '15, now prof bot, dir bot garden; edn cons U Philippines since '47. Bot Soc Am—Am Soc Naturalists—Mich Acad Sci—Wash Acad Sci—AAAS—Am Philos Soc—New Eng Bot Club—Sigma Xi. 1601 Brooklyn Av., Ann Arbor.©

15 BARTLETT, Luis Hamilton. Food refrigeration and technology; Quick freezing; Thermodynamics; Soaps and detergents; Waste disposal. b'95. BS '34—MS '35 (U Tenn); PhD '43 (U Tex). Holds five patents in field. Co-author: Handbook of Refrigerating Engineering '48; also articles in field. Dir Engring Expt Sta La State U since 48. Am Chem Soc—ASME—Am Soc Refrigerating Engrs—ASEE—Am Inst Chem Engrs—Sigma Xi. Engineering Experiment Station, Louisiana State University, Baton Rouge, La.

16 BARTLEY, Samuel Howard. Vision (Neurophysiology; perception; fatigue). b'01. BS '23 (Greenville Coll); MA '28—PhD '31 (U Kan). Research on related cortical response to alpha rhythm in brain, optic nerve discharge; Studied visual fatigue situations reflex conflict in pupillary mechanisms, monocular and binocular vision. Author: Fatigue and Impairment in Man '47; Vision—A Study of Its Basis '41. Author articles: Vision in Ency Brit.; and others. Research asso Washington U Med Sch '32-42; asst prof and prof research in visual scis Dartmouth Eye Inst '42-47; prof psychol Mich State Coll since '47. Am Psychol Assn(F)—Am Acad Optometry(F)—Optical Soc Am—Am Physiol Soc—Midwestern Psychol Assn. Fellowship NRC '31 '32. Psychology Dept. Michigan State College, Lansing, Mich. H: P.O. Box 763, East Lansing, Mich.

17 BARTON, Fred Hubert. Propaganda; Psychological warfare; International Relations; Folklore (Musical). b'19. License des lettres '38 (U Paris); License Sc Mus '39 (Conservatoire de Paris); '39 (Charles U, Prague); LLB '51 (George Washington U). Research on Theoretical and technical aspects of propaganda, mass media for information and propaganda activities; research on folk music of Europe and Latin America. Broadcasting cons Interallied Com and Co-ordinator Inter-Am Affairs '40-43; cons Pan-Am Union '43-44; overseas program planning officer Dept State (VOA) '46-48) dep dir radio unit UNESCO '48-49; mem Operations Research Office Johns Hopkins U since '50. Am Folk-lore Soc—Am Soc Internat Law. Awarded Grand Prix d'Autriche '37, Prix d'Honneur du Conservatoire '38. Operations Research Office, Johns Hopkins University, Fort Lesley J. McNair, Washington 25.

18 BARTON, Jackson Mounce. Petroleum geology. b'17. Student 34-36 (Phillips U); BS '38 (U Okla); '39-41 (Yale). Research on subsurface geological maps, microscopic examination of rock fragments from drill holes, mapping of surface exposures of sedimentary rocks, coordination of geophysical and geological data. Author articles in field. Geol Magnolia Petroleum Co '41-46; div geol Coop Refinery Assn '46-49, chief geol '49-50; mgr geol dept Deep Rock Oil Corp since '50. AAAS—Am Assn Petroleum Geol—Am Geophys Union—Soc Exploration Geophys—AIMME. Deep Rock Oil Corp., Box 1051, Tulsa.

19 BARTON, John Rector. Rural adult education. b'97. AB '21 (Central Coll Fayette Mo); BD '26 (Yale). Lecture tours in Denmark, Sweden, Canada, United States; community organizer in mining camps of north Idaho '23-24. Author: Rural Artists of Wisconsin '48. Prof rural sociol U Wis Coll Agr since '35. 314 Agricultural Hall, University of Wisconsin, Madison, Wis.

20 BARTON, Lela Viola. Seed physiology (Germination, storage). b'01. BA '22 (U Ark); MA '27—PhD '39 (Columbia U). Author articles: Some Special Problems in Seed Dormancy '42; Effect of Moisture Fluctuations on the Viability of Seeds in Storage '43; The Storage of Citrus Seeds '43; Viability of Seeds of Fraxinus After Storage '45; and others. Plant physiol Boyce Thompson Inst Plant Research Inc Yonkers NY. Sigma Xi—Bot Soc Am—Torrey Bot Club—AAAS. Boyce Thompson Institute for Plant Research, Inc., 1086 N. Broadway, Yonkers 3, N.Y.

21 BARTON, Millard Vernon. Stress analysis; Aircraft structures; Aeroelasticity. b'10. BSE '32 (Calif Inst Tech); MS '37 (U Colo); PhD '40 (Cornell U). Author: Elementary Aircraft Structures '43; Fundamentals of Aircraft Structures '48; also articles in field. Research engr defense research lab U Tex since '45. ASME (aviation div com)—Inst Aeronautical Scis(asso F)—American Society of Engineering Education. Department of Aeronautical Engineering, University of Texas, Austin, Tex.†

22 BARTON, Samuel Goodwin. Double stars; Constellations; Astronomical history. b'82. BA '03 (Temple U); PhD '06 U Pa). Research on Halley's Comet, properties of normals to parabolas, interrelations of asteroid elements, declinations of stars, determination of true meridian, measures of double stars, proper motion in double stars, Dürer and early star maps. Co-author: (with Wm H Barton) A Guide to the Constellations '43; also articles in field. Asso prof astron U Pa '31-50. Am Astron Soc—Astron Soc Pacific. Sigma Xi. Research fellow U Pa '06-07. 33 N. 61 St., Phila 39.

23 BARTOW, Edward. Water purification; Sewage treatment; Treatment and utilization of trade wastes. b'70. BA '92—DSc '23 (Williams Coll); PhD '95 (U Goettingen). Work in water supply, methods of analysis, and mineral content of waters; sewage purification, activated sludge process; waste disposal and preparation of useful compounds from organic trade wastes, inositol, and sodium glutemate; member commission to investigate cause coal mine explosions Kansas '05; member and secretary Lake Michigan Water Commission '08, commission Standards of Water for Interstate Carriers '13, '22; assistant editor Chem Abstracts since '11; delegate 9th International Congress Chemistry Madrid '34, 10th congress Rome '38. Author: Reports on Chemical and Biological Survey of Waters of Illinois (14 volumes) '06-20; also articles in field. Prof, head dept chem and chem engring State U Ia '20-40, prof emeritus since '40; research cons Johns-Manville Corp '40-41. Internat Chem Union (mem council '22-25, '27-30, '33-38, vp US '34-38)—Am Chem Soc (dir '33, pres '36)—AAAS—Am Water Works Assn (trustee '13, vp '21, pres '22)—Am Inst Chem Engrs (dir '23-25, '36-39)—ASCE AAUP—Franklin Inst—Am Pub Health Assn—Am Soc Testing Materials—Am Soc Engring Edn—Am Pub Works Assn—Nat Inst Social Sci—Sigma Xi—Phi Beta Kappa—Tau Beta Pi. Medaille d'Honneur des Epidemics d'Argent. France '17-19. Chemistry Building, Iowa City, Ia. H: 304 Brown St.©

10 BARTSCH, Alfred Frank. Sanitary biology (Stream pollution, aquatic nuisance control). b'13. BA '36 (U Minn); PhD '39 (U Wis). Research in stream pollution, progressive biological changes occurring downstream from points of pollutant entry, activities of stream organisms leading to sanitary recovery of polluted streams; use of certain key organisms as indicators of stream condition; aquatic nuisance control; factors leading to occurrence of nuisances caused by swimmers' itch, excessive growths of algae, rooted vegetation; programs preventing aquatic nuisances and in controlling them mechanically or chemically. Author articles in field. Sanitary biologist Wis State Bd Health '39-45; Sr biol state com water pollution Madison Wis '45-49; Pac NW River Basin biologist, WPC PHS Portland Ore '49-50; cons to Chief WPC PHS of FSA and coordinator Division's biol activities since '50. Wis Acad Sci, Arts Letters—Mycol Soc Am—Am Soc Limnol Oceanog—Am Fisheries Soc—Torrey Bot Club—Ecol Soc—Fed Sewage Research Assn. Won Thomas F Andrews prize undergraduate research U Minn '35, awarded Gus H Radebaugh Award Cent States Sewage Works Assn '47. Federal Security Building, S. Washington 25.

11 BARTSCH, Paul. Malacology; Ornithology; Botany; Medical zoology. b'71. BS '96—MS '99—PhD '05 (State U Ia); ScD '37 (George Washington U). Smithsonian representative Philippine Expedition '07-09; conducts breeding experiments with Cerions on Florida Keys under Carnegie Institute and Smithsonian Institution since '12; scientific explorations Gulf California, Bahamas, West Mexico, Florida, Cuba, Haiti, Santo Domingo, Puerto Rico, all West Indian Islands between Puerto Rico and Trinidad, Gulf St Lawrence; Smithsonian delegate 2d Pan-American Scientific Congress Washington '16; delegate 1st Pan-Pacific Scientific Congress Honolulu '20; dir Johnson Smithsonian Deep-Sea Expedition to Puerto Rican Deep '32; Smithsonian Roebling Exploring Expedition '37; furnished the poison gas detector to Chemical Warfare Service '18. Author articles in field. Asso div Mollusks US Nat Mus since '46; prof emeritus George Washington U since '39. AAAS(F)—Washington Acad Sci—Washington Biol Soc—Am Ornithol Union—Am Assn Anatomist—Am Soc Zoologists—Am Genetic Assn—Malacol Soc Gt Britain and Ireland—Am Malacol Soc—Sigma Xi. Smithsonian Institution, Washington. H: Lebanon, Lorton, Va.◉

12 BARTUNEK, Paul Franklin. Spectroscopy; Thermodynamics; Statistical mechanics; Electricity; Magnetism. b'03. PhD '35 (U Mich). Author articles: Zeeman Effect in Cobalt Spectrum '35; Infrared Spectra of Carbonyl Sulphide and Deutruim Cyanide '35; Photographic Recording of Heavy Particles '40; Expt with Current Pendulum '42; Gyroscope Expt for Dyn Lab '42. Asst prof physics Allegheny Coll summer '43; asst prof physics U Maryland '43-44; physicist Nat Bureau Standards '44-46; asst prof physics Lehigh U '46-50; asso prof physics Colo School Mines since '50. Am Phys Soc—Am Assn Physics Teachers—AAAS—Sigma Xi. Physics Dept, Colo. School of Mines, Golden, Colo.

13 BARUCH, Sydney Norton. Radio engineering (Mercury tubes); Electronics; Supersonics; Film sound recording; Submarine signalling; Servo mechanisms. b'90. EE '11 (Cooper Union) DSc '21 (Royal, Eng); spl study elec phenomenon (U Calif). Builder high power radio broadcast chain '25; designer broadcasting stations, CHCR, WBNY, WKBK, WKBQ, LIY (France); designer 300,000 volt direct current transmission system for Bonneville Project US Dept Interior '41. Inventor thermo relay and other devices, thyratron and nortron type mercury rectifier tubes and sound recording on film '34; depth bomb successfully used in destruction of submarines in World War I and II. Cons engr spl weapons div US Air Force since '43; chief engr Fed Telephone Co, radio div Postal Telegraph Co '19-20, Gen Petroleum Co of Am '21; pres Pub Service Corp of Calif '16-20; condr pvt research labs NYC since '30; dir and controller United Broadcasting chain of radio stas; chief research engr Gen Arc Lighting Co. Royal Soc of London(F)—Am Inst Radio Engrs—Soc Motion Picture Engrs. Awarded gold medal Internat Jury of Scientists '15. 1476 Broadway, NYC.◉

14 BARWICK, Arthur Richardson. Economic minerals; Paleontology; Stratigraphy. b'96. BSc '17 (Coll City NY); MSc '23—PhD '26 (NY U). Government consultant on metals, ores, and other economic minerals; field work and mapping of Atlantic Coastal Plain; studies on fossils of coastal plain formations Maryland. Asso prof geol Catholic U Am '29-40; prof geol and head dept Howard U since '46. Paleontological Soc Am—Am Inst Mining Engrs—AAAS—Geol and Biol Socs of Washington. Howard University, Department of Geology, Washington.

15 BASCOM, William Russell. African and Micronesian Ethnology (Ifa, Yoruba). b'12. BA '33—MA '36 (U Wis); PhD '39 (Northwestern U). Field studies in West Africa, Caroline Islands, and Cuba; research on Ifa divination, principle of seniority in social structure of Yoruba, legacy of unknown Nigerian Donatello, complexity of African cultures. Author articles in field. Fulbright grant research Yoruba of Nigeria, '50-51; associate prof anthrop Northwestern U since '49. Phi Beta Kappa—Sigma Xi—Am Anthrop Assn—Am Folklore Soc—Am Ethnol Soc—Internat African Inst (London)—Internat Inst Afroam Studies (Mex City)—AAAS—Nat Research Council. Fellow Social Sci Research Council '38-39; grant-in-aid, Northwestern U '39-42, Viking Fund, Cuba summer '48. Northwestern University, Evanston, Ill.

16 BASSETT, Cecil Emerson. Metallurgy of lead and magnesium. b'04. AB '25 (Neb Wesleyan U); extension U Chicago, LaSalle Extension U, U Nev, U Calif. Chief chem, asst supt Atencingo Central Puebla Mexico '26-34; chem, metall Am Metal Co Ltd Monterrey and Torreon Mexico '35-41; unit supt Basic Magnesium Inc Henderson Nev '42-44; pres Schuylkill Products Inc since '44; dir Bayou Chem Co Inc since '44. AIMME. P.O. Box 178, Baton Rouge, La.

17 BASSETT, Charles Francis. Breeding habits, nutrition, and factors affecting fur quality of foxes, mink, and martens. b'99. BS '21—MS '26 (Ia State Coll). Research on vitamin and protein requirements for red, cross, black, silver, platinum, and white face foxes, natural, Blufrost, Kohiner, pastel and white mink, and marten; effect of altered day length on fur growth, primeness, and molting for adult and growing foxes and minks, and its effect on gestation and reproduction of silver foxes; desirability of substitutes for horsemeat in diet of foxes and mink. Supt expt animal husbandry sect Ia Expt Sta '26-30; dir US Fur Animal Expt Sta since '35. Alpha Zeta—Gamma Sigma Delta. US Fur Animal Experiment Station, Saratoga Springs, N.Y.

18 BASSETT, Leon Burdette. Ceramics (Control analysis); Spectrochemistry. (Emission spectroscopy). b'92. BS '16 (Alfred U). Research in use of spectrograph in study of soild state diffusion at high temperatures '46-49; commercial experimental work with refractory bonds and whiteware glazes '32-38; development and research studies in emissivity of ceramic mix-(H. C. Harrison) Emiission Spectrotures '28-32). Co-author articles: (with scopy and its Application in the Investigation and Solution of Problems in Ceramics '41; (with V D Frechett) Note on Microsampling of Ceramic Materials for Analysis '48; (with Frechett) Some Notes on the Use of the Spectrograph in the Study of Solid State Reactions '49. Enamels research Roper Corp Rockford Ill '26-28; development and research Burdick Corp Milton Wis '28-32; asst in chem Alfred U '32-38; research asst NY State Coll of Ceramics '38-46, prof ceramic engring since '46; asso prof research State U of NY College of Ceramics Alfred Univ. Am Ceramic Soc—Ceramic Ednl Council—AAAS—Sci Service Asso—Keramos—Spectroscopy Soc Pittsburgh. Alfred, N.Y.

19 BASSETT, Robert Cochem. Newspaper industry (Labor relations). b'11. AB '32 (U Wis); LLB '35 (Harvard). Author: Wisconsin Laws Affecting Newspapers '38; Labor Guide for Italy '44. Author articles in field. Admitted Wis bar '35; gen counsel Wis Daily Newspaper League '36-43; spl counsel Inland Daily Press Assn Chicago '37-43; labor counsel Hearst Corp since '46; vis lectr grad sch bus Columbia since '49. Head labor relations div Office of Sec Navy '44-46, gen counsel '44-45; liaison officer Navy Dept and US Maritime Commn to Nat War Labor Bd '43-44. Citation of Merit with Commendation Ribbon (Navy). Newspaper Personnel Relations Assn—Phi Kappa Phi. 326 W. Madison St., Chgo. 6.◉

20 BASSETT, William Varick. Mechanical engineering (Heavy machinery design). b'15. ME '37 (Cornell); MS '39 (Mass Inst Tech). Research on heavy machinery design, turbine design, stress analysis with resistance wire gages, torsional vibration in marine geared-turbine propulsion units, electric resistance strain gage for ship structural tests, impact strains by carbon-strip extensometer. Author articles in field. Mech engr Bethlehem Steel Co since '38. ASME—Soc Naval Architects Marine Engrs—Soc Exptl Stress Analysis. Bethlehem Steel Co., Bethlehem, Pa.

21 BATCHELDER, Marjorie Hope. Puppetry. b'03. BA '33 (Fla State Coll Women); MA '34—PhD '42 (Ohio State U). Toured England, France, Italy, Germany, Austria, Czecho-Slovakia seeing puppet shows and puppeteers for 3 months; work on rod-puppets, a special type worked from below the stage floor. Author: The Puppet Theatre Handbook '47; Rod-Puppets and the Human Theatre '47. Co-author: Hand and Rod Puppets '47; also articles in field. Teacher Sch Fine and Applied Arts Ohio State U '34-48. Puppeteers of Am (charter mem founded '37, hon pres '39, active pres '40, ed bd '42-47.) 4426 North High St., Columbus 2, Ohio.†

22 BATCHELLER, Willis Tryon. Hydro-electric, hydraulic, steam engineering; Rates and valuations. b'89. BS '11—EE '15 (U Wash). Served engineer design and construction three 10,000 kilowatt units Lake Union steam electric plant, 18,000 hp hydro-elect development Cedar Falls, preliminary work, design Skagit River power project; report and survey 2,800,000 hp development Columbia River Grand Coulee, 1,800,000 acre Columbia Basin irrigation project, chief of Joseph Power Project, Nimpkish River pulp, paper and power project International Harvester Co north end Vancouver Island, Quincy Valley Irrigation Dist, and others. Cons government war indsl projects, incl 1,-000,000 kw steam-elec plant to supply power shortage, burning local coal after processing for chemicals. Pres and chief engr Can Alaska Ry Co; mem State Development Com, Indsl Com Seattle Chamber of Commerce, chairman Reclamation Com; Seattle Light and Power System '12-21; pres, chief engr Portland Canal Power Co since '30. Am Concrete Inst—AIEE—Am Water Works Assn—Nat Soc Profl Engrs. 814 Arctic Building, Seattle. H: 1848 N. 51st St.†⊚

10 BATCHELOR, Leon Dexter. Horticulture (Citrus). Research in agriculture under arid conditions. Coeditor: The Citrus Industry (2 vol). b' 84. BS '07 (U NH); PhD '11 (Cornell U). Dir U Calif Citrus Expt Sta Riverside Calif since '29. AAAS—Am Hort Soc. Citrus Experiment Station, University of California, Riverside, Cal.⊚

11 BATEMAN, Alan Mara. Economic geology. b'89. BA—BS '10 (Queens U); PhD '13 (Yale). Head special United States mission to Mexico '42; editor-in-chief Journal of Economic Geology. Author: Economic Mineral Deposits; also articles in field. Prof econ geol Yale U since '25; director metals and minerals Foreign Economic Administration '42-45; cons geol Kennecott Copper Corp since '16. Inst Mining Metall—Geol Soc Am—Soc Econ Geol (pres '41-42)—Mineral Soc Am—Am Assn Petroleum Geol—Washington Acad Sci—Am Acad Arts Sci—Chile Soc Mineral and Geol (hon)—Soc Geologique de Belgique (corr)—Sigma Xi. 450 St. Ronan St., New Haven.⊚

12 BATES, Arthur Crocker. Design and stress analysis; Metal working; Vibration; Photoelasticity; Needle bearing behavior. b'05. BS '29 (Purdue U); MS '33 (U Mich); PhD '41 (U Pa). Research on properties of moist air, crankshaft designs, riding qualities of automobiles; invented accelerometer. Co-author: (with M J Zucrow) Bibliography of Crankshaft Design; also articles in field. Prof mech engring Lehigh U since '48; cons design of special devices. ASME—SAE—Sigma Xi. Mechanical Engineering Department, Lehigh University, Bethlehem, Pa.†

13 BATES, Charles Carpenter. Ocean waves; Meteorology; Oceanography. b'18. BA '39 (De Pauw U); MA '43 (Calif U); '43 (U Chicago). Conducted reflection seismograph surveys; forecast wave conditions for invasions (Army); naval technician Bikini atomic bomb test; member panel on geographic environment, Research and Development Board, National Military Establishment; secretary, sub-committee on oceanography Joint Meteorological Committee; discovered quantitative relationship between wave heights and tonnage unloaded daily at military beachhead '44. Developed methods for utilizing tabulated sea

and swell data to determine best sea routes, number of operational days for given area at sea, surf information, and index of sea roughness, rapid method of forecasting ocean swell from standard weather maps. Author articles: Meteorological Engineering and the Oil Industry '47; Oceanography and the Offshore Drilling Campaign '48; Utilization of Tabulated Sea and Swell Data '48, and others. Jr geophysicist Carter Oil Co Okla '39-41; spl asst to pres Am Meteorolog Soc '45-46; oceanographer '46, US Hydrographic Office '46-48 and since '48; mem Bates and Glenn Meteorol Engrs '47; cons A H Glenn and Assocs, meteorol cons since '48. Private to capt US Army, oceanographer '41-45. Am Meteorol Soc (chmn com business, agrl and industrial meteorol)—Geol Soc Wash—Am Assn Petroleum Geol—Soc Exploration Geophysicists—Am Geophys Union. Box 7215 College Station, Tex.

14 BATES, Richard Waller. Naval operations in Pacific (World War II). b'92. BS '15—post grad student '20-21 (US Naval Acad); MS '22 (Columbia); student '40-41 (Naval War Coll). Commissioned ensign USN '15, advanced through grades to rear adm '49; comdg officer USS Buchanan '32-33, USS Ramapo '33, USS Long '34-35, USS Clark '38-40, USS Minneapolis, Pacific waters '43-44; on staff Comdr in Chief Pacific Fleet '44; chief staff Bombardment and Fire Support Group 3rd Fleet Palau '44 and 7th Fleet '44-45, participating in battles Leyte Gulf and Surigao Strait; chief staff Battleship Squadron 1, Lingayen and Okinawa '45; comdr motor torpedo boats Pacific Fleet '45; chief staff Philippine Sea Frontier '45-46; mem staff Naval War Coll '41-42, chief strategy '42-43, head dept analysis '46-50, retired for phys disability '49, recalled and on active duty as head special projects sect since '49; now preparing critical analyses of major naval battles of World War II. Decorated Navy Cross, Legion Merit with 2 gold stars, Victory medal WWI Asiatic-Pacific Area Campaign with 10 bronze stars, Philippine Liberation medals, Victory medal WW II, others. Naval War College, Newport, R.I.⊚

15 BATES, Robert Hicks. Mountaineering; Arctic and mountain equipment; Mountain literature. b'11. AB '33—AM '35 (Harvard); PhD '47 (U Pa). With Harvard Institute of Geographical Exploration expedition to Mt Crillon Alaska '32; National Geographic Society Yukon expedition wintered in Yukon and mapped 10,000 square miles mountainous terrain in Yukon Territory and received congratulations of King George V '35; American Karakoram expedition, expedition reached 26,000 feet on Mt K₂, second highest mountain in world, personally reached 24,800 feet; American Geographical Society Wood Yukon expedition '41. Co-author: Five Miles High '39; also articles in field. Instr Eng Phillips Exeter Acad since '39. Capt later lt col World War II US Army charged with development arctic and cold climate clothing and equipment OQMG War Dept, exec officer Alaska test expedition to Mt McKinley, midwinter flights to Hudson's Bay Great Slave Lake and Cambridge Bay. Appalachian Mountain Club—Am Alpine Club (council '37-47, co-ed Am Alpine Journ since '46). Exeter, N.H.†

16 BATES, Robert Wesley. Pituitary hormones; Hormonal preparations and assay. b'04. AB '25 (Simpson Coll); PhD '31 (U Chicago). Preparation, assay and physiology of anterior

pituitary hormones, method for determination of tryptophane. Author articles in field. Head endocrine development dept E R Squibb & Sons since '45. Am Chem Soc—Am Soc Biol Chem—Assn Study Internal Secretions—AAAS. NY Acad Si. E.R. Squibb & Sons, New Brunswick, N.J.

17 BATES, Sanford. Penology; Criminology; Crime and delinquency prevention. b'84. LLB '06—LLD '37 (Northeastern U). Official delegate US government to International Prison Congress London '25, Prague '30; chairman, delegate to International Penal and Penitentiary Congress Berlin '35; member Committee to Investigate Criminal Law; White House Conference on Children in a Democracy '39-40; pres Internat Penal and Penitentiary Commn since '50. Author: Prisons and Beyond '38. Commr Penal Instns '18-19, Mass Dept Correction '19-29; supt Fed Prisons '29-30, dir Bur of Prisons '30-37; exec dir Boys Clubs of Am '37-40; tchr NY Sch Social Work '37-44; commissioner institutions and agencies State NJ since '45; bd dirs NJ Welfare Council since '45; trustee Nat Probation Assn since '39; chmn Nat Advisory Com on Prisoners and Parolees to Selective Service since '44; cons War Dept on restoration military prisoners since '44. Am Pub Welfare Assn—Am Hosp Assn—Nat Conf Juvenile Agencies—Nat Conf Social Agencies—Fed Prison Industries (pres)—Am Bar Assn—Am Prison Assn (pres '26)—Am Parole Assn (pres)—Nat Acad Arts Sci. State Bldg., Trenton, N.J.⊚

18 BATSON, Avery Aloysius. Engineering; Water resource development. b'03. AB '26—BS archtl engring '28 (U Neb). Conservation control and use water and land resources. Asst dir fiscal and adminstrv management, asst dir region 7 Bur Reclamation, Washington and Denver '44-47, dir region 7 Denver since '47. Bldg. 46, Denver Federal Center, Denver.⊚

19 BATTIN, Isaac Lucius. Architectural acoustics; Pipe organ design. b'03. AB '25—AM '26 (Swarthmore Coll); PhD '49 (NYU); B Mus '28 (U Pa); FAGO '26 (Am Guild Organists); grad work (U Mich, Nat Conservatory Munich Germany, U Pa, Princeton U). Chmn courses in math Brothers Coll Drew U since '41; organist-choirmaster Stanley Congregational Ch Chatham N J since '45; acoustical cons since '41. Acoustical Soc Am—Am Inst Physics—Math Assn Am—Am Math Soc—Inst Math Statis — Sigma Xi — Phi Beta Kappa. Brothers College, Drew University, Madison, N.J.†

20 BATTISON, John Henry. Radio Engineering; TV Production; Television engineering. b'15. Research on design of television stations, production of television films, designed double-single system film photographing equipment, ultra and very high frequency television transmitters. Author: Movies for TV '50; An Introduction to TV '51; Special Effects for TV and Films '51; also articles in field. Research engr EKCO Radio Co '34-37; mem tech div Brit Air Ministry '37-39; tech dir Midland Broadcasting Co '45-47; asst chief allocations engr Am Broadcasting Co '47-49; asso ed Tele-Tech magazine '49-50; faculty NY U '50-51 Div TV Commercial Production Dancer-Fitzgerald-Sample Inc since 51. Inst Radio Engrs (sr mem) —Brit Inst Radio Engrs—Soc Motion Picture and Television Engrs. NYC 17. Dancer-Fitzgerald-Sample, Inc. 347 Madison Ave., H: B 53 Hudson View Gardens, NYC 33.

10 BAUDIN, Maurice. French theater; French philosophy (Eighteenth century). b'92. AB '15 (Washington U); AM '26 (Ohio State U); PhD '31 (Johns Hopkins). Student (U Chicago). Author: Les Batards au Theatre; The Profession of King in French Drama of the 18th Century; also articles in field. With NYU since '31, now prof French '31. Mod Lang Assn—Math Soc—Math Assn. 37-36 86th St., Jackson Heights, L.I., N.Y.

11 BAUER, Carl August. Meteoritics; Astrophysics. b'16. BA '42 (Minn U); MS '44 (Chicago U); PhD '49 (Harvard). Astrophysical and photometric research at Yerkes and McDonald observatories; revised ages of meteorites from previously accepted values of up to 7 billion years down to a new value of about sixty million years; developed proposal that meteorites originated from disruption of planet-sized body within solar system, reconstructed model for parent planet; proposed that meteorites are not associated with comets but related to asteroids. Proposed production of helium in meteorites by cosmic radiation. Author articles in field. Instr astron Mich U since '47. Sigma Xi—Am Astronomical Soc—International Astronomical Union—Meteoritical Soc. Academy of Time Fellowship, Harvard '47. Observatory, University of Michigan, Ann Arbor.

12 BAUER, Catherine (Wurster). Housing; City and regional planning. b'05. AB '26 (Vassar); '24-25 (Cornell U). Travel and study in Europe '26, '30, '32, '39, '46; council member of International Housing and Town Planning Fedn since '48. Author: Modern Housing '34; also articles in field. Visiting lectureships U Calif '40, U Wis '46, Cornell U '48; vp Nat Pub Housing Conf since '42; lecturer on housing dept regional planning Harvard '46, '47, '48; U Calif '50. Received grant Carnegie Corp '33; Guggenheim fellow '36. 2683 Buena Vista Way, Berkeley 8, Cal.†

13 BAUER, Harry Charles. Technology (Literature); Library administration. b'02. BA '27—MS '29 (Washington U); grad '31 (St Louis Library Sch). Co-editor: Public Administration Libraries: A Manual of Practice '41; also articles in field. Dir libraries U Washington since '47. ALA — Spl Libraries Assn — Pacific Northwest Library Assn—Washington Library Assn. University of Washington Library, Seattle 5.

14 BAUER, William Malcolm. Electric circuits. b'06. BS '27—EE '28 (Northwestern U); MS '29—ScD '39 (Harvard). Specializes in electronic circuits and tubes as applied to radio and radar; development of special amplifiers and servo motor control. Author: The Power Equations and Circle Diagrams of the Synchronous Motor '36; Recovery Strength of Alternating Current Arcs '41; Electrical Laboratory Experiments (2 vol) '41. Lecturer elec engring U Minn '39-41; prof elec engring, head dept U SC '41-44; development engr Curtiss-Wright Corp '44-46; prof electronics engring US Naval Postgraduate Sch Monterey Cal. AIEE—Inst Radio Engineers—Am Soc Engineering Edn—Sigma Xi—Phi Beta Kappa. U.S. Naval Postgraduate School, Monterey, Cal.©

15 BAUGHMAN, George W. Railroad signals and communications; Remote and automatic train control. b'00. BEE '20—EE '24 (O State U). Development and field engineering on a number of automatic train control and cab signal installations on both electrified and non-electrified territories; research in remote control and relay code systems, subway signaling; development of brake systems for use on streamlined high-speed trains, coded wayside signaling; largely responsible for centralized traffic control being practical for very long territories and requiring only one pair of line wires. Holds nearly 100 patents. Author articles in field. Labs Bell Telephone System NYC '20-23; development and field engr Union Switch & Signal Co '23-32; development studies for The Westinghouse Air Brake Co '33; development engr Union Switch & Signal Co '33-44, asst chief engr in charge of electronics '44-45, chief engr '45-49, assistant vp engineering since '50. AIEE-IRE—Am Assn RR (Signal and Communications sect) Am Ry Engring Assn—Franklin Inst—Tau Beta Pi—Sigma Xi. Union Switch & Signal Company, Pittsburgh 18.

16 BAUGHMAN, John Lafferty. Texas fish; History of Texas; Oyster and Caribbean fisheries literature. b'02. Grad '20 (Lake Forest Acad Ill). Has made collections of Gulf fishes for museums numerous places in US and for British Museum of Natural History London. Author: An Annotated Bibliography of Oysters With Pertinent Material on Mussels and Other Shellfish and an Appendix on Pollution '48; An Annotated Bibliography for the Student of Texas Fish and Fisheries With Material on the Gulf of Mexico and the Caribbean Sea '47; also articles in field. Curator fishes Houston Mus Nat Hist since '43; chief marine biol State of Texas charge Marine Lab since '46; asso prof marine fisheries U Houston since '48; research asso marine fisheries A & M Coll Texas since '48. Texas Acad Sci (conservation sect '47; ed Proceedings and Transactions '48-49)—Am Soc Ichthyology and Herpetology—North Am Wildlife Conf (vice-chmn wildlife and bus sect San Antonio '47. Texas Game, Fish and Oyster Commission, Rockport, Tex.

17 BAUM, Custer Charles. Galactic star clusters; Ballistics (Exterior). b'14. BS '36 (Carroll Coll); MA '40—PhD '47 (U Calif). Measured distances of 14 galactic star clusters. World War II exterior ballistics of rockets Calif Inst Tech '43-46. Research physicist electronics dept Hughes Aircraft Co since '46. Am Astron Soc—Astron Soc Pacific—Sigma Xi. Hughes Aircraft Co., Culver City, Calif.†

18 BAUM, Harry Lester. History of Freemasonry; Masonic playwriting. b'87. MD '10 (Pa U). Research and writing on relation of Freemasonry to democracy, world crises and the future, history of Freemasonry in various geographical sections, George Washington as a Freemason, missions and creeds of Masons; author Masonic plays for amateur performance including John Brent '34, Prelude to Victory '46, When the Red Army Marches '32; Fifty-Nine '30, Vigilante '30. Author: History of Freemasonry in Colorado '36; also articles in field. Mason (33°, Grand Master Grand Lodge Colo '37-38. 510 Republic Building, Denver 2. H: 900 Bonnie Brae Blvd., Denver 9.

19 BAUMANN, Frederick L(ewellyn). Ancient and modern Utopias (Sir Thomas More's); Sixteenth century Renaissance England. b'89. PhB '17 —MA '24 (U Chicago); PhD '28 (Cornell U). Prof hist, chmn hist dept and div social studies Grinnell Coll. Am Acad Polit Social Sci—AHA—State Hist Soc Ia—Far Eastern Assn—Phi Beta Kappa. Grinnell College, Grinnell, Ia.

20 BAUMANN, Herman P. Textiles (Chemistry of printing and dyeing). b'02. Chem E '23 (Rensselaer Poly Inst). Co-translator: Chemical Technology of Dyeing and Printing (by L Diserens). Textile chem Gen Dyestuff Corp '26-33; textile chem Willaim Wilheim Co '33-39; textile chem Allied Textile Printers Inc '39-48; textile chem United Piece Dye Work since '48. Am Assn Textile Chem and Colorists. United Piece Dye Works, Lodi, N.J.

21 BAVER, Leonard D. Soil physics, fertility and conservation; Physical chemistry of soil; Colloidal chemistry. b'01. BS '23—M Sc '26 (O. State U); PhD '29 (U Mo). Head dept agron and asso dir NC Agrl Expt Sta, NC State Coll '40-41, dir '41-48, asso dean '44, dean sch agr and forestry '45-48; dir exp sta Hawaiian Sugar Planters' Assn since '48. Am Soc Agron(F)—Soil Sci Soc Am—Am Geophys Union—Sigma Xi—Gamma Sigma Delta. 2047 Wilhelmina Rise, Honolulu, Hawaii.†©

22 BAXTER, Dow Vawter. Forest pathology (Fungi); Plant exploration and geography (Silvics); Alaska, northern North America and northern Europe; Plant photography (Environmental). b'98. BS '21—MS '22—PhD '24—fellow '23-24 (U Mich); National Research Council fellow to Europe '34. Discovered first infection of white pine blister rust on Ribes in Michigan, fungus Cronartium occidentale on Ribes in Wyoming; discovered and described new mechanical method for handling moldy staves, and described a number of new species of fungi for North America that decay wood; Director University of Michigan expeditions Alaska and Yukon '34, Kodiak Island '38, Bering Sea '40, Prov[...]es of Quebec and New Bru[...]ck '43, Puerto Rico '44, Newfoundland '46, Labrador '47 and Yukon '48. Author: On and Off Alaskan Trails '37; Pathology in Forest Practice; also articles in field. Div forest path US Dept Agr, field worker and collaborator since '24; with U Mich since '19, now prof forest path. Soc Am Foresters—Wash Acad Sci—Soc Foresters Gt Britain—Mycol Soc Am—Mich Acad Sci Arts Letters (sec '33-34)—Eugene Field Soc—Am Phytopath Soc—Explorers Club—Sigma Xi (sec '33-34)—Phi Kappa Phi. Pres Forest Botany Section, VII International Botanical Congress, Stockholm, Sweden, '50. School of Natural Resources, University of Michigan, Ann Arbor.©

23 BAXTER, John Franklin. Hydrated metallic ions; Beryllium (Aqueous solution). b'09. AB '32 (Bethany Coll); PhD '42 (Johns Hopkins U). Research at Johns Hopkins on acidity of the hydrated beryllium ion. Author articles in field. Professor chem Washington and Lee Univ since '49. Am Chem Soc—AAAS—Va Acad Sci—Sigma Xi. Department of Chemistry, Washington and Lee University, Lexington, Va.

24 BAXTER, John Lincoln. Potato processing (Dehydration, canning, quick freezing); Vegetable dehydration. b'96. AB '16 (Bowdoin Coll). Chairman committee coordinating activities for dehydrated food production and procurement program WPB '40-42; pioneered in potato dehydration, quick frozen French fried potatoes, whipped potatoes, canned potatoes; member potato research advisory committee Research and Marketing Act. Author articles in field. Chief

52633

processed foods sect WPB '40-42; established potato dehydration plant H C Baxter & Bro '42 facilities for quick frozen, canned potatoes since '46. Phi Beta Kappa. H. C. Baxter & Bro., Box 319, Brunswick, Me.

10 BAY, Helmuth. Cartography (Map literature, nomendature, history and techniques); History of logging, sawmilling and wood working tools and equipment. b'95. Student forest engring '13-17 (U Mont). Forester and research associate with Museum of Science and Industry, Chicago, '28-48, specializing in history of logging, sawmilling, and wood working tools and equipment. Author: History and Technique of Mapmaking '48; World Flags '42; many Rand McNally maps and atlases. Map cons, head Washington office, Rand McNally since '42. 1104 National Press Building, Washington.†

11 BAYER, Frederick M(erkle). Taxonomy of Alcyonaria and marine mollusks. b'21. Cert '41 (Palm Beach Jr Coll); BS '46 (U Miami); '47 (US Dept Agr Grad Sch). Field studies of reef-dwelling Crustacea, coelenterates, field work in southern Florida, biology of Alcyonarian Corals of the Florida-West Indies region; Bikini Scientific Resurvey Expedition of the Marshall Islands '47. Author: Observations on Marine Mollusca with Descriptions of New Species '43; The Florida Species of the Family Chamidae '43; The Alcyonaria of Bikini and other Atolls in the Marshall Group '49. Research asst Fla State Mus '39-40, asst dir '42-46; research asst charge biol mus U Miami '46-47; research asst U Miami Marine Lab '50; asst curator div marine invertebrates, US Nat Mus Washington since '47. AAAS—Am Genetic Assn—Am Malacol Union—Am Soc Limnol and Oceanog. U.S. National Museum, Washington 25.

12 BAYLIS, John Robert. Water purification. b'85. BS '05 (Miss State Coll). Research on chemical treatment of water for clarification, odor removal, and to lessen corrosion of water pipe; studies on care and maintenance filter beds; engineering and chemical work on design and construction largest water treatment and filtration plant in the world. Civil engr RRs Tex '05-15; mgr Jackson Miss Water Works '15-16; bact and chem Baltimore City water works '17; prin san chem '18-26; chemist in charge research in water purification City Chicago '26-38, engr on design S Dist Filtration Plant '38-45, engr water purification Dept Pub Works since '42. Author: Elimination of Taste and Odor in Water '35. Author 145 tech articles in field. ACS—Am Water Works Assn—Am Soc CE—Am Pub Health Assn—Am Pub Works Assn—ASTM—NE Water Works Assn—Central States Sewage Works Assn. Engineer of Water Purification, 3300 East Cheltenham Pl., Chgo. 49. H: 1643 East 86th St., Chgo 17.⊙

13 BEACH, Frank Ambrose. Sexual behaviour in animals (Hormonal control, Instinctive behaviour). b'11. BS '32—MS '34 (Kan State Teachers Coll); PhD '40 (U Chicago). Prof psychol Yale U since '46. NY Zool Soc—NY Acad Sci (F); AAAS—Am Psychol Assn—Am Soc Naturalists—Nat Acad Scis—Soc Exptl Psychologists. Sigma Xi. Department of Psychology, Yale University, New Haven.⊙

14 BEACH, Walter Spurgeon. Vegetable diseases (Tobacco, lettuce, tomato, fungicides); Mushroom diseases. b'90. BS '14 (U Minn); MS '15 (Mich State Coll); PhD '18 (U

Ill). Author articles in field. With Pa State Coll since '18, now prof plant pathology. AAAS—American Phytopath Soc—Sigma Xi. Buckhout Laboratory, Pennsylvania State College, State College, Pa.†

15 BEACHER, Lawrence Lester. Contact lenses. b'05. OD '27 (Pa State Coll Optometry); DOSc '37 (Northern Ill Coll Optometry); PhD (hon) '33 (First Nat U Naturopathy); ScD '46 (Dearborn Coll Phys and Surgeons); LittD (hon) '47 (Sem St Francis of Assisi); '48 (McCormick Med Coll); PhD (hon) '45 (Phila Coll Infirmary of Osteopathy). Author: Ocular Refraction and Diagnosis '31; Practical Optometry '34; Contact Lens Technique '46; also articles in field. Chief of staff head ed div Bronx Co Optometric Clinic Service '29-31; lecturer on contact lens impression methods Optometric Foundation since '45; dir Am contact lens research labs; optometric practitioner and cons. Am Acad Optometry(F)—Internat Acad Optometry Contact Lens Practitioners(F)—Distinguished Service Foundation Optometry (F)—Essex Co Optometric Soc—Am Optometric Assn. 1127 Delynn Way, San Jose 25, Cal.

16 BEALL, Chandler Baker. Comparative literature (Franco-, Anglo-, and Hispano-Italian literary relations); French and Italian literature. b'01. BA '22—PhD '30 (Johns Hopkins U); diplome '21 (U Paris). Editor Comparative Literature since '48. Author: Chateaubriand et le Tasse, Baltimore '34; Un Italofilo americano di cent'anni fa, Richard Henry Wilde, con versioni inedite di poemi italiani '39; La Fortune du Tasse en France '42; also articles in field. Asso prof '29-36, prof French and Italian U Ore since '36. Modern Lang Assn—Philol Assn Pacific Coast—Am Assn Teachers Italian. Am Council Learned Socs(F) '35-36; grant from Am Philos Soc '47. University of Oregon, Eugene, Ore.

17 BEALL, Geoffrey. Entomology (Statistical method, ecology); Insect migration. b'08. BA '31 (U British Columbia); MSc '32 (U Ill); PhD '38 (U London). Author articles in field. Investigation and consultation Preston Labs Butler Pa '48-49; professor statistics U Conn since '50. Am Statis Assn—Inst Math Statis—Biometrics Soc. Statistical Lab., Univ. of Conn., Storrs, Conn.

18 BEALS, Ralph L(eon). Ethnology of Latin America; American Indians. b' 01. AB '26—PhD '30 (U Calif). Study Yaqui-Mayo Indians Mexico '30-32, Mixe Indians '32-33, Nisenan Indians California '29, Tarascan Indians Mexico '40-41, Quichua Indians of Ecuador '48-49. Author articles in field. With U Calif since '29, now prof; mus tech Nat Park Service '33-35; dir Latin American Ethnic Studies Smithsonian Instn '41-42. Am Anthrop Assn(F)—AAAS(F)—Soc Am Archaeol—Am Folklore Soc—Inter-American Soc Anthrop and Geog—Sociedad Mexicana de Antropologia—Sociedade Brasileira de Antropologia—Social Sci Research Council. Nat Research Council fellow '30-32; Southwest Soc fellow '32-33. University of California, Los Angeles 24.⊙

19 BEAM, Robert E(dwin). Electronics; Microwaves; Antennas. b'14. BEE '37 (O State U); PhD '40 (Ia State Coll). Research on dielectric rod and dielectric tube waveguides, open-ended waveguide radiators, slot antennas, folded dipole antennas and microwave optics; one of founders of National Electronics Conference, on board of

directors inception to '48. Editor Proceedings of National Electronics Conference '44, '46, '47. Co-author: (with A B Bronwell) Theory and Application of Microwaves '47; also articles in field. Asst prof elec engring So Meth U '41-42; asst prof elec engring Northwestern U '42-47, associate prof '47-50, tech dir Microwave Research Lab (sponsored by US Army Signal Corps) since '47, professor since '50. National Electronics Conference (founder '44, member board dir since '44, vp and chmn pub com '45-46, sec '47) —Inst Radio Engrs (mem edn com since '45, membership com '47)—AIEE (chmn exec com Gt Lakes Dist student br activities com '47-48)—Am Soc Engring Edn—Sigma Xi. Electrical Engineering Department, Northwestern University, Evanston, Ill.†

20 BEAMER, Parker Reynolds. Yeast (Heat resistance); Poisoning (Food); Stains (Bacteriologic). b'14. Student '31-32 (U Louisville); AB '35—MS '37 —PhD '40 (U Ill) MD '43 (Washington U). Research on heat resistance certain yeasts and non-spore forming, pathogenic bacteria; study of development Clostridium botulinum in refrigerated foods; investigation public health bacteriologic problems; histopathology of infectious diseases. Faculty sch med Washington U '42-49, asst prof path '46-49; asst path Barnes Hosp St Louis '46-49, also St Louis Children's Hosp, St Louis Maternity Hosp and McMillan Hosp; bact and asso path NC Baptist Hosp Winston-Salem since '49; prof and dir dept microbiol and immunology, asso prof path Bowman Gray Sch Med since '49. Asst chief and chief lab services US Army hosps '44-45; chief med bact and parasitol divs and Commanding Officer Antilles Gen Med Lab San Juan PR '45-46. Am Assn Path and Bact—Am Pub Health Assn—Soc Am Bact—Soc Exptl Biol and Med—AAAS —AMA (F)—Am Soc Clin Path (F)— Sigma Xi—Alpha Omega Alpha. Bowman Gray School of Medicine, Winston-Salem 7, N.C.

21 BEAMER, Scott. Lighting design (Commercial, industrial). b'14. BS (elec engring) '36 (U Calif). Research on interior lighting with cold cathode and neon, neon displays, roof signs and structures, commercial and industrial wiring installations. Granted patent on neon dimming transformer. Author 15 articles in field. Elec engr Luminad Neon Corp '37-38; jr elec engr Pacific Elec Motor Co '38-40; elec engr USDA Farm Security Adminstrn '40-42; elec engr Clyde E Bentley '46-48; lecturer U Calif '48-50; cons engr since '50. Am Inst EE—Illuminating Engring Soc. 1012 Bank of Commerce Building, Oakland 12, Calif.

22 BEAN, Ernest F. Highway materials; Engineering and glacial geology; Economic geology of pre-cambrian. b'82. Member Alaska Glacial Expedition '09, '10. Author: Manual of Physical Geography '13; Laboratory Manual of College Geography '13; Mineral Lands of Northern Wisconsin '15, '29. Geol Wis Geol Survey '11, chief of field parties '13-19; geol in charge road material surveys Wis '20-25; Wis state geol since '26. Geol Soc Am(F)—Soc Econ Geol—Am Inst Mining Metall Engrs—Wis Acad Sci, Arts Letters— Wis Hist Soc—Sigma Xi. Science Hall, Madison 6, Wis.

23 BEAN, Frederic Roland. Photographic chemicals; Fine organic pharmaceuticals; Cosmetics; Oxidation dyes (Fur, wool, hair); Antioxidants; Organic synthesis; Herbicides; Insecticides. b'04. AB '27—Rector Scholar (Depauw); PhD '31 (Cornell). Author articles in field. Mem tech staff engaged in research development work Eastman Kodak Co NY since '31. Am Chem Soc—Shuttlecraft Guild—AAAS —Am Inst Chem(F)—Phi Beta Kappa. Scottsville, N.Y.†

10 BEAN, Howard S(tewart). Gas and fluid meters. b'93. BS '17 (U Calif). Research on orifice meters, flow nozzles for fluid meters, viscosity of gases. Author: Gas Measuring Instruments '26; Measurement of Flow of Air and Gases With Nozzles '28; Developments in the Application of Orifice Meters to the Measurement of Fluids, Especially Gases '36; Fluid Meters, Their Theory and Practice '37. Inspector weighs and measures Nat Bur Standards '17-20, chief gas measuring instruments sect '20-48, chief capacity density and fluid meters sect since '48. ASME (dir research programs)—Am Gas Assn (dir research program '26-31)—Sigma Xi. National Bureau of Standards, Washington 25.

11 BEAN, Walton Elbert. American history (Early national, Jacksonian, twentieth century). b'14. BA '35—MA '37 (U So Calif); PhD '41—fellow hist '40-41 (U Calif). Research in US government information policies and effects public opinion World War I; money, banks, and politics, Jacksonian era; historical interpretation and historiography of US; labor in US politics. Author: Boss Ruef's San Francisco; the Story of the Union Labor Party and the Graft Prosecution, 1901-1911 '49. Author articles: Revolt Among Historians '39; The Accuracy of Creel Committee News, 1917-1919 '41; James Warren and the Beginnings of Agricultural Institutions in California '44; and others. Instr hist U Calif '41-46, asst prof since '46. AHA —Pacific Coast Branch Am Hist Assn —AAUP—Phi Beta Kappa. Department of History, University of California, Berkeley 4.

12 BEAN, William Bennett. Internal medicine; Cardiology; Coronary artery disease; Human nutrition; Chronic liver disease; Human environmental physiology. b'09. AB '32—Med '35 (U Va). Research on infarction of heart, relation weather and climate to incidence heart failure and myocardial infarction, syndrome of neurologic disturbance in acute myocardial infarction, aortic stenosis; clinical aspects human pellagra; vascular spiders and palmar erythema in liver disease and pregnancy; environmental physiology demonstrating water and salt requirements at various levels of temperature and work, limits of heat and humidity tolerable for working men, process and significance of aclimatization and evaluation physical fitness; critique of rations and ration testing. Author articles Infarction of the Heart II, Symptomatology of Acute Attack, III Course and Morphological Findings; Coronary Occlusion, Heart Failure, and Environmental Temperatures; Acquired Palmar Erythema and Cutaneous Vascular "Spiders"; The Cutaneous Arterial Spider; Anticoagulents in the Treatment of Acute Myocardial Infarctions and Its Complications. Asso editor Jour Clin Investigation since '47. Prof medicine and head dept internal med State U Ia since '48; med examiner Draft Boards '41-42; sr med cons VA since '47. Dir hot room research Armored Med Research Lab, Ft Knox, Ky '42-43, dir med research '43-45, commanding officer '45-46. Am Bd Internal Med (diplomate)—Central Soc Clin Research (pres '50-51)—Am Soc Tropical Med— Am Heart Assn—AAAS—AMA(F)— Am Soc Clin Investigation—Am Coll

Physicians (F)—World Med Assn— Alpha Omega Alpha. John Horsley Memorial prize U Va '44. Department of Internal Medicine, University Hospitals, Iowa City, Ia.

13 BEAR, Firman Edward. Growing plants. b'84. BSc '08—MSc '10 (Ohio State U); PhD '17 (U Wis). Author: Soils and Fertilizers '24; Theory and Practice in Use of Fertilizers '29. Editor-in-chief Soil Science since '40. Contbr to Practical Guide to Successful Farming '44, Grounds for Living '46. Indsl research Stickstoff Syndicat Berlin Germany '27; head soil dept U WVa '14-16, Ohio State '16-29; dir agrl research Am Cyanamid Co NYC '29-38; sci editor Country Home mag Crowell Pub Co NYC '38-40; prof agrl chem and chmn soils dept Rutgers U since '40. AAAS(F)—Am Soc Agron(F, pres '49)—Nat Research Council (mem-at-large)—Am Chem Soc—Am Soc Plant Physiol—Soil Sci Soc Am (pres '43)—Soil Conservation Soc Am—Sigma Xi—Phi Beta Kappa—Alpha Zeta. Rutgers University, New Brunswick, N.J.◎

14 BEAR, Richard S(cott). Natural polymers and tissues (X-ray diffraction); Chemistry of starch; Structure of protein and nerve fibers. b'08. BS '30 (Princeton); PhD '33 (U Calif). Author articles in field. Asst prof chem Ia State Coll Ames '38-41; asso prof biol MIT Cambridge '41-46, prof since '46. Am Chem Soc—Crystallographic Soc Am—Am Soc for X-ray and Electron Diffraction—NY Acad Sci. Voted among ten outstanding starch chem of US by readers of Chemical Bulletin, Am Chem Soc Chicago '47. Department of Biology, Massachusetts Institute of Technology, Cambridge 39, Mass.

15 BEARD, Mary Ritter (Mrs Charles A Beard). History; American history; History of Women in America; Historical women. b'76. PhB '97 (DePauw U) grad study (Columbia). Author: Woman's Work in Municipalities '15; A Short History of the American Labor Movement '20; On Understanding Women '31; Woman as a Force in History '46. Editor: America Through Women's Eyes '33; Co-Author (with husband) numerous volumes history on American Civilization and culture. H: New Milford, Conn.◎

16 BEARDEN, Joyce Alvin. Physics (X-rays, physical constants, radioactivity). b'03. AB '23 (Furman U); PhD '26 (U Chicago). Physicist Applied Physics Lab Washington '42-46. Prof physics Johns Hopkins U since '39, chmn dept '47-48, dir Radiation Lab since '43. Am Phys Soc(F)— AAAS(F)—Inst Radio Engrs (sr mem) —Am Phys Soc (council '46-50)— Sigma Xi—Phi Beta Kappa. Johns Hopkins University, Balt 18.◎

17 BEARDSLEY, Harry M. Mormonism; Midwestern history and politics (United States). b'93. Student (U Chicago). Author: Joseph Smith and His Mormon Empire '31. Co-author: Kanguk, A Boy of Bering Strait '39; also articles in field. Ed writer Chicago Daily News since '36. Ill Library Assn—ALA. Daily News Plaza, Chgo.

18 BEARDSLEY, Richard King. Japanese ethnography; Inner Asia (Archeology). b'18. PhD '47 (U Calif). Research on village culture of Japan. With U Mich since '47, asst prof anthrop from '48. Sigma Xi—Phi Beta Kappa—Am Anthrop Assn—Soc Am Archeol—Far E Assn—Asiatic Soc Japan. F Soc Sci Research Council '50-51. Department of Anthropology, University of Michigan, Ann Arbor, Mich.

19 BEATTY, Willard Walcott. American Indians (Education, affairs, arts and crafts); Progressive, rural and teacher education; School building design. b'91. BS '13—AM '21 (U Calif); '24-31 (U Chicago); '26-28 (Teachers Coll Columbia); EdD (hon) '37 (Reed Coll Portland). Editor: Indian Education. Co-author: Mathematics of Everyday Life '36; Education for Action '45; also pamphlets on Indian Life. Dir edn Office Indian Affairs US Dept Interior since '36. Progressive Edn Assn (dir '29-38, pres '33-37, treas '41-44)—NEA. Bureau of Indian Affairs, Department of Interior, Washington 25.◎

20 BEAUDETTE, Fred R(obert). Poultry pathology. b'97. DVM '19 (Kans State Coll). Discovered cause of laryngotracheitis and developed method of active immunization; first to diagnose swine erysipelas and pseudotuberculosis in birds in United States; made first diagnosis of Newcastle disease on east coast and developed live virus vaccine for disease; made first cultivation of virus of infectious bronchitis in developing egg; demonstrated egg transmission of fowl typhoid; identified fowl plague in US '29. Author articles in field. Asst prof poultry path Rutgers U '23, asso prof '25, prof since '29. Am Vet Med Assn —Poultry Sci Soc—Am Soc Parasito —Am Micros Soc—Research Workers in Animal Diseases in NA—Sigma Xi —Gamma Sigma Delta—Phi Kappa Phi—Alpha Zeta—US Livestock Sanitary Assn. Borden award '44. New Jersey Agricultural Experiment Station, New Brunswick, N.J.

21 BEAUMONT, Andre Alden. History of the Crusades and medieval France. b'00. BA '21 (Yale); MA '22 —Boudinot fellow history '22-23— Proctor fellow history '24-25—PhD '25 (Princeton). Author articles in field. Instr hist Washington Sq Coll '23-24, asst prof '26-28, asso prof '28-46, prof since '46. AHA—Mediaeval Acad Am —Phi Beta Kappa. New York University, Washington Sq., NYC 3.†

22 BEAUMONT, Jane Graville Lightfoot. Early American silverplated ware. b'00. Student '17-20 (Devon Manor Jr Coll); '20-23 (NY Sch Fine and Applied Art). Co-author: (with G. L. Freeman) American Plated Silver '48; also articles in field. Independent research. NY State Hist Soc. 314 Clinton St., Penn Yan, N.Y.

23 BEAUMONT, John Herbert. Horticulture (Nursery and field); Tropical fruits and nuts; Apples; Pecans. b'94. BS '17 (W Va U); PhD '25 (U Minn); student (U Chicago, Cornell U, U Cincinnati). Agricultural mission to Philippines auspices of State Department and Office Foreign Agricultural Relations '46. Author articles in field. Prof hort and head dept U Hawaii '36-38, dir Hawaii Agrl Exptl Station since '38. AAAS(F)—Am Soc Hort Sci —Am Soc Plant Physiol—Am Genetics Soc—Hawaiian Acad Sci—Hawaiian Bot Soc—Sigma Xi—Phi Kappa Phi. Hawaii Agricultural Experiment Station, Honolulu, T.H.

24 BEAVEN, G(eorge) Francis. Oyster biology (Eastern United States); Crabs; Chesapeake Bay fisheries. b'03. Student '21-22 (U Md); BS '25 (Washington Coll); MA '37 (Duke U). Author articles in field. Fishery biol Chesapeake Biol Lab since '40. Nat Shellfisheries Assn—Ecol Soc Am—Am Soc Limnol and Oceano—AAAS. Solomons, Md.

25 BECHET, Paul Esnard. Medicine (History); Medical exhibits (Historical, technical). b'81. MD '03 (Tulane U). Exhibits relating to early American dermatologists (awarded special certificate of merit by American Medical Association Cleveland Session '41); exhibit of memorabilia referring to early American dermatologists (awarded special commendation American Medical Associal Centennial Session Atlantic City '47). Author: Napoleon, His Last Illness and Postmortem; Arsenic, History of Its Use in Dermatology; Psoriasis, a Brief Historical Review; Jean Nicholas Corvisart, Physician to the Emperor Napoleon; The Early History of American Dermatology; The Last Few Hours of Nelson's Life; also articles in field. Cons dermatologist Hosp for Spl Surgery since 18; cons derm Bellevue Med Center. Am Bd Dermatology (diplomate)—Med Soc NJ—NY Acad Med—AMA—Manhattan Dermatol Soc (pres '17-19)—Am Acad Dermatology Syphilogy (dir '38-41)—NY Dermatol Soc (sec '27-29, pres '29, '36)—Am Dermatol Assn (historian)—Am Assn Hist Med—NY Soc Med Hist. 1364 North Av., Elizabeth, N.J.

10 BECHTEL, Albert Reiff. Taxonomy of seed plants and fungi (Urticales, flowers of Central Indiana). b'82. AB '12 (U Pa); PhD '21 (Cornell U). Author articles in field. Prof bot and gen biol Wabash Coll since '20. AAAS(F)—Bot Soc Am—Mycol Soc Am—Am Soc Plant Taxonomists—Ind Acad Sci(F). Wabash College, Crawfordsville, Ind.†

11 BECHTEL, Welker George. Rheology of starches; Starch chemistry. b'02. BA '24 (U Dubuque); MS '28 (U Chicago); '31-32, '42 (Ia State Coll); '30 (State U Ia). Author articles in field. Inventor of Corn Industries Viscometer (with C C Kesler). Research fellow Corn Industries Research Foundation since '43. Soc Rheology—An Inst Physics—Am Chem Soc—Sigma Xi. Am. Inst. of Baking, 1135 Fullerton Ave., Chgo.†

12 BECHTNER, Paul. Clays (Bentonite). b'82. Ed pub schs. Numerous patents on bentonite usage. Contributor: Industrial Minerals and Rocks (2nd edit) '49. Operation silicate mines and plants since '11; organized Am Colloid Co '26, pres since '36. ACS—Am Ceramic Soc—AIMME—Am Foundrymen's Soc. 222 N. Bank Drive, Chicago 54.

13 BECHTOL, Charles Orville. Orthopaedic surgery; Artificial limbs. b'11. BS '34 MD '40 (Stanford U). Cons VA for artificial limbs and braces; med cons com on artificial limbs of Nat Research Council. Asst clin prof Orthopaedic surgery U Calif since '50. Diplomate Am Bd Orthopaedic Surgery—Am Acad Orthopaedic Surg—Am Phys Therapy Assn. 1624 Franklin St., Oakland 12, Cal.

14 BECK, Clifford Keith. Isotope separation; Radioactive tracers (Technique). b'13. AB '33 (Catawba Coll); MS '40 (Vanderbilt U); PhD '43 (U NC). Author articles in field. Dir research labs Gaseous Diffusion Plant Carbide & Carbon Oak Ridge Tenn '46-49; Head dept phys NC St Col '49. Am Phys Soc (dir SE Sect)—NC Acad Sci—AAAS—Sigma Xi. N C State College, Raleigh.

15 BECK, Clyde. Language and literature. b'84. AB '07 (Earlham Coll); AM '16 (U Ill). Book collecting; bibliography. Literary editor Detroit News since '26; special instr book reviewing Wayne U since '46. Program chmn Friends Detroit Pub Library. The Detroit News, Lafayette and 2d Blvd., Det. 35†◎

16 BECK, George Frederick. Petrified wood; Paleontology and Geology of the Columbia Basin. b'92. BS '31 (Wash State Coll); MS '48 (U Wash). Author: Tertiary Coniferous Woods of Western North America '45; Pine and Pine-like Woods of the West American Tertiary '48. Prof geol Central Wash Coll since '25. Central Washington College, Ellensburg, Wash.

17 BECK, Henry Gabriel Justin. Medieval church history. b'14. BA '34 (Seton Hall Coll); SThL '38—DHist '48 (Gregorian U Rome). Author articles in field. Prof church hist Immaculate Conception Sem Darlington NJ since '40. AHA—Am Catholic Hist Assn—Societe d'Histoire de L'Eglise de France. Immaculate Conception Seminary, Darlington, N.J.†

18 BECK, Hubert Park. Research Administration; Personnel Research. b'07. Parmenter scholar '25-26—AB '29 (Harvard); MA '31 (U Chicago); Romiett Stevens scholar '34—PhD '45 (Columbia). Director and consultant on educational psychological and industrial research. Author: Men Who Control Our Universities '47. Contributor: The Educational Yearbook, 1935 '35. Prof and head dept edn and psychol Limestone Coll '36-38 and RI State U '41-45; indsl personnel research Am Type Founders and Personnel-Management Service '45-46; Pan-Am Airways '45-47 and cons '47-48; co-ordinator research City Coll NY since '48 and dir instnl research from '49. Am Ednl Research Assn—Am Psychol Assn—E Psychol Assn—NY Psychol Assn—Nat Soc Study of Edn—Soc Advancement Edn—NEA—Nat Council Ednl Travel—AAAS—Phi Delta Kappa—Kappa Delta Pi. City College of New York, NYC 31. H: 523 W. 121st St., NYC 27.

19 BECK, Lyle Vibert. Cellular and mammalian physiology. AB '28 (Wabash Coll); MS '30 (Washington U); PhD '33 (U Pittsburgh); Eli Lilly F, '33-34 (NYU); Cancer Biol., '34-35 (U Pa); Van Camp F, '35-36 (L I Coll Med); Commonwealth F, '36-38 (U Pa); instr to asso prof physiol Hahnemann Med Coll '38-47; Physiol Nat Cancer Inst '47-51; asso prof physiol and pharmacol U Pittsburgh since '51. Research on permability and intracellular oxidation-reduction reactions, effects of poisons on kidney function; glucose absorpt by intestine and kidney; pyrogenic and circulatory effects of tumor-necrotizing bacterial polysaccharide; protective effects of adrenal hormones against certain toxic substances. Phi Beta Kappa—Sigma Xi—AAAS—ACS—Am Physiol Soc—Am Soc Cancer Research—Am Soc Zool—Corp Marine Biol Lab—Soc Exptl Biol and Med. Dept. of Physiol and Pharmacol., Univ. of Pittsburgh, Pittsburgh 13, Pa.

20 BECK, Paul Adams. Physical metallurgy; Recrystallization; Grain growth in Metals; Nonferrous alloys. b'08. MS '29—research fellow '28-29 (Mich Coll Mining and Tech); '25-28, '29-30 mech engring (Budapest U Engring); research fellow '30-31 (Kaiser Wilhelm Institut f. Metallforschung, Berlin); '33-35 (U Paris, France). Research on cosmic rays, neutrons, instrumentation, Geiger-Mueller counters, electronic coincidence selecting and registering devices, barrier layer photocells, recrystallization of tin and of aluminum single crystals, effect of reversed deform on recrystallization, precipitation hardening, recrystallization of lead alloys, development of bearing alloys, grain growth in metals and alloys, high temperature alloys; development and fab-

rication of copper-beryllium alloys, properties, casting, fabricating of bearings, problems of bonding metals, porosity in metals. Author articles in field. Prof, head dept metall U Notre Dame. Am Inst Mining Metall Engrs—Am Soc Metals—Am Soc Testing Materials—Am Foundrymen's Soc—Am Phys Soc—Am Soc X-ray Electron Diffraction. Department of Metallurgy, University of Notre Dame, Notre Dame, Ind.†

21 BECK, Richard. Scandinavian languages and literatures; Icelandic literature, history and culture; Icelandic-American history; Norwegian literature and culture; Poetry. b'97. AB '20 (State Coll Iceland); AM '24—PhD '26 (Cornell U). Gave address at festivities in Iceland commemorating re-establishment of Icelandic Republic '44. Co-author: The History of Scandinavian Literatures '38. Editor: Icelandic Lyrics '30; Icelandic Poems and Stories '43; selected poems by J A Sigurdsson '46; also articles in field. Prof Scandinavian langs and lits U ND since '29; hon vice consul Iceland for ND since '42. Modern Lang Assn Am—Am Scandinavian Foundation—Medieval Acad Am—Soc Advancement Scandinavian Study (vp '38-40, pres '40-42)—Lit Soc Iceland—Icelandic Soc for Sci (corr). Decorated Knight Order of Icelandic Falcon by King of Iceland and Denmark '39, Knight Commander '44; Knight Order of St. Olaf by King of Norway '39; special medal commemorating founding of Icelandic Republic '44; Danish Medal of Liberation '46. University Station, Grand Forks, N.D.◎

22 BECKENBACH, Joseph Riley. Subtropical olericulture; Mineral nutrition of plants. b'08. AB (Antioch Coll); MSc (Ohio State U); PhD (Rutgers U). Author articles in field. Hort charge Vegetable Crops Lab Bradenton Fla since '39; asso dir Fla Agrl Expt Sta Gainesville since '50. Am Soc Plant Physiol—Am Soc Hort Sci—Sigma Xi—Gamma Sigma Delta. Agrl. Expt. Sta., Univ. of Fla., Gainesville, Fla.

23 BECKER, Arman Edward. Fuels (Motor and Diesel). b'86. AB magna cum laude '09 (Marietta Coll); AM '10—PhD (Physics)'17 (Harvard). Research on knock rating of aviation and motor fuels; surface action effect lubrication. Author articles: Surface action and fluid film lubrication; An index of Diesel fuel performance; Certified Isooctane by the carload. Editor: Methods of Testing Petroleum Products. With Aluminum Castings Co Cleveland '19-'20; with Standard Oil Co (NJ) and Standard Oil Development Co NJ since '20. Editor: Technical Publications, S.O. Co. (N.J.) & Affiliated Companies since '48. Phi Beta Kappa—Am Petroleum Inst—Soc Automotive Engrs—ASTM. 129 Brightwood Ave., Westfield, N.J.

24 BECKER, Elery Ronald. Protozoology (Coccidia, malaria, parasitic ciliates of ruminants, Trypsonosomes). b'96. AB '21 (U Colo); DSc '23 (Johns Hopkins). Author: Coccidia and Coccidiosis '34; also articles in field. Prof zool Ia State Coll since '35. Ia Acad Sci (sec-treas '41-43)—Am Soc Zool—Am Soc Parasitol—Am Soc Protozool—AAAS—Soc for Experimental Biol and Medicine—Sigma Xi—Phi Beta Kappa—Phi Kappa Phi—Gamma Sigma Delta. 413 Lynn Av., Ames, Ia.◎

25 BECKER, John G. Persian art (Rugs, brasses). b'05. AB (Yale); AM (Columbia). Author articles in field. Vice pres Fitch Publs Co NYC; pres Bible Magazine Inc Phila since '37,

Revelation Magazine; lecturer on Persian art. Pa Chautauqua (chancellor, mem bd dirs Mt Gretna Pa)—Haji Baba Soc (Oriental)—Am Tract Soc (mem finance com). 120 Wall St., NYC.

10 **BECKER, Joseph Aloysius.** Statistics (Agricultural). b'91. BSA '14—MS (Agrl econ) '16 (U Wis). Research on crop and livestock estimating methodology; member technical committee on statistics Interim Commission Food and Agricultural Organization United Nations, also standing advisory committee on statistics; consultant on agricultural statistics Mexican Ministry of Agriculture '46, Cuban Ministry '48. With Bur Agrl Econ '22-35, in charge tech work '25-35; chmn com agrl statis USDA Yearbook '27-44; chmn Crop Reporting Bd '35-38 and '43-44; chief internat commodities br Office Fgn Agrl Relations since '44. Am Farm Econ Assn—Am Statis Assn—Alpha Zeta. Office of Foreign Agricultural Relations, U.S. Department of Agriculture, Washington 25.†

11 **BECKER, Kurt.** Chemistry and technology of brewing and malting; Fermentation industries. b'98. Student Columbia U. Author articles in field. Chemist, then dir research div and vp J E Siebel Sons' Co Chicago since '34. Am Assn Cereal Chem—Am Soc Brewing Chem—Master Brewers Assn Am. J. E. Siebel Sons' Co., 741 W. Jackson Blvd., Chicago 6.†

12 **BECKER, Raymond Brown.** Dairy production; Animal nutrition; Dairy cattle (Breeding, history). b'92. BS '16—MS '20 (Ia State Coll); PhD '25 (U Minn). Author articles in field. Dairy husbandman U Fla Agrl Expt Sta since '29, on leave summer '38 for study of dairy cattle in Europe. Am Dairy Sci Assn—Am Soc Animal Prodn—Fla Acad Sci—Sigma Xi—Phi Kappa Phi. Florida Agricultural Experiment Station, Gainesville, Fla.†

13 **BECKER, Robert Henry.** Dogs (Care, feeding, training); Setter; Spaniel; Retriever. b'90. AB (Beloit Coll Wis). Care and training of dogs especially sporting breeds; judging of spaniel and retriever field trials. Author: Bob Becker's Dog Digest. Author: It's Easy to Raise and Train your Puppy; Feeding the Dog; How to Make your Dog Behave. Outdoors ed Chicago Tribune since '21; ed Outdoorsman magazine since '44; writer syndicated column Mostly About Dogs. Dog Man of the Year award '47. Outdoors Editor, Chicago Tribune, Chicago.

14 **BECKETT, Grace.** International economics and trade; Reciprocal trade agreements program (United States); American foreign commercial policy. b'12. AB '34—AM '35 (Oberlin Coll); PhD '39 (Ohio State U). Author: Reciprocal Trade Agreemnts Program '41; also articles in field. Asst prof econ U Ill since '45. Am Econ Assn—Am Acad Polit Social Sci—Am Market Assn—Phi Beta Kappa. 323 David Kinley Hall, University of Illinois, Urbana, Ill.

15 **BECKMAN, Theodore N.** Economics; Marketing; Credit; Wholesaling. b'95. BSc '20—AM '22—PhD '24 (Ohio State U). Author: Wholesaling '26; Credits and Collections in Theory and Practice '39. Co-author: Democracy in Transition '37; Principles of Marketing '46; Wholesaling Principles and Practice '37; The Chain Store Problem '37; also articles in field. Prof marketing O State U since '32. Nat Assn Credit Men (adv council)—Am Econ Assn—Am Marketing Assn (ex vp and dir)—Am Statis Assn (ex vp)

—Beta Gamma Sigma. Ohio State University, Columbus, O.

16 **BECNEL, Irwin Joseph.** Economic entomology (Cotton and citrus insects control). b'09. Research fellow '37-38—BS '31—MS '32 (La State U); hon fellow '38-39 (Ohio State U). Author articles in field. Dir agrl research Freeport Sulphur Co New Orleans since '47. Am Assn Econ Entomol—Tex Entomol Soc—Am Soc Hort Sci—Assn So Agrl Workers—Am Phytopath Soc—Am Rose Soc—Am Soc Agron—Phi Kappa Phi—Gamma Sigma Delta. Freeport Sulphur Co., 1804 American Bank Bldg., New Orleans.†

17 **BEDDIE, James Stuart.** Diplomatic history; Mediaeval libraries; Germany since 1918. b'02. AB '22 (U Minn); AM '25—PhD '28 (Harvard U); traveling fellow for research in Europe, American Council of Learned Societies '31-33; Editor for Department of State of American and captured German diplomatic documents. Author articles: Libraries in the XIIth Century '29; The Ancient Classics in the Mediaeval Libraries '30; Books in the East in the Period of the Crusades '33. Editor: (with Raymond J. Sontag) Nazi-Soviet Relations 1939-1941, '48. Prof hist Upper Ia U '28-30; prof social sci ND St Teachers Coll Minot ND '30-31; research asso and historian US Dept State since '36. Phi Beta Kappa—AHA—Mediaeval Acad Am. Division of Historical Policy Research, Department of State, Washington 25. H: 9 West Washington St., Kensington, Md.†

18 **BEDELL, Ralph Clairon.** Educational psychology (Testing, measurement, guidance, counseling, teaching methods). b'04. AM '29—PhD '32 (U Mo); BS '29 (Central Mo State Coll). Co-author: Workbook to General Science for Today '37; Unit Tests for General Science for Today '37; Learning and Test Activities in General Science '31. Editor: Basic Guidance '47; also articles in field. Prof ednl psychol and measurements U Neb '46-50; chmn dept psychol and edn Am U Washington 50— on leave as chief tech assistance, international educational programs US Office Edn since '52; test officer Central Examining Bd US Navy '43-44; training manuals officer staff Chief Naval Air Training '44; research psychol Office Naval Research '44-45. Am Psychol Assn(F)—Am Ednl Research Assn—Psychometric Soc—Am Statis Assn—Nat Assn Research Sci Treaching—Midwestern Psychol Assn—Nat Soc Study Edn—Nat Council Ednl Measurements—NEA—Neb State Edn Assn—Kappa Delta Pi. Diplomate in counseling and guidance, Am Bd of Examiners in Profl Psychology. 3140 Wisconsin Av., NW, Washington 16.†⊚

19 **BEDNAR, William Carr.** Petroleum wells (Temperature measurement, pressure measurement). b'09. Student '30-31 (Tex A&M Coll); BS '35 (U Okla). Research on measuring subsurface pressures in conjunction with drill stem tests and measurement of temperature anomalies. Petroleum engr Amerada Petroleum Corp '35-38; asso prof petroleum engring U Okla '38-43; petroleum engr in charge operations N Ordnance Inc '43-47; cons petroleum, engr from '47, partner Meyer and Achtschin since '49. Tau Beta Pi—Sigma Tau—Sigma Gamma Epsilon—AIMME—Am Assn Petroleum Geol—Am Petroleum Inst. 1600 M and W Tower, Dallas 1.

20 **BEEBE, Lucius Morris.** Railroading history and photography; Western Americana (Express com-

panies, stage coaches). b'02. AB '27 (Harvard U). Author: High Iron, a Book of Trains '38; Highliners, A Railroad Album '40; Trains in Transition '41; Shoot If You Must '43; Highball, A Pageant of Trains '45. Co-author: (with C M Clegg) Mixed Train Daily, A Book of Short Line Railroads '47. Formerly corr, NY Evening Post; staff feature writer Boston Telegram '24; staff NY Herald Tribune '29-50; writer syndicated column This New York '33-44. A and Union Sts., Virginia City, Nev.

21 **BEEBE, William.** Ornithology; Pheasants. b'77. BS '98 (Columbia) Sc D LLD '28 (Tufts and Colgate U). Curator ornithology NY Zool Soc since '99 also dir dept tropical research. Author: Two Bird Lovers in Mexico '05; The Bird '06; Log of the Sun '06; Our Search for a Wilderness (with wife) '10; Monographs of the Pheasants '18; Galapagos, World's End '23; Pheasants-Their Lives and Homes '26; Pheasant Jungles '27; Field Book of the Shore Fishes '32; Book of Naturalists '44. Author many articles and monographs on birds fish and evolution. AAAS—Soc Am Ornithol—Linnaean Soc—Soc Mammalogists—Ecol Soc—Audubon Soc—Zool Soc London. Holds Elliot and John Burroughs medals. Zoological Park, Bronx, NYC 60.⊚

22 **BEECHEM, Henry A(lbert).** Lithographic chemistry. b'06. BS (Mich State Coll). Holds patents on automatic liquid dispenser, method of destroying thermophylic bacteria. Author articles in field. Dept ed Graphic Arts Monthly since '42. With Beechem Labs since '44. AAAS. Beechem Laboratories, St. Johns, Mich.†

23 **BEELEY, Arthur Lawton.** Social psychology; Criminology; Mental hygiene. b'90. AB '13 (Brigham Young U); AM '18—PhD '25 (U Chicago). White House Conference on Child Health and Protection '29-30. Author: An Experimental Study of Left-Handedness '18; The Bail System in Chicago '27; Boys and Girls in Salt Lake City '29; Social Planning for Crime Control '35; also articles in field. Prof sociol U Utah since '27, dean sch social work since '37; lecturer Nat Police Acad (FBI) '43-45; dir Inst World Affairs since '46. Am Ortho-Psychiatric Assn(F)—Am Sociol Soc—Am Assn Social Workers—Utah Soc Mental Hygiene (pres '38-39)—Phi Beta Kappa—Phi Kappa Phi. Grant Am Social Sci Research Council for criminol research in Eng '32-33. Univ of Utah, Salt Lake City.

24 **BEERS, Roland Frank.** Geophysics; Geology; Seismology; Sedimentology. b'99. EE '21 (Rensselaer Poly Inst); SM '28—PhD '43 (MIT; Tech); '40-41 (Harvard Grad Sch Arts and Sci). Geophysic consultant US Geologic Survey Washington '43-46; member Committee on Seismic Effects of Detonations National Research Council '45-46, Committee on Measurement of Geologic Time since '45. Author articles in field. Pres and dir Geotech Corp Dallas since '35, chmn bd and dir since '47; pres and dir Geotech Corp of Canada Ltd, Montreal, since '44; dir Goetech Service Corp Dallas Tex since '45; partner Beers and Heroy Dallas since '46. Chmn Comm on Geophys Sci Research and Development Board The National Military Establishment since '46; dir W & L E Gurley Troy, NY '48. b'48. Geol Soc Am(F)—Am Geog Soc(F)—Am Acad Arts Sci(F)—Am Assn Petroleum Geol—AAAS—Soc Exploration Geophysicists—Acoustical Soc Am—Am Inst Mining Metall Engrs—Inst

Radio Engrs—Am Geophys Union—Seismol Soc Am—Franklin Inst. 282 River St., Troy, N.Y.ⓒ

10 BEESON, Malcolm Alfred. Education; Agronomy. b'79. BSc '00 (Ala Poly Auburn); student '01-03 (Johns Hopkins); DSc hon '10 (Meridian Miss Coll); LLD '33 (Oklahoma City U). Prof agronomy and agronomist Okla Agrl and Mech Coll '14-21, dean agrl div and dean sch agr '21-23, also dir Experiment Sta '23; pres Central State Tchrs Coll Edmond Okla '31-35; field rep George Peabody Coll Tchrs Nashville '35-37. AAAS(F)—Kappa Delta Pi—Sigma Tau Delta. H: 311 S Duck St., Stillwater, Okla.ⓒ

11 BEETLE, Alan Ackerman. Grasses; Plant distribution; Scirpus. b'13. AB '36 (Dartmouth Coll); '36-37 (Harvard Coll); MA '38 (U Wyo); PhD '41 (U Calif). Collector University of California second botanical expedition to the Andes '38-39. Author articles in field. Faculty, asso prof range management U Wyo since '46. Bot Soc Am—Calif Bot Soc—Colo-Wyo Acad Sci—British Grassland Soc—Am Soc Range Managers—Am Soc Plant Taxonomists—Am Soc Agron—Grassland Research Foundation—Sigma Xi. Department of Range Management, University of Wyoming, Laramie, Wyo.

12 BEGG, John Murray. International information and radio; Documentary films. b'03. AB '24 (Harvard Coll); BA '25 (Magdalen Coll Oxford U); '25-26 (Harvard Law Sch). Department of State representative Office of Inter-American Affairs Radio Conference Lima Peru '43; expert consultant US Delegation London Preparatory Commission United Nations Educational, Scientific and Cultural Organization '46; vice-chairman US Delegation to International High Frequency Broadcasting Conference Atlantic City '47. With Dept State since '41; spl asst to dir since '48. Am Fgn Service Assn. Department of State, Washington 25.

13 BEGGS, Thomas Montague. Heraldic art; Medieval tapestry and woodcarving; Portraiture (purposes); Artistic relations (resident artists and colleges, art and science). b'99. BFA '24 (Yale); 20-21 (Art Students League NY); student (Ecole Americane des Beaux Arts Fontainebleau); Carnegie scholar '28-29 (Harvard). Author: The Amazon and the Gothic Weaver '29; Weather in Art '46 and others. Instr '26-30, asst prof '30-36, asso prof '36-44, prof '44-47 art dept Pomona Coll; dir Nat Collection Fine Arts Smithsonian Inst since '48. Coll Art Assn—Am Fed Arts—Assn Am Mus—Western Coll Art Assn. John W Alexander medal, Ludwig Nissen medal, silver and bronze medals mural paintings Beaux Arts Inst Design. National Collection of Fine Arts, Smithsonian Institution, Washington 25.ⓒ

14 BEHAR, M(anoel) F(elix de Mayo). Instrumentation (Instrumentology); Industrial physics; Measurement and control. b'89. Ed France, Switzerland and Eng; grad '09 (Pratt Inst). Formulator of science of instrumentation; founder and gen dir Instrumentation Manual Project. Author: Handbook of Measurement and Control '48; Fundamentals of Instrumentation '32; Temperature and Humidity Measurement and Control '32; Pressure and Vacuum Measurement and Control '31, and others; also articles in field. Tech and sci writer, lecturer, cons engr since '20; vp, ed The Instruments Pub Co since '33. AAAS—Am Assn Physics Teachers—

AIEE—Am Phys Soc—Am Soc Metals—ASME—Natl Soc Profl Engrs—Assn Pittsburgh Scientists—Fedn Am Scientists—Inst Aero Sci—Pittsburgh Phys Soc—Instrument Soc Am—Franklin Inst. 245 Melwood St., Pittsburgh 13.

15 BEHLEN, Walter Dietrich. Buildings (Frameless sheet metal). b'05. Ed pub schs. Developed single shell type of structural strength in sheet metal buildings. Pres Behlen Mfg Co since '36. Behlen Manufacturing Co., Columbus, Neb.

16 BEHRENDT, Lee A. Clay-graphite and carbon-bonded crucibles; High temperature refractories. b'96. Student '14-17 (U Ill). Author articles in field. Lab asst Midland Terra Cotta Co '11, ceramics dept '14-17, '20-21, asst chem '18-20; mfr porcelain articles '21; mining chem Combined Terra Cotta Ind '20-23; asst supt Midland Terra Cotta Co '22-25; asst dir tech control Northwestern Terra Cotta Co Chicago '25-26; supt Chicago Crucible Co '26-30; gen supt, vp and plant mgr Chicago-Naugatuck Crucible Co, now Am Crucible Co '30-41; dir crucible and refractories div Joseph Dixon Crucible Co Jersey City '41-48, vp since '48. Crucible Mfrs Assn (pres). Wayne and Monmouth Sts., Jersey City.

17 BEHRENS, Otto Karl. Biosynthesis of penicillin; Virus; Enzymes; Proteins; Amino acids; Biochemistry. b'11. AB '32 (DePauw U); MA '33—PhD '35 (U Ill). Discovered compounds which stimulated yield of penicillin by acting as precursors; discovered method of inducing mold to make new penicillin. Now holds 17 patents in field. Author articles in field. Research chem Lilly Research Labs Indianapolis since '40. Am Chem Soc—AAAS—Ind Acad Sci—NY Acad Sci—Sigma Xi—Phi Kappa Phi—Phi Beta Kappa. Lalor Found fellow '39-40. Lilly Research Laboratories, 740 S. Alabama St., Indianapolis 6.†

18 BEHRMAN, A. Sidney. Water treatment; Ion exchange; Siliceous gels. b'92. BS '14 (U Ky). Holder patents in fields of water treatment, ion exchange, siliceous gels and gel catalysts. Author: Philippine Water Supplies '18; also articles in field. Chem cons since '47. Capt San Corps US Army '17-19, lt col '42-44. Am Chem Soc—Am Water Works Assn—AAAS. Voted by poll Chicago Sect Am Chem Soc as one of ten ablest chem in US in water sewage and sanitation '47. 9 S. Clinton St., Chicago 6.

19 BEICHNER, Paul Edward. Literature (Middle English, Peter Riga, Chaucer). b'12. AB '35—MA '41 (U Notre Dame); '35-39 (Holy Cross Coll, Washington); PhD '44—research fellow '44-45 (Yale). Discovered that Old French verse Bible of Mace de la Charite is a free translation of Latin Aurora of Peter Riga. Author articles in field. Asst head dept Eng U Notre Dame since '47. Mediaeval Acad Am—Mod Lang Assn Am. Department of English, University of Notre Dame, Notre Dame, Ind.†

20 BEIER, Delton C. Psychology (Clinical tests, test construction, selection procedures, abnormal). b'15. BA '38—MA '39 (Wis U); PhD '43 (La State U). Author articles in field. Asso prof and dir psych clinic Ind U since '45. AAAS—Am Assn Mental Deficiency(F)—Am Psych Assn(F)—Midwestern Psych Assn—Southern Soc Phil and Psych—Ind Acad Sci—Ind Assn Clinical and Applied Psychol—Sigma Xi—Psi Chi. Psychological Clinic, Indiana University, Bloomington, Ind.†

21 BEIJ, K(arl) Hilding. Hydraulics, BS '14 (Trinity Coll). Editor: Bibliography of Hydrology for the United States '35-36, '37, '38, '40; also articles in field. Research asso Copper and Brass Research Assn '25-29; asst engr Nat Bur Standards '20-25; Engr and physicist, asst chief Nat Hydraulic Lab Nat Bur Standards since '30. Philos Soc Wash—Wash Soc Engrs—Wash Acad Sci—Am Meteorol Soc—Am Geophys Union (gen sec since '47)—Internat Assn Hydraulic Structures Research. National Bureau of Standards, Washington 25.

22 BEILHARZ, Edwin Alanson. Medieval and contemporary history. b'07. AB '31 (U Creighton); MA '34—seminars in field '33-34 (U Neb); seminars in field '34-35 '35-36 (U Calif). Research on life of Fray Juan de Zumarraga, first Bishop and Archbishop of Mexico; 11th century German chronicles; medieval French metrical romances; 13th century Flanders, medieval art and architecture and pre-Columbian Mexico. Author articles in field. Instr hist U Santa Clara '36-41, chmn dept hist since '41, asso prof since '48. AHA—Am Catholic Hist Assn. University of Santa Clara, Santa Clara, Calif.

23 BEISHLAG, George Albert. Map evaluation and cataloging. b'07. AB '30 (Wayne U); MA '37 (Clark U). Developed and installed new map cataloging system for Office Strategic Services which was adopted by United States Department State '45; helped develop State Department methods of evaluating maps. Author, reviewer of map evaluations for official govt circulation only, undistributed catalog manual '44. Chief map analysis unit map div OSS '44; ed and reviewing officer Map Div US Dept State since '45. Assn Am Geog—Am Geog Soc—Inter-Am Soc Anthrop and Geog. H: 2044 Ft. Davis St. S.E., Washington 20.

24 BEISLER, Walter H(erman). Lithographic inks and coatings; Chemical products of Florida; Azo and vat dyes. b'96. BS '18—MS '19 (Rutgers); MS—DSc '22 (Princeton). Holds US patents (with Williamson) on manufacture of varnish from tung oil and crude turpentine gum in one operation, manufacture of ester gum from crude turpentine gum and glycerine in one operation; individual patent on prevention of checking of tung oil films. Author articles in field. Head prof chem engring U Fla since '39. Am Inst Chem Engrs (asso)—Am Chem Soc (sec-treas Fla Sect '26-27, chmn '38)—Am Soc Engring Edn—Fla Engring Soc (F, sec '43-46, dir since '48, pres '51-52)—Phi Kappa Phi—Sigma Tau. College of Engineering, University of Florida, Gainesville, Fla.

25 BEITLER, Samuel Reid. Hydraulic machinery; Flow measurement and nozzles; Fluid measurement. b'99. BME '20—ME '32 (Ohio State U). Co-author: Hydraulic Machinery '42, '47; also articles in field. Patents on apparatus for measuring pulsating fluid flows, for compensating gas meter readings. With Ohio State U since '21, prof hydraulic engring since '44. Cons engr Bailey Meter Co since '31; gen cons practice in flow measurement since '28, on hydraulic machinery since '35; research supervisor Ohio State U Research Found since '41. ASME (vp '46-47)—Am Soc Eng Edn—Nat Assn Power Engrs (hon)—Tau Beta Pi—Sigma Xi. Mechanical Engineering Department, Ohio State University, Columbus 10, O.†

26 BEITO, Edwin Arne. Celestial navigation; Astronomical instruments.

b'91. AB '14 (St Olaf Coll); MA '28 (U Minn); '29-31 (Columbia). Research to determine shape of apparent celestial sphere in estimating altitudes of stars and planes, designed surveying and astronomical instruments including chronoastrolabe or sky dial, combination surveying instrument, sextant, angle mirror, sun dial, level, and link chain. Author: Supplement to Navigation and Nautical Astronomy (9th edit) '50. Revised: Navigation and Nautical Astronomy (10th edit) '51. Prof nav Civilian Pilot Training Program U Wichita '38-41; instr and head nav dept Midshipmen Sch Northwestern U '41-42; nav officer US Nav Personnel '43-45; proctor Nav Dept Nav Acad since '46. Am Astron Soc—Kan Astron Soc (past pres). US Naval Academy, Annapolis, Md.

10 BEKKEDAHL, Norman. Chemistry of rubber. b'03. BS '25 (U Minn); MS '29 (Geo Washington U); PhD '31 (American U). Research on physical and chemical properties natural and synthetic rubber, thermodynamics of rubber; established and directed rubber research and testing laboratory for Brazilian Government '42-45. Author articles in field. Rubber sect Nat Bur Standards Washington since '31, asst chief rubber sect since '48. Am Chem Soc (councilor '45-49, membership com '47-49)—Chem Soc Washington (treas '38, '39, sec '40, '41, pres '42)—AAAS—Washington Acad Sci—Am Phys Soc—Philos Soc Washington—Washington Rubber Group (sec-treas '48, '49). National Bureau of Standards, Washington 25.†

11 BELCHETZ, Arnold. Petroleum refining. b'04. BSc '22—MSc '24 (U South Africa); PhD '28 (Cambridge U Eng). Research and development on catalytic cracking, hydroforming, polymerization, gasoline treating, hydrogenation, dehydrogenation, and alkylation. Holds 12 patents in field. Chief tech oil refineries E Chicago Ind and Arkansas City Kan Royal Dutch Shell Group '29-38, dept head in charge isooctane plants; head new processes dept M W Kellogg Co '38-43 and '46-48; pvt cons chem and petroleum industries since '48. ACS—AICE—Am Inst Chem—APS—AAAS—Soc Chem Ind—Am Tech Soc. Professional engr NY, NJ, Del. 125 Woodbine Av., Larchmont, N.Y.

12 BELKENGREN, Richard Oliver. Processing and canning chemistry of vegetables and tropical fruits. b'13. Student '31-32 (Duluth Jr Coll); BS '39—PhD '41 (U Minn). Research on chemistry and technology of canned peas and canned sweet corn, nutritional value of these two products, changes in nutritional values upon heat processing; breeding sweet corn with increased nutritional quality, determining corn maturity by means of a refractometer; research on pineapple products, quality factors in pineapple, homogenization of pineapple juice; research on papaya products and Macadamia nuts. Biochem Armour Research Found '41-42; chief chem Minn Valley Canning Co '42-47; head food research sect Hawaiian Pineapple Co Honolulu '47-49; asso prof bot and plant path dept Ore State Coll since '49. Gamma Sigma Delta—Phi Lambda Upsilon—Sigma Xi. Oregon State College, Corvallis, Ore.

13 BELKIN, John N(icholas). Mosquitoes; Biting flies; Ticks and disease. b'13. Student '31-33 (Harvard Coll); BS '36 (N Y State Coll Agr); PhD '46 (Cornell). Author: A Laboratory Manual for Invertebrate Biology '49. Co-author: (with F H Wilson) A Laboratory Manual for Vertebrate Biology '48. Jr entomologist Tenn Valley Authority '42; asso prof biol Associated Colleges Upper NY '46-48; asst prof and asst entomol U Calif since '49. San Corps US Army '42-45. AAAS—Am Soc Profl Biol—Entomol Soc Am—Am Soc Parasitol—Am Soc Zool—Entomol Soc Washington—Sigma Xi—Phi Kappa Phi. Division of Entomology, College of Agriculture, University of California, Los Angeles 24.

14 BELKNAP, Ralph L. Greenland (Geology). b'99. BS '23—MA '24—ScD '29 (U Mich); '41-42 (U Chicago). Exploration in Greenland as geologist summers '26, '27, '28; director Michigan Pan-American Airways Greenland Expedition '32-33. Associate professor geol and meteorol U Mich since '36. Am Geol Soc—Am Assn Petroleum Geol—Am Meteorol Soc—Am Geophys Union — AAAS — Arctic Inst NA — British Glacier Soc. University of Michigan, Department of Geology, Ann Arbor.

15 BELL, Alfred H(annam). Petroleum geology. b'95. BA '17 (U Toronto); PhD '26 (U Chicago). Paper of '31 entitled Relation of Geology to the Petroleum Industry in Illinois, forecast major discoveries made in Illinois basin beginning in '37. Author articles in field. Asso geol Ill State Geol Survey '26-27, geol '27-29, geol and head oil and gas div since '30. AAAS(F) — AIME — AAPG — GSA — Am Geophys Union—Ill Acad Sci—Ill Geol Soc—Sigma Xi. State Geological Survey, Urbana, Ill.†

16 BELL, Bernard Iddings. Education administration; Religious education. b'86. AB '07 (U Chicago); STB '12—DD '21 (Western Theol Sem Chicago); STD '23 (U of South); LittD '29 (Columbia); LLD '31 (Colo Coll); PedD '33 (U State of NY); LHD '50 (Coe Coll). Author: Common Sense in Education '28; Preface to Religion '35; A Catholic Looks at His World '36; Understanding Religion '41; Crisis in Education '49. Editor: The St. James Lessons in Religion '40-45. Canon of Cathedral of SS Peter and Paul Chicago; cons to Bishop of Chicago on edn since '46; gen cons on religion and edn, pastor of Episcopalians U Chicago since '48. Phi Beta Kappa. H: 1321 E 56th St., Chgo 37.

17 BELL, Frank Coffman. Aircraft navigation; Missile guidance. b'11. AB '33 (Harvard). Invented system of automatic celestial-inertial navigation for aircraft, developed differential geometric theory of space navigation by line-of-sight, developed geometric theory of position by star lines and other directions; member and technical consultant of Institute of Navigation and panel on long-range guidance and committee on guided missiles, Research and Development Board. With Northrop Aircraft Inc '46-50; prof mem tech staff guided missile dept Hughes Aircraft Co since '50. Guided Missile Department, Research and Development Laboratories, Hughes Aircraft Co., Florence and Teale Sts., Culver City, Calif.

18 BELL, James Washington. Money and banking (Policies and practice); Business cycles; Public and international finance. b'90. BA '12—MA '13 (U Colo); teaching fellow—PhD '18 (Harvard). Author: A Guide to the Study of Money and Banking; Taxation of Railways in New England; also articles in field. Prof money and banking Northwestern U since '29, dir grad div sch commerce '32-'36, head dept finance '26-'41, acting dean grad sch '37-41, chmn dept econ since '42.

Royal Econ Soc(F)—Am Econ Assn (sec-treas, ed proc since '36)—Beta Gamma Sigma—Econ Nat Com on Monetary Policy. Awarded Norlin Achievement medal U Colo '38. 1745 Chicago Av., Evanston, Ill.

19 BELL, Kenneth Eldon. Leather technology; Fibrous material drying. b'94. SB '17—research asso '19-20 (Mass Inst Tech). Research and development on tanning and finishing upper and sole leathers; development and design of driers for all types leather. Author articles in field. Vice-pres, tech dir A C Lawrence Leather Co. Am Chem Soc—AICE—Am Leather Chem Assn. A.C. Lawrence Leather Co., Peabody, Mass.

20 BELL, Robert Smith. Grass (Turf); Soil conservation. b'11. BS '34—PhD '39—NY Florist Club fellow, Bancroft fellow '35-38 (Cornell U). Research in influence of fertilizers on accumulation of roots from closely clipped bent grasses and on quality of turf, control of wind erosion by establishment of turf under airport conditions, turf management in Rhode Island, killing weed seed in the grass seed bed by use of fertilizers and chemicals; turf consultant to Quonset Naval Air Station during World War II. Author articles in field. Asst prof agron RI State Coll since '43. Am Soc Agron—Soil Sci Soc—Soil Conservation Soc Am. University of Rhode Island, Kingston, R.I.

21 BELL, Roscoe E(arnest). Phosphate fertilizer industry; Land management (public). b'05. BS '27—MS '30 (State Coll Wash); grad work (U Idaho, U Calif). Author articles in field. Coordinator western phosphate program US Dept Interior since '47, now asso dir Bur Land Managment. Sigma Xi. Phi Sigma. Bureau of Land Management, Interior Building, Washington 25.†

22 BELL, Walter Andrew. Paleobotany. b'89. BSc '11 (Queens U); PhD (Yale). Author articles in field. Asst to chief paleontol sect Geol Survey of Can '20-38, chief since '38. Can Inst Mining and Metall—Royal Soc Can(F) Medal Profl Inst Civil Service Can '44, Internat Nickel Co CIMM '45. Geological Survey of Canada, Ottawa, Ontario, Can.†

23 BELL, Whitfield Jenks, Jr. Medical history. b'14. AB '35 (Dickinson Coll); AM '38—PhD '47 (Penn U). Research for bibliography of American history for American Association of Medical History since '41; also research in early American science. Author: Suggestions for Research in the Local History of Medicine in the United States '45; also articles in field. Instr hist '37, '38-39, '41-43, professor hist Dickinson Coll since '50. AHA—Am Assn Med Hist (com on Bibliography Am Med Hist). Dickinson College, Carlisle, Penn.†

24 BELLAMY, Ben Charles. Engineering. b'87. BS '10 (U Wyo). Sr partner Bellamy & Sons engineers since '36. Am Math Soc—Math Assn Am—Am Phys Soc—Am Chem Soc—Am Soc Photogrametry—Congress Mapping and Surveying—AAAS—AIM ME—AIEE—Nat Soc Profl Engrs. Box 37 Lamont, Wyo.

25 BELLAMY, John Cary. Instrumentation; Meteorological and navigation techniques. b'15. BS '36 (U Wyo); PhM '38 (U Wis ; PhD '46 (U Chicago). Developed special surveying procedures and mapping techniques, research in artificial radioactivity for commercial application, developed concepts of use of pressure-altitude and altimeter corrections in meteorology, conceived and tested drift determinations with pressure and radio altimeters in overwater flights, conception design and direction development of instrumentation with emphasis on aircraft navigation and meteorological instruments and automatic data processing equipment. Author articles in field. Partner Bellamy & Sons Engrs Wyo '38-42; asst prof U Chicago '43-47; spl cons US AAF '43-45; asso dir Cook Research Labs Chicago since '47. Internat Meteorol Orgn—Am Meteorol Soc—Inst Navigation—Wyo Engring Soc. Received Losey award Inst Aero Soc '44, Thurlow award Inst Navigation '46. Cook Research Laboratories, 1457 Diversey Parkway, Chicago 14. H: 431 June Terrace, Barrington, Ill.

10 BELLINGER, Frederick. Fruit juice (High pressure filtration); Cellulose; Propellants, chemical; Explosives; Chemical warfare; Chemical plant design; Food preservation (Freezing process). b'04. BS '26 (Ga Sch Tech); MS '35 (Emory U); Dr Engring '40 (Yale). Research sweet potato starch plant design, preservation of foods by freezing, chemical propellants and experimental explosives, cellulosic plastics; research dir on chemical propellants. Holds patents on container closures, production of filaments. Author articles in field. Chem engr development dept R & H Chem Co Perth Amboy NJ '28-32; chief plants design dept Army Chem Center Md '40-41; chief chem engr Huntsville Arsenal Ala '41-43, chief FRED Project, chm propellant research since '45; prof chem engring and research project dir Ga Inst Tech Atlanta since '45. Chem engr US Army '40-45. Am Inst Chem Engrs—Nat Soc Profl Engrs—Am Chem Soc—Ga Engring Soc—Sigma Xi—Tau Beta Pi—Alpha Chi Sigma—Armed Forces Chem Assn. School of Chemical Engineering, Georgia Institute of Technology, Atlanta.

11 BELLQUIST, Eric Cyril. Scandinavia; Comparative government. b'04. AB '27—MA '28—PhD '32 (U Calif). Author: Some Aspects of the Recent Foreign Policy of Sweden '29; also articles in field. Instr polit sci U Calif since '36; principal regional specialist area chief for Scandinavia and regional dir western Europe OWI '43-45; chief area div I Dept State '45-47; public affairs officer United States Embassy Stockholm since '49. Am Political Science Assn—Am Acad Polit Social Sci—Am Soc Internat Law —Am Soc Pub Adminstrn—Baltic Inst —Am-Scandinavian Found—Augustana Inst Swedish Culture. Knight Order of Vasa, First Class Sweden '41; King Christian X's Medal of Liberation Denmark '46. U.S. Embassy, Stockholm, Sweden.

12 BELLROSE, Frank Clifford, Jr. Wildlife research; Ornithology. b'16. BS '38 (U Ill). Research primarily on waterfowl and marsh ecology, secondarily on muskrats. Author articles: Quail and Pheasant Studies in an Orchard County '40; Duck Food Plants of the Illinois River Valley '41; Relative Values of Drained and Undrained Bottomland in Illinois '45; Analysis of Methods Used in Determining Game Kill '47. Asso game tech Ill Natural Hist Survey since '38. Wildlife Soc—Am Ornithol Union— Wilson Ornithol Club—Am Soc Mammalogists. Illinois Natural History Survey, Natural Resources Building, Urbana, Ill.

13 BELOCK, Harry David. Fire control systems; Computers; Automatic tracking radar. b'08. Student (Pratt

Inst). Engaged in design and development of equipment such as servo controls, automatic control instruments, aircraft frequency shifting devices, special recording systems and photographic systems for expeditions and major motion picture laboratories fifteen years; design and development automatic gun fire control equipment such as computers, servos, automatic tracking radar, latest type fire control systems; designed and developed Reeves Electronic Analog Computer being used throughout country by all major aircraft companies for stability control analysis. Holder patents in field. Engr and designer Columbia Pictures Studios '31-32; engr Paramount Motion Picture Studios NY '32-35; design engr CBS '35-37; pres, chief engr Am Teletimer Corp NY '37-41; sr engr, head data control sect Camp Evans Signal Lab Belmar NJ '41-44; exec vp Reeves Instrument Corp since '44. ASME—AIEE—Soc Radio Engrs —Soc Motion Picture Engrs—Am Ordnance Assn—Armed Forces Communications Assn—Nat Soc Prof Engrs. Reeves Instrument Corporation, 215 E. 91 St., NYC 28. H: 78-29 221 St., Bayside, N.Y.

14 BELTER, Paul A. Oils (Vegetable extraction); Soybean (Oils). b'20. Student '38-40 (Bradley U Peoria Ill); BS (Chem engring) '42 (U Ill). Research on soybean protein production, soybean oil extraction. Holds patents in field, including process and equipment for recovery oil and by-products from alcoholic solutions oleaginous materials. Co-author articles: (with A C Beckel and A K Smith) Laboratory Study of Continuous Vegetable Oil Extraction '46; (with A C Beckel and A K Smith) Solvent Effects on the Products of Soybean Oil Production '48; (with A C Beckel and A K Smith) The Nodistillation Alcohol Extraction Process for Soybean oil '48. Chem engr USDA Northern Regional Research Lab Peoria Ill '42-49, chem since '49. Northern Regional Research Laboratory, 825 N. University St., Peoria 5, Ill. H: 804 Park Av., Pekin, Ill.

15 BELZER, Jack. Fundamental astronomy; Punch card methods in science. b'10. BEE (Cooper Union); grad work (Catholic U). Expert in field of scientific computations by punch card methods; devised many new methods of obtaining solutions to scientific problems; helped in preparation of material for publications of American Air Almanac, American Nautical Almanac and American Ephemeris. General astron USN Observatory '37-39, in charge punch card methods '39-45; in charge Scientific Computing Lab Ohio State University '47-51; in charge Scientific Computing Lab Battelle Memorial Institute since '52. Am Astron Soc. Battelle Memorial Institute, 505 King Av., Columbus 1, O.†

16 BEMIS, Alan Cogswell. Meteorology (Radar, airborne instruments, fog, cloud, precipitation, infrared radiation); Housing and building construction (Applied modular design); Guided missiles. b'06. Student '19-24 (Milton Acad); AB '28 (Harvard); MS '30 (Mass Inst Tech). Research asso meteorol MIT since '38; pres Housing Co, dir Bemis Industries Inc; dir Boott Mills Inc, chmn exec bd Modular Service Assn. Am Meteorol Soc— American Phys Soc—AAAS—Sigma Xi. Massachusetts Institute of Technology, Cambridge Mass.

17 BEMIS, Edwin Arnold, Jr. Radiological physics. b'19. BA '41—'42-44 and '46-47 (U Colo). Measurement of nuclear radiations; estimates of bio-

logical hazards of externally and internally deposited radioactive materials; design and construction of instruments for measurement, and efficiency tests on existing instruments; participant Nevada and Eniwetok atomic bomb tests '51; technical advisor on training interim civilian defense monitoring teams Santa Fe office Atomic Energy Commission. Contributor: Effects of Atomic Weapons. Research asst advancing to staff mem biophysics sect Health Div Los Alamos Sci Lab since '47. Am Inst Physics— Am Assn Physics Teachers—Pi Mu Epsilon—Sigma Pi Sigma. Los Alamos Scientific Laboratory, P.O. Box 1663, Los Alamos, N.M.

18 BENBROOK, Charles H. Chemistry (Diazotype, diazo, dyeing theory). b'05. BS '29 (Neb U); MS '33 (Colo U). Research on diazo compounds, reactions, kinetics and mechanism of decomposition, exhaust and diffusion rates into cellulosic materials of direct dyes, vat and sulfur colors, chemistry and physics of Ozalid, dry-developing diazo-type material. Holds patent for Dyeometer. Author articles in field. Research chem, Gen Aniline and Film Corp '43-49, now mgr research and development Ozalid div. Ozalid Division, General Aniline and Film Corporation, Johnson City, N.Y.†

19 BENCOWITZ, Isaac. Sulphur chemistry; Book restitution (War areas). b'96. BA '21—vis PhD '26 (U Chicago); MA—PhD '24 (Columbia); Nat Research fellow '24-26 (NYU). Holds patents in sulphur recovery, sulphur burners and grinder, road material, sulphur insecticides, sulphur metering. Author articles in field. Research chem and chem engr Texas Gulf Sulphur Co since '27. Capt mil govt '43-47, collected, classified, and restored millions of books in many languages looted from many countries. Am Chem Soc—AICE—NY Acad Sci —Mil Govt Assn—Phi Beta Kappa— Sigma Xi. Newgulf, Tex.

20 BENDA, Wladyslaw Theodor. Masks. Student (Sch Tech and Acad Art, Cracow), art schs Vienna, San Francisco, NY. Creator of new type of masks used on stage under name Benda masks. Author: Masks '45; also articles in field. Illustrator and painter; lectures on masks, gives stage demonstrations of his masks. Soc Illustrators. 2 W. 67th St., NYC 23.

21 BENDER, Edward Krug. Vegetable crops; 2, 4-D weed killer. b'19. BS (Penn State Coll); MS (U Md). Research and writing on broccal culture in Maryland, spinach growing, preparation of vegetables for exhibit. Specialist in vegetable crops, 2, 4-D weed killer, U Md since '46. Am Soc Hort. Horticulture Department, University of Maryland, College Park, Md. H: 403 Clayborne Av., Takoma Park, Md.

22 BENDER, Howard Leonard. Plastics; Resins (Phenolic). b'93. Research and patents on polymeric synthetic resins of phenolic type. Asst research dir Bakelite Co. 7 Carteret St., Bloomfield, N.J.

23 BENDER, James F(rederick). Psychology; Training (Executive, sales). b'05 BS '28—PhD '39 (Columbia). Author: The Technique of Executives Leadership '50; Your Way to Popularity and Personal Power '50; How to Sleep; Personality Structure of Stuttering; N.B.C. Handbook of Pronunciation; How to Talk Well; Salesman's Mispronunciations. Adjunct prof psychol Brooklyn Polytech Inst '28-40; chmn dept speech dir Queens Speech and Hearing Center, Queens Coll. '37-

44; dir Nat Inst for Human Relations since '44; cons Sales Tng Corp '49. AAAS(F)—Am Speech and Hearing Assn (F)—Am Speech Correction Assn—NY State Assn Applied Psychology (exec com '42-44)—NY Soc Clin Psychologists—nat Vocational Guidance Assn. 545 Fifth Av., NYC 17.†☉

10 BENDER, Wesley Charles. Mercantile credits; Marketing analysis. b'08. AB '29 (Cornell U); MA '31 (U Pittsburgh); student (Northwestern U, Columbia). Editor: The Credo, national credit monthly. With U Notre Dame since '31, now prof marketing, head dept marketing since '46; instr Am Inst Banking since '46; mgr Northern Ind Adjustment Bur since '45. Am Econ Assn—Am Marketing Assn—Nat Bur Econ Research (asso)—Ind Acad Social Sci (vp '40-41, pres '41-42)—Nat Assn Credit Men (exec sec St Joseph Valley Chap). University of Notre Dame, Notre Dame, Ind.

11 BENDER, William, Jr. American ballads and folk songs. b'16. Student '34-35 (Wesleyan U); BA '47 (U Colo). Attended Ballad Conference University of Colorado '47; Western Folklore Conference University of Denver '48 participating in each; has recorded 36 traditional western ballads on commercial platters; folksong programs for US State Department Voice of America '49. Author: Trail Song, Univ of Colo radio series on origin traditional western ballads. Radio dept U Colo since '47-49; Folksinger NBC-KOA '36-40, KOB '45-46; publicist since '46. University of Michigan, Ann Arbor.†

12 BENEDETTI-PICHLER, Anton A(lexander). Microchemistry; Chemical analysis. b'94. DSc '22 (Technische Hochschule Graz Austria). Author: Introduction to the Microtechnique of Inorganic Analysis '42; also articles in field. With Queens Coll NY since '40; asso prof chem since '47; cons microanalysis and analytical chemistry. Am Chem Soc (chairman microchem sect '36)—Metro Microchem Soc NY (pres '48-49)—Am Soc Testing Materials. Received the Pregl prize in microchem Acad Sci Vienna '33. Chemistry Department, Queens College, Flushing, N.Y.†

13 BENEDICT, Manson. Thermodynamics; Diffusion; Extractive distillation; Equations of state. b'07. MS '32—PhD '35 (MIT); BChem '28 (Cornell U). Author articles in field. In charge process design gaseous diffusion plant for U-235 Kellex Corp '43-'46; dir process development Hydrocarbon Research Inc since '46; engring adv com Brookhaven Nat Lab, reactor safeguard com US Atomic Energy Commission. American Chemical Soc—Sigma Xi. Walker award Am Inst Chem Engrs; Nat Research fellow '35-36. Hydrocarbon Research Inc., 115 Broadway, NYC 6. H: 465 Topping Rd., Westfield, N.J.

14 BENEDICT, Paul Charles. Fluvial sediments; Hydrology. b'06. BS '29—CE '44 (U Colo). Research on methods used in measurement and analysis of sediment loads in streams, including design and development of sediment sampling equipment and methods and equipment for determination of sedimentation diameters of fluvial sediments; investigations of fluvial sediments and mineral quality of waters with Missouri River Basin Departmental Program. Author: Preliminary Field Tests of the United States Sediment-Sampling Equipment in the Colorado River Basin '44; A Study of the Errors Resulting from the Use of Turbidity in Computing the Suspended Sediment Discharge of Iowa Streams '45; Determination of the Suspended Sediment Discharge of Streams '48. Co-author: Discharge and Sediment Loads in the Boise River Drainage Basin, Idaho '39-40; Comparative Field Tests on Suspended Sediment Samplers '44. Hydraulic engr US Geol Survey Boise Ida '30-40, rep at U Iowa Hydraulic Lab '41-45, dist engr since '45. ASCE—Am Geophys Union—Ia Acad Sci—Am Water Works Assn—Sigma Xi. 510 Rudge & Guenzel Building, Lincoln 8, Neb.

15 BENEDICT, Ralph C. Ferns; History of science; Science education. b'83. PhB '06 (Syracuse U); PhD '11 (Columbia). Founder, editor American Fern Journal since '10. Prof biol Brooklyn Coll since '31; resident investigator Brooklyn Bot Garden since '15. AAAS(F)—Am Fern Soc—Hist Sci Soc—Am Biol Teachers Assn—NY Assn. Biol. Teachers. 1819 Dorchester Rd., Bklyn 26.

16 BENIS, Anthony Augustus. Antique European clocks and watches; Internat banking and economics. b'01 BA '19 (Coll Neuchatel, Switzerland); '19-20 (U Geneva); MA '23 (Sch Polit Sci, Cracow Poland); LLD '24 (U Cracow). Special horological research in museums Cracow, Vienna, Paris, Berlin, Augsburg, Nuremberg, London, Warsaw. Author articles in field. With Banca Commerciale Italiano '24-39, in various capacities; pres Harmonia Records Corp '41-50 financial cons various firms. National Assn Watch and Clock Collectors (council, mus and exhbn commn, head spl com on market antique clocks). Hon horological advisor to Polish Nat Museums '30-39. 411 Forest Av., Rye, N.Y.†

17 BENJAMIN, Edward B(ernard). b'97. Economic clichés. AB '18 (Harvard). Author: The Larger Liberalism '18. Author articles: Programme for Plenty '48; Economic Cliché and Economic Nonsense '43. Pres Bay Chemical Co '38-47, Myles Salt Co '40-47; pres Starmount Co, Benjamin Minerals Co. 1050 Constance St., New Orleans.

18 BENJAMIN, Mary Avezzana. Autographs. b'05. BA '25 (Barnard Coll). Author: Autographs: A Key to Collecting '46; also articles in field. Owner and dir Walter R Benjamin Autographs since '43; publisher ed The Collector, since '43. Nat Soc Autograph Collectors. 18 E 77th St., NYC 21.

19 BENNE, Kenneth Dean. Group development. b'08. BS '30 (Kan State Coll); MA '36 (U Mich); PhD '41 (Columbia). Assisted in founding National Training Laboratory in Group Development '47; study of methodological and ethical bases of group training and group decision in relation to social action; investigation process of change in human relations at institutional level, especially the school. Author article: Democratic Ethics and Human Engineering '49; Human Relations in Curriculum Change '49; Group Dynamics and Social Action '50. Asso Social and Philos Found Edn Teachers Coll Columbia U '38-41, asso prof edn Teachers Coll '46-48; asst prof edn U Ill '41-46, prof since '48; research asso Horace Mann-Lincoln Inst Sch Expt '46-48; ed bd Educational Theory, and Progressive Education. Am Philos Assn—Philos Edn Soc (pres '50-51)—Soc Psychol Study Social Issues—Phi Delta Kappa—Kappa Delta Pi. Kilpatrick award for outstanding contbn to Am Philos Edn '43. University of Illinois, Urbana, Ill.☉

20 BENNETT, Alva Herschel. Applied optics. b'95. BA '18 (O State U); MA '26 (George Washington U); '19-29 (Ednl Courses Nat Bur Standards). Research on optical glass and optical instruments, aberrations of optical systems, optical instrument and lens design, microscopic apparatus and techniques; holder numerous patents in field of optical instruments and their applications. Author: Binocular Instruments; Aberrations of Long Focus Anastigmatic Photographic Objectives. Lab asst Nat Bur Standards '18-20, asst physicist '20-22, asso physicist '22-29; chief physicist and asst sci dir Spencer Lens Co Buffalo '29-37; dir research Am Optical Co sci instrument div since '37. Optical Soc Am (dir at large)—Am Ceramic Soc—Am Phys Soc—Inst Phys—Sigma Xi. AAAS. American Optical Co., Buffalo, N.Y.

21 BENNETT, Archibald Synica. Marketing research, Psychology of selling; Sampling. b'77. BS '02 (Lawrence Coll); grad student (U Wis, Columbia). Conducted publicity for Oystermen's Committee of diphtheria epidemic '25; completed first broad survey of frozen food industry for promotion '30-31; conducted first inventory survey of a national pool of 2000 part-time research interviewers and supervisors entitled Researching Researchers part II '48; introduced many new methods of securing accurate reports from field interviewers and supervisors, including checks and devices; methods of eliminating and checking fabrication of reports and of validating reports; conducted random precision research survey on a national scale and depth interviewing of top executives as well as consumers on a national scale; made survey of reasons for success or failure of 91 national and regional trade associations; analyzed and compared various effects of written or spoken word vs use of eye in controlling reactions of prospect's mind; operated campaigns to improve public relations between corporations and the public. Author articles: The Framework of Consumer Thinking Need No Longer be a Mystery; Marketing Research the Radar of the Sales Division; Some Aspects of Preparing Questionnaires; Twelve Ways to Improve Field Research, and others. Am Assn Pub Opinion Research — Am Marketing Assn. 347 Madison Ave., NYC 17.

22 BENNETT, Carlyle Wilson. Plant virus diseases (Sugar beet, deciduous fruits, tristeza disease of citrus). b'95. BS '17 (U Ky); MS '19 (Mich State Coll); PhD '26 (U Wis). Special mission to Argentina '40-41, to study sugar beet virus diseases; Brazil '46-47 to study tristeza disease of citrus. Author articles in field. With US Dept Agr since '29, principal path since '46. AAAS—Am Phytopath Soc—Bot Soc Am. U.S. Department of Agriculture, Box 31, Riverside, Calif.

23 BENNETT, Charles Abel. Cotton ginning processes and machinery. b'89. BSc '11 (U Neb). Developed, obtained public patents on, seed cotton drying processes and driers now used annually on eight million bales of American cotton at cotton gins, also used around the world. Author articles in field. Mech and agrl engr cotton drying research US Dept Agr La '26-30, principal engr charge agrl research adminstrn US Cotton Ginning Lab Stoneville Miss and Mesilla Park NM since '30. Am Soc Agrl Engrs(F). Awarded McCormick Gold Medal award '45, Nebraska Medal award '46. Box 426, Leland, Miss. H: Rt. 1, Box 240.

24 BENNETT, Donald Menzies. Industrial thermal expansion; Acoustics.

b'97. BA '21—MA '22—PhD '26 (U Wis); seminars in radio-isotopes and their med uses (Vanderbilt U and U Wis). Author: Physical Basis of Music; Fundamentals of Physics '36; also articles in field. Prof and head engring physics Speed Sci Sch U Louisville since '44. Am Phys Soc—AAAS—Ab Acoustical Soc—Am Assn Physics Teachers—Am Soc Engring Edn—Ky Assn Physics Teachers—Phi Beta Kappa—Sigma Xi. University of Louisville, Louisville 8. H: 1810 Fleming Rd., Louisville 5.

10 BENNETT, D w i g h t Granville. High temperature resistant ceramic coatings for metal. b'94. BS '30—student '48 (U Ill); '36 (U Pittsburgh). Author articles in field. Industrial fellow Mellon Inst '31-43; spl research prof U Ill since '43. Am Ceramic Soc(F)—Inst Ceramic Engrs—ASTM—Sigma Xi—Tau Beta Pi. Department of Ceramic Engineering, University of Illinois, Urbana, Ill.

11 BENNETT, George William. Management of fish in artificial lakes. b'08. AB '29 (Doane Coll Crete Neb); AM '31 (U Neb); PhD '39 (U Wis). Development of techniques for managing warm water fishes for angling in lakes and ponds in Illinois. Author papers on fish management. Instr zool McCook Jr Coll Neb '31-36; limnologist Ill Natural Hist Survey '38-43, head aquatic biol sect since '43. Phi Sigma —Gamma Alpha—Sigma Xi—Am Fish Soc—AAAS—Wildlife Soc—Ill Acad Sci. Ill. Natural History Survey, Nat. Resources Bldg., Urbana, Ill.

12 BENNETT, H(arry). Chemical specialties formulation; Chemical trade-marks; Technical definitions; Emulsions; Synthetic waxes. b'95. BS Chem '17 (NYC). Compiler and publisher, The Chemical Formulary (8 vols) '33-48. Holds 11 US patents, 1 Canadian, 1 British. Pres, dir research, Glyco Products Co Inc Brooklyn since '26. Am Inst Chem—Soc Chem Industry—Am Chem Soc—Am Assn Textile Chem and Colorists—AAAS—Am Soc Test Materials—Electrochem Soc—NY Acad Sci. 26 Court St., Bklyn 2.

13 BENNETT, Herbert S. Electronic Systems and Equipment (Military and Industrial Application); Systems and Operational Analysis; Quality Control; Technical Art Air Navigation; Radar, and Communications electronic equipment and systems. b'17. BS (Elec engring) '38—MS (Elec engring) '39 (Coll City NY Sch Tech); MS (Physics) '47—Dr Elec Engring '51 (Poly Inst Brooklyn). Has planned, directed, and coordinated research and development, production, quality control, and methods of engineering. Author articles: Transmission line characteristics of the sectoral horn; Sectoral horn as a component of the microwave transmission system, and others. Tech adv comdg officer Signal Corps Procurement Dist '39-'42; officer in charge inspection planning at hdqrs Signal Corps Inspection Agency '42-'46; asst chief engr plans office US Air Force Watson Labs '46-50. Presently Chief Engr Engring Branch Hq EWC US Army Signal Corps and President of Bennett-Klayton Associates, Consulting Engineers. Sci Research Soc Am—IRE—Am Inst EE—Nat Soc Prof Engrs—Sigma Xi—Tau Beta Pi —Eta Kappa Nu. US Army Signal Corps Fort Monmouth, N.J.; H: 31 Cedar Av., Long Branch, N.J.

14 BENNETT, H o w a r d Franklin. American economic history; Early American railroads. b'11. BA '33 (Amherst Coll); MA '39—MA teach-ing '38—PhD '51 (Harvard University). Research on railroad land policy, westward movement; study of general history Hannibal and St Joseph Railroad Co. Author articles in field. Asst professor business history School Commerce Northwestern since '46. AHA—Miss Valley Hist Assn—Mo Hist Soc—Am Econ Assn—Phi Beta Kappa. 307 Commerce Building, Northwestern University, Evanston, Ill.

15 BENNETT, Hugh Hammond. Soil conservation; Southern and Alaskan agriculture. b'81. BS '03—LLD '36 (U NC); DSc '37 (Clemson Coll). Research in meaning of sheet erosion, resistance of lateritic soils to erosion, susceptibility of clay soils of high silica content and relatively low content of sesquioxides of iron and aluminum; secretary Agriculture and Conservation Eighth American Scientific Conference Washington '40; in charge North American Technical Mission Venezuela '41-42; surveyed erosion conditions Union South Africa '44; consulting delegate first, second, third Inter-American Conferences Agriculture '30, '42, '45. Author: Soils of the US '13; Agricultural Possibilities of Alaska '16; Soils and Agriculture of the Southern States '21; Soils of Cuba '28; Soil Conservation '39; This Land We Defend '42; Elements of Soil Conservation '47; also articles in field. Chief soil conservation service US Dept Agr since '35. Can Conservation Assn (hon)—Am Geog Soc(F)—Am Soc Agron(F) — AAAS(F) — Soil Conservation Soc Am (F, founder)—Assn Am Geog (pres '43)—Am Forestry Assn—Friends of the Land. Department of Agriculture, Washington 25. H: Eight Oaks, RFD 2, Falls Church, Va.◎

16 BENNETT, Josephine W a t e r s. English literature (Edmund Spenser, Sir John Mandeville); Renaissance in England. b'99. BA '24—MA '25—PhD '36 (Ohio State U); '28-31 (Radcliffe Coll). Author: The Evolution of the Faerie Queene '42. Editor: A Revelation of the True Minerva '41; also articles in field. With Hunter Coll since '42, now asst prof Eng. Mod Lang Assn Am—New Eng Conf on Renaissance Studies, Phi Beta Kappa. Asso in U Seminar on Renaissance in Columbia U. Dorothy Bridgman Atkinson fellow Am Assn U Women for study in England '34-35, Guggenheim fellow '45-46, Am Council Learned Socs grants '41. Hunter College of the City of New York, 695 Park Av., NYC 23. H: 501 W. 113 St., NYC 25.

17 BENNETT, Logan J. Vertebrate ecology; Wildlife management; Hunting and hunting dogs. b'07. BS '30 (Central Coll); MS '32—PhD '37 (Ia State Coll). Breeder and trainer of ruffed grouse and woodcock bird dogs; composed bird collections of Nissen Island, Bismarck Archipelago and Admiralty Islands north of New Guinea for Smithsonian Institute; led Iowa and Pennsylvania Cooperative Wildlife Research Units; research on ecology and management of various types of North American birds. Author articles: The Blue-winged Teal, Its Ecology and Management '38; (with others) The Ring-necked Pheasant and Its Management in North America '45; and others. Game tech Ia Fish and Game Commn '34-35; asso biol US Biol Survey Ia State Coll '35-38; biol US Fish and Wildlife Service Pa State Coll '38-43, '45-47, in chge Cooperative Wildlife Research Units Wash DC '47-48; chief branch wildlife research US Fish and Wildlife Service since '48. Wildlife Society (past sec, pres '47-48)—Outdoor Writers Assn Am— Wilson Ornithol Club—Am Ornithol Union—Am Soc Mammalogists. Fish and Wildlife Service, Department of the Interior, Washington 25.†

18 BENNETT, Merrill Kelley. Agricultural economics (Food). b'97. PhB '20—AM '21 (Brown U); AM '26 (Harvard); PhD '27 (Stanford). Author: Farm Cost Studies in the United States: Their Development, Applications and Limitations '28; Food for Postwar Europe: How Much and What? '44; International Commodity Stockpiling as an Economic Stabilizer '49. Co-author: (with W D Wickizer) Rice in Monsoon Asia '41; also articles in field. Exec dir and prof econ geog, Food Research Institute Stanford U since '42. Am Statis Assn(F)—AAAS(F)—Am Econ Assn—Am Farm Econ Assn—Assn Am Geog. Food Research Institute, Stanford University, Stanford, Cal.◎

19 BENNETT, Ralph Decker. Electrical measurements; O r d n a n c e; X-rays; Cosmic rays. b'00. BS '21—MS '23—ScD (hon) '45 (Union Coll); PhD '25 (U Chicago); Nat Research Fellow '26-27 (Princeton); Nat Research Fellow '27-28 (Calif Inst Tech). Author articles in field. Lt comdr, comdr, capt USNR, chief mine and depth charge div Naval Ordnance Lab '41-44, tech dir since '44. Am Phys Soc(F)—AIEE(F)—SPEE—Washington Philos Soc—Inst Radio Engrs (sr mem)—Sigma Xi. Naval Ordnance Laboratory, White Oak, Md.

20 BENNETT, Victor W. Marketing; Consumer economics. b'95. BA '17—MA '18 (Gettysburg Coll); MA 24 (U Pittsburgh); PhD 37 (U Washington). Co-author: Current Economic Policies '34; Agricultural Credit Legislation of 1933 '34; also articles in field. Prof marketing chmn marketing dept U Miami since '46. Am Marketing Assn —Tau Kappa Alpha. Delta Sigma Pi—Alpha Delta Sigma. University of Miami, Miami, University Branch, Fla. H: 3709 Monserrate St., Coral Gables 34, Fla.†

21 BENNETT, Willard Harrison. Cathodes; Mass spectrometry. b'03. Student '21-22 (Carnegie Inst Tech); AB '24 (O State U); MSc '26 (U Wis); PhD '28 (U Mich); NRC fellow physics '28-30 (Calif Inst Tech). Study physics of composite cathodes using pulsed vapors; development method for production of intense focussed beams of negative atomic hydrogen ions; examination of negative ion formation at solid surfaces and in gas phase; research on field currents from various metal cathodes, and theory of field emission breakdown due to magnetically self-focussing steams; inventor of non-magnetic radio frequency mass spectrometer. Co-author: (with H G Heil) Fundamental Principles of Physics '38. Author articles: Pulses in Negative Point-to-Plane Corona '41; Mobilities in Some Free Electron Gases '42; A Cold Cathode Rectifier '47; Radio Frequency Mass Spectrometer '50, and others. Dir research Electronic Research Corp '38-41; physicist Nat Bur Standards since '46. APS (F)—AAUP—Sigma Xi. National Bureau of Standards, Washington 25.

22 BENNETT, William Ernest. Nuclear Physics. b'07. BA '32—MA '34 (Queens U); PhD '37 (Cambridge U). Research on stopping power of mica for Alpha-particles, Gamma ray resonances from bombardment of carbon by deuterons, resonances in emission of neutrons and protons from reaction $C 12 + D$, disintegration of carbon by deuterons, neutron-proton and neutron-carbon scattering cross sections for fast neutrons, resonances in disintegration of fluorine by protons. Author articles: High Energy Gamma Ray from Li + D '41. Co-author: (with Bonner, Richards and Watt) The Disintegration of Li 7 by Deuterons '47; (with Richards) Neutrons from C 12 + D '47; and others. Instr physics Rice Inst '38-46; prof Ill Inst Tech since '46. Am Phys Soc—AAAS —Sigma Xi. Illinois Institute of Technology, 3300 Federal St., Chicago.

10 BENNETT, William Holmes. Old Germanic languages (Gothic). b'07. AB '30—PhD '42 (U Pittsburgh); AM '32 (Harvard). Author: Skeireins aiwaggeljons thairh Iohannen '42; also articles in field. Asso prof U Notre Dame since '42, apptd to teach in The Mediaeval Inst since '46. Linguistic Soc Am—Mod Lang Assn—Mediaeval Acad Am—Kappa Phi Kappa. University of Notre Dame, Notre Dame, Ind.; H: 2005 Marquette Blvd., South Bend 16.†

11 BENNETT, William Tapley, Jr. United States relations with Panama and Central America. b'17. AB '37 (U Ga); '38 (U Freiburg Germany); '40 (Am U); LLB '48 (George Washington U). Civil attache US Embassy Ciudad Trujillo Dominican Republic '41-44, attache Panama '44; aide to US del UN conf on internat orgn San Francisco '45; with US Dept State since '46, officer in charge Central Am and Panama affairs since '50; adv to orgn of Am states mission in Costa Rica-Nicaragua incident '48; adv to US del fifth session gen assembly of UN '50. Ateneo Dominicano Am Fgn Service Assn—Phi Beta Kappa—Phi Delta Phi—Phi Kappa Phi—Georgia Historical Society—Am Society of International Law.

12 BENSIN, Basil Mitrophanovich. Agronomy; Agroecology; Forage crops; Alaskan agriculture (Grain, grasses, legumes). b'81. BD '05 (Moscow Theol Acad); BS '10 — MS '12 (U Minn); DS '30 (Czechish Poly Agrl Sch). Expedition to Central Asia, Turkestan, for collection of drought-resistant cereals '12, discovered new species of native rye (Secale turkestanicum Bensin); organizer of Russian Institute of Agricultural Cooperation in Prague '22; agroecological exploration Sotola Marina region Mexico '31; acclimitization of cereals, grasses and legumes in Alaska, Alaska Agricultural Experiment Station, College, Alaska, since '45; originated dehydration of vegetables by dry-freezing process '46. Author articles in field. Ecol Soc Am—Am Soc Agronomy—Am Geog Soc—Am Geophys Union — Calif Acad Sci—AAUP. Received award for distinguished service to Alaska from Jessen's Weekly, Fairbanks Alaska '48. Agricultural Experiment Station, College, Alaska.

13 BENSON, Adolph Burnett. History of Swedes in America; Swedish literature; American-Scandinavian literary and historical relations. b'81. BS '07—MS '10—Litt D '42 (Wesleyan U Conn); AM '10—PhD '14 (Columbia); AM '32 (Yale); Litt D '43 (Upsala Coll); LLD '47 (Augustana Coll). Author: The Old Norse Element in Swedish Romanticism '14; Sweden and the American Revolution '26. Co-author: (with J L Deen) Swedish-English Vocabulary for Foresters '35; (with Naboth Hedin) Americans from Sweden '49; also articles in field. Prof German and Scandinavian Yale U since '32, emeritus '47; fellow Silliman Coll since '33. Modern Lang Assn Am

(mem exec council '47)—Linguistic Soc Am—Soc Advancement Scandinavian Study—Swedish Colonial Soc—Am-Scandinavian Found—Am Swedish Hist Found (vp)—Phi Beta Kappa (asso '42). Berlin, Conn.⊙

14 BENSON, Homer Edwin. Synthetic liquid fuels. b'18. BS '41 (Case Inst Tech). Author articles in field. Chem engr charge pilot plant operations of synthetic liquid fuel plants US Bur Mines since '42. Am Inst Chem Engrs—Am Chem Soc. U.S. Bureau of Mines, Bruceton, Pa.

15 BENSON, Lyman (David). Botany of United States (Taxonomy, plant distribution, floristics). b'09. AB '30—MA '31—PhD '39 (Stanford U). Classification, distribution and floristics of Ranunculaceae especially in North America, Cactaceae of US Gramineae especially Pleuropogon, Prosopis in US, trees and shrubs of southwestern deserts of US, vascular flora of western NA especially California, Arizona and Pacific northwest. Author: The Cacti of Arizona '40; manual of Southwestern Desert Trees and Shrubs '45; A Monograph of the North American Ranunculi '48, and others; also articles in field. Research fellow NY Bot Garden summer '35, collaborator since '35; instr U Ariz '38-40, asst prof bot '40-44, asst bot Agrl Exdpt Sta '38-44; asso prof bot and head dept Pomona Coll since '44, professor since 49; asso prof bot Claremont Grad Sch '44-49; professor since '49. AAAS(F)—Am Soc Plant Taxonomists—Soc Study Evolution—Am Biol Soc—Calif Bot Soc—Torrey Bot Club—So Calif Acad Sci—AAUP—Western Soc Naturalists—Am Fern Soc—Cactus and Succulent Soc Am(F) —So Calif Bot—Phi Beta Kappa— Sigma Xi. Department of Botany, Pomona College, Claremont, Calif. H 455 University Circle.

16 BENSON, Seth B(ertram). Systematics and ecology of North American mammals. b'05. AB '28—PhD '33 (U Calif). Author articles in field. Curator mammals Mus of Vertebrate Zool and asso prof zool U Calif. Am Soc Mammal—Wildlife Soc—Sigma Xi —Phi Beta Kappa. Museum of Vertebrate Zoology, Berkeley 4.†

17 BENSON, Sidney William. Physical and photochemistry; Reaction rates. b'18. BA '38 (Columbia); MA—PhD '41 (Harvard). Author: Outline of General College Chemistry '38; Laboratory Manual — Instrumental Methods of Analysis and Control '44; Syllabus for General Chemistry '47; also articles in field. Patents on thermoregulators '43, manufacture of cyclobutane and derivatives '47; patent pending thermoplastic hook '48. Asso prof chem U So Calif since '48. Research asso and cons Chem Warfare Service '44-46. Am Chem Soc—NY Acad Sci—AAAS—Phi Beta Kappa— Sigma Xi—Phi Lambda Upsilon. Certificate of Merit Nat Defense Research Council; Guggenheim Found fellowship '50-51. University of Southern California, Los Angeles 7.†

18 BENTLEY, Gerald Eades. Drama; Theater; Shakespeare; Ben Jonson. b'01. AB '23 (DePauw U); AM '26 (U Ill); PhD '29 (U London). Delegate International Shakespeare Conference, England '47. Author: The Jacobean and Caroline Stage (2 vols) '41; Shakespeare and Jonson (2 vols) '45; The Swan of Avon and the Bricklayer of Westminster '48; Shakespeare and the Blackfriar's Theatre, Shakespeare Annual '48. Editor: (with Fred B Millett) The Play's the Thing '36; The Alchemist (Jonson) '47; Development

of English Drama, '50; also articles in field. Instr Eng U Chicago '29 advanced to prof '44; prof Eng Princeton U since '45; lecturer Post Grad Sch Elizabethan Studies U Birmingham Eng summer '47. Modern Humanities Research Assn—Modern Lang Assn Am —AAUP — Nat Council Teachers Eng—Eng Literary Hist (bd editors). Awards: Rector scholar DePauw U '19-23; research fellow Huntington Library '38-39; Guggenheim Found '44-45. 119 Fitz Randolph Rd., Princeton, NJ.⊙

19 BENTON, Pauline. Chinese and Occidental shadow plays (Materials, history, figures, scenery). b'98. AB '20 (Barnard Coll). Animator and demonstrator color motion picture The Chinese Shadow Play. Author: Chinese Shadow Plays '38; China's Old Shadow Plays in a Modern Setting '40; The Red Gate Players Introduce the Actors and Plays of the Chinese Shadow Theatre '40; Turning a Gay Hobby Into a Full-Time Job '41; The Twenty-Four Stories of Filial Piety are Chinese Nursery Tales '43; also plays and articles. Dir and owner Red Gate Players, prod Chinese Shadow Plays and Red Gate Arts, prod shadow play materials since '32. Internat House Alumni Assn (vp '45-46, pres '46-47) —Pen and Brush. 454 Riverside Dr., NYC 27.

20 BENZINGER, Theodor Hannes. Physiology (Environmental, stress, altitude, respiration, metabolism); Instrumentation (Scientific); Instruments (Calorimetry, radiometry). b'05. MS '27—DSc '29 (U Tuebingen Germany); MD '32 (U Freiburg Germany). Assisted development aluminum foil suit for protection from fire radiation; devised method for recording alveolar gases and gaseous metabolism; research on respiratory stimulants other than blood gases, mechanisms of altitude adaptation altitude unfitness, pressure demand system for high altitude oxygen breathing, demand breathing apparatus separating supply and control; study arterial air embolism as main cause of death in air or underwater blast. Author articles: New Aspects of the Control of Respiration '40; Detonation Death Induced by Arterial Air Embolism '44. Co-author articles: (with C Kitzinger) Direct Calorimetry by Means of the Gradient Principle '49; a 4 ? Radiometer '50. Head aeromed lab German Air Forces Materiel Command Rechlin Germany '34-44; with Naval Med Research Inst Bethesda Md since '47. Deutsche Physiologische Gesellschaft—Gesellschaft Deutscher Naturforscher—Am Physiol Soc. Naval Medical Research Institute, National Naval Medical Center, Bethesda 14, Md.

21 BERANEK, Leo Leroy. Acoustics (Architectural); Speech communication; Sound control. b'14. BA '36— DSc (hon) (Cornell Coll); MS '37— DSc '40 (Harvard U); Guggenheim Fellow '46 (jointly at Harvard and MIT). Author: Acoustic Measurements '49. Co-author: Principles of Sound Control in Airplanes '44; also articles in field. Instr physics Harvard U '40-43, dir research on sound '43-45, dir electro-acoustics and systems research '45-46; asso prof communication engr and tech MIT since '47; co-partner acoustical cons firm Bolt Beranek Newman. Acoustic Soc Am (F, mem Exec Council '44-47, chmn commn on standards '47, biennial award for outstanding contributions to acoustics '44)—Am Phys Soc(F)— AAAS(F)—Inst Radio Engrs (sr mem) —Am Standards Assn (chmn com on fundamental measurement and terminology in acoustics). Acoustics

Laboratory, Massachusetts Institute of Technology, Cambridge, Mass.

10 BERBERIAN, Dicran Abraham. Lebanon and Syria (Health conditions). b'03. BA '26—MD '30 (Am U Beirut); Student '35-36 (London Sch Hygiene and Tropical Med, Malaria Inst Rome, U Paris). Research on incidence and distribution of helminthic infections in Lebanon and Syria, artifical immunization of dogs and sheep against echinococcus and hydatidosis, mechanism of invasiveness of streptococci, antityphoid-paratyphoid immunization, oriental sore transmission immunization and treatment, cheese poisoning in Syria and the Lebanon; prophylaxis of malaria; treatment lambliasis and menolepidisis with acranil; amebiasis with milibis. Author articles in field. Adj prof bacteriol and parasitol Am U Beirut '35-45; asso prof chmn dept bacteriol and parasitol Am U Beirut '45-47; municipal health council City of Beirut '41-47; asst prof tropical med Albany Med Coll since '47. Royal So Hygiene and Tropical Med—Am Soc Bacteriologists—Nat Malaria Soc. Gold medal for meritorious services to Republic of Lebanon '43; Rockefeller fellow '35-36. Sterling-Winthrop Research Inst., Rensselaer, N.Y. H: 439 Loudonville Road, Loudonville, N.Y.

11 BERDAHL, Clarence Arthur. Government; Political parties; International organization; American government. b'90. AB '14 (St Olaf Coll Northfield Minn) AM '17 (U SD) PhD '20 (U Ill). Instr polit sci '20-22 U Ill asso '22-25 asst prof '25-29 asso prof '29-30 prof since '30 chmn div social scis '35-39 chmn dept polit sci '42-48; consultant US Dept State '42-45; on London staff OSS '44; mem internat secretariat UN Conf '45. Am Polit Sci Assn—Am Hist Assn—Am Soc Pub Admin—Am Soc Internat Law—Fgn Policy Assn—Phi Beta Kappa. Author: War Powers of the Executive in the United States '20; The Policy of the United States with Respect to the League of Nations '32; Regionalism and World Organization '44. 1103 S. Douglas Av., Urbana, Ill.⊙

12 BERELSON, Bernard. Communication; Public opinion. b'12. BA '34 (Whitman Coll); BA '36—MA '37 (U Washington); PhD '41 (U Chicago). Author: Content Analysis '52. Co-author: The Peoples' Choice '48; What Reading Does to People '40; also articles in field. Co-editor: Reader in Public Opinion and Communication '50. Research dir Bur Applied Social Research Columbia U '44-46; prof library sci, social scis, U Chicago '46-51, dean grad library sch '47-51; sr staff officer Ford Found since '51. Am Assn Public Opinion Research (pres '51-52) —Am Sociol Soc—ALA—AAAS—Am Psychol Assn. Pasadena, Cal.†⊙

13 BERESFORD, Hobart. Agricultural Engineering (Education). b'96. BS '24 AE '41 (Ia State Coll). Author: Agricultural Engineering Reference (revised) '39; also articles in field. Agrl engr Ida Power Co Boise '27-28; faculty U Ida '28-46; faculty Ia State Coll since '46, prof agrl engring head dept. research prof agrl engring. Am Soc Agrl Engrs (F)—Soc Engring Edn — AAAS — Sigma Xi — Gamma Sigma Delta. Profl engr Ia and Ida. H: Skunk Hollow, Ames. Ia.†⊙

14 BERESFORD, Rex. Beef cattle (Production and marketing). b'85. BS '11 (Ia State Coll). Author articles in field. Ext prof animal husbandry Ia State Coll '16-48, ext prof livestock marketing since '48. Am Soc

Animal Production. Extension Service, Iowa State College, Ames, Ia.

15 BERG, Clifford O(sburn). Diptera (Immature stages and biology). b'12. AB '34 (Luther Coll Ia); MS '39— PhD '49 (U Mich). Developed a technique to project images of living animals onto a screen using miniature aquaria and 2x2 projection lantern '40-48; extensive studies and collections of Solomon Islands Diptera '44-45; research on fresh water insects related to plants of genus Potamogeton '39-42. Author articles in field. Asso prof zool O Wesleyan U since '50. Limnol Soc Am—Ecol Soc Am—Am Micros Soc—Mich Acad Sci Arts Letters—O Acad Sci—Sigma Xi—Phi Kappa Phi—Entomol Soc Am. Department of Zoology, Ohio Wesleyan University, Delaware, O.

16 BERGDOLL, John George, Jr. Refrigeration and air conditioning engineering. b'98. ME '20 (Lehigh U). Research in, development of portable room cooling, adaption of refrigerating equipment to lower temperature, investigation high altitude flying, particularly strato-chambers; pioneer work automatic control by use of float valves. Draftsman engring div York Corp '20-23, engr mech engring dept '23-27, chief development engr '27-35, product engr '35-37, asst chief engr '37-39, chief engr '39-43, dir engring and manufacturing, gen works mgr '43 vp since '49. Am Soc Refrigerating Engrs (f, pres '50). York Corporation, York, Pa.

17 BERGENDOFF, Ruben N. Bridges-long span and movable Expressways; Turnpikes. b'99. BS (CE) '21 (U Pa). Bridges, Long Span and Movable: Design of major bridge projects; nine over Mississippi River; three over Ohio River; Two over Delaware River; seven over Missouri River; eighteen over Welland Canal. Expressways: Toledo, Ohio; Akron, Ohio; Columbus, Ohio; Kansas City, Missouri. Turnpikes: Maine; New Jersey; West Virginia; Colorado. Author articles: Turnpike Economics '43; Mississippi River Bridge-Dubuque Iowa '50; Notable Bridges in United States '37; Privately Financed Superhighway in Maine '47. With NC State Highway Dept '21-22; cons engr Harrington, Howard & Ash '22-28, Ash, Howard, Needles & Tammen '28-39, Howard, Needles, Tammen & Bergendoff since '40; mem Kansas City Planning Commn. Am Soc CE—Am Inst Cons Engrs. Am Inst Steel Constrn awards for beautiful bridges. 921 Walnut St., Kansas City 6, Mo.

18 BERGER, Elmer. Zionism; Relation of American Jew to American life. b'08. AB '30 (U Cincinnati). Rabbi '32 (Hebrew Union College). Lecturer on Palestine, Zionism, Israel and the Problem of Integration of the American Jew. Author: The Jewish Dilemma '45; The Palestine Dilemma '46; Anti Semitism, Britannica Book of the Year, '47, '48, '49, '50. Exec dir Am Council for Judaism since '43. Phi Beta Kappa. 201 E. 57th St., NYC 22.

19 BERGER, Evelyn Miller. Education; Psychology. b'96. grad State Normal Sch San Jose Cal '19; special student '15-16 and '20 (Coll of Pacific Stockton); '16-17 (U So Cal); summer '26 (U Mexico); Centro de Estudios Historicos Madrid Spain; AB '21 AM '30 (Stanford) PhD '32 (Columbia). Dean women U Ida '38-39, State Coll, San Diego '38-39; lectr adult study groups, mental hygiene, child guidance Almeda, Berkeley, Albany Schs '42-44; dir Family Counseling Center Oakland Cal since '44; radio program Successful Parents sta KLX '44-46. Diplo-

mate Am Bd Examiners Profl Psychol. Am Psychol Assn(F)—Nat Council Women Psychol—Cal Assn Applied Psychol—Mental Hygieen Soc No Cal —Am Assn U Women—Phi Beta Kappa — Kappa Delta Pi — Pi Lambda Theta—Phi Sigma Iota. 315 14th St., Oakland 12, Cal.†⊙

20 BERGER, Kermit Carl. Agronomy; Soil fertility and chemistry. b'10. BS '37—PhD '41 (U Wis). Research on boron determination in soils and plants, boron deficiencies revealed by plant, soil tests; beets; boron availability in relation soil reaction and organtic matter content, boron tests, determinations and fixation, magnesium-phosphorus relationships in plant nutrition, manganese toxicity to potatoes in relation strong soil acidity. Author articles: Soil Profiles of Natural Appearance Mounted with Vinylite Resin '45; Soil Profiles and Materials Embedded in Transparent Plastics '46; Stem Streak Necrosis of Potatoes in Relation to Soil Acidity '47; Soil Fertility Investigations with Potatoes in Wisconsin '48; Thin Sections of Soils and Friable Materials Prepared by Impregnation with the Plastic "Castolite" '47. Asst soils dept U Wis '40-41, instr soils '41-43, asst prof '43-45, professor since '49. Soil Sci Soc Am—Am Soc Agron—Am Chem Soc—AAAS—Wis Acad Arts, Letters, Sci—Sigma Xi. Soils Department, University of Wisconsin, Madison 6, Wis.

21 BERGER, Raoul. Administrative, constitutional and corporate law. b'01. AB '32 (University of Cincinnati); JD '35 (Northwestern); LLM '38 (Harvard). Author articles in field. Handled appellate matters with Securities Exchange Commn Washington '38-40; spl asst to Atty Gen Washington '40-42; asst asso and gen counsel to Alien Property Custodian Washington 42-47. Order of Coif—Am Law Inst. Ring Bldg, Washington.†⊙

22 BERGER, Rolf M(ikael). Plastics; Vulcanized fiber; Resins; Cellulose. b'01. BS Chem Engr, Chem '17-21 (orebro Tech Coll Sweden); '23 (Leopold Cassella Farbfabrike, Frankfort Am Main Germany). Chief chem Spaulding Fibre Co since '34. Spaulding Fibre Company, Tonawanda, N.Y. H: P.O. Box 204, Tonawanda, N.Y.

23 BERGMAN, Lester V. Motion pictures (Educational); Design of Photo-optical research equipment. b'09. BS '31—MA '31 (Columbia). Produced research and clinical films involving color, animation, microscopy, and time-lapse; research proving rubber stamps lapse; research in questioned documents, physiology, and photo-optics. Illustrator 25 medical texts, others in science. Designed and built clinical research cameras, endoscopic still and motion picture cameras, research cameras for vitamin studies under OSRD grant (World War II). Self-employed since '29. Soc Motion Picture and Television Engrs—AAAS—Photog Engrs— Biol Photog Assn—Optical Soc Am— NY Micros Soc—Photog Soc Am. 732 Eastern Parkway, Bklyn 13.

24 BERGMAN, Ray. Fresh water fishing; Trout; Trout and salmon flies, leaders, hooks; Bass; Pikes. b'91. Ed public schools. Traveled over 160,000 miles specifically for fishing. Author: Just Fishing '32; Trout '38; Fresh Water Bass '42; With Fly, Plug and Bait '47. Angling ed Outdoor Life Mag since '33. Nyack 5, N.Y.†

25 BERGMANN, Werner. Chemistry (Organic, marine). b'04. Student '14-23 (Gymnasium Bielefeld Germany); '25-26 (U Tubingen); PhD '28 (U Gottingen); Rockefeller fellow '30-31 (Edinburgh U, U Heidelberg). Research and field work on chemistry of silk and silkworm, marine products in France, Italy, Puerto Rico, Bahamas, Bermuda, Florida. Author articles in field. With Yale U since '39, now prof chem; sci cons Bingham Oceanographic Lab; trustee Bermuda Biol Sta. Conn Acad Sci—Soc Biol Chemists—AAAS— Am Chem Soc—Sigma Xi. Department of Chemistry, Yale University, New Haven, Conn.†

10 BERK, Sigmund. Industrial mycology; Mildewproofing materials. b'15. BS '35 (Temple U); MA '39 (U Pa). Author articles in field. Am Phytopath Soc—Am Chem Soc—Am Inst Biol Sci. Pitman-Dunn Laboratory, Frankford Arsenal, Phila. 37.†

11 BERKELEY, Edmund Callis. Cybernetics; Automatic computing machinery. b'09. AB summa cum laude '30 (Harvard). Research, schematic design, specifications, appraisal, market, applications, automatic computing machinery, robots, logical machines. Author: Giant Brains or Machines That Think '49. Actuarial clk Prudential Ins Co Am '34-42, methods analyst '46-48; partner Edmund C Berkeley and Assos since '48. Served as 1t (jg) to 1t comdr USNR '42-'46, Harvard Computation Lab '45-46. Assn Computing Machinery—Soc Actuaries (F)— Assn Symbolic Logic—Am Cryptogram Assn—Phi Beta Kappa. 36 West 11th St., NYC 11; 19 Mild St., Boston 9.

12 BERKELEY, Francis L(ewis), Jr. History of Virginia. b'11. BS '34— MA '40 (U Va). Research in Virginia history and manuscript records, archives and history University of Virginia; collecting of Virginia manuscripts; in course of compiling guide to manuscript collections of University of Virginia, checklists of writings of Jefferson, Madison, Monroe, and Revolutionary Lees; member special committee investigating Horn Papers Institute Early American history and Culture '47; U of Va records adminstr since '49. Author: Checklist of Bound Business Records '38; Dunmore's Proclamation of Emancipation '41. Co-compiler Annual Report on Historical Collections U Virginia Library since '40; also articles in field. Acting dir rare books and manuscripts, curator Tracy W McGregor Lib '41-42, curator manuscripts since '45. Va Hist Soc—So Hist Assn—AHA—Bibliog Soc Am—Soc Am Archivists (mem com memberships)—Va Teachers Assn—Va Lib Assn—ALA—Sigma Xi. Curator of Manuscripts, University of Virginia Library, Charlottesville, Va.†

13 BERKLEY, Earl E(sco). Fiber technology (Cellulose, Cotton, abaca); Physical and structural properties of southern yellow pine. b'02. Diploma '26 (Alderson Jr Coll); AB '29 (West Va U); MS '30—PhD '33 (Washington U). Patented a low density carbonaceous ingredient for dynamite filler. Author articles in field. Head cotton fiber lab Anderson Clayton and Co since '49. Am Chem Soc—AAAS—Am Bot Soc—Textile Research Inst (asso ed)—Fiber Soc—Sigma Xi. Anderson Clayton & Company, P.O. Box 2538, Houston 1, Tex.

14 BERKNER, Lloyd Viel. Geophysics; Meterology; Electronics; Radar; Radio engineering; Ionosphere. b'05. BS '27—grad student '27 (U Minn); '33-35 (George Washington U). Engaged in studies of the ionosphere since '30; chairman section on geophysics of the atmosphere, dept terrestial magnetism Carnegie Instn Washington, also acting dir '48, re-

search asso since '51; cons Sec State '50; pres Asso Univs Inc (Brookhaven Nat Lab) since '51. Author articles in field. Comd Naval Res Aviation Sqdn VS-6R '35-36; active aviation duty Bur Aeronautics '41 as organizer and head aircraft radar sect and electronics material br; field assignments aboard USS Enterprise during Okinawa operations. Am Phys Soc(F)—Inst Radio Engrs(F)—AIEE(F, mem com on research)—Nat Acad Sci (mem com on the Antarctic)—Nat Research Council (mem com internat unions)—Internat Union Geodesy and Geophysics—Internat Assn Terrestrial Magnetism (mem exec com, mem internat commn on ionosphere, rep Edinburgh Congress '36, Washington Congress '39)—Washington Acad Sci—Philos Soc Wash— Am Geophys Union—Internat Sci Radio Union (mem exec com US nat com) —Eta Kappa Nu. Recipient sci award Washington Acad Sci in recognition of ionospheric research '41. Associated Universities, Inc., 350 5th Ave., NYC 1.◎

15 BERLAU, Abraham Joseph. Germany (Social democratic party). b'17. BS '44—MA '45—PhD '49 (Columbia). Research on recent German history, German Socialism, and period of World War I, of the Revolution and post-war period. Author: The German Social Democratic Party 1914-1921 '49. Acad Polit Sci—Nat Council Social Studies. H: 632 Columbus Av., NYC 24.

16 BERLIN, Theodore H. Stochastic processes (Theory); High energy accelerators. b'17. BChE '39 (Cooper Union Inst Tech); MS—PhD '44—Rackham fellow '41-43 (U Mich). Author articles in field. Asso prof physics Johns Hopkins U since '49. Am Phys Soc—Sigma Xi. Department of Physics, Johns Hopkins University, Baltimore.

17 BERLINER, J(ulius) F(rederick) T(homas). Plastics; Wood Technology; Fiber products. b'02. BS '22—MS '23 —PhD '26 (George Washington U). Engaged product and process development; research on water treatment, mirror manufacture, high power fuels, plastics, metallurgy, hydrogenated oils, treatment of wood, industrial application of chemicals, improvement and utilization forest products, pulp and fiber products. Author: Potash Bibliography '30. Asst physicist metall research US Bur Standards Washington '18-23; asso chem phys-organic chem research US Bur Chem '23-26; asso engr investigation potash tech US Bur Mines '26-28; cons engr surveying potash resources Poland, Germany, France for Blair & Co, Chase Bank, US govt '28-29; research and development engr E I duPont de Nemours & Co '29-45; chem and engring cons since '45. AAAS(F)—Am Chem Soc—Am Forestry Assn—TAPPI. 539 S. Franklin St., Chicago 7.

18 BERLINER, Victor Richard. Physiology and endocrinology of reproduction; Artificial insemination; Animal breeding. b'01. Dipl Agr '29 (U Berlin); MSc '34 (U Alberta); PhD '36 (U Mo). Research on estrous cycles of jennets and jacks, effects of feeds on sperm production of jacks and stallions, diluters for stallion and jack semen; reproductive capacity of rams, effects of pituitary and thyroid on sperm production of rams. Author: The Biology of Equine Spermatozoa '46; The Problem of Fertility '46; Artificial Insemination of Horses and Jackstock '48; Artificial Insemination of Farm Animals '48; also articles in field. Dir div animal industry Ortho Research Found. Am Soc Animal

Prodn—Am Dairy Sci Assn—NY Acad Sci—Sigma Xi. Ortho Research Foundation, Raritan, N.J.

19 BERMAN, Eleanor Davidson. Philosophy (Aesthetics, psychology); Thomas Jefferson in relation to the arts. b'04. AB '24 (U Calif); DSSc '46 (New Sch for Social Research NY). Author: Thomas Jefferson Among the Arts '48; also articles in field. Am Soc Aesthetics—Met Mus Art (women's com). 26 Ogden Rd., Scarsdale, N.Y.

20 BERMAN, Morris. Structures (Model analysis). Prof engr '29 (U State NY) LLB '30 (NY Law Sch). Invented instrument measuring stresses directly in pounds in structural models and bending in inch-pounds. Granted patent on instrument. Author articles in field. Cons engr Engring Instruments Co since '50. NY Soc Engrs (pres). 393 Central Park West, Box 402, NYC 25.

21 BERMAN, Morton Mayer. Judaism (Role of Rabbi). b'99. BA '21 (Yale); MHL '26—DD '46 (Jewish Inst Rel '46. Author: History of Inwardness, 1926 Jew's View of the Crucifixion '29; Index to Nielziner's Introduction to the Talmud '25; Role of the Rabbi '41. Editor Jewish material for Collier & Sons New Encyclopedia. Guggenheim fellowship Jewish Inst Religion '26. Am Oriental Soc—Am Acad Jewish Research—Am Acad Polit Social Sci—Phi Beta Kappa. 1100 Hyde Park Blvd., Chgo.◎

22 BERNHARDT, Joshua. Economics. b'93. AB '16 (U Rochester); PhD '21 (Johns Hopkins). Research on government control sugar industry, government organization. Author: A Statistical Survey of the Sugar Industry and Trade of the United States '20; Government Control of the Sugar Industry of the United States; The Federal Government and the Sugar Industry (1917-47) '49. Chief sugar div US Tariff Commn '23-24; statistician group sugar cos NY '25-26; dir Sugar Statistics Service and sec Palestine Econ Corp '27-33; chief economist sugar sect AAA '33-35, chief sugar sect '35-43; chief sugar br War Food Adminstrn '43-45; US mem combined Food Bd Sugar Com and successor orgn '43-48. Am Econ Assn—Phi Beta Kappa.◎

23 BERNREUTER, Robert Gibbon. Psychology of personality (Testing). b'01. AB '24 (Coll of The Pacific); PhD '31 (Stanford). Author: The Personality Inventory '31; Manual for the Personality Inventory '35; also articles in field. Prof psychol Penn State Coll since '39; technical director Klein Institute for Aptitude Testing since '46. American Psychol Association—Pa Psychol Assn—AAAS—Sigma Xi. Department of Psychology, Pennsylvania State College, State College, Pa.†◎

24 BERNSTEIN, Isidor Mayer. Printing inks; Drying oils; Pigments (Printing inks). b'96. Student '18 (Armour Inst Tech); '19-20 (U Chicago); '31-38 (U Cincinnati). Holder of nine US Patents, four patents pending. Author articles in field. Chief chem Standard Printing Ink Co Cincinnati '30-36; chief research and development lab Internat Printing Ink Southern Div Cincinnati '36-40; dir research HD Roosen Co Brooklyn '40-46; dir Nat Printing Ink Research Inst Lehigh U '46-48; tech dir Gotham Ink & Color Co Long Island since '48. Am Chem Soc — AIC(F) — Am Inst Phys—Am Oil Chem Soc—Tech Assn Pulp and Paper Ind—NY Printing Ink Prodn Club (pres '47)—AAAS—Assn Research Dirs—Sigma Xi—NY Ac

Scis—NY Paint and Varnish Prodn Club—NY Micros Soc—Chemists Soc. 18 86th St., Brooklyn 9.

10 **BERNSTEIN, Samuel.** The Digger movement; Babeuf and Babouvism. b'98. BA '19 (Coll City NY); MA '20—PhD '33 (Columbia); '26-27 (La Faculte de Droit U Paris). Research on the Digger movement, Babeuf and Babouvism, Buonarroti and the Risorgimento, Marxism, Fabianism, the French Utopians, French labor after the Commune. Author: The Beginnings of Marxian Socialism in France '33; Filippo Buonarroti '46; A Centenary of Marxism '48; also articles in field. Societe des Etudes Robespierristes—Societe D'Histoire de la Revolution de 1848—Econ History Soc. Science and Society, 30 East 20 St., N YC 3. H: 4j-720 Riverside Drive, NYC 31.

11 **BERRY, Charles Thompson.** Fossil ophiuroidea; Teritiary deposits of the Atlantic Coast; Paleontology. b'06. PhD '34 (Johns Hopkins). Author articles in field. Asst prof U Conn '47-50; research asst Conn Geol and Nat Hist Survey '47-50. AAAS(F)—Geol Soc Am(F)—Phi Beta Kappa—Sigma Xi. Al Harvey Rd., Stonington, Conn.

12 **BERRY, Edward Willard.** Coastal plain geology; Coal; Petroleum. b'00. AB '24—PhD '29 (Johns Hopkins). Vice-president paleobotany section International Botany Congress '35; attended various geological congresses. Author articles in field. Professor geol and chmn dept Duke U since '38; asst geol NC Dept Econ Geol since '43; cons various companies. AAAS(F)—Geol Soc Am(F)—AIME—Am Assn Petroleum Geol—Geophys Union—Soc Geol de France—Pan-American Soc Engr Geol—Geol Soc Peru—Sigma Xi. Department of Geology, Duke University, Durham, N.C. H: 1003 N. Gregeson St.†

13 **BERRY, George W(illard).** Petroleum geology (Rocky Mountains). b'15. AB '36 (Colgate U); MS '38—PhD '41 (Cornell U). Author articles in field. Dist geol Sun Oil Co Casper Wyo since '48. AAAS—Am Inst Mining Metall Engrs—Am Assn Petroleum Geol—Geol Soc Am—Soc Econ Geol—Am Geophys Union—Sigma Xi—Phi Kappa Phi. Sun Oil Company, Box 1166, Casper, Wyo.†

14 **BERRY, John W(illiam).** Flame photometry; Instrumentation. b'16. AB '37 (Ind U); PhD '42 (State U Ia); student (Northwestern U). Author articles in field. Research physicist Am Cyanamid Co since '42. Am Chem Soc—Sigma Xi. American Cyanamid Co., Stamford, Conn.

15 **BERRY, William Julius.** North American geography; Geomorphology; Conservation of natural resources. b '91. AB '21 (Ia State Teach Coll); SM '26—PhD '38 (U Chicago). Author articles: Capacity of United States for Population '43; Arabs of Kordofan '29, and others. Asso prof geog West Mich Coll Edn '30-38; prof since '38; prof geog Peabody Coll '47; prof Northwestern U '44, '50; Eastern Washington Coll '52. Nat Council Geog Teach (sec '32-36)—Assn American Geog—Mich Acad Sci—AAAS—Sigma Xi—Assn Am Geog. Western Michigan College of Education, Kalamazoo, Mich.

16 **BERTALANFFY, Ludwig von.** General and theoretical biology and physiology; biophysics; philosophy of biology. b'01. PhD '26 (U Vienna). Research on comparative physiology of metabolism and growth in vertebrates and invertebrates, tissue metabolism, quantitative theory of metabolism and growth, kinetics and thermodynamics of open systems and steady states organismic biology. Author: Modern Theories of Development '33; Theoretische Biologie (2 vol, 2nd edit) '51; Problems of Life: An Evaluation of Modern Biological Thought '52; numerous papers sci jours. Editor: Handbuch der Biologie, since '42; Biologia Generalis, since '49. Privatdozent then prof biol U Vienna '34-48; research prof biol U Ottawa since '49. AAAS—Can Physiol Soc. F Rockefeller Found '37-38. Department of Biology, Faculty of Medicine, University of Ottawa, Ont., Can.

17 **BERTHOLF, Lloyd Millard.** Apiculture; Tunicates. b'99. BA '21 (Southwestern Coll); MA '24—PhD '28 (Johns Hopkins); '30-31 (Munich U). Research on honeybees with emphasis on moults, utilization of carbohydrates by larvae, reactions to light, distribution of relative stimulative efficiency in U-V spectrum and its physiological effects, toxicity of insecticides; extent of spectrum for Drosophila. Author articles in field. Dean and prof zool Coll Pacific since '48. AAAS(F)—Am Soc Zool—Am Assn Econ Entomol—Sigma Xi—Phi Beta Kappa—Beta Beta Beta (nat pres). Nat Research Council fellow, Munich '30-31. College of the Pacific, Stockton 4, Cal.†

18 **BERTRAND, Kenneth J.** Geomorphology; Geographical names. b'10. '32-33 (Syracuse U); BS '32—'33-35—'36-37 PhD '40 (U Wis). Supervised and collaborated on several publications of US Board on Geographical Names, major contributor to Special Pub No 86; Geographical Names in Antarctica. Instr geog Oklahoma AM '37-39, asst prof '39-41, asso prof 41-43; regional geog US Bd Geog Names '43-44, chief research div '44-46; asst prof geog Catholic U Am '46-48, asso prof since '48. Special cons OQMG '46-47. Am Geog Soc—Am Soc Profl Geog—Assn Am Geog—Nat Council Geog Teach—Assn Pacific Coast Geog—Brit Glaciological Soc—Special Com Antarctic Names, US Bd Geog Names. Catholic University. Washington 17.†

19 **BESHAR, Herbert K.** Woolen fabric mercerization; Floor coverings. b'97. Student '14-16 (DeWitt Clinton Coll); '16 (Columbia). Perfected process of mercerizing wool under trade mark of Besharizing. Author: Life Story of Ispahan '27. Asst mgr, later pres A Beshar and Co, Inc since '21; pres Carpet Servicing Co Inc; vp NY Carpet Inst; lecturer on rugs of the Orient. 23 E. 49th St., NYC 17.

20 **BESLEY, Harry E(lmer).** Rural electrification; Farm power and machinery. b'09. BS '29 (Va Poly Inst); MS '31 (U Md). Asst agrl engr Md Agrl Expt Sta Coll Pk Md '31-32, asst agrl engr NJ Agrl Expt Sta New Brunswick NJ '32-41; instr and asst prof agrl engring Rutgers U '32-41, prof and chmn dept since '46. Am Soc Agrl Engrs (chmn North Atlantic sect '46)—Phi Kappa Phi. College of Agriculture, New Brunswick, N.J.

21 **BESTOR, Arthur Eugene, Jr.** Communitarian socialism in America; New Harmony Movement. b'08. PhB '30—PhD '38 (Yale). Research on Robert Owen, the experiment at New Harmony, Fourierist movement of 1840's, Brook Farm Community. Author: Chautauqua Publications: An Historical and Bibliographical Guide '34; David Jacks of Monterey, and Lee L. Jacks, His Daughter '45; Education and Reform at New Harmony: Correspondence of William Maclure and Marie D. Fretageot, 1820-1833 '48; Backwoods Utopias: A History of Communitarian Socialism in America '49. Asso hist Columbia '36-37, asst prof hist '37-42; asst prof humanities Stanford U '42-45, asso prof hist '45-46; professor hist U Ill since '51; AHA—Miss Valley Hist Assn—AAUP—NY State Hist Soc—Ill State Hist Soc—Ind Hist Soc—Wis Hist Soc—Phi Beta Kappa. Newberry fellow Newberry Lib Chicago '46; Albert J. Beveridge memorial fellowship AHA '46. 315 Lincoln Hall, University of Illinois, Champaign, Ill.†

22 **BETH, Richard Alexander.** Physics; Mechanical effects of light; Terminal ballistics; Elasticity; Magnetic Phenomenon. b'06. BS '27 MS '29 (Worcester Poly Inst) Dr Phil-Nat in Math '32 (U Frankfort Am Main). Asso prof applied math '39-40 Mich State Coll; physicist Com on Passive Protection against Bombing Nat Research Washington '40-42; mem div 2 Nat Defense Research Com Princeton '42-44 dept head '42-46; prof chmn physics dept Western Reserve U since '46 Perkins Prof physics since '47; mem council reps Argonne Nat Lab Chicago since '47. Author numerous reports for coms Office Scientific Research and Development and Nat Research Council. Experimental discovery of angular momentum of light '34-35; scale effect of projectile penetration of targets '41-42. Am Phys Soc(F)—AAAS(F)—Am Math Assn—Optical Soc Am—Am Assn Physics Teachers—Sigma Xi—Tau Beta Pi—Pi Mu Epsilon. Physics Dept., Western Reserve U., Cleveland 6.†☉

23 **BETHEL, John P.** Lexicography. b'04. BA '24 (McGill U); AM '25—PhD '27 (Harvard). Dir G & C Merriam Co Springfield Mass, gen ed Merriam-Webster dictionaries since '39. 224 Ellington Rd., Longmeadow, Mass.☉

24 **BETHKE, William.** Business administration. b'85. AB '10—AM '11 (U Minn). Author: The Private School in Modern Education. Editor: Business Administration (18 volumes); Salesmanship, (9 vols). Gen ednl dir, vp and sec La Salle Extension U, Chicago; sec Stenotype Co and Nat Stenotype Inst. Chicago Assn Commerce—Am Econ Assn—NEA—Phi Beta Kappa. 417 S. Dearborn St., Chicago.*

25 **BETHMANN, Erich Waldemar.** Islamics. b'04. Ed German gymnasium and theol sem; postgrad work Livingstone Coll London, and Am U, Cairo; Research on Arabic, Urdu and Persian languages, extensive travel in Egypt, Trans-Jordan, Iraq, Syria, Lebanon, Palestine, India. Author: Bridge to Islam '50. Dir mission, Amman '33-37; regional dir Iraq, Baghdad '38-39; in India '39-46; with Wash Theol Sem '46-50; Director of Publications & Research Am Friends Middle E since '51. Middle E Inst. 139 E. 57th St., NYC 22.

26 **BETTELHEIM, Edwin Sumner, Jr.** Military analysis, information and procedure. b'87. BS '11 (Columbia); LLB '24—LLM '25—AB '26— AM '27 (George Washington U); grad '38 (Command and Gen Staff Sch). Author: My Experiences in Northern Russia '29; Army Mobilization '34. Ed and pub Nat Bulletin of Mil Order World Wars; 1st lt 104th and 17th FA Res '19, advanced to col; asst chief staff Mil Dist Washington; mil analyst US Dept State; mil biog Inter-Am Mil Assn; adj gen and exec officer (treas gen) Mil Order of World Wars since '31. Res Officers Assn (past pres). 1700 "I" St., N.W., Washington 6.†

27 **BETTEN, Cornelius.** Trichoptera (North America). b'77. BA '00—MA '01—DSc '23 (Lake Forest Coll); PhD

'06 (Cornell U). Author: The Trichoptera of New York State '34. Vice dean resident instruction NY State Coll Agr Cornell U '20-22, dir '22-40, acting dean '24-26, '31-32, dean U faculty Cornell '32-45, prof emeritus since '45. AAAS(F)—Entomol Soc Am (F)—Sigma Xi—Phi Kappa Phi. 177 Woodland Rd., Asheville, N.C.◎

10 BETTERS, Paul V(ernon). Federal-city relations. b'06. BS '28 (U Minn); MS '29 (Syracuse U); '31 (George Washington U)—'32 (Selwyn Coll, Cambridge, Eng). US delegate International Congress of Local Authorities, London '32, Lyon, France '34, Paris, France '47; Hague '48, Geneva, Switzerland '49; US delegate Pan-American Congress of Cities, Havana Cuba '39. Author: Personnel Classification Board '31; Federal Services to Municipal Governments '32; State Centralization in North Carolina '32; Recent Federal-City Relations '36. Editor: City Problems (12 volumes) '33-'50; The United States Municipal News, since '33; also articles in field. Staff NY Commn on Revision of Pub Service Laws, State of NY, Washington '30; staff, The Brookings Instn, Washington '30-32; exec dir United States Conference Mayors, Washington since '32. Am Acad Polit Social Sci—Am Polit Sci Assn—Govtl Research Assn—Nat Municipal League—Internat City Mgrs Assn—Am Pub Welfare Assn—Am Soc Planning Officials—Nat Assn Housing Officials—Civil Service Assembly of US and Can—Municipal Finance Officers Assn—Nat Planning Assn—Urban Land Inst—Nat Tax Assn—Am Soc Pub Adminstrn—Nat Pub Housing Conf—Tax Inst—Am Com for Internat Union of Local Authorities. Awarded Citation and Award for Distinguished Service to Am Cities, US Conf of Mayors '42, '47. 730 Jackson Pl., N.W., Washington 6.

11 BETTERSWORTH, John K(nox). American history (Mississippi, Civil War). b'09. AB '29 (Millsaps Coll); PhD '37—grad fellow '35-37 (Duke U). Research on Confederate exiles in Mexico, Edward Hyde and the Church of England, American exposition in cultural history. Author: Confederate Mississippi: The People and Policies of a Cotton State in Wartime '43; also articles in field. Prof hist and govt since '37 and head dept Miss State Coll since '48, chmn soc sci research cntr since '50. Miss Hist Soc—So Hist Assn—Miss Valley Hist Assn—AHA—So Polit Sci Assn—Phi Beta Kappa. Box 148, State College, Miss.

12 BETTINGER, A(lvin) K(ilian). Mathematics. b'93. Author: Commerce Algebra '47; articles in field. BA '26 MA '27 (U Wis) student '33-36 (U Neb). Dir dept math Creighton U Omaha since '27. Mem Math Assn Am.◎

13 BETTS, Emmett Albert. Educational psychology (Reading, semantics); Psycho-physiology of vision. b'03. BS '25 (Des Moines U); AM '28—PhD '31 (U Ia). Associate editor Journal of Educational Research, Journal Exceptional Children and Journal of Experimental Education. Author: Prevention and Correction of Reading Difficulties; Betts Ready to Read Tests; Betts-Arey Directed Spelling; Betts Basic Readers; Foundations of Reading Instruction; also articles in field. Prof psychol and dir Reading Clinic Temple U since '45; Pa Assn Blind (hon mem adv bd)—Internat Council for Study Exceptional Children (hon mem adv com)—Distinguished Service Found Optometry(F)—Assn for Childhood Edn (F)—Am Assn Applied Psychol(F)— AAAS(F)—Am

Ednl Research Assn (dept supervisors and dir instrn)—NEA (life mem dept elementary sch prins)—Am Psychol Assn—Nat Soc Study Edn—Pa State Edn Assn—Pa Ednl Research Assn—Progressive Edn Assn—Soc Advancement Edn—Am Assn Sch Adminstrs (life mem dept supt). Temple University, Philadelphia 22.

14 BETTS, Robert Edward. Libraries (Special). b'07. BA '32 (U NC); BS (library sci) '42 (George Peabody Coll). Research on serials and monographs for use in colleges and universities offering courses in geography. Chief os tacks Dept Agr Library; head librarian Ia Wesleyan Coll '47-48; engring librarian Tex Engrs Library since '48. ALA—Assn Coll and phy. Chief of stacks Dept Agr Library; Assn. Texas Engineers Library, College Station, Tex.

15 BEVAN, Ralph M. Rationalization of religion. b'81. AB '04 (Brown U); BCL—Rhodes scholar '06 (Oxford U). Research for enlightening and inspiring effectual religion in prospective leaders. Author articles in field. Studied Am Law '07-14, specialized in rationalizing religion since '14; commission World Fedn Edn Assns on Feasibility of a World U '24-25. Phi Beta Kappa. 235 Hope St., Providence, R.I.

16 BEVER, Wayne M(ellville). Cereal crop pathology (Smut and rust). b'04. BS '27—MS '28 (U Idaho); PhD '40 (U Wis). Author articles in field. Jr path, later path Bur Plant Ind Soils and Agr Engring US Dept Agr since '29; asso prof crop path dept agron U Ill. Am Phytopath Assn—Sigma Xi—Gamma Sigma Delta. Department of Agronomy, University of Illinois, Urbana, Ill.

17 BEYER, Arthur Frederick. Paleobotany; Petrified trees. b'22. BS '43 MS '45 (O State University) PhD '50 (U Cincinnati). Paleobotany; plant morphology wood anatomy; fossil woods of Yellowstone Park. Asso prof botany Midwestern Univ Wichita Falls Tex since '50. AAAS—Sigma Xi. Midwestern University, Wichita Falls, Tex.

18 BEYER, Glenn H. Housing. b'13. AB '35 (Augustana Coll Sioux Falls SD); MA '39 (George Washington U). Analysis urban housing market; community studies housing situation in southeastern US; determination housing requirements Oak Ridge Tenn; in charge farm housing research project northeastern US; housing consultant on problems of mortgage financing and marketability, on development of new federal housing research program '50; member National Housing Council since '50. Author: Farm Housing in the Northeast '49; Housing and Journey to Work '51. Housing econ Fed Housing Adminstrn Washington and Atlanta '39-41; econ Div Defense Housing Coordination Washington '41-42; econ and dep regional rep Nat Housing Agency Atlanta '42-46, chief market analysis div Washington '46-47; prof housing and design Cornell U since '47, dir housing research center since '50; housing cons govt and industry since '47. Am Econ Assn—Am Statis Assn—Nat Econ and Polit Sci—Acad Polit Sci—AAUP. Cornell University, Ithaca. H: 221 Bryant Av.

19 BEYER, H(enry) Otley. Philippine peoples (History, archeology, ethnology); Tektites. b'83. Student '01-03 (Ia State Coll); AB '04—AM '05 (U Denver); Winthrop scholar '08-09 (Harvard). Conducted Rizal-Bulakan archeological survey '26-30 securing a collection of more than a half-million specimens, Batangas archeological

survey '32-41 resulting in a collection of about 250,000 specimens; discovered first Philippine tektites '26, first Philippine remains of Palaeolithic man '28-29. Author: Population of the Philippines in 1916 '17; Philippine Tektites '42; Outline Review of Philippine Archaeology by Islands and Provinces '47; Philippine and East Asian Archeology '48. Co-author: A History of the Orient '26. Compiler and editor: Philippine Ethnographic Series; Philippine Customary Law Series; Philippine Archaeological Series; Philippine Tektite Series; also author articles in field. Prof anthropol U Philippines and ethnologist Philippine Bur Sci since '14. Am Hist Assn—Philippine Acad—Philippine Nat Research Council—Philippine Geol Soc (pres 2 terms). Presidential Medal of Honor for 45 years scientific work for the Government and people of the Philippines '49. University of the Philippines, Quezon City, Philippines.

20 BIBB, Thomas William. American education (College administration, history); Economic theory. b'84. AB '08 (William Jewell Coll); AM '26—Denny fellow '27-28—PhD '28 (U Washington). Author: History of Early Common School Education in Washington '29; Challenge to the College '47. Co-author: History of Education in Washington '34; also articles in field. Prof econ and business Whitworth Coll. Am Palestine Com—Com for Jewish Army Stateless and Palestinian Jews — Nat Edn Assn. Whitworth College, Spokane, Wash.

21 BIBBER, Harold Whitney. Electric Power System and Engineering (Machinery); Electric Power (Japan); Engineering education. b'99. SB '20 (MIT); grad '20 (Universite de Besancon France); '20-21 (Ecole Superieure d'Electricite U Paris); '22-23 (Boston U). Spent three years in Japan as General Electric Company engineer specializing in power systems; research in power system analysis; developed new teaching methods in engineering education. Author: Synchronous Machines '36; Alternating Current Machinery '41. Office engr Internat Gen Elec Co '23-29; engr Gen Elec Co '29-32; prof elec engring Ohio State U '32-42; prof elec engring and chmn div engring Union Coll since '42. AIEE—Am Soc Engring Edn—AAUP—Newcomen Society—Soc Francaise des Electriciens—Sigma Xi—Tau Beta Pi—Eta Kappa Nu. Union College, Schenectady 8, N.Y.

22 BICE, Ernest Gordon. Meteorology (Weather forecasting, atmospheric pressure changes, statistical correlations). b'06. BS '31 (North Tex State Teachers Coll); MS '44 (U Chicago). Author articles in field. Weather observer and meteorol since '37; Meteorol in charge US Weather Bur Nashville Tenn since '47. Am Meteorol Soc—Nat Assn Weather Forecasters. Weather Bureau Airport Station, Nashville 4.†

23 BICE, Harry Voorhies. Psychology of crippled children; Mental deficiency. b'95. BA '24 (Temple U); BD '28 (Drew U); MA '35—PhD '38 (U NC). Assisted in reorganization of educational work in State Institution for Mentally Deficient at Austin, Texas; research on mentally deficient child in residential school, religious work with mental defectives, moron level, psychological examination of cerebral palsied. Author: A Study of Negro and White Pupils in Piedmont, North Carolina '38; also articles in field. Cons on psychol problems of crippled children, NJ State Crippled Children Commn since '46. Am Psycho'

Assn—Am Assn Mental Deficiency (F, past vp). Diplomate American Psychol Assn. 732 Broad St., Bank Building, Trenton 8, N.J.

10 BICKLEY, William Elbert. Entomology. b'14. BS '34—MS '36 (U Tenn); PhD '40 (U Md). Research on Japanese beetle, Chrysopidae, stomodael nervous system of insects, malaria control. Author articles in field. Asso professor entomology University of Maryland since '49. Mosquito Control Assn—Am Assn Econ Entomol—AAUP —Entomol Soc Wash—Entomol Soc Am —Am Soc Profl Biol—Sigma Xi. University of Maryland, College Park, Md.

11 BIDDLE, Arthur. Adhesives. b'97. Student (Chem) '16-18 (Drexel Inst Tech). Holds 50 patents on adhesives, based on dispersed colloidal systems. Author articles: Laminating Adhesives and their Applications '46; Types of Adhesives '46. Chief chemist Union Casein Co Phila. '19-20; gen mgr. vp United Products Co Phila '20-29; pres Biddle Labs Trenton NJ '29-42; tech dir research and developmental lab Reynolds Metals Co Richmond Va since '42, tech asst to vp in charge research and operations '46-50; now tech dir J. M. Fry Co Richmond Va. Tech Assn Paper and Pulp Industries—Am Chem Soc—AAAS. J. M. Fry Co., Richmond, Va. H: 3311 North Av.

12 BIDDLE, William Wishart. Community dynamics. b'00. BA '23 (Pomona Coll); MA '28—PhD '32 (Columbia). Research on processes by which communities grow in ability to direct own growth, studies of conflict, such as inter-religious, social, and industrial, and their resolution as essential to community growth, rural development and small cities and their role in international contact, basic social processes. Head dept psychol and edn State Teachers Coll (Milwaukee) '35-44; sr health spl and chief community and coop services Farmers Home Adminstrn USDA '44-47; dir community dynamics Earlham Coll since '47. Am Psychol Assn—Am Council for Community (exec bd)—Nat Assn Adult Educators—Nat Assn Fgn Student Advisers. Earlham College, Richmond, Ind.

13 BIDDULPH, Orlin Nathan. Plant physiology; Radioisotopes. b'08. BS '29—MS '33 (Brigham Young U); Hutchinson fellow '33-34—PhD '34 (U Chicago). Research on photoperiodic response; absorption, translocation, and metabolism of phosphorus and iron; chlorosis. Author articles in field. Asst prof, head dept bot U SD '34-37; asst prof bot Washington State Coll '37-41, asso prof '41-46, prof since '46. AAAS(F)—Nat Research Council(F)— Am Soc Plant Physiol—Bot Soc Am— Sigma Xi. State College of Washington, Pullman, Wash.

14 BIEBER, Ralph Paul. American history (Frontier in Trans-Mississippi West: 1803-1893; Colonial period). b'94. AB '14 (Muhlenberg Coll); AM '15—PhD '20—Harrison scholar and fellow '15-18 (U Pa). Research California gold rush, Santa Fe trail, frontier life in army, Texas cattle trails, overland trails to the Pacific, Mexican War in the Southwest, Mormon battalion, Indians of the Great Plains, history of Missouri. Author: Lords of Trade and Plantations 1675-1696 '19. Editor: Southwest Historical Series; also articles in field. Prof hist Wash U since '40. Miss Valley Hist Assn (exec com '31-34 and since '47, pres '47-48)—AHA—Pacific Hist Assn—Am Cath Hist Assn—Mo Hist Soc—State Hist Soc Mo—Kan State Hist Soc— State Hist Soc Ia—Hist Soc NM(F)— Royal Hist Soc(F)—Am Antiquarian

Soc—Phi Beta Kappa. Grant-in-Aid Social Sci Research Council '40, Rockefeller Found '44-48. Department of History, Washington University, St. Louis 5.†◎

15 BIEBERDORF, Gustav Adolph. Apiculture; Pecan insects; Insect photography. b'98. BS '22—MS (Okla A & M Coll). Author articles in field. Asst prof and asst entomol Okla A & M Coll since '24. Am Soc Hort Sci—Okla Acad Sci—Am Assn Econ Entomol— Phi Sigma. Oklahoma A. & M. College, Stillwater, Okla.†

16 BIEL, William Collins. Human engineering; Physiological and industrial psychology. b'09. BA '31 (Oberlin Coll); MA '33 (Western Reserve U); PhD '37 (Stanford). Engaged research and writing on human engineering, physiological conditions as they affect learning, emotional and regressive behavior, effects of intentional and incidental learning on retention, selection and training of military and industrial personnel. Research psychol psych br, Aero Med Lab Wright-Patterson Air Force Base since '48. Sigma Xi—AAAS—Am Psychol Assn—Midwestern Psychol Assn—O Psychol Assn. Psychology Branch, Aero Medical Laboratory, Air Materiel Command, Wright-Patterson Air Force Base, Dayton, O.

17 BIER, Justus. History of medieval and Franconian sculpture; Tillmann Riemenschneider. b'99. PhD '24 (U Zurich); student (U Munich, U Erlangen, U Jena, U Bonn). Author: Nurnbergisch-Frankische Bildnerkunst '22; Tilmann Riemenschneider Die fruhen Werke '25; Tilmann Riemenschneider Die reifen Werke '30; Tilmann Riemenschneider Die spaten Werke '49; Tilmann Riemenschneider Ein Gedenkbuch '48, and others; also articles in field. Asst prof art hist and acting head dept fine arts U Louisville '37-41, head dept since '41, prof since '46, dir Allen R Hite Art Inst since '46. Coll Art Assn Am. Travel fellow Notgemeinschaft der Deutschen Wissenschaft '28. University of Louisville, Louisville 8, Ky.†

18 BIERCK, Harold Alfred, Jr. Latin American history. b'16. BA '38—MA '40—PhD '44 (U Calif). Author: Vida Publica de Pedro Gual '47; Selected Writings of Bolivar (2 vols) '49. Asst prof hist U NC since '48. Department of History, University of North Carolina, Chapel Hill, N.C.

19 BIERER, Andrew Gordon Curtin. Jr. Examination and licensure for admission to the bar. b'99. AB '21 (U Okla); LLB '25 (Harvard). Member State Bar Commission and Committee of State Bar Examiners '27-39; executive committee National Conference Bar Examiners '31-41, chairman '38, '39; committee of experts bar examinations and admission to practice law American Bar Association Survey of the Legal Profession '48. Author articles in field. Firm Bierer & Bierer since '26. Am Bar Assn—Okla State Bar Assn. Bierer Building, Guthrie, Okla.

20 BIERER, John M(ichael). Chemicals; Technical development of rubber. b'88. BS '08 (Washington & Lee U) BS '10 (Mass Inst Tech). With Boston Woven Hose & Rubber Co Boston since '11 vice pres '44-50 exec vice pres '50 pres and gen mgr since '51. Instn Rubber Industry—Am Chem Soc—ASTM. 29 Hampshire St., Cambridge 39, Mass.◎

21 BIESANZ, John. Life and culture of Costa Rica, Panama and the Canal Zone; Sociology of marriage and

the family; Youth hostels. b'13. BA '37 (U Chicago); PhD '41 (State U Ia). Research on youth hostels throughout world, on specific aspects of Costa Rican life such as education and standards of mate selection. Coauthor: (with Mavis Biesanz) Costa Rican Life '44; also articles in field. Asso prof sociol and anthrop Wayne U since '50. Wayne University, Det.†

22 BIESELE, John Julius. Cancer (Chromosomes, nuclei); Phosphatases; Cancer tissue culture. b'18. BA '39— PhD '42 (U Tex). Research on multiple-stranded condition of cancer chromosomes, activity of alkaline phosphatase, toxicities of drugs to normal and cancerous mouse cells using tissue cultures. Author articles in field. Research asso dept genetics Carnegie Inst '44-46; with Sloan-Kettering Inst Cancer Research since '46, asso and head cell growth sect from '48; asst prof anatomy Cornell U Med Coll since '50. Phi Beta Kappa—Sigma Xi—AA AS—Am Assn Cancer Research—NY Acad Sci—Tissue Culture Assn—Histochem Soc. Internat Cancer Research Found F '42-43, '43-44. Sloan-Kettering Institute, 410 E. '68th St., NYC 21.

23 BIESELE, Rudolph Leopold, Jr. Illuminating engineering; School lighting; Daylighting. b'15. BS '36 (U Tex). Conducted extensive research on daylight control methods for schools. Author articles in field. Asst prof elec engring So Meth U Dallas '43-44, asso prof '44-46, prof, chmn dept elec engring '46-52; vp Toff Illuminating Engring Soc—Am Soc Engineering Edn—AIEE—Tex Acad Sci —Tex Soc Profl Engrs. Toff Corporation, Dallas.

24 BIETZ, Arthur Leo. Psychosomatics; Non-directive technique and therapy. b'13. BA '42—MA '44—PhD '46 (U So Calif). Author: Guideposts to Happiness '42; Conquering Personal Problems '44; In Quest of Life '47. Prof Coll Med Evangelists Los Angeles since '43; psychol cons White Memorial Clinic since '43. Am Psychol Assn. 312 N. Boyle, Los Angeles. H: 732 Fay St., Glendale 6, Calif.

25 BIGELOW, Arthur Lynds. Bells and carillons. b'09. Lic Phil '40 (U Louvain). Laureate, Carillon School, Mechlin. Bell-master, Princeton U; architect and designer of several new carillons in the US; designed, moulded, tuned, treble bells for carillon of Princeton U and others; tonal designer of electronic carillon. Author: Carillon '48; Music from the Belfry '49; also articles in field. Faculty Princeton U since '41. Am Guild Organists—North Am Guild Carillonneurs — Am Soc Engring Edn. Department of Engineering, Princeton University, Princeton, N.J.

26 BIGELOW, Karl Worth. Teacher education; Higher education. b'98. AB '20—LHD '38 (Clark U); PhD '29 (Harvard); LL D '41 (Parsons Coll). Coauthor: A Manual of Thesis-Writing '34; General Education in the American College, '39; The Social Studies in General Education '40; Teachers for Our Times '44; The Improvement of Teacher Education '46 General Education '52. Consultant in social studies Gen Edn Board NYC '37-38; director Commn on Teacher Edn Am Council on Edn '38-44; chmn com on function of social studies in gen edn Commn on Secondary Sch Curriculum, Progressive Edn Assn '36-40; del at large Council on Cooperation in Teacher Edn Am Council on Edn since '41, chmn '45-51; cons and lecturer UNESCO Seminar on Edn for Internat Understanding France '47; dir UNESCO

Seminar on teacher edn and training Eng '48. Asst prof econ U Buffalo '30-31, prof '31-37, dir tutorial instrn '35-37; vis prof edn Teachers Coll Columbia, '36-37, prof since '37. AAUP—Am Econ Assn—NEA—Am Assn Sch Administrs—Nat Soc for Study of Edn —Assn for Student Teaching—Phi Delta Kappa—Kappa Delta Pi. 525 W. 120th St., NYC 27.©

10 BIGELOW, Maurice Hubbard. Plastics; Glass; Microscopy; Acetylene chemistry. b'03. BS '24 (Northeastern U); PhD '33 (U Pittsburgh). Author: Modern Acetylene Chemistry; Handbook of Plastics; New Plastics. Holder five patents relating to plastics. Tech dir plaskon div Libbey Owens Ford Glass Co since '34. Lt col US Army Chem Corps '42-46. Am Chem Soc— Soc Plastics Ind—ASTM—Ill Engring Soc—Sigma Xi. 2112 Sylvan Av., Toledo 6, Ohio.

11 BIJLAARD, Paulus Pieter. Stability; Plasticity; Plates; Shells. b'98. CE '20 (Tech U Delft Holland). Studies in theory of local plastic deformations; plastic stability of thin plates; local plastic deformations with respect to deformations of earth's crust. Bridge engr Netherlands East Indies State Rwys '20-28; prof bridge and structural engring Tech U Bandoeng Netherlands East Indies '28-47; prof applied mechanics Tech U Delft Holland '47-50; asso prof structural engring Cornell U since '49. Internat Assn Bridge and Structural Engring —Royal Inst Engrs (Dutch)—Am Soc CE—Am Geophys Union. Lincoln Hall, Cornell University, Ithaca, N.Y.

12 BIKERMAN, Jacob Joseph. Surface chemistry. b'98. Diploma '21 (U Petrograd); hon research fellow '36-37 (U Manchester); '23-33 (Kaiser Wilhelm Inst f Physik Chemie, Berlin-Dahlem; '37-39 (U Cambridge). Research in adhesion, electrocapillarity, electrophoresis, foaminess, friction and lubrication, membranes, organosols, surface films, surface roughness, tensile strength, wetting. Author: Surface Chemistry for Industrial Research '47; Co-author: (with H Freundlich) Kapillarchemie '31-32; also articles in field. Staff mem research and development div Merck & Co Inc Rahway NJ since '46. Am Chem Soc— Soc Rheology—NY Acad Sci—Brit Rheologists' Club—Faraday Soc. Merck & Co., Inc., Rahway, N.J.†

13 BILGER, Earl Matthias. Physical and biochemistry; Colloids. b'98. BS '20—AM '21 (Wesleyan U); PhD '25 (Yale); '28-29 (U Cincinnati); '35-36 (Cambridge U Eng). Research on iodine and copper content of Hawaiian food products, on pathology of blood, and on water, soils and rocks. Author articles in field. Prof chem U Hawaii since '42. Am Chem Soc (chmn Hawaii sec)—Hawaiian Acad Sci—Phi Beta Kappa—Sigma Xi—Phi Kappa Phi. 2425 University Av., Honolulu 5, T.H.

14 BILGER, Leonora Neuffer. Chemistry; Organic chemistry. AB '13— MA '14—Ph D '16 (U Cincinnati); Sarah Berliner Fellowship, AAUW; chem research Cambridge U '24-25, '35-36. Author articles in field. Prof chem U Hawaii '25-28, and since '37, chmn dept since '43, chmn research com '42-47. Sec Labor and Indsl Relations Commn Ter Hawaii since '46. Nat Sci Teacher Assn (Hawaii dir since '46)—Am Chem Soc—AAUP—AAAS—NEA—Hawaiian Acad Sci—Phi Beta Kappa—Phi Kappa Phi—Sigma Xi—Iota Sigma Pi. (Nat hon Woman's Chemical). 2425 University Av., Honolulu 5, T.H.

15 BILLETT, Roy Oren. Education (Secondary). b'91. BSc '23—MA '27— PhD '29 (Ohio State U). Program of studies: core curriculum including group guidance; supervision, methods teaching, provisions for individual differences. Author articles in field. Specialist sch. adminstrn US Office Edn '30-32; With Boston U since '35, prof since '35, chmn dept edn grad sch since '44; staff Survey Pub Schs Cincinnati '35; dir Survey Pub Edn Harford Co Md '45-46; dir Two-Year Revision Program Coop Study Secondary Sch Standards '48. Am Assn Sch Adminstrs—Nat Assn Secondary Sch Prins—NEA—AAUP—Am Ednl Research Assn—Nat Soc Study Edn—Phi Delta Kappa. 332 Bay State Rd., Boston.©

16 BILLIG, Albert LeRoy. Tests (Intelligence, personality evaluation). b'06. BS '30 (Muhlenberg Coll Allentown Pa); '31 (U Pa); AM '36 (Columbia); EdD '41 (Temple U). Developed a commercial arithmetic attitude scale; study emotional factors, and effect on student intelligence; investigation effect of physical handicap on student intelligence and morale, also effect of treatment of such handicap. Author articles: Nervous Habits and Morale '42; Emotionalized Mental Tests '43; Approaches in Learning '44; A Study of the Learning Process in the Classroom '49, and others. Contributor: Genetic Psychology Monographs '41. Psychol recruiting and induction sta Allentown Pa '42; private practice psychol since '43; psychol for cleft palate, speech, and cerebral palsy clinics Lehigh Co Crippled Children's Soc since '49. Am Psychol Assn (F)—Eastern Psychol Assn—Pa Acad Sci—Kappa Phi Kappa—Phi Delta Kappa. 1328 Gordon St., Allentown, Pa

17 BILLINGER, Robert Dominick. Early Pennsylvania industries (Iron and steel, zinc, pottery, paper manufacturing). b'99. ChE '21—MS '25 (Lehigh U); '26-27 (Yale); PhD '29 (U Cincinnati). Co-author: Experiments in Inorganic Chemistry; General Chemistry Experiments; also articles in field. Asso prof Lehigh U since '39. Am Chem Soc—Newcomen Soc— Tau Beta Pi—Sigma Xi. Lehigh University, Bethlehem, Pa.

18 BILLINGS, Bruce H. Crystal optics; Infrared physics; Evaporated films. b'15. AB '36—AM '37 (Harvard); PhD '43 (Johns Hopkins). Radiology safety section atomic bomb test Bikini '46; research on scalar polarization fringes produced by superposition of crystalline plates, haidinger interference fringes in plane-parallel crystalline plates, a study of efficiency of carbon microphone hearing aids, investigation of the properties of evaporated metal bolometers, construction and characteristics of evaporated nickel bolometers, the infrared refractive index and dispersion of evaporated stibnite films, a comparative study of some possible systems of polarized headlights. Physicist Polaroid Corp Cambridge; dir research Baird Assos Inc Cambridge since '47. NY Acad Sci—Am Phys Soc—Acoustical Soc Am—Optical Soc Am—AAAS —Sigma Xi. Baird Associates, Incorporated, 33 University Rd., Cambridge 38, Mass.

19 BILLINGS, William Dwight. Quantitative plant ecology (Desert, forest); Plant distribution (Trees, grasses); Nevada trees and grasses). b'10. AB '33 (Butler U); MA '35— PhD '36 (Duke U). Research on quantitative correlations between vegetational change and soil development, factors affecting vegetational zonation on coastal dunes, Great Basin; grasses and clovers of Nevada. Author articles in field. With U Nev since '38, now chmn dept biol. AAAS(F)—Ecol Soc Am (exec com Western sec '46-48)— Am Soc Range Management—Sigma Xi —Phi Kappa Phi. Department of Biology, University of Nevada, Reno, Nev.†

20 BILLINGTON, Lillian. Methods of spelling and handwriting. AB '32 (San Jose State Coll); AM '34—EdD '47 (Stanford U). Author: Laurel Handwriting Series, Grades 1-9 '37; 8 manuals for spelling series '44; Using Words '45. Asso prof edn supervisor student teachers San Jose State Coll since '32; cons langs art. Am Assn Sch Adminstrs—Am Assn Supervisors— Nat Arts. C/o Silver, Burdett Co., 45 E. 17th St., NYC.

21 BILLINGTON, Ray Allen. United States history. b'03. PhB '26 (U Wis); MA '27 (U Mich)—PhD '33 (Harvard). Research on history of American frontier, anti-Catholicism in US. Author: The Protestant Crusade, 1800-1860 '38; Westward Expansion: A History of the American Frontier '48; Editor: Massachusetts, A Guide to its Places and People '37; and others; Schouler lecturer Johns Hopkins '43; John Simon Guggenheim memorial fellow '43-44; prof hist Northwestern U '44-49; William Smith Mason prof hist since '49. Econ Hist Assn—Chgo Hist Soc—AHA—Miss Valley Hist Assn—Ill Hist Soc—Phi Beta Kappa. Northwestern University, Evanston, Ill.©

22 BILSING, Sherman Weaver. Pecan insects; Pecans. b'85. BS '12 (Otterbein Coll); AB '12—MA '13—PhD '24 (O State U). Study life history, habits, and methods of control pecan twig girdler (Oncideres Cingulata); biological study, anatomy, relationships to temperature, and control methods pecan nut casebearer (Acrobasis caryse); research on obscure scale, pecan leaf casebearer, pecan phylloxera, and other insects. Author articles: The Type of Damage Caused by Common Pecan Insects '32; The Control of the Obscure Scale by Oil Sprays '35; Combination Sprays for the Control of the Common Insects of the Pecan '39; Review of the Experimental Work on the Pecan Nut Casebearer '50, and others. Contributor: Southern Vegetable Crops '37. Faculty A&M Coll Tex since '13, prof entomology since '18, head of dept '18-46. Entomol Soc Am (F)—Tex Acad Sci (F)—AAAS (F)—Am Assn Econ Entomol—Sigma Xi. College Station, Tex.

23 BIMMERMAN, H(arry) G(ordon). Rubber technology. b'01. BS ChE '22 (A&M Coll Tex). Chem Am Cotton Oil Co '22-23, Miller Rubber Co '23-28; rubber lab EI duPont de Nemours & Co since '28, dir since '41. Am Chem Soc—Am Soc for Testing Materials— Tau Beta Pi. DuPont Company, P.O. Box 525, Wilmington, Del.

24 BING, Franklin Church. Foods; Drugs. b'02. BA '24 (U Pa); PhD '30 (Yale). Member food and nutrition board National Research Council '41-45; consultant to Congressional committee investigating chemicals in food products '50. Editor various monographs on foods and nutrition. Instr to asst prof biol chem Western Reserve U Sch Med Cleveland '29-36; sec Council on Food and Nutrition AMA. '36-43; dir Am Inst Banking Chicago '43-49; cons biochem since '50. Am Pub Health Assn (F)—AMA (F)—Am Soc Biol Chem—Soc Exptl Biol and Med— Inst Food Tech—Am Inst Nutrition. 30 W. Washington St., Chicago 2. H: 2651 Hurd Av., Evanston, Ill.

10 BINGHAM, Walter Van Dyke.
Aptitude testing; Personnel psychology; Interviewing; Accident reduction. b'80. BA '01—ScD '29 (Beloit Wis Coll); MA '07 (Harvárd); PhD '08 (U Chicago). Chairman committee on classification of military personnel '40-46; chairman board on clinical psychology advisory to Surgeon General US Army '44-47; chairman council advisory to director personnel and adminstrn Army Gen Staff '46-50 personnel consultant Sec of Defense since '50. Author: Aptitudes and Aptitude Testing '37. Co-author: Procedures in Employment Psychology '26; How to Interview '31; Psychology Today '32. Chief psychol Adj Gen's Office War Dept '40-47; bd Psychol Corp since '20 (pres '26-28); Lt col Personnel Br Gen Staff US Army '18-19. AAAS (F, sec council '17)—Am Psychol Assn (sec '11-14)—Am Assn Applied Psychol (pres '41)—Psychometric Soc—Sigma Xi—Phi Beta Kappa—and others. 1661 Crescent Pl., Washington 9.†

11 BINGHAM, Woodbridge. History of China. b'01. BA '24 (Yale); Chinese lang stud '26-27 (Yenching Inst Chinese Studies, Peking); MA '29 (Harvard); PhD '34 (U Calif); '39 (Far East Inst U Mich). Research on history and civilizations Asia, social and political conditions China; member advisory editorial board Far Eastern Quarterly from founding '41-48, editor Notes and News section '46-48; member board editors Pacific Historical Review since '46. Author: Modern China—Research Topics, report for research advisory committee Conference Institute Pacific Relations San Francisco '39. The Founding of the T'ang Dynasty: The Fall of Sui and Rise of T'ang, A Preliminary Survey '41; History and Civilizations of Asia (syllabuses University of California) '47; also articles in field. Hon traveling fellow north China and Japan U Calif '35-37; with U Calif since '37, now associate professor, Far East hist and director Institute of East Asiatic Studies since founding '48. Lieut comdr USNRF, research Japanese lang materials at Pearl Harbor and Guam '43-44; research and analysis br Far Eastern div OSS '44-45. AHA—Am Oriental Soc—Am Inst Pacific Relations—World Affairs Council Calif—Social Sci Research Council (mem Pacific Coast sub-com on World Area Research—Am Council Learned Soc (mem com Far Eastern studies). University of California, Berkeley 4.

12 BIRCH, Raymond Embree.
Ceramic engineering; Refractories; Mineral utilization. b'05. B Ceramic Engring '27—Ceramic Engr '37 (O State U). Holder US patents on refractories and mineral uses. Author articles in field. Dir research Harbison-Walker Refractories Co since '46. Am Ceramic Soc (F, trustee '38-41)—AAAS (F, chmn Pittsburgh sect '35, chmn refractories division '36)—American Institute Ceramic Engineers—Keramos (nat pres '36-37)—Am Society Testing Materials—Soc Glass Tech (Gt Britain)—Pittsburgh Geol Soc (vp '45)—Am Inst Mining Metall Engrs. 1800 Farmers Bank Building, Pittsburgh 22.

13 BIRCH, Raymond Russell. Brucellosis (Man, animals); Infectious diseases (Animals). b'81. BS '06 (Kan State Agrl Coll); DVM '12—PhD '16 (Cornell). Author: Hog Cholera '22; also articles in field. With Cornell U since '12, now research prof of vet medicine vet expt sta. Am Vet Med Assn—NY State Vet Med Soc—US Livestock Sanitary Assn—Sigma Xi. Awarded Rockefeller fellowship for

European study '26. R.F.D. 2, Ithaca, N.Y.†

14 BIRD, Emerson Wheat. Dairy chemistry (Butter manufacture, fats); Glass blowing. b'01. BS '23 (Pa State Coll); PhD '29 (Ia State Coll). Granted patent with others on butter composition control device. Author articles in field. With dept dairy industry and Ia Agr Expt Sta Iowa State Coll since '28, prof dairy industry and chem since '48; also cons. Am Chem Soc—AAAS—Am Dairy Sci Assn—Am Oil Chem Soc—Inst Food Tech—Sigma Xi—Phi Kappa Phi—Gamma Sigma Delta. Department of Dairy Industry, Iowa State College, Ames, Ia.

15 BIRD, Herbert Roderick. Poultry husbandry (Nutrition feeds, vitamins, physiology and diseases of chicks). b'12. BS '33—MS '35—PHD '38 (U Wis). Research in chick nutrition; growth; curled toe paralysis; increasing yellow pigmentation in shanks of chickens; time of origin, factors influencing gizzard lesions in chicks, and the possibility of controling gizzard disorders by dietary control; relation of grit to development gizzard lining. Author articles in field. Poultry husbandman charge poultry investigations Bur Animal Industry US Dept Agrl since '48. Am Chem Soc—AAAS—Am Inst Nutrition—Poultry Sci Assn—Sigma Xi. Received Am Feed Mfgrs award in poultry nutrition '48. Bureau of Animal Industry, U.S. Department Agriculture, Beltsville, Md.

16 BIRDSELL, Joseph Benjamin.
Physical anthropology (Australian aborigines, human genetics). b'08. SB '31 (MIT); PhD '41 (Harvard). Co-director Harvard-Adelaide Universities Australian expedition '38-39. Author articles in field. Asst prof anthrop and sociol U Calif since '47. Am Anthrop Assn(F)—Am Assn Phys Anthrop—Soc Study Evolution—Human Genetics Soc Am—Soc Am Archaeol. Guggenheim fellow '47. University of California, Los Angeles.†

17 BIRDSEYE, Clarence. Food preservation (Freezing, dehydration). b'86. Grad '10—MA (hon) '41 (Amherst Coll). Holder of over 250 US and foreign patents covering inventions in fields of preserving foods by freezing and dehydration, Birds Eye Frosted Foods, and incandescent lighting (inside silvered lamps and heat lamps). Author articles in field. Pres and dir Mechanical Research Inc and Dehydration Inc since '39. Am Soc Refrigerating Engrs(F)—Inst Food Tech—Am Chem Soc—Am Dairy Assn—Am Fisheries Soc—AFA—Am Genetic Assn—Am Soc Agrl Chem—Am Soc Indsl Engrs—ASME—Am Soc Mammalogists—Boston Market Gardeners Assn—Illuminating Engrs Soc—Internat Assn Milk Sanitarians—Mass Hort Soc—Nat Dehydration Assn—Nutrition Found Inc—QM Assn (chmn food industries com New Eng chapter)—Soc des Gentilshommes Chefs de Cuisine. Eastern Point Blvd., Gloucester, Mass.†

18 BIRKELAND, Charles John. Plant genetics and physiology; Pomology (Apple leaf). b'16. '35-37 (ND State Coll); BS '39 (Mich State Coll); MS '41 (Kan State Coll); PhD '47 (U Ill). Research on internal structure and chlorophyll content apple leaves, spray material effects, plant genetics and breeding; in charge of fruit breeding, University of Illinois. Author articles in field. Asst later asst prof pomol hort dept U Ill '46-48, asst prof plant breeding '48-49; prof hort head dept hort since '50. AAAS—American Soc Hort Sci—Am Pomol Soc—Ill Hort Soc

—Phi Kappa Phi—Sigma Xi—Gamma Sigma Delta—Alpha Zeta. Department of Horticulture, University of Illinois, Champaign, Ill.

19 BIRKHAUG, Konrad Elais. Tuberculosis control; Tuberculosis-Vaccine; Bacteriologist; Medicine; Medical bacteriology; BCG. b'92. AB '17 (Jamestown Coll) MD '24 (Johns Hopkins) MS '27 (Rochester U). Asst in medicine Johns Hopkins Hosp '24-25; asso in bacteriology '25-26 (U Rochester) asst prof '25-28 asso prof '28-34; resident bacteriologist Strong Memorial Hosp Rochester '25-32; sous chief Inst Pasteur Lab Tuberculosis Paris '32-35; mem Christian Michelsen Inst Bergen Norway '35-45; dir Norwegian Nat Tuberculosis Vaccine (BCG) Lab Bergen '37-45; bacteriol adv Sahlgrenska Hosp Gothenburg Sweden '45-46; asso med bacteriol dir Tuberculosis Vaccine (BCG) State Dept Health Albany '46-50 prin med bacteriol since '50. Vice pres 1st Internat BCG Cong Paris '48. Gold Medal Norwegian Nat Tuberculosis Assn '45. Am Assn Immunologists—Am Trudeau Soc—Internat Leprosy Assn—Am Assn Path and Bacteriol—Am Soc Bacteriol—Soc Exptl Biol and Med-Norwegian Pathol Soc—Internat Union against Tuberculosis—Norwegian Acad Scis—Phi Chi—Pi Gamma Mu—Sigma Xi. New York State Dept. Health, Albany 1, N.Y.†⊙

20 BIRNBAUM, Martin. Art (Nineteenth century, contemporary, English, seventeenth and eighteenth century Venetian school, Khmer [Indo-China] art; history); Greek and Asiatic archaeology. b'78. AB '97 (Coll City NY); AM '98—LLB '01 (Columbia). Ethnological and artistic research in Asia, Africa, South Seas, etc., and writing since '26; arranged for art exhibitions in United States of foreign artists, wrote catalogues in connection with exhibitions '10-20. Author: Introductions: Painters, Sculptors and Graphic Artists '19; John Singer Sargent: A Conversation Piece '40; Vanishing Eden '42; Jacovleff and other Artists '46; Angkor and the Mandarin Road '52, articles in field. Explorer's Club—Asia Institute (life)—Phi Beta Kappa. Decorated Commandatore of Royal Crown of Italy in recognition of service in connection with Biennial Art Exhbns Venice '32. 117 E 81st St., NYC 28.⊙

21 BIRNEY, (Herman) Hoffman.
Military and sporting rifles and revolvers; Rockets. b'91. Student '08-12 (Dickinson Coll Carlisle Pa). Author articles in field. Ed rocket research and development Ft Bliss Tex since '47. US Army Aviation Sec Signal Corps '17-20; attached to Phila regional office OWI '42, editor, ammunition and small arms research and development US Army Ordnance Dept '42-47. Ordnance Guided Missiles Center, Redstone Arsenal, Huntsville, Ala.

22 BIRNIE, James Jr. Designing on aluminum foil. b'06. Student '25-27, '29-30 (Yale). Experimentation in drawing and painting techniques on varied surfaces and reproduction results; research in preparation of surface of aluminum foil for water color painting and establishing the design to take advantage of the beauty and reflectivity of foil without sacrificing legibility of reading matter on packages, labels, displays, etc; assisted in development of printing on aluminum foil for rotogravure, letterpress, analine and silk screen. Art dir and chief designer in charge of customer art activity Reynolds Metals Co since '45. National Soc of Art Dir—Art Dir Club of NY. Reynolds Metals Company, 2500 S 3rd St., Lsvl.

10 BIRO, Sydney Seymour. History of the French Revolution; Comparative jurisprudence. b'01. AB '23 (U Calif); MA '26 (Harvard); D Phil '28 (Oxford U, Eng); JD '31—JSD '33 (U Chicago). Research on status of the alien in French law, the Congress of Rastatt; research in London, Paris, Berne, Oxford, Vienna, elsewhere aboard and US since '23. Author: Revolutionary France, Germany and the Rhine during the War of the First Coalition: A Study in French Diplomacy (2 vols) '49; also articles in field. Phi Beta Kappa—Am Acad Polit Social Sci—AHA—Acad Pol Sci—Foreign Policy Assn—Council Foreign Relations. 125 California Av., Santa Monica, Cal.

11 BISHOP, J. Paul. Chemical engineering; Food technology (Processes, equipment). b'98. BS '22 (Ia State Coll); student (Parsons Coll, U Ia). Author: Karo Baby Book; also articles in field. Holder 23 US patents issued on food products, processes and equipment. Pres and dir J Paul Bishop and Assos since '47. Inst Food Tech—Am Inst Chem Engrs—Am Chem Soc. 105 N. 2nd St., Champaign, Ill.

12 BISHOP, Sherman Chauncey. Spiders, phalangids, amphibians and reptiles (Taxonomy, ecology); Fishes. b'87. BS '13—PhD '25 (Cornell U). Okefenokee expedition '12; expedition to Alaska, all states, and Mexico '36. Author books, articles in field. Prof vertebrate zool U Rochester since '41. AAAS(F)—Mammalogy Soc—Soc Ichthol and Herpetol (vp '32-34)—Fisheries Soc—Entomol Soc Am(F)—Soc Naturalists—Soc Zool—Biol Soc Washington—Sigma Xi—Phi Kappa Phi. Department of Biology, University of Rochester, Rochester, N.Y.

13 BISHOPP, Fred Corry. Entomology (Medical, ticks, insecticides). (b'84. BS '02—MS '26 (Colo State Coll); grad student '23-24 (So Meth U); PhD '32 (Ohio State U). Research in identification of ticks; the chemistry, toxicology and effectiveness of insecticides. Editor sections on Insects Affecting Animals and Sanitary Entomology of Biological Abstracts. Author articles in field. Asst prof entomol and zool Md Agrl Coll '04-05; spl field agt Bur Entomol US Dept Agr '05-08, asst entomol '08-11, entomol '11-26, chief Div of Insects Affecting Man and Animals '26-41, asst chief of bur in charge research since '41. Herman Biggs Memorial Lecture NY Acad Med '45. AAAS(F)—Entomol Soc Am (vp '32)—Am Pub Health Assn(F)—Am Assn Econ Entomol (pres '37)—Am Soc of Parisitol (pres '38)—Washington Acad Sci—Entomol Soc Washington (pres '32)—Am Soc Tropical Med Acad Tropical Med—Nat Malaria Soc—Biol Soc Washington—Phi Kappa Phi—Sigma Xi. Awarded His Majesty's Medal for Service in the Cause of Freedom (Great Britain '48). U.S. Department of Agriculture, Washington 25.☉

14 BISSLAND, Howard Ross. Game fish management; Water weed (Control). b'12. BS '35 (Mich State Coll). Research and development of management measures on natural pond and lake waters in Florida for protection of freshwater game fish including chemical means of eradicating objectionable species of fish, seine analysis of water, determination of stocking ratio and species of game fish to be used, chemical fertilization of water; effective application of chemical and mechanical methods of water weed control and eradication of such pests as water hyacinths and parrot feather. Biol US Soil Conservation Service since '35. Soil Conservation Soc Am—Am Fisheries Soc—

Wildlife Soc. Postoffice Box 3149, Orlando, Fla.

15 BITKER, Bruno Voltaire. Public regulatory commissions. born '98. LLB '21 (Cornell). Mem Sewerage Commn Milwaukee since '31; spcl counsel Wis State Banking Commn '38; cons OPM '41; Wis counsel dist dir OPA '42-44; chmn state pub utility arbitration Bd '47; chmn Milwaukee com Living Costs and Food Conservation 47; chmn Commn Econ Study Milwaukee '48; mem Mayor's Commn Human Relations since 48. Author numerous reports and surveys of governmental agencies. 208 Wisconsin Ave., Milw 2.☉

16 BITTER, Francis. Magnetism; Mine warfare (Operation analysis). b'02. AB '24—PhD '28 (Columbia); '24-25 (U Berlin); '19-23 (U Chicago). Author: Introduction to Ferromagnetism '37; Nuclear Physics '50. Associate prof physics (MIT) since '35. Operation analysis mine warfare USN '40-45. Am Phys Soc—Phi Beta Kappa—Sigma Xi. Nat Research fellow '28-30, Guggenheim fellow '33. Massachusetts Institute of Technology, Cambridge 39, Mass.☉

17 BITTNER, Walton Simon. Education (University extension, Adult education, Correspondence teaching. b'84. AB '09—AM '28 (U Chicago). Co-author: (with Mallory) University Teaching By Mail '33; (with Duncan) Guide to Correspondence Study; also articles in field. Asso dean div adult edn and pub services, prof sociol Ind U since '45; sec Nat U Ext Assn since '28. Dir teaching materials staff US Armed Forces Inst '42; adv com USAFI joint Army and Navy com on recreation and welfare '41-45. AAAS—Am Sociol Soc—Am Anthrop Assn. Indiana University, Bloomington, Ind.

18 BITTSON, Anthony John (Anthony Jan Anatole Leopold, Prince Liniewski). Electrical treatment concrete works under zero and sub-zero temperatures; American exports; Communism; Soviet Union (Government organization); Lenin; Stalin. b'95. Student '15 (Imperial Inst Tech, Tomsk Siberia); '20 (Sorbonne, Paris). Inventor folding fan, movable transforming sub-stations, electrical treatment of concrete, electrically heated concrete constructions in sub-zero temperatures; construction supervision and engineering Russia, Ukraine, Lithuania, France '14-35. Owner A John Bittson Engring Co since '37; pres World Distributors Corp since '40; pres Orion Assos Inc since '47; pres Peggy Equities Corp since '47. Am Inst Mining Metall Engrs—NY Acad Sci—Am Mus Natural Hist—AAAS—Acad Polit Sci—AIEE—Am Geog Soc(F). 11 Broadway, NYC

19 BJORK, Kenneth O. Norwegian-American history; American industrial history. b'09. BA '30 (St Olaf Coll); MA '31—PhD '35 (U Wis); '33-34 (London and Berlin). Research on Norwegian engineers in America, Norwegian immigration to and life on Pacific Coast, including Canada and Alaska. Author: Saga in Steel and Concrete, Norwegian Engineers in America '47. Author articles: A School and Language Controversy in 1858 (with Arthur C Paulson '38; 'A Doll's House' on the Prairie; The First Ibsen Controversy in America '40; The Unknown Rolvaag '40; Ole Evinrude and the Outboard Motor '41; A Migration of Skills '44; Pioneering on the Technical Front '44. With St Olaf Coll since 37; visiting prof U Mich '40-41, U Wis '43-44. AHA—Am-Scandinavian Found—Minn Hist Soc—Miss Valley Hist Assn—Nor-

wegian-Am Hist Assn(F)—AAUP. St. Olaf Coll, Northfield, Minn.†

20 BJORKSTEN, Johan Augustus. Plastics (Chemistry); Proteins (Chemistry). b'07. MS '27—'29-31—PhD '31 (U Helsingfors Finland); student '27-28 (U Stockholm Sweden); Rockefeller fellow '31-32 (U Minn). Study of raw material conditions in Asia, Africa and South America '36-37; development surface treatments for plastics; research and patents on hydrocarbon resins, protective coatings, friction reducing coatings, low pressure lamination and resins. Holds patents in field. Chem dir Quaker Chem Products Corp '41-44; pres Bjorksten Research Labs Inc since '44; chmn bd Bee Chem Co since '45. Soc Plastics Industry—ACS—Farm Chemurgic Council — Chem Arts Forum—Am Inst Chem—Franklin Inst—Am Assn Cereal Chem—AAAS—NY Acad Sci—Tech Assn Pulp and Paper Industry—ASTM—Sigma Xi—Gamma Alpha. 323 W. Gorham St., Madison, Wis.; also 50 E. 41st St., NYC 17.

21 BJORNSTAD, William Bernard. Jonathan Swift; Restoration and eighteenth century English literature. b'07. BA '29—MA '30—PhD '45 (U Minn). Author: Politics in Restoration Poetry 1660-1689 '30; A Swift Handbook: the Biography (1667-1745) and the Poetry through 1714 '45. Asso prof Eng Drake U since '48. Modern Lang Assn Am—Nat Council Teachers Eng—Coll Eng Assn—Modern Humanities Research Assn. Awarded Moses Marston prize in Eng U Minn '29. Drake University, Des Moines 11, Ia.

22 BLACK, Alvin Percy. Water supply and treatment; Ground water law. b'95. BA '17 (Southwestern U); PhD '33 (U Ia). Research on chemistry of water treatment, coagulants, water conservation and control, basic concepts in ground water law, geo-chemistry of natural waters. Author articles in field. Prof chem U Fla since '23. Am Water Works Assn (dir '36-39, Fuller Award '39; vp '49, pres '50)—Am Chem Soc (ch water sewage and sanitation div '37-39)—Am Inst Chem Engrs—Brit Soc Chem Industry—Am Inst Chem(F)—Am Geophys Union—Am Pub Health Assn—Aso Interamericana Ingenieria Sanitaria (charter)—Sigma Xi—Sigma Tau—Phi Kappa Phi. Head Department of Chemistry, University of Florida, Gainesville, Fla.†

23 BLACK, Charles A. Water supply treatment. b'20. BS (CE) '47 (U Fla). Consultant on design water treatment plants; research on small chlorine plants, and on new methods for chemical determinations; studies on growth promoting characteristics of main packing materials. City chem Gainesville Fla since '42; pres Black Labs Inc Gainesville since '47; cons civil engr since '47; asso engr Goin & Co (architects, engrs, chem) since '51. Am Water Works Assn (chmn subcom on methods of determining fluorides)—Am Soc CE—Nat Soc Professional Engrs—Am Soc Am Mil Engrs—Fedn Sewage Works Assn—Am Pub Health Assn—Fla Engring Soc—Asociacion Interamericana de Ingenieria Sanitaria. Professional engr Fla, Ala, SC. 700 S. East Third St., Gainesville, Fla.

24 BLACK, Charles Allen. Soil fertility and phosphorus. b'16. BS '37 (Colo State Coll); MS '38—PhD '42 (Ia State Coll). Research on reaction of phosphorus with soil clays, organic phosphorus in soils, fertilizer requirements of soils, soil management practices and hemp production, statistical studies of crop sampling. Author articles in field. Research asso prof Ia

State Coll since '46. Soil Sci Soc Am—Am Soc Agron—Sigma Xi. Department of Agronomy, Iowa State College, Ames, Ia.†

10 BLACK, Cyril Edwin. Diplomatic and constitutional history of east and southeast Europe (Russia, Adviser, United States delegation, United Nations Security Council Balkan Commission of Investigation '47; Balkans). b'15. AB '36 (Duke U); AM '37—PhD '41 (Harvard). Research in Balkan diplomatic and constitutional history in London, Vienna, Sofia '39; contributing editor Current History '41-43. Author: The Establishment of Constitutional Government in Bulgaria '43; coauthor: Handbook of Slavic Studies '49; Twentieth Century Europe '50; Negotiating With the Russians '51; also articles in field. Research div Dept State Washington specializing in southeastern Europe '43-44; special asst to US Polit Rep Allied Control Commn Bulgaria '44-45; Div Southeastern European Affairs Dept State Washington '45-46; asso prof hist Princeton U since '49. APSA—AHA—Am Geog Soc—AA UP. Department of History, Princeton University, Princeton, N.J.†

11 BLACK, Glenn Albert. American archaeology and anthropology; Prehistory of Indiana and Ohio valley. b'00. Research in Indiana and Ohio Valley prehistory since '31. Author: Archaeology of Greene County Indiana '33; Archaeology of Dearborn and Ohio Counties '34; Excavation of the Nowlin Mound '35; The Angel Site '44. Dir Ind U Field Sch Archeol since '45; dir archaeol Ind Hist Soc since '31. Ind Acad Sci(F)—Am Anthrop Soc(F)—Soc Am Archaeol (one of founders, vp '38-39, pres '41-42, treas '47-51). Indiana Historical Society, Indianapolis 4.

12 BLACK, Hayse Henry. Pollution control. b'06. BS (Civil engring) '29 (State U Ia); MS '33—CE '38 (U Ill). Study liquid wastes from new manufacturing processes and investigation stream pollution attributed to industrial wastes; strikes to determine toxic characteristics, taste-and odor-producing substances and compounds which exert high chlorine demand; pioneered in development Diatomite Water Filtration and Thermocompression Distillation. Sr san engr Ill San Water Bd '34-42; chief water supply equipment br Engr Bd Corps of Engrs Ft Belvoir Va '42-45; asso prof san engring State U Ia '47-48; officer in charge US Sect Internat Joint Commn Boundary Waters Pollution Investigation '46-49; chief indsl wastes sect Environmental Health Center USPHS since '49. Am Soc CE—Fedn Sewage and Indsl Wastes Assn—Am Water Works Assn—Am Pub Health Assn—Nat Soc Profl Engrs—O Soc Profl Engrs Inc—Engring Soc Cincinnati—Permanent Internat Assn Navigation Congresses—Sigma Xi. U. S. Public Health Service. 1014 Broadway, Cincinnati 2, O.

13 BLACK, John David. North American vertebrates (Taxonomy, zoogeography and ecology of Greater Mississippi Valley); Ecology of robin in winter; Zoology of northern Arkansas (Birds, mammals, reptiles, fishes); Mammals of Kansas; Ecology of minnows, darters and carp. b'08. BA '35 (U Kan); MA '37 (U Ind); PhD '40 (U Mich). Author articles in field. Prof zool NE Mo State Teachers Coll since '48. Am Soc Ichthyol Herpetol—Wis Acad Sci—Phi Beta Kappa—Sigma Xi. Julius Rosenwald fellow for investigation Ark fishes '38-40; research grant Am Philos Soc '40. North East Missouri State Teachers College, Kirksville, Mo.

14 BLACK, John Donald. Economics (Agricultural, food, production), Marketing; Agricultural policy, Population and food supply; Land utilization; Farm management. b'83. BA '09—MA '10—PhD '19 (U Wis). Author: Introduction to Production Economics '26; Agricultural Reform in the United States '29; Production Organization '29; A Food and Nutrition Program for the Nation '44; Rural Economy of New England '50. Co-author: Farm Management '47; Sugar: Produce or Import? '47; Future Food and Agricultural Policy '48. Editor: Social Science Research Council Series on scope and method of research in agricultural economics and rural sociology. Prof econ Harvard since '27; cons econ Tenn Valley Authority since '40. Am Farm Econ Assn (pres '32)—Am Econ Assn—Food and Nutrition Bd of Nat Research Council—Adv Com on Econ and Marketing of FAO—Am Statis Assn—Phi Beta Kappa. 12 Lambert Rd., Belmont, Mass.◉

15 BLACK, Lindsay MacLeod. Plant pathology and viruses. b'07. BSA '29 (U Brit Columbia); PhD '36 (Cornell U). Research on multiplication of plant viruses in insect vectors, genetic variation in ability of insect vectors to transmit, varieties of plant viruses with different specific insect vectors, plant tumors caused by virus. Author articles in field. Nat research fellow Rockefeller Inst Med Research '36-37, asst plant path '37-41; asso '41-46; curator plant path Brooklyn Bot Garden since '46. Am Phytopath Soc—Can Phytopath Soc—Bot Soc Am—Soc Study Development Growth—AAAS—NY Acad Sci—Sigma Xi. Brooklyn Botanic Garden, Brooklyn 25.

16 BLACK, Mary Ellouise. Weaving (Hand); Nova Scotia (Early textile handcrafts). b'95. Student '11-15 (Acadia Sem & Acadia U Wolfville NS Can); (Occupational therapy) '19 (McGill U). Research on old types Nova Scotia weaves, tartans, homespun wool and its uses, vegetable dyeing of native yarns. Author: Key to Weaving '45. Occupational therapist various hospitals '20-43; dir handcrafts div Dept Trade and Industry Province NS since '43. An Occupational Therapy Assn — Mich Occupational Therapy Assn (pres '36-38)—Halifax Weavers Guild—NS Craftsmens Guild—Guild Can Weavers (vp since '49). Department of Trade and Industry, Handcrafts Division, Halifax, N.S., Can. H: Box 14, Bedford, N.S.

17 BLACK, Robert Foster. Permafrost; Arctic (Geomorphology); Ice (Formation and structure). b'18. AB '40 (Coll Wooster O); MA '42 (Syracuse U); '42-43 (Calif Inst Tech); '46-47 and '48-49 (Johns Hopkins). Field study geomorphology and petrofabrics of Huntington Forest in Adirondack Mountains '41-42; in charge geologic research expeditions to Alaska; research on character, temperature, distribution and genesis of permafrost and its relation to Arctic geomorphic processes, terrain features and climate; microscopic study of ice masses in permafrost utilizing petrofabric techniques and polarizing microscope. Author: Eolian Deposits of Alaska '50. Contributor: Applied Sedimentation '50. Geol Roosevelt Wildlife Commn NY State '41-42, Geol Survey Alaska '43-45, geol in charge Alaska terrain and permafrost sect '46-49, research geol permafrost and Arctic geomophology since '49. Geol Soc Am (F)—Arctic Inst NA (F)—Am Geog Soc (F)—AA AS—Geol Soc Washington—Am Geophys Union—Brit Glaciological Soc—Sigma Xi. U. S. Geological Survey, Washington 25.†

18 BLACK, Rodney Elmer. Electrodeposition of alloys; Synthesis of heterocyclic compounds; Properties of pure hydrocarbons. b'16. BS '38 (Okla A&M Coll); MS '40—PhD '42 (Wis U); '40 (Cornell U). Research on electrodeposition of iron-tungsten alloys from acid plating bath, and of cobalt-tungsten alloys. Holder of patent on electrodeposition of iron-tungsten alloys (with Holt). Author articles in field. Prof chem and dept chmn Morningside Coll since '47. Am Chem Soc—Electrochem Soc — AAAS — Sigma Xi — Phi Kappa Phi. Weston fellow Electrochem Soc '41-42. Morningside College, Sioux City 20, Ia.

19 BLACKALL, Frederick Steele, Jr. Machinery and tool manufacturing; Gages and gaging; Standardization; Economics and banking; Industrial history; Depreciation. b'96. BA '18 (Yale); SB '22 (MIT). Member advisory committee precision tools and machine tool industry War Production Board during World War II; chairman '46 technical mission to England on Unification Anglo - American Screw Threads; member Gage Industry Advisory Committee United States Army Industrial College, American Gage Design Committee (chairman editorial committee, member standing committee); Author: Report of the American Gage Design Committee '30 (editor all subsequent editions); also articles in field. Pres, treas Taft-Peirce Mfg Co Woonsocket RI since '33; dir Fed Reserve Bank of Boston; vp, exec com Am Wringer Co Woonsocket; dir Am Research and Development Corp Boston; dir, exec com N.Y. N.H. & H. RR; vp Nat Mach Tool Bldrs Assn. ASME (dir, exec com)—Am Soc Metals—Am Soc Tool Engrs. Taft-Peirce Manufacturing Co., Woonsocket, R.I.†◉

20 BLACKMON, G(ulie) H(argrove). Horticulture; Nutrition; Pecan and tung oil production; Deciduous fruits and ornamentals. b'86. BS '10 (Tex A&M); MS '27 (U Fla). Research in micro elements, pecan and tung oil production, deciduous fruits and ornamentals, pecan industry, pecan orchards, cold storage, fertilizing, roses, nitrogen content. Author articles: Yield, Sizes and Kernel Percentages of Nuts Produced in a Cover Crop Experiment . . . '35; Nitrogen Content of Dormant Pecan Twigs '41; Boron in Pecan Nutrition '41; The Tung Oil Industry '43; Effect of Nitrogen and Potash on Pecans '46; Fertilizer Ratio Experiments with Tung '46, and others. Asst prof hort Tex A&M Coll '10-14; comml hort Texas '14-23; pecan culturist Fla Agr Exp Sta '23-34, hort '34-35, asso head dept '35-36, acting head '36-37, head dept since '37. AAAS—Am Soc Hort Sci—Fla Hort Soc—Fla Acad Sci—Soil Sci Soc Fla—SE Pecan Growers Assn—Am Tung Oil Assn. Florida Agricultural Experiment Station, Gainesville, Fla. H: 214 NE, 7th Ave.◉

21 BLACKWELDER, Eliot. Pleistocene and Tertiary history of the southwestern United States. Sedimentation; Geomorphology (arid and semiarid regions). b'80. AB '01—PhD '14 (U Chicago). Paleontologist Carnegie Institution expedition to China '03-04. Author: Research in China (with B Willis) '06; Regional Geology of the United States '12. Head dept geol Stanford U '22-45. Geol Soc Am (F, vp '33, '39, pres '40)—AAAS (vp '21)—Nat Acad Sci—Wash Acad Sci—Calif Acad Sci—Am Philos Soc—Am Assn

Petroleum Geol—Assn Am Geog—Seismol Soc Am (pres '47-49)—Sigma Xi. Stanford, Cal.

10 BLACKWELDER, Richard Eliot. Coleoptera; Systematic zoology. b'09. AB '31—PhD '34 (Stanford); Walter Rathbone Bacon traveling scholar '35-38 (Smithsonian Instn). Expedition to Panama '30, West Indies '35-37. Morphology of insects, principles of classification, zoological nomenclature, taxonomy of staphylinidae. Author: Morphology of the Coleopterous Family Staphylinidae '36; West Indian Staphylinidae '43; Checklist of Coleoptera of Latin Am '44-49. Asst curator entomol Am Mus Nat Hist '39-40, asst curator insects US Nat Mus '40-42, asso curator since '42; agt white-fringed beetle identification unit US Dept Agr '38. AAAS—Pacific Coast Entomol Soc—NY Entomol Soc—Entomol Soc Washington—Washington Acad Sci—Soc Systematic Zool—Soc Brasil Entomol (corres). Division of Insects, US National Museum, Washington 25. H: 3728 Second Street South, Arlington, Va.

11 BLACKWELDER, Ruth. North Carolina history. b'01. AB '22 (Wittenberg Coll); MA '30 (U NC); '34 (Columbia U); '37-40 (U NC). Author articles in field. Research fellowship Inst Research in Soc Sci U NC '38-41; asso prof hist Lenoir Rhyne Coll since '45. AHA—So Hist Assn. Lenoir Rhyne College, Hickory, N.C.

12 BLACKWELL, Gordon Williams. Community organization; Culture of southern United States. b'11. BA '32 (Furman U); MA '33 (NC U); MA '37—PhD '40 (Harvard). Author: Toward Community Understanding '43; New Farm Homes for Old '46; also articles in field. Dir Inst Research in Social Sci, research prof sociol U NC since '44. Am Sociol Soc—So Sociol Soc—Rural Sociol Soc. Box 1171, Chapel Hill, N.C.†◉

13 BLACKWELL, H(arold) Richard. Psychophysiology of vision; Atmospheric optics. b'21. BS '41 (Haverford Coll); MA '42 (Brown U); PhD '47 (U Mich). Author articles in field. Asst prof psychol U Mich '47, now also asst prof physiological optics in ophthalmology, dir Vision Research Lab since '46; now exec sec Armed Forces Nat Research Council Vision Com. Optical Soc Am—Am Psychol Assn (asso)—Sigma Xi. Mason Hall, University of Michigan, Ann Arbor.

14 BLACKWELL, Thomas Joseph. Medical jurisprudence. b'96. City atty North Miami '32-34; municipal judge Miami Shores '36-45; sr mem Blackwell Walker and Gray Miami since '26. Am Judicature Soc—Am Bar Assn—Internat Assn Ins Counsel. 100 N.E. 1st Ave., Miami 32, Fla.†◉

15 BLAIN, Alexander William. Bird behavior (Under stress). b'85. MD—MS (Wayne U). Mich Hort Soc (pres)—AAAS (F)—NY Acad Sci—Sigma Xi—Am Ornith Soc—Wilson Ornith Soc—Cooper Ornith—Audubon Soc. Alexander Blain Hospital and Clinic, 2201 E. Jefferson, Detroit.

16 BLAIR, Albert Patrick. Toads (Taxonomy, evolution). b'13. BS '36 (U Tulsa); PhD '40 (Ind U); Nat Research fellow '40-41 (Columbia). Resch in relationships of toads of fowleri-woodhousii-americanus-terrestris complex. Author articles in field. Asso prof dept zool U Tulsa since '48. AAAS—Am Soc Zool—Genetics Soc Am—Am Assn Ichthyologists Herpetologists—Soc Study Evolution—Sigma Xi. Department of Zoology. University of Tulsa, Tulsa, Okla.†

17 BLAIR, Bertha. Economic analysis; American labor history; Railroad labor history. b'96. BA '19 (Macalester Coll); Certificate '29 (Bryn Mawr Coll). Research on state laws, regulations on sanitary facilities in places of employment; field investigation of employment of women in various business institutions Chicago, Philadelphia, Atlanta; investigation of home work in lace industry RI, unemployment in South Bend Indiana, effect of six-hour shift in certain industries in Michigan, power laundry industry Washington. Author articles in field. With women's bur US Dept Labor Washington '29-36; US Railroad Retirement Bd '36-42; War Labor Bd, WPB, Civilian Prodn Adminstrn '42-47. AHA. 1892 Ontario Pl., Washington.†

18 BLAIR, Dorothy (Lilian). Arts of the Orient; Art and culture of Japan; Ancient Korean art; East Asiatic glass. b'90. AB '14—Mary E Woolley fellow '32 (Mount Holyoke Coll); '27 (Kyoto Imperial U); '33 (Courtauld Inst U London); '37-42 (U Mich). Studied in Japan Korea and Manchuria '27-28; survey of East Asiatic art in European Museums and private collections '37, individual lectures on arts of Orient. Author, co-author catalogues and articles in field. Asst dept Oriental art Art Inst Chicago '22-23; asst dir John Herron Art Inst Indianapolis '23-26; asst curator Oriental Art Toledo Museum of Art since '28. Soc Japanese Studies NY—Japan Soc NY—Japan Soc London—Asiatic Soc Japan (life)—Japan Meiji Soc (life)—Far Eastern Assn. Third prize Internat essay contest Kokusai Bunka Shinkokai Tokyo in commemoration of 2600th anniversary of Founding of Japanese Empire '40. The Toledo Museum of Art, Toledo 2, O.

19 BLAIR, George Yeomans. Boron and salt investigations (In soils); Water availability; Management and irrigation of soils. b'95. BS '19 (Kan State Coll). Conducted experiments in soils, water, and sand cultures for boron and salt tolerance, conducted experiments with plants relating to water availability and use, with soils relating to water retention against forces equal to plant extraction and evaporation forces, tested soil amendments and influence on soil to water permeability and release of salts for reclamation purposes. Asst supt US Field Sta BPISAE '24-28; with US Regional Salinity and Rubidoux Lab since '28. W Assn Soil Sci. US Regional Salinity and Rubidoux Laboratories, Box 672, Riverside, Calif.

20 BLAIR, Glenn Myers. Educational and adolescent psychology; Education (Remedial reading, diagnostic and remedial teaching). b'08. AB '30 (Seattle Pacific Coll); AM '31—research fellow '31-32 (U Wash); PhD '38—fellow '37-38 (Columbia U). Author: Diagnostic and Remedial Teaching in Secondary Schools '46; also articles in field. On faculty of U Illinois since '38. Am Psychol Assn(F)—Midwestern Psychol Assn—Ill Assn for Applied Psychol—Am Ednl Research Assn—Nat Soc of Coll Teachers of Edn (mem com ednl psychol and child development). College of Education, University of Illinois, Urbana, Ill.

21 BLAIR, Walter. American literature, humor and folklore; Mark Twain. b'00. PhB '23 (Yale); MA '26—PhD '31 (U Chicago). Author: Two Phases of American Humor '31; Native American Humor (1800-1900) '37; Horse Sense in American Humor '42; Tall Tale America '44. Co-author: (with F J Meine) Mike Fink '33; (with W K Chandler) Approaches to Poetry '35.

Co-editor: (with Theodore Hornberger and Randall Stewart) The Literature of The United States (2 vols) '46-'47. Instr Eng U Chicago '26-30, asst prof '30-39, asso prof '39-44, prof since 44, chmn dept since '51. Modern Language Assn. University of Chicago, Chgo.◉

22 BLAIR, William Franklin. Mammalian speciation and ecology; Population dynamics. b'12. BS '34 (U Tulsa); MS '35 (U Fla); PhD '38 (U Mich). Described new forms of marsh rabbit, prairie pocket mouse, eastern cottontail from Texas Panhandle, pocket-mice from western Texas, short-tailed shrew, meadow vole, jumping mouse, deer-mouse, red-backed vole, collared lizard, woodland deer-mouse, eastern chipmunk. Author articles in field. Asst mus zool U Mich '35-37, research asso lab vertebrate biol '37-43; asst prof zool U Tex '46-47, asso prof since '47. Am Soc Mammalogists—Ecol Soc Am—AAAS—Genetics Soc—Wildlife Soc—Soc Study Evolution—Am Soc Ichthyology and Herpetology—Texas Acad Sci. Department of Zoology, University of Texas, Austin 12, Tex.†

23 BLAKE, Archie. Periodicity; Inverse probability; Boolean algebra. b'06. BS—MS PhD (U Chicago). Editor: Health of The Army; also articles in field. Dir and treas Mechanical Research Corp since '41; mathematician Commerce Dept '31-44; ballistician and statistician US Army Dept since '44. Am Math Soc—Math Assn Am—Philos Soc Wash—Assn Symbolic Logic—Inst Math Statis—Am Statis Assn—Am Soc Quality Control—Soc Adv Management—Am Acad Polit Social Sci—Am Econ Assn—Biometric Soc—Am Pub Health Assn—Am Finance Assn—Phi Beta Kappa. 241 Campus Dr., Buffalo 21, N.Y.

24 BLAKE, Irving H(ill). Animal ecology; Fish histology. b'88. AB '11 (Bates Coll); AM '13 (Brown U); PhD '25 (U Ill). Author articles in field. Prof zool and anat U Nebr since '26, chmn dept since '46. AAAS—Ecol Soc Am—Limnol Soc Am—Wildlife Soc (asso)—Sigma Xi. 102 Bessey Hall, University of Nebraska, Lincoln, Nebr.◉

25 BLAKE, John Twiss. Rubber; Dielectrics; Synthetic resins. b'01. BS '21 (Tufts Coll); PhD '24 (MIT). Research on rates of reaction, theories and chemistry of vulcanization, pigment reinforcement, dielectrics, oxidation of rubber, deproteinized rubber, synthetic rubber in electrical insulation, effects of soil microorganisms, light, and ozone on rubber. Holds patents on improved cables, especially submarine cables. Co-author: (with Davis) Chemistry and Technology of Rubber '37; also articles in field. Research chem Simplex Wire & Cable Co Cambridge '24-35, in charge chem development '35-40, dir research since '40; mem various technical adv com WPB and armed forces. Am Inst Chem(F)—NY Acad Sci(F)—Inst Rubber Industry, Eng(F)—AAAS(F)—Boston Rubber Group (F, chmn '36—Am Chem Soc (F, chmn rubber div '43, councilor since '46, dir Northeastern sect since '46, chmn-elect '49)—Am Soc Testing Materials (chmn wire and cable sect since '48)—Nat Research Council (mem insulation com)—Soc Chem Industry, Eng—Am Inst Chem Engrs (chmn Boston sect '44-45). Simplex Wire & Cable Co., 79 Sidney St., Cambridge 39, Mass.

26 BLAKE, Nelson Manfred. Diplomatic and social history of the United States; United States history since 1900. b'08. BA '30 (Dartmouth Coll);

MA '31 (Brown U); PhD '36 (Clark U). Also research on Anglo-American relations since 1895, influence of organized pressure groups on US foreign policy; interrelations of nineteenth century religious development and humanitarian reform movements. Co-author: Since 1900: A History of the United States in Our Times (with Oscar T. Barck, Jr) '47. Author articles: Background of Cleveland's Venezuelan Policy '42; The Olney-Pauncefote Treaty of 1897 '45. Instr hist Syracuse '36-39, asst prof '39-46, asso prof since '46. AHA. History Department, Syracuse University, Syracuse 10, N.Y.†

10 BLAKE, Nelson Morehouse. History of Southern United States; United States Navy records. b'01. AB '26 (George Washington U); MA '29—PhD '32 (Duke U). Research on Virginia political and constitutional history 1775-1895. Author: William Mahone of Virginia; Soldier and Political Insurgent '35. Manuscript div Duke U Library '32-34; deputy examiner Nat Archives Washington '35-37; chief division Navy Dept Archives Nat Archives '38-42; Naval Records and Library Washington '42-46; World War II Records Project National Archives '46-47; asst dir War Records Div Nat Archives since '47. AHA—So Hist Assn—ALA—Soc Am Archivists—Naval Hist Found. The National Archives, Washington 25.†

11 BLAKE, Sidney Fay. Systematic botany (Compositae); Bibliography of Floras of world. b'92. AB '12—AM '13—PhD '17 (Harvard). Author: Revision of the Genus Viguiera '18; Geographical Guide to Floras of the World '42; also articles in field. Asst bot, later sr bot Bur Plant Industry US Dept Agr since '17. Bot Soc Am—New Eng Bot Club—Calif Bot Soc—Wash Acad Sci—Biol Soc Wash (rec sec)—Wash Biol Field Club (past pres)—Am Soc Plant Taxonomists (p pres)—Linnean Soc (London). Plant Industry Station, Beltsville, Md.†

12 BLAKE, Warren Everett. Language and literature; Greek language and literature; Classical philology. b'00. Mem faculty U Mich since '25 prof Greek language and literature since '46 chmn Greek dept '44-46. Author Charitonis Aphrodisiensis De Chaerea et Callirhoe Amatoriarum Narrationum Libri '38; Chariton's Chaereas and Callirhoe '39. Editor Transactions and Proceedings of the Am Philol Assn '44. Am Philol Assn—Archaeol Inst Am—Soc Promotion Hellenic Studies—AAUP—Phi Beta Kappa. H: 916 Olivia Ave., Ann Arbor.†◉

13 BLAKESLEE, Myra Allen. Human relations (Civil rights, race relations, education, State agencies, anti-discrimination and civil rights laws). b'92. Student '09-13 (Pa State Coll). Dir Good-Will Commn of NJ, first ofcl agency in field of human relations, '38-45. Dir edn div against discrimination NJ State Dept of Edn since '45. 1060 Broad St., Newark 2, N.J.

14 BLAKEY, Roy Gillispie. Taxation. b'80. Student '00-01 (U Mo); PhB '05 LLD '40 (Drake U); MA '10 (U Colo); PhD '12 (Columbia). Tax adviser to governor of West Virginia '30; director Minnesota tax survey '31-32; director tax and public expenditure division Minnesota and US Department of Agriculture land utilization survey '33; chairman Minnesota Income Study State Resources Commission '38-42; tax and research consultant Council of State Governments '43-44; consultant National Resources Planning Board

'39-42; member advisory tax committee US Civil Aeronautics Board '44-45; many other state and national posts. Author: The State Income Tax '32. Co-author: Taxation in West Virginia '31; Taxation in Minnesota '32; Studies in State and Local Finance '35; The Federal Income Tax '40; State Income Taxes '42; Sales Taxes and Other Excises '45; also articles in field. Prof econ U Minn since '19. Am Statis Assn—Minn Statis Assn (p pres)—Am Econ Assn—Nat Tax Assn (vp '42-43, pres '43-44)—Minn State Tax Assn (past pres)—Tax Research Found—Royal Econ Soc(F) — Royal Hist Soc(F) — Beta Gamma Sigma — Phi Beta Kappa. University of Minnesota, Mpls 14.

15 BLANCHARD, Arthur Horace. Highway engineering; Traffic control (Pedestrian). b'77. CE '99 (Brown U); AM '02 (Columbia). Studies in every phase of pedestrian traffic control and safety. Author: Don't Walk to Death '51. Co-author: (with Henry B Drowne) Highway Engineering '15; (with Roger L Morrison (Elements of Highway Engineering '28. Editor: American Highway Engineers Handbook '19; Traffic Engineers Handbook (in compilation) Prof highway engring Columbia '11-17; prof highway engring and highway transport U Mich '19-27; pres commn Inst Transport U Md since '46; cons engr since '10. Am Soc CE—Automobile Old Timers and RH Truck Owners' Assn—Am Soc ME—Inst Traffic Engrs—Soc Automotive Engrs—Nat Highway Traffic Assn (pres '18-33, exec dir since '33)—Am Road Builders Assn—Nat Pedestrians' Assn (exec dir since '32). P.O. Box 561, Lake Mohawk, Sparta, N.J.

16 BLANCHARD, Jay Lyle. Floriculture (Lilies, Iris). b'19. BS '41 (NE Mo State Teachers Coll); MS '48 (Cornell U). Author articles in field. Instr ornamental hort and coll landscape architect NE Mo State Teachers Coll since '48. Am Soc Hort Sci—AAAS—Am Iris Soc. Northeast Missouri State Teachers College, Kirksville, Mo.

17 BLANCHARD, Phyllis (Mrs. W.W. Lucasse). Child and adolescent psychology (Emotional factors and attitudes). b'95. BS '17 (NH State U); MA '18—PhD '19 (Clark U). Research on role of emotional factors in etiology of reading disabilities of children, influence of emotional attitudes on intelligence test results, techniques of psychotherapy with children; special work in psychoanalysis '33-36. Author: The Adolescent Girl '20; The Child and Society '26. Co-author: (with Groves) Introduction to Mental Hygiene '30; also articles in field. Psychol Phila Child Guidance Clinic since '27; guest lecturer Phila Psychoanalytic Inst '45-50; lecturer Inst of Phila Assn for Psychoanalysis since '50. Am Psychol Assn(F)—AAAS(F)—Am Orthopsychiatric Assn(F, vp '46)—Phila Psychoanalytic Soc (affiliate '41-50)—Phila Assn for Psychoanalysis. Philadelphia Child Guidance Clinic, 1711 Fitzwater St., Phila. 46.

18 BLANCHARD, William Godwin. Pipe organ design; Choral music; Fire truck specifications. b'05. BMus '30 (DePauw U); MMus '33 (U Mich). Has drawn up specifications for a number of pipe organs; prepared plans and specifications for fire-trucks. Organist, Claremont Community Ch since '39; connected with Wicks Pipe Organ Co '28-29; music faculty Pomona Coll since '36, now asso prof music and college organist, taught engring drawing during World War II. Am Guild

Organists (exec com Los Angeles chap) —Phi Kappa Psi, Phi Mu Alpha. Bridges Hall of Music, Pomona College, Claremont, Calif. H: 1495 Via Zurita.

19 BLANCK, Jacob Nathaniel. American literature (Bibliography, children's books). b'06. Research on bibliography of American literature, bibliographical study of American juvenile books; editor Bibliography of American Literature since '44. Author: Jonathan and the Rainbow '48; Harry Castlemon: Boy's Own Author '41; Peter Parley to Penrod: A Bibliographical Study of America's Best-Loved Juvenile Books '38; King and the Noble Blacksmith '50. Editor: Merle Johnson's American First Editions '42; American Book-Prices Current '38; also articles in field. Ind Hist Soc—Bibliog Soc Am. 62 W. 45th St., NYC 36.†

20 BLANK, Eugene William. Microanalysis of soap. b'07. BS '33 (Pa State Coll); '34-35 (Brooklyn Poly Inst). Research on semi-micro analysis of soap, determination of borax in soap and synthetic detergents. Research chem Colgate-Palmolive-Peet Co '33-41, supervisor analytical research lab '41-48, head analytical research div since '49. Am Oil Chem Soc—Am Chem Soc—NY Mineral Club. Colgate-Palmolive-Peet Company, Jersey City 2, N.J. H: 9 Woodwild Terrace, Metuchen.

21 BLANKENSHIP, Albert B. Questionnaires; Opinion and market measurement; Market research. b'14. AB '35 (Franklin & Marshall Coll); AM '36 (U Ore); PhD '40 (Columbia). Author: Consumer and Opinion Research '43. Co-author: Market and Marketing Analysis '47. Editor: How to Conduct Consumer and Opinion Research '46; also articles in field. Dir A B Blankenship & Associates since '48. Am Marketing Assn (chmn com on questionnaire design since '47)—Am Psychol Assn—Sigma Xi. Rockefeller fellow '40-41. 1649 N. Broad St., Phila. 22.†

22 BLANKNER, Frederika. Psychology of art; Coordination of the arts with science; Vibration design. PhB '22—MA '23—grad honor scholarship '22-23, fellow '23-24, grad student '22-25 (U Chicago); Litt D '26 (Royal U Rome); student '19-20 (Abel Sch Music); '21-23 (Am Conservatory Music). Experimented with and applied theory of Chladni figures to biological and physical domains; has applied theory through interpretation of art and poetry. Author: Art as Vibration Design '40; A New Psychology of the Arts Integrating the Arts and the Sciences and Proposing a New Orientation for Art Method, Education and Criticism Derived Therefrom '41; The Unity of Art with Science '41; A New Explanation of the Structural Characteristics of Classical Literature '43; Literary Pattern as a Graph of Social Evolution, An Inquiry into a New Field '46; A New Method of Education for the Creative Artist Based on a New Psychology of the Arts '47; also articles in field. Prof and chmn dept classical civilization, langs and lits Adelphi Coll since '43. Phi Beta Kappa—Foundation for Integrated Edn (Charter sponsor) — Am Philol Assn — Am Classical League—Classical Soc Am Acad Rome—Vergilian Soc—Medieval Acad Am—Dante Soc Am—Mod Humanities Research Assn—Nat Art Edn Assn—AAAS—Poetry Soc Am—Modern Language Assn Am—Am Musicological Soc—College Art Assn. Adelphi College, Garden City, N.Y.†

10 BLASINGAME, Ralph Upshaw. Farm machinery. b'86. SB (civil engring) '08 (Ala Poly Inst); SB (agr) '10—SB (agrl engring) '13 (Ia State Coll). Organized industry seminar Farm Equipment Inst '38. Author: Relations of Mechanical Progress in Agriculture to Land Development and Land Policy '34; Home Electrification '41. Co-author: Report of an Inquiry into Changes in Quality Values of Farm Machines 1910-14 '32. Head dept agrl engring Pa State Coll since '17. Am Soc Agrl Engrs (F, chmn power and machinery div, 1st vp, chmn S., N Atlantic sect, pres '35-36)—Alpha Zeta. Received B F Goodrich award for distinguished pub service '40. State College, Pa.©

11 BLAU, Ludwig W(ilhelm). Oil research. b'94. AB '25 (West Tex STC); AM '26—PhD '29 (U Tex). Author articles in field. Humble Oil and Refining Co. since '29, research geophysicist '29-30, in charge geophysics research '30-37, in charge geophysics and production research '37-42, research consultant since '42. Tex Acad Sci (F, ed '43-45)—AAAS—Soc Exploration Geophysicist (vp '35-36, pres '36-37)—Am Physical Soc—Am Assn Petroleum Geologists—Am Inst ME—Am Petroleum Inst—Am Geophys Union—Tex Soc Prof Engrs. Humble Oil and Refining Co., Houston, Tex.

12 BLAUVELT, Ralph Coe. Crystal circuits (High frequency); Vibrator power supplies (Interference reduction); Radio receivers (High frequency crystal circuits). b'04. Ed pub schs. Research in design of high frequency circuits creating operation of piezo-electric cyrstals up to 100 megacycles, methods for direct frequency modulation of a crystal, design of equipment. Granted patents on high frequency circuits, hearing aid. Design engr Wells Gardner Mfg Co '33-40; project engr Zenith Radio '40-42; chief engr Radiart Corp '42-46; chief engr Elec Research and Mfg Corp since 46. Inst Radio Engrs (sr mem). Electronic Research and Manufacturing Corp., 1420 E. 25th St., Cleveland 14.

13 BLAYDES, Glenn William. Morphology and histology of plants; Mutations. b'00. BA '24 (Ind U); MA '26 —PhD '31 (O State U). Study of mutations resulting in chimeras and segregation of new plant varieties. Author articles in field. Instr bot Ohio Wesleyan U '24-26, asst prof '26-28; Instr bot O State U '28-32, asst prof '32-37, asso prof '37-45, prof since '45; AAAS Coop Com on Teaching Sci and Math since '45. Sigma Xi—Bot Soc Am—AAAS(F)—O Acad Sci(F)—Am Genetic Assn—Gamma Sigma Delta—Am Soc Plant Taxonomists. Department of Botany, Ohio State University, Columbus 10, O.

14 BLEECKER, William Hill. Powder metallurgy. b'17. BS (U Pittsburgh); (Trinity Coll). Research on cemented carbides and development metallographic technique and nomenclature. Asso dir research Allegheny Ludlum Steel Corp since '50. Allegheny Ludlum Steel Corp., Ferndale 20, Mich.

15 BLEIFUSS, Donald J. Hydraulic engring. b'96. BS (CE) '20 (U Minn). Design and construction hyroelectric plants; consultant test and construction engineering. Asst hydraulic engr Minn Power & Light Co Duluth Minn '23-26, Aluminum Co Am Pittsburgh '28-42; chief engr constrn Naval Ordnance Testing Sta Inyokern Calif '45; vp and chief engr Internat Engring Co Inc San Francisco since '46. Am Soc CE—Am Conc Inst—Tau Beta Pi. International Engineering Co., Inc., 74 New Montgomery, San Francisco 5.

16 BLIESNER, Gustav Henry. Irrigation (Sprinkler systems); Pacific Coast (Rural electrification). b'10. BS (EE) '33—MS '34—AE '39 (State Coll Wash); '43-46 (Ia State Coll). Assisted in installation and operation of sprinkler irrigation systems utilizing electrical energy; application of electrification to farm operations; public instruction and demonstration of new developments in use of electricity. Elec engr US Dept Interior '39-40, agrl engr '40, power utilization repr '40-43; asst prof agrl engring State Coll Wash '44-46; asst prof phys sci Farragut Coll and Tech Inst '46-49; mgr Malheur Coop Elec Assn Rural Elec Adminstrn '48; Elec engr US Dept of Interior, '49-50; US Dept of the Army since '51. AAAS—Am Assn Engrs—Am Inst Elec Engrs—Am Soc AE—Am Soc Engring Edn—AAUP—Tau Beta Pi—Sigma Tau. 48L, Franklin Apartments Savannah, Georgia.

17 BLISS, C(hester) I(ttner). Biometry; Biological assay; Entomology. b'99. BA '21 (O State U); MA '22— PhD '26 (Columbia); '25 (Marine Biol Lab); '26 (Harvard); '33-35 (U Coll London); '40 (NC State Coll). Research on life history and insecticidal control of camphor scale, Mexican fruit fly and citrus red scale at laboratories in New Orleans, Mexico City, Whittier, California '26-33; and on entomological problems, biological assay in Leningrad, USSR '36-37; consultant in biometry to government agencies and industrial organizations; advisor on design and analysis of experiments and biometrical research. Author articles in field. Consultant biometrician since '38; biometrician Conn Agrl Expt Station and Storrs Agrl Expt Station since '40; lecturer, later prof biometry Yale Grad and Med Schs since '42; US Pharmacopoeia coms on insulin, digitalis and biol assay. AAAS(F)—Inst Math Statis(F)—Am Statis Assn (F, past vp, past dir)— Am Assn Econ Entomol—Am Soc Pharm and Exptl Therapeutics— Animal Nutrition Research Council (exec com)—Am Soc Qual—Biometric Soc (sec)—Conn Acad Arts Sci—Nat Research Council—com on Appl Math Stat—Phi Beta Kappa—Sigma Xi. Box 1106, New Haven 4.

18 BLISS, Donald E(verett). Pathology of dates and citrus. b'03. BS '25 (Colo A&M Coll); MS—PhD '31—research fellow '26-27 (Ia State Coll). Research on cedar-apple rust; omphalia root rot of the date palm; structural, chemical and handling factors in date fruit spoilage; rhizosis of the date palm; nutrition and physiology of the date palm; armillaria root rot of citrus. Author articles in field. Path U Calif since '48. AAAS(F)—Am Phytopath Soc—Mycol Soc Am—Sigma Xi. University of California Citrus Experiment Station, Riverside, Calif.†

19 BLITZER, Leon. Spectroscopy; Astrophysics; Rocket ballistics. b'15. BS '38—MS '39 (U Ariz); PhD '43 (Calif Inst Tech). Research theoretical rocket ballistics, stellar spectroscopy; studied spark spectroscopy with United States Navy, NOTS, Pasadena California summers '46-50. Author articles in field. Research fellow astron Steward Obs U Ariz '39-40, asst prof physics '46-48, asso prof physics since '48; research asso OSRD '41-46. Am Phys Soc—Am Astron Soc—Sigma Xi. Department of Physics, University of Arizona, Tucson, Ariz.†

20 BLIVAISS, Ben Burton. Endocrinology; Poultry reproduction. b'17. BS '38—MS '40—PhD '46 (Chicago U); '34, '37 (Central YMCA Coll, Wright Jr City Coll). Principal investigator, research grant to University of Chicago, Committee on Growth of National Research Council acting for American Cancer Society '46; research on modification of feather growth of thyroidectomized roosters after thyroxin and estrogen administration, development of secondary sexual characteristics, male copulatory behavior in hens as result of implantation of testosterone propionate pellets, results of sex hormone administration in fowl and relation of thyroid gland to plumage pattern and gonad function. Author articles: Plumage and Other Sex Characters in Thiouracil Treated Brown Leghorn Fowl '48; Interrelations of Thyroid and Gonad in Development of Henney Plumage in Brown Leghorns '47; Feather Growth Rates in Thyroidectomized Brown Leghorn Fowl '44; and others. Guest investigator Chicago U '47-48; instr physiol and pharmacology Chicago Med Sch since '48. AAAS—Am Soc Zool— Sigma Xi. Sheldon Fellow in Zool U Chicago '43-44. Chicago Medical School, 710 Wolcott Av., Chicago. H: 1942 E. 74th St., Chicago 49.

21 BLOCH, Bernard. Linguistics; American dialects; English grammar; Japanese grammar. b'07. AB '28— MA '29 (U Kan); PhD '35 (Brown U); grad study (Harvard, Columbia, Northwestern); fellow '42 (Nat Sch Mod Oriental Langs and Civilizations); research fellow '32-33 (U Vt). Field work in American English dialects; phonetic and grammatical analysis of English and Japanese; research in theory of descriptive linguistics; editor Language since '40. Co-author: (with Hans Kurath and others) Linguistic Atlas of New England '39, '41, '43; Handbook of the Linguistic Geography of New England '39; (with George L. Trager) Outline of Linguistic Analysis '42; (with Eleanor Harz Jorden) Spoken Japanese (2 vols) '45-46; also articles in field. Field worker Linguistic Atlas of New England '31-33, asst ed '33-42; instr Eng Brown U '37-38, instr Germ '39, asst prof Eng '39-43; asst prof linguistics Yale '43-45, asso prof since '45. Linguistic Soc Am (ed since '40)—Am Oriental Soc—Am Acad Arts Sci—Am Dialect Soc—Internat Phonetic Assn. Yale University, New Haven.

22 BLOCH, Herman S. Petroleum chemistry (Catalytic reactions of hydrocarbons). b'12. BS '33—PhD '36 (U Chicago). Holds about 60 patents in field of catalytic reactions of petroleum hydrocarbons. Author articles: Reactions of Hydrocarbons in Presence of Metal Oxides; Proximate Analysis of Gasoline; Catalytic Cracking of Aliphatic Hydrocarbons; Catalytic Cracking of Cyclic Hydrocarbons; Dehydroisomerization of n-Butane; Mechanism of Paraffin; Isomerization. Gustavus Swift Fellow U Chicago '35-36; research chem '36-39, group-leader '39-45, coordinator chem research div since '45 Universal Oil Products Co Riverside Ill. Am Chem Soc (councilor—Am Inst Chem (F, Chmn Chicago Chapter)—Ill Acad Sci—Phi Beta Kappa—Sigma Xi. Universal Oil Products Co., Riverside, Ill. H: 8443 S. Michigan Av., Chicago 19.

23 BLODGETT, Earle Comstock. Stone fruit virus and potato diseases. b'06. BS '29 (U Ida); MS '30 (U Ida); PhD '34 (U Wis). Author articles: Some Obscure Peach Diseases in Idaho '39; Studies on Peach Viruses in Idaho '41; Peach Wart '43; Rasp Leaf of Cherry '43; Peach Calico '44; Transmission of Peach Wart by Graft Inoculations with Affected Fruit Tissue '46. Asst hort U Ida '29-30; research asst

U Wis '30-35; asso plant pathol U Ida '35-43; path US Dept Agr Moscow Ida '43-45, State of Ida Aberdeen Ida '45-46; pathologist Wash State Dept Agr and Washington State College Prosser Washington since '46. Phytopath Soc —Hort Entomol and Plant Path Assn—Wash Hort Assn—Sigma Xi. Irrigation Experiment Station, Prosser, Wash. H: 1309 Patterson Rd.

10 BLOMQUIST, Hugo Leander. North Carolina botany (Flora, ferns, marine algae, grasses); Sphagna of North America. b'88. BS '16—PhD '21 (U Chicago). Co-author: (with H L and N F Wilkerson) A Laboratory Manual for General Botany '24; The Ferns of North Carolina '34; (with H J Oosting) A Guide to the Spring Flora of the Lower Piedmont of NC '34; The Grasses of North Carolina '48. Asst prof biol Trinity Coll (now Duke U) '20-23, prof bot since '23, chmn dept since '35. AAAS(F)—Bot Soc America—Am Bryological Soc—Am Fern Soc—Sigma Xi. Duke Station, Durham, N.C.

11 BLOOM, Leonard. Race relations; Acculturation; Ethnic groups. b'11. BS '33—AM '34 (Boston U); PhD '37—research fellow '36-37 (Duke U). Research on acculturation of Eastern Cherokee, ethnic groups (especially Jews) in a midwest community and Japanese Americans on West Coast. Co-author: (with Ruth Riemer) Removal and Return: The Socio-economic Effects of the War on Japanese Americans '49; also articles in field. Vis prof sociol Clemson Coll '37-38; asst prof sociol U Calif '41-48, asso prof since '48. Am Sociol Soc—Pacific Sociol Soc — Am Anthrop Assn(F). Recipient of grant-in-aid Social Sci Research Council. University of California, Los Angeles 24.

12 BLOOM, Mortimer Charles. Physical chemistry of solids; Corrosion; Electrical insulating papers. b'99. Student '16-17 (Harvard); '17-18 (Northeastern U); BS '22—PhD '38 (MIT). Research on phase transitions in solids, electrodeposition of antimony as anticorrosive and decorative coating, electroplating, crystallization, corrosion, processing jute and manila fibres, electrical insulating papers. Holds patents on electrochemical processes. Author articles in field. With Hollingsworth & Vose Paper Co '22-25, chief research chem '24-25; dir research Tide Water Oil Co '25-28; with MIT '29-34; research asso mineralogy MIT '35-37, research asso semiconductors '41-45; research consultant General Communication Co, Fed Telephone and Radio Corp '45-49; cons metall div Naval Research Lab Washington since '49. Am Chem Soc—Crystallographic Soc Am—Electrochem Soc—Sigma Xi —Alpha Chi Sigma. Naval Research Laboratory, Washington 25.

13 BLOOMER, Robert Oliver. Stratigraphy, structural geology and petrology of the Blue Ridge Province (Virginia); Petrography. b'12. BS '37 —MS '38 (U Va); PhD '41 (U NC); National Research Council fellow '47-48 (Harvard Univ). Author: Catalogue of Topographic and Geologic Maps in Virginia '40; A Laboratory Manual for Elementary Physical Geology '48; also articles in field. Prof geol, head dept St Lawrence U since '47. Va Acad Sci—Elisha Mitchell Sci Soc—AAAS—Am Geophys Union—Geol Soc Am(F)—Sigma Xi. Department of Geology, St. Lawrence University, Canton, N.Y.†◎

14 BLOOMFIELD, Gerd M. Asbestos goods; Insulating materials; Industrial packings (Development, production,

marketing). b'06. Grad '26 (State Coll Textile Tech, Reutlinger, German); '26-27 (U Munich); '41-42 (Ill Inst Tech). Author articles in field. With Frankfurt Asbestwerke, Frankfurt/M Germany '28-38; Union Asbestos and Rubber Co Cicero Ill since '40, mgr specifications since '47; '46-47 sci cons office Tech Services US Dept Commerce. 518 Diversey Pkwy., Chicago 14.†

15 BLOSSOM, Philip Moss. Mammals (Ecology, taxonomy). b'03. Student '29-30 (U Mich). Biological field investigations in mammalian ecology; collection of specimens for studies in mammalian taxonomy and genetics; expeditions to Arizona, Nebraska, Idaho, Michigan and California; investigation colors of desert mammals. Hon asso curator div mammals Mus Zool U Mich since '31, collaborator Inst Human Biol since '49. AAAS—Am Soc Mammalogists—Am Ornithol Union—Ecol Soc Am—Mich Acad Sci Arts and Letters—Soc Study Evolution—Wilson Ornithol Club. Museum of Zoology, University of Michigan, Ann Arbor. H: 10969 Rochester Ave., Westwood Hills, Los Angeles 24.

16 BLUESTEIN, Ben A(lfred). Organic chemistry (Organo-metallic chemistry). b'18. BS '38—PhD '41 (U Chicago). Research in synthesis of organo-metallic monomers and polymers, effects of ionizing radiations on various materials; organo-silicon chemistry and polymers; worked on atomic bomb project. Author articles in field. Chem Gen Electric Co since '46. Am Chem Soc—Sigma Xi. General Electric Co., Waterford, N.Y.

17 BLUM, Victor Joseph. Geophysics; Study of magnetic fields. b'07. AB '31 (Xavier U); MA '33—MS '36—PhD '44 (St Louis U); STL '40 (St Mary's Coll). Author articles in field. Asst dean Inst Tech St Louis U since '44, asst prof geophysics since '48, dir dept engring since '48. Am Geophys Union —Seismol Soc Am—Soc Exploration Geophysicists—Am Meterol Soc—AAAS —Am Phys Soc—Sigma Xi. 3621 Olive St., St. Louis 8.

18 BLUMBERG, Roland Krezdorn. Seismology; Gravimetry; Instrument design. b'11. AB '35—BS '38—AM '42 (U Tex); PhD '48 (Harvard). Adapted the LaCoste-Romberg gravimeter for continuous recording of the variation of gravity; developed a displacement seismograph with electronic magnification and giving an ink-written record; development represented an increase in sensitivity and decrease in cost previously designd instruments; development and improvement instruments and machines listed as classified by armed services; development of a phase-modulated combination-transducer-amplifier; distance measuring device using electromagnetic waves—indication of distance is made as a function of an audio frequency. Research in seismol and geophys Humble Oil and Refining Co '40-42; research fellow Harvard '47-49; Served in AUS in Underwater Sound Lab Harvard '42-45. AAAS—Seismol Soc Am—Soc Exploration Geophysicists—Sigma Xi. H: 414 N. Milam St., Seguin, Tex.

19 BLUME, John August. Structural design (Earthquake resistant structures). b'09. AB '32—engr '34 (Stanford U). Research in vibration characteristics of buildings and other structures, design and construction of dynamic building model and original machine for forced vibration of structures and ground, design and supervisor construction of diversified projects including plants, buildings, foundations, wharves. Author: A Machine

for Setting Structures and Ground into Forced Vibration '35; also articles about Earthquake Engineering Research Institute. Inspector and constrn engr San Francisco-Oakland Bay Bridge '35-36; pvt practice structural engr since '45. Structural Engrs Assn Northern Calif (pres '48, pres state assn '49)—Cons Engrs Assn Calif—ASCE (chmn joint com seismol soil mechs and found div)—Seismol Soc Am—Soc Am Mil Engrs—Adv Com Engring Seismol (sec)—Earthquake Engring Research Inst (sec)—Sigma Xi—Tau Beta Pi. 45 2nd St., San Francisco 5.

20 BLUMENSTEIN, Robert R. Wood technology. b'17. BS '40 (Pa State Coll). Research and laboratory evaluation of wood preservatives, stabilization efficiencies of various coatings, dip treatments, and impregnating resins on wood, coatings for wood requiring high solvent resistance and high moisture vapor barrier efficiency, evaluation of wood adhesives; laminating of wood for marine or maximum exposure use, hardboard from wood waste. Author articles in field. Treating supervisor wood preserving div Koppers Co '42-44; wood tech Timber Engring Co Research Lab since '44. Soc Am Foresters—Forest Products Research Soc. 4812 Minnesota Av., N.E., Washington 19.†

21 BLUMER, Herbert. Sociology of movies; Labor arbitration. b'00. AB '21—AM '22 (U Mo); PhD '27 (U Chicago). Editor American Journal of Sociology since '40. Author: Movies and Conduct '33; Movies, Delinquency and Crime '33; Appraisals of Social Research '39. Editor: Human Side of Social Planning '35; also articles in field. Research staff Motion Picture Research Council '29-31; pub panel chmn War Labor Bd '43-44; permanent arbitrator Armour & Co '44-45; chmn bd arbitration US Steel Corp '45; instr sociol U Chicago '25-30, asso prof '31-47, prof since '47. Am Sociol Soc (sec '31-36)—Am Polit Sci Assn—Am Econ Assn—Institut International de Sociologie. University of Chicago, Chicago.◎

22 BLYTHE, Rudolph Hamma. Pharmaceutical research; Industrial pharmacy. b'10. PhC '31 (Union U); BS '32 —PharD '34 (Columbia U). Formulation of medicinal products drug standardization, drug manufacturing, labeling drug products. Developments and/or inventions: vasoconstrictor plus antibiotics, hydrophilic colloid laxative, medication formulated to provide timed release, medicinal tar preparations; methods of sterilizing sulfonamide suspensions and of preparing microcrystalline suspensions. Author: Industrial Pharmacy, Opportunities and Training '48, also articles in field. Successively Research pharmacist, coordinator of development labs, head pharm research sect Smith, Kline & French Labs since '34. Am Pharm Assn—Am Chem Soc—AAAS—Am Soc Hosp Pharm. Award: Grand chapt scholarship medal Kappa Psi. 1530 Spring Garden St., Phila. 30.

23 BOAK, Arthur Edward Romilly. Papyrology. b'88. MA '07 (Queen's U); AM '11—PhD '14 (Harvard); '12-14 (U Berlin); '13 (Am Sch Classical Studies Rome). Staff University of Michigan archaeological expeditions in Egypt '24-25, '31-32; Comite international de papyrologie since '48. Author: The Master of the Offices in the Late Roman and Byzantine Empires '18, 2nd edit '24; A History of Rome to 565 AD '21, 3rd edit '43; articles in field. Instr ancient hist U Mich '14, asst prof '17, asso prof '18, prof '20. Richard

Hudson prof '40. Am Philol Assn—AHA (bd ed '38-'42, council since '48)—Medieval Acad Am (council '46-49)—Archaeol Inst Am—Societe royale egyptienne de papyrologie—Assn internat de papyrologues. University of Michigan, Ann Arbor.◎

10 BOAST, Warren B. Electrical engineering (Illumination; Network analyzers; Magnetic circuits. b'09. BS in EE '33—MS '34 (U Kan); PhD '36 (Ia State Coll). Author: Illumination Engineering '42; Principles of Electric and Magnetic Fields '48; Principles of Electric and Magnetic Circuits '50. Consultant practice as registered engineer; Research prof Engring Expt Sta Ia State Coll since '48; Am Inst Elec Engrs—Illuminating Engring Soc—Am Soc Engring Edn—Sigma Xi—Tau Beta Pi—Phi Kappa Phi—Sigma Tau—Eta Kappa Nu. Department of Electrical Engineering, Iowa State College, Ames, Ia.†

11 BOATNER, Edmund Burke. Education of the deaf. b'03. CE '25 (U Miss); AM '33 (Gallaudet Coll). Supt and prin American School for the deaf Hartford Conn since '35; sec conf execs American Schools for the Deaf since '39. 139 N. Main St., West Hartford. Conn.

12 BOATRIGHT, Mody Coggin. American folk humor and folklore. b'96. BA '22 (West Tex State Coll); MA '23—PhD '32—Research Fellow '40 (U Tex). Author: Tall Tales from Texas '34; Gib Morgan, Minstrel of the Oil Fields '49; Folk Laughter on the American Frontier '49; also articles in field. Asso prof Eng Sul Ross State Teachers Coll '23-26; instr, asst prof, asso prof Eng U Tex '26-49. Am Dialect Soc (dir work in Tex on Dictionary of Am and Can Proverbs)—Am Folklore Soc—Tex Folklore Soc (asso ed '37-42, sec and ed since '43); Tex Inst Letters—Authors League. Main Building, 2405, University of Texas, Austin 12, Tex. H: 1419 Newning Av.

13 BOBULA, Ida. Magyars; Chaldeans; Magians; Medes; Sumerian culture; Babylonian mythology; Near Eastern divinities; Hungarian Women: Women in History. b'01. PhD '23 (Budapest U); certificate '25 (Bryn Mawr Coll); '25-26 (W Reserve U); '29-30 F (Vienna Hist Inst). Research on origins, history, laws, institutions, folklore, culture and literature of Magyars, Magians, Medes, Sumerians. Author: History of Women '30; Sarolt (A Princess in the Xth Century) '31; Veres Pálné (A Woman Leader in the XIXth Century) '32; Hungarian Women in the XVIIIth Century '33; Sumerian Affiliations '51; and others in field. Asst ed Szabadság '22-23; soc worker Am Young Women's Christian Assn '24-26; case worker Hungarian Red Cross '26; exec Ministry Pub Instruction '26-32; dir Servolta Coll '32-47; dozent Debrecen U '39-47; chief librarian Am Library Budapest '47; lecturer NJ Coll Women '48; librarian Mid-European Study Group '49-51; asst ed Library of Congress since '51. Assn Hungarian Hist—Hungarian Soc Sociol—Hungarian Fedn U Women (pres '46-48). Received Pasquich prize for history '23, gold medal Pro Hungariae Juventute '29. Library of Congress, Washington 3. H: 321 First St., S.E.

14 BOCKSTAHLER, Harold William. Sugar beet pathology. b'06. BS '28—MS '30 (Purdue U); PhD '47 (U Minn). Experiments on control root rot disease, leaf spot by dusting, spraying, breeding. Author articles in field. Jr path, later path US Dept Agr sugar plant investigations since '30, field coordinator black root project E Lansing Mich since '48. Am Phytopath Soc—Am Soc Agron—Am Soc Sugar Beet Tech—Sigma Xi. P.O. Box 226, East Lansing, Mich. H: 4723 Woodcraft Rd.

15 BODENSTEIN, Dietrich H.F.A. Insect hormones; Morphology and physiology of insects and lower vertebates (Growth and differentiation). b'08. Author articles in field. Research asst Kaiser Wilhelm Inst Biol Berlin '28-33; research asso German-Italian Inst marine biol Rovigno d'Istria Italy '33-34; research asso Stanford U sch biol '34-41; fellow John Simon Guggenheim Memorial Found Columbia U dept zool '41-43; asst entomol Conn Agrl Expt Sta New Haven '44; insect physiol Army Chem Center med div Md since '45. Am Soc Zool—Genetics Soc Am—Sigma Xi—NY Acad Sci. Army Chemical Center, Medical Division, Md.

16 BODER, David Pablo. Psychology of displaced persons; Cultural anthropology; Telegraphy. b'86. AM '27 (U Chicago); PhD '34 (Northwestern U); Study of displaced persons of Europe in France, Switzerland, Italy and Germany summer '46; collection verbatim recordings of stories of displaced persons by means of magnetic wire recorder. Inventor Boder voice keys and, with Joseph H Stonekin, of metascope and disloscope. Author: La Education el Maestro y el Estado Mexico '21; Stanford-Binet Tests for Mexico '24; Concomitant Activity and Fatigue '35. III Morse Code Training Forms, 43; I Did Not Interview the Dead '49; also articles in field. Prof Ill Inst Tech since '30. Am Psychol Assn—Sigma Xi (vp Ill Inst Tech chap '42-43). 4880 Sheridan Rd., Chicago 40.◎

17 BODINE, Marcy Gordon. Social science curriculum construction. b'05. BS '28 (Bradley U); MA '35—PhD '38 (U Ia). Curriculum consultant Illinois Secondary School Curriculum Revision Project '49; study of effect of social studies in high school curriculum. Author articles: Curriculum Revision for More Effective Living; An Adventure in More Effective Living, and others. Faculty Western Ill State Teachers Coll since '38, head dept social sci since '43, prof since '49. Am Polit Sci Assn—Nat Council Social Studies—Ill Council Social Studies—Ill Edn Assn—NEA—Ill Soc Mental Health—Midwest Polit Sci Assn—Pi Gamma Mu—Kappa Delta Pi—Phi Delta Kappa. Western Illinois State College, Macomb, Ill. H: 321 W. Murray St.

18 BOEHNE, Eugene Wheelock. Electrical engineering (Circuit breakers, fuses, protective devices, appearance design). b'05. BS '26—EE '40—DEng '48 (Tex A&M Coll); MS '28 (MIT). Holder of 15 US patents. Author articles in field. Asso prof, dir coop course elec engring MIT since '47. AIEE(F)—Franklin Inst (sci and arts com)—CIGRE—ASEE—Eta Kappa Nu—Sigma Xi. Received two Coffin awards. Massachusetts Institute of Technology, Cambridge 39, Mass.†◎

19 BOELL, Edgar John. Embryology (Biochemical development); Enzyme systems (Development, growth); Metabolism (Morphogenesis, Protozoa). b'06. Fellow Rockefeller Found '37-38 (Cambridge U); BA '29 (U Dubuque); PhD '35 (U Ia). Author articles in field. With Yale U since '38, now Ross Granville Harrison prof exptl zool. Am Soc Zool—Am Physiol Soc—AAAS—Soc Study Growth and Development NY Acad Sci—Conn Acad Arts Sci—Am Soc Gen Physiol—Sigma Xi. Osborn Zoological Laboratory, Yale University, New Haven.†◎

20 BOERNER, Eugene S. Rose breeding. b'93. '13 (U Wis); BS '17 (U Ill). Commercial plant breeding since '35, perennial plant breeder, originator of northern NY strain of delphiniums; rose breeder specializing in floribunda and climbing roses, hybrid tea roses, everblooming climbers. Author articles in field. Am Rose Soc—Mass Hort Soc—Royal Hort Soc, Eng—Brit Rose Soc—Am Delphinium Soc. Winner gold medals, other awards, for roses. Jackson and Perkins Co., New ark, N. Y.

21 BOGERT, Clinton Lathrop. Sanitary engineering; Water supply; Flood control. b'83. CE '05 (Cornell U). Author: Glossary of Terms for Hydrology and Sanitary Engineering. Co-author: Waterworks Handbook (Flinn, Weston & Bogert), three editions. Independent practice since '23. Am Inst Cons Engrs—ASCE—Am Water Works Assn—Am Soc Mil Engrs—Am Soc Testing Materials — N.E. Water Works Assn., 624 Madison Av., NYC.

22 BOGGS, Elizabeth Monroe (Mrs. F. W.). Chemical quantum mechanics; Physics of high explosives. b'13. BA '35 (Bryn Mawr Coll); PhD '41 (Cambridge U). Author articles in field. Research asso Explosives Research Lab (NDRC) Bruceton Pa '43-45. Am Chem Soc—Am Phys Soc—Am Math Soc. Margaret E Maltby fellow Am Assn U Women '38-39. 75 Edgemont Rd., Upper Montclair, N.J.

23 BOGGS, Fitzhugh Willets. Physics (Instrumentation electronics, applied mathematics). b'11. BS '38 (Columbia); PhD '44 (Cornell U); student (NYU, Brown U). Research in measurement of dielectrics at ultra high frequencies, the resnatron, dielectric heating. Author articles in field. Physicist Gen Labs US Rubber Co since '46. Am Phys Soc—ACS—NY Acad Sci—Sigma Xi. General Laboratories, U.S. Rubber Co., Passaic, N.J. H: 75 Edgemont Rd., Upper Montclair, N.J.

24 BOGGS, Ralph Steele. Hispanic-American folklore; Folklore (Spain, Latin-America, US). b'01. PhB '26—PhD '30 (U Chicago). Studied and lectured in Germany, France, Spain, Morocco, Santo Domingo, Haiti, Cuba, Mexico, Panama, Ecuador, Peru, Bolivia, Chile, Argentina, Uruguay, Paraguay and Brazil; research in Hispanic-American folklore; organized curriculum of folklore at University of North Carolina, and folklore studies in the Universities of Mexico and Santo Domingo; organized Folklore Americas, a Pan-American society of folklorists '40. Author articles in field. Prof Spanish and folklore U NC '29-50; vis prof U Mex '45-46, professor Spanish and folklore U Miami and dir Hispanic-American Inst since '50. Folklore Americas (dir)—Am Folklore Soc (councillor)—Folklore Soc of Mexico (hon mem)—Argentine Folklore Assn (corr mem)—Acad Guarani Culture of Paraguay (corr mem) — Folklore Athenaeum of Buenos Aires (corr mem)—Nat Commn of Folklore of Brazil (corr mem)—Bolivian Folklore Soc (corr mem)—Folklore Soc of Uruguay (corr mem)—Acta Anthropologica of the Nat Sch of Anthropology and History of Mexico (councillor). Box 8, Miami (Univ. Branch), Fla.

25 BOGGS, S(amuel) Whittemore. Geography; Toponymy; Cartography. b'89. BL '09 (Berea Coll); MA '24 (Columbia U). Author: International

Boundaries—A Study of Boundary Functions and Problems '40. Co-author (with Dorothy C Lewis) Classification and Cataloging of Maps and Atlases '45; also articles in field. Geog US Dept State since '24; Special adviser on geog since '46; chmn US board on geog names, '49-51. AAAS(F)—Royal Geog Soc(F)—Assn Am Geog (councillor '41-'42)—Am Soc Profl Geog—Am Council Learned Socs (sec-treas '42-48, treas since '48)—Mexican Soc Geog and Statis (hon mem)—Lima Geog Soc (corr mem). U.S. Department of State, Washington 25.⊙

10 BOGGS, Winthrop Smillie. Postage stamps and postal history of Newfoundland and Canada; Philately (Australia, Afghanistan, Kashmir, Formosa). b'02. Author: Postage Stamps and Postal History of Newfoundland '42; Postage Stamps and Postal History of Canada '46 (Crawford Medal of Royal Philatelic Society '47); Foundations of Philately, a Manual for Stamp Collectors '49; also articles in field. Philatelist asso with Eugene N Costales '36-45; dir Philatelic Found since '45. Royal Philatelic Soc—Am Philatelic Soc—Assn for Stamp Exhibitions. Philatelic Foundation, 22 E. 35th St., NYC.

11 BOGUE, Robert Herman. Chemistry (Hydraulic cements, gelatin, glue). b'89. BS '12 (Tufts Coll); MS '15 (Mass State Coll) PhD '20 (Pittsburgh U). United States delegate to second International Symposium on Chemistry of Cements, Stockholm '38, third Symposium, London, '52; research on chemistry of gelatins and cements, phase equilibria, hydration, constitution. Author: The Chemistry and Technology of Gelatin and Glue '22; Colloidal Behavior (2 vols) '24; The Chemistry of Portland Cement '47. Asst prof chem Mont State Coll '15-17; asso prof Lafayette Coll '22-24; dir Portland Cement Assn Fellowship since '24. Am Chem Soc—Am Concrete Inst—Phi Beta Kappa—Sigma Xi. Fellow Mellon Inst Industrial Research '17-22; fellow Nat Bur Standards since '24. National Bureau of Standards, Washington 25.†

12 BOGUSCH, Edwin R(obert). Ecology; Wildlife management; Botany of south Texas. b'05. BA '28—MA '28—PhD '43 (U Tex); '28-30 (U Ill). Collecting, color photography of phanerogams and ecologic habitats, south Texas. Author: Keys to 2500 Texas Plants '44. Faculty A&I Coll Tex since '41, dept chmn since '47, curator herbarium. AAAS—Am Soc Plant Taxonomists—Sigma Xi—Phi Beta Kappa. Texas College of Arts & Industries, Kingsville, Tex.

13 BOHN, Ernest John. Housing; Regional planning. b'01. AB—LLB '26 (Western Reserve U). Member International Housing Commission which toured American cities advising on housing '34; organized Regional Association Cleveland '37; chairman first National Conference on Slum Clearance '33; technical advisory committee of National Conference on Family Life Washington '48. Author: Ohio Housing Authority Law '33. Co-author: A Housing Program for the United States '34; also articles in field. Dir Cleveland Met Housing Authority, Regional Assn Cleveland; chmn City Planning Commn Cleveland; cons to US Housing Authority, Resettlement Adminstrn and Defense Housing div Fed Works Agency; planning com Cleveland Welfare Fedn, chmn health and welfare needs com '48. Nat Assn Housing Officials first pres, bd govrs since '47)—AIA (hon asso)—Am Soc

Planning Officials—Nat Conf Social Work. Recipient $1,000 Am Design award by Lord & Taylor for work in housing and slum clearance '46. Housing Center, W. Mall Dr., Cleveland 14.⊙

14 BOHREN, Bernard B(enjamin). Poultry genetics and physiology. L'14. BS '37 (U Ill); MS '40 (State Coll Wash); PhD '42 (Kans State Coll); '43 (Purdue U). Research on factors affecting fertilizing capacity of fowl sperm. Author articles in field. With Purdue U since '43, now asso poultry husbandry and prof. Poultry Sci Assn—Am Genetic Assn—Genetics Soc Am—Am Soc Animal Prodn—Sigma Xi—Phi Kappa Phi—Gamma Sigma Delta. Received Poultry Sci Research award '44. Department Poultry Husbandry, Purdue University, Lafayette, Ind.†

15 BOK, Bart Jan. Milky Way. b'06. Student '24-27 (U Leiden Holland); '27-29 (U Groningen Holland). Author: The Distribution of the Stars in Space '37. Co-author: The Milky Way '41; Basic Marine Navigation '44; also articles in field. R. W. Wilson fellow in astronomy Harvard U '29-33, asst prof '33-39, asso prof '39-46, prof, asso dir Harvard Coll Observatory since '46; mem Nat Research Council com on UNESCO. Am Astron Soc—Am Assn Sci Workers—AAAS—Sigma Xi. Harvard Observatory, Cambridge 38, Mass.⊙

16 BOLENDER, Milferd Henry. US coins; Silver dollars. b'94. Ed pub schs. Research on early US silver dollars from 1794-1803, US trade and pattern dollars. Author: The United States Early Silver Dollars from 1794 to 1803 '50; Rare coin dealer since '27. Am Numismatic Assn—Am Numismatic Soc. P.O. Box 63, San Marino, Calif.

17 BOLIN, Oren Edgar. Corn breeding; Crop quality. b'10. BS '35—MS '36 (Ia State Coll). Did corn breeding for Illinois Agricultural Experiment Station '38-45; developed high protein hybrids '47. Co-author: Crop Quality '49; also articles in field. Research dir Lowe Seed Co since '45. AAAS—Am Soc Agron—Am Genetics Assn—Alpha Zeta—Phi Sigma—Gamma Sigma Delta. Lowe Seed Company, Aroma Park, Ill.

18 BOLLEY, Donald Sheldon. Oils (Drying); Coatings (Protective); Castor Oil Chemistry. b'08. BS '29 (ND Agrl Coll); MS '34 (Poly Inst Brooklyn); '34-'44 (NYU). Research on air oxidation drying linseed oil film; fundamental investigation chemistry heat polymerization of linseed oil and other drying oils; preparation and study various synthetic and modified drying oils as improved vehicles for protective coatings; solvent extraction linseed oil from flaxseed and utilization of meal; formulation and testing new types of paints as protective coatig materials; preparation and utilizaing of resins and varnishes in protective coatings; investigation new sources of drying oils; preparation Castor Oil derivatives. Issued patents in field. Research chem Nat Lead Co '29-34, head organic research dept '35-49, head protective coatings dept '50; dir research Baker Castor Oil Co since '51. ACS—Am Oil Chem Soc—ASTM. 40 Avenue A, Bayonne, N.J.

19 BOLLINGER, Clyde John. Climatology (Southwest United States); Climatic cycles. b'88. AB '15 (U Mich); SM '20—post grad work '28 (U Chicago); '29 (Clark U). Engaged in research climate of southwest since '21, sunspot and solar radiation cycles

since '30, Caribbean Sea and Gulf temperatures since '33, cyclic variation of rainfall and crop yields. Author articles: Relation of Solar Radiation to Sunspot Cycles '35; The Role of Caribbean Sea and Gulf Temperatures in the Solar Control of Seasonal Weather and Crop Yields in the Southwest '35; The Cycle Pattern of Wheat Yields in the Great Plains '47. Planetary Precession Coordinates in Solar-Climatic Cycle Analysis '48. Asso prof geog U Okla since '21. Am Meteorol Soc—Assn Study Cycles—Am Geog Soc—Sigma Xi. Box 63, University of Oklahoma, Norman, Okla.

20 BOLT, Richard H(enry). Acoustics (Architectural, material properties, measurement, studio). b'11. AB '33—MA '34—PhD '39 (U Calif); '33-34 (Heinrich Hertz Inst Berlin Germany). Delegate Acoustical Society America to World Congress celebrating fiftieth anniversary of the discovery of radio by Marconi Rome Italy '47. Author articles in field. Dir acoustics lab Mass Inst Tech since '45, asso prof since '46; cons in acoustics since '40. Sci liaison officer OSRD London '43-44; chief tech aide NDRC Div 6 NY '44-46. Acoustical Soc Am (F), exec council '44-46, pres '48-49)—Am Inst Physics (policy com '45-48)—AAAS—Am Phys Soc—Sigma Xi—Phi Beta Kappa. Houghton memorial research award UCLA '39, Nat Research Council fellow '39-40; Biennial award Acoustical Soc Am '42. Massachusetts Institute of Technology, 77 Massachusetts Avenue, Cambridge 39, Mass.†

21 BOLTON, Ethel (Stanwood). American antiquarians (Samplers, wax portraits). b'73. AB '94 (Wellesley). Author: The Stanwood Family in America '98; Some Descendants of John Moore '04; Clement Topliff and his Descendants '06; Farm Life a Century Ago '09; Shirley Uplands and Intervales '14; Wax Portraits and Silhouettes '15; Immigrants to New England 1700-1775 '27; American Wax Portraits '29. Co-author: (with Mrs E J Coe) American Samplers '21. Registrar Mass Soc Colonial Dames since '13. NE Hist Geneal Soc. Pound Hill Pl., Shirley, Mass.

22 BOMHARD, Miriam Lucile. Palms (Taxonomy, economic values); Southeastern United States range plants. b'98. BS '21—MA '21—PhD '26 (U Pittsburgh). Delegate Fifth International Botanical Congress Cambridge '30; travel and study Europe and England, British Malaya and Sumatra; taxonomist for recent United Nations Food and Agricultural Organization vegetable oil mission to Venezuela '48. Author articles in field. Prof Tulane U '26-32; bot, ecol, present range conservationist (resch) US Forest Service Dept Agr Washington since '34. AAAS(F)—Washington Acad Sci—Soc Am Foresters—Bot Soc Washington (corres sec '40)—Bot Soc Am—Ecol Soc Am—Am Soc Plant Taxonomists. U.S. Forest Service, Washington 25.

23 BONAR, Lee. Systematic mycology. b'91. Fellow '20-22—BA '18—MA '20—PhD '22 (U Mich). Co-author: A Laboratory Guide for a Course in General Botany '38; also articles in field. Prof bot, chmn dept U Calif '46. Bot Soc Am—Mycol Soc Am—Am Phytopath Soc—Calif Bot Soc—AAAS(F).

24 BOND, Boyce Chupp. Textile dyeing and finishing. b'97. BS in textile engring '17 (Ga Sch Tech). Inventor Bond Continuous Dyeing and Scouring Machine patented '48. Supt dyeing and finishing Farr Alpacca Mills Holyoke Mass '31-33; textile chem and sales Gen Dyestuff Corp Phila '33-53; sales supervisor Eastern Coast Pitts Coke & Chem Co. Pitts since '52. Am Assn Textile Chem and Colorists (charter mem, a founder, past officer). Box 853 Kenilworth Rd., Villanova, Pa.

10 BOND, Chauncey David. Piano acoustics and design; Plywood. b'84. Inventor Weaver B and other piano improvements. Author articles in field. Dir Weaver Piano Co since '34. Nat Piano Mfg Assn Am Inc (past pres) — Acoustical Soc Am — AAAS — York Engring Soc. 1805 W. Macheb Street, York, Pa.†

11 BOND, Fred. Scenic color photography. b'93. Student '11-13 (Friends U); '14 (John Herron Art Inst Indpls); '15-16 (Acad Fine Arts, Art Inst Chgo). Author: Kodachrome and Ektachrome From All Angles '42; Westward Howthrough the Scenic West '47; Better Color Movies '48. Professional color photographer since '37. Photog Soc Am (asso)—Amateur Cinema League—Color Soc Cal. 1007 Broxton Av., LA 24. H: 616 23rd St., Santa Monica, Cal.

12 BOND, James. Birds of West Indies, Peru and Bolivia. b'00. BA '22 (Cambridge U). Expedition to Lower Amazon '25; continuing ornithological survey of West Indies since '27, taxonomic studies birds of Peru, Bolivia since '40. Author: Birds of the West Indies '36; Check-List of Birds of the West Indies '50; Field Guide to Birds of the West Indies '47. Co-author: The Birds of Bolivia '42-43. Formerly research asso now asso curator birds of the Americas Acad Nat Sci Phila. Am Ornithologists Union(F)—Sociedad Cubana de Historia Natural (corres)—Wilson Ornithol Club—Del Valley Ornithol Club(F). 1900 Race St., Phila. 3.

13 BOND, Lora. Soil bacteriology; Plant morphology; Root nodules. b'17. BA '38 (U Tenn); MA '41 (Wellesley Coll); PhD '45 (U Wis). Research on colchicine induction of polyploidy in petunia, origin and developmental morphology of root nodules of Pisum sativum and of the responses of pea roots to the application of certain growth substances. Author articles: Origin and Developmental Morphology of Root Nodules of Pisum sativum '48; Responses of Pea Roots to Application of Certain Growth Regulating Substances '48. Asso prof biol Drury Coll since '48. Bot Soc Am—Ecol Soc Am—AAAS—Tenn Acad Sci—Sigma Xi—Phi Kappa Phi. Biology Department, Drury College, Springfield 2, Mo. H: 1707 Highland Av., Knoxville 16, Tenn.

14 BOND, Ned James, Jr. Grain driers (Design). b'21. BS (AE) '43 (U Ga); MS '51 (La State U). In charge design and production grain driers and drying plants, including driers for rice and corn. Research rice and small grain drying La State U '46-48; chief engr grain driers Hawthorne Inc since '49. Am Soc AE—La Soc AE—La Engring Soc. P.O. Box 765, Welsh, La.

15 BOND, Otto Ferdinand. Foreign language methodology; Visual education (Oral-aural aids in language study). b'85. AB '07 (Clark Coll Worcester Mass); MA '12 (Ohio State U). Author: Introduction to Study of French; Sounds of French; Terre de France; Review Essentials of French Grammar; La Terre qui meurt; En Route; Première Etape; Deuxiéme Etape; Graded French Readers, Books I-X, Alternate Series I-VII; Fifty Foreign Films. Co-author: (with Michael West) Grouped Frequency French

Word List; (with Carlos Castillo) Spanish-English, English-Spanish Dictionary; also articles in field. Prof and chmn Romance langs U Chicago Coll since '34. Modern Lang Assn—AAUP—AAAS—Fedn Mod Lang Teachers. 5307 University Av., Chgo 15.◎

16 BOND, Richmond Pugh. English literature (Eighteenth century; Joseph Addison, satirical poetry); History of British periodicals. b'99. AB '20 (Vanderbilt); AM '23—Dexter traveling fellow '27, '28-29—PhD '29 (Harvard); Sterling research fellow '37-38 (Yale). Editor The Periodical Post Boy since '48. Author: English Burlesque Poetry 1700-1750 '32; Chesterfield: Letters and Other Pieces '35; English Literature 1660-1800; A Current Bibliography, Philiological Quarterly '38-41; Studies of British Newspapers and Periodicals from their Beginning to 1800. Co-author: (with K K Weed) A Bibliography '46; also articles in field. Asst prof Eng U NC '29-34, prof since '39. Modern Lang Assn Am—Eng Assn (London)—Phi Beta Kappa. Chapel Hill, N.C.◎

17 BONDE, Reiner. Potato pathology and disease control. b'96. BS '22—PhD '38 (U Minn). MS '26 (U Maine). Research on potato degeneration diseases '26, effect of virus diseases on yield, resistance to virus diseases, seed plots in northeastern Maine, components of potato mild mosaic '33; potato ring rot '41, '44; spraying and dusting potatoes '31; rate of spread and effect on yield of potato virus diseases '43. Author articles in field. Neb Potato Improvement Assn '22-23; asst plant path Maine Agrl Expt Sta '24-28, asso '28-46, plant path since '47. AAAS—Phytopa Soc—Am Potato Assn. Maine Agricultural Experiment Station, Orono, Me.

18 BONDS, Alfred Bryan, Jr. Higher education; Scientific personnel. b'13. BA '35 (Henderson Coll); MA '36 (La State U); '40-41 (U NC). Chief educational surveys sect, National Roster Scientific and Specialized Personnel, War Manpower Commission '42-43; assistant executive secretary President's Commission on Higher Education '46-48; special consultant UNESCO Paris '48 to lay ground work for annual world-wide inventory of scholarships, fellowships, etc., for study in other countries; mem US Ednl Mission to Israel '51; mem Council of Advisors US Office Edn. Author: Essays on Southern Life and Culture '41; also articles in field. Director training US Atomic Energy Commn '48-49; state commr edn Arkansas since '49. Am Political Sci Assn—Am Soc Internat Law—Omicron Delta Kappa. Julius Rosenwald Fellow U NC '40-41. State Dept of Education, Educational Bldg., Little Rock, Ark.

19 BONE, Evan Paul. Highway visibility; Automotive headlighting. b'83. ME(EE) '05 (O State U). Research on optical principle of ellipsoidal reflector focused with projection lens for headlighting, and development of light reflecting autocollimating device to enhance reflecting efficiency; design of long range visibility headlighting, and reflex reflectors for highway markers; experiments in electronic glare control. Holds numerous patents in field. Pvt researcher since '20. Illuminating Engring Soc—O Soc Professional Engrs. H: 1163 Beverly Hills Drive, Cincinnati 26.

20 BONER, Charles Paul. Acoustics. b'00. BA '20—MA '22—PhD '29 (U Tex); Whiting fellow '27-28 (Harvard). Research in acoustical properties of plywood panels and cylinders, organ

pipes; design of auditorium and broadcast studios; acoustical design of churches and pipe organs. Editorial board Review of Scientific Instruments '47-49. Author: Laboratory Manuals for General Physics '30-36; also articles in field. Instr physics U Tex '22-25, 26-27, asst prof '28-35, asso prof '35-36, prof since '36, chmn dept '41, dir defense research lab since '45; exec dir office govt sponsored research since '49; Dean Coll A&S since '49; cons acoustics Austin since '37; asso dir underwater sound lab Harvard '42-45. Acoustical Soc Am (F, mem exec council '47-50)—AAAS—Am Phys Soc—Am Assn Physics Teachers—Tex Acad Sci—Philos Soc Tex—Sigma Xi—Phi Beta Kappa. Physics Department, University of Texas, Austin, Texas.◎

21 BONILLA, Charles Francis. Chemical engineering (Unit operations, thermodynamics, electrochemistry, corrosion, heat transfer, distillation, filtration. b'09. AB '25 (Madrid U); AB '28—BS in EE '30—ChE '32—PhD '33 (Columbia). Member US industrial mission to Brazil, US technical mission to Cuba. Holds U.S. patent on rechargeable dry cells. Author articles in field. Employed Bakelite Corp, Bell Telephone Labs, Aerovox Corp, US Industrial Chemicals Inc '27-39; with John Hopkins U '37-48, instr, later prof and head dept chem engring; prof Columbia since '48; cons since '34; prin and chief cons Bd Econ Warfare and Foreign Econ Administrn '42-46; supervisor research projects Office Rubber Reserve, Foreign Econ Admnstrn and Air Tech Command '43-48; cons Phillips Petroleum Co since '45, US Naval Engring Expt Station since '46 and Brookhaven Nat Lab since '48; dir Hedwin Corp. Am Inst Chem Engrs —Am Chem Soc—Electrochem Soc—Am Soc Engring Edn. Columbia University NYC 27.†◎

22 BONNER, Campbell. Greek religion (Superstition, magic); Greek literature; Papyrology. b'76. AB '96—AM '97 (Vanderbilt U); AM '98—PhD '00 (Harvard); '00-01 (U Berlin). Traveled and studied in Greece and Italy '01. Author: A Papyrus Codex of the Shepherd of Hermas '33; The Last Chapters of Enoch in Greek '37; The Homily on the Passion by Melito, Bishop of Sardis '40; Studies in Magical Amulets '48; also articles in field. Prof Greek lang and lit U Mich '12-46, now emeritus. Am Philol Assn (pres '33)—Classical Assn Middle West and South ('18-19)—Archaeol Inst Am —Mich Acad Sci Arts Letters (pres '23-24)—Am Acad Arts Scis(F)—Am Philos Soc—Brit Acad (CorrF)—Am Sch Classical Studies (mng com, annual prof '27-28)—Phi Beta Kappa. 1025 Martin Pl., Ann Arbor.◎

23 BONNER, Hubert. Paranoia; Personality; Social psychiatry; Social psychology (Creative genius). b'01. AB '25—AM '26 (Ohio State U); AM '29 (Harvard); fellow '38-40, PhD '49 (U Chicago). Research paranoia and paranoid conditions, paranoid personality; sociology of art, social psychology of creative genius; integration of sociology, psychology, and anthropology in social psychology. Author articles in field. Prof psychol and sociol Ohio Wesleyan U since '48. AAAS(F)—Am Psychol Assn—Am Sociol Soc—Am Philos Assn—Am Acad Polit Social Sci —Nat Council on Family Relations—AAUP. Department of Psychology, Ohio Wesleyan University, Delaware, O.

24 BONNER, James. Plant biochemistry and physiology. b'10. AB '31 (U Utah); PhD '34 (Calif Inst Tech).

Research in plant growth hormones, vitamins in plants, plant respiration, rubber formation in plants; physiology of flower production. Author articles in field. Nat Research Council fellow Holland, Switzerland '34-35; prof biol Calif Inst Tech since '35. Am Chem Soc—Bot Soc Am—Am Soc Plant Physiol. California Institute of Technology, Pasadena 4, Calif.⊚

10 BONNER, John Franklin, Sr. Land use problems of small municipalities; Planning and zoning; Land classification and valuation. b'94. BS '16 (Pa State Coll). Research on problems created by premature subdivision of urban lands. Author articles in field. Dir vocational agr Churchville NY '21-29; sec-dir regional planning Monroe Co NY '29-46; planner Endicott NY '47; municipal cons since '48; planning and zoning specialist Ky Agrl and Industrial Development Bd '51-52. NY State Fed Ofcl Planning Bds (exec sec '38-47)—Am Soc Planning Officials (chmn sect on problems in planning of small municipalities)—Nat Assn Officials—Soil Conservation Soc Am. Churchville, N.Y.

11 BONNER, Tom Wilkerson. Nuclear physics; Neutrons; Airborne radar; Atomic energy. b'10. BS '31 (So Meth U); MA '32—PhD '34 (Rice Inst); Nat Research fellow '34-36 (Calif Inst Tech). Author articles in field. Prof physics Rice Inst since '45; cons Los Alamos Lab since '48. Asso head airborne div Radiation Lab MIT '41-45. Am Phys Soc—AAAS—Am Geophys Union. Rice Institute, Houston.†

12 BONNER, Willard Hallam. Pirate and buccaneer literature; Thomas De Quincey. b'99. AB '20 (Coll of the Pacific); MA '21 (Stanford U); PhD '31 (Yale). Author: Captain William Dampier—Buccaneer Author '34; Pirate Laureate: The Life and Legends of Captain Kidd '47; DeQuincey at Work '36; also articles in field. Prof Eng U Buffalo since '22. Phi Beta Kappa. University of Buffalo, Buffalo 14, N. Y.⊚

13 BOOGE, James Eliot. White and colored pigments; Titanium. b'90. PhG '09—Phc '10—AB '14 (U Ia); PhD '16 (Columbia). Chem E I du Pont de Nemours & Co '17-'28; tech dir lithopone Grasselli Chem Co Newark NJ '28-31, Krebs Pigment & Color Corp Newark NJ '31-36; research dir white pigments E I du Pont de Nemours & Co Krebs Dept '36-43, pigments dept '43-46, chem dir since '46. Am Chem Soc—Am Soc Testing Materials—Am Phys Soc—Am Inst Physics—AAAS—Soc Chem Ind, Brit. Pigments Department, E. I. du Pont de Nemours & Co., Wilmington, Del.

14 BOOHER, Lela Evangeline. Biochemistry of nutrition. b'98. BS '20 (Ohio State U); MS '22 (State U Ia); PhD '28—research fellow '28 (Columbia); research fellow '46-48 (U Minn). US delegate committee of the technical commission on nutrition Health Organization League of Nations Geneva '38. Co-holder two US patents on vitamin concentration. Author articles in field. Chief nutritionist since '43 and dir nutrition labs Gen Mills Inc since '48. Am Inst Chem(F)—Am Chem Soc—Am Soc Biol Chem—Am Inst Nutrition—Soc Exptl Biol and Med—AAAS—Sigma Xi. General Mills, Inc., 1081 21st Av., S.E., Minneapolis 14.

15 BOOKHOUT, Cazlyn Green. Invertebrate embryology (Marine polychaetes); Cytology (Germ cells of mammals). b'07. AB '28 (St Stephen's Coll); MA '29 (Syracuse U); PhD '34 (Duke U). Author articles in field.

With Duke U since '35, now asso prof zool. Department of Zoology, Duke University, Durham, N.C.

16 BOONE, Gladys. Labor economics; International relations. b'95. BA '16—MA '17 (Birmingham U); PhD '41—fellow '19-20, '27-28 (Columbia). Delegate to First International Workers' Education Conference Brussels '22, second Oxford '24; associate editor Encyclopedia of the Social Sciences '28-29, '44-45; public panel member National War Labor Board, Region IV. Author: The Great Poor Law of 1601 '17; Labor Laws of 12 Southern States '34; Household Employment '37; Labor Laws of Virginia '40; The Women's Trade Union Leagues in Great Britain and the United States '41; also articles in field. Prof econ Sweet Briar Coll since '31, chmn div social studies. Am Econ Assn—So Econ Assn (vp '44-45)—Fgn Policy Assn. First holder Rose Sidgwick Memorial fellowship International Relations '19-20. Sweet Briar College, Va.†

17 BOORSE, Henry A. Low temperature physics; Gases (Liquefaction). b'04. Grad '26 (US Naval Acad); AM '33—PhD '34 (Columbia); '34-35 (Cambridge Eng). Delegate Federation of American Scientists to International Conference of Atomic Scientists at Oxford '46, and observer for Carnegie Endowment for International Peace. Author: Prof physics Barnard Coll Columbia U since '48, chmn dept since '37, on leave of absence for war research Manhattan Dist Project '42-45; cons Brookhaven Nat Laboratory; US Atomic Energy Commn since '46. Am Phys Soc—Am Assn Physics Teachers—Sigma Xi. Milbank Hall, Barnard College, Columbia University, N YC 27.⊚

18 BOOS, C(harles) Maynard. Petroleum geology; Geophysics. b'98. BS '21—MS '24 (U Chicago); '32-33 (U Wis). Research in geology of underground gas storage, photo-geologic interpretation, geologic data in Rocky Mountain region, geologic interpretation of seismic data, oil and gas development in Colorado. Author articles in field. Petroleum geol Empire Gas & Fuel Co '25-32; petroleum geophysicist Phillips Pet Co '32-33, Independent Exploration Co '34-38; cons geol Denver, part time teaching Denver U '38-42; indsl analyst WPB '42-44; petroleum geol Barnsdall Oil Co '44-47; photogeol Geophoto Service '47-48; geol cons since '48. Am Assn Petroleum Geol—Soc Econ Geophysicists—Rocky Mntn Assn Geol—Colo Sci Soc—Colo-Wyo Acad Sci. 2036 S. Columbine St., Denver.

19 BOOTH, Ernest Sheldon. Mammals (Pacific Northwest); Birds (Western US). b'15. BA '38 (Pacific Union Coll); MS '40 (U Wash); PhD '47 (Wash State Coll). Author: Birds of Southeast Washington '42; Laboratory Anatomy of the Cat (4th edit) '48; Birds of the West '50; How to Know the Mammals '50; Biology, the Story of Life '50. Head dept biol sci Walla Walla Coll since '38, dir Walla Walla Coll Biol Sta since '47. Am Soc Mammalogists—Am Ornithol Union—Cooper Ornithol Club—Pacific NW Bird and Mammal Soc—Soc Systematic Zool—Biol Photog Soc—Am Soc Parasitol—Am Assn Biol Teachers—Phi Kappa Phi. Department of Biological Sciences, Walla Walla College, College Place, Wash.

20 BOOTH, Harold Simmons. Inorganic chemistry; Fluorides; Gases; Chemical microscopy. b'91. AB '15—AM '16 (Western Reserve U); PhD '19 (Cornell U). Co-author: Text on Quantitative Analysis '40. Editor-in-chief:

Inorganic Syntheses, Vol I, associate editor, Vol II. Prof chem Western Reserve U since '37, head dept chem Cleveland Coll since '25, head div sci since '26, Hurlbut prof chem since '47. Dir Western Reserve Sta US Naval Research Lab '41-44. Am Acad Arts Sci(F)—Am Chem Soc (council, hon chmn convention '43)—AAAS—Electrochem Soc—Phi Beta Kappa—Sigma Xi. 10940 Euclid Av., Cleveland. Died June 23, 1950.

21 BORDEN, Avis. Underwater explosions. b'10. AB '31 (Vassar Coll); MA '33 (Yale); PhD (U Mich). Research on pulsations of gas globe from underwater explosions and on incompressible flow. Author articles in field. Asst prof Newcomb Coll '41-42; physicist David Taylor Model Basin Washington since '42. Am Phys Soc. David Taylor Model Basin, Washington.

22 BOREN, James Basil. Role of United States government in education. b'05. BA '36—BE '36 (Okla City U); ME '36 (Okla State U); PhD '40 (U Tex). Organized and established Mangum Junior College, Oklahoma '37; active lecturer in the field of education since '36. Author: The Federal Government and Education '47. Pres SW Inst Tech Weatherford Okla '39-42; pres Midwestern U Wichita Falls Tex since '42. NEA—Tex State Tchrs Assn. Midwestern University, Wichita Falls Tex.†⊚

23 BORGERHOFF, Joseph L(eopold). Sylvestre Bonnard; French drama (Nineteenth century). b'68. MA '02 (Vanderbilt U); PhD '13 (U Paris). Author: Le Theatre Anglais a Paris ous la Restouration '12; Nineteenth Century French Plays '31; modernized French version of Aucassin et Nicolette '21. Editor: Memoires d'un Collegien by Laurio '08; France's Sylvestre Bonnard '21; also articles in field. Head dept Romance langs Western Reserve U '03-39, prof emeritus since '39. Chevalier Crown of Belgium; Cavaliere Crown of Italy. 134 E. New Hampshire Av., Orlando, Fla.

24 BORGHETTY, Hector Charles. Textile chemistry; Surface active chemicals; Fibres and fabrics; Synthetic detergents. b'06. MSc '28 (TURIN). Author articles in field. Holder various US patents. Mgr textile chem div Gen Dyestuff Corp NY. Am Assn Textile Chem and Colorists—Am Chem Soc—AAAS. 2 Brooklands, Bronxville, N.Y.

25 BORGLIN, Joseph Nathaniel. Terpenes (Chemistry); Resins (Acid chemistry). b'99. BS (Chem engring) '24 (U Washington). Research on rosins, including new applications for rosins, modifications and purification; research on industrial and engineering applications and production terpenes. Holds numerous patents in field, including process for purification wood rosin, conversion rosin to rosin oil, removal metals from rosin and derivatives, halogenated derivatives terpene and resin acids, terpene mercaptan preparation, mfr and use terpene thiocyanoacetate for insecticides, modified rosins for use as emulsifiers in mfr synthetic rubber by emulsion polymerization. Author articles; Terpene Furoates '36; Oxidation of Terpenes in Petroleum Solvents '38; Rosin—Use in Salt Water Soap '44; Terpene Esters by Direct Addition of Aliphatic Acids, and others. Chem and research dept Republic Creosoting Co Seattle '24-26; with Hercules Powder Co since '26, chief chem Hattiesburg Miss '27-28, research and development expt sta Kenvil NJ and Wilmington Del '28-

39, tech service and development since '46. ACS—Oil Chem Soc—Econ Entomol — ASTM — Am Wood Preservers Assn. Naval Stores Dept., Hercules Powder Co., Wilmington, Del. H: 215 W. 37th St.

10 BORING, Edwin Carriques. Psychology (Experimental); Consciousness (Physical dimensions). b'86. ME '08 AM '12 PhD '14 (Cornell). History of Experimental Psychology '29; physical dimensions of consciousness '33; sensation and perception in the history of experimental psychology '42. Co-editor. Psychology for the Fighting Man '43; Psychology for the Armed Services '45; Foundations of Psychology '48. AAAS(F)—Soc Exptl Psy—Am Acad Arts & Scis—Am Psycol Assn. Memorial Hall, Cambridge 39, Mass.⊚

11 BORNEMANN, William. Photography (Equipment). b'97. Student spl courses U Goettingen, Germany, U Rochester. Development and research specialized photographic equipment as cameras for high-speed photography, sensitometers, sound and color printers for motion picture film, equipment for one-step process photography, documentary copying machines; equipment used in connection with manufacture and inspection motion picture film. Issued patents in field. Author articles: A method of dimensional gaging with photoelectric cells; Printer light control; and others. Development and design engr Goerz Optical Co Berlin Germany '23-27, Eastman Kodak Co since '27. Optical Soc Am—Rochester Acad Sci. Eastman Kodak Co., Rochester 4, N.Y. H: 108 Frankland Rd., Rochester 17, N.Y.

12 BORROR, Donald J(oyce). Odonata (Morphology, taxonomy, ecology); Bird-banding; White-throated sparrow (Migratory behavior). b'07. BS '28—PhD '35 (Ohio State). Author articles: The genus Oligoclada '31; The genus Erythrodiplax '42; Checklist Birds of Ohio '50, and others. Grad asst in zool O State U '28-30, instr 30-42, asst prof zool and entomol '42-46, asso prof since '47; research entomol Atlas Powder Co '42; instr entomol Audubon Nature Camp Maine summers '38-41, '46, '48. Entomol Soc Am(F)—Ohio Acad sci(F)—Wilson Ornithol Club—Am Ornithol Union—Widlife Soc—Nat Audubon Soc—Sigma Xi. Department Zoology and Entomology, Ohio State University Columbus 10, O.†

13 BORSODY, Stephen. Hungarian-Slovak relations; Political and historical problems of Eastern Europe. b'11. D Laws and Polit Sci '34 (Charles U Prague). Author: Magyarok Csehszlovakiaban '38; A Magyar-Szlovak Kerdes Alapvonalai '39; Benes '43; Magyar-Szlovak Kiegyezes '45; also articles in field. Prof hist Pa Coll Women since '47. Pennsylvania College for Women, Pittsburgh.†

14 BORSOOK, Henry. Biochemistry (Multi-purpose food). b'97. BA '21—MA '22—PhD '24—MB '27—MD '40—fellow '27-28 (U Toronto). Author: Vitamins: What They Are and How They Can Benefit You '40; also articles in field. Prof biochem Calif Inst Tech since '35; mem food and nutrition bd and com on nutrition in industry Nat Research Council. Am Soc Biol Chem—Am Soc Exptl Biol and Med—Am Assn Sci Works (vp)—Hist Sci Soc. 1201 East California, Pasadena, Cal.

15 BORTON, Hugh. Japanese history. b'03. BS '26 (Haverford Coll); MA '33 (Columbia U); PhD '37 (Rijks Universiteit Leyden Holland); '28 (Harvard); '28-29 (Tokyo-Japanese Lang Sch); '33-35)Rijks Imperial U Leyden Holland); '35-36 (Tokyo Imperial U Tokyo). Author: Peasants Uprisings in Japan of the Tokugawa Period '38; A Survey of Japanese Historiography '38; Japan Since 1931: Its Political and Social Developments '40; War and the Rise of Industrialization in Japan '41; Korea: Internal Poltical Structure '44; The Administration and Structure of Japanese Government '44; United States Occupation Policies in Japan Since Surrender '47. Co-author: A Selected List of Books and Articles on Japan '40; Formosa '45. Rep Am Friends Service Com Tokyo '28-31; mem faculty Columbia U since '37, on leave for gov't service '42-48; various positions Dept State since '42; spl asst dir Far Eastern Affairs for Treaty of Peace with Japan; chief Div Northeast Asian Affairs, alternate State mem and acting chmn Sub-Com for Far East State-War-Navy Coordinating Com, US mem Com Constl and Legal Reform of Far East Commn; asso prof Japanese, asst dir East Asian Inst, Clumbia U. AHA—Am Oriental Soc—Asiatic Soc of Japan—Am Council Learned Socs Com Far Eastern Studies—Far Eastern Association (treas)—Phi Beta Kappa. East Asian Institute, Columbia University, NYC 27. H: R.F.D. 1, Neshanic Station, N.J.⊚

16 BOSCH, Leon A. Meat distribution; Rationing and economic controls. b'07. BA '29 (Hope Coll); MA '30 (Ill U); PhD '48 (Northwestern U). Assisted in formation of meat rationing program for Office of Price Administration, later deputy administrator for rationing; research on World War II meat rationing contributing toward administrative policy for direction of future emergency programs. Faculty mem Northwestern U Sch Commerce since '31, now chmn dept bus adminstrn. Am Management Assn., Beta Gamma Sigma. School of Commerce, Northwestern University, Evanston, Ill.†

17 BOSS, William. Agricultural engineering. b'69. Student (agr) '90-92 (U Minn). Studies on farm structures and mechanics; development and improvement farm implements. Co-author: (with J G Dent, H B White) Mechanical Training '32, and others. Faculty sch agr U Minn '92-38, prof agrl engring and chief dept '19-38, prof emeritus since '38; chief conselor Boss Engring Co (cons and development engrs) since '29; pres Boss Foundry Bayport Minn since '44. AAAS(F)—Am Soc AE (F, past pres)—Soc Promotion Engring Edn—AAUP—Minn Soc Professional Engrs—Nat Soc Professional Engrs—Alpha Zeta—Gamma Sigma Delta. Am Soc AE John Deere medal for distinguished achievement in application of sci and art to soil. Professional engr Minn. H: 1439 Raymond Av., St. Paul.⊚

18 BOSSLER, Robert Burns. Secondary recovery of petroleum. b'94. Grad (Petroleum Engr) (U Pittsburgh). Research in rejuvenation of oil wells and fields by water flooding and air and gas drive processes of secondary recovery; theoretical investigation of mechanics of water flooding process. Author articles in field. Geol, engr Brundred Oil Corp since '35. Am Inst Mining Metall Engrs. National Transit Building, Oil City, Pa.

19 BOSTICK, Vernon Brower. Range management. b'14. BS (Forestry) '35 (Colo A&M Coll). Developed methods, techniques conducting range condition surveys, for judging range condition and trend in condition; initiated studies to determine grazing capacities and proper management practices for reseeded ranges; experiment for determination influence of gophers and ground squirrels on range recovery and establishment of reseeded stands; study of deer-livestock forage relationships, including stomach analyses deer and cattle, forage utilization measurements, physical condition of deer in relation to forage condiitions; collection and identification of western range plants. With US Forest Service since '37, range ecol since '45. Ecol Soc Am—Soc Am Foresters—Am Soc Range Management—Beta Beta Beta. Box 1310, Albuquerque, N.M.

20 BOSWELL, George Worley. Folksongs. b'19. BA '39—MA '40 (Vanderbilt U); PhD '51 (George Peabody Coll for Teachers). Collector folksongs and fiddle tunes in Tennessee; research on interplay between poetry and music in folksong; study literature and music folksongs and ballads in the South. Co-author: (with Charles F Bryan) Tennessee Folk Songs '50. Author articles: Usage in the Southern Ballad and Folksong '49; Shaping Controls of Ballad Tunes over their Texts '51; Reciprocal Influences of Text and Tune in the Southern Traditional Ballad (thesis) '51. Asso prof English Austin Peay State Coll since '50. Tenn Folklore Soc—Southeastern Folklore Soc—Am Folklore Soc—Tenn Philol Assn—South Atlantic Modern Lang Assn—Coll Eng Assn—Internat Folk Music Council—Phi Delta Kappa—Kappa Delta Pi. Jo Stafford prize in American Folklore '50. Austin Peay State College, Clarksville, Tenn. H: 1001 Lawrence Av., Nashville 4.

21 BOSWELL, James Louis. Oyster biology and mortality. b'11. BS '36 (E Central State Coll Okla); MS '38 (U Okla); grad study (U Okla, Rocky Mt Biol Labs, U Mich). Research on effects of various organic chemicals on oysters and associated fauna to determine degree of tolerance to pollution in natural habitat and to establish pollution-indicator organisms on oyster beds. Asso prof biol E Central State Coll Oklahoma '42-46; asso prof biol Oklahoma City U '46-47; biol Texas A&M Research Found since '48. Limnol Soc Am—Okla Acad Sci—Phi Sigma—Beta Beta Beta. Texas A&M Research Foundation, Grand Isle, La.

22 BOSWELL, Victor R(ickman). Vegetable crop growth and physiology. b'00. BS '22 (U Mo); MS '23—PhD '26 (U Md). Author articles in field. Sr hort charge vegetable investigations '28, now prin hort, asst head div US Dept Agr since '28. AAAS(F)—Am Soc Hort Sci (pres '39)—Sigma Xi—Phi Kappa Phi. Plant Industry Station, Beltsville, Md.

23 BOSWORTH, Welles. Architecture; Architectural groupings; Architecture (dwelling and commercial). b '69. MA LLD Ecole des Beaux Arts. Designed dwellings and gardens numerous outstanding mansions in vicinity of New York City; architect for groups of buildings for educational institutions; office buildings for several large corporations. Am Inst Arch—Soc Beaux Arts Arch—Am Soc Arts & Scis—Academie des Beaux Arts. Locust Valley, N.Y.†⊚

24 BOTKIN, Benjamin Albert. American folklore. b'01. AB '20 (Harvard); AM '21 (Columbia); PhD '31 (U Neb)u Author: The American Play-Party Song '37. Editor: Folk-Say, A Regional Miscellany, 4 vols '29-32; The Southwest Scene '31; A Treasury of American Folklore '44; Lay My Burden Down: A Folk History of Slavery '45; A Treasury of New England Folklore '47; A Treasury of Southern Folklore '49; Pocket Treasury of Am Folklore

'50. Contbr Collier's Encyclopedia; Standard Dictionary of Folklore, Mythology, and Legend; contbr ed NY Folklore Quart. Instr Eng U Okla '21-31, asst prof '31-38, asso prof '38-40; folklore ed Federal Writers' Project '38-39; chief ed writers' unit Library of Congress project '39-41, asso fellow in folklore '40-41, fellow library in folklore since '41, chief archive Am folk song '42-45. Am Dialect Soc — The Westerners — Am Folklore Soc—Okla Folklore Soc (pres '28-40)—Am Folk Song Soc—Nat Folk Festival—Nat Com on Folklore Arts of the US (expert consult)—Nat Council Teachers Eng (com on folk song and folklore '42)—Com on folk music Music Educators Nat Conf '43—Phi Beta Kappa. 45 Lexington Dr., Croton-on-Hudson, N.Y.

10 BOTSET, Holbrook Gorham. Petroleum production and reservoir engineering; Radioactivity; Fluid flow. BS '22 (Purdue); indsl fellow '28-29 (Mellon Inst). Author articles in field. Research engr Gulf Research and Develop Co '30-46; prof, head petroleum engring dept U Pittsburgh. AAAS(F)—Am Chem Soc—Am Soc Eng Educ—Am Inst Min Engrs—Amer Petroleum Inst—Sigma Tau—Sigma Xi —Phi Lambda Upsilon. University of Pittsburgh, Pittsburgh 13.

11 BOTTGER, Gilbert Ted. European corn borer (Chemical control, nutrition); Insecticides (Testing). b'05. BS '27 (Ia Wesleyan Coll); '27-28 (U Ill). Studies of relationship between chemical constituents and resistance to corn borer; development of synthetic food medium for rearing larvae of European corn borer; screening tests to find new and more effective commercial insecticides for various types insects. Entomol div cereal and forage insects Bur Entomol and Plant Quarantine USDA '29-43, with div control investigations since '43, now in charge Bur Insecticide Testing Lab Anaheim Cal. AAAS—Am Assn Econ Entomol. P.O. Box 511, Anaheim, Cal.

12 BOUCHER, Chauncey Samuel. Antebellum history of South Carolina and southern United States. b'86. AB '09—AM '10—PhD '14 (U Mich); LLD '36 (Washington and Jefferson Coll); '11-12 (Harvard Grad Sch). Author: The Nullification Controversy in SC '16; Correspondence addressed to John C. Calhoun 1837-1849; also articles in field. Abraham Lincoln lecturer in Am civilization Knox Coll since '47. AHA—Miss Valley Hist Assn (pres '20-21)—Royal Hist Soc(F)—Phi Beta Kappa. Knox College, Galesburg, Ill.

13 BOUNDY, Ray Harold. Plastics; Hydrocarbon chemistry; Electrochemistry; Instrumentation; Styrene and synthetic rubber. b'03. BS '24 (Grove City Coll); BS '26—MS '30 (Case Inst Tech). Holder patents in above fields. Author articles in field. With Dow Chem Co since '26, mgr plastics div since '45. Am Chem Soc—Midland Engring Soc—Am Inst Chem Engrs—Electro-chem Soc — Detroit Engring Soc. Dow Chemical Co., Midland, Mich.

14 BOURKE, Vernon Joseph. Thomistic and Augustinian philosophy. b'07. BA '28—MA '29—PhD '37 (U Toronto). Associate editor: The Modern Schoolman since '44. Author: Augustine's Quest of Wisdom '45; Thomistic Bibliography 1920-40 '45; also articles in field. Prof philos St Louis U since '46. Mediaeval Acad Am—Am Philos Assn —Am Cath Philos Assn (pres '48-49)— Catholic Com Intellectual and Cultural Affairs (vice chmn '48-49)—Pontifical Inst Mediaeval Studies (Toronto). Gov General's gold medal philos and Eng

'28; Cardinal Mercier gold medal in philos '28. St. Louis University, 221 N. Grand, St. Louis.†

15 BOUTROSS, James Joseph. Pearls (Natural, cultured, simulated); Puzzles. b'12. LLB LLD (Kansas City Law Sch); J D (Blackstone Coll Law); (Gemological Inst Am). Research to determine effects heat, cold, quick temperature changes to layers calcium, carbonate and vegetable matter; effects acid conditions of humans which chnge appearance of pearls; causes black pearls; causes different sizes, shapes, colors. Collection and solution 500 varied puzzles. Author articles in pearl field. West coast mgr Pearl Syndicate '44-46; pres Empress Pearl Syndicate since '46. Am Soc Tech Appraisers. Empress Pearl Syndicate, 315 West 5th St., Los Angeles 13.

16 BOVEY, Wilfrid. French Canada. b'82. BA '03 (McGill U) LLB '06 (Cambridge) DLitt '35 (U Montreal) LLD '41 (U Ottawa). French Canada trends and developments; Canadian history particularly pioneering and military; Quebec history and people. Mem legislative council Province Quebec; pres Herbert Reddy Meml Hosp mem cons com Province Quebec Dept Health; parliamentary lawyer; pres Can Assn Adult Edn. Legislative Council Quebec —Chartered Inst Secs. Legislative Council, 1374 Sherbrooke St. W. Montreal, Ontario, Can.

17 BÖVING, Adam G(iede). Beetles (Immature stages); Insect morphology. b'69. MS '94—PhD '06 (U Copenhagen, Denmark). Danish Government Zoological Geological Expedition to Iceland '08. Author: Natural History of the Larvae of Donaciinae '10; A Classification of Larvae and Adults of Genus Phyllophaga '42. Co-author: An Illustrated Synopsis of the Principal Larval Forms of the Order Coleoptera '31, and others; also articles in field. Entomol, sr entomol Bur Entomol Plant Quarantine US Dept Agr '13-39, 43-45. Entomol Soc Am(hon F)—Entomol Soc Copenhagen (hon) —Entomol Soc Stockholm (hon)—Finnish Zool-Bot Soc (corres)—Royal Danish Soc Sci and Art—Washington Acad (hon F) '24-30)—Entomol Soc Wash (pres '23) —Sigma Xi. Commander, Order of Dannebrog, Denmark. 221 Rock Creek Church Rd., Washington 11.

18 BOWDITCH, Henry LaReau. Education (Epileptic children); Emotional stresses under modern educational processes. b'92. MD—PhD. Author articles in field. Founder and dir Eric Bowditch Hosp Sch since '37; lecturer. Am Assn Mental Deficiency (F)—Nat Assn Control Epilepsy. Ruxton, Baltimore 4.

19 BOWEN, Ira Sprague. Astronomy; Atomic structure; Spectra of gaseous nebulae. b'98. AB '19—ScD '48 (Oberlin Coll); '19-21 (U Chicago); PhD '26 (Calif Inst Tech), '50 (Lvnd). Articles in field. Instr in physics Calif Inst Tech '21-26, asst prof '26-28, asso prof '28-31, prof '31-45, dir Mt Wilson Observatories '46-48, dir Mt Wilson and Palomar Observatories since '48. Nat Acad Sci—Am Philos Soc—Am Phys Soc—Am Astron Soc—Astron Soc Pacific (pres '48)—Royal Astron Soc (asso). Draper Medal Nat Acad Sci '42; Potts Medal Franklin Inst '46. 2388 N. Foothill Blvd., Altadena, Cal.◉

20 BOWEN, Norman Levi. Mineralogy (High temperature and pressure, refractories, slags, glass, ceramics). b'87. AM '07—BS '09—LLD '41 (Queens U); Ph D '12 (MIT); ScD (hon) (Harvard Tercent); Yale '51. Joint discoverer mullite, fundamental

constituent fire clay refractories. Author: The Evolution of the Igneous Rocks '28; also articles in field. Charles L Hutchinson distinguished service prof petrology U Chicago '37-'47; petrologist Carnegie Inst Washington since '47. Geol Soc Am (vp '38, '45, pres '46, Penrose Medallist '41) —Mineral Soc Am (pres '37)—Mineral Soc London—Am Geophys Union—Am Acad Arts and Sci—Washington Acad Sci—Am Philos Soc—Nat Acad Sci— Indian Acad Sci (hon)—Kaiserlich deutsche Akademie der Naturforscher (Halle)—Soc geol Belgique—All-Russian Mineral Soc. Awarded Bigsby medal, Geol Soc London Eng '31; Miller medal, Royal Soc Can '43. Geophysical Laboratory, 2801 Upton St., Washington 8.◉

21 BOWEN, Richard LeBaron. New England (Seventeenth century history). b'78. Student (Brown U); grad '98 (RI Sch of Design). Research on history of Rehoboth; life of Reverend Samuel Newman, history of Swansea. Author: Early Rhode Island Colonial Money and Its Counterfeiting 1647-1726 '42; The Providence Oath of Allegiance and Its Signers 1651-2 '43; Early Rehoboth '49; Index to Early Providence Town Records '49; also articles in field. Vice-pres and gen mgr O'Bannon Corp '12-22; founder Coated Textile Mills Inc Providence '23, pres and treas since '23; founder, pres, treas Bowen Mills Inc Pawtucket since '29. New Eng Hist Genealog Soc (colonial mem, com on heraldry since '35, fgn and Eng research since '43, com on publications since '46, asst editor Register '46, '47, councilor '48, RI up '49)—Colonial Soc Mass—Am Antiquarian Soc — Soc Genealogists London—Am Soc Genealogists(F). 173 Columbus Av., Pawtucket, R.I.

22 BOWEN, Wilfrid Wedgwood. Birds of Anglo-Egyptian Sudan and Africa; Bird distribution (Ecological factors). b'99. BA '21 (Cambridge U Eng). Gray African expedition '29. Author: Catalogue of Sudan Birds '26-31; also articles in field. Curator since '34, dir since '46 Museum Dartmouth Coll, asst prof zool Dartmouth Coll '36-46, prof since 46. AAAS—Am Ornithol Union — British Ornithol Union—Soc Study Evolution—Acad Nat Sci Phila—Biol Soc Wash—NH Acad Sci. Dartsmouth College Museum, Hanover, N.H.

23 BOWERMAN, Mary L(eolin). Taxonomy of flowering plants of California and British Columbia. b'08. Student '26-28 (Pasadena City Coll); AB '30—PhD '36 (U Calif); Gen Sch Certificate with Matriculation Exemption '23 (U London). Awarded a trust scholarship by Girls' Public Day School Trust Ltd London. Author: The Flowering Plants and Ferns of Mount Diablo California; Their Distribution and Association Into Plant Communities '44. Research asso in bot U Calif since '46. Calif Acad Sci— Calif Bot Soc—Am Soc Plant Taxonomists—Soc Study Evolution—Ecol Soc Am—AAAS—Sigma Xi—Phi Beta Kappa. Herbarium of the University of California, Berkeley 4.†

24 BOWERS, Alfred William. Mandan and Hidatsa Indians (Archaeology and ethnology). b'01. BS '28 (Beloit Coll); MA '29—PhD '48 (U Chicago). Surveys and discoveries of ancient Indian archeological sites on Upper Missouri River and tributaries; ex-cavations in aboriginal Mandan, Hidatsa and Arikara Indian village sites; archeological researches Mimbres Valley, New Mexico; ethnological studies of the Mandan and Hidatsa. Author: A History of the Mandan and Hidatsa

'48; Mandan Social and Ceremonial Organization '50. Asst prof anthrop sociol and Dir prog in anthrop U Ida since '49. Am Anthrop Assn—Soc Am Archeol—Am Sociol Soc—Sigma Xi. Department of Social Sciences, University of Idaho, Moscow, Ida.

10 BOWERS, Clement Gray. Plant breeding; Floriculture (Rhododendrons). b'93. BS '23—MS '25 (Cornell U); PhD '30 (Columbia). Author: Rhododendrons and Azaleas '36; also articles in field. Tech cons hort trade since '32; lecturer and writer hort and bot; professorial lectr, head bot div Harpur Coll State Univ of New York; research associate Cornell U since '48. AAAS(F) — Torrey Bot Club — Royal Hort Soc—Am Hort Council (dir)—Am Hort Soc—Am Genetic Assn—Am Rhododendron Soc. Box 181, Maine, N.Y.†

11 BOWERS, Douglas Albert. Traffic engineering. b'09. BS (Civil engring) '38 (Okla A&M Coll); Certificate in transportation '39 (Yale). Geometric design streets and highways; planning or selection signals, markings, signing of traffic facilities; analysis accidents to reduce vehicle accidents through correction or modification physical design of roadways and/or installation of traffic control devices; to find driver defects or weaknesses for education of drivers, originated graphical method for computing progressive timing of traffic signals. Contributor: Traffic Engineering Handbook '50. Supervisor Okla Statewide Highway Planning Survey '36-'42; asst highway engr traffic engring dept Calif Div Highways '45-46; asst gen mgr and traffic engr City Bus Co since '47. Inst Traffic Engrs—Nat Soc Profl Engrs—Okla Soc Profl Engrs—Yale Traffic Research Assn. Received Am Soc CE ("Outstanding Civil Engineer Graduate" award of jr membership in Am Soc CE '38; Alfred P Sloan Fellowship graduate study Yale '38-39. City Bus Co., 1206 Exchange Av., Oklahoma City 4, Okla. H: 2468 N.W. 38th St., Oklahoma City 12, Okla.

12 BOWERS, Fredson Thayer. Analytical bibliography; Elizabethan and Restoration drama. b'05. PhB '25 (Brown U); PhD '33 (Harvard). Research in analytical bibliography on printing house techniques and effect on textual problems in 16th and 17th centuries, with special reference to drama; post-Restoration drama 1660-1700; plays of Thomas Dekker. Author, Elizabethan Revenge Tragedy '40; The Fairy Knight, a Manuscript Play Attributed to Thomas Randolph '42; Principles of Bibliographical Description '49. Co-author A Bibliography (with R B Davis) of the English Editions of George Sandys before 1700 '48. Editor: Papers, University of Virginia Bibliographical Society. Asst prof Eng Va U '38-45, asso prof '46-49, prof since '50, professor lect Eng U Chi '51. Bibliog Soc (London)—Bibliog Soc Am —Modern Lang Assn—Eng Inst. Colonnade Club, Charlottesville, Va.†◎

13 BOWERS, Neal Monroe. Pacific islands (Geography). b'06. BS '38 (Western Mich Coll Edn); MS '39— PhD '51 (U Mich). Problems of Resettlement on Saipan Tinian and Rota, Mariana Islands; Resources of the Trust Territory, Mariana, Volcano and Bonin Islands. Contributor: Geography of the Pacific, 1951. Geographer OSS '42-45; asst prof geog Mich State Normal '45-46; instr Amherst Coll '46-47; field study Marianas Islands, Pacific Sci Bd '47-48; asso prof geog U Hawaii since '49. Asso Am Geographers— AAAS—Assn Am Geog—Hawaii Acad Sci—Am Geog Soc—Mich Acad Arts Sci Letters—Phi Kappa Phi—Sigma Xi. Department of Geography, University of Hawaii, Honlulu, T.H.

14 BOWLES, Edward Lindley. Electrical engineering; (Electrical communications, patents); Electronics. b'97. BS '20 (Wash U); MS '22 (MIT); DSc (hon) '45 (Norwich U). Over-all responsibility for communications and radar acting with power for Commanding General AAF, responsibilities broadened to include operational and organizational problems and other technical fields '43-44, scientific adviser US Air Forces since '47; Radio Technical Committee for Aeronautics of Department of Commerce; Radio Advisory Committee for US Bureau of Standards. Asst dept Elec Engring MIT '20, prof '37-42, now cons prof Elec Commn; apptd expert cons to Sec of War '42. Sci Adv Com on Safety at Sea—Nat Acad Sci—Natl Research Council Bd for Natl Security—AIEE(F)—AAAS—Soc Promotion Engring Edn—Am Phys Soc—Inst Radio Engrs(F)—Am Acad Arts Sci— Sigma Xi. Awarded DSM '45. Massachusetts Institute of Technology, Cambridge, Mass.◎

15 BOWLES, Ella Shannon. American folkways and folk arts; New Hampshire history and handcrafts. b'86. Grad '05 (NH State Normal Sch). Author: Practical Parties '26; Geography Outlines of the Continents '27; Handmade Rugs '36; About Antiques '29; Children of the Border '38; Homespun Handicrafts '31; Let Me Show You New Hampshire '38; Supervised Hands That Built New Hampshire '40. Co-author: (with Dorothy Towle) Secrets of New England Cooking '47; also articles in field. Publications ed U NH. Nat League Am Penwomen— NH Hist Soc—Soc Am Folklore. University of New Hampshire, Durham, N.H.

16 BOWLES, Gordon Townsend. Ethnography (Asian). b'04. AB '25 (Earlham Coll); PhD '35 (Harvard). Field expeditions collected comparative racial and ethnographic data on more than 100 contagious ethnic groups inhabiting Tibetan Plateau, the Himalayas and adjacent mountainous and plains areas of East Afghanistan, North India, North Burma, and West China; evacuation of Polynesian sand dune burial site on north coast of Oahu, Hawaii involved skeletal collection of over 600 individuals with comparative racial and archaeological study; studies in Japan, Korea, Formosa, etc. Author article: Linguistic and racial aspects of the Munda problem; and others. Research asso anthrop Harvard '37-38; asst prof anthrop U Hawaii '38-42; sr econ analyst Far East Fgn Econ Adminstrn US Govt '42-44, specialist Japanese Affairs Dept State '44-47, exec sec com Internatl Exchange of Persons Ednl Exchange Program under Fulbright Act since '48. Am Anthrop Assn (F)— Am Assn Phys Anthrop—Sigma Xi—A AAS. 2101 Constitution Ave., Washington 25. H: 3708 Quebec St., N.W. Washington 16.

17 BOWLES, James Ten Broeck. Petroleum technology; Panama canal (Sanitation). b'82. BS '07 (U Mich); '07-09 (U Wis). Research on use of oils and oil products; superintendent filtration plants and water supplies during construction of Panama Canal; lecturer on sanitation of Panama Canal at eastern and southern universities. Asst to vp Lederle Labs NYC '15-17; asst to gen mgr Mayer & Lage NYC '19-20; tech Tide Water Oil Co Bayonne NJ '21-25; with Crown Central Petroleum Corp Baltimore since '25, now petroleum tech. Sanitary expert US AEF Vera Cruz Mex '14; with water supply engrs Sanitary Corps AUS World War I. Inst Petroleum London (F)—ACS—Am Petroleum Inst—Soc Automotive Engrs—A STM—Panama Canal Soc Washington. Crown Central Petroleum Corp., American Bldg., Baltimore 2.

18 BOWMAN, Donald H(outs). Breeding for resistance to corn diseases. b'11. BS '33—MS '35 (Kan State Coll); PhD '39 (U Wis). Author articles in field. Agron charge corn and small grains breeding Delta Expt Sta since '48. Am Phytopath Soc—Am Soc Agron—AAAS(F)—Sigma Xi—Gamma Sigma Delta. Delta Branch Experiment Station, Stoneville, Miss.

19 BOWMAN, Le Roy Edward. Community organization; Race relations; Discussion techniques; Adult and parent education. b'87. BA '11—grad work '11-12 (U Chicago), '13-16 (Columbia). Author: Wilderness of American Prosperity '29; Parenthood in a Democracy '35; Community Programs for Summer Play Schools '36; How to Lead Discussion '39; Organization and Leadership of Group Discussions and Forums '43; Discrimination in the Building Trades in New York '48. Mem dept social sci Columbia '17-31, dir training sch community workers '20-23, organized summer exptl schs various cities on Rosenwald Fund grant under Child Study Assn Am '31-35; organized discussion project US Dept Agr '35; dir United Parents Assn Greater NY '35-38; forum leader and dir SC and Vt state forum demonstrations US Office Edn '38-39; free-lance lecturer '40-41; supervisor bur adult edn training forum leaders, organizing intercultural community leagues NY State Edn Dept '42-46; asst prof sociolanthrop Brooklyn Coll since '46; bd dirs Eastern Coop League since '41. Nat Community Center Assn (aec, editor)—Am Sociol Soc (sec sect on community '24-29)—Am Assn Study Group Work (central com '41-43). 112 Waverly Pl., NYC 11.†◎

20 BOWMAN, Mary Jean. Income distribution; Consumption economics; Chinese economy; Resource allocation. BA '30 (Vassar Coll); MA '32 (Radcliffe Coll); PhD '38 (Harvard-Radcliffe). Contract job US Bureau Labor Statistics to expand study of Chinese levels and patterns of consumption '45-46. Co-author: (with G L Bach) Economic Analysis and Public Policy '49; also articles in field. Case work, research on life hist of inmates Mass State Reformatory for Women '32-34; City supervisor NH, Bureau Labor Statis study of expenditures of families of wage earners and low salaried workers '34, regional supervisor NW central region on study consumer purchases '36; instr, asst prof econ Ia State Coll '37-42; research Ia State Coll on part-time war emergency appointment for dept econ pamphlet series on wartime food strategy '42-43; Internat Labor Office '44; econ Bureau Labor Statis '45; working on income distribution theory and statistics, free lance writing since '48. Am Econ Assn—Economonetric Soc—Phi Beta Kappa. Virginia Swinaburne Brownell Prize in Economics, Vassar Coll '30; Radcliffe graduate scholarship '31-32; Vassar graduate fellowship for research on the life histories of reformatory women '33-34. Department of Sociology, University of Kentucky, Lexington, Ky.

21 BOWN, Ralph. Research engineering (Radio broadcasting, radio-telephony). b'91. ME '13—MME '15—PhD '17 (Cornell U). Granted 30 patents. Author articles in field. With Am Telephone & Telegraph Co dept of development and research '19-34, engaged in development of radio broadcasting and transoceanic comml radio-telephony; dir radio research Bell Telephone Labs NYC '34-37, dir radio and television research '37-46, dir research since '46; mem microwave division Defense Research Com; expert cons to Sec War '41. Inst Radio Engrs (F, vp '25; pres '26)—A I E E—AAAS—Sigma Xi—Eta Kappa Nu. Awarded Morris Liebmann Memorial prize by Inst Radio Engrs '26. Bell Telephone Laboratories, Murray Hill, N.J.◎

10 BOWSHER, Arthur L(eRoy), Sr. Paleontology (Mississippian). b'17. BS '41 (U Tulsa); '41-42, '46-48 (U Kan). Author articles in field. Asso curator upper paleozoic invertebrates US Nat Mus Washington since '48. Am Assn Petroleum Geol—Geol Soc Wash—Sigma Xi—Sigma Gamma Epsilon. U.S. National Museum, Washington 25.

11 BOWYER, John Wilson. Victorian and Renaissance English literature; Shakespeare. b'01. BA '21—MA '22 (Washington & Lee U); PhD '28 (Harvard). Author and editor: (with C H Thurman) Annals of Elder Horn '29; (with John O Beaty) Famous Editions of English Poets '31; (with Beaty, David L Clark and J L Neu) Form and Style, '35; (with John Lee Brooks) The Victorian Age '38. Co-author: Better College English '50; also articles in field. Instr Eng Va Poly Inst '22-23, asst prof '23-24; acting prof Eng Coll Charleston SC '24-25; asso prof Eng So Meth U '28-32, prof since '32. Modern Lang Assn Am—AAUP—Tex Inst Letters—S Central Modern Lang Assn—Phi Beta Kappa (asso). 3521 Milton Av., Dallas 5.

12 BOYCE, A(lfred) M(ullikin). Agricultural entomology (Citrus and subtropical fruits, Persian walnuts, Insecticides). b'01. BS '26—MS '27 (Cornell U); PhD '31 (U Calif). Author: Bionomics of the Walnut Husk Fly, Rhogoletis completa Hilgardia '34; The Citrus Red Mite, Paratetranychus citri in California and its Control '36. Co-author: Studies with dinitro-o-cyclo-hexylphenol '39; The Citrus Bud Mite, Aceria sheldoni '41. Asst prof, asst entomol U Calif Citrus Expt Sta '31-39, asso prof and asso entomol '40-42, prof and chmn div entomol since '43. AAAS—Am Entom Soc—Am Assn Economic Entomol (1st vp '48, pres '49)—Nat Research Council—Crop Protection Inst—Sigma Xi. University of California, Riverside, Calif. H: 7125 Delaware St.

13 BOYCE, Aline Abaecherli. Roman coins. AB '27 (U Cincinnati); AM '28—PhD '32—scholar in Latin '27-29—fellow in Latin '29-30 (Bryn Mawr Coll); fellow '33-35 (Am Acad in Rome). Author articles in field. Staff mem Am Numismatic Soc '41-44, asst to curator '45-47, curator Roman and Byzantine coins since '47. Am Numismatic Soc—Am Philol Assn. Taft grant-in-aid for study in Paris, U Cincinnati '32. American Numismatic Society, Broadway and 155th St., NYC 32.

14 BOYCE, Arthur Clifton. Persian writing scales, Adult Persian literacy. b'84. PhB '07 (Lafayette Coll); MA '11 (U Ill); PhD '33 (U Chicago). Research studies in teaching Persian adults to read according to Laubach methods, author and co-author two primers for purpose. Author articles in field. Asso prin Am High Sch Teheran '15-25; vp Am Coll of Teheran (Alborz Coll of Teheran '25-40; now educational missionary of Presbyterian Bd Fgn Missions. Developed two scales for measuring quality of Persian writing. Nat Soc Study Edn—Iran-Am Relations Soc—Phi Delta Kappa. Received Scientific Medal Ministry Edn Iran '41, Edn Medal '48. Presbyterian Board of Foreign Missions, 156 Fifth Av., NYC 10.†

15 BOYCE, Gray Cowan. History of Middle Ages. b'99. BA '20—MA '21—PhD '25 (U Calif); '22-23 (Harvard); '25 (U Grenoble, France); '25-26 (U Gand, Belgium). Research in medieval intellectual history, medieval education, schools, universities in Belgium, France, Germany, Italy; board editors American Historical Review since '47. Author: The English-German Nation in the University of Paris during the Middle Ages '27. Co-author: (with D C Munro) Paetow's Guide to the Study of Medieval History '31; (with W H Dawson) The University of Prague '38; also articles in field. Teaching and U fellow U Calif '20-22, '23-25; George and Martha Derby Scholar Harvard '22-23; CRB fellow Belgium '25-26; instr hist Princeton '26-29, asst prof '29-45, Shreve fellow '34-35; prof hist Northwestern U since '46, chmn dept hist since '48. AHA—Mediaeval Acad Am—Econ Hist Assn—Department of History, Northwestern University, Evanston, Ill.†◎

16 BOYCE, Joseph C(anon). Spectroscopy; Astrophysics. b'03. AB '22—AM '23—PhD '26 (Princeton). With Harvard-MIT Eclipse Expedition to Soviet Central Asia '36; research on spectroscopy of the vacuum ultraviolet and its applications to astrophysics. Editor: New Weapons for Air Warfare '47; served as technical aide and section chief for National Defense Research Committee '41-46; prof physics, chmn dept Coll Engring NYU '44-50; asso lab dir Argonne Nat Lab since '50. Am Phys Soc (F, sec treas NE sect '36-41, councilor '41-44)—AAAS (F, sec sect B '45-48)—Royal Astron Soc, London (F)—Am Astron Soc—Am Soc Engring Edn—Am Geophys Union. Argonne Nat. Lab., P.O. Box 5207, Chgo 80.

17 BOYD, Catherine Evangeline. Mediaeval Italian and European history. b'04. AB '26—AM '29—PhD '34 (Radcliffe Coll). Research on canon law in Middle Ages, Cistercian order, taxation in Middle Ages, the Renaissance in France. Author: The French Renaissance '40; A Cistercian Nunnery in Mediaeval Italy '43; also articles in field. Research fellow Am Council of Learned Societies '35-36; research asso Boston Mus Fine Arts '37-42; lecturer Wells Coll '42-43; asso prof, prof hist and polit sci, chmn dept Cedar Crest Coll '43-46; asst prof hist womens' coll U NC '46-47; asso prof hist Carleton Coll since '47. AHA—Mediaeval Acad Am—Am Soc Church Hist—AAUP—Phi Beta Kappa. Carleton College, Northfield, Minn.†

18 BOYD, Elizabeth Margaret. Ornithology (Parasitology); Invertebrate zoology. b'08. BSc '30 (Edinburgh U); MA '33 (Mt Holyoke Coll); PhD '46 (Cornell U). Research on food of sea trout (for Fishery Board of Scotland), tissue culture, human and bird parasitology, studies and writing on starlings as non-distributors of gapes in North America, changes in adrenals of newts following hypophysectomy or thyroidectomy, external parasites and parasites of digestive tract and derivatives of starling. Discovered new mite from respiratory tract of starlings. Author articles in field. Asso prof Mt Holyoke Coll since '48, faculty mem since '37. AAAS—Brit AAS—Cooper Ornithol Soc—Wilson Ornithol Club—Am Ornithol Union — Nat Audubon Soc — Mass Audubon Soc—Entomol Soc Wash—Am Soc Zool—Am Soc Parasitol—Sigma Xi. Class medalist in zool Edinburgh U '27, '29, Vans Dunlop Scholarship '30; Allen Seymour Olmstead Scholarship, Cornell U '45-46. Zoology Department, Mt. Holyoke College, S. Hadley, Mass.†

19 BOYD, Julian Parks. Declaration of Independence; Indian treaties; Land companies (Eighteenth Century); Federalism (American). b'03. AB '25—AM '26 (Duke U); Litt D '27 (Franklin and Marshall Coll). Author: The Susquehannah Company Papers (4 vols) '30; Miner's Essays of Poor Robert the Scribe '30; (with C Van Doren) Indian Treaties Printed by Benjamin Franklin '38; Anglo-American Union '41; Declaration of Independence '45, and others. Editor Wyo Hist and Geol Soc, Wilkes-Barre Pa '28-32; dir NY State Hist Assn '32-34; asst librarian Hist Soc Pa '34-35, librarian '35-40; librarian Princeton U Library since '40; mem adv com Franklin D Roosevelt Library; chmn adv council NJ State Mus. ALA—Am Antiquarian Soc—Bibliog Soc Am—Hist Soc Pa—NY Hist Soc—Mass Hist Soc—Soc Am Archivists — Am Phil Soc — AAAS — Phi Beta Kappa. Princeton University Library, Princeton, N.J.◎

20 BOYD, Robert A. Daylight engineering. b'01. AB '25 (Carleton Coll); MS '27 (Wash U); PhD '40 (U Mich). Development daylighting laboratory; research on daylighting design of prismatic glass block extensive study of daylighting development of photocell, brightness meter, reflectometer and other laboratory equipment. Staff Western Res U '27-37; research physicist Engring Research Inst U Mich since '40. Sigma Xi—AAAS—Optical Soc—Illuminating Engring Soc. East Engineering Building, University of Michigan, Ann Arbor, Mich.

21 BOYD, William I. Vegetable production (Growing regions); Canning company and farmer relations. b'10. BSA '32 (Purdue U). Conducted agricultural survey of eastern US and Ontario to determine best locations for growing tomatoes, asparagus, pears and sweet corn for canning; included studies of climate, soil and ancestral nationalities of farmers in better agricultural areas. Agrl tech service rep Grasselle Chem Dept du Pont de Nemours & Co. Am Soc Hort Sci—AAAS. N. Brookfield, Mass.

22 BOYD, William Sprott. Mining and metallurgical engineering; Copper mining. '79. BE '01 (U Sydney). Asst mine supt Boston Consol Mining Co Bingham U '06-10; mgr Ray Consol. Copper Co '19-22 gen mgr '22-30; vice pres Kennecott Copper Co Nevada Northern Ry Gallup Am Coal Co '42-45; cons engr Kennecott Copper Corp '45-47. AIMME—Mining and Metall Soc Am—Inst Mining and Metall. 220 Bush St., SF◎

23 BOYER, Benjamin Franklin. Education; Education administration; Legal education administration; Law school administration. b'04. Asso prof law U Kan '37-42 prof law '42-47 Asst to dean law sch '38-39 chmn law faculty '39-40 dean sch law '40-47; dean prof law Temple U Sch Law Phila since '47; mem Mo Supreme Ct Com Civil Procedure '39-41. Am Arbitration Soc—Phi Delta Phi—Alpha Pi Zeta—Sigma Nu—Phi Beta Kappa. Temple Univ. Law School, 35 S. Ninth St., Phila.†◎

10 BOYER, Ralph L. Internal combustion engines. (Diesel and dual fuel types). b'01. BME '24—ME '30 (O State U). Co-author: Wear Book '48; also articles in field. Diesel engr Cooper-Bessemer Corp '26, asst chief engr '29, chief engr '38, vp director and chief engr. SAE—Sigma Xi—Tau Beta Pi. Cooper-Bessemer Corporation, Mt. Vernon, O.

11 BOYER, Raymond F(oster). Physical chemistry of plastics and high polymers (Cast styrene and resins). b'10. BS '33—MS '35 (Case Inst Tech). Research on, development of cast styrene, divinyl-benzene copolymer rods for high-temperature service in radar equipment, casting resins for potting electrical equipment. Holds patents on light and heat stabilizers for Saran, polystyrene. Author articles in field. With Dow Chem Co since '35, group leader '41-45, asst dir phys research lab '45-48, dir since '48, mem exec research com '49. Am Chem Soc —Am Phys Soc—NY Acad Sci—Sigma Xi—Tau Beta Pi. Dow Chemical Company, Midland, Mich.

12 BOYER, William Preston. Phosphorus (Chemistry); Protein fibers; Fertilizers; Pesticides. b'18. BS (chem) '38 (Va Mil Inst); PhD (chem) '42 (U Va). Research on organic compounds of phosphorus with emphasis on phosphites, phosphates, and phosphoric acids and related esters. With Va-Carolina Chem Corp since '47, dir research from '51. ACS—Va Acid Sci—Sigma Xi—Alpha Chi Sigma. Research Department, Virginia-Carolina Chemical Corp., Richmond, Va.†

13 BOYERS, William Hayden. Nineteenth century French literature; Dante. b'00. AB '22—MA '24 (O Wesleyan U); PhD '29 (U Chicago); student (U Paris). Author articles in field. Instr and asso prof Romance languages Oberlin Coll since '28. Mod Lang Assn Am. Oberlin College, Oberlin, O.

14 BOYKIN, Garland Lester. Extension (Agricultural); Conservation. b '00. BS Animal husbandry '22 (A&M Coll Tex); '24-26 (Colo A&M Coll). Beef cattle, swine, cotton, conservation soil and water; irrigation farming dry land agriculture Great Plains. County agent Hansford Co Tex '34-37; asso dir extension State Coll NM '46-50, acting dir since '50. Epsilon Sigma Phi. State College, New Mexico.

15 BOYLAN, Louis D(aniel). College fraternity and publications accounting. b'06. BSC '29 (U Ala); '24-25 (Spring Hill Coll). Developed uniform system of accounting for 41 undergraduate chapters of national collegiate fraternities University of Alabama accepted by headquarters of each; standardized accounting procedure for the publications; invited to convention of National Scholastic Press Association in Chicago as a speaker on accounting for college publications. Advisor and accountant 41 undergrad chapters nat college Frats U Ala. L. D. Boylan & Co., P.O. Box 1225, University, Ala.

16 BOYLE, Lytton Wesley. Plant diseases and prevention (Flax, cereal root rot, virus, potato rot and root knot nematode, peanut). b'99. BS '23 —MS '24 (Wash State Coll); PhD '32 (U Wis). Author articles in field. Asst plant path US Dept Agr '26-43, plant path emergency plant disease prevention project '43-46; Idaho crop pest control and research found '46-48; asso bot Ga Agrl Expt Sta since '48. AAAS—Phytopath Soc—Sigma Xi. Department of Botany, Georgia Agricultural Experiment Station, Experiment, Ga.†

17 BOYLES, James McGregor. Herpetology. b'26. BS '51 (U Ala). Herpetology, snakes and salamanders. Am Soc Ichthyologists and Herpetologists. Box 2154, University, Ala.

18 BOYNTON, Arthur J. Industrial iron and steel engineering (Production methods, technical economics, metallurgical processing). Student (O State U). Author articles in field. Pres A J Boynton & Co engrs, tech counselors. Am Inst Mining Metall Engrs—ASME —Am Iron Steel Inst—Assn Iron Steel Engrs—Am Soc Metals—Blast Furnace Coke Assn. 109 N. Wabash Ave., Chicago 2.

19 BOYNTON, Damon. Pomology (Fruit plant growth and nutrition). b'08. BS '31—PhD '34 (Cornell U); '26-27 (Amherst Coll); '28 (Chicago U). Made collection of tropical fruits, Puerto Rico; research on influence of mulching apple trees on moisture holding capacity of topsoil, soils in relation to fruit growing in New York, capillary tension as measure of pore space occupied by water in dense orchard subsoils, orchard fertilization, magnesium deficiency, leaf analysis in estimating potassium, magnesium and nitrogen needs of fruit trees, mineral nourishing of fruit trees, acidification of soil in northeastern apple orchards. Author article: Recent Developments in Nitrogen Fertilizers and Ways of Applying them to Orchards '48. Co-author articles: (with Cain) Some Effects of Season, Fruit Crop and Nitrogen Fertilization on the Mineral Composition of McIntosh Apple Leaves '48; (with Fisher and Skodvin) Fertilization of the McIntosh Apple Tree with Leaf Sprays of Urea '48. Farm mgr '31-34; instr pomol Cornell U '34-40, asst prof '40-42, asso prof '42-45, prof since '45. Am Soc Hort Sci—Bot Soc Am—Soil Sci Soc Am—Am Soc Agron —Sigma Xi. Coll Agr fellow, Eng '39; Guggenheim fellow, Calif '45-46. Pomology Dept, Cornell University, Ithaca, N.Y.†

20 BRAATHEN, Sverre O. Circus history. b'95. Owns extensive collection of literature and pictures concerning circuses. Author articles in field. Lecturer on circus; state chmn circus div Wis State Centennial '48. Circus Fans Assn Am (Central States vp). 110 E. Main St., Madison, Wis.

21 BRACELIN, N. Floy (Mrs. H. P.). Ynes Mexia; Cultivated plants of South America and Mexico. Collections of the genus Salix with C R Ball, assisted the University of California Botanical expedition to the Andes collecting 20,000 specimens of cultivated plants. Author articles in field. Asst U Calif Herbarium '28-32, bus mgr and complete responsibility for Ynes Mexia botanical collections in Mexico, Alaska, Brazil, Argentina, Chile Tierra del Fuego, Peru and Ecuador since '28; asst in Calif Acad Herbarium San Francisco '35, '39-43; draftsman sci graphs US Dept Agr Western Regional Research Lab Albany Calif since '43. Bot Soc Am—Calif Bot Soc—Calif Acad Sci (life)—Am Forestry Assn—AAAS —Am Geog Soc—Cooper Ornithol Club. Botany Department, University of California, Berkeley 4.

22 BRADBURY, Norris Edwin. Atomic physics; Atmospheric physics; Ionization in gases. b'09. BA '29 (Pomona Coll); PhD '32 (U Calif); Nat Research Council fellow in physics '32-34 (MIT); ScD '51 (Pomona Coll). Prof physics U Calif since '50; director Los Alamos Sci Lab Los Alamos NM since '45. Am Phys Soc(F)—Nat Acad Scis. Decorated Legion of Merit. Box 1663, Los Alamos, N.M.⊙

23 BRADFIELD, Richard. Agronomy; Soil chemistry, management and physics; Fertilizer usage. b'96. AB '17—DSc(hon) '41 (Otterbein Coll, Westerville, O); PhD '22 (O State U). US delegate to third International Congress of Soil Science, Oxford England '35. Member Rockefeller Foundation Mexican Agricultural Commission since '41; advisor US delegate third Inter-American Conference on Agriculture, Caracas '45; US Food and Agriculture Organization Committee on Agricultural Production, Copenhagen '46; editorial board Journal American Society Agronomy since '40, consulting editor Soil Science since '35. Asst prof, asso prof soils U Mo '20-30; prof soils O State U '30-37; prof soil tech head dept agron Cornell U since '37. Am Soc Agron (vp '41, pres '42)—Soil Sci Am (pres '37)— Internat Soc Soil Sci—Am Chem Soc— AAAS—Sigma Xi. 711 Triphammer Rd., Ithaca.⊙

24 BRADFORD, Donald Comnick. Microseisms; Instruments (Meteorological). b'10. BS (geol) '32 (U Wash); F '32-35—MS '34 (St Louis U); '41-42 (U Pittsburgh). Research on nature and possible origin of various types of microseisms, relationship of meteorological phenomena to occurrence of microseismic storms; research on accuracy and producability of chronometric type radiosonde equipment; humidity measurement. Seismol and geophys '35-42; dir geophys lab U Pittsburgh '39-43; chief radiosonde subsect US Signal Corps Lab '43-44; chief engr Serdex Corp '45-47; management engr Raytheon Mfg Corp since '47. Seismol Soc Am—Soc Exploration Geophys—Am Meteorol Soc —Sigma Xi—Am Geophys Union. Raytheon Manufacturing Corp., 100 River St., Waltham, Mass.

25 BRADLEY, Daniel Frederick. Typography; Book design and production. b'03. Prodn mgr Harper and Bros NYC since '42. Am Inst Graphic Arts (chmn textbook clinic '46-47). Harper and Brothers, 49 East 33rd St., NYC.†

26 BRADLEY, Francis Wright. German word formation; Contemporary proverbs. b'84. BS '07—MA '09 (U SC); PhD '26 (U Chicago). Author articles in field. Head dept modern langs USC since '21, dean faculty since '46. Modern Lang Assn—Phi Beta Kappa. 800 Sumter St., Columbia. S.C.

27 BRADLEY, George Hirst. Entomology; Insect control. b'93. BS '16, '17, '24-25, PhD '49 (Cornell). Research biology and control of insects affecting man; organization and administration insect control phases malaria, typhus and other disease control programs. Author articles in field. Chief entomol div communicable disease center USPHS since '42. AAAS(F)— Entomol Soc Am(F)—Nat Malaria Soc (pres '44)—Washington Entomol Soc—Am Pub Health Assn—Am Assn Econ Entomol—Fla Entomol Soc—Am Soc Prof Biol—Am Mosquito Control Assn—Am Soc Trop Medicine and Hygiene (councillor '52). U.S. Public Health Service. Communicable Disease Center, Atlanta.

28 BRADLEY, Harold Whitman. History of Hawaii and the Pacific. b'03. BA '25—MA '26 (Pomona Coll); PhD '32 (Stanford U). Author: The American Frontier in Hawaii: The Pioneers 1789-1843 '42. Dean and prof hist Claremont Grad Sch since '45; bd ed Pacific Hist Review since '40; bd ed Miss Valley Hist Review '46-'49. AHA —Miss Valley Hist Assn—So Hist

Assn—Am Assn State and Local Hist (bd ed since '47)—Phi Beta Kappa. Recipient Albert J Beveridge Memorial prize '43. Harper Hall, Claremont, Calif. H: 488 W. Sixth St.†☉

10 BRADLEY, Hazel Louise. Ornithology. b'01. BS (Agr) '25 (Mich State Coll); MS (Biol) '42 (U Mich). Research projects on study of nesting chipping sparrows, nesting indigo buntings. Author article: A Life history study of the indigo bunting; and others. Teacher biol Jackson (Mich) High Sch since '34. Am Ornithol Union —Wilson Ornithol Club—Mich Audubon Soc. 908 W. Michigan Av., Jackson, Mich. H: Route 1, Springport, Mich.

11 BRADLEY, John Hodgdon. World geology and geography. b'98. AB laude '21 (Harvard); PhD '24 (U Chicago). Author: The Earth and Its History '28; Parade of the Living '30; Fauna of the Kimmswick Limestone '30; Autobiography of Earth '35; Farewell Thou Busy World '35; Patterns of Survival '38; The World at War '43; World Geography '45. Co-author: Exploring Our World '40; Our World Changes '40; Using Our World '41; Our World and Science '41; also articles in field. Prof geol U Sou Calif '29-35; presently engaged as geog and author. AAAS(F) — Geol Soc Am — Paleontol Soc Am—Sigma Xi. Route 1, Box 650, Escondido, Cal.☉

12 BRADLEY, (Edward) Sculley. American literature (Nineteenth and twentieth century); Social history; Edgar Allen Poe; Walt Whitman; Mark Twain; English versification. b'97. AB '19—AM '21—PhD '25 (U Pa). Editor The General Magazine and Historical Chronicle since '45. Author: George Henry Boker, Poet and Patriot '27; Henry Charles Lea '31; Walt Whitman's Backward Glances (with John A Stevenson, qv) '47; Lowell's "Pioneer" '47. Editor: Boker's Nydia '29; Boker's Sonnets '29; Boker's Glaucus and other Plays '40; Whitman's Leaves of Grass '48; also articles in field. Instr Eng U Pa '19-26, asst prof '26-27, asso prof '37-40, prof since '40. Soc Am Studies(F)— Modern Lang Assn Am (sec Am lit group '28-36, chmn '37-38)—Phi Beta Kappa. Apartment D9, Pastorius Ct., Germantown, Phila. 19.

13 BRADLEY, Theodore Franklin. Chemistry of coating materials; Drying oils and resins. b'01. Student '19-21 (Rensselaer Poly Inst); '33-34 (Rutgers U). Research on synthetic resins, coating compositions, and chemical intermediates, research on chemistry of drying oils. Granted numerous US and foreign patents in field. Contributor: Soybean and Soybean Products '50; Chemistry of Heat-Bodied Drying Oils (vol 3) '43; Protective and Decorative Coatings (vol 5) '46. Research group leader Am Cyanamid Co '28-43; head organic and applications dept Shell Development Co since '45; chem cons War Dept since '46. ACS—Fedn Paint and Varnish Clubs (Award '50 for distinguished scientific achievement in field of paint technology). Shell Development Co., Emeryville, Calif.

14 BRADLEY, William Frank. Clay mineralogy; X-ray diffraction; Clastic sediment minerals (Crystallization and crystallochemical properties). b'08. AB '30—PhD '35 (U Ill). Research in constitution of bond clays and its influence on bonding properties, identification of minerals in clays by X-ray diffraction, effect of heat on illite and montmorillonite, amenability of various types of clay minerals to alumina extraction by lime sinter and lime-soda processes, rehydration and dehydration of clay minerals, etc. Author articles in field. Chem Ill State Geol Survey since '34. Am Chem Soc—Am Soc X-ray and Electron Diffraction — Am Geophys Union — Mineral Soc (London) — Geol Soc Am(F). Illinois State Geological Survey, Urbana, Ill.†

15 BRADLEY, Wilmot H. Geology of Rocky Mountain Tertiary formations (Microfossils); Non-glacial varves; Deepsea sediments. b'99. PhB '20—PhD '27—ScD '47 (Yale). Author articles in field. Geol US Geol Survey since '22, chief geol since '44. Nat Acad Sci—Linnol Soc Am—Geol Soc Am—AAAS—Am Assn Petroleum Geol —Geol Soc Washington—Sigma Xi. Recipient award of merit in phys sci Washington Acad Sci '40. U.S. Geological Survey, Washington.☉

16 BRADT, Glenn Warner. Wild life management; Beaver management. b'89. BS '25—MS '26 (Mich State Coll); PhD '36 (U Mich). Extension, administration, research on beaver, wildlife management since '26; field work and travel in British Guiana, Mexico, Canada, southwestern US; studies on coloration of lava bed mammals. Author: Study of Beaver Colonies in Michigan '38; Michigan Wildlife Sketches '47; Michigan Beaver Management '47; also articles in field. Ext biol Mich State Coll '26-27, instr zool '27-36; game biol Mich Dept Conservation '36-46, dir Rose Lake Expt Sta '46-49; prof wildlife management Mich State Coll since '49. Am Soc Mammalogists—Am Wildlife Soc. Marcellus, Mich.†

17 BRAGDON, Charles Ridgaway. Varnishes; Enamels; Printing inks. b'84. AB '05 (Northwestern U); SB '07 (MIT). Holds patents on adhesive lacquer and wrinkle finish. Author articles in field. Mgr spl services dept research labs Interchemical Corp since '47. Am Chem Soc (chmn Cincinnati sect '30, chmn elect div paint varnish and plastics chem)—Am Oil Chem Soc. 432 W. 45th St., NYC 19.†

18 BRAGDON, John Stewart. Engineering; Flood control and river and harbor engineering. b'93. Commd 2nd lt. '15 advanced through grades to maj gen '50; asst div engr N Atlantic Div '35-37 dist engr Providence RI '37-41 div engr S Atlantic Div '41-44 dir military constrn Office Chief of Engrs since '44 dep chief engrs since '49. Office of Chief Engr., US Army, Gravelly Point, Arlington, Va.†☉

19 BRAGG, Arthur N(orris). Animal habits and environmental evolution (Amphibia); Protozoology; Embryology; Oklahoma amphibians. b'97. BS '24 (Bates Coll, Lewiston, Maine); MA '34 (Boston U); PhD '37 (U Okla). Principal research for past 14 years consists in study for which there is yet no adequate name; essentially it attempts to answer question, "How do the habits of amphibians (and incidentally of other animals) aid in adjusting them to various environments and what evolutionary history is involved in the individual cases?". Author articles in field. Asst prof zool Marquette U '25-33; instr zool U Okla '35-42, asst prof '42-46, asso prof since '46; herpetologist, U Okla Biol Survey, several summers research collection and study of Okla amphibians. AAAS(F)—Okla Acad Sci— Phi Sigma—Am Soc Zool—Sigma Xi. Department of Zoology, University of Oklahoma, Norman, Okla.

20 BRAIDECH, Mathew M(ichel). Fire prevention and protection. b'02. Student '21-22 (Baldwin-Wallace Coll); BChEng '22-25—Chem Engr '31 (O State U). Research on fire gases, ovens and furnaces, ignitability and flamability of industrial materials, role of water in fire control, hazards of synthetic rubber production. Author articles in field. Dir research div Nat Bd Fire Underwriters NYC since '45; safety cons civil defense planning Office Sec Defense '48-49. Am Inst Chem Engrs—Am Chem Soc— Am Inst Chem(F)—Am Soc Testing Materials—Nat Fire Protection Assn (com indsl ovens, furnaces, com toxic fire gas research). 85 John St., NYC 7. H: 172 High St., Hastings-on-Hudson, N.Y.

21 BRAINERD, George W(alton). Northeastern Arizona archaeology; Mayan archaeological ceramics (Yucatan); Aerial mapping. b'09. MSc '35 —PhD '37 (Ohio State U); BSc '30 (Lafayette Coll). Assistant to director Persian expedition University of Pennsylvania Museum '34; Archaeological work in Arizona '35-'39; excavation and research Maya archaeological ceramics of Yucatan Mexico '39-43. Invented Photomapper, a device for aerial mapping from oblique and vertical photographs. Author articles in field. Asso prof anthrop U Calif since 50; archaeol Southwest Museum Los Angeles. Am Anthrop Assn(F)—Sigma Xi. Southwest Museum, Los Angeles 42.

22 BRAINERD, Henry Bowen. History of street and electric railways (New England). b'07. AB in physics '29 (Harvard); spl courses '46-52 (MIT). Study street railways, particularly in New England since '38; collected photographs, post cards, guidebooks, maps relating to field; interviews with old-time employees; study engineering problems of an electric railway museum. Author articles: Stepbrother to the Iron Horse '52; others in railroad mag, hist bulls. New Eng Electric Ry Hist Soc (bd dirs, chief engr since '41, vp '51-53, exec vp since '53)—Nat Ry Hist Soc(pres Boston chpt '39-50, nat pres '41-43). Instrumentation Laboratory, Mass Inst Technology, 68 Albany St., Cambridge 39, Mass. H: 10 Upland Rd., Wellesley 81, Mass.

23 BRAINERD, John W(hiting). Ecological habitat-mapping; Vegetation mapping and description; Aerial photos (Botanical interpretation); Wild life habitats; Plant-bird relationships. b'18.. AB '40 (Harvard); MA'42; PhD' 49 (Harvard Grad Sch). Author articles in field; illustrations in books and miscellaneous maps. Asst prof biol Springfield Coll since '49. Ecol Soc Am—Bot Soc Am—New Eng Bot Club —Am Forestry Assn—Am Ornithol Union—NE Bird-Banding Assn—Mass Audubon Soc—Sigma Xi. Springfield College, Springfield 9, Mass.†

24 BRALEY, Silas Alonzo. Acid mine water. b'89. AB '13 (Morningside Coll); MS '15—PhD '17 (U Ill). Research on acid mine drainage, including properties, methods of elimination, its function as pollution agent. Instr U Ill '17-19, asso prof '19-20, asst prof '20-27; sr fellow Mellon Inst since '27. Am Chem Soc—ASTM (comm D19, sec sub 7)—Pa Chem Soc. Mellon Institute, 4400 5th Av., Pittsburgh 13.

25 BRANCH, Harold Francis. Egyptology; History of the Bible; Palestinian history and geography; Biblical archaeology; Religious art. b'94. AB '19 (Park Coll); BD '22 (McCormick Theol Sem); DD '27 (Buena Vista Coll). Made two study and lecture trips of an archaeological nature to Palestine, Egypt and parts of Asia '31, '35, explored and studied excavations at Jericho, Baalbeck; lecturer, party leader Travel Inst Bible Research '31. Author: The Trial of Jesus '24; Christ's Ministry and Passion in Art '29; Travel Notes on the Mediterranean and Bible Lands '31; Keeping Life Fresh '40; The Status of Biblical Archaeology Today '50; also articles in field. Pastor Grace Presbyn Ch Kansas City since '39. 314 S. Lawn Av., KC 1 Mo.◎

10 BRANCH, Houston. Opera management; Training films. b'03. Asso with Fortune Gallo in management of San Carlo Opera Co '25; writer film stories since '26; expert cons on training films US Army Signal Corps '42-43. Authors League Am—Motion Picture Acad Arts and Scis—Screen Writers Guild. 1250 Hilldale Ave., LA 46.

11 BRAND, Donald Dilworth. Latin America (Geography); Agricultural geography. b'05. AB '29—PhD '33 (U Calif). Studies in regional and topical geography Latin America; vegetation and fauna of Mexico; history, techniques, economics agriculture from prehistoric times to present; New World plants and agricultural origins; world agricultural patterns; field research and expeditions into Mexico. Author: Quiroga '51. Co-author (with C O Sauer) Aztatlan '32. Author more than 100 articles in field. Asst prof, prof anthropo-geog U NM '34-47, head dept anthrop '35-47; cultural geog Inst Social Anthrop of Smithsonian Inst Mexico '44-46; prof geog U Mich '47-49; prof and chmn dept geog U Tex since '49. Am Geog Soc—Assn Am Geog—AAAS—Inter—Am Soc Anthrop Geog — Am Anthrop Assn — Ethnol Soc Am—Soc Mexicana de Antropolgia—Agrl Hist Soc. Department of Geography, University of Texas, Austin 12, Tex.

12 BRAND, Katharine Edith. Papers of Woodrow Wilson. b'00. BA '21 (Smith Coll). Author: Books in the Woodrow Wilson Field publ in (L S Turnbull) Woodrow Wilson Bibliography '48; The Papers of Oscar S. Straus publ in (G S Hollman) The Oscar Straus Memorial Volume '49; also articles in field. Asst to Ray Stannard Baker '25-39; curator Woodrow Wilson Papers div Manuscripts Library of Congress '39-44, asst div Manuscripts since '44. AHA—Soc Am Archivists. Division of Manuscripts, Library of Congress, Washington. H: R.F.D. 1, Vienna, Va.

13 BRAND, Louis. Vector and tensor analysis; Mechanics. b'85. ChE '07—EE '08—MA '09 (Cincinnati U); PhD '19 (Harvard). Research on first systematic treatment of motor algebra by means of dual vectors. Author: Vectorial Mechanics '30; Vector and Tensor Analysis '47; Advanced Calculus '50. Author articles in field. Head dept math Cincinnati U since '36, prof math since '20. AAAS—Am Math Soc—Am Math Assn—Sigma Xi—Tau Beta Pi—O Acad Sci(F). Fellow Grad Sch Arts and Sciences U Cincinnati '38. Department of Mathematics, University of Cincinnati 21. H: 2603 University Court, Cincinnati 19.†

14 BRANDES, Elmer Walker. Plant pathology; Physiology; Sugar, rubber, and tropical crops production. BS '13—MS '15 (Mich State Coll); PhD '19 (U Mich). b'91. Director various scientific expeditions in Central and South America, Asia, Africa and Pacific Islands; leader US Department Agriculture airplane explorations, New Guinea '28; appointed to organize research and stimulate plantation rubber production in 15 countries of Latin America for national preparedness '40. In charge divs sugar plant investigations and rubber plant investigations US Dept Agr since '40. Proefstation voor de Java-Suikerindustrie, Pasocroean, Java (hon)—Am Sugarcane League (hon life) — AAAS(F) — Am Phytopath Soc—Sigma Xi.◎

15 BRANDOW, (Brandeaux), Ada Grace van Loon. Suffrage movement (Memorabilia). b'89. Exhibition custodian suffrage mementos placed in National Smithsonian Institution '42. Educator and poet. Am Poetry Circle—League of Women Voters—Nat Women's Party (former vp)—Susan B Anthony League Found—Eugene Field Soc—Am Geog Soc. Apt 301, 2501 Calvert St., Washington.

16 BRANDT, Allen D(emmy). Industrial hygiene and ventilation. b'08. BS '31 (Pa State Coll); MS '32—DSc '33 (Harvard). Author: Industrial Health Engineering '47; also articles in field. Chief indsl hygiene sect med dept Bethlehem Steel Co since '46. Asst chief indsl hygiene br safety and security div Office Chief Ordnance War Dept Chicago '42-45. Am Indsl Hygiene Assn (bd dirs, pres)—Am Soc Heating Ventilating Engrs (tech adv com)—Am Pub Health Assn (F, chmn com indsl ventilation, com air sanitation)—AAAS. Bethlehem Steel Company, Bethlehem, Pa.†◎

17 BRANDT, Bartholomew Brandner. Ecology and distribution of Amphibia; Taxonomy of water snakes; Migration and conservation of Anadromons fishes. b'98. BSc '17 (Miss State Coll); AM '34—PhD '35 (Duke U). Author: Syllabus in Economic Zoology '47; Syllabus in General Zoology '48; Laboratory Manual in General Zoology '48; Laboratory Manual in Economic Zoology '48. Co-author (with C F Walker) A New Species of Pseudacris from the Southeastern United States '33; also articles in field. Prof zool NC State Coll since '46. cons biol on problems of pollution effects on wildlife since '44. NC Acad Sci—Am Soc Ichthyologists Herpetologists — Soc Systematic Zool—AAAS(F)—Am Soc Zool—Herpetologists League(F)—Am Soc Limnol Oceanog—Sigma Xi. Department of Zoology, North Carolina State College, Raleigh, N.C.†

18 BRANDT, Weldon H(enry). Magnetic materials; Glass-metal sealing. b'10. BA '31 (N Central Coll); MS '33—PhD '36 (U Ill). Holds patents on immersion heaters, insulation for silicon irons, ferromagnetic material, magnetic core. Author articles in field. Research engr Westinghouse Elec Corp East Pittsburgh '36-39, sect engr magnetic development of materials engr dept '39-45, asst mgr materials engr dept '45-46, mgr spl products engr dept since '46. Am Phys Soc—ASME. Westinghouse Electric Corporation, 1844 Ardmore Blvd., Pittsburgh 21.

19 BRANDT, William Otis. Ceramic research. b'14. BS in ceramic engring —MS (U Wash). With Gladding McBean & Co since '37, dir research and development since '46. Am Ceramic Soc(F)—Inst Ceramic Engrs—AIMME—Tau Beta Pi(F). 2901 Los Feliz Blvd., LA 39.

20 BRANDWEIN, Paul Franz. Science education (Methods, curriculum); Smuts (Cereal diseases); Culture of Algae and Protozoa. b'14. BA '34—MSc '36 (NYU); PhD '39 (Columbia). Co-author: (with D A Marsland) Manual of Biology '39. Senior author: Science for Better Living; articles and films in field. Chmn sci Forest Hills High Sch since '40, lecturer Teachers College Columbia since '42, sci ed Harcourt Brace & Co since '45. Nat Assn Research in Sci Teaching—Nat Assn Sci Teachers (dir)—Phi Beta Kappa—Sigma Xi. Teachers College, Columbia University, NYC.†

21 BRANNER, George C. Economic geology (Bauxite and non-metallic minerals); Mineral economics; State planning. b'90. AB '15 (Stanford U); AM '20 (U Chicago). Author articles in field. Dir geol survey Ark '23-42, cons economic geol; vice chmn, chmn exec com Ark State Planning Bd '34-42; SW Regional Planning Com '40; state representative Ark Mining Div OPM and later WPB '41-42. Active duty US Army lt col World War II, Mining Div Allied Control Commn Naples and Rome Italy; dep chief coal and non-metallic mining sect Office Mil Govt (US) Berlin, alternate US mem Quadripartite Coal Com Allied Control Authority Berlin 10 months; left service as col; re-entered service as lt col Corps of Engrs, Engr Sch Ft Belvoir Va since '47. Geol Soc Am —Am Inst Mining Metall Engrs—Soc Econ Geol—Assn Am State Geol (pres '34-37). The Engineer School, Fort Belvoir, Va.

22 BRANNON, Clarence Ham. Entomology (Insect paleontology). b'00. MS '21 (Miss State Coll); '24 (U Va); MS '28 (NC State Coll); '31-32 (Duke U). Research US Bur Entomol '21-23; ext entomol NC State Coll '25-36; state entomol State NC since '37. AAAS—NC Acad Sci. North Carolina Department of Agriculture, Raleigh, N.C. H: 1321 Canterbury Rd., Raleigh, N.C.

23 BRANNON, Victor DeWitt. Local government (Charters); Taxation (Intangible Personal Property). b'09. Student '27-29 (Phoenix Jr Coll); BA '31 —MA '32 (U Ariz); '35-36 (U Wis); PhD '38 (U Mo). Served as research consultant to St. Louis (Mo) Board of Freeholders and University City (Mo) Charter Commission in writing new city charters. Author articles: Employers' Liability and Workmen's Compensation in Arizona '34; State Auditor and Fiscal Control in Missouri Counties '39; Missouri's Apportionment Key '46. Research asst inquiry on cost and character pub edn NY Bd Regents '36-37; researcher and statis Mo State Highway Dept, Mo State Planning Bd '38-39; asst dir Gov Research Inst St Louis '39-46, dir since '47. Govt Research Assn—Am Polit Sci Assn—Nat Tax Assn—Phi Kappa Phi—Phi Delta Kappa. 769 Paul Brown Bldg., St. Louis 1. H: 7 Hillard Rd., Glendale 22 Mo.†

24 BRANSON, Carl Colton. Upper Paleozoic stratigraphy; Paleozoic paleontology. b'06. BA '26—MA '27 (U Mo); PhD '29 (U Chicago). Author articles in field. Research geol Shell Oil Co '44-50; professor geol U Oklahoma since '50. Geol Society America—Paleontol Soc Am—Am Assn Petroleum Geol—Soc Econ Paleontol Mineral —AAAS—West Tex Geol Soc—Midland Geol Soc—Ill Acad Sci—Sigma Xi— Phi Beta Kappa. Dept. of Geology, Univ. of Oklahoma, Norman, Okla.

25 BRANT, Joseph H(enry). Textile chemistry and technology. b'08. AB '30 (Ohio Wesleyan U); PhD '35 (Cornell U). Author articles in field. Dir research Inst Textile Tech '44-47; acting dir research Tennessee Eastman Corporation '35-44; dir research Bates Mfg Co '48-50; sub-com National Research Council on textile problems for QMC since '45. Am Chem Soc—British Chem Soc—Soc Chem and Ind London —Soc Rheology—The Fiber Soc— AAAS(F)—Va Acad Sci—Am Assn

Textile Chem Colorists—Sigma Xi. The Toni Co., Merchandise Mart, Chicago 54.

10 BRANTLEY, Lee Reed. Adhesion (Organic coatings); Oxygen fluoride; Fluorine (Handling); Hardness (Plastics). b'06. AB '27 (U Calif Los Angeles); MS '29—PhD '30 (Calif Inst Tech). Research on measurement of adhesion, adhesion of organic coatings to non-ferrous metals, adhesion of lacquers to aluminum, preparation and reaction of oxygen fluoride and its chemistry, methods of hardening plastics and properties of coating on plastics. With Occidental Coll since '30, chmn dept chem from '40, prof chem from '42, dir Office Nav Research contract since '49; research asst and cons Calif Inst Tech '42-44; cons Nat Bur Standards since '51. ACS (past chemn S Calif sect '47-48, councilor)—AAAS —Sigma Xi—Electrochem Soc—Pacific SW Assn Chem Teachers (pres '51)— Pacific Rocket Soc (hon)—Alpha Chi Sigma. Research F phys Calif Inst Tech '36-42. Occidental College, 1600 Campus Rd., Los Angeles 41.

11 BRASHEARS, Maurice Lyman, Jr. Ground water geology. b'08. '27-28 (U Md); SB '33 (MIT). Field investigations of ground water resources throughout New York and New England, locating potential supplies of ground water, determining quantity available, developing means for proper utilization and improvement of methods of extraction water from ground, also development of exploratory equipment. Author articles in field. Jr geol to sr geol US Geol Survey '36-52, dist geol charge ground-water investigations NY, NE '42-52; partner Leggette & Brashears, cons ground water geologists since '52. Am Geophys Union—Am Water Works Association—NE Water Works Assn—AS CE—Soc Econ Geol—Am Assn Petroleum Geol—Geol Soc Am(F). 551 5th Av., NYC 17.

12 BRASOL, Boris. Criminology; Russian law; History of Russian literature; Pushkin, Dostoievsky; Wilde. b'85. BL '08 (U Petrograd); spl police scientifique training '12 Lausanne U). Expert in Russian law Criminological Commission, Columbia, '29-32, International Criminalistic Academy, Lausanne, since '30. Author: Critical Essays '10; History of Russian Prosecuting Attorneys '14; Methods of Criminal Investigation '15; Socialism vs Civilization '20; World at the Crossroads '21; Balance Sheet of Sovietism '22; Institute of Scientific Criminology '25; Elements of Crime '27; Essay on Russian Religious Philosophy '30; Pushkin, the Shakespeare of Russia '31; Mighty Three—Pushkin, Gogol, Dostoievsky '34; Russian Wonderland '36; Oscar Wilde, the Man, the Artist, the Martyr '38; Crime, Criminology and Criminological Institutes '38; translated Dostoievsky's A Writer's Diary (3 vols); also articles in field. Expert in Russian law, practicing in NYC since '18; chmn, Pushkin Com in the USA since '35; dir, Pushkin Fund, Inc.; Pushkin Soc of Am (chmn) —Am Geog Soc(F)—AHA—Acad Polit Sci—Comite Cultural Argentine (hon mem)—Academia Mexicana de Ciencias Penales (corr mem)—Institut Litteraire et Artistique de France. Awarded gold medal by Institut Litteraire et Artistique de France for critical biog of Oscar Wilde '39. 1841 Broadway, NYC. 23.†◉

13 BRATT, Elmer C. Economic forecasting; Business cycles; Statistical measurement. b'01. AB '25—AM '26 (Nebraska U); '26-27 (Calif U); PhD

'35 (Wisc U). Research on mechanization and productivity, factors responsible for economic growth, regional distribution of industry, possibilities of business-cycle forecasting by use of distribution of total expenditures, and potentialities of stabilizing secondary trend. Author: Problems of Economic Change '36; This Unbalanced World '40; Business Cycles and Forecasting '48. Statis cons Bethlehem Steel Co '30-31; econ cons Central Statis Bd US govt '34; indsl econ Nat Bur Econ Research '36; chief econ analyst Bur Fgn and Domestic Commerce '42-45; prof econ Lehigh U since '29. Am Econ Assn—Am Statis Assn—Econ Soc—Royal Econ Soc(F). Lehigh University, Bethlehem, Pa. H: 1521 W. Broad St.†◉

14 BRATTER, Herbert Max. Currency; Silver (Monetary). b'00. Student '17-19 (Coll City NY); '19-21 (Columbia U Sch Bus). Research and investigation Far Eastern currency and exchange problems, especially question of silver '21-23 and '29-35, Japanese financial trends relative future of yen '34, monetary use of silver in Far East and effect of American government silver purchases, English and French gold and silver markets, and currency of US; testified before Senate Banking Committee on bill to repeal silver purchase act of 1934 '39; member J H Roger's financial mission to Far East for US government '34; member Economists National Committee on Monetary Policy '36-40; director monetary standards inquiry New York City '43-44. Author: Japanese Banking '31; The Monetary Use of Silver in 1933 '33; Silver Market Dictionary '33; The Committee for the Nation—A Case History in Monetary Propaganda '41; "Hard Money" Examined '44, and others; also articles in field. Contributor: Encyclopedia of Social Sciences; Dictionary of American History. Statis Bur Econ Information Chinese Govt '21-23; investment banker NYC '28; sr econ analyst US Treas Washington '34; asst comml attache US Embassy Tokyo '34; corr UN Monetary and Financial Conf Bretton Woods NH '44, first session of preparatory com UN Conf on Trade and Employment London '46, and boards of governors' conferences on internat monetary fund and internat bank for reconstrn and development; Washington corr Banking Magazine NYC since '37, also Norges Handels og Sjöfartstidende (Norwegian Journ Commerce and Shipping) Oslo, Algemeen Handelsblad (Gen Jour Commerce) Amsterdam, Indian Finance Calcutta, South African Financial News Johannesburg, Commercial Financial Chronicle NYC '44-47, Financial Times London '46-47. Nat Press Club—Am Econ Assn—Beta Gamma Sigma. 3000 39th St., N.W., Washington 16.

15 BRATTSTROM, Bayard Holmes. Herpetology (Snakes, lizards); Osteology and Reptiles; Ecologic distribution of reptiles. b'29. BS '51 (San Diego Coll). Asst curator reptiles Natural History Museum San Diego Soc Natural History. Natural History Museum, Balboa Park. San Diego, Cal.

16 BRAUN, Daniel Carl. Hazards to health in the steel and coal mining industries. b'05. BS '35—MD '37 (U Pittsburgh). Participated in President's conference on industrial safety '49 and '50; Clinical Observation of 8000 workers over 12 years, with periodic examinations to determine effects of working environment; special attention to dust, heat, toxic fumes & vapors. Administration of medical, industrial hygiene and com-

pensation work. Med examiner Pittsburgh Coal Co '38-44, med dir '44-49; med dir Universal-Cyclops Steel Co Bridgeville Pa since '49. Am Coll Chest Phys—Pa State Med Soc (co-chmn commn on indsl health and hygiene)—Am Assn Indsl Physicians and Surgeons—Am Indsl Hygiene Assn—AIMME—AMA—Alpha Omega Alpha. Pittsburgh Consolidation Coal Co., Koppers Bldg., Pittsburgh. H: 731 Kewanna Av., Pittsburgh 34.

17 BRAUN, Milton L(au). Creep in, and mechanics of, stretched rubber. b'92. Student '12-13 (O State U); BA '15 (Wake Forest Coll); MA '24—PhD '30 (U NC). Author articles in field. Prof, head dept physics Catawba Coll NC. NC Acad Sci (vp '37-38, pres '44-46, various coms)—AAAS(F)—Am Phys Soc (chmn SE sect '47-48)—Am Meteor Soc (regional dir)—Am Assn Phys Teachers—Sigma Xi. Catawba College, Salisbury, N.C.

18 BRAUNS, Friedrich Emil. Lignin; Polysaccharides; Wood pulp. b'90. '10-12 (U Goettingen, U Munich); PhD '15 (U Berlin). Abstractor of organic chemistry for Chemical Abstracts since '36. Author: The Chemistry of Lignin '52; also articles in field. Research chem Koholyt Aktien-Gesell Konigsberg and Berlin pulp mills '22-26; Zellstoff-Fabrik Waldhoff '26-30; Canadian Pulp and Paper Assn fellow dept cellulose and ind chem McGill U '30-35; research asso Inst Paper Chem Appleton Wis since '35. Am Chem Soc —Swiss Chem Soc—AAAS—Am Inst Chem(F)—Wis Acad Arts Sci Letters —Sigma Xi—Forest Products Research Soc—TAPPI. 306 E. S. River St., Appleton, Wis.†

19 BRAVERMAN, Shelley. Firearms; Ballistics; Projectiles (High velocity). b'10. Inventor and research physicist; editor and pub The Firearms Directory; research lab Columbia County ultra high velocity projectiles and silent firearms. Internat Assn for Identification—Am Ordnance Assn—Am Rifle Assn(life)—US Revolver Assn. 207 E. 31st St., NYC 16.

20 BRAYMAN, George. Bridges (Reinforced concrete); Walls (Retaining). b'01. CE '22 (Cornell U). Research and construction of concrete structures for highways. Project engr J G White Engring Corp '22-24; engr and construction supt F R Weller '24-27; engr NY State Dept Highways '27-30; supt Albany Bridge Co '31-32; with Brayman Construction Co since '32. 67 N. Harrison Av., Pitts 2.

21 BRAYMAN, Harold. Public relations; American political campaigns and conventions. b'00. AB '20 (Cornell U). Accompanied Alfred E Smith through 1928 campaign and F D Roosevelt through 1932 campaign as correspondent; covered all national conventions and national political campaigns '28-40. Asst dir pub relations dept E I du Pont de Nemours & Co '42-44, dir since '44; dir Nat Press Bldg Corp. Nat Press Club (pres '38)—Gridiron Club (pres '41). Chm 5th Nat Conf Bus Public Relations Execs '48. Du Pont Building, Wilmington, 98, Del.

22 BRAYNARD, Frank Osborn. Merchant shipping; Passenger liners; Marine history. b'16. AB '39 (Duke U); AM '40 (Columbia). Author: Lives of the Liners '47; also articles in field. Research Am Merchant Marine Inst NYC since '43, asst ed marine dept NY Herald Tribune since '48. Steamship Hist Soc Am (bd dirs, exec com, ed Steamboat Bill of Facts '46-49). New York Herald Tribune, 230 W. 41st St., NYC.

10 BRAYTON, Margaret Morrison. Children's museums. b'96. PhB '20 (U Chicago); MA '21 (U Ill); '22 (Boston ·U); '37-39 (U Mich). Chairman children's section International Council Museums under UNESCO Paris '48. Author: Work with Children in Museums. Editor: Small Sprouts; also articles in field. Mus teacher Children's Mus Detroit '27-39, now curator; supervisor mus edn Detroit Pub Sch; vis lect U Mich '46-48; asst prof edn Wayne U '39-49. Am Council Mus —Am Assn Mus (vp '49-52)—Mich Edn Assn (chmn internat relations sect '48-49)—Mich Acad Sci. 5205 Cass Av., Detroit 2.

11 BRAZELL, Nicholas Joseph. Hydrofoil propellers. b'95. BS '24—Marine Engr '24 (U Mich); '45 (U Md); '44 (Dept Agr). Developed CLYBEN and NACABS hydrofoil propeller design techniques. Author articles in field. Prin engr Bur Ships Navy Dept, civilian head of design of propellers and shafts since '37. Soc Naval Architects and Marine Engrs—Am Soc Naval Engrs. Navy Department, Bureau of Ships, 18th and Constitution Av., Washington 25.

12 BREAKEY, Herbert Abner. Petroleum economics (International policy, requirement forecasts). b'96. BS '24—MS '27 (U Denver); PhD '34 (Am U, Washington); '30 (U Calif); '33 (Grad Sch, Dept Agr). Research in trends, seasonal variations, measurement, and forecasting of gasoline and crude oil requirements. Co-author Minerals Yearbook chapter on Crude Petroleum and Petroleum Products for many years. Author articles in field. Asst chief general policy br petroleum div Dept State '45-49; chief Requirements Sec, Munitions Bd '49. Munitions Board, Petroleum Div., Washington 25.†

13 BREARTY, Charles Ross. Inspection of manufactured products; Quality control sampling. b'02. BS '23 (U Calif). Author: The Signal Corps Inspection Manual. Co-author: Acceptance Procedures with Applications of Statistical Quality Control, and others. Special concern with defects per unit methods for large complex equipment; engaged directly and indirectly in inspection communications supplies, general problems maintenance of quality in Bell System since '23. Officer Signal Corps US Army '42-46, lt col Signal Reserve Corps. Tau Beta Pi. Army Commendation Ribbon. Bell Telephone Laboratories, Inc., 463 West St., NYC 14.†

14 BRECKENRIDGE, Walter John. Birds, reptiles and amphibians of Minnesota. b'03. BA '26 (U Ia); MA '34—PhD '41 (U Minn). Author: Reptiles and Amphibians of Minnesota '44; illustrated in part: Birds of Minnesota '36; also articles in field. With Minn Mus Nat Hist U Minn since '26, now dir Am Ornithol Union—Am Soc Mammalogists—Wilson Ornithol Club (2nd vp '47-48)—Minn Acad Sci (pres '47-48)—Minn Ornithol Union (pres '45-46)—AAAS.

15 BREED, John Brewster. Four Corners (Geography); Indians (Hopi, Navajo, Havasupai); Kachina dolls. b '17. Student '36-40 (Harvard); '42 (USN Photo Intelligence Sch). Exploration of Four Corners area; research on arts and crafts especially silversmithing of Navajo and Hopi Indians; Navajo sandpainting ceremonies; representations of masked dancers of Hopi Indian tribe called Kachina dolls. Contributor of illustrations: Hopi Kachinas '49. Mem field expedition Children's Mus Indianapolis to western US

and Mexico '33-36; dir expeditions into unknown sectors western US, Canada '37-41; dir Escalante and Central Utah Expeditions '48-50. Explorers Club—Inst Geog Exploration—Am Soc Magazine Photographers — Photographic Soc Am—Soc Colonial Wars. 42 Longview Dr., Marblehead, Mass.

16 BREEN, Quirinus. History of rhetoric to 1600 A.D.; Roman law in the Middle Ages. b'96. AB '20 (Calvin Coll); PhD '31 (U Chicago). Author: John Calvin: A Study in French Humanism '31; also articles in field. Professor hist U Ore. Am Soc Reformation Research. AHA—Med Acad Am—Am Soc Church Hist. Department of History, University of Oregon, Eugene, Ore.

17 BREESE, Edward Yarde. History of industrial management. b'12. AB '34 (Princeton U); '34-35 (Harvard). Author articles in field. Instr Sch Indsl Mgt Ga Inst Tech; personnel cons. Am Soc Engring Edn—Ga Edn Assn. Georgia Institute of Technology, Atlanta.†

18 BREGGER, John Taylor. Soil conservation (Orchard crops); Orcharding (Fruit varieties). b'96. BS '17 (Mich State Coll); '17-18 (Ore State Coll); MS in Agr '22 (Cornell U). Stock-scion relationships, tree fruit propagation; fruit varieties. Editor-in-chief American Fruit Growers Magazine Cleveland O '33-35. Author: Manual of Modern Orcharding '23; Guide to Profitable Orcharding '27. Co-author: (with G S Brown) Soil and Moisture Conservation in Orchards and Vineyards '45. Head orchard research and spl service depts Stark Bros Nurseries Louisiana Mo '23-37; supt Luther Burbank Exp Farms Sebastopol Calif '27-29; ext hort Wash State Coll Pullman Wash '29-32; prof ext pomol Cornell U '32-33; project mgr Soil Conservation Service Waynesboro Pa '35-37; project supervisor Evaluation Surveys Williamsport & Upper Darby Pa '38-39; orchard erosion investigations Clemson SC since '39, work covers nine SE States. Soil Conservation Soc Am—Am Soc Hort Sci—Am Pomol Soc (pres '49-51). P.O. Box 952, Clemson, S.C.

19 BREITUNG, Charles Adelbert. Chemical engineering (Oil and natural gas). b'92. Student '09-10 (Wittenberg Coll); BS in Chem Engring '17 (U Mich); DSc (hon) '45 (Laval U). Cons gas engr since '22; asso with natural gas enterprises in Shreveport, La; cons engr on natural gas pipe lines in La, Tex, Okla; producer of oil and natural gas. 407 W. 18 St., The Ambassador, Austin, Tex.◎

20 BREITWIESER, Charles John. Electrical engineering; Electronics; Aircraft electrical engineering; Electro-mechanical design. b'10. BS in EE '30 (U ND); '30-31 (Chicago Central Sta Inst); MS '33 (Calif Inst Tech). Elec engr Public Service Northern Ill '30-31; engr United Sound Products Corp Los Angeles '33-34; cons engr, mfg comml research Pasadena Calif '34-37; chief engr, and vp Caldo Corp '37; sec-treas Conducto-Therm Corp of Los Angeles '39; cons engr DeForest Labs and chief engr DeForest Research; former staff engr in charge radio-elec engring, head development labs and chief electronics Consolidated-Vultee Aircraft Mfg Co '40-50; with P R Mallory Co since '51, dir engring since '52. AIEE—Inst Radio Engrs—AAAS—Am Physics Soc. 3029 E. Washington St., Indpls 6.

21 BREITZKE, Charles Frederick. Hydraulic and Sanitary Engineering.

b'84. BS '06 (MIT). Research and consultation in engineering and economic aspects of state and regional problems in water supply, stream pollution, flood control, coast protection, federal submerged lands legislation. Research engr NJ State Bd Commerce since '37, now div planning and development Dept Conservation and Economic Development. ASCE—AAAS—Am Assn Engrs. 1060 Broad St., Newark 2, N.J.

22 BRELAND, Osmond Philip. Mosquitoes; Parasitic wasps; Preying mantids. b'10. BS '31 (Miss State Coll); PhD '36 (Ind U). Author: Manual of Comparative Anatomy '43; Animal Facts and Fallacies '48; also articles in field. Professor zool U Tex since '50. First lt and capt San Corps Med Dept US Army '43-46. AAAS—Am Zool Soc—Am Entomol Soc—Mosquito Control Assn—Sigma Xi. Department of Zoology, University of Texas, Austin, Tex.†

23 BREMNER, Raymond Wilson. Iron (Occurrence in sea water); Smog (Effects of constituents); Metals (In solution); Spectrophotometry (Interferences). b'04. Grad '30 (W Wash Coll Edn); BS '28—MS '32—fellow '31-37—PhD '37 (U Wash). Research on interference of impurities in flame spectrophotometric determination of metals in solution, effects of smog constituents on flame spectrophotometric determination sodium and potassium and chemical determination of sulfur therein, effects of interfering substances on determination of organic compounds by infrared and ultraviolet spectrophotometry, salt effects in determination of iron in sea water by colorimetry. Instr to asso prof chem Tex A&M Coll '37-44; lab project leader Dow Chem Co '44-47; asso prof analytical chem Fresno State Coll '47-53, professor analytical chem since '53; analytical research chemist Stanford Research Institute '48. Sigma Xi—ACS—Phi Lambda Upsilon—Pacific SW Assn Chem Teachers—AA UP—Assn Calif State Coll Instr. Fresno State College, Fresno 4, Calif.

24 BRENNAN, Cornelius Patricius. Child welfare. AB (Phila Theol Sem Phila); AM—PhD (Royal and Pontifical U Santo Tomas Manila). Co-chairman of church group of Philadelphia Conference for the prevention and control of juvenile delinquency since '47; rural extension committee work Pennsylvania State Department Welfare '37-40. Sec to Bishop of Jaro '25-32; vicar-gen Jaro Diocese PI '32-33; named Domestic Prelate with title of Rt Rev Monsignor by Pope Pius XI '33; dir charities Archdiocese of Phila since '34; rector All Saints Chaplaincy, Phil Gen Hosp; Dir Cath Children's Bur Inc, Archdiocese of Phila, Alliance of Catholic Women; parole adviser Phila Protectory for Boys since '44. 1706 Summer St., Phila 3.

25 BRENNAN, James Marks. Trombiculid mites; Ticks; Tick repellents; Ectoparasites. b'05. AB '26 (Dickinson Coll); MA '31—PhD '33 (U Kans). Author articles in field. Asst, asso entomol, entomol Rocky Mountain Lab USPHS since '44. Prin sanitary technician, entomol US Army Med Dept '42-44. AAAS—Am Soc Parasitol—Soc Systematic Zool—Sigma Xi. Rocky Mountain Laboratory, U. S. Public Health Service, Hamilton, Mont.†

26 BRENNAN, John Earl. Petroleum industry (Commercialization of new tools and equipment). 1414 W. Clay St., Houston 19, Tex. H: 2413 Stanmore Drive, Houston 19.

10 BRENT, Bernard J. Endocrinology; Physical chemistry (Molecular beams, spectroscopy, elementary reactions). b'02. Engring diploma '25 (Breslau U); '25-28 (Kaiser Wilhelm Inst Phys Chem); PhD '28 (Berlin U); research fellow '31-32 (Hamburg U) —'32-33 (Utrecht U). Research and production hormones, vitamins, pharmaceuticals; research on carotenoids, enzymes, molecular beams, collisions of second kind in fluorescence and in chemiluminescent elementary processes; made first demonstration of Vitamin C in cerebrospinal fluid, in vitreous fluid and in lens; established structural formula of testosterone: achieved maintenance of spermatogenesis in adult hypophysectomized rats with 5-pregnenol-3-one-20. Author articles in field. Hon prof endocrinology Rutgers U Sch Pharmacy; sci dir Roche-Organon Inc N.J. Assn Study Internat Secretions—NY Acad Sci—AAAS—Am Chem Soc—Am Pharm Assn—Sigma Xi. Roche-Organon Inc., Nutley 10, N.J. H: 127 Essex Av., Montclair, N.J.

11 BRETZ, Theodore Walter. Shade tree diseases (Elms, Juniper); Plant viruses. b'08. BSc '30—PhD '37 (Ohio State U); MSc '31 (Ia State Coll). Co-author: Shade Trees for the Plains States '49; also articles in field. Path div forest path US Dept Agr since '45; asso prof bot U Mo since '48. Am Phytopath Soc—AAAS—Am Forestry Assn—Sigma Xi—Gamma Sigma Delta. Department of Botany, University of Missouri, Columbia, Mo.

12 BREUER, Frederick William. Rubber technology; Plastics; German industries; Physiological chemistry. b'03. PrD '30 (U Vienna); undergrad work (U Munich); Austro-Am Exchange fellow '30-32 (Ia State Coll). Chief American delegate Interallied Commission on Reparations, Office of Military Government in Germany '47; research in organo metallic compounds, aliphatic chemistry, heterocyclics, organo deuterium compounds; development of quantitative organic microanalytical methods; isolation of minute quantities of physiologically active compounds from biological materials, preparation of hormone extracts from the adrenal cortex, chemical study of adrenal medulla, studies on precursors of adrenaline. Holds patents on separation and purification unsaturated hydrocarbons by methods other than distillation, utilization of unsaturated hydrocarbons; low temperature fractionation, development of analytical methods for determination of unsaturated hydrocarbons as well as for estimation of traces of impurities; work in the field of emulsion polymerization and on synthetic rubber derivatives, development of special synthetic rubbers, survey of German synthetic rubber plastics paint and varnish industry. Author articles in field. Research chem under Rockefeller grant in physiol dept O State U '36-37; research chem United Gas Improvement Co Phila '37-42; spl project leader Copolymer Research Br Office Rubber Dir WPB Washington '43-44; head synthetic sect Research Lab Armstrong Cork Co Lancaster Pa since '44. ACS—Am Inst Chem(F). Armstrong Cork Company, Lancaster, Pa. H: Lititz, R.D. 4, Pa.

13 BREUHAUS, Waldemar Otto. Flight test measurements. b'18. BS '40 (Carnegie Inst Tech); '47-49 (Cornell U, U Buffalo). Research on stability and control aerodynamics, flight test measurements. Author: Summary of Dynamic Stability and Control Flight Research Conducted Utilizing a B-25 Airplane; also articles in field. Aero-dynamics engr Chance Vought Aircraft Div United Aircraft Corp '40-46; head engring br flight research dept Cornell Aero Lab since '46. Inst Aero Sci—Tau Beta Pi. Cornell Aeronautical Laboratory, 4455 Genesee St., Buffalo 21.

14 BREUKELMAN, John (William). Fish, amphibia and reptiles of Kansas. b'01. AB '23 (Yankton Coll); MS '29—PhD (State U Ia). Editor American Biology Teacher since '42. Author articles in field. Head dept biol State Teachers Coll Emporia Kan since '29, acting dean grad div '44-47; Kan Acad Sci (pres '45) — Okla Acad Sci—AAAS(F)—Nat Assn Biol Teachers—NEA—Am Soc Ichthologists Herpetologists—Herpetologist's League. Am Soc Limnol Oceanog. State Teachers College, Emporia, Kan.†

15 BREWER, George Eugene Francis. Electricity (Frictional). b'09. PhD (chem) '32 (U Vienna). Research on frictional electrical phenomena and development of electronic amplifiers. Granted patent on electrically neutral organic solvent compositions. Prof analytical chem and head dept chem Marygrove Coll since '44; research chem Gage Products Co since '45. ACS (chmn ednl com Detroit sect). Department of Chemistry, Marygrove College, Detroit 21.†

16 BREWER, Given Ankeny. Stress analysis. b'13. BS '38 (MIT). Studies in measurement stresses in fifty foot Hortonsphere; rocket blast pressures Mark X Launcher; landing gear drop test load factors; mechanical punch press tonnages; torsion trailer spring stresses during road testing; stress distribution and sealing load on gas valve; static and dynamic stress distribution SGVI Helicopter; impact loads 900 lb drop hammer; loads torques and stresses 30 ton cam rolling mill; inventor Equilateral Fleximeters and Photogrid process. Sr research engr Lockheed Aircraft '38-42; asst chief structures Willow Run Bomber Div Ford Motor Co '42-44; structures project engr Consol Vultee '44-46; cons engr since '46. Inst Aeronautical Scis—Am Soc Metals—Am Soc ME—AST M—Soc Exptl Stress Analysis. P.O. Box 664, New Bedford, Mass.

17 BREWER, Howard Eugene. Plant ecology (Adaptation); Physiology of seeds. b'10. BA '31—BS '32 (Simpson Coll); PhD '42 (Ia State Coll). Author articles in field. Asso prof bot and asso bot Ala Poly Inst '47-48; asso prof bot State Coll Wash since '51. Ecol Soc Am (Council '47-48)—AAAS(F) — Brit Ecol Soc — Am Soc Plant Physiol—Am Soc Plant Taxonomists—Sigma Xi—Phi Kappa Phi—Gamma Sigma Delta. State College of Washington, Pullman, Wash.

18 BREWER, John Hanna. Medical equipment (Pipetting machine). b'09. AB '30—AM '31 (Simmons Coll); '33-35 (U Tex); PhD '38 (Johns Hopkins U). Granted patents on pipetting machine, method of washing ampoules, sterile surgical package, apparatus for cultivation of anaerobic and microaerophilic organisms, dispensing apparatus for powders, pipette washer, anaerobe jar. Author articles in field. Dir biol research Hynson, Westcott and Dunning since '38. Soc Am Bact—Am Pharm Assn—AAAS—Am Assn Immunologists—Am Pub Health Assn(F). Hynson, Westcott & Dunning, Charles and Chase Sts., Baltimore 1. H: 505 Dogwood Lane, Towson 4, Md.

19 BREWER, Wilmon. Ovid's Metamorphoses; History of the sonnet, sestina, triolet, villanelle, pantoum; American poetry. b'95. AB '17—AM '20—PhD '25 (Harvard). Author: Shakespeare's Influence on Sir Walter Scott '25; Dante's Eclogues '27; Ovid's Metamorphoses in European Culture, vol 1 '33, vol 2 '41; Sonnets and Sestinas '37; Life and Poems of Brookes More '40; About Poetry and Other Matters '45; Adventures in Verse '46; Talks About Poetry '48. Editor: Twentieth Anniversary Volume of American Poetry Association '42, also anthologies. Writer and lecturer. Am Poetry Assn (pres '39-41, treas since '43) Sovereign Colonial Soc—Shakespeare Assn Am—Modern Lang Assn—Mass Audubon Soc—Salon Allied Arts. Great Hill, Hingham, Mass.

20 BREWSTER, Paul G. Folklore. b '98. BS (Oakland City Coll Ind); MA (U Okla); Student (U Ill-U NC-Ind U). Consultant National Conference American Folklore for Youth; collector of Turkish games, children's games in Indiana, Illinois, Missouri, Arkansas; lecturer on children's games and rhymes Folklore Institute of America-Indiana University '46. Author: Ballads and Songs of Indiana '40. Author articles: Two Games from Africa '44; Forfeit Games from Greece and Czechoslovakia '48; Some Traditional Games from Roumania '49; Ten Games from Other Lands '49; Some Indian Games of Tag—with American and other Analogues '50; An Attempt at Identification of Some of the Games Mentioned in Basile's Il Pentamerone (Italy) '50; A String Figure Series from Athens (Greece) '50, and others. Co-editor: Brown Collection of North Carolina Folklore (4 vols). Prof Eng and head dept Shurtleff Coll Alton Ill '48-49; asso prof Eng Henderson State Teachers Coll Arkadelphia Ark since '49. Am Folklore Soc—Am Anthrop Assn —La Sociedad Folklorica de Mexico—La Sociedade Brasileira de Folklore—Instituto Interamericano de Musicologia—Internat Folk Music Council—Internat Commn for Folk Arts and Folklore—Centro de Folclore de Piracicaba —Sigma Tau Delta. Department of English, Henderson State Teachers College, Arkadelphia, Ark.

21 BRICKMAN, William Wolfgang. Education (History of). b'13. BA '34 —MS (Edn) '35 (Coll City of NY); PhD '38 (NY U). Brown University President's research fellowship on history of international education '50-51; research in major libraries of Europe. Author: Guide to Research in Educational History '49. Contributor: Encyclopedia of Educational Research (2nd edit) '50; Encyclopaedia Britannica Yearbook; Collier's Encyclopedia Yearbook. Faculty dept edn NY U '40-42 and since '46, asst prof since '50, asso prof since '51. AHA—Am Acad Polit and Social Sci—Nat Soc Coll Teachers Edn (com hist found). School of Education, New York University, Washington Sq., N.Y.C. 3. H: 1325 Edward L. Grant Highway, Bronx 52, N.Y.

22 BRIDGMAN, Percy Williams. High pressures; Thermodynamics; Philosophy of physics. b'82. AB '04—AM '05—Ph D '08—Fellow '08-10—Sc D '34, 39, 41 (Harvard). Author: Dimensional Analysis '23; The Logic of Modern Physics '27; The Physics of High Pressure '31; Thermodynamics of Electrical Phenomena in Metals '34; The Nature of Physical Theory '36; The Intelligent Individual and Society '38; The Nature of Thermodynamnics '41; Reflections of a Physicist '50. Hollis prof math and natural philos Harvard U '26-50; Higgins Univ prof at Harvard since '50. Am Academy Arts and Sci (F, Rumford medalist '17) — Am Philos Soc — Washington Acad Sci—Nat Acad Sci (Comstock prize '33)—Am Phys Soc—Academia Nacional de Ciencias (Mex, corr mem) —Phi Beta Kappa—Sigma Xi. Awarded Cresson medal, Franklin Inst '32; Roseboom medal Royal Acad Sci of Amsterdam '33; Research Corporation award '37; Nobel prize in physics '46. Lyman Laboratory of Physics, Cambridge, Mass.◉

10 BRIEGLEB, Philip A. Forest management research; Forest resources; Douglas fir, Ponderosa pine and northeastern regions of United States. b'06. BSF '29—MF '30 (NY State Coll Forestry); '24-26 (Drury Coll), '26 (Minn U); seminars '36 (Calif U). Member US Forestry Mission to Chile '43-44; in charge US Forest Service forest survey northeastern region US '45-46. Author articles in field. Chief div forest management research Pacific NW Forest and Range Expt Station since '46. Soc Am Foresters—NW Sci Assn—Ore Acad Sci—Phi Kappa Phi. 423 U. S. Courthouse, Portland 5, Ore.†

11 BRIER, Glenn Wilson. Meteorological statistics. b'13. BS '35 (Parsons Coll); AM '40 (George Washington U). Author: Verification of Prognostic Pressure Patterns '43; 40-year Trends in Northern Hemisphere Surface Pressure '47; also articles in field. Chief verification sect US Weather Bur '42-47, statis chief meteorol statis sect since '48. Am Meteorol Soc—Am Geophys Union—Inst Math Statis—Am Statis Assn. U. S. Weather Bureau, Washington 25.

12 BRIERLEY, Wilfrid G. Horticulture (Raspberries, strawberries, cold resistance of fruit plants, fruiting habits, water movement). b'85. BS '06 (Cornell U); MS '13 (Wash State Coll); PhD '29 (Mich State Coll); '19-28 (U Minn). Author articles in field. Asst prof hort U Minn '13-17, prof since '37. Am Soc Hort Sci—Am Soc Plant Physiol—AAUP—Sigma Xi—Gamma Alpha—Gamma Sigma Delta. Horticulture, University Farm, St. Paul 1.◉

13 BRIERLY, William Biggar. Medical geography; Speleology; Western European maps. b'12. BA '34—MA '36—PhD '42 (Clark U); fellow hygiene and preventive med '36-38 (Geo Washington U Sch Med); '35 (Harvard). Research on incidence and distribution diseases Western Hemisphere, cartography of disease and geographical factors distribution of typhus fever in US, malaria and socio-economic conditions in Mississippi, influence surface features on distribution of malaria northwestern Mississippi; investigations of hydro-geological conditions caves of Maryland, Virginia and West Virginia; member Bowdoin-MacMillan Arctic Expedition '34. Discovered first oil shale deposits and first fossils Collingwood formation Middle Ordovician age Labrador. Author: The Influence of Geographical Factors Upon the Prevalence and Distribution of Malaria, with Special Reference to the United States '42; An Atlas of Diseases of the United States '50; also articles in field. Dir World Survey of Incidence and Distribution of Diseases Geo Washington U, Clark U '36-42; geog OSS Washington '42-45; geog US Dept State '44-46; geog chief west European research Army Map Service US War Dept Washington since '46; lecturer geog dept U Md since '47. Nat Speleology Soc—Va Acad Sci—Am Soc Profl Geog—Am Polar Soc—Arctic Inst No Am—Internat Congress Tropical Med and Malaria—Am Congress Surveying Mapping. Army Map Service, Washington 25.†

14 BRIESEMEISTER, William. Cartography. b'95. Student '12 (Columbia). Specializes in projections and map compilation. Asst cartographer Am Mus Natural Hist '09-12; cartographer Am Geog Soc '13-40, sr cartographer since '40. American Geographical Society, Broadway at 156 St., NYC 32.†

15 BRIGGS, Charles Willers. Steel castings; Radium radiography; Testing (Non-destructive). b'03. AB '26—Engr D '28 (Stanford U). Research and consultant on metallurgy, technology, manufacture, steel making, testing, properties and uses of steel castings; member of Technical Industrial Intelligence Committee '45 reporting on steel casting manufacturing in Germany and Austria; research on use of radium and radon for radiography of castings and welds and gamma ray radiography. Author: Metallurgy of Steel Castings '46; Steel Castings Handbook '41, '50. Author articles in field. Contributor: Metals Handbook '48; Marks' Handbook '51; ABC of Iron and Steel '51. Sr phys metall US Nav Research Lab '30-38; tech and research dir Steel Founders Soc Am since '38. AIMME (Elec Furnace Steel Award '47)—Am Foundrymen's Soc (McFadden Gold Medal '37)—Am Soc Metals—Am Soc ME—Non-destructive Testing Soc—ASTM—Welding Soc—Soc Nav Engrs—Sigma Xi. 920 Midland Bldg., Cleveland 15.

16 BRIGGS, Glen. Agricultural administration and economy; Agronomy. b'90. BS '16 (Okla A&M Coll); MS '21 (Okla A&M Coll) grad student (Colo State Coll, US Dept Agr Grad Sch). Traveled in Philippine Islands, Japan, Cuba, Haiti, Australia, New Zealand, Netherlands East Indies, New Guinea, Korea, China, Formosa, England and Scotland, Ceylon and India, British West Indies and United States Possessions. With US Dept Agr since '31, research coordinator since '48, on loan '44-47 to UNRRA as chief Agr Rehabilitation Div SW Pacific, deputy chief China office. Am Soc Agron—Australia Geog Soc—Royal Asiatic Soc—China Agrl Soc—Tex Acad Sci—Tex Agrl Workers Assn—Friend of the Land—Crop Improvement Assn. Agricultural Research Administration, U. S. Department of Agriculture, Washington 25.

17 BRIGGS, Harold Edward. History of the Dakotas and the American Northwest; The American frontier. b'96. BA '23—MA '24 (U SD); PhD '29 (U Ia). Author: Frontiers of the Northwest; A History of the Upper Missouri Valley '40; also articles in field. Head dept soc sci, prof hist Culver-Stockton Coll Canton Mo '28-35; chmn dept hist, prof Am hist U Miami Coral Gables Fla '35-45, Southern Ill U Carbondale since '45. AHA (life)—Miss Valley Hist Assn—Agrl Hist Soc—Ill State Hist Soc—Mo State Hist Soc—Southern Ill Hist Soc. Awarded grant-in-aid from Soc Sc, Research Council to work on western hist '36; Southern Illinois University, Carbondale, Ill.◉

18 BRIGGS, John Ely. Iowa history and politics. b'90. AB '13—LLD '46 (Morningside Coll). MA '14—PhD '16 (State U Ia). Author: Iowa Old and New '39; Biography of William Peters Hepburn '19; Interpretation of Iowa Primary '22; History of Social Legislation in Iowa '15; History of the Iowa Legislature '16. Editor: Palimpsest '22-45; State Historical Soc Iowa publs '40-43; also articles in field. Prof State U Ia since '37. Am Polit Sci Assn (chmn com on regional societies '42-48)—Am Acad Polit Social Sci—

State Hist Soc Ia—So Polit Sci Assn—Western Polit Sci Assn—Midwest Conf Polit Sci (chmn '42). 336 Beldon Av., Iowa City, Ia.

19 BRIGGS, Lawrence Palmer. Southeast Asia (Ancient Cambodia). b'74. AB '05 (U Mich); AM '08 (U Chicago); teaching F '10-11—traveling F '11-12 (U Calif). Research on ancient Khmer empire. Author: A Pilgrimage to Angkor '43; The Ancient Khmer Empire '51. H: Manton, Mich.

20 BRIGHAM, Clarence Saunders. History of Rhode Island; American newspaper history; Early American bibliography. b'77. AB '99—AM '09—Litt D '34 (Brown U); Litt D '48 (Clark U). Author: History of Rhode Island '02; Bibliography of Rhode Island History '02; Report on the Archives of Rhode Island '04; The Narragansett Indians '05; Bibliography of American Newspapers '13; Wall-paper Newspapers of the Civil War '24; Cabon's History of Hayti Journalism '40; History and Bibliography of American Newspapers (2 vols) '47, and others; also articles in field. Librarian RI Hist Soc '99 dir Am Antiq Soc since '08. 34 Cedar St., Worcester, Mass.

21 BRIGHAM, Henry Randolph. Sociology; Housing; Real estate investment. b'80. With US Dept Labor '18-20; asst mgr Home Registration Div later mgr Real Estate Div US Housing Corp charge appraisal and sale 6000 parcels real estate; investigated housing conditions Washington '22; former lectr Boston U on real estate methods. 53 State St., Boston 9.†◉

22 BRIGHOUSE, Gilbert. Industrial psychology (Physically handicapped). b'06. Student '25-27 (U Ore); PhB—MS '34 (U Chicago); PhD '36 (U Ia). Member mission on industrial psychology sent by United States Department of Commerce to Germany '46-47. Author: The Physically Handicapped in Industry '46; The Physically Handicapped in German Industry '47; also articles in field. Prof Occidental Coll since '42; clinical psychol San Marino Pub Sch since '45. Am Psychol Assn(F)—So Calif Psychol Assn—Sigma Xi. Occidental College, Los Angeles 41.

23 BRIGHT, Willard Mead. Polymer chemistry; Adhesives. b'14. BS '36—MS '37 (U Toledo); '37-38 (U Pittsburgh); AM '40—PhD '42 (Harvard). Research on, development of, plastic and other special industrial adhesive tapes; attended Gordon Research Conference Textiles '48-49. Author articles in field. Research cons Peabody Mus '40-41; research chem Kendall Co '42-44, lab dir since '48; research chem Bauer & Black '44-48. Am Chem Soc—AAAS. 140 Federal St., Boston 10. H: 272 Tappan St., Brookline 46.

24 BRIGHTMAN, Edgar Sheffield. Philosophy (Personalistic, religion, axiology, metaphysics, Hegel). b'84. AB '06—AM '08—Litt D '36 (Brown U); STB '10—PhD '12 (Boston U); LLD '29 (Neb Wesleyan U); LLD '42 (Ohio Wesleyan U). Author: The Sources of the Hexateuch '18; An Introduction to Philosophy '25; Immortality in Post-Kantian Idealism '25; Religious Values '25; A Philosophy of Ideals '28; The Problem of God '30; Moral Laws '33; A Philosophy of Religion '40; The Spiritual Life '42; Nature and Values '45; and others. Prof philos Boston U Grad Sch since '19. Am Philos Assn (pres Eastern div '36)—Am Theol Soc (pres '33-34)—Natl Assn Bibl Instrs (pres '41-43)—Am Acad Arts Sci(F)—Kant-Gesellschaft (hon)—Phi Beta Kappa. 725 Commonwealth Av., Boston 15.◉

10 BRIL, Jacques L. Criminology; Scientific and lie detection. b'06. Installed lie detection laboratory NJ State Hospital Trenton Cons to district attorneys, Kings County, Westchester County, Summit County, atty gen state NJ, NY Police Department, City of Yonkers. Collaborated with Father Summers, professor of psychology, Fordham University in development of pathometer (lie detector) '36; invented Bri] ograf and devised technique known as Bril deception test; inventor of listening-in and recording devices. Established firm Jacques L Bril criminology cons and investigators NYC '31. Am Inst Criminal Law Criminology—Internat Assn Identification — Am Radio Relay League—Internat Assn Chiefs Police—NY State Assn Chiefs Police. 222 W. 77th St., NYC; Smithtown, L.I.◎

11 BRIMLOW, George Francis. Bannock Indian War (1878); American military and western history; History of the Pacific Northwest (Livestock rangeland, Indian affairs). b'98. AB '33—MA '36 (U Ore). Author: The Bannock Indian War of 1878 '38; Cavalryman Out of the West '44; also articles in field. Hist research and writing since '36. Miss Valley Hist Assn—Ore Hist Soc—Phi Beta Kappa. Blue River, Ore.

12 BRINJAC, John Joseph. Fuels; Furnaces. b'21. BS (ME) '48 (Villanova Coll Pa). Design and building of industrial heating furnaces; design, application, and installation of industrial instruments; industrial burner design for various fuels; application of fuels, method of conveyance, and storage; piping layout design and installation; research on fuel injection for reciprocating engines. Fuel engr Central Iron & Steel Co. Am Soc ME—Iron and Steel Engring Soc. Central Iron & Steel Co., Harrisburg, Pa.†

13 BRINKER, Robert Durie. Scottish-American colonial history; Eighteenth century English literature; George Washington (Biography). b'01. BA '28 (Marshall Coll); AM '31 (George Washington U); student (Columbia, Johns Hopkins, Catholic U Am). Author: Scottish Friends of George Washington '44, also articles in field. Teacher journalism and Eng McKinley High Sch Washington since '31. McKinley High School, Washington.

14 BRINKER, William Earle, Jr. Chemical engineering; Process development. b'06. BS '28—PhD '40 (U Pittsburgh. Thermal engr Am Dressler Tunnel Kilns Inc '28-29; instr chem engring U Pittsburgh '29-35, asst prof '35-36; indsl fellow Mellon Inst Indsl Research Pittsburgh '36-37; asso prof chem engring U Pa '37-42; asso prof, chmn chem engring dept Northwestern Tech Inst Evanston '42-44; dir engring chem div Corn Products Refining Co Argo Ill '44-48; asst chief engineer Corn Products Refining Co Chicago Ill since '48. Institute Chem Engrs—Am Chem Soc—Am Soc Engring Edn—Sigma Xi. Corn Products Refining Co., 201 N. Wells St., Chgo 6.

15 BRINKLEY, Homer Lee. Farmer cooperative organizations; Rice economics and distribution; Agricultural production, economics and finance. b'98. BS '19—grad work '22 (La State U). Consultant to American delegation at UN Conference on International Organization San Francisco; member US Delegation UN FAO Conference Geneva Switzerland '47; member US Delegation to third Inter-American Conference on Agriculture Caracas, Venezuela '45. Directed operations since '28 rice producers organization engaged in extensive operations La and Tex in selling, packaging, milling, warehousing, drying, irrigating, financing and distributing in domestic and foreign markets. Author articles in field. Gen mgr Am Rice Growers Coop Assn and Exchange (covering La, Ark, Tex) Lake Charles La since '28; dir Central Bank for Coops Farm Credit Adminstrn Washington; trustee, vice chmn, exec com Am Inst Cooperation Phila; Council Farmer Coops (pres, exec com, chmn labor-management com); dir Gulf Coast Agrl Credit Corp; Asso Coops Inc; Nat Rice Research (chmn adv com). 414 Pujo St., Lake Charles, La.

16 BRINLEY, Floyd John. Fish embryology. b'97. BS '19 (Colo A&M Coll); MA '26—PhD '27 (U Pa). Research and physiological studies of fish embryology, including development and innervation of elasmobranch and teleost fish hearts, origin of muscular movement in fish embryos, action of drugs on embryonic fish heart and somatic muscular movement, transplantation of embryonic tissues in fish,, metabolism of fish embryos. Prof physiol Battle Creek Coll '28-30; asso prof zool and physiol ND State Coll '30-39; aquatic biol USPHS '39-43; asso prof zool U Toledo since '46. AAAS—Am Soc Zool—O Acad Sci—Mich Acad Sci—Sigma Xi—Beta Beta Beta. NRC F '27-38. University of Toledo, Toledo 6, O.

17 BRINTON, Paul Henry Mallet-Prevost. Chemistry; Chemistry of rare elements. b'82. BS '12 MS '13 PhD '16 (U Minn). Prof head div analytical chem '21-27 U Minn; cons chem; vis prof chem U Southern Cal '32-42; capt chem warfare service US Army chief analytic chem '18. Author: Numerous papers and reports on analytic chemistry and chemistry of rare elements. AAAS—Am Inst Chem—Am Chem Soc—AAUP—Phi Kappa Phi—Phi Lambda Upsilon—Sigma Xi. Madre del Oro Mine, Oracle, Ariz.†◎

18 BRISCOE, Lester Ernest. Electrical mining engr. b'02. BSEE. '25 (Purdue. Supt Patoka mine Ayrshire Collieries Corp '40-44 electrical engr since '44. AIEE—Open Pit Mining Assn. 430 Big Four Bldg., Indpls.

19 BRISLEY, Harold R(oy). Sulphur dioxide injury to vegetation; Insects and plant disease. b'95. BS '20 (U Ariz); MS '22—'23-24 (U Calif). Research on effect of sulphur dioxide gas from industrial plants on vegetation with special reference to its influence on the yield of agricultural crops; insects and plant diseases injurious to Arizona agriculture. Author articles in field. Dir dept agrl research United Verde Ext Mining Co Jerome Ariz '20-33; cooperating dir smelter smoke research and dir smelter smoke research Phelps Dodge Corp Douglas Ariz since '33. AAAS—Sigma Xi. Douglas Reduction Works, Phelps Dodge Corporation, Douglas, Ariz.

20 BRISON, Fred Robert. Horticulture (Pecans). b'99. BS '21 (Tex A&M Coll); MS '31 (Mich State U). Co-author: Propagation of Horticultural Plants '39; also articles in field. Prof hort Tex A&M Coll since '26. Am Soc Hort Sci—Tex Pecan Growers Assn (past pres). Texas A&M College, College Station, Tex.

21 BRITT, Kenneth William. High wet strength paper. b'07. BChem '29 (Cornell U); '34-35 (Inst Paper Chem Lawrence Coll). Holds US patents on high wet strength paper and paper product, Canadian patent on paper production. Author articles in field. Research chem Scott Paper Co since '31. Am Chem Soc—Tech Assn Pulp and Paper Ind (chmn wet strength com). Scott Paper Company, Chester, Pa.

22 BRITT, Steuart Henderson. Social psychology; Personnel; Administration; Public opinion. b'07. BA '31—MA '32—fellow '31-32 (U Wash St. Louis Mo.);—PhD '35—fellow '32-35 (Yale); '28-30 (Kan City Sch Law); '35-36 (Columbia Law Sch). Member board editors Psychological Bulletin since '42, Journal of Marketing since '46. Author: Social Psychology of Modern Life '41. Co-author: (with I Graeber) Jews in a Gentile World; The Problem of Anti-Semitism '42. Sec emergency com psychol Nat Research Council '42-43; exec sec com wartime requirements specialized personnel Nat Resources Planning Bd '42; cons and chief mil advisory sect nat roster sci and specialized personnel War Manpower Commn '41-43; asst prof psychol Geo Washington U '36-42; prof psychol Mt Vernon Sem Washington '37-43; asso dir research McCann-Erickson Inc NYC '46-48, mgr research and merchandising department '48-49; dir of personnel '50-51; vp and dir research Needham Louis & Brorby. Lt comdr USNR problems selection, training, psychol warfare Commdr in Chief's Hdqrs '43-46. AAAS(F)—Am Psychol Assn (F, sec div personality and social psychol '45-47—NY Acad Sci(F) —Am Marketing Assn—Am Sociol Soc—Soc Psychol Study Social Issues—Eastern Psychol Assn—Eastern Sociol Soc—So Soc Philos and Psychol—Sigma Xi—Phi Delta Phi—Am Edn Res Assn. Diploma in personnel psychology (Industrial) by Am Bd Exam in Profl Psychol '48. Needham, Louis & Brorby, Inc., 135 S La Salle St., Chgo 3.◎

23 BRITTON, Ralph Royal. Housing technology (Building construction, standards, structure, materials, codes, prefabrication, special methods, lightweight concrete). b'93. BS (Dartmouth Coll); CE (Thayer Sch Civil Engring). Author articles in field. Chief Structural Sect Div Standardized Building Codes, Housing and Home Finance Agency since '47; cons on bldg constrn, bldg codes, standards for housing. Am Soc Testing Materials—Am Standards Assn. Housing and Home Finance Agency, Washington 25.

24 BROCK, Ignatius W. French sixteenth century bibliography and modern literature. b'01. PhB '27 (Emory U); PhD '38—dept fellow '36-37—U fellow '37-38—Markham Memorial Grad Travel fellow '38 (U Wis); certificat '28 (Institut de Touraine). Author articles in field. With Emory U since '26, now prof Romance lang, registrar since '48. Am Bibliog Soc—Mod Lang Assn Am—Am Assn Teachers French — Am Assn Teachers Spanish—So Atlantic Mod Lang Assn (sec-treas, asso ed bull)—Phi Beta Kappa—Kappa Phi Kappa. Emory University, Ga.

25 BROCK, Leslie Van Horn. American history (Colonial and revolutionary). b'03. BS '28 (Waynesburg Coll, Waynesburg, Pa); AM '32—PhD '41 (U Mich). Research in colonial finance and imperial relations 1700-75. Instr hist, econo govt Waynesburg Coll '28-36, prof '36-47; prof hist, head dept Coll Ida Caldwell Ida since '47. AHA—Am Econ Assn—Am Polit Assn —Tau Kappa Alpha—Phi Kappa Phi—Phi Alpha Theta. College of Idaho, Caldwell, Ida.

26 BROCK, Vernon Eugene. Biology of the albacore tuna. b'12. BA '35—MA '44 (Stanford U). Research on

Hawaiian fish and fisheries with emphasis on tunas; in charge fisheries investigations for Operations Crossroads and Bikini Resurvey '46, 47, emphasizing lagoon fishes. Biol, chief biol Ore Fish Commn '36-43; dir Div Fish and Game of Hawaii since '44; lecturer U Hawaii; collaborator US Fish and Wildlife Service. Sigma Xi—Am Fisheries Soc—Wildlife Soc—Oceanog Soc Pacific—Biometric Soc—Hawaiian Acad Sci—Am Soc Ichthyologists and Herpetologists. Postoffice Box 5425, Pawaa Substation, Honolulu, Hawaii.

10 BROCKMAN Frank G(ottlieb). Chemistry and magnetism (techniques of analysis, materials). b'05. PhG '26—PhC '27—BSc '29 (Phila Coll Pharm and Sci); MS '31—PhD '34 (U Pa). Research in physical methods of analysis, X-ray diffraction methods, insulating oils, spectrography, magnetic resonance effects in non-metallic magnetic materials, chemistry of photoflash lamps. Author articles in field. Research chem Philips Labs Inc since '44. Am Chem Soc—Electrochem Soc — Sigma Xi. Philips Laboratories, Inc., Irvington-on-Hudson, N.Y.

11 BROCKUNIER, Samuel Hugh. Roger Williams; US history (Political, 1790-1860). b'03. AB '26—AM '28—PhD '37 (Harvard). Research on congressional practices, party politics and political theory in US 1790-1860, American political theories and practices relating to problem of democracy and leadership, 17th century origins of American democratic ideas. Author: The Irrepressible Democrat: Robert Williams '40. Co-author: The United States: American Democracy in World Perspective '47; The Making of American Democracy '50. Author articles in field. With Wesleyan U since '30, prof since '44. Soc Sci Research Council (sec, mem com historiography since '48)—AHA (officer Carnegie Revolving Fund '42-48, hon mention Dunning prize '40)—Miss Valley Hist Assn. Wesleyan University, Department of History, Middletown, Conn.

12 BRODE, Wallace Reed. Chemical spectroscopy; Color analysis; Dyes. b'00. BS '21 (Whitman Coll); MS '22 —PhD '25 (U Ill). American delegate 12th International Chemical Union Zurich Switzerland '36; Harvard-MIT eclipse of sun expedition to Siberia '36. Author: Chemical Spectroscopy '43. Co-author: Organic Chemistry '38; Scott's Standard Method of Analysis '39; Advances in Enzymology '44; Applications of Instruments in Chemistry '45; Physical Methods in Chem Analysis '50. Co-author and editor: Laboratory Outlines for Organic Chemistry '49. Asso dir Nat Bur Standards since '47; Physics division National Research Council since '48; editor Journal Optical Society of America since '50. Am Chem Soc (Councilor, chmn, sec, Columbus sect)—Optical Soc Am (mem bd dirs)—Am Institute Physics (bd governors) — Inter-Soc Color Council—Wash Acad Sci—Phi Beta Kappa—Sigma Xi—AAAS(board directors). Guggenheim Memorial Found fellow Leipzig, Zurich, Liverpool '26-28; National lecturer, Sigma Xi, '52-53. National Bureau of Standards, Washington 25.◎

13 BRODERICK, Thomas M. Mining geology (Copper, iron ore). b'89. AB '13—PhD '17 (U Minn); MS '14 (U Wis); '19 (MIT, Harvard). Author articles in field. Field geol Minn and Wis Geol Surveys '13-19; asst prof geol U Minn '13-20; geol Calumet & Hecla Consol Copper Co since '20. Geol Soc

Am(F)—AAAS(F)—Soc Econ Geol—Am Inst Mining Metall Engrs—Sigma Xi. Calumet, Mich.†◎

14 BRODIE, Bernard. Military and naval history and strategy; Atomic energy (Military uses); International relations. b'10. PhB '32—fellow in internat relations '39-40—PhD '40 (U Chicago); Carnegie fellow '40-41 (Inst Advanced Study, Princeton). Technical expert American delegation to San Francisco Conference '45; editor World Politics. Author: Sea Power in the Machine Age '43; Layman's Guide to Naval Strategy '42-43; A Guide to Naval Strategy '44. Editor, co-author: The Absolute Weapon '46; also articles in field. Asso prof Yale Inst Internat Studies since '45, dir grad studies Dept Internat Relations since '47; cons expert Dept State, Library Congress since '46; prof Nat War Coll '46, sometime lecturer Air War Coll, Nav War Coll, Nat Defense Coll (Can). Soc Am Historians(F)—Naval Hist Found—Am Polit Sci Assn—Am Acad Polit Social Sci. Institute of International Studies, Yale University, New Haven.

15 BRODKORB, Pierce. Taxonomy, distribution and natural history of birds of North, Central and South America; Geography of Mexico. b'08. Student '26-28 (Northwestern U); AB '33 (U Ill); PhD '36 (U Mich). Zoological expeditions to Northern Rockies '31-32, '34, Black Hills '35, Mexico '37, '39, '41. Author articles in field. Asso prof biol U Fla since '46. Am Ornithol Union—Cooper Ornithol Club—Biol Soc Washington—Fla Acad Sci—Mich Acad Sci—Sigma Xi. Department of Biology, University of Florida, Gainesville, Fla.†

16 BRODSHAUG, Melvin. Audiovisual materials. b'00. AB '23 (ND Agrl Coll); MA '27 (U Chicago); PhD '31 (Columbia). Research asso Erpi Picture Cons '30-36; dir research Erpi Classroom Films Inc '36-45; vp charge research Ency Brit Films Inc '45-48, vp charge product development since '48. Encyclopaedia Britannica Films Inc., Wilmette, Ill. H: 601 Lake Av.

17 BRODY, Samuel. Dairy husbandry; Metabolism; Physiology (Environmental); Agricultural chemistry. b'90. BA '17—MA '19—life teaching certificate '19 (U Calif); PhD '28 (U Chicago). Research on growth and energy metabolism, animal and dairy husbandry, nutrition, environmental physiology, energetic efficiency of growth, milk production, egg production, muscular work, and effect of climate and its meteorological factors on efficiency. Author: Bioenergetics and Growth '45; also articles in field. Asst biochem U Calif Med Sch '19-20; asst prof dairy and agrl chem U Mo '20-25, asso prof agrl coll '25-45, prof dairy husbandry since '45. AAAS(F) —Am Soc Biol Chem—Am Inst Nutrition — Am Dairy Sci Assn — Am Animal Sci Prodn—Soc Development and Growth—Mo Hist Soc—Mo Acad Sci—Czechoslovak Acad Agr—Sigma Xi—Gamma Sigma Delta. Recipient several Nat Research Council grants nutritional research '25-28; fellow Guggenheim Mem Found for work in Europe '30-31; recipient Borden Award '50. Eckles Hall, University of Missouri, Columbia, Mo.

18 BROEK, Jan O(tto) M(arius). Indonesia (Social and political geography). b'04. Student '24-29—PhD '32 (U Utrecht Netherlands); '29 (London Sch Econs); '30-31 (U Calif). Research and writing on Indonesia and the Netherlands, the future of Southeast Asia, the economic significance of the Netherlands Indies. Asst

and asso prof U Calif '37-46; prof and dir social geog inst U Utrecht '46-48; prof and chmn dept geog U Minn since '48; research asso Inst Pacific Relations '42-44; dir Southeast Asia Inst '42-46; vis prof U Indonesia Batavia '47. Far Eastern Assn—Assn Am Geographers (Asia com) — Royal Netherlands Geog Soc (editorial bd jour '46-48). Department of Geography, University of Minnesota, Minneapolis, 14◎

19 BROEL, Albert. Frog meat (Canning); Frog raising. b'89. BS—MD '14 (U Warsaw); LLB (St Petersburg Acad). Research on raising and marketing of giant bull frogs for food, canning of frogs. Author: Frog Raising for Pleasure and Profit '50. 1035 Marlborough Av., Detroit 15.

20 BROLYER, Cecil Robert. Civil service. b'00. AB '23—'24-26 (Stanford U); '23-24 (Columbia). Coll entrance examination bd Princeton U '27-36; prin personnel tech N State Civil Service Dept since '48. Psychometric Soc—Soc Personnel Adminstrn—Civil Service Assembly. New York State Department of Civil Service, Albany 1, N.Y.

21 BROMLEY, Helen Brown. Algae (Vaucheriaceae; United States coastal plain region, Desmids, commercial uses); Ornamental gardening. b'03. Student '21-23 (U Buffalo); BA—MA '25—PhD '29 (Ohio State U); '26, '27, '32 (Woods Hole Biol Station, Puget Sound Biol Station, Naples Zool Lab Italy). Author: The Algal Family Vaucheriaceae '29; also articles in field. Instr bot Ohio State U '29-36; pvt research since '36. AAAS(F)—Ohio Acad Sci(F)—Am Microscopical Soc—Sigma Xi. 17 Knollwood Avenue, Stamford, Conn.†

22 BROMLEY, Stanley Willard. Economic entomology; Insecticides; Arboriculture; Asilidae; Robber flies. b'99. BSc '22—MSc '24 (Mass Agrl Coll); PhD '34 (Ohio State U). Inventor insecticidal spray STYX, fumigants SWB77 and SWB 93 for control of pine crown weevil; has largest private collection of robber flies. Editor: Index of Economic Entomology. Author articles in field. Entomol Bartlett Tree Research Labs since '29. AAAS(F)—Entomol Soc Am(F)—Assn Econ Entomol—NY Entomol Soc—Brooklyn Entomol Soc—Entomol Soc Wash — Nat Shade Tree Conf — Phi Kappa Phi—Sigma Xi. Bartlett Tree Research Laboratories, Stamford, Conn.†

23 BRONEER, Oscar Theodore. Ancient and modern Greece; Corinth; Athens; Eleusis; Ancient lamps; Greek theater. b'94. AB '22 (Augustana Coll); AM '23—PhD '31 (U Calif); '24-27 (Am Sch Classical Studies Athens Greece). Author: Terracotta Lamps '30; The Odeum '32; The Lion Monument at Amphipolis '41; also articles in field. Act dir Am Sch Classical Studies Athens '47-'48; professor archaeol Chicago U since '49. Archaeol Inst Am—German Archaeol Inst—Greek Archaeol Soc—Geographical Soc NY. Department of Greek, University of Chicago, Chgo 37.◎

24 BRONSON, Bertrand Harris. Folk music. b'02. AB '21 (U Mich); AM '22 (Harvard); BA '24 (Oxford U); PhD '27 (Yale). Research in popular music abroad and in United States '38-52. Author articles in field. Instr Eng U Calif '27, now prof Guggenheim fellow research popular ballad and ballad music '43, '44, '48. MLA—PAPC—AFLS—Calif Folklore Soc. Department of English, University of California, Berkeley 4.†

10 BRONWELL, Arthur B. Electronics; Communication. b'09. BS '33—MS '36 (Ill Inst Tech); MBA '47 (Northwestern U); '39-40 (U Mich). Organized and supervised Army Signal Corps School in radio and ultra-high frequencies at Northwestern U '42-43; supervised wartime research project on microwave generators; research on transmission-line analogies of plane electromagnetic waves. Holds patent on chromoscope, color television tube. Author: Theory and Application of Microwaves (with Beam) '47; also articles in field. Prof engring Northwestern U since '47; cons Galvin Mfg Co, Dumont Co and others. Am Soc Engring Edn (sec)—Inst Radio Engrs—Nat Electronics Conf (past pres)—AIEE—Eta Kappa Nu—Sigma Xi. 1539 Lake Av., Wilmette, Ill.

11 BROOKER, Floyde Elroy. Audiovisual education. b'05. BA '28 (Marietta Coll); MA (Columbia). Representative of US government to First International Congress on Educational and Instructive Films Paris '48; consultant in visual education preparatory commission UNESCO London and Paris, advisor in education US delegation; director visual aids for war training US Office Education and produced 472 sound motion pictures and 432 filmstrips. Author articles in field. Vice-chmn social studies panel ednl adv com Motion Picture Producers Distributors Assn Am '37-38; sr specialist visual aids US Office Edn '41-42, now chief; adjunct prof Am U Wash since '49; cons and script writer Erpi Classroom Films of NY. Soc Motion Picture Engrs (com for 16 and 8 millimeter motion pictures)—Film Council Am (Board Trustees)—Phi Beta Kappa. U.S. Office of Education, Washington 25.

12 BROOKES, William R. Phenolic resins; Photographic emulsions. b'18. BS '38 (Coll City NY); MS '39 (U Colo). Co-author article: (with Julian M Blair) Sodium Hydrosulfite as a Photographic Developer '41, and others. Head emulsion dept Gevaert Co of Am Williamstown Mass '41-44; tech specialist Fercleve Corp Oak Ridge Tenn Manhattan Project '44-45; development chem Gen Elec Co Pittsfield Mass since '45. Am Chem Soc—AIC—AAAS. General Electric Co., Chemical Department, Pittsfield, Mass. H: Lanesboro, Mass.†

13 BROOKFIELD, Charles Mann. Birds (South Florida); Florida (Historical marine wrecks and salvage). b '03. Student '22-24 (U Minn). Co-author: (with Oliver Griswold) They All Called It Tropical '49. US Coast and Geodetic Survey Fla '34-36. So Fla Hist Soc (pres). 13 McAllister Arcade, Miami.

14 BROOKS, Arthur Minard. Paper manufacturing (Pigments, lime products, sodium compounds). b'97. AB '20 (Yale); '25, '41 (Cornell U); '34, '43, '47 (MIT); '21-22 (Northeastern U Law Sch). Research and development in pulp and paper industry, paper and rubber fillers, pigments and sizes, alkalis and alkaline earths. Holder US and foreign patents on pigments and paper manufacture. Author: Pigments for Paper Coating '48. Chem Raffold Co Am Andover Mass '20-28; vp and dir Raffold Process Corp and asso companies since '28. Am Chem Soc—Am Forestry Assn—Tech Assn Pulp and Paper Industry—Sigma Xi. 16 Haverhill St., Andover, Mass.

15 BROOKS Benjamin Talbott. Chemistry; Petroleum chemistry; Alkali chemistry. b'85. AB '06 (Ohio State U) PhD '12 (Göttingen U). Prof chem engring U Pittsburgh '13-17; chief chem Comml Research Co NY '17-18; cons '18-19; chem engr Mathieson Alkali Works '19-24; cons chem since '24; petroleum cons Venezuela '40-41; cons chem US-Mexican Oil Commn '42. Author: Non-Benzenoid Hydrocarbons '22; Peace, Plenty and Petroleum, '44. Co-Author: Crude Oils, '50. Am editor The Science of Petroleum. Am Chem Soc—Am Inst Chem Engrs—Inst Petrol Tech—Soc Chem Industry—Phi Beta Kappa—Sigma Xi—AAAS. 405 Lexington Ave., NYC 17.†

16 BROOKS, Berry Boswell. Big game hunting. b'02. Student '20-22 (Washington and Lee U). Has made explorations and expeditions into virtually all countries of Europe, Near East, most sections of Africa, and in US; led new explorations into Abyssinia, Portuguese East Africa, Angola, other parts of Africa '49. Explorers Club—Camp Fire Club—Adventurer's Club Chicago. 161 South Front St., Memphis.

17 BROOKS, David William. Cotton marketing. b'01. BS in Agr '22—MS '23 (U Ga). Gen mgr Cotton Producers Assn Atlanta Ga since '33, dir since '40 Am Cotton Coop Assn; (mem exec comm '44-46, vp since '46) (Natl Council of Farmers Coop Washington; dir Asso Coops Inc; pres since '40 Ga Coop Council; Trustee Am Inst Cooperation; mem Cotton Advisory Com of Research and Marketing Act to Sec Agr '47; Textiles Industry Advisory Com of Army-Navy Munitions Board '47. Phi Kappa Phi. 308½ Ivy St. NE, Atlanta.☉

18 BROOKS, Edward Morgan. Synoptic and dynamic meteorology (Tropic-polar front); Equations of atmospheric motion; Tornadoes. b'16. AB '37 (Harvard); SM '39—ScD '45 (MIT); '41 (U Miami); research fellow '38 (Woods Hole Oceanog Inst). Author articles in field. Asst prof meteorol Inst Tech St Louis U '46-49, asso prof since '49. Meteorol Soc (sec-treas St Louis Chap '47-48, chmn '48-49)—Pi Mu Epsilon—Am Geophys Union—AAAS—Sigma Xi. Institute of Technology, St. Louis University, St. Louis 8.†

19 BROOKS, Frank Gary. Parasitology; Helminthology; Embryology; Conservation. b'93. BS '15 (Allegheny Coll); MA '22 (U Okla); ScD '28 (Johns Hopkins). Research on parasitology with emphasis trematode germ cell cycles, trematode life histories, control of trematode diseases of fish, taxonomy of larval trematodes. Author: Biological Science '44; Charles Wardell Stiles, Intrepid Scientist '47. Editor Proceedings Iowa Academy Sci since '48. Ed BIOS since '30; prof biol Cornell Coll Mt Vernon Ia since '36; parasitol for jt research project U Wis and Wis Conservation Dept '45-49. A AAS(F)—Ia Acad Sci(F)—Am Society Zool—Am Soc Parasitol—Am Microscopical Soc—Helminthological Soc Washington—Sigma Xi—Am Soc Taxonomists—Phi Kappa Phi—Beta Beta Beta. Cornell College, Mt. Vernon, Ia.

20 BROOKS, Frederick A(ugustus). Frost protection; Atmospheric radiation; Microclimatology. b'95. BS '17—ME '27 (U Ill); SM—ScD '20 (MIT). Field dusts raised by agricultural implements, cyclone dust separators, water heating by solar energy, smokiness of orchard heaters, frost protection by heaters and wind machines, atmospheric radiation, density flow of chilled air, heat transfer in soil, atmospheric turbulence, dispersion of aerosols over ground and sea, heat transfer in agricultural climatic environment. Author articles in field. Research in agrl engring U Calif since '31. ASME—Am Soc Agrl Engrs (chmn research com '45-48) — Am Meteorol Soc — Am Geophys Union. University of California Agricultural Experiment Station, Davis, Calif.

21 BROOKS, Lester Eugene. Field crops; Irrigation studies; Soils management; Vegetable growing; Orchard management. b'02. BS (agr) '48 (Tex Tech Coll). Research on soil and crop management, adaptability studies with major field crops, tests on vegetable adaptability, tree fruit varieties and home orchards and gardens. Hort Tex Agrl Expt Sta '31-36, supt substa 16 from '36. Am Soc Agron—Tex Agrl Workers Assn. Texas Substation No. 16, Iowa Park, Tex.

22 BROOKS, Maurice. Wild life management; West Virginia birds; Ecology of Appalachian region. b'00. Student '18-21 (W Va Wesleyan Coll); AB '23—MS '35 (W Va U); '39-41 (U Mich). Author articles in field. Prof wild life management and forester W Va U and Agr Expt Sta since '47; dir W Va Conservation Sch since '45; on W Va Conservation Commn since '45. Wildlife Soc—Soc Am Forester—AAAS—Am Ornithol Union—Wilson Ornithol Club (sec '41-46, first vp since '47)—Am Soc Ichthyology and Herpetology—Am Fern Soc—W Va Acad Sci—Va Soc Ornithol. West Virginia University, Morgantown, W. Va.†

23 BROOKS, Philip Coolidge. Archival economy; United States diplomatic history. b'06. BA '28 (U Mich); '29 (U Chicago); MA '30—travelling fellow Spain, France, England '32-33—PhD '33 (U Calif). Special research and emphasis archives on evaluation of records for retention and disposal considering administrative, legal, and research utilization, planned records programs in administrative agencies; research Spanish-American diplomacy early 19th century. Author: Diplomacy and the Borderlands '39; Public Records Management '49. Author articles: Pichardo's Treatise and the Adams-Onis Treaty '35, Pacific Coast's First International Boundary Delineation 1816-19 '34, Spanish Royalists in the US 1809-21 '36, Spain's Farewell to Louisiana '03-21 '40; What Records Shall We Preserve '40; Retirement and Disposal of Federal Records '40; The Archivist's Concern in Records Administration '43; and others. Special examiner Nat Archives Washington '35-41, staff officer records administrn '42-46, acting director general records division, '47-48, chief archivist war records branch '50, records officer National Sec Resources Bd, '48-50, guest lecturer archival econ Am U since '42. Am Archivists (founding mem, sec '36-42, council mem '42-47, chmn com records administrn '43-46, since '47)—AHA—Am Assn State and Local Hist—Brit Records Assn. National Archives, Washington 25.†

24 BROOKS, Reid Merrifield. Morphology and anatomy of pomological fruits; Register of new fruit varieties; Cherries (Breeding, culture); Climate in relation to fruit production. b'08. BS '29 (U Chicago); MA '33—PhD '38 (U Calif). Author articles in field. Asso prof pomol, asso pomol expt sta U Calif since '48. Am Soc Hort Sci—AAAS(F)—Bot Soc Am—Sigma Xi—Gamma Alpha. Division of Pomology, University of California, Davis, Calif.†

25 BROOKS, Virginia Field Walton (Mrs.). Big game hunting (Africa). b '04. Student '22-24 (Lindenwood Coll Mo). Expedns by air in Europe, Asia Minor, Africa, Middle East, Central

America, Canada, throughout US; participated in Berry B Brooks big game hunting and photographic expedition in Africa '47, '49. Genealogist, explorer, author. Archeol Inst Am—Nat Geog Soc. Epping Forest Manor, James Rd., Memphis.

10 BROPHY, John Joseph. Varnished surfaces (Drying); T r e a t m e n t of leather. b'88. Student (Harvard, MIT). Inventor electronic devices, ultra-violet radiation process for rapid drying of varnished surfaces, machines for measuring sheet material, machines for treating leather and other processes. Engr and inventor Turner Tanning Machinery Co Mass '12-33; United Shoe Machinery Corp since '33, now head phys sect research div. AIEE—Soc Am Mil Engrs—Am Chem Soc. United Shoe Machinery Corporation, Beverly, Mass.

11 BROSCHÉ, Lyle E. Weather (Long-range temperature forecasting); Air navigation (Average drift-correction method). b'14. U.S. Naval Aerographers' School. Developed new tehcnique in long-range temperature forecasting based on extended study of habits and peculiarities of surface temperatures over US, technique averages 90 per cent accuracy for forecasts of up to six months in advance. Originated and developed average drift-correction method of air navigation designed to increase payload factor and minimize fuel consumption. Supervisor, instr US Weather Bur (on loan from Pan Am Airways) '42-45; meteorol in charge Pan Am World Airways '45-50, now asst sta mgr. First prize 1948 Nat Meteorol Contest sponsored by Air Transport Asso Am. H: 47-28 215th Place, Apartment 2B, Bayside, N.Y.

12 BROTHERS, Mary Hudson. South west U.S. episodes and history. b'87. Author articles and stories historical episodes of southwestern U.S.. from first hand experience and as recounted by ancestors. 301 N. Allen Ave., Farmington, N.M.

13 BROUGHAM, Royal. Sports (Rowing). Ed in pub schs. Chose All-Am rowing crew; covered rowing events US and abroad since '30, also Olympic events. Author articles in field. Sports ed Seattle Post-Intelligencer; rowing writer Internat News Service. Seattle Post-Intelligencer, Seattle.

14 BROWN, Alexander Crosby. Maritime history. b'05. BA '28 (Yale). Sailed around the world '28-30 as master of the small schooner yacht Chance, hydrographic and ethnological work as amateur. Author: Horizon's Rim '35; Twin Ships '39; The Old Bay Line 1840-1940 '40; The Dismal Swamp Canal '46; Newport News' 325 Years '46; Steamboat CODORUS, First Iron Hull Built in America, '50. Chief publications The Mariners' Museum Newport News Va since '46; a founder and asso ed The American Neptune: A Quarterly Journ of Maritime Hist since '41. Active duty comdr USNR '42-46. Steamship Hist Soc (chmn publications com since '47). Naval Hist Foundation—US Naval Inst—AHA. H: 228 James River Dr., Hilton Village.

15 BROWN, (Mrs) Bonnie Taber. American history of hand spinning and spinning wheels. b'09. Student pub schs. Rearing of angora rabbits, utilization wool for hand spinning and knitting into sweaters. Author: History and Art of Hand Spinning '50. Mgr angora farm Mastic NY; hand spinning, lecturing and exhbn Colonial Williamsburg. Internat Fedn Hand Arts. Wythe Spinning House, Colonial Williamsburg, Williamsburg, Va.

16 BROWN, Bruce K. Petroleum technology (100 octane aviation gasoline, military petroleum supply, synthetic liquid fuel). b'98. BS '18—MS '20 (U Ill). Author: A Survey of Nitrocellulose Lacquers '26; also articles in field. Granted several patents. Pres and dir Pan-Am Southern Corp. since '49. Chmn Mil Petroleum Adv Com. 944 St Chas. Ave., New Orleans.

17 BROWN, Charles Bradner. Seismic exploration; Proximity fuses; Wave transmission (Electromagnetic); Semi-conductors. b'10. BS (elec engring) '31—MS (phys) '33—EE '38 (U Kan). Developed electromagnetic methods of exploration for oil, improvements in semi-conductor amplifier devices or transistors; research on transmission of seismic waves through earth in connection with seismic exploration for oil; granted patent on fluorescent method of detecting oil by soil sample analysis. Research engr First Nat Television Corp '31-33; research phys McCollum Exploration Co '33-40, Nav Ordnance Lab since '41. Sigma Xi—Am Inst EE (chmn semiconductor com of electronics com, chmn solid state com of basic sci com) —Soc Exploration Geophys—Seismol Soc Am. Naval Ordnance Laboratory, White Oak, Silver Spring, Md. H: 1402 Elson St., Carole Highlands, Takoma Park, Md.

18 BROWN, Charles Harvey. Library Service. b'75. BA '97—MA '99—Litt D '37 (Wesleyan U Conn); '99-01 (NY State Library Sch). Author: Report to Iowa State Planning Board on Library Service in Iowa '35. Co-author: (with H G Bousfield) Circulation Work in College and University Libraries; also articles in field. Librarian emeritus Iowa State Coll Library '46; vis bibliographer La State U '49-50; vis prof U Ill '50-51. Ia Library Assn (pres '28-29)—ALA (pres '41-42)—Phi Kappa Phi. 317 Lynn Av., Ames, Ia.

19 BROWN, Charles Owen. Nitrogen fixation; Synthetic ammonia. b'88. BS '11—D Eng '44 (NH U); AM '13 (Cornell); fellow '13-17 (Mellon Inst). Assisted in design and construction of first synthetic ammonia plant in US '19; constructed large plants for US Army '17 making chemicals for war; designed, built first synthetic methyl alcohol plant in US; recently built several munitions plants for US Army; built first explosives ammonium nitrate plant, war program for Ordnance Dept, Wilson Dam, Alabama '40. Cons chem engr NYC since '38. Capt, lt col Army Ordnance Dept '17-19. Am Chem Soc—Am Inst Chem Engrs—Cons Chem Chem Engrs (asso mem)—Sigma Xi. 331 Madison Av., NYC 17.

20 BROWN, Charles Philip. Wildlife management; Economic biology. b'13. BS '35 (NY State Coll Forestry); MS '44 (U Me). Research on census methods, life histories small mammals; small mammals central New York; food habits Maine ruffed grouse; food habits game birds, mammals, predators. Author articles: Food of Maine Ruffed Grouse by Seasons and Cover Types '46. Co-author article: Alternative Methods in Upland Gamebird Food Analysis '46. Game tech US Forest Service Clark Nat Forest Mo '35-37; asst leader Me Coop Wildlife Research Unit U Me, instr game management '41-44; game research investigator NY state conservation dept since '44. Wildlife Soc—Am Soc Mammalogists. New York State Conservation Department, Wildlife Research Laboratory, Delmar, N.Y.†

21 BROWN, Claudeous Jethro Daniels. Freshwater fisheries; Limnology. b'04. BS '27—MS '28 (Brigham Young U); PhD '33 (U Mich). Author articles in field. Professor zool Mont State Coll since '47. Am Fisheries Soc—Am Soc Ichthyology Herpetology—Am Micros Soc—Limnol Oceanog Soc Am—Wildlife Soc. Department of Zoology and Entomology, Montana State College, Bozeman, Mont.†

22 BROWN, Corder Travis. Bullet-sealing fuel cells; Packaging. b'15. AB '37 (U Kan). Compound development of fuel-resistant inner liners and synthetic bullet-sealing layers, synthetic fuel barriers; paper converting for automatic wrapping machinery, functional p a c k a g i n g for overseas shipment-manufacturing, a l u m i n u m foil converting. Holds patent in field. Development chem US Rubber Co '41-45; mgr research Rapinwax Paper Co since '47. Packaging Inst, Inc. Rapinwax Paper Co., 150 26th Av., S.E., Minneapolis 14.

23 BROWN, D. A. Historical photographs of western America. b'08. BS '37 (George Washington U); MS '51 (U Ill). Assembled and published collections of historical photographs with narrative texts on cattle trade and Indian wars of western America. Co-author: (with Martin F Schmitt) Fighting Indians of the West '48, Trail Driving Days '52. Librarian USDA '34-42; librarian War Dept '45-48; librarian coll agr U Ill since '48. 226 Mumford Hall, University of Illinois, Urbana.

24 BROWN, Dillon Sidney. Pineapples; Apples; Peaches. b'11. BS '35 (U Ill); MS '39 (W Va U); PhD '44 (Ohio State U). Author articles in field. Sr hort research dept Hawaiian Pineapple Co Ltd '47-49. Am Soc Hort Sci—AAAS—Sigma Xi. Division of Pomology, University of Cal., Davis, Cal.†

25 BROWN, Douglas MacNeil. Glaciers. b'01. BS (Civil engring) '22 (Lafayette Coll). Organized five glacier expeditions into Prince William Sound Alaska and other parts of Alaska; Austrian Swiss and French Alps; measurement of movements and peculiarities of glaciers to determine their relationships with each other and world history of ice. Leader of expeditions; lecturer on expeditions. Am Geog Soc (F)—Am Polar Soc (F)—British Glacialgical Soc(F)—Am Geophys Union (F)—Arctic Inst. H: 296 Bradley Av., Meriden, Conn.

26 BROWN, Earle B. Optical, astronomical and electronic instruments; Computing devices. b'09. Student '26-28 (Bentley Sch Accounting, Boston)—'39-42 (NYU)—'47—(Columbia U). Editor Gleanings for Amateur Telescope Makers, Sky and Telescope Magazine, Harvard Observatory since '38. Author: Optical Instruments '45; Basic Optics for the Sportsman '49. Design engr Farrand Optical Co NYC since '47. US Army '42-45, instr optics and optical instruments Ordnance Dept '43-44, optical engring '44-45, Cons engring '45-47. 60 Haven Ave., Bergenfield, N.J.

27 BROWN, Edna Mae. Libraries (Cataloguing). b'00. BS '26 (Purdue U); (Library sci) '28—AM '30 (U Ill); summer '38 (U Mexico), summer '39 (U PR). Collaborator in preparation of code of descriptive cataloging rules; studies on procedures for handling serial publication. Cataloger U Ill Library '31-41; head serials sect descriptive cataloging div Library Congress since '42. Am Library Assn—DC Library Assn. Library of Congress, Washington.

10 BROWN, Edward Mitchell. Caverns (Commercial); Caverns (Development). b'89. AB '12 (U Ga). Developed and operated Endless Caverns, New Market, Va.; expert witness condemnation Mammoth Cave National Park; consultant National Bridge of Va. Endless Caverns, New Market, Va.

11 BROWN, Frank Arthur, Jr. Comparative physiology; Invertebrate zoology. b'08. AB '29 (Bowdoin Coll); MA—PhD '34—Austin teach fellow '29-32 (Harvard). Research in animal reactions, physiology of pigmentary systems, color perception in lower animals, physiology of fish swim bladders, Phototaxes, influence of light on seasonal cycles of animals, diurnal rhythms in invertebrates, and endocrinology of invertebrate animals. Author articles in field. Prof zool Northwestern U since '46; instr charge zool Marine Biol Lab Woods Hole summers since '45. AAAS(F)—Am Soc Zool (treas '48-51)—Soc Limnol Oceanog—Am Physiol Soc—Soc Study Development Growth—Union Am Biol Socs (sec '40-46)—Ill Acad Sci—Am Biol Soc—Soc Exptl Biol and Med—Human Genetics Soc—Soc Gen Physiol—Am Soc Naturalists. Department of Biology, Northwestern University, Evanston, Ill.

12 BROWN, F(rank) E(merson). Catalysis; Surface tension; Reactions under pressure: Vanadium oxytrichloride; Potassium chlorate. b'82. AB '11 (Kans State Teachers Coll); BS '13—PhD '18 (U Chicago). Invented automatic Toepler pump and device for distillation of corrosive liquids, research in decomposition of potassium chlorate, preparation and solvent properties of vanadium oxytrichloride, tests for arsenic, mercury and zinc, and cuprous oxide as a catalyst. Author: A Short Course in Qualitative Analysis '32; Qualitative Analysis Work Book '37; also articles in field. With Ia State Coll since '17, now prof chem. Am Chem Soc—Ia Acad Sci—Am Inst Chem(F)—Sigma Xi—Phi Kappa Phi. Department of Chemistry, Iowa State College, Ames, Ia.†☉

13 BROWN, F(rank) N(ewton) M(ithery). Aerodynamics; Flow visualization. b'02. BSE '28—MSE '32 (U Mich). Inventor space time recorder for study of acceleration, capacity pickup for torsional vibration indicator and recorder, instrumentation for damping capacity evaluation; residency on Johns Hopkins supersonic wind-tunnel (Bumblebee Project) '45-46; consultant Minister of Education, China '43. Author: The Space Time Recorder '42; The Brown Navigator '42. Head dept aero engring U Notre Dame since '35. Tech ed US Army Air Corps '31-33, research engr attached to USS Macon '33-35. Inst Aero Sci(asso F)—ASEE. University of Notre Dame, Notre Dame, Ind.†

14 BROWN, Frederick Martin. Pieridae and Satyridae of western hemisphere; Zoo-geography of Andes and Rockies; Microscopy of animal hair. b'03. Student '23 (Columbia). Author: America's Yesterday '37; also articles in field. Head sci dept Fountain Valley Sch Colo Springs since '30. Royal Entomol Soc (F, London)—AAAS(F)—NY Entomol Soc—Entomol Soc Am—Am Soc Mammal—Colo-Wyo Acad Sci. 305 Out West Building,

Colorado Springs, Colo. H: Fountain Valley School.

15 BROWN, George Bosworth. Nucleic acids. b'14. BS '34 (Ill Wesleyan U); MS '36—PhD '38 (U Ill). Investigation of metabolic precursors of nucleic acids, including purines, pyrimidines, nucleosides, and nucleotides; research on chemotherapeutic treatment of cancer with nucleic acids. Author articles: Studies of Purine Metabolism '48; Biosynthetics of Nucleic Acids in the Mammal '50, and others. Faculty Cornell '38-51 now prof biochemistry Sloan-Kettering Div Cornell U Med Sch; head protein chem div Sloan-Kettering Inst for Cancer Research since '46. Am Soc Biol Chem—ACS—Harvey Soc—AAAS—NRC protein panel com on growth since '49, chmn since 50)—Sigma Xi—Phi Kappa Phi. Sloan-Kettering Institute for Cancer Research, 444 E. 68th St., NYC 21.

16 BROWN, George Granger. Chemical engineering (Thermodynamics, gasoline, petroleum). b'96. BS Chem Engring '17 (NYU)—MSE '22—PhD '24 (U Mich). Motor fuel and petroleum refining consultant; technical expert appearing before government bodies and in patent and damage litigation for numerous petroleum companies. Author articles in field. With dept chem engring U Mich since '20; chmn dept chem and metall engring U Mich since '42. Dir engring Atomic Energy Commn '50. Am Inst Chem Engrs (pres '44). Received William H Walker award Am Inst Chem Engrs '39; Hanlon award Natural Gasoline Assn Am '40; citation by Chem Bull Chicago Sect Am Chem Soc for work in gas and fuel chemistry '48; Edward DeMille Campbell, University (distinguished) prof '47. 2028 East Engineering Building, University of Michigan, Ann Arbor.☉

17 BROWN, George Harold. Radio antennas, transmitters, and radio-frequency heating; Wave propagation; Television transmission. b'08. BS '30—MS '31—PhD '33—EE '42 (U Wis). Holder of 75 US patents covering radio circuits. Author articles in field. Co-author: Theory and Application of Radio-Frequency Heating '47. Research engr RCA Labs Princeton NJ since '42. Inst Radio Engrs(F)—AIEE(F)—Sigma Xi—Tau Beta Pi. Recipient Am Mfrs Assn Modern Pioneer award '40. RCA Laboratories, Princeton, N.J.

18 BROWN, George H(ay). Marketing; Advertising and preference measurement; Area sampling; Price determination. b'10. AB '29 (Oberlin); MBA '31 (Harvard); PhD '45 (U Chicago). Research in measurement of advertising effect and consumer preference; designed sample for Chicago Tribune sample census. Author: The International Economic Position of New Zealand '46; author articles in field. Divisional sales mgr Mallinckrodt Chem Works St Louis Mo '31-38; instr marketing U Chicago '38-41, asst prof, asso prof '41-47, prof since '47, dir bus problems bur since '42, dir development Social Sci Bus and Social Service Adminstrn since '47, part time cons market research. Am Econ Assn—Econometric Soc—Am Marketing Assn. 8453 Constance Av., Chicago 17.†

19 BROWN, Gordon Stanley. Servomechanisms. b'07. Diploma '25 (Melbourne Tech Sch Australia); SB—MS—ScD (MIT). Co-author: Principles of Servomechanisms '48; also articles in field. With MIT since '31, now prof elec engring, head dept elec engring, dir Servo-mechanisms Labora-

tory 40-52. AIEE—ASA—ASEE—Am Acad Arts and Sci—Sigma Xi—Eta Kappa Nu—Tau Beta Pi. Certificate for exceptional service for development of Naval Ordnance Equipment by Bur of Naval Ordnance '45; Presidential Certificate of Merit '48; George Westinghouse award in engring edn '52. Massachusetts Institute of Technology, Cambridge, Mass.

20 BROWN, Harley Procter. Protozoology; Invertebrate zoology. b'21. AB—AM '42 (Miami U); PhD '45 (O State U). Research in structure and mechanics of protozoan flagella by means of electron microsope, life history of Climacia areolaris. Author articles in field. Asst prof zool sci U Okla since '48. AAAS—Phi Sigma—Nat Hist Soc—AAUP—Phi Sigma—Wilderness Society—Am Soc Zool—Am Soc Protozool—Okla Acad Sci—Phi Beta Kappa—Sigma Xi. Zoological Sciences, University of Oklahoma, Norman, Okla.

21 BROWN, Harrison Scott. Nuclear chemistry; Meteoritics; Atomic energy; Planet evolution. b'17. BS '38 (U Calif); PhD '41 (Johns Hopkins). Executive vice chairman Emergency Committee of Atomic Scientists since '47. Author: Must Destruction Be Our Destiny? '46. Asso prof Inst Nuclear studies U Chicago since '48. Fedn Am Scientists—Phi Beta Kappa—Sigma Xi. University of Chicago, Chicago 37.

22 BROWN, Herbert C. Chemistry (Reaction mechanisms, boron, compounds of hydrogen, addition compounds). b'12. Asso Sci '35 (Wright Jr Coll); BS '36—PhD '38 (Chicago U). Research in reactions of atoms and free radicals, steric strains, alkali metal borohydrides; presently engaged research volatile compounds of uranium, materials for field generation of hydrogen, effects of steric strains on stability of addition compounds, reaction mechanisms, effects of steric strains on rates of chemical reactions, chemistry of Friedel-Crafts catalysts, directive effects in aliphatic substitution. Author articles in field. Prof chem Purdue U since '47. Am Chem Soc—Sigma Xi—AAAS. Eli Lilly postdoctoral fellow Chicago U '38-39. Department of Chemistry, Purdue University, Lafayette, Ind.†

23 BROWN, Herbert Ross. Early American popular novels. b'02. BSc '24—LittD '49 (Lafayette Coll); AM '28 (Harvard); PhD '39 (Columbia). Managing editor New England Quarterly since '45. Author: The Sentimental Novel in America: 1789-1860 '40 (Duke U prize). Editor: Hannah Webster Foster's The Coquette '40; also articles in field. Prof Eng Bowdoin Coll since '25. Colonial Soc Mass (corres). Hubbard Hall, Bowdoin College, Brunswick, Me.

24 BROWN, Hiram. Alloys (High-temperature and light metal). b'14. BS in metall engring '37 (Fenn Coll); student '41-44 (Niagara U). Research on casting of light and non-ferrous alloys including sand, permanent mold, die casting, plaster casting, and precision investment casting; fabrication of stainless steel and other corrosion and heat-resistant alloys. Co-author: Aluminum and its Applications '48. Foundry metall Aluminum Co Am '33-40; chief metall Frontier Bronze Corp '41-44; asst works mgr Aluminum Industries Inc '45-46; chief metall Solar Aircraft Co since '46. Am Foundrymen's Soc (chmn aluminum-magnesium div)—Am Soc Metals—ASTM (mem light alloy specification com)—Soc Automotive Engrs (mem corrosion and heat resistant alloy specification com). Solar Aircraft Co., Des Moines 5, Ia.

10 BROWN, Howard Dexter. Horticultural technology; Vegetable gardening. b'91. BS '14—MS '17 (U Ill); PhD '27 (Mich State Coll). Research on greenhouse soil sterilization, effect of paper wrappers on preservation of horticultural products, vegetable forcing, hydroponics, seed purity, effect of DDT on cucurbits, several aspects of potato and tomato culture and preservation; described types of American variety of tomatoes. Co-author: Frozen Foods, Processing and Handling '46; (with Hutchinson) Vegetable Science '48; also articles in field. Prof hort products Ohio State U since '46. Am Soc Advancement Hort Sci—American Society Plant Physiology—Institute Food Techn—Ohio Academy Sci—Vegetable Growers Assn Am (sec since '33)—Nat Assn Hot House Vegetable Growers (sec-treas '40-45)—Sigma Xi — Gamma Sigma Delta. Second recipient Kelsey award outstanding contributions to commercial vegetable gardening industry. Horticulture Department, Ohio State University, Columbus 10, O. H: 123 W. New England Av., Worthington, O.

11 BROWN, Hylton R(oller). Industrial dust explosions; Uses of inert gas in fire prevention; Metal powders (Flammability and fire safety measures). b'95. BS '16—ME '23 (Pa State Coll). Co-author: Handbook of Fire Protection '48; National Fire Codes for the Prevention of Dust Explosions '46; also articles in field. Engr, later chief dust explosion sect US Dept Agr '17-40; sr engr US Bur Mines since '40; cons tests and research War Dept Civilian Protection Sch, Fed Specifications Bd fire extinguisher com. Nat Fire Protection Assn (chmn dust explosion hazards com and combustible metals com). U.S. Bureau of Mines, College Park, Md.

12 BROWN, Ina Corinne. Negro (History, education). AB '36—PhD '40 (U Chicago). Travel in Cuba studying problems of race contact '28, Central Africa and Orient '29-30. Author: Story of the American Negro '36; Race Relations in a Democracy '49; also articles in field. Prof anthropol Scarritt Coll since '42; cons edn Fisk U since '42. Am Anthropol Assn(F)—Am Geog Soc—AAAS—Internat African Inst—So Sociol Soc—Sigma Xi—Phi Beta Kappa. Rosenwald fellow engaged in research in Brit Mus '38-39. Scarritt College, Nashville 4, Tenn.

13 BROWN, James Wilson. Plant physiology (Growth regulators, respiration, methods). b'13. BS '35 (Md U); MA '37—PhD '38 (Duke U). Research on physiological effects of 2, 4-dichlorophenoxyacetic acid (2, 4-D), effects of organic chemicals on growth responses of plants including alteration of chemical composition of plants, environmental conditions affecting translocation of compounds or stimuli within plants, environmental conditions affecting potency of compounds; development of bio-assays and tests for activity of compounds, and plant mechanisms involved in their action; engaged research in use of Warburg respirometers in plant physiology investigations. Author articles: Respiration of Acorns as Related to Temperature and After-Ripening '39; Effect of 2, 4-Dichlorophenoxyacetic Acid on the Water Relations, the Accumulation and Distribution of Solid Matter, and the Respiration of Bean Plants '46; Inactivation of 2, 4-D in Soil as Affected by Soil Moisture,

Temperature, the Addition of Manure and Autoclaving '47, and others. Asst plant physiol Bur Plant Industry Soils and Agrl Engring US Dept Agr, Md '44-47; plant physiol Chem Corps Camp Detrick Frederick Md since '47. AAAS—Am Soc Plant Physiol—Sigma Xi. Chemical Corps, Camp Detrick, Frederick, Md.

14 BROWN, Jesse Edward. Design of radio and television receivers. b'02. Student (Cornell). Performance characteristics of radio and television apparatus. Holds patents on radio and television equipment. Radio insp radio div US Dept Commerce, Fed Radio Commn, FCC '24-37; engr Zenith Radio Corp since '37, now chief engr. Inst Radio Engrs (F). 6001 Dickens Av., Chicago 39.

15 BROWN, John Bernis. Biochemistry; Physiological and fat chemistry; Nutrition. b'93. BS '15—MS '17—PhD '21 (U Ill). Research in yeast metabolism, anti-enzymes, chemistry endocrine products, fats and oils, chemistry of saliva. Asso chem in pharmacol U Pa Med Sch '21-22; research chem Swift & Co Chicago '22-24; with O State U '24-30, prof physiol chem since '41. Am Chem Soc—Am Oil Chem Soc—Am Leather Chem Soc—Internat Assn Dental Research—Am Inst Nutrition—O Acad Sci—Soc Exptl Biol and Med—Am Soc Biol Chem. College of Medicine, Ohio State University, Columbus, O. H: 1190 Lincoln Rd., Columbus 8, O.

16 BROWN, John Herbert Jr. Military and Naval Science; Military submarines. b'91. BS '14 (US Naval Acad). Commd ensign US Navy '14 advanced through grades to rear admiral '43; served in submarines 17 yrs; dep comdr submarine forces Pacific Fleet comdr submarine force '49-51, comdt 4th Naval Dist US Naval Base since '51. US Naval Base. Phila. 12.©

17 BROWN, John Stafford. Mining geology; Ore deposits. b'94. BS '17 (Mo Sch Mines and Metall); MS '22 (George Washington U); PhD '25 (Columbia). Introduced Herzberg principle from European literature into America; researches on porosity and ore deposition; originator of new (metallurgical) interpretation of ore genesis. Author: Ore Genesis '48. Co-author: Interpretation of Topographic and Geologic Maps '25; also articles in field. Geol St Joseph Lead Co '25, chief since 46. Geol Soc Am(F)—Mineral Soc Am(F)—Am Inst Mining Metall Engrs. St. Joseph Lead Co., Bonne Terre, Mo.

18 BROWN, Meta Suche. Plant cytology and genetics; Gossypium; Drosophila. b'08. BA '31—MA '33—PhD '35 (U Tex). Study of relationships between species of cotton, fertility of species hybrids, chromosome pairing and inheritance in species hybrids and their application to improvement of cultivated cotton. Author articles in field. Cytologist dept agron A&M Coll Coll Station Tex. Tex Acad Sci—Genetics Soc Am—Am Genetic Assn—Bot Soc Am—Soc Study Evolution—Sigma Xi. Department of Agronomy, Texas A&M College, College Station, Tex.

19 BROWN, Morden Grant. Optical instrument design; Physiology of encystment of protozoa. b'06. AB '29—AM '36—PhD '38 (Stanford U). Research in analysis of the physiology of the excystment and excystment phenomena of protozoa, analysis of the physiology of early development of amphibian embryos, experimental embryology, research basic design of new optical instruments. Author articles in

field. Research asst Sch Biol Sci Stanford U 1934-37; research asso dept zool Wash U St Louis 1938-41; research physicist Am Optical Co sci instrument div Buffalo 1941-45, chief development physicist '45-49, mgr development '46-49, supervisor instrument research since '49. AAAS—American Soc Zool—Am Oil Chem Soc—Optical Soc Am—Western Soc Naturalists. American Optical Company Research Lab., Box 137, Stamford, Conn. H: 44 Phillips Lane, Darien, Conn.

20 BROWN, Oral Ala. Tobacco curing equipment; Farm machinery and electrification. b'93. BSEE '24 (W Va U); MSEE '24—PhD '32 (Ia State Coll). Invented machine for mechanically digging and shaking peanuts, sheller for shelling seed peanuts, temperature and humidity control systems for tobacco curing barns. Author articles in field. Asso elec engr, later sr agrl engr US Dept Agr since '39. Am Soc Agrl Engrs. Tobacco Station, Oxford, N.C.

21 BROWN, Ralph Thompson. Tung production. b'15. BS '37—MS '38 (La State U). Studies on relation between nutrition and growth, yield, and fruit composition; length of stigma receptivity; pollen viability; progeny studies and selection propagation. Author articles in field. Agt, later jr pomol US Dept Agr field lab for tung investigations Cairo Ga '39, '47, asst hort charge lab Spring Hill Ala '47, '49; supt plaguemines Parish Br Sta Diamond La since '49. American Soc Adv Hort Sci—Am Genetics Assn—AAAS. Plaguemines Parish, Branch Experiment Station, Diamond, La.

22 BROWN, Randolph Milton. Forestry (Forest mensuration). b'96. BS '21—MF '24 (Cornell U). Author articles in field. With U Minn since '27, now asso prof forestry. Soc Am Foresters—Am Statis Assn—Sigma Xi. Division of Forestry, University Farm, St. Paul 1.

23 BROWN, Robert Benaway. American history (Mexico and America). b'16. AB '37—AM '46 (Univ Mich); '38 (Marquette U); '48 (Nat U Mex). Author: The Netherlands and America '48; The Fourth Americanist '49; also articles in field. Newspaper reporter '37-41; curator printed books William L Clements Library since '45. Bibliog Soc Am—AHA—Ind, Mich Hist Socs—Hispanic Assn—Phi Kappa Phi. William L. Clements Library, University of Michigan, Ann Arbor. H: 555 Packard St.

24 BROWN, Roland Wilbur. Paleobotany of the United States. b'93. BS '17 (Lafayette Coll); PhD '26 (Johns Hopkins). Editor Journal of the Washington Academy of Sciences '34-37; chairman committee on paleobotany National Research Council '35-40. Author articles in field. Geol, paleobot US Geol Survey Washington since '29. Geol Soc Washington—Washington Acad Sci—AAAS—Poleontol Soc Am—Am Soc Plant Taxonomists—Geol Soc Am—Phi Beta Kappa—Sigma Xi. U.S. National Museum, Washington 25.†

25 BROWN, Russell Guy. Vascular plants of Maryland; Ecology, taxonomy and physiology of plants. b'05. BS '29—MS '30 (W Va U); PhD '34 (U Md). Co-author: A Catalog of the Vascular Plants of Maryland '46; also articles in field. Asst and asso prof bot U Md since '36. Bot Soc Am—Washington Bot Soc—Southern Appalachian Bot Club. University of Maryland, College Park, Md.†

26 BROWN, Sanborn C(onner). Electrical discharge in gases; Detection of radioactivity. b'13. AB '35—MA '37 (Dartmouth Coll); PhD '44 (MIT). Author articles in field. Teaching fellow, later asso prof physics MIT since '38. Am Phys Soc—Am Inst Phys Teachers—Sigma Xi. Department of Physics, Massachusetts Institute of Technology, Cambridge 39, Mass.†

10 BROWN, Seymour William. Refrigeration and air-conditioning for passenger and cargo ships and naval combat vessels. b'14. BME '37 (Coll City of NY). Engineering application and design of ships' stores plants for merchant marine and naval combatant vessels, air conditioning systems of passenger vessels and naval combatant vessels, hospital ships, and yachts, refrigeration and air conditioning for submarines, cargo refrigeration for quick frozen foods, frozen beef, precooled fruits and vegetables, hot fruits and vegetables and bananas. Holds patent on compressor apparatus to improve lubrication of compression-type refrigerating compressor, also other devices for air distribution systems. Author articles: Modern Developments in Marine Refrigeration '48; Modern Practice in Marine Refrigeration '49; Refrigeration on the High Seas '50, and others. Contributor: American Society of Refrigerating Engineers Data Book '50. Engr Carrier Corp since '37, chief engr marine dept since '43. Am Soc Refrigerating Engrs—Am Soc Heating and Ventilating Engrs—Soc Naval Architects and Marine Engrs—Am Soc Naval Engrs. Carrier Corp., 385 Madison Av., N.Y.C. 17.

11 BROWN, Vernon Lee. Numismatics. b'04. AB '27 (George Washington U); MBA '41 (NYU). Research on emergency currency issued in the US during the depression years '31-34. Author articles in field. Asst curator Chase Nat Bank Collection Moneys World NYC '32-39, curator since '39. Am Numismatic Assn (bd govs '40-42, since '47)—NJ Numismatic Soc (pres '39-40) — Am Numismatic Soc(F). Chase National Bank Collection of Moneys of the World, 46 Cedar St., NYC 15.

12 BROWN, Vinson. Natural history of Panama and American Pacific coast. b'12. BA '39—MA '47 (Stanford). Made three trips Chiriqui Province Panama collecting wild animals '31-35. Author: The Amateur Naturalist's Handbook '48. Sci cons San Mateo Co Calif Schs '48, Santa Clara Co Calif Sch '48-49; dir research Naturegraph Co Los Altos since '46. Am Assn Icthyologists Herpetologists—Amateur Naturalists Assn (founder). Naturegraph Co., P.O. Box 62, Los Altos, Calif.

13 BROWN, V(irgil) K(enneth). Recreation; Playgrounds; Parks (Community service programs, organization, administration). b'83. '02-03 (Cornell Coll); '04-06 (Northwestern U); '09-11 (U Chicago). Field judge Olympic games Los Angeles '32; board of directors Athletic Institute, Billiard Congress of America; recreation committee International Labor Office Geneva; editor recreation section Parks and Recreation Magazine 12 yrs; editorial board Youth Leader's Digest. Coauthor: (with James O'Rourke) Recreation Manual '32. Editor: Modern Recreation Series '36-42; Sports Analysis Series '36-42. Mgr Eckhart Park West Park Commrs Chicago '07-08; dir Cornell Square South Park Commrs Chicago '08-13, asst supt playgrounds and sports '13-16; supt recreation city playgrounds Newark NJ '16-18; supt community relations also morale officer Air Nitrates Corp

Muscle Shoals Ala '18-19; supt recreation South Park commrs Chicago '20-34; dir recreation Chicago Park Dist, cons indsl recreation, emeritus since '48. Am Inst Park Execs (past pres) —Nat Recreation Policies Com—Am Recreation Soc (past pres)—Am Soc Health Phys Edn and Recreation(F). 10042 Prospect Av., Chgo.

14 BROWN, Virginius Elholm. Malariology; Helminthology; Parasitology. b'02. BS '25—MS '26 (Emory U); PhD '31 (U Calif). Author: Cytology of Perama; Neuromotor Apparatus of Paramecium; also articles in field. Prof biol Taylor U '38-43; asst prof biol Marquette U since '46. Capt US Army, malaria control work and survey So Pacific and Luzon Army and Navy units '43-46. AAAS—Am Soc Mammalogists —Am Malaria Soc—Am Genetics Soc —Am Assn Mus—Linnean Soc NY— NY Acad Sci—Sigma Xi. Biology Department, Marquette University, Milwaukee. H: 601 N. 25th St.

15 BROWN, Walter Creighton. Herpetology of North America and Pacific Islands. b'13. AB '35—MA '38 (Coll Puget Sound); student (U Rochester, Stanford U). Author articles in field. Teaching and research Nat Hist Mus Stanford U '47-50; Northwestern University since '50. Am Soc Ichthyologists Herpetologists— Soc Systematic Zool—AAAS—Biol Soc Washington—Sigma Xi—Am Soc Zools. Dept. of Biology, Northwestern Univ., Evanston, Ill.

16 BROWN, Walter John. Electronic Controls; Radio (Very high frequency, frequency modulation). b'00. BSc '20 (Manchester U Eng). Pioneer experiments on very high frequency radio communication and vacuum tubes; development, tooling, and testing mass production radios and radio-phonographs; development of pocket-size miniature four-tube broadcast receiver; research on wide-angle phase modulation for frequency modulation mobile and multiplex systems; simplified phase shift control development on thryatrons and mercury arc rectifiers producing variable direct current power controlled by small signal. Holds patents in field. Author articles: Ultra-Short Waves for Limited Range Communication '30; Miniature Pocket Radio Receiver Design '45, and others. Supervision broadcasting and research Metropolitan Vickers Elec Co Eng '21-29; chief engr Elec & Mus Industries Ltd Eng '29-36; vp in charge prodn electronic and piezo-elec devices Brush Development Co Cleveland '39-43; cons engr since '43. Inst EE—Am Inst EE (F)—Inst Radio Engrs. Seventeenth Floor, 100 Broadway, N.Y.C. 5.

17 BROWN, Walter Lindsay. Legal ethics; Federal legislation. b'03. BS '24 LLB '26 (U Va) BA '28 (Oxford U). Vice-pres, gen counsel, director Western Electric Co since '41. Am Bar Assn (com professional ethics and grievances, special common law lists) —Assn Bar City NY (com fed legislation)—Phi Delta Phi—Phi Beta Kappa. 195 Broadway, NYC. 7.©

18 BROWN, Walter Nicholas, Jr. Bone density; Acoustics (General). b '17. BS (elec engring) '40—MS (elec engring) '40 (MIT) PhD (phys) '49 (Pa State Coll). Developed physical analysis, computational equipment, and computational procedures for Mack technique for bone density determination; research on loudspeakers and absorption coefficient measurement in acoustics. Research asso and F phys Pa State Coll since '46; research cons Haller, Raymond, and

Brown Inc since '46. Inst Radio Engrs (sr mem)—APS—Am Assn Phys Teachers—Sigma Xi—Pi Mu Epsilon —Sigma Pi Sigma—Am Inst EE (student paper prize '39). Pennsylvania State College, State College, Pa.

19 BROWN, Wenzell. West Indies; Stanley Prison. b'12. AB '32 (Rollins Coll); AM '40 (Columbia); '32-33 (King's Coll, U London). Served with Hong Kong Civilian Defense throughout siege, captured by Japanese at fall of city, interned Stanley prison, exchanged in '43. Author: Hong Kong Aftermath '43; Dynamite on Our Doorstep '44-45; Angry Men—Laughing Men '47; Murder Seeks an Agent '47; also articles in field. Defense security promotion specialist US Treasury '43-45. Soc of Friends. C/o Margaret Christie, 65 University Pl., NYC 3.

20 BROWN, Willard Cowles. Lighting. b'95. BS '14—EE '25 (Va Mil Inst); BS '16 (Harvard); BS '16 (MIT). Special lecturer Case School Applied Science; American delegate and director secretariat on lighting practice International Congress Illumination, The Netherlands '39, director for Paris meeting '48. Holds patents on lighting devices. Author articles in field. Mgr engring div lamp dept Gen Electric Co since '48. Illuminating Engring Soc (vp '39-41, pres '41-42). Nela Park, Cleve.©

21 BROWN, William F. Sporting dogs; Field trials. b'03. Ed DePaul U. Author: The Field Trial Primer '34; How to Train Hunting Dogs '42; Rod and Gun Calendar since '44; Retriever Gun Dogs '45; Field Trials '47; also articles in field. With The American Field since '22, pres Am Field Pub Co since 43. 222 W. Adams St., Chgo.

22 BROWN, W(illiam) Horatio. Zinc deposits. b'99. BS '20 (Va Poly Inst); EM '21 (Colo Sch Mines); PhD '24 (U Minn). Author: Quantitative Study of Ore Zoning '35. Instr, asst prof geol U Ariz '25-29; chief geol Bertha Mineral Co '29-34; Empire Zinc Div NJ Zinc Co '34-40, Empire Zinc Co '40-46; Bertha Mineral Div NJ Zinc Co since '46. AIME—GSA—SEG—Sigma Xi.

23 BROWN, William Lacy. Cytogenetics and evolution of grasses; Multiple factor genetics; Maize breeding. b'13. AB '36 (Bridgewater Coll Va); MS '38—PhD '42 (Washington U St Louis); Spl Research Fellow '37-41 (Mo Bot Garden). Research on cytogenetics of Poa pratensis, turf and forage grass, sweet corn breeding, history and evolution of corn belt maize, multiple factor inheritance in maize. Author articles in field. Geneticist US Golf Assn '41-42; collaborator US Dept Agr '41-42; geneticist Rogers Bros Seed Co '42-45; geneticist Pioneer Laboratory; Pioneer Hybrid Corn Co since '45. Genetics Soc Am—Bot Soc Am—Am Soc Plant Taxonomists— AAAS—Sigma Xi. Pioneer Laboratory, Johnston, Ia.

24 BROWN, William Randall. Igneous and metamorphic geology; Mineralogy; Pegmatites. b'13. BS—MA '39 (U Va); PhD '42 (Cornell U). Author articles in field. Asst and asso prof geol U Ky since '45. Am Inst Mining Metall Engrs—Am Mineral Soc —Ky Geol Soc—Va Acad Sci. Department of Geology, University of Kentucky, Lexington 29, Ky. H: 125 Edgemoor Dr., Lexington 1.†

25 BROWNE, Frederick L(incoln). Colloid chemistry; Technology of painting wood; Wood preservation. b'95. BC '17 (Cornell); MS '20—PhD '21—Nat Research fellow '21-22 (U

Wis). Developed a classification of woods for painting and system of classifying house and barn paints, improved methods of testing paints for durability and of priming woods for painting; developed principles for optimum maintenance of paint coatings; set forth mechanism of wood weathering and use of coatings for preventing it. Co-author: Casein and Its Industrial Applications '39; also articles in field. Chem Forest Products Lab since '22. AAAS(F)—Am Chem Soc—Am Soc Testing Materials—Wis Acad Arts Sci Letters—Sigma Xi. Forest Products Laboratory, Forest Service, U.S. Department of Agriculture, Madison 5, Wis.†

10 BROWNE, Secor Delahay. Aircraft (Heating, pressurization, ventilation). b'16. BA '38 (Harvard); '45 (U Birmingham). Research on control of pressurization, heating and ventilating of aircraft. Engr Barber-Colman Co since '39. Am Soc Heating and Ventilating Engrs—Soc Automotive Engrs (mem com A-9 aeronautical standards). 152 Grove St., Waltham 54, Mass.

11 BROWNE, William Ward. Bacteriology and sanitation of foods (Fish and fish products, oysters, frozen eggs, canned foods, cold storage). b'84. AB '08—AM '09—PhD '12 (Brown U). Author articles in field. With Coll City NY since '12, now prof bact. Am Pub Health Assn(F)—AAAS(F)—Soc Am Bact—Soc Am Naturalists—Inst Food Tech—Internat Assn Milk Sanitarians—Sigma Xi. Department Biology, College of the City of New York, 139th St., NYC.†

12 BROWNING, Glenn H. Frequency modulation (Tuner design); Power factor (Meters); Radio frequencies (Transformer design, measurement); Relays (Capacitance); Alarm systems (Capacitance). b'97. BA '21—DSc (hon) '50 (Cornell Coll); '21-22 (Harvard). Design of frequency modulation receivers; special power factor meters; radio frequency transformer incorporated in circuit known as Browning-Drake circuit; capacitance relays and capacitance alarm systems. Asst Cruft Lab Harvard '22-23; radio and research engr Nat Co '24-26; pres Browning Drake, cons engr Nat Co '26-28; cons engr '28-37; pres Browning Lab Inc since '37. Inst Radio Engrs (sr mem)—Am Inst EE. Research F elec engring Harvard '23-24. Browning Laboratories, Inc., 750 Main St., Winchester, Mass.

13 BROXON, James William. Cosmic rays. b'97. AB '19 (Wabash Coll); MA '20—teaching fellow physics '19-22—PhD '26 (U Minn). Author articles in field. With U Colo since '22, prof physics since '29. Am Phys Soc(F)—AAAS(F)—Am Assn Physics Teachers—Am Soc Engring Edn—Am Geophys Union—Colo-Wyo Acad Sci—Phi Beta Kappa—Sigma Pi Sigma—Sigma Xi. 945 14th St., Boulder, Colo.

14 BRUBAKER, Paul Mays. Electric filters; Transformers; Amplifiers. b'16. BS '38 (Lehigh U); '46-47 (Newark Coll Engring). Developed improved designs on high quality audio transformers and magnetic tape recorders; special magnetic components for servomechanism use. Sr engr research and design Rangertone Inc since '48. Audio Engring Soc—Inst Radio Engrs. Rangertone, Inc., 73 Winthrop St., Newark, N.J.†

15 BRUCK, Eberhard Friedrich. History of Law and Religion; Roman, Greek, Civil Law; Patristics. b'77. JD '04 (U Breslau); Prof L. Mitteis

seminar '07-08 (U Leipzig). Research on history Roman, Greek and civil law antiquity and middle ages in connection pagan and Christian religion, patristics, general civilization; defined evolution last will and testament Greek and Roman law, ancestor worship and immortality in relation to development law of inheritance and property, influence Church-fathers on law. Author: The Donation mortis cause in Greek Law (Germ) '09; On the History of the Last Will in Greek Law (Germ) '08; On the Evolution of the Executor of the Will in Roman Law (Germ) '14; Dead Man's Part and Foundations for the Deceased in Greek Law, a Study in the Relationships between Law and Religion, with Special Regard to the History of Property and Law of Inheritance (Germ) '26; also articles in field. Instr Roman and civil law U Breslau '09-13, prof '16-29, dean law sch '28-29; prof Roman and civil law U Geneva Switzerland '13-16, U Frankfurt-on-Main '29-32, dean law sch '30-31; prof Roman and civil law U Bonn '32-35; research asso law Harvard since '39. Greek Archaeol Soc Athens (hon mem)—Riccobono seminar Roman law Am—AHA. 10 Langdell Hall, Harvard University, Cambridge, Mass. H: 72 Foster St., Cambridge 38, Mass.

16 BRUCKER, Herbert. American newspaper history; Journalism (History, techniques, functions). b'98. AB '21 (Williams Coll); B Litt '24 (Columbia U); Pulitzer traveling scholar '24. Author: The Changing American Newspaper '37; Freedom of Information '48. With The Hartford Courant since '44, ed since '47. Hartford Courant, Hartford 1, Conn.

17 BRUCKNER, J(acob) Herbert. Poultry genetics; Genetics of pheasant. b'05. BS '30 (Purdue U); PhD '35 (Cornell U). Prof, head poultry dept Cornell U since '42. Genetics Soc—Poultry Sci Assn—Sigma Xi. Rice Hall, Cornell University, Ithaca, N.Y.

18 BRUMAN, Henry John. Cultural geography and pioneer settlement of Latin America; Mexican Indian cultures; Aboriginal beers, wines; Coconuts; Vanilla. b'13. '30-31 (Calif Inst Tech); AB '35 (U Calif LA); Predoctoral fellow Mexico and Central Am Social Sci Council '38-39; PhD '40 (U Calif). Research on Mexican and Central American native beverages, possibilities refugee settlement Brazil, early history coconut, Mexican vanilla industry; field work various parts rural Mexico and Central America. Author articles in field. Instr geog Pa State Coll '40-41, asst prof '41-44; cultural geog Inst Social Anthrop Smithsonian Inst '44-45; asst prof geog U Calif '45-49, assoc prof since '49. Assn Am Geog—Am Geog Soc—AAAS—Am Acad Polit Social Sci—Sigma Xi. University of California, Los Angeles 24.†

19 BRUMFIELD, Robert Clarence. Jet propulsion; Hydro-propulsion; Turbomachinery. b'19. BS '40—MS '41—PhD '43—Cole scholar '41-42, '43-44 (Calif Inst Tech). Author articles in field. Research and development engr Aerojet Engring Corp '43-45; head propulsion unit US Naval Ordnance Test Sta Pasadena '46-47, head engring research sect '47-48, head propulsion sect '48-49, head propulsion div underwater ordnance dept since '49; chief engr MK 40 Torpedo Test Vehicle since '46; cons power and propulsion panel, com on undersea warfare Nat Research Council '48-50. Inst Aero Sci—Sigma Xi—Tau Beta Pi. 3600 Greenhill Rd., Pasadena 8, Cal.

20 BRUMLEY, David Joseph. Water supply; City planning; Sewage treatment. b'09. BS '31—MS '32 (U Ill). Research, planning, and construction of water supply and sewage treatment facilities for army camps and government projects; municipal improvements and plans for proper growth. Post engr Columbia Army Air Base '42-44; staff engr Maxwell Field '44-45; chief mech and utilities sect Engring and Construction Div Atomic Energy Commn since '47. Am Soc CE—Am Geophys Union—Soc Am Mil Engrs. Atomic Energy Commission, Box 550, Richland, Wash.

21 BRUNAUER, Stephen. High explosives; Adsorption of gases; Catalysis. b'03. AB '25 (Columbia U); MS '29 (George Washington U); PhD '33 (Johns Hopkins). Research on catalysis adsorption reaction kinetics and chemical equilibria, contributed to the theory of chemical adsorption and heterogeneous catalysis. Invented with P H Emmett a new and now widely used method for determination of surfaces of finely divided solids; with P H Emmett, Edward Teller and W E Deming advanced new theory of physical adsorption of gases now called the BET theory; holds patent with J F Shultz on oxidation of phosphorous. Author: Adsorption of Gases and Vapors '43; also articles in field. Jr chem Dept Agr '28-36, asst chem '36-39, asso chem '39-42, chem '42; lt USNR '42-43, lt comdr '43-45, comdr Bur Ordnance since '45, chief tech administr explosives research and development since '46. Am Chem Soc—Washington Acad Sci—Philoso Soc Washington—Nat Research Council (div chem and chem tech since '48). Hillebrand prize Chem Soc Washington '45. Bureau of Ordnance, Navy Department, Washington. H: 3417 Quebec St., Washington 16.

22 BRUNETTI, Cledo. Research administration; Electronics; Radio; Television; Printed electronic circuits. b'10. BEE '32—PhD '37 (U Minn). Research on electronics, vacuum tubes, various elements radio equipment, operational calculus, radio proximity fuze, ultrahigh frequency radiation, radio meteorograph, acoustical and production engineering; invented sub-miniature radio transmitters and receivers, resistance-tuned oscillators, printed circuits on non-planar surfaces, world authority on printed electronic circuits. Author articles in field. Nat Research Com '42-46; mem com electronics Research and Development Bd since '47, com vacuum tube development OSRD '43, com aircraft radio and electronics Aeronautical Bd '47. Instr dept elec engring Lehigh U '37-39, asst prof '39-41, dir research radio, electronics and elec engring '37-41; research and develop engr Nat Bur Standards '41-42, alternate chief radio and electronics development sect '42, organizer and chief Production Engineering Sect '43-45, chief ordnance engring sect '45-47, organizer, chief engring electronics sect '47-49; asso dir Stanford Research Inst since '49; lecturer Stanford University since '50. Inst Radio Engrs—Sigma Xi—Tau Beta Pi—Eta Kappa Nu. Chosen America's Outstanding Young Elec Engr Eta Kappa Nu '41, received Grand Award, Materials and Methods Achievement Award, Materials and Methods Magazine '47. Stanford Research Institute, Stanford, Cal.

23 BRUNHOUSE, Robert Levere. United States history (Revolution, Pennsylvania). b'08. AB '30 (Dickinson Coll); AM '35—PhD '40 (U Pa). Author: Counter-Revolution in Pennsylvania, 1776-90, '42. Co-author: Writings on Pennsylvania History, A Bibliography '46; edited series of film pictures for teaching American history; also articles in field. Teacher at Drew U since '42, asso prof since '47. Phi Beta Kappa—AHA—Pa Hist Assn. Drew University, Madison, N.J. H: 39 Green Village Rd.

10 BRUNNIER, Henry J. Structures and construction. b'82. BCE '04—CE '13 (Ia State Coll). Consulting engineer low level Broadway tunnels between Almeda and Contra Costa counties, and on construction buildings for earthquake safety to boards of education San Francisco, San Rafael, Redwood City, San Leandro, University California, Pedro Corcuera y Mier Estate; member consulting board engineers San Francisco-Oakland Bay Project, numerous other buildings and structures in western US, Canal Zone. Structural engr Ford-Bacon and Davis Co NYC '06-08; cons and structural engr private practice San Francisco since '08. ASCE—Pacific Assn Cons Engrs—Structural Engrs Assn No Calif—Seismol Soc Am—Concrete Inst. Awarded Marston Medal Ia State Coll '41. 55 New Montgomery St., San Francisco 5.

11 BRUNO, Charles. Aluminum welding. b'07. Student '36-38 (Lawrence Tech Coll); '42-43 (U Detroit); '39 (Detroit Sch Tech); '49 (U Louisville). Developed method of welding heat treated aluminum alloy 20-ton dump truck bodies without loss of strength; developed method of flash welding extruded aluminum sections; designed and improved welding methods for high production lines for light metal industries in all phases of welding. Welding supt and design engr Lincoln Div Ford Motor Co '37-44; welding engr and cons Reynolds Metal Co since '44. Am Welding Soc—Am Soc Metals. 2500 S. Third St., Louisville 1.

12 BRUNO, Michael H. Lithographic technology. b'11. BS '31 (Yale). Author article in field. Research mgr Lithographic Tech Found Chicago since '45; Research officer Army Map Service US Army '41-45. Tech Assn Lithographic Industry (pres)—Am Optical Soc—Photographic Soc Am—Sigma Xi. 1800 South Prairie Av., Chicago 16.

13 BRUNS, Hank (Henry P.). Amsport fishing and fish breeding (Fly and bait casting, fishing tackle merchandising; black bass); Nomenclature of fishes. b'04. Privately tutored. Fished all of US catching every major sport fish many times. Author: The Making of a Fisherman '47; Know Your Fishing Tackle '49. Instr fly and bait casting since '36; lectr on sport fishing and fish breeding since '32; SE rep South Bend Bait Co since '46. Winner various prizes for unusual light tackle catches of both salt and fresh water fish. South Bend Bait Company, South Bend, Ind.

14 BRUNSKI, Michael. Fruit trees (Grafting). b'87. Grad (Krizevci Agrl Coll Croatia Austria). Specialist in regrafting methods producing blooms or fruit during first season, and in grafting and budding for unusual results. Chief hort RKO Studio nursery since '43. Am Landscape Soc—So Cal Hort Soc. 5500 Melrose Av., Hollywood 38, Cal. H: 10740 Woodbine St. Palms, LA 34.†

15 BRUNSMAN, Howard George. Statistics of housing; Population. b'04. BCS '27—MA '29 (O State U); '30-31 (Columbia U). Author articles in field. Asso dir Financial Survey Urban Housing, Bur Fgn, Domestic Commerce

'34; asso dir Div Econ and Statis FHA '35-39; chief housing statis sect Population Div Bur Census '39-43, asst chief Population and Housing Div '43-48, chief since '48. Am Statis Assn—Am Sociol Soc—Population Assn Am—Nat Assn Housing Officials—Royal Statis Soc(F). Population and Housing Division, Bureau of the Census, Washington 25.

16 BRUNTON, Paul. India (Yoga, mysticism); Oriental religions; Abnormal psychology; Comparative philosophy; Mystical cults. b'98. Student (Central Foundation Sch London); PhD (St George's Coll London). Traveled extensively throughout Europe and Asia as student of literature and art, religion, mysticism, philosophy; investigated ideas and practices of Oriental yogis and holy men, lived in hermitages retreats monasteries as practicing yogi; carried out special research in Asiatic philosophy under auspices of Maharajah of Mysore with assistance of University of Mysore and Mysore Government Oriental Manuscript Library. Author: A Search in Secret India '35; A Search in Secret Egypt '36; A Hermit in the Himalayas '37; Discover Yourself '39; The Hidden Teaching Beyond Yoga '41; The Wisdom of the Overself '43 and others; also articles in field. c/o E. P. Dutton & Co., 300 Fourth Ave., NYC 10.

17 BRUTCHER, Henry Eric. Metallurgical terminology. b'97. Student '18-23 (Maximilians U, Munich). Research on technical terms in ferrous metallurgy. Author articles in field; translator 3000 articles from 15 languages. Compiler of over 100 glossaries. Tech translator Rep (Steel) Research Corp '30-31 and patent dept Sun Oil Co '31-41; self-employed since '41. Am Soc Metals—Am Welding Soc—Am Foundrymen's Soc—Am Ceramic Soc (refractories div)—Brit Iron and Steel Inst. Postoffice Box 157, Altadena, Calif.

18 BRUUN, Geoffrey. Modern European history; French Revolution; Napoleon; Clemenceau, Twentieth century world history. b'98. AB '24 (U Brit Columbia); AM '26—PhD '27 —White fellow in hist and Boldt fellow (Cornell U). Author: The Enlightened Despots '29; St Just, Apostle of the Terror '32; Survey of European Civilization, Vol II '36; Europe and the French Imperium '38; Clemenceau '43; Europe in Evolution '45; The World in the Twentieth Century '48. AHA. Forest Home Dr, Ithaca, N.Y.

19 BRYAN, Alice Isabel. Library personnel; Reader psychology; Communications; Research methods. b'02. BS '29—MA '30—PhD '34 (Columbia); MA '49—fellow (U Chicago). Author: The Public Librarian '49; also articles in field. Head dept psychol Sch Fine and Applied Arts Pratt Inst '35-39; cons psychol and asso in library service Sch Library Service Columbia '36-39, asst prof Sch Library Service since '39; dir personnel project Pub Library Inquiry Social Sci Research Council NYC '47-48; cons library ext div NY State Library '46-48. American Psychol Assn (F)—NY Acad Sci(F)—Internat Council Women Psychol(F)—NY Psychol Assn—Eastern Psychol Assn—ALA—NY Library Assn—Sigma Xi. School of Library Service, Columbia University, NYC 27.

20 BRYAN, Edwin H(orace), Jr. Geography, natural history, and bibliography of Pacific Islands (Polynesia and Micronesia). b'98. BS '20 (Coll Hawaii); PhB '21 (Yale); MS '24 (U Hawaii); '29-30 (Stanford U). Member scientific expeditions various

Pacific Islands since '23; associate in bibliography South Pacific Commission since '49; during World War II compiled gazetteer of place names in Pacific; prepared geographic section, maps and gazetteer of Economic Survey of Micronesia reports. Author books and articles in field. Entomology Bernice P Bishop Mus '19-27, curator of collections '27-41, asso in Pacific geog since '47; research Econ Survey Micronesia US Comml Co '46-47; Honolulu officer Nat Research Council, Pacific Sci Bd '47-48, cons in Pacific geog and bibliog since '48. Am Geog Soc—Hawaiian Entomol Soc (pres '28) — Hawaiian Bot Soc — Hawaiian Anthrop Soc — Hawaiian Meteorol Soc — Hawaiian Acad Sci (pres '34). 2721 Ferdinand Av., Honolulu 54, Hawaii.

21 BRYAN, John Albury. American architecture; History of ironmaking; History of the Mississippi Valley. b'90. Student '13-15 (Atelier St Louis Arch Club); '15-17 (Columbia U). Author: Missouri's Contribution to American Architecture '28; also articles in field. Research arch with Nat Park Service US Dept Interior since '36. AIA—Soc Arch Historians—Mo Hist Soc. Old Courthouse, 415 Market St., St. Louis.

22 BRYAN, Joseph Gerard. Statistical meteorology. b'16. SB '38 (MIT); EdM '42 EdD '50 (Harv). Co-author: Short Range and Extended Weather Forecasting by Statistical Methods. Div indsl coop MIT since '42, asst dir statis lab since '47; weather research US AAF; supervisor MIT unit Washington and connected with Weather Div USAAF '42-45. Inst Math Statis—Am Statis Assn—Psychometric Soc — Am Meteorol Soc. Massachusetts Institute of Technology, Cambridge 39, Mass.

23 BRYAN, Leslie Aulls. Aviation economics; Water transportation; Traffic management. b'00. BS '23—MS '24—LLB '39 (Syracuse U); PhD—30—Security Owner Fellow '29-30 (Am U). Author: Aerial Transportation '25; Industrial Traffic Management '29; Principles of Water Transportation '39, also articles in field. Transportation cons Nat Resources Planning Bd '42-44, Syracuse and Onondaga County Planning Bd '43-44, NY State Dept Commerce '44-46; aviation advisor Joint Legislative Com Interstate Cooperation '45-46, dir of aviation, state of New York, '45; cons Inst Air Age Activities since '46; aviation com for Ill State C of C '46-49; dir Institute Aviation Univ Ill since '46; cons Air Cargo Research since '47; dir Flying Farmers of Prairie Farmer Land since '47; cons and adv bd Funk and Wagnall's New Standard Ency since '47. NY State Aviation Council (pres '44-46, hon mem '47)—Nat Aeronautics Assn—Aircraft Owners and Pilots Assn—Am Assn Airport Execs—Nat Assn U Adminstrs Aviation Edn (pres '48-49) —Am Soc Traffic and Transportation (bd examiners since '47)—Am Soaring Soc—Aviation Writers Assn. University of Illinois, 318 Engineering Hall, Urbana, Ill.

24 BRYAN, William A. Physical geography; Climatology; Land use; Pleistocene geology. b'17. AB '40 (Princeton)—MS '42 (Northwestern). Studies on polio and climate, land use in central Pennsylvania, collaborator on Navy course, Foundations of National Power. Author articles in field. US Army Map Service supervisor at Chicago branch '42; Prof geog and geol Marlboro college since '49. Sigma XI—Am Soc Profl Geog—Soc Am Mil

Engrs—AAUP. Marlboro College, Marlboro, Vt.†

10 BRYANT, Billy. American theater (Ohio and Mississippi showboats). b'85. Member troupe known as Four Bryants, owned showboats Princess and Valley Belle, touring all river valley towns '01-42, Cincinnati '30-42, Chicago winters '32-34 and NYC '33; licensed master and pilot from Pittsburgh to New Orleans and all tributaries. Author: Children of Old Man River '44; also articles in field. Lecturer since '45. Point Pleasant, W. Va.

11 BRYANT, Harold Child. Western American mammals, birds and reptiles (Food habits, economic value); United States national parks; Natural resource conservation; California game birds. b'86. BS '08 (Pomona Coll); MS '10—PhD '13 (U Calif). Author: Outdoor Heritage '29. Co-author: (with Joseph Grinnell and Tracy M Storer) The Game Birds of California '18; also articles in field. Supt Grand Canyon Nat Park since '39; advisory bd Greater Ariz Inst since '45. Am Nature Study Soc (vp '45-46)— AAAS(F)—Am Ornithol Union—Calif Acad Sci—Biol Soc Washington—Am Soc Mammalogists — Wildlife Soc — Cooper Ornithol Club (bd govs since '27)—Audubon Soc Washington (hon vp)—Audubon Assn Pacific—Ariz Nat Hist Soc—Phi Beta Kappa—Sigma Xi. Grand Canyon, Ariz.†

12 BRYANT, Louis Ralph. Pomology (sour cherries, grapes, tomato fruit rot, fruit tree pollination, fertilization). b'95. BS '31—MS '32—PhD '34 (U Ill). Author articles in field. Asst prof hort Colo A&M Coll '34-38, asso prof '38-44, prof '44-45; asso prof hort State Coll Wash since '45. Am Soc Hort Sci—Sigma Xi. Department of Horticulture. State College of Washington, Pullman, Wash.†

13 BRYANT, Margaret M. Linguistics; Folklore; Proverbs; English language (Grammar, usage, dialects); Semantics. b'00. AB '21 (Winthrop SC State Coll for Women); AM '25— PhD '31 (Columbia); student (U Mich, U Wis); Traveled British Isles, Europe, Africa, North and South America, Guatemala, Mexico, Japan and China. Author: English in the Law Courts '30; Essays Old and New '40; A Functional English Grammar '45; Proverbs and How to Collect Them '45; Modern English and Its Heritage '48. Co-author: Psychology of English '40; Prose Pieces '41. Also articles in field. Asso prof Eng Brooklyn College; mem advisory bd American Speech '43-44. Linguistic Soc Am—Nat Council Teachers Eng (dir '46, now Chairman College Section, Chairman Current English Usage Com)—Am Folklore Soc (mem council)—Coll Eng Assn—Modern Lang Assn (mem com Proverbs in Comparative Lit II: Popular Lit Group, past sec, chmn, Present Day Eng Sect)— AAUW—AAUP—Eng Inst—Dialect Soc (chmn com proverbial sayings)— NY Folklore Soc—Philol Soc England —Internat Soc General Semantics. Granted scholarship by Am Council Learned Socs '39. 1 Montague Terrace, Brooklyn.☺

14 BRYANT, Reece L(awrence). Poultry husbandry and genetics. b'98. Student '19-21 (Western Ky State Teachers Coll); BS '23 (U Ky); MS— PhD '27 (Cornell U). Research on use of peanut meal as a source of protein in starting mashes for chicks, comparison of mortality of single comb white leghorn growing pullets and laying hens, breeding leghorn chickens to increase life span, effect

of washing on keeping quality of hen's eggs, fishy flavor in turkey meat caused by feeding menhaden fish meal, a study of egg cooling methods, a forced-air system for poultry house ventilation. Author articles in field. Asst and asso prof poultry husbandry Va Polytechnic Inst '28-46; asst and asso poultry husbandman Va Agrl Expt Sta '29-46; prof poultry husbandry and chmn dept ND Agrl Coll since '46, poultry husbandman ND Agrl Expt Sta since '46. Poultry Sci Assn—ND Acad Sci. State College Station, Fargo, N.D.

15 BRYDER, Christian Jensen. History, identification, appraisal, and repair of rare violins. b'89. Ed pub schs Denmark. Research on repair of violins and bows, advisor to US Treasury, Smithsonian Institute on violin appraisals, advisor to Chicago Police Department and Federal Bureau of Investigation on ancestry and value of stolen violins. Author: articles in field. Curator Lyon and Healy since '45. 6044 S. Justine St., Chicago 36.

16 BRYSON, Lyman (Lloyd). Adult education; Radio communications. b'88. AB '10—AM '15 (U Mich); LLD '43 (Occidental). Traveler and lecturer on Junior Red Cross America, Europe and Asia. Author: Adult Education '36; Which Way America? '39; The New Prometheus '41. Co-author: Working for Democracy '41; Science and Freedom '47. Editor The People's Library; also articles in field. Ext lecturer U Calif '25-32; asso dir San Diego Mus '28, dir '29-30; dir U Calif Summer Sch Adult Edn '31-32; vis prof Edn Teachers Coll Columbia '34-35; prof Edn since '35; chief Bur Spl Operations OWI '42, counsellor pub affairs CBS. AAAS(F)—Am Assn Adult Edn (pres '44-46)—Inst Intercultural Studies (pres)—Phi Beta Kappa. Winner Nelson C Field poetry prize U Mich '09. 450 Riverside Dr., NYC 27.☺

17 BRYSON, Vernon. Bacterial genetics; Aerosols; Chemotherapy; Mutation; Antibiotics. b'13. AB '34 (U Calif); AM '36—PhD '44 (Columbia). Research on aerosols for Chemical Warfare Service, on decontamination of atmospheres containing pathogenic bacteria, aerosolization and inhalation of medicinal agents, including penicillin, chemotherapy of bacterial infection in bone, synergism of antibiotics and synthetic detergents, chemical induction of mutations in bacteria and genetics of microorganisms, bacterial resistance. Research asso dept genetics Carnegie Inst Washington Cold Spring Harbor NY '42-43; research biol The Biol Lab since '43; mem cons staff Huntington Hosp. Genetics Soc Am—Am Soc Zool—Soc Am Bact—Soc Study Evolution—NY Acad. Awarded Newberry Prize Columbia '39. The Biological Laboratory, Cold Spring Harbor, N.Y.☺

18 BUC, George Leo. Spectrophotometry. b'12. BS '33—PhD '39 (Rutgers U); MA '34 (Columbia). Research on direct spectrographic determination of copper and manganese in dyestuff, uses of retardation plates in spectrophotometry, determination of slit shape and width, calibration of wave length, measurement of dichroic samples, phenomenon of bronze in surface coatings. Granted patents (with Stearns) on photometric apparatus and spectrophotometers, photometric apparatus giving reading and invariant with azimuth on polarizing samples, flickering beam spectrophotometers for measurement of bronze. Author articles in field. Asst chief physicist Calco Chem Div Am Cyana-

mid Bound Brook NJ since '46; instr Rutgers U Coll since '46. Optical Soc Am—Am Inst Physics—Soc Applied Spectroscopy (ed since '46)—AAAS— Sigma Xi.

19 BUCHANAN, Ben F(ranklin). Corn products; Wheat products; Monosodium glutamate. b'08. AB '33 (U Kan); PhD '38 (Ia State Coll). Research and product development starch, sugars, syrups, proteins, amino acids and oils from corn and wheat, development expanded uses for monosodium glutamate and derivatives in all types food preparations. With Am Maize Products Co '38-46, dir research '45-46; tech service dir Amino Div Internat Minerals and Chem Corp since '46. ACS—AAAS—Am Assn Cereal Chem—Inst Food Tech. International Minerals and Chemical Corp., 20 N. Wacker Dr., Chgo 6.

20 BUCHANAN, David Maclachlan. Plastics (Chemical, electrical, and mechanical properties). b'98. Student (Pratt Inst). Research in proper selection of plastic material (Chemical, electrical, mechanical physical properties) for industrial uses; Product design, mold engineering, molding processes and fabricating methods. Cons Bakelite Div, Union Carbide and Carbon Corp since '25. Soc Plastics Industry. Bakelite Division Union Carbide and Carbon Corp., 30 E. 42nd St., New York 17. H: 41-12 68th St., Woodside Long Island, N.Y.

21 BUCHANAN, Marion Alexander. Chemistry of wood. b'08. BA '30 (Ill Coll); MS '31—PhD '33 (U Ia). Author articles in field. Research asso Inst Paper Chem Appleton Wis since '34. Am Chem Soc—Tech Assn Pulp and Paper Ind—Am Leather Chem Assn— AAAS. Institute Paper Chemistry, Appleton, Wis.†

22 BUCHANAN, Mark Twain. Agricultural economics; Farming (Modern methods). b'15. BS '37 (U Mo); PhD '40 (Cornell). Research on price flexibility, international price movements, marketing, marketing and agricultural economics, apple and turkey production Washington, modern methods specialized and diversified farming. Author articles in field. Asst agrl econ State Coll Wash '40-42, ext marketing specialist '42, asso prof agrl econ, asso agrl econ exptl sta '42-43, head dept agrl econ, chmn div exptl sta '43-46, v-dir Inst Agrl Sci, dir agrl expt stas since '46. Am Econ Assn— Am Farm Econ Assn—Am Assn Farm Mgrs and Rural Appraisers—West Farm Econ Assn—AAAS—Sigma Xi. State College of Washington, Pullman, Wash.

23 BUCHHOLTZ, Walter Frederick. Plant pathology (Soil-borne pathogens, root diseases). b'08. BS '29—MS '30 —PhD '35—research fellow '29-30 (Ia State Coll); '30-31 (U Chicago). Author articles in field. Asso prof bot and plant path Ia State Coll since '45. Am Phytopath Soc—Canadian Phytopath Soc—Ia Acad Sci—Sigma Xi— Phi Kappa Phi—Gamma Sigma Delta. Department of Botany, Iowa State College, Ames, Ia.†

24 BUCHSBAUM, Ralph. Tissue culture (Radiation); Photomicrography; Invertebrate zoology. b'07. BS '28— PhD '31 (U Chicago). Work in growing living tissues outside body (in vitro), cine and ordinary photomicrography, photography of small living animals, research on effects of radiations on living cells and other tissue culture studies. Author: Animals Without Backbones; Readings in Ecology; Methods of Tissue Culture in Vitro. Research asso dept zool and Inst Radiobiol and Biophysics U Chicago '45-47, asst prof zool '31-47; prof zool dept biol sci U Pitt since '49. Am Soc Zool —Ecol Soc Am—AAAS—AAUP—Biol Photographers Assn—Sigma Xi. University of Pittsburgh, Pitts 13.†

10 BUCHTA, J. William. Physics (Metallic crystals, properties of single crystals). b'95. BS in EE '17—AM '21 (U Neb); PhD '25 (U Minn). Author articles in field. With U Minn since '25, prof and chmn dept physics since '38, chmn U Coll since '41, asst dean senior coll sci lit and arts since '45; asst ed Phys Rev and Rev Modern Physics '31-40, acting ed '41-46. Am Phys Soc(F)—Acoustical Soc Am—Optical Soc Am—AAAS—Am Assn Physics Teachers (pres, '48). Physics Department, University of Minnesota, Mpls 14.☉

11 BUCK, John Lossing. Chinese agriculture (Land utilization, prices and currency, agricultural economics, farm management). b'90. BS '14—MS '25—PhD '33 (Cornell). Monetary advisor to Secretary of Treasury US '34-35; US Treasury representative in China '35-39; advisor Ministry Finance Republic of China '39-40; economic advisor Farmer's Bank of China '45-46; agricultural economist (technical advisor) office foreign agricultural relations US Department of Agriculture '45-46; member China-US Agriculture Mission '46; head land use branch, agriculture division UN Food and Agriculture Organization since '47. Author: Chinese Farm Economy '30; Land Utilization in China (3 vols) '37; Co-author: (with W M Curtiss) Farm Management in China '38. Prof dept agrl econ U Nanking '40-44, on leave since '44; UN FAO since '47. Ministry of Industry Nat Govt China—Chinese Statis Assn—Nat Econ Council—Sigma Xi—Phi Kappa Phi. Decorated with White Cravat with Red and Blue Borders of the Order of Brilliant Jade, Chinese Govt '38; commendation for book '37. Food and Agriculture Organization of United Nations, 1201 Connecticut Av. N.W., Washington.

12 BUCK, Paul Herman. American history (Civil War, history of the South, historiography); University administration and educational policy. b'99. AB '21—AM '22—LLD '43 (Ohio State U); AM '24—PhD '35—LittD '46 (Harvard); LLD '45 (Coe Coll); LLD '46 (Tufts Coll); LittD '47 (Princeton U). Sheldon Traveling Fellow '25-26 (London and Paris). Author: The Road to Reunion '37. Co-author: General Education in a Free Society '45; also articles in field. With Harvard U since '26, prof hist since '42, dean since '42, provost of U since '45. AHA—Mass Hist Soc—Miss Valley Hist Assn—So Hist Assn—Am Agrl Soc—Phi Beta Kappa. Awarded Pulitzer prize in hist '38. 5 University Hall, Cambridge, Mass.☉

13 BUCK, Pearl Sydenstricker (Mrs. Richard J. Walsh). China. b'92. AB '14 (Randolph-Macon Woman's Coll, Lynchburg, Va); MA '26 (Cornell); MA '33 (Yale); LittD '39 (W Va U); LLD '42 (Howard U); LLD '42 (St. Lawrence U). Author: East Wind-West Wind '30; The Good Earth (awarded Pulitzer prize) '31; Sons '32; The Mother '34; A House Divided '35; The Exile '36; This Proud Heart '38; Today and Forever '41; The Chinese Children Next Door '42; What America Means to Me '43; Pavilion of Women '46; Far and Near '47; Peony '48; Kinfolk '49, and others. East and West Assn (pres since '41)—Am Inst Arts Letters — Phi Beta Kappa. Awarded William Dean Howells medal

1935; Nobel award in lit '38. John Day Co., 62 W. 45th St., NYC.

14 BUCK, Peter Henry. Ethnology (Technology); Polynesian arts and crafts. b'80. Student '96-98 (Te Aute Coll, New Zealand); MB '04—ChB '04 —MD '10—DSc '37 (Otago Med Sch U New Zealand); MA '36 (Yale); DSc '39 (U Rochester). Author (under Maori name of Te Rangi Hiroa); Evolution of Maori Clothing '26; Ethnology of Tongareva '32; Introduction to Polynesian Anthrology '45; and others. Dir Bishop Mus Honolulu since '36; prof anthrop Yale U since '36. Royal Soc New Zealand(F)—Royal Anthrop Inst — AAAS — Am Anthrop Assn—Polynesian Soc—Sigma Xi. Decorated Knight Comdr St Michael and St George; received Hector medal anthrop New Zealand; Rivers Memorial medal Royal Anthrop Inst London. B.P. Bishop Museum, Honolulu 17, T.H.

15 BUCK, Richard David. Painting (Restoration, conservation, examination). b'03. MA '34 (Harvard). Research in dimensional response of wood to atmospheric humidity, effectiveness of moisture-excluding coatings suitable for use on painted wood panels, treatment of wood panel paintings, effect of age on hygroscopicity of wood, use of stereo-radiography in examination of paintings; studies on original and later paint in pictures, methods and materials of pre-Raphaelite painters. Author articles in field. Conservator dept conservation Fogg Mus Art since '47; advisor in conservation Nat Gallery London on leave Fogg Mus '49. Fogg Museum of Art, Cambridge 38, Mass.†

16 BUCK, Solon Justus. American history, archives, and historical manuscripts. b'84. AB '04—Am '05 (U Wis); PhD '11 (Harvard). Delegate eighth International Congress Historical Science '38; chairman US delegation 14th International Federation for Documentation '38; United States representative UNESCO International Conference on Archives '48. Author: The Granger Movement '13; Travel and Description 1765-1865 '14; Illinois in 1818 '17; The Agrarian Crusade '19. Co-author: Stories of Early Minnesota '25; Planting of Civilization in Western Pennsylvania '39; also articles in field. Archivist of US '41-48; chief MSS div Library Congress '48-51, asst librarian and cons on manuscripts since '51. AHA (treas)—American Antiquarian Soc—Soc Am Archivists—Agricultural History Society—British Records Assn—Miss Valley and Pa Hist Assns—Hist Socs of Minn, Wis, Okla, and Western Pa—Phi Beta Kappa. 321 "A" St., S. E., Washington 3.

17 BUCKINGHAM, Earle. Mechanical engineering (Gears, dimensions, tolerances and gages). b'87. Student '04-06 (US Naval Acad. Author: Interchangeable Manufacturing '21; Spur Gears '28; Manual of Gear Design—Machinery '37; Production Engineering '42; Analytical Mechanics of Gears '49. Prof mech engring MIT. ASME—SAE. Massachusetts Institute of Technology, Cambridge 39, Mass.

18 BUCKLEY, Charles Robert. Music; Music criticism. b'10. MusB '32 (Am Conservatory Music) AM '41 (U Chicago). Pvt teacher violin since '29; string coach asst condr U Chicago Symphony '31-43; music critic Chicago Herald Am since '45; instr instrumental music Washington High Sch East Chicago Ind since '46. Chicago Herald American 326 W. Madison St., Chicago.†☉

19 BUCKMAN, Stanley J(oseph). Biochemistry and microbiology of wood preservation and paper manufacture. b'08. BS '31—PhD '33 (U Minn). Research in movement of liquids in wood, preservation and other factors affecting durability of wood, nonpressure treatment of wood, microbiology of paper manufacture. Author articles in field. Pres Buckman Labs Inc since '45. ACS—Am Soc Testing Materials—AAAS—Am Wood-Preservers Assn—Soc Am Foresters—Tech Assn Pulp and Paper Ind—Am Pulp and Paper Mill Supts Assn—Sigma Xi —Gamma Sigma Delta—Xi Sigma Pi. Buckman Laboratories, Inc., Memphis 8.

20 BUDDINGTON, Arthur Francis. Petrology; Mineral deposits; Geology (Alaska, Adirondacks New York, Magnetite ore); Igneous rocks (Origin). b'90. PhB '12—ScM '13—ScD (hon) '42 (Brown U); PhD '16 (Princeton U). Author articles in field. Chmn dept geol Princeton U '36-50; prin geologist (part time) US Geol Survey since '45. Geol Soc Am (F, councillor '39-42, vp '43 and '47)—Soc Econ Geol(F)—Am Geophys Union (F, pres volcanol sect '41-44)—Am Mineral Soc (F, councillor '36-40, pres '42)—Am Philos Soc(F)—Nat Acad Scis(F)—AAAS(F). 185 Prospect Av., Princeton, N.J.☉

21 BUDENHOLZER, Roland Anthony. Thermodynamics; Heat pump. b'12. BS in ME '35 (NM State Coll); MS '37—PhD '39 (Calif Inst Tech). Research on Joule Thomson coefficient of methane, of gaseous mixtures of methane and ethane, and methane and n-butane, and in methane-propane systems; losses in cycle of heat pump using ground coil. Author articles in field. Prof mech engring Ill Inst Tech since '47; cons in thermodynamics Armour Research Found since '47; dir, Midwest Power Conf since '48. ASME—Am Soc Engring Edn—Sigma Xi—Tau Beta Pi. Research fellow Am Petroleum Inst, Calif Inst Tech '37-40. Illinois Institute of Technology, 3300 Federal St., Chicago 16.†

22 BUECHLER, Peter R. Tanning (Chemistry of fibrous proteins); Cystine content of hair. b'19. BS '41 (Fordham U); '41-42 (NYU); MS '46 (Denver U); PhD '49 (Cinc U). Resch on cystine content of hair of tuberculous patients; sulfur distribution studies on cattle hair and epidermis, chemical modification of collagen to improve its water resistance, specific group reagents, their application to collagen and subsequent effects on tanning action. Author: The Cystine Content of the Hair of Tuberculous Patients '46; also articles in field. Analytical chem NY Quinine and Chem Works '41-43; asst prof tanning research dept U Cincinnati since '46, Herman Schneider fellow '48; dir surgical biochemistry lab and research asso U Cincinnati since '49. AAAS —Am Chem Soc—Am Leather Chem Assn—Sigma Xi. Surgical Biochemistry Lab., College of Med., University of Cincinnati, Cincinnati 29.†

23 BUECHNER, Helmut Karl. Ecology; Wildlife management. b'18. BS '41 (NY State Coll of Forestry); MS '43— (A&M Coll Tex)—PhD '49 (A&M Coll Okla). Research on relationship of range vegetation to livestock and white-tailed deer '42, on life history, ecology and range use of pronghorn antelope in Trans-Pecos Region of Tex '46-47. Biol Roosevelt Wildlife Forest Exptl Sta Newcomb NY '46; Pisgah Nat Forest Game Preserve Asheville NC '41; dept wildlife management A&M Coll Tex '47; teaching, research dept zool (wildlife) State Coll

Wash since '48. Ecol Soc Am—Am Soc Mammalogists—Wildlife Soc — Pacific Northwest Bird and Mammal Soc— Northwest Sci Assn—Wilderness Soc —Am Soc Range Management. Department of Zoology (Wildlife) State College of Washington, Pullman, Wash. H: 1609 Charlotte St., Pullman, Wash.†

10 BUELL, Carleton Eugene. Synoptic meteorology (Thunderstorms, down drafts). b'10. AB '31 (Oberlin Coll); MA '32 (O State U); PhD '35 (Wash U). Research on determination of vertical velocities in thunderstorms, phase relations between temperature and streamline waves, occurrence of hail in thunderstorms, down drafts caused by heavy rain. Author articles in field. Meteorol Ft Worth Am Airlines Inc '38-39, system chief meteorol NY '39-46; research and development div NM Sch Mines '46-48; div leader Sandia Lab '48-49; asso prof math and astron, U NM since '49. Am Meteorol Soc (Councilor '42-45, '46-49)—NY Acad Sci—Am Math Soc—Math Assn Am. University of New Mexico, Albuquerque, N.M.

11 BUELL, William Collins, Jr. Steel (Liquid). b'83. Student (RI State Coll). Metallurgy of raw steel from pig iron, steel scrap, ferro alloys, and other raw materials, and design of apparatus used in production. Author: The Open-Hearth Furnace (3 vols) '35-39. Cons on prodn and econ of raw steel. AIMME. 2300 Chester Av., Cleveland 1.

12 BUERGER, Martin Julian. Crystallography (X-ray, structure); Mineralogy. b'03. BS '25 — MS '27 — PhD '29 (MIT). Explored central Newfoundland, making mineral and glaciation surveys, Frobisher Bay, Baffin Island with attention to southern ice caps and glaciers; research on crystallography, mineralogy, X-ray diffraction, crystal structure, geology. Holds US patents on articles of nonmetallic mineral compounds and method of producing same; inventor of cameras and apparatus used in X-ray diffraction and crystal structure analysis. Author: Crystal Structure Analysis '50; X-Ray Crystallography '42; Optical Identification of Crystalline Substances '39; also articles in field. Instr geol MIT '28-29, asst prof mineralogy and petrography '29-35; asso prof '35-44, prof mineralogy and crystallography since '44. American Crystallographic Assn—Am Phys Soc—Mineralog Soc Am(F)—Geolog Soc Am(F)—Am Acad Arts Sci(F). 77 Massachusetts Av, Cambridge 39, Mass. H: Lincoln, Mass.☉

13 BUERGER, Newton Weber. Crystallography; Mineralogy; X-ray diffraction. b'07. SB '33—SM '34—PhD '39 (MIT). Research in crystallographic relations between cubanite segregation plates, chalcopyrite matrix and secondary chalcopyrite twins, low-chalcocite and high-chalcocite. Author articles in field. Asst dept geol MIT '34-35; lecturer mineral and petrography Queen's U '37-39, mineral and crystallography '39-41, asst prof '41-46; asso prof crystallography and metall US Naval Postgrad Sch since '46. Lt comdr USNR '42-46. Mineral Soc Am(F)—Crystallographic Soc Am (councillor)—Am Soc X-ray and Electron Diffraction—Sigma Xi. U.S. Naval Postgraduate School, Monterey, Cal. H: Pebble Beach, Cal.†

14 BUFF, Karl Edward. Adhesives. b'07. BS '30 (Elmhurst Coll); MS '31 —student '32-34 (Inst Paper Chem, Lawrence Coll); Research on adhesives, plastic and rubber compounds, paper, textiles and fibrous materials related to automotive production work. Granted patents. Chem Alton Box Board & Paper Co Carlyle Ill '34-36; exec chem Nat Automotive Fibres Inc Detroit. Tech Assn Pulp & Paper Industry—Am Assn Textile Chem and Colorists—Am Soc Quality Control. 19925 Hoover Av., Detroit 5.

15 BUFFUM, Charles Walbridge. Cartography; Map classification and cataloging. b'00. AB '22 (Amherst Coll); BS '31 (Syracuse U). Developed map classification scheme Library Congress, collaborated development map cataloging practice Library Congress. Instr lib sci Syracuse U '31-33; Library Congress since '35, map cataloger '41-43, head map processing sect since '44. ALA—Spl Lib Assn—DC Lib Assn—Assn Am Geographers. Library of Congress, Washington.

16 BUFFUM, Douglas Labaree. Romance languages; Old French literature; French texts. b'78. AB AM '98. (U Va) PhD '04 (Johns Hopkins). Prof romance languages Princeton '12-44 prof emeritus since '44; chief examiner French Coll Entrance Examining Bd '16-26. Editor: French Short Stories '07; Hugo's Les Miserable '08; Michelet's Histoire de France '09; Contes Francais '15; Stories from Balzac '17; Stories from Merimee '20; Le Roman de la Violette '28; Roman d'Alexandre '37. Modern Lang Assn—AAUP—Societe des Anciens Textes Francais—Phi Beta Kappa. 60 Hodge Rd., Princeton, N.J.†☉

17 BUGBEE, Percy. Fire prevention; Fire protection. b'98. BS '20 (MIT). Research on fireproof construction, fire hazards, fire waste control, fire prevention education. With Nat Fire Protection Assn since '24, gen mgr from '40. Soc Fire Protection Engrs— Brit Inst Fire Engrs (hon mem)— French Nat Soc des Sapeurs—Pompiers (hon Mem)—Dominion Fire Prevention Assn (hon mem). 60 Batterymarch St., Boston 10.

18 BULBULIAN, Arthur H. Medical museums; Facial prosthesis. b'00. BS '25—MS '26 (Middlebury Coll); DDS '31 (U Minn). Co-invenor (with Lovelace and Boothby) BLB Oxygen Mask for oxygen therapy and high altitude flying; designer A-14 oxygen mask used by USAAF during World War II. Author: Facial Prosthesis '45; co-author Atlas of Congenital Anomalies of the Heart and Great Vessels; also articles in field. Dir Mayo Found Mus Hygiene Med since '36; mem staff Mayo Clinic since '35. Am Coll Dentists(F) — Am Asso Museums — Am Dental Assn—Sigma Xi. Mayo Clinic, Rochester, Minn.

19 BULEY, R. Carlyle. Recent United States and midwestern American history; American economic history (Life insurance, Midwest industries). b'93. AB '14—AM '16 (Ind U); PhD '25 (U Wis). Author: The Old Northwest; Pioneer Period, 1815-1840, two volumes, '50; The American Life Convention—A Study in The History of Life Insurance, two volumes, '53; co-author: The Midwest Pioneer: His Ills, Cures and Doctors '47; also articles in field. With Indiana U since '25, now prof Am hist. AHA—Indiana Hist Soc—Miss Valley Hist Assn. Awarded Pulitzer Prize in history, '51. Indiana University, Bloomington, Ind.

20 BULL, Edith Hellman. Vertebrate paleontology, evolution, and taxonomy (Fossil fish). b'14. BA '32 (Skidmore Coll); MA '33—grad work '33-34 (Columbia U). Author articles in field. Cataloger fossil fish collection Am Mus Nat Hist NY '44-46, dept sec div fishes and aquatic biol '46-47; editor Scientific Manuscripts and bibliog since '47. Soc Vertebrate Paleontol. 49 Merrall Road, Far Rockaway, N.Y.†

21 BULL, John Lewis, Jr. Birds of Westchester County and Long Island, New York; Feathers; Artificial flowers; Butterflies (New York City region). b'14. Spl research work (Am Mus Nat Hist NY). Author articles in field. Research dept ornithol Am Mus Nat Hist since '35; specialist in feathers and artificial flowers US Customs NY since '42. Linnaean Soc NY (sec '43, '44)—Am Ornithol Union —Eastern Bird Banding Assn. 49 Merrall Road, Far Rockaway, N.Y.†

22 BULL, Ludlow (Seguine). Ancient Egypt (History, language, hieroglyphic script, hieratic script, religion); Classical Arabic language. b'86. AB '07 (Yale); LLB '10 (Harvard); PhD '22 (U Chicago). Expeditions Oriental Institute University of Chicago to Egypt, Mesopotamia, Syria '19-20, Egypt '23. Co-author: The Rhind Mathematical Papyrus, vol II '29. Editor: Publications of the Egyptian Department Metropolitan Museum (12 vols); also articles in field. Asso curator Egyptian dept Met Mus NYC since '28; research asso rank prof Egyptology Yale since '36, curator Yale Egyptian Collection since '25. Am Geog Soc(F)—Am Oriental Soc (del to centenary Royal Asiatic Soc '23, rec sec '25-26, vp '38-39, pres '39-40)— Archeol Inst Am—Soc Bibl Lit—Egypt Exploration Soc (London)—Palestine Exploration Soc (Jerusalem) — Soc Reine Elisabeth (Brussells). Litchfield, Conn.☉

23 BULL, Storm. Johann Sebastian Bach (Comparative analysis of various editions of works); Bela Bartok. b'13. Student '19-31 (Am Cons Music); '27, '28, '30 (Chicago Musical Coll)—'31, 33 (Sorbonne)—'31-33 (Ecole Normale de Musique); '33-35 (U Budapest). Author articles in field. Private teacher music '35-40; Chicago Conserv Music '40-42; Baylor U '45-47; prof music U Colo since '47. Am Coll Musicians. College of Music, University of Colorado, Boulder, Colo.

24 BULLARD, Fred Mason. Vulcanology; Sedimentary petrography; Stratigraphy (Cretaceous); Geology of western United States. b'01. BS '21— MS '22 (U Okla); PhD '28 (U Mich). Author articles in field. With U Tex since '24, now prof geol, grad faculty since '42. Geol Soc Am(F)—Mineral Soc Am(F)—Am Assn Petroleum Geol. Studied Central American volcanoes under grant from U Tex Research Inst '46, Paricutin Volcano under grant Geol Soc Am and U Tex Research Inst '44-45. Department of Geology, University of Texas, Austin, Tex.†

25 BULLEN, Adelaide Kendall. Fatigue (Nervous and mental); Social anthropology; Physical anthropology. b'08. '25-26, '29 (Simmons Coll Sch Pub Health); AB '43 (Radcliffe Coll); '43-46, '47-48 (Harvard). Research, Anthropological study female Army personnel '46; industrial studies on nervous and mental fatigue '49. Author: A Cross-Cultural Approach to the Problem of Stuttering '45; also articles in field. Research anthrop Health Center Radcliffe Coll '43-44; research anthrop Fatigue Laboratory Harvard U '44-46; civilian cons anthrop to War Dept '46; analysis of data collected and writing of report dept anthrop Peabody Museum Harvard U '46-48. Am Anthrop Assn(F)—Royal Anthrop Inst(F)—Am Assn Physical Anthrop—Soc Applied Anthrop—Soc for Research Psychosomatic Med—Soc Research Child Development — Am

Acad Polit Social Sci—Sigma Xi. Florida State Museum, Gainesville, Fla.

10 BULLIET, Clarence Joseph. Modern art; Art masterpieces (Italian; French). b'83. AB '05 (Ind U). Author: Apples and Madonnas '27; Venus Castina '28; The Courtezan Olympia '30; Art Masterpieces of the World's Fair '34; The Significant Moderns '36; Masterpieces of Italian Art '39; French Art from David to Matisse '41; Eccentrics in Modern Art '49; Art Treasures from Vienna '50, and others. Art critic Chicago Daily News since '32, motion picture critic '39-42, music critic since '41; contbg critic Art Digest NY since '46. Phi Beta Kappa. Chicago Daily News, Chgo.⊙ Deceased.

11 BULLOCK, B(enjamin) F(ranklin). Education (American rural, Southern Negro). b'88. BS '13 (U Minn); MA '31 (Columbia); student (Cornell U, Rutgers U). Author: Practical Farming for the South '46; A Survey of Rural Education in America, With Suggestions for the South '49; The Rural School and its Community '49; also articles in field. Prof rural edn Atlanta U since '32. Am Teachers Assn (first dir dept rural life activities)— Ga Teachers Edn Assn—Am Country Life Assn—NEA. Atlanta University, Atlanta 3.

12 BULLOCK, Harry Leslie. Plastics fabrication; Separation of dry materials; Colloid milling. b'95. Student '14-17 (Columbia U). Research on grinding, dispersion, and emulsions of colloids, processes and equipment for difficult separations of dry materials, formation of emulsions of plastic solutions, production of polished surface on continuous lengths of plastic, methods and machinery for forming articles of large diameter in large quantity, improved methods of plastics extrusion employing high frequency heating and on insuring uniform chemical reaction in columns and application of columns to fume and dust collections. Granted patent on dielectric electrostatic separator for dry solids, other equipment. Author articles in field. Development engr Celluloid Co '19-26; cons '28-31; chief engr Tech Sales Corp '31-34; investigations colloid milling '34-42; director Bullock-Smith Assocs. Society Plastics Industry — ASME. 136 Liberty St., NYC 6. H: 468 Riverside Dr., NYC 27.

13 BULOT, Francis Henry. Water supply; Sewage treatment. b'90. BS '14 (U Ill). Research on population trends; water supply for industrial housing projects. With Green and Opper, Altis, Seaberg and Bulot '23-26; Gordon and Bulot '26-37; Consoer, Townsend and Assos '37-39; private practice '39-42 and since '46. Am Soc CE—Am Waterworks Assn—Nat Sewage Works Assn — Engrs and Archts Assn—W Soc Engrs—Tau Beta Pi—Sigma Tau. 411 W. 5th St., Los Angeles 13.

14 BUMPUS, Dean Franklin. Oceanography; Hydrography; Productivity of marine areas. b'12. AB '35 (Oberlin Coll); '35-37 (Brown U); '39 Harvard). Reconnaissance Mediterranean Sea hydrography, chemistry, productivity '47-48; senior scientist, oceanography in support of radiological safety section, Operation Crossroads '46; codesigner the plankton sampler, instrument for quantitative plankton investigations. Author articles in field. Oceanographer Woods Hole Oceanog Inst since '37. Am Soc Limnol Oceanog —AAAS—Am Geophys Union. Woods Hole Oceanographic Institution, Woods Hole, Mass. H: Quissett Av,†

15 BUNCE, E(arl) H(amlin). Zinc metallurgy. b'91. BS '13 (Cornell). Invented zinc vapor condensors, reheating furnaces for zinc oxide, mechanical furnaces for production zinc oxide, use of zinc pigments, briquetting of charges for metallurgical furnaces, vertical retort process for production slab zinc. Author articles in field. Research investigator and metallurgist The New Jersey Zinc Co '13-17, asst chief research div '18-27, chief research div '27-28, gen mgr tech dept since '28. Technical Department, New Jersey Zinc Co. (of Pa.), Central Laboratory, Palmerton, Pa.

16 BUNCH, Marion E. Psychology of learning and memory. b'02. AB '25 (Ky U); AM '26 (Wash U); PhD '34 (Chicago U). Research in human learning and memory, learning, memory and abnormal behavior in animals. Author articles in field. Prof psychol U Ill '48-49; prof psychol Washington U since '49. Am Psychol Assn — A A A S — Midwestern Psychol Assn—So Soc Philos and Psychol— Sigma Xi. Department of Psychology, Washington University, St. Louis.

17 BUNCHE, Ralph Johnson. International organization and trusteeship; Colonial policy; Africa; Palestine; Indonesia; Race relations. b'04. AB '27 (U Calif LA); AM '28—PhD '34 (Harvard). Staff member Carnegie Corporations Survey of Negro in America, southern US '39; adviser US Delegation 27th Session International Labor Conference Philadelphia '45; top-ranking director Department Trusteeship United Nations since '47; principal secretary United Nations Palestine Commission since '47, acting mediator since '48. Instr polit sci Howard U '28-29, prof since '38, head dept since '29; co-dir Inst Race Relations Swarthmore '36; sr social sci analyst in charge research on Africa and other colonial areas Brit Empire sect OSS '41-44, deputy chief Near East-Africa sect '43; asso chief div dependent area affairs Dept State '45-47. Department of State, Washington; Department of Trusteeship, United Nations, N.Y.⊙

18 BUNGER, Mills Emerson. Water (Uses, evaporation). b'86. EM (Colo Sch Mines); (U Denver). Design and construction irrigation structures and distribution water to users; engineer on Gila Project, Big Thompson Project; prepared plan and made preliminary survey for bringing 1,000,000 acre feet water from Colorado River to Central Arizona; determination water supply for certain industrial purposes in about 170 counties in 22 states; research to determine evaporation from land areas and reprecipitation within Colorado River Basin. Expert on water problems US Corps Engrs.; sr engr, planning engr, asst supervising engr US Bur Reclamation Denver; asst chief engr Van Sant Houghton Constrn Co San Francisco; engr mgr Model Land and Irrigation Co Colo; cons engr for water problems Ford Bacon and Davis. Am Geophys Union—Colo Soc Engrs. Ford, Bacon and Davis, Inc., 39 Broadway, N.Y.C. 6.

19 BUNKER, Milton Newman. Grapho analysis. b'92. Grad several penmanship schls, bus colls. Developed grapho analysis starting '10; developed law of evaluation and strokes values in relation to handwriting. Author: Case Book Number 1 '36; You Wrote It Yourself '39; Grapho Analysis Dictionary '47; also articles in field. Founded Am Inst Grapho Analysis '29, inc '31. 2 Wilhoit Bldg., Springfield, Mo.

20 BURCALOW, Frank Victor. Grassland farming; Heavy duty turf (Air-

ports, highways). b'09. BS '32—MS '38 (U Wis). Representative Fourth International Grassland Congress Aberystwith Wales '37. Ext agron and soil conservationist dept agron Wis Coll Agr U Wis since '35. Am Soc Agron (adv com to FAO UN since '48). Agronomy Building, Madison 6, Wis.

21 BURCH, Guy Irving. Population; Human migrations; Natural resources conservation; Eugenics. b'99. Student '14-16 (Culver Mil Acad); '19-23, '25 (Columbia U). Supplied Joint Army and Navy Selective Service Committee with age group data for original draft bill '40; chairman Population-Resources Roundtable '47. Author: Human Breeding and Survival '47. Co-author: (with E Pendell) Population Roads to Peace or War '45; also articles in field. Editor Population Bulletin since '40; founder, dir Population Reference Bur since '29; mem Council on Population Policy '35-36. Population Assn Am (F '31-35, charter and organizing mem)—Am Eugenics Soc (dir '32-47, sec '33-36). 1507 M St., N.W., Washington 5.

22 BURCH, John Quincy. Sea shells. b'94. Student '10-15 (U Tex); '15-16 (U Calif). Editor of Minutes of Conchological Club of Southern California since '41; research on taxonomy of mollusks and described number of new species. Am Malacological Union (pres Pacific div '50)—Malacological Soc London—Conchological Soc Gt Brit and Irleand—Calif Acad Sci—S Calif Acad Sci—Soc Systematic Zool—Conchological Club S Calif (pres '40). 1584 W. Vernon Av., Los Angeles 62.

23 BURCH, Paul Randolph. Conchology; Herpetology (Allegheny Plateau); Snails and toads of Virginia. b'98. BS '20 (Randolph Macon Coll); MS '27—teaching fellow '26-28—PhD '30—research fellow Mt Lake Biol Sta '35-46 (U Va). Discovered and named Polygyra virginiana, a new mollusc Author articles in field. Prof biol Radford Coll since '28. Va Acad Sc— AAAS(F)—Am Genetic Assn. Radford College, Radford, Va. H: 614 W. Fourth St.

24 BURCHFIELD, Louise H. Portrait miniatures. Author article: Portrait Miniatures, Origin and Technique '50. Asst curator of paintings Cleve Mus Art '41-49, asso curator paintings since '50, prepared catalogue Portrait Miniatures, The Edward B Greene Collection '51; Guggenheim fellowship for study portrait miniatures '52. Royal Society Miniature Painters Sculptors and Gravers London (hon). The Cleveland Mus of Art, Cleve 6.

25 BURD, Edward Wasson. Steel (High carbon). b'05. BS (Met E) '30— BA '30 (O State U). Hardenability studies effecting high and medium carbon alloy steels. Metall engr Wheeling Steel Corp '30-33; product metall Am Steel & Wire Co '34-40; metall dir Trico Products Corp '41-47; metall engr and sales rep Ajax Engring Corp since '48. Soc Automotive Engrs—Am Ordnance Assn—Am Soc Metals—Alpha Chi Sigma. Professional engr O. 42 Ivy Lea Rd., Kenmore 23, N.Y.

26 BURDEN, William Armistead Moale. Commerce (Aviation); Latin American airways. b'06. AB '27 (Harvard). Author: The Struggle for Airways in Latin America '43; also articles in field. Charge of analysis of aviation financing Brown Bros., Harriman & Co, NYC '28-32; aviation research in Europe, Far East, S Am preparing basic surveys on air transportation and mfg industries Scudder, Stevens & Clark NYC '32-39; vp and dir Nat Aviation Corp, aviation investment trust '39-41; dir United Airlines Transport Corp '35-39; vp Defense Supplies Corp (subsidiary RFC) Washington, in charge div Am Republics Aviation (active in eliminating Axis influence in Latin Am air transportation) '41-42; spl aviation asst to Sec Commerce with supervision of Civil Aeronautics Admnstrn, Weather Bur, Coast and Geod Survey '42-43; asst Sec Commerce '43-47; now aviation cons Smith, Barney & Co. Inst Aeronautical Sci—SAE—Council Fgn Relations. Mus of Modern Art Foreign Service Ednl Found. William A M Burden & Co., 75 West St., NYC.

10 BURDETTE, Franklin L. American politics and political science. b'11. BA '34 (Marshall Coll); MA '35 (U Neb); '35-36 (U NC) '36 (U Chicago); MA '37—PhD '38 (Princeton). Author: Filibustering in the Senate '40; Political Parties: An American Way '45; Lobbyists in Action '50; Election Practices in Maryland '50. Editor: Education for Citizen Responsibilities '42. Co-editor An American Way of Life since '47; exec sec Nat Found Edn Am Citizenship '40-46, ed publ since '46; ed pol sci textbooks Van Nostrand Co since '48; also articles in field. Instr politics Princeton '36-37, '38-39, fellow polit '37-38, research asso Princeton Local Govt Survey '39-40; asst prof hist polit sci Butler U '40-43, asso prof '43-46; asso prof govt and politics U Md '46-47, prof since '47, department head since '50. Academy Political Sci—Am Acad Polit Social Sci—AHA—Am Polit Sci Assn (ed biog directory '45, '48)—Am Soc Pub Adminstrn—Nat Council Social Studies—Nat Ednl Assn—Nat Municipal League—Ind Merit System Assn (mem bd '41-46)—Ind War Hist Commn (mem bd '43-46)—Fgn Policy Assn (sec Ind br '44-46)—Soc Advancement Edn—So Pol Sci Assn—Pi Sigma Alpha (nat sec since '46). Awarded Bryan prize polit sci U NC '36. University of Maryland, College Park, Md.◎

11 BURDICK C(harles) Lalor. Chemical engineering; Chemistry of high polymers; Nitrogenous fertilizers. b'92. BS '11 (Drake U); BS '13—MS '14 (MIT); PhD '15 (U Basel, Switzerland). Chemistry and chemical engineering of nitrogenous fertilizers; technical development of high polymers. Research asso chem MIT and Calif Inst of Tech '16-17; metall engr Guggenheim Bros, NY and Chile '19-24; vp and cons engr Anglo-Chilean Consol Nitrate Corp '24-28; with E I du Pont de Nemours since '29, now sec high polymer committee; dir Equitable Trust Co, Haskell Research Found, Lalor Found, Del Academy Med. AAAS—Am Inst Chem Engrs—Am Chem Soc—Phi Beta Kappa. Nemours Bldg., Wilmington 98, Del.◎

12 BURDICK, E. Douglass. Statistics (Alcoholism, vital, hospital facilities). b'05 BA '26—MA '28 (Wesleyan U); PhD '35 (U Penn). Instr econ and social statis U Pa '30-36, asst prof '36-44, asso prof since '44; asst prof vital statis and biometry U Pa Med Sch since '40; statis research cons Com Hospital Facilities Orgn and Standards Dept of Welfare Pa '46-48; statis C Dudley Saul Found (on alcoholism) since '48. Am Statis Assn—Am Econ Assn—Phi Beta Kappa. Wharton School, University of Pennsylvania, Philadelphia 4, Pa.†

13 BURDICK, Everette Marshall. Citrus processing; Submerged combustion. b'13. BS '35 (U Miami); MS '37—PhD '43 (Purdue U). Research on citrus processing, citrus oils, en-

zymes, sugar, fermentation, submerged combustion in waste utilization, and on naringin, the bitter principle found in grapefruit. Holds patents covering saccharification and separation of wheat starch and gluten, naringin, butylene glycol, ethyl alcohol fermentations, diastatic enzymes, and others. Author articles in field. Research chem US Dept Agr No Regional Research Lab '41-45; research chem US Fruit and Vegetable Lab '45-46; dir research Texsun Citrus Exchange since '46. Am Chem Soc—Am Inst Chem(F)—Inst Food Technol—AAAS —Sigma Xi—Phi Lambda Upsilon. Texsun Citrus Exchange, Weslaco, Tex. H: P.O. Box 26.

14 BURDICK, Raymond Terry. Sugar beets; Economics of ranching; Field crop labor. b'89. BS '12 (Cornell U); MS '32 (Colo A&M Coll); PhD '46 (U Chicago). Research on economics of irrigated agriculture, cattle and sheep ranching; development of equation for estimating field crop labor requirements. Author: Landlord and Tenant Income in Colorado '38; The Economics of Sugar Beet Production in Colorado '39; Possibilities for Cattle Income '40; Factors that Affect Sheep Income '41; Buying a Farm in Colorado '44; Father-and-Son Farm Agreements '46; A New Technique of Field Crop Labor Analysis '47. Asso prof Colo A&M Coll '19-43, prof and head dept econ sociol and hist since '43. AAAS—Am Econ Assn—Am Farm Econ Assn. Colorado A.&M. College, Ft. Collins, Colo.◎

15 BURDICK, William Elliott. Stress analysis; Trucks and castings (Railroad). b'01. AB '25 (Stanford). Studies in static load stresses obtained through use of stresscoat and SR-4 strain gauges; points maximum stress; dynamic stress measurements using electronic recording; inventor spring suspensions; anti-nosing devices; driving wheel counterbalance. With Gen Steel Castings Corp since '26, engr tests since '48. Am Soc ME—Soc Exptl . Stress Analysis. General Steel Castings Corp., Granite City, Ill.†

16 BURFORD, William B., III. Physical and fluorine chemistry; X-ray diffraction. b'16. Student '34-35 (Ind U); PhD '42 (Johns Hopkins). Research on poisoning of nickle hydrogenation catalysts by water vapor, development and use of 600-ampere fluorine cell, synthesis of fluorocarbons, pilot plant synthesis of perfluoro-n-heptane, metallic fluorides in fluorocarbon synthesis. Author articles in field. Asso prof chem Johns Hopkins '47-49; dir Inst for Coop Research since '50. Am Chem Society. Department of Chemistry, Johns Hopkins University, Homewood, Baltimore 18.†

17 BURGER, Alfred. Medicinal chem. b'05. PhD '28 (U Vienna). Research on synthesis of various experimental drugs, their theoretical development, anti-tubercular drugs, anti-malarials, functional drugs, especially analgetics. Author articles in field. Research asso drug addiction lab Nat Research Council U Va '29-38, synthetic analgetics, morphine substitutes, phenanthrene derivatives, asst prof chem '38-46, asso prof since '46. Am Chem Soc—Sigma Xi. Cobb Chemical Laboratory, University of Virginia, Charlottesville, Va.

18 BURGER, Alvin A(rthur). Governmental and municipal budge'ng; Education financing; Public pensions. b'98. '19-20 (Washington U, St Louis); '40-42 (NYU). Served with various state legislative commissions dealing with state budget, tax, education and

pension problems. Author: How to Study Your Municipal Budget; also articles in field. Research dir NJ State C of C since '36, Council of State C's of C, Washington since '47. Governmental Research Assn (treas since '45)—Tax Inst (bd dir since '46)—Am Econ Assn—Am Soc Pub Adminstrn—Acad Polit Sci—Am Acad Polit Social Sci—AAAS—Am Finance Assn—Nat Tax Assn. 1722 H St. NW, Washington.

19 BURGER, Emmett Earl. Electrical engineering (Sealing glass to Metal, lightning arresters). b'93. BS '16 (Penn State Coll). Author articles: Lightning Arresters for Transmission and Distribution Circuits '25; The Expansion Characteristics of Some Common Glasses and Metals '34. Co-author articles: Glass-to-Metal Seals '34; Glass-to-Metal Seals II '41, and others. Entire career with General Electric Co, test course '16-17, switch gear dept '17-18, cons engr dept '18-28, research lab since '28. General Electric Co., Schenectady 5, N.Y.

20 BURGESS, Blandford C. Copper mines (Seepage problems); Chemical control of mineral processing; Mineral resources and mining laws of Guatemala; Mica deposits, mining and processing; Economics of industrial minerals. b'93. Student '13-15 (U Calif). Research on ore milling and water seepage problems pioneer in design and construction feldspar plant providing chemical control of products; consultant ore deposits, asbestos, beryl, kyanite, manganese, talc, tin, tungsten. Author: Mineral Resources of Guatemala '46; Mica Buyer's Guide '49; Tuscaloosa Kaolins of Georgia '50. Contributor: chapters on feldspar and pyrophyllite in Industrial Minerals and Rocks '49. Efficiency engr Old Dominion Co Copper Globe Ariz '18; chief engr Iron Cap Copper Co Copper Hill Ariz '19; field mgr Tenn Mineral Products Co '26-36; vp and dir United Feldspar & Minerals Corp '36-43; vp and gen mgr Appalachian Minerals Co since '47; mining cons since '43; chief Johannesburg dist Def Materials Procurement Agy, Region 3, Johannesburg, S. Africa. AIMME—Am Ceramic Soc (F)—Ga Soc Professional Engrs. Registered professional engr Ga and NC. care American Consulate General, Johannesburg, Union of South Africa.

21 BURGESS, Ernest Watson. Sociology (Human adjustment prediction, human ecology, family, criminology). b'86. AB '08 (Kingfisher Okla Coll); PhD '13 (U Chicago). Editor Marriage and Family Living '39-49. Editor: The Urban Community '26; Personality and the Social Group '29. Author: The Function of Socialization in Social Evolution '16. Co-author: (with R E Park) Introduction to the Science of Sociology '21; (with Park) The City '25; (with A A Bruce, A J Harno and John Landesco) The Workings of the Indeterminate Sentence Law and the Parole System in Illinois '28; (with Leonard S Cottrell) Predicting Success or Failure in Marriage '39; (with H J Locke) The Family '45, and others. AAAS—Chicago Recreation Comm — Chicago Crime Commn—Am Statis Assn—Social Sci Research Council—Sociol Research Assn. 1126 E. 59th St., Chicago 37.◎

22 BURGESS, Harold H. Tropical forestry; Wildlife management; Liberia (People, wild rubber, birds, timber, mammals, history and government, customs); South Korea (Forestry, agriculture, sociology); Pheasants (US and Korean Varieties). b'17.

BS '40—MS '46 (Mich State Coll). Collected various birds and mammals for American Museum of Natural History New York City '42-44; traveled by foot through Kru, Bassa, Kpellie, Buzzi, Mano, Gola and Vai hinterland tribal lands of Liberia; studied plantation rubber; studied, promoted production and purchased wild rubber on trips of 7000 miles through the 17 tribal lands of Liberia '44-46; studied Korean and Oriental forestry techniques '48. Author articles in field. US forestry advisor to Forestry Sect Chungchong Pukto Korea and cpl US Army '48-49. Refuge manager Prairie du Chien since '49. Soc Am Foresters —Soc Wildlife Management. Box 87, Prairie du Chien, Wis.

10 BURGESS, Hovey Mann. Dehydration. b'16. BS '38 (Bowdoin Coll); MA '40 (Columbia). Research in gelatin desserts, pectins, processing changes, dehydration of rice and potatoes, soluble coffee. Chem Gen Foods Corp central labs since '40, now head process tech sect. Central Research Laboratories, General Foods Corp., 1125 Hudson St., Hoboken, N.J.

11 BURGESS, Perry. Leprosy. b'86. Grad—LLD (Baker U). US delegate International Congress on Leprosy Cairo '38; chairman US delegation second Pan American Conference on Leprosy Rio de Janeiro '46: chairman US delegation fifth International Conference on Leprosy, Havana Cuba '48. Author: Who Walk Alone. awarded Discovery Book of '40 by Booksellers Assn, gold medal Soc for Libraries of NY; also articles in field. Elected nat dir Leonard Wood Memorial for Eradication of Leprosy Am Leprosy Found '25, pres and exec officer since '30; cons Office Coordinator Inter-American Affairs '43-45; cons sec of War on Epidemic Diseases (spl mission to Philippines '45). Authors League of Am—Eugene Field Society (hon)—Mark Twain Soc (hon). 1 Madison Av., NYC.

12 BURGESS, Robert Wilbur. Business statistics and economics; Mathematics of statistics. b'87. BA '08 (Brown U); Rhodes scholar '08-11— BA '10 (Oxford); PhD '14 (Cornell). Actuarial studies of company pension plans and machinery depreciation rates, forecasts industrial activity and commodity prices. Author: Introduction to the Mathematics of Statistics '27; also articles in field. Statis, econ Western Elec Co since '24. Maj NA statis br Gen Staff Washington US Army '18-19. Am Math Assn—Am Econ Assn — Econometric Soc — Inst Math Statis—Conf Business Econ—Am Statis Assn(F)—Sigma Xi. 195 Broadway, NYC 7.◉

13 BURKE, Arvid James. Public financing of schools. b'06. BA '28— MA '30 (NY State Coll Teachers); EdD '36 (Columbia); student (Cornell U, Harvard). Research on surveys of public school systems, personnel problems in schools. Author: Defensible Spending For Public Schools '43; A Postwar Program of State Aid for Schools '46. Co-author: (with F W Cyr and P R Mort) Paying For Our Public Schools '38; (with P R Mort and W W Schmidt) An Improved System of State School Finance for New York State '40; (with P R Mort) A Study of Educational Programs Relative to Expenditure Levels '43; also articles in field. Co-dir study financing rural schs NY State '35-36; dir studies NY State Teachers Assn since '36; cons Nations Schs since '39, Ednl Conf Bd NY State since '39, NY State Civil Service Com '43, '47, '49. Am Statis Assn—Am Ednl Research

Assn (com to prepare Review of Ednl Research '49)—NEA (tax edn com since '36)—Tax Inst—Nat Soc Study Edn—Nat Municipal League—Am Soc Pub Adm. 152 Washington Av., Albany 6, N.Y.

14 BURKE, Frances Hart (Mrs Arthur). Quakerism. b'94. AB '16 (Mt Holyoke Coll). Quaker faith (including Mysticism), practice, and past and present objectives, activities, including the American Friends Service Committee Speaker on Quakerism '21-42; exec sec NY Friends Center Assn since '42. New York Friends Center Association, 144 E. 20th St., N.Y.C. 3.

15 BURKE, Mary E. Physically handicapped children (Spastics). Conducted schools over period of 45 years for spastic children; public relations work on the same problem. Co-author: The Exceptional Child '17. Burke School for Exceptional Children, Box 759, Santa Cruz, Cal.

16 BURKHARDT, Charles Henry. Automatic oil heat. b'15. BSc '38 (St John's U); '48 (Pratt Inst). Author: Principles of Automatic Oil Heating '49; Basic Oil Burner Service Procedures '48. Instr heat engring Walter Hervey Jr Coll since '48; cons to various oil burner mfg concerns. Am Soc Heating and Ventilating Engrs. 188-02 64th Ave., Flushing, N.Y.

17 BURKHART, Leland. Fruit physiology and quality (Citrus and pecan culture, temperature and growth); Plant chemistry and nutrition; Subtropical horticulture. b'09. BS '31 (O State U); MS '33 (U NH); PhD '35 (U Chicago). Author articles in field. Asso plant nutrition NC Agr Expt Sta '39-45; head dept hort U Ariz since '49; hort Ariz Agr Expt Sta since '49; asso hort (agent) US Dept Agr Bureau Plant Industry since '45. Am Soc Plant Physio—Am Soc Hort Sci—Soil Sci Soc Am—Sigma Xi. Department of Horticulture, University of Arizona, Tucson, Ariz.†

18 BURKHEAD, Charles Edwin. Agricultural statistics; Popcorn. b'05. AB '38 (Oklahoma City U Okla); '41-42 (U Md). Study of corn yields in Alabama '48; statistical study corn acreage; yield, and production North Carolina and Virginia; analysis and improvement methods for crop production estimates; research on history of policies and programs of US Department of Agriculture; studies on production, marketing, processing, and utilization of popcorn. Author articles: American Soybean Output in the Spotlight '45; Estimating the Corn Corp '46; Crop Yields Push Upward '47; Popcorn Dollars '47. Co-author article: (with J C Scholl) Agricultural Economics Research '49. With crop reporting service USDA since '29, in charge grain crops '43-46, in charge div field crop statis since '46. Am Statis Assn— Nat Grange— Am Farm Econ Assn. Bureau of Agricultural Economics, U. S. Department of Agriculture, 2427 South Bldg., Washington 25.

19 BURKS, Richard Voyles. Eastern European history; Ideological conflict. b'13. '30-31 (Franklin Coll); AB '34 (Miami U Ohio); MA '35—PhD '37 (U Chicago). Research in history of Slavic world, Soviet occupied areas Europe, ideological conflict. Co-author: (with W J Bossenbrook and others) Foundations of Western Civilizations (2 vol) '39-40; also articles in field. Asst prof hist Wayne U Detroit since '37. Capt US Army polit econ analyst Research and Analysis Br OSS '42-46. AHA—Social Sci Research Council (twice fellow)—Phi Beta Kappa. De-

partment of History, Wayne University, Detroit 1.

20 BURLAGE, Henry Matthew. Pharmacy; Pharmaceutical analysis. b'97. BA '19 (Ind U); MA '21 (Harvard); PhG and BS '24 (Purdue U); PhD '29 (U Wash). Research on filtering aromatic elixir, preparation of lotio flava, rhus dermatitis, stabilized hypochlorite solutions as source for chlorine test solution and application in testing for bromide and iodine ions, pharmaceutical applications of isopropyl alcohol; chromatographic analysis of Nux vomica; studies on bentonite. Author: Fundamental Principles and Processes of Pharmacy '49; A Study Guide and Problems to the Literature of Pharmacy '48; A Laboratory Manual to Principles and Processes of Pharmacy '49; also articles in field. Prof U NC '31-47; dean Coll Pharmacy and prof Tex U since '47. Am Pharm Assn—Am Chem Soc— AAAS—Phi Beta Kappa—Sigma Xi. (pres NC chapt). College of Pharmacy, University of Texas, Austin, Tex. H: 702 E 43d St., Austin.

21 BURLINGAME, Robert Sparks. Australia; Australian foreign policy. b'07. AB '28 (Grinnell Coll); grad work (U Mich, Drake U, U Neb). Author: Australia and the United States, '49. Chief for Australia US OWI '44-46; chief Pub Affairs Officer Am Embassy Australia '46-47; news dir radio sta KIOA Des Moines since '48. Australian Inst Internat Affairs. Radio Station KIOA, Onthank Building, Tenth and Mulberry Sts., Des Moines 9, Ia.

22 BURNELL, Max R. Women (Health problems of industrially employed). b'93. MD (U Mich). Author articles: Placement and Health Maintenance '42; Health of Women in Industry '43; Gynecological and Obstetrical Problems of the Industrial Physician '47. Med dir AC Spark Plug Div Gen Motors '31-49, med dir Gen Motors Corp from '49. Am Coll Surgeons—Am Assn Indsl Phys and Surgeons. General Motors Building, Det.

23 BURNETT, Mary Clarke. Social work education; Community organization. b'92. BA '14 (U Toronto); AM '18 (Columbia U). Author articles in field. Head dept social work Carnegie Inst Tech since '22. Am Assn Social Workers—Pittsburgh Fedn Social Agencies—Pa Assn for Blind (vp Pittsburgh br)—Pub Charities Assn Pa (bd dirs)—Am Acad Polit Social Sci—Nat Conf Social Work. Carnegie Institute of Technology, Pittsburgh 13.†

24 BURNETT, Philip Mason. International Organization; Technical Assistance; Point Four; International Children's Emergency Fund. b'08. AB '31 (Yale U); AM '33—PhD '40 (Columbia U). Author: Reparation at the Paris Peace Conference (2 vols) '40. US Dept State divisional asst '42-44, specialist hist research '44, asst internat orgn '44-46, specialist internat orgn affairs since '46; adviser tech problems US del Gen Assembly UN London '46, NY '47; adviser US mem UNRRA Geneva '46, Washington '46. AHA—Am Polit Sci Assn — Am Soc of Internat Law. Awarded hon mention for George Louis Beer Prize, AHA, for work European diplomatic hist '40. Department of State, Washington 25. H: 7212 Ramsgate Road, Washington 16.†

25 BURNHAM, Charles Russel. Corn genetics, cytology and inheritance; Wilt resistance in flax; Barley and wheat cytogenetics. b'04. Student '20-22 (U Minn); BA '24—MS '25—PhD

'29 (U Wis); Nat Research Council fellow '29-31; Sterling fellow '33-34 (Yale); Gosney fellow '47-48 (Calif Inst Tech). Author articles in field. Asso prof, then prof plant genetics U Minn since '39. University of Minnesota, University Farm, St. Paul 1.†

10 BURNHAM, John. Chemistry of electrical insulation; Electrolytic capacitors; Semi-conductors; Dielectrics; High-voltage p h e n o m e n a; Raman spectra. BS '32 (Pomona Coll); MS '33—student '33-36 (Stanford U). Research on Raman spectra of liquids and solutions, mechanism of electrolytic oxidation reaction of metals and structure and properties of films formed, mechanism of rectification in electrolytic and dry rectifiers, and on various aspects of capacitors, such as nature of dielectric absorption, electrothermal e q u i l i b r i u m, mathematical relation between leakage resistance and temperature and field strength. US patents on capacitors, airplane de-iceing antenna, other items. Author articles in field. With Sprague Elec Co since '36, now chief engr. Am Chem Soc—AAAS—Phi Beta Kappa—Sigma Xi — Phi Lambda Upsilon. Sprague Electric Co., Marshall St., N. Adams, Mass.

11 BURNHAM, Wilbur Herbert. Art and craft of stained glass. b'87. Student '04-08 (Mass Sch Art). Travel and study in France, England, Italy and Spain; stained glass represented in outstanding churches and cathedrals throughout country including Cathedral of St John the Divine, Washington Cathedral, Princeton University Chapel, St Mary's Cathedral Peoria Ill, and many others. Designer of stained glass since '06, in business alone since '22. Med Acad Am—Am Fed Arts—Stained Glass Assn of Am (pres '39, 40, 41) — Boston Soc Arts Crafts. Awarded gold medal Boston Tercentenary Art Exhbn 1930; awarded craftsmanship gold medal Am Inst Architects '47; Diplome de Medaille d'Argent, Paris Exhbn 37. 1126 Boylston St., Boston.

12 BURNS, Dennis Francis. Theology and religion; Philosophy. b'89. AB '14 AM '15 (St Louis U) PhD STD '31 (Gregorian U). Prof philosophy Loyola U '25-26; prof sacramental theology Mundelein Sem '26-27; prof fundamental philosophy John Carroll U Cleveland '31-33 prof philo '40-44 dir laymen's retreats '44-46; prof Loyola U '33-34; regent law sch prof jurisprudence Loyola '34-34; pres Xavier U Cincinnati '35-40; prof philo and religion U Detroit since '46. St Thomas Aquinas Acad. Univ. of Detroit, McNichols Rd. at Livernois, Det 21.†◎

13 BURNS, Norman. Education in Georgia. b'07. BS '29 (Buffalo U); MBA '33 (Northwestern U); PhD '45 (Chicago U). Assisted in surveys of institutions and systems of higher education; research on unified control of state-supported higher education in Georgia, state-controlled junior colleges in Georgia; dir of survey of State-Controlled Higher Education in Arkansas, '49-50. Editor: The Administration of Higher Institutions Under Changing Conditions '47; also articles in field. Sec Commn Colls and Univs, No Central Assn Colls and Secondary Schs since '46, asso prof edn U Chicago since '47. University of Chicago, Chicago 37.

14 BURNS, Robert Homer. Sheep and wool breeding and nutrition; Fleece improvement and performance; Wool preparation and marketing. b'00. BS '20 (Wyo U); MS '21 (Ia State Coll); PhD '31 (Edinburgh U). Pioneer in domestication of mink and marten '27; China-US Agricultural Mission '46; initiated wool shrinkage work US Department Agriculture '37-39; Overseas Consultants Mission Iran '49. Author articles in field. Wool specialist, head dept wool tech U Wyo since '47. Department of Wool Technology, University of Wyoming, Laramie, Wyo.

15 BURPEE, David. Seeds (Flower, vegetable, mail order business, plant breeding). b'93. Student (Culver Mil Acad); '13 (Cornell U). Developed marigolds with odorless foliage. Pres W Atlee Burpee Co since '17; chmn bd James Vick's Seeds Inc; dir Agr Missions Inc NY, Nat Agr Coll Phila. Am Seed Trade Assn (ex-pres)—Nat Sweet Pea Soc Gt Britain (vp). 18th and Hunting Park Av., Phila. 32.

16 BURR, George Oswald. Photosynthesis; Fats; Biochemical effects of light; Plant saps (Physico-chemical properties). b'96. BA '16—LLD '37 (Hendrix Acad and Coll, Conway Ark); MA '21 (U Ark); PhD '24 (U Minn). Associate editor Journal Nutrition, Journal Physical Chemistry. Editor: Physico-Chemical Properties of Plant Saps '34; also articles in field. Head dept phys and bio-chem Expt Sta Honolulu since '46. Nat Research Council—Am Chem Soc—Am Soc Biol Chem — Am Inst Nutrition — AAAS — Sigma Xi. Guggenheim fellow for European study '34-35. Experiment Station, Hawaiian Sugar Planters Assn., Honolulu, T.H.

17 BURR, Samuel Engle, Jr. Progressive education; Military psychology; Army education; Aaron Burr. b'97. LittB '19 (Rutgers U); MA '25 (U Wis); MA '27 (Teachers Coll Columbia U); EdD '36 (U Cincinnati). Author: A School in Transition '37; An Introduction to Progressive Education '33; Our Flag and Our Schools '37. Dir ednl research pub schs Lynn Mass '27-30; supt schs Glendale Ohio '30-33, New Castle Del '34-39, Rye Neck Mamoroneck NY '39-42; chmn dept edn Coll Arts Sci Am U Washington since '47, director summer session '47-48; director Institute on Position of United States in World Affairs since '48. Lt col US Army, personnel cons, personnel staff officer, edn officer '42-47. Aaron Burr Assn (founder and exec dir)—Am Psychol Assn—NEA—Am Assn Sch Adminstrs—Am Ednl Research Assn. Hurst Hall, American University, Washington 16.†◎

18 BURRELL, Robin Charles. Phytochemistry; Biochemistry. b'96. BS '18 (Mt Union Coll); MA '21—PhD '25 (O State U). Research on isolation of compounds from Ohio weeds, effects of boron and manganese on quality of beets and tomatoes, ascorbic acid content of cabbage as influenced by variety, season and soil fertility, chemical composition of soybeans during maturation, vitamin C content of spring greens. Author: An Introduction to Phytochemical Research '31; Chemistry for Students of Agriculture and Home Economics '31; Organic Chemistry '36; Organic Chemistry for Students of Biological Sciences '47. Co-author: (with Almy) Elementary Quantitative Biochemistry '39; also articles in field. Prof agrl chem O State U since '40. Am Chem Soc—AAAS—Am Soc Plant Physiol—O Acad Sci—Sigma Xi. Ohio State University, Columbus 10, O.

19 BURRIS, Robert Harza. Plant biochemistry; Biological nitrogen fixation; Potatoes (Cooking, potato chips). b'14. BS '36 (SD State Coll); MS '38—PhD '40 (U Wis). Research on biological nitrogen fixation, respiratory systems of organisms concerned, application of isotopic nitrogen to studies in biological nitrogen fixation, mode of action of herbicides, nitrogen nutrition of plants, folic acid content and preservation in plant materials, control of blackening of potatoes on cooking, control of quality in manufacture of potato chips. Co-author: Manometric Techniques and Related Methods for the Study of Tissue Metabolism '45; also articles in field. Research asst dept agrl bact U Wis '36-40, instr agrl bact '41-44, asso prof biochem since '46. AAAS—Am Soc Biol Chem—Bot Soc Am—Am Soc Am Bact—Am Chem Soc —Sigma Xi. Nat Research Council fellow Columbia '40-41. Department of Biochemistry, University of Wisconsin, Madison 6, Wis.

20 BURRIS-MEYER, Harold. Sound (Theatrical, military, psychological uses). b'02. BS '23 (Coll City NY); AM '25 (Columbia). Accomplished first complete control of sound in theatre; applied to concert stage Carnegie Hall '40, to opera Metropolitan opera '41; first analytical studies which led to development and general acceptance of music in industry '43; first development of music service for railroads '46, developments for military purposes such as project battle noise, mass psychological screening, projection of speech from combat types of aircraft. Co-author: (with Edward C Cole) Scenery for the Theatre '38; Theatres and Auditoriums '49; also articles in field. Dir Muzak Corp '43-47, vp '45-47; dir Associated Program Service '45-47, Magnetic Programs Inc '48, Control Inc '49; Professor Stevens Inst Tech since '29, dir Stevens Theatre, dir research on sound in theatre; cons. Cmdr USNR World War II. Acoustical Soc Am (F, chmn music com)—Am Inst Phys—Am Television Soc—Audio Engring Soc—Am Nat Theatre and Acad. Stevens Institute of Technology, Hoboken, N.J.†

21 BURROUGHS, Raymond Darwin. Wild life management (Population dynamics, upland game and water fowl). b'99. AB '24 (Neb Wesleyan U); MA '25 (Princeton U); '29-30, '33 (Ia State Coll), '31, '36-37 (Minn U). Aided in setting up projects, inspection and supervision of research, land acquisition, habital restoration, management and development of state game lands acquired under provisions of Federal Aid in Wildlife Restoration Act; study of cooperation of farmers and hunters, analysis of hunting records for prairie farms, and game areas. Author articles: Game Refuges and Public Hunting Grounds in Michigan '46; Untilled Gardens '47; Rewards of the Hunt '47, and others. Biol Game Div Mich Dept Conservation '37-38; coordinator Fed Aid Wildlife Restoration Program '38-46; regional game supervisor Game Region III Mich since '47. Wildlife Soc—Am Soc Mammologists—Wilson Ornithol Club —Ecol Soc Am—Mich Acad Sci Arts Letters. P.O. Box 451, Jackson, Mich.†

22 BURROUGHS, Wise. Animal nutrition. b'11. BS '34—PhD '39 (U Ill). Research on protein requirements in swine, amino acids in adult nutrition, nutrition in reproduction in swine, vitamin needs of pigs in relation to swine entiritis. Author articles in field. Asst O Agrl Expt Sta '39-45, asso since '45; asso prof vet research O State U since '44. Am Soc Animal Prodn—Sigma Xi—Phi Kappa Phi. Reynoldsburg, O.†

23 BURROWS, Charles N(icholl). Sociology; Marriage and family; Crime and delinquency; Social welfare. b'94. AB '18 (Mo Wesleyan Coll) STB '21

(Boston U) MA '27 (Harvard) PhD '30 (U Ia). Prof sociol Simpson Coll Indianola Ia '23-46 Trinity U San Antonio since '46; forum leader Adult Pub Forums sponsored by Fed Office Edn '36-37; mem bds Community Settlement Houses San Antonio. Author: Criminal Statistics in Iowa '30; Ten Questions about the American Crime Problem '38; Ten Questions about the American Family '39. Mental Hygiene Soc—Community Welfare Council—Gudiance Inst. Trinity University, San Antonio 1.☉

10 BURROWS, Edwin Grant. Anthropology (Cultural); Pacific Islanders; Primitive music. b'91. AB '13 (Cornell U); AM '33—PhD '37 (Yale). Author: Native Music of the Tuamotus '33; Ethnology of Futuna '36; Ethnology of Uvea '37; Songs of Uvea and Futuna '45; Western Polynesia '38; Hawaiian Americans '47. With U Conn since '39, now professor anthropology. Research analyst Pacific br Mil Intelligence '42-44. Sigma Xi. University of Connecticut, Storrs, Conn.†

11 BURT, Charles Earle. Herpetology (Lizards); Biological supplies (Preserved plants and animals). b'04. BS '26—MS '27 (Kan State Coll); PhD '30 (Mich U). Made expeditions to southeastern US for Smithsonian Institution '32-35, other biological exploration in US, Canada, and Mexico '36-48; research on South American and Kansas lizards, key to lizards of US and Canada, amphibians and reptiles of South Seas, sexual dimorphism of collared lizard Crotaphytus collaris, occurrence of throat-fan in sand lizard Uma notata Baird, phylogenetic relationships of teiid lizards of genus Cnemidophorus, lizards, snakes, frogs, and toads of various regions. Author articles in field. Prof biol Southwestern Coll '31-44, mgr Quivira Specialties Co since '45. Phi Kappa Phi—Sigma Xi—Am Soc Ichthyologists Herpetologists—Herpetologists League—Biol Soc Washington—Am Soc Zool(F)—Kan Acad Sci (life)—Kan Entomol Soc—Am Microscopical Soc—Mich Acad Sci (life)—Ecol Union—Soc Systematic Zool—British Herpetological Soc. 4010 W. 21st St., Topeka, Kan.

12 BURT, Gordon Lansing. Water supply; Sewage treatment. b'13. BS (civil engring) '35 (Rose Poly Inst). Research, design, construction and operation of sewers, sewage pumping stations and sewage treatment works, design, construction and operation of water supply, water purification works and water distribution systems. Chief Div Water and Sewer Utilities US Army Ordnance Dept '40; prin design engr Camp Breckinridge '41; asst to archt engr Camp Atterbury '42; city mgr Hayward, Calif '48-49; sewage disposal engr Portland Ore since '49 at present Engr Mgr Bur of Sewage and Refuse Disposal. Am Soc CE—Pacific—NW Sewage Works Assn—Calif Sewage Works Assn—Am Water Works Assn—Am Pub Works Assn—Am Concrete Inst—Tau Beta Pi. 5001 N. Columbia Blvd., Portland 3, Ore. H: 5326 N.E. 39th Av., Portland 11.

13 BURT, Wayne Vincent. Oceanography. b'17. BS '39 (George Fox Coll) '39, '46 (U Ore); MS '48 (U Calif). Survey Chesapeake Bay and tributaries for determination physical and chemical conditions; penetration of light in turbid natural waters. Asst Scripps Inst Oceanog of U Calif '46-48, asso oceanog '48-49; asst prof oceanog and asso oceanog Chesapeake Bay Inst Johns Hopkins U since '49. Am Meteorol Soc—Am Geophys Union—Am Soc Limnol and Oceanog—Atlantic Estuarine Research Soc—Sigma Xi—Phi Mu

Epsilon. The Chesapeake Bay Institute, 1315 St. Paul St., Baltimore 2.

14 BURT, William H(enry). Mammalogy (United States, Michigan, gophers, woodpeckers, mice and rats); Population dynamics. b'03. AB '25—MA '27 (U Kan); PhD '30 (U Calif). Described several new species of gophers, rats, shrews, skunks; editor Journal of Mammalogy since '47. Author: Territorial Behavior and Population Densities in Mammals '37; The Mammals of Michigan '46; Territorial Behavior and Populations of Some Small Mammals in Southern Michigan 40; also articles in field. Research fellow Calif Inst Tech '30-35; asst curator mammals U Mich '35-38, curator since '38, asst prof zool '41-45, professor since '49. Am Soc Mammalogists—Gesellschaft fur Saugetierkunde—Wildlife Soc—Ecol Soc—Soc Study Evolution—Biol Soc Washington—Am Soc Ichthyologists Herpetologists—Northwest Bird and Mammal Soc — Am Ornithol Union — Cooper Ornithol Club—Wilson Ornithol Club—Am Naturalists—Phi Beta Kappa—Sigma Xi. Museum of Zoology, University of Michigan, Ann Arbor. H: 1305 Henry St.☉

15 BURTON, Glenn Willard. Agronomy; Grass Breeding; Turfs. b'10. BSc '32 (U Neb); MSc '33—PhD '36 (Rutgers U). Research in genetic improvement through breeding of grasses best adapted for improved pastures and Piney Woods revegetation in South, studying cytology and genetics of species and hybrids of Bermuda, Bahia, Dallis, Sudan, and Napier grasses, and Cattail millet; studies of physiology and genetics of seed production; work on increase and distribution of superior germ plasm; Coastal Bermuda and Tift Sudan grasses developed in this research. Author articles in field. Geneticist div forage crops US Dept Agr Tifton Ga since '36. Am Soc Agron—AAAS—Am Genetic Assn—Bot Soc Am—Sigma Xi. Experiment Station, Tifton, Ga.

16 BURTON, John Edward. Public administration and budgeting. b'08. BA '28 (Hiram Coll); MBA '29 (Northwestern U). Author articles in field. Dir budget NY State '43-50; vp bus Cornell U since '50; chmn NY State Power Authority since '50; chairman Post-war Pub Works Planning Commn '43-47; mem State Veterans Commn since '44; mem Gov's Com on State Edn Prog '45-48; mem State U Commn '46-48; mem com on fed-state relations of Commn on Org. Exec Branch of Govt '48. Nat Assn State Budget Officers (pres '46)—Am Soc Pub Adminstrn—Nat Tax Assn. Adminstrn Bldg. Cornell U., Ithaca.†☉

17 BURTON, Linus Homer. Horticultural zones of midwestern and southwestern states. b'08. BS (Hort) (Kan State Coll). Author articles: Landscape Planning; Arkansas Garden Calendar; Arbor Day in Arkansas; Big Trees in Arkansas, and others. Supt Bartlett Arboretum Belle Plaine Kan '29-34; ext landscape specialist Kan State Coll '41-43; ext hort U Ark since '46. Kan Assn Landscape Architects—Alpha Zeta. University of Arkansas, Fayetteville, Ark.

18 BURTT, Harold Ernest. Industrial psychology (Advertising; Employment). b'90. AB '11 (Dartmouth); AM '13—PhD '15 (Harvard). Author: Principles of Employment Psychology '42; Psychology and Industrial Efficiency '29; Legal Psychology '31; Psychology of Advertising '38; Applied Psychology '48, abridged edition '52. Expert cons to War Dept in connec-

tion planning separation centers World War II; with O State U since '19, prof psychol since '22, chmn dept since '39. Am Psychol Assn—Am Assn Applied Psychol—AAAS—Ohio Acad Sci(F)—Phi Beta Kappa—Sigma Xi. Ohio State University, Columbus, O.

19 BUSCH, Daniel Adolph. Petroleum geology. b'12. Bownocker scholar '36-37, '37-38—MA '36—PhD '38 (O State U); BS '34 (Capital U). Research on oil-bearing sands in southwestern Pennsylvania, subsurface techniques. Author articles in field. Instr geol U Pittsburgh '38-42; petroleum geol Pa Topographic and Geol Survey '42-43; cons geol Huntley and Huntley Pittsburgh '43-46; sr research geol Carter Oil Co Tulsa Okla since '46. Am Assn Petroleum Geol—Tulsa Geol Soc—Geol Soc Am(F)—Sigma Xi. The Carter Oil Company, Box 801, Tulsa, Okla. H: 3757 S. Wheeling Av.†

20 BUSCHMANN, Charles Severin. Law. b'96. AB '17 (Indiana University); LLB '21 LLM '31 (Yale). Partner firm Buschmann, Krieg, DeVault & Alexander. Phi Delta Phi. Circle Tower, Indpls 4.☉

21 BUSH, Chilton Rowlette. American journalism; Opinion and media measurement. b'96. BA '25—MA '27—PhD '35 (U Wis); Litt D '40 (Georgetown Coll). Author: Newspaper Reporting of Public Affairs '40; Editorial Thinking and Writing '32. Co-author: Reading Interests of Business Executives '36; Five Western Newspapers '45-52. Prof, dir Inst for Journalistic Studies Stanford U since '34; tech cons measurement of public opinion, media and employee attitudes. Assn for Edn in Journalism—Am Assn Schs, Departments Journalism (chmn council research '39-42, pres '42-44), Am Marketing Assn, Am Assn Public Opinion Research—Kappa Tau Alpha. 669 Cabrillo, Stanford University, Cal.

22 BUSH, George Pollock. Public administration. b'92. Student '31—33—MBA '46 (Harvard); MA '46—PhD '49 (Am U). Research on public administration, public personnel administration, organization and management. Co-editor: (with Lowell H Hattery) Scientific Research: Its Administration and Organization '50. With US Army Signal Corps '12-44; faculty Am U since '47. Am Soc Pub Adminstrn—Soc Personnel Adminstrn—Am Mil Inst—Inst Radio Engrs (sr mem)—A AAS. The American University, 1901 F St., N.W., Washington.

23 BUSH, Lucius M. Sinusitis, Asthma, Hayfever and their corrections; Corrections of the eustachian tubes by manipulation. b'87. Student '07-09 (Syracuse U); DO '12 (Am Sch Osteopathy). '20 (Phila Coll Osteopathy). Author: Common Sense Health; Secret of Sinusitis and Headaches. Am Osteopathic Assn (chmn ear nose throat sect '21-22—Am Osteopathic Soc of Ophthalmology Rhinology and Otolaryngology. 551 Fifth Av., NYC.

24 BUSHMAN, Edwin Francis Arthur. Low pressure molding of reinforced plastics (Bottle pouring handles, arch supports). b'19. BS '41 (U Ill); grad student (Calif Inst Tech). Invented first plastics interchangeable pouring handles for large glass bottles and jugs; developed a complete line of such handles for mass production at low cost by injection or transfer molding; developer of new process for low pressure molded arch supports from polyester resins and glass fabric; holder 10 US patents. Owner Edwin F Bushman Co cons engr product design and development in plastics and synthetic rubber since '46. 715 Spring St., Aurora, Ill. H: 1146 E. Spencer St.

10 BUSIGNIES, Henri Gaston. Electronics; Radio aids to navigation (Direction finder equipment, instrument landing systems). b'05. Degree Elect Engring '26 (U Paris). Granted patents in US and France '26 for an aerial direction finder device. Holds total of 117 patents in field. Author articles in field. With Internat Telephone and Telegraph Co since '28, Fed Telecommunication Labs Inc, affiliated companies, since '40, now tech dir labs. Radio Mfgrs Assn (chmn aeronautical radio com)—Inst Radio Engrs (chmn radio navigation com)—Radio Tech Commn Aeronautics (mfgrs adv com). Awarded Presidential Certificate of Merit for NDRC work during World War II, '48. Federal Telecommunication Laboratories, Inc., 500 Washington Av., Nutley, N.J.

11 BUSS, Irven O. Wisconsin wildlife; Wildlife management; Pheasants. b'08. BS '33 (Stout Inst); MS '38—PhD '43 (U Wis). Research on Wisconsin pheasant survival, wildlife restoration, pheasant populations. Author articles in field. Leader Wis pheasant research project '40-43; chief wildlife research Wis Conservation dept '45-48; prof wildlife management Wash State Coll since '48. Wildlife Soc—Am Ornithol Union—Soc Am Mammalogists—Wis Acad Sci Arts Letters—Sigma Xi. Department of Zoology, Science Hall, State College of Washington, Pullman, Wash.†

12 BUSS, Robert Rumsey. Vacuum tubes; Feedback amplifiers; Radio receivers (Very high frequency); High Power Klystrons; Moving-Target Indicator Radar. b'13. AB '35 (San Jose State Coll); EE '37—PhD '40 (Stanford). Research on stabilized feedback at radio frequencies, design on research basis of wide-tuning-range very high frequency radar countermeasures receivers, research on control of electron beams, design of highpower pulsed triode tubes, vacuum systems, and special-purpose tubes. Co-author, assistant editor: Very High Frequency Techniques '47. Design engr Heintz and Kaufman '39-40; with Litton Engring Lab '40-42; design group leader, cons AAF radio research lab Nat Defense Research Council '42-46; asso prof radio and elec engring Northwestern U '46-51; Research Asso and Research Group dir Stanford since '51. Inst Radio Engrs (sr mem)—Am Inst EE—Sigma Xi—Eta Kappa Nu—Tau Beta Pi—Nat Elec Conf (sec '48, treas '49). Electronics Research Laboratory, Stanford University, Stanford, Cal.

13 BUSSART, James Everett. Insecticides. b'03. BS '26—MS '35 (U Ill). Research and Development on new insecticides and their uses. Entomol Ill State Dept Agr '24-44; entomol Calif Spray Chem Corp '44-47; entomol Velsical Corp since '47. Kappa Phi Kappa—Am Assn Econ Entomol—Entomol Soc Am—Entomol Soc Can—Fla Entomol Soc—Am Soc Tropical Med. H: 215 W. Harrison St., Wheaton, Ill.

14 BUSSOW, Carl. Manufacture and applications of asphalt and other bitumens. b'99. BS (chem) '22 (Cooper Union); BS (chem engring) '30—'30-33 (Poly Inst Brooklyn). Designed air field runway pavements for US Army, Civil Aeronautics Administration designed paving mixtures for governments and private companies in North, Central, and South Americas, Europe, and Asia, designed red and green asphalt paints. Author articles in field. Chem Am Synthetic Dye Corp '18-22; chief chem Dow & Smith '22-35; tech

dir A W Dow Inc since '35. Highway Research Board—ASTM (chmn subcommittees)—ACS—AAAS—NY Acad Sci—Marine Chem Assn—AIC—ACC & Ch E—AAPT—NSPE. 801 Second Av., N.Y.C. 17.

15 BUSWELL, Arthur Moses. Chemistry (Water and sanitation); Bacteriology (Industrial waste treatment). b'88. AB '10 (U Minn); AM '12 (U Me); PhD '17 (Columbia). Holds numerous patents on fermentation. Author: The Chemistry of Water and Sewage Treatment '28. Editor: Mason's Water Examination '31; chem referee: Standard Methods of Water Analysis, 5th, 6th, 7th, 8th, 9th edits; also articles in field. Chief Ill State Water Survey since '20; research prof U Ill since '45. Officer San Corps US Army '17-19; maj San Corps Med Research Edgewood Arsenal '43-45. NY Acad Sci(F)—AAAS(F)—Am Pub Health Assn(F)—Am Inst Chem(F)—Am Chem Soc—Am Water Works Assn—Am Micros Soc—Soc Chem Industry—Sigma Xi. Box 232, Urbana, Ill.⊚

16 BUTCHER, Devereux. United States national parks; Nature and wilderness preservation; Nature photography. b'06. Student '26-28 Pa Acad Fine Arts. Engaged extensive photography of botanical subjects. Author: Exploring Our National Parks and Monuments '47; Exploring Our Prehistoric Indian Ruins, '50. Editor Nat Parks Mag since '42; also articles and photographs in field. Nat Parks Assn (exec sec)—Wilderness Soc—Save-the-Redwoods League—Am Nature Assn—Nat Audubon Soc—Am Forestry Assn. 1214 16th St., N.W., Washington 6. H: 3133 Connecticut Av.

17 BUTCHER, Frank Charles. Medieval pageantry; Community singing; Church music. b'82. Ed (Canterbury Cathedral Choir); B Mus '11 (Durham U, Eng); fellow (Royal Coll Organists). Composer of church music and incidental music for pageants and plays. Head music dept Hill School. Friends Canterbury Cathedral—Royal Coll Music, London (asso mem)—Royal Acad Music, London (licentiate)—Am Guild Organists—Am Ch Union. Manufacturers National Bank, 4th and Grand Sts., Troy, N.Y.

18 BUTLER, Charles Edward, Jr. Electrical porcelains (Whiteware); Titanate ceramics for radio and radar parts. b'19. BS '42 (Va Poly Inst). Research and development on electrical porcelains and titanate ceramics. Holds patents in field. Ceramic engr US Signal Corps '42; ceramic research engr Centralab Globe-Union '45, A O Smith Corp Milwaukee '47; in charge ceramic research Line Material Co since '48. Am Ceramic Soc—Inst Ceramic Engrs. Professional engr Wis. Line Material Co., 9th and Marion, South Milwaukee, Wis.

19 BUTLER, G(urdon) M(ontague). Mining engineering and geology (Crystallography, mineralogy); Gemmology. b'81. EM '02—ScD '22 (Colo Sch Mines). Taught first college course in gemmology given in this country at Colorado School of Mines, beginning in 1909; student and collector of gems since that time. Author: A Pocket Handbook of Minerals '08; A Manual of Geometrical Crystallography '18, and others; also articles in field. With Colo Sch Mines '03-13; prof mining engring, dean Coll Mines and Engring U Ariz 15-40, dean Coll Engineering '40-51; dean emeritus since '51; director Arizona Bureau Mines '18-40. Geol Soc Am(F)—AAAS(F)—Mineral Soc Am(F)—Am Inst Mining Metall Engrs—ASEE—Am Assn Engrs

—Gemmological Inst Am (ednl advisory bd)— Tau Beta Pi—Phi Kappa Phi —Sigma Xi—Phi Delta Kappa. 2820 E. 6th St., Apt. 33, Tucson.⊚

20 BUTLER, Joe Beaty. Highway Engineering. b'95. BS in CE '15—BS in Edn '24 (Okla A&M Coll); MS in CE '24—CE '22 (Mo Sch Mines). Author articles in field. Engring asst railroad maintenance and valuation surveys in Middle West '15-17; highway survey and constrn '19-20; with dept civil engring Mo Sch Mines since '20, prof and head dept since '31. ASCE—Am Road Builders Assn (div dir, vp)—MSPE (past pres)—NSPE (nat dir)—ASEE—Phi Kappa Phi—Theta Tau—Chi Epsilon. Missouri School of Mines, Rolla, Mo.

21 BUTLER, Mary (Mrs. Clifford Lewis, 3rd). American archaeology (Mayan, northeastern). b'03. AB '25 (Vassar Coll); Certificate '25 (Sorbonne, Paris); AM '30 (Radcliffe Coll); PhD '36 (U Pa). Field work on Maya pottery Piedras Negras, Guatemala; Monongahela woodland culture of southwestern Pennsylvania; Highland Maya culture in Alta Verapaz and Quiche, Guatemala; coastal woodlands of Broomall, Pa. Author: Piedras Negras Pottery '35; Three Archaeological Sites in Somerset County '41; also articles in field. Research asso Am sect U Mus Phila since '35. Am Anthrop Assn(F)—Soc Am Archaeol—Pa Archaeol Soc — Inter-Am Soc Anthrop and Geog—Sociedad de Geografia e Historia de Guatemala (hon) —Sigma Xi. University Museum, Phila. 4.†

22 BUTLER, Ruby Stainbrook. Hoosierana; Midwest folklore. b'03. Student '45-47 (Ind U Grad Sch). Research on North American manners, customs and speech, discovered Hoosier folk characters Old Man Edmonds and Sassafras George. Free-lance writer since '41. Hoosier Folklore Soc—Am Folklore Soc—Am Anthrop Assn. Received Theta Sigma Phi award '48. 148 N. Jackson St., Franklin, Ind.

23 BUTLER, Ruth Lapham (Mrs. Pierce). United States history (Indian and Hispanic American). b'96. BA '18—MA '19—PhD '25 (Northwestern U). Author: Checklist of American Revolutionary Pamphlets '22; Doctor Franklin, Postmaster General '28; Checklist of Manuscripts in the Edward E Ayer Collection '37; A Bibliographical Checklist of North and Middle American Indian Linguistics (2 vols) '41. Translator and editor: The Journal of Paul Du Ru '34. Editor: (with S. Pargellis) N F Moore's "A Trip from New York to the Falls of St Anthony" '46; Guide to Hispanic American Historical Review, 1st 25 years; also articles in field. Historian Wm. Smith Mason Collection Frankliniana '22-24; librarian and asso prof hist Hillsdale Coll '25-26; Newberry Library Chicago '20-22, '27-31, custodian Edward E Ayer Collection since '31. AHA—Hispanic Am Conf—Bibliog Soc Am—Am Archivists Ill Hist Soc. Newberry Library, 60 W. Walton Pl., Chicago 10.

24 BUTTERFIELD, Harry Morton. Horticulture (Ornamental); California (History, horticulture). b'87. BS '14—MS (Pomol) '16 (U Calif). Specialist ornamental horticulture old and new plants, history horticulture in California; studied history deciduous fruits in California; consultant plant identification, nomenclature; in charge judges ornamentals Golden Gate International Exposition '39-40; supervisor judges spring garden show Calif '30-49. Author articles: Home Floriculture in California '43; Bush Berry

Culture '47; Easter Lily Production '47; Rose Culture '48, and others. Faculty agrl dept U Calif since '18, prof agr since '49. Calif Garden Clubs (state chmn hort)—Nat Council Garden Clubs (hort cons)—Gourd Soc of Am—Calif Hort Soc (pres)—Am Begonia Soc (nomenclature dir). 121 Giannini Hall, University of California, Berkeley, Calif.

10 BUTTERWORTH, Charles Collier. English versions of the Bible (1340-1611); History of English primers (1525-1545). b'94. AB '15 (U Pa). Author: Literary Lineage of the King James Bible '41; The English Primers, 1529-1545, '53; also articles in field. Instr Eng U Pa '19-27; since '33 specializing in Eng versions of the Bible 1340-1611. Phi Beta Kappa. 1028 W. Upsal St., Phila. 19, Pa.†

11 BUTTERWORTH, Julian Edward. Educational administration (Rural schools). b'84. AB '07—AM '10—PhD '12 (U Ia). Member Committee of 21 for study of rural education in New York, director division grounds and buildings; member staff for state school surveys of Virginia '27, New Jersey '28; member New York State Council on Rural Education since '43; member National Commission on School District Reorganization since '46; dir New Haven Conn Sch Survey '47; chief cons Intermediate District NY State '44-47. Author: Problems in State High School Finance '18; School Buildings and Grounds in Rural New York '22; Principles of Rural School Administration '26; The Parent-Teachers Association and Its Work '27. Co-author: (with V Rueggedger (Administering Pupil Transportation '41; (with H Dawson et al) The Modern Rural School '52. Professor of rural education Cornell U since '19, dir Grad Sch Edn '31-44. N Central Assn Colls Secondary Schs (mem bd insps '13-19)—Nat Soc Coll Teachers Edn—Nat Soc Sci Study Edn —Phi Beta Kappa. 101 Irving Pl., Ithaca.†◎

12 BUTTS, Allison. Mining and metallurgical engineering; Metallurgy (Copper); Metallurgical calculations. b'90. AB '11 (Princeton); SB '13 (MIT). Author: Textbook of Metallurgical Problems '32. Co-author: (with Prof Bradley Stoughton) Engineering Metallurgy '26. Editor: Methods of Nonferrous Metallurgical Analysis; asso editor The Mineral Industry '16-27; spl editor on metallurgy 2d edit Webster's New Internat Dictionary. With metallurgy dept Lehigh U since '16, prof since '38. Mem jury of award Lincoln Welding Found '42, '47; investigator and tech rep Nat Def Research Com '44-46. AIMME (dir '50-52)—Electrochem Soc—Am Soc Metals—Inst Metals Gt Britain—Am Soc Engring Edn (sec div mineral tech '37-40)—Sigma Xi. H: 1343 Montrose Av., Bethlehem, Pa.◎

13 BUYS, John L. Zoology; Insect taxonomy; Cicadellidae. b'97. BS '19—MS '21—PhD '22 (Cornell U). Author: The Cicadellidee of the Vicinity of Ithaca, N.Y., '24; Leafhoppers of Mt. Marcy and Mt. MacIntyre, Essex County, N.Y. '31. Prof. biology and head dept St Lawrence U Canton NY since '23. Entomol Soc Am(F)—Beta Beta Beta—Sigma Xi. Department of Biology, St. Lawrence University, Canton, N.Y.◎

14 BYARS, L(oren) Freeland. Ants of southwestern United States (Ecology and distribution). b'08. AB '30 (Central Coll Fayette Mo); MA '36—fellow '31-32 (U Colo). Author articles in field. Agt Bur Entomol and Plant Quarantine US Dept Agr '39-41, plant quarantine inspector div fgn quaran-

tines since '41. Entomol Soc Wash—Am Assn Econ Entomol—Entomol Soc Am—AAAS. 641 Washington St., Room 844, NYC 14.

15 BYE, Arthur Edwin. Art History (Painting, drawing); Art restoration (Paintings). b'85. BSc '11 (U Pa); MA '13—PhD '18 (Princeton U); '11-12 (Oxford). Author: Pots and Pans '20; also articles in field. Asso prof hist art and drawing UNC '47-48; specialist in restoration of works of art various univs '26-48. Antiquarian Soc—Numismatic Soc. Byecroft, Holicong, Pa.†

16 BYERLY, Perry. Seismology; Vibration measurement. b'97. BA—MA—PhD '21—grad sch '21-24 (U Calif). Author: Seismology '42; also articles in field. Asso prof, prof seismol U Calif since '25. Nat Acad Scis—Seismol Soc Am—Geol Soc Am—Am Geophys Union. Bacon Hall, University of California, Berkeley 4, Cal.◎

17 BYERS, Charles Francis. Odonata (Taxonomy, ecology, and geographic distribution). b'02. AB '25—MS '26—PhD '29 (U Mich). Author: Laboratory Manual in Invertebrate Zoology '45. Co-author: A Handbook of the Dragonflies of North America (with Needham and Heywood) '29; Man and the Biological World (with Rogers and Hubbell) '41; also articles in field. Head prof Div biol sci U Fla since '42. AAAS—Entomol Soc Am—Fla Acad Sci—Assn SE Biol—Fla Entomol Soc—Limnol Soc Am—Sigma Xi. Awarded Achievement Medal Fla Acad Sci '41. Department of Biology, University of Florida, Gainesville, Fla.†

18 BYERS, Douglas Swain. Archaeology (New England Indians). b'03. AB '25—MA '28 (Harvard). Studies of catalogue systems, treatment of museum specimens; research on archaeology of southwestern US, New England, primitive agriculture and forest cover, environment aboriginal inhabitants of northeastern North America. Co-author: The Year Bearer's People '31; Two Sites on Martha's Vineyard '40; also articles in field. Asst to dir Peabody Mus Harvard '31-33; Robert S Peabody Found, asst dir '33-38, dir since '38. Am Anthrop Assn (rep Nat Research Council '45-48)—Soc Am Archaeol (asso ed '38-39, ed '39-46, pres '46-47)—Mass Archaeol Soc (ed '39-40, since '41)—Archaeol Socs Conn, NY, Del. Robert S. Peabody Foundation, Phillips Academy, Andover, Mass.

19 BYLER, William Henry. Luminescent materials (Preparation, properties). b'04. BS '27—AB '27 (Central Mo State Coll); MA '31—PhD '37 (U Mo). Research on fluorescent materials especially zinc sulfide, zinc cadmium sulfide phosphors, and their practical application in x-ray screens, cathode ray tube screens for television, radar, radium luminescent materials, fluorescent, phosphorescent, infra-red; study fluorescent calcium phosphate and photocell measurement radium luminescent materials. Holds patents in field. Author articles: Inorganic Phosphors Without Metallic Activator '38; Emission Spectra of Some Zinc Sulfide and Zinc Cadmium Sulfide Phosphors '47; Methods of Evaluating X-Ray Screen Quality and Performance '50. Co-author articles: Method for Determining Chromaticity of Fluorescent Material '45; On Decay of Phosphorescence and Mechanism of Luminescence of Zinc Sulfide Phosphors '49. Research chem Gen Electric Co '37-38; dir research US Radium Corp NYC since '39. ACS—Am Inst Chem—Electrochem Soc—AAAS—Sig-

ma Xi. U.S. Radium Corp., 535 Pearl St., N.Y.C. 7.

20 BYRD, Elon Eugene. Parasites (Birds, Amphibians, reptiles). b'05. Research on taxonomy and life history helminth parasites of amphibians and reptiles, morphology and taxonomy of helminth parasites of birds; studies on excretory flame cell pattern in digenetic trematodes, and on parasitic protozoa; investigation reproductive potentialities of trematode egg. Author articles: The Helminth Parasites of Birds—A New Species of Acanthocephala from North American Birds '49; Alloglyptus crenshawi—A New Genus and Species of Digenetic Trematode (Plagiorchiinae) '50; The Helminth Parasites of Amphibia—Studies on Loxogenoides bicolor '50, and others. Co-author articles: (with J Fred Denton) The Helminth Parasites of Birds—A Review of the Trematode Genus Tanaisia Skrjabin '50; (with Denton) The Helminth Parasites of Birds—The Dicrocoeliid Trematodes of North American Birds, and others. Faculty biol dept U Ga since '34, prof since '45, member of graduate faculty since '38. Officer in charge epidemiological unit (filariasis) South Pacific USN '43-45; Bronze Star, '44. AA AS (F)—Am Micros Soc—Am Soc Parasitol—Am Soc Tropical Med—Assn Southeastern Biol—Tenn Acad Sci—Sigma Xi—Soc Syst Zool. Michael award in research Helminth Parasites of Georgia Vertebrates '48. Biology Department, University of Georgia, Athens, Ga.◎

21 BYROM, Mills Herbert. Technology of processing long vegetable fibers. b'00. BS '28—MS '34 (Tex A&M Coll). Invented cotton stripping machinery, bur extractor, cotton cleaner, planting attachments, fiber decorticator, process and equipment for drying long vegetable fibers, fiber burnishing machine, improvements in long fiber harvesters, process and equipment for degumming ramie fiber. Co-author: Progress in the Study of the Mechanical Harvesting of Cotton '32; Calibration of Cotton Planting Mechanisms '35. Agrl engr Tex Agrl Expt Sta '31-42; sr agrl engr charge Spl Fibers Lab US Dept Agr Fla since '43. U.S. Department of Agriculture, Belle Glade, Fla.

C

22 CABLE, Louella E. Fishery biology and management. b'00. AB '26—MA '27 (U SD). Research in food of bullheads, life history of fish, taxonomy of fish and other marine animals, rearing larval salt water fish, food of juvenile fishes; investigation of shad fishery of Atlantic Coast of US, racial characteristics resulting from homing proclivity of species, population trends and causes thereof; fishery management problems. Author articles in field. Fisheries research biologist United States Fish and Wildlife Service since '47. American Fisheries Society—AAAS—Am Soc Zool—Sigma Xi—Phi Beta Kappa. 1220 E Washington St., Ann Arbor.

23 CADWALLADER, Henry, Jr. Machine shop methods and management; Machine tools. b'81. Student '96-00 (Temple U); '07-08 (U Pa). Invented CAD bolt for T-slots of machine tools; engr Jamaica Govt Ry '09; equipment design Panama Canal, Culebra, Gatum, Canal Zone, Rep Panama '10-11; indsl engr Continental Motor Mfg Co Muskegon Mich '13-16; organizer Standard Shop Equipment Co Phila '19, pres since '19. ASME—Am Soc Tool Engrs. Recipient Panama Canal Medal '11, two Sesquicentennial Expn Medal awards '11. 82nd and Timicum Av., Phila.

10 CADWELL, Sidney March. Rubber (Chemistry, accelerators, antioxidants, abrasion resistance). b'93. BS '14—PhD '17 (U Chicago). Development antioxidants for rubber products to increase serviceability; assisted in development of golf ball cover highly resistant to cuts and slicing. Author article: Correlation of Various Aging Tests with Natural Shelf Aging. Co-author articles: (with O H Smith) A Laboratory Burning Test for Accelerators; (with Merrill, Sloman, Yost) Static Fatigue —Life of Rubber, and others. With US Rubber Co since '19, dir research and development dept since '46. ACS (past chmn div rubber chem)—AICE— Am Inst Physics—APS—Indsl Research Inst—Chem Soc London(F)— Soc Automotive Engrs—Tire and Rim Assn (past pres)—Gamma Alpha (past pres)—Sigma Xi. U.S. Rubber Co., 1230 Av. of the Americas, N.Y.C. 20.

11 CADY, Willoughby Miller. Spectroscopy; Optics; Radar. b'07. AB '27 (Brown U); '27-28 (Yale); PhD '32 (Harvard); NRC fellow '32-34 (Calif Inst Tech). Research on spectra of manganese, oxygen, and nitrogen in the extreme ultraviolet; analysis of the ultra-soft x-ray emission spectrum of sodium, magnesium, aluminum, and sulfur; development of methods in photography, especially sensitometry and spectrophotometry; study of spectrum changes during a single electric spark; photography of acoustic and shock waves in air; development of airborne radar scanners. Co-author and co-editor: Radar Scanners and Radomes '48. Contributing author: Radar Systems Engineering '48. Radar Aids to Navigation '48, Experimental Methods in High Speed Aerodynamics. Asst prof physics Clark U '34-36; asst prof physics U Wash '41-42; staff radiation lab MIT '42-46, leader airborne scanner group '43-46; with US Naval Ordnance Test Sta '46-50, head physics div since '48; group leader fundamental developments North American Aviation Inc since '50. APS(F)—Optical Soc Am—Am Asso Phys Teachers —AAAS—Sigma Xi. North American Aviation Inc., Downey Calif.

12 CADZOW, Donald A. Anthropology of American Indians and Eskimo; Pennsylvania history and archaeology; Indians of Western Arctic and Sub-arctic. b'94. Student '19-23 (Columbia U). Anthropological staff Museum American Indian. Leader of two Expeditions to western Arctic, three to northern Canada, one to south Baffinland; anthropologist with Hendriks Hodge expedition to New Mexico; archaeological surveys New York, south central states; special research Loucheux Indians north Alaska, Canada. Anthropologist for Pennsylvania. Author: books and articles in field. Sec Pa Hist and Museum Commn, exec dir since '45. Royal Anthrop Soc of Brit(F) — Soc Americanists(F) — Pa Archaeol Soc (pres). State Museum Building, Harrisburg, Pa.

13 CAEMMERER, H(ans) Paul. History of Washington D.C. (Architectural, social). b'84. AB '16—AM '17 (George Washington U); LLB '24 (Georgetown U); '26 (Wittenberg Coll); PhD '38 (American U); special work in Archaeology; Architectural engineering. Author: Washington, The National Capital '32; The George Washington Bicentennial Frieze '32; Origin and Development of Washington '39; The Sesquicentennial of the L'Enfant Plan '40; The Sesquicentennial of the United States Capitol '43; Architects of the Capitol '46; Early Washington and Its Art '47; Historic Washington '48; also articles in field. Clk Nat Commn Fine Arts '19-20, sec since '22. Am Fed Arts—Am Planning Civic Assn—Columbia Hist Soc (life) —Washington Bldg Congress—Am Soc Archtl Hist—Archaeol Inst Am (life). 2114 N St., Washington.

14 CAFFEE, Nathaniel Montier. American language (Southern dialect). b'09. AB '28 (Coll William and Mary); MA '33—PhD '35 (Va U); '28 (Harvard), '34-35 (Brown U), summer '38 Jena U). Research and writing on consonant pronunciation in South, Southern '1' plus consonant, Negro speech, foreign language curriculum. Author articles in field. Asso prof Eng La State U '42-52, Professor since '52. So Central Modern Language Association—Gen Edn Bd, Linguistic Atlas of New Eng(F) '34-35. English Department, Louisiana State University, Baton Rouge 3.†

15 CAGLE, Fred R. Zoology (Herpetology). b'15. BEd '37 (S Ill U); MS '38—PhD '43—Rackham fellow '42-43 (U Mich). Research on vertebrate populations, growth in poikilothermic vertebrates, specialized growth rates and life histories of turtles. Author articles in field. Asst prof zool '40-42, dir Museum '38-43; asso prof zool Tulane U since '46. Capt AAF aviation physiol '43-45. AAAS—Ichthyologists and Herpetologists—Soc Mammalogists — Wilson Ornith Club — Wildlife Soc—NY Acad Sci—Sigma Xi. Biology Department, Tulane Univ, New Orleans. H: 1307 Audubon St.†

16 CAHEN, Alfred. Textile economics; Market research. b'07. BA '27 (O State U); MA '29—PhD '31 (Columbia). Statistician, International Association of Garment Manufacturers '34-35; Textile Analyst U.S. Bureau of Census, '37-42; Apparel economist War Production Board '42-45. Co-author: Report on Productivity in the Cotton Garment Industry. Author articles in field. Textile economist Dun and Bradstreet Inc '45-49; Quality Home Products Co since '49. American Statis Assn (treas N Y Met chap)—Am Marketing Assn (com on sampling indsl markets) — Textile Analysts Group (sec-treas '46-47). Quality Home Products Co., 54 Franklin St., NYC 13.

17 CAILLIET, Emile. Pascal; Christian Philosophy; Symbolism. b'94. PhD '26 (U Montpellier, France); ThD '37 (U Strasbourg, France); MA '46 (Wesleyan U). Author: The Life of the Mind '42; La Tradition Litteraire des Ideologuos (vol 19, Memoirs Am Philos Soc '43); The Clue to Pascal '43; Pascal: Genius in the Light of Scripture '45; The Beginning of Wisdom '47; Great Shorter Works of Pascal '48. Prof Christian philosophy Princeton Theol Sem since '47. French Acad Colonial Scis (Nat F '32). Officier d'Academie (France) for service in field of letters '34. Add: 31 Alexander St., Princeton, N.J.◉

18 CAIRNS, Huntington. Legal philosophy; Jurisprudence; Aesthetics; Obscenity in literature and works of art. b'04. LLB '25 (U Md). Author: Law and the Social Sciences '35; The Theory of Legal Science '41; The Limits of Art '48. Co-author: (with Allen Tate and Mark Van Doren) Invitation to Learning '41; (with John Walker) Masterpieces of Painting from the National Gallery of Art '44; Legal Philosophy from Plato to Hegel '48; also articles in field. Lectr in criticism Johns Hopkins U; spl adviser to Treas Dept on obscenity in works of art and literature since '34. Mem com on practice Treas Dept since '44; sec treas and gen counsel Nat Gallery Art since '43. National Gallery of Art, Washington 25.◉

19 CAIRNS, Robert William. Chemistry of explosives, propellants, rosin and cellulose. b'09. Student '27 (U Calif); AB '30 (Oberlin Coll); PhD '32 (Johns Hopkins U). Synthesis of organic accelerators and antioxidants; electron scattering theory; research on high explosives and smokeless powder, rosin, cellulose; administration of research; member Division 8 National Defense Research Committee propellant research '42-44, explosives research '42-44; dep chmn Panel on Ammunition and Explosives, Committee on Ordnance, Research and Development, National Military Establishment since '48. Author articles in field. Research chem Firestone Tire and Rubber Co '30-33 part-time; research chem Hercules Powder Co '34-40, asst to dir research '40-41, dir expt sta '41-45, dir development Radford Ordnance Works '42-43; asst dir research since '45. Fellow Bartol Research Found '33-34. Am Chem Soc— Am Phys Soc—Indsl Research Inst— Am Inst Physics—Am Soc for X-ray and Electron Diffraction—Forest Products Research Soc—Armed Forces Chem Assn—Army Ordnance Assn— Sigma Xi—Phi Beta Kappa. Research Department, Hercules Powder Company, Wilmington, Del.

20 CALABRESE, Giuseppe. Probability method of determining electric power system reserve; electric power circuit protection and analysis; Power system planning. b'97. Dr Eng '21 (Poly Inst Turin); '35-37 (Columbia). Lightning research and investigations, protection of transmissions and generating facilities, electric and gas system planning, development of out-of-step and fault protection of 132 KV interconnection lines, pioneer use of propane-air peak plants. Author articles in field. Transmission engr Westinghouse Elec Mfg Co '26-28; asst and div engr Consol Edison Co NYC '28-48; prof elec engring NYU since '48. AIEE (chmn sub com on application probability methods to reserve capacity problems, sec power generation com). New York University, University Heights, NYC 53. H: 188-01 Dormans Rd., St. Albany 12, L.I.◉

21 CALAVAN, Edmond Clair. Citrus diseases (Lemon, orange, grapefruit). b'13. BS '39—MS '41 (Ore State Coll); PhD '45 (U Wis). Author articles in field. Asst plant pathologist U Calif Citrus Expt Sta since '47. Am Phytopathol Soc—AAAS—Sigma Xi—Phi Kappa Phi—Phi Sigma. Citrus Experiment Station, Riverside, Calif.†

22 CALAWAY, Paul Kenneth. Organic chemistry (Quinolines, aryloxyketones, arylthioketones). b'10. BA '31 (Ark Coll); MS '33 (Ga Tech); PhD '38 (Tex U). Prof and head chem dept Ga Tech since '48. Am Chem Soc —Ga Acad Sci(F)—Sigma Xi.†

23 CALCOTT, William Stansfield. Industrial organic chemistry (Rubber and petroleum chemicals, antioxidants, dye intermediates and processes). b'92. ChE '13 (U Va); hon LLD (Notre Dame U). Holder 110 U S patents resulting from chem research, 43 British patents, 32 Canadian patents. Author articles in field. Asst editor: Chemical Engineer's Handbook '34. With du Pont Co '15-48, dir gen organic div Jackson Lab '31-43. Am Chem Soc— Inst Chemists Soc—Am Inst Chem Eng —Soc Chem Ind (London)—Soc Dyers and Colorists—AAAS—Am Soc Testing Materials. Nemours Building, Wilmington, Del.

10 CALDWELL, John S. Leafhoppers and planthoppers of West Indies; Psylliidae of Mexico. b'11. BS '33—MS '34—PhD '38 (O State U); '47 (Puerto Rico U). Research in taxonomy of Ohio specialist responsible for identification in restricted groups in order Homoptera to carry on taxonomic studies in the order to improve classification for US Department Agriculture Division Insect Identification '44-45; identified Puerto Rican and Virgin Island Homptera with special reference to Cicadellidae and Fulgoroidea. Author articles in field. Specialist, Govt of Puerto Rico since '47. Entomol Soc Am(F). 535 So. Court St., Circleville, O.

11 CALDWELL, Colonel Lyle. Electronics; Geophysics. b'06. BS (elec engring) '29 (Wash State Coll). Shift engr RCA Communications '29-30; elec tester Westinghouse Elec '30-33; geophys Gulf Research and Development Co '33-42; engring rep Bendix Aviation Corp since '50. 1333 G St., Washington.

12 CALDWELL, Ralph Merrill. Phytopathology; Plant breeding; Cereal pathology. b'03. BS '25 (S D State Coll); MS '27—PhD '29 (U Wis). Author articles in field. Chief dept bot and plant pathol Purdue U Agrl Expt Sta since '37, head dept agrl bot Purdue U '43-50; head dept bot and plant path since '50. AAAS(F)—Am Phytopath Soc (treas, bus mgr Phytopathol '44-46)—Am Soc Agron—Ind Acad Sci—Bot Soc Am—Sigma Xi—Phi Sigma. 628 Terry Lane, West Lafayette, Ind.

13 CALDWELL, Robert Graham. Criminology. BS '28—MA '34—PhD '39 (U Pa); BL '47 (Jackson Sch Law). Author: The New Castle County Workhouse '40; The Penitentiary Movement in Delaware '46; Red Hannah, Delaware's Whipping Post '47; also articles in field. With Fed Security Agency '43-45; prof sociol and research criminologist State U Ia since '48. Am Sociol Soc—Va Social Sci Assn—Pi Gamma Mu—Va Bar Assn. Sociology Department, State University of Iowa, Iowa City, Ia.

14 CALDWELL, Samuel Hawks. Computing machinery; Industrial control; Electronic application. b'04. SB '25—SM '26—ScD '33 (Mass Inst Tech). Author articles in field. Asso prof elec engring Mass Inst Tech '40-47, prof since '47, dir resch Graphic Arts Research Found. Am Inst Elec Engrs—AAAS—Sigma Xi. Massachusetts Institute of Technology, Cambridge 39, Mass. H: 135 Newbury St., Boston.⊚

15 CALEY, Earle Radcliffe. Chemical analysis; Reagents and tests; Archaeological chemistry; Composition of ancient materials; Ancient technology; Ancient coins and coinage. b'00. BS '23 (Baldwin-Wallace Coll); MSc '25—PhD '28 (Ohio State U). Agora excavation staff Athens Greece '37, established chemical laboratory at excavation site in Athens, conducted research on ancient materials; developed methods for restoration and preservation of antiquities. Invented new forms of chemical apparatus, filtration pipet, microdensimeter. Discovered new chemical reagents. Author: analytical Factors and Their Logarithms '32; The Composition of Ancient Greek Bronze Coins '39; also articles in field. Asso prof chem Ohio State U since '46; advisory ed staff Numismatic Review since '43. AAAS(F)—Ohio Acad Sci—N Y Acad Sci—Am Chem Soc (chmn '31)—Hist Sci Soc—Am Numismatic Soc — Royal Numismatic

Soc(F). Department of Chemistry, Ohio State University, Columbus 10, O.

16 CALHOUN, Fred Harvey Hall. Geology; Mineral deposits of South East states. Author geological monographs. Asst prof geology and mineralogy Clemson Coll SC since '04, dir agr dept '15-33, dean sch chemistry and geology since '33; cons geologist Seaboard Air Line RR; asst geologist US Geol Survey '03-15. Geol Soc Am(F)—AAAS(F)—SC Acad Sci (pres)—Alpha Chi Sigma—Phi Kappa Phi. Clemson, S.C.†⊚

17 CALHOUN, John B(umpass). Vertebrate population ecology. b'17. BS '39 (U Va); MS '42—PhD '43 (Northwestern U). Research in activity rhythms of animals during the 24 hour daily period, time factor in natural selection; bird migration, nesting behavior in doves and robins; sociality of wild rats. Author articles in field. Research asso rodent ecol Johns Hopkins U '46-49; spec fellow Nat Inst Mental Health to the Hamilton Sta Jackson Mem Lab. Am Soc Mammalogists—Am Ornithol Union—Sigma Xi. Hamilton Station Box 847, Bar Harbor, Me.†

18 CALHOUN, Mary Lois. Chickens (Histology of digestive tract); Cow and horse (bone marrow); Comparative histology (Urinary tract). b'04. BS '24—MS '31—Dr Veterinary Med '39—PhD '46 (Ia State Coll). Author articles: The microscopic anatomy of the digestive tract of Gallus domesticus; A cytological study of the costal marrow of the adult horse and cow, and others. Histological and embryological technician, asst and instr Ia State Coll '28-43; with Mich State Coll since '43, prof and head dept since 1948. AAAS—Biol Photographic Assn—Internat Assn Med Mus—Am Veterinary Med Assn—Womens Veterinary Med Assn—Sigma Xi—Phi Kappa Phi—Sigma Delta Epsilon—Gamma Sigma Delta—Phi Zeta. Anatomy Bldg., Michigan State College, East Lansing, Mich.

19 CALIVER, Ambrose. Negro education. b'94. MA(hon) '36 (Tuskeegee Inst). BA '15 (Knoxville Coll); MA '20 (U Wis); PhD '30 (Columbia U). Conducted annual radio broadcast on education of Negroes Office of Education '30-40; pub '37-40 National Educational Outlook Among Negroes. Author articles in field. Specialist in edn of Negroes US Office Edn '30-50; asst to US commr of educ since '50; profl lecturer in grad dept Howard U since '38; dir project for Adult Edn of Negroes since '46. Nat Assn Collegiate Deans and Registrars in Negro Schs (pres '28)—NEA—Nat Vocational Guidance Assn (chmn com spl groups '38-42)—Am Ednl Research Assn—Am Assn Adult Edn—AAAS—Am Acad Polit and Social Sci—Southern Edn Foundation (bd dirs and exec com)—Assn Study Negro Life and Hist—NAACP. U.S. Office of Education, Washington.⊚

20 CALKIN, Homer Leonard. American history (Colonial, revolutionary, foreign-born groups, Irish-American); Propaganda, public opinion and pressure groups in United States since '35; British Empire history (Great Britain-Ireland relations). b'12. BA '35—MA '36—PhD '39 (State U of Ia). National Archives Washington; at present with US Dept of State. AHA—Miss Valley Hist Assn—Ia State Hist Soc. Dept. of State, Washington 25.

21 CALKIN, John B(urgess). Pulp and paper chemistry and technology; Fire prevention technology; Food technology; Chemical marketing research; Wood and Naval stores chem-

icals. b'04. Student '18-22 (York Collegiate Inst); SB '26—AM '27 (Haverford Coll); fellow '27 (Cornell U); MS '28 (U Maine); Arkwright textile fellow '31-32 (MIT). Author articles in field. Micros Brown Co '27-29, chem engr '42-43; research chem Dennison Mfg Co '29-31, chem engr '35-39; own constrn bus '39-42; coordinator research Union Bag & Paper Corp '43-48; dir dept indsl coop and asso prof chem engring U Maine since '49; cons pulp and paper chem process ind. Tech Assn Pulp and Paper Ind—AICE—Am Chem Soc—AIC—Am Oil Chem Soc—Chem Market Research Assn—Comml Chem Development Assn—AAAS—Am Soc Testing Materials—NY Acad Sci. 500 Fifth Av., NYC 18.

22 CALL, Ara Om. Process cheese production; Lactose production. b'09. Student '27-29 (Brigham Young U); BS '33 (Ia State Coll); '41-42 (Utah State Agrl Coll); MS '44 (U Wis). Tech dir Queseria de Dublan, S A '31-40; with Call Cheese Co '40-41; mgr control lab W Condensing Co since '44. Am Dairy Sci Assn—ACS (chmn NE Wis sect '50)—Wis Milk Sanitarians—Internat Assn Milk and Food Sanitarians—Animal Nutrition Research Council—AAAS—Nat Cheese Institute (mem research com)—Phi Sigma—Gamma Alpha. Research F diary industry U Wis '42-44; received Walker Award in dairying Ia State Coll '33. Western Condensing Co., 935 E. John St., Appleton, Wis. H: 911 E. Hancock St.

23 CALLAGHAN, Edna S (Mrs Eugene). Educational Guidance; Population Movements; Consumer Economics; Adolescent psychology; Social legislation. b'08. BS '31—MA Honors '33 (U Ore). Research on adolescent psychology and guidance in fields of secondary school education and community youth organization, child labor legislation, Oregon Population Movements. Guidance dir and dean girls high schs '31-35; asso econ U.S. Temp Nat Econ Com '39; chmn Com Legislation and Soc Studies Wash branch Am Assn U Women '39-41; chmn Com Pub Affairs Young Women's Christian Assn '41-45; pres League Women Voters Wash '42-44; chmn Wash Legislation Com Nat Congress Parents and Teachers '49-51, chmn Women's Joint Congressional Com and delegate Nat Congress Parents and Teachers '50-51. Nat Congress Parents and Teachers—Am Assn U Women—Nat League Women Voters—Pi Lambda Theta—Alpha Kappa Delta. 600 S. Michigan Av., Chicago.

24 CALLAGHAN, Eugene. Nonmetallic mineral resources of the United States (Indiana). b'04. BA '26—MA '27 (U Ore); PhD '31 (Columbia). Barton expedition to Iran '28; field studies of metallic and non-metallic minerals in western and northwestern states; tin, tungsten and antimony resources in Bolivia; engineering geology and stone resources in Puerto Rico; clays, building stone, crushed stone, sand and gravel and other resources in Indiana. Author articles in field. With US Geol Survey '30-45; prof econ geol and econ geol Ind U '46-49; dir N.M. Bur of Mines and Resources since '49. Geol Soc Am(F)—Soc Econ Geol—Am Geophy Union—Nat Research Council — Am Inst Mining Met Engr. New Mex Bur Mines and Mineral Resources, Socorro, N. M.†

25 CALLANDER, William Forrest. Economic agricultural statistics (United States). b'80. LLB '12 (Georgetown U); spl studies '15-16 (U Wis); spl studies '12-24 (George Washington U). Author articles in field. Chief statis for agr US Bur Census

Washington, asst chief in charge statis Bur Agrl Econs, also chmn crop reporting bd to '49; lecturer and dir Statistical Laboratory U Fla since '50. Am Statis Assn—AAAS—Am Farm Econ Assn. Statistical Lab., Univ. of Florida, Gainesville, Fla.

10 CALLAWAY, Cason Jewell. Southern farming (United States); Soil conservation. b'94. Pres and chmn bd Callaway Mills, LaGrange, Ga. '20-38. Experiments in cash crops for South; orgn Georgia 100 Better Farms; dir, Nutrition Foundation, N.Y. Cotton Mfrs Assn of Ga. (past pres)—Am Cotton Mfrs Assn. Blue Springs Farms, Hamilton, Ga.

11 CALLIHAN, A(lfred) Dixon. Nuclear reactions; Boron. b'08. AB '28 (Marshall); MA '31 (Duke); PhD '33 (NY). Co-author: (with E O Salant) Modified Scattering by Crystalline HC1 and HBr '34; (with Waldman et al) Disintegration of Boron by Protons '38. Instr physics Coll City NY '34-38, asst prof '48 (on leave '42); research physicist Columbia U Div of War Research '42-45; research physicist Carbide and Carbon Chem Co since '45. Am Phys Society—Am Assn Physics Teachers—Sigma Xi—Sigma Pi Sigma. Carbide and Carbon Chemicals Corporation, P.O. Box P, Oak Ridge, Tenn.

12 CALLON, Ross William. Aluminum alloys; Magnesium alloys. b'17. BA '38 (McMaster U); MA '39 (U Toronto). Research and development of physical methods of analysis with emphasis on spectrochemical methods for determination of constituents in aluminum and magnesium alloys, their raw materials and intermediate products. Chief spectroscopist Aluminum Co Can Ltd '40-45; with Aluminum Lab Ltd since '46, head analytical div from '50. ASTM (chmn subcom I, com E-2 since '47)—Chem Inst Can—Can Assn Phys—APS—Optical Soc Am (asso mem). Aluminum Laboratories, Ltd., Postoffice Box 645, Arvida, Que., Can.

13 CALVER, Homer Northup. Health education and exhibits; Public relations. b'92. BS in Sanitary Engring '14 (Mass Inst Tech). Sec pub health com Paper Cup and Container Inst since '34; ed Health Officers News Digest since '36; sec Am Mus of Health Inc since '38; sec-treas Internat Inst of Health Edn since '46; cons in health edn Inst Inter-Am Affairs. Internat Assn of Med Mus—Municipal Art Soc (bd dirs since '38)—Child Study Assn Asm (bd dirs since '42)—Pub Relations Soc of Am (bd dirs, exec com since '48)—Am Pub Health Assn(F, v chmn Pub Health Edn Sect '34-36, chmn '36-37; chmn com on scil exhibits '32-42)—AAAS—Royal San Inst(hon F)—AMA(asso F)—Soc Am Bact. 1790 Broadway, NYC 19.

14 CALVERLEY, Edwin Elliott. Arabic; Islamics. b'82. AB '06—AM '08 (Princeton U); PhD '23 (Hartford Sem Found). Missionary in Arabia of Reformed Church in America '09-30; co-editor of The Moslem World '38, editor '47. Author: The Arabian Readers '20, 25; Worship in Islam '25. With Kennedy Sch of Missions of the Hartford Seminary Found since '30, prof Arabic and Islamics since '37. Am Council Learned Soc (mem Comm on Near Eastern Studies) — Royal Asiatic Soc—Mediaeval Acad Am—Royal Central Asian Soc—Am Oriental Soc—Oriental Soc of Hartford Sem Found (sec)—Linguistic Soc Am—Phi Beta Kappa. 143 Sigourney St., Hartford 5, Conn.

15 CALVERT, O(scar) H(ugh). Plant pathology (Vegetables). b'18. Stu-

dent '39-40 (San Antonio Jr Coll); '40-41 (Wheaton Coll); BS '43 (Okla A&M Coll); PhD '48—MS '45 (U Wis). Research in cabbage, tomato, and spinach diseases, resistance in spinach to Albugo occidentalis, causal organism of white rust; assisted in discovery of the high penicillin yielding strain Q176 through ultra-violet irradiation. Author articles in field. Vegetable path Tex Agr Expt Sta since '48. Am Phytopathol Soc—Sigma Xi. Texas Agricultural Experiment Station, Winter Haven, Tex.

16 CALVIN, Dea Bailey. Physiological chemistry (Blood volume, water balance). b'00. AB '23 (Rice Inst); AM '25 (Tex U); PhD '28 (Yale). Research on loss of bases in diuresis and effect upon alkali reserve of blood, water balance and acid-base regulation, carbohydrate metabolism, medical education. Author articles: Glycogen Storage by Fresh Water Mussels (with Ellis) '32; Plasma Protein Changes Following Intravenous Saline Administration '39; Chemistry in the Premedical Curriculum, The Viewpoint of the Medical College '46; and others. Instr physiol, Mo. U Sch Med '28-29, asst prof '29-33, asso prof '33-37; asso prof biol chem and asso dean Tex U Med Sch '37-44, prof and asso dean '44-45, prof and dean students and curricular affairs since '45. AAAS(F) —Am Physiol Soc—Am Soc Biol Chem —Am Chem Soc—Soc Exptl Biol and Med—Tex Acad Sci—Sigma Xi. University of Texas, Medical Branch, Galveston, Tex.

17 CALVIN Melvin. Photosynthesis; Organic and biochemistry. b'11. BS '31. (Mich Coll Mining and Tech); PhD '35 (U Minn). Co-author: (with G E K Branch) Theory of Organic Chemistry '40; also articles in field. With U Calif since '37, now prof chem, dir bioorganic group Radiation Lab since '46. Official investigator and dir NDRC project '42-44, Manhattan Dist Project 48B '45. Rockefeller Foundation fellow '35-37. Department of Chemistry, University of California, Berkeley.†

18 CAMERON, Charles F(ranklin). Electrical engineering. b'98. Diploma '19 (Northwestern (Okla) State Coll); student '20-21 (U Okla); BS '23—EE '36 (Okla A and M Coll); MSE '39 (Purdue). Research predicting performance induction motors, polyphase and single-phase. Author engring dept bulls. Prof elec engring specializing in power machinery Okla A and M Coll since '47; cons elec projects; registered profl engr Wyo, Okla. AIEE— Illuminating Engring Soc—Am Soc Engring Edn—Nat Soc Profl Engrs— Okla Soc Profl Engrs—Eta Kappa Nu —Sigma Xi. Oklahoma A and M College, Stillwater, Okla.†Ⓖ

19 CAMERON, Eugene Nathan. Economic geology; Pegmatite mineral deposits. b'10. BS '32 (NYU); MA '34— PhD '39 (Columbia). Author articles in field. Asso later sr geologist US Geol Survey since '42; asso prof geol U Wis since '47. Mineral Soc Am(F) —Geol Soc Am(F)—Soc Econ Geol(F) —Sigma Xi—Phi Beta Kappa. Samuel F Emmons Memorial fellow '35-36. Science Hall, Madison 6, Wis.

20 CAMERON, Francis. Geology (Metal mining). b'02. AB '24 (Leland Stanford U). Asst foreman and engr Chief Consol Mining Co Eureka Utah '24-25; asst geologist Internat Smelting Co Salt Lake City '26-28, Anaconda Copper Mining Co NY, various US and Fgn cities '28-45; adviser Metals Reserve Co Washington '42-45; asst to exec vp St Joseph Lead Co NYC '45-46, vp since '46. Geol Soc Am(F)

—AIMME—Soc Econ Geol. 250 Park Av., NYC 17.Ⓖ

21 CAMERON, George Glenn. Ancient Persian history and languages; Babylonian-Assyrian history and languages; Semitic, Persian and Elamic languages. b'05. AB '27 (Muskingum Coll); MA '30—PhD '32 (U Chicago). Research on cuneiform languages, member Persepolis Expedition of Oriental Institute '39, director expedition to Behistun monument (Iran) of Darius, King of Persia, '48, editor American Journal of Semitic Languages and Literatures and Journal of Near Eastern Studies '40-48. Author: History of Early Iran '36; Persepolis Treasury Tablets '48. Editor: They Wrote on Clay '37. Faculty, asst and asso prof U Chicago Oriental Inst '33-48; chmn dept Near Eastern studies, prof Near Eastern cultures U Mich since '48; annual prof Am Sch Oriental Research (Baghdad Sch) '48-49. Am Oriental Soc —AHA—Middle E Inst—Phi Kappa Phi. Received Order of Homayoun from govt of Iran. University of Michigan, Ann Arbor, Mich.

22 CAMERON, John Andrew C(ameron). Reproduction; Artificial fever; Carbon monoxide physiology. b'02. BA '25—MA '26 (Neb U); PhD '34 (Mo U). Research on origin of new cells in epidermis, mitosis during healing of X-ray burns, termination of early pregnancy by artificial fever, artificial fever as contraceptive. Coauthor article: (with Fisher) The Effect of Light on the CO Poisoned Embryonic Fundulus Heart '36; also articles in field. Prof anatomy Baylor U Coll Dentistry since '44. Am Assn Anat—Am Soc Zool—Am Soc Parasitol—Soc Exptl Biol and Med—Sigma Xi. Fellow Gen Edn Bd, Rockefeller Found, and research fellow, Harvard '36-37. Baylor University, Dallas 1.

23 CAMERON, Kenneth Walter. Ralph Waldo Emerson; John Heywood; Early Tudor drama; American transcendentalism. b'08. AB '30—AM '31 (W Va U); STB '35 (Gen Theol Sem NYC); PhD '40 (Yale). Author: Emerson the Essayist, 2 vols '45; Ralph Waldo Emerson's Reading '41; John Heywood's Play of the Wether: A Study in Early Tudor Drama '41; John Heywood's Play of Love '44, and others; also articles in field. Asst prof Eng Trinity Coll since '46. Mod Lang Assn Am—Coll Eng Assn—Oxford Biblio Soc—So Atlantic Mod Lang Assn — Church Hist Soc — Mod Humanities Research Assn—Shakespeare Assn Am. Trinity College, Hartford 6, Conn.†

24 CAMERON, S(idney) H(erbert). Subtropical horticulture; Fruit tree physiology; Plant Propagation. b'97. PhD '27 (U Calif); '28-29 (U Leeds, Eng). Instr subtropical hort U Calif '23-28, prof since '46. Am Soc Hort Sci—Am Soc Plant Physiol—Bot Soc Am. University of California, 405 Hilgard Av., Los Angeles 24.

25 CAMMANN, Schuyler van Rensselaer. Far Eastern symbolism; Oriental religions; Chinese textiles; Tibet. b'12. BA '35 (Yale); MA '41 (Harvard); PhD '49 (Johns Hopkins); spl lang study (U Tours, U Munich, Peking Lang Sch). Anthropological research west China, Tibetan borders, Burma, and northern India '37-38; west China and Mongolia '45; associate editor Journal of the American Oriental Society '48. Asst curator Chinese dept University Museum Phila '48-50; asso curator since '50; asst professor Chinese U Pa since '48. Am Oriental Soc — Am Anthropol Assn — Archeol Inst Am—Medieval Acad Am—Phila

Anthropol Soc. University Museum, 33rd and Spruce, Phila 4.†

10 CAMP, Arthur Forrest. Citrus culture. b'96. AB '20 (U Calif); PhD '23 (Wash U). Research on minor elements in citrus nutrition, incorporation of minor elements in citrus fertilization and spraying, eradication of Mediterranean fruitfly. Head dept hort Fla Agrl Expt Sta '26-36; in charge Citrus Expt Sta U Fla from '35; v-dir Fla Agrl Expt Sta and Tech Adv Fla State Plant Bd from '44. Sigma Xi—Am Soc Hort Sci—Fla State Hort Soc. Citrus Experiment Station, Lake Alfred, Fla.

11 CAMP, Cecil Cicero. Gold mining; Mineral exploration. b'93. BS '28 (Wash State Coll). Research on economical operation of gold mines, metallurgy of gold for small gold mines, exploration of mineral deposits in Canada, US, Mexico and Colombia, coal mining exploration in Pennsylvania, West Virginia, Kentucky and Oklahoma. Research Dept Anaconda Copper Mines Great Falls, Montana '29-31; supt Morning Star Mine '33-37; mill supt and metall Privateer Gold Mine '38-42; exploration engr Butler Brothers Iron Ore miners '42-48, on exploration work since '48. Can Inst Mining and Metall—Prof Engrs BC—Phi Kappa Phi—Sigma Tau. Lane Hotel, Morrilton, Ark.

12 CAMP, W(endell) H(olmes). Taxonomy of blueberries, cranberries, azaleas and rhododendrons; Forest tree species (Beeches, oaks); Luffa gourds (Breeding, culture); Quinine (Wild stands); Plant species (Origin, evolution); History and development of horticultural plants. b'04. BSc '25 (Otterbein Coll); PhD '32 (Ohio State U); spl work (Oberlin Coll, Cornell U). Exploration for and production of essential fiber and drug plants '42-45 in Haiti, Honduras, Salvador, Guatemala, Mexico, and Ecuador under auspices various governmental agencies and private concerns; chairman, editorial board, for International Rules of Botanical Nomenclature '47 edition. Founder and editor: The Taxonomic Index; author articles in field. Sci staff NY Bot Garden '36-49; grad faculty Columbia U '37-49; cur exptl bot Phila Academy since '49. Am Society Plant Taxonomists (sec-treas '48, pres '49)—Bot Soc Am—Soc Study Evolution—Am Hort Council (president '49). Philadelphia Academy of Natural Sciences, 19th and Parkway, Phila. 3.

13 CAMPAIGNE, Ernest E(dwin). Medicinal chemistry (Antihistaminics, local anesthetics, hypnotics); Organic sulfur compounds; Substituted thiophenes and thiocarbonyls. b'14. BS '36—MS '38—PhD '40 (Northwestern U). Author articles in field. Asso prof chem Indiana U since '49. American Chem Soc (medicinal div, organic div) —AAAS—Ind Acad of Sci—Sigma Xi. —NY Acad Sci—Soc Exptl Biol Med. Department of Chemistry, Indiana University, Bloomington, Ind.†

14 CAMPAU, Edward Junior. Insecticides; Fungicides. b'16. AS '36 (Grand Rapids Mich Jr Coll); BS '38 (Mich State Coll); MA '40 (Stanford U); PhD '42 (U Wis). Research in toxicity of rotenone dust mixtures, and effects on toxicity of such diluents as clay when used in pea aphid control. Author articles in field. Group leader Research Dept Standard Oil Co since '46; Served US Army malaria survey unit '43-46. AAAS—Am Assn Econ Entomol—Sigma Xi—Phi Kappa Phi. Research Department, Standard Oil Co., Whiting, Ind.†

15 CAMPBELL, Arthur Shackleton. Recent and fossil Radiolaria, Tintinnoina and Foraminifera; Aquarium fishes. b'98. AB '21 (Pomona Coll); AM '24 (Harvard); PhD '26 (U Calif). Author articles in field. Prof zool St Mary's Coll since '26, chmn sch sci since '48. Am Soc Zool—Paleontol Soc —Geol Soc Am(F)—Am Genetic Assn —AAAS(F)—Sigma Xi. St. Mary's College, Contra Costa, Calif. H: 3011 Regent St., Berkeley 5.

16 CAMPBELL, Berry. Brain anatomy, physiology and pathology; Virus diseases; Poliomyelitis; Histology of allergy; Behavior (Neurological). b'12. AB '32 (U Calif); PhD '35 (John Hopkins U); research fellow in neurology '42-43 (Columbia U); Nat Research Council Fellow in medical sci '35-36, '36-37 (Western Reserve U). Research on morphological problems of locomotion, integrative mechanisms of the nervous system. Author articles in field. Asst prof anat U Okla '37-42; visiting asst prof anat U Tenn Med Sch '42; asst prof anat U Minn '43-45, asso prof since '45. Am Soc Herpetologists and Ichthyologists—AAAS—Am Soc Mammalogists—Am Assn Anat— Am Assn Hist Med—Harvey Soc—Am Physiol Soc—Am Assn Phys Anthrol— Sigma Xi. Fellow John Simon Guggenheim Memorial Found at Rockefeller Inst for Med Research '40-41, '41-42. University of Minnesota Institute of Anatomy, Minneapolis.

17 CAMPBELL, Charles Duncan. Petrology; Geology of Washington. b'05. '25-27 (U Ariz); PhD '34 (Stanford); BS '30—MS '31 (U Mich). Research genesis of Kruger alkaline syenites of Washington-B.C. border; petrology of the east border of the Colville batholith Ferry County Washington and of adjacent metamorphic rocks; stratigraphy, structure and ore deposits of the Northport district and other parts of northern Stevens County Washington, mylonites from the San Andreas fault zone, lead-zinc deposits of northeastern Washington. Author articles in field. Prof and chmn dept State Coll Wash since '50; geol US Geol Survey '42-45. Geol Soc Am(F)—Mineral Soc Am(F)—Am Geophys Union—Northwest Sci Assn. Department of Geology, State College of Washington, Pullman, Wash.†

18 CAMPBELL Donald Atwood. Furnace equipment; Burners (Industrial); Combustion (Industrial gas); Mixers (Gas and air). b'94. BS (elec engring) '16 (Colo U). Research and development of industrial gas burners, air and gas mixing equipment, automatic gas and air proportioning equipment; granted patents on electric and gas igniters for tunnel burners, flo mixer for gaseous fuels, and entrainment device. Indsl sales mgr Kan City Gas Co '25-28; mgr combustion dept Eclipse Fuel Engring Co '28-39, v-pres (Eng & Research) from '51; mgr NY dist office Wheelco Instrument Co '39-44; mgr Bryant Ind Div-Affiliated Gas Equipment Co '44-51. Am Soc Metals —Gas Appliance Mfrs Assn—Am Gas Assn—Gild Ancient Suppliers. Eclipse Fuel Engineering Co., Rockford, Ill.

19 CAMPBELL, George Ashley. Telephone engineering (Electric wave filters, telephone cable loadings, Fourier integrals, electrical units, antenna arrays). b'70. BS '91 (Mass Inst Tech); AB '92—AM '93—PhD '01 (Harvard). Pioneering research in connection with loading, crosstalk, 4-wire repeater circuits, sidetone reduction, electric wave filters, inductive interference, antenna arrays, maximum output networks, Fourier integrals and electrical units. Author: Collected Papers '37. With Am Telephone & Telegraph Co '97-34; Bell Telephone Labs '34-35. Am Acad Arts Sci—Math Soc—Math Assn Am—Phys Soc—AAAS. Awarded Distinguished Service medal by Inst Radio Engrs '36; Elliott Cresson medal by Franklin Inst '39; Edison medal by AIEE '40. Upper Montclair, N.J.

20 CAMPBELL, Ian. Petrology; Industrial minerals. b'99. AB '22—AM '24 (U Ore); '23-24 (Northwestern U); PhD '31 (Harvard). Author articles in field. Prof Calif Inst Tech since '46, asso chmn div geol sci since '40. Soc Econ Geol—Am Ceramic Soc—Am Inst Mining Metall Engrs (western vice-chmn indsl minerals div '48)—Geol Soc Am(F) — Mineral Soc Am (vp '40) — AAAS (exec com Pacific div '39-47). California Institute of Technology, Pasadena 4, Cal.†⊙

21 CAMPBELL, John C. Irish Potatoes; Plant pathology. b'05. Student '26-27 (Rutgers U). Research on nutrient value of new phosphatic materials used on potatoes, potato growing in New Jersey, wireworm control, new varieties, irrigation, fertilizer placement, minor elements, sprout inhibitors, storage problems; evaluation of sludge-acid and alkylation acid superphosphates as sources of phosphorus in potato fertilizers, effect of various amounts of spindle tuber and leaf roll on yields of Irish potatoes; tests of fungicides and insecticides; field comparisons of colloidal phosphate and superphosphate as sources of phosphorus. Co-author articles: (with Hawkins, Brown and Chucka) Fertilizer Placement for Potatoes, A Comparison on Level-Band and Hi-Lo Methods '45; (with Martin) Fertilizer Placement in America '46; (with Pepper) Promising New Chemicals for the Control of Diseases and Insects '48, and others. Jr asst plant path NJ Agrl Expt Station, Rutgers U '27-31, asst plant path '31-44, research asso in agr '44-45, asst research specialist plant path since '45. Am Phytopath Soc—NJ State Potato Assn (secretary, editor Hints to Potato Growers)—Potato Assn Am (treas, asso ed Am Potato Yearbook). Rutgers University, N.J. Agricultural Experiment Station, New Brunswick, N.J.†

22 CAMPBELL, Joseph. Mythology; Hinduism; James Joyce. b'04. AB '25— MA '27 (Columbia); Proudfit F Letters (Columbia) '27-28 (U Paris) and '28-29 (U Munich). Author: Grimm's Fairy Tales, Folkloristic Commentary '44; The Hero with a Thousand Faces '49. Co-author: (with Maud Oakes and Jeff King) Where the Two Came to their Father, a Navaho War Ceremonial '43; (with Henry Morton Robinson) A Skeleton Key to Finnegan's Wake '44. Editor: The Portable Arabian Nights '51; The Philosophies of India '51; The King and the Corpse '48; Myths and Symbols in Indian Art and Civilization '46. Contributor: James Joyce, Two Decades of Criticism '48. Faculty Sarah Lawrence Coll since '34. Am Folklore Soc—Am Oriental Soc—Medieval Acad Am—James Joyce Soc. Received Nat Inst Arts and Letters Award for The Hero with a Thousand Faces '49. Sarah Lawrence College, Bronxville, N.Y.

23 CAMPBELL, Robert Argyll. Economics. b'79. AB '06—Asst '06-08—Fell '09-10 (U Wis); Fell '08-09 (Cornell). Prof econ Rochester U '19-22; with Inst Econs Washington '23-27; head dept econs Vanderbilt U '27-40, prof econs '40-49 prof emeritus since '40; vis prof econs George Pepperdine Coll since '50. Am Econ Assn—Phi Delta Epsilon. 1121 W 79th St LA 44. H: 917 W 81st St.†⊙

24 CAMPBELL, Robert Samuel. Range ecology, management and utilization; Forest grazing. b'04. BS '25—MS '29—PhD '32 (U Chicago). Research in range seeding and chemical control of scrub hardwoods. Author articles in field. Jr Range Examiner US Forest Service Jornada Exptl Range Las Cruces NM '25-27; asst and asso range examiner Southwestern Forest and Range Expt Sta '27-34; sr forest ecol US Forest Service Washington, asst to chief div range research '34-36, in charge western study range utilization standards Berkeley '36-38, asst chief div range research Washington '38-43; chief div range research Southern Forest Expt Sta New Orleans since '43. AAAS(F)—Ecol Soc—Soc Am Foresters—Am Soc Range Management—Am Forestry Assn—Washington Acad Sci — New Orleans Acad Sci — New Orleans Bot Soc—Phi Beta Kappa—Sigma Xi. Award for sci achievement in biol sec, Wash Acad Sci '42. Southern Forest Experiment Station, 1008 Federal Office Bldg., New Orleans 12.

10 CAMPBELL, Roy Elliott. Vegetable crop insects (California). b'90. BS '13—MS '25 (U Calif); '30 (U Minn). Author articles in field. With Calif Bur Entomol and Plant Quarantine US Department Agriculture since '14. AAAS—Am Assn Econ Entomol (sec Pacific Slope Br '24-30, since '39)—Entomol Soc Am—Ecol Soc Am. 1208 E. Main St., Alhambra, Cal.⊙

11 CAMPBELL, Thomas Nolan, Anthropology; Archaeology of Texas. b'08. BA '30 (U Tex); MA '40—PhD '47 (Harvard). Has made archaeological expeditions in Texas and Arizona. Author articles in field. Chmn dept anthropol and dir research in anthropol U Tex since '47, asso prof anthropol since '47. Am Anthropol Assn(F)—Soc Am Archaeol — AAAS(F) — Tex Acad Sci(F) — Tex Archaeol and Paleontol Soc (vp '47-48). Department of Anthropology, University of Texas, Austin, Tex.

12 CAMPBELL, Walter Stanley (pen name Stanley Vestal). Trans-Mississippi West (Great Plains); Plains Indians (History, ways, warfare); The Old West; Fur trade; Southwestern literature. b'87. Rhodes Scholar '08-11—MA '11 (Oxford U). Author twenty-one books in field. Tchr male high schs Louisville '11-14; research among Indians '14; prof English '15; director courses profl writing U Okla since '38, research prof English since '45. Fellow Guggenheim and Rockefeller Founds.; mem Okla Hall Fame—Soc Am Historians. University of Oklahoma, Norman.⊙

13 CAMPBELL, William Andrew. Forest pathology (Tree diseases, fungi). b'06. BS '29 (Mansfield State Teachers Coll Pa); MA '31 (U Colo); PhD '35 (Penn State Coll). Author articles in field. Path div forest path Dept Agr Bur Plant Industry Soils and Agrl Engring, Athens Ga since '46. Am Phytopathol Soc—Mycol Soc Am—Am Soc Foresters—AAAS. School of Forestry, University of Georgia, Athens, Ga.†

14 CAMPEN, William Hershey. Civil engineering; Highway engineering. b '97. Student (Omaha U); BS in Chem (U Neb). Design flexible pavements for strength and durability; evaluation material deposits, and testing building and paving materials; soil surveys and foundation evaluation; field inspection bituminous and concrete mixtures for strength and durability. Chief testing engr City Omaha '19-21, city chem '30-33; chief chem and testing engr Omaha Testing Labs '21-30 since '33. ASTM—Am Soc CE—Assn Asphalt Paving Tech—Nat Highway Research Bd. 511 S. 20th St., Omaha, Neb.

15 CAMPISI, Paul John. Minority groups (Italian, Portuguese, French-Canadian). b'12. BA '38 (U Ariz); MA '42—PhD '47 (U Chicago). Survey adjustment of Italian-Americans to war crisis '42; Social Science Research Council fellowship for construction of index to measure extent to which foreign background peoples are assimilated into American culture; studies on structure, functions, and changes of minority groups in America. Author: Ethnic Family Patterns–The Italian Family in the United States '48. Head sociol sect AUS University Florence Italy '45-46; asst prof sociol Washington U '46-47, asso prof since '47. Am Sociol Soc—Am Folklore Soc—Am Acad Polit and Social Sci—Midwest Sociol Society. Department of Sociology-Anthropology, Washington University, St. Louis.

16 CAMPUZANO, Elizabeth Pound. Spanish-English and English-Spanish translations (Scientific, literary, historical); Spain: Spanish education and archaeology. b'08. AB '28 (U Kan); MA '44 (U Mo); '28 (U Madrid)—'29 (U Barcelona)—'42 (U Mexico). Research and translations for individuals and companies in varied technical fields, including medicine, archaeology and philosophy; lecturer on Spain, Spanish education and Spanish archaeology. Author articles in field. Asso prof Spanish, chmn dept, Mo Valley Coll since '47. Am Assn Teachers of Spanish—Modern Lang Soc—Big Bend Archaeol Soc—Phi Sigma Iota—Sigma Delta Pi—Phi Beta Kappa. Awarded first prize La Prensa Spanish essay contest '25. Missouri Valley College, Marshall, Mo. H: 303 E. Mitchell.

17 CAMRAS, Marvin. Radio; Magnetic and sound recording; Magnetism; Electronics. b'16. BS '40 (Armour Inst Tech); MS '42 (Ill Inst Tech). Perfected wire recorder now widely used in home and office; invented magnetic belt dictating machine; Stereophonic (three dimensional) sound on tape recorder; holds numerous US and foreign patents; developed method recording sound magnetically on motion picture film for profl and amateur use. Author articles in field. Research physicist Armour Research Found Ill Inst Tech since '40. Am Inst EE—Inst Radio Engrs — Soc Motion Picture Engrs — Acoustical Soc Am—Am Radio Relay League—Sigma Xi—Tau Beta Pi—Eta Kappa Nu. Armour Foundation, 35 W. 33rd St., Chicago.

18 CANDELA, Pompeo B. Physical anthropology (Blood grouping, human and racial origins). b'06. Student '23-25 (Columbia), '25-28 (LI Coll); MD '29 (Rome U). Research in blood groups as applicable to problems in racial origins and human evolution; devised and perfected method of determining blood group factors present in human bones, ancient and recent, used in criminal investigation; traced spread of blood group B from Asia to Europe during Mongol invasions; discovered presence of group B factor in lowland gorilla by use of blood grouping tests upon urine, confirmed by tests on blood and secretions of same animals; discovered (with Wiener and Goss) that blood group factor in monkeys was present in tissues and secretions, but not blood cells. Author articles in field. Research asso anat NY Med Coll since '38; private practice med and surgery. Am Anthropol Assn (F) — Am Assn Phys Anthrop — Am Ethnol Soc—Am Assn Anat—AMA(F)—Am Soc Human Genetics. 1094 D St., San Bernardino, Cal.

19 CANDOR, Robert Ross. Patent law (refrigeration, air conditioning, elec-

trical ranges, washing machines, driers, ironers). b'91. SB (Wooster Coll). Asst examiner US Patent Office '17-25; patent atty Gen Motors Corp since '25. Holds 36 patents in field. Frigidaire Div., Gen. Motors Corp., Dayton, O.

20 CANNADAY, Daniel Aldredge. Western Virginia history and literature; English literature. b'99. BA '18—MA '19 (Roanoke); MA '22 (Harvard) '32-33 (U Va); '33-34 (Stanford U). Member advisory committee Virginia Historical Commission, Committee to Establish State Historical Markers. Author articles in field. Prof Eng Wash Coll Chestertown Md '22-23; prof Eng, head dept Tusculum Coll Greeneville Tenn '24-28; acting prof Eng Randolph-Macon Coll Men '29-32; asso prof Eng U Richmond '29-32; asso prof Eng and hist Radford Coll '34-48, prof since '48. AHA—Am Acad Polit and Social Sci—Nat Geog Soc—Va Edn Assn. English prize Roanoke Coll '47, Loomis research fellowship Stanford U '33-34. Radford College, Radford, Va.

21 CANNON, Harry B(eard). Beach sand placers. b'07. BS '28 (Princeton U); '44 (T C U). Patent pending on separation of granular mixtures, advanced design and methods for unconsolidated sand sampling. Author articles in field. Geologist pigments dept E I duPont Co '45-49; geologic cons Nat Lead Co since '49; owner and mgr Old Kent Nursery Md '37-48. AIME. 701 E. Charles St., Lakeland, Fla.†

22 CANNON, Melvin Croxall. Synthetic sapphires and rubies; Diamond powder. b'13. BS '33—MS '36 (U Utah); PhD '41 (Boston U); student (U Pittsburgh, Ill Inst Tech). Research and work on manufacture of sapphire (special rod forms) and ruby in all pilot plant phases; investigation of mechanical, chemical, other properties; fabrication of sapphire articles; application of sapphire in industry in gauges, dies, wear surfaces, nozzles, etc; preparation of graded diamond powder, diamond powder pastes. Two patents granted on manufacture of sapphire. Author articles in field. Professor dept chem Utah State Agrl Coll since '47. Am Chem Soc—AAAS—Sigma Xi. Department of Chemistry, Utah State Agricultural College, Logan, Utah.†

23 CANNON, Orson S(ilver). Disease resistance in tomatoes and cucumbers; Vegetable breeding. b'08. BS '35—MS '37 (Utah State Agrl Coll); PhD '43 (Cornell U). Plant path US Bur Plant Ind Soils and Agrl Engring Logan Utah since '48. Am Phytopath Soc—Am Soc Plant Physiol—Am Soc Hort Sci—Sigma Xi—AAAS. Utah State Agricultural College, Logan, Utah.†

24 CANNON, Ralph S(myser), Jr. Copper deposits. b'10. BS '31—PhD '35 (Princeton); MS '33 (Northwestern U). Research in copper deposits, their geology, geochemistry, origin, distribution, resources, discovery. Author articles in field. With NJ Zinc Co '35-37; US Geol Survey '37-41, copper investigations '42-46, staff since '46. Soc Econ Geol—Mineral Soc Am—Geol Soc Am—Am Inst Mining and Metall Engrs. U.S. Geological Survey, Washington 25.

25 CANSE, John Martin. Early history of western U. S. (Pacific area). b'69. PhB '99—DD '18 (DePauw U). Author: The Hope That Sings '15; Colonizing the Pacific Northwest '26; Pilgrim and Pioneer '30; Jason Lee and his Associates '34; William Roberts and Pioneer Builders of Pacific States '37; Civilizing Foundations Along the Pacific '47; and others. Curator Wash

State Hist Soc '17-44; exec sec Puget Sound Hist Soc '08-29; pres Hist Soc Pacific Northwest Conf since '29. Robert Gray Memorial Assn. 3324 N.E. 18th Av., Portland 12, Ore.

10 CANTRALL, Irving J(ames). Entomology (Orthoptera and dermaptera); Ecology. b'09. AB '35—PhD '40 (U Mich). Author: The Ecology of the Orthoptera and Dermaptera of the George Reserve, Michigan '43. Asst aquatic biol TVA '42-43, asst prof biol U Fla '46-49; curator U Mich Edwin S George Reserve since '49. Fla Acad Sci—Fla Entomol Soc. Edwin S. George Reserve, Pinckney, Mich.†

11 CANTRIL, (Albert) Hadley. Social psychology; Public opinion; Propaganda; Mass media. b'06. BS '28 (Dartmouth Coll); student '29-30 (U Munich and U Berlin); PhD '31 (Harvard U). Special consultant US Secretary of War and Office War Information '42-45; advisory editor Public Opinion Quarterly. Author: The Invasion from Mars '41; The Psychology of Social Movements '41; Gauging Public Opinion '44. Co-author: (with G Allport) Psychology of Radio '35; (with M Sherif) The Psychology of Ego Involvements '47; Understanding Man's Social Behavior '48. Editor: Tensions That Cause War '50. With Princeton U since '36, prof since '45, dir Office Pub Opinion Research dept psychol since '40; dir UNESCO tension studies '48. Am Psychol Assn—Soc Psychol Study Social Issues. 124 Mercer St., Princeton, N.J.◉

12 CAPERS, Gerald Mortimer, Jr. American history (Cities, southern, economic history of Mississippi Valley). b'09. AB '30 (Southwestern Coll); PhD '36 (Yale U). Author: Biography of a Rivertown—Memphis: Its Heroic Age '38; Our Fair City '47. Asst prof hist Newcomb Coll Tulane U New Orleans '40-41, asso prof '41-42, '45-48, prof since '48. AHA—So Hist Assn. Egleston Prize Yale '36. Tulane University, New Orleans 18.

13 CAPLAN, Albert Joseph. Sir Walter Scott (Bibliography). b'08. BS '29 (Temple U). Author: For You and other poems '25; Manuscript Making and Illuminating in the Middle Ages '26; Bibliography of Sir Walter Scott '27. Gen partner Albert J Caplan & Co. 1500 Walnut St., Phila. 2. H: 7913 Montgomery Av., Elkins Park, Pa.†

14 CAPPON, Lester Jesse. History of Virginia and the South; Archives; American historical manuscripts. b'00. BA '22—MA '23 (U Wis); MA '25—PhD '28 (Harvard U). Author: Bibliography of Virginia History Since 1865 '30; Virginia Newspapers, 1821-1935; A Bibliography '36; 1st-15th Annual Reports on Historical Collections, University of Virginia Library '31-45. Editor: New Market, Virginia Imprints, 1806-1876; A check-list '42; The War Records Collector (monthly) '44-45. Research asso hist Inst Research Social Sciences U Va '26-30, archivist Library '30-40, asst prof hist '30-45, asso prof '45, cons hist and archives '40-45 hon cons since '45; dir Hist Records Survey Va '36-37; dir Va World War II History Commn '44-45; archivist Colonial Williamsburg, Inc since '45; research ed Inst Early Am Hist and Culture Williamsburg since '45; lecturer hist Coll William and Mary since '45. AHA—So Hist Assn (vp '48)—Miss Valley Hist Assn— Va Hist Soc—Econ Hist Assn— Soc Am Archivists (sec sinc '42)—Am Assn State Local Hist (mem council since '42). Francis Parkman fellow Harvard '27-28. Pi Delta Epsilon (hon). Colonial Williamsburg, Inc, Williams-

burg, Va. H: Prentis House, Duke of Gloucester St.

15 CAPPS, Edward, Jr. Early Christian ivory carvings; Sculpture (Greek and Roman). b'02. AB '24—MFA '27—PhD '31—fellow Inst for Advanced Study '40-41 (Princeton); jr fellow '41 (Dumbarton Oaks Research Library and Collection); Princeton U travel fellow '25-26 (Am Acad Rome); '20-21, '37-38, '49 (Am Sch Classical Studies Athens); MA '27 (Harvard). Research on Corpus of early Christian ivory carvings, Consular Diptychs. Author articles in field. Asst prof fine arts Oberlin Coll '27-46, asso prof since '46, annual prof to Am Sch Classical Studies at Athens '37-38, prof Greek lit and archaeol to the Am Sch at Athens '49. Mediaeval Acad Am—Archaeol Inst Am—Coll Art Assn. Fellow in medieval and renaissance studies Archaeol Inst Am. Allen Memorial Art Building, Oberlin, O. 139 Morgan St., Oberlin, O.†

16 CAPPS, Robert Waldron. Fats and oils. b'90. Student '09-10 (Yale); '11-12 (U Washington Law Sch). Vice-pres, dir Archer - Daniels - Midland Co Minneapolis since '47; advisory com US Dept Agr, Linseed Crushers Industry, Soybean and Flaxseed Advisory Com, Research and Marketing Admn. NY Produce Exchange (mem '24-42, pres '35-36). 600 Roanoke Building, Minneapolis.

17 CAPRON, John Dodge, Steel industry history. b'94. PhD '14-'15 (Yale). Compiled data on ownership, capacities, production, sources of raw material, and location of iron furnaces in Virginia. With US Pipe & Foundry Co '15-29, research engr '20-29; pres Glamorgan Pipe & Foundry Co Lynchburg since '30. Am Soc ME—Am Iron and Steel Inst—Cast Iron Pipe Research Assn (chmn corrosion com)—Am Standards Assn (council, mem ed com). Glamorgan Pipe & Foundry Co., Box 740, Lynchburg, Va.

18 CAPRON, Louis. Seminole Indians of Florida; Florida history (Seminole War 1835-42, Territorial period). b'91. PhB '13 (Yale). Intimate contact with the Seminoles 20 years, has taken part in ceremonies, first eye-witness account Green Corn Dance, first report Seminole Medicine Bundles. Author: The Gold Arrowhead '48; also articles in field. Fla Hist Soc—Fla Anthrop Soc. 218 Westminster Rd., West Palm Beach, Fla.

19 CARDINAL, Paul Joseph. Vitamins (Synthetic). b'04. BS '24 (MIT). Food enrichment and pharmaceutical use; marketing. Author: Vitamins by the tons. With Hoffmann-La Roche Inc since '24, vp in charge vitamin div since '48. Am Pub Health Assn—Am Soc Bakery Engrs—Sci Research Soc Am. Hoffmann-La Roche, Inc., Nutley 10, N.J. H: 195 Midland Av., Montclair, N.J.

20 CARDOZO, Manoel da Silveira. History of Brazil and Spanish America. b'11. BA '31—MA '34—fellow '33-35—PhD '39 (Stanford U). Research Brazilian and Spanish-American history Portugal '36-38, Brazil '41, Mexico '45, England, Vatican City, Spain, Portugal, '48; special studies of colonial Minas Gerais, nineteenth century Brazilian church history; advisory editor The Catholic Historical Review, The Americas; mem national advisory board Who's Who in Latin America; co-author (with P A Martin) Who's Who in Latin America '35; also articles in field. Lecturer hist Cath U Am '40-43, asst prof '43-47, asso prof since '47; curator Oliveira Lima Lib since '40. AHA—Am Cath Hist Assn—Geog Soc

Lisbon—Inst Ibero-Am Studies. Decorated Rio Branco Medal Brazilian Ministry Fgn Affairs '45; grant-in-aid Social Sci Research Council '41, fellowship Inst Para a Alta Cultura Lisbon '36-38. Catholic University of America, Washington 17, NE.†

21 CARDWELL, A(lvin) B(oyd). Physics; Solid state (Photoelectricity and thermionic emission). b'02. BS '25 (U Chattanooga); MS '27—PhD '30 (U Wis). With Kan State Coll since '36, head physics dept since '37; research physicist Manhattan Project '44-46; asso editor Transactions Kan Acad Sci since '42; council rep Argonne Nat Lab since '47; physicist in charge Kan Agrl Expt Sta since '47. Am Phys Soc (F)—AAAS(F)—Kan Acad Sci—Am Assn Physics Tchrs—Sigma Xi—Phi Kappa Phi—Gamma Alpha—Gamma Sigma Delta. Dept Physics Kansas State Coll., Manhattan, Kan.†◉

22 CAREY, Andrew Galbraith. Machine tools; Metal cutting tools. b'99. AB '21 (Princeton U). Staff on machine tools Office Deputy Director Office War Mobilization and Reconversion '45; expert consultant to Secretary of War Machine Tool Committee, Army Navy Munitions Board '41-42. Sales mgr Carey Mach and Supply Co Baltimore '26-30, vp '30-46: pres Rudel Carey and Briggs Inc NYC '46-49; spl cons Barrington Assos NYC since '49; cons NPA '51. Nat Supply and Machinery Distributors Assn (exec com '37-39, vp '39-41). 230 Park Av., NYC 17. H: RFD No. 2, Westport, Conn.

23 CAREY, Henry Ames. Ancient civilization (Egypt). b'95. '18-20 (U Wash); BA '22—MA '25 (U Calif); PhD '29 (Columbia). Exploratory and anthropological research Near East, exploration in Mexico, archeological excavation Mexico and American Southwest, research and classification Indian antiquities, studies of antiquities in museums of Europe and US. Author articles in field. Asst curator Metropolitan Museum of Art '28-35; supervisor U Ky Archeol Survey '38-42, museum curator Nat Park Service Mammoth Cave Nat Park '42: prof sociol and anthrop Morehead State Coll Ky since '44, now head dept. Am Ethnol Soc—Am Oriental Soc—Soc Archeol—Am Sociol Soc—Ky Archeol Soc. Morehead State College, Morehead, Ky.

24 CAREY, James William. Civil and electrical engineering (Hydro-electric, water, sewerage, dams, irrigation; Highway). b'88. Ed various schs of Minn, Ohio, NY. Member National Rivers and Harbor Congress; outlined public service laws of Oregon '28-33; member Alaskan International Highway Commission since '38; consulting engineer rebuilding City of Renton, Washington. Chief engr State Wash. Dept Pub Works and Tax Comm '22-28; constrn engr Portland Ore and Tacoma Wash engaged in valuation, reports on water power sites, etc, including present Bonneville power site; aptd by President chief engr insp Fed Pub Works Adminstrn State Wash '36-38; cons civil and elec engr Seattle and Tacoma since '38. Alaska Trades Building, 1917 First Av., Seattle 1.

25 CARHART, Arthur Hawthorne. Public lands of western United States; Hunting and fishing (Techniques, Methods, economics); Conservation (Renewable resources); Wildlife management. b'92. BS '16 (Ia State Coll). Considered to have been first to direct significant attention to important role of wildlife in national economy; leader in movement to preserve public estate in West; authority on history policies, management, resources, etc., of western public lands, national forests, national parks, monuments and Taylor Grazing lands. Author: The Last Stand of the Pack '28; Colorado '31; Planning the Home Grounds '34; Trees and Shrubs for the Home Grounds '34; The Outdoorsman's Cook Book '44; Hunting North American Deer '46; Fresh Water Fishing '49; Fishing is Fun '50; Fishing in the West. Editor: Conservation Please!; also articles in field. Engaged as author, conservationist, landscape arch. Colo Author's League (1st pres) —Gamma Sigma Delta. 2591 Eudora St., Denver 7.

10 CARHART, George Cook. Gear design. b'80. EE '03 (Syracuse U). Research and development automatic transmissions, hydrodynamic torque converters; inventor automatic gear tooth grinding machine, automatic gear tooth chamfering machine, automatic gear tooth lapping or shaving machine; and others. Issued patents in field. Chief engr Brown-Lipe Gear Co '12-28; div engr Buick Motor Co '28-32, Gen Motors Truck Co '33-35, overseas Opel plant Germany '37-39; spl engr Detroit Diesel Engine Div '42-45; reg prof engr since '48. Soc Automotive Engrs. 212 North Bridge St., San Gabriel, Calif.

11 CARHART, Raymond T. Hearing; Deafness; Speech correction. b'12. AB '32 (Dak Wesleyan U); MA '34—PhD '36 (Northwestern U). Research on psychophysics of hearing loss, hearing aids, education of the acoustically handicapped, training non-medical specialists in audiology. Author articles in field. Dir edn deaf and hard of hearing Northwestern U since '42, prof audiology and acting chmn dept speech correction and audiology '47-48, asst prof otolaryngology since '48. Capt Med Administrv Corps US Army, acoustic physicist Deshon Gen Hosp Pa '44-46, cons on aural problems Surg Gen US Army since '46 to Am Acad Ophthalmology and Otolaryngology. Am Speech Correction Assn(F)—AAAS(F) —Acoustical Soc Am. School of Speech, Northwestern University, Evanston, Ill.

12 CARITHERS, Ward. Cobalt; Pumice; Cascade Mountains. b'13. BS (Geol) '37 (State Coll Wash). Mapping cobalt deposits of Blackbird District Idaho; studies economic pumice and pumicite deposits of Washington; studies in geology of Cascade Mountains particularly Holden Mine. Geol Wash State Div Mines and Geol '42-46; mine geol Howe Sound Co Holden Wash '46-49, Calera Mining Co since '49. AIMME. Cobalt, Ida.

13 CARLANDER, Kenneth Dixon. Fishery biology (Fish growth, pond management). b'15. BA '36—MS '38— PhD '43 (U Minn). Author: Handbook of Freshwater Fishery Biology '50. Associate prof zool entomol Ia State Coll since '48; leader of projects of Ia Coop Fishery Research Unit. Am Fisheries Soc—Am Soc Limnol Oceanog— Wildlife Management Inst—AAAS— Sigma Xi—Wildlife Soc—Am Soc Ichthyology and Herpelology—Biometrics Soc—Ga Acad Sci. Department of Zoology and Entomology, Iowa State College, Ames, Ia.†

14 CARLIN, Jack Raymond. Radioactivity (Applications and instrumentation); Beta Ray absorption. b'24. BS (Coll City of NY). Design ionization chambers for special applications; development of industrial control equipment employing radioisotopes; design of instrumentation for civil defense against atomic attack. Author articles: Application of Beta Ray Backscattering to Industrial Gauging; Radioactive Thickness Gage for Moving Materials; Industrial Applications of Radioactivity. Res asst Canadian

Radium & Uranium Corp '46-47; project engr Tracer Lab Inc '47-50 NY sales mgr since '50. Tracer Lab., Inc., 1775 Broadway, N.Y. City 19.

15 CARLISLE, James Mallory. Pharmacology, toxicology and clinical use of vitamins and antiarthritic, antibacterial, and antishock drugs. b'04. AB '27 (U Ala); MD '32 (Temple U). Clinical and physiological research on vitamins, sulfa drugs, cortisone, penicillin, streptomycin, neomycin, amino acids; pulmonary edema and chemical burns; uses in clinical medicine; study of workmen exposed to the manufacturing of the above drugs. Author: Essential Procedures in the Immediate Care of Fresh Major Traumatic Wounds '43; Crystalline Vitamin B-12 in the Treatment of Megaloblastic Anemias '49; Cortisone (Compound E) Pharmacology and Clinical Use '50, and others. Contributor: Principles and Practice of Industrial Medicine '43; Musser's Textbook of Internal Medicine '50. With Merck & Co since '34, med dir since '36; head dept clin research Rahway Mem Hosp since '46; subcom nutrition and toxic reactions in industry NRC. NY Acad Sci(F) —Am Pub Health Assn(F)—Am Coll Chest Physicians(F)— AMA(F)— Am Assn Indsl Physicians and Surgeons (F, dir '48-50)—NY Acad Med(F)—Med Soc NJ (chmn adv com indsl health and hygiene)—NJ Assn Indsl Physicians and Surgeons—Assn Mil Surgeons US—Am Soc Tropical Med—Mfrs Chem Assn (med adv com) —Am Drug Mfrs Assn (med adv sect) —Am Trudeau Soc (med adv com)— Am Acad Gen Practice—Am Acad Occupational Med (F, dir '49-52)—Am Indsl Hygiene Assn—Gorgas Med Soc —Alpha Tau Omega—Alpha Kappa Kappa. Merck & Co., Inc., Rahway, N.J.

16 CARLS, Erwin William. Wood specimens. b'07. Student '33-34, '34-35 (U Ida). Research and collection of wood specimens for study of wood anatomy, occurrence of ripple marks, hardness. Cons Desert Woods Co '39; faculty mem Calif Inst Men since '49. Wood Collectors Soc—Lepidopterists Soc. H: 1985 E. Phillips Blvd., Pomona, Calif.

17 CARLSON, James Gordon. Cytology; Radiation biology. b'08. AB '30— PhD '35 (U Pa). Research on effects of X-ray and ultra-violet exposure on mitosis in grasshoppers. Author articles in field. Instr zool U Ala '35-39, asst prof '39-45, asso prof '45-46; sr biol Nat Inst Health USPHS '46-47; prof zool, head dept zool and entomol U Tenn since '47; participant 4th Pacific Sci Congress Java '29; guest investigator dept genetics Carnegie Instn of Washington summers '37, '38; asso biol Nat Inst Health USPHS summer '43, biol summers '45-46, spl cons biol '43-46, since '48; cons biol div Oak Ridge Nat Lab since '47. AAAS(F)— AAUP—Am Soc Naturalists—Am Soc Zool—Assn SE Biol—Genetics Soc Am —Soc Exptl Biol and Med—Tenn Acad Sci—Ala Acad Sci (vp '38)—Phi Beta Kappa—Sigma Xi. Awarded grant-in-aid Com on Radiation Nat Research Council, U Research Com U Ala, cancer research grants branch USPHS. Department of Zoology and Entomology, University of Tennessee, Knoxville 16, Tenn.†◎

18 CARLSON, John Wilford. Alfalfa (Seed production, breeding, culture and management). b'92. BS '22—MS '27 (Utah State Agrl Coll); PhD '39 (U Wis). Research on alfalfa seed production, insects and disease; culture and management; found toxicogenic injury by lygus bugs a cause of declining yields of alfalfa seed in Utah and western states, DDT as a

control measure. Supt Utah Basin Alfalfa Seed Exptl Farm, Utah State Agrl Expt Sta '25-34; with U Wis '35-37; agron Div Forage Crops and Diseases USDA since '37. AAAS(F)—Am Soc Agron—Phi Kappa Phi—Sigma Xi (charter mem Utah State Agrl Coll chapter). Legume Seed Research Laboratory, Utah State Agricultural Experiment Station, Logan, Utah.

19 CARLSON, Leland Henry. Alaskan history (Gold Rush period); English Restoration history. b'08. BA (Beloit Coll); BTh '34—BD '38 (Chicago Theol Sem); PhD '39 (U Chicago); '36 (U Grenoble, Cambridge U). Author: The History of An Alaskan Gold Mine; also articles in field. Asst prof Northwestern U since '42. AHA—Am Ch Hist Soc—Am Theol Soc—Ill Hist Soc—Soc Advancement Scandinavian Study—Phi Beta Kappa. 214 Harris Hall, Northwestern University, Evanston, Ill. 9460 Lincolnwood Dr., Skokie, Ill.

20 CARLSON, William Samuel. Arctic meteorology and aviation. b'05. AB '30—MS '32—PhD '38 (U Mich); LLD '48 (Dickinson Coll); Henry Goddard Leach Fellow Am-Scandinavian Found '31-32. Lived 30 months and traveled extensively in Greenland and Baffin Land; research on glaciology and Greenland weather; war experience related to planning air activities in Arctic and participating in Arctic operations of Air Forces; Field leader University Michigan Greenland Expedition '28-29. Author: Greenland Lies North '40; Report of the Northern Division of the Fourth University of Michigan Greenland Expedition '41; also articles in field. Asst dept geol U Mich '29-30, leader fourth expdn to Greenland '30-31, instr geol '32-33, grad fellow '33; asst prof U Minn '37-39, asso prof '39-41, dir admissions and records '41-45, dean and prof '46; pres U Delaware '46-50; president U Vermont since '50. Spl cons on arctic problems to comdg gen US AAF '41; commd maj Air Corps '42, advanced through grades to col '45; asst chief spl projects br plans div Hdqrs AAF '42-43, exec western hemisphere br plans div '43-44, dir Artic, Desert and Tropic br AAF Tactical Center '44-45; col ORC since '45. AAAS — Minn Acad Sci — Am Swedish Hist Mus—NEA—Soc Advancement Edn— Sigma Xi—Phi Kappa Phi—Sigma Gamma Epsilon. 25 Colchester Ave., Burlington, Vt.◎

21 CARMICHAEL, Colin. Mechanical engineering (Machine design analysis, dynamics of machines, internal combustion and marine engines). b'05. BSc '26 (Glasgow U); MS in ME '34 (U NC). Editor: Kent's Mechanical Engineers' Handbook (12th edit, Design and Production vol); also articles in field. Engr, draftsman Alexander Stephen & Sons Ltd Glasgow Scotland '22-29; draftsman Sun Shipbuilding and Drydock Co, Chester Pa '29-31; instr, asst prof mech engring U NC '31-36; asst prof machine design Cornell U '36-37; asst prof mech engring Rutgers U '37-42; asso ed Machine Design '42-49; ed since '49. ASME—SAE—Am Soc EE—Inst of Engrs and Shipbuilders (Scotland)—Tau Beta Pi. Penton Building, Cleveland 13.

22 CARMICHAEL, Emmett Bryan. Biochemistry; Toxic proteins (Rattlesnake venom, ricin, tetanus toxin); Anesthetics (Barbiturates, paraldehyde); Enzymes. b'95. AB '18—MS '22 (U Colo); PhD '27 (U Cincinnati). Editor: Journal of the Alabama Academy of Science '42-48. Author articles in field. Prof biochem Med Coll Ala since '32. AAAS(F, chmn acad conf '33)— Am Inst Chem — Internat Coll Anesthetists—AMA (asso F)—Am Chem

Soc (vice chmn Ala sect '32-34, chmn '34-35) — Am Soc Biol Chem — Assn Study Internal Secretions—Soc Exptl Biol and Med (vice chmn so sect '46-47)—Am Physiol Soc—Ala Acad Sci (pres '30-31) — Am Assn Hist Med — Sigma Xi (1st pres, Ala chapter '39-40). 3028 13th Av. S., Birmingham, Ala.†⊚

10 CARMICHAEL, Leonard. Sensory psychology and physiology; Manpower mobilization. b'98. BS '21 (Tufts Coll); PhD '24 (Harvard). Research on mobilization of scientists, organized and directed Nat Roster of Scientific and Specialized Personnel '40-44. Contbr: Civil Service in Wartime '45. Pres Tufts College, director research lab sensory psychology and physiology since '38. Am Psychol Assn (pres '39-40, treas '30-36)—Nat Acad Sci—Am Philos Soc. Tufts College, Medford 55, Mass.⊚

11 CARMICHAEL, Robert Daniel. Mathematical theory (Functions, numbers, groups); Differential and difference equations; Philosophy of science. b'79. AB '98 (Lineville Coll, Ala); PhD '11—fellow '09-10—Jacobus fellow '10-11 (Princeton). Author: Theory of Relativity '13, '20; Theory of Numbers '14, French edit '29; Diophantine Analysis '15, French edit '29; The Logic of Discovery '30; Theory of Groups of Finite Order '37. Co-author: A Debate on Relativity '27; Calculus '27; Plane and Spherical Trigonometry '30; also articles in field. Prof math U Ill since '20, dean grad sch '34-47, emeritus '47. AAAS(F)—Am Math Soc (vp '22)—Math Assn Am (vp '21-22, pres '23)—Am Philos Assn—Nat Research Council — Sigma Xi — Phi Beta Kappa—Phi Kappa Phi. S. Corey St., P.O. Box 278, Griggsville, Ill.⊚

12 CARMODY, Francis James. Arabico-Latin astronomy; Celtic languages; Phonetics of modern Scottish-Gaelic and Manx Gaelic; Animal lore. b'07. AB '29—MA (U Calif); PhD '32 (Harvard). Editor mediaeval texts in astronomy: Thabit ibn Qurra, Four Astronomical Tracts in Latin '41; Gerard of Sabbioneta, Theorica Planetarum '41; Al-Farghani, Differentiae '43; Leopold of Austria, Li Compilacions de le scienche des estoilles '48; two editions of the Latin Physiologus (bestiary, animal lore), '39 and '41. Prof French U Calif Berkeley. Guggenheim fellow for Arabic-Latin astron '48-49. University of California, Berkely.†

13 CARMONY, Donald Francis. History of the United States (Mid-west); Indiana history (Public finance, newspapers, education); Adult education. b'10. BA '29 (Ind Central Coll); MA '31—PhD '40 (Ind U); '37 (Butler U). Author: Indiana '41. Co-author: (with H W Peckham) A Brief History of Indiana '48. Author articles: Indiana Territorial Expenditures 1800-1816 '43; Highlights in Indiana Newspaper History (series 8 articles) '44-45; Indiana's Newspaper Heritage '45; Fiscal Objection to Statehood in Indiana '46; and others. Instr. Am and European hist Ind U '39-42, asst prof '42-48, asso prof since '48; dir So Bend-Mishawaka center Ind U '44-50; asso dean Ind U div adult education, and public services since '50; board trustees Indiana Cent Coll. AHA—Miss Valley Hist Assn—Ind Hist Soc—North Ind Hist Soc (mem bd dirs)—Am Acad Polit Social Sci—Hist Soc—Ind Assn Adult Education—NEA. Indiana University, Bloomington, Ind. 223 S. Bryan Street, Bloomington, Ind.

14 CARNOVSKY, Leon. Surveys of libraries; Library education. AB '27 (U Mo); certificate (St Louis Library Sch); PhD '32 (U Chicago). Associate

director survey Westchester County, New York, libraries '35, Michigan State Library '37, Chicago Public Library '38, Los Angeles Public Library '48; director survey Cleveland Public Library, '39; US Education Mission to Japan '46; managing editor The Library Quarterly. Author: (with E A Wight) Library Service in a Suburban Area '36; (with D Waples) Libraries and Readers in the State of New York; (with C B Joeckel) A Metropolitan Library in Action. Co-editor: (with L Martin) The Library in the Community '44. Instr Grad Library Sch U Chicago '32-36, asst prof library sci '36-41, asso prof '41-43, prof since '43, asst dean '42-45, asso dean and dean students '45-47. Assn Am Library Schs (pres '42-43)—ALA (council)—Am Library Inst —Phi Beta Kappa. 1424 E. 58th St., Chgo 37.

15 CARNS, Harry Robert. Plant growth substances; Cotton (Insecticide effects); Abscission. b'17. BS '39 —MS '41 (U Ia); PhD '51 (U Cal). Research on insect attack and insecticide applications to cotton, phytotoxicity of insecticides to cotton plant, effect insecticides on quality of lint and seed, possible adulteration of cottonseed oil and cake, residual insecticide toxicity which may accumulate in soils; relationships of auxin to development square, bloom and boll. Research asst div bot U Cal '48-50; plant physiol US Cotton Field Station BPI SAE Delta Branch Expt Sta since '50. Sigma Xi—AAAS. Delta Branch Experiment Station, Stoneville, Miss.

16 CARPENTER, Arthur Howe. Geology; Mineral deposits. b'77. AM '14 (Ohio U); student 2 yrs (Northwestern U). Photographs of Macro-structures or Evanesce structures of metals, mountains and geologic structures; paintings of geologic structures and interpretations; geologic reconnaissance surveys; treatment of ores of rare metals; preparation of parabolic mirrors. Inventor methods of covering pipe with lead. Author articles in field. Prospector Nev '10-11; research metallurgist Am Vanadium Corp '18-20; asst prof metallurgy Armour Inst Tech (Ill Inst Tech) Chicago '20-28, asso prof '29, head metallurgy div, lectr geology astronomy meteorology, prof emeritus since '44; staff cons metallurgy Armour Research Found. AAAS(F)—AIMME—Ill Acad Sci—AS TM—Soc Promotion Engring Edn— Astron Soc Pacific—Am Assn Variable Star Observers—Chicago Astron Soc— Soc Amateur Telescope Makers of Chicago—Phi Lambda Upsilon—Alpha Chi Sigma—Pi Gamma Mu. Illinois Institute Technology, Technology Center, Chgo 16.†⊚

17 CARPENTER, Clarence Ray. Social and comparative psychology; visual education (Films). b'05. AB '28— AM '29 (Duke U); PhD '32 (Stanford). Research on societies of free-ranging primates under natural conditions in Panama, Canal Zone, Costa Rica, relation of psychology to medical studies; developed experimental laboratory, Columbia U, associate director Asiatic Primate Expedition '37-38; directed expeditions to Far East; established laboratory for medical and behavioral research in Puerto Rico; director Instructional Film Research Project (ONR); studies on problems of German reconstruction, social behavior of Rhesus monkeys; field studies in Siam of behavior and social relations of gibbons; editor Psychological Cinema Register since '40; associate editor Behavior. Author articles in field. Prof psychol, acting dir research Sch Edn, Pa State Coll; Officer US Army Air Forces '43-46, on staff Desert and Tropic Section of Arctic Desert and Tropic Informa-

tion Section, Air Corps; head psychol and sociol dept and research Biarritz Am U, France, organizing German youth program '45-46. Am Psychol Assn—Am Anthrop Soc—NY Zool Soc (F)—AAAS. Stanford U Research fellow '32; Yale U, Nat Research fellow '31-34; fellow Bard Coll of Col U '32-38. Dept of Psychology, Pennsylvania State College, State College, Pa.†

18 CARPENTER, Dwight Clark. Protein chemistry; Amino acids; Vitamins; Monolayers. b'90. BS '11 (Mich State Coll); MS '20—PhD '21 (U Mich); Internat Edn Bd fellow '27-29 (U Upsala, U Vienna). Also research in molecular weights, effect of ultraviolet light, chromatography. Author articles in field. Prof chem Cornell since '30; chief chem research NY State Exptl Sta Geneva NY since '30. Am Chem Soc — Electrochem Soc — Sigma Xi — Gamma Alpha—Phi Lambda Upsilon— Alpha Chi Sigma. 78 Maple St., Geneva, N.Y.

19 CARPENTER, John Melvin. Ecology of insects (Drosophila, biotic potential, intraspecific and interspecific competition, evolution). b'10. BA '36— MA '40—Phd '46 (U Tex). Research on culture media in regard to oviposition and mass production of Drosophila melanogaster '41; effect of population density on productivity of the parasite Microbracon mellitor Say '44. Author articles in field. Research asso entomol Clayton Found for Research U Tex '38-45, tutor dept zool '42-45, instr zool '45-46; asst prof zool U Tenn since '46. AAAS—Am Soc Zool—Am Soc Study Evolution—Assn SE Biol—Tenn Acad Sci. Department of Zoology and Entomology, University of Tennessee, Knoxville, Tenn.†

20 CARPENTER, Mildred Evangeline Carver. Massachusetts history (Heraldry). b'90. Inst Am Geneal—Nat Geneal Soc—Huguenot Soc New England—Nat Soc Daughters Founders and Patriots Am—Old Plymouth Colony Descendants—Nat Soc US Daughters of 1812—George and Ann Borodell Denison Soc—Roger Williams Family Association, and others. 12 Rexhame Rd., Worcester, Mass.

21 CARPENTER, William Kemble. Zoological collecting. b'19. Ed pub schs. Research on natural history with emphasis on large mammals, discovered genera of fish subspecies of animals. Collector and naturalist with Phila Acad Natural Sci since '32. NY Zool Soc—Acad Natural Sci (mem bd trustees). Nemours Building, Wilmington, Del.

22 CARR, Archie Fairly, Jr. Turtles. b'09. BS '33—MS '34—PhD '37 (U Fla). Research on identity and status of US turtles; Thomas Barbour fellow Museum Comparative Zoology Harvard summers of '37-43; compiler of handbook on turtles of US; research associate American Museum of Natural History. Author articles: Pseudemys Nelsoni—a New Turtle from Florida '38; Notes on Sea Turtles '42; Sea Turtles on a Tropical Island '48, and others. Co-author articles: (with T Barbour) Another Bahamian Fresh-Water Tortoise '38; Antillean Terrapins '40; (with Lewis J Marchand) A New Turtle from the Chipola River, Florida '42. Asst prof biol sci U Fla '40-43, asso prof '43-45, prof since '49; prof biol Escuela Agricola Panamericana Honduras '45-49; biol United Fruit Co Lake Yojoa Honduras '49. Soc Ichthyology and Herpetology (vp '41, gov since '42)—Herpetologists League—Soc Vertebrate Paleontology —Sigma Xi—Phi Sigma. Department of Biology, University of Florida, Gainesville, Fla.

10 CARR, Hugh H. Piping (Thermal stresses, fluid flow, fabrication, installation). b'99. ME '23 (Syracuse U); night sch '42-44 (Del U), '46-48 (Rochester Inst Tech). Devised methods for simplified use of Walker-Crocker Grapho-Analytical method of calculating thermal stresses in piping; designed devices for simplifying accurate piping installation, research on weights, dimensions and behavior of materials and components of piping systems as related to stresses, flow restriction, heat transmission and creep. Successively test engr Chile Exploration Co; chief engr Robinson Engring Corp; design engr Du Pont Power Dept; cons Rochester Gas and Elec Co; now chief engr Dollinger Corp. ASME—Nat Soc Profl Engrs. Dollinger Corp., 11 Centre Park, Rochester 3, N.Y. H: 24 Britton Rd., Rochester 12.

11 CARR, Isaac Newton. Mexican history (Catholic church, Maximilian regime); Inter-American relations (Cuba, Panama Republic). b'92. AB '16 —MA '25 (U NC); student '27-29 (Duke U). LLD '41 (Carson-Newman Coll). Author articles in field. Prof hist, dean Mars Hill Coll '23-41; dean Carson-Newman Coll Jefferson City Tenn. Am Hist Assn—Miss Valley Hist Assn —So Hist Assn—East Tenn Hist Soc. Carson-Newman College, Jefferson City, Tenn.⊙

12 CARR, Martha Ensign Strait. Iron ores; Geology of the District of Columbia. b'94. BS '22 (Russell Sage Coll). Co-author: Iron-ore Deposits of the Western United States '47. Author: The District of Columbia—Its Rocks and Their Geologic History '49. Geol USGS Washington DC since '42. Washington Geol Soc. US Geological Survey, 18th and F Sts., N. W., Washington 25.

13 CARR, Percy Hamilton. Electron microscopy. b'04. BS '25 (Furman U); MS '26 (U NC); PhD '30 (Cornell U). Research in effect of electrons on metals, X-ray diffraction of oscillating quartz; devices for teaching physics and applications of electron microscope. Author articles in field. Res Gen Elec Lab Schenectady NY '29; prof physics Ia State Coll since '30, dir coll photographic service since '38. Am Physics Soc—Optical Soc Am—Sigma Xi. Physics Department, Iowa State College, Ames, Ia.†

14 CARR, William H(enry). American natural history and conservation; Outdoor education. b'02. Naturalist and past lecturer national conferences on state and national parks. Author: Stir of Nature '29; Glimpses of Familiar Birds '30; Trailside Actions and Reactions '35; Signs Along the Trail '30; Desert Parade '47; also articles in field. Asst and asso curator dept edn Am Mus Nat Hist NYC '26-45; dir Bear Mountain Trailside Mus '26-45; ret '45. Am Ornithol—Am Soc Mammalogists—NY Linnean Soc—Tucson Natural Hist Soc (pres '48)—Ariz Wildlife Fedr (pres '48). 1708 N Santa Rita, Tucson, Ariz.

15 CARRIERE, Joseph Medard. French literature (18th Century, Modern); French civilization and travelers in US; French folktales and literature (Canada, Missouri); French dialects (Canada, Louisiana). b'02. AB '21—Docteur es lettres, hon '47 (Laval U, Quebec); AM '25 (Marquette U); AM '26—PhD '32 (Austin scholar romance langs '25-26 (Harvard); student '29-30 (Ecole Pratique des Hautes Etudes, Ecole des Chartes, Sorbonne, Paris, Sheldon traveling fellow Harvard). Author: Tales from French Folklore of Missouri (awarded prize by French Acad '39) '37. Co-author: D'Annunzio

Abroad, vol 1 '35, vol 2 '37; Transition to Writing and Reading French '40; Folk Songs of Old Vincennes '46. Prof romance langs U Va since '46; trustee Inst Francais of Washington since '45. Officier d'Academie '38—Institut d'Histoire de L'Amerique Francaise (corr mem)—Societe Francaise de Folklore (corr mem)—Inst Internat d'Archeocivilisation—Societe de l'Histoire de l'Eglise au Canada—Modern Lang Assn—Nat Fedn Modern Lang Teachers—South Atlantic Modern Lang Assn—Am Dialect Soc—Am Folklore Soc (vp '45-46, pres since '46) —Linguistic Soc Am—Am Assn Teachers Italian, of French (vp since '46)— Alliance Francaise de Paris—Comite France-Acadie, Paris—Am Cath Hist Soc—Can, Am, So, Miss Valley hist assns—Bibliog Soc Am—French and Southeastern folklore socs. 1410 Gordon Av., Charlottesville, Va.

16 CARRIKER, Melbourne Romaine. Malacology; Oyster drill; Bivalve larvae; estuarine ecology. b'15. BS '39 (Rutgers U); PhM '40—PhD '43 (U Wis). Assistant on ornithological expedition to Bolivia '35. Author articles in field. Asst prof zool Rutgers U since '47; research on hard clam, Venus mercenaria. Am Micros Soc—AAAS—Am Mus Nat Hist—Am Zool Soc—Wis Acad Arts Sci—Nat Shell-fisheries Assn—Soc Limonology and Oceanography. Zoology Department, Rutgers University, New Brunswick, N.J.†

17 CARRINGTON, Omar Raymond. South American agriculture. b'04. BA '28 (U Md). Editor: Agriculture in The Americas, pub office Fgn Agrl Relations US Dept Ag '44-47. Louis Tiffany Foundation fellow '36. 107 Taylor St., Chevy Chase, Md.

18 CARROLL, Eber Malcolm. Diplomatic history (European); History (Germany, France); Public opinion (19th, 20th centuries). b'93. AB '16— AM '17 PhD '22 (U Mich). Author: Origins of the Whig Party '25; French Public Opinion and Foreign Affairs 1871-1914 '31; Germany and the Great Powers 1866-1914; A Study in Public Opinion and Foreign Policy '38; also articles. Joint editor: Das National-sozialistische Deutschland und Die Sowjet Union '48. Prof history Duke U since '37; deputy editor in charge Berlin operations German War Documents Project Dept State. Am Hist Assn— AAUP—Am Polit Sci Assn—Acad Polit Sci—Phi Beta Kappa. Awarded John Simon Guggenheim Memorial Fellowship '27-28. 406 Library Tower, Duke University, Durham, N.C.†⊙

19 CARROLL, Horace Bailey. History and bibliography of Texas; Southwest trails. b'03. AB '28—MA '28 (Tex Tech Coll); PhD '35 (Tex U). Editor: Guadal P'a '41; Texas County Histories: A Bibliography '43. Co-editor: Three New Mexico Chronicles '42. Instr Tex Tech Coll '28-29, asso prof '29-30, '31-32; prof Lamar Coll '34-35; prof Hillsboro Coll '35-36; prof West Tex State Coll '36-37; prof Eastern N.M. Coll '37-38; prof N. Tex Agrl Coll '38-40, '41-42; prof since '46. Panhandle-Plains Hist Soc (asso ed Panhandle-Plains Hist Review)—AHA—Tex State Hist Assn (asso dir)—Tex Folklore Soc—Bibliog Soc Am—Hist Soc in US and Can. (corr mem)—Am Assn State Local Hist. 2100 Sharon Lane, Austin 3, Tex.†⊙

20 CARROLL, Howard. Early Christian martyrdom. BA (U Richmond); U Fellow '43-46—BD '43—PhD '46 (Duke U). Author: The Conception of the Ecclesia in the New Testament '43; Polycarp of Smyrna—With Special Reference to Early Christian Martyrdom '46; also articles in field. Minister

in Md and NC since '41. Soc Biblical Lit and Exegesis—Phi Beta Kappa. Easton, Md.

21 CARROLL, J. Cleve. Plant biochemistry; Ecology of turf grasses; Lawn grasses. b'98. BSc '20 (Wilmington Coll); MSc '28—PhD '41 (O State U). Research on effect of drought temperature and nitrogen on turf grasses. Author articles in field. Asst prof Eastern Ky Teachers Coll '28; research chem O Agrl Expt Sta '29-46; asso prof chem MacMurray Coll '46-47, Kent State U since '47. ACS—Am Soc Plant Physiol—Sigma Xi. Department of Chemistry, Kent State University, Kent, O.†

22 CARROLL, John Bissell. Factor analysis (Psychological tests); Mental tests (Statistical theory of); Language (Psychology of); Personnel psychology. b'16. BA '37 (Wesleyan U); PhD '41 (U Minn). Development factor analysis tests to determine mental abilities; evaluation importance of speed in mental tests; statistical study validity of mental tests as affected by variations in item difficulty and examinee's success by mere guessing; theoretical study psychology of language; research on personnel psychology, including test construction and statistical analysis. Author articles: A Factor Analysis of Verbal Abilities '41; The Effect of Difficulty and Chance Success on Correlations between Items or between Tests '45. Now asst prof edn Harvard. Aviation psychol USN '44-46; research psychol Dept of Army '46-49. Am Psychol Assn(F)—Psychometric Soc—Linguistic Soc Am. Graduate School of Education, Harvard University, Cambridge 38, Mass.

23 CARROLL, Mitchell Benedict. Tax systems (Foreign). b'98. BA '20 (Johns Hopkins); student (U Grenoble)(Ecole Libre des Sciences Politiques U Madrid) (U Geneva) (Academie de Droit International The Hague); Licencie en Droit '22 (Universite de Paris); Dr Juris '23 (U Bonn Germany); LLB '27 (George Washington U). Mem conf Tech Experts on Double Taxation, London '27, Govtl Experts on Double Taxation, Geneva '28, Law Commn of Fed Aeronautique Internationale '29-31; spl atty US Treasury Dept in internat tax matters '30-31; mem Am Commn to negotiate double taxation treaty with France '30; dir survey tax systems in 35 countries for Fiscal Com League Nations '31-33, Am. mem. Fiscal Com '34-46; pres Internat Fiscal Assn '48-52, Tax Congresses The Hague '47, Rome '49, Monte Carlo '50, Zurich '51, Brussels '52. Am Bar Assn —Am Fgn Law Assn—Am Soc Internat Law—Academie Diplomatique Internat—Bar Assn City NY. 67 Broad St., NYC 4.†⊙

24 CARROLL, Mollie Ray. Social insurance; Labor economics. b'90. PhB—MA—PhD (U Chicago). Author: Labor and Politics; Unemployment Insurance in Germany; Our Wants and How They Are Satisfied; Unemployment Insurance in Austria; American Workers' Education; What Is Collective Bargaining?; also articles in field. Indsl econ Div of Labor Standards, US Dept of Labor '37-42; training specialist Social Security Adminstrn since '42. Am Econ Assn. John Simon Guggenheim Found fellow '27-28. McLean, Va.⊙

25 CARROLL, William Richard. Legume inoculation; Serology; Undulant fever; Typhus. b'96. BS '22 (Miss State Coll); MS '25 (U Wis); student '25-27 (Ill U); PhD '32 (Minn U). Research on occurrence of a red pigment in corn meal mash, measurement of heat resistance of bacteria, use of living tissue for securing favorable condition for development anaerobic bacteria. Author articles in field. Jr bact Comml Solvents Corp '23; asst prof bact Fla U '27-35, asso prof '35-39, prof since '39; approved bast US Civil Service. Soc Am Bact—Am Pub Health Assn—Fla Acad Sciences—AAAS—Sigma Xi. Bacteriology Dept, University of Florida, Gainesville, Fla.

10 CARRUTH, Laurence Adams. Economic entomology (Crops); Insect control. b'07. BSc '29 (Mass Agrl Coll); MSc '31 (SD State Coll); PhD '35 (Cornell U). Research on taxonomy of Meloidae, biology of Blattidae '29-31; apiculture, control of grasshoppers and crickets '31-33; insect ecology and physiology, effect of reduced air pressures on insect development '31-35; biology and control of insect pests of sweet corn '41; evaluation of insecticides used on cultivated crops '45; biology and control of insects affecting vegetable crops, phytotoxicity of insecticides to cucurbits and other cultivated crops, varietal and specific resistance of cultivated crops to insect attack, control of insects affecting food processing establishments. Author articles in field. With NY State Agrl Expt Sta '39-49; prof and head dept entomol, Coll Agric U Ariz since '49. Am Assn Econ Entomol—Entomol Soc Am—Sigma Xi. Awarded gold medal and cash award by eastern br Am Assn Econ Entomol '41. University of Arizona, Tucson, Ariz.

11 CARRUTHERS, John Litster. Ceramic engineering; Pyrometric cones; Refractories; Clay wares; Drying kilns. b'95. BCerE '21—'34 (Ohio State U). Author articles in field. Cons engr Drier, Kiln & Factory Design Mfr problems since '25; part time mgr Edward Orton Jr Ceramic Found Columbus O since '44; chmn and prof cer engr Ohio State U since '46. Am Ceramic Soc (vp '39-40, pres '40-41, bd trustees '36-43)—Inst Ceramic Engrs (vp '38-39, pres '39-40)—Ceramic Ednl Council—Am Soc Engring Edn—Am Soc Testing Materials—Sigma Xi—Tau Beta Pi. Lord Hall, Ohio State University, Columbus 10, O. H: 2029 Collingswood Rd., Columbus 12.†◎

12 CARSNER, Eubanks. Sugar beet diseases and physiology. b'91. BA '12 (U Texas); MS '14—PhD '17 (U Wis). Author articles in field. Path US Dept Agrl '17-48. Am Phytopathol Soc—Bot Soc Am—Am Soc Sugar Beet Technol—Washington Acad Sci—AAAS. In charge Unit Group which received US Dept Agrl Superior Service Award '47. U.S. Department of Agriculture, Box 31, Riverside, Calif.

13 CARSON, Gerald Hewes. Merchandising, retail (Country store); Advertising copy (Development and history); Food (Cereals and breakfast foods). b'99. AB '21—Ma '22 (U Ill). Author: Country Store '54. Author articles: Early Days in the Breakfast Food Industry '45; New Uses for Advertising '46; Copy Trends of the Future '48. Copy writer Calkins & Holden, Inc., '24-27, J Walter Thompson Co Inc 28, Batten Barton Durstine & Osborn Inc '29-32; vp William Esty & Co Inc '37-40 Benton & Bowles Inc since '40; pres Copy Research Council '46-47; writer on social and econ history. AHA—Bus Hist Soc—NY State Hist Assn—NY Vt hist socs—The Manuscript Soc(bd dirs). 87 Perry St., NYC 14.

14 CARSON, Max Howard. Water resources of Hawaiian Islands. b'89. BS (civil engring) '16 (Throop Coll Tech). Research on surface and ground water supplies of Hawaii. Author articles in field. With US Geol Survey since '19, dist engr Water Resources Div from

'24. Engring Assn Hawaii—Hawaiian Acad Sci—Am Meteorol Soc (Mid-Pacific sect). 225 Federal Building, Honolulu 13, Hawaii.

15 CARSON, William Glasgow Bruce. Stage history. b'91. AB '13—MA '16 (Wash U); grad work (Columbia). Research history of St. Louis stage, life and diaries of Matthew C Field. Author: The Theatre on the Frontier '32; Letters of Mr and Mrs Charles Kean Relating to Their American Tours '45; St Louis Goes to the Opera '46. Co-author: Tested One-Act Plays '39. Instr Eng Ia State Coll '16-19, Washington U '19-23, asso prof Eng since '35. Mo Hist Soc (bd trustees sec and ed The Bulletin)—Mod Lang Assn—Am Ednl Theatre Assn—Theatre Library Assn—Am Nat Theater and Acad. Washington University, St. Louis 5. H: 7006 Maryland Ave.

16 CARSWELL, Thomas S(mythe). Phenoplasts. Industrial organic chemistry; Organic plastics and pharmaceuticals. b'97. BS '18 (U Del). Holds about 40 patents. Author: Phenoplasts '46; also articles in field. Research chemist Nat Aniline & Chem Co '18-23, Rohm & Haas Co '23-25, Monsanto Chem Co '26-34, development engr '34-36, dir development '36-39, dir research '39-44, exec rep '44-46; mgr research and development dept Comml Solvents Corp Terre Haute Ind since '46. AICE—ACS—Soc Chem Ind—Tau Beta Pi—Phi Kappa Phi. Commercial Solvents Corporation, Terre Haute, Ind.

17 CARTER, Charles Webb. West African native life, religion, and culture; (Themne; Loko); West African Wild Life. b'05. ThB '33—AB '47 (Marion Coll); MA '33 (Winona Lake Sch Theology); student '23-24 (Dakota Wesley U), '25-28 (God's Bible Sch and Coll), '46 (O State U and Otterbine Coll), '47-48 (Butler U); BD '49. (Asbury Theolog Sem). Pioneer missionary to Themne and Loko tribes of Sierra Leone, W Africa; travelled through W African colonies of French Guinea, French Sinegal and Portuguese Guinea; engaged research and writing on Religion of Crescent (Mohammedanism). Author: A Half Century of American Weslyan Missions in West Africa '40; Transformed Africans of the Conversion of an African Village '38. Co-editor and co-translator: Akafa Ka Maleng Ma Themne (hymn book) '48. Asso prof philos, anthrop and missions, Marion Coll since '46. Nat Geographic Soc. Marion College; Marion, Ind. H: 4308 So Wigger St.

18 CARTER, Deane G. Farm structures; Farm and rural housing. b'94. BS '15—MS '26 (Ia State Coll). Co-author: Farm Buildings, '41; also articles in field. Prof agrl engring U Ark '22-41; prof farm structures U Ill since '41. Am Soc Agrl Engrs(F)—Tau Beta Pi—Sigma Xi. University of Illinois, Urbana, Ill.

19 CARTER, Edward P(endleton). Weed control; Plant pigments; Storage of cereal grains. b'11. BS '36—MS '39 (U Md). Research on effect of moisture content temperature and length of storage on development of sick wheat in sealed containers '45; role of fungi in the heating of moist wheat; sugar production and pigment analysis in sorghums. Articles in field. Asst plant physiol US Dept Agr, BPISAE '36-39; plant pathologist US Dept Agric, PMA Beltsville, Md.†

20 CARTER, Edwin Morton. Solvent vapor recovery; Distillation; Cellophane. b'09. MS equivalent in Chem Eng. Assisted in the development of methods and equipment for testing physical properties of cellophane; de-

signed equipment for testing toxicity of hazardous mixtures of air; engineering equipment for recovery of solvent vapors on activated carbon and their purification by distillation. Basic research directed toward a more efficient use of adsorption equipment and fractionating columns. Author articles in field. With E I Dupont since '36; chem engr technical section since '40. E. I. du Pont de Nemours & Co, Inc, Cellophane Division, Old Hickory, Tennessee.†

21 CARTER, George Francis. Anthropogeography; Ethnobotany (United States; California); Archeology (California). b'12. AB '34—PhD '42 (U Calif). Special research and field work ethnobotany American southwest '38-42, ethnobotany American Indians; antiquity of men in America and relationships of archeology to late Pleistocene geomorphology, climatology, soils of California. Author: Plant Geography and Culture History in the American Southwest '45; also articles in field. Curator anthrop San Diego Mus '34-38; asst social sci analyst Latin Am Div OSS Wash '42-43; instr geog Johns Hopkins U '43-44, asso prof '44-45, '46-48; prof since '48; chmn dept since '44. Assn Am Geog(F)—Am Geog Soc—Am Soc Profl Geog—Soc Am Archeol—Inter-Am Soc Anthop and Geog—Am Anthrop Assn—Sigma Xi. Department of Geography, Johns Hopkins University, Baltimore 18.◎

22 CARTER, Homer L. J. Projective testing technique; Psychogalvanic response; Corrective and remedial reading. b'94. BS '26 (Wayne U); AM '31 (Ohio State U). A combined projective and psychogalvanic response technique has been used to discover locus of emotional conflicts and relative importance of each. Co-author: (with E J McGinnis) Reading Manual and Workbook for College Students '48; also articles in field. Asso dir research Western Mich Coll '28-36, dir psychoednl clinic since '36, asso prof psychol since '41, prof since '47. Midwestern Psychol Assn—Am Psychol Assn—Mich Acad Arts, Sci, and Letters—Mich Psychol Assn. Western Michigan College, Kalamazoo, Mich.

23 CARTER, Hubert Adams. Mountaineering; Mountain warfare. b'14. AB '36 (Harvard); student (Sorbonne, Middlebury Coll French and Spanish Sch, U Chile). Ascents in Alps '29-31, '37-39 first ascent of Mt Dagelet Alaska '33 and Mt. Crillon Alaska '34; first successful winter crossing of Alaskan Coast Range from upper Alsek River Yukon Territory to Nunatak Fiord Alaska '35; British Himalayan Expedition which made first successful ascent Nanda Devi, India, highest summit yet reached '36, ascents in Chilean Andes '46. Research in mountain and winter warfare for G-3 War Dept Gen Staff, charge tech intelligence OQMG War Dept '42-45; spl intelligence surveys in Germany and Japan. Am Alpine Club—Swiss Alpine Club—Himalayan Club. Commendation for meritorious civilian service '45. Milton Academy, Milton, Mass.†

24 CARTER, Hugh S. Immigration. b '95. AB '16 (Southwestern U); AM '22 (U Minn); PhD '27 (Columbia). Author: Displaced persons—location and activity in the United States; Migration of aliens in the United States. Co-author: Crime and the foreign born; Social characteristics of naturalized Americans from Mexico: age and marital status. Staff U Pa '24-45; chief gen research sect research edn and information div Immigration and Naturalization Service US Dept Justice since '45. Am Sociol Soc—Am Statis Assn

—Population Assn Am—Am Acad Polit and Social Sci. Immigration and Naturalization Service, Department of Justice, Washington 25. H: 2015 N St., N.W., Washington 6, D.C.

10 CARTER, J(ames) C(edric). Plant pathology; Arboriculture; Fungicides; Antibiotics. b'05. BS '28—MS '32—PhD '34 (Purdue U). Author articles in field. Plant path Ill Natural Hist Survey since '34. Nat Shade Tree Conf (vp '47, pres '48)—Am Phytopath Soc —Ill Acad Sci—Crop Protection. Inst —Sigma Xi. Nat Arborist Assn award for work on wetwood disease of elm as outstanding research during '45 on shade tree preservation. Natural Resources Building, Urbana, Ill.

11 CARTER, James Maurice. Corrosion (High temperature); Propellants (Rocket); Propellants (Jet). b'03. BS '26 (Calif Inst Tech); PhD '29 (W Reserve U). Research and development of rocket and jet propellants and engines, corrosion and related phenomena in fused salt systems. Granted 30 patents in field. Contributor: Encyclopedia of High-Speed Aerodynamics and Jet Propulsion '52. Chem helium plant US Bur Mines '30-31; dept head Linde Air Products Lab '31-38; dir research Jergins Oil Co '38-42; supervising chem Radiation Lab U Calif '42-43; asst chief chem Aerojet Engring Corp '43-44; dir research Bone Engring Co '44-46; cons since '46; owner Carter Laboratories '51. ACS—AICE—Electrochem Soc—Tau Beta Pi —Sigma Xi. 250 N. Vinedo Av., Pasadena, Calif. H: 2418 Mayflower Av., Monrovia, Calif.†

12 CARTER, Jerry (Williams). Mental Health (Community); Psychological Services (Community programs); Education (Mental health). b'08. ABE '32 (U Fla) MA '34 PhD '38 (Ind U). Planning organization development administration, staffing and operation of state and local mental health programs; utilization of psychological services to meet community mental health needs; teacher education for vocational rehabilitation programs. Asst dir '40-41 dir '41-48 Wichita Guidance Center; br chief clin psychologist '47-48 VA; chief clin psychologist since '48 Community Services Br Nat Inst Mental Health USPHS. AAAS(F)—Am Psy Assn—Am Orthopsychiat Assn—Soc Research Child Development—Am Group Therapy Assn—Sigma Xi. Nat. Inst. Mental Health, U.S. Pub. Health Service, Bethesda 14, Md.

13 CARTER, Leonard Leroy. Overhead line wires; Electrical conductors; Weatherproof coverings; Accelerated aging. b'03. BS '27—MS '29 (Purdue U). Author articles in field. Asst chief engr Anaconda Wire and Cable Co. AIEE—Am Soc Testing Materials—Am Transit Assn—Am Standards Assn —Engring Soc W Pa—Sigma Xi—Assn Am RR—Eta Kappa Nu. Anaconda Wire & Cable Co., Hastings-on-Hudson 6, N.Y. H: 57 Circle Dr.

14 CARTER, Mary Duncan. Library organization; Library training; Libraries of the Near East. b'96. PhB '17 —PhD '42 (U Chicago); BLS '23 (NY State Library Sch). Prof library sci and dir grad sch library sci U So Calif '37-46; in charge OWI outpost library Cairo Egypt '45-46, regional librarian US Information Service for Middle East and cultural relations attache Am Embassy Cairo Egypt since '47. ALA—Spl Libraries Assn—Calif Library Assn—Can Library Assn. Recipient Cameyie grant-in-aide '31-32. 10 Trafalgar Pl., Montreal 25, Can.

15 CARTER, T. Donald, Mammalogy; Ornithology. b'93. Co-author: (with J E Hill and G H H Tate); also articles in field. Asst NY Zool Soc '13-16; asso with NY State Conservation Commn '16-17; with Am Mus Natural History since '20, asst curator world mammals since '28. Am Soc Mammologists—Am Ornithol Union—Linnaean Soc—Eastern Bird Banding Assn — NY Zool Soc(F). American Museum of Natural History, NYC 24. H: 204 Church St., Boonton, N.J.†

16 CARTLEDGE, J(oseph) Lincoln. Corn breeding; Plant cytogenetics; Human heredity. b'95. AB '18—MA '21 (U Pa); PhD '28 (U Pittsburgh). Research on sex in mucorales, cytogenetics of Datura, pollen abortion, mutation rate, heat treatments, age of seed and pollen, genetics and breeding of corn; human inheritance. Author articles in field. Prof and geneticist West Virginia U since '49. AAAS(F)—Bot Soc Am—Genetics Soc Am—Am Soc Naturalists—Am Soc Agron—W Va Acad Sci—Sigma Xi. Research grants Am Philosophical Soc '34-35. Department Agronomy and Genetics, West Virginia University, Morgantown, W. Va.

17 CARTWRIGHT, C(harles) Hawley. Glass (Non-reflecting, mechanical properties); I n f r a r e d spectroscopy; Vacuum thermocouples; High sensitivity galvanometers. b'04. BS '26—PhD '30 (Calif Inst Tech); research fellow in astro-physics Calif Inst Tech '30-31; Nat Research fellow physics U Wis and Physikalisches Inst Berlin '31-32; research with Prof M Czerny Berlin '32-33; CRB fellow in physics U Brussels Belgium '33-35. Research in development of radiometric instruments, thermocouples, galvanometers, infrared spectroscopy, molecular structure, evaporation of metals in high vacuum; developed non-reflecting glass especially valuable for high-speed lenses. Author articles in field. Physicist RCA Hollywood Calif '36-37; member research staff Corning Glass Works '40-44 and since '45; cons physicist Paramount Pictures Inc '44-45. Am Phys Soc(F)—Am Optical Soc—Sigma Xi. 109 East 4th St., Corning, N. Y.

18 CARTWRIGHT, Leonard Carl. Product evaluation; Packaging. b'06. BS ChE '27 (U Fla); MA '35—Austin teaching fellow '27-28 (Harvard); '37-40 (NYU). Various patents. Author articles in field. Cons chem, account exec Foster D Snell Inc NYC since '36. Am Inst Chem(F)—Am Chem Soc—Soc Chem Industry—Tech Assn of the Pulp and Paper Industry—AAAS—Phi Kappa Phi. 29 West 15th St., NYC 11.

19 CARTY, Donald Joseph. Drama (Play reading); American literature. b'08. Student '25-26 (Boston College); BLI '30 (Emerson Coll Boston); summer '30 (Harvard); AM in speech '34 (Marquette U); AM in edn '38 (Columbia); PhD '47 (Fordham U); summer '48 (NYU). Drama consultant; tournament adviser Hearst National Tournament of Orators NY. Instr speech St Edward's U '30-31; lectr speech Boston Coll '34; instr speech Augustinian Acad SI '41; instr English Horace Mann Sch for Boys, Tchrs Coll Columbia '44-45; vis asst prof English Coll Mt St Vincent NYC '43; asst prof English US Army Specialized Tng Program Manhattan Coll NYC '43-44; field supervisor '41-45, head dept of speech, dir drama since '34; dir Manhattan Coll Players since '34, Manhattan Coll Exptl Theatre since '48. AAUP—Speech Assn Am. Manhattan College, NYC 71.†⊚

20 CARVAJAL, Fernando Mycology; Antibiotics; Bacteriology. b'13. BS '38 (U Costa Rica); MS '41 (Cornell U); PhD '43 (La State U). Discovered sexual stage of fungus Omphalia flavida occurring freely in nature; discovered perfect stage of Colletotrichum falcatum. Author articles in field. Sr research mycol Schenley Research Labs Inc Lawrenceburg Ind since '44. AAAS —Mycol Soc Am—Am Phytopath Soc —Soc Am Bact—Electron Microscope Soc Am—Bot Soc Am—Sigma Xi. Certificate of Merit La State U '42. Schenley Research Labortories, Inc., Research and Development Division, Lawrenceburg, Ind.

21 CARVER, Gail L(uke). Natural resources conservation. b'79. Grad '00 (Mich State Normal Coll); AB '07—AM '08 (U Mich); '12-13 (Columbia); summers '11-15, '17, '23 (Woods Hole). Research in genetics and on conservation of soil, timber, wild life. Prof biol Mercer U '08-18, since '24. AAAS —Am Assn Anatomists—Marine Biol Assn—AAUP—NEA—Ga Ednl Assn—Am Inst Biol Sci—Ga Acad Sci—Assn SE Biol—Forest Products Research Soc—Sigma Xi—Sigma Mu—Audubon Soc—Cooper Ornithol Club—S Assn Sci and Industry—Am Soc Prof Biol—Ga Forestry Assn. Head Department Biology, Mercer University, Macon, Ga.

22 CARVER, James Edward. Northern English homily cycle. b'02. BA '26 (U Richmond); MA '30 (UNC); PhD '38 (NYU); student (US Naval Acad, U Louisville, Columbia). Author: The Northern Homily Cycle '40; The Date of the Northern Homily Cycle and Missionaries to the Saracens. Asso prof and act chmn dept Eng Shorter Coll '28-29; Mt Holyoke College '30-33; Eng dept NY City Coll '33-50; prof and head eng dept William Jewell Coll since '50. Mod Lang Assn—Medieval Acad —NY Soc Medievalists. Research at Oxford, Cambridge, Nat Library Wales, Brit Mus under grant Am Philos Soc '39-40. New York City College, NYC 31. H: 229 Wilmore Rd., Little Falls, N.J.

23 CARVER, William Angus. Peanut breeding. b'95. BS '21 (Clemson Coll); MS '22 (U Wis); PhD '25 (Ia State Coll). Research on peanut breeding by hybridization and selection. With Fla Agrl Expt Sta since '25, asso agron from '32. Phi Sigma—Sigma Xi—Fla Acad Sci. Florida Agricultural Experiment Station, Gainesville, Fla.

24 CASAGRANDE, Arthur. Control of soils (Civil engineering); Dams and foundations. b'02. Ing (civil engr) '24 —Dr techn '33 (Tech U, Vienna, Austria); SM(hon) '42 (Harvard). Presently engaged as consulting engineer by Federal, State, Municipal, private engineering organizations in US and other countries on foundations and earth works since '32; consultant US Army Engineers on earth dam projects and special investigations, research on design of airfields; consultant to Panama Canal on design of Third Locks Project and study of Sea-Level Canal Project; consultant on international airports in Boston and Philadelphia; designed foundations for several insurance companies and other large buildings and steam power plants. Author articles in field. Lecturer soil mechanics Harvard U '32-34, asst prof '34-40, asso prof '40-46, Gordon McKay prof soil mechanics, found engring since '46. AAAS—ASCE—Am Soc Engring Edn—Am Concrete Inst—Highway Resch Bd—Am Geophys Union—Am Acad Arts Sci—Sigma Xi. Awarded Boston Soc Civil Engrs Clemens Herschel Prize; Desmond Fitzgerald Medal, Constr Sect Prize. Pierce Hall, Harvard University, Cambridge 38, Mass.⊚

25 CASAMAJOR, Robert. Orchids (Cymbidiums, cypripediums); Camellias. B'85. BS '06 (Columbia). Pres Pasadena Flower Show Assn '38-46; pres So Calif Hort Inst '43-45; trustee Rancho Santa Ana Bot Garden since '47; vp and trustee Calif Arboretum Found since '48. Am Camellia Soc (vp '47)—Cymbidium Soc (dir since '46, ed News since '46)—Orchid Soc So Calif (dir since '44.). 385 E. Green St., Pasadena 1, Calif. H: 2036 Pasadena Glen Rd., Pasadena 8.

10 CASANOVA, Richard Louis. Paleontology (Cambrian fossils and stratigraphy); Archaeology (Panama). b '18. DSC '49 (Duke). Compiling Cambrian fossil faunas for a bibliography; research on history of pre-Columbia Indian tribes of Chiriqui Province. Led archaeological expedition into interior of Panama for the location and unearthing of pre-Columbian Indian relics; Surveyed Atlantic Sect of Panama for fossil material and made several collections of same. Dir Cambrian Research Lab. Paleontological Soc Am—Rochester Acad Sci—Earth Sci Inst. Cambrian Research Laboratory, Statesville, N.C.

11 CASE, Leland Davidson. Western American history (Black Hills). b'00. SD '20—Litt D'41 (Dakota Wesleyan U); BA '22 (Mancalester Coll); MA '26 (Northwestern U). Informal exploration Bear Butte region early life; personal acquaintance with early settlers of period following discovery gold by Custer expedition '74; collection books, photos, lore of region; co-founder Friends of Middle Border, Mitchell, South Dakota, center for history, indigenous art, music, literature. Author: Lee's Official Guidebook to Black Hills and Badlands '49. Ed Rotarian Mag since '35. SD Hist Soc—Westerners. 35 E. Wacker Dr., Chgo 1.

12 CASE, Lynn Marshall. European history (Diplomatic); French history (Since 1789). b'03. BA '2₀ (Hamilton Coll); Harrison F '29-30—MA '29—PhD '31 (U Pa). Research on European diplomatic history since 1815, modern French history; associate editor Southwestern Social Science Quarterly '37-38, member editorial board of Historian. Author: Franco-Italian Relations, 1860-1865 '32; French Opinion on United States and Mexico '36. Coauthor: (with C E Smith) Short History of Western Civilization '40. Faculty Rice Inst '30-37; asst and asso prof European hist La State U '37-46; asso prof European hist U Pa since '46. AHA—Soc d'Hist Moderne —Phi Beta Kappa—Phi Alpha Theta —AAUP—S Hist Assn (mem council). History Department, University of Pennsylvania, Phila. 4.

13 CASE, Virginia (Mrs. W. B.). Jungian psychology; Introversion-extraversion; Human relations in ethics. b'99. Student psychology with C G Jung Zurich '32-34; student (Washington U, St Louis); student Gestalt psychology '40-41 with Dr Max Wertheimer. Lecturer on contribution of Swiss school to child and adolescent psychology St Louis '32-34; work on simplified interpretation of Jung's work on marriage. Author: Your Personality—Introvert or Extravert? '41, and others. Writer since '34. NY Soc Ethical Culture. 29 Valley Rd., Larchmont, N.Y.†

14 CASEY, Albert Eugene. Familial leprosy; Epidemiology; Blood cytology (Standard breeds of rabbits); History (Amite County Miss). b'03. AB '22 (Spring Hill Coll). MD '27 (St Louis U). Asst and asso path and bacteriol Rockefeller Inst '27-34; asso prof path Va U '34-36; asso prof chmn dept St Louis U dir lab U Hosp '36-38 asst prof path and bacteriol La State U '38-42; asso prof path Med Coll Ala since '48. Author: County History

(Amite County, Miss, 1699-1865) '48; The Churches '50; Nohavaldaly & Kilcummin Parishes and the Keeffe Country, Ireland 300 B.C.-1865. 2236 Highland Av., Birmingham, Ala.

15 CASEY, Robert S(abert). Writing inks; Punched cards (Scientific); Chemical literature. b'98. BS '19—MS '20 (Trinity Coll); '21 (Columbia). Developed Skrip writing fluid and production methods. Author articles in field. Chem W A Sheaffer Pen Co since '19, dir research since '43. Am Chem Soc (punch card com since '47, sec chem literature div since '48)—Am Inst Chem(F)—AAAS(F)—Ia Acad Sci(F) —Am Inst Chem Engrs—Ia Engring Soc—Soc Am Mil Engrs—Am Documentation Inst (classification com since '48). Received Anson Marston award Ia Engring Soc '46. W. A. Sheaffer Pen Co., Ft. Madison, Ia.

16 CASH, William Thomas. Florida newspaper and political history. b'78. Ed pub schs Taylor Co Fla. Member Florida State House of Representatives '09, 15, 17, State Senate '18-20. Author: History of the Democratic Party in Florida '36; Story of Florida (4 vols) '38; One Hundred Years of State Library History (in biennial report of State Library Bd) '47; contbr Library Quarterly, Library Journal, Fla newspapers. Librarian Fla State Library since '27. Nat Assn State Libraries— Fla Hist Soc—Fla Acad Sci—Fla Library Assn—Tallahassee Hist Soc. New Supreme Ct Bldg, Tallahassee, Fla.†

17 CASKEY, John Langdon. Aegean archaeology; Greek literature; Homer. b'08. BA '31 (Yale); PhD '39 (U Cinn). Staff University of Cincinnati Excavations at Troy, Dardanelles Turkey '32-38; appointed assistant director of American School of Classical Studies Athens Greece '48-49, dir since '49. Coauthor, asso ed: Troy, vol I '50, vol II '51, succeeding vols scheduled; also articles in field. Am Philol Assn—Archaeological Inst Am—Phi Beta Kappa —Hellenic Soc. American School Classical Studies, 54 Souidias St., Athens, Greece.

18 CASPARI, Fritz. Renaissance humanism; Sixteenth century English political thought. b'14. Diploma econ and polit sci '34—BLitt '36—Rhodes scholar '33-36 (Oxford U); PhD '39 (U Hamburg). Author articles in field. Asst prof German and humanities U Chicago since '46 AHA. Faculty Exchange, University of Chicago, Chicago 37.

19 CASSADY, John Tom. Forest grazing and range revegetation research. b'09. BS '32—MS '37 (U Ariz). Research range revegetation, range cattle management, forest grazing, sheep, poisonous plant control. Co-author: (with George E Glendening) Revegetation Semi-desert Range Lands in the Southwest '40; (with C W Doran) Management of Sheep on Range Infested with Orange Sneezeweed '44. Author articles: Management for Prevention of Sneezeweed Poisoning '40; Feed, Forage and Forests—the Need for Winter Feed '47, and others. Jr range examiner US Forest Service NM '33-36, asst forest ecol '37, asso forest ecol '38-41, forest ecol La '46, forester since '47. Ecol Soc—Soc Am Foresters —Am Soc Range Management—Sigma Xi. P. O. Box 1192, Alexandria, La.

20 CASSELL, Robert Calder. Plant Diseases (Cereal and vegetable crops). b'06. BS '30 (Ia State Coll); MS '32 (U Ida); PhD '38 (U Minn). Author articles in field. Plant path biol br Chem Corps War Dept since '48. Ill

State Hort Soc—Am Phytopath Soc— AAAS — Bot Soc Washington — Sigma Xi. Camp Detrick, Frederick, Md.

21 CASSENS, Frank Paul. Tests (Psychological); Merit rating; Employee selection and evaluation; Vocational Guidance. b'18. BA '38 MS '42 (Tulane U). Performance tests in academic and trade areas; standardized tests for industrial personnel; merit rating blanks. Research psychologist Dept of the Army '42-45; chief psychol measurements, Occupational Opportunities Service O State U '45-48; indsl psychol Lago Oil & Transportation Co Ltd Aruba Netherlands W.I. since '48. Am Psychol Assn—AAAS(F) —Indsl Relations Research Assn. Lago Oil & Transport Co., Ltd., Aruba, Netherlands West Indies.

22 CASTAÑEDA, Carlos Eduardo. History and culture of Spain; War between Texas and Mexico. b'96. AB '21 —MA '23—PhD '32 (U Tex); LLD '40 (St Edwards U); (Coll of William and Mary, U Havana, U Mexico). Author: The Mexican Side of the Texas Revolution '28; Early Texas Album, Fifty Illustrations with Notes '29; Our Catholic Heritage in Texas (6 vol); The End of the Spanish Regime '42; The Fight for Freedom '49; A History of Latin America for Schools '44; The Lands of Middle America '48. Asso editor: Hispanic American History Review '40-46. Bd editors: The Americas since '44. Asso prof Spanish and hist Coll William and Mary '23-27; librarian Latin American collections U Tex '27-46, prof hist of Spain and Latin America since '46. Acad Am Franciscian Hist—Hispanic Soc Am—Sociedad Mexicana de Geografia and Estadistica —Ateneo Nacional de Artes Ciencios— Academia Mexicana de la Historia— Centro de Estudios de Buenos Aires. Box 1633 University Station, Austin, Tex. H: 301 W. 37th St.

23 CASTER, Kenneth E(dward). Invertebrate paleontology; Paleogeography; Stratigraphy; Evolution. b'08. AB '29—MA '31—PhD '32 (Cornell U). Author articles in field. Curator Paleontol Mus U Cincinnati '36-40, professor geol paleontol since '52, fellow Grad Sch Arts and Sci since '39; dir dept geol U Sao Paulo Brazil '45-48. Geol Soc Am—Paleontol Soc—Soc Vertebrate Paleonotol(F)—Paleontol Research Inst(pres '51-53)—Am Association Petrol Geol—Inst Est Sup Montevideo — Sociedade de Geologia de Brasil(F)—Soc Geologique de France —Evolution Soc. Guggenheim fellow '48; grants-in-aid Geol Soc Am '40, '42, Nat Research Council '34, '35. Department of Geology, University of Cincinnati, Cincinnati 21.†

24 CASTETTER, Edward Franklin. Ethnobiology; Primitive Indian agriculture; Origin and development of cultivated plants. b'96. BS '19 (Lebanon Valley Coll); MS '21 (Pa State Coll); PhD '24 (Ia State Coll); '21-23 (Chicago U). Research on comparative cytology of annual and biennial varieties of Melilotus alba, species crosses in genus Cucurbita, prehistoric seeds, early tobacco utilization and cultivation in American southwest. Author: Ethnobiological Studies in the American Southwest I-VII '35-41. Co-author (with Bell) A Laboratory Manual of General Botany '35; (with Bell) Pima and Papago Indian Agriculture '42; also articles in field. Prof, head dept biol U NM since '28, dean graduate school since '50. Botanical Society Am—Am Anthrop Assn(F) — AAAS(F) — NM Acad Sci. University of New Mexico, Department of Biology, Albuquerque, N.M.†

10 CASTLE, Benjamin Frederick. Distribution of milk. b'94. BS (US Mil Acad West Point NY). Wrote Introduction to Milk Marketing Under Federal Control. Exec dir Milk Industry Found Washington since '40. 1625 Eye St., N.W., Washington 6.

11 CASTLE, Samuel Northrup. Electro-sidurgy; Hydraulics; Fluids and gases; Diesel engines. b'80. AB '01 (Harvard); '02-04 (Cornell). Investigated European shop practices '08-09; research in electrical steel furnace work '16-18. Invented centrifugal oiling device for Corliss engines, centrifugal gas cleaner, non-inductive method of leading-in conductors on arc furnaces, commercial searchlight. Commercial engr Gen Elec Co NY '09-19; private practice since '19; dir, sec Honolulu Rapid Transit and Land Co '26-29, since '38; dir Castle and Cooke Ltd, Hawaiian Pineapple Co Ltd; dir vp Ewa Plantation Co Ltd, Waialua Agrl Co Ltd, Kohala Sugar Co Ltd, dir Advertiser Publishing Co Ltd since '37. AIEE — ASCE — ASME(F)—Am Inst Mining Metall Engrs — SAE — AAAS(F) — Am Inst Chem Engrs—Am Iron Steel Inst—Am Math Soc—Soc Am Mil Engrs—Am Ordnance Assn—Harvard Eng Soc — NY Elec Soc — Engring Assn Hawaii. Mamalu, Waimanalo, Oahu, T.H.☉

12 CASTLE, William A(ugustus). Planaria. b'04. BSc '24 (Denison U); PhD '28 (U Chicago). Author articles in field. Prof Mary Washington Coll U Va since '41, head dept biol since '47. AAAS—Am Soc Zool—Ecol Soc Am (sec '48-50)—Sigma Xi. Box 1331 College Station, Fredericksburg, Va.

13 CATAN-ROSE, Richard. Anatomy for artists. b'05. Student '42-43 (Coll City NY); cert '34 (Cooper Union Inst); MFA '37 (Royal Acad Fine Arts Sicily). Research in general artists' anatomy. Founder and dir Institute of Fine Arts, Inc, Forest Hills LI since '40; painting instr, drawing anatomy sculpture etching; lecturer on anatomy. 72-72 112th St., Forest Hills, L.I., N.Y.

14 CATHCART, William H. Biochemistry (Electronics); Bread and baking. b'11. AB '33—AM '34 (Ind U); PhD '36 (NY U). Developed electronic processes for high-speed defrosting of frozen foods, for eliminating mold spores in bread without affecting its nutritive value. Author articles in field. Dir bakeries lab Great Atlantic & Pacific Tea Co NYC since '41. Am Chem Soc—AAAS—Am Assn Cereal Chem—Inst Food Tech—NY Acad Sci—Phi Beta Kappa—Sigma Xi. Great Atlantic & Pacific Tea Co., 420 Lexington Av., NYC 17.

15 CATION, Donald. Fruit pathology; Stone fruit virus diseases. b'96. BS in agr '25—MS '29 (Ia State Coll). Co-author: (with E M Hildebrand and G H Berkeley) Handbook of Virus Diseases of Stone Fruits in North Ameirca '42; also articles in field. Research asso dept bot and plant path Mich State Coll since '41. Am Phytopath Soc—Sigma Xi. Botany Department, Michigan State College, East Lansing, Mich.

16 CATTELL, Roscoe Arnold. Petroleum engineering; Helium production; Natural gas; Oil shale. b'92. BS in CE '16 (Calif U). Author articles in field. Petroleum engr US Bur Mines Okla '17-18, engr, asst supt, supt Petroleum Expt Sta '21-25, chief helium div '25-33, chief petroleum and natural gas div since '33. Am Inst Mining Metall Engrs—Am Petroleum Inst—Am Gas Assn. U.S. Bureau of Mines, Washington.

17 CAUGHEY, Robert Andrew. Concrete (Prestressed); Grain and material storage bins (Lateral pressures); Composite beams; Impact stresses. b'85. BS '07—CE '16 (Penn State Coll). Author: Reinforced Concrete '36. Prof civil engring Ia State Coll since '30. ASCE (pres Ia sect '35-36)—Am Concrete Inst—Am Soc Engring Edn—Ia Engring Soc—Phi Kappa Phi—Sigma Xi—Tau Beta Pi. Dept Civil Engineering, Iowa State College, Ames, Ia.

18 CAVE, Marion Stilwell (Mrs). Plant embryology; Cyto-taxonomy; Latin American forest laws and economic woods. b'04. AB '24; AM '25 (U Colo); '26-27 (U Kan); PhD '36 (U Calif). Research in plant embryology with special reference to Liliales, chromosome numbers in Hydrophyllaceae, microchemical tests for white pine blister rust on Ribes; work in translation and abstraction forest laws Latin American countries and listings of their woods in economic use. Author articles in field. Research asso bot U Calif since '36; asst econ analyst Office Coordinator Inter-Am Affairs Washington '44-45. Bot Soc Am—Calif Bot Soc. Botany Department, University of California, Berkeley 4.†

19 CAVENY, Charles Claire. Aeronautics; Diesel; Electronics; Technician training and school administration. b'97. BS in EE '28 (U Pittsburgh); MS '40 (Pa State Coll). Co-editor US Navy Diesel engines texts; directing editor US Navy manuals, Aviation Machinist Mates, Aviation Metalsmiths Series, etc., and electronic technician manuals. Prof, exec dean Chicago undergrad div U Ill since '46. NEA—Pa State Ednl Assn—Ill Vocational Assn — Am Vocational Assn. — AIEE State College, Pa.

20 CAVERT, Samuel McCrea. Theology and religion. b'88. Religious organizations, national and international; Inter-church cooperation and unity. BA '10 (Union Coll); MA '14 (Columbia); BD '15 (Union Theol Sem); DD '28 (Lawrence Coll) '35 (Union Coll); LLD '42 (Yale); D Theol '48 (U Gottingen). Author: Securing Christian Leaders for Tomorrow '26; The Adventure of the Church '27. Co-author or editor: Christian Unity, Its Principles and Possibilities '21; (with Henry P Van Dusen) The Church Through Half a Century '36; Church and State in the Modern World, '37; The Church Faced the World '39. Gen sec Fed Council Chs Christ in Am. since '21; del World Conf Chs Jerusalem '28, Oxford '37, Edinburgh '37, Utrecht '38; apptd Protestant liaison ofcl between German chs and Am Mil Govt authorities in US zone of occupation '46. Internat Council Religious Edn (exec com). 297 4th Av., NYC. H: 161 Boulder Trail, Bronxville, N.Y.☉

21 CAVETT, Jesse William. Biochemistry of poultry; Vaccine production on eggs. b'00. AB '21 (Hanover Coll); MA '24 (Ind U); PhD '30 (Ia State U). Studies in histology, hemotology and biometry; research on racinization curves of urinary, edema fluids and blood plasma proteins, modification of Van Slyke nitrogen distribution method, tyrosine and tryptophaneanalysis for normal and goiterous human thyroglobulin, determination of alcohol in blood and other body fluids. Author articles: Ammonia Formation by the Kidney (with Foster) '38; Non-Fermentable Reducing Substance of Chicken Blood '39, Feather Follicle Method of Vaccinating with Fowl Laryngotracheitis Vaccine (with Molgard) '47; and others. Head sci dept LaGrange Coll '24-28; biochem Dr Salsbury's Labs since '37. Am Chem Soc—AAAS. Dr Salsbury's Laboratories, Charles City, Ia.†

22 CAWLEY, Elizabeth Hoon. English customs system; Eighteenth century British economic and administrative history and colonial relations. b'06. BA '26 (Northwestern U); MA '30 (Yale); PhD '34 (U London); '31-32 (Columbia). Research on the English customs systems of the eighteenth century, American diaries of Richard Cobden. Author: The Organization of the English Customs System, 1696-1786 '38. Asso prof hist, act chmn hist dept Albany Coll '30-31; dean Mary Baldwin Coll. Pi Gamma Mu—AHA. Julia C G Piatt memorial fellow Am Assn U Women '34, fellow NJ Fed Women's Clubs '33. 111 Fitz Randolph Rd., Princeton, N.J.

23 CAYLOR, Richard Lee. Algae (Panama Canal, Mississippi); Tropical ferns. b'94. AB '22 (Miss Coll); MA '31 (George Peabody Coll); PhD '44 (La State U). Author articles in field. With Delta State Coll since '31, now prof, head div sci; dir Gulf Coast Research Lab. Miss Acad Sci (pres '48-49)—AAAS—Phycological Soc Am. 900 Court St., Cleveland, Miss.†

24 CAZIER, James Henry. Mine development; Mine operation. b'12. BS (mining engring) '35 (U Nev). Research on reopening and pioneer operation of nonferrous metal mines. With Internat Smelting and Refining Co '35-41; asst gen supt Lexington Mining Co and gen supt Callahan Consol Mines Inc '41-43; with Mine Loan Sect RFC '43-48; gen supt Goodwin Mining Co '48-49; gen supt Bagdad Copper Corp since '49. AIMME. Bagdad, Ariz.

25 CAZIER, Mont A. Beetles (Biology, classification, distribution). b'11. BS '35—PhD '41 (U Cal). Specialized in entomology and more specifically in Coleoptera (beetles); published numerous papers dealing with classification, speciation, biolody, distribution and ecology in the order Coleoptera, families Cicindelidae, Scarabaeidae, Cleridae, Buprestidae, Cerambycidae; order Diptera, family Apioceratidae. Author articles: New West Indian Scarabaeidae and Cerambycidae '52; The Cerambycidae of the Bahama Islands, B.W.I. '52; A review of the scarab genus Acoma '53. Asst curator dept insects and spiders Am Mus Natural History '41-46, chmn and asso curator dept insects and spiders '46-52, chmn and curator dept insects and spiders since '52. Am Entomol Soc—NY Entomological Soc. American Museum Natural History, 79th St. at Central Park W., NYC 24.

26 CEAGLSKE, Norman Hugo. Chemical engineering (Unit operations); Instrumentation and controls. b'07. BS '28—MS '29—PhD '36 (U Wis). Author articles in field. Instr and asst prof head div met State U Ia '36-40; engr research Universal Oil Products Co Chicago '37; engr Scullin Steel Co St Louis '41; asst and asso prof Washington U '40-46; research engr Anheuser-Busch Inc St Louis '42-46; prof chem engring U Minn since '46. Am Inst Chem Engrs—ASEE—Am Chem Soc—AAUP—Instrument Soc Am—Tau Beta Pi—Sigma Xi. Division of Chemical Engineering, University of Minnesota, Mpls 14.☉

27 CELLA, Francis Raymond. Statistical economics and methodology; Business statistics. b'09. AB '33 (Ky

Wesleyan Coll); MA '37—grad student '37-42 (Ky U). Research in agricultural economics, social security, labor problems, employment service, statistical analyses of Air Force operations, statistical methodology; studies on further cooperative arrangements between federal agencies and bureaus of business research, upper limits of real roots of real algebraic equation. Author articles: An Analysis of the Proposed Federal 3% Diversion '41; A Benefit Formula Based Upon Annual Earnings '40; The Dynamics of Employment and Unemployment '42, and others. Statis Ky Agrl Expt Station '34-37; dir research and statis Ky Unemployment Compensation Commn '37-42; dir Bur Business Research, prof business statis Coll Business Admnstrn Okla U since '46. Statis analyst, capt US Army Air Force '42-46. Am Statis Assn—Am Econ Assn—Econometric Soc—Inst Math Statis SW Social Sci Assn. University of Oklahoma, Norman, Okla.†

10 CENTER, Stella Stewart. Education (Reading); Reading clinics. b'78. AB '94 (Monroe (now Bessie Tift) Coll); AB '01 (Peabody Coll Nashville); PhB '11 (U Chicago) AM '13 (Columbia) LittD '29 (U Ga). Author: (with collaborator) Teaching High School Students to Read. Editor: (with collaborator) Reaching and Thinking '40, Reading Today '47. General editor: Junior Academy Classics. Lectr on edn and dir reading clinic NYC '36-50 H: 51 Fifth Av., NYC.†⊚

11 CHACE, Fenner Albert, Jr. Biology, taxonomy, and distribution of decapod Crustacea. b'08. AB '30—AM '31—PhD '34 (Harvard). Author articles in field. Curator marine invertebrates US Nat Mus Washington since '46. AAAS(F)—Boston Soc Nat Hist—Bermuda Biol Sta for Research—Wash Acad Scis—Sigma Xi. U.S. National Museum, Washington 25.

12 CHACO-DANGLEY, Nicholas Carol Victor. Theoretical physics (Electron optics, acoustics); Crystal physics; Byzantine education, universities, and institutions. b'10. Bachelier '28 (U France); PhD '34 (Johns Hopkins); student (Am Coll and Gym, Salonica; Harvard, Robert Coll, Univs Mich, Paris, and Marseille). Author: Emperor Anastasius I; Theory of Crystal Vibrations '48; Mathematical Theory of Electron Optics '45; also articles in field. Councilor, adviser sci tech affairs, Ministry Nat Edn Albania, prof and head depts math, physics, State Gymnasium Albania, '36-37; asso prof physics and research asso Ala Polytech Inst and Auburn Research Foundation since '47. Tech adviser chief signal officer 6th Service Command US Army '42, also chief instr; cons OSS Joint Chiefs of Staff Washington '42. Am Phys Soc—Am Math Soc—NY Acad Sci. Box 608, Lynn, Mass.

13 CHADA, Harvey Lorenzo. Japanese beetles (Milky disease); European corn borer (Biology and control); Rhodes-grass (Scale control). b'03 BS '26—MS '31—PhD '47 (U Wis). Japanese beetle research included biological control with the milky disease organism (Bacillus popillae Dutky) European corn borer research: biology, ecology, and evaluation of the factors affecting its abundance. Research on the Rhodes-grass scale (Antonina graminis Maskell): biology, ecology, biological control, insecticidal control, and host resistance studies. Ext and research entomol U Del '42-44; entomol corn borer research US Bur Entomol and Plant Quarantine Muscatine Ia '44-49, in charge Rhodes-grass

scale research since '49. Am Assn Econ Entomol—AAAS. U.S. Bureau of Entomology & Plant Quarantine, P.O. Box 144, Weslaco, Tex

14 CHADWICK, Lewis C. Ornamental horticulture; Plant Propagation; Arboriculture; Soils and fertilizers. b'02. BS '25 (U Vt); PhD '31 (Cornell). Research in vegetative propagation of ornamental plants; selection, planting, maintenance ornamentals; soil and fertilizer studies. Co-author: (with Alex Laurie) The Modern Nursery '31; (with Laurie); Commercial Flower Forcing '33; also articles in field. Asst ornamental hort Cornell U '25-27, instr '27-28, investigator '28-29; asst prof hort O State U '29-38, asso prof '38-47, prof since '47; prof hort O Agr Expt Sta since '47. Am Soc Hort Sci—Sigma Xi—Gamma Sigma Delta. Department of Horticulture, Ohio State University, Columbus, O.

15 CHALKLEY, Harold William. Cancer research; Cell physiology. b'87. BSc '24 (Miss State Coll); MA—PhD '27 (Johns Hopkins). Research on chemistry of cell division and cell physiology. Author articles: The Chemistry of Cell Division II. The Relation Between Cell Growth and Division in Amoeba Proteus '31; Control of Fission in Amoeba Proteus as Related to the Mechanism of Cell Division '49; (with Carl Voegtlin) The Chemistry of Cell Division I. The Effect of Glutathions on Cell Division in Amoeba Proteus '31; The Chemistry of Cell Division III. Inhibitions of Cell Division of Amoeba Proteus by High Dilutions of Copper Salts '32; and others. Asso physiol Hygiene Lab USPHS '28-30, physiol '30-42; sr physiol Nat Cancer Inst '42-47, prin physiol '47-48, act asst chief Cancer Grants Br Nat Cancer Inst '48-49, asst chief since '49. Am Soc Zool—Am Physiol Soc—Soc Study Growth and Development—Washington Acad Sci—Soc Exptl Biol and Med (asso)—Phi Beta Kappa—Sigma Xi. National Cancer Institute, Bethesda 14, Md.

16 CHALLIS, John. Harpsichord construction. b'07. Student four year with Arnold Dolmetsch. Dolmetsch Found scholar '26-30 (Arnold Dolmetsch Haslemere Eng). Developed split-proof, non-wearing tuning pin blocks of phenolic resin, all aluminum structural frame not dependent on wooden substructure, special piano for playing music of Mozart and Haydn patterned on ideals of 18th century, light metal wrest plank eliminating alterations caused by weather changes, moisture resistant action jacks. Started harpsichord bldg Ypsilanti Mich '30, now in Detroit. 549 E. Jefferson Av., Detroit 26.

17 CHALMERS, Gordon Keith. Seventeenth Century thought and letters; Education. b'04. AB '25—Litt D '46 (Brown); BA '28—MA '34 (Oxford Eng); MA '33—PhD '33 (Harvard); LLD '38 (Hobart Coll Geneva NY); Litt D '41 (Rockford Coll); LHD '45 (Ripon Coll). Studies of liberal higher education: definition, aims, curriculum, place, purpose and limits of literary, philosophical and historical studies; chairman Commission on Liberal Education of Association of American Colleges. Author articles in feld. Pres Kenyon Coll since '37; ed Am Oxonian '46-49. Modern Lang Assn America—Oxford Soc—Newcomen Soc of Eng—Coll Eng Assn—O Coll Assn—Mediaeval Acad Am—Am Assn Rhodes Scholars—Phi Beta Kappa. Cromwell House, Gambier, O.†⊚

18 CHALMERS, Harvey II. Mohawk Valley history; Indian lore; Iroquoian

history; Bird dogs. b'90. AB '13 (Yale). Author: West to the Setting Sun '43; Drums Against Frontenac, '49; also articles in field. R. 31 E. Main St., Amsterdam, N.Y.

19 CHAMBERLAIN, Donald William. Plant pathology; Diseases of soybeans and forage crops. b'05. BA '29 (St Norbert Coll, DePere Wis); MA '32; PhD '43 (U Wis). Studies on identification of diseases soybeans, grasses, red clover, other forage crops, and evaluating for disease resistance research on brown stem rot, brown leaf spot; presently engaged research on nature of disease resistance to bacterial pustule and bacterial blight in soybeans, and surveying soybean field in Illinois during season to determine kind and amount of diseases present. Author articles in field. With Wis State Highway Dept as soils surveyor and inspector '32-34, survey party '35-36, resident engr '37-39; asst in agron Ky Agrl Expt Sta Lexington Ky '45-46; agent (asst path) US Dept Agr Div Forage Crops and Diseases, U Ill Urbana Ill '46-48, asso path since '48. Am Phytopath Soc—Sigma Xi. 205 Davenport Hall, University of Illinois, Urbana, Ill.

20 CHAMBERLAIN, Katherine McFarlane. Physics; Color photography; Spectrochemical analysis. b'92. AB '14—AM '19—ScD '24 (U Mich); postdoctoral research student Cavendish Lab '25-26 (U Cambridge). Lecturer on the social implications of atomic energy. Author: Darkroom Handbook '47; An Introduction to the Study of Photography '51. With Wayne U since '33, prof physics since '45. Am Assn Physics Tchrs—Optical Soc Am—Engring Soc Detroit—Phi Beta Kappa—Sigma Xi—Sigma Pi Sigma. Ellen Richards Research grant '25; Bronze medal Distinguished Service Found Optometry '37. Wayne University, Det 1⊚

21 CHAMBERLAIN, Neil Wolverton. Labor economics. b'15. AB '37—AM '39 (Western Reserve U); PhD '42 (O State U). Research on financial and internal governmental policies of labor unions, collective bargaining procedures; studies of judicial process in labor unions, organized business in America, grievance proceedings. Author: Collective Bargaining Procedures '44; The Union Challenge to Management Control '48; also articles in field. Research dir Labor and Management Center since '46, asst prof econ Yale '47, assoc '49. Am Econ Assn—Industrial Relations Research Assn—Phi Beta Kappa. Brookings Inst Research Fellow '41-42. 333 Cedar St., New Haven.†

22 CHAMBERLAIN, Robert Stoner. Spanish history; Spanish colonial and Latin American history. b'03. AB '25 (Stanford U); BSc '27 (Ohio State U); PhD '36 (Harvard). In charge Project A in Mexico for Library of Congress '30-31, photostating of documents concerning history of US in Mexican archives; studies of the conquest of Yucatan and of Honduras; research in Spanish archives, 32-34, on fellowship from Harvard; staff member Division Historical Research, Carnegie Instn of Washington '36-41, '45-47; research in Mexican and Central American archives, '36-37. Author articles in field. Cultural relations officer US Embassy, Guatemala City, (Auxiliary Fgn Service) '41-45; asso prof hist U Miami '47-48; US Govt Service since '48. AHA—Sociedad de Geografia e Historia de Guatemala—The Railway and Locomotive Hist Soc—Hakluyt Soc (London). 804 Grand View Dr., Beverly Hills, Alexandria, Va.

10 CHAMBERLAIN, Thomas K(night). Fish population management (Freshwater mussel, trout-stream fish, farm-pond fish, large impoundment fish). b'95. BS '20 (Cornell U); MA '27 (Stanford); student (U Mo). Author articles in field. Aquatic biol US Fish and Wildlife Ser since '22. Sigma Xi. 254 Faculty Exchange, Texas A & M College, College Station, Tex.†

11 CHAMBERLIN, Joseph C(onrad). False scorpions (Morphology, taxonomy, geographical distribution); Citrus insects and their control; Oil sprays; Biology and control of beet leafhopper and pea weevil and aphids; Alaskan insects of agricultural importance (Cutworms, rootmaggots). b'98. U fellow '24—AB '23—MA '24—PhD '29 (Stanford); student (U Utah, U Calif). Author: The Arachnid Order Chelonethida '31; also articles in field. Entomol US Dept Agr since '29, charge studies on biol and control of the pea aphid and the development and improvement equipment for the application of insecticides since '48. AAAS(F) —entomol Soc Am(F)—Pacific Coast Entomol Soc—Am Assn Econ Entomol —Sigma Xi—Phi Beta Kappa. 2330 Elm St., P.O. Box 278, Forest Grove, Ore.

12 CHAMBERLIN, Noel Stillwell. Sanitary chlorinaton. b'06. BS '28 (U Pa); '28-31 (Rutgers U). Research on trickling filter performance, effect of enzymes on sewage solids, chlorination of activated sludge and studies on odors in sewage; practical applications and uses of chlorine in water treatment, sewage treatment, industrial waste disposal and industrial waters, development of methods of treatment, control of chlorination. Author articles in field. Chem dept sewage investigation State of NJ '23-31; san chem Fed Water Service Corp '31-33, chem in charge North Atlantic Div Lab '33-37, supt sewage treatmen't plant Farrell Pa '37-40; san chem tech service dept Wallace & Tiernan Co Inc since '40. Am Chem Soc—Fed Sewage Works Assn—Am Water Works Assn—Pa Water Works Operators Assn—AAAS. Co-winner with JR Glass of John M. Goodell prize Am Water Works '43. Wallace and Tiernan Company, Incorporated, Newark 1, N.J. H: 9 Sherman Av., Pompton Plains.

13 CHAMBERLIN, Thomas Roscoe. Economic entomology; Hymenopterous parasites. b'89. BA '20 (Utah U). Engaged investigations of alfalfa weevil in Utah and intermountain states; parasites of alfalfa weevil, Europe and intermountain States; cereal and forage insects and their parasites, Pacific Northwest; white grubs (Phyllophaga species), corn insects; legume insects; research and writing on wheat jointworm in Oregon, host plants of Grapholitha coversana, life history and parasites of Hypera rumicis, proportion of sexes in June beetles in Wisconsin, oviposition of June beetles and survival of offspring in grasses and legumes, control of fall armyworm in sweet corn and popcorn with DDT. Co-author articles: (with Rockwood) The Western Spotted Cucumber Beetle as a Pest of Forage Crops in the Pacific Northwest '43; (with Rockwood and Zimmerman) The Wheat Stem Maggots of the Genus Meromyza in the Pacific Northwest '47; (with Fluke) White Grubs in Cereal and Forage Crops and Their Control '47; and others. Entomol US Dept Agr Bur Entomol and Plant Quarantine since '13, in chge legume insect lab Wis U since '46. AAAS(F) —Wash Entomol Soc—Am Assn Econ Entomol—Sigma Xi. 424 University Dr., Madison 6, Wis.

14 CHAMBERS, Carl C. Electronic circuits and control; Digital computers; Graphic arts (Photographic processes). b'07. BS '29 (Dickinson Coll); DSc '34 (U Pa). Research on conduction of electric current vacuum-tube oscillators. Invented vacuum tube measuring set, electronic control system, and photographic processes in graphic arts. Author articles in field. Cons Brooke Engring Co Phila since '34, Internat Resistance Co since '47; cons dir Edward Stern & Co Phila since '36; prof Moore Sch U Pa since '41; acting dean Moore Sch since '49. Am Phys Soc—AIEE—IRE. Moore School of Electrical Engineering, University of Pennsylvania, Phila.†⊙

15 CHAMBERS, Francis T., Jr. Psychotherapy of chronic alcoholism. b'97. Lecturer in post-graduate instruction. Co-author: (with E A Strecker) Alcohol: One Man's Meat '38; also articles on alcoholism. Asso in therapy Inst Pa Hosp Phila since '35; cons on alcoholism; mem bd dirs Phila Child Guidance Clinic. The Institute of Pennsylvania Hospital, Phila.†

16 CHAMBERS, Merritt Madison. Administration (University, local and state government, philanthropic foundations, public, school); Foreign universities; Law of higher education; Public school law; Youth welfare and education. b'99. BA '22)Ohio Wesleyan U); MA '27—PhD '31 (O State U). Author: Military Training in American Universities '27; State Educational - Administrative Organization '36; Youth-Serving Organizations '47. Co-author: The Government of Higher Education '35; The Colleges and the Courts '36; Charters of Philanthropies '48; and others; also articles in field. With Am Council on Edn. '35-'42 and since '45, now dir Fgn Univs Project; asso prof sch administrn (O State U, summers) '38-40, prof summer '47. AAAS(F)—Am Polit Sci Assn—Am Soc Pub Adm—Am Acad Polit Social Sci—NEA (life)—Am Assn Sch Administrs—Am Ednl Research Assn— Nat Soc Study Edn. R.D. 4, Mt. Vernon, O.†⊙

17 CHAMPE, John Leland. Anthropology (American). b'95. AB '21 (U Neb); PhD '46 (Columbia). Author articles in field. Associated with U Neb and Neb State Hist Soc in field work in Central Plains archaeol since '30; asso prof anthropol U Neb since '50, Dir lab anthrop since '41. AAAS(F) —Am Anthropol Assn(F)—Plains Conf Archaeol (sec '40-47) — Sigma Xi. Laboratory of Anthropology, University of Nebraska, Lincoln 2, Neb. H: 1917 S. 27th St.

18 CHAMPIE, Clark (Lafayette). Desert plants (Ecology and taxonomy); Photography (Desert plants and insects). b'16. BS '51 (NM Coll A and M) Discovered rare desert species of moth-apatelodes angelica race serathica Dyar, family Zanolidae. H: 140 Champie Lane, El Paso, Tex.

19 CHAMPNEY, William Brooks. Wind tunnel design and operation. b'16. BS '38—MS '40 (Case Inst Tech). Author articles and reports in field. Section head Curtiss Wright Corp Research Lab Buffalo '43-46; asst dept head wind tunnel dept Cornell Aero Lab Buffalo since '46. Daniel Guggenheim Airship Inst wind tunnel engr '40-43. 4455 Genesee St., Buffalo 21.

20 CHAN, Shau Wing. Chinese language. b'07. AB '27 (Lingnan U China); AM '32—PhD '37 (Stanford U). Consultant international secretariat UN conference San Francisco '45; member sub-committee on Chinese, committee on foreign languages State of California since '47. Author: Chinese Reader for Beginners '42; Concise English-Chinese Dictionary '46; Elementary Chinese '51. Lecturer Chinese Kwangtung Provincial Normal Sch for Women Canton China 1928 to 1930; faculty Stanford U since '38, prof Chinese since '50. Am Oriental Soc—Stanford Philol Assn. Stanford University, Stanford, Calif.

21 CHAN, Wing-tsit. Chinese philosophy, culture and religion; Oriental and twentieth century philosophy; Buddhism. b'01. AB '24 (Lingnan U, Canton China); PhD '29 (Harvard). Chinese delegate to several international conferences; chairman Council of Christian Higher Education in China '34. Author: Twentieth Century Philosophy '43; Philosophy East and West '44; Approach to National Unity '45; China '46; Religion in the Twentieth Century '48. Editor: The Essentials of Buddhist Philosophy (by J Takakusu) '47. Prof Chinese culture Dartmouth Coll since '42. Am Oriental Soc—Far Eastern Assn—Phi Kappa Phi. Awarded Guggenheim Fellow '48. 6 Tyler Rd., Hanover, N.H.

22 CHANCE, Britton. Enzyme mechanisms; Electronic time measurements. b'13. BS—MS '35—PhD '40 (U Pa); PhD '42 (Cambridge U). Author: Waveforms '48; Electronic Time Measurements '49; also articles in field. Act dir Johnson Found '40-41; staff Radiation Lab '41-46; prof biophys and dir Johnson Research Found U Pa since '49. Am Phys Soc(F)—Inst Radio Engrs—Nat Research Council (com on blood and blood substitutes)—Tau Beta Pi—Sigma Xi. Guggenheim fellow Med Nobel Inst and Molteno Inst '46-48. Johnson Research Foundation, University of Pennsylvania, 3508 Hamilton St., Phila 4.⊙

23 CHANDLEE, Edward Earl. Horology; American tall clocks. b'84. Student '07 (Princeton U). Author: Six Quaker Clock Makers, 1682-1813 '43. Chmn bd, Edw. K. Tryan Co., 817 Arch St., Phila. 5.

24 CHANDLER, Asa Crawford. Parasitology (Taxonomy, life cycles, immunology); Helminthology; Medical entomology; Tropical medicine; Immunology. b'91. AB '41 (Cornell); MS '12—PhD '14 (U Calif). Made helminthological survey of India '24-27; in charge Aedes aegypti control work in Texas, '42-'45; research in parasitology, Rice Institute, '19-'23, '27. Author: Animal Parasites and Human Disease '18; Hookworm Disease '29; Introduction to Parasitology, '49; The Eater's Digest '41. Co-author: (with R N Chopra) Anthelmintics and Their Uses '28. Instr zool, later prof Oregon Agrl Coll '14-16; instr biol Rice Inst Houston Tex '19-24, prof since '27; in charge hookworm research lab Sch of Tropical Medicine Calcutta India '24-27; spl cons USPHS '42-47. Served as 2d lt Sanitary Corps US Army '18-19. AAAS(F)—Am Soc Parasitol—Am Soc Tropical Med—Am Acad Tropical Med—Am Micros Soc—Am Soc Naturalists—Sigma Xi. 6315 Vanderbilt Av., Houston 5.

25 CHANDLER, Clyde. Plant genetics and cytology. b'01. BA '23—Licensed Instructor '23—Diploma in Music '23 (Ark U); MA '27—PhD '40 (Columbia). Research on forest genetics, cinchona, colchicine and its effect on flowering plants; studies on breeding of irises, iris seedlings, pollen-tube behavior in Hemerocallis, microsporogenesis in diploid and triploid types of Lilium tigrinum and of Hemerocallis fulva, number of chromosomes in species of Amorphophallus. Co-author articles: (with Stout) Report on the Breeding Work with Irises at the New York Botanical Garden '29; and others. Geneticist Boyce Thompson Inst Plant Research since '48. Torrey Botanical Club—Sigma Xi—Genetics Soc Am. Boyce Thompson Institute, 1086 N. Broadway, Yonkers, N.Y.†

10 CHANDLER F(rederick) B(arker). Mineral nutrition; Composition and uses of blueberries. b'03. BS '28 (U Maine); '28-29 (Mass State Coll); '29-30 (U Chicago); '30-35 (U Minn); '36-38 (U Md); PhD '39 (U Md). Author articles: Mineral Nutrition of the Genus Brassica with particular reference to Boron '41; The Effect of Mulch on Soil Moisture '42; Nutrition of Brassica and Potatoes '43; Composition and Uses of Blueberries '44; The Effect of Boron on the Vitamin C Content of Rutabagas '46; Blueberry Weed in Maine and Their Control '46. Asst Expt Sta Maine '28-31, asst biol '31-38, asso physiol '38-43; research staff MIT '43-44; hort US Dept Agr '44-46; research prof U Mass since '46. Soc Hort Sci—Soc Plant Physiol—AAAS. East Wareham, Mass.

11 CHANDLER, Stewart Curtis. Entomology; Fruit insects of Illinois. b'89. BS '15 (U Wis). Special research on peach diseases and insect enemies, including peach borer, causes of cat-facing in peaches; also research on apple flea weevil, Oriental fruit moth and mosquitoes in Illinois. Author articles in field. Entomol Ill State Natural Hist Survey since '17; cons entomol agr dept Souther Ill U. 607 W. College St., Carbondale, Ill.†

12 CHANEY, Newcomb Kinney. Petroleum chemistry; Chemical engineering (Dry batteries, carbon problems, synthetic resins). b'83. BS '04 —MS '05 (Carleton Coll); Rhodes scholar '07-10—BA (hon) '10 (Balliol Coll, Oxford U); Harrison fellow in chem '10-11—PhD '12 (U Pa). Invented processes for manufacture of activated carbon, a toxic gas absorbent first employed by American army during World War I, which later achieved industrial importance; holds US and foreign patents on dry batteries, carbon products, synthetic resins, processes for ultra-violet irradiation of foods, petroleum cracking, chemical processing. Author articles in field. Cons chem Bur Mines war gas investigations '17-18, Chem Warfare Service '18-19 and since '25; asst dir research and development labs Nat Carbon Co '19-21; with Union Carbide & Carbon Research Labs Inc '21-25; asst dir research labs Nat Carbon Co Inc '25-35; asst dir research United Gas Improvement Co '35-36, dir research since '36; research cons Am Gas Assn since '47. Chem Soc. London(F)—Am Inst Chem Engrs—Am Chem Soc—Am Gas Assn—Am Phys Soc—Soc Chem Industry—Inst Petroleum Engrs, London — Phi Beta Kappa. Awarded Potts gold medal Franklin Inst '39, Modern Pioneer award NAM '40. United Gas Improvement Co., 1401 Arch St., Phila. 5.⊙

13 CHANNING, George. Theology and religion; Christian Science. b'88. AB '11 (Brown U); student '11-12 (Yale Law Sch) '12-13 (Boston U Law Sch); CSB '34 (Mass Metaphysical Coll). First Reader Fifth Ch Christian Science San Francisco '26-29; Christian Science Com on Publ for No Calif '32-38; Christian Science Tchr '34, lectr '38-41; first reader Christian Science Mother Ch '41-42; editor Christian Science Jour, Sentinel and Herald

since '49. 107 Falmouth St., Boston 15.†⊙

14 CHAO, Yuen Ren. Phonetics. b'92. AB '14 (Cornell U); PhD '18 (Harvard); LittD (Hon) '46 (Princeton U). Assisted in design National Romanization of Chinese; survey dialects of seven Chinese provinces; development techniques for teaching Chinese to Occidentals; translator English literature into Chinese. Author: Phonetics of the Yao Folksongs '29. Author English Intonation and its Chinese Equivalents '32; The Non-Uniqueness of Phonetic Solutions of Phonetic Systems '34; The Logical Structure of Chinese Words '47, and others. Co-editor: Harvard-Yenching Dictionary '41-46. Prof Chinese Nat Tsing Hua U '25-29; chief linguistic sect Academia Sinica since '29; consultant Bell Telephone Labs '43-47; prof Oriental langs and linguistics U Calif since '47. Sci Soc China—Am Oriental Soc—Acoustical Soc Am—Linguistic Soc Am (pres '45)—Am Acad Arts and Sci (F)—Internat Phonetic Assn (council) —Phi Beta Kappa—Sigma Xi.

15 CHAPANIS, Alphonse. Experimental psychology (Color vision). b'17. AB '37 (U Conn); MA '42—PhD '43 (Yale). Co-author: Applied Experimental Psychology '49; also articles in field. Research asso and asst prof dept psychol Johns Hopkins U since '46; research psychol Aero Med Lab AAF Tech Service Command '42-46. Am Psychol Assn(F)—AAAS(F)—Optical Soc Am—Inter-Soc Color Council —Am Physiol Soc—Eastern Psychol Assn—Sigma Xi. Mergenthaler Hall, Johns Hopkins University, Baltimore 18.

16 CHAPEL, Charles Edward. Aeronautical and ordnance engineering; Guns (Gunsmithing, markmanship); Finger Print Identification; Electronics; Radio; b'04. Student '22-25 (US Naval Acad); AB '26 (Mo U); BS '41 (Poly Coll Engr Oakland Calif). Author: Forensic Ballistics '33; The Gun Collector's Handbook of Values '46; Finger Printing: A Manual of Identification '41; Aircraft Electricity for the Mechanic '46; Aircraft Weight, Balance and Loading '48; The Boy's Book of Rifles '48; Shotgun Field, Skeet and Trap Shooting '48; Simplified Rifle Shooting '50; Jet Aircraft Simplified '50; Simplified Pistol and Revolver Shooting '50. Chief research and development Northrop Aeronautical Inst '45-48. Nat Rifle Assn (hon life)—Inst Aeronautical Sci—AIEE. 135-A W. Manchester, Inglewood, Cal.

17 CHAPLINE, William Ridgely. Range and watershed management; Range reseeding and ecology; Erosion and shrub control; Grazing. b'91. BS '13 (U Neb). Delegate International Congress Soil Scientists '27, Inter-American Conference Agriculture '30, International Grassland Congress, Wales '37, Inter-American Conference Renewable Natural Resources '48; member President's advisory committee on water flow '33-34. Author articles in field. Grazing asst US Forest Service '13-16, examiner '16-20, insp '20-25, chief div range research since '35. Forest Service, U.S. Department of Agriculture, Washington 25.

18 CHAPMAN, Carl Haley. American archaeology. b'15. AB '39 (U Mo); MA '46 (U NM). Investigation of Missouri and Osage Indian sites; editor The Missouri Archeologist. Author articles in field. Dir Am archaeol, instr sociol and anthrop U Mo since '46, asst prof sociol and anthrop since '51, also dir summer field session Midwestern archaeol. Am Anthrop

Assn—Soc Am Archeol—AAAS—Mo Archeol Soc (sec-treass, dir Archeol Survey of Mo). Department of Sociology and Anthropology, University of Missouri, Columbia, Mo.

19 CHAPMAN, Carleton A(bramson). Petrology; Structural geology; Mineralogy. b'11. BS '33 (U NH); AM '35—PhD '37 (Harvard). Author articles in field. Asso prof geol U Ill '47-48, prof since '48. Boston Geol Soc—Geol Soc Am(F)—Geol Soc London(F)—Mineralogical Soc Am(F)—Ill Acad Sci—AAAS—Sigma Xi—Geol Soc Norway(F). Department of Geology, University of Illinois, Urbana, Ill.†

20 CHAPMAN, Edward Mortimer. New England village life and history. b'62. AB '84—BD '90 (Yale). Author: The Dynamic of Christianity '04; English Literature in Account with Religion '10; Companions of the Way '18; A Modernist and His Creed '26; New England Village Life '37; also articles in field. Lecturer Bibl lit Conn Coll for Women '17-28. Phi Beta Kappa. Old Saybrook, Conn.

21 CHAPMAN, Everett. Welding failures; Vibration; Impact; Investigation aircraft crashes; High temperature metallurgy. b'01. BS (EE)—MS (U Mich). Study and development welding equipment and processes; welding design of diesel engine frames, marine propulsion units, and hydraulic machinery; supervision of manufacturing processes to insure against failure of fabricated welded steel construction; laboratory diagnosis welding failures; use of photoelastic and strain gage methods for determining adequacy of a structure for imposed loads; diagnosis failures due to vibration of airplane propellors and impact on steam hammer foundations. Holds ten patents on electrical methods of brazing, welding, diesel frame design, high tonnage hydraulic presses, bridges, and heat exchangers for high temperatures. Author articles in field. Development welding equipment and processes exptl lab Lincoln Elec Co '25-30; head development and research Lukenweld Inc Coatesville Pa '30-33, in charge design and fabrication Welded Steel '33-36, pres '36-43; consulting engr since '43. Am Soc Metals—Am Soc ME—Inst Aeronautical Sci—Soc Exptl Stress Analysis—Sigma Xi. P.O. 207, West Chester, Pa.

22 CHAPMAN, Floyd B. Wildlife Management; Ecology. b'11. BA '32 —MA '33—PhD '38 (O State U). Research in ornithology, mammalogy, bird and mammalian ecology, myxomycetae and periodicity of freshwater algae; investigated game birds (ruffed grouse), gray squirrel, whitetailed deer; administered and supervised wildlife research, development and utilization of wildlife resources. Discovered new variety of freshwater algae: Vaucheria geminata D. C. variety longistipata Chapman. Author articles in field. Field ecol O Div Conservation '35-40; regional inspector US Fish and Wildlife Serv '40-42; forest game tech O Div Conservation '46-48; Asst Chief game management since '48. Am Soc Mammalogists—Soc Am Foresters—Wilson Arnithol Club—O Acad Sci(F)—Am Ornithol Union—Sigma Xi. Ohio Division of Wildlife, State Office Building, Columbus 15, O.

23 CHAPMAN, George H(erbert). Bacteriology; hematology and toxicology of chronic disease. b'96. Developed methods of isolating and testing staphylococci, for isolating and testing streptococci, for isolating and testing food poisoning staphylococci, for preparing highly specific vaccines for most chronic idiopathic and obscure diseases. Discovered method for determining effect of any method of treatment on progress of streptococcus infection. Dir Clinical Research Lab NYC since '24. Soc Am Bact (com path methods of com on bact technic)—NY Acad Sci(F)—AAAS(F)—Biol Stain Commn (cons ed Stain Technology). 604 5th Av., NYC 20.

10 CHAPMAN, Homer Dwight. Soils and plant nutrition; Citrus nutrition. b'98. BS '23—MS '25—PhD '27 (U Wis). Author articles in field. With U Calif since '27, prof agrl chem, chem in expt sta '44-47, chmn div agrl chem '37-47, chmn div soils and plant nutrition since '46. AAAS—Am Soc Plant Physiol—Am Soc Agron—Soil Sci Soc Am—Western Soc Soil Sci—Am Chem Soc. University of California Citrus Experiment Station, Riverside, Calif.†

11 CHAPMAN, Jeff Watson. Trypanosomes. b'03. AB '24 (Presbyn Coll SC); MD '28 (Med Coll SC). Research in African sleeping sickness; work in Belgian Congo Camps; surveys and experimental work in treatment. In charge Presbyn Hosp Bulape Kasai Dist Belgian Congo '29-39 chief surgeon Bulape Hosp '29-34; medicin Agree Cong Colonial Govt '29-39; surgeon Chapman Clinic Walterboro SC. Am Soc Trop Med—Am Soc Parasitol—Coastal Med Soc—Nat Rehabilitation Assn. Chevalier Royal Order of Lion by Leopold III Belgium. Chapman Clinic, Walterboro, S.C.

12 CHAPMAN, John Holbrook. History of Siam (Pre-World War II). b'91. Student '14-17 (George Washington U). Served US State Dept '19-47, second sec Legation and consul Bangkok Siam '36-42, on duty Washington '44-47; ret since '47. 3323 Wisconsin Av., N.W., Washington.

13 CHAPMAN, Joseph Roy. Georgia caves. b'98. Student '19-20 (Emory U). Research on more than 100 Georgia caves, stereoscopic photography; extensive collection of cave literature, photographs, speleological data. Author articles in field. Nat Speleological Soc—Ga Mineral Soc. 425 State Capitol, Atlanta.

14 CHAPMAN, Randolph Wallace. Petrography. b'07. AB '29 (U NH); AM '32—PhD '34 (Harvard). Geological excursions in England, Scotland, Wales, Hawaiian Islands, and US; special study of lithified clay on Oahu and volcanic rocks of Kilauea on Hawaii and Haleakala on Maui. Author articles in field. Asst prof geol Marshall Coll '37-39; instr petrography Johns Hopkins U '39-41, '46, asst prof geol '46-47, asso prof petrography since '47. Geol Soc Am(F)—Geol Soc London(F)—Mineral Soc Am(F)—Am Geophys Union—Geol Soc Washington—Sigma Xi. Department of Geology, Johns Hopkins University, Baltimore 18.†

15 CHAPMAN, Seville. Thunderclouds. b'12. AB '34—PhD '38 (U Calif). Thundercloud studies dir Office Naval Research '47-48. Author articles in field. Instr and asst prof phys Stanford U '41-48; prin physicist Cornell Aero Lab since '48. Am Phys Soc—Am Meteorol Soc—Inst Radio Engrs—AAAS. Cornell Aeronautical Laboratory, Buffalo 21.†

16 CHAPMAN, Wilbert McLeod. Fisheries (International law); Fishes. b'10. BSc '32—MSc '33—PhD '37 (U Wash Seattle). Classification and anatomical studies of fish; formation and implementation US policy on international fisheries; chief US delegation for negotiation International Convention for the Northwest Atlantic Fisheries, convention with Mexico for establishment of International Commission for Scientific Investigation of Tuna, convention for establishment of Inter-American Tuna Commission, convention with Canada for extension of port privileges to halibut fishing vessels. Biologist with Wash State Dept Fisheries to '42; curator Calif Acad Sci '42-47; Chief, South Pacific Fish Mission, Econ Warfare '43-44; dir sch fisheries U Wash '47-48; spl asst to undersec US Dept State since '48, dir research Am Tuna Boat Assn since '51. Calif Acad Sci—Am Fisheries Soc—Am Soc Ichthyologists and Herpetologists—Pacific Fishery Biol—Am Soc Int Law. Department of State, Washington.ⓒ

17 CHAPPELL, Warren. Book illustration; Type designing and typography; Calligraphy. b'04. BA '26 (U Richmond); '26-28 (Art Students League NY); '31-32 (Offenbacher Schreibwerkstatt, Germ); '35-36 (Colo Springs Fine Arts Center). Work in various graphic media, especially wood-engraving; designed Lydian and Trajanus type faces; thought to be only American artist trained as punch-cutter; contributed to revival of use of calligraphic forms in contemporary letter design. Author: The Anatomy of Lettering '35. Author articles: Illustrations Made with a Tool '35; Illustration in These United States '41; The Anatomy of Printing '41. Teacher graphic media Art Students League NYC '33-35; free-lance artist, designer, illustrator. Phi Beta Kappa. 54 W. 53rd St., NYC 19.

18 CHAPPELL, William Everett. Horticulture (Herbicides, vegetables). b'17. BS (La Poly Inst); MS '41 (La State U); PhD '47 (Cornell U). Research on commercialization of hybrid tomatoes, plant physiology and breeding, effects of various minerals on yield and keeping qualities of onions and effect of certain weed control practices, testing herbicides. Author articles in field. Ext vegetable specialist Conn U '47-48; agron US Dept Agr Beltsville Md since '48. Am Soc Hort Sci—Northeastern Weed Control Congress—AAAS. Fungicide and Herbicide Section, PMA, Beltsville, Md.†

19 CHARANIS, Peter. Medieval history; The Byzantine Empire; Southeastern Europe. b'05. BA '31 (Rutgers U); MA '32—PhD '35 (U Wis); '36-38 (Oriental Inst U Brussels). Studies of church and state, social conflicts, population shifts and changes, economic organization, institutions. A u t h o r: Church and State in the Later Roman Empire '39; The Monastic Properties and the State in the Byzantine Empire; also articles in field. With Rutgers U since '39, asso prof hist '46-49, prof since '49; fellow Harvard U Dumbarton Oaks '44-46; visiting prof history U Wis '50-51. Medieval Acad Am—AHA—Am Soc Church Hist—Phi Beta Kappa. Belgian-Am Ednl Found fellow '36-38. Department of History, Rutgers University, New Brunswick, N.J.†

20 CHARLES, Lucile Hoerr. American folklore. b'03. MA '42—PhD '43—U scholar '42-43—fellow '41-42 (Yale); MA '41 (Columbia U). Author: Regeneration Through Drama at Death; The Clown's Function. Drama dir Am Peoples Sch NYC '34-36; coordinator Land of Plenty radio drama series Columbia Broadcasting System '37; asso in drama speech New Coll Columbia U '37-39; asst prof dramatic arts Mary Washington Coll U Va; asso prof Eng and dir dramatic arts East Carolina Coll since '46. American Folklore Society—NEA—NC Education Assn. East Carolina College, Greenville, N.C.†

21 CHARLES, T. Burr. Poultry husbandry (Turkey production). b'90. BS '15—MS '38 (Cornell U); '21-23 (Pa State Coll). Studies of poultry farm management, breeding, and housing; research on disease control. Prof and head poultry dept U NH since '28. Poultry Sci Assn (past pres)—World's Poultry Sci Assn—Am Poultry Assn—NH Poultry Growers Assn—Nat Turkey Fedn—Phi Kappa Phi. University of New Hampshire, Durham, N.H.

22 CHARLESWORTH, James Clyde. Public Administration (Management analysis, executive director); Local and state government (Organization, administrative methods, personnel); Political theories (Ancient and Medieval, American). b'00. Student '19-22 (Carnegie Inst Tech) '28 (Harvard); AB—AM—PhD (U Pittsburgh). In charge educational program for city managers and state government officials Institute Local and State Government; associate and acting editor Annals of American Academy Political and Social Science. Author: Governmental Administration '51; also articles in field. Prof polit sci U Pa since '39, in charge governmental service course '33-35. Am Soc Pub Adminstrn (pres Phila regional chapt)—Am Polit Sci Assn—So Polit Sci Assn—Western Polit Sci Assn—Pa Polit Sci Assn—Am Acad Polit and Social Sci. 3437 Woodland Av., Phila 4.†ⓒ

23 CHASE, Alice Elizabeth. History of art. b'06. AB '27 (Radcliffe); MA '43 (Yale). Docent Yale U Art Gallery since '31; curator edn Brooklyn Mus '46-47; asst prof hist art Sch Fine Arts Yale U since '47. College Art Assn. Yale University, New Haven.

24 CHASE, Aurin M(oody), Jr. Bioluminescence; Physical chemistry of vision; Blood storage and preservation. b'04. AB '26—AM '29 (Amherst Coll); PhD '35 (Columbia). With Princeton U since '39, asso prof since '48. AAAS(F)—Am Physiol Soc—Am Soc Zool—Optical Soc Am—NY Acad Sci—Soc Gen Physiol—Sigma Xi. Biology Department, Princeton University, Princeton, N.J.

25 CHASE, Eugene Parker. British history (Modern, English constitution and politics). b'95. AB '16 (Dartmouth); Rhodes Scholar from NH, BA '19 (Magdalen Coll Oxford U); MA '21—PhD '24 (Harvard). Author: Democratic Governments in Europe—England '38; Government in Wartime Europe—England '42. Editor, translator: Barbe-Marbois ' Our Revolutionary Forefathers '29; also articles in field. Professor of government Lafayette Coll '26-29, prof since '29; with Dept State Washington '43-46. Am Polit Sci Assn (bd ed '42-45)—AHA—Fgn Policy Assn—AAUP—Phi Beta Kappa. Easton, Pa.

26 CHASE, George Clinton. Calculating and adding machines. b'84. Ed Worcester High Sch. Holds about 100 US and foreign patents. Inventor and patentee since '06 of many widely used adding and calculating machine mechanisms. Monroe Calculating Machine Co.. Orange, N.J. 373 Melrose Place, So. Orange, N.J.†

27 CHASE, Warren W. Wild life management; Soil conservation; Forestry. b'02. AB '26 (Macalester Coll); MS '28—PhD '33 (U Minn); student '28-29 (U Calif). Research in tree physiology; relation of wild life to forestry. Author articles in field. Biol Soil Conservation Service '34-45; prof wild life management Sch Forestry and Conservation U Mich since '45. Soc Am Foresters—Wildlife Soc—Soil Conservation Soc Am—Wilderness Soc—Sigma Xi. School of Forestry and Conservation, University of Michigan, Ann Arbor.†

10 CHATELAIN, Verne Elmo. Preservation and use of United States historical sites and buildings; American social-economic history (Spanish contribution). b'95. AB '17 (Neb State Teachers Coll); MA '25 (U Chicago); PhD '43 (U Minn). First to hold position of chief historian, National Park Service, US Dept of Interior, '31, deputy asst dir in charge of Branch of Historic Sites and Buildings, extensive research dealing with nationally important historic sites; sponsored legislation providing for first National Historical Park, Morristown, NJ, '32, winter camp ground of Washington's Revolutionary Army; secretary National Advisory Board for Historic Sites, '35-36; sponsor of legislation creating National Historic Sites program, '35; member Joint National Committee on Materials for Research, representative American Historical Society, Social Science Research Council and American Council of Learned Societies, '35-36. Author articles: The Defense of St. Augustine 1565-1763, '41; Spanish Contributions in Florida to American Culture '41; The Land Officer in the Northwest '31; The Federal Land Policy and Minnesota Politics 1854-60, '41; Archeological and Historic Sites '36; Perpetuating our Military Past '36; Making American History Live at Yorktown '35. Prof hist chmn dept State Teachers' Coll Peru Neb '25-31; chief hist Nat Park Service Washington '31-36; research asso in hist Carnegie Instn Washington dir St Augustine Hist Program Fla, exec sec Nat Adv Com for St Augustine Program '38-42; prof hist U Md Coll Park since '45. AHA—Miss Valley Hist Assn—Naval Hist Found—Minn Hist Soc—Fla Hist Soc—Am Nat Trailways Assn—Am Assn U Profs. 6101 5th St. N.W., Washington 11.

11 CHATTERS, Carl Hallack. Government (Local administration); municipal finance. b'98. AB '19—LLD '43 (Kalamazoo (Mich) Coll); student '19-20 (U Chicago). Research on municipal finance, public administration, municipal accounting. Co-author: (with A M Hillhouse) Local Government Dept Administration '39, Tax Reverted Properties in Urban Areas '42; (with Irving Tenner) Governmental Accounting '40. City auditor Flint Mich 23-29; dir Municipal Advisory Council Mich '31-32; exec dir Municipal Finance Officers Assn US and Can '32-45; prof municipal adminstrn and finance Northwestern U '47-48; exec dir Am Municipal Assn since '48; chief pub finance br Office Mil Govt for Germany '46. Del Internat Union Local Authorities Berlin '36, Internat Inst Adminstry Scis Warsaw '36. Municipal Officers Assn (hon life)—Nat Assn Assessing Officers—Internat City Mgrs Assn—Am Polit Sci Assn. 1313 E 60th St., Chgo 37.†☉

12 CHEADLE, Vernon I(rving). Monocotyledoneae (Vascular tissue, anatomy); Salt pond vegetation. b'10. AB '32 (Miami U); PhD '36 (Harvard). Author articles in field. Prof and head dept bot RI State Coll since '42, dir grad studies since '43. Bot Soc Am—AAAS—New Eng Bot Assn—Am Assn Plant Taxonomists—Soc Study Development and Growth—Sigma Xi—Phi Beta Kappa—Phi Kappa Phi. Atkins scholar for collecting in Cuba '36; grant-in-aids from Am Acad Arts Sci, Am Philos Soc for research on vascular tissues of Monocotyledoneae. Botany Department, Rhode Island State College, Kingston, RI.

13 CHEATHAM, Owen Robertson. Plywood (Manufacture); Veneers. b '00. Grad '21 (Hargrave Mil Acad Chatham Va); LLD hon '50 (Presbyn Coll Clinton SC); spl studies (Va Polytech Inst) (U Ga). Founder pres Ga-Pacific Plywood & Lumber Co as Ga Hardwood Lumber Co home office Augusta since '27; chmn bd Wash Veneer Co Olympia since '47, Springfield (Ore) Plywood Corp since '47, Dir So Research Inst. Southern Finance Bldg., Augusta, Ga.; also Maritime & South Dock sts., Port Newark, NJ.

14 CHEATUM, Elmer Phillip. Zoology, limnology of reservoir lakes; Fish culture. b'01. AB '24 (Southwestern Coll); MS '25 (Kan State Coll); PhD '33 (U Mich). Research on freshwater and land gastropods and limnology of reservoir lakes; limnological investigations on respiration and annual migratory cycle of fresh-water pulmonate snails; fish culture in north-central and northeast Texas '43; gastropods of Davis Mountains in west Texas '35. Author articles in field. Asst prof zool So Meth U '25-34; instr zool U Mich '31-33; asso prof zool So Meth U '35-43, prof since '43. AAAS—Limnol Soc Am—Am Microscopical Soc—Tex Acad Sci (pres '43-44)—Sigma Xi. Biology Department, Southern Methodist University, Dallas.

15 CHEESEMAN, Joseph Andrew. Communications engineering. b'97. High school and Bell Systems student course and Bell Systems training. Directs and coordinates engineering activities pertaining to communications facilities systems and networks for all civilian Federal agencies of US government. Traffic Engring Bell Systems '20-39; asst telephone engr War Dept Panama '40-41; sr telephone engr Army Signal Corps '42-44; communications specialist Treas Dept since '45. Am Soc Elec Engrs—Soc Am Mil Engrs (mem com '44-45)—Armed Forces Communication Assn—Independent Tel Pioneer Assn. Apt 1015, 2800 Quebec St., Washington 8.

16 CHEN, Ko Kuei. Poisoning (Toad, cyanide); Chinese drugs. b'98. BS '20—PhD '23 (U Wis); MD '27 (Johns Hopkins); ScD (hon) '46 (Phila Coll Pharmacy and Sci). New treatment of cyanide poisoning; Chinese drugs; Senecio alkaloids, synthetic analgesics. Co-author: (with C F Schmidt) Ephedrine and Related Substances '30; also articles in field. Sr asst Peking Union Med Coll '23-25; research pharmacologist U Wis '25-26; asso Johns Hopkins '27-29; dir pharmacologic research Eli Lilly and Co Indianapolis since '29; prof pharmacology Ind U since '33. Academia Sinica(F)—AMA(F)—AAAS(F)—Am Soc Pharmacology and Exptl Therapy—Am Physiol Soc—Am Pharm Assn—Am Heart Assn—Assn Study Internal Secretions — Soc Exptl Biol and Med—Chinese Med Assn—Chinese Pharm Assn—Phi Beta Kappa—Sigma Xi—Sigma Sigma—Phi Sigma. First prize China Found for Promotion Edn and Culture '28. C/o Eli Lilly and Co., 740 S. Alabama St., Indpls 6.

17 CH'EN, Shou-yi. Chinese history and culture. b'99. AB '20 (Lingnan); PhD '28 (U Chicago). Board directors Sino-Swedish Scientific Expedition to Chinese Central Asia '32-35. Author articles in field. Instr Chinese lit Lingnan U '20-22, asst prof '22-24, asso prof '24-25; lecturer Far Eastern hist U Chicago '27; head dept and prof Chinese Lingnan U '28-31; head dept and China Found research prof hist Nat Peking U '31-37; research prof Chinese hist Oriental Inst U Hawaii '37-41; visiting prof U Calif LA summers

'44, '45; Stanford summer '51. Chairman dept and prof Chinese culture Pomona Coll and Claremont Grad Sch since '41. Inst Hist and Philos(F)—Academia Sinica(F)—Am Oriental Soc—AHA—Far Eastern Assn—Inst Pacific Affairs. Sumner Hall, Claremont, Calif. H: 690 Indian Hill Blvd.

18 CHEN, T(ze)-T(uan). Protozoology; Cytology. b'06. BA '23 (Fukien Christian U China); MA '30 (Oberlin Coll); PhD '34 (U Pa); Sterling research fellow '34-36 (Yale); research fellow '36-39 (Johns Hopkins). Research on chromosomes in opalinid ciliate infusorians; endamoebae parasitic in the opalinids; chromosomes in Paramecium; mating reaction, mating types and conjugation in Paramecium; mating reaction of enucleate fragments of Paramecium; antibiotics produced by Paramecium; nuclei in malaria parasites; microscopical technique; nervous system of annelids. Author articles in field. Instr zool Fukien Christian U '26-28, U Pa '30-34; research asso protozool Johns Hopkins '39-40; lecturer zool U Calif Los Angeles '40-46; sr mem Academia Sinica Shanghai '46-47; prof biol '47-49, director inst biol research '49 State Teachers Coll Minn; visiting prof zool summer '49, asso prof zool U So California since '49. Am Soc Naturalists—Soc Exptl Biol and Med—Am Soc Zool—Am Soc Protozool—Nat Marlaria Soc—AAAS—NY Acad Sci—Genetic Assn—China Sci Soc—Chinese Nat Sci Assn—Chinese Zool Soc—Sigma Xi. Walker prizes Boston Soc Nat Hist '31, '35; research grants USPHS Nat Research Council, AMA, Nat Acad Sci, Am Philos Soc, Am Acad Arts Sci, Sigma Xi, NY Acad Med, AAAS, Elizabeth Thompson Fund, Milbank Memorial Fund, John and Mary Markle Found, Ella Sachs Plotz Found, China Found. University of Southern California, Los Angeles.

19 CHENEA, Paul Franklin. Stress analysis; Vibration analysis; Plastic flow. b'18. BS '40 (U Calif); MS '46—PhD '49 (U Mich). Research work in above on bridges, tunnel lining, aircraft structures, power transmission systems, helicopters, die-casting machines, turbine rotors, reciprocating engines. Co-author: (with H M Hansen) Mechanics of Vibration (in press). Project engr for contractors Pacific Naval Air Bases '40-41) staff U Mich since '46, asso prof mech engring since '50. Served at lt col Ordnance Dept AUS on stress and vibration analysis '41-46. Am Soc CE—Am Soc Engring Edn—Soc Exptl Stress Analysis—Tau Beta Pi—Chi Epsilon—Sigma Xi. Department of Engineering Mechanics, University of Michigan, Ann Arbor, Mich.

20 CHENERY, William Ludlow. Sociology; Public information. b'84. AB '07 (Randolph-Macon Coll) Fellow sociology '08-09 (U Chicago); Research fellow '09 (Chicago School Civics). In charge labor publicity for US Committee on Public Information '18, representative Paris France '18-19. Author: Industry and Human Welfare '22. Editor: Ideals of America '19; Standards of Child Welfare '19. RFD 1, Winsted, Conn.; 608 Westridge Dr., Redwood City, Cal.

21 CHENETTE, Edward Stephen. Acoustics; Theory of sound; Band arrangements. MA (Highland Park Conservatory Des Moines Ia); post grad (Bush Temple Conservatory Chicago); diploma (Société Academique Paris). Composer 300 pieces for band, orchestra, and voice; band contest judge; professional arranger; studies on tone colors of dynamics, practical acoustics, band ethics, and interpretation. Dir band and orchestra, also condr own band; dir mus Ia State Coll '19-21, also Chicago Regimental Band, and Ill State Legion Band. Condr Am Band (concert band of Can Army) Can Expeditionary Forces '16-19. Fla Bandmasters Assn (hon life pres)—Am Fedn Musicians—Am Bandmasters Assn—Am Soc Composers, Authors and Publishers. Durham, Okla.

10 CHENEY, Elliott Ward. Light (Measurements in physical optics). Consumer goods quality testing. b'99. AB '20 (Dartmouth Coll); MS '25 (Brown U); PhD '29 (Princeton U). Author: Consumers Test Manual '38; also articles in field. Asso prof physics Middlebury Coll '26-27; acting prof physics Gettysburg Coll '27-29, prof '29-34; physicist Consumers Research Inc '34-42; asso prof physics Lehigh U since '42. Charles A Coffin Fellow Princeton U '24-26, measurement of index of refraction of gases at higher temperatures. Am Phys Soc—AAAS—Am Assn Physics Teachers—Am Inst Physics. Lehigh University, Bethlehem, Pa.

11 CHENEY, Ralph Holt. Physiological effects of caffeine and nicotine; Beverages; Medicinal plants; Cellular physiology. b'96. BS '19—MA '19 (Boston U); MS '22—ScD '23 (Harvard). Engaged in monographic studies of world beverages, their plant sources, chemistry and physiological effects on man, purine compounds (mono-di-trimethylated purines), histo-physiological effects of caffeine on muscle and nerve tissue including striated, smooth and cardiac muscle, nicotine-caffeine antagonism in cardiac pharmacology, influence of caffeine on cellular physiology with respect to permeability, cell division, reproduction and growth, plants of northeastern US as sources of drugs. Author: Economic Monograph of the Genus Coffea '25; also articles in field. Prof biol Brooklyn Coll Pharm since '32; asso prof biol Brooklyn Coll City NY '46-48, prof since '49; cons to beverage industry since '30; res investigator econ plants Brooklyn Botanic Garden since '30; investigator Marine Biol Lab since '29; advisory ed Economic Botany (journal applied botany) since '47. Am Soc Pharmacology—Soc Exptl Biol and Med—Am Soc Zool—Bot Soc Am—Am Soc Plant Physiol—Torrey Bot Club (council)—Brooklyn Inst Arts Sci—AAAS (F, council)—NY Acad Sci (F chmn biol sect, vp, council mem)—Phi Beta Kappa—Sigma Xi. Biology Department, Brooklyn College, Bedford Av. and Av. H, Bklyn. 10.†

12 CHENEY, Sheldon (Warren). Modern art and architecture; History of art; Theatre; Mysticism. b'86.' AB '08 (U Calif). Collected and edited Isadora Duncan's papers published as The Art of the Dance. Author: The New Movement in the Theatre '14; Open Air Theatre '18; Stage Decoration '27; The New World Architecture '30; A World History of Art '37; Men Who Have Walked with God '45, and others. Lecturer many universities and art mus '35-47; author. Authors League of Am—Soc Am Historians—Royal Soc Arts London(f). Pt. Pleasant, Bucks Co., Pa. (Mail, Route 2, Doylestown, Pa.)◎

13 CHERMOCK, Ralph L(ucien). Butterflies (Rhopalocera); Biological staining. b'18. BS '39 (U Pittsburgh); MS '41—grad research fellow '39-41 Duquesne U); PhD '47 (Cornell); '42 (U Pa). Research in Rhopalocera classification and phylogeny of this group of insects with particular emphasis on North American species, descriptions of

over 40 new species, discoveries of unknown life histories of six butterflies, migration, evolution; staining technique for demonstrating tuberculosis producing organisms, use of vacuum in microtechnique, use of detergents such as the tergitols in various biological stains and fixatives. Author articles in field. Asst prof biol U Ala since '47. AAAS—Soc Study Evolution —Entomol Soc Can—Lepidopterists Soc—Biol Stain Commn—Am Soc Ichthyologists Herpetologists—Sigma Xi—Am Mus Nat Hist (hon). Nat Research Council fellow '46-47. Department of Biology, University of Alabama, University, Ala.

14 CHERRINGTON, Ernest Hurst Jr. Stellar spectrophotometry. b'09. AB '31—MS '32 (O Wesleyan U); PhD '35 (Calif U). Research on repulsive forces in comets, profiles of magnesium b lines in solar spectrum; spectrophotometric research on Be stars. Discovered remarkable luminosity increase of Gamma Cassiopeiae '36, emission lines in spectrum of Epsilon Orionis '37, emission lines in spectrum of Zeta Orionis '38, variable hydrogen emission in spectrum of Gamma Ursae Majoris '38, relationship between super-shell stars and novae '39. Author: The Motion of Matter in the Tail of the Comet Morehouse '34; Photometry of the Magnesium b Group in the Solar Spectrum '35; astronomer Perkins Observatory '36-46; asst prof astron and physics O Wesleyan and O State Univs '36-46; asst dean and asso prof physics Centenary Coll of La '46-47; dean of coll, prof, dept head physics and astron Centenary Coll of La '47-48; dean Coll Liberal Arts, prof astron U Akron since '48. Am Astron Soc—Astron Soc Pacific—AAAS—Sigma Xi—Phi Beta Kappa—Ohio Academy Sci—American Physical Society. Fellow Perkins Obs Delaware O '31-32; fellow Lick Obs Cal U '33-35. University of Akron, Akron 4, O.◎

15 CHESTER, Allan Griffith. English literature (Tudor period; Bible); English Church history. b'00. AB '22 —AM '24—PhD '30 (U Pa). Thomas May, Man of Letter, 1595-1650 '31 Asst to asso prof Eng U Pa since '36. Mod Lang Assn—Mod Lang Research Assn. Bennett Hall, University of Pennsylvania, Phila 4.

16 CHESTER, Kenneth Starr. Wheat rust; Plant virus diseases (Serology). b'06. AB '28—SM '29 (Boston U); SM '30—PhD '31 (Harvard). Work on classification of plant viruses by serological means; forecasting wheat rust epidemics; appraisal of plant disease losses. Author: The Nature and Prevention of Plant Diseases '47; The Cereal Rusts as Exemplified in Wheat leaf Rust '46; also articles in field. Adv ed Chronica Botanica Publs; staff mem Rockefeller Inst Med Research '32-37; now supervisor Batelle Memorial Inst. Am Phytopath Soc—AAAS(F)—Bot Soc Am—Okla Acad Sci—Phi Beta Kappa—Sigma Xi—Phi Sigma—Pi Gamma Mu. Recipient Sheldon Traveling Fellowship (Harvard), two USPHS research grants. Battelle Memorial Institute, Columbus 10, O.◎

17 CHESTNUT, A(lphonse) F. Biology of shellfish (Oysters, molluscs). b'17. BSc '41 (Coll William and Mary); MSc '43, PhD '49 (Rutgers U). Oyster specialist charge sci studies concerning molluscs Inst Fisheries Resch since '48. Nat Shellfisheries Assn NC Acad Sci—Am Soc Limnol Oceanog —Sigma Xi. Institute of Fisheries Research, Morehead City, N.C.†

18 CHEVALIER, Elizabeth Pickett. History of the American Red Cross. b'96. AB '18 (Wellesley Coll); Litt D '43 (Transylvania Coll). Author: Official History of the American Red Cross Nursing Service '21; The American Red Cross: Its Origin, Purposes and Service '22; and others. Mem bd governors Am Nat Red Cross. 1065 Charles St., Pasadena, Cal.

19 CHEVALIER, Stuart. International organization; Federal taxation. b'79. AB '98—LLD '28 (King Coll Bristol Tenn); LLB '03 (Washington and Lee U). Author: The World Charter and The Road to Peace '46. Prof law Washington and Lee U '03-04; partner law firms Chicago and Washington, DC, since '20, Los Angeles since '27. Title Insurance Bldg., LA 13.◎

20 CHEW, Tobias Otterbein. Spelling. b'85. BS '08—MS '12 (Adrian Coll); AM '28 (U Pittsburgh). Author: Practical High School Speller '31; Practical Speller '38; Refresher Speller '46; also articles in field. Prof psychol State Teachers Coll Indiana Pa since '25. NEA—Pa State Edn Assn—Acad Polit Sci—AHA—Phi Delta Kappa. State Teachers College, Indiana, Pa. H: 401 S. 13th St.†

21 CHEYNEY, LaVerne E(merson). Rubber; Plastics; Adhesives; Packaging materials; Paper and fabric coatings; Hydraulic packings; Sealants; Plasticizers. b'11. BS '33 (U Akron); MS '35 (U Pa); PhD '38 (Ohio State U). Inventor of water-vapor-resistant coatings, chemical derivatives of natural and synthetic rubbers, methods of vulcanizing synthetic rubbers, plasticizers for synthetic rubbers and vinyl resins, gas-impermeable compositions, sealant compositions, flame-resistant rubber, oil packages, frozen food packaging materials, laminating adhesives, fabric coatings, paper-softening treatment, waterproofing compositions, hydraulic packing compositions, hot melt compositions; holder several US patents. Author articles in field. Research dir Pollock Paper Corp since '48. Am Chem Soc (chmn polymer symposium Columbus sect '47)—Soc Plastics Engrs—Am Soc Testing Materials (com D-11 on rubber)—Tech Assn Pulp and Paper Ind—Am Inst Chemists—AAAS. Pollock Paper Corporation, 1601 Plum St., Middletown, Ohio.

22 CHIDESTER, Lawrence William. European and American band instrumentation; School bands. b'06. AB '27 (Hamline U); AM '29—EdM '36 (Tufts Coll); PhD '43 (State U Ia); student (Harvard, U Minn, Ecole Normale de Musique Paris). Author: International Wind-Band Instrumentation '46. Co-author: Getting Results with School Bands '38; arrangements of fgn band lit; also articles in field. Prof music and chmn dept fine arts Tex Coll Arts and Industries since '45. Texas College of Arts and Industries, Kingsville, Tex.

23 CHIERI, Pericle A. Aircraft (Design and development); Helicopters; Jet Propulsion; Gas turbines. b'05. D Eng in naval arch and mech engring '27 (U Genoa Italy); ME '27 (U Naples Italy); D Aero Eng '28 (U Rome Italy). Aeronautical engr, tech advisor to Chinese Govt Commn on Aeronautical Affairs Nat Govt Republic of China, Loyang, '35-36, Nanchang '36-37; engr exec Nat Aircraft Works Nanchang Kiangsi, China, as dir aircraft materials test lab and supt factories tech instrn '37-49; aero engr Office Air Attache Italian Embassy Washington '39-41; prof aero engring Tri-State Coll Angola Ind and dir aero lab and wind tunnel '42; aero engr research and development Helicopter design Aero Products Inc Detroit '43-44; sr aero engr aircraft design and development ERCO Engring and Research Corp Riverdale Md '44-46; asso prof mech engring U Toledo '46-47; asso prof mech engring Newark Coll Engring, also mem faculty grad div teaching grad course in gas turbines and jet propulsion, internal combustion and aircraft engines since '47. Inst Aeronaut Sci (asso F)—AAAS—AAUP—Am Soc EE—Am Soc ME—Soc Automotive Engrs—Soc Exptl Stress Analysis. Profl engr Italy and NJ. Newark College of Engineering, 367 High St., Newark 2.

10 CHILD, Edward Rushmore. Aerodynamics; Aerophysics; Gas turbine, simulator, and computer design; Nuclear power engineering. b'02. BS in ME '24 (U of Pa); student (Columbia, NYU). Work in aerodynamic analysis of flight simulator for guided missiles, research on performance characteristics of long-range pilotless aircraft. Holds patents on slot and flap operating mechanism, irreversible control device, wing flaps, control surface tab mechanism, airplane control balancing system. Author articles in field. With Fredric Flader Inc since '45, gen cons engring physics dept since '49. Inst Aero Scis (asso F). Fredric Flader Inc., Toledo Division, 1330 Laskey Rd., Tol. 12.

11 CHILDE, Cyril Edward. Transportation (Economics). b'87. Member Federal Transportation Board of Investigation and Research to study and report to President and Congress on economy and fitness of country's transportation agencies and methods which should be adopted to provide national transportation system adequate for commerce and national defense '41-44; consultant on transportation and economics US Senate Committee to Study Problems of Small Business '44-46. Transportation cons Washington since '48. Nat Indsl Traffic League (past pres)—Nat Hwy Users Conf (past mem exec bd). 905 Washington Building, Washington 5.

12 CHILDS, Geoffrey Stafford. Beet sugar industry. b'92. BCS '12 (NYU). Author articles in field. Vice pres Michigan Sugar Co Saginaw Mich since '34, pres since '40; pres Farmers and Mfrs Beet Sugar Assn. Second National Bank Building, Saginaw, Mich.

13 CHILDS, James Bennett. Sixteenth century books. b'96. AB '18—BLS '21 (U Ill). Author: Sixteenth Century Books '25; Account of Govt Document Bibliography in US and Elsewhere '42; Memorias of Republics of Central America and Antilles '32; Guide to Official Publications of Other American Republics '45; also articles in field. Chief documents officer Library of Congress '25-30 and since '34, chief catalog div '30-34. ALA—Bibliog Soc Am—Inter-Am Bibliog and Library Assn (mem council)—Phi Beta Kappa. Library of Congress, Washington 25.

14 CHILDS, James Henderson. Electrical engineering. b'83. BS (civil engring) '04 (Ala Poly Inst); PhB '08 (Yale); '42-44 (Tex Tech Coll). Research design and construction of electric transmission lines and substations. Engr Dept Army '30-44; asst div engr RFC '44-48; formerly with US Bur Reclamation, now consulting engineer. Am Soc CE—Am Soc Safety Engrs—Nat Soc Profl Engrs. Postoffice Box 452, Auburn, Ala.

15 CHILDS, William Henry. Small fruits. b'07. BS '30—MS '31 (U Ill); PhD '40 (Cornell U). Research concerned chiefly with cultural and varietal studies of strawberries, raspberries, grapes, currants, gooseberries, and blueberries; hybridization and propagation studies with blueberries. Author articles in field. Instr, later asso prof hort and asso hort expt sta W Va U since '31. Am Soc Hort Sci—Sigma Xi. Department of Horticulture, West Virginia University, Morgantown, West Va.†

16 CHILLMAN, James, Jr. Western painting and architecture; History of art. b'91. BS '13—MS '14 (U Pa); fellow in architecture '19-22 (Am Acad Rome). Staff member, southwestern representative, now with Intercollegiate Tours, spending nine summers in Europe and eight in Mexico lecturing in art; special fields of interest in architecture Rome and Italian Renaissance painting 14th-15th centuries in Italy. Author articles in field. Instr architecture Rice Inst Houston Tex '16-19, asst prof '22-45, asso '45-48, prof since '48; dir Mus Fine Arts Houston since '24; cons architect Houston since '24. Research work in German-speaking countries Europe under Carl Schurz Memorial Found Fellowship summer '36. Tex Fine Arts Assn (ex-pres, vp)—Am Assn Mus—Am Assn Art Mus Dirs—Am Fed Arts —AIA. Museum of Fine Arts, Houston 5.

17 CHILTON, St. John P(oindexter). Plant diseases (Forage crops, rice, sugarcane); Seed treatment; Genetics of fungi. b'09. BS—MS (La State U); PhD (U Minn). Asst prof, later head dept plant path and chmn dept bot bact path La Agrl Expt Sta La State U since '40. Am Phytopath Soc (councillor)—Am Soc Agron—Am Soc Mycol —AAAS(F)—Am Bot Soc—La Acad Sci (permanent sec)—Sigma Xi. Department Botany, Bacteriology, and Plant Pathology, Louisiana State University, Baton Rouge, La.†

18 CHITTENDEN, Edward Wilson. Mathematics (Analysis, topology); Theory of operations. b'85. AB '09—AM '10 (U Mo); Fellow '10-12 PhD '12 (U Chicago). Mathematical analysis topology and theory of operations. With State U of Ia since '19 prof mathematics since '25; mem bd editors Am Jour Mathematics '28-37; mem Inst for Advanced Study '35-36. Am Math Soc—Math Assn Am (chmn com on tests '35-40)—Phi Beta Kappa—Sigma Xi. Physics Bldg., Iowa City, Ia. H: 1101 Kirkwood Av.◉

19 CHITTICK, Howard Allen. Biological control of Japanese beetles and other insects. b'07. BS '35 (George Washington U). Production of milky disease spores (bacteria) for control of grubs of Japanese beetle; discovery of grubs of Cotinus nitida being controlled by Metarrhizium anisopliae, a fungus, Norfolk County, Virginia. Accompanied Walter Rathbone Bacon Expedition to West Indies to collect biol specimens for Nat Mus Washington '30; project analyst Nat Park Service US Dept Interior '31-42; owner, operator Fairfax Biol Lab hdqrs and lab Clinton Corners NY, field lab Lynnhaven Va since '45. AAAS—Entomol Soc Am—Nat Shade Tree Conf. Fairfax Biological Laboratory, Clinton Corners, N.Y.

20 CHITTICK, Martin Burton. Automotive lubrication; Chemicals from petroleum. b'92. BA '16 (U Nebr); MX '17 (U Minn). Holder numerous patents covering petro-chemicals. Author: Automotive Lubrication '39; also articles in field. Tech dir and dir tech sales Am Mineral Spirits Co since '48. Am Chem Soc—Am Inst Chem Engrs — SAE — Am Petroleum Inst (chmn lubrication com)—Nat Lubricating Grease Inst (past chmn)—Am Soc Testing Materials. 155 E. 44th St., N.Y.C. 17.†

21 CHITWOOD, Benjamin G(oodwin). Nematodes (Anatomy, physiology, systematics, soil fumigation, plant therapy). b'06. BA '28 (Rice Inst); MS '29—PhD '31 (George Washington U). Author: An Introduction to Nematology '41; also articles in field. Asso nematologist US Dept Agr Bur Plant Ind '37-49; asso prof Catholic U Am since '49. Am Soc Parasitol—Am Phytopath Soc—Helminthol Soc Washington. Box 104, Catholic University of America, Washington 17.

22 CHOLAK, Jacob. Industrial Hygiene; Chemical Analysis; Spectrography. b'00. ChE '24—grad student '32-34 (Cincinnati U). Engaged research and writing on microchemical methods in industrial hygiene and industrial toxicology; lead in biological material spectrographic determinations of beryllium lead, antimony, cadmium, copper, aluminum, in biological material and air; spectrochemical analysis with air-acetylene flame. Author articles in field. Asso prof indsl hygiene, Inst Indsl Health, Cincinnati U since '48. Am Chem Soc—AAAS—Am Optical Soc—Am Indsl Hygiene Assn—Sigma Xi. Kettering Laboratory of Applied Physiology, Medical College, University of Cincinnati, Cincinnati 19, O.†

23 CHOQUETTE, Charles Auguste. French literature, grammar and phonetics. b'02. AB '26 (Clark U); MA '32—PhD '35 (Cornell U). Author: French Vocabulary and Idiom Builder '39. Co-author: A Short Review of French Grammar '48. Translator: A Short History of French Literature '35; also articles in field. Prof Romance langs Colgate U since '46; chmn Romance langs since '52; prof-in-charge Sweet Briar Coll Jr Yr in France '51-52. Modern Language Assn Am—Am Assn Tchrs French (former pres Central NY)—NY State Fed Mod Lang Teachers (pres '46-50)—Phi Beta Kappa. Colgate University, Hamilton, N.Y.†

24 CHRAKIAN, Elisha B. Ethics; Social psychology; Seventeenth century English philosophy; History of English Utilitarianism. b'01. AB '25 (Boston U); MA '27 (Brown U); student (Harvard); EdD (Calvin Coolidge Coll). Sponsor and first ed Armenian Mirror. Lectr philos Northeastern U since '45; prof philos and psychol Calvin Coolidge Coll Boston since '45. Am Philos Assn — Nat Council Social Studies—New Eng Assn Social Sci Teachers—Nat Council Teachers Eng. 83 Barnard Av., Watertown 72, Mass.†

25 CHRIST, Jay Finley. Sherlock Holmes; Federal courts and organized labor. b'84. AB '18 (Morningside Coll); JD '20 (U Chicago). Author: An Irregular Guide to Sherlock Holmes '47; Flashes by Fanlight '46; Sherlock's Anniversaries '49; An Irregular Chronology of Sherlock Holmes '47; five textbooks in field of business law. Co-author: Outlines of Economics '29 and others; also articles in field. With U Chicago since '20, asso prof law and business since '32. 9551 Longwood Dr., Chicago 43.

26 CHRISTENSEN, Erwin Ottomar. Art (Tests, psychology). b'90. BS '14 (U Ill); M Arch '16—MA '27 (Harvard). Research on decorative arts and sculpture and folk art; development of test for art appreciation; application of psychology to art. Author: Popular Art in the United States '49; The Index of American Design '50; Early

American Woodcarving '51. Faculty art dept O State U '15-19, UND '19-26; staff Gardner Mus Boston '28-31; Asst Dir Am Fed of Art '31-34; Director of Educational Work, Dir Ednl Work art dept Syracuse U '34-36; Lectr Fine Arts U Pa '37-39; with Nat Gallery of Art since '40, now Curator Index of American Design and of Decorative Arts; art dept Am U '45-46, Lecturer in Art history; NY State Hist Assn (teaching staff seminar on Am culture '49-50). National Gallery of Art, Washington 25. H: Box 82, Lanham, Md.†

10 CHRISTENSEN, Leo M(artin). Fermentation industry; Motor fuels; Xylose and levulose manufacturing and use; Vegetable oil crops (Agronomy, economics); Synthetic rubber; Farm products marketing; Evaporation, dehydration, distillation and solvent extraction equipment. b'98. BSc '23—PhD '26—indsl fellow '23-26 (Ia State Coll). Holder or co-holder 33 US and 3 Canadian patents in fermentation processes; co-holder two US patents on plastics. Co-author: Power Alcohol and Farm Relief '35; also articles in field. Cons chemical engr. Am Inst Chem(F)—Tau Beta Pi—Sigma Xi—Gamma Sigma Delta—Phi Lambda Upsilon. 3115 N. 70th St., Lincoln 5, Neb.

11 CHRISTIAN, John Edward. Organic medicinal synthesis; Radioactive tracers. b'17. BS '39—post doctorate fellow '44-45—PhD '44 (Purdue); '39-40 (Kalamazoo Coll). Holder US patents on quinoline thiols, quinoline disulfides. Author articles in field, aluminum methionate. Professor pharm chemistry Purdue U since '50. Adv com isotope distbn US Atomic Energy Commn. Am Pharm Assn (ed advisor journal since '47)—Am Chem Soc—Am Soc Bact—AAAS—Ind Acad Sci—Am Assn Coll Pharm (chmn com grad instruction since '46, chmn com teachers conf since '48)—Sigma Xi. Purdue University, School of Pharmacy, West Lafayette, Ind.†

12 CHRISTIE, John Watson. American church history (Presbyterian, church attitude toward slavery). b'83. AB '04—AM '08 (Princeton); '07-08 (United Free Church Coll Glasgow and Marburg Germany); DD '22 (Coll of Wooster); LLD '51 (Univ Delaware). Dir Presbyn Hist Soc Phila; special lecturer in Am ch hist U Del '47-48. Am Soc Ch Hist—Western Sect Alliance of Reformed Chs Throughout the World, Holding the Presbyn System. 2308 Madison St., Wilmington 259, Del.

13 CHUBATY, Nicholas. History of eastern Europe (Nationalities; Religious Ukrainian problems). b'89. Student '09-13 (U Lviv Sch Divinity); PhD '17 (U Lviv). Seminar on East European history with Prof M Hrushevsky U Lviv '11-14; editor Ukrainian Quarterly since '44; director undersecretariat Pro Oriente on International Catholic Organization Pax Romana '37-44. Author: Western Ukraine and Rome in the 13th Century '17; History of the Ukrainian Law (2 vols) '22; Status of Ukrainian Lands in the Lithuanian Federation '26. Asst prof hist Ukrainian law Ukrainian State U Kamenetz '19, asso prof Ukrainian U Lviv '20-24; asso prof eastern European ch hist Greek-Cath Theol Acad Lviv '24-32, prof '32-39; prof Ukrainian hist St Basil's Coll '39-41. AHA—Am Assn Teach Slavonic and East European Lang—Ukrainian Congress Com Am. Ukrainian Quarterly, 50 Church St., NYC. H: 250 Franklin Mahwah, N.J.

14 CHURCH, Austin Harris. Centrifugal pumps and blowers; Pump and compressor design; Mechanical vibration. b'06. ME '28 (Cornell U); MS '34 (NYU). Author: Centrifugal Pumps and Blowers '44; Elementary Mechanical Vibrations '48. Asst prof, later prof machine design and mech engring NYU since '40, chmn mech engring dept since '46. ASME—ASEE—SESA—AAAS—Sigma Xi. New York University, University Heights, N.Y.C. 53†

15 CHURCH, Clifford Carl. Micropaleontology; Gemmology; Optics. b'99. AB '23 (U Okla); MA '25 (Stanford U). Research in Foraminifera, description of new species, stratigraphy; collection and research in malacology, optical work. Author articles in field. Mineral Marland Oil Co San Francisco '25-26; asst paleontol Tide Water Assd Oil Co San Francisco '26-48, paleontol since '48. Am Assn Petroleum Geol—Soc Econ Paleontol Mineral (vp '30, pres '52)—Geol Soc Switzerland—Paleontol Soc—Geol Soc Am(F)—Sigma Xi. 79 New Montgomery St., San Francisco.

16 CHURCH, Earl Frank. Photogrammetry (Mathematical calculations); Geodesy. b'90. CE '11 (Syracuse U). Assn prof mathematics and civil engring Pa Mil Coll '19-20 prof '20-23; asst prof applied mathematics Syracuse '27-31 asso prof '31-39 prof '39-50 retired '50. Author: Triangulation in Rhode Island '20; Analytical Computations in Aerial Photogrammetry '36; Elements of Photogrammetry '44; 19 pamphlets on aerial photogrammetry. Photogrammetry award '47. Soc Am Mil Engrs—Am Geophysical Union—Theta Tau—Sigma Xi—Pu Mu Epsilon. H: Parish, New York.

17 CHURCH, George Lyle. Grasses (Phylogeny). b'03. ScB '25 (U Mass); AM '27—PhD '28 (Harvard). Author articles in field. With Brown U since '28, now professor and curator of herbarium. Bot Soc Am—Soc Plant Taxonomists—Soc Study Evolution—Growth Soc—NE Bot Club—RI Bot Club (pres). Department of Botany, Brown University, Providence 12, R.I.†

18 CHURCH, Randolph Warner. Library building (Planning and equipping). b'07. BS '29—MS '32 (U Va); AB '33 (Emory U). Author: articles in field. State librarian Richmond Va since '47; advisor and cons. ALA (library arch and bldg planning com '41)—Assn Coll and Research Libraries (bldg com '47-48). Virginia State Library, Richmond 19, Va.

19 CHURCHILL, Rogers Platt. Russian and eastern European diplomatic history since 1870. b'02. AB '24—AM '26 (Cornell U); PhD '34 (U Chicago). Author: The War, the Peace and the New Europe (with L R Gottschalk) '38; The Anglo-Russian Convention of 1907, '39. Acting head dept hist Allegheny Coll '37-38, Brooklyn Coll '39-42; hist analyst USSR fgn polit sect OSS '43-45, Dept State '45-46; fgn relations hist Div Hist Policy Research Dept State since '46. Phi Beta Kappa—AHA. Division of Historical Policy Research, Department of State, Washington 25. H: 622 S. Stafford St., Arlington, Va.

20 CHURCHILL, Warren S. Fishery biology. b'15. BS '36—MA '40 (George Washington U); '40-42 (Ill U). Made biological survey of trout streams; research on diseases of fish and their control, fish management in lakes and streams, fish populations with reference to age and growth, chemistry of natural waters, pollution of waters and biological effects. Author bulletins: The Food of Trout '44; The Brook Lamprey in the Brule River '45; also articles in field. Fishery biol Wis Conservation Dept since 42. Am Fisheries Soc—Wis Acad Sci Arts Letters—Sigma Xi. Northeast Area Fishery Headquarters, Woodruff Wis.†

21 CHUTE, Aaron Hamilton. Retailing; Marketing. b'91. BA '16 (U Mich); MA '31—PhD '35 (O State U). Special assistant to chief Compliance Division War Food Administration Washington '43-45. Author: Employee Discounts and Vacations with Pay in Ohio Department and Dry Goods Stores '32; Marketing Burned-Clay Products '39; Retailing by Pharmacists '41; Use of Income Data as a Guide to Marketing in Minneapolis '42; Marketing by Manufacturers '46; also articles in field. Prof retailing Coll Bus Adminstrn U Tex, retailing specialist in Bur Bus Research Austin Tex since '47. Am Marketing Assn—Am Econ Assn—Phi Beta Kappa—Beta Gamma Sigma. Waggener Hall, University of Texas, Austin 12, Tex.

22 CHUTE, George Maynard. Electronics. b'00. BS '22—EE '47 (U Mich). Special work in coordination of electronic units with magnetic controls. Author: Electronic Control of Resistance Welding '43; Electronics in Industry '46. Elec test course Gen Elec Co Schenectady '22-23, indsl engring dept Schenectady '23-27, application engr Detroit since '27; lecturer industrl electronics U Mich since '43. AIEE (fellow, chmn Mich sect '46-47)—Am Soc Profl Engrs—Engring Soc Detroit. General Electric Co., 700 Antoinette St., Detroit 2.

23 CHYZ, Yaroslav J. Nationality groups in the United States; Slavonic languages and literature. b'94. Grad '22 (Czech Karlova U, Prague); '36-37 (NYU). Author: The Ukrainian Immigrants in the United States '39; also articles in field. Dir fgn lang press div Info Service, asso dir Common Council for Am Unity NYC since '42. Common Council for American Unity, 20 West 40th St., N.Y.C. 18.†

24 CIAMBRONE, Fred Pershing Jr. Electroplating; Insulation materials. b'19. B Chem E '41 (Clarkson Coll Tech Potsdam NY). Development equipment and methods for application electroplate and organic finishes; design layouts for conveyorized electroplating departments; research on plating processes for plastic; test and specifications on electroplate coatings. Holds patents on wire insulating apparatus, and method and apparatus for moisture proofing electrical devices. Process finishing engr Stromberg-Carlson Co '43-51, was asst chief materials engr. AICE—ACS—Soc Plastic Engrs—Electrochem Soc—Tau Beta Pi. Stromberg Carlson Co., Rochester, N.Y. H: 255 Genesee Park Blvd.

25 CLAAR, Elmer Allen. Day-lilies. b'91. AB '15 (U Ill); '15-16 (Harvard); LLB '20 (Northwestern U). Hybridizer of daylilies since '36; author and lecturer on Hemerocallis, irises and peonies. Am Plant Life Soc (chmn Hemerocallis com); Men's Garden Clubs Am (Chief Hemerocallarian). 1400 Lake Shore Dr., Chicago 10. H: 617 Thornwood Lane, Northfield, Ill.

26 CLAASSEN, Cornelius Jansen. Farm management for absentee owners. b'83. '03-04 (Haverford Coll); student (Ames and Neb Agrl Coll). Originated a new system of farm management for absentee owners that combines modern agricultural principles and modern business organization, now operating 1377 farms in seven midwestern states. Author: Better Tenant Farming '30; Making Farms Pay '31;

Successful Farming for Absentee Owners '41; also articles in field. Mgr Farm Investment Co '21-29; founder and pres Farmers Nat Co Omaha since '29; dir Neb Taxpayers Fedn since '38; dir Assn Omaha Taxpayers Inc since '40. Nat Farm Chemurgic Council (bd govs NY since '37)—Neb Bankers Assn—(organizer and chmn publicity com '22-29) Mortgage Bankers Assn—Neb Grain Improvement Assn (dir '38-45). Farmers National Co., Omaha, Neb. H: 405 S. Happy Hollow Blvd.

10 CLAIBORNE, Mildred Frost Brown. Bacteriology (Milk and water); Food (Bacteriology). b'17. AB '39 (U Tenn). Effect of age and storage temperature on bacteriological water samples; direct microscopic counts on perserved milk samples as an effective measure for uniform standard control. Supervisor Sanitation Bacteriol Unit WVa State Health Dept. Am Soc Prof Biologists. W.Va. State Health Dept., Charleston, W.Va.

11 CLANCY, Donald Washburn. Insect natural enemies; Biological control of insects. b'09. BS '31—MS '32 —PhD '38 (U Calif). Engaged fruit insect investigations; research biological control of insects using natural enemies to control harmful species; in charge biological control of Comstock mealybug; studies on effect of insecticides on natural enemies of fruit insects. Author articles in field. Entomol agrl research adminstrn bur entomol and plant quarantine US Dept Agr Charlottesville Va '42-48; sr entomol in charge biol control fruit flies in Hawaii US Dept Agr since '48. Am Assn Econ Entomol—Sigma Xi. Box 2280, Honolulu 4, T.H.

12 CLAPP, Charles William. Non-contacting thickness gages; Metal detectors; Magnetic recording. b'09. BSc '32—MSc '36 (Queen's U); PhD '39 (U Mich). Patents issued or pending on magnetic recording head, magnetic recording system, X-ray thickness gage, distortion and noise analyzer, metal detector, filter network, counter circuit and others. Author articles in jours field. Development engr Gen Engring and Cons Lab Gen Electric Co since '43. AAAS(F)—Acoustical Soc Am—Inst Radio Engrs (asso)—Phi Beta Kappa—Sigma Xi. General Electric Company, Schenectady, N.Y.†

13 CLAPPER, Russell B(yron). Forest tree breeding and genetics; Blight-resistant chestnuts; Chestnut blight. b'92. Student '15 (Purdue U); '28 (George Washington U). Author articles in field. Path US Dept Agr since '43. AAAS—Am Phytopath Soc. U.S. Forest Pathology Field Laboratory, Southeast Forest Experiment Station, Post Office Building, Lake City, Fla.†

14 CLARK, Andrew Hill. Historical and agricultural geography; Geography of vegetation and soils; Geography of New Zealand. b'11. BA '30 (McMaster Coll, Ont); MA '38 (U Toronto); PhD '44 (U Calif). Field work in agricultural geography Algeria and Tunisia, historical-agricultural geography maritime Canada, New Zealand; government service in India, China; one of few geographers concerned with problems migration and spread domesticated plants and animals through world in post-Columbian times; engaged research and field work on historical geography of Mediterranean, comparative utilization world's temperate grasslands; landforms, vegetation and soils North Canada; agricultural geography of British Empire (non-tropical); Rutgers University research council fellowship grant pursue historical geography

maritime Canada summers '47-49. Author: Invasion of New Zealand by Exotic Plants and Animals '48; also articles in field. Geog OSS '43-45; Geog State Dept '45-46; asso prof geog Rutgers U '46-49; prof and chmn geog dept since '49. NZ Geog Society—Agr Hist Soc—Econ Hist Assn—Am Geog Soc—Am Geophys Union—Am Soc Profl Geog—Assn Am Geog—Sigma Xi. Geography Department, Rutgers University, New Brunswick, N.J.

15 CLARK, Donald Lemen. Rhetoric; Milton. b'88. AB '11 (DePauw U); MA '12—PhD '20—scholar 2 yrs (Columbia). Author: Rhetoric and Poetry in The Renaissance '22; John Milton at St. Paul's School '48. Co-author: Thinking, Speaking, and Writing '37; Sentence Building '37; Modern English Readings '34. Editor: Columbia Poetry '31-40; Renaissance Literary Theory and Practice '39; The Familiar Letters of John Milton and the Prolusions '36; also articles in field. Prof rhetoric Columbia U since '47, dept rep charge courses in writing for publication since '18. Mediaeval Acad—Modern Lang Assn—Am Assn Adult Edn—Coll Eng Assn (sec '46-47). Guggenheim fellow '44-45. 301 Business, Columbia University, NYC 27.ⓒ

16 CLARK, Dudley Bowen. Selenium in electronics; Acyclic generators. b'92. Developed electronic transmissions, motor controls, silver-selenium rectifiers, mercury tubes, acyclic generators, selenium rectifier sub-stations for coal mines, electronic transformer controls. Cons White Motor Co; engr Navy Dept; pres Electron Equipment Corp; now dir Clark Electronic Labs. Box 165, Palm Springs, Calif. H: Pioneer Ranch.

17 CLARK, Elmer Talmage. Church history (Small sects in America); Psychology of religion; History of Methodism. b'86. student '05-06 (West Plains (Mo) Coll) '06-09 (Hendrix Coll Ark) '09-11 (Vanderbilt); AB '26 (Birmingham So Coll); AM '27 (George Peabody Coll for Tchrs); BD—STD '25 (Temple U); LLD '27 (Southern Coll); LittD 40 (Southwestern U). Author: Educational Survey of the M.E. Church South, '20; Year Book of Methodist Missions, annually '27-40; The Psychology of Religious Awakening '29; The Small Sects in America '37 (rev edit '49); The Warm Heart of Wesley '50; An Album of Methodist History '52; ed-in-chief Who's Who in Methodism '51. Nat publ dir Centenary Commn ME Ch S '19-20, Christian Edn Commission since '20; editorial secretary Board Education ME Ch S and editor Christian Education Monthly '20-23; publicity and editorial secretary Centenary Commn '23-26; editorial sec Bd Missions and Ch Extension Meth Ch and editor World Outlook '26-52; sec World Methodist Council since '51; exec sec Assn Methodist Hist Societies since '44; press representative World Council Churches Amsterdam '48; delegate Ecumenical Meth Conf Oxford '51. 150 5th Av., NYC 11; Lake Junaluska, N.C.

18 CLARK, Ernest Dunbar. Pacific fisheries. b'86. AB '08 (Harvard); MA '09—PhD '10 (Columbia). Served as fisheries expert with the US Food Administration California during World War I. Author articles in field. Food investigation chem asst to chief US Bur Chem Dept Agr '13-19; dir Nat Canners Assn Seattle since '19; sec Assn Pacific Fisheries since '21. Am Chem Soc (chmn Puget Sound sect '25-26)—Am Soc Biol Chem—AIC(F) —Am Fisheries Soc—Inst Food Technol (regional dir '39-40)—AAAS(F). 826 Skinner Building, Seattle 1.

19 CLARK, Francis Eugene. Soil microbiology; Medical bacteriology; Serology. b'10. AB—BDE—MA—PhD '38 (U Colo). Author articles in field. Collaborator agrl expt sta since '46, now prof agron; bact US Dept Agr since '36 now senior bact. 1st lt San Corps U S Army '43-44, maj '45, now reserve. Soc Am Bact—Soil Sci Soc Am—Am Soc Agron—Kans Acad Sci—Sigma Xi —Phi Beta Kappa. Department of Agronomy, Iowa State College, Ames, Ia.†

20 CLARK, Frances N. Fisheries (Biology). b'94. AB '18 (Stanford U); MA '24—PhD '25 (U Mich). Biology and dynamics of marine fish popolations, especially sardines. Author bulletins: The life history of Leuresthes tenuis, an artherine fish with tide controlled spawning habits; Maturity of the California sardine (Sardinops caerulea) determined by ova diameter measurements; Interseasonal and intraseasonal changes in size of the California sardine (Sardinops caerulea). Librarian and lab asst Cal State Fisheries Lab '21-23, fisheries biol '26-41; supervisor Cal State Fisheries Lab Cal Dept Fish and Game since '41. AAAS—Am Soc Ichthyologists and Herpetologists—Biometric Soc—Western Soc Nationalists — Sigma Xi. California State Fisheries Laboratory, Terminal Island Station, San Pedro, Cal.

21 CLARK, George Lindenberg. Chemistry (Analytical); X-Rays; Electron Microscopy. b'92. BA '14—ScD '37 (DePauw U); MS '14—PhD '18 (U Chicago). Pioneered installation and direction industrial X-ray research laboratory. Author: Applied X-Rays '27; also articles in field. Prof chemistry U Ill since '27. AAAS(F)—Am Phys Soc (F)—Am Chem Soc—Radiol Soc Am—ASTM (Marburg Meml lectr '27)—Phi Beta Kappa—Sigma Xi—Phi Lambda Upsilon — Alpha Chi Sigma — Electron Microscope Soc Am (founder '43). Grasselli medal '32, Mehl medal '44, Orton Lectureship award '46. 305C Noyes Laboratory, Urbana, Ill.ⓒ

22 CLARK, Howard Selby. Organic microchemical analysis. b'06. BA '37 (Ohio State U). Author articles in field. Asso chem Ill State Geol Survey since '43; dir Clark Microanalytical Lab since '47. Am Chem Soc—AAAS—Ill Acad Sci. Illinois State Geological Survey, University of Illinois, Urbana, Ill.†

23 CLARK, Hugh. Embryology; Herpetology; Physiology. b'14. BA '34 (Clark U); PhD '41 (Mich U). Research in embryology of snakes and lizards, homogamy in earthworms, respiration snake and lizard embryos. Author articles in field. Asst prof U Conn since '47. Am Soc Zool—Herpetologists League—AAAS—Am Soc Ichthyologists and Herpetologists—Sigma Xi. Department of Zoology, University of Conn, Storrs, Conn.†

24 CLARK, James Lippitt. Animal sculpturing and museum preparation; Big game photography and hunting; Natural history (Africa, Asia). b'83. Student (RI Sch of Design). Toured Europe studying museums and zoological parks '08; hunting, photographing and collecting expedition East Africa '08; co-leader Modern Clark expedition Bombay crossing Himalayas and Central Asia '26; Africa '28, '31; Indo-China expedition '36; leader Central African Expedition of American Museum of Natural History '47-48; also in North America hunting and collecting. Author: Trials of the Hunted. Dir emer preparation and install Am Museum Nat Hist. Am Game Protective Assn—Am Bison Soc—Am Geographical Soc(F)—Nat Assn Audubon

Socs—Nat Sculpture Soc—NY Acad Sci —NY Bot Garden—NY Zool Soc(F)— Soc Animal Painters and Sculptors— Soc Mammalogist. Received Speyer Memorial prize by Nat Acad Design '30. American Museum of Natural History, NYC 24.

10 CLARK, Kenneth Willis. Greek manuscripts; Rare Bibles; History of English Bible. b'98. BA '24 (Yale); BD '27 (Colgate-Rochester Divinity Sch); PhD—fellow New Testament '29-31 (U Chicago). Author: Codex 2401-The Theophanes Praxapostolos '34; A Descriptive Catalogue of Greek New Testament Manuscripts in America '37; Eight American Praxapostoloi '41. With Duke U Divinity Sch since '31, now prof New Testament; Western NC Meth Conf since '43; asso as dir editor-in-chief or surveyor Manuscript Filming Project Jerusalem, Mt Sinai, Mt Athos '49-50. Society Biblical Lit (Sec since '46)—Nat Assn Biblical Instrs—Am Oriental Soc—Am Schs Oriental Research—Archaeol Inst Am. Received grant-in-aid from Am Council Learned Socs '37. 4684 Duke Station, Durham, N.C.†

11 CLARK, LeRoy Vincent. Industrial explosives; Blasting supplies and accessories. b'02. BSc in chem engring '25 (Grove City Coll); fellow Mellon Institute '34-36 (U Pittsburgh). Holder of patents on explosives, blasting methods, manufacturing equipment and absorbents for liquid oxygen explosives. Author articles in field. Asst dir research Explosives Dept Am Cyanamid Co '36-47, plant mgr New Castle Pa since '48. AAAS(F)—Am Inst Chemists(F)—Am Inst Chem Engrs—Am Chem Soc. American Cyanamid Co., Box 270, New Castle, Pa.

12 CLARK, Lois. Taxonomy of Hepaticae (Frullania). b'84. AB '07—MA '10 (U Washington); '07-08 (Yale); PhD '20 (U Minn). Co-author: Liverworts of Washington; Hepaticae of North America. Research asso U Washington since '33. Sullivan Moss Soc —AAAS—Sigma Xi. Botany Department, University of Washington, Seattle 5. H: Lakota Beach, Tacoma, Wash.

13 CLARK, Melville. Harps. b'83. Ed high sch and bus coll, Syracuse U. Invented improvements which have made possible a perfect portable harp and mark an epoch in harp manufacturing industry; developed improved method of pedaling concert harp. Author: How to Play the Harp '45; Audiotricity '6; singing Strings. In music bus Syracuse since '99; pres Clark Music Co. Nat Assn Music Merchants. Received silver medal Turin Italy '11. Clark Music Building, 416-420 Salina St., Syracuse, N.Y.

14 CLARK, Orin Ray. Grass ecology; Rainfall interception. b'92. AB '16— MA '21—PhD '39 (U Neb). Work in ecological studies of grassland formation '21; ecological comparison of two types of woodland '26, interception of rainfall by herbaceous vegetation '37, by prairie grasses '40. Author articles in field. Prof nat sci Ia State Teachers Coll '22-33; prof biol Sterling Coll since '42. Kan Acad Sci—Ecol Soc Am— Sigma Xi—Phi Beta Kappa—AAAS. Sterling College, Sterling, Kan.†

15 CLARK, Ralph Albert. Radar; Television metallurgy; Guided missiles; Helicopters (Jet propelled); Jets (Rocket and turbine). b'06. Grad '18 (Marconi Inst); BS in elec engring '22 (Worcester Poly Inst); MS in Phys '25 (Clark U); student (Columbia, NYU, Ga Tech, MIT). Research on V2 type rocket projectile, jet helicopters, gas turbines, television, radar metallurgy, iron, titanium,

zirconium, hafinium and germanium; electro and pyro metallurgy. Designer builder and operator WCN radio station '21-25; pres Standard Radio Corp '25-28; exec vp Television Corp Am '30-37; pres Clark Electronics and Aviation Corp since '38. Inst Radio Engrs —NACA. Clark Electronics and Aviation Corp., Treasure St., Indian Rocks Beach, Fla.

16 CLARK, Robert Campbell. Paper (Business and government forms, printing, standardization). b'96. AB '17 (U Calif). Administrative consultant to Office Chief of Ordnance Transportation Corps Army Service Forces and Bureau of Budget Executive Office of the President Washington '44. Author: Federal Manual on Forms. Pres Paper Associates Inc NY since '45. Suite 2207-9 Henry Hudson Hotel, 353 57th St., NYC 19.

17 CLARK, Thomas Dionysius. American frontier; Kentucky (History). b '03. AB '29 (U Miss); MA '29 (U Ky); PhD '32 (Duke U); DLitt '49 (Lincoln Memorial U). Managing editor Journal of Southern History since '48. Author: The Beginning of the L&N '33; A Pioneer Southern Railroad '36; A History of Kentucky (revised) '50; The Rampaging Frontier '39; The Kentucky (Rivers of America series) '42; Simon Kenton, Kentucky Scout '43; Pills, Petticoats and Plows '44; The Southern Country Editor '48. Coauthor: (with Lee Kirkpatrick) '39. With U Ky since '34, prof from '42, head hist dept from '45; vis prof U Vienna '50; lecturer Sem Am Studies Salzburg '48; State Department's cultural program in India and Pakistan '52. AHA—Miss Valley Hist Assn— Southern Hist Assn—Phi Alpha Theta —Phi Beta Kappa. Department of History, University of Kentucky, Lexington, 29, KY.†

18 CLARKE, Alfred E(rnest). Onions (Genetics, cytology, breeding); Nature of cytoplasmic inheritance. b'03. BA '24—MSc '27 (U Alberta); PhD '31 (U Wis). Author articles in field. Cytologist US Dept Agr since '36. AAAS(F)— Bot Soc Am—Am Soc Hort Sci—Am Genetic Assn—Genetic Soc Am—Agrl Inst Can—Sigma Xi. Awarded Nat Research fellowship '31-33; co-winner Vaughan Research award in hort '43. Utah Agricultural Experiment Station, Logan, Utah.†

19 CLARKE, Alfred Grant. Tobacco research. b'03. PhG '22—PhC '24 (U Pittsburgh). Dir med and tech reseach William Esty & Co NYC since '41. Med Exhibitors Assn Inc (pres '48-49). 100 E. 42d St., NYC17.

20 CLARKE, Beverly Leonidas. Analytical and physical chemistry. b'00. BS in Chemistry '21 (George Washington U); fellow of Chemists Club NYC '19-21; traveling fellow Am-Scandinavian Foundation, Nobel Inst., Stockholm, Copenhagen, Sorbonne, Paris, U Vienna; MS '23—PhD '24 (Columbia). Deviser of method of separating certain rare earths; research on instrumental and electrochemical methods of analysis and product quality control. Associate editor Analytical Chemistry, Microchimica Acta (Vienna). Author: The Romance of Reality '27; Marvels of Modern Chemistry '32. Co-author: The Doctor Looks at Murder '37; also articles in field. Tech asst to special US comml attache Paris and London '22; mem faculty Coll NYC and Columbia U '23-24; special research on colloid chem of vital processes Carnegie Inst of Washington '24; Nat Research Council fellow in phys chem Stanford '25-26; mem tech staff Bell Telephone Labs NYC '27-45, materials chem '38-44, anal res chem '44-45; dir chem

control Merck & Co Inc Rahway NJ since '45; cons US Dept Nat Defense since '47. AAAS(F)—Am Chem Soc (mem bd dirs, NY sec '40-41, chmn '44-45)—Micro Chem Soc (pres '36-37) —Am Pharm Assn—Am Soc Statis Control—ASTM—NY Acad Sci. 126 Lincoln Av., Rahway, N.J.©

21 CLARKE, Charles Walter. Veneral diseases; Social hygiene; Public health. b'87. AB '12 (U Wash); AM '23 (Harvard); MB, Chir B '28—grad work '29 (Edinburgh U); '35 (U Vienna). Advisory editor American Journal of Syphilis; medical editor Journal of Social Hygiene. Dir health edn League, Red Cross Socs, Switzerland '19-22; sec Nat Health Council '22-23; European sec Am Social Hygiene Assn '23-28; rep sociol sect League of Nations '25; med dir Am Social Hygiene Assn '28-35; ass syphilologist NY Skin and Cancer Hosp '30-35; dir Bur Social Hygiene NY Dept Health '35-37; exec dir Am Social Hygiene Assn since '37; lecturer Army Med Sch '40-46; clin prof public health practice Harvard U since '43; vis prof U Puerto Rico '40; cons US Office Indian Affairs since '34, USPHS since '36, Sec War '42-46; mem com venereal diseases Nat Research Council '41-45; cons NY State Health Dep since '45; mem exec com Nat Social Welfare Assembly since '46. Served as 1st lt, later capt, Sanitary Corps US Army, with AEF '17-19. Am Coll Physicians(F)—AMA(F)—Am Pub Health Assn(F). Awarded fellowship Harvard '13-14, Carl Schurz Foundation '35; medalist in clinical med Edinburgh '28. 1790 Broadway NYC.

22 CLARKE, Charles W(arrington) E(arle). Mechanical engineering; Public utility and industrial power engineering. b'82. Student Lewis Inst Chicago. Engr elec NYC&HR Ry NY; mech engr Stone & Webster Boston; power and cons engr United Engrs and Constructors Inc Phila '28-35 since '37, vp and cons engr since '45. Am Iron and Steel Inst—ASME(F)—Inst Mech Engrs. 1401 Arch St., Phila 5.†©

23 CLARKE, George L. Marine ecology. b'05. BA '27—MA '28—PhD '31 (Harvard); '28-29 (Cambridge U). Research on physiology of plankton; transparency of natural waters; utilization of solar energy by aquatic organisms; seasonal production, nutritional value, and diurnal vertical migration of zooplankton; poisoning and recovery in barnacles and mussels; ecology of salt ponds; dynamics of production in marine areas. Author articles in field. Asso prof zool Harvard since '40; marine biol Woods Hole Oceanographic Inst since '40. Limnol Soc Am (past pres)—Am Soc Limnol and Oceanog (sec treas)—Am Soc Zool —Ecol Soc Am—Am Fisheries Biol— AAAS—Sigma Xi. Biological Laboratories, Harvard University, Cambridge, Mass.

24 CLARKE, J. Calvitt. Child welfare; Social problems of the Orient. b'87. MA '16 (Washington and Jefferson Coll); DD '17 (Bellevue Coll); STB '18 (Western Theol Sem Pittsburgh). Author: Melissa '34; Castles in the Sand '35; The True Light '35; Dream No More '37; Graduate Nurse '38; also articles in field. Asso state dir Near East Relief Pittsburgh '19; survey famine situation Russian Caucasus, Armenia, Greece, Turkey '20; asso regional dir Near East Relief Pittsburgh '20-21; campaign cons north central region Near East Relief Milwaukee '22-23; state dir Near East Relief Cleveland O '24-26; sou dir Near East Relief Richmond Va '27-30; nat sec and sou dir Golden Rule Found Richmond '31-33; sou dir Save the

Children Fund Richmond '34-37; campaign work Am Found for Blind and other orgns '37-38; founder China's Children Fund '38, also nat dir. China Building, Richmond, Va.

10 CLARKE, W(alter) F(ieldhouse). Chemistry and physics of lime and gypsum; Alumina (Phase rule studies, clay recovery); Organic and inorganic analytical methods. b'86. AB '03 (Hampden-Sydney Coll); PhD '14 (Johns Hopkins). Research on use of hydrogenated oils in manufacture of tin plate; work with systems involving alumina and calcium oxide; determination of metals in foods; analysis of "certified" dyes; separation of alumina from ardinary clay as well as from bauxite. Author articles in field. Nat Bur Standards US Dept Commerce since '30. AAAS(F). National Bureau of Standards, Washington 25.

11 CLARKE, William Sloan. Orchard culture (Fruits, apple, nuts); Relation of temperature to fruit growing. b'02. BS '25 MS '26 (Penn State Coll); '26-28 (U Pa). Research on effects of cultural treatments on growth of apple trees, relations of orchard cultural treatments to soil moisture, effects of low temperatures on fruit plants, orchard sites in relation to their freedom from frost damage, rootstocks for deciduous fruit trees, culture of nut trees. Author articles in field. Asst prof pomology Penn State Coll since '49. Am Soc Hort Sci—Am Pomol Soc—Pa Nut Growers Assn—Northern Nut Growers Assn—Am Forestry Assn——Am Genetic Assn. Department of Horticulture, State College, Pa.

12 CLARKSON, Paul Stephen. William Sydney Porter (O. Henry); Law in Elizabethan drama (Shakespeare); Henry Fielding; Thomas DeQuincey; Fictional piracy and treasure. b'05. BA '25 (Clark); LLB '28 (Harvard). Research O. Henry, law as revealed in Shakespeare's and 18 other Elizabethan dramatists' plays, Fielding's Tom Jones, Samuel Chase, Rufus Choate, Luther Martin, Daniel Webster, other famous American lawyers; compiled bibliographies Thomas DeQuincy, piracy and treasury trove in fiction, American historical fiction. Author: A Bibliography of William Sydney Porter (O Henry) '38. Co-author: The Law of Property in Shakespeare and the Elizabethan Drama (with C T Warren), '42; also articles in field. Atty Consol Gas Elec Light and Power Co Baltimore since '29. 1707 Lexington Building, Baltimore 1.†

13 CLAUDEL, Calvin André. French-American folklore. b'09. BA—MA '32 (Tulane U); '34 (U Chicago)—'45-46 (Washington U); PhD '47 (U NC). Author: Creole Folk Tales '42; Louisiana Tales of Jean Sot and Bouqui and Lapin '44; Snow Bella: A Tale from the French Folklore of Louisiana '42; Foolish John Tales from the French Folklore of Louisiana '48; also articles in field. Instr modern lang St Louis U '45-46; asst prof modern langs Beloit Coll Wis '46-47; instr modern lang Phoenix Coll '48-49, on curriculum com for Phoenix schs; asst prof modern lang Miss State Coll '49; acting head div of language literature art Kentucky Wesleyan College. Awarded Smith Fund Grant for research in La folklore and recording of folktales in Avoyelles Parish La. Am Folklore Soc—Southeastern Folklore Soc—Western Folklore Soc—Medieval Acad—Mod Lang Assn—Am Assn Teachers of Fr—Soc for Advancement of Edn—Phi Beta Kappa. Kentucky Wesleyan College, Winchester, Ky.

14 CLAUDY, Carl Harry. Freemasonry in the United States. b'79. LittD hon '49 (Wake Forest Coll). Author: The Old Past Master '24; The Master's Book '35; These Were Brethren '47; Introduction to Freemasonry (3 vols) '31; Washington's Home and Fraternal Life '31; United Masonic Relief '31; The Unknown Mason '34; Masonic Service Association '39; Masonic Harvest '48. Editor: Little Masonic Library '46. Author Masonic plays: Greatest of These '34; He That Believeth '35; Greater Love Hath No Man '36; A Rose Upon the Altar '37; Judge Not '38; Hearts of the Fathers '39; And Not Forsake Them '40; To Entertain Strangers '41; A Gift in Secret '42; Treasures of Darkness '43; He Which Is Accused '44; If a Man Die '45; also articles in field. Ed Cathedral Calendar '21-27; asso ed Master Mason '24-30; exec sec Masonic Service Assn since '29. Mason 33°, Past Grand Master Dist Col '43. 700 10th St. NW, Washington.†

15 CLAUS, Edward P(raegner). Pharmacognosy; Pharmaceutical botany; Allergy; Hay-fever. b'08. PhG '29—BS '30—MS '35—PhD '40 (U Pittsburgh). Research on allergenic plants of Pennsylvania, anemophilous plants of Puerto Rico, medical, poisonous, and allergenic plants; phytoconstituents. Author: A Study of the Anemophilous Plants of Puerto Rico '48; also articles in field. Instr pharmacognosy U Pittsburgh Sch Pharmacy '30-42, asst prof biol '42-44, prof pharmacognosy since '46; asso prof pharmacy U Puerto Rico Coll Pharmacy '44-45; asst prof bot and pharmacognosy U Ill Coll Pharmacy and bot allergy unit U Ill Coll Med '45-46. Am Pharm Assn—Pa Pharm Assn—Pa Acad Sci (vp '48-49)—Am Acad Allergy (Herbarium com)—Pittsburgh Allergy Soc (chmn pollen commn)—Am Assn Coll Pharmacy (sec conf teachers biol scis '48-49)—AAAS(F)—Bot Soc Am—Am Soc Plant Taxonomists—Plant Sci Seminar (pres '46-47; sec since '47). University of Pittsburgh School of Pharmacy, Pittsburgh 19.

16 CLAUSEN, Robert Theodore. Vascular plant taxonomy; Plant cytology; Horticulture. b'11. BA '33—MA '34—PhD '37 (Cornell U). Work in classification, distribution and culture of ferns, succulents, legumes and trees; research on taxonomy of Ophioglossaceae, Crassulaceae, Leguminosae, Najadaceae, Gentianaceae. Author: Studies in the Genus Najas in the Northern United States '36; A Monograph of the Ophioglossaceae '38; Aquatic Vegetation of the Lake Ontario Watershed '39, '40; Studies in the Crassulaceae III, Sedum, subgenus Gormania, section Eugormania, '42; A Botanical Study of the Yam Beans '45; Selaginella, Subgenus Euselaginella, in the Southeastern United States '46; also articles in field. Asst dept bot Cornell U '33-35, asso prof since '44, asst Bailey Hortorium '35-37, asst prof '39-41. AAAS—Bot Soc Am—Am Soc Plant Taxonomists—Torrey Bot Club—Am Fern Soc (pres '39-42)—Cactus and Succulent Soc Am—NE Bot Club—So Appalachian Bot Club—Am Soc Study Evolution—Sigma Xi—Phi Kappa Phi. Department of Botany, Cornell University, Ithaca, N.Y.

17 CLAYBOURN, John Geronold. Harbor, river and canal engineering; Dredging. b'86. Student 3 yrs (Coll of Engring U Minn). Designed layout for new town and Dredging division headquarters, Gamboa Canal Zone, including docks, shops, harbor and location of quarters for employees and Civic Center '35; design of first floating relay pump barge used in connection with section dredging; design of floating hydraulic grader and floating air compressor; collaborated in design of diesel-electric pipe-line suction dredge Las Cruces, diesel-electric tugs and rehabilitating 15 yard dipper dredges and 1000 yard dump scows; design of subaqueous drill boat; design of docks for Ports of Aguadulce, Republic of Panama and Puntarenas, Costa Rica; design of bridge over Barranca River, Costa Rica. Author: Dredging on the Panama Canal '14; The Dredging Division of the Panama Canal, Its Function, Organization and Equipment 37; Streamlining the Panama Canal for Maximum Safety and Unlimited Capacity '46; Suggested Methods and Equipment, Dredging and Mining, for Converting the Present Locktype Canal to Sea Level '46, and others; also articles in field. With dredging div of Panama Canal '14, supt of div and mem staff gov Canal Zone '22-48. Retired June 1948. ASCE—Soc Am Mil Engrs. Decorated by Panama Govt La Orden Vasco Nunez de Balboa Comendador '45 and Gran Oficial '46. 327 E. Jackson St., Orlando, Fla.⊙

18 CLAYPOOL, Lawrence Leonard. Post-harvest physiology of deciduous fruits (Storage, transportation, marketing); Horticulture. b'07. '25-27 (Chaffey Jr Coll); BS '27-28—'29 (U Calif); PhD '35 (State Coll Wash). Research on irrigation and fertilization fruits and vegetable crops; influence on deciduous fruits of ethylene treatments, methyl bromide fumigation, fungicidal fumigants and washes, waxes, film and metal foil fruit wraps and box liners; modified atmosphere storage relating to carbon dioxide and oxygen during transit and long storage periods; temperature relating to rate of ripening various fruits; pre-cooling and storage clingstone peaches in relation to quality and canned product; respiration various fruits; aided in setting up loan policies for crop production loans, supervised several production credit associations in Washington, Idaho. Developed rapid coloimetric method for determining carbon dioxide and respiration studies with R M Keefer, developed simple method determining amount carbon dioxide in fruit tissue. Author articles in field. Asst hort in charge research irrigation br expt sta Yakima Valley State Coll Wash '30-34; hort, assn supervisor prodn credit corp farm credit adminstrn US Dept Agr Spokane '34-37; instr pomol jr pomol agrl expt sta U Calif '37-39; asst prof pomol '39-45, asso prof, pomol since '45. Lt comdr supply corps US Navy '42-45. AAAS—Am Soc Hort Sci—Am Soc Plant Physiol—Sigma Xi. University of California, Davis, Calif.

19 CLAYTON, Edward Eastman. Economic plant pathology and breeding (tobacco). b'95. BS '16 (O State U); MS '17 (Chicago U); PhD '20 (Wis U). Ext plant path O State U '20-22; research asso NY Expt Station '22-31, plant path '31-35, sr path '35-47, prin path since '47 Div Tobacco Med and Spl Crops, Bur Plant Industry Soils and Agrl Engring US Dept Agr. Sigma Xi—Phytopath Soc—Am Genetic Assn—Bot Soc—Wash Acad Sci. Plant Industry Station, Beltsville Md.†

20 CLEAVES, Arthur Bailey. Pennsylvania geology and paleontology; Engineering and field geology. b'05. PhB '27—MA '29 (Brown U); MA '30 (U Toronto); MA '32—PhD '33 (Harvard). Research and investigations Pennsylvania geology, paleontology, and Devonian, sedimentation, surface, subsurface and Appalachian region geology, oriskany sandstone; field work Greenland and Iceland '33, Brazil '34; consulting geologist barium sulphate deposits Cuba '36, geologist for board consulting engineers Philadelphia

Water Commission '46, damsites Albright & Friel '46, Wabash Railroad '47, condemnation project Big Inch Missouri '47; permanent consulting geologist Pennsylvania Turnpike Commision; field service consultant OSRD '44-45; cooperative geologist topographic and geological survey Pennsylvania Department Internal Affairs '47, committee applied sedimentation National Research Council. Author: A Guidebook to the Geology of the Pennsylvania Turnpike (with G H Ashley) '42; Geology of the Pennsylvania Turnpike (Irwin-Middlesex) '48; Geology in Engineering Practice '50; Applied Sedimentation '50. Prof geol Wash U St Louis since '46. Geol Soc Am (F, councillor engr geol sect '47, 49)—Am Inst Mining Engrs (sec-treas St Louis chapt '48)—Am Paleontol Soc (F)—Mo Soc Profl Engrs (mem com ethics and practice, sec-treas '49 St Louis chapter)—Pa Conf Field Geol (sec-treas '36-38, pres '39)—Sigma Xi. Department Geology and Geological Engineering, Washington University, St. Louis 5.†⊚

10 CLEGG, Charles Myron, Jr. Railroad photography; History of western America; History of American transportation. b'16. Special photographic student J Ghrislain Lootens. Pictorial collaborator: (with Lucius Beebe) Highball, A Pageant of Trains '45; Mixed Train Daily, A Book of Short Line Railroads '47; co-author with Lucius Beebe: The Saga of Wells Fargo '49, Virginia and Truckee '49; Legends of the Comstock Lode '50. Coeditor: (with Lucius Beebe) Dreadful California '48; also articles in field. Railway and Locomotive Hist Soc—Virginia City, Nev.

11 CLELAND, Emily Wadsworth (Mrs Herdman F Cleland). Classical archaeology. b'92. AB '15 (Smith Coll); AM '16 (Columbia); fellow '19-21 (Am Acad, Rome). Author: Stucco Reliefs of the 1st and 2d Centuries Still Extant in Rome; also articles in field. Teacher Latin Pine Cobble Sch Williamstown Mass '44-47. Archaeol Institute Am—Class Assn NE—Prehistoric Soc, Gt Britain—Societe Prehistorique Francaise. 2 Lynde Lane, Williamstown, Mass.

12 CLELAND, James Edwin. Caramel color manufacture and usage; Specific gravity and refractive indices of solids; Carbohydrates (Moisture methods, conversion tables). b'11. BSc '31 (Dalhousie U); '35-36 (Dalhousie-Kings U); SM '37 (London U). Research on methods of analysis and construction of tables relating to dry substance, specific gravity, reducing sugars and refractive indices of corn starch hydrolysates; specific gravity solids relationship of starch suspensions. Author articles in field. Asst chief chem Acadia Sugar Refining Co '33-37; research chem Union Starch and Refining Co '38-43, research dir since '43, exec com since '44 vp since '52. Am Chem Soc—Inst Food Technol—TAPPI. Awarded silver medal City and Guilds of London Inst '37. Union Starch and Refining Company, Granite City, Ill.†

13 CLEMENCE, Gerald M. Celestial mechanics; Art of computation. b'08. PhB '29 (Brown U). Worked in determination of accurate time, fundamental star positions; constructed almanacs. Devised optimum interval tables (with Paul Herget). Author: The Motion of Mercury 1765-1937 '43. Jr astron US Naval Obs '30-37; asst astron '37-40, astron '40-45, head astron US Naval Obs and dir Nautical Almanac Office since '45. Am Astron Soc—Inst of Navigation—AAAS(F)—

Royal Astron Soc(F). U.S. Naval Observatory, Washington 25.⊚

14 CLEMENCE, LeRoy W. Organic medicinals (Chemotherapy, metalloorganics, sulphas). b'06. BS '26 (U Pa). Work in synthesis of compounds effective in bacterial and protozoan infections; research in determination activity in vitro and in vivo. Co-inventor bismuth and arsenic compounds used in syphilis, diasone used in treatment of leprosy; bactericidal alkylphenols; holds many patents. Author articles in field. Sr research chem Abbott Labs since '26. Am Chem Soc—Sigma Xi. Abbott Laboratories, North Chicago, Ill.

15 CLEMENCE, Richard Vernon. National income; Business cycles. b'10. PhB '34—AM '36 (Brown U); AM '40—PhD '48 (Harvard). Development of new technique for income analysis; research in economic development and economic theory. Author: The Theory of Economic Maturity (unpub thesis) '47; Income Analysis '51. Editor: Readings in Economic Analysis '50; Co-editor: (with A H Hansen) Readings in Business Cycles and National Income. Asst in econ MIT '39-42; research asso Nat Bur Econ Research '42; head dept econ Pine Manor Jr Coll since '45; asst prof econ Wellesley Coll since '47. Am Econ Assn —Econometric Soc —Royal Econ Soc (F). Department of Economics, Wellesley College, Wellesley 81, Mass.

16 CLEMENS, Cyril. Mark Twain. b'02. AB '28—MA '48 (Washington U); grad work (Stanford, Cambridge). Led parties to California, Nevada, Hawaii, Europe and Asia following various itineraries of Twain; assembled Mark Twain collection of books inscribed in memory of Twain and presented them to Library of Congress as permanent memorial; has assembled a large collection of Mark Twain letters and books personally inscribed by Twain, including a very rare edition of Huck Finn; editor Mark Twain Quarterly since '36. Author: Mark Twain the Letter Writer '32; Mark Twain and Mussolini '34; My Kinsman Mark Twain '39; Young Sam Clemens '42; Mark Twain Wit and Wisdom '35; Mark Twain's Religion '35; Mark Twain and Franklin D Roosevelt '48. Edited: Republican Letters by Mark Twain '41; Washington in 1869 by Mark Twain '43. Pres Internat Mark Twain Soc since '30; chmn Mark Twain Centenary Com '35, chmn judges for annual Mark Twain Contests, chmn Mark Twain Medal Com. International Mark Twain Society, Webster Groves, Mo. H: 841 N. Kirkwood Rd., Kirkwood, Mo.

17 CLEMENS, Eli Winston. Public utilities. b'09. BS (engring) '30 (Va Poly Inst); MS '34 (U Ill); PhD (econ) '40 (U Wis). Research on economics, regulation, rate of return, and depreciation of public utilities. Author: Economics and Public Utilities '50. With U Md since '42, prof econ and bus adminstrn from '44; pub utility cons. Am Econ Assn—Royal Econ Soc—Phi Kappa Phi. College of Business and Public Administration, University of Maryland, College Park, Md.†

18 CLEMENTS, George P. Agricultural economics (Irrigation); Water, land and forest conservation; Drainage; Water polution. b'67. MD '96 (U Neb); LLB '44 (U Calif). Author articles in field. Counselor on agr and conservation Los Angeles Chamber of Commerce '39-47, retired '47. Pacific Geog Soc (dir, vp treas '21-31)—So Calif Conservation Assn (dir)—Sigma Xi. 4805 Alta Canyada Rd., La Canada, Cal.

19 CLEMENTS, Harry Frank. Croplogging of sugar cane; Plant nutrition. b'01. BS '24—MS '25 (U Wis); PhD '29 (U Chicago). Research on plant nutrition and drought resistance, translocation, transpiration, freezing resistance, sugar cane physiology of growth and mineral nutrition, crop-logging. Author: Factors affecting the germination of sugar cane '40; Crop-logging Sugar Cane in Hawaii '48. Asst prof bot Wash State Coll '29-33, asso prof '33-37; asso prof bot U Hawaii '37-38, prof and plant physiol since '38; agrl cons Castle and Cooke Ltd since '43, Hawaiian Commercial and Sugar Co since '47. Am Soc Plant Physiol—Bot Soc Am—Hawaiian Acad Scis—Sigma Xi—Phi Kappa Phi. University of Hawaii, Honolulu 10, T.H. H: 3264 Oahu Av., Honolulu 54, T.H.

20 CLEMENTS, Robert John. Pléiade. b'12. AB '34 (Oberlin); PhD '39 (U Chicago); student (U Bordeaux, U Florence). Author: Critical Theory and Practice of the Pleiada '42. Assisted in foreign language editing Pocket Book Basic English '46; also articles in field. Prof and chmn dept Romance langs and lit Pa State Coll since '47; adv modern lang ed Ginn and Co Boston since '44. Modern Lang Assn Am (officerships in French II, Italian I, and Portuguese I sects)—Am Council Learned Socs (editorial bd Renaissance com since '44)—Société des Amis du Louvre —Am Assn Teachers Italian (councilor)—Dante Alighieri Soc—Mazzini Soc—Mediaeval Acad (sec publ '40-47) —Phi Beta Kappa. Pennsylvania State College, State College, Pa.⊚

21 CLEMENTS, Thomas. Geology (Petroleum, mining; desert, southern California); Petrography. b'98. EM '22 (Tex Sch Mines); MS '29—PhD '32 (Calif Inst Tech). Author articles in field. Teaching staff dept geol U So Calif since '29, Hancock prof geol since '45, head dept since '33; cons geol and mining engr various companies since '30. Geol Soc Am(F)—Am Assn Petroleum Geol—Soc Econ Geol—Seismol Soc Am—Am Inst Mining Metall Engrs —Sigma Xi—Soc Econ Paleontologists and Mineralogists. Univ of Southern California, 3518 University Av., Los Angeles 7. H: 2171 Vista del Mar Av., Hollywood 28, Calif.

22 CLEMONS, E. Jay. Milk preservation. Research on role of carbon dioxide in bacterial growth in milk. Granted patents on containers for transportation of raw milk, and on means for removal of carbon dioxide from milk. Author articles in field. 5425 Brynhurst Av., Los Angeles 43.

23 CLEMONS, Harry. Virginia libraries (Rsch materials). b'79. AB '02—AM '05—Litt D '42 (Wesleyan U); AM '05 —Scribner fellow '03-04 (Princeton U); Jacobus fellow of Princeton '06-07 (Oxford U. Eng). Offical representative ALA in charge library war service AEF, Siberia '18-19. Author: The ALA in Siberia '19; A Survey of Research Materials in Virginia Libraries '36-37 and '38. Editor: (with M W Croll) Lyly's Euphues, the Anatomy of Wit, Euphues and His England '16. Librarian U Va '27-50; cons in research since '50. ALA—Va Library Assn (pres '31-32)—Am Geog Soc—Phi Beta Kappa. Alderman Library, University of Virginia, Charlottesville, Va.

24 CLENCH, William James. Mollusks. b'97. BS '21 (Mich State Coll); MS '23 (Harvard); Hinsdale fellow '22-25 (U Mich); fellow '40-41 (Yale). Biological survey work in Kentucky, Tennessee and Alabama '25-32, in southern Florida, Cuba, Hispaniola and Bahama Islands since '30; medically important Mollusk survey in Cuba '46. Author articles in field. Curator Mollusks Mus Comparative Zoöl Harvard U since '26. Mich Acad Arts Sci—Am Malacological Union. Museum of Comparative Zoölogy, Cambridge 38, Mass. H: 48 Avon Hill St., Cambridge 40.

10 CLEVELAND, Forrest F(enton). Spectroscopy; Spectra (Molecular, Raman, infra-red). b'06. AB '27 (Transylvania Coll); MS '31—PhD '34 (U Ky); student (U Chicago). Author: General Physics Laboratory Manual (with others) '43-48; Experiments in Physics '38; also articles in field. Prof physics and dir spectroscopy research Ill Inst Tech since '43. Am Phys Soc(F)—AAAS(F)—Am Assn Physics Teachers—AAUP—Sigma Xi—Sigma Pi Sigma. Received with M J Murray Va Acad Sci research prize '39. Illinois Institute of Technology, 3300 Federal St., Chicago 16.†

11 CLEVELAND, Reginald McIntosh. American aviation; German shepherd dogs; Guernsey cattle. b'86. AB '08 (Yale). Author: Cop, Chief of Police Dogs '26; Guard, Son of Cop '31; Young America's Aviation Annual (with Frederick P Graham) '41, 42 and '43; America Fledges Wings '42; Air Transport at War '45; The Aviation Annual for '44 (with Frederick P Graham '45, '46) and '47; also articles in field. Indsl adv mgr New York Times since '41. Inst Aeronautical Sci—Wings—German Shepherd Dog Am—Aviation Writers Assn—Phi Beta Kappa. Recipient four Transcontinental and Western Air newspaper writers awards for editorials on air transport, NY times. Times Annex, NYC.

12 CLEWELL, Dayton Harris. Petroleum exploration; Electronics, Instrument design. b'12. BS in physics '33—PhD '36 (MIT). Research in optical properties of paints and pigments, geochemistry, seismic, gravity, electrical prospecting and catalysis; developed instruments to measure gravity, brightness and color of pigments. Author articles in field. Research physicist CK Williams Co Easton Pa '35-38; research geophysicist Magnolia Petroleum Co '38-42, in field research labs '42-49, asst dir since '46. AIME—API (project 43 Adv Com, Central Com on Radio Facilities)—Am Phys Soc—Am Geophys Union—Am Soc X-ray and Electron Diffraction—Electron Micros Soc Am—AIEE—Sigma Xi. Magnolia Petroleum Company, Box 900, Dallas 1.

13 CLIFF, Ivan S(paulding). Petroleum cracking. b'98. BA '26 (Carleton Coll); PhD '33 (MIT). Research on thermal and catalytic cracking, commercial catalytic cracking plants. Author articles in field. Research chem Shell Oil Co '33-43, sr tech '43, tech cons since '46. Am Chem Soc—Inst Chem—Phi Beta Kappa. Shell Oil Company, Wood River, Ill.

14 CLIFT, Garrett Glenn. Kentucky history. b'09. Student '29-31 (U Ky); grad '47-48 (Pratt Inst Library Sch). Research on pioneer history of Kentucky to 1824, Indian wars and War of 1812, biographies and state documents of governors' administrations to General John Adair, research on Isaac Shelby, historical literature of period with emphasis on Kentucky Gazette 1787-1848. Author: History of Pioneer Kentucky '33-34; History of Mason County (vol I) '36; Governors of Kentucky 1792-1842 '42. Asst librarian Lexington Pub Library '35-42; staff mem NY Pub Library '42, '46-48; ref librarian Univ Miami '48-49; asst sec Ky Hist Soc '46, since '50. Ky Hist Soc—ALA. Kentucky Historical Society, Old State House, Frankfort, Ky. H: 215 Capital Av.

15 CLINARD, Outten Jones. Naval history. b'00. BA '36 (Colo U), MA '37 —PhD '42 (Calif U). Author: Japan's Influence on American Naval Power 1897-1918 '47; also articles in field. Historian Office of Chief of Engrs War Dept '44-45; chief hist branch Office Chief of Engrs '45-45; asst chief Engr Hist Div '46-49; air intell analyst Navy Dept since '49. AHA—Phi Beta Kappa. 24th and Maryland Av., Baltimore 18. H: 3700 39th St., Washington 16.

16 CLINE, Isaac Monroe. Tropical cyclones (Hurricanes, typhoons); Storm tides; Summer hot winds on United States Great Plains; American Painting. b'61. AB '82—AM '85 (Hiwassee Coll); MD '85 (U Ark); Phd '96 (Tex Christian U) ScD '34 (Tulane U). In Mississippi flood of '27 issued flood warnings predicting area and depth 2 weeks in advance of arrival of flood and for this was commended by President Hoover, and presented by Southern Pacific Company with bronze tablet eulogizing work; studies of climate of Southwest, its effect on health and agriculture. Author: Storms Floods and Sunshine '45; also articles in field. Prin meteorol US Weather Bur, ret '35. Am Meteorol Soc (F, pres '34-35)—Am Geog Soc(F)—AAAS(F)—Nat Inst Social Sci—Union Geodesique et Geophysique—Commn pour l'Etude des Raz de Maree. 633 St. Peter St., New Orleans 16.◎

17 CLOPPER, Edward Nicholas. Child welfare and labor; Social legislation; Community organization; History of social work; Puerto Rico (History). b'79. BS '97 (Bethany Coll, W Va); AM '10—PhD '12 (U Cincinnati). Director of child welfare surveys in Oklahoma '17, Alabama '18, Kentucky '19, Tennessee '20, West Virginia '21. Author: Facts of Porto Rican History '05; Course of Study for Graded Schools of Porto Rico (with C A Perry) '06; Child Labor in City Streets '12; Society and the Child '29; Child Welfare in Ohio '39; also articles in field. Sec Cincinnati Council Social Agencies '22-25; Exec sec Pittsburgh Fedn Social Agencies '25-33; prof social administrn O State U '42-45. 4254 Spring Grove Av., Cin.◎

18 CLOUSING, Lawrence Adrian. Aeronautical engineering (Airplane testing, flight). b'06. B Elec Engring '28—B Aeronaut Engring '32—MS Aeronaut Engring '33 (U Minn). Editor Minnesota Techno-Log magazine '27-28. Author articles in field. Engr and test pilot Nat Advisory Com for Aeronautics Langley Lab since '38, at Moffett Field Calif since '41, head flight research sect Ames Aeronaut Lab since '42. Officer and pilot USN attached to fleet air squadron US battlefleet '28-30, at Moffett Field '45-46, lt comdr USNR. Inst Aeronaut Sci (asso F)—ASME—Tau Beta Pi—Eta Kappa Nu—Sigma Delta Chi. Received Octave Chanute Award Inst Aeronaut Sci '47. National Advisory Committee for Aeronautics, Moffett Field, Calif.

19 CLUGSTON, Katherine Woods. Library cataloging of motion pictures. b'06 AB '26 (Carleton Coll); MA '28 (Colo U); grad study (Am U). Collaborated on library code for cataloging motion pictures. With Library of Congress '26-27, since '40; in charge preparation of bibliographies of motion pictures and dramas registered for copyright, head motion picture and drama unit, Copyright Cataloging Div since '46. Ednl Film Library Assn—Washington Film Council — Theatre Library Assn (regional chmn Middle Atlantic States '49). Library of Congress, Washington 25.

20 CLUGSTON, William George. Historical essays (Political). b'89. LLB '10 (U Ky). Author: Facts You Should Know About Kansas '45; Politics in Kansas '44; Rascals in Democracy '41; also articles in field. Newspaper reporter, ed, corr The Topeka, Kan State Journ, Kansas City Journal-Post, NY Post, Baltimore Sun, NY Times '15-44. Ky State Bar Assn. 209 W 6th St., Topeka, Kan. 300 Country Club Drive, Topeka.

21 CLUTE, Walker Stillwell. Geology and economics of petroleum industry; Oil development. b'91. AB in Geol and Mining '15 (Stanford U). Oil exploration in Colombia, South America, Gulf coast and mid-continent US. Oil and gas valuation engr US Treasury Dept; field mgr Wyo and Mont Properties; US Geol Survey Washington and Tulsa Okla; chief oil and gas sect Calif Tax Research Bur, State Bd Equalization; cons practice Los Angeles '33-44, specializing in appraisals and taxation of oil properties. Am Inst Mining Metall Engrs—Am Assn Petroleum Geol— 509 Havenstrite Oil Bldg., 811 West 7th St., Los Angeles 17.†

22 CLYDE, Paul Hibbert. United States Foreign Policy (Far East). b'96. AB '20—AM '22—PhD '25 (Stanford U). Travel, historical research in Far East '29, '33-34, '38-39. Author: International Rivalries in Manchuria '28; Japan's Pacific Mandate '35; A History of the Modern and Contemporary Far East '37; United States Policy toward China '40; The Far East: A History of the Impact of the West on Eastern Asia '48; also articles in field. Prof hist Duke U since '37; Bur Research and Analysis OWI '43; AAF Evaluation Bd SW Pacific area '45; academic adviser ASF '45-46; dir Duke U Summer Session since '50. AHA— Far Eastern Assn—Miss Valley Hist Assn—So Hist Assn—Am Polit Sci Assn—Phi Beta Kappa. Duke University, Durham, N.C.◎

23 COATS, Robert Roy. Alaska (Tin deposits, volcanoes); Aleutian Islands (Geology, volcanoes). b'10. BS (geol and mining) '31—MS '32 (U Wash); PhD '38 (U Calif). Study of tin deposits Seward Peninsula and Yukon Basin, Alaska '40-43; survey geology and volcanoes of western Aleutian Islands, Adak, Kanaga, Amchitka, Tanaga, Gareloi, Semisopochnoi, and Kiska '46-47. Author articles: Geology of Northern Adak Island '47; Geology of Northern Kanaga Island; Reconnaissance Geology of Some Western Aleutian Islands. Co-author article: (with J C Reed) Geology and Ore Deposits of the Chicago Mining District, Alaska '41. Asst prof geol U Alaska '37-39; geol US Geol Survey since '39. Geol Soc Washington—Soc Econ Geol— Mineral Soc Am—Geol Soc Am. U.S. Geological Survey, Washington 25.

24 COATS, Ruth Emily. Mollusks (Fresh water). b'11. BS '35—MS '38 (U Wash). Research on marine mollusca of Pacific Northwest; Am Malacological Soc (chmn Pacific div since '48) — Paleontological Soc—AAAS— Ore Acad Sci—Geol Soc Ore Country— Geol Soc Am—Malacological Soc London—Phi Sigma. H: 702 E. First St., Tillamook, Ore.

25 COBB, Allen L(ochheed). Fire protection. b'05. BS '26 (MIT). Research on development controls for automatic safe operation gas and oil fired ovens, industrial furnaces and boilers, fire protection devices for nitrocellulose and similar fast-spreading fires, design bursting discs, safe methods storage and use fuel gases and flammable liquids, development new standards fire protection using wager spray systems, use inert gas, foam and vaporizing liquids; member President's Conference on Industrial Safety, chairman subcommittee on safeguarding machines, tools and equipment. Author articles in field. Mem bd ed: Handbook of Fire Protection (10th edit). With Factory Mutual Engring Div '28-36, engr of spl hazards; with Kodak Park works Eastman Kodak Co since '36, dir fire protection and safety. Nat Fire Protection Assn (first vp, bd dir, chmn com on industry, chmn spl extinguishing methods, pres '42-53)—Soc Fire Protection Engrs (charter mem, exec bd, qualifications bd)—Nat Soc Prof Engrs—NY State Soc Prof Engrs (chmn code panels Monroe Co area)—Nat Safety Council (indsl conf, past gen chmn chem sect, spl com machinery safe-guarding)—Am Soc Safety Engrs—Veterans of Safety. Eastman Kodak Co., Kodak Park Works, Rochester 4, N.Y.

10 COBB, William Montague. Ageing of adult human skeleton; Physical anthropology of American Negro; American Negro medical and health history. b'04. AB '25 (Amherst Coll); certificate in embryology '25 (Marine Biol Lab Woods Hole Mass); MD '29 (Howard U); PhD '32—fellow anat '33-39 (Western Reserve U). Author: What Is Man: Synopses of Lectures on Human Anatomy '35; The Laboratory of Anatomy and Physical Anthropology of Howard University '36; The First Negro Medical Society '39; The Physical Anthropology of the American Negro '42; Medical Care and the Plight of the Negro '47; also articles in field. Prof anat Howard U Washington since '42, head dept since '47. AAAS(F)—Am Assn Anat—Anat Soc Gt Brit and Ireland—Am Assn Phys Anthrop (vp '48-50)—Am Soc Mammalogists—Nat Med Assn—Medico-Chirurgical Soc DC (sec '35-41, pres since '45)—Am Anthrop Assn—Anthrop Soc Washington (bd mgrs '44-46, vp '48). 520 W St., N.W., Washington.†⊚

11 COBBAN, William Aubrey. Cretaceous paleontology and stratigraphy; Mesozoic; Cephalopoda. b'16. BA '40 (Mont State U); grad work, PhD '49 (Johns Hop). Field studies on Missouri River in North and South Dakota, north flank Black Hills, Montana, Utah, and Great Plains of Kansas, Nebraska, Wyoming, Dakotas, Montana. Author articles in field. Geol US Geol Survey since '46. Am Assn Petroleum Geol—Paleontol Soc—Soc Econ Paleontol and Mineralogists—Soc Vertebrate Paleontol. U.S. Geological Survey, Washington 25.

12 COBINE, James Dillon. Conduction in gases. b'05. BS '31 (U Wis); MS '32—PhD '34 (Calif Inst Tech); '34-35 (Harvard). Author: Gaseous Conductors '41; Electronic Circuits and Tubes '47; also articles in field. Research physicist Gen Elec Research Lab since 45. Group leader Radio Research Lab NDRC Div 15 Harvard U '43-45; asst prof grad sch engring Harvard U '41-45. AIEE—Am Phys Soc—Am Soc Engring Edn—Inst Radio Engrs (bd ed)—Sigma Xi—Tau Bet Pi. General Electric Research Laboratory, Knolls I, Schenectady, N.Y.†

13 COCHRAN, Alexander McKie. Fogging; Insect control; Weed control; Rodent control. b'23. Student '40-42 (Va Mil Inst). Research and development of aerosol fogging from ground equipment, airplanes and helicopters, methods of application of commercial weed killers, application and mixture of prepared baits for rodent control. Pres Fogging and Dusting Service Inc since '47. Inst Aeronautical Sci—Am

Helicopter Soc—Am Rocket Soc—Am Mosquito Control Assn—Nat Agrl Chem Assn—Custom Foggers Assn NJ. 56 Greenwood Av., Montclair, N.J. H: 3 Park Terrace, Upper Montclair, N.J.

14 COCHRAN, Hamilton. History and economic condition of the Virgin Islands and West Indies; History of piracy and buried treasure. b'98. AB '22 (U Mich). Established native handicraft industries in Virgin Islands and created markets for them in US, thus improving economic condition of Virgin Islanders. Author: These are the Virgin Islands '37; Buccaneer Islands '41; Windward Passage '42; Captain Ebony '43; Silver Shoals '45; Rogues Holiday '47; the Dram Tree '49; also artciles in field. Commr Pub Welfare for islands of St Thomas and St John, govt of Virgin Islands of US '32-33; advt and promotion work for Saturday Evening Post Phila since '44. Saturday Evening Post, Independence Square, Phila 5.

15 COCKADAY, Laurence Marsham. Naval electronics and radio engineering. b'94. Student St John Cathedral Sch, NYC; private tutors; Acad Design. Member Hoover First Radio Conference '24. Granted numerous radio patents. Author articles in field. Tech ed Popular Radio '22-28, NY Herald-Tribune '28-31; ed Radio News '31-38; mem adv board Radio Ednl Commn of NYC '36-40; cons radio engr Bodnar Radio Labs '39-40; research cons Telecommunications Inc '40; cons physicist E E Free Labs. Commd lt comdr USNR '36, active duty since '40, capt and dir radio and electronics US Naval Acad since '45. Radio Club Am(F)—AIEE—AAAS—Acoustical Soc Am—Inst Radio Engrs—Am Soc Naval Engrs—Soc Mil Engrs—US Naval Inst—Am Acad Air Law—Internat Broadcasting Club. Department of Electrical Engineering, US Naval Academy, Annapolis, Md.⊚

16 CODDINGTON, Broughton Edwin. US history (Civil War). b'05. AB '29 (Dartmouth Coll); MA '35—PhD '39 (Clark U). Research on Southern Confederacy during Civil War, Reconstruction period. Contributor: Essays in History and International Relations in Honor of George Hubbard Blakeslee '49. Faculty Allegheny Coll '37-38; faculty, asst and asso prof soc sci Teachers Coll Conn '39-46; visiting professor history Clark University '45-46; now prof and head dept hist Lafayette Coll. AHA—Miss Valley Hist Assn—S Hist Assn—Phi Alpha Theta—Pa Hist Assn. Lafayette College, Easton, Pa.

17 CODWISE, Philip Witt. Paper (Chemistry, sizing). b'92. BS (Chem engring) '15 (Mass Inst Tech). Investigation paper manufacture, water resistance processes. Chief chem fine paper mfr Byron Weston Co Dalton Mass '18-23; chem engr Beaver Products Co Buffalo '23-27, Certainteed Products Corp Ardmore Pa since '27. Tech Assn Pulp and Paper Industry (chmn com water resistance, roofing felt, paperboard coms)—Can Pulp and Paper Assn (tech sect standards com)—ASTM—Am Pulp and Paper Mill Supts Assn. Certainteed Products Corp., Military Rd., Buffalo.

18 COE, Elbert Hart. Radiant heating; Small house design. b'93. BS '17 (Syracuse U). Holder US patent on warm wall house heating. Author articles in field. Mech engr Research Mathieson Chem Corp since '34 NY State Soc Profl Engrs—Tau Beta Pi—Phi Kappa Phi. Mathieson Chemical Corporation, Niagara Falls, N.Y. H: 8656 Champlain Av.†

19 COE, Maynard Henry. Farm safety. b'95. BS '17 (U Minn); '27-29 (Kan State Coll). Research and investigations in White Pine blister rust, located first infection of pines in the wild in Minnesota; studies and testing of community and commodity organizations in rural field; developed first nation-wide program for farm accident prevention; originator Annual National Farm Safety Week. Author articles in field. Research Bur Plant Ind '16-17; ext agt U Minn '18-22; state 4-H Club leader Kan State Coll '22-44; first dir farm safety programs Nat Safety Council Chicago since '44. Nat Orgn State Club Leaders (organizer, nat chmn). Received citation and medal US Dept Agr '46. National Safety Council, 425 N. Michigan Ave., Chgo 11.

20 COENEN, Clement Henry. Stream pollution; Chemistry of waste disposal; Aquatic nuisance control. b'13. Student (St Norbert Coll); certificate (U Wis). Research and development work on disposal of sulphite wate liquor, paper coatings laminating materials, control of aquatic nuisances such as algae, swimmers' itch and rooted vegetation. Plant control chem Union Bag & Paper Corp Wis and NY '35-38; supt and chem Chem Precipitation Sewage and Indsl Waste Treatment Plant City of DePere Wis '38-42; resident fellow and tech asst Sulphite Pulp Mfgrs Com on waste disposal and Inst of Paper Chem Appleton Wis '42-45; pres and mgr De Pere Development Lab Inc since '45. 345½ Main St., West De Pere, Wis. H: 504 Lande St.†

21 COFFMAN, Franklin Arthur. Agronomy (Cereal crops, oats). b'92. BS '14—MS '22 (Kan State Coll). Travelled Orient and Philippines; research on oats, corn, wheat, sorghum, barley; specialist in oats, their production, improvement, adaptation, varieties, etc., also origin, physiology, genetics, histology, and pathology. Agron US Dept Agr '37-43, sr agron since '43. AAAS(F)—Am Genetic Soc—Am Soc Agron—Wash Genetic Club—Sigma Xi. Division of Cereal Crops and Diseases, Plant Industry Experiment Station, Beltsville, Md.

22 COFFMAN, George Raleigh. Language and literature; mediaeval literature and culture (English 1350-1400); Drama (Mediaeval and early English Renaissance); English literature (Tradition and heritage); Relations between literature and society. b'80. AB '03 (Drake U Des Moines Ia); AM '09 (Harvard); PhD '13 (U Chicago). Author: A New Theory Concerning the Origin of the Miracle Play '14. Editor: A Book of Modern Plays '25; Five Significant English Plays '30. Editor of Studies in Philology; advisory editor College English. Kenan prof English U NC since '30. Mediaeval Acad Am(F, pres '45-48)—Am Acad Arts and Sciences(F)—Modern Lang Assn—Modern Humanities Research Assn—Phi Beta Kappa. University of North Carolina, Chapel Hill, N.C.⊚

23 COFFMAN, Harold Coe. Intercultural Relations. b'89. AB '15 (U Kan); '16-17 (George Williams Coll Chicago); fellow '16-17 (U Chicago); AM '22 (U Mich); PhD '36 (Columbia). Advisory committee US Office Education on recreation training, Chicago Recreation Commission; chairman 8th Annual Chicago Recreation Conference; Delegate to World's Committee of YM CA Plenary Meeting and Consultation on Leadership Training Denmark '50; Southeast Chicago Commission; Advisory Selection Committee, Fulbright Act. Author: American Foundations—A Study of Their Role in the Child

Welfare Movement '36; also articles in field. Profl lectr since '36; pres and trustee George Williams Coll Chicago since '36; mem Citizens Advisory Com on Racial and Intergroup Relations in Chicago. Nat Council Religion in Higher Edn(F)—Am Psychol Assn—Nat Com Mental Hygiene—Am Assn Study Group Work—Progressive Edn Assn. Presented Danish Medal Kong Christian den Tiendes Frihedsmedaille for contribution to Denmark's cause during Nazi occupation. 5315 Drexel Av., Chgo. 15.

10 COFFMAN, John Daniel. Forest fire control; Recreational forestry. b'82. '05-07 (Cornell U); MF '09 (Yale). Organized Civilian Conservation Corps program for National Park System '33-35. Author: Opportunities in Park Work '32; also articles in field. Deputy forest supervisor US Forest Service Trinity Nat Forest Calif '11-16, forest supervisor Calif Nat Forest '16-28; fire control expert Nat Park Service US Dept Interior Berkeley Calif '28-33; chief forester Nat Park Service Washington since '33. Soc Am Foresters (F, council '46-47, chmn div forest recreation '46-47)—Am Forestry Assn—Wildlife Soc—Nat Geo Soc—Am Planning and Civic Assn—Save-the-Redwoods League—Sigma Xi. National Park Service, 3310 Interior Building, Washington 25.

11 COFFMAN, L Dale. Jurisprudence. b'05. BA '26 JD '28 (State U of Ia); LLM '29 SJD '35 (Harvard). Editor: Cases on Nebraska Trial Practice '33. Contbr articles to law publs since '28. Prof law U Neb '31-37; counsel Gen Electric Co Schenectady NY '37-46; dean sch law Vanderbilt U '46-49, U Cal at Los Angeles since '49. Phi Delta Phi—Phi Beta Kappa—Order of Coif. Law School, U of California, LA. H: 10760 Weyburn Av., LA 24.⊚

12 COGGESHALL, Arthur Sterry. Museum administration; Mounting of specimens. b'73. Ed pub schs New Haven; Hon DSc Occidental College '50. Designed and perfected cast steel method of mounting large Dinosaurs '04; specialized work Dinosaurs British Museum Natural History Branch '05, Natural History Museum Jardin des Plantes Paris '07, Museum Natural History Vienna '09, Museo Geologico Bologna Italy '09, Imperial Museum St Petersburg Russia '11, National Museum Argentina '12, National Museum Spain '13. With Am Mus Nat Hist NY '96-99; curator pub edn and preparator-in-chief dept paleontol Carnegie Mus Pittsburgh '99-29; dir St Paul Inst '29-31; chief Ill State Mus '31-37; dir Santa Barbara Mus Nat Hist since '37; instr U Calif Nature Sch. Western Museums Conf—AAAS(F)—Am Assn Mus (Council) Officier deL'instruction Publique de France '08; Francis Joseph Order of Merit with Golden Crown Austria '09; Cavaliere della Corona d'Italia '09; Order of St Anne Russia '10; Caballero de la Orden civil de Alfonso XII Spain '14; Caballero de la Real Orden de Isabel la Catolica Spain '14. 653 Mission Canyon Rd., Santa Barbara, Calif.⊚

13 COGHILL, Robert DeWolf. Pharmaceutical and immuno-chemistry; Fermentation; Penicillin production; Anti-toxins. b'01. AB '21—MS '22 (U Kan); PhD '24 (Yale). Author articles in field. Dir research Abbott Labs, North Chicago since '46; mem board of directors since '52. Am Chem Society—AAAS—Soc Am Bact—Am Soc Biol Chem—Sigma Xi. Abbott Laboratories, North Chicago, Ill.⊚

14 COHEE, George Vincent. Paleozoic geology of the Michigan Basin. b'07. BSc '31—MSc '32—PhD '37 (U Ill). Author articles in field. Geol fuels br Geol Survey Dept Interior since '43. Geol Soc Am(F)—Am Assn Petroleum Geol—Am Geophys Union—AAAS—SOC Econ Paleontol and Mineralogists Geol Society Wash—Sigma Xi. U.S. Geological Survey, Washington 25.

15 COHEN, Arthur LeRoy. Cell physiology; Microbiology. b'16. AB '37 (Stanford U); MA '39—PhD '40—Sheldon travel fellow '40-41 (Harvard); research fellow '42-46 (Calif Inst Tech). Research on nutrition of myxomycetes, yeast metabolism, experimental wound healing; immunological studies on tumor, effect of bacterial products on destruction of animal tumors, chemical aspects of morphogenesis. Author articles in field. Research asso Cedars of Lebanon Hosp '45-47; prof biol Oglethorpe U since '47. Am Bot Society—Soc Study of Growth and Development—Sigma Xi—Phi Beta Kappa. Oglethorpe University, Ga.†

16 COHEN, Felix S. Jurisprudence; Anthropology and ethnology; Government; Philosophy. b'07. AB '26 (City Coll NY); AM '27 PhD '29 (Harvard); LLB '31 (Columbia). Author: Ethical Systems and Legal Ideals '33; Handbook of Federal Indian Law '41; Combating Totalitarian Propaganda: A Legal Appraisal '44; Readings in Jurisprudence and Legal Philosophy '51; also articles in field. Asst solicitor US Dept Interior '33-48, mem bd appeals '36-48, chmn '40-48; spl asst to Atty Gen '39; chief Indian Law Survey US Dept Justice '39-40; asso solicitor US Dept Interior Washington '43-48; vis lectr (prof) Yale Law Sch since '46, City Coll NY since '48. Am Philos Assn—Inst of Living Law (research cons)—Inst Ethnic Affairs (dir)—Phi Beta Kappa. 810 18th St NW, Washington 6.†⊚

17 COHN, Morris Mandel. Sanitary engineering and chemistry (Sewage and industrial wastes treatment; water purification, milk, food and environmental sanitation, smoke abatement, refuse incineration, household food wastes grinding). b'98. Editor Municipal Sanitation since '36, Sewage Works Engineering and Municipal Sanitation since '40; adviser-at-large on pollution abatement State of Vermont since '46; consultant New York State Legislature Joint Committee on Interstate Cooperation. Author: Grit and Grist '44; Sewage Treatment Practice '46; also articles in field. San testing and public health engr Schenectady NY since '28; lecturer on sanitary engring Union Coll '30-45; Am Pub Health Assn(F)—NY State Sewage Works Assn (pres '35)—Fedn Sewage Works Assn (vp '36)—ASCE (pres Mohawk-Hudson sect. '43)—Conf Municipal Public Health Engrs—AAAS—Soc Am Mil Engrs—Am Geophys Union—NJ Sewage Works Assn—Central States Sewage Works Assn—Md-Del Water-Sewage Conf—Mohawk Valley Sanitation Council—City Hall, Schenectady, N.Y. Or: 24 W. 40th St., NYC.

18 COIT, John Eliot, Avocado culture. b'80. BAgr '03 (NC State Coll); MS '05—PhD '07 (Cornell U). Author: Citrus Fruits '15, since translated into Spanish and Hebrew; also articles in field. Hort Ariz Agrl Expt Sta '07-09; asst prof pomol U Calif '09-11, asso prof charge citrus expt sta Riverside '11-12, prof citriculture '13-20; co agrl agt Los Angeles Co '18-19, head Coit Agrl Service since '19. Calif Avocado Assn (dir '15-46, pres '23-30, ed year-

books since '30)—Calavo Growers of Calif (dir '24-44). P.O. Box 698, Fallbrook, Calif.

19 COKE, C Eugene. Viscose rayon. b '05. BSc (chem) '27—MSc (organic chem) '30 (U Toronto); research F textiles '32-36 (Ont Research Found); Worshipful Co Clothworkers Research Scholar '36-38—PhD '38 (textile chem) (U Leeds). Research and development on quality control of viscose rayon, improvements in manufacturing methods of viscose rayon, design and testing of articles of protective personal equipment for Royal Canadian Air Force, physical and chemical properties of viscose rayon in relation to new end uses, development of new industrial and textile and uses for high tenacity viscose rayon. Contributor: Chemistry in Canada '51. In charge research Courtaulds (Can) Ltd '39-42, mgr indsl yarn sales and development from '48. Royal Inst Chem Gt Brit (F)—Chem Inst Can (F)—Textile Inst Gt Brit (F)—AAAS (F)—Am Assn Textile Chem and Colorists (sr mem)—Can Assn Textile Chem and Colorists (mem council). 1420 Sherbrooke St., W., Montreal, Que., Can.

20 COLBERT, Edwin H. Vertebrate paleontology; Comparative anatomy; Herpetology; Mammalogy. b'05. BA '28 (U Neb); AM '30—PhD '35 (Columbia U). Research asst Am Mus Natural Hist '30-32, asst curator '33-42, acting curator '42, curator '43, chmn dept amphibians and reptiles '43-44, curator fossil reptiles, amphibians, fishes since '45; lecturer dept zool Columbia U '38-39, prof vertebrate paleontol dept geol since '45; research asso geol and paleontol Acad Natural Sci Phila since '37. AAAS(F)—Geol Soc Am(F)—Paleontol Soc(F)—Soc Vertebrate Paleontol—Soc Mammalogy—Soc Ichthyology Herpetology—Soc Study Evolution—Sigma Xi. Awarded John Strong Newberry Prize Columbia U '31; Daniel Giraud Elliot Medal Nat Acad Sci '35. American Museum of Natural History, NYC.⊚

21 COLBETH, Ivor Milton. Castor oil. b'94. BS '18 (Coll CCNY). Research designing processing liquid fats, petroleum emulsions, wetting agents, castor oils. Originator and owner 31 US patents, several foreign. With Baker Castor Oil Co since '20, pres since '49. Am Inst Chem(F)—Assn Research Dirs—Am Chem Soc—AAAS—Am Soc Testing Materials—Am Oil Chem Soc. 40 Av. A, Bayonne, N.J.

22 COLBURN, Allan Philip. Heat transfer; Diffusional operations research. b'04. '22-24 (Marquette U); BS '26—MS '27—PhD '29 (U Wis). Research on heat transfer, distillation, extraction, fluid flow, thermo-dynamics. Holder US patent on cooling aircraft engines. Author articles in field. Research chem engr E I duPont de Nemours & Co Del '29-38; prof chem engring U Del since '38, actg pres '50, provost since '50, advisor resch since '47. American Institute Chem Engineers—American Chemical Soc—ASME—AAAS. Recipient Walker award AICE '36, profl progress award '48. University of Delaware, Newark, Del.⊚

23 COLBY, Arthur Samuel. Fruits (Small); Nuts (Culture). b'87. BS '11 (U NH); MS '15—PhD '19 (U Ill). Originator of new varieties, including Vermilion strawberry; studies on growth and fruiting habits, pruning and training practices; breeding for disease resistance. Co-author: Horticulture Enterprises (rev edit) '39, Faculty U Ill since '13, prof hort since '29. AAAS (F)—Am Soc Hort Sci—Ill State Hort Soc—Minn State Hort Soc

—Northern Nut Growers Assn (pres '40)—Am Pomol Soc (vp '50)—Ill Nurseryman's Assn—Gamma Sigma Delta—Sigma Xi—Phi Delta Kappa. 102 Horticulture Field Laboratory, University of Illinois, Urbana, Ill.

10 COLBY, Charles Carlyle. Land classification; land planning; urban research and planning. b'84. BPd '08—MEd hon '22 (Mich State Normal Coll); BS '10—PhD '17 (U Chicago). Land committee National Resources Planning Board '38-42, chairman sub-committee National Resources Planning Board '38-42, chairman sub-committee on land classification '39; Geography consultant on planning staff of Headquarters Commission of General Assembly of United Nations. Author: Source Book for the Economic Geography of North America '21. Co-author: (with V Roterus) A Method of Public Works Planning '42. Editor: Geographical Aspects of International Relations '37; Land Classification in the United States '41; also articles in field. Asso prof geog George Peabody Coll for Teachers '14-16; instr, asst prof and asso prof U Chicago '16-25, prof since '25, chmn department '42-49. AAAS(F)—Assn Am Geog (sec '23-29, pres '35)—Ill Acad Sci—Sigma Xi. 5737 Kimbark Av., Chgo.37.⊙

11 COLE, Arch Evan. Anatomy; Stream pollution. b'95. BA '16 (O Wesleyan U); PhD '20 (U Wis). Made biological survey of Wisconsin rivers, and of Little Miami River; studied toxic effects of paper mill wastes and their various components on fish; engaged research on physiology of fresh water invertebrates, anatomy of inguinal region, regeneration of peripheral nerves. Author articles in field. Prof anat U Louisville Sch Med since '48. AAAS—Am Assn Anat—Ky Soc Natural Hist—Sigma Xi. University of Louisville School of Medicine, 101 W. Chestnut St., Louisville 1.

12 COLE, Arthur Charles, Jr. Insect taxonomy and ecology (Ants). b'08. AB '29—MS '30—Phd '33 (O State U); '35 (Mich State Coll). Author articles in field. Instr entomol U Tenn '37-39, prof since '47; research fellow Gen Edn Bd Mt Lake Biol Sta U Va summer '41, prof entomol summer '42, '48; staff mem Bikini Sci Resurvey Bikini Atoll summer '47; collaborator Insect Pest Survey US Dept Agr '39-49. Assn SE Biol—Entomol Soc Am(F)—Tenn Acad Sci—Gamma Alpha—Sigma Xi—Entomol Soc Wash—Soc Systematic Zool. Department of Zoology and Entomology, University of Tennessee, Knoxville 16, Tenn.†

13 COLE, Charles Woolsey. European history (Modern, economic, Mercantilism, seventeenth century). b'06. AB '27—LHD '42 (Amherst Coll); AM '28—PhD '31 (Columbia U); LLD (hon) '46 (Wagner Coll Wesleyan U and Williams Coll); LittD '48 (Hamilton Coll). Author: French Mercantilist Doctrines Before Colbert '31; Colbert and a Century of French Mercantilism (2 vols) '39; (with S B Clough) Economic History of Europe '41; French Mercantilism 1688-1700 '43. Prof hist Columbia U '40-46; pres Amherst Coll since '46. Am Econ Assn—Econ Hist Assn—AHA—Council Fgn Relations—Phi Beta Kappa. 175 S. Pleasant St., Amherst, Mass.⊙

14 COLE, Everett Leland. Biological engineering design of biological laboratories and equipment (refrigeration and low temperature control). b'90. BS '18 (U Wis). Biol engr USPHS since '34. AIEE—Instrument Soc Am—Mont Soc Engrs—Asso Engrs Spokane. Rocky Mountain Laboratory,

U. S. Public Health Service, Hamilton, Mont.

15 COLE, Fay-Cooper. Southeastern Asia (Ethnology, history); Archaeology of Illinois and the Middle West; Early Man (Pre-history). b'81. BS '03—ScD '28 (Northwestern U); '04-05 (U Chicago); '06 (U Berlin); PhD '14 (Columbia); LLD '44 (Beloit Coll). Member various archeological expeditions in American southwest; conducted two expeditions among pagan tribes of Philippines; leader Field Museum Expedition to Malay Peninsula, Sumatra, Java, and Borneo '22-23. Author: Chinese Pottery in the Philippines '12; The Wild Tribes of Davao District, Mindanao '13; Traditions of the Tinguian '15; (with others) The Nature of the World and of Man '26; (with others) Making Mankind '29; (with T Deuel) Rediscovering Illinois '37; Peoples of Malaysia '45; also articles in field. Prof anthrop U Chicago since '27, emeritus since '47; research asso Malayan ethnol Chicago Mus Natural Hist. AAAS(F)—Am Geog Soc—Soc Am Archeol—Am Anthrop Assn (pres '33-35)—Social Sci Research Council ('25-30)—Nat Research Council (v chmn anthrop and psychol '27-29, chmn '29-30)—Am Philos Soc—State Museum (dir)—Ill State Acad Sci (pres '31)—Sigma Xi—Phi Beta Kappa. University of Chicago, Chgo. 37.⊙

16 COLE, Fred (Carrington). American history. b'12. AB '34—MA '36—PhD '41 (La State U). Asso ed Miss Val Historical Review since '46. Managing editor Journal Southern History '41-42. Co-editor: Southern Biography Series '38-42; also articles in field. Asso prof, later prof hist Tulane U since '46, dean Coll Arts Sci since '47. So Hist Assn—AHA—Miss Valley Hist Assn (asso ed Historical Review since '46)—So Polit Sci Assn—Phi Kappa Phi—Omicron Delta Kappa—Phi Beta Kappa. Tulane University, 6823 St. Charles Av., New Orleans 18. H: 6325 Freret St.⊙

17 COLE, Ira Albert. Folklore (Rocky Mountains). b'83. Ed in pub schs. Life study prairie and mountain legends, folklore. Author: Ibe of Atlan '47; The Golden Antelope '49; El Cuartelejo '50, and others. Cowhand on early day ranches, trailed cattle out of Tex over old Chisholm trail; traveling missionary Great Plains country; in charge White Rock excavations Boulder Archeol Soc for Colo U Museum '41-45. Wagon Wheel Lodge, Boulder, Colo.

18 COLE, James Webb, Jr. Complex and organo-metallic compounds; Pharmaceutical chemicals. b'10. BS '32—MS '35—PhD '36 (U Va). Co-author: Laboratory Course in General Chemistry '39; Introduction to Chemistry '40; also articles in field. Asso prof chem U Va since '46; chem cons various industries. Am Inst Chem(F)—Va Acad Sci—Am Chem Soc (chmn Va sect '43-44)—AAAS—So Assn Sci Indstry—Sigma Xi. DuPont research fellow '35-36. Cobb Chemical Laboratory, University of Virginia, Charlottesville, Va.

19 COLE, Kenneth Stewart. Biophysics (Electrophysiology). b'00. BA '22 (Oberlin); PhD '26 (Cornell). Research on physical properties and phenomena of living systems, alternating current impedance of cells and tissues, electrical characteristics of nerve membrane. Author articles in field. Asst prof physiol Columbia '29-37, asso prof '37-46; prin biophysicist metall lab U Chicago '42-46, prof biophysics '46-49; scientific dir Naval Med Res Inst since '49. AAAS—Am Phys Soc—Am Math Soc—Am Physiol Soc—NY Acad

Sci—Harvey Soc—Soc Philomatique de Paris—Sigma Xi. Nat Research Council fellow Harvard '26-28, Leipzig '28-29; Guggenheim fellow Inst Advanced Study Princeton '41-42. Naval Medical Research Institute, Bethesda 14, Md.⊙

20 COLE, LaMont Cook. Reptiles (Distribution, ecology, temperature toleration, lizards, Navajo country); Ecology of invertebrates; Ectoparasitia; Biometry (Statistical methods, animal populations). b'16. SB '38—PhD '44—fellow and asst '40-44 (U Chicago); fellow '39-40—MS '40 (U Utah). Herpetologist on expeditions to Navajo country northern Arizona and southern Utah summers '34-39. Author: Herpetology of The Navajo Country '35; also articles in field. Instr zool Ind U '46-48, asst prof, asso prof zool Cornell U since '51 Ecol Soc Am (ed bd). Department of Zoology, Cornell University, Ithaca, N.Y.

21 COLE, Mabel Cook (Mrs. Fay-Cooper Cole). Philippine folklore; Primitive societies. AB '03 (Northwestern). Traveled in Orient, spent four years in interior of Philippines, studying sociology and mentality of primitive tribesmen; in Dutch East Indies studying matriarchal form of government of Menangkabau Malays '22-23. Author: Philippine Folk Tales '16; Savage Gentlemen '29. Co-author: The Story of Man '37; also articles in field. 3229 Calle Cedro, Santa Barbara, Calif.

22 COLE, O(tis) D(emmitt). Rubber (Chemistry, plantations, chemicals). b'06. BA '27 (Neb Wesleyan U); MS '28 (U Akron); PhD '31 (Ia State Coll). Research on accelerators and antioxidants for rubber vulcanization, research on latex compounds, dipped goods and foam, latex production problems on plantations and improvement of quality of latex concentrate. With Firestone Tire and Rubber Co since '30, asst dir chem and phys research lab, '45-52, asst to dir of labs since '52. ACS—Am Inst Chem—Alpha Chi Sigma—Phi Kappa Phi—ASTM (temporary mem com D-11 on rubber).

23 COLE, Randall Knight. Animal genetics (Disease resistance, poultry, avian neoplasms). b'12. BS '34 (Mass State Coll); PhD '39 (Cornell U). Research in development through breeding of strains of poultry resistant to disease, especially avian lymphomatosis; study of avian neoplasms, genetics of fowl, and genetics of spontaneous mouse leukemia since '39. Author articles in field. Instr poultry husbandry Cornell U '35-39, professor poultry husbandry and animal genetics since '39. Am Assn Cancer Research—World's Poultry Sci Assn—Poultry Sci Assn—Am Genetic Assn—Genetic Soc Am—Sigma Xi. Department of Poultry Husbandry, Cornell University, Ithaca, N.Y.†

24 COLE, Robert C. Educational and vocational guidance. b'03. AB '29 (Syracuse U); AM '35 (Clark U); spl grad study in guidance (Columbia U, Boston U). Author: An Evaluation of the Vocational Guidance Program in Worcester Boys Club '39; Vocational Guidance for Boys '41; also articles in field. Dir edn and guidance Worcester Boys Club '30-43, asst exec dir since '43, counselor and consultant in ednl and vocational guidance Worcester Acad since '39, vocational guidance dir Worcester Veterans Service Center since '43. Nat Vocational Guidance Assn (profl mem and mem ethical practices com)—Mass Conf Social Work—Am Assn Study of Group Work—Boys' Clubs Am Exec Assn—Am Boys' Clubs Assos. Worcester, Mass.

10 COLE, Sam G. Orthodontics. b'99. DDS (Emory U Dental Sch). Orthodontics practice. Com Dentistry Nat Research Council Nat Acad Scis. Medical Arts Bldg., Atlanta, Ga.

11 COLE, Stewart G(rant). Intercultural education; Sociology (Culture). b'92. AB '16—ThB '18 (McMaster U Toronto); AM '19—BD '20—PhD '29 (U Chicago); '29-30 (Oxford and Marburg Univs). Author: History of Fundamentalism '30; Leisure in Our Time '34; Character and Christian Education '36; Liberal Education in a Democracy '40. Co-author: Intercultural Education in American Schools '43; also articles in field. Executive director Pacific Coast Council on Intercultural Edn Los Angeles since '44; intercultural edn cons to schools colleges and univs. AAAS(F)—Am Acad Polit Social Sci—Religious Edn Assn (bd dirs). Awarded second prize for manuscript The Cutting Edge of Democracy: The Direction of Its Social Growth by Inst Religious Social Studies NYC '48. Room 209, 3757 Wilshire Blvd., Los Angeles 5.

12 COLE, W. Storrs. Micropaleontology. b'02. BS '25—MS '28—PhD '30 (Cornell). Author articles in field. Research asso Scripps Instn Oceanography U Calif summers '31-35; instr geol Ohio State U '31-37, asst prof '37-43, asso prof '43-45, prof '45-46; prof geol Cornell U since '46, chmn dept since '47; geol US Geol Survey since '47; cons paleontol Fla Geol Survey since '29. Geol Soc Am(F)—Paleontol Soc—AAAS—Sigma Xi. McGraw Hall, Cornell University, Ithaca, N.Y. H: 310 Fall Creek Dr.†☉

13 COLE, William Earle. Regional and rural planning; southern United State problems. b'04. BSA '26 (U Tenn); AM '28—PhD '30 (Cornell U). Consultant, social science analyst, etc., Tennessee Valley Authority. Author: Teaching of Biology '34; Recent Trends in Rural Planning '37. Co-author (with C S Montgomery) Sociology for Schools '43; (with Marvin Kemp) Guidebook in Sociology '39; (with Wm H Combs) Tennessee: A Political Study '40; (with Clyde B Moore) Sociology in Educational Practice '52; also articles in field. Professor, head dept sociol U Tenn since '36; dir Knoxville Co-op Assn; dir Farmers State Bank Mt City Tenn; dir Tenn Crippled Children's Commn. Am Sociol Soc—So Sociol Soc—Tenn Conf Social Work (pres '37)—So Sociol Soc (pres '40-41)—Tenn Maternal Health Assn (pres '40-44)—Newcomen Soc Eng. Knoxville, Tenn.†☉

14 COLE, William Harder. Animal physiology; Marine biology; Invertebrate blood chemistry; Research administration. b'92. Root fellow—AB '14 (Hamilton Coll); MA '16—PhD '21—Thayer scholar '15-16—Austin Teaching Fellow '20-21 (Harvard); guest investigator '37-38 (Calif Inst Tech). Author articles in field. Prof physiol and biochem Rutgers U since '28, dir research council since '44; trustee Mt Desert Island Biol Lab since '31; bd dirs LI Biol Assn since '33. AAAS(F)—Am Soc Zool (sec '30-33)—Am Soc Naturalists—Soc Exptl Biol and Med—NY Acad Sci—Phi Beta Kappa—Sigma Xi. Rutgers University, New Brunswich, N.J.†☉

15 COLEAN, Miles Lanier. Housing; Construction economics; Real estate finance. b'98. '16-17 (U Wis); BArch '22 (Columbia). Chairman American delegation 16th International Congress on Planning and Housing Mexico City '38; Central Housing committee '36-40; consultant Advisory Committee on National Defense '40, National Resources Planning Board '42; advisor on housing Senate and House Postwar Policy and Planning Com '44-45; Business Res Advisory Committee Bureau of Labor Statistics. Author: Can America Build Houses? '38; Housing for Defense '40; The Role of the Housebuilding Industry '42; American Housing: Problems and Prospects '43; Stabilizing the Construction Industry '45; Impact of Govt on Real Estate Finance '50; articles in field. Tech dir Fed Housing Adminstrn '34-37, asst administr '37-40; dir Housing Survey Twentieth Century Fund '40-42; vp Starrett Bros and Eken Inc '42-45; cons construction, finance since '45. AIA(F)—Am Statis Assn. Transportation Building, Washington 6.

16 COLEMAN, George Ephraim, Jr. Poultry breeding. b'06. BS '28 (U NH). Establishment of need for progeny tests in meat breeding; breed improvement and development of new strain of birds, Maine Reds. Founder Coleman Farms '28; poultry specialist Charles M Cox Co '31-41, also mem research council; gen mgr Christie Poultry Farms '41-44; gen sales mgr in charge breeding Nichols Poultry Farm Inc since '44. World Poultry Sci Assn—NH Poultry Growers Assn—Me Poultry Improvement Assn—Internat Baby Chick Assn (dir Me hatchery div). Nichols Poultry Farm, Inc., Kingston, N.H.

17 COLEMAN, George Hopkins. Carbohydrates; Chloroamines; Chromotography. b'91. AB '15 (Greenville Coll); MS '19—PhD '21 (U of Ill). Author: Laboratory Manual of Organic Chemistry; also articles in field. Prof organic chem State U of Iowa '30-46; dean grad work Inst Textile Tech Charlottesville '46-50; now prof organic chemistry, acting chmn dept Wayne Univ since '50. American Chemical Soc—AAAS—Phi Beta Kappa—Sigma Xi. Guggenheim fellow study in France and Germany '28-29. Chemistry Department, Wayne University, Detroit 1.☉

18 COLEMAN, Howard S. Optics (Fluid, application for supersonic airflow, metal); Intermetallic diffusion; Gaseous diffusion through metals; Photography. b'17. BS '38—MS '39—PhD '42 (Penn State Coll). Author articles in field. Asso prof physics University of Texas since '47, director Optical Research Lab since '47. Am Meteorol Soc—Am Phys Soc—Am Astron Soc—Astron Soc Pacific—Am Meteor Soc—Astron Soc Can—Inst Aeronautical Sci—Am Soc Metals—Am Optical Soc. The Optical Research Laboratory, Department of Physics, The University of Texas, Austin, Tex.

19 COLEMAN, James Bruce. Mathematics of finance; Continued fractions; Correlation in statistics. b'86. BS '06 (U SC); AM '14 (Columbia U); PhD '29 (U Calif). Author: Mathematics of Finance '47. Instr math U SC '09-18, Prof '19-42; prof math Presbyterian Coll Clinton SC '47-48. Econometric Soc—Am Math Soc—Math Assn Am—SC Acad Sci. 620 Boll St., Columbia, S.C.

20 COLEMAN, Jesse E(lwood). Early American clock history. b'98. Student '15-16 (Middle Tenn State Teachers Coll). Special research in early American clock history, coupled with assembling horological library over nearly a quarter century; board technical editors, columnist, The American Horologist & Jeweler. Author articles in field. Operator special clock repair service Nashville since '32. United Horological Assns Am—British Horol Inst—British Watch and Clockmakers' Guild—Nat Assn Watch Clock Collectors (pub com). 64 Arcade Building, Nashville 3, Tenn.

21 COLEMAN, John Winston, Jr. Kentucky (History and bibliography). b' 98. BS in ME '29—Litt D (hon) '47 (U Ky); Litt D '45 (Lincoln Memorial U). Author: Masonry in the Bluegrass '33; Stage-Coach Days in the Bluegrass '35; The Court-Houses of Lexington '37; Lexington During the Civil War '38; Slavery Times in Kentucky '40; A Bibliography of Kentucky History '48; also articles in field. Owner and operator Winburn Farm, Lexington Ky since '36. Miss Valley Hist Assn—So Hist Assn—Biblio Soc Am—Hist and Philos Soc of O. Winburn Farm, Lexington, Ky.

22 COLEMAN, Joseph Johnston. Dry batteries. b'07. AB '31—MA '34—PhD '36 (U Colo). Author articles in field. Research chem, physicist Burgess Battery Co '36-40, chief engr since '40. Am Phys Soc—Electrochem Soc—Sigma Xi. Burgess Battery Company, Freeport, Ill. H: 304 N. Chicago Av.

23 COLEMAN, Robert Boisseau, Jr. Cement; Blast furnace slag; Lime; Acids for explosive production. b'16. BS (Chem E) '39 (NC State Coll); '39-40 (MIT); '43 (U Cincinnati); '47-50 (Birmingham Sch Law). Research on concrete with respect to alkali aggregate reaction; study of lime production and hydration in search for method to increase plasticity; utilization of slag from blast furnaces, in bloating, and other applications; development methods for production and concentration of sulfuric and nitric acid. Co-author articles: (with Norman F Williams) Program to Prevent Alkali-Aggregate Reaction in Concrete Structures '49; (with Locke White Jr, Herbert Cox) Blast Furnace Slag in Alkali-Aggregate Reaction '50. Metall research Am Cast Iron Pipe Co '40-41; training and prodn supt acid dept Kankakee Ordnance Works '41-43; metall engr Kings Mills Ordnance Works '43-44; chem engr Belle Works DuPont '44-46, So Research Inst '47-49; research engr So Cement Co since '49. ACS—AICE—Am Concrete Inst—Sigma Delta Kappa. Southern Cement Co., 608 Protective Life Bldg., Birmingham, Ala.

24 COLEMAN, Robert Hemphill. South Carolina land mammals. b'93. AB '15 (Coll Charleston); summer '26 (U Chicago). Research on distribution, life histories South Carolina land mammals as avocation since '24; collecting trips southern, western, southwestern states to secure comparative specimens genera mammals also occurring South Carolina; skin collection numbers about 1600; recorded additions to South Carolina fauna: Scalopus aquaticus aquaticus (Linn), Sorex fumeus fumeus (Miller), Dasypterus floridanus Miller, Peromyscus polionotus polionotus (Wagner), Neotoma floridana haematoreia (Howell), Napaeozapus insignis roanensis (Preble). Author articles in field. Prof math Coll Charleston since '19, head dept since '26. AAAS(fellow)—Am Soc Mammalogists—SC Acad Sci(F)—SC Natural Hist Soc—Carolina Bird Club—Charleston Nat Hist Soc—Ecol Soc Am—Soc Systematic Zool. Trustee and honorary curator zool Charleston Mus. College of Charleston, Charleston 10, S.C.

25 COLEMAN, Russell. Soils; Fertilizers; Plant nutrition. b'13. BS '36—MS '37 (Miss State Coll); PhD '41—research fellow '39-41 (U Wis). Research on plant response to fertilizers, soil fertility, and plant nutrition with particular attention given to phosphate and its reaction in soil. Author articles in field. Asso prof agron Miss State Coll '41-46, asso dir Agrl Sta '46-47, dir, adminstr charge agrl research program for State of Miss '47-48; pres Nat Fertilizer Assn Washington since '48. Am Soc Agron—Soil Sci Soc Am. 616 Investment Building, Washington. H: 20 E. Woodbine St., Chevy Chase, Md.

10 COLEMAN, William Beecher. Castings; Furnaces (Steel manufacturing). Student (U Pa, MIT). Research and improvements in steel manufacturing in furnaces; in charge casting some of largest ingot and casting made in world. Supt foundry and open hearths Midvale Steel So '14-15, supt O H shell steel mfg '16-18; cons Ordnance Dept charge gun steel melting '18; gen supt Tacony Steel Co '19-21; owner W B Coleman & Co metall chem engrs since '22. Am Soc Metals (pres '33) — Am Foundrymen's Soc (dir) — Am Chem Soc—Nat Assn Corrosion Engrs—Franklin Inst—Am Inst Mining Metall Engrs—Am Council Comml Labs. 9th and Rising Sun Av., Phila. 40. H: 6635 McCallum St., Phila. 19.

11 COLEMAN, William Jackson. Latin American history; Church history (Catholic). b'11. '26-32 (St Joseph's Coll); BA '34 (St Gregory's Sem); '35-39 (Cath Foreign Mission Sem); '39-40 (U Ill); MA '41-PhD '48 (Cath U). Research on papal relations with Latin America during and after era of revolution, restoration of hierarchy in Argentina, Uruguay, Chile, Peru, Bolivia, activities of papal nunciature located Rio de Janeiro with secret apostolic delegation for Spanish America; work in Vatican archives Rome '45-47; study tour South America '45. Instr modern European and Latin Am hist Maryknoll Coll Clarks Summit Pa '41-44, Lakewood NJ '47-50. AHA—Cath Hist Assn. Catholic Foreign Mission Society, Maryknoll, N.Y. Padres de Maryknoll, Colegio Gonzalo Correa, Casilla 196, Molina, Chile.

12 COLES, Donald K. Spectroscopy; Molecular and atomic physics; Electronics; Microwave. b'11. Student '27-28 (Northhampton Engring Coll London); BS '32 (Ill Wesleyan U); '34 (U BC); MS '37 (Calif Inst Tech); PhD '44 (U Okla). Author articles in field. Physicist dept electronics and nuclear physics Westinghouse Research Labs since '46. AAAS—Am Phys Soc—Am Chem Soc—Optical Soc Am—Sigma Xi. Westinghouse Research Laboratories, East Pittsburgh, Pa.

13 COLES, Harold William. Carbohydrates (Chemistry, fermentation, utilization of by-products); Plastics (Optical); Films; Adhesives; Gels; Medicinal preparations (Organic). b '98. BS (chem) '23 (Syracuse U); MS (bact) '26—PhD (chem) '27 (Ia State Coll). Research on structure, purification and recovery of dextrines from stillage, in carbohydrates, new glycosides, levulinic acid compounds, pharmacologically active compounds from sugars; developed new optical cements, method for spin-coating lenses, films for optical instruments, plasticizer migration, plastic lenses, synthetic fibers; research on local anesthetics including development of metycaine and corneal method of testing, antimony compounds for tropical diseases, new method for making ephedrine, barbituric acids; devised new techniques for determining impurities in alcohol and for making very pure alcohol, utilization of fermentation by-products. Granted patents in field. Research chem Lilly Research Lab '27-33; F Mellon Inst Indsl Research '33-42; head plastics and organic lab Bausch and Lomb Optical Co '42-48; dir QM Research and

Development Chem Lab since '48. AC S—AAAS—NY Acad Sci—Optical Soc Am—Am Inst Phys—Am Pharm Assn —Sigma Xi—Alpha Chi Sigma—Phi Lambda Upsilon—Gamma Sigma Delta—QM Assn—Nat Geog Soc Received Crary Scholarship ('19-23). Phila. Quartermaster Depot, 2800 S 20th St., Phila. 45.

14 COLES, James Stacy. Physical chemistry of starch; Underwater explosives. b'13. BS '34 (Mansfield State Teachers Coll); AB '36—AM '39—PhD '41 (Columbia). Research group leader and supervisor Underwater Explosives Research Laboratory Woods Hole Oceanographic Institute '43-46. Author articles in field. Asst prof chem Brown U '46-49, asso prof '49-52, '47-52, acting coll dean '51-52, pres Bowdoin Coll since '52. exec officer dept chemistry. Am Chem Soc—AAAS—New England Assn Chem Teachers—Sigma Xi. Bowdoin College, Brunswick, Me.†

15 COLIN, Edward Cecil. Animals (Genetics, pharmacology); Human genetics and evolution. b'90. AB '13— LLB '14 (U Kan); PhD '30 (U Chicago). Research on genetic effects of lead poisoning in male guinea pigs; investigations on the origin and development of hair direction in mammals through a combination of histological studies and genetic data; research on inheritance of human characteristics and on human evolution. Author: Elements of Genetics (2d edit) '46. Co-author: Introductory Biology '49. Author articles: A Comparison of the Descendants of Lead-Poisoned Male Guinea Pigs with those from Untreated Animals of the Same Closely Inbred Strains '31; Hair Direction in Mammals—Embryogenesis of Hair Follicles in the Guinea Pig '43. Faculty zool and genetics dept Chicago Teachers Coll since '39, now prof. Genetics Soc of Am—Eugenics Soc Gt Brit—Am Soc Human Genetics —Soc Study Evolution—Am Assn Phys Anthrop—Am Anthrop Assn—AAAS— Am Soc Zoologists. Chicago Teachers College, 6800 Stewart Av., Chicago 21. H: 6567 Harvard Av.

16 COLLBOHM, Franklin Rudolf. Engineering. b'07. '28 (U Wis). With Douglas Aircraft Co Inc Santa Monica Cal '29-48, asst to vp engring '42-48; cons to Sec of War, Def Dept '44-45; mem at large on engring OSRD '44-45; dir The Rand Corp since '48. Inst Aeronautical Sciences(F)—Tau Beta Pi—Eta Kappa Nu. 1500 Fourth St., Santa Monica, Cal.☉

17 COLLIER, Donald. Archaeology and ethnology (Peru, Ecuador and Plains Indians). b'11. AB '33 (U Calif); fellow '34-35—research fellow '38-39 (U Chicago). Editor South American Archaeology Handbook of Latin American Studies '43-46. Field work in Arizona, New Mexico, Washington, Oklahoma, Montana, Peru, and Ecuador. Author: Peyote—A General Study of the Plant, the Cult and the Drug '37. Co-author: Archaeology of the Upper Columbia Region '42; Indians Before Columbus '47; Survey and Excavations in Southern Ecuador, and others; also articles in field. Curator Chicago Nat Hist Mus since '43. Am Anthrop Assn—Soc Am Archaeol—Inst Andean Research. Chicago Natural History Museum, Chicago 5.☉

18 COLLIER, James E. Economic geography; Aluminum. b'13. BS '36 (West Ky Teach Coll); MA '38 (U Cincinnati); '42-43 (U Mo); '45-46, '47 (U Neb). Author articles: Aluminum Industry of Western Hemisphere '44; Aluminum Industry of Europe '46; Aluminum Resources of the United States '48; Artesian Water and Aus-

tralia's Pastoral Industry '45. Instr geog U Mo '42-45, asst prof since '47; asst prof geog Fresno State (Calif) Coll '46-47. Nat Council Geog Teach(F) —Am Soc Profl Geog—Assn Pacific Coast Geog—AAAS—Assn Am Geog— Sigma Xi. Geography Department, University of Missouri, Columbia, Mo.†

19 COLLINS, Donald Clark. Appendicitis. b'02. AB '23 (U Calif Berkeley); MD '27—ScD '47 (U Calif Med Sch San Francisco); MS (Path) '32—MS (Surgery) '34 (U Minn). Author: Historic phases of appendicitis; Adenomatous polyps of vermiform appendix; Length and position of the vermiform appendix; The chronic inflammation and obliteration reactions of veriform appendix; Acute retrocecal appendicitis; The grave prognosis of appendicitis in the aged. Cons surgeon Hollywood '35-'40, since '45. Am Coll Surgeons (F)— Internat Coll Surgeons (F)—Nat gastroenterological Assn (F)—Internat Acad Practology (F)—Am Geriatrics Soc (F)—AMA(F)—British Med Assn —Canadian Med Assn—Am Ethnol Soc —NY Acad Sci—Calif Acad Sci—Am Soc Study Arteriosclerosis—Assn for Study Internal Secretions—Am Anthrop Assn—Gerontological Soc—AA AS (F). 7046 Hollywood Blvd, Hollywood 28, Calif.

20 COLLINS, Ellen, Latin American affairs (Ecuador, Venezuela, Peru). b'16. BS '39—certificate journalism (St Joseph's Coll); MA '41 (Columbia U); student '41-42 (U San Marcos, U Mexico). Author articles in field. Dir Inter-Am Seminar, Mexico '42; asst cultural attache Am Embassy Quito Ecuador '43-44, Caracas Venezuela '45-46. Centro Venezolano-Norteamericano—2900 Adam Mill Rd., Washington.

21 COLLINS, Henry B(ascom). Eskimo and Arctic people (Art, archaeology, anthropology, ethnology, caries, anthropometry); Southeastern U.S. Indians (Archeology, anthropology; anthropometry). b'99. AM '25 (George Washington U). Assistant Pueblo Bonito expedition National Geographic Society '22-24; director Smithsonian expeditions to Florida, Mississippi, Louisiana '25-29, Nunivak Island and Bering Sea '27, Punuk Island and Bering Strait '28, St Lawrence Island, Norton Sound and Arctic coast '29, St Lawrence Island '30; director National Geographic Society Smithsonian expedition Bering Strait '36; dir Nat Museum of Canada—Smithsonian expeditions Baffin Island '48, Cornwallis Island, NWT, '49, '50. Chairman Board of Governors, Arctic Institute of North America '48. Ethnology and Anthropology Sciences Copenhagen '38; Author: Prehistoric Art of the Alaskan Eskimo '29; Archeology of St. Lawrence Island Alaska '37; co-author: The Aleutian Islands, their People and Natural History '46; also articles in field. Sr ethnol Bur Am Ethnol since '39. Am Anthrop Assn—Anthrop Soc Washington (pres '38, 39)—Am Assn Phy Anthrop—Soc Am Archeol (vp '42) —Wash Acad Sci. Awarded gold medal Royal Danish Acad Sci Letters '36. Smithsonian Institution, Washington 25.☉

22 COLLINS, Marcus Whitford. Human relations; Ethnic and religious group tensions; Family; Housing; Criminology. b'04. AB '29 (U Ala); AM '37 (George Washington U) AM— PhD '43 (Harvard). Author: Life, Labor and Sorrow, A Study of the Negro in the Santee-Cooper Area of South Carolina; Forward Steps in Democracy; The Clinical Approach to the Alleviation of Prejudice Regarding Minority Groups in the United States;

Evidence of Influences Which Have Served as Retarding Forces in the Process of Disintegration in a Cumulative Community. Former dir Transient Homes, Greenville SC; met dir Nat Conf Christians and Jews NY City; sociol cons Com on Unity NY City; community service specialist Fed Council of Churches of Christ in Am; prof sociology U Ga Atlanta Div; cons in human relations; ednl specialist Dept of State Europe. AAAS—Am Social Soc—AAUP—So Social Soc—Phi Alpha Theta—Alpha Psi Omega—Sigma Delta Pi—Phi Alpha Delta—Kappa Phi Kappa—Sigma Tau Delta—Pi Gamma Mu. Grad Bowdoin prize Harvard '43; 1948 award Fla Acad Sci for outstanding research. University of Georgia, Atlanta Division, Atlanta.†

10 COLLINS, William Dennis. Water (Industrial, agricultural); Analytical reagents; Laboratory apparatus. b'75. AB '95—AM '97 (Harvard). Author articles in field. Chem US Geol Survey '06-08; US Dept Agrl '08-20; US Dept Interior '20-46. AAAS(F)—Am Chem Soc—Am Water Works Assn—Am Soc Testing Materials. 1924 Belmont Rd., Washington.†⊚

11 COLLINS, William Leighton. Mechanical properties of metals (Cast iron). b'06. BS '28—MS '32 (U Ill). Research on mechanical properties of cast iron under fatigue and static loads at room and elevated temperatures. Author: Fatigue and Endurance Limit of Gray Cast Iron, Summary for Cast Metals Handbook '44; co-author: Statics and Strength of Materials (with Draffin) '50; Resistance of Materials Laboratory Manual (with Draffin) '48. Professor theoretical and applied mechanics Univ Ill since '49. Am Soc Testing Materials—ASCE—Am Soc Metals—Am Soc Engring Edn—Sigma Xi. Department of Theoretical and Applied Mechanics, University of Illinois. H: 206 Indiana Av., Urbana, Ill.†

12 COLMAN, James Douglas. Health economics; Morbidity statistics. b'10. ME (Cornell U); student (Johns Hopkins Sch Hygiene and Pub Health). Sec Hosp Council Essex Co Inc; dir Hosp Service NJ Inc, Md Hosp Service Inc; sec Med Care Sect Md State Planning Com; chmn Blue Cross Com Am Hosp Assn; lecturer Sch Hygiene and Pub Health Johns Hopkins, Am Hosp Assn—Am Pub Health Assn—Am Statis Assn. 15 E. Fayette St., Baltimore 3.

13 COLTON, Dudley T. Building materials. b'07. BS '28 (Harvard). Research in building materials specifically asbestos-cement pipe, shingles and sheets, asphalt floor tile, roofing. Inventions building materials field. Engring and research dept US Gypsum Co '28-32; research div Johns-Manville Corp '33-48, asst to vp since '48. Am Soc Testing Materials—Bldg Officials Conf Am—Nat Fire Protection Assn—Producers Council (com chmn constr methods)—Tau Beta Pi. Johns-Manville Corporation, 22 East 40th St., NYC 16. H: Washington Valley Rd., Martinsville, N.J.

14 COLVIN, Charles Herbert. Aeronautical engineering; Aircraft instruments; Engineering administration. b'93. ME '14 (Stevens Inst Tech). With Curtiss Aeroplane and Motor Companies '13; mgr Aircraft Instrument dept Sperry Gyroscope Co '14-19; founder '19 Pioneer Instrument Co, pres, gen mgr '19-32; dir Colvin Labs since '33; asst to pres Kollsman Instrument Co '37-40; spl asst to chief US Weather Bur '40-41; dir Guggenheim Sch Aeronautics '41-44, dir En-

gring Research Div Coll Engring NYU '43-44; research cons, Bur Aeronautics Navy Dept, '44, Adv President's Air Policy Commn '47. Inst Aeronautical Sciences(F)—Royal Aeronautical Soc(F)—Soc Automotive Engrs—ASME(F)—Am Meterol Soc—AAAS—Franklin Inst—Am Soc Engring Edn. Egbert Hill, Morristown, N.J.⊚

15 COLWELL, Robert Cameron. Physics; Radio waves (Propagation); Gyros (High speed); Motors (Electric); Chaladni plates. b'84. AB '04—AM '08 (U NB); AB '07 (Harvard); student '08-10 (U Chicago); PhD '18 (Princeton); student '23-24 (Cambridge U Eng). Research on radio waves, spinning tops and gyroscopes, vibrating plates, velocity of sound. Author articles in field. Prof physics W Va U since '24; asst commr weights and measures State WVa since '24. Am Phys Soc—Franklin Inst—Inst Radio Engrs—AAAS—Optical Soc Am—Acoustical Soc Am—Sigma Pi Sigma—Sigma Xi. H: 426 Jefferson St., Morgantown, W.Va.⊚

16 COMAN, Dana. Psycho-Physiological adaptation; Expeditionary nutrition. b'95. AM '20 (Harvard); MD '24 (Johns Hopkins); LLD '40 (Florida Southern). Medical assistant Sir Wildred T Grenfell, Labrador '22-24; medical director Byrd Antarctic Expedition '28-30, Ellsworth Transantarctic Expedition '34-35; leader Coman Pacific Oceanographic Expedition '36-37; developed food products, colloidally dispersed dietary supplements, concentrated special purpose polar airforce and navy survival rations, pemmican; studies of adaptation to extreme environment, techniques of effective performance, motivation and morale; General Staff observer task forces Frigid, Williwaw, Furnace '46-47; US delegate representing Department of Army at Seventh Pacific Science Congress New Zealand '49. Author articles in field. Anat, surg, psychiat faculty Johns Hopkins U '24-39; prof nutrition Fla So Coll since '39; sci advisor War Dept Gen Staff since '46; chmn panel expdn Research and Development Bd since '47; cons AAF '40-41, WPB '41-42, OQMG '42-46, Strategic Air Command since '50. American Assn Anat—AAAS—Am Pub Health Assn—Am Geog Soc—Am Antarctic Assn (sec)—Am Polar Soc (Pres)—Arctic Inst NA (acting dir)—Nat Acad Sci (com on antarctic sci)—Nat Research Council (com on QM environmental problems). 145 W. 57th St., NYC 19. H: Hotel Statler, NYC 1.

17 COMBS, Joseph Franklin. Pasture crops; Grasses; Soil; Gardening. b'92. Self educated. Discovered new species of pasture grass '29 recognized by National Herbarium '32 and named Combs Paspalum. Author: Growing Pastures in The South '36; also articles in field. Co agrl ext agt Tex A&M Coll and US Dept Agr since '19. Nat Geog Soc—Am Mus Nat Hist—Coastal Cattle Assn (sec). 604 Courthouse Building, Beaumont, Tex. 2255 Park St., Beaumont.†

18 COMFORT, Howard. Ancient Roman ceramics; Latin and Greek language and literature. b'04. AB '24 (Haverford Coll); AM '27—PhD '32 (Princeton); Fellow '27-29 (Am Acad Rome). Author: Terra Sigillata in Pauly Wissowa's Realenc; also articles in field. Teacher classical langs Haverford Coll since '32, actg cultural attaché Rome Italy '50. Am Philol Assn (dir, sec-treas since '46)—Osborne Assn (dir)—Archeol Inst Am—Classical Assn Atlantic States—Deutsch Archeol Inst. Haverford College, Haverford, Pa.

19 COMPTON, Arthur H(olly). Physics (X-rays; Cosmic rays; Nucleonics). b'92. BS '13—ScD '27 (Coll Wooster); MA '14—PhD '16—ScD '34 (Princeton); ScD (Ohio State U, Yale, Brown, Harvard, U San Marcos, U Arequipa); LLD (Wash U, U Cal, Lehigh, Texas Christian U); MA '34 (Oxford); LHD (U Tampa); Litt D (Jewish Theol Sem Am). Discovered change in wave-length of X-rays when scattered; total reflection of X-rays; with CH Hagenow, complete polorization of X-rays; with R L Doan, X-ray spectra from ruled gratings; electrical character of the cosmic ray; directed world cosmic ray survey '31-34; directed work resulting in first atomic chain reaction. Author: Secondary Radiations Produced by X-rays '22; X-rays and Electrons '26; The Freedom of Man '35; Human Meaning of Science '40; also articles in field. Chancellor Washington U St Louis since '45. Am Phys Soc (F, vp '33, pres '34)—AAAS (F, pres '42)—Western Soc Engrs (hon)—Am Assn Sci Workers (pres '39-40)—Am Philos Soc (pres '34 vp '48-49)—Nat Research Council (chmn Com X-rays and Radioactivity '22-25)—Sigma Xi—Phi Beta Kappa. Guggenheim fellow '26-27; awarded Rumford gold medal '27; Nobel prize '27; gold medal Radiological Soc '28; Matteucci gold medal Italian Acad Sci '33; Hughes Medal Royal Soc London '40; Franklin Gold Medal of Franklin Inst '40; Wash award Western Soc Engrs '45; Franklin Medal Am Philos Soc '46; St Louis Distinguished Service Award '46; Medal for Merit US Govt '46.⊚

20 COMPTON, Karl Taylor. Physics b'87. PhB '08—MS '09—hon degree (Coll of Wooster); PhD '12 (Princeton); hon degrees (Stevens Inst Tech, Lehigh, Princeton, Clarkson Coll, Boston U, Columbia, W. Virginia, NYU, Harvard, U Wis, Middlebury Coll, Williams Coll, Johns Hopkins, Franklin & Marshall Coll, Northeastern U, St Lawrence U, U Calif, Northwestern U, Tufts Coll, Norwich U, William & Mary, Rollins Coll., U. of Hawaii, Brooklyn Poly Inst, Case Sch Applied Sci, Rutgers, Worcester Poly Inst, Ecole Poly Montreal, Cambridge U). Dir Pacific branch OSRD and Sci Intelligence Mission to Japan '45; chairman US Radar mission to United Kingdom '43; special representative of Secretary of War in Southwest Pacific Area '43-44; chairman joint chiefs of staff evaluation board on Atomic bomb test '46. Pres Mass Inst Tech '30-48; vis com US Bureau of Standards '31-47. Aeronautical engr Signal Corps US Army '17; asso scientific attache Am Embassy Paris '18. Am Physical Soc (F, councillor, vp '25-27, pres '27-29—Optical Soc Am—AAAS (exec Com '31-40, pres '35-36)—Am Philos Soc—Am Chem Soc—Inst Aeronautical Scis—Franklin Inst—AIEE—ASME—Nat Acad Sci—Am Acad Arts Scis—Am Soc Engring Edn (vp '37, pres '38-39)—Phi Beta Kappa—Sigma Xi—Tau Beta Pi. Massachusetts Institute of Technology, Cambridge 39, Mass.⊚

21 COMPTON, Mary T. (Mrs. O. C. Compton). Apple trees (Winter injury, anatomy); Plant translocation. b'04. BS '33—MS '37 (U NH); PhD '41—Goldwyn Smith fellow '38-39—grad scholar '39-40 (Cornell U). Author articles in field. Prof bot Milwaukee-Downer Coll '46-51. Am Soc Hort Sci—Bot Soc Am—Sigma Xi. 433 N. 17th St., Corvallis, Ore.†

22 COMPTON Wilson Martindale. American forestry and forest conservation; Lumber industry. b'90. PhB '11—AM '12—LLD '35 (Coll Wooster O); PhD '15—LLB '17 (Hamilton Coll

Law Chicago). Assisted in drafting NRA and administrative regulations, lumber and forest products industries code. Author: The Organization of the Lumber Industry '16; Forest Conservation—A Task in Engineering '39; also articles in field. Med adv com Forest Products Div US Dept Commerce since '29; chmn survey com US Timber Conservation Bd since '31; apptd chief cons Lumber and Timber Products Office Prodn Management '41; mem adv bd Materials and Equipment QM Gen US Army since '42; cons research com OSRD since '43; hon dir Am Forest Products Industries Inc since '45; hon dir Timber Engring Co since '45; chmn adv com Wash State Resources Bd '47; pres State Coll Washington and State Expt Sta since '45. Royal Econ Soc(F)—Am Econ Assn—Am Econometric Soc—Am Bar Assn—Am Statis Assn—Am Polit Sci Assn—Acad Polit Sci—Am Trade Assn Execs (awarded medal '37)—AFA (vp '46)—AAAS—Soc Am Foresters (hon mem)Comite Internationale du Bois, Brussels (mem exec com, dir Dept D'Utilisation '39)—Phi Beta Kappa—Sigma Xi—Sigma Tau (hon). State College of Washington, Pullman, Wash.⊚

10 COMSTOCK, Daniel Frost. Physics (Industrial applications, electricity, magnetism, optics, heat) b'83. SB '04 (Mass Inst Tech); PhD '06 (U Basel); student '05 (U Berlin), '05-06 (U Zurich), '06-07 (U Cambridge, Eng). Directed scientific work on development of means for detection of hostile submarines, World War I. Co-inventor of new refrigeration process owned by Stator Co; director scientific work on and principal inventor of the process for producing motion pictures in natural color known as Technicolor process, developed by Kalmus Comstock & Wescott Inc for Technicolor Motion Picture Corp '14-25. Author: (with L T Troland) Nature of Matter and Electricity '17; also articles in field. Pres Comstock & Wescott Inc (indsl research) since '25; pres and dir Stator Co. AAAS(F)—Am Phys Soc(F)—Am Chem Soc. Comstock & Wescott, Inc., 1430 Massachusetts Av., Cambridge 38, Mass.⊚

11 COMSTOCK, Gregory Jamieson. Powder metallurgy. b'93. PhB '17 (Yale). The preparation of alloy powder products from fully alloyed powders; types of metal powder products —a classification. Dir research and mgr factory Internat Silver Co Meriden Conn '21-26; dir research Firth-Sterling Steel Co McKeesport Pa '26-31; mgr metal powder div and asst mgr research and development Handy and Harmon Fairfield Conn '31-38; dir Powder metallurgy Stevens Inst Tech Hoboken NJ since '38, prof powder metallurgy since '51. Am Soc Metals —AIMME—Engring Soc Western Mass —Soc Carbide Engrs. Stevens Institute of Technology, Powder Metallurgy Laboratory, 1 Elysian Park, Hoboken, N.J.

12 CONANT, Roger. Geographical distribution, life history and taxonomy of North American reptiles and amphibians; Water snakes (genus Natrix). b'09. Student '27-28 (U Pa). Editor Parks and Recreation, Zoo section, '33-51; editor Fauna 1939-48. Author: Reptiles of Ohio '38-51. Co-author: (with William Bridges) What Snake Is That? '39; also articles in field. Curator Phila Zool Garden since '35. Am Soc Ichthyol and Herpetol—NY Zool Soc—Am Inst of Park Executives— Am Assn Zool Parks Aquariums (past chmn, past sec)—Zool Soc (London). Philadelphia Zoo, 34th St. and Girard Av., Phila 4.

13 CONARD, Henry S(hoemaker). Mosses; Waterlilies. b'74. BS '94—MA '95 (Haverford Coll); PhD '01—fellow '99-04 (U Pa); Johnston scholar '05-06 (Johns Hopkins); ScD (hon) (Grinnell Coll, Haverford Coll). Travel in New Mexico and Washington '02, Europe '02-03, '35, moss collecting in most of US and in Ontario. Author: Waterlilies '05; How to Know the Mosses '44; Plant Sociology '32; also articles in field. Prof bot Grinnell Coll '06-44, prof emeritus since '44; prof bryology Ia Lakeside Lab '46-49; visiting research prof bot State U Ia since '44. Ia Acad Sci (life)—Ia State Hort Soc (life)—Minn State Hort Soc (life)— AAAS(F)—Bryological Soc Am (hon life)—Am Soc Plant Taxonomists—Soc Linn de Lyon (life). Grinnell College, Grinnell, Ia. H: 1310 Elm St.

14 CONDAX, Louis M. Photography (Color); Violin varnishes. b'96 Grad (Gymnasium-Lyceum, Salonika Greece); student (Sch Indsl Art, Phila, Wagner Inst, Phila). Experimented with violin making and varnish since '21; research in artistic, scientific and chemical functions affecting violin tone, analyzed scientifically the Old Master Varnishes using modern scientific methods. Research Eastman Kodak Co color field since '42. Research Laboratory, Eastman Kodak Company, Rochester, N.Y. H: 87 East Parkway, Rochester 5.

15 CONDON, Edward U. Quantum mechanics; Atomic and nuclear physics. b'02. AB '24—PhD '26 (U Calif). Co-author: Quantum Mechanics '29; Theory of Atomic Spectra '35. Dir Nat Bur of Standards Washington since '45; Nat Adv Com for Aeronautics. Nat Acad Sci—Am Phys Soc (pres '46) —AAAS—Am Assn Physics Teachers— AIEE—Inst Radio Engrs—Phi Beta Kappa—Sigma Xi. National Bureau of Standards, Connecticut Av. and Upton St., Washington.⊚

16 CONE, Russel G. Suspension bridge construction; Ordnance shell and bomb loading; Ammonium nitrate; Fertilizer manufacturing. b'96. BS in CE '22 (U Ill). Successively junior engineer, assistant engineer and resident engineer in charge construction of main span Delaware River Bridge Philadelphia '22-27; resident engineer in charge construction for Modjeski and Chase, constulant on construction Ambassador Bridge Detroit '27-30; general manager Tacony-Palmyra Bridge Philadelphia '30-33; resident engineer in charge construction Golden Gate Bridge (longest span in world) San Francisco '33-37; engineer in charge maintenance of the structure Golden Gate Bridge and Highway District '37-41; member board of investigation Tacoma-Narrows Bridge collapse State of Washington, consulting engineer; numerous engineering reports and inspections of bridges throughout US since '27; associate engineer with Modjeski and Masters on report and engineering study of passenger tramway Palm Springs California and other projects '39-41; assistant chief engineer on design, construction Louisiana Ordnance Plant, general manager Silas Mason Co on operation of Louisiana Ordnance Plant and others; consultant on design and construction of Green River Ordnance Plant Dixon Ill. Auhtor articles in field. ASCE—Am Toll Bridges Assn—Am Soc for Testing Materials—Am Concrete Inst—Tau Beta Pi. La Ordnance Plant, Shreveport, La.†⊚

17 CONFER, Carl Vincent. History of France (Third Republic, Imperialism). b'13. AB '34 (DePauw U); AM '35—PhD '39 (U Pa). Special study in

French imperialism in North Africa, especially Morocco and French international relations 1870-1914; analyzing attitudes toward colonial imperialism in France since 1870. Author articles: The Social Influence of the Officer in the Third French Republic '39; Divided Counsels in French Imperialism; the Ras-el-Ain Incident in 1904 '46. Harrison Fellow U Pa '38-39; Guggenheim Fellow '49-50; asso prof hist Syracuse U since '46. AHA—Phi Beta Kappa. Maxwell Hall, Syracuse University. Syracuse 10, N. Y.†

18 CONGER, Paul S(idney). Diatoms. b'97. BS '20—MS '21 (U Wis); grad sch (U S Dept Agrl). Author articles in field. Diatom research Carnegie Inst Washington '22-43; asso curator charge diatom collection US Nat Museum since '43. AAAS(F)—Washington Acad Scis(F)—Am Soc Limnol Oceanog— Am Microscopical Soc—Phycol Soc Am. U. S. National Museum, Washington 25.

19 CONKLIN, Albert Edward. Paper (Creping, adhesives, laminates). b'04. Student '22-24 (U Pa); BS (Chem E '26—Chem E '36 (Bucknell U). Tests on creping and embossing of tissues and light weight papers; adhesive research for cellophane, cellulose acetate, cardboard, and tissues; tests on laminating crepe to paperboard, tissue, paper, cellophane, and to itself. Research chem viscose process DuPont Rayon Co Buffalo '26-30; research chem engr on creping problems Dennison Mfg Co Framingham Mass '30-31; research on creping, laminating and adhesive problems C A Reed since '31. Tech Assn Pulp and Paper Industry—Am Inst Chem (F)—Pa Chem Soc. Professional chem engr Pa. C. A. Reed Co., Williamsport 62, Pa.

20 CONKLIN, Dwight Burr. Plant physiology; Industrial microbiology. b'15. AB '40—AM '42 (Syracuse U); '43-45 (State U Ia). Research on influence climatic and edaphic factors, nutritional requirements. Research and development div Wyandotte Chemicals Corp Wyandotte Mich since '45. AAAS—Bot Soc Am—Am Soc Plant Physiol. Wyandotte Chemicals Corporation, Wyandotte, Mich.

21 CONKLIN, Groff. Housing; Building construction; Science fiction. b'04. '23-25 (Dartmouth Coll)—'26 (Harvard); AB '27 (Columbia). Analyses of postwar housing problems; studies of building construction elements; articles in field science fiction. Author: How to Run a Rental Library '34; All About Subways '38; All About Houses '39; Editor: Best Science Fiction '46; Treasury of Science Fiction '48; also articles in field. Vicepres Tauxemount Development Corp, Alexandria Va since '46. Am Soc Profl Geog—Nat Assn Housing Officials—Nat Pub Housing Conf—The Authors League. 432 W 22 St., NYC 23.

22 CONKLIN, Leurance Ross. US fruits (Adaptation of foreign, adaptation of tropical); Pawpaw. b'90. Ed pub schs. Calif Acad Sci. Route 1, Box 475, Chico, Calif.

23 CONLEY, Albert Rolland. Dairy industry (History of research); Milk (Marketing). b'13. BS '36—MS '41 (Okla A and M Coll); PhD '49 (O State U). Research on history dairy industry, seasonal milk pricing plans Kansas City and St Louis, economics of federal order milk markets, pricing of non-fat milk solids; development graduate course in agricultural economics research. Author articles: History of Research of Problems Confronting the Dairy Industry which have been Conducted by Agricultural Experiment Stations 1881-1947 '49; Effect of Base and Surplus Plan on Seasonal Pattern of Milk Deliveries in Ohio '49. Co-author article: (with C G McBride) Effect of Price Plans on the Seasonal Pattern of Milk Deliveries from Ohio Farm '49 Research asst dept agrl econ O State U; asso prof agrl econ U Mo '49-50; dir sales Sanitary Milk Producers St Louis since '50. Am Farm Econ Assn—Western Agrl Econ Assn—Can Agrl Econ Soc—Internat Agrl Econ Soc. Sanitary Milk Producers, 2208 Washington Ave., St.L. 3.

10 CONMY, Peter Thomas. History of California. b'01. AB '24—MA '27—EdD '37—BLS '47 (U Calif); MA '41 (Stanford). Author: Aids to the Study of Government '28; History of Public School Finance in California '37; Public School-Public Library Relationships '45; The Date of the Founding of San Francisco '47; A Centennial Evaluation of the Treaty of Guadelup Hidalgo 1848-1948 '48; and others. Appt city librarian of Oakland Calif '43, charge Oakland Pub Library dept including Oakland Pub Museum, Snow Museum and Oakland Art Galley. Am and Calif Library Assns—NEA—Calif Teachers Assn—Calif Hist Soc—Am Polit Sci Assn. 659 14th St., Oakland 12, Cal.

11 CONN, Arthur Leonard. Petroleum refining; Pilot plant development (Petroleum procedures). b'13. SB '34—SM '35 (MIT). Holder US patents relating to fluid catalytic cracking. Author articles in field. With Standard Oil Co since '39, now div dir in charge pilot plant development. Am Inst Chem Engrs—Am Chem Soc. Standard Oil Co (Indiana), Research Dept., Whiting, Ind. H: 7450 Euclid Pkwy., Chgo. 49.†

12 CONN, Harold Joel. Biological stains; Soil bacteriology; Microtechnique. b'86. PhD '08 (Wesleyan U); PhD '11 (Cornell U). Studies of bacterial flora of soil; standardization of biological stains, with special attention to making US independent of other countries in that field; development of methods in microtechnique. Chairman Commission on Standardization of Biological Stains '22-44; president Biological Stain Commn '44-51, sec since '51. Ed Stain Technology since '26. Author: Bacteriology (with H W Conn) '23; Biological Stains (with others) '46; Laboratory Guide in General Bacteriology '27; History of Staining '33; (with others) Staining Procedures '33; (with others) Manual of Methods for Pure Culture Study of Bacteria '36. Soil bact since '08; asso bact NY Agrl Expt Sta '11-20, chief in research '20-48. AAAS(F)—Soc Am Bact (chmn com on bact technique '20-47 vp '47 pres '48)—Sigma Xi—Phi Beta Kappa. 458 Castle St., Geneva, N.Y.◎

13 CONNER, Herbert W(esley). Chewing gum. b'06. PhD '33 (U Chicago). Research chem Pacini Labs '33-34; civilian chem US Army QMC '34-35; prof bot DePaul U '35-36; research chem and chief chemist Wm Wrigley Jr Co research dept Chicago since '36. William Wrigley Jr. Co., 410 N. Michigan Av., Chicago 11.

14 CONNETTE, Earle. Music education (Supervision and administration). b'10. BS '33—MS '35 (Ind State Teachers Coll); PhD '44 (Ind U). Co-author: The Supervision and Administration of Music Education '48; also articles in field. Asso prof mus edn Syracuse U since '46. Music Teachers Nat Assn—Am Musicol Assn—Music Educators Nat Conf—Am Soc Aesthetics—Am Ednl Research Assn. School of Music, Syracuse University, Syracuse 10, N.Y.†

15 CONNOLLY, Vera. American social malajustments (Juvenile detention and delinquency, child labor; American Indian; Prisons and reformatories; Narcotics; Jail and court conditions). Veteran crusading journalist known for thorough investigations in field of social problems such as conditions among Indians, kidnapping and racketeering in Chicago, St Louis and Kansas City, child labor, schools for mountain children, juvenile delinquency and many others; investigated county jails and wrote for Woman's Home Companion "Get the Children Out of the Jails", resulting in bills being framed and passed in New York, Maryland and New Hampshire forbidding jailing of children; studied Buffalo's juvenile detention system and wrote "No Place Like Home"; investigated county corruption and wrote for Collier's "Kangaroo Courts", "County Pork Barrel" '45-46, resulting in bill being framed and passed in West Virginia to abolish fee system. Author: No Straps, No Paddles '47. Nat Probation Assn—Author's League. 405 E. 54th St., NYC 22.

16 CONNOR, George Alan. Esperanto; International language. b'00. Student intermittently '19-36 (Hunter Coll, NYU). Research work on use of universal language, delegate to international conferences on use of Esperanto. Author: Ten in One Dictionary of Basic Language '45. Co-author: (with Doris T Connor, Dr W Solzbacher, V Rev Dr J B Se-Tsien Kao) Esperanto: The World Interlanguage '48. Pres Esperanto Soc NY '37-38; pres Pan Am Interlang Assn '39-42; ed Am Esperanto Mag Amerika Esperantisto since '44; gen sec Esperanto Assn N Am since '45; Am del World Esperanto Congress '36-39; mem Internat Com Universal Esperanto Assn since '47. Esperanto Assn of N Am. 114 W. 16 St., NYC 11.

17 CONNORS, John Duffy. Worker and adult education; Labor relations. b'03. BBA '23 (Boston U). As director of Workers Education Bureau, in charge of adult education program for American Federation of Labor and affiliated unions. Author: Workers Education—What? Why? How?; Workers Education and the Atomic Age; A New Frontier: Workers Education and the University; also articles in field. Sec New Bedford Central Labor Union '38-40; vp Mass State Fedn of Labor '39-41; nat field rep Am Fedn of Labor '40-43; nat vp Am Fedn of Teachers '37-47; v-chmn Hudson Shore Labor Sch since '46; dir Workers Edn Bur of Am since '43. Mem exec council Am Assn for Adult Edn; bd dir Asso Hospital Service NY; bd dir Save the Children Federation. Am Acad Polit Social Sci—ALA (com on library service to labor). 1440 Broadway, NYC.

18 CONOVER, Robert Armine. Plant diseases (Vegetables, sub-tropical). b'16. BS '39 (Culver-Stockton Coll); MS '41 (State U Ia); PhD '47 (U Ill). Author articles in field. Plant pathologist U Fla Sub-Tropical Expt Sta since '48. Am Phytopath Soc—Bot Soc Am—AAAS—Fla State Hort Soc—Sigma Xi. Sub-Tropical Experiment Station, Homestead, Fla.

19 CONQUEST, Victor. Meat and meat products; By products from packing industry (Biologicals, glandular products, pharmaceuticals, fats and oils). b'96. With Armour and Co since '26, now general mgr Research Division. Am Chem Soc—Am Oil Chem Soc—Inst of Food Technologists.

20 CONRAD, John P(eter). Enzymes in soils; Soil relations in field crop production; Plant nutrition. b'93. Hon fellow '34 (O State U, U Minn); BS '17 —PhD '33 (U Calif). Research in the effects of different field crops and crop residues upon the soil and upon crops which follow '26-48, enzymes and other organic constituents and their role in soil and crop relationships since '47, physico-chemical soil relationships '33-34. Author articles in field. Asso in agron U Calif '21-25, research asst in agron '25-27, asst agron expt sta '27-31, asso agron expt sta '31-43, lecturer agron '35-39, asso prof agron '39-43, agron prof agron since '43. Am Soc Agron—Am Soc Plant Physiol—Soil Sci Soc Am—Western Soc Soil Sci—Phi Beta Kappa—Sigma Xi. 109 Hunt Hall, University of California, Davis, Calif.

21 CONRATH, Philip A. Medical illustration. b'92. Student '11-12 (U Mo) '12-15 (Washington U Sch Fine Arts). Illustration surgical procedures, pathological conditions for publication; preparation exhibits still and motion photography for scientific meetings. Illustrations: Operative Gynecology '32; Textbook of General Surgery '36; Neuro-Anatomy '50; and others. Artist, Washington U Sch Med '19-36, St Louis U Sch Med '36-49; asst prof anatomy and med illustration and dir sect med illustration since '49. Assn Med Illustrators—Biol Photog Assn—Photog Soc Am. St. Louis University School of Medicine, 1402 S. Grand St., St.L. 4.

22 CONROY, Jack. American humor, folklore and literature; Labor history and problems; Writing (technique); American Negro history (Northward migration). b'99. Author: The Disinherited '33; A World to Win '35; They Seek a City (with A Bontemps) '45 (with Bontemps) The Fast Sooner Hound '42; (with Bontemps) Slappy Hooper, the Wonderful Sign Painter '46. Editor: The Rebel Poet '31-32; The Anvil '33-37; The New Anvil '39-41; Unrest (with R Cheyney) '20-31; Midland Humor, A Harvest of Fun and Folklore '47; also articles in field. Asso editor and director Standard Edn Soc. Awarded John S. Guggenheim fellowship '35. 6012 S. Green St., Chicago 21.

23 CONSIDINE, Douglas Maxwell. Weighing and scales; Instruments and automatic controls. b'15. BS '37 (Case Inst Tech). Author: Industrial Weighing '48. Mgr. market ext dept ind div Minneapolis-Honeywell Regulator Co Philadelphia since '46, with same since '41. Am Chem Soc—Am Inst Chem Engrs (chmn instrumentation com)—Instrument Soc Am. Minneapolis-Honeywell Regulator Co., Wayne and Roberts Avs., Phila., 44.†

24 CONSTANCE, Lincoln. Taxonomy of flowering plants (Umbelliferae, Hydrophyllaceae); Plant geography. b'09. AB '30 (U Ore); MA '32—PhD '34 (U Calif). Author articles in field. Prof bot and curator seed plant collections U Calif since '47. Asso geo-bot geobot and research analyst OSS Washington '43-45; vis lectr biol and acting dir Gray Herbarium Harvard U '47-48. Cal Academy Sci(F)—Soc Study Evolution—Am Society Naturalists—American Society Plant Taxonomists (pres '50)—Bot Soc Am—Torrey Bot Club—Calif Bot Soc—New Eng Bot Club—AAAS—Sigma Xi—Phi Beta Kappa. Department of Botany, University of California, Berkeley 4.†

25 CONSTANT, Clinton. Chemical engineering; Astronomy (Theory). b'12. BSc '35—student '36 (U Alberta); '39 (West Reserve U). Engaged research, manufacture, and handling anhydrous HF, fluorides, processes; analytical research special industrial application; research theory astronomy particularly planets, conditions, life thereon; photographed solar eclipse (partial) '30, '31, lunar eclipse '34; commercial methods all types photography finishing; dissemination principles rocketry lectures, news items '30-36. Aurthor: War of the Universe '31. Chem engr Harshaw Chem Co Cleveland '36-38, foreman HF dept '38-43; supt HF dept Nyotex Chem Inc Houston '43-47, chief develop engr '47-48; mgr engring Ferro Chem Corp Bedford '50-52; tech asst mfg dept Armour Fertilizer Works Bartow Fla since '52. Am Chem Soc Soc—AAAS. P.O. Box 726 Lakeland, Fla.

10 CONSTANTINIDES, Constantine. Endocrinology (Hormones-adrenal endocrinology). b'20. MD '41 (Vienna U). Effect of nutrition on production of defense hormones by the adrenal glands; effect of sugar on ACTH; inhibiting undesirable effects of estrogens. Asst prof anatomy dept U Brit Columbia Vancouver, BC since '50. Can Physiol Soc-BC Acad Scis. Anatomy Dept., Medical Sch., University of British Columbia, Vancouver, B.C.

11 CONVERSE, Joseph Brandly. Port development. born '88. CE '10 (Rensselaer Poly Inst Troy NY). Development design and construction of docks and wharves, terminals, and shipyards. Cons engr New Orleans '19-28; pres J B Converse & Co (engrs) since '28. Am Soc CE—Am Water Works Assn —Am Concrete Inst—Newcomen Soc —Tex Soc Professional Engrs—La Engring Soc. P.O. Box 1084, Mobile 6, Ala.

12 CONWAY, J. Gregory. Flower arrangement; Japanese Art. b'09. Ed St Vincents Sch Los Angeles Calif, U Calif, Ohara Ryu Osaka Japan. Studies of Japanese gardens, architecture, drama, tea ceremony. Author: Flowers East-West '38; Flowers: Their Arrangement '40. Teacher Long Beach Public Schs since '33; lecturer on flower arrangement U Southern Calif since '35; lecturer on Japanese culture U Hawaii '45-46; traveled extensively in Orient and South Seas. 757 No. Carhart Av., Fullerton, Cal.

13 CONWAY, Martin John Thomas. Fuel engineering (Gas manufacturing, applied oxygen generation in large quantities, open hearth and steel heating furnace design). b'93. Student '11-12 (Hanley, Staffordshire); '14-18 (Oxford U). Inventor recuperative open hearth furnace, improved methods in manufacture wrought iron, improved metallic mine prop. Author articles in field. Fuel engr Lukens Steel Co '26-46. Royal Soc Arts(F)— Nat Assn Profl Engrs(F)—Inst of Fuel, London(F)—AIME—Assn Iron and Steel Engrs—ASME—Army Ord Assn—Iron and Steel Inst—NY Iron and Steel Inst, London—Am Mil Engrs. Hill Top Farm, Gap, Pa.

14 CONWELL, John William. Rayon viscose (Raw materials, by-products). b'10. BS '32—MS '34 (Ia State Coll); '40-47 (Poly Inst Brooklyn). Author articles in field. American Viscose Corp Nitro W Va '46-51; process engr, Tide Water Associated Oil Co '35-46. Am Chem Soc—Am Inst Chem Engrs—Sigma Xi. c/o General Delivery, Ponca City, Okla.†

15 COOK, Charles H. Electrical insulating varnishes. b'96. Student '14-18, '19-20 (Carnegie Inst Tech). Research, development, production of varnishes especially for insulation of electrical equipment. Holds patent. Vice-pres, chief chem Sterling Varnish Co Haysville Pa. Am Inst Chemists(F). Haysville, Pa.

16 COOK, Clarence Sharp. Nuclear Physics; Electronics; Astrophysics.

b'18. BA '40 (De Pauw U); MA '42— PhD '48 (Ind U). Engaged resch equipment design and constrn for beta ray spectroscopy, coincidence counting, cyclotron. Beta and Gamma Spectra N13, C14, S35, Cu61, I131 Ti45, Se75, Ce141, Pr143. Articles: Energies of the Beta and Gamma Rays from Antimony '48; A High Resolution Nuclear Spectrometer '48; The Beta Spectra of Cu64 as a Test of the Fermi Theory '48; On the Alleged Gamma-Ray of N13 '47; On the Disintegration Scheme of Na24 '46; Radiations from Radioactive Co56 '42. Asst prof physics dept Washington U since '48. Am Phys Soc—Am Assn Physics Teachers—Sigma Xi—Phi Beta Kappa. Physics Department, Washington University, St Louis 5.†

17 COOK, David B. Forestry; Wildlife management. b'01. BS '24 (Cornell U). Interested in production and utilization low-grade wood and planting and silviculture of genus Larix, also ecological relationships between small mammals and forest. Supervising forester NY State Conservation Dept since '46. Soc Am Foresters (NY sect sec '46-51)—Ecol Soc Am—Am Soc Mammalogists—Wildlife Soc Am. Conservation Department, 488 Broadway, Albany 7, N.Y.†

18 COOK, Earle Stanley. Mechanical engineering (Pneumatic and electropneumatic control systems). b'90. Student '13 (Purdue U). Credited with about 60 inventions. Test engr Westinghouse Air Brake Co '13-28, asst research engr '28-39, asst to chief engr '39-44, asst to vp in charge engring since '45. ASME—Air Brake Assn (com approved maintenance practices). Westinghouse Air Brake Co., Wilmerding, Pa.

19 COOK, Ellsworth B(arrett). Pharmacology; Sensory psychology; Personnel selection. b'16. BS '38 (Springfield Coll); '38-39 (Duke U); '39-41 (Clark U); since '49 (Tufts Med Sch). Methods of bioassay; sources of variance in visual testing; visual test standards psycho-physical aspects of stereoscopic vision; psychological and physiological studies in submarine personnel selection. Author articles in field. Officer USN Div Scis Allied to Med since '41, Harvard Fatigue Lab '41-45, Med Research Lab Submarine Base New London Conn '45-49, dept pharmacology Tufts Med Sch since '49. AAAS—Am Psychol Assn—Eastern Psychol Assn—Optical Soc Am—Am Statis Assn—Inst Math Statis—Psychometrics Soc—Biometrics Soc—Am Standards Assn (sub-com on visual acuity) (sub-com on visual standards of the Armed Forces) NRC Vision Committee. Department of Pharmacology, Tufts Medical School, Boston 11.

20 COOK, Emory Giddings. Sound recording. b'13. Student '30 to '31 (MIT); EE '38 (Correll U '40-41 (Columbia). Development stabilized Feedback disc recording cutter; production in commercial quantities disc recording system; development systems methods for disc recording at double-speed; co-inventor anti-noise-modulation stylus for micro-groove recording; producer Sounds-of-our-Times specialty and demonstration records. Construction engr CBS '40-42; training aids supervisor Western Electric Co '42-45; owner Cook Labs since '45. Audio Engring Soc. Cook Laboratories, R. 2, Stamford, Conn.

21 COOK, Harold Thurston. Agricultural plant pathology (Vegetable). b'03. AB '26 (DePauw U); PhD '31 (Cornell U). Investigated shipping and handling fresh food supplies to island bases in South Pacific; re-

search on diseases of vegetable crops, vegetable seed treatments, vegetable breeding for disease resistance; forecasting epiphytotics; transportation, storage and market diseases of vegetables; military food supplies; research on nature of powdery mildew disease of snap beans, downy mildew of onions and causal organism, occurrence of oospores of Peronospora effusa with commercial spinach seed, cabbage seed treatment, watermelon wilt and resistant varieties for control, influence of acid-forming and non-acid-forming fertilizer on development of potato scab. Author articles: Forecasting Tomato Late Blight '47; 1947 Results, Late Blight Forecasting '47; Fusarium Wilt of Spinach and the Development of a Wilt Resistant Variety (with Nugent, Parris and Porter) '47; and other in field. Head plant path dept Va Truck Expt Sta '30-48; sr plant path US Dept Agr since '48. Lt, 1t comdr USNR, officer in chge Fruit and Vegetable Sect Food Inspection Div US Joint Purchasing Bd New Zealand, cmdg officer FEA Naval Unit Tinian, Mariannas '42-46. AAAS(F)— Am Phytopath Soc—Mycol Soc Am— Va Acad Sci—Sigma Xi. Plant Industry Station, U.S. Department of Agriculture, Beltsville, Md. H: 6512 40th Av., University Park, Hyattsville, Md.

22 COOK, John Call. Geophysics (Rockets, radar). b'18. BS with honors (Physics) '42 (U Utah); '43-44 (Harvard Extension); '45 (MIT); MS '47 (Physics) PhD 1951 (Geophysics) (Pa State Coll). Research on liquid-fueled rockets; microwave radar; quantitative interpretation of oil-well electric logs; airborne surveys of gamma-ray field; production and measurement gravitational waves; new type vertical teleseismograph. Issued patent in field. Research staff mem MIT Radiation Lab '42-45; with Pa State Coll since '45, research asso since '49. Sigma Pi Sigma—AAAS— Am Geophys Union—Soc Explor Geophys—Sigma Xi. Awarded 3d prize Gravity Research Found essay contest '49. Geophysics Division, Pennsylvania State College, State College, Pa.

23 COOK, Lloyd Allen. Intergroup education; School and community relations). b'99. AB '22 (Franklin Coll); fellow '26-27 (U Chicago); PhD '32 (Ohio State U). Director National College Study in Intergroup Relations American Council on Education '45-49. Author: Community Backgrounds of Education '39; Community Action and the School '41; The Study of Group Relations; also articles in field. Prof and chmn dept educational sociology Wayne U since '47. Am Sociol Soc —Am Ednl Research Assn — Soc Psychol Study Current Social Issues. Wayne University, 5272 Second Av., Detroit 2.

24 COOK, Melvin Alonzo. Physical Chemistry (Explosives). b'11. BA '33 —MA '34 (U Utah); PhD '37 (Yale). Developed the theory of detonation process; carried out theoretical and experimental research on bazooka, research on flotation, adsorption of gases on solids, quantum theory, rates of reactions. Holds patents on ammonium nitrate, oil well, and coal mine explosives, induction heater for shooting explosive rivets. Author articles in field. Prof metall U Utah since '47; cons DuPont Co since '47; cons Western Assn Railroad Executives since '47. Am Chem Soc—Am Inst Metall Engrs —AAAS—Sigma Xi. Loomis fellow '37. 211 Mines Building, University of Utah, Salt Lake City.☉

25 COOK, Norman L. Personnel identification (High speed photographic systems). b'08. '26-30 (Earlham Coll). Granted patent on high speed identification camera. Visual aids cons Kaufmann-Fabry Co '36-37; tech dir Technigraphic Inst '38; indsl photographer since '39. Photographers Assn Am. 111 East 11th St., Anderson, Ind.

10 COOK, Richard K. Sound (Theory, measurement). b'10. BS '31—MS '32—PHD (Physics) '35 (U Ill). Experimental and theoretical research on absolute measurement sound intensity, absorption sound by porous materials, piezoelectric effect in cyrstalline materials, alternating-current bridges. Physicist Nat Bur Standards since '35, chief sound section since '42; instr math physics and applied math US Dept Agr Grad Sch since '41, NBS Grad Sch since '42. Am Phys Soc—Phil Soc Washington — Washington Acad Sci—Acoustical Soc Am—AAAS. Recipient Washington Acad Sci 1949 Award in the Engineering Sciences. National Bureau of Standards, Washington 25. A: 8517 Milford Av., Silver Spring, Md.

11 COOK, Robert C(ecil). Psychology; Education; Biology (Botany). b'03. BS '24 (Mississippi State); AM '33—EdD '42 (Columbia). Editor: Current Science Review '26-28; Presidents in American Colleges and Universities '34. Pres Miss So Coll since '45; Staff officer ASTP Stanford U '43-44; chief curriculum and advisement sects Army Edn Program, United Kingdom Base Hdqrs ETOUSA 44-45. NEA—Am Assn Sch Adminstrs—Pol Sci Assn—AAAS — Phi Delta Kappa—. Mississippi Southern College, Hattiesburg, Mississippi.†☉

12 COOK, Warren Ayer. Air (Determination and control of industrial contaminants); Toxic dusts and gases (Control); Silicosis (Control of contributory conditions); Industrial Hygiene. b'00. AB '23 (Dartmouth); '23-24 (Yale). Member medical advisory committee on healthful working conditions National Association of Manufacturers '41-46, committee on chemistry and toxicology Industrial Hygiene Foundation of America, committee on toxic dusts and gases American Standards Association; chairman engineering control committee National Silicosis Conference '36-37. Author articles: Occupational Disease Hazards—Evaluation in the Field '42; Maximum Allowable Concentrations of Industrial Atmospheric Contaminants '45; Review of Automatic Indicating and Recording Instruments for Determination of Industrial Atmospheric Contaminants '47, and others. Chief indsl hygienist Bur Indsl Hygiene Conn State Dept Health '28-37; dir div indsl hygiene and engring research Zurich-Am Ins Co Chicago since '37; ed Am Indsl Hygiene Assn Quarterly '40-50; asso ed Jour Indsl Hygiene and Toxicology '47-49. Am Indsl Hygiene Assn (past pres)—ACS—Am Pub Health Assn (F, chmn com standard methods of determination atmospheric contaminants '35-37, com on volatile solvents) —Am Soc Safety Engrs. 135 S. La Salle St., Chicago 3.

13 COOK, William Carmichael. Insect ecology and physiology (Cutworms, beet leafhopper, wireworms, pea aphid); Climatic relations of insects. b'95. Student '13-16 (Syracuse U); BS '17 (Cornell U); MS '20—PhD '22 (U Minn). Author articles in field. Entomol div truck crop and garden insects Bur Entomol and Plant Quarantine US Dept Agr since '30. AAAS—Am Assn Econ Entomol—Entomol Soc Am—Ecol Soc Am—Sigma Xi. P.O. Box 616, Walla Walla, Wash.†

14 COOKE, Dennis Hargrove. Education (Principles, teacher education and teacher personnel, school administration). b'04. AB '25—M Ed '28 (Duke U); PhD '30 (George Peabody Coll for Teachers). Served in advisory capacity to large number of university, college and public school boards, administrative officers and presidents; on educational surveys: South Carolina High School Conditions; Greenwood Mississippi City Schools; all North Carolina Baptist Colleges; Baton Rouge parish and city schools; Louisiana State Educational survey; Louisville city schools; Athens Georgia city schools; Darlington County South Carolina city and country schools; Crossett Arkansas city schools. Author: The White Superintendent and the Negro Schools in North Carolina '30; Problems of the Teaching Personnel '33; Practical Problems in Managing Teachers '34; Minimum Essentials of Statistics as Applied to Psychology and Education '36; Principles of School Administration (with Proctor and Hamon) '38; Administering the Teaching Personnel '39; Using Arithmetic, Grades 1-8 '48; and others; also articles in field. Head dept edn, dir summer session The Woman's Coll U NC Greensboro NC since '47. Sou Soc for Philos Psychol Edn—Am Psychol Assn—Am Ednl Research Assn—NEA—NC Edn Assn—Kappa Delta Pi. The Woman's College, University of North Carolina, Greensboro, N.C.☉

15 COOKE, Giles Buckner. Cork and composition cork (Chemistry and properties); Cork trees (Culture). b'97. BS '23 (Coll William & Mary); MS '26 —PhD '29 (U Md). Research on composition cork and cork; developed special liners and coatings for use in closures; special research on adhesives, metal coatings, paper coatings and rubber jar rings; experimental planting of cork trees in United States, studies on growth and stripping. Holds 14 patents in field. Contbr material on cork for Ency of Chem Tech. Research chem Armstrong Cork Co '29-32; asst in chem U Md '32-34; research chem Crown Cork & Seal Co '34-41, dir research and analytical dept since '52. ACS—Alpha Chi Sigma—Sigma Xi—Phi Kappa Phi. Research and Analytical Dept., Crown Cork & Seal Co., Balt 3.

16 COOKE, Morris Llewellyn. Civil engineering; Labor organizations and production. b'72. ME '95—ScD '22 (Lehigh U). Author: Academic and Industrial Efficiency '10; Snapping Cords '15; Our Cities Awake '18; Brazil on the March '44. Co-author: (with Philip Murray) Organized Labor and Production '40. Editor: Public Utility Regulation '22; What Electricity Costs '33. Dir Giant Power Survey Pa '23; chmn Miss Valley Com Pub Works Adminstrn '33; dir water resources sect Nat Resources Bd '34; administr Rural Electrification Adminstrn '35-37; chmn Great Plains Com '36-37; agement '40-41; US expert adjudication Mexican Oil dispute, head Am Tech Mission to Brazil '42; chmn President's Water Resources Policy Commn '50-51. AAAS(F)—ASME(F, council '15)—Franklin Inst—Sigma Xi—Delta Phi. H: St. Georges Rd., Mt. Airy P.O., Phila 19; also New Hope, Bucks County, Pa.☉

17 COOKE, Theodore Frederic. Pigments, dyes, textile finishes. b'13. BS '34 (U Mass); PhD '37 (Yale). Physical chemical research on pigments, including studies of formation mechanisms of inorganic and organic pigments; effect of pigment size, size distribution and crystal form on the optical properties of pigmented films; effect of size and degree of dispersion of pigments on the rheological properties of pigmented vehicles, and effect of adsorbed materials on wetting and dispersion properties of pigments; work on textile finishes including coloring of fabrics with resin-bonded pigments, flame-proofing of textiles, water repellent finishes, mildew-proofing of textiles, and shrinkage control of fabrics; on dyes including studies of mechanism of dyeing, the effect of dyeing assistants on the mechanism of dyeing; spectrophotometric measurements of colors of nature in both visual and infra-red regions of spectrum and methods of duplicating these colors with camouflage paints; also work on protective coatings, coated fabrics. Author articles in field. Research chem Std Oil Dev Co '37-40; research chem Calco Chemical Div Am Cyanamid Co '40-42; dir Materials Lab Engr Bd War Dept '42-45; asst dir phys chem research Calco Chemical Div, Am Cyanamid Co '45-50; asst dir appl research dept since '50. American Inst Chem—Am Chem Soc—Am Assn Textile Chem Colourists—Sigma Xi—Phi Kappa Phi. Calco Chemical Division, American Cyanamid Co., Bound Brook, N.J.†

18 COOKE, William Bridge. Fungi (Ecology and Classification); Mount Shasta (Calif ornia fungi and flora). b'08. BA (U Cincinnati); MS (Ore State Coll); PhD State Coll Wash. In Tropical Deterioration Research Laboratory Philadelphia Quartermaster Depot maintaining culture collection of, doing taxonomic and assay work on, molds isolated from fabrics exposed to tropical conditions '45-46; ten summers' study of fungi and flora of Mount Shasta; research asso dept plant path. Mycol Society Am—Society Plant Taxonomists—Sullivant Moss Soc—Calif Bot Soc—Am Fern Soc—Northwest Sci Assn—Sigma Xi—Gamma Sigma Delta—Phi Sigma. 1014 Broadway, Cincinnati 2.

19 COOKE, W(illiam) Henry. International relations; Intercultural education. b'92. '11-14 (Lawrence Coll); BA '20—MA '21 (Pomona Coll); PhD '28 (Stanford U). Author articles: Joseph Caillaux, Statesman of the Third Republic '44; International Understanding '46; History and International Understanding '46. Co-editor: Readings in European International Relations since 1879 '31. Dir survey of teaching international and intercultural understanding in pub schools California '45; sec Calif Federation Civic Unity '47-48; chmn Los Angeles Conference on Community Relations '47-48; advisory council Pacific Coast Council Intercultural Education '47-48. Asst prof social sci Calif State Coll San Jose '26-27; instr history Pomona Coll Claremont Calif '23-24, asst prof '27-33, asso prof '33-38; prof hist Claremont Grad Sch since '38, dir studies '38-41, dir summer sch '36. AHA—Am Acad Pol Social Sci—Nat Council Social Studies—Phi Beta Kappa. The Claremont Graduate School, Claremont, Calif.

20 COOLIDGE, Harold Jefferson. Primate mammalogy; International conservation; Great apes. b'04. BS '27 (Harvard); student (U Ariz, Cambridge U). Assistant zoologist Harvard African expedition to Liberia and Belgian Congo '26-27; leader Indo-China Division of Kelley-Roosevelt's Field Museum Expedition '28-29; organizer and executive of the Asiatic Primate expedition to Siam and Borneo '37-38; assistant Curator of Mammals MCZ '29-46; chairman panel on nature protection US National Commission for UNESCO since '48; vice president International union for the Protection of Nature. Author: A Revision of the Genus Gorilla; Three Kingdoms of Indo-China; also articles in field. Exec dir Pacific sci bd Natl Research Council, collab Nat Parks Serv '48; asso in mammal Mus of Comparative zool Harvard since '46. Am Geophy Union—Am Soc Phys Anthrop—Am Soc Applied Anthrop—Artic Inst Am—Wildlife Soc—Am Nature Assn—Wilderness Soc—Am Found Tropical Med—Am Soc Mammalogists—Sigma Xi. 2101 Constitution Ave., Washington.

10 COOLIDGE, Warren Algernon. Building materials. born '99 BS (Civil engring) '24 (U Kan); MS '32 (Vanderbilt U). Mortar Studies, Graduation of Sand and Gravel for Concrete Aggregate, Shrinkage of Cinder Block for use in Wall Construction, Weathering tests on Lime Stone Aggregates; method for finding the equation of the elastic line for a beam or column loaded with transverse and longitudinal loads. Staff Vanderbilt U since '25, prof civil engring since '33; dir pub works and city engr Nashville since '45. Am Soc CE—Am Rd Bldrs Assn—Am Pub Works Assn—Nat Soc Profl Engrs—Am Concrete Inst. 300 City Hall, Nashville, Tenn.

11 COOLIDGE, William David. Physical chemistry (Metallurgy of tungsten, Roentgen rays). b'73. BS '96 (MIT); PhD '99 (U Leipzig); and nine honorary degrees US and fgn schools. Author articles in field. Instr in phys chem '01-03, asst prof physicochem research '04-05 MIT; research in physico-chem General Electric Co Schenectady NY '05-07, asst dir research lab '08-28, asso dis '28-32, dir '32-40, vp and dir research '40-44, cons since '44. Am Chem Soc—Am Electrochem Soc—Am Phys Soc—AIEE—Nat Acad Sci—Am Acad Arts and Sci(F)—AAAS—Am Roentgen Ray Soc (hon mem)—Radiol Soc NA—Am Coll Radiology—Am Radium Soc—Nat Acad Exact Phys and Nat Sci. Awarded Rumford medal '14 for invention and application of ductile tungsten; Howard N Potts medal for development of new and improved X-ray tube; Louis Edward Levy medal of Franklin Inst; gold medal of Am Coll of Radiology; medal of award Panama-Pacific Internat Expn '15; Hughes medal of Royal Soc (London) '27; Edison medal, '27; Washington award, Western Soc Engrs '32; John Scott award '37; Faraday medal, Institution of Electrical Engrs of Eng '39; Modern Pioneer award, Nat Assn Mfrs '40; Duddell medal, Phys soc Eng '42; Franklin medal '44; K.C. Li Medal and Award '52. General Electric Co., Schenectady, N.Y.☉

12 COOMBES, Ethel Russell. Coal. Student (George Washington U). Editor the Mining Congress Journal '23-37. Organized national standardization movement to eliminate waste and promote efficiency and economy in mineral production; organized industrial cooperation division American Mining Congress. Est Mechanization Inc '37, publishers of Mechanization the Magazine of Modern Coal, Mechannual the Book of Mechanization Progress, Utilization, magazine of coal uses. 2500 Q St., Washington.

13 COOMES, Ralph Edwin. Power plants (Hydroelectric). b'01. Student '21, '23 (Worcester Poly Inst); '22 (MIT); '51 (Am U). Co-author: Electric Rate Uniformity '35. Hydraulic engr Fed Power Commn '35-42, since '45. Am Mil Engrs—Am Soc CE. H: 4212 46th St., N.W., Washington 16.

14 COON, Carleton Stevens. Ethnology of the Middle East. b'04 AB '25 —MA—PhD '28 (Harvard). Field work in Morocco '24-25, '26-27, '28, '39, '47,

Albania '29, Ethiopia Yemen '33-34; Iraq Iran '48-49; discovered Neanderthal remains in High Cave Tangier Morocco '39. Author: Flesh of the Wild Ox '33; The Riffian '34; Measuring Ethiopia '35; The Races of Europe '39; Principles of Anthropology '42; A Reader in General Anthropology '48; also articles in field. With dept anthrop Harvard '28-48; curator ethnol and prof anthrop U Mus U Pa since '48. Am Anthrop Assn—Am Assn Phys Anthrop—Am Acad Arts Scis. University Museum, Phila.☉

15 COON, Celia Wilson (Mrs). Holly. BS '22 (Ore State Coll); '44-45 (George Washington U). Research on taxonomy, distribution, culture and uses of Ilex genus. Biol teacher high schs '22-27; forest service herbarium '44-51. Am Bot Soc—Wash Bot Soc—Holly Soc Am. H: 428 N. Monroe St., Arlington 1, Va.

16 COON, Nelson. Historical materials on the blind and blindness; Tactual museums for the blind; Growth and culture of fragrant violets. b'95. Student (Union Coll NY). Grower, introducer new varieties of violets to US; curator-librarian Tactual and Historical Museums at Perkins Institution for the Blind Watertown Mass; assists resch workers in all phases relating to education of the blind and social problems. Author: Practical Violet Culture '25; Nursery Sales and Management '31. Author monograph and articles on work with the blind. Partner Rhinebeck Floral Co NY 15 yrs; with Perkins Instn for the Blind Watertown Mass 22 yrs, now librarian. Perkins Institution for the Blind, Blindiana Reference Library, Watertown, Mass.

17 COONS, Arthur Gardiner. Economics (Orient, international); Corporations. b'00. AB '20 (Occidental Coll); AM '22—PhD '27 (U Pa). Member, U. S. Reparations Mission to Japan, '45-46; trustee, American Institute of Pacific Relations since '46; trustee, The Haynes Foundation. Author: The Foreign Public Debt of China '30; Economic Reconstruction in China '34; Five Years of National Finance (China) '34; An Economic and Industrial Survey of the Los Angeles and San Diego Areas '41. Pres Occidental Coll since '46; Ednl Film Research Inst (pres '46-47)—Pacific Coast Econ Assn (pres '40)—Am Econ Assn—Am Acad Polit Social Sci—Social Sci Research Conf (Pacific Coast group, pres '41)—Phi Beta Kappa. Awarded research fellow Calif Coll in China Found '33-34. Occidental College, LA 41.☉

18 COOPER, Alfred Morton. Yachting; Automobile trailering. b'90. Student U Wash '18-20. Conversion of small yachts sail and power into comfortable homes afloat and cruising in ocean or inland waterways. Trailer travel and equipment of trailer coach for comfortable living. Author: The Cruising Yacht '45; Cruising to Florida '46; Coast-wise Yacht Cruising '48; The Cruising Book '51; The Trailer Book '50. Free-lance author since '38. Postoffice Box 444, Desert Center, Calif.

19 COOPER, Byron Nelson. Geology and mineral resources of the Appalachian Valley region; Engineering and Economic Geology of Virginia; Stratigraphy. b'12. AB '34 (DePauw U); MS '35—PhD '37 (U Ia.). Geological consultant on development of natural resources of Virginia, studies of economic geology of high-calcium limestone. Author articles: Lower Middle Ordovician Stratigraphy of the Shenandoah Valley, Virginia '46; Geology

and Mineral Resources of the Burkes Garden Quadrangle, Virginia '44; Industrial Limestones and Dolomites of Virginia '45; Industrial Limestones and Dolomites of the Clinch Valley District, Virginia '48, and others. Asst prof geol U Wichita '37-42; field geol Va Geol Surveys summers '38-42; asso geol Va Geol Survey '42-45; paleontol US Natl Mus '45-46; prof and head geol dept Va Poly Inst since '46. Geol Soc Am(F)—AAAS(F)—Sigma Xi—Paleontol Soc—Va Acad Sci—SPEE. Virginia Polytechnic Institute, Blacksburg, Va.†☉

20 COOPER, Chalmer L(ewis). Micropaleontology and stratigraphy; Geology of Oklahoma and Illinois. b'98. BS '23—MS '26 (U Okla); PhD '45 (U Chicago). Supervised construction of engineering projects related to geologic features in state and national parks in Michigan, Wisconsin, Illinois and Indiana. Author: Coal in Oklahoma '26; Chester Ostracodes '42, Pennsylvania Ostracodes '46; Kinderhook Micropaleontology '47, and others. Chief geol, asst dir Okla Geol Survey '25-31; geol supervisor Nat Park Serv '35-37; geol Ill Geol Survey '37-46; geol US Geol Survey since '46, chmn publns com. Geol Soc Am(F)—AAAS(F)—Paleontol Soc(F)—Geolog Soc Washington—Am Assn Petroleum Geologists—Society Economic Geologists and Paleontol—Paleontol Society Washington—Sigma Xi—Ill and Okla Acads Sci. U.S. Geological Survey, Washington 25. H: 9012 2nd Av., Silver Spring, Md.

21 COOPER, D(elmer) C(lair). Cytology. b'96. AB '16 DSc '48 (Morningside Coll); MS '26 (Purdue U); PhD '30 (U Wis). Research in endosperm and seed development in certain angiospems. Author articles in field. With U Wis since '30, now prof genetics. Bot Soc Am—Genetics Soc Am—Ind Acad Sci —Wis Acad Sci Arts Letters—AAAS— Sigma Xi. 103 Genetics Building, University of Wisconsin, Madison 6, Wis.

22 COOPER, Franklin Dixon. Dams (Earth, concrete construction, design); Floods (Control engineering, dams, channels); Factories (Rehabilitation). b'09. BS '31—MS '31 (Civil engring) '32 (Case Tech Cleveland); '32-33 (Stanford); '33-35 (O State U); '34 (Carnegie Tech). Design and development cantilever type sheet pile flood walls, reinforcement around openings in gravity dams, earth dams on previous foundations, earthquake dam, gravity concrete and earth dams; development stress analysis by photoelasticity; rehabilitation abandoned factories, redesign factories for manufacture new products; precise altimeter surveys for flood control, pipe-lines, transmission lines. Author articles: Conveyors Their Design and Application; Stress Analysis by Photoelasticity, and others. Asst plant engr Easy Washing Machine Corp Syracuse NY; now cons engr De Witt NY. Civil engr corps AUS World War II. Am Soc CE—Am Soc ME—Nat Soc Professional Engrs—Am Soc Mil Engrs—Internat Navigation Assn Congress—Sigma Xi. 321 Lansdowne Rd., De Witt, N.Y.

23 COOPER, Franklin Seaney. Speech analysis and synthesis; Blind aids. b '08. BS '31—'31-34 (U Ill); PhD '36 (MIT). Research on sensory devices and design and testing of guidance aids and reading machines for blind. Co-author: (with P. A. Zahl) Research on Guidance Devices and Reading Machines for the Blind '47. Contributor: Blindness: Modern Approaches to the Unseen Environment '50. Research engr Gen Elec Research Lab Schenectady NY '36-39; asso research dir Haskins Labs since 39; sr liaison officer OSRD '41-46. AAAS—APS—Acoustical Soc Am—Inst Radio Engrs—Sigma Xi. Haskins Laboratories, 305 East 43d St., N.Y.C. 17.

10 COOPER, G(ustav) Arthur. Fossil brachiopods; Devonian and Ordovician stratigraphy. b'02. BS '24—MS '26 (Colgate U); PhD '29 (Yale). Co-author: (with Charles Schuchert) Brachiopod Genera of the Suborders Orthoidea and Pentameroidea '32; (with E O Ulrich) Ozarkian and Canadian Brachiopoda '38. Research asst and asso Yale U '28-30; asst curator stratigraphic paleontol US Nat Mus '30-43, curator div invertebrate paleontol and paleobot since '43. Geol Soc Am(F). U.S. National Museum, Washington 25. H: 3425 Porter St., Washington 16.†

11 COOPER, La Mar Smith. Refrigerators (Household); Home freezers. b'98. BS (elec engring) '21 (Pa State Coll); '30-31 (U Pa). Research, design, development and testing of two-temperature refrigerators with one and two units, butter conditioners, refrigerator and freezer door strikes and door breaker strips, lightweight refrigerator cabinets. Engr Gen Elec Co '23-28, '34-47; engr Phila Rural. Transit Co '28-32; automotive engr Hoffmann Beverage Co '32-34; chief engr Amana Refrigeration Inc since '47. Am Inst EE—Am Soc Refrigeration Engrs (chmn A-1 tech com '51). Amana Refrigeration Inc., Amana, Ia. H: 724 19th St., S.E., Cedar Rapids, Ia.

12 COOPER, Weldon. Local government (Finance, civil service, police administration, charters, university research programs); Texas (Local government); Alabama (Local government); Virginia (Local government). b'06. BA '26 (Abilene Christian Coll); MA '32 (U Tex); PhD '39 (U Chicago). Studied government of metropolitan area of Birmingham and Jefferson County, Alabama; Study of urban local government in Texas, consultant to several Texas cities on problems of organization and administration; Consultant for Virginia cities and departments of state government, particularly on state and local revenues and expenditures and organization and methods. Asst dir Bur Municipal Research U Tex '35-37; asst prof polit sci U Ala '38-40, prof '46-47; administrative analyst US Bur Budget '41-44, '45-46; prof polit sci and asso dir bur pub administration U Va since '47; exec asst Gov Va since '50. Am Polit Sci Assn—Am Soc Pub Administration—So Polit Sci Assn (vice pres '47-48)—Nat Municipal League—Va Social Sci Assn. 29 Rotunda, University of Virginia, Charlottesville, Va.☺

13 COOPER, William Cecil. Plants (Root-forming hormones); Citrus fruits (Salt tolerance. growth hormones, forcing). b'09. BS '29 (U Md); MS '36—PhD '38 (Calif Inst Tech). Research on existence of root-forming substances other than conventional plant growth substances; use of growth substances for rooting ornamental plants, citrus and sub-tropical fruits, cinchona, derris, and cube; distribution of auxin in citrus; comparative salt tolerance of various citrus rootstocks and scions; comparative influence of excess added salt on uptake of anions and cations; induced premature flowering of pineapples with ethylene and acetylene, and of cube and juvenile citrus seedlings by girdling. With BPISAE USDA since '29, physiol from '46, hort Office Foreign Agrl Relations Puerto Rico, Peru for USDA '43-44. Am Assn Hort Sci—Am Bot Soc—Am Soc Plant Physiol—Fla State Hort Soc—Calif Avocado Soc

—Tex Avocado Soc. Box 241, Weslaco, Tex.

14 COOVER, Mervin S. Electrical Engineering (Brush wear, special problems, foreign electrification, inductive interference, load dispatching). b'90. EE '14 (Rensselaer Poly Inst). Research on theory of speed-time curve, automatic electrical equipment, measures of electrical brush disintegration. Author articles: Lighting for Highway Safety '38; New Developments in Street and Highway Lighting and Their Importance in a Highway Safety Program '36; and others. Prof and head dept elec engring Ia State Coll since '35. AIEE—Am Soc Engring Edn—Ia Engring Soc—Phi Kappa Phi—Tau Beta Pi—Eta Kappa Nu—Sigma Tau. Received John Dunlap Meml Award, Ia Engring Soc '38. Electrical Engineering Department Iowa State College, Ames, Ia.†

15 COPE, Oliver Brewern. Fishery biology (Insecticides); Entomology. b'16. AB '38—MA '40—PhD '42 (Stanford U). Represented US Fish and Wildlife Service summer '47 with Alaska Mosquito Control Project. Author articles in field. Aquatic biol US Fish and Wildlife Service since '46. Now chief Rocky Mountain Investigations US Fish and Wildlife Service, Logan Utah. Entomologist US Navy World War II. Society American Fisheries—Limncl Society Am—Entomol Society Am—Sigma Xi. Forestry Bldg., Utah State Agricultural College, Logan, Utah.†

16 COPE, Stanley R. Die design. b'07. Student pub sch. Specialize in design, building and operation of all types of sheet-metal dies for cutting, bending, forming, drawing, etc; authority on deep drawing all shapes of shells from steel, stainless steel, nickel and nickel alloys, aluminum, magnesium, copper, brass, and other metals. Author: Die Design Engineering: Vol 1 Cutting Dies; Vol 2 Bending and Forming Dies; Vol 3 Drawing Dies; Vol 4 Squeezing Operations, Assembling Dies, Estimating; Tool Design Engineering: Vol 1 Drill Press Operations; Vol 2 Milling and Surfacing Oprations; Vol 3 Turning, Boring, Grinding, and Threading Operations; Vol 4, Assembly Fixtures, Welding and Gaging Practices; also articles in field. Die engr Acklin Stamping Co Toledo O '28-31; chief die engr Bendix Products Div Bendix Aviation Corp South Bend Ind '31-36; founded Acme Sch Die Design Engring '36; schs South Bend, Dayton O, Chicago, Detroit, courses in tool and die design engring resident schs or by correspondence; founded Colfax Tool Engring Co South Bend '38; cons engr pressed-metal and stamping industries. Am Soc Tool Engrs (past chmn Chap No. 30)—Soc for Engring Edn. 129 W. Colfax Av., South Bend 1, Ind. H: 519 Parkovash Av., South Bend 17.

17 COPELAND, Frederick Cleveland. Corn genetics (Growth rates in inbred and hybrid embryos). b'12. BA '35 (Williams Coll); MA '37—PhD '40 (Harvard); '35-36 (U Munich Germany). Research in connection with growth rates in inbred and hybrid corn embryos, chromosome aberrations in endosperm of maize '40, Instr biol Trinity Coll Hartford '40-46; ast prof biol and dir admissions Williams Coll since '46. Genetics Soc Am. Williams College, Williamstown, Mass.†

18 COPELAND, John Andrew. Climate (Summaries); Weather (Machine tabulation of data). b'08. BA '29 (Daniel Baker College); MA '33 (Texas Tech College). Developed new types of cli-

matological summaries giving more specific and detailed weather and climate information to industry, commerce, business and agriculture, developed new techniques for handling large volumes of weather data. Meteorol US Weather Bur since '37. Am Meteorol Soc—Am Geophysical Union. US Dept Commerce Citation for "Outstanding leadership in design and implementation of machine tabulation program for climatological records." United States Weather Bureau, 24th and M Sts., N.W., Washington 25.

19 COPELAND, John Thomas. Soil and water (Conservation); Erosion pattern (Principles of). b'91. BSA '15 (Purdue U); summer '30 (U Mo); '32, '49 (State Coll Miss). Interval and direction pattern in terrace grade relation; mechanical and physical relationship with erosion pattern. Extension agrl engr State Coll Agr and US DA since '19. Am Soc Agrl Engrs. Agricultural Extension Service, Mississippi State College, State College, Miss.

20 COPELAND, Morris A. Money flows; National income; Value theory. b'95. AB '17 (Amherst Coll); PhD '21 (U Chicago). Research on national income; impact of war on civilian consumption in United States, United Kingdom, Canada; Sources and uses of railroad funds; income size distribution; wholesale prices; monopolistic competition; equation of exchange; government procurement; development of War Production Board and combined indexes of war production. Author articles in field. With Cornell U '21-30, last position prof econ; prof econ U Mich '30-36; cons fellow Robert Brookings Grad Sch Econ and Govt '27-28; spl staff mem nat income Nat Bur Econ Research Inc '27-28; price analyst Fedl Reserve Bd '29; exec sec Central Statis Bd '33-35, '36-39; dir research US Bur Budget '39-40; chief munitions branch WPB and predecessor agencies '40-45; mem staff Nat Bur Econ Research Inc '45-47; spl cons Fedl Reserve System '47-48; prof Johns Hopkins U '47-48; Cornell U since '49. Am Econ Assn (vp '48)—Am Statis Assn (F, vp '36)—Nat Planning Assn—Inst De Science Economique Appliquee, Paris (fgn corr mem)—US Conf on Resch in Income and Wealth—Internat Assn Research in Income and Wealth. Cornell University, Ithaca, N. Y.

21 COPELAND, Paul L. Electrons (Secondary emission, microscopy). b'05. BA '27 (Neb Wesleyan U); MS '30—PhD '31 (Ia State U). Research in secondary emission of electrons '27-31, anode effect '38-40, stability of mercury arcs since '39, application of the electron microscope since '42; cooperative programs with Metallurgical Laboratory University of Chicago '44-45, Burgess Battery Company '45-46, Elgin National Watch Company '46-47; electron diffraction studies of sapphire crystals '46-47 Co-inventor of pool type cathodes for use at low currents. Asst professor phys Mont State Coll '34-37; asso prof phys Armour Inst '37-42; phys Armour Research Found '37-39; prof phys dir electronics research Ill Inst Tech since '43. Am Phys Soc(F) — Am Assn Phys Teachers — Phi Kappa Phi—Sigma Xi. Illinois Institute of Technology, Chicago 16.☺

22 COPENHAVER, James Earl. Industrial organic chemistry. b'06. AB '20 (Emory and Henry Coll); MS '23 (Vanderbilt U); PhD '26 (Johns Hopkins). Research paper chemistry, textile carriers, cones tubes. Author articles in field. Assoc prof chemistry U SC '26-37, prof '37-42; chemist

Sonoco Products Co Hartsville SC '42-47, chief chemist since '47. Am Chem Soc—SC Acad Sci (vp '41 '46)—So Assn Sci and Industry—Sigma Xi, Phi Beta Kappa—Gamma Alpha. Sonoco Products Co Hartsville, SC.©

10 CORBETT, James Arthur. Paleography; Alchemy. b'08. AB '29 (Georgetown U); archiviste-paléographe '35 (Ecole Nationale des Chartes, Paris); '30-32 (L'école des Hautes Etudes, Paris). Author: Catalogue des manuscrits alchimiques des bibliothèques publiques de France. Vol. I. Les manuscrits des bibliothèques publiques de Paris '39. Co-editor: Allegoriae super Tabernaculum Moysi Petri Pictaviensis '38. Co-translator: La Grande crise de la troisième république by Yves R Simon published as The Road to Vichy '42. Instr and asso prof medieval hist U Notre Dame since '35. Am Catholic Hist Assn—Com de Bibliographie, Académie internationale de l'histoire des sciences. 818 E. Miner St., South Bend 17, Ind.

11 CORBIN, Ludlow Vincent. Chemistry of preparing biological specimens. b'15. ThB—AB '44 (Marion Coll); '46 (Ball State Coll); '42-43 (Harvard). Research on clearing, staining and plastic embedding of biological specimens. Asso prof sci Cascade Coll since '47. 705 N. Killingsworth, Portland 11, Ore.

12 CORBIN, Milford Howard. Chemistry of protective coatings. b'02 ChemE '25 (Lehigh). Author articles: Electrodeposition of Non-Metallic Materials '29; Application of .Finishing Materials on Zinc '33; Decorative Effects with Organic Finishes '37; and others. Dir research Electro Chemical Engraving Co '27-29; dir lacquer lab Ault & Wiborg Corp Div Interchemical Corp '29-32; dir research Arco Co '32-37; vp and dir research Standard Varnish Works-Toch Brothers Inc '37-49, pres since '49; mem bd dir Metal Litho Co, Standard Varnish Works. Am Inst Chem(F)—Am Soc Testing Materials (D1 com)—NY Paint, Varnish, Lacquer Assn. Standard Varnish Works, 2600 Richmond Terrace, Staten Island 3, N.Y. H: 6 West 77th St., NYC 24.

13 CORBITT, David Leroy. Archives; North Carolina history. b'95. BA '24 (U NC). Compiler, editor historical collections; history of public buildings; assistant managing editor, North Carolina Historical Review '26-35; managing editor since '35. Author The Formation of North Carolina Counties, 1663-1943. Calendar clk state dept archives and hist Raleigh NC '24-25, chief library asst '25-45, in charge archives '26-45, head div publs since '45; Soc Am Archivists—Am Assn State and Local Hist—So Hist Assn—Soc Co Hist—Hist Soc NC. Box 1881, Raleigh, N.C.

14 CORBITT, Duvon Clough. Colonial history of Cuba and Latin America, Tennessee and the Old Southwest. b'01. Student '18-20 (Meridian Coll); AB '23 (Asbury Coll); MA '26 (Emory U); '26-27 (Ga Sch Tech); PhD '38 (U NC). Research in Cuban libraries and archives on colonial history of Latin America and Spanish influence on U.S. research projects on population changes in Cuba before and after independence; since '37, translating and editing documents from Spanish archives on Tennessee and Old Southwest, for East Tennessee Historical Society. Author: The Colonial Government of Cuba '38; The Chinese in Cuba '44; also articles in field. Prof Candler Coll Habana Cuba '27-29, '31-43, 45-46; head hist dept

Columbia Coll, Columbia SC '43-45; chmn div social studies Asbury Coll Wilmore Ky since '46; fraternal del for Duke U and The Hispanic Am Hist Review to El Primer Congreso Nacional de Historia, Habana, Cuba, '42. AHA—So Hist Assn—Royal Soc Arts—Sociedad Cubana de Estudios Historicos é Internacionales—Academia de la historia de Cuba—Ga Hist Soc. Asbury College, Wilmore, Ky. H: Hughes Av., Bromley Addition.†

15 CORBITT, Willis Gregg. Surveying. b'92. BS '20 (U Wash Seattle). Location and restoration section corners; identification timber cruisers and surveyor's marks found at section corners in California, Oregon, and Washington. Logging engr Cherry Valley Timber Co Carnation Wash '20; logging and forestry engr Pacific Lumber Co Scotia Calif '21-33; forest tech Calif Div Forestry Sacramento '34-35; foreman forestry USDA and US Dept Interior Mendocino Calif '35-39; logging engr Crown Zellerbach Corp since '39. Xi Sigma Pi—Soc Am Foresters. Licensed engr and land surveyor Calif, Ore. Crown Zellerbach Corp., Molalla, Ore.

16 CORCORAN, George Francis. Electrical networks. b'00. BS '23 (SD State Coll); MS '26 (U Minn); '37 (U Mich); '42 (MIT). Research in induction motor design and non-linear circuit behavior. Author: Basic Electrical Engineering '49. Co-author: Introduction to Electric Transients '36; Alternating-Current Circuits '38; Electrical Engineering Experiments '39. Asst prof elec engring Kan State Coll '29-31; asso prof elec engring State U Ia '31-39, prof '39-41; prof and chmn elec engring U Md since '41; adv ed Pitman Pub Corp '47-49. AIEE—Inst Radio Engrs—Instrument Soc Am—ASEE—Sigma Xi—Tau Beta Pi. Electrical Engineering Department, University of Maryland, College Park. Md.†©

17 CORCORAN, Thomas Francis. Latin America (Census and statistics). b'07. AB '29—AM '32 (Yale); Certificate '31 (U de Toulouse), '39 (U Calif). Organization and administration statistical and census offices in Panama, Paraguay, Guatemala, Costa Rica, Honduras, El Salvador. Author: Statistics in Guatemala '45; Statistics in Costa Rica '47. Author articles: Crecimiento de la Poblacon de la Republica de Panamá; An agricultural census in Panama. Dir gen statis and census Panama '41-44; prof statis Inter-Am U Panama, '42-44; statis assignments for Office Coordinator of Inter-Am Affairs Paraguay and Honduras '45, Inter-Am Development Commn Guatemala '45, Panama and Paraguay '46; chief consultation and training Office Coordinator Internat Statis Bur Census since '46. Am Statis Assn—AAAS—Population Assn Am—Cath Econ Assn. Bureau of the Census, Department of Commerce, Washington 25.

18 CORDASCO, Francesco. Tobias Smollett; Junius. AB '42 (Columbia); B en L '43 (U de Madrid); PhD '44 (U de Salamanca); MA '45 (NYU). Author: Ensayo sobre las obras de Smollett y la Gil Blas de Le Sage '44; Handbook for Research: a Bibliographical Manual '48; A Junius Bibliography '49; also articles in field. Editor: Smollett en Espana '43. Asso paleography and com lit U de Salamanca '42-44; asst prof Eng LI U '46-49, asso since '49. Mod Lang Assn Am—Instituto de Filologia Espanola—Nat Assn Teachers Eng—Am Assn Teachers Eng—Am Assn Teachers Spanish and Portuguese—Academia Reale Espanola.

Long Island University, Brooklyn. H: 6606 Jackson St., West New York, N.J.

19 CORDELL, Richard Albert. Literature (Dramatic); Modern drama. b'96. BA '17—MA '25 (Ind U); '30-31 (U London). Author: Representative Modern Plays '28; Henry Arthur Jones and the Modern Drama '32; Twentieth Century Plays '34; W Somerset Maugham '37; Twentieth Century Plays, British, American, and Continental, 47; also articles in field. Staff Purdue U since '19, prof Eng since '38. Purdue University, West Lafayette, Ind. H: 2001 Union St., Lafayette.©

20 CORE, Earl L(emley). West Virginia vascular plants; Genus Scleria and Paronychia in North America; Siphonychia. b'02. AB '26—MA '28 (W Va U); PhD '36 (Columbia). Botanist Colombian Cinchona Mission Foreign Economic Administration Bogota Colombia '43-45; Editor: Castanea since '36; Wild Flower since '46. Author: (with others) Common Seed Plants of the Mid-Appalachian Region '31; (with B R Weimer) A New Manual for the Biology Laboratory '44; also articles in field. Prof bot W Va U since '40; chmn dept biol since '48. AAAS—Bot Soc Am—W Va Acad Sci. Department of Biology, West Virginia University, Morgantown W. Va.†©

21 COREY, Albert Bickmore. New York history; Canadian-American relations. b'98. AB '22—AM '23 (Acadia U); AM '24 (Harvard); fellow '24-25 (U Toronto); fellow '31-32—PhD '34 (Clark U). Author: The Crisis of 1830-1842 in Canadian-American Relations '41; also articles in field. State Hist NY State since '44. NY State Hist Assn (trustee)—Am Assn State and Local Hist (dir)—Am Scenic and Hist Preservation Soc (trustee)—NY Hist Soc. Education Building, Albany, N.Y.†

22 COREY, Cyrus Stanley. Interstate commerce. b'08. AB '28 (Colby Coll); AM '31—PhD '33 (U Ill). Studies in legal decisions and economic background state taxation of interstate commerce. Asso prof bus and econ Keuka Coll '34-35, prof 31-37; asso prof econ Kent State U '37-43, prof since '46. Am Econ Assn—Nat Tax Assn—Tax Inst. Kent State University, Kent, O.

23 COREY, Stephen Maxwell. Educational psychology (Curriculum, American high school, adolescence). b'04. BS '26 (Eureka Coll Ill); fellow '26-28—MA '27—PhD '30 (U Ill); '35 (U Chicago). Author: (with others) Adolescence '44; The American High School '46; Schools for a New World '47; General Education in the American High School '42; also articles in field. Prof edn, exec officer Horace Mann-Lincoln Inst Sch Experimentation Teachers Coll Columbia U since '48. Am Psychol Assn(F)—Nat Soc Study Edn—NEA (bd dirs Asso Supervision and Curriculum Dir '44-48; pres dept audio-visual instrn '47-48)—Sigma Xi. 170 Reldyes Av., Leonia, N.J.©

24 CORFITZEN, William Edward. Land reclamation; Irrigation; Sedimentation. b'08. BS '32 (Worcester Poly Inst) LLB '39 (U Denver). Studies of sedimentation and silting of irrigation canals and reservoirs; density current studies Lake Mead; engineering financial and legal analysis of reclamation projects. With US Bur Reclamation '33-47; US State Dept '47-48; US Economic Cooperation Administrn since '48. U.S. Embassy, Rome, Italy.

10 CORKUM, Howard David. Textile industrial research. b'93. PhB '17 (Brown U). Research on cloth finishing; technician in dyestuff laboratory; superintending dyeing and finishing; reseach in dyestuffs, thread finishes, fibre strengths, seam strengths; manufacturing viscose rayon. Chief chem supt Sayles Finishing Co Saylesville RI '17-19; tech rep dyestuff lab EI du Pont de Nemours & Co Wilmington Del '19-'22; chief chem supt dyeing finishing Amoskeag Mfg Co, Manchester NH '23-36; dir research Am Thread Co NYC since '43. Am Chem Soc—Assn Research Dirs—Am Assn Textile Chem and Colorists—Am Soc Testing Materials. American Thread Company, Willimantic, Conn. H: 332 Prospect St.

11 CORLISS, Carlton Jonathan. Railway history. b'88. Student '04-05 (Ricker Classical Inst). Research on history of Illinois Central Railroad, transportation progress in Illinois. Author: Main Line of Mid-America '50; Trails to Rails '35; The Human Side of Railroading; The Story of American Railway Development '46; also articles in field. Contributor: Americana Annual '45, '46, '47; World Book Cyclopedia '47, 48. Asso ed Ill Central Magazine '25-34, asst pub relations '34-36, hist '48-50; mgr pub sect Assn Am RR '37-47, since '50. Ry and Locomotive Hist Soc—Ia Hist Soc—Miss Hist Soc. 735 Transportation Building, Washington 6.

12 CORNELIUS, Donald Risdon. Forage crops; Range reseeding. b'14. BS '35—MS '38 (Kans State Coll Agr and Applied Sci); PhD '49 (U Nebr). Studies of grasses and legumes with view to use in revegetation of cultivated or abandoned land for control of erosion, production of forage; research on methods of producing seed of native and recently introduced foreign forage plants, on eradication of range brush and weeds. Author articles in field. Range conservationist Calif Forest and Range Expt Sta US Forest Service since '46. Ecol Soc Am—Am Soc Agron—Soc Range Management—Gamma Sigma Delta—Sigma Xi. California Forest and Range Experiment Station, University of California, Forestry Building, Post Office Box 245, Berkeley 1.

13 CORNELIUS, Roberta Douglas. Medieval allegory; English Romantic movement. b'90. AB '09 (Randolph-Macon Woman's Coll); AM '16 (U Chicago); PhD '30 — resident fellow '26-27 (Bryn Mawr Coll). Editor: The Castell of Pleasure, an early sixteenth-century poem by William Nevill '30; Le Songe du Castel, an Old French allegorical poem, PMLA '31. Author: The Figurative Castle '30; also articles in field. Prof Eng Randolph-Macon Woman's Coll since '37. Modern Lang Assn Am—Medieval Acad Am—Coll Eng Assn—Poetry Soc Va—Phi Beta Kappa. Helene and Cecil Rubel fellow for study abroad '27-28. Randolph-Macon Woman's College, Lynchburg, Va. H: No. 4, Parkmont Apartments.

14 CORNELL, Francis Griffith. Education (School administration and finance). b'06. Student (Ohio Wesleyan U); AB '27—MA '31—PhD '36 (Columbia). Education expert US Senate committee on labor and public welfare '47. Author articles in field. Prof edn and dir Bur Research and Service Coll Edn U Ill since '47. NEA—Am Ednl Research Assn—Nat Soc Study Edn—Am Assn Sch Adminstrs—AAAS —Am Statis Assn—Inst Math Statis— Am Acad Polit Social Sci—Soc Adv Edn—Ill Edn Assn. College of Education, University of Illinois, Urbana, Ill.

15 CORNELL, Herbert Watson. Civil Service law (Judicial interpretation). b'84. Student '04-07 (U Pa); AB '08 (U Colo); LLB '19 (George Washington U). Chief examiner and sec Colo Civil Service Commn '09-12; tech examiner US Civil Service Commn '12-20; admitted Wis bar '20; asst chief examiner and sec City Civil Service Commn Milwaukee '20-24, chief examiner since '24; vp Civil Service Assembly US and Can '26-27; chmn Central States Regional Conf Civil Service Commns '29-31. Am Soc Pub Adminstrn—Milwaukee Bar Assn (com on adminstrv tribunals)—Am Polit Sci Assn City Hall, Milw 2.

16 CORNELL, James Irving. Electronic components (Capacitors, transformers, rectifiers). b'03. BS '25 (Worcester Poly Inst); '39-41 (Stevens Inst Tech); '26-28 (Union Coll). Author articles in field. Sect engr receiver div RCA Victor div Camden NJ '29-34; dir, chief engr Magnavox Co Fort Wayne '34-38; vp engring, chief engr, dir Solar Mfg Corp N Bergen NJ '38-49; mgr prodn, prodn engring div Vickers Electric Div since '49. Am Inst EE—St Louis Engrs Club —Inst Radio Engrs. Vickers Electric Division, 1815 Locust St., St. Louis 3. H: 930 Wood Ave., Kirkwood 22.

17 CORNELL, Russell Todd. Lead and Zinc (Mining, exploration, mine evaluation); production Sulphuric acid and Smelting of Zinc. b'79. EM '01 (Columbia). Development and operation of Aquilar Mine, Province Jujuy Argentina; vp and dir Compania Minera Aquilar Compania "Sulfacid" and Compania "Austral", Argentina '41-50. Contributor: International Encyclopedia (2nd edit). Mine evaluation L Vogelstein & Co '05-08; mine examinations Adolph Lewisohn & Sons '08-14; mgr exploration dept St Joseph Lead Co '17-41. AIMME—Mining and Metall Soc Am. H: 157 Brewster Rd., Scarsdale, N.Y.†

18 CORNETT, Richard Orin. Electronics; Acoustics. b'13. BS '34 (Okla Baptist U); MS '37 (U Okla); PhD '40 (U Tex); '38-39 (U Ill). Instr physics Okla Baptist U '35-37, advanced to prof '41; asst supervisor physics Pa State Engring, Sci, Management, Defense Training Program '41-42; lecturer electronics Harvard '42-45; spl research asso OSRD '45; asst to pres Okla Baptist U '45-46, vp since '46. Author: Practical Physics (with White, Weber, Manning) '43; Electron Tubes and Circuits (with ten others) '47. Am Assn U Profs— Acoustical Soc Am. Am Assn Physics Teachers. 624 University Parkway, Shawnee, Okla.

19 CORNWELL, Ralph Thomas Kline. Cellophane. b'98. BChem '18— PhD '25 (Cornell U); '26-27 (Inst for Chem, U Munich)—'27 (U Graz). Research on organic syntheses, quantitative organic microanalysis, moisture vapor transmission testing, research, organization and management. Holds 35 patents related to regenerated cellulose films and/or moisture vapor proof coatings and miscellaneous subjects. Asst prof organic chem U Pittsburg '27-29; sr microanalyst quantitative organic Nat Inst of Health USPHS Washington '29-30; dir research Sylvania Indsl Corp Fredericksburg Va '30-46, mem bd dirs '44-46; dir research Sylvania Div Am Viscose Corp Marcus Hook Pa since '46. Am Inst Chem(F)—AAAS(F)—Am Chem Soc—Soc Chem Industry—Indsl Research Inst—Chem Club of NY—Sigma Xi—Phi Kappa Phi—Gamma Alpha. —Union League Phila. Sylvania Division, American Viscose Corporation, Marcus Hook, Pa.

20 CORRE, Mary Price. Vocational guidance; Occupational research. b'94. BA '18 (U Cincinnati); MA '27 (U Mich); '21-22 (NY Sch Social Work). Served as research worker White House Conference study on vocational guidance '32; staff associate National Occupational Conference '37-38. Author: Metal Industries in Cincinnati '24; Metal Industries in Cleveland '25, and others; also articles in field. Supervisor div counseling services Cincinnati Pub Schs since '26. Nat Vocational Guidance Assn (pres '40)— O Edn Assn—NEA—Am Assn Social Worker. Board of Education, 216 E. Ninth St., Cincinnati 2, O.

21 CORRELL, Donovan Stewart. Orchids (North Carolina, Florida, Texas, West Indian, Guatemalan, North and South American, Taxonomy); Ferns (Florida, Texas, southeastern United States, North Carolina, Louisiana, taxonomy); Louisiana plants; African oil palm; Vanilla; Mexican wild potatoes. AB '34 —AM '36—PhD '39 (Duke U); '38 (U Vt), '38-39—Anna C Ames Memorial Scholarship (Harvard). Author articles in field. Bot Bur Plant Industry Soils and Agrl Engring Div Plant Exploration and Introduction US Dept Agr since '47. Am Fern Soc— NE Bot Club—Am Hort Soc—Am Soc Plant Taxonomists. Received NC Acad Sci award '36; Guggenheim Memorial Fellowship '46-47. Bureau of Plant Industry, Soils and Agricultural Engineering, Division Plant Exploration and Introduction, U.S. Department of Agriculture, Beltsville, Md.†

22 CORRY, Andrew Vincent. Economic geology and mineral economics. b'04. Student '22-24 (Carroll Coll); AB '26 (Harvard); BA '29 (Rhodes Scholar)—BS '30—MA '34 (Oxford); MS '31 (Mont Sch Mines). Made special studies in field School of Metalliferous Mining, Camborne, Cornwall, England; extensive research in Latin American and Asian mineral deposits; investigated gold deposits in various areas; studied mineral industry in relation to output. Author articles in field. Engr in chge prospecting parties Argentina, Brazil, Bolivia for Arminas, Buenos Aires Argentina '39-40; cons price stabilization unit Advisory Commn Council Nat Defense '40; Office Coordinator Comml and Cultural Relations between Am Republics Washington '40-41 mem mission foreign liaison div Lend-Lease Admnstrn '43; Far East Enemy Br Foreign Econ Admnstrn '43-44; spl asst and chief mineral advisor US Foreign Econ Admnstrn New Delhi office '44-46; cons and special asst office Dir Am Republic Affairs Dept State, '46-47; Minerals Attaché, American Embassies in India, Pakistan, Burma, Ceylon, and Legation in Nepal since '47. Am Inst Mining Metall Engrs—AAAS—NY Acad Sci—Oxford Soc—Geol Soc London(F). c/o American Foreign Service, Department of State, Washington.☉

23 CORT, William Walter. Parasitology; Hookworm disease; Helminthology; Trematodes; Tropical medicine, Ascariasis. b'87. AB '09 (Colo Coll); AM '11—fellow '13-14—PhD '14 (U Ill); ScD (hon) '46 (U NC). Director commission International Health Division Rockefeller Foundation for investigation of hookworm disease Trinidad BWI '21, Puerto Rico '22, China '23-24, Panama '26; director five-year program '27-32 for study of ascariasis in children National Research Council and American Child Health Assn. Co-author: (with R W Hegner) Diagnosis of Protozoa and Worms Parasitic in Man '21; (with

R W Hegner and F M Root) Outlines of Medical Zoology '23; also articles in field. Asst prof zoology U Calif '16-19; cons helminthologist Calif State Bd of Health '17-19; asso prof helminthology Sch Hygiene and Pub Health Johns Hopkins '19-25, prof helminthology '25-42, prof parasitol since '42; vis prof parasitol Peking China Union Med Coll '23-24; mem staff U Mich Biol Station summers '27-42; cons in tropical medicine to Sec War '41-46; chmn ed com Jour of Parasitology '32-37; AAAS(F)—Am Soc Parasitol (secy '25-29; pres '30)— Am Soc Tropical Med—Am Acad Tropical Med (treas '34-37; vp '38; pres '39)—Am Soc Zool—Am Micros Soc (pres '37)—Am Soc Naturalists (pres '41)—Phi Beta Kappa—Sigma Xi. 5000 Norwood Av., Balt. 7.

10 CORWIN, Elbert F. Meteorology; Aerological engineering. b'06. ME '30 —MME '34—'34-38 (Rensselaer Poly Inst). Investigation stratosphere winds up to 100,000 feet including the jet stream; study of tail method for obtaining data on winds aloft; development of electronic anemometer; design and development of aerological equipment; weather reconnaisance investigations. Author: Weather Station Handbook for the Observer '45. Faculty Rensselaer Poly Inst '30-42, asst prof aeronautical engring '39-42; observer US Weather Bur Albany NY summer '37; dir Mount Whiteface Meteorol Observatory Lake Placid NY '37-42; aerological engr Aerology Br Bur Aeronautics Dept of the Navy since '47. Am Meteorol Soc—AAAS— Inst Aeronautical Sci—Am Soc ME— Nat Aeronautics Assn—NY State Aviation Assn—Sigma Xi. Bureau of Aeronautics, Department of the Navy, Washington 25.

11 CORY, David Munroe. Indians (Mohawk language) (Iroquois language). b'03. AB with honors '23 (Columbia Coll); certificate '26—(New Coll Edinburgh); MST '28 ThD '31 Union Theol Sem). Co-editor (with Mrs Margaret Lahache and Mrs Josephine Skye Schmidt) Kanawake Teieriwakawata (The Caughnawaga Hymnal) '39; Reviser (with Mrs Louise Diabo) Rok (The Gospel according to St Luke) '31. Am Soc Church Hist— Am (Hymn Soc—National Fellowship Indian Workers. Cuyler Presbyterian Church, 360 Pacific St., Brooklyn 2, N.Y.

12 COSS, Harold Thornton. Thermal insulation (Ramie and asbestos textiles). b'00. BS '22 (U Ill); '23 (Rutgers). Studies in insulating materials such as Bentonite, Ramie, refractory cements; insulating results obtained from mineral wool, ceramics, insulating bricks and asbestos materials. Holds 12 patents on insulating brick, mineral wool. Author articles in field. Ceramic engr Celite Co Lompoc Calif '23-29; cermaic engr Johns-Manville Manville NJ '29-32, sect chief mineral wool '32-41, mgr insulations and textiles research dept since '41. Am Ceramic Soc(F)—Inst Ceramic Engrs— NJ Ceramic Assn—AAAS. Johns-Manville Research Center, Manville, N.J.

13 COSTELLO, David F(rancis). Range ecology (Wyoming, Colorado); Range vegetation (Condition, trends); Range plants (Utilization standards); Plant succession. b'04. AB '25 (Nebr State Teachers Coll); MS '26—PhD '34 (U Chicago). Chief division range mgt Rocky Mt Forest and Range Expt Sta Forest Service since '36; spl lecturer Colo A & M Coll since '42. Ecol Soc Am (ab bd)—Am Soc Range Management (council, editorial board) —AAAS—Sigma Xi. Rocky Mountain

Forest and Range Experiment Station, Ft. Collins, Colo. H: 502 Peterson.†

14 COTNER, Frank B(oyd). Physiology and cytology of the lower fungi; Serology of certain proteins. b'91. Diploma '13 (Bloomsburg State Normal Coll Pa); AB '16—AM '17—PhD '30 (U Mich). Acting chief of fundamental research branch of Scientific and Technical Division Economic and Scientific Section, General Headquarters Supreme Commander of Allied Powers Tokyo '46-47. Author articles in field. Prof bot Puerto Rico Coll Agr and Mech Arts '19-20; asst prof biol Albion Coll Mich '21-22; asst prof bot and bact, ext bot Mont State Coll '22-24, asso prof '25-30, prof since '31, asst dean div sci and dir student health service '43-44, also head dept bot and bact; dean science division since '44. MEA (life)—AAAS—Bot Soc Am—Am Bact Soc—Am Mycol Soc—Sigma Xi—Phi Kappa Phi. Montana State College, Bozeman, Mont.

15 COTNER, Robert Crawford. American history (Social, West); Personnel planning. b'06. AB '28 (Baylor); MA '29—U Jr fellow '28-29 (Brown); Austin scholar '33-34—Rosenwald fellow '39-40 (Harvard). Editor: Minutes of the Rhode Island Constitutional Conv 1790 '29; asst prof dept hist U Tex since '40, asst to dean of coll of arts sci on personnel matters since '46. Cmdr USN '42-46, assigned Bur Naval Personnel, later demobilization officer on staff Chief Naval Operations. AHA—Southwestern Hist Assn—Am Acad Polit Social Sci—Fla Hist Soc (mem bd dirs '37-39) —So Hist Assn. Department of History, University of Texas, Austin, Tex.

16 COTNER, Thomas Ewing. Mexican and Latin-American history; Texas history. b'16. BA '37 (Baylor U); MA '39 PhD '47 (U Tex). Author: The Military and Political Career of José Joaquin de Herrera, 1792-1854 '49. also articles in field. Lecturer Latin-Am hist and govt Tulane U '40-41, and George Washington U '47-48, '48-49; specialist Am Rep Sect Div Internat Ednl Relations Office Edn '46-48, exec sec adv com on exchange of students and profs since '46. NEA—Hispanic Am Assn—SW Hist Soc—Phi Kappa Sigma. Selected as exchange fellow to Mexico under the Buenos Aires Convention '42. American Republics Section, Division of International Relations, U.S. Office of Education, Washington 25.†

17 COTTER, Ralph U(lysses). Stem rust (Barberry susceptibilty, hybridization). b'96. MS '24—PhD '29 (U Minn). Author articles in filed. Jr agron later path US Dept Agr since '22, now with office barberry edn Bur Entomol and Plant Quarantine. AAAS(F) — Phytopath Assn Am— Sigma Xi. Plant Pathology Department, University Farm, St. Paul 1.

18 COTTON, Richard Thomas. Control by fumigation of insect pests of stored grains, seeds, and their milled products; Insectiproof packages. b'93. BS '14—MS '18 (Cornell); PhD '24 (George Washington U). Research and development industrial and commercial fumigants and fumigant mixtures for use in vacuum vaults, atmospheric chambers, warehouses, elevator bins and on farms; assisted in development insect-proof cotton bag; head US delegation FAO International Conference on Infestation of Foodstuffs London '47. Holds patents on commercial fumigants and fumigant mixtures. Insect Pests of Stored Grain and Grain Products '41; Insects in Relation to National Defense '41;

Pests in Stored Products '47. Co-author articles: Chemical Control of Insects '43; (with A I Balzer) Insect Pests of Rice and Their Control '47; Preservation of Grains and Cereal Products in Storage from Insect Attack '48, and others. Entomol US Bur Entomol and Plant Quarantine since '19, in charge field research on control stored grain and grain products since '34. AAAS(F)—Entomol Soc Am (F)—Am Assn Econ Entomol—Entomol Soc Wash—Kan Acad Sci—Kan Entomol Soc (pres '40)—Sigma Xi— Gamma Sigma Delta. NAM Modern Pioneer award for work with fumigants '40. 520 N. Juliette St., Manhattan, Kan.

19 COTTON, Robert H(enry). Citrus and sugar beet food technology; Analytical chemistry ; Plant nutrition (Fertilization); High vacuum technique. b'14. BS '37 (Bowdoin Coll); MS '39—research fellow '38 (Mass Inst Tech); PhD '44 (Penn State Coll). Developed new techniques for leaf analysis as a guide in plant nutrition; commercial development frozen orange juice concentrate; patent applied for new technique of stabilizing dehydrated foods. Author articles in field. Dir research Holly Sugar Corp Colo Springs since '47. Am Inst Chem(F) —Am Chem Soc—AAAS—Inst Food Chem—Am Soc Hort Sci—Am Soc Plant Physiol—Sigma Xi. Holly Sugar Corporation, Research Department, 318 Colorado Av., Colorado Springs, Colo.

20 COTTRELL, Casper L(ehman). Illumination; Bio-electric measurements. b'95. AB '20 (George Washington U); PhD '28 (Cornell U). Author articles in field. Asst prof, later asso prof elec engring Cornell U since '42. AAAS(F)—Am Assn Phys Teachers— Inter Soc Color Council—ASEE—IES —AIEE (asso)—Sigma Xi. Eta Kappa Nu. Franklin Hall, Cornell University, Ithaca, N.Y.†

21 COUCH, John Nathaniel. Fungi (Water, soil, symbiosis with insects). b'96. AB '19—AM '22—PhD '24 (U NC); '14-17 (Trinity Coll); '19 (Universite de Nancy France); DSc '46 (Catawba Coll). Discovered bisexual strains in water fungi '24; worked out symbiosis between scale insects and Septobasidium '29; developed technic for culturing certain chytrids in pure culture '39; with Johns Hopkins bot expedition Jamaica '26. Editor: Journal of the Elisha Mitchell Scientific Society since '46. Author: The Gasteromycitis of the Eastern U.S. and Canada (with W C Coker); The Genus Septobasidium '38; also articles in field. Prof U NC since '32, Kenan prof since '45, chmn dept since '44 Nat Acad Sci — NC Acad Sci — Bot Soc Am—Mycol Soc Am—AAAS—Soc Naturalists—Elisha Mitchell Sci Soc —Sigma Xi. Jefferson medal NC Acad Sci '37; Walker Grand Prize Nat Hist '38. Department of Botany, University of North Carolina, Chapel Hill, N.C.©

22 COUCH, Leo King. Wildlife management; Rodent control; Beavers; Ornithology. b'96. BS '18 (Oregon State Coll). Research in control methods of injurious field rodents, protected mammals and injurious birds; operational work in control of injurious rodents and predators; inspector Civilian Conservation Corps operations affecting wild bird and mammal populations in National Forests; administration of research on wildlife in US and possessions. Co-inventor trap for trapping and transplanting live beavers. Author articles in field. Biol US Biol Survey '30-38; asst chief Div Wildlife Research US Fish and Wildlife Serv since '39. Coordinator research on migratory waterfowl for Pacific Flyway since '49. Am Soc Mammalogists—Wildlife Society. U.S. Fish and Wildlife Service, Interior Building, Washington 25.

10 COUCH, Robert de Schweinitz. Food packaging. b'14. BS '36 (Lehigh U). Worked on the development and wrote specifications for the packaging of combat rations. Author articles in field. Control and research labs paper mills Riegel Paper Corp NYC '36-39, rar packaging lab '39-42; QMC Subsistance Research and Development Lab Chicago '42-46; head packaging research sect Gen Foods Corp Central Labs Hoboken NJ since '46. Tech Assn Pulp and Paper Ind—Packaging Inst—Am Management Assn (packaging council). Central Laboratories, General Foods Corporation, 11th & Hudson Sta., Hoboken, N.J.

11 COULBORN, Rushton. Theoretical history; Prehistory; Synthesis of social sciences. b'01. BA '26 (McGill U); PhD '31 (Lond U); '28 (Ecole Libre des Sciences Politique Paris); '29 (Hochschule fur Politik, Berlin). Research on mediaeval history of England and France, especially breakdown of church and society. Contributing editor Phylon '42-48. Author: International Security (with E Benes, A Feiler) '39. Author articles: The Individual and the Growth of Civilizations '40; The American Culture: the Polity '41; The Meaning of History '44; Civilized and Primitive Culture '47; The Concept of the "Conglomerate Myth," and others. Lecturer hist Sussex House London '27-29, chief lecturer '29-34, v-principal '34-38; prof European hist, chmn dept hist and prehist Atlanta U Atlanta '39-45, prof hist and prehist since '45. Norman Wait Harris memorial lecturer U Chicago '39; Arnold Found lecturer So Methodist U '39, '41; Joseph H Larwill lecturer Kenyon Coll '41; research grants Social Scis Research Council '43-46, Am Philos Soc '46, Carnegie Found '47; Shreve fellow Princeton U '45-46. AHA —Am Pol Science Assn—Inst Hist Research—Royal Inst Internat Affairs. Department of History and Prehistory, Atlanta University, Atlanta.†

12 COULTER, Ellis Merton. Georgia (History); Antebellum South (History); Civil War (History); Reconstruction (History). b'90. AB '13 (U NC); AM '15—PhD '17 (U Wis). Author: Civil War and Readjustment in Kentucky '26; College Life in the Old South '28; William G Brownlow—Fighting Parson of the Southern Highlands '37; John Jacobus Flurnoy—Champion of the Common Man in the Antebellum South '42; Georgia—A Short History (rev edit; '47; The South During Reconstruction 1865-1877 '47; Confederate States of America 1861-1865 '50. Editor: Georgia's Disputed Ruins '37. Prof hist and polit sci Marietta Coll O '17-19; asso prof hist U Ga '19-23, prof since '23; visiting prof hist U Tex '29-30, '43-45, La State U '35-36. Ga Hist Soc—So Hist Assn—Miss Valley Hist Assn—AHA. University of Georgia, Athens, Ga.⊙

13 COULTER, John Wesley. Human geography (Pacific area). b'93. Student '05-10 (Methodist Coll Belfast Ire); AB '17—AM '21—Teach fellow '19-20 (U Calif); PhD '26 (U Chicago); '27-41 (U Hawaii). Pacific Anthropological and Educational Seminar Conference Honolulu '36; rapporteur International Geography Congress Amsterdam '38; committee on land classification and land utilization Pacific Science Congress Berkeley '39, New Zealand '49; Institute Pacific Relations Conference Hot Springs Va '45.

Author: Fiji: Little India of the Pacific; Land Utilization in the Hawaiian Islands; also articles in field. With U Hawaii '27-41, prof '41; prof geog U Cincinnati since '46, Pacific-Asia specialist trusteeship dept UN secretariat '49-50. Am Geog Soc(F)—Assn Am Geog—Am Assn Profs Geog—AAAS—Am Assn Prof Anthrop—Pacific Sci Assn—Hawaiian Hist Soc—Ohio Acad Sci—Sigma Xi. Dept Geol. and Geog., Univ. Cincinnati, Cin. 21.†

14 COULTER, Samuel Todd. Dry milk products; Butter. b'03. BS '25 (Ore State Coll); MS '30—PhD '33 (U Minn). Author articles in field. Instr, later prof U Minn since '30; research dir Maple Island Farm Inc Stillwater Minn since '46; dairy products adviser since '47. Cons and coordinator US Army Food and Container Inst for Chicago QM Depot '44-47. Am Dairy Sci Assn—AAAS—Assoc Internat Assn Milk and Food Sanitarians (asso). University of Minnesota, Dairy Division, St. Paul Campus, St. Paul 1.†

15 COUNT, Earl Wendel. Physical and cultural anthropology; Raciology; Human growth. b'99. BA '22 (Williams Coll); BD '26 (Garrett Biblical Inst); PhD '35 (Calif U). Research on mythopoea as social integrator of culture, Eurasiatic-North American datable cultural diffusion, mathematical expression of behavior of anthropometric measurements and indices during time; discovered that Indians of North America received diffusion-impulse from old world of third century AD central Asia, that ratio of human brain weight to body weight not phylogenetically aberrant but describable mathematically as part of total primate pattern. Author: This Is Race '50; also articles in field. Prof anthrop, dept head Hamilton Coll since '46. Am Assn Phys Anthrop—Am Anthrop Assn (council)—Am Assn Applied Anthrop—Am Folklore Soc—Am Assn Anat—AAAS—Am Sociol Assn—NY Acad Sci(F)—Inst Antrop Tucuman (hon). Department of Anthropology, Hamilton College, Clinton N.Y.

16 COUPER, William. History of Pennsylvania Railroad tunnels and terminals. b'84. Grad '04—CE '26 (Va Mil Inst); SB '06 (MIT). Consulting engineer War Department '40-41, expert consultant on War Department contract work '43, member advisory committee on education House of Representatives '44-45. Author: History of the Engineering, Construction and Equipment of the Pennsylvania Railroad New York Tunnels and Terminal '12, and others. Sec bd engrs in charge constrn NY Tunnel and Terminal Project Pa RR NYC '06-09; exec officer Va Mil Inst since '25. Assn Mill Colls and Schs of US (past pres)—Va Hist Soc. Virginia Military Institute, Lexington, Va.

17 COURLANDER, Harold. Folklore and music in Haiti, West Africa, Eritrea, Ethiopia, Cuba, and Indonesia. b'08. AB '31 (U Mich); '39 (Columbia). Recorded music in Africa and West Indies, folk music in US; collection, analysis, and presentation folk tales, legends, and folk music; research expeditions to Haiti, Cuba, and Africa '32-43. Author: Haiti Singing '39; The Caballero '40; Uncle Bouqui of Haiti '42; Kantchil's Lime Pit (Indonesian folklore) '50. Co-author: (with George Herzog) The Cow-tail Switch (W African folklore) '47; (with Wolf Leslau) The Fire on the Mountain (Ethiopian folklore) '50. Author articles: Musical Instruments of Haiti '41; Musical Instruments of Cuba '42; Notes from an Abyssinian Diary '45, and others. Ed in chief India operations OWI '43-45;

regional ed for Far East Voice of Am since '46; now ed recordings world folk music Ethnic Folkways Library. Research grants from Am Council Learned Soc '39, 41, Franz Boas fund Columbia U '39, Am Philos Soc '46, Viking fund Inc '50; Guggenheim fellow '48. U.S. Department of State, 251 W. 57th St., N.Y.C.

18 COURT, Arnold. Polar regions climatology; Glaciology and geography. b'14. AB '34 (U Okla); MS '49 (U Wash). Meteorol US Antarctic Service 1939-41, at Little America 1940-41; meteorol Dept Army since '46. Served as officer US Army Air Force weather service Alaska '43-45. AAAS—Am Geog Soc—Am Geophys Union—Am Meteorol Soc—Am Soc Profl Geog—British Glaciol Soc—Arctic Inst NA. 312 Livingston Terrace, S.E., Washington 20.

19 COURTIS, Stuart Appleton. Measurement of growth; Educational psychology (Tests, measurements, methods, cooperation techniques). b'74. BS '19—MA '21 (Teachers Coll Columbia U); PhD '25 (U Mich). Originated Curtis "standard tests," a system of measuring efficiency of school work; member staff of experts Hanus Committee on School Inquiry New York '11, The Gary Survey '16, New York Survey '24; in charge of testing work Boston public schools '12. Author: Why Children Succeed; The Measurement of Growth. Co-author: (with Otis W Caldwell) Then and Now in Education; (with Mrs G Watters) A Picture Dictionary for Children; also articles in field. Prof sch edn U Mich '21-44, emeritus '44. AAAS(F, sec sect L '13-17, pres '18-19, 32-33)—Nat Assn Dirs Ednl Research (pres '17-18)—Nat Soc Sci Study Edn Coll Teachers Edn (sec '25-31)—Phi Kappa Phi. 9110 Dwight Av., Det. 14.

20 COUTINHO, Joaquim de Siqueira. Portugal (Language, history); Brazil (History); Geopolitics; Political geography; Economic geography. b'85. CE '06—ScD '07 (Tech U Lisbon); travel fellow Portuguese Govt '07-09 (U London, U Oxford). Came to United States as official agent of Portuguese Commerce '16; in charge Brazilian Section Pan-American Union '16-20. Co-author: Portuguese Grammar '25; also articles in field. Prof geog Sch Fgn Service Georgetown U Washington '20-40; Curator museum Cath U Am since '40. Awarded Order of Santiago for Merit, Knight '10, Knight Officer '20, Knight Commdr '23. 1890 Ontario Pl. N.W., Washington 9.

21 COUTLEE, Douglas Wakefield. Drugs (Merchandising) b'94. Ed pub schs. Author articles in field. With various advt agencies '10-33, dir advt Merck & Co Inc NYC '33-49. Advertising and editorial cons in drug and pharmaceutical field since '49. 45 Oak Ave., Larchmont, N.Y.

22 COVEN, Glenn Ellis. Resinography; Microscopy. b'10. AB '33—MA '39 (Oberlin Coll). Author articles in field. Microscopist American Cyanamid Co Stamford Conn since '44. Am Assn Textile Technologists—Am Association Textile Chemists and Colorists. American Cyanamid Co., 1937 W. Main St., Stamford, Conn.†

23 COVER, Harry Ralph. Food processing (Methods, machines). b'92. AB '10 (Western Md Coll); LL B '13 (Harvard Law Sch). Development and manufacture of inventions, machines and methods employed in food processing industry. Inventor various machines and methods, director technical experts in development of such machines. Author articles in field.

Pres The United Company and The United Products Co., Westminster Md since '14. Charter mem Inst Food Technologists. Old Guard Soc of Canning Industry. Tuc Road, Westminster, Md.

10 COVINGTON, Cecil Lyons. Apprentice training (Facilities). b'11. AB cum laude '33 (Baylor U); LLB '39—MPL—SJD '40 (Nat U Washington). Administrative asst Pub Works Adminstrn Washington '33-40; spl asst on contracts Office Sci Research and Development U S Govt '41-43; chief training facilities div Vets Adminstrn Dist 10 Dallas since '46. Lt US Navy '44-45. 9403 Waterview Rd., Dallas 18.

11 COWAN, J Milton. Linguistics; Acoustical analysis. b'07. AB '31—AM '32 (U Utah); fellow '32-33 (U Calif); PhD '35 (U Ia); '29-30 (U Leipsig Germany). Special consultant War Department in charge language phase of Army Specialized Training Program and other such training programs in War, State departments and other government agencies. Author: Monograph in Archives of Speech-Pitch and Intensity Characteristics of Stage Speech '36; also articles in field. Asst prof German U Ia '38-41, asso prof '42; dir intensive language program Am Council Learned Socs '42-46; prof linguistics and dir div Mod Langs Cornell U since '46; dir linguistic Research Fund Am Council Learned Socs; sec-treas business mgr publs Linguistic Soc Am '39-50. Acoustical Soc Am(F)—Sigma Xi. Cornell University, Ithaca, N.Y.☉

12 COWAN, John Charles. Organic chemistry (Vegetable oils, proteins). b'11. '29-33 (U Colo); AB '34—PhD '38 (U Ill). Research on reactions and polymers of gamma bromo-propylalkyl amines; preparation and structure of a-haloacrylates; polymers from optically active sec-butyl a-bromo-acrylate; polyesters, polyamides, polyesteramides and polymeric salts from dimeric and polymeric fat acids; rubber substitutes and synthetic rubbers from vegetable oils; composition of polymeric fat acids; catalytic isomerization of vegetable oils; heat-sealing and moisture proofing resins from vegetable oils; reaction of tertiary butyl hypochlorite with vegetable oils; studies on after-tack in soybean oil films, flavor stability of soybean oil and methods of organoleptic evaluation, alcoholic extraction of soybean oil, composition of soybean lecithin, reactions of vegetable proteins, fibers from vegetable proteins; symposium on drying oils '47; symposia on flavor stability soybean processors '46, '47, '48; Holder with others five US patents, ten to fifteen pending. Author: Catalytic Conjugation of Linseed and Soybean Oils '45; also articles in field. Asso chem No Regional Research Lab Peoria Ill '40-41, chem '42, sr chem '43-44, principal chem since '45, chief oil and protein div. ACS—Am Oil Chem Soc—Soybean Research Council —Sigma Xi. Superior service award Dept of Agr '48. Northern Regional Laboratory, 825 N University, Peoria 5, Ill.†

13 COWELL, Henry Dixon. Extra-European music (Iceland, Albania, Persia, Turkey, Korea, Japan, China, India, Java, Bali, Thailand, Burma, Armenia, Oriental Russia, Spain, Balkans); Latin American music; Primitive music of Incas; Modern music materials (Tone clusters, atonality, polytonality, polyrhythm, dissonant counterpoint, polyharmony); Comparative music theory. b'97. Made five European tours since 1923 and tour of US each year. Author: New Musical Resources 30; American Composers '33; The Na-

ture of Melody; also articles in field. Dir music New Sch for Social Research, NYC '30-36 and since '40, also Mills Sch for Teachers NYC '41-45; lecturer in music. New Music Soc (dir-in-chief)—Pan Am Assn Composers (exec bd)—League of Composers (exec bd) —Am Composers Alliance (bd govs). Awarded Guggenheim Fellowship for research extra-European music, Berlin, 1931-32. c/o The New School, 66 W. 12th St., NYC 11.☉

14 COWGILL, George Raymond. Foods (Vitamin fortification); Vitamins (Biochemistry). b'93. AB '16 (Stanford U); PhD '21 (Yale); DSc (hon) '47 (U So Cal). Research on vitamin B-complex, improvement of staple foods; editor Journal of Nutrition, member Food and Nut Board of National Research Council, '40-46. With Yale U since '21, prof nutrition since '44. AMA (council on foods)— Am Inst Nutrition—Am Physiol Soc— Am Soc Biol Chem. Received Mead Johnson annual award for research on vitamin B-complex '42, annual sci award of Grocery Mfrs Am '48. Yale Nutrition Laboratory, 333 Cedar St., New Haven 11. H: 70 Brookside Dr., Hamden 14, Conn.

15 COWIE, Alexander. American novels. b'96. AB '19—AM '20—grad scholar '19-20 (U Minn); grad scholar '23-24—PhD '30 (Yale). Author: John Trumbull; Connecticut Wit '36; William Gilmore Simms' The Yemassee '37; The Rise of the American Novel '48; also articles in field. With Eng dept Wesleyan U since '24, now prof. Mod Lang Assn Am (sec treas Am lit group '41-45)—Coll Eng Teachers. Received Marston prize in Eng U Minn. 160 Wesleyan Station, Middletown, Conn.†

16 COWIE, Dean Bruce. Artificial radio activity; Permeability (Living cells); Cosmic rays; Tropical diseases. b'13. BS (Swarthmore Coll); student (U Calif, George Wash U). Author articles in field. Physicist and biophysicist Carnegie Inst Wash since '44; research fellow Georgetown Med Sch since '48. Am Phy Soc—AAAS(F) —Tex Radio Soc (hon)—Am Soc Tropical Med—Wash Acad Sci—Philos Soc Wash—Soc Exptl Biol and Med. Department of Terrestrial Magnetism, Carnegie Institute of Washington, 5241 Broad Branch Rd., Washington 15.

17 COWLES, Alfred. Security market indexes. b'91. AB '13 (Yale). Author: Common Stock Indexes '38; also articles in field. Economist since '33; pres Cowles Commn for Research in Econ; dir Tribune Co, Chicago Tribune Bldg Corp, WGN Inc; Ontario Paper Co Ltd, Ill Atlantic Corp, Marlhill Mines Limited, News Syndicate Co and others. Econometric Soc (F, treas)— AAAS. 435 N. Michigan Av., Chgo.☉

18 COWLES, LeRoy Eugene. American education (Utah). b'80. Student '00-03 (Weber Acad); Phb '10—AM '13 (U Chicago); PhD '26 (U Calif); Dr Humanities (Hon) '46 (U Utah). Author: Utah Educational Program of 1919 '26; Organization and Administration of Education in Utah '46. Co-author: Building Needs and Transportation Program Carbon School District, Utah '29, and others; also articles in field. Pres U Utah '41-46, pres emeritus since '46; pres Utah Teachers' Retirement Board '35-41. NEA—Am Assn Sch Adminstrs—Utah Edn Assn—Phi Kappa Phi. 124 University St., Salt Lake City 2.

19 COWLIN, Robert William. Pacific Northwest (Forest economics and forest resources). b'99. BS '22—MS '28

(U Cal). Land Taxation, land use, forest land ownership; financial aspects management and economics forest industries; ponderosa pine and douglas fir. Author government reports and articles in field. Sr forest economist US Forestry Service '38-42, chief div Pacific NW Expt Station '42-51, dir Pacific NW Expt Sta since '51. Soc Am Foresters—Forest Products Research Soc—AAAS—Phi Sigma—Alpha Zeta—Xi Sigma Pi. US Courthouse, Portland 5, Ore.

20 COWPER, Frederick Augustus Grant. Old French literature; Gautier d'Arras. b'83. BA '06—MA '11 (Trinity Coll); PhD '20 (U Chicago); student (U Strassburg, U Geneva, McGill U). Prof Romance langs Duke U '20-52; professor emeritus since '52. Duke-Carnegie resch grant '47 work on Gautier. Mod Lang Assn—Mediaeval Acad —So Atlantic Mod Lang Assn—Am Assn Tchrs French—Societe des Anciens Textes Francais. Duke University, Durham, N.C.☉

21 COX, Alonzo Bettis. Cotton economy and marketing; Texas resources. b'84. AB '11—Am '14 (U Tex); PhD '20 (U Wis); LLD '38; (Abilene, Tex, Christian Coll). Visited all European countries as research economist for Edward T Robinson & Son, Havre, France '28; appointed by Lions International to study business cycles of US '33; invited to address international Cotton Congress, Prague '35, Cairo '37. Author: Cotton Prices and Markets '26; services in Cotton Marketing '26; Cotton Marketing in England '28; Marketing American Cotton on the Continent of Europe '28; Cotton Markets and Cotton Merchandising '48; The Cottonseed Crushing Industry in its National Setting 49. Assistant Univ Texas '17-18, in charge div farm and ranch econs agrl expt sta '19-22, prof bus administrn, dir bur bus research, '26-45; prof cotton marketing, cotton research, since '26. AAAS(F)— Am Farm Econ Assn—Am Statis Assn —Am Econ Assn. 2700 Cherry Lane, Austin 3, Tex.☉

22 COX, Carroll E. Vegetable diseases (Seed-borne and soil-borne). b'11. AB '38 (U Del); MS '40 (Va Poly Inst); PhD '43 (U Md). Research on tomato late blight, stem and collar rot of tomato, storage diseases of sweet potatoes and their chemical control. Author articles in field. With U Md and Md Agr Expt Sta since '40, asso prof plant path since '48. Am Phytopath Soc—Bot Soc Am—Bot Soc Washington. University of Maryland, College Park, Md.

23 COX, Doak Carey. Geology (Ground-water, Hawaiian, fluorspar deposits, Tidal waves). b'17. BS '38 (U Hawaii); MA '41 (Harvard). Author articles in field. Geol expt sta Hawaiian Sugar Planters Assn since '46. Geol Soc Am—Econ Geol—Seismol Soc Am—Am Inst Mining Metall Engrs— Hawaiian Acad Sci—Engring Assn Hawaii. Experiment Station, Hawaiian Sugar Plant Association, Honolulu 4, Hawaii.

24 COX, Gertrude Mary. Statistics (Experimental designs, methodology). b'00. BS '29—MS '31—'33-38 (Ia State Coll); '32-33 (U Calif). Author articles in field. Dir Inst Statis U NC since '44. Am Statis Assn(F)—Inst Math Statis(F)—AAAS(F)—Biometrics Soc —Psychometric Soc—Sigma Xi—Phi Kappa Phi. Institute of Statistics, Raleigh, N.C.

25 COX, Grady. Music (Education) Musicology (Trends in Modern music). b'95. Artist Diploma '20 MusM in musicology '38—PhD hon '43 (Cincinnati Conservatory Music); MusB in piano—MusB in theory and composition '32 (American Conservatory); private study '22-23 (Berlin). Research in 16th Century Counterpoint. Author articles on music form and theory. Head piano dept Miss Coll Clinton since '46; judge Miss Fedn Music Clubs. Jackson Music Tchrs Assn (pres '50-51)—Music Edn Assn. Madison St., Clinton, Miss.

10 COX, James Alton. Insects of grapes; Oriental fruit moth control; Codling moth. b'04. BSc '30—MSc '32 —PhD '37 (O State U). Research on Oriental fruit moth parasites, grape and cherry insects. Author: Ascogaster carpocapsae An Important Parasite of the Codling Moth and Oriental Fruit Moth '32; Biological Control of The Oriental Fruit Moth '33; Oriental Fruit Moth Control in Quince Plantings '36, and others. Spl investigator NY Agrl Expt Sta '30-36; asst entomol charge deciduous fruit insects Va Agrl Expt Sta '36-44; entomol charge Erie Co research lab Pa Agrl Expt Sta since '44. Am Assn Econ Entomol—Sigma Xi. Erie County Research Laboratory, North East, Pa.

11 COX, Leland G. Plant physiology; Chewing gum. b'12. BS Agr '36 (U Calif); PhD '42 (Cornell U). Co-author articles: Factors Influencing the Germination of Iris Seed and the Relation of Inhibiting Substances to Embryo Dormancy '43; Preliminary Studies on Catkin Forcing and Pollen Storage of Corylus and Juglans '43; A Germination Inhibitor in the Seed Coats of Certain Varieties of Cabbage '45; A Remarkable Tree-fall and an Unusual Type of Graft Union Failure '45. Research asst forestry Cornell '38-41, instr floriculture, plant propagation teaching and research '41-42, research asso botany since '42, research on analysis and comml extraction of rubber from rubber bearing plants; tech projects Beech-Nut Packing Co Canajoharie NY since '46. Soc Am Foresters—Assn Hort Sci—Am Soc Plant Phsyiol—Am Chem Soc—Inst Food Tech—AAAS—Xi Sigma Pi—Sigma Xi. Co-recipient '43 Vaughan Award for best paper in field of floriculture. Beech-Nut Packing Co., Canajoharie, N.Y.

12 COX, Paul E. Pottery; Grinding wheels. b'79. BS '05 (Alfred U). Research on use of bentonites in pottery bodies, many phases of ceramics from structural clay products to fine art wares, mold making; expert on production of light weight concrete aggregate made from clays. Author: Potteries of The Golf Coast; Possibilities of Pottery from Iowa Clay; also articles in field. Foreman, asst to supts com on stoneware plants Ind and Ill '98-10; tech expert Newcomb Pottery of Newcomb Sch of Art Tulane U '10-18; tech adviser La Compagnie Generale des Mueles Paris '18-20; head dept ceramic engring Ia State Coll '20-39; operator small pottery New Orleans '39-42; research work Phila '42-45; ceramic expert La Geol Survey since '45. Am Ceramic Soc(F)—Phi Kappa Phi. Louisiana Geological Survey, Baton Rouge 3, La. H: 520 N. 10th St., Baton Rouge 8, La.

13 COX, Richard Threlkeld. Bioelectricity; Electric fish; Electrons (Scattering, polarization). b'98. BA '20—PhD '24 (Johns Hopkins). Expedition to Brazil for study of electric eels '37. Author: Time, Space and Atoms' 33; also articles in field. Prof physics Johns Hopkins U since '46, acting dean Coll Arts and Sci '48-51, dean Coll Arts and Sci since '51. Am Phys Soc(F)—AAAS(F)—NY Zool Soc(F)—Phi Beta Kappa—Sigma Xi. Johns Hopkins University, Balt 18.☉

14 COXE, Wallace Hammond. Ballistics (Small arms). b'91. CE '13 (Princeton); MA '36 (Temple U). Conducted proof tests and experiments on propellant powders for use in small arms, machine guns, cannon since '13; research forensic ballistics since '25. Inventor ball-type target disjunctor, monoptograph and technique for testing shooter's eye dominance; co-inventor device for holding all sizes small arms barrels for velocity, pressure, accuracy tests. Author articles: Smokeless Shotgun Powders; Exterior Ballistic Charts; Eye Dominance of Shooters, and others. Ballistic engr E I du Pont de Nemours & Co since '13, spl asst to dir Burnside lab since '45. Nat Rifle Assn Am—Am Ordnance Assn. Burnside Laboratory, Box 152, Penns Grove, N.J. H: 18 B St., Carney's Point, N.J.

15 COYKENDALL, Claud Carlisle. Highway administration. b'86. BS (civil engring) '10 (Ia State Coll). Research on highway grading and paving, public highway administration, finance and construction; executive secretary Iowa Legislative Interim Highway Study Committee '48, highway consultant to Commission to Study State Government, Illinois, '50, executive secretary Legislative Interim Municipal Statutes Study Committee Iowa '49-50. With Ia State Highway Commission since '23. Ia Good Roads Assn (exec sec since '49). 326 State Finance Building, Des Moines, Ia. H: 460 Westwood Dr., Ames, Ia.

16 CRABB, Alfred Leland. History of Nashville, Tennessee. b'84. Student '03-04 (Bethel Coll); '04-06 (Sou Normal Sch); '08-10 (Western Teachers Coll); BS '16 (George Peabody Coll for Teachers); MA '21 (Teachers Coll Columbia); PhD '25 (G. Peabody Coll), DLitt '42 (U Ky). Editor Peabody Jour of Education. Author: Supper at The Maxwell House '43; Breakfast at the Hermitage '45; Lodging at the Saint Cloud '46; Home to the Hermitage '48; A Mockingbird Song at Chickamauga '49; Reunion at Chattanooga '50. Prof edn George Peabody Coll for Teachers since '27. 1701 18th Av. S., Nashville.

17 CRABB, George Arthur, Jr. Solar radiation (Measurement, effects, geographical patterns, effects of land-cover on ground temperature); Reservoirs (Sedimentation); Rivers (Sedimentation); Soils (Moisture and temperature measurement); Caves (Mapping). b'15. BS (AE) '40 (U Ga); MS '50 (Va Poly Inst). Author articles: Solar Radiation Investigations in Michigan '50; The Normal Pattern of Solar Radiation at East Lansing '50. Co-author articles: (with T W Edminster) Losing Farms by the Truckload '43; (with G J Bouyoucos) The Electrical Resistance Method of Soil Moisture Determination '49; (with James Tyson) Tillage Studies in Michigan '52; (with James L. Smith) Hydrologic Report on the Wooded Watershed '52. With Soil Conservation Service '39-42, since '43, now supervisor hydrologic research station. Mich Acad Sci Arts and Letters—Am Soc AE—Nat Speliologic Soc—Sigma Xi—Alpha Zeta. Soil Conservation Service, 404 Agricultural Bldg., East Lansing, Mich. H: 806 Bretton Rd., Lansing 15.

18 CRABTREE, August F. Ship models (Building); Miniature sculpture; Nautical archaeology. b'05. Has spent most of life constructing 15 exact scale models showing the evolution of water craft from pre-historic times to end of the sailing ship, which form nucleus of personal museum; authority on qualities, seasoning, curing woods used in carving model construction. Author articles in field. Soc Nautical Research. Rte 2, Box 548, Miami 43, Fla.†

19 CRAFT, Jesse Herman. Mental defectives (Social control), psychological services). b'97. AB '21 (Southeast Mo State Teachers Coll); MA '25 (Columbia); PhD '37 (Colo State Coll Edn); '33-34 (U Minn). Author articles in field. Clinical psychol Hertzler Clinic since '48. Clinical Psychol US Army 43-46. Am Assn Mental Deficiency—Am Assn Social Workers (chmn SD chap '39-41)—Am Psychol Assn(F)—SD State Conf Social Workers (pres '38). Hertzler Clinic, Halstead, Kan.

20 CRAFT, William Arthur. Animal husbandry and genetics; Swine production. b'94. BS '22—MS '23 (Ia State Coll); PhD '32 (U Wis). Research on effects of inbreeding animals; hemogloben and white blood cells in pigs varying as to breeding, feeding and management; inheritance of defects; variation in activity and production of spermatozoa in male chicken; factors influencing quality and quantity of fleece in sheep; sex ratio in mule and other hybrid mammals; variations in free choice intake of components of rations by pigs; significance of weight changes in sows during gestation and lactation. Editor Animal Production, Biological Abstracts since '48. Director Regional Swine Breeding Lab since '37. Ia Acad Sci—AAAS—Genetics Soc Am —Am Soc Animal Prodn (past pres)—Sigma Xi—Phi Sigma. 108 Curtiss Hall, Ames Ia.

21 CRAFTON, William Louis. Electrical measurements. b'02. Ed pub schs. Installation and operation of meter laboratory and maintenance shop; in charge of carrier current and telemetering installations; carrier current control and power relaying. Meter engr Ark-Mo Power Co since '26, now supt meter dept. Am Inst EE. Arkansas-Missouri Power Co., Blytheville, Ark. H: 913 Holly St.

22 CRAFTS, Alden Springer. Plant Physiology; Chemical weed Control. b'97. Research fellow biol '38 (Harvard); BS '28—PhD '30 (U Calif); Nat Research Council Fellow '30-31 (Cornell U). Co-author: Weed Control '42; Water in the Physiology of Plants '49. Bot, prof bot U Calif since '46; visiting prof U Puerto Rico '47-48. Bot Soc Am—Am Soc Plant Physiol—Calif Bot Soc—AAAS—Am Soc Range Mgt—Phi Beta Kappa—Sigma Xi. Guggenheim fellow '38. Botany Division, University of California, Davis, Calif. H: 626 B St.†

23 CRAIG, Gerald Spellman. Science for the elementary schools. b'93. BS '15 (Baylor U); AM '17—PhD '27 (Columbia). Consultant elementary science public school systems since '29; developed natural science field centers Alabama, Connecticut, New York '34-35. Author: Horace Mann Course of Study in Elementary Science '27; Pathways in Science '32; New Pathways in Science '40; Science for the Elementary School Teacher '40; Science in Childhood Education '44; Our World of Science '46; also articles in field. Cons elem sci Horace Mann Sch Teachers Coll Columbia '25; asso natural sci Teachers Coll Columbia U '27-29, prof since '41; dir Natural Sci Field Center Plymouth NH summer '47, U Puerto Rico Summer '48. AAAS(F)—Nat Council Supervisors Elementary Sci (pres '35-36)—Teachers in Sci (sec conf on edn '36-40)—

Edn Research Assn—NY Acad Sci. 460 Riverside Dr., NYC 27.◉

10 CRAIG, Homer Vincent. Tensor Analysis. b'00. BA '24 (U Colo); PhD '29 (U Wis). Application of extensor theory to tensor analysis, differential geometry, and mechanics; study of invariance in geometry and mathematical physics; tensor analysis of spaces when involving derivatives of coordinates with respect to curve parameter of higher order than the first. Author: Vector and Tensor Analysis '43. Co-author: Dictionary of Mathematics '49. Prof applied math U Tex '42, grad prof since '43, math mil physics research lab '45-47; ed Mathematics Magazine since '47. AAAS (F)—Am Math Soc—Am Math Assn—AAUP—Circolo Matematico di Palermo—Sigma Xi—Sigma Pi Sigma. Department of Applied Mathematics, Univ. of Texas, Austin, Tex. H: 3104 Grandview St., Austin 5.

11 CRAIG, Palmer Hunt. Industrial electronics and gaseous rectifiers; Television; Enriched fuels; Fruit preservation (Electro-chemical); Storage batteries; Voltage regulators. b'01. AB '23—MA '24—PhD '26 (U Cincinnati); Hanna grad fellowship physics '24, Hanna, Baldwin, and Taft fellowships in physics '24-26. Inventor Kathetron, Photodync, and Pyradyne tubes, Craig system of television, Craig hermetically sealed storage battery; also work and patents in preservation fruits and vegetables, fuel enrichment by ozonides and organic peroxide. Author articles in field. Vice pres. lab dir Invex Inc since '30; head dept elec engring U Fla '41-46, supervisor war research lab '43-46; prof engring and dir Electronics Res Lab, U Miami Coral Gables since '47. AIEE(F)—Am Phys Soc(F)—AAAS(F)—Fla Engring Soc—Inst Radio Engrs—Phi Beta Kappa—Sigma Xi—Sigma Tau. P. O. Box 56, University Branch, Miami, Fla.

12 CRAIGHEAD, Frank Cooper. Forest entomology. b'90. AB '12 (Pa State Coll); AM '15—PhD '19 (George Washington U). Author articles in field. Forest entomol '12-48, in charge forest insect investigation US Dept Agr, except three years with Can govt. Am Soc Econ Entomol—Am Forest Soc. R.F.D. 6, Carlisle, Pa.

13 CRAIN, Clark Nixon. Geomorphology (Water). b'14. BA '39—MA '40 (U Colo); '41-42 (Clark U). Research on problems water irrigation, irrigated regions, relationship structure to water supply; formulated thesis on geographic factors relating to Hispano-American minority problem Rocky Mt West, indicating correlation between soils, water supply, socio-cultural stresses, frequently consultant on this phase minority problem; established relative inability subterranean escape of water from Laramie River Valley. Author: Backgrounds of Present Inter-State Disputes Over Water Resources '48. Co-author: (with P M Harris) Handbook of Weather and Climate '49. Author article: Physical Aspects of the Laramie River Dispute '46. Dist Supervisor US Census Bur '44-45; Asst prof geog U Denver '45-46, asso prof, chmn dept since '46. Am Soc Profl Geog—Sigma Xi. University of Denver, Denver.†

14 CRALL, James Monroe. Soybean and forage legumes diseases. b'14. BS '39 (Purdue U); AM '41—PhD '48 (U Mo); '33-34, '34-35 (Washington and Jefferson Coll). Research on Fusarium wilt of tomato '39-42, charcoal rot of soybean '46-48, investigations on diseases of soybean and forage legumes since '48; brown stem rot of soybean in Missouri '47. Author articles in field. Research asst Mo Agrl Expt Sta '39-42; jr path US Dept Agr, Mo Agrl Expt Sta '46-48; asso path US Dept Agr and Ia Agrl Expt Sta since '48. Am Phytopath Soc—Sigma Xi. Botany Section, Iowa State College, Ames, Ia.†

15 CRALLEY, Lewis J. Industrial hygiene. b'11. BS '33 (McKendree Coll) PhD '42 (U Ia). Environmental factors effecting health of industrial workers; efficiency of hospital masks. Indsl hygiene research and investigation div indsl hygiene USPHS '43-47 chief cooperative health services Br '48-49 chief environmental investigations br Div Indsl Hygiene USPHS Cincinnati since '49. Am Pub Health Assn—Am Indsl Hygiene Assn—Sigma Xi—Phi Lambda Upsilon. 1014 Broadway, Cincinnati 2.

16 CRAMER, Archie Barrett. Carbohydrate chemistry; Candy technology; Wood chemistry. b'09. BSc '34—MSC '35 (U Manitoba Can); PhD '39 (McGill U). Holder patents in wood and sugar chemistry. Author articles in field. Chief chem F & F Labs Chicago since '45. ACS—Am Inst Chem—Am Assn Candy Tech—Am Inst Food Tech—AAAS. F & F Laboratories, 3501 W. 48 Pl., Chicago 32. H: 1126 Hyde Park Blvd., 15.†

17 CRANDALL, Bruce Nichols. Outboard motorboat designing. b'04. Student (Northwestern U, Lake Forest Coll); PhB '27 (U Chicago). Over 50 world's records for speed have been established with boats from his designs. Author articles in field. Free lance designer since '33, now engaged in applying new developable-surface designing technique to new types of small pleasure boats for construction with sheet plywood. Naval architect for Navy Dept Bur of Ships small boat design sect Washington '42-46. Three Lakes, Wis.†

18 CRANDALL, Lynn. Water (Allocation and distribution): Idaho (Water resources). b'88. CE '10 (Cornell U). Study use and distribution of water for irrigation, investigation effect of water storage and use on supply, for irrigation rights involved in litigation; collection of steam flow records. Engr water supply investigation US Geol Survey '10-15, dist engr and watermaster Snake River Ida since '30; commr dist ct on water distribution, surface and ground water Big Lost River Valley Ida '20-29. Am Soc CE—Soc Am Mil Engrs. Cornell U Fuertes gold medal for study on use of water for irrigation. Box 697, Idaho Falls, Ida.

19 CRANDALL, Norris Ingersoll. Art (Analysis, appreciation). b'91. BArch '14—MArch '15 (Cornell U); student '18 (Mass Inst Tech). Author: Art as You See It '40. Prof architecture and head dept George Washington U '23-28, dir div fine arts '28-37, exec officer dept art since '37; registered architect DC. AIA—AAUP—Scarab. George Washington U, 2013 G St., Washington 6. H: Baileys Cross Rds., Alexandria, Va.†◉

20 CRANE, Harley Lucius. Nut production; Mineral nutrition of plants. b'91. BS '14—MS '18 (West Va U); PhD '29 (Cornell U). Member China-United States Agricultural Mission '46. Author articles in field. Principal hort US Dept Agr charge nut production investigations since '35. Am Soc Hort Sci—Northern Nut Growers Assn—Tex Pecan Growers Assn—SE Pecan Growers Assn—Am Tung Oil Assn—Sigma Xi. Plant Industry Station, Beltsville, Md.

21 CRANE, Harry Wolven. Adjustment problems; Mental deficiency; Mental hygiene; Abnormal behavior. b'85. AB '09—AM '10—Phd '13 (U Mich); diplomate in Clinical Psychology '48 (Am Bd Examiners Profl Psychology). Chief investigator Michigan Legislative Commission on Feeblemindedness, Epilepsy and Insanity '13-15. Instr psychol O State U '15-18, asst prof '18-21; field worker Ark State Com on Feeblemindedness and Eugenics Record Office '15; staff psychol mental survey Nassau Co NY '16; asso prof psychol U NC '21-23, prof since '23; psychol, dir Div Mental Hygiene NC State Bd Charities and Pub Welfare '21-38; psychol con U NC since '38; br cons clin psychol VA since '48; cons practice. American Psychol Assn (F) — AAAS(F) — Am Assn Mental Deficiency(F)—Am Orthopsychiat Assn—Phi Beta Kappa—Sigma Xi. P.O. Drawer 809, Chapel Hill, NC.†◉

22 CRANE, Julian Coburn. Fig culture; Plant hormones. b'18. BS '39—PhD '42 (U Md). Research on various tropical fiber plants '42-44; coffee culture, fruits, and vegetables '44-45, fig culture since '46. Author: Economic plants of interest to the Americas '43; Roselle as a fibre crop '43; also articles in field. Agron US Dept Agr at Havana Cuba '42-44, hort at El Salvador Central America '44-45; asst prof pomol, pomologist Expt Sta U Calif since '46. Am Soc Hort Sci—Sigma Xi. Division of Pomology, University of California, Davis, Calif.†

23 CRANE, William G(arrett). Literature (Renaissance, English sixteenth and seventeenth centuries); Rhetoric; American civilization. b'97. AB '19—MA '20 (State U Ia); PhD '37 (Columbia); Roberts traveling fellow '24-25; field service fellow for French Us '28-29 (U Paris, Sorbonne). Research in Bodleian Library, Oxford '29-31. Author: Wit and Rhetoric in the Renaissance '37; Twelve Hundred Years '48 (in collaboration) American Literature and Civilization in the College Curriculum '48; Models and Values '28; How to Think and Write '50. Prof Eng City College NY. Acad Polit Sci—Am Acad Polit Social Sci—AAAS—Am Geog Soc—Coll English Assn — English Assn, London — Fgn Policy Assn—Modern Humanities Research Assn, London—Modern Lang Assn—Nat Council Teachers of English (com on coll study of Am lit and culture '45-48) — NEA — NY Council Coll Teachers of Eng (pres '46-47)—Pub Engl Assn—Soc Advancement Edn—Steamship Hist Soc Am—Phi Beta Kappa. 35 Hamilton Pl., NYC.◉

24 CRAVER, Bradford North. Pharmacology (Privine, radioactive emanations). b'10. AB '32 (Cornell U); Am '36—PhD '41 (Boston U); MD '44 (Wayne Coll Med). Research on vascular and respiratory effects of privine, on vascular effects of epinephrine, on nature of radioactive emanations, their mechanism of action, biological effects, tolerance limits, and effects of adrenal cortical injury on toxicity, on apparatus for and effects of perfusion of mammalian hearts with common drugs, and on dynamics of histamines and antihistamines. Author articles in field. Research asso in pharmacology Wayne Coll Med Detroit '41-44; research asso Manhattan Engring Project Rochester U '44-45; sr pharmacologist Ciba Pharm Prod Inc since '45. Am Soc Pharmacology and Exptl Therapeutica—NY Acad Sci—Assn Analytical Chem — Am Indsl Hygiene Assn — AAAS. Ciba Pharmaceutical Products, Inc., Summit, N.J.

10 CRAVER, John Kenneth. Plasticizers; Synthetic lubricants and hydraulic fluids. b'15. BE '37 (U So Ill); MS '38 (Syracuse U). Plasticizers and synthetic hydraulic fluids, emphasis on vinyl plasticizers, non-toxic plasticizers and non flammable hydraulic fluids. Holds eight patents in field. Author article: The Mechanism of Plasticization in Plastics '48. Co-Author article: (with HS Bergen) The Sulfonamide Plasticizers and Resins '47. Contbr: A Cyclopedia of Plastics. Development mgr, plasticizers, resin intermediates and functional fluids, organic div Monsanto Chemical Co St Louis. ACS—ASTM—Soc Automotive Engrs—Am Inst Physics—Soc Plastics Industry—Soc Rheology—Alpha Chi Sigma. 1700 S 2d St., StL 4.

11 CRAWFORD, Arthur Whipple. Money and banking; International and public finance; Federal fiscal policies (United States). b'85. AB '06 (Beloit Coll); AM '35—PhD '40 (Am U). Autor: Monetary Management Under the New Deal '40; also articles in field. Staff econ, financial specialist US C of C '42-50; Citizens Com for Hoover Report '50; member Econ Nat Com on Monetary Policy. Phi Beta Kappa. 6325 Woodside Pl., Chevy Chase 15, Md.

12 CRAWFORD, Bartholow Vincent. Thoreau; Major New England authors. b'88. AB '10 (Cornell Coll); AM '13—PhD '18 (Harvard). Also research in non-dramatic prose dialogue in English before 1750. Author: Representative Selections: Henry David Thoreau '34; Outline History of American Literature (with Kern and Needleman) '45. Prof Eng Ia U since '37. Modern Lang Assn. 101 F, University Hall, University of Iowa, Iowa City, Ia.

13 CRAWFORD, Bryce Low, Jr. Molecular spectroscopy and structure; Kinetics of propellants. b'14. AB '34 —AM '35—PhD '37 (Standford U). Nat Research fellow '37-39 (Harvard). Author articles in field. Prof phys chem U Minn since '46. Directed OSRD work on propellant burning at U Minn in contact with NDRC Div 3, research continuing under Navy sponsorship. Am Chem Soc—Optical Soc Am—AAAS—Sigma Xi—Phi Beta Kappa. School of Chemistry, University of Minnesota, Minneapolis 14⊚

14 CRAWFORD, Claude C. Education (Study, curriculum, statistical and teaching methods). b'97. BA '18— MA '19 (U Tex); '21-23 (Carnegie Inst Tech); '20-24—PhD '24 (U Chicago). Author: Methods of Study '26; The Technique of Study '28. Co-Author (with E W Tiegs) Statistics for Teachers '30; (with L P Thorpe and Fay Adams) The Problems of Education '38; (with Francis Grant Bartlett) Art for All '42; and others. Prof edn U So Calif since '26; curriculum lab work in cooperation with Los Angeles city and county schs, with state depts of edn Calif, Nev and with Civil Aeronautics Adminstrn. National Soc for Study of Edn—NEA. 3832 W. Vernon Av., LA 8.⊚

15 CRAWFORD, Lawrence Caldwell. Stream gaging. b'06. BS (CE) '30—CE '42 (Purdue U). Administration and management of state cooperative programs for collection and publication basic data on surface water resources; design, construction, and operation of gaging stations; analysis and computation of records of stream flow; evaluation of present utilization and future potential development of water resources; planning of stream gaging network to provide data on adequacy of present and future water supplies; study of artificial and natural factors influencing stream flow; preparation of reports on rare hydrologic occurrences, including floods and droughts. Co-author articles: Maximum Discharges in the United States; Summary of Yearly and Flood Flow Relating to Iowa Streams 1873-1940, and others. Asso dir Ia Inst Hydraulic Research '40-49; dist engr US Geol Survey Ia '40-49, now O. Am Soc CE—Am Water Works Assn—Ia Engring Soc —Sigma Xi—Tau Beta Pi—Chi Epsilon. 1509 Hess St., Columbus 12, O.

16 CRAWFORD, Nelson Antrim. Cats. b'88. BA '10 (U Ia). MA '14 (U Kan). Editor: Cats '47. Ed-in-chief Household mag since '28. Am Assn Agrl Coll Editors (ex-pres)—Am Assn Teachers of Journalism—Phi Kappa Phi. Household, 912 Kansas Av., Topeka, Kan.

17 CRAWFORD, Robert Platt. Japanese money and banking; Farm land prices (United States). b'93. AB '17 (U Neb); AM '26 (Columbia). Investigation farm land boom for Barron's and other publication '46; prepared monograph on Japanese money and Banking for SCAP '48. Author: These Fifty Years '25; also articles in field. Prof journalism U Neb since '26; SCAP Tokyo '46-48, finance hist '48. Royal Econ Soc(F)—Am Econ Assn—Am Acad Polit Social Sci—Am Assn Teachers Journalism—Neb Writers' Guild (sec '25-26, pres '28-29). Burnett Hall, University of Nebraska, Lincoln, Neb.

18 CRAY, Raymond E(dgar). Egg and poultry marketing; Poultry production. b'00. BS '22 (Rutgers U); MS '30—part time grad work '30-42 (Ohio State U). Largely responsible for development of cooperative egg marketing programs in Ohio '32-42. Author articles in field. Mgr egg marketing dept Ralston Purina Co St Louis '42-49. Poultry Sci Assn. Champion Inter-Collegiate poultry judging team '22. Poultry Dept Ohio State University, Columbus, O.

19 CREAMER, Walter J. Electrical and communication engineering. b'96. BS '18—EE '21—AB '23 (U Me). Author: Elements of Electrical Engineering '48; also articles in field. Prof communication engring U Me since '38, head dept elec engring since '45. Am Soc Engring Edn—Inst Radio Engrs —AIEE—Tau Beta Pi—Phi Kappa Phi. 331 Center St., Bangor, Me.⊚

20 CREASER, Charles William. Zoology; Ichthyology. b'97. AB '20—MS '21—PhD '24 (Mich U); '16-19 (Alma Coll). Engaged research in lampreys, species specificity of gonadotropic factors in vertebrates, accumulation of radio-active iodine by vertebrates, scale structures in relation to life history in fishes (sunfish, smelt, grayling); field studies for Michigan Department of Conservation '21-31; studied distribution of venomous snakes, other animals, classification of Lampreys and fishes, conditions of habitat selection by brook trout. Author articles: Species specificity of the Gonadotropic Factors in Vertebrates (with Gorbman) '39; Guide to Zoological Experiences (with Metcalf) '46; Accumulation of Radio-Active Iodine by the Endostyle of Larval Lampreys and the Problem of Homology of the Thyroid (with Gorbman) '42, and others. Asst curator fishes Mus Zool Mich U '21-23, prof vertebrate field zool U Mich, Biol Sta, summers since '25; prof Wayne U since '24, chmn dept biol since '35. AAAS—Am Soc Zool—Soc Ichthyology and Herpetology —Soc Exptl Biol and Med—Detroit Physiol Soc (past pres)—Sigma Xi (past pres Wayne chapt)—Mich Acad Science (past vice pres). Wayne University, Detroit 1.

21 CREELMAN, George Douglas. Synthetic fuels; Fluidized solids. b'08. AB '31 (Harvard). Holder patents petroleum refining and fluidized solids. Dir research synthetic fuels M A Hanna Co Cleveland since '46. ACS— API—AIMME—AIC. M. A. Hanna Company, Leader Building, Cleveland 14.

22 CREER, Leland Hargrave. History (Utah, Mormonism, nationalism). b'95. AB '16—AM '20 (U Utah); PhD '26 (U Calif). Author: Utah and the Nation '29; Nationalism and World Peace '44; The Founding of an Empire '47; also articles in field. With U Utah since '37, prof hist since '43, head dept hist polit sci since '42, Reynolds Memorial lecturer '44. AHA— Utah Hist Soc—Pioneer Trails and Landmarks Assn. University of Utah, Salt Lake City.⊚

23 CREIGHTON, Harriet Baldwin. Plant cytogenetics and growth hormones. b'09. BA '29 (Wellesley Coll); PhD '33 (Cornell U). Collaborator in translation and revision: Boysen-Jensen Growth Hormones in Plants '36; also articles in field. Professor bot dept Wellesley Coll since '52. AAAS (F)—Bot Soc Am—Genet Soc Am—Am Soc Naturalists—Soc Exptl Study Growth and Development—Sigma Xi— Phi Beta Kappa. Botany Department, Wellesley College, Wellesley 81, Mass.

24 CREIGHTON, John T. Agricultural entomology; Insects of men, animals and plants (Control technique). b'05. BSA '26—MS '29 (Fla U); PhD '35 (O State U); '22-24 (Clemson Coll); '29 (Cornell U). Field research in US for Bureau Entomology and Plant Quarantine US Department Agriculture, and in Central America. Head prof U Fla since '33, head pest control div since '35; indsl cons. Am Assn Econ Entomol (vp)—Entomol Soc Am —Fla Entomol Soc (sec)—Sigma Xi. P.O. Box 2845, University Station, Gainesville, Fla.

25 CREIGHTON, John Wallis. History. b'82. AB '04 (Westminster Coll); PhD '17 (U Mo); LLD '36 (Coll Wooster). Prof, chmn dept history, dir summer session Westminster Coll Pa since '46. AAUP—Econ Hist Assn—Am Hist Assn—Am Oriental Soc. Westminster College, New Wilmington Pa. H: 155 Beechwood Rd.⊚

26 CREITZ, Ellis Erwin Titanium (Chemistry); X-ray (Diffraction); Spectroscopy (Emission); Petrography; Minerals (Artifical). b'08. BS '41 (U Ala). Holds patent on mfr of artificial ilmenite. Co-author article: (with T N McVay) A Study of Opaque Minerals in Trail Ridge, Florida Sand Dunes '48. Chem Nat Bur Standards '28-37; with So Expt Sta US Bur Mines since '38, now head phys services sect. Am Inst Physics—ACS— Mineral Soc Am—Ala Acad Sci—So Assn Spectrographers (pres '51). P.O. Box L, University, Ala.

27 CRENSHAW, Ollinger. Southern United States history. b'04. AB '25— MA '26 (Washington and Lee U); PhD '45 (Johns Hopkins U). Author: The Slave States in the Presidential Election of 1860 '45. Author articles: The Knights of the Golden Circle: The Career of George Bickley '41; Christopher G Memminger's Mission to Virginia, 1860 '42; The Speakership Contest of 1859-1860 '42; The South, Old and New '47; and others. Instr hist Washington and Lee U '26-29, asst prof '30-41, asso prof, '41-47, prof since '47. AHA—Miss Valley Hist Assn—So Hist Assn—Md His Soc—Phi Beta Kappa. Washington and Lee University, Lexington, Va.†

10 CRESSMAN, Luther Sheeleigh. Great Basin archaeology Early man in North America; Oregon anthropology. b'97. AB '18 (Pa State Coll); STB '23 (Gen Theol Sem NY); AM '23—PhD '25 (Columbia). Author: Social Composition of the Rural Population of the US '25; Archaeological Survey of the Guano Valley Region in Southeastern Oregon '36; Petroglyphs of Oregon '37; Studies in Anthropology '40; Archaeological Researches in the Northern Great Basin, '42; also articles in field. Prof anthrop U Ore since '29, Head dept, dir Mus Natural Hist. AAAS(F)—Soc Am Archeol—Am Assn Phys Anthrop—Am Anthrop Assn—Sigma Xi—Phi Kappa Phi. John A King travelling fellow in Europe '25-26; Guggenheim Memorial fellow '40-41; '49-50. University of Oregon, Eugene, Ore.☉

11 CRESSWELL, John Reginald. Franciscan philosophy (Thirteenth and fourteenth centuries); Contemporary Arab affairs. b'02. BA '22 (Brandon Coll); PhD '26—Sage scholar '23-26 (Cornell U); student (Columbia U, U Bonn). Cultural relations attache Am Legations in Beirut and Damascus '45-47. Author: A Study of Certain Logical Procedures '36. Professor philos W Va U since '49. Am Oriental Soc—Middle East Inst—Am Philos Assn—So Soc Philos Religion—Phi Kappa Phi. Am Council Learned Socs grant-in-aid '43. West Virginia University, Morgantown, W. Va.†

12 CREUTZ, Edward C. Nuclear physics; Atomic energy. b'13. BS '36—PhD '39 (U Wis). Author articles in field. Prof, head Dept Physics, director Nuclear Research Center Carnegie. Inst Tech '49. Physicist OSRD, Manhattan Project '42-46. Am Phys Soc—AAAS. Carnegie Institute of Technology, Pittsburgh 7.†☉

13 CRICKMAY, Geoffrey William. Geology (Appalachian tectonics and stratigraphy; Georgia). b'05. BA '27 (U Brit Columbia); PhD '30 (Yale). Author articles in field. Sr geol Venezuelan Atlantic Refining Co since '46. Am Assn Petroleum Geol—Am Geog Soc—Geol Soc Am—Ga Mineral Soc—NY Acad Sci—Sigma Xi. Aptdo. 893, Caracas, Venezuela, S. A. H: 48 Hubinger St., New Haven 11.

14 CRISCUOLO, Luigi. Italian affairs; Greek and Roman numismatics; Ancient gems; Heraldry and orders of knighthood. b'87. Ed (pub schs and pvt tutors). Chairman of American Italian Congress '46; delegate in US of Montenegrin Government of which the late Queen Milena was regent '21-24. Author: The Italo-American Entente '25; Montenegro's Right to Live '28; also articles in field. Pres and dir Midland Bldg Corp '38-48; dir Mernat Trading Co Inc NY until '48. Italy-Am Soc—Royal Italian Geog Soc—Italian Acad Sci Letters (hon, gold medalist)—Am Numismatic Soc NY(F)—Soc Acad Histoire Internat. Diploma from Dante Alighieri Soc Italy for 25 yrs service for Italian culture '37; Silver Medal Italian Geog Soc '48; decorated Chevalier Order of Crown Italy '21; Grand Cordon Order of Danilo I '22; Grand Officer Holy Sepulchre (Vatican); Knight Order N S de la Mercede; Knight Constantinian Order of St George; and other decorations. 50 Broadway, NYC 4.

15 CRISSEY, Walter Ford. Ruffed grouse. b'15. BS '37 (Cornell U). Co-author: The Ruffed Grouse, Its Life History, Management and Propagation (with others); also articles in field. Ruffed grouse investigation NY State Conservation Dept '37-42, studies of waterfowl woodcock and pheasant '45-49; asst chief sect waterfowl management investigations US Fish and Wildlife Service Washington since '49. Wildlife Soc. Section of Waterfowl Management Investigations, Branch of Wildlife Research, Fish and Wildlife Service, Washington 25.

16 CRISSY, William Joseph Eliot. Applied and vocational psychology; Executive personnel selection and development; Educational psychology (Testing, measurement, guidance). b'12. BS '35 (West Chester State Teachers Coll); EdM '37—fellow psychometry (Harvard); PhD '42 (U NC). Author articles in field. Cons in measurement and guidance Cooperative Test Service Am Council Edn; personnel cons; lecturer applied psychol grad sch Fordham U, grad sch arts sci NYU; asst prof psychol Queens Coll. Am Psychol Assn(F)—Am Coll Personnel Assn—Psychometric Soc—Eastern Psychol Assn—NY State Psychol Assn—Sigma Xi. Room 1919, 122 E. 42nd St., NYC 17. H: Apt. R-25, 51-01 39th Av., Long Island City 4, N.Y.

17 CRITTENDEN, Christopher. American history (North Carolina; Colonial and Revolutionary). b'02. AB '21—AM '22 (Wake Forest Coll); PhD '30 (Yale). Author: North Carolina Newspapers before 1790 '28; The Commerce of North Carolina 1763-1789 '36; co-editor: The Historical Records of North Carolina, 3 vols, '38-39; compiler and editor: Historical Societies in the United States and Canada; A Handbook '44; contbr articles and revs to jours. Prin pub sch Roxobel NC '22-23; instr history Yale '24-26; instr history U NC '26-29, asst prof '30-35; dir NC State Dept Archives and History since '35; on leave '46-47 serving as asst dir World War II Records Project of Nat Archives Washington; state dir Hist Records Survey '36-37; regional dir Survey of Fed Archives '36-37; chmn Conf Hist Socs '38-40; pres Am Assn for State and Local History '40-42; editor NC Hist Rev since '35. Am and So Hist Assn—Soc Am Archivists (pres '40-42)—NC Folk-Lore Soc—Phi Beta Kappa. Add: 1537 Caswell St., Raleigh, N.C.☉

18 CRITTENDEN, Walter Marion. Eighteenth century English literature. b'00. AB '23 (Baylor U); AM '25—PhD '31 (U Pa). Author: Sarah Scott, Novelist 1723-1795. Asso prof Eng U So Calif. Modern Language Association—Nat Teachers Speech—AAUP. University of Southern California, Los Angeles 7.

19 CROASDALE, Hannah T(hompson). Freshwater algae; Latin diagnoses (New plant species); Plastic (Biological materials embedded). b'05. BS '28—MS '31—PhD '35 (U Pa). Author: Freshwater Algae of Woods Hole, Mass; also articles in field. Asso in zool Dartmouth Coll since '46. NH Acad Sci—Sigma Xi—Phi Beta Kappa. Department of Zoology, Dartmouth College, Hanover, N.H.†

20 CROCKER, Lionel George. Speech; Rhetoric; Oratory. b'97. AB '18—MA '21—PhD '33 (Mich U). Research and writing on rhetorical influence and training of Henry Ward Beecher, rhetorical theory of Harry Emerson Fosdick, influence of Robert Green Ingersoll on American oratory, and Charles Haddon Spurgeon's theory of preaching. Author: Henry Ward Beecher's Speaking Art '37; Argumentation and Debate '44; Effective Speaking '48; Public Speaking for College Students (rev edit) '49. Co-author: (with Eich) Oral Reading '47, Business & Professional Speech '51; Basic Concepts in Oral Reading, '52. Head dept speech Denison U since '28; lecturer on speech subjects; asso ed Quarterly Journ Speech '37-44; ed The Speaker; ed Central Speech Assn Journal '49-50; Nat Assn Teachers Speech—Speech Assn Am. Denison University, Granville, O. H: 423 E. College St.

21 CROCKFORD, Horace Downs. Electrochemistry of aqueous solutions. b'98. BS '20 (NC State Coll); MS '23—PhD '26 (U NC). Research in thermodynamics of aqueous solutions, particularly in connection those magnitudes determinable by electromotive force measurements. Author articles in field. Asst prof chem U NC '26-30, asso prof '30-39, prof since '39. Am Chem Soc. University of North Carolina, Chapel Hill, N.C.†

22 CROFT, Harry Packard. Metallurgy of copper, copper alloys, and titanium. b'97. ChemE '21 (Rensselaer Poly Inst); MS '38—PhD '42 (Case Inst Tech). Research on casting (including centrifugal casting), fabrication, properties, uses of copper, brass, other copper alloys, and titanium. Author: Copper Tech Book. Author articles: Influence of Lead and Copper Alloys; Machining of Copper Alloys; Fabrication of Copper and its Alloys; Stress Corrosion Cracking of Cartridge Brass '40. Co-author article: (with Dr D K Crampton) Copper-Nickel-Aluminum Alloys. Dir research Chase Brass & Copper Co Cleveland Div; copper cons OPM; vp in charge development centrifugal casting Wheeling Bronze Casting Moundsville WVa '48-49; now research engr on titanium Kennecott Copper Corp. Am Soc for Metals—AIME—Brit Inst Metals—Soc Automotive Engrs—ASTM. Kennecott Copper Corp., 120 Broadway, NYC 5.

23 CROFTS, Alfred. China, Korea, Japan. b'03. PhD '36 (Stanford); MA '44 (Columbia). Educational development, religious history and contacts, contemporary politics and military operations, geography and economics of Far East, Korea, Japan, China. Author: (annual vols) Journeys Behind the News '47-50. US Naval Intelligence and Mil Govt '42-46; with dept history U Denver since '46, broadcaster world affairs Social Sci Found Denver '47-50; broadcast commentary tour world (especially Far East) '49-50. Inst Pacific Relations—Am Acad Polit Sci (F)—Soc Am Historians (F). Department of History, University of Denver, Denver.

24 CROMWELL, Norman Henry. Organic nitrogen compounds; Reaction mechanisms; Isomerism; Drugs; Absorption spectra. b'13. BS in Chem Engring '35 (Rose Poly Inst); PhD '39 (Minn U). Research on mechanisms and drug synthesis, such as antimalarials; cons in field; discussion leader in nitrogen chemistry for Conference on Current Problems in Organic Research, Stanford '48. Author articles in field. Professor of organic chem Neb U since '48; Guggenheim F Fulbright Scholar '50-51. Am Chem Soc—Chem Soc London—Sigma Xi—Sigma Tau. Department of Chemistry, University of Nebraska, Lincoln, Neb.†

25 CRONIN, Eugene Joseph. Ultrasonics; Telecommunications; Biophysics. b'11. AB '34 (Boston Coll); '37-38 (McGill U); '48-49 (Johns Hopkins); '49-50 (Stanford). Development instrumentation and techniques for operating on fundamental above 200 KC; dial tuning magnetostriction over broad bands in ultra high ranges; focusing magnetostriction at point of wave propergation; instantaneous extraction of yeast cell contents. Development instrumentation and technique for automatically charting ocean currents while collecting and recording various oceanographic data at land stations as temperature, salinity, light. Direction of research on fish movement control by electronics; athermal sterilization of liquids in radio frequency field; sterilization of eggs in shell to prolong edible life; extraction and purification of enzymes; cancer detection by protein level determination in blood; effects of nonionizing radiation on living tissue; application of ultrasonics in medical research; instrumentation in blood cell counting. Co-inventor color-television system operating on fraction of presently assigned TV band. Observer and computer instrumentation Nat Geophys Co Dallas '38-41; spl agt supervisor acoustics and elec sect FBI '41-47; research cellular physiol Johns Hopkins Hosp '48-49; research dir Am Inst Radiation since '49. Soc Exploration Geophysicists. American Institute of Radiation, Belmont, Calif.

10 CRONIN, Lewis Eugene. Blue crab (Biology, fishery, populations, histology). b'17. AB '38 (Western Md Coll); MS '42—PhD '46 (U Md). Author articles in field. Research biol blue crabs Md Dept Research and Edn; at present asso prof and marine biol U Del. Am Micros Society—Biol Photog Assn—Am Soc Limnol Oceanog—Sigma Xi. University of Delaware, Newark, Del.

11 CRONQUIST, Arthur. Taxonomy of North American Compositae; b'19. BS '38—MS '40 (U State Coll.); PhD '44 (Minn U); '34-36 (Ida State Coll). Research on taxonomy of Simarubaceae for antimalarials in some species, and Sapotaceae for latex content of group; special studies in genera Aster, Erigeron and Solidago; research on revisions of western North American species of Aster centering about Aster foliaceus, North American species of Erigeron, and Oreastrum group of Aster. Author articles in field. Asst prof Wash State Coll since '48. Am Soc Plant Taxonomists—Torrey Bot Club—So Appalachian Bot Club. Washington State College, Pullman, Wash.†

12 CROOKS, Donald M(undell). Translongitome; Drug plants. b'02. BS '27 (Ball State Coll); MS '29—PhD '33 (U Chicago). Specializes in Plant Anatomy, Morphology, Production tobacco and special (medicinal etc.) crops. Holds patent on translongitome, a continuous sectioning device. Author: Histological and Regenerative Studies on the Flax Seedling '33; Plants for Special Uses '48; Investigations with the Castor Bean Plant '45. Asst prof biol Ball State Teachers Coll '29-35; prof and chmn bot and range ecol U Ariz '35-40; sr plant anat US Dept Agr '40-41, principal plant hort charge div drug and related plants '41-45, head hort charge div tobacco, medicinal and special crops since '45. AAAS—Wash Bot Soc—Sigma Xi. Plant Industry Station, Beltsville, Md.

13 CROSBY, Elizabeth Caroline. Neuroanatomy (Comparative). b'88. BS '10—DSc '39 (Adrian Coll); '12—fellow '14-15—PhD '15 (U Chicago); '26 (University Coll London); '26 (Inst Brain Research Amsterdam). Co-author: (with Ariens Kappers, G Carl Huber) Comparative Anatomy of the Nervous System of Vertebrates. Faculty dept anatomy U Mich since '20, prof since '36; lectr Mich U Hosp Ann Arbor '49; edit bd Jour Comparative Neurology, Anatomical Div of Excerpta Medica. Am Assn Anatomists

—Am Neurological Assn—Alpha Omega Alpha—Phi Kappa Phi. E. Medical Bldg., University of Michigan, Ann Arbor.◉

14 CROSBY, Everett Uberto. Nantucket (History, architecture). b'71. Chairman Nantucket Art Center Kenneth Taylor Gallery since 1943. Author: Ninety-Five Per Cent Perfect (Nantucket houses) '37; Early American Silver Spoons '41; Eastman Johnson at Nantucket '44; Nantucket in Print '46, and others. AIA (Hon mem)—Nantucket Hist Assn. H: (winter) 133 E. 64 St., N.Y.C. 21; (summer) 28 Orange St., Nantucket, Mass.

15 CROSBY, Sumner McK(night). History of art; Medieval art. b'09. AB '32—PhD '37 (Yale); '34-35 (Ecole des Chartes Paris). Excavated in Abbey Church of St Denis north of Paris summers '38-39, '46-48; special adviser American Commission for the protection and salvage of artistic and historic monuments in war areas '44-46; special adviser on restitution cultural materials Department of State '45. Author: Abbey of St. Denis I '42; also articles in field. Asso prof, chmn hist art dept Yale since '47, curator medieval art Yale Art Gallery since '46. Col Art Assn (dir '39-45 and since '47, pres '40-44)—Medieval Acad Am Archaeol Inst—Societe d'Archeologie Francaise—Soc Nat des Antiquaires de France. Yale Art Gallery, New Haven.◉

16 CROSIER, Willard Francis. Seedborne fungi; Seed analysis; Cereal diseases; Chemical seed treatments. b'04. AB '27 (U Kans); PhD '32 (Cornell U). Author articles in field. Asso prof seed investigations Cornell U since '46. Am Phytopath Soc—Assn Official Seed Analysts (exec com since '47, research com chmn since '47)—Internat Seed Testing Assn (chmn com seed sanitation since '47). New York State Agricultural Experiment Station, Cornell University, Geneva, N.Y. H: R.D. 1, Waterloo, N.Y.†

17 CROSS, Aureal T(heophilus). Paleobotany (Geology of coal); Botany (Spore flora, pollen analysis). b'16. BA '39 (Coe Coll); MA '41—PhD '43 (U Cincinnati). Author articles in field. Asst prof bot and coal geol U Cincinnati '48-49; geol Geol Survey of Ohio; at present geol Geol Survey of W. Virginia and asst prof geol West Virginia Univ. Bot Society Am—Paleontol Soc—Am Geophys Union—AAAS(F)—Am Geog Soc—Ohio Acad Sci(F)—Sigma Xi. Nat Research Council Fellow '43. W.Va. Geologic Survey, Morgantown, W.Va.

18 CROSS, Ephraim. Latin and Indo-European language and linguistics; Romance languages; Origin and history of personal names. b'93. AB '13 (Coll City NY); AM '14—PhD '30—2 annual scholarships in Latin, Romance langs and linguistics (Columbia); JD '29 (NY U). Author: Syncope and Kindred Phenomena in Latin Inscriptions; Your Name: Its Origin and History; also articles in field. Staff, lang inst Coll City NY '32. Linguistic Soc Am—Modern Lang Assn Am—Am Philol Assn—Am Soc Internat Law—Nat Lawyers Guild—Am Oriental Soc—The Mediaeval Acad Am—Am Geog Soc(F). Awarded OWI citation for Lang Study and the Armed Forces '44. The City College, St. Nicholas Terrace, NYC.

19 CROSS, Harold Fred. Painting (Conservation, restoration); Color and light (Visibility). b'07. AB '30-31, '36-37 (Harvard). Research on properties of surface coatings, and methods for treatment on works of art; examination and treatment of Old Master and

other paintings; study use of color and light in influencing visibility; development and specification of low and high visibility color systems for use on aircraft, or in connection with aircraft activities. Conservator Isabella Stewart Gardner Mus Boston '32-38; independent professional conservator '39-41, and since '46; in charge development visibility measures for use on naval aircraft '42-45; staff conservator Corcoran Gallery of Art Washington '49-50. Founding fellow Internat Inst for Conservation Mus Objects London. 1820 Jefferson Pl., N.W., Washington 6.

20 CROSS, Samuel Avery. Public utilities engineering. b'97. PhB '18 (Yale); LLB '39 (Hartford Coll Law); LLD '42 (Blackstone Coll Law). Asst elec engr, utility engr Pub Utilities Commn Conn since '32; admitted Conn bar '41. Conn Soc Civil Engrs. Public Utilities Commison, State of Connecticut, Hartford, Conn. 24 Edgehill Rd., New Haven 11.

21 CROSSEN, George Edward. Manufacture of pharmaceuticals. b'05. BS '33—MS '37—PhD '40 (U Minn). Development of dosage types and forms for new drugs; correction of unsatisfactory formulae or products. Co-author: (with C H Rogers) Laboratory Manual of Inorganic Pharmaceutical Chemistry '41; (with Karl J Goldner) Pharmaceutical Preparations '42; (with Justin L Powers) The Art of Compounding '48; member Revision Committee US Pharmacopeia '50-60. Instructor College Pharmacy University Minnesota '31-41, asst professor '41-42; dean and prof pharmacy Drake U '42-45; dean and prof pharmacy Ore State Coll since '45; tech cons since '41; dir analytical lab Ore Bd Pharmacy since '45. Am Pharm Assn (chmn pract sect '44-46)—Am Chem Soc—AAAS—Minn, Ia, Ore, State Pharm Assns—Sigma Xi. Oregon State College, Corvallis, Ore.

22 CROSSLEY, Archibald Maddock. Public opinion (Radio audience measurement); Marketing. b'96. AB '17 (Princeton U). Originated measurement of radio audiences (Crossley Ratings) '29. Crossley presidential poll '36, measurement of weekly magazine readers '38; member advisory council, department of psychology, and chairman of committee for archives of radio, Princeton University; dollar-a-year consultant for Office of Civilian Requirements of War Production Board. Author: Watch Your Selling Dollar '30; also articles in field. Research mgr advt agency J H Cross Philadelphia '18-22; asst dir and dir research Literary Digest '22-26; pres and treas Crossley Inc since '26; pres Radiograph Corp; guest lecturer pub opinion Princeton U, NYU, U Calif, Stanford, Chicago U; chmn tech Com Econ Development. Market Research Council (past pres)—Am Marketing Assn (past pres, treas)—Am Statis Assn. Awarded Bok Prize for research, Harvard '31, silver medal for service to radio Annual Advt Award '43. Crossley Inc., 330 W. 42d St., NYC.*

23 CROSSMON, Germain Charles. Biological and chemical microscopy; Microscopical technique. b'05. BS '28 (Alfred U, NY); '31-33 (U Rochester). Research on refractive index determination of tissue, textiles, minerals and chemicals by dispersion coloration. Developed new applications dispersion staining. Author articles: A Paraffin Block Cooler for Use with the Microtome '35; The Isolation of Muscle Nuclei '37; Modification of Mallory's Connective Tissue Stain '37; Separation of Acidophilic Elements of Tissue into

Two Groups '39; Selective Staining of Red Blood Cells '40; Optical Staining of Tissue '48, and others. Instr and tech histological technique Sch Med Dentistry U Rochester '31-42; indusl hygiene chem biol and chem microscopist Bausch and Lomb Optical Co Rochester since '42. Am Indsl Hygiene Assn —Am Chem Soc—AAAS. Bausch and Lomb Optical Co., Rochester N.Y.†

10 CROUCH, Kenneth Elwood. Folklore. b'24. Research on state songs of the U.S., national songs for foreign countries. The Bedford Democrat, Bedford, Va. H: Twin View Farm.

11 CROUSE, Charles Stevens. Low temperature processing of carbonaceous materials; Production metallurgy; Matting of nickel oxide cres; electric smelting (Kentucky iron ores). b'88. EM '11 (U Minn). Developed process for treating coals and shales, now in pilot plant stage; developed process for matting of nickel oxide ores. Author articles in field. Prof metal engring U Ky since '19, head dept mining and metal engring since '29. Am Inst Mining Metal Engrs—British Inst Metals—Sigma Xi—Tau Beta Pi—Am Soc Engring Edn—Ky Acad Sci. Recipient medallion from U Louisville for work on the development of Kentucky. University of Kentucky, Lexington 29, Ky.†

12 CROUTER, John Yale. Education of the deaf; Lip reading; Speech for the deaf; Hearing aids. b'00. BS '32 (NYU); MEd '40 (Harvard). Author articles in field. Prin RI Sch for Deaf Providence since '32. NEA—Volta Speech Assn for Deaf—Conf Am Instrs Deaf—Conf Execs Am Sch Deaf. 520 Hope St., Providence.

13 CROW, Leonard Roy. Rectifiers; Electromagnets (Non-ferrous attracting); Servomechanisms. b'93. Ed pub schs. Research and invention of electromagnets for attracting aluminum, copper and other non-ferrous metals, axial air gap electric motors. electrical levitators, polyphase electric guns, traveling magnetic field ring motors. Author: Learning Electricity and Electronics Experimentally '49; Saturating Core Devices—Operating Principles and Applications '49; Design, Construction and Operating Principles of Electromagnets for Attracting Copper, Aluminum and Other Non-Ferrous Metals '51; Synchros, Self-Synchronous Devices and Electrical Servo-Mechanisms '52; Metallic Rectifiers, Principles and Applications '52. Dir elec research and development Universal Sci Co Inc since '40. 11th and Shelby Sts., Vincennes, Ind.

14 CROWE, Lawrence K(enneth). Dairy technology. b'98. BSc '22 (Colo State Coll); MSc '25 (U Neb); PhD '47 (U Minn). Author: Testing Ice Cream for Butterfat; Why Milk Tests Vary '37; Babcock Testing and other Methods of Analyzing Dairy Products '41; Some Changes Occuring in Dry Whole Milk During Storage '47. Co-author: (with H P Davis) Emergency Rations for Dairy Cows '36; Feed Comparision —Which Feed will Furnish Protein and Total Nutrients at Lowest Cost '36; (with M N Lawritson) Approximate Food Values for Dairy Cows '36. Asst prof dairy husbandry U Neb '25-34, asso prof '34-47, prof since '47; research asso U Minn '45-46. Am Dairy Sci Assn (chmn mfg sect '45-46) —Am Soc Animal Prodn—Inst Food Technologists — Am Chem Soc — Neb Dairy Tech Soc—Sigma Xi—Gamma Sigma Delta. University of Nebraska, Lincoln, Neb.

15 CROWELL, Walter S. Cements and resins. BS '11 (U Pa). Holds five patents on dental cement, art of molding composite resins and molding resins of the vinyl type. Author articles in field. Research dept S S White Dental Mfg Co since '11, supervising chem engr since '30. Am Chem Soc— Am Inst Chem Engrs—Am Soc Metals — Brit Inst Metals—Internat Assn Dental Research. The S.S. White Dental Manufacturing Company, 211 S. 12th St., Phila 5.

16 CROWLEY, Francis Michael. Catholic education in America. b'93. AB '16—Litt D '41 (Holy Cross Coll); AM '23 (Georgetown U); PhD '30 (George Washington U); LLD '48 (Boston Coll). Compiler of Directory of Catholic Colleges and Schools '26, '28 edit with Edward P Dunne. Author: The Catholic High School Principal '32; also articles in field. Dean Fordham U Sch of Edn since '38; mem bd ed Catholic Sch Jour, bd advisers Modern Ency of Edn. Nat Soc of Coll Teachers of Edn. 302 Broadway, NYC 7.©

17 CROWNOVER, Arthur, Jr. Military law. b'07. AB '29—AM '30—LLB '32 (Vanderbilt U); student summers '26, '27 (Peabody College). Co-author: (with Joseph Higgins) Tennessee Procedure in Law Cases '37. Co-editor (with Joseph Higgins) Higgins and Crownover's edit Gibson's Suits in Chancery '37. Grad Officer Candidate Sch Adj Gen Sch, Ft Washington Md; co-instr mil law dept Adj Gens Sch, also sch legal assistance officer and supervisor dept '42-45. Am Bar Assn— Tenn State Bar Assn (vp Jr bar sect '38-39)—Nashville Bar Assn—Internat Assn Ins Counsel—Phi Beta Kappa —Delta Theta Phi. Stahlman Bldg., Nashville.©

18 CROWSON, Benjamin Franklin, Jr. Latin America (Politics). b'18. AB '39 (Wm. and Mary Coll); summer '38 (U Mexico). Travels in all 20 Latin American Countries. Research in lives of political leaders of various countries, particularly Latin American; analysis historical patterns to attempt to forecast who will be political leaders in future; biographical information political leaders of all Nations. Founder '51 Amer Acad Language Research. Author: Our Southern Neighbors in Review (annual); Inter-Nations Biographical Record (3 vols). Dir Pan Am Edn Center '40-44; organizer research Crowson Inst Global Research '47. Received Eloy Alfaro decoration for Pan Am Activities '49. Am Acad Polit Sci. Crowson Institute of Global Research, Box 6188, Washington.

19 CROXTON, Frank Cutshaw. Petroleum refining, catalysis, organic synthesis and materials utilization. b'07. BA '27—MA '28—PhD '30 (Ohio State U). Author articles in field. Research engr later asst dir Battelle Memorial Inst since '39. Am Chem Soc —AICE—AAAS—Rheol Soc—Chem Soc —Soc Chem Ind—Am Pet Inst—Am Coke and Coal Chem Inst—Soc Auto Engrs—Sigma Xi. 505 King Av., Columbus, O.

20 CROXTON, Fred(erick) C(leveland). Labor; Economic statistics; Immigration. b'71. LLB '97—LLM '98 (Columbian U). Author articles in field. Clk later spl agt US Dept of Labor '93-07; chief statis US Immigration Commn '07-10; supervising spl agt in charge preparation of reports US Bur Labor Statistics '10-13; chief mediator, chief statis O Indsl Commn '13-16; chmn Nat Adv Com on Welfare Work Among Arriving Immigrants apptd by commr gen '21; mem Pres Emergency Com for Employment '30-31; asst dir Pres Emergency Orgn on Unemployment Relief '31-32; in charge of Federal emergency relief under RFC '32-33; spl commr of conciliation US Dept Labor '35-36; cons econ Social Security Bd '36-37, chief Div Administrative Aid Bur Unemployment Compensation '37-39; asst to dir Bur Employment Security '39-41; spl commr US Conciliation Service '42-43; private arbitration since '43; member fair employment board US Civil Service Commission since '48. American Statis Assn(F)—AAAS(F)—Am Acad Polit Social Sci—Am Econ Assn. 3200 16th St., N.W., Washington 10.

21 CRUICKSHANK, Allan (Dudley). Wildlife photography; North American birds. b'07. BS '31 (NYU). Considered outstanding bird photographer in US; has studied bird wildlife all parts North America, rural and urban; has collection 30,000 negatives representing over 300 different species North American birds; lecturer on ornithology on radio, before groups, organizations since '32; photographs appearing US Camera Yearbooks, periodicals, books. Author: Birds Around New York '42; Wings in the Wilderness '47. In charge nature work Camp Menatoma Kents Hill Me '26-32; ornithol Am Mus Natural History '34-35; official lecturer ornithol Nat Audubon Soc, head bird instruction Soc Nature Camp Me since '35. Nat Audubon Soc—Wilson Ornithol Club—Linnaean Soc NY (Pres '40)—Am Ornithol Union—Am Nature Study Soc. 1000 5th Av., NYC.

22 CRUIKSHANK, James W. Southern and southeastern forest resources. b'08. BS '30 (Cornell U). Author articles in field. Jr forester US Dept Agr '30, forest econ since '42, Chief div forest econ SE Sta since '46. Soc Am Foresters—NC Forestry Assn— Forest Farmers Assn Coop. Southeastern Forest Experiment Station, Box 252, Asheville, N.C.†

23 CRUM, Earl LeV(erne). Language and literature; Archaeology. b'91. AB '13 (St John's Coll Annapolis Md); AM '16 (Johns Hopkins); PhD in classics '24 (NYU). Author articles in field. Prof and head dept Greek Lehigh U since '29; vis prof Heidelberg U '49; lectr U Coimbra Portugal '35-36; pres Classical Assn Lehigh Valley '32-33, Atlantic states '34-35; lectr Archaeol Inst Am since '37. Officer in charge opening Heidelberg U '45-46, lectr '49; directeur du Foyer Retrouve Lyon France '19-21. Am Philol Assn— Archaeol Inst Am. Lehigh U, Bethlehem, Pa. H: 717 7th Av.†

24 CRUM, Mason. Negro in southern United States; Gullah Negro of Carolina Coast; Marriage and the family; Religious pageantry. b'87. AB '09 (Wofford Coll); '09-10 (Vanderbilt U); '11-12 (Harvard); PhD '25 (U SC). Attended White House Conference on Family Relations '48. Author: Gullah Negro Life in the Carolina Sea Islands '40; A Guide to Religious Pageantry '23; The Project Method in Religious Education '25; The Negro in the Methodist Church '51; also articles in field. Teacher and specialist in undergrad instrn Duke U. NC College Teachers Religion (past pres) — Soc Afro-American Studies—Nat Council Family Relations —Nat Conf Ch Leaders (co-chmn). Duke University, Durham, N.C.

25 CRUMB, Frederick Waite. New York state folklore. b'09. AB '30—AM '35 (NY State Coll for Teachers); EdD '42 (Columbia). Appeared in frequent radio broadcasts on American folklore '34-38, Army education programs, World War II. Served in War Department and overseas theaters, organizing and administering dissemination of information and education to

American troops. Author: Tom Quick, Early American '34; also articles in field. Pres NY State Teachers Coll Potsdam since '46. Nat Soc for Study Edn—Nat Ednl Assn—Kappa Delta Pi. 69 Pierrepont Ave., Potsdam, N.Y.

10 CRUMPLER, Thomas Bigelow. Roulette color comparator; Photoelectric colorimeter; Photoelectric polarimeter. b'09. BS '31—MS '32 (Va Poly Inst); PhD '36—post-doctoral F '36-37 (U Va); Ford Found Faculty F '51-52 (on leave from Tulane U). Co-inventor of roulette color comparator, photoelectric colorimeter and photoelectric polarimeter, research on instrumental chemical analysis relating to use of these instruments. Co-author: (with John H Yoe) Chemical Computations and Errors '40. With Tulane U since '37, prof and head chem dept from '43. ACS—Sigma Xi—Alpha Chi Sigma. Department of Chemistry, Tulane University, New Orleans 18.

11 CRUSE, Andrew William. Telecommunications (International); Television; Radio and landline communications (Telephony, telegraphy). b'98. BS '22 (US Naval Acad); grad Navy schs for optics (Washington), torpedoes (Newport), chem warfare (Edgewood Arsenal), submarines (New London). Author articles in field. Asst vp charge radio operating dept International Telephone and Telegraph Corp since '46 vp and dir Radio Corp of Cuba; pres and dir Radio Corp of Porto Rico. Active duty as capt USN '41-46. AAAS(F)—Am Geog Soc(F)—Soc Am Mil Engrs—Acoustical Soc Am—Acad Polit Sci—Sociedad Colombiana De Ingenieros (hon)—Am Inst Physics. Inst Radio Engrs (sr mem) —AIEE. 67 Broad St., N.Y.C. 4.†◉

12 CRUSIUS, Paul Nicholas. Medieval history; History of the medieval church; early monastic cartularies. b'85. BA '09—MA '16—PhD '36 (Harvard); summers '12-14 (U Chicago Div Sch); '16-17 (Columbia U); summers '24-25 (U Chicago). Teacher Eng Elmhurst (Ill) Coll '10-15, prof hist since '19. AHA—Medieval Acad Am—Am Church Hist Soc. Elmhurst College, Elmhurst, Ill.

13 CRUTHIRDS, Archie Edward. X-ray burns; Burns of eye, ear, nose and throat and adjacent tissues (Treatment with sulfhydryl solution). Author articles: The Treatment of Face and Eye Burns '42; Burns of the Ear, Nose, Mouth and Adjacent Tissues '43; Importance of Sulfhydryl in the Treatment of Corneal and X-ray Burns '46; Sulfur Metabolism and its Relation to Wound Healing in Ophthalmology and Otolaryngology '49; The Role of Sulfhydryl in Tissue Respiration and Repair as Applied to Burns in Ophthalmology '49; Use of Sulfhydryl Preparations in Treatment of Burns in Ophthalmology and Otolaryngology '50; Use of Sulfhydryl in the Treatment of Corneal Scars Following Chemical Eye Burns and Ulcers (instruction course) '50 Suplfhydryl Treatment as Applied to Burns in Ophthalmology '50; Treatment of Eye Burns with the Sulfhydryl Solution '50. 1011 Professional Building, 15 E. Monroe St., Phoenix.

14 CSANYI, Ladis Henry. Highway engineering; Asphalt paving technology. b'03. CE—MCE (Polytech Inst Brooklyn). Research rainfall, sewer runoff, pile and caisson foundations; traffic studies Harlem River Drive, East River Drive, West Side elevated highway NYC, design tunnel lighting, traffic signs, interchanges, highway repair equipment and operations, highway routings, parking lots, pavements and materials, design asphalt plants and asphalt technology. Author articles in field. Asst engr DPW Manhattan NYC '32-36, engr research '36-40, asst maintenance engr '40-44; engr charge Municipal Asphalt Plant '44-46; cons engr since '46; asso with Edwards & Kelcey '47-48; prof civil engring Ia State Coll since '49. ASCE —Assn Asphalt Paving Technol—Highway Research Bd—Inst Traffic Engrs —Am Rd Builders Assn—Am Soc Engring Educators—Sigma Xi—Tau Beta Pi. Iowa State College, Ames, Ia. H: 427 North Franklin Av.

15 CUATRECASAS, Jose. Colombia (Flora); Botany. b'03. Explorations and studies on Spanish plants and west-European plants made in Barcelona Madrid, Geneva, Paris, and Berlin '21-39, South American plants '32-47. Author books and articles in field. Asst prof systematic bot U Barcelona Spain '24-30; prof systematic bot U Madrid '31-39; chief curator sect tropical plants Bot Garden Madrid '32-39, dir '37-39; prof Inst de Ciencias Naturales Nat U Bogota Colombia '39-42; prof bot Sch Agr Cali Colombia '42-47; dir Comision Botanica del Valle Cali Colombia '43-47; curator Colombian Bot Chicago Natural Hist Mus since '47. Sociedad Geografica de Colombia (hon)—Academia Colombiana de Ciencias Exactas Fisicas y Naturales (hon). Chicago Natural History Museum, Chicago.

16 CUBER, John F(rank). American social problems; Sociology of marriage. b'11. AB '32 (Western Mich Coll); PhD '37 (U Mich). Author: Marriage Counseling Practice '48; Sociology '47. Co-author: (with Robert A. Harper) Problems of American Society '48, rev '51; ed Sociol Series Appleton Century Crafts since '50. Prof sociol O State U since '46, dir marriage counseling clinic '48-50; pvt counseling practice since '37. Nat Council Family Relations (chmn sect marriage counseling '48-50)—National Conf Family Life (research com '48) — Am Assn Marriage Counselors — AAAS—Am Sociol Soc. Ohio State University, Columbus, O.

17 CULBERT, Fred J. Diesel engine (Development, combustion). b'94. Ed in pub schs. Research on improved service stability of high speed diesels; directing development light weight dimensional engines. Holds patent on internal combustion engine, also liquid-cooled muffler with plural expansion chambers eliminating back pressure. Chief inspector Continental Motors Corp '17-22, Buda Co '22-32; in charge diesel engring and development Norfolk Naval Shipyard Portsmouth Va since '34. Code 353 Norfolk Naval Shipyard, Portsmouth, Va. H: 1516 Holland Av., Norfolk 9.

18 CULBERTSON, William Smith. International law; Latin American and Middle Eastern economics; Geopolitics. b'84. AB '07—LLD '18 (Emporia Coll); AB '08—PhD '11 (Yale); LLD '31 (Georgtown U); '08-10 (Berlin U, Leipzig U). Studied trade conditions and tariffs in Brazil, Uruguay, Argentina, Chile, Peru and Panama '15; chairman with rank of ambassador of economic mission to French North Africa, Middle East, Italy and France '44; technological intelligence mission to Germany '45; technical adviser in charge of economic questions for American delegaton Conference on Limitation of Armaments '21; delegate to Copenhagen Congress International Chamber of Commerce '39, Montreux '47. Author: Raw Materials and Food Stuffs in the Commercial Policies of Nations '24; International Economic Policies: A Survey of the Economics of Diplomacy '25; Reciprocity, A National Policy for Foreign Trade '37; Political Economy of Toal War '42, and others. Apptd by Pres Wilson mem US Tariff Commn '17, reapptd by Pres Harding '21, vice chmn '22-25; EE and MP to Rumania '25-28; AE and P to Chile '28-33; mem law firm Culberston, Briggs and Pendleton; prof head dept econ, mem exec faculty Sch Fgn Service Georgetown U. Lt col, col Gen Staff Corps US Army '42-45, chief Geopolit Sect MID; Planning Group Office Strategic Services; asst to Comdr Army Industrial Coll. Am Fed Pa State (chmn sect labor and industry) — Council Fgn Relations — Am Soc Internat Law—Internat Law Assn (pres Am br '43-49)—Am Econ Assn — Phi Beta Kappa. Awarded Grand Cross from Chile, Peru, Rumania, Ecuador, and Sultan of Morocco. Stoneleigh Court, 1025 Connecticut Av., Washington.

19 CULLEN, Max O'Rell. Meat cutting; Meat carving; Knives (Carving); Knives (Stoning and steeling). b'03. Student pub schs LaGrande Ore. Meat and animal carving to provide best and most economical use and cuts; knives for carving; use, care, honing, stoning and steeling of carving knives. Author: How to Carve Meat, Game and Poultry '41. Meat cutter, market mgr, meat equipment salesman '15-28; meat specialist Nat Live Stock and Meat Bd '29-31, dir dept meat merchandising and lectr demonstrator improved meat cutting and carving methods since '31. QMC Food and Container Inst(asso)—Am Marketing Association—Nat Cleaver Club. 407 S. Dearborn St., Chgo 5.

20 CULLIMORE, Clarence. Adobe Architecture. b'85. BS '10 (U Calif); M Arch '42 (U Southern Calif). Specializes in scientific design and construction of adobe buildings made fireproof, waterproof and earthquake-proof. Author: Old Adobes of Forgotten Fort Tejon '42; Adobe Architecture '47; Santa Barbara Adobes '48; also articles in field. Certified practicing architect Calif since '25; teacher architecture Bakersfield College since '30; mem City Planning Commn Bakersfield. Kern County Hist Soc (pres '43-44)—Kern County Museum (pres '44-45) — AIA(F) — Calif Assn State Architects. 10 Oleander Av., Bakersfield, Cal.

21 CULLINAN, Frank P. Pomology (Nutrition). b'95. BS '17 (Cornell U); PhD '31 (U Chicago). Sr and Principal pomol div fruit and vegetable crops and diseases Plant Ind US Dept Agr since '31, now asst chief bur. AAAS(F) —Am Soc Plant Physiol—Am Soc Hort Sci—Am Bot Soc—Wash Acad Sci— Am Inst Biol Sci. Bureau of Plant Industry, Soils and Agricultural Engineering, Plant Industry Station, Beltsville, Md.

22 CULVER, Kenneth Leon. History of French Revolution; Eighteenth Century France. b'03. AB '29—MA '30— PhD '35 (U Calif). Research on Jacques Rene Hebert and origins of Worship of Reason, the Brissotin-Robespierrist struggle during the legislative assembly with reference to fear of a dictator, Edmund Burke and the French Revolution. Asso prof history, Chico State Coll; coll rep D C Heath & Co, since '39. AHA—Am Acad Polit Social Sci—Societe des Etudes Robespierristes. 182 Second St., San Francisco 5.

23 CUMINGS, Glenn A(rthur). Fertilizer placement. b'94. BS '17 (Ia State Coll). Author: Placement of Fertilizer for Cotton '38; Fertilizer Placement for Potatoes '39; Methods of

Applying Fertilizer '48; also articles in field. Project leader research on fertilizer distributing machinery US Dept Agr since '27, sr agr engr since '43. Am Soc Agrl Engrs—AAAS(F)—Nat Joint Com Fertilizer Application (gen chmn '40, '41). Bureau of Plant Industry, Soils and Agricultural Engineering, Agricultural Research Center, U.S. Department of Agriculture, Beltsville, Md.†

10 CUMMINGS, Harold Neff. Engineering education. b'84. AB '06 (Bates Coll, Lewiston, Me); SB in CE '10 (Mass Inst Tech). Prin asst engr Great Northern Paper Co Millinocket Me '11-13; head civil engring dept Mechanics Inst Rochester NY '13-14; asso prof civil engring and acting head of dept U Delaware '18-20; prof applied math and head of dept Newark (NJ) Coll Engring '20-26, prof civil engring and head of dept, 27-42, vp coll '42-50, emer '50. AAAS(F)—ASCE—Am Soc Engring Edn—Phi Beta Kappa—Tau Beta Pi 367 High St., Newark 2.

11 CUMMINGS, Osmond Richard. History of street and electric railways (New England). b'23. Student '40-42 (Bates Coll Lewiston Me); '46-48 (Bentley Sch Accounting and Finance Boston). Compilation historical data on electric railways of New England, particularly Mass, New Hampshire and Maine. Author features for Transportation, ann publ Conn Valley chpt Nat Ry Hist Soc Inc, also Turnout monthly bull Boston chpt.; histories of electric railways for publ by various railroad fan orgns. Elec Railroaders' Assn—Central Electric Railfans' Assn—New Eng Electric Ry Hist Soc Inc—Nat Ry Hist Soc—Conn Electric Railfans' Assn. Newburyport Daily News, Box 191, Newburyport, Mass. H: 13 Parsons St.

12 CUMMINS, Arthur Benson. Diatomite; Asbestos; Filtration. b'95. BS '20 (U Chicago); PhD '26 (U Calif). Research industrial minerals particularly diatomite, magnesia, asbestos, filter aids, insulations. Holds various patents. Author articles in field. Research chem Celite Co '25-26, development engr '26-27, research engr '27-29; mgr celite research Johns-Manville '30-43, research div supervisor '44-48, research dept mgr since '48. AAAS—Am Chem Soc—AICE—Am Inst Mining Engrs—Am Ceramic Soc—Calif Acad Sci—Am Soc Testing Materials—Mineral Soc Am. Research Center, Johns-Manville, Manville, N.J. H: Cedar Crest Rd., Bound Brook, N.J.†

13 CUMMINS, George Baker. Mycology (Uredinales); Taxonomy (Tomato). b'04. BS '27 (Mont State Coll); AM '29 (Mich U); PhD '35 (Purdue U). Research in biology, morphology and taxonomy of plant rusts, disease resistance in the tomato; studies of differential teliospore and aeciospore characters of Phragmidium species, phylogenetic significance of pores in urediospores; compiled index of rusts of Guatemala. Author: Workbook in Fundamentals of Plant Science (with Gries) '48. Author articles: The Genus Prospodium (Uredinales) '40; Revisionary Studies in the Tropical American Rusts of Panicum, Paspalum, and Setaria '42, and others. Asst in bot Purdue U '31-36, asso bot since '36, asso prof '45-47, prof agrl bot since '47; agt US Dept Agr since '47; in chge Arthur Herbarium Plant Rusts since '36. Mycol Soc Am (past sec, treas, vp, pres)—Am Phytopath Soc—Ind Acad Sci—Sigma Xi. Purdue University Agricultural Experiment Station, Lafayette, Ind.☉

14 CUMMINS, Harold. Finger prints; Dermatoglyphics. b'93. AB '16 (U Mich); PhD '25 (Tulane U). Managing editor American Journal Anatomy; adv ed board Radiology; adv ed bd Am Journ Human Genetics. Author: Finger Prints, Palms and Soles '43; also articles in field. Prof anat and chmn dept Tulane U. AAAS—Am Assn Anat—Am Assn Phys Anthrop Soc Exptl Biol and Med—Internat Assn for Identification—New Orleans Acad Sci—Phi Beta Kappa—Sigma Xi—Alpha Omega Alpha. 310 Audubon St., New Orleans 18.☉

15 CUNNIFF, Hilda Spink. Soil conservation botany; Siamese language. b'04. BA '25 (U Wis); MS '34 (Pa State Coll). Asst bot Soil Cons Service US Dept Agr '36-46 research on erosion controlling plants of economic value; translator Army Map Service War Dept during '46, loaned from US Dept Agr to War Dept '43 to translate Siamese. AAAS—Am Phytopath Soc—Nat Aud Soc—Soil Conservation Soc Am—Acad World Econ—Am Forestry Assn—Gamma Sigma Delta. 404 South St., Key West, Fla.

16 CUNNINGHAM, Bess Virginia. Psychology; Child development; Parent education; Preschool education. b '82. BS '17 (U Toledo) AM '21 (O State U) PhD '23 (Columbia). Author: Family Behavior (awarded Parents Mag medal '37) '36; Psychology for Nurses '46. Co-author: (with R. Pintner) Pintner-Cunningham Primary Test '23. Research and teaching asst teachers coll Columbia U '21-22, Grace Dodge fellow '22-23, exec sec Child Development Inst '23-24, asso prof edn and supervisor ednl clinic '24-26, asso prof edn tchrs coll '26-34; asso prof edn U Toledo '36-38, prof edn '38-51, emeritus prof edn since '51. Am Psychol Assn(F)—AAAS(F)—Kappa Delta Pi. U of Toledo, Tol 6.☉

17 CUNNINGHAM, Frederick William. Servomechanisms; Non-circular gears; Spectrophotometers; Computers (Analogue); Color reproduction. b '02, SB '24—ScD '36 (MIT). Devised automatic photoelectric spectrophotometer with others; servomechanisms for electro-mechanical computers, for gun controls machine tools, non-circular gears; theory of color reproduction; advocated use of red light for preservation of dark adaptation, applied it to numerous instruments. Author articles With Arma Corp since '34, sr development engr in charge servomechanisms '44-49, gen cons since '48. APS—Optical Soc Am. 254 36th St., Bklyn 32. H: 56 Hubbard Av., Stamford, Conn.

18 CUNNINGHAM, Mary Elizabeth. History of New York state. AB (Cornell U); MA (State Coll for Teachers, Albany NY). Editor The Yorker, New York History, American Heritage. Author articles in field. With NY State Hist Assn Cooperstown NY, supervisor sch service and librarian '39, advanced to asso in publs and edn. AHA—Am Assn for State and Local Hist—Am Acad Polit Sci—Nat Council Social Studies—Middle States Council for the Social Studies—NY State Hist Assn—Phi Beta Kappa—Phi Kappa Phi. Awarded grant-in-aid by NY State Hist Assn, '47-48. Cooperstown, N.Y.

19 CUNNINGHAM, Raymond W. Development of new drug compounds. b'03. BS '29 (U Neb Coll Pharm); MS '31-'32 (U Neb Grad Sch); PhD '36 (U Minn Grad Sch Med). Research on new compounds with special reference to antispasmodics, anticonvulsants, antibiotics, analgesics, local anesthetics, and pharmacology of folic acid, hetra-

zan, aureomycin and artane. Author articles in field. Instr, later asso prof pharmacology Temple U Med Sch '38-43; dir pharmacology research Lederle Labs Div Am Cyanamid Co since '43. Am Soc Pharmacology and Exptl Therapeutics—Am Pharm Assn—AAAS—NY Acad Sci. Lederle Laboratories Division, Pearl River, N.Y.

20 CUNNINGHAM, Thomas M. Air conditioning; Refrigeration; Industrial relations; Sheet metal construction. b'00. Student '05-16 (Clydebank Tech Sch, Scotland). Industry committee member National War Labor Board Washington '45-46. Author articles in field. Dir indsl relations Carrier Corp Syracuse NY '45-50; exec sec Heating, Piping and Air Conditioning Contractors' Chicago Assn since '50. Am Soc Heating and Ventilating Engrs. 228 N. LaSalle St., Chgo 1.

21 CUNNINGHAM, William A(aron). Adsorption; Gypsum plaster; Water treatment. b'04. PhD '41 (U Tex). Prof chem engring U Tex since '42, chmn dept chem engring since '47. chmn dept chem engring '42-45, '47-49. Chemical Engineering Bldg., University Texas, Austin 12, Tex.

22 CUNZ, Dieter. Germans in Maryland. b'10. Student '20-29 (Humanistisches Gymnasium Wiesbaden); PhD '34 (U Frankfurt). Author: History of the Germania Club Baltimore '40; The Maryland Germans, A History '48. Editor annual bibliography Americana-Germanica since '45. Staff German department U Md since '39, prof German since '49, resident dean U Md fgn study center Zurich '47-48. AAUP—Modern Lang Assn Am—Am Assn Tchrs German—Goethe Soc Md—Soc History of Germans in Md (sec since '44). H: 7501 Rhode Island Av., College Park, Md.☉

23 CUPLER, John Adwin, II. Microdrilling. b'12. Student (Potomac State College). Design and production precision drills. Holds patents in field. Author articles: Microscopic Precision Tools '43; Micro Tools Drill Tiny Holes '49; The Technique of Micro-Drilling '50, and others. Founder and pres Nat Jet Co (mfr drills) since '33. NAM—Am Soc Tool Engrs. National Jet Co., 115 Milton Pl., Cumberland, Md.

24 CURETON, Edward Eugene. Psychometrics; Educational and psychological statistics. b'02. AB '25 (San Jose State Teachers Coll); MA '27 (Stanford); PhD '31 (Columbia). Directed college testing programs; designed reporting systems and forms in US Office of Education; surveyed civilian personnel testing needs in Army Service Forces and directed development of over 100 tests, questionnaires, check-lists and rating forms; engaged in research on analysis of causation, errors of measurement and correlation, validation against fallible criterion, accomplishment quotient technique, factor-analysis, clerical and mechanical aptitudes tests, testing in college personnel service. Author articles in field. Prof psychol U Tenn since '48; head dept phil and psych since '50. AAAS(F)—Am Psychol Assn(F)—Sigma Xi—Phi Kappa Phi—American Statistical Assn—Inst Math Statis—Am Edn Research Assn—Kappa Delta Pi — Psychometric Soc (past pres). University of Tennessee, Knoxville, Tennessee.†

25 CURETON, Thomas Kirk, Jr. Physical education and Health. b'01. BS (Elec engring) '25 (Yale); BPE '29—MPE '30 (Springfield Coll Mass); MA (Health, phys edn) '37—PhD (Edn) '39 (Columbia). Research on physical fitness Olympic athletes '32 and '36; research consultant US Navy, US Army Air Forces. Physical fitness test construction; fitness tests, treadmill run tests, flexibility tests, fat tests, posture tests, foot tests, physique tests, aquatic tests, endurance tests, center of gravity. Author: How to Teach Swimming and Diving 34; Physical Fitness Workbook (3rd edit) '47; Physical Fitness Appraisal and Guidance '47; Research Methods Applied in Health, Physical Education and Recreation '49, and others. Dir athletics and phys edn Suffield Acad Conn '25-29; prof health and phys edn Internat YMCA Coll Springfield Mass '30-41, dir grad health and phys edn '39-41; visiting prof phys edn and recreation U Calif Berkeley '39, U So Calif '40; now prof phys edn U Ill, dir phys fitness research lab, exec com sch of phys edn; cons phys training sect US Navy Washington '43-44; asso ed Research Quarterly; bd dirs Scholastic Coach since '47. AAAS (F)—Am Assn Research in Child Development (F)—Am Assn Health Phys Edn and Recreation—Am Heart Assn—Am Physiol Soc—APHA—Am Edn Research Assn—Am Stat Assn—NEA—Nat Collegiate Athletic Assn—AAUP—Phi Delta Kappa—Pi Gamma Mu. 213 Huff Gymnasium, University of Illinois, Urbana, Ill. H: 501 E. Washington St.

10 CURME, George Oliver, Jr. Synthetic organic chemistry; Hydrocarbon gases; Plastics. b'88. BS '09—DSc '33 (Northwestern U); PhD '13 (U Chicago). Research on organic synthesis based on natural hydrocarbons on behalf of companies which later became units of Union Carbide and Carbon Corporation, later commercialized results of preceding research. Vice-pres Union Carbide and Carbon Research Lab Inc since '38; vp Bakelite Corp since '39, dir since '44; vp Carbide and Carbon Chemicals Corp since '29, dir since '44; vp, dir Carbide and Carbon Chem Ltd since '44. Am Chem Soc—Am Inst Chem Engrs—Soc Chem Industry—AAAS—Nat Acad Sci—NY Acad Sci—Phi Beta Kappa—Sigma Xi. Chandler medalist '33; Perkin medalist '35; Elliott Cresson medalist '36; Willard Gibbs medalist '44; recipient Nat Modern Pioneer Award '40. 30 E. 42d St., NYC 17.◎

11 CURRAN, C. Howard. Clinical entomology; Insects of Pacific regions; Diptera; Medical entomology; Insect control. b'94. BS '16 (U Toronto); MA '31 (U Kan); DSc '34 (U Montreal). Research on diptera, insects and insect control, other entomological subjects; demonstrated first commercial use calcium cyanide in mill fumigation, uses of DDT in camp areas, stables and public buildings; accessory control measures; conducted research with paradichlorobenzene for pest control in grain and seeds. Author: Families and Genera of North American Diptera '34; The Diptera of Kartabo, British Guiana '34; Insects of the Pacific World '45. Co-author: (with C Kaufeld) Snakes and Their Ways '36; (with F E Lutz) Insects, Tick and Human Disease '42; also articles in field. Cons entomol US Testing Co '37-42; collaborator flight of diptera Sperry Gyroscope Co since '44; entomol cons Civilian Defense Volunteer Office '41-45; dir insect control Palisades Interstate Park Commn since '45; dir and treas Bakon Yeast Co NYC since '37; curator Am Mus Natural Hist NYC since '47. Calif Acad Sci(F)—AAAS(F)—Entomol Soc Am(F)—Am Mosquito Control Assn(F)—Am Soc Econ Entomol(F)—NY Entomol Soc (pres '36)—Panama Soc Natural Hist

(hon). American Museum of Natural History, 79th St. & Central Park West, NYC 24.†

12 CURRAN, George Perry. Coal carbonization; Carbonization of liquid hydrocarbons. b'98. Met Engr '21 (O State U). Directed research on coal carbonization, coal use, maximum use of fuels, air drafts, fuel mixtures; carbonization of liquid hydrocarbons; high temperature coking, production and yields of metallurgical coke or Electrode Carbon, oils, light distillate and gas. Vice pres Coal Carbonizing Co '35-47; vp Curran Carbonizing & Engring Co since '47; partner and dir research MD Curran & Co since '44. Registered profl engr Mo. Mo Soc Profl Engrs. Curran Carbonizing and Engineering Company, St. Louis 2.

13 CURRENCE, Troy Mansell. Tomato, melon, bean and asparagus breeding and genetics (Northern conditions). b'97. BS '23—MS '25 (W Va U); PhD '30 (Cornell U). Author articles in field. Prof U Minn since '28. Am Soc Hort Sci—Genetics Soc Am—Minn Acad Sci—Sigma Xi. Division of Horticulture, St. Paul Campus, University of Minnesota, St. Paul 1.†

14 CURRENT, Richard N. American history (Nineteenth century, Civil War and Reconstruction); Political science; Social science. b'12. AB '34 (Oberlin Coll); MA '35 (Fletcher Sch Law and Diplomacy); PhD '39 (Wisconsin U). Author: Old Thad Stevens '42. Co-author: Public Men In and Out of Office '46; also articles in field. Asst prof hist and polit sci Rutgers U '42-43; asst prof hist Hamilton Coll '43-44; prof hist Northern Mich Coll of Edn '44-45; asso prof hist Lawrence Coll '45-47; May Treat Morrison prof Am hist Mills Coll since '47. AHA—Miss Valley Hist Assn—Wisc Hist Soc—Phi Beta Kappa. 331 Lincoln Hall, University of Illinois, Urbana, Ill. H: 1215 W. Springfield Ave., Champaign, Ill.

15 CURRIE, Chester C(arlyle). Organo-silicon fluids and lubricants. b'17. BS '39 (Alma Coll). Engaged in basic research on chemistry of organo-cilanes, organo-silicon polymers, development silicone fluids, methods polymerization and synthesis; developed antifoam compound; associated with development silicone diffusion pump fluids, silicone mold release agents, silicone emulsions, greases, compounds. Several patents issued and pending in field. Author articles in field. Charge development group silicone fluids lubricants and compounds Dow Corning Corp since '47. Am Chem Soc. Dow Corning Corporation, Midland, Mich. H: 204 W. Carpenter.†

16 CURTIN, Leonora Scott Muse. Ethnobotany, ethnology and folklore of the American Southwest. Ed pvt schs (England France Switzerland). Author: Healing Herbs of the Upper Rio Grande '47; By The Prophet of The Earth '48; also articles in field. Research asso Pueblo Grande Phoenix Ariz since '40. Archaeol Inst Am (exec com Sch Am Research)—Instituto Nacional de Antropologia e Historia Mexico (hon). 614 Acequia Madre, Santa Fe, N.M.

17 CURTIS, Brian C(utler). Fishery biology; Fish management and conservation. b'93. AB '15 (Harvard); MA '34 (Stanford U). Editor California Fish and Game '42-46. Author: The Life Story of the Fish '38; The Life Story of the Fish: His Morals and Manners, '49; also articles in field. Supervising fisheries biol Calif State Div Fish and Game '40-48. Am

Fisheries Soc (asst ed)—Am Soc Ichthyologists and Herpetologists — Pacific Fisheries Biol. H: Faradawn, St. Helena, Calif.†

18 CURTIS, Charles Pelham. Law (Education). b'91. AB '14—LLB '17 (Harvard). Co-author: (with George C Homass) Introduction to Pareto '34; (with Ferris Greenslet) The Practical Cogitator '45. Admitted Mass bar '19; spl asst US atty Mass '22-23; spl asst to Under Sec of State '41; mem Mass Constitutional Conv '17; lectr in govt Harvard '28; mem com continuing legal edn Am Law Inst; mem council Survey of the Bar. Am Bar Assn—Mass Bar Assn—Boston Bar Assn—NY City Bar Assn. 30 State St., Boston.◎

19 CURTIS, Henry Stoddard. Recreation (Parks and playgrounds); Retirement. b'70. AB '94 (Olivet (Mich) Coll); AB '95 (Yale); PhD '98 (Clark U). Surveyed recreational facilities southeastern Michigan by canoe on Huron River; toured county poorhouses and infirmaries; proposed retirement home for teachers on campuses of American universities; motor tour surveys Florida state facilities for retired oldsters. Author: Play and Recreation in the Open Country '14; Education Through Play '15; Practical Conduct of Play '15; The Play Movement and Its Significance '17; Recreation for Teachers. Author article: Why Retire at Sixty-five? Asst dir, dir and gen dir playgrounds NY City summers '98-01; student playgrounds Germany and England '05-09; dir Huron Valley Recreation Survey U Mich; organizer '06 later sec and vp Playground Assn of Am; exec sec Huron-Clinton Parkway Com. Play Assn Am. H: 1100 Hill St., Ann Arbor.◎

20 CURTIS, James Frederick. Phonetics; Speech pathology. b'14. BA '35 (Ia State Teachers Coll); MA '40—PhD '42 (U Ia). Studies on voice disorders, articulation disorders, and methods for improvement of oral reading; auditory tests on relation of hearing ability to voice volume, and effects of background noise; tests on voice training techniques. Co-author: (with Johnson, Brown, Edney, Keaster) Speech Handicapped School Children '48. Author articles: A Study of the Effects of Muscular Exercise Upon Stuttering '42; Intelligibility Related to Microphone Position '46. Co-author article: (with D C Spriestersbach) Misarticulation and Discrimination of Speech Sounds '51. Contributor: National Society Study of Education Yearbook '49. Instr speech and acting dir speech clinic Purdue U '42-43; research asso psycho-acoustic lab Harvard U '43; dir voice communication lab Voice Communication Research Project OSRD and National Defense Research Com Waco Tex '43-44; prof speech in charge exptl phonetic labs and grad training exptl phonetics U Ia since '46. Am Speech and Hearing Assn (F)—Speech Assn Am (F)—Acoustical Soc Am (F)—AAAS—Central States Speech Assn—Sigma Xi. State University of Iowa, Iowa City, Ia.

21 CURTIS, John Thomas. Orchids (Physiology); Plant ecology and physiology. b'13. BS '34 (Carroll Coll); MA '35—PhD '37 (U Wis). Author articles: Non-Specificity of Orchid Mycorrhizal Fungi '37; Growth of Fruits in the Orchidaceae '43; Germination in Five Species of Cypripedium '43; Latex and Rubber Characteristics of Cryptostegia '46; Fruit Production by the Cryptostegia Rubber Plant '46; Undifferentiated Growth of Orchid Embryos on Media Containing Barbiturates '47; Studies on the Nitrogen Nutrition of Orchid Embryos I, II, III '47, and others. Instr bot U Wis '37-39, asst prof '40-41, asso prof since '45; research dir Societe Haitiano-Am de Developpement Agricole Gonaives Haiti '42-45. Wis Acad Sci—Bot Soc Am—Ecol Soc Am—Am Soc Plant Taxonomists—AAAS. Awarded Guggenheim Fellowship U Minn '42. Department of Botany, University of Wisconsin, Madison 6, Wis.

10 CURTISS, John Shelton. History of Russia. b'99. AB '21 (Princeton U); MA '29—PhD '40 (Columbia U); seminars in field '32, 33-34. Research in Leningrad '34, elsewhere in Europe '48. Author: Church and State in Russia; The Last Years of the Empire '00-17; '40; An Appraisal of the Protocols of Zion '40. Archival staff Franklin D Roosevelt Library Hyde Park NY '41-42; mem Research and Analysis Branch USSR Div OSS '42-45; asso prof hist Duke U since '45; senior fellow Russian Inst Columbia U '47-48. Awarded Herbert Baxter Adams Prize from AHA for dissertation '40. Duke University, Durham, N.C.

11 CURTISS, Leon Francis. Nuclear physics. b'95. AB '17—PhD '22 (Cornell U). Investigation of beta and gamma ray spectra of nuclear radiation; development of instruments for measurement of radioactivity and cosmic radiation; preparation and calibration of standards for radioisotopes; study of methods for measurement intensities of neutrons; examination of standard neutron sources and methods for calibrating instruments for measurement of intensity of neutrons; member commission on standards, units, and constants of radioactivity International Council Scientific Unions; chairman committee on nuclear science National Research Council since '46. Author article: Radioactive Standards and Methods of Testing Instruments used in Measurement of Radioactivity '49. Contributor: Industrial Hygiene and Toxicology '48. Chief radioactivity sect Nat Bur Standards '40-49, cons radioactivity and chief neutron measurement sect since '49. APS (F)—AAAS—Washington Acad Sci—Washington Acad Med—Sigma Xi —Cosmos Club. National Bureau of Standards, Washington.

12 CURTISS, William Marshall. Agricultural marketing. b'04. BS '27 (U Ill); PhD '36 (Cornell). Co-author: (with J Lossing Buck) Chinese Farm Management '42; also articles in field. Economist Found for Econ Edn since '46. Internat Conf Agrl Econ—Am Farm Econ Assn—Acad Polit Sci—Am Econ Assn—Sigma Xi—Phi Kappa Phi—Gamma Sigma Delta. 30 S Broadway, Irvington-on-Hudson, N.Y.

13 CUSHMAN, Paul Allerton. Bearings (Hardening); Hardening (Induction). b'89. SB elec engring '11—SM mech engring '27 (MIT); ScD mech engring '32 (U Mich). Research on hardening cam followers and ball bearing races by electrical induction process, hardening roller bearing rolls, hardening of bearing races and rolls by salt bath process, developed bearing testing machines to test ball and roller bearings. Designer, engr and metall McGill Mfg Co '39-47; chief engr and metallurgist L and S Bearing Co since '47 part time since '49; prof mech engring, thermodynamics and refrigeration U Okla since '49. AS ME—Am Soc Metals—AAAS—Pi Tau Sigma—Sigma Tau. 1212 Marlboro Lane, Nichols Hills, Oklahoma City 14.

14 CUSTIS, Eleanor Parke. Dynamic symmetry in photography. Student (Corcoran Sch Art, Pa Acad Fine Art,

Henry B Snell). Author: New Method in Composition (8 vol) '29-32. Author articles: Dynamic Symmetry for Photographers '47, and others. Free lance illustrator and author. Royal Photographic Soc Gt Britain(F)—Photographic Soc Am(F). 115 B Mt. Pleasant Av., Gloucester, Mass.

15 CUTHBERT, F. Leicester. Clay mineralogy; Foundry sand technology; Oil and gas well drilling fluids. b'13. BA '35—MA '37 (U Buffalo); PhD '40 (Ia State Coll). Author articles in field. Mgr research and development Baroid Sales Div Nat Lead Co since '45. Am Mineral Soc—Geol Soc Am(F) —Am Foundrymen's Soc—Am Petroleum Inst—Sigma Xi. Nat Research Council fellow '45; State NJ Dept Conservation research fellow '45. Baroid Sales Division, National Lead Company, City National Bank, Houston, Tex.†

16 CUTHBERTSON, Frank G. Seed genetics. b'87. Student (Rothesay Acad, Scotland). Responsible for breeding and introducing many vegetables and flowers, Red Cored Chantenay carrot, Morse's Detroit dark red Beet, White Boston lettuce, Sulfur Resistant 91 muskmelon, Cuthbertson sweet peas. Apprentice seedgrowing '04-11; worked seed farms CC Morse & Co '11, sec '17-29; vp CC Morse & Co merged with DM Ferry & Co '30, sr vp. Ferry-Morse Seed Company, 500 Paul Av., San Francisco 24.

17 CUTLER, David Roy. Rubber manufacturing, technology and latex. b'10. Student (Thayer Acad); '28-32 (Mass Inst Tech). Vice pres and dir to pres and dir Alfred Hale Rubber Co since '30; treas gen mgr Am Curatex '32-33. Am Chem Soc. Alfred Hale Rubber Company, North Quincy 71, Mass.

18 CUTLER, Hugh C(arson). Economic botany (Maize, curcurbits, palms, rubber-bearing plants); Breeding and taxonomy of economic plants. b'12. BA '35-MA '36 (U Wis); PhD '39 (Washington U). Research on grasses related to maize in Mexico and southwest, on cultivated American plants, especially maize and curcurbits, and their wild relatives, and palms and plants of Andes in Central and South America; exploration for and production of secondary rubbers in extra-Amazon Brazil; study of plant distribution in Colorado River Basin '36-46. Author: Monograph of the North American Species of the Genus Ephedra '39. Author articles: Races of Maize in South America '46; Chicha, a native South American beer '47 (with M Cardenas). Research asso Washington U '40, Bot Mus of Harvard '41-47; field technician Rubber Development Corp '43-45; curator econ bot Chicago Natural Hist Mus since '47. Guggenheim Fellow '42-43, '46-47. Chicago Natural History Museum, Roosevelt Rd. and Lake Shore Dr., Chicago 5.

19 CUTLER, James Elbert. Human relations; American folkways and culture; Professional education. b'76. BA '00—LLD '34 (U Colorado); PhD '03 (Yale). Author: Lynch Law '05. Co-author: Study in Professional Education at Western Reserve University —the School of Applied Social Sciences '16-30 (with M R Davie) '30; also articles in field. Prof emeritus sociol Western Reserve U since '46. Am Acad Polit Social Sci—Am Sociol Soc. 2040 Stearns Rd., Cleve 6.

20 CUTLER, Theodore Harold. Industrial psychology; Labor and industrial relations. b'07. AB '29 (Drake U); PhD '48 (U Colo). Author: A Study of Unemployment in St. Louis '31; 1947 Labor

Relations in Denver Manufacturing '48; also articles in field. Indsl psychol Ralston Purina Co St Louis '30-31; asst Denver mgr Colo State Employment Service '33-35; regional personnel advisor Resettlement Adminstrn San Francisco '35-37; dir testing bur U Denver '37-41; civil service cons Colo State Civil Service Commn '41-42; regional personnel officer OPA Denver '42-43; labor relations officer USNR Mare Island Calif '43-46; dir bur personnel, indsl relations, prof psychol U Denver since '46. Am Psychol Assn—Colo-Wyo Acad Sci—Indsl Relations Research Assn—Sigma Xi. Diplomate in indsl psychol, Am Bd Examiners in Professional Psychol. University of Denver, 211 15th St., Denver 2.

21 CUTLER, Thomas Henry. Highway engineering, administration, and design. b'82. BS in ME '03—CE '38 (U Ky). Author articles in field. Supt constrn Powers, Thompson Constrn Co Joliet Ill '19-22; engr with Mo State Highway Commn from '23, constrn engr for state and chief engr from '27; state highway engr Ky Dept Highways to '48, now cons engr. Served as capt engrs US Army. Am Soc Mil Engrs—ASCE—Nat Soc Professional Engrs—Ky Soc Prof Engrs—Tau Beta Pi. State Highway Bldg., Frankfort, Ky. H: R.R. 9, Frankfort, Ky.

22 CUTLER, Wallace Milton. New product machinery; Hydraulic and marine machinery. b'87. Student '00-03 (U NY); grad '05 (Pratt Inst). Designed, patented, introduced Horton Differential Lathe Chuck for E Horton & Sons Co Conn '21-24; designed and built machinery and plants for Birdseye Freezing System of General Foods Co. Cons engr at Wallace M Cutler Assos Cambridge since '30, designing machinery for numerous indsl concerns; also with research dept United Shoe Machinery Corp and for Boston Ordnance Dist US Army designing ordnance machinery during World War II. ASME—Am Military Eng Army Ordnance Assn. 53 Hampshire St., Cambridge 39, Mass.

23 CUTRIGHT, Clifford Reginald. Economic entomology. b'93. BA '21 MS '22—PhD '25 (O State U). Author articles: Through the Year with Spray Materials 35; Experiments with Apple Pests in 1939 '40; Programs for Codling Moth Control '41; Economic Insect Control '43; DDT on Ohio Apples '46. Asst entomol O Agr Expt Sta research in control deciduous fruit insects '22-28, asso entomol deciduous fruit insect investigations since '28; Asso prof O State U '47. Am Assn Econ Entomol—Am Entomol Soc—O Acad Sci—Sigma Xi. Ohio Agricultural Experiment Station, Wooster, O.

24 CUTRIGHT, Paul Russell. Zoology; General biology; Animals of North and South America. b'97. AB '21—AM '23 (W Va U); PhD '32 (U Pittsburgh). Author: The Great Naturalists Explore South America '40. Head of biol dept Geneva Coll Beaver Falls Pa '23-29; instr in zool U Pittsburgh '29-33; head biol dept Beaver Coll Jenkintown Pa since '33; travel and study Carnegie Instn Labs on Dry Tortugas Islands '37; Lab of Inst for Research in Tropical Am on Barro Colo Island Gatun Lake, Canal Zone '39. AAAS(F)—Sigma Xi. 312 Summit Av., Jenkintown, Pa.

25 CUTRIGHT, Prudence. Social studies; Elementary education. b'92. PhB '23 (U Chicago); MA '27 (U Minn). Director research and curriculum construction, public schools Minneapolis '27-33. Author: The Day Before Yesterday in America '46. Co-author: (with W W Charters and G I Sanchez) Latin

America—Twenty Friendly Nations '44. Co-editor: Democracy Series '39; also articles in field. Acting supt public schools Minneapolis '43-44; lecturer various university summer schools. NEA (Ednl policies comm)—Am Assn Sch Adminstrs—Childhood Edn Assn—AAUW. Macalester College, St. Paul.

10 CUTSHALL, Alden. Economic geography (Urban, manufacturing, Far Eastern, midwestern United States); Philippines; Origin of Illinois place names. b'11. B Edn '32 (Eastern Ill State Coll); MA '35 (U Ill); PhD '40 (Ohio State U). Research in economic geography, urban geography, and geography of manufacturing in Wabash Valley, with specialization in economic geography of Philippine Islands. Instr geog '40, head dept geog Chicago undergraduate div U Ill since '47; research analyst, acting section chief, Ports and Urban Studies Section Far East Div OSS and State Dept '44-46. Asso Am Geog—Internat Geog Union—Am Geog Soc—Nat Council Geog Teachers—Phil Geog Soc—AAUP—Ill State Acad Sci—Sigma Xi. University of Illinois, Chicago Undergraduate Division, Navy Pier, Chicago.†

11 CUTSHALL, Elmer Guy. Philosophy of Methodism. b'90. AB '13—DD '28 (Cornell Coll Ia); AM '14 (State U Ia); BD '18—ThM, DD '31 (Garrett Bibl Inst); Swift fellowship '19-20—PhD cum laude '22 (U Chicago); post grad in psychology '23 (U Pa); LLD '31 (Kan Wesleyan U). Organizer Wesley Foundation of Philadelphia; has held forums in 110 cities, given 5600 lectures to high schools, colleges and universities. Author: Philosophy of Methodism. Chancellor Neb Wesleyan U '32-37. Phi Beta Kappa—Phi Kappa Phi. 203 W. Cheyenne Rd., Colorado Springs, Colo.

12 CUTTER, Victor Macomber, Jr. Mycology (Physiology, cytology, taxonomy, fungicide and antibiotic action); Native American plants (Latex production). b'17. AB '38 (Dartmouth Coll); PhD '41 (Cornell). Author articles in field. Asst prof microbiol Yale since '47. Am Mycol Soc—Bot Soc Am—Sigma Xi—Phi Kappa Phi. Osborn Botanical Laboratory, Yale University, New Haven.†

13 CUTTS, Elmer Henry. Indian and Oriental history; Education (India) Indic studies. b'08. BA '29—MA '32 (U Wash); PhD '40 (Harvard). Author: Source Book for the History of Civilization, part 1 '47; Basic Bibliography for Indic Studies '39. Author articles. Asst prof hist Northeast U Boston '41-43, '45-47, asso prof '47, prof since '47, chmn dept hist and govt since '48. Am Oriental Soc—AHA. Northeastern University, Boston 15.☉

14 CUTUJIAN, Frances C(atharine). Child and social psychology; Psychological testing. b'97. AB '20—AM '22 (Vassar Coll); PhD '37 (Yale); '29-31 (Radcliffe Coll). Author articles. Asst prof psychol Hood Coll '39, acting head dept '45-46, head of dept and prof psychol since '47. Am Psychol Assn—Eastern Psychol Assn—Md Psychol Assn—AAAS. Hood College, Frederick, Md.

15 CYR, Frank W. Rural education and rural life in the United States. b'00. BS '23 (U Neb); PhD '33 (Columbia). Author: Responsibility for Rural School Administration '33; The Small School in Wartime '42; Rural Education in the United States (translated into Spanish and Portuguese) '43. Co-author: The Small High School at Work '36; An introduction to Modern Education '37; Paying for Our Public Schools '38; Schools in Small Communities '39; A Policy for Rural Edu-

cation in the United States '40. Prof rural edn Teachers Coll Columbia since '41; cons on rural edn Am Inst Cooperation '45-51. Am Assn Sch Administrators—NEA (pres rural dept '40). Teachers College, Columbia University, NYC 27.†☉

D

16 DABNEY, Virginius. Social, political and economic history of southern United States; History of prohibition in Virginia and United States. b'01. AB '20—AM '21 (U Va); DLitt '40 (U Richmond); LLD '44 (Lynchburg Coll, Coll William and Mary). Author: Liberalism in the South '32; Below the Potomac '42; also articles in field. Ed Richmond Times-Dispatch since '36. Phi Beta Kappa—Am Soc Newspaper Editors. Awarded Pulitzer prize for editorial writing '47; winner Lee Editorial award of Va Press Assn and Lee School Journalism Washington and Lee U for distinguished editorial writing during '37. Times-Dispatch, Richmond 11, Va.

17 Da CUNHA, Mario Wagner Vieira. Public administration. b'12. MA '38 (U Sao Paulo Brazil); MA '44 (U Chgo). Research in Brazilian political orgn and public adminstrn; human relations in industry; bureaucracy in government and business. Author: A Burocratizacáo das Emprezas Industriais '51; Educacao Para a Administracão No Brazil '51. Co-author: (with A P Canabrava) A Administracao de Sant'ana de Parnaiba 1839-1867 '51. Prof sociology and anthropology Escola Sociologia e Politica Sao Paulo; prof bus and pub adminstrn U Sao Paulo; dir Instituto de Administracao Sao Paulo; chmn Civil Service Commn State of Sao aulo. Rua Dr Vila Nova, 268.

18 DAHL, Adrian Hilman. Nuclear radiation detection (Civilian defense instrumentation); Industrial radiography. b'19. BA '41 (St Olaf Coll); '50 (U Rochester Grad Sch). Research on development, procurement, evaluation of radiation detection instruments (conducted spectral sensitivity studies); Instrumental in establishing United States Atomic Energy Commission interim program for civilian defense; Studied photographic films and techniques in radiography of aluminum spot-welds with low voltage x-rays and of heavy castings with million volt x-rays. Cons to Nat Mil Establishment on radiation detection instrumentation requirements. Head radiation health phys sect Tennessee Eastman Corp-Clinton Engr Works, Oak Ridge Tenn '44-46; asst chief radiation instruments branch, div prodn US Atomic Energy Commn '46-47, chief '47-49; chief instrumentation sect U Rochester Med Sch Atomic Energy Project since '50. Am Inst Phys—Am Phys Soc—Am Assn Phys Teachers—Inst Radio Engrs—Sigma Pi Sigma. Atomic Energy Project, University of Rochester Medical School, Rochester, 20, N.Y.

19 DAHL, Crete. Education (Hotel, restaurant, retail store). BS '17 (O State U); MS '23 (Prince Sch Retailing Simmons Coll Boston). Publisher hotel and restaurant books; instruction in hotel equipment, textiles, and management; chief infants and childrens' section Office Civilian Requirements '43-44. Author: How to Get and Keep Restaurant Employees '45; How to Buy Bedding (rev edit) '49; Housekeeping Management and Organization in Hotels and Institutions (4th edit) '50. Publisher: Blueprints for Training Employees in Retail Stores '50. Ednl dir Esmond Mills NYC and Providence '24-29; copywriter Ander-

son, Davis & Platte NYC '29-30; tech and contbg ed Hotel Management since '29; ed in chief Infants and Childrens' Wear Review '32-43; womens personnel dir Waldorf Astoria NYC '43; asso ed My Baby '43-48; pres Dahl Pub Co (pub hotel and restaurant books, and Little Gold Gus Books) since '45; instr hotel housekeeping management hotel adminstrn dept Cornell since '45; organized Dahl Book Club for Hotel and Restaurant Executives '46. Am Home Econ Assn —Nat Training Dirs Assn—Nat Exec Housekeepers Assn—Nat Office Mgrs Assn. Dahl Publishing Co., 74 W. Park Place, Stamford, Conn.

20 DAHLE, Chester Distad. Dairy manufacturing. b'96. BS '20—MS '21—PhD '37 (U Minn). Invented high pressure homogenizing valve for homogenizer; originator of methods of making certain types of cheese; research in manufacture and processing of ice cream. Author: A Manual for Ice Cream Makers '27. Co-author: Manual for Dairy Manufacturing Short Courses '46; also articles in field. Prof charge dairy mfg Pa State Coll since '29. Am Dairy Sci Assn—Milk and Food Tech Assn—Dairy Industries Soc Internat—Sigma Xi—Gamma Sigma Delta. Received Borden award and gold medal in dairy mfg research '47. Dairy Department, Pennsylvania State College, State College, Pa. H: R. D. #1, Centre Hall, Pa.

21 DAHLE, Dan. Cosmetics; Coal-tar colors. b'94. ChE '19 (Chalmers Inst Tech Gothenburg Sweden); MS '34—PhD '36 (Am U). Author articles in field. Chief cosmetic div US Food and Drug Adminstrn '38-46; dir research Bristol-Myers Co Hillside NJ since '46. Bristol-Myers Co., Hillside 5, N.J.

22 DAHLE, Joseph. Resins (Synthetic); Glass (Laminated). b'00. MS '25 (Chalmers Poly Inst); '30-31 (Brooklyn Poly Inst); '42-43 (Case Sch Applied Sci). Research on polyvinyl esters, alcohols, acetals and furane resinification, applications of natural and synthetic polymeric materials for adhesives, protective coatings and liners, corrosion proofing materials, synthetic fibers and bristles, laminated glass, textile finishes, packaging materials of low vapor permeability, molding compounds. Granted US and foreign patents on processes, equipment and uses for vinyl resins and new types of laminated glass. Chief chem and tech adv Triplex Safety Glass Co '29-32; asst development dir Fiberloid Corp '35-39; project leader Gustavus J Esselen Inc ' 39-42; research dir Aspinook Corp '43-46; Woods Plastics Inc '46-49 and Atlas Mineral Products Co '49-50; cons since '50. ACS—AAAS—Am Assn Textile Chem & Colorists—ASTM. Box 611, Allentown, Pa.

23 DAHLEN, Miles Augustinus. Chemistry of dyes, pigments, and organic chemicals. b'04. BS '24—PhD '28 —duPont fellow '27-28 (U Minn). Author articles in field. Research chem EI duPont de Nemours Co Wilmington '28-30, div head Jackson Lab intermediates div '30-34, miscellaneous dye div '34-38, asst dir tech lab '38-46, asst dir sales domestic dyestuff div '46-49, dir sales fine chem div since '49. Am Chem Soc (chmn Del sect '36, councillor '37) —AICE—Am Assn Textile Chem and Colorists—Textile Research Inst (dir since '45)—Sigma Xi—Tau Beta Pi. Du Pont Company, Nemours Building, Wilmington, Del.

24 DAHLGREN, Elmer George. Conservation, economics, statistics and history of oil and gas; Marginal oil wells; Underground natural gas storage. b'03. AB '29 (U Wis). Chairman Production Review committee, American Institute Mining and Metallurgical Engineers. Author: Surveys of Underground Natural Gas Storage '43, '44, '45. Co-author: (with George Pasquella) National Stripper Well Surveys '41, '42, '44; also articles in field. Field gauger and office mgr Okla City Producers Assn '31-33; dep proration umpire and chief clerk oil and gas conservation dept Okla Corp Comm '33-37; dir oil and gas conservation div Kan Corp Commn '37-39; oil and gas valuation engr oil and gas unit SEC Washington '39-41; sr petroleum development analyst prodn div Petroleum Adminstrn for War Washington '41-42; tech sec Interstate Oil Compact Commn Okla City '42-48. Am Assn Petroleum Geol—Am Inst Mining Metall Engrs—Okla Soc Petroleum Engrs—Okla City Geol Soc. Oil and gas cons. 910 Braniff Bldg., Oklahoma City 2, Okla. H: 715 N.W. 49th St.

10 DAHLSTRAND, Hans P. Steam and gas turbines; Lubrication. b'74. Student (Boras Tech Coll Sweden). With Allis-Chalmers Mfg Co since '04, engr in chge steam turbine dept '15-42, cons engr '42-48; dir steam turbine engring since '48. ASME—Nat Assn Power Engrs. Allis-Chalmers Manufacturing Co., Milw.

11 DAILEY, Manvel C(lair). Building materials; Lime, gypsum. b'01. BSc '29 (U Washington). Research on plaster, lime, gypsum products; developments include new process for hardboard from wood fiber, new process for production high-strength cements from calcined gypsum, adaptation of such cements to industrial uses. Holder numerous patents in field. Author articles in field. Research asso Bur Standards Gypsum Assn '26-29; research engr US Gypsum Co since '29, now research supervisor charge of development work on plaster, lime, and gypsum products. ASTM (com Cll). 1253 Diversey Blvd., Chicago.

12 DAKE, Henry C. Uranium minerals; Gemology. b'96. DMD '19 (North Pacific Coll Portland). Author: Quartz Family Minerals '38; Fluorescent Light '41; Uranium and Atomic Power '41; Ultra-Violet Light '42; Art of Gem Cutting '43; Rarer Metals '46; Handbook of Uranium Minerals '47; Editor The Mineralogist Magazine since '32. NW Federation Mineral Soc (hon pres)—Mich Mineral Soc (hon)—Am Federation Mineral Soc. 329 S.E. 32nd Av., Portland 15, Ore.

13 DALE, Edward Everett. American frontier history (Indians, ranching, pioneer life, Oklahoma). b'79. AB '11 (U Okla); AM '14—PhD '22 (Harvard). Collaborator in historical research US Department Agriculture '25; member Indian Survey Commission US Institute for Government Research '26-27. Author: Territorial Acquisitions of the U.S. '12; A History of Oklahoma '24; The Range Cattle Industry '30; Cow Country '42; (with J S Puchanan) Tales of the Teepee '19; (with D L Drumond, E B Wesley) History of United States '48; (with M L Wardell) History of Oklahoma '48; and others. Research prof hist U Okla since '43. AHA—Miss Valley Hist Assn—So Hist Assn—Okla Hist Assn—Okla State Folk Lore Assn—Phi Beta Kappa. University of Oklahoma, Norman, Okla.

14 DALE, Ernest. Labor relations and economics. b'17. BA '39—MA '43 (Cambridge U); MA '46—fellow and asso fellow Jonathan Edwards Coll, PhD '50 (Yale). Author: The Unionization of Foremen '45; The Development of Foremen in Management '45; Guaranteed Wages and Employment Stabilization Techniques '45; The Preparation of Company Annual Reports '46; Increased Productivity Through Labor Management Cooperation '49; Criteria and Sources of Wage Determination '50; Planning and Developing the Company Organization Structure '52; also articles in field. Lecturer labor relations Columbia since '46 and asst prof indsl relations since '50; econ and research advisor Am Mgt Assn. Royal Econ Soc(F). Grad School of Business, Columbia University, NYC 27.†

15 D'ALELIO, Gaetano Francis. Plastics; Fibers; Resins (Synthetic). b'09. AB '31 (Boston Coll); PhD '35 (Johns Hopkins). Research and inventions in outstanding ion exchange resins; synthetic fibers; molding and laminating compositions; radar insulations; rocket launchers; heat resistant polystyrene. Issued about 275 patents in field. Author: A Laboratory Manual of Plastics and Synthetic Resins '43; Plastics and Synthetic Resins '46; Substancias Plasticas Experimentales y Resinas Sinteticas '48; Fundamental Principles of Polymerization—Polymers, Plastics and Resins (in press). Research chem Gen Elec Co '36-39, dir plastics lab '39-43; dir research Pro-phy-lac-tic Brush Co '43-44, vp in charge research '44-46; mgr high polymer research Indsl Rayon Corp '46-47; asst dir research Koppers Co Inc '47-49, vp and mgr research since '49. ACS—AAAS—Am Inst Chem (F)—NY Acad Sci (F)—Textile Inst —Nat Farm Chemurgic Council—Soc Chem Industries (London)—Hist Sci Soc—Indsl Research Inst—Am Ordnance Assn—Phi Lambda Upsilon—Phi Beta Kappa—Sigma Xi. Received Nat Bur Ordnance Individual Citation for War Research and Development '46. Koppers Company, Inc., Pitts 19.

16 DALEY, Arthur. Sports. b'04. BA '26 (Fordham U). Sportswriter specializing in track and field since '28. Author: Times at Bat '50. Co-author: (with John Kieran) The Story of the Olympic Games '52, also articles in field. Sports staff NY Times since '26, sports columnist since '42. The New York Times, 229 W. 43rd St., NYC 18.

17 DALGIN, Ben. Typography; Quality of printing. b'92. Member Joint Mechanical Committee of American Newspaper Publishers Association and American Association of Advertising Agencies since '47. Author: Advertising Production '46; also articles in field. Advt prodn mgr NY Times '20-34, dir art and reproduction since '34; member teaching staff Employing Printers Assn NY '26-35; lecturer universities and other ednl instns, and before profl and tech groups; cons. New York Times, Times Building, 229 W. 43rd St., NYC.

18 Da LIE, David A. Herpetology; Okefenokee Swamp; snakes. b'19. Student '37-39 (U Dayton). Research on breeding habits, habitat control, social aspects sexes and general attitude and reactions on contact with man of American alligator; venoms, treatment of bites, feeding habits, range, hibernation of diamond back rattlesnake and cottonmouth moccasin; topography, history, flora, fauna, geological composition Okefenokee Swamp. Author articles in field. Asst Curator Dayton Pub Mus '36-'39; mgr and wild life dir Okefenokee Swamp Park since '46. Herpetologists League —Am Soc Icthyologists and Herpetologists. P.O. Drawer-860, Waycross, Ga.

19 DALKE, Paul David. Wildlife management; Forestry. b'01. BSF '25 —MSF '28—PhD '34 (Mich U). Research on food habits of young pheasants in Michigan, and of adult pheasants based on crop analysis method; cover maps; home and seasonal ranges of eastern cottontail in Connecticut; use and availability of more common winter deer browse plants in Missouri Ozarks; census techniques for upland game; ecology and management of wild turkeys in Missouri Author articles in field. Biol Fish and Wildlife Service since '35, Mo Coop Wildlife Research Unit '37-47, Ida Cooperative Wildlife Research Unit since '47. Soc Am Foresters (sr)—Am Soc Mammalogists—Am Ornithol Union—Wildlife Soc (treas)—Sigma Xi—Phi Sigma. Fish and Wildlife Service, School of Forestry, Moscow, Idaho. H: 642 North Hayes St.⊙

20 DALLA VALLE, J(oseph) M(aria). Micromeritics (Technology of fine particles); Industrial ventilation and health. b'06. BS '27—MS '28—ScD '30 (Harvard). Author: Micromeritics '48; The Industrial Environment '48; also articles in field. Asso prof chem engring Ga Inst Tech since '48. Georgia Institute of Technology, Department of Chemical Engineering, Atlanta.

21 DALLIN, David J. Soviet foreign relations; Forced labor. b'89. Student (U St Petersburg and U Berlin); grad '13 (U Heidelberg). Participated in Russian Revolution '17-21, was member of Moscow Soviet as representative of an anti-Communist party, in exile since '22, in US since '40. Author: Soviet Russia's Foreign Policy '42; Russia and Postwar Europe '43; Real Soviet Russia '44; Big Three '45; Forced Labor in Soviet Russia '47; Russia and the Far East '48; The Rise of Russia in Asia '49. Asso ed The New Leader in New York since '45. 50 Manhattan Av., NYC 25.

22 DALQUEST, Walter Woelber. Mammalogy (Washington, California, Mexico). b'16. BS '40 — MS '41 (U Washington). Author: Mammals of Washington '48; also articles in field. Research Mexican mammals U Kan Mus Nat Hist since '45. Am Soc Mammalogists—Biol Soc Wash. University of Kansas, Museum of Natural History, Lawrence, Kan.

23 DALTON, Van Broadus. Dental bibliography and history. b'85. DDS '07 (Ohio Coll Dental Surgery); Diplomate '48 (Am Bd Oral Surgery). Chairman of history and museum commission Ohio State Dental Association; Chairman history committee Cincinnati Dental Society. Author: Essentials of Orthodontia (including chpt on history of orthodontic terminology) '14; The Genesis of Dental Education: its struggles, triumphs and achievements '46; History of the Ohio College of Dental Surgery '46. Oral surgeon since '16. Charter mem and 1st sec Cincinnati Dental Research Soc '14—State Hist Soc Mo—Fedn Dentaire Internat —ADA(Assoc)—AMA. 116 Garfield Pl., Cin 2.†

24 DALY, Lloyd William. Greek mythology. b'10. AB '32 (Knox Coll); AM '33—PhD '36 (U Ill); '37-38 (Am Sch Class Studies, Athens Greece). Author articles in field. Asso prof classical studies U Pa since '47. Am Philol Assn—Archaeol Inst Am—Class Assn Atlantic States. University of Pennsylvania, Phila 4. H: 310 Morton Av., Ridley Park, Pa.

25 DALY, Robert Welter. Hispano-americanism; Russian naval history (1651-1815). b'16. PhB '39—MA '40— PhD '49 (Loyola U); student (Northwestern U, Georgetown, Yale). Author articles in field. Instr gen studies US Coast Guard Acad '41-43, research in Russian naval hist since '39; asso prof

Eng hist and govt US Naval Acad since '46. Department of English History and Government, U. S. Naval Academy, Annapolis, Md.

10 DAMANN, Kenneth Eugene. Plankton periodicity. b'15. BS '38 (Kent State U); MS '40—PhD '43 (Northwestern U). Research on plankton of Lake Michigan, and automatic recording of residual chlorine as related to water purification '43-47. Author articles in field. Prin filtration bact City of Chicago '43-47; asso prof bot Eastern Ill State Coll since '47. AAAS — Limnol Soc Am — Phycol Soc Am—Bot Soc Am—Am Water Works Assn. Awarded Sigma Xi Prize for best PhD dissertation of year Northwestern U '43. Eastern Illinois State College Department of Botany, Charleston, Ill.†

11 DAMBACH, Charles A(rthur). Conservation of wildlife; Insect and animal ecology. b'11. BS '37—MS '41 —PhD '45 (O State U). Author articles in field. Asso prof zool entomal O State U, instr animal ecol and dir O Conservation Lab O State U since '48; collaborator US Soil Conservation Service since '45; collaborator US Fish and Wildlife Serv since '45; chief div wildlife Ohio Dept Nat Rescs. AAAS—Am Entomol Soc—Am Ornithol Union— Friends of Land—O Acad Sci—Soc Am Foresters—Soil Conservation Soc Am— Wildlife Soc—Sigma Xi. Ohio State University, Columbus 10, O.†

12 DAME, Lawrence. Modern and ancient Yucatan; French and German wines. b'98. Student (Harvard, Ecole des Hautes Etudes Sociales, Paris, U of Grenoble and Toulouse, France, Instituto de Burgos, Spain). Author: New England Comes Back '40; Yucatan '41; also articles in field. Feature writer, art ed Boston Herald and Boston Traveller since '43. SAR—Wine and Food Soc, London and Boston—League NA Indians (hon mem). 74 Pinckney St., Boston.

13 DAMON, Norman Clare. Traffic safety. b'97. BA '22 (U Mich). Staff organizers Automotive Safety Foundation '37; secretary committees National Conference Street and Highway Safety '24, '26, '30; chairman Committee on Economic Costs of Motor Vehicle Accidents, Highway Research Board, National Committee Traffic Training; member executive and advisory committees National Committee Traffic Safety; consultant President's Highway Safety Confs. Author: Let's Face the Facts About Accidents '44; Let's Look at the Record '46. Co-author: Standard Highway Safety Program '39; Wartime Highway Traffic Program '42. Asst to Washington rep Automobile Mfrs Assn '22-36; sec safety com '30-37; dir Automotive Safety Found '37-42, vp and dir grants since '42. SAE—Inst Traffic Engrs — Internat Assn Chiefs Police (hon life)—Nat Sheriffs Assn. Automotive Safety Found., 700 Hill Bldg., Washington 6.

14 DANA, Bliss F. Plant pathology, Virus diseases; Curly top vegetables; Breeding beans and beets for disease resistance. b'91. BS '16—MS '17 (Wash State Coll); '32-36 (Ore State Coll). Author articles in field. Plant path US Dept Agr at Ore State Coll since '31. Am Phytopath Soc (pres Pacific div '40)—AAAS(F)—Sigma Xi—Phi Kappa Phi. Botany Department, Oregon State College, Corvallis. Ore.†

15 DANHOF, Clarence Henry. American economic history (Agricultural); American economy (Government and business, World War II). b'11. MA '33—PhD '39 (U Mich); AB '32 (Kalamazoo Coll); '33-34 (U Ia). Author articles in field. Editor: Survey of Current Business '44-45; staff Bur of the Budget '45-46; asst prof Woodrow Wilson Sch Pub Affairs Princeton U since '46; econ War Manpower Commn '42-43, Nat War Labor Bd '43. Am Econ Assn—Econ Hist Soc (London)— Agrl Hist Soc—Business Hist Soc— Econ Hist Assn. Woodrow Wilson School, Princeton University, Princeton, N.J.

16 DANIEL, Dorothy. History and identification of early American cut and engraved glass. b'05. Student (Simpson Coll Indianola Ia). Pennsylvania. Author: Cut and Engraved Glass 1771-1905 '50. Author article: First Glass House West of the Alleghenies '49, and others. 5707 Lynne Haven Rd., Pitts 17.†

17 DANIEL, Earle H. Artificial limbs (design, materials, training of amputees in use). b'88. Ed pub schs. Research since '19 on artificial limbs and devices, perfected ankle, knee and hip joints, developed new type metal limb, soft adjustable socket for below-the-knee limbs, new method of taking casts of stumps for socket duplication, consultant to all city hospitals in New York City on prosthetic service. Author: Looking Ahead '47; Amputation Prosthetic Service '50; also articles in field. Research, design, prodn and fitting artificial limbs and devices '19-45; prosthetic spl Veterans Adminstr '45-47; dir prosthetic service NY U Inst Rehabilitation and Phys Med since '48; lecturer NY U Med Sch. NY Acad Sci. Director of Prosthetic Service, Institute of Physical Medicine and Rehabilitation, New York University-Bellevue Medical Center, 34th St. and 1st Ave., N.Y.C.

18 DANIEL, Hawthorne. Geopolitics; Islands of the Pacific; Logistics; Ships. b'90. '08 (US Naval Acad); '09-10 (Ia State Coll); '14-15 (NYU, Columbia). Research on political and economic development of nations in modern times, rise of US and Canada to power, decline of Great Britain; studies of Pacific islands (Oceanic, Philippines, East Indies); military supply, communications, transport, quartering, influence of logistics on war from American revolution to present, history and development of ships and clipper ships; traveled Artic coast of Canada '21, islands of Pacific, East Indies, Australia, China, India, World War II. Author: Ships of the Seven Seas '25; The Clipper Ship '28; North America: Wheel of the Future '42; The Islands of the Pacific '43; Islands of the East Indies '44; For Want of a Nail (The Influence of Logistics on War) '48; and others. Ed Natural History Mag, curator printing pub Am Mus Natural History '27-35; mng ed The Commentator '36-39; now writer, lecturer. War corr with Army and Navy in Pacific, Asiatic, Mediterranean and European areas '41-45. H: 37 Standish Av., Tuckahoe 7, N.Y.

19 DANIEL, Ruby Kathryn. Rehabilitation of the blind. MD '28 (Baylor U); MS '38 (U Minn); fellow in ophthalmology '34-36 (Mayo Clinic Found). Initiated and incorporated two philanthropic organizations for salvaging eyes and rehabilitating after eye difficulties, president both organizations. Author articles in field. In private practice ophthalmology Dallas Tex since '39. Am Bd Ophthalmology (diplomate) — ACS(F)—AM —AAAS— Am Acad Ophthalmology and Otolaryngology (past pres). Medical Arts Building, Dallas.

20 DANIEL, Theodore William. Silviculture; European forestry; Plant physiology; Range management; Erosion control; Plant ecology. b'07. BS '34—MS '36—PhD '42 (U Cal). Research on Spruce-fir type of Utah; study plant transpiration, stream flow, grasses for grazing. Author articles: Comparative Transpiration of Several Western Conifers under Controlled Conditions '42; Coniferous Root Exudate '49, and others. Jr forester US Forest Service Cal Forest Range Expt Sta '36-41; grazing specialist Wash State Agrl Coll '41-44; prof silviculture Utah State Agricultural Coll since '44; Fulbright research scholar in Austria studying European forestry practices '51-52. Soc Am Foresters—Am Soc Range Management—Am Soc Plant Physiol—Phi Beta Kappa—Sigma Xi—Xi Sigma Pi. School of Forestry, Utah State Agricultural College, Logan.

21 DANIEL, Walter Green. Negro and intergroup education. b'05. AB '26 (Va Union U); BE '27—AM '28 (U Cincinnati); PhD '41 (Columbia). Author: Reading Interests and Needs of Negro College Freshmen Regarding Social Science Materials; Study of Requirements and Achievements in College English; also articles in field. Mem editorial staff: Journal of Negro Education. Prof edn Howard U since '46. AAAS(F)—ALA—Soc for Advancement Ednl Assn for Study of Negro Life and History—Pleasant Plains Civic Assn. Howard University, Washington.

22 DANIELS, Robert Martin. Sugar chemistry; Beet sugar processing. b '90. Student '09-10 (U Colo); '10-11 (Colo Sch Mines). Research on methods of analysis for use in manufacture of beet sugar. Gen supt Holly Sugar Corp since '36. Am Soc Beet Sugar Tech. Holly Sugar Corp., Colorado Springs, Colo.

23 DANIELS, Robertson Balfour. English literature (Seventeenth and fourteenth century, contemporary). b'00. AB '22 (Princeton U); LLB '25— MA '32—PhD '34 (Yale). Author: Some Seventeenth-Century Worthies '40; To the Dark Covert '47; and others; also articles in field. Prof eng, chmn Eng dept U Houston since '47; asso dean School Arts and Sciences. Modern Lang Assn Am—Coll English Assn— Nat Council Teachers Eng—Tex Conf Coll Teachers Eng. University of Houston, Houston 4, Tex.

24 DANIELSON, Loran Leroy. Chemical weed control; Plant tissue tests. b'13. BA '38—MS '40—PhD '41 (State U Ia). Author articles in field. Head plant physiol dept Va Truck Expt Sta Norfolk since '45. Am Soc Plant Physiol—Am Chem Soc—Am Soc Hort Sci—AAAS—Ia Acad Sci—Va Acad Sci—Sigma Xi. P.O. Box 2160, Norfolk, Va.

25 DANIELSSON, Bengt Emmerik. Tuamotus (Anthropology, history, geography); Raft navigation; Ecuador (Jibaro Indians, anthropology). b'21. Graduate degree Fil. Kand. 1945 (U Upsala Sweden) research fellow social '47-48 (U Wash). Delegate UNESCO Amazonian Congress at Iquitos Peru-'48; study of rafts used on Guayas River in western Ecuador; participation in Kon-Tiki expedition across Pacific from Peru to Polynesia on balsa raft of prehistoric type to test its capacities '47; examination reed rafts on Lake Titicaca '48; museum studies on raft navigation; balsa raft voyages on Amazon River '46; expedition to Santiago Ecuador for study of Jibaro Indians; expedition to French Oceania '49-51 for anthropological studies. Author: Tuamotu '51. Author article: Attraction-Repulsion Patterns among Jibaro Indians '49, and others. Soc Geog Peru—Societe des Estudes Oceaniennes—Alpha Kappa Delta.

Ostgöta Nation, University of Upsala, Sweden.

10 DANNELLY, Clarence Moore. Methodism; Souvenir spoons. b'89. BPd '07 (State Normal Sch Troy Ala); AB '12—LhD '31 (Birmingham Southern Coll); AM '26 (George Peabody Coll Teachers); PhD '33 (Yale); Litt D '32 (Southwestern U); LLD '32 (Centenary Coll). Has collection 1300 souvenir spoons of many varieties from all continents. Supt Sunday sch work Ala Conf ME Ch S '19-28; pres Ky Wesleyan Coll '28-32; prof edn U Ala '34-36; supt city and co schs Montgomery Ala since '36; past pres Gen SS Council ME Ch S; mem Gen Bd Edn, Gen Bd Lay Activities; lay leader Ala Conf Meth Ch; mem ed bd The School Executive '39-43. NEA (vp '46-47)—Am Assn Sch Adminstrs (adv council '46-49)—Ala Edn Assn—Kappa Delta Pi —Kappa Phi Kappa—Phi Delta Kappa. 301 S. Lawrence St., Montgomery 5, Ala. H: 207 Magnolia Curve.

11 DANTON, J(oseph) Periam. Library education; Microphotography. b '08. Student '25-26 (U Leipzig Germany); AB magna cum laude '28 (Oberlin Coll); BS '29 (Columbia); AM '30 (Williams Coll Williamstown Mass); PhD (Carnegie fellow '33-35) '35 (U Chicago). Delegate to International Library Meeting The Hague '39; member executive board Philadelphia Bibliographical Center and chairman committee on microphotography '40-46. Author: Education for Librarianship '46. Compiler: (with others) Library Literature 1921-32 '34; (with M F Tauber) Theses and Dissertations '42; Union List of Microfilms '42-46. Translator sections on German libraries in Popular Libraries of the World '33; Librarian and asso prof biblography Temple U Phila '36-46; dean sch librarianship and prof U Cal since '46; nat library cons. US Works Progress Adminstrn '37); vis. prof grad library sch U Chicago '42, Columbia '49. ALA—Assn Coll and Ref Libr—Cal Library Assn—Assn Am Library Schs—AAUP —Bibliog Soc Am. Office of the Dean, School of Librarianship, University of California, Berkeley 4, Cal.

12 DARBY, Hugh H(ackland). Biochemistry; Biophysics; Spectrography. b'95. BSc '26—AM '26—PhD '28 (Columbia). Developed (with E M Kapp) basic methods for control Mediterranean fruit fly applied successfully in Florida '29. Author articles in field. Cons Carnegie Instn Washington since '47. AAAS—Am Chem Soc—Am Soc Zool—Biochem Soc—Marine Biol Assn United Kingdom—Optical Soc Am—Sigma Xi Carnegie Institution of Washington, Department of Terrestrial Magnetism, 5241 Broad Branch Rd., Washington 15.

13 DARGUSCH, Carlton Spencer. Taxation; Selective service in World War II. b'00. Student '21-22, '24 (Ind U)—'22-25 (O State U). Co-author: Estate and Inheritance Taxation (with J R Cassidy) '30. Tax commissioner O '33-37; private practice taxation law '37-40 since '47; mem group which prepared plans for Selective Service prior World War II; drafting bills and planning Universal Military Training since '45; lt col Judge Adv Gen Dept US Army '40-47, advanced to brig gen '46, dep dir nat hdqrs Selective Service System '40-47. Am. O Bar Assns—Phi Delta Phi. 44 E. Broad St., Columbus, O.☉

14 DARKEN, Marjorie A(lice). Plant physiology; Antibiotics. b'15. BS '36 (St Lawrence U); MA '37—Newcombe fellow '36-38 (U Mich). Author articles in field. Research microbiol Heyden Chem Corp Princeton since '43. NY Acad Sci—Am Soc Plant Physiol—Am

Chem Soc—Bot Soc Am—Phi Beta Kappa—Sigma Xi—Soc Am Bact—AAAS. Heyden Chemical Corporation, Princeton, N.J. H: Allendale, N.J.

15 DARLAND, Raymond Winston. Grasslands ecology. b'11. BSc '33—MS '36 (Ft Hays Kan State Coll); PhD '47 (U Neb). Research grasslands ecology; yields, consumption of forage; vigor; effects of clipping; soil and root relations. Author articles: (with J E Weaver) Yields and Consumption of Forage in Three Pasture-Types: An Ecological Analysis '45; A Method of Measuring Vigor of Range Grasses '47; Changes in Vegetation and Production of Forage Resulting from Grazing Lowland Prairie '48. Instr ecol U Neb '41-44, asst professor '46-48; asso prof bot U Minn Duluth br since '48; head dept biol Duluth Br since '49. AAAS —Bot Soc Am—Ecol Soc Am—Neb Acad Sci—Sigma Xi. University of Minnesota, Duluth Branch, Duluth 5, Minn.†

16 DARLING, Frederick Warren. Figure of the earth; Gravity; Isostasy; Deflection of the vertical; Geodetic astronomy. b'79. BA '02—student '13-14 (Cornell); '04-05 (U Mich). Author: Latitude Redeterminations; also articles in field. Geodetic computer US Coast and Geodetic Survey '19-49. Am Geodetic Union—Math Assn Am—Am Geog Soc—AAAS—Am Forestry Assn—Nat Audubon Soc. 45 Kenilworth Av., Garrett Park, Md.

17 DARLINGTON, Oscar G. Medieval history of France (Tenth and thirteenth centuries). b'09. BA '32—MA '33 (Penn State Coll); PhD '38 (U Penn): '31 (Harvard): '32 (Temple U). Field studies in France: made only study to date on Odo Rigaud, Archbishop of Rouen in 13th-century Normandy; author only published articles on Gerbert, first French pope; made first translation into English of work of Richer, 10th-century French historian; studies of social and economic influence of relics in Middle Ages and Renaissance; made 21 original maps tracing travels year-by-year of Rigaud through France, listing hundreds of 13th-century places and modern equivalents Author articles: Gerbert, Obscuro Loco Natus '36; The Travels of Odo Rigaud, Archbishop of Rouen '40; Gerbert the Teacher '47, and others. Instr '38, asst prof '39, asso prof '40, chmn dept '41-50, prof hist '42-50 Hofstra Coll NY; prof hist and pol sci and head dept Champlain Coll since '50. AHA—Medieval Acad Am—Am Soc Church Hist—Am Acad Soc and Pol Sci. Champlain College, Plattsburgh, N.Y.

18 DARRAH, Helen Hilsman. Early American woodenware; Microscopy of woods; American frontier diets and nutrition. b'09. BS—MS '32—grad study '33-34 (U Pittsburgh). Author articles in field. Collector, lecturer, cons. Sigma Xi. 122 Lincoln Rd., Medford 55, Mass.

19 DARRAH, W. A. Ceramics; Metallurgy; Electrochemistry. b'89. Research and development special casting process, enameling furnaces, complete vitreous enamel plant, tunnel kiln, glass lehr, terra cotta and glass fiber equipment, special processes for carburizing, heat treating, descaling; design of chemical and electrochemical plants. Holder over 100 patents in field. Author articles in field. Plant mgr Noble Electric Steel Co Heroult Calif since '17; pres Continental Indsl Engrs Inc and Intercontinental Engrs Inc since '19; cons engr Owens-Ill Glass Co and Owens-Corning Fiberglas Corp. AIEE—ASME—Am Chem Soc—Am Electro-Chem Soc—Am Cera-

mic Soc—AAAS—Am Soc Metals—Sigma Xi. 176 W. Adams St., Chicago 3.

20 DARRAH, William Culp. Coal (Structure and constitution); History of science in America; Oil shales. b'09. BS '31 (U Pittsburgh). Research on paleobotany, coal, oil shales, industrial raw materials, fossil plants; also studies of scientific aspects photography in early exploration; has prepared comprehensive checklist of stereographs taken 1850-1860 by government and railroad surveys. Author: Textbook of Paleobotany '39; Principles of Paleobotany '39; Introduction to the Plant Sciences '42; Paleobotany of Coal '48; also articles in field. Fellow Carnegie Mus '31-33; instr, tutor div biol Harvard '34-42, research curator paleobot Harvard Bot Mus '34-42; materials engr Raytheon Development Labs since '42; assistant head Magnetron Research and Development Labs since '48. AAAS(F)—Sigma Xi. Development Laboratories, Raytheon Manufacturing Co., Waltham, Mass. H: 122 Lincoln Rd., Medford 55, Mass.☉

21 DARRIN, Marc de Lepine. Chromium chemicals (Manufacturing, uses); Corrosion inhibitors; Anodizing; Metal finishes; Pigments. b'91. BS '12—MS '13 (U Washington). Holder numerous US and fgn patents. Author articles in field. Asso director research Mutual Chem Co Am since '36. AIC(F)—Am Chem Soc—AAAS—Md Acad Sci—Electro-Chem Soc—Am Soc Testing Materials — Am Soc Refrigerating Engrs—Nat Assn Corrosion Engrs—Sigma Xi. Mutual Chemical Company of America, Balt 31. H: 4401 Wickford Rd., Balt 10.

22 DARROW, George McMillan. Fruit production and breeding (Berry). b'89. AB '10 (Middlebury Coll); AM '11 (Cornell U); PhD '27 (Johns Hopkins). Originated many strawberry, blueberry, raspberry and blackberry varieties, including Blakemore strawberry; research on response of strawberries to photoperiodism. Author: Improvement of Small Fruits '37; also articles in field. Scientist US Dept Agr since '11, prin pomol in chge deciduous fruit prodn since '46. Am Soc Hort Sci (vp). Bureau of Plant Industry, Beltsville, Md.†☉

23 DARROW, Robert A(rthur). Southwestern desert trees and shrubs (United States); Range management and ecology. b'11. BS '32 (NY State Coll Forestry); MS '35 (U Ariz); PhD '37 (U Chicago) Co-author: Manual of Southwestern Desert Trees and Shrubs '45; also articles in field. Professor range and forestry dept Tex A&M Coll since '51. AAAS(F)—Ecol Society Am (chmn western sect '45-47)—Am Soc Plant Taxonomists—Am Soc Range Management—Sigma Xi. Range and Forestry Department, Texas A&M College, College Station, Tex.†

24 DASHER, P(aul) J(ames). Rubber technology (Reclamation, processing, development). b'12. BS '34 (U Ill); MA '35—PhD '37 (Ind U). Inventions include many process patents in reclaim industry field, chemical processing of rubber balata, use high frequency currents in processing high molecular weight rubbers, two basic inventions in bullet sealing tank for aircraft. Research chem BF Goodrich Co '37-39, asst dir rubber research '39-41, dir development and engring fuel cell div '41-44, tech supt fuel cell div '44-45, cons to reclaim div '45-46, mgr new process development '46; pres Merit Chem Co '46-47; Summit Indsl Products Co since '46; vp and sec Lowmans Inc since '47; pres Dasher Rubber Chem Co '49. Am Chem Soc —AIC(F)—AAAS(F)—Sigma Xi. Recipient Navy Dept award in field of tech development '46. Dasher Rubber & Chemical Co., Fairport, O.

10 DATER, Henry Murray. History of naval aviation. b'09. BA '31—PhD '36 (Yale); '33-34 (U Lyon, France). Instr, asst prof, asso prof hist Kent State U Kent O; mil service '43-46; aviation hist sect, Office Chief Naval Operations Navy Dept Washington since '46. AHA—Miss Valley Hist Assn—Naval Hist Found—Am Mil Inst.

11 DAU, Frederick W. History of Florida; Real estate history of Chicago and New York. b'80. Author: American State Histories; Florida Old and New; also articles in field. In real estate bus NYC since '11. 15 E. 40th St., NYC.

12 DAUBENMIRE, Rexford F. Forest and range ecology. b'09. BS '30 (Butler U); MS '32 (Colo U); PhD '35 (Minn U). Research on classification of forests in northern Rockies, plant succession due to overgrazing in grasslands southeastern Washington, vegetational zontation in Rocky Mountains, diameter growth in deciduous and evergreen trees. Author: Plants and Environment '47; also articles in field. Asso prof bot Wash State Coll since '46. Ecol Soc Am—Soc Am Foresters—Am Soc Plant Taxonomists—Sigma Xi— Phi Kappa Phi. Awarded research grants from Northwest Scientific Assn. Department of Botany, State College of Washington, Pullman, Wash.†

13 DAUBERT, Bernard Forbes. Chemistry and physiology of fats and oils. b'05. PhG '25—BS '30—PhD '39 (U Pittsburgh). Author articles in field. Research prof dept chem U Pittsburgh since '46, research adminstr chem since '47. Am Chem Soc—Am Oil Chem Soc—Am Pharmaceutical Assn— Am Soc Biol Chem—AAAS—Sigma Xi. 220 Alumni Hall, University of Pittsburgh, Pittsburgh 13.

14 DAUGHERTY, Marion Roberts. National income. b'05. AB '27 (U New Zealand); '28-29 (London Sch Econ); F '30 (Brookings Instn); PhD '41 (U Chicago). Research on factual bases and validity of Keynsian approach to problems of national income and economic stability, methods of estimating national income in Japan, New Zealand, flow of capital in US. Co-author: (with Carroll R Daugherty) Principles of Political Economy '50. Asst econ US Treasury '37-40; statis Fed Reserve Bank NY '41-42; mem faculty Sarah Lawrence Coll '42; mem faculty Am U '43-44; research Dept State '43-44; asst prof Loyola U since '50. Am Econ Assn. Loyola University, Lewis Towers, 820 N. Michigan Av., Chicago 11.

15 DAUME, Lloyd Emil. Metal mining industries of South America, Africa, and southwestern United States. b'03. BS '34—EM '34 (Mich Coll Mines). Management, operational and technical work in Utah, Michigan, California, Arizona, Texas, Mexico, Bolivia, Argentina, Brazil, South Africa, Southern Rhodesia, Tanganyika, and French Equatorial Africa. Mining and Metall Soc Am—AIMME—Geol Soc So Africa—Instituto Boliviano de Ingenieros de Minas y Geologos—Theta Tau. Professional engr Ariz; Ingeniero certificado Bolivia. Managing dir Southern Minerals & Marketing Corp., Ltd., P.O. Box 9782, Johannesburg, South Africa. H: 44, The Valley Rd., Westcliff, Johannesburg.

16 DAVENPORT, Charles Henry. Chemical pilot plants; fertilizers phosphates phosphoric acid. Lub-

ricating oils and greases; Chemical utilization of low grade ores; Fractional distillation and crystallization. b'16. BASc '38—MASc '39 (U British Columbia); ScD '42 (MIT); grad '45 (Alexander Hamilton Inst). Author articles in field. Patent applications pending. Sr group leader in pilot plant operations Lion Oil Co since '48. Am Chem Soc—Am Inst Chem Engrs—Sigma Xi. Research Division, Lion Oil Co., El Dorado, Ark.

17 DAVENPORT, Francis Garvin. History of the United States (Upper southern region); History of American culture. b'05. BA '27—MA '28 (Syracuse U); PhD '36 (Vanderbilt U). Engaged research frontier in relation American culture, cultural development of Nashville Tennessee, of Kentucky before 1860, cultural forces in relation Tennessee and Kentucky frontier, southern travel books 1852-1860, cultural interests upper south 1870-90 with special attention Alexander Winchell and conflict between Darwinism and fundamentalism late 19th century, Alexander and Newton Winchell in relation scientific history upper Mississippi Valley. Developed special course history of American culture introduced Transylvania '45, taught Colgate '45-46. Author: Cultural Life in Nashville on the Eve of the Civil War '41; Ante-Bellum Kentucky: A Social History '43; also articles in field. Prof, head dept hist Transylvania Coll '36-47; prof hist, head dept Monmouth Coll since '47. AHA—Miss Valley Hist Assn—So Hist Assn—Ill State Hist Soc—NEA— AAUP. Social Science Research Council grant '41, Rockefellow grant U Ky '45. Carnegie fellowship Transylvania Coll '47. Monmouth College, Monmouth, Ill.†

18 DAVENPORT, Willard Eugene. Retailing. b'04. AB '29 (Ia State Teachers Coll); MCS '36 (U Colo). Research in buying habits; retail trade territories; trade potentials; consumer studies for Decatur Illinois, Buffalo New York and others. Head dept bus adminstrn Kan Wesleyan U 40-42; asso dir research Inst Transit Advertising Chicago '44-45; head dept marketing and management U ND '42-44; since '46; prof retailing Shrivenham (Eng) Am U '45. Biarritz (France) Am U '46. Am Marketing Assn—AA UP. Box 577, University of North Dakota, Grand Forks, N.D.

19 DAVID, Lore Rose. Paleo ichthyology (Cretaceous, Tertiary); Fish scales. b'05. Maturum '25 (Nikolai Real Gym Leipzig Germany); PhD '32 (U Berlin). Author articles in field. Paleontologist Richfield Oil Corp '43-47; asst prof dept zool U Vt since '48. Geol Soc Am—Am Soc Ichthyol and Herpetol—Soc Vertebrate Paleontol. Zoology Department, University of Vermont, Burlington, Vt.

20 DAVID, Ralph Roosevelt. Foods (Prepackaging); Plastics. b'10. BA '32 (U Ore). Conducted first national forums on prepackaging for National League of Fresh Fruit and Vegetable Distributors; editor regional publication Pacific Plastics. Ed Plastics Industry since '44; established and ed Pre Pack Age '48, editor-in-chief since '49. Artists and Writers Assn—Soc Plastics Industry—Produce Prepackaging Assn—ACS. Miller Freeman Publications, 370 Lexington Av., N.Y.C. 17.

21 DAVIDSOHN, Israel. Pathology Serum diseases; Mononucleosis; Hemagglutination. b'95. MD '21 (U Vienna). Researches and studies of heterophilic antigen and antibody, with special reference to serum diseases; infectious mononucleosis and

differential tests; blood groupings; bacteriogenic hemagglutination. Author and co-author several books and many articles in the field. Am Assn Blood Banks—Am Assn Path Bact— Am Soc Clin Path—Coll Am Path— Internat Soc Hemat. 2750 W. 15th Place, Chicago 8.

22 DAVIDSON, Arthur William. Nonaqueous solutions (Solutions of electrolytes in acetic and sulphuric acid). b'96. BS '15 (Coll City NY); AM '17— PhD '21 (Columbia). Author articles in field. Prof chem U Kan since '37. Asso ed, Journal of the Amer Chem Soc. Chem Warfare Service US Army '17-19. Am Chem Soc (chmn Kan City sect '29)—Kan Acad Sci—AAAS—Phi Beta Kappa—Sigma Xi. Department of Chemistry, University of Kansas, Lawrence, Kan.†

23 DAVIDSON, C(row) Girard. Jurisprudence; Natural resources (Pacific Northwest). b'10. AB '30 (Southwestern La Inst); LLB '33 (Tulane U); Sterling fellowship for grad study '33-34—JSD '36 (Yale). Author articles in field. Atty Tenn Valley Authority Knoxville Tenn '34-37; cons atty Bonneville Power Adminstrn Portland Ore '40-42, gen counsel '43-46; cons Office Prodn Management Washington '41-42, asst gen counsel '44-45; asst sec of interior '46. Am Bar Assn—La State Bar Assn—Ore State Bar Assn— Order of Coif—Phi Alpha Delta. Equitable Bldg., Portland, Ore.†⊙

24 DAVIDSON, Daniel Sutherland. Ethnology and archeology of Australia and the American Indian. b'00. BS '23 —MA '24—PhD '28—U scholar '23; Harrison scholar '24 (U Pa). Leader Lock Haven Expedition University of Pennsylvania Museum '29, Australian Expedition '30-31, West Australia '38-40; anthropological field work eastern United States, eastern Canada; research in ethnology and archeology of Australia, New World, Oceania. Author: Aboriginal Australian and Tasmanian Rock Carvings and Paintings '36; A Preliminary Consideration of Aboriginal Australian Decorative Art '37; Snowshoes '37; A Preliminary Register of Australian Tribes and Hordes '38; Aboriginal Australian String Figures '41; Oceania '47; The Interlocking Key Design in Aboriginal Australian Decorative Art '49. Editor: Twenty-Fifth Anniversary Studies Publications of the Philadelphia Anthropoligical Society '37; also articles on Australian boomerangs, watercraft and fire-making. Asst Prof anthrop U Pa '36-45, asso prof '45-46, Oregon U '47-48, Washington U '48-49, prof since '49; curator Oceania sect U Museum '42-47. Am Anthrop Assn(F, council, asso ed '45-46)—Am Folklore Soc (Sec-treas '41-43, 1st vp '44)—Soc Des Am (Fr)— Polynesian Soc (NZ)—Soc Am Archaeol (F)—Anthrop Soc New South Wales— Sigma Xi. Department of Anthropology, University of Washington, Seattle 5.

25 DAVIDSON, Donald Miner. Mining geology (Precious and base metals evaluations involving Africa, Europe, North Am & Far East. Mineral economics of copper, gold, titanium lithium. b'02. AB Magna Cum Laude '25—MSc '26—PhD '28 (U Minn). Author: The Animikie Slates of Minnesota '27; Geology and Ore Deposits of Lemhi County, Idaho '28. Geol and chief geol Rhodesian Selection Trust '28-33; sr engr Selection Trust Ltd London '33-40; chief geol E J Longyear Co Minneapolis since '40, chief geol mgr exploration and vp and dir since 1943. AAAS—Am Inst ME (chmn min goel com)—Can Inst Min Engrs— Geophys Union—Soc Econ Geol—Geol Soc Am (F)—Sigma Xi—Gamma Alpha. 1701 Foshay Tower, Minneapolis 2.

10 DAVIDSON, J. LeRoy. Art (Chinese, Far Eastern, modern); Jade (Chinese). AB '30 (Harvard); AM '36 (Inst Fine Arts, NYC); '35-36 (Inst Art and Archaeology, U Paris). Author: Unpopular Art '41; Chinese Paintings '42; Catalogue T B Walker Jade Collection '44; also articles in field. Asst dir Walker Art Center Minneapolis '39-42; asst prof art hist Yale U since '47. Soc Japanese Studies—Am Oriental Soc—Coll Art Assn. Department of Art History, Yale University, New Haven.

11 DAVIDSON, John H(unter). Agriculture chemicals; Bird banding. b'14. BS '36—MS '40 (Mich State Coll). Holder US Patents on plant treatment composition containing ethylene bromide, herbicide. Author articles in field. Hort Dow Chem Co since '46; US Fish and Wildlife Service bird banding permit since '29. Am Chem Soc—Am Soc Hort Sci—Inland Bird Banding Assn—Phi Kappa Phi. 225 Broadway, South Haven, Mich.

12 DAVIDSON, Lyndall Phillips. Zinc (Electrolytic production). b'94. BS '15 —Chem E '39 (Mont State Coll). Asst research engr Anaconda Copper Mining Co '16-26; metall engr Giesche Spolka Akcyjna Polish Silesia '26-38; supt elecytrolytic zinc plant Am Zinc Co of Ill since '40. Am Inst Mining Engrs—Am Inst Chem Engrs. P.O. Box 222, Monsanto, Ill.

13 DAVIDSON, Ward Follett. Electrical and mechanical engineering; Electrical power generation and transmission; High voltage electrical cables; Metallurgy of power plant equipment; Coordination of electrical power and communication systems. b'90. BS '13 —MS '20 (U Mich). Member US delegation International Electrotechnical Commission, Torquay 1938. Instr elec engring U Mich '16-17, '10-20, asst prof '20-22; dir research Brooklyn Edison Co and Consolidated Edison Co NY '22-42; research engr since '42. Served as lt, later capt, Corps of Engrs US Army '17-19; maj Engr Res '19-42; cons to chmn deputy exec officer, Nat Defense Research Com '42-46; Sec '27-39, chmn '39-47 conf on elec insulating materials Nat Research Council; chairman Joint Coord Comm EEI-Bell system '33-37. AIEE (chmn com basic sci '36-38, chmn com on research '38-40)—ASME—IEE (London)—Inst Aero Sci—Inst Radio Engrs—Am Meteor Soc—Sigma Xi—Tau Beta Pi. 4 Irving Pl., NYC 3.◉

14 DAVIDSON, William Lee, Jr. Rubber (Radioactive tracers); Cyclotron; Neutron diffraction. b'15. BS '36 (Coll William and Mary); PhD '40 (Yale). Research on radioisotope tracers in rubber; helped construct Yale cyclotron. Co-author: Applied Nuclear Physics '42, '51. Contributor: Physical Methods in Chemical Analysis '50. Research phys B F Goodrich Co '40-46, dir phys research '48-52; dir office indsl development US AEC '52; research phys Oak Ridge Nab Lab '46-47. APS—ACS—Sigma Xi—Phi Beta Kappa. US Atomic Energy Commission, 1901 Constitution Av., Washington.†

15 DAVIE, Maurice R(ea). Sociology; Race relations; Refugees; Immigration; Human ecology (Urban); City problems. b'93. AB '15—AM '17—PhD '18 (Yale). Author: Directory of Community Activities '21; A Constructive Immigration Policy '23; Problems of City Life '32; World Immigration? '46; What Shall We Do About Immigration? '46; Refugees in America '47; Negroes in American Society '49. Coauthor: The Refugees Are Now Americans '45. Del Internat Sociol Congress Paris '37; dir study recent immigration from Europe '44-47; editor Am Sociol Review since '48; sociol faculty Yale since '21, prof since '32, dir grad studies in sociol and chmn dept. AAUP—Am Sociol Soc—Eastern Sociol Soc (pres '40-41)—Nat Council Naturalization and Citizenship—Phi Beta Kappa—Sigma Xi—Pi Gamma Mu. Yale University, New Haven.◉

16 DAVIES, Joseph Edward. International affairs; Russian relations; Financial economics and anti-trust laws. b'76. AB '89—LLF '01—LLD '41 (U Wis); six honorary degrees US, fgn universities. Economic adviser to President Wilson at Versailles Conference '18; counsel for Government of Mexico '20; counsel for Government of Peru in arbitration proceedings before President of US in Tacna Arica controversy with Chile; ambassador to Belgium and minister to Luxembourg '38-39; special envoy of President Roosevelt with rank of ambassador to confer with Marshal Stalin '43; special envoy of President Truman with rank of ambassador to confer with Prime Minister Churchill '45; special adviser to President Truman and Secretary of State Byrnes to Potsdam Conference '45. Author: Mission to Moscow '41; also articles in field. Law practice Washington '18-36 and since '41. Phi Beta Kappa. 815 15th St., Washington 5.

17 DAVIES, Raymond Arthur. Soviet and Canadian North; Soviet Asia. b'08. Ed primary and high schs. Author: Soviet Asia '42; This is Our Land '43; Canada and Russia, Friends and Allies '43; Arctic Eldorado '44; Truth About Poland '45; Odyssey Through Hell '46; The Great MacKenzie '47. Writer on background World War II for Saturday Night, Toronto Star Weekly, MacLean's, Montreal Standard, Mag Digest; in USSR as spl corr Saturday Night, Religious News Services, Transradio; mng ed, Pres World News Services; ed World Newsletter '46-50. Am Geog Soc(F)—Arctic Institute. 5820 Terrehonne Ave., Montreal, Can.

18 DAVIS, Alton Frank. Arc welding (Hand and automatic). b'89. ME in elec engring '14 (Ohio State U). Development of arc welding hand and automatic, development of its uses in industry farming and home. Pub and gen editor: Design for Welding; Studies in Arc Welding, Design Manufacture and Construction; Arc Welding in Design, Manufacture and Construction; Welded Deck Highway Bridges; Maintenance Arc Welding; Welding Helps for Farmers; Arc Welding Lessons for School and Farm Shop; Manual of Farm Arc Welding; others. With Lincoln Electric Co since '14, dir and vp '26, sec '38; organizer sec The James F Lincoln Arc Welding Found since '46. Am Welding Soc (dir) —Am Soc Agrl Engrs—ASME(asso)— Am Soc Engring Edn—Am Soc Metals. 22801 St Clair Av., Cleve 17.◉

19 DAVIS, Ben Arthur. Hemerocallis (Hybridizing); Azaleas; Camellias; Gardenias; Horticulture (Ornamental Southern). b'88. Student '10-11 (S Miss Coll); '11-12 (Clarke Memorial Coll). Research on life of ornamental plants with reference to their responses to varying conditions of soil, climatic conditions and cultural attention. Author: Azaleas—Camellias—Gardenias; Holland's Handbook for Southern Gardeners; also 400 articles in field. Garden ed Holland's Magazine since '35. Royal Hort Soc (F). Box 443, Meridian, Miss.

20 DAVIS, Benjamin Harold. Vegetable crop diseases. b'05. AB '28 (Wabash Coll); PhD '34 (Cornell U). Author articles in field. Asso prof plant pathol Rutgers U since '39. Am Phytopath Soc—Mycol Soc Am—Sigma Xi. Department of Plant Pathology, Rutgers University, New Brunswick, N.J.

21 DAVIS, Charles Carroll. Plankton (Marine and fresh water). b'11. AB '33 (Oberlin Coll); MS '35—PhD '40 (U Washington). Author articles in field. Asst prof biol Cleveland Coll, Western Reserve U since '48. Am Micros Soc— Am Soc Limnol and Oceano—AAAS. Cleveland College, Western Reserve University, 167 Public Sq., Cleveland 14.†

22 DAVIS, Charles Freeman. Colonial American history (Economic). b'90. BA '22—MA '23 (McGill U, Montreal); BD '23 (Wesleyan Theol Coll, Montreal); '23-24 (Union Theol Sem and Columbia U); '25-29 (U Chicago). Prof hist and head dept social sci Nat Coll Edn Evanston Ill '29-45, dir pub relations since '45. AHA—Ill Hist Soc— Am Acad Polit Social Sci—Am Sociol Soc. National College of Education, Evanston, Ill. H: 1208 Ashland Av., Wilmette, Ill.

23 DAVIS, Charles Shepard. Alabama history; World War II military history (African and European theatres). b'10. BS '31—MS '32 (Ala Poly Inst); '34 (U Calif, Berkeley); PhD '38 (Duke U). Author: The Cotton Kingdom in Alabama '39. Editor: The Seventh United States Army, Report of Operations (3 vols) '46 (Bronze Star); also articles in field. Asso prof hist Fla State U since '47. So Hist Assn— Ala Hist Assn—Newcomen Soc of Eng. Florida State University, Tallahassee, Fla.

24 DAVIS, David E(dward). South American mammalogy and ornithology; Rodent control. b'13. BA '35 (Swarthmore); MA '36—PhD '39 (Harvard). Engaged research ornithology Cuba and Argentina '37-40, relation mammals to yellow fever Brazil '42-44, typhus fever and rat control '44-45, principles rat control since '46; engaged as consultant rat control. Author articles in field. With Rockefeller Found (Brazil) '42-44, USPHS (Texas) '44-45, Johns Hopkins School Hygiene and Public Health (Baltimore) since '45. Am Soc Mammalogists—Am Ornithol Union—Am Soc Zool—Sigma Xi. 615 N. Wolfe St., Baltimore 5.†

25 DAVIS, Delbert Dwight. Anatomy of vertebrates; Herpetology; American snakes. b'08. BS '30 (No Central Coll); '41-42 (Chicago U). Member of Field Museum Texas Expedition '37, Field Museum-Mandel Caribbean Expedition '40. Research on anatomy of treeshrew Dendrogale, anatomy of babirusa, arteries of forearm in carnivores, carotid circulation in domestic cat. Author: Field Book of Snakes of the United States and Canada (with K P Schmidt) '41; also articles in field. Curator div vertebrate anat. Chicago Natural Hist Mus since '41. Am Soc Mammalogists —Am Soc Ichthyologists and Herpetologists—Soc Study Evolution—Soc Vertebrate Paleontol—Am Soc Zool. Department of Zoology, Chicago Natural History Museum, Chicago 5.

26 DAVIS, Frederick Barton. Psychological test construction; Educational tests and measurements; Psychology of reading. b'09. BS Ed '31 (Boston U); EdM '33—EdD '41 (Harvard). Author: Item-Analysis Data: Their Computation, Interpretation and Use in Test Construction '46; Utilizing Human Talent '47; The AAF Qualifying Examination '47. Dir Test Resch Serv Bronxville since '46; prof psychol, head dept psychol Peabody Coll since '47; prof educ dir Educ Clinic Hunter Coll since

'49; spl cons Sec Air Force since '47. Aviation psychol US AAF '42-46, asst dir AAF aviation psychol program '46. 47. Am Psychol Assn—Psychometric Soc—Am Ednl Research Assn—Nat Soc Study Edn. Educational Clinic, Hunter College, 695 Park Ave., NYC 21.†

10 DAVIS, Gordon E(rnest). Ticks. b'89. Certificate '16 (Marine Biol Lab Woods Hole); AB '17 (Oberlin Coll); SM (U Chicago); ScD '30 (Johns Hopkins U); cert trop med '43 (Army Med Sch). Special member West African Yellow Fever Commission International Health Division Rockefeller Foundation '28-30. Author articles in field. Research Rocky Mt Lab USPHS '30-43, '46-48, since '48. Teaching staff Army Med Sch Washington '43-44, typhus com China-Burma-India '44-46. AAAS(F)—APHA(F)—Am Soc Parasitol—Am Soc Tropical Med—Helm Soc Wash—Mont Acad Sci—Northwest Sci Assn—Sigma Xi. Rockefeller Foundation fellow '28. Rocky Mountain Laboratory, Hamilton, Mont.†

11 DAVIS, Harold E. Latin American history and government; Inter-American education. b'02. AB '24 (Hiram Coll); AM '27 (Chicago U); '23-24 (Western Reserve U Law Sch); '28 (Calif U); workshop General edn '40 (Chicago U); PhD '33 (Western Reserve U). Research and travel in Mexico, Peru, Central America; directed conference on Educational Problems of the Southwest, Santa Fe, New Mexico '43; conducted National Conference of Educational Leaders on Permanent Bases of Inter-American Education, Columbus O '44. Author: History of Western Hemisphere '40; Makers of Democracy in Latin America '45; also articles in field. Prof hist and polit sci '27-47, dean admnstrn '44-47 Hiram Coll; lecturer Cleveland Coll Western Reserve U '41; liaison officer Cooperative Study in Gen Edn '39-41; dir Div Edn and Tech Aids Office Inter-Am Affairs '43-45; prof hist, chmn dept hist and govt, dir Inter-American studies, Am U Washington since '47. AHA—O Acad Hist—Inter-Am Soc Geog and Anthrop—Am Assn State and Local Hist—Instituto Indigenista Interamericano—Am Soc Internat Law. American University, Washington 16.†

12 DAVIS, Harold Simmonds. Acrylonitrile; Petrochemistry. b'89. BA '10 —MA '12 (Dalhousie); PhD '14 (Harvard). Research sulfur, benzol, chemicals from petroleum gases, reactions of olefin hydrocarbons, acrylonitrile. Holds patents in field. Author: Fractioning Columns '29 Lectr, asst prof U Manitoba '14-18; research asso Arthur D Little Inc. '22-26; dir research MIT '26-30; div leader Vacuum Oil Co '30-34; group leader Am Cyanamid Co '34-45, sci advisor since '45. Fellow Mellow Inst '18-22. Am Chem Soc. Stamford Laboratories, American Cyanamid Company, Stamford, Conn. H: 218 Palmer Hill Rd., Riverside, Conn.

13 DAVIS, Harvey Henry. Educational administration. b'94. Student '16-19 (Drake U) summers '19 '20 (Ia State Coll); AB—AM '23—PhD '28 (State U Ia). Author articles in field. Auditor Ohio State Dept Edn and asst prof sch admnstrn Ohio State U '28-31, asso prof sch admnstrn '31-35, prof edn since '35, chmn dept edn '37-42, vp '42-48, exec dean div research and training, dean grad coll since '48; asso dir project research in univs US Office Edn '36; research asso Am Council Edn '37; participated sch surveys Cleveland. Am Assn Sch Adminstrs— Phi Delta Kappa. Old Capitol Bldg., Iowa City, Ia.☉

14 DAVIS, Harvey Nathaniel. Steam engineering; Thermodynamics. b'81.

AB '01 AM '02 ScD '28 (Brown U); AM '03 PhD '06 (Harvard); ScD '38 (Northeastern U) '40 (Columbia); LLD '28 (Rutgers); ED '48 (Stevens Inst Tech); DEng '36 (NYU) '38 (Rose Poly Inst) '49 (Rensselaer Poly Inst). Thermal properties of steam, locomotives (particularly locomotive accessories) and liquefaction of air; associated with development locomotive booster; an organizer first conference at Cambridge from which ASME Steam Research Program has grown. Holds five patents on liquefaction of air. Author: Elementary Practical Physics '38. Co-author: (with L S Marks) Steam Tables and Diagrams '08; (with H Henry Black) Practical Physics for High Schools '13. Pres Stevens Inst Tech '28-51; regent Smithsonian Inst since '38. Am Acad Arts and Sci(F)— Am Phys Soc (F)—AAAS(F)—ASME (hon; pres '37-38)—Am Math Soc(life) —Franklin Inst(hon)—Inst of ME (London)—Washington Acad Sci—Phi Beta Kappa—Sigma Xi. H: Hoxie House, Castle Point, Hoboken, N.J.☉

15 DAVIS, Hiram S(immons). Textile economics. b'03. BS '24 (Kan State Teachers Coll); MS '27 (U Denver); student (U Pa). Co-author: Analysis of Production of Worsted Sales Yarn '30; Production and Equipment Trends in American Worsted Yarn Manufacture, 1919-1932 '33; Vertical Integration in the Textile Industries '38; Inventory Policies in the Textile Industries '41. Author: Economic Issues in Textiles '45; The Industrial Study of Economic Progress '47; Productivity Accounting '49. With Indsl Research Dept Wharton Sch Finance and Commerce U Pa since '29, now dir. Industrial Research Department, 3440 Walnut St., Phila. 4.†

16 DAVIS, Howard Smith. Refractories (High temperature). b'00. BS (Mining Engineering) '25 (Pa State Coll); MS (Mining Engineering) '27 (U Wash) —Bur Mines fellow '26-27—BS (Ceramic Engineering) '29 (U Wash). Development of high alumina refractories (Diaspore, cyanite, topaz); Basic refractories (Magnesite); Neutral refractories (Alumina spinel); Beneficiation of refractories minerals (Clays, cyanite). Ceramic engr Lacled Christy Co St Louis '29-40; Chas Taylor Sons Co Cincinnati '41-42; ceramic engr, gen mgr Portsmouth Clay Products Co '43-46. AIMME—Tau Beta Pi —Sigma Gamma Epsilon. H: R.D. No 1, Smithfield, Pa.

17 DAVIS, Jerome. Soviet Union; Jails; Labor; Social ethics. b'91. AB '13—DD '33 (Oberlin); grad '20 (Union Theol Sem); MA '19—Gilder Fellow '20-21—PhD '22 (Columbia); LLD '33 (Hillsdale); Litt D '47 (Fla Southern). First in Russia '16-18 for YMCA, in charge prisoner of war camps '16-17; independent investigations in Russia '21, '26, with Edward A Filene '27, with others '32, '37, '38, '39, war correspondent in Russia '43-45; in charge prisoner of war camps Canada '40-43; impartial arbitrator in garment trade in Connecticut; president American Federation of teachers (AFL) '36-39; largely wrote Statement of Social Ideals of Congregational Church. Author: The Russians and Ruthenians in America '21; The Russian Immigrant '22; (with H E Barnes) Introduction to Sociology '27; Labor Speaks for Itself on Religion (with others) '29; The New Russia (in collaboration) '33; The Jail Population of Connecticut '35; (with E Stein) Labor Problems in America '40; Behind Soviet Power '46; Character Assassination '50; Peace, War and You '52; also articles in field. War correspondent and lecturer since '43; director Promoting Enduring Peace. Am Social Soc (com on internat relations

'22-24)—Am Econ Assn—Nat Conf Social Work. 489 Ocean Av., West Haven, Conn.†☉

18 DAVIS, John Blackwell. Water conditioning. b'98. BS '20 (Beloit Coll); MS '22 (U Ill). Evaluation quality various water supplies based on analyses; selection, design, application primary treating equipment, establishment control tests, limits of operation covering power plants; research in water conditions for industrial use for steam generation, Diesel engine operation, heat exchange cycles. Research dir Chicago Milwaukee St Paul and Pacific Ry '29-35; field engr water conditioning dept Allis Chalmers Mfg Co '35-43. engr in charge chem sales since '43. Water Conditioning Section, Mechanical Power Department, Allis Chalmers Co., Milwaukee.

19 DAVIS, John F(rederick). Soil science (Muck and peat). b'08. BS— MS—PhD (Mich State Coll). Fertility work on mineral soils and organic soils investigations; agricultural statistics connected with field plot experiments. Author articles in field. Asso prof dept agron U Del '43-44; asst prof div vegetable crops Cornell U '44-46; asso prof dept soil sci Mich State Coll since '46. Am Soc Hort Sci—Soil Sci Soc—Phi Kappa Phi—Alpha Zeta—Sigma Xi. Soil Science Department, Michigan State College, East Lansing, Mich.

20 DAVIS, John H(enry), Jr. Florida botany (Vegetation, Everglades, mangrove swamps, Dry Tortugas Islands); Peat (Origin, kinds, uses). b'01. BS '24—MA '24 (Davidson Coll); PhD '29 (U Chicago). With American Philosophical Society, Carnegie Institute of Washington and National Research Grant investigated in Florida summers '35-40, concerning mangrove vegetation and botany of Dry Tortugas Islands; as research associate of the Florida Geological Survey Tallahassee Florida, completed investigations of Everglades region and other parts of southern Florida, also completed an investigation of peat deposits of Florida. Author articles in field. Prof bot U Fla since '46. Fla Acad Sci (chmn biol Sect)— Ecol Soc Am—Bot Soc Am (sec se sect)—Sigma Xi—Phi Beta Kappa. Department of Botany, University of Florida, Gainesville, Fla.

21 DAVIS, John Warren. Education (Higher); Educational adminstration. b'88. AB '11—AM '29 (Morehouse Coll Atlanta); student '11-13 (U Chicago); DLitt '31 (State Coll Orangeburg SC); LLD '39 (Wilberforce U) '40 (Howard U) '52 (Morgan State Coll) (VA State Coll). Member National Advisory Committee on Education '29, Commission on Institutions of Higher Education of North Central Association of Colleges '36-48; executive committee North Central Association College and Secondary Schools '47, vp '51-53; member National Education Association for Defense of Democracy Through Education since '45, chmn nat com since '50; North Central Assn Committee on Evaluation of Accrediting Procedures since '48. Pres WVa State Coll since '19. NEA—Nat Assn Tchrs Colored Schs (pres '28)—. Harmon award in Edn '26. Institute, W.Va.☉

22 DAVIS, Kingsley. International population; Social stratification; Family; India; Latin America. b'08. BA '30 —MA '31 (Tex U); MA '33—PhD '36 (Harvard). Studied relation of population to social organization; directed research project on Puerto Rican population problems for University of Puerto Rico and Princeton University; engaged research on sociology of parent-youth conflict, intermarriage in caste societies, political ambivalence in Latin America, human fertility in India, future migration into Latin America. Author: Youth in the Depression '35; Urbanization in Latin America (with Casis) '46; Human Society '49; Modern American Society '49; The Population of India and Pakistan '50; also articles in field. Asso prof sociol dir Bur Applied Social Research and dir Div Population Research, Columbia since '48. Am Anthrop Assn—AAAS (F)—Am Sociol Soc—Am Statis Assn—Eastern Sociol Soc—Inter-Am Soc Anthrop Geog—Phila Anthrop Assn—Population Assn Am—Sociol Research Assn. Oldright Fellow in philosophy, Tex U '31-32; Henry Bromfield Rogers Meml Fellow in sociology, Harvard '32-33; field investigator in rural edn, Julius Rosenwald Fund '35; post-doctoral fellow, Social Science Research Council '40-41. Department of Sociology, Columbia University, NYC 27. H: 5 Southgate Av., Hastings-on-Hudson, N.Y.

10 DAVIS, Olive G Stull (Mrs Loy E Davis). Herpetology; Poultry pathology. b'05. BA '26 (Smith Coll); MA '28—PhD '29 (Mich U); '43-46 (Purdue U). Research on avian leukosis, particularly study of visceral lymphomatosis, variations and relationships in snakes of family Boidae. Author articles in field. Asst vet sci Purdue U since '43; agent in poultry path Bur Animal Industry US Dept Agr since '44. Am Soc Ichthyologists and Herpetologists—Herpetologists League(F)—Annual Conf Research Workers Animal Diseases NA—Phi Beta Kappa—Sigma Xi. Museum fellow Mich U '27-29; Nat Research Council fellow Harvard '30-31. Department of Veterinary Science, Purdue University, Lafayette, Ind.†

11 DAVIS, Pearce. Industrial relations; Labor (United States); American industries. b'08. BS '29 (U Pa); AM '31—Sanders teaching fellow '31-32 (George Washington U); Fellowship '33-34—PhD '38 (Harvard). Co-chairman National Meat Packing Commission, chmn N Eng Wage Stabilization Board '46-47; member Presidential board of inquiry into labor dispute in meat packing industry '48. Co-author (with H J Meyer): The War Labor Board and the Telephone Industry; Report on Wage Stabilization Policy in the Operating Telephone Industry '45; Labor Dispute Settlement in the Telephone Industry 1942-1945 '46. Collaborator: Fiscal Policy for Total War '42; The Development of the American Glass Industry '48. Joint-author: Report to the President on the Labor Dispute in the Meat Packing Industry '48; also articles in field. Prof and chmn dept bus and econ Ill Inst Tech Chicago since '46. Am Econ Assn—Am Arbitration Assn (national labor panel). Illinois Institute of Technology, Technology Center, Chicago.

12 DAVIS, Ralph Currier. Management and organizational problems. b'94. ME '16 (Cornell U); MA '26 (O State U). Consultant organization and management. Author: Principles of Factory Organization and Management '28; Purchasing and Storing '31; Principles of Business Organization '37; Principles of Industrial Organization and Management '40; Fundamentals of Top Management '51; also articles in field. Prof bus orgn, head management div, Coll Commerce and Adminstrn, Ohio State U since 36; head management dept Gen Motors Inst '27-30; adminstr and organizational planning AAF Lt Col '42-46. Soc Advancement Management (vp '42-43, '46-47)—Am Management Assn—Acad Management (pres '48)—Beta Gamma Sigma. Ohio State University, Columbus, O. H: 1994 North Edgemont Rd.†⊙

13 DAVIS, Raymond Tilton. Adsorption of gases by solids; Catalysis; Gas kinetics. b'18. BS '40—MS '41 (Va Poly Inst); PhD (Johns Hopkins). Author articles in field. Asst prof chem Juniata Coll since '47. Am Chem Soc—Am Soc Metals—Sigma Xi. Department of Chemistry, Juniata College, Huntington, Pa.†

14 DAVIS, Richard Beale. American literature culture; Virginian and southern literary culture of Jeffersonian era. b'07. BA '27 (Randolph-Macon Coll); MA '33—PhD '36 (Va U). Research on George Sandys, first English poet writing in America, treasurer of Virginia colony; studies on literary tastes in Virginia befor ePoe, scientists in old Virginia. Author: Correspondence of Thomas Jefferson and Francis Walker Gilmer, 1814-1826 '46; Francis Walker Gilmer: Life and Learning in Jefferson's Virginia '39; also articles in field. Prof Eng in chge Am lit Tenn U since '47. Bibliograph Soc Am—Modern Lang Assn—So Atlantic Modern Lang Assn—Va Hist Soc—So Caroliniana Soc—Phi Beta Kappa. DuPont teaching fellow U Va '33-36, Huntington Library fellow '47, Guggenheim Research fellow '47-48; awarded Cincinnati Medal and Prize, U Va '36. Department of English, University of Tennessee, Knoxville, Tenn. H: 607 Cherokee Dr.⊙

15 DAVIS, Robert Tyler. Indians of the northwest coast of America; Art education. b'04. AB '26—MA '28 (Harvard). Dir edn Albright Art Gallery Buffalo NY '34-39; dir Portland Art Mus Ore '39-47; dir Montreal Mus Fine Arts Can '47-52, prof fine arts McGill U '47-52 Research in London and Paris since '52. South Providence House, Lelant, Cornwall, Eng. H: 19 Sommer Av., Maplewood, N.J.

16 DAVIS, Roland Clark. Electrical recording; Muscular and electrodermal responses. b'02. Student '20-22 (Lafayette Coll); AB '24 (Harvard U); PhD '30 (Columbia). Author: Ability in Social & Racial Classes '32; also articles in field. With Ind U since '31, now prof. Am Psychol Assn(F)—Midwestern Psychol Assn—Sigma Xi. Department of Psychology, Indiana University, Bloomington, Ind.†

17 DAVIS, Spencer H., Jr. Ornamental plant pathology; Tropical deterioration; Organic fungicides. b'16. BS '37 (Westminster Coll); PhD '44 (U Pa). Author articles in field. Asso research specialist NJ Agrl Expt Sta since '48. Am Phytopath Soc—Nat Shade Tree Conf—Bot Soc Pa (sec '41-43)—Holly Soc Am—NJ Fed Shade Tree Commissions—Sigma Xi. Koppers research fellow '46-47. New Jersey Agricultural Experiment Station, New Brunswick, N.J.†

18 DAVIS, Watson. Science (Popularization, documentation, history); Properties of concrete; Microfilm. b'96. BS in CE '18—CE '20 (George Washington U). Author: The Story of Copper '24; Science Picture Parade '40. Editor: Science Today '31; New World of Science Series '31; also articles in field. Dir Sci Service since '33; ed Science News Letter since '22; ed THINGS of Science since '40; ed Chemistry (magazine) since '44. AAAS (F)—Am Soc Testing Materials—Am Eugenics Soc—Am Polar Soc—Am Concrete Inst—Philos Soc Washington—Geol Soc Washington—Washington Soc Engrs—Seismol Soc Am—Brit Assn Advancement Sci—Hist Sci Soc—Sigma Xi. Awarded Syracuse University Journalism medal '44; Westinghouse Sci Writing Award '46. 1719 N St., Washington 6.

19 DAVIS, William B. Mammalogy; Ornithology; Ecology; Wild life management. b'02. BA '33 (Calif State Coll); MS '36—PhD '37 (U Calif). Editor Journal Mammalogy '40-47. Bighorn investigations Texas '38; ecological survey Big Bend National Park '44; field work Mexico '41, '42, Colorado '47, '48. Author: Mammals of Idaho '39; Mammals of Western United States '49; also articles in field. Prof, acting head dept instruction fish and game Tex A&M Coll '37-44, acting head dept wildlife management '44-46, head dept since '46; asst leader Tex coop wildlife research unit since '38; curator Tex coop wildlife collections since '38. Am Soc Mammalogists (corr sec '39-40)—Wildlife Soc—Am Ornithol Union—Cooper Ornithol Club—Wilson Ornithol Club—Pacific Northwest Bird and Mammal Club Soc Study Evolution. Box 254FE, College Station, Tex.

20 DAVIS, William Lyle. Colonial American history; Catholic history (De Smet). b'93. AB '12—MA '24 (Gonzaga U); STL '31 (Weston Coll); PhD '43 (U Calif). Research on missions of St Ann and St Rose on Middle Columbia, 1847-48; life of Father P J DeSmet, SJ; and history of the Catholic Church in Oregon Country. Advisory editor Catholic Historical Review since '45. Head dept hist Gonzaga U since '37; archivist Ore Province Soc Jesus since '42. AHA—Am Geog Soc—Mediaeval Acad Am—Am Catholic Hist—Wash State Hist Soc. Gonzaga University, Spokane 11, Wash.

21 DAWE, Harold Joseph. Graphite; Pigments. b'12. BS '32 (Central Mich Coll Edn); MS '34—PhD '40 (U Mich). Graphite dispersions in all types of media formulated to possess characteristics suitable for applications involving lubrication, electrical conductivity, and opacity; dispersion of pigments in water, plasticizers, resin solutions, and plastics, for use as master batches. Dir product research Acheson Colloids Corp since '40. AC S—Am Inst Chem (F)—Engring Soc Detroit—Soc Rheology—ASTM—Sigma Xi—Phi Lambda Upsilon. Acheson Colloids Corp., Port Huron, Mich.

22 DAWSON, Alden Benjamin. Biology. b'92. '08-10 (Prince of Wales Coll); AB '15—DSc (hon) '38 (Acadia U); PhD '18 (Harvard). Developed several new methods of preparing specimens for microscopical study; associate editor Journal of Morphology '42-45. Asso prof biol NYU '25-28, prof '28-29; asso prof zool Harvard '29-38, prof zool since '38, dir Harvard Biol Labs '35-40, chmn dept biol '40-45; trustee Biol Abstracts '38-46. Am Acad Arts Sci(F)—Soc Naturalists— Soc Zool (vp '46-47)—Assn Anat—Soc Development Growth—Micros Soc (pres '48)—Hist Sci Soc—Sigma Xi—Gamma Alpha. 12 Scott St., Cambridge 38, Mass.⊙

23 DAWSON, Charles R. Enzymes and organic chemistry; Poison ivy. b'11. BS '33—MS '35 (U NH); PhD '38 (Columbia); Cutting traveling fellow '38-39 (Cambridge U, Eng). Author articles in field. Asst to dean Columbia Coll since '44; asso prof organic chem Columbia U since '46. Am Chem Soc (nat councillor NY sect)—AAAS—Am Soc Biol Chem—Sigma Xi—Phi Kappa Phi. 177 Lakeview Av., Leonia, N.J.

24 DAWSON, E(lmer) Yale. Taxonomy and morphology of marine algae; Taxonomy of cactaceae; Marine algae of the Pacific Coast of North America (California, Mexico); Herbarium procedure (Algae, cacti). b'18. AB '40—PhD '42 (U Calif). Allan Hancock expedition to Gulf of California '40. Author articles in field. Research asso marine bot Allan Hancock Found U So Calif since '45. Engr bd US Army '42; research asso hydrography US Navy at Scripps Inst '43-45. AAAS—Phycol Soc—Am Bot Soc—Western Soc Naturalists—So Calif Acad Sci—Am Assn Plant Taxonomists—Cactus and Succulent Soc Am—Phi Beta Kappa—Sigma Xi. Guggenheim fellow '46-47. Allan Hancock Foundation, University of Southern California, Los Angeles 7.†

10 DAWSON, Joseph Martin. Religion in the southwest United States; Separation of church and state; Religious liberty. b'79. AB '04—DD '16 (Baylor U); LLD '36 (Howard Payne Coll). Chairman Southern Baptist World Peace Committee and representative of Baptists of US at San Francisco Conference of United Nations; executive secretary Joint Conference Committee on Public Relations of Baptists of US. Author: The Light That Grows '23; The Spiritual Conquest of the Southwest '27; Brooks Takes the Long Look '31; Souls Aflame '32; Christ and Social Change '37; A Century With Texas Baptists '47; Separate Church and State Now '48; also articles in field. Pastor First Ch Waco Tex '15-46. 2904 P St., N.W., Washington.

11 DAWSON, Lyle Ramsay. Electrochemistry; Nuclear, analytical and physical chemistry. BEd '28 (Ill State Normal U); MS '32 (U Ill); PhD '35 (U Ia). Research on colored solutions, cement products, analytical methods, electrochemistry of non-aqueous solutions, nuclear chemistry, atomic bomb. Author articles in field. Acting head dept chem State Teachers Coll Eau Clair Wis '35-36; asst prof chem U Omaha '36-37; research chem Universal Atlas Cement Co '37-39; asst prof, asso prof, prof chem La Poly Inst '39-43; research chem metall lab U Chicago '43-45; prof, head dept chem U Ky since '45. Am Chem Soc—AAAS—Ky Acad Sci—AAUP—Sigma Xi—Kappa Delta Pi. University of Kentucky, Lexington, Ky.☉

12 DAWSON, Ray Fields. Plant chemistry; Biochemistry and biological production of the alkaloids; Nutritional improvement of cereal crops. b'11. AB '35 (DePauw U); PhD '38 (Yale). Botanical exploration in Honduras '36; visiting botanist Cinchona Developments Guatemala '46. Author articles in field. Asso prof bot Columbia since '46. Ind Acad Sci—AAAS(F)—Bot Soc Am—Am Chem Soc—Am Soc Plant Physiol—Sigma Xi—Phi Beta Kappa. Stephen Hales award '45; Nat Research Council fellow '38-39. Columbia University, Botany Department, NYC 27.†

13 DAWSON, Roy Carlton. Factors affecting number and distribution of soil microorganisms; Earthworm microbiology. b'07. BS '37—MS '39 (U Md); PhD '47 (U Neb). Distribution of microorganisms in the soil shown to be associated with method of handling and kind of plant materials used, rate of decomposition of plant materials varied with kind of plant materials and microorganisms involved; studied method for controlling amount and time of release of soil nitrates by regulation kind of crop plowed under and date of plowing; earthworm casts shown to contain larger numbers bacteria than soil from intestinal tract of worm, increase in number microorganisms in excreted casts accompanied by decrease in water stability of casts; distribution of microorganisms in soil as affected by plowing and subtilling crop residues; decomposition of wheat straw by fungi; earthworm microbiology and the formation of water-stable aggregates. Bact Soil Conservation Service USDA '41-50;

Cons internat programs agrl research adminstrn US dept agr since '51. Soc Am Bact—Soil Sci Soc Am—Soil Conservation Soc Am—Am Soc Agron—Am Soc Agrl Engrs—AAAS—Am Soc Professional Biol—Sigma Xi. U.S. Department of Agriculture, Washington 25.

14 DAY, Cameron Donald. Embryology; Histology. b'90. AB '10 (Central Wesleyan Coll); AM '25—PhD '27 (U Kan). Research on descent of the testes, function of the mesonepheros. Author articles in field. Prof biol Central Wesleyan Coll '19-21, Trinity U '21-28, Westminster Coll Fulton Mo since '28. Am Soc Anat—Soc Mammalogists—Tex Biol Soc—Am Genetics Assn—Sigma Xi. 17 E. 9th St., Fulton, Mo.

15 DAY, Cyrus Lawrence. English literature (Songs); Knots. b'00. BS '23 —PhD '30—Sheldon fellow '30-31 (Harvard); MA '25 (Columbia. Author: The Songs of John Dryden '32; The Songs of Thomas D'Urfey '33; Sailors' Knots '35; The Art of Knotting and Splicing '47. Co-author: English Song-Books 1651-1702: A Bibliography '40. Asst prof, later prof Eng U Del since '31.☉

16 DAY, Daniel D. Personal counseling (Supervision); Psychotherapy; Social attitudes (Measurement techniques). MA '29 (U Chicago); PhD '31 (Ohio State U). Constructed scale for measuring social attitudes based on psychophysical method; supervision nation wide personal counseling services in rehabilitation veterans; supervised procedures for use recording equipment in training for personal counseling interviews. Author articles: Methods for Measuring Attitudes; The Nature of Attitude; Attitudes toward the Professional Training of Social Workers; Methodological Problems in Attitude Research. Clin psychologist and personnel cons US Army '43-45; with VA Washington since '46, sr advisement and guidance officer since '47. Am Psychol Assn (F counseling and guidance)—Am Psychol Assn (F)—Soc Sigma Xi. Advisement and Guidance Service, VR & E, Veterans Administration, Washington 25.

17 DAY, Frank, Jr. Glass chemistry. b'14. AB '36 (O State U); PhD '41 (U Pittsburgh). Research on high temperature reactions in glass, chemistry of melting. Author articles in field. Research chem Corning Glass Works since '41. Am Ceramic Soc—Soc Glass Tech—Am Chem Soc—Sigma Xi. Corning Glass Works, Corning, N.Y.†

18 DAY, Karl S. Aeroneautics (Instrument and radio flying, air line flight operations). b'96. BA '17 (Ohio State U). Author: Instrument and Radio Flying '38. Operations mgr Curtiss-Wright Flying Service '29-32; successively instrument instr, pilot, check pilot, asst flight supt, system flight supt Am Airlines, Inc since '32. American Airlines, Inc., LaGuardia Field, NYC.

19 DAY, Paul Louis. Vitamin biochemistry; Nutritional aspects and experimental production of cataracts; Nutritional Aspects of Blood Cell Production. b'89. AB '21 (Willamette U); AM '23—PhD '27 (Columbia). Research on role of riboflavin and tryptophane deficiency in cataracts and keratitis, cataracts resulting from xylose feeding, folic acid deficiency in monkeys. Author 50 articles in field. Contributor: Biological Symposia (vol 12) '47. Prof biochm U Ark Sch Med since '27. Am Soc Biol Chem—Am Inst Nutrition—ACS—Soc Exptl Biol and Med —S Soc Clin Research. Received Midwest Award in chem '48, Mead Johnson Vitamin B Award '47. 1209 McAl-

mont St., Little Rock, Ark. H: 2525 Chester St.

20 DAY, Ralph K(ohlrausch). High temperature processes; Glass tempering; Glass furnace instrumentation and control. b'04. PhB '25 (Yale); PhD '30 (Cal Inst Tech). Research on properties of glass and technology of glass manufacture. Author: Glass Research Technology) '52. Research phys Corning Glass Works '30-37; glass research and control prodn Spencer Lens Co '37-42; foreman optical insp Nat Cash Register Co '42-44; research supervisor glass tech sect Libbey-Owens-Ford Glass Co since '44. Am Ceramic Soc (F)—Inst Ceramic Engrs—Brit Soc Glass Tech—Am Soc Quality Control —Alpha Chi Sigma—Sigma Xi. Libbey-Owens-Ford Glass Co., 1701 E. Broadway, Tol 5.

21 DAYTON, William Adams. Dendrology; Range forage; Forests of Costa Rica; Plant names; Oaks (OC). b'85. BA '05—MA '08 (Williams Coll). Appointed to represent US Department of Agriculture on Editorial Committee on Standardized Plant Names '39; representative Ecology Society of America to Institute of Biological Science. Author: Important Western Browse Plants '31; Range Plant Handbook (with others) '37; Standardized Plant Names (with H P Kelsey and others) '42; The Forests of Costa Rica (with others) '43. With US Forest Service since '10, charge range forage investigations since '11, prin dendrologist since '42; Nat Research Council since '47. AAAS (F)—Am Forestry Assn—Am Genetic Assn—Am Nature Assn—Am Soc Plant Taxonomists—Bot Soc Am—Ecol Soc Am (charter mem)—Soc Am Foresters (sec-treas Washington sec '33-36; chmn '30-41)—Wildlife Soc (charter mem). Awarded gold medal by Mass Hort Soc '40. c/o Forest Service South Building, U.S. Department of Agriculture, Washington 25.☉

22 DEAL, Laurie Joe. Radiation protection. b'24. BS (Lenoir Rhyne Coll Hickory NC). Study health physics problems of atomic energy installations. Research asst Oak Ridge Nat Lab '44-48; health physicist US Atomic Energy Commn Oak Ridge Operations Office '48-49, now biophysicist div biol and med Washington. APS. Division of Biology and Medicine, U. S. Atomic Energy Commission, Washington.

23 DEAN, David Parks. Waterflooding of shallow oil fields; Petroleum engineering. b'98. AB '20 (U Okla). Water flood projects in north and west central Texas shallow oil fields. Geol Barnsdall Oil Co and Waite Phillips Co '21-31; independent oil operator, geol, petroleum engr operating in Texas as partner firm Dean Bros since '31. Am Assn Petroleum Geol—Am Petroleum Inst. W.T. Waggoner Building, Fort Worth 2, Tex.†

24 DEAN, Ernest W(oodward). Petroleum (Specifications and tests); Hydrolysis of aliphatic esters. b'88. BA '08 (Clark U); MA '12—PhD '14 (Yale). Author articles in field. Lab asst Yale '11-14; petroleum chem US Bur Mines Pittsburgh '14-22; dir stan inspection lab '22-'50, cons chem Stan Oil Devel Co since '50. Am Chem Soc—Am Soc Testing Materials—Am Petroleum Inst —Inst Petroleum (Gt Britain)—Sigma Xi. Standard Oil Development Co., 15 W. 51st St., NYC 19.

25 DEAN, George Rhoades. Sugar chemistry; Dextrose manufacturing. b'09. AB '32 (Hiram Coll); PhD '37 (Pa State Coll). Co-author Advances in Carbohydrate Chemistry '49; also articles in field. Development of improved processes for dextrose manufacture; discovery of chemical reactions of dextrose. Research chem Corn Products Refining Co Argo Ill since '37. Research chem Manhattan Project U Chicago '43-44. ACS—Phi Kappa Phi. Corn Products Refining Co., Argo, Ill.†

10 DEAN, Herman Palmer. Firearms (Antique, historical); Powder horns (American engraved); Eskimos. b'97. Student '14-18 (Bethany Coll); '20 (O State U). Research on Arctic travel of Eskimos. Nat Rifle Assn—Nat Muzzle Loading Rifle Assn (dir). Postoffice Box 1240, Huntington 14, W.Va.

11 DEAN, John Peebles. Housing research; Home ownership. b'14. AB '36 (Dartmouth Coll); MA '38—PhD '44 (Columbia). Author: Home Ownership: Is It Sound '45. Co-author: The Book of Houses '46; also articles in field. Dir Cornell Field Research Office Elmira NY since '48. Am Sociol Soc—Nat Assn Housing Officials—Phi Beta Kappa. Rockefeller fellow '38-39; Social Sci Research Council fellow '47-48. Cornell Field Research Office, Federation Bldg., Elmira, N.Y.

12 DEAN, Ralph W(illard). Insect control and anatomy. b'07. BSc '30—MSc '32—PhD '39 (O State U). Author articles in field. Tech asst, later professor NY State Agrl Expt Sta since '31. AAAS—Am Assn Econ Entomol—Entomol Soc Am. New York State Agricultural Experiment Station, Cottage Rd., Poughkeepsie, N.Y.

13 DEAN, Reginald Scott. Metallurgical engineering (Alloys, electroplating, rare metals, batteries); Manganese alloys; Smelter smoke control. b'97. BS '16—MS '16—Metall Engr '20 (Sch Mines U Mo); '16-18 (Harvard, U Chicago); PhD '36 (U Md). Inventor high expansion and hardenable manganese alloys, alternating current magnetic separation process; others. Author: Theoretical Metallurgy '24. Translator: Physical Chemistry of the Metals '19; Textbook of Metallography '25. Development engr West Elec Co Chicago '20-29; chief engr metall div US Bur Mines Washington '29-42, asst dir '42-46, cons metall since '46. Am Inst Mining Metall Engrs—Am Chem Soc—Am Soc Steel Treating—Assn Cons Chem—Electrochem Soc—Faraday Soc. 6900 Oak Ridge Rd., College Heights, Md.⊙

14 DEAN, Robert B(erridge). Colloids; Ion physiology; Diffusion (through membranes). b'13. AB '35 (U Calif); PhD '38 (Cambridge U Eng); '31-33 (Stanford); '37-38 (U Copenhagen). Author: Modern Colloids '48; also articles in field. Asst prof dept chem U Ore since '47. Am Chem Soc—Soc Freedom in Sci—Sigma Xi—Phi Beta Kappa. Department of Chemistry, University of Oregon, Eugene, Ore.†

15 DEAN, Ruth J(osephine). Anglo-Norman paleography and literature. BA (Wellesley); MA—PhD (Oxford U); mem Institute for Advanced Study, Princeton '43-44, '50-51. Mt Holyoke Coll since '34, now prof French. Mediaeval Acad Am—Mod Lang Assn Am—Am Assn Teachers French—Mod Humanities Research Assn. Fanny Bullock Workman scholar Wellesley '37-38, Alice Freeman Palmer Memorial fellow Am Assn U Women '43-44, Guggenheim fellow '48-49, Officier d'Academie. Mt Holyoke College, South Hadley, Mass.

16 DEAN, William Tucker, Jr. Legal aspects of atomic energy; Conflict of laws Legal history; Trade Regulation; International law. b'15. AB '37—MBA '47 (Grad Sch Bus Adminstrn Harvard); JD '40—student '38-40 (div humanities U Chicago); Diploma '44 (Sch Mil Govt U Va). Author articles in field. Intelligence officer Bd Econ Warfare '42; spl atty antitrust div US Dept Justice '43; asst prof law U Kan '46-47; asst prof law NYU sch law since '47. Am Bar Assn (mem adv bd Journal, chmn committee on international control of atomic energy. Am Soc Internat Law—AHA—Am Mil Inst. Awarded Ross Essay award Am Bar Assn '47. New York University School of Law, 100 Washington Sq. E, NYC 3. H: 340 Pelhamdale Av., Pelham 65, N.Y.†

17 DEARBORN, Curtis H. Nutrition of cauliflower; Weed control; Vegetable breeding. b'12. BS '35 (U NH); PhD '39 (Cornell U). Conceived and introduced idea using cold water spray on outside glass of cold frames to prevent frosting of plants under the glass. Author articles: Boron Nutrition of Cauliflower in Relation to Browning; Magnesium Deficiency in Cauliflower in Delaware, New York '39; Weed Sweet corn with 2,4-D: Effects of Timing, Rates and Varieties '48, and others. Research assistantship vegetable crops dept Cornell U '35-39; plant breeder W Atlee Burpee Seed Co Phila '41-42; mem staff vegetable crops dept Cornell U Agrl Expt Sta Geneva NY '46-50. AAAS—Sigma Xi—Alpha Zeta —Phi Sigma. Horticulturist, ARA, Palmer, Alaska.

18 DEARBORN, Ned Harland. Safety (Education). b'93. BS Edn '21—MA '24 —PhD '25 (Columbia U). Author: The Oswego Movement in American Education '25; Once in a Lifetime '36; (with Earl Rugg) Social Studies in Teachers Colleges '28. Exec vp Nat Safety Council '42-44, pres since '44. Am Assn Adult Edn—Am Edn Fellowship—Indsl Hygiene Found—Am Museum Safety—Kappa Delta Pi. 425 N Michigan Ave., Chgo.

19 DEARING, LeRoy Matthew. Photography, (Color); Molecules (Shapes, sizes). b'08. BS '30—MS '33 (Antioch Coll); PhD '35 (O State U). Research on sizes and shapes of organic molecules. Tech supervisor cine-kodak processing Eastman Kodak Co '35-42; dir research Technicolor Motion Picture Corp since '47. ACS—Optical Soc Am —Photog Soc Am—Soc Motion Picture and Television Engrs—Photogrammetric Soc Am — AAAS — Phi Lambda Upsilon — Gamma Alpha— Sigma Xi. Technicolor Motion Picture Corp., 6311 Romaine, Hollywood, Calif.

20 DEARLE, Denis Arthur. Plastics. b'02. '27 (MIT). Author: Plastic Molding '41; Plastic Molding and Plant Management '44; Comprehensive Course in Plastics '49; also articles in field. Established and mgr plastics div North and Judd Mfg Co New Britain Conn since '38; lecturer and instr plastics Plastics Industries Tech Inst since '42; instr Hillyer Coll Hartford Conn. 259 Lincoln St., New Britain, Conn.

21 DEASY, George F. Military geography; World vegetable oils and fats; Manchuria and northern Japan. b'12. AB '25—MA '36 (U Cincinnati); PhD '48 (Clark U). Work on physical and economic conditions Manchuria and north Japan; extensive personal research geography and economics of world vegetable oils production. Author articles in field. Instr, asso prof geog U Cincinnati '36-40; Cent Mich Coll '39, '42; Pa State Coll since '47. Geog topographic br Intell Div US War Dept '42-47, contractee geog environmental protection sect since '47. Am Soc Profl Geo (treas)—Assn Am Geog—Am Geog Soc—Nat Council Geog Teach. Division of Geography, Pennsylvania State College, State College, State College, Pa.†

22 DEATHERAGE, Fred E. Food processing (Chemistry); Processing of fresh meat and edible fats. b'13. AB '35 (Ill Coll); AM '36 (U Ill); PhD '38 (State U Ia); Kroger research fellow '40-42 (O State U). Research on chemistry of quality in meat, chemical changes in preparation, processing, storage of foods. Granted US patent '48 on lard rendering method. Author articles in field. Research chem Kroger Food Found Cincinnati '42-43, charge research lab '43-46; asso prof agrl biochem O State U since '49; asso in animal science O Agrl Expt Sta since '49. Am Chem Soc—Am Oil Chem Soc—AAAS—Inst Food Tech—Inst Nutrition Food Techn—O Valley Assn Food Tech —Sigma Xi—Phi Beta Kappa. Department of Agricultural Biochemistry, Ohio State University, Columbus 10, O.

23 DEAVER, Chester Franklin. Flora of northern Arizona. b'98. AB '20 (North Central Coll); MS '30 (U Ariz); student (U Minn). Teacher biol and bot Ariz State Coll and asso prof sci since '24. Sullivant Moss Soc—Am Assn Biol Teachers—Ecol Soc Am—Am Soc Plant Taxonomists. Arizona State College, Flagstaff, Ariz. H: 62 Grand Canyon Av.†

24 DeBACH, Paul. Economic entomology; Field ecology (Biological control). b'14. BS '37—PhD '40 (U Calif). Conducted investigations on anopheline mosquitoes in California to determine malaria vectors for US Public Health Service '42-43; supervised field operations and test on white fringed beetle project for US Department of Agriculture '43-45. Author articles in field. Asst entomol Div Biol Control U Calif since '45. Am Assn Econ Entomol—AAAS—Entomol Soc Am—Sigma Xi. Citrus Experiment Station, Riverside, Calif.†

25 de BEAUMONT, Pierre Stuart. Automobiles (History). b'15. BS '38 (Harvard). Assistant editor The Antique Automobile. Contributor: The Sports Car, The Bulb-Horn. Assistant chief engineer Bostitch Inc since '48. Soc Automotive Engrs—Antique Automobile Club Am (Thomas McKean Memorial Award for hist research '50)—Veteran Motor Car Club —Horseless Carriage Club — Sports Car Club Am—Veteran Car Club Gt Brit. R.F.D. 1, N. Stonington, Conn.

26 DeBECK, Hubert Oakley. Ceramic materials; Mica. b'04. Geol Engr '30 (U Cincinnati). Design and outline of government strategic mica program for war effort '41-42; development of process for production of commercial froth flotation concentrates of ceramic raw material mineral, kyanite. Author: Clay Grinding Equipment '49; Hammer Mill Grinding of Clays '50; Primary Kaolin-bearing Wilcox Sands of Texas '51. Geol and geophys engr Ducktown Chem & Iron Co Isabella Tenn '29-33; cons geol engr '32-41 and since '45; geol engr in charge mines prodn and froth flotation research Celo Mines Burnsville NC '36-40; field engr and western mgr Colonial Mica Corp '43-44, tech asst to pres '44-45; geol engr Research Lab Ceramics U Tex since '46, instrn raw materials and mineral processes ceramic engring dept since '46; cons mining engr US Bur Mines since '51. Nat Soc Professional Engrs — AIMME — Am Ceramic Soc—Ceramics Soc SW—Tex Soc Professional Engrs—Sigma Gamma Epsilon. Professional engr and land surveyor SD, professional mining, geol, and metall engr Tex. P.O. Box 264, Johnson City, Tenn.

27 de BECZE, George Imre. Fermentation; Microbiology. b'03. Doctor Rerum Technicarum '27 (Jozsef Tech U Budapest); '31 (Inst fur Angewandte

Botanic Hamburg); '44 (U Cincinnati); '48-49 (St Xavier U). Holder three US four foreign patents. Author articles in field. Asst, later prof fermentation Jozsef Tech U '23-27; chief engr Krauss Moskovits R T Budapest '27-38; chem advisor Schenley Distilleries Inc Ind '36-46, asso dir biochem lab Schenley Dist '46-47, mgr distillery central control lab since '47; lecturer on indsl microbiol Inst Divi Thomae Cincinnati '47-48. ACS—Soc Am Bact—Assn Vitamin Chem—Distillers Feed Research Com. Schenley Distilleries, Inc., Lawrenceburg, Ind.

10 de BEER, Edwin John. Biological assay; Pharmacology; Biometrics. b'02. BS '25—MS '27—PhD '32 (U Pa); '28 (Harvard U). Development new drugs; relation of drug structures to action; muscle paralysants. Author articles in field. Acting director research and head department pharmacology The Wellcome Research Labs since '46. Biometric Soc (co-organizer)—Am Soc Pharm Exptl Therapeutics—Am Chem Soc—AAAS—NY Acad Sci—Am Statis Assn—Sigma Xi. The Wellcome Research Laboratories, Tuckahoe 7, N.Y.

11 DeBELL, John M(ilton). Plastics; Synthetic resins; Polymers. b'95. BSc '17 (Mass Inst Tech). Holder patents in field. Author: (with others) German Plastics Practice '46. Pres DeBell & Richardson cons and plastics lab Hazardville Conn since '46; cons, dollar-a-year man, advisor WPB, QMG, World War II; reviewed Germ plastics industry for Army. Am Chem Soc—Plastics Industry Soc—Soc Plastics Engrs—Plastics Pioneers. DeBell and Richardson, Hazardville, Conn.†

12 DEBENHAM, William Stuart. Ceramic engineering (Steel plant refractories). b'10. '29-31 (U Colo); BS '35 (U Ill). With Carnegie-Ill Steel Corp since '36, research asso research and development div Pittsburgh since '47. Am Ceramic Soc—Am Soc Testing Material—British Ceramic Soc—Am Iron Steel Inst—Am Inst Mining Metall Engring. 714 Frick Building, Pittsburgh 30.

13 DEBYE, Peter Joseph William. Chemistry; Physical chemistry; Plastics (Polymers). b'84. EE (Engring Sch Aachen); PhD (U Munich); hon degrees (Oxford, Brussels, Liege, Sofia, Harvard, Brooklyn Poly, St Lawrence). Prof theoretical physics U Zurich '11; prof univs Utrecht, Gottingen, Leipzig, Berlin; Todd prof chemistry Cornell U since '40. Fgn mem Royal Soc—Acad Amsterdam—Pont Acad—Royal Irish Acad. Nat Acad Washington. Awarded Lorentz, Faraday, Rumford and Franklin medals; Nobel award in chemistry '36; Willard Gibbs medal '49. Chemistry Dept., Cornell University, Ithaca.†⊚

14 DECHERT, Robert. Life insurance law; French-American exploration bibliography. b'95. AB '16—LLB '21 (U Pa); '19 (St John's Coll Oxford U). Collector of books and author on subjects related to French and other explorations in North America, especially on Jesuit relations; owner one of largest private collections in America on subject Jesuit relations, their contacts with Indians 1632-1673, allied material. With Penn Mut Life Ins Co since '27, now gen counsel; counsel Am Coll Life Underwriters, Am Inst Property and Liability Underwriters Inc; with Barnes, Dechert, Price, Myers & Clark since '30. Bibliog Soc Am—Am Pa Bar Assns—Assn Life Ins Counsel (pres '46-47)—Phi Beta Kappa. Packard Building, Phila. 2.

15 DECKER, Carmen Clyde. West African languages and customs; Sociology of religion. b'96. ThB '31—AM '33—AB '46 (Marion Coll); AM '47 (Ind U). Missionary Sierra Leone West Africa '21-24, '25-28, '38-41; research on impact of World War II on culture of Temne people of Sierra Leone. Author: This is the Word of God '37; also articles in field. Minister Wesleyan Meth Ch since '19; prof sociol Taylor U since '47. Am Sociol Soc. Taylor University, Upland, Ind. H: 601 N. College Av., Bloomington.

16 DECKER, Elbert Leroy Land reclamation; Irrigation; Drainage. b'87. BS '14 (Colo A&M Coll) Research, design, and construction of concrete and earth fill dams and canals. With Bur Reclamation '14-22, project engr '22-24; with Bur Indian Affairs since '24, project engr Flathead Project from '50. Am Soc CE. Postoffice Box 37, St. Ignatius, Mont.

17 DeCOURSEY, Elbert. Ophthalmic pathology; Pathologic anatomy of ionizing radiation (Atomic). AB '24 (U Ky); MD '28 (Johns Hopkins); grad '29 (Army Med Sch). Member Joint Commission for study of effects of atomic bomb in Japan and director of Army group in Nagasaki '45, Naval Medical Research Section and Radiologic Safety Section, Operation Crossroads (Bikini) '46; research on pathologic anatomy of lethal ionizing radiation (late developments), effects of atomic bomb explosions. Author: Atlas of Ophthalmic Pathology (with Ash) '42; Radiologic Defense Vol III (with Lapp) '50; Pathology of Atomic Bomb Casualties (with Liebow and Warren) '49. Colonel, Medical Corps, US Army since '28, laboratory service Brooke Gen Hosp Ft Sam Houston Tex since '47; cons to Div Biol and Med US Atomic Energy Comms since '48; dir Armed Forces Inst Path since '50. Coll Am Path(F)—ACP(F)—Am Soc Clin Path(F)—Nat Bd Med Examiners. Diplomate Am Bd Path Adjutant Gen. Department of the Army, Washington 25. H: 1014 Gorgas Circle, Fort Sam Houston, Tex.

18 DEDRICK, Calvert L(ampert). Registration procedures for special population groups; Foreign population census procedures. b'00 BA '24—PhD '33 (U Wis). Assisted in design social security registration system; set up forms and procedure for alien registration '40; developed census technique US and Panama '40; designed registration and reporting forms for Japanese evacuation from West Coast; chairman committee Census of America's '50; adviser foreign governments on statistical organization and census procedures; trainer foreign statisticians. Co-author article: The Emunerative Check Census '37, and others. Social statis Central Statis Bd Washington '34-35; with US Bur Census since '35, coordinator internat statistics since '46; econ Office Asst Sec of War '42-45. Am Statis Assn(F)—Inter—Am Statis Inst—Internat Union for Sci Study Population—Population Assn Am—Am Sociol Soc. Bureau of the Census, Washington 25.⊚

19 DEEN, Joshua Lee. Silviculture. b'96. Student '14-16 (St Olaf Coll); BS '27 (U Minn); MF '29—PhD '31 (Yale). Author: Silvical Characteristics of American Trees '37. Co-author: Colorado Forest Resource Appraisal '44. Dean forestry and range management Colo A&M Coll since '38. Soc Am Foresters (sec div edn '46, chmn '48)—Soc Range Management—Am Wildlife Soc—Ecol Soc—Sigma Xi. Division of Forestry and Range Management, Colorado A.&M. College, Ft. Collins, Colo.†

20 DEEN, Lucile. William III; English Revolution of 1688. b'04. BA '25 (Carleton Coll); MA '27 (Columbia); PhD '36 (Radcliffe). Research on career William III Stadholder of Netherlands and King of England with special reference relationship to Revolution 1688; English Revolution 1688 on thesis was actually palace revolution; detailed study persons involved to discover motivation; importance character of revolution determining English attitude toward revolutions elsewhere; use of propaganda in revolution; study in Europe grant Social Science Research Council '37. Instr hist Carleton Coll '34-37, asst prof '37-42, asso prof '42-46, prof, chmn hist dept since '46. AHA—Phi Beta Kappa. Carleton College, Northfield, Minn.

21 DEEVEY, Edward Smith, Jr. Postglacial stratigraphy (Radiocarbon dating); Limnology. b'14. AB '34—PhD '38 (Yale). Author articles: Biostratonomy of Linsley Pond; Biogeography of the Pleistocene. Co-author article: (with R F Flint) Radiocarbon dating of late-Pleistocene events; zool ed Ecology '50. Research asso biol Woods Hole Oceanographic Inst '43-46; asst prof biol Yale since '46. Ecol Soc Am—Am Soc Limnol and Oceanog—Am Geog Soc. Osborn Zoological Laboratory, Yale University, New Haven, Conn.

22 DEFANDORF, James Holmes. Chemical and anti-personnel warfare. b'92. AB '15—AM '16 (Wesleyan U); PhD '34 (Am U). Author articles in field. Pharmacologist Edgewood Arsenal '38-39, sr pharmacologist since '41. Enlisted army '17, 1st lt San Corps AEF '18-19; called to active duty Chem Warfare Service '41, still col on active duty with Chem Corps. Am Soc Pharm and Exptl Therapeutics—Soc Exptl Biol and Med—Sigma Xi. Office Chief Chemical Corps, Gravelly Point, Va.

23 DeFOREST, F. Ray. Automechanics. b'92. BS '19 (Ia State Coll); MEd '37 (U Cincinnati). Invented two-stroke-cycle engine with specially designed cylinder head. Author articles in field. Asst prof edn Teachers Coll U Cincinnati since '42; supervisor vocational edn for sw O '42-46. Am Vocation Assn—Ohio Vocation Assn—Ohio Ednl Assn—SW O Teachers Assn—SW O Assn Trades and Inds—Am Assn Indsl Teacher Trainers—Am Soc Agrl Engrs—Phi Delta Kappa. Department of Vocational Education, Teachers College, University of Cincinnati, Cincinnati 21, O.

24 de FUNIAK, William Quinby Community property. b'01. LLB '24 (U Va); LLM '47 (U San Francisco). Author: Principles of Community Property '43; Cases and Materials on Community Property '47; Handbook of Modern Equity '50. Prof law U San Francisco since '41; cons on community property. University of San Francisco, SF 17.⊚

25 DEGENER, Otto. Hawaii (Plants). b'99. BS '22 (Mass State Coll Amherst); MS '23 (U Hawaii); '25 (NY Bot Garden-Columbia U); DSc '52 (U Mass Amherst). Conducted botanical explorations islands of Hawaii; botanist Archbold Expedition to Melanesia '40; discoverer new species of plants Hawaiian and Fiji Islands, including flowering plant family Degeneriaceae. Author: Plants of Hawaii National Park—with Descriptions of Ancient Hawaiian Customs and an Introduction to the Geologic History of the Islands '45; Flora Hawaiiensis (New Illustrated Flora of the Hawaiian Islands) (Vol IV last edit) '46; Naturalists South Pacific Expedition—Fiji '49. Bot U Hawaii '25-27; naturalist Hawaii Nat Park '29; collaborator in Hawaiian bot NY Bot Garden since '35. AAAS—Hawaiian Bot Soc—Nature Conservancy—Save-the-Redwoods L e a g u e. Mokuleia Beach, Waialua, Oahu, T.H.

10 DEGERING, Ed(ward) F(rank-lind). Carbohydrates; Organic nitrogen compounds; Medicinals; Surface active agents; Organic syntheses. b'98. AB '24 (Union Coll); MA '29—PhD '30 (U Neb); '31 (Cornell U). Holder nine patents in field. Instr Purdue U '30-31, prof since '42; asst chmn chem and chem engring Armour Research Foundation '49-50. Author: An Outline of the Chemistry of the Carbohydrates '43; An Outline of Organic Nitrogen Compounds '45; The Quadri Service Manual of Laboratory Work in Organic Chemistry '38; Work Book of Fundamental Organic Chemistry '41; The Tri Service Manual of Laboratory Work in Organic Chemistry; also articles in field. AAAS—Am Chem Soc —Ind Acad Sci (vp '40-41, pres '45-46) —Ind Chem Soc (vp '39-40, pres '40-41) —Amt Inst Chem—Am Sci Teachers Assn—NY Acad Sci—Am Assn Sci Workers—Am Inst Chem Engrs—Sigma Xi. George Washington Inn, New Jersey and C St., S.E., Washington.

11 DE GOLYER, E(verette) L(ee). Petroleum geology; History of Spanish Southwest. b'86. AB '11 (U Okla); DSc (hon) '25 (Colo Sch Mines); DSc (hon) '45 (So Methodist U); LLD (hon) '47 (Trinity Coll); DEng (hon) '49 (Princeton). President, general mgr Amerada Corp, Amerada Petroleum Corp, Amerada Refining Corp '26-29, chmn bd '29-32, vp, gen mgr Geophys Research Corp, pres Felmont Corp '34-39; adv com Atomic Energy Commn '48; mem US Dept Interior Petroleum Advisory Commn; sr mem DeGolyer and MacNaughton since '37. Geol Soc Am(F)—AAAS(F)—NY Acad Sci(F)— Inst of Petroleum(F)—Am Assn Petroleum Geologists (hon mem)—Am Inst Mining Metall Engrs—Am Petroleum Inst—Am Geophys Union—Soc Exploration Geophysicists (hon mem) —Nat Research Council—Phi Beta Kappa—Tau Beta Pi. Distinguished prof geol U Texas '40; Fritz medalist '42; Anthony F Lucas Medalist '41. Sidney Powers medalist '50. H: 8525 Garland Rd., Dallas 18.©

12 DE GRAFF, Herrell Franklin. Economic geography (Food economics, farm management). b'08. BS '37—PhD '41 (Cornell U); '41-42 (U Chicago). Research in land economics; farm management, farm accounting procedures, economic geography; special studies agricultural development of Mexico. Co-author: The Business of Farming (with Haystead); also articles in field. With Cornell U since '40, prof land econ since '46; Am del Internat Conf Agrl Econ in Great Britain '47; special fellow of Rockefeller Found in Mexico '49. Am Farm Econ Assn—Western Farm Econ Assn—Am Soc Farm Mgrs and Rural Appraisers —NY State Agrl Soc—Internat Conf Agrl Econ. Cornell University, Ithaca, N.Y. H: 107 Brandon Pl.

13 De GROTE, Irwin A. Quality control. b'10. Student '28 (Ia State Coll). Practical application of quality control system to production machining operations; installation statistical quality control system in automotive manufacturing operations. Chief process insp US Cartridge Co St Louis '41-45; chief insp Deepfreeze Div Motor Products Corp '45-49; supervisor quality analysis Ford Motor Co since '49 Am Soc Quality Control. Ford Motor Co, 3000 Schaefer Rd., Dearborn, Mich.†

14 de HAAS, Elsa. Bail (History of); Political theory; Legal history of the Middle Ages. b'01. AB '23 (Hunter Coll); MA '25—PhD '39 (Columbia U);

'26-27 (London Sch Econs Polit Sci). Presently engaged editing Registra Brevium reigns of Henry III and Edward I. Author: Antiquities of Bail '40. Author articles: Concepts of the Nature of Bail in English and American Criminal Law '46; An Early Thirteenth-Century Register of Writs '47. Asst prof Brooklyn Coll since '47. Am Polit Sci Assn—Acad Polit Sci—Nat Municipal League—Selden Soc—AAUP —AAUW. Brooklyn College, Bedford Av. and Av. H., Brooklyn 10.

15 DeHAAS, John Christian. Aircraft motors. b'02 Student '20-25 (Tech Coll Netherlands); EE '32 (Stanford U). Design and development of aircraft motors with magnetic brakes, including direct current, and 400 cycle alternating current; co-inventor of coilless magnetic motor brake. Holds patent in field. Asst engr electronics lab Philips Lamp & Radio Works Netherlands '25-28; engr Shell Chem Co Pittsburg Calif '37-42; elec engr AiResearch Mfg Co Phoenix Ariz '42-46, engr Central Ariz Light & Power Co since '46; cons elec engr Metalcraft Mfg Co Phoenix since '51. Nat Soc Professional Engrs—Am Inst EE. H: Route 2, Box 1200, Phoenix, Ariz.

16 De HOFFMANN Frederic. Nuclear physics; Chain reactors. b'24. BS (phys) '45 — MA (phys) '47 — PhD (phys) '48 (Harvard). Research on statistical aspects of nuclear chain reactions, criticality experiments, delayed neutrons from fission, theory of nuclear scattering, magnetohydrodynamics; consultant US Atomic Energy Commission '46-48. Author articles in field. Contributor: Science and Engineering of Nuclear Power '48. Staff mem Los Alamos Lab Manhattan Dist '44-46; alternate asst dir Los Alamos Sci Lab since '49. APS—Sigma Xi. NR CF phys '46-48. Postoffice Box 1663, Los Alamos Scientific Laboratory, Los Alamos, N.M.

17 de HOSTOS, Adolfo. Puerto Rico (History), ancient Spanish military architecture); Antillean pre-Colombian archaeology and ethnology. b'87. Student (S Jersey Inst); teachers degree (Normal Sch Santo Domingo City, Dominican Rep). Executive committee for investigating the Caparra ruins Puerto Rico, director Caparra excavations '37; First National Congress of History Havana '42; official delegate First International Conference Archaeologists Honduras '46. Author: Investigaciones Historicas '38; Anthropological Papers '41; Indice Hemero-Bibliografico de Eugenio Maria de Hostos '40; Industrial Applications of Indian Designs '41; Al Servicio de Clio '42; Ciudad Murada '48. Editor: Tesauro de Datos Historicos '48; also articles in field. Official historian of Puerto Rico '36-51. AAAS—Am Anthrop Association—Societe des Americanistes de Paris—Inter-Congress Americanists. 1859 Odette St., Santurce, Puerto Rico.

18 DEIBLER, Frederick Shipp. Economics (General theory); Labor and industrial relations. b'76. Special agent US Commission on Industrial Relations '14-15; chairman advisory board Illinois Free Employment Offices '17-29; assistant examiner for Shipbuilding Labor Adjustment Board Great Lakes District '18; chairman special committee to study effect of NRA on boot and shoe industry '35; public mediator National War Labor Board '42. Author: Principles of Economics '29. Economics faculty Northwestern U since '04, prof emeritus since '42. H: 2306 Marcy Av., Evanston, Ill.†©

19 DEIGNAN, Herbert G. Siamese natural history, language and affairs; Ornithology. b'06. Student '23-24 (Mer-

cersburg Acad); AB '28 (Princeton U). Asiatic Primate Expedition North Borneo '37; National Geographic Society - Smithsonian - Commonwealth of Australia expedition to Arnhem Land '48; zoological field studies in Siam '28-32, '35-37. Author: Birds of Northern Thailand; also articles in field. Asso curator div birds US Nat Mus since '42. Am Ornithol Union(F)—Biol Soc Washington—British Ornithol Union— Royal Australasian Ornithol Union— Siam Soc—Washington Acad Sci. Walter Rathbone Bacon scholar '39. Smithsonian Institution, Washington.

20 DEINDORFER, Robert Greene. Uranium mine (Belgian Congo); Lower Africa. b'22. Student '40-43 (U Mo). Research on uranium mining in Belgian Congo. Author articles in field. Free-lance author. Soc Magazine Writers—Sigma Delta Chi—Explorers Club—Polar Club. Box 566, Stony Brook, L.I., N.Y.

21 DEINES, Ernest Hubert. Wood engraving; Print-making; Typographical, book and magazine design. b'94. Student '14-17, '20-21 (Kansas City Art Inst); '19 (Academie Julien Paris). Exhibited principal graphic art exhibitions and museums in US including Contemporary American Art Good Will Exhibition tour of British Isles '44-45; permanent collection located at Library of Congress, Vanderpoel Memorial Gallery Chicago, Philadelphia Museum Art and others. Established studio Kansas City Mo for wood engravings, printmaking, typographical design, book and magazine design and illustrations '32. Am Inst Graphic Arts—Soc Am Wood Engravers—Am Fed Arts—Nat Acad Design (asso)—Soc Print Connoisseurs. Awarded Henry Putzel prize; 1st prize graphic art '42; Atwood prize for wood engraving '40; Northwest Printmakers' 15th Annual Purchase Prize '43. 1st J and E R Pennell prize '43, '46. 621 E. 31st St., Kansas City, Mo.

22 DEITZ, Victor Reuel. Solid adsorbents; Bone char. b'09. PhD '33 (Johns Hopkins U); fellow Nat Research Council '33-35 (U Ill). Research on bond energies of the hydrocarbons '35, vapor pressure of potassium chloride and cesium iodide crystals '36. Holds US patent on method of treating char bone '45. Author: Bibliography of Solid Adsorbents '44; Preliminary Survey of Bone Char Revivification and Filtration '47; also articles in field. Research chem Gen Elec Co '37-38; in charge bone char research Nat Bur of Standards since '39. Am Chem Soc— Sigma Xi—Phi Beta Kappa. National Bureau of Standards, Washington.

23 DeKAY, Henry George. Industrial pharmacy and radiography; Pharmaceutical chemistry. b'98. BA '23 (Wayne State Teachers Coll); BS '28 (Neb U); MS '30 (Chicago U); PhD '34 (Purdue U). Research in industrial drying of tablet granulations with infra red light and high frequency current, tablet coating and triturates by rotary presses, prevention and cure of athlete foot organisms, radiographic opaques. Author: Qualitative Analysis for Students of Pharmacy and Medicine '38; also articles in field. Prof pharm Purdue Sch Pharm since '43. Am Pharmaceutical Assn (life)—Ind Pharmaceutical Assn—Ind Acad Sci—Sigma Xi. School of Pharmacy, Purdue University, Lafayette, Ind. H: 711 Meridian St., W.

24 DE LA ROZA, Joaquin, Sr Pulp digesters; Bagasse; Sugar cane (Cellulose pulp). b'92. ME '16 (Cornell U). Invented pre-hydrolysis pulping process to produce high grade cellulose pulp from any fibrous vegetable material, invented continuous digester to digest fibrous vegetable material in production of cellulose and paper pulp, research and production of commercial bagasse cellulose and paper pulp. Granted 70 patents in field. Cons engr Celulosa Cubana Corp '18-25, pres '27-39; pres Bagasse Products Corp '25-39, dir since '25; pres and dir de la Roza Corp since '32; pres United Bagasse Cellulose Corp since '51. Asociacion de Tecnicos Azucareros de Cuba. 106 Wall St., NYC.

10 de la RUE, Sidney. Turkey, Liberia, Haiti, and Dominican Republic (Economic and financial administration); French Code. b'88. Grad '07 (Farnum Prep Sch Beverly NJ); '07-09 (U Pa). Adviser to Minister of Finance, Turkey; US official in economic and financial administrations in Liberia, Dominican Republic, Haiti; president National Bank of Haiti. Author: Land of the Pepper Bird '31; also articles in field. US govt official '19-47, last post Lend-Lease officer; adv Office Near Eastern and African Affairs since '47; sr vp Stettinius Asso Inc and Liberia Co Washington since '48. Geog Soc NY(F). 3834 Macomb St., N.W., Washington 16.

11 DE LAUBENFELS, Max Walker. Porifera; Sponges. b'94. BA '16 (Oberlin Coll); summers '21, '23 (U Calif); MA '26—PhD '29 (Stanford). Research and investigations classes of Porifera (Demospongiae, Hyalospongiae (Hexactinellida) and Calcispongiae (Calcarea); Keratosa, or Horny sponges; systematic zoology; physiology of sponges. Sect ed Biological Abstracts. Author: Life Science '49; also articles in field. Prof zool U Hawaii '47-50; prof zool Oregon State Coll Corvallis since '50. AAAS(F)—Sigma Xi—AAUP —Soc Systematic Zoologists—Am Soc Limnol & Oceanog. Oregon State College, Corvallis, Ore.☉

12 De LEUW, Charles E. Urban transportation, traffic highway, and railway engineering. b'91. BS CE '12—CE '16 (Ill U). Directed highway planning surveys, expressway, railway, and urban transportation improvements. Pres De Leuw, Cather and Co, cons engrs since '29. Am Inst Cons Engrs—Am Pub Works Assn—ASCE—Am Transit Assn—Am Water Works Assn—Engring Inst Can—Ill Soc Engrs —Inst Traffic Engrs—Soc Am Mil Engrs—Western Soc Engrs. 150 No. Wacker Dr., Chicago 6.☉

13 DELLINGER, John Howard. Radio (Communication, aviation); Telecommunications; Electronic. b'86. Student '03-07 (Western Reserve U); AB '08 (George Washington U); PhD '13 (Princeton U); DSc '32 (George Washington U). US representative Inter - American Telecommunication Conference Rio de Janeiro '45, Five-Power Telecommunication Conference Moscow '46; delegate International Radio and Telecommunication Conference Atlantic City '47, and others. Physicist Nat Bur Standards '07-48, chief radio sect '18-46; sometime chief of work in field for various govt labs, commns, including Fed Radio Commn, Dept Commerce, Nat Defense Research Com, Joint Chiefs of Staff, and others. Chmn US govt Interdept Radio Adv Com '41-43, '46-48, Radio Tech Com for Aeronautics since '41, for Marine Services since '46. Chmn tech subcom Telecommunications Coordinating Com '44-48, Washington Liaison Com Provisional Frequency Bd '48. Inst Radio Engrs (F, vp '24, pres '25)—Am Geophys Union—Internat Sci Radio Union (vp)—Phi Beta Kappa. 618 Pickwick Lane, Chevy Chase, Md.☉

14 De LONG, George Cass. Economic and regional geography. b'10. BA '39 —student '46-47 (U Ill); MA '41 (Columbia U); '40-41 (Ill State Normal U); '48 (Mich U). Engaged research in dairy region of northeastern Illinois and Wis, tung oil industry; buffalo in US. Author articles in field. Asst prof geog Mich State Normal Coll since '47. Am Soc Profl Geog—AAAS—Ill Acad Sci. Michigan State Normal College, Ypsilanti, Mich. H: 1204 Pearl St.

15 de LUCCIA, Emil Robert. Hydroelectric engineering (River basins, Hydraulic structures, dams; Hydroelectric plants, locks, flood walls, industrial construction, electric power production and use). b'04. BS in CE '27 (MIT). Member Technical Industrial Disarmament Committee for German electric power industry; consultant on electric power to National Security Resources Board; US delegate to international Conference on Large Dams, Stockholm '48, to International Conference on Large Electric High Tension Systems at Paris '48. With Fed Power Commn since '38; asst dir Nat Defense Power staff and chief Bur Elec Engring, Bur of Power since '44; consultant on power for OPM and WPB. Served as lt col US Army '42-45 in charge aircraft plant and modification center program Office Chief Engrs; with SHAEF European theater '44 as operations engring officer. ASCE—Washington Soc Engrs —Am Geophysics Union—Internat Conf on Large Elec High-Tension Systems —Soc Am Mil Engrs. Federal Power Commission, Washington.☉

16 DeMARCO, Roland R. History; Italian colonies and education; Imperialism. b'10. BS '34 (NY State Coll Teachers, Albany); MA '37—PhD '42 (Columbia U). Author: Italianization of African Natives; Government Native Education in the Italian Colonies, 1890-1937 '43; also translations various articles from Italian. Prof hist, head dept social sci State Teachers Coll Florence Ala '40-43; vis prof hist Columbia U Teachers Coll '46-47; head hist dept, chmn faculty Finch Jr Coll NYC '46-49, pres dep during '49, dean '49 president College since '50. AHA—Am Acad Polit Social Sci—Am Sociol Soc—Nat Council Social Studies— Kappa Delta Pi (scholar '40). 52 East 78th St., N.Y.C. 21. H: 58 East 78th St.

17 DEMAREE, Juan Brewer. Small fruit and pecan diseases. b'85. BS '10 (Purdue U). Author articles in field. With US Department Agriculture '18-51. Am Phytopath Society—Phytopath Soc (Potomac Div)—Wash Bot Soc. Plant Industry Station, U.S. Department of Agriculture, Beltsville, Md.

18 De MENT, Jack Andrew. Luminescence; Radio chemistry; Uranium minerals; Atomic energy. b'20. Student '38-41 (Reed Coll). Official US observer and consultant to Secretary of War on Project Crossroads, Bikini atomic bomb tests '46; named and established fluorochemistry '42; investigated and catalogued 20,000 luminescent substances; formally enunciated First Law of Fluorescence (DeMent's Absorption Law) '42, Third Law of Fluorescence '43, Law of Precharged Luminescence '45. Invented invisible tattooing (with H C Dake) visible under X-rays, black light picture projector and television tube, test for death on battlefield, artificial teeth made natural enamel; holds or filed 100 patents. Author: Fluorescent Light and Its Applications (with H C Dake) '41; Uranium and Atomic Power '45; Fluorescent Chemicals and Their Applications '42; Fluorochemistry '45; Handbook of Uranium Minerals '47; Applied Fluorochemistry '47; Diction-

ary of Luminescent Substances '47; Fluorescent Minerals '48; also articles in field. Research chem, asso ed Mineralogist Mag since '40; research chem, head De Ment Labs Portland Ore since 41. Lectrochem Soc—Am Chem Soc— London Chem Soc—NY Acad Science —US Naval Inst—Soc Illuminating Engrs—Ore Mineral Soc—London Faraday Soc—AAAS. New Fliedner Bldg., Portland 5.†☉

19 DEMERATH, Nicholas Jay. American society (Sociology); Planning; Housing. b'13. AB '34 (DePauw U); MA '38—PhD '42 (Harvard). Adviser to resident commissioner from Philippines to US; on Philippine delegation to UNRRA Assembly '46. Co-author: Building Atlanta's Future '48; Toward a Housing Program for the Philippines '45; also articles in field. Prof sociol and research prof Inst Research in Social Sci U NC since '48; mem Planning Associates Chapel Hill NC since '48. Ensign, later lt jg USNR '44-46, staff Philippine Nat Planning Commn '45-46. Am Sociol Soc—So Sociol Soc— Am Inst Planners—Am Soc Planning Officials—Nat Assn Housing Officials —Assn Planning and Regional Reconstruction (British). 307 Alumni Building, Chapel Hill, N.C.

20 de MILLE, Agnes George. Choreography. AB (U Calif Los Angeles). Choreographed and danced The Black Crook '29; choreographed film Romeo and Juliet '36; choreographed and directed Allegro '47; choreographed musicals Nymph Errant '33, Hooray for What '37, Oklahoma '43, One Touch of Venus '43, Bloomer Girl '44, Carousel '45, Brigadoon '47, Gentlemen Prefer Blondes '49; Out of This World '50; choreographed ballets Obeah Black Ritual '40, Three Virgins and a Devil '41. Drums Sound in Hackinsack '41, Rodeo '42, Tally-Ho '44, Fall River Legend '48.

21 DE MILLY, Adolphe. French journalism, economics, and politics. b'10. Licencie es Lettres '31 (Sorbonne Paris). Author: L'ecole romane '27; La Vie de Mata Hari '32; also articles in field. Lecturer in US since '40; founder, ed La Voix de France NYC since '40, first Fighting French newspaper in US having direct connection with French underground. Editions A De Milly, 119 W. 57th St., NYC.

22 DEMING, Milo Henry. Range forage surveys (Western United States); Range ecology, watershed, conservation). b'94. BS '20 (Ia State Coll Agr). Developed forage value index for native flora of intermountain region, US); originated primary forage species method of checking range utilization; designed erosion and sedimentation experimental installations; developed range and dependent property survey methods and procedures. Author articles in field. With US Forest Service '20-30, Intermountain Forest and Range Experiment Station '31-35; US Grazing Service asst act chief Range Surveys '38-46, western US; US Bur Land Mgt Squaw Butte-Harney Range and Livestock Expt Sta Burns Ore as range ecol range research '46-49. Soc Am Foresters (chmn Intermountain sect, exec com range mgt subdiv)—Ecol Soc Am—Am Soc Range Mgt (council)— Utah Acad Sci Arts Letters—Am Forestry Assn—AAAS. U. S. Bureau of Land Management, P.O. Box 659, Salt Lake City, Utah.

23 DEMING, W(illiam) E d w a r d s. Mathematical statistics (Sampling, quality control). b'00. BS '21 (U Wyo); MS '24 (U Colo); PhD '28 (Yale). Author: Least Squares '38; Statistical Adjustment of Data '43; Theory of Sampling '49. Instr physics

Colo Sch Mines '22-23, asst prof '23-24; asst prof U Colo '24-25; physicist US Dept of Agr '27-39; math adv Bur of Census since '39; adviser in sampling Bur of the Budget since '42; spl lecturer mathematics Nat Bur of Standards since '30; head dept math statis Grad Sch US Dept Agr since '33; cons to Sec of War since '40; adj prof in math statis NYU since '46; cons in sampling to Govt of India '47, Supreme Command Tokyo '47. Inst Math Statis (F, pres '45)—Royal Statis Soc (F, London)—Am Statis Assn(F)—AAAS—Population Assn—Philos Soc of Washington—Washington Academy of Sci—Math Assn (London)—Am Soc for Quality Control(F)—Biometric Soc—Assn for Pub Opinion Research—Market Research Council—Sigma Xi—Phi Beta Kappa—Phi Kappa Phi. Bureau of Budget, Washington 25.©

10 de MOND, Willy. Hosiery (Theatrical, period). b'05. Grad (NY Textile Coll NYC). Production of specialty hosiery for motion picture musicals and costume dramas; research on hosiery history, and production of period and contemporary stockings; development of hosiery innovations, including black heel, black bottom lace toe and heel, iridescent hosiery, jeweled stockings, ombre hosiery, panel seam, mitten toe, pleated and mesh styles. Designer Leigh Silk Hosiery Mills '23-29; designer costume and high-fashion hosiery Willys of Hollywood since '29; now with Sanson Hosiery Mills Inc Hollywood. Calif State Fair gold medal award '49 and '50, innovation and creation award 39; Boot and Shoe Recorder Magazine outstanding fashion creative personality award '49 '51. Willys of Hollywood, 7626 Santa Monica Blvd., Los Angeles 46.

11 deMONSABERT, Winston Russel. Ziroconium. b'15. BS '37 (Loyola U of the South); MA '45 (Tulane U). Investigation structure of complexes of zirconium, and nature of these complexes with regard to use in electroplating; hydroxy, hydroxy-carboxy, hydroxy amino, and carboxy amino complexes of ziromium with respect to their preparation, stability, structure, and field of application in both aqueous and non aqueous solvents. Prof physics Warren Easton Boys High Sch New Orleans La '40-44; prof chem and physics Behrman High Sch New Orleans La '44-48; asso prof chem Loyola since '48. Am Inst Chem (F)—AAAS— Nat Geog Soc—ACS. Loyola University, 6363 St. Charles Av., New Orleans.

12 DEMPSTER, Richard Roy. Theoretical physics. b'08. AB '30—MA '31—PhD '42 (U Calif). Author: The Calculation of Transition Probabilities for Photoionization of Sodium from the 3P State; The Magnetic Field of an Interrupted Solenoid (with E U Condon); The Path of an Ion in an Approximately Uniform Magnetic Field '44; and others. Physicist armor and projectile lab Naval Proving Ground '42-43; theoretical physicist Radiation Lab (Manhattan Project) U Calif '43-44; asso prof physics Ore State Coll since '44; cons Radiation Lab since '48. Am Phys Soc—Am Assn Physics Teachers—Am Astron Soc—Sigma Xi.

13 DEMRICK, Carl. Translating (Technical). b'95. Informal study foreign langs and terminologies. Translator of about 10,000 articles, theses, books, etc from Bohemian, Croatian, Czech, Danish, Dutch, Flemish, French, German, Italian, Norwegian, Polish, Portuguese, Rumanian, Russian, Serbian, Slovak, Spanish, Swedish, Ukrainian and Yugoslavian into English; supervised translation of about 90,000 more items; knowledge of about 1,000,000 foreign technical terms and 6,000,000 non-technical words. Founder technical-translating service '36. 53 S. Broadway, Yonkers 2, N.Y.

14 de NAVARRE, Maison Gabriel. Chemistry of cosmetics. b'09. PhC—BS '30 (Wayne U). Technical editor American Perfume and Essential Oil Review since '39; American editor Journal of Society Cosmetic Chemists. Author: Chemistry and Manufacture of Cosmetics '41; Production Control and Analysis of Cosmetics '44; also articles in field. One patent pending. Cons chem various drug, cosmetic mfgrs '30-47; vp charge mfg and research Cosmetic Labs Inc since '47; vp Beauty Counselors Inc since '47; spl instr cosmetics Wayne U since '39; Soc Cosmetic Chem—Allied Drug Cosmetic Assn Mich—Am Oil Chem Soc—Am Chem Soc—Am Pharm Assn (com experts)—Soc Pub Analysts (London)—Analytical Chemists Soc—Am Inst Chem(F)—Engring Soc Detroit—Mich Acad Pharm—Phi Delta Chi. Cosmetic Laboratories, Inc., 5850 Second Av., Detroit 2. H: 404 Lothrop Rd., Grosse Pointe Farms 30, Mich.†

15 DENDY, John Stiles. Limnology; Fishery biology (Tennessee impounded waters). b'09. BS '30 (Presbyn Coll); MA '32 (U NC); PhD '43—teaching fellow '38-42 (U Mich). Author articles in field. Asso prof zool Ala Poly Inst Auburn Ala since '47. Tenn Acad Sci—Ecol Soc Am—Am Soc Limnol Oceanog—Am Fisheries Soc—Am Soc Ichthyologists and Herpetologists—Sigma Xi. Zoology and Entomology Department, Alabama Polytechnic Institute, Auburn, Ala.†

16 DENHARDT, Robert Moorman. Horses. b'12. AB '36—MA '37—Rockefeller fellow '41-42 (U Calif). Research on history of the Spanish horse in the New World and present day offspring, cowboy horse and gear, present day and historical. Author: The Quarter Horse (3 vols) '41, 45, '50; The Horse of the Americas '47. Author articles: The Southwestern Cowhorse '39; Horse Lore of the Conquest '40. Editor: The Horses of the Conquest '49. Contributor: Dictionary of American History '40; Agricultural History '50. Asst prof agrl econ Tex A&M '37-41; agrl analyst USDA Porto Algere Brazil '42-45; ed The Western Horseman since '47. Am Quarter Horse Assn (dir)—Tex Horse and Mule Assn (dir)—Am Quarter Racing Assn (dir). Western Horseman, 3850 N. Nevada, Colorado Springs, Colo.

17 DENISON, A(lbert) Rodger. Petroleum geology. b'97. BS '21—MS '25 (Okla U). Author articles in field. Geol, later chief geol Amerada Petroleum Corp since '22. Am Assn Petroleum Geol (sec-treas '29-30, pres '43-44)—Geol Soc Am(F)—AAAS(F)—Am Inst Mining Metall Engrs—Am Geophys Union. Box 2040, Tulsa 2, Okla.

18 DENISON, Archibald Campbell. Maritime and architectural history. b'95. BA '17—BArch '20 (Columbia). Author: America's Maritime History '44; also articles in field. Cons practice Glendale Ohio since '42; asso prof arch Ohio U since '46. Marine Hist Assn—US Naval Inst—Newcomen Soc Eng in N Am. Ohio University, Athens, O.

19 DENISON, Robert Howland. Primitive fossil fishes. b'11. AB '33 (Harvard College); MA '34—PhD '38 (Columbia). Resch creodonts whale shark, primitive fossil fishes, early lower Eocene mammals Wind River Basin Wyoming, anatomy head and pelvic fin of the whale shark; field work in western states and Canada. Author articles in field. Asst curator Dartmouth Coll Museum '37-47; paleontol U Calif African Expedition '47-48; curator fossil fishes Chicago Nat Hist Mus Chicago since '48. Soc Vertebrate Paleontol—Soc Study Evolution. Chicago Natural History Museum, Chicago 5.

20 DENNIS, Earl A(ubrey). Embryology and developmental physiology of birds and reptiles; International educational exchange. b'02. AB '25 (Coll of Wooster O); PhD '34 (U Chicago). Asst prof dept biol Am U Washington '35-40, prof '42-46, chmn dept '35-46, dean coll arts sci '44-45; on leave to serve as civilian instr biol Biarritz Am U France '45-46; adviser sci and tech sect Office Internat Information Cultural Affairs US Dept State '46; acting asst chief Div Internat Exch Persons Office Information and Ednl Exch Dept State '47-49; chief British Commonwealth and N European Br Internat Information Administration Department of State since '52. AAAS—Am Soc Zool—Genetics Soc Washington—Sigma Xi. U.S. Department of State, Washington.

21 DENNIS, Lawrence. Contemporary social, political and economic systems (Capitalism, communism, fascism, totalitarianism, functionalism, instrumentalism). b'93. AB '20 (Harvard). Conducted peace conference and first phase American intervention in Nicaragua '26 during revolution. Author: Is Capitalism Doomed? '32; The Coming American Fascism '36; The Dynamics of War and Revolution '40; A Trial on Trial (with M J St George) '46. In diplomatic service '20-27; writer since '30; propr, ed, pub Appeal to Reason (weekly news analysis) since '46. R.F.D., Becket, Mass.

22 DENNISON, Jackson Belden. Economics; Finance. b'91. AB '12 (Lenox Coll Hopkinton Ia); AM '15—grad student '19-21 (U Wiks); grad Student '15-17 (U Minn). Asso prof economics Miami U '21-22, asso prof economics and business '22-37, prof business '37-39, prof finance since '39; dir Bur Business Research since '39; research asso Cincinnati Bur Govtl Research '31 and '45-46. Am Statis Assn—Am Finance Assn—Delta Sigma Pi—Beta Gamma Sigma. Miami University, Oxford, O. H: 327 E. Vine St.©

23 DENNY, Frank Earl. Plant dormancy and respiration. b'83. AB '06 (U Neb); PhD '16 (U Chicago). Research on methods of hastening and inhibiting sprouting, and of measuring respiration rate. Granted US patents on method of coloring citrus fruits '23, process of sprouting buds and plants '27. Author articles: Factors influencing the pH equilibrium known as the isoelectric point of plant tissue '26; Chemical treatments for controlling the growth of buds of plants '28; The twin-leaf method of studying changes in leaves '30; Changes in leaves during the night '32; Improvements in methods of determining starch in plant tissues '34; Gas content of plant tissue and respiration '46; The role of the surface micro-flora in measurements of the respiration rate of germinating seeds '48, and others. Asst hort U Neb '06-08; plant physiol US Dept Agr '16-18, asso chem '19-23; plant physiol Boyce Thompson Inst for Plant Research since '24. AAAS (F, v chmn sect G '37)—Bot Soc Am (treas '36)—Torrey Bot Club (vp '36)—Am Soc Naturalists. Boyce Thompson Institute for Plant Research, Inc., 1086 N. Broadway, Yonkers 3, N.Y.

24 DENNY, George Hutcheson. Language and literature. b'70. AB '91—AM '92 (Hampden Sydney Coll); PhD '96 (U Va); LLD '03 (Furman U) '05

(Washington Coll Md) '12 (Tulane U) '13 (Washington and Lee U) '37 (U Ala); DCL '14 (U of South). Author: The Subjunctive Sequence After Adjective and Substantive Predicates and Phrases '96; also articles in field. Contbr to Library of Southern Literature. Prof Latin and German Hampden-Sydney Coll '96-99; prof Latin '99-11, acting pres '01-02, pres '02-11; pres U Ala '12-37, '42-43 chancellor '37 since '43. Ala Edn Assn (life) So Univ Conf—Phi Beta Kappa. University, Ala.⊙

10 DENNY, Henry Wadhams. Chemistry. b'86. BS '08 (Worcester Poly Inst). Chemist NJ State Dept Health Trenton '08-15, chief chemist '15-17; dir research Schoenhoffen Co Chicago '17-20; gen mgr Sugola Co Am Orange NJ '20-24; research tech Sun Maid Raisin Growers Assn Fresno Cal '24-26; mgr sales development Comml Solvents Corp NY City '26-37, vp charge sales '37-50, dir '43-50. Soc Chem Industry—Am Chem Soc. H; 214 Parkside Av., Trenton 8, N.J.⊙

11 DENOMY, Alexander Joseph. Origins of courtly love; Spanish-southern French relations (Twelfth century); Medieval saints' lives (Vernacular versions). b'04. BA '23 (U Western Ontario); MA '28 (U Toronto); MA '32—PhD '34—Thayer fellow '33-34—Shelden Travel fellow '34-35 (Harvard); '34-35 (Ecole des Chartes, Coll de France, Ecole des Hautes Etudes). Managing editor Medieval Studies since '42; advisory board Speculum since '47. Author: Medieval Studies in Honor of J D M Ford '48; The Heresy of Courtly Love '47; The De celo et de Mundo of Nichole d'Oresme '42-44; The Old French Lives of St Agnes and Other Vernacular Versions of the Middle ages '38; also articles in field. Ordained Catholic priest '28; prof comparative lit Middle Ages Pontifical Inst Medieval Studies since '35; prof dept Romance lang and lit U Toronto since '35. Mod Lang Assn—Royal Soc Canada(F)—Medieval Acad Am—Guggenheim fellow '47-48. Pontifical Institute of Medieval Studies, 59 Queen's Park Cn., Toronto 5, Can.†

12 DENSLOW, Ray Vaughn. Freemasonry; Masonic history. b'85. AB '07 (U Mo). Representative Grand Lodge of England in Missouri since '25; chairman Masonic Relief Commission to Europe '45; chairman special Masonic Mission for Investigation Conditions in Germany '49; represented conference of Grand Masters USA at Inter-American Masonic Conference of Latin-American Grand Lodges Mexico City '52. Author: Territorial Masonry '25; The Masonic Conservators; Civil War and Freemasonry; A Missouri Frontier Lodge; Freemasonry and the Santa Fe Trail '49; History of Missouri Commanderies of Knights Templar '49, and others; also articles in field. Ed Royal Arch Mason '43-52; editor Transactions of Missouri Lodge of Research '52, head Royal Arch Masons of US and Ter '42-46. Nat Masonic Research Soc—Mo Lodge Resch. Me Grand Lodge Freemason's Josiah H Drummond medal; NC medal for Royal Arch achievement; Hon First Grand Prin Grand Chapter of Royal Arch Masons Scotland '44; award for establishment United Grand Lodge of Germany '50; Grand Lodge of Austria special plaque for services rendered. 305 W. 12th, Trenton, Mo.

13 DENTON, James Fred. Platyhelminthes; Birds of Georgia and Newfoundland. b'14. BS '35—MS '38 (U Rice Inst); Markle fellow '43—certified-Ga); PhD '41—research fellow '38-41 cate post grad course tropical med '43 (Tulane U). Collected birds for US

Fish and Wildlife Service in Newfoundland '47. Author articles in field. Asst prof microbiol U Med Coll Ga since '42. Am Soc Parasitol—Am Soc Tropical Med—Helminthol Soc Washington—Am Microscopical Soc—Ga Ornithol Soc (founder '36, ed The Oriole since '43)—Sigma Xi. The Medical College of Georgia, Augusta, Ga.†

14 DeOME, K(enneth) B(enton). Animal and Avian pathology (Cancer, tumors, oncology); Airborne bacteria viruses. b'06. BA '28 (Albion Coll); MS '34 (Mich State Coll); PhD '38 (U Calif). Author articles in field. Instr animal path, jr animal path exptl sta dept vet sci U Calif '38-43, asst prof, asso prof Animal Pathol '43-48, asso Animal Pathol '49; dir Cancer Research Genetics Lab; asso prof zoology U Cal since '50. AAAS—Am Assn Cancer Res—Sigma Xi. Univ of Calif, Berkeley.

15 De POSTELS, Theodore Frederic August. Architectural perspectography; Perspectoscopy; Delineation. b'73. Diploma '00 (Imperial Beaux Arts Acad St Petersburg); Diploma '00 (NYU). Invented practical perspectographical devices '18, '20, practical perspectoscopic graphical and mechanical devices '20, '44. Author: Architectural and Engineering Lettering '22; Fundamentals of Perspective '44; also articles in field. Cons, designer, illustrator, owner private studio for art and architecture since '23. AIA—AAAS—NY State Assn Architects—Municipal Art Soc. Second prize for design shrine in memory of Czar Martyr Nicholas II '37. 644 Riverside Dr., NYC.

16 DERLETH, August (William). American regional literature; History of comics in America; Wisconsin history. b'09. BA '30 (U Wis). Professor of world's largest selected collection of comics, newspaper Sunday, daily, strips, panels, 500 volumes together with adjunctive material; presently engaged research on comprehensive study and history of comics in America. Author: Country Growth '40; The Wisconsin: River of a Thousand Isles '42; Sac Prairie People '48; Milwaukee Road '48; also articles in field. Guggenheim fellow '38. Ed, dir Arkham House Publishers; Mycroft and Moran; Stanton and Lee, Sauk City Wis. Midland Authors—Poetry Soc Am—Am Folklore Soc—Author's Guild—Wis State Hist Soc. Sauk City, Wis.

17 der MATEOSIAN, Edward. Nuclear physics; Geiger-Muller counters. b'14. BA '35—MA '40 (Columbia); '41-42 (Ind U). Co-holder US patent on methylene bromide quenched Geiger-Muller tubes '47. Author articles: Electrolytic Polishing of Electron Microscope Samples '47; Multiple Nuclear Isomerism (with others) '47. Research physicist Naval Research Lab Washington '42-46; physicist Argonne Nat Lab Chicago since '47. Am Phys Soc. Argonne National Laboratory, P.O. Box 5207, Chicago 80.

18 DERMEN, Haig. Cytology of fruit plants. b'95. BS '25 (U Conn); MS '27 (U Maine); MS '31—PhD '33 (Harvard). Research on use of colchicine in inducing polyploidy in such fruit plants as strawberries, cranberries, peaches, pears, apples. Author articles in field. Cytologist US Plant Ind Beltsville Md since '37. AAAS—Am Soc Naturalists—Am Genetic Assn—Am Soc Hort Sci—Bot Soc Am—Genetics Soc Am—Wash Acad Sci. U.S. Department of Agriculture, Plant Industry Station, Beltsville, Md.†

19 DESBARATS, George Henry. Marine engineering; Electrical engineering. b'00. Marine engr '19 (Royal Naval Coll Can); BSc (EE) '22 (McGill

U). Construction and operation large hydroelectric plants; improvements in automatic load, frequency, and time control; exploratory water power survey Newfoundland and Labrador; operation of marine railways, floating docks, graving docks, and machine shops. Author articles: Newfoundland Water Power '49; Water Power Possibilities of the Hamilton River, Labrador '50, and others. Sta supt Farmer's Rapids Hydro-Elec Plant Que Can '27-28, Paugan Hydro-Elec Plant '28-42; water power surveys Newfoundland and Laborador '47-51. Engring Inst Can—Am Soc Me—Am Soc Civil Eng—Am Inst EE—Professional Engrs Que—Am Geog Soc. Frost Bldg., Harvey Rd., St. John's, Newfoundland.

20 DESMOND, Robert William. Mass communications; International news gathering. b'00. AB '22 (U Wis); certificate '29 (Sch Internat Studies Geneva Switzerland); MA '30 (U Minn); PhD '36 (U London Sch Econ Polit Sci). Member UNESCO Commission on Technical Needs in Mass Communications Paris '47. Author: Newspaper Reference Methods '33; The Press and World Affairs '37. Co-author: (with F J Brown, Charles Hodges, J S Roucek, others) Contemporary World Politics '39; Professional Training for Journalists '49; also articles in field. With New York Herald (Paris) '26-27; instr and asst prof journalism U Minn '28-32; various positions Christian Science Monitor US and abroad '33-38; act asso prof journalism Stanford '38; prof journalism Medill Sch Journalism Northwestern U '38-39; prof journalism, chmn dept U Calif since '39. Commd maj US Army '43 assigned to Sch Mil Govt; assignments in N Africa, Sicily, Italy, England; attached to OWI and UN Information Office '44-45. Am Assn Schs Depts Journalism (pres '47)—Am Assn Teachers Journalism—Sigma Delta Chi. University of California, Berkeley 4, Cal.

21 DESSAUER, John H. Photochemistry (Xerography, photo emulsion, photo paper, sensitizing dyes). b'05. BS '26 (Inst Tech Munich); MS '27—DSc '29 (Inst Tech Aachen Germany). Chem Ansco Binghamton NY '29-35; chief chem The Haloid Co Rochester '35-37, dir research '37-46, vp charge research and product development since '46. Holds six patents in field. ACS—Optical Soc Am—Soc Motion Picture Engrs—Photog Soc Am. The Haloid Company, 6 Haloid St., Rochester 3, N.Y.

22 DESTLER, Chester McArthur. American history (Recent, agrarianism, radicalism, liberalism, Populism, historiography); Early history of the petroleum industry. b'04. AB '25 (Coll Wooster); AM '28—PhD '32—Henry Milton Wolf Fellow in Am hist (U Chicago). Author: American Radicalism 1865-1901; Essays and Documents '46. Senior collaborator: Studies in Social Progress '38; also articles in field. Prof, chmn dept hist Conn Coll since '42. AHA—Agr Hist Assn—Econ Hist Assn—Miss Valley Hist Assn—So Hist Assn—Phi Beta Kappa. 111 Nameaug Av., New London, Conn.

23 DE TERRA, Helmut. Ice Age geology, archaeology and geography. b'01. PhD '25 (U Munich). Conducted scientific expeditions India, Kashmir, Tibet, Burma, Malaya, Java, Central Asia; Viking Fund research in Mexico '46-48; gave first modern geographical-geological account of west Tibet and of southern Chinese Turkestan; discovered and dated earliest pre-historic cultures in India, Burma, Mexico; discovered Tepexpan man Mexico '47. Author: Ice Age in India and Associated Cultures '39; Durch Urwelten am Indus '39; Research on Early Man in Burma '43; Early Man in Mexico '48; also articles in field. Instr, asst prof geol Yale '30-36; asso Carnegie Instn Washington '36-40, '45; chief regional research geog bd US Dept Interior '43-44; vis lecturer US Dept Agr '40-41, U Md '43; vis prof geog O State U '44-45; research asso Viking Fund Inc NYC since '45. Assn Am Geog—Geol Soc China—Geo Soc Am(F)—Am Anthrop Assn—SE Asia Inst. Viking Fund, Inc., 14 E. 71st St., NYC.

10 DETHIER, Vincent Gaston. Sensory physiology (Insects); Lepidoptera (Life history). b'15. BA '36—MA '37 —PhD '39 (Harvard). Research on gustation and olfaction in lepidopterous larvae, and taste thresholds, antennae, and function of antennal receptors; chemical factors determining choice of food plants by Papilio larvae; dioptric apparatus of lateral ocelli; studies of testing methods of attractants and repellants. Author: Chemical Insect Attractants and Repellants '47; also articles in field. Asso prof biol Johns Hopkins since '48. AAAS—Am Soc Zool—NY Acad Sci—So Calif Acad Sci —Entomol Soc Am—Sigma Xi. Research fellow, Harvard grant, Woods Hole Marine Biol Lab '35, Harvard Sch Forestry '36, Clark U '37, Atkins Inst Cuba '39-40. Department of Biology, Johns Hopkins University, Baltimore 18.

11 DETJEN, Louis Reinhold. Fruit plants (Physiological drop); Pollination (Cane fruits, grapes, peaches); Grape, cabbage and beet breeding. b'84. BS '09 (U Wis); MS '11 (U NC). Author articles in field. Prof hort, asso research prof U Del since '45. ASHS (F)—Phi Kappa Phi—Alpha Zeta. Department of Horticulture, Agricultural Experiment Station, Newark, Del.

12 de TOLNAY, Charles Erich. Life and works of Michael Angelo; Hist of art. b'99. Student '18-19 '23-25 (U Vienna); '20-21 (U Berlin); '22 (U Frankfurt am Main); PhD '25 (U Vienna). Travel and study in Austria, Belgium, England, France, Germany, Greece, Holland, Hungary, Italy, Portugal, Spain, Switzerland. Author: The Youth of Michael Angelo '42; also 6 other books pub in Belgium, Germany and Hungary. Contbr articles on art to US and European jours. Research Rome and Florence '25-28; lecturer history of art U Hamburg '29-33, Sorbonne Paris '34-39; vis lectr fine arts U London '35, U Gand '36, U Utrecht '37; mem Inst for Advanced Study, Princeton since '39. Coll Art Assn, Athenaeum. Laureat de L'Academie des Inscriptions et Belles-Lettres Inst de France Paris '37. H: 293 Nassau St., Princeton, N.J.◎

13 DEUEL, Thorne. Archeology (Illinois, Central and Eastern US). b'90. BS '12 (US Mil Acad); PhD '35 (U Chicago). Reconstruction of Hopewellian and other central US aboriginal cultures by field work and comparison with reports already published on similar sites and on cultures (both existent, recently existent, or extinct) in the same cultural stage and substage. Editor: Hopewellian Communities in Illinois '52. Assistant editor American Antiquity '35-39. Co-author: (with Dr Fay-Cooper Cole) Rediscovering Illinois '37. Asst prof Syracuse U '29-33; asst anthrop U Chicago '31-34; dir Archeol Survey Miss Valley '31-38; research asso U Chicago '34-38; dir Ill State Mus since '38. Soc Am Archeol (sec-treas '40-42)—Ill Archeol Soc (mem adv bd)—Ill State Acad Sci (pres '49-50, librarian)—Midwest Mus Conf (pres '50-51). Illinois State Museum, Springfield, Ill. H: 2150 Illini Rd.

14 DEUTSCH, Karl Wolfgang. Nationalism; communications theory; Cybernetics. b'12. DSc (Polit '38 (Charles U Prague Czechoslovakia); MA (Govt) '41—PhD '51 (Harvard). Application of communications theory to social sciences. Author Nationalism and Social Communication '52; articles The Value of Freedom '48; Innovation, Entrepreneurship and the Learning Process '49; Models in the Natural and Social Sciences '49; Mechanism, Teleology and Mind '51. Sumner Prize in Political Science. Instr hist and internat relations MIT '42-44, asst prof hist '44-47, asso prof '47-52, prof hist and polit sci since '52. Am Hist Assn —Am Acad Polit and Social Sci— Medieval Acad—Econ Hist Assn. Room 14-N-417, Massachusetts Institute of Technology, Cambridge 39, Mass. H: 81 Kilburn Rd., Belmont 78, Mass.

15 DEUTSCH, Zola Gotthard. Manufacture of Alkalis. b'99. Chem E '23 (U Cincinnati). Consultant ammonia-soda process for manufacture of alkali; design and improvement of factories for production of alkalis, including sodium carbonate, caustic soda, and chlorine. Contributor: Encyclopedia of Chemical Technology; Thorpe's Dictionary of Applied Science. Project engr in charge plant design Mathieson Alkali Works '30-38; cons engr on alkali mfg '39-41 and since '45; indsl specialist alkali, chlorine and heavy chem plants, with US State Dept in Germany '45. Am Soc ME—Am Inst Chem Engrs—ACS—Soc Am Mil Engrs—Sigma Xi. 70 E. 45th St., N.Y.C. 17. H: Rural Delivery, Hackettstown, N.J.

16 deVALINGER, Leon, Jr. Archives; Document restoration; Microfilming; Delaware history. b'05. AB '30—MA '35 (U Delaware); '41-47 (U Pa). Author: Colonial Military Organization in Delaware 1638-1776 '38. Co-author: George Washington and Delaware '32; also articles in field. Asst state archivist '30-41, archivist since '41; director of Delaware State Museum. Soc Am Archivists (co-founder, chmn com publication policies '40-47, ed bd '45-48) Hist Soc Del (dir, mag com, library com)—Archaeol Soc Del (co-founder, organizing sec and dir '38-48)—Del Swedish Colonial Soc (sec '41-47, vp '47-48). Hall of Records, Dover, Del.

17 DE VANE, William Clyde. Language and Literature. b'98. student '15-16 LLD '50 (Furman U Greenville SC); AB '20—PhD '26 (Yale); LittD '44 (Wooster Ohio Coll); LHD '48 (Washington and Lee U); LLD '51 (Brown U). Research on English literature of the 19th Century; Educational administration. Author: Browning's Parleyings—The Autobiography of a Mind '27; Browning's Shorter Poems, '34; A Browning Handbook '35; Tennyson '40. Co-author: (with Fanny Ratchford) Charlotte Bronte's Legends of Angria '33; (with K L Knickerbocker) New Letters of Robert Browning '50. Prof English and head dept Cornell U '34-38, Goldwyn Smith prof English '37-38; prof English and dean Yale Coll since '38, dir div humanites and social sciences since '46; Scholar English Literature of the 19th Century. Pres Coll English Assn '39-40. Modern Lang Assn Am (exec council '38-40 '43-48)—Am Council Learned Soc (chmn since '47), Phi Beta Kappa—Phi Kappa Phi. Yale College Dean's Office, Yale University, New Haven.◎

18 de VAZEILLE, Bruce Randanne. French heraldry. AB '25 (U Cal); diploma '26 (U Grenoble); diploma Doctorat en Droit '26-27 (U Lyons); student '27 (Ecole des Sciences politiques Paris). Active duty US Air Force since '41. Export Mgrs Assn. Chief Liaison

Office Chateauroux Air Depot, Chateauroux (Indre), France.

19 DEVER, Henry F. Industrial recording instruments and automatic controls. b'01. BS '23—EE '24 (Northwestern U). Testing in central station steam and combustion efficiency; safety and fire hazard testing of electrical equipment and appliances. Salesman Minneapolis-Honeywell Regulator Co '31-35, branch mgr Phil terr '36-39, vice pres engring '39-45, president Brown Instrument Division Minneapolis-Honeywell since '45. Am Soc Heating Ventilating Engrs—Franklin Institute, Wayne and Roberts Avs., Phila. 44.

20 DEVEREUX, George. Anthropology (Cultural, social, relationship of culture and personality, anthropology and psychiatry, anthropology and psychoanalysis, anthropology of Hopi and Mohave Indians, Moi of Indo-China); Sociology (Pathology, criminology, marginal men, family, sociology and psychiatric theory); Psychiatry and psychoanalysis in sociological and anthropological research. b'08. Diploma '31, licence '32 (U Paris, Inst d'Ethnologie); diploma '31 (Ecole Nationale des Langues Orientales Vivantes, Paris); PhD '32 (U Calif); research candidate since '48 (Topeka Inst Psychoanalysis). Anthropological field work among Hopi Indians '32, Mohave Indians '32-33, '35, '36, '38, Karuama Pygmies and Roro Melanesians, Papua '33, Moi of Indo-China '33-34; studies on Hopi rabbit hunt; on Mohave soul, paternity, homosexuality, witchcraft, relationship of culture and personality, incest, infanticide, coyote tales, pregnancy, obstetrics, etiquette, zoophilia, function of alcohol, magic substances, narcotics, heterosexual behavior, profanity, gestures, male puberty rite; on Moi divination; also work on mental hygiene of American Indian, psychotherapy of marginal men, social aspects of neurosis, sociological theory of schizophrenia, social structure of hospitals and prisons, motivation and control of crime, classical Chinese penology '44, and other subjects. Faculty U Wyo '41-43, Columbia U '44, Wellesley Coll '45, U Haiti '45, Menninger Found Sch Psychiat and Topeka Inst Psychoanalysis since '46; research com Winter Vets Adminstrn Hosp since '46, exec sec since '48. Am Ethnol Soc (adv ed bd Journ Clinical Psychopathol). Winter Veterans Administrations Hospital, Topeka, Kan.

21 DEVOE, Alan. Natural history; Animal psychology; Animalizing; Animal behaviour; Foxes (Diets). born '09. Student '27-30 (Columbia University). Author: Phudd Hill '37; Down to Earth '40; Lives Around Us '42; Speaking of Animals '47; also articles in field. Author monthly dept Down to Earth in American Mercury since '37; contbg ed Audubon Magazine; spl contbr and ed cons in natural hist for Reader's Digest. Phudd Hill, Hillsdale, N.Y.

22 DeVORE, Lloyd Thomas. Radiation (Measurement); Electromagnetism (Theory); Mechanics (Nonlinear); Communications systems (Electronic). b'09. BS '30—MS '31—PH D '33 (Pa State Coll). Faculty, asst prof (phys) Pa State Coll '34-42; chief engr spl projects lab Wright Field '42-46; asso prof, prof elec engring U Ill '46-50; mgr elec lab Gen Elec Co since '50. Phi Kappa Phi—Sigma Xi—Sigma Pi Sigma—Pi Mu Epsilon—APS—Inst Radio Engrs. Research F Pa State Coll '30-34; War Dept Exceptional Civilian Service Medal '46 for direction of research in Radio and Radar Countermeasures and Guided Missile Control Systems. Electronics Laboratory, General Electric Co., Electronics Park, Syracuse, N.Y.

10 DEWEY, Bartlett Taggart. Chemical microscopy; Sanitary chemistry; Identification of organic acids and alcohols. b'02. '21-23 (U Vt); BA '26—MA '34—PhD '35 (U Colo). Research on identification of organic acids by use of p-Chlorobenzyl Pseudothiuronium Chloride '39; identification of alcohols by means of optical properties of esters of carbanilic acid '40. Author articles in field. Prof chem, acting head dept Stephen F Austin State Teachers Coll Tex '35-37; asso prof chem John Tarleton Agrl Coll Tex '35-37; prof chem head dept North Pacific Coll of Oregon '37-41; asst prof chem U Colo '41-43; prof chem Eastern New Mexico U since '43, chmn div nat sci and math since '45. Am Chem Soc—Am Pharm Assn—AAAS—Sigma Xi. Eastern New Mexico University, Portales, N.M.†

11 DEWEY, Ralph Lawrence. Transportation economics (Rates, discriminations, services, finances); Public utilities; Monopolies. b'01. Student '19-21 (Oberlin Coll); AB '23—AM '24—scholar '23-24 (Ohio State U); PhD '29 (U Mich); research fellow '28-29 (Brookings Inst). Author: The Long and Short Haul Principle of Rate Regulation '35; also articles in field. Prof econ, asst dean grad sch O State U since '46. Am Econ Assn (chmn transportation and pub utilities sect '48). Graduate School, Ohio State University, Columbus 10, O.†

12 DEWHURST, J(ames) Frederic. Economics research (Natural resources, labor, marketing). b'95. BS '18 (U Wash); AM '22—PhD '28 (U Pa). Technical adviser to American delegation to International Conference on Government Statistics League of Nations Geneva '28, and to Preparatory Commission for World Economic Conference Geneva '32. Co-author: University Education for Business (with J H S Bossard) '31; Does Distribution Cost Too Much? (with P W Stewart) '39; America's Needs and Resources (with others) '47; also articles in field. Econ 20th Century Fund '33-35 and since '37. Social Research Council (dir com social security '35-37, staff cons '37-45, bd dirs and exec com since '46)—Am Statis Assn (vp '39)—AM Econ Assn—Acad Polit Sci—Am Marketing Assn. 330 W. 42d St., NYC.⊙

13 DEWITT, Clyde Colvin. Surface chemistry; Separation of materials; Process design. b'93. BS '25—PhD Chem Engring '27 (U Mich). Co-author: Partial Oxidation of Light Hydrocarbons at Atmospheric Pressure '47. Author articles: Colloidal Ferric Hydroxide as a Cause of the Bond in Molding Sands '28; Improved Bartell-Osterhof Cell '30; The Recovery of Iodine from Waste Solutions '37; The Discriminant Function in the Comparison of Fuel Analyses '44, and others. Chmn dept chem and metall engring Mich State Coll '40-48; dir Engineering Expt Station since '48; coordinator Solid Fuels Administrn Fuel Conservation Div World War II. Am Inst Chem(F)—Am Inst Chem Engrs—Am Chem Soc—Am Soc Engring Edn—Am Inst Mining Metall Engrs—Sigma Xi. Olds Hall, Michigan State College, East Lansing, Mich.⊙

14 DeWITT, Paul B(urton). Judicial administration. b'10. AB—AM '31 (University of Iowa); AM '34 (Harvard); LLB '37 (U Mich). Secretary National Conference Judicial Councils since '41; secretary special committee on improving judicial administration and chairman section bar activities Am Bar Assn since '47. Editor: Annual Handbook National Conference of Judicial Councils. Chief legislative drafting bur and state law librarian State Ia '39-40; asst sec Am Judicature Soc Ann Arbor '41; reporter rules com Supreme Ct Ia Des Moines '41-42; exec sec Assn Bar City of NY since '45. Am Bar Assn—Ia Bar Assn—Phi Beta Kappa. 42 W 44th St., NYC 36.†⊙

15 DeWITT, Roscoe Plimpton. Architecture (Hospitals; public housing). b '94. AB '14 (Dartmouth); MA Arch '17 (New School of Design). Approved hospital architect by American Hospital Association. AIA. 2025 Cedar Springs Av., Dallas 1.⊙

16 DEXTER, Ralph Warren. Marine ecology (Phyllopod Crustacea; lobster, mollusks); Chimney swift (Life histories). b'12. BS '34 (U Mass); PhD '38 (U Illinois). Author articles in field. Prof biol Kent State U Kent O since '37. Ecol Soc Am—Am Soc Limnol Oceanography—Nature Conservancy—AAAS(F)—Ohio Academy Sci(F—American Ornithological Union—Am Society Mammalogy—Society Systematic Zoology—Inland Bird-Banding Soc —American Malacological Union—Phi Beta Kappa—Phi Kappa Phi—Sigma Xi. Department of Biology, Kent State University, Kent, O.†

17 DEXTER, Stephen Torrey. Winter hardiness in plants; Quack grass; Forage crops (Quality); Grain and forage curing and storing (Moisture relations). b'97. BS '19—MS '24—PhD '30(U Wis); Fellow Nat Research Council '30-32 (U Chicago, U Minn). Holder patents covering methods of conditioning popcorn to proper moisture for optimum popping; device for rapidly determining moisture content in hay; rapid colorometric method for determining moisture in dry materials; device for curing crops by use of drying agents. Author articles in field. Prof farm crops dept Mich State Coll since '34. Prof crops in Army universities '45-46. AAAS(F)—Am Soc Agron—Am Soc Plant Physiol—Sigma Xi. Farm Crops Department, Michigan State College, East Lansing, Mich.†

18 deZEEUW, Donald J(ohn). Mushroom culture. b'11. BS '33 (Mich State Coll); MS '40—PhD '49 (U Minn). Research on method for obtaining single spore cultures of Agaricus campestris, pathological and cultural differences in isolates of Rhizoctonia solani. Research asst plant path U Minn '38-41, '45-47; asst prof research vegetable and cucurbit diseases dept bot and plant path Mich State Coll since '48. Am Phytopath Soc. Department of Botany and Plant Pathology, Michigan State College, East Lansing, Mich. H: 533 Evergreen Ave., East Lansing, Mich.

19 DIACHUN, Stephen. Tobacco diseases; Virus and bacterial diseases of plants. b'12. BS '34 (RI State Coll); MS 35'—PhD '38 (U Ill). Research on method of entry of bacteria into plants, over-wintering of plant pathogenic bacteria in soil and on roots, movement of tobacco mosaic virus, methods of inoculation with tobacco streak virus, inhibition of streak virus with healthy juice. Author articles in field. Grad work penicillium seedling disease of corn U Ill '34-37; asst, asso and plant path agrl expt sta U Ky since '37. AAAS—Bot Soc Am—Am Phytopath Soc—Ky Acad Sci—Phi Beta Kappa—Phi Kappa Phi—Sigma Xi. Kentucky Agricultural Experiment Station, Lexington 29, Ky.

20 DIAMOND, Grant S. Refractories; Abrasives; Silicon carbide; Electrically fused alumina. b'01. AC '23 (U Buffalo); Profl Ceramic Engrs '40 (Alfred U). Obtained patents for method of making refractory articles and materials; process of glazing refractory articles; kiln furniture. Author articles in field. Pres Electro Refractories & Abrasives Corp since '43: vp and dir Strategic Mat Corp; dir Dominion Silica Corp. New York State Ceramic Association(dir)—Am Ceramic Soc(F) —Inst Ceramic Engrs—NY State Coll Ceramics (mem bd mgrs). 344 Delaware Av., Buffalo 2.

21 DIAMOND, Randolphe William. Differential flotation of complex ores. b'91. BASc '13 (U Toronto Can); LLD (Hon) '48 (Queens U); DSc (Hon) '50 (U BC). With Anaconda Copper Mining Co Anaconda Mont '13-17, in charge exptl flotation '14-17 (copper & zinc); mill supt Ohio Copper Co Lark Utah '17; in charge exptl differential flotation Consol Mining & Smelting Co of Can Ltd Trail BC '17-19 (lead-zinc-iron), supt concentration '17-29. AIM ME—Engring Inst Can—Inst Mining and Metall (London)—Australasian Inst Mining and Metall—Can Inst Mining and Metall (pres '48-49)—Assn Professional Engrs BC. U Toronto McCharles medal and award for work on differential flotation of ore '34; Engring Inst Can Leonard Medallist award '35, Julian C Smith medal for achievement in development of Can '48; Selwyn G Blaylock medal for distinguished service to Can in field metall '48. H: Trail, B.C., Can.

22 DIBBLE, Barry. Electrical engineering; Generating stations (Hydroelectric and diesel); Electricity transmission and distribution; Power markets; Pumping for irrigation. b'81. Student '99 (Washington State Coll); EE '03 (U Minn); '05-06 (St Paul Law Sch). Consultant on various projects, including San Carlos Irrigation Project (Arizona), Wapato Project (Washington), Flathead Project (Montana), National Irrigation Commission (Mexico), Pensacola Dam and hydroelectric development (Oklahoma), Bonneville Project (Washington-Oregon), Denison hydro-electric development (Texas), Chief Joseph Dam (Washington), Columbia River and tributaries. With US Reclamation Service '09-24, asst engr Los Angeles '09-10, elec engr in charge constrn and operation and pump system Minidoka project (Ida) '10-15, project mgr '16-23, chief elec and mech engr Bur Reclamation Denver '23-24; pvt practice since '24. AIEE—ASCE—Am Soc Agrl Engrs—Am Assn Engrs. 120 E. Palm Av., Redlands, Cal.⊙

23 DICHTER, Ernest. Application of psychoanalysis to advertising and mass communications. b'07. PhD (U Vienna) licencie en lettres (Sorbonne). Work in depth-interviewing, psychological analysis of advt and industrial problems and of radio and television with help of modern psychological techniques. Author: The Psychology of Everyday Living '46; also articles in field. Research psychol J Stirling Getchell Inc advt agency NY; cons psychol on programs to CBS; cons indsl psychol. Montrose, N.Y.

24 DICHTER, Harry. Sheet music (Early American). b'98. Ed pub schs. Author: Handbook of American Sheet Music '47. Co-author: (with Elliott Shapiro) Early American Sheet Music, Its Lure and Its Lore '41. Assembled for libraries and collectors. 5458 Montgomery Av., Phila. 31.

25 DICK, Hugh Gilchrist. History of superstition; Renaissance literature; Bibliography. b'09. AB '30 (Union Coll); MA '36—PhD '37—fellow '36-37 (Cornell U). Engaged research on reference guide to Sir Francis Bacon since 1700. Author: Thomas Tomkis, Albumazar (1614) '44; A Survey of Humanistic Research in Progress on the Pacific Coast '46; also articles in field. Asst prof Eng U Calif '42-48; asso prof since '48. Mod Lang Assn Am—Pacific

Coast Philol Assn—Hist Sci Soc—Am Council Learned Soc (see Pacific Coast com for humanities). Rockefeller Found fellow '47-48. 405 Hilgard Av., Los Angeles 24.†

10 DICKEN, Samuel N. Economic and physical geography (Pacific Northwest, Mexico, Kentucky). b'01. BA '24 (Marietta Coll); PhD '30 (Calif U). Studies of population redistribution, surface configuration; research on Kentucky barrens, Mexican highland community of Galeana, cotton regions of Mexico, soil erosion in Karst Lands of Kentucky, Kentucky solution cuesta, basin settlements of middle Sierra Madre Oriental, Mexico. Author: Economic Geography '49; also articles in field. Head dept geol geog Ore U since '47. Am Geog Soc(F)—Assn Am Geog. Geology and Geography Department, Condon Hall, University of Oregon, Eugene, Ore.☉

11 DICKERSON, Gordon Edwin. Population genetics and breeding (Animal). b'12. BS '33 (Mich State Coll); MS '34—PhD '37 (U Wis). Research dealing with application population genetics to problems in improvement livestock, including use of dairy production records in evaluating breeding animals, experimental design testing inbred strains, effectiveness alternative methods selecting breeding animals (evaluation progeny tests as supplement to information obtained earlier in life), evidence for genetic or physiological correlation between different functional characters effecting breeding methods, evidence from results inbreeding and crossbreeding relating to potential importance hybrid vigor livestock production, and effectiveness different methods improving over-all performance in livestock. Author articles: Effectiveness Selection on Progeny Performance as Supplement to Earlier Culling in Livestock '44; Hereditary Obesity and Efficient Food Utilization in Mice '47; Composition of Hog Carcasses as Influenced by Heritable Differences in Rate and Economy of Gain '47, and others. Geneticist regional swine breeding lab US Dept Agr Ames Ia '40-47; professor animal husbandry animal breeding lab U Mo since '47. AAAS—AAUP—Am Dairy Sci Assn—Am Soc Animal Prodn—Am Genetic Assn—Genetics Soc Am—Biometrics Soc—Am Statis Assn (mem biometrics sect). Animal Breeding Laboratory, Schweitzer Hall, University of Missouri, Columbia, Mo.

12 DICKERSON, Oliver Morton. Prerevolutionary American history. b'75. AB '03—AM '04—PhD '06 (U Ill). Author: History of the Illinois State Constitutional Convention of 1862 '05; American Colonial Government '12; Boston Under Military Rule, 1768-1769 '36; Writs of Assistance as a Cause of the Revolution '39; John Hancock, Notorious Smuggler or Near Victim of British Revenue Racketeers?. Prof emeritus hist and polit sci Colo State Coll Edn '40. AHA—Am Acad Polit Social Sci—Nat Council Social Studies —Phi Beta Kappa. 1700 7th Av., Greeley, Colo.

13 DICKERSON, Roy Ernest. Family life education; Social hygiene; Sex education. b'86. LLB '09 (U Denver); LLM '10 (George Washington U). Author: So Youth May Know '30; Growing Into Manhood '33; Action Guide on Preparation for Marriage (written for United Christian Youth Movement of NA) '37; Understanding Myself '42; Home Study Course in Social Hygiene Guidance '44; Straight from the Shoulder '44. Co-author: (with Fritz Kunkel) How Character Develops '39; (with George Gould) Digest of Laws Dealing with Prostitution '41. Asst dir

Div Social Protection Fed Security Agy '41; exec sec Cincinnati Social Hygiene Soc since '41; asso dir Am Inst Family Relations; acting asso prof tchrs coll U Cincinnati. Cons Nat Conf on Edn for Marriage and Family Social Relations NY City '34; scout commr dir Nat Conf on Family Relations; chm com Edn for Family Life in the Schools; bd mgrs dept family life Nat Council Chs. Am Social Hygiene Assn—Nat Assn Social Hygiene Execs (pres)—Ohio Social Hygiene Soc (pres)—Nat Conf Family Relations. 312 W. 9th St., Cin.†☉

14 DICKEY, George Daman. Filtration. b'98. BS '19 (Pa State Coll); grad study (Pratt Inst, Columbia U). Patents cataphoric filter, dewatering filter. Author: Theory and Practice of Filtration '47. Co-author: Textbook of Filtration '23; also articles in field. Vice-pres Indsl Filtration Corp '22; market analyst Gen Motors Corp '27; dryer mgr Carrier Corp '30; organized Conkey Filter Co '24, now partner; cons. Am Inst Chem Engrs—Am Chem Soc. 10 E. 49th St., NYC.

15 DICKEY, Ralph Davis. Tung oil production. b'04. BSA '27 (U Fla); MSA '39 (Cornell U). Author: Proper Tung Orchard Methods Pay '41; The Importance of Tung Seed Selection '42; Correct Tung Tree Bronzing '48. Instr dept entomol and plant path U Fla '27-29, asst prof '29-33; asso hort Fla Agrl Expt Sta since '51. Am Soc Hort Sci—Fla State Hort Soc—Assn So Agrl Workers. Department of Horticulture, Florida Agricultural Experiment Station, Gainesville, Fla.

16 DICKINSON, Charles Alexius. Psychology; Mental health. b'79. Student '07-10 (Internat YMCA Coll Springfield Mass); AM '22—PhD '25 (Clark U Worcester Mass): Research fellow '25-26 (Cornell U). Member national committee and national council for Mental Hygiene. Editor: The Vibratory Sense and Other Lectures (by David Katz) '30. Contbr. to profl jours. Prof psychology U Me since '26, prof emeritus of psychology '51; chmn Coe Research Fund Com. AAAS(F)— Am Psychol Assn—Eastern Psychol Assn—Me Tchrs Assn (organizer and sec dept mental hygiene)—Me Pub Health Assn—Me Tchrs Hygiene Assn (organizer and sec-treas)—Phi Kappa Phi. H: 91 Bennoch Rd., Orono, Me.

17 DICKINSON, Helena Adell (Mrs. Clarence Dickinson). Lituriology: Ancient Christmas carols; Anglo-Saxon philology: Greek and medieval philosophy. b'75. MA '95 (Queens U. Can); PhD '01 (Heidelberg U). Author: Metrical Translations of 150 Ancient Carols '30: (with C Dickinson) Excursions in Musical History '17; A Book of Antiphons '19; The Troubadours and Their Music '20; A Nativity Play in Ancient Christmas Carols '19; The Technique and Art of Organ Playing '21, A Choirmaster's Guide '23; A Treasury of Worship '26; Metrical Translations of 50 Ancient Carols '35; The Choir Loft and the Pulpit '43. Lecturer liturgics, hist sacred music, hist church architecture. Union Theol Sem NYC since '28. 7 Gracie Sq., NYC 28.

18 DICKINSON, Malcolm G(ibson). Marine zoology (California Gulf sponges). b'09. AB '31 (Pomona Coll); MA '32 (Claremont Coll); PhD '41 (U So Calif). Author: Sponges of the Gulf of California '45. Headmaster Flintridge Prep Sch since '35. Phi Kappa Phi. 301 Foothill Blvd., Pasadena 3, Cal.

19 DICKINSON, Robert Eric. Regional geography of western Europe (Historical, economic, urban, political);

City and regional planning; Methodology of geography; History of geographic thought. b'05. BA '26—MA '28 (Leeds U, Eng); PhD '32 (U London). Co-author: The Making of Geography '32; The Regions of Germany '45; City Region and Regionalism '47; The West European City '49, and others. Prof geog Syracuse U since '47. Intelligence Service cons Ministry Home Security London Royal Air Force '41-45. Royal Geog Soc—Assn Am Geog—Inst British Geog. Rockefeller travelling fellow '31-32, '36-37. Syracuse University, Syracuse, N.Y.

20 DICKINSON, Thomas Albert. Plastics; Electrets. b'17. Spl student (Washburn Coll). Investigated electrochemical methods of polarizing dielectrics for production of plastic electrets; developed phenolic plastic casting resin '46; new application for silicone plasticizers '47. Author: Experimental Casting Plastics '47; Electrets '48; Plastics Dictionary '48; also articles in field. Aircraft inspector USN Ryan Aero Co '37-43; ed-in-chief W Coast Lit Enterprises '45-48. Am Soc Tool Engrs—Authors League Am—Bus Writers Guild. Box 67, Station M, Los Angeles 32. H: 4361 O'Neil St.

21 DICKINSON, Wesley Howard. Herpetology; Mosquito control. b'20. Student '39-40 (Long Beach City Coll); '40-41 (U Calif Los Angeles); '43 (Sch Tropical Med); '44 (Haffkine Inst). Lecturer on life history and habits of reptiles since '41; photographer motion and still pictures life history and habits of reptiles. Author articles in field. Curator reptiles Long Beach Zool Soc '41-45, since '45; sanitarian Calif State Dept Pub Health '46-47; entomologist Consolidated Mosquito Abatement Dist Selma Calif since '47; dir Long Beach Zool Garden since '49. AAAS—Am Museum Nat Hist (asso) —Herpetologists League—Am Soc Ichthyologists and Herpetologists— Am Mosquito Control Assn. 2510 Olive Av., Long Beach 6.

22 DICKINSON, William Edmund. Amphibians, reptiles, mosquitoes, craneflies, snakes, and lizards of Wisconsin. b'02. BS '32 (U Wis); MS '46 (Marquette U). Author: Snakes and Lizards of Wisconsin '49. Mus asst Milwaukee Public Mus '23-37; dir Kenosha Mus '37-40, curator lower zool Milwaukee Mus since '40. AAAS— Midwest Mus Assn. Public Museum, Milwaukee, Wis.†

23 DICKSON, James G. Plant pathology and physiology; Agronomy (Forage and cereal crops). b'91. BS '15 (Wash State Coll); MS '17—PhD '20 (Wis U). Special research England, Russia, Germany '29-30. Author: Outline of Diseases of Cereal and Forage Crops of the Northern Part of the United States '41; Cereal Disease Studies of Europe and Asia '30; Diseases of Field Crops '48. Co-author: (with M B Jacobs) The Chemistry and Technology of Food and Food Products; also articles in field. Asst bot U Wis '16-17, instr '17-18, asso prof plant path '19-26, prof since '26; agent div cereal crops and diseases US Dept Agr since '18. AAAS(F '29)—Am Phytopath Soc (vp '32)—Bot Soc Am—Am Soc Agron —Am Statis Assn—AAUP—Sigma Xi. Department of Plant Pathology, University of Wisconsin, Madison 6, Wis.

24 DI CYAN, Erwin. Drug and cosmetic chemistry; Federal drug regulation. b'08. PhD '33 (Rheinische Friederich Wilhelm U). Consultant on evaluation of research and development of drugs and cosmetics, nature and propriety of therapeutic claims in advertising; technical expert on prosecutions for violations of Federal Food

Drug and Cosmetic Act. Author articles in field. Independent cons chem dir firm Di Cyan & Brown NYC since '36. NY Acad Sci—Am Chem Soc—Assn Cons Chem and Chemical Engrs. 12 East 41 St., NYC 17.†

10 DIDUSCH, Joseph Stephen. Pollen allergens; Hemoglobin. b'79. AB '98 (Loyola Coll); MA '10 (Woodstock Coll); grad work (Columbia). Author articles in field. Prof biol, head dept Loyola Coll Baltimore since '35. AAAS —Am Assn Jesuit Sci—Am Genetic Assn—Ecol Soc Am—Am Mus Nat Hist —Nat Geog Soc—Md Acad Sci—Nat Hist Soc Md. Loyola College, 4501 N. Charles St., Baltimore 10.ⓒ

11 DIEHL, H(elmut) C(harles). Food technology (Fruit and vegetable handling, storage and harvesting, frozen foods, refrigeration of perishables); Food preservation (Freezing). b'94. BSc '18 (Mich Agrl Coll); '19-20 (Johns Hopkins); '23-24 (U Md); '38-39 (State Coll Wash). Established US Horticultural Field Laboratories at Wenatchee Washington '24, Yakima Washington '28, US Frozen Pack Laboratory in Seattle '31. Author articles in field. Dir, sec Refr Resch Found Berkeley. AAAS(F)—Am Inst Chem(F)—Am Chem Soc—Am Soc Hort Sci—Am Pub Health Assn(F)—Nat Assn Practical Refrig Engrs—Am Soc Refrig Engrs (council-at-large) — Inst Food Tech (pres). Refrigeration Research Foundation, 410 Mercantile Building, Berkeley 4.

12 DIENNER, John Astor. Atomic Energy Act (Patent provisions). b'86 BSEE '10—EE '13—DrE(hon) '39 (Purdue U); LLB '13 (George Washington U); MLD '13 (Georgetown U). Mem Brown, Jackson, Boettcher & Dienner since '27; sec and dir various cos and corps; mem Patent Office Adv Com; Patent Adv Panel, Atomic Energy Commn; spl lecturer John Marshall Law Sch. Am Inst Chem (life)—AIEE —Am Pat Law Assn (pres '45)—Am Bar Assn (chmn patent sect '42-43)—Am Judicature Soc—Acad Polit Sci— Franklin Inst—Tau Beta Pi. 53 W. Jackson Blvd., Chgo 4.ⓒ

13 DIETRICH, William Francis. Hungarian and Central European current affairs. b'93. Student (City Coll NY, NY State Maritime Acad); grad '17 (US Naval Acad). US naval member Allied Control Commission for Hungary '45, specialized in middle Danube hydrographic and hydraulic matters, and shipping. Commd ensign USN 17, RADM (ret) '49. 2125 34th St., SE, Washington 20 DC.

14 DIETZ, Albert George Henry. Plastics research (Mechanical properties); Wood research; Housing construction. b'08. AB '30 (Miami U); SB '32—ScD '41 (MIT). Author: Dwelling House Construction '47; Construction Materials: Wood, Plastics, Fabrics '49; Engineering Laminates '49; also articles in field. Asst, later professor dept bldg engring and constrn MIT since '34. ASCE—ASME—Am Soc Testing Materials—Forest Products Research Soc—Soc Plastics Engrs— Soc Plastics Ind. Desmond Fitzgerald Medal Boston Soc Civil Engrs, Richard L Templin award Am Soc Testing Materials. Room 5-209, Massachusetts Institute Technology, Cambridge, Mass.ⓒ

15 DIETZ, Robert Sinclair. Marine geology; Oceanography. b'14. PhD '41 (U Ill). Author articles in field. Oceanog research div Oceanog Studies sect USN Electronics Lab since '46. Geol Soc Am—Am Geophys Union— Sigma Xi—Phi Beta Kappa. Oceanographic Studies Section, U.S. Navy Electronics Laboratory, San Diego 52, Calif.†

16 DIGGS, Ellen Irene. Negro in Latin America; Race relations. b'06. Student '23-24 (Monmouth Coll); AB '28 (U Minn); AM '33 (Atlanta U); PhD '45—Roosevelt fellow '43-44 (U Havana, Cuba); exchange scholar Uruguay '46-47 (US Dept State, Div Internat Exchange Persons). Research for Department of Special Research on Color and Democracy, Colonies and Peace Institute International Education University Havana '44-46. Author articles in field. Prof sociol Morgan State Coll Baltimore since '47. Am Anthrop Assn—Am Sociol Soc—Am Sociol Soc—Am Assn Teachers Spanish and Portuguese—AAUP. Morgan State College, Baltimore 12. H: 409 Edgecomb Av., NYC 32.†

17 DIJKMAN, Marinus Johannes. Tropical agronomy. b'07. PhD '34 (Utrecht Holland). Food and rubber research in Sumatra and Java '35-47. Author: Identification Characteristics of the Most Important Hevea Clones Under Commercial Cultivation '39; also articles in field. Asso prof applied tropical bot U Miami since '47. Reserve 1st lt for food research in NEI army in Sumatra and Java World War II. Botany Department, Office B 103, University of Miami, Miami, University Branch, Fla.

18 DIKE, Paul Harrison. Instrumentation (Industrial); Pyrometry. b '78. BS '01—MS '03 (Northwestern U); '05-06 (U Berlin); '06 (Cambridge U); PhD '11 (U Wis). Development radiation pyrometer for industrial use; supervision development of potentiometric optical pyrometer; test and development alternating current resistors of woven type; devised production method for stable direct current resistors; design alternating and direct current bridges. Holds four patents in field. Author articles: A Bridge for the Measurement of the Conductance of Electrolytes '31; The Effect of Atmospheric Humidity on Unsealed Resistors, Causes and Remedy '36. Co-author article: (with A J Williams Jr) New Instrumentation for Unidirectional Current Measurement in Dielectrics, '46, and others. Contributor: Metals Handbook '39. Prof physics Cornell Coll '11-13, Robert Coll Constantinople '15-23, U NC '23-24, U Vt '24-25; research engr Leeds & Northup Co since '25, research cons since '48. AAAS (F)—APS (F)—Inst Metals Brit. Leeds & Northup Co., 4901 Stenton Av., Phila 44.

19 DIKE, Sheldon Holland. Theory and design of antennas and proximity fuzes. b'16. Student '34-35 (Colgate U); BS '41 (elec engring)—'42-43 (U NM); since '47 (Johns Hopkins). Research on absorption and scattering gain and scattering cross section of loaded dipole antennas, theory, design, development and testing of proximity fuzes with emphasis on utilization of electromagnetic radiation in radio sense. Several patents in field. Asst phys Carnegie Instn '41-42; radio engr U NM '42-43; research asso U Mich '43-44; sci Los Alamos '44-45; research engr Glenn L Martin Co '46-47; research phys Johns Hopkins U since '47. Am Inst EE—APS—Inst Radio Engrs—Sigma Xi. Radiation Laboratory, Johns Hopkins University, 1315 St. Paul St., Baltimore 2.

20 DILLE, Glenn Scott. Stratigraphy. b'96. BA '21 (Coe Coll); MS '24—PhD '29 (U Ia). Research on anticlines of Iowa, oolitic limestone in Otis bed of Devonian, paleontology and stratigraphy of Mississippian of Black Hills South Dakota, pre-Pennsylvanian stratigraphy of Western Nebraska.

Instr geol Coe Coll '21-24, asst prof '24-27; geol and paleontol Texas Co Tulsa Okla '29-36; cons geol Tulsa '36-44; vp charge land and exploration Deep Rock Oil Corp Tulsa '44-46; cons geol and oil producer Tulsa since '46; dir Great Plains Oil and Gas Co since '41. Am Assn Pet Geol—Tulsa Geol Soc (pres '41-42)—Tulsa Stratigraphic Soc (pres '35-36)—AIMME—Sigma Xi. 512 Atlas Building, Tulsa, Okla.

21 DILLEHUNT, Harry B., Jr. Wood restoration, designing, and art. b'98. Student (Md Inst Fine and Practical Arts). Work in restoration wooden objects d'art for museums; designer in wood for industrial and interior decorating concerns, individuals. Instr, adviser MacLea Sch Wood Art; instr Md Inst Fine and Practical Arts since '46; cons. 214 W. Read St., Baltimore 1.†

22 DILLON, Mary Earhart. American political parties, pressure groups and public opinion. b'05. PhD '39 (Northwestern U). Author: Frances Willard: From Prayer to Politics '44; also articles in field. Faculty Northwestern U '40-48, Queens Coll since '48. Queens College, Flushing, N.Y.†

23 DILTS, Marion May. Japanese culture and history. b'03. BA '24 (Wellesley Coll); grad work in Japanese cultural hist '32-36 (Columbia U); Rockefeller Found fellow Japan '37. Spent six months as member Japanese household studying customs and traditions of Japanese culture, also six months in Korea, China, Philippines, Java, Singapore. Author: The Pageant of Japanese History '38; To Japan for a Year '48; also articles in field. Lecturer, author on Japanese hist since '34. 1305 N. Adams St., Arlington, Va.

24 DIMMICK, Forrest Lee. Vision (Night; Color). b'93. AB '15—PhD '20 (Cornell U). Relative efficiencey of goggles for dark adaptation, mapping the central scotoma of the dark adapted retina, relation of dark adaptation to duration of prior red adaptation. Head gen and night vision sect USN Med Research Lab since '47. Am Psychol Assn—Optical Soc Am—Sigma Xi. U.S. Naval Medical Research Laboratory, U.S. Navy Submarine Base, New London, Conn.

25 DIMMICK, Walter Franklin. Photometry; Radiometry; Night visibility. b'21. BS '46 (U Calif). Research in design of fluorescent luminaires, automotive lighting, reflex-reflector photometry, nuclear radiation detection. Author: Designing a High-Efficency Fluorescent Luminaire. Inventor Radiation Detector Tube. Engr Radiation Lab U Calif Berkeley since '50; Illuminating engr Indsl Testing Engrs since '47. Illuminating Engring Soc—Am Inst EE—Pi Tau Pi Sigma— Radiation Laboratory, University of California, Berkeley 4, Calif. H: 3792 Mosswood Dr., Lafayette, Calif.

26 DIMMITT, Luther Mason. Educational method; Eudcational psychology; Religious education. b'89. Student '11-12 (U Mo); AB '20 (Westminster Coll Fulton Mo); ThM '22 (Princeton Theol Sem); MA '24 (U Tex); grad study '27 (U Pa) '26-28 (Columbia). Sec Presbyn Com of Christian Edn, Louisville, '21-22; student pastor U Tex '22-24, instr ednl psychol '24-26; asst editor young people's publs, Bd Christian Edn Presbyn Ch USA '26-27, gen dir dept ednl research '30-39, dir dept student aid '37-39; asst prof edn Duke U '28-30; research specialist and writer since '40. Am Assn Adult Edn—Internat Council Religious Edn—Gen Edn Bd Fellowship— NEA—AAUP—Phi Delta Kappa—Kappa Delta Pi. 156 Fifth Av., NYC 10.†ⓒ

10 DIMOCK, Hedley S(eldon). Adolesence; Summer camps. b'91. AB '20 (U Saskatchewan); MA '25—BD '26—PhD '26 (U Chicago). Author: Rediscovering the Adolescent '37. Co-author: Camping and Character '29. Talks to Counselors '39; Supervision Group Work and Recreation '49. Ed: Adminstrn of the Modern Camp '48. Prof religious edn Geo Williams Coll Chgo '27-34, dean and prof since '34. Am Assn Group Workers—Am Acad Social Polit Sci—Am Assn Adult Edn—Am Camping Assn—Nat Council Religion in Higher Edn—Nat Conf Social Work—Religious Edn Assn. 5315 Drexel Av., Chgo 15.

11 DIMOND, Albert E. Plant pathology and physiology; Fungi and fungicides; Chemotherapy of plant diseases. b'14. BA '36—MA '37—PhD '39 (U Wis). Research on control of Dutch elm disease and other vascular wilt diseases by chemotherapy; work in evaluating significance of dosage-response curves, nutrition of plants in relation to disease susceptibility, test methods evaluating fungus resistance of materials, clothing, electrical equipment under tropical conditions. Author articles in field. Fellow Crop Protection Inst '40-42; asst prof bot U Neb '42-45; asso in research U Pa '44-45; asso path Conn Agr Expt Sta since '46; asst chief dept plant path and bot since '48. Bot Society Am—AAAS (F)—Am Phytopath Soc. Connecticut Agricultural Experiment Station, P.O. Drawer 1106, New Haven 4. H: 25 Marlin Dr., New Haven 15.

12 DIMSDALE, Bernard. High speed computing equipment. b'12. BCh '33 MA '35—PhD '40 (U Minn). Author articles in field. Math Ballistic Research Labs Aberdeen Proving Ground Md since '47. Am Math Soc—Math Assn Am—Inst Math Statis—Sigma Xi. Ballistic Research Laboratories, Aberdeen Proving Ground, Md.†

13 DINGMAN, Charles Francis. Buildings (Construction cost). b'85. Preparation budget and contract estimates for government, investors, contractors since '25; litigation testimony regarding building costs, state and federal courts. Author: Construction Job Management '28; Building Estimators' Data Book '29, Estimating Building Costs '23; and others. Cons archtl engr Palmer Mass since '25. Am Soc CE—NJ Soc Arch—Engring Soc Western Mass. 34 Maple St., Palmer, Mass.

14 DINNEEN, Gerald Uel. Shale oil chemistry; Adsorption; Mass spectrometry; Organic sulfur compounds. b'13. BS '34 (U Denver). Author articles in field. Research chem US govt since '38, Bur Mines Interior Dept since '45. Am Chem Soc. U.S. Bureau of Mines, Petroleum and Oil Shale Experiment Station, P.O. Box 621, Laramie, Wyo.†

15 DINSMORE, Ray Putnam. Synthetic rubber (Use estimates, quality and performance). b'93. BS '14 (MIT); DEng (hon) '40 (Case School Applied Sci). Rubber use estimates based upon overall demand, cost-quality relationship of natural and synthetic rubbers, effects government regulation. Author articles in field. With the Goodyear Tire and Rubber Co since '14, vp since '43, vp, dir Goodyear Synthetic Rubber Corp; asst dep rubber dir '42-43 US Govt; visited Europe inspecting rubber and chem plants '28 '32 '35 '38 '48 '51; trustee Midwest Research Inst since '46. Royal Soc Arts(F) — Inst Rubber Industries (Brit) (Colwyn Medal for work on synthetic rubber '47)—AAAS—ACS (councilor '22-25, v-chmn rubber div '25-26, chmn rubber div '26-27)—AIC

E—Soc Automotive Engrs. Goodyear Tire and Rubber Co., Akron 16, O.☉

16 DINSMORE, Wayne. Horses; Mules; Livestock pastures. b'79. BS '04—MS '16 (Ia State Coll); JD '32 (John Marshall Law Sch). Co-author: A History of the Percheron Horse '17; Livestock Farming '47; also articles in field. Instr, asso prof animal husbandry Ia State Coll '03-10; sec Percheron Soc Am '10-20; exec sec Horse and Mule Assn Inc '20-49. Town and Country Equestrian Assn. Awarded certificate of merit by Ia State Coll '44. 9318 Longwood Dr., Chicago 20.

17 DIRKS-EDMUNDS, Jane Claire. Bio-ecology of Oregon coast range mountains. b'12. AB '37 (Linfield Coll); PhD '41 (U Ill). Author articles in field. With Linfield Coll since '46, now asso prof biol. Ecol Soc Am—Am Soc Mammal—Pacific North West Bird and Mammal Soc—Ore Acad Science—AAAS—Sigma Xi. Linfield College, McMinnville, Ore.

18 DIRKSE, Thedford P(reston). Alkaline batteries. b'15. AB '36 (Calvin Coll Grand Rapids Mich); AM—PhD '39 (Ind U). Research on electrolytic dissolution and oxidation of zinc in alkaline solutions; charge group doing research and developmental work on alkaline batteries at Naval Research Laboratory Washington '42-46. Author articles in field. Asso prof chem Calvin Coll since '47. Am Chem Soc—Electrochem Soc. Calvin College, Grand Rapids 6, Mich.†

19 DISTAD, Merril Francis. Physics of insulators and semiconductors; Sliding electrical contacts; Electronics systems (Military applications); Radar oscillators. b'10. BA '31 (Concordia Coll); MA '34—PhD '38 (U Minn). Staff U Minn '31-37; faculty Va Jr Coll '38-39; radio engr and phys Nav Research Lab since '39; chief sci Chesapeake Bay Annex '43-46. APS—Inst Radio Engrs—Phys Soc London—Am Inst EE—Sigma Xi. Naval Research Laboratory, Washington 20. H: 4720 Edgefield Rd., Bethesda 14, Md.

20 DITTMER, Howard J. Plant morphology (Subterranean plant parts, roots and root hairs); Lawns and plants (Alkaline soils). b'10. BA '33—MA '34 (U NM); PhD '38 (U Ia). Quantitative studies of roots and root hairs and their relation to physics of soil; application of these studies in absorption, soil-binding, systematic botany; use of such parts in taxonomic botany. Author articles in field. Asso prof U Chicago Teachers Coll Chicago '38-43, acting dean upper div '42-43; asst prof U NM '43-47, asso prof since '47. Phi Kappa Phi—Sigma Xi—Phi Sigma—Bot Soc Am—AAAS—NM Acad Sci. Biology Department, University of New Mexico, Albuquerque, N.M.

21 DIVELBISS, James Dennis. Petroleum exploration. b'15. BS '36 (W Tex State Coll); MS '38 (U Okla). Research in geophysical exploration for oil; exploration with seismograph. Seismic party chief Nat Geophys Co '42-44; Atlantic Refining Co '44-46; seismic supervisor, gravity-magnetics coordinator Sun Oil Co since '48. Soc Exploration Geophysicists—Am Assn Petroleum Geols. Sun Oil Co., P.O. Box 1798, Denver, Colo.

22 DIXON, George P. Communications engineering. b'12 (Worcester Poly Inst). Engr Western Elec Co NYC '19-20; traffic supervisor and insp NY Telephone Co '20-25, dist mgr '27-29; communications engr Nat City Bank and Asso Cos '29-49; vp Internat Telephone & Telegraph Corp '45-49; exec sec Armed Forces Communications Assn since '50. Served in Signal Corps

AUS and AUSR '17-49, dir communications USAF Europe '42-45. Armed Forces Communications Assn—US Vet Signal Corps Assn—Inst Radio Engrs —Radio Engring Soc Great Britain— Telephone Pioneers Am—Brazilian Telecommunication Assn. A r m e d Forces Communications Association, Washington.

23 DJANG, Chu. Chinese political thought and frontier problems. b'10. BA '31 (Shanghai U); MA '32 (U Mich); PhD '35 (Johns Hopkins). Author: Chinese Suzerainty; also works in Chinese. Lecturer Central Polit Inst Nanking '35-36; asst prof Soochow Comparative Law Sch Shanghai '36-38; asso sec gen New Life Movement Chungking '38-46; spl lecturer Sch Advanced Internat Relations Washington '46-48; instr grad sch Dept Agr Washington since '48. 153-21 77th Road, Flushing, N.Y.

24 DOBBS, Wallace E. Professional photography (costs, equipment, materials). b'90. BSc '12 (O State U). Author: Beginners Book of Photography '41; Costs in Professional Photography, The Complete Photographer '41; Photographic Lenses '47; Toning and Fixing Printing-Out Papers '46; also articles in field. Co-author: (with Charles A Savage) Your Camera and How It Works '39. Dir div photog Buick Motor Co '18-32; Photog Assn Am (chmn comml sect '30-31, sec-treas '32-33) tech rep Eastman Kodak Co since '44. Eastman Kodak Company, Rochester 4, N.Y.

25 DOBIE, James Frank. Folklore (West); Folklore (Southwest). b'88. AB '10 (Southwestern U); MA '14 (Columbia); MA (hon) '44 (Cambridge U). Research on folklore of Southwest, including Mexico, and West and range life, cowboys and ranches of West and Southwest. Author: A Vaquero of the Brush Country '29; Coronado's Children '31; Tongues of the Monte '35; Apache Gold and Yaqui Silver '39; The Longhorns '41; Guide to Life and Literature of the Southwest '43; A Texan in England, '45; The Voice of the Coyote '49; The Ben Lilly Legend '50; The Mustangs '52. Sec and ed Tex Folklore Soc '21-43; faculty U Tex '27-47; visiting prof Am Hist Cambridge Univ '43-44. H: 702 Park Pl., Austin, Tex.☉

26 DOBRIANSKY, Lev Eugene. Thorstein Veblen; Ukraine. b'18. BS '41—teaching F econ '42-43—MA '43—Hirshland polit sci F '43-44—PhD '51 (NY U). Research on socio-economic thought of Thorstein Veblen; research on history and politics of Ukraine. Author: A Philosophico-Economic Critique of Thorstein Veblen '43; The Social Philosophical System of Thorstein Veblen '50. Faculty NY U '45-48; asso ed Ukrainian Quarterly since '46; asst prof econ Georgetown U since '48. Am Acad Polit and Soc Sci—Am Econ Assn—Shevchenko Sci Soc—Common Cause Inc—Beta Gamma Sigma—Ukrainian Congress Com Am (pres since '49)—Fedn Am Central and E European Descent (exec v-pres since '51). Georgetown University, Washington 7.

27 DOBROVOLNY, Charles George. Parasitology; Malariology; Anti-malarial drugs. b'02. BA '28 (U Mont); MS '33 (Kan State Coll); PhD '38 (U Mich). Research on helminthes, and on effects cobalt on cattle and sheep. Author articles in field. Prof zool U NH Durham '40-48; scientist chemotherapy of malaria under field conditions USPHS Guatemala '48-50. Project for control blood flukes in man USPHS Brazil and World Health Org. Am Soc Parasitol — Nat Malaria Soc — Am

Micros Soc—Am Soc Tropical Diseases Kan Acad Sci—Mich Acad Sci—NH Acad Sci—Am Soc Zool—Gamma Sigma Delta—Phi Kappa Phi—Sigma Xi. Nat. Institute of Health, Bethesda 14, Md.

10 DOBRY, L(addie) F(rancis). Chemical engineering (Plastics, gas absorbents). b'07. BS '30—PhD '35 (U Ill); MS '32 (Purdue U). Research on removal of SO_2 from stack gases, filtration and decolorization of oils by activated clays, special lubricants and greases, waxes, solvent extraction; activated charcoal absorption studies, canister gas life studies, rigid plastic containers; design special equipment for cold water dispersible starch building; three chemical and physical testing laboratories. Author articles in field. Asso prof chem engring Miss State Coll '38-39; chief engr, chief chem engr, dir research Johnson & Johnson Gas Mask Div '40-45; chief chem engr, chem engring cons DeLeuw Cather & Co '46-49. Sen chem engr and head special materials lab Argonne Nat Lab since '49. Am Chem Soc—Western Soc Engrs—Sigma Xi. P.O. Box 5207, Chgo 80. H: 3828 S. Maple Av., Berwyn, Ill.

11 DODD, Charles Mitchener. Ceramic engineering; Refractories; Structural clay products; Kiln and drier design. b'95. Student '14-16 (Hiram Coll); BCeramic E '27—Ceramic E '33 (O State U). Author articles in field. Head ceramic engring dept Ia State Coll since '39. Am Ceramic Soc (F, trustee '47-50)—Inst Ceramic Engrs (sec '38, vp '45, pres '46)—Ceramic Ednl Council (sec '43, pres '44)—Am Soc Testing Materials—Am Soc Engring Edn—Sigma Xi—Tau Beta Pi—Phi Kappa Phi—Keramos. Department of Ceramic Engineering, Iowa State College, Ames, Ia.†©

12 DODD, Dorothy. History of Florida. b'02. BS '23—MA '29 (Fla State Coll Women); B Litt '25 (Pulitzer Sch Journalism Columbia); PhD '33 (Chicago U). Editor: Florida Becomes a State '45. Asst dir Survey Fed Archives for Fla '36-37; public records ed Fla Hist Records Survey '38-41; archivist Fla State Library since '41. Phi Beta Kappa—AHA—Soc Am Archivists —Am Assn State Local Hist—So Hist Assn—Fla Hist Soc—Fla Acad Sci. Florida State Library, Tallahassee, Fla.

13 DODD, Paul A(lbert). Labor economics. b'02. AB '24—LLD '50 (Park Coll); Harrison grad fell '30-31—PhD '32 (U Pa); Rockefeller Found fellow to Australasia '40-41. Arbitrator various industrial disputes including agricultural, aircraft, furniture, hosiery, jewelry, lumber, motion picture, newspaper, petroleum, shipbuilding and textile industries. Author: Financial Policies in the Aviation Industry '33; California Medico-Economic Survey '37; Management of Labor Relations (with G S Watkins) '38, and others; (with G S Watkins, W McNaughton and P Prasow) The Management of Personnel and Labor Relations (2d edition) '50. With University Calif since '32, prof since '45; dir Inst Indsl Relations '45-47; mem President's Emergency Railway Labor Bd '47. Am Arbitration Assn—Am Econ Assn—Am Acad Polit Social Sci—Am Statis Assn— Pacific Coast Econ Assn. 405 Hilgard Av., LA. 24.

14 DODD, Stuart Carter. Sociology (Systematics, statistics, public opinion research). b'00. BS '22—MA '24—PhD '26—Nat Research fellow 23-26 (Princeton U); Nat Research fellow, Rockefeller fellow, '26-27 (London U). Adj prof sociol Am U Beirut '27-30, **asso**

prof '30-36, prof '36-47, dir Social Sci Research Sect '29-47; Walker Ames lecturer U Washington '46, research prof sociol and dir Washington Pub Opinion Lab. Author: International Group Mental Tests '26; Social Relations in the Middle East '46; A Controlled Experiment on Rural Hygiene in Syria '34; Dimensions of Society '42; A Pioneer Radio Poll in Lebanon, Palestine and Syria '43, Systematic Social Science '47; also articles in field. Lt col, dir surveys, cons, Psych Warfare Br Allied Force Hdqrs, Sicily '43-44. Sociol Research Assn—Sociometric Assn—Am Sociol Soc—Am Psych Soc—Am Statis Assn—World Congress Pub Opinion Research. Award: decoration by Lebanese Republic with Gold Order of Cedar for pub instrn. POL, University of Washington, Seattle.©

15 DODD, Stephen Harrison, Jr. Electronic digital computers (Storage tubes). b'20. BS '43—SM '43 (MIT). Research and development of electrostatic storage tube with capacity of 1000 digits and access time of ten-millionths of second; design and construction of circuits, power supplies and physical equipment necessary to operate 32 of those tubes in computer with system studies and maintenance methods; in charge operation and maintenance of 5000 tube computer. With MIT since '42, research engr from '45. AAAS—Sigma Xi. Massachusetts Institute of Technology Digital Computer Laboratory, 211 Massachusetts Av., Cambridge, Mass.

16 DODDS, John Wendell. English literature and civilization (Nineteenth century); English and American drama. b'02. BA '24—LittD (hon) '45 (Coll Wooster); MA '27—PhD '32 (Yale). Author: Thomas Southerne, Dramatist '33; Thackeray: A Critical Portrait '41. Co-editor: An Oxford Anthology of English Prose '35; Types of English Fiction '40; Modern British and American Plays '47. Prof Eng Stanford U since '39. Guggenheim Found fellow '47-48. Modern Lang Assn—Phi Beta Kappa. Stanford University, Cal.

17 DODGE, Adiel Yeaman. Transmissions (Variable speed). Gears (Differential). Arrangements and calculations on differential gears and their use in connection with Infinitely Variable Speed Transmissions. Holds patents in field—also on automobile brakes. Inventor, chief engr Bendix Products Div '21-37; development engr Borg-Warner Corp '37-42; free lance since '42. Soc. Automotive Engrs. 307 S. Main St., Rockford, Ill.

18 DODGE, Alexander. Dams; Locks; Fishways; Electric Foundations. b'99. BS '28—MS '32—CE '39 (U Wash). Criteria for dam design and assumptions to be used in analysis; dynamic forces acting on major hydraulic structures. Contributor: Engineering Manual for Civil Works. Designer of fishways for Bonneville Dam Corps of Engineers '35-37, Fern Ridge, Cottage Grove, Dorena Dams Ore '39-45; in charge structural design Detroit, McNary, Big Cliff Dams Ore since '45. Am Soc CE—Soc Profl Engrs Ore. 628 Pittock Block, Portland 5, Ore.

19 DODGE, Ernest Stanley. Oceania; Maritime history (U.S.); Iroquois; Algonquian. b'13. Studies on ethnology of Polynesia, especially material culture, arts and crafts, and religion; field trips for study of arts and crafts, and knowledge of plants and animals of Iroquois and Algonquian Indians in eastern US and Canada; maritime history studies of New England. An Account of the Marquesas Islands in 1825 '40; Gourd Growers of the South Seas '43; Notes from Six Nations on

the Hunting and Trapping of Wild Turkeys and Passenger Pigeons '45; A Canoe from the Penobscot River '48; A Cayuga Bear Society Curing Rite '49, and others. Mus asst advancing to dir Peabody Mus since '31. Am Anthrop Soc (F)—Mass Hist Soc (council)—Colonial Soc Mass—Mass Archeol Soc—Royal Anthrop Inst(F). Peabody Museum, 161 Essex St., Salem, Mass.

20 DODGE, Harold French. Quality control; Sampling inspection methods. b'93. SB '16 (MIT); AM '22 (Columbia U). Consultant Secretary of War on quality control and sampling inspection procedures Office Chief of Ordnance '42-44; chairman ASA war committee Z1 on quality control since '41, ASTM committee E-11 on quality control of materials since '46, ASQC standards committee since '47; editorial board Annals of Mathematical Statistics '43-since, Industrial Quality Control since '46; member sub-committee number 4 Engineering and Scientific Graphs of Sectional Committee on Standards for Graphic Presentation sponsored by ASME, American Standards Association. Co-author: Sampling Inspection Tables; also articles in field. Mem tech staff and quality results engr Western Elec Co '17-25 and Bell Telephone Labs since '25. Am Soc for Qual Control(F)—Inst Math Statis (F)—Am Statis Assn—ASTM. ASQC Shewhart Medallist '49. Bell Telephone Laboratories, Inc., 463 West St., NYC 14. H: 96 Briarcliff Rd., Mountain Lakes, N.J.

21 DODGE, Homer Levi. Physics (Electrical measurements and instruments); American higher education (Military, graduate, engineering). AB '10—ScD '32 (Colgate U); PhD '14 (State U Ia); LLD '45 (Middlebury Coll); ScD '45 (U Vt). Extensive travel in Europe visiting laboratories, universities and engineering colleges '26, England '28-29, US '32-33. Holder US Patents on Dodge Design Rheostat and porous dampers for acoustical instruments. Author: Problems in Physics Derived from Military Situations and Experience '19. Co-author: Laboratory Manual of Physics '26; also articles in field. President Norwich Univ Vt '44-50; director James Jackson Cabot Fund Program in Aviation since '50. academic adv bd US Merchant Marine Acad since '47. AAAS(F)—Am Phys Soc(F)—Am Assn Physics Teachers— Newcomen Soc, Eng—Am Soc Engring Edn—Sigma Xi—Phi Beta Kappa. Norwich University, Northfield, Vt.

22 DODGE, Theodore Ayrault. Mining geology of Southwestern United States, Mexico, and Peru; Diamond drilling. b'11. AB '32—AM '35—PhD '36 (Harvard); MA '33 (U Wis). Exploration of mineral deposits by diamond drill in Mexico. Author articles in field. Mining geol Homestake Mining Co, Cerro de Pasco Copper Corp, Am Metal Co, and Anaconda Copper Mining Co '33-45; cons mining geol Tucson since '45. Phi Beta Kappa— Sigma Xi—Geol Soc Am—Soc Econ Geologists — Mineral Soc Am — Am Assn Advancement Science—Am Inst Mining & Metall Engrs—Geol Soc Am —Am Soc Econ Geol—Mineral Soc Am—AAAS—AIMME. 635 N. Third Ave., Tucson, Ariz.

23 DODSON, Joseph Curtis. Statistics (Economics). b'15. BA '37 (Henderson State Coll Ark); '41-42 (Ia State Coll); '46 (U So Cal). Design, operation, and analysis of market and general economic surveys; consultant on sampling methods for obtaining agricultural statistics in Japan. Co-author: (with V B Buckley) Real Property Inventory of Little Rock,

Arkansas '40. Author article: The Statistical Program of Iowa State College '48. Statis Allied Mission to Observe Greek Elections '46; research asso and asst prof statis Ia State Coll '46-48; statis Econ Survey Crete Rockefeller Found '48; agrl econ and statis natural resources sect GHQ Supreme Comdr Allied Powers since '48. Am Statis Assn. Department of Statistics, Iowa State College, Ames, Ia.

10 DODSON, Leonidas. American Colonial history; History of the British Empire since 1783. b'00. AB '23 (Whittier Coll); AM '24 (U Wis); PhD '27 (State U Ia). Author: Alexander Spotswood, Governor of Colonial Virginia 1710-1722 '32. Co-editor: Philip Vickers Fithian Journal 1775-1776 '34; also articles in field. Instr, asst prof U Pa since '30, U archivist since '45. AHA—Soc Am Archivists—Pa Hist Assn—Hist Soc Pa—Va Hist Soc—Econ Hist Soc. 115 Bennett Hall, University of Pennsylvania, Phila. 4.

11 DODSON, Richard W(olford). Radiochemistry. b'15. BS '36 (Calif Inst Tech); PhD '39—Am Can Co fellow '39-40 (Johns Hopkins). Author articles in field. Asso prof chem Columbia U since '47; act chmn chem dept Brookhaven Nat Lab since '47, chmn '48; Nat Research fellow '40, NDRC research on chem warfare '41-43, Manhattan project 43-45. Am Phys Soc—Am Chem Soc—AAAS. Chemistry Department, Brookhaven National Laboratory, Upton, L.I., N.Y.

12 DOELLE, Henry E. British Columbia (Mineral deposits). b'89. BS in mining '12 (State Coll Wash). Author articles in field. Engr St Joseph Lead Co '20-23; mgr Akerite Gold Mines Ltd '24-27; mine supt Bonanza Mine Granby Consol MS&P Co '28-34; mng dir Sheep Creek Gold Mines Ltd since '34. Am Inst Mining Engrs—Can Inst Mining and Metall. Sheep Creek, B.C.

13 DOERING, John Frederick. Correlation of arts; Eighteenth century literature; Western Ontario folklore. b'12. Fellow '34-36—AM '35 (Duke U); BA '33 (U Western Ontario); MA '39 (U Toronto); PhD '45 (U Ottawa). Research since '45 on correlations of the arts (literature, music, and art), using common narratives. Author: Speech in Church and School '39; also articles in field. Dean Coll Mo Valley Coll '47-50, interim chief adminstr '48-49; prof eng East Tennessee State College since '49. Victoria Inst, London(F). East Tennessee State College, Johnson City, Tenn.

14 DOERNER, Henry Alfred. Metallurgy (Nonferrous). b'89. BS '13 (U Colo). Research and development processes for treating carnotite ore to recover radium, uranium, vanadium; refining radium salts and research to reveal fundamental principles involved; recovery vanadium from descloiste ore; research centrifugal concentration ores; electrothermic reduction magnesia, refining by distillation; pilot plants for continuous carbothermal process and bicarbonate leaching process; research on zinc electrowinning; production ductile titanium and zirconium; reduction magnesia by ferrosilicon; reaction rates and equilibria in formation nickel carbonyl; thermodynamic study of anhydrous chromium chlorides. Contributor: Liddells Handbook Nonferrous Metallurgy '45. Radium tech US Bur Mines Denver '14-21, research chem Reno and Berkeley Cal '21-36, metall and engr in charge research lab Pullman Wash '36-48, metall chief nonferrous metals sect Albany Ore '48-50, chief metall Region III since '50. Tau Beta Pi—Sigma Xi—Alpha Chi Sigma—Electrochem Soc—Am Inst Mining Engrs. U.S. Bureau of Mines, U.S. Customs House, 555 Battery St., S.F. 11.

15 DOHRENWEND, Clayton Oliver. Stress analysis. b'09. CE '31—MCS '35—MS '37 (Rensselaer Poly Inst); PhD '40 (U Mich). Author articles in field. Research cons, later asst dir Midwest Research Inst since '46; prof and head department mechanics Rensselaer Poly Institute since '50, director of graduate division '52. ASME—ASCE—Am Welding Society—Am Society Metals—Am Society Engring Edn—Soc Exptl Stress Analysis (past pres). Rensselaer Polytechnic Institute, Troy, N.Y.⊚

16 DOLE, Charles Minot. Ski patrol system. b'99. BA '23 (Yale). Editor: National Skiing Guide '47; also articles in field. Founder Nat Ski Patrol System '38, nat dir '38-50. Originator of training in mountain and winter warfare in War Dept '40 resulting in 10th Mountain Division. Can Nat Ski Patrol System (hon)—Ski Club Andino, Bolivia. Awarded spl war dept citation '46, Eastern Safety Trophy '41, Am Ski Trophy '41. 113 Patterson Ave., Greenwich, Conn.

17 DOLKART, Leo. Power distribution. b'81. BS (elec engring) '03 (U Ill); '36 (Northwestern U). Research, design and construction of power distribution systems substations and underground loop network distribution systems in US, Mexico, and Russia. Contributor: Illuminating Engineering Society Lighting Handbook '48. Owner and managing engr Moline Elec Co '19-30; chief elec engr Albert Kahn Inc '30-31; chief engr Cons Engring '31-42; chief elec engr, chief engr and dir purchases Leonard Constrn Co '42-45; engr cons and chief elec engr Cementos Portland del Bajio S A '45-47; chief engr Latin Am Export Service '47-51; elect engr Coml Lighting Co since '51. Am Inst EE (mem indsl power systems com since '49)—Illuminating Engring Soc (mem hist com '50-52 rep on industry com in connection with revision of Handbook of Interior Wiring Design '43-46)—Soc Am Mil Engrs—Am Technion Soc. George W Fleming Safety Plaque Award '36, '37. 222 E. Chestnut St., Chicago 11.

18 DOLLEY, James Clay. Investment theory and analysis; Commercial and Central banking; Foreign exchange. b'00. AB '19 (McKendree Coll); AM '23 (U Ill); PhD '28—teaching fellow econ '26-28 (U Calif). Econ adviser Fed Reserve Bank Dallas '43-44, dir research '44-45. Author: Principles of Investment '40; also articles in field. Prof banking and vp U Tex since '45. Am Econ Assn—Royal Econ Soc (Eng)—SW Social Polit Sci Assn—Am Finance Assn—Am Finance Assn (vp '40-41)—Beta Gamma Sigma. 2106 Elton Lane, Austin 21, Tex.

19 DOLLEY, William Lee, Jr. Eristalis (Physiology, vision); Phototropism; Light reactions. b'87. AB '07—AM '08 (Randolph-Macon Coll); PhD '14 (Johns Hopkins). Research on reactions to light in Vanessa antiopa with reference to circus movements, relative stimulating efficiency of continuous and intermittent light in tachina fly, dark adaptation in eye of eristalic Tenax, relative sensitivity to light in different parts of compound eye, rate of light adaptation in Eristalis tenax. Author articles: Factors Involved in Stimulation by Intermittent Light '32; The Effect of Sex and Age on the Temperature at Which Reversal in Reaction to Light in Eristalis tenax Occurs (with Golden) '47; The Relation Between the Reversal and the Lethal Temperatures in the Drone Fly, Eristalis tenax '48; and others. Investiga-

tor Marine Biol Lab '24-34; prof biol Buffalo U since '25. AAAS(F)—Soc Exptl Biol and Med—Am Soc Zool—Phi Beta Kappa—Sigma Xi. University of Buffalo, Buffalo 14, N.Y.

20 DOMAS, Isaiah Jonathan. Race relations; Labor relations. b'09. BS '39 EdM '41 (Springfield Coll); STB '41 (Tufts Coll); '45-47 (Harvard). Israel: Problems in Emergent Nationalism. Asso prof social work Atlanta U '47-50. Alpha Kappa Delta—Pi Gamma Mu—Soc for Psychol Study Sociol Issues. All Souls Unitarian Church, 12th and H Sts., Lincoln, Neb.

21 DOMINGO, Emil. Sanitation (Milk, food). b'96. Diploma '19 (Coll Agr and Mech Arts, Puerto Rico); Student (Bellevue Med Sch NYC) (U PR) (Coll City NY) (NY U). Promotion new operational methods and improved sanitary designs equipment and utensils for production of milk; investigation food poisoning outbreaks, and techniques and equipment for their control; inventor milking machine eliminating contamination of milk during milking; development method for detection small amounts of organic matter on surface of utensils, and evaluation efficiency of detergents and washing machines. Holds patents in field. With NYC Dept Health since '28 now chief supervisor and in charge milk sanitation and quality control research; cons sanitation food equipment mfrs and milk and food industries. AAAS—NY Acad Sci—Soc Am Bact—Internat Assn Milk and Food Sanitarians—Assn Food and Drug Ofcls of US. New York City Department of Health, 125 Worth St., N.Y.C. 13. H: 248 W. 105th St., N.Y.C. 25.

22 DOMOGALLA, Bernhard P(aul). Applied biochemistry (Water treatments for bacteria, algae, weeds, waterborne diseases). b'96. BS '22—MS '23 —PhD '25 (U Wis). Specializes in biochemical treatment of lakes, bathing beaches, fish hatcheries; treatment for removal industrial odors; industrial waste water treatments; also work in biological investigations, treatments, bathing beach and industrial skin diseases, golf course problems. Author articles in field. Biol chem City Madison Wis and Dane Co '25-47; pres Applied Biol Chem Co Madison since '47. 723 W. Johnson St., Madison, Wis.†

23 DONAHUE, Charles. Medieval Irish literature. b'08. BA '30—PhD '33 —fellow '33-34 (Yale); '33-34 (U Copenhagen). Investigation of spoken Scottish Gaelic of Mabou Nova Scotia '38, spoken Gaelic of Carraroe Co Galway Ireland '39. Author: The Testament of Mary, the Gaelic Version of the Dormitio Mariae '42; also articles in field. With Fordham U grad sch since '35, now asso prof and chmn dept Eng. Mod Lang Assn Am (see Celtic group '42-47, chmn '48). Fordham Graduate School, NYC 58.

24 DONAHUE, Francis Michael. Christianity (Eastern); Catholicism (Old, Jansenism); Russian Orthodox church. b'13. MA '48—Hinman F '51-52 (Mich State Coll); STD '50 (St Francis Sem). Editor The Augustinian; research on history and theology of Jansenists in Netherlands and ecclesiastical bodies derived from Jansenist Church in 18th and subsequent centuries. Author: Historical and Doctrinal Sketch of the Old Roman Catholic Church '51. Chaplain State Prison S Mich '41; pastor St Peter and Paul Ukrainian Orthodox Church '42-46; prof Mich State Coll since '47. Am Philos Assn—Mich Acad Arts Letters and Sci—Soc Psychol Study Soc Issues—AAUP—Nat Chaplains Assn. Received grant from

Rockefeller Found for Midwestern Studies '51.

10 DONINI, Ugo. Italian history; '36-39 (Penn U). Editor: Romanica '35-36. Author articles in field. Asst prof Political science. b'01. Student '15-18 (Ginnasio di Modena); '21 (Naval Acad Prep Sch); '22-23 (Perkiomen Prep Sch); AB '29—AM '33—grad student '36-40, asso prof '40-42 La Salle Coll; asst prof polit sci hist '45-48, asso prof Drexel Inst '48-49; asso prof hist La Salle Coll since '49. AHA. La Salle College, Phila.

11 DONOGHUE, David. Petroleum geology. b'91. BS '09 (St Mary's Coll San Antonio); '09-'12 (U Tex). Reservoir studies and commercial appraisals in connection with geological and engineering phases of oil gas and water production. Geol Gulf Prodn Co '14-21; dir Tex Pacific Coal and Oil Co '25-29; pres Fed Royalties Co Inc since '33; cons petroleum geol; cons Consejo Nacional de Petroleos, Ministerio de Mines y Petroleos, Republic Colombia '48-49. Am Assn Petroleum Geol—AIMME—Inst Petroleum (London) — AAAS—Am Soc Tech Appraisers. Fort Worth National Bank Building, Fort Worth 2, Tex.

12 DONOHUE, Arthur Thomas. Language and culture of Pottawatomie Indians. b'93. AB '20 (Columbia Coll); '20-21 (Ia State Teachers Coll)—'22-27 (U Ia); MA '27 (Creighton U); PhD '32 (U Kan). Author: The History of the Early Jesuit Missions in Kansas '40; also articles in field. Chmn sch social sci St Mary (Kan) Coll '24-31, Marymount Coll Salina Kan '31-36; prof sociol, chmn dept Loyola U New Orleans since '37; prof sociol, acting dir dept social sci Marquerette U Milwaukee '47. Am Sociol Soc—Am Cath Sociol Soc (bd ed)—So Sociol Soc—Am Rural Sociol Soc—Kan State Hist Soc —Alpha Kappa Delta. 406 N. 70th St., Wauwatosa 13, Wis.

13 DONOHUE, Francis J(oseph). American education (Church-state relations, history, higher, Catholic and religious public schools). b'34. AB '34 —MA '36 (Fordham U); PhD '44—seminars higher edn and sch adminstrn '41-44 (U Mich). Volunteer work of National Conference of Christians and Jews since '37; research on problems in administration of Catholic parochial schools, legal and extra-legal control by public authorities, canon law pertaining to schools, national survey of administrative practices and procedures in Catholic schools receiving state aid; conducted survey of minority-group problems in Detroit school system for Bureau of Administrative Research Detroit Public Schools '44-45. Author articles in field. Prof edn and head dept edn Villanova C since '49. Am Assn Sch Adminstrs—Am Catholic Philos Assn—Am Ednl Research Assn —Nat Soc Study Edn—Religious Edn Assn—Phi Kappa Phi. Villanova College, Villanova, Pa. H: 570 Barrett Ave., Haverford, Pa.

14 DONOVAN, Richard Julian. Hydraulic structures; Foundations; Electronics (Airborne operation). b'17. BS (CE) '38 (Worcester Poly Inst Mass). Operation and instruction operation of radio and radar in carrier-based aircraft. C T Main Inc Boston '46-48; civil engineer F H Whelan Boston '48-50; civil engineer Pierce Cons Engring Co since '50. Am Soc CE—Mass Soc Professional Engrs. Professional engr Mass, NH. Pierce Consulting Engring Co., 683 Atlantic Av., Boston. H: 8 Horn Pond Brook Rd., Winchester, Mass.

15 DONOVAN, Thomas Leroy. Highway location surveys; Railroad location surveys; Oil field surveys. b'98. Student '20-22 (Washington and Lee U); 22-23 (Colo Sch Mines). Research and geodetic surveys in Ethiopia and Northeast Africa. Jr engr W Va State Rd Commn '24-27; jr engr Pa State Highway Dept '27-28; transitman Montour RR Co '28; field engr Venezuelan Petroleum Co '28-34, supervising engr '35-39; field engr Venezuela Gulf Oil Co '34-35; chief engr Tex Petroleum Co '39-47; chief engr Sinclair Petroleum Co since '47. Am Soc CE. Sinclair Petroleum Co., Dire Dawa, Ethiopia. H: New Cumberland, W.Va.

16 DOOLEY, William Germain. American art and antiques; Old Sandwich glass. b'03. Student '26-30 (Harvard Coll). Author: Old Sandwich Glass '34; also articles in field. Ed antiques and art critic Boston Transcript since '34; head div edn Mus Fine Arts Boston since '41. Pewter Collectors' Soc (founder). Division of Education, Museum of Fine Arts, Boston.

17 DOOLEY, William Paul. Viscose rayon. b'15. BS '38 (U Richmond); MS '40 (MIT). Research in viscose rayon production, production control, cost analyses relative to selling price changes and location of source of excess costs, market surveys determining outlets for by-product chemicals, administration of wage rates and policies; process and product development of viscose rayon staple fiber, design specifications for new equipment, trial of experimental and semi-commercial equipment. Tech, adminstrv asst to gen mgr Viscose Mfg Div '40-45, staple development plant asst supt '45-46, supt since '46. Am Chem Soc—AAAS—Am Inst Chem Engrs— Phi Beta Kappa—Sigma Pi Sigma. American Viscose Corporation, Nitro, W.Va. H: 1509 West Virginia Av., Dunbar, W.Va.

18 DOOLITTLE, S(ears) P(olydore). Virus diseases of vegetable crops (Tomatoes, cucumbers, celery, peppers); Breeding for resistance to virus diseases. b'90. BS '14—MS '15 (Mich State Coll); PhD '18 (U Wis). Research dealing with virus properties, dissemination by insects, overwintering hosts, seed and soil transmission and development of resistant varieties; breeding for resistance to bacterial and fungus disease of cucumbers; studies of antibiotic substances in relation to disease resistance in tomatoes; conducted research on virus diseases of cucumber and related crops '19-30, virus diseases of celery, tomatoes, pepper, and lettuce '25-48. Author: Tomato Diseases '43. Author articles: The Mosaic Disease of Cucurbits '20; Control of Cucumber Mosaic in the Greenhouse '24; Control of Cucumber Mosaic by the Eradication of Wild Host Plants '25, and others. Bur Plant Ind US Dept Agr since '15, prin path since '52. AAAS—Am Phytopath Soc—Washington Acad Sci —Wis Acad Sci—Washington Bot Soc —Sigma Xi. Plant Industry Station, Beltsville, Md.†

19 DORMAN, Keith W(illiam). Silviculture (Southern United States forests); Forest genetics; Pines; Naval stores. b'10. BS '34 (Ia State Coll); '37-38 (U Calif). Author articles in field. With SE Forest Expt Sta Asheville NC since '48. AAAS—Am Forestry Assn—Soc Am Foresters—Forest Farmers Assn—Fla Forest and Park Assn—Sigma Xi. Southeastern Forest Experiment Station, Box 252, Asheville, N.C.

20 DORN, John E. Metallurgy; Aircraft materials engineering. b'09. BS '31—MS '32 (Northwestern U); PhD '36 (U Minn). Research on X-ray structure of metals, diffusion in metals, heat treatment, properties, plastic flow, fracture, creep, damping capacity, fatigue and formability of metals, light alloys; member War Metallurgy Committee; official investigator National Research Council Projects NRC 21, 44, 548. Author articles in field. Phys chem and research fellow Battelle Memorial Inst '36-38; asst prof mech engring U Calif '38-44, asso prof phys metall since '44; research metall Dow Chem Co '40. Am Soc Metals (chmn Golden Gate chapter '45-46, trustee since '46)—Am Inst Mining Metall Engrs—Sigma Xi. University of California, Berkeley.

21 DORNBUSCH, Charles E. World War II (US regimental history). b'07. Research on regimental histories published by American units and allies; projection of checklist of American unit histories for World War I. Author: Unit Histories of World War II, United States Army, Air Force, Marines, Navy '50. Asst NY Pub Library since '26. Am Mil Inst—ALA. H: 50 Chauncy Av., New Rochelle, N.Y.

22 DORNER, Alexander. History of art; Modern art. b'93. PhD (U Berlin). Author: Romanesque Architecture in Saxony and Westphalia; Catalogue of Paintings and Drawings in the State Museum, Hannover, Germany; One Hundred Years of Art in Hannover, and others. Dir State Mus Hannover Germany, prof hist art Hannover U '20-36; dir mus RI Sch Design '38-41; lecturer hist art Brown U '41-48; faculty Bennington Coll since '48. Bennington College, Vt.

23 DORNFELD, Ernst John. Cellular biology; Cytochemistry; Developmental physiology. b'11. BS '33 (Marquette U); MA '35—PhD '37 (U Wis). Research on ultra-centrifugation of cells and tissues, cytology and developmental physiology of ovary, nucleic acids in cellular proliferation and histogenesis. Author articles in field. Instr histol and embryol U Okla Med Sch '37-38; instr zool, asst prof, asso prof Ore State Coll since '38. AAAS—Am Soc Zool—Ore Acad Sci—Sigma Xi. Carter award for distinguished teaching Ore State Coll '47. Department of Zoology, Oregon State College, Corvallis, Ore.

24 DORSEY, LeRoy Howard. Sport Fishing Rodeos. b'87. Originated International Deep Sea Fishing Rodeos throughout Mexico. Founded National Better Fishing Rodeos for Boys and Girls under license age, working through Municipal Authorities throughout U.S.A. U.S.A. Honorary Representative, Federal Fishing Commission of Mexico; President Better Fishing, Inc. and Four Corporations; Member of various Foreign and U.S.A. Fishing Clubs. Awarded Aztec Eagle by Mexican Government '49. 509 S. Wabash Ave., Chicago 5.

25 DORSEY, Stephen P. Architecture of early American houses and churches (Colonial and Federal periods). b'13. AB '35 (Dartmouth Coll); MBA '37 (Harvard); '51 (Am U Beirut). One of those responsible for presentation to Congress and passage of law requiring approval by architectural bd of review any proposed building changes in Old Georgetown section of Washington; also instrumental in formation Historic Georgetown, Inc to restore certain old buildings on commercial basis; government service in economic reconstruction following war; economic development and international technical assistance Latin America and Near East. Author: Georgetown Houses of the Federal Period, 1750-1830 '44; Alexandria Houses, 1720-1820 '46; Early English Churches in America, 1607-1807 '52. With Dept of State '44-53, dep dir Office of Nr Eastern Affairs '53. Department of State, Washington 25.☺

10 DORWEILER, Paul. Casualty actuarial mathematics; Casualty statistics. b'80. BS '04 (State U Ia); grad work (U Chicago, U Mich). Research on compensation and liability loss reserves, American remarriage, mortality of disabled, relations between compensation losses and wage levels. Author articles in field. Casualty actuary Aetna Life Affiliated Cos since '28. Casualty Actuarial Soc (pres '32-34)—Am Statis Assn—Inst Math Statis. Aetna Casualty and Surety Company, 151 Farmington Av., Hartford 15, Conn.

11 DOTSON, John Andrew. Education (Curriculum); Public education in Alabama and South Carolina. b'95. AB '16—PhD '43 (George Peabody Coll); MA '31 (U Ky). Author articles in field. Dir div teacher edn Emory U since '47; curriculum cons Candler Coll and Buena Vista Coll Havana since '48. Nat Soc Coll Teachers of Edn—Assn Supervision and Curriculum Development (adv ed '46)—Nat Soc Study Edn —NEA—Ga Edn Assn—So Assn Colls and Secondary Schs (commn curricular problems and research)—Kappa Phi Kappa. Emory University, Ga.

12 DOTTERWEICH, Frank Henry. Natural gas. b'05. BS (Engring) '28—PhD '37 (Johns Hopkins U). Studies on production, transmission, and utilization of natural gas; processing of natural gas condensate reservoirs, including studies of retrograde condensation phenomenon and use of electrolytic model studies as applied to processing of natural gas reservoirs. Author articles: Removal of Entrained Materials from Natural Gas '49; The Production, Transmission, and Utilization of Natural Gas '51. Asso prof natural gas engring Tex Coll Arts and Industries Kingsville Tex '37-41, prof and dir div engring '41-51; tech cons natural gas gasoline div Petroleum Adminstrn for War Washington '41-45; now cons petroleum and natural gas engr. So Gas Assn—Am Gas Assn (mfr gas tech adv and natural gas adv com)—AIMME. Texas Coll Arts and Industries, Kingsville, Tex.

13 DOTY, Lorenzo Donald. River control. b'03. BS '25 (Denison U); MS '33—CE '37 (U Ill). Research on watershed potential, flood hydrograph and routing; instigating documentation of floods via sound film. Author articles in field. Acting prof engring sci Denison U '32-33; state park supt US Dept Interior '33-34; civil engr River Control Works US Corps Engrs (Civilian), War Dept '34-42; asso prof, head dept hydraulic engring Cornell U '42-46; prof hydraulic engring U Ia '46-48; cons engr NY, O, Calif; harbor planning engring US Corps Engrs San Francisco Dist since '49. Am Society Engring Edn—Am Mil Engrs—Am Geophys Union. 180 New Montgomery St., SF.†

14 DOUD, Donald Budlong. Examination of questioned documents; Forgery detection. b'16. Student '41-43 (U Calif); '44-45 (Sch Govt U So Calif). Research on color photography for accurate reproduction of inks, methods for deciphering charred documents, visual infrared ray instrument. Author article: Photography Foils the Forger '47. Engaged in questioned document work since '41; head Tyrrell & Doud (questioned document examiners) since '50. Am Soc Questioned Document Examiners—So Calif Acad Criminology Tyrrell & Doud, 312 E. Wisconsin Av., Milwaukee, Wis.

15 DOUDOROFF, Peter. Ichthyology (Physiology, ecology); Water pollution; Fishery biology. b'13. BA '35 (Stanford); PhD '41 (U Calif); '30-32 (San Mateo Jr Coll). Research in ecology and physiology of marine fishes, pigmentation, temperature relations and acclimatization, behavior and metabolism of fishes; investigated stream pollution in relation to aquatic life and fisheries, toxicity of industrial wastes to fish; studied reservoirs and reservoir sites in Pacific Northwest and limnology in relation to fishery management and conservation. Author: The Resistance and Acclimatization of Marine Fishes to Temperature Changes, Part I '42, II '45; Reactions of Marine Fishes to Temperature Gradients '38; The Evaluation of the Toxicity of Industrial Wastes, Chemicals and Other Substances to Fresh-Water Fishes (with W B Hart and J Greenbank) '45; also articles in field. Biol Environmental Health Center USPHS since '47. Am Soc Ichthyologists Herpetologists —Am Fisheries Soc—Am Soc Limnol Oceanog—Fed Sewage Research Assn—Western Soc Naturalists—AAAS—Sigma Xi. U.S. Public Health Service, 1014 Broadway, Cincinnati 2.†

16 DOUGLAS, Clarence Joseph. Railroad and highway bridges. b'07. BS '29—CE '46 (U Vt). Design reinforced concrete and steel bridges and highways; engineer in charge construction main line railroad tracks; highway paving both through and clover leafs, under and overpasses. Engr NY State '36-40; asst prof civil engring U Vt '46-47; engr and engr in charge John F Casey Co since '47. Served as capt to col AUS Corps Engrs '40-45. Am Soc CE—Soc Am Mil Engrs—AAUP. John F. Casey Co., P.O. Box 1888, Pittsburgh 30. H: 5520 Fifth Av., Pittsburgh 32.

17 DOUGLAS, Frederic Huntington. American Indian Arts and crafts (Styles, techniques, history, development). b'97. Research in design, styles, techniques appearing in work of Indian tribes north of Mexico in last 150 years, special emphasis on history each; special studies in beadwork, quillwork, Pueblo textiles, Woodlands silk applique embroidery. Co-author: (with Rene d'Harnoncourt) Indian Art of the United States '41. Editor: (since '30) Indian publications of Denver Art Museum—Indian Leaflet, Indian Design series; also articles in field. Curator dept native arts Denver Art Mus since '47; commr Fed Indian Arts and Crafts Bd since '46; sec Clearinghouse for Southwestern Mus since '38; asst prof anthrop U Denver since '34. AA AS (F, vp southwest div '42-47, pres '47-48)—Royal Anthrop Soc Gt Britain —Am Anthrop Assn—Soc Am Archaeology—Am Folklore Soc—Societe des Americanistes de Paris. 1300 Logan St., Denver.☺

18 DOUGLAS, George Anthony. Family Relations; Social agencies; Juvenile delinquency. b'04. AB '26 (U Mich); '26 (Chicago Theol Sem); '28-29 (Floating U); '29 (Columbia); PhM (Sociol) '30 (U Wis); '31 (U Chicago); PhD '39 (Johns Hopkins U). Traveling educational secretary Intercollegiate Prohibition Association '26-28; member American Social Science Committee to Russia '32; executive secretary National Religion and Labor Foundation New Haven '32-33; chairman organizing committee county council of social agencies Appleton Wisconsin '39-40, chm Montevallo Recreation com '45-48. Author: The Community Chest Movement '30; The Life of the Worker—The New Russia '33; Juvenile Delinquency in Appleton, Wisconsin '41. Asst prof sociol Lawrence Coll

Appleton Wis '38-42; with regional studies dept and personnel dept TVA '42-44; prof and head dept sociol Ala Coll Montevallo Ala '44-49; prof and chm sociol dept Davidson Coll '49-51; Coordinator Family Life Education Charlotte NC since '51; executive secretary Charlotte Family Life Council since '51. AAAS—AAUP—Am Sociol Soc —Southern Sociol Soc—Nat Council Family Relations—Southeaster Council Family Relations. North Carolina Family Life Council, 2209 Colony Rd., Charlotte 7, N.C.

19 DOUGLAS, James. Mining engineering and geology (Copper, zinc). b'03. AB '25 (Amherst Coll); student (Stanford U, Ecole National des Mines, France). Mining engr So Rhodesian Base Metals Corp so Rhodesia '27-28, Roan Antelope Copper Co no Rhodesia '28, S African Copper Co Union S Africa '28-30; profl and cons mining and geol Mexico, SA, Can, US '31-40; with copper and mining div WPB '41-43, dir zinc div, '43-44, dep v-chmn for metals and minerals WPB '44-45; with Phelps-Dodge Corp '45, sec since '47. Am Inst Mining Metall Engrs—Mining Metall Soc Am. 10 Gracie Sq., NYC 28.

20 DOUGLAS, Kenneth Neilson. French Existentialism; Modern French literature (Paul Valéry). b'10. BA '37 (Trinity Coll, Dublin); MA '40 (U Toronto); PhD '43 (Yale); student (U Coll, Dublin; Sorbonne; London U). Author articles in field. Dept French Yale U since '40, asst prof since '45. Mod Lang Assn—Am Assn Teachers French. Moderator and ex-scholar House Trinity Coll Dublin; spl Gold Medal and research prize on graduation '37, also French govt's Bronze Medal. Department of French, W. L. Harkness Hall, Yale University, New Haven.†

21 DOUGLAS, Lester. History of graphic art, printing and design; typography. b'93. Books designed at Library of Congress, Columbia University Library, Princeton University Library, private collections, exhibited in 50 books of the year, American Book Illustration, Printing for Commerce, AIGA. Author: Color in Modern Printing '31; Modernizing Business Print '29; The Battle of the Fifty Books '32; also articles in field. Free lance and advt agency exec '15-28; dir art, typography and printing, C of C US, Nation's Bus since '28; founder Am Book Illustration, traveling exhibitors, '26. Am Inst Graphic Arts (dir, hon vp)—AHA—Soc Am Hist—Newcomen Soc Eng—Typophiles—Art Dir Club. 1615 H St., Washington 16. H: 21 Duvall Dr., Washington 16.

22 DOUGLAS, Marjory Stoneman (Mrs.). History of southern Florida, the Everglades, and the West Indies. b'90. AB '12 (Wellesley Coll). Author: The Everglades: River of Grass '47; Road to the Sun '52. Book ed Miami Herald '42-49. c/o Rinehart & Co., 232 Madison Av., NYC 16.

23 DOUGLAS, Mary Stahlman. Cumberland River history. b'95. BA '16 (Randolph-Macon Woman's Coll). Research in collaboration with Byrd Douglas on history Cumberland River. Lit ed Nashville Banner since '35. Nashville Banner, Nashville, Tenn.†

24 DOUGLASS, Andrew Ellicott. Dendrochronology; Climatology; Age of prehistoric ruins; Astronomical photography (Zodiacal light, shadow bands, Mars); Cycles (Cycloscope). AB '89—DSc (hon) '08 (Trinity Coll); DSc (hon) '38 (U Ariz). Dated southwestern prehistoric ruins by tree rings; invented cycloscope for climatological and cycle studies of tree-ring chronologies. Author: Annals of Lowell Observatory (Vol I, pt II and vol II); Climatic Cycles and Tree Growth (3 vol) '19, '28, '36. Prof astron U Ariz since '06; director Steward Observatory '18-38; prof dendrochronology since '36, dir Lab Tree-Ring Research since '37. Royal Astron Soc(F)—AAAS—Am Philos Soc—Am Meteorol Soc (vp '24-25)—Ariz Archaeol and Hist Soc (pres '29-30)—Am Astron Soc—Astron Soc Pacific—Nat Geog Soc (hon life)—Phi Beta Kappa (pres Ariz chapter '34-35)—Phi Kappa Phi—Sigma Xi (pres Ariz chapter '30-31). Received award Research Corp NY for studies in tree rings and chronology '31. Research asso Carnegie Instn of Washington '25-38. Laboratory of Tree-Ring Research, University of Arizona, Tucson, Ariz.

10 DOUGLASS, J(ames) R(obert). Entomology (Mexican bean beetle, beet leafhopper). b'94. BS '18 (Clemson Agrl Coll); MS '23 (Kans State Coll); student (Ohio State U, Cornell U). Author articles in field. With Bur Entomol and Plant Quarantine US Dept Agr since '21, charge Twin Falls Ida Field Sta since '35, sr entomol since '48. AAAS—Entomol Soc Am—Am Soc Econ Entomol—Am Soc Sugar Beet Tech—Ecol Soc Am—Sigma Xi—Gamma Sigma Delta. Box 1100, Twin Falls, Ida.†

11 DOUTT, J Kenneth. Mammalogy; Travel and camping in Arctic and desert climates. b'05. AB '29 (U Pittsburgh); MS '30—ScD '49 (Calif). Field studies in western US, British Guiana, Gulf St Lawrence, Labrador, Ungava, Hudson Bay; spent one one-half years with Hudson Bay Eskimo, has speaking knowledge Eskimo language; studied, collected, photographed, largely in movies, large and small mammals of areas visited. Author articles: A Review of the Genus Phoca '42; List of Types of Mammals in Carnegie Museum '34; A Systematic Study of a Collection of Mammals from Southern Arizona '34; The Expedition to Hudson Bay '39; Collecting in the Vinta Basin '38; Mammal Collections of North America '45, and others. Curator of mammals Carnegie Mus since '38. Am Soc Mammalogists—Wildlife Soc. Carnegie Museum, 4400 Forbes St., Pittsburgh 13.†

12 DOVE, Walter E. Insect control; Insecticides. b'94. BS '13 (Miss State Coll); ScD '29 (Johns Hopkins). Directed cooperative insect control southern state against screw-worms in livestock '35-37, grasshopper control 24 western states '38-39; engaged war time developments insecticides for armed forces, including DDT; presently engaged research and development insecticides non-toxic to warm blooded animals. With US Bur Entomol Plant Quarantine '24-35, in charge div insects affecting man and animals '42-45; dir entomol development US Indsl Chem Inc (Dodge & Olcott Inc) Baltimore since '46. Am Assoc Econ Entomol—Entomol Soc Am—Am Soc Parasitol—Am Soc Tropical Med—Washington Acad Sci—US Livestock Sanitary Assn—Nat Pest Control Assn (hon). U.S. Industrial Chemicals Co., Box 1956, Baltimore.

13 DOVE, W(illiam) Franklin. Food acceptance; Food habits and nutritional behavior; Appetite levels; Taste tests; Psychophysics; Army rations; Climate-soil-plant-animal-man relations; Individuality; Tissue transplantation; Horns and unicorns. b'97. BS '22 (Ia State Coll); MS '23—PhD '27 (U Wis). Author articles in field. Head biol lab Exptl Sta Me '31-43; chief Food Acceptance Research Br QM Food and Container Inst Armed Forces '44-50; biol nutrition br USPHS dir food ac-

ceptance studies dept public health Coll Medicine U Illinois since '50. AAAS—Soc Growth and Development—Genetics Soc Am—Am Statis Assn (Biometrics)—Inst Food Tech—Sigma Xi. Univ. of Ill., College of Medicine, Dept. of Public Health, 808 S. Wood St., Chgo. 12.

14 DOW, Alden Ball. Architect. b'04. Student 1923 to 26 (U Mich); BArch 1931 (Columbia). Residences, churches, schools, public and commercial buildings, based upon the natural use of materials. Established own archtl bus '33. AIA—Nat Council Archtl Registration Bd. Awarded Paris Internat Exposition Diplome de Grand Prix for residential architecture in this country '37. 315 Post St., Midland, Mich.

15 DOW, Peter Staub. Highways and sanitary municipal improvements; Graphic methods; Descriptive geometry and graphics. b'87. Student '06-08 (Tenn U). CE '11 (Dartmouth Coll). Instr Dartmouth Coll '12-17, asst prof '17-25, prof '25-52, dept chmn 20 yrs. Soc Am Mil Engrs—SAR—ASCE—AP HA—NH Acad Sci—AAAS(F). 4 W. Wheelock St., Hanover, N.H.☉

16 DOW, Raymond. Lost treasure; Lost gold mines. b'98. Student '21-23 (Cornell U, Coll CE). Has collections of data on lost treasures and lost gold mines number over 2,500 items, records of sources of many additional items; writes The Mining Record column consisting of material on lost gold mines. Author articles in field. Civil engr with US Army Engrs, Merritt, Chapman & Scott, and others since 24. 2922-164th St., Flushing 58 N.Y.

17 DOW, Sterling. Greek epigraphy; Greek constitutional history. b'03. AB '25—AM '28—PhD '36 (Harvard); '25-26 (Trinity Coll Cambridge); '31-36 (Am Sch Classical Studies Athens). Excavated at Corinth '34; Research on Hymettian quarries, evidence for dating Polyeuktos, panathenaic amphorae from Hellenistic period, Athenian decrees of 216-212 BC, Egyptian cults in Athens, Athenian law code of 411-401 BC, Aigaleos-Parnes wall, Demetrios of Phaleron, Athenian tribute lists. Discovered Greek allotment machine '35. Author: Prytaneis: A Study of the Inscriptions Honoring the Athenian Councillors '37; also articles in field. Prof hist and Greek Harvard U '46-49, Hudson prof archaeology since '49. Archaeological Inst Am (hon pres)—Am Philol Assn (life)—Classical Assn New Eng—Am Classical League (vp)—Phi Beta Kappa (hon)—Soc Promotion Hellenic Studies (hon life). Fellow Harvard, Am Sch Classical Studies, Athens '31-33, '35-36, Guggenheim fellow '34-35. Widener Library 690, Cambridge 38, Mass.☉

18 DOW, William Gould. Electrical engineering; Electronics; Microwaves; Radar. b'95. BS in EE '16—EE '17 (U Minn); MSE '29 (U Mich). Investigation of destructive effects of wind storms on ice-loaded electric power distribution lines '28-32, ignition of electric arcs '29-35; theory of thermionic vacuum tube design '37-40; use of high-frequency power for welding sheet metal '41-43; industrial applications of electronics '38-52; generation of continuous-wave power at power levels above 500 watts and frequencies above 300 megacycles '43-45, research and development on radar countermeasures equipment '44-45; direction of research and development of continuous wave vacuum tubes for use at microwave frequencies; direction of research toward measurement of pressure and temperature of upper atmosphere by means of rockets '45-52. Author: Fundamentals of Engineering Electron-

ics '37; Loading and Strength of Wood Pole Lines '36; Very-high Frequency Techniques (with others) '47; also articles in field. Cons Nat Bur Standards '45-52; prof elec engring U Mich since '26. AIEE—Inst Radio Engrs—Am Soc Engring Edn—Am Welding Soc—Am Phys Soc—Engring Soc Detroit—Tau Beta Pi—Sigma Xi—Eta Kappa Nu. Department of Electrical Engineering, University of Michigan, Ann Arbor.†☉

19 DOWD, David Lloyd. Theory, historiography, and bibliography of revolutions, especially the French Revolution; History of Art (neoclassicism) and propaganda. b'18. BA '40—MA '43—PhD '46 (U Calif); '44-45 (Harvard). Author: Jacques-Louis David: Propagandist of the French Revolution '48. Instr hist U Neb '46-49; teaching fellow U Calif '43-44, Amy Bowles Johnson travelling fellow '44-45; research French Archives grant Am Philos Soc and U Neb '48; asst prof U Fla since '49. AHA—Hist Assn, London—Société d'histoire moderne, Paris—AAUP—Phi Beta Kappa. University of Florida, Gainesville, Fla.

20 DOWDY, Andrew Hunter. Radiation biology. b'04. AB '29 (Central Coll); MD '31 (Washington U). Research cancer control, permissible external dose radiation. With U Rochesprof, chmn dept radiology sch medicine and dentistry, dir AEC project '46-48, dir Manhattan project '43-46; prof, chmn dept radiology sch med9cine U Cal at Los Angeles since '48; chief radiation biology div AEC since '48; cons div biology and medicine AEC Washington since '48; cons Rand Douglas Aircraft Corp '49, Nuclear Energy Powered Aircraft, Fairchild Engine & Airplane Corp '48-51, VA Washington since '48, on radiology and isotopes VA Los Angeles since '48; responsible investigator Am Cyanamid Co (Lederle) since '41; research contract Office Sci Research and Development '42-45, U Cal at Los Angeles cancer research grant since '48; cancer control grant USPHS since '49, adv com radiation tolerance mil personnel '48-50, research guidance com '50-51, chmn subcom radiation physics, com radiation studies USPHS since '51; subcom permissible external dose, com radiation protection Nat Bur Standards '46-47; com radiology Nat Research Council since '48. Am Bd Radiology (Diplomate)—AAAS(F)—Am Coll Radiology—AMA(F); Am Cancer Soc (med and sci adv bd Los Angeles Co br)—Am Assn Cancer Research—AAUP—Am Indsl Hygiene Assn—Nat Rehabilitation Assn—Radiol Soc NA—Sigma Xi—Phi Rho Sigma. H: 1325 Warnall Av., L.A. 24.☉

21 DOWN, Eldon Eugene. Plant breeding. b'92. BS '15—MS '30 (Mich State Coll); PhD '40 (Cornell U). Research and breeding of new types wheat, barley, beans, oats and hybrid corn. With Mich State Coll since '16, research prof from '41. Am Soc Agron—AAAS—Sigma Xi. 304 Agriculture Hall, Michigan State College, East Lansing, Mich.

22 DOWNEY, Glanville. Byzantine history and literature; Near Eastern antiquities. b'08. AB '31—PhD '34 (Princeton U). Archaeological expedition for excavation of Antioch Syria '32. Co-translator: Procopius "Buildings" '40; Chronicle of John Malalas '40; ed-in-chief American Journal of Archeology, associate editor Archeology; also articles in field. Asst prof Byzantine lit Dumbarton Oaks Research Library Washington since '46. Am Philol Assn—Washington Soc Archaeol (sec '47-48, treas since '48). Dumbarton Oaks, 3101 R St., Washington 7.†

10 DOYLE, Frank Butler. Vacuum processing of foods and tobacco. b'95. BS (elec engring) '20—ME '32 (U Ill); MS (exptl physics) '23 (Cornell). Equipment design for food freezing and dehydration, for tobacco moistening, development work steam ejector and condenser design, puffing of cereals and tobacco into vacuum. Research engr Ingersoll Rand Co '30-46; research engr Guardite Corp since '48. Soc Prof Engrs—Inst Food Tech. 9535 Cottage Grove Av., Chicago 28.

11 DOYLE, Henry Grattan. Spanish and Latin American literature; Inter-American educational and cultural relations. b'89. AB '11—AM '12 (Harvard); LLD '48 (George Washington U). Editor Modern Language Journal '34-38, Hispania '42-48. Author: Spanish Studies in the United States '26; A Tentative Bibliography of the Belles-Lettres of Central America '35; (with G Rivera) En España '21; (with F Aguilera) New World Spanish (on RCA Victor records) '45. With George Washington U since '16, prof since '21, dean Columbian Coll since '34; lecturer, vis prof various universities; dir Washington Inter-Am Training Center '42-44. Am Assn Teachers Italian—Am Assn Teachers Spanish and Portuguese (pres '30)—Modern Lang Assn Am (chmn com on trends in edn since '39) —Hispanic Soc Am—Am Acad Arts Sci—US Nat Comm for UNESCO—Phi Beta Kappa. George Washington University, Washington 6. H: 5500-33rd St., N.W., Washington 15.†

12 DOYLE, Price. Curriculum for music schools. b'96. BS '24 STC, Maryville, Mo.; MA '30 U Cincinnati); MusD '50 (Am Conservatory Chgo). Studies concerning curriculum for training of teachers of music in public schools, certification for teachers of music in public schools. Author articles in field. Dir dept fine arts Murray Ky State Coll since '30. NASM (chmn com on teachers colleges since '40, offical examiners since '40, com on curriculum since '43, pres since '48). College Station, Murray, Ky.†◎

13 DOYLE, William Lewis. Histochemistry; War gases (Toxicology). b'10. MA '32—PhD '34 (Johns Hopkins U). Studies on origin and cellular localization of enzymes, toxicology of war gases, behavior of dusts (airborne particles) in respiratory tract, and hydrolytic enzymes in protozoa and higher organisms. Author articles in field. Asst prof biol Bryn Mawr Coll '37-42; research asso dept pharmacology U Chicago '42-45, dir toxicity lab '45-46, asso prof anat since '46. Am Soc Zool —Am Physiol Soc—Am Assn Anat. Department of Anatomy, University of Chicago, Chicago 37.◎

14 DOYLE, Wilson Keyser. Government; Governmental administration. b'03. AB '24 (U NC); PhD '36 (Johns Hopkins). Technical consultant to Florida Legislative Committee on Governmental Reorganization '49, to Florida Advisory Council of County Officers and Employees '51, to the Governor of Florida '49-51. Author: Independent Commissions in The Federal Government, Head dept pub adminstrn Fla State U '47-49, dean sch pub adminstrn since '49. Am Acad Polit and Social Sci—So Polit Sci Assn —Internat City Mgrs Assn (affiliate mem), Am Soc Pub Adminstrn—Phi Beta Kappa. H: 1702 Golf Terrace, Tallahassee.◎

15 DOZIER, Herbert L. Marsh management (Muskrat); Economic and systematic entomology; Dahlia and iris breeding. b'95. BS '15 (U SC); MS '17 (U Fla); PhD '22 (O State U). Research on biology of muskrat, marsh ecology, management fur resources, especially muskrat Ondatra zibethica; dahlia breeder since '29, bred and introduced some 25 new varieties including consistent medal winners; iris breeding since '44 of amoena-neglectas and onco hybrids. Author articles in field. Entomol, chief entomol various stations Puerto Rico, Haiti, US since '20, dir fur animal field sta Blackwater Natl Wildlife Refuge Cambridge Md. Fish and Wildlife Service, '37-49; wildlife research biol Fish and Wildlife Service Lafayette since '50. Wildlife Soc—Am Assn Mammalogists— Assn Econ Entomol—Sigma Xi—Am Dahlia Soc—Am Iris Soc. Fish and Wildlife Service, Lafayette, La.

16 DRABKIN, Israel Edward. History of science and mathematics; Science, medicine and philosophy in classical antiquity. b'05. AB '24 (Coll City NY); MA '26—PhD '30 (Columbia). Co-author: (with Morris Cohen) A Source Book in Greek Science '48; also articles in field. Instr City Coll NY asst prof since '49. Hist Sci Soc—Am Philos Assn—Am Philol Assn—Am Assn Hist Med—Classical Assn Atlantic States—Phi Beta Kappa. Guggenheim fellow '45, Carnegie fellow '41-43. City College, Convent Av. and 139 St., NYC.†

17 DRAIN, Brooks D(aniel). Fruit breeding; Mutations; Enzymes; Pyrethrum; Strawberries; Raspberries. b'91. BSc '17 (Ohio State U); SM '25 (U Chicago); PhD '33 (Mich State Coll). Pyrethrum survey in Republic of Haiti sponsored by strategic materials sect US Navy '45. Author articles in field. Hort, head sta dept hort U Tenn Agrl Expt Sta since '32. Sigma Xi. University of Tennessee Agricultural Experiment Station, Knoxville 16, Tenn.

18 DRAKE, Thomas Edward. American social and religious history; Quaker history (Antislavery movement). b'07. BA '28 (Stanford U); MA '30 (U Mich); PhD '33 (Yale)—Bulkeley fellow '31-32, Sterling fellow '32-33; '30 (U Grenoble France); '30-31 (Munich Germany); '31 (Heidelberg). Editor: Quakeriana Notes '36-42; Bulletin of Friend Historical Association '45-49. Author articles: Quakers in Minnesota '37; Cadwalader Morgan, Antislavery Quaker of the Welsh Tract '41; William Penn's Experiment in Race Relations '44; Elihu Coleman, Quaker Antislavery Pioneer of Nantucket '44; Joseph Drinker's Plea for the Admission of Colored People to the Society of Friends '47. Asst prof Am hist and curator Quaker collection Haverford Coll '36-39; chmn dept of history. AHA —Hist Soc Pa—Friends Hist Assn— Phi Beta Kappa. Haverford College, Haverford, Pa.†

19 DRAPEAU, Joseph Edward, Jr. Powder metallurgy; Paint pigments. b'99. ChE '22 (Rensselaer Poly Inst); MS '23 (U Utah). Dir research, later tech dir Glidden Co Div Metals Refining Co since '31. Am Inst Mining Metall Engrs—Am Soc Metals—Am Chem Soc—British Inst Metals—Electro-chem Soc—Am Soc Testing Materials—Sigma Xi. 1717 Summer St., Hammond, Ind.†

20 DRAPER, Alfred Avery. Intestinal flora; Bacterial metabolism. b'99. BS '23 (Middlebury Coll); MS '24— PhD '26 (U Cincinnati). Author articles in field. Bact Steffen Biol Labs Inc NYC '26-45, dir gen since '26, bd dirs since '29, sec-treas since '29, in practice as cons since '30. Soc Am Bacteriol—AAAS—Am Chem Soc—NY Assn Clin and X-ray Labs (pres '29-31, '46, exec com since '29—Am Soc Professional Biol. 121 E. 60th St., NYC.

21 DRAPER, Charles Stark. Aeronautical engineering (Instrumentation); Control systems. b'01. Student '17-19 (U Mo); AB '22 (Stanford U); BS in elec chem engring '26—MS in aeronautical engring '28—ScD in physics '39 (Mass Inst Tech). Research and development improvements in antiaircraft fire control; gun fire, flight control; gyroscopic instruments; infra-red signaling devices for Navy. With Mass Inst Tech since '29, prof since '39, head aeronautical engring dept, dir instrumentation lab; cons editor Jour Aeronautical Scis '38; cons to USN, US Air Force and comml orgns in field aeronautics and control. Am Phys Soc (F)-Inst Aeronautical Sci (F)—AAAS—Am Soc Engring Edn— NY Acad Sci—ASME—Soc Automotive Engrs—Army Ordnance Assn— Am Inst Conf Engrs—Sigma Xi. Awarded Sylvanus Albert Reed award Inst Aeronaut Scis, Medal for Merit, Naval Ordnance Development award, Engring Socs NE '47 award. Massachussetts Institute of Technology, Cambridge, Mass. H: 62 Bellevue St., Newton 58.†◎

22 DRAUGHON, Ralph Brown. Higher education; Political history of southern United States. b'99. BS '22—MS '29 (Ala Poly Inst); LLD (hon) '48 (Birmingham Southern Coll). Author articles in field. Act pres Ala Poly Inst '47-48, pres since '48. SE Conf (exec com)—Assn Ala Colleges (pres '44-45) — So Assn Colleges Secondary Schs (Ala com on post-war edn, exec council commn on higher institutions '44, evaluation commn higher edn)—Ala Edn Assn (legislative com, com on ethics)—NEA—Am Acad Polit Social Sci—Tau Kappa Alpha—Kappa Delta Pi. Alabama Polytechnic Institute, Auburn, Ala.

23 DRAVNIEKS, Andrew. High temperature corrosion; Lubrication; Bleaching earths; Polarography; Paint technology. b'12. Author: Friction, Lubrication, Lubricants (in Latvian) '40; also articles in field. Asst U Latvia '39-40, lecturer '40-41, research asso '41-44; tech mgr Riga Paint Factory '41-44; lecturer, Riga State Technicum '40-44; analyst Osram (fluorescent coatings) Berlin '45; State Inst Metal Chemistry Philipps U, Marburg Germany '46; research asso Ill Inst Tech '47-49; Standard Oil Co (Ind) since '49. Am Chem Soc—Latvian Chem Soc— Soc Latvian Engrs—Sigma Xi—Phi Lambda Upsilon—Electrochem Soc— Nat Assn Corrosion Engrs. Standard Oil Co. (Ind.) Eng. Research Dept., 910 S. Michigan, Chicago.

24 DRECHSLER, Charles. Fungi (Grass leaf spot, root rots, nematode and amoeba capturing, nematodes and protozoa parasites). b'92. BS '13—MS '14 (U Wis); PhD '17 (Harvard). Author articles in field. Plant path Bur Plant Ind Soils and Agrl Engring US Dept Agr since '19. Wis Acad Sci Arts Letters—Washington Acad Sci—Bot Soc Washington—Torrey Bot Club— Bot Soc Am—Am Phytopath Soc—Am Micro Soc—Mycol Soc Am—Nat Geog Soc—AAAS—Sigma Xi. Division of Fruit and Vegetable Crops and Diseases, Plant Industry Station, Beltsville, Md.†

25 DREIER, Katherine Sophie. Contemporary art concepts. b'77. Privately ed US and abroad. Assembled with Marcel Duchamp since '20 a unique international collection known as Collection of the Societe Anonyme of new trends in art from '09 to present day for educational purposes and therefore not based on personal taste but on fundamentals of art; collections given to Yale University '41; personal contribution to new concepts in art were psychological portraits in color and abstract forms which were created since '18. Author: Kandinsky '20; Western Art and the New Era '23; Burliuk '44, and others. Trustee Fine Arts Adv Yale U Art Gallery '46. 130 W. River St., Milford, Conn.

10 **DREISBACH, Robert Rickert.** Hymenoptera Spider Wasps (Psammocharidae). b'88. AB '12—AM '13 (W Reserve U). Taxonomy of spider wasps. Has described about 60 species along with keys for separating genera and the species in the genera. With Dow Chem Co '13-20, since '49 dir chem res. Mich Acad Sci Arts and Letters (past chmn sect zool)—Am Entomol Soc—Wash Entomol Soc—Soc Systematic Zool—Am Soc Plant Taxonomists—Ont Entomol Soc—Kan Entomol Soc—Phi Beta Kappa—ACS. Received silver medal of Hyatt Award '47. Dow Chemical Co., Midland, Mich.

11 **DRENNON, Herbert.** English literature (18th century). b'93. AB '15 (Henderson-Brown Coll Arkadelphia); AM '19 (Vanderbilt U Nashville Tenn); PhD '28 (U Chicago) Newtonian influence on religious, ethical, philosophical and literary work of eighteenth century, especially on James Thompson. Author articles in field. Prof, head Eng dept Murray Ky State Teachers Coll '28-38; prof, head Eng dept, dean grad sch Miss State Coll since '38, dean Coll since '47. Conf Deans So Grad Schs (pres '43, mem com cooperative study teacher edn)—Assn Land Grant Coll U (mem exec com grad sect '44-46, senate standing com grad council '46-47)—S Central Modern Lang Assn (pres '42-46, on exec com '46-47)—Coll Eng Assn—AAUP. State College, Miss.

12 **DREPPERD, Carl William.** Early American art (Prints, advertising); American antiques; Psychology (Publicity, radio, public attitudes, advertising). b'96. Privately educated. Co-founder American Foundation '43; author radio programs. Author: Early American Prints '30; American Pioneer Arts and Artists '42; American Advertising Art '43; Primer of American Antiques '44; The Conestoga '49; First Reader for Antiques Collectors '46; Handbook of Antique Chairs '48; New Geography American Antiques '48 (with Lurelle Guild); American Clocks and Clockmakers '47; Three Centuries of American Antiques '48; also articles in field. Co-owner with Matthew N Chappell of office specializing in psychological analyses and cons on publicity, radio, public attitudes and advertising NYC since '39. 51 E. 42d St., NYC.

13 **DRESCH, Francis W.** Ballistics (Exterior); Mathematical economics. b'13. AB '32—AM '34 (Stanford U); PhD '37—fellowship for Cambridge U and U Paris '37-38 (U Calif). Research on problem of aggregation, problem of passing from micro-economic theories of individual enterprises to micro-economic systems or models relating to aggregative variables defined as index numbers. Author articles in economic field. Asst dir computation and ballistics dept USN Proving Ground with responsibility for directing research in exterior ballistics and related mathematical analysis in ballistic aerodynamics and in use of large scale rapid computing machinery on solution of Navy problems since '47. Asst exterior ballistics officer USNR '41-46. Econometric Soc—Am Math Soc—Inst Math Statis. Naval Proving Ground, Dahlgren, Va.†

14 **DRESCHER, William James.** Ground water hydrology. b'18. BS in CE '40 (U Colo). Hydraulic engineer with US Geological Survey '41-44. Miami ground water studies salt water encroachment in drainage everglades,

establishing water supplies for municipalities, armed forces; Baton Rouge study of quantitative ground water for development large supplies army camps, war industries, municipalities, rice irrigation; registered prof eng Wis. Author: Results of Pumping Tests on Artesian Wells in Milwaukee-Waukesha Area, Wisconsin '48. Co-author articles in field. Quantitative groundwater studies Madison since '46. Am Geophys Union—ASCE —Am Water Works Assn. Room 116, Science Hall, Madison 6, Wis.

15 **DRESSER, Louisa.** New England painting (Seventeenth-nineteenth centuries); Handicrafts of New England. b'07. AB '29 (Vassar Coll); '32 (Fogg Art Mus Harvard); '34 (Courtauld Inst U London); '36-37 (Clark U). Author: XVIIth Century Painting in New England '35; Early New England Printmakers '39; also articles in field. Asso in decorative arts Worcester Art Mus '32-36, asso curator decorative arts '37-41, curator since '42, acting dir '43-46, ed News Bulletin and Calendar '35-43; adv com acquisitions of dept fine arts Amherst Coll since '48. Am Assn Mus —Am Fed Arts—Soc Preservation NE Antiquities—Mass Assn Handicraft Groups (chmn edn com '45-46, chmn assn '47-49)—Soc Arts Crafts (asso, asst to dir Boston '46-47)—Mass Dept Edn (state-wide adv com for handicraft edn since '44). Worcester Art Museum, 55 Salisbury St., Worcester 2, Mass.

16 **DREW, Thomas Bradford.** Heat transfer; Nuclear process design. b'02. BS '23—MS '24 (MIT). Research in fluid mechanics and heat transfer especially condensation boiling and convection in streamline flow, mass transfer and diffusion, development of nuclear piles. Author articles in field. Chem engr EI duPont de Nemours & Co '34-40, '43-44; asso prof and prof chem engring Columbia since '40, exec officer dept chem engring since '48; cons and chem engr adv com Brookhaven Nat Lab since '47. AICE—ASME —Am Chem Soc—NY Acad Sci(F). William H Walker award AICE '37. Department of Chemical Engineering, Columbia University, NYC 27.◉

17 **DREW, William Brooks.** Botany (Ecology, taxonomy, bryology). b'08. ScB '30 (Mass State Coll); AM '31— PhD '34 (Harvard U). Botanist Louise A Boyd East Greenland Expedition; taxonomist and ecologist charge all botanical work expedition on Jan Mayen Island and Scoresby Sound region of eastern Greenland; collected and studied vegetation of Norway; studied Royal Botanic Garden, Kew England; exploration and research in Ecuador and Columbia in connection with cinchona program. Author articles in field. Prof bot, head dept bot and plant path Mich State Coll since '48. Am Assn Plant Taxonomists—Bot Soc Am —Ecol Soc Am—Mich Assn Native Plant Protection (treas)—New Eng Bot Club—Mich Acad Sci Arts Letters —Instituto Ecuatoriano de Cinencias Naturales Quito Ecuador—Sigma Xi. Department of Botany and Plant Pathology, Michigan State College, East Lansing, Mich.

18 **DREWES, Harm.** Vegetable varieties (Cabbage), cauliflower, broccoli, radish, spinach); Stock seed production. b'91. Diplomas (Royal Hort Bot Soc; State Teachers Coll The Netherlands). Co-worker in development spinach varieties Juliana, Long Standing Bloomsdale, Nobel, from monoecious single plants, and in production Snowball cauliflower seed in America, considered impossible before experimental work done since '28. Co-author: Snowball Cauliflower—History, Cul-

ture, and Seed Production in America '46; also articles in field. Supt, chief plant breeder Oakview Seed Breeding Sta Ferry-Morse Seed Co since '40; pres All-American selections '46-47. Am Soc Hort Sci—Am Vegetable Growers Assn —Mich Vegetable Council—Old Guard Nat Canners Assn. Oakview Seed Breeding Station, Ferry-Morse Seed Co., Rochester, Mich.

19 **DREWSEN, Pierre.** Roofing felt; Corrugated paper; Container liner. b '89. BS '10 (Amherst Coll); BS (Chem engring) '12 (MIT); '19 (Coll City NY); '20 (NYU). Developed use of crop fiber raw materials, chemical processing of same; theory roofing felt quality-composition; instrument for testing saturating capacity of dry felt; practical control method and instrument for pre-determining compression resistance of straw paper, nine point corrugating and container liner to establish box making quality; chemical methods preparing straw for manufacturing into corrugating paper; chemical processing cornstalks, sugar cane bagasse, sorghum bagasse, flax straw, soy bean straw, cotton stalks, other crop fibers; process manufacturing nine point corrugating paper from mixed paper stock; established testing stations in paper machine rooms for quality control paper during manufacture; process and chemical means surface coloring paper and container liner. Issued patents in field. Research chem The Barrett Co '23-28; chief chem and chem engr The Hinde and Dauch Paper Co Sandusky O '28-44; mgr and tech dir Amherst Blanket Co since '44. Tech Assn Pulp and Paper Industry—Canadian Pulp and Paper Assn—Am Inst Chem (F). P.O. Box 104, Northampton, Mass.

20 **DREYER, Robert M.** Petrography; Economic geology; Geophysics. b'14. BS '34 (Northwestern U); MS '37—PhD '39 (Calif Inst Tech). Research on mutual interference in microchemical analysis of ore minerals, geochemistry of quicksilver mineralization, geophysical investigations in Tri-State zinc and lead mining district. Author articles in field. Prof geol, chmn dept U Kan since '48. Geol Soc AM(F)—Am Inst Mining Engrs—Mineral Soc—Soc Econ Geol—Sigma Xi—Phi Beta Kappa. Department of Geology, University of Kansas, Lawrence, Kan.†◉

21 **DREYER, William A(lbert).** Ecology; Insect physiology; Ants. b'04. AB '26 (U Ill); PhD '31 (U Chicago). Author articles: Effect of Hibernation and Seasonal Temperature on the Respiratory Exchange of Formica ulkei Emery '32; Seasonable Weight and Total Water Content of the Mound Building Ant, Formica exsectoides Forel '38; Further Observations on the Occurrence and Size of Ant Mounds with Reference to Their Age '42. Instr dept zool U Cincinnati '31-37, asso prof since '45. Research fellowship Edmund Niles Huyck Preserve '48. AAAS(F)—O Acad Sci(F)—Am Soc Zool—Ecol Soc Am (sec '42-47, vp '48)—Soc Study Evolution—Sigma Xi. Zoology Department, University of Cincinnati, Cincinnati 21.

22 **DRISCOLL, Charles Benedict.** Social history (Buried treasure, pirates, sea lore); History of New York City; Kansas. b'85. AB '12—Litt D '37 (Friends U). Travels widely, following treasure clues; owns large library devoted to treasure and pirates. Author: Doubloons, the Story of Buried Treasure '30; Treasure Aboard! '31; Driscoll's Book of Pirates '34; Pirates Ahoy! '27-28. Newspaper work various publs '12-24; asso ed McNaught's Monthly NYC '25-27; exec ed McNaught Syndicate '25-28. Authors' League Am —Am Writers. Lincoln Building, NYC.

10 DROLET, Godias J. Public health statistics. b'82. Student (St. Ann's Acad NYC, Columbia U, Cooper Union, NYU, U and Bellevue Hosp Med Coll). Delegate Eighth American Scientific Congress Washington. Author articles in field. Asst dir NY Tuberculosis and Health Assn since '37; statis Assn Tuberculosis Clinics Greater NY since '19; mem com Health and Hosps NYC Planning Commn; cons statis Conf Metropolitan NY since '26, Com Neighborhood Health Development Dept Health NYC since '29. Am Geog Soc(F)—Biometric Soc—Am Statis Assn—Am Epidemiol Soc—Am Pub Health Assn(F)—Nat Cancer Foundation—NY Acad Med (Asso F). 386 Fourth Av., NYC.

11 DROSDOFF, Matthew. Soil chemistry and fertility; Tung trees (Mineral nutrition). b'08. BS '30 (Ill U); MS '32—PhD '34 (Wis U). Research on chemical and physical properties of colloidal clays; classified and mapped soils in Ohio, Alabama, Georgia, Oregon, California; studies genesis and morphology of claypan soils of Oregon and Mojave Desert; research in method for removing and determining free iron oxide in soil colloids, action of hydrogen peroxide on weathered mica, leaf analyses, soils and mineral nutrition problems,, of tung trees, and minor element deficiencies in tung trees. Author articles in field. Jr soil surveyor US Dept Agr '35-38, asst soil chem '38-40, asso soil tech '40-45, soil tech '45-51, sr soil scientist since '51. Research adviser in Colombia SA on problems of soils and mineral nutrition in coffee production '52. Am Soc Agron—Soil Sci Soc Am—AAAS(F)—Am Hort Soc—Am Chem Soc—Fla Soil Sci Soc—Sigma Xi. U.S. Tung Laboratory, Box 2817, Gainesville, Fla.

12 DROUET, Francis. Cryptogamic botany. b'07. AB '28—MA '29—PhD '31 (U Mo); Theresa Seessel research fellow in bot '36-38 (Yale). Author articles in field. In charge herbarium U Mo '31-35; bot Commissao Technica de Piscicultura, Brazil '35. Research asso cryptogamic bot Northwestern U since '46; curator cryptogamic bot Chicago Natural Hist Mus since '38. Bot Soc Am—Am Assn Plant Taxonomists—Am Micros Soc—Am Limnol Soc. Chicago Natural History Museum, Chicago 5.

13 DRURY, Clifford Merrill. History of the Chaplain Corps, United States Navy; Missionary and Presbyterian history of Pacific Northwest; Religious history of Pacific Slope; California church history. b'97. AB '18—DD '41 (Buena Vista Coll); BD '22—STM '28 (San Francisco Theol Sem); PhD '32 (U Edinburgh). Author: Henry Harmon Spalding, Pioneer of Old Oregon '36; Marcus Whitman, MD, Pioneer and Martyr '37; Mary and Elkanah Walker, Pioneers Among the Spokanes '40; History of the Chaplain Corps, United States Navy (3 vols) vol 3 '48; vol 1 '49; vol 2 '50. Ordained to ministry of Presbyn Ch '22; pastor various churches '22-38; prof ch hist San Francisco Theol Sem '38; historian Naval Chaplain Corps. Commd in Chaplain Corps USNR '33, active duty '41-46 attaining rank of capt. Am Ch Hist Soc—Phi Beta Kappa. 118 Bolinas Av., San Anselmo, Cal.

14 DRURY, John. Chicago and midwestern United States (Architecture, social and economic history, early life). b'98. Research on twelve states American Midwest, Midwestern pioneer social and economic life, pictorial representations early life of region revealed old periodicals, gazetteers, books, town and county histories, history and architecture outstanding Chicago, Illinois and Midwestern houses; covered all activities north Ill unit Historic American Buildings Survey US government for Chicago Daily News '35-44, author weekly series on old Chicago houses '39-41, weekly illustrated articles old Illinois houses '41-43. Author: Arclight Dusks '25; Chicago in Seven Days '28; Dining in Chicago '31; Guide to Chicago (official Century of Progress guidebook '33; Old Chicago Houses '44; Historic Midwest Houses '47; Midwest Heritage '48; Old Illinois Houses ("book of year" Ill State Hist Soc) '48; also articles in field. With Chicago Daily News '26-44; now writer and author. Ill State Hist Soc—Am Newspaper Guild. Awarded regional writing fellowship U Minn '44; scroll for distinguished service to literature, Chicago Found Lit '46. "Hawthornden", R.F.D. No. 2, Chesterton, Ind.

15 DRYDEN, Hugh Latimer. Aeronautical engineering; Fluid mechanics; Aerodynamics (Turbulence and boundary layer). b'98. AB '16—AM '18—PhD '19 (Johns Hopkins). Co-author: (with H Bateman and F D Murnaghan) Hydrodynamics '32; Fluid Mechanics and Statistical Methods in Engineering (with others) '41; also articles in field. With Nat Bur Standards '18-47, head physicist, chief mechanics and sound div '38-47, asso dir '46-47; National Advisory Commission Aeronautics, director since '47. Nat Academy science—Inst Aeronautical Sci (pres '43, F)—ASME—Phi Beta Kappa—Sigma Xi. Received award Inst Aeronautical Sci '40. National Advisory Committee for Aeronautics, Washington.ⓒ

16 DUANE, John Prioleau. Chemistry and marketing of pigments, colors, synthetic resins, and protective coatings; Role of infra-red radiation in mate location of moths. b'09. AB '32—(Engring) '33—MBA '35 (Harvard). Author: Market Research in Industrial Fields '46; Market Research on Industrial Finishes '47; Opportunities in Chemical Market Research '48. Mgr trade analysis div pigments dept E I duPont de Nemours & Co '37-42; dep chief plastics and protective coatings br chem div WPB '43-45; dir market research Interchem Corp since '46. Soc Plastics Industry (policy com reinforced plastics div)—Nat Paint Varnish and Lacquer Assn—Nat Security Indsl Assn (plastics adv com)—Am Marketing Assn—Chem Market Research Assn—Am Management Assn. Interchemical Corp., 67 W. 44th St., N.Y.C. 18.

17 DUBBERSTEIN, Waldo Herman. Ancient history; Chronology and economic, social, cultural history of the Ancient World. b'07. Diploma '24-27 (St John's Coll); BD '27-30 (Concordia Sem); MA '31—PhD '34 (U Chicago). Member field expedition Persepolis Iran (Persia) University of Chicago '39; 1934-35 assisted in compiling the Assyrian Dictionary, a continuing linguistic research project of University of Chicago. Author: Babylonian Chronology 626 BC-AD 45 '42. Author articles: Comparative Prices in Later Babylonia '39; Chronology of Cyrus and Cambyses '38; Assyrian Babylonian Chronology (669-612 BC) '44. Research asst linguistic and hist dept Oriental lang and lit U Chicago '34-38, research asso '38-47, instr Oriental hist '39-47, instr home study dept since '34; research specialist US govt Washington since '47. Am Oriental Soc—AHA—AAUP. Fellow dept Oriental lang and lit U Chicago '33-34. 707 N Overlook Dr., Alexandria, Va.

18 DUBBS, Clyde Andrew. Guayule essential oil and rubber; Micro-laboratory apparatus. b'20. Student '38-39 (U Calif); BS '43—PhD '46 (Calif Inst Tech). Chemical and physiological investigations on guayule essential oil and rubber including design of apparatus for micro-determination of essential oils in plant tissues, precision fractionation of essential oil, essential oil production by the growing leaf, quantitative ozonization apparatus, thermoperiodicity studies on guayule leaf growth; preparation of radioactive C^{14} glucose; design of universal micro-apparatus for filtration, extraction, reflux, distillation, homogenization, centrifugation and drying in the same apparatus. Research asst Kerckhoff Biol Labs Calif Inst Tech '46; research asso U So Calif Med Sch and on attending staff Los Angeles Co Hosp '47-48; biochem Gen Med Research Lab Vets Adminstrn Center Los Angeles since '48. Am Chem Soc—AAAS—Bot Soc Am. General Medical Research Laboratory, Veterans Administration Center, Los Angeles 25. H: 1814 West Boulevard.

19 DUBESTER, Henry Joachim. Demographic statistical sources. b'17. BSS '39 (Coll City NY); MA '46 (Columbia). Gives reference services to scholars, advising on historical as well as current source materials in field of demographic and related socio-economic statistics, paritcularly in realm of multilingual official publications. Author: National Censuses and Vital Statistics in Europe 1918-1939 '48; State Censuses. An Annotated Bibliography of Censuses of Population Taken after the Year 1790 by States and Territories of the United States '48. Chief census library project Library Congress since '45. Population Assn Am. Library of Congress, Washington 25.

20 Du BOIS, Arthur E. Heraldry; Uniforms; Flags; Insignia; Seals. b'00. Student (Boys Voc Sch Newark NJ, McKinley Tech, Corcoran Art Wash). Designer District of Columbia Flag and writer flag code pertaining to same '38; designer numerous medals, ribbons, decorations, insignia, uniforms and regimental coats of arms used by State and Federal military services; designer Philippine High Commander Flag and Seal, Secretary of State's, Attorney General's, Postmaster General's flags, National Gallery of Art seal. Author articles in field. Successively mech draftsman, chief draftsman, chief heraldic branch, Dept of the Army. Temporary Building A, 2nd and V Sts. S.W., Washington 25.

21 DU BOIS, Cora. Cultural anthropology; Sociology of southeastern Asia; Personality and culture; Wintu mythology and ethnography. b'03. BA '27 (Barnard Coll); MA '28 (Columbia U); PhD '32 (U Calif). Author: People of Alor '44; Social Forces in Southeast Asia '49; also articles in field. Chief so areas br Div Research for Far East Dept State since '45; chief Pacific Islands Sect OSS '42-43, chief research and analysis br '44-45 in Ceylon. Am Anthrop Assn (exec bd)—Am Ethnol Soc—Nat Research Council (com on Oceania)—Inst Pacific Relations—Inst Ethnic Affairs—Social Sci Research Council (com World Area Fellowship) —Phi Beta Kappa—Sigma Xi. Social Sci Research Council of Columbia fellow '37-39; Nat Research Council fellow '35-36.

22 DU BOIS, Cornelius. Marketing research; Public opinion. b'04. AB '26 (Harvard). Research through sampling surveys into public opinion, consumer preferences, and group attitudes; devised standard method of measuring magazine audiences, originated card-sort or psycho-physical method of interviewing as applied to research problems. Author: (with Charles J. V. Murphy) The Life and Opinions of a Colllege Class. Contributor: How to Conduct Consumer and Opinion Research '46. Promotion mgr Time Inc '31-37, research dir '37-41, '43-48; dep chief Bur Intelligence OWI and Office Facts and Figures '42-43; with Cornelius Du Bois & Co since '48. Am Marketing Assn—Market Research Council (past pres)—Am Assn Pub Opinion Research—World Assn Pub Opinion Research—Soc Psychol Study Soc Issues Soc Analysis High and Low Statistics. 17 E. 42nd St., NYC 17.

10 Du BOIS, J(ohn) Harry. Plastics engineering; Transfer molding; Plastics product design. b'03. BS '27 (U Minn). Author: Plastics; (with W I Pribble) Plastics Mold Engineering. Comml engr plastics div General Elec Co '28-44; exec engr Shaw Insulator Co Irvington NJ since '44; tech cons plastics ednl films US Office Edn. Soc Plastics Engrs (nat pres '48, dir)—Soc Plastics Industry—Plastics Pioneers—Am Soc Testing Materials—Nat Farm Chemurgic Council. 160 Coit St., Irvington, N.J.

11 DUBOSCLARD, Paul Pierre Michel. Metal-forming machines; Milling machines. b'92. BS '13—BPh '13 (U Paris). Designed forming rolls and forming machine for aircraft skins, spar millers for high production of wing spars. Granted patents in field. In charge research Lidgerwood Mfg Co '20-29; chief cons engr Am Hoist and Derrick Co '29-31; chief engr Internat Milling Co '31-34; pres and chief engr Farnham Mfg Co '34-42; pres Paragon Research Inc '42-45; cons engr since '45. ASME(F)—Soc Automotive Engrs—Am Soc Metals—Inst Aeronautical Sci. Postoffice Box 126, Topanga, Cal.

12 DuCHARME, Ernest Peter. Citrus and vegetable pathology. b'16. BSc '38 (St Mary's Coll); MS '43 (De Paul U); PhD '49 (U Minn). Research vegetable diseases, wilts of melons and Peas, fusarium wilts; Tristeza and citrus disease investigations in Argentina '46-51. Co-author: The Cephaleuros Disease of Citrus '46; Citrus Decline '47. Research asst U Minn '43-46; plant path Citrus Expt Sta U Fla since '46. AAAS —Phytopath Soc Am—Am Soc Bot— Am Soc Mycol—Torrey Bot Club. Citrus Experiment Station, Lake Alfred, Fla.

13 DUCOFF, Louis Joseph. Farm labor. b'09. BS '33 (Rutgers U); PhD '49 (Am U). Author: Wages of Agricultural Labor in the United States '45; co-author: Rural life in the United States '49; also articles in field. Agrl econ, later prin labor econ Bur Agrl Econ US Dept Agr since '35; Fed Interdepart com on labor supply, employment, unemployment statis since '42; Am Statist Assn—Am Econ Assn— Am Farm Econ Assn—Am Sociol Soc —Population Assn Am—Rural Sociol Soc. Social Sci Research Council fellow '47-48. Division of Farm Population and Rural Life, Bureau of Agricultural Economics, U.S. Department of Agriculture, Washington 25. H: 305 Mansfield Rd., Silver Spring, Md.

14 DUDLEY, Horace Chester. Bromides (Organic); Warfare (Chemical); Poisons (Industrial); Isotopes (Radioactive); Gallium. b'09. AB '31 (Mo State Coll); '31-34 (Md U); '34-36 (Johns Hopkins); PhD '41 (Georgetown U). Research in effective use methyl bromide as a fumigant; effect of chemical warfare agents and industrial poisons; development proper control of industrial use methyl bromide, acrylonitrile, phenyldichlorarsine, selenium; application radiogallium to diagnostic and therapeutic clinical trials in bone malignancies. Chem Chem Warfare AUS

'34-36; toxicologist USPHS '36-42; with USN as lt to commdr since '42, head biochem div Naval Med Research Inst since 1947. ACS—AAAS— Soc Exptl Biol and Med. Awarded ACS Prize '29. Naval Medical Research Institute, Bethesda, Md.

15 DUELL, Prentice. Etruscan and ancient Mediterranean art; Classical archaeology; Ancient painting (Technique, pigments). b'94. AB '16 (U Calif); AM '17 (U Ariz); M Arch '24 (Harvard); '19 (Paris); '19-20 (U Pa). Field director Sakkarah Egypt Expdn Oriental Institute University of Chicago '30-36; research London and Vienna '36-38; exhibitions of water colors and photographs of Etruscan wall paintings Metropolitan Museum New York City and other museums and universities. Author: Mission Architecture, Exemplified in San Xavier del Bac '19; The Tomba del Triclinio, at Tarquinia '27; The Mastaba of Mereruka at Sakkarah (2 vols) '38; also articles in field. Research fellow in Etruscan Art Fogg Mus Art Harvard U since '39; mem vis com dept Egyptian art Mus Fine Arts Boston. NY State Assn Architects—Archaeol Inst Am— AHA—AIA—Am Acad Rome—College Art Assn Am—Istituto di Studi Etruschi (Florence Italy)—Sigma Xi—l'Association Internat d'Arch classical (Rome)—Internat Inst for Conservation Museum Objects (London). Awarded: Charles Eliot Norton fellowship Am Sch Classical Studies Athens '23-25; Guggenheim fellowship Etruscan tomb painting Italy '29-30. Fogg Museum of Art, Harvard University, Cambridge 38, Mass.

16 DUEY, Philip Alexander. History of Singing (Ancient and medieval, Bel Canto period, Castrati). b'01. AB '24— M Mus '38 (Ind U); AM '43—PhD '50 (Columbia U); '26-29 (Juilliard Grad Sch). Professor music, dir U Mich Men's Glee Club since '47. Am Musicol Soc—Phi Beta Kappa—Kappa Delta Pi. School of Music, University of Michigan, Ann Arbor.

17 DUFFENDACK, Ora Stanley. Gases (Electrical conduction); Spectrochemistry (Analytical techniques, apparatus development). b'90. BS '17 (U Chicago); AM '21—PhD '22 (Princeton); Guggenheim fellow for research electrical phenomena in gases '29-30 (Gottingen Germany). Investigated characteristics and discovered mechanism low voltage arcs; demonstration usefulness of low voltage arcs in determination of critical potential in atoms and molecules; devised method using working curve for spectrochemical analysis; development technique for calibration of spectroscopic plates. Co-author articles: The Conductivity Produced in Neon and in Helium by Irradiation with their Own Resonance Radiations and the Effect of Foreign Gases on this Conductivity '35; (with R A Wolfe) The Quantitative Spectrochemical Analysis of Mixtures of Gases '39; (with Richard G Fowler) Radiative Processes in Thermionically Controlled Discharges in Helium '49, and others. Faculty physics dept U Mich '22-44, prof to '44; pres Philips Labs Inc since '46. APS(F)—Am Optical Soc—NY Acad Sci—AAAS(F)—Phi Beta Kappa—Sigma Xi. Philips Laboratories, Inc., Irvington-on Hudson, N.Y.

18 DUFFORD, Mamie Ericson (Mrs R T Dufford). Music (History, composition). b'98. Music grad '22—MusB '50 (Northwestern U). Experience in teaching, study and performance of music, especially the works of J S Bach. Instr music Stephens Coll '22-26, Christian Coll '44, Mo Valley Coll since '44. Am Guild Organists—Music

Tchrs Nat Assn—Mo Music Tchrs Association—Mu Phi Epsilon—Am Assn U Women. Missouri Valley College, Marshall, Mo.

19 DUFFORD, Ray Theodore. Physics; Luminescence; Photo-voltaic effect. b'91. BS '18—MS '21 (Northwestern U); PhD '31 (U Mo). Author articles in field. Prof phys Mo Valley Coll since '44. Am Phys Soc(F)—AAAS (F)—Am Geog Soc(F)—Am Physics Teachers Assn—Electron Microscope Soc AM—Mo Acad Sci—Mo Archaeol Soc—Phi Beta Kappa—Sigma Xi. Missouri Valley College, Marshall, Mo.

20 DUFFY, Carl Edward. Virology. b'06. BA '34 (Ohio U); MS '38—PhD '40 (Cincinnati U). Research on correlation of reaction to Schick test and diphtheria antitoxin content of blood serum in children with scarlet fever, Japanese B type encephalitis virus and vaccines, isolation of virus from saliva in rabies. Author articles in field. Prof, head dept bact parasitol U Ark Sch Med since '48. AAAS—Am Assn Path Bact Am Pub Health Assn—Phi Beta Kappa—Society American Bact —Soc Exptl Biol and Med—Sigma Xi. Fellow in biol Ohio U '35-36. University of Arkansas School of Medicine, Little Rock, Ark.

21 DUFFY, Elizabeth. Psychological theory; Emotion (Psychology); Personality development. b'04. AB '25 (Womans Coll U NC); AM '26—NRC fellow emotional responses '28-29 (Columbia); PhD '28 (Johns Hopkins U). Experimental investigation of individual differences in muscular tension and their relation to emotional tendencies; development implications of concept of energy mobilization; studies on determinants of personality. Faculty social sci dept Sarah Lawrence Coll '29-37; prof psychol Woman's Coll U NC since '37. Am Psychol Assn (F)— Soc Psychol Study Social Issues—AA AS (F)—So Soc Philos and Psychol (council '44-47, '50, pres '49-50)—NC Psychol Assn—NC Acad Sci (chmn psychol sect '44-45)—Sigma Xi—Phi Beta Kappa. The Woman's College, University of North Carolina, Greensboro, N.C. H: 1412 W. Lake Drive.

22 DUFFY, Francis Kiernian. Fibre containers. b'91. Student '08-10 (Rochester Bus Inst); '10-14 (U Rochester) grad '37 (Command and Gen Staff Sch Ft Leavenworth Kan); grad '41 (Army Indsl Coll). Dir indsl bur Commerce and Ind Assn NY since '44; gen sales mgr and research dir Carpenter Container Corp '46-48. Exec asst Greif Bros Coop Corp since '49. Indsl and management engring US Army '41-43. 147 41st St., Brooklyn 32.

23 DUGGAN, Reo Eldred. Foods (Measurement of filth, decomposition). b'16. BS '37—MS '38 (La State U). Development analytical methods for detection and measurement cow dung in milk, and milk products, for chicken excrement in frozen eggs, tryptophane in milk, cream, and butter as index of decomposition; detection and measurement indices of decomposition in shrimp; investigation to determine normal and adulterated products, and surveys to determine incidence and extent of adulteration. Chem US Food and Drug Adminstrn since '39, chief chem New Orleans dist since '50. Assn Ofcl Agrl Chem—ACS. Food and Drug Administration, Customhouse, New Orleans. H: 6864 Milne St., New Orleans 19.

24 DUGGINS, Oliver Hervey, Jr. Human hair (Identification). b'13. BS '34 —MS '36 (Northwestern U); '50-53 (Washington U St Louis). Study of age changes in human hair from birth to maturity; Identification of hair specimens with reference to their particular source. Author articles in field. Supervisor hair and fiber sect FBI Lab '44-46; research asst Washington U Sch Medicine St Louis '46. Am Assn Phys Anthrop. Washington University School of Medicine, St. Louis 10.

10 DUKER, Abraham Gordon. Jewish social history and bibliography; Palestine; Labor movements among Jews; Zionism; Polish history; Minority problems and foreign language groups (United States); Community organization. b'07. BA '30 (Coll City NY); '30-33 (Columbia). Founding editor Contemporary Jewish Record '38-41. Author: Jews in the Post War World (with Gottschalk) '45; Jews in World War I '39; Jewish Survival in the World Today '39. Editor: Study Course on Jewish Post War Problems '43; pamphlet series Jews and the Post War World '42-45. Research librarian Grad Sch Jewish Social Work '34-38; research cons Training Bur Jewish Communal Service; ed Research Inst Peace and Post War Problems of Am Jewish Com '41-43; managing ed Jewish Social Service Quarterly '42-43; asso ed Reconstructionist '40-43, '45-48; ed Jewish Book Annual since '46; instr hist Seminary Sch Jewish Studies '40-47, Hebrew Union Sch Religious Edn since '46; inst hist NYU since '50; lect hist New Sch for Soc Research since '50. Am Hist Soc—Am Jewish Hist Soc—Yiddish Sci Inst—Conf Jewish Relations—Palestine Hist-Ethnographic Soc. Research fellow, Columbia '33-34. 315 W. 98th St., NYC 25.

11 DULING, Hugo Bruce. Electrical power machinery. b'92. BS '18—BS EE '19 (W Va U); MS '28 (Ga Sch Tech). Research in correction for opposition method, bridge type RPM counter. Author: Electrical Engineering Laboratory Manual '26. Prof elec engring, in chge power lab Ga Inst Tech since '19. AIEE—Eta Kappa Nu —Tau Beta Pi. Georgia Institute of Technology, Atlanta 3.

12 DULL, Paul S. Japanese political science. b'11. BA '35—PhD '40 (U Wash); '29-30 (Stanford U); '40-41 (Harvard); '41 (U Hawaii). Author articles in field. Asst prof polit sci hist U Ore since '46. Japanese lang officer US Marine Corps '41-44, acting chief Japanese Intelligence Sect OWI '44-46. Am Polit Sci Assn—AHA. University of Oregon, Eugene, Ore. H: 1862 Madison St.

13 DUMAN, Maximilian George. Sedge. b'06. AB '32 (St Vincent Coll); MS '37—PhD '41 (Catholic U). Arctic expedition to northern Hudson Bay region '38, Catholic University Arctic expedition '39. Discovered Carex dutillyi O'Neill and Duman, type Duman 1506 Churchill Manitoba; Taraxacum dentifolium Hagl type Duman 2652 Wakeham Bay Ungava; Pertusaria atra lynge type Duman 2795 Churchill Manitoba. Author articles in field. Instr biol St Vincent Coll Latrobe Pa '37-39, asso prof since '41 AAAS(F)—Bot Soc Am—Am Soc Plant Taxonomists—Arctic Inst NA. St. Vincent College, Latrobe, Pa.

14 DU MONT, Allen Balcom. Television; Oscillography; Broadcasting; Electronic; Cathode ray tubes. b'01. EE '24—Engring D '44 (Rennsselaer Poly Inst Troy NY) Engring D '49 Brooklyn Poly Inst). Inventor of magic eye tube, cathautograph photovision, electron turbine, has recd patents on cathode ray tubes, television. Pres Allen B Du Mont Labs Inc cathode ray and television equipment Clifton NJ since '31. Radio Club Am(F)— Inst Radio Engrs(F)—Am Inst Elec Engring(F)—Television Society Eng

—Soc Motion Picture and Television Engineers—Sigma Xi. Westinghouse award for most outstanding accomplishment '27; American Television Soc award for advancement commercial televn; Televn Broadcaster award development cathode ray tube '33-44; Marconi Mem Medal Achievement for pioneer work in field of Communication'45; AAAA gold medal award for contributions to advancement ot television as new service to public '47. Chevalier French Legion of Honor. 750 Bloomfield Av., Clifton, N.J.⊙

15 DUMONT, Paul Emile. Sanskrit; Indology; Comparative philology of Indo-European Languages. b'79. PhD '03 (U Bologna). Studies on Vedic ritual, Vedic religion, Indian philosophy, Sanskrit grammar. Author: Histoire de Nala '23; L'Asvamedha '27; L'Illumine '33; L'Isvaragita '34; L'Agnihotra '39; The Horse-Sacrifice in the Taittiriya-Brahmana '48. Charge de cours U Brussels '24-29; visiting lecturer in Indology Johns Hopkins '29, prof Sanskrit and Indology since '31. Am Oriental Soc— Linguistic Soc Am—Société Belge des Etudes Orientales — Provincial Utrechtsch Genootschap van Kunsten en Wetenschappen. Decorated Chevalier Order of Leopold (Belgium). 4 W. Highfield Rd., Balt 18.

16 DuMONT, Raymond Peaslee. Ship trials; Vessel acceptance procedure. b '10. BS '32 (Webb Inst Naval Architecture and Marine Engring NY). Assisted in development and administration ship and vessel acceptance procedure US Maritime Commission. Preliminary design and trials US Navy Dept Bur Ships '35-38; chief ship acceptance trial bd US Maritime Commn '38-47; marine ins surveyor Marine Office of Am '48. Soc Naval Architects and Marine Engrs—Propeller Club of Am. H: 212 Carmel Av., Piedmont 11, Calif.

17 DUNAR, E. Helen. Home Furnishings; designing. b'06. Student (U Chicago) (Art Inst Chicago) (Columbia). Study of color; research surveys for new colors to be used in current style trend, and to create new style trends; creator wide line of colors for blankets and sheets. original colors for mass production in home furnishings, painted fabrics, wall paper, china. Cons creative colors. Inter-Soc Color Council — Home Fashion League — Fashion Group Inc. 530 E. 88th St., NYC 28.

18 DUNBAR, Clarence Peckham. Universities (Budgets, finances, statistics); Petroleum (Statistics, bibliography); Natural gas (Statistics, bibliography). b'07. S '27—MS '31 (La State U); '27-28 (U Ore). MBA '34-'34-35 (Harvard). Chief statis Bur Ednl Research La State U '40-43, dir '43-47; dir Bur Institutional Research U Louisville '47-50, Div Institutional Services since '48. Am Statis Assn— Am Assn Petroleum Geol—AIMME— Nat Oil Scouts Assn. University of Louisville, Louisville.

19 DUNBAR, Ralph Edwin. Organic chemsitry; Plastics; Paints. b'95. BS '21 (Dakota Wesleyan U); AM '26 (Columbia U); PhD '33 (U Wis); grad work (Ia State Coll) (Northwestern U) (U Minn). Author: The Quadriservice Manual of Organic Chemistry 38; Visual Outline of General Chemistry '39; The Work Book of Fundamental Organic Chemistry '41; Encyclopedia of Chemical Reactions, Vol I '46, Vol II '48, Vol III '49, Vol IV '51; State High School Course of Study for Chemistry '52. Prof organic chemistry ND Agrl Coll '37-43, dean sch chem tech and chmn grad council since '43. Am Chem Soc (Nat councillor)—

ND Acad Sci—AAAS—Sigma Xi—Phi Kappa Phi—Pi Gamma Mu. N.D. Agricultural College, Frago, N.D. H: 1350 9th St. N.†⊙

20 DUNBECK, Norman Joseph. Foundry sands and binders. b'02. BS ChE '24 (Catholic U Am). Pioneered in use of foundry bond clays and synthetic foundry sands in US, Southern bentonite clay and use of chemically bonded molding sands. Holds patents in field. Author articles in field. Established lab Eastern Clay Products Inc Hutchins Pa '26-27, prodn supt '27-28, field service work foundry clays and sands '28-31, prodn mgr Eifort O '31-36, vp and gen mgr Jackson O '36-49. Am Foundrymen's Soc (nat dir)—Am Inst Mining Metall Engrs—Am Ceramic Soc. 223 Main St., Jackson, O.

21 DUNCAN, Carl Dudley. Vespine wasps; Insect morphology; Agricultural entomology; Medical entomology; Insect-human relations; Botany of flowering plants (California); Physiography of California. b'95. AB '23— AM '28—PhD '31 (Stanford U). Author: Biology of North American Vespine Wasps '39. Co-author: World of Insects '39; also articles in field. Instr, later prof entomol and bot San Jose State Coll since '22, head natural sci dept since '49; ed work Calif State Dept Edn since '36, Quarrie Corp Chicago since '44, Pacific Books Palo Alto since '46; advisor Palo Alto Jr Mus since '38; Calif State Subcom Conservation Edn since '44, chmn since '45. Entomol Soc Am—Am Assn Econ Entomol—Pacific Coast Entomol Soc— AAAS—Calif Acad Sci—Western Soc Naturalists—Am Assn Biol Teachers— NEA—Calif Teachers Assn—Phi Beta Kappa—Sigma Xi. San Jose State College, Calif.†

22 DUNCAN, Sydney Ford. Mechanical engineering (Machine and product design, jet propulsion). b'04. BS '24— BS '25—MS '39 (Calif Inst Tech). Instr, later prof mech engring U So Calif since '29, head dept since '48, coordinator Navy Research on jet propulsion problems since '46. ASME—Am Soc Engring Edn—Am Soc Metals—Sigma Xi—Tau Beta Pi. University of Southern California, Los Angeles 7.†

23 DUNCAN, Wilbur H. Plant ecology and taxonomy; Mosquito control; Poisonous plants; Trees, flora and poisonous plants of Georgia. b'10. AB '32—MA '33 (Ind U); PhD '38 (Duke U). Instr bot U Ga '38-40, asst prof '40-42; chief engring aide USPHS dog fly control Panama City Fla '42, Aedes Aegypti Control Key West Fla '42-43, dir Charleston SC '43-44, asst to nat dir Atlanta '44-45; asst state entomol malaria control Paducah Ky '45-46; asso prof bot U Ga since '46, curator herbarium since '41. AAAS—Bot Soc Am—Ecol Soc Am—Assn SE Biol—So Appalachian Bot Club—Am Soc Plant Taxonomists—Tenn Acad Sci — Ind Acad Sci—Sigma Xi. Department of Botany, University of Georgia, Athens, Ga.

24 DUNHAM, Arthur Louis. Economic history of England, France, United States. b'91. AB '14—AM '17—PhD '23 (Harvard); '19 (Paris U). Author: The Anglo-French Treaty of Commerce and the Industrial Revolution in France '30. Co-editor: Facts and Factors in Economic History '32; also articles in field. Instr hist '23, asst prof '26, asso prof '32, prof since '41 U Mich. AHA—Econ Hist Soc (Eng)— Econ Hist Assn—Soc d'Histoire Moderne—Mich Acad. Department of History, University of Michigan, Ann Arbor. H: 2017 Vinewood Blvd.

10 DUNHAM, Dows. Egyptian archaeology (Sudan). b'90. AB '13 (Harvard); '16 (Oriental Inst U Chicago). Assistant to director Harvard University-Boston Museum of Fine Arts Egyptian Expedition '14-16, '20-24, '26-28, dir expedition '46-47; excavations at Giza Naga-ed-Der and Coptos, Gammai, Gebel Barkal, Nuri and Meroe. Author: Naga ed-Der Stelae of the First Intermediate Period '37; Royal Cemeteries of Kush I '50; articles in field. Asst dept Egyptian Art Mus Fine Arts Boston '15-19, asst curator '20-24, '26-35, asso curator '36-42, curator since '43; vis com on Semitic and Egyptian civilizations Harvard since '40. Egypt Exploration Soc London (life)—Boston Soc—Archaeol Inst Am—Am Oriental Soc. Museum of Fine Arts, Boston 15.

11 DUNHAM, Franklin. Radio; Audiovisual education and music. b'92. Ed '11-12 (Poly Inst Brooklyn); '12-15 (Columbia U); '15-16 (Columbia Law Sch); '16, '17 (NYU Sch Music); D Mus '35 (NY Coll Music); D Litt '37 (St Bonaventure Coll); Fellow '39 (Trinity Coll Music London). Inventor embossed piano keyboard '29, audiographic music '27. Author articles in field. Lecturer in audio edn Columbia U since '38. Inst Radio in Edn—Am Econ Assn—Assn Edn by Radio—Music Teachers Nat Assn—NEA—Nat Music Supervisors Conf (bd bus adminstrn)—Nat High Sch Orchestra (bd mgrs)—Am Acad Polit Sci—Am Acad Polit Social Sci—Music Educators Nat Conf—Am Assn Sch Adminstrs. Decorated Officier de l'Instruction Publique (France); Cross with Palms of d'Academie (France). U.S. Office of Education, Washington 25.©

12 DUNHAM, Theodore, Jr. Astrophysics; Optics; Instrument design. b'97. AB '21 (Harvard); MD '25 (Cornell U Med Coll); AM '27—PhD '27 (Princeton U); Nat Research fellow in physics '27-28. Research on stellar and planetary atmospheres, application of Schmidt cameras to spectroscopy, application of physical techniques to studies of biological and medical problems. Discovered (with W S Adams) carbon dioxide in atmosphere of Venus, and interstellar titanium and iron; developed high dispersion stellar spectrograph at 100-inch telescope, photoelectric recording microphotometer, photoelectric solar spectrum microphotometer; confirmed presence of ammonia and methane in atmospheres of Jupiter and Saturn, spectrophotometric studies of bird cells; articles in field. Sci dir Fund Astrophys Research Inc since '36; research asso Harvard Coll Obs since '47, MIT '47-48. Res Asso U Rochester since '49. Am Astron Soc—Am Phys Soc(F)—Optical Soc Am—Royal Astron Soc(F)—Astron Soc Pacific. 234 Castleman Rd., Rochester 20, N.Y.

13 DUNHOLTER, Russell. Vibration and stress analysis. b'08. CE '30—PhD '39 (U Cincinnati). Research aeroelasticity Air Corps Material Center, Cincinnati '49. Author articles in field. Asso prof mechanics U Cincinnati since '46; cons on math and vibration analysis for Aero Products Div Gen Motors Corp Vandalia. Am Math Soc—Am Soc Engring Edn—Sigma Xi. College of Engineering, University of Cincinnati, Cincinnati 21.†

14 DUNKELBERGER, Benjamin Walter, Jr. Fantasy fiction. b'13. EE (ND State Coll). Visited Orient studying Oriental philosophies and folklore '34-35; has one of most complete science fiction collections in world, covering all English-speaking publications. Author articles in field. Pub and asst ed Fantasy Fiction Field '43-44, Fanews since '44. AIEE—

NDEA (pres visual instr sect '36-37)—Minn-Dak Fantasy Soc (sec-treas '43, pres '44-45)—Nat Fantasy Fan Fedn (sec-treas '43-45, pres '46)—Fantasy Amateur Press Assn. Towne Theatre, Fargo, N.D. H: 1443 4th Av. S.

15 DUNKIN, Paul Shaner. Books (Rare), Bibliography. b'05. AB '29 (DePauw U); AM '31—BLS '35—PhD '37 (U Ill). Author: Post Aristophanic Comedy—Studies in the Social Outlook of Middle and New Comedy '46; How to Catalog a Rare Book '51. Author articles: Issues of The Fairy Queen 1692 '44-45; Foxe's Acts and Monuments, 1570, and Single Page Imposition '47-48; The State of the Issue '48. Sr cataloguer Folger Shakespeare Library Washington '37-48, head cataloguer since '48. Bibliog Soc London—ALA—Bibliog Soc Am—Phi Beta Kappa. Folger Shakespeare Library, Washington 3.

16 DUNKLE, David Hosbrook. Fossil fishes; Comparative vertebrate anatomy, stratigraphy and paleontology. b'11. BA '35 (Kan U); PhD '39 (Harvard U). Participation in collecting expeditions including trips to many parts of US, Mexico, principal objectives being collection of vertebrate fossils from Devonian, Permian, Triassic, Cretaceous, Eocene, and Oligocene formations. Asst curator-in-charge dept geol paleontol Cleveland Mus Natural Hist '39-46; asso curator div vertebrate paleontol US Nat Museum Washington since '46. AAAS—Am Soc Zool—Am Soc Ichthyologists Herpetologists—Kan Acad Sci—O Acad Sci—Sigma Xi—Soc Vertebrate Paleontol. Division of Vertebrate Paleontology, U.S. National Museum, Washington 25.†

17 DUNKLEY, Ferdinand (Luis). Pitch control. b'69. Student '85-86 (Trinity Coll Music London); fellow '86 (Royal Coll Organists); '86-90 (Royal Coll Music London). Composer and teacher of music; discoverer of pitch control of the voice. Author: The Buoyant Voice, Acquired by Correct Pitch-Control '42; Nature's Law of Voice '46. Prof of music Loyola U Coll Music New Orleans since '31; dir Ursuline Coll Glee Club. ASCAP—Nat Assn Singing Teachers. H: 1915 Calhoun St., New Orleans 18.©

18 DUNLAP, Earl Sylvester. Cotton circular knit goods (Dyeing); Synthetic textile dyeing. b'02. BS in chem engring '24—Chem E '34 (Bucknell U). Research on dyeing cotton circular knit goods, nylon, orlon, acetate, etc. Chief chem Thal Dyeing Co since '46. Am Assn Textile Chem and Colorists. Thal Dyeing Co., Indian Orchard, Mass. H: 21 Puritan Rd., Springfield 9, Mass.

19 DUNLAP, Jack Wilbur. Human factor in equipment design; Psychometry (Statistical); Plant personnel problems. b'02. BS '24—MS '26 (Kan State Coll); PhD '31 (Columbia). Editor: Journal of Educational Psychology; member editorial board: Psychometrika, Personnel Psychology. Author: The Computation of Descriptive Statistics '37; Workbook in Statistical Method '39; (with A K Kurtz) Handbook of Statistical Nomographs, Tables and Formulas '32; also articles in field. Pres Dunlap, Morris and Assos Inc since '48. AAAS(F)—NY Acad Sci (F, vp '36-37)—Am Ednl Research Assn—Am Psychol Assn (dir eastern br, pres div cons psychol '47)—Am Statis Assn—Am Assn Applied Psychol (treas)—NY Vocational Assn—Psychometric Soc (treas '35-36, sec '36-40, pres '40-41)—Nat Research Council (dir research Com on Pilot Selection and Training '41-42)—Tau Kappa Alpha—Phi Kappa Phi—Kappa Delta Pi—Sigma Xi. Dunlap, Morris and Associates, NYC.†©

20 DUNLAP, Lawrence Hallowell. Drying oils; Synthetic resin chemistry; Linoleum. b'10. AB '31—BS '33—MA '35 (U Mo); PhD '39 (U Illinois). Author articles in field. Granted US patents on drying oil and resins in linoleum. Research lab Armstrong Cork Co since '39, head drying oil and resins sect since '46; adj prof chem dept Franklin & Marshall Coll '47-48. Am Chem Soc—Sigma Xi. Research Laboratory, Armstrong Cork Company, Lancaster, Pa. H: 1315 Quarry Lane.

21 DUNLOP, Andrew P. Furan chemistry; Furfural. b'14. BS '38 (U Chicago). Research on mechanism of oxidation of furan compounds; hydrogenation of furan compounds, particularly furfural; kinetics of formation of furfural from pentoses; characterization and identification of new furan products and of non-furan products obtained from furans; synthesis of new types of furan resins; development research process for producing furoic and fumaric acid, holds patents for process. Author articles: Furfural, Formation and Behavior '40; Nature of Furfuryl Alcohol '42. Co-author: Furan Resins '46; Autoxidation of Furfural '46; Liquid-Vapor Equilibria in Furan Systems '40; Recovery of Furfural from Aqueous Solutions '40; Thermal Stability of Furfural '40; Determination of Furfural in Furfural-Furfuryl Alcohol Solution '39. With Quaker Oats Co since '31, asst dir chem research since '47. Am Chem Soc. Quaker Oats Company Research Laboratories, 345 E. 25th St., Chicago 16.

22 DUNN, Cecil Gordon. Industrial microbiology; Food technology and sanitation; Germicides; Dehydration; Fermentations; Irradiation of foods and micro-organisms. b'04. BS '30—PhD '34 (MIT). Author: Industrial Microbiology (with S C Prescott) '40; also articles in field. Asso prof indsl microbiol MIT since '47. Served as capt and instr QMC Res US Army '38-41, col '46, col QMC Res since '46. Am Pub Health Assn(F)—Soc Am Bact (sec-treas ne br '48-49)—Am Chem Soc—AAAS—QM Assn—Mass Pub Health Assn—Sigma Xi—Delta Omega. Massachusetts Institute of Technology, Cambridge 39, Mass.

23 DUNN, David B. Lupinus (Micranthi); Speciation ecology. b'17. AA '38 (Los Angeles City Coll); BA '40—MA '43—PhD '48 (U Calif). Asst in charge bot research Atomic Energy Project U Calif since '48. Soc Study Evolution—AAAS—Am Soc Plant Taxonomists—Western Soc Naturalists—Sigma Xi. Atomic Energy Project, University of California at Los Angeles, Los Angeles.

24 DUNN, Emmett Reid. Amphibians and reptiles; Zoogeography. b'94. AB '15—MA '16 (Haverford Coll); PhD '21 (Harvard). Prof biol Haverford Pa Coll since '35; curator reptiles and amphibians Phila Acad Natural Sci since '37. Acad Colombiana de Ciencias—Am Soc Ichthyologists Herpetologists. Fellow Guggenheim Memorial Found '28. Haverford College, Haverford, Pa.©

25 DUNN, Karl Lindemann. Heat (Radiant); Instruments (Glass). b'13. Ed pub schs and spl work. Research on radiant heat as a hazard or nuisance in high temperature industry; development protective hand creams to reduce effects on skin; system combination radiant heat shielding and ventilation to reduce temperature effects on workers in glass industry; design clothing to permit working in extreme exposures; studies to determine exposures and effects to the eye; development easily cleaned microscope cell for counting dusts; portable flow-meter for use with air sampling instruments; all-glass Greenburg-Smith impinger for determination dusts and toxic materials in air. Tech Phys Research Lab Corning Glass Works '31-35, indsl hygienist med dept since '35. Am Indsl Hygiene Assn —Am Pub Health Assn—NY State Pub Health Assn. Corning Glass Works, Corning, N.Y. H: 282 East First St., Corning, N.Y.

10 **DUNN, Robert W(illiams).** World labor conditions; Civil rights; Trade and company unions. b'95. AB '18 (Yale). Author: American Foreign Investments '26; Company Unions '27; Americanization of Labor '27; Soviet Trade Unions '28; Labor and Automobiles '29; The Palmer Raids '48. Co-author: Labor Spy '24; (with Stuart Chase and Rexford G Tugwell) Soviet Russia in the Second Decade '28; Labor and Textiles '31. Exec sec Labor Research Assn and ed Labor Fact Books since '36. Civil Rights Congress —Internat Workers Order. 80 E. 11th St., NYC 3.

11 **DUNN, Stuart.** Magnesium nutrition of plants; Utilization of wood wastes in agriculture. b'00. BS '23— PhD '31 (U Minn); MS '25—fellow '24-25 (Ia State Coll). Research in dye adsorption by hydrophilic colloids as related to plant hardiness, fertilizer placement for potatoes, control of apple scab, influence of soil texture on plant growth, uses of lignin, sawdust and other industrial wastes as soil builders, propagation of sugar maple by cuttings, control of magnesium leaf scorch of apple, effects of ultrasonic waves on seeds. Author articles in field. Instr bot and asst bot expt sta U NH '26-37, asst prof bot and asst bot Agrl Expt Sta '37-41, asso prof bot and plant physiol Agrl Expt Sta since '47. Am Soc Plant Physiol—AAAS(F)— Phi Kappa Phi. Botany Department, University of New Hampshire, Durham, N.H.

12 **DUNN, Thomas Franklin.** Semantics. b'06. AB '29—AM '30 (Washington U); PhD (U Chicago). Author: The Facetiae of the Mensa Philosophica '34; Learning Our Language '44. Co-author: (with C A Ranous) Learning Our Language '44; Our World in Words '46. Professor and head Eng Drake Univ since '36. Co-author: (with C A Ranous and H B Allen) Learning Our Language '50. Mod Lang Assn—Nat Council Teachers Eng—Am Dialect Soc—Linguistic Soc Am. Fellow Am Council Learned Socs '49. Drake University, Des Moines, Ia.◎

13 **DUNTON, Sewell Nightingale.** Bamboo (Utilization); Conservation of natural resources. b'94. AB '18 (Harvard). With Montague Rod and Reel Co Montague City Mass since '31, treas, sec and dir; treas, sec, dir Mohawk Sales Corp; comptroller and dir Ocean City Mfg Co. Nat Parks Assn—Associated Industries Mass—Mass Forestry and Park Assn. Montague Rod and Reel Co., Montague City, Mass.

14 **DU PUIS, Robert Newell.** Organic chemistry of glycerine and wax. b'10. AB '31 (U Ill); PhD '34 (NYU). Research on substituted cinchophens; presently engaged research on chemistry of waxes and surface coating resins. Holds five US, seven foreign patents on various organic chemical subjects. Author articles in field. Research chem Miner Labs Chicago '35-45, asst dir '45-47; asst research and development dir S C Johnson & Son Inc Racine Wis since '47. Am Chem Soc—Am Oil Chem Soc —AAAS— Comml Chem Development Assn—Phi Beta Kappa—Sigma Xi—Phi Lambda Upsilon. S. C. Johnson & Son, Inc., Racine, Wis.

15 **DUPUY, Leon William.** Prospect drilling (Sampling techniques mine development & production). b'96. BS (mining and metall) '21 (U Ariz). Developed drilling procedures including vacuum drill sampling with wagon drill, use of power auger and Baker core barrel. Mining engr '21-40; with US Bur Mines since '40, spl asst to regional dir from '50. AIMME. US Bureau of Mines, Amarillo, Tex.†

16 **DURAND, Loyal, Jr.** Economic geography (Dairy regions, Wisconsin). b'02. BA '24—MA '25—PhD '30 (U Wis). Special land planning consultant for Wisconsin National Resources Planning Board '41; member National Research Council Committee Advisory to the Office of Naval Research since '51. Co-author: An Economic Geography '48; also articles in field. Professor geography U Tenn since '46. Assn Am Geographers—Nat Council Geog Tchrs (2d vp '48)—Wis Acad Sci Arts Letters—Tenn Acad Sci—Phi Beta Kappa —Sigma Xi. University of Tennessee, Knoxville, Tenn.◎

17 **DUREA, Mervin Arnold.** Abnormal child psychology; Juvenile delinquency; Behavior problems; Personality (Dynamic aspects); Psychoses. b'92. BA '22—MA '24—PhD '28 (O State U). Research on method of appraising seriousness of delinquent careers, criteria for diagnosing potential delinquent, personality characteristics of juvenile offenders. Author articles in field. Prof psych O State U since '45. Am Psychol Assn(F)—Sigma Xi. Diplomate Am Bd Examiners Profl Psych '48. Department of Psychology, Ohio State University, Columbus 10, O.†

18 **DURHAM, Henry Welles.** Highway, municipal, and hydraulic engineering (Highway and street paving, municipal improvements, water works and sewers). CE '95 (Sch Mines Columbia U). Author: Street Paving and Maintenance in European Cities '15; also articles in field. Asst engr in charge constrn NYC subway '00-04; resident engr in charge design, constrn all municipal improvements City of Panama '04-07; resident engr charge surveys, constrn Cape Cod Canal '07-12; design, survey, constrn work local and natl govts Central and SA '20-22, '35-38, designed and constructed first modern highway in Paraguay '39-41; research Mil Intelligence Div Engr Corps '43-45. Commanded 41st Engrs World War I. ASCE—Permanent Internat Assn Road Congresses—AAAS—Am Road Builders Assn—Am Pub Works Assn—Soc Am Mil Engrs—Am Geog Soc(F)—Sociedad de Ingenierus del Peru. Conspicuous Service Cross NY State; Officier du Merite Agricole of French govt. Sandwich, Mass.

19 **DURHAM, J(ohn) Wyatt.** Tertiary Mollusca (Stratigraphy, corals, Echinoids). b'07. BSc '33 (U Wash); MA '36—PhD '41 (U Calif). Paleontologist E W Scripps expedition to Gulf of California '40. Author articles in field. Asso prof paleontol U Calif since '47. Geol Soc Am(F)—Paleontol Soc(F)— Sigma Xi. Department of Paleontology, University of California, Berkeley.†

20 **DURHAM, Oren C.** Aerobiology as related to allergy; Pollen. b'89. Supervised first coordinated atmospheric and field pollen research '25; conducted coordinated atmospheric pollen surveys in more than 100 cities in US, Canada, Mexico, with cooperation US Weather Bureau, Canadian and Mexican meteorological services; participated in establishment at University of Illinois of type collection air-borne pollens and wind-pollinated plants for American Academy of Allergy. Developed standard exposure device for gravity slide pollen research. Author: Your Hay Fever '36; also articles in field. Chief bot Abbott Labs since '25; tech dir pollen com Aero-allergen Council Am Acad Allergy since '45; asst prof and special lecturer aerobiol U Ill Coll Med since '46. AAAS—Am Acad Allergy—Chgo Allergy Soc. Abbott Laboratories, North Chicago, Ill.

21 **DuROSE, Arthur H.** Plating; Corrosion. b'12. Student '30-32 (Graceland Coll); BS '34 (Mich State Coll); MS '37 (U Cincinnati); '41 (Western Reserve U). Holder patents covering plating solutions; nickel, alloy, manufacture nickel and copper compounds. Author articles in field. Supervisor plating research; tech service; indsl cons; chem mfg since '44. Am Soc Testing Materials—Am Chem Soc—Electrochem Soc —Am Electroplaters Soc—Tau Beta Pi —Phi Kappa Phi. Harshaw Chemical Co., 1945 East 97th St., Cleveland 6.†

22 **DuSHANE, Graham Phillips.** Embryology (Development of pigmentation, nervous system, behaviour). b'10. AB '30 (Wabash Coll); PhD '34 (Yale); fellow Nat Research Council '35-36 (Stanford U). Author articles in field. Instr, asst prof asso prof U Chicago '36-46; prof biol Stanford U since '46. AAAS(F)—Am Soc Zool—Am Assn Anat—Sigma Xi—Phi Beta Kappa. Received Campbell award Wabash Coll '30; award for excellence in under-grad teaching U Chicago '45. Department of Biology, Stanford University, Stanford, Calif.◎

23 **DUTTON, Bertha P.** Archaeology (Indians of the Southwest and Latin America; State of New Mexico). b'03. BA '35—MA '37 (U NM); '45-46 (Columbia). Archaeological excavation and survey Jemez Canyon New Mexico '33-34, Chaco Canyon '34; archaeological reconnaissance and investigations Peru and Bolivia '35, Guatemala '37; archaeological studies in Guatemala and Mexico. Co-author: Excavations at Tajumulco, Guatemala '43; The Pueblo Indian World '45. Editor: New Mexico Indians Pocket Handbook '48; also articles in field. Curator ethnol and research asso Mus NM and Sch Am Research since '36. Am Anthrop Assn(F)—Soc Am Archaeol—Am Ethnol Soc(F)—Sociedad Interamericana de Antropologia y Geografia—Phi Kappa Phi. Museum of New Mexico, Box 1727, Santa Fe, N.M.

24 **DUTTON, Donnell Wayne.** Aircraft structures; Rotary wing design; Aeronautical research. b'13. BS '35 (Mo Sch Mines Metall); MS '40 (Ga Sch Tech). Member subcommittee helicopters National Advisory Committee on Aeronautics '45-46; scientific advisor (on leave) Research and Develop Division US War Department '46-47. Draftsman designer engring dept Allis Chalmers Mfg Co '35-38; student asst Daniel Guggenheim Sch Aeronautics Ga Sch Tech '38-40, asst prof '40-43, prof, dir sch since '43; stress analyst Curtiss Wright Corp Robertson Mo '40. Inst Aeronautical Sci—Am Soc Engring Edn—Am Helicopter Soc—Ga Engring Soc. 483 E. Wesley Rd., N.E., Atlanta.

25 **DuVAL, Miles P., Jr.** Marine operational problems; Diplomatic and political history of Panama Canal. b'96. BS '19 (US Naval Acad); MFS '37 (Fgn Service Sch, Georgetown U). In charge marine operations of Pacific subdivision of Panama Canal '41-44; developed high level terminal lake plan for improvement of Panama Canal '43; designated Navy Department liaison officer and coordinator for modernization studies of Panama Canal by Secretary of Navy '46. Author: Series on Panama Canal; Cadiz to Cathay '40;

And the Mountains Will Move '47; The Future Canal (in preparation). Commd ensign USN '18, capt since '45. US Naval Inst—Soc Am Mil Engrs—AAAS—Panama Hist Soc (corr mem)—Panama Canal Soc, Washington—Panama Canal Natural Hist Soc (past vp)—Naval Hist Found—Phi Alpha Theta. H: 4017 Clinton Ave., Richmond, Va.⊚

10 DUVALL, Evelyn Millis. Youth, marriage, sex and family life education. b'06. BS '27 (Syracuse U); MS '29 (Vanderbilt); '38 (Columbia); '39-40 (Northwestern U); PhD '46 (U Chgo). Organization secretary National Conference on Family life '46-48, co-chairman committee on dynamics of family interaction '48; originator marriage course Town Hall New York City '47, '48. Author: Family Living '50; Facts of Life and Love '50. Co-author: (with Reuben Hill) When You Marry '45; (with S M Duvall) Leading Parents Groups '46. Author articles: Conceptions of Parenthood '46, and others. Contributor: Courtship and Engagement in Successful Marriage '47; What Holds a Marriage Together in The Marriage Reader '47; Roles of Men and Women as Causes of Sex Conflict in Sex in Our Culture '50. Dir Assn for Family Living Chicago '34-44; cons family life edn since '38; asso ed Marriage and Family Living since '45; exec sec and cons Nat Council on Family Relations since '45; dir original Workshop on Marriage and Family Research U Chicago summer '50. Am Assn Marriage Counselors (exec com)—Am Sociol Soc—Child Study Assn Am (adv bd)—Fed Council Churches (commn on marriage and home)—Soc for Research Child Development. 1126 E. 59th St., Chicago 37. H: 5453 Woodlawn Av., Chicago 15.⊚

11 DVORAK, Beatrice Jeanne. Aptitude tests; Trade tests. b'08. BA '29—MA '30—PhD '34 (U Minn). Development of US Employment Service general aptitude test battery. Author articles: Differential Occupational Ability Patterns '35. Research asst employment stabilization research inst U Minn '31-34; chief testing br US Employment Service US Dept Labor Washington since '47. AAAS (F)—Am Psychol Assn—Phi Beta Kappa. U.S. Employment Service, U.S. Department of Labor, Washington 25.

12 DWYER, Richard Clement. Marine engineering. b'86. Student '02-04 (WVa U Tech Inst); LLD (hon) '42 (Calif Maritime Acad). Author: Marine Steam Engineering (courses I, II, III) '40-42. Staff chief engr and chief engr various ships; with Calif Maritime Acad '30-52, supt and comdg officer of training ship '34-37, dean edn '44-52. Soc Naval Architects and Marine Engineers. 505 Drake St., Antioch, Cal.

13 DYCE, Elton James. Beekeeping; Honey. b'00. BSA '23 (U Toronto); MSc '28—Macdonald scholar '25 (McGill U); Schuyler fellow '30—PhD '31 (Cornell U). Inventor of honey process, secured product patent for honey spread, later donated it to Cornell University. Author articles in field. Demonstrator, later prof apiculture Ontario Agrl Coll Can '24-40; mgr Finger Lakes Honey Producers Coop Groton NY '40-42; ext apiarist Cornell '42-45, asso prof, prof apiculture since '45. Am Assn Econ Entomol—Empire State Honey Producers Assn (field sec)—Sigma Xi. Comstock Hall, Ithaca, N.Y.†

14 DYE, Alexander Vincent. International economics; History of Latin America; Foreign trade. b'76. AB '01—AM '02 (William Jewell Coll); PhD '04 (U Leipzig, Germany). Am consul Nogales Mexico '09-13; spl asst US

Dept States and rep War Trade Bd Norway '17-19; rep Am Internat Corp '19-21; US trade commr London '21-33; commercial attache Mexico City '23-26, Buenos Aires '26-35; dir Bur Fgn Domestic Commerce Washington '36-39; commercial attache London '39-41; ret from fgn service '41; econ cons Nat Fgn Trade Council '41-45; mem Com on Internat Econ Policy; chmn Organizing Com Internat Business Conf Rye NY '44; mem adv bd Com for Econ Development; mem Council Fgn Relations. Boxwood Terrace, Tyron, N.C.⊚

15 DYEN, Isidore. Linguistics; Malay; Malayo-Polynesian languages; Indo-European comparative grammar. b'13. BA '33—MA '34—PhD '38 (U Pa); '38-39 (Columbia U); '39-42 (Yale). Linguist in Coordinated Investigation of Micronesian Anthropology sponsored by Pacific Science Board of National Research Council at Truk and Yap '47. Author articles in field. Instr Malayan langs Yale '42-43, asst prof '43-48, asso prof since '48. Linguistic Soc Am—Am Oriental Soc. Hall of Graduate Studies, Yale University, New Haven.

16 DYER, Hubert Jerome. Mineral nutrition of plants; Maturity of vegetables; Plant growth regulators. b'14. Student '32-37 (Quigley Prep Sem, St Patrick's Sem, DePaul U); SB '39—SM '40—PhD '46 (U Chicago); '40-41 (Ohio State U). Author articles in field. With Libby McNeill & Libby in quality control research '43-47, head research dept '47-48; instr Brown U since '48. AAAS—Am Soc Plant Physiol—Bot Society of Am—Biometric Society Am—Inst Food Tech—Sigma Xi. Department of Botany, Brown University, Providence, R.I.

17 DYKSTERHUIS, Edsko J(erry). Grassland and savannah ecology; Range management; Forest grazing. b'08. BS '32 (Ia State Coll); PhD '45 (U Neb). Author: The Vegetation of the Fort Worth Prairie; The Vegetation of the Western Cross Timbers; also articles in field. With US Forest Service and US Dept Agr '33-38, now regional conservationist Soil Conservation Service for Northern Great Plains. Ecol Society America—Soc Am Foresters (sr)—Am Soc Range Management—Soil Conservation Soc Am—Soil Sci Soc Am—Am Soc Agron—Tex Acad Sci(F)—AAAS—Sigma Xi. United States Soil Conservation Service, P.O. Box 713, Lincoln 1, Neb. H: 5342 Cleveland Ave., Lincoln 4.

18 DYKSTRA, Kenneth G. Foods (Technology). b'11. AB '33 (Central Coll); PhD '37 (Ia State Coll . Research on improvement canning techniques for vegetables and fruits; improvement condiments particularly tomato condiments. Research chem Am Can Co '37-42; chief chem Snider Packing Corp '42-44; plant mgr Birds Eye-Snider Div Gen Foods Corp '45-46, dir labs since '46. ACS—AAAS—Inst Food Tech—Sigma Xi. 162 S. Main St., Albion, N.Y.

E

19 EADES, Jack Arthur. English peas (Breeding); Plants (Cold resistance). b'18. AB '40 (Fort Hays State Coll Kan). Research on breeding English peas for adaptability to the South by incorporating factors of cold and disease resistance into desirable horticultural types; chairman Southern Co-operation Pea Trials, and coordinator research on peas in the South; developed method artificially freezing plants in cold liquids to determine cold resistance. Co-author article: (with B L Wade) Frost Resistance Tests with Cold Liquids. Hort US Regional Vegetable Breeding Lab Charleston SC

since '49. Am Soc Hort Sci. P.O. Box 177, St. Andrews Branch, Charleston, S.C.

20 EADIE, William Robert. Economic mammalogy; Rodent control. b'09. BS '32—MS '33 (U NH); PhD '39 (Cornell). Research on mammalian life histories and ecology, control of injurious mammals, mammalian morphology. Rodent control specialist USNR '44-46. Author articles in field. Asst zool U NH '33-35, instr '35-39, asst prof '39-42; asst prof Cornell '42-47, asso prof since '47. AAAS—Am Soc Mammalogists—Wildlife Soc Am—Am Soc Zool—Sigma Xi. Fernow Hall, Cornell University, Ithaca, N.Y. H: 1402 Hanshaw Rd.†

21 EADS, Laura K(rieger). Tests (Psychology, educational); Mathematics (Elementary and Junior high school). b'02. BS '24 (U Buffalo); MA '26—PhD '30 (Columbia). Research test construction, administration and supervision educational tests for elementary and junior high grades, administration, interpretation, and research with Rorschach and Szondi psychological tests and intelligence and thematic apperception tests. Contributor: The Educational Talking Picture '37. Sch psychol '28-29; research and prodn Ednl Sound Films '30-37; research Bur Curriculum Research NYC Bd Edn since '37. Kappa Delta Pi—Am Psychol Assn—Am Ednl Research Assn. Bureau of Curriculum Research, Board of Education of City of New York, 110 Livingston St., Bklyn 2. H: 141 Joralemon St.

22 EADS, Richard Bailey. Entomology; Insect vectors (Taxonomy). b'19. BS '39—PhD '49 (Tex A and M Coll). Studies taxonomy and ecology relative to insect vectors of disease organisms necessary for efficient control measures; research on plague and typhus; arthropod reservoirs of Q fever; identification insects responsible for transmission disease organisms with emphasis on determination ectoparasites particularly fleas and mites. Author articles: The fleas of Texas; A new species of flea from the field mouse, Baiomys taylori; A new species of Jellisonia Traub from Mexico; and others. With Tex State Dept Health since '40, prin entomol since '49. Served as entomol Med Service Corps USNR '43-45. Am Assn Econ Entomol—Entomol Soc Am—Am Soc Parasitol—Am Soc Tropical Med—Am Mosquito Control Assn—Entomol Soc Wash—Sigma Xi. State Dept of Health, Austin 1, Tex.

23 EAGLE, Jacob Eugene. Ceramic colors. b'98. BS '23—profl ceramic engr '37 (Alfred U). Author articles in field. Mgr color sales Pemco Corp since '46; sect chief non-metallic minerals War Prodn Bd '43-46. Am Ceramic Soc(F)—Inst Ceramic Engrs. Pemco Corporation, Baltimore 24.†

24 EAKER, J(ay) Gordon. Victorian literature; Pater; Meredith; Bridges; Galsworthy; English novel. b'04. AB '28—AM '31—PhD '32 (Ia State U); '49-50 (NY U). Research on methods of Walter Pater, Robert Bridges' concept of nature, modernism in Victorian fiction, comedy of Meredith, Galsworthy and the modern mind. Author: Walter Pater: A Study in Methods and Effects '33; also articles in field. From asst prof to prof and head Eng dept State Teachers Coll (Pittsburg, Kan) '32-46; head Eng dept Jersey City Jr Coll since '46. Phi Beta Kappa—MLA—Coll Eng Assn—AAUP. Jersey City Junior College, Jersey City 4. H: 217 Audley St., South Orange, N.J.

25 EARDLEY, Armand John. Continental tectonics; Structural geology (Utah, Wyoming, Montana, sedimentation, Paleozoic cordilleran geosyncline); Petroleum geology. b'01. PhD '30 (Princeton U). Author: Aerial Photographs; Their Use and Interpretation '42; Structural Geology of North America '51; also articles in field. With U Mich since '30, prof, director geol field work '43-49, dir div of earth sciences, chmn dept of geology. Geol Society America(F)—American Assn Petroleum Geologists—Geophys Union America. Department of Geology, University of Utah, Salt Lake City.†

10 EARHART, Kenneth Allen. Alkyd resins; Drying oils. b'07. BS '30—MS '32 (Lehigh U); '44-47 (Polytech Inst Brooklyn). Director research on alkyd, phenolic, urea, silicone and related resins for use in coatings field. Author articles in field. US Indsl Chem Inc since '39. ACS—AIC—Am Soc Testing Materials—Am Oil Chem Soc—Tau Beta Pi.

11 EARLE, Clarence Edwards. Chemical engineering (Lubricants, coupling devices, special greases). b'93. BS '23 (George Washington U). Discovered and developed lithium soap lubricating greases used in aircraft manufacturing US and foreign World War II; originated, developed all-purpose hydraulic oil, chemical polar compounds for thin film preservation of metallic surfaces against corrosion, aircraft carbon monoxide detector; pioneered discovery and development of chemical compounds known as phenyl-amino salts used as mycotic drug in South Pacific. Dir Earle Research Lab since '39; research dir Baltimore Engring and Chem Co; dir Medical Chem Inc, Breco Mfg Co; chief tech cons B-R Engring Co, Baltimore. Am Chem Soc—Soc Automotive Engrs—Washington Soc Engrs. 309 E. Saratoga St., Balt 2.

12 EARLE, Wilton R(obinson). Tissue Culture; Experimental Cancer Research. b'02. BS '23 (Furman U); MS '24 (U NC); PhD '28 (Denison fellow '27—Nat Research fellow '27 (Vanderbilt U). Author: numerous articles in jours. Cytologist Nat Cancer Inst US Pub Health Service '28-41, sr to head unit cytol tissue cult unit cytol biol sect since '41. AAAS—Am Assn Anatomists—American Society Experimental Pathol—NY Acad Sciences—Wash Academy Scis—Soc Exptl Biology and Med—Am Assn Cancer Research—Soc Study Development and Growth—Photographic Soc Am—Gerontol Soc. National Cancer Institute, Bethesda, Md.

13 EARLEY, James Stainforth. British finance; Economic stabilization. b '08. BA '32 (Antioch Coll); MA '34—PhD '39 (U Wis); Soc Sci Field F '36-37 (U London). Research on US and British stabilization policies during World War II, price-restraining subsidies, interest rates and policies of British financial institutions. Author: British Wartime Price Administration and Price Movements (2d edit) '44. Co-author: (with K Boulding, L Seltzer, and A Gruchy) Economic Theory in Review '50. Author articles in field. With U Wis since '37, prof econ since '47; econ Nat Defense Adv Commn and OPA '40-42; head econ OPA '43-45; adv Brit Commonwealth financial affairs to Dept State '45; cons State Dept. Nat Bur Econ—Am Econ Assn—Royal Econ Soc. Department of Economics, University of Wisconsin, 317 Sterling Hall, Madison 6, Wis.

14 EARLY, Harold C. Aluminum (Resistance welding ; Microwaves (Waveguides); Wind tunnels (Supersonic low-pressure); Gases (Pulsed arc electrical discharges in). b'12. AB '39 (Mich State Coll); MS '41—'46-47 (U Mich). Assisted design of devices for resistance welding of aluminum; design equipment for microwave guide apparatus; inventor ionic wind tunnel for production supersonic wind at low pressure; development industrial applications gaseous electrical discharges by use of pulsed arc. Holds patents in field. Research engr welding U Mich '41-43, gaseous elec discharge since '47; research asso microwave electronics Harvard '43-46. APS—Inst Radio Engrs. Engineering Research Institute, University of Michigan, Ann Arbor.

15 EARLY, Joseph. Glass manufacturing (Bulbs for fluorescent lamps, tubing used in incandescent lamps). b'03. BS in mech engring '26—ME '41 (Washington U). Engr Amsler Morton Co Pittsburgh '27-36; Phoenix Glass Co Monaca '36-40; Bridgeville Glass Co '40-45; supt Westinghouse Elec glass div since '45. Inst Ceramic Engrs—Am Ceramic Soc—Soc Glass Tech (Eng). Box 1312, Fairmont, W. Va.

16 EARP, Unus F. Electrification (Rural); Farms (Refrigeration). b'15. BS '39—MS '50 (Va Poly Inst). Designed and operated experimental two-compartment walk-in farm refrigerator, organized and conducted experimental work dealing with one and two compressor operation, evaporators, insulation, vapor-sealing methods and materials, and miscellaneous refrigeration components. Author: Rural Electrification Engineering '50. Author article: The Virginia Walk-in Farm Refrigerator. Faculty Va Poly Inst '39-42; engr Air Tech Service Comd Wright Field '42-45; asst, then asso prof agrl engring Va Poly Inst since '45 and asso agrl engr Va Agrl Expt Sta. Am Soc Agrl Engrs. Agricultural Engineering Department, Virginia Polytechnic Institute, Blacksburg, Va.

17 EAST, Ben. Wildlife conservation; Natural history. b'98. Student (U Mich). Free-lance writer since '25; illustrated lecturer since '30, sometime lecturer appearing on platforms of National Geographic Society, American Museum of Natural History, Columbia University, University of Michigan, Chicago Museum of Natural History and others, and on radio and television. Contributor: Natural History Magazine, Nature Magazine, American Forests, Outdoor Life, Field and Stream, National Geographic Magazine, Fisherman's Encyclopedia, Outdoor Life Cyclopedia. Outdoor ed Booth Newspapers Inc Detroit '26-46; field ed Outdoor Life Magazine since '46. Outdoor Writers Assn Am—Mich Outdoor Writers Assn. Annual award of Boone and Crockett Club in big game photography for Alaskan bear film '48. 353 Fourth Av., NYC 10.

18 EASTER, George Jones. Abrasives; Refractories; Silicon carbide. b'93. BS '15 (MIT). Fused cast refractories, crucibles for metal melting, ceramic engineering education, thermal conductivity. Issued about 60 patents relating to abrasives, refractories, furnaces. Research engr Carborundum Co Niagara Falls '20-47, dir '44-47; research engr Electro Refractories and Abrasives Corp since '47. Am Ceramic Soc—Electrochem Soc—ACS—AAAS—Inst Ceramic Engrs (pres '51-52)—Canadian, British ceramic socs. Electro Refractories and Abrasives Corp., Buffalo 19.   ''

19 EASTER, Stephen S. Control of stored products, insects, rodents and fungi. b'05. BS '27—MS '29 (U Minn). Organized international meeting of United Nations on control of stored products, insects, rodents and fungi at London England '47; on special mission of grain storage conditions Egypt and Italy '48; conducted School on Infestation Control in Europe '48. Editor: Preservation of Grains in Storage '48. Entomol FAO since '47. Food and Agriculture Organization of the United Nations, 1201 Connecticut, Washington 6.

20 EASTON, Jason Clark. Modern European history. b'92. BA '15 (Yale); MA '32 (Northwestern U); PhD '37 (U Wis). Author articles in field. Statistician in Chicago investment banks '25-31; asso prof W Va U since '38. Am Assn U Profs—AHA—W Va Hist Soc. History Department West Virginia University, Morgantown, W. Va.

21 EASTON, Robert Dean. Book binding. b'94. BS (ME) (U Cal). Design and development high-speed equipment for bookbinding; improvement of gathering machines, catalog binders, automatic stitching machines, mailing, casing-in, rounding, backing, and back lining machines; development book trimmer for stitching machines; collaborated in design side sewing machine and stitcher feeder. Holds patents in field. Printing press design Brewer-Stone Inc '24-27; design and development engr R R Donnelley & Sons Co '27-44; cons engr graphic arts industry '44-47; chief engr Pacific Press Inc since '47. Soc Automotive Engrs. H: 413 W. Gurdon Av., San Gabriel, Cal.

22 EASTWOOD, Sidney Kingman. Mosses (Buxbaumia); Numismatics (British token coinage, bibliography); Liturgics. b'90. ME '13 (Cornell U); student (U Pittsburgh). Made studies of rare mosses, especially genus Buxbaumia, and their habitats, increased known sources Buxbaumia from four to fifty, authenticated by specimens deposited Carnegie Museum; studies of British token coinage including coffee tokens of Ceylon, booksellers', bank, Bath tokens, and others; comparative study various English, Scottish, American versions of Book of Common Prayer with Book of 1549 and pre-Reformation missals and service books, including changes and probable errors in Trinity Preface. Author articles in field. With Am Bridge Co Pittsburgh since '16, asst to vp. Am Soc Mammalogists—Am Geog Soc—Pa Acad Sci—Medieval Acad Am—Western Pa Numismatic Soc (vp '38, pres '46-48)—Am Numismatic Soc. Frick Building, Pittsburgh.

23 EASUM, Chester Verne. German history. b'94. AB '14 (Knox Coll); AB, AM '20 (Oxford U); PhD '28 (U Wis). Author: The Americanization of Carl Schurz '29; Carl Schurz; Vom Deutschen Einwanderer Zum Amerikanischen Staatsmann '37; Prince Henry of Prussia, Brother of Frederick the Great '42; Half-Century of Conflict '52. With University Wisconsin since '30, prof since '41. Am Hist Assn—Am Acad Political and Social Science. 115 N. Allen St., Madison, Wis.

24 EATON, Frank Morris. Cotton plant physiology; Boron and salt toxicity to plants. b'93. Student '11-13 (U Neb)—'15-16 (George Washington U); BS '23—MS '25—PhD '26 (U Minn). Special cropping advisor Food and Agricultural Organization of United Nations '47-48 Egypt, Syria, Iraq, Lebanon, Turkey, also salinity consultant on causes and remedies of salinity and alkali problem along Indus and tributary rivers in Pakistan; studies of relation of water quality to irrigation developments and selection crop plants; growth and fruiting; UN '50 Haiti opinion on reclamation of artibonite plain. Prin physiol cotton plant US Dept Agr since '49. AAAS(F)—Am Soc Plant Physiol—Bot Soc Am—Am

Soc Agron—Sigma Xi—Gamma Sigma Delta. Experiment Station, College Station, Tex.

10 EATON, Herbert N(elson). Hydraulics of building drainage systems. b'92. AB (civil engring) '16 (Worcester Poly Inst); AM '23 (Johns Hopkins); John R Freeman traveling scholarship in hydraulics '27. Designed National Hydraulics Laboratory at National Bureau of Standards '29-31. Co-author: Aeronautic Instruments '27. Author articles in field. With Nat Bur Standards '19-26, chief aeronautic instruments sect '23-26; development engr W A Baum Co '26-27; with Nat Bur Standards since '27, chief Hydraulics Sect from '33. Am Soc San Engrs—Am Soc ME—Wash Acad Sci—Wash Philos Soc—AAAS—Am Geophys Union—Internat Assn Hydraulic Structures Research—Sigma Xi—Tau Beta Pi. National Bureau of Standards, Washington 25.

11 EATON, Hubert. Metal engineering. Cemetery development. b'81. AB '02—LLD (hon) '37 (William Jewell Coll, Liberty Mo.). Known as "The Builder" of Forest Lawn Memorial Park, Glendale Calif; created a new park-plan of development of cemeteries, originated ('16) name "Memorial Park" as applied thereto. Author articles in field. Asst chief chem, Boston & Mont Consol Copper Co, Great Falls, Mont; chief metall chem, Teziutlan Copper Co, Mexico; gen mgr Adaven Mining & Smelting Co, Nev; pres Am Security & Fidelity Corp; pres and gen mgr Forest Lawn Co, Glendale, Calif; chmn Bd Forest Lawn Life Ins Co. 837 Greenway Drive, Beverly Hills, Cal.

12 EATON, James Tucker. Chemicals (Surface active). b'07. AB (Central Coll); AM '31—PhD '34 (U Ill). Research and development in alkyl aryl sulfonates, sulfated esters, sulfated hydroxy amides, alkyl aryl sulfopropionic esters, alkyl aryl sulfonamides, application of detergents and wetting agents, nonionic agents of Polyoxyethylene ester and fatty acid alkylolamine condensate type, textile fiber lubricants, leather oils, emulsifiable cutting oils, impregnated hydraulic and industrial leathers. Contributor: Houghton Line '42 et seq. Issued several patents in field. Research chem Nat Aniline Div Allied Chem and Dye Corp '34-37; group leader textile specialties A F Houghton and Co '38-45, mgr research '46-49, dir research and dir since '50. ACS—AAAS—Am Leather Chemists Assn. 303 W. Lehigh Av., Phila. 33.

13 EATON, Joseph Wechsler. Urban and rural sociology; Psychological warfare; Land settlement; Social planning and ecology. b'19. BS '40 (Cornell U); PhD '47 (Columbia). Specialist in city planning and ecology. Author: Exploring Tomorrow's Agriculture '43; Research Guide for Cooperative Farming '42; also articles in field. Asst prof sociol Wayne U since '49. Dir US Pub Health study Cultural and Psychiatric Factors in the Mental Health of the Hutterites since '49. Served US Army psychol warfare '42-46. Editor: Regensburger Post newspaper of US Army in Germany for civilian population '45-46. Am Sociol Soc—Rural Sociol Soc. Department of Sociology, Wayne University, Det. 1.

14 EATON, Merrill T(homas). Measurement and research in education. b'98. BS '25 (Ind State Teachers Coll); MS '30—EdD '32 (Ind U). Research in learning, especially broad studies of abilities and achievement of school children elementary and secondary. Studies of the abilities and achievement of students enrolled in certain state colleges for Negroes. Extensive

travel and study of various aspects of the eucational program in Mexico. Research and Measurement consultant to the State Department of Public Instruction. Author: The Relation of Retention of Speed of Learning '39; One Hundred and Fifty Years of Arithmetic Textbooks '45; also articles in field. With Ind U since '30, now prof sch edn and dir bur measurement. Nat Edn Assn—Am Research Assn—Am Psychol Assn—Midwestern Psychol Assn—Nat Vocational Guidance Assn—Kappa Delta Phi. Indiana University, Bloomington, Ind.⊚

15 EATON, Paul Blaine. Textile machinery. b'92. AB '17 (UNC) LLB '23. Preparation and prosecution of patent applications on textile machinery, including full-fashioned and circular knitting machines. With Eaton & Bell since '24, now sr member. 904 Johnston Bldg., Charlotte, N.C.

16 EATON, Samuel Edward, Jr. Radioactive tracers (Industrial applications); Electropolishing; Printing methods. b'15. Student '33-34 (Davison Coll); BA '37 (Wesleyan U); grad study '39-47 (MIT). Application of radioactive tracer techniques in research on corrosion, electroplating, manufacture of coke; granted patents on methods of electropolishing silver, copper, brass and cadmium; developed new methods of printing. Contributor: Nucleonics '51, Industrial and Safety Problems of Nuclear Technology '50; Metals Technology '48; Metal Finishing '47. Group leader Arthur D Little Inc since '37. Mem Isotope Distribution Com US AEC. ACS—Am Optical Soc—Electro-chemical Soc. 30 Memorial Dr., Cambridge 42, Mass.

17 EBEN, Christian Frederick, Jr. Dams. b'03. Student (Keystone Inst). Design and construction. Wells Engineering Co Reading '24-32; engr County of Berks Reading '32-36; engr Nat Park Service Birdsboro Pa '36-42; now chief engr Michael Baker Jr Inc. Nat Soc Professional Engrs—Am Soc CE. Professional engr Pa. Michael Baker, Jr., Inc., Harrisburg, Pa.

18 EBERHARD, Wolfram. China (Folktales, ancient and modern social structure, ancient astronomy and science); Turkey (Folktales, ancient and modern social structure, early Chinese histories). b'09. PhD '33 (U Berlin). Collected more than 3,000 Chinese folktales, research in assimilation and acculturation of foreign tribes into Chinese society, collected 3,000 Turkish folktales, field work in China and Turkey. Author: Kultur und Siedlung der Randvölker Chinas '42; Lokalkulturen im alten China (2 vols) '43; Chinese Fairy-tales and Folk-tales '37; A History of China '50; Contributions to the Astronomy of the Han Dynasty (3 parts) '33-34; also articles in field. Research asst Mus Anthrop (Berlin) '29-34; fieldwork in China, asst prof Nat U (Peking) and Hopei Province Med Coll '34-35; dir Asiatic Dept Mus Anthrop (Leipzig) '36; traveled China and Japan '37; prof U Ankara '37-48; with U Calif since '48, professor since '52. Field research in Southern Turkey on Guggenheim Grant '51-52. Internat Soc Oriental Research California, Department of Sociology, Berkeley 4.

19 EBERZ, (William) Ferdinand. Petroleum emulsions. b'09. BS '31—PhD '34 (Cal Tech). Resolution of petroleum emulsions into their components by means of electrical fields or chemical demulsifiers. Development coloring and processing glass fabrics. Chief chem Petroleum Rectifying Co Long Beach Cal '37-47; research chem Tretolite Co of Cal '47-49. ACS—Sigma Xi. H: 1023 Wapello St., Altadena, Cal.†

20 EBY, Edwin Harold. American transcendentalists; Nineteenth century American literature. b'00. PhB '23 (U Chicago); PhD '27 (U Washington). Research and writing on American transcendentalists, Emerson, Thoreau, Hawthorne, Melville and Whitman, American romantic critics 1815-1860. Editor: Main Currents in American Thought (vol 3) '30. Prof Eng dept U Washington since '47. Modern Lang Assn—Pacific Coast Philol Assn (chmn Am lit sect '40)—Phi Beta Kappa. University of Washington, Seattle 5.

21 ECCLES, Mark (Williams). Shakespeare, Elizabethan Drama. b'05. BA '27 (Oberlin Coll); MA '28—PhD '32 (Harvard); student '29-30 (U Coll London). Author: Christopher Marlowe in London '34. Co-author: Thomas Lodge and Other Elizabethans '33. Editor: Othello '46; Twelfth Night '48. Asst to prof Eng U Wis since '36. Mod Lang Assn — Folger Shakespeare Library (adv council). Am Council Learned Socs fellow '33-34; research fellow Huntington Library '40-41. Bascom Hall, Madison 6, Wis.

22 ECHOLS, Dorothy Jung. Stratigraphy (Gulf Coast); Micropaleontology; Ostracodes. b'16. AB '36 (NYU); AM '38 (Columbia). Specializing tertiary ostracodes; Stratigraphic correlations. Co-author articles: (with D S Malkin) Transgressive marine overlap; Regressive marine offlap and overlap-offlap; Wilcox (Eocene) stratigraphy, A key to production. Geol Am Republic Corp Houston '38-'41; filing and geol fgn div Tex Co NYC '41-42; cons Pond Fork Oil and Gas Co since '46; research asso micropaleontology Washington U St Louis. Am Assn Petroleum Geol—Soc Econ Paleontologists and Mineral—Sigma Xi. Box 535 R.R. 10, Ferguson 21, Mo.

23 ECKARDT, Robert Edward. Industrial toxicology and hygiene. b'16. BS '37 (Antioch Coll); MS '39—PhD '40—MD '43 (Western Res U). Research on occupational cancer; Toxicity of insecticides, petroleum products; Vitamins (Riboflavin). Spl research physician Standard Oil Co NJ '48-50; med research dir Standard Oil Development Co., Esso Research Center Linden NJ since '51. Am Bd Internal Med (diplomate)—AMA—Am Assn Indsl Physicians and Surgeons—Am Indsl Hygiene Assn—Sigma Xi—Alpha Omega Alpha. Standard Oil Development Co., Esso Labs., Esso Research Center, P.O Box 51, Linden, N.J.

24 ECKEL, Edwin B(utt). Geology (Engineering, quicksilver deposits). b'06. BS '28 (Lafayette Coll); MS '30 (U Ariz). Examined entire quicksilver industry of Italy '45; examined geology and mineral resources of Paraguay '52. Author of articles in field. Geologist United States Geological Survey since '30, chief engring geol branch since '45. Geol Soc Am(F)—Mineral Soc Am(F)—Soc Econ Geology—Geology Society Washington—Colo Sci Soc(pres '50-51)—Colo Engring Council—New Mex Geol Soc (hon life)—Sigma Xi—Phi Kappa Phi. Engineering Geology Branch, U.S. Geological Survey, Denver Federal Center, Denver.†

25 ECKEL, Paul E(dward). History of the Far East. b'08. AB '29 (U Miami); AM '36—PhD '41 (U So Calif). Japanese language and general Far Eastern History since 1500 with special emphasis on cultural and economic approach. Author: Revival of Western Economic Interest in Japan from 1800 to 1855 '40; The Far East since 1500 '47; also articles in field. Prof social studies U Commerce Kobe Japan '29-30; prof Eng and Hist Coll of Fgn Langs Nara Japan '30-35; part time lecturer econs and hist Coll Commerce Tarumi Japan '30-35; asst prof History U Miami '36-43; polit analyst and chief Japan desk fgn broadcast intelligence service Fed Communications Comm '44-45; Far Eastern desk Office Strategic Services '45-46; chief Eastern Asiatic desk Strategic Services Unit, War Dept '46; spl lecturer in Far Eastern Hist U Pa '46-48; cons on Far Eastern Affairs United States government since '48. AHA—Far Eastern Assn—Am Acad Polit and Social Sci—Phi Beta Kappa—Phi Kappa Phi—Phi Alpha Theta. H: 9112 Lindale Dr., Bethesda, Md.⊙

10 ECKELS, John H. Embalming chemicals. b'94. Student '13-17 (Lehigh U, U Pa). Author: Modern Mortuary Science '44. With Eckels & Co Phila since '19, pres and owner since '37; teacher Eckels Coll Mortuary Sci Inc Phila '23-28, dean since '28, pres and owner since '37. Franklin Inst—Am Chem Soc. 231-35 N. 16th St., Phila 2.

11 ECKER, Enrique E(dward). Medical biology. b'87. Student (Wageningen the Netherlands); PhD '17 (U Chicago); post grad '24 (Lausanne) '27 (Cambridge). Research in immunology, bacteriology and experimental pathology. With Western Res U since '18, prof immunology since '42; vis immunologist and bact U Hosps Cleveland City and St Luke Hosps; asso med dir Cleveland Regional Blood Center Am Nat Red Cross since '51. Soc Microbiologists—Soc Clin Path Am Assn Immunologists—Soc Am Bact—Am Chem Soc—Am Soc Exptl Path—AAAS—Soc Exptl Biol and Med—NY Acad Sci. Inst of Path Western Reserve University, 2085 Adelbert Rd., Cleve 6.⊙

12 ECKER, Lawrence. Linguistics. b'01. PhD '33 (U Berne Switzerland). Research in Mexican Indian languages (Otomi, Aztec, Maya and Tarascan) for Instituto de Investigaciones Linguisticas Mexico City. Prof comparative Indoeuropean linguistics U Mexico Mexico City '36-38; research analyst specializing geography vegetation economics Soviet Union, Intelligence div Dept of Army, Washington '41-50. Linguistic Soc Am. 7969 Melrose Av., Los Angeles 46.†

13 ECKERT, Ernst Rudolf Georg. Gas turbines (Cooling); Steam boilers; Heat transfer; Jet propulsion. b'04. Ing '27—Dr Ing '31 (U Prague); Dr habil '38 (U Danzig). Research on thermal radiation of steam boilers and furnaces. heat transfer at high velocities in gas turbines and rockets, aerodynamics of gas turbines, designed Zehnder-Mach interferometer for use in research on heat transfer and turbulence, cooling problems in gas turbines. Granted patents on steam boilers, air conditioning and turbine cooling. Author: Technische Strahlungsaustausch rechungen '37; Warme-und-Stoffaustausch '49; Introduction to Transfer of Heat and Mass '50; also 97 articles in field. Lecturer Univ Danzig '34-38; chief thermodynamics sect Aeronautical Research Inst 38-45; prof and dir Inst Thermodynamics U Prague '43-45; research engr Wright-Patterson Air Force Base '45-49; cons Nat Adv Com Aeronautics '49-51; prof mech engring U Minn since '51. ASM E. Institute of Technology, University of Minnesota, Mpls. 7.

14 ECKERT, J. Presper, Jr. Computers (Automatic high speed). b'19. BS '41—MS '43 (U Pa). Holder numerous US patents mostly digital computer field. Author articles in field. Partner-

ship with Mauchly known as Eckert-Mauchly Computer Corp now Remington Rand Eckert-Mauchly Division for purpose designing and building large scale all electronic high speed digital computing devices since '46. Inst Radio Engrs—Sigma Xi. 2300 W. Allegheny Av., Phila. 29.

15 ECKERT, John Edward. Apiculture; California honeys, nectar and pollen plants. b'95. BS '16—MS '17—PhD '31 (Ohio State U). Author articles in field. Prof entomol and apiculturist U Calif since '45. Entomol Soc Am—Am Assn Econ Entomol—Sigma Xi. University of California, Davis, Calif.†

16 ECKERT, Ralph. Parent, sex and marriage education; Family relations; Adolescence. b'06. AB '31—PhD '40 (U Calif); AM '34 (U So Calif). President Northern and Southern California Councils on Family Relations; committee chairman National Council on Family Relations; member technical advisory committee Conference on Family Life '48. Author articles in field. Cons in Parent Edn Calif State Dept Edn since '46. 809 State Building, Los Angeles 12.

17 ECKERT, Wallace J. Scientific computation; Celestial mechanics. b'02. AB '25 (Oberlin Coll); MA '26 (Amherst Coll), '25 (Univ of Chicago), '28 (Columbia U); PhD '31 (Yale). Author: Punched Card Methods in Scientific Computation '40. Instr Columbia U '27, asst prof '32, prof '40; dir US Nautical Almanac US Naval Obs '40-45; dir dept pure sci Internat Bus Machines Corp since '45; dir Watson Sci Computing Laboratory since '45; prof celestial mechanics Columbia U '46. Am Astron Soc (councillor)—Internat Astron Union—Washington Acad Sci—Am Math Soc. 612 W. 116th St., NYC. H: 216 Leonia Av., Leonia, N.J.

18 ECKEY, Eddy William. Oils (Chemistry). b'02. Student '19-20 (U Ia); '20-22 (Principia Coll); AB '23 (Wash U); MA '26 (Harvard). Research on fats and oils; directed interesterification in glycerides. Holds patents in field. Author articles: Oil and Soap '46; An Oxygen Absorption Method for Examination of Fat '48, and others. Research chem Procter & Gamble Co '26-45, in charge oil research lab '30-45; operator E W Eckey Research Lab Cincinnati since '46. Am Chem Soc—Am Oil Chemists Soc—AAAS—Nat Farm Chermurgic Council. E W Eckey Research Laboratory, 338 Crescent Av., Cin. 15.

19 ECKHARDT, Henry. Pilot plant design. b'05. BS '27 (Cooper Union Inst Tech). Development and design small plants for processing industry; special equipment for operation and test purposes in pilot plants. Staff engr pilot plant development Lithaloys Corp '45-46; design engr Squibb '46-48; cons engr '48-51; project engr Chem Plants Div Blaw Knox Constrn Co since '51. Am Inst Chems—Nat Soc Profl. Engrs. 930 Duquesne, Pitts. 22.

20 ECKHARDT, Robert C. Maize breeding. b'13. BS '36 (U Ill); MS '38—PhD '44 (Ia State Coll). Research on maize breeding for South and Corn Belt of US) development inbred lines of maize prepotent for high yield, resistant to lodging, insects and diseases. In charge Ia corn performance tests '37; asst Ia corn breeding program '38-41; in charge corn breeding program Tenn '41-43, Miss since '43; cons Econ Cooperation Adminstrn and Office European Econ Coop on corn breeding Europe and Near East '49-50. Am Soc Agron—Genetics Soc Am—Biometrics Soc—AAAS—Sigma Xi—Alpha Zeta—Phi Kappa Phi. Box 486, State College, Miss.

21 ECKIS, Rollin (Pollard). Petroleum geology and stratigraphy in California; Hydrology. b'05. AB '27 (Pomona Coll); MS '30—research fellow '27-29 (Calif Inst Tech); research fellow '29-30 (Claremont Coll). Engineering geologist in charge ground water studies State California Division Water Resources South Coastal Basin Investigation '30-34. Author articles in field. Petroleum geol The Tex Co in Calif '34-37; dist geol San Joaquin Valley Calif Richfield Oil Corp '37-43, asst chief geol '43-46, chief geol since '46. Am Assn Petroleum Geol—Geol Soc Am(F)—Am Geophy Union—Sigma Xi.

22 ECKLER, A(lbert) Ross. Population and labor-force statistics. b'01. BA '22 (Hamilton Coll); MA '28—PhD '34 (Harvard). Adviser sixth International Conference Labor Statisticians International Labor Office '47; United States delegate to 28th meeting International Statistical Institute New Delhi '51. Author articles in field. Statisn, dir statis lab Harvard Econ Soc Cambridge '24-31; instr pub util econs Harvard Bus Sch Boston '31-35; chief spl inquiries, asst dir resch WPA Washington '35-39; chief econ statistics population div, asst chief population div, chief spl surveys div Bur Census '39-45, chief social sci analyst '45-47, dep dir since '49. Am Statis Assn(F)—International Population Union—Am Econ Assn—Population Assn America Am Nat Bur Econ Research (conf research income and wealth)—Phi Beta Kappa. Bureau of the Census, Washington 25. H: 3643 Brandywine St., N.W., Washington 8.

23 ECKMAN, James Russell. Medical and scientific editing; History of science and medicine; Typographic research. b'08. BA '32—seminars in field '39-43 (U Minn); MA '44—PhD '46—seminars in field '43-45 (Georgetown U). Research in history medicine of frontier, development science University Padua 1250-1600, history medicine Minnesota, Anglo-American hostility medical literature 19th century, life Jerome Carden 1501-1576, early addresses Sir William Osler; typography and typographic design. Author: Jerome Cardan '46; Development of Science at the University of Padua 1250-1600 (treatise) '45; also articles in field. Asso editor The Journal-Lancet Minneapolis '38-38; asso editor div pub Mayo Clinic Rochester since '38. Medical intelligence officer med intelligence div preventive med service Office Surgeon Gen US Army Wash '43-45. Am Hist Assn—Medieval Acad Am—Econ Hist Assn—Hist Sci Soc—Am Inst of Graphic Arts—Miss Valley Hist Assn—South Hist Assn—AAAS. Mayo Clinic, Rochester. H: 921 8th Av., S.W., Rochester, Minn.†

24 EDDY, C(lifford) O(tis). Insecticides; Fungicides; Pest control. b'94. AB '20—BSc '20—MSc '23—PhD '29 (O State U). Dir research Niagara Chem Div Food Machinery Chem Corp Midleport NY since '44. Niagara Chemical Division, Food Machinery and Chemical Corp., Middleport, N.Y.

25 EDDY, Milton Walker. Identification of hair, fur, and wool in criminal cases; Determination of paternity from hair. b'84. BS '10—MS '12 (Northwestern U); PhD '28 (U Pa). Expert testimony in crime cases involving hair identification since '34. Author articles: Hair Classification '38; Technique in Hair, Fur and Wool Identification '41. AAAS—Am Assn Zool—Pa Acad Sci—Sigma Xi. Dickinson College, Carlisle, Pa.

26 EDDY, Samuel. Microbiology; Aquatic biology; Limnology; Comparative anatomy. b'97. BA '24 (James

Millikin U); '24 (U Wash); MA '25—PhD '29 (U Ill). Limnological research on Minnesota lakes; research on deep water fishes and plankton of Lake Superior; consulting biologist Minnesota emergency conservation work '36-37, Minnesota Department Conservation fisheries investigations '37-40. Co-author: Guide to the Study of the Anatomy of the Dogfish Shark, Necturus, and the Cat (with C P Oliver and J P Turner) '47; Atlas for Comparative Anatomy (with C P Oliver) '47; Northern Fishes (with T Surber) '47; Comparative Anatomy: An Introduction to the Vertebrates (with L A Adams) '48; Taxonomic Keys to the Common Animals of Minnesota (with A C Hodson) '47; also articles in field. Asst prof zool U Minn '29-38, asso prof '38-44, prof since '44. Am Microscopical Soc—Ecol Soc Am—Am Fisheries Soc—Limnol Soc Am—Sigma Xi. University of Minnesota, Department of Zoology, Minneapolis.☉

10 EDELMAN, Norman B. Feathers; Glass wool; Cotton batting; Wool batting; Rubber bonded hairs; Spanish moss; Kapok; Milkweed floss; Plastics (Molded); Adhesives; Glues: Textiles (Organic finishes). b'12. BS '35 (Phila Coll Pharm and Sci); (Phila Textile Inst); (U Pa, Drexel Inst Tech, Temple U). Research and development on feathers and filling materials, including method of imparting permanent curl into chicken feathers, chicken feather yarn and fabric, chicken feather fiberglass mixture; glues for musical instruments, special adhesives and sealers. Granted patents in field. Textile tech Phila QM Depot '42-48; dir Phila Research Labs '48-50; materials engr Frankford Arsenal since '50. ASTM—ACS—Am Inst Phys. Frankford Arsenal, Bridge and Tacony Sts., Phila. 37.

11 EDGAR, Samuel Allen. Parasitology (Poultry). b'16. BA '37 (Sterling Coll); student '34-35 (Fresno State Teachers Coll); MS '39 (Kan State Coll); PhD '44 (U Wis). Author articles in field. Research asst zool and veterinary science depts U Wis '41-44; animal path poultry dept of Ala Agrl Expt Sta Ala Poly Inst since '46; served US Army '44-46, as parasitol on Saipan '44-45, CO of 17th Malaria survey detachment in the Philippines '45-46, chief entomol and parasitol depts and Theater malariologist 19th Med Gen Lab Manila '46. Tour of duty with US Public Health Department in Tahiti in connection with filarasis of man. American Society Parasitology American Micro Soc—Poultry Sci—Philippine Malaria Soc (bd dirs life)—Worlds Poultry Congress—AAAS—Sigma Xi—Gamma Sigma Delta—Am Soc Trop Medicine—Am Soc Zool. Poultry Department, Alabama Polytechnic Institute, Auburn, Ala.

12 EDGECOMBE, Samuel Wheeler. Vegetable and flower seed growing; Fruit, vegetable and flower breeding; Apple orchards; Thin wood pruning. b'07. BSA '30 (U Manitoba); MSc '31—PhD '36 (Ia State Coll). All-American selections vegetable judge '46-47. Author articles in field. Head and prof hort Utah State Agrl Coll since '47. AAAS—Am Soc Hort Sci—Agrl Inst Can—Western Can Soc Hort—Am Pomol Soc—Soc Econ Entomol—Am Hort Soc—Ia Acad Sci—Ia State Hort Soc—Utah State Hort Soc—Sigma Xi. Department of Horticulture, Utah State Agricultural College, Logan, Utah.☉

13 EDGELL, George Harold. History of art (American architecture, Sienese painting). b'87. AB '09—PhD '13—Art D (hon) '48 (Harvard). fellow '10-12 (Am Acad in Rome). Author: The American Architecture of Today '28; A History of Sienese Painting '32. Co-author: A History of Architecture '18; also articles in field. Dir Mus Fine Arts Boston since '35. Am Acad Arts Sci(F)—Archaeol Inst Am—Coll Art Assn Am—Phi Beta Kappa (pres Harvard chapt '40-42). Decorated Chevalier of Legion of honor '37. Museum of Fine Arts, Boston 15.☉

14 EDGERTON, Franklin. Indologist; Sanskrit language and literature; India (Philosophy, religion, culture); Comparative Indio-European linguistics. b'85. AB '05 (Cornell); fellow in Sanskrit '07-09—PhD '09 (Johns Hopkins); (hon) MA '26 (Yale). Research and travel in India '26-27, '38. Author: The K-Suffixes of Indo-Iranian '11; The Panchatantra Reconstructed (2 vols) '24; The Bhagavad Gita or Song of the Blessed One '25; Vikramas Adventures or the Thirty-two Tales of the Throne (2 vols) '26; The Mimansa Nyapa Prakasa '29; The Elephant Lore of the Hindus; The Bhagavad Gita (transl and interpretation) '44; Buddhist Hybrid Sanskrit Grammar, Dictionary and Reader (3 vols) '53. Editor: The Mahâbhârata, Book 2 '44; also articles in field. Salisbury '26-46, Sterling prof Sanskrit comp philol Yale '46. Bhandarkar Oriental Research Inst Poona India (hon)—Bihar Research Soc Patna India (hon)—Am Acad Arts Sci(F)—Am Philos Soc—Am Oriental Soc (corr sec '15-19, vp'26-28)—Linguistic Soc Am (pres '34)—Royal Asiatic Soc of Great Britain (hon)—Phi Beta Kappa. 1007 Sheridan St., Laramie, Wyo.☉

15 EDGERTON, Harold Eugene. High speed photography apparatus. b'03. BSc '25 (U Neb); MSc '27—DSc '31 (Mass Inst Tech). Invented stroboscopic high-speed motion and still photography apparatus. Author: Flash! '39; also articles in field. Prof elec engring Mass Inst Tech. AIEE—Am Phys Soc—Sigma Xi. Awarded medal of Royal Photog Soc, Modern Pioneer Award and Potts Medal of Franklin Inst. 205 School St., Belmont, Mass.☉

16 EDGERTON, William Franklin. Egyptology (Ancient Egyptian language, history and law, Demotic, Coptic). b'93. AB '15 (Cornell); PhD '22 (U Chicago); '19 (U Pa); '23-24 (Columbia); '27 (U Munich). Archeological survey in Mesopotamia and Syria for Oriental Institute '20; field work in Egypt for Oriental Institute, University of Chicago, '26-29, '31-33. Author: Notes on Egyptian Marriage, Chiefly in the Ptolemaic Period '31; The Thutmosid Succession '33; Medinet Habu Graffiti Facsimiles '37. Co-author: Historical Records of Ramses III, The Texts in Medinet Habu '36; Michigan Papyri from Tebtunis (part II) '44; also articles in field. Chmn dept Oriental lang and lit U Chicago since '48. AHA—Am Oriental Soc (pres '44-45)—Linguistic Soc Am—Egypt Exploration Soc—Phi Beta Kappa. Oriental Institute, University of Chicago, Chicago 37.☉

17 EDINGER, Tilly. Brain (Fossil); Vertebrate paleontology. b'97. Student (U Heidelberg, U Munich); PhD '21 (U Frankfurt); ScD (hon) '50 (Wellesley Coll). Author: Die Fossilen Gehirne '29; Evolution of the Horse Brain '48; also articles in field. Research paleontologist Museum of Comparative Zool Harvard Coll since '40. Soc Verteb Paleon—Soc Study Evolution—Sigma Xi—Senckenbergische Naturforschende Gesellschaft. Guggenheim fellow '43-44. Museum of Comparative Zoology, Harvard College, Cambridge 38, Mass.†

18 EDISON, Oskar E(dwin). A-C circuits and machines; Power transmission. b'92. BSc '14—MSc '15—EE '24 (U Neb); SPEE '28 (U Pittsburgh). Research on regulation of open-delta connected transformers, phase advancer for power factor correction, grid-controlled thyratron rectifier, cathode ray oscillograph. Co-author: (with Norris) Electrical Engineering Laboratory Practice '28. Asst prof elec engring dept U Neb '19-25, asso prof '25-44, prof since '44; summer employment Central Neb Pub Power & Irrigation Dist since '45. AIEE(F)—ASEE—Neb Engring Soc—Sigma Xi—Sigma Tau. University of Nebraska, Electrical Engineering Department, Lincoln 8, Neb.

19 EDLER, George C(hristian). Seed statistics and marketing specialisms. b'89. BS '11 (U Ill). Delegate to International Institute of Agriculture Rome Italy '24; collaborated with W A Wheeler in devising and starting seed verification service in US Department of Agriculture '27. Author article: The Use of Explosives in Blasting Stumps and Boulders, in Breaking up Hard Pan, and in Tree Planting (article awarded first prize by Dupont to student in Midwestern Universities '10); The Farm Boy of Tomorrow (first prize students U Ill '09); also others in field. Traveling seed salesman and buyer Albert Dickinson Co Minneapolis '12-16; seed marketing splst and principal agrl statist Bur Agrl Econs US Dept Agr since '16. Am Statis Assn—Alpha Zeta. Bureau of Agricultural Economics, U.S. Department of Agriculture, Washington 25. H: 5428 31st St., Washington 15.

20 EDMINSTER, Frank C(uster). Soil conservation; Wildlife management; Land-use study; Ecology. b'03. BS '26—MS '30 (Cornell U). Supervisor game management New York State Conservation Department '30-37, research on ruffed grouse, wildlife ecology, development and management of game lands; regional biologist United States Soil Conservation Service since '37, research and program planning in soil conservation biology, studies of land-use biology. Author: The Ruffed Grouse '47; Fish Ponds for the Farm '47. Co-author (with G Bump, R Darrow, W Crissey): The Ruffed Grouse—Life History, Propagation and Management '47. Wildlife Soc—Soil Conservation Soc Am. U.S. Soil Conservation Service, Upper Darby, Pa.

21 EDMINSTER, Lynn Ramsay. Tariffs; International trade. b'93. AB '16 (Harvard U); PhD '30 (Brookings Inst). Principal economist, Division Foreign Service, US Deptartment Agriculture '31-33; chief Import-Export Division Agriculture Adjustment Administration '33-36; chief economic analyst, Division Trade Agreements, US Department of State '36-38; special assistant to Secretary of State '38-42; member, vice chairman US Tariff Commission since '42; chairman, Committee for Reciprocity Information since '42; member, Filipino Rehabilitation Commission '44-48; US delegation Preparatory Commn for International Conference on World Trade and Employment, London '46, Geneva '47. Author: The Cattle Industry and the Tariff '26. Co-author: International Control of Raw Materials '30; World Trade Barriers in Relation to American Agriculture '33. Prof political science Kansas State Normal University '17-18, member econ staff United States Shipping Board '19, US Tariff Commn '19-22; adj prof Sch Fgn Service Georgetown U '21-33; mem econ staff Brookings Instn '22-30; exchange prof commerce and bus administrn U Va '26-27; adj prof Grad Sch Am U '34-38. Am Econ Assn. U.S. Tariff Commission, Washington.☉

10 EDMISTER, W a y n e Clinite. Process engineering; Thermodynamics; Petroleum refining. b'09. BS (Mech engring) '32—CE '42 (Okla A&M Coll); M (Mech engring) '34 (Cornell U). Design aviation gasoline, toluene, synthetic rubber plants; research thermal and catalytic petroleum refining. Author articles: Applications of thermodynamics, fractional distillation. Chem engr Whiting Research Lab Standard Oil Co Ind '34-43; process engr Foster Wheeler Corp NYC '44-47; prof chem engring Carnegie Inst Tech '48-51; res engr Cal Resch Corp since '52. Am Inst Chem Engrs—ACS —Sigma Xi—ASME.

11 EDMOND, Joseph Bailey. Vegetable crops. b'94. BS '23 (Mich State Coll); MS '24 (Ia State Coll); PhD '33 (U Md). Work in physiology and breeding of sweet potatoes; horticulture and vegetable crop production. Author: (with Alex Laurie) Fertilizers for Greenhouse and Garden Crops '29; (with A M Musser, F S Andrews) General Horticulture '41; (with G W Ware) Southern Vegetable Crops '37. Asso prof and asso hort Miss State Coll '31-35, Clemson Coll '35-44; agr specialist Fgn Econ Adm '44; asso hort Ga Agrl Expt Sta '45-46; chmn div agr Berry Schs Mt Berry Ga '46-47; asso hort La Agr Expt Sta '47-48; prof hort Miss State Coll since '48. AAAS(F)— Am Soc Hort Sci (sec so sect '36-46, vice-chmn '47-48, chmn '48-49)—Sigma Xi—Phi Kappa Phi. Department of Horticulture, State College, Miss.

12 EDMONDSON, W. Thomas. Ocean waves; Ecology of rotatoria. b'16. BS '38—PhD '42 (Yale); '38-39 (U Wis). Research in field at American Museum Natural History, Woods Hole Oceanographic Institution. Author articles in field. Lecturer biol Harvard '46-49; asso prof zool U Wash '51. Am Soc Zool—AAAS—Am Ecol Soc—Am Micros Soc—Am Soc Limnol Oceanog—Sigma Xi. Department of Zoology, University of Washington, Seattle.†

13 EDMONSTON, William Jesse. Geophysical exploration. b'00. BS '22 (SW Tex Tchrs Coll); MS '31 (S Methodist U). Research on positions for seismograph crews, topographical surveying, computation of records in geophysical exploration for petroleum. Surveyor-computer Nat Geophys Co '42-44; sr surveyor Sun Oil Co '44-45 engr Geotech Corp since '45. Soc Exploration Geophys. Geotechnical Corp., Postoffice Box 7166, Dallas 9.

14 EDMUNDS, George Francis. Mayflies, Ephemeroptera. b'20. BS '43—MS '46 (U Utah)—PhD '52 (U Mass). Author articles in field. Asst prof biol div U Utah since '45. Biol Soc Wash —Society Systematic Zoology—Entomol Soc Am—Entomol Soc Wash— Pacific Coast Entomol Soc—Sigma Xi. Department of Invertebrate Zool., University of Utah, Salt Lake City 1.†

15 EDMUNDS, Gerald Humfrey. Brass (Season cracking); Zinc (Metallurgy). b'04. BS (chem engring) '26 (U Colo); MS '29 (Yale); '37-38 (Princeton). Research on rolling, alloying, die casting, testing and structure of zinc and zinc base alloys. Granted patents on alloys. Research metall NJ Zinc Co '26-45; non-ferrous metall Am Brake Shoe Co since '45. AIMME— Inst Metals (London) — Sigma Xi. Metallurgy Department, American Brake Shoe Co., Mahwah, N.J.

16 EDMUNDS, Palmer Daniel. Procedures (Federal); Laws (Conflict); Laws (Administrative). b'90. AB '12 —LLD '45 (Knox Coll); LLB '15 (Harvard). Author: Edmunds Common Law Forms '31; Illinois Civil Practice Forms '23; Edmunds Federal Rules of Civil Procedure '38; Cyclopedia of Federal Procedure Forms '39. Co-author: (with W F Dodd) Illinois Appellate Procedure '29; Encyclopedia of Federal Procedure (2d edit) '44; Edmunds Conflict of Laws '48. Editor and compiler: Jones Illinois Statutes Annotated (vols 18-22) '24. Admitted Ill bar '15; commr Supreme Court Ill '29-32; lectr conflict of laws and Ill practice John Marshall Law Sch Chicago since '26, lectr on federal practice since '38; vis prof law Knox Coll since '44; compliance commr WPB and Civilian Prodn Adminstrn '44-47. Am Ill Chicago and Internat bar assns. 30 N. La Salle St., Chgo.◉

17 EDSALL, John Tileston. Biochemistry (Proteins, amino acids, spectroscopy, Raman effect, double refraction of flow, blood clotting). b'02. AB '23 —MD '28 (Harvard). Member ed board Journal of the American Chemical Society '48. Author articles in field. Editor: (with M L Anson) Advances in Protein Chemistry, 4 vols pub through '48. Tutor biochem sci Harvard since '28, asso prof biol chem since '38. NY Acad Sci(F)—Am Chem Soc (sec div biol chem '46-48, chmn '48-49)—Am Soc Biol Chem—Am Acad Arts Sci—AAAS —Sigma Xi. John Simon Guggenheim Memorial Found fellow Calif Inst Tech '40-41. Harvard University, 25 Shattuck St., Boston 15.◉

18 EDSON, Alden P(otter). Metallurgy (Steel, physical); Metal failures. b'14. BS '37 (U Kan). Alloy steel research and development, development of gaseous fluxes for brazing and power metallurgy applications, investigation in chemical and electrochemical processing of metals; studies of causes and prevention of metal failures, weldability and machinability of steels. Author: Weld Hardening and Steel Composition. Metall International Nickel Co '37-43; Hamilton Standard Div United Aircraft Corp since '43, chief metall '45-51, chief materials engr since '51. Am Soc Metals. Hamilton Standard Division, United Aircraft Corporation, Windsor Locks, Conn. H: 49 Mountain Rd., West Hartford, Conn.

19 EDSON, William Alden. Oscillators (Vacuum Tube); Cavity resonators (Microwave); Quartz Crystals. b'12. Summerfield scholar '33-34—grad fellow '34-35—BS '34—MS '35 (U Kan); Gordon McKay scholar '35-37—Sci Dr '37 (Harvard). Holder two patents on theory of linear oscillators, several patents on resonators. Prof elec engring Ga Inst Tech since '46. Am Phy Soc—Inst Radio Engrs—AAAS—Am Soc Engring Edn—Ga Soc Profl Engrs—Tau Beta Pi—Sigma Xi. Electronics Research Laboratory, Stanford U, Cal.

20 EDWARDS, Cecil Byron. Numismatics. b'84. Student '31-34 (Am Inst Banking). Authority and public speaker on rare coins and counterfeiting; appraiser old coins. Am Numismatic Assn. Fourth National Bank, Wichita, Kan. H: 406 N. Estelle, Wichita 8.

21 EDWARDS, Harlan Hammond. Earthquake engineering; Building project construction and planning. b'93. BS '17—CE '22 (U Ill). Member board of consulting engineers and architects investigating Long Beach earthquake of '33, research on earthquake in Western Washington '49. Cons engr since '27, specializing in advisory services as owner's representative and cons in planning and construction of building projects. Am Soc CE (chmn Seattle earthquake com '49-52)—Am Concrete Inst—Structural Engrs Assn Wash— Earthquake Engring Research Inst— Sigma Xi. 715 Hoge Bldg., Seattle 4.

H: 3509 W. Laurelhurst Dr., Seattle 5.

22 EDWARDS, Junius David. Aluminum; Aluminum paint and powder; Metals (Anodic coating); Film permeability (Gases). b'90. BS 12—ChemE '13 (U Minn). Author: Aluminum Paint and Powder '36. Co-author: Laboratory Glass Blowing (with Frary and Taylor) '28; The Aluminum Industry (with Frary and Jeffries) '30; also articles in field. Asst dir research Aluminum Co Am Aluminum Research Labs since '21. Am Chem Soc (Pittsburgh sect award '43)—Electro-chem Soc (vp '31-33, '35-37 and '39-41)—Am Inst Chem Engrs—Pa Chem Soc—Am Soc Heating Ventilating Engrs—Illuminating Engring Soc—Sigma Xi. Aluminum Research Laboratories, Aluminum Co of America, Box 772, New Kensington, Pa.

23 EDWARDS, Leroy Delos. Pharmacology; Toxicology; Pharmacognosy. b'97. BS '23 (U Wis); AM '31—PhD '36 (Western Reserve U). Research on action of soaps and drugs on human skin, drug action of new organic synthetics. Author articles in field. Instr Western Reserve U Cleveland '29-33, teaching fellow pharmacology '34-36, asst prof pharmacognosy and pharmacology '36-39, prof '39-40; prof pharmacognosy and pharmacology U Fla '40-45; prof pharmacology Purdue U Sch Pharmacy since '45. Am Pharm Assn— Phi Beta Kappa—Phi Kappa Phi—Sigma Xi. School of Pharmacy, Purdue University, Lafayette, Ind.

24 EDWARDS, Philip Rarick. Salmonella and related enteric bacteria. b'01. BS '22 (Ky U); PhD '25 (Yale). Associate editor Journal of Bacteriology since '45; research on streptococci and diseases of horses. Author articles in field. Prin bact Communicable Disease Center USPHS since '48. Soc Am Bact—Soc Exptl Biology and Med— Sigma Xi. USPHS research grant '45-48. Communicable Disease Center, U.S. Public Health Service, P.O. Box 185, Chamblee, Ga.

25 EDWARDS, Ray Lee. Mechanics; Liquid viscosities; Magnetism; Physics teaching (Methods). b'85. AB '08 (Oberlin Coll); BS '09 (O Wesleyan U); AM '11 (O State U); PhD '25 (U Ia). Asociate editor American Journal of Physics '45-48. Author articles in field. Prof and head dept physics Miami U Oxford O since '26. O Acad Sci(F, vp '33, '43, '48)—Am Phys Soc —Am Assn Physics Teachers—AAAS— Sigma Xi. Oersted medalist '45 for notable contbns to teaching physics. 414 E. Chestnut St., Oxford, O.◉

26 EDWARDS, Warrick Rigeley, Jr. Organic chemistry (Alicyclic and nitroso compounds, furans, ion-exchange resins, viscose process, okra seed oil); Sonar. b'01. BS '22—PhD '28 (Johns Hopkins). Research in furan compounds, alicyclic compounds, nitroso compounds, okra seed oil, properties of homologous series, use of synthetic resins in water treatment. Author articles in field. Chem US Indstl Chem Co '22-23, James P Hooper Mfg Co '23-24; with La State U Dept Chem since '28, prof since '42; L Cdr USNR, specialist in anti-submarine warfare, sonar tactics and devices '43-45. Sigma Xi— Omicron Delta Kappa—Am Chem Soc— AAAS—La Acad Sci. Department of Chemistry, Louisiana State University, Baton Rouge, La. H: 512 Cornell Av., Baton Rouge 14, La.

27 EELLS, John Shepard, Jr. Romantic and Victorian literature. b'06. BA '28 (Yale); LLB '31 (Stanford); MA '39—PhD '43 (U Calif). Prof Eng Sage Found, chmn dept Beloit Coll since '45. Mod Lang Assn—Coll Eng Assn—State

Hist Soc Wis—Wis Acad Sci Arts Letters—Phi Beta Kappa. Beloit College, Beloit, Wis. H: 757 Milwaukee Rd.

10 EERNISSE, James Guy. Water distribution; Water pumping equipment; Water wells; Hydraulic controls. b'86. BS (mech engring) '13 (U Wash). Research on water well construction, design, installation, maintenance and operation, hydraulic controls for wells, deep and large water well construction. Chief asst engr Tacoma City Water Div Dept Pub Utilities '22-51. 402 City Hall, Tacoma 2.

11 EGAN, James E(verett). Fats and oils; Soaps; Synthetic detergents; Glycerine. b'86. AB '08 (DePauw U); AM '10—PhD '12 (U Ill). Chem advancing to chem engr Procter & Gamble Co since '18. ACS—Am Inst Chem (F). Procter & Gamble Mfg. Co., Port Ivory, S.I., NY.

12 EGBERT, Donald Drew. History of architecture and art. b'02. AB '24—MFA '27 '27-29 (Princeton U). Author: The Tickhill Psalter and Related MSS '40; Princeton Portraits '47. Lecturer in ancient architecture Bryn Mawr Coll '30-31; instr art, archeol, architecture Princeton '29-34, asst prof '34-44, asso prof '44-46, prof since '46, curator Am art Art Mus since '45, exec soc Program in Am Civilization '42-44, acting chmn '44-45. Soc for Am Studies(F)—Medieval Acad Am (Haskins Medal '43). 233 McCormick Hall, Princeton, N.J.

13 EGE, Otto. Medieval manuscripts. b'88. Grad '11 Pa Mus Schl Indsl Arts); '10 (NYU)—Europe summers '11, '21, '25, '28. Organized traveling exhibits of medieval manuscripts, early printing, rare Bibles; private press printing; several large traveling units arranged for Am Federation Arts, two large collections leaves selected and annotated dealing with 60 Famous Bibles, Nine Centuries and 40 Famous Books, Nine Centuries, distributed to educational institutions, museums and collectors here and abroad; Bible set issued '35, Famous Books '48; manuscript collection totals over 100 volumes and 1000 individual leaves. Author: Story of the Alphabet '23; Pre-Alphabet Days '23; also articles in field. Lecturer grad sch library sci Western Reserve '24; lecturer Internat Cong for Art Edn Prague '28; dean Cleveland Inst of Art since '45. Am Inst Graphic Arts (hon pres 2 yrs)—Am Soc of Aesthetics—NEA. Cleveland Institute of Arts, Cleve, 6.†

14 EGELSON, Louis I. History of reform Judaism. b'85. AB '04 (Coll City NY); AM '07 (Columbia); rabbi '08 (Jewish Theol Sem). Studies on the part played by laymen in promotion of reform Judaism, confirmation in the religious school. Co-author: A Layman's Jewish Library. Adminstr sec Union Am Hebrew Congregations since '42; sec Com on Chaplain Procurement since '42-45; Com on Emergency Placement of Chaplains '43-45; secretary Commn Information about Judaism; exec com Central Conf Am Rabbis '46-49. Editor: Liberal Judaism '49-50. 32 W 6th St., Cincinnati.☺

15 EGGAN, Frederick Russell. Anthropology (Hopi, Choctaw, Cheyenne and Arapaho Indians); Philippines; Social organization. b'06. PhB '27—MA '28—PhD '33 (University Chicago). Author: Social Organization of the Western Pueblos. Editor: Social Anthropology of North American Indians '37; also articles in field. With U Chicago since '35, now prof anthrop, chmn dept '48-52. Am Anthrop Assn (pres-elect '52)—National Research Council (chmn com on Asian anthrop '48-49, '52-53, Philippine com Pacific Sci Bd

'47)—Social Sci Research Council (chmn com on Social Sci Personnel '48-49, bd dirs '50-54, problems and policy com '50-53). 1126 E. 59th St., Chicago 37.☺

16 EGGERTSEN, Claude Andrew. History of American education; Administration (Higher education). b'09. AB '30—MA '33 (Brigham Young U); PhD '39 (U Minn). Editor: History Edn Journ since '50. Author articles in field. Asso prof U Mich since '49; USNR ednl services officer NAS, Kaluliu Maui; ednl officer 14th Naval Dist Pearl Harbor, Oahu; officer-in-charge Navy Pacific U Pearl Harbor '44-46; ednl cons, sec selection bd Professional Books Inc. AHA—AAAS—Am Ednl Research Assn—Nat Soc Study Edn—Soc Coll Teachers Edn (co-chmn hist edn sect)—Phil Edn Soc—Phi Kappa Phi. Awarded bronze star US Navy for adminstrn ednl program. School of Education, University of Michigan, Ann Arbor.

17 EGGLER, Willis Alexander. Volcanology and plant life. b'04. AB '23-27 (Northland Coll); MS, PhD '34-39 (U Minn). Ecological research on deciduous forests in northwestern Wisconsin '35, on manner of vegetation of lava areas and cinder cones in southern Idaho '36-39, in Michóacán, Mexico, on effects of activity of volcano, El Paricutin, on plant life '45, on bottomland hardwoods of Mississippi River flood plains '48-49. Author articles: The Maple-Basswood Forest Type in Washburn County '38; Primary Succession on Volcanic Deposits in Southern Idaho '41; Paricutin '45; The Effect of Paricutin upon Vegetation '46; Plant Communities in the Vicinity of the Volcano El Paricutin, Mexico, After Two and a Half Years of Eruption '48. Prof biol Alma Coll Mich '42-45; asso prof biol Central Mich Coll '45-47; asso prof biol Tulane U since '47. Ecol Soc Am—Am Geophys Union — AAAS(F) — Sigma Xi. Department of Biology, Newcomb College, Tulane University, New Orleans.

18 EGGLESTON, Harla Ray. Zoology; Fresh-water Mollusca. b'90. BS '12—Elihu Root fellow '12 (Hamilton Coll); MA '13 (Harvard); student (U Chicago). Prof biol Marietta Coll since '15; bact in charge Marietta Water Treatment Plant since '18, City Bd Health since '20. AAAS(F)—O Acad Sci(F)—W Va Aca Sci—Am Water Works Assn—Ecol Soc Am—Am Malacol Union—Am Soc Limnol Oceanog—Am Soc Profl Biol—Nat Assn Biol Teachers—Friends of the Land—Sigma Xi. Marietta College, Marietta, O.

19 EGGLETON, Frank E(gbert). Limnology; Sphaeriidae. b'93. AB '22 (Hillsdale Coll); MA '23—PhD '30 (U Mich). Research in Gulf coast and west coast institutions '39, Sphaeriidae eastern universities and museums '49; work on morphology and ecology of Sphaeriidae, Benthic fauna of fresh-water lakes. Author articles in field. Instr zool U Mich '26-30, asst prof '30-37, prof since '52; with U Mich Biol Sta since '27, staff since '31. AAAS(F, council '46-52)—Am Micros Soc (vp '38, sec since '46, ed '48-51, pres '52)—Am Society Zool—Ecol Society Am (chmn com on nomenclature '40-48)—Am Soc Limnol Oceanog—Am Fish Soc—Wilderness Soc—Mich Acad Sci—Wis Acad Sci—Sigma Xi—Phi Kappa Phi—Soc System Zoology. Department of Zoology, University of Michigan, Ann Arbor.☺

20 EGGLETON, Leonard Zerah. Poultry (Production, processing). b'17. BS '40 (Mich State Coll); MS '47 (Ia State Coll). Development systems of production and growing poultry; education

on poultry production and marketing especially quality programs; work in processing poultry—eviscerating, freezing, merchandising ready-to-cook-poultry. Grower advisor Crown Poultry Co '46-47; mgr Shenandoah Plant, Crown Poultry Co. '47-48; ext poultry marketing specialist Ia State Coll since '48. Alpha Zeta—Gamma Sigma Delta. Poultry Department, Iowa State College, Ames, Ia.

21 EGLER, Frank E(dwin). Plant ecology; Vegetation (West Indies, Hawaii, North America, regional bibliography). b'11. BS '32 (U Chicago); MS '34 (U Minn); PhD '36 (Yale); Certif '37 (Sorbonne). Travel in Europe, Africa, Asia, Cent and S America. Charge Aton Forest for ecol research since '44; tech advisor R/W Maintenance Corp since '50; research asso Am Mus Nat Hist NYC since '51. Author articles in field. AAAS(F)—Ecol Soc Am—Soc Plant Taxonomists—Cons Bot Soc—Am Geo Soc(F)—Soc Study Evolution. Aton Forest, Norfolk, Conn.

22 EGLOFF, Gustav. Oil chemistry and technology. b'86. AB '12 (Cornell U); MA '13—PhD '15—fellow '15 (Columbia). Appointed oil expert War Department '42; member National Research Council's tour of industrial exploration South America, permanent council for World Petroleum Congresses; went to China as head oil mission at request of Chinese government '46; Scandinavian research and industry tour '46; appointed by US Commissioner of Patents as mem US Patent Office Advisory Committee. Holds about 300 patents. Author: Catalysis '40; Emulsions and Foams '41; Physical Constants of Hydrocarbons and others; also articles in field. Dir research Universal Oil Products Co. American Chem Soc (selected as one of 10 ablest chemist and chemical engrs by Chicago sect '47)—Am Inst Chem Engrs—Am Inst Chem (F, pres '42-46, hon mem)—AAAS(F)—American Petroleum Inst—ASME—Am Soc Testing Materials—Am Inst Mining Metall Engrs—SAE—Ill Soc Engrs. Received Gold Medal Am Inst Chemists '40; Octave Chanute Medal Western Soc Engrs '39-40; distinguished service award Nat Research Council '41; named Modern Pioneer, NAM '40; Columbia U Medal for Excellence '43; Certificate Appreciation, War Dept '46. 310 S. Michigan Av., Chgo 4.☺

23 EHLERS, Joseph Henry. Japan (Civil engineering); China (Civil engineering). b'92. BS '14—MS '16 (Trinity Coll Conn); MS (CE) '15 (U Cal); MCE '16 (Cornell); law student (George Washington U); LLB '45 (Southeastern U). Construction engineer on dam across Yellow River; studies of Far Eastern engineering and heavy industry developments; delegate first World Engineering Congress Tokyo '29; chairman committee on engineering US Civil Service Commission; sec joint cooperative com of Am Soc CE—Am Inst Arch; member national engineers committee Engineers Joint Council. Author articles: Reconstruction Tokyo-Yokohama District '29; Japanese Iron and Steel Industry '29; Engineer and Architect in National Affairs '52. Prof structural engring Pei Yang U Tientsin China, also dir engring materials lab '29-24; engr on diversion of Yellow River Asia Dev Co '23; engring trade commr '26-30 and acting comml attache '29 Am Embassy Tokyo; tech dir Nat Conf on Constrn Washington '31-33; asst to dep adminstr Pub Works Adminstrn Washington '33-38; cons engr '38-41; chief cons engreg div Fed Works Agency '44-46; now field rep Am Soc CE, cons engr and atty. Chinese Inst Engrs—Assn Ch and Am Engrs (sec '23-24)—

DC Bar Assn (com on internat law). Kellogg Bldg., Washington 4. H: Westchester Apts., Washington 16, D.C.

10 EHRENFELD, Louis. Foods (Chemistry). b'00. BS (Chem engring) '21 (Rice Inst); MS '22 (Northwestern U). Research in alcoholic fermentation; technology of cereals; non-medical chemistry of brewing enzymes; manufacture of fermented beverages. Mgr Pabst Brewing Co '38-44; tech cons Red Top Brewing Co since '44. ACS—Inst Food Tech—Inst Brewing (Gt Britain)—Am Soc Brewing Chems. 1747 Central Av., Cin. 14. H: 933 Avondale Av., Cin. 29.

11 EHRENFRIED, George. Color photographic processes; Photographic sensitometric testing. b'13. AB '35 (Harvard). Improvement dye transfer and selective dye bleaching color photographic processes for prints on paper) development of methods and apparatus for tests on rapid processing Land camera. Photographic chemist Kodak Research Labs Rochester NY '36-42; with Polaroid Corp since '46, now physicist. Optical Soc Am—Photog Soc Am—AAAS. Polaroid Corp., 730 Main St., Cambridge 39, Mass.

12 EHRENSPERGER, Edward Charles. Early English language and literature (Anglo-Saxon, middle English, place names). b'95. AB '16—AM '18—PhD '21—Sheldon prize fellow Eng, France, Italy '16-17—Sheldon fellow Bonn U '21-22 (Harvard); Am-Scandinavian fellow '22-23 (Lund Sweden). Author: Dreams in Middle English Literature '21. Editor: South Dakota Place Names '41; also articles in field. Prof Eng, head dept U SD since '32. Modern Lang Assn (life)—Am Dialect Soc—Am-Scandinavian Found. University of South Dakota, Vermillion, S.D.

13 EHRICH, Robert William. Prehistoric archaeology (Europe, near East); Physical anthropology; Race. b'08. AB—MA '33—PhD '46 (Harvard). Exploratory excavations in Czechoslovakia with Fewkes for Peabody Museum '29; excavations Nuzi Iraq as Peabody representative '29-30, associate field director Neolithic excavations at Homolka '30-31; archaeological reconnaissance in Jugoslavia '32-33; excavations at Starcevo '32; physical anthropological reconnaissance in Montenegro '32; assistant field director excavations Tarsus Turkey '34-39. Author articles in field. Assistant professor of anthropology Brooklyn College since '52; instr anthrop Hunter College since '48. Am Anthrop Assn(F)—Am Assn Phys Anthrop—Archaeol Inst Am —Am Soc Human Genetics. Department of Sociology and Anthropology, Brooklyn College, Brooklyn 10.†

14 EICHBERG, Joseph. Lecithin (Soybean). b'06. BS '26 (Ga Sch Tech). Pres Am Lecithin Co since '34. 57-01 32 Ave., Woodside, L.I., N.Y.

15 EICHELBERGER, Frank. Nonferrous metallurgy. b'85. Student '02-06 (O State U); BSc—EM '08 (Mich Coll Mines). Mgr Alexandria Mining Co Cobalt Ont '08; supt Gold Hill Mining Co Butte Mont '10-14; mgr Custom Milling Plant Helena Mont '14-20; cons engr '20-26; gen mgr Base Metals Mining Corp '27-34; vp and dir Sunshine Mining Co '35-36; gen mgr, dir and vp Callahan Zinc Lead Co '36-39; pres Livengood Placers, and Kalunite Inc; vp and dir North Am Mining Corp; pres Standard Metals Inc, San Juan Metals Corp; pres Tacoma Powdered Metals Co '46-50; cons engr '46-49. Symons Bldg., Spokane 4, Wash.†

16 EICHER, George John. Salmon biology. b'16. BS '40 (Ore State Coll). Research on red and pink salmon to discover reasons for fluctuating abun-

dance. Party leader Bristol Bay Red Salmon Investigation '39-41; freelance author '42-43; state fisheries biol Ariz Game and Fish Dept '43-47; aquatic biol Alaska Investigations US Fish and Wildlife Service since '47. Am Fisheries Soc—Am Soc Limnol and Oceanog—Wildlife Soc—Pacific Fisheries Biol. 2725 Montlake Blvd., Seattle 2.

17 EICHNER, L(aurits) C(hristian). Instrument design. b'94. ME (Maskinteknicum Odense Denmark). Construction and development astrophotometer; development seismometers; designer two-circle goniometer; optical instruments; instruments for nuclear physics. Cons mech design. Am Optical Soc—Am Geophys Union—Am Inst Physics. 19 Sebago St., Clifton, N.J.

18 EIDE, Carl John. Plant pathology; Diseases of fruit and vegetables. b'04. Research on pathogenicity and genetics of Gibberella saubinetii, wood decay in Minnesota apple trees, inheritance of reaction to common scab in potatoes. Author articles in field. Prof plant path Minn U since '47. Division of Plant Pathology, University Farm, St Paul 1, Minn.◎

19 EIFLER, Gus Kearney, Jr. Geology of Texas; Norden bombsight; Bombing principles. b'08. BA '29—MA '30 (U Tex); PhD '41 (Yale). Author articles in field. With U Tex since '29, now prof geol; ground sch instr bombing Midland Army Air Field '42-45, dir '45. Geol Soc Am(F)—Am Geophys Union—Am Assn Petroleum Geol Phi Beta Kappa—Sigma Xi—Geol Soc Am. Consulting Geologist, Nash Building, Austin, Tex.

20 EIGENBRODT, Harold John. Drosophila (Environmental effects). b'98. Scholar '21-22—fellow '22-23, '24-25— MA '22—PhD '25 (U Ill); AB '21 (North Central Coll). Author articles in field. Prof zool North Central Coll since '25. AAAS—Am Soc Zool—Sigma Xi. North Central College, Naperville, Ill.†

21 EIGSTI, Orie J. Pollen-tube cytogenetics; Colchicine pollen-tube technique. b'08. Student '27-29 (Bradley U); BA '31 (Goshen Coll); PhD '35 (U Ill). Author articles in field. Prof bot Northwestern U '45-49; research bot Funk Brothers Seed Co since '50. Am Assn Sci—Bot Soc Am—Genetics Soc Am—Am Naturalist Soc—Soc Study Evolution—Ill Acad Sci—Sigma Xi. Fulbright Award, Pakistan, '52-53. Funk Bros. Seed Co., Bloomington, Ill. 1005 Hovey Ave., Normal, Ill.

22 EILERTS, C(harles) Kenneth. Chemistry (Phase relations of hydrocarbons, corrosion in gas wells). b'04. BS '26 (Okla A&M Coll). Experimented with process for cracking natural gas and light oil; measured properties of gas-condensate fluids by means of especially designed mobile laboratory; developed windowed cell for observing critical state phenomena of natural hydrocarbon mixtures; determined characteristics of metals and inhibitors for controlling corrosion in gas wells. Author articles in field. Supervisor research US Bur Mines Bartlesville Okla since '30. Am Chem Soc—Am Gas Assn —Nat Assn Corrosion Engrs—Am Inst Mining Metall Engrs. Award of Excellence from Dept Interior '44 with personal approval of Harold L Ickes. Bureau of Mines, Bartlesville, Okla.

23 EISELEN, Malcolm Rogers. United States history and government; Political science. b'02. AB '24—MA '25 (Northwestern U); Harrison fellow '25-27—PhD '31 (U Penn). Studies of US politics and public opinion, and of history, structure, functions of President

and Congress. Author: Franklin's Political Theories '28; The Rise of Pennsylvania Protectionism '32; also articles in field. Asso prof '27-33, prof since '33, chmn dept hist, polit sci since '34 Coll Pacific. Phi Beta Kappa —AHA—Am Polit Sci Assn. College of Pacific, Stockton 4, Cal.

24 EISELEY, Loren C(orey). Early man (Floral and faunal problems); Folsom culture; Algonkian hunting territory systems; Paleo-archaeology; Human evolution. b'07. AB '33 (U Neb); AM '35—PhD '37—Harrison scholar and fellow '34, '36 (U Pa); Social Sci Research Council post-doctoral fellow '40-41 (Columbia, Am Mus Natural Hist). Author articles in field. Asst prof sociol and anthrop U Kan '37-42, asso prof '42-44; prof and head dept sociol and anthrop Oberlin Coll '44-47; chmn dept anthrop U Pa since '47; curator of early man U Pa Mus since '48. Am Anthrop Assn (F, vp '48-49)— Soc Study Evolution—Am Inst Human Paleontology (president since '49)— AAAS(F) — Society Am Archaeol — Am Assn Phys Anthrop—Sigma Xi. Box 14, Bennett Hall, University of Pennsylvania, Phila. 4.◎

25 EISELSTEIN, Herbert L(ouis). Nickel metallurgy. b'19. Chem E '41 (U Cincinnati). Research on composition variable involved in machineability of nickel alloys, methods of measuring machineability. Fatigue, creep and stress rupture tests of high temperature alloys and superalloys. Metall Internat Nickel Co since '41. Soc Exptl Stress Analysis. International Nickel Co., Inc., Huntington, W.Va.

26 EISENBERG, Phillip. Cavitation; Mechanics of materials; Model basins. b'19. BS '41 (Wayne U); CE '48 (Calif Inst Tech); '41-42 (State U Ia); '46-47 (U Md). Research in fluid mechanics, cavitation, turbulence; US Naval Technical Mission in Europe for investigation of continental model basin research '45. Invented tension dynamometer. Author papers in field of hydrodynamics. Head of fluid phenomena sect David Taylor Model Basin '42-45, '45-47, since '48; research asst State U Ia '41-42. Am Soc ME—Soc Naval Architects and Marine Engrs—Schiffbautechnische Gesellschaft. Inst Aero Sci. David Taylor Model Basin, Washington 7.

27 EISENBERG, Sylvan. Baking (Technology); Dehydration (Vacuum and atmospheric drying of fruits); Electrolytes (Activity coefficients); Tropical fish (Transportation). b'13. BA '34—MS '36 (U Pa); PhD '42 (Stanford). Investigation of panary fermentation, mineral solids of water, wheat blending and flour selection, new bakery products; dehydration processes and equipment design, development new products; theory and practical applications for electrolytes with regard to concentrated aqueous solutions; development oxygen generator and means for use in shipping tropical fish by air. Author articles: The Baking Test '41; Concentrated Solutions of Strong Electrolytes '42; Fermentation Losses '48. Lab dir and cons Western Foods Lab Lactol Corp Cal '36-41; dir chem engring and food tech Anresco San Francisco since '41; tech dir Desiccated Foods Co Lyons NY '43-47, AAAS—ACS—Am Assn Cereal Chem—Inst Food Tech—Sigma Xi —Phi Lambda Upsilon. 693 Minna St., SF 3.

28 EISENBERG, William Victor. Microanalysis of food and drugs. b'13. BA '34 (Brooklyn Coll); MA '42 (George Washington U); Grad work (Catholic U, US Dept Agr Grad Sch). Author articles in field. Chief microanalytical branch Division Microbiol Food & Drug

Adm since '47. Assn Official Agrl Chemists—Bot Soc Washington—Am Chem Soc. Food and Drug Administration, F.S.A., Washington.

10 EISENBUD, Merril. Industrial hygiene; Air pollution. b'15. EE '36 (NYU). Research into causes of occupational diseases and means of engineering control; responsible for health and safety in installations of Atomic Energy Commission. Author articles in field. Indsl hygienist Liberty Mutual Ins Co '36-46; chief health and safety br US Atomic Energy Comm NYC since '46; asst prof san engring grad div NYU since '45; asso prof Indsl Hygiene Post-Grad Med Sch NYU since '50, dir div health and safety NY Operations Office AEC since '49. Am Indsl Hygiene Assn—Am Pub Health Assn. 70 Columbus Ave., NYC 23.†

11 EISENHART, Churchill. Accuracy and precision of measurement; Statistics of correlation and regression in biology and industry; Sampling of wool and textiles. b'13. AB '34—AM '35 (Princeton); PhD '37 (U London). Instructor mathematical statistics and statistical method as applied to research in natural sciences and engineering; active cooperation with biological and physical scientists in application statistical principles and techniques; research in statistical theory, method, and application to natural sciences and engineering; editorial board Industrial Quality Control since '48. Author articles: The Interpretation of Certain Regression Methods and their Use in Biological and Industrial Research '39; The Statistical Consultant in a Research Organization '48, and others. Co-author articles: (with Frieda S Swed) Tables for Testing Randomness of Grouping in a Sequence of Alternatives '43; (with P W Wilson) Statistical Methods and Control in Bacteriology '43, and others. Co-editor: (with Millard W Hastay, W Allen Wallis) Selected Techniques of Statistical Analysis for Scientific and Industrial Research and Production and Management Engineering '47. Biometrician Wis Agrl Expt Sta '37-47; with U Wis '37-47, asso prof math '45-47; research asso math Tufts '43; research math and statis div war research Columbia U '43-45; chief statis engring lab Nat Bur Standards since '46. AAAS(F)—Am Math Soc (council '46-48)—Am Soc Quality Control (edit bd since '48)—Am Statis Assn (F; com for development statis applications in engring, mfg '38-49)—Biometrics Soc—Econometric Soc (37-38)—Inst Math Statis (F, vice pres '48, mem council '49-51, chmn war preparedness com '40, chmn tabulation com '46-49)—Royal Statis Soc Gt Brit(F)—Wash Acad Sci. Statistical Engineering Laboratory, National Bureau of Standards, Washington 25.

12 EISENMAN, Herschel I. Fur (Dressing, dyeing); Seals (Hair). b'99. BS in chem '22—MS '23 (Rutgers U). Specialist in hair seals processing and dyeing. Chem A Hollander and Son Newark '24-40; operator own fur dressing and dyeing bus since '40. 37 Bogart St., Bklyn. 6.

13 EISENSCHIML, Otto. Lincolniana (Assassination); Civil war history; Chemistry of vegetable drying oils. b'80. ChemE '01 (Polytech Sch Vienna); LittD (hon) '37 (Lincoln Memorial U). Author: Why Was Lincoln Murdered? '37; In the Shadow of Lincoln's Death '40; The Art of Worldly Wisdom '47. Co-author: (with Ralph G Newman) The American Iliad '47; (with E B Long) As Luck Would Have It '48; The Celebrated case of Fitz John Porter '52; also articles in field. Chmn bd Sci-

entific Oil Compounding Co Inc Chgo. Am Chem Soc—Paint Oil and Varnish Assn US—Am Inst Chem—Nat Soybean Oil Mfrs Assn (founder, 1st pres). 1637 S. Kilbourn Av., Chgo.

14 EISENSON, Jon. Psychology of speech and physically handicapped; Speech pathology; Psychological changes accompanying brain injury. b'07. BS '28 (City Coll NY); MA '30—PhD '35 (Columbia). Author: The Psychology of Speech '38; Examining for Alphasia '46; Basic Speech '50. Co-author: The Psychology of the Physically Handicapped '40; The Defective in Speech '42; also articles in field. Asso prof Queens Coll since '49, dir speech and hearing center; cons psychol Vets Adm since '46; US Naval Hosp St Albans LI since '50; lecturer in otolarygo Coll Physicians and Surgeons Columbia since '48. American Speech and Hearing Assn(F)—Am Psychol Assn(F)—Diplomate Am Bd of Examiners in Professional Psychol—Speech Assn Am—NY State Psychol Assn. Queens College, 65-30 Kissena Blvd., Flushing, N.Y.†

15 EKHOLM, Gordon Frederick. Archaeology (Middle America). b'09. BA '33 (U Minn); PhD '41 (Harvard). Author articles in field. With Mexican and Central America archaeol Am Mus Natural Hist since '42, now asso curator; lecturer anthrop Columbia U since '44. Inst Andean Research (sectreas)—Sociedad Mexicana de Antropologia. American Museum of Natural History, Central Park W. at 79th, NYC.†

16 EKLUND, John Manley. International teacher organizations; Educational legislation; Federal aid (Education). b'09. AB '31 (Bethany Coll); MA '36 (U Denver); ThM '36 (Iliff Sch Theol). Research on pension, tenure and salary legislation for teachers; delegate 15th Conference of Peace, Paris, November '49; adviser American delegation to sixth General Conference of UNESCO; consultant state teacher groups. V-pres Am Fedn Teachers '46-48, pres since '48. Phi Delta Kappa—Am Council Edn (constituent del)—Nat Vocational Guidance Assn. 210 Denham Bldg., Denver.

17 EKSERGIAN, C. Levon. Automotive and railroad engineering; Brakes; Wheels. b'98. BS '21 (MIT). Invented artillery steel wheel adopted by entire automobile industry; composite cast iron and steel brake drum extensively adopted by automobile industry; railroad disc brake, first successful highspeed railroad brake, now used many modern trains; designed, developed hot rolling mill for rolling automobile wheel discs; designed one of world's largest dynamometers for testing heavy-duty brakes; many other inventions and developments in automotive and railroad equipment and processes; holds 200 patents. Author articles in field. Mech engr metall lab and process and machinery development Edward G Budd Mfg Co Phila '23-27, exec engr charge research and prodn since '46; chief engr in charge all engring and labs Budd Wheel Co Detroit '28-46; exec engr assistant to vp since '46. Am Welding Soc (past vp, mem various com)—ASME (founder plasticity com, mem exec com Detroit chapter)—SAE (mem brake com)—Am Soc Testing Materials—Am Soc Metals—Engring Soc Detroit (mem spl com). Budd Company, Phila. 32. H: Rock House, Rose Tree Rd., Media, Pa.

18 EKSERGIAN, Rupen. Railway engineering (Dynamics of machinery, engine and turbine design, electrical machinery, fluid and electro-mechanical transmission systems, high pressure chemical equipment, welding design).

b'89. SB '14—SM '15 (Mass Inst Tech); SM '15 (Harvard); fellow '16-17—PhD '28 (Clark U). Developed methods of analysis on locomotive design; responsible for technical phase of stainless steel train developments including Pioneer Zephyr. Author articles in field. Chief cons engr E G Budd Mgr Co, now the Budd Co, since '34; sr staff adviser and cons Franklin Inst Research Labs since '41; cons engr Lukens Steel Co since '45; served as 1st lt maj Ordnance Dept US Army World War I; spl cons to Chief of Research Development Ordnance Dept US Army. ASME(F). Recipient George R Henderson medal Franklin Inst '37, Worcester Reed Warner medal ASME 539, Louis E Levy medal '45. Rose Tree Rd., Media, Pa.☉

19 ELBERT, Samuel Hoyt. Polynesian languages and folklore. b'07. AB '28 (Grinnell Coll); '28-29 (U Toulouse); BL '31 (Columbia); '47-48 (Yale); PhD '50 (U Ind). Author: Chants and Love Songs of Marquesas Islands, French Oceania '41; Trukese-English and English Trukese Dictionary '47; Grammar and Comparative Study of Language of Kapingamarangi '48; The Chief in Hawaiian Mythology '50; Conversational Hawaiian '51. Linguist with Coordinated Investigation of Micronesian Anthrop by Pacific Sci Bd Nat Research Council in coop US Navy '47; asst prof Pacific lang U Hawaii since '49. Linguistic Soc Am—Am Folklore Soc—Polynesian Soc (New Zealand)—Anthrop Soc Hawaii—Hawaiian Hist Soc. University of Hawaii, Honolulu, TH.

20 ELCHIBEGOFF, Ivan Mamikon. International timber trade; World forest resources and industries; Land economics. b'99. Student '17-20 (Tomsk U, Russian Naval Acad, Far Eastern U); '23-24, '37 (Sch Bus Columbia); BBA '34 (Coll City NY); MSS '38—DSS '42 (New Sch for Social Research). Independent research in international forest economics since '35 and special research in forest resources and timber trade of 26 Pacific Countries. Author: United States in the Pacific Area '49; also articles in field. Econ geog US Bd Econ Warfare '41-43; econ US Fgn Econ Adm '44-45; Food and Agr Orgn UN '45-46; econ US State Dept '46-47. 4206 Kaywood Drive, Mount Rainier, Md.†

21 ELDER, Francis B. Public health administration; Military sanitation. b'06. BS '30 (Rutgers U); MSPH (U Mich). Pub health br Army European Civil Affairs Div '43-44, san engr cons pub health br Div Mil Govt Supreme Hdqrs AEF and US Forces European Theatre '44-46; col (res) San Corps US Army; engring asso Am Pub Health Assn since '46. Am Pub Health Assn (F)—ASCE (asso)—Am Water Works Assn—Nat Soc Profl Engrs—Nat Malaria Soc. American Public Health Association, 1790 Broadway, NYC 19.

22 ELDER, James Lowry. Underground gasification of coal. b'09. BS in chem engring '31 (Pa State Coll). Chem, asst pulp mill supt W Va Pulp and Paper Co '31-35; with US Bur Mines since '35. ACS—Phi Lambda Upsilon. Bureau of Mines, Gorgas, Ala.

23 ELDER, Lucius Williams, Jr. Food and coffee technology; Taste testing (Statistical); Packaging. b'00. AB '20 (Haverford Coll); PhD '26 (Harvard); student (Cambridge U). Research on instrumental methods of analysis especially glass electrode for pH measurement. Author articles in field. Asso in chem U Ill '27-30; supt process lab EI duPont Co ammonia div Charleston W Va '30-32; analytical chem research dept Gen Foods Corp '32-39, head phys chem div Hoboken

'39-42, dir phys research lab '42-46, dir product evaluation lab since '46. Am Chem Soc—Am Assn Textile Chem and Colorists—Inst Food Technol—Sigma Xi—Phi Beta Kappa. General Foods Corporation, Central Laboratories, 1125 Hudson St., Hoboken, N.J.

10 ELDERFIELD, Robert Cooley. Organic chemistry (Heterocyclic, antimalarials, glycosides, alkaloids, steroids). b'04. AB '26—DSc '52 (Williams Coll); PhD '30 (Mass Inst Tech). Editor and co-author six-volume Heterocyclic Compounds since '50. Prof Columbia '46-52 U Mich since '52; cons various industries since '45, USPHS since '46, Sloan-Kettering Found since '52. Am Chem Soc (chm organic div '52)—Nat Acad Sci—Am Soc Biol Chem. Department of Chemistry, University of Michigan, Ann Arbor, Mich.

11 ELDREDGE, Laurence Howard. Law of torts and equity. b'02. BS '24 (Lafayette College); LLB '27 (U Pa). Adviser on Torts and Evidence to Am Law Institute '32-42; reporter on decs of Supreme and Superior Cts of Pa since '42; revising reporter Restatement of the Law of Torts '42-47. Author: Eldredge on Modern Tort Probs '41; Pennsylvania Annotations to Restatement, Torts vols I and II '38. Ed Pa Bar Assn Quarterly '38-42. Prof law Temple U '28-33, adj prof since '47; asso in law U Pa '33-34, '37-38, prof law '38-44; lectr med jurisprudence U Pa Med Sch; spl dep atty gen Pa '48-49. Am Law Inst—Am Bar Assn—Phi Beta Kappa—Delta Theta Phi—Order of Coif. 1500 Walnut St., Phila 2.†

12 ELGIN, Joseph Clifton. Solvent extraction (Chemical engineering); Solutions (Separation methods, chemical engineering); Rubber (Reclaiming, polymerization processes for synthetic); Textiles (Finishing chemistry). b'04. Chem E '24—MS '26 (U Va); PhD '29 (Princeton U). Engineering development industrial applications of solvent extraction and separation methods; equipment and process development emulsion polymerization for synthetic rubber; co-inventor process for reclaiming vulcanized rubber. Patents in field, including processes for extraction of polyhydric alcohols, glycerine, separation ethylene and ethane by liquid extraction, and rubber reclaiming. Author articles: Design and Principles of Liquid—Liquid Extraction '42; Solvent Extraction '47, '48, '49, '50, and others. Contbr: Chemical Engrs Handbook (3rd edit) '50. Resch cons textile finishing since '36; prof chem engring Princeton since '33; research cons rubber reclamation '39-42 since '45; chief polymer equipment br and polymer development br Rubber Dirs Office WPB '42-44; indsl cons solvent extraction and separation methods since '46. ACS—AICHE—Soc Chem Industry—NRC (div chem and chem tech). Dept. of Chemical Engineering, Princeton University, Princeton, N.J. H: 218 Prospect Av.

13 ELIASON, Norman Ellsworth. English language; Old & Middle English Literature. b'07. BA '27 (Luther Coll); MA '31 (U Ia); PhD '36 (Johns Hopkins); fellow summer '37 (Linguistic Inst U Mich). Author monograph and articles in field. Asso editor: Southern Folklore Quarterly '37-47; adv editor: American Speech '39-40. Prof English U NC since '46. Modern Lang Assn (chm Practical Phonetics Group '37-39, sec Exptl Phonetic Group '42-44)—Linguistic Soc Am (exec com '40)—S Atlantic Modern Lang Assn (chmn Com on English Lang Study '41-42)—Am Dialect Soc. Dept. of English, University of North Carolina, Chapel Hill, NC.

14 ELICKER, Paul Edgar. American education (Secondary, student councils, school activities, school honor societies). b'94. AB '14 (Ursinus Coll); AM '21 (Columbia); EdM '31 (Harvard); ScD '41 (Boston U). Editor: The Bulletin, Student Life, Educator. Co-author: Planning for American Youth '44. Nat Assn Secondary Sch Principals (pres '38-39, exec sec since '40)—New Eng Assn Colls Secondary Schs (chmn)—Nat Assn Student Councils (sec since '44)—Nat Honor Soc (sec since '40)—Nat Jr Honor Soc—Nat Youth Adminstrn—Nat Com Edn and Defense—Phi Delta Kappa. 1201 Sixteenth St., N.W., Washington 6.

15 ELION, Edward. Fermentations; Cereal chemistry; Enzymes. b'00. Chem Engr '25 (U Inst Tech Delft Holland); PhD '27 (U Paris France); Hon Prof '37 (Inst Fermentations Ghent Belgium). Industrial research in fermentation industries, cereal chemistry; developed new processes and inventions in fields baker's yeast, bread baking, enzymes, food products; improvements in yeast testing methods; sugar production by enzymes; fermenting power of yeast, baking salt; studies on proteolytic enzymes, catalase, discoloration fruit juices, wines, cut surfaces fruits. Mng dir Lab Fermentation Tech and Applied Chem The Hague '28-39; cons and research chem USA '39-43; head med and sci sect Commonwealth Australia War Supplies Procurement Mission Washington '43-46; pres Tech Representations Inc since '46, E A van Esso's Fabrieken Rotterdam since '46. Royal Soc Arts (London)—ACS—Soc Am Bact—Am Assn Cereal Chems—Inst Food Tech—AAAS—Soc Chem Industry (London)—Inst Brewing (London)—Netherlands Chem Soc—Netherlands Soc Microbiol—Netherlands Soc Biochem — Société de Chimie Biologique (Paris)—Assn des Chimistes de Sucrerie, Distillerie et Industries Agricoles (Paris)—Am Soc Sugar Beet Tech. 1622 Juniper St., Washington 12.

16 ELISOFON, Eliot. Photography. b '11, BS '33 (Fordham U). Photography of primitive man and his environment, especially ancient cultures such as Egyptian, Cambodian, Indian; photographic essay on study of racial mixtures in Hawaii '48; photographic study Andean man South America, art of India. Author articles: Documentary Photography '40; Underwater Photography '40; Flash Photography '41; War Photography '44; Paradise that Was (Pacific Trust Ter) '50. Comml photog '35-39; staff photog Mus Modern Art '39, Life Mag since '42. War photog North Africa, Europe, Arctic, and Pacific '42-46. Am War Correspondents Assn. Life Magazine, 9 Rockefeller Plaza, N.Y.C.

17 ELKINS, Lloyd Edwin. Petroleum reservoirs (Mechanics); Petroleum (Secondary recovery); Natural gas (Secondary recovery); Petroleum appraisal. b'12. Prof degree (petroleum production engring) '34 (Colorado School Mines). Research in prediction of oil and gas recoveries possible under both natural and manmade processes to which reservoir can be subjected, fluid displacement processes. With Stanolind Oil and Gas Co since '34, prodn research dir since '49. Am Petroleum Inst (v-chmn adv com on fundamental research on occurrence and recovery of petroleum '50)—AIMME—Tau Beta Pi—AAPG—Sigma Gamma Epsilon. Research Department, Stanolind Oil and Gas Co., Box 591, Tulsa 2, Okla.

18 ELLIOTT, Alice. Fish ecology; Nematodes. b'19. BS '42 (Kan State Tchrs Coll); MS '47—PhD '50 (Kan State Coll Agr and Applied Sci). Research on ecology of Kansas fishes, aging and infectivity of embryonated Ascarid eggs of nematodes. Asst prof biol dept Kan State Teachers Coll '50-51. Kappa Delta Pi—Gamma Sigma Delta—Beta Beta Beta—Phi Kappa Phi—Sigma Xi—Kan Acad Sci—Am Soc Parasitol—Am Micros Soc—AAUP—AAAS. H: 323 N. Poplar, Eureka, Kan.

19 ELLIOTT, Bruce Walter. Legerdemain; Witchcraft; Comic magazines. b'14. Ed pub schs. Specialist in small magic, subtleties and strategems; philosophy and practice of witchcraft, its historical import, its rise and fall; complete history of comic magazines from inception to the present, how they came into being; editor and publisher The Phoenix, trade paper for magicians. Author: Magic as a Hobby '48. The Phoenix, 284 W. 70th St., N.Y.C. 23.

20 ELLIOTT, Byron Kauffman. Corporate administration; b'99. AB cum laude '20 (Indiana U); '23 (Harvard). Ed Monthly Legal Bulletin '29-34. Mgr and gen coun Am Life Conv (assn 132 Legal reserve life ins cos) '29-34; pres Am Service Bur '29-33, chmn bd '33-34; gen solicitor law dept John Hancock Mut Life Ins Co '34-35, gen counsel '36, vp, gen counsel and dir '37-47, exec vp, dir since '48. Am Bar Assn—Am Law Inst—Am Judicature Soc—Assn Life Ins Counsel (pres '49).

21 ELLIOTT, Charles Newton. Wildlife and forestry management; Southern forestry. b'06. Student U Ga '24-27. Author: Key to Georgia Trees '31; Conservation of American Resources '40; Careers in Forestry '41; Careers in Wildlife Management '42. Co-author: Southern Forestry '38; American Conservation '38; also articles in field. Forester Ga State Forest Service '28-35; asso forester Nat Park Service '35-37; dir div state parks State Dept Natural Resources '37-39; dir div wildlife '39, commr '39-41; spl asst in charge pub relations, Region 1 Nat Park Service and editor Regional Review '41-42; editor Outdoor Georgia '40-41. Soc Am Foresters—Eugene Field Soc (hon mem). 412 State Capitol, Atlanta.

22 ELLIOTT, Claude. Texas (History); Texana (Postal cancellations); Texas (Cultural conflict). b'96. Student (W Tex State Tchrs Coll) (Abilene Christian Coll) (Simmons Coll); BS '23 (SW Tex State Tchrs Coll); AM '28—PhD '34 (U Tex). Collector of Texana (including Texas postal cancellations relating to postal history of Republic of Texas) as related to cultural background of Texas, especially as to Anglo-Spanish cultural conflict). Author: Leathercoat, Life of a Texas Patriot '38; Union Sentiment in Texas, 1861-1865 (monograph) '48, Alabama and Texas Revolution (monograph) '47. Mem faculty SW Tex State Tchrs Coll since '29, prof history '29-42. registrar, dir personnel '42-40, coordinator vets affairs '42-45, dean grad studies since '49. Tex State Hist Assn (F, life mem, vp '50)—NEA—So Hist Assn—Tex State Tchrs Assn—Tex Classroom Tchrs Assn—Tex Assn Collegiate Registrars (pres '47)—Hays County Tchrs Assn. Rockefeller grant for Tex history research '45, '47. H: 434 N. Comanche St., San Marcos, Tex.

23 ELLIOTT, Harold Farley. Radar (Design); Radio (Design). b'92. AB '16—EE '25 (Stanford U). Development push button and remote control mechanisms for automatic tuning radio apparatus; design timing mechanism for automatic control radio, and other apparatus with preselected time function patterns. Holds 75 patents in field. Engr Fed Telegraph Co San Francisco '16-22; cons engr San Francisco and Del '23-25; research engr Radio Corp Am Camden NJ '30-31; development and cons work Palo Alto Cal '32-41, specializing automatic remote control and timing devices since '46; cons Radio Research Lab Harvard '42-45. Am Inst EE—Inst Radio Engrs(F) — AAAS — Sigma Xi — Tau Beta Pi. 1216 Webster St., Palo Alto, Cal.

10 ELLIOTT, Mabel Agnes. Social disorganization (Criminology, sociology, penology, delinquency). b'98. AB '22—AM '23—PhD '29 (Northwestern U); Wieboldt Research Fellowship in Sociology '24; Carola Woerishoffer Memorial Fellowship in Social Economy '24-26. Author: The Correlation Between Racial Heterogeneity and Juvenile Delinquency '26; Correctional Education and the Delinquent Girl '29; Conflicting Penal Theories and the Statutory Criminal Law '21; Coercion in Penal Treatment; Past and Present '47; Disaster Relief Services of the American Red Cross; Crime in Modern Society '52. Co-author: Social Disorganization '41; Our Dynamic Society '35; Marriage and the Family '48; also articles in field. Asso prof sociol U Kan '38-47; cons sociol Am Nat Red Cross '46-47; chmn Dept of Sociol Pa Coll for Women Pittsburgh since '47. Am Sociol Soc (chmn criminology div '43-44)—Midwest Sociol Soc—Am Assn Social Workers—Ohio Valley Sociol Soc—Soc Sci Study Social Problems—Phi Beta Kappa. Pennsylvania College for Women, Pitts.

11 ELLIOTT, Stanley Bennett. Metallic soaps; Cobalt salts. b'16. AB '39 (Western Reserve U). Research incendiary fuel; presently engaged research on alkaline-earth and heavy metal soaps and salts. Holds two US patents. Co-author: Paint and Varnish Technology (with W Von Fischer) '48; The Encyclopedia of Chemical Technology (with R Kirk, D Othmer) '49; also articles in field. Research chem Harshaw Chem Corp '39-41, tech dir metallic soap research direction '41-43; project dir Nat Defense Research Com '43-45; asst to pres Ferro Chem Corp '45-48, vp research and prodn dir since '48. Am Chem Soc—Am Oil Chem Soc —Armed Forces Chem Assn—Am Inst Chem—Am Soc Lubrication Engrs— Am Wood Preservers Assn—Am Soc Testing Materials. Ferro Chemical Corporation, Box 76, Bedford, Ohio.

12 ELLIS, Albert. Family relations. b'13. BBA '34 (Coll City NY); AM '43 —PhD '47 (Columbia). Love, marriage, sex counseling and research; member editorial board of Marriage and Family Living. Author articles: Love and family relations of American college girls; Some significant correlates of love and family attitudes and behavior; The value of marriage prediction tests. Author: The Folklore Of Sex '51. Marriage counselor NYC since '43; sr clin psychol NJ State Hosp '48-49; chief psychol Diagnostic Center Menlo Park NJ '49-50, NJ Dept Institutions and Agencies since '50. Am Psychol Assn—Am Orthopsychiat Assn —Am Assn Marriage Counselors—Nat Council Family Relations—AAAS—Am Group Psychotherapy Assn—Assn Advancement Psychotherapy. New Jersey Dept Institutions and Agencies, Diagnostic Center, Menlo Park, N.J. H: 56 Park Av., N.Y.C. 16.

13 ELLIS, Brooks Fleming. Micropaleontology; Geology; Foraminifera. b'97. AB '23 (Marietta Coll); MS '29— PhD '32 (NYU). Author articles on Foraminifera; senior author: Catalogue of Foraminifera; editor: The Micropaleontologist. Prof geol and dept chmn NYU since '46; curator and chmn micropaleontology Am Mus Natural Hist since '44. AAAS—Paleontol Soc—Soc Econ Paleontol and Mineralogists—NY Acad Sci(F)—Am Assn Petroleum Geol—Am Geog Soc—Geol Soc Am(F)—Am Geophys Union—Soc for Study of Evolution—Nat Inst Social Sci—Am Assn Petroleum Geol— Soc Study Evolution—Schweizerischen Palaontologischen Gesellschaft — Societe Geologique, Suisse—Societe Geologique de France—Phi Beta Kappa— Sigma Xi. New York University NYC.☉

14 ELLIS, David Maldwyn. History (Economic, American); History of Transportation; New York (History); Railroad Land Grants. b'14. BA '38 (Hamilton Coll); MA '39—PhD '42 (Cornell); post-doctoral fellow '44-45 (U Mich). Engaged research land grants to railroads, public aids to transportation, history New York State (econ and transportation); grant research transportation Social Science Research Council '44-45, Dixon Ryan Fox Memorial fellowship to write history NY state for state hist assn '48. Author: Landlords and Farmers in the Hudson-Mohawk Region 1790-1850 '46 (won John H Dunning Award Am Hist Assn '46); author articles: Forfeiture of Railroad Land Grants '46; Railroad Land Grant Rates '45; Troy and Albany, Commercial Rivals '43; papers antirentism, railroad land grants before membership societies. Asst hist dept Cornell '39-41, asst prof hist '44; instr hist U Vt '42-44; asst prof hist Hamilton Coll since '46. Am Hist Assn—Miss Valley Hist Assn— NY Hist Assn—Econ Hist Soc. Messinger Prize, Boldt fellowship Cornell '42. Hamilton College, Clinton, N.Y. H: 12 Observatory Rd.

15 ELLIS, Don Edwin. Vegetable crop diseases (Lettuce, cucurbits); Root-knot control; Fungi imperfecti. b'08. AB—BS '29 (Neb Central Coll); MS '33 (La State U); PhD '45 (U NC). Author articles in field. Asso prof plant pathol NC State Coll since '45. Am Phytopathol Soc—Am Mycol Soc— NC Acad Sci—Sigma Xi. Plant Pathology Section, North Carolina State College, Raleigh, N.C.†

16 ELLIS, Edgar Watson. Petroleum refining; Water treatment. b'05. BS (Chem E) '29—MS '30 (U Tex). Tests and analyses of crude oil and its products; Industrial water treatment. Author articles: Determination of Lead in Doctor Solution '36; Determination of Thiols in Hydrocarbon Gases '51. Chief chem Panhandle Refining Co Wichita Falls Tex '33-41; sr chem engr Hdqrs Eighth Service Command ASF '43-46; chief chem Atlas Oil & Refining Co Shreveport La '46-47; chief chem East Chicago Ind refinery Cities Service Oil Co since '47. AICHE—ACS —Tau Beta Pi—Phi Lambda Upsilon. Cities Service Oil Co., P.O. Box 718, East Chicago, Ind.

17 ELLIS, Elmer. American history; Education administration. Social studies teaching. b'01. AB '24—AM '25 —LLD '46 (U ND); PhD '30 (U Ia). Author: Henry Moore Teller, Defender of the West '41; Mr. Dooley's America, a Life of Finley Peter Dunne '41. Editor: Education Against Propaganda '37. Mem editorial bd Miss Valley Hist Review since '47. Prof history and govt ND State Tchrs Coll '25-28; asst, asso and prof history U Mo since '30, acting dean grad sch summers '36, '39 '41, vp '45-46, dean coll arts and sci since '46. Maj US Army Hist Br, War Dept Gen Staff. Phi Beta Kappa. 210 Jesse Hall, U Mo., Columbia, Mo.☉

18 ELLIS, Emory Leon. Rocket ordnance. b'06. BS '30—MS '32—PhD '34 (Calif Inst Tech). Author articles in field. Chem US Food and Drug Adminstrn '35-36; research asst Calif Inst Tech '36-41; development engr Rocket Ordnance Calif Inst Tech '42-45, Research and Development Adminstrn US Naval Ordnance Test Sta since '45. Am Chem Soc—AAAS—Am Ordnance Assn—Tau Beta Pi—Sigma Xi. Received Naval Ordnance Development Award '45. Rocket Department, U.S. Naval Ordnance Test Station, China Lake, Cal.

19 ELLIS, Greer. Experimental stress analysis; Dynamic instrumentation; Coatings (Brittle). b'10. BS (Physics) '34 (Geo Wash U); MS (aeronautical engring) '38 (MIT). Development Stresscoat brittle coatings, instruments, methods. Patents in field. Co-author article: (with A V de Forest, F B Sertn Jr) Brittle coatings for quantitative strain measurements. Mgr Stresscoat div Magnaflux Corp '38-46, mgr Zyglo div '42-46; owner Ellis Assos since '46. Am Soc ME—Soc Exptl Stress Analysis. Awarded Franklin Inst Certificate of Merit for work on Stresscoat. Ellis Associates, Box 77, Pelham 65, N.Y.

20 ELLIS, John Tracy. American church history (Catholic). b'05. AB '27 (St Viator Coll); AM—PhD '30 (Catholic U Am). Author: Anti-Papal Legislation in Medieval England 1066-1377 '30; Cardinal Consalvi and Anglo-Papal Relations 1814-1824 '42: The Formative Years of the Catholic University of America '46; The Life of James Cardinal Gibbons (2 vols) '52. With Catholic U Am since '35, now professor of American church history; managing editor Cath Hist Review since '41. AHA—Am Cath Hist Assn (Sec since '41)—Miss Valley Hist Assn —US Cath Hist Soc—Am Cath Hist Soc —Cath Assn Internat Peace. The Catholic University of America, Washington 17.†

21 ELLIS, Lacoste George. Petroleum exploration (Seismic). b'04. BA '27— MA (phys) '29 (Rice Inst). Research on development, construction, and maintenance of seismograph instruments and equipment, seismic method of petroleum geophysical exploration. Chief seismograph dept Sun Oil Co since '33. Soc Exploration Geophys— APS—Am Geophys Union. Sun Oil Co., Box 2831, Beaumont, Tex.

22 ELLIS, Nathan Kent. Horticulture; Peppermint oil and vegetable crops production. b'09. BS '32—MS '35 —PhD '50 (Mich State Coll). Articles in field. Research asst Purdue U '35-40; asst prof hort '40-47, asso prof hort since '47, head dept horticulture since '50. American Soc Hort Sci—AAAS. Department of Horticulture, Purdue University, West Lafayette, Ind.☉

23 ELLIS, Richard B(assett). Solid adsorbents (Surface area measurements); Alcoholic beverage analysis (Fusel oil). b'15. BA '36—MS '37— PhD '40 (Vanderbilt U). Research on fusel oil analysis, surface areas of solid adsorbents. Supervisor analytical div research and development dept Jos E Seagram and Sons Inc Louisville '40-42; research chem Corning Glass Works '42-46; asst prof chem U Miami since '47. ACS (phys and inorganic div). Chemistry Department, University of Miami, Miami, University Branch, Fla.†

24 ELLIS, Wayne Philip, Jr. Adhesives and coatings; Acoustical materials. b'15. BS '37 (U Md). Research on development of synthetic resinous and asphaltic adhesive cements, sealing compounds, sound and vibration deadeners for metal, protective coatings especially such products having properties of fire-retardance, moisture vapor impedance, chemical resistance and very low temperature resistance. Developed first known fire-retardant adhesives for thermal insulation used by USN World War II. Tech dir Benjamin Foster Co Phila since '39. Am Chem Soc—Franklin Inst—AAAS—Am Soc Testing Materials. Benjamin Foster Company, Phila 31.

10 ELLIS, Wells E(ugene). Ferrous metallurgy. b'22. Student '43-44 (Purdue U); student '40-43, '47-48—BS (Metall) '47—MS '48 (U Ill). Production, forging, constitution, and metallography studies of high temperature turbine alloys; application of nitriding to bearing production; carburizing and heat treatment of steels for bearings; studies on hardenability of bearing steels, annealing of nickel-chromium steels, bearing preservation and packaging research, weldability of low carbon structural steels, and notch toughness and impact properties of steels; ballistic tests of armour; weldability studies of submarine steels. Author articles: Strain Aging in Welding Structural Steel '48, and others. Research metall Navl Research Lab Anacostia Sta Washington '45-47; research metall phys metall Timken Roller Bearing Co since '48. Am Welding Soc—Am Soc Metals—Sigma Xi. Registered profl engr Ohio. Timken Roller Bearing Co., Canton, O.

11 ELLISON, Joseph Wald. U.S. History (Western); Samoa. b'91. AB '17—AM '19—PhD '23 (U Cal at Berkeley). Author: California and the Nation, 1850-1869 '27; Samoa in World Politics: A study in imperialism and International Relations '38. Author articles: The struggle for civil government in California, 1846-1850; The Currency question on the Pacific Coast during the civil war period; The partition of Samoa: A study in imperialism and diplomacy; The adventures of an American premier in Samoa, 1874-1876. Prof, head hist dept Ore State Coll; vis prof U Wash '31, Pa State Coll '39. AHA. History Dept., Oregon State College, Carvallis, Ore.☆

12 ELLISON, Lincoln. Ecology of vegetation (Range management, mammalian ecology, soils). b'08. BA '33 (U Calif); MS '38—PhD '48 (U Minn). Co-author: Range Plant Handbook '37; also articles in field. Range examiner, forest ecol, range conservationist Intermountain Forest and Range Expt Sta Ogden Utah since '38. Ecol Soc Am—Soc Am Foresters—Northwest Sci Assn—Soil Conservation Soc Am—Am Soc Range Management —Wilderness Soc—Sigma Xi.

13 ELLISON, Walter David. Splash erosion process; Measurement of soil erosion and sedimentation hazards; Infiltration of rainfall into soil. b'98. BS in CE '26 (Mont State Coll). Developed equipment, proceedures for splash erosion investigations, techniques for measuring soil erosion hazards and for evaluating sedimentation hazards as affected by splash; demonstrated infiltration of rainfall into the land most sensitive to impact energy of raindrops; supervised design N Appalachian Hydrologic Sta, dir '35-44; made preliminary plan and supervised design first large weighing water-cycle, in-situ lysimeters. Author: Studies of Raindrop Erosion '44; Factors That Affect Infiltration and Sealing of Exposed Soil Surfaces '45; Soil Erosion Studies '47; Protecting The Land Against The Raindrop's Blast '48; Soil Erosion by Rainstorms '50. Asst chief div drainage and water control Soil Conservation Service Dept Agr '44-48; charge soil conservation Bur Yards and Docks US Navy since '48.

Am Soc Agrl Engrs—Am Geophys Union—Range Soc Am. Awards from Am Soc Agrl Engrs for paper on infiltration '45, on soil erosion '47; from Soil Conservation Soc Am for paper on soil erosion '50. Bureau of Yards and Docks, U.S. Navy, Washington.

14 ELLS, Victor Raymond. Spectroscopy. b'14. AB '35 (Kalamazoo Coll Mich); MS '38 (Brown U); PhD '39 (U Rochester). Application physical chemical methods and Spectrophotometry to research and new analytical methods in organic, biological, pharmaceutical, food, and medicinal chemistry, including nitrofurans; establishment of laboratory for application spectroscopy to crime detection. Faculty U Mo '39-43; research phys chem Norwich Pharm Co & Eaton Labs Inc since '43. ACS—APS—Optical Soc Am —AAAS—NY Acad Sci—Sigma Xi—A AUP—Gamma Alpha. Norwich Pharmacal Co. & Eaton Laboratories, Inc., Norwich, N.Y. H: 121 S. Broad St.

15 ELLSBERG, Edward. Marine salvage. b'91. EngD '29 (Colorado University); ScD '52 (Bowdoin); BS '14 (US Naval Academy); MS '20 (Mass Inst Tech). Salvage work in Red Sea, Western Mediterranean; raised US submarine S-51 from sea bottom; installed artificial harbors on Normandy coast '44. Invented under water torch for cutting steel, improved method in fields of dehydrating and dewaxing lubricating oils and in cracking crude oil for anti-knock gasoline; designed system used by US Navy for salvaging submarines. Author: Salvage Operations on S-51 '27; Thirty Fathoms Deep '30; Men Under the Sea '39; Treasure Below '40; Under the Red Sea Sun '46 and others; also articles in field. US Navy until '26 advancing to lt comdr; salvage officer initial operations on S-4 '27; promoted comdr Special Act of Congress for work on S-51 and S-4 '29; reappointed US Navy World War II; officer in charge United States Naval Repair Base Massawa Africa '42 captain USNR '42, rear admiral '51; principal salvage officer Western Mediterranean for Allied Expeditionary Force '42-43; supervisor shipbuilding Cleveland area '45; chief engineer Tide Water Oil Co '26-35, cons engr '35-41. NJ Soc Professional Engrs—Am Petroleum Inst—Naval Inst—Am Polar Soc. Awarded DSM US Navy; awarded Legion of Merit '42 and '44; awarded CBE British Empire; officially stated by Naval Court of Inquiry on S-4 disaster as foremost authority on submarine rescue. Southwest Harbor, Maine.Ⓖ

16 ELLSBERG, Harry. Structural and civil engineering. b'89. BS in civil engring '13 (U Colo); grad study '38-39 (U Mich). Structural steel and reinforced concrete; designs and direction commercial and industrial buildings. Mem Am Concrete Inst Com 317 for '39 edit of Reinforced Concrete Design Handbook. Author article: Ribbed Concrete Arch Roof Construction. Structural engr and Corn Products Refining Co '16-23, Holabird & Root '23-32, Albert Kahn architects and engrs '37-47; chief structural engr Giffels & Valet Inc '47-50. Am Soc CE—Engr Soc Detroit—Nat Soc Profl Engrs—Am Concrete Inst—Tau Beta Pi.

17 ELLWOOD, Walter Breckenridge. Switches (Electric); Ferromagnetic materials. b'02. AB '24 (U Mo); AM '26—PhD '33 (Columbia). Research and development glass-enclosed switches; underwater warfare devices; ferromagnetic materials, instrumentation, measurements. Issued about 20 patents in field. Research physicist Bell Telephone Labs '30-40, since '43; sci cons Bur Ordnance Navy Dept '40-43.

APS(F)—AAAS(F)—Sigma Xi—Epsilon Chi—Am Soc Metals—NY Acad Sci. 463 West St., N.Y.C. 14.

18 ELMENDORF, William W. Indians (Pacific Northwest). b'12. BA '34 —MA '35 (U Wash); PhD '49 (U Cal). Research on cultures of Spokane and Lakes Indians, culture and language of Twana Indians. With U Wash since '46, asst prof anthrop from '50; Carnegie teaching asso anthrop Northwestern U '50-51. Am Anthrop Assn(F)— Am Ethnol Soc—Linguistic Soc Am —Sigma Xi. Dept. of Anthropology, University of Washington, Seattle 5.

19 ELMSTROM, George Pierpont, II. Optometry; Color blindness; Color vision. b'25. AA (U Co Cal); BS (Visual sci)—Dr Optometry (Los Angeles Coll Optometry). Development modified self-ophthalmoscope. Author articles: Evidence of Frequency and Correlations of Defective Color Vision; We Came, We Saw, We Conquered; A Comparative Analysis and Limitations of Pseudo-Isochromatic Tests for Color Vision Testing; asso editor: Optometric World. Cons and aid to practitioners in surveys on illumination and color vision. Optical Soc Am —Am Inst Physics—Illuminating Engring Soc—Phys Soc London (color and optics group)—Nat Soc Prevention Blindness—Am and Cal Optometric assns—Omega Delta—AAAS. 325 Richmond St., El Segundo, Cal.

20 ELSENSOHN, Sister M. Alfreda. Idaho history and flora (Idaho County). b'97. '24 (Northern Ida Coll of Edn); BS '27 (Gonzaga U); MS '39 (U Ida). Established Museum at St Gertrude's Academy '32. Author: Pioneer Days in Idaho County Vol I '47 Vol II '51; also articles in field. Instr journalism St Gertrude's Acad Cottonwood Idaho. Idaho Edn Assn—Idaho Writers' League. St. Gertrude's Convent, Cottonwood, Idaho.

21 ELSTAD, Leonard M. Education (Schools for the deaf). b'99. AB '22 (St Olaf Coll Northfield Minn); AM '23 (Gallaudet Coll Washington). Associate editor: American Annals of the Deaf. Prin Kendall Sch Columbia Instn for Deaf Washington '24-25; asst prin Wright Oral Sch NY City '25-26, prin and mgr '26-32; supt Minn Sch for Deaf Fairbault Minn '32-45; pres Gallaudet Coll (only coll for deaf students in the world, est 1864) since '45. Pres Conv Am Instrs of Deaf; treas Conf Execs Am Schs for Deaf. Gallaudet College, Washington 2.†Ⓖ

22 ELVEY, Christian Thomas. Night sky (Light); Photoelectric photometry; Stellar spectroscopy. b'99. AB '21— AM '23 (U Kan); PhD '30—fellow astron '25-26 (U Chicago). With McDonald Obs Ft Davis Tex '35-42 astron in charge; on leave of absence to work with Office of Sci Res and Dev '43-45, head research dept Naval Ordnance Test Sta '47-49, sr research scientist, '49-52, head of staff '51-52; dir Geophysical Inst, U Alaska since '52. AA AS. Geophysical Institute, U of Alaska, College, Alaska.Ⓖ

23 ELWELL, Cyril Frank. Complete continuous wave radio transmission systems antenna and tower design; Motion picture sound systems; Zamboni cell; Liquid magnetic clutches; Magnetic amplifiers; Evaporation of metals; Printed circuits. b'84. BA (EE) '07—EE '08 (Stanford U). Developed recording and projecting talkie equipment. Author The Poulsen Arc Generator '23, also articles in field. Chief engr Fed Telegraph Co '10-13, Poulsen Radio London '13-14; designer and contractor high power arc stations in Eng, France and Italy '14-19; cons engr Ste Francaise Radioelectrique '19-24; mng dir and tech adv DeForest

Phonofilms Ltd London '23-29; cons engr Radio Communication Co Ltd London '20-36; tech adv Cie Radio Cinema Paris '29-30; cons engr Bur Electronics Navy Dept Washington '43-45, Hewlett-Packard Co since '46. Am Inst EE—Inst Radio Engrs (F)—Sigma Xi—Tau Beta Pi. Hewlett-Packard Co., Palo Alto, Cal. H: Route 1, Box 516A, Los Altos.

10 ELWOOD, Everett Sprague. Medical examinations and licenses. b'81. '04-05 (U Mich); PhB '08 (Syracuse U). Mayor's committee on survey of Philadelphia Mental Hospital '31; chairman Governor's committee on survey of Pennsylvania State Mental Hospitals '32-33. Editor: The Diplomate since '28. Exec sec com on mental hygiene NY State Charities Air Assn '10-15, asst sec '12-15; sec NY State Hosp Commn '15-21; managing dir Nat Bd Med Examiners '15-28, exec sec treas and editor since '28. AAAS(F)—Am Pub Health Assn(F)—Am Psych Assn (hon)—Am Occupational Therapy Assn (vp '31-38, pres '38-46)—NY State Commn on Mental Hygiene—Nat Com for Mental Hygiene—Pub Charities Assn Pa (pres '45-49). 225 S. 15th St., Phila. 2.

11 ELY, Richard Royal. Philippines (Government, economy). b'92. AB '15 (Wash and Jefferson Coll). Studies Philippine government and economy covering period between Spanish-American war and present. Teacher and high sch prin Philippines '17-25; asst sec to Gov-Gen to Philippines '25-35; staff US High Commn to Philippines '35-37; supervisor Philippine Affairs Div Territories and Island Possessions Dept Interior '39-42; exec asst to US High Commr to Philippines Washington '44-46; asst chief and chief div Philippine Affairs Dept State '46-49; dep dir Office Philippine and SE Asian Affairs Dept State since '49. Dept. of State, Washington 25.

12 EMBERSON, Richard Maury. Radiometry; Marine radar; Research coordination. b'14. AB '31—AM '32—PhD '36 (U Mo). Research stellar radiometry, artificial radioactivity and its therapeutic applications. Developed preliminary designs cyclotron; microwave radar and associated equipment, particularly for marine navigation. Staff mem Harvard Coll Obs '36-39; staff mem Radiation Lab MIT '41-46; staff mem Naval Research Lab '46; secretariat (Joint) Research and Development Bd Washington '46-51; asst to pres Associated Universities since '51, asst sec Associated Universities Inc since '52. Am Astron Soc—Am Physical Soc—Am Asso Phys Teach—AAAS—Sigma Xi. Associated Universities, Inc., 350 5th Av., NYC 1. H: Anondale Dr., RFD 2, Huntington, N.Y.†

13 EMBODY, Daniel Robert. Biometry; Limnology; Entomology (Statistics). b'14. BS '38—MS '39—'39-42 (Cornell U); summer '41 (UNC). Statistical analysis of width measurements on a New Hampshire stream, biological survey of the Merrimack Watershed; methods of measuring the quantity of insect habitat in streams; method of estimating number of fish in given section of stream; effect of cresol on brook-trout; method of measuring number of ectoparasites infesting hatchery fish, particular application to gyrodactylus; effect of full moon on trout fishing. Author articles in field. Sr math analyst Arnold Bernhard and Co NYC '47-48; dir Embody Statis Lab Spirit Lake Ida '48-49; statis analyst Wash Water Power Co Spokane since '49, statis cons Ida Fish and Game Dept. Nat Farm Chemurgic Council—Am Statis Assn—

Gamma Alpha—Sigma Xi. P.O. Drawer 1445, Spokane, Wash.

14 EMBREE, John Fee. Southeastern Asia (Japan, Indochina, Siam, cross-cultural acculturation and administration, dependent and colonial peoples); Anthropology. b'08. BA '31 (U Hawaii); MA '34 (U Toronto); PhD '37 (U Chicago). Delegate University of Hawaii to Pacific Science Conference Washington '46; US Cultural Attache in Siam and Indochina '47-48. Author: Suye Mura, A Japanese Village '39, British edit '43; The Japanese '43; Japanese Peasant Songs '44; The Japanese Nation '45 and others; also articles in field. Asso prof Yale since '48; research asso ethnol Bishop Mus since '46. Head community analysis sect War Relocation Authority '42-43, psychol warfare supervisor OWI Pacific Area '45. Soc Applied Anthrop—Am Anthrop Assn—Royal Anthrop Inst (London)—The Far Eastern Assn—Siam Soc—Societe des Etudes Indochinoises (Saigon)—Sigma Xi. Yale University, New Haven.

15 EMBREE, Norris D. Chemistry of oil-soluble vitamins; Chemistry of fatty oils; Molecular distillation. b '11. BA '31 (U Wyo); PhD '34 (Yale). Research on drying oils, edible oils, monoglycerides, fatty acids, unsaponifiable fractions, and on high-vacuum equipment, vacuum and molecular stills, and applications; discovered several products related to vitamin A. With Distillation Products Industries Div Eastman Kodak Co since '34, dir research since '48; WPB (vitamin A adv com '44); US Pharamcopoeia (vitamin A informal com '47-50). ACS (nat council '49-51)—Am Oil Chem Soc (chmn vitamin com '45-50)—Am Soc Biol Chemists—AICE—Vitamin Oil Producers Assn (chmn techn com '43). Distillation Products Industries, Rochester 3, N.Y.

16 EMCH, Arnold Frederick. Management consultant. b'99. AB '25—MA '26 (U Ill); PhD '34 (Harvard). Author articles in field. Partner Booz Allen and Hamilton since '45. Comdr management cons to Surgeon Gen US Navy '42-45. Am Hosp Assn—Ill Hosp Assn. Booz, Allen and Hamilton, 135 S. La-Salle St., Chicago.

17 EMERICK, Robert Henderson. Heating and air conditioning (Heat exchange apparatus, system concealment); Power plants (Casualty investigations, design steam generators, all mechanical components of complete plants; Power plant valuation studies, including district steam properties and artificial gas systems. b'97. Student '20-21 (U Pa Teachers Coll). Invented multistream tube for heat exchange, research on boiler explosions and boiler and turbine casualties for US Navy, insurance companies; investigations air pollution. Author: Basic Refrigeration and Air Conditioning '48; Heating Design and Practice '51; Power Plant Management. With Phila Elec Co '23-37; engr Phoenix Engring Corp '37-38; cons mech engr since '46. Am Soc ME—Fla Engring Soc (sr mem). 109 Jenkins Av., N. Charleston, SC.†

18 EMERSON, Alfred Edwards. Termites; Social insects; Speciation; Zoogeography; Instinct; Biology and society; Ecology and genetics; Taxonomic theory. b'96. BS '18—AM '20—PhD '25 (Cornell U). Co-author: Termite City '37; also articles in field. Research asso Chicago Natural Hist Mus since '42. NY Zool Soc(F)—Am Soc Naturalists—Am Soc Zool—Ecol Soc Am (sec-treas '31, pres '41)—Am Entomol Soc—Am Genetics Assn—Soc Study Evolution (vp '46, '48)—AAAS (vp sect F '46)—Sigma Xi. **Guggenheim fellow**

'26-27. University of Chicago, Department of Zoology, Chicago 37.◉

19 EMIG. Elmer Jacob. Opinion analysis. b'98. BA '22 (Canterbury Coll); MA '26 (U Wis). Author: Reading Habits of Newspaper Readers '28; Survey of University Presses '31; Union List of Newspapers in the Libraries of the US and Canada '37. Co-editor: Headlining America '40; also articles in field. Prof dept journalism U Fla since '49. Fla Press Assn—Nat Editorial Assn (publ com '48-49). Department of Journalism, University of Florida, Gainesville, Fla. H: 2120 N.W. 3rd Pl.†

20 EMLEN, John Thompson, Jr. Bird behavior; Mammal populations. b'08. BA '31 (Haverford Coll); PhD '34 (Cornell U). Scientific expeditions to Haiti and Santo Domingo '27, Honduras '30. Author articles in field. Professor zoology U Wis. AAAS—Am Ornithology Union—Am Soc Mammal—Ecol Soc Am—Wildlife Soc Am—Sigma Xi—Phi Beta Kappa—Phi Kappa Phi.

21 EMMART, Emily Walcott. Folklore medicine of Mexico; Chemotherapy of tuberculosis (Nocardin). AB '22 (Goucher Coll); MA '24—PhD '30 (Johns Hopkins). Author and translator: The Badianus Manuscript, Codex Barberini Latin 241, 1552 published '40, a translation, annotated, and illustrated herbal, first medical text of New World, containing earliest illustrations of Mexican plants, descriptions, medical treatments known to Aztecs; also articles in field. Cytologist Fed Security Agency Nat Inst Health since '36. AAAS—Wash Acad Sci—Soc Exptl Biol and Med—Soc Am Bact—Am Soc Pharm and Therapeutics—Am Trudeau Soc—Soc Indsl Microbiology. National Institute of Health, Bethesda, Md.†

22 EMMERT, Emery Myers. Plant tissue testing; Mineral nutrition of plants. b'00. PhD '31 (Ia State Coll). Developed methods for analyzing plant tissues to detect deficiencies or excesses of nutrients in plants; determined nitrogen, phosphorus and potassium curves showing needs of tomatoes, potatoes at various stages of growth. Author articles in field. With U Ky since '28, prof hort since '46. Horticulture Department, University of Kentucky, Lexington, Ky.

23 EMMONS, Howard Wilson. Supersonic aerodynamics; Heat transfer (Theory); Numerical solutions by relaxation methods; Fluid mechanics; Aerodynamics. b'12. ME '33—MS '35 (Stevens Inst Tech); SD '38 (Harvard). Member joint chiefs of staff temporary guided missiles committee '46; NACA subcommittees on compressors high speed aerodynamics, internal aerodynamics, fluid mechanics; scientific advisory board NOTS; chairman NOL Aeroballistic Panel. Collaborating editor Quarterly of Applied Mathematics. Author: Gas Dynamics Tables for Air '47; also articles in field. Research engr Westinghouse Elec and Mfg Co '37-39; asst prof U Pa '39-40; with Harvard U since '40, now prof; cons Pratt and Whitney Aircraft, Thompson Products Co, Naval Ordnance Lab, Ballistics Research Lab. AAAS—Am Phys Soc (fluid mechs com)—ASME (chmn appl mech div '47)—Math Assn Am—Am Acad Arts Sci—Sigma Xi—Tau Beta Pi. 303 Pierce Hall, Harvard University, Cambridge 38, Mass.◉

24 EMRICH, Duncan Black Macdonald. American folklore; History of Nevada. b'08. AB '32 (Brown U); MA '33 (Columbia); Doctor en Letras '34 (U Madrid); PhD '37—Shattuck scholar and Austin fellow (Harvard); student (U Aix-en-Provence, Sorbonne, U Cologne, Escuela de Estudios Arabes). Author: Who Shot Maggie in the Freckle and other ballads of Virginia City, Nevada '40; Casey Jones and other ballads of the mining West '41; It's an Old Wild West Custom '49; Comstock Bonanza '50. Asst prof Eng U Denver '40-42; chief Archive of Am Folksong Library of Congress '45-46, chief folklore sect since '46. Am Folklore Soc (exec council)—Internat Commn on Folk Arts and Folklore (vp)—Internat Folk Music Council (exec council). Fellow Nat Council on Religion in Higher Edn, John Simon Guggenheim fellow '49-50. Folklore Section, Library of Congress, Washington 25. H: 1517 30th St., N.W., Washington 7, and Virginia City, Nevada.†

10 EMRICH, Raymond Jay. Shock waves; Chronographs; Terminal ballistics (Armor piercing projectiles). b'17. AB '38—PhD '46 (Princeton U); '39 (Cambridge U); '40 (Cornell U). Work in velocity measurements and dissipation studies in shock tube. Author articles in field. Div 2 NDRC Princeton U '41-45; asso prof physics Lehigh U since '46. Am Phys Soc. Department of Physics, Lehigh University, Bethlehem, Pa.†

11 EMSWELLER, Samuel Leonard. Lilium cytology and genetics; Floricultural plant breeding. b'98. BSc '22 (U West Va); PhD '33 (U Calif). Work in breeding floricultural plants as Antirrhinum, lilium and chrysanthemum; studied induced polyploidy in lilium, cytology of lilium polyploids and lilium interspecific hybrids; research in use of growth-promoting substances to overcome self-incompatability in lilium, inheritance of resistance to rust in Antirrhinum, crossing-over, fragmentation and formation of new chromosomes in allium specie hybrid. Co-author: The Vegetable Industry '32; also articles in field. Prin hort charge floricultural investigations US Dept Agr since '35. Washington Acad Sci—Am Bot Soc—Am Genetics Soc—Washington Bot Soc—NY Bot Soc—Sigma XI. Awarded gold medal by NE Gladiolus Soc, $500 Vaughan Memorial Prize. Plant Industry Station, Beltsville, Md.†

12 EMURIAN, Albert Diran. Radio and television communications engineering; Electronic meteorological instruments; (including Weather Radar) Radio navigation systems. b'08. BS (elec engring) '30 (U Pa). Designed and developed radio receivers, television video circuitry, microwave television transmitting and relay equipment; designed and developed radio direction finding sytems, invented microwave radiosonde transmitter. With Philco Corp '31-41; with Signal Corps Engring Lab since '41, dep chief radar equipment sect since '50. Inst Radio Engrs (sr mem)—Armed Forces Communications Assn—Am Inst EE. Received Meritorious Civilian Achievement Award '47. Evans Signal Lab., Signal Corps Engineering Laboratories, Belmar, N.J. H: 1074 Broadway, Long Branch, N.J.

13 ENDERS, Robert Kendall. Mammalogy (Physiology of reproduction). b'99. Student '21-23 (Wooster Coll); AB '25—PhD '27 (U Mich). Research in physiology reproduction with special reference to delayed implantation fur seals, mustelids; controlled length pregnancy mink and marten by shortening delay in implantation. Field work and collecting in tropical America and southeast Asia and India; work in mink farming and other fur animals. Author: Mammalian Life Histories

from Barro Colorado Island, Panama '34. Asst prof zool Union Coll '27-28; prof biol Mo Valley Coll '28-30; mammalogist O State Conservation Com '30; fellow Nat Research Council '30-32; asst prof zool Swarthmore Coll '32-37, asso prof '37-44, prof since '44; chmn zool dept since '48; biol US Biol survey or Bur Animal Industry since '38. Am Soc Mammalogists—Wildlife Soc—Soc Zool Am—Am Assn Anat Soc Vert Paleontol—AAAS(F)—NY Acad Sci(F)—NY Zool Soc(F). Swarthmore college, Swarthmore, Pa. H: 311 Elm Av.†

14 ENDLICH, Philip Jacob. Wind bracing; Bridges; Tunnels; Subways; Hangars. b'84. BS (CE) '09 (U Mich). Consultant on wind bracing tall buildings; computation temperature stresses of bridge arch, and erection stresses; design of floor system and bridge approach spans; assisted in design of Detroit River tunnel, also statically indeterminate steel highway bridge. Supervising engr Lockwood-Greene Engrs Inc NYC Detroit office '20-22; structural engr A E Yokom (cons engr) Detroit '27-28, Albert Kahn Asso Architects & Engrs Inc Detroit '29-32; chief draftsman and sr civil engr USN Shipyard Portsmouth NH '39-45; practice as structural engr Detroit since '47. Am Soc CE—Nat Soc Professional Engrs — Internat Assn Navigation Congresses—Soc Am Mil Engrs—Internat Assn Bridge and Structural Engring. 1806 Oakman Blvd., Det. 6.

15 ENGBERG, George Barker. History of labor. b'12. BS '34—MA '39 —PhD '49 (University of Minnesota). Research in labor unions and rise of organized labor especially in Minnesota, history of labor supply for lumber industry in Lake States. Author: Activities Notebook for America's Road to Now '39; also articles in field. Asst prof hist U Cincinnati since '47. AHA—Miss Valley Hist Assn—Econ Hist Assn—Minn Hist Soc—Nat Council Social Studies—Phi Beta Kappa. Research fellow Forest Products Hist Found Minn Hist Soc '46-47. University of Cincinnati, Cincinnati 21.†

16 ENGDAHL, Richard Bott. Combustion; Fuels (Industrial); Gas turbine; Heat transfer. b'14. BS (ME) '36 (Bucknell U); MS '38 (U Ill). Studies on combustion of coal and oil, application pulverized coal to metallurgical furnaces, combustion in radiant tubes, and application pulverized coal to gas turbines; measurement of flow of pulverized coal in air. Co-author articles: Development of Instruments for Study of Air Distribution '40; Temperature Drop in Ducts for Forced Air Heating Systems '44; Pulverized Coal for Forge Furnaces '43; Overfire Air Jets '43; Meter for Flowing Mixtures of Pulverized Coal '48, and others. Research engr Battelle Memorial Inst '41-45, asst supervisor fuels '45-46, now supervisor fuels. Am Soc ME—Am Soc Heating and Ventilating Engrs—Sigma Xi—Tau Beta Pi—Pi Mu Epsilon. Battelle Memorial Institute, 505 King Av., Columbus 1, O.

17 ENGEL, Albert Edward John. Petrology; Structural geology; Stratigraphy. b'16. AB '38—AM '39 (U Mo); PhD '44 (Princeton). Research on origin and evolution rocks, expecially Pre-Cambrian rocks and mineral deposits; occurrence deposits quartz crystals, lead, zinc, talc. Geol US Geol Survey since '42; asst prof geol U Mo '42; asst prof Cal Tech Inst '48-49, asso prof since '49. Geol Soc Am(F)—Mineral Soc Am—Soc Econ Goel. Dept. of Geology, California Institute of Technology, Pasadena, Cal.†

18 ENGELMAN, Uriah Zevi. Jewish education; Jewish population research; Jewish social history. b'96. BA '20 (U Cal); MA '21 (Columbia); PhD '36 (U Buffalo). Annual survey of Jewish educational developments; in charge community self-studies for Jewish education, and several Jewish demographic studies; research on Jewish emancipation. Author: The Rise of the Jew in the Western World '44. Co-author: The Jews of Charleston '50. Author monographs: A Study of Size of Families in the Jewish Population of Buffalo '38; Hebrew Education in America—Problems and Solutions '46; Jewish Statistics in the US Census of Religious Bodies 1850-1936 '47, and others. Contbr: Encyclopedia Americana; The Jews '50. Exec dir Bur Jewish Edn Buffalo '39-45; head dept research information and publications Am Assn Jewish Edn since '45. 1776 Broadway, NYC 19.

19 ENGHOLM, Frank Goldie. Bridges (Reinforced concrete). b'85. CE '06—ME '06. Establishment system of working drawings and lists giving detailed dimensional bending size, weight, and length each reinforced steel rod used in concrete construction; engineering design and construction first combined arch-cantilever bridge of reinforced concrete in Canada. Cons engr design and constrn Toronto Hamilton Highway Commn '11-24, Detroit-Windsor Vehicular Tunnel '24-33; pres and gen mgr Macoth Co of Can Ltd since '36, vp F C Russell Co of Can Ltd Seerboro Ont since '36. Am Inst CE—Am Inst ME—Mining Engrs Inst Can. Professional engr Can. Macoth Co. of Canada, Ltd., 85 Main St. S., Weston, Ont., Can.

20 ENGLEMAN, Rolf. Petroleum geology. b'00. AB '21 (U Okla). Studies of petroleum geology in Mexico, Venezuela, Cuba, Mid-continent US, Ohio, Louisiana, Oklahoma since 1921. With Carter Oil Co since 1935. Am Assn Petroleum Geol—Am Geophys Union —Am Geog Soc. The Carter Oil Co., 1300 Apco Tower, Oklahoma City 2.

21 ENGLERTH, George Henry. Decay in conifers and wood products. b'07. BSF '33 (U Wash); MF '35 (U Mich); PhD '40 (Yale). Research in decay of fire-killed timber, cultural studies of wood destroying fungi, decay of western Conifers and wood products. Author: Decay of Western Hemlock in Western Oregon and Washington '42; also articles in field. Jr path Bur Plant Ind '34; asst U Mich '35; asst path Bur Plant Ind '35-42; asso path Bur Plant Ind Soils and Agrl Engring since '42. Soc Am Foresters—Sigma Xi. Forest Products Laboratory, Madison 5, Wis.

22 ENGLISH, Earl Franklin. Newspaper typography; Facsimile newspaper; Journalism education. b'05. AB '28—BS '32 (Western Mich Coll); MA '37—PhD '44 (State U Ia); SS '33 (Purdue U). Inspected 48 schools of journalism in recent years while serving on accrediting committees. Author: Exercises in Journalism '37. Co-author: An Intr to Journalism Research '49; Scholastic Journalism '50. Prof U Missouri since '44, dean since '51; exec sec accrediting com Am Council Edn Journalism since '46. AAAS—Am Psychol Assn—Council Research in Journalism (chmn)—Am Assn Teachers Jour—Soc General Semantics—Association Edn Journalism (pres '52)—Sigma Xi. Nat Scholastic Press Assn awards '36-37; Sigma Delta Chi research award '44. University of Missouri, Columbia, Mo. H: 930 Highway 63 South.†

23 ENGLISH, Horace B(idwell). Psychology (Terminology); Child psychology. b'92. AB '14 (Oxford U England); PhD '16 (Yale). Author: A Student's Dictionary of Psychological Terms (4th edit) '34; Child Psychology '51. Prof psychol Ohio State U since '30. Adv bd Warren's Dictionary of Psychology. Am Psychol Assn (council '40-42)—Sigma Xi—Brit Psychol Soc(F). Dept. of Psychology, Ohio State University, Columbus 10, O.†

10 ENGLISH, Pennoyer Francis. Wildlife management (Game). b'94. BS '19 (Ore Agrl Coll); MS '25 (Tex A&M Coll); PhD '34 (Mich U). Research on game bird flushing apparatus, winter feeding of wildlife, food habits of red and gray fox in Pennsylvania, ring-necked pheasant, conservation and habits of various animals. Author articles in field. Prof wildlife management Pa State Coll since '45 directing work grad students, acting head dept zool and entomol since '52. AAAS(F)—Am Soc Mammalogists—Am Ornithol Union—Wilson Ornithol Club—Am Forester Soc (sr mem)—Wildlife Soc (charter, chmn membership com, past sec, past pres). Frear Laboratory, State College, Pa.†

11 ENGLISH, Van Harvey. Cartography (Physiographic maps); Geography of Soviet Russia. b'14. BA '36 (Colorado State Coll Edn); PhD '42 (Clark U, Worcester, Mass). Author: Map Library; also maps and map illustrations for various books and papers. Cartographer OSS '42-45; spl cartographer to Chief of Staff '43-45; geog US Dept State '45-46; prof geog, chmn dept Dartmouth Coll since '52. Am Geog Soc—AAAS—Am Soc Profl Geog. Dartmouth College, Hanover, N.H.

12 ENOS, George Magee. Corrosion. b'96. BS (Met E) '21—Met E '22 (SD Sch Mines); MSc '22 (Carnegie Inst Tech); PhD '25 (U Cincinnati). Research on causes and prevention of failures in metals; development methods for surface treatment of steels. Author: Visual Examination of Steels '38. Jr metall corrosion research US Bur Mines '22-23; asso prof metall engring U Cincinnati '23-39; prof metall engring Purdue since '46; cons metall engr. Dir engring Cincinnati Ordnance Dist AUS '39-46. AIME—Am Soc Metals — Sigma Gamma Epsilon — Phi Lambda Upsilon—Sigma Xi—Tau Beta Pi. Purdue University, Lafayette, Ind.

13 ENSKO, Stephen G. C. Colonial American silver and silversmiths. b'96. Author: American Silversmiths and Their Marks '48; English Silver 1675-1825 '37. 682 Lexington Av., NYC 23.

14 ENSMINGER, Marion Eugene. Beef cattle husbandry; Sheep and goat husbandry; Swine husbandry; Horse husbandry. b'08. BS '31—MS '32 (U Mo); PhD '42 (U Minn). Research on nutrition, breeding, production, and management. Author: Animal Science '50; Horse Husbandry '51; Beef Cattle Husbandry '51; Sheep Husbandry '52; Swine Husbandry '52. Prof and chmn dept animal husbandry State Coll Wash since '41. Am Soc Animal Production—Soil Cons Soc Am—Am Southdown Breeders Assn (dir)—Am Soc Range Management—Sigma Xi—Alpha Zeta. State College of Washington, Pullman, Wash.ⓒ

15 ENTEMANN, Charles E. Agricultural pesticides; Peroxides (Organic); Mothproofing agents. b'06. AB '29—PhD '33 (Cornell). Research and development methods for synthesis and applications organic peroxides in polymerization and flour bleaching; studies and development mothproofing agents, including phenol condensation products (except resinous), aromatic sulfur compounds, nitrogen and sulfur heterocycles, and inorganic fluosili-

cates and fluorides. Research chem organic synthesis and mothproofing agts Zonite Products Corp New Brunswick NJ '36-41, Gen Chem Co LI City NY '41-44; chem Lucidol Div Novadel-Agene Corp Buffalo since '44, chief chem '46-51; research chemist Diamond Alkali Co Painesville since '51. ACS—Am Inst Chem—AAAS. Diamond Alkali Co., Technical Center, Painesville, O. H: Painesville, O.

16 ENTRIKIN, John Bennett. Qualitative organic analysis; Steam pollution. b'99. AB '22—MA '23 (Southwestern U); PhD '29 (Ia State U). Research on effect of stream pollution on soils, plant and animal life. Co-author: (with N D Cheronis) Semimicro Qualitative Organic Analysis '47. Mem faculty Centenary Coll since '29; cons stream pollution Internat Paper Co since '48. Am Inst Chem(F)—ACS—AAAS—Alpha Chi Sigma—Phi Lambda Upsilon—La Acad Sci (past pres). Dept. of Chemistry, Centenary College, Shreveport, La.

17 ENY, Desire Marc. Biochemistry; Plant physiology. b'15. BS '35 (U Algiers France); EE '38 (Institut Breguet Paris); PhD '48—Clinton DeWitt Smith fellow '46—Henry Strong Dennison fellow '47 (Cornell U). Author articles in field. Research biochem Vets Adm Northport LI NY since '49. Am Chem Soc—AAAS—AAUP—Am Soc Bact—Am Soc Plant Physiol—Sigma Xi—Phi Kappa Phi. Biochemical Research Division, Veterans Administration, Northport, L.I., N.Y.†

18 EPPERSON, Joseph Bolen. Television coverage (Computing); Television (Signal range and quality); Radar (Interference). b'10. Student (U Tenn); Grad (Capitol Radio Engring Inst Washington). Supervised installation Ohio's first commercial television station; research and improvement in operation of radar equipment, especially elimination of interference to radar systems; developed slide rule for calculating TV coverage. Author: Characteristics of Resonant Transmission Lines '43; Television Field Intensity Survey '49. Co-author articles: Radar Electronic Fundamentals; Radar System Engineering. Cons to chief signal officer on radar Pentagon Washington '42-44; tech ed Broadcast News Radio Corp of Am Camden NJ 44-46; chief engr Scripps-Howard Chain Television and Radio Broadcast Stas since '46. Inst Radio Engrs (US, Australia)—Am Inst Elec Engrs—Soc Motion Picture and Television Engrs—Fed Communications Cons Engrs. Scripps-Howard Radio, Inc., 1816 E. 13th St., Cleveland 14.

19 EPPLEY, Garrett G. Recreation (College, public). b'96. AB '19 (Manchester Coll); AM '47 (U Chicago); student '40, '42 (NYU). American Olympic Baseball Committee '36; board directors and tournament committee American Baseball Congress '35-41; organized Midwest Hiking Club Association '40; organized Great Lakes Park Training Institute '46, dir since '46; instigated National Association Recreation Educators '47. Author articles in field. Asso prof recreational edn and field recreation Ind U since '45, also chmn dept recreation, sch health phys edn and recreation since '47; cons State Parks Cities and Schs since '45. Am Recreation Soc—Nat Recreation Assn—Am Inst Park Exec—Am Assn Pub Administrs—Am Camping Assn—Am Assn Health Phys Edn and Recreation—NEA. Indiana University, Bloomington, Ind.

20 EPPS, Ernest Allen, Jr. Soil chemistry. b'17. BS '36 (La Poly Inst); MS '38 (La State U). Research on

soils, fertilizers, economic poisons. Faculty La State U '39-40; asst soil tech US Bur Reclamation '40-42; chem Esso Standard Oil Co '43-46; chief chem La Dept Agr and La Agrl Expt Sta since '46. ACS—Phi Lambda Upsilon—Alpha Chi Sigma—Assn Ofcl Agrl Chem—Assn Am Feed Control Ofcls—Assn Am Fertilizer Control Ofcls—Assn Am Econ Poison Control Ofcls—Assn S Feed and Fertilizer Control Ofcls—Assn Ofcl Racing Chemists (asso). Box 589, Baton Rouge.

21 EPPS, William Monroe. Vegetable diseases. b'16. BS '37 (Clemson Coll); PhD '42 (Cornell U). Author articles in field. Asso plant path Clemson Coll Truck Expt Sta since '46. Officer US Army 42-46, conducted research with spl projects div chem warfare service '43-45. Am Phytopath Soc—Sigma Xi—Phi Kappa Phi. P.O. Box 158, St. Andrews Branch, Charleston, S.C.

22 EPSTEIN, David William. Television; Electronics; Cathode ray tubes; Geometrical optics. b'08. BS '30 (Lehigh U); DSc '37 (U Pa). Author: Electron Optics in Television '38; also articles in field. Research engr RCA Labs Princeton NJ since '30. Am Phys Soc—Optical Soc Am—Inst Radio Engrs—Sigma Xi. Radio Corporation of America Laboratories, Princeton, N.J.

23 EPSTEIN, Emanuel. Mineral metabolism of plants; Radioactive isotopes (Application to biological research). b'16. BS '40—MS '41—PhD '50 (U Calif). Research on plant absorption of clay-adsorbed micronutrient elements, such as iron, manganese, zinc, and copper; separation, identification, and assay of radioactive iron, manganese and zinc in tracer studies involving absorption and utilization of these elements by plants; research on mechanism of ion absorption by plants. Research asst plant nutrition U Cal '46-49; plant physiol USDA Beltsville Md since '50. American Society Plant Physiologists—Sigma Xi—Gamma Alpha. U.S. Department of Agriculture, Plant Industry Station, Beltsville, Md.

24 EPSTEIN, Fritz Theodor. European and Slavic history; Historical bibliography. b'98. PhD '24 (Berlin U). Research in School Slavonic Studies, Institute Historical Research, Royal Institute International Affairs, London '34-36; Hoover Library Stanford U '37 and '41. Editor: Heinrich von Stadens Aufzeichnungen über den Moskauer Staat '30; Das national-sozialistische Deutschland und die Sowjetunion 1939-1941 (with E Malcolm Carroll) '48. Sub-editor Minerva (Yearbook Learned World) '24-26; also articles in field. Research asst Hamburg U '26-31; German lecturer Institut Français de Londres '34-36; research asst Bur Internat Research Harvard and Radcliffe Coll '39-41; vis prof NY City Coll '41; research asst Harvard Coll Library '41-44; bibliog asst Harvard School Overseas Adminstrn '42-44; OSS '44-45; research div Dept State '45-46; mem Am group Berlin Team Inter-Allied German War Documents Project '46-48; vis prof Berlin (Germany) Free University '50; curator Central and East European Collections Hoover Library Stanford U '48-51; dir research War Documentation Project '51; USSR and East European Area specialist Library of Congress since '52; lect American U Sch of Social Sciences of Public Affairs '52-53. AHA. Grant-in-aid Acad Assistance Council '34-36. Research fellow Notgemeinschaft der Deutschen Wissenschaft and William Kerkhoff Found '31-33. Slavic Division, The Library of Congress, Washington 25, D.C.

10 EPSTEIN, Lenore Alice. Family expenditures in relation to income. b'14. BA '35 (Wellesley Coll); MA '36 (Columbia U). Studies of Variations in levels of living with family size, occupation, place of residence, and other factors. Author: Family Expenditures in Selected Cities, 1935-36: Medical Care '40; Travel and Transportation '40; Wartime Earnings and Spending in Honolulu, 1943 '44; Wartime Food Purchases '45. Social sci analyst US Bur Labor Statis, consumer purchases study '36-39, price econ and chief income and expenditure sect '42-47, research asst survey of Negro in Am Carnegie Corp of NY '39-40; statis for price and labor data Div Statis and Reports Econ Coop Admin '48-51; now Reports and Statistics officer Mutual Security Agency Special Mission to France. American Statistics Association—Am Acad Polit Social Sci—Phi Beta Kappa. MSA/MF, American Embassy, Paris, France.

11 EPSTEIN, L(udwig) Ivan. Phase contrast; Thin films (Optics); Optics (Geometrical). b'18. BS '40—MS (phys) '41 (Cal Inst Tech). Research on resolving power optical instruments, aberrations of decentered optical systems, image formation in phase contrast microscopy, design thin film combinations for use as color filters. With US Navy Rocket Project Cal Inst Tech '43-46; with Bausch & Lomb Optical Co since '47. Optical Soc Am—APS. Scientific Bureau, Bausch and Lomb Optical Co., Rochester 2, N.Y.†

12 EPSTEIN, Samuel Sidney. Food technology; Bacteriology; Coliform bacteria; Germicides; Brewing technique; Flavor chemistry. b'06. BS '29 (RI State Coll); MS '32—PhD '34 (Ia State Coll). Author articles in field. Cons bact since '38; cons Foster D Snell Inc Bklyn, Food Res Lab Long Island City; chief chem and vp Kirsch's Beverages Inc since '42. Am Pub Health Assn—Inst Food Tech—Am Soc Bact—Phi Kappa Phi—Sigma Xi. Chesterton Award outstanding scientific contribution to bottling industry '50. 919 Flushing Av., Bklyn 6.

13 ERDÉLYI FAZEKAS, John Alexander. Petroleum geology: Exploration spotty oil fields. b'12. Diplomeconomist '39—Dr Econ Geol '40 (Palatine Joseph Tech and Econ U Budapest); Exploration Geophys '39 (Baron Roland von Eötvös Geophys Inst). Research on combined geological and geophysical technique of location of spotty oil fields. Inventor, developer new effective technique in this exploration. Author: Application of Geology, Geophysics and Photogeology in Microtectonical Exploration '43. Exploration geol and geophys Hungarian Am Oil Indsl Co '40-47; exploration geol and geophys Danish Am Prospecting Co '47-48; asso prof structural geol and petroleum geophys U Okla. Sigma Xi—Am Assn Petroleum Geol—Soc Exploration Geophys—Am Geophys Union—Okla Acad Sci. Dept. of Geology, University of Oklahoma, Norman, Okla.

14 ERDMAN, Lewis W(ilson). Legume inoculation; Legumes (Nitrogen-fixing bacteria); Seeds (Inoculation with nitrogen fixing bacteria). b '95. BS '16 (U Md), MS '21—PhD '22 (Ia State Coll). Research on bacteria active in fixation of nitrogen when grown in symbiosis with various leguminous plants; efficiency of various strains of legume organism, involving the isolation and propagation of strains of bacteria that produce maximum benefits when applied to particular legumes; selection of strains that have ability to inoculate more than one variety of legume; iso-

lation and development strains for successful inoculation foreign importations and newly introduced legumes; propagation, storage and distribution of legume nodule bacteria. Author articles: Studies on Inoculation of Soybeans; The Rise of Inoculation; Legume Inoculation—What It Is—What It Does, and others. Sr bacteriologist USDA, Plant Industry Station Beltsville Md since '46. AAAS(F)—Soc Am Bacteriologists—Soil Sci Soc Am—Am Soc Agronomy—Sigma Xi. Plant Industry Station, Beltsville, Md. H: 120 Springbrook Dr., Silver Spring.

15 ERDMANN, Charles Edgar. Coal, natural gas, and petroleum (Rocky Mountain states); Dam and reservoir sites (Northwestern states); Structural geology and tectonics of Montana; Stratigraphy (Montana). b'97. EM '23—MS '24 (U Minn); '25-26 (Yale). Author articles: Problems of Petroleum Geology '34; Geology of Natural Gas '35; Stratigraphic Type Oil Fields '41; Application of Geology to the Principles of War '43, and others. Co-author articles: (with C E Dobbin) Structure Contour Map of the Montana Plains '46; Geologic Occurrence of Oil and Gas in Montana, and others. Geol US Geol Survey since '24, regional geol ND, Mont, northern Ida, and Wash mineral classification br conservation div since '49. AAAS(F)—Geol Soc Am(F)—Am Assn Petroleum Geol—Soc Econ Geol—Am Mining Soc—Geol Soc Wash—Am Geophys Union—Sigma Xi—Gamma Alpha—Sigma Gamma Epsilon. U.S. Geological Survey, 417 Electric Bldg., P.O. Box 1827, Great Falls, Mont.

16 EREKSON, Arthur Beau. Cheese (Bacteriology, enzymes, packaging). b'06. BA '28 (U Utah); BS '31 (Utah State Agrl Coll); MS '32 (U Wis). Bacteriological studies brick and Swiss cheese; development new packaging methods for natural and processed cheese; research on new methods for enzyme curing of cheese. Author articles: A Comparative Study of Packaging Materials for Process Cheese '40; Should Cheese be Priced on a Solids and Butterfat Basis? '46; Standards of Identity for Cheese '46; Shelf Curing of Cheese—What are the Facts '46, and others. Research Swiss Fed Expt Sta Liebefeld Switzerland '33-34; research fellow U Wis '34-35; dir research Swiss and Cheddar cheese, and process cheese Borden Co since '35. Am Dairy Sci Assn—Inst Food Tech—Soc Am Bact—Wis Dairy Tech Soc—Nat Cheese Inst Research Com. Lakeshire Marty Co., Plymouth, Wis.

17 ERGANG, Robert Reinhold. Modern European history; Germany (Nationalism, militarism). b'98. '15-17 (Concordia Coll); BA '19—BD '21 (Concordia Sem); MA '22—PhD '31—seminars in field '21-23, 30-31 (Columbia). Research in medieval history, early Germanic languages and literature, modern nationalism. Author: Herder and the Foundations of German Nationalism '31; Europe from the Rennaissance to Waterloo '39; The Potsdam Fuehrer: Frederick William I, Father of Prussian Militarism '41; Europe in Our Time '48; Europe Since Waterloo '50. Teaching fellow Columbia '22-24; instr hist NYU '25-29, asst prof '38-43; historical research '31-38; now exec vp Pocono Crest Corp. Am Hist Assn—Am Acad Pol Sci. 11 W. 42nd St., NYC 18. H: Holly Chambers, 33 Washington Sq., W., NYC 11.

18 ERGLE, David Ramsey. Chemistry and physiology of cotton plant and cotton root-rot. b'03. BS'26 (Clemson Coll); MS '28—PhD '30 (U NC). Author articles in field. Chem US Dept Agr since '30. Am Chem Soc—AAAS—

Am Soc Agron—Sigma Xi. Agricultural Experiment Station, College Station, Tex.†

19 ERICKSON, Arnold Burton. Wildlife ecology (Terrestrial); Ornithology; Mammalogy; Game parasitology. b'09. BS '35—MA '37—PhD '42 (U Minn). Made wildlife surveys St Croix Park Minnesota '36-37; research on cycles and game parasitology '39-45, effects DDT on bird and mammal populations '45-46, cycles and game populations since '46. Developed method for censusing white-tailed deer; perfected holder for confining small mammals while tagging, sexing and aging; editor The Flicker (Minnesota Ornithological Journal) '39-45. Author articles in field. Wildlife tech Nat Park Service '36-37; asst ornithol U Minn '37-39, research asso game parasitol and wildlife '39-45; biol USPHS '45-46; game biologist Minn Div Game and Fish '46-51, game research supervisor since '52. Wildlife Soc Am—Am Soc Mammalogists—Am Soc Parasitol—Am Ornithol Union—Minn Acad Sci—Minn Ornithol Union—Sigma Xi. Minnesota Division of Game and Fish, 1005 Commerce Building, St. Paul, Minn. H: Rt. 3, Excelsior.

20 ERICKSON, C(harles) Telford. Albania and the Balkans; Ecumenical religion. b'67. BA (DePauw U); MA '93—LLD '32—STB '95 (Boston U); MA '02 (Yale); DD (Drury Coll). Honor delegate for Albania at Paris Peace Conference '19-20; special commissioner for Albania to US '20-21; delegate Pan-Albanian Federation America to United Nations Conference San Francisco '45; Good-will Mission sponsored by World Council of Churches, International Missionary Council, National Council Congregational Churches, to New Zealand, Australia, England, Sweden '47; Commissioned by Albanian Government to build American-Albanian College of Agriculture, trades school for boys, school domestic arts for girls with American charter and trustees '24-35, retired '35; engaged lit work '48. Comdr Order of Scanderbeg. 360 N. Quaker Lane, W. Hartford, Conn.

21 ERICKSON, Franklin Carl. Cartography; Economic geography of North Carolina; Land utilization. b'03. BA '28—MA '30—PhD '35 (Clark U); '32-33 (Zurich U). Research on transhumance in land economy of Schachental, land utilization of various areas, cotton and tobacco belts of North Carolina, broken cotton belt, Swiss neutrality. Author articles in field. Prof geog Boston U since '47. Am Assn Geog—Am Soc Profl Geog—Sigma Xi. Swiss-Am Exchange Student '32-33. Boston University, Boston.†

22 ERICKSON, John Gerhard. Nitrogen compounds. b'17. BA '38 (St Olaf Coll); MS '40 (ND Agrl Coll); PhD '44 (U Minn). Research on preparation and reactions of nitriles, preparation various types of nitrogen heterocycles, preparation acrylamides, reactions of hydrogen cyanide, fatty amides, amines, B-aminocrotonic esters, and triazines, tetrazines, and pentazines. Co-author: The 1, 2, 3-and 1, 2, 4- Triazines, Tetrazines and Pentazines '53. Granted patents in field. Research chem Am Cyanamid Co '44-50; research chem Gen Mills Inc since '51. ACS—AAAS—Sigma Xi—Phi Lambda Upsilon. General Mills, Ind., 2010 E. Hennepin Av., Mpls. 13.

23 ERICKSON, Myrtle Catherine. Education of exceptional children. b'06. BS '48 (Winona State Teachers Coll Minn). Teacher academic and indsl work at Colony for Epileptics Cambridge Minn '29-33; spl classes for subnormal children Austin Minn Pub

Schs since '36. NEA—Am Childhood Edn—Am Assn Mental Deficiency(F). 310½ W. College, Austin, Minn.

10 ERICKSON, Ole Peter. Dredge design. b'90. ME '17 (Internat Corr Schs). Specialist in hydraulic dredge design; subaqueous excavation problems; rock cutter design; design largest Diesel electric portable hydraulic dredge. Issued patents on Y-valve and quick release flexible connection for hydraulic dredge pipelines, special dredge pump liners. Supt Standard Dredging Co NYC '24-27; mech engr Great Lakes Dredge and Dock Co Chicago '27-32; civil, mech engr and gen mgr Hendry Corp Tampa Fla '33-47; cons engr US Bur Reclamation, also cons engr since '47; pres Erickson Engring Co. Am Soc CE—ASME—Am Inst EE—Am Soc Naval Engrs—Nat Soc Profl Engrs—Fla Engring Soc. Erickson Engineering Co., 819 Grove Park Av., Tampa 9, Fla.†

11 ERICKSON, Ray Charles. Waterfowl management; Marsh ecology. b '18. AB '41 (Gustavus Adolphus Coll); MS '42—PhD '48 (Ia State Coll). Research into agriculture relationships waterfowl; studies marsh management; improvement for waterfowl and fur-bearers. Collaborator with Fish and Wildlife Service Br Wildlife Research at Patuxent Research Refuge Laurel Md '39-41; wildlife management biol Malheur Refuge since '48. Am Ornithol Union—Wildlife Soc—Wilson Ornithol Club—Ecol Soc Am—Cooper Ornithol Club. Malheur Refuge, Box 113, Burns, Ore.

12 ERICKSON, Roland Irvin. Mining engineering. b'07. EM '30 (U Minn). Research on geology and milling of tin, open pit mining of nitrate, and mining and milling of iron. Co-author article: (with L E Daume) Working Tin Dumps and Fills in Cerro Rico de Potosi '44. Mine engr and foreman Anglo-Chilean Nitrate Corp Chile '30-32; asst gen supt Bolivian Tin and Tungsten Mines Corp Bolivia '36-38; supt and acting gen mgr Cia Minera Unificada Potosi Bolivia '39-48 supt Cleveland Cliffs Iron Co '48-51; chief of engring and mining Reserve Mining Co since '51. Am Inst Mining Engrs — AAAS — SAME. 300 Christie Bldg., Duluth, Minn.☆

13 ERICSSON, Eric Oscar. Pulp mills (By-products). b'12. BS in chem engring '35 (U Wash). Manufacture alcohol from sulfite waste liquor. Puget Sound Pulp and Timber Co since '35, now gen supt. ACS—AICE—Tech Assn Pulp and Paper Industry. Puget Sound Pulp and Timber Co., Bellingham, Wash.

14 ERLANDSON, Paul M. Radio direction finders; Cathode ray tubes; Frequency scanning; Industrial process instrumentation. b'20. BS '41 (MIT); MA '49—PhD '50 (U Tex). Design shipboard high frequency, very high frequency, and ultra-high frequency radio direction finders; investigation rapid data presentation methods, study frequency scanning receivers for electronic counter-measures; design units employing cathode ray tubes as light sources for dimensional measurements, counters, and generation of complex voltages; research basic requirements for improvement quantitative qualities of cathode ray tubes; design devices for industrial process measurements using electronic, acoustic, and nuclear techniques. Holds patents on systems using electronic switches and systems for simultaneous recording of bearings and related data. Project officer Electronics Div Navy Bur Ships '42-46; research physicist Defense Research Lab U Tex '46-50; Chmn Physics Dept

Southwest Research Inst since '50. APS—Inst Radio Engrs—Optical Soc Am—Sigma Xi—Sigma Pi Sigma—Eta Kappa Nu. Physics Dept, Southwest Research Institute, San Antonio 6.

15 ERNST, Robert Craig. Chemical engineering (Unit operations, tobacco technology, marine oil refining). b'00. BS '21 (NC State Coll); MS '23—PhD '30 (U Minn). Holds five patents in field. Author articles in field. Dean Speed Sci Sch U Louisville since '47, pres and dir Inst Indsl Research since '47; cons various govt agencies, Fish Products Co Lewes Del since '40, Brown and Williamson Tobacco Corp Ky since '43, British Am Tobacco Co since '44; mem Council Oak Ridge Inst Nuclear Studies. Nat Research Council (mem com on design, constrn, and equipment of labs)—Am Inst Chem Engrs—Nat Acad Sci—Am Chem Soc—Sigma Xi—Phi Kappa Phi. University of Louisville, 3rd and Eastern Parkway, Louisville 8.

16 ERNST, Thomas Edward. Railroads (Passenger terminal consolidation). b'06. Student '24-26 (Tulane U); BS in civil engring '31 (U Ala). Engineer in charge Union passenger terminal survey City New Orleans resulting consolidation five stations into one. Engr in charge survey 36-40; cons engr since '46. Am Soc CE—Am Pub Works Assn—La Engring Soc—Soc Am Mil Engrs. 822 Perdido St., New Orleans 12.

17 ERNST, Walter. Hydraulics. b'01. Dipl Ing (ME) '23 (Techn Hochschule Dresden Germany). Design and development high speed presses and machine tools, pumps, variable and constant delivery rotary, vane and plunger, controls and valves, hydraulic drives and systems, and servomechanisms. Author: Oil Hydraulic Power and its Industrial Applications '49. Author article: Commercial and Industrial Applications of Hydraulic Servomechanism '49. Dir engring Hydraulic Press Mfg Co Mt Gilead O '26-44; vp and dir engring Commonwealth Engring Co since '44. Commonwealth Engineering Co., 1771 Springfield St., Dayton, O.

18 ERRINGTON, Paul L(ester). Zoology (Vertebrate ecology, predation, population mechanics). b'02. BS '30 (SD State Coll); PhD '32 (U Wis). Research on population principles, ecology of game birds, fur bearing animals, and habits of predatory birds and mammals; writings on threshold of security in prey populations, vulnerability of prey as conditioned by over-population tensions, emergencies and disease; intercompensatory or automatically adjusting trends in rates of loss or gain of populations; and manifestations of periodic depression phases affecting populations. Author monographs: The Northern Bob-white's Winter Territory (with F N Hamerstrom Jr) '36; The Great Horned Owl and Its Prey in North Central US '40; An Analysis of Mink Predation upon Muskrats in North Central US '43; Predation and Vertebrate Populations '46. Indsl fellow U Wis '29-32; research asst Iowa State Coll '32-38, research asso prof '38-48, research prof '48. AAAS—Am Soc Zool—Am Ornithol Union — Wilson Ornithol—Cooper Ornithol—Am Soc Mammalogists—Ecol Soc Am—Wildlife Soc—Iowa Acad Sci—Wis Acad Sci Arts Letters — Ottawa Field - Naturalists. Wildlife Soc award for outstanding publs in wildlife ecol and management '40-46. Insectary, Iowa State College, Ames, Ia. H: 2850 Arbor St.†

19 ERSELCUK, Muzaffer Mehmet. Petroleum utilization; Iron utilization;

Resources. b'16. BS '38 (Robert Coll); MA '40—PhD '45 (Ind U); '40 (U Wis); '41-42 (Clark U). Consultant to US government on evaluation of iron and steel industries of Japanese Empire '41-45, member American Delegation of Resources '49. participant Conference on Conservation and Utilization of Resources '49. participant Centennial Conference on Science, Technology and World Resources at Northwestern University '51. With Purdue U since '45, prof since '50. Am Econ Assn—Acad Polit and Soc Sci—Assn Am Geog—Far E Assn—Ind Acad Soc Sci—Ind Acad Sci—Am Geog Soc. Economics Dept., Recitation Bldg., Purdue University, West Lafayette, Ind. H: 2238 Union St., Lafayette.

20 ERSKINE, Archibald Montimer. Pigments; Building materials; Industrial research. b'92. BS in chem '14—PhD '21 (Cornell). Director industrial research on pigments, especially pigment colors; application research for pigments for paints and lacquers, printing inks, cold water paints, rubber, and linoleum; study asphalt refining, roofings, linoleum, felt-base floor covering, magnesia insulations, and gypsum wallboard. Holds seven patents on pigments and their uses. Prof chem Hamilton Coll Clinton NY '22-28; asst dir pigment research DuPont Co Newark '28-44; dir research and development Paraffine Companies San Francisco '45-48; cons chem since '49. ACS—Sigma Xi—Tau Beta Pi—Alpha Chi Sigma. 2321 Derby Street, Berkeley 5, Cal.

21 ERSKINE, Hazel Gaudet (Mrs. Graham Erskine). Public opinion measurements. b'08. AB '30—AM '30 (Geo Wash U); summer '31 (U Minn); '33-35 (Columbia). Co-author: (with Paul Lazarsfield, Bernard Perelson) The People's Choice ' 48. Research psychol OWI NYC and London '42-45, CBS NYC '45-46; free-lance research psychol since '46. Am Psychol Assn (asso)—Soc Psychol Study Social Issues—World Assn Pub Opinion Research—Acad Polit and Social Sci. H: Route 1, Box 644, Reno.

22 ERSPAMER, August Severn. Pulp chemistry. b'12. BS in chem engring '34—MS in chem '35 (Wash U); PhD '39 (Inst Paper Chem). Studies in flocculation and dispersion pulp fibers; problem of curl; treatment pulp waste. Issued patents on paper sizing. Asst tech dir P H Glatfelter Co Spring Grove Pa '39-42, tech dir since '45. Served as asso chem engr Edgewood Arsenal AUS '42-45. ACS—Tech Assn Pulp and Paper Industry. P. H. Glatfelter Co., Spring Grove, Pa.

23 ESCHMAN, Karl Henry. Modern Music (Forms). b'91. PhB '11 (Denison U); MA '13 (Harvard); student '29-30 (Vienna U). Rhetoric, morphology and sentence structure of modern music, piano sonatas and problem of modern form, especially Scriabine. Author: Changing Forms of Modern Music '45. Composer: Masque in Time's Garden. Dir Granville Festival Assn since '13; prof music and dir Conservatory Music Denison U since '13; faculty mem summer sessions Northwestern U since '36; pianist and organist. Am Musicolog Soc—Am Guild Organists (F). Naumberg Fellowship, Harvard '19-20. Denison University, Granville. O.

24 ESHLEMAN, Silas Kendrick. Industrial and metallurgical engineering (Materials, automotive). b'86. AB '25—MA Edn '27—JD '36 (Ta U); MS '10 (Harvard); ME '08—EE '09 (Lehigh U). Research on materials such as ferrous metals and alloys used in guns and ordnance materiel, and on selection, manufacture, heat treatment, fabrication and adaptation of metals for automotive industry. Author articles in field. Metall engr, gen purchasing agent Columbia Steel and Shafting Co '12-18; mill supt Crucible Steel Co Am '20-22; prof Fla U since '22. Officer US Army Ordnance Dept, chief TW sect '18-19. ASME—AIEE—SAM—AAUP—Phi Alpha Delta—AIIE—Phi Kappa Phi—Kappa Delta Pi. College of Engineering, University of Florida, Gainesville, Fla. H: 543 N.E. 6th Ave.†

10 ESKEW, Garnett Laidlaw. Mississippi and Ohio River steamboating. b'95. Student '17-21 (NY U). Publicized completion of Lakes-to-Gulf Waterway connecting Great Lakes and Mississippi system '30-33. Author: Pageant of the Packets—a Book of American Steamboating; Salt, The Fifth Element '48; Engineering Administration Afloat; Activating Ships of the Reserve Fleet. also articles in field. Writer USN since '49. Ice Bldg., Washington.†

11 ESKEW, Roderick K(oenig). Nitrocellulose (Viscosity reduction); Agricultural wastes (Utilization); Food flavor; Rutin (Methods of manufacture); Rubber (Domestic source); Potatoes (Utilization of surplus). b '97. Research on stabilization and viscosity reduction by pressure digestion cellulose nitrate; directed research on utilization agricultural residues especially preparation of high-protein, high-carotene feeds from vegetable field wastes; directed research of recovery and utilization volatile aromas of fruit juices especially in preparation frozen concentrated fruit juices; developed process for producing drug rutin from buckwheat leaves; directed research on recovery natural rubber from domestic plants especially guayule, cryptostegia grandiflora, taraxacum kok-saghyz, chrysothamnus nauseosus and pingue; directed research on utilization surplus white potatoes for production flour and dried product for feed; survey in Europe potato processing methods for starch, flour and feed. Holds patents on processes for nitrocellulose stabilization and viscosity reduction. Author articles: Natural Rubber from Russian Dandelion '46; European Methods for the Utilization of Potato Starch Factory Wastes '48; Conversion of Potatoes to Stable Form '49. Coauthor articles: (with David A Colker) Processing Vegetable Wastes for High-Protein High-Vitamin Leaf Meals; (with Howard P Milleville) Recovery and Utilization of Natural Apple Flavors), and others. Research cellulose nitrate E I duPont de Nemours & Co Arlington NJ '25-34; head chem engring and development div Eastern Regional Research Lab USDA Phila since '40. AICE. Eastern Regional Research Laboratory, Chestnut Hill Station, Phila. 18.

12 ESKIN, Sam. Folksongs. born '98. Collector, singer, and recorder of folksongs since '20. Recorded folksong record albums: Sierra; Sounds of our Times; Folkways (logger's songs and sea shanties). Am Folklore Soc—NY Folklore Soc—Western Folklore Soc—So Folklore Soc—Tenn Folklore Soc—Ozark Folklore Soc—W Va Folklore Soc—Internat Folkmusic Council. Box 506, Woodstock, N.J.

13 ESKIN, Samuel George. Thermostats and automatic controls for domestic appliances. b'04. BS '26 (MIT); MS '39 (Northwestern U); '27-28 (U Chicago). Research on thermostats and control circuits for electric heating devices, controls for gas and electric heating and cooking appliances and house heating equipment, electric ignition of gases. Holder numerous patents on thermostats and safety controls. Author articles in field. Research and development engr Edison Gen Elec Appliance Co Chicago '27-32, '37-39; chief eng Am Thermometer Co St Louis '36-37; dir research Robertshaw Thermostat Co Pittsburgh '39-44, Robertshaw-Fulton Controls Co Los Angeles since '44. ASME—Am Soc Heating and Ventilating Engrs—Am Soc Metals—Am Soc Testing Materials—Inst Aeronautical Sci—Instrument Soc Am—Pacific Coast Gas Assn—Am Gas Assn. 833 N. Highland Av., Los Angeles 38. H: 9271 Flicker Way, LA 46.

14 ESLICK, Leonard James. Predication (Logic); Thomistic philosophy; Platonic logic. b'14. AB '34 (U Chicago); MA '36 (Tulane U); PhD '39—du Pont fellow philos '36-39 (U Va). Comparison of logic of Plato and Aristotle and relation to other types of philosophies. Author: Recent Theories of Universals '36; Scientific Abstraction and the Unity of Essence '39; The Current Conception of Truth '42; also articles in field. Asso prof philos St Louis U since '48. So Soc Philos Psychol—Am Cath Philos Assn—Ia Philos Soc—U Va Philos Club (past pres). Philosophy Department, St. Louis University, St. Louis, Mo.

15 ESPENSHADE, Edward B., Jr. Cartography; Regional geography of Asia. b'10. BS '30—MS '32—PhD '43 (U Chicago). Built research collection of maps University of Chicago; preliminary planning for enlargement of map collection and acquisition of vital map materials; set up specifications and plans for reproduction and drafting of large number of foreign topographic series for various parts of world in service of War Department; cartographic intelligence work in Germany and other areas; established place-names procedures on Roman, non-Roman alphabet, non-alphabet languages for War Department; worked with US Board on Geographical Names in establishing procedures for other government agencies. Editor: Goode's School Atlas. Curator maps U Chgo '34-39; fgn map ed Army Map Service, Corps Engrs, War Dept '41-44; engr intelligence Corps Engrs '44-45; teacher cartography Northwestern U since '45; cons Rand McNally Co Chicago since '45. Assn Am Geog—Am Soc Profl Geog—Am Geophys Union—Am Congr Surveying Mapping. Department of Geography, Northwestern University, Evanston, Ill.

16 ESPINOSA, J. Manuel. Latin and western American folklore and history; Inter-American cultural relations. b'09. AB '30—MA '31 (Stanford U); PhD '34 (U Calif). Author: Spanish Folk-Tales From New Mexico '37; First Expedition of Vargas into New Mexico '40; Crusaders of the Rio Grande '42; also articles in field. Instr hist '34-37, asst prof St Louis U '37-39; prof hist and lit '39-44 Loyola U; lecturer in hist Cath U Am '45-49; chief professional programs sect Div Internat Exch of Persons Dept of State since '44. AHA—Am Assn Teachers Spanish and Portuguese—Phi Beta Kappa. Division of International Exchange of Persons, Department of State, Washington. H: 4224 Albemarle St., N.W.

17 ESPY, Melvin Paul. Airframe (Design, testing). b'13. BS (ME) (Pa State Coll); '30-34 (Johns Hopkins). Plan and direction performance aircraft structural tests in fields of development, operation, proof, fatigue, and destruction testing; stress analysis airframe structure; co-inventor of oil-spring landing gear drag strut for twin-engine airplanes; inventor all-hydraulic closed loop servo system for structural testing. Test engr Glenn L Martin Co Baltimore '38-50; missile engring Bendix Products Div Bendix Aviation Corp '50-51 test engr Canadair Ltd Montreal '51. Am Soc ME—Soc Exptl Stress Analysis. Professional engr Md. Engring. Dept., Canadair Ltd., P.O. Box 6087, Montreal, Que., Can.

18 ESSICK, Charles Rhein. Lens grinding. b'83. AB '05 (Yale); MD '09 (Johns Hopkins); DSc '36 (hon) (Albright Coll). Mgr lens grinding plant Pa Optical Co Reading Pa '15-30, propr since '30, pres since '46. Capt Med Corps US Army '17-19. AAAS—Am Assn Chem—Am Ceramic Soc. 234 S. 8th St., Reading, Pa.

19 ESSIG, Edward Oliver. Agricultural insect pests; Aphids; Irises; History of entomology. b'84. Prep edn (Kildale Normal and Pomona Coll); BS '09—MS '12 (Pomona Coll). Author: Injurious and Beneficial Insects of California '13; Insects of Western North America '26; A History of Entomology '31; College Entomology '42; also articles in field. Prof entomol U Calif since '27; entomol Calif Agrl Expt Sta since '28; head div entomol and parasitol since '43; Nat Research Council '41-47. AAAS—Am Assn Econ Entomol (pres)—Entomol Soc Am (pres)—Am Iris Soc (dir, award for hybridizing)—Am Fuchsia Soc—Pacific Coast Entomol Soc (pres)—Calif Acad Sci—Sigma Xi. Awarded rank of Chevalier du Merite Agricole '32, Dykes medal '35. 744 Creston Road, Berkeley.†

20 ESTES, Stanley Goddard. Psychotherapy. b'01. AB '23 (Colby Coll); AM '30—PhD '37 (Harvard). Member editorial board Journal Abnormal and Social Psychology since '40. Author articles in field. Lecturer clin psychol dept social relations Harvard since '47. Mass Civic League (dir '43-45, chmn bd '40-45)—Am Psychol Assn—Mass Soc Clin Psychol (sec '37-42, pres '43)—Am Orthopsychiat Assn—Eastern Psychol Assn—Diplomat in Clinical Psychology. Harvard Psychological Clinic, Cambridge, Mass.

21 ETHEREDGE, M(ahlon) P(adgett). Chemical analysis (starch, fertilizer, cottonseed meal). b'97. BS '18 (Clemson Coll); MS '40 (Miss State Coll); PhD '45 (MIT). Investigational work on potash and nitrogen for Association Official Agricultural Chemists '23-43, research on methods for determining starch '38-44, on methods for nitrogen determination in fertilizers, appointed associate referee '47-50; research on organic sugar Massachusetts Institute of Technology '43-45; special investigational methods on determination of oil and ammonia in cottonseed meal under auspices of American Oil Chemists' Society '26-39. Author articles in field. Head dept chem, prof chem Miss State Coll since '45; state chem Miss since '45. Am Chem Soc—Am Oil Chem Soc (helped win six cups for work on oil and ammonia '26-39)—Assn Official Agrl Chem—Assn Food and Drug Officials USA—Am Feed Control Ofcls (pres)—Am Fertilizer Control Officials (investigator on nitrogen)—Am Soc for Testing Materials—NEA—Council Oak Ridge Inst for Nuclear Studies. Awarded grant-in-aid Gen Edn Bd MIT. Mississippi State Chemical Laboratory, State College, Miss.†◎

22 ETKES, Perez Willard. Israel (Reconstruction) b'92. BS in civil engring '15—CE '25 (Cooper Union Inst). Construction roads, bridges and public buildings, Haifa airport in Israel; rebuilt famous antique walls Acre.

Dist engr and sr exec engr N of Palestine '20-48; now cons engr. Profl. engr NY State. Am Soc CE—Israeli Soc Engrs and Architects. Received British King's Medal for services in the cause of freedom. P.O. Box 422, Haifa, Israel. H: 213 West 66th St., N.Y.C. 23.

10 ETTAWAGESHIK, Jane Willets. Ottawa Indians. b'15. AB '36 (Barnard Coll); scholarships '46-47, '47-48—MA '48 (U Pa). Research on ethnology of Ottawa Indians and their legends, songs, crafts, religious beliefs, social customs, superstitions, and effect of acculturation on relationship system. Am Anthrop Assn—Am Folklore Soc. H: 146 E. Lake Rd., Harbor Springs, Mich.†

11 ETTENBERG, Eugene M(artin). Typography; Typographic history. b'03. Grad '25 (Fine and Applied Arts Sch of Pratt Inst); student (NYU, Columbia). Designed over 200 books for Scribners, Metropolitan Museum of Art, The Pierpont Morgan Library and others. Author: Types for Books and Advertising '48. Editor: Graphic Arts Production year book '36-41; also articles in field. Typog and manager Gallery Press since '45; instr typog Pratt Inst since '47; dir and vp Am Inst Graphic Arts—Typophiles (trade book judge). Gallery Press, 225 Varick St., NYC 14. H: 450 W. 24th St., NYC 11.

12 ETTINGHAUSEN, Richard. Persian miniatures; Islamic ceramics and art. b'06. PhD '31 (U Frankfurt); student (U Munich, Cambridge University). Editor Ars Islamica '38-51; Near Eastern editor Ars Orientalis since '52. Author: Antiheidnische Polemik im Koran '34; Studies in Muslim Iconography, I: The Unicorn '49. Co-author: Iranian and Islamic Art '41; also articles in field. Research asso Near Eastern Art Freer Gallery Art Smithsonian Inst since '44; also research prof Islamic art U Mich since '49. Am Oriental Soc—Coll Art Assn Am—Am Council Learned Soc (com Near Eastern studies '47-49)—Archeol Inst Am). Freer Gallery of Art, Smithsonian Institution, Washington 25.†

13 EUBANK, John Augustine. Aeronautical law and history. LLB (St Lawrence U); LLM (Brooklyn Law Sch). US delegate to First Inter-American Bar Association Conference Havana '41 and author of resolution advocating and initiating modern conception of a United Nations organization with an international police force composed largely of air power; conducted 3 national symposiums on aeronautical law '33, '38, '46; developed doctrine of airspace zone of effective possession accepted by US Supreme Court '45; analysis and research legal aspects aerial warfare: study domestic and international air transportation. Author articles in field. Prof aeronautical law Brooklyn Law Sch since '32. Fed Bar Asso NY-NJ-Conn (chmn com on air law)—NY County Lawyers Assn (com aeronautical law)—Aircraft Industries Assn—Am Bar Assn (com on treaties agreements)—NY State Bar Assn (com aeronautical law)—Aeronautical C of C Am—Nat Aeronautic Assn—Inst Aeronautical Sci—Am Mus Natural Hist—Am Soc Internat Law —Soaring Soc Am (charter mem). 32 Broadway, NYC.†⊙

14 EUBANK, William Roderick. Ceramic chemistry; Refractories; High temperature measurement; Paint technology; Ferroelectrics. b'19. BS '40—MS '41 (U Ky); PhD '47 (Johns Hopkins); special courses paints (ND Agrl Coll) '51. Research on ceramic chemistry including refractories, insulations, enamels, cements, ferroelectrics and clays; design and construction

high-temperature furnaces for operation under oxidizing conditions; research on Georgia clays for use as extender pigments and coating agents; formulation of paints. Research fell ceramics Pa State Coll '41-42; research phys chem Keasbey and Mattison Co '42-43; fell indsl research Mellon Inst '43-44; research asso Nat Bur Standards '44-48; ceramic cons US Nav Ordnance Testing Sta '48-51; head paint laboratory Edgar Brothers Co since '51. ACS—Am Ceramic Soc—AAAS —Am Inst Chem—Research Soc Am—Nat Paint Varnish & Lacquer Assn—Fed Paint Varnish Prodn Clubs—Sigma Xi—Alpha Chi Sigma. Edgar Brothers Co., McIntyre, Ga.

15 EURICH, Alvin Christian. American higher education; Educational psychology. b'02. BA '24 (North Central Coll); MA '26 (U Maine); PhD '29 (U Minn); LLD '44 (Hamline U). On Problems and Policies Committee of American Council on Education '45-49; served on Truman's Commission on Higher Education; Personnel Policy Committee Hoover Commission on Reorganization Executive Branch of Federal Government. Author: The Reading Abilities of College Students '31. Co-author: Educational Psychology '35; Federal Aid for College Students '37; Social Education '39; The Improvement of College Instruction '40; Modern Education: An Evaluation '42; also articles in field. Acting pres Stanford U '48-49; pres State U NY '49-51; vp Ford Fund for Advancement of Edn since '51; Comdr USNR '42-44, later comdr dir div standards and curriculum Bur Naval Personnel. AAAS (council '41-45)—Am Edn Research Assn (vp pres '45)—Phi Delta Kappa—Sigma Xi. 575 Madison Ave., NYC 22.⊙

16 EUSTIS, Warner. Non-woven and elastic fabrics; Surgical dressings; Elastomeric adhesives. b'95. SB '18 (Harvard). Research non-woven fabrics, elastic fabrics, surgical dressings, elastomeric adhesives; automatic player pianos; patent law, trade-mark law. Patentee in metal goods manufacture, surgical dressings and allied products. Contbg author: Research in Industry (Furnas D Van Nostrand) '48; also articles in field. AAAS(F)—Am Chem Soc—Am Phys Soc—Indsl Research Inst—Textile Research Inst. The Kendall Co., 140 Federal St., Boston 10.

17 EUVERARD, Maynard Ray. Physics (Protective coatings and electronics). b'17. BA '38 (Miami U); MS '40 (U Cincinnati). Invented interchemical inclined tube viscometer, interchemical wet film thickness gage. Author: Interchemical Inclined Tube Viscometer '48; The Efflux Type Viscosity Cup '48; Surface Tension Measurements '49. Dir phys engring Interchemical Corp since '49. Officer charge radar planning div plans and policies headquarters US Marine Corps '41-45, charge ground radar planning, staff commander in chief Pacific '45-46. Am Soc Testing Materials—Fed Paint Varnish Prodn Clubs—AAAS—Sigma Xi. Interchemical Corporation, 67 W 44th St., NYC 36. H: 300 Lupine Way, Short Hills, N.J.

18 EVANOFF, Vlad. Surf fishing. b'16. Certificate '37 (Cooper Union Night Art School). Surf angler for past 15 years. Author: Surf Fishing '48; also articles in field. Free lance writer and illustrator. Outdoor News Assn. Box 35, Vanderveer Station, Brooklyn 10, N.Y.

19 EVANS, Charles Tyndale, Jr. High temperature alloys. b'17. BS Met E '40 (U Mich). Developed heat resisting

alloys for use in gas turbins, jet propelled aircraft, rockets; research in fabrication, processing heat resisting alloys. Contributor: Gas Turbins and Jet Propulsion '48. Metall engr Universal-Cyclops Steel Corp Titusville Pa '40-45; chief metall Elliott Co Jeannette Pa since '45. ASTM (chmn gas turbine panel——ASME (chmn gas turbine panel)—Am Soc Metals—Nat Assn Corrosion Engrs. Elliott Co., Jeannette, Pa. H: P.O. Box 136, Delmont, Pa.

20 EVANS, Clifford, Jr. South American archeology. b'20. AB '41 (U So Cal); PhD '50 (Columbia). Member Viru Valley archeological expedition to north coast of Peru '46; field research lower Amazon Brazilian Guiana, islands Marajo, Caviana, and Mexiana '48-49; British Guiana '52-53. Co-author: Cultural Stratigraphy in the Viru Valley, Northern Peru '51. Author articles: The Archeology of the Territory of Amapá, Brazil '50; A Report on Recent Archeological Investigations in the Lagoa Santa Region of Minas Gerais, Brazil '50. Co-author article: (with B J Meggers) Preliminary Results of Archeological Investigations at the mouth of the Amazon '50. Research asst anthrop Columbia '46-48; archeol and asso curator US Nat Mus Smithsonian Inst since '51. Am Anthrop Assn(F)—Soc Am Archeol—Phi Beta Kappa—Phi Kappa Phi. Division of Archeology, U.S. National Museum, Smithsonian Institution, Washington 25.

21 EVANS, Elma Theora. Literature of aeronautical research. b'12. AB '34 (U Pittsburgh); BS '35 (Columbia); govt certificate '41 (U Delaware). Author articles: Special Libraries After the War '41; A Teaching Experiment '45. Research librarian Atlas Powder Co Wilmington Del '39-42; librarian Curtiss-Wright Corp Buffalo '42-45; Cornell Aeronautical Lab Inc since '46. Spl Libraries Assn (dir '46-49)—ALA —Inst Aero Sci. Cornell Aeronautical Laboratory, Incorporated, Buffalo 21.

22 EVANS, F(rancis) Gaynor. Comparative osteology; Human bone (Physical properties, mechanical behavior). b'07. AB '31 (Coe Coll); MA '31—PhD '38 (Columbia). Research on structure and function of vertebral column; comparative osteology of Amphibia and mammals; laboratory tests of strength, elasticity, and energy absorbing capacity of bones. Author: A Laboratory Manual for Gross Anatomy '50. Author articles: The Morphology and Functional Evolution of the Atlas-Axis Complex from Fish to Mammals '39; Stresscoat Studies on Femur '50, and other . Coauthor articles: (with Helen Rockwell, Homer C Pheasant) The Comparative Morphology of the Vertebrate Spinal Column—Its Form as Related to Function '38; (with Vernon E Krahl) The Torsoin of the Humerus—A Phylogenetic Survey from Fish to Man '45; (with H R Lissner and H E Pedersen) The role of tensile stress in the mechanism of femoral fractures '51; and others. Asst prof gross anatomy U Md '43-45; faculty coll med Wayne U since '45, asso prof since '50, now in charge course in gross anatomy. Am Assn Anatomists—Am Assn Phys Antrop—AAAS—NY Acad Sci—Soc Vertebrate Paleontology—Sigma Xi-Phi Kappa Phi—Phi Sigma. NY Acad Sci A Cressy Morrison prize for research on morphology and functional evolution atlas-axis complex. Wayne University, College of Medicine, 1512 St. Antoine, Det. 26.

23 EVANS, James William. Starches. b'08. BS '28 (Central Mo State Coll); PhD '40 (U Minn). Holds US Patent on non-gelling starch solution '46. Author articles in field. Research dept project leader General Mills Inc '43-46, head food and carbohydrate research sect '47-50; dir research American Maize Products Co since '50. Am Chem Soc—Assn Cereal Chem—Inst Food Technol—Sigma Xi. American Maize-Products Co., Roby, Ind.

10 EVANS, O(rron) D(rayton). Farm (Erosion). b'86. Student (Benton (Mo) Coll of Law). Member Rocks and Minerals Assn—St Louis Friends of the Land—Mo Ill and Greater St Louis archaeol scos—Conservation Fedn Mo—Am Forestry Assn—St Louis Farmers—Amatuer Archaeologists of St Louis. Pierce Bldg., St.L. 2.

11 EVANS, Robert John. Amino acids; Eggs (Biochemistry); Poultry nutrition. b'09. BS '34—MS '36 (Utah State Agrl Coll); PhD '39 (U Wis). Research in heat inactivation of amino acids in proteins; changes in nutritive composition shell eggs during storage; different phases nutrition to prevent turkeys and chickens from illness. Asst poultryman Wash Agrl Expt Sta '40-42, asst chem '42-44, asso chem '44-47; prof agrl chem Michigan State Coll since '47. ACS—Poultry Sci Assn—AAAS—Sigma Xi—Phi Kappa Phi—Phi Lambda Upsilon—Gamma Alpha. Dept. of Agricultural Chemistry, Michigan State College, East Lansing, Mich.

12 EVANS, Willa McClung. Influence of music on poetry (English); Elizabethan music. b'99. BA '21 (Coe Coll); MA '23—PhD '30 (Columbia). Research on aspects of influence of music on poetry in seventeenth century England, especially verse of Richard Lovelace, Milton's use of music; made available several facsimile reproductions of manuscript songs from collection autographed by Henry Lawes. Author: Ben Johnson and Elizabethan Music '29; Henry Lawes, Musician and Friend of Poets '41; also articles in field. Asso prof Eng Hunter Coll since '43. Modern Lang Assn Am. Grad fellowship in Eng Ia U '21-22; Lydia C Roberts fellow in Eng Columbia '22-23, '23-24. 501 W. 113th St., NYC 25.†

13 EVENDEN, James Cawston. Entomology (Forest). b'89. BS in foestry '14—FE '37 (Ore State Coll). Research in forest insect control primarily with bauh beetles of genus Dendroc vonus; direction entomological service in solution of insect problems to all land managing agencies. With Bur Entomol and Plant Quarantine USDA since '14, charge forest insect lab since '19. Soc Am Econ Entomol—Soc Am Forestry—Phi Kappa Phi—Xi Sigma Pi. P.O. Box 630, Federal Bldg, Coeur d'Alene, Ida.

14 EVEREST, David Clark. Paper and pulp chemistry and manufacturing (Sulphite, sulfate, bleaching, waste sulphite, liquor, lignin); Forestry; Packaging food products. b'83. Dr Bus Adminstrn '46 (Northland Coll). Chairman bd Wausau Paper Mills Co since '50, chairman bd Marathon Corp since '50; pres and dir various companies. Am Paper and Pulp Assn (past pres '27-28, '37-38)—Inst Paper Chem (vp). Awarded Gold Medal for Advancement Tech Research and Development, Tech Assn Pulp and Paper Industry '44. Marathon Corp., Rothschild, Wis.

15 EVERETT, Guy M. Pharmacology of antiepileptic drugs; Pharmacology of neuromuscular paralytic agents; Neurophysiology of epileptic seizure activity. b'15. AB '40 (U Ia); PhD in physiology '43 (U Md). Author: Pharmacological Studies of D-Tubocurarine and other Curare Fractions. Co-author: Comparative Anticonvulsive Action of 3, 5, 5-Trimethyloxazolidine-2, 4-Dione (Tridione), Dilantin and Phenobarbital; Observations on the Alpha (Orthocresol) Ether of Glycerol (Myanesin); The Search for New Drugs Against Epilepsy; Pharmacological Studies of Phenacetylurea (Phenurone) an Anticonvulsant Drug. Sr research pharmacologist Abbott Labs N Chgo since '43. Am Soc Pharmacol and Exptl Therapeutics—Soc Exptl Biology and Med—Sigma Xi. Abbott Labs., N. Chicago, Ill. H: 7606 North Bosworth, Chgo.

16 EVERHART, Donald Lough. Quicksilver deposits (California); Uranium deposits (North America). b'17. AB '39 (Denison U); MA '42 (Harvard). Geologic and mineralogic study of quicksilver deposits of California Coast Ranges; collaborated in determination structural control of ore bodies and recommendations for finding new ore bodies; investigation and appraisal uranium deposits Northwest Territories and Ontario, Colorado, Utah, New Mexico, Arizona, California, and Michigan; study geologic environment of primary uranium depoits. Jr geol advancing to geol US Geol Survey '42-49; asst chief gen exploration br and staff geol US Atomic Energy Commn since '49. Geol Soc Am(F)—Phi Beta Kappa. U.S. Atomic Energy Commission, Box 30 Ansonia Station, N.Y.C. 23. H: 283 Jamaica Blvd., Carle Pl., L.I., N.Y.†

17 EVERHART, John Laurence. Impact extrusion of aluminum, lead, and tin; Mechanical and physical properties of metals, including liquid metals. b'03. Chem E '25 (Lehigh U). Development of impact extrusion process for aluminum, including investigation of pressure requirements, lubrication, tool angles, annealing of materials, and suitable alloys; layout of a plant for production of aluminum collapsible tubes by impact extrusion; investigation of room and high temperature properties of ferrous and nonferrous metals and alloys; examination of properties of liquid low-melting heavy alloys; tensile, impact and creep at room and elevated temperatures; freezing points, expansion and viscosity of liquid metals. Co-author: Mechanical Properties of Metals and Alloys '43. Author article: Significanee of Proportional Limit and Yield Strength '48, and others. Co-author article: (with E L Van Nuis) Development of New Low-Melting Alloys for Heat Transfer Applications '50. Contributor: Metals Handbook '48. Metallographer US Metals Refining Co Carteret NJ '33-38, asst dir research '38-41; engr Nat Bur Standards '41-44; research metall engr Battelle Memorial Inst '44-48; research metall Am Smelting & Refining Co '48-51; asso ed Materials & Methods since '51. AIM ME—ASTM—Am Soc Metals. Professional metall engr Ohio and New Jersey. Reinhold Publishing Co., NYC.

18 EVERLY, Robert Edward. Municipal park and recreational planning. b'05. Author articles in field. Landscape engr parks, estates, golf courses '25-30; supt Glencoe Ill Parks '30-47; partner landscape architects, engineers, community planners McFadzean, Everly, Rose & Asso Winnetka Ill since '35. Midwest Park Exec Inst (pres '36-37)—Am Inst Park Exec (vp '46-47)—Am Soc Planning Ofcls—Chicago Hort Soc (vp '46-47)—West Soc Engrs—Nat Shade Tree Conf—Nat Recreation Assn—Park and Recreation Council Am (pres '50). 675 Vernon Av., Glencoe, Ill. 874 Green Bay Rd., Winnetka, Ill.

19 EVJEN, Victor Harald. Probation; Parole; Delinquency; Crime prevention and control. b'06. BA '26 (Wittenberg Coll); BAS '29 (George Williams Coll); MA '30 (U Chicago). Managing editor Federal Probation Quarterly. Editor: Army's military prison program during World War II '46; Statistical Study of 24,000 Military Prisoners '46. Author: The Case Record and Case Recording '42; Schools and Delinquency '36; Leisure-Time Guidance and Delinquency '37. Co-author: The Presentence Investigation Report '43; also articles in field. US probation officer Chicago '36-40, asst chief US Probation System Washington since '40; officer US Army '43-46, asst to Chief of Army's military prison program. Am Assn Social Workers. Supreme Court Building, Washington.

20 EWAN, Joseph (Andorfer). Botanical biography and bibliography; Delphinium; Gentianaceae; Ferns. b'09. AB '34 (U Calif). Author Rocky Mountain Naturalists; Bibliography of Botany of Arizona '36; Botanical Explorers of Colorado '41; Synopsis North American Delphiniums '45, and others; also articles in field. Asso prof bot Tulane U since '52. Torrey Bot Club—Am Fern Soc (vp '41-47 pres '48-50)—California Bot Soc—Biol Soc Washington—Cooper Ornithol Club—Washington Acad Sci—Sigma Xi. Department of Botany, Tulane University, New Orleans 18.†

21 EWART, Roswell H(orr). Emulsion polymerization; Molecular weights of polymers. b'03. ChE '25 (Lehigh U); PhD '33 (U Ill). Research on kinetics of emulsion polymerization, sedimentation equilibria of polydisperse non-ideal solutes. Co-author articles: The Significance of Viscosity Measurements on Dilute Solutions of High Polymers '46; The Determination of Polymeric Molecular Weights by Light Scattering in Solvent-Precipitant Systems '46; and others. Research chem US Rubber Co since '33. Am Chem Soc. U. S. Rubber Company, General Laboratories, Passaic, N.J.

22 EWERS, John Canfield. Plains Indians of North America. b'09. AB '31 (Dartmouth Coll); '31-32 (Art Students League NY); MA '34 (Yale). Research in general ethnology of the Plains Indians, and studies of costumes of and paintings by North American Indians, paintings of North American Indians by white artists, use of horses by North American Indians. Author: Plains Indian Painting '39 (selected as one of 50 books of year '40 by American Graphic Arts Institute); The Story of the Blackfeet '44; Blackfeet Crafts '45; also articles in field. Asso curator ethnol US Nat Mus Smithsonian Inst Washington since '46. Am Anthrop Assn(F)—Anthrop Soc Washington—Washington Acad Sci—Am Assn Mus. Smithsonian Institution, Washington 25.

23 EWERS, Lela A. Freshwater copepoda (Crustacea); Crustacean food of fishes. b'93. BS '16—AB '17 (Ohio U); MSc '23—PhD '29 (Ohio State U). Author articles in field. Instr biol Cottey Jr Coll for Girls since '33. Am Limnol Soc—AAAS(F)—Am Fisheries Soc—Sigma Xi. Cottey College, Nevada, Mo.

24 EWERT, Willian Van Velsor. German propaganda in United States (1914-1917); St. Augustine of Hippo (Mysticism); European social democratic parties. b'03. BA '26—MA '37 (Stanford U). European study '47, '48. Instr and chmn social sci dept Bakersfield Coll since '28. AHA—NEA—Am Acad Polit Social Sci. Bakersfield College, Bakersfield, Calif.

25 EWING, Alfred M. Chemical eduuon. b'00. BA '21 (Rio Grande Coll O); MSc '28—PhD '34 (O State U); Ed D '45 (U Colo). Author: Experimental Chemistry for the Beginning Student;

Qualitative Chemical Analysis Q-A-Easy Way (rev edit) '49; Individualized Chemical Experiments '50. Author article: Scientific Progress Through Accidental Discoveries '36. Chem div soils Bur Forestry USDA '34-35; prof chem Tex Wesleyan Coll Ft Worth '35-46, chmn div sci '41-46 asso prof chem U Ga '46-48; chmn dept chem U Alaska; asso prof chem ND Agrl Coll, US Dept State exchange prof Seoul Nat U and Christian Chosen U Korea, U PI and Adamson U Indsl Chem and Engring PI. ACS—Nat Sci Teachers Assn—NEA—Tex State Assn Sci—Am Assn Univ Profs—AAAS—Alpha Chi Sigma—Phi Delta Kappa—Kappa Delta Pi. H: 3300 Purington Av., Ft. Worth.

10 EWING, Dressel Dewitt. Electric railways (Power transmission & distribution). b'83. EE '05—ME '06—ED '36 (Ohio Northern U); grad study Purdue U, '12-13. Consultant railway electrification, motor applications, transmission lines. Author: (with C F Harding) Electric Railway Engineering, '15; also univ bulls; contbr numerous tech articles; contbg editor Electric Ry Jour, '15-21. Asst prof elec engring Purdue U, '13-16, prof since '18, head sch elec engring and dir elec div engring expt sta since '42; dir research Am Electric Ry Assn, '25-30, Internat Steel Tie Co, Cleveland, '29-32; cons engr. AIEE(F)—Am Soc Engr Edn—Am Transit Assn—Tau Beta Pi—Eta Kappa Nu—Sigma Xi. 321 University St., West Lafayette, Ind.⊚

11 EWING, Dwight Tarbell. Electroplating (Chromium); Electrochemistry; Spectroscopy; Colloid chemistry; Adsorption. b'88. BS '11 (Parsons Coll); MS '15—PhD '20 (U Chicago). Du Pont fellow also National Research Council work on mustard gas World War I; worked on Manhattan project '43-44. Holds seven patents on electroplating of chromium and other electro-chemical processes. Prof phys chem Mich State Coll since '30. Am Chem Soc—Phys Soc — Electrochem Soc — Optical Soc Am—Electrophys Soc—Sigma Xi—Phi Kappa Phi. 513 Ardson Rd., East Lansing, Mich.

12 EWING, J(oseph) Franklin. Anthropology. b'05. AB '28—AM '29 STL '36 (Woodstock Coll); PhD '47 (Harvard); '37-38 (U Vienna). Member Boston College—Fordham University archaeological expedition in Lebanon '38-40, '47-48, palaeolithic excavation of Ksar 'Akil; Ateneo de Manila anthropological expedition in Mindanao '40-41. Author articles in field. Asst prof anthrop Fordham U since '49. Am Anthrop Assn(F) — Am Assn Phys Anthrop— Far Eastern Assn—Sigma Xi. Medaille d'Honneur pour la Merite Republic of Lebanon. Fordham University, NYC 58.

13 EWING, (William) Maurice. Ocean basins; Geophysics. b'06. Hohenthal scholar '23-26—fellow '26-29—BA '26—MA '27—PhD '31 (Rice Inst). Author articles in field. Prof geol Columbia U since '47; research asso Woods Hole Oceanog Inst since '40, dir Lamont Geol Obs Palisades NY. Am Phys Soc — Am Math Soc — Geol Soc Am— Seismol Soc Am—Am Geophys Union— NY Acad Sci—AAAS—Am Geog Soc— Bermuda Biol Assn—Nat Acad Sci— Soc Exploration Geophysicists — Nat Geog Soc—Sigma Xi. Guggenheim fellow '38-40. Lamont Geological Observatory, Palisades, N.Y.†⊚

14 EYERDAM, Walter Jacob. Botany (Alaska, South America); Conchology of the Pacific area; Birds of Solomon Islands; Humming birds of Ecuador and Bolivia. b'92. Student (U Wash). Collected biological material for various institutions in over 60 countries during three excursions around the

world, including 5 excursions to USSR before '31 and 16 excursions to Alaska since '17. Author articles in field. 7531 19th Av., Seattle 5.

15 EYRING, Henry. Radioactivity; Theory of liquids; Reaction rates; Quantum mechanics. b'01. BS '23—MS '24 (U Ariz); PhD '27 (U Cal); chem research asso '28-29 (U Wis); NRC fellow '29-30 (Kaiser Wilhelm Inst Berlin Germany); Dr Science '52 (U of Utha). Research on theory of reaction rates; application of quantum mechanics to chemistry. Co-author: (with Glasstone, Laidler) Theory of Rate Processes; (with Walter, Kimball) Quantum Chemistry; (with Johnson and Polissar) The Kinetic Basis of Molecular Biology. Assistant advancing to asso prof chem Princeton U '31-38, prof '38-46; chem dean grad sch and prof chem U Utah since '46, also professor metallurgy since '48. Nat Acad Sci—AAAS—ACS—Am Philos Soc—Textile Research Found—Soc Rheology—Utah Acad Sci Arts and Letters—APS—Sigma Xi—Phi Kappa Phi—Phi Lambda Upsilon—Tau Beta Pi. Soc Rheology 2nd Bingham medal '49; Wm H Nichols Medal for outstanding work in field of rate processes '51. University of Utah, Salt Lake City.

16 EYSTER, H. C. Photosynthesis; Enzymes; Auxins; Adsorption; Chlorophyll; Hybrid vigor. b'10. AB '32 (Bucknell U); AM '34—PhD '36 (U Ill); fellow bot '35-36 (U Ill). Author articles in field. Asst prof bot, head dept U SD '37-44, asso prof '44-46; research plant physiol Charles F Kettering Found Antioch Coll Yellow Springs O since '46. AAAS(F)—Bot Soc Am—Am Soc Plant Physiol—Genetics Soc Am—SD Acad Sci—O Acad Sci. Charles F. Kettering Foundation, Antioch College, Yellow Springs, O.†

17 EYSTER, William H(enry). Corn (Hybrid seed corn); Marigolds (Red and gold hybrid); Organic gardening; Compost (Bacterial starters, plant shredding equipment). b'89. AB '14—AM '15 (Bucknell University); PhD '20 (Cornell University); '22 (Harvard); '27-28 (U Berlin, U Erlangen). Creator of Penn-hybrid seed corns, red and gold hybrid marigolds and other plants. Author: College Botany '32; Genetics of Zea Mays, Bibliographia Genetica '34; also articles in field. Asst prof bot U Mo '20-24; research specialist Mo Agrl Expt Sta for researches in Indian corn '20-24; prof bot U Maine '24-27; prof bot Bucknell '28-41, research prof genetics '41-45; pres Eyster Hybrid Seed Co '45-46; prof bot Baldwin-Wallace Coll '46-47; managing ed Organic Gardening Publishers '47-51; sec Soil and Health Found Pa '47-51; soil scientist John L Roper Lumber Co Roper NC '51-52; vp The Soil-Tone Corp Plymouth NC '52. A AAS(F)—Am Naturalists—Am Genetic Soc—Am Bot Soc—German Bot Soc— Pa Acad Sci—NC Acad Sci. P.O. Box 218, Plymouth, N.C. H: 235 Harrison St.⊚

18 EZEKIEL, Mordecai Joseph Brill. Agricultural economics and statistics. b'99. BS '18 (U Md); MS '24 (U Minn); PhD '26 (Robert Brookings Grad Sch Econ and Govt Washington). Developed methods of analyzing data; pioneered in methods of curvilinear multiple correlation and price forecasting for farm products; assisted in formulating plans for farm relief and drafting Agricultural Adjustment Act. Author: Methods of Correlation Analysis '30; $2,500 A Year—from Scarcity to Abundance '36; Jobs for All '39. Co-author and editor: Toward World Prosperity '47; also articles in field. With div farm management US Dept Agr '22-30; asst chief econ Fed Farm Bd '30-33;

econ adv to Sec Agr '33-44; econ adv bur of agrl econ US Dept Agr '44-'47; asst to exec vice-chmn WPB '42-43; econ FAO since '47. Am Statis Assn (F)—Am Farm Econ Assn—Am Econ Assn—Econometric Soc(F). Food and Agriculture Organization, 1201 Connecticut Av., Washington.

19 EZEKIEL, Walter N(aphtali). Experimental mycology; Moisture and fungus proofing. b'01. BS '20 (Md State Coll); MS '21—PhD '24 (U Md). Moisture and fungus proofing of electrical and electronic equipment; development test methods for moisture and fungus resistance; fruit rotting Sclerotinias; physiology of resistance to Puccinia graminis tritici; Phymatotrichum root rot; diseases of cotton plants; soil fungicides. Author articles in field. Plant path Tex agrl expt sta '28-44; prin exptl mycol Naval Ord Lab '44-46; head mycologist in charge moisture and fungus proofing, Bur Ordnance since '46. AAAS(F)— Am Phytopath Soc—Mycol Soc Am. —Sigma Xi—Texas Acad Sci(F)— Wash Bot Soc—Soc Indsl Microbiol. Bureau of Ordnance Navy Department, Washington 25.

F

20 FABERGÉ, Alexander Cyril. Genetics (Botany, cytology). b'12. BSc '33 (U Reading, Eng); PhD '36—DSc '45 (U London, Eng). Research on chromosome breakage and mutation, genetics of several species of papaver, sweet peas and other plants, unstable genes, mutation produced by ultraviolet radiation. Author articles in field. Research John Innes Hort Instn London '33-37; asst lecturer Galton Lab U Coll London '37-45; research Rothamsbed Exptl Sta on bees in connection with crop pollination '41-42; research asso bot dept U Wis '45-47; asso prof U Mo since '47. Genetics Soc, Eng—Genetics Soc Am—Soc Exptl Biol. Awarded Guggenheim fellowship '46. Genetics Bldg., University of Missouri, Columbia, Mo.

21 FABIAN, Frederick William. Food and dairy products; Fermented foods and products (Vinegar, wine, beer, pickles). b'88. BS '14 (Allegheny Coll); MS '24 (Mich State Coll); PhD '29 (Yale). Author articles in field. Instr '17, now research prof bact Mich Agrl Expt Sta, prof bacteriology and pub health Mich State Coll. Internat Assn Milk Sanitarians (pres '41)—Am Pub Health Assn (chmn food and nutrition sect '40)—Inst Food Tech (chmn Great Lakes sect '44-46) — AAAS — Soc Am Bact—Am Dairy Sci Assn—Mich Pub Health Assn — Mich Assn Dairy and Milk Inspectors—Sigma Xi—Alpha Chi Sigma—Phi Kappa Phi—Delta Omega —Phi Sigma. Michigan State College, East Lansing, Mich.

22 FABRI, Ralph. Art (Education). b '94. AB '12 (Royal State Gymnasium Budapest); student 2 yrs (Royal Inst Tech Budapest); Prof degree '18 (Royal Acad Fine Arts Budapest). Author: Learn to Draw '45. Received etching prize Am-Hungarian Cultural Fedn '32; John Taylor Arms prize NY '43; 3 Pennell prizes Library of Congress '43-45; 5 prizes in nat competition for Patriotic Designs '42-43; Ringius prize Hartford Conn '45. Paintings and etchings exhibited Nat Acad NY City, Pa Acad Fine Arts Phila, Art Inst Chicago, Carnegie Inst, Am Water Color Soc, museums of Denver, San Francisco, Seattle; one-man shows US Nat Mus Washington, Honolulu Acad, Phila Art Alliance, Alliance NY City, Budapest. Soc Am Etchers—Conn Acad Fine Arts—Audubon Artists—Cal Soc Etchers—Nat Acad—Brooklyn Soc Artists. 54 W. 74th St., NYC 23.†⊚

10 FAGADAU, Simion H(aralamb). Petroleum engineering. b'99. Student '18-19 (Sorbonne Paris); '19-20 (Poly Inst Grenoble France); PE '23 (U Pittsburgh). Studies of valuation oil and gas properties in US, Canada, South America; management, exploration, and production oil and gas properties. Engr Ralph E Davis '23-28; resident engr Venezuelon-Mexican Oil Corp '20-31; valuation engr and producer of oil '31-33; cons petroleum engr since '34. AIMME—Tex Soc Profl Engrs (dir '49-50 pres N Central Chpt '48)—Am Petroleum Inst. 208-10 Hamilton Bldg., Wichita Falls, Texas.

11 FAGER, E(dward) W. Photosynthesis; Biochemistry (Tracers). b'17. BA '39—PhD '42—Alexander and So Calif Yale Alumni scholar—Annie G K Garland fellow (Yale); resident fellow '42-45 (Branford Coll); Frank B Jewett fellow '46-47 (U Chicago). Author articles in field. Research asso U Chicago since '47. AAAS—Am Chem Soc—Sigma Xi—Phi Beta Kappa. Received NY Yale Club award. Institute of Radiobiology and Biophysics, University of Chicago, Chgo 37.

12 FAGIN, N. Bryllion. American literature; Drama; Theater (History); Short story (Methods). b'92. AB '23—AM '24 (George Washington U); PhD '31 (Johns Hopkins); '24 (Columbia), '25 (Harvard). Critic judge of Drama Festival, University of Delaware '48; holds American Philosophical Society grant for research on Edgar Allen Poe; studied theater in Moscow; research on expressionism, short story writing, Stephen Crane, Eugene O'Neill, O Henry, Sherwood Anderson, drama, playwriting, history of theater; conducted seminar in American drama at Salzburg Seminar in American Studies January-February '52. Author: Short Story Writing '23; The Phenomenon of Sherwood Anderson '27; William Bustram '33; America Through the Short Story '36; Poe as a Literary Critic '46; Histrionic Mr. Poe '49. Asst prof Md U '24-25; prof Baltimore U '25-31; dir playshop and instr drama Johns Hopkins '31-32, asso in Eng and dir playshop '33-46, asso prof Eng and drama since '47. Authors League Am—Modern Lang Assn—Am Edn Theatre Assn—Writers League Wash (past pres)—Md Conf Dramatic Organizations (past pres)—Edgar Allen Poe Soc Baltimore (pres). Johns Hopkins University, Baltimore 18.

13 FAHEY, James Charles. United States Navy and Air Force; Naval vessels; Warships; Naval and military aircraft. b'03. Author, editor, compiler and publisher: The Ships and Aircraft of the United States Fleet '39, '41, '42, '44, '45 and '48; United States Army Aircraft '08-46 '46 and '49; also articles in field. US Naval Inst (asso mem). 3812 18th St., N.E., Washington 18.

14 FAHNESTOCK, James Murray. Automobiles (Automotive spring suspensions and leaf springs, Ford cars, trucks and tractors). b'85. Student '08-09 (Carnegie Inst Tech); '12-13 (U Pittsburgh). Author: Secrets of Ford Engineering '27; Know the Ford '28; The Model A Ford '30; The Service Handbook '34; L'Auto Ford Modele A (in French); Automotive Springs '46. Ed Ford Field Mag since '29; dir engring Leaf Spring Inst Detroit Mich since '43, also speaker and writer on automotive spring suspensions and automobiles. Nat Soc Automotive Engrs (councillor '39-40, chmn Pittsburgh sect '33). 524 S. Murtland Av., Pittsburgh 8.

15 FAHNESTOCK, John Sheridan. Primitive music; South Pacific bird groups. b'12. Ed (St Aloysius Sch and Chaminade Sch Garden City NY). Leader Fahnestock South Seas expedition of American Museum Natural History on voyage throughout South Pacific in 65 ft schooner '34-37, second expedition '40, discovered Ndakunimba Stones on Vanua Levu Island Fiji believed to be first discovered example of Pacific written language '36. Co-author: Stars to Windward '38. Ed and pub St Mary's Enterprise since '46; dir internat pub relations Trans World Airline since '47. Received Carnegie grant for musicological research. 630 Fifth Av., N.Y.C.

16 FAHS, Charles Burton. Far Eastern affairs; Japanese studies; Political science. b'08. BS '29—MA '31—PhD '33 (Northwestern U); '29-30 (U Berlin); '33-34 (Ecole Nat des Langues Orientales Vivantes Paris); '34-35 (Kyoto, Japan, Imperial U); '35-36 (Tokyo Imperial U). Author: Government in Japan: Recent Trends in its Scope and Operation '40; also articles in field. Instr Oriental affairs Pomona Coll and Claremont Coll '36-39, asst prof '39-46 (on leave '40-46); vis prof Coll Chinese Studies Peiping '40-41; research analyst Office Coordinator Information '41-42; research analyst research and analysis br OSS '42-45, chief Far East div '44-45; acting chief div research for Far East US Dept State '45-46; asso dir humanities Rockefeller Found '49-50, dir since '50. Am Pol Sci Assn—Japan Soc NY—Soc Japanese Studies. 49 W. 49th St., N.Y.C. 20.

17 FAILLA, Gioacchino. Atomic energy; Radiological physics; Radiobiology. b'91. EE '15—AM '17 (Columbia); DSc '23 (U Paris). Developed automatic radon collection apparatus and other devices for safe handling of radon and radium, gold radon seeds used in the treatment of cancer '36, first radium bomb with shutter '28, two-tube self-rectifying x-ray circuit '34, rotating potentiometer compensator '37, x-ray dosimeter with flexible leads '39, instruments for measuring tissue dose of radioactive isotopes, protection of personnel against ionizing radiations, and others. Author articles in field. Prof radiology and dir radiological research lab Coll Phys and Surgs Columbia U since '43; physicist Marine Biol Lab since '31; cons USPHS since '38, Vets Adminstrn since '42; chmn com isotope distribution Atomic Energy Comm since '48, and others. Am Phys Soc—Am Radium Soc—AAAS—Radiology Soc NA—Am Radium Soc—Optical Soc Am—Am Roentgen Ray Soc—NY Elec Soc (pres '40)—NY Acad Sci—Am Geophys Union—Sigma Xi. Leonard prize Am Roentgen Ray Soc '23, '25; Janeway medal Am Radium Soc '39; gold medal Radiology Soc NA '47. 630 W. 168th St., N.Y.C. 32.⊙

18 FAIN, Jacob Mitchell. Bitumens; Emulsions. b'01. AB '21—ChE '23—PhD '32 (Columbia). Research in asphalt products; devised and accomplished necessary modifications of B-25 aircraft to adapt them to carry British smoke tanks. Holds patents. Author articles in field. Chem engr Flintkote Co E Rutherford NJ '26-31; asso Foster D Snell Inc NYC '33-36, chem '36-41, research dir '41-42, since '46. Chem officer US Army and AAF, maj '42 advanced to col '46. Am Chem Soc—AICE—Sigma Xi. Awarded Pulitzer Scholarship '17-21. Foster D. Snell Inc., 29 W. 15th St., NYC 11. H: 201 Crown St., Bklyn 25.†

19 FAIRBANKS, Henry N(athaniel). Photography; Cinematagraphy. b'05. ME '27 (Cornell U). Holds about 30 patents. Author articles in field. Mem gen engring staff Eastman Kodak Co since '47, in charge development and design motion picture apparatus since '48. Soc Motion Picture Engrs. 333 State St., Rochester, N.Y.

20 FAIRCHILD, David. Tropical plants; Useful plants of the world. b'96. Student (Kan State Agrl Coll); hon degrees (Oberlin Coll, Fla State Coll), Kan State Agrl Coll). In charge scientific work Fairchild Garden expedition to Philippines, Celebes, Java, Bali and Moluccas, '39-40; collected plants in Colombia, Panama, and Guatemala '41, Guatemala and Yucatan '44; introduced rare plants into the US; Fairchild Tropical Garden Coconut Grove Fla named in his honor. Author: Book of Monsters '14; Exploring for Plants '30; The World Was My Garden '38; Garden Islands of the Great East '45; The World Grows Round My Door '47. Agrl explorer. Nat Geog Soc (bd dir)—Am Genetic Assn (pres). Received Thomas Barbour medal '48. 4013 Douglas Rd., Coconut Grove, Fla.

21 FAIRCHILD, Hoxie Neale. English poetry (Eighteenth and nineteenth century); Romanticism; Religious thought in English literature. b'94. AB '17—PhD '28 (Columbia). Author: The Noble Savage '28; The Romantic Quest '31; Religious Trends in English Poetry (3 vols); also articles in field. Instr, asso prof Columbia U '28-40; prof Hunter Coll since '40. Modern Lang Assn William Bayard Cutting Traveling fellow '25-26. Hunter College, 695 Park Av., N.Y.C. 21.

22 FAIRCHILD, Iler James. Standards and standardization. b'90. BS '14—ME '28 (Mich State Coll). Designed lathes and shapers; designed first hydro-pneumatic recoil system for Navy broadside gun mounts; work in specification writing and commercial standards. Author articles in field. Mech engr Nat Bur Standards '22-28, chief div trade standards '29-45; sec Enameled Cast Iron Plumbing Fixtures Assn and Vitreous China Plumbing Fixtures Assn since '46. Am Soc Testing Materials. 1709 M St., N.W., Washington 6.⊙

23 FAIRHALL, Lawrence Turner. Chemistry, toxicology, physiology, and trace methods of analysis industrial poisons; Lead poisoning. b'88. BS '11—MS (chem) '12 (U Ill); MA (phys chem) '15—PhD (phys chem) '18 (Harvard). Research on localization industrial poisons in various organs and tissues of body, modes of action, metabolites formed, and detoxification mechanism in general. Author: Industrial Toxicology '49. Co-author: Lead Poisoning '26. Author 95 articles in field. Faculty Sch Pub Health Harvard '21-38; with USPHS since '36, now scientist dir, chief lab sect, div indsl hygiene. ACS—Soc Biol Chem—Am Inst Chem(F)—AAAS—Am Indsl Hygiene Assn—Royal Microscopic Soc (F)—Alpha Chi Sigma—Gamma Alpha—Sigma Xi—Am Conf Govt Indsl Hygienists. US Public Health Service, Washington. H: 406 Fairfax Rd., Bethesda, Md.

24 FAISON, Haywood Renick. Waterway transportation. b'84. '99-01 (UNC); '05-06 (Lehigh U). Economic studies and reports on river and harbor and public improvements; member World Bank mission on water transportation to Colombia '49. Co-author: The Rationale of Waterway Transportation '41; also articles in field. Engr US Army Corps Engrs Gulf of Mexico Div '30-36, sr prin engr US Bd Engrs for Rivers and Harbors Washington '36-40, head engr, chief engr-econ since '40. Waterway Transp Com President's Water Resources Policy Commn '50. ASCE. Cosmos Club, Washington 5.

10 FAISON, Samson Lane, Jr. Sienese painting; Fourteenth and fifteenth century art. b'07. AB '29 (Williams); MA '30 (Harvard); MFA '32 (Princeton). Author articles: Barna and Bartolo di Fredi '32; Note on a Sienese Resurrection '41. Research medieval Italian painting Princeton '30-32; faculty hist art Yale U '32-36; asst prof Williams Coll '36-40, asso prof '40-46, prof since '46, chmn art dept since '40; dir Lawrence Art Mus Williamstown since '48; art critic The Nation since '52. College Art Assn (pres '52-54). Lawrence Art Museum, Williamstown, Mass.†

11 FAITH, William Lawrence. Chemical engineering (Organic chemical technology, agricultural products processing, manufacture starch and starch products). b'07. BS '28 (U Md); MS '29—PhD '31 (U Ill). Co-author: Applications of Chemical Engineering '40; Industrial Chemicals '50; Laboratory Design '51. Special research assistant in chemical engineering Engineering Experimental Station U Ill '31-33; chem Nat Aluminate Corp Chicago '33; asst prof chem engring Kan State Coll Manhattan Kan '33-36, head dept chem engring '39-42; prof chem engring State U Ia, Ia City Ia (on leave) '42-44; cons Office Production Research and Development WPB Washington '42-43, dep dir '44-45; dir development engring chem div Corn Products Refining Co Argo Ill '45-48, dir engring since '48. Am Chem Soc—AICE—Sigma Xi. Corn Products Refining Co., Argo, Ill.☺

12 FALCK, Edward. Public utilities engineering and economics. b'11. AB '30—BS '31—MS '32 (Columbia). Dir rates and research TVA '33-37; special asst to vice pres Consol Edison Co of NYC '37-43; cons to power branch WPB '41-42; asst dept dir gen for distribution WPB '42-43; dep dir Office War Utilities '43-44, dir '44-45; established cons firm, Edward Falck and Company since '45. Am Econ Assn—AIEE—Sigma Xi. 1625 I St., N.W., Washington 6.

13 FALES, Walter. Theory of knowledge; Pestalozzi. b'96. PhD '22 (U Berlin). Editor of Pestalozzi's Works and Letters 1923-1940. Author: Der Einfluss Jacob Boehmes auf Novalis, Emil Ebering '22; Entdecke Dein Ich, Quelle und Meyer '25; Wisdom and Responsibility '46; also articles in field. Prof philos Lincoln U since '48. Am Philos Assn. Lincoln University, Pa.

14 FALES, William David. Textile design; Art in industry. b'93. Diploma '14 (RI Sch Design); MS (hon) '38 (RI Coll Pharm and Allied Scis). Author articles in field. Instr, lecturer, cons on textile design and art in industry, RI Sch Design since '15, now head textile sch; cons Fgn Econ Administrn, Germany '45. Am Soc Testing Materials—Textile Found—Providence Engring Soc. Rhode Island School of Design, Providence, R.I.

15 FALK, Isidore Sydney. Medical economics (Social security, public health, vital statistics, bacteriology, immunology). b'99. PhB '20—PhD '23 (Yale). Research in eugenics of infant welfare, theory of microbic virulence, microbic cause of influenza, economics of medical care and public health and social insurance. Adjunct staff member Health Section, League of Nations '35; staff member President Roosevelt's (cabinet) Committee on Economic Security '34-35; member various government advisory committees World War II. Author: Principles of Vital Statistics '23; Laboratory Outlines in Bacteriology and Immunology (with J F Norton) '26; The Costs of Medical Care (with C R Rorem and M D Ring) '33; Security Against Sickness '36; and

others; also articles in field. Now director Division of Research and Statistics Social Security Adminstrn Washington. Am Pub Health Assn(F)—AAAS(F)—Am Acad Polit Social Sci—Am Pub Welfare Assn — Am Statis Assn — Am Econ Assn — Sigma Xi. Awarded Selective Service medal. Social Security Administration, Washington.

16 FALK, Melvin Leroy. Airframes; Aircraft fatigue problems. b'10. BS (mech engring) '34 (U Colo); MS (aeronautics) '48 (Wichita U). Research on strength analysis of airplane airframes, including deriving loads on airframe from known or assumed conditions both in flight and in landing attitude, research on fatigue of metals. Author articles in field. Structures engr Beech Aircraft Corp '40-47; engr White Eagle Div Socony-Vacuum Oil Co '47-51; structural design engr Boeing Aircraft Co since '51. Am Soc ME—Soc Aircraft Structural Engrs. Boeing Aircraft Co., Wichita, Kan.

17 FALK, Sawyer. Drama; Educational theatre; Community theatre; Non-commercial theatre. b'98. BS '21 (NYU); AM '22 (Columbia). Contributor to Handbook of Adult Education in US, Producing the Play, Oxford Companion to the Theatre; articles in theatrical publs. Prof drama, chmn dept drama and dir dramatic activities Syracuse U since '27, dir Civic U Theatre Syracuse since '35; Rockefeller Found fellowship, survey Brit theatre '48. Nat Theatre Conf (pres since '44)—Am Nat Theatre and Acad (bd dirs since '46)—Phi Beta Kappa—Delta Upsilon. Syracuse University, Syracuse, N.Y.☺

18 FALLS, Eugene Kelty. Mechanical engineering (Safety valve flow problems, apparatus design). b'09. ME '32 (U Akron); MSc '38—PhD '41—fellow '40-41 (O State U). Personally conducted fundamental research on factors affecting flow through safety valves, devised methods to represent test results; aided in design of test apparatus, development new steam safety valve having maximum capacity for any size; patent in course of development; designed and constructed apparatus to test water relief valves for capacity and performance, etc. Author articles in field. Asso mech engr Argonne Nat Lab since '49. ASME (jr mem)—AAAS—Am Soc Engring Edn—Sigma Xi—Tau Beta Pi—Sigma Tau—Sigma Pi Sigma. Argonne National Laboratory, P.O. Box 5207, Chicago 80.

19 FALNES, Oscar J. Scandinavian and European intellectual history; Research administration. b'98. BA '21 (St Olaf Coll); MA '22 (Stanford); PhD '33—U Fellow '25-26 (Columbia). Author: National Romanticism in Norway '33; Norway and the Nobel Peace Prize '38; also articles in field. Instr, later prof his NYU since '27. Research Office Coordinator Information, later OSS '41-44; UNRRA '44-47, in charge fellowship program. AHA — Norwegian-Am Hist Assn — Am Scandinavian Found (asso)—Acad Polit Sci. Travelling fellow to Norway of Am-Scandinavian Found '26-27; also fellow contemporary Scandinavian Library Congress '43-45. New York University, 738 E, N.Y.C. 3.†

20 FAN, Edwin Hsing Yun. Insect physiology; Insecticides; Biochemistry; Organic chemistry. b'14. BS '35 (Nat Tsing Hua U, China); PhD '45 (U Minn). Research on Chinese citrus fruits, Chinese tobacco. Author articles in field. Research asst Nat Tsing Hua U China '35-40, China Found fellow '40-45; research fellow U Minn '45-46, research asso '46-48. Am Chem Soc—

Am Assn Econ Entomol—Chinese Chem Soc—Sigma Xi. Research Dept., Julius Hyman Co., Denver.

21 FANKHAUSER, Gerhard. Salamanders (Fertilization, embryology, cytology, development genetics). b'01. PhD '24 (U Berne, Switzerland); Rockefeller Found fellow '29-31 (U Chicago, Yale). Author articles in field. Asst, later prof biol Princeton U since '31. AAAS(F)—Am Soc Zool—Am Assn Anat—Genetics Soc Am—Am Genetic Assn—Am Soc Human Genetics—Soc Study Development and Growth—Am Soc Naturalists — Sigma Xi. Department of Biology, Princeton University, Princeton, N.J.†☺

22 FANNING, Ralph S. History of fine arts. b'89. B Arch '12 (Cornell U); MS '17—M Arch '21 (U Ill). Lecturer in European Galleries for Bureau of University Travel summers '22-38; research in colonial architecture in Mexico summer '40. Author: Outline for Study of the History of Art '25; Churches of the Meuse '21. Author articles: Reconstruction Problems in Devastated France '19; The Della Robbias '29; Mystery of Ionic Volute '17; Eastern Long Island Doorways '18. Prof hist fine arts O State U since '24. Am Fed Arts — Coll Arts Assn — Soc Archtl Historians — Am Water Color Soc—Phi Beta Kappa—Sigma Xi. History of Fine Arts, Ohio State University, Columbus, O.

23 FANO, U. Theoretical, atomic, and molecular physics; Radiobiology; Biophysics. b'12. DSc '34 (U Torino). Research on atomic spectra, action of radiations on matter, genetic effects of radiation, penetration of high energy radiations. Author articles in field. Resch asso Washington Biophys Inst Bethesda Md '39-40; research fellow, asso, physicist, math dept genetics Carnegie Inst Washington Cold Spring Harbor NY '40-45; research asso Carnegie Inst Washington at Columbia U '46; physicist Radiation Physics Laboratory of the National Bureau of Standards since '46. Am Phys Soc—Genetic Soc Am—Am Soc Naturalists. National Bureau of Standards, Washington 25.

24 FANT, Handy Bruce. History; Colony of Georgia; Archives. b'03. AB '24 (U Ga); AM '27 (Mercer U); AM '30 (Harvard U). Archivist Nat Archives since '46. Author articles in field. AHA—Ga Hist Soc—So Hist Assn—Soc Am Archivists—Phi Beta Kappa—Phi Kappa Phi. The National Archives, Washington 25.

25 FARBER, Eduard. Wood chemistry. b'92. Dr Phil '16 (U Leipzig). Research on methods of producing carbohydrates, lignin, synthetic resins; fermentations and by-product recovery in organic acids; yeast; development of processes and machinery in wood processing. Author articles in field. Developed many patents in other countries, over forty in US. Chief chem Deutsche Bergin AG, Holzhydrolyse AG '20-38; dir research Polyxor Chem Co '39-43; chief chem Timber Engring Co since '43. AAAS—Am Chem Soc—Am Inst Chem — NY Acad Sci — Hist Sci Soc — Forest Research Soc — Am Forestry Assn—TAPPI. 4812 Minnesota Av., N.E., Washington 19. H: 4530 Brandywine St., N.W., Washington 16.

26 FARBER, Marvin. Logic; Phenomenology; Social and modern philosophy; Philosophy of education. b'01. BS '22—PhD '25—Sheldon fellow '22-23—Parker fellow '23-24 (Harvard). Member Committee of Experts on Philosophy and Humanities of UNESCO at Paris '47; member UNESCO Philosophical Conference at Mexico City '47.

Author: Phenomenology as a Method and as a Philosophical Discipline '28; The Foundation of Phenomenology '43. Editor: Philosophy and Phenomenological Research. Editor and co-author: Philosophical Essays in Memory of Emund Husserl '40; Philosophic Thought in France and the US '50. Chmn dept philos U Buffalo since '37. Internat Phenomenol Soc (pres since '40)—Am Philos Assn—Symbolic Logic Assn (mem exec com '46-49)—Phi Beta Kappa. Guggenheim Found fellowship '44-45. University of Buffalo, Buffalo 14.◉

10 FARLEY, Arthur J(ames). Peach; Apple. b'85. Grad '08 (Mass Agrl Coll). Director and member executive committee National Peach Council; secretary-treasurer NJ Peach Council since '28; sec NJ Peach Industry committees '42-49; secretary NJ Apple Institute. With NJ Coll Agr and Expt Sta since '08, also prof pomology Rutgers U. NJ Hort Soc (sec treas since '27; awarded citation '48)—Am Pomology Soc—Soc Hort Sci. Judge annual fruit exhibits. Rutgers University, The State University, New Brunswick, N.J.†◉

11 FARMER, Edward Willard. Snakes; Reptiles. b'25. Student '46-47 (Wharton County Coll). Snakes and reptiles of Texas Gulf Coast, snake venom. Author: So You Saw A Snake '52; also articles in field. Owner Dixon-Farmer Reptile Ranch since '46. Am Soc Ichthyologists and Herpetologists—Herpetologists League—NY Zool Soc. Dixon-Farmer Reptile Ranch, Pierce, Tex.

12 FARMER, Malcolm F(rench). Navaho and southern California archaeology; Early man in the far western United States. b'15. AB '40 (U Ariz). Author articles in field. Dir San Diego Mus of Man; now dept anthrop U Washington. Am Anthrop Assn(F)—Soc Am Archaeol—San Diego Hist Soc (dir). Dept. of Anthropology, University of Washington, Seattle 5, Wash.

13 FARNAM, Helen Rayley. Puppets; Marionettes (Television). b'92. Student (Wellesley Coll, Morningside Conservatory Music). Inventor (with B Wheeler) of the patented doll Looby-Loo. Co-author: Let's Make a Puppet. Producer of classic marionette shows for children in schools, churches, etc; weekly television show on KSTP, instr dept art education U Minn. Puppeteers of Am. c/o Webb Publishing Co., 55 E. 10th St., St. Paul 2.†

14 FARNER, Donald S(ankey). Avian physiology; Bird migration. b'15. BS '37 (Hamline U); MA '39—PhD '41 (U Wis). Research in physiology of digestion in birds, physiology of fat metabolism, physiology of migration, precision of migration, age-group structures of avian populations; associate editor of Bird-Banding. Author articles in field. Faculty U Wis '41-43; asst prof zool, asst curatr birds U Kan '46-47; asst prof biol U Colo '47; asso prof zoophysiol Wash State Coll '47-52 prof since '52; vis prof zool U Mont '49. Am Soc Zool—Am Ornithol Union—Biol Soc Wash. Department of Zoology, Washington State College, Pullman, Wash.

15 FARNSWORTH, Alice Hall. Astronomy (Photographic photometry, occultations). b'93. AB '16 (Mount Holyoke Coll); MS '17—PhD '20 (U Chicago). Joined expedition in Brazil sent by Brown University and Skyscrapers of Providence to photograph eclipse of sun '40; later went to South America to photograph spectrum of night-sky. With Mt Holyoke Coll since '20, prof astron since '37; dir John Payson Williston Obs since '36. AAAS—Am Astron Soc—Am Assn Variable Star Observers—Phi Beta Kappa. Mt. Holyoke Coll., South Hadley, Mass.

16 FARNSWORTH, C(linton) Eugene. Silviculture of northeastern United States; Forest surveying. b'04. BSF '26 (Ia State Coll); MF '28 (Yale); PhD '45 (U Mich). Research on elongation of tree species in northern New York. Author articles in field. Tech asst Targhee Nat Forest Ida '26-30; sr instr NY State Coll Forestry '30-31, asst prof '31-36, asso prof '36-'47; professor teaching silviculture, seeding, planting. Society Am Foresters—AAA S—Ecol Soc Am—Phi Kappa Phi—Sigma Xi. New York State College of Forestry, Syracuse 10, N.Y.†

17 FARNSWORTH, Helen Elliott Cherington. Grain (Economics). b'03. BSc '24—MA '24 (O State U); PhD '30 (Stanford U). Studies of world grain production, trade, prices, and consumption; research on problems of consumption of major foods in different countries. Author: Wheat Growers and the Tariff '46; Grain Saving for United States Export '47. Co-author: (with V P Timoshenko) World Grain Review and Outlook '45. Author articles: World Wheat Stocks 1890-1914 and 1922-1939 '39; Wheat in the Post-Surplus Period 1900-1909 '41; Wheat in the Fourth War Year '43; European Recovery Program and the American Farmer '49. Co-author articles: (with M K Bennett) World Wheat Acreage, Yields, and Climate '37. Staff Food Research Inst Stanford since '30, econ since '45, prof since '50. Am Econ Assn—Am Farm Econ Assn—Am Statis Assn. Food Research Institute, Stanford University, Stanford, Cal.◉

18 FARQUHAR, Donald W(ells). Vertebrate anatomy; Lepidoptera (New England); Forest insects (Parasites). b'07. BS '29—Ostend teaching F '26-29 (Tufts Coll); MS '30—PhD '34 (Harvard). Research on distribution of Lepidoptera of New England and Tachinid parasites of forest insects. Author articles in field. Seasonal worker gipsy moth lab US Bur Entomol and Plant Quarantine '26-32; asst in zool Harvard and Radcliffe Coll '31-34; with Coll City NY since '34, asst prof from '47. Geog Soc Am (F)—AAAS(F)—Entomol Soc Am—Am Mus Natural Hist—Lepidopterists Soc. Department of Biology, College of City of New York, Convent Av. at 139th St., NYC 31. H: 185 Claremont Av., NYC 27; 83 Long Beach Av., York Beach, Me.

19 FARQUHAR, Henry Hallowell. Industrial organization; Management; Industrial relations; Employee cooperation. b'84. AB '09 (U Mich); MBA '16 (Harvard Grad Sch Bus Administrn). Author: Factory Stores-Keeping '22; Positive Contributions of Scientific Management (Scientific Management Since Taylor) '24; Functional Organization (Scientific Management in American Industry) '29; also articles in field. Dir, mem exec com, controller Smith Iron Works Boston '23-28; owner and mgr Electracraft Corp Boston '24-28; cons and exec work with various NY firms and govt agencies '28-43; head engr prodn research and development, and scheduling WPB '43-45; dir indsl research Army Indsl Coll '45-47. Taylor Soc—Soc Advancement Management—Am Soc Pub Adminstrn—Am Management Assn. 13200 3rd St., St. Petersburg 6, Fla.

20 FARR, Lee Edward. Radiation (Biological effects); Nitrogen (Metabolism); Amino acids (Physiology); Kidneys (Physiology); Protein (Nutritional requirements). b'07. BS '29—MD '33 (Yale). Author: Treatment of the Nephrotic Syndrome '50; also articles in field. Contributor: Advances in Internal Medicine (vol I) '42. Asst pediatrics Yale U Sch Med and New Haven Hosp '34-37; asst, asso in med Hosp of Rockefeller Inst '34-40; dir research, phys-in-chief Alfred I duPont Inst, vis asso prof U Pa Sch Med '40-49; chmn med dept Brookhaven Nat Lab, phys-in-chief Brookhaven Nat Lab Hosp since '49. AAAS—AMA (F)—Am Acad Pediatricians(F)—Am Pediatrics Soc—Am Soc Clin Investigation—Am Soc Exptl Biol—Am Soc Exptl Path—Am Soc Pediatric Research—Harvey Soc—NY State Med Soc. Mead Johnson Award '40 for research in pediatrics. Brookhaven National Laboratory, Upton, Long Island, N.Y.

21 FARR, Robert Nikolaus. Radar. b'20. BA '38 (U Cal). Preparation scientific papers for popular consumption. Author article: Radar—How it Works and What it Does '45. Feature writer and war corr Scripps-Howard Sci Service '42-46; writer and producer CBS radio show "Adventures in Science" '44-45. AAAS—Aviation Writers Assn—Sci Writers Am—Optical Soc Am. 870 Park Av., NYC.†

22 FARR, Wanda Kirkbride. Cellulose: Pollen mother cell and root hair development; Plant cell membranes (Formation, structure): Micro-chemistry: Cotton fiber growth and development. b'95. BS '15 (Ohio U); MA '18 (Columbia); '21-24 (U Ia). Discovered formation of cellulose in plastids of living cells; made identification of cellulose in living protoplasm. Author articles in field. Dir Cellulose Lab Chem Found, Boyce Thompson Inst Plant Research '36-40; research chem Am Cyanamid Co '40-43; research chem Celanese Corp Am Research Labs since '43. AA AS(F)—Roy Microscopical Soc, London(F)—Bot Soc Am—Am Chem Soc—Optical Soc Am—NY Microscopical Soc—Am Soc Naturalists—Nat Inst Social Sci—Torrey Bot Club—Phi Beta Kappa—Sigma Xi. Celanese Corporation of America, Summit, N.J. H: Manley Court, Locust Dr.

23 FARRALL, Arthur William. Milk products (Processing equipment); Frost (Control equipment): Farm Machinery and Equipment. b'99. BS '21—MS '22 (U Neb): '26 (U Calif). Designed and patented ice cream manufacturing equipment including continuous ice cream freezer and continuous fruit feeder, designed homogenization equipment, process for continuous manufacture butter, designed equipment for application refrigeration to processing dairy and food products, operation experimental plant for spray drying milk, eggs and other food products, supervised general research dealing with development of equipment and methods for prevention of frost damage to farm products, official delegate from US to 12th annual International Dairy Congress, Stockholm '49. Holder patents on electronic ice cream freezer controller, continuous ice cream freezer, fruit feeder, continuous butter machine, radiant type frost prevention equipment. Author: Dairy Engineering '42; also articles in field. Faculty U Calif '22-28, asst prof '28-29; research engr, then supt spray drying lab Douthitt Engring Co '29-32; research engr. dir research Creamery Package Mfg Co '32-45; head dept agrl engring Mich State Coll since '45. Am Soc Agrl Engrs—Am Soc Engring Edn—Am Assn Coll Prof—Inst Food Tech—Am Dairy Sci Assn—Gamma Sigma Delta—Sigma Xi. Agricultural Engineering Department, Michigan State College, East Lansing, Mich.

24 FARRAR, Clayton (Leon). Apiculture (Bee behavior and management for production, honeybee stock improvement, testing, selection, breeding). b'04. BS '26 (Kan State Coll); PhD '31 (Mass State Coll). Research on winter wax secretion, pollen, pollination, influence of colony's strength on brood rearing and production, flight range of honeybees, two-queen and single-queen colony management, supersedure or loss of queen bees, nosema disease in relation to queen supersedure, winter losses, artificial insemination of queen bees, stock testing for selection and breeding. Author articles: Influence of Colony Populations on Production '37; The Use of Pollen Traps and Pollen Supplements in Developing Honeybee Colonies '46; Productive Management of Honeybee Colonies in the Northern States '44; Two-Queen Colony Management '46; Overwintering of Productive Colonies (in The Hive and the Honeybee) '46; More Honey from Bees (in Yearbook of Agriculture) '47, and others. Apiculturist div bee culture US Dept Agr Somerset Md '31, Laramie Wyo '31-38, in charge Madison Wis sta, prof dept econ entomol U Wis, since '38. Am Assn Econ Entomol—AAAS— Nat Fed Beekeepers — Sigma Xi — Phi Kappa Phi. U.S. Bee Culture Laboratory, 105 King Hall, University of Wisconsin, Madison, Wis.

10 FARRAR, Victor John. Alaskan history. b'86. AB '11—AM '12—PhD '27 (U Wis). Author: The Annexation of Russian America to the United States '37. Research asst Dept of State since '30, head Am Republics Sect Fgn Relations Br Div of Hist Policy Research since '46. Department of State, Washington 25.

11 FARRELL, Gabriel. Blind (Education, legislation, deaf-blind). b'86. BS '11—DD '35 (Dartmouth Coll); BD '15 (Episcopal Theol Sch Cambridge Mass). Author articles in field. Dir Perkins Instn and Mass Sch for Blind Watertown Mass '31-52, director emeritus since '52; lecturer Graduate School Education Harvard University '41-52; mem advisory com for war-blinded Vets Adminstrn since '46; consultant on blindness UN, Nat Soc for Prevention Blindness. Am Found for Blind (sec and dir)—Am Found Overseas Blind (dir)—Am Assn Instructors of Blind—Am Assn Workers for Blind —Mass Assn for Adult Blind—Mass Council Orgns for Blind (past pres). Hon chmn Internat Conf Educators of Blind Youth since '52. Perkins Institution, Watertown 72, Mass.⊙

12 FARRELLY, Theodore Slevin. History of Alaska. b'83. Student '02-06 (Harvard); '29-35 (Columbia U). Conducted research on Russian settlement of Alaska and identification of ruins of lost colony of Novgorod, 1571, on Kenai Peninsula '29-45. Author articles in field. Pres and dir Farrelly and Co, ins brokers since '23. Am Geog Soc (F)—Fedn Francais de la Natation et de Sauvetage (France). 110 East 42nd St., NYC 17.

13 FARRIER, Clarence Winfield. Sociology and technology of housing (Regional planing, zoning and building regulation); Television. b'93. BS '16 (Armour Inst Tech). Asso Bennett Parsons & Frost cons archs and city planners '24-29; asst dir of works, asst dir operations and asst gen mgr A Century of Progress Expn Chicago '29-34; asst gen mgr TVA '34-37; television coordinator NBC NYC '37-40; regional coordinator Defense Housing Washington '41; tech dir Nat Housing Agency '42-46; dir research Gunnison Homes Inc New Albany Ind since '46. Collaborator: Television Broadcasting '40; Housing Costs '44. AIA—Am Pub Health Assn — Forest Products Research Society. Ambridge Housing

Experimental Laboratory, American Bridge Co., Ambridge, Pa.

14 FARRIN, James Moore. Warship design. b'08. BS '29 (US Naval Acad); MS '34 (MIT). Various assignments in ship design construction and repair, battle damage repairs. Head preliminary design Bur Ships Navy Dept. Soc Naval Architects Marine Engrs— Soc Naval Engrs. Bureau of Ships, Navy Department, Washington 25.

15 FARRINGTON, S(elwyn) Kip, Jr. Salt water fishing; Duck and upland hunting; American railroads, merchant marine, steamships (History); Ice hockey. b'04. Ed '20 (Lawrenceville Sch NJ). Member committee that designed emergency fishing kits to be placed in all life boats and rafts of US Army, Navy and Coast Guard; captain US team in International Fishing Matches England and Cuba '37; holder 6 world fishing records. Author: Atlantic Game Fishing '37; Bill, the Broadbill Swordfish '42; Pacific Game Fishing '42; Railroading from the Head End '43; Railroads at War '44; Giants of the Rails '44; The Ducks Came Back '45; Interesting Birds of Our Country '45; Railroading from the Rear End '46; A Book of Fishes '46; Ships of the US Merchant Marine '47; Railroad of Today '47; Fishing the Atlantic Offshore and On '49; Fishing Boats of the World '48. In advt Kelly Nason Inc NYC since '40; writer on outdoor sports, especially salt-water fishing, since '34, salt-water ed Field & Stream since '37. Am Soc Ichthyologists. 247 Park Av., N.Y.C.

16 FARRIS, Edmond J. Anatomy; Reproduction; Male and female sterility; Ovulation timing. b'07. BA '28 (U Buffalo); PhD '38 (U Pa); fellow in anat '36-38 (Wistar Inst). Author: Anatomy and Physiology Laboratory Guide '48; Art Students' Anatomy '49; Care and Breeding of Laboratory Animals '49. Co-author and co-editor: (with J Q Griffith) The Rat in Laboratory Investigation '41, 2nd edition '49; Human Fertility and Problems of the Male '50. Exec dir and associate mem anat Wistar Inst since '38. Am Assn Anat—Internat Assn Med Mus— Biol Photog Assn (dir, pres '48)—NY Acad Sci—Am Soc Zool—AAAS—Am Soc Study Sterility—Phi Beta Kappa— Sigma Xi—Brazilian Soc Ster (corr mem)—Geront Soc—Soc Panamena de Obstet y Ginec. Spl award from Nat Research Found for Alleviation of Human Fertility '45. Wistar Institute, 36th St. and Woodland Av., Phila.⊙

17 FASSETT, Norman Carter. Native flora of the middle west. b'00. SB '22— MA '23—PhD '25 (Harvard). Author: Manual of Aquatic Plants; Spring Flora of Wisconsin; Leguminous Plants of Wisconsin; Hayfever Plants of the Middle West; also articles in field. Prof bot and curator herbarium U Wis. AAAS—Am Soc Plant Taxonomists— NE Bot Club—Am Soc Naturalists— Wis Acad Sci. Biology Building, Madison 6, Wis.†⊙

18 FAULKNER, Fred Lewis. Automotive equipment (Lubrication, maintenance). b'93. BS (mech engring) '15 (Armour Inst Tech—now Ill Inst Tech Armour Coll). Motor vehicle fleet operation; motor vehicle maintenance, industrial lubrication; extreme pressure lubricants; refrigerated transport. Author articles in field. Automotive engr, mgr automotive dept Armour & Co '26-46; regional automotive cons Office Defense Transportation, gen chmn regional maintenance commn, chmn truck rationing appeal bd (Ill, Ind Mich); v-pres, mgr operations Nelson Chevrolet Sales Inc since '46. Soc Automotive Engrs (v-pres

transportation and maintenance div '38, chmn transportation and maintenance standards div '38-46, fuels and lubricants div '40-50, highway research com, truck rating com, etc.). Nelson Chevrolet Sales Inc., 1002 Diversey Parkway, Chicago 14. H: 1606 Hinman Av., Evanston, Ill.

19 FAULL, J. Horace, Jr. Rubber latex; Rubber (Synthetic); Polymers (High). b'04. Student '21-23 (Phillips Exeter Acad); AB '27—AM '29—PhD '31 (Harvard); F '33-34 (U Munich). Developed processes and control procedures for synthetic rubber with emphasis on carbonblack masterbatching; research on latex colloid stability. Author articles in field. Latex research chem Firestone Tire and Rubber Co '37-40; tech supt Baytown Synthetic Rubber Plant '43-46; head sci sect Office Nav Research Boston '46-48; air research Gen Latex and Chem Co '40-43 '48; chem cons Officer Rubber Reserve Adv Com, adv Office Nav Research, and Gen Tire and Rubber Baytown since '48. ACS—Am Inst Chem— Sigma Xi. H: 72 Fresh Pond Lane, Cambridge 38, Mass.

20 FAUNCE, Wayne Moody. Museum administration. b'99. BS '21 (Brown U). Asst sec Am Mus Natural Hist '25-27, asst to dir '27-30, asst exec sec and asst dir '30-34, v dir and exec sec since '35; pres Hudson River Mus Yonkers since '50. Am Assn Mus— AAAS—NY Acad Science—Sigma Xi. American Museum of Natural History, N.Y.C. 24.

21 FAUSET, Arthur Huff. Intercultural relations (Negro folklore). AB— MA—PhD (U Pa). Research on Negro folklore Nova Scotia '23, southern US '25, West Indies '27. Author: For Freedom '27; Folk Lore of Nova Scotia '31; Sojourner Truth '38; Black Gods of the Metropolis '42. Prin Phila pub schs '26-46; ed Phila edition People's Voice '45-46. Am Anthrop Assn(F). 4948 Walnut St., Phila. 39.†

22 FAUST, Lawrence Yoder. Seismology (Exploration). b'04. BS '25 (Franklin and Marshall Coll); PhD '30 (U Pa). Studies in seismic velocities in sedimentary rocks; seismic interpretations in locating oil fields; research on near surface low velocity layer. Author article: Seismic velocity as a function of depth and geologic time. Geophysicist Sun Oil Co '26-27; geophys supervisor Amerada Petroleum Corp '34-50, cons geophysicist since '51. Soc Exploration Geophysicists— Am Geophys Union. Box 2040, Tulsa 2, Okla.

23 FAUSTMAN, Daniel Jackson. Traffic engineering (Traffic control); Highway design. b'16. BS '37 (U Calif); Certificate in transportation '38 (research F '37-38) (Harvard). Planning and design of streets and highways; traffic operation; design traffic control devices and facilities; research on magnetic and electro-mechanical devices to guide and control vehicular traffic. Author articles in field. Transportation engr Calif Pub Utilities Commn '47; city traffic engr Sacramento since '48; lectr traffic engring U Calif since '49, Northwestern U '50, Sacramento State Coll '50. Served as lt to maj traffic control br The Engr Bd Fort Belvoir Va AUS '42-45. Am Soc CE—Inst Traffic Engrs —Traffic Research Assos—Highway Research Bd. City Hall, Sacramento, Calif.

24 FAWCETT, Howard Hoy. Accident prevention; Safety education. b '16. BS '40 (U Md); '45-47 (U Del). Extension of accident prevention and utilization of safety principles in scientific circles and among technical personnel, safety aspects of chemistry and chemical engineering courses in colleges. Author articles in field. Chem, foreman, supervisor of standardization and safety coordinator Mil Explosives Mfg '40-44; research asso Manhattan Dist Atomic Project '44-45; research and development chem E I du Pont de Nemours and Co '45-48; safety supervisor research lab Gen Elec Co since '48. Alpha Chi Sigma (mem nat safety com '44-50, chmn from '50)—Nat Safety Council (mem exec com chem sect since '49)—ACS —AAAS—Am Indsl Hygiene Assn. Research Laboratory, General Electric Co., Postoffice Box 1088, Schenectady, N.Y.

10 FAY, Arthur Cecil. Dairy products (Chemistry, bacteriology); Food bacteriology and technology; Sanitation. b'96. BS '20 (U Mo); MS '21 (U Wis); PhD '33 (Ia State Coll). Author articles in field. Dir labs H P Hood & Sons Boston since '37. Am Dairy Sci Assn—Am Soc Bact—Am Pub Health Assn—Inst Food Tech (pres NE sect '47-48, nat councillor since '48)—Sigma Xi—Phi Kappa Phi. H. P. Hood & Sons, 500 Rutherford Av., Boston.

11 FAY, George Emory. Mexican archeology; European paleolithic archeology. b'27. AB '48 (U Mo); '48-49 (U NM); AM '51 (U Mich). Research on archeology of Sonora, Mexico; Old World fossil man. Asst archeol research U Mo '47-48; archeol expeditions U Mo '47 '47, U NM '49; personal archeol investigation Great Britain and Eire '51; field asst Neb State Hist Soc Expdn '51; research chem Eagle Picher Co since '51. AAAS—Am Anthrop Assn—Soc Am Archeol—Archeol Inst Am—Middle Am Research Inst—Internat Soc Am Linguistics—Archeol Soc Colo, Conn, Ill, Ia, Mo, Wis, NC—Hist Soc Mo and Okla—Kan Acad Sci—Antiquity (Eng)—Phi Beta Kappa—Alpha Phi Omega. Eagle Picher Co., Joplin, Mo. H: 1035 Crest Dr.

12 FAY, Sidney Bradshaw. Prussian history (1640-1786); German History (1870-1939); World War I (Causes). b'76. Author: Origins of the World War (2 vols) '28, rev edit '30; Rise of Brandenburg—Prussia to 1786 '37. Author articles: The Idea of Progress; and others. Prof history Dartmouth '02-14; prof European history Smith Coll '14-29; prof history Harvard '29-46. Am Hist Assn (pres '46)—Am Polit Sci Assn—Am Philos Soc—English Hist Soc—Verein fur Geschichte der Mark Brandenburg—Societe d'Histoire Moderne—Societe de L'Histoire de la Guerre. H: 194 Brattle St., Cambridge, Mass.†◎

13 FAYE, Christopher Urdahl. Zulu Language; Medieval and Rennaissance bibliography. b'86. BA '09 (Luther Coll); cand theol '12 (Luther Sem St Paul); MA '24 (U Minn); BS '29—MS '30 (U Ill); F L Jonsson scholar '00 (Eng). Missionary in Church of Norway Mission in Natal and Zululand South Africa '12-22; appointed by American council of learned societies to edit supplement to De Ricci-Wilson Census of Medieval and Rennaissance manuscripts in US and Canada. Author: The influence of hlonipa on the Zulu clicks; Fifteenth Century Printed Books at the University of Illinois '49. Staff U Ill library since '26, now bibliog cons and cataloger, rank of asst prof. ALA—Medieval Acad Am—Heimskringla. University Library, Urbana, Ill. H: 710 S. Foley, Champaign, Ill.

14 FEARING, Franklin. Psychology (Social, human communication, mass media); Content analysis (Radio, film); Public opinion and propaganda analysis; Group dynamics; Psychoreflexology; Race prejudice; Education (Audio visual). b'92. AB '23—AM '24—PhD '26 (Stanford U). Member board editors special issue The Motion Picture Industry, Annals American Academy Political and Social Science '47, Hollywood Quarterly since '45, Journal of Psychology since '37; advisory editorial board Journal of Social Issues, editor special issue Mass Media of Communication '47; managing editor Comparative Psychology Monographs; member advisory council of commission on community inter-relation American Jewish Congress. Author: Reflex Action '30; also articles in field. Asso prof psychol O Wesleyan U '26-27, Northwestern U '27-36; prof psychol U Calif Los Angeles since '36; vis prof U Ore '27-28, U Calif '30. AAAS(F)—Am Psychol Assn(F)—Soc Psychol Study Social Issues—Soc Exptl Biol and Med—AAUP—Phi Beta Kappa—Sigma Xi. University of California, Los Angeles 24.

15 FEARON, Edwin H. Forgery (Detection). b'77. LLB '02 (Western Ky State Normal); BCS '12 (Kinman Bus Inst); grad '04 (Ohio Bus Inst), '00 (Zanerian Art Coll); post grad law '15 (Gonzaga U). Research on age and composition inks, paper, typewriting, and questioned handwriting; use measuring instruments, photography, ultra violet, infra red. Author articles: The Document Examiner's Laboratory '47; Camera Dick '41; and others. Supervisor handwriting, teacher law accounting Spokane Pub Schs '13-28; operator lab investigation research The Fearon Questioned Document Research Laboratory since '28. Am Soc Questioned Document Examiners (charter mem, dir). Bessemer Bldg., Pittsburgh 22.

16 FEARON, Robert Earl. Geophysics; Well logging; Neutron bombardment; Atmosphere radioactivity. b'12. BS '33—MS '34—'34-36 (U Pittsburgh). Research and investigation of electrical conductance of very short gaps under non-arcing conditions, discoverer of methods of appraising rock structures penetrated by borings employing neutron bombardment. Inventor of an especially sensitive direct current amplifier for nuclear work (patented); coordinator and co-author of some non-governmental studies on atmosphere radioactivity associated with atomic bombs; patentee of many US and foreign patents employing neutron bombardment. Author articles: Gamma Ray Well Logging '49; Neutron Well Logging '49. Research engr Eng Lab Inc Okla '38-39, Well Surveys Inc Tulsa '39-41, Stanolind Oil & Gas Co '41-44; dir research Well Surveys Incorporated '44-52; organizer Electro-chemical Laboratories Tulsa '52. Society of Exploration Geophysicists—American Geophysicists Union—American Institute Mining and Metall Engrs—Am Chem Soc—Am Phys Soc—Sigma Xi. 2207 E. 6th St., Tulsa 4. H: 1430 S. Terrace Dr.

17 FEATHERSTONHAUGH, (James) Duane. Ornithological and speleological photography. b'13. AB '36 (Union Coll). Co-leader with Paul A Zahl of expedition to take first color photographs of roseate flamingo nesting colonies in West Indian salt swamps '46; leader of expedition to take first color and black and white photographic study of trumpeter swans northern Alberta '48; chief photographer of Canadian government expedition to study and photograph whooping crane '49. Author: Press Photography With the Miniature Camera '38; Photography for All '47; Nature for All '48; also articles in field. Photographer, reporter various papers Schenectady, Albany '36-46; photographer and author since '46; contbr to photographic and gen mags since '36. Nat Speleological Soc (publicity chmn)—NY Acad Sci—Photographic Soc Am—Am Ornithol Union—Audubon Soc—Authors League Am. Mount Maria, Duanesburg, N.Y.

18 FEDERIGHI, Henry. Oysters; Chromatophores; Tropisms. b'00. BS '23 (Rutgers); MA '24—PhD '26—Gorham Thomas Scholar '23-24—Thayer fellow '24-26 (Harvard). In charge oyster investigation Texas Coast '36. Author articles in field. Prof biol Antioch Coll since '29. AAAS—Soc Bact—Soc Study Evolution—Phi Beta Kappa —Sigma Xi. Grant AAAS '31, grant-in-aid Nat Research Council '31. Antioch College, Yellow Springs, O.

19 FEDERN, Walter. Egyptology (Egyptian texts and grammar). b'10. Dr Phil '34 (U Vienna). Author: Egyptian Bibliography '39-47 '48. Lecturer for Egyptian lang Sch for Asiatic Studies NYC since '47. Inst fur Agyptologie und Afrikanistik an der Universitat Wien—Am Oriental Soc. 105-20 66 Av., Forest Hills, N.Y.

20 FEINBERG, Richard. Vision (Occupational). b'11. BS (Optometry) '33 (U Rochester); D Ocular Sci (hon) '44 (Northern Ill Coll Optometry) PhD (applied psychol) '48 (Purdue U). Author articles: New advances in occupational seeing; Viewpoints in occupational seeing; The nurse in an industrial vision program; Conservation of child and adult vision. Supervisor vision program Sperry Gyroscope Co '43-46; research asso Indsl Vision Inst Purdue U '46-48; prof psychol and optometry Pacific U dean coll since '48. Am Optometric Assn—Am Acad Optometry—Am Psychol Assn—AAAS—Am Pub Health Assn—Nat Soc Prevention Blindness—Am Assn Safety Engrs—Illuminating Engring Soc—Sigma Xi. Pacific University, Forest Grove, Ore. H: 1813 Ash St., Forest Grove, Ore.

21 FEJER, Andrew Akos. Aircraft propulsion; Aero-thermodynamics; Gas turbines. b'13. ME '36 (Czech Tech U Prague); MS '39—PhD '45 (Calif Inst Tech). Internal aerodynamics propulsion systems, axial compressors, turbines; development and testing supersonic compressors; design high speed wind tunnels. Head gasdynamics and advanced design sects Aircraft Engine Div Packard Motor Car Co '45-49; prof and chmn dept aeronautical engring U Toledo since '49, also engring cons. Am Soc Engring Edn—Inst Aeronautical Scis—Sigma Xi. University of Toledo, Toledo 6, O. H: 3328 Chelteham Rd., Toledo 6, O.

22 FEJOS, Paul. Anthropology; Ethnology; Archaeology. b'97. Ed U Budapest '20. Author: Ethnography of the Yagua '44; Archaeological Explorations in the Cordillera Vilcabamba, Peru '44; also articles in field. Dir research The Viking Fund Inc since '41; cons prof anthrop Stanford U since '43. Am Geog Soc(F)—Royal Danish Geog Soc—Am Acad Polit Social Sci—Am Anthrop Assn(F)—AAAS—Am Assn Phys Anthrop—Am Ethnol Soc—Am Folklore Soc—Am Sociol Soc—Geog Soc of Lima Peru (Orellana medal '42)—Inst Ethnic Affairs—Royal Soc Natural Sci (Budapest)—Soc for Am Archaeol—Soc for Applied Anthrop. Decorated Knight Comdr Order of the Sun Peru '41. c/o The Viking Fund, Inc., 14 E. 71st St., NYC 21.

23 FELD, Bernard Taub. Nuclear physics; Nuclear moments; Neutron physics; Mesons. b'19. BS '39 (City Col NY); PhD '45 (Columbia). National Research Council committee on nuclear science, subcommittees on nuclear constants and neutron physics '46-52; consultant in nuclear physics Brookhaven National Laboratory since '47. Co-author: Science and Engineering of Nuclear Power '47; also articles in field. Research asso Columbia uranium project '41-42; Metall Lab U Chicago '42-44, group leader '43-44; physicist, asst group leader Los Alamos Sci Lab '44-46; asso prof phys MIT since '52. Am Phys Soc(F)—Sigma Xi—Phi Beta Kappa. Physics Department, Massachusetts Institute of Technology, Cambridge, Mass.†

10 FELD, Jacob. Soils (Engineering control); Retaining walls; Cables. b '99. BS '18 (City Coll NY); CE—MA '21—PhD '22 (U Cincinnati). Lateral earth pressure and soil foundations; research on retaining walls and abutments; design analysis on cables for long span cableways and guyed radio towers. Chairman committee on highway bridge abutments, Highway Research Board of National Research Council. Author: Lateral Earth Pressure '23; Unbraced Cables '30; Foundation Primer '38; Camp Construction '26; also articles in field. Designer and cons since '24; site project mgr Sampson Nav Training Sta '42; cons postwar highway program Bronx since '44; archt-eng Nav Amm Depot Earle '50. AAAS(F)—Am Soc CE—NY Acad Sci—Am Concrete Inst—Nat Soc Prof Engrs—Phi Beta Kappa—Sigma Xi. Baldwin research F U Cincinnati '19-22. 60 E. 23rd St., NYC 10.

11 FELDMAN, Albert William. Elm (Dutch elm disease). b'18. AA '38 (Wright Coll); AB '42 (U Ill); MS '44 (NC State Coll); PhD '47 (U Minn). Development plant chemotherapy related to Dutch elm disease; study of nature and effects produced by Dutch elm fungus toxins, separation toxin components and analysis of effects on host, determination of mechanism by which these toxins adversely affect host; technique for screening toxin neutralizing chemicals; study on physiology of host-pathogen relationship. Holds 4 patents in plant chemotherapy. Author articles: Physiological and Chemotherapeutic Investigations of Ceratosromella ulmi '49; Physiology of Toxin Production by Ceratosromella ulmi '50; Chemicals for Dutch Elm Disease Therapy '50; Dutch Elm Disease in Seedling Elms '50. Research fellow physiol path U Minn '44-47; asst research prof plant path RI Agrl Expt Sta '47-51; research biologist US Rubber Co since '51. Am Phytopath Soc—AAAS—Soc Plant Physiol—Soc for Growth and Development—Ill Acad Sci—Sigma Xi. Naugatuck Chemical Div., United States Rubber Co., Bethany 15, Conn.

12 FELDMAN, Hyman. Buses (Maintenance). b'18. BS (mech engring) '39 (Va Poly Inst). Author articles in field. Supervisor automotive maintenance Capital Transit Co since Nov 1946. Soc Automotive Engrs—Am Transit Assn (chmn subcommittee on vehicle cleaning)—Wash Soc Engrs. Capital Transit Co., 3222 M St., N.W., Washington 7.

13 FELDMESSER, Julius. Nematodes; Parasitology. b'18. AB '40 (Brooklyn Coll); '41 (George Washington U); MS '51 (NY U). Research on biology of plant parasitic nematodes and effects of temperature and humidity on larvae, cytology of nematodes. Author articles in field. Asst nematologist Div Nematology Bur Plant Industry USDA since '47. Am Soc Parasitol—Sigma Xi. Nematode Research Laboratory, RFD 2, Hicksville, N.Y.

14 FELLAND, Nordis Adelheid. Geographical bibliography. b'01. BA '23 (St Olaf Coll); BLS '27 (Pratt Inst Lib Sch); '31-32 (Columbia U Sch Lib Service). Cooperation with Bibliographie Géographique Internationale, Paris. Editor Current Geographical Publications since '43. Cataloger Am Geog Soc NYC '27-44, librarian since '44. ALA—Spl Lib Assn—Am Documentation Inst—Bibliog Soc Am—NY Regional Catalog Group—Assn Am Geographers—Soc Women Geographers. American Geographical Society, Broadway at 156th St., NYC 32.

15 FELLER, Alexander. Labor economics and law (Relations, fair standards, management-employee relations, arbitration, industrial collective bargaining). b'04. LittB '24 (Rutgers U); LLB '27 (Columbia); AM '27 (Columbia Grad Sch). Co-author: How to Deal with Organized Labor '37; How to Operate Under the Wage-Hour Law '38. Lawyer pvt practice New Brunswick and Newark NJ specializing in labor relations since '36. Am Bar Assn—NJ Bar Assn—Middlesex County Bar Assn—Am Judicature Soc—Assn of ICC Practitioners — Am Arbitration Assn (mem nat panel arbitrators since '40). 390 George St., New Brunswick, N.J.

16 FELLER, Robert Livingston. Art conservation (Chemistry). b'19. AB '41 (Dartmouth); MS '43—PhD '50 (Rutgers U). Research on artists' varnishes. Nat Gallery of Art F Mellon Inst since '50. ACS—Phi Lambda Upsilon—Sigma Xi—AAAS. Mellon Institute, Pitts. 13.

17 FELLERS, Carl Raymond. Food technology; Bacteriology. b'93. BA '15 (Cornell U); MSc '16—PhD '18 (Rutgers U). Research on sanitation, food technology, food law enforcement, seafoods, canned foods, food preservation, fish and marine products, human and animal nutrition; member editorial board Food Research and Quick Frozen Foods. Invented methods pasteurizing dried foods, canning Atlantic crabs, ascorbic acid antioxidants in food. Author articles in field. Research bact Nat Canners Assn Seattle and State Wash '21-23; asso prof food preservation U Wash Seattle '24-25; research prof food tech Mass State Coll and Exptl Sta Amherst since '26, head dept since '41; dir Blue Channel Corp packing marine products. Lt col QMC US Army '42-45; col '52. Dir QM Associates since '51. AAAS(F)—Am Pub Health Assn (gov council 6 years, chmn food and nutrition sect '36)—Am Chem Soc (councillor, sec-treas agr and food sect '41-42, vice-chmn '47)—Soc Am Bact—Am Soc Hort Sci—Am Fisheries Soc—NY Academy Sci—Inst Food Tech (founder, councillor sec-treas '47-48)—Sigma Xi. Babcock Award '50. University of Mass., Amherst, Mass.†☺

18 FELLOWS, Hurley. Wheat diseases (Foot rot, speckled leaf blotch). b'91. BS '20 (Ore State Coll); MS '21—PhD '23 (U Wis). Path US Dept Agr. Am Phytopath Soc. Botany Department, Kansas State College, Manhattan, Kans.

19 FELLOWS, John Albert. Steel melting; Steel (Manganese); Heat resistant alloys; Copper melting; Creep testing; Abrasion testing. b'06. AB '28 (Williams Coll); MS '32—ScD '42 (MIT). Austenite-ferrite transformation in alloy steels; improved alloy compositions for high temperature service; studies of structure versus abrasion resistance of alloyed steels and irons, with development new commercial alloy grades; creep testing steels and pure metals at elevated and room temperatures; studies analysis, heat treatment, and melting practice austenitic manganese steel for service conditions of high impact and abrasive wear. Co-author articles: (with E Cook, H S Avery) Precision in Creep Testing '42; (with E Cook, H S Avery) Engineering Properties of Heat-Resistant Alloys '42; (with R A Flinn, E Cook) A Quantitative Study of Austenite Transformation '43, and others. Metall Am Brake Shoe Co '37-43 since '48, research metall since '50; with Carbide & Carbon Chem Corp '43-48, metall '46-48. Am Soc Metals—Inst Metals London—AIMME—Am Foundrymen's Soc—Phi Beta Kappa. Am Soc Metals Henry Marion Howe medal '44. Metallurgical Department, American Brake Shoe Co., Mahwah, N.J. H: 216 Highland Rd.

20 FELS, Irving Gordon. Sulfur (Intermediate metabolism); Detoxification of selenium compounds. b'16. BA '41 (Brooklyn Coll); MA '41 (U Minn); PhD '49—Swift fellow '47-48 (Ore State Coll). Author articles in field. Research asst Oregon State Coll since '47. Am Chem Soc—Sigma Xi—Phi Lambda Upsilon. Department of Chemistry, Oregon State College, Corvallis, Ore.†

21 FELSENFELD, Oscar. Epidemic control. b'06. MD '30 (Charles U Prague); CPH '36 (Czechoslovak State); '40-41 (Scarritt Coll Nashville); laudatory decree '37 (Govt Iran); laudatory decree '36 (Czechoslovak Govt); fellow '30 (Ferran Inst Barcelona). Surveys and scientific trips in the tropics; described new media for detection and differentiation of Salmonellae and Shigellae, methods for isolation and identification of Salmonellae, Shigellae, Vibrio comma and intestinal protozoa, described a new method of vaccination against cholera and dysentery; devised new method for evaluation of antiamebic drugs and antibiotics; studied geographical distribution and animal-human relationship of Salmonellae. Author articles in field. Dir bacteriol Hektoen Inst Cook Co Hosp since '48. Royal Soc Tropical Med and Hygiene (London)—Soc Exptl Biol and Med—Am Soc Path Bact—Am Assoc Immunol. Received Schroeder award '31, Romanian Cross of Merit '35. Hektoen Institute, Cook County Hospital, Chicago 12.†

22 FELTEN, Charles John. Typography; Design. b'98. Grad '15 (Augustinian Acad Staten Island). Author: Layout, The Practical Application of the Principles of Design to Advertising and Printing; also articles in field. Instr layout and typography Fordham U and other schools since '47. Printing liaison officer and chief printing div Bur Overseas Pubs OWI '42-46. Internat Assn Printing House Craftsmen—NY Typog Union No 6—Printing Navigators—Type Directors Club of NY. 515 E. Fordham Rd., NYC.†

23 FELTON, George Edwin. Ion exchange resins; Carbohydrate chemistry. b'09. BS '31—PhD '35 (Ia State Coll). Research chemistry of corn starch, food flavors, production and use of modified starches, use of ion exchange resins in recovery of organic acids and purification of sugar containing waste, frozen pineapple production. Author articles in field. Research chem Ia State Agrl Expt Sta '35-36; Gen Foods Corp Battle Creek '36-38; Am Maize Products Ind '38-43; Hawaiian Pineapple Co Honolulu '43-49, tech dir since '49. Am Chem Soc—Sigma Xi. Hawaiian Pineapple Company, Ltd., Honolulu 1, T.H.

24 FELTON, Jean Spencer. Atomic energy research (Health hazards). b '11. AB '31—MD '35 (Stanford). Research on industrial health practices and methods, preventive medicine procedures, mental health in industry, utilization of the handicapped, job adjustment of the veteran, development of industrial dispensary facilities. Author articles: Industrial Health and Medical Rehabilitation at an Atomic Energy Laboratory '47; The Effect of New Forms of Energy on Industry and Medical Service '48; The Unusual in Industrial Health at an Atomic Energy Research Lab '50, and others. Now med dir Oak Ridge Nat Lab. Indsl med officer AUS 40-46. AMA(F, sec preventive and indsl med and pub health sect)—Am Acad Compensation Med(F)—Am Pub Health Assn(F)—Am Assn Indsl Physicians and Surgeons(F)—So Med Assn—Tenn State Med Assn (cons indsl med, com indsl health). Oak Ridge National Laboratory, P.O. Box P, Oak Ridge, Tenn.

10 FELTON, Mathias William. Potato and vegetable crop diseases. b'13. BA '36—PhD '42 (U Wis). Research on downy mildew diseases of cruicifers, bacterial diseases of bean and tomato, Fusarium wilts of tomato and potato, leaf roll of potato '40-46, virus diseases of potato since '46. Author articles in field. Teaching asst plant pathol U Wis '36-40; asst prof plant path and asst plant path Expit Sta U Neb '40-46; plant path Neb Certified Potato Growers Assn, dir Found seed program since '46. Am Phytopath Soc. Drawer 71, Alliance, Neb.†

11 FENNELL, Richard A(dams). Zoology. b'03. BA '27 (Birmingham-So Coll); '28-30 (Duke U); PhD '36 (Johns Hopkins U). Research in biological cell physiology including cytopathology of chorioallantoic lesions induced with saline suspensions of Tetrahymena geleii; influence of temperature, salts, hydrogen-ion concentration, and of attachment to substratum on ingestion of amoeba; also on relation between heredity, sexual activity, and training to dominance-subordination in game cocks; avian hematology; function vermiform appendix herbivora. Author articles in field. Asst biol Birmingham So Coll '25-27, grad asst '27-28, instr '30-32, grad asst '32-33; instr Mich State Coll '36-41, asst prof '41-44, asso prof '44-47, prof since '47. Am Soc Study Evolution—Am Soc Zool—Am Soc Protozool—AAAS—Mich Acad Sci Arts Letters—Sigma Xi—Gamma Alpha—Delta Sigma Phi. Michigan State College, East Lansing, Mich.

12 FENTON, Faith. Food and nutrition; Frozen and dehydrated foods; Vitamin and palatability retention (Home and large-scale cooking). BS (Ia State Coll); MS '23 (Teacher's Coll Columbia U); PhD '38 (U Chicago). Responsible investigator on emergency dehydration project relating to Lend-Lease in cooperation with US Bureau Home Economics '42, on National Research Council project on vitamin and palatability retention in large-scale cooking for Army '42-45; chairman national committee on recommendations for cookery and processing procedures in connection with US Experiment Station nat cooperative project Conservation of Nutritive Value of Food '42-46; chmn research dept Am Home Ec Assn '50. Author articles in field. With State Coll Home Econ Cornell U since '22, teaching and research since '36. AAAS(F)—Am Home Econ Assn—Inst Food Tech—AAUP—NY Acad Sci —Sigma Xi—Phi Kappa Phi—Omicron Nu—Sigma Delta Epsilon—Pi Lambda Theta. Alumni Merit Award Ia State Coll '47. Brook Lane Apartments, Ithaca, N.Y.

13 FENTON, Mildred Adams. Fossil algae, invertebrates and paleoecology. b'99. BS '22 (U Chicago). Co-author: The Rock Book '40; Mountains '42; The Land We Live On '44; Worlds in the Sky '50; Rocks and Their Stories '51; Giants of Geology '52; also articles in field. Research on fossil invertebrates, algae and paleoecology since '29. Sigma Xi. 404 Livingston Av., New Brunswick, N.J.†

14 FENTON, William N(elson). Indian Ethnology (Iroquois, Six Nations, herbalism, place names, political organization, masks, ceremonies, music); Foreign area and language study programs in American universities. b'08. AB '31 (Dartmouth Coll); PhD '37 (Yale). Author articles: Seneca Ceremonies at Coldspring Longhouse '36; Seneca Society of Faces (Masks) '37; Problems Arising from the Historic Northeastern Position of the Iroquois '40; Iroquois Suicide '41; Contacts between Iroquois Herbalism and Colonial Medicine '42; Installing Cayuga Chiefs '45; Area Studies in American Universities '47, and others. Sr ethnol Bur Am Ethnol Smithsonian Instn '43-51; US del Internat Congress Anthrop '52; member US Nat Commn UNESCO panel on language. National Research Council (Com International Coop in Anthrop, exec sec Div Anthropology and Psychol since '52)—Am Anthrop Assn—Am Folklore Soc—Soc Am Archaeol—Anthrop Soc Wash (sec '43-46, vp '47, pres '48)—Wash Acad Sci (asso ed jour '43-44, bd ed '45, sr ed '47, bd mgrs '48-51)—Sigma Xi. National Research Council, Washington 25.⊚

15 FERDON, Edwin Nelson, Jr. Archeology of Ecuador. b'13. Student '31-33 (Marietta Coll); AB '37 (U NM); MA '39 (U So Calif). Archeological and geographical explorations in Ecuador '39-45. Author articles: Reconnaissance in Esmeraldas '40-41; Characteristic Figurines from Esmeraldas '45. Curator of Br Museums, Mus of NM '37-38, curator Middle Am Archeol '38-40; research asso in Hispanic Studies Sch Am Research and Mus NM '46-47, research asso in charge Hispanic Studies since '47. AAAS—Am Anthrop Assn(F)—Am Geog Soc(F). School of American Research, Santa Fe, N.M.

16 FERENCE, Michael, Jr. Physics of the upper atmosphere (Meteorology, geophysics, clouds, rockets, hydrodynamics, radar weather, atmospheric electricity). b'11. BS '33—MS '34—PhD '37 (U Chicago). Associate editor Journal of Meterology. Co-author: (with Harvey B Lemon) Analytical Experimental Physics '43; also articles in field. Instr physics U Chicago '37-40, asst prof physics meterol '40-44, asso prof '44-46; chief meterol br Signal Corps Engring Labs Ft Monmouth NJ '46-48, chief scientist since '48. Inst Radio Engrs (sr)—Am Meterol Soc—Am Geophys Union—Am Phys Soc—Phi Beta Kappa—Sigma Xi. Evans Signal Laboratory, Belmar, N.J. H: 102 Deal Esplanade, Deal, N.J.

17 FERGUS, Ernest Newton. Forage crops and pastures. b'92. BS '16 (O State U); PhD '31 (U Chicago). Research in red clover adaptation, improvement, forage crop seed production, pasture production and management. Author articles in field. Asst in soils and crops Purdue U Agrl Expt Sta '18-20; instrs soils and crops U Ky '20-23, asst prof farm crops '23-28, asso prof '28-38, prof since '38; asst agron Ky Agrl Expt Sta '20-36, agron charge pasture and forage crops investigation since '36; agt Bur Plant Ind US Dept Agr '18-20, collaborator since '36. AAAS—Ky Acad Sci—Am Soc Agron—Sigma Xi—Alpha Zeta. Kentucky Agricultural Experiment Station, Lexington 29, Ky.

18 FERGUSON, Alfred Lynn. Electrochemistry. b'84. BPd '04 (Mich State Normal Coll); AB '08—AM '09—PhD '15 (U Mich). Research in mechanisms electrode reactions; adhesion electroplated deposits; electroplating alloys; electrochemical preparations. Member faculty U Mich since '11, prof chem since '44. ACS—Am Electrochem Soc (pres '49-50)—Am Electroplaters Soc—AAAS—Mich Acad Sci—Chem Tchrs Assn—Alpha Chi Sigma—Gamma Alpha—Phi Lambda Upsilon—Sigma Xi. Chemistry Building, University of Michigan, Ann Arbor, Mich. H: 11505 East Dunlavy Lane, Whitmore Lake, Mich.⊚

19 FERGUSON, (John) DeLancey. Robert Burns; Mark Twain; Rudyard Kipling. b'88. BA '11—MA '12 (Rutgers U); fellow '13-14—PhD '16 (Columbia). Author: American Literature in Spain '16; The Letters of Robert Burns (2 vols) '31; Pride and Passion: Robert Burns '39; Robert Burns, His Associates and Contemporaries '43; Mark Twain: Man and Legend '43. With O Wesleyan U '18-30, prof '24-30; prof Western Reserve U '30-44; prof and chmn Eng dept Brooklyn Coll since '44. Guggenheim fellow '28-29. Brooklyn College, Bklyn 10.⊚

20 FERGUSON, Milton James. Library planning and buildings; Library surveys; American library laws. b'79. AB '01—AM '06 (U Okla); certificate '02 (NY State Library Sch); HLD '33 (New York U). Made library survey Union South Africa, Rhodesia and Kenya Colony, for Carnegie Corporation '28-29. Editor: American Library Law '30, Dewey Decimal Classification 15th ed '51. Chief librarian Brooklyn Pub Library '30-49. ALA (exec bd '25-26, '33-37, pres '38-39)—Calif Library Assn (pres '18-19, '26-27)—Nat Assn State Libraries (pres '18-19)—NY Library Assn (pres '32-33)—NY Acad Public Edn—Trustee Edn Foundation Lake Placid since '37—Phi Beta Kappa. 115 Willow St., Bklyn 2.

21 FERGUSON, Thomas Stuart. Mayas; Toltecs; Olmecs; Nahuas; Itzas. b'15. AB '37—LLB '42 (U Cal). Research on origins, history, and religion advanced peoples of ancient Mexico, Guatemala, and Central America; manager '48 expedition of Brigham Young University department of archeology to southern Mexico. Co-author (with Milton R Hunter): Ancient America and the Book of Mormon '50. With Brown, Smith and Ferguson since '46. Soc Am Archeol. 1305 Franklin St., Oakland 12, Cal. H: 1 Irving Lane, Orinda, Cal.

22 FERGUSON, Wallace Klippert. History of the Renaissance. BA '24 (U Western Ontario); MA '25—PhD '27 (Cornell U). Author: Erasmi Opuscula: A Supplement to the Opera Omnia '33; A Survey of European Civilization (with G Bruun) '36; The Renaissance '40; The Renaissance in Historical Thought '48. Fellow Social Sci Research Council, Europe, '27-28; instr hist NYU '28-30, asst prof '30-36; asso prof '36-45, prof since '45. Fellow Guggenheim Mem Found '39-40. Phi Beta Kappa. New York University, NYC.⊚

23 FERLAINO, Frank R. Boxing (Medical aspects); Industrial pulmonary diseases, traumatic diseases, injuries. b'00. BA '22—MS '23 (Princeton); MD '27 (Johns Hopkins). Asst phys Am Telephone & Telegraph '30-38; indsl med cons '38-41; asso med dir Schenley Labs '44-45; med dir Gen Motors Corp NYC since '45; now asst attending physician and asst clin prof indsl med NYU-Bellevue Med Center

Hosp; chmn med adv bd NY State Boxing Commn since '48. NY State Med Soc—AMA—AAAS—NY Acad Sci—Am Coll Chest Physicians(sec)—Am Pub Health Assn—Am Heart Assn—Am Trudeau Soc—Nat Tuberculosis Assn—Am Assn Indsl Physicians and Surgeons—Johns Hopkins Med and Surg Assn—NY Acad Sci. General Motors Corp., 1775 Broadway, NYC; also 580 Park Av., NYC. H: 519 Ocean Parkway, Brooklyn.

10 FERNELIUS, W(illis) Conard. Inorganic chemistry (Nitrogen and coordination compounds, rare elements, radio-chemistry). b'05. AB '25—AM '26—PhD '28 (Stanford U); '30 (U Munich); '37 (Western Reserve U). Also research on reactions in liquid ammonia, rare elements, nitrogen compounds, coordination compounds, recovery of elemental sulfur, chlorosulforic acid, radio-chemical problems. Co-author: A Course in Inorganic Preparations '35; Inorganic Syntheses vol I '39, vol II '46; Chemistry, a Textbook for Colleges '40; Fundamentals in Chemistry for the Laboratory '41; Introduction to College Chemistry '42; also articles in field. Instr O State U '28-32, asst prof '32-36, asso prof '36-40, prof '40-42; prof Purdue U '42-47; atom bomb project Monsanto Chem Co '43-46, atom bomb test Bikini '46; prof and chmn dept chemistry Syracuse U '47-49; prof and head dept chem Pa State College since '49. AAAS(F)—Am Inst Chem(F)—Am Chem Soc. Department of Chemistry, Pennsylvania State College, State College, Pa. H: 305 Adams Av.◉

11 FERNOW, Karl Herman. Potato diseases (Rot); Mosaic diseases of plants. b'93. BS '16—PhD '25 (Cornell U). Asst prof, asso prof dept plant path Cornell U since '25; chief seed potato inspector NY since '23. AAAS—Am Phytopathol Soc. New York State College of Agriculture, Ithaca, N.Y.†

12 FERNSWORTH, Lawrence A. Spain; Catalonia (Customs, language); Andorra. b'91. Student '19-21 (U Calif); '23 (Columbia); '25-29 (U Montpellier France); Nieman fellow '43-44 (Harvard). Made archaeological studies in southern France; investigated customs of Andorra. Author: Protestants under Franco '39; Nothing But Danger '39; Dictators and Democrats '41. Pres Fgn Correspondents Assn in Spain; governing council the Nieman Soc, editorial bd the Nieman Report. Formerly staff corresp London Times in Spain; author US Army booklet Spain, World War II. Harvard Club, 27 W. 44th St., New York 18, N.Y.†

13 FERRIER, Ben. Canoes; Canadian exploration. b'03. Student '24-28 (U Minn); BS '33 (Northwestern U); '34-35 (Ia State Coll)—'40 (Cornell U)—'41 (Boston U); MA '46 (Ia State Coll). Leader of expeditions by canoe Fuller-Ferrier Expedition down Berens and Severn Rivers to Hudson Bay for Northwestern University '32, Mackenzie Arctic Alaskan Expedition '35; to Hudson Bay '34, '37, '39, '40, '41; other expeditions in conjunction universities and museums. Author articles in field. Licensed Can canoe guide '27-32; chief guide Border Lakes Outfitting Co Ely Minn; wildlife lyceum and extension lecturer, wildlife and canoe explorations in Far North '39-42, U Wis and U Minn extension and lecture bur '45-48; U Kan '49, U Wis '50, U Minn '51, N D Agricultural College '52; dir Outing Club Norwich U Northfield Vt '48-49. Outdoor Writers Assn — Explorers Club of NY—Wilderness Soc. Lake Saganaga, Grand Marais, Minn.

14 FERRIS, Gordon Floyd. Scale and parasitic insects; Lice. b'93. AB '16—

AM '18 (Stanford U). Research at Molteno Institute for Research in Parasitology Cambridge University England '30-31. Author articles in field. Prof entomol Stanford U since '37. AA AS(F)—Calif Acad Sci—Entomol Soc Am—Sigma Xi—Phi Beta Kappa. Fellow Guggenheim Memorial Found traveling in Mexico '25-26. 667 Melville Av., Palo Alto, Cal.

15 FERRIS, Ruth. Steamboating on western waters (History, literature); History of early St. Louis. b'97. BS '22—AM '24 (U Mo). Author articles in field. Teacher and asst principal Community Sch St Louis since '22. Missouri Hist Soc—State Hist Soc Mo. Community School, 900 Lay Rd., Clayton 24, Mo.

16 FERRIS, Walter. Hydraulic transmission of power; Design of positive displacement pumps and motors. b'68. ME '95 (Lehigh U). Oilgear hydraulic broaching machine, Oilgear crosshead type and rolling piston multiple piston pumps and motors, Oilgear system of hydraulic machine tool feeds. Holder 150 patents on hydraulic pumps and other applications hydraulic power. V-pres, dir The Oilgear Co since '21. Am Soc ME(F)—AAAS. The Oilgear Co., 1560 W. Pierce St., Milw 4.

17 FERRON, Robert Daniel. South America (Metal mining industry). b '92. BS (U Utah). Mill metall Braden Copper Co Rancagua Chile SA '15-18; cons mining engr and geol Santiago Chile '19-21; metall supt Cia Minera Huanchaca Pulacayo Bolivia '22-25; cons mining engr and geol Bolivia '25-35; gen mgr Bolivian Internat Mining Corp Huanuni Bolivia '36-45; SA rep exploration dept Kennecott Copper Corp since '46. AIMME. Apartado Aereo 1197, Medellin, Colombia, S.A.

18 FERRY, John Douglass. High polymer chemistry; Proteins. b'12. AB '32—PhD '35 (Stanford U). Research on physical chemistry, especially mechanical properties, of proteins and other natural and synthetic polymers of high molecular weight; mechanical properties of gels; action of antifouling shipbottom paints. Attached worker Natl Inst Medical Research London '32-34; research asst Hopkins Marine Sta Stanford U '35-36; instr and tutor, biochem sci Harvard U '36-38, Soc Fellows '38-41; asso chem Woods Hole Oceanographic Instn '41-45; research asso Harvard U '42-45; asst prof chem U Wisconsin '46, asso prof '46-47, prof since '47. Am Chem Soc—Am Soc Biol Chem—Soc Rheology—Phi Beta Kappa—Sigma Xi. Received Eli Lilly Award in biol chem from Am Chem Soc '46. Department of Chemistry, University of Wisconsin, Madison 6, Wis.

19 FERTIG, George J(oseph). Industrial chemistry; Metallurgy. b'99. BSChE '21 (Purdue); '22 (Harvard); '24 (MIT). Author articles in field. Metall Tennessee Coal Iron & RR Co '26-27; lecturer indsl chem and metall Birmingham So Coll '27-35; chem engr Birmingham Slag Co '28-29; dir Pittsburgh Testing Labs so div '30-33; pres George J Fertig cons chem and metall since '33. Am Chem Soc (chmn Ala sect '30-32)—Ala Acad Sci (pres '32-33)—Tau Beta Pi. Comer Building, Birmingham 3, Ala.

20 FESSENDEN, Seth Arthur. Speech education; Group dynamics; Sociometry. b'03. BS '34—MS '35 (UIll); PhD '40 (NYU); student (U Tex, Mont, Ia, USCLA, Cornell U). Author: The Speech Inventory '42; Speech and the Teacher '46; Basic Experiences in Speech '49; Designed for Listening '51; also articles in field. Associate professor speech, coordinator research Sch of Speech U Denver since '48. Western

Speech Assn—Nat Assn Teachers Speech—Nat Collegiate Players—NEA—Phi Delta Kappa. School of Speech, Denver University, Denver.†

21 FETHERSTON, Edith Hedges. Chinese gardens; Hydrocotyle Fetherstoniana. b'85. PhB '05—AM '08 (Bucknell); '08 (U Berlin); '18, '19 (Columbia U); '31-32 (Carnegie Inst Tech); '40-45 (Bucknell University). Exhibition of garden art by Garden Club Alleghany County Carnegie Institute '34; The Garden Club of America exhibition of paintings Arden Gallery '35; Garden of the Nations '35; made plant discovery which was named hydrocotyle Fetherstoniana; designer and planter Chinese gardens. Author articles in field. Bot Soc Western Pa—Sullivant Moss Soc. Packwood House, Lewisburg, Pa.

22 FETROW, Ward Willard. Agricultural cooperation. b'93. Student '13-14 (Baker U Baldwin Kan); BS '20 (Kan State Coll); PhD '24 (U Wis). In charge cotton section Federal Farm Board '31-33; in charge cotton section cooperative division Farm Credit Administration '33-34; chief cooperative research and service division '38-48, in charge cotton and oilseeds section since '48. Am Farm Econ Assn—Alpha Zeta—Gamma Sigma Delta. South Bldg., Dept. of Agriculture, Washington.◉

23 FETTER, Charles Harold. Precision timing; Frequency standards. b'95. BS—EE '17 (Pa State Coll). Research on radio-telephone interference, sound recording methods and sound motion pictures; work in design and operation precision timing devices for races, watch rate recorder for timing watches. Holder patents on telephone transmission systems, timing devices. Research engineer Elec Research Prod Inc NYC '29, development mgr '31-37; European recording manager Western Elec Co '29-31; pres Am Time Prod NYC since '37. 580 Fifth Av., NYC 19. H: 94 Dover Rd., Manhasset, L.I., N.Y.

24 FEVOLD, Harry Leonard. Hormones; Proteins. b'02. BA '25 (St Olaf Coll); MS '26—PhD '28 (U Wis). Research chemistry and physiology ovarian and pituitary hormones and their separation and identification, pituitary-gonadal relationships, protein hormones of pituitary, blood proteins, egg proteins. Author about 80 articles in field. Contributor: Sex and Internal Secretions (2d edit) '39; The Chemistry and Physiology of Hormones '44; Advances in Food Research (vol I) '48; (Greenberg) Amino Acids and Proteins '50; Recent Advances in Protein Chemistry, Vol VI '50. Research asso U Wis '28-35; asst prof biol chem Harvard '35-41; sr chem USDA W Regional Research Lab '41-47; chief Food Research Div Dept Defense QM Food and Container Inst for Armed Forces '47-51; dir biochem research Baxter Lab Inc since '51. ACS—Soc Biol Chem—AAAS—Proc Soc Exptl Biol and Med—Sigma Xi—Pi Lambda Upsilon—Phi Sigma—Gamma Alpha—NY Acad Sci—Alpha Chi Sigma. Received Honor Award USDA '50. Baxter Laboratories, Inc., 6301 Lincoln Av., Morton Grove, Ill.

25 FFOLKES, David. Stage and costume designing. b'12. Student (Sebright's, Worcestershire Eng; Birmingham Sch Architecture, Eng). Designer New York and London since '34, including costumes and/or sets for Thracian Horses, The Day After Tomorrow, What Every Woman Knows, Brigadoon, Man and Superman, and others; costumes for Globe Theatre, New York World's Fair '39. 926 Park Av., NYC.

10 FICARRA, Bernard Joseph. Intestinal tract (Physiology, surgery). b 14. AB magna cum laude '35—ScB '35 (St Francis Coll Brooklyn); MD '39 (Georgetown U). The role of the serosal arterioles in resuscitation of small bowel; protective physiology of small intestine following traumatic perforation; effect of anoxia on small bowel; use of oxidized cellulose in the control of hemorrhage from liver; research in phobia as a new symptom in hyperthyroidism; method of removing T tube from the common bile duct; migratory polyphlebitis; method of skin care following colostomy; importance of physio-chemical studies in surgery. Author: Diagnostic Symbols of Acute Surgical Abdomen '50. Surgical editor contemporary progress dept Medical Times. With Kings County Hosp Brooklyn '39-44; fellow in surgery Lahey Clin Boston '44-45; prof research physiol St Johns U Brooklyn since 1949. Am Bd Surgery(D)—Internat Bd Surgery(D)—Nat Bd Med Examiners(D)—Internat Coll Surgeons (F) — AMA(F) — Nat Gastroenterological Assn(F)—Am Geriatric Soc (F)—Am Acad Comparative Med(F)—NY Acad Med(F) — AAUP — World Health Assn. 567 First St., Bklyn 15.

11 FICKLEN, Joseph Burwell III. Industrial safety; Explosion hazards. b'02. Student '18-20 (U Va); BS (chem engring) '28 '41-42 (Cal Inst Tech); '32-34 (Yale). Research and development of methods for detection and estimation small amounts of benzene, lead, and carbon monoxide in air and tin in solution; explosion hazards in ordnance manufacture and hazards in guided missiles and nuclear energy research. Co-inventor three instruments for estimation particulate matter in air. Author: Manual of Industrial Health Hazards '40; also 20 articles in field. Chem engr Travelers Insurance Co '28-41; spl health officer indsl hygiene and cons Div Indsl Hygiene Los Angeles '41-42; asst mgr in charge med, fire and safety Charlotte Ordiance Plant US Rubber Co '42-44; major indsl hygiene div US PHS '44-46; spl health officer Div Indsl Hygiene Los Angeles County since '46; spl NA Aviation Inc since '47. Am Inst Chem(F)—So Cal Acad Sci—ACS—AICE—AAAS—Am Assn Engrs—Am Assn Mil Engrs—Am Inst Indsl Hygienists—Am Rocket Soc—Soc Chem Industry (London)—Am Soc Prof Engrs—Am Inst EE (asso mem). Los Angeles County Health Department, 808 N. Spring St., LA 12. H: 1848 E. Mountain St., Pasadena 7, Cal.; or University Club, 30 Lewis St., Hartford 2, Conn.

12 FIEGER, Ernest (August). Agricultural chemistry. b'97. BS '20—BChE '21—PhD '24 (U Minn). Holder patent on vitamin enrichment of rice '45. Instr, later prof biochem and agrl chem La State U since '24, head depts since '44. Am Chem Soc—Inst Food Tech—La Acad Sci—Sigma Xi. Louisiana State University, Baton Rouge, La.†

13 FIELD, Byron D(ustin). Spectrochemical analysis. b'18. BS '39—MS '42 (Mich State Coll). Development spectrochemical analytical methods for determination of trace impurities in high-purity chemicals. Asst spectroscopist Wyandotte Chem Corp Wyandotte Mich '41-43; chief spectroscopist Mallinckrodt Chem Works since '43. ACS—Optical Soc Am—Sigma Xi—Sigma Pi Sigma.

14 FIELD, Crosby. Electrical and mechanical engineering (Electric, chemical, mechanical, and refrigerating processes and equipment). b'89. BS '09 (New York U); ME '12 (Cornell U); MS '14 (Union Coll, Schenectady, NY).

Inventor oxide film lightning arrestor '12, continuous ice ribbon freezing process '16, continuous steel wool manufacturing process '23; holder over 100 US patents in field. Author articles in field. Chief engr Standard Aniline Products Inc '15-17; engring mgr Nat Aniline & Chem Co in charge all engring '19-23; vp, dir, sec Brillo Mfg Co '23-42; also pres Flakice Corp 23, Chem Machinery Corp '23-37. ASME(F)—AIEE(F)—AAAS(F)—Am Soc Refrigerating Engrs (past pres)—Am Chem Soc—Am Inst Chem Engrs (past mem council)—Am Soc Tool Engrs—Am Ordnance Assn—Soc Exptl Stress Analysis—Soc X-ray electron diffraction—NY Soc Professional Engrs—Phi Beta Kappa. Flakice Corporation, 360 Furman St., Bklyn 2.☉

15 FIELD, Henry. Physical anthropology and pre-history of southwestern Asia. b'02. BA '25—diploma in Anthropology '26—MA '29—DSc '37 (Oxford U). Research '26 University Heidelberg '36-37 Research Fellow, Peabody Mus, Harvard. Member archaeological expeditions in Europe and Southwestern Asia; leader Marshall Field Archaeological Expeditions to Europe '27, '29, '30, '32 for Hall of Stone Age of Old World, also research for Hall of Races of Mankind; leader first and second Marshall Field North Arabian Desert Expeditions '27-28; member staff Field Museum-Oxford University Expedition to Kish Iraq '27-28; leader Field Museum Near East Expedition to Iraq, Iran and Caucasus USSR '34; University of California African Expedition to Faiyum, Sinai, Sudan and Kenya 47-48; leader Peabody Museum-Harvard Expedition to Syria, Iraq, Iran, Persian Gulf, and Saudi Arabia '50. Author: Arabs of Central Iraq, their History, Ethnology and Physical Characters '35; Contributions to the Anthropology of Iran '39; The Anthropology of Iraq '52: (with David Hooper) Useful Plants and Drugs of Iran and Iraq '37. Govt research on Near East, Library of Congress Washington '41-45; pvt research SW Asia and anthrop work Morelos Mexico '46-47. AAAS(F)—Eng Royal Geog Soc (F)—Royal Central Asian Soc(F)—Royal Anthrop Inst Gt Brit and Ireland (F)—Am Assn Phys Anthrop, and others. 3551 Main Highway, Coconut Grove, Fla.☉

16 FIELD, John. Tissue metabolism (Drug and temperature effects). b'02. AB '23—AM '24—PhD '28—food research fellow '24-25 (Stanford). Panel on physiology committee on geographical exploration Research and Development Board '48; attended International Physiological Congresses Boston '29, Rome '42; developed moist cold box technique for preparing tissues for metabolic study '43. Author articles in field. Asso prof '35-42, prof since '42; acting dir Arctic Research Lab Office Naval Research '48; cons physiol Office Naval Research '48-49, cons physiol and biochem since '49; head biol br Office Naval Research '49-51; exec sec Arctic Research Lab Adv Bd '49-51; asst dir National Sci Found '52-53; cons National Science Found since '52. Chairman Dept Physiology U Cal Los Angeles since '51. Cosmos Club Washington—American Physiology Soc—Soc Exptl Biol and Med—Western Soc Naturalists—Western Soc Clinical Med—AAAS(F)—Sigma Xi. Department of Physiology, UCLA School of Medicine, Los Angeles 24, Cal.☉

17 FIELD, Theodore Estes. Refractories (Fusion cast). b'08. BS '29 (Bates Coll); PhD '34 (Johns Hopkins U). Inventor compositions of commercial fused cast refractories. Patentee

of techniques and compositions for melting and casting refractories. Chief chemist Corhart Refractories Co '35-38, research dir '38-45, tech dir since '45. Am Chem Soc—Am Inst Chem(F)—Electro-Chem Soc—Am Ceramic Soc—Brit Ceramic Soc—AAAS—Ky Acad Sci. 1600 West Lee St., Louisville.

18 FIELD, Thorold Farrar. Metal mining industries of United States, Canada, Latin America, Central Africa, Spain, Portugal, and Australia; Economics of gold, silver, copper, lead, zinc, aluminum, and iron. b'84. EM '05 (U Minn); '11-12 (Harvard). Metallurgical consultant to government agencies, including US Metals Reserve Company, and War Production Board; advisory committee raw materials operations Atomic Energy Commission since '48; appraisals metalliferous deposits and metallurgical operations. Cons mining engr since '16; explored Central Africa '20-30; dir Roan Antelope Copper Mines Ltd, Mufulira Copper Mines Ltd, and Rhodesian Selection Trust Ltd '20-30, Bendigo Mines Ltd Australia '34-36, Case Pomeroy Co Inc since '47. AIMME—Mining and Metall Soc. 807 Lonsdale Bldg., Duluth 2.

19 FIELD, William Dewitt. Butterflies. b'14. AB '36—MA '38—grad work '38-40 (U Kan). Author articles in field. Entomol div insect identification Bur Entomol and Plant Quarantine US Dept Agr '40-47; asso curator div insects US Nat Museum Smithsonian Inst since '47. Entomol Soc Am(F)—Kan Entomol Soc—Washington Entomol Soc—Kans Acad Sci—Sigma Xi. Division of Insects, U.S. National Museum, Washington.†

20 FIELDHOUSE, H(orace) Noel. English history (1700-1750); British foreign policy since 1815. b'00. BA '21—MA '22 (U of Sheffield); BA '24 (U Oxford). Asst prof hist U Manitoba '28-30, prof, head dept hist '30-45; Kingsford prof history McGill U since '45, chmn dept since '47, dean faculty arts sci since '48. Research in British and French archives summers '28-39, grant-in-aid for this work Social Sci Research Council '35, 39-40. Royal Soc Can(F)—Canadian Hist Assn (past pres)—Hist Assn Gt Britain—AHA—Canadian Inst of Internat Affairs. Department of History, McGill University, Montreal, Quebec, Can.†

21 FIELDS, Ellis Kirby. Medicinal and petroleum chemistry. b'17. SB '36—PhD '38 (U Chicago). Research on polysulfones, liquid ammonia reductions, free-radicals in solution, polyhalogen compounds, antimalarials, insect-repellants, economic poisons, leukemia, hypertension, organic phosphorus compounds, anti-oxidants, deactivators. Holder two patents on deactivators; seven patents pending on phosphorus compounds. Author articles in field. Postgrad Lilly fellow U Chicago '38-41, research dir development lab since '41. AAAS—Am Chem Soc—Ill Acad Sci—Sigma Xi. Development Laboratory, 1525 E. 53rd St., Chicago 15.†

22 FIELDS, Victor Alexander. Diction; Voice and speech training and therapy. b'01. BS '26 (Coll City NY); MA '30—PhD '46 (Columbia U). Member New York City Board of Education committee surveying handicapped children in public schools '36-39. Author: Training the Singing Voice '47; The Singer's Glossary '52. Co-author: Voice and Diction '48; Phonetic Readings '39; Taking the Stage '39; Principles and Practices of Speech Correction '38. Professor of voice and diction College of City of New York since '26, director voice and speech clinic since

'32, departmental supervisor evening session since '41; speech rehabilitation of disabled war vets Vets Adminstrn Army Hall Speech Clinic '46-49. NY Singing Teachers Assn—Music Educators Nat Conf—Nat Assn Teachers singing—Music Teachers Nat Assn—NEA—NY State Sch Music Assn—Speech Assn Am. College of the City of New York, Convent Av. and 139th St., NYC 31.

10 FIESENHEISER, Elmer Irving. Structural engineering; Stress analysis. b'06. BS '30—CE '45 (Purdue U); MS '46 (Ill Inst Tech). Has completed following projects as consulting engineer: timber airplane hangers, steel airplane hangers, structural design paper mill in Chicago, complete design truck crane; stress analysis of tall guyed towers 500 ft high for Wincharger Co; consultant on design of cyclotron at Institute for Nuclear Studies University of Chicago; on reinforced concrete bulk plant in Chicago; irrigation well installation in Texas, structural design blast furnace plant in Indiana. Author articles in field. Professor civil engring Ill Inst Tech since '46; cons engr. ASCE—Am Concrete Inst—Inst Aeronautical Scis—Inter Assn Bridge and Structural Engrs—AAAS. 9512 South Lowe Av., Chicago 28.†

11 FIESER, Louis Frederick. Organic chemistry (Cancer, chemotherapy). b'99. AB '20—DSc '39 (Williams Coll); PhD '24 (Harvard); '24-25 (Frankfort-on-Main)—'25 (Oxford U). Author: Experiments in Organic Chemistry; Organic Chemistry. Sheldon Emery prof organic chem Harvard since '39. Nat Acad Sci(F). Awarded Katherine Berkan Judd prize for work on cancer-producing hydrocarbons, Memorial Hosp '41. 27 Pinehurst Rd., Belmont, Mass.☉

12 FIFE, Austin Edwin. Folklore (Western United States). b'09. AB '34—AM '35—PhD '39 (Stanford U); AM '39 (Harvard). Collector and contributor to the Archive of American Folklore Library of Congress since '46. Author: The Bear Lake Monsters '48; Folk Belief and Mormon Cultural Autonomy '48; Folk Songs of Mormon Inspiration '47; The Legend of the Three Nephites Among the Mormons '40. Co-author: (with James M. Fife) Hay Derricks of the Great Basin and Upper Snake River Valley '48. Asso ed Western Folklore Quarterly since '48; asso prof Romance langs and organizer and teacher Am folk music Occidental Coll Los Angeles since '46; lecturer on Am folklore for the French National Museums '50. American Folklore Society (councilman since '47)—California Folklore Soc—Modern Lang Assn. Occidental College, Los Angeles 41.

13 FILLER, Louis. American liberalism, abolition and related subjects; Arts projects of Works Progress Administration; Quartermaster General operations. b'12. BA '34 (Temple U); MA '41—fellow '41-42—PhD '43 (Columbia U). Book Review Editor, Antioch Review. Author: Crusaders for American Liberalism '39; Randolph Bourne '43. Author articles: Edward Bellamy and the Spiritual Unrest '46; An American Odyssey: The Story of Susan Lenox '40; Parker Pillsbury: An Anti-Slavery Apostle '46; California and Henry George '47, and others. Research historian Am Council Learned Socs Washington '42-44; historian hist sect OQMG US War Dept '44-46; asso prof Am civilization and lit Antioch Coll since '46; visiting prof Am hist U Wyo '47, City Coll NY '48. AHA—Miss Valley Hist Assn—Soc Am Historians—Modern Lang Assn. Fulbright

Award in history '50-51 U Bristol (England). Antioch College, Yellow Springs, O.

14 FINCH, Alton Harold. Fruit and vegetable growing in arid regions; Citrus fruiting (Irrigation, fertilization); Vegetable fertilization, breeding and seed production; Pecan fruiting (Rosette, zinc nutrition); Grape maturity; Physiological economic horticulture. b'00. BS '25 (Ore State Coll); MS '26—fellowship '25-26 (Ia State Coll); PhD '29 (U Wis). Author articles in field. Sr hort US Dept Agr since '45-48. Established own business, especially grape and citrus production '49. Sigma Xi. 756 6th Av., Yuma, Ariz.†

15 FINCH, Ruy Herbert. Volcanic processes. b'90. Student (George Washington U, U Chicago). Independent studies in meteorology, seismology and volcanology with W J Humphreys and T A Jaggar Jr; delegate 4th Pacific Science Congress Java '29; geophysical studies of Kilavea and Mauna Loa. Author articles in field. With US Weather Bureau '10, meteorol '19; asso volcanologist US Geol Survey '24; established observatory for study of Cascade Volcanoes at Lassen Peak Calif '26, orchardist Watsonville Calif '36-39; volcanologist Hawaiian Volcano Observatory since '40. Instr meteorol US Navy and forecaster at Naval Air Sta Ireland during World War I. AA AS(F)—Geophys Union—Geol Soc Am—Seismol Soc Am. U.S. Geological Survey, Hawaii National Park, Hawaii.☉

16 FINCH, William George Harold. Radio engineering (Radiotypewriter press circuit, radio printing systems [FAX]). b'95. Completed spl course radio engring and patent law Columbia '23. Established first radiotypewriter press circuit between New York City and Chicago '32, first international radiotypewriter circuit between New York City and Havana '33. Inventor automatic high speed radio printing system, radio relay and recorder, high fidelity facsimile transmission system, both black and white and in natural colors. Holder 160 patents in electronics and radar. Radio engr, radio ed Internat News Service since '21; radio ed NY American; patent adviser for Popular Radio and Wireless Age since '25. Inst Radio Engrs—AIEE—AAAS. Elfin, Newtown, Conn.☉

17 FINCHER, John Albert. Porifera (Cell behavior in regeneration and development). b'11. BS '33—MS '35 (U SC); PhD '39 (U NC). Research on gemmule cells of fresh water sponges, phagocytic behavior in eggs of sponges, origin of germ cells in Stylotella heliophila Wilson, formative cells of marine sponge on double duty following excess rainfall. Author articles in field. Prof and head dept biol Howard Coll since '46. AAAS—Assn SE Biol—Ala Acad Sci—Phi Beta Kappa—Sigma Xi (assoc). Department of Biology, Howard College, Birmingham 6, Ala.†

18 FINCK, Joseph Louis. Thermodynamics; Heat transfer. b'93. BS '15 (MIT); MA '21 (Harvard); PhD '22 (Johns Hopkins U). Invented reflective type of heat insulation commonly referred to as aluminum foil heat insulation. Author articles in field. Founded J L Finck Labs Brooklyn '33. Am Phys Soc—ACS—AAAS. 440 Rogers Av., Brooklyn 25.

19 FINDLEY, Warren George. Educational testing. b'06. AB '27 (Princeton); MA '29—PhD '33 (Columbia). Author articles in field. Dir Test Development Ednl Testing Service Princeton since '48; Supervisor test constrn US Armed Forces Inst '44; chief eval br ednl adv staff Air U '46-48; asst dir

exams and testing NY State Edn Dept '38-46. Am Ednl Research Assn (com on psychol tests and their uses '44-50)—Nat Soc Study Edn—Am Statis Assn—Psychometric Soc—NY State Assn Applied Psychol (pres '42-43)—Am Psychol Assn(F)—AAAS(F)—National Council on Measurements Used in Edn (vp '52-53)—Phi Beta Kappa. Educational Testing Service, Box 592, Princeton, N.J.

20 FINDLEY, William Nichols. Plastics (Mechanical testing and properties, fatigue, creep); Metals (Mechanical testing, fatigue); Materials (Low and high temperature properties); Stress analysis; Applied mechanics. b'14. AB '36 (Ill Coll, Jacksonville Ill); BSE in math '37—BSE in ME '37 (U Mich); McMullen research scholar '37—MS '39 (Cornell). Author articles in field. Research asso prof theoretical and applied mechanics U Ill since '47. Am Soc Testing Materials (chmn com on fatigue of plastics; chmn com on creep of plastics; Charles B Dudley medal for paper Creep Characteristics of Plastics pub '44 plastics symposium)—American Society for Metals—Soc Experimental Stress Analysis—Am Soc Engring Edn—Soc Rheology—Am Inst Physics—Sigma Xi—Phi Kappa Phi. 105 S. Draper St., Champaign, Ill.

21 FINEBERG, S. Andhil. Community relations; Anti-semitism. b'96. BA '20 (U Cincinnati); PhD '32 (Columbia U). Author: Biblical Myth and Legend; Project in American History; Overcoming Anti-Semitism; Punishment Without Crime '50. Director community service Am Jewish Com since '39; lecturer. Natl Assn Intergroup Officials—Central Conf Am Rabbis—Am Jewish Com. 386 Fourth Av., NYC 16.

22 FINK, Arthur Emil. Sociology (Crime); Sociol work (Public welfare). b'03. AB '24—AM '30—PhD '36 (U Pa); MSW (Pa Sch Social Work). Author: Causes of Crime '38; The Field of Social Work '49; also articles in field. Dean Sch Social Work U NC since '50. Fulbright prof U of Birmingham, Great Britain, '51-52. Am Assn Social Workers—So Sociol Soc—NC Conf Social Service—Nat Conf Social Work—Nat Probation Parole Assn—Am Pub Welfare Assn. University of North Carolina, Chapel Hill, N.C.

23 FINK, Donald Glen. Television engineering; Radar; Radio navigation. b'11. BSc '33 (MIT); MSc '42 (Columbia). Editor-in-chief Electronics since '46. Author: Engineering Electronics '38; Principles of Television Engineering '40; Microwave Radar '42; Radar Engineering '47. Editor: Television Standards and Practice '43; also articles in field. Bd dirs McGraw-Hill Book Co Inc since '46. Expert cons Office Sec of War Loran and radar '43. Inst Radio Engrs (F, bd dirs since '49, chmn television system com '47-48)—Am Inst Elect Engrs—Sigma Xi—Tau Beta Pi. McGraw-Hill Publishing Company, Inc., 330 West 42nd St., NYC 18. H: 2 Knoll Rd., Tenafly, N.J.

24 FINK, W(illiam) L(aVilla). Physical metallurgy and corrosion of aluminum alloys; X-ray methods. b'96. BSE—MSE—PhD '25 (U Mich). Author articles in field. Chief phys metall div Aluminum Research Labs New Kensington Pa since '43. Am Chem Soc—AAAS—Am Inst Mining and Metall Engrs—Am Soc Metals—Inst Metals (British)—Am Soc Testing Materials—Soc Non-Destructive Testing—American Crystallographic Assn. Aluminum Research Laboratories, Box 772, New Kensington, Pa.

25 FINKELSTEIN, Sidney W(alter). History of jazz; Contemporary movements in the fine arts. b'09. BA '29 (Coll City NY); MA '31 (Columbia). Author: Art and Society '47; Jazz: A Peoples Music '48. Instr Jefferson Sch Social Sci since '46; music ed Masses and Mainstream since '48. Masses and Mainstream, 832 Broadway, NYC 3.†

10 FINN, Fenton H. Natural gas (Geology and underground storage). b'04. BS '28—EM '42 (Carnegie Inst Tech). Instrumental in discovery and development Oriskany gas pools in Northern Pa and Southern NY; shallow gas pools Southwestern Pa, Wyoming and McDowell Counties, West Virginia; responsible for design and development of 16 underground storage pools in Pennsylvania, including the largest (Oakford) pool in United States. Field geol Columbia Gas and Elec Co Pittsburgh and Binghamton NY '28-32; geol NY State Natural Gas Corp and Peoples Natural Gas Co Wellsboro Pa '32-39, chief geol and prodn engr '39-42; system geol Consol Natural Gas Co since '42; vp NY State Natural Gas Corp since '51. Geol Soc Am(F)—AA AS(F)—Am Assn Petroleum Geol—Am Petroleum Inst—Am Gas Assn—AIM ME—Am Geophys Union—Tau Beta Pi. 545 William Penn Place, Pitts 19.

11 FINNELL, Henry Howard. Agronomy (Dryland); Wind erosion control. b'94. BS '17 (Okla A&M Coll). Member Great Plains Agricultural Council since its establishment '35; research in soils, moisture conservation, crop management and wind erosion control, technical and administrative charge of Soil Conservation Service program for southern Great Plains including Old Dust Bowl of Colorado, Kansas, Oklahoma, New Mexico, Texas. Author articles in field. Asst agron Okla Expt Sta Stillwater '17-20, Goodwell Okla '23-24; regional dir US Dept Agr Soil Conservation Service Amarillo Tex '34-42, research specialist '42-48, and at Panhandle A&M Coll Goodwell Okla since '48; asst dir Okla Expt Sta in charge Panhandle work. Am Soc Agron —Soil Conservation Soc Am—Friends of Land—Am Geophys Union—AAAS— Am Geog Soc. Panhandle A&M College, Goodwell, Okla.

12 FINNERUD, Clark Wylie. Vinegarone (False scorpion family) Hodag (Legendary timbering-days animal). 55 E. Washington St., Chgo 2.

13 FINZI, Leo Aldo. Electrical engineering machinery. b'04. Elec Engr '26 (U Naples); doktor ingenieur (Inst Tech Aachen Germany). Research and development special motors, magnetic amplifiers, non-linear devices. Holder patents in field. Author articles in field. Professor elec engr Carnegie Inst Tech since '46. AIEE—ASEE— Sigma Xi. Borchers Medal '32. Carnegie Institute of Technology, Pittsburgh 13.†

14 FIREMAN, Milton. Alkali and saline soils; Permeability of soils to water. b'10. BS '33—MS '34 (U Ariz); PhD '43—fellow '36-39 (U Calif). Author articles in field. Jr soil scientist, sr soil scientist US Salinity Laboratory since '41. Western Soil Sci Soc—Soil Sci Soc Am—Sigma Xi. U.S. Salinity Laboratory, Riverside, Cal.†

15 FIREMAN, Peter. Chemistry. b'63. Grad '81 (Gymnasium Charkov Russia); student (U Odessa Konigsberg, Zurich and Berne); PhD '93 (Berne). Prof chemistry Mo Sch Mines '01-02; chem geologist US Nat Mus '01; in charge Chem Research Lab Alexandria Va '04-06; mfg chemist '06-51, pres Magnetic Pigment Co '11-42; chmn adv com Magnetic Pigment Co., Div Columbia Carbon Co since '43. Lambertville, N.J.☉

16 FIRMIN, Albert Bancroft Wilcox. Postal history (American). b'68. Student pub schs. Research on postal history, ancient, colonial and current. Entered postal service Manhattan '83, advanced to supt Money Order and Postal Savings NY Post Office; postmaster Brooklyn '24 until retirement; served with Joint Commn on Postal Service of US Senate and Ho of Reps and various other nat commns and coms for improvement of postal system. Nat Assn Postal Supervisors (past pres NY chpt, editor nat bull; regional dir)—Assn Postal Supervisors of NY and Brooklyn. H: 788 Mac Donough St., Bklyn 33.

17 FIRTH, Frank Edward. Fishing gear; Manila hemp (Substitute); Haddock; Mackerel; Tuna; Redfish. b'05. Student part time '28-36 (Boston U) (Harvard). Research on life histories of haddock, mackerel, tuna and redfish; research on substitutes for manila hemp and preservatives to lengthen life of scarce cordage. Co-author: (with Tressler and Lemon) Marine Products of Commerce '51. Author articles in field. Contributor: Gloucester Master Mariner's Year Book '42; Official Year Book New England Fishing Industry '41, '42. Biol Bur Fisheries and Fish and Wildlife Service '28-42, fisheries tech '42-44; fisheries spl Econ Coop Adminstrn since '51. Am Inst Chem(F)—Am Soc Ichthyologists and Herpetologists (asso)—Inst Textile Chem and Colorists(F)—NY Acad Sci—Biol Soc Wash—N Atlantic Fisheries Biol. H: 1100 Randolph Av., Milton 86, Mass.

18 FISCH, Max Harold. Philosophy of law; History of science; American philosophy. b'00. AB '24 (Butler U); PhD '30 (Cornell U). Member editorial board Journal of the History of Medicine and Allied Sciences since '45. Author: Nicolaus Pol Doctor 1494 '47. Co-author: (with Paul Russell Anderson) Philosophy in American from the Puritans to James '39 (with others) Classic American Philosophers '51. Translator: (with Thomas G Bergin) The Autobiography of Giambattista Vico '44, The New Science of Giambattista Vico '48. Curator rare books Army Med Library '42-45, chief hist medical division '46; prof philos U Ill since '46. Am Philos Assn—Hist Sci Society. University of Illinois, Urbana, Ill.†

19 FISCHEL, Henry Heinz Albert. Biblical literature and rabbinics; Semitic languages, history and religion. b'13. PhD '44 (U Edinburgh); rabbi '39 (Berlin). Author: The First Book of Maccabees '48; Prophet and Martyr '47; also articles in field. Lecturer U Ala dept religion, linguistics, hist since '48; dir Hillel Foundation since '48. Soc Biblical Lit and Exegesis, Can sect (pres)—Am Oriental Soc—Nat Association Biblical Instructors—American Acad Jewish Research—Rabbinical Assembly Am. Winner Heinemann Vogelstein prize '36; Nathanson Memorial Award '42. E4 Stoneleigh Apartments, Tuscaloosa, Ala.

20 FISCHEL, Walter J. Islamic civilization; Orientalist; Semitic languages and literature; Arabic, Hebrew, Persian languages and literature. b'02. Travel to countries of Middle East, Iraq, Persia, Kurdistan, India, Turkey, Egypt '30, '36, '40; specialized in economic and cultural aspects of medieval Islam and Judaeo-Persian literature; International Congress of Orientalists, Leydon '30, Rome '35, Paris '48. Author books and articles in field. Faculty Hebrew U Jerusalem, lecturer in Sch Oriental Studies '26-43; guest lecturer various universities in US and Can '43-44; lecturer Semitic langs U Calif '45, prof Semitic langs and lit since '46, chmn dept Near Eastern langs since '48. Soc Biblical Research (vp Pacific br)—Royal Asiatic Soc Gt Britain(F)—Am Oriental Soc—Am Acad Jewish Research—Am Assn Jewish Edn (bd gov). University of California, Berkeley 4. H: 2419 Durant Av., Berkeley 5.

21 FISCHELIS, Robert Philipp. Pharmacy; Drug laws and regulations; History of pharmacy; Inter-professional relations. b'91. PhG '11—PhC '12—PharmD '13 (Medico-Chirurgical Coll of Phila); BSc '12 (Temple U); PharmM '18—ScD (hon) '45 (Phila Coll of Pharmacy); PharmD (hon) '34 (Conn Coll of Pharmacy); ScD (hon) '42 (Rutgers U). Founder Pennsylvania Pharmacist, New Jersey Journal of Pharmacy. Editorial director Journal American Pharmaceutical Association. Author: (with C Rufus Rorem) Costs of Medicines '32; (with H V Arny) Principles of Pharmacy '37; also articles in field. Cons pharmacist and chem since '19; profl lecturer George Washington U Coll Pharmacy since '47. AAAS(F)—Am Pub Health Assn (F)—Am Social Hygiene Assn (sec '45-49)—Am Pharm Assn (exec sec, gen mgr since '45, chmn conf of pharm law enforcement officials '39-42) — Am Chem Soc — AMA — Nat Assn Bds Pharmacy—Am Acad Polit Social Sci —Pa Pharm Assn Assn (sec '16-19, pres '19-20)—NJ Pharm Assn (sec '26-29, pres '42-45)—Am Assn Colls Pharmacy. Awarded Remington Medal by Am Pharm Assn '43. 2215 Constitution Av., Washington 7.☉

22 FISCHER, Carl Hahn. Pension plans. b'03. BS '23 (Washington U); MS—PhD '32 (U Iowa). Studies of teacher retirement plans, retirement plans for municipal employees, firemen, and policemen, banking and industrial pension trusts. Co-author: (with C J Nesbitt) Mathematics of Life Insurance '43; (with P R Rider) Mathematics of Investment '50; also articles in field. Actuarial research Northwestern Nat Life Ins Co '33-34; asst prof math Wayne U '34-41; asso prof math U Mich '41-50; prof ins and prof act math since '50; cons actuary various public retirement systems, pension trusts, and ins cos. Actuarial Soc Am (asso)—Am Inst Actuaries (asso)—Mich Actuarial Soc (pres '45-46)—Instituto Brasileiro Atuario—National Council Teacher Retirement—Am Assn U Teachers Ins—Inst Math Statis (sec since '49)—Am Statis Assn—Am Math Soc. 720 Bus Admin Bldg., University of Michigan, Ann Arbor.

23 FISCHER, Edward Lee. Gas (Natural, pipelines). b'89. BS (EE)—EE (Ia State Coll). Economic study and design underground storage system for gas; design of first interstate pipeline utilizing sufficient storage to produce full daily use of capacity without sale of interruptible gas; research natural gas operated heat pump. Inventor large volume electrically operated natural gas meter. Author articles: Natural Gas Pipeline Rates '39; Underground Storage of Natural Gas '47. Gas engr United Light & Power Co '25-49; natural gas cons since '50. Am Gas Assn. 206 E. Second St., Davenport, Ia.

24 FISCHER, Hugo C. Architectural concrete (Exposed aggregate). b'91. BS '13 (O U). Research on architectural exposed aggregate concrete. Author article: Architectural Concrete on the New Naval Medical Center (Wason medal). Civil engr corps officer US Navy '17-48; own bus since '48. Am Soc CE—Am Concrete Inst. Marland Rd., Broadmoor, Colorado Springs, Colo.

10 FISCHER, LeRoy Henry. American Civil War and Reconstruction. b'17. BA '39—MA '40—PhD '43 (U Ill); student summer '41 (Columbia U), '45 (Oxford U, Eng), '45 (Cambridge U, Eng). Author articles in field. Research asst in history specializing in Lincoln and Civil War studies under Professor J G Randall U Ill '40-43; asst prof hist Ithaca Coll NY '46; asst prof hist Okla A&M Coll '46-49; asso prof since '49, part time on staff of Okla A&M Coll Resrch Found. AHA—Miss Valley Hist Assn—So Hist Assn — Abraham Lincoln Assn — Ill State Hist Soc—Southwestern Social Sci Assn—AAUP. Department of History, Oklahoma Agricultural and Mechanical College, Stillwater, Okla.†

11 FISCHER, Richard P(hilip). Uranium and vanadium resources; Mineral resources. b'10. BA '32 (O Wesleyan U); MA '34—PhD '36 (Princeton U). Research on geology of sedimentary deposits of uranium, vanadium, copper, and silver in southwestern US '33-36, exploration for and geologic study of uranium and vanadium deposits of Colorado, Utah, Arizona, New Mexico. Author articles in field. Geol US Geol Survey since '37. Geol Soc Washington—Geol Soc Am—Soc Econ Geol—Am Assn Petroleum Geol—Colo Sci Soc—Sigma Xi. U.S. Geological Survey, Washington 25.

12 FISCHTHAL, Jacob Henry. Fish parasites; Fishery biology. b'17. BS '37 (LIU); MS '38 (State U Ia); PhD '50 (U Mich). Author: Parasites of Northwest Wisconsin Fishes '47; also articles in field. Aquatic biol US Fish and Wildlife Service Cambridge '43, Wis Conservation Dept Fish Management Div '43-48; instr biol dept Triple Cities Coll Syracuse U '48-50, asst prof biology dept Harpur College State U of New York since '50. American Soc Parasitology—Am Micros Society—Wis Acad Sci Arts Letters—Sigma Xi. Biology Department, Harpur College, State University of New York, Endicott, N.Y.

13 FISH, Charles John. Biological oceanography (Marine ecology and populations, zooplankton). b'99. PhB '21—ScM '22—PhD '23 (Brown U). Member International Committee on Oceanography of the International Council of Scientific Unions since '46; member United State Committee on the Oceanography of the Pacific National Research Council since '47; Oceanographer on Arcturus Expedition '25; director International Joint Survey Lake Erie '28-29, cooperative survey Gulf Maine '29; director Federal and State Cooperative Investigation of Narragansett Bay '35-36; oceanographer International Bahama Expedition '30; made biological survey of Woods Hole Mass Region '22-23; oceanographic survey of Massachusetts Bay and Grand Banks '24-25. Marine biol Woods Hole Oceanographic Inst since '46; cons marine biol since '46 and dir Narragansett Marine Biol Lab since '48; prof marine biol RI State Coll since '48. AAAS—Am Geophys Union (ed oceanog sect)—Officer de Acad Republic France—Phi Kappa Phi—Phi Beta Kappa—Sigma Xi—Phi Sigma. Kingston, R.I.⊚

14 FISH, John Charles Lounsbury. Engineering economics; Engineering method. b'70. CE '92 (Cornell U). Author: Engineering Economics '23; The Engineering Profession (with T J Hoover) '41. Instr civ engring '93-94, asst prof '94-98, asso prof '98-05 Stanford U; resident engr '05-07, div engr '07-09, LS&MS RR, prof railroad engring '09-25, prof civil engring '25-35, exec head civil engring dept '28-35, emeritus prof civil engring since '35, Stanford U. ASCE—Am Ry Engr Assn

—Sigma Xi—Sigma Delta Xi. Awarded Fuertes gold medal for original research Cornell U '15. 131 S. Carmelina Av., LA 49.

15 FISH, Marie Poland. Marine biology; Fishes (Early life history); Underwater sound; Sonic marine mammals. b'02. BA '21 (Smith Coll). Arcturus Oceanographic expedition Sargasso Sea Galapagos and Cocos Island '25, Bermuda '29; International Expedition Andros '29-30, Passamaquoddy Bay '31-33, North Atlantic '36-41. Author articles in field. Ichthyologist Pacific Oceanic Biol project Woods Hole Oceanog Inst since '47; Research Office of Naval Research since '47. Research asso Narragausett Marine Lab Kingston RI since '48. Soc Women Geo—Phi Beta Kappa—Sigma Xi. Received Women's Centennial Cong award. Woods Hole Oceanographic Institution, Woods Hole, Mass.

16 FISHEL, Vinton Crews. Groundwater engineering (Kansas). b'07. BS '31 (So Ill U); '30-35 (George Washington U). Research in determination of availability and utilization ground water for municipal, industrial, domestic, and stock use. Physicist in charge hydrologic lab US Geol Survey Washington '29-41, engr with ground water br Lawrence (Kan) '41-45, dist engr since '45. Am Geophys Union—Am Water Works Assn—Kan Acad Sci—Washington Philos Soc—Sigma Xi. US Geological Survey, University of Kansas, Lawrence, Kan.

17 FISHER, Charles E(mil). Mesquite control; Range improvement. b'11. BS '34 (Kan State Coll); MS '36 (Tex A&M Coll). Research on mesquite problem in the Southwest '48; developed soil tube jack to remove soil tubes from the soil with ease and minimum of equipment. Author articles: Factors Affecting Action of Oils and Water-soluble Chemicals in Mesquite Eradication '46; Present Information of Mesquite '47, and others. Asst soil conservationist Tex Agrl Expt Sta and Soil Conservation Service US Dept Agr '36-40, asso agron since '40. Am Soc Agron—Ecol Soc Am—Am Soc Range Management—Phi Kappa Phi—Delta Sigma Gamma. Texas Agricultural Experiment Station, Spur, Tex.

18 FISHER, Edna M(aria). California mammals and reptiles (Sea otter, snakes, lizards). BA '20—MA '21 (U Calif); '26 (Stanford). Research on California sea otter's life history, habits, fur trade, anatomy, adaptations; California reptiles especially snakes and lizards; Indian shell mounds along California coast, records of vertebrates shown in bones; director field school natural history, San Francisco State Coll. Author: Osteology and Myology of the California River Otter; also articles in field. Asst curator osteology Mus Vertebrate Zool U Calif '22-30, teaching fellow dept zool '23-24; instr biol sci San Francisco State Coll '30-36, asst prof '36-41, asso prof since '41. AAAS(F)—Am Soc Mammalogy—Cooper Ornithol Club—Am Soc Ichthyol and Herpetol—Sigma Xi. San Francisco State College, San Francisco 2.

19 FISHER, Elwood George. Fertilizers (Nitrogen). b'16. BS '38 (U Md); PhD '49 (Cornell U). Research on foliage nitrogen sprays. Pomol USDA Tung Lab '38-42; with pomol dept Cornell U since '45. Phi Kappa Phi—Sigma Xi—Alpha Zeta. Pomology Department, Cornell University, Ithaca, N.Y.†

20 FISHER, F(rancine) E(leanore). Diseases of citrus insects. b'24. BS '45 (Fla State Coll for Women); MS '46 (Mich State Coll). Research in identifying bacterial and fungal di-

seases of insects injurious to citrus to determine what methods can be used to increase efficiency of these diseases in coordination with artificial control measures. Author: Insect Disease Studies '47; Diseases of Citrus Insects '48. Asst plant path Citrus Expt Sta U Fla since '46. AAAS—Am Inst Biol Sci—Am Phytopath Soc—Mycol Soc Am—Fla Entomol Soc—Fla State Hort Soc—Ancient Order of Ranales (hon)—Seminarium Botanicum. University of Florida, Citrus Experiment Station, Lake Alfred, Fla.

21 FISHER, Gerhard Richard. Navigation (Radio instruments); Minerals and metals (Electronic exploration instruments). b'99. MA '23 (U Dresden). Granted patents on aircraft radio compass, directional radio receiver, radio antenna system, radio receiving system, visual indicating direction finder, light indicating system, metalliscope instrument. Author: Geophysical Prospecting for the Layman '46. Research engr DeForest Co '23-25; with Kolster Radio Corp '26-30; charge research Radiore Co '31-32; cons engr Heintz & Kaufman '33-35; Western Air Express '33-35; research radio navigation Bur Aeronautics '34-35; research engr, owner Fisher Research Lab Inc since '36, pres since '46. Inst Radio Engrs. Fisher Research Laboratory, Inc., Box 640, Palo Alto, Cal.

22 FISHER, Granville Chapman. Psychology (Psychotherapy, personality, hypnosis). b'06. PhB '44 (U Chicago); BD '45 (Meadville Theol Sch); MA '46—PhD '48 (U Chicago). Author articles in field. Asso prof psychol, chmn dept U Miami since '48. Am Psychol Assn—Fla Acad Sci—Psi Chi—Sigma Xi. Department of Psychology, University of Miami, Miami, Fla.

23 FISHER, Harry Johnstone. Food (Analysis); Drugs (Analysis). b'96. AB '17 '18-20 (Harvard); PhD '31 (Yale). Analysis foods, drugs, insecticides and fungicides; research on composition of foods; studies food and drug law regulations and standards. Editor: Official Methods of Analysis of the Association of Official Agricultural Chemists '45 '50. Chem div food and drugs Mass State Dept Health '20-21; asst chem to chief chm dept analytical chem Conn Agrl Expt Sta since '21. ACS—Sigma Xi—Assn Ofcl Agrl Chems—Assn Food and Drug Ofcls US—Assn Am Feed Control Ofcls—Assn Am Fertilizer Control Ofcls—Assn Econ Poison Control Ofcls. Connecticut Agricultural Experiment Station, P.O. Box 1106, New Haven. H: 615 Westwood Rd., Mt. Carmel, Conn.

24 FISHER, Harvey Irvin. Ornithology (Bird anatomy); Vertebrate natural history; Game and wild life management. b'16. BS '37 (Kan State Coll); PhD '42 (U Calif). Field work in Micronesian Islands of Pacific, western North America, Hawaiian Islands; assistant editor The Condor: A Magazine of Western Ornithology '42-46; vertebrate zoology editor Pacific Science since '46; editor The Auk: A Quarterly Journal of Ornithology since '49. Author: Adaptations and Comparative Anatomy of new World Vultures '46; also articles in field. Teaching fellow zoology U Calif '37-41; research asst Museum Vertebrate Zool Berkeley Calif '41-42, tech curator '42-45; asst prof vertebrate zool U Hawaii '45-48; exchange prof U Nev '47-48; asst prof U Ill since '48. Am Ornithol Union—Cooper Ornithol Club—Am Soc Mammalogists—Hawaiian Acad Sci—Soc Study Evolution—Sigma Xi—Phi Kappa Phi. Department of Zoology, University of Illinois, Urbana, Ill.

25 FISHER, John Wesley. Agriculture; Horticulture; Sociology. b'07. BS in agr '32 (So U Baton Rouge); MS in vocational agr '38 (Ia State Coll); grad student (U Ill). Author: Year Around Vegetable Gardening in Louisiana '38. With So U Baton Rouge since '32, asst dir agr '38-39, dir div agr since '39; cons state farmers' orgns. Southern University, Southern Branch P.O., Baton Rouge.†☉

10 **FISHER, Joseph Frederick.** Television (Color systems, ultra-high frequency propagation). b'11. Grad '36 (Drexel Inst Tech). Design of specialized television equipment, propagation tests ultra-high frequency television, development work on color television. Author articles in field. With Philco Corp since '34, project engr research div since '45. Inst Radio Engrs. Philco Research Division, C and Tioga Sts., Phila. H: 1517 Powder Mill Lane, Wynnewood, Pa.

11 **FISHER, Lillian Estelle.** Latin-American history. b'91. BA '12 (Susquehanna U); MA '18 (U South Calif); PhD '24 (U Calif). Engaged research on American influence on movement for Mexican independence; commercial conditions in Mexico at eve of independence; downfall of Spanish monarchy; early masonry in Mexico; totalitarianism in South America; Latin American culture. Secretary, conference on Latin-American History, American Historical Association '34-39; member executive committee Conference Latin American Relations for Southwest '38-42. Author: Viceregae Administration in the Spanish American Colonies '26; The Intendant System in Spanish America '29; The Background of the Revolution for Mexican Independence '34; Priestley's Franciscan Exploration in California (editor) '46; also articles in field. Prof hist U Calif ext div '43-46; lecturer seminar conference Spanish-Am hist Geo Washington U '35; visiting prof Latin Am hist Hunter Coll NYC '42. AHA. Awarded fellowship research Spanish archives Spanish govt '29-30. Bancroft Library, University of California, Berkeley.

12 **FISHER, Morris Albert.** Chemical analysis (Dusts, smokes, fumes, fine particles, colloids). b'13. BS '35—MS '36—grad study '38-42 (Carnegie Inst Tech). Research on particle size measurement, microscopy, dust sampling, production and properties finely divided particles, aerosols, filters, atmospheric pollution. Author articles in field. Supervisor analytical sect dir fine particles Lab Armour Research Foundation since '47. Manhattan Dist Atomic Project Columbia U '43-45. Am Chem Soc—Sigma Xi. Armour Research Foundation, 35 W. 33rd St., Chicago.

13 **FISHER, Raymond Henry.** History of Russia; Slavic and European history. b'07. '25-27 (Yale); '27-28 (U Calif LA); BA '29—MA '32—PhD '37 (U Calif) '35 (Russ Lang Sch Columbia U). Origin present Polish government, Americans in Siberia, Russian fur trade 1700-1900, Russian eastward expansion, Curzon line. Author: The Russian Fur Trade: 1550-1700 '43. Author articles: Mangazeia: a Boom Town of Seventeenth Century Siberia; Agreements and Treaties Concluded by the USSR in 1945 '46. Asso prof hist Humboldt State Coll Arcata Calif '37-44; Russia specialist US Dept State Washington '44-46; asst prof hist U Calif LA '46-48, asso prof '48. AHA. Awarded Herbert Baxter Adams prize European history AHA '44. Department of History, University of California, Los Angeles 24.†

14 **FISHER, Sydney Nettleton.** History of Near East (Turkey); European history. b'06. AB '28—MA '32 (Oberlin Coll); PhD '35 (U Ill); Islamic seminar—'35 (Princeton); '38 (Brussels U). Author: The Foreign Relations of Turkey, 1481-1512 '48. Author article: Civil Strife in the Ottoman Empire 1481-1503 '41. Asst prof hist O State U '42-47, asso prof since '47; asso chief Econ Analysis Sect Middle East Div Fgn Econ Admnstrn Washington DC '43-44; country specialist Commercial Policy Div Dept State Washington '44-45, chief Eastern Europe Sect '45-46; chmn Special Microcopying Program Comm for Turkey and Lebanon AHA since '47. AHA—Phi Beta Kappa—Phi Kappa Phi. Grants from Am Council of Learned Socs '35, '38. Ohio State University, Columbus 10, O.

15 **FISHER, Thomas Russell.** Social legislation; Public law. b'95. PhB '21 (U Chicago); AM '28—PhD '38 (Columbia); LLB '37 (Syracuse U). Author: Federal Legislation Regulating Industrial Disputes '37. Prof social legislation Syracuse U since '30, chmn dept sociology, anthropology since '41, professorial lectr since '30; chief spl projects sect, div Exchange Persons, Dept State. Mem Selective Service Bd '42-43, NY State Bd Mediation '35-43, Nat Bd Arbitration '37-43, Prison Industries Reorgn Admnstrn Washington '37. AAAS—Am Acad Polit Social Sci—Eastern Social Sci Assn—Am Sociol Soc—Phi Delta Phi—Alpha Kappa Delta—Phi Delta Kappa. Dept of State, Pennsylvania Av. N.W., Washington.☉

16 **FISHER, Waldo Emanuel.** Industrial and labor relations; Economics of fuels and minerals. b'91. AB '17 (Columbia U); AM '24—PhD '39 (U Pa). Author: Economic Consequences of the Seven-Hour Day and Wage Changes in the Bituminous Coal Industry; Production and Distribution Costs and Sales Realization in Deep, Commercial Mines of the Bituminous Coal Industry; Wage Rates in the Bituminous Coal Industry and Wage Rates in the Anthracite Coal Industry. Co-author: Wage Rates and Working Time in the Bituminous Coal Industry; Manual on Collective Bargaining for Professional Employees; also articles in field. Prof indsl relations Wharton Sch of Finance and Commerce U Pa since '44. Am Econ Assn—Acad Polit Social Sci—Am Mgmt Assn—Econ Hist Assn. University of Pennsylvania, 3440 Walnut St., Phila. 4.

17 **FISHER, William Halder.** Regional economics; Tobacco; Peanuts; Cotton; Fisheries; Population; Business expectation; National income. b'14. BS '34 (U Richmond); MA '43—PhD '45 (U Va). Author: Economics of Flue-Cured Tobacco '45; Peanuts in the Fifth Federal Reserve District '46; also articles in field. Free lance research tech Va State Planning Bd, Dept Edn, WPA, NYA, Va Population Study '39-41; research worker on tobacco for Va Bur Indsl Res and Fed Res Bank Richmond '41-43; econ Fed Res Bank of Richmond '43-46; asst prof econ bus adm, econ Bur Econ and Bus Res U Del '46-52; bus economist Fed Trade Commn since '52. Federal Trade Commission, Washington. H: 1320 N. Frederick St., Arlington, Va.

18 **FISHLEIGH, Clarence Turner.** Patent experting; Automobile engineering. b'95. BS in elec engring '17 (U Mich); JD '39 (Detroit Coll Law). Planned organized and developed engineering defenses in patent litigation; organized extensive comparative tests of engineering equipment. Author papers: The Tear Drop Car '31; The Car of the Future '36. Asso engr Walter T Fishleigh '30-47; cons engr Detroit since '47. SAE—Engring Soc Detroit—Nat Mich and Ohio socs profl engrs—Am Mich Detroit bar assns—Am Mich patent law assns. 18074 Ohio Av., Det 21.

19 **FISHWICK, Marshall William.** Southern Culture heroes, myths, and legends. AB '43 (U Va); MA '46 (U Wis); PhD '49 (Yale). Author: The Face of Jan; Isle of Shoals; Robert E. Lee, A Bibliography; Virginians on Olympus. Editor: Rockbridge County, Va.; Since I Was Born. Asso prof Am studies Washington and Lee U since '52. Am So Va hist socs—So Sociol Assn—Jefferson Soc—Guild of Scholars—Phi Beta Kappa—Elizabethan Club. Washington and Lee University, Lexington, Va. H: 5 University Pl.

20 **FISK, Harold Norman.** Geology (Stratigraphic, petroleum, alluvial, Louisiana). b'08. BS '30—MA '31 (Ore U); PhD '35 (Cincinnati U). Research on depositional terrace slopes in Louisiana, investigation of alluvial valley of Lower Mississippi, fine-grained alluvial deposits and effect on Mississippi River activity. Author: Geology of Grant and La Salle Parishes, Louisiana '38; Geology of Avoyelles and Rapides Parishes, Louisiana '40; also articles in field. Chief, geol research section, Humble Oil and Refining Co since '48. Sigma Xi—Geol Soc Am—Am Assn Petroleum Geol—Soc Econ Paleontol Mineral—Am Geophys Union. Humble Oil and Refining Company, P.O. Box 2180, Houston, Tex.☉

21 **FISK, Henry Grunsky.** Wyoming (Mineral resources); Refractories (Calcium oxide); Cements (Portland and alumina, constitution and petrography). b'01. BS '23 (Occidental Coll); MS '24 (U Ill); PhD '27 (O State U). Author articles: Refractories for Cement Kilns '40; Ceramics and Industrial Minerals in the War Effort '42; Refractories as they Relate to the Steel Industry '43. Petrographer Universal Atlas Cement Co '29-36; dir Wyo Natural Resources Research Inst since '43. Am Ceramic Soc—ACS—AIMME—Am Mineral Soc. Natural Resources Research Institute, University of Wyoming, Laramie, Wyo.

22 **FITE, Alexander Green.** Language and literature. b'92. AB '13, MA '14 (Vanderbilt); Rhodes scholar '14-17—BA '17 (Oxford U Eng); student '19-20 (univs Paris, Madrid and Rome); PhD '22 (U Wis). Editor: Le Repas du Lion (by F. de Curel) '26; Contemporary One-Act Plays (French) '31; Le Missel d'Amour (Alberic Cahuet) '37. Associate editor The French Review '30-42. Contributor to Modern Lang. Forum, French Review. Professeur de lettres Ecole des Yvelines France '15-16; instr French and Spanish U Wis '18-22; asst prof French U Cal at Los Angeles '22-26, asso prof since '26. Awarded Les Palmes Academiques by French Government and named Officier d'Academie '37.☉

23 **FITE, Daniel Harley.** Education (Teacher, rural, resource-use, workshop techniques, curriculum). b'02. BS '27 (State Teachers Coll Tenn); MA '31—PhD '42 (George Peabody Coll). Steering committee for improvement of instruction program in Tennessee four years; Alabama curriculum committee since '47; conducted eighteen education workshops; invited to participate in Southwide Curriculum Conference Peabody College five times. Author articles in field. Pres Carson-Newman Coll since '48. Am Acad Polit Social Sci—Nat Edn Assn—Am Assn Sch Admnstrs—Tenn Pub Sch Officers Assn—Ala En Assn. Scholar Rosenwald Found and Tenn Edn Dept. Carson-Newman College, Jefferson City, Tenn.

24 **FITTING, Ralph Ulf, Jr.** Limestone petroleum and natural gas reservoirs. b'10. BA '32 (geol) (Stanford U); '32-33 (U Cal). Basic research on limestone reservoirs of West Texas and Southeast New Mexico, improvement techniques of securing basic petroleum reservoir data, co-inventor basic methods employed in one method of determining fluid flow in bore holes, fluid flow differences between sand and limestone oil and gas reservoirs. Co-author: (with A C Bulnes) An Introductory Discussion of the Reservoir Performance of Limestone Formation. Geol engr Shell Oil Co '33-43; cons petroleum geol and engr since '43. AIMME—Am Assn Petroleum Geol—Am Petroleum Inst. 223 S. Big Spring St., Post Office Box 1637, Midland, Tex.†

10 FITTON, Edith M. Geographic nomenclature; Maps (Modern and historical). AB '24 (Smith); MA '29 (Clark U). Research on place names for US and foreign countries, assembling data on published and local usage of disputed place names; participates monthly and special bulletins listing place-name decisions of US Board on Geographic names. Asst, div maps Lib Cong '31-43; case work US Bd Geog Names '43-44, chief case research sect since '44. Soc Woman Geog—Assn Am Geog. Department of the Interior, Washington 25.

11 FITZGERALD, George Stephen. Social welfare. b'01. AB '23 (Holy Cross Coll); LLB '26 (U Detroit). Delegate Council Social Agencies since '45; member Social Welfare Commission Michigan since '43. Legal advisor US Customs '26-28; asst US atty '28-31; asst prosecuting atty Wayne County Mich '31-34; prof law U Detroit '32-35. Am Bar Assn—Am Assn Social Workers—Gamma Eta Gamma. 2418 Guardian Bldg., Det 26.

12 FITZGERALD, James Anderson. Group insurance (Hospital, medical, surgical). b'83. AB '01 (Georgetown Coll); AM '07—PhD '25 (U Chicago). With U Tex '18-21, since '25, prof since '25; trustee Am Inst for Property and Liability Underwriters Inc '42-49; dir Group Hosp Service Inc since '43; dir Group Med and Surg Service since '45. Am Asso U Teachers Ins (mem exec com '40-43, vp '46-47, pres '48)—Am Econ Assn—Am Assn Collegiate Schs Bus (sec-treas '30-35, chmn com membership standards '36-38, pres '39-40)—Nat Bus Research Council—Economists' Nat Com Monetary Policy—Beta Gamma Sigma (mem nat exec com '30-39, grand pres '33-36). University of Texas, Austin 12, Tex.

13 FITZGERALD, Lloyd Greenworth. Coal mining (Hazards of explosives and blasting devices, safe blasting practices). b'96. BS '22 (U Ky). Surveys on explosives to determine hazards and to make suggested improvements in blasting practices using explosives and blasting devices in coal mines. Conducts accident prevention training courses for mine ofcls US Bur Mines; mining engr, foreman, supt John P Gorman Coal Co and Four Seam Coal Corp '22-38; dist engr Cardox Corp '38-42; coal mine insp, mining engr explosives US Bur Mines since '42. AIMME—WVa Mining Inst—Ky Mining Inst—Mine Insp Inst Am—WVa Soc Profl Engrs. Registered profl engr Ky and WVa. Mount Hope, W.Va.

14 FITZGERALD, Ruth. Education. b '85. Diploma '05 (NC State Normal and Indsl Coll); BS '25—AM '26 (Columbia); student child development center '40-41 (U Chicago). Prof edn Woman's Coll U NC since '31, chmn elementary edn '31-47, summer sessions '31-49, dir reading clinics summer sessions '41-49; collaborator Teacher Edn Commn;

Nat Council on Edn U Chicago '40-41. NEA—Soc Coll Tchrs Edn—Assn Supervision and Curriculum Development—Dept Higher Edn—Nat Council Tchrs English—AAUP—Am Edn Fellowship—Assn Supervisors Student Teaching (chmn NC '37-40)—Assn for Childhood Edn—NC Edn Assn (pres NW dist '34)—AAUW—Kappa Delta Pi. H: 308 S. Aycock St., Greensboro, N.C.†◎

15 FIVAZ, Alfred E(dward). International trade in forest products; Forestry in soil conservation. b'00. BS '21 (Syracuse U). Author: Forestry in Soil and Moisture Conservation; also articles in field. Asst to chief export controls, chief pulp and paper sect Office Internat Trade Forest Products Br US Dept Commerce since '48. Soc Am Foresters—Ecol Soc Am—Washington Acad Sci. Forest Products Branch, Office of International Trade, Department of Commerce, Washington 25. H: 804 Dale Dr., Silver Springs, Md.†

16 FLACK, Alonzo, II. Industrial management engineering (Efficiency). b'85. ME '08 (Syracuse U). Representative American Society Mechanical Engineers and Association consulting management engineers eighth International Management Congress Stockholm '47. Author articles in field. Chmn trustees and treas Emerson Engineers NYC since '33; cons management engr to oil industry since '41. Assn Consulting Mgmt Engrs (past dir, vp)—Soc Advancement of Mgmt (vp, past nat vp NY chapter)—ASME (sec mgmt div, life mem '49)—Indsl Mgmt Soc—Acad Polit Sci—Am Ordnance Assn—Tau Beta Pi. The Emerson Engineers, 30 Rockefeller Plaza, NYC 20.

17 FLANAGAN, John C(lemans). Psychological evaluation, measurement and test construction (Scholastic achievement, interest, personality, aptitudes); Personnel and social psychology. b'06. BS '29—AM '32 (U Washington); PhD '34 (Harvard). Author articles in field. Prof psychol U Pittsburgh; pres Am Institute for Research; cons US Air Force; chief psychol branch Air Surgeon's Office AAF and dir aviation psychol program '41-46. Am Statis Assn—Am Assn Sch Admnstrs—Am Ednl Research Assn—NY Acad Sci—AAAS(F)—Am Psychol Assn(F)—Psychometric Soc—Nat Vocat Guidance Assn. Department of Psychology, University of Pittsburgh. H: 415 Morewood Av., Pittsburgh 13.

18 FLANAGAN, John T(heodore). American literature (Midwest, Sinclair Lewis, E L Masters, O E Rolvaag, W M Reedy). b'06. BA '27—MA '28—PhD '35 (U Minn); '31 (Columbia). Author: James Hall '41. Editor: Tales of the Northwest '36; America is West '45; also articles in field. Instr Eng U Minn '29-38, asst prof '38-45; prof Eng So Meth U '45-46; prof English, U Ill since '49; Fulbright lectr Am Lit and Civilization at U Bordeaux and U Montpellier '52-53; Midwest book reviewer Chicago Sun Book Week '44-47. Mod Lang Assn—Miss Valley Hist Assn—Ill Hist Soc—Wis Hist Soc—Minn Hist Soc (life)—Phi Beta Kappa. Awarded Guggenheim fellowship '43-44, Newberry Library fellow '44. University of Illinois, Urbana, Ill.

19 FLANAKIN, Hubert Agee Mike. Planning (Regional). b'05. BCE '27—CE '33 (La State U) '40-41 (Yale). Research for long range programs improvement for Louisiana Highway Department; coordination local planning agencies for programs of expansion and development. Highway planning and traffic engr La Highway Dept '36-41; state, regional, city planning State

La '41-42; area dir National Housing Agency Dallas '42-43 '46-47; asso prof civil engring and acting dir engring expt sta La State U since '47, also cons engr. Inst Traffic Engrs—Highway Research Bd., Am Road Builders Assn—Am Soc Refrigerating Engrs—Am Soc Engring Edn—Tau Beta Pi—Phi Kappa Phi. Registered profl engr La and Tex. Engineering Experiment Station, Atkinson Hall, Louisiana State University, Baton Rouge.

20 FLANDERS, Stanley Ellsworth. Bionomics of parasitic insects. b'94. AB '23—PhD '35 (U Calif). Explored eastern Australia for parasites of citrus pests '31; originated and developed methods of mass culture of entomophagous insects on factitious hosts; propagated and released introduced parasites that attack European earwig and elm beetle, citrus mealybug, alfalfa and vegetable weevils, codling and oriental fruit moths, many types of scale; definitely proved occurrence of ovisorption in insects and described role of ovisorption in economy of parasitic hymenoptera; originated hydrostatic theory sex control in honeybee and ovisorption theory for caste formation in ants. Author articles in field. Parasite collector, later entomol and professor biological control University Calif Agrl Expt Sta since '29. Entomol Soc Am(F). Citrus Experiment Station, Riverside, Calif.

21 FLEMER, Henry Lewis. Photography (Documentary). b'92. PharmD '18 (George Washington U). Application mass production principles to photo duplication; design equipment for photo duplication. Am Documentation Inst '37-49; With bibliofilm service USDA since '41, now chief copying section Library. U.S. Department of Agriculture, Washington 25. H: 2714 S. Dakota Av., Washington 18.

22 FLEMER, John Adolph. Topography (Photo); Heraldry. b'59. Grad '78 (Poly Sch Cassel Germany); course in civ engring '78-81 (Royal Tech High Sch Berlin). Engineer to Commissioner for dimarcation of Alaskan boundary 1904-1906; topographer, engineer to Commission on Improvement and Development of Jamaica Bay New York '09-10. Author: Treatise on Phototopographic Methods and Instruments '06; also articles in field. Topographical engr. AAAS(F)—Am Geog Soc—Washington Soc Engrs—US Naval Inst—Soc Am Mil Engrs—Am Soc Engrs—Va Acad Sci. Oakgrove, Va.

23 FLEMING, Harold Kenneth. Temperate zone tree and small fruit orcharding. b'02. BS '24—MS '35 (Pa State Coll). Research on soil management in sweet and sour cherry orchards, Concord grape vineyards; work in renovation old Concord vineyards, breeding improved varieties raspberries, improvement understocks for fruits, fruit variety testing; studies of low temperature injury of fruit plants. Author articles in field. Full time research Erie Co Field Research Lab North East Pa since '43. Am Soc Hort Sci—Sigma Xi—Gamma Sigma Delta. Erie County Field Research Laboratory, North East, Pa.†

24 FLEMMING, Edwin George. Personnel tests; Aptitude tests. b'89. LLB '10 (U Buffalo); AB '15 (Cornell); AM '20 (U Wis); PhD '28 (Columbia). Personnel selection procedures for employers of salesmen, sales managers, office and shop executives with emphasis upon use psychological tests, patterned analytical interviews and weighted application blanks; development individual company norms for application blanks and psychological tests; analysis and interpretation results of psychological tests taken by individual applicants. Asso prof psychol Coll William and Mary '28-30; cons in psychol '30-45; dir div for sales personnel selection Burton Bigelow Organization since '46. Am Psychol Assn (F div bus and indsl psychol and div cons psychol)—NY State Psychol Assn—Conn State Psychol Soc—Conn Valley Assn Psychol—Metropolitan NY Assn for Applied Psychol. Certified psychologist Conn. 274 Madison Av., NYC 16.

10 FLENNER, Albert Lawrence. Seed disinfectants; Fungicides. b'99. BS '20 (Gettysburg Coll); MS '24—PhD '27 (U Md). Development of seed disinfectants and fungicides containing mercury compounds, principally ethyl mercury compounds '30-32, formulations of insecticidal and fungicidal materials since '32. Author articles in field. Research chem EI duPont de Nemours since '27. Am Chem Soc—Sigma Xi. DuPont Experimental Station, Wilmington, Del.

11 FLESCH, Rudolf. Readability. b'11. Dr jur '33 (U Vienna); BS '40—MA '42—PhD '43 (Columbia). Developed statistical formula to estimate readability of prose '43, revised '48; engaged by Associated Press to simplify copy for newspaper publication; editorial consultant to publishers and business organizations. Author: Marks of Readable Style '43; The Art of Plain Talk '46; The Art of Readable Writing '49. Co-author: (with A H Lass) The Way to Write '47; also articles in field. Research asst Readability Lab Am Assn for Adult Edn '40-41, edn dept CBS '42-44; information specialist OPA '44-46; lecturer grad sch US Dept Agr '44-46, NYU since '46. Am Psychol Assn—Linguistic Soc Am—Nat Council Teachers Eng—Am Assn Adult Edn—ALA—AAAS. 534 Broadway, Dobbs Ferry, N.Y.†

12 FLETCHER, Charles Henry. Handwriting (Identification); Lie detection; Polygraph. b'97. Grad '35 (Internat Soc Grapho Analysis Inc); Grad (Sci crime detection) '41 (Inst Applied Sci Chicago). Practical application handwriting analysis and identification since '35, polygraph tests since '46; confidential character reports for banks and business executives; instr bank employees and officers in detection forgeries; confidential lie detector tests civil and criminal court cases; research on human character as revealed by handwriting and proven by polygraph tests. Author: Six Easy Ways to Recognize a Bad Check '50; Personology '51. Author articles: Why and How Forgeries can be Detected '48; How Personal Character is Revealed by Handwriting '48; How to Recognize a Raised Check, Draft or Money Order '49; Every Employee May Learn to Recognize Forgeries '49, and others. Author, writer and lecturer handwriting identification since '36 and polygraph tests since '46. Internat Assn Identification—Am Judicature Soc—Internat Grapho Analysis Soc—Internat Sheriffs' Assn—Nat Assn Bank Auditors and Comptrollers. 2515 W. 82d St., Chgo. 29.

13 FLETCHER, Harvey. Acoutics (Musical and general); Noise; Speech; Hearing. b'84. BS '07 (Brigham Young U); PhD '11 (U Chicago); DS hon '35 (Columbia U) '42 (Kenyon College) (Stevens Inst) (Case Sch); DS '44 (U Utah). Research on audition, electronic charge and theories of hearing. Author: Speech and Hearing '29. Head dept physics Brigham Young U '11-16; on engring staff research dept Bell Telephone Labs since '16, dir physical research since '33. Am Inst Physics(exec Council)—AAAS(F, vp

'37-38)—Am Phys Soc(F, pres '45)—AIEE(F)—Am Soc Hard Hearing(pres '29-30)—Acoutical Soc Am(pres '29-30)—Nat Acad Scis—Phi Beta Kappa—Sigma Xi. Awarded Louis Edward Levy medal for physical measurements of audition '24. H: 5 Westminster Rd., Summit, N.J.†⊙

14 FLETCHER, Richard De Leon, Jr. Public employment services; Unemployment insurance. b'09. PhB '31—grad work '31-34 (U Chicago); grad fellow '38-39 (U Minn). Studied systems of public employment service and unemployment insurance in France, England, Belgium, Holland '37. Chief standards and methods US Employment Service Fed Security Agency Washington '45-49, assistant chief US Employment Service US Dept of Labor since '49. Am Econ Assn —Am Soc Pub Adminstrn—Nat Vocational Guidance Assn. US Department of Labor Washington 25. H: 2800 Quebec St. N.W.

15 FLETCHER, Saxton Woodbury. Ventilation; Heating; Drying; Air Conditioning. b'95. Student '14 (Phillips Acad Andover Mass); SB '18 (MIT); BS '18 (Harvard). Air systems for paper industry. Sales engring to pres J O Ross Engring Corp since '23; vp and sec and dir Ross Industries Corp since '30; dir and sec Ross Engring of Can Ltd '27, pres and dir since '44; dir John Waldron Corp. Indsl Furnace Mfrs Assn(dir)—Textile Research Inst—Tech Assn Pulp and Paper Ind—Am Soc Heating and Ventilating Engrs. Office: 444 Madison Av., NYC 22.

16 FLETT, Lawrence H. Chemistry (Detergents, dyes, coal tar intermediates, engineering, petroleum, organic, azo, oils-paints-varnish, food preservation and wrapping, surface active agents). b'96. BS '18 (MIT). Developed first synthetic detergent from petroleum, first stable commercial synthetic detergent. Holder many patents. Author articles in field. Dir new products div Nat Aniline Div Allied Chem Dye Corp since '44. AAAS—Soc Chem Ind—NY Acad Sci—Chem Market Research Assn (vp)—Commn Chem Div Assn (com)—Am Assn Textile Colorists and Chem—Am Chem Soc—Am Inst Chem (F, pres)—Chem Metall Mining Soc, S Africa (hon mem). Schoellkopf Medalist '42. 40 Rector St., NYC 6.⊙

17 FLICK, Hugh Meredith. Archives; New York history. b'05. PhB '28 (Wesleyan U); PhD'47 (Columbia); Cert '27 (U Berlin). Associate editor Quarterly Journal New York State Historical Association '36-39. Author articles: The Council of Appointment in NY State '34; Public Records in NY State '36; Harry A Ogden, Military Artist '34, and others. Asst pub records NY State '28-31, supervisor pub records '36-40, archivist '40-49, director Motion Picture Div since '49, acting dir Div Archives and Hist '39-40; mem staff NY Hist Soc NYC '33-36; chief War Dept Records Br AGO Washington '43-46. AHA—NY State Hist Assn —Soc Am Archivists—Am Acad Pol Social Sci—Am Mil Inst. Edward H Perkins Scholar Am history Columbia U '30. State Education Department, Motion Pictures Div., 80 Centre St., NYC.

18 FLINT, Robert Newton. Seeds technology. b'04. BS '31—MS '32 grad study '35, '37 (Miss State Coll) '41 (Tex A&M); '49 (La State U). Identification of crop and weed seeds; purity and germination analysis 15,000 seed samples annually. Head dept agr East Central Jr Coll Decatur Miss '35-45; chief inspector Miss Seed Improvement Assn State Coll Miss '45-

47; dir La State Seed Lab since '47. Assn Ofcl Seed Analysts NA—Assn So Seed Control Ofcls—Internat Crop Improvement Assn. State Department of Agriculture, Box 4063, Baton Rouge.

19 FLINT, Winston Allen. Vermont history. b'06. BA '28 (Norwich U); MA '34 (U Vt); internat law certificate, fellow Carnegie Found inst internat law and relations '36—PhD '40 (U Mich). Research in American progressive movements, designed to show strength of movement of 1900-1917, by its penetration of ultra-conservative rural Vermont. Author: The Progressive Movement in Vermont '41; also articles in field. Instr hist Norwich U Northfield Vt '30-34, asst prof '34-36, asso prof '36-40, prof '40-46, acting head dept '43-46; sr instr hist US Merchant Marine Acad Kings Point NY '46-47, asst head dept hist and lang since '47. AHA. United States Merchant Marine Academy, Kings Point, L.I., N.Y.

20 FLOE, Carl Frederick. Physical metallurgy. b'08. BS '30—MS '32 (Washington State Coll); ScD '35 (MIT). Author articles in field. Asst prof, asso prof metall MIT since '39, now prof metall and asst provost; cons in fields of heat treatment, surface hardening of steel and service behavior of metals. Am Inst ME—ASM—Inst Metals (British)—Iron and Steel Inst (British)—Sigma Xi—Tau Beta Pi—Phi Kappa Phi. Department of Metallurgy, Massachusetts Institute of Technology, Cambridge 39, Mass.⊙

21 FLOOD, Merrill M(eeks). Management counsel; Military engineering; Operations research; Statistics (Industrial) Photogrammetry. b'08. AB '29—MA '30 (U Neb); PhD '35 (Princeton). Engineering consultant to industrial firms, government agencies, and educational institutions; statistical analysis and economic forecasting; ordnance and quality control engineering; inventor military range finder optical systems; gunsight design and testing. Tech adv adminstrn, finance, and econ Gov WVa '36-40; dir statis state and local govt sect Princeton U '36-40, dir fire control research sect '40-46; pres Merrill Flood & Asso (photogrammetry and indsl statis) '42-49; expert cons research planning and adminstrn Sec War '46; asst dep dir research and development Dept Army '47; project officer Rand Corp since '49. Am Statis Assn (exec officer '48-49)—Am Math Soc—Inst Math Statis—Econometric Soc—Biometric Soc—Royal Econ Soc—AAAS. The Rand Corp., 1500 Fourth St., Santa Monica, Cal. H: 308 Alta Av.

22 FLORA, Carroll Cephas. Dairy manufacturing; Nutrition. b'10. BS '33 (Va Poly Inst); MS '35—PhD '38 (Pa State Coll). Author articles in field. Asso prof dairy mfgring dairy dept Va Poly Inst since '38. Am Dairy Sci Assn—Va Acad Sci—Gamma Sigma Delta. Dairy Department, Virginia Polytechnic Institute, Blacksburg, Va.

23 FLORY, Leslie E. Electronics; Television; Vacuum tubes. b'07. BS EE '30 (U Kan). Development of television pick-up tubes, electron multipliers, electronic computers, and sensory devices. Co-author articles: Theory and Performance of the Iconoscope '37 (Overseas Award from Instn Elec Engrs, Eng); An Electronic Reading Aid for the Blind '46; An Infra Red Image Tube and Its Military Applications '46; Barrier Grid Storage Tube and Its Application '48, and others. In charge research on industrial television since '50. RCA Labs Princeton NJ since '42. Inst Radio Engrs (sr)—Sigma Xi. R.C.A. Laboratories, Princeton, N.J.

10 FLORY, Paul J(ohn). Polymer chemistry (Plastics, rubber). b'10. BSc '31 (Manchester Coll); MSc '31—PhD '34 (O State U). Research on high polymers, their constitution, properties, mechanism of formation, theories. Esso Labs Standard Oil Development Elizabeth NJ '40-43; in charge fundamental research Goodyear Research Lab Akron O '43-48, prof chemistry Cornell U Ithaca since '48. Am Chem Soc—Sigma Xi. Awarded Joseph Sullivant Medal '45 O State U; Leo Hendrik Baekeland Award '47 N Jersey Sect Am Chem Soc. Goodyear Research Laboratory, Akron 16, O.⊚

11 FLORY, Walter S., Jr. Horticultural plant breeding and genetics; Cytogenetics and phylogeny of flowering plants. b'07. BA '28 (Bridgewater Coll); MA '29—PhD '31 (U Va); Nat Research Council fellow '35-36 (Harvard). Consulting editor Fruit Varieties and Horticultural Digest since '47. Author articles in field. Prof exptl hort U Va, vice-dir Blandy Expt Farm since '47. AAAS (council '41, since '47, sect O com '46-50)—Va Acad Sci (sec agrl sect '46-47)—Am Soc Hort Sci (chmn exec com So Sect '46-47, chmn program com '46)—Bot Soc Am—Genetics Soc Am (councilor '41)—Am Plant Life Soc—Soc Study Evolution—Sigma Xi—Tau Kappa Alpha. Blandy Experimental Farm, University of Virginia, Boyce, Va.

12 FLOSDORF, Earl William. Medical research. b'04. BS '25 (Wesleyan); PhD '29 (Princeton); fellow nat research council '33-34 (med sch U Pa). Research on blood plasma, penicillin, tobacco, whooping cough, production and measurement of high vacuum, super-sonics, drying by sublimation, freeze drying, orange juice, immunology, immuno-chemistry and bacteriology, supersonic disintegration and frationation micro-organisms, studies with hemophilus pertussis, agglutinogen skin test, biologicals and foods from frozen state; indsl research consultant several companies. Holds 65 patents. Author: Drying by Sublimation '48; (co-author) Qualitative Analysis of Inorganic Materials '38; Semi-Micro Qualitative Analysis '39; also articles in field. Sec, dir, mem bd Lyophile-Cryochem Co Phila '41-46; dir research and development F J Stokes Co Phila since '41. AMA(F)—Am Chem Soc—Pa Chem Soc—Am Human Serum Assn—Am Soc Immunol—AAAS—Soc Am Bact—Am Assn Pub Health (F)—Am Assn Food Tech—Am Inst Chem Engrs—NY Acad Sci—Pa Pub Health Assn—Pa Acad Sci—Sigma Xi. Forest Grove, Pa.

13 FLOSS, Carl William. Internal combustion engines (High compression); Gears. b'95. BS (elec engring) '24 (U Mich). Design internal combustion engines making use of new materials and advanced techniques; design extreme accuracy gearing and adaptation to gun fire control mechanisms. Asst chief engr Detroit Gear Div Borg Warner Corp '45-46, gear spl in charge nav gun fire dir; design engr Ford Motor Co since '46. Am Ordnance Assn—Society Automotive Engrs. Ford Motor Co., Engineering Laboratory, Dearborn, Mich. H: 897 Rivard Blvd., Grosse Pointe 30, Mich.

14 FLOWER, Rousseau H(ayner). Paleozoic Nautiloidea; Stratigraphy and paleontology of Older Paleozoic and eastern North American graptolites. b'13. AB '34—AM '35 (Cornell U); PhD '39 (U Cincinnati). Author articles in field. Asst state paleontol NY State Museum since '45. Geol Soc Am(F)—Paleontol Soc Am(F)—AAAS (F)—Societe Geologique de France—

Paleontol Research Instn. New York State Museum, Albany 1, N.Y.†

15 FLOWERS, John Wilson. High voltage physics; Lightning; Underwater sound. b'10. BS '31 (Southwestern at Memphis); MS—PhD '35—Du Pont fellow '31-35 (U Va). Author articles in field. Physicist General Elec Co '37-47; asso prof physics U Fla since '47. University of Florida, Gainesville, Fla.†

16 FLOWERS, Seville. Bryology (Mosses); Algae; Pteridophytes; Vegetation of Great Salt Lake Region; Ferns and hepatics of Utah. b'00. AB '25 (U Utah); AM '26 (Brigham Young U); PhD '32 (U Chicago). Author articles in field. Asso prof bot U Utah since '36. Am Bryological Society—Am Fern Soc—Algalog Soc Am—Sigma Xi. University of Utah, Salt Lake City 1. H: 208 Douglas St., Salt Lake City 2.†

17 FLUCK, William Zeidler. Industrial hygiene; Health physics (Radiation). b'14. BS (Chem engring) '35—MS '37 (U Wis). Research on control health hazards dust, fumes, vapors, gases, noise, ionizing radiations. Author articles: in field. Engr Indsl Hygiene Div Wis State Bd Health '37-43, chief engr '46-48, acting dir '49; indsl hygienist US Naval Air Sta since '50. Served as Indsl Hygiene Officer AUS Indsl Hygiene Lab Baltimore '43, USAAF '44-46. Am Conf Governmental Indsl Hygienists—Am Indsl Hygiene Assn — San Diego Safety Council. Building 14, U.S. Naval Air Station, San Diego 35, Calif.

18 FLUKE, Charles Lewis. Syrphidae; Fruit insects. b'91. BS '16 (Colo State Coll); MS '18—PhD '28 (U Wis). Research discoveries concerning Syrphidae, control of fruit insects and white grubs. Prof econ entomol U Wis since '30. Am Assn Econ Entomol—Entomol Soc Am—Sigma Xi (awarded research grant '30-31). 3003 Harvard Dr., Madison 5, Wis.

19 FLYNN, Clarence Edward. Testing programs (Education). b'90. Grad (Shepherd State Teachers Coll W Va); grad (David and Elkins Coll); post grad work (Marshall Coll, WVa U). State supervisor under AAA program; prin schs Circleville WVa since '43. WVA State Edn Assn (exec com)—Central WVa Supts Assn (past pres). Circleville, W.Va.

20 FLYNN, Vincent Joseph. Renaissance Latin grammar; William Lily; Anglo-Italian cultural relations (Fifteenth century). b'01. AB '23 (Coll St Thomas); STB '27 (Catholic U Am); AM '29 (U Minn); PhD '39 (U Chicago). Traveled and worked in libraries in England, France, Italy, Germany and Belgium '34-35; discovered manuscript relating to history of Anglo-Italian relations and general cultural history in last half of 15th century Venerable Eng Coll Rome. Editor: A Shorte Introduction of Grammar (by William Lily, 1567) '45. Pres St Thomas Coll since '44. Modern Lang Assn—Medieval Acad Am—Bibliog Soc Am. College of St. Thomas, St. Paul 1.

21 FOBES, Eugene William. Logging. b'08. BS (Forestry) '32 (U Mont). Research in timber harvesting including logging and related equipment. Author articles: Bark peeling machines and methods; Status of portable wood choppers. Forest ranger US Forest Service '36-42, asst area forester timber prodn. war project '43-45; asst forest econ Central States Forest Expt Sta '42-43; forester Forest Products Lab since 1946. Soc Am Foresters—Phi Sigma—

Druids. Forest Products Lab., Madison 5, Wis.†

22 FODOR, Nandor. Psychical research. b'95. LLD '17 (Royal Hungarian U Sci, Budapest). Author: Encyclopedia of Psychic Science '34; These Mysterious People '35; The Search for the Beloved '49; Dictionary of Psychoanalysis '50. Dir research Internat Inst Psychical Research London '34-38; London editor Jour Am Soc Phys Research '35-39; practicing psychoanalyst NYC. NY Acad Sci—Danish Soc Psychical Research (hon)—Magyar Metafizikai Tarsasag Budapest(hon)—Assn Advancement Psychotherapy. Park Sheraton Hotel, 870 Seventh Av., NYC 19.

23 FOHS, Ferdinand Julius. Petroleum geology of United States (Mid-continent, Gulf Coast), Middle East and Russia; Middle East (Water problems and irrigation, natural resources). b'84. Post graduate course (Columbia '09). Recommended in advance and assisted in development of more than 75 important oil and gas pools; investigated natural and water resources of Palestine, directed development of water '19, '30, '36, '37; investigated oil possibilities of Sicily '27; has made maps and private report on natural resources of Palestine in behalf of World Zionist Organization and British War Office '19 which led to development of cement plant, Dead Sea potash and bromine plant. Author articles in field. Asst state geol of Ky '05-12; lecturer Sch of Mines U Ky '06-08; actively identified Humphreys Fohs group of companies '14-31, serving as cons geol and vp Humphreys Corp; pres Fohs Oil Co '32-45; independent oil operator since '45; dir Palestine Econ Corp, Refugee Econ Corp, Independent Petroleum Assn Am; cons engr water supply for Palestine for Jewish orgns since '30. Geol Soc Am(F)—Am Inst Mining Metall Engrs—Am Assn Petroleum Geol—AAAS—Brit Inst Petroleum Tech. Commerce Building, Houston, Tex. H: Lamar Hotel.⊚

24 FOLEY, John Porter, Jr. Industrial psychology. b'10. AB (with distinction) '31 (Ind U); AM '32—PhD '35 (Columbia). Research in selection of personnel; executive, sales and supervisory evaluation; training; merit rating and performance review; interview training; test construction; employee attitude and management and personnel audits. Author over 80 articles and monographs in wide range psychol jours. Co-author: Differential Psychology: individual and group differences in behavior '49; Human Relations and the Foreman '51. Tchr psychol and dir lab exptl psychol Geo Washington U '36-34; cons psychol The Capital Transit Co Washington '43-44; cons staff Indsl Div The Psychop Corp '44, asso dir div '45, dir since '45. Am Psychol Assn(F)—Eastern Psychol Assn—NY State Psychol Assn—Am Anthropol Assn—Am Ethnol Soc—NY Acad Sci (psychol sect)—AAAS (F)—Am Bd Examiners Profl Psychol (Dip indsl psychol)—Phi Beta Kappa—Sigma Xi. Industrial Division, The Psychological Corporation, 522 5th Av., NYC 18.

25 FOLK, Marion Hayne, Jr. Botany. b'99. BS '19 (Clemson Agrl Coll); MS '29—summer student '42 '49 (La State U). Author: Methods of Delinting Cotton Seed for Early Germination '19; A New Method for Preparing Sulfonphthalein Indicators '29. Asst dept biology La Poly Inst '26-36, asso prof '36-42, prof '42-47, prof, head dept botany and dean sch agr and forestry since '44. Mem La Fruit Growers Assn—La Tchrs Assn. Louisiana Polytechnic Institute, Ruston, La.†⊚

10 FOLLETT, Prescott H(arrison F(ownes). Japanese sword blades and other edged weapons. b'97. Grad '23 (Tulane U). Antiquarian research regarding edged weapons since '15, studied Ken Do or Japanese swordsmanship. Author: Souls and Swords '32; Maya War and Weapons '33; also articles in field. Received the Palms of Officer d'Academy and later Officer Order of Nichen Ifticar of Tunis for relocating the site of first French Fort on the Mississippi from French Govt. Nippon Token Honzon Kai (Japan Sword Research Soc). Times-Picayune Publishing Company, North St., New Orleans.

11 FOLMSBEE, Stanley John. History of Tennessee; Southern and American history. b'99. AB '22 (Dickinson Coll); AM '26—PhD '32 (U Pa). Research on history of Tennessee, including general history of state, transportation, University of Tennessee. Author: Sectionalism and Internal Improvements in Tennessee '33. Co-author: The Story of Tennessee '52. Author articles: The Beginnings of the Railroad Movement in East Tennessee '33; The Origins of the Nashville and Chattanooga Railroad '34; The Turnpike Phases of Tennessee's Internal Improvement System of 1836-38 '37; The Founding of Knoxville '41; others. U Tenn since '28, now prof hist; managing ed Publs E Tenn Hist Soc since '35. AHA—Miss Valley Hist Assn—So Hist Assn—Tenn Hist Soc—E Tenn Hist Soc. Department of History, University of Tennessee, Knoxville, Tenn

12 FOLSOM, Donald. Phytopathology; Potato diseases (Tubers, virus). b'91. AB '12 (U Neb); AM '14—PhD '17 (U Minn). Author articles in field. Plant path Me Agr Expt Sta since '23. Am Phytopath Soc—AAAS(F)—Canada Phytopath Soc—Am Potato Assn—Phi Beta Kappa—Sigma Xi—Phi Kappa Phi. Agricultural Experiment Station, Orono, Me†⊚

13 OLSOME, Clair Edwin. Gynecic pathology. b'03. MS in gynecic pathology '38 (U Mich Grad Sch). Research on water balance in pregnancy, genital carcinoma, fetal and maternal mortality; use of color film earlier detection genital carcinoma. Abstractor Am Jour Obstetrics and Gynecology since '34. Post grad tng U Mich Med Sch '33-41; in charge post grad obstetrics and gynecology Mich State Med Soc and U Mich Grad Sch '38-41; cons Children's Bur Dept Labor '38-41; exec dir Nat Com on Maternal Health NYC '41-42; comdg officer charge venereal disease control Greater Atlanta area USPHS '42-43; exec dir Ortho Research Found Raritan NJ since '44. Am Bd Obstetrics and Gynecology (Diplomate)—Nat Bd Med Examiners (Diplomate)—Am Society Study Human Sterility—Am Coll Surgeons(F)—Sigma Xi. Ortho Research Foundation, Raritan, N.J.

14 FONCK, Charles M(arie). Internat trade fairs; World's Fairs; Internat conferences and conventions; Auditoriums. b'97. M Philosophy and Letters '22—LLD '25 (U Brussels); Licentiate in Econ and Finance '37 (Solvay Bus Sch Brussels). Expert on principal World's Fairs and Internat Trade Fairs since '27, organization, management, adviser on planning, financing and promoting; International conferences and conventions, adviser on technical and building requirements for efficient and profitable utilization for exhibition purposes and civic activities. Author articles: Exhibit News, Fairs to Spur Our Exports, International Trade Fairs, Now Implement Economic Recovery, and others. Expert and adviser to public and pvt instns since '35. Nat Assn Exhibit Mgrs—Am Soc Planning Ofcls—Society Advancement Management—Belgian Nat Com Sci Orgn—Internat Chamber of Commerce (com on fairs and exhibits). H: 1005 Brickell Av., Miami 32, Fla.

15 FONDA, Gorton R(osa). Luminescence (Incandescent, sodium vapor and fluorescent lamps); Thermionic emission; X-ray spectroscopy; Phosphorescent materials. b'84. BS '07—MA '08 (NYU); Dr Ing '10 (Technische Hochschule-Karlsruhe Germany). Editor: Preparation and Characteristics of Solid Luminescent Materials '48; also articles in field. Research chem research lab Gen Electric Co '10-50. Am Chem Soc—Am Phys Soc(F)—Am Optical Soc—Electrochem Society. 1028 Parkwood Blvd., Schenectady, N.Y.†

16 FONDILLER, Richard. Workmen's compensation (Tables of valuation). b'84. BS '03 (Coll City NY); MA '12—LLB '13 (Columbia U). Author tables for valuation of workmen's compensation awards; also articles in field. Asst actuary, other positions various companies '06-22; cons actuary since '22; actuarial and accounting work for ins companies, US War Dept '46-48, and for various states; surveyed actuarial work as mem Safety and Indsl Health Adv Bd apptd by US Atomic Energy Commn '47. Casualty Actuarial Soc (sec-treas since '18 F)—Society of Actuaries(F)—Inst Inst Am(F)—Fraternal Actuarial Assn(F)—Internat Congress Actuaries—Internat Assn Indsl Accident Bds and Coms. 524 West 57th St., NYC 19.

17 FONTAINE, Thomas Davis. Biochemistry (Antibiotics, proteins, enzymes, plant disease, amino acids). b'16. AB '37 (Miss Coll); PhD '42 (U Pittsburgh). Research on solubility characteristics cottonseed proteins, amino acids, nutritional studies, enzymes, peanut and cottonseed proteins, solubility characteristics, proteinphytic acid relationship, proteolytic enzymes, electrophoretic investigations on proteins; studies of plant disease, antibiotics from plants, natural and synthetic plant-growth regulators and their mechanism of action; isolated fungistatic agent tomatine from tomato plant. Fellowship asst Cotton Research Found Mellon Inst Pittsburgh '38-41; asst chem oil, fat, and protein div So Regional Research Lab US Dept Agr New Orleans '41-44, asso chem '44-45; asso chem biologically active compounds div Bur Agrl and Indsl Chem Agrl Research Center Beltsville Md '45-46, chem '46-47, sr biochem '47-48, principal biochem and head biologically active compounds div '48-52; head biologically active compounds div Eastern Regional Research Lab, US Dept Agr '52. Am Chem Soc—Am Soc Biol Chem—Soc Exptl Biol and Med—NY Acad Sci—Sigma Xi. Eastern Regional Research Laboratory, Phila. 18.

18 FONTANA, Mars G. Metallurgical engineering (Corrosion). b'10. BS '31—MS '32—PhD '34 (U Mich). Holder three patents on corrosion testing, alloys and indicating devices. Author articles in field. Prof metall research engring expt sta, prof engring dept metallurgy Ohio State U since '45; head dept since '48; cons metall engr since '45. Am Soc Metals—Nat Assn Corrosion Engrs—Electrochem Soc—AAAS—Soc Promotion Engring Edn—Am Inst Chem Engrs—Am Inst Mining Metall Engrs—Tau Beta Pi—Sigma Xi. Ohio State University, Columbus 10, O. H: 2086 Elgin Rd.

19 FONTENROSE, Joseph. Greek and Roman religion; Mythology. b'03. AB '25—MA '28—PhD '33 (U Calif); Sterling fellow '36-37 (Yale); resident '35-36 (Am Sch Classical Studies Athens). Research on the Delphic Oracle since '35, creation, flood and other themes of Greek mythology, Ovid's Metamorphoses Assistant prof Greek and Latin U Ore '33-34; instr Greek U Calif '34-35, Latin '37-41, asst prof classics '41-47, asso prof since '47. Am Philol Assn—Philol Assn Pacific Coast—Mod Lang Assn. Am Council Learned Socs Fellow '35-36 Am Acad in Rome fellow '51-52. Classics Department University of California, Berkeley 4.

20 FOOSE, Richard Martin. Mineral deposits. b'15. BS '37 (Franklin and Marshall Coll); MS '39—turtorial fellow '38-39 (Northwestern U); U scholar '41-42—PhD '42 (Johns Hopkins). Research on manganese oxide ores and their identification, genesis and occurrence of iron ores in Appalachian Mountain area and of high-alumina clays, new photogeologic techniques for mineral exploration. Author articles in field. Prof and head dept geol Franklin and Marshall Coll since '46; cons geol since '42. Pa Acad Sci (ed '44-48, pres '49-50)—Geol Soc Am—NJ Mineral Soc—Soc Econ Geol—Am Inst Mining Engrs (chairman indsl minerals div '49-50)—AAAS (chairman Lancaster Branch '51-53)—Sigma Xi —Phi Beta Kappa. Recipient Pa Acad Sci research grant '43. Department of Geology, Franklin and Marshall College, Lancaster, Pa.⊚

21 FOOTE, Charles Lee. Embryology: Physiology of Reproduction. b'12. BS '34 (N Tex State Teachers Coll); MA '36 (A&M Coll Tex); PhD '40 (State U Ia). Research on effects sex hormones on gonads and sex characteristics Rana Clamitans and Ambystoma larvae, synthetic hormones on sex development in marbled salamander; embryology of golden hamster. Asso prof dept zool So Ill U since '47. AAAS—Sigma Xi. Zoology Department, Southern Illinois University, Carbondale, Ill.

22 FOOTE, Paul D(arwin). Petroleum technology; Geophysical prospecting; Physics in industry. b'88. AB '09 (Western Reserve U); AM '11 (U Neb); PhD '17 (U Minn); sr fellow '27-29 (Mellon Inst Indsl Research). Lecturer and teacher. Editor-in-chief Journal Optical Society America; Revue of Scientific Instruments '21-32; associate-editor Journal Franklin Institute. Co-author: Pyrometric Practice '21; (with Fred Loomis Mohler) The Origin of Spectra '22; Physics in Industry '37. Exec vp Gulf Research & Development Co Pittsburgh; vp Gulf Oil Corp and Gulf Refining Co; lecturer U Pittsburgh. Am Phys Soc (F, pres '33)—AAAS(F)—Optical Soc Am —Am Philos Soc—Nat Acad Sci—Am Petroleum Inst—Washington Acad Sci (vp '36)—Inst Petroleum Tech—Am Inst Mining Metall Engrs—Am Geophys Union—Phi Beta Kappa—Sigma Xi—Sigma Pi Sigma. Gulf Research & Development Co., Drawer 2038, Pittsburgh 30.⊚

23 FOOTE, Perry A. Pharmaceutical and plant chemistry; Essential oils; Synthetic drugs. b'99. BS '22—MS '26 —PhD '28 (U Wisconsin). Prof pharmaceutical chemistry U Fla since '39, dean coll pharmacy since '49, dir bur of professional relations since '40. Am Pharmaceutical Assn (chmn com for Ebert Award '37-38, mem com on profl relations since '44)—Am Chem Soc (v chmn Fla sect '30-32, chmn '32, dir radio programs '31)—Sigma Xi—Phi Kappa Phi—Rho Chi (nat president '50-52). Received Dr J Leon Lascoff Award for promotion of professional pharmacy in US '46, Am Coll Apothecaries; James H Beal Pharmacist of the Year Award Fla '47, State Pharmaceutical Assn. University of Florida, Gainesville. Fla.

10 FORBES, Allan W(hite). Vocational guidance. b'86. AB '08 (Amherst); BS '10 (Worcester Polytechnic). Research on influence of education on i n d u s t r i a l management, effect of schools on unemployment, vocational guidance. Author articles in field. Owner Forbes and Myers electrical mfgrs since '13. 172 Union St., Worcester 8, Mass.

11 FORBES, Clarence Allen. Ancient Greek education and athletics. b'01. AB '22 (Bates Coll); AM '24—PhD '28 (U Ill). Author: Greek Physical Education '29; Neoi, a contribution to the Study of Greek Associations, and others. Prof classical langs Ohio State U since '48. Am Philol Assn—Classical Assn Middle West and South. Ohio State University, Columbus, O.†

12 FORBES, Ian, Jr. Turf and pasture grasses (Cytology and genetics). b'20. BSc '41—MSc '49 (U Md). Research on fertilizers, grass species, establishment and maintenance practices in the production of turf for lawns, athletic fields, airports, cemeteries, playgrounds, golf courses, road shoulders; cytological genetic and breeding studies on Zoysia japonica and other turf grasses species. Author articles: Urea-Form-A Nitrogenous Fertilizer of Controlled Availability—Experiments with Turf Grasses '48; Effect of Strain Differences, Seed Treatment, and Planting Depth on Seed Germination of Zoysia '48; Observations on the Zoysia Grasses '47; The Beltsville Turf Gardens '47. Research asst turf grasses US Golf Assn Green sect Arlington Va '41-42, Beltsville Md '45-47; agronomist turf investigations Div Forage Crops and Diseases Bur Plant Ind US Dept Agr since '47. Bot Soc Am—Am Soc Agron. Division of Forage Crops and Diseases, Bureau of Plant Industry, USDA Coastal Plains Experiment Station, Tifton, Ga.

13 FORBES, James. Insect morphology, anatomy and histology (Ants, house-fly, life-histories and biology of mosquitoes). b'10. Biol fellow '32-36—BS '32—MS '34—PhD '36 (Fordham U). Author articles in field. Instr, asst prof biol Fordham U since '36. NY Entomol Soc—Entomol Soc Am—Am Soc Zool—Am Soc Profl Biol. Biological Laboratory, Fordham University, NYC 58.†

14 FORBES, John Douglas. American architectural history; American economic history. b'10. AB '31 (Calif U); AM '32 (Stanford); AM '36—PhD '37 (Harvard). Biography of Irish Victorian architect William Tinsley (1804-85) who practiced in Co. Tipperary, Ireland, and Indiana, Ohio, Wisconsin; biography of Israel Thorndike (1755-1832), merchant-shipowner of Boston, Mass. Contbr of articles: Port of Boston 1783-1815 '38; European Wars and Boston Trade '38; The Art Museum and the Am Scene '42; Crawfordsville, U.S.A. (architecture) '48; Lew Wallace, Romantic '48; Boston Smuggling (1807-15) '50. Research eonomist John F Forbes and Co, '37-38; curator paintings, asst to dir fine arts Golden Gate Internat Exposition San Francisco '38-49; chmn dept of art U Kansas City '40-42; asso architecture editor Dictionary of the Arts '41; prof polit, econ hist Bennington Coll '43-46; asso editor Am Enterprise Assn NY '45-46; asso prof history and fine arts Wabash Coll Crawfordsville Ind since '46. Phi Beta Kappa—Soc of Architectural Hist —Am Hist Assn—College Art Assn. Wabash College, Crawfordsville, Ind.

15 FORBES, William Hathaway. Environmental physiology (Physical effects of clothing, heat, cold, altitude, muscular work, carbon monoxide poisoning). b'02. AB '23—teaching fellow physiol Med Sch '28-29—MA '31 (Harvard Univ); PhD '31 (Cambridge U); MD '52 (Johns Hopkins Univ). National Research Council sub-committees on clothing, nutrition, and industrial fatigue '43-46, Research and Development Board Panel on Environmental Physiology '47. Asst Fatigue Lab Harvard U '32-36, research fellow '38-41, acting dir '41-42, asst dir since '42, asst prof indsl physiology since '42, research asso Harvard Sch Pub Health; lecturer Wellesley Coll '38-39. Harvard School of Public Health, 55 Shattuck St., Boston 15.

16 FORBUSH, Bliss. Religion (Educator). b'96. AB '36—AM '47 (U Chicago); student '14-15 (Oberlin Coll) '26-28 (Johns Hopkins); travel fellowship '39 (Europe). Author: Study Guide to Old Testament '31; Study Guide to New Testament '32; Gospel of Mark '35; Toward Understanding Jesus '39 (rev edit '46). Instr Bible Friends Sch Baltimore '25-37 since '40, acting headmaster '41, headmaster since '43; chmn bd Friends Sch. '28-43; instr Bible Baltimore Sch Christian Edn '24-36; chmn leadership training com Baltimore Council Chs '27-41, mem bd dirs since '36; chmn leadership tng com Friends Gen Conf '29-41. Friends Council on Edn—Quaker Headmasters. 5014 Embla Av., Balt. 10.☉

17 FORD, Guy Stanton. History (Modern European). b'73. LittB '95—LittD '33 (U Wis); '99-00 (U Berlin) '00-01—PhD '03—LittD '39 (Columbia); LLD '27 (Lawrence Coll); LHD '38 (U Rochester); LLD '39 (U Mich) '46 (U Minn). Author: Hanover and Prussia '03; Stein and the Era of Revolution Reform in Prussia '22; Science and Civilization '33; Dictatorship in the Modern World '35, rev '39. Editor Harper History Series. Prof modern European history U Ill '06-13; prof history and dean grad sch U Minn '13-38; exec sec Am Hist Assn and editor Am Hist Rev since '41. Am Hist Assn— (pres '37)—Miss Valley Hist Assn— Minn Hist Soc (pres '30-33, exec council since '14)—Gamma Sigma Delta— Phi Beta Kappa—Gamma Alpha—Phi Alpha Theta—Kappa Delta Pi. Library of Congress Annex, Washington 25.☉

18 FORD, James Alfred. Archaeology of the Americas (Southeastern United States, Peru, Columbia, Alaskan Eskimo). b'11. AB '36 (La State U); MA '38 (U Mich); PhD '49 (Columbia). Field work on pre-historic Indian cultures, southeastern US '27-29, '32-36, '38-40; on pre-historic Eskimo cultures of arctic coast of Alaska '30-32, '36; on pre-historic cultures of Andean region Colombia SA '41-42; expedition to Peru '46-47. Author articles: Ceramic Decoration Sequence at an Old Indian Village Site near Sicily Island La '35; Analysis of Indian Village Site Collections from Louisiana and Mississippi '36; The Tchefuncte Culture, An Early Occupation of the Lower Mississippi Valley '45. Asst curator NA arch Am Museum Natural Hist NY since '46. Soc Am Archaeology. American Museum of Natural History, 79th St. and Central Park, NYC.

19 FORD, Nick Aaron. American Negro literature. b'04. AB '26 (Benedict Coll); MA '34—PhD '45 (State U Ia). Author: The Contemporary Negro Novel '36; also articles in field. Prof and head dept Eng Morgan State Coll since '45. Nat Council Teachers Eng. Awared Gen Edn Bd fellowship '44-45. Morgan State College, Baltimore 12.†

20 FORESTER, Don Montell. Water (Conservation); Land (Reclamation); Flood control. b'90. BS (Civil engring) '14 (Ga Inst Tech). Investigation and planning irrigation, flood control and hydroelectric developments, both project and river basin-wide, various dams. Author articles in field. Flood control and drainage engring Lower Miss Valley '19-26; engr US Bur Reclamation since '32. Am Soc CE—Tau Beta Pi. 611 Ave. D, Billings, Mont.

21 FORKNER, Hamden Landon. Vocational education; Business Education; Secondary education. b'97. AB '29 —MA '36—PhD '39 (U Cal). Co-author: 20th Century Bookkeeping and Accounting; Correlated Dictation and Transcription: Developing a Curriculum for Modern Living. Head comml dept Marysville High Sch '21-25; vocational counselor and dept head Castlemont High Sch Oakland '29-32; acting head Merritt Bus Sch Oakland '32-37; head dept vocation and bus edn tchrs coll Columbia since '37. Nat Council for Bus Edn (pres '40-44)—Nat Assn Bus Tchr-Tng Instns (pres '45-46)— United Bus Edn Assn (pres '46-48)— Nat Assn Secondary Sch Prins—Am Assn Sch Adminstrs—Nat Bus Tchrs Assn—Eastern Comml Tchrs Assn—So Bus Edn Assn—Comml Edn Assn NY City—NEA—Phi Delta Kappa—Delta Pi Epsilon. 525 W. 120th St., NYC 27.†☉

22 FORMAN, Harrison. History (Asia, Far East, China, Tibet); Documentary motion pictures. b'04. BA '29 (U Wis). Organized and led motor caravan expedition to Central Asia '32; made three expeditions to Tibet, on second expedition took first motion pictures of the Panchen Lama at a ceremony attended by more than half million pilgrims, on third expedition took motion pictures of Jamv Japa, fourth in the hierarchy of Living Buddhas of Tibet; also motion pictures of Chinese Communist Red Army and of bombardment of Shanghai 1937, Warsaw 1939, etc; private collection over 30,000 negatives on Far East; authority current social, economic, and political developments of China. Author: Through Forbidden Tibet '35; Horizon Hunter '40; Report from Red China '45; Changing China '48; Blunder in Asia '50; How to Make Money with Your Camera '52; also articles in field. Formerly foreign corr New York Times, London Times, NBC; now free-lance writer, lecturer. c/o Explorers Club, 10 W. 72d St., NYC. H: 6 Colby Rd., Port Washington, N.Y.☉

23 FORMAN, Henry Chandlee. American and Latin American art and archeology. b'04. AB '26 (Princeton); PhD '42 (U Pa). Research in American colonial archeology, history of Mexican painting, creative landscape painting; conducted archeological excavations St Mary's City, birthplace religious freedom America; edited national records historical surveys; excavated foundation of 1st permanent English settlement in America. Author: Jamestown and St. Mary's: Buried Cities of Romance '38; The Architecture of the Old South '48; Early Manor and Plantation Houses of Maryland '34, and others. Prof fine arts Agnes Scott Coll since '45; chief architect Jamestown Archeol project US Dept Interior '35-36; ed hist Am Bldgs Survey Library of Congress '36. Am Inst Architects—Archeol Inst Am— Am Council Learned Soc. George Barnard White prize in architecture at Princeton. Agnes Scott College, Decatur, Ga.

24 FORMAN, Jonathan. History of medicine; Allergy; Soil-health. b'87. AB '10 (O State U); MD '13 (Starling-O Med Coll). Co-founder Annual Forums on Allergy; editor Directory of Physicians Interested in Clinical Allergy '42. Author: History of the First Hundred Years of the College of Medicine of Ohio State University '34; also articles in field. Med practice Columbus O since '20; with O State U since '33; prof hist med since '45; member board trustees and exec dir Friends of the Land since '42, mem Nat Policy Forestry Bd of Review. AMA (F)—Am Coll Allergy—Am Acad Allergy—Am Bd Internal Med (diplomate)—Internat Corr Club of Allergy (dir gen, ed Letters since '37)—Am Assn Anat—O State Med Assn—O Hist and Archaeol Soc (chmn med hist and archives com since '35)—Am Assn Med Hist (treas '48, mem exec com)—O Valley Soc Allergy. 394 E. Town St., Columbus 15, O.

10 FORNEROD, Marcel Francis. Concrete (Prestressed). b'03. BS MS '26 (Fed Poly Inst Zurich). Theory, design, development, construction practice in prestressed concrete; structural design prestressed concrete bridges, circular reservoirs, spherical shell dome roofs. Author articles: Prestressed concrete shell roof construction; Prestressing safety factors; Factors in prestressed concrete design. Contributor: Modern Bridges '49. Design engr Robert Maillart Switzerland '31-33; cons engr '33-36; asst gen mgr Borsari Tank Corp Am '37-41; with Preload Corp since '43, chief engr since '46. Am Soc CE—Am Concrete Inst—Nat Soc Profl Engrs—Internat Assn Bridge and Structural Engring. Preload Enterprises, Inc., 211 East 37th St., N.Y.C. 16.

11 FORNOFF, Frank Junior. Inorganic chemistry of rare elements. b'14. Fellow '38-39—MSc '37—PhD '39 (Ohio State U); AB '36 (U Ill). Author articles in field. Chem engr Western Electric; asso prof Lehigh U since '47. Am Chem Soc—AAAS—Sigma Xi—Phi Beta Kappa—Phi Kappa Phi. Nat Research Council fellow '39-40. Department of Chemistry, Lehigh University, Bethlehem, Pa.†

12 FORREST, Linn Argyle. Totemic art and literature; Alaska. b'05. Student '27 (U Ore); '28 (MIT). Author: Tourist Recreation Possibilities in Alaska '47; Significance of the Totem '40. Co-author: (with Viola E Garfield) Totemic Stories Southeastern Alaska Indians '49. Architect Ore since '37, Alaska since '44; architect Timberline Lodge Mt Hood Ore US Forest Service '36-38, Alaska Region since '38; reconstrn Tlingit and Haida, Southeastern Alaska Indians, totems and community houses '38-41, compilation of lit and custom data of above groups '38-42; study entire territory of Alaska with reference to recreation resources and their potentials '47; development of archtl styles best suited to Alaska '38-49. Territorial Bd Engrs and Architects (sec since '45). U.S. Forest Service, Juneau, Alaska. H: Box 995.

13 FORRESTER, James Donald. Mining and economic geology; Mining engineering. b'06. BS '28 (U Utah); MS '29—PhD '35 (Cornell). Author: Principles of Field and Mining Geology '46; also articles in field. Prof, chmn dept mining engring Mo Sch Mines Metallurgy since '44; cons commissions mines and mineral deposits in west and midwest US. Geol Soc Am(F)—Soc Econ Geol—Am Inst Mining Metall Engrs—Am Assn Petroleum Geol—Am Soc Engring Edn—Mo Soc Profl Engrs—Sigma Xi. Department of Mining Engineering, Missouri School of Mines, Rolla, Mo.†

14 FORRESTER, Jay W(right). Digital computers; Servomechanisms; Control systems. b'18. BS '39 (U Neb);

MS '45 (Mass Inst Tech). Teaching and research in high voltage engring on x-ray equipment MIT '39-40, cofounder Servomechanisms Lab for remote control '40, asso dir Lab '44, now dir MIT digital computer laboratory. AIEE—Inst Radio Engrs—AA AS—Sigma Xi. Massachusetts Institute of Technology, Cambridge 39, Mass.†

15 FORSBERG, Junius Leonard. Plant pathology; Diseases of ornamental plants. b'07. BS '30 (Colo A&M Coll); MS '32 (Mich State Coll). Author: Diseases of Ornamental Plants '46; also articles in field. Asso plant path Ill Nat Hist Survey since '44. AAAS—Am Phytopath Soc—Ill State Acad Sci—NA Gladiolus Council—NE Gladiolus Soc—Ill Gladiolus Soc—Sigma Xi. Illinois Natural History Survey, 381 Natural Resources Building, Urbana, Ill.†

16 FORSLING, Clarence L(uther). Forestry (Range management, natural resources conservation, hydrology of soil erosion). b'93. BS '15 (U Neb). In charge of all forest and range research US Department of Agriculture including 12 regional forest and range experimental stations and forest products laboratory, throughout continental US and Puerto Rico '37-44; was responsible for administration of 142,000,000 acres Federal land in grazing districts in western states '44-46. Author articles in field. With US Dept Agr '15-44, special asst to Sec Interior '46 to '48, chmn Dept Interior Southwest Field Com since '48. Soc Range Management—Soc Am Foresters. Recipient of Oberlaender Trust fellowship to study forestry in Central European countries '35. U.S. Department of Interior Program Staff, Albuquerque, N.M. H: 307 S. Solano Av.©

17 FORSYTH, William Holmes. Medieval sculpture, tapestries, ivories and enamels. b'06. AB '30 MFA '33 (Princeton U). Research on medieval sculpture, particularly on statues of the Virgin and Child of the fourteenth century in France; art of the period of tribal migrations, fourth to eighth centuries in Europe. Author: A Brief Guide to the Medieval Collection, Metropolitan Museum of Art; The Virgin and Child—A Picture Book of Medieval Sculpture; also articles in field. Mem staff Metropolitan Museum of Art since '33, now asso curator dept Medieval Art. Metropolitan Museum of Art, NYC.

18 FORT, William Edwards, Jr. Philosophy of history and religion; Ethics; History of philosophy; Abnormal psychology. b'05. BS '30 (Ga Sch Tech); AM '32—PhD '34—U Fellow (Duke U). Author: A Philosophical Examination of Some Contemporary Theories of History '34; also articles in field. Chmn human relations div since '48, prof philos and psychol Rollins College since '46. Am Philos Assn—Southern Soc Philos Psychol—Phi Kappa Phi—Beta Gamma Sigma. Received M L Brittain award Ga Tech, Duke University Graduate Fellowship in Philosophy '32. Box 126, Rollins College, Winter Park, Fla.

19 FORTNEY, William Hugh. Industrial instrumentation and measurements; Control systems and valves. b'04. Student '20-23 (U Tex). Holder US patent on gravity indicator or recorder for fluids. Author articles in field. With the Humble Oil and Refining Co since '27, foreman instrument dept Baytown Refinery since '37. Instrument Soc Am (chmn recommended practices com, convention com '51 (Houston). Humble Oil and Refining Co., Baytown, Tex.

20 FOSBERG, F(rancis) Raymond. Botany of Pacific islands (Taxonomy, floristics, vegetation); Taxonomy of Rubiaceae (Cinchona). b'08. Morris fellow '37-39—PhD '39 (U Pa); BA '30 (Pomona Coll); MS '35 (U Hawaii). Organized Honolulu Conference on Conservation in Micronesia '48; International Symposium on Plant Taxonomy and Nomenclature Utrecht Holland '48. Author articles in field. Profl lecturer George Washington U since '48; research asso Catholic U Am since '48. AAAS(F)—Bot Soc Am—Am Soc Plant Taxonomists—New Eng Bot Club—Hawaiian Acad Sci—Calif Bot Soc—Biol Soc Washington—Soc Study Evolution—Am Geog Soc. Guggenheim fellow '47-48. Room 400, Building C, George Washington University, Washington.†

21 FOSCUE, Edwin Jay. Geography of the United States & Mexico; Southwest United States (Resort centers). b'99. BA '22 (So Meth U); MS '25 (U Chicago); PhD '31 (Clark U). Coauthor: Regional Geography of Anglo-America '42; contbg editor: Economic Geography. Instr Geography So Meth U '23-24, asst prof '24-31, asso prof '31-38, prof since '38, chmn dept geography since '46; vis prof Geography U Neb summers '37 and '38; vis prof Geography Western Reserve U summers '39 and '41; vis prof Geography U Colo summers '40 and '42; asst dir US Bd on Geog Names '43-44; vis prof U Washington summer '46; vis prof Geography U Virginia summer '48. AA AS(F)—Assn Am Geographers (councillor '43-45)—Nat Research Council ('47-49)(del Internat Geog Cong Lisbon, 1948)—Sigma Xi. Add: 3225 Hanover. St., Dallas.©

22 FOSHAG, William Frederick. Mineralogy; Gemology; Meteoritics; Vulcanology. b'94. AB '19—PhD '23 (U Calif). Co-author: Minerals from Earth and Sky. Head curator US Nat Mus since '48. Mineral Soc Am (F, pres '40)—Geol Soc Am (vp '41)—Soc Research on Meteorites (vp '33-34)—Washington Acad Sci—Geol Soc Mexico—Sociedad Cientifica Antonio Alzate de Mexico—Sigma Xi—Soc Econ Geologists. U.S. National Museum, Washington.©

23 FOSS, Noel E. Pharmaceutical chemistry. b'05. Student '23-24 (So Dakota State Sch Mines) 24-25 (So Dakota U); PhC—BS in Pharmacy '29 (SD State Coll); 40-42 (Columbia), '42-43 (Wash U), '44-45 (Brooklyn Poly Inst); MS '32—PhD '33 (Md U). Inspected, examined, and directed preparation of specifications of all drugs and chemicals purchased by Medical Dept US Army, consultant to buyers in awarding contracts, made survey of drugs and chemicals used by German Army, France and Germany '45; represented Army during preparation of joint Army-Navy catalogue list of chemicals and drugs; engaged organic chemical research, pharmaceutical research and development, manufacturing control, new drug application and production; research on unsymmetrical aryl sulfides, physiological action of disalicyl aldehyde and physiological effect of quinolyl-ethanol, inks for printing on ampuls. Author articles in field. Tech dir pharm dept Calco Chem Div Am Cyanamid Co NJ '46-47; asst dean, prof of pharm Ill U '47-49; dean, prof pharm U Md since '49. Army Med Purchasing Office '42-46, receiving and warehouse office St Louis '42-43, lab officer NY '43-46. Am Pharm Assn—Sigma Xi. Dunning fellow Md U '30-34. University of Maryland School of Pharmacy, 32 & Greene St., Balt.†

24 FOSSUM, Charles Peter. Agriculture economics (Korea, India, Holland). b'19. BS '40 (Ia State Coll).

Increasing food and agricultural production utilizing existing arable lands, equipment, fertilizers, improving scientific farming practice, meeting requirements for food in relation to standard of living and its relationship to increased productivity. Author articles in field. Chief advisor Minister Agr South Korean Interim Govt '46-48; mem US Delegation UN Food and agr World Conf New Delhi and Trivandrum (India) '47; Area Specialist Benelux, Scandanavia, China, Korea food and agr div Econ Coop Adminstrn '48-49, chief technical assistance br ECA, '49-50; food and agriculture dir, ECA Mission to Netherlands since '50. American Embassy, The Hague, Netherlands.

10 FOSSUM, Mennick Truman. Economics of floriculture and ornamental horticulture. b'12. Certificate (N Dak Sch Forestry); BSc '40 (Cornell U); MSc '41 (Ohio State U); Certificate (Royal Bot Garden Kew; NY Bot Garden); '42-43 (U Md); '47-48 (Purdue U). Presently engaged specifically in developing economics for floriculture and ornamental horticulture as has previously been done for rest of agriculture and industry, dir research and member services Soc Am Florists since '49. Asso prof Cornell U since '45. Royal Hort Soc—AAAS—Am Soc Hort Sci—Am Farm Econ Assn—Assn Kew Gardeners Am (pres)—Sigma Xi—Gamma Sigma Delta—Pi Alpha Xi. Society of American Florists, 600 S. Michigan Ave., Chicago 5, Ill. H: 223 Vidal Drive, Parkmerced, SF.

11 FOSTER, Arthur Crawford. Plant pathology, physiology and biochemistry; Non-parasitic diseases; Plant toxicology (Insecticides, fungicides); Crop growth. b'93. BSc '17 (NC State Coll); Heinz Research Fellow '19-20—MSc '20 (U Wis). Author articles in field. Sr plant path Hort Field Sta Beltsville Md since '34. AAAS—Am Bot Soc—Phytopath Soc—Am Soc Plant Physiol—Am Chem Soc—Wis Acad Sci, Arts Letters—Washington Bot Soc—Sigma Xi. Bureau of Plant Industry Station, Beltsville, Md.

12 FOSTER, Aubrey Alfred. Plant diseases (Celery, vegetables, bulbs, ornamental crops). b'12. Student '32-33 (NYU); BS '39—PhD '46 (Cornell U). Author articles in field. Asso prof dept plant pathol Cornell U '48-50. AAAS—Am Phytopath Soc—Am Soc Hort Sci—Am Chem Soc. Macedonia Co-op, Clarkesville, Ga.

13 FOSTER, Aurel Overton. Helminthology (Anthelmintics). b'06. AB '29—AM '30 (Wesleyan U Conn); ScD '33 (Johns Hopkins Sch Hygiene Pub Health). Research on hookworm anemia, immunity, verminuous aneurysm, phenothiazine, sodium fluoride, borax, sulfaguanidine, treatments and control livestock parasites. Author articles in field. Helminthologist Gorgas Memorial Lab Panama '34-39; parasitol US Dept Agr since '39. AAAS—Am Soc Parasitol—Am Soc Trop Med—Am Micr Soc—Helminthological Soc Washington—Insecticide Soc Washington—Washington Acad—Sigma Xi. Zoological Division, Bureau of Animal Industry, Agricultural Research Center, Beltsville, Md.

14 FOSTER, Charles Howell. Harriet Beecher Stowe; New England theology; Ralph Waldo Emerson; Robert Frost; Nathaniel Hawthorne. b'13. BA '36 (Amherst Coll); MA '37—PhD '39 (U Ia). American literature with emphasis on New England writers of 19th century, work of Harriet Beecher Stowe as expression of New England culture. Author: Emerson's Theory of Poetry '39; also articles in field. Dir Sch Letters Hour Am Heritage U Ia

'39-44; asso prof Eng U Colo '44-47; prof Eng Grinnell Coll since '47. MLA—Soc Am Hist(F). Awarded scholarship by Am Council Learned Soc for research in NE theol and intellectual hist '51-52. Grinnell College, Grinnell, Ia.

15 FOSTER, Edgar Eugene. Hydrology (Power plants, flood control). b'94. BS (Civil engring) '22 (U ND). Studies in stream gaging collecting data of surface stream flow; field research of hydroelectric projects; investigation proposed projects; determination power possibilities of streams under investigation for government development; hydrologic, hydraulic, economic studies of flood control projects in various parts of US including power, navigation, irrigation development; investigations and studies for drainage, flood control, water supply, storm and sanitary sewers. Author: Rainfall and Runoff '48. With US Geol Survey '22-24; engr US Corps Engrs '24-44; Stanley Engring Co '45-46; US Bur Reclamation since '46. Am Soc CE—Am Geophys Union—Am Meteorol Soc—Am Geog Soc—AAAS—Permanent Internat Assn Navigation Congresses. U.S. Bureau of Reclamation, Denver Federal Center, Denver.

16 FOSTER, Francis Apthorp. History of the United States; The American Revolution; History of the Society of the Cincinnati. b'72. '91-92 (Lawrence Sci Sch). Research on French volunteer officers in American Revolution, officers of French Auxiliary Army, American Revolution, Society of the Cincinnati; editor publications New England Historical and Genealogical Society '07-12. Author: Materials Relating to the History of the Society of the Cincinnati in the State of Georgia '34; The Society of the Cincinnati '44; The Burning of Harvard Hall '21; also articles in field. Am Geog Soc(F)—AAAS—Soc Cincinnati (asst sec-gen '20-32, sec-gen since '32)—Mass Hist Soc—Colonial Soc Mass—Me Hist Soc (corres mem)—Ga Hist Soc—AHA—New Eng Hist Geneal Soc—Legion of Honor (officer). Vineyard Haven, Mass.

17 FOSTER, George McClelland, Jr. Social anthropology. b'13. Student '31-32 (Harvard); BS '35 (Northwestern U); PhD '41 (U Calif). Author: A Summary of Yuki Culture '44; Sierra Popoluca Folklore and Beliefs '45; Empire's Children: The People of Tzintzuntzan '48; also articles in field. Charge Mexican sta Mexico City Inst Social Anthropol Smithsonian Inst '43-46, dir of Inst Washington since '46. Am Anthrop Soc—Wash Acad Sci—Sigma Xi. Smithsonian Institution, Washington 25.†

18 FOSTER, James William. Maryland history (Bibliography, maps, prints). b'90. BA '12—MA '13 (U Va). Editor, Maryland Historical Magazine '38-50. Author articles in field. On staff Enoch Pratt Free Library Baltimore '31-42, asso head, local hist dept '36-42; dir Md Hist Soc since '41. Am Antiquarian Soc—AHA—Am Association State and Local Hist—Md Library Assn. Maryland Historical Soc., 201 W. Monument St., Baltimore 1.

19 FOSTER, Leon Victor. Optical engineering. b'95. BS '17 (Syracuse U). Holder 15 US patents on lens and optical system, sound reproducing apparatus, microscope and others. Now with Bausch and Lomb Optical Company. Author articles in field. Optical Society America — AAAS — Am Micros Society — Biol Photographic Assn—Am Soc Testing Materials—Am Standards Assn—Soc Motion Picture Engrs—Electron Micros Soc Am. 635 St. Paul Street, Rochester 2, N.Y.

20 FOSTER, Richard Fredric. Pollution (Columbia River); Trout (Yellowstone Lake); Sockeye salmon (Fraser River, migration); Chinook salmon (Sacramento River, salvation); Radiobiology (Aquatic organisms). b'17. Student '34-35 (U Utah); BS (fisheries) '38—PhD (fisheries) '48 (U Wash). Research on life history and abundance of trout in Yellowstone Lake, migration sockeye salmon of Fraser River, salvation salmon of upper Sacramento River, pollution rivers and harbors of Washington, effects X-radiation and atomic materials on aquatic life. Biol State of Wash Pollution Commn '42-43; research asso Applied Fisheries Lab U Wash '43-45; mem Bikini Resurvey '47; head aquatic biol unit Radiological Sci Dept, Nucleonics Div Gen Elec Co since '45. Wildlife Soc—Am Fisheries Soc—Soc Ichthyologists and Herpetologists—Pacific Fisheries Biol—AAAS—Sigma Xi—Phi Sigma. Biology Section, General Electric Co., Richland, Wash.

21 FOSTER, Robert Edward, II. Pathology of vegetables (Disease resistance); Vegetable breeding; Hop diseases. b'20. Student '37-39 (San Diego State Coll); BS '41 (U Calif); PhD '45 (U Wis). Research on ways changes in environment variously predispose plants to disease; development of several new disease-resistant cabbage varieties, seed treatments for canning crop vegetables; breeding for disease resistance. Author articles in field. Inspr State Dept Agr Calif '41; research asst dept plant pathol U Wis '41-46; asst prof div plant pathol NY Agrl Expt Sta '46-50; associate prof U Arizona since '50. Am Phytopath Soc—Sigma Xi. Salt River Valley Vegetable Research Station, Mesa Arizona.

22 FOSTER, Thomas Henry. Rare Books and Manuscripts. b'75. Student '93-94—hon BS '29—hon D Letters (Parsons Coll) LLD '47 (Westminster Coll). Author: Bookplates in Iowa (with Wyer) '14; A Letter from the Fire '23; A Little Journey to the Valley of the Loire '45; Shakespeare: Man of Mystery '46. Asso John Morrell and Co since '94, chmn bd since '44; pres Yorkshire Creamer Co. Ia State Historical Soc—Beta Gamma Sigma. H: 1560 N. Elm St., Ottumwa, Ia.

23 FOWKES, Robert A(llen). Indo-European linguistics; Welsh language and literature. b'13. AB '34—MA '35 (NYU); Ottendorfer Memorial Fellow '36-37 (U Bonn, Germany); PhD '47 (Columbia U). Author: Gothic Etymological Studies '49; also articles in field. Instr NYU dept German '39-47, asst prof since '47; lecturer in Indo-Iranian Columbia U since '47, gen and comp linguistics since '49. Modern Lang Assn Am—Linguistic Soc Am—St David's Soc State NY (chmn com on Welsh lit and music). New York University, University Heights, NYC 53.

24 FOWLER, George Bingham. Medieval and Asiatic history. b'03. BS '25 (US Naval Acad); MA '29—seminars in field '27-29 (U Calif); '29-37—fellow Chinese and Japanese studies Far East Sect '35—Japanese lang '43-44—PhD '46 (Columbia); Fulbright research scholar in Austria '51-52. Engaged research and study medieval Latin; medieval heresy and the inquisition; Paris University in 13th century; papacy from false decretals to Innocent III; Monumentum Ancyranum; period of Ptolemy II; Zenon Papyri; intellectual hist closing medieval and early mod centuries. Author: Intellectual Interests of Engelbert of Admont '47; also articles in field. Instr hist Briarcliff Jr Coll '45-48, academic dean '47-48; prof hist U Pitts since '48. Medieval Acad Am—AHA—Am Oriental Soc—Soc Jap Studies—Hist Sci Soc. Department of History, University of Pittsburgh, Pittsburgh 13.

10 FOWLER, James Abbott. Herpetology; Speleology. b'16. BS '40—MA '43 (George Washington U). Author articles in field. Dir edn Acad Natural Sci Phila since '47. American Society Ichthyologists Herpetologists — Nat Speleological Soc—Am Nature Study Soc—Pa Acad Sci—Sigma Xi. Academy of Natural Sciences, 19th & The Parkway, Phila. 3.

11 FOWLER, William Alfred. Nuclear physics. b'11. BEng Physics '33 (O State U); research fellow '36-39— PhD '36 (Calif Inst Tech). Tech observer OSRD S Pacific '44; prof physics Calif Inst Tech since '46. Sigma Xi—Tau Beta Pi. 1201 E. California, Pasadena 4, Cal.◎

12 FOWLIE, Wallace. French literature. b'08. AB '30—AM '33—PhD '36 (Harvard). Author: Rimbaud; Clowns and Angels; Jacob's Night, The Clown's Grail. Asso prof French lit U Chicago '46-50; head dept French Bennington College since '50. Guggenheim fellow '48-49. Bennington College, Bennington, Vt.

13 FOWLKES, John Guy. Education (Accounting systems). b'98. AB '16 (Ouachita Coll Ark); AM '21—PhD '22 (Columbia). Author: Evaluating School Text Books; School Bonds; Financial Accounting System for Schools; Pupil Accounting Systems for Schools; Practical Unit Lesson Plan Books; Principles and Practices of Financial Accounting for Schools '34. Co-author: Practice Tests in Arithmetic; Modern Life Arithmetics; Practical Arithmetic Work-Books; Algebra Work-Book; Healthy Life Series of health textbooks; various bulls of Bur of Ednl Research, U Wis. Mem cons editorial bd The Nations Schools. With U Wis since 22, prof since '27, vis prof edn U Cal '26-27; spl asst to commr of edn US Office Edn '42; dean sch edn and dir summer session U Wis since '47. AAAS(F)—NEA—Phi Delta Kappa— Alpha Kappa Lambda. 88 Cambridge Rd., Madison, Wis.◎

14 FOX, Arthur L. Taste; Dyes, detergents and dispersing agents. b'99. BA '23—MS '23 (U Ill); PhD '27 (Northwestern U). Research in the relationship of chemical constitution and taste; specialized in dyes and detergent and dispersing agents; also photography, photo sensitive diazo compounds and aliphatic chemicals derived from acetylene. Received 50 US patents on various chemical subjects related to dyes, intermediates, flotation agents, rubber chemicals, detergents etc. Author: The Relationship between Chemical Constitution and Taste; Our Different Taste Worlds. Research chemist US Bur Chemistry '23-24; research chemist DuPont Co '27-38, group leader '38-42; section leader Gen Aniline & Film Corp '42-46, dir research '46-48; dir research Colgate-Palmolive-Peet Jersey City since '48. Am Chem Soc—Soc Chem Industry—Am Assn Textile and Color Chem—NAM (patents and research com)—Am Ord Assn. Colgate-Palmolive-Peet Co., Jersey City, N.J.

15 FOX, Charles Kirby. Irrigation. b '83. Ed pub schs. Design over 3,000 standard irrigation structures. Author articles in field. Cons engr hydraulic design and construction since '12. Am Soc CE—Am Soc Mil Engrs—Am Geog Soc(F). 301 Douglas Bldg., 257 S. Spring St., LA 12.

16 FOX, Denis Llewellyn. Animal pigments; Marine biochemistry. b'01.

AB '25 (U Calif); PhD '31 (Stanford); Rockefeller fellow '38-39 (Cambridge U). Research on nutrition, growth rate, general metabolism of marine invertebrates, and on animal pigments. Author articles in field. Asst prof physiol marine organisms SIO U Calif '36-37, asst prof marine biochem '37-42, asso prof '42-48, prof since '48; cons on fouling by marine sedentary animals and on antifouling measures since '41. Western Soc Naturalists (sec-treas '39-43, pres '48)—San Diego Soc Nat Hist (pres of fellows '36)—AAAS (F, council)—American Society Naturalists— Society Gen Physiologists—Am Soc Limnol and Oceano—Sigma Xi. Grants-in-aid Nat Research Council '34-35, Am Philos Soc '46-47, Rockefeller Foundation '47-49, '49-53; Guggenheim fellow '45-46. Scripps Institution of Oceanography, La Jolla, Calif.†

17 FOX, Irving. Medical entomology. b'12. AB with distinction '37—AM '38 (Geo Wash U); PhD '40 (Ia State Coll). Studies on insects and related forms of medical importance; special aspects of population in relation to disease; discovery and description new species of fleas, mites, ticks, biting flies, spiders. Author articles in field. Contributor: Encyclopedia Britannica '46, '48. Instr biol U PR '41-42; asst prof med entomol Sch Tropical Med since '46. Served as lt to maj san corps AUS as malaria control officer in PR '42-46. Am Assn Econ Entomol —Am Soc Parasitol—Am Pub Health Assn—Entomol Soc Am—AAAS—Entomol Soc Wash—Biol Soc Wash—Am Soc Profl Biol—Am Soc Tropical Med —Soc Systematic Zool—Am Mosquito Control Assn—Royal Soc Tropical Med and Hygiene. School of Tropical Medicine, San Juan, P.R.

18 FOX, John Cameron. Mining. b'12. BS (Mining) '40 (Columbia). Study underground and surface mining methods; consultant on mineral exploration, mine surveying and management and use of explosives. Author article: Metal Mining Practice '49. Contributor: Canadian Mining Journ '47-50. Engr NJ Zinc Co '40-42; engr in charge stripping office and cost engr Nicaro Nickel Co Oriente Cuba '42-45; tech rep explosives dept E I DuPont de Nemours '46; asso mining School Mines Columbia U '46-50; ed Mining Congress Journ since '50. AIMME— Soc Bus Magazine Ed. Mining Congress Journal, 1102 Ring Bldg., Washington 6.

19 FOX, Marvin. Nuclear physics (Mass spectroscopy, radar). b'10. BS '31 (Carnegie Tech); MA '32—PhD '35 (Columbia U). Author articles in field. Chairman Reactor dept sci and engring Brookhaven Nat Lab since '46. Brookhaven National Laboratory, Upton, N.Y.†

20 FOX, William Basil. Dendrology; Taxonomy and distribution of native legumes and woody plants in North Carolina. b'15. Student '32-33, '34-35 (Concord State Teachers Coll); BS '39 —MS '40 (W Va U); PhD '42 (State U Ia). Research weed control '45-46, dendrology and plant taxonomy since '46. Author: The Leguminosae in Iowa '45; also articles in field. Asst agron Agrl Expt Sta State Coll Wash '45-46; asst prof bot NC State Coll since '46. Bot Soc Am—Am Soc Plant Taxonomists—NC Acad Sci—Sigma Xi. Botany Department, North Carolina State College, Raleigh, N.C.†

21 FRAAS, Arthur Paul. Combustion engines. b'15. BS '38 (Case Inst Tech); MS (Aeronautical engring) '43 (NY U). Research and development aircraft power plants, including work on cycle analysis, heat transfer, fluid flow, vibration, pumps, and compressors. Au-

thor: Aircraft Power Plants' 43; Combustion engines '48. Exptl test engr Wright Aeronautical Corp '38-40; exptl project engr aircraft engine div Packard Motor Car Co '43-45; asst prof automotive engrs Case Inst Tech '45-47; asso prof motors Instituto Tecnologico de Aeronautica Rio de Janeiro Brazil '47-50; prin design engr aircraft nuclear propulsion program Oak Ridge Nat Lab since '50. Am Rocket Soc—Inst Aeronautical Sci—Am Soc ME—Soc Automotive Engrs—Am Soc Engring Edn—Soc Exptl Stress Analysis. Oak Ridge National Laboratory, Oak Ridge, Tenn.

22 FRAIKIN, Leon Arthur. Soil mechanics; Piling; Caissons; Sand drains; Prestressed concrete. b'07. CE '29 (Y Ghent Belgium); MS '31 (MIT). CE La Sté des Pieux Franki Liege Belgium '31-35; cons engr found Braithwait and Co London '35-37; asst to chief engr McDonald Gibbs and Co Mohammed Ali barrages Cairo Egypt '37-38; vp mng dir Franki Compressed Pile Co Let Montreal since '38; dir Franki Found Co Pittsburgh since '51; prof applied soil mech Poly Sch U Montreal since '50. Association des Ingénieurs sortis de l'Université de Gand Belgique—Engring Inst Can—Profl Engr Quebec. Received Belgian Am Found Ednl Found Award 1930.

23 FRALICK, Samuel. Soccer. b'10. Grad '31 (Chicago Teacher's Coll); BE '35 (Northwestern U); '40 (Loyola U Chicago). Professional soccer player ten years, high school coach 12 years; publicity writer National Soccer League in Chicago; dir boy camp Eagle River Wis '46 asst dir Minocqua Wis '41 counselor boys camp Rhinelander Wis '43 operates Camp Big Chief for Boys Hayward Wis since '50; mem sports staff Chicago Herald American; basketball golf soccer coach Sullivan High School. Author: Soccer '44. Soccer ed Chicago Herald American '31-41; member rules com Chicago Pub High Schs; soccer referees unit US Nat Cup Tournament. Nat Soccer Coaches Assn —Midwest Camping Assn. Sullivan High School, 6631 N. Bosworth Av., Chicago.

24 FRAMPTON, Merle Elbert. Rehabilitation education of the blind and physically handicapped. b'03. B Religious Edn '25—AM '27—MS '28 (Boston U); AM '35—PhD '35 (Harvard); LLD '32 (Coll of the Ozarks Ark); LittD '40 (Missouri Valley Coll, Marshall Mo). Vice-chairman President's Committee on Employment of Physically Handicapped. Author: Family and Society '35; The Education of the Handicapped (vol I) '38, (vol II) '40; Methods of Teaching the Blind '40; Our Present Revolution '43; Rehabilitation in Theory and Practice '47. Prof edn and head dept Teachers Coll Columbia since '35; prin NY inst for Edn of Blind since '35; professor Hunter College NYC; director Am Printing House for Blind. NEA—Am Sociol Soc—Am Assn of Instrs and Workers for Blind (chmn findings com, chmn com war blinded)—Social Service Soc. 999 Pelham Parkway, NYC 67.◎

25 FRANCIONI, John Baptiste. Farm meats; Food preservation (Canning, curing sharp freezing); Animal husbandry. b'91. BS '14—MS '25 (La State U); '23, '30-31 (Ia State Coll). Did special meat work for National Livestock and Meat Board, organized and established School Community Food Preservation centers in Louisiana and Arkansas. Co-invented steam blancher and peeler for food preservation centers; developed cattle skinning cradle to speed up and facilitate skinning cattle regardless of size. Author articles in field. Professor, department animal industry Louisiana State University since '31. AAAS—Am Soc Animal Prodn—Am Genetics Assn—So Agrl Workers—Alpha Zeta—Phi Kappa Phi—Omicron Delta Kappa—Theta Zi. Received commendation from War Dept for assisting in developing overseas slaughtering outfit in World War II. Animal Industry Department, Louisiana State University, Baton Rouge, La.

10 FRANCIS, Richard J(ohn). Plastics (Reinforced, laminated, design and tooling); Fibrous glass; Printed Circuits; Adhesives. b'10. ChE '34 (U Cincinnati). Co-author: Low-Pressure Laminating of Plastics '47; also articles in field. Consulting engineer. Nat Soc Profl Engrs—O Soc Profl Engrs—Soc Plastics Ind—Am Inst Chem Engrs—Am Chem Soc—Soc Plastics Engrs—Am Soc ME—Sigma Xi—Alpha Chi Sigma. Received two individual Navy citations for developing methods of molding reinforced plastics and reinforcements for plastics. 105 South 33rd St., Newark, Ohio.☉

11 FRANK, John (Geisenberger). Medieval and modern German literature; German-American relations. b'96. Student (Gymnasium, U Munich); PhD '31 (U Mich). Author: Hans Carossa '43; Two Modes of Minnesong '41; Tristan and Isolde '47; Parzifal '48; The Old South in French and German Literature '46; Hessian Letters from the War of Revolution '48. Prof Germ Am U Wash since '48. Mod Lang Assn—Assn Teachers Germ—Assn Teachers Russian. American University, Nebraska and Massachusetts Av., Washington.

12 FRANKENSTEIN, Alfred. American art history (Nineteenth century still-life paintings); Music history. b'06. PhB '32 (U Chicago); '30 (Yale). Managed 19th Festival International Society for Contemporary Music Berkeley California '42; discovered pictures by Hartmann, Russian architect and water color painter, on which is based well known musical composition Pictures at an Exhibition by Moussorgsky. Music and art ed San Francisco Chronicle since '34; inst music, art U Cal Ext Div. Am Fedn Musicians—Am Musicol Soc. Awarded Guggenheim fellowship '47 for research in Am still-life painting resulting in volume: After the Hunt '51. 901 Mission St., SF.☉

13 FRANKFORT, Henri. Ancient history; Egyptology; Assyriology. b'97. MA '24 (U London); PhD '27 (U Leiden). Director of excavations for Egypt Exploration Society London at Abydos, Tell El Amarna and Erment '25-29; field director Iraq Expedition of Oriental Institute University of Chicago '29-37. Author: Studies in Early Pottery of the Near East, I '24, II '27; Archaeology and the Sumerian Problem '32; Cylinder Seals, A Documentary Essay on the Art and Religion of the Ancient Near East '39; Sculpture of the Third Millennium BC from Tell Asmar and Khafajah '39; Kingship and the Gods, An Essay on Ancient Near Eastern Religion as the Integration of Society and Nature '47; Ancient Egyptian Religion '48; The Birth of Civilization in the Near East '51; also articles in field. Professor U Chicago '32-49; now Warburg Inst director, professor of pre-classical antiquity Univ London. Royal Anthrop Inst Gt Brit and Ireland—Am Philos Soc—Royal Netherlands Acad Sci (foreign member)—Egypt Exploration Soc. Warburg Inst., Univ of London, Imp. Inst. Buildings, London, S.W.7, Eng.†

14 FRANKFORTER, Weldon DeLoss. Pleistocene geology; Fossil bison. b'20. BSc '44—MSc '49 (U Neb). Articles in field. Asso curator paleontol U Neb State Mus and instructor geology, dept U Neb since '50. Society Vertebrate Paleontol—Am Soc Mammal—Soc Am Archaeol—Neb Acad Sci—Geol Soc Am—Ia Archeol Soc—Ia Acad Scis—Am Assn Museums—Sigma Xi. Sanford Museum, 117 E. Willow St., Cherokee, Ia.

15 FRANKLIN, DeLance Flournoy. Vegetable seed production; Hybrid onion breeding. b'09. BS '42 (U Idaho). Author articles in field. Supt U Ida Br Expt Sta since '42, asso hort Ida Agrl Expt Sta since '46, collaborator US Dept Agr Bur Plant Industry Soils Agrl Engring since '43. Am Soc Hort Sci—AAAS—Sigma Xi. Branch Experiment Station, Parma, Ida.

16 FRANKLIN, John Hope. American Negro; History of the southern United States. b'15. AB '35 (Fisk U); AM '36—PhD '41 (Harvard). Author: The Free Negro in North Carolina, 1790-1860 '43; From Slavery to Freedom: A History of American Negroes '47. Editor: The Civil War Diary of James T Ayers '47; also articles in field. Prof hist St Augustines Coll '39-43, NC Coll '43-47, Howard U since '47. Social Sci Research Council(F)—AHA—So Hist Assn—Assn Study Negro Life and Hist—Ill State Hist Soc—Am Acad Polit Social Sci. Awarded Frederic Bancroft Prize Journal Negro History '45, second place Stern Essay Contest Ill State Hist Soc '47; Edward Austin fellow Harvard '37-38; Rosenwald fellow '37-39. Howard University, Washington.

17 FRANKLIN, Mitchell. Law (European, Latin-American, comparative, Roman, civil, history, commercial, international, constitutional, conflict). b'02. AB '22—LLB '25—SJD '28 (Harvard U). Legal adviser United Nations Relief and Rehabilitation Administration southeastern Europe, Middle East, headquarters Rome '46; US Reporter Congresses of Comparative Law The Hague; member Legal Secretariat of United Nations to codify international law '48. Author articles in field. Law sec Supreme Judicial Ct Mass '25-28; pvt law practice NYC '28-30; W R Irby prof law Tulane U New Orleans La since '30. NY, La, Am Bar Assns—Nat Lawyers Guild. Awarded Guggenheim fellowship '46; Rosenwald fellow (Paris) '39; Fulbright lectureship (France) '50. Tulane Law School, New Orleans 15.

18 FRANKLIN, Raymond Earl. Alluvial mining (Gold, tin). b'85. EE '07 (Oakland Tech Inst); spl courses '08-09 (U Calif, Stanford). Exploration and examination placer mining projects in Yukon Territory, Alaska, British Columbia; Malaya, Siam, Burma, Indonesia, Philippines; Chile, Peru, Bolivia, Ecuador, Colombia, Venezuela, Guianas, Amazon Country, Central America, Mexico, West Indies; Western US; West and Central Africa. Design and construction gold and tin dredges. Co-author article: (with John B. Huttl) Aluminum dredge designed for difficult placer job. Supt power and water supply Yukon Gold Co Yukon Ty '07-17, chief engr and asst gen mgr Yukon Gold Co Malay Peninsula '19-23; gen mgr Pato Consol Gold Dredging Ltd since '37, Asnazu Gold Dredging Ltd since '37, Nechi Consol Dredging Ltd since '46; dir cons engr Placer Development Ltd since '39, Bulolo Gold Dredging Ltd since '39. Am Inst EE—AIMME—Soc Am Mil Engrs. Russ Building, San Francisco 4.

19 FRANKLIN, Wallace Collin. Law. Prep education (So Normal Bowling Green Ky); LLB '02—LIM '03 (George Washington University). Atty Tidal Oil Co '17, vp and gen counsel '22-30; now engaged pvt practice law. Am Bar Assn—Tulsa County Bar—Okla Bar Assn—Am Petroleum Inst. Mayo Bldg., Tulsa.☉

20 RANKLIN, Woodrow Wilson. Alfalfa (Pollinating and injurious insects); Soil insects. b'18. BS '42 (McPherson Coll); PhD '50 (Kan State Coll). Methods of control injurious insects, and increase of population of pollinating insects; determination varieties of soil insects injurious to wheat plants in Kansas, and study of methods for their control. Author articles: Control of Injurious Insects in Alfalfa Fields Being Left for Seed; Insects Affecting Alfalfa Seed Production in Kansas. Faculty Kan State Coll since '48, asst prof entomol since '50. Kan Acad Sci—Sci Research Soc Am—Biometric Soc—Am Assn Econ Entomol—AAAS—Gamma Sigma Delta—Sigma Xi. Fort Hays Experiment Station, Hays, Kan.

21 FRANQUIZ, Jose Antonio. Personalism; Borden Parker Bowne; Philosophy in Latin America; Latin American cultural affairs; Juvenile and adult delinquency (Puerto Rico). b'06. AB '30 (Colgate U); STB '33 (Boston U Sch Theol); PhD '40 (Boston U Grad Sch); '26-27, '38 (U Puerto Rico). Author: Introspection as Fundamental Method '34; Personalism and Spiritual Values '36; Place of Man in the Cosmos '38; Delinquency in Puerto Rico in the Light of Abnormal Psychology '35; Abnormal Psychology and Human Suffering '38; In Nature of Mind '35; Dewey's Logic and Epistemology '40; Koehler's Philosophy of Science '44, and others; also articles in field. Head dept, prof philos W Va Wesleyan Coll since '46. Am Philos Assn—Am Acad Polit Social Sci—AAAS—Nat Edn Assn—AAUP—Internat Phenomenal Assn—Philos Soc W Va (pres '48-49)—W Va Assn Higher Edn. Hostos Memorial Medal '39 and others. Department of Philosophy, West Virginia Wesleyan College, Buckhannon, West Va.†

22 FRANTZ, Horace Gawthrop. Trout breeding. b'91. Ed pub schs. Research and experiment in proper breeding of rainbow trout for the market. Owner largest trout farm in the world. Frantzhurst Rainbow Trout Co., Salida, Colo.

23 FRANTZ, Samuel Gibson. Magnetic separation. b'97. CE '18—MS '23 (Princeton). Inventor of hydraulic coal breaker, various separation and radio inventions. Author articles in field. Cons engr since '27; organized S G Frantz Co '36, pres since '36. Am Ceramic Soc—Am Ordnance Assn—Phi Beta Kappa—Sigma Xi. c/o S. G. Frantz Co. Inc., Trenton N.J.

24 FRANZÉN, Carl Gustave Frederick. Secondary education (Curriculum, especially English, foreign language, mathematics); Teacher education. b'86. AB '08 (U Pa); MA '12—PhD '20 (Ia State U). Author: (with A T Stanforth) Observation and Study Manual '41; Improvement Sheets for teaching high sch subjects '49; Principles of Secondary Education '51. Joint author: The High School Curriculum '47. Prof secondary edn Ind U since '27. AAAS(F)—Am Assn Sch Administrs—NEA—Nat Assn Secondary Sch Principals—Nat Soc Study Edn (mem nat comm for Coop Study Sec Sch Standards)—Phi Beta Kappa. School of Education, Indiana University, Bloomington, Ind.†☉

25 FRANZEN, Raymond. Public health (School children); Advertising (Effectiveness); Marketing research. b

'95. AB '17 (Harvard); PhD '20 (Columbia). Research on prevention of loss of 6-year molars in children, research on general physical examinations for cancer, development of scale for measuring susceptibility to advertising influence; consultant National Research Council. Author: Health Education Tests '29; Physical Measures of Growth and Nutrition '29; Public Health Aspects of Dental Decay in Children '30; Influence of Social and Economic Factors on Health of School Child '32; An Evaluation of School Health Procedures '33; Physical Defects; The Pathway to Correction '34. Co-author: (with F B Knight) Textbook Selection '22. Author articles in field. Dir research Des Moines Pub Sch '19-22; asst prof psychol and edn U Calif '22-25; research dir Am Child Health Assn '25-31; dir research J David Houser Asso '31-35, cons since '35. Sigma Xi—Am Psychol Assn(F)—Am Statis Assn—Soc Psychol Study Soc Issues—Inst Math Statis—Am Marketing Assn — Market Research Council. 10 Rockefeller Plaza, NYC 20.

10 **FRASER, Andrew.** Surveys (Business, economic and statistical). Engring diploma '20 (Dundee Tech Coll); BSc in civil elec and mech engring '20-24 (U Coll Dundee of St Andrews U); '25-27 (U London Sch Economics); AM in economics and edn '36 (George Washington U). Preparation and direction studies and reports on salaries, wages, hours, labor requirements, occupational pattern, employment and unemployment; institution systems for coordinating, evaluating and utilizing economic data; organization and administration surveys chemical and engineering professions; organization adminstrn and analyses questionnaire data for architectural profession. Author articles and reports of surveys. Joined US Bur Labor Statistics '35, sect chief to '42; sr economist and statistician UW US War Dept '42-45; acting dir operational planning div State Dept Office Fgn Liquidation Commr '45-48; internat economist and statistician Econ Cooperation Adminstrn '48-50; pvt cons practice Washington since '50 as Andrew Fraser Associates. Econometric Soc. 3125 38th St., Washington 16.

11 **FRASER, Donald Alexander.** Forests (Ecology). b'18. BA '40—PhD '50 (U Toronto Ont Can); '41-43 (U London Eng). Author articles: Production of Spring Wood with Heteroauxin '49; Soil Types of Balsam Fir in Northern Ontario '49; Seasonal Growth of Some Trees in Ontario '51. Soils surveyor research div Ont Dept Lands and Forests '45-48; demonstrator dept bot U Toronto '45-48; lecturer dept bot U Alberta '48-49; forest col Forest Insect Lab Dominion Dept Agr Sault Ste Marie since '49. Bot Soc Am—Am Soc Plant Taxonomists—Ecol Soc Am—Can Soc Forest Engrs—Brit Ecol Soc—Am Fern Soc—Arctic Inst NA. Forest Insect Laboratory, Sault Ste. Marie, Ont., Can.

12 **FRASER, Gladys Spicer.** Folk customs; Festivals. AB '16 (Vassar Coll); AM '18 (Radcliffe Coll); '24-25, '31, '33 (Columbia); '37 (Coll City NY). Research on folk customs and European village life of Scandinavia, Finland, Russia, France, Spain, Italy, and other countries; research on traditional foods and ceremonies. Author: Folk Festivals and the Foreign Community '23; Book of Festivals '37; Holiday Parties '39; Parties for Young Americans '40; Latin American Costumes '41; Windows Open to the World '46; From an English Oven '48. Folklore and folk art spl Dept Immigration and Fgn Communities, Nat Bd Young Women's Christian Assn '19-29; dir Nat Communities Dept Brooklyn Young Women's Christian Assn '45-47; program and resch cons Am Fedn Internat Inst '51; ed asst Lewis Hist Pub Co '51. Brit Folklore Soc. H: 1 Greenridge Av., White Plains, N.Y.

13 **FRASER, Henry S.** International and constitutional law. BA '22 (Haverford Coll); LLB '26 (Cornell Law Sch). Technical advisor on territorial waters to League of Nations committee of experts for progressive codification international law '25-27; obtained royal pardons Belgrade under religious minority treaty for 150 conscientious objectors imprisoned by Yugoslav government '27; director research Constitutional Convention Albany revising New York State Constitution '38; chief counsel US Senate Special Committee Investigating Petroleum Resources '45-47. Author: Treaties and Executive Agreements '44; Diplomatic Protection of American Petroleum Interests in Mesopotamia, Netherlands East Indies, and Mexico '45; Questions and Answers as to Legal Aspects of the Anglo-American Petroleum Agreement '47; Civilian Defense Manual on Legal Aspects of Civilian Protection '43; also articles in field. Mem bar US Supreme Ct since '30; mem Frazer Brothers law firm since '38; ed Lawyer Service Letter NY State Bar Assn since '36. Am Bar Assn—NY State Bar Assn—Harvard Research Internat Law (mem advs com)—Am Soc Internat Law—AHA—Phi Beta Kappa. Chamber of Commerce Bldg., Syracuse 2, N.Y.†⊚

14 **FRASER, Hugh Russell.** American history (Andrew Jackson, R J Walker, Martin Van Buren, John Tyler); American education (Statistics, secondary curriculum). b'01. Ed Mt Hermon Mass Prep Sch '17-19. Author of plan for, co-designer with Allan Nevins Columbia University of Pulitzer prize-winning New York Times American history survey of 7000 college freshmen in 36 colleges '43. Author: Democracy in the Making: The Jackson-Tyler Era '38; also articles in field. Asso ed Pathfinder mag since '46. 1829 Summit Pl., N.W., Washington.

15 **FRASER, Ian Forbes.** French literature; French-Canada. b'07. BA '29 —MA '33—PhD '39 (Columbia); diploma '30 (U Paris). Author: Bibliography of French-Canadian Poetry '35; The Spirit of French Canada '39. Instr dept French Columbia U NYC '30-47, dir Maison Francaise '40-46, asst to dean '37-47; dir Am Lib in Paris France since '47. Modern Lang Assn Am—Am Assn Teachers French. Chevalier de la Legion d' Honneur, Officier de l'Instruction Publique. 149 W. 12th St., NYC 11.

16 **FRASER, R. Lee.** Power plants (Electric). b'14. Student '31-32 (Ark Poly); '32-33 (Tulane); BS (CE) '37 (U Ark). Construction designs and alterations. Engr and insp constrn hydro dams and power plants Grand River Okla and Santee Cooper SC '38-40; engr and supt constrn steam-elec power plants since '42. Am Soc CE. Ebasco Services, Two Rector St., N.Y.C. H: McCrory, Ark.

17 **FRASER, Samuel.** Fruit production, distribution. b'76. Student '96-98 (Cheshire Agrl Coll Holmes Chapel Eng); MS in agr '05 (Cornell U). Apple, pear, world statistics, production, marketing distribution, transportation, tariffs and problems in world trade. Author: The Potato '05; American Fruits '24 (rev edit) '27; The Strawberry '27. Co-author: (with R G Phillips) Distribution of Fruits and Vegetables '22. Fruitgrower, Nurseryman

since '06; economist Internat Apple Assn '19-41, sec '41-51, exec vp since '51. Royal Soc Arts London(F)—AAAS (F)—Sigma Xi. 1302 18th St., Washington 6.⊚

18 **FRAYNE, Nathaniel Zebulon.** Worms (Parasitic). b'11. BS '34—MS '35 (U Va); DDS '39 (U Pa). Discovered new specie Ectoparasitic Trematode, Choricotyle reynoldsi; redescribed related speci Choricotyle cynosioni. Author article: The morphology of two monogenetic Trematodes. Am Micros Soc—AAAS—Alpha Omega. 85 Van Reypen St., Jersey City 6, N.J.

19 **FRAZER, Robert Walter.** History of Latin America and the United States; Inter-American relations 1860-1890. b'11. BA '36—MA '40—PhD '41 (U Calif Los Angeles). Author articles: The Ochoa Bond Negotiations '42; Maximilian's Propaganda Activities in the United States '44; Trade Between California and the Belligerent Powers During the French Intervention in Mexico '46; The Truce of Altmark '47; Latin American Projects to Aid Mexico during the French Intervention '48. Asst prof hist Adams State Teach Coll Alamosa Colo '40-42; asst prof hist Wichita (Kan) U '46-48, prof since '50. AHA—Latin American Conf—Am Geog So (F). University of Wichita, Wichita 14, Kan.

20 **FRAZIER, John C(arroll).** Plant physiology; Weed control. b'00. AB '25 (Depauw U); MA '26 (U Neb); PhD '39 (U Chicago). Research on nature of root systems of such noxious perennial weeds as field bindweed, hoary cress; Russian knapweed, and on food reserves of such weeds in relation to control; studies of low and high temperatures and drought effects on hard red winter wheat. Author articles in field. Asst prof bot and bact Ill Wesleyan U '27-36; instr bot Kan State Coll Agr Applied Sci '36, prof plant physiol since '47; plant physiol Kan Agrl Expt Sta since '45. AAAS (F)—Bot Soc Am—Am Soc Plant Physiol—Am Chem Soc—Am Soc Agron—Am Soc Hort Sci—Kan Acad Sci (sec '41-44)—Ill Acad Sci—Sigma Xi—Gamma Sigma Delta. Department of Botany, Kansas State College, Manhattan, Kan.

21 **FRAZIER, John Earl.** Mechanical engineering (Glass, ceramic, and steel industries, furnace arches and doors, heat treating ovens). b'02. BS '22 (Washington and Jefferson Coll); '22-24 (MIT); ScD '38 (Academie de Sciencias e Artes, Brazil). Co-author: Glass Sand and a Glass Industry in Puerto Rico; also articles in field. Pres and sec Frazier-Simplex Inc Washington Pa since '45. Am Ceramic Soc(F) —Royal Soc Arts of England(F)—AA AS—Am Inst Min & Met Engrs— Am Chem Soc—Am Soc Mil Engrs— Nat Soc Profl Engrs—Am Soc Heating Ventilating Engrs (mem tech adv com on glass)—Inst Ceramic Engrs— Soc Glass Tech, Eng—Pa Atomic Scientists—Pa Ceramics Assn (dir, mem pub relations com)—Phi Chi Mu—Phi Beta Kappa. 436 East Beau St., Washington, Pa.

22 **FRAZIER, Richard Henry.** Guided missiles (Problems of flight and control); Electric circuit analogs. b'00. SB '23—SM '32 (MIT). Author: Elementary Electric Circuit Theory '45; also articles in field. Elec engr Ry and Indsl Engring Co Pa '23-25; instr elec engring MIT '25-31, asst prof '31-37, asso prof since '37; instr elec measurements The Lowell Inst Sch '26-31, charge elec measurements lab '31-35; cons engr. AIEE — ASEE. Massachusetts Institute of Technology, Cambridge 39, Mass.†

10 FRAZIER, Russell G. Climatology; West United States rivers explorations. b'93. DSc (hon) '38 (Morris Harvey Coll); MD '19 (U Louisville). Head expedition by boat Green River Utah '33; head expedition from Grand Canyon Colorado River to Boulder Dam '34; member archaeological and geological expedition middle and main fork Salmon River '36; memmer archaeological and historical expedition establishing route and Colorado River crossing of Father Escelante, first white man in Utah '37; head expedition discovering most northern American cliff dwellings near Yampa River Colorado '38; physician and surgeon United States Antarctic Expedition (Byrd's third expedition) studying climatology and physiology '39-41. Chief mine surgeon Utah Copper Co Bingham Canyon Utah '21-52. Royal Geog Soc(F)—Am Geog Soc(F)—Am Polar Soc—Am Med Soc—Utah Acad Arts Sci. 4177 S. 23d E., Salt Lake City.

11 FREAD, Bernard. Refractive errors (Etiology and symptomatology); Eye (Muscle exercise). b'04. BS '25 (Coll City NY); MD '29 (Cornell U). Founder orthoptic (eye muscle exercise) clinic Bellevue Hospital '32. Asst clin prof ophthalmology Med Coll NYU since '43, former grad instr refraction and optics; dir eye service psychopathic div Bellevue Hosp. Am Bd Ophthalmology (Diplomate)—NY Acad Med (F eye sect)—Nat Bd Med Examiners (Diplomate)—Ophthalmol Soc United Kingdom (Am mem)—Societe Francaise d'ophthalmologie—Am Optical Soc—Am Inst Physics—NY Clin Ophthalmol. 45 E. 85th St., NYC 28.

12 FREAR, Donald Elisha Harding. Pest control chemicals (Insecticides, fungicides, herbicides, rodenticides). b'06. BS '26—PhD '37 (Pa State Coll); MS '28 (Univ NH). Research in relation of chemical structure to biological properties, pyridine derivatives as insecticides, fungicides and bactericides; developed first course in US on chemistry of insecticides and fungicides for college students. Author: Chemistry of Insecticides and Fungicides '42; Chemistry of Insecticides, Fungicides, Herbicides '48; Catalogue of Insecticides and Fungicides, vol I '47, vol II '48; Agricultural Chemistry, vol I '50, vol II '51; also articles. Prof agrl chem Pa State Coll since '41. Gamma Sigma Delta—Sigma Xi—Phi Lambda Upsilon — Alpha Zeta — Am Chem Soc—Am Soc Hort Sci—Am Soc Biol Chem—Am Assn Econ Entomol—Nat Research Council. Department of Agricultural Biochemistry, Pennsylvania State College, State College, Pa. H: 311 E. Park Av.

13 FRECHETTE, Van Derck. Petrography; X-ray diffraction; Ceramic technology. b'16. Student '34-36 (U Toronto); BS '38 (Alfred U); MS '40—PhD '42 (U Ill). Participated in International Congress on Vitreous Enameling London '48, Colloquium on Solid State Reactions Paris '48, International Symposium on Reactivity of Solids Sweden '52. Author articles in field. Professor ceramic technology NY State Coll of Ceramics at Alfred U since '44. Am Ceramic Soc—Brit Ceramic Soc—Can Ceramic Soc—Soc Glass Tech—Mineral Soc Am—Am Crystallographic Assn—Sigma Xi. New York State College of Ceramics, Alfred University, Alfred, N.Y.†

14 FREDENHAGEN, Victor Byron. Soil conservation; Flood control. b'88. BS (CE) '10 (U Ill). Land management for control of run-off and soil erosion; rainfall, evaporation and transportation, infiltration, ground waters, flood control, cropping practices, and contour farming; control of erosion by irrigation and drainage facilities, and building of terraces, dams, and gully control structures. Engr Kan Highway Commn Topeka '20-21; co engr Jewell Co Kan '21-29, Republic Co Kan '29-33; with Soil Conservation Service USDA since '33, now zone conservationist. Soil Conservation Service, U.S. Department of Agriculture, Post Office Bldg., Lincoln, Neb.

15 FREDERICKSON, Edward Arthur. Paleontology (Upper Cambrian Trilobites). b'08. BA '30—PhD '42 (U Wis). Author articles in field. With U Okla since '40, prof geology since '51. Geol Soc Am—Okla Acad Sci—Paleontol Soc —Soc Econ Paleontol Mineral—Am Assn Petroleum Geol — Sigma Xi. Dept. of Geology, University of Oklahoma, Norman, Okla.†

16 FREDERIKSEN, Oliver Jul. Russian history and language. b'94. AB '16 (Dartmouth Coll); MA—PhD '34 (Cornell U); '26 (Columbia). Research on Virginia tobacco in Russia under Peter the Great '43, Alexander I and his league to end wars '43, the Soviet and foreign relations '46. Translator and editor: Michael Hrushevsky, History of Ukraine '40; also articles in field. Fgn work sec Internat Council YMCA relief work and YMCA organization in Russia and Eastern Europe '22-32; asso prof hist Miami U Oxford O '34-43, '45-49; head Eastern European sect Fgn Nationalities Br OSS '43-45; chief historical consultant Headquarters European Command '49-52. AHA—Am Assn Teachers Slavic and East European Langs (sec-treas O chap)—Phi Beta Kappa. Miami University, Oxford, O.†

17 FREEDLEY, George. History of the theater and drama; Films; Radio. b'04. AB '25 (U Richmond); MFA drama '36 (Yale). Author: Theatre Collections in Libraries and Museums, An International Handbook '36. Co-author: A History of the Theatre '40. Collaborator: Bernard Sobel's Theatre Handbook and Digest of Plays '40; Theatrical Designs from the Baroque through Neo-Classicism '40; A History of Modern Drama '47; also articles in field. Actor and dir '28-31; in charge theater collection NY Pub Library '31-38, curator '38-47, cons '48-49, curator since '50; head Play Dept A&S Lyons Inc '48-49, dramatic critic Morning Telegraph '40-49, book and record editor, columnist since '49. New York Drama Critics Circle (fgn corr sec)—Theatre Library Assn (pres)—US Centre Internat Theatre Inst (mem Am delegation Paris Conf '47)—Am Nat Theatre and Acad (bd dirs). Awarded Carnegie ALA traveling fellowship '34-35. 19 E. 55th St., NYC 22.⊚

18 FREEMAN, Ethel Cutler (Mrs. Leon S. Freeman). Seminole Indians of Florida; Primitive peoples (Americas, Mexico, West Indies); Cultural dynamics and change (Laws); Indians of North America and Mexico (Kickapoo, Pueblo, Navajo, Papagos). Grad (Miss Dana's Sch Morristown NJ); student (Mlle Souvestre's Sch Allenswood Wimbledon Eng). Author: Seminole Indians in Florida; also articles in field. Asso with Am Mus Nat Hist NYC dept anthrop since '38, yearly field trips for Mus to study various tribes. Archaeol Inst Am (trustee)—Society of Woman Geographers—Am Ethnol Soc—Fla Hist Soc—Hist Soc So Fla—Seminole Indian Assn Fla (2nd vp)—Nat Council Historic Sites and Bldgs (asso). Department of Anthropology, American Museum of Natural History, Central Park West at 79th St., NYC. H: Blue Mill Rd., Morristown, N.J.

19 FREEDMAN, Louis. Processing and biochemistry of vitamins. b'94. PhB '15—MS '17—Sheffield fellow '15-16—Indsl fellow '16-17 (Yale); PhD '22 (Columbia). Inventor vitamin and mineral composition, preparation of fat soluble vitamins, co-inventor suprarenin derivatives, vitamin-free products, process for extraction of fat-soluble vitamins, extraction apparatus for fat-soluble vitamins, fat-soluble vitamin solutions, all patented. Author articles in field. Research chem Calco Chem Co '17-19, HA Letz Labs Brooklyn '19-32, Winthrop-Metz Research Labs '32-36; dir research US Vitamin Corp since '36, vp since '47. Soc Exptl Biol and Med—Am Chem Soc—AIC(F) —AAAS—NY Acad Sci—Yale Engring Assn—Chem Club NY. 250 E. 43rd St., NYC 17. H: 1 Parkway East, Mount Vernon.†

20 FREEMAN, Ira Henry. Sail yachting; Long-distance cruises in sailing yachts. b'06. LittB '28 (Columbia). Author: White Sails Shaking '48, also articles in field. News Department, New York Times, 229 W. 43rd St., N.Y.C.

21 FREEMAN, Ira Maximilian. Theoretical physics; Science interpretation. b'05. BS '25—MS '26—PhD '28 (U Chicago); fellow Inst Internat Edn and Von Humboldt Found '28-30 (J Wolfgang Goethe U, Germany). Research on spectrum of hydrogen, astronomical spectroscopy, meson, optics, physiological mechanics; research associate US National Defense Research Committee Princeton '42-45; member Princeton Solar Eclipse Expedition '45. Author: Elementary Survey of Physics (with A Haas) '38; Invitation to Experiment '40; Physics (with W F G Swann) '41; Practical Physics (contributor) '43; Modern Introductory Physics '49. Collaborating author: Theoretical Physics (eng trans Joos') '49; also articles in field. Asso prof physics Rutgers U since '47. AAAS(F)—Sigma Xi—Phi Beta Kappa. Department of Physics, Rutgers University, New Brunswick, NJ.†

22 FREEMAN, James Nelson. Agricultural education; Soil technology. b '04. BSA '25 (Hampton Inst); MS '34 (Ia State Coll); PhD '45 (Cornell U). Studies program education in agriculture for negroes of Missouri based on analysis of economic factors and social activities in selected rural communities; research on drainage of crop lands in the Missouri river bottoms. Author articles in field. Instr agrl edn and poultry NC A&T Coll '26-29, SC State Coll '29-33, Prairie View State Coll Tex '34-35; supervisor agrl edn state dept edn Tex '35-39; head dept agr, dir u farms Lincoln U since '39. Sigma Alpha—Phi Delta Kappa—Am Vocational Assn—Soc for Agron—AA UP—Mo State Teachers Assn—Nat Negro Bus League—dirs and leaders Negro Land-Grant Colls. Awarded Modern Farmers and Superior Farmers Degree by Nat Assn New Farmers Am. Lincoln University, Jefferson City, Mo.

23 FREEMAN, Joseph. Novel (Proust, Flaubert); Poetry; European history (French revolution, Soviet Russia, Germany); Socialism; Modern painting; United States civil liberties. b'97. AB '19 (Columbia). Co-founder New Masses '26; active in founding of Theatre Union. Author: (with Scott Nearing) Dollar Diplomacy '25; (with Joshua Kunitz, Louis Lozowick) Voices of October '30; The Soviet Worker '32; An American Testament '36; Never Call Retreat '43; The Long Pursuit '47; also articles in field. Lecturer since '22. Authors League Am—PEN—Phi Beta Kappa. 301 E. 38th St., NYC 16.

10 FREEMAN, Otis Willard. Geography and economic geology (Pacific Northwest, Hawaii, Pacific area). b'89. AB '10 (Albion Coll); MS '13 (U Mich); PhD '29 (Clark U). Specialist for geography in higher education Office of Education Washington '48; geography editor Education since '41. Author: Geography of Washington '32; Economic Geography of Hawaii '27; The Story of the Hawaiian Islands '35; Essentials of Geography '49; Geography of Pacific '51. Co-author: The Pacific Northwest. Prof geog, head dept phys sci Eastern Wash Coll Edn '24-50, pres since '51; acting state geol Ind '45. Assn Am Geog—Assn Pacific Coast Geog (pres '34, editor '35-39, sec '46-48)—Am Meteorol Soc—Nat Council Geog Teachers—Northwest Sci Assn (sec '38-43, pres '48)—AAAS—Am Geophys Union —Sigma Xi. Eastern Washington College of Education, Cheney, Wash.⊚

11 FREEMAN, Roslyn Weller. Music (Psychology). b'02. Grad '22 (Jamaica Training Sch for Teachers); spl courses (Rutgers, Pa State, Columbia, NYU, U So Calif) '27 (Bklyn Law Sch). Composer, pianist. Author: Music for the Maladjusted '48; Motion and Music for the Maladjusted '49. Teacher Adjustment Sch for Delinquent Boys NYC since '46. 113 E. 87th St., N.Y.C.

12 FREEMAN, Sarah Elizabeth. Numismatics; Medals (Medical, American development, early American engravers and medallists); Classical archaeology. b'06. BA '28 (Mount Holyoke Coll); '28-29 (Bryn Mawr Grad Sch); PhD '34 (Johns Hopkins); fellow '31-32 (Am Sch Classical Studies Athens). Staff American excavations at Corinth '32-33. Author articles in field. Curator fine arts Johns Hopkins U since '44. Arch Inst Am (sec Baltimore chap)— Am Numismatic Soc(F)—Photographic Soc Am—Phi Beta Kappa. Johns Hopkins University, Baltimore 18.

13 FREEMAN, Theodore Russell. Dairy chemistry; Cheese manufacture. b'06. BS '29 (Kan State Agrl Coll); MS '33 (Okla A&M Coll); PhD '37 (Pa State Coll). Research on storage of dairy products, wartime problems in ice cream manufacture, composition of milk and certain physical-chemical properties, cheese ripening, methods of analysis and methods of accelerating ripening. Author: New Methods of Preparing Invert Sirup. Co-author: Dairy Manufacturing Processes '48; Rate of Ripening in Cheddar Cheese; Storing Frozen Cream; also articles in field. Asso prof dairy husbandry A&M Coll Tex '37-41; asso in dairy manufactures Fla Agrl Expt Sta '41-46, U Ky since '48. Am Dairy Sci Assn—Internat Assn Milk and Food Sanitarians—Inst Food Tech—Sigma Xi. Dairy Section, University of Kentucky, Lexington 29, Ky.

14 FREEMAN, Thomas Nesbitt. Butterflies. b'11. BSA, MSc, PhD. Specializing in insect taxonomy and evolution. Author articles in field. Insect pest investigator Dept Agr Can '35-36; agrl asst dept agr div entomol Ottawa '41, agrl sci '45-47, co-ordinator No Insect Survey Dept Agr div entomol Ottawa since '48. Am Entomol Soc— Ontario Entomol Soc—Sigma Xi. Room 335 Science Service Building, Division Entomology, Department of Agriculture, Central Experiment Farm, Ottawa, Ontario, Can.

15 FREEMAN, Warren Samuel. Photograph recordings; Music education. b'11. MusB '32—MEd '37 (Boston U); student '38 (Harvard). Author: Story of Music '37; The Key '41; How to Teach Children to Know Music '40; Children's Record Book '44; Recordings for Elementary Schools '49; Songs

to Sing '46; Time and Tune '38; Children's Book of Composers '51; Adventures in Singing '51. Dir music edn pub schs Haverhill Mass '32-35, State Tchrs Coll Hyannis Mass '35-37, Belmont Mass '37-46; with Boston U since '46, dean coll music since '49; mgr Eastern Music Camp '33-34. Dir NE Philharmonic Orchestra, Boston Esplanade Children's Concerts '40-41, NE Opera Theatre, All Newton Music Sch, NE Music Festival Assn. Mass Music Educators Assn—Music Educators Nat Conf—Musicians Protective Assn—Phi Delta Kappa—Sinfonia. 85 Newbury St., Boston 16. H: 15 Williston Rd., Auburndale 66, Mass.†⊚

16 FREITAS, Moacyr G. Animal parasitology. b'14. DVM (Escola Superior da Agricultura e Veterinaria do Estado de Minas Gerais, Vicosa); MSc (Mich State Coll). Research on parasites of domestic animals of Minas Gerais; overwintering nematode parasites of sheep; bionomics of rice fever, Boophilus microplus and habronemiasis of horse. Prof animal parasitology Veterinary Sch Rural U State Minas Gerais Brazil since '42. Biol Soc State Minas Gerais—Am Soc Parasitologists—Sigma Xi. Escola Superior de Veterinaria, Caixa Posta, 567 Belo Horizonte Minas Gerais, Brazil.

17 FRENCH, Arthur Perkins. Fruit varieties (Trueness to name); Genetics of the peach. b'95. BSc '21 (O State U); MSc '23 (U Mass); PhD '50 (U Minn). Author articles in field. Prof pomol and plant breeding U Mass '36-47, head dept pomol since '47. Am Soc Hort Sci—Genetics Soc Am—Sigma Xi—Phi Kappa Phi. French Hall, University of Massachusetts, Amherst, Mass.†

18 FRENCH, C(harles) Stacy. Biochemistry (Plant physiology, photosynthesis). b'07. '21-25 (Loomis Inst); BS '30—MA '32—PhD '34 (Harvard). Author articles in field. Guest worker with O Warburg Kaiser Wilhelm Inst Berlin-Dahlem Germany '35-36; asst prof dept bot U Minn '41-45, asso prof '45-47; dir div plant biol Carnegie Inst Washington Stanford U since '47. Am Soc Plant Physiol—Bot Soc Am—Am Chem Soc—Am Soc Biol Chem—Am Assn Sci Workers—AAAS. Carnegie Institution of Washington, Stanford, Calif.

19 FRENCH, Chester D. Enzymes (Chemistry); Papaya (Products, experimentation, agricultural development). b'87. Student '17 (U Calif Berkeley). Papaya in its native habitat; development Papaya products for commercial marketing; established experimental Papaya plantation from virgin jungle Muncipality Santiago de Esquinta, State Nayarit Mexico '36-46; member economic division US Navy instituting interest in Papain production in Micronesia; exploration Papaya districts Pacific area, Orient, Mexico, Central and South America, East Africa and Brazil Ceylon since '27. Frenco Laboratories, P.O. Box 977, Nogales, Ariz. H: 531 Morley Av.

20 FRENCH, J(oseph) Milton. Seventeenth century English literature; John Milton. b'95. AB '17—AM '21— PhD '28 (Harvard). Author: Milton in Chancery '39. Editor: History of the Pestilence (by George Wither) '32; Charles Lamb: Essays and Letters '37; Bibliography of the Theophrastan Character in English (with Chester N Greenough) '47; The Life Records of John Milton vol I '49; vol II '50. Contrib ed: The Works of John Milton '31-38; also articles. Prof and head dept Eng Rutgers U since '40, acting dean coll arts and sci '44-45. Modern Lang Assn Am—Phi Beta Kappa. Rutgers University, New Brunswick, N.J.⊚

21 FRENCH, Reginald Foster. Italian Renaissance literature; Minstrel technique. b'06. AB '27 (Dartmouth); MA '28—PhD '35 (Harvard); student (U Rome). Author articles in field. Professor Romance langs Amherst Coll since '37. Phi Beta Kappa. 20 Grosvenor House, Amherst, Mass.

22 FRENCH, Sidney James. Inorganic chemistry; Indium and gallium fusible alloys; Science in education. b'94. BS '22 (U Chicago); MS '27—PhD '28 (U Wis). Author: The Drama of Chemistry '44; Atoms, Rocks and Galaxies (with others) '42; Torch and Crucible, The Life and Death of Antoine Lavoisier '41; The American Idea (with others) '42; also articles in field. Prof chem Franklin Coll '28-32; asst prof chem Colgate U '32-38, prof since '38, dean faculty since '45. Am Chem Soc —Phi Beta Kappa. Colgate University, Hamilton, N.Y.

23 FRESCOLN, Wilson Lysle. Old French Arthurian romance. b'12. AB '36—MA '38 (U Pa); CEF '38 (U De Grenoble). Instr Romance lang Villanova Coll since '47; ed J B Lippincott Co Phila '47-52; Modern Lang Assn Am—Medieval Acad Am—Societe des ancines textes francais—Internat Arthurian Soc. R.D. 3, Media, Pa.

24 FRETTER, William B(ache). Nucleonics; Radar. b'16. AB '37—PhD '46 (U Calif). Research on atomic physics, cosmic rays; research and development micro-wave radio, radar, high power radar jamming equipment, measured mass of meson. Author articles: Successive Multiple Production of Penetrating Particles (with W E Hazen) '46; The Mass of Cosmic Ray Mesotrons '46. Research asso MIT '41; research engr Westinghouse Elec Corp '41-45; asso Manhattan Project '45; Whiting fellow physics U Calif '45-46, instr physics '46, asso prof since '50. Am Phys Soc—Sigma Xi. University of California, Berkeley.

25 FREUND, Ludwig (Franz). Political philosophy; International relations. b'98. Student '18-19 (U Goettingen); '19-20 (U Heidelberg); '20-21 (U Munich); PhD '22 (U Leipzig). Research on relativism in social and political philosophy, relation of power and democratic processes, relation between freedom, equality and authority and between ethics and politics, relation of ethics and power in US and foreign policy. Author: Boundaries of Philosophy '30; Insoluble Problems of Philosophy '33; The Threat to European Culture '35; Sources of US-Foreign Policy '51; also articles in field. Prof polit sci and sociol Ripon Coll '38-47, chmn dept polit sci '46-47; prof polit sci Roosevelt Coll since '47, chmn dept polit sci from '50; guest prof polit sci U Erlangen and Coll Polit Sci Munich '51 and US spl polit sci US State Dept '51. Am Assn Polit Sci—Acad Polit Sci. Roosevelt College, 430 S. Michigan Av., Chicago 5. H: Hotel Webster, 2150 Lincoln Park W., Chicago 14.

26 FREUNDLICH, Leo. Cocoa and chocolate. b'99. Student '19-20 (U Heidelberg); PhD '23 (U Wuerzburg). Author articles in field. Research on control methods, improvement of yield, purity, use of by-products. With Eckroth Labs '24-29, Runkel Bros '29-31, Hooton Chocolate Co '31-51. American Assn Candy Tech—Am Chem Soc—Am Inst Chem(F). H: 129 N. Walnut St., East Orange, N.J.

27 FREVERT, Richard Keller. Soil permeability; Land drainage; Erosion control. b'14. BS '35—MS '40—PhD '48 (Ia State Coll); Certificate meteorology '43 (U Chicago). Developed field method of measuring permeability of soil below a water table. Research asst, and now assistant director Ia Agr Expt Sta since '46. Am Soc Agr Engring—Ia Engring Soc—Am Geophys Union—Sigma Xi—Phi Kappa Phi—Gamma Sigma Delta. Agricultural Experiment Station, Iowa State College, Ames, Ia.

10 FREY, Albert Jean. Pharmaceutical production; Extraction (Alkaloids). b'92. PhD '14 (U Berne). Large-scale production of pharmaceuticals such as synthetic vitamins and barbiturates, research on plant extraction and production of alkaloids, liquid-liquid extraction both simple and fractional. Granted patent on producing morphine and codeine. Co-author: (with Scheibel) Encyclopedia of Chemical Technology '51; Liquid-Liquid Extraction '51. Mfg and development chem '20-42; v-pres and dir Hoffmann-La Roche Inc since '45. NRC—ACS—AICE—Soc Chem Industry—Am Inst Chem—AAAS—Sci Research Soc Am. Hoffmann-La Roche Inc., Nutley, N.J.

11 FREY, David G(rover). Limnology; Pollen analysis; Fishery biology; Atyidae and Palaemonidae. b'15. BA '36—MA '38—PhD '40 (U Wis). Investigation Columbia River system to determine present abundance of salmon, possible causes of decline, means of increasing populations; surveys of ecological relationships of oysters in Potomac River and Chesepeake Bay, fresh water biota Japanese Mandated Islands to determine which vectors or intermediate hosts of human diseases are present; research on age, origin, productive history North Carolina lakes. Author articles in field. Aquatic biol US Fish and Wildlife Service '40-45; asso prof zool U NC '46-50; asso prof zool Indiana U and dir Indiana Lake and Stream Survey since '50. Am Soc Limnol Oceanog—Soc Study Evolution — Soc Zool Systematics — NC Acad Sci—Elisha Mitchell Sci Soc—Sigma Xi. Biology Hall, Bloomington, Ind.

12 FREY, Fred E. Petroleum chemistry (Hydrocarbon). b'99. BS '22 (Coll Wooster); MS '24 (O State U). Research on hydrocarbon analytical methods and hydrocarbon pyrolysis chemistry, reaction mechanism of hydrocarbon pyrolysis, thermodynamics, hydrocarbon catalytic reactions, process development. Holder patents in field. Author articles in field. Asst chem US Bur Mines '24-27; with Phillips Petroleum Co since '27, now asst dir research. Am Chem Soc—Sigma Xi—Phi Beta Kappa. Phillips Petroleum Co., Bartlesville, Okla.

13 FREY, Harold Alfred. Florida (Tourist industry). b'00. BA '23—MA '25—PhD '42 (U Wis); '26-27 (Harvard); MBA '28 (Northwestern U). Research on tourist trade of South Florida covering such items as point of origin, method of transportation, length of stay, preferences in amusements, lodgings, food, money spent. Author: The South Florida Visitor '48. Co-author: (with Dr Victor H Bennett) Survey of Tourist Industry of Greater Miami '49. Prof marketing U Toledo '30-41; free-lance market research '30-42; pres O Thermeron Co '36-39; dist econ OPA '42-43; prof marketing U Miami '45-49; head Market Research Asso '48-50; prof U Ark since '50. Phi Beta Kappa—Artus—Phi Kappa Phi—Alpha Delta Sigma—Advertising Fedn Am—Am Marketing Assn. 133-College of Business Administration, University of Arkansas, Fayetteville, Ark.

14 FREY, John William. Pennsylvania Dutch language and customs; Folklore. b'16. AB '37 (Dickinson Coll); '37-38 (Giessen U, Germany); MA '39—PhD '41 (U Ill); scholarship

linguistics and dialect geog '41 (Linguistic Inst); exchange-fellowship '37-38 (to Germany from Inst Internat Edn). Author: A Simple Grammar of Pennsylvania Dutch '42; also articles in field. Asst prof German French Russian Presbyn Coll Clinton SC '41-43; asst prof German ASTP Lehigh U '43-44; asst prof German Franklin and Marshall Coll Lancaster Pa '44-48, asso prof German and Russian since '48, head dept German since '45, dir Pa Dutch Folklore Center Inc since '49; co-ed The Pennsylvania Dutchman since '49. Pa German Soc—Pa German Folklore Soc—Modern Lang Assn Am—Linguistic Soc Am—Am Assn Teachers of German. Pennsylvania Dutch Folklore Center, Franklin and Marshall College, Lancaster, Pa.

15 FRIAUF, James J(oseph). Insect ecology; Invertebrate zoology. b'14. BS '36 (U Toledo); MA '37 (U Mich); PhD '42 (U Fla). Ecological and taxonomic studies of Orthoptera of southeastern US. Author articles in field. Asso prof zool Vanderbilt U since '46. AAAS—Am Ecol Soc—Ecol Union—Am Entomol Soc—Tenn Acad Sci—Assn SE Biol—Sigma Xi—Phi Kappa Phi. Department of Biology, Vanderbilt University, Nashville 4, Tenn.

16 FRICK, Thomas Adam. Plant ecology; Ferns (Taxonomy). b'01. AB '23 (Newberry Coll); AM '28 (U SC); PhD '37 (Peabody Coll). Author articles in field. Head biol dept Lincoln Memorial U since '42, also dean. Ecol Soc Am—Am Fern Soc—So Appalachian Bot Soc—Tenn Acad Sci. Lincoln Memorial University, Harrogate, Tenn.

17 FRIEDEL, Robert Augustine. Mass spectrometry; Infrared and ultraviolet absorption spectrometry; Reaction mechanism (Tracer Isotope applications); Instrumentation; Analysis of synthetic and natural hydrocarbon fuels, jet fuels, organic chemicals, air pollution. b'17. BA '39 (O State U); MS '40—DSc '43 (Carnegie Institute Technology). Author articles in field. Section leader spectrometric section research and development br Office Synthetic Liquid Fuels US Bur Mines since '45. Am Chem Soc—Am Phys Soc—Optical Soc Am—Sigma Xi. Synthetic Fuels Laboratory, U.S. Bureau of Mines, Bruceton, Pa.

18 FRIEDERICH, Werner Paul. Comparative literature (Literary relations western European countries, Renaissance to romanticism, United States and western Europe eighteenth to nineteenth century); Dante; literature (Swiss, German, Baroque). b'05. Maturitatszeugnis '24 — Schweizerisches Staatsexamen '31 (Bern U); MA '29—PhD '32 (Harvard); '25-27 (Sorbonne). Associate editor Comparative Literature since '48. Author: Die Schweiz '38; Kurze Geschichte des Deutschen Volkes '39; An Outline-History of German Literature '48; Werden und Wachsen der USA in 300 Jahren '39; Spiritualismus und Sensualismus in der englischen Barocklyrik '32; also articles in field. Professor German and comparative lit U NC since '35; Am rep Commn Internat d'Histoire Littéraire Moderne, Paris since '46. Modern Lang Assn Am (founder comparative lit sect)—Dante Soc Am. Box 775, Chapel Hill, N. C.

19 FRIEDLANDER, Gerhart. Radiochemistry; Nucleonics. b'16. BS '39—PhD '42 (U Calif). Research on nuclear reactions induced by high energy X-rays. Co-author: Introduction to Radiochemistry '49; also articles in field. Chem and group leader radiochem research and development Los Alamos Lab U Calif '43-46; research asso Gen Elec Co Research Lab

Schenectady NY '46-48; chem radiochem research Brookhaven Nat Lab Upton LI NY since '48. Am Chem Soc—Am Phys Soc—Phi Beta Kappa—Sigma Xi. Designated as one of ten ablest chemists in US in field of nucleonics, Chicago Sect Am Chem Soc poll in '47. Brookhaven National Laboratory, Upton, L.I., N.Y.

20 FRIEDMAN, Aaron. Food and rare earth chemistry. b'96. ChE '17 (Columbia); profl engr '34 (NY State). First person to make metallic lithium in US '19; research on food processing, ice cream, dried eggs, thorium, cerium. Holder US Patents in food technology. Editor Patent Reporter '32-41. Supt New Process Metal Works NJ '21-24; supt Kamchatka Fur Dyeing Co Brooklyn '24-26; research Wolff Alport Chem Co Brooklyn '26-30; pvt practice cons engr NYC '30-41; dir research and chem engr Joe Lowe Corp NYC since '41. Am Inst Chem(F)—Am Inst Food Tech—Am Assn Cereal Chem—Am Dairy Sci Assn—AAAS. 601 W. 26th St., NYC 1. H: 327 Central Park West, NYC 25.

21 FRIEDMAN, Leonard Seymour. Adult education. b'02. Student '19-32 (NYU); '23 (Columbia U); DD '35 (Coll Divine Metophysics); LLD (Webster U). Inaugurated half day school, half day work plan, adopted by many school systems and by US Department of Education in its war training program. Author: Fundamentals of Typewriting '42; Friedman Shorthand '43; also articles in field. Organized Abbe Inst '34. Am Assn Comml Coll—Eastern Comml Teachers Assn. 1697 Broadway, NYC.

22 FRIEDMAN, Maurice. Electrochemistry; Batteries; Galvanic cells. b'15. AB '36—MS '38 (NYU). Research and development on primary alkaline cells, materials for components used in electronic equipment; engineered miniature dry cell batteries used in hearing aids, geophysical instruments, personal radios, military electronic equipment; research on electrochemistry and technology of Ruben cell, new alkaline primary dry cell battery. Invented improved methods of manufacturing alkaline dry cells and batteries. Chief engr battery div P R Mallory and Co Inc '46-49. Am Chem Soc—Electrochem Soc—Faraday Soc, Eng—NY Acad Sci—AAAS—Army Signal Assn. Vice-pres of engineering, National Catalytic Battery Co., St. Paul.

23 FRIEDMAN, William Frederick. Cryptology; Communication security; Signal intelligence; Crypto-mechanisms; Cryptanalysis. b'91. BS '14 (Cornell U). Inventor of many cryptographic machines. Author: Riverbank Publications on Cryptography and Cryptanalysis '17-20. Prin cryptanalyst War Dept Washington since '21; dir communications research Army Sec Agency '42-49; chief tech div Armed Forces Sec Agency since '49. Act and inactive mil service '18-41. Medal for Merit, US govt highest award and decoration for exceptional civilian service '46. 424 N. Geo Mason Drive, Arlington, Va.

24 FRIEDMANN, Herbert. Birds of the world; Systematic ornithology; Animal symbolism in art. b'00. BSc '20 (Coll City NY); PhD '23 (Cornell U). Author: The Cowbirds: A Study in the Biology of Social Parasitism '29; The Parasitic Cuckoos of Africa '48; The Symbolic Goldfinch '46; The Birds of North and Middle America pt 9 '41, pt 10 '46, pt 11 '49; Birds Collected by Childs-Frick Expedition in Ethiopia and Kenya Colony pt 1 '30, pt 2 '37; Birds of Tropical East Africa '37, and others; also articles in field.

Curator div birds US Nat Mus since '29. AAAS(F)—Am Soc Zool—Am Soc Naturalists—Am Ornithol Union (pres '38-39)—Washington Acad Sci—Biol Soc Washington (ed since '32)—Coll Art Assn—Hist Sci Soc. Nat Research Council fellow '23-26. U.S. National Museum, Washington 25.⊙

10 FRIEDMANN, Robert. Mennonite, Anabaptist and Hutterite history. b'91. PhD '24 (U Vienna); hon fellow '40 (Yale Divinity Sch); research fellow '40-42 (Goshen Coll). In Europe was member commission for editing Anabaptist records of 16th and 17th centuries. Author: Mennonite Piety Through the Centuries '49; also articles in field. Prof European hist Western Mich Coll since '45, head dept philos since '47. Am Soc Church Hist—Mennonite Hist Soc (asso ed Mennonite Quarterly Review). Western Michigan College, Kalamazoo, Mich.

11 FRIEDRICH, William George. Industrialization and economic development: Econometric analysis. b'97. M Ind Engring '23—D Tech Sci '26 (U Prague); Engenieur Diplome '24 (U Paris); CE '27 (Govt authorization); grad study (Paris, London, NY, Washington). Consultant United Nations Relief and Rehabilitation Administration, Industrial Rehabilitation Division, '45 as adviser on technical assistance to liberated countries and on industrial rehabilitation; consultant Office Foreign Economic Development and Industrialization, US Department of Commerce '46, preparing development and industrialization projects, agenda for United Nation Economic and Employment Reconstruction and Economic Development Commissions; attended reconstruction and development conference Paris '46; survey industrial and economic trends Europe '46-47. Devised advanced econometric charting system suitable for analysis of complex economic interrelationships, forecasting and economic planning, management controls. Author: Engineer's Task in Economic Depression '33; Public Works and Their Financing '34; A Rational View of Economic Problems '36; Economic Policies of the Roosevelt Administration '37; also articles in field. Cons econ, engr, researcher various corporations and organizations in US and abroad '30-41; vis prof industry U NC '41-45; sometime cons War Labor Bd, Bd Econ Warfare, Fgn Econ Adminstrn. Sec War '42-45; cons Office Internat Trade Dept Commerce '47, Econometric Inst '47-48. Nat Research Council—Inst World Econ—Internat Econometric Soc—Am Econ Assn—Am Statis Assn—Nat Planning Assn. c/o Cosmos Club, Washington 5.†

12 FRIEND, Albert W(iley). Television (Color); Electron beam deflection; Magnetic recording and reproduction; Troposphere (Meteorological soundings). b'10. BSEE '32—MS '36 (WVa U); SD '48 (Harvard). Wave propagation; Vibration of plates and membranes, electric power distribution, radio interference elimination, lightning protection, short wave communication. Holds patents in field. Author articles: Television Deflection Circuits; Continuous Topospheric Soundings by Radar; Theory and Practice Topospheric Sounding by Radar; Further Comparisons of Meteorological Soundings by Radio Waves with Radiosonde Data; Ionospheric Sounding; Magneto-Optic Transducers; and others. Co-author articles: (with R C Colwell) The Daylight Variation of Signal Strength; Vibrating Membranes; and others. Staff mem RCA Labs Div Radio Corp Am since '47. Inst Radio Engrs—AIEE—Acoustical Soc Am—AAAS—Am Geophys Union—Am Meterol Soc (asso mem)—Tau Beta Pi—Sigma Pi Sigma—Sigma Xi. Dir. Engineering and Development, Magnetic Metals Co., Hayes Ave at 21st St., Camden 1, N.J.

13 FRIEND, Roger Boynton. Forest insect biology and control. b'96. BSc '23 (U Mass); PhD '27 (Yale). Author articles in field. Conn State entomol since '39; professorial lecturer forest entomol Yale U since '41. Am Assn Econ Entomol—Entomol Soc Am—Am Soc Zool—Soc Am Foresters—AAAS—Conn Acad Arts, Sci Letters. 123 Huntington St., New Haven.

14 FRIERSON, William Coleman. History of the modern English novel. b'97. BA '20 (Vanderbilt U); BA '22 (Oxford U); Docteur de l'Université '25 (U Paris). Research on development of English novel since 1885. Author: L'Influence du naturalisme francais sur les romanciers anglais, 1885-1900 '25 (mention très honorable); The English Novel in Transition 1885-1940 '42; also articles in field. Asso prof Eng U Ala '45-47, prof since '47. Modern Lang Assn. Rhodes Scholar from Tenn '21-23, '24-25. Box 2012, University, Ala. H: Rt. 2, Cottondale, Ala.

15 FRIES, Karl W. Glassine and greaseproof paper (Manufacture); Semi-chemical pulping of poplar. Student mech engring '20-23 (U Berlin); chem engring '23-25 (U Darmstadt); PhD '40 (Inst Paper Chem-Lawrence Coll). Research in various types of paper for peculiar uses; methods of manufacturing paper; chemical pulping of poplar wood; mechanical difficulties of paper manufacture, such as boiler feed problems, recovery of white water, hydrating pulp wood. Author articles in field. Engr paper bd mill Gross-Saerchen Germany '25-26; research Oxford Paper Co Rumford Me '26-38; tech dir Rhinelander Paper Co Rhinelander Wis since '40. Forest Products Research Soc—Tappi. Rhinelander Paper Company, Rhinelander, Wis. H: Rt. 1.

16 FRIESNER, Ray Clarence. Taxonomy (Solidago); Tree growth; Indiana plant distribution. b'94. AB '16 (O Wesleyan U); PhD '19—research fellow '17-19 (U Mich). Author articles in field. Prof bot Butler U since '25, dir div grad instrn '44-47, dean Coll Liberal Arts and Sci since '47. Ind Acad Sci (sec '26-35, pres '36)—Bot Soc Am—O, Mich, Wis, Ill Acads Sci—Eugenics Research Assn—Am Eugenics Soc—Am Genetic Assn—Biol Soc Washington—Am Soc Plant Taxonomy—AAAS—Sigma Xi—Phi Beta Kappa—Phi Kappa Phi. Butler University, Indpls 7. H: Brendonwood, Indpls 44.†⊙

17 FRIIS, Herman Ralph. Cartography (Statistical); Geography (Historical). b'05. BA '31—MA '34 (U Calif); '31 (Imperial U Tokyo) (Stanford); research fellow geog '34-36 (U Wis). Strategic geographic studies in Asia, USSR, North America, Greenland, and Arctic; preparation geographic monographs and cartographic studies of Japan, Greenland, Spitsbergen, and Arctic. Author articles in field. Asst chief cartographic records br Nat Archives Washington since '38; lecturer (geography and cartography) Cath U Am Washington '47-51. Chief map sect Arctic, Desert and Tropic Br Air Intelligence AAF '43-44, chief map div Strategic Services Unit Office Asst Sec War China Theatre '44-45. Assn Am Geog—Soc Am Archivists—Arctic Inst NA—NRC. Cartographic Records Branch, National Archives, Washington.

18 FRITZ, Percy Stanley. American history. b'95. AB '17 (Franklin and Marshall); MA '27—PhD '33 (U Colo); '21-22 (U Chicago). Special interest in Colorado and history of Trans-Mississippi west, especially early mining districts and their laws, development of mining law, mining methods, water rights, irrigation, and Cliff Dwellers. Author: Colorado: The Centennial State '41; also articles in field. Asst in hist '25-31, instr '31-38, asst prof U Colo since '38. AHA—Miss Valley Hist Assn—Colo-Wyoming Acad Sci—State Hist Soc Colo—Phi Beta Kappa. University of Colorado, Boulder, Colo. H: 1018 Pine St.

19 FRIZZELL, Don(ald) L(eslie). Micropaleontology. b'06. BS '30—MS '31 (U Wash); PhD '36—Jacobs fellow '31-32—U scholar '33-34—Jordan fellow '34-35 (Stanford U). Author articles in field. Asso prof geol Mo Sch Mines Metall since '48. Geol Soc Am(F)—Paleontol Soc(F)—Sociedad Geologica del Peru (corres)—Am Assn Petroleum Geol—Soc Econ Paleontol Mineral—Sigma Xi. Department of Geology, Missouri School of Mines, Rolla, Mo.

20 FRIZZELL, Harriet Exline. Zoology (Spiders). b'09. BA '30 (Reed Coll); MS '32—PhD '36 (U Wash); Sterling fellow '37-38 (Yale). Made field studies of spiders of Ecuador and Peru '38-43, studies of American spiders '45-48. Author articles in field. Guest worker U Tex '45-48, independent research since '38. Am Soc Zool—Entomol Soc Am—AAAS—Calif Acad Sci. 6 Rolla Gardens, Rolla, Mo.†

21 FROELICH, Herman Christian. Fluorescent materials. b'07. Dr Chem Eng '31—MA '29 (Inst Tech Berlin). Research in development of catalysts for hydrogenation, development and production of fluorescent materials, study of their performance characteristics, development of new fluorescent lamp colors. Author articles in field. Research asst Inst Tech Berlin '31-33; with Harshaw Chem Co Cleveland '34-41, Gen Elec Co since '41. Am Chem Soc—Electrochem Soc. General Electric Company, Nela Park, Cleveland 12. H: 3424 Bradford Rd., Cleveland Heights 18.

22 FROLIK, Elvin Frank. Agronomy; genetics of crop plants. b'09. BS '30—MS '32 (U Neb); PhD '48 (U Minn). Research on genetic effects of irradiation pollen and seeds of crop plants with therma neutrons. Assistant ext agron U Neb '36-45; asso prof agron U Neb '46, now prof and chmn dept. Genetics Soc Am—Am Soc Agron—AAAS. College of Agriculture, Lincoln 3, Neb.

23 FROMAN, Darol Kenneth. Atomic physics (Cosmic rays, X-rays, supersonics, atomic weapons). b'06. BSc '26—MSc '27 (U Alberta); PhD '30 (U Chicago). Author articles in field. Group and div leader Los Alamos Sci Lab since '43, sci dir Eniwetok Atomic Energy Proving Ground '48; tech asso dir Los Alamos Scientific Lab. P.O. Box 1663, Los Alamos, N.M.

24 FROMM, Fritz Wilhelm. Organic and biochemistry (Weedkillers, textile fibers, waste utilization, pyrrole). b'04. PhD '28 (Munich U). Research on tetramolecular fulminic acids, unsaponifiable matter of liver, proteins, and NaOBr, textile fibers, herbicide and plant studies, pyrrole in tobacco and coffee, pyrrole blue, technology and uses of wastes. Author articles in field. Head dept chem Mount Mercy Coll Pittsburgh since '48. Am Chem Soc—AAAS—Penna Acad Sci. Mount Mercy College, Fifth Av., Pittsburgh 13.

10 FROST, Donald Karne. Motors (Highspeed); Machinery (Metal working, wood working). b'80. BS—EE (U Wis). Development of built-in type high speed motors, and constant and variable speed frequency changers for wood shapers, four and five head wood moulders, tenoners, and internal and way grinders. Author articles in field. With Gen Elec Co '06-27, head application dept '16-27; development wood working and way grinders utilizing high frequency motors Mattison Machine Works since '27. Am Inst EE. Mattison Machine Works, Blackhawk Park Av., Rockford, Ill.

11 FROST, Douglas Van Anden. Nutritional aspects of intravenous feeding. '10. AB '33 (U Ill); MA '38—PhD '40 (U Wis). Investigations in new nutritional factors nicotinic acid, cobalt, vitamin B12, antithyrotonic factor; intravenous feeding development partial acid hydrolysate of fibin (Aminosol), work on fat emulsions, invert sugar; repletion assay for amino acid value of hydrolysates; measurement decomposition of pantothemic acid, relation to thiamin instability; differential method for determining vitamin B12b and vitamin B12 by reaction with ascorbic acid; rat assay for vitamin B12; safety of arsonilic acid as a growth stimulant for use in poultry and swine feeds, mechanism of action for growth and for disease control. Author publications in field. Chemist Rival Packing Co Chgo '35; biochemist Abbott Labs N Chgo '40-45, head nutritional research since '46. ACS—Am Inst Nutrition—Am Soc Biol Chem—Soc Exptl Biol and Med—Poultry Sci Assn—Sigma Xi—NY Acad Sci (F)—Assn Vitamin Chemists (pres '53-54)—Am Nutrition Research Council —Alpha Xi Zeta. Abbott Labs., North Chicago, Ill.

12 FROST, Frederick Hazard. Paper printing. b'02. BS '23 (U Chicago); PhD '27 (U Calif) Nat Research F '27-29 (Harvard). Resrch studies on coated surfaces for letterpress and lithographic printing, and on development Army wet strength maps, lithographic paper printing plates, starch adhesives, coating pigments. Author articles in field. Supervisor coating dept S D Warren Co Cumberland Mills Me '36-40, dir research '41, bd dirs since '49; research adv com U Me. Lithographic Tech Foundation. S. D. Warren Co., Cumberland Mills, Me.

13 FROST, Reuel Bryan. Geography of Ohio; Conservation in short grass. b'97. BA '26 (U Okla); MA '28—PhD '33 (U Wis). Author articles: Lorain, Ohio: A Study in Urban Geography '33; Distribution of Cities on the Lake Plain of Ohio '35; Distribution of Population on the Lake Plain '36; The Pattern of Land Occupance in Northern Ohio '32; The Distribution of Sheep in Wisconsin '28. Now asso prof geol geog Oberlin Coll. Acad Sci(F)—O Council Geog Teach—Nat Council Geog Teach—Am Soc Profl Geog—AAUP—Sigma Xi. Geography Building, Oberlin College, Oberlin, O.

14 FROST, Stuart Ward. Entomology; Frog motif in art. b'91. BS '15—PhD '28 (Cornell U). Research in entomology in Pennsylvania, Central and South America, West Indies, Canada. Author: Leaf Mining Insects '28; Ancient Artisans, the Wonder of the Insect World '36; General Entomology '42. With US Dept Agr '16-37; prof entomol Pa State Coll since '37. Am Assn Econ Entomol—Entomol Soc Am —Am Entomol Soc—NY Entomol Soc—Pa Soc Archaeol—Royal Linnaean Soc de Lyons—AAAS—Nat Speleological Soc—Sigma Xi—Gamma Sigma Delta—Pi Gamma Mu. Department of Zoology

and Entomology, Pennsylvania State College, State College, Pa.

15 FROST, Wilfrid Tuttle. Snow surveys; Snow profiles (Flood potentials); Water supply forecasting. b'05. AB '33 (U Calif). Research, administration and extension of Oregon Snow Survey network to obtain depth and water content of snow, making of bimonthly snow measurements on Willamette River Basin to indicate flood potentials of snow cover, forecasting of water supplies based on snow surveys as modified by temperature, precipitation, wind, ground storage. Author articles in field. Park ranger '36-42; hydraulic engr Soil Conservation Service since '42, in charge Ore Coop Snow Surveys and Water Forecasting from '44. Am Geophys Union (hydrology sect)—W Snow Conf—Ore Reclamation Congress. Soil Conservation Service, Division of Irrigation, Postoffice Box 1149, Medford, Ore.

16 FROTHINGHAM, Alice Wilson (Mrs Coleridge S). Ceramics (Spanish); Glassware (Spanish); Majolica. b'02. BA '24 (Mt Holyoke Coll). Author: Catalogue of Hispano-Moresque Pottery '36; Hispanic Glass '41; Sigillate Pottery of the Roman Empire '37; Talavera Pottery '44; Lustreware of Spain '51. Contributor: Handbook: Museum and Library Collections '38; Notes Hispanic (5 vol) '41-45. Curator of ceramics Hispanic Soc Am since '37. Hispanic Soc Am (Mitre Medal '40) —Com Internazionale di Patronato of Mus Internazionale delle Ceramiche of Faenza, Italy. Hispanic Society of America, 156th St. and Broadway, NYC 32.

17 FRUTH, Hal Frederick. Metallizing on insulators; Photoengraving; Lithographic plates; Precision tumbling methods. b'90. BA '14—BS '22 (St John's U); MS '23 (U Minn); PhD '27 (U Mich). Research on metallizing on insulators by cathode sputtering, making of printed circuits, use of bimetallic lithographic plates. Granted patents in fields. Author articles in fields. Research and development engr W Elec Co '23-32, research engr '37-42; research, exec engr P R Mallory and Co '32-37; research dir Elec Mfg Co '42-43; asst chief engr Galvin Mfg Co '43-45; research dir electromed div Raytheon Mfg Co '45-46; private cons since '46; res dir Newman Rudolph Litho Co. Sigma Xi—APS—AAAS(F) —Am Inst EE (chmn elec sect)—Inst Radio Engrs (sr mem, chmn program com). 5032 Morse Av., Skokie, Ill.

18 FRYE, Ozro Earle, Jr. Bobwhite quail; Florida game birds and mammals. b'17. BS '39—MS '41—post grad work (U Fla). Wildlife biol, later chief wildlife biol and assistant director Fla Game and Fresh Water Fish Commn since '46. Wildlife Soc—Ecol Soc—Am Ornithol Union—Wilson Ornithol Club. Game and Fresh Water Fish Commission, Tallahassee, Fla.

19 FRYE, Richard Nelson. Iran; Armenia. b'20. PhD '46—fellow '40 (Harvard); '46-47 (London U). Author articles in jours. Jr fellow Soc of Fellows Harvard U since '46, asst prof Middle East studies Harvard since '49. Research analyst Near East sect research and analysis OSS '41-45. Am Oriental Soc (life)—Internat Soc Oriental Research. 546 Widener Library, Harvard University, Cambridge, Mass.

20 FRYLING, Charles F(rederick). Synthetic rubber; Emulsion polymerization. b'97. BS '20 (Lafayette Coll Easton Pa); MS '23—PhD '24 (NYU); National research fellow '24-26 (Princeton). Research on emulsion polymerization of sythetic rubber; redox initiated polymerizations; development of

low temperature polymerized synthetic rubber; variables which influence properties of chemical rubbers prepared by emulsion polymerization. Holds 32 US patents on synthetic rubber. Author articles in field. Research chem BF Goodrich Co Akron '37-43, resident dir Kent labs '43-44; asst chief Polymer Research Br Office Rubber Director Washington '44-45; supervisor emulsion polymerization research Phillips Petroleum Co Texas since '45. Am Chem Soc—Am Inst Chem Engrs—Armed Forces Chem Assn—Phi Beta Kappa—Sigma Xi—Alpha Chi Sigma. Phillips Petroleum Co., Box 968, Phillips, Texas. H: 10 Jopling St.

21 FUCHS, Abraham Wallerstein. Sanitary engineering (Milk and food sanitation). b'92. CE '13 (Cornell U). Editor all editions USPHS milk ordinance and code since '33, restaurant ordinance and code, frozen desserts ordinance and code. Author articles in field. With USPHS since '16, san engr dir with rank of col since '42. Internat Assn Milk and Food Sanitarians (pres '49)—Fed Sewage Research Assn—Nat Sanitation Foundation (tech research com)—Am Pub Health Assn(F). Public Health Service, Washington 25. H: 5420 Connecticut Av., Washington 15.

22 FUCHS, Henry Otten. Springs; Vibrations. b'07. BL '29 (U Strasbourg France); ME '29—D Eng '33 (Karlsruhe Inst Tech Germany). Design and production springs; research on distribution of stress in springs, on measurement of residual stresses of torsion bar springs; study of methods for reducing vibrations; shock absorber design. Author articles: A Design Method for Volute Springs '43; Secondary Stresses in Volute Springs '43; Trapped Stress—How They Can Improve Machine Parts '48. Contributor: Experimental Stress Analysis '46. Engr Gen Motors Corp '33-45; chief resch engr Preco Inc since '45. Soc Automotive Engrs—Am Soc ME. Preco, Inc., 6300 E. Slauson Av., Los Angeles 21.

23 FUCILLA, Joseph Guerin. Comparative literature (Renaissance). b '97. AB '21—MA '22 (U Wis); PhD '27 (U Chicago). Author: Forgotten Danteiana '39. Co-author: D'Annunzio Abroad (two vols) '35, '37. Editor: Grazia Deledda, Il Vecchio della Montagna '32; Alarcon, Novelas Cortas '52. Asst prof Romance langs Northwestern U '28-32, asso prof '32-36, prof since '36. Modern Lang Assn—Am Assn Tchrs Italian (past pres)—AAUP —Am Assn Tchrs Spanish—Phi Beta Kappa—Phi Kappa Phi. H: 1108 Hinman Av., Evanston, Ill.⊙

24 FUDGE, Joseph Franklin. Soil chemistry and fertility; Fertilizer law enforcement; Feed and insecticide laws. b'97. BS '24 (U Ill); MS '25—PhD '28 (U Wis). Author articles in field. Chem, later state chem and prof agron Tex Agrl Expt Sta since '29. Am Chem Soc—Am Soc Agron—Soil Sci Soc Am—AAAS—Assn Am Fertilizer Control Officials—Assn Econ Poisons Control Officials—Assn Am Feed Control Officials—Assn Official Agrl Chem. College Station, Tex.†

25 FULCHER, Paul Milton. The Novel; Contemporary literature; Bernard Shaw. b'95. AB '16 (U WVa); AM '17 (Harvard); study '19 (Oxford U Eng '20 (U Mo); PhD '25 (U Wis). Author: Guests of Summer (novel) '30. Compiler: Foundations of English Style '27; Descriptive Passages '28; Short Narratives '28. Editor: Wuthering Heights (by Emily Bronte) '29; Literary Masters of England (with Bushnell and Taylor) '36 rev edit '50. With U Wis since '20, prof English since '43. Modern Lang Assn Am—Phi Beta Kappa. University of Wisconsin, Madison 6, Wis. H: Frost Woods, R.F.D. 5, Madison 4.⊙

10 FULD, Leonhard Felix. Nursing education: Student nurses (Health). b '83. AB '03—AM '04—LLB '05—LLM '06—PhD '09 (Columbia). Author: Student Nurses Health Record Book '38. Editor: Journal Helene Fuld Health Foundation. Expert US Bur Edn '15-19; ednl dir Henry L Doherty & Co '19-23; dir Med Center Jersey City. Am Pub Health Assn(life F)—Phi Beta Kappa. Medical Center, Jersey City.†⊙

11 FULFORD, Margaret H. Hepaticae (Liverworts); Tropical American Hepatics (Leafy). b'04. AB '26—BE '27—MA '28 (U Cincinnati); PhD '35 (Yale). Asso editor Bryologist since '47. Author: The Genus Bazzania in Central and South America '46. Author articles: Recent Interpretations of the Relationships of the Hepatics '48; Leucolejeunea—Its Habit and Structure '48. and others. Instr and curator bot U Cincinnati '27-40, asst prof '40-46, asso prof since '46. AAAS(F)—Bot Soc Am—Am Soc Plant Taxonomists—Sullivant Moss Soc—Brit Bryological Soc—Torrey Bot Club—O Acad Sci(F)—Ind Acad Sci—Sigma Xi—AAUP. Guggenheim Fellowship '41-42. Botany Department, University of Cincinnati, Cincinnati.

12 FULLER, Claud Edgar. History and development of United States Army shoulder arms: Confederate Army firearms; United States arms makers; Brick manufacturing and handling equipment. b'77. Research on early American firearms and arms makers; study types of arms used by Confederacy. Holds 48 patents on brick making and brick handling machines. Author: Springfield Shoulder Arms '31; The Breech Loader in the Service '33; Whitney Firearms '46. Co-author: (with Stewart) Firearms of the Confederacy '44, Confederate Currency and Stamps '49; also articles in field. H: R.R. No. 7, Box 339, Chattanooga 4, Tenn.

13 FULLER, Errett Otto. Indian tribal land appraisal. b'75. Original research in Indian land and tribal history and preparation of reports showing results of such research and land appraisals used as evidence in several court suits before the US Court of Claims, land values fixed for the Shoshone tribe in Wyoming, several Oregon Indian tribes; fiscal agent emer U Wyoming Clerk US Land Offices and spl agt US Pub Land Service 18 yrs. Box 858, Laramie, Wyo.

14 FULLER, Harry James. Photoperiodism; Plant response and growth (Environmental effects); Physiology of rubber trees: Plant geography of Latin America. b'07. AB '29—MS '30—PhD '32 (Washington U and Mo Bot Garden). Rubber specialist for US Government in Venezuela and British Guiana '43-45. Author: The Plant World '41; Outlines of General Botany '47; (with O Tippo) Textbook of General Botany '48; also articles in field. On faculty U Ill since '32, now professor bot. Botanical Soc Am—AAAS—Nat Assn Biol Teachers—Venezuelan Acad Sci—Phi Beta Kappa—Sigma Xi. Department of Botany, University of Illinois, Urbana, Ill.

15 FULLER, John Langworthy. Animal behavior; Aquatic biology. b'10. BS '31 (Bates); PhD '35 (MIT). Research on fouling; studies on physiology, ecology, and distribution of various New England woodlice, season of attachment and growth of sedentary marine organisms, feeding of calanus finmarchicus, accommodation of marine invertebrates to reduced osmotic pressure; made biological survey of lakes in lower Penobscot River and Union River drainage systems, and Mt Desert Island. studied emotional reactions of dogs. Co-invented Radio Inductograph for psycho-physiological research. Author articles in field. Research asso Roscoe B Jackson Meml Lab since '47. Sigma Xi—Phi Beta Kappa—AAAS—Am Soc Zool—Am Genetics Soc. Fellow Wood's Hole Oceanog Inst summers '35-36. Box 78, Hamilton Station, Bar Harbor, Me.†

16 FULLER, Raymond Harold. Waterworks design; Sewerage design. b '10. BS (CE) '32 (Ohio U). Participated in National Research Council survey of sewage treatment military installations; supervision of design and construction; outline of course on waterworks operation and management for Army Engineers School; studies on processing phase of water treatment. Author articles: Stretching Waterworks Income to Survive Inflation; Relocation and Cleaning of Fifty Year Old 16" Cast Iron Water Transmission Main. Asso engr Burgess & Niple (cons engrs) 35-42, partner specializing in waterworks and sewerage since '46. Sanitary engr in charge operation waterworks and sewerage systems Corps Engrs AUS '43-46. Am Soc CE—Nat Soc Professional Engrs—Am Water Works Assn—Fedn Sewage Works Assn. 584 E. Broad St., Columbus 15, O.

17 FULLER, Richard Eugene. Far Eastern art: Petrogenesis; Basalt (Aqueous chilling). b'97. PhB '18 (Yale); BS '24—MS '25—PhD '30 (U Wash); LLD '44 (Wash State Coll). Member US Committee of National Research Council for study of Paricutin Volcano. chairman since '44; president and director Seattle Art Museum since '33. Author articles in field. Research prof geol U Wash since '40. Geol Soc Am(F)—Mineral Soc Am—AAAS—Am Geophys Union (pres volcanology sect '44-47)—Phi Beta Kappa—Sigma Xi. King's medal Gt Brit for service in cause of freedom '47. Seattle Art Museum, Seattle 2.⊙

18 FULLER, Wallace Hamilton. Soil chemistry (Microbiological transformation of organic carbon, nitrogen, and phosphorus); Cellulose (Microbiological decomposition); Hemp (Retting). b'15. BS '37—MS '38 (Wash State Coll); PhD '42 (Ia State Coll). Investigation of extent organic phosphorus compounds of plant residues are utilized by succeeding crops, also utilization of phosphorus of biological tissues; research on influence of hemicellulose and lignin on microbiological decomposition of cellulose; pioneer in research on methods for controlled retting of hemp (Cannabis sativa). Author articles: Decarboxylation Rate of Uronic Groups Contained in Soil Organic Matter, Plant Gums of Known Constitution, Plant Materials and Microbial Products '47; Influence of Some Cropping and fertilizing Practices on the Uronides of Soil '47. Co-author articles: (with Katznelson, S C Vandecaveye) Bacteriophage of Rhizobia in Relation to Symbiotic Nitrogen Fixation by Alfalfa '40; (with A G Norman) The Retting of Hemp—Biochemical Changes Accompanying Retting of Hemp '46; (with L A Dean) Utilization of Phosphorus from Green Manures '49, and others. Research asso Wash State Coll '37-38, Ia State Coll '40-45; bact and soil sci Bur Plant Industry Beltsville Md '45-48; asso prof and asso biochem agrl chem soils dept U Ariz since '48. Am Soc Agron—Soil Sci Soc—Sigma Xi—Phi Lambda Upsilon—Alpha Zeta—Phi Sigma. University of Arizona, Tucson, Ariz.

19 FULLING, Edmund Henry. Economic botany. b'03. BS '26 (NY State Coll Forestry Syracuse U); PhD '35 (Columbia). Founder. manager, editor, publisher Botanical Review. Economic Botany. Author: A Guide to the Pinetum '34; also articles in field. Bot Soc Am—Torrey Bot Club—AAAS—Sigma Xi. New York Botanical Garden, NYC 58.

20 FULLING, Kay Painter. Contemporary Latin American art. b'16. Student '38 (Ecole Normale de Musique Paris France); BA '40 (Northwestern U); '41 (San Marcos U Lima Peru)—'42 (Vassar Coll); MA '43 (Columbia); fellowship Inst Internat Edn and Pan-Am Airways '47 (Central U Quito Ecuador). Author: The Cradle of American Art, Ecuador (Its Contemporary Artists) '48; also articles in field. Asst dir Casa Panamericana Mills Coll Oakland Calif summer '44; asst to Dir Fine Arts Dept Teachers Coll Columbia U, lecturer contemporary art in Hispanic Am countries '45-47. Brooks Art Gallery (past mem exec bd Memphis Tenn)—Sigma Alpha Iota. 59 Guilford Road, Port Washington, L.I., N.Y.

21 FULTON, Charles Clarke. Narcotics (Chemistry and identification). b'00. BS '22 (MIT). Research on chemistry of identification of alkaloids, especially narcotics; precipitating agents, chemical tests for, crystal tests for alkaloids. Author articles in field. Chem Treasury Dept US Govt '24-48; office Secretariat UN Narcotic Div since '48. Narcotics Division, United Nations, New York, N.Y.

22 FULTON, Robert Avery. Chemical control of insects affecting fruits and truck crops; Aerosol insecticides. b'03. BS '25 (Ore State Coll); MS '27 (U Wis); PhD '29 (Stanford). Chemical research and development insecticides for control crop insects; in charge development liquified gas propelled aerosols USDA since '46. Author articles: Biochemical Studies of Insects; Development of Fumigants; Development of the Liquified Gas-Aerosol Method for the Control of Disease Carrying Household, Greenhouse and Field Crop Insects, and others. Sr chem Bur Entomol and Plant Quarantine USDA since '46. AAAS(F)—Am Assn Econ Entomol—Washington Insecticide Soc—Phi Lambda Upsilon—Sigma Xi—Alpha Chi Sigma—Gamma Sigma Delta. Agriculture Research Center, Beltsville, Md.

23 FUNK, Charles Earle. Lexicography. b'81. BS '04 (U Colo); Litt D '37 (Wittenberg Coll). Editor: (with Frank H Vizetelly) New Comprehensive Standard Dictionary '37; Standard Junior Dictionary '39; New Practical Standard Dictionary '46; New College Standard Dictionary '47. Author: What's the Name, Please? '36; A Hog on Ice, and Other Sayings '48; Thereby Hangs a Tale: stories of curious word origins '50. Engaged as lexicographer, editor, writer. Mt. Dora, Fla.⊙

24 FUNK, John Benjamin. Public works; State taxation. b'05. BS '26 (Washington and Lee U). Planning in field mental hospitals, correctional institutions, teachers colleges, tuberculosis hospitals, chronic disease hospitals, schools and other public institutions; distribution state revenues to political sub-divisions, reorganization revenue collecting agencies and tax appeal courts, financing public education. Author: Maryland Builds '50; Report of Commission on State Office Building by the State of Maryland '51. Co-author: Report of Tax Survey Commission of 1949-1950 '50; Report of Commission on Distribution of Tax Revenues by the State of Maryland

'46. Mem Md Ho of Dels '35-38, Md State Senate '39-46, chmn senate finance com '44-46, sec of state Md '47, chief engr '47-51; chmn Md State Planning Commn since '49; dir pub works Baltimore Co since '51. Am Soc CE—Nat Soc Profl Engrs (dir)—Phi Beta Kappa—Engrs Club of Baltimore. Director of Public Works, Towson 4, Md.

10 FUNKE, Erich. German literature (Eighteenth century); German language (Aesthetics, pedagogy, phonetics). b'91. PhD '21 (Halle U Germany). Author: Die Umgangssprache '45; also articles in field. Prof, head dept German State U Ia since '37. Am Modern Lang Assn—Am Assn Teachers of German. Department of German, University of Iowa, Iowa City, Ia.☺

11 FUOSS, Raymond Matthew. Polymers; Electrolytes; Dielectrics. b'05. ScB '25 (Harvard); '25-26 (U Munich); PhD '32 (Brown U); '34-35 (U Leipzig, Cambridge). Author articles in field. Research prof Brown U '34-36; research chem Gen Elec Co '36-45; Sterling prof chem Yale since '45. Am Chem Soc—Sigma Xi—Phi Beta Kappa—Nat Acad Sci. Received Am Chem Soc award in pure chem '35. Yale University, New Haven.†☺

12 FURBER, Henry Jewett. Phonotelemetry. b'65. BS '86 (U Chicago); '86-89 (U Vienna, U Berlin, U Leipzig); AM—PhD '91 (U Halle); law student (Northwestern U); AM '89 (Bowdoin Coll). Inventor of method of mathematically locating masked batteries and detecting submarines and aircrafts by sound waves, and automatic sales system and calculating apparatus. Member law firm Furber and Wakelee, now ret. Nat Inst Social Sci. c/o Bank of Montreal, 27 S. LaSalle St., Chgo.

13 FURMAN, N(athaniel) Howell. Analytical chemistry (Electroanalysis, potentiometric titrations, uranium). b'92. BS '13—AM '15—PhD '18 (Princeton). Associate editor Industrial Engineering Chemistry, Journal American Chemical Society, Chemical Reviews. Also research on polarography, new volumetric processes. co-author: Textbook in Quantitative Analysis; Standard Methods of Chemical Analysis; Potentiometric Titrations; also articles in field. Asst chem Princeton '13-16, asst prof '19-27, prof since '37, Russell Wellman Moore Prof chem since '45, chairman dept chemistry since '51; Charlotte Elizabeth Procter fellow Princeton '16-17. Am Chem Soc—Electrochem Soc—Am Soc Testing Materials—AAAS(F)—Phi Beta Kappa—Sigma Xi. Awards: among ten leaders in analytical chem in US, Am Chem Soc '47; first recipient Fisher Award in Analytical Chem, Am Chem Soc '48. Frick Chemical Laboratory, Princeton, N.J.☺

14 FURR, Joe Roudolph. Date production. b'00. BS '24 (Miss State Coll) PhD '32 (Cornell U). Asst, later sr hort US Dept Agr since '30, date prodn investigations since '46. AAAS—Am Soc Hort Sci—Am Soc Plant Physiol—Bot Soc Am—Soil Soc Am—Sigma Xi. U.S. P.O. Box 737, Indio, Calif.†

15 FUSFELD, Irving Sidney. Special education (Education of the deaf). b'93. BS '15—MA '17 (Columbia U); BPd '16—MA '21—LittD '46—Normal Fellow '15 (Gallaudet Coll). Author: A Study of Teacher Certification Requirements Among Public Residential Schools for the Deaf '48. Co-author: (with Day and Pintner) A Survey of American Schools for the Deaf '28. Prof psychol and edn Gallaudet Coll since '25, dir research dept since '38, dean since '39; survey cons schools for deaf in Ala, Ga, Ill, Md, NJ, Tex, and Wash. Conv Am Instructors of Deaf—Am Psychol Assn. 4314 Argyle Terrace, Washington 11.☺

16 FUSSLER, Herman H. Library science (University library administration); Microphotography; Scientific literature. b'14. AB '35—AB LS '36 (U NC); MA '41—PhD '48 (U Chicago). Head demonstration microphotography Paris International Expedition '37; World Congress on Documentation, Paris '37; 14th International Conference on Documentation, Oxford and London '38; associate editor Journal of Documentary Reproduction '38-42; American Documentation since '50. Author: Photographic Reproduction for Libraries: A Study of Administrative Problems '42. Editor: Library Building for Library Service '47; also articles in field. Head dept photographic reproduction U Chicago Library '37-46, sci librarian '41-46, asst dir '46-47, asso dir '47-48, dir since '48; instr U Chicago Grad Library Sch '41-43, asst prof '44-48, prof since '48; asst dir information div and librarian Metall Project U Chicago '42-45; member board directors Midwest Inter-Library Center since '50. ALA—Assn of College and Reference Libraries—Ill Library Assn—Spl Libraries Assn. University of Chicago, Chicago 37.

17 FYFE, Robert Andrew. Boat and small craft design. b'10. BS '32 (MIT). Research, design and development of laminated plastic boats, inflatable boats made of rubberized fabric, wood and metal boats; design of all boats and small craft for US Navy, including inflatable boats, ship service boats, landing and rescue craft, and mine sweeping boats; research on construction materials, components and equipment, lightweight diesel engines, power plants and drives, basic research on hull form, planing action, and wave motion. Jr designer Burgess & Donaldson '32-34; hull draftsman Newport News Shipbuilding and Drydock Co '34-36; asst nav archt Phila Nav Shipyard '36-37; asst nav archt NY Nav Shipyard '37-38; nav archt Bur Ships Navy Dept since '38, in charge design of boats and small craft from '42. Soc Nav Archts and Marine Engrs. Bureau of Ships, Navy Department, Washington 25.

G

18 GABLE, J. Harris. Bibliography; Robin Hood; Photography. b'02. AB '26 (U Neb); AB LS '32—Carnegie fellow for research '32-33 (U Mich). Author: Learned and Scholarly Publications of the University of Nebraska '26; Bibliography of Robin Hood '39; Complete Introduction to Photography '48; Subject Index to United States Stamps '49; also articles in field. Writing, producing and directing ednl and tech motion pictures since '41. Screen Writers Guild—Authors Guild—Authors League. 1676 N. Sycamore, Hollywood 28, Calif.

19 GABLE, Luther Stansbury Hooper. Radioactivity; Fluorescence. b'80. Dr Physiotherapy '28 (Ashland Phys Therapy Coll); MA Electrotherapy '30 (Waddington Sch Electrotherapy Detroit); PhD '42 (Poly Coll Liberal Arts Ft Wayne Ind). Assisted refinement radium, and production first radium watch-dials in America; design and construction first radioactive drinking fountains and radium emanators, and director experimental clinics for physicians; experiments with radioactivity to promote plant growth; production of radioactive exhibit of nuclear fission simulating explosion of atomic energy as visible aid for classroom demonstrations; development use high frequency invisible radiation (black-light) for factory inspection, and night hunting for tungsten ore, calcite, and whilimite for plain and color television; development first units of fluorescent pictorial advertising, as window cards and shadowbox exhibits activated by black-light. Author: Miracle of Television 1949. Author articles: Crime Detection by Black-Light '47; Electromagnetic Radiations '48, and others. Radium research and development Standard Chem Co Pittsburgh '06-20, also Radium Co Am Phila, Denver Radium Co; prospector for uranium ore US and Arctic region; lectr and instr physiol application radioactivity, superficial, comml, agrl, and by inhalation. Soc Am Mil Engrs—AAAS. Signal Corps AUS citation for black-light application in fungus prevention at Squire Lab Ft Monmouth NJ. Professional engr. Adventurers Club, 111 W. Jackson Blvd., Chgo.

20 GABRIEL, Vittaly Gavrilovich. Geophysics (Gravity, magnetic, seismic). b'95. BS (Mining) '25 (U Cal Berkeley); MS '31—ScD '33 (Colo Sch Mines). Seismic, gravitational, magnetic explorations United States. Asst seismol Mt Wilson Obs Pasadena Cal '25-27; seismol Shell Oil Co '27-28; lectr geophys MIT '28-29; geophys Fohs Oil Co Houston '35-37; asst geol US Engring Dept Los Angeles '41-43; research analyst Vultee Aircraft Corp San Diego '46-48; asso prof geophys and structural geol Mo Sch Mines and Metals U Mo since 1949. AAAS—Soc Exploration Geophys—Am Geophys Union—Am Mil Engrs. Dept. Geology, Missouri School of Mines, University of Missouri, Rolla, Mo.

21 GABRIELSON, Ira N(oel). Oregon birds; Alaska birds; Wildlife (Conservation, management); Wildlife refuges. b'89. BS '12—LLD hon '41 (Morningside Coll); Dr Sc hon '36 (Ore State Coll). Author: Western American Alpines '32; Wildlife Conservation '41; Wildlife Refuges '43; Wildlife Management '50. Co-author: (with Stanley A Jewett) Birds of Oregon '40. With US Biol Survey '15-46, chief Bur Biol Survey '35-40; chief Fish and Wildlife Service '40-46; pres Wildlife Management Inst since '46. Wilderness Soc—Am Ornithol Union—Wilson Ornithol Club—Cooper Ornithol Club—Pacific NW Bird and Mammal Club—Ecol Soc Am—Wash Biol Field Club—Ore Audubon Soc—Zaak Walton League—Wash Acad Sci—NA Wildlife Found—Cosmos Club. 709 Wire Bldg., Washington 5.☺

22 GADDIS, Merrill Elmer. American history (Small holiness sects, old Southern domestic architecture). b'91. BD '24 (Iliff Sch Theology, Denver); AB '26 (U Denver); fellow '27-29—PhD '29 (U Chicago). Research on history and sociological explanations of small holiness sects; research and picture collections on Southern houses of antebellum period. Author: Christian Perfectionism in America '47; also articles in field. Minister Colo Conf ME Church '21-24; prof hist and chmn dept hist and polit sci Central Coll Fayette Mo since '29; chmn div social sci since '44. AHA—Hist Soc Mo—Am Soc Ch Hist. Central College, Fayette, Mo. H: 400 N. Church St.

23 GADDIS, Porter L. Farmland appraisal. b'85. AB '08 (Greenville, Ill, Coll); BSc Agr '16—AM '20 (U Neb); PhD '40 (Am U). Author articles in field. Chief appraisal sub-division Farm Credit Adminstrn Washington '33-44; asst mgr farm loan service Equitable Life Assurance Soc US since '44. Am Farm Econ Assn—Alpha Zeta—Gamma Sigma Delta. Equitable Life Assurance Soc of the United States, 393 7th Av., NYC 1.

10 GAEBELEIN, Frank Ely. Christian education; English Bible. b'99. AB '20 (NYU); AM '21 (Harvard); LittD '31 (Wheaton Coll). Member national prep school committee and commission on education National Association Evangelicals. Author: A Brief Survey of Scripture '29; Exploring the Bible '29; From a Headmaster's Study '35; The Christian Use of the Bible '46; Christian Education in a Democracy '50. Organizer Stony Brook Sch '21, headmaster since '22; Griffith Thomas Meml lectr Dallas Theol Sem '44; Bible conf speaker. Headmasters Assn—Nat Assn Bibl Instrs—Soc Bibl Lit and Exegesis — Phi Beta Kappa — Kappa Sigma. H: Grosvenor House, Stony Brook, L.I., N.Y.†◎

11 GAFFNEY, Francis J. Microwave measurements. b'12. BS (Elec engring) '35 (Northeastern U); '41-42 (MIT); '45-47 (Poly Inst Brooklyn). Development signal generators, frequency meters, impedance measuring devices. Applied for patents on multiple pulse generator; range or time measuring circuit; coding circuit for selective signalling; broad range high frequency oscillator. Chief engr Browning Labs Inc Winchester Mass '37-41; head test equipment group MIT Radiation Lab '41-45; chief engr Poly Research and Development Co '45-50, gen mgr since '50. Am Inst EE—Inst Radio Engrs (chmn com on measurements and instrumentation) — APS — Research and Development Bd. Polytechnic Research and Development Co., 55 Johnson St., Bklyn.

12 GAFFRON, Hans. Plant physiology (Photosynthesis); Biochemistry (Microbiology, purple bacteria metabolism). b'02. PhD '25 (U Berlin). Author articles in field. Professor biochem Inst of Radiobiology and Biophysics U Chicago since '52. AAAS(F) —Am Soc Biol Chem—Am Bot Soc—Soc Exptl Biol and Med—Soc Gen Physiol —Sigma Xi. Inst of Radiobiology and Biophysics, 57th St. and Ellis Av., University of Chicago, Chgo 37.

13 GAGLIARDI, Domenick Donald. Textiles (Creaseproofing, shrinkproofing resins); Fabrics (Cellulose, waterproofing, fireproofing). b'19. BS (Chem) '42 (Yale); Seminar in high polymers '46 (Nat Bur Standards). Study physical, chemical and mechanical properties of fibers and fabrics; testing and evaluation fabric properties; supervising and directing research in textiles and chemicals. Co-author articles: Properties of Water Repellent Fabrics; Analysis of Tear Strength; Creasing and Creaseproofing of Textiles; Modification of Cellulose by Reaction with Formaldehyde, and others. Research asso Textile Found Washington '43-44; training, research chem warfare service Camp Detrick Md '44-45; testing of fabrics Nat Bur Standards Washington '45-46; staff research lab Rohm & Haas Co Phila '46-51; dir products development labs Warwick Chem Co since '51. ACS — ASTM — AAAS — Am Assn Textile Chem and Colorists. Warwick Chemical Co., Wood River Junction; R.I. H: Shore Rd., Westerly, R.I.

14 GAIL, Floyd Whitney. Photosyntheses (Red and brown algae); Douglas Firs (Northwest); Cell sap (Osmotic pressure and pH). b'84. AB '11 AM '12 (U Neb); PhD '20 (U Wash); study (U Cambridge Eng). Research in deep sea illumination, osmotic pressure and pH of cell sap, vertical distribution of fucus, photosynthesis of red and brown algae, distribution of Douglas fir and other trees and plants of the Northwest. Contbr to Botanical Gazette, Gail and Long's Ecology (Vol 16) '35. With U Ida since '13, prof and head dept botany since '22; visited leading botanical institutions and gardens in Norway, Sweden, Germany, France, Italy and England '37-38. AA AS(F)—Bot Soc Am—NW Sci Soc (councillor since '31, vp '39-40, pres '40-41)—Sigma Xi (treas '28-29)—Moscow Garden Soc (pres '28-29). University of Idaho, Moscow, Ida. H: 623 Urquhart Av.◎

15 GAINES, Francis Pendleton. Comparative literature; American literature (Southern United States). b'92. AB '12 (Richmond Coll Va); AM '14 (U Chicago); PhD '24—LittD '31 (Columbia U); LittD '28 (Duke); LLD '30 (Wake Forest), '30 (Mercer), '32 (Furman), '34 (Richmond), '35 (Baylor), '38 (William Jewell); DCL '39 (Sewanee U of S). American literature and history. Author: The Southern Plantation '24; Lee—The Final Achievement '33; Southern Oratory '45. Pres Washington and Lee U since '30. Phi Beta Kappa. Lexington, Va.◎

16 GAINSBRUGH, Martin R. Industrial economics; Inflation. b'08. AB '28 (U Rochester); '29-32 (Columbia) Author: Basic Data for Excess Profits Tax Relief '43; Pattern of Inflation '45; Economics of the Cotton Textile Industry '46; Retail Cost Absorption '45; Wages in the Transition Period '46; Public vs Private Housing '45. Co-author: High-Level Consumption '35; Behavior of Wages '48; War and Defense Economics '52. Editor: Studies in Income and Wealth vol 14, '51; also articles. Economics Trade-Ways '32-39; mem research staff Nat Indsl Conf Board '39-42, chief econ since '43; adjunct professor School Business NYU; tech cons Bur Census, Bur Labor Statistics. Econometric Soc—Am Finance Assn—Am Econ Assn—Am Statis Assn —Phi Beta Kappa. 247 Park Av., NYC. H: 4 Wakeman Pl., Larchmont, N.Y.†

17 GALE, Esson McDowell. China and Far East (Language, literature, history, politics). b'84. BA '07—MA '08 (U Mich)—Litt PhD '31 (U Leyden Sinologisch Inst Holland). Author: Basics of the Chinese Civilization '34. Translator: Discourses on Salt and Iron 'Yen T'ieh Lun 83 BC; also articles in field. Counselor to fgn students and dir Internat Center U Mich since '43. Am Council Learned Soc— Chinese Social Polit Sci Assn—Royal Asiatic Soc—Am Oriental Soc—AHA— Am Polit Sci Assn—Inst Pacific Relations—Phi Beta Kappa. Decorated 4th and 3rd grades Order of the Chia Ho Republic of China '15, '17; 3rd Grade 1st Rank Finance Ministry decoration (China) '36. International Center, University of Michigan, Ann Arbor.◎

18 GALE, Louis Clyde. Syrian golden hamsters. b'99. DD '50 (Burton Coll). Author: The Laboratory Hamster Manual '45; Raising Hamsters for Science '46; The Golden Hamster Manual '49, also articles in field. 723 Main St., Larned, Kan.

19 GALL, John Christian. Law. b'01. Student '17-18 (The Citadel Charleston SC); LLB '23 (George Washington U). Author booklets on legal and legislative subjects; contbr to mags in mfg field. Bookkeeper cotton mfrs '19-20; employee US Treasury Dept US Govt '20-21; legal dept Nat Assn of Mfrs '21-41; now in pvt practice; admitted to Dist Columbia bar '23, Va bar '27. Am Bar Assn—DC Bar Assn—Am Bldg., Washington 6. H: Amandale Farm, Upperville, Va.

20 GALLAGHER, David. Korea (Mineral resources); Uranium (Colorado deposits); Mercury (Mexican deposits). b'06. BS '29—PhD '35 (Yale). Project chief in charge exploration uranium resources of Colo Plateau for Atomic Energy Commn US Geol Survey '47-50. Geol Soc Am(F)—Am Mineral Soc(F)—Soc Econ Geol—Pan-Am Inst Mining Engrs and Geol—Am Geophys Union—Geol Soc Washington. U.S. Geological Survey, Washington 25.

21 GALLAGHER, Robert Taylor. Mining and geophysical engineering; Mine safety (Roof conditions); Anthracite coal (Sizing, dewatering). b'05. BS '27 (Penn State Coll); MA '38 (U Mo); Dr engr mines '41 (Colo Sch Mines). Author articles in field. Asst prof advancing to prof and head dept of engineering Lehigh Univ since '42; cons on mineral dressing, coal preparation and geophysics. Am Inst Mining Metal Engrs—Soc Exploration Geophys—Am Soc Engr Edn—Sigma Xi. Coxe Mining Laboratory, Lehigh University, Bethlehem, Pa.†

22 GALPIN, William Freeman. History of grain trade; New York history. b'90. BA '13—MA '14 (Northwestern U); '14-15 (Yale); PhD '17—Harrison fellow '15-17 (U Pa). Engaged research, work, articles American grain trade to Spanish peninsula 1810-14, under embargo of 1808, New Orleans 1804-14, source of exports to England 1801-06, Alexandria Va; early peace efforts of Rhode Island, Geritt Smith Miller, Elizabeth Cady. Author: Grain Supply of England During the Napoleonic Era (awarded Herbert Baxter Adams prize Am Hist Assn '28) '26; Pioneering for Peace '33; 100 Years Delta Upsilon Fraternity '34; A History of England '28; Central New York: An Inland Empire (4 vols) '41; Reform Movements (in History of State of NY) '34; Instr history NYU summer '17; instr hist Carnegie Inst Tech '17-18; asst prof hist Hamline U '19-20; instr hist U Mich '20-24, U Neb summer '25-26; asso prof hist U Okla '24-26; prof Eng hist Syracuse U since '26, chmn hist dept Syracuse U since '48. Am Hist Assn— Miss Valley Hist Assn—NY State Hist Soc—Onondago Co Hist Soc—NC Hist Soc—Am Agrl Hist Soc (vp '28-30). Maxwell Building, Syracuse University, Syracuse, N.Y.◎

23 GALT, William Egleston. Phylobiology. b'04. BS '31—MA '32—PhD '39 (Columbia). Research on principle functional unity and solidarity activating behavior of individuals and species; investigation divisive self-reflective type of response which characterizes individual's habitual social adaptation, and the organism's total, integrative adaptation in relation to social and physical environment; instrumental recording characteristic features of respiration, brain waves, and eye movements accompanying tensional patterns. Author: Phyloanalysis —A Study in the Group or Phyletic Method of Behavior-Analysis '33. Author articles: The Principle of Cooperation in Behavior '40; Note on the Psychoanalytic Concept 'Polymorphous Perverse' '41; The Male-Female Dichotomy in Human Behavior—A Phylobiological Evaluation '43; Our Mother Tongue—Etymological Implications of the Social Neurosis '43. Co-author article: (with Trigant Burrow) Electroencephalographic Recordings of Varying Aspects of Attention in Relation to Behavior '45. With Lifwynn Found '27-42 and since '46, dir Psychol Lab '39-42 and since '46, research asso since '46. Aviation psychol AAF '42-46. Am Anthrop Soc— AAAS—Am Psychol Assn—Am Psychopath Assn—NY Acad Sci—So Soc Philos and Psychol—Sigma Xi. The Lifwynn Foundation, South Morningside Drive, Westport, Conn.†

24 GALTSOFF, Paul Simon. Marine biology (Regeneration, oysters, shellfisheries, sponges, sea water pollution). b'87. Diploma First Degree '10 —research fellow '10-13 (Imperial Moscow U); PhD '24 (Columbia). Extensive study of effect of dam construction on life of Mississippi River '21-22; leader government expedition to explore pearl oyster resources of Hawaiian Islands '38-39; at request of British Government studied sponge disease in West Indies, studied pearl fishery for Panama Government '48; biological explorations around Margarita Venezula '48. Author: Limnological Observations in the Upper Mississippi River '24; Regeneration After Dissociation '25; Pearl and Hermer Reef Hawaii '33; Culture Methods for Invertebrate '37. In charge sect shellfishery investigation US Fish and Wildlife Service '25-48, dir US Shellfish Lab Woods Hole since '49. Nat Shellfisheries Assn (past pres)—AAAS—Washington Acad Sci—Am Soc Zool—Am Naturalists—Sigma Xi. Awarded Moscow U gold medal for research '10; Bogandov Prize of Moscow Soc Friends Natural History '14. U.S. Fishery Laboratory, Woods Hole, Mass.†◎

10 GAMBRELL, Herbert Pickens. History (Texas, Latin America). b'98. Student '16-18 (Baylor U); AB '21—AM '24 (So Meth U); PhD '46 (Tex U); '25 (U Nacional Mex); fellow '28-29 (U Chicago). History director Texas Centennial Exposition '35-36, Greater Texas and Pan American Exposition '37; commissioner, Texas Centennial of Statehood '45. Author: A Social and Political History of Texas (with Newton) '35; Mirabeau Buonaparte Lamar, Troubadour and Crusader '34; Anson Jones, The Last President of Texas '48. Editor: Memoirs of Mary Israel Ellet '39. Mem hist faculty So Meth U since '23; staff Inst Politics Mass '28; mng ed Southwest Review '24-27; chmn U Press Dallas since '30; curator Dallas Hist Soc since '31; dir mus Hall of State since '38. Soc Am Hist(F)—Tex State Hist Assn (F, vp)—Tex Folklore Soc—SW Com Latin Am Culture (past pres)—Counseil Historique et Heraldique de France (hon corr)—Phi Alpha Theta—Phi Beta Kappa. Decorated Officer d'Academie France '38. 3543 University Blvd., Dallas 5.

11 GAMBRELL, Mary Latimer. History of American Colonial culture. b'98. BA '17 (Greenville Woman's Coll); MA '31—PhD '37 (Columbia). Research on American history, Colonial culture, Samuel Finley. Author: Ministerial Training in Eighteenth-Century New England '37. Co-author: Human Liberty in a Universe of Reason and Order '43. Author article: Old Wine in New Bottles '42. Instr hist Hunter Coll NYC '37-43, asst prof '44-49, asso prof since '49, chmn dept since '48. AAUP—AHA. 695 Park Av., NYC 21.◎

12 GAMMON, Nathan, Jr. Soil fertility; Plant physiology (Mineral nutrition). b'14. BS '36—MS '39 (U Md); PhD '41 (O State U). Research on ion exchange as related to soil fertility and plant nutrition, soil chemistry, production pasture and horticultural crops on light sandy soils. Asst agron U Md '36-38; asst agron O Agrl Expt Sta '38-42; soil chem Fla Agrl Expt Sta since '46. Alpha Chi Sigma—Phi Lambda Upsilon—Phi Epsilon Phi—Gamma Alpha—Sigma Xi—ACS—AAA S—Soil Sci Soc Am—Am Soc Agron—Soil Sci Soc Fla. Dept of Soils, Florida Agricultural Experiment Station, Gainesville, Fla.

13 GANAHL, Richard Gregory. Engineering; Naval operations. b'02. BS '24 (US Naval Acad). Navigator, operations officer, participated in assaults and captures of Saipan, Guam, Tinian, Leyte, Mindoro, Lingayen, battles Leyte Gulf, Lingayen Gulf. Sulu Sea aboard US Colo '44-45; executive officer Salt Lake City participated in assault and capture Okinawa, China Sea Sweeps, offensive strikes against China Coast, Kyushu; occupation operations Ominato, Aomori, Hakodate, Otaru '45; comdg officer Material Reservation Schs US Naval Tng Center, Naval Base, Phila '46, ret as brig gen '48; coordinator engineering design constrn Ebasco Services, Inc NY City since '48. Decorated Bronze Star (2), Purple Heart Navy Expeditionary medal, Philippine Liberal medal with 3 stars, Victory medal.◎

14 GANDERS, Harry Stanley. Higher education; Teacher education; Philosophy of education. b'94. BEd '20 AM '22 (U Wash); PhD '26 (Columbia). Author: A System of School Records and Reports '26; Personnel and Organization in Schools of Small Cities '26; (with C E Reeves) School Building Management '28; (with others) A Functional Program in Teacher Education '40. Tchr and adminstr pub schs Wash '19-22; prof sch adminstrn Colo State Coll Edn '24-26; prof ednl adminstrn U Cincinnati '26-29; dean sch edn Syracuse U since '30, acting dean grad sch since '43; mem NY State Regents advisory council on tchr edn since '42. Nat Council Edn—NEA —Nat Soc Coll Tchrs Edn—NY State Ednl Research Assn (pres '34)—Nat Assn Tchr Ednl Instns Met Dists (pres '40)—Kappa Phi Kappa—Kappa Delta Pi—Phi Delta Kappa. Syracuse University, Syracuse 10, N.Y. H: 208 Berkeley Dr.†◎

15 GANS, David Manus. Surface and colloid chemistry. b'05. BS '26—MS '27—PhD '29 (U Chicago). Research in surface and colloid chemistry, pigments, coatings, nucleonics, spectroscopy, textile coloring. Granted several patents. Author articles in field. Asst dir research Interchem Corp NYC '35-45; tech dir Quaker Chem Products Co Conshohocken Pa '45-48; dir research Arco Co Cleveland since '48. Am Chem Soc—Am Phys Soc—Am Inst Chem—Am Soc Metals—Soc Rheology—Electron Microscope Soc—Am Assn Textile Colorists and Chem. Arco Co., 7301 Bessemer Av., Cleveland 27.

16 GARBER, Clark McKinley. Ethnology (Alaska Eskimo). b'91. BS '16 (Wittenberg Coll); '17 (Ohio State U). Research among Eskimos of Alaska for eight years. Author: Stories and Legends of the Bering Strait Eskimos '40; Folktales of the Alaska Eskimos '42. Supt native edn and med relief in Alaska US Bur Edn '25-33; lectr, writer since '33. AAAS—Am Folklore Soc—Arctic Inst NA—Am Ethnol Soc—NEA. Butler, O.

17 GARBUNY, Max. Atomic physics; Microwave tubes; Solid state optics. b'12. Dipl Ing '36—Dr Ing '38 (Tech Hochschule Berlin). Research and development reflex resnatron, a high power wide band ultra-high frequency transmitter tube. Phys Allen-Bradley Co '39-43; faculty Princeton U '43-44; with Westinghouse Research Lab since '45. APS. Westinghouse Research Laboratories, East Pittsburgh, Pa.

18 GARCEAU, (Ernest) Lovett. Electrophysiology; Electroencephalography. b'06. BA '28 (Harvard). Research in engineering, cancer, application of electroencephalography to epilepsy, schizophrenia; research and development electrophysiological apparatus, electroencephalograph, manufacturing electroencephalographic and neurological instruments. Designed Garceau electroencephalograph, chronaximetre, dermohmeter for medical use, Garceau chronograph, velograph for ordnance and industrial measurements. Author articles in field. Engring research Harvard '28-30, research engr med sch '31-35; engr Internat Telephone Corp '30-31; founder, pres Electro-Med Lab Inc since '35. AIEE—Inst Radio Engrs (asso). Registered professional engineer, Massachusetts '45, Vermont '52. Electro-Medical Laboratory, Inc., South Woodstock, Vt.

19 GARCEAU, Oliver. Pressure group politics. b'11. AB '33—MBA '35—AM '39—PhD '40 (Harvard); student (Oxford U, U Chicago). Author: The Political Life of the American Medical Association '41; The Public Library in the Political Process '49. Professor govt Bennington Coll since '48. Social Sci Research Council fellow '45-46. Bennington College, Bennington, Vt. H: East Boothbay, Me.

20 GARD, Richard A. Buddhism (Madhyamika school); Chinese Taoism; Japanese philosophy. b'14. BA '37 (U Wah); MA '40 (Hawaii U); '45-47 (U Pa); PhD '51 (Claremont Graduate Sch). Mem Japanese study seminar on related problems in Buddhist philosophy, Japanese thought and Western physical science conducted by Prof Takakusu Junjiro at Musashino, Kichijoji, Tokyo '39-40; research in Chinese San-lun-tsung; studies and writing on political philosophy of Lao Tzu as expressed in Tao Te Ching; Japanese language officer for Amphibious Forces South Pacific and First Marine Amphibious Corps, Japan staff planner for Office Strategic Services while major, USMCR. Author: Buddhist Political Thought '52; also articles in field. Lectr Young Buddhist League Conf and Japanese Buddhist temples since '45; research chmn So Calif Dist Young Buddhists League since '47, lecturer on Far East Affairs and participant in Southeast Asia Conference, Sch of Advanced International Studies Johns Hopkins U '52; lecturer on Buddhism Otani U Kyoto since '53. Am Oriental Society—Claremont Soc Oriental Studies—Buddhist Soc London—Los Angeles Young Buddhist Assn. Awarded Japanese Buddhist o-kesa recognition Phila '46; Oriental Inst fellow, Hawaii U '37-39; Kokusai Bunka Shinkokai research fellow Tokyo '39-40; Rockefeller Found fellow Pa U '46-47. 115 Valle Vista, Chino, Cal. and Otani University, Kyoto, Japan.

21 GARDINER, William Cecil. Mercury cells; Alkali-chlorine. b'04. BA '26—MA '27 (Queens U); PhD '29 (Princeton U). Patents on brine treating, mercury-type alkali-chlorine cells and magnesium cells; development of magnesium cell, stationary mercury cell. Author articles in field. Asso dir electrochemical engineering Mathieson Chem Corp since '52. Am Chem Soc—Electrochem Soc—AICE. Electrochem Soc Prize to Young Authors '29. Mathieson Chemical Corporation, Niagara Falls, N.Y.†

22 GARDNER, Horace Tillman. Hepatitis; Infectious mononucleosis. b'13. BA '35 (U NM); MD '41 (Yale). Research on infectious hepatitis and mononucleosis; director hepatitis research European Theater Operations for US Army Epidemiological Board, Commission on Virus and Rickettsial Diseases '47-48. Contributor: The Oxford System of Medicine '50; Official History of Medicine in World War II '52. Bact NM State Lab Pub Health '35-37; faculty Cornell U Med Coll '46-47; faculty Yale U Sch Med '47-50; sr phys Brookhaven Nat Lab '50-51. Conn State Med Soc—AMA—Soc Am Bact—Am Soc Tropical Med—Alpha Omega Alpha—AAAS.

23 GARDNER, James Linton. Transplanted plants (Environmental factor effects); Range and crop plants (Sediment-laden water effects); Vegetation

(Arroyos control). b'01. AB '27 (Colo Coll); AM '30 (U Colo); '28-29 (U Neb); PhD '35 (U Tex). Author articles in field. Plant ecol Soil Conservation Service research div US Dept Agrl since '35. Soil Conservation Service, Box 127, State College, N.M.

10 GARDNER, Lester Durand. Aeronautics. b'76. BS '98 (MIT); Post Grad '00 (Columbia); LLD (hon) '43 (Brooklyn Poly Inst). Author articles in field. Pres Aviation Magazine '16-26; chmn bd Inst Aeronautical Sci '32-46; cons '46. Inst Aeronautical Sci (F)—Royal Aeronautical Soc (hon F)—Nat Aeronautic Assn—Aeronautical Med Assn—Gamma Alpha Rho. H: 875 W. End Av., NYC 25.

11 GARDNER, Percy W. Trusts (Instituting, supervision and revision); Corporation investment portfolios (business and charitable). b'81. PhB '03 (Brown U); student '03-05 (NY Law Sch). Author: Lawyer's Philosophy of Life '35. Former investment counsel, chairman finance committee and director Am Unitarian Assn; chairman investment committee South County Hosp. Bd mgrs and counsel Wakefield Trust Co; pres, dir chmn finance com Providence Mut Fire Ins Co. Am Bar Assn—Internat Law Assn—Am Judicature Soc—RI Bar Assn. Turks Head Bldg., Providence.†◎

12 GARDNER, Robert Edward. Gunmakers (American, foreign); Fire arms. b'91. Compiled 10,600 listings of gunsmiths, bladesmiths, armourers (defensive armour), bowyers and cannon founders, with pertinent data; research on location, dates, period of activity, developments and identity of mark employed by craftsmen. Compiler: Arms Fabricators Ancient and Modern '34; American Arms and Arms Makers '38; Five Centuries of Gunsmith, Swordsmith and Armourer '47. O State Archeol and Hist Soc—O State Museum. 538 Rowland Bldg., Columbus 15, O. H: 1189 W. First Av., Columbus 12.

13 GARDNER, Sterling Marshall. Transformers. b'85. Grad '07 (Oakland Poly Coll Engring). Research and design neon transformers. Pres Gardner Elec Mfg Co since '17 also pres Elec Facilities Inc. Am Inst EE—Nat Assn Mfrs (mem research trade com, com coop community leaders). Gardner Electrical Manufacturing Co., 4227 Hollis St., Emeryville 8, Cal.

14 GARDNER, Thomas Samuel. Gerontotherapeutics; Gerontology; Organic chemical synthesis (Compounds having possible chemotherapeutic and pharmacological activity); Sugar derivatives; Cellulose chemistry (Ester and ether derivatives). b'08. BS '31 (State Coll Johnson City Tenn); MS '36 (U Tenn); PhD '41 (O State U); duPont F '41-42 (MIT). Research effect of nucleic acid on prolongation of life of mice, effect thyroid inhibitors and nucleic acid on length of life of mice, screening chemical factors of royal jelly, longevity factors of pantothenic acid and pyridoxin in royal jelly, effect on length of life of Drosophila of pantothenic acid, pyridoxin and sodium yeast nucleate. Research with Tenn Eastman Corp '33-35, '36-38, group leader '42-46; sr research chem Hoffman-La Roche Inc since '46. AAAS — ACS — NY Acad Sci — Tenn Acad Sci—Am Rocket Soc—Gerontological Soc—Internat Soc Gen Semantics—Sigma Xi—Research Soc Am—Phi Lambda Upsilon. Hoffman-La Roche Inc., Nutley, N.J.

15 GARDNER, W(illiam) Howlett. Shellac; Synthetic resins, plastics and high polymers. b'02. BChem '23—PhD '27 (Cornell U); MS '25 (Dartmouth Coll). Holds nine US patents. Author

articles in field. With New Products Div Nat Aniline Div Allied Chemical & Dye Corp since '44; now dir materials engr and chief Chem Materials Per Conservation Div WPB Washington '42-44. Am Inst Chem(F)—AAAS (F)—Am Soc Testing Materials—Am Chem Soc—Am Inst Chem Engrs—NY Acad Sci—Sigma Xi—NY Paint and Varnish Production Club—Phi Lambda Upsilon. 29 Merriam Av., Bronxville, N.Y.

16 GARFIELD, Viola Edmundson. Ethnology (Alaskan Indians); Art of North American Indians (Northwestern coast). b'99. BA '28—MA '31 (U Wash); PhD '39 (Columbia U). Author: Tsimshian Clan and Society '39; The Wolf and the Raven '49; Meet the Totem '51; also articles in field. Teaching staff department of anthropology U Washington since '33; field trips to BC and Alaska. Am Anthrop Assn—Am Folklore Soc—Inter-Am Soc Anthrop and Geo. University of Washington, Seattle 5.†

17 GARMAN, Raymond Leroy. Television; Radar; Chemical instrumentation; Hydrogen (Isotopic); Nuclear moments. b'07. BS '29 (Franklin and Marshall Coll); MS '31—PhD '32 (NY U). Research on photometry of spectra of isotopic hydrogen, helped develop titrator and ph meter instruments. Granted patents in field. Author: Experimental Electronics (2d edit) '45. With NYU '29-42, asst prof chem '40; group leader Radiation Lab MIT '42-46; dir research Gen Precision Lab '46-48, v-pres and tech dir since '48. ACS—APS—Optical Soc Am—AAAS—Acoustical Soc Am—Instrument Soc Am—NY Acad Sci—Inst Radio Engrs —Soc Motion Picture and Television Engrs. Received Pentathlon Award in chem '29. General Precision Laboratory, 63 Bedford Rd., Pleasantville, N.Y. H: Manville Lane.

18 GARMAN, Willard Hershel. Soils; Fertilizers; Plant nutrition and physiology. b'12. BS '33—MS '34—PhD '39 (Pa State Coll). Availability of soil and fertilizer, potassium, sodium, magnesium, calcium to plants; potassium-sodium relationships in nutrition of cotton plant. Asso prof agron U Ga '39-42; soil sci SC Agrl Expt Sta '42-47; head dept agron U Ark '47-49; prin research adminstr Office Expt Sta US DA since '49. Sigma Xi—Am Soc Agron—Soil Sci Soc Am—ACS—AAAS (F)—Gamma Sigma Delta. Office of Experiment Stations, US Department Agriculture, Washington 25.

19 GARNER, James Ryan. Posture (Seating); Posture research; Industrial fatigue; Industrial health. b'77. MD '00 (U Va). Research on Posturosis and posturasthesia and description of new operation for reducing fractures of malar bone and zygomatic arch. Author articles: Man Power; Industrial Man Power; Man Power as Affected by Posture; Circulation; The Back Bone of Industry; Cataracts in Locomotive Engineers; Postural Changes in the Spine; Posture In Its Relation to Industrial Fatigue, and others. Vice-pres directing med research Posture Research Inst Inc Elkhart Ind since '47. AMA(F)—Am Assn Indsl Physicians Surgeons(F)—Am Assn Ry Surgeons—So Med Assn—Am Ry Assn—Am Medico-Legal Assn (life mem). H: 794 Springdale Rd., N.E., Atlanta.

20 GARRETT, Henry E(dward). Psychology. b'94. AB '15 (U Richmond); MA '21—PhD '23 (Columbia). Research on learning, mental organization, experimental design, individual differences; associate editor Journal Abnormal and Social Psychology; general editor American Psychology Series.

Author: Statistics in Psychology and Education '47; Great Experiments in Psychology '41; Psychological Tests, Methods and Results '33. With Columbia U since '23, asst prof psychol '26-35, asso prof '35-43, prof since '43, head dept psychol since '41. AAAS(F)—Eastern Psychol Assn (dir '43, pres '44)—Psychometric Soc (pres '43)—NY State Assn Applied Psychol (pres '40)—Nat Inst Psychol—Am Psychol Assn (pres '46)—Nat Research Council—AAUP—Phi Beta Kappa—Sigma Xi. 35 Claremont Av., NYC 27.◎

21 GARRETT, Sherman Scott. Human pregnancy (Tests, complications, eclamptic toxemia); Human sterility (Treatment). b'00. AB '21 (U Ill); MD '25 (Johns Hopkins). Research test for human pregnancy using injections of estrone; use hydriodic acid for relieving obstruction of Fallopian tubes in treatment sterility; etiological mechanism of eclamptic toxemia of pregnancy based on hyperactivity of adrenal steroid hormones; use of testosterone, choline and digitalis glycosides as specific treatment of eclamptic toxemia; inventor new utero-tubal insufflator for treatment human sterility. Am Soc Study Sterility. 311 W. University Av., Champaign, Ill. H: 1206 W. University Av.

22 GARRISON, Karl Claudius. Psychology of adolescence; Growth and development; Educational psychology; Aptitude testing. b'00. Student '17-18, '19-21 (Lenoir-Rhyne Coll); BS '22—PhD in psychol (George Peabody Coll). Original research on different phases of growth and development, adolescent psychology. Author: Adolescence psychology '34; Psychology of Exceptional Children '40, revised edit '50; A Growth and Development '52. Co-author: Fundamentals of Psychology in Secondary Education '36; Workbook in Adolescent Psychology '51. Contributor: Skinner's Educational Psychology (revised edit) '45; Gray's Psychology in Use '51. Asso prof edn Tchrs Coll Conn '41-46; prof psychol Ga State Coll Women '46-47; dean of instrn State Tchrs College Frostburg Md '47-48; asso prof and prof edn U Ga since '48. Am Ednl Research Assn—AAAS(F)—So Society Philos and Psychol—Phi Kappa Phi—Phi Delta Kappa—Kappa Delta Pi—Kappa Phi Kappa. College of Education, University of Georgia, Athens, Ga.

23 GARRISON, Olen Branford. Vegetable crops; Plant breeding (Asparagus, sweet potatoes); Irrigation; Varieties. b'10. Fellow '36-39—PhD '39 (Cornell U); BS '33 (Clemson Agrl Coll); MS '34 (La State U). Author articles in field. With Clemson Coll since '45, now prof hort and horticulturist. Am Soc Hort Sci—So Agrl Workers—SC Acad Sci. Clemson Agricultural College, Horticultural Department, Clemson, S.C.‡

24 GARTLEIN, Carl W(itz). Aurora borealis; Spectroscopy. b'02. BA '24 (DePauw U); PhD '29—Heckscher research grant '29 (Cornell). Author articles in field. With Cornell U since '26, now supt tech service personnel; dir Nat Geog Soc Cornell U Study of Aurora Borealis since '38. Am Phys Soc—Optical Soc Am—Am Geophys Union—Am Assn Variable Star Observers—Sigma Xi—Phi Beta Kappa. Department of Physics, Cornell University, Ithaca, N.Y.†

25 GARTNER, William Louis. Airplanes (Engines, propellors, hydraulic mechanisms, instruments); Automobiles (Engines, steering mechanisms, alignment, brakes). b'06. Student '26-27 (U Kan). Owner and mgr Gartner Motors and Safety Service since '29;

administrative procurement inspector Air Tech Service Command '42-45. Soc Automotive Engrs — Am Ordnance Assn. 1318 W. 1st St., Coffeyville, Kan.

10 GARVE, T. Walter. Ceramics; Dryers; Kilns; Clayware plants. b'80. ME (State Inst Tech Chemnitz, Germany) '03; B Ceramic Engring '16— Ceramic Engr '40 (O State U). Design, construction, performance and efficiency of structural clayware plants, kilns, and dryers. Author: Factory Design and Equipment and Manufacture of Claywares (3rd edit) '51. Cons engr since '26. Nat Soc Prof Engrs—Inst Ceramic Engrs—Am Ceramic Soc(F). Clay Testing Laboratory, Engineering Office, Columbus. H: 69 W. Weisheimer Rd., Columbus 14, O.

11 GASOREK, Kathryn Eleanor Albert. Mental deficiency (Projective techniques). b'19. AB '41 (NJ Coll for Women); AM '42—PhD '51 (Columbia U). Research on effects of glutamic acid administration on mental defective individuals, effect of amino acid evaluated by means of psychological tests and case histories; study reliability and consistency of certain characteristics of one projective technique, practical application of projective techniques principally Rorschach and drawings. Author: The Reliability and the Consistency of Formal and Structural Aspects of Childrens Drawings '51. Research asst dept biochemistry NY State Psychiatric Inst '45; asst chief clin psychologist Halloran VA Hosp. Am Psychol Assn—Soc for Projective Techniques—Am Statis Assn— AAAS. H: RFD 1, Plainfield, N.J.

12 GAST, Paul F(rederick). Atomic energy. b'16. AB '37 (Ohio State U); PhD '41 (U Wash). Contributor articles to Physical Review on cosmic rays and on nuclear fission. Physicist research lab Remington Arms Co. Bridgeport Conn '41-43; engaged tech liaison and development work in connection with design of nuclear reactors for DuPont Co, Hanford works of Manhatten Project '43-44; chief physics sect Hanford works for Gen Electric Co Richland Wash since '46. Am Phys Soc—Am Inst Physics—AAAS— Phi Beta Kappa. General Electric Co., Richland, Wash.⊚

13 GATES, Arthur Irving. Educational psychology (Reading disabilities, scholastic abilities, intelligence tests, spelling difficulty). b'90. BL '14—MA '15 (U Calif); PhD '17 (Columbia). Author: Interest and Ability in Reading '30; Reading for School Administrators '31; Generalization in Spelling '35; Improvement of Reading '47; Spelling Difficulties '37; Teaching Reading to Slow Learning Pupils '43; (with D E Russell) Diagnosis of Disabilities in Spe'ling '37; (with A T Jersild, T R McConnell, R C Challman) Educational Psychology '48, and others; also articles in field. Prof ednl psychol Teachers Coll Columbia since '24; exec officer dept Psychol and research methods since '33. AAAS (F)—Am Assn Ednl Research (pres '43)—Am Assn Applied Psychol (chmn edn sect '40-42)—NEA—Am Psychol Assn (council). Teachers College, Columbia University, NYC 27.⊚

14 GATES, Charles Marvin. History of western United States; War of 1812 (Diplomacy). b'04. BA '26 (Yale); MA '28 (Harvard); PhD '34 (U Minn). Research on inter-relations of frontier and metropolitan centers of US during nineteenth and early twentieth centuries, economic colonialism in West, pattern of metropolitan expansion, dispersion of urban culture in West, diplomacy of war of 1812. Editor: Five Fur Traders of the Northwest '33; Messages of the Governors of the

Territory of Washington to the Legislative Assembly, 1853-1889 '40; Readings in Pacific Northwest History: Washington, 1790-1895 '41; also articles in field. Acting curator manuscripts Minn Hist Soc '34-35; regional hist Nat Park Service Indianapolis '35-36; instr hist U Washington '36-39, asst prof '39-43, asso prof since '43. AHA— Miss Valley Hist Assn—Am Assn State and Local Hist. Awarded grant-in-aid for research on hist of Am westward expansion Hist Am Civilization Lib Congress '46-47. University of Washington, Seattle 5.

15 GATES, Gordon Enoch. Earthworms. b'97. BA '19—DS (hon) '48 (Colby Coll); MA '20—PhD '33 (Harvard). Research on taxonomy, zoogeography, morphology, physiology of earthworms at museums and laboratories in US and foreign countries. Author articles in field. Prof biol and dept head Colby Coll since '48. AAAS —Sigma Xi—Washington Acad Sci— Soc Systematic Zool. Research fellow Mus Comparative Zool Harvard '47-48. Biology Department, Colby College, Waterville, Me.

16 GATHMAN, Albert. Solvents; Coatings (Surface); Lubricants; Antifreezes. b'10. BS in chem '43 (Poly Inst Brooklyn). Research on industrial solvents for surface coatings field, cleaning solvents and extractants, purification and recovery of solvents, impregnants and glues for wallboard. Granted six patents on solvents. With Synthetic Resins div Am Cyanamid and Chem Co '33-36; with Chem Products Div Esso Standard Oil Co since '36. ACS—ASTM (com D-1 and D-2) —Fedn Paint Varnish and Prodn Clubs —Phi Lambda Upsilon. Esso Standard Oil Co., Linden, N.J.

17 GATKE, Robert Moulton. Pacific Northwestern United States history; Rhodendrons. b'96. AB—AM (Willamette U); BD (Kimball Sch Theol); PhD (Am U). Editor The Rhododendron Yearbook. Author: Chronicles of Willamette: The Pioneer University of the West '43; also articles in field. Instr hist, later prof polit sci and hist Willamette U since '20. Am Rhododendron Soc. Willamette University, Salem, Ore. H: 280 Richmond Av.†

18 GAUDET, Frederick Joseph. Psychology (Personality, human nature); Industrial; Vocational guidance. b'02. AA '27—EdM '28 (Harvard U); PhD '38 (Columbia); student Washington Sch Psychiat since '47. Author articles in field. Asso prof psychol Stevens Inst since '40, dir dept psychol studies since '45; cons VA Mental Hygiene Div since '47. NY State Psychol Assn—NJ Psychol Assn (exec sec '47-50)—Am Psychol Assn—Nat Vocational Guidance Assn—NJ Guidance and Personnel Assn. Stevens Institute, Hoboken, N.J. H: 150 Claremont Av., NYC 27.

19 GAUL, Albro T. Wasps; Hornets; Yellowjackets; Insects in stored products. b'17. BS '40 (Long Island U); '42 (NYU). Research on the biology and sociology of Vespine wasps during the active season, maintenance of wasp colonies in hives, sex and egg deposition habits, nest structure and utility, geographic distribution, interspecific and intraspecific toleration, taste sensitivity comparisons between adults and larvae, social and individual parasites, castes and labor divisions and specialties in the nest, chemistry and physics of the nest and nest paper, position of social wasps in the general ecological picture, economic importance of social wasps. Author articles in field. Entomol NYC Dept Parks '41-42; with US Dept Agr '42-46; head sci dept Adelphi Acad

since '46. Royal Entomol Soc (London F)—Am Assn Econ Entomol—Entomol Soc Am—AAAS. 282 Lafayette Ave., Bklyn 5.†

20 GAVER, Kenneth Merlyn. Starch derivatives; Food, dairy and carbohydrate chemistry. b'08. AB '30—PhD '45 (O State U); student (W Va U, Charleston Coll). Holder numerous patents on soap, wetting and emulsifying agents, oil emulsions, powdered flavors, mildew-proofing carbohydrates, flavoring materials and others. Author articles in field. Research Asso Keever Starch Co since '45. Am Chem Soc—Am Assn Cereal Chem—AAAS— Soc Plastics Engrs—Sigma Xi. Keever Starch Company, 324 Dering Rd., Columbus 7, O.

21 GAW, Harold P. Metallurgy and production of flat-rolled steel. b'03. AB '28 (Stanford). Research on chemical reaction and sulphur removal in open hearth furnaces and on hot rolling, cold reduction, and annealing. With Armco Steel Corp since '28, now works metallurgist. AIMME—Alpha Chi Sigma. East Works Metallurgical Dept., Armco Steel Corp., Middletown, O. H: 218 Bellemonte St.

22 GAY, Cecil H(ardin). Penstock (Design); Pressure vessel (Design); Steam boilers (High pressure); Machine tools (Design). b'05. BS (elec engring) '28 (U Nev). Research and development design for large branch connections and supporting systems on penstocks, special high pressure high temperature vessels including steam drums for large power boilers, accumulator vessels for hydro-pneumatic systems for large hydraulic presses, pressure vessels for oil refineries; research on machine frame weldments and casting design, structural design of plattens for heavy presses, welded frames for large upsetting machines; design high pressure high temperature steam power generating units. Granted patents in field. With Babcock and Wilcox Co since '28. O Soc Prof Engrs—Am Soc ME—Engring Found (welding research council)— Newcomen Soc—Phi Kappa Phi.

23 GAYTON, A(nna) H(adwick). Indian pottery; Folklore; Indians of western United States. b'99. AB '23— MA '24—PhD '25 (U Calif). Research on ethnography of California Indians, especially Yokuts and Western Mono '28-30, Espirito Santo festivals of the California Portuguese '47. Author: The Festa da Serreta at Gustine '48; The Uhle Collections from Niveria '27; Yokuts and Western Mono Potterymaking '29; Yokuts and Western Mono Ethnography '48. Co-author: (with A L Kroeber) The Uhle Pottery Collections from Nazca '27; (with S S Newman) Yokuts and Western Mono Myths '40. Asst Yale U Publications in Anthrop '35-40; lecturer dept decorative art U Calif '48; asso prof '49. Am Anthrop Assn (F, exec bd western br '48)—Am Folklore Soc (ed asst '35-40, vp '46, chmn com on research '46-48)—Soc Am Archaeol — Calif Folklore Soc — NM Folklore Soc. Nat Research Council fellow '28-30, John Guggenheim fellow '47. Department of Decorative Art, University of California, Berkeley.†

24 GAZDA, Antoine. Cannon (Automatic rapid-firing); Helicopters (Jet). b'95. ME '26 (Vienna Tech Coll). Inventor 20 mm automatic anti-aircraft Gazda cannon and of first jet-propelled helicopter. Granted 284 patents in aviation, armament and automotive fields. Owner Gazda Engring Vienna Austria '18-28; owner Establissement Gazda Paris France '28-34; armament engr, export mgr Swiss Oerlikon Works '35-39; founder, v-pres Pilatus Swiss Aircraft Works '39; founder, v-pres Am Oerlikon Gazda Corp '40; founder, pres Am Octanator Corp '44. Gazda Engineering, 2107 Industrial Trust Bldg., Providence.

10 GEARY, James A. Algonquian Indian languages (Phonetics, grammar); Celtic languages; Comparative linguistics. b'82. AB '03 (Coll Holy Cross); PhD '31 (Cath U Am); '03-06 (St Sulpice, Paris); '06-07 (Am Coll, Louvain, Belgium); Author: An Irish Version of Innocent III's De Contempti Mundi; also articles in field. Asso prof Celtic langs and comparative linguistics Cath U Am since '44. Catholic University of America, Washington.

11 GECK, Francis Joseph. Interior design; French and Italian art. b'00. Diploma '25 (Paris Atelier, NY Sch Fine and Applied Arts); MFA 46 (Syracuse U). Exhibited water colors oils designs in National Regional and Local Jury Shows, numerous one-man exhibitions. Author: French Interiors and Furniture: The Historical Development '32; Bibliographies of Italian Art (6 vols) '32-41; Art: Period Styles '45; Exercises in Perspective '48; Introduction to Interior Decoration '52; articles in field. Instr fine arts U Colo '30, asso prof since '44. Boulder Artists Guild—Medieval Acad Am—Biblio Soc Am—Am Artists' Profl League—Delta Phi Delta (natl first vp '48). Arts 319, University of Colorado, Boulder, Colo.

12 GEDDES, Jos(eph) A(arch). Utah (Social problems); Social institutions. b'84. AB '07 (Brigham Young Coll); summer student (U Chicago); AM '13 —PhD '24 (Columbia); student '38 (NY Sch Social Work). Author: United Order Among the Mormons '24; The Community High Road to Better Things '35. Asso prof econs and sociology Utah State Agrl Coll '26-28, prof and chmn dept sociology since '28, dir grad div social work since '38. Director various cooperative associations; pres Utah State Conf Social Work '33-34; mem exec com Nat Assn Sch for Social Adminstrn since '45; bd dirs Cooperative League USA since '48. Utah Acad Sci Arts and Letters(F)— Am Sociol Soc—Rural Sociol Soc—AA AS—Am Acad Social and Polit Sci. Utah State Agricultural College, Logan, Utah. H: 644 E. 6th N.☉

13 GEDDES, Ray Llewellyn. Bubble plate efficiencies; Petroleum distillation, plant design, conversion, synthesis. b'05. BS '27 (Kan State Agrl Coll); MS '28—PhD '30—research fellow '29-30 (O State U). Developed method of prediction of ASTM distillation analysis curves from true boiling analyses, method of prediction of plate efficiencies from fundamental diffusion phenomena. Author articles in field. Cons Stone & Webster Engring Corp Boston since '39. Am Chem Soc—Am Inst Chem Engrs— Sigma Xi—Phi Kappa Phi. Stone & Webster Engineering Corp., 49 Federal St., Boston 7. H: 272 Quinobequin Rd., Waban 68, Mass.†

14 GEDDES, William Findlay. Agricultural biochemistry; Food technology (Cereal, carbohydrates, amylases). b'96. BSA '18—MA '25 (U Toronto); MS '28—PhD '29 (U Minn). Editor: Cereal Chemistry since '43. Author articles in field. Chief div agrl biochem U Minn since '45; com on food research OQMG '45-48. sub-com on foods Com on QM Problems Nat Research Council since '48. Can Inst Chem(F)—AAAS— Agrl Inst Can—Am Assn Cereal Chem (chmn com standardization of lab baking '32-34, vp '37-38, pres '38-39, ed Transactions since '42, chmn com on monographs since '44)—Am Chem Soc (councillor for Minn '40-42, '47-48, chmn Minn sect '43-44)—Am Oil Chem Soc—Inst Food Tech (com edn '46-47)

—Sigma Xi. Awarded Coronation medal by King George VI; Osborne Medal by American Association of Cereal Chemists '50. University Farm, St. Paul 1.☉

15 GEER, C. Willard. Television (Color). b'02. BS '27—MS '30 (U Washington); PhD '39 (U Cal Berkeley). Research on color screen processes; advisor color television Technicolor Motion Picture Corp since '50. Holds patent for three-color tube and screen for color television. Head dept physics Long Beach City Coll Cal '38-43; faculty U So Cal since '43, dir labs since '44, asst prof since '46. Am Assn Physics Tchrs—Phi Beta Kappa—Sigma Xi—Phi Delta Kappa—Sigma Pi Sigma. University of Southern California, LA 7.

16 GEHMAN, Harry Merrill. Mathematics. b'98. AB '19—AM '20—PhD '25 (U Pa). Prof and head mathematics dept U Buffalo since '20; head math dept Shrivenham (Eng) U US Army '45. AAAS(F)—Math Assn Am(sectreas)—Am Math Soc—Inst Math Statistics—Canadian Math Congress—Phi Beta Kappa—Sigma Xi. H: 163 Winspear Av., Buffalo 15.†☉

17 GEIGER, Charles Francis. Silicon carbide, fused alumina, and mullite refractories; Rocket refractories. b'93. Student '12-13 (Crane Jr Coll Chicago); BS (Ceramic engring) '15 (U Ill). Developed products, manufacturing processes, and techniques in field of special and rocket refractories; devised high temperature tunnel kilns employed in production. Holds 21 patents in field. Author articles: The History of the Development of Silicon Carbide Refractories '23; A New Type of Dried Heater '26. Co-author articles: Notes on Use of Silicon Carbide Kiln Furniture '47; Applications of Super Refractories made from Electric Furnace Products '48. Tech supervisor refractories dept Carborundum Co Niagara Falls NY '19-20, refractories engr refractories div Perth Amboy '20-46, tech mgr refractories div since '46. Am Ceramic Soc (F, chmn refractories div '30)—Ceramic Assn NJ (pres '37)—Inst Ceramic Engrs (pres '48)—ASTM—Am Rocket Soc. The Carborundum Co., P.O. Box 268, Perth Amboy, N.J. H: 176 Maple Av., Metuchen.

18 GEIRINGER, Karl. Joseph Haydn; Johannes Brahms; Musical instruments; Bach & Family; Seventeenth century Austrian music. b'99. Student '18-22 (U Berlin); PhD '22 (U Vienna). Editor of previously unknown works by Haydn, Schubert, Schumann, Brahms and others. Author: Brahms '47; Musical Instruments '43; Haydn '46. Prof hist and theory of music Boston U Coll Music since '41; chmn dept music hist theory and literature; chmn div grad studies. Am Musicol Society (bd) —Music Teachers Nat Assn. 25 Blagden St., Boston.

19 GEISLER, Walter Charles. Gemmology. b'08. BS '29 (Butler U); MA '36 (Ind U). Research Indiana University on cutting and polishing sapphires, nature of finished polished surface as affected by particle sizes; construction of diamond saws for cutting quartz crystal, electrical deposition of silver and production of a finish without polish. Co-discoverer with F B Wade on cause and color of turquoise; patents on lapidary cement, final polishing agent for gem cutting. Research chemist Indianapolis Water Co '27-29; asst dir research Ball Brothers '29-30; Shortridge High Sch chem dept since '30; prof Chem Ind U Ext. Am Chem Soc—Ind Acad Sci—AAAS— North Central Assn Sci and Math Teachers. Shortridge High School, 34th

and Meridian Sts., Indianapolis. H: 3632 Drexel.

20 GELB, I(gnace) J(ay). Hittite hieroglyphics; Assyriology; Near East (Ancient history); Grammatology. b '07. PhD '29 (U Rome). Research on deciphering Hittite hieroglyphics; editor Chicago Assyrian Dictionary since '47. Author: Hittite Hieroglyphs I-III '31-42; Inscriptions from Alishar '35; A Study of Writing or The Foundations of Grammatology '51; Hurrians and Subarians '44. Co-author: (with P M Purves and A A MacRae) Nuzi Personal Names '43. With U Chicago since '29, prof Assyriology since '47. Am Oriental Soc—Am Schs Oriental Research — Linguistic Soc Am — Soc Asiatique (hon mem)—Finnish Oriental Soc (corresponding mem). 1155 E. 58th St., Chgo 37.☉

21 GELHAUS, Henry Ferdinand. Ships (Repair, construction). b'86. Student (Humboldt Mech and Naval Archtl Coll). In shipbuilding business since '01, supt machinery shipbldg plant Craig Shipbuilding Co '17-19; supt engr, marine supt Swayne & Hoyt Inc '19-40; vp, mgr shipbuilding, drydocking and repair Todd Shipyards Corp Brooklyn '41-46, mgr sales, shipbuilding and repair Pacific Coast '46-51; pres The Log '23-40. Soc Naval Architects and Marine Engrs—Soc Naval Engrs. Pier 36, SF 4. H: 2930 25th Av., SF 16.

22 GELTZ, Charles Gottlieb. Silviculture: Dendrology; Silvics. b'96. BSF '24 (Pa State Forest Sch); MSF '27 (Calif U); PhD candidate '40-41 (Duke U). Work on forest fire prevention and suppression, study of causes of forest fires, distribution of Clarke-McNary funds for forest protection purposes; research on control of damping-off in beds of sugar pine seedlings by use of uspulin and semesan, silvicultural systems, regional silviculture, planting problems with slash and longleaf pine under various conditions of site, cutting system applicable to young second growth stands. Jr forester US Forest Service Calif, Ida, Ark, dist forest ranger Ouachita Nat Forest Ark '27-29; asst prof Purdue U '30-35; asso prof and dir Purdue Forestry Camp '35-40 and '46; prof silviculture Fla U since '46. Fla Acad Sci—AAAS—Soc Am Foresters—Xi Sigma Pi—Am Forestry Assn—Fla Forestry Assn—Am Geographic Soc(F). School of Forestry, University of Florida. Gainesville, Fla.☉

23 GENSAMER, Maxwell. Metals (Properties). b'02. BS '24—MS '31— DSc '33 (Carnegie Inst Tech). Research on constitution of alloys of iron, carbon, and manganese, properties of steels as affected by composition and distribution of constituents in microstructure, effects of alloying elements in solution in otherwise pure iron, texture of rolled and drawn steel and directional properties, forming properties of steel and aluminum alloy sheets and testing for formability, brittle behavior of steel in large structures and testing for susceptibility, yield point and strain aging in mild steel; consultant Atomic Energy Commission Division of Research. member of subcommittee on materials for aircraft structures for National Advisory Committee for Aeronautics. Author articles in field. Plant metall Am Chain and Cable Co, Page Steel and Wire Co '24-29; research metall to prof Carnegie Inst Tech '29-45; head dept min tech Pa State Coll '45-47; asst to dir of research Carnegie Ill Steel Corp '47-50; prof metall Sch Mines Columbia since '50. Am Soc Metals (Howe medal '32, Campbell lectr '45, chmn pub com '41-43)—AIMME (chmn inst metals div, dir inst '50). School of Mines, Columbia University, NYC 27.⊙

10 GENSTEIN, Edgar S. Emulsifying agents; Rayon sizing compounds; Locust bean gum. b'99. BS '18 (Coll City NY); '18 (Carnegie Inst Tech, George Washington U). Research on and development of technical process materials and industrial chemical specialties including emulsifying agents, soluble oils, gums, glues, sizings, adhesives. Holder patents in field. Pres and tech dir Kem Products Co Inc Newark NJ since '22. Am Inst Chem(F)—Phi Beta Kappa. c/o Kem Products Co., 229 High St., Newark 2, N.J.

11 GENTRY, Glenn. Herpetology of Tennessee. b'95. AB '23—DPE '25 (YMCA grad sch, Vanderbilt U); MS '37 (Peabody Coll for Teachers). Author articles in field. Aquatic biol Tenn Div Game and Fish since '41. Acad Sci—Am Fisheries Soc—Am Soc Ichthyology Herpetology. Received Tenn Acad Sci research grant '38. 14 Colonial Circle, Donelson, Tenn.

12 GENTRY, Howard Scott. Botany of Mexico; Plant geography. b'03. BA '31 (U Calif); PhD '47 (U Mich). Biologic field exploration in southwestern US and Mexico '33-41. Author: Rio Mayo Plants '42; Land Plants Collected by the Allan Hancock Expedition of 1939 '48; Land Plants Collected by A Hancock Pacific Expedition '49; also articles in field. Research asso bot Allan Hancock Found U So Calif since '46. Am Geog Soc NY—Calif Bot Soc—Am Soc Plant Taxonomists—Torrey Bot Club—Soc Vertebrate Paleontol—Sociedad Botanica de Mexico.

13 GEORGE, John Lothar. Sandhill crane; Great Blue Heron; Effect of DDT on birds. b'16. Student '34-36 (U Wis); BS '39—MS '41 Rackham spl fellow '47-50—PhD '52(U Mich). Author: Dance of the Sandhill Crane '39; Great Blue Heron Spearing Fish '39; also articles in field. Biol US Dept Interior Fish and Wildlife Service Md '46-47; lect dept zool Vassar Coll since '50. Wilson Ornithol Club —Am Ornithol Union—Sigma Xi. Department of Zoology, Vassar College, Poughkeepsie, N.Y.

14 GEORGE, Percy Frederick. Magnesium metallography and metallurgy; Primary cells. b'11. BS '32 (Mich Coll Mining and Tech). Holder three patents preventing corrosion of light metal gasoline tanks '40-44. Author articles in field. With Dow Chem Co since '34, now in magnesium primary cell research. Am Soc Metals. Spl award for series of photomicrographs and first prize in light metals classification metallographic exhibit Nat Metal Congress '46; $1500 award for paper on arc welding magnesium James F Lincoln Arc Welding Foundation '47. Magnesium Laboratories, Dow Chemical Co., Midland, Mich.†

15 GEORGE, W(esley) C(ritz). Vertebrates (development); Comparative hematology; Philosophy of science. b '88. AB '11—AM '12—PhD '18 (U NC); Hinton Maule fellow '17-18 (Princeton). Co-editor Journal of Elisha Mitchell Science Society. Prof biology Guilford Coll NC '16-17; adjunct prof zoology U Ga '19; asso prof histology and embryology U Tenn Med Sch '19-20, asso professor U NC '20-24, prof since '24, head dept anatomy since '40; investigator marine biology summers US Fisheries Biol Sta Beaufort NC, Bermuds Biol Sta, Bass Biol Sta Fla. AAAS(F)—Am Assn Anatomists—Am Soc Zoologists—Am Soc Human Genetics—Elisha Mitchell Sci Soc (pres '26)

—NC Acad Sci—Sigma Xi—Phi Chi. University of North Carolina Medical School, Chapel Hill, N.C.⊙

16 GEORGI, (Frederick) Carl Eduard. Micro-organisms (Biochemistry, physiology); Fermentation biochemistry; Fungistatic and fungicidal agents. b'06. BS '30—MS '32—PhD '34 (U Wis). Co-author: Laboratory Manual for General Bacteriology '46; also articles in field. With U Neb since '35, now prof bact; cons Smith-Dorsey Pharm Co. AAAS(F)—Am Chem Soc (chmn Neb sect '42, '47, sec-treas '44, '45)—Soc Am Bact (pres Mo Valley Br '42-43, councilor '43-44)—Soc Exptl Biol and Med—Soc Gen Microbiol, Brit —Neb Acad Sci (pres '44-45, councilor '46-47)—Sigma Xi (pres Neb chap '48-49). Fulbright Scholar (France) '51-52. Department of Bacteriology, University of Nebraska, Lincoln 8, Neb†

17 GEORGIA, Frederick Raymond. Water chemistry; Chlorination of water. b'92. BChem '15—PhD '22 (Cornell U). Research in coagulants and coagulation and flocculation of water, sedimentation; filtering media and filter construction, flow control, bacteriological culture media. Prof chem Rollins Coll '26-33; rector sec and prof chem Black Mt Coll '33-37; supervisor water works Cornell U since '38. ACS —Am Water Works Assn—Soc Am Bact—Am Pub Health Assn(F)—AAA S(F)—Sigma Xi. Forest Home, Ithaca, N Y.

18 GEPPERT, Otto Emil. Maps; Map mountings; Globes (Geographical, astronomical); Models (Anatomical, botanical, zoological). b'89. Student '10-11 (Lewis Inst); '12-14 (Young Men's Christian Assn Coll); '15-16 (Northwestern U). Research on foreign and domestic maps, use of slated outline globes. Sec-treas, gen mgr Denoyer-Geppert Co since '16. Assn Am Geog—Nat Council Geog Teachers —Nat Council for Soc Studies—Am Assn School Administr—NEA (life). Denoyer-Geppert Co., 235 Ravenswood Av., Chicago 40. H: 225 Central Av., Wilmette, Ill.

19 GERARD, George. Metals (Plasticity). b'22. B Aeronautical Engring '43—M Aeronautical Engring '48—ScD '50 (NYU). Directed research program on transonic thick skin aircraft structures concerned with buckling of tapered skins, stress distribution at root of a swept wing and structural arrangements for thin wings; investigations of formability of metals, plastic buckling, buckling of sandwich construction and experimental stress analysis. Prin research engr Republic Aviation Corp '43-47; asst prof aeronautical engring NYU since '47. AS ME—Soc Exptl Stress Analysis—Aeronautical Sci—Sigma Xi—Tau Beta Pi. New York University, University Heights 53, N.Y.

20 GERARD, Ralph Waldo. Brain (Physiology). b'00. BS '19—PhD '21 (U Chicago); MD '25 (Rush Med Coll). Research electrical and chemical studies on nerve and brain; relation brain to behavior and mental traits and the social interaction of men. Author: Unresting Cells '40; The Body Functions '41; Methods in Medical Research '50; Food for Life '52. Editor: Jour Electroenceph. U Chicago '28-52; prof neurophysiol U Illinois School of Medicine since '52. Am Physiol Soc —Chicago Inst Medicine—Brit Physiol Soc—Biochem Soc—Am Neurological Assn—AAAS—Phi Beta Kappa— Sigma Xi—Alpha Omega Alpha. Medal of Charles U (Prague); Order of White Lion 4th Class (Czech government). 912 S. Wood St., Chgo 11. 1209 Astor St., Chgo.⊙

21 GERBERICH, Albert Horwell. Genealogy (Pennsylvania German). b '98. AM '18 (Dickinson Coll); AM '26 (U Pa); PhD '32 (Johns Hopkins). Research and compilation cyclopaedia immigrant ancestors Pennsylvania German families and their lives. Author: The Gerberich Family '25; The Brenneman History '33; The Backenstoss Family '50; others in ms. Nat Genealogical Soc — Genealogical Soc Pa—Am Soc Genealogists—Pa German Soc—Huguenot Soc Pa—Pa Junto —Phi Beta Kappa. Room 4215, Department of State, Washington.

22 GERDES, John. Corporate law; Bankruptcy. b'86. BLitt '07 (Berea Coll); AM '18—LLB '10—LLM '11—JD '12 (NYU). Member National Bankruptcy Conference, chairman committee on reorganizations; adviser Restatement of the Law of Business Associations of American Law Institute; member rules committee Federal Court in NY. Author: Gerdes on Corporate Reorganization (3 vols). Prof law of corporate finance and corporate reorgn NYU since '22. Am Judicature Soc—Am Law Inst—Am Bar Assn (chmn com on reorgn, sec on corp banking and mercantile law)—NY State Bar Assn—Assn Bar City NY— Phi Delta Phi. 1 Wall St., NYC 5.†⊙

23 GERIG, John Lawrence. Celtic and Romance languages and literatures; Romany (Gypsy) language. b'78. BA '98—MA '99—LLD '41 (U Mo); PhD '02 (U Neb); Eléve Titulaire de l'Ecole des Hautes-Etudes '03-05 (U Paris); LittD (hon) '27 (U Rome). Research on Celtic literature and philology, Old Irish, Manx, Scottish Gaelic, Old Welsh, Cornish, Old Breton, Gaulish, Romance languages philology and phonetics, Old French literature, French Renaissance literature, Italian, Provençal, and Spanish language and literatures; founder Instituto di Coltura Italiana negli Stati Uniti, president '23-29; president Institute Rumanian Culture since '26; American member International Committee Experts in Linguistic Bibliography and International Committee of Literary History; assistant editor Edgren's Italian Dictionary '02, co-founder and associate editor '10-25; editor-in-chief Romanic Review '25-37, advisory editor '37-46; associate founder Revista de Estudios Hispanicos; founder, advisory editor Celtic Digest since '38. Author: Antoine Arlier and the Renaissance at Nimes '29; also articles in field. With Williams Coll since '06, prof emeritus since '44; exec officer dept Romance langs Columbia '19-29. Italian Hist Soc Am (pres '27-33)—India Acad Am (pres '30-33)—India Soc Am (vp since '30)—Italian Inst Culture (vp since '34)—Am Irish Hist Soc (exec council since '39 and hon)—Modern Lang Assn Am (life)—Am Philol Assn (life)— Am Iona Society—Phi Beta Kappa, and other Am and fgn organizations. Decorated Cavaliere della Corona d'Italia for distinguished services Italian culture in Am '25. Chevalier Legion of Honor '27; cmdr Crown of Rumania '31; awarded gold medal Am Irish Hist Soc '44. 39 Claremont Av., NYC 27.†⊙

24 GERKING, Shelby Delos. Indiana and Midwestern fish distribution; Fish populations in lakes and streams. b'18. AB '40 (DePauw U); PhD '44 (Ind U). Studied distribution of Midwestern fishes in relation to their migration northward after ice retreat. Author article: The Distribution of the Fishes of Indiana '45; and others. Physiol research asso in war project Ind U '44-46, instr zool since '46. Am Soc Zool (asso)—Wild Life Soc (asso)—Am Soc Ichthyology Herpetology — Am Soc Limnol Oceanog—Ind Acad Sci—Am

Fisheries Soc—Sigma Xi. Department of Zoology, Indiana University, Bloomington, Ind.†

10 GERLA, Morton. Rockets (Solid propellant); Machine guns. b'16. BS (ME) '37 (Coll City of NY); spl course '41 (George Washington U); '44 (Cal Inst Tech). Production of 11-¾ inch aircraft rocket; initiated design rapid firing five inch spinner rocket launcher for aircraft; test and production experimental prototypes of expendable multiple rocket launchers for aircraft; production early type rocket accelerated bomb; in charge design, development, and testing new machine guns for aircraft; development improved feed mechanism for machine guns. Design and development naval ordnance advancing to ordnance engr in charge aircraft machine guns, rocket launchers, rockets and testing USN Gun Factory Washington '38-45; asst chief engr in charge design automatic naval and aircraft machine guns Industro-Matic Corp Am NYC '45-47; in charge design high-speed automatic machinery Superior Development Corp NYC '48-51. Am Soc ME—Am Rocket Soc—Am Soc Metals—Soc Exptl Stress Analysis—Tau Beta Pi. Professional engr NY, Conn. Screw Corporation of America, 34 Meadow St., New Britain, Conn. H: 30 Arnold Way, W. Hartford 7.

11 GERLACH, George Henry. Menthol; Alkaloids (Chemistry). b'10. PhC '31—BS '32—MS '37—PhD '41 (Western Res U). Studies in production menthol from natural and synthetic sources in US, Latin America, China, Japan; developed commercial method of preparation of alkaloid Scopolamine from new plant source. Contributor: Economic Botany '48. Sci dir Strong Cobb and Co Inc Cleveland '34-38, vp '38-41; tech adv Vick Chem Co NYC since '41. ACS—Am Pharm Assn—AA AS—Sigma Xi—Rho Chi. Vick Chemical Co., 122 E. 42d St., NYC.

12 GERLETTI, John Dominic, Jr. Juvenile delinquency (Police training). b'15. BS '39 (La Crosse State Tchrs Coll Wis); MS '47—EdD '49 (U So Cal). Development curriculum for in-service training program of juvenile police officers; evaluation and improvement present methods for treatment juvenile problem; check surveys of existing problems in selected areas, and analysis of duties of juvenile officers. Author syllabus: Materials for the Study of the Problems of Juvenile Police Officers '49. Lecturer Delinquency Control Inst Sch Pub Adminstrn U Cal since '46, research asso '49-50, now asst prof pub adminstrn. Am Soc Pub Adminstrn—Nat Soc Study Edn—Phi Delta Kappa—Pi Sigma Alpha. School of Public Administration, University of Southern California, LA.

13 GEROW, Milo Robert. Plastic films. b'07. BS '31 (U Del). Research on low gauge plastic film development and its uses, film handling, heat sealing, low gauge film tube development. Tech engr Esso Standard Oil Co '33-41; tech rep Cellulose Products Div Hercules Powder Co '41-47; gen mgr plastic films div Reynolds Metal Co '47-50; pres and tech engr Kemtek Corp and gen mgr Lyndhurst Chem Corp since '50. Soc Plastics Engrs—Society Plastics Industry—Plastics Engineers Assn Am—Salesmans Assn Am Chem Industry. Kemtek Corp., 210 Sylvan Av., Newark.

14 GERSBACHER, Willard Marion. Ecology; Bottom fauna. b'06. EdB '26 (So Ill U); AM '28—PhD '32 (U Ill). Study development animal communities on stream bottom and bottom artificial impoundments of water; evaluation rank of communities existing in these areas, studies of habitats. Asst prof So Ill U '36-38, asso prof '38-47, prof since '47, head dept since '38. AAAS—Am Micros Soc—Wildlife Soc —Am Soc Limnol and Oceanog—Ecol Soc Am—Ill Acad Sci—Tenn Acad Sci. Southern Illinois University, Carbondale, Ill.ⓒ

15 GERSHINOWITZ, Harold. Petroleum technology. b'10. BS '31 (Coll City NY); AM '32—U scholar '32-33—PhD '34 (Harvard); Parker traveling fellow '34-35 (Princeton U). Research on reaction kinetics, spectroscopy, quantum mechanics, cracking and reforming of hydro carbons. Holds patents in field. Author articles in field. Sr research tech Shell Oil Co Inc '38-'39, at Houston research lab '40-42, research dir mfg dept '43-45. vp exploration and prodn research tech div since '51. Am Chem Soc—SAE—Inst Aeronautical Sci—AAAS—Am Petroleum Inst—Phi Beta Kappa—Sigma Xi. Thayer fellow '33-34. 3737 Bellaire Blvd., Houston 25, Tex.

16 GERSTELL, Richard. Wildlife management; Avian and mammalian physiology; Radiological aspects of atomic warfare. b'10. AB '33 (Dartmouth); PhD '42 (U Mich). Served in radiological safety section Operation Crossroads '46, later as instructor in Navy School of instruction on radiological aspects of atomic warfare. Author articles: The Pennsylvania Bounty System '37; Physiological Variations in Wild Turkeys and their Significance in Management '39; The Place of Winter Feeding in Practical Wildlife Management '42; How You Can Survive an A-Bomb Blast '50. Chief div resch Pa Game Commn '33-42; dir sales research Animal Trap Co Am '46-48. Aviation physiol USN '42-46; cons radiological defense Office Sec Defense '48-49. Am Soc Mammalogists—Am Ornithol Union—Wildlife Soc Am. 355 N. West End Av., Lancaster, Pa.†

17 GERTH, Maude Chatfield (Mrs. Ralph Eugene). Thoroughbred horses and pure bred Guernsey cattle. Student (Coe Sch of Oratory). Collaborator and director Tercentenary Horse Show and Pageant. Author: The Horse 300 Years Development in Connecticut —Entrance with Thomas Hooker to Present Day. Owner Longue Vue Farms West Hartford Conn. Homes: Longue Vue Farms and Whitman Hooker House, West Hartford, Conn.

18 GETTY, Robert. Veterinary anatomy and histology; Histopathology; Cytology; Histochemistry. b'16. DVM '40 (Ohio State U); MS '45—PhD '49 (Ia State Coll). Research on histopathology of focal hepatitis and its termination; Histocytological studies on normal bovine livers and bovine livers exhibiting focal hepatitis and telangiectasis. With dept veterinary anatomy and histology Ia State Coll since '41, prof and head dept since '51. Am Ia vet med assns—AAAS—Am Assn Anatomists—Am Genetic Assn—Phi Zeta—Phi Kappa Phi—Gamma Sigma Delta—Sigma Xi. Iowa State College, Dept. Veterinary Anatomy, Ames, Ia.

19 GEVECKER, Vernon Arthur Charles. Soil mechanics (Foundations and general); Structures (Concrete and steel); Hydraulics (Open channels). b'09. BS in CE '31—CE '50 (Mo Sch Mines Rolla); MS in CE '37 (Cal Inst Tech Pasadena ; '51 (Ia State Coll Ames). Surveys, investigations, design pertaining to rivers; supervised graduate research and thesis investigations in soil mechanics and hydraulics; professional witness flood damage lawsuit; consultant on foundation problems for power generating station and other structures; concerned with airfield, structures, soils and drainage Air Service Command. With US Engr Dept St Louis '31-35; dept civil engring Mo Sch Mines Rolla since '46. Asst constrn officer San Bernardino Air Service Command US Army '41-46. ASCE—Am Soc Engring Edn—Permanent Internat Assn Nav Congresses—US Nat Council on Soil Mechanics and Found Engring—Mo Soc Profl Engrs—Engrs Club of St Louis—Phi Kappa Phi—Chi Epsilon (hon). Dept Civil Engineering, Missouri School of Mines, Rolla, Mo. H: 1101 State St.

20 GHOSH, Stanley S. India; South Asia; Geography (Economic). b'21. BA '42—MA '44 (U Calcutta); PhD '50 (Ind U). Research on international economic and political relations of South and Southeast Asia, agricultural economics and geography of South Asia and Middle East, geography of India. Author: Economic and Commercial Geography '45; also articles in field. Econ UN FAO '46-50; lectr Am U '50-51; ed India Unit Internat Broadcasting Div US Dept State since '51. Am Polit Sci Assn—Assn Am Geog—Am Geog Soc. International Broadcasting Division, US Department of State, 250 W. 57th St., NYC 19.

21 GIANELLA, Vincent P(aul). Mineral deposits; Seismology. b'86. BS '11 (Ore State Coll); grad study '14-15 (U Ariz); MS '20 (U Neb); PhD '37 (Columbia). Author articles on seismology, economic geology and mineralogy. Member faculty Mackay Sch of Mines U Nev since '23, prof and chmn dept geology and mineralogy since '35; geologist Nev State Bur Mines '29-42; geologist and mineralogist Nev State Analytical Lab since '28; curator Mackay Mus '35-37; cons seismology for Nev, US Coast and Geodetic Survey since '38. AAAS(F)—Geol Soc Am—Soc Econ Geologists—Mineral Soc Am—Seismol Soc Am—AIMME —Sigma Xi—Phi Kappa Phi. University of Nevada, Reno. H: Valley Road.†ⓒ

22 GIANNINI, Gabriel Maria. Airplanes (Automatic control systems and computers); Guided missiles (Guidance systems). b'05. PhD (phys) '29 (Royal U. Rome). Designer automatic flight equipment, two-way loudspeaking telephone equipment, guidance systems, automatic aircraft controls, computer components. Holder 16 patents. Designer Automatic Elec Co '36-39; pres G M Giannini & Co Inc '35-50. Inst Aeronautical Sci(asso F)—APS—Acoustical Soc Am—Soc Automotive Engrs—Inst Radio Engrs—Am Soc ME—Am Rocket Soc—Instrument Soc Am. 254 W. Colorado St., Pasadena, Cal.

23 GIBBONS, Walter Joseph. Dairy cattle (Mastitis, X-disease). b'03. DVM '25)—MS '28 (Cornell). Asst prof NY State Veterinary Coll, Cornell, '26-46; prof surgery, med, head dept surgery and med Sch Veterinary Med Ala Poly Inst since '47, head prof surgery and med from '48; disease investigator in charge hyperkeratosis (X-disease survey) US Bur Animal Industry (temporary appointment) '48. Am Veterinary Med Assn—Sigma Xi—Phi Kappa Phi—Phi Zeta (charter mem, past pres)—Omega Tau Sigma (internat pres '49)—Omicron Delta Kappa. Cary Building, School of Veterinary Medicine, Auburn, Ala.

24 GIBBONS, William Joseph. Rural welfare; Population problems. b'12. AB '36—PhLic '37—STL '44 (Woodstock Coll); BS '38 (Drexel Inst Tech); '38 (U Pa); since '47 (NYU). Research on agriculture and rural problems '45-48; field work in rural areas of Maryland and Pennsylvania organizing discussion groups with rural pastors '43-44. Co-author: (with Walter Dushnyck) Refugees are People '47. Legislative work on agr for Nat Cath Rural Life Conference in Washington since '47; cons on displaced persons for War Relief Services. Nat Cath Rural Life Conf—Am Farm Econ Assn—Friends of Land. '30 W. 16th St., NYC 11.

10 GIBBS, Carlin Frary High polymers; Rubber antioxidants. b'08. BS '30 (Knox Coll); MS '32—PhD '35 (U Ill). Research on rubber chemicals, chiefly rubber antioxidants, and on high polymers, including thermoplastic, thermosetting, elastomeric types. Holds 13 patents, chiefly on rubber antioxidants. With B F Goodrich Co since '36, dir polymerization research since '44. Am Chem Soc. B. F. Goodrich Research Center, Brecksville, O.

11 GIBBS, Helen Marilla. Business history. b'06. AB '27 (Sioux Falls Coll SD); AM '32 (Stanford U). Research on economic development of California; study historical aspects Western shipping and lumber 1850-1950; analyst San Francisco Bay shipping. Co-author: (with E T Coman Jr) Time, Tide, and Timber—A Century of Pope and Talbot '49. Teaching specialist Grad Sch Bus Stanford U '44-45, research asso '47-49. Care Carl E. McDowell, 28 Woodland Av., Bronxville 8, N.Y.

12 GIBSON, James J(erome). Visual, space, depth perception; Motion picture testing and research. b'04. BS '25—AM '26—PhD '28 (Princeton U). Basic research on visual perception and human learning '27-42; wartime research on depth-perception in aviation and on psychological use of motion pictures '42-46 in AAF aviation psychology program; member of National Research Council Vision Committee since '47. Co-author and editor: Motion Picture Testing and Research '47; author: The Perception of the Visual World '50; also articles in field. Asst professor '29-36, asso prof '36-49 Smith Coll; prof Cornell U since '49. Am Psychol Assn—Soc Exptl Psychol. Department of Psychology, Cornell University, Ithaca, N.Y.

13 GIBSON, John McClure. Fertilizer and soil chemistry. b'98. BS '23 (U Ill); '28-31 (Ga Inst Tech, Columbia). Special study nitrogen production and land use of fertilizer Limburgherhof and Oppau, Germany with I G Farben Industrie A G '27. Dir production and research Cotton Producers Assn since '42. Am Soc Agron—Soil Sci Soc Am. 746 Glenn St., S.W., Atlanta. H: 885 Clifton Rd., N.E., Atlanta 6.

14 GIBSON, Joshua Sullivan. Land utilization; Climatology. b'01. BA '26 (Abilene Christian Coll); PhM '29 (U Wis); PhD '34 (Clark U). Research on agricultural geography, land utilization mapping and analysis, climatic studies, conservation natural resources, physiography, field mapping. Author: Studies in Economic Geography (with D C Ridgley) '35; Climate of the Earth '37; Atlas of the Tennessee Valley Region '36; Climate and Weather for Flight in Naval Operational Zones (with Bureau Aeronautics staff) '44; also articles in field. Prof geog West Ky Teach Coll '30-32; research geog TVA '34-37; prof geog, head dept Ala Teach Coll '37-42; instr climatology and aerology US Navy '42-43; asst prof geog Ind U '43-44; asst prof geog U Wis '45-47; asso prof geog U NC since '47. Assn Am Geog—Am Soc Profl Geog—Nat Council Geog Teach—Am Meteorol Soc—AAAS(F)—AAUP. Department of Geology and Geography, University of North Carolina, Chapel Hill, N.C.

15 GIBSON, Kasson Stanford. Spectrophotometry; Colorimetry; Photometry. b'90. AB '12—PhD '16 (Cornell U). Research, development, testing relating to lamp testing, aviation lighting, atmospheric optics, and related subjects. Author articles in field. Physicist Nat Bur Standards since '16, chief colorimetry and spectrophotometry sect '33-41, chief photometry and colorimetry sect since '41, asst chief elect and optics div since '47, optics div '41-46. Am Phys Soc(F)—Optical Soc Am (pres '39-41)—AAAS—Am Oil Chem Soc—Washington Acad Sci—Illuminating Engring Soc—Washington Philos Soc—Phi Beta Kappa—Sigma Xi. Journal Award, Soc Motion Picture Engrs '37. National Bureau of Standards, Washington '25.

16 GIBSON, Ralph Edward. Physical chemistry; Internal ballistics of rockets; Supersonic missiles. b'01. BSc '22—PhD '24 (Edinburgh U). Research on compressibilities of dunite and basalt glass and their bearing on composition of earth '26, nature of solutions and their behavior under high pressures '38. Author articles: The System Sodium Sulphate-water '27; Physical Reflections in a Chemical Mirror '41. Co-author articles: (with A Kossiakoff) The Launching of Guided Missiles; The Compressibility of Rubber '30; (with L H Adams) Changes of Chemical Potential in Concentrated Solutions of Certain Salts '33. Phys chem Carnegie Instn Washington '24-46, on leave with div 3 and 8 Nat Defense Research Com '41-44, dir research Allegany Ballistics Lab Geo Washington U '44-46; Applied Phys Lab Johns Hopkins '46, act dir Applied Physics Lab '47, dir since '48. Am Chem Soc (pres Wash sect '31)—Philos Soc Wash (vp '36-38, pres '40)—Washington Acad Med (vp '39-40)—Sigma Xi. Hillibrand prize Chem Soc Washington '39. Applied Physics Laboratory, Johns Hopkins University, 8621 Georgia Av., Silver Spring, Md.†⊙

17 GICLAS, Henry Lee. Astrometry; Photometry. b'10. BS '37 (U Ariz); '40-41 (U Calif). Search and detection of comets and asteroids, measurement of their position; brightness measurements of stars and planets; instrument maintainance. Research asst Lowell Obs since '31. Am Astron Soc—AAAS(F). Lowell Observatory, Flagstaff, Ariz.†

18 GIDDENS, Joel Edwin. Soil chemistry (Georgia). b'17. BS '40—MS '42 (Ga U) PhD '50 (Rutgers U). Soil analysis, effects cultivation on piedmont soils of Georgia, stabilization of cellulose nitrate with ammonia, mechanism of ammonia stabilization of cellulose nitrate. Holds patent (with Reeves) on stabilization of nitrocellulose. Author articles in field. Dir Soil Testing Service Ga U since '46, asso prof agron U Georgia. Sigma Xi—Phi Kappa Phi—Am Chem Soc—Am Soc Agron. Department of Agronomy, University of Georgia, Athens, Ga.†

19 GIDDINGS, James Louis Jr. Arctic archaeology; Dendrochronology (Tree-ring dating). b'09. Student '26-27, '28-29 (Rice Inst); BS '32 (U Alaska); MA '41 (U Ariz). Archaeological field trip to Kobuk River region '47, Norton Sound '48, Kotzebue Sound '40-41, Mackenzie River '46. Author articles in field. With U Alaska since '46, now asso prof anthrop. Soc Am Archaeol—Tree-Ring Soc (asso ed bull)—Am Anthrop Assn(F)—Am Geog Soc—Arctic Inst NA—Sigma Xi. University of Alaska, College, Alaska.

20 GIDDINGS, N(ahum) J(ames). Plant pathology (Virus diseases); Virus diseases of sugar beet. b'83. BS '06—MS '09 (U Vt); PhD '18 (U Wis). Discovered a new muskmelon rot and described causative organism; made detailed studies of potato late blight and of apple rust; discovered several strains of Curly-Top virus and methods of differentiating them from one another; developed methods and equipment for various phases of work with insect vector and host plants. Author articles in field. Sr path div sugar plant investigations US Dept Agr since '29. AAAS—Am Phytopath Soc (council '21, '41, vp '22)—Bot Soc Am—W Va Sci Soc—Sigma Xi—Phi Beta Kappa. 3949 Lime St., P.O. Box 31, Riverside, Calif.†

21 GIER, Herschel Thomas. Intracellular symbiosis; Cockroaches; Herpetology and mammalogy of southeastern Ohio; Foxes (Population, reproduction, food, rabies); Coyotes (Reproduction, embryology). b'07. AB '31 (Kan State Teachers Coll); PhD '36 (Ind U); research fellow '36-37 (Harvard U). Author articles in field. Asso prof zool Kan State Coll since '47. AAAS—Soc Zool—Sigma Xi. Department of Zoology, Kansas State College, Manhattan, Kan.

22 GIER, L(eland) J(acob). Botany (Ecology, taxonomy); Missouri and Kansas flora and fauna. b'04. BS '28—MS '31—AB '34 (Kan State Teachers Coll); PhD '40 (Duke U). Research on geographical distribution of mosses of Missouri; ecological relations of plant roots; taxonomy of mosses and flowering plants. Author articles: Peridermium Gall on Western Yellow Pine '38; Root Systems of Bright Belt Tobacco, and others. Sci prof Campbell Coll NC '34-41; prof biol William Jewell Coll since '41. AAAS—Bot Soc Am—Ecol Soc Am—Am Soc Plant Taxonomists—Am Bryological Soc—Kan Acad Sci. William Jewell College, Liberty, Mo.

23 GIES, William John. Tissue chemistry; Metabolism; Nutrition; Dentistry. b'72. BS '93—MS '96—ScD '14—LLD '24 (Gettysburg); PhB '94—PhD '97 (Yale); and other honorary degrees. Editor Journal Dental Research '19-36; editor Journal American College of Dentists '34-40. Author: Biochemical Researches (8 vols) '03-27; Laboratory Work in Biological Chemistry '06, and others; also articles in field. Prof biol chem Columbia since '07. AAAS (F, organizer, sect K '05-09)—Am Acad Periodontology—Exptl Biol and Med (sec '03-09, vp '09-10, '14-15, pres '17-19)—Am Soc Biol Chem (sec '06-10)—Internat Assn Dental Research (hon pres '22-28, sec '28-33, pres elect '38-39, pres '39-40)—Am Physiol Soc—Soc Pharm and Exptl Therapeutics—Phi Beta Kappa—Sigma Xi—Omicron Kappa Upsilon. Award of merit Rhode Island State Dental Soc '27; Callahan medal O State Dental Soc '28; permanent ann fellowship in biol chem Columbia founded in his honor '28 by pupils and colleagues; permanent dental research awards and fellowship founded in his honor '37 by Am Coll Dentists; Gies Foundation for Advancement of Dentistry established by dentists '50; recipient of distinguished service award, Gettysburg Coll '38. 632 W. 168th St., NYC 32.⊙

24 GIESE, Arthur C(harles). Cellular and comparative physiology; Photobiology. b'04. BS '27 (U Chicago); PhD '33 (Stanford U). Research on effects of ultra-violet radiation on life activities; associate editor Annual Review of Physiology since '47. With Stanford U '30-39, '40-47, prof biol since '47; Rockefeller Found fellow Princeton and Woods Hole '39-40; Guggenheim fellow Calif Inst Tech, Kerckhoff Marine Lab and Biochem Lab Northwestern U '47. AAAS—Am Soc Zool—Western Naturalists—Soc Gen Physiol—Sigma Xi. Biology Department, Stanford University, Cal.⊙

10 GIESE, Henry. Farm structures. b'90. BS '19—MS '27—Archtl Engr '30 (Ia State Coll). Directed Farm Structures Research Survey for US Department Agriculture '29-30. Author books and articles in field. With agrl engring dept and sect Ia State Coll since '23. Am Soc Agrl Engrs—Ia Engring Soc—Phi Kappa Phi—Sigma Xi—Tau Beta Pi—Gamma Sigma Delta. Recipient Cyrus Hall McCormick gold medal for exceptional and meritorious engring achievement in agr. Iowa State College, Agricultural Engineering Department, Ames, Ia.†⊙

11 GIESECKE, Albert Anthony. Peruvian culture and archaeology. b'83. BS '04 (U Pa); BS '05-06 (U Berlin, Paris, Lausanne); PhD '08 (Cornell U); Prof law (hon) (U Cuzco). Appointed special expert in commercial education for government of Peru '09; appointed by President of Peru as Peruvian counselor to Plebiseitary Commission of Tacna-Arica '25; third Pan-American Scientific Congress Lima '24; president educational section of sixth Pan-American Child Welfare Congress Lima '30; staff US delegation to Inter-American Peace Conference Buenos Aires '36; secretary US delegation to eighth International Conference of American States Lima '38; delegate US government to 27th Congress of Americanists Lima '39, third Pan American General Assembly of the Institute of Geography and History Lima '41; delegate to second Inter-American Indian Congress Cuzco, Peru '48. Author: The Commercial Policy of the US before 1789; Municipal Civics; also articles in field. Educator, tech adv to minister of edn Peru since '30. Am Econ Assn—Am Acad Polit Social Sci—Am Anthrop Soc—Sociedad Geografica de Lima—Sociedad de Anticuarios del Cuzco—Hispanic Soc Am—Archaeol Soc NM (hon)—Centro Geografico del Cuzco. Enon Valley, Pa.

12 GILBERT, Fabiola Cabeza de Baca. New Mexico (Foods, folklore, history . b'98. AB (Edn) '21 (Highlands U Las Vegas NM); BS (Home econ) '29 (NM Coll A&M Arts); '20 (Centro de Estudios Historicos Madrid Spain). Research on New Mexican foods, history and rural folklore '30-49; extension worker New Mexico. Author articles: Los Alimentos y su Preparacion '33; Historic Cookery '34; Native New Mexican Diets, and others. Home demonstration agt Santa Fe Co NM '29-47, home demonstration agt at large NM since '47. Epsilon Sigma Phi —Delta Kappa Gamma. Certificate recognition from Epsilon Sigma Phi for outstanding service as extension worker NM '44; Nat Home Demonstration Agts Assn award for distinguished service '46. Agricultural and Mechanical Arts College, State College, N.M.

13 GILBERT, Frank A(lbert). Physiology and taxonomy of slime moulds; Flora of West Virginia; Plant growth substances; Plant nutrients (Copper); Mineral nutrition of plants and animals. b'00. BS '22 (U Mass); MA '25—PhD '27 — teach fellow '23-24 (Harvard). Botanical expedition to Newfoundland and Labrador '25. Author: Mineral Nutrition of Plants and Animals '48; also articles in field. Research bot Battelle Memorial Inst '45-48, asst supervisor agr res '48-50. Sigma Xi—Bot Soc Am—Mycol Soc Am—Soc Plant Taxonomists—AAAS— W Va Acad Sci—So Appalachian Bot

Assn (pres). Battelle Memorial Institute, Columbus 1, O.†

14 GILBERT, Lew. Welding electrodes (Procedures, techniques). b'10. Student '28 (John Marshall Law Sch); (Rutgers U Ext Sch) (Internat Corr Schs). Special studies of behavior of moisture and characteristic moisture pickup in the lime-ferritic, low hydrogen type electrodes; operating characteristics and mechanical properties of deposited weld metal from every known type of mild steel and stainless steel welding electrodes; detailed investigation of welding procedures and techniques for all types, ferrous and non-ferrous welding electrodes; research and development various thermit welding compounds. Author articles: Better Welding at Lower Cost; How to Choose and Use the Correct Electrode, and others. Chief test welder Metal and Thermit Corp '40-44; asst welding engr M W Kellogg Co '44-47; welding instr in NJ '48-49; tech sales engr, trouble shooter Champaion Rivet Co '47-49; now editor Industry and Welding Mag. Industry and Welding, Am Welding Soc. 1240 Ontario St., Cleve 13.

15 GILBERT, Perry Webster. Vertebrate anatomy. b'12. AB '34 (Dartmouth College); PhD '40 (Cornell University). Resch on functional anatomy of vertebrates; locomotor adaptations of aquatic birds. Author articles: The Morphology of the Male Urogenital System of the Frilled Shark, Chlamydoselachus anguineus '43; The Alga-Egg Relationship in Ambystoma maculatum, a Case of Symbiosis '44; The Origin and Development of the Extrinsic Ocular Muscles in the Domestic Cat '47, and others. Asst prof Zool Cornell U '43-46; professor since '52. Am Soc Zool—AAAS—Am Soc Anat—Am Soc Ichthyologists Herpetologists —Am Ornithol Union—Soc Study Evolution—Gamma Alpha (sec '43-46)— Sigma Xi—Phi Kappa Phi. Awarded Cramer Fellowship in Zool '36. Department of Zoology, Cornell University, Ithaca, N.Y. H: 316 The Parkway.†

16 GILBERT, Russell W. Pennsylvania-Germans: G e r m a n literature (Medieval short story, Heinrich Heine). b'05. BA '27 (Muhlenberg Coll); MA '29—PhD '43 (Pa U); '31 (Middlebury Coll) Research on almanac in Pennsylvania German homes, Pennsylvania German wills; scope of Heine's reading based on his correspondence. Author: Jacob Appet, Der Ritter unterm Zuber '43; A Picture of the Pennsylvania Germans '47, Pennsylvania German Wills '51. Editor: Brush; Walk the Long Years (with Arthur Herman Wilson) '46; also articles in field. Prof German Susquehanna U since '30. Tau Kappa Alpha—Pa German Folklore Soc (dir)—Pa German Soc—Pa Hist Assn—Speech Assn Am. Susquehanna University, Selinsgrove, Pa.†

17 GILBERT, S e y m o u r G(eorge). Plant and tung tree physiology and biochemistry. b'14. BS '35—MS '38— PhD '41 (Rutgers U). Author articles in field. With US Dept Agr since '42, now asso plant physiol; interim instr chem U Fla since '46. Am Soc Plant Physiol—Am Chem Soc—Am Soc Hort Sci—Sigma Xi. Box 2817, Gainesville, Fla.

18 GILBERT, William Harlen. India (Caste system); Cherokee Indians (Culture); American Indians (Welfare, sociology and geographical distribution of mixed blood). b'04. AB '27 (U Cincinnati); MA '30—PhD '34 (U Chicago). Linguistic and ethnological research at Umatilla Reservation, Oregon, and Cherokee, North Carolina; specialist on clans, ceremonies, dances, marriage customs, kinship, sweat-

houses and new fire rites of Indian culture; mixed bloods of Maryland and West Virginia. Author: Caste in India '48; Peoples of India '44; Racial Discrimination and Governmental Policy in Foreign Countries '45. Co-author: Compilation of Materials Relating to Indians of the United States and Alaska '50; Apsects of Indian Policy '45; and others. Faculty U Cincinnati '35-36; asso prof Ala Poly Inst '36-37; faculty NY State Tchrs Coll '38-39; asst prof Am U '39-40; analyst Indian Affairs Library of Congress since '41; asso prof Polycultural Instn Am since '49. Am Anthrop Assn(F)—Anthrop Soc Washington (sec '50)— Washington Acad Sci. Legislative Reference Service, Library of Congress, Washington 25. H: 9209 First Av., Silver Spring, Md.†

19 GILBERTSON, Lyle I(thiel). Analytical and electro chemistry; Inorganic chemistry (Selenium, tellurium); Peroxyacids of sulfur; Electrodeposition of silver; Rare gases. b'03. BA '25 (Augustana Coll); MA '26 (U Wis); PhD '40 (Ind U). Author articles in field. Adminstrv mgr research labs Air Reduction Co Inc since '51. Electrochem Soc—Am Inst Chem(F)—Sigma Xi. Air Reduction Research Laboratories, Murry Hill, N.J.

20 GILE, Bueford Monroe. Agricultural economics, finance and education; Louisiana rural economics. b'89. BSA '13 (Wis U); MA '25—PhD '27 (Minn U). Work in selection and training of graduate students and curricula for undergraduate students majoring in agricultural economics; research on farm credit situation in Minnesota, functioning of Federal Intermediate Credit Banks and on research methods in farm finance, organization and management of agricultural credit corporations and indicators of condition of banks and bank failures. Author articles: Economic Utilization of Rural Land Resources in Beauregard Parish '40; State Tax Collections and Allocations by Parishes '42; Farmers' Cooperative Business Organizations in Louisiana (with Baker) '45, and others. Prof agrl econ Ark U '27-34; regional dir Fed Land Program Ark '34-38; econ and prof agrl econ La State U since '38, dept head since '41; asso ed Louisiana Rural Economist; mem La State U Research Council, La State Land Use Planning Com, SW Land Tenure Research Com; chm Coll Agr Adjustment Com for Agrl Prodn in La. Am Farm Econ Assn—SW Social Sci Assn —Am Econ Assn. Department of Agricultural Economics, Louisiana State University, Baton Rouge 3, La. H: 2195 Kleinert Av., Baton Rouge 11.†⊙

21 GILES, George Wallace. Farm machinery. b'10. BS '33 (U Neb); MS '35 (U Mo). Design and development two dynamometers for use in measurement of power required for operation farm machinery; development one-row combination fertilizer distributor and seed planter; devised new principle for windrowing hay permitting flexibility in conforming to uneven terrain; analysis and design hay rakes for improved efficiency. Author articles: The Electric Ultramicrometer Circuit as a Drawbar Dynamometer '40; A New Fertilizer Distributor and Planter for the Southern Farmer '45, and others. Asst prof agrl engring advancing to prof NC State Coll since '36, now head dept. Am Soc AE—Sigma Xi—Gamma Sigma Delta. Department of Agricultural Engineering, North Carolina State College, Raleigh, N.C.†

22 GILES, Norman Henry, Jr. Cytogenetics (Radiation induced changes, X-ray effects). b'15. AB '37 (Emory U); MA '38—PhD '40—Parker fellow

'40-41 (Harvard). Author articles in field. Asso prof bot Yale since '46; prin biol Oak Ridge Nat Lab since '47. Genetics Soc Am—Bot Soc Am—AAAS (F)—Am Ornithol Union—Am Naturalists Soc—Phi Beta Kappa—Sigma Xi. Osborn Botanical Laboratory, Yale University, New Haven.†

10 GILKEY, George Leland. Dogs (Rare breeds, origin of common breeds). b'82. BA '05 (U Wis). Research on Basenji, Boris Hound, Plott Hound, several strains of Fox Hound, and others. Author articles: Another Newcomer (Rhodesian Ridgeback dog) '44; He Didn't "Stay Dead" (Basenji dog) '45, and others. Merrill, Wis.

11 GILKEY, Herbert James. Civil engineering; Construction materials (Plain and reinforced concrete). b'90. BS '11 (Ore State Coll); SB '16 (MIT); BS '16 (Harvard); MS '23 (U Ill); ScD (hon) '39 (Buena Vista). Concrete consultant Eleven Mile Canyon Dam, City of Denver; member special board consulting engineers on concrete problems for Hoover (Boulder) Dam; member third Joint Commission on Specifications for Concrete and Reinforced Concrete. Author: (With J L Savage, Ivan E Houk and Fredrik Vogt) Engineering Foundation Arch Dam Investigation (vol II) '34; A Manual of Materials Testing (with Glenn Murphy and E O Bergman) '39; Materials Testing '41; also articles in field. Civil engr state, fed, private surveys '11-21; dept civil engring U Colo '23-31; head dept theoretical and applied mechanics Ia State Coll since '31. Awarded Wason Medal by Am Concrete Inst '39. AAAS(F)—ASCE—Am Soc Testing Materials—Am Concrete Inst (vp '48, pres '49)—Soc Am Mil Engrs (charter)—Western Soc Engrs — Ia Soc Engrs — Am Soc Engring Edn (vp '43-44) — Nat Research Council (Highway Research Bd)—Ia Acad Sci—Sigma Xi—Tau Beta Pi—Phi Kappa Phi. 2328 Donald St., Ames, Ia.⊚

12 GILL, Denzell Leigh. Azalea and camellia diseases. b'09. BS '31 (La State U); PhD '35—fellow '31-35 (Cornell). Research diseases potted plants, azalea petal blight, camellia wilt and root rot. Author articles in field. Instr and asst prof La State U '35-41; asso path US Dept Agr '41-42, asso path since '46. Am Phytopath Soc—Am Soc Hort Sci. Georgia Coastal Plain Experiment Station, Ga.

13 GILL, James Presley. Metallurgical engineering; Applied metallurgy; High speed, tool, and special steels. b'96. BS '18—MS Metall Engring '19 (U Mo Rolla Sch Mines); '18-20 (Columbia U Sch Mines); Dr Engring (hon) '46 (U Mo). Member Foreign Economic Administration Commission to investigate German steel industry '45. Holder 10 patents on compositions of special steels. Author: Tool Steels '34. Coauthor: Modern Steels '39; Tool Steels '44; also articles in field. Research metall Vanadium Alloys Steel Co '20, chief metall since '21, mem bd dir, vp '43, chmn exec com '45; chief metall Anchor Drawn Steel Co since '26, vp '45, president Colonial Steel Co since '29. Am Soc Metals (pres '39-40)—Am Inst Mining Metall Engrs—Am Soc Testing Materials—Am Standards Assn—Am Soc Testing Engrs—Am Soc Tool Engrs—Am Iron Steel Inst—Tau Beta Pi. Vanadium-Alloys Steel Co., Latrobe, Pa.⊚

14 GILL, Richard C(ochran). Pharmacognosy; Ethnobotany; Pharmacology; d-Tubocurarine and curare. b'01. BA '24 (Cornell); '26-27 (Columbia and NYU). Leader Gill-Merrill expedition and other South American (upper-Amazonian) expeditions in ethnobotany, tropical American pharmacog-

nosy; ethnographic exploring chiefly in ethnobotany of drug curare and research on its clinical application to spastic paralysis and its accepted clinical application in shock-therapy method of treating mental diseases, more recently used as adjuvant in anesthesia and anti-convulsant in other fields; also private research in evolution and clinical application of new therapeutic curare variant of higher alkaloidal potency. Author: Manga '37; White Water and Black Magic (a history of curare) '40; Scientific Bibliography of Curare (1595-1948) '48; also articles in field. Writer and lecturer since '30; pres and founder SA mfg base Transandino Co of curare and other tropical drugs; pres Gill Miller Co Ecuador since '30. Am Geog Soc (F)—AAAS—Am Polar Soc—Hakluyt Soc, Gt Brit—Am Acad Polit Social Sci—Am Pharm Assn — Torrey Bot Club — Sigma Phi Sigma. Recipient two citations from Republic of Ecuador. Palo Alto, Calif. H: 10 Coburn St., Presque Isle, Me.†⊚

15 GILL, Thomas G(lick). Wood (Seasoning). b'06. BS (forestry) '30—MF '31 (U Mich). Research on timber seasoning and dry kiln operation, seasoning, preservation treatment, chemical and mechanical modofications of wood to lengthen service life of railroad crossties. Farm forester USDA '38-42; wood tech Air Force Air Materiel Command Dayton O '45-46, Timber Engring Co since '46. Soc Am Foresters (sr mem)—Forest Products Research Soc. Timber Engineering Co., 1319 18th St., Washington 6.†

16 GILLASPY, Carrie G. Nerve cells (Degeneration); Neuro-anatomy; Gross anatomy. b'06. BA '28 (Ia State Teachers Coll); MS '40 (U Okla); '33-35 (U Ia); '35-37 (U Minn); '37-38 (Washington U); '38 (U Mich); '41-43 (U Kans); '44-47 (U Chicago). Research in zoology, neuro-anatomy, gross anatomy, microinsineration, facial nucleus in reptiles. Author articles in field. Fellow in gross anat Chicago Med Sch '43-47, asst prof anat, chmn anat dept Still Coll Des Moines Ia since '47. Ia Acad Sci—AAAS. Still College, 6th Av., Des Moines, Ia.

17 GILLETT, Glenn Dewey. Radio transmission e n g i n e e r i n g (Field strength surveys, directive antenna systems, interference measurements). b'98. AB '19—SB (Elec engring) '21 (Harvard); '22-25 (Columbia). Development techniques for field strength surveys of broadcast stations and originated use field strength contours for depicting results; techniques for use field strength measurements to determine effective conductivity of terrain in any direction from broadcast transmitter; design directive antennas for broadcast stations, introduced use vertical radiation patterns as definite criterion which determined protection characteristics; development and use expanded metal ground screen about base towers to reduce ground losses and increase stability of operation of broadcast antennas; simple and accurate means measuring co-channel intereference received by broadcast stations without shutting down or interfering with operation. Issued patents in field. Research engr devel development and research Am Telephone and Telegraph Co '22-29, Bell Telephone Labs '29-32; cons engr '32-42, since '45. Inst Radio Engrs(F)—Assn Fed Communications Commn. 982 National Press Bldg., Washington 4.

18 GILLINGHAM, Thomas Ellwood, Jr. Solubility of silica in steam; Ore deposits of Hong Kong, Malaya and Idaho. b'12. BS '34 (mining engring) (Harvard); MS '36 (geol) (U Ariz); PhD '46 (geol) (U Minn). Performed over 100 experiments to prove that

superheated steam is an active solvent of several non-volatile substances, particularly silica; examination mining properties throughout Malaya and Siam '36-38, studied lead mines of Hong Kong '38-39, study ore deposits and geology of Coeur d'Alene district northern Idaho; development methods of finding metallic ores through applications geological principles and utilization geological data to increase mining efficiency. Mining engr Nielson & Co Inc '36-39; research F U Minn '39-42; regional tech adv WPB '42-43; geol Bunker Hill & Sullivan Mining and Concentrating Co since '46. AIMME—Soc Econ Geol—Mineralogical Soc Am—Sigma Xi—Tau Beta Pi—Gamma Alpha—Sigma Gamma Epsilon. Bunker Hill & Sullivan Mining and Concentrating Co., Box 29, Kellogg, Ida.

19 GILLIN, John (Philip). Anthropology (Latin American ethnology, United States culture). b'07. AB '27—AM '30 (U Wis); AM '31—PhD '34 (Harvard); '28 (U Berlin); '28 (U London). Anthropological field work in Algeria '30, Europe '30, New Mex '31, British Guiana '32-33, Ecuador and Eastern Peru '34-35, Utah '36-37, Wisconsin '38-39, Guatemala '42, 46, 48, Peru '44-45, Columbia '46, modern culture of South '46-48, Central America and Ecuador '51. Author: The Barama River Caribs of British Guiana '36; Archaeological Investigations in Nine Mile Canyon '38; Archaeological Investigations in Central Utah '41; The Quichua Speaking Indians '41; Introduction to Sociology '42; The Ways of Men '48; Moche: A Peruvian Costal Community '47; Cultural Sociology '48; The Culture of Security in San Carlos '51; also articles. With Peabody Mus '34-35; faculty Sarah Lawrence '33-34, U Utah '35-37; staff O State U '37-41, Duke U '41-46; attached to US embassy Lima Peru '43-44; prof anthrop and research S U NC since '46, head soc sci mission S Am UNESCO '50. AAAS(F)—Am Anthrop Assn(F)—Society for Applied Anthropology (regional vice president '51-52)—NC Archaeol Society (exec board '45, president '46-47)—Am Sociol Soc — Nat Research Council — Sigma Xi—Phi Kappa Phi. 204 Alumni Building, Chapel Hill, N.C.⊚

20 GILLMOR, Frances. Folklore of American Southwest and Mexico. b'03. AB '28—MA '31 (U Ariz); student (U Chicago, U Nacional de Mexico, Ind U). Author: Dance Dramas of Mexican Villages '43; (with L W Wetherill) Traders to the Navajos '34; Fruit Out of Rock '40; Flute of the Smoking Mirror '49; also articles in field. Editor: Opportunities in Arizona Folklore '45. Asst prof Eng U Ariz '34-44, asso professor '44-52, professor since '52, chmn faculty interdeptmental committee on Ariz Folklore. Am Folklore Soc (council)—American Anthrop Assn—Phi Beta Kappa—Phi Kappa Phi. Department of English, University of Arizona, Tucson.

21 GILLULY, James. Tectonic and metamorphic geology; Petrology; Copper deposits. b'96. BS '20 (U Wash); PhD '26 (Yale). Editorial board Copper Resources of the World 16th International Geological Congress Washington '33. Author articles in field. Prof U Calif '38-50, chmn dept geol '45-47, research lecturer '48; research geol US Geol Survey since '50. Mineral Soc AM(F) — Nat Research Council — Am Geophys Union—Geol Soc Am (chmn Cordilleran sect '40, councillor '43-45, vp '47, pres '48)—Soc Econ Geol—Nat Acad Sci—AAAS—Am Assn Petroleum Geol—Soc Econ Paleontol and Mineral—Seismol Soc Am—Sigma Xi—Am Acad Arts & Sci. U.S. Geological Survey, Denver 14.⊚

10 GILLY, Charles L(ouis). Phytogeography; Speciation; Plant phylogeny; Cinchona (Guatemala); Insecticides (Rotenone, pyrethrum); Flora of Iowa, Michigan; Tropical plants (Cyperaceae, sapotaceae); Physiography (Mexico and Central America); Vegetation of Mexico and Guatemala; Teosinte; Maize (Origin, classification). b'11. BS magna cum laude '36 (Parsons Coll Ia); MA '42 (Columbia); PhD '50 (Iowa State Coll). Botanical collecting southeastern US and Cuba '37, Mexico '42-45, '51-52, Guatemala '44, '47, Nicaragua '45. Author articles in field. Asst prof and curator herbarium dept bot Mich State Coll, affiliated with Ia State Coll-Guatemala Tropical Research Center. Bot Soc Am—Am Soc Plant Taxonomists (ed Taxonomic Index '42-43)—Torrey Bot Club—So Appalachian Bot Soc—Soc Study Evolution—Ia Acad Sci (chmn biol survey com '46-48)—Ind Acad Sci—Mich Acad Sci Arts Let—Mich Bot Club—Am Forestry Assn—Phi Kappa Phi—Gamma Sigma Delta—Sigma Xi. Department of Botany and Plant Pathology, Michigan State College, East Lansing, Mich.

11 GILMAN, Charles Sherrill. Weather (Heat theory of pressure changes); Weather forecasting (Improvements); Rainfall (Estimates intensities, areal distribution, relation to topography); Snow surveys (Melt yield estimates); Floods (Prediction, hydrometeorology). b'15. BS '40 (U Pittsburgh); SM '43—ScD '49 (MIT). Author articles: An Expansion of the Thermal Theory of Pressure Changes; Large-Scale Synoptic Aspects of Forecasting Freezing Weather in Florida. Co-author article: A Numerical Solution for Irrotational Flow over a Mountain Barrier. With US Weather Bur since '37, at Inst Tropical Meteorol '43-45, now in charge hydrometeorol research unit in cooperation with Bur Reclamation. Am Geophys Union—Am Meteorol Soc—Sigma Xi. US Weather Bureau, Washington 25. H: 2636 N. Powhatan St., Arlington, Va.

12 GILMAN, Henry. Compounds (Organo-metallic aliphatic); Heterocycles; Drugs and chemical constitution; Furans: Grignard reagents; Reaction mechanisms. b'93. BS '15—AM '17—PhD '18 (Harvard); '16 (Zurich Poly and Oxford). Co-author: Organomagnesium Compounds in Synthetic Chemistry '22. Editor: Organic Syntheses (Vol VI and collective Vol I): Organic Chemistry '43; also articles in field. Prof organic chem Ia State Coll Agr and Mech Arts since '19; nat defense research work Manhattan Project and NDRC since '40. AAAS (F, vp, chmn sect chem '30)—Am Chem Soc (councillor at large '39-41, '42-44, chmn organic div) — Nat Acad Sci—Phi Beta Kappa—Sigma Xi—Phi Kappa Phi. 3221 Oakland St., Ames, Ia.☉

13 GILMAN, Joseph C(harles). Soil fungi. b'90. BSA '12—MS '14 (U Wis); PhD '15 (Washington U). Author: A Manual of Soil Fungi '45. With Ia State Coll since '21, now prof bot. AAAS (F, council '32-40, acad conf vp '38, pres '39)—Am Phytopath Soc—Am Soc Plant Physiol—Bot Soc Am—Ia Acad Sci (sec '30-32, sec-treas '32-41, vp '44, pres '45)—Mycol Soc Am (council '47-48, sec-treas '48-50, vp '51, pres '52)—Sigma Xi—Gamma Sigma Delta—Phi Kappa Phi. Botany Department, Iowa State College, Ames, Ia.†

14 GILMAN, Lauren Cundiff. Protozoon genetics; Mating types in paramecium. b'14. AB '36 (Baker U); PhD '40—research grant Brooks Fund (John Hopkins). Author articles in field. Asso prof zool U Miami since '47. Sigma Xi—Phi Beta Kappa. Depart-ment of Zoology, University of Miami, Miami, University Branch, Fla.

15 GILMAN, Wilbur E(lwyn). Speech; Public speaking and address; Rhetoric. b'02. AB with honors in English '23—PhD '37 (Cornell). Author: Milton's Rhetoric, Studies in His Defense of Liberty '39; (with Aly) A Course Book in Extemporaneous Speaking; (with Aly and Reid) A Course Book in Public Speaking '37-39; (with Aly and Reid) Speech Preparation '46; also articles in field. Chmn dept speech U Mo '40-42; chmn dept speech Queens Coll NY since '45; asso ed Quarterly Journal of Speech, '44-47; sec sub-com on English and Speech, High Sch-Coll Articulation Com, Bds of Edn and Higher Edn NYC since '46. Speech Assn Am (exec council '40-41, 43, 46-49, finance com '46-49, chmn '48-49, com history of speech edn since '43) — Am Speech and Hearing Assn — Modern Lang Assn Am—NY State Speech Assn—NEA—Phi Beta Kappa. Queens College, Flushing, N.Y.

16 GILMER, B(everly) von Haller. Toy design. b'09. BS '30 (King Coll); MS '32—PhD '34 (U Va). Research on relation of toys to child development. Author: How to Help Your Child Develop Successfully '51. Asso prof psychol U Va '46-47; prof psychol Carnegie Inst Tech since '47. Am Psychol Assn(F)—Am Soc Engring Edn—Sigma Xi. Carnegie Institute of Technology, Pittsburgh 13.

17 GILMORE, Edward Robert. Gas (Distribution systems, meters). b'97. ME '20 (Rensselaer Poly Inst). Research design, construction, operation, and maintenance gas distribution systems with emphasis on pressure control, measurement, utilization, and leak detection equipment; invented complete gas meter, meter mechanisms and diaphragms, and gas leak detecting stethoscope. Gas engineer and supt Cities Service Co '20-36; with Rockwell Mfg Co since '36, chief engr since '45. Am Gas Assn—Midwest Gas Assn. Postoffice Box 1761, Tulsa 1.†

18 GILMORE, Harlan Welch. Sociology of southern United States (Disorganization, Negro relations); Human ecology. b'01. BA '23 (Hendrix Coll); MA '25—PhD '31 (Vanderbilt U); student (Northwestern U, U Chicago). Author: Social Disorganization in a Southern City '31; The Beggar '40; also articles in field. With Tulane U since '31, now asso prof sociol. Am Sociol Soc—So Sociol Soc—Population Assn Am. Social Sci Research Council (F, '29-31). Tulane University, New Orleans 15.†

19 GILMORE, Myron Piper. European history (Fifteenth and sixteenth centuries, political thought and institutions). b'10. AB '32 (Amherst Coll); PhD '37 (Harvard U). Author: Argument from Roman Law in Political Thought 1200-1600 '41. Instr and tutor Harvard U since '37, asso prof hist since '43. AHA—Medieval Acad. Widener Library 274, Cambridge 38, Mass.

20 GILMORE, Raymond Maurice. Whales, dolphins, porpoises. b'07. AB '30—AM '33 (U Cal Berkeley); PhD '42 (Cornell U). Field work in Alaska on arctic mammals; research and field work on biology of Cetacea and technology of whaling industry; research and field work on South American vertebrates and public health. Contributor: Colliers New Encyclopedia, 1949; Marine Products of Commerce, 1951. Biol Office Fgn Activities Fish and Wildlife Service Dept Interior since 1946. Am Soc Mammal—Biol Soc Washington—Washington Acad Scis—Soc Systematic Zool—Am Soc Limnol and Oceanog—Sigma Xi. Office of Foreign Activities, Fish and Wildlife Service, Dept. of Interior, Washington 25.

21 GILMOUR, Charles Hoffman. Heat exchange equipment design. b'02. BS '24—MS '26 (Syracuse U); MS '27 (Carnegie Inst Tech); '27-31 (MIT). Research on mechanism of heat transfer from condensing vapor to water through solid retaining wall, rate of combustion of coal dust particles, measurement of total radiation of carbon dioxide gas and water vapor. Research fellow US Bur Mines Expt Sta Pittsburgh Pa '26-27; asst dir Boston Sta MIT Sch Chem Eng Practice '28-29; chem engr Carbide and Carbon Chem Corp since '33. Am Inst Chem—Am Inst Chem Engrs—Am Acad Sci (com on heat transmission by radiation—Sigma Xi. Nat Research Council fellow '31-33. Carbide and Carbon Chemicals Corporation, Box N, South Charleston 3, W. Va.

22 GILMOUR, George Peel. Religious education. b'00. BA '21—BTh '23—BD '29 (McMaster U Toronto Can); AM '29 (Yale); student '24-25 (Oxford U); DCL '49 (Acadia U); DD '42 (Victoria U Toronto Can). Author: The Bible and The Christian Religion '36; A Handbook of the Gospels '44. Editor: Hymnary For Use In Baptist Churches '36. Pastor Baptist chs of Canada '23-28; lectr ch history McMaster U '29-30, asst prof '30-34, asso prof '34-38, prof '38-41, chancellor '41-50, pres and vice chancellor since '50. Can Council Chs (pres '46-48; mem exec com)—Nat Conf Can Univs (pres '51-52). McMaster University, Hamilton, Ont., Can.☉

23 GINGERICH, Melvin. Mennonite history in America. b'02. BA '26 (Goshen Coll); MA '30—PhD '38-'39, '40 (U Ia); '41 (U So Calif). Managing editor The Mennonite Quarterly Review, co-editor The Mennonite Historical Bulletin, associate editor Mennonite Life, managing editor The Mennonite Encyclopedia. Author: The Mennonites in Iowa '39; Mennonite Civilian Public Service '48; Service for Peace '49; What of Concombatant Service '49. Assistant editor: Who's Who Among the Mennonites '43. Asso prof Bethel Coll North Newton Kan '41-47; dir research Mennonite Research Found Goshen Ind since '47; custodian archives Mennonite Hist Library Goshen Ind since '48. Ia State Hist Soc—Miss Valley Hist Assn—Am Soc Ch Hist—Mennonite Hist Soc. 1613 S. Eighth, Goshen, Ind.

24 GINSBURG, Jekuthiel. History of mathematics. b'89. MA '16—DSc (hon) '42 (Columbia); '13-15 (Cooper Union). Co-author: (with D E Smith) History of Mathematics in America '34; Numbers and Numerals '38. Editor: Scripta Mathematica '32; also articles in field. Asso in math Teachers Coll Columbia '17-39; prof and head dept math Yeshiva Coll since '29, dir Yeshiva Institute Mathematics. Hist Sci Soc—Am Math Assn—Am Math Soc—French Math Soc — AAAS(F) — Internat Hist Sci (corres). Yeshiva University, 186th St. and Amsterdam Av., NYC 33. H: 610 W. 139 St., NYC 31.

25 GIRVIN, Harvey Frank. Applied mechanics; Strength of materials. b'86. BME '11—'24-25 (U Mich). Author: Applied Mechanics '38; Strength of Materials '44; A Historical Appraisal of Mechanics '48. Prof eng mech Purdue U since '42. ASME—Am Soc Engring Edn—AAUP. Purdue University, West Lafayette, Ind.†

26 GISH, Oliver Holmes. Atmospheric electricity; Geo-electricity. b'83. BSc '08 (Kan State Coll); AM '13 (U Neb); student '13-14 (U Gottingen Germany); summers '15-17 (U Chicago). Member sub committee on lightning hazards to aircraft National Advisory Committee for Aeronautics. Research engr Western Electric and Mfg Co E Pittsburgh '18-21; asso physicist dept terrestrial magnetism Carnegie Instn Washington '22-25, physicist '26-29, chief sect terrestrial electricity '30-33, asst dir '34-48; cons geophysics since '48. AAAS(F)—Am Phys Soc(F)—Washington Acad Scis(past pres)—Am Geophys Union(past pres sect terrestrial mag and elec)—Sigma Xi—Am Meteorol Soc(profl mem)—Internat Meteorol Commn. H: 2626 Sewell St., Lincoln 2, Neb.†☉

10 GITLOW, Abraham Leo. Labor relations; Economic anthropology. b'18. BA '39 (U Pa); MA '40—PhD '47 (Columbia U); Seminar '41 (Columbia). Research on economic life of primitive tribes in interior at Mt Hagen New Guinea. Author articles: Union Welfare Funds '47; Economics of the Mount Hagen Tribes, New Guinea; also others in field. Econ cons Profl Linen Service Inc NYC since '41; asst prof econ Sch Commerce NYU. Am Econ Assn—Am Acad Polit Social Sci—Am Anthrop Assn—Nat Geog Soc. School of Commerce, New York University, Washington Square, NYC.

11 GITTER, Alice Josephine. Ceramic raw materials; Non-metallic minerals. b'12. B Ceramic Engring '34 (O State U). Study economics, applications, available production facilities, and mines of non-metallic minerals; consultant control raw materials and sales engineering of ceramics, including talcs, china clays (kaolin), ball clay, feldspar, bentonite, fire clays, flint, and pyrophyllite. Ceramic engr W H Loomis Talc Corp Zanesville O and Gouverneur NY '35-40; supt ceramic workshop Nat Youth Adminstrn Denison O '40-42; chief clay-talc unit WPB Washington '42-45; dir market research Whittaker, Clark & Daniels Inc NYC since '45. Am Ceramic Soc—NJ Ceramic Assn—O Ceramic Industry Assn—Am Management Assn—Inst Clay Tech (Eng)—Brit Ceramic Soc. Professional ceramic engr O, Pa. Whittaker, Clark & Daniels, 260 W. Broadway, NYC 13.

12 GIVLER, Robert Chenault. Motor psychology; Chevilles and cliches; Chord sequences in music. b'84. AB '06 (Hamline U); AM '13—PhD '14 (Harvard). Composer of String Quartet in E-minor '31. Inventor of chimes practice console '27. Author: Psychophysiological Effect of the Speech Elements in Poetry '16; Psychology, the Science of Human Behavior '22; The Ethics of Hercules '24; Amateur Composer's Notebook '50; Chord Sequence Finder and Keys to Unlock Chords '48; (with others) History and Prospects of the Social Sciences '25. Head dept aesthetics and creative imagination Tufts Coll since '44. Phi Beta Kappa (hon). Tufts College, Medford 55, Mass.

13 GJULLIN, Claude Melvin. Insects affecting man and animals. b'03. BS '30 (Mont State Coll); MS '37 (Ore State Coll). Research on ecology, taxonomy and insecticides in relation to mosquitoes of Oregon, Washington, Idaho, and Alaska. Articles in field. Entomol US Bur Entomol and Plant Quarantine since '30. AAAS—Am Assn Econ Entomol—Entomol Soc Wash—Am Mosquito Control Assn. Box 332, Corvallis, Ore.†

14 GLANCY, Warren Eugene. Rubber footwear (Testing). b'90. BS '13 (MIT). Author articles: Influence of Certain Compounding Ingredients in Hard Rubber '24; Rate of Combination of Sulfur with Rubber in Hard Rubber (with D

Wright and K H Oon) '26; Testing of Rubber Footwear '36. Chem and tire chem Hood Rubber Co '14-17, chief chem and lab mgr '19-46, mgr development since '46. Am Chem Soc—AAAS—Am Soc Testing Materials. Hood Rubber Co., Watertown 72, Mass.

15 GLANVILLE, Leo Henry. Ventilation (Mines, industrial plants). b'96. Ed pub schs. Studies general metal and coal mine ventilation; industrial application ventilating systems for removal injurious dusts and fumes. Author article: Ventilation of the Climax Mine. Ventilating engr Owl Creek Coal Co Gebo Wyo '32-37; ventilation and indsl hygiene engr Climax Molybdenum Co since '37. Am Indsl Hygiene Assn—Am Inst Mining Engrs. Climax Molybdenum Co., Climax, Colo. H: 216 Bartlett St.

16 GLANZ, Rudolf. Jews in America; European lower classes; History of European punishment. b'92. Dr juris utriusque ('18—)—'18-23 (U Vienna). Research on history of Jewish immigration to US to 1880, Jews in California, Jews in early German-American literature, Jewish peddling in America, historic comparison of Jews and Yankees, Jews in colonial and 19th century America, Jewish execution in medieval Germany, Yiddish elements in early German thief jargon. Author: Jews in Relation to the Cultural Milieu of the Germans in America up to the Eighteen Eighties '47; The History of the Jewish Community in New York '47; The Lower Classes of German Jewry in the 18th Century '37; also articles in field. Research Asso Am Jewish hist, Yiddish Scientific Inst NYC since '39, lecturer training div since '36, mem bd dirs since '44. Am Jewish Hist Soc—AHA. Yiddish Scientific Institute, 535 W. 123rd St., NYC 27.

17 GLASER, Lewis. Geese; Animal, poultry and goose husbandry. b'98. BS '22 (U Ill). Visited Hungary, Germany, and France to study European methods of goose production, introduced system to American producers. Author: Successful Goose Raising '48; Geese Management '49; also articles in field. Operator of Yankee Goose Farm New Haven since '43. Am Embden Assn (pres). Box 123, New Haven.

18 GLASSER, Otto. Radiological and atomic physics; Biography. b'95.' PhD '19 (U Freiburg). Research on application of physical theories, principles and techniques to medical problems and practice, notably clinical dosage determinations of and protection measurements against all types of ionizing radiations; member council on physical medicine and rehabilitation of the American Medical Association. Invented condenser dosemeter for measurement of X-Rays and radiations from radioactive substances. Author: Wilhelm Conrad Roentgen '34; Dr W C Roentgen '45; Science of Radiology '34. Collaborator and editor: Physical Foundations of Radiology '44. Compiler and editor: Medical Physics '44; Medical Physics II '50. Biophysicist Cleveland Clinic '23-25, resch div since '27; prof biophysics Frank E Bunts Ednl Inst Cleveland since '37; cons biophysicist US Veterans Adminstrn since '46; special examiner American Board of Radiology since '36. AAAS(F)—Am Phys Soc(F)—Am College Radiology (F)—Am Roentgen Ray Society—Am Radium Society—Radiol Society NA—Assn Hist Med—Hist Sci Soc—Sigma Xi. Awarded spl certificate honor Roentgen exhbn AMA Detroit '30, gold medal achievement award Radiol Soc NA '36, Olympia Decoration '38, Janeway medal Am Radium Soc '50, Roentgen honor plaque Roentgen Museum

Lennep '51. Cleveland Clinic, 2020 E. 93rd St., Cleveland 6.☉

19 GLATZER, Nahum Norbert. Classical Hebrew literature; Jewish history; Bible exegesis. b'03. PhD '31 (Goethe U Germany); student (Talmudic Acad Frankfort). Author: Sendung und Schicksal '31; Geschichtslehre der Tannaiten '33; Geschichte der Talmudischen Zeit '37; Maimonides Said '41; Kitzur Toledoth Yisrael '47; In Time and Eternity: A Jewish Reader '46; The Language of Faith '47; Hammer on the Rock '48; Franz Rosenzweig: His Life and Thought '52. also articles in field. Prof Hebrew literature Yeshiva U NY '48-51; asso prof Jewish history Brandeis U since '51. ed Schocken Books since '45. Am Acad Jewish Research—Am Hist Soc. Brandeis University, Waltham, Mass. H: 379 School St., Watertown, Mass.

20 GLAZE, Roland Aerhart. Framed (timber) structures (Engineering). b '05. BS '28 (Wash State Coll). Research on timber joints, fastenings, house framing, storage structures, glued laminated arches; designer large timber structures such as hangars, grain storage bins. Co-editor: (with Howard J. Hansen) Timber Engineers Handbook, '48. Structural research product development engr Timber Products '30-40; chief engr Weyerhauser Forest Products Co since '40. Am Soc Agrl Engrs—Am Soc Civil Engrs—ASTM—Sigma Tau. 3353 University Av. S.E., Mpls 14. H: 4166 Forest Ct., White Bear Lake 10, Minn.

21 GLAZER, Sidney. Michigan history. b'05. AB '27 (Wayne U); AM '29—PhD '32 (Mich U). Author: Syllabus for History of Michigan '41; Michigan: From Primitive Wilderness to Industrial Commonwealth (with Milo Qauife) '48; The Secret of Serenity '51; also author articles in field. Asso prof hist Wayne U since '48. Am Acad Arts Sci—AHA—Miss Valley Hist Soc—Agrl Hist Soc—State Hist Soc Mich. Wayne University, Detroit.

22 GLEASON, Robert Patrick. Beryllium (Health hazards); Lead (Health hazards); Mercury (Health hazards). b'17. BS '38—MS '42 (U Mass). Investigation control of health hazards in fluorescent lamp industry; studies on lead and mercury health hazards, evaluation and control in industry. Co-author article: (with Ruotolo, Tabershaw) Plumbism Resulting from Oxyacetylene Cutting of Painted Structural Steel '43. Indsl hygiene chem Mass Dept Labor and Industries Boston '41-43; indsl hygienist Fidelity & Casualty Co NYC '44-47; indsl hygiene engr Sylvania Elec Products Inc since '47. ACS—Am Indsl Hygiene Assn—Am Pub Health Assn. Sylvania Electric Products, 1740 Broadway, NYC 19. H: 26-17 157th St., Flushing, N.Y.

23 GLICK, Carl. Chinese in America; American community theaters. b'90. BS '15 (Northwestern U). Director of several community and college theaters at intervals from '17-35; participated in building of San Pedro Playhouse, city-built and city-owned San Antonio Tex '30. Author: Shake Hands with the Dragon '41; Three Times I Bow '43; Double Ten, Captain O'Banion's Story of the Chinese Revolution '45; (with Hong Sheng-Hwa) Swords of Silence, The Secret Societies of China '47; (with Albert McCleery) Curtains Going Up '39; also plays and articles in field. Instr playwriting div gen edn NYU since '43; chmn Com Community Theaters for National Drama Week, Drama League America '40-43. Dramatists Guild—Chinese Athletic Club—Drama League of NY (adv com)—Phi Kappa Psi. 21 Bethune St., NYC 14.

10 GLICK, Dudley Peters. Agricultural bacteriology. b'05. AB '27—MA '32—PhD '37 (O State U). Author articles in field. Mgr standardization dept div biol control Sharp & Dohme Inc '47, dir div biol control '48 to '49. Am Pub Health Assn (F)—AAAS(F)—Soc Am Bact—Am Dairy Sci Assn—Inst Food Tech—Internat Assn Milk Food Sanit. Now: Biolog. Dept, Camp Detrick, Frederick, Md.

11 GLICK, Perry A(aron). Insect migration. b'95. Student '15-16 (Park Coll); '19-20 (U Kan); AB '21—MS '22 (U Ill); (U Colo); (U Mich Biol Sta). Research on insect damage to cotton, relation of insecticides in insect population of cotton fields, collecting insects by airplane, insect populations and migration in the air; invented and adapted insect collecting traps for monoplanes and biplanes '26. Author articles in field. Asst entomol Ariz Comm Agr & Hort '22-23; jr plant quarantine insp Fed Hort Bd NY and Washington '23-25; asst entomol Bur Entomol La '25-36; asst entomol Ga Coastal Plain Exp Sta Bur Entomol and Plant Quarantine '36-39; asso entomol Tex since '43. AAAS(F)—Entomol Soc Am—Am Assn Econ Entomol—Texas Acad Sci(F)—Tex Entomol Soc—Royal Entomol Soc London(F)—Sigma Xi—Kappa Delta Pi—Kappa Alpha Mu. Bureau Entomolgy and Plant Quarantine, U.S. Department of Agriculture, Box 1218, Waco, Tex.

12 GLIDDEN, Horace Knight. Airports (Design, construction). b'01. BS '25 (Kan U). Research, design and construction emergency landing fields along federal airways, construction airports for Civil Aeronautics Administration. Co-author: Airports—Design, Construction and Management '48. With Bur Air Commerce '28-33; with Civil Aeronautics Adminstrn '37-46; Civil Aeronautics Adminstrn dist airport engr for Ida '46-50; private practice since '50. Am Soc Prof Engrs. P.O. Box 954, Boise, Ida.

13 GLOCK, Waldo Sumner. Tree rings; Climate. b'97. BA '20 (State U Ia); PhD '23 (Yale). Member Fiji-New Zealand Expedition '22; discovery of methods of absolute dating of growth layers in branches of trees and their application to growth-layer problems; with R A Studhalter constructed apparatus to induce artificial frost injury in living tissues of trees. Author: Principles and Methods of Tree-ring Analysis '37; also articles in field. Head dept geol Macalester Coll since '48, in charge Tree-Ring Research Lab, also Wilkie Astronomical Observatory. Geol Society Am(F)—AAAS(F)—Bot Soc Am—Am Geophys Union—Am Meteorol Soc—Sigma Xi—Phi Beta Kappa. Macalester College, St. Paul 5.†

14 GLOCKLER, George. Physical chemistry; Chemical engineering (Electro chemistry of gases, molecular structure, light scattering, electron affinity). b'90. BS '15—MS '15 (U Wash); PhD '23 (U Calif). Associate editor Journal of Physical Chemistry. Co-author: The Electrochemistry of Gases and Other Dielectrics (with S C Lind) '39; Chemistry in our Time (with Ruby C Glockler) '47; also articles in field. Nat research fellow Calif Inst Tech Pasadena '23-26; research asso Am Petroleum Inst Minn '26-29; asso prof U Minn '29-36, prof phys chem '36-40; head dept chem and chem engring and prof phys chem U Ia since '40. Am Phys Soc(F)—AAAS—Am Chem Soc—Am Electrochem Soc—Faraday Soc, London—Deutsche Bunsen Gesellschaft—Phi Beta Kappa—Sigma Xi. 621 Holt Av., Iowa City, Ia.◎

15 GLOSTER, Hugh Morris. American Negro literature. b'11. Diploma '29 (LeMoyne Coll); BA '31 (Morehouse Coll); MA '33—fellow '31-33 (Atlanta U); PhD '43—fellow '38-39, '40 (NYU). Author: Negro Voices in American Fiction '48. Co-editor: The Brown Thrush: An Anthology of Verse by Negro College Students '35; also articles in field. Instr and asso prof Eng LeMoyne Coll '33-41; ext prof Eng Lincoln U Mo '37, '39, '40; prof Eng Morehouse Coll and Atlanta U '41-43; USO asso regional exec charge Services to Negroes Atlanta '44-46; prof Eng, chmn Communications Center Hampton Inst since '46; vis prof NYU '49. Nat Council Teachers Eng—Mod Lang Assn—Speech Assn Am—Am Ednl Theatre Assn — Coll Lang Assn (founder and pres). Hampton Institute, Hampton, Va.

16 GLOVER, Charles Arthur. Corporation finance, statistics, accounting. b'90. BS '21 (U Cal); MBA '23—Sheldon traveling F in finance (Europe) '23-24 (Harvard); research on corporation finance (Western Europe). Long-range planning and statistical and accounting control in business. U prof econ, statis and accounting '24-29; econ-statis Am Telephone and Telegraph Co since '29; cons. Royal Econ Soc(F)—Am Econ Assn—Am Finance Assn—Am Statis Assn—Econometric Soc. 195 Broadway, NYC 7.

17 GLOVER, Conrad Nathan. Systematic theology; Church history (Baptist). b'95. ThB '25—DD (hon) '31 (Missionary Bapt Coll); DCH '41—BD '41 (Missionary Bapt Inst). Author articles in field. Served as sec bd trustee Missionary Baptist Coll '29-36; moderator Pine Bluff Miss Bapt Assn since '38; co-moderator Ark State Bapt Assn 2 yrs; moderator Ark State Bapt Assn of Chs since '43, co-founder '34, now vp Missionary Bapt Inst Little Rock Ark. Am Bapt Assn (pres '41-47). P.O. Box 25, Sheridan, Ark.

18 GLOYD, Howard Kay. Herpetology; North American snakes. b'02. BSc '24—DSc (hon) '42 (Ottawa U); MS '29 (Kan State Coll); PhD '37 (U Mich). Field work, museum and laboratory studies on Kansas and Louisiana reptiles '23-29, Arizona '37, '40-41, '43-44, Misouri '38, '46-47, Texas '39, toured southwest and west coast for field and museum studies '35-36; special studies on taxonomy and zoögeography of crotalid snakes, ecology of desert reptiles. Author: The Rattlesnakes, a study in zoogeography and evolution '40; also articles in field. Dir mus Chicago Acad Sci since '36. AAAS (F)—Am Soc Ichthyologists Herpetologists (vp '39-40)—Wilson Ornithol Club (sec '25-28)—Cooper Ornithol Club—Am Ornithol Union—Am Soc Mammalogists—Tex Acad Sci—Ill Acad Sci—Ill Natural Hist Survey (cons herpetology '41-47)—SW Monuments Assn (adv herpetology since '38). Chicago Academy of Sciences, 2001 N. Clark St., Chicago 14.

19 GLUCK, Samuel Emanuel. Coal preparation. b'25. Student '46 (U Colo); BA '47 (O State U); '48 (Rackham Inst U Mich). Design beneficiation equipment; studies on weight control in coal preparation; design of mineral processing plant installations for nonmetallics other than coal; solution of mineral industry materials-handling problems. Author article: Weight Control in Coal Preparation 49. Geol Bonded Scale & Machine Co Columbus since '42, research chief, asst mgr since '50. Can Inst Mining and Metall—AIM ME—Geol Soc South Africa—Royal Can Inst—Can Geog Soc—Franklin Inst. Bonded Scale & Machine Co., 2176 S. Third St., Columbus 7, O. H: P.O. Box 566, Columbus 16†

20 GLUCKMAN, Arcadi. History of US Army small arms (Late 18th century and 19th century. b'96. Research on construction, manufacture, description and historical data of black powder burning hand and shoulder small arms 1785-1889. Author: United States Martial Pistols and Revolvers '39; Catalogue of United States Martial Short Arms '39; United States Muskets, Rifles and Carbines '48; Supplement of American Gun Makers '49. Co-author: (with L D Satterlee) American Gun Makers '40. Col US Army retired. Silver Star, Legion of Merit, Commendation Ribbon, Purple Heart with Cluster; Spl Breast Order Pao Ting (China). P.O. Box 644, Carmel, Cal.

21 GLUDE, John Bryce. Oysters; Clams; Shellfish ecology. b'18. Student '35-36 (Wash State Coll); BS (fisheries) '39—'39-40 (U Wash). Effect of sulfite waste liquor from pulp mill on decline in abundance of Olympia oysters, restoration of oyster industry through installation evaporator by mill, spawning and setting of Pacific oysters, developed methods of predicting setting itme and abundance, inspection Japanese seed oyster shipments to US to prevent entry of oyster drills; Japanese clam industry; US clam farming, histology and bacteriology, catch records, spawning, setting, growth, mortality, predators, geological studies of beaches. Biol Internat Pacific Salmon Fisheries Commn '39; sr biol Wash State Dept Fisheries '40-41, '45-48; chief clam investigations US Fish and Wildlife Service since '48. Sigma Xi—Phi Sigma—Am Fisheries Soc—Am Soc Limnol and Oceanog—Nat Shellfisheries Assn—Atlantic Fisheries Biol—Ecol Soc Am. US Department of Interior, Fish and Wildlife Service, US Fishery Laboratory, Boothbay Harbor, Me.

22 GLUECK, Nelson. Biblical archaeology; Trans-Jordan; Civilizations (River Jordan, Ammon, Moab, Edom, Gilead, Nabataean); Ancient Near East, pottery and agriculture; Copper (Solomon's mines); Palestine. b'00. BH '18—Rabbi '23 (Hebrew Union Coll); '23-24 (U Berlin and Heidelberg U); PhD '26 (U Jena Germany); Morgenthau fellow '28-29 (Am Sch Oriental Research Jerusalem); LLD '36 (U Cinn); DHL '47 (Jewish Theol Sem, Jewish Inst Religion). Excavations and important archaeological discoveries in Palestine and Transjordan '32-47. Author: Das Wort hsd im Alten Testament '27; Explorations in Eastern Palestine, Vol I '34, Vol 2 '35, Vol 3 '39; Vol 4 '52; The Other Side of the Jordan '40; The River Jordan '46; also articles. Pres Hebrew Union Coll '47; president Jewish Institute of Religion '48. Central Conference American Rabbis—Archaol Inst Am—Am Oriental Soc—Palestine Oriental Soc—Sigma Xi—Phi Beta Kappa. Awarded Cincinnati Fine Arts Award '40. Hebrew Union College, Cin.◎

23 GOBLE, Frans Cleon. Parasitology; Comparative pathology; Chemotherapy. b'13. BS '33 (Battle Creek Coll); '30 (U Colo); '34-35 (Rice Inst); MS '34—ScD '39 (U Mich). Work in testing for activity such new compounds as antimalarial, trypanocidal, antileishmanial and anthelminthic agents. Numerous articles on lungworms and other parasites of mammals and birds. Path NY State Conservation Dept '38-45; path and parasitol chemotherapy sect Sterling-Winthrop Research Inst since '45, in charge path and hematological studies on effects of new drugs. Am Soc Parasitol—Nat Malaria Soc—Sigma Xi—NY Acad Sci. Sterling-Winthrop Research Institute,

Rensselaer, N.Y. H: Star Route, Delmar, N.Y.

10 GODBEY, John Campbell. Water treatment. b'82. AB '04—AM '05 (Central Coll); DSc (hon) '43 (McMurry Coll). Research on water analysis and treatment. Author: General Chemistry (revised) '48; General Chemistry Laboratory Manual '48. Head dept chem Southern U '13-17; head dept chem Southwestern U since '17; cons since '42. Tex Acad Sci—AAAS—ACS—Am Inst Chem—Tex League Municipalities. Southwestern University, Georgetown, Tex.

11 GODDARD, Calvin H(ooker). Firearm identification (Forensic ballistics); Criminology; Military history; Ordnance engineering and history; Small arms and ammunition. b'91. BA '11—MD '15 (Johns Hopkins); grad '17 (Army Med Sch). Research on ordnance and small arms practice, scientific crime detection, legislation on use of firearms, firearm identification, history of ordnance, armored car, and artillery; also on use of balloons and smoke in war, cannon, canteen, cantonment, engines of war, flamethrower, various guns and rocket apparatus, development small arms, tanks, armor, and fortifications; owns ordnance technical library over 1,000 volumes, large small arms and ammunition collection, and reference material; managing editor American Journal Police Science '30-32; military editor Encyclopaedia Britannica since '44. Developed instruments and techniques now employed world-wide in identifying weapon which has discharged a given bullet or empty shell '25-29. Author articles in field. Chief criminal investigation lab Provost Marshall Sect Far East Command '48-51; chief historical unit Army Medical Service Washington DC since '51; director science crime detection lab Northwestern U '29-33, dir research '33-34, prof police sci '30-34. Soc Internat Criminalistique, Stockholm—Internat Assn Identification (past dir)—Am Ordnance Assn—Soc Am Mil Engrs (bd dir '39-42)—AHA—Nat Rifle Assn—Am Acad Forensic Sciences—International Assn for Detection of Deception. Awarded for contributions to firearm identification Guggenheim Found fellowship '35, Carl Schurz Found fellowship '36, decoration of Order of Crown of Italy (rank Commander) '46. Main Navy Bldg., Washington 25. H: 3533 Quebec St., N.W.

12 GODDARD, Henry Herbert. Abnormal psychology; Mental deficiency; Moron; Eugenics; Feeblemindedness. b '66. AB '87—AM '89—LLD '32 (Haverford Coll); F in psychology '96-99— PhD '99 (Clark U); LLD '43 (Ohio State U); ScD '46 (U Pa); student (German univs). Research on eugenics, feeblemindedness, abnormal psychology; originator word moron. Author: The Kallikak Family '12; Feeble-Mindedness '14; The Criminal Imbecile '15; School Training of Defective Children '15; Psychology of the Normal and Subnormal '19; Human Efficiency and Levels of Intelligence '20; Juvenile Delinquency '21; Two Souls in One Body? '27; The School Training of Gifted Children '27; How to Raise Children in the Atomic Age '48. Contbr to Jeliffe and White's Modern Treatment of Nervous and Mental Diseases '13; The New Century Dictionary '27; Ency Britannica 14th edit; Warren's Dictionary of Psychology '33. Founder first lab for psychol study of feeble minded Training Sch for Feeble Minded Children Vineland NJ '06, dir '06-18; dir State Bur Juvenile Research Columbus O '18-22; prof abnormal and clin psychology Ohio State U '22-38, emeritus since '38; lectr

on psychology of mental defectives NYU '07-16. AAAS—Am Psychol Assn —Hungarian Psychol Soc(hon)—Am Assn on Mental Deficiency—Phi Beta Kappa. 1618 De la Vina St., Santa Barbara, Cal.⊚

13 GODFREY, Alfred Laurance. Holstein cattle. b'88. AB '14—LLB '19 (U Wis). Breeder Holstein cattle, specializing in Burke and Marto blood lines; law practice Elkhorn Wis since '21. First National Bank Building, Elkhorn, Wis.

14 GODFREY, George Harold. Nematode diseases of plants; Soil fumigation for plant disease control; Cantaloupe breeding; Citrus and vegetable diseases. b'88. BS '13 (Wash State Coll); MS '17 (Ia State Coll); PhD '23 (U Wis); student (George Washington U). Author articles in field. Plant pathol Lower Rio Grande Valley Substa Texas Agrl Expt Sta Weslaco Tex since '37. AAAS—Am Phytopath Soc (asso ed '30-32)—Hawaiian Bot Soc (pres '30)—Rio Grande Hort Soc (ed proc Citrus and Vegetable Inst '46-47) —Texas Avocado Soc—Nat Com Soil Fumigation. Texas Agricultural Experiment Station, Weslaco, Tex.

15 GODING, Maurice Wilfred. Alaska (Government, transportation, business, industry). b'11. AB '33 (Yankton Coll); '40-43 (George Wash U Sch Law). Author articles in field. US customs service Skagway Alaska '38-39; sec to del in congress from Alaska '40-42; econ analyst, asst to chief, econ potential div Bd Econ Warfare Washington '42-43; intelligence officer, asst to chief Econ Intelligence Div Fgn Econ Adminstrn '43-44; asst chief, acting chief Alaska Br div Terr and Island Possessions Dept Interior Washington '44-47, exec sec Fed Inter-Agency Alaskan Development Com Washington '48-51; staff asst to Asst Sec of the Interior since '51. Dist mgr Dept Commerce Field Service Juneau Alaska '47-48; asst chief Alaska Division Office of Territories. Office of the Secretary, Department of the Interior, Washington.

16 GODSEY, Frank Waldman, Jr. Electric control devices. b'06. BS '27 (Rice Inst); MS '29—EE '33 (Yale). Mgr new products div in development and mfr spl products and mil armament devices Westinghouse Elec Corp since '40. AIEE(F)—Inst Aeronautical Sci—SAE—Sigma Xi. Westinghouse Electrical Corporation, Pitts.

17 GODWIN, Francis Wood, Jr. Industrial and economic development of South America. b'10. AB '33 (San Diego State Coll Cal); MS '34—PhD '37 (State U Ia). Studies and advisory services since '42 to governments, central banks, development corporations, United Nations groups and World Bank; travel over 11 years in 36 countries of North and South America, Europe, Scandinavia, Middle East and Asia; missions to Argentina, Mexico, El Salvador, Cuba, Ceylon. Author: The Technical Needs of Latin American Countries '49. Co-author: Report on Cuba '51; The Economic Development of Ceylon '53. Editor and co-author: Technological and Economic Suvey of Argentine Industries '43; Technological Audit of Selected Mexican Industries '45. Editor: The Economic Development of Guatemala '51. Conf Internat Bank for Reconstrn and Development '50, chief tech research inst program since '52; advisor Lab Nacional de Fomento Industrial Mexico '50; advisor on internat development Armour Research Found since '50. Am Chem Soc—Am Inst Chem Engrs—Sigma Xi—Alpha Chi Sigma— Phi Lambda Upsilon. 1818 H St., Washington 25.

18 GOESSL, Elmer Anthony. Glass (Historical development, hollow forms). b'98. 4 yrs (Sch Engring U Wis). Study historic development of glass as world commodity, its influence in history, effects of design, taste, fashion, technology; investigation of theory of hollow forms as they reflect art, taste, fashion. Author article: Historical Development of Glass '49. Asst curator hist Milwaukee Pub Museum since '41. Far Eastern Assn—Oriental Soc. Public Museum, Milw 3.

19 GOETZ, Alexander. Physics of small particles including microbiological matter; Microscopy; Low temperature physics (Cryogenics). b'97. PhD '21—Habil '23 (U Goettingen). Granted patents on self-regenerating source of oligodynamic silver for sterilization of liquids, emergency desalination of sea-water. Author: Physik und Technik des Hochvakuums '26; also articles in field. Asso prof physics Calif Inst Tech since '30. Sci cons to Navy Dept '41-42, War Dept since '46—Am Phys Soc—Inst Metals—AAAS—Sigma Xi. California Institute of Technology, Pasadena 4, Calif.†

20 GOETZE, Albrecht. Cuneiform studies; Assyriology. b'97. Student (Gymnasium Leipzig, Darmstadt, U Munich, U Leipzig, U Berlin); PhD '21 (U Heidelberg). Editor Journal of Cuneiform Studies. Author: Kulturgeschichte Kleinasiens '33; Hethiter Churriter and Assyrer Oslo '36; Tunnawi '38; Kizzuwatna '40; Old Babylonian Omen Texts '47; also articles in field. Laffan prof Assyriology Yale since '35. Royal Danish Acad—Inst Comparative Research in Human Culture (Oslo)—Am Oriental Soc—Linguistic Soc Am—Archaeol Inst Am—Am Schs Oriental Research. 306 Yale Graduate School, New Haven.⊚

21 GOETZEL, Claus Guenter. Powder metallurgy. b'13. ME '35 (Technische Hochschule Berlin); PhD '39 (Columbia). Research on powder metallurgy of copper and copper alloys; production development on powder metallurgy of iron and steel, porous nickel filter elements for proximity fuse; development technique for infiltrating iron and steel powder sponges with molten copper and copper alloys for jet engine compressor blades; consultant on powder metallurgy problems, and on high temperature heat resistant alloys and metal-nonmetal composites. Holds eight patents in field. Author: Treatise on Powder Metallurgy I and II, '49 and '50. Author articles: Some Properties of Sintered and Hot Pressed Copper-Tin Powder Compacts '45; The Pressing of Complicated Shapes from Iron Powders '46; Cemented Steels-Infiltration Studies with Pure Iron and Copper '46; Trends in Powder Metallurgy '48, and others. Head powder metall lab Hardy Metall Co '36-39; with Electro Metal Corp Yonkers NY '39-47, tech dir '44-47; adjunct prof chem engring NYU since '46; exec vp, dir research Sintercast Corp of Am NYC since '47. AIMME— Am Soc for Metals—Inst of Metals (London). Sintercast Corp. of America, 570 Lexington Av., NYC 22 and 134 Woodworth Av., Yonkers 1, N.Y.

22 GOFF, Charles Weer. Physical anthropology (Analysis burial material); Archaeology (Mayan). b'97. BS '20— MD '23 (U Ill); grad study '44-45 (Columbia), '46-48 (Yale), since '49 (Harvard). Analysis large Army series photographs for body types; assisted United Fruit Project Zaculen, Quatamala CA on analysis material from burials; measured and analyzed Indians of Quatamala CA; analysis congenital malformations in USA. Author article: Anthropometry of A Mamspeaking Group of Indians of Quatemala. Training in physical anthropology and asst to United Fruit Co. Zaculen project '46-50. Am Assn Phys Anthrop—Am Assn Anthrop—Soc Study Evolution. 30 Farmington Av., Hartford 5, Conn.

10 GOFF, Frederick Richmond. Rare books; Incunabula. b'16. BA '37—MA '39 (Brown U). Author: The Dates in Certain German Incunabula '40. Editor: Catalogue of Exhibitions Held at the Library of Congress in Honor of Bicentennial of Thomas Jefferson '43; A Catalog of Important Recent Additions to the Lessing J Rosenwald Collection Selected for Exhibition at the Library of Congress '47; also articles in field. Asst to editor Incunabula in Am Libraries '37-40; asst to curator rare books div Library Congress '40-41, acting chief '41-45, chief since '45. Bibliog Soc Am—Phi Beta Kappa. Library of Congress, Washington 25.

11 GOGGIN, William C. Plastics (Fabrication, molding, extrusion). b'11. BS '33 (Alma Coll); BS '35—MSE '36 (U Mich). Co-author: German Plastics Practice '46; also articles in field. With Dow Chemical Co on plastics since '36, mgr plastics tech service since '47; tech cons War Dept QMC in Germany investigating German plastics industry '45. Am Soc Testing Materials—Soc Plastics Engrs—Soc Plastics Industry—Midland Engring Soc—Am Chem Soc—Tau Beta Pi—Phi Kappa Phi—Sigma Xi. Dow Chemical Company, Midland, Mich.

12 GOLDBERG, Edward David. Sea water composition; Meteorites (Composition). b'21. BS '42 (U Calif); PhD '49 (U Chicago). Research on concentration of vanadium directly from its ionic state in marine waters by tunicates, transfer of phosphate from sea water to marine plants; research on trace element content of meteorites and concentration of minerals in meteorites. Author articles in field. Research asso Inst Nuclear Studies U Chicago '47-49; asst marine chem Scripps Instn Oceanog since '49. Sigma Xi—ACS—Am Soc Limnol and Oceanog—Meteoritical Soc—Am Geophys Union. Scripps Institution of Oceanography, La Jolla, Calif.

13 GOLDBERG, John Edward. Structural theory (Aircraft, buildings, and bridges); Stress analysis; Dynamics of Structures; Vibrations; Elastic stability. b'09. BS '30—CE '31 (Northwestern U). Developed methods for analysis wind stresses and vertical load stresses in continuous structures and building frames, stress analysis of monocoque, semi-monocoque, and space framework aircraft structures, vibrations of structures and shells, dynamic response and stresses of structures, elastic stability, elasticity, thermal stresses, pressure waves, reinforced concrete. Structures engr Waco Aircraft Co '42-43; structures engr Consol Vultee Aircraft Co '43-47; research asst prof, asso dir fundamental mech research Ill Inst Tech '47-50; asso prof Sch Civil Engring and Engring Mech Purdue U since '50. Tau Beta Pi—Sigma Xi—Am Soc CE. School of Civil Engineering and Engineering Mechanics, Purdue University, Lafayette, Ind.†

14 GOLDBLITH, Samuel Abraham. Food technology; Radiobiology of foods. b'19. BS '40—MS '47—research fellow '46-49—PhD '49 (MIT). Research in effects of ionizing radiations on foods and their chemical components. Author articles in field. Asst professor MIT since '52. US Army '41-46, studied malnutrition in Japanese Prisoner of War Camps as result of fall of Bataan PI. NY Acad Sci—

Am Chem Soc—Am Pub Health Assn—Inst Food Technol—Assn Vitamin Chem—Soc Am Bact NE Sect—Sigma Xi. Massachusetts Institute of Technology, Cambridge 39, Mass.

15 GOLDMAN, Marcus Selden. Elizabethan and Jacobean literature (Prose fiction, poetic theory); Neo-Latin literature; Non-dramatic literature of the English Renaissance (Sir Philip Sidney, Sir John Harington, Spenser, prose fiction). b'94. Grad '12 (Culver Military Acad); AB '16 (Miami U); AM '17—PhD '31 (U Illinois); AM Field Service fellow '19-21 (U Paris); AM '26 (Harvard). Author: Sir Philip Sidney and the Arcadia '34. Co-author: A Progressive Study of English Composition '41. Translator: St Anne and the Govty Rector and Other Plays '50. With Eng dept U Ill since '26. Modern Lang Assn Am (life)—Medieval Acad Am—Modern Humanities Research Assn—Phi Beta Kappa. 334 Gregory Hall, University of Illinois, Urbana, Ill.

16 GOLDMAN, Stanford. Electronics; Electrocardiography. b'07. BA '36—MA '28 (U Cincinnati); PhD (Physics) '33 (Harvard). Development of fundamental theory of random fluctuations and its application to radio engineering; research on electrical transient problems in radio design; originated method of area display for study electrical activity of heart and brain. Author: Frequency Analysis, Modulation and Noise '48; Transformation Calculus and Electrical Transients '49. Author article: Some Fundamental Considerations Concerning Noise Reduction and Range in Radar and Communication '48. Co-author article: (with W E Vivian, C K Chien, H N Bowes) Electronic Mapping of the Activity of the Heart and Brain '48. Electronics engr Gen Elec Co '35-46; research asso MIT '46-49; prof elec engring Syracuse U since '49. Inst Radio Engrs—APS—Sigma Xi. Electrical Engineering Department, Syracuse University, Syracuse 10, N.Y.

17 GOLDRING, Winifred. Devonian paleontology; stratigraphy crinoids and paleobotany. b'88. BA '09—MA '12 (Wellesley Coll); student (Teachers Sch Sci Boston, Harvard, Columbia, Johns Hopkins); DSc (hon) '37 (Russell Sage Coll). Author articles in field. State paleontol NY State Mus since '38. Paleontol Soc Am (pres '48-49)—Geol Soc Am(F)—AAAS(F)—Paleontol Soc Am(F)—NY Acad Sci—Bot Soc Am—Am Assn Mus—Am Mus Nat Hist—Phi Beta Kappa—Sigma Xi. New York State Museum, Albany 1, N.Y. H: Font Grove Rd., Slingerlands, N.Y.†

18 GOLDSMITH, Philip Harold. Paper machines (Cylinder). b'99. Student '18-19 (US Naval Acad); '21-23 (U Mich). Inventor improvements in cylinder paper machines permitting better quality formation at higher speeds. Issued patents in US, Can, United Kingdom, France, Norway, Denmark, Sweden, Finland. Resident engr paper mill constrn Mead Corp '28-30; field engr Black-Clawson Co '30-39; development engr Pusey & Jones Corp Wilmington Del since '39. Am Soc ME—Tech Assn Pulp and Paper Industry.

19 GOLDSMITH, Sidney Wilmot, Jr. Education; Theology and religion. b '16. AB '40 (Williams Coll); BD '48 (Va Theol Sem). Asso Christian edn Pasadena (Cal) Presbyn Ch '41-42; asst minister Whittle and Piedmont (Va) parishes '46-48; chaplain to Episcopalian students Williams Coll Williamstown Mass '48-50; rector, headmaster Shattuck Sch Faribault Minn since '50; canon Cathedral of Our Merciful Saviour Faribault since '51. Shattuck School, Faribault Minn.◎

20 GOLDSMITH, Thomas Toliver, Jr. Television; Cathode ray tubes. b'10. BS '31 (Furman U); PhD '36 (Cornell). Author articles in field. Dir research Allen B DuMont Labs since '36, now charge of development in cathode ray tubes, cathode ray oscillographs, oscillograph recording cameras, television receiving equipment, motion picture apparatus. Inst Radio Engrs—Soc Motion Picture Engrs—Am Phys Soc—Sigma Xi. 2 Main Av., Passaic, N.J.

21 GOLDSTEIN, Milton. Television (Engineering, production and programming); Electronics (in industry and medicine); Radar. b'21. BS '42—MS '45 (Northwestern U); grad study 5 yrs (Northwestern) (U Chicago) (Ill Inst Tech). Research on receiver and transmitter circuits TV design problems; developed new studio and camera techniques; developed circuit for blood pressure tumor brain wave and heart studies, temperature measurements. Research engr Am Television Inc '41-51; prof radio engring Chicago Tech Coll '41-43; dean engring Am Television Inst of Tech since '42; chief engr Engring Services Co since '45; cons television engr. Inst Radio Engrs—Soc Motion Picture and Television Engrs—AIEE—Acad TV Arts and Sciences—Am Television Soc—Eta Kappa Nu—Sigma Xi. 5050 N Broadway Chgo 40. H: 1111 Ainslie St.

22 GOLDSTINE, Herman Heine. Computing devices; Applied mathematics (Calculus of variations, numerical analysis). b'13. BS '33—MS '34—PhD '36 (U Chicago). Author articles in field. Asst project dir Electronic Computer Project Institute Advanced Study since '46, permanent mem the Institute since '51; cons Ballistic Research Labs Aberdeen Proving Ground since '47, Los Alamos Sci Lab since '48, Wright Air Development Center since '52. Am Math Soc—Math Assn Am—Inst Math Statis (sub-com A-1 on computing centers of Inst). Institute for Advanced Study, Princeton, N.J. H: Cold Soil Rd.†

23 GOLDSWORTHY, Marion Charles. Fungicides; Plant disease control; Industrial fumes. b'93. BS '24—MS '25—PhD '28 (U Calif). Author articles in field. Path US Dept Agr since '46. AAAS—Am Phytopath Soc—Mycol Soc Am—Bot Soc Washington—Insecticide Soc Washington—Sigma Xi. U.S. Horticultural Station, Beltsville, Md.†

24 GOLDSWORTHY, Vernon. Cranberries. b'05. BS (Entomol and hort) '29—MS '31 (U Wis). Assisted development cranberry industry in Wisconsin. Author (thesis): Cranberry false blossom. Cranberry specialist State Wis '29-33, cons for cranberry industry in Wis '33-50; gen mgr Wis Cranberry Sales Co '33-45; Wis ed Cranberries (nat pub '33-47; gen mgr Fruit Grower's Co-op Sturgeon Bay Wis since '49. Wis Cranberry Growers Assn (sec '33-45)—Michigan Hort Soc—Am Cranberry Exchange—National Cranberry Grower Council—Wis Hort Soc. Fruit Grower's Cooperative, Sturgeon Bay, Wis. H: 936 Memorial Dr.

25 GOLEMAN, Irving. Cultural history (Goleman cycle); History of civilization. b'98. AB '23—MA '25 (U Calif); '25-26 (U London). Research and discoveries on literature as autobiography of civilization, Goleman cycle theory of cultural history. Author articles in field. Asst prof Eng James Millikan U '27-30; prof Eng and religious edn Coll of Pacific and chmn div humanities Stockton Coll since '37. NEA—Eng Assn—Phi Beta Kappa. Stockton College and College of the Pacific, Stockton, Calif. H: 1843 N. Concord Av., Stockton 11.

10 GOLOMSHTOK, Eugene A. Siberian anthropology; Permafrostology. b'97. AB '22—MA '23 (U Calif); '14-16 (U Kazan Russia); PhD '35 (U Pa); '31 (Am Sch Prehistoric Research in Europe). Field director first joint Soviet-American Expedition in Crimea for University Museum Philadelphia '33; field director archaeological excavations Indian Site Survey of New Jersey '36-39. Author: The Yakut Religion '49; contributor to Encyclopedia Arctica on Siberian ethnology and archaeology; also articles in field. Research asso U Mus Phila '30-36; lecturer prehist and ethnol Siberia Columbia U '38-39; lecturer in anthrop Brooklyn Coll '39-40; permafrost studies research analyst since '47; bibliog analyst Arctic Inst Am since '49. Am Anthrop Assn(F)—Am Geophys Union —Sigma Xi. Research fellow Viking Fund Inc '46-47.

11 GOMMEL, Carl Frederick. Tin; Tungsten. b'08. Student '33 (Mackay Sch Mines); PhD '40 (Acad Arts and Sci, Rio de Janeiro). Research on metallurgy, design and supervision of tin and tungsten ore concentrating plants. Mill supt Cie Aramayo de Mines en Bolivia '35-46, chief metall since '48; engr Standard Oil Cal '47. AIMME. Casilla No. 674, La Paz, Bolivia. H: 1220 N. Cedar St., Glendale 7, Cal.

12 GONDOS, Victor, Jr. Archives (Architecture). BSc (Architecture) '25 (U Mich); AM '41 (Hist (U Pa); '42-46 (Am U). Specialist on appraisal of government records for administrative, legal, and historical content; research and writing on functional planning and design of archival architecture; studies on bombproof archives of Stockholm, Sweden, and plans for archives of Archdiocese of New York; description history of records retirement plans, organization, and activity incident to disposition of World War II records of federal government. Author articles: Building and Equipment for Archives '45; Collaboration Between Archivists and Architects in Planning Archives Buildings '46; American Archival Architecture '47, and others. Architect Treas Dept '27-29; tech staff Puerto Rican Hurricane Relief Commn '29; pvt practice architecture Phila and Atlantic City NJ '30-41; archivist Nat Archives of US since '42, records retirement supervisor war records div '43-47, in charge bus econ sect since '48. AIA—Soc Am Archivists (chmn com archival bldgs). Registered architect Pa, NJ. National Archives, Washington 25.

13 GOOCH, Robert Kent. Parliamentary history (French). b'93. AB '14—AM '15 (U Va); AB '20—AM '20—PhD '24 (Oxford U London). Research in history parliamentary government and related matters in France. Author: The French Parliamentary Committee System '35. Petain Government and the Vichy Regime. Prof U Va since '24. Internat Polit Sci Assn. Received Fulbright award for advanced research in France '50-51. East Lawn, University Station, Charlottesville, Va.⊙

14 GOOD, Albert Irwin. Birds and stamps of Cameroun; Bulu and Mabea tribe language; Folklore of Bulu tribe. b'84. AB '06—DD '26 (Coll Wooster); BD '09 (Western Theol Sem Pittsburgh). Author: Book of Forms for Ministers in Bulu '34; Bulu Handbook Supplement '34. Translated and revised greater part of Old Testament in Bulu language; revised New Testament in Bulu language. Editor: Hymns in Bulu (with music) '28; Banok Hymns

'36; Mabea Hymns '38; also articles in field. Presbyn missionary since '09; collector sci material (insects mammals etc) for Carnegie Mus Pittsburgh since '09; collector birds for Cleveland Mus Natural Hist since '30; head Mission Lang Sch '33-43, '49. Royal Geog Soc(F)—Am Ornithol Union—Phi Beta Kappa. 819 Quinby Av., Wooster, O.

15 GOOD, Charles Winfred. Internal combustion engines and machine design. b'93. BSE '18 (U Mich). Mechanical and combustion studies, research on internal combustion engine fuels at high compression rations, effect of valve timing and other factors on volumetric efficiency, effect of hydrogen as a fuel when used alone and in combination with other fuels; design of clutches and development of equipment to test clutches and gears; design of permanently-lubricated bearings. Co-author: Internal Combustion Engines. Instr auto mechanics U Mich '18, instr mech engring '18-25, asst prof '25-33, asso prof '33-43, prof since '43, asst to dir dept engring research '23-36, asst dir since '36. ASME—SAE—Detroit Engring Soc—ASEE—Tau Beta Pi. University of Michigan, Ann Arbor.

16 GOODALL, Cecile Roberta. History and government of West Virginia. b'03. BA '28—MA '37 (U W Va); '29 (U Colo); '38 (Cambridge U, Eng); '42 (Inst World Orgn). Author articles in field. Asso ed West Virginia Review Charleston '33-35; ed West Virginia History since '41. NEA (life)—AHA—W Va Hist Soc—Nat Council Social Studies—Phi Beta Kappa. Charleston High School, Charleston 1, W. Va.

17 GOODALL, Robert Aldrich. Pipe lines (Elimination of corrosion); Instruments (Mechanical cleaning); Soldering (Highspeed electric); Crystals (Frequency control by etching); Condensers (Miniature, shock-proof, plastic). b'91. BS '13—DSc '50 (Doane Coll Crete Neb); Degree optometry '14 (Omaha Watch and Optical Coll). Oil type clutch drums for motion picture projectors; sound absorption and acoustics; fireproofing wood structures; electronic firing of shells. Author articles in field. Pres and operator Goodall Elec Mfg Co Ogallala Neb since '25; operator Ogallala Industries and Goodall Industries since '25. Nat Assn Corrosion Engrs—Nat Mfrs Assn —Radio Mfg Assn. 112 W. First St., Ogallala, Neb.

18 GOODBAR, Isaac. Motors (Electric); Bells (Electric); Illumination (Theatrical, airport). b'18. CE '41 (U Buenos Aires); MS (elec engring)—F '43-45 (MIT). Research on dynamic balancing of electric motors, starting devices for single-phase induction motors. Granted Argentine patents in field. Managing dir Goodbar and Cia and partner since '45; tech dir and partner Wilson Tecnica S R L since '50; tech dir Estelar '47-50; cons. Am Inst EE—Sigma Xi—Optical Soc Am —Illuminating Engring Soc Am and Gt Brit—Asociacion Argentina de Elctrotecnicos—Centro Argentino de Ingenieros—Centro Estudiantes de Ingeniera. Wilson Tecnica, S.R.L., Hernandarias 2081, Buenos Aires, Argentina; Goodbar and Cia., S. en C., Sarmiento 2849, Buenos Aires. H: Beauchef 322, Buenos Aires.

19 GOODBAR, Joseph Ernest. Business cycles; Creative capitalism; Causes and cure of depression; Money. b'90. AB '10 (U Ark); LLB '30 (Boston U); LIM '31—SJD '33 (Harvard). Lectured in Berlin, Munich and Budapest '38 on money and banking; testified before House and Senate Committees on banking measures '37, '38; before Ways and

Means Committee on taxation '42; special consultant United States Department of Commerce '42. Author: Managing the People's Money '35; A Creative Capitalism '48; also articles in field. Legal practice and research in money, banking and econ Boston and NYC '33-46; lecturer Boston U Sch Law '33-48; now atty, author, head dept bus adminstrn U Tampa since '49. AAAS —Am Econ Assn—Phi B Kap. 1501 Bayshore Blvd., Tampa, Fla. Summer: P.O. Box 840, Portland, Me.†⊙

20 GOODDING, Leslie N(ewton). Southwestern plants (Taxonomy, poisonous range); Gymnosporangia and other tree fungi; Land abuse (Plant indicators); Medicinal plants; Wild life in southwestern United States. b'80. BA '03 (U Wyoming); BS in forestry '04 (U Neb). Author articles in field. Govt service '19-46, soil conservation service '34-40, bot Bur Plant Industry US Dept Agr rubber investigations '42-46, ret '46; extensive plant collections in West '99-48. AAAS(F)— Soc Am Foresters—Phi Beta Kappa— Sigma Xi. R No. 1, St. David, Arizona.

21 GOODER, Seth MacDonald. Underpinning. b'90. Research and engineering on underpinning of printing plant for new deep foundations, deep foundations to replace piles tilting to river, new method for skyscraper foundation, tunnel beneath theaters, underpinning to protect large buildings during subway construction, and caisson underpinning on waterfront. Holds patents in field. With L P Friestedt Co (underpinning and bldg moving specialists) '18-26; pres Gooder Henrichsen Co Inc since '26. 1247 Deerfield Av., Deerfield, Ill.

22 GOODHART, Robert Stanley. Alcoholism (Nutritional deficiencies); Thiamine (Nutritional deficiencies, measurement and identification in humans); Industrial feeding; Nutrition (Chronic deficiencies). b'09. BS '30 (Lafayette Coll); MD '34—DSc '40 (NY U). Co-author: Nutritions in Industry '46. Contributor: Medical Clinics of North America '43, '48; Dietotherapy '45; Clinical Nutrition '50. Asst prof med NY U '42-47; passed asst surgeon advancing to surgeon USPHS '42-46; chief indsl feeding programs div War Food Adminstrn USDA '43-46; sci dir Nat Vitamin Found Inc since '46; asso chief nutrition clinics NYC Dept Health since '46; mem food and nutrition bd NRC '46-50. AMA(F)—Am Pub Health Assn(F)—NY Acad Med(F)— Am Soc Clin Investigation—Harvey Soc—NY Acad Sci—NY State Med Soc. 150 Broadway, NYC 7.

23 GOODHUE, Lyle D(avid). Insecticides; Aerosols. b'03. AB '28—MA '29 —PhD '34 (Ia State Coll). Research on, testing of insecticides, herbicides, and fungicides, and other agricultural chemicals; developed and perfected Aerosol bomb method of dispersal of insecticides. Has 33 patents on insecticides and related items. Author articles in field. Insecticide research Bur Entomol and Plant Quarantine Beltsville Md '34-46; dir research Airosol Inc Neodesha Kan '46-47; research chem Phillips Petroleum Co since '47. Am Chem Soc—Assn Econ Entomol— AAAS—Sigma Xi—Phi Kappa Phi— Phi Lambda Upsilon. John Scott Award Phila '45; Ia State Coll Alumni Award '48. Research Department, Phillips Petroleum Co., Bartlesville, Okla. H: General Delivery.

24 GOODIER, James Norman. Elasticity (Engineering). b'05. BA '27—PhD '31 (U Cambridge Eng). Solution mathematical problems of calculation of stress and strain, tendency to buckling, and application such results to engineering problems. Author articles: Applicability of Similarity Principles to Structural Models '44; The Cylindrical Buckling of Sandwich Plates '46; Elastic Torsion in the Presence of Initial Axial Stress '50 Coauthor article: Loosening of Threaded Fastenings by Vibration '45. Research fellow Ont Research Found Toronto Can '31-38; prof engring mech and head dept Cornell '38-47; prof engring mech Stanford since '47. Am Soc ME —Am Math Soc—Inst Aeronautical Sci. Stanford University, Stanford, Cal.†☉

10 GOODMAN, Robert Joseph. Iron mining (Marquette range); Water supply (Southern California); Climate (Chicago). b'18. BS '40—MS '41 (U Chicago); PhD '48 (Northwestern U). Research on discovery, early mining, and future of iron mining of Marquette Range, problem of water supply of Southern California, weather and climate studies of Chicago. Chief compilation div Army Map Service '41-42; research geog US War Dept '45-46; rsearch asst Northwestern U '46-48; asst prof geog Wayne U since '48. Assn Am Geog—Am Geog Soc—Nat Council Geog Teachers—Mich Acad Sci, Arts and Letters (chmn geog sect) —Sigma Xi. Department of Geography, Wayne University, Detroit 1.

11 GOODNIGHT, Clarence James. Arachnids; Ecology, zoogeography. b'14. AA '34 (Blackburn Coll); AB '36 —AM '37—PhD '39 (Ill U); '32-33 (Ill Coll). Research on effect of pentachlorphenol on aquatic organisms, especially fish; study of taxonomy, ecology, and zoogeography of Phalangida (Arachnida), and Branchiobdellidae of North American crayfishes; research trips to Mexico '46-50. Author articles in field. Asso prof zool Purdue U since '48; research asso Am Mus Nat Hist NY. Phi Beta Kappa—Sigma Xi—AA AS—Am Soc Zool—Am Micros Soc— Ecol Soc Am—Am Soc Study Evolution— Ecol Union—Soc Syst Zoologists—Am Geog Soc. Research fellow Monsanto Chem Co Ill U '39-40. Department of Biological Sciences, Purdue University, W. Lafayette, Ind.

12 GOODRICH, Arthur L(eonard). Kansas birds; Embryology of isopods. b'05. BS '28 (Coll Ida); MS '29 (U Id); PhD '38 (Cornell U). Author and illustrator: Birds in Kansas; also articles in field. With Kans State Coll since '29, now prof zool. Am Micros Soc—Sigma Xi—Phi Kappa Phi. Department of Zoology, Kansas State College, Manhattan, Kans.

13 GOODRICH, Lloyd. American art; Art forgery (Detection). b'97. Student '13-15, '16-18 (Art Students League NY); '15-16 (Nat Acad Design). Research on twentieth-century American art, problem of authenticity and forgery in American field; member New York Regional Committee, Public Works of Art Project '33-34, chairman editorial board Magazine of Art '42-50, member editorial board Art Bulletin, Art in America and Magazine of Art; chairman Committee on Government and Art since '49, member Smithsonian Art Commission. member Advisory Committee Huntington Hartford Foundation. '51-52, member Art Jury, Opportunity Fellowships, John Hay Whitney Foundation; member Advisory Committee Skowhegan School Painting and Sculpture. Author; Kenneth Hayes Miller '30; H E Schnakenberg '31; Thomas Eakins '33; American Genre '35; Century of American Landscape Painting '38; Problem of Authenticity in American Art '42; Winslow Homer '44; American Watercolor and Winslow Homer '45; Pioneers of Modern Art in America '46; Robert Feke '46; Ralph Albert Blakelock '47; Albert P Ryder '47; Yasuo Kuniyoshi '48; Max Weber '49; Edward Hopper '50; John Sloan '52. Editor: Research in American Art '45. With Macmillan Co '23-25; asso ed The Arts '25-27, '28-29, European ed '27-28, contrib ed '29-31; asst art critic NY Times '29; with Whitney Mus Am Art since '35, asso dir from '48. Am Art Research Council (dir '42)—Am Fedn Arts—Coll Art Assn Am—Soc Am Studies—Soc Am Historians—Am Inst Decorators (hon mem)—Am Assn Mus—Internat Inst for Conservation Museum Objects (asso). Whitney Museum of American Art, 10 W. 8th St., NYC 11.☉

14 GOODRICH, Luther Carrington. Sinology. b'94. AB '17 (Williams Coll); AM '27—PhD '34 (Columbia); William Straight Fellow Peking '30-32. Author: The Literary Inquisition of Ch'ien-lung '35; A Short History of the Chinese People '43; (with Henry C Fenn) Syllabus of the History of Chinese Civilization and Culture '47; also articles in field. Editor: Japan in the Chinese Dynastic Histories '51. Professor of Chinese Columbia University since '45. China Society America (dir)—Royal Asiatic Soc (N China br) —Am Oriental Soc (vp '45-46, pres '46-47). Columbia University, NYC 27.☉ Columbia University, NYC 27.☉

15 GOODRICH, Ralph Dickinson. Hydraulic engineering (Rivers, floods, irrigation and drainage, water supply). b'78. BS '03—CE '13 (U Mich). Designed and built systems for river regulations and flood control; made investigations and reports on water supplies for irrigation, power, and municipal uses; special investigations of flood frequencies and magnitudes and effect of reservoirs on reduction and control of floods. Author articles in field. Hydrographer Grand Canal Shantung and Chihli, Grand Canal Improvement Bd Tientsin China '18-19; engr flood relief and river regulating works Chihli River Commn Tientsin '19-27; asso prof Civil engring U Wyo '27, dean '36-48, sr hydraulic engineer for flood control problems US Engr Office Sacramento Dist '30-31; cons engr N Pacific Div US Engrs Office '35-37; chief engr Upper Col River Commn. ASCE—Am Soc Engring Edn —Wyo Engrs Soc—Sigma Xi—Phi Kappa Phi—Sigma Tau—Tau Beta Pi. City Administration Building, Grand Junction, Colo.

16 GOODRICH, Sidney Pullman. Ancient classical civilization; Greek literature; Papyrology. b'05. AB '28—AM '29—PhD '37 (Princeton U); '31-33 (Cincinnati U). Author articles in field. Professor classics Ripon College since '44. Am Philol Assn—Am Classical League—Classical Assn Middle West and South—Latin League Wis Colls—Guild Scholars. 26 Ingram, Ripon College, Ripon, Wis.†

17 GOODSPEED, Thomas Harper. Tobacco; Plants (South America). b '87. AB '09—DSc (Hon) '40 (Brown U); PhD '12 (U Calif); DSc (Hon) '39 (U La Plata Argentina). Research on origin and evolution genus Nicotiana, geographic distribution, morphology, and cytogenetics, including wild and cultivated species; director University of California Botanical Garden expeditions to Andes for collection specimens and seeds South American crop and ornamental plants; discovery five new species Nicotiana; collector Nicotiana specimens and seeds South American species; study nature and distribution floras of temperate South America; president cytology and genetics section Second South American Botanical Congress Argentina 1948; honorary president experimental taxonomy section Seventh International Botanical Congress Stockholm '50. Author: Plant Hunters in the Andes '41, also articles in field. Prof bot U Calif Berkeley since '28, dir bot garden since '34; hon dir Jardin Bot Lima Peru; hon mem faculty Nat Peruvian Coll Agr since '42, Nat Sch Subtropical Agr Colombia since '43. Nat Acad Sci Argentina, Peru, Chile, Colombia—Internat Assn Sci Tobacco Research. Department of Botany, University of California, Berkeley 4.☉

18 GOODWIN, DuWayne LeRoy. Plants (Ecology, taxonomy). b'19. BS '42 (U Ida); MS '45 (U Wis); '46-47 (U Minn); '49-52 (State Coll Wash). Studies on ecological life history of Artemisia tridentata; long term study vegetation of Snake River Plains. Agrl aid range research US Forest and Range Expt Sta summers '41 '42 '46 '49; asst prof bot Ida State Coll '47-49, research bot summer '50. Bot Soc Am—Brit Ecol Soc—Ecol Soc Am— Sigma Xi. Botany Department, The State College of Washington, Pullman, Wash.

19 GOODYEAR, Trevor S. Forests. b '93. BS (forestry) '16 (Wash State Coll). Research and development of forest fire detection system and forest fire fighting organization, established largest state owned and operated forest nursery west of Mississippi River, development of logging management plans on sustained yield basis, contributed to strengthening forest fire code and forestry protection laws of Washington. Asst state forester '17-33, state forester '33-49; dir state sustained yield forest No 1 since '49. Assn State Foresters (pres '47)—Soc Am Foresters (sr mem). Room 118, Old Capitol Building, Olympia, Wash.

20 GORANSON, Roy Waldemar. Properties of materials at high pressures. b'00. BS '22 (U BC); AM '23—PhD '31 (Harvard). Research work ·primarily concerned with high pressures, and design, development of apparatus for such experimentation; recently extended range of high prssure research to nine million pounds per square inch; rsearch on atomic bomb development Los Alamos '44-45. Geol Soc Am(F)—Am Phys Soc(F)—Am Geophys Union—Nat Geog Soc—Am Chem Soc—Sigma Xi. University of California, P.O. Box 1663, Los Alamos, N.M.

21 GORDER, Leslie O. Radio engineering; Television engineering. b'01. BS '26 (Armour Inst Tech and Chicago Tech Coll). Author: Whys and Wherefores of Television '51; television transpondence course. Co-author: Radio Cyclopedia; Fundamentals of Radio. Editor: Radio Dictionary. Chief instr Chicago Radio Inst '26-30; chief instr Chicago RCA Inst '30-34; dept head radio div Chicago Tech Coll '34-45; dir training Am Television Inst Tech and v-pres DeForest-Sanabria Corp since '45. Inst Radio Engrs (asso mem)—Soc Mil Engrs. H: 1340 Ashland Ave., Wilmette, Ill.

22 GORDON, Arthur Ernest. Latin epigraphy. b'02. AB '23 (Dartmouth Coll); PhD '29 (Johns Hopkins); fellow Dartmouth '23-25 (Am Acad in Rome), '27-28 (Johns Hopkins); fellow Johns Hopkins '28-29, Am Acad in Rome '48-49. President Philol Assn. Pacific Coast '52. With U Calif since '30, now prof Latin. 5215 Dwinelle Hall, University of California, Berkeley 4.

23 GORDON, Clement Davis. Poultry genetics. b'09. BS '30 (Rutgers U); MS '31 (Kan State Coll); PhD '38 (U Wis). Tests on hormone additions to feed as means of altering sex-ratio; study relationship of known inheritance factors with non-isolated factors governing economic qualities; breed crosses of closed flocks for concentration of desired economic qualities in one line. Asst advancing to asso poultry husbandman Ala Poly '36-39; poultry husbandman animal husbandry div USDA Beltsville Md '39-48; asso advancing to animal husbandman Brooksville Fla; poultry coordinator Nat Poultry Improvement Plan Washington '48-49; now inspector Livestock Sanitary Bd Poultry Service Div Tallahassee Fla. Phi Kappa Phi. Poultry Sci Soc prize for best publication '48. Livestock Sanitary Bd., Poultry Service Division, Tallahassee, Fla.

10 GORDON, John Boyle. Vegetable oil. b'89. BS '09 (U Mo); '09 (U Wis). Research on vegetable and animal oils and fats, oil seeds, copra; with US Vegetable Oil Mission inspecting vegetable oil industry and oil seed producing region Brazil as guests federal and state governments '42; secretary Copra Export Management Company Inc organized as procurement agency for US Commercial Company for copra Philippines '45, set up copra purchasing organization Philippine Islands '45. Author articles in field. Gen mgr Capital Refining Co S Washington Va '20-21; Washington rep Bur Raw Materials Am Veg Oils and Fats Industries since '21, sec since '23. Am Econ Assn —Nat Bur Econ Research—NY Oil Trades Assn—Acad Polit Sci. National Press Building, Washington.

11 GORDON, Robert B(enson). United States natural vegetation (Northeastern forest trees, wild flowers and freshwater plants). 'b'01. BSc '22— MSc '28—PhD '31 (Ohio State U). Author articles in field. Head dept sci Pa State Teachers Coll since '44. AA AS(F)—O Acad Sci(F)—Pa Acad Sci —Ecol Soc Am—Am Soc Plant Taxonomists—Acad Nat Sci—Nat Audubon Soc—Sigma Xi. State Teachers College, West Chester, Pa.†

12 GORDON, Seth (Edwin). Wildlife conservation and surveys; Conservation administration and legislation. b'90. Student (New Bloomfield Acad, Pa Bus Coll). Author articles in field. Cons Calif Wildlife Conservation Bd '48-51; dir Cal Dept Fish and Game since '51; vp N Am Wildlife Found Washington. Internat Assn Game Fish and Conservation Commrs (past pres) —Am Fisheries Soc—Wildlife Society (hon)—Outdoor Writers Am. Ferry Building, San Francisco; also Capitol, Sacramento.†

13 GORE, Wilbert Lee. Applied statistical chemical methods (Design of experiments, correlation analysis); Plastics. b'12. BS '33—MS '35 (U Utah). Developed methods for quality control and application statistical principles to research and development work; processing of plastics, especially extrusion and molding. Author articles in field. Sr supervisor plastics and elastomer research duPont Co since '45, cons on statis applications. Am Chem Soc—Am Statis Assn—Am Soc Quality Control. E. I. DuPont Co., Wilmington, Del.‡

14 GORELY, Jean (Mrs Charles P. Gorely, Jr). Wedgwood ware; Eighteenth century English ceramics and ceramic portraits. b'94. BA '16 (Wellesley). Co-founder with Charles P Gorely in '33 of Wedgwood Club. Author: Portraiture in Relief with Special Reference to Wedgwood's Portraits '43; Old Wedgwood (14 vols) '34-49; Old Wedgwood (Catalog of Winthrop Collection) '44; Wedgwood '50; also articles in field. Contributor: Encyclopedia Americana '51. Wedgwood Club (sec since '33). H: Gore Lea, Weston 93, Mass.

15 GORIS, Jan Albert. Belgium (Modern art, literature, and history). b'99. PhD (Hist sci) '25 (U Louvain); '25 (Sorbonne U Paris); '26 (London Sch Econ); Student (U Fribourg Switzerland); '26-27 (U Wash). Author: Belgium in Bondage '43; Belgium '46. Co-author (with Julius Held) Rubens in America '47; Belgian Letters (3d edit) '50; Modern Belgian Woodengravers '49. Dep comr gen for Belgium World's Fair NYC '39-40; commr of information for Belgium in US since '41. Belgian Government Information Center, 630 5th Ave., NYC 20.

16 GORNICK, Alan Lewis. Tax law; Estate taxes; Federal taxation. b'08. AB '35—LLB '37 (Columbia). Member federal finance committee US Chamber of Commerce since '51; national vice president Tax Executives Institute since '52. Author: Divorce, Separation and Estate Taxes '52; Arrangements for Separation or Divorce '52; Partnerships, Estates and Trusts (rev edit) '52. Asso counsel charge tax matters Ford Motor Co Dearborn Mich '47-49, dir tax affairs, tax counsel since '49; lectr tax matters NYU Inst on Fed Taxation since '47, Am Bar Assn and Practicing Law Inst courses on fundamentals in federal taxation since '46. Am Bar Assn(sect on taxation)— Am Law Inst—Tax Inst Inc (adv council '47-50, dir since '51)—Nat Tax Assn —Internat Fiscal Assn. 300 Schaefer Rd., Dearborn, Mich.☺

17 GORTNER, Willis A(lway). Foods (Biochemistry, freezing, processing). b'13. BA '34 (U Minn); PhD '40 (U Rochester). Biochemist on Bikini Scientific Resurvey '47. Co-author: Principles of Food Freezing '48. Co-editor: Outlines of Biochemistry; also articles in field. Head dept chem Pineapple Research Inst Hawaii. Am Soc Biol Chem—Inst Food Tech—Am Chem Soc—AAAS—Sigma Xi. Pineapple Research Institute, Honolulu, T.H.†

18 GOSNELL, Charles Francis. Statistical bibliography; Book obsolescence; Spanish personal names; Latin-American cultural relations. b'09.' AB '30 (U Rochester); BS '32—MS '37 (Columbia U); PhD '43 (NYU); certificate '34 (Centro de Estudios Historicos Madrid Spain). US delegate UN ESCO Conference on Library Service São Paulo Brazil '51. Author: Spanish Libraries under the Republic '35; Spanish Personal Names '38; Obsolescence of Books in College Libraries '44; also articles in field. State librarian and asst commissioner of education NY State since '45. Am Geog Soc(F)—ALA (chmn com library cooperation with Latin Am '39-41, mem Council since '45)—Assn Coll and Reference Libraries—Bibliog Soc Am—Inter-Am Bibliog and Library Assn—NY Library Assn— NEA—Am Assn State and Local Hist —Am Statistic Assn—Joint Microcard Com—Am Council on Edn (com materials for teachers in internat relations '40-41)—Nat Assn State Librarians (pres)—Mohawk Valley Hist Assn— NY State Bd Geog Names—Soc Am Archivists. State Library, Albany 1, N.Y.

19 GOSS, Warren Hand. Oilseeds; Fats; Oils. b'12. BS '33 (U Wash); '34-37 (U Md); '38-40 (U Ill). Chemistry and technology of oilseed processing, solvent extraction, refining, edible fats and oils. Author: The German Oilseed Industry '46. Co-author: Soybean Chemistry and Technology '44. Chem Nat Bur Standards Washington '33-37; chem engr Regional Soybean Lab Urbana Ill '37-42, chem engr, later asst to dir No Regional Research Lab Peoria Ill '42-47; asso dir research Pillsbury Mills Inc Minneapolis since '47; Soybean Research Council, dir Inst of Oilseed Technology. AICE—Am Oil Chem—Am Chem Soc—Am Soybean Association—Inst Food Tech. Pillsbury Mills, Inc., Minneapolis 2.

20 GOSSARD, Atherton Clark. Culture and production of pecans and Chinese chestnuts. b'04. BS '27 (O State U); MS '29 (U Wis); '38 (U Chicago). Research in pecan production, culture, nutrition, variety testing, Chinese chestnut production and breeding. Author: (with H L Crane) A Method of Studying Germination Problems of Pecan Nuts '40; (with Chesley Hines) Pecan Production in Mississippi '46; also articles in field. Asst pomol U Dept Agr US Pecan Field Lab Albany Ga '30, US Pecan Field Sta Spring Hill Ala '31-35, US Hort Field Sta Meridian Miss '35-48, hort US Hort Field Station since '50. sta supt since '49. Am Soc Hort Sci. U.S. Horticultural Field Station, Rt. 6, Meridian, Miss.†

21 GOTLIEB, Albert Irwin. Atomic energy (Civil defense). b'22. BBA '45 —BE '45 (U Ariz); MA '47 (Columbia). Summary of news and developments for civilian defense groups; preparation of outline for first civil defense film produced; consultant to first joint community-college seminar on civil defense problems University of Southern California. Author: Achieving International Control of Atomic Energy; also articles: Critical Thinking for a New Age '47; Teaching Atomic Education—A Collection of Units, Reports of Teaching Experiences and Sources '48; The Atom Enters the Social Structure—A Survey '50. Co-author: The Challenge of Atomic Energy—A Resource Unit and Discussion Guide for Teachers and Group Leaders '48. In charge atomic edn program Teachers Coll Columbia '47, '48; exec sec Council on Atomic Implications Inc '48-51; ed Civil Defense News (bi-monthly) since '50. Soc Psychol Study Social Issues (atomic energy com)—Nat Council Social Studies—NEA. Civil Defense News, 1811 E. Foothill, Altadena, Cal. H: 3501 S. La Brea, Los Angeles 16.

22 GOTTLIEB, David. Microbiology; Plant pathology and Physiology (Fungi); Antibiotics. b'11. BS '37 (Coll City NY); MS '40 (Ia State Coll); PhD '42 (U Minn); fellow U Minn '43-44, U Del '44-46. Studies of physiology of plant disease, fungi, obligate parasitism, fungicide development. Discovered phosphorus relations in wheat rust, toxins in tomato wilt, antibiotic, chloromycetin, mechanism of fungicide activity. Author articles in field. Asso research prof U Ill since '50. Am Phytopath Soc—Am Bot Soc (microbiol sect)—Ill Acad Sci—Sigma Xi. University of Illinois, Urbana, Ill.†

23 GOTTMAN, I Jean. Economic and political geography. b'15. AB '32; License es Lettres '36—Diplome d'Etudes Superieures '34 (U Paris). Chief studies and research Department of Social Affairs United Nations '46-47; member International Port Commission for study of industrial ports '47-48. Author: Les Relations Commerciales de la France '44. Co-author: Le Probleme des Matieres Premieres (with E Dennery) '39; La Federation Francaise (with J de la Roche) '45; Readings in the Geography of the Mediterranean Region '43; Makers of Modern Strategy '43; Studies on War '43; Doctrine Politiques Modernes '47. Exec sec human geog sect U Paris '36-41, asst econ geog '37-40; mem Inst Advanced Study '42-44; con Bd Econ Warfare Washington '42-44; vis lecturer Johns Hopkins '43, asst prof '44, asso prof '46; member Inst for Advancued Study '49-50; adv French Ministry Nat Econ Paris '45; French Supply Council

Washington '45-46; mem commn Franco-Am pour la Reforme de l'Etat Washington '45-46; con Centre de-Etudes de Politique Etrangere Paris since '37; chmn Commission on Regional Planning of Int Geog Union since '49. Assn Am Geog—Am Geog Soc—Am Soc Profl Geog—Soc de Geog Montreal—Soc de Geog de Paris—Assn de Geog Francais—Soc Languedocienne de Geog (Montpellier). Laureate in geog of Concours General of France '31. Bronze Medal of U Brussels '47. Institute for Advanced Study, Princeton, N.J.

10 GOTTSCHALK, Louis. Modern European history; French revolution; Historiography; Franco-American relations. b'99. AB '19—AM '20—PhD '21 (Cornell U). Associate editor of various historical periodicals. Author: Jean Paul Marat—A Study in Radicalism '27, French translation '29; The Era of the French Revolution '29; Lafayette Comes to America '35; Lafayette between the American and the French Revolution '50; Understanding History: A Primer of Historical Method '50. Articles in field. Asst prof hist U Louisville '23-25, asso prof '25-27; asso prof modern hist U Chicago '27, prof since '35, chmn dept hist '37-42. AHA (pres modern hist sect '47-48)—AAUP—Am Friends of Lafayette (exec com)—Soc Am Hist—Phi Beta Kappa. Awarded Guggenheim Fellowship '28-29; Newberry Library Fellowship '46; Princeton U Bicentennial Medal '46; U Louisville Sesquicentennial Medal '47; James Hazen Hyde Prize '49. 5551 University Av., Chgo.◎

11 GOULD, Bruce Anthony. Mercury (Geology, mining, extraction). b'12. Student '30-33 and '34 (Mackay Sch Mines U Nev). Exploration and development of quicksilver mines Alaska, Canada, US, Colombia, and Peru; supervision installation of quicksilver mines; assisted in improvement of rotary quicksilver furnace. Pres and gen mgr mines Cal and Nev since '35; pres H W Gound & Co San Francisco since '50. AIMME. 1000 Mills Bldg., SF 4. H: 30 Woodacre Dr., SF 27.

12 GOULD, Charles J(ay), Jr. Diseases of ornamental bulbous plants (Narcissus, iris, tulip, gladiolus). b'12. AB cum laude '34 (Marshall Coll); MS '37—PhD '42 (Iowa State College). Fulbright Scholar to the Netherlands on bulb research '51. Author articles in field. With Western Wash Experimental Station State Coll Wash since '41, now plant path; collaborator US Dept Agr since '47. Am Phytopath Soc—Am Plant Life Soc—Sigma Xi. Gen Edn Bd scholar '37. Western Washington Experiment Station, Puyallup, Wash.†

13 GOULD, Donnell Hunting. Weather (Analysis, Alaska). b'09. AB '43 (Berea Coll); MS '47 (Calif Inst Tech). Studies and analysis of weather conditions in Alaska. Author: Preliminary Report on Relationship between North American Weather Types and the Weather of Juneau, Alaska. Weather observer US Weather Bureau Rock Springs Wyo '38-38, weather observer, forecaster, insp and administrative asst Juneau Alaska '38-47, analyst and prognostic analyst Weather Bur-Air Force-Navy Analysis Center since '47. Am Meteorol Soc—Am Geophys Union. U.S. Weather Bureau, Honolulu, T.H.

14 GOULD, Gerald Blenkiron. Economics of coal and coke fuels. b'89. AB '10 (Yale); MA '11 (U Pa). Author: Judging Coal Values; Steam Generation Steps Ahead. Pres Fuel Engring Co NYC since '28; fuel power cons since '38. AIMME (chmn joint com with Am Soc ME fuel values '34-41)—Am Society ME—ASTM. 215 Fourth Av., NYC 3.

15 GOULD, Gordon Ingraham. Mercury. b'11. AB '32 (U Calif). Geological studies and examinations all important American deposits for purpose advising on mining and treatment methods; development and design Gould Rotary furnace and condensing system. Author article: Modern Quicksilver Reduction Plants. Contributor: Handbook of Non-ferrous Metallurgy. Gen supt Klau mine New Idria Mine '34-35, '36-37; design engring and management several properties '38-45; mgr New Idria Quicksilver Mining Co and New Idria Honduras Mining Co since '45. AIMME—Mining and Metall Soc Am. 58 Sutter St., San Francisco 4.

16 GOULD, Laurence McKinley. Polar region geology and geography; Glacial geology (Upper Mississippi valley, Cordilleram areas). b'96. BS '21—MA '23—DSc '25 (U Mich); ScD (hon) '31 (Poly Inst Brooklyn); LLD '45 (Coe Coll); LLD '46 (Macalester Coll). Assistant director and geologist University of Michigan Greenland Expedition '26; assistant director and geographer Putnam Baffin Island Expedition '27; second in command and geologist-geographer Byrd Antarctic Expedition '28-30; delegate International Congress of Geodesy and Geophysics Edinburgh '36, 17th International Geology Congress Moscow '37. Author: Cold—the Record of an Antarctic Sledge Journey '31; also articles in field. Pres Carleton Coll since '45. Chief Arctic Sect Arctic Desert and Tropic Information Center Army Air Forces '42-44. Geol Soc Am(F)—AAAS—Am Geog Soc—Am Geophys Union—Phi Beta Kappa—Sigma Xi. Awarded Congressional gold medal '31; David Livingston gold medal '30; Geog Soc Chicago gold medal '31; Cross First Class Royal Norwegian Order of St. Olaf '49. Carleton College, Northfield, Minn.◎

17 GOVAN, Gilbert Eaton. Contemporary literature; Confederate military history; Local and Eastern Tennessee history. b'92. Student '08-11 (Ga Sch Tech). Co-author: University of Chattanooga; Sixty Years '47; also articles in field. Librarian U Chattanooga since '34; literary ed Chattanooga Times since '31, ed writer since '42. ALA—SE Library Assn—Tenn Library Assn—Tenn Hist Soc—Southern Hist Assn. University of Chattanooga, Chattanooga 3, Tenn.

18 GOVIN, Gustavo Lawrence. Refineries (Engineering); Irrigation engineering; Highway engineering; Municipal engineering. b'95. CE '20 (Brooklyn Poly Inst). Research on engineering and structures of power houses, pump houses, small dams, oil separators, piping, water supply, sewers, irrigation and drainage projects, waterfront improvements, etc. Engr various co since '26; with Raymond Concrete Pile Co since '51. Am Soc CE—Soc Mil Engrs. Raymond Concrete Pile Co., 140 Cedar St., NYC 6.

19 GOWARD, Frank Kenneth. Synchrotrons (Electron accelerators); Aerials (Radio). b'19. MA '47 (St John's College Cambridge Eng). Constructed first synchrotron electron accelerator; assisted in construction machines producing voltages of up to three hundred million volts; discovered and studied new nuclear disintegrations, especially splitting of oxygen into four alpha particles; improved centimetre-wavelength aerial systems using linear arrays. Co-author: (with D W Fry) Aerials for Centimetre Wavelengths '50, also articles in field. Radio aerial development Telecommunications Research Establishment Malvern Eng '42-45; with Atomic Energy Research Establishment since '46, now head synchro-tron group. Inst EE London. Atomic Energy Research Establishment, Harwell, Didcot, Berkshire, Eng.

20 GOWEN, John Whittemore. Genetics (Inheritance); Animal physiology; Animal pathology. b'93. BS '14—MS '15 (U Me); PhD '17 (Columbia). Author: Milk Secretion '24; Manual of Dairy Cattle Breeding '25; also articles in field. Editor: Heterosis '52. Prof genetics Ia State Coll since '37. AAAS—Am Naturalists—Genetics Soc Am (pres '52)—Am Soc Zool—Sigma Xi—Phi Kappa Phi—Phi Beta Kappa. 2014 Kildee St., Ames, Ia.◎

21 GRABER, Laurence Frederick. Crop and pasture problems; Grazing (Renovation and reseeding of pastures); Seed distribution; Alfalfa problems. b'87. BS '10—MS '12 (U Wis); PhD '30 (U Chicago). Member Fourth International Grassland Congress Oxford England and Aberysthwyth Wales '37; member committee Agricultural Board National Research Council '45; chairman Seed Practices Committee North Central States since '47. Author: Laboratory Manual for Students of Agronomy; Agronomy, Principles and Practices; also articles in field. Prof agron U Wis since '21. Wisconsin Hist Soc—AAAS(F)—Am Soc Agron (F, pres '48)—Am Soc Plant Physiol—Wis Acad Sci Arts Letters—Alpha Zeta—Sigma Xi. 1138 Waban Hill, Madison 5, Wis.◎

22 GRAEFF, Arthur D(undore). Pennsylvania history; Pennsylvania German history. b'99. AB '20 (Franklin and Marshall Coll); MS '32—DSc '35—Seminar '29-35 (Temple U); Seminar '26 (U Pa); Carl Schurz Memorial Found and Oberlander Trust Fellow '39; Fellow '43 (Franklin Inst). Research mission to England, Holland, Germany securing 2500 microfilm copies of documents in foreign archives which pertain to Pennsylvania history. Author: Old World Backgrounds '41; The Pennsylvania Germans—A Study in Stability '43; Lebanon County Through the Centuries '44; Conrad Weiser, Pennsylvania Peacemaker '45; The History of Pennsylvania '44; It Happened in Pennsylvania '47; The Pennsylvania Germans in Ontario '47; Industrial Berks County '48; History of Steel Casting Industry '49. Co-author: The Pennsylvania Germans '42; also articles in field. Head dept hist Overbrook Sr High Sch Phila since '42. Pa German Folklore Soc (mem bd dirs). Awarded Phi Delta Kappa Medal for excellency in research. Overbrook Senior High School, 59th and Lancaster Av., Phila. 31.

23 GRAFF, Paul W(eidemeyer). North American fungi; Systematic botany and mycology; Plant diseases. b'87. BS '07 (U Conn); AM '16—PhD '32 (Columbia). Author articles in field. Prof, head dept biol Appalachian State Teachers Coll since '47. Bot Soc Am—Am Mycol Soc—Am Micros Soc—AAAS(F)—Tenn Acad Sci—NC Acad Sci—So Appalachian Bot Soc—NCEA—Sigma Xi—Phi Sigma. Department of Biology, Appalachian State Teachers College, Boone, N.C. H: 405 Stanbury Circle.

24 GRAHAM, David Crockett. Chinese (Recent history, art, culture); Tibet (Ethnology); Ch'uan Miao; Lolos; Ch'iang. b'84. AB '08—DSc (hon) '30 (Whitman Coll); BD '11 (Colgate-Rochester Divinity Sch); AM '20—PhD '27 (U Chicago). Anthropology, ethnology and folklore of non-Chinese ethnic groups central Asia; history Chinese art and culture as represented in archaeology, pottery, porcelains, religion, art, burial customs and superstitions. Author: Religion in Szechwan Province, China; The Ancient

Caves of Szechwan Province, China. Curator Mus Archaeol and Ethnol West China Union U '32-42. Am Anthrop Assn—Am Folklore Soc—Am Oriental Soc—China Inst Am—Royal Geog Soc (London, F). H: 904 Fifth St., Wenatchee, Wash.

10 GRAHAM, Edward Harrison. Ecology: Land use; Soil conservation. b'02. BS '27—PhD '32 (U Pittsburgh). Head Carnegie Museum expeditions to southern Arizona '27, Sonora Mexico '28, Uinta Basin Utah and Colorado '31, '33, '35. Author: Flora of the Kartabo Region, British Guiana '34; Botanical Studies in the Uinta Basin of Utah and Colorado '37; Natural Principles of Land Use '44; The Land and Wildlife '47. Chief biol div Soil Conservation Service US Dept Agr since '42. Wildlife Soc—Soil Conservation Soc—Sigma Xi. Soil Conservation Service, U.S. Department of Agriculture, Washington 25.†

11 GRAHAM, Herbert Winfield. Steel making processes (Bessemer); Steel (Intermediate manganese). born '91. Degree electrometall '14 (Lehigh U). Chairman first steel group of Nelson Mission to China. Author articles in field. Asso with Jones & Laughlin Steel Corp since '14, charge all tech activities as vp and dir tech since '47. Indl Research Inst (co-founder, first pres)—Am Soc Metals—SAE—AAAS—Am Iron Steel Inst—British Iron Steel Inst—Am Inst Mining Metall Engrs (chmn iron and steel div '43). 5437 Ellsworth Av., Pittsburgh.

12 GRAHAM, John Meredith. Early American pewter, chinaware, and glass. b'04. Student '27-28 (Leigh U); (Columbia). Adviser to Bartow Mansion Museum, adviser to Decorative Arts Department, Brooklyn Museum. Author: American Pewter '49; Popular Art in America '39. Co-author: Wedgwood, A Living Tradition. Contributor: Handbook of Old Pottery and Procelain Marks; The Handbook of American Silver and Pewter Marks; Fine Points of Furniture, Early America '50. Curator Decorative Arts Brooklyn Mus '38-50; curator collections Colonial Williamsburg since '50. Pewter Collectors Club Am (regional v-pres)—Soc Preservation Long Island Antiquities. Curator of Collections, Colonial Williamsburg, Williamsburg, Va.

13 GRAHAM, Robert Clark. Optics (Variable focus lenses; Multifocals; Contact lenses; Plastic optics; Aspheric lenses). b'06. AB '33 (Mich State Coll BSc '37 (Ohio State U). Inventor variable focus lens; director research which developed hard plastic lenses. Author articles: A Variable Focus Lens '40; Plastic Lenses made of Thermosetting Resins '49; The Corneal Lens '49; and other articles in field. With Bausch & Lomb Optical Co '37-40; western mgr Univis Lens Co '40-44, sales mgr '44-46; vp and dir research Plastic Optics Co since '46; asso prof Los Angeles Coll Optometry since '47; spl lectr phys optics Coll Med Evangelists since '49. Optical Soc Am—Am Inst Physics—Am Acad Optometry—Am Ordnance Assn. 117 E. Colorado St., Pasadena 1, Calif.

14 GRAHAM, Samuel Alexander. Forest entomology and ecology; Wildlife management. b'91. BS '14—PhD '21 (U Minn); MF '16 (Cornell U). Author: Forest Entomology '52. Co-author: On Your Own'43; also articles in field. Professor economic zoology Sch Forestry and Conservation U Mich since '29, research asso Mus Zool since '29. AAAS—Am Assn Econ Entomol—Entomol Soc Am—Ecol Soc Am—Soc Am Foresters—Wildlife Soc—Sigma Xi. School of Natural Resources, University of Michigan, Ann Arbor.

15 GRAMMER, Allen L. Color printing (Prevention of offset). b'89. Industry advisory committee magazine and periodical printing and publishing WPB '41. Inventor of Grammer wax spraying process for prevention of offset in color printing and machines and improvements in magazine manufacture. Sec dir Curtis Pub Co '15-37; pres Street & Smith '38-48, chmn bd '48-49; sec, dir Grammer Dempsey & Hudson Inc Newark since '40. 790 Broad St., Newark, N.J.

16 GRANBERY, John Cowper. Greek language literature and culture (New Testament and modern). b'74. AB '96 (Randolph Macon Coll); BD '99 (Vanderbilt U); AM '08—PhD '09 (U Chicago); DD '13 (Ky Wesleyan). Head dept history Tex Tech Coll '25-32; travel, study, writing and speaking in Brazil '32-34; acting prof philosophy and polit sci Southwestern U '34-35, head dept philosophy '35-38; prof govt and history Trinity U '44-45, prof Greek '44-45, classical langs '45-46. War work under YMCA with Am French and Greek armies '17-20. Golden Cross of Order of Saviour, Mil Merit (Greece). Author: Outline of New Testament Christology '09; Students' Prolegomena to Philosophy '31. 3305 W Ashby, San Antonio 1.†◎

17 GRANDSTAFF, James O(kley). Sheep (Breeding, Navajo). b'07. BSA '30 (O State U); '35-36 (US Dept Agr Grad Sch); '39 (Mass Inst Tech). Technology animal fibers, adaptation to environment and breeding factors of sheep; evaluation fleece quality sheep wool; US delegate International Symposium on High Altitude Biology Lima Peru '49. Author articles: Breeding for Quality Wool '40; Evaluating Fleece Characteristics of Navajo Sheep from a Breeding Standpoint '41; Wool Characteristics in Relation to Navajo Weaving '42; Fertility and Reproduction in Sheep in Relation to Breeding and Environment '49, and others. Co-author article: Improvement of Wool for Navajo Hand Weaving '45, and others. Jr animal fiber tech Bur Animal Industry US Dept Agr '31-33; asst animal fiber tech in charge wool research Southwestern Range and Sheep Breeding Lab '36-39, dir lab since '44; animal husbandman Navajo service Bur Indian Affairs '44-49. Am Soc Animal Prodn—AAAS. Southwestern Range and Sheep Breeding Laboratory, P.O. Box 758, Fort Wingate, N.M.

18 GRANGE, Wallace Byron. Wildlife research and management (Grouse, snowshoe rabbits, deer, wildlife cycles, minnow propagation). b'05. Student '26-27 (U Mich); 24-25—grouse fellow '33-34 (U Wis). Also research on semi-natural game farms for wildlife, feeding wildlife in winter, improvement of farm environment for wildlife. Author: Practical Beaver and Muskrat Farming '47; Wisconsin Grouse Problems '48; also articles in field. Asst regional game mgr for Wis, Minn, Mich US Resettlement Adminstrn '35; game biol Wis Conservation Commn '40-41; founder, pres since '37 Sandhill Game Farm Inc Babcock Wis. Wildlife Soc—Wis Soc Ornithol—Wilson Ornithol Club—Am Soc Mammalogists—Wilderness Soc—Am Ornithol Union (asso). Babcock, Wis.†

19 GRANT, Arthur William. Electroforming (Molds). b'08. BS (Detroit Inst Tech). Developed important inventions, discoveries, patents relating to electro-forming and heat treating of metals and dies. Engr mold div US Rubber Co Detroit plant. Electrochem Soc—Electro Plater's Soc—Am Chem Soc. 9800 Somerset, Detroit 24.†

20 GRANT, Chapman. Ornithology; Herpetology; Biogeomorphology. b'87.

AB '10 (Williams Coll Williamstown Mass). Scientist, expedition of American Museum to Yucatan and Mexico '10; scientist US Navy and Bishop Museum USS Tanager expedition to Leeward Islands (Hawaiian group) '23; private herpetological expeditions to Jamaica, Puerto Rico, Santo Domingo, Virgin Islands, Cayman Islands, others; bio-geomorphological expeditions to study Carolina bays, polished rocks of Cornudas Mountains of New Mexico, Mima mounds of southern California, other changes in earth's surface caused by biological agencies; founder, editor Herpetologica since '36. Author articles in field. Avacado grower Escondido Calif '39-46. AAAS (F)—Herpetologists League (F, founder '46)—Am Soc Ichthyologists Herpetologists—Am Ornithol Union. 2970 Sixth Av., San Diego 3, Calif.†◎

21 GRANT, J(ames) A(llan) C(lifford). Law (Constitutional). b'02. Student '20-22 (U Calif); BA '24—MA '25 —PhD '27 (Stanford U); Social Sci Research Council fellow '31-32; Guggenheim fellow Latin America '42-43. Field study of federalism, and rights of persons accused of crime US, Canada, Europe, and Mexico; study judicial control of legislation in Colombia; research on judicial control of legislative procedure. Author articles: Immunity from Compulsory Self Incrimination in a Federal System of Government '35; The Search for Uniformity of Law '38; Constitutional Basis of the Rule Forbidding the Use of Illegally Seized Evidence '41; Contract Clause Litigation in Colombia—A Comparative Study in Judicial Review '48; Judicial Control of the Legislative Process—The Federal Rule '50, and others. Contributor: Selected Essays on Constitutional Law '38. Clk judiciary com Calif Assembly '27; instr polit sci U Wis '27-29, asst prof '29-30; faculty polit sci dept U Calif since '30, prof since '40, chmn dept '39-42, dean div social sci since '50; vice chmn tenth region War Labor Bd '43-45. Am Polit Sci Assn (bd eds '38-41, exec council '44-46)—Western Polit Sci Assn (bd eds '50)—Am Fgn Law Assn. University of California, 405 Hilgard Av., Los Angeles 24.◎

22 GRANT, James Josiah. Rifles (Target, history). b'08. Research on design, manufacture and use of single shot breechloaded sporting and target rifle; personal tests and experimentation of existing specimens to ascertain relative strength of various breech locking mechanisms, ignition time and certainty; exhaustive loading and reloading of cartridges to determine correct bullet temper, primer strength and powder charge for maximum velocity, ultimate accuracy, correct powder type and charge to prolong barrel life. Author: Single Shot Rifles '47. Author article: Single Shot Rifles '50. Nat Rifle Assn—Nat Muzzle Loading Rifle Assn—O Gun Collectors Assn—Single Shot Rifle Assn. 112½ W. Main St., Van Wert, O.

23 GRANT, Martin L. Vascular plant taxonomy (Polynesia, Iowa, Middle America); Iowa ornithology. b'04. BA '27 (Oberlin Coll); MA '29—PhD '36 (Minn U); Bishop fellow '30-31 (Yale). Made botanical explorations in Society Islands, Hawaii, Mexico, Central America and Colombia. Author articles in field. Asso prof bot Ia State Teachers Coll since '36. AAAS(F)—Ecol Soc Am—Bot Soc Am—Am Soc Plant Taxonomists—Ia Ornithol Union (past pres)—Ia Acad Sci—NEA—Am Ornithol Union—Wilson Ornithol Club—Phi Beta Kappa—Sigma Xi—Inland Bird Banding Assn. Science Department, Iowa State Teachers College, Cedar Falls, Ia. H: 417 Olive St.

10 GRANT, Ulysses S., IV. Paleontology; Mollusks; Echinoids. b'93. AB '15 (Harvard); PhD '29 (Stanford). Research in dynamical geological processes, shore processes, surface subsidence in oil fields; marine invertebrates. Author articles in field. Instr geol U Calif '31, asst prof '31, asso prof '34, prof since '40. Geol Soc Am(F)—AA AS(F)—Am Geophys Union—Am Assn Petroleum Geol—Soc Econ Paleontol Mineral—Am Math Soc. 405 Hilgard Av., Los Angeles 24.

11 GRANVILLE, Walter Clark. Color standards; Color systems; Colorimetric analysis. b'12. Ed pub schs. Research, development and application of color systems and standards, application of colorimetric analysis to paints, printing inks, and other pigmented media, color selection, harmony, names and control in printing, interior color planning. Author articles in field. In charge color room Internat Printing Ink Co '29-37; phys in charge colorimetry lab Interchem Corp Research Lab '37-45; asst dir dept design Container Corp Am since '45. ASTM—Illuminating Engring Soc—Am Designers Inst—Inter-Soc Color Council—Optical Soc Am—Soc Typographic Arts. 38 S. Dearborn St., Chicago 3.

12 GRAS, Norman Scott Brien. History of American business; English economic history; Public relations. b'84. BA '06—MA '06 (Western U London Ont); MA '09—PhD '12 (Harvard); LLD (hon) '24 (U Western Ontario); Harvard travel fellow '10-12 (Europe). Author: Evolution of the English Corn Market '15; An Introduction to Economic History '22; Industrial Evolution '30; Casebook in American Business History '39 (with H M Larson); Shifts in Public Relations '45; Are You Writing a Business History? '47. Prof bus hist Harvard '27-50. Medieval Acad Am(F)—AHA—Am Econ Assn—Business Hist Soc. Harvard School of business, Soldiers Field, Boston.☉

13 GRATON, Louis Caryl. Ore deposition and microscopy; Volcanism. b'80. BS '00—PhD '30 (Cornell); AM (hon) '41 (Harvard); '00-02 (McGill U). Research in geology of mining districts, principles of ore deposition, and processes relating to volcanos, hot springs and geysers; associate editor Economic Geology. Author articles in field. Mem US Geol Survey '03-09; sec-treas Copper Producers Assn NY '09-15; prof mining geol Harvard '12-49; cons geol various mining companies, dir Cerro de Pasco Copper Corp. Mexican Nat Acad Sci (foreign asso)—Geolog Soc Belgium (hon)—Penrose Gold Medal Soc Econ Geol—Am Inst Mining Metall Engrs—Can Inst Mining and Metall Engrs—Geol Soc Am—Geol Soc Washington — AAAS — Washington Acad Sci—Mining Metall Soc Am—Soc Econ Geol—Am Geophys Union—Chem Metall Mining Soc So Africa—Geol Soc So Africa—Mineral Soc Am—Am Acad Arts Sci(F). Vanserg Laboratories, Harvard University, Cambridge 38, Mass.☉

14 GRAUBARD, Mark. Biochemistry (Pigments, food); Genetics (Hormones); History of science. b'04. Research on pigment reaction, relation to hormones, oxidases, and hormone metabolism; studies and writing on history and psychology of magic, witchcraft, alchemy and astrology, scientific hypotheses and culture matrix, ancient superstitions. Author: Biology and Human Behavior '36; Man the Slave and Master '38; Man's Food: Its Rhyme or Reason '43; Science and Superstition in Our Daily Food '42; also articles in field. Asso prof natural sci U Minn since '47. Physiol Soc—Genetics Soc Am—Am Soc Zool—

Hist Sci Soc. Fellow Nat Research Council '31-33, Finney-Howell Cancer Research Fund '40-41. University of Minnesota, Minneapolis 14.†

15 GRAUMONT, Raoul. Knots; Rope work. b'96. Author: Encyclopedia of Knots and Fancy Rope Work '39; Square Knot, Tatting, Fringe and Needlework '43; Splicing Wire and Fiber Rope '45; Handbook of Knots '45; Fisherman's Knots and Nets '48. Writer since '38. Authors' Guild of Authors' League Am. c/o Cornell Maritime Press, Box 109, Cambridge, Md.

16 GRAVATT, George Flippo. Diseases of chestnut and pine. b'91. BS '11—MS '12 (Va Poly Inst); '14 (U Calif); '26-28 (George Washington U). In charge investigation of chestnut blight, pine blister rust and international forest disease work. With div forest path US Plant Industry Sta Beltsville Md since '12, now sr path. Bot Soc Washington (past pres)—Washington Acad Sci. Division of Forest Pathology, Plant Industry Station, Beltsville, Md.

17 GRAVATT, Marshall. Handicrafts (Veteran training). b'87. Student (Mining geol) '15 (U Va); '49 (Sch for Am Craftsmen). Instruction of crafts for benefit of combat sustained physical handicaps; in charge establishment of arts and crafts program, including instruction, production, and marketing. Specialist in handicrafts since '45; now arts and crafts supervisor Spl Services AUS Alaska. AIMME. H: 83 Fenner Av., Asheville, N.C.

18 GRAVES, Alvin Cushman. Nuclear physics (Energy). b'09. BS '32 (Univ Va); PhD '39 (U Chicago). Deputy scientific director Operation Sandstone (Atomic weapon tests) '48. Author articles in field. Staff Los Alamos Sci Lab U Cal, scientific dir all atomic weapons tests since '48. Am Phys Soc—Tau Beta Pi—Sigma Xi. P.O. Box 1663, Los Alamos Scientific Laboratory, Los Alamos, N.M.

19 GRAVES, Arthur Roselle. Design of mill buildings and wind bracing. b'95. Rensselaer Poly Inst. Supervised structural design Presbyterian Eye and Ear Hospital Pittsburgh; continuous hot strip mill, cold mill, bar mill, Lackawanna NY; two continuous hot strip mills, two cold mills, two rod mills, Sparrows Point Md, and others. Draftsman to sr designer Bethlehem Steel Co since '19. ASCE. 701 E. Third St., Bethlehem, Pa.

20 GRAVES, Edgar Baldwin. English medieval law courts; Sacra Romana Rota 1464-1530. b'98. AB '19—AM '22 (Haverford Coll); PhD '29 (Harvard U). Research in Public Record Office London, British Museum and English episcopal archives '26-27, '29, '32, '35; research in Vatican archives Rome '32. Author articles in field. Asst prof hist Hamilton Coll '27-28, prof since '36. Medieval Acad Am—AHA—Am Council Learned Soc. Awarded research fellowships by Harvard, Am Council Learned Soc, Medieval Acad Am. Hamilton College, Clinton, N.Y.

21 GRAY, Alice. Insects (Methods of capture, preservation, and mounting) b'14. BS '37 (Cornell); MA '51 (Columbia). Design and construction scientific insect exhibits; development of methods for safe use of insect nets and insect killing jars; preservation and mounting of moths and butterflies. Author articles: How to Collect Insects and Spiders for Scientific Study; How to Mount and Label Hard-Bodied Insects; How to Make and Use Spreading Boards for Insects; How to Preserve a Collection of Soft-Bodied Insects and Spiders, and others. Spl

tech dept insects and spiders Am Museum Natural Hist since '37, sci asst since '50. AAAS—NY Entomol Soc. Department of Insects and Spiders, American Museum of Natural History, Central Park W. at 79th St., N.Y.C. 24.†

22 GRAY, Chester H(arold). Agricultural and transportation economics; Taxation; Government debts; Lobbying. b'79. Student '94-96 (Stanberry Mo Normal Sch); '96-97 (U Mo). Early advocate of nation-wide highway system, road maintenance; consultant in transportation and agricultural relations. Author articles in field. Dir Am Farm Bur Fedn '19-23, Washington rep '25-37; dir Nat Highway Users Conf '38-45; master Potomac Grange No 1, Washington DC '40-42, gen chmn '43-46; Grange research coms post-war agrl planning, transportation, edn, agr, farm econ. Wash Trade Assn Execs. Given award for distinguished services to agriculture, U Mo '32. "The Wayside," R.F.D. No. 1, Nevada, Mo.

23 GRAY, David. Power plants (Hydroelectric). b'19. BS (elec engring) '42 (U Ariz). Research, supervision and erection of waterwheel generators and hydroelectric power plants. With Westinghouse Elec Corp since '42, zone engr Caracas, Venezuela, since '51. Am Inst EE. Westinghouse Electric Co., S.A., Caracas, Venezuela.

24 GRAY, Frank. Electronic Commutators. Switches, Tubes (Storage). b '87. BS '11 (Purdue U); AM '13—PhD '16 (U Wis). Studies on mathematical theory electron streams and beams. Issued patents in field. Author article: Electrostatic electron optics. Tech staff USN Exptl Sta '18-19; research TV Bell Telephone Labs '24-36, electronics since '36. AAAS—APS—Inst Radio Engrs—Sigma Xi—Gamma Alpha. Bell Telephone Laboratories, Murray Hill, N.J.

25 GRAY, Fred Edwin. Ore concentrating mill design and operation. b'96. Student '16-30 (U NM); BS '22 (Mo Sch Mines Metall). Author articles in field. Manager, superintendent, cons various mining companies since '26; cons Oglebay, Norton & Co USSR '30-32; bd dirs Summit King Mines Ltd and metall cons '40-47. Am Inst Mining and Metall Engrs—Can Inst Mining Engrs—Mining and Metal Soc Am. R.R. 2, Box 145-B, Mission, Tex.

26 GRAY, George Francis. Microfilm. b'87. ME '09 (O State U); fellow '16-17 (Mellon Inst Indsl Research). Pioneered in microfilming industry, developing new machines and processes; work in manufacture aniline dyes, photographing and photograming, reduction of newly discovered processes to practical use in manufacturing. Vice pres and tech dir Pratt & Gray Co Inc Norwalk Conn and preceding companies engaged in microfiling since '33. AAAS—Photographic Soc Am—Am Soc Photogrammetry—Soc Motion Picture Engrs—Am Phys Soc—Optical Soc Am—Sci Research Soc Am—Sigma Xi. Pratt & Gray Lab. of Diebold, Inc., Norwalk, Conn.

27 GRAY, James Arthur. Sheep and wool; Goats; Wool and mohair marketing. b'12. BS '32—MS '39 (U Wyo). Research on wool shrinkage, core sampling and preparation of raw wool for marketing; sheep and goat culling for wool and mohair production; preparation of mohair for marketing. Author articles: Compressed Volume of Raw Wool as an Indicator of Yield '39; The Future of Texas Wool and Mohair '45; Sheep Production a Science '49; Sheep on those Displaced Acres '50, and others. Co-author articles: Lamb Feeding '48; Sorghum Gluten Meal and Feed in Rations for

Fattening Lambs '49; The Calcium Magnesium and Potassium Contents of the Serum of Ewes Fed High Levels of Potassium '49, and others. Asso prof animal husbandry Tex A&M '40-49; animal husbandman, sheep and goat specialist Tex Ext Service since '49. Tex Acad Sci—Am Soc Animal Prodn—Tex Agrl Workers Assn. San Angelo College, San Angelo, Tex.

10 GRAY, Joseph Burnham. Gas-solid mixtures (Flow behavior); Chemical processes (Automatic control); Catalytic processes. b'15. AB '36 (St Johns Coll); BE '39—PhD '41 (Johns Hopkins U). Holds US patent. Research on hydrogenation of olefines on iron catalysts, crystallization, process design and development of fluid catalytic cracking process, flow behavior of gas-liquid mixtures, automatic control of chemical processes. Author articles in field. Chem engr Standard Oil Co (Ind) '41-47; asst prof chem engring Syracuse U since '47. Am Chem Soc—Am Inst Chem Engrs—Sigma Xi. Department of Chemical Engineering, Syracuse University, East Syracuse, N.Y.†

11 GRAY, Peter. Microtomy; Tropical deterioration; Experimental embryology. b'08. ARCS '29—BSc '29—PhD '31—DIC '33 (U London); Rockefeller '38-39 (U Rochester). Author articles in field. Head dept biol sci U Pittsburgh '46. AAAS(F)—Am Assn Anat—Am Soc Zool—Biometric Soc—Pa Acad Sci—Sigma Xi. Department of Biological Sciences, University of Pittsburgh, Pittsburgh 13.†©

12 GRAY, Philip P(aul). Chemistry of enzymes, fermentation, brewing, beer, cereals and foods. b'96. BS '17 (Coll City NY). Research on factors influencing the quality and shelf life of beer. Author articles in field. Dir chem dept Pease Lab '19-34; chief chem Wallerstein Lab since '34. ACS (councillor NY sect)—Am Inst Chem (F)—Assn Cons Chem and Chem Engrs (twice past mem council)—Inst Food Tech—Am Soc Brewing Chem (pres '48-50). Wallerstein Laboratories, 180 Madison Av., NYC 16.

13 GRAY, William D(udley). Physiology of fungi; Industrial mycology. b'12. AB '33—Rector Scholar '29-33 (DePauw U); PhD '38 (U Pa); Nat Research Council Fellow '38-39 (U Wis). Author articles in field. Asso prof bot O State U since '47. Ind Acad Sci(F)—Mycol Soc Am—Bot Soc Am—Sigma Xi. Department of Botany, Ohio State University, Columbus 10, O.

14 GRAYZEL, Solomon. Jewish history and literature; Medieval history. b'96. BA '17 (Coll City NY); MA '20 (Columbia); PhD '27 (Dropsie Coll); Rabbi '21—Dr Hebrew Letters honoris causa '48 (Jewish Theol Sem). Research in Europe '26-28. Author: The Church and the Jews in the Thirteenth Century '32; A History of the Jews '47; also articles in field. Editor Jewish Publication Soc Am since '39; pres Gratz Coll b overseers since '48. Medieval Acad—Acad Jewish Research—Am Jewish Hist Soc—AHA—Jewish Book Council Am. 222 North 15th St., Phila. 2.†

15 GREATHOUSE, Glenn Arthur. Plant biophysics and biochemistry; Material deterioration prevention. b'03. BS '27 (Ill State Normal U); MS '30 (U Ill); fellow in chem, physics, bot '30-31—PhD '31 (Duke U). Research on physico-chemical properties of plant juices, chemistry of disease resistance and immunity, chemical compounds as preservatives for various materials, mechanism of degradation of cellulose by microorganism and ultraviolet radiation, isolation and identification of organic compounds from plants, development of scientific apparatus. Author articles in field. Dir Prevention of Deterioration Center, National Research Council, Nat Acad Sci since '45. AAAS(F)—Am Chem Soc—Washington Acad Sci—Mycol Soc Am—Sigma Xi—Phi Sigma. Awarded King's Medal for Service in Cause of Freedom. 2101 Constitution Av., Washington.

16 GREAVES, Thomas Guy. Dyes (Natural); Wetting agents. b'88. BS '10—MS '23 (U Va). Dispersed colors fortinting high grade writing paper; organic dry colors; bright colored printing inks; tannins and syntans. Author articles: The tannin analysis and the Parker effect, The iron contamination of chestnut extract; and others. Plant chem E I Du Pont Co '11-13; control chem J H Heald Co '13-18; chem Am Dye and Chem Corp since '18; research chem United Dye and Chem Corp since '41. ACS—Am Leather Chems Assn. American Dye and Chemical Corp., 374 Main St., Belleville 9, N.J.

17 GREEN, Elizabeth Adine Herkimer. Orchestral bowings; Violin pedagogy. b'06. BS '28 (Wheaton Coll); MMus '39 (Northwestern U); violin study (Gordon String Quartet School Conn) (Ivan Galamian Meadowmount Westport NY). Research in teaching materials and classification necessary bowings of violin with directions of down-bow and up-bow to the music. Author: Orchestral Bowings and Routines '49. Author articles: Orchestral Bowings for High School Students; Strings, the Strength of the Orchestra; Eyes to See. Instr violin pub schs Waterloo Ia '28-42, orchestra dir '33-42; staff viola player WMT '30-32; asst prof music edn U Mich since '44. Music Educators Nat Conf Assn—Am String Tchrs Assn—Pi Kappa Lambda. Burton Tower, University of Michigan, Ann Arbor.

18 GREEN, Ferris M(ilton). Fruit tree nutrition. b'94. BS '22 (Ore Agrl Coll). Author articles in field. Supt Western Slope Br Sta Colo Agrl Sta since '41. AAAS(F)—Am Pomol Soc—Am Soc Hort Sci—Wash State Hort Assn—Va State Hort Soc—Western Colo Hort Soc. Western Slope Branch Station, Austin, Colo.

19 GREEN, George Kenneth. Nuclear physics; Accelerators; Cyclotrons; Proximity (VT) fuses, radio countermeasures. b'11. BS '33—MS '35—PhD '37 (U Ill); Nat Research fellow '38-39 (U Calif). Participated in design, construction and use of major accelerators. Author articles in field. Sr physicist Brookhaven Nat Lab since '47. Capt Office Chief Signal Officer US Signal Corps '42-44, signal corps engring labs '44-46. Am Phys Soc—Sigma Xi—Tau Beta Pi. Brookhaven National Laboratory, Upton, N.Y.†

20 GREEN, Melvin W(illiam). Drug standardization. b'10. PhG '31—BS '32—PhD in chem '37 (U Pittsburgh). Author articles in field. Asstd revision monographs of organic chem and research asst Mellon Inst Pittsburgh '36-38; asst prof Cincinnati Coll Pharmacy '38-40; instr pharmacology Georgetown Med Sch '40-42; pharm chem Am Pharm Assn Lab '42-46, dir lab '46-49; asso prof Pharm Chem U Wis Sch Pharmacy since '49. AAAS—Am Pharm Assn—Am Chem Soc—Soc Exptl Biol Med—Sigma Xi—Phi Lambda Upsilon. University of Wisconsin, School of Pharmacy, Madison, Wis

21 GREEN, Norman Bayard. West Virginia amphibia and reptiles; Pseudacris brachyphona. b'05. BS '26 (Davis and Elkins Coll); MS '31 (W Va U); PhD '52 (Ohio State University). Author articles in field. Associate prof, head dept zool Marshall Coll since '47. Sigma Xi—Am Soc Ichthyologists Herpetologists—Wilson Ornithol Club—Herpetologists League—W Va Acad Sci (pres '51-52). Marshall College, Huntington 1, W. Va.†

22 GREEN, Thomas Henning. Structural geology. b'15. AB (Geol) '39 (U Colo); Profl Cert (Physics Meteorol) '43 (U Calif Los Angeles). Studies in geologic structural interpretation from bore holes and geophysical data. Geology of Eola Area Garvin County, Okla. Geophysicist Shell Oil Co Inc '40-43, geol '46-48; dist mgr Sunray Oil Corp since '48. Am Assn Petroleum Geol—Soc Exploration Geophysicists—Am Geophys Union. Sunray Oil Corp., First National Bldg., Oklahoma City, Okla.

23 GREEN, Warren Kimball. Photometry (Astronomical, photographic, photoelectric); Navigation (Development). b'91. AB '13—AM '14 (Harvard); PhD '16 (U Calif); AM (hon) '34 (Amherst Coll); Martin Kellogg fellow '16-17 (Lick Obs). Research on internal motion of nebulae, brightness of asteroids and of stars. Prof astron Amherst Coll since '26, dir Amherst Coll Obs since '21. AAAS(F)—Royal Astron Soc, London—Am Astron Soc—Am Phys Soc—Internat Astron Union—Phi Beta Kappa—Sigma Xi. 46 Snell St., Amherst, Mass.

24 GREEN, William John. Agricultural economics; Agricultural extension. b'92. BS '16—MS '31 (Okla A and M Coll); '34-35 (Brookings Institution); ext courses '36-40 (Tex A and M Coll). Dist agt ext service Okla A and M Coll '28-34; asst regional dir Farm Security Adminstrn Dallas '35-44; chief agrl rehabilitation div China Office UNRRA '45-47; asst chief US Food Supply Mission in Peru '48-50; agr officer US Tech and Econ Mission to Burma since '50. Alpha Zeta—Am Agrl Econ Soc—Farmers Assn China. Decorated Order of the Brilliant Star by Republic of China for assistance in rehabilitating agr in China. Food and Agriculture Division, Economic Cooperation Administration, Washington 25. H: 1106 Bolivar St., Denton, Tex.

25 GREENBANK, George Richard. Fats and oils; Antioxidents; Dairy product deterioration. b'92. BA '17 (O State U); PhD '30 (Am U). Holder patents on antioxidants. Author: Fundamentals of Dairy Science (with others) '35; The Relationship of Structure to Antioxygenic Activity '47; also articles in field. Bur Dairy Ind research labs US Dept Agr since '22. Am Chem Soc—Am Dairy Sci Assn—Washington Acad Sci. Borden Award for work on chemistry of milk '49; Superior Service Award Dept. of Agriculture '50. Bureau of Dairy Industry, Department of Agriculture, Washington.†

26 GREENBANK, John T(homas). Fresh-water fisheries (Winter-kill, toxicity, population studies, Mississippi River); Stream pollution. b'06. BS '35—MS '37 (U NM); PhD '43 (U Mich). Research on fish populations, effect of environmental factors on fish, pollution of streams by pulp mills, oil well brine and sugar mills, water suffocation of fish in shallow lakes. Author articles in field. Formerly fish biol Wis Cons Dept. Am Fisheries Soc—Limnol Soc Am—Sigma Xi. Olathe, Colo.

27 GREENBAUM, Ervin. Steel (Fabrication); Armor plate (Manufacture). b'12. BS (civil engring) '32 (U Mich). Research and management of plants producing fabricated and welded steel products, conversion of existing automobile spring and bumper plants and stove and furnace plants to manufacture of armor plate for tanks and armored vehicles. Civil engring '32-37; state dir Pub Works Commn '38-40; ordnance US Army '40-46; cons since '46. 12919 Broadstreet Blvd., Detroit 4.

10 GREENBERG, Bernard Samuel. Animal behavior and sociology; Herpetology. b'13. BS '35 (Coll City NY); MS '41 (NYU); PhD '47 (U Chicago); '41-42 (State U Ia). Author articles: Some Effects of Testosterone on the Sexual Pigmentation and Other Sex Characters of the Cricket Frog '42; Social Behavior of the Western Banded Gecko, Coleonyx Variegatus Baird '43; Some Relations Between Territory, Social Hierarchy and Leadership in the Green Sunfish '47. Co-author: Induction of Female Behavior in Male Anolis Carolinensis with Testosterone '41; Effects of Seasons, Castration and Crystalline Sex Hormones Upon the Urogenital System and Sexual Behavior of the Lizard '41; Social Behavior of the American Chameleon '44. Research asst Am Mus Natural Hist NY '36-41; Fellow zool U Chicago '42-43, asst zool '43-46; instr biol Roosevelt Coll Chicago '46-47, asso prof since '49. Am Soc Zool—Ecol Soc Am—Am Soc Herpetologists Ichthyologists—Sigma Xi. Department of Biology, Roosevelt College, 430 S. Michigan Av., Chicago 5.†

11 GREENBERG, Joseph H. African anthropology and linguistics. b'15. BA '36 (Columbia); PhD '40 (Northwestern U); '37-38 (Yale). Social Science Research Council pre-doctoral fellow '36-37, field fellow '38, field research in Nigeria, British West Africa on native Negro culture and language of the Hausa as a study of Mohammedan influence on African native peoples. Author: Influence of Islam on a Sudanese Religion '46. Asst prof anthrop U Minn '46-48, Columbia '48-52; associate prof since '52. Am Anthrop Assn—Linguistic Soc Am—Internat African Inst Lang and Cultures—Phi Beta Kappa—Sigma Xi. Anthropology Department, Columbia University, NYC.†

12 GREENE, Harry Washington. Collegiate research. b'97. BA—MA—PdD '47 (Lincoln); '18-20 (Yale); MA '27 (Columbia). Author: Criteria of Teaching Excellence; Negro Leaders; Experimental Cooperative Teaching; Two Decades of Research; Holders of Doctorates Among Negroes; Educating for Community Participation: Re-directing the Teacher Education Program Through Studies of Intergroup Relations. Dir W Va State Coll since '30. W Va State Teachers Assn—NEA—Am Teachers Assn—Soc Adv Edn—Am Assn Sch Administr—Prog Edn Assn—AAAS—Am Acad Polit Social Sci—Nat Assn Authors and Journalists (hon)—John Dewey Soc(F). Institute, W. Va.

13 GREENE, Hoke Smith. Electrochemistry; Resonance; Organic medicinals. b'06. BA '27 (Mercer U); MS '28—PhD '30 (Cincinnati U); '31-32 (Tech Hochschule Karlsruhe Germany). Research on electric moments of organic compounds, industrial fermentation (patents), synthesis of herbicide, organic and inorganic phosphates, electrolytic oxidations and reductions. Author articles in field. Prof chem and dept head Cincinnati U since '45, dean Grad Sch Arts and Sci since '47. Am Chem Soc—AAAS—Soc Am Bact—O Acad Sci—Sigma Xi. Am-German Exchange Fellow to Karlsruhe '31-32. University of Cincinnati, Cincinnati 21.†◎

14 GREENE, James Edward. Educational, clinical and child psychology; Guidance. b'00. AB '22 (Henderson Coll); MA '24 (Vanderbilt U); PhD '31 (Peabody Coll); '30-31, '40-41 (U Chicago). Author articles in field. Prof edn head dept ednl psychology U Ga since '37, chmn div grad studies coll education since '50. Am Assn Applied Psychol(F)—Am Physchol Assn(F)—AAAS—So Soc Psychol Philos—Am Ednl Research Assn—So Sociol Soc—Phi Kappa Phi. Department of Education, University of Georgia, Athens, Ga.†◎

15 GREENE, Richard Leighton. English literature (Medieval lyric). b'04. AB '26 (U Rochester); AM '27—PhD '29 (Princeton). Editor: The Early English Carols '35; also articles in field. Pres Wells College '46-50. Modern Lang Assn Am—Medieval Acad Am—Phi Beta Kappa. Research fellow Am Council Learned Socs '31-32. 19 Amherst St., Rochester 7, N.Y.☆

16 GREENFIELD, Alfred. Choral music. Pub anthem: The Earth is The Lords '50. New York University, University Heights, NYC 53.

17 GREENFIELD, Sydney Stanley. Plant physiology and growth; Mineral nutrition and toxicity in plants; Photosynthesis. b'15. BA '36 (Brooklyn Coll); MA '37—PhD '41 (Columbia U). Research on responses of stock seedlings to heteroauxin applied to soil, differential inhibition of photochemical and dark chemical reactions in photosynthesis by inorganic compounds, inhibitory effects of inorganic compounds on photosynthesis in chlorella, and others. Author articles in field. Asst prof biol Newark Coll of Rutgers U since '46, asso since '49. AAAS—Bot Soc Am—Sigma Xi. Newark Colleges, Rutgers University, Newark 2, N.J.

18 GREENHALL, Arthur M. Zoological curatorship; Herpetology; Vampire bats. b'11. BA '34—MS '35 (Mich U); '39-41 (Columbia); '40-41 (NYU). Made expeditions (some with Raymond L Ditmars) to collect animals for New York Zoo and Museum of Zoology, for University of Michigan to Costa Rica, West Indies, Trinidad, British Guiana, Panama, Colombia, Cuba; worked in health and welfare of zoological collection, planning, and construction of new exhibits, recordings of animal sounds; prepared plans for proposed new Portland Zoo; staff member of Office Civilian Defense in charge of animal protection, City of Portland and Multnomah County; taught first aid treatment of snake bite and personal care in tropical jungles to Armed Forces, wartime diets of animals; member of general committee of first International Snake Exposition, New York City; engaged research on bushmaster and vampires. Author articles: The Vampire Bat (with Ditmars) '35; A Cannibalistic Hog Nosed Snake '36; The Care of the Bushmaster and of Certain Lizards in the New York Zoological Park '36; and others. Research asst dept zool Mich U '30-34; asst dept herpetology Am Mus Natural Hist NY '30; mem Panamanian and Canal Zone Govt Vampire Bat Commn '33, Trinidadian Govt Vampire Bat Commn '34; redesigner Nat Zool Park Costa Rica '35; asst to R L Ditmars curator mammals and reptiles NY Zool Park '28-42; inspector fgn birds and mammals US Fish and Wildlife Service Port of Portland '43-47, Port of Detroit since '47; dir Portland Zool Park '42-47; gen curator Detroit Zool Park since '47, cons Pan Am Sanitary Bureau (div UN World Health Orgn) on vampire bats and diseases they carry; cons Toronto (Can) Zoo, Zoo of Port of Spain Trinidad BWI. New York Zool Soc—Am Museum Natural Hist—AA

AS—Am Assn Mus—Am Inst Park Execs(F)—Am Assn Zool Parks Aquariums—Am Soc Mammalogists—Am Soc Ichthyologists Herpetologists — Herpetologists—Herpetologists League Am. Detroit Zoological Park, Royal Oak, Mich. H: 42 Oakdale Blvd., Pleasant Ridge, Mich.

19 GREENING, Edward Owen. Railway engineering (Location and construction). b'88. Diploma '07 (Wye Coll U London Eng). Railway reconnaissance, location and construction Northern Quebec '07-14; field engr ry project Peace River Outlet '28-31; construction engring RCAF Dept Nat Def since '46. W&B, RCAF Station, Whitehorse, Y.T., Can.

20 GREENLEAF, Walter Helmuth. Breeding adapted to Southern growing conditions (Pepper, tomatoes, peas, pumpkins). b'12. Student '32-34 (Chaffey Jr Coll, Calif)—'34-35 (U Calif, Davis); BS '36—PhD '40 (U Calif, Berkeley). Research in hybridizations between varieties of muscadine grapes with emphasis on developing superior quality varieties that are self-fertile, breeding of tomatoes adapted to South with special emphasis on resistance to Fusarium wilt and other diseases, breeding winter-hardy English peas especially adapted to southern growing conditions; developed all-double petunias; discovered new method of producing polyploids in certain tobaccos, pepper resistant to bacterial leaf spot and initiated breeding program to transfer this resistance to commercial pimiento pepper. Author articles in field. Prof hort and vegetable breeder Ala Agrl Expt Sta Auburn Ala since '47. Am Phytopath Soc—Am Soc Hort Sci—Sigma Xi. Department of Horticulture, Alabama Agricultural Experiment Station, Auburn, Ala.†

21 GREENLEE, William Brooks. History of Portugal; Brazilian and Latin-American history; Historical geography. b'72. BS '95 (Cornell); LittD (hon) '46 (Dickinson Coll). Research on Portuguese history and bibliography, Brazilian and Latin-American history; consultant and collector Portuguese books and periodicals for Newberry Library Chicago, trustee since '32. Author: The Voyage of Pedro Alvares Cabral to Brazil and India '38; also articles in field. Chmn bd Greenlee Bros & Co since '44; chmn bd Northwestern Stove Repair Co, Greenlee Foundry Co, Northwestern Foundry Co since '26. Royal Geog Soc(F)—Am Geog Soc(F)—Hakluyt Soc—Instituto Historico e Geografico de Sao Paulo, Brazil (hon). 1100 Lake Shore Dr., Chicago 11.

22 GREENLY, Albert Harry. Michigan historical literature and bibliography; Western American history (Overland trail, emigration, Pacific coast). b'81. Student public schools. Special study in Western Americana and Grizzly Adams, the bear hunter in the Sierras. Chmn Official Classification Com, railroad frt since '31. 143 Liberty St., NYC 6.

23 GREENSHIELDS, Bruce Douglas. Transportation and traffic engineering. b'93. BS '20—CE '27 (U Okla); MS '32—Detroit Edison fellow '32-33—PhD '34 (U Mich). Originator of photographic method of traffic analysis '33, developed theory of probability (statistical analysis) in traffic analysis '47; inventor of process for preparing bituminous paving materials '48. Author articles: Traffic Performance at Urban Street Intersection. Head dept and prof civil engring George Washington U since '48. ASCE (asso)—Inst Traffic Engrs (com traffic engring training, ed Traffic Engineering '37-

40)—Am Soc Engring Edn—Sigma Xi. George Washington University, Washington 6.†

10 GREENSTEIN, Jesse Leonard. Astrophysics. b'09. AB '29—AM '30—PhD '37 (Harvard). Research in absorption and scattering of light in dust and gas clouds of interstellar space to determine nature of matter in space, analysis by spectrographic means of constitution of star atmospheres, by theory and observation establishing similarity in constitution of stars and sun; study of peculiar stars with abnormal chemical compositions; optical design and construction of high-altitude spectrographs for observation from V-2 and other rockets; design of ultra high-speed photofluorographic cameras. Nat Resch fellow Yerkes Obs '37-39; instr, asst prof, asso prof U Chicago '39-48, stationed at Yerkes Obs; prof, head grad sch in astron Calif Inst Tech, on staff Mt Wilson and Palomar Obs since '48. AAAS(F)—Am Astron Soc (councillor)—Royal Astron Soc—Internat Astron Union—Phi Beta Kappa. Mount Wilson and Palomar Observatories, 1201 E. California St., Pasadena 4, Calif.☉

11 GREER, James Kimmins. Trans Mississippi history; Texas history; Southern history. b'96. AB '18—AM '22—grad F '25-27—PhD '27 (U Tex). Research on Louisiana politics and Alabama history, Texas Declaration of Independence. Author: Louisiana Politics '29; Grand Prairie '35; Bois D'Arc to Barb'd Wire '36; Early in the Saddle '36; Alabama's Tragic Decade '40; also articles in field. Prof hist and head dept Howard Coll '28-44; prof hist U Tex '47-48; prof and chmn dept hist Hardin-Simmons U since '48. AHA—Miss Valley Hist—S Hist Soc—Tex State Hist Assn—W Tex Hist Assn—Pi Gamma Mu—Kappa Phi Kappa. Received Rockefeller Grant for research in '46. Hardin-Simmons University, Abilene. Tex.†☉

12 GREET, William Cabell. Phonetics; American language; English language and literature; Lexicography. b'01. AB '20 (U of South); AM '24—PhD '26 (Columbia). Author: War Words, Recommended Pronunciations '43; World Words '48; also articles in field. Editor: Pecock's Reule of Crysten Religion '27. Ed American Speech Magazine since '33; speech cons CBS since '37; chmn ed adv com Funk and Wagnalls Coll Standard Dictionary since '42; adv ed Am Coll Dictionary since '46; prof Eng, head dept Barnard Coll Columbia U since '46; cons Walt Disney Prodn '47; adv ed Century Cyclopedia of Names since '48. Modern Lang Assn Am—Am Dialect Soc—Nat Council Teachers Eng—Linguistic Soc Am. Fulbright Exchange Professor (France) '50-51; Guggenheim Fellow '51-52. Barnard College, Columbia University, NYC 27.☉

13 GREEVER, William S(tClair). Railroad history. b'16. AB '38 (Pomona Coll); AM '41—PhD '49 (Harvard). Research on western land grant of Santa Fe railway and comparison of railway land-grant policies. Author articles in field. Instr and asst prof hist U Ida since '49. AHA—Miss Valley Hist Assn—Ry and Locomotive Hist Assn. University of Idaho, Moscow, Ida.

14 GREGG, Donald C. Metals (Lead, Zinc, Gold, Silver, Copper in Mexico, Bolivia, Philippines). b'99. EM (Colo Sch Mines). Mining engr Am Metal Co Republic of Mex '22-25, examining engr '26-32; examining engr Tin Mines Bolivia SA '25-26; examining engr and geol US Smelting Refining & Mining Co Mex '32-37; geol PI '37-41; cons geol Mexican govt since '45; faculty geol dept Colo Sch Mines since '45.

AIMME—Theta Tau. Colorado School of Mines, Golden, Colo.

15 GREGG, Robert Edmond. Taxonomy, biology and distribution of ants. b'12. SB '35—PhD '41 (U Chicago). Author articles: The Origin of Caste in Ants with Special Reference to Pheidole morrisi Forel '42; The Ants of Northeastern Minnesota '46, and others. Instr U Colo '44-46, asst prof since '46. Entomol Soc Am—Ecol Soc Am—Cambridge Entomol Soc—Entomol Soc Wash—Am Soc Zool—Sigma Xi—Phi Beta Kappa. Department of Biology, University of Colorado, Boulder, Colo.

16 GREGORIUS, Joseph Scott. Flat glass manufacturing; Glass technology. b'96. BE '20 (O State U). Research in compounding, melting and processing of glass; studied modulus of rupture and thermal shock resistance of glass at elevated temperatures. Patents granted on glass melting tank and apparatus for drawing sheets of glass; glass melting tank and apparatus for manufacture of window glass by upward drawing. Author articles in field. Research engr Pittsburgh Plate Glass Co '24-38, asst dir research glass div '38-42, tech adv mfg dept glass div since '42. Inst Ceramic Engrs—Sigma Xi (hon). Am Ceramic Soc (F, trustee '45-47). Pittsburgh Plate Glass Co., 2315 Grant Building, Pittsburgh.

17 GREIBACH, Emil Henry. Scientific instruments (Acoustics, radio, X-ray). b'98. EE '21—ME '21 (German U Prague); PhD '29 (U Pittsburgh); Seminars in advanced math '34-40 (NYU). Inventor bone conduction receivers for hard of hearing, throat microphones, electrical and X-ray measuring instruments, systems for sound and sound movie reproduction; holder about 30 patents and applications. Author articles: Vaporization Under the Influence of an Electric Field '29; A Generating Voltmeter of Extremely High Sensitivity '41; Inertia Throat Microphones '46; Laboratory Method for Objective Testing of Bone Receivers and Throat Microphones '46; and others. Research on elec instruments, radio and sound movies Westinghouse Elec & Mfg Co '24-29; in charge research and prodn hearing aids Sonotone Corp '29-32, cons since '29, dir research '42-45; pres Greibach Research and Development Labs since '32, Beechmont Electric Corp since '48; vp Columbus Products Corporation. Am Phys Soc—American Acoustical Soc—AIEE—Inst Radio Engrs—Instrument Soc Am. 80 Pryer Terrace, New Rochelle, N.Y.†

18 GRESHAM, Luveta Williams. History of Negro colonization and migration; History of meat packing industry. b'97. AB '21—AM '27 (Howard U); grad study (Am U). Research on status of American Negro, Negro exodus to Kansas 1879, Negro colonization projects in the Americas and the West Indies during the nineteenth century; American meat packing industry, refrigeration as a link between the producers and the consumers. Author articles in field. Teacher social studies Randall Jr High Sch Washington '28-48, Garnet-Patterson Jr High Sch since '48. AHA—Nat Council Social Studies—Assn Study Negro Life and Hist—NEA—Nat Council Negro Women. 763 Kenyon St. N.W., Washington.

19 GRETTIE, Donald P. Proteins; Fat and oil chemistry. b'00. BA '24 (Williamette U); MA '27 (Ore U); PhD '29 (Pittsburgh U). Research on absorption of organic compounds on hydrous oxides and Fullers earth, concentration and properties of Vitamin C,

antioxidants for fats and oils, methods of testing fats and oils, hydrogenation and catalysts, modification and improvement of gelatin for special uses. Holds patents on methods for extraction of glue and gelatin, fundamental studies on hides, skins and gelatin, new methods for measurement of acid and basic groups on protein molecules. Author articles in field. Research chem Swift and Co since '29. Am Chem Soc.

20 GREULACH, Victor A. Plant growth; Photoperiodism; Radioactive tracers; History of botany. b'06. AB '29—Rector scholar '25-29 (DePauw U); MS '33—PhD '40 (O State U). Author articles in field. Asso prof bot U NC since '49. AAAS(F)—Bot Soc Am—Am Soc Plant Physiol—AAUP—Sigma Xi—Phi Sigma—Elisha Mitchell Sci Soc—Assn Southeastern Biologists. Univ. of N.C. Chapel Hill, N.C.☉

21 GREULICH, Gerald Gregory. Construction of pile foundations, piers and wharves, bridges and bridge floors, airplane runways, bank vaults. b'96. Student '14-17 (Carnegie Inst Tech). Research on steel bearing piles, developed bank vault reinforcement, bar joists, zee-shaped sheet piling, and prefabricated concrete reinforcement. Granted more than 100 patents on piles, structural members, I-beam-lok steel bridge floors, pierced steel plank mats for airplane runways. Author articles in field. Associate editor: Pocket Companion (24th edit) '34. Design engr Walker and Weeks Archts '20-23; gen mgr Concrete Reinforcing and Engring Co and Rivet-Grip Steel Co '24-31; partner J Willis Dalzell Co '32; cons engr Carnegie Ill Steel Corp '33-50; cons engr since '51. Am Iron and Steel Inst (mem concrete research com)—Am Inst Cons Engrs—Am Soc CE (mem pile foundns and pile structures com)—Engrs Soc W Pa—Soc Am Mil Engrs—Am Concrete Inst. 778 Osage Rd., Pittsburgh 16; 610 DuPont Circle Building, DuPont Circle and Connecticut Av., Washington 6.

22 GREVILLE, Thomas N(all) E(den). Actuarial mathematics. b'10. BA '30 (U of South); AM—PhD '33 (U Mich); student (Berlitz Sch Langs, George Washington U). Author: United States Life Tables and Actuarial Tables 1939-1941 '46. Statis editor: Journal of Parapsychology since '44. Chief actuarial analysis branch Pub Health Service Fed Security Agency since '47. Soc Actuaries (F)—Am Math Soc—Math Assn Am. Triennial prize Am Inst Actuaries '48. National Office of Vital Statistics, Public Health Service, Federal Security Agency, Washington 25.

23 GRIBBINS, Myers Floyd. Soils chemistry. b'16. BS (chem) '38 (U Miami); MS (agr, biol chem) '40—PhD (agr, biol chem) '42 (Pa State Coll). Research on manufacture of fertilizer mixtures and nitrogen fertilizer, nitrogen foliage feeding of plants, nitrogen fertilization of agricultural crops. Field supervisor anti-mosquito dist '35-38; faculty Pa State Coll '38-42; biochem E I du Pont de Nemours and Co since '42. ACS—Sigma Xi—Phi Lambda Upsilon—Am Agron Soc—Am Soc Hort Sci. E I du Pont de Nemours and Co., Wilmington, Del.

24 GRIER, Albert Oliver Herman. History of Wilmington, Delaware. News-Journal Building, Wilmington 99, Del.

25 GRIES, George Alexander. Physiology of parasitic fungi; Host-parasite relations (Plant); Plant physiology. b'17. AB '38 (Miami U); MS '40 (Kan State Coll); PhD '42 (U Wis). Research on root diseases of plants, relation of amphoteric metals in soil to potato scab, physiology of parasitic fungi and host-parasite relations. Co-author: Fundamentals of Plant Science '48; Laboratory Problems in Plant Sciences '48; Textbook of Intermediate Plant Science; also articles in field. Asso plant physiol Purdue Agr Expt Sta and asso prof botany since '45; asso prof biol Purdue U since '48. Am Phytopath Soc—Bot Soc Am—Am Soc Plant Physiol—AAAS. A.E.S. Building, Purdue University, Lafayette, Ind. H: 1028 Tulip Lane.

10 GRIES, John Paul. Mineral, fuel, and water resources of South Dakota. b'11. AB '32 (Miami U); MS '33—PhD '35 (U Chicago). Study of ore deposits, oil possibilities, and ground water supplies Black Hills area, with special emphasis on manganese, mica, beryl, lead and zinc, bentonite, petroleum, and lignites. Author articles: Exploration in the Dakota Basin '48; Sampling of the Helen Beryl Pegmatite, Custer County, South Dakota '49; Investigation of the Beecher No. 2 Pegmatite, Custer County, South Dakota '50, and others. Co-author article: (with E P Rothrock) Manganese Deposits in the Lower Missouri Valley in South Dakota '41. Prof geol engring SD Sch Mines since '36; cons Carter Oil Co '47-50; cons minerals tech US Bur Mines since '36; cons Carter Oil Co great plains area. Am Assn Petroleum Geol—AIMME—Geol Soc Am. South Dakota School of Mines and Technology, Rapid City, S.D.†

11 GRIFFENHAGEN, Edwin O. Public administration; Public finance. b '86. BS in civil engring '06—CE '09 (Ill Inst Tech). Reorganized Canadian Government departments '18-21; chief counselor to US Commission Reclassification of Salaries '20; consultant to over more than 25 states and numerous large cities. Sr partner Griffenhagen & Assos, management engrs and cons in pub adminstrn; chief cons War Dept Manpower Bd '43-44. Inst of Management (past pres)—Assn Cons Management Engrs (charter mem, pres)—Am Soc CE—Western Soc Engrs—Am Econ Assn—Am Polit Sci Assn—Am Acad Polit and Social Sci—Nat Tax Assn—Nat Municipal League—Governmental Research Assn—Am Soc Pub Adminstrn—Civil Service Assembly—Chicago Civil Service Assn(past pres)—Nat Civil Service Reform League—Tau Beta Pi. 333 N Michigan Av., Chgo 1.☉

12 GRIFFENHAGEN, George Bernard. Pharmacy (History). b'24. BS '49—MS in Pharm '50 (U S Calif). Research on history of pharmacy in California including Indian, Spanish, Mexican and gold rush periods, biographies of pioneer California pharmacists, history of Oregon pharmacy, established traveling museum of early California drug store. Author of The Story of California Pharmacy and articles in field. Lecturer hist pharm U S Calif Sch Pharm since '49; dir pharm research Nion Corp since '50. Am Pharm Assn (sec hist sect)—Am Inst Hist Pharm (Calif rep)—Am Coll Pharm—AAAS—Rho Chi—Phi Kappa Phi. University of Southern California School of Pharmacy, Los Angeles. H: 7710 Isis Av., Los Angeles 45.

13 GRIFFIN, Donald R(edfield). Birds (Navigation); Bats (Sensory mechanisms); Sounds (Animal); Human vision. b'15. BS '38—AM '40—PhD '42 (Harvard). Homing ability of several species of wild birds and homing pigeons, tracing actual routes flown by following and observing birds from airplane; radioactive tagging of birds to permit instrumental recording of their return to nests. Investigations of migrations, homing and activity cycles, metabolic rates and ability of bats to avoid obstacles dur-

ing flight by a process called echolocation. Acoustical studies of the ultrasonic sounds produced by bats for purposes of echolocation; studies of underwater sounds of fish and other aquatic animals. Author articles in field. Research asso Harvard '42-45; asst prof dept zool Cornell U '46-47, asso prof since '47. Phi Beta Kappa—Sigma Xi—Soc Gen Physiol—Am Soc Zool—Ecol Soc Am—Am Soc Mammalogists—Am Ornithol Union. Department of Zoology, Cornell University, Ithaca, N.Y.

14 GRIFFIN, Eldon. External relations of Pacific areas; Philosophy of higher education. b'95. B A'16 (Harvard); PhD '37 (Yale). Incorporator, trustee North Pacific Research Institute to promote studies of American and Asiatic areas bordering on North Pacific. Author: Notes on English '19; Clippers and Consuls: American Consular and Commercial Relations with Eastern Asia, 1845-1860 '38; China's Railways as a Market for Pacific Northwest Products, a Study of a Phase of the External Relations of a Region '46; Clinching the Victory '43; Oysters Have Eyes: or the Travels of a Pacific Oyster '41; also articles in field. Co-author: The Progress of Chinese Studies '31. Assistant Professor of Oriental studies U Wash '26-31, special research prof '44; part-owner Willapoint Oysters Inc. Far Eastern Association—Asiatic Society Japan. Award in Pacific History for book Clippers and Consuls, Pacific Coast Br AHA '39; Seabury fellow Stanford '19-20; Currier fellow Yale '24-25. 1211 21st Av., N., Seattle 2.

15 GRIFFIN, James Bennett. Archaeology; Prehistoric cultures of eastern United State. b'05. PhB '27—MA '30 (U Chicago); PhD '36—fellow '33-36 (U Mich). Archaeological field work Illinois '28, '29, '48, Pennsylvania '30, Indiana '33, Mississippi and Arkansas '40, '41, Central Mexico '46, Michigan '48. Author: The Fort Ancient Aspect: Its Cultural and Chronological Position in Mississippi Valley archaeology '43; also articles in field. Research asso Mus Anthrop U Mich '36-41, asst curator '37-42, asso curator '42-45, curator archaeol, made full prof '49, dir since '46 Am Anthrop Assn—AAAS—Mich Acad Arts Sci and Letters—Sociedad Mexicana de Anthropologia—Soc Am Archaeol. Museum of Anthropology, University of Michigan, Ann Arbor.☉

16 GRIFFIN, William Raymond. Gravity (Residual). b'07. AB '36 (Baylor U); MS '38 (Tex A&M Coll). Investigation and discovery order of sensitivity of several variables entering into computation of residual gravity as calculated in practice; quantitative definition of residual gravity as applied to prospecting art; derived equations and prepared curves for lateral variation of residual gravity due to a frustrum of a vertical cone; designed, supervised, operated gravity integrator. Author article in field. Geophys research in residual gravity Robt H Ray Co '45-50; research geophysicist Chance Vought Aircraft Corp since '50. Inst Aeronautical Scis—Soc Exploration Geophysicists—Tex Acad Sci. Engineering Department, Chance Vought Aircraft Corp., Dallas.

17 GRIFFITH, Ernest Stacey. Local American history; Municipal government; Congress. b'96. AB '17 (Hamilton Coll); Rhodes Scholar—DPhil '25 (Oxford U). Author: Modern Development of City Government in United Kingdom and United States '27; Current Municipal Problems '33; History of City Government—The Colonial Period '38; The Impasse of Democracy '39; The Modern Government in Action '42.

Research in Political Science (Edit.) '48. Dir legislative reference service Library Congress since '40. Am Polit Sci Assn (exec council '39-42, chmn research com '42-47)—Nat Municipal League—Am Soc Pub Adminstrn—Wilderness Soc (council since '37, treas since '40)—DC Planning Commn—Phi Beta Kappa—Phi Kappa Phi. Library of Congress, Washington 25.☉

18 GRIFFITH, James Prather. Ohio (Government). b'02. AB '24 (Muskingum Coll); LLB '29 (Youngstown Coll); EdM '50 (U Pittsburgh). Author: Ohio—The State and its Government (revised) '49. Mem O State Senate '39-40, '43-44; teacher law, govt E High Sch since '26. O Ednl Assn—NEA—O Bar Assn. East High School, East High Av., Youngstown, O.

19 GRIFFITH, Melvin E(ugene). Entomology; Public Health. b'12. AB '34—AM '35—PhD '38—fellow '35-38 (U Kan). Author: Alconeura of the United States '36; The Environment, Life History and Structure of the Water Boatman '45; also articles in field. Instr zool ND State Coll '38-39, asst prof '39-41, asso prof '41-42; entomol USPHS '42-46; asso prof zool sci U Okla '46-51; prof since '51; US PHS chief malariologist MSA Mission to Thailand '51-53. cons entomology Okla State Dept Health since '46; research asso U Okla Museum since '48. Entomol Soc Am—AAAS—Nat Malaria Soc—Am Pub Health Assn—Am Mosquito Control Assn—Am Soc Limnol and Oceanog—Okla Pub Health Assn—Kan Entomol Soc—Sigma Xi—Phi Beta Kappa. Department of Zoological Sciences, University of Oklahoma, Norman, Okla.

20 RIFFITH, Sanford. Industrial economics; Governmental economics. b'93. Student (Dartmouth); PhB '15 (U Chicago); grad '17 (Ecole des Sciences Politiques Paris). Research on industrial and general economics for foundations, government agencies and industry. European rep and corr Wall Street Jour and other Dow Jones & Co publs '23-27; Dillon Read & Co Paris '28-30; engaged in underwritings, brokerage and indsl reorgns NY '30-37; project dir Marketing research Miller Franklin & Co '38; pres Market Analysts Inc, Research Surveys Inc. 8 W. 40th St., NYC 18.☉

21 GRIFFITHS, Farnham Pond. Admiralty and maritime law. b'84. BL '06 (U Calif); BA '10—MA '25 (Oxford Coll Eng). Practicing law McCutchen, Thomas, Matthew, Griffiths, & Greene and predecessor firms San Francisco since '13, partner since '19. Marine Exchange San Francisco (pres '40-41)—Maritime Law Assn US (vp '38-41). Balfour Building, San Francisco 4. H: 1590 La Vereda, Berkeley 8.

22 GRIFFITHS, John Cedric. Sedimentary petrography (Petroleum applications). b'12. BSc '33—MSc '34—PhD '37 (U Coll Swansea U Wales); PhD '40—DIC '40 (Imperial Coll Sci U London). Author articles in field. Asso prof petrography dept earth sci Penn State Coll since '50. Geol Soc Am(F)—Geol Soc London(F)—Mineral Soc Am—Mineral Soc London—Assn Am Pet Geol—Inst Petroleum, London—Sigma Xi. Grant Royal Soc research on glacial deposits of South Wales '39. Department of Earth Sciences, Division of Mineralogy, Pennsylvania State College, State College, Pa.†

23 GRIFFITTS, Fred Albert. Vanadium compounds; Catalytic poisons. b'03. BA '25 (Maryville Coll); MS '34 (Ia State Coll); PhD '36 (Ind U). Author articles in field. Prof chem Maryville Coll since '25. Am Chem Soc—NY Acad Sci—Sigma Xi. Maryville College, Maryville, Tenn.†

10 GRIGAUT, Paul L. France (Art). b'05. Ancien eleve '32 (Ecole du Louvre); Certificate de Licence '32 (U Sorbonne); '41 (U Chicago); '46-47 (Fogg Art Mus). Research on 18th century French painting and sculpture, especially Fragonard, Watteau, Aubry, and Boucher; engraving and graphic arts of 18th and 19th cneutires with emphasis on engravings by Delacroix, Meryon, and Whistler; editor of Detroit Institute of Art Bulletin, assistant editor Art Quarterly since '47. Coauthor: Initiation a la Culture Francaise 45. Author articles in field. Asso prof Humanities div U NH '27-43, '46-47; div asst World Trade Intelligence Dept State '43-45; asst curator Western Art since Renaissance Detroit Inst Arts since '47. AAUP—Archeol Soc Am—Am Assn Mus—Coll Art Assn. Detroit Institute of Art, Detroit 2.†

11 GRIGGS, Charles Clifton. Mine valuation. b'75. BSc (U Neb); student (George Washington U, Nat Law Sch). Author articles in field. Valuation engr Bur Internal Revenue Washington '21, chief non-metals sect '22, asst head engring div '23, office tech advisor to head income tax unit '26, tech advisor tech staff '33-46, ret from govt service '46; now tax consultant with Olvany, Eisner & Donnelly. AIM ME. 20 Exchange Place, NYC. 42 Bar Beach Rd., Port Washington, L.I., N.Y.

12 GRIGGS, David Tressel. Rock deformation under high pressure. b'11. AM '33 (O State U); jr fellow '34-41 (Harvard). Author articles in field. Expert cons Office Sec War '42-45, adv specialist group USSTAF, chief adv specialist group FEAF, prof geophysics U Calif since '48; chief Nuclear Energy Sect Project RAND '46-48; chief scientist USAF '51-52 (on leave). Institute of Geophysics, University of California, Los Angeles 24.

13 GRIGGS, Edward Fry. Structural frameworks. b'94. BS in civil engring '15 (Purdue U). Research and design structural steel and reinforced concrete structures. Partner Topper and Griggs since '23. Tau Beta Pi—Am Soc CE—Nat Soc Prof Engrs—Am Concrete Inst. Topper and Griggs, 10 N. Main St., West Hartford, Conn.

14 GRIGGS, William Holland. Pomology; Deciduous fruits and olive (Pollination); Cultural problems and breeding of pears. b'16. BS '37 (NE Mo State Teachers Coll); MA '39 (Mo U); PhD '43 (Md U). Research on fruitfulness of Delicious apple, fertilizer and soil management studies with apples, peaches, strawberries and blueberries, pollination of deciduous fruits and olive, stimulation of parthenocarpy in pears. Asst prof pomol Calif U since '47, asst pomol expt sta since '47. Sigma Xi—Am Soc Hort Sci—Biometric Soc. Department of Pomology, University of California, Davis, Calif.†

15 GRIGSBY, Buford H. Weed control; Pollen; Hay-fever. b'09. BS '30 (Ala Poly Inst); MS '32—PhD '37 (Mich State Coll). Pollen surveys, principally on ragweed, in cooperation with Michigan Department of Health on state-wide basis '40-47; research on weed control in vegetable crops and sugar beets; board directors North Central State Weed Control Conference, vice chairman Northeastern States Weed Control Conference. Discovered stoddard solvent for carrot weeding '43, rate of application of 2, 4-D to prevent pollen formation in ragweed without destruction of plants '44, developed chemical which is specific for crabgrass control and one or two other annual grasses '47. Author: Death to Weeds with 2, 4-D '46. Author articles: Some Effects of 2, 4-D on Ragweed and Certain Woody Plants '46; Selective Control of Crabgrass '48; Michigan's 1945 State-Wide Pollen Survey '45, and others. Asso physiol US Dept Agr '42; research asso, asso prof Mich State Coll '43, part-time research asso and asso prof bot '48; agt physiol part-time research on weed control in sugar beets US Dept Agr '48. AAAS—Bot Soc Am—Sigma Xi. Department of Botany, Michigan State College, East Lansing, Mich.†

16 GRIMALDI, John V. Safety engineering; Industrial engineering. b'16. BS '39—MA '41—PhD '49 (NYU); student (Brooklyn Poly Inst). Organization of loss prevention programs utilizing industrial engineering techniques; member President's committee on National Employ the Physically Handicapped Week; member President's Conference on Industrial Safety. Cons indsl safety edn '41-42; safety dir Grumman Aircraft Engring Corp Bethpage NY '42-44; research fellow Am Mus Safety; asst Center of Safety NYU '44-45; research engr accident prevention div Assn Casualty and Surety Companies NYC '45-47, dir indsl engring div since '47. Am Soc ME—Am Soc Safety Engrs. Association of Casualty and Surety Companies, Accident Prevention Department, 60 John St., NYC.

17 GRIMES, Henry Dustin. Wool (Dyeing and finishing). b'97. Student '16-20 (Lowell Textile Inst Mass); '32 (Mit). Author articles on textiles and textile chemistry and processing in Am Dyestuff Reporter and The Textile World. Consulting editor: Textile World. Chief chemist Washington mills Am Woolen Co Lawrence Mass '21-30, Wood Worsted mills, '30-36, asst chief chemist main labs '36-52. Assigned by War Dept as scientific cons, on mission to Germany to obtain tech information regarding advances by textile industry during the war. Am Assn Textile Chemists and Colorists (charter mem). H: 25 Quincy St., Lawrence, Mass.

18 GRIMM, Harold John. History of the Reformation; Luther; Germany. b'01. AB '24 (Capital U); AM '28—PhD '32 (O State U). Author: Martin Luther as a Preacher. Co-author Western Civilization: Decline of Rome to the Present; American editor Archiv fuer Reformations geschichte. Asst prof O State U '37-42, asso prof '42-47, prof since '47. AHA—Am Soc Ch History—Soc Am Historians—Phi Beta Kappa—Phi Alpha Theta—Fgn Policy Assn—British Royal Historical Society (F). Department of History, Ohio State University, Columbus 10, O.

19 GRIMSHAW, Ivan Gerould. Libraries (Buildings, equipment); Bibliography (Spanish-American); Revivalism. b'00. AB '24 (Hiram Coll); BD '26 (Yale); MA '27—teaching F '27-28 (U Chicago); DPhil '33 (U Edinburgh); BSc (library sci) '45 (Colombia U). Research and building of college libraries, consultant on college libraries; research on religious revivals and their psychology; research and bibliography on life and works of Eduardo Barrios of Chile. Author articles in field. Prof comparative lit Am Internat Coll '40-45; research Colombia and Chile '45-47; dir libraries Youngstown Coll '47-50; dir libraries and chmn dept library sci Beloit Coll since '50. ALA—Coop Com Library Bldg Plans—Assn Coll and Research Libraries—Inter-Am Bibliog and Library Assn—Philatelic Library Assn—AAUP—Wis Hist Soc. Beloit College Libraries, Beloit, Wis.

20 GRINNALDS, Jefferson Cleveland. City planning and zoning (Laws). b'84. Student '04-07 (U Va); LLB '15 (U Md); '21-23 (Johns Hopkins). Designer and author of zone plans and ordinances Baltimore, Frederick, Salisbury, Cumberland (Maryland), Raleigh, Burlington, Rocky Mount (North Carolina), Seaford (Delaware); appointed city planning expert dept commerce by Herbert Hoover '21-25. Author articles in field. Engr city planning topog survey commn '10-23, zoning commn, sec eng bd zoning appeals Baltimore since '23; city planning and zoning cons. Am Soc Planning Officials—Am City Planning Inst—Nat Conf City Planning—Nat Housing Assn—Am Hort Soc—Am Soc Municipal Improvement—Am Civic Assn—Nat Conf St Hwy Safety. Municipal Building, Balt 2. H: Ruxton 4, Md.†

21 GRINSFELDER, Henry. Synthetic resins; Coatings; Inks; Plastics; Laminates; Binders; Plywood and metal adhesives; Coated fabrics; Statistical analysis; Chemical cost accounting. b'08. Student '26-28 (U Ida); BS '31 (MIT); '43 (St Joseph's Coll Phila). Granted US patent on mending tape. Author articles in field. Laboratory head Rohm and Haas Company since '41. Econometric Soc—Am Chem Soc—Am Soc Testing Materials. 5000 Richmond St., Phila. 37. H: 8250 New Second St., Elkins Park 17, Pa.

22 GRINTER, Linton E. Structural engineering; Theoretical and applied mechanics. BS '23—CE '30 (U Kan); MS '24—PhD '26 (U Ill). First chairman graduate division American Society for Engineering Education '45; official delegate to International Technical Congress and International Congress of Applied Mechanics Paris '46; developed method of determining wind stresses in skyscrapers; presented an early explanation on how to design reinforced concrete pavements; recent studies in design of continuous frames for stresses beyond the elastic limit; also a statistical approach to problems usually analyzed by mathematical theory of elasticity. Author: Theory of Modern Steel Structures (vol I) Determinate Structures '49, (vol 2) Indeterminate structures '49; Automatic Design of Continuous Frames '39; Design of Modern Steel Structures '41; Elementary Structural Analysis and Design '42. Co-author: Engineering Preview '45. Editor and co-author: Numerical Methods of Analysis in Engineering '49; also articles in field. Asso prof engring Tex A&M Coll '28-29, prof structural engring '29-37; dean grad div and dir civil engring Armour Inst Tech Chicago '37-39, vp and dean grad div '39-40; vp and dean Grad Sch Ill Inst Tech '40-46, research prof civil engring and mechanics since '46; member governing council Argonne Nat Lab since '46. ASCE—ASME—Western Soc Engrs—Am Concrete Inst—Internat Assn Bridge and Structural Engrs—Am Soc Engring Edn—Tau Beta Pi—Sigma Xi. 5749 S. Kenwood Av., Chgo 37.☺

23 GRISCOM, Ludlow. Birds (Distribution and origin); Conservation. b'90. AB '12 (Columbia); AM '15 (Cornell). Research birds of Central America. field identification of North American Birds, conservation. Author: Birds of the NY City Region '23; Distribution of Bird Life in Guatemala '32; Ornithology of the Republic of Panama '35; Birds of Nantucket '48; Birds of the Concord Region, a Study in Population Trends '49; Distribution and Origin of the Birds of Mexico '51; Distributional Check-List of the Birds of Mexico, Part I, '51. Contbg editor Nat Audubon Mag; asso editor Audubon Field Notes. Research curator zoology Mus Comparative Zoology, Harvard '27-48, research ornithologist and editor since '48; mem zool exploration parties, Panama, Yucatan,

Nicaragua, Guatemala; vol asst Gray Herbarium Expdn to Arctic Newfoundland and Gaspé Penissula. AAAS (F)—Am Ornithologists Union(F)—NY Acad Scis(F)—Ecol Soc Am—Brit Ornithol Union—Nat Audubon Society (chmn bd dirs)—Boston Soc Natural History (hon curator birds)—Mass Fish and Game Assn—Am Mus Natural History—Sigma Xi. 21 Fayerweather St., Cambridge 38, Mass.†☉

10 GRISMER, Raymond Leonard. Spain (Literature). b'95. AB '16 (U Vt); Rhodes scholar '16-17 (Oxford U Eng); MA '22 (O State U); PhD '30 (U Calif). Study classical influence on literatures of Spain and Spanish America; compilation bibliography of literatures of Spain and Spanish America. Author: A Reference Index to Twelve Thousand Spanish American Authors '39; A New Bibliography of the Literatures of Spain and Spanish America (7 vols) '41; The Influence of Plautus in Spain Before Lope de Vega '44; Cervantes—A Bibliography '46. Prof modern langs Oklahoma City U '24-27; asso in Spanish U Calif '27-31; faculty U Minn since '31, now prof. Modern Lang Assn—Am Assn Teachers of Spanish—Phi Beta Kappa. University of Minnesota, Minneapolis 14.

11 GRISWOLD, John. Distillation (Extractive); Solvent extraction. b'06. BS (Chem engring) '28 (U Ill); ScD '32 (MIT). Research on extractive distillation and vapor-liquid equilibria; solvent extraction and liquid-liquid equilibria; recovery pure hydrocarbons from petroleum and oxygenated organic compounds from aqueous mixtures by above processes. Author articles in fields. Prof chem engring U Tex '36-49, Ill Inst Tech '49-51; fulltime cons Gen Chem Div since '51; dir research RFC Office Rubber Reserve U Tex project '45-49. ACS—AICE—Tau Beta Pi. General Chemical Div., NYC 6.

12 GROCE, George Cuthbert. Early American art and artists; American history (Eighteenth century). b'99. BA '21 (Trinity U); MA '23 (Tex U); PhD '37 (Columbia); private study US and abroad. National consultant for American Portrait Inventory of Works Progress Administration '40-41. Author: William Samuel Johnson '37. Editor: 1440 Early American Portrait Artists '40. Compiler: Dictionary of 8000 Early American Artists '49; also articles in field. Historian War Dept since '45. Office of the Chief Chemical Officer, Department of the Army, Washington.

13 GRONER, Miriam Georgia. Phosphor chemistry; Plant physiology and breeding (Maize, tetra snapdragons). b'10. BS '31—MS '31 (Bucknell U); PhD '34 (U Mich). Author articles in field. Chem Nat Union Radio Corp since '43, known as Lansdale Tube Co since '47. Bot Soc Am—Sigma Xi. Lansdale Tube Co., Lansdale, Pa.†

14 GROSCH, Daniel S(wartwood). Wasps (Genetics, cytology, behavior); Cytology (Developmental); Parasites (Intestinal, human); Sulfonamide and biologicals (Bacteria resistance). b'18. BS '39 (Moravian Coll); MS '40 (Lehigh U); PhD '44 (U Pa). Author articles in field. Asso prof zool NC State Coll Agr and Engring U NC since '50. AAAS—NC Acad Sci—Genetics Soc Am—Am Soc Parasitol—Sigma Xi—Marine Biol Lab, Woods Hole, Mass. Zoology Department, North Carolina State College, Raleigh, N.C.†

15 GROSS, Alfred Otto. Ornithology (Control, North American life histories, migrations); Wildlife conservation; Cyclic fluctuations of birds and mammals. b'83. AB '08 (U Ill); PhD '12—Edward Austin research fellow '11-12 (Harvard); research scholar '10-11 (Bermuda Biol Sta); DSc (Bowdoin) '51. Author: The Heath Hen '28; also articles in field. Prof biol Bowdoin Coll since '22; biol US Dept Int Fish and Wildlife Service since '40; director Bowdoin Sci Sta since '35, Josiah Little prof of natural science Bowdoin '50. Nat Assn Audubon Socs (Me state adviser)—Am Zool(F)—Am Ornithol Union (F, council)—AAAS(F)—Am Geog Soc(F)—NE Bird Banding Assn (pres)—Brit Ecol Soc—Me Audubon Soc (pres, ed bull '45)—Sigma Xi—Arctic Inst NA (charter mem)—Wildlife Society. 11 Boody St., Burnswick, Me.†☉

16 GROSS, Bernard. Aircraft materials. b'05. BS '34 (Poly Inst Brooklyn). Research and development materials relating to metal fabrication; processes of forming, joining, sealing, finishing. Issued patents in field. Staff San Diego State Coll Ext '39-41; U Cal Ext '41-42; process engr Ryan Aeronautical Corp '39-40; dir labs Rohr Aircraft Corp since '40. ACS—Am Soc Metals—Am Welding Soc—Inst Aeronautical Scis—AAAS—Sigma Xi. Rohr Aircraft Corp., Chula Vista, Calif.

17 GROSS, Eric T(uras) B(enjamin). Electrical engineering (Power system grounding, electric system protection, power circuit analysis). b'01. BME—MEE—EE '23—DSc '32 (Inst Tech, Vienna Austria). Studies and patents concerning resonant neutral grounding of electric power systems, sensitive ground relaying, short circuits in systems. Author articles in field. Prof elec engring grad sch and Coll Engring Ill Inst Tech since '45, acad adv grad students in power systems engring curriculum; cons to utility cos participating in A-C network calculator project Armour Research Found Ill Inst Tech, cons engr. AIEE(F)—AAAS(F)—Inst Elec Engrs, London—Swiss Inst Elec Engrs—Sigma Xi—Tau Beta Pi—Eta Kappa Nu. 3319 Federal St., Chicago 16.†

18 GROSS, Feliks. Social anthropology; Political sociology; International relations; History of Eastern Europe. b'06. LLM '29—LLD '30 (U Cracow, Poland); Carnegie Scholarship for Internat Studies Paris '30. Member Polish delegations at UNRRA and international labor conferences; active in workers educational movement Poland '25-39; member delegation of Polish Socialist Party and Polish Trade Unions in US '41-47. Author: (with Z Gross) Sociology of the Political Parties '45; Nomadism '36; Workers are Writing (with Z Myslakowski) '38; Proletariat and Culture '38; Crossroad of Two Continents '45; The Polish Worker '45; Humanistic Socialism '46. Editor and co-author: European Ideologies '48. Asso ed Ency Slavonica Philos Library '47-48; editor New Europe '42-45; vis prof Regional Studies Grad Sch NYU since '45; dir inst of Internat Relations; vis prof U Wyo since '45; asst prof sociol and social anthrop Brooklyn Coll since '46; sec gen Central and Eastern European Planning Bd '41-45; co-ed, asso ed Encyclopedia Slavonica '47-48. Am Soc Internat Law—Am Sociol Assn—Eastern Sociol Soc—Am Acad Polit Sci—Polish Inst Arts Sci—Am Pol Sci Assn. New York University, Washington Square, NYC.

19 GROSS, Paul Magnus. Physical and agricultural chemistry (Tobacco, flourine); Electrochemistry. b'95. BS '16 (Coll City NY); MS '17—PhD '19 (Columbia). Research on development of cigarette paper, new tobacco types, dielectric investigations, solution theory. Author: Elements of Physical Chemistry (with J M Bell) '29; also articles in field. Prof chem Duke U '22-47, dean Grad School '47-52, vp Duke U since '49, dean of University since '52, dir tobacco resch since '21, pres Oak Ridge Inst Nuclear Studies. Am Phys Soc(F)—Am Chem Soc—AA AS—AAUP—Sigma Xi—Phi Beta Kappa. Herty Medal '45, Presidential Medal of Merit '48, So Assn Sci and Industry award '51, Fla sect Am Chem Soc award '52. Hope Valley, Durham, N.C.☉

20 GROSSCHMID-Z S O G O D, Geza Benjamin. Economics; Heraldry. b'18. LLB '43—JUD '43 (Royal Pazmany Peter U Budapest). Itensive research in field continental heraldry with special emphasis on illuminated armorial bearings on patents of nobility of the 15th century. Author articles in field. AAUP—Nat Genealogical Society. Duquesne University, Pittsburgh 19.

21 GROSSE, Aristid V. Catalytic chemistry (Radioactivity, atomic energy, isotopes); Chemistry (Fluorine, metal organic). b'05. Dr Engring '27 (Technische Hochschule Berlin-Charlottenburg Germany). Research on catalytic chemistry of hydrocarbons; discovered with V N Ipatieff reactions of paraffins with olefins, aromatic, dehydrogenation of paraffins to olefins; with W Mattox and J C Morrell cyclization of straight chain hydrocarbons to aromatics; with J C Morrell and J Mavity dehydrogenation of n-butane and n-butenes to butadiene; with C Linn hydrogen fluoride catalytic alkylation process for production of aviation gas; isolated element 91, protoactinium '27; proved with A O Nier, J Dunning and E Booth slow neutron fission of uranium 235 '40; associated with Dunning and Booth in development of K-25 gaseous diffusion plant for separation of U235 '40-42; discovered with Libby cosmic radio carbon '47. Co-author: Chemie der Metallorganischen Verbindungen '37. Dir research Houdry Labs Pa '43-48; cons '48; pres research inst Temple U '48. Am Chem Soc—AAAS—Soc Am Mil Engrs—Sigma Xi. 1926 N. Park Av., Phila.; 456 Glynwynne Av., Haverford, Pa.☉

22 GROSVENOR, Gilbert Hovey. American ornithology; Alaskan and polar exploration; World geography. b'75. AB '97—AM '01—LittD '26 (Amherst Coll); seven other honorary degrees. Country home holds Audubon Society and US Biology Survey record for greatest number of land birds nesting in one acre adjacent house in US, 59 pairs in '15; lake 28 miles long discovered in Alaska '19 named Grosvenor Lake in recognition of his encouragement of Alaskan explorations; Gilbert Grosvenor Range in Antartica discovered and so named by Admiral Byrd '29. Author: Young Russia '14; The Hawaiian Islands '24; A Maryland Pilgrimage '27; Maps for Victory '42; The Society's Maps of Europe '44. Editor: Book of Birds '39; also articles in field. Ed-in-chief Nat Geog Mag since '03, dir Nat Geog Soc since '99, pres since '20. Calif Acad Sci(F)—AAAS(F)—Assn Am Geog (hon)—Geog Socs Australasia, Edinburgh, Gautemala, Uruguay, Rio de Janerio, Michoacan and Lima—Phi Beta Kappa—Sigma Xi. Awarded Culver gold medal Geog Soc Chicago '27; Bryant medal Geog Soc Phila '41; Grosvenor Medal of Nat Geog Soc; Samuel F. B. Morse Medal of Am Geog Soc '52; Distinguished Service award Nat Council Geography Teachers '44. National Geographic Society, 16th and M St., Washington.☉

23 GROTE, Irvine Walter. History of cordials and liqueurs. b'99. BS '22 (U Chattanooga); AM '23 (Columbia); PhD '25 (U Cincinnati); '29 (U Pittsburgh).

Author articles in field. Holder patents in pharmaceutical chemistry and related fields. Prof chem U Chattanooga since '31; cons chem drug and allied fields since '31. Am Chem Soc—Am Pharm Assn—AAAS—Sigma Xi. University of Chattanooga, Chattanooga 3, Tenn.

10 GROUPÉ, Vincent. Microbiology; Virology; Immunology; Antibiotics; Chemotherapy. b'17. AB '39 (Wesleyan U Conn); PhD '42 (U Pa). Research in Virus diseases, chemotherapy, antibiotics, electron microscopy, immunology. Author articles in field. Research asso Squibb Inst Med Research '44-47; asso prof virology in animal diseases U Conn '47-49; asso prof microbiol Rutgers U since '49. Soc Exptl Biol and Med—Soc Am Bact—Am Assn Immunology—Sigma Xi. Department of Microbiology, Rutgers University, New Brunswick, N.J.

11 GROUT, Donald Jay. History of opera; Musicology. b'02. AB '23 (Syracuse U); AM '32—PhD '39 (Harvard). Author: A Short History of Opera '47; also articles in field. Prof music Cornell U since '45, chmn dept music '47-49. Am Musicol Soc—Internat Musicol Soc—Société française de Musicol—Music Library Assn—Phi Beta Kappa. Department of Music, Cornell University, Ithaca, N.Y.◎

12 GROUT, Roy A. Beekeeping; Beeswax. b'08. BS '29—MS '31 (Ia State Coll). Author articles in field. Editor: The Hive and the Honeybee '46. Employed by Dadant & Sons mfrs beeswax comb foundation since '31, co-partner since '37. Am Assn Econ Entomol—Nat Fed Beekeepers Assn. Dadant & Sons, Hamilton, Ill.

13 GROVE, Cornelius Sherman, Jr. Textile engineering. b'05. BA '25 (Lenoir Rhyne Coll); BS '28—ChE '32 (NC State Coll); MS '34 (MIT); PhD '42 (Minn U). Research on rayon development, determination of drying rates of thin films, viscose rayon, chemistry of ink stain removal from fabrics, codification of materials, crystallization. Author: Laboratory Manual of Applied Electrochemistry (with Montillon) '39; also articles in field. Prof chem engring Syracuse U since '47; cons chem engr W A Sheaffer Pen Co since '45; cons textile engr G*and H Hosiery Co since '30. Am Inst Chem Engrs—Am Chem Soc—Am Soc Engring Edn—NC Acad Sci—AAAS—So Assn Sci Industry—Sigma Xi—Tau Beta Pi. Department of Chemical Engineering, College of Applied Science, Syracuse University, Syracuse 10, N.Y.†

14 GROVER, Dana Irving. Range management; Pastures; Forage plants; Field crops; Livestock. b'10. AB '35 (Pomona Coll); BS '37 (U Calif). Research on ecology of plant life in annual grass and weed type of range land in California; methods of improving grazing capacity of annual type range by grazing management, fertilization, and mechanical means. Author articles in field. Asst farm adv U Calif Agrl Ext Service since '47. Agricultural Extension Service, P.O. Building, Napa, Calif.†

15 GROVER, Elliott Brown. Textiles (Physical testing, manufacture, cotton and synthetic). b'06. BS '28 (MIT). Research on time studies and mill cost system, design of novelty yarns and equipment for manufacture, spinning tests of Sea Island and other long staple cottons, developed and patented tester for controlling density of wound yarn for package dyeing, patented automatic conveyor and yarn marker for winders; London and deputy European representative to Technical Industrial

Intelligence Committee, textile and leather division '45; special consultant to Puerto Rico Economic Development Administration on textile plants. Author: Fundamentals of Textiles, Part II '50; Mill Organization '48. Co-author: Fundamentals of Textiles '47; Textile Processing Continuous Filament Yarns '49; Quality Control Through Textile Testing '51. Research engr Pinemah Mills '28-33; quality control to gen supt Manville Jenckes Corp '33-44; head yarn mfg dept Sch Textiles NC State Coll since '44. NC Soc Engrs—Fiber Soc—ASTM—Am Soc Quality Control—S Textile Assn—Sigma Xi (pres)—Theta Tau. North Carolina State College, School of Textiles, Raleigh, N.C. H: 804 Lake Boone Trail.

16 GROVES, Walter Alexander. Education (Near East). b'98. AB '19 (Lafayette Coll); MA '22 (Princeton Theol Sem, Princeton U); PhD '25 (U Pa). Special commission on secondary education Ministry of Education of Iran '33; special trip to Iran to investigate postwar conditions, especially education, for Presbyterian Board of Foreign Missions '45; Committee for Justice and Peace in the Holy Land since '48. Pres Centre College of Ky since '47. Royal Asiatic Geog Soc(F). First degree sci medal Iranian govt for services to edn in Iran '44. Centre College of Kentucky, Danville, Ky.†◎

17 GRUENBERG, Frederick P(aul). Public administration; Governmental research. b'84. BCS '11 (NYU); post grad study '16-18 (U Pa). With Philadelphia Bureau of Municipal Research 10 years, director 8 yrs; member Philadelphia Charter Revision Committee '17-19, exec sec City Charter Committee '38-40; directed nation-wide study of governmental research for Social Research Council '37-38; area rent dir Philadelphia Defense Rental Area, OPA '42-44. Dir Phila Housing Assn, Crime Prevention Assn Phila. Am Polit Sci Assn—Am Acad Polit and Social Sci—Nat Municipal League—Governmental Research Assn (chmn 2 terms)—Am Soc Pub Adminstrn—Pa Polit Sci and Pub Adminstrn Assn—Phila Com on Pub Affairs—Phi Alpha Sigma—1315 Walnut St, Phila 7.†◎

18 GRUENHAGEN, Richard H(amilton). Fungicides; Forest pathology. b'15. Student '33-36 (State Teachers Coll Oshkosh Wis); BS '38 (U Minn); MS '39—PhD '44 (U Wis). Research on diseases of forest trees, burn blight disease of jack and red pine, plant disease control through use of chemicals, developing organic fungicides. Author articles in field. Asst path US Dept Agr div forest path '44-46; plant path Dow Chem Co since '46. Am Phytopath Soc—Sigma Xi. Dow Chemical Co., Midland, Mich.†

19 GRUITCH, Jerry Morris. Mechanical engineering; Refrigeration (Self-contained systems); Heating and ventilating equipment; Aviation armament design. b'04. BS '33—Donovan scholar '32 (U Mich); MME, MSAE '40 (Chrysler Inst Engrs). Research on radial cylinder type refrigeration compressors, reverse cycle heating, unitary split system heating and cooling, bomb and fuse, high cyclic rate machine gun. Author articles in field. Dir research development Am Car & Foundry Co NYC since '47; mem Nat Mil Est Com on Ordnance. SAE—Am Soc Heating Ventilating Engrs—ASME—Am Soc Refrigerating Engrs—Soc Advancement Management—Inst Metals, London—Am Soc Testing Materials—Navy Indsl Assn—Am Ordnance Assn—Tau Beta Pi. American Car & Foundry Co., 30 Church St., NYC 8.

20 GRUNBERG, Emanuel. Chemotherapy (Fatty acids, penicillin). b'22.

BA '43 (U Ala); '44 (Washington U); PhD '46 (Yale); '48 (Harvard). Author: The Fungistatic and Fungicidal Effects of the Fatty Acids on Species of Trichophyton. Co-auth: Mechanism of the Topical Effect of Penicillin G in Experimental Local Streptococcal Infections. Med mycol New Haven Dispensary New Haven Hosp '44-46; sr bact dept chemotherapy sci div Hoffmann-LaRoche Inc Nutley NJ since '46. NY Acad Sci—AAAS (speaker Gordon research conf)—Soc Am Bact—Mycol Soc—Bot Soc Am—Sigma Xi—Phi Beta Kappa. Department of Chemotherapy, Hoffmann-LaRoche, Inc., Nutley, N.J.

21 GRUNBERG, Emile S. Cartels. b '05. MA '29—PhD '30 (U Frankfurt). Research on international cartels in raw material markets, quantitative effect of cartels including methods of statistical measurement of demand, supply, and income elasticities. Author: Der Mittelstand in der kapitalistischen Gesellschaft '32; also articles in field. Faculty U Kan City '42-43; research asso New Sch Soc Research '43-46; asst prof econ U Akron '46-48; asso prof econ Carnegie Inst Tech since '48. Am Econ Assn—AAUP. Carnegie Institute of Technology, Pittsburgh 13.

22 GRUNTFEST, I(rving) J(ames). Textiles (Crase resistance, wetting, detergency); Paper (Wet strength). b '17. BS '37—MS '38 (Brown U); PhD '41 (Cornell). Research on crease resistance cotton and rayon, wet strength of paper, mechanism of wetting textiles, mechanism of detergency, design wet-end additives for paper. Author articles: Wetting of Textiles '47; Reaction Cellulose Formaldehyde '48; Wrinkle Resistance of Fabrics '49; Chemistry of Detergency '49, and others. Research chem since '41; research chem resin treatment textiles and paper, wetting and detergency Rohm & Haas Co Phila since '43. AA AS—Am Assn Textile Chem Colorists —Am Chem Soc—Tech Assn Pulp Paper Industry (wet strength com)—Sigma Xi. Rohm & Haas Co., 5000 Richmond, Phila. 37.

23 GUARD, A(rthur) T(homas). Botany (Hybrids of wheat, soybean). b'97. AB '24 (DePauw U); MS '29—PhD '35 (Purdue U). Research on cytology and resistance to leaf rust of inter-specific and inter-generic hybrids of wheat, development of floral organs of soybean, seed production in tulip poplar. Author articles in field. Asso prof bot Purdue U since '43. Ind Acad Sci(F)—AAAS—Bot Soc Am. Purdue University, West Lafayette, Ind.†

24 GUBA, Emil Frederick. Plant pathology (Fruit, vegetable, floricultural and greenhouse crops, trees); Taxonomy of the fungi; Industrial and medical molds and plant poisons. b'97. BS '19 (U Mass); PhD '23 (U Ill). Author articles in field. Research prof bot U Mass since '37. Am Phytopath Soc—Sigma Xi. Waltham Field Station, University of Massachusetts, Waltham 54, Mass.†

25 GUDDE, Erwin Gustav. California place names and history; German literature. b'89. MA '18—PhD '22 (U Calif). Author: Social Conflicts in Medieval Poetry '34; Sutters Own Story '36; Edward Vischer First Visit to California '40; California Place Names: A Geographical Dictionary '49, and others; also articles in field. German dept U Calif since '22. Modern Lang Assn—Calif Hist Soc—Philol Assn Pacific Coast. University of California, Berkeley 4.†

26 GUENTHER, Ernest. Chemistry (Essential oils). b'95. PhD '21 (U Zurich Switzerland). Field surveys for many years in almost every country of world. Author: The Essential Oils 6 vols. since '48; and other articles. Tech dir and vp Fritzsche Brothers Inc NY since '24. Fritzsche Brothers Inc., 76 Ninth Av., NYC.

10 GUERLAC, Henry. History of radar development; History of science (1600-1800). b'10. AB '32—MS '33 (Cornell U); PhD '41—Soc of Fellows '35-38 (Harvard). Author articles in field. Asst prof and chmn dept hist sci U Wis '41-46; prof hist sci Cornell since '46; historian Radiation Lab and radar development program Radiation Lab MIT '43-46. AAAS(F, council)—Hist Sci Soc—AHA —Sigma Xi. Department of History, Cornell University, Ithaca, N.Y. H: 3 Fountain Pl.⊙

11 GUERRANT, Edward Owings. US Latin-American relations. b'11. BA '33 (Davidson Coll); MA '39—PhD '42 (U S Calif). Research on Good Neighbor policy of US toward Latin America. Author: Roosevelt's Good Neighbor Policy '50; also articles in field. Mem faculty Calif Inst Tech '42-44; polit analyst Dept State '45-46; asso prof Davidson Coll since '46. S Polit Sci Assn—Am Soc Internat Law—AHA. Davidson College, Davidson, N.C.

12 GUEST, Henry G(rady). Petroleum geology (Applied electrical logging and physical measurements). b'08. BS '31 (Miss State Coll); MA '33— PhD '35 (U Ia). Engr Schlumberger Well Surveying Corp since '35. Am Assn Petroleum Geol—Miss Geol Soc— AAAS—Am Inst Mining Metall Engrs.

13 GUHL, Alphaeus M. Animal behavior and sociology. b'98. BA '22 (N Central Coll); MS '39—PhD '43 (U Chicago). Research on social and sexual behavior of domestic chicken. Author articles in field. Asso prof Kansas State Coll since '43. Am Soc Zool —Ecol Soc Am—AAAS—Sigma Xi— Gamma Sigma Delta. Department of Zoology, Kansas State College, Manhattan, Kan.

14 GUILLEMIN, Ernst Adolph. Electrical network theory. b'98. BS '22 (U Wis); SM '24 (MIT); PhD '26 (U Munich). Author: Communication Networks, vol I and II, '31-35; Mathematics of Circuit Analysis '49; also articles in field. With MIT since '26, now prof elec engring; cons Radiation Lab during war, now for Raytheon Mfg Co. AIEE—Inst Radio Engrs—Am Soc Eng Education—Tau Beta Pi—Sigma Xi—Eta Kappa Nu. Massachusetts Institute of Technology, Cambridge, Massachusetts.†

15 GUISE, Arthur Barnes. Fire control equipment. b'03. BS '27 (MIT). Development and design of dry chemical fire extinguishing equipment, including piped systems and crash fire trucks; assisted in development of fire prevention and fire protection standards for magnesium, synthetic rubber manufacture, water spray, foam, and carbon dioxide. Author articles: Protecting Industrial Plants from Magnesium Fires; Dry Chemical Fire Extinguishers '48. Co-author articles: Magnesium and its Alloys '40; Artillery Ammunition Manufacture 41. Development engr refining companies '27-35; fire protection engr '35-42; chief engr mfr dry chem extinguishing equipment Ansul Chem Co since '43. Nat Fire Protection Assn—Compressed Gas Assn—Fire Extinguisher Mfrs Assn—Liquefied Petroleum Gas Assn. Ansul Chemical Co., Marinette, Wis.

16 GUITERAS, Albert Francis. Antiseptics (Testing). b'05. BS (chem) '26 (Lafayette Coll); '28-30 (Columbia); PhD (chem) '32 (U Goettingen). Au-

thor articles in field. With US Food and Drug Adminstrn '27-28; NYC Health Dept '28-30; Wallace and Tiernan Products Corp '33-34; Interchemical Corp '34-36; H D Roosen Co '36-39; Winthrop Chem Co '39-40; Foster D Snell Inc '40-51; with Hudson Lab Inc since '51. ACS—AAAS—Am Inst Chem (F)—NY Acad Sci—Alpha Chi Sigma —Soc Cosmetic Chemists. Hudson Laboratories, Inc., 117 W. 13th St., NYC 11.

17 GULICK, Leeds. Japan (Culture, language, education, religion); Community organization; Motion pictures (Documentary, educational); Organized camping. b'94. BAS '21 (YMCA Coll); MAS '29 (George Williams Coll); diploma '26 (Sch Japanese Lang and Culture, Tokyo). Author: Programs for Boys and Young Men '30; Christian Camp—Conference Leader's Manual '36; Japanese Language, Japanese Word List '45; Erziehung in den Vereinigten Staaten '47. Co-author: Amerika no Kyoiku '48; also articles in field. Chief Japanese-Korean affairs reorientation Br, Civil Affairs Div, Dept Army Special Staff '47-48, deputy chief Edn and Religion Policy Sect '48. NEA—Far Eastern Assn—Kappa Delta Pi. Pentagon Building, Washington.⊙

18 GULLIKSEN, Harold. Aptitude and achievement tests; Theory of tests; Psychology and theory of learning. b'03. BA '26—MA '27 (U Wash); PhD '31 (U Chicago); '27-29 (O State U). Author articles in field. Prof psychol Princeton since '45; research adviser Ednl Testing Service since '48. Directed NDRC war research project '42-45. Am Psychol Assn—Inst Math Statis—Psychometric Soc—Am Statis Assn.⊙

19 GUNDERSON, Harold. Economic entomology and rodent control. b'13. BSc '34—MSc '35 (Mont State Coll); PhD '39 (Ia State Coll). Author articles in field. Ext entomol Ia State Coll since '39. Am Assn Econ Entomol—Ia Acad Sci—Ia Pest Control Assn (hon)—Nat Fly Control Com—Ia Hort Soc—Phi Kappa Phi—Sigma Xi—Gamma Sigma Delta. Extension Service, Iowa State College, Ames, Ia.

20 GUNN, Charles L. Hybrid corn. b'86. Research and experimental hybrid testing plots, selection, purification, production and distribution of grasses, legumes cereal grains, soybeans and corn. Author: Proceedings of the New York Farmers '46-47; also articles in field. Seedsman and corn breeder DeKalb Agrl Assn Inc and DeKalb Hybrid Seed Co Ill since '17, dir hybrid corn breeding research in No and N central corn belts since '25. Am Soc Agron—AAAS—Ill Acad Sci —Friends of The Land. 310 N. Fifth St., DeKalb, Ill.

21 GUNN, Edward Mansfield. Audiovisual aids. b'13. Student '31-35 (RI State Coll); MD '39 (Syracuse U Coll Med). Medical educator with responsibility for planning, preparation, evaluation, and utilization of integrated teaching materials in the medical and allied scientific sciences. Chief training doctrine br edn and training div Office Surgeon Gen US Army Washington '45-47, chief med illustration service Armed Forces Inst Pathol since '47; chmn interdepartmental com med training aids Army Navy Air Force Vets Adminstrn USPHS '46-48. AMA (F)—Assn Mil Surgeons US—Biol Photographic Assn Inc—Assn Med Illustrators—Washington Film Council —Am Assoc Health, Physical Education, and Recreation—Am Publ Health Assoc. Medical Illustration Service, Armed Forces Institute of Pathology, 7th St. and Independence Av., S.W., Washington 25.

22 GUNN, Ross. Mountain structure; Isostasy; Earths crust (Equilibrium); Electricity (Atmospheric); Terrestrial Magnetism. b'97. BS (Elec engring) '20 —MS '21 (U Mich); PhD '26 (Yale). Research physicist US Naval Research Lab '27-33; tech adviser '33-47, supt mech and elec div '38-46, supt aircraft elec div '43-46; tech dir Army-Navy Precipitation Static Project '43-46, supt physics div '46-47; tech dir Army-Navy Atmospheric Elec Project '46-47; dir Air Force-Weather Bur Cloud Physics Project '47-49; dir phys research div US Weather Bur since '47. APS(F)—Inst Radio Engrs(F)—Nat Acad Sci. Physical Research Division, U.S. Weather Bureau, Washington 25.†⊙

23 GUNTER, Gordon. Marine biology (Oysters, mammals); Fisheries; Ichthyology (Texas); Ecology. b'09. BA '29 (La State Normal Coll); MA '31—PhD '45 (U Tex). Area consultant Officer Coordinator of Fisheries '42-45; vice-chairman Committee on Treatise on Marine Ecology National Research Council. Author articles in field. Marine biol Tex Game Fish and Oyster Commn '39-44; research asso marine fisheries Inst Marine Sci U Tex since '45; acting dir '49; vis prof zool and research asso Marine Laboratory Univ Miami '47; sr mar biol Scripps Institute Oceanography '48. Am Soc Zool—AAAS—Am Soc Limnol Oceanog—Am Soc Ichthyologists Herpetologists—Am Soc Mammalogists— Soc Systematic Zool—Am Ornithol Union—Am Fisheries Soc—Wildlife Soc— Ecol Soc Am—Am Soc Nat—Sigma Xi. Institute of Marine Science, University of Texas, Port Aransas, Tex.

24 GUNTHER, Erna. Anthropology (American Indians). b'96. PhD '28 (Columbia U). Author articles in field. Dir Washington State Mus U Wash since '29, prof anthrop since '41. Am Anthrop Assn(F)—Am Folklore Soc (vp)—Sigma Xi. Washington State Museum, University of Washington, Seattle 5.

25 GURIN, Samuel. Physiological chemistry (Metabolism); Radioactive isotopes. b'05. BS '23—MS '30—PhD '34 (Columbia U). Research on isolation of Chorionic Gonadotrophins of pregnancy urine, intermediary metabolism with stable and radioactive isotopes. Discovered thiazole nature of vitamin B1. Author articles in field. Prof U Pa since '47 Am Soc Biol Chem —Am Chem Soc—Assn Study Internal Secretions—NY Acad Sci—Sigma Xi. Nat Research Council fellow '35-37. Medical School, University of Pennsylvania, Phila.

26 GURINSKY, David Harris. Metallurgy (Vacuum furnaces, iron-tin system, argon arc welding of aluminum); Plastic deformation. b'14. BS '36— PhD '42 (NYU). Patents on welding of aluminum. Author articles in field. Group leader in metall Brookhaven Nat Lab since '47. Am Soc Metals—Am Inst Mining Metall Engrs—Phi Beta Kappa—Sigma Xi. Brookhaven National Laboratory, Associated Universities, Inc., Upton, L.I., N.Y.†

27 GURLEY, Martin Henry, Jr. Textiles (Cellulose Fiber, vinyl fiber). b '05. AB '27 (Harvard). Synthetic fiber production and utilization; textile finishing research and production; chemical pulp production by nitric acid process; fabric manufacture of lace, broad goods, and linoweaves. Contributor: Roger's Manual of Industrial Chemistry (6th edit); Casein and Its Industrial Applications '51. Viscose research Amoskeag Mfg. Co '27-35; textile and paper research Esselen Research Corp '36-49; cons fibrous materials and products since '49. ACS—

Am Assn Textile Chem and Colorists —Textile Inst Gt Brit—Textile Research Inst—AAAS—Soc Rheology—Am Assn Textile Tech. P.O. Box 637, Pawtucket, R.I. H: 91 S. Angell St., Providence 6.

10 GURNEE, Herbert Social psychology and learning; Human learning in social situations. b'95. AB '22—MA '23 (Wesleyan U); '22-23 (Boston U); PhD '29 (Harvard). Author: Elements of Social Psychology '36; also articles in field. Prof psychol Ariz State Coll since '46. Am Psychol Assn (F)—Western Psychol Assn. Arizona State College, Tempe, Ariz. H: 244 E. 15th St.†

11 GUSHEE, Charles Harold. Finance mathematics. b'03. AB '24 (Harvard). Director computation and publication books of tables on compound interest, bond values. Pres Financial Pub Co Boston since '29. 82 Brookline Av., Boston 15.

12 GUSHEE, Edward T. Electric (Manufacturing); Purchasing (Scientific). b'95. Student (Pomona Coll). Co-author: (with L F Boffey) Scientific Purchasing. Exec vp and dir Electromaster Inc '29-33; with Detroit Edison Co '20-39, vp '35-39, dir '36-39; exec vp and dir Union Electric Co of Mo and subsidiaries '39-42; chief Purchase Policy br Army Ordnance '42; chmn Prodn Urgency Commn WPB '43-45; dist chief Detroit Ordnance Dist '47-53; asst to chmn Detroit Edison Co '45-48, vp since '48. Recipient Shipman Gold medal '37. 2000 2d Av., Det.

13 GUSTAFSON, Alton H(erman). Fresh water biology (Algae, taxonomy, ecology, relation of algae to fish production). b'04. BSc '26 (U Mass); MA '28—PhD '30 (Harvard). Author: Notes on the Algal Flora of Michigan '42; Notes on Some Fresh-water Algae from New England '42. Instr, asst prof, asso prof, prof biol Williams Coll '30-46, acting dean '44-46; head dept biol Bowdoin Coll since '46. Bot Soc Am—Limnol Soc—NE Bot Club—Phi Kappa Phi. Department of Biology, Bowdoin College, Brunswick, Me.

14 GUSTAFSON, Felix Gustav. Plant physiology (Growth hormones). b'89. AB '15 (Wis U); MA '19—PhD '21 (Harvard); '11-13 (Northland Coll); '12 (Marine Biol Lab). Research on respiration of cacti, growth hormones in fruits and flowers. Discovered that seedless fruits can be produced by treating flowers with synthetic growth hormones '36. Author articles in field. Instr bot U Mich '20-25, asst prof '25-34, asso prof '34-43, prof since '43. AAAS—Am Bot Soc—Am Soc Plant Physiol—Mich Acad Sci—Torrey Bot Club—Am Soc Naturalists. Dept of Botany, University of Michigan, Ann Arbor.◎

15 GUSTAFSON, John Kyle. Mining geology; Atomic energy raw materials. b'06. AB '27 (Washington U); AM '28 —PhD '30 (Harvard). Author articles in field. Dir raw materials US Atomic Energy Commn '47-48; mgr raw materials operations '48-50; mem adv com on raw materials since '50; cons geologist M A Hanna Co. Am Institute Mining Metall Engrs—Can Inst Mining and Metall—Soc Econ Geol—Geol Soc Am(F)—Sigma Xi—Phi Beta Kappa. M. A. Hanna Co., 1300 Leader Bldg., Cleve.◎

16 GUSTAVSON, Carl Gustav. German enlightenment (Political thought); Psychology of Lutheranism; Leon Bourgeois. b'15. AB '37 (Augustana Coll); AM '38 (U Ill); PhD '42 (Cornell U). Author articles in field. Asst prof modern European hist Ohio U '45-

48, asso prof since '48. AHA—Miss Valley Hist Assn—O Acad Hist—Phi Beta Kappa. Awarded Ill Grad Scholarship '37-38; Pres White Fellowship Modern European Hist Cornell '38-40. Department of History, Ohio University, Athens, O.

17 GUTENBERG, Beno. Geophysics (Seismology, atmosphere and earth structure, elastic waves, microseisms). b'89. PhD '11 (U Göttingen). Made first exact determination of radius of earth's core. Co-author: (with C F Richter) Seismicity of the Earth '41. Editor: Internal Constitution of the Earth; also articles in field. Prof geophys Calif Inst Tech since '30, dir Seismol Lab. Seismol Soc Am (pres '45)—Am Meteorol Soc—Geol Soc Am —Am Phys Soc—American Acad Sci and Arts—Royal Swed Acad Sciences (fgn mem)—Am Assn Petroleum Geol— Am Geophys Union—AAAS—Royal Astron Soc(F)—Soc Exploration Geophys —Nat Acad Sci—Royal Soc New Zealand (hon)—Finnish Geog Soc (hon)— Acad Lincei Rome (fgn mem)—Finnish Acad Letters Sci (fgn mem). Seismological Laboratory, Pasadena 2, Cal.◎

18 GUTERBOCK, Hans Gustav. Hittites (Excavations, texts and seals, sculptures); Western Asia (Ancient history). b'08. Abiturium '26 (Humanist Gymnasium); Dr phil '34 (U Leipzig). Research on Hittite cuneiform texts and hieroglyphic seals, Hittite sculpture and excavations. Author: Keilschrifturkunden aus Boghazkoi (vol 25, 28) '30, '35; Siegel aus Bogazkoy '40, '42; Kumarbi '46. Co-author: (with Kurt Bittel) Bogazkoy Neue Untersuchungen in der Hethitischen Hauptstadt '35. Contributor: Forgotten Religions '50. Prof Hittitology U Ankara '35-48; vis lecturer U Uppsala '48-49; asso prof Hittitology Oriental Inst U Chicago since '49. Deutsche Orient-Gesellschaft—Internat Society Oriental Research—Am Oriental Soc— Am Sch Oriental Research. Oriental Institute, University of Chicago, Chicago 37.

19 GUTERMUTH, Clinton Raymond. Wildlife and natural resource management. b'00. Grad '27—student '27-28 (Am Inst Banking). Author: Where to Go in Indiana, Official Lake Guide '38; also articles in field. Dir div edn Ind Dept Conservation '34-40, dir div fish and game '40-42; exec sec Am Wildlife Inst '45-46, vp Wildlife Management Inst (successor to former instn) since '46; program chairman annual NA Wildlife Conf. Outdoor Writers Assn Am—Wildlife Soc—Wilderness Soc— Am Fisheries Soc—Zool Soc (NY)— Izaak Walton League Am—Soil Conservation Soc Am—Am Nature Assn— Friends of Land. 709 Wire Bldg., Washington 5.†◎

20 GUTHE, Carl Eugen. North American archaeology; Pueblo pottery making. b'93. BS '14 (U Mich); AM '15— PhD '17—Austin teaching fellow '15-17 (Harvard U). Has made excavations in New Mexico, Guatemala, and Philippine Islands; chairman committee on State Archaeological Surveys of National Research Council '27-37, division anthropology and psychology '38-41; chairman board Laboratory of Anthropology, Sante Fe '36-39; president Midwest Museum Conference '40-43. Author: Pueblo Pottery Making '25; also articles in field. Dir NY State Mus since '44. Soc Am Archaeol—Am Anthrop Assn—AAAS—Am Assn Mus— Sigma Xi—Phi Kappa Phi. New York State Museum, Albany 1, N.Y.†◎

21 GUTHRIE, John D(aulton). Chemical composition of plants (Cotton fiber, physiology of potato tubers). b'03. BSc '25—PhD '29 (O State U). Re-

search on chemical composition of cotton fiber, cotton seed, peanuts and sweet potatoes; isolation of l-malic acid and citric acid from cotton fibers; aminization of cotton fabrics for dyeing with wool dyes; methods of chemical analysis of plants. Author articles in field. Sr chem charge new products sect So Regional Resch Lab-US Dept Agr since '49. Am Chem Soc —AAAS—Bot Soc Am. Southern Regional Research Laboratory, 2100 Robert E. Lee Blvd., New Orleans 24†

22 GUTHRIE, Mary Jane. Cytology; Embryology; Endocrinology. b'95. AB '16—AM '18 (Mo U); PhD '22 (Bryn Mawr Coll). Research on cleavage and mesenchyme formation in Toxopneustes variegatus, cytoplasmic inclusions in cross-activated eggs of teleosts, seasonal movements and habits of cave bats, cytology of ovaries and hypophysis of bat Myotis lucifugus lucifugus, histo-chemistry of ovary of Fundulus heteroclitus with reference to differentiating oocytes, reproductive cycles in animals, growth of follicles in ovaries, ovaries in Myotis lucifugus lucifugus after injection of hypophyseal extract, transplanted and explanted ovaries of new-born mice. Author: Laboratory Directions in General Zoology (with Curtis) '48; Textbook of General Zoology (with Curtis) '47; also articles in field.With U Mo '22-51, professor '37-51; with Detroit Institute of Cancer Research since '51. AAAS—Am Soc Zool—Am Soc Naturalists—Am Soc Mammalogists—Am Assn Anat—Genetics Soc Am—Sigma Xi. Detroit Institute of Cancer Research, 4811 John R St., Detroit 1.†

23 GUTKIN, Sydney A. Federal taxation (Law and practice). b'07. BS '27 (Coll City NY); LLB '29 (Columbia). Author: Security Transactions. Co-author: Estate Tax Handbook, Handbook of Tax Techniques. Contbr law and tax jours. Revisor NJ Law Revision Commn '29-32; asso Office Chief Counsel, US Bur Internal Revenue '36-38; asso prof law Rutgers U since '51; lectr on taxation Tax Inst of NYU, Pa State Coll, U Miami, U Pittsburgh, RI State Coll, Marquette U, NJ and NY insts for Practicing Lawyers; chmn Rutgen Fed Tax Inst. Am Bar Assn. 744 Broad St., Newark 2.†◎

24 GUTTMACHER, Manfred S. Crime (Psychiatric aspects). b'98. AB '19—MD '23 (Johns Hopkins U). Psychiatric advisor to UN Social Section Committee on causes and prevention of crime; consultant to judges on disposition criminal offenders. Gimbel Lectr Sex Offenses. Author articles in field. Co-author: (with Henry Weihofen) Psychiatry and the Courts. Chief psychiatric cons 2nd Army AUS. Group for Advancement of Psychiatry (mem former chmn Forensic com)— Am Psychiat Assn (chmn legal aspects com '48-51). Court House Baltimore 2.

25 GUTZEIT, Gregoire. Flotation (Mineral beneficiation); Chelates; Spot test analysis. b'01. AB '19 (Calvin Coll, Geneva, Switzerland); MS Chem Engring '27—MS Econ Geol '27—PhD '29 —DS '32 (U Geneva). Published first systematic semi-micro qualitative method for more common ions; developed chromite flotation, new flotation reagents, chemical and flotation processes and equipment, flotation machines, contact print method for localization and determination of minerals, methods for flotation of oxide and nonmetallic ores, waste treatment methods, process for chemical nickel plating. Holds patents. Author articles in field. Dir research and testing labs Gen Am Trans Corp since '44. Am Inst Mining Metall Engrs—Am Inst Chem Engrs—Am Chem Soc—Am Soc Testing Materials—AAAS. General American Transportation Corporation, Research and Testing Laboratories, 300 West 151st St., East Chicago, Ind.†

10 GUY, Raymond Frederick. Television and radio engineering. b'99. Student Pratt Inst Brooklyn '21. Author series of articles The Why and How of Frequency Modulation '40-41. Mem engring staff research labs RCA, NY City '24-29; head mgr radio and allocations engrs NBC since '29. Signal Corps US Army '18-19. Ships radio officer '16-17; radio officer and insp Marconi Wireless Telegraph Co NY City '16-17, Ind Wireless Telegraph Co NY City '20, Shipowners Radio Service NY City '21; staff radio sta WJZ Westinghouse Newark '21-23, dir field activities WJZ-WJY '23-24; Radio Club Am(F)—Inst Radio Engrs(pres '50)—Television Broadcasters Assn—Vets Wireless Operators Assn—Radio Tech Planning Bd—Soc Profl Engrs—Radio Executives Club—Radio Pioneers. 30 Rockefeller Plaza, NYC 20.†⊙

11 GUYOD, Hubert Charles. Well logging. b'99. EM (Sch Mines, St Etienne France). Author articles: Electrical Well Logging (30 articles) '44; Caliper Well Logging (4 articles) '45; Temperature Well Logging (7 articles) '46. Research engr Halliburton Oil Well Cementing Co Houston Tex '40-45; cons Houston since '46; pres Well Instrument Development Co. Am Assn Petroleum Geol—Am Inst Mining Metall Engrs—Soc Exploration Geophysicists —Am Geophys Union. 1754 Marshall, Houston 6, also P.O. Box 282, Bellaire, Tex.

12 GUYTON, F. E. Bee venom (Medicinal uses). b'93. BS '20—MS '21 (Ohio State U). Research in bee venom therapy for arthritis, neuritis, fibrositis; experiments with treatment rheumatoid arthritis in cooperation with local doctors. Author articles in field. With Ala Poly Inst since '21, prof zool and entomol since '38. Gamma Sigma Delta—Phi Delta Kappa—Phi Kappa Phi—Sigma Xi—Ala Beekeepers Assn—Am Assn Econ Entomologists. Alabama Polytechnic Institute, Auburn, Ala.

13 GUZE, Henry C. Physiological psychology; Constitution and Behavior; Maternal and sex behavior; Hypnosis; Fertility. b'19. AB '42 (U Newark); grad work (NYU Grad Sch Arts and Scis). Research on effects of early nursing deprivation on later maternal and sex behavior of rats; research on repression in hypnosis; posthypnotic behavior and personality. Psychologist NY State Vocational Inst '45; teaching fellow Coll City NY '46; research worker, maternal and sex behavior Am Mus Natural History '46-47; instr psychology LI U since '48. Am Anthropol Assn—Am Assn Applied Anthropol—AAAS—Soc Clin and Exptl Hypnosis(vp)—Am Psychol Assn—Nat Council Family Relations. Long Island University, 380 Pearl St., Bklyn.

14 GWALTNEY, Frederick William. Alcoholism. b'91. Student (Massey Bus Coll Richmond; Pace and Pace Inst NY; Va Mech Inst Richmond; William & Mary; U Richmond). Author articles in field. Exec sec Va State Hosp Bd and Dept Mental Hygiene and Hosps since '38; exec sec Mental Hygiene Soc Va since '41. Am Assn Mental Deficiency(F)—Va Conf Social Work—Am Soc Pub Admnstrn. Main Street Office Building, 9 N. 12th St., Richmond 19, Va.

15 GWYNN, Price Henderson, Jr. Religion (Weekday teaching in public schools). b'92. AB '12—AM '13 (U NC); BD '28—PhD '30 (Yale). Research on religion in public schools, examining

U.S. Constitution, state constitutions, legislation and all court decisions. Author: Leadership Education in the Local Church (in process of publ). Author articles: Weekday Religious Education in North Carolina; The responsibility of the Church in education for the future, and others. Supt Weekday Church Schs Bridgeport (Conn) '28-30; dir Christian Edn Synod of NC '44-46; dir leadership edn Presbyterian Church USA since 1946. AAAS—Am Acad Polit and Social Sci —Internat Council Religious Edn— Fed Council of Churches—Phi Beta Kappa—Kappa Delta Pi. Flora Macdonald College, Red Springs, N.C.

H

16 HAAG, William George. Ethnozoology; North American archeology. b'10. BS '32—MS '33 (U Ky); PhD '48 (U Mich). Research in ethnozoology on relation of domestic dog to prehistoric inhabitants of North America, research in North American archeology in early cultures in southeast area. Field archeol Tenn and Ala TVA '34, '36-37; asst prof dept anthrop, curator Mus U Ky '37-49; asso prof sociol, anthrop U Miss '49. Soc Mammalogists—Am Anthrop Assn—Soc Am Archeol—Sigma Xi. University of Miss, University, Miss.

17 HAAKE, Alfred Paul. Industrial economics; Community development; Municipal and community problems; Economic principles (Reconciliation with religion); National affairs (Prosperity). b'85. BA '14—MA '16—PhD '22 (U Wis). Author model code for NRA '33. Author: (with others) Industrial Government '20; also articles in field. Ed Furniture Management magazine; sec-treas, gen mgr Nat Furniture Credit Bur Chicago; pres Furniture Management Pub Co; chmn Nat Trade Executives Com against Govt Competition with Business; co-founder, trustee, chief econ Am Econ Found since '39; cons General Motors Corp. Nat Wholesale Furniture Assn (mng dir)—Nat Council—Nat Econ League —Am Trade Assn Executives (exec com)—Am Econ Assn—Am Acad Polit Social Sci—Furniture Club Am—Nat Small Bus Mens Assn—Phi Beta Kappa —Phi Kappa Phi—Beta Gamma Sigma. Rm. 1243, 33 S. Clark St., Chicago 3. H: 426 N. Prospect Av., Park Ridge, Ill.†⊙

18 HAAGEN-SMIT, Arie Jan. Chemistry of natural volatile flavors and essential oils; Chemical characteristics of plant growth hormones. born '00. AB '22—AM '26—PhD '29 (U Utrecht). Chemical analysis of volatile flavor constituents of Zinfandel wine, and pineapple; analysis and characterization essential oils from pines, guayule, and desert plants; isolation of plant growth hormones and chemical characterization of such hormones. Co-author article: (with F N Hirosawa, T H Wang) Chemical Studies on Grapes and Wines '49, and others. With Calif Inst Tech since '37, prof bio-organic chemistry since '40. ACS—Swiss Chem Soc—Dutch Chem Soc—Soc Exptl Biol and Med—Soc Plant Physiol—Inst Food Tech—Bot Soc Am—AAAS—Sigma Xi. ACS Fritzsche award '50. California Institute of Technology, Pasadena 4, Calif.⊙

19 HAAS, Fritz. Malacology; Ecology of land and fresh water Mollusca (Palaearctic regions, Africa, central and South America); Unionidae. b'86. PhD '10 (Heidelberg Germany). Scientific voyages and expeditions Norway '06, Pyrenees and Northeastern Spain '14-19; South and Central Africa '31-32, Northeastern Brazil '37, Bermuda '47-48; biological survey of Lake Bang-

weolo Central Africa. Author: (with A Bofill y Poch) Fauna Malacologica del Pirineu Catala; The Abidas and Chondrinas of the Pyrenees and the Iberian Peninsula, and others; also articles in field. Curator lower invertebrates Chicago Nat Hist Mus since '38. Institucio Catalana d'historia natural Barcelona Spain—Peiping Soc Nat Sci Peiping China—Acad Nat Sci Philadelphia—Senckenbergische Naturforschende Gesellschaft Frankfurt am Main Germany. Chicago Natural History Museum, Roosevelt Rd., Chicago 5.†

20 HAAS, Theodore Harold. Indians (Law and culture). b'05. AB '28 (Coll City NY); LLB '31 (Columbia U). Investigation of claims to lands of all native villages of the southeastern Alaska '46; adviser to policy board National Indian Institute for Second Inter-American Conference on Indian Life Cuzco Peru '49. Author: Should Indians Vote '48; Transfer of Functions from Federal Government to Indian Tribes; The Indian and the Law '49; also articles in field. Coauthor: Possessory Rights of the Natives of Southeastern Alaska '46. Spl atty Dept Justice and asst chief Indian Law Survey '39-40; asst solicitor Dept Interior and atty Bur Indian Affairs '40-41; project atty War Relocation Authority for Colo River Relocation Center Ariz '42-44; chief counsel Bur Indian Affairs; asst chief claims div Office Solicitor Dept Int since '51. 25 Ft. Washington Av., NYC 32.✦

21 HAASE, Eric. Public relations. b'21. Grad '39 (Taft Sch Conn). Co-author: You and Your Brand '43; Grade Labeling and the Consumer '44; A Plan for Action '47; also articles in field. In charge public and govt relations Assn Nat Advertisers '41-47; pres and treas Public Policy Inc since '47; cons Assn of National Advertisers, Distribution Council Nat Advertisers since '47. cons War Finance Div US Treasury Dept '42-45, Bur of Campaigns Domestic Br OWI '43-44. Am Trade Assn Executives. 61 East 66 St., NYC 17.

22 HABACH, George Frederic. Centrifugal pumps and compressors. b'07. ME '29 (Stevens Inst Tech); MME '36 (Brooklyn Poly Inst). Development of chemical pumps of stainless steel, porcelain, and other corrosion resisting materials, standardized lines of centrifugal pumps for general service, compressors for air, steam and refrigerants, viscosity effects in centrifugal pumps, stuffing boxes and their operation, multi-stage and large capacity pumps. Author articles in field. Patent on pump impeller assembly. With Worthington Pump and Machinery Corp since '29, chief engr centrifugal engring div since '45; adj prof mech engring Polytech Inst of Brooklyn since '46. ASME—Hydraulic Inst—Am Standards Assn—Adv Com Engrs Digest. c/o Worthington Pump & Machinery Corp., Harrison, N.J. H: 69 Osborne St., Glen Ridge.

23 HABER, Ernest Straign. Vegetable crop breeding (Hybrid sweet corn). b'96. BS '18 (O State U); MS '22—PhD '28 (Ia State Coll). Author: Laboratory Manual of Horticulture '49; also articles in field. Asst prof hort, later head dept Ia State Coll since '20. Am Soc Hort Sci—Ia Acad Sci—Ia State Hort Soc—Sigma Xi—Gamma Sigma Delta. Department of Horticulture, Iowa State College, Ames, Ia.†⊙

24 HABER, Heinz. Space medicine; Optics. b'13. Dr rer nat (phys) '39— Dr rer nat habil (astron) '44 (U Berlin). Space medicine (human problems of flights in upper atmosphere and space); physiological optics, diffraction gratings, spectroscopy. Asst Kaiser Wilhelm Inst Phys '37-39; chief dept spectroscopy Kaiser Wilhelm Inst Phys Chem '42-45; asst prof astrophysics US Air Force Air U '51. Space Med Assn—Optical Soc Am—Sigma Xi. Dept Space Medicine, US Air Force School of Aviation Medicine, Randolph Field, Tex.

10 HABERLY, Loyd. Printing (History). b'96. BA '18 (Reed Coll); '19-21 (Harvard); Rhodes scholar—MA '24 (Oxford). Discoverer specimens printing from wooden types made by tilemakers two centuries before Gutenberg; research on pictured pavements of medieval England; study life of George Catlin, painter and recorder of American Indians. Author: Medieval English Pavingtiles '36; Pursuit of the Horizon—a Biography of George Catlin '48. Dir private presses Eng, Wales, and St Louis; excavator of Notley Abbey; lecturer Monastic arts Harvard '38-40; writer, illustrator, printer and binder private press books since '26; now chmn English Dept., Fairleigh Dickinson College, Rutherford, N.J.

11 HABERMAN, Sol. Blood banks (Immuno-chemical problems); Rh factor. b'14. AS '34 (N Tex Agr Coll); AB '36—MA '37 (U Tex); PhD '41 (Ohio State U). Research in immunochemistry and blood group problems of blood banking; investigations in the nature of antibodies and antigenantibody reactions, antibiosis in human disease, blood groups, Rh-Hr types, diseases of the blood (erythroblastosis). Author articles: The Clinical Significance of the Rh Factor: Its Importance in Transfusion Reactions: The Preparation of Potent Anti-Rh Typing Serum by Injection of Rh Positive Blood into Previously Isoimmunized Individuals; others. Bact and serologist Baylor U Hosp since '41; prof grad research inst Baylor U '48-51; asso prof Southwestern Med Sch '48-51, clin asso prof '52; asst dir Wadley Research Inst and Blood Center '52. Internat Soc Hematology—AAUP—SAB—Am Assn Immunologists—AAAS—Sigma Xi—Sigma Pi Sigma—Beta Beta Beta—Phi Delta Epsilon—Am Soc Human Gentics. Award of Merit, Tex Soc Path '46; hon mention Sci Exhibit on Blood, AMA Conv '49 Baylor Hospital and College of Dentistry, Dallas. H: 4929 Wenonah Dr.

12 HACKENSMITH, Charles William. Secondary school health programs. b'06. BS '30 (U Ill); MA '35 (U Ky); PhD '48 (O State U). Prepared a syllabus for health instruction and to guide planning health programs for Kentucky secondary schools. Author articles in field. Asso prof phys edn and dir grad research '41-42; Commr AAU Bluegrass Area Lexington '41-45; act head dept phys edn and dir phys training Army specialized training program U Ky '42-45, asso prof and dir grad research '46-48, prof phys edn and dir grad research since '48. Am Assn Health Phys Edn and Recreation—Coll Phys Edn Assn—Kappa Phi Kappa. Department of Physical Education, University of Kentucky, Lexington, Ky.

13 HADDOCK, Jay Lamar. Potatoes (Cooking quality); Sugar beets (Factors affecting chemical composition, yield, quality); Soils (Identification clay minerals); Alfalfa (Chemical composition). b'03. BS '30 (Brigham Young U); MS '32 (Mass State Coll); PhD '42 (Ia State Coll). Development quick and accurate method for determining cooking quality of potatoes by specific gravity; field study interrelation of soil moisture, plant population and soil fertility; identification predominant clay minerals, Montmoril-

lonite in Iowa soil types, Illite in New England soils; soil fertilization tests to determine relation of boron, potassium and sulphur content of soil to yield and chemical composition of alfalfa. Author article: The Influence of Plant Population, Soil Moisture, and Nitrogen Fertilization on the Sugar Content and Yield of Sugar Beets '49. Co-author articles: (with P T Blood) Variations in Cooking Quality of Potatoes as Influenced by Varieties '39; (with P T Blood) Variations in Cooking Quality of Potatoes as Influenced by Fertilizers '49; (with M B Russell) The Idnetification of Clay Minerals in Fine Iowa Soils by the Thermal Method '40, and others. Ext argon U NH '35-44; asso agron Wash State Coll '44-45; soil sci USDA since '45. Am Soc Agron—Coll Soil Soc Am—Sigma Xi. Sigma Xi special commendation for excellence in research '33. Utah Experiment Station, Logan, Utah.†

14 HADLEY, Egbert Charles. Ballistics. b'88. Grad '06 (Gunnery Sch Washington Conn); BA '10 (Middlebury Coll); '10-11 (Harvard); BS '14 (MIT). Chairman technical committee Sporting Arms and Ammunition Manufacturers Institute '26-48; chairman Committee on small arms ammunition of Am Ordnance Assn '46-48. Laboratorian NY Navy Yard '14-15; elec engr Remington Arms Co Bridgeport Conn '15-16, ballistician '16-17, asst ballistic engr '17-19, ballistic engr '19-30, asst to pres '30-31, tech dir '31-39, '40-43, asst to vice pres and asst gen mgr '43-48. Delta Kappa Epsilon—Phi Beta Kappa. H: Golf Course Rd Middlebury, Vt.†☺

15 HADLEY, Thomas Erle. Wildlife photography; Industrial architecture. b'03. BArch '25 (U Mich). Research and production colored motion pictures of wildlife and nature subjects with natural sound taken directly in field with parabolic sound reflector; research on industrial architecture using ideas from growth patterns of Nature, use of designs based upon fundamental biology of man and living growing things such as trees, design of steel trusses based on structure of living tree and man. Produced: Zoolandia, Happy Valley, America the Beautiful, and others. Archtl engr Smith Hinchman and Grylls '26-29; exec engr Gen Motors Corp '29-48, chief archt Fisher Boyd Div; free lance conservation lectr since '48; mgr U Mich Hiawathan Wildlife Series. Nat Audubon Soc—Am Inst Archt. Received Lion of St Mark award '51 in collaboration with Walt Disney for Nature's Half Acre; 1st award Detroit Soc, Cinematographers '39. H: 306 S. Saginaw St., Holly, Mich.

16 HAENISCH, Edward L(auth). Quantitative analysis. b'11. BS '30—PhD '35 (U Chicago). Co-author: (with W C Pierce) Quantitative Analysis (3rd edit) '48. Faculty Villanova Coll '36-49, prof and head chem dept '44-49; prof chem and chmn dept Wabash Coll since '49. ACS (chmn div chem edn)—Am Inst Chem (F)—Electrochem Soc—Ind Acad Sci—Sigma Xi—Phi Beta Kappa. Wabash College, Crawfordsville, Ind.

17 HAFEN, LeRoy R. History of Colorado and western United States; The Overland Trails. b'93. AB '16 (Brigham Young U); MA '19 (U Utah); PhD '24 (U Calif); LittD '35 (U Colo). Author: The Overland Mail '26; Colorado—The Story of a Western Commonwealth '33; Colorado and Its People (2 vols) '48. Editor: Pike's Peak Gold Rush Guide Books of 1859 '41; Diaries of the Gold Rush 1859 '42; also articles in field. Exec dir, state historian State Hist Soc Colo since '24; prof hist U Denver, vis prof Am Hist U

Glasgow Scotland '47-48; ed Colorado Magazine since '25. AHA—Miss Valley Hist Assn—Colo Authors League. State Museum, Denver.☺

18 HAFSTAD, Katharine C. Climatology. b'03. BS '26 (Northwestern U); MA '30 (Clark U) Compiled meteorological results of cruises of the Carnegie; research in relationships between climate and soil conservation, and between climate and types of military operations. Author: Meteorological Results of the Last Cruise of the Carnegie (with W C Jacobs). Carnegie Inst Washington '30-34; Soil Conservation Service div Climatic and Physiographic Research '36-42; hdqrs. Air Weather Service '42-48; hq USAF 1009th Spl Weapons Squadron '48-49; Operations Research Office The Johns Hopkins University since '49. Am Meteorol Soc—Am Geophys Union —Am Soc Profl Geog—Soc Women Geog. Operations Research Office, Johns Hopkins Univ., Ft. Lesley J. McNair, Washington 25.†

19 HAFSTAD, Lawrence Randolph. Nuclear physics; Geophysics; Electronics. b'04. BS '26 (U Minn); PhD '33 (Johns Hopkins). Conducted research and development in regard to propagation of radio waves, measurement of height of radio-reflecting layer and its relation to magnetic storms, high-voltage vacuum tubes, atomic disintegrations, and artificial radioactivity, while with Carnegie Institution of Washington '27-45; also helped carry out research and development of VT radio proximity fuse for Army and Navy. Author articles in field. Dir research Applied Physics Lab '45-47 and dir Inst for Cooperative Research, Johns Hopkins U '47-50; exec sec Research and Development Bd Nat Mil Establishment '47-49; dir Div Reactor Development US Atomic Energy Commn Washington since '49; chmn Interdepartmental Com Sci Research and Development '49. Am Phys Soc(F) —Am Geophys Union—Washington Acad Sci—Washington Philos Soc—Sigma Xi—Tau Beta Pi. Recipient (with M A Tuve) AAAS award for research and development 1,000,000-volt vacuum tube '31; Medal for Merit from Sec Navy for major contbn in development of significant improvements in ordnance for Army and Navy '46. Atomic Energy Commission, Washington.†☺

20 HAGAR, Donald. Ceramic industry (Talc utilization, materials). b'87. BS Ceramic Engring '19—Profl Ceramic Engr '37 (Coll Ceramics NY, Alfred U). Research on talc to stop crazing, effect of a tremolitic talc in whiteware bodies, lengthening sagger life with talc. Holder US and British patents. Author articles in field. With Cambridge Tile Mfg Co since '27; cons ceramic engr since '31; vp and tech dir W H Loomis Talc Corp since '48. Am Ceramics Soc(F)—Inst Ceramic Engrs —O Ceramic Industries Assn—Ceramic Assn NJ—Ceramic Assn NY. Room 310 Richards Building, Zanesville, O. H: 1315 Blue Av.

21 HAGEMAN, Richard Harry. Plant biochemistry (Root respiration and saline toxicity, minor element requirements). b'17. BS '38 (Kan State Coll); MS '40 (Okla A&M Coll). Research on effects saline and alkaline toxicity on greenhouse plants; biochemical studies on effects deficient, optimum, and toxic concentrations of minor elements on greenhouse and field crops, on root respiration of Derris plants; agronomic, chemical and biological evaluation of rotenone-bearing plants; vanilla processing. Author articles in field. Research fellowship Okla A&M Coll '38-40; asst chem Agr Expt Sta

U Ky '40-42, '46-47; biochem Fed Expt Sta Mayaguez Porto Rico '47-50; Atomic Energy Commission fellowship in plant nutrition U Calif since '50. Am Chem Soc—Plant Physiol—AAAS—Am Soc Agron. 3048 Life Science Bldg., Univ. of California, Berkeley, California.

10 HAGEN, Karl Walter, Jr. Chinchilla (Diseases); Rabbits (Bacteriology). b'18. AB '40 (U Cal Los Angeles). Research on bacterial and parasitic infections of South American Chinchilla; studies on enteric bacteria and protozoa and Toxoplasmosis; development polyvalent vaccine for enteric infections in Chinchilla; research in general bacteriology and virology of diseases of domestic rabbit. Author: Serological and Biochemical Relationship of Saccharomycopsis guttulatus in the Chinchilla and Rabbit (unpublished thesis). Bact Chapman Chinchilla Research Lab Inglewood Cal '40-42, '48-49; asso expt sta dept veterinary sci U Cal Berkeley '46-47; bact Bur Animal Industry path div USDA US Rabbit Expt Sta since '50. Soc Am Bact—AAAS—Cal Acad Sci—Biol Photog Assn—Am Pub Health Assn. U.S. Rabbit Experiment Station, 210 N. Cypress, Fontana, Cal.

11 HAGENGUTH, Julius H. High voltage phenomena; Lightning; Lightning protection; Transients. b'01. Diplom Ingenieur '25 (Inst Tech Munich Germany). Research in transient phenomena in transformer windings; measuring technique with cathode-ray oscillograph at high voltages and short times; shielded resistance divider; lightning investigations; crater-lamp oscillograph; high speed automatic oscillographs; shunts; breakdown phenomena in air, oil and solids; transient phenomena in transformers and other apparatus and on transmission lines; perfecting of impulse tests on transformers; lightning recording instruments. Author articles in field. With Gen Electric Co since '26, in charge high voltage engring lab since '45. AIEE—Internat Conf Large Elec High Tension Systems. General Electric Co., 100 Woodlawn Av., Pittsfield, Mass.

12 HAGERTY, William Walsh. Fluid dynamics. b'16. B Mech Engring '39 (U Minn); MS '44—PhD '47 (U Mich). Research on fluid mechanics and thermodynamics and their relation to viscous fluids including phenomena of secondary flows, entrance effects, lubrication, resistance, flow patterns, drying of solids by hot gases, sprays, flows through porous media. Operating engr Gt Lakes Pipe Line Co '35-39; engr and foreman US Gypsum Co '39-40; factulty Villanova Coll '40-41; faculty U Cincinnati '41-42; with U Mich since '42, asso prof engring mech since '49. Sigma Xi—Phi Kappa Phi—Am Soc Engring Edn. College of Engineering, University of Michigan, Ann Arbor.

13 HAGOOD, Margaret Jarman. Statistical and rural sociology (Statistics, population, level of living, labor, social research methods). b'07. AB '29 (Queens Coll NC); AM '30 (Emory U); PhD '37 (U NC). Research on methods of estimating annually farm population and migration to and from farms, improving official definition of farm population, use of component analysis in index construction and in statistical sampling, labor force concepts, fertility differentials among farm women. Author: Mothers of the South: Portraiture of the Southern White Tenant Farm Woman '39; Statistics for Sociologists '41. Co-author: Rural Life in the United States '49; also articles in field. Sr social scientist Div Farm Population and Rural Life Bur Agrl Econ US Dept Agr Washington '42-45,

principal social scientist '45-47, principal statis '47-52, head since '52. Internat Union Sci Invest Popul Probs —Population Assn Am (bd dirs '42-47, treas '49-50)—Am Sociol Soc (com social statis, 2nd vp, exec com)—Am Statis Assn—Rural Sociol Soc—So Sociol Soc—DC Sociol Soc (pres '46-47). Division of Farm Population and Rural Life, Bureau of Agricultural Economics, U.S. Department of Agriculture, Washington 25.

14 HAGUE, Wesley McLaren. Management relations; Industrial relations. b'97. BS '19 (US Naval Acad); MS '23 (MIT). Mgr Boston Naval Shipyard '46-49; chief of indsl relations Navy Dept '49-52; commandant Indsl Coll of Armed Forces, Fort Lesley I McNair, Washington since '52. Soc Naval Engrs. Legion of Merit with gold star. Commandant Industrial College of the Armed Forces, Ft Lesley J. McNair, Washington 25.⊚

15 HAHN, E. Adelaide. Language (Hittite, Greek, Latin, Indo-European); Syntax; Literature (Greek and Latin); Vergil. AB '15 (Hunter Coll); AM '17—PhD '29 (Columbia); post doctoral work (Columbia, Yale, Linguistic Inst of Linguistic Soc and Linguistic insts of Univs of Mich, NC, Wis, Am Acad at Rome. Author: Coordination of Non-Coordinate Elements in Vergil '30. With Hunter Coll since '15, prof and head dept Latin and Greek since '36. Am Philol Assn—Archaeol Inst Am—Linguistic Soc Am (pres '46)—Am Oriental Soc—Am Classical League —Classical Assn Atlantic States—NY Classical Club (pres '39-41) chmn forum '41-47)—AAUP—Am Sch Classical Studies—Classical Soc Am Acad Rome—Linguistic Circle of NY—Phi Beta Kappa. Drisler fellowship in classical philology Columbia '16-17, hon fellowship in linguistics Yale '34-35 '36-37. Hunter College, 695 Park Av., NYC 21.†⊚

16 HAHN, Harry. Art authenticity and restoration. b'96. Engaged in establishing authenticity old masters, restoration techniques; microscopic identification and classification of pigments; X-ray plate analysis; infra-red and polarized light effects on over-painted surfaces; specialist in documentary research as applied to art of high Renaissance; research art French Nat Archives Bibliotheque Nationale '22-32. Author: The Rape of La Belle 46. P.O. Box 465, Wichita, Kan.

17 HAHN, Lewis Edwin. Metaphysics of contextualism; Theory of knowledge (Perception); Theory of value. b'08. BA—MA '29 (U Tex); PhD '39 (U Calif). Author: A Contextualistic Theory of Perception '42. Co-author: A Symposium On Value '49; also articles in field. Instr, later asso prof U Mo since '36. Am Philos Assn (com placement, available personnel since '49, chmn since '51)—Am Soc Aesthetics—AAAS—SW Philos Conf—Phi Beta Kappa. University of Missouri, Columbia, Mo.⊚

18 HAHNE, Ernest Herman. Special assessments; Public expenditures; Taxation. b'90. AB '11—LLB '13 (U Neb); AM '14 (Harvard); PhD '30 (U Chicago). Administration national code authority under NRA for cotton cloth glove, academic costume and household ice refrigerator industries, special assessment and federal tax consultant. Author articles in field. Pres Miami U since '46. Am Econ Assn—Farm Econ Assn—Nat Tax Assn—Mid-West Econ Assn (vp '47-48)—Beta Gamma Sigma —Phi Beta Kappa. Miami University, Oxford, O.

19 HAHNERT, William F(ranklin). General invertebrates; Bottom fauna; Protozoa. b'01. AB '27 (DePauw U);

PhD '31—Bruce fellow '30-31 (Johns Hopkins). Author articles in field. Prof zool O Wesleyan U since '47, chmn dept since '41. Am Soc Zool—AAAS—O Acad Sci (chmn zool sect '49-50)—Am Soc Limnol Oceanog—Sigma Xi—Phi Beta Kappa. Nat Research Council fellow '31-33. Department of Zoology, Ohio Wesleyan University, Delaware, O.⊚

20 HAIG, Irvine Theodore. Forest management; Western white pine silviculture; Chilean forests and forest industries. b'01. BS '23 (Pa State Coll); MF '28—PhD '35 (Yale). Chief Chilean Forest Mission Washington '43-44. Author articles in field. Dir SE Forest Expt Sta Asheville NC since '44. Soc Am Forestry—AAAS(F)—Gamma Sigma Delta—Sigma Xi—Phi Kappa Phi. Southeastern Forest Experiment Station, 223 Federal Building, Asheville, N.C. H: The Bonnie Farm, Route 2.†

21 HAIGH, John Thomas. Enzymes; Paper Textiles; Dry Cleaning; Sewage Disposal; Adhesives; Industrial New Product Development; Sales; Machinery for Ultarafine Grinding. b'17. BS '39—MS '41 (U ND). Research on protected enzyme preparation and method of enzymic conversion of starch. Granted patents in field. Development of special cereal products for industrial use. Tech adv G-2 mil intelligence '41-44; group leader Nat Distillers Products Corp '44-46; with Pillsbury Mills Inc since '46, tech sales dir, Mechanical Div from '51. ACS—Chem Market Research Assn—Tech Assn Pulp and Paper Industry—Am Assn Textile Chem and Colorists—AAAS— Minn Indsl Chem Forum—Nat Paint Varnish and Lacquer Assn. Pillsbury Mills, Inc., Pillsbury Building, Mpls. 2.

22 HAINES, Francis. Nez Perce Indians (History, culture); American western horses (Appaloosa). b'99. BS '23 (Mont State Coll); MA '32 (Mont State U); PhD '38 (U Calif). Author: Nez Perce Indians in Northwest History 1805-1895 '38; Red Eagles of the Northwest '39; Story of Idaho '42; also articles in field. Asso prof hist No Idaho Coll Edn since '46. Appaloosa Horse Club (pres). Northern Idaho College of Education, Lewiston, Ida. H: 1211 14th Av.

23 HAINES, Lewis Francis. Charles Reade (Criticism of). b'07. AB '30— PhD '41 (U Mich). Research in social criticism in the novels of Charles Reade. Author articles in field. Asst prof Eng U Fla '42-46, prof humanities since '46, ed U Press since '45, dr since '49. Modern Lang Assn Am— Fla Hist Soc—Phi Kappa Phi. University of Florida, Law Building, Gainesville, Fla. H: Hibiscus Park, Rt. 5.†⊚

24 HAKANSON, R(ichard) C. Forensic Photography. b'06. Student '23-24 (U Pittsburgh). Photography of People and things taken under varying conditions and by differing processes to show imperishably the temporal state of things for adjucation of disputes. Forensic photographer since '46. Photog Soc Am—Royal Photog Soc Gt Britain. 10322 Lake Shore Blvd., Cleve 8.

25 HALBACH, Edward Anthony. Auroras (Northern lights); Variable stars. b'09. BEE '31—MS '33 (Marquette U); '31-33 (Milwaukee State Teachers Coll). Regular observer on variable star program for American Association of Variable Star Observers Harvard College Observatory since '32; participant in National Geographic Society program investigating and photographing auroras since '38; headed party of six amateur astronomers into Northern Canada for solar eclipse of July '45 to obtain photographic data in collaberation with astronomers in Stockholm; headed expedition six scientists into Burma '48 to photograph solar eclipse of May 9 '48 for National Geographic Society; member editorial advisory board Sky and Telescope. Author articles in field. Research engr Perfex Corp since '46; dir Milwaukee Astron Soc Obs since '40. Milwaukee Astron Soc—Am Meteor Soc—Am Assn Variable Star Observers (life). 2971 S. 52 St., Milwaukee 14.†

10 HALBOUTY, Michel Thomas. Petroleum geology and engineering (Oil operations and production). b'10. BS '30—MS '31 (Tex A&M Coll). Aided in discoveries of new oil fields in Texas and Louisiana. Author articles in field. Owner firm cons geol and petroleum engrs Houston Tex since '37. Reserve office US Army '30-42, active duty '42-45, overseas as 1t col inf for Army-Navy Petroleum Bd. Am Assn Petroleum Geol—Am Petroleum Inst—Am Inst Mining Metall Engrs—Soc Palontol Mineral—Soc Econ Geol—Mineral Soc Am—NY Acad Sci—Tex Acad Sci — AAAS. Shell Building, Houston, Tex.

11 HALDEMAN, William S(trubhar'). Chemistry (Teaching). b'81. Diploma '04 (Pa State Normal Sch); BS '14 (U Pa); AM '20 (Harvard); student summer sessions '20-24 (U Ill). Professor and head chemistry department Monmouth (Ill) Coll since '18. AAAS(F)—ACS (councilor)—Ill State Acad Scis—Alpha Chi Sigma. Gold medal Midwest award from St Louis sect Am Chem Soc for meritorious contribution to chemistry '50. 228 S. Eighth St., Monmouth, Ill.◎

12 HALE, Hugh Ellmaker. Railway engineering (Investment, valuation, maintenance). CE '97 (Lehigh U). Engring positions with B&ORR '02-08, Mo Pacific RR '08-14; engr Eastern group, Presidents' Conf Com Federal Valuation of RRs in US '14-26, v chmn same '26-31; sr mem H E Hale & Co, cons engrs '31-36; rr engr investment dept Equitable Life Assurance Soc US '36-45; cons engr since '45. ASCE—Am Ry Engring Assn—Soc Am Mil Engrs. 1165 Fifth Av., NYC 29.

13 HALE, William J. Chemurgy; Fermentation; Chlorphyll. b'76. AB—AM '97—LLD '37 (Miami U); AB '98—AM '99—PhD '02 (Harvard); travel fellow '02-03 (Technische Hochschule Berlin and U Gottingen). Patentee of new process for manufacture phenol, aniline, acetic acid, butadiene and their derivatives. Author: The Calculations of General Chemistry '09; A Laboratory Manual of General Chemistry '17; Chemistry Triumphant '32; The Farm Chemurgic '34; Prosperity Beckons '36; Farmward March '39; also articles in field. Research cons Dow Chem Co since '34; pres Nat Agrol Co Washington since '39. AAAS(F)—London Chem Soc—Am Chem Soc—Societe Suisse de Chimie—Societe Chimique de France—Deutsche Chemische Gesellschaft—Phi Beta Kappa — Sigma Xi. Midland, Mich.◎

14 HALL, Benedict Arthur. Floral anatomy and morphology (Phylogenetic implications). b'06. BA '38 (NY State Teach Coll Albany); MA '41—Scholarship '38-39—Goldwin Smith fellow bot '46-47—PhD '47 (Cornell). Research on floral anatomy Droseraceae, Aceraceae, related families. Asst prof biol Hartwick Coll Oneonta NY '44-45; asst prof biol Westminister Coll New Wilmington Pa '45-46; asst prof biol Denison U '47-48; asst prof State Teach Coll Cortland NY since '48. Bot Soc Am—AAAS. State Teachers College, Cortland, N.Y.†

15 HALL, Edward T(witchell), Jr. Cultural anthropology (Interpersonal relations). b'14. BA '36 (U Denver); MA '38 (U Ariz); PhD '42 (Columbia). Director Columbia University Governador Expedition '41; Anthropologist US Commercial Company economic survey of Micronesia '47; Staff dendrochronologist Peabody Museum-Awatovi expedition '38-39. Author: Early Stockaded Settlements in Governador '44; also articles in field. Social studies faculty Bennington Coll since '48. Am Anthrop Assn(F)—Soc Am Archaeol(F)—Tree-Ring Soc(F)—Am Ethnol Soc (affiliate). Bennington College, Bennington, Vt.†

16 HALL, E(ugene) Raymond. Mammals (North American). b'02. AB '24 (U Kan); AM '25—PhD '28 (U Cal Berkeley). Classification mammals of North America; economic relations wild mammals to man. Author: Mammals of Nevada '46. Author articles: Mustelid mammals from the Pleistocene of North America, with systematic notes on some recent members of the genera Mustela, Taxidea, and Mephitis; and others. Curator mammals Mus Vertebrate Zool U Cal Berkeley '27-44, also asst and asso prof '30-44; dir Mus Natural Hist, prof and chmn dept zool U Kan since '44. Am Soc Mammalogists—Am Soc Anatomists—Am Soc Zool. Museum of Natural History, University of Kansas, Lawrence, Kan.◎

17 HALL, James Edmund. Fruit, Vegetables (Canning, preservation, product control); Foods (Standards). b'10. Student (Notre Dame) (Northwestern U). Research on effect of blanching on vegetables for canning, brine density separation of peas, size grading of peas; development method for prevention browning of fruit; effect of in-plant chlorination food plant water supplies; study control procedures quality and cost for canned and frozen vegetables, frozen fruits and methods for predetermining quality of canned, frozen foods; investigation Food and Drug Administration mandatory standards for canned peas, corn, tomatoes, frozen fruits and berries, industry grades and standards for canned and frozen fruits, vegetables. Holds patents on size grading of peas, (with E A Heiss) on method for prevention browning of fruits. Author articles: Organization of Quality Control in Canneries; Use of Sterilized Water in Canning and Freezing Plants; Technical Problems Facing Frozen Food Industry, and others. Research dept Am Can Co '33-39; dir research and product control, mgr prodn Pictsweet Foods Inc '43-49; food cons US since '47; pres Hall Packing Co Ltd Ladner BC since '50. Inst Food Tech—NA Assn Food Products (research, standards com); NW Canners Assn (research com)—NW Frozen Foods Assn (research com). P.O. 139, Ladner, B.C. H: 916 S 11th, Mt Vernon, Wash.

18 HALL, John Scoville. Photoelectric photometry. b'08. AB '30 (Amherst); PhD '33 (Yale). Research in photoelectric photometry including colorimetry and absolute spectrophotometry of bright stars. Developed photoelectric polarizing photometer and device for measuring brightness of stars in full daylight. Author articles in field. Editor: (book 2) MIT Radiation Laboratory series: Radar Aids to Navigation. Instr, asst prof Amherst Coll '38-41; radar work radiation lab MIT '42-46; asso prof astron, physics Amherst Coll '46-48; head Equatorial Div US Naval Obs since '48. Am Astron Soc — Internat Astron Union. Awarded portion of Boyden Premium, Franklin Inst '39. U. S. Naval Observatory, Washington, 25.

19 HALL, Lawrence B(abcock). Malaria control; Airborne pathogens. b '09. BS '35 (ND State Coll); MS '36 (Ore State Coll); '37 (U NC); '49-50 (Johns Hopkins U). Administration national malaria control program covering 13 states; member US Medical Mission to China on Burma Road; consultant malaria control program to Imperial Ministry of Health Iran '49; in charge research group investigating improved equipment for malaria control, equipment and methods for detection and quantitation of airborne pathogenic pollens, spores, bacteria and viruses; member expert panel on insecticides World Health Organization. Author article: Malaria Control Recommendations to Imperial Iranian Government. Co-author article: (with R L Stenburg) A Continuous Recording Particle Sampler. Regional engr Ga Dept Pub Health '37-41; sr asst sanitary engr US Med Mission to China USPHS '41-43, sr sanitary engr Communicable Disease Center UPHS since '43. Nat Malaria Soc—Am Soc CE—Sci Research Soc Am—Am Pub Health Assn. U.S. Public Health Servic, P.O. Box 769, Savannah, Ga.

20 HALL, Lloyd A. Food technology; Meat curing products; Protein hydrolysates; Sterilization of spices and cereals. b'94. PhC—BS '16 (Northwestern U); grad study (U Chicago); ScD '44 (Va State Coll); ScD '47 (Tuskegee Inst). Developed unusual processes for sterilization of spices, cereals, other food materials widely used during last war; work on meat curing products, seasonings, emulsions, bakery products, protein hydrolysates. Patentee and co-patentee approximately 80 US and foreign patents. Author articles in field. Chem dept Health Labs Chicago '16, later sr chem; chief chem John Morrell & Co Ottumwa Ia, Boyer Chem Lab; pres and chem dir Chem Products Corp Chicago; chem cons, chief chem, dir research Griffith Labs Inc '29-46, tech dir since '46. AAAS(F)—Am Pub Health Assn(F)—Am Inst Chem(F)—Am Chem Soc—Am Assn Cereal Chem—Ill Acad Sci—Inst Food Tech (councilor)—Food Advisory Council Ill Inst Tech—Research Com Quartermaster Food and Container Inst—Soc Chem Ind—Sigma Xi—Beta Kappa Chi. 1415-31 W. 37th St., Chicago. H: 420 E. 65th St.

21 HALL, Newman A(rnold). Flight propulsion (Jet); Thermodynamics (Gases); Fluid flow; Aerodynamics; Heat transfer. b'13. AB '34 (Marietta Coll); PhD '38 (Calif Inst Tech). Research on flight propulsion, thermodynamic properties of gases, fuel-air ratio required for constant pressure combustion hydrocarbon fuels and ideal temperature rise in such combustion; analysis of performance aircraft gas turbine power plants, thermodynamic matching and performance calculation of aircraft turbine engines; theoretical performance of ram-jets and convergent-divergent nozzles; thrust and drag jet propulsion systems. Author articles in field. Research math Chance Vought div United Aircraft Corp Stratford Conn '41-42, supervisor engring personnel '42-43, research engr power plant analysis E Hartford '43-45, head analysis sect research engr '45-47; prof thermodynamics U Minn since '47. Am Math Soc—Math Assn Am—SAE—Inst Aeronautical Sci(asso F)—ASME—Phi Beta Kappa—Sigma Xi. University of Minnesota, Mechanical Engineering Department, Minneapolis 14.◎

22 HALL, Norris Folger. Acids and bases (Electrochemistry); French translation (Scientific); Analytical chemistry). b'91. Certificat d'études francoises '08 (Grenoble); AB AM '13 (Haverford Coll); AM '15—PhD '17

(Harvard). Research in electrochemistry of non-aqueous solutions; chemistry of technetium, exchange reactions; acid-base equilibria, particularly in glacial acetic acid and other non-aqueous solvents; potentiometric and conductivity titrations, colorimetric acidity; separation, purification and inorganic chemistry of technetium; studies in exchange reactions between oxyanions and water, nickel complexes in solution. Author articles in field. From asst prof to prof chem U Wis since '29, prof since '34; sr chem Argonne Nat Lab '48-49. AAAS (F)—ACS—Wis Acad Sci. Chemistry Bldg., University of Wisconsin, Madison 6, Wis.†☉

10 HALL, Ralph Corbin. Forest entomology; Silviculture (Logging deterioration, locust borer, bark beetles, forest insects in northeastern California). b'99. BS '25 (NY State Coll Forestry, Syracuse U); MF '27 (Harvard); '29-30 (U Minn); '36 (Ia State Coll); PhD '31 (U Mich). Research on fire weather studies, on logging areas to study deterioration of reserve stand under various methods of cutting in New England and Lake states, on locust borer and other forest insects, effect of climatic factors on tree killing insects. Author articles in field. Asst entomol US Dept Agr '31-42, entomol since '42 Bur Entomol and Plant Quarantine Forest Insect Lab Berkeley Calif, in charge Hat Creek Field Lab. Soc Am Foresters—Sigma Xi—Gamma Sigma Delta. 29 Forestry Building, University of California, Berkeley 4. H: 72 Davis Rd, Route 1, Orinda.

11 HALL, Richard P. Protozoology. b'00. AB '19 (Henderson-Brown Coll); AM '22—PhD '24 (U Cal). Mem faculty NYU since '26, prof biology since '38. AAAS(F)—NY Acad Sci (asso editor biology '37-42)—Am Soc Zoologists—Am Soc Naturalists—Am Micros Soc—Am Soc Parasitologists (editorial bd '41-43)—Am Soc Protozool (pres '50-52)—Am Soc Tropical Medicine—Soc Exptl Biol and Medicine—Internat Congress Microbiology (sec sect V '39). New York University, NYC 53. H: Scarsdale, N.Y.☉

12 HALL, Richard N. Geographic nomenclature (Japanese Empire, Latin America); Japanese settlement in Mexico. b'07. AB '32 (Western Mich Coll Edn); MA '34 (U Mich). Chief, Regional Research Section, US Board on Geographic Names since '44, specializing on Japanese Empire and Latin America; research at University of Michigan, Washington, and Mexico on Japanese settlement in Mexico '37-43; collaborator US Board on Geographic Names publications on Korea, Latin American countries, Bahama Islands, British possessions in Lesser Antilles '47; research on problems connected with State Department publication on Administrative Subdivision of Japan, with an appendix of 47 prefectural maps '46. Arctic Inst NA—Am Soc Profl Geog. U. S. Board of Geographic Names, Department of Interior, Washington.†

13 HALL, Robert Green. Marine refrigeration; Cargo Vessel design. b '16. Student '34-37 (US Naval Acad); BS '40 (MIT). Installation specialist of refrigerated cargo spaces for 480,-000 cubic feet of cargo at 100 below zero Fahrenheit; liquid cargo spaces and pumping machinery for molasses; revision cargo handling gear. Naval arch Bur Ships Navy Dept '42-44; naval arch freighter reconversion Matson Navigation Co '44-48, vessel replacement program Am Pres Lines since '49. Soc Naval Archs and Marine Engrs—Am Soc Refrigerating Engrs. Box 945, R.F.D. 1, Redwood City, Cal.

14 HALL, Robert King. Comparative education; Latin America; Japan; Islam; Japanese relocation. b'12. AB '34 (Lake Forest Coll); AM '35 (Harvard); AM '36 (Chicago); AM '44 (Columbia); PhD '41 (Michigan); '37 (Mexico); Research in Brazil '40, Buenos Aires '35, School for Asiatic Studies '47, South America '40, '42, '48, '49, '50; made study of unassimilated German and Japanese national groups in Brazil; research in Iran '49. Co-author: (with J O Gauntlett) Kokutai no Hongi '49; Education in the New Japan '49; Shushin: The Ethics of a Defeated Nation '49; Teaching of English '42; Federal Control of Secondary Education in the ABC Republics '42; Basic English for South America '43; Ingles Basico para Brasil '43. Co-editor: Report of Workshop of Latin American Studies '41. Asso prof Teachers Coll Columbia U; staff Nat Japanese-Am student Relocation Council; chief edn sub-sect SCAP Japan first months of occupation. Associaçao Brasileria de Educaçao—Inst Nacional de Estudos Pedagogicos. Pan Am Airways fellow to Argentina '39; Itamarati exchange fellow '40; Guggenheim fellow '46-47. 106 Morningside Dr., NYC 27.☉

15 HALL, William Earle Brandon. Forensic medicine (Pathology); Medical jurisprudence; Legal medicine. b '04. MB '28—MD '29 (U Toronto); LM CC '29 (Med Council Can); grad study '31-32 '45 '46 (U Pa) (Harvard). Chairman section on pathology Am Acad Forensic Sci '51-53; organizer and president Seminar on Forensic Medicine for Police Officers coroners and pros attys Pa '51; expert witness pathologist and coroner's physician various courts since '49. Author articles: Medico-Legal Topics and Questions requiring Clarification; Medico-Legal Aspects of Autopsies and Pathological Specimens in Missouri; Some Signs, Findings and Interpretations of Criminal Abortion. Coll Am Path—International Assn for Identification—Nat Sheriffs Assn—Am Acad Forensic Scis (chmn sect on pathology '51-52). Pathologist and dir labs Port Huron Hosp '41-48, Sarnia (Ont Can) Hosp '46-48, Mo Bapt Hosp St Louis '48-50, Chambersburg Pa Hosp and Waynesboro Pa Hosp since '50. Chambersburg Hospital, Chambersburg, Pa. H: Lincolnway East, R.F.D. 2, Fayetteville, Pa.

16 HALLBERG, Charles W. History (Suez Canal, Austro-French relations 1852-64). b'99. BS '23 (Trinity Coll); MA '24—PhD '31 (Columbia U). Research Austria, England, France '28-29, Austria and France '32-33. Author: The Suez Canal, Its History and Diplomatic Importance '31; also articles in field. Instr hist Syracuse U '29-31, professorial lecturer hist U Minn '21-32; asst prof hist U Mo '33-34, grad div Brooklyn Coll '34-37, Queens Coll since '37. AHA. Department of History, Queens College, Flushing, N.Y.

17 HALLDEN, Karl William. Flying shears (Automatic). b'84. BS '09—MS (hon) '48 (Trinity Coll). Pres and treas Hallden Machine Co, designers and builders of spl machinery automatic sheet metal wire and tube straightening and cutting machinery since '17; asso The W H A Robertson Co Ltd Bedford Eng, The Wean Engring Co Warren O. River St., Thomaston, Conn.☉

18 HALLEN, John Edward. Slander; Libel. b'94. BA '16—LLB '18 (Yale). Author articles in field. Asso prof law U Kan '22-24, prof '24-25; prof U Tex '25-30, O State U since '30. Order of the Coif. Ohio State University College of Law, Columbus 10, O.

19 HALLER, George Louis. Electronics; Radar; Missile guidance. b'07. BS '27 — EE '34 — MS '35 — PhD '42 (Pa State Coll). Author articles in field. Educator, asst dean, later dean sch chem and physics Pa State Coll since '46; cons and bd dirs Haller, Raymond, and Brown Inc and Central Pa Corp; chmn panel on countermeasures against guided missiles research and development bd Nat Defense Establishment. Radio engr War Dept Wright Field '35-42; maj, later col Signal Corps and Air Corps '42-46, chief development of Air Corps radar countermeasures and missile guidance. Am Phys Soc(F) —Inst Aeronautical Scis(asso F)—Inst Radio Engrs (sr) — AIEE — Franklin Inst — Newcomen Soc, England — Am Assn Engring Edn — Sigma Xi — Tau Beta Pi—Sigma Pi Sigma. School of Chemistry and Physics, The Pennsylvania State College, State College, Pa.

20 HALLER, Herbert Ludwig Jacob. Chemistry and formulation of insecticides. b'94. Chem E '18 (Cincinnati); PhD '26 (Columbia). Research on chemistry and formulation of insecticides effective against agricultural insect pests and disease-carrying insects, insect attractants and repellents, economic entomology, biochemistry, stereochemistry, photosensitizing, dyes, chemical constitution and optical activity, chemical structure and insecticidal action. Author articles in field. Asso chem '23-29 Rockefeller Inst; sr chem US Dept Agr '29-40, prin chem '40-47, asst to chief Bur Entomol and Plant Quarantine since '47. Assn Econ Entomol—Chem Soc Washington (treas '35, pres '41)—Entomol Soc Washington — Washington Acad — Insecticide Soc Washington (pres '41). Hillebrand prize Chem Soc Washington '33. Bureau of Entomology and Plant Quarantine, U. S. Department of Agriculture, Washington 25. H: 4407 38th St., Washington 16.

21 HALLER, William. History of Puritanism in England and America; Life and works of John Milton; English poetry of the sixteenth and seventeenth centuries. b'85. BA '08—LHD '40 (Amherst); PhD '16 (Columbia). Author: Tracts on Liberty in the Puritan Revolution '36; Rise of Puritanism '38. Co-author: (with Godfrey Davies) The Leveller Tracts '44. Co-editor: Works of John Milton (Columbia edit) '31-38. Faculty, prof Eng Barnard Coll, Columbia '09-50; prof emeritus since '50; research asso Folger Shakespeare Library since '50; vis prof Eng U Rochester '50-51. MLA—Am Soc Church Hist. Research F Huntington Library '40-41; Guggenheim F '47-48, '50. Folger Shakespeare Library, Washington 3.☉

22 HALLOCK, Richard Treadwell. Persepolis; Elamite (Language); Darius I; Sumerian-Akkadian (Language). b'06. AB '29 (U Toronto); PhD '34 (U Chicago). Preparation administrative documents from Persepolis period of Darius I in Elamite language for publication; Sumerian-Akkadian syllabary texts in connection with projected dictionary. Author: The Chicago Syllabary and the Louvre Syllabary AO 7661 '40. Asso Assyrian Dictionary Project Oriental Inst U Chicago '31-41, since '47. Am Oriental Soc. Oriental Institute, University of Chicago, Chgo 37.

23 HALMBACHER, Paul. Enzymes (Commercial); Fermentation. b'09. BA '32 (James Millikin U); '32-34 (U Ill); '38-39 (Marquette U). Vice-pres and tech dir Paul-Lewis Labs since '37. AAAS—Am Chem Soc—Soc Brewing Chem. 4253 N. Port Washington Rd., Milwaukee 12. H: 1208 Grant St., Waukesha, Wis.

10 HALSETH, Odd S(igurd). Prehistoric desert cultures (Irrigation, farming, adobe architecture); Hohokam prehistory; Pueblo ethnology; Norwegion language and literature; Indian and Mexican folk art (Religious). b'93. MSc '31 (U So Calif). Spent five years world travel, studied folkways in European countries, South America, Africa, Asia. Author articles: Saints of The New World '29; Primitive Copyrights '32; Arizona's 1500 Years of Irrigation History '47, and others. City archeol Phoenix since '29. AAAS—Am Anthrop Assn—Am Soc Archeol—Inter-American Soc Anthrop Geog—Awarded medal of St Olav by King Haakon '29. Pueblo Grande, 4619 E. Washington St., Phoenix, Ariz.

11 HALVORSON, (Henry George) Homer. Bibliography; Onomatology; English philology. b'08. AB '30 (Whittier Coll); certificate librarianship '31—MA '34 (U Calif); AM '36—PhD '37—Dexter Travel fellow '37 (Harvard). Author articles in field. Asso U librarian U Ill '41-43; librarian Johns Hopkins U since '43. ALA (joint com on govt publs chmn)—Biblio Soc Am—Calif Library Assn—Md Library Assn (pres '46-47)—Spl Library Assn—Am Assn State and Local Hist—Am Geog Soc—Md Hist Soc—Mod Lang Assn—Norwegian-Am Hist Assn—Eng Place Name Soc. Johns Hopkins University Library, Baltimore 18.†

12 HAMBURGER, Ferdinand, Jr. Radio frequency measurements; Instrumentation; Dielectrics. b'04. BE '24—DE '31 (Johns Hopkins). Research on impregnated paper insulation, tests of electrical equipment as radio receivers, transmitters and compasses, radar, banding of 105 MM shells, radar target simulating equipment, instrumentation for psychological and climatological research. Author articles in field. Prof Johns Hopkins since '47, asso dir Systems Research since '45. AIEE(F)—Inst Radio Engrs (sr)—Sigma Xi—Tau Beta Pi. Charles A Coffin Fellow, Johns Hopkins U '30-31. Johns Hopkins University, Baltimore 18.©

13 HAMER, Philip May. Federal archives as materials for research in American history; Documentary publication in American history. b'91. AB '12—LittD '36 (Wofford Coll); MA '15 (Trinity Coll (now Duke); PhD '18 (U Pa). Author: The Secession Movement in South Carolina, 1847-52, '18; Tennessee, a History '33. Editor and part author: The Centennial History of the Tennessee State Medical Association '30. Mem bd editors Miss Valley Hist Review '32-35, Jour So Hist 35-36. Editor: Guide to Records in the National Archives '48. Dep examiner The Nat Archives '35, chief div of the library '36-38, chief div accessions '38, chief div reference '38-41, dir reference '38-41, dir reference service '41-44, now dir records control; nat dir Survey of Fed Archives '36-37; sec Nat Hist Publs Commn since '46; vis prof history George Peabody Coll for Tchrs summer '20, Ind U summer '26. Am Hist Assn—Miss Valley Hist Assn—So Hist Assn (pres '38)—East Tenn Hist Soc (pres '26-28, mng editor publs '31-35)—Soc Am Archivists—Phi Kappa Phi. National Archives Bldg., Washington 25.©

14 HAMER, Walter J(ay). Galvanic cells and batteries; Electrolytes; Hydrogen-ion concentration; Thermodynamics; Standard cells. b'07. BS '29 (Juniata Coll Huntingdon Pa); PhD '32—Usn Research Fellow '32-34 (Yale); Research Asso '34-35 (MIT). Research on thermodynamics and electrode potentials of lead-acid storage battery, vapor pressures by isotonic method, standardization of scale of hydrogen-ion concentration or activity and initia-

tion of a new method for this standardization, eletrochemistry of uranium and uranium salts and isotopes. Author articles in field. Asst, later sr chem Nat Bur Standards since '35, chief electrochemistry section '50; lecturer, phys and electrochem US Dept Agr Grad Sch since '40; lecturer physics Georgetown U since '47. Am Chem Soc (councilor Washington sect)—Electrochem Soc—AAAS—Washington Acad Sci—Am Inst Chem(F)—NY Acad Sci(F)—Sigma Xi—Alpha Chi Sigma. National Bureau of Standards, Washington 25.†

15 HAMERMESH, Morton. Neuclear physics. b'15. BS '36 (Coll City NY); PhD '40 (NYU). Research and writing on magnetic scattering of neutrons, scattering resonance neutrons in parafin, neutron polarization and ferromagnetic saturation. Author articles in field. Instr City Coll NY '41, Stanford U '41-43; research asso OSRD Cyclotron Project '42-43, Radio Research Lab Harvard '43-46; asst prof phys NYU '46-47, asso prof '47-48; cons Brookhaven Nat Lab '47-48; sr physicist Argonne Nat Lab since '48. Am Phys Soc(F)—Sigma Xi. Argonne National Laboratory, Box 5207, Chicago 80.

16 HAMERSTROM, Frances. Predation of owls; Management of grouse and prairie chickens. b'07. Student '26-28 (Smith Coll); '31-32 (Game Conservation Inst); BS '34 (Ia State Coll); MS '39 (U Wis). Co-author articles: The Great Horned Owl and Its Prey in North-Central United States (Wildlife Society Award for '41); Daily and Seasonal Movements of Wisconsin Prairie Chickens '49; Ecology of Seasonal Movements of Sharp-tailed Grouse '49, and others. Asst leader grouse research and management project Wis Conservation Dept since '49. Wilson Ornithol Club—Cooper Ornithol Club—Am Soc Mammalogists. Plainfield, Wis.

17 HAMERSTROM, Frederick Nathan, Jr. Vertebrate ecology; Wildlife management and conservation; Grouse. b'09. Student '27-29 (Dartmouth Coll); AB '31 (Harvard); MS—research '32-35 (Ia State Coll); PhD '41—research fellow '38-40 (U Wis). Author articles in field. Curator Edwin S George Reserve Museum Zool U Mich '41-49; with Game div Wisc conserv dept. Am Ornithologists Union (chmn comm for relief of European ornithologists '47-48)—British Ecol Soc—Ecol Soc Am—Wildlife Soc—Wilson Ornithol Club (chmn wildlife conservation commn '41-43, '46-47; asso ed Wilson Bull '42-48). Conservation Dept., Game Division, Plainfield, Wis.†

18 HAMID, George Abou. Circus and Outdoor Amusements. b'98. Ed pub schs. Associated with circuses, amusement parks, piers and fairs as performer and entrepreneur since '20; founder National Showmen's Association. Co-author: Circus '49. Owner George A. Hamid & Son outdoor booking and gen theatrical co. since '24; owner and operator Guilford County Fair Greensboro NC since '37; pres and operator NJ State Fair since '36; owner and operator Steel Pier Atlantic City since '45; and others. Decorated presidential citation for outstanding achievement Lebanon, Horatio Alger award, '48. Steel Pier, Atlantic City.

19 HAMILL, William Henry. Chemical kinetics; Isotopes. b'08. '26-27 (St Bonaventure Coll); BS '30—MS '31 (U Notre Dame); PhD '36 (Columbia). Research on chemical kinetics in heavy water and isotopic exchange '33-36, use of heavy hydrogen in animal metabolism studies '36-38, solubility of acety-

lene, cryogenic recovery of acetylene '38-41, thermodynamics of rubber '42-43, radiation chemistry '42-43, radioactive carbon '46; kinetic studies in allied field of nuclear chemistry, radiation chemistry and photochemistry since '46. Co-holder US patent for recovery of acetylene by a cryogenic method. Author articles in field. Instr chem Fordham U '31-36, asst prof '36-38; asst prof chem U Notre Dame '38-41, asso prof since '41, on leave of absence at Argonne Nat Lab '46, spl assignment with USN for Bikini Survey '47. Am Chem Soc—Sigma Xi. Chemistry Department, University of Notre Dame, Notre Dame, Ind.†

20 HAMILTON, Charles Horace. Social statistics; Population; Rural life; Health economics. b'01. AB '24 (Sc Meth U); MS '25 (Tex A and M Coll); PhD '32 (U NC); student '25 (U Chicago) '30-31 (Harvard). Managing editor Rural Sociology Journal of Rural Sociology Soc since '40; Social Science Research Council fellow '30-31; sec rural sub-committee Governors Commission on Hospital and Medical Care, also chairman statistics and publications sub-committee. Asst rural sociologist Va Poly Inst Blacksburg Va '27-30, NC State Coll Raleigh '31-36; state supervisor rural research FERA and WPA '34-36; economist in rural life Tex Agrl Expt Sta '36-39; sr social scientist bur agrl econs USDA Washington '39-40; head dept rural sociology NC State Coll since '40; on leave as dir sociol research Commn on Hosp Care Chicago '45-46. Am Rural Social Soc—AAUP—Am Sociol Soc—Am Statis Assn—Population Assn Am—So Sociol Soc—Am Pub Health Assn. Box 5428 State College Station, Raleigh, N.C.†Ⓖ

21 HAMILTON, Daniel Edward. Automotive maintenance. b'92. Ed pub schs; spcl subjects '43 (Northwestern Inst Tech). Special studies on mortality of automotive parts; maintenance procedures for military vehicles; safety regulations; operational efficiency in combat. Author articles in field. Automotive maintenance engring specialist Maxwell Motor Co, Chrysler Corp, and Chalmers Motor Co '22-28, Ethyl Gasoline Corp '31-39; head instr ordnance automotive sch '41-43; automotive adv First Air Force Selfridge Field '43-44; automotive engr Office Chief of Ordnance '44-47, dep chief parts mortality and usage br '47-49, automotive maintenance engring specialist since '49. Soc Automotive Engrs—Am Ordnance Assn. Ordnance Tank Automotive Center, 1500 Baird St., Detroit. H: 6980 Bulwer St.

22 HAMILTON, Donald William. Entomology; Insect control. b'06. BS '29 (U Ill Coll Agr). Research on fruit insects, including codling moth Carpocapsa pomonella, Oriental fruit moth Grapholetha molesta, pear psylla Psylla pyricola, insects attacking apples, cherries. Author articles in field. Entomol F Rynveld & Sons NYC '29-30, US dept Agr Bur Entomol and Plant Quarantine Div Fruit Insect Investigations Cornelia Ga '30-33, Orleans Ind '34-36, US Dept Agr Agrl Research Adminstrn Bur Entomol and Plant Quarantine Div Fruit Insect Investigations Poughkeepsie NY '36-49; US Dept Agr Agrl Research Adminstrn Fruit Insect Investigations Vincennes '49-50. Am Assn Econ Entomol. 1237 Washington Ave., Vincennes, Ind.

23 HAMILTON, Holman. Zachary Taylor; Compromise of 1850; Whig party. b'10. BA '32 (Williams Coll). Research in US political and military history with special reference to Zachary Taylor 16 years. Author: Zachary Taylor: Soldier of the Republic '41; also articles in field. Reporter Fort Wayne Journal-Gazette '32-34, editorial writer '35-42, '46, '47-49. Pvt to maj U S Army World War II. Guggenheim fellow '46. 3711 Indiana Av., Fort Wayne 6, Ind.

10 HAMILTON, Joseph. Irrigation agriculture; Oil seed crops. b'06. BS '28 (U Ariz). Author articles in field. With US Dept Agr since '30, work in hort and field crops grown under irrigation Yuma Ariz since '45. AAAS— Am Soc Hort Sci—Potato Assn Am— Fla Hort Soc. P.O. Box 1710, Yuma, Ariz.

11 HAMILTON, Milton Wheaton. History of American newspapers. b'01. AB '24—AM '25 (Syracuse U); PhD '36 (Columbia). Author: The Country Printer, New York 1785-1830 '36; Anti-Masonic Newspapers 1826-1834, a bibliography '40; Adam Ramage and His Presses '42. Prof hist Albright Coll Reading Pa '26-49. Pa Hist Assn— AHA—Miss Valley and New York State Hist Assns—Bibliog Soc Am—Am Inst Graphic Arts—Am Assn State and Local Hist. Albright College, Reading. Pa.

12 HAMILTON, William Baskerville. American history (Federal period, Old South); English constitutional history. b'08. BA '28—MA '31 (U Miss); PhD '38 (Duke U). Research on eighteenth century English history London summers '35, 38, American and English history various US libraries since '28; compiling critical bibliography travel in Southern US 1783-1805; studies on history of Mississippi territory; board editors Journal of Southern History since '46; asistant editor Journal Mississippi History since '39. Author articles: The Southwestern Frontier 1795-1817: An Essay in Social History '44; The Dynamics of Politics in the Mississippi Territory '48; and others. Fellow hist dept Duke U '35-46, instr hist '37-42, asst prof '42-47, asso prof since '47. AHA (com Am legal records)— So Hist Assn—Miss Valley Hist Assn— NC Lit and Hist Assn. Duke University, Durham, N.C.

13 HAMLETT, Iona Cuyler. Mental deficiency; Child guidance (Infancy, pre-school); Primary behavior disorders. b'01. AB '22—AM '23 (U Tex); PhD '34 (Ind U). Psychol Ft Wayne State Sch since '34. Am Psychol Assn (F, clinical and abnormal sect, cons sect, psychol Pub Service sect)—Am Assn Mental Deficiency—Ind Acad Sci —Ind Psychol Assn. 801 East State Blvd., Fort Wayne 1, Ind.

14 HAMMER, Jacob. Classical and medieval Latin; Hellenistic poetry; Political prophecy in England. b'94. AM '22—PhD '26 (Columbia). American correspondent Latomus (Revue d'Etudes Latines) Brussels; American editor Scriptorium (International Review of Manuscript Studies) Brussels. Author: Prolegomena to an Edition of the Panegyricus Messalae '25; A Variant Version of Geoffrey of Monmouth's Historia Regum Britanniae '51. Co-translator: Koerte's Hellenistic Poetry; also articles in field. Instr, later prof Latin Hunter Coll since '26; research prof Inst Advanced Study '44-45. Polish Inst Arts Sci in Am—Am Philol Assn—Am Classical League— Classical Assn Atlantic States—Mod Lang Assn—Medieval Acad Am—NY Classical Club—Société pour le Progrèss des Études Philologiques et Historiquer (Brussels)—Phi Beta Kappa. Guggenheim research fellow '29-30, '31, '38-39; grants Am Council Learned Socs '31-32, '34-35; publication grant Inst Advanced Study, Guggenheim Found. Hunter College, N.Y. H: 2757 Claflin Av., Bronx, NYC 68.

15 HAMMERQUIST, William Lauran. Manganese (Electrolytic). b'05. B ChE '30 (U Minn). Research on corrosion, electro deposition, organic coatings; studies on cathode potential, ore reduction furnaces, electrolyte purification, effect of various factors upon electrolysis, development of analytical procedures. Holds patents relating to electrolytic manganese. Research chem Bell Telephone Labs Inc '30-33; asso ed Steel '35-37; research engr Electro Manganese Knoxville Tenn since '39, head dept research. Electrochem Soc —Alpha Chi Sigma. Electro Manganese Corporation, Knoxville 4, Tenn.

16 HAMMETT, Fredrick Simonds. Growth chemistry. b'85. AB '08 (Tufts Coll); MS '11 (RI State Coll); AM '14 —PhD '15 (Harvard). Research on inverse relation between starch and inorganic phosphorus in living plant cells, inverse relation between human birth weight and postnatal weight increase, growth and m·k factor in human placenta, role of naturally occurring chemical groups in growth, of sulfur groups in cell multiplication; hemopoetic action of germanium dioxide, role of thyroid apparatus in growth. Author: The Nature of Growth '36. Asst prof biochem Winstar Inst Anat Biol '20-27; sci dir Lankenau Hosp Research Inst '27-47, emeritus since '47. AAAS(F)—Am Soc Biol Chem—Am Soc Physiol—Am Soc Zool — Am Genetics Assn—Soc Study Growth and Development (founder, hon life mem)—Phi Beta Kappa Sigma Xi. 493 Commercial St., Provincetown, Mass.

17 HAMMOCK, Earl Garland. Symbolic art of southwestern United States Indians (Ceremonial decorations); Indian culture of the American Southwest. b'96. Special study and painting of decorative pieces using ceremonial motifs of Indians; over fifty art exhibits and lectures in 35 towns and cities; painted two Indian studies for Ford Motor Co Dearborn. Author articles in field. Tech dir Art Assn Colo '38-48. Artists Profl League Am. Eight first awards by popular vote in Art Festival annual exhibits Western State Coll Colo; two first awards by jury Colo Art Assn annual art exhibits '40-45; first and second awards Colo Fed Womens Club State exhibit '38-39. Gunnison, Colo.

18 HAMMOND, Bayard Louis. Genetics and breeding of guayule and root-rubber plants. b'00. AB (Lebanon Valley Coll Pa); PhD (Johns Hopkins). Research asso cytogenetics of oenothera Goucher Coll and Ind U '34-41; charge goldenrod rubber breeding program Bur Plant Industry US Dept Agr Savannah Ga '41-44, charge guayule rubber research project Saltillo Coahuila Mexico '44-46, geneticist US Nat Rubber Research Sta Salinas Calif '46-49; research fellow Calif Inst Tech '50. Bot Soc Am—Genetics Soc Am— Sigma Xi. 1340 First Avenue, Salinas, Calif.

19 HAMMOND, Charles Percy. Rolling mills; Steel metallurgy. b'95. Student (ME) (Temple U) (Drexel Inst) (Carnegie Inst Tech) (Columbia). Development installation and operation mill layouts; research on rolling of tool, alloy, and carbon steel bars. Holds patent on hollow drill section forming in steel. Author articles: Rolling of Alloy Steel; Art of Rolling Rounds; Art of Rolling Hexagon and Octagon; Art of Rolling Flats. Roller advancing to supt mills Crucible Steel Co '25-33; supt mills Atlas Steel Ltd Wellard Ont Can '33-48, Rotary Elec Steel Co since '48. Assn Iron and Steel Engrs. Rotary Electric Steel Co., Det. H: 519 Harmon, Birmingham, Mich.

20 HAMMOND, Datus Miller. Animal parasitology; Protozoology (Morphology, protozoan diseases of turkey, cattle diseases). b'11. BS '32 (Utah State Agrl Coll); MA '34—PhD '36 (U Calif). Author articles in field. Prof, head dept zool Utah State Agrl Coll since '45; collaborator Zool Div Bur Animal Ind USDA since '50. Am Soc Zool—Am Soc Parasitol—Phi Kappa Phi—Phi Beta Kappa—Sigma Xi. Utah State Agricultural College, Logan, Utah.⊙

21 HAMMOND, George Peter. Latin American history; Southwestern United States. b'96. AB '20—AM '21—PhD '24 (U Cal). Traveling fellow Pacific Coast history of Native Sons of Golden West in Spain '22-23; member US delegation to 4th Assembly of Pan-American Institute of Geography and History Caracas '46. Author: Don Juan de Onate and the Founding of New Mexico 27; Coronado's Seven Cities '40. Co-author: (with T C Donnelly) The Story of New Mexico '36; (with E F Goad) The Adventure of Don Francisco Vasquez de Coronado '38, A Scientist on the Trail '48. Translator and editor (with Agapito Rey) The Gallegos Relation of the Rodriguez Expedition to New Mexico '27; Obregon's History of the 16th Century Explorations in Western America '28; Expedition into New Mexico—Made by Antonio de Espejo, 1582-1583 '29; New Mexico in 1602 '38; Narratives of the Coronado Expedition 1540-1542 (with Agapito Rey) '40; Fray Alonso de Benavides' Revised Memorial of 1634 (with F W Hodge and Agapito Rey). Editor with foreword, My Life on the Frontier, 1882-1897 (by M A Otero) '39. Editor Coronado Hist Series since '40; editor county archieves of several counties of New Mexico. Prof history, head dept and dean grad sch U NM '35-46, dean upper div coll arts and scis '35-38, dir Bancroft Library and prof history U Cal Berkeley since '46. Bancroft Library, University of California, Berkeley 4, Cal.⊙

22 HAMMOND, John Hays, Jr. Radio control; Radio engineering, telephony and telegraphy; Musical reproductions. b'88. BS '10 (Sheffield Sci Sch—Yale); ScD '10 (George Washington U). Pioneered radio control moving objects since '10; engaged invention and research on systems for radio control torpedoes, ships, aeroplanes, rockets, aeroplane drone targets, musical developments; contructed privacy telephone communication system Italian government '26, organ with 150 stops embodying many new principles; contributed first practical systems using gyro-stabilization modified by selective radio control; radio-control inventions applied boats and planes in Bikini tests; demonstrated target seeking controls and principles proximity fuse US government '14; US delegate Radio Telegraphic Convention London '12, delegate Radio Conference Washington '27; member advisory board US Naval Board Inventors, advisory committee Langley Aerodynamic Laboratory Smithsonian Institute. Invented aluminothermic incendiary projectiles used World Wars I and II, automobile torpedo firing, hard vacuum tubes (co-operatively), thyratron, intermediate frequency selective receivers used in superheterodyne receivers, uni-control superheterodynes, multiplex, single-side band and privacy telephony systems, selective radar and multiplex radio systems, variable pitch propulsion system for ships, reflector piano, "Pirafon" piano, improved methods phonographic reproduction, pipe organ mechanisms and tonal principles, and others; holder over 800 US and foreign patents, largest number any living inventor. Pres Radio Engring Co NYC since '16, Hammond Research Corp Am since '28; dir and cons engr Radio Corp Am; constructor, curator Hammond Medieval Mus Gloucester since '26. Aero Club Am (gov, mem aerodynamic tech pub safety, map, landing places com)—Am Soc Aeronaut Engrs (vp)—Inst Radio Engrs (past treas)—ASME (hon)—AIEE—Nat Inst Inventors. Hesperus Av., Glucester, Mass.☉

10 **HAMMOND, Lansing Van der Heyden.** Eighteenth century English literature; Laurence Sterne; International education. b'06. PhB '30—PhD '40 (Yale); '34-35 (Harvard U Grad Sch). Author: Laurence Sterne's Sermons of Mr. Yorick '48; also articles in field. Asst prof Eng lit Russell Sage Coll Troy NY '46-47; asso dir div edn Commonwealth Fund since '47. Mod Lang Assn Am. Commonwealth Fund, 41 E. 57, NYC 22. H: Yale Club, Vanderbilt Av.

11 **HAMMOND, Mason.** Roman literature and history. b'03. AB '25 (Harvard U); BA '27—BLitt '30—Rhodes scholar Mass '25 (Oxford U). With military government in Italy and Germany for work in monuments, fine arts and archives (protection, preservation and restitution of works of art, monuments, historical archives and other cultural materials) '43-45. Author: The Augustan Principate '33; The Menaechmi of Plautus (with N Moseley) '33; also articles in field. Instr, later prof Greek, Latin, hist Harvard U since '28, Radcliffe Coll '28-42 Pope prof Latin lang and lit '50; prof in charge classical studies Am Acad in Rome '37-39. Am Philological Assn—AHA—Archaeol Inst Am. Widener Library 575, Harvard University, Cambridge, Mass.

12 **HAMMOND, Merrill Clyde.** Wildlife and waterfowl management. b'12. AB '35 (Brigham Young U). Research dealing with waterfowl, upland game, mammals, marsh management. Author articles in field. Wildlife biol Lower Souris Nat Wild Life Refuge Upham ND since '37. Wildlife Soc—Wilson Ornithol Club—Am Soc Mammalogists —Am Ornithol Union. Lower Souris Refuge, Upham, N.D.†

13 **HAMMOND, Russell Irving.** Educational administration (Methods); Education in Wyoming. b'08. BA '29 (Morningside Coll); MA '34 (U Colo); EdD '42 (Columbia U). Author: Age-grade Practices in Wyoming Schools; Teacher Supply and Demand in Wyoming; also articles in field. Asso prof edn, dir bur ednl research and service U Wyo since '47. NEA—Wyo Edn Assn —Colo Edn Assn—AAUP—ASCD—Phi Delta Kappa. University of Wyoming, Laramie, Wyo.

14 **HAMOR, William Allen.** Industrial research, hygiene, human relations; Professional and public relations of research. b'87. MA '13—DSc (hon) '35 (U Pittsburgh); ScD (hon) '32 (Grove City Pa Coll); DSc (hon) '47 (U Louisville); LLD (hon) '47 (U Miami). Co-inventor of cellulosic food products and of processes of preserving foods and of distilling and plasticizing sulphur; studies on fuels, petroleums and oil-shales of America, chemistry of anesthetics; specialist in professional and public relations of industrial research and in human relations in management. Author: History of Chemistry '09. Co-author: The American Petroleum Industry (2 vols) '16; Examination of Petroleum '20; American Fuels (2 vols) '22; Science in Action '31; Glances at Industrial Research '36; also articles in field. Asst dir Mellon Inst Industrial Research Pittsburgh since '16; lecturer on chem U Pittsburgh since '42; ed adv Nutritional Obs since '40; contbg ed Pitts Quarterly since '39, ed Chem Mono-

graphs Am Chem Soc since '47; mem research adv com Industrial Hygiene Found Am since '42; mem sci personnel com US Atomic Energy Commn since '47. AAAS(F)—Am Inst Chem—Chem Soc London—Am Chem Soc—Pa Chem Soc—Electrochem Soc—Am Mgmt Assn—Am Dairy Sci Assn—Soc Advancement Mgmt—Am Pharm Assn —Hist Sci Soc—Inst Food Tech—Sigma Xi. Mellon Institute, 4400 Fifth Av., Pitts 13.☉

15 **HAMPEL, Clifford A(llen).** Flourides and fluosilicates (Chemistry and uses); Chlorine (Compounds); Natural salts (Recovery); Bleaching of pulp, paper, textiles. b'12. BS (Chem engring) '34 (Minn). Research on inorganic and organic heavy chemicals derived from alkalis and chlorine, methods of production and use of chlorine, inorganic and organic chlorine compounds, sea water evaporation and chemistry, natural salts and their recovery, bleaching pulp, paper, textiles; study separation of salts from heterogeneous solutions. Holds patents in field. Author articles: Fresh Water from the Sea '48; Modern Laundry Practice '48; Sodium Fluosilicate —A Neglected Chemical '49; Densities of Sea Water Concentrates '50. Co-author articles: Chlorine Products '42; (with P W Leppla) Production of Potassium Perchlorate '47. Associate editor: Encyclopedia of Chemical Reactions. Research chem Mathieson Alkali Works Niagara Falls NY '36-42, Diamond Alkali Co Painesville O '42-43, SAM Labs Columbia U '43-44, Minn Mining & Mfg Co St Paul '44-45; asst chief chem Cardox Corp Chicago '45-46; research chem Armour Research Found Chicago '46-48, supervisor inorganic tech '48-49, supervisor extraction metall since '49. ACS—AA AS—Am Inst Chem (F)—Electrochem Soc — Alpha Chi Sigma — Chemists' Club NY. Armour Research Foundation, Chgo 16. H: 18246 Gottschalk Av., Homewood, Ill.

16 **HAMPTON, Burt Laurent.** Terpenes; Resins and resin acids. b'09. BS '34—PhD '37—research scholarship (U Fla). Research on constituents of turpentine; developed new ways to polymerize and stabilize rosin, new resins from terpenes, synthesis of chemotherapeutical derivatives from terpenes, molecular rearrangements in terpene series, chlorination of turpentine; theoretical work on resin acids, organic synthesis, alpha amino ketones and alcohols. Holds 11 patents. Author articles in field. Research chem with G&A Labs '37-41; in charge rosin research Glidden Co Naval Stores Div Jacksonville Fla '41-47; asst research dir Crosby Chemicals Inc De Ridder La. Am Chem Soc—Sigma Xi—Phi Kappa Phi. Crosby Chemicals, Inc., Box 32, De Ridder, La.

17 **HAMPTON, Virginia Taylor.** American railroad and industrial history. b'10. AB '35 (U Cincinnati); certificate '32 (Geneva Sch Internat Relations). Author: The Nickel Plate Road '48; also articles in field. Free lance publicity research and writing since '35. Phi Beta Kappa. 13415 Shaker Blvd., Cleveland 20.†

18 **HANABURGH, David Henry.** Forest appraisals; Forest products (Marketing). b'10. BS (Forestry) '32 (U Me); MF '39 (Yale). Private forest land survey to determine kind, quality, and volume of timber products; analysis of land for purpose timber production; location existing markets for products of forest, and development markets for forest products in low demand. Forest land appraisals US Forest Service '33-38; private cons forester '39-42 and since '46. Soc Am Foresters—Can Pulp and Paper Assn—

Forest Products Research Soc. Buchanan, N.Y.

19 **HANACHE, Jean Elie.** Food chemistry; Food bacteriology; Meat and meat by-products (Technology). b'00. BS '29 (U Miami Fla); '31 (Loyola U); '36 (U Chicago). Research on methods for food spoilage prevention and correction; development of new items; study legal food compliance. Author: Food Industries. Chem in charge Stahl-Meyer '34-38; cons food chem since '38. Inst Food Tech—ACS —Soc Am Bact—Nat Independent Meat Packers Assn. 82-03 165th St., Jamaica 3, N.Y.

20 **HANCE, Robert Theodore.** Mammalian, plant and avian cytology; X-ray effects; Emulsions; Microscopical technique; Histological instrument design. b'92. AB '13—MA '14 (U Cincinnati); PhD '17 (U Pa). Author: The Machines We Are '32. Co-author: Laboratory Experiments in General Zoology '31; also articles in field. Invented (with Harold C O'Brien) a machine tool coolant. Research biol Cincinnati Milling Machine Co since '43. AAAS(F)—Am Soc Zool—Am Micros Soc (first vp for two terms)—Pa Acad Sci (pres '29, ed '39-42). CIMCOOL Division, Cincinnati Milling Machine Company, Cincinnati 9. H: Box 220, R.R. No. 3, Loveland.†

21 **HANCKEL, Robert Champney.** Structural designs. b'94. BS (civil engring) '17 (Worcester Poly Inst). Research on concrete, structural steel and wood designs, precast concrete units for bridges and buildings. Prin designer Thompson and Lichtner Co Inc '44-48; own bus since '48. Am Soc CE—Am Concrete Inst—Mass Soc Prof Engrs—Nat Soc Prof Engrs. 294 Washington St., Boston 8.

22 **HANCOCK, John M.** International control of atomic energy. AB '03—LLD '32 (U ND). Alternate to Bernard M Baruch as US representative on UN Atomic Energy Commission '46. Partner Lehman Bros; chmn exec com or dir various indsl, retail, insurance companies. 1 William St., NYC 4. H: Scarsdale, N.Y.

23 **HAND, Ellsworth Joseph.** Electrical engineering. b'01. BS (EE) '33 (George Washington U). Study foreign and domestic power supplies; utility and power consultant on exports of equipment; advisor specifications for federal procurement, priority, and allocation problems. Sr elec engr defense power staff Fed Power Commn '41-43, sr elec engr elec resources and requirements div '47-48; utility and power cons with US Dept Commerce '48-50, asst dir power equipment div Bur Industry Operations Nat Prodn Authority '50, now dep dir engine and turbine div. Am Inst EE—Theta Tau.

24 **HAND, Harold Curtis.** Secondary school curriculum; Guidance and administration. b'01. BA '24 (Macalester Coll); MA '30 (Minn U); PhD '33 (Columbia); '37-38 (London Sch Econ Polit Sci). Author: What People Think About Their Schools '48; An Appraisal of the Occupations or Life-Career Course '34; Neutrality in Social Education '40; The Role of the Public Junior College in Illinois '47. Co-author: General Education in the American High School '42; Appraising Guidance in Secondary Schools '41; Social Education '39; Guidance in Educational Institutions '38; Designs for Personality '38; Beyond High School '38; School and Life '37; The Challenge of Education '37; The Changing Curriculum '36, and others. Prof edn Ill U since '46; supervisor basic research studies, Ill Secondary Sch Curriculum Program since '47. Am Assn Sch Administrators

—Assn Supervision Curriculum Development—NEA—Nat Soc Study Edn—John Dewey Soc. College of Education, University of Illinois, Urbana, Ill.ⓒ

10 HAND, Wayland D. Folklore of miners. b'07. AB '33—AM '34 (U Utah); PhD '36 (U Chicago). Assistant director Folklore Institute of America '46; associate editor Journal of America Folklore '46, editor since '47. Research on folklore from Utah's silver mining camps '41, California miners' folklore '42, also work in other field American folklore, German folklore, superstitions. Author articles in field. Instr German U Calif '37-42, asst prof '42-46, asso prof since '46. Mod Lang Assn Am—Am Folklore Soc (first vp '45)—SE Folklore Soc US—Calif Folklore Soc—NY Folklore Soc—Philol Assn Pacific Coast (exec com since '48). Winner Chicago Folklore Soc Prize '42. University of California, Los Angeles 24.†

11 HANDLEY, Charles Overton. Wildlife management; Ornithology (Bird banding); Mammalogy. b'97. BS '22 (Washington & Lee U). Research on fish-eating birds, food habits of grebes and bald eagle, and on life history, food habits, breeding, and natural enemies of bob-white quail. Invented chimney swift trap used principally in trapping chimney swifts for banding. Author articles in field. Supt game propagation, in charge game management div Commn Game and Inland Fisheries Va '29-35; biol, leader Va Coop Wildlife Research Unit US Fish and Wildlife Service, cons Commn Game and Inland Fisheries Va, and prof conservation Va Polytech Inst '35-47; Pittman-Robertson coordinator Conservation Commn W Va '47-49; chief Div Game Mgt, Cons Comm since '47. Am Soc Mammalogists—Nat Audubon Soc—Wildlife Management Inst—Am Ornithol Union—Wildlife Soc—Wilson Bird Club—NE Bird Banding Assn—Phi Beta Kappa. Recipient Wildlife Soc award of merit '43. Conservation Commission of West Virginia, Charleston, W. Va. H: 6571 Roosevelt Av.†

12 HANDY, E(dward) S. Craighill. Ethnology (Polynesian, Asiatic); Genethnics; Personality appraisal. b'92. AB '15—AM '16—PhD (anthrop) '20 (Harvard); '28-29 (Sorbonne). Investigation Polynesian religion and ethnology; exploratory research basis phases of Polynesian living, Japan, China, Southeast Asia and India; for a systematic comprehensive technique applicable to biological, ecological, ethnological appraisal of individual persons against background of heredity and in setting of family, society and locale; research and experimentation with Genethnic technique in Virginia and Hawaii. Author monographs and articles in field. Contributor: An Introduction to Unified Science '50. Ethnol Bishop Mus Honolulu TH '20-35, vis prof to Yale '35-37, asso in ethnol since '37; pres Genethnics Inc since '49. Va Acad Sci—Am Anthrop Assn—Am Assn Phys Anthrop—Inst Ethnic Affairs (Washington)—Polynesian Soc (Wellington)—Inst Pacific Relations (Honolulu)—Kern Institut (Leiden). P.O. Box 3685, Honolulu, T.H. H: P.O. Box 57, Oakton, Va.

13 HANDY, George William. Acoustical engineering (Treatment, materials); Gypsum (Manufacturing, chemistry, uses). b'02. BS '26 (U Buffalo). Mgr acoustical div Nat Gypsum Co since '39. Nat Noise Abatement Council (dir)—Acoustical Material Assn (dir)—Acoustical Soc Am. 325 Delaware Av., Buffalo 2.

14 HANES, Leigh (Buckner). Lyric poetry. b'93. BA '16—LittD '36 (Hamp-

den-Sydney Coll); LLB '20—MA '38 (Washington and Lee U). Research on emotional effect of vowel sounds in tonal variations, communication of poetic imagery dependent upon some common ground of actual or vicarious experience, subconscious sources of imagery such as animism, rhythm or empathy, poetry as intuitive synthesis, enrichment of American poetry through preservation of sectional characteristics; editor The Lyric '29-49. Author: Song of New Hercules and Other Poems (2nd edit) '33; Green Girdle '39; The Star That I See '50. Lectr Hollins Coll '32, '33, '36, '37; U Va Ext '39-42; title attorney Peoples Fed Savings and Loan Assn since '42. Poetry Soc Am—Poetry Soc Va (exec bd). Postoffice Box 2552, Roanoke 10, Va.

15 HANEY, John Louis. Bibliography of English literature; Shakespeare; Samuel Taylor Coleridge. b'77. Harrison scholar '98-99—Fellow English '99-12 BS '98—PhD '01 LLD '39 (U Pa). Author: The German Influence on Coleridge '03; Early Reviews on English Poets '04; The Name of William Shakespeare '06; Good English '15; English Literature '20; The Story of Our Literature '23 (rev edit) '39; Shakespeare and Philadelphia '36; others. Editor: Shakespeare's MidSummer Night's Dream '11; Bok's A Dutch Boy Fifth Years After '21; The Boy Who Followed Ben Franklin '24; Barnwell Addresses, 3 vols '31, '37, '43. With Central High Sch Phila '00-43, head English dept '16-20, pres '20-43, ret. Modern Lang Assn—Am Dialect Soc—Authors League Am—Headmasters Assn—Am Philos Soc—Phi Beta Kappa—Pi Gamma Mu. H: 6419 Woodbine Av., Phila 31.†ⓒ

16 HANKE, Lewis Ulysses. History of Latin America. b'05. BS '24—MA '25 (Northwestern U); PhD '36 (Harvard). Mem editorial boards Hispanic-American Review, The Americas; Amherst Memorial Fellow '33, Archibald Cary Coolidge Fellow '34, for research in Spanish archives; Milton Fund of Harvard University grant '35 for research in Bolivian archives; Social Science Research Council Post Doctoral Fellow '38 for research and travel in Latin America. Author: The Struggle for Justice in the Spanish Conquest of America (awarded Albert J Beveridge Memorial Fellowship AHA '47); The First Social Experiments in America '35; Las Teorias Politicas de Bartolome de las Casas '35. Dir Hispanic Found Library Congress since '39. Am Council Learned Socs '48 (sec) —AHA—Academia Nacional de la Historia—Sociedad de Historia Argentina—Academia Colombiana de Historia—Sociedad de Historia y Geografia de Guatemala. Library of Congress, Washington 25.ⓒ

17 HANKS, Jane Richardson (Mrs. Lucien, Jr.). Indians (Blackfoot, Kiowa). b'08. AB '29 (U Cal); PhD '42 (Columbia). Studies in ethnology of Blackfoot and Kiowa Indians. Author: Law and Status among the Kiowa Indians '40. Co-author: (with L M Hanks, Jr) Tribe under Trust '50. H: North Bennington, Vt.

18 HANKS, Lucien Mason, Jr. Indians (Blackfoot); Burma (Sociology). b'10. BA '31 (U Wis); PhD '37 (Columbia). Research on individual differences of culture and personality in certain primitive groups. Co-author: (with Jane R Hanks) Tribe Under Trust '50. Author article: The Quest for Individual Autonomy in Burmese Personality, Psychiatry '49. Co-author articles: (with Jane R Hanks) Observations on Blackfoot Kinship '45; The Physically Handicapped in Certain Non-Occidental Societies '48. Contrib-

utor: Culture and Personality '49. Prof social sci Bennington Coll since '42; psychol OSS '44-45. Am Psychol Assn—Soc Psychol Study Social Issues—Far Eastern Assn—Am Anthrop Assn—Rural Sociol Soc—Sigma Xi. Bennington College, Bennington, Vt. H: North Bennington.

19 HANMER, Hiram Rupert. Tobacco and tobacco smoke; Biology of cigarette smoking; Technology in cigarette and tobacco manufacture. b'96. BS '18 (U Vt); '21-22 (Columbia); '22-23 (Brooklyn Poly Inst). Research on nature of cigarette smoke, volatile bases and acids in cigarette smoke, variation in chemical composition of cured tobacco leaves according to position on stalk, effect of ultraviolet radiation on nicotine. Author articles in field. Dir research Am Tob Co since '32, dir since '38. Chem Soc, London(F)—AAAS(F) —Am Inst Chem(F)—Am Chem Soc (councillor '44-45, chmn Va sect '42-43)—Va Acad Sci (pres '45-46)—So Assn Sci Industry (trustee since '45)—NY Acad Sci—Soc Chem Industry—Tech Assn Pulp Paper Industry. 400 Petersburg Turnpike, Richmond 24, Va.

20 HANN, Gordon E. Glazing and caulking compounds; Masonry waterproofing and dampproofing compounds; Asphalt emulsions. b'10. BS '32 (Case Inst Tech); student (Western Reserve U). Research in gun and tool consistency caulking compounds for buildings, glazing compounds and putties for wood, steel and non-ferrous sash, roof preservatives, asphalt emulsions for industrial floor repairs and waterproofings, waterproofings and dampproofings for masonry buildings including oleo resinous, pigmented oleo resinous, resin solution, wax solution, asphalt cutback, asphalt emulsion; developed one of first elastic glazing compounds for use instead of hard setting putties; high quality non-bleeding caulking compound, a successful technique for application of asphalt emulsion flooring under many industrial conditions. With Tremco Mfg Co Cleveland since '32, dir research since '34, dir mfg Cleveland plant since '40, Toronto plant since '49. Tremco Manufacturing Co., 8701 Kinsman Rd., Cleveland.

21 HANN, Victor Adams. Ozone. b'13. BS '35 (Columbia). Research in the generation of ozone, design and development of ozone generating machines, design of ozone plants and the utilization of ozone; designed and supervised construction and initial operation of world's largest ozone plant; research and writing on ozone treatment of water, water quality improvement with ozone, ozone treatment for the removal of taste, odor and color from water. Engr Bethlehem Steel Co '35-38; research engr Ozone Processes Inc '38-39, supervisor field testing '39-40, dir research '41-46; dir ozone processes div The Welsbach Corp since '46.' 1500 Walnut St., Sixth Floor, Phila. 2.

22 HANNA, Alfred Jackson. Florida and Latin-American history. b'93. AB '17—LHD '45 (Rollins Coll); grad work (U Madrid, U Mexico). Author: Fort Maitland '35; Founding of Rollins College '36; Flight into Oblivion '38; A Prince in Their Midst '46; Introduction to Letters of Don Juan McQueen '43; Bibliography of the Writings of Irving Bacheller '39. Co-author: The St Johns (Rivers of America Series) '43; Recommended Readings on Florida '46; Lake Okeechobee (American Lakes Series) '48; also articles in field. Weddell prof hist Americas Rollins Coll Winter Park Fla since '17, also dir Inter-Am studies since '42. So Hist Assn—AHA—Hispanic Inst Fla (pres '33-40)—Fla Acad

Sci (vp '45)—Fla Audubon Soc (pres '43-47). 235 Sterling Av., Winter Park, Fla.◉

10 HANNA, Kathryn Abbey. American history (Florida). b'95. AB '17—AM '22—PhD '26—fellow '24-26 (Northwestern U); LHD (hon) '47 (Rollins Coll). Author: Florida, Land of Change '41; Lake Okeechobee '48; also articles in field. Asso prof Fla State Coll for Women '26-27, prof since '27, head dept hist geog polit sci '30-41; dir Survey Fed Archives Fla '36-37; prof hist ext div U Fla since '41; lecturer adult edn series Rollins Coll since '42; Fla Acad Sci (chmn social sci sect '41)—AHA—So Hist Assn (dir '34-35 and '39-41)—Fla Hist Soc (vp '36-39 and dir '39-41)—Am Acad Social Sci—Fla Citizens Com Edn (sec since '44)—Am Scholar (mem adv council '41-44)—Journal So Hist (editorial bd '44)—State Library Bd (chmn since '43)—Fla Lib Assn (2d vp since '46)—Phi Beta Kappa (sec So Atlantic dist '40)—Phi Kappa Phi—Phi Alpha Theta (nat vp '38-40). 235 Sterling Av., Winter Park, Fla.

11 HANNA, Lester W. Entomology (Poliomyelitis, insect vectors); Hannaturmycin. b'09. BS (Colo Agrl Coll). Research in growing pyrethrum plants in Colorado; studies and experimental tests with drosophilinae (pomace flies) as possible insect vector carrying poliomyelitis virus; discovered material han-naturmycin; developed new strain of Coypu (South American beaver), produced breeding stock; worked out insect control technique on dendroctonus species of barkbeetles. Developed H M 204 insecticide and fungicide, which can be used successfully on nearly all insect pests, mildews, rusts, blights. Author: Bones of the Golconda; Battling Barkbeetles in Western Farm Life '37; Coypu Fur Farming booklet '42; also articles in field. Served with US Forest Service as special entomol, with Bur Entomol and Plant Quarantine for work in blister rust control; western div entomol Birds Eye-Snyder Div General Foods Corp controlling over 50 detrimental insect pests on 40,000 acres fruits and vegetables in western US. Am Assn Econ Entomol—AAAS. Birds Eye-Snider Division of General Foods Corp., Hillsboro, Ore. H: R No. 1, Forest Grove.

12 HANNA, Paul Lamont. History; Middle East and Palestine (Political policy). b'13. BA '35 (George Washington U); MA '36—PhD '39 (Stanford U). Special research analyst Anglo-American Committee Inquiry on Palestine '46; political adviser US Cabinet Committee on Palestine '46; managing editor Journal of Politics '44-46. Author: British Policy in Palestine '42; also articles in field. Asst prof social sci U Fla '39-44, asso prof '44-46, prof since '46. AHA—So Hist Assn—Middle East Inst—Am Polit Sci Assn—So Polit Sci Assn (treas '44-46). University College, University of Florida, Gainesville, Fla. H: 1021 S.W. 3rd Ave.†

13 HANNAU, Hans Walter. Photography (Color). b'04. PhD '28 (U Vienna). Colorphotography for general advertising; advertising brochures of cities, resorts, hotels; illustration books and magazines. Author: (pictorial book) Florida, A Photographic Journey '48. Pres Natural Color Pubs Inc since '48. 605 Lincoln Rd., Miami Beach 30, Fla.; 948 Madison Av., NYC 21.

14 HANNUM, Alberta Pierson. Southern highland life and people (Smokies and Blue Ridge); Navajo life. b'06. BA '27 (O State U); '28 (Columbia). Author: Thursday April '31; The Hills

Step Lightly '34; The Gods and One '41; The Mountain People in the Great Smokies and the Blue Ridge '43; Spin a Silver Dollar '45; Roseanna McCoy '47 (Italy '48); also articles in field. Moundsville, W.Va.

15 HANNUM, C(lair) A(rthaud). Platyhelminthes (Cestodes and trematodes); Nemathelminthes (Nematodes). b'00. Student '19-21 (Monmouth Coll); BS '23—MS '24—PhD '41 (U Washington). Author: Laboratory Manual of Animal Histology '39, '47; Laboratory Manual in Elementary Zoology '39; Comparative Chordate Anatomy '41; also articles. Instr U Ariz '28-34, asst prof '34-40; acting prof Seattle Coll '41; asso prof U Wichita since '46. Am Micros Soc—Am Soc Parasitol—Am Soc Zool—Phi Sigma—AAAS—Am Soc Profl Biol—Sigma Xi. Department of Zoology, University of Wichita, Wichita 14, Kan.

16 HANSBERRY, (Theodore) Roy. Insecticides. b'10. BS '31—MS '32 (Wash State Coll); PhD '36 (Ia State Coll). Work in development of insecticidal spray oils; research on insecticidal properties of nicotine and related compounds and of Latin American and Chinese plants, toxicology of insecticides, agricultural uses of petroleum chemicals. Author articles in field. Sr chem Shell Petroleum Corp Wood River Ill '36-37, dir agrl lab Modesta Calif since '44; asst, asso prof Cornell Univ '37-44. AAAS—Am Assn Econ Ent. P. O. Box 1531, Modesto, Calif.

17 HANSBROUGH, John Raymond. Forest pathology and management; Mycology; Wood rots. b'03. Marston scholar '24-25—Grand Army Repub fellow '26—PhB '25—AM '26 (Brown U); AA '23 (La Grange Jr Coll); PhD '36 (Yale). Studies of canker diseases of forest trees, heart rots of forest trees in relation to management, significance of defects in aircraft woods, rate of deterioration of killed trees and forest products in service. Author articles in field. With US Dept Agr since '24, sr path since '48. Soc Am Foresters—Mycol Soc Am—Sigma Xi—Phi Beta Kappa. 360 Prospect St., New Haven 11.†

18 HANSBOROUGH, Louis Armstead. Vitamins in embryological development of chick. b'08. BS '28 (Howard U); MS '31 (U Chicago); PhD '38 (Harvard). Author: The Influence of Vitamins on the Development of the Chick '38; also articles in field. Coauthor: Autoradiography Illustrated with P32 in the Chick Embryo '48; Metabolism of P32 in the Presence of Vitamin D in the Early Chick Embryo '49. Asso prof zool Harvard U since '47; prof and head sci dept Fort Valley State Coll Ga '46-47. AAAS—Am Soc Zool—Nat Assn Biol Teachers—Washington Assn Sci—Nat Inst Sci. Department of Zoology, Howard University, Washington 1.

19 HANSELL, Clarence Weston. Radio communication (International); Microwave relay systems. b'98. BS (elec engring) '19 (Purdue U). Research, invention, development and design of Alexanderson alternators, low frequency multiple tuned antennas, high frequency vacuum tube transmitters, highly directional antenna systems for use in international radio communication; use of microwave relay systems for long distance transmission of television, facsimile record communication, telephony and telegraphy. Granted 275 US patents in field. With RCA since '20. Inst Radio Engrs(F)—Am Inst EE(F)—Franklin Inst—AAAS—Electrochem Soc. Received Nat Modern Pioneers joint award Nat Assn Mfrs '40. Radio Corp.

of America, RCA Laboratories Division, Rocky Point, L.I., N.Y.

20 HANSEN, Asael T(anner). Society and culture of modern Yucatan and Mayas; Japanese-Americans. b'03. BS '26 (Utah State Coll); PhD '30 (Univ of Wis). Research field work in Yucatan, Mexico on study of social and cultural change with emphasis on Merida; community analyst on relocation of Japanese ancestry persons; community analyst on study of readjustment of resettled Japanese American evacuees on the Pacific Coast. Author several articles in field. Research field worker Carnegie Instn of Washington '31-34; asst and asso prof Miami Univ Oxford Ohio '35-47; community analyst War Relocation Authority '44-46; asst prof Mich State Coll '47-49; professor Univ of Ala since '51. Am Anthropol Assn(F)—Soc Applied Anthropol—AA AS—Inter-Am Soc Anthropol and Geography—Instituto Indigensia—Am Sociological Soc. Department of Sociology and Anthropology. University of Alabama, Tuscaloosa, Ala.

21 HANSEN, Carl Joseph. Fruit plants (Boron nutrition, propagation). b'04. AB '28 (Stanford U); MS '39 (U Calif). Articles: The Effect of Boron on Deciduous Fruit Trees '45; Boron Content of Olive Leaves '45; (with E R Eggers) Propagation of Fruit Plants '46; and others. Asst in pomol U Calif '31-33, asso '33-42; asso in pomol and asst pomol in expt sta U Calif '42-48, asst prof pomol and asso pomol since '48. Am Soc Hort Sci—Western Soc Soil Sci—Sigma Xi. Division of Pomology, University of California, Davis, Calif. H: 240 A St.

22 HANSEN, Elmer Neil. Dairy cattle (Breeding). b'98. BS '23 (U Minn); MS '25 (Ia State Coll). Author articles in field. Staff dairy husbandry dept Calif State Poly Coll San Luis Obispo Calif since '47. Am Dairy Sci Assn—Am Soc Animal Production—Am Vocational Assn—Calif Agrl Teachers Assn. California State Polytechnic College, San Luis Obispo, Calif.

23 HANSEN, Howard James. Timber engineering and design; Beach erosion; Plywood; Structural engineering; Mechanics. b'09. BS CE '30 (Purdue U); CE '39 (Tulane U). Research on strength of materials, elementary and indeterminate structures, timber and plywood design, theory and design reinforced concrete, masonry and foundations, fluid mechanics, hydraulics, hydrology; design and construction wooden buildings; studies of physical and mechanical properties wood and plywood, wooden roof trusses, plywood beams. Author: A Course in Modern Timber Engineering '41; Southern Pine Manual of Wood Construction '41; Modern Timber Design '48; Plywood Engineering Data '43; Timber Engineers Handbook '48; Beach Erosion Studies in Florida '47; also articles in field. Engr So Pine Assn '37-41; cons engr '41-42; chief research Tech Plywoods '42-43; asso prof civil engring Tex A&M Coll '42-43, '46; asso prof civ engring U Fla '46-47, prof, acting head indsl engring dept '47-50, head structures research dept US Naval Civil Engring and Eval Lab. ASCE (asso, chmn com timber structures structural div)—Am Shore Beach Preservation Assn—Am Soc Engring Edn—Fla Engring Soc. U.S. Naval Civil Engineering Research and Evaluation Lab., Port Hueneme, Cal.◉

24 HANSEN, James Edward. Porcelain enamels. b'98. BS '20 (U Ill). Author: The Technique of Vitreous Enameling '27; The Advanced Technique of Porcelain Enameling '32. Editor: A Manual of Porcelain Enameling '37. With Ferro Enamel Corp Cleveland since '26, mgr Los Angeles plant since '48. Am Ceramic Soc (trustee '40-43, vp '45-46, pres '46-47)—Sigma Xi. 5309 South District Blvd., Los Angeles 22.

10 HANSEN, Niels Sandager. Welding; Bridges (Repair, design). b'14. Student '37-38 (Coyne Elec Sch); '39-43 (U Wis). Design of all welded steel bridge; design new bridges and temporary bridges required during construction; supervision welded repair old bridges and moving to temporary supports. Pres Ruckman and Hansen Inc since '45. Am Welding Soc—Nat Fedn Independent Bus—Kappa Eta Kappa. 3617 Leo Rd., Fort Wayne 8, Ind.

11 HANSER, Hugo E. Exploitation of natural resources; Design and construction industrial plants, public utilities, public works, and transportation systems. b'89. BS '11—CE '36 (U Nev); LLB '13 (Lincoln-Jefferson U Ind); MAdE '44—MBA '45—MPA '46—AM '47 (NYU). Consultant production, transportation and marketing problems of natural resources; consultant industrial economics and administrative engineering. Author: Transit Unification and the Credit of the City of New York '35; Transportation Needs of South Korea '48; Sources and Aspects of Canadian Administrative Law '46. Contributor: Wage Incentive Methods '42. Sundry engring activities '13-19; development engr Barrett Div Allied Chem Dye Corp '19-22 and '30; dep supt industries State NY '26-28; econ and cons engr Gertler & Co Inc '32-37; engr-accountant NY Bd Transportation '40-51; statis econ and indsl cons USA Mil Govt in Korea (USAMGIK) '48; mem Sandberg & Co cons since 1941. AIM ME—S Bar Nev—Sigma Xi. Admitted to Nevada Bar '13; Reg prof engr Pa '22. H: 277 Eastern Parkway, Bklyn 16.

12 HANSING, Earl Dahl. Plant pathology and breeding; Mycology. b'08. Special studies in cereal smuts, cereal and forage crop diseases, potato yellow dwarf; research on influence of environmental conditions at planting time on sorghum kernel smut infection; reactions of oat varieties and selections to four races of loose smut; viability and seed treatment of flax; reaction of varieties, selections, inbred lines and hybrids to black-stem of alfalfa. Author articles in field. Prof plant path Kan State Coll since '47; plant path Kan Agrl Expt Sta since '47; collaborator Bur Plant Industry US Dept Agr since '40. Am Phytopathol Soc—Potato Assn Am—Am Soc Agron—Kan Acad Sci—Sigma Xi—Gamma Sigma Delta. Department of Botany and Plant Pathology, Kansas State College, Manhattan, Kan.

13 HANSON, Clarence Herman. Breeding of alfalfa and lespedeza. b '13. BS '40 (U Minn); MA '42 (U Mo). Development productive, disease resistant varieties alfalfa and lespedeza for Southeastern US; basic studies on reproductive morphology and cytology of lespedeza. Author article: Cleistogamy and the Development of the Embryo Sac in Lespedeza stipulacea '43. Agron div forage crops and diseases BPISAE since '41. Am Soc Agron—Sigma Xi. Agronomy Department, North Carolina State College, Raleigh, N.C.

14 HANSON, Earl Parker. Regional planning; Latin America; The Tropics. b'99. BS '22 (Wis U); '33 (Chicago U). Exploratory research Iceland '27; made expedition to Amazon and Orinoco basins for Carnegie Institute

Washington to study fluctuations of earth's magnetic field '31-33; research in subarctic Canada '29. Author: Journey to Manaos '38; Highroad to Adventure '41; Chile, Land of Progress '41; Stefansson, Prophet of the North '41. Editor: New World Guides to Latin America '47; Index to Millionth Map of Hispanic America '42 '43. Research tech Nat Resources Com '34-35; planning cons and mem exec bd PR Reconstruction Admnstrn San Juan PR '35-36; cons OQMG US Army on clothing and equipment for jungle warfare '42-44; cons US Army Air Force '44; special rep Fgn Econ Adminstrn in Liberia, special asst US Minister Liberia and special agent US Commercial Co '44-46; cons research and development bd since '47; adv and mem US Army Engrs expedition to Rio Orinoco and Rio Negro '43; chmn dept geog U Del since '49. Assn Am Geog—NY Acad Sci—Am Geog Soc(F). Knight Official Liberian Humane Order of African Redemption '46. University of Delaware, Newark, Delaware.

15 HANSON, Earle William. Plant diseases (Forage and cereal crops, wheat, rubber plants). b'10. BS '33—MS '39—PhD '42 (U Minn). Studies on parasitism and physiologic specialization in Fomes lignosus, on cytology of Urocystis waldsteiniae, on certain insects in relation to root rot and basal stem rot of cereals and grasses, on effect of fertilizers on development of bunt of wheat, on effect of bunt on development of seedling blight, etc. Author articles in field. Path div cereal crops and diseases Bur Plant Ind US Dept Agr '37-46, div forage crops and diseases since '46. Am Phytopath Soc—Minn Acad Sci—Sigma Xi—Gamma Sigma Delta. Department of Plant Pathology, University of Wisconsin, Madison 6, Wis.

16 HANSON, Herbert C(hristian). Grassland ecology; Grasslands of America; Ecology of Alaska. b'90. AB '14 (U Minn); AM '16—PhD '25 (U Neb). Author articles in field. Agrl specialist UNRRA Washington, chief div agr Czechoslovak mission UNRRA Prague '45-47; vis prof plant ecol Catholic U Am Washington since '48. AAAS(F)—Ecol Soc Am (pres '38)—Am Soc Agron—Brit Grassland Soc—Czechoslovak Acad Agrl—Sigma Xi. Department of Biology, Catholic University of America, Washington 17.†

17 HANUS, Francis. Church history. b'08. Grad '29 (Humboldt Coll, Berlin)—'33 (Munich U, Germany)—'35 (Breslau U, Germany)—'43 (Catholic U Am). Research Columbia University '39-42, Catholic University America '42-43; independent research historian since '43, Paris, Fribourg (Switzerland), Rome, London, Berlin, Zurich. Editor: Texts, Documents and Studies in Medieval and Modern Church History: No I, Church and State in Silesia under Frederick II, 1740-1786 '44, No II, Die Aeltere Geschichte der Zisterzienser, Abtei Leubus in Schlesien bis zur Mitte des 14 Jahrhunderts '47. Prof Liceo aleman Concepcion Chile '35-39, Colegio aleman de Santiago, Los Guindos, and Colegio de Santiago, Los Leones, Chile '37-39; sec gen Liga de los Alemanes Catolicos de America del Sur, Buenos Aires '39. AHA—Am Acad Polit Social Sci—Am Catholic Hist Assn—Mediaeval Acad Am—Am Soc Church Hist—Canon Law Soc. Brookland Station, Box 4442, Washington 17, D.C. H: 5003 13th St., N.E., Washington 17.

18 HAPPEL, John. Petroleum chemicals (Butadiene, ethylene, acetylene). b'98. BS '29—MS '30 (MIT); DChE '48 (Poly Inst Brooklyn). Member petro-

leum industry war council; member technical committee in charge construction and operation world's largest butadiene plant for synthetic rubber '42-47; consultant on petrochemicals. With Socony Vacuum Oil Co various tech capacities '30-48; prof chem engring NYU, chmn chem engring dept since '49. Am Inst Chemists(F)—Am Chem Soc—Am Inst Chem Engrs—Sigma Xi—Alpha Chi Sigma—Phi Lambda Upsilon—Tau Beta Pi. New York University, University Heights, NYC 53.†⊙

19 HARA, Hatsuji James. Otology; Rhinology; Laryngology. b'88. Student '08-12 (Walla Walla Coll); MD '18 (Coll Med Evangelists); MS '28—DSc '34 (Pa U); PhD '35 (Hokkaido Imperial Univ). Made comparative study of pollen air contents of cities of Tokyo, Kobe and Sapporo, Japan, and Los Angeles, made clinical observation that average of 5 years in women and 10 years in men are required before immigrant Japanese in US develop hayfever, a disease unknown in Japan; associate editor Journal Medical Arts and Sciences since '47. Author article: Hayfever Among the Japanese in the United States, and others. Clinical prof otolaryngology Coll Med Evangelists since '39, dir Div Otolaryngology Grad Sch since '47. Awarded Research Prize, Calif Med Assn '30. 436 S. Boyle Av., Los Angeles 33.

20 HARBAGE, Alfred Bennett. Shakespeare; Cavalier drama; Elizabethan drama. b'01. AB '24—MA '26—PhD '29 (U Pa). American delegate Shakespeare Conference England '47. Member Editorial Board PMLA. Author: Thomas Killigrew '29; Sir William Davenant '35; Cavalier Drama '36; Annals of English Drama '40; Shakespeare's Audience '41; As They Liked It: On Shakespeare and Morality '47. Instr Eng later prof and grad chmn dept U Pa '24-47; prof Eng and comparative lit Columbia U since '47. Modern Lang Assn (ed bd)—Modern Humanities Assn—Phi Beta Kappa. Columbia University, NYC 27.

21 HARBER, William Irving. Organic products; Synthetic rubber; Cosmetics; Vegetable, tall and sulfonated oils; Organic, rubber and aliphatic chemicals; Fatty acids and amines; Factice; Metal soaps; Flavors; Chewing gum. b'15. AB '36 (Brooklyn Coll); PhD '40 (Ia State Coll). Author articles in field. Dir Research and Develop Corp since '49. Am Inst Chem(F)—Am Chem Soc—Ia Acad Sci. 21 E. Van Buren St., Chgo 5.

22 HARBERT, Lloyd. Vapor phase cooling and waste heat recovery. b'95. Granted three US patents on high temperature cooling of internal combustion engines, or vapor phase cooling. Pres Engineering Controls Inc since '32. 2835 East 11th St., Los Angeles 23.

23 HARCOURT, George Alan. Metallurgy of nickel and copper; Flotation of nickel and copper ore. b'05. BS '30 (U Alberta); MS '32—Royal Soc Can scholarship '33-34 (Queen's U); Scholarship '34-35—PhD '36 (Harvard). Research on miner constituents igneous rocks, x-ray powder patterns ore minerals, improvements in flotation of nickel copper ores, co-inventor method to separate nickel from copper in smelter products by slow cooling to promote crystal growth followed by flotation. Granted patents in field. Research engr Internat Nickel Co of Can since '37, now asst to gen mgr. Can Inst Mining and Metall—AIMME—Am Mineral Soc—Sigma Xi. Nat Research Council bursary '31-32 and studentship '32-33; award of Prof Engrs Alberta '30. International Nickel Co. of Canada, Copper Cliff, Ont.

10 HARD, Walter. Vermont history and folklore. b'82. Student '94-00 (Burr and Burton Sem Manchester); '00-03 —AM hon '33 (Williams Coll). Author: Some Vermonters '28; Salt of Vermont '31; A Mountain Township '33; Vermont Vintage '37; Vermont Valley; Walter Hard's Vermont '41; The Connecticut (Rivers of America Series) '47. Co-author: (with Margaret Hard); This is Vermont '36. Contbr column Manchester Jour, Rutland Herald. Vt state senator '36-37, '41-43, '45; village trustee; trustee Mark Skinner Library; pres bd Burr and Burton Sem. So Vt Artists(dir)—Vt League of Writers— Vt Hist Soc—Delta Upsilon. Manchester, Vt.

11 HARDEN, Milton Jones. Photogrammetry. b'95. Student '23-25 (Mo Sch Mines and Metall); BS (Civil engring) '26 (U Mo). Research in form line delineation on aerial photographs; research and application aerial photographs to stereoscopic principle map production by use Multiplex aeroprojector. Author artcles: Photo image points and their measurement with the Gaertner comparator; and others. Asst engr Brock and Weymouth Inc Phila '27-28; topographic engr US Geol Survey '28-46, photogrammetric engr since '49. Am Soc CE—Am Soc Photogrammetry—Am Congress on Surveying and Mapping —Mo Soc Profl Engrs. US Geological Survey, Rolla, Mo.

12 HARDESTY, John Oliver. Granulation and ammoniation of fertilizers. b'99. AB '24 (DePauw U); MS '28 (Mich State Coll); '31-33 (US Dept Agr Grad Sch). Chemical research on preparation and properties of fertilizer materials and mixed fertilizers. Holds patents covering various process methods of commercial fertilizers. Author articles in field. Asst chem Bur Chem and Soils '30-37, asso chem '38-43, chem Bur Plant Industry Soils and Agrl Engring US Dept Agr since '43. Am Chem Soc—Assn Official Agrl Chem—Sigma Xi. Division of Fertilizer and Agricultural Lime, Bureau of Plant Industry Station, Beltsville, Md.†

13 HARDGROVE, Ralph M(artin). Fuels. b'91. ME '14 (O State U). Holder over 100 patents on meters, automatic controls, pulverizers, furnaces, boilers such as cyclone furnace, pebble heater. Author articles in field. Research consultant Babcock & Wilcox Co Alliance Lab since '48. ASME— Sigma Xi. Babcock & Wilcox Co., Box 835, Alliance, O.†

14 HARDIN, Clifford M(orris). Agricultural economics. b'15. BS '37—MS '39—PhD '41 (Purdue U); student '39-40 (U Chicago). Farm Foundation fellow U Chicago '39-40; US delegate to International Conference Agricultural Economists England '47. Author articles on agricultural marketing. Asso prof agrl econs Mich State Coll '44-46, prof and chmn agrl econs dept '46-48, asst dir agrl expt sta '49, dir since '49. Am Farm Econ Assn—Western Farm Econ Assn—Indian Soc Agrl Econs—Am Country Life Assn—Sigma Xi—Alpha Zeta. School of Agriculture, Michigan State College, East Lansing, Mich.◉

15 HARDING, Harold Friend. Rhetoric; Speech. b'03. AB '25 (Hamilton Coll); AM '29—PhD '37 (Cornell U); post-war fellowship in the humanities '46 (Rockefeller Found). Author articles in field. Prof speech O State U since '46; cons instr training sect Command & Gen Staff Coll Ft Leavenworth Kan since '47; lectr Army War Coll '50; editor Quarterly Jour of Speech '48-51. AAAS—Internat Phonetic Assn — Modern Lang Assn —

Speech Assn Am. 1699 Essex Rd., Columbus 12, O.†

16 HARDING, Lowry Waring. Education (Reading, adult illiterates, literacy training); Attitudes and values; Educational psychology; Testing. b'07. BA '29 (Lynchburg Coll); MA '35 (U Va); PhD '41 (O State U). Devised technique and assisted in developing tests for selection of school administrators for Cincinnati; conducted elementary school sections of comprehensive school surveys in Ohio and New York; author six books for use in Armed Forces concerning literacy development. A u t h o r: Arithmetic Through Experience '43; Arithmetic In Action '43; also articles in field. Professor dept edn O State U since '50. AAAS—Assn Supervision and Curriculum—Assn Childhood Edn— Nat Soc Coll Teachers Edn—O Edn Assn—NEA. Department of Education, Ohio State University, Columbus 1, O.

17 HARDING, Samuel William. Physical optics. b'15. BS '39 (Utah State Agrl Coll); MS '42—PhD '47 (Pa State Coll). Studies on resolving power of optical instruments. Co-author articles: A Method for Making Precise Resolution Measurements '47; The Loss in Resolving Power Caused by Primary Astigmatism, Coma, and Spherical Aberration in Telescopic Systems '48; Coefficient of Specific Resolution of the Human Eye for Foucault Test Objects Viewed Through Circular Apertures '49; Influence of Magnification on Resolving Power of Telescopic Systems for Foucault Test Objects of Different Inherent Contrast '49. Asst prof physics U Wyo '47-50, asso prof since '50; research physicist Optical Research Lab U Tex summer '48, cons '48-51. APS—Optical Soc Am —Colo-Wyo Acad Sci—Am Assn Physics Teachers—Sigma Xi—Phi Kappa Phi—Sigma Pi Sigma. Physics Department, University of Wyoming, Laramie, Wyo.

18 HARDING, T. Swann. Rare sugars; Carbohydrates; Nutrition; Agricultural history and social implications of natural science advances. b'90. BS '10 (Md Agrl Coll). Author: Degradation of Science '31; The Popular Practice of Fraud '45, Two Blades of Grass '47, and others. Free lance writer with US Dept of Agrl since '10, now Information Specialist. Am Chem Soc—AAAS. Division of Special Reports, Office of Information, Department of Agriculture, Washington 25.

19 HARDING, William Harry. Paper chemicals; Pulp mill by-products. b'03. BS '23 (MIT). Holder several patents on paper chemicals. Author articles in field. Dir Tech Service and Development Div Am Cyanamid Co since '42. Tech Assn Pulp and Paper Ind— Soc Chem Ind—Am Chem Soc—Am Inst Chem Engr—Am Inst Chem. American Cyanamid Co., 1937 W. Main St., Stamford, Conn.†

20 HARDINGE, Harlowe. Pulverizing and grinding systems; Separations (Ores and materials). b'94. ME '16 (Cornell). Research on grinding and pulverizing mills and systems for treating ores, cement, coal, ceramics, chemical and industrial materials; granted patents and developed equipment for liquid solids separation, apparatus and systems, developed equipment for making particle size separations by use of air or water, developed heavy media separator to separate light from heavy materials. Contributor: Taggart's Handbook of Mineral Dressing '45; Non-Ferrous Metallurgy '45; Plant Engineering '50. Pres Hardinge Co Inc and Hardinge Mfg Co

since '39. AIMME—Mining and Met Soc—Am Ceramic Soc—Canadian Inst Mining and Metall—Sigma Xi. Hardinge Co., Inc., 240 Arch St., York, Pa.

21 HARDWICKE, Robert Etter. Oil and gas (Law, conservation). b'89. LLB '11 (U Tex); student (Va Mil Inst). Specialized in law of oil and gas since '11; Texas representative on legal committee Interstate Oil Compact Commission '39-48. Author books: Petroleum and Natural Gas Bibliography '37; Antitrust Laws, et al. v. Unit Operation of Oil or Gas Pools '48. Author articles: Penalties as Affected by Good Faith Litigation '34; The Rule of Capture and its Implication as Applied to Oil and Gas '35; The Tidelands and Oil '49. Co-author: The Constitution and the Continental Shelf '48. Contributor: Legal History of Conservation of Oil and Gas, A Symposium, '39; Conservation of Oil and Gas, A Legal History—1948 '48; First Annual Institute on Oil and Gas Law '49. Assisted atty gen of Tex on oil and gas conservation litigation '30-34; asso, advancing to chief, counsel Petroleum Adminstrn for War '43-46; lectr govtl regulation oil prodn Sch Law So Methodist U '51. Am Law Inst —Am Bar Assn (chmn sect mineral law '39-40)—Tex Bar Assn (chmn sect mineral law '50-51)—Am Petroleum Inst—AIMME—Independent Petroleum Assn Am—Phi Delta Phi. Hardwicke & Hardwicke, 1214 Sinclair Bldg., Ft. Worth 2.

22 HARDY, Arthur C. Optics; Spectrophotometry; Color reproduction. b'95. AB '17—AM '19 (U Calif); ScD '38 (St Lawrence U). Inventor recording spectrophotometer. Author articles in field. Prof optics and photography MIT since '33. Optical Soc Am (life mem, pres '35-37, sec since '40)— Am Phys Soc (F)—Am Acad Arts Sci —Soc Motion Picture Engrs—Sigma Xi. 15 Kenilworth Rd., Wellesley, Mass.

23 HARDY, Cecil Ross. Ecology of desert vertebrates; Taxonomy of Rodentia; Desert tortoise; Conservation. b'08. BS '33—MS '38 (Utah U); PhD '43 (Mich U). Research on ecology of birds of pinon-juniper areas of eastern Utah, relationships between distribution of plants and small mammals and soils of southwestern Utah, ecology and life history of desert tortoise (Gopherus agassizii), bats, birds of southwestern Utah, ecology of desert bighorn sheep; made observations on status of big game herds in southern Utah. Author articles in field. Head biol dept Dixie Jr Coll '38-46, Weber Coll '46-49; professor biology Long Beach State Coll since '49. Wildlife Soc—Am Ornithol Union—Cooper Ornithol Club—Wilson Ornithol Club—Am Soc Ichthyologists Herpetologists (past western div vp)—Ecol Soc Am— Herpetologists League (charter)—U Acad Sci Arts Letters (life, F, exec council '48-50, chmn conservation com)—Western Soc Naturalists—Sigma Xi. 5400 E Anaheim Blvd., Long Beach 4, Cal.†

24 HARDY, John Ira. Wool and animal fibres. b'88. BS '10 (Rhode Island State Coll); MS '15 (U Tenn); PhD '17 (U Mo). Research on relation of nutrition to production of hides and wool, types of fur fibers, feather coloring, tests for wool fineness and shrinkage, and wool blends. Holds patents in field. Co-author: (with T M Plitt) Feathers from Domestic and Wild Fowl '49. With Bur Animal Ind Dept of Agr since '23 as dir research on wool, mohair, furs and other animal fibers. AAAS — Sigma Xi. USDA Distinguished Service Honor Award '48. Agricultural Research Center, Beltsville, Md.†

10 HARDY, Thora Marggraff Plitt. Microscopy; Fibers (Plant and animal, especially fur). b'02. BA '25 (Barnard Coll); PhD '32 (U Chicago). Directed research of US government Fur Fiber Laboratory, developed microscopic and macroscopic methods of analyzing furs in order to establish objective criteria for judging quality of furs, to relate findings to physiology and genetics of fur animals in cooperation with experiment stations and other agencies to promote production of better quality of furs, and to relate findings to conservation practices as applied to wild fur animals. Author articles in field. With Dept Interior '39-46, US Dept Agr since '38. Sigma Xi —Am Soc Plant Physiol (life). U.S. Department of Agriculture, Production and Marketing Administration, Grain Branch, Agriculture Research Center, Beltsville, Md.

11 HARE, Mary Louise Eckles (Mrs. W. W. Hare). Begonias (Cytology, genetics). BS '36 (Miss State Coll for Women); MS '38—PhD '42—Alumni research fellow '39-41 (U Wis). Research in cytology chromosome counts especially in Begonia. Author articles in field. Research asso dept plant pathol U Wis in '43. Bot Soc Am—Sigma Xi. Box 125, State College, Miss.

12 HARE, Robert Converse. Hydroponics; Selenium in plants; Greenhouse flowers growth (Chrysanthemum). b'16. BS—MS '40 (U Akron); '40-41 (State Coll Wash). Plant physiol Yoder Bros Inc since '46. Yoder Brothers, Inc., Barberton, O.†

13 HARE, Weston Andrew. Synthetic fibers. b'08. BSc '29 (U Akron); PhD '32 (O State U). Research chem E I duPont de Nemours & Co '38-43, research group leader since '43. Am Chem Soc—Sigma Xi. E. I. duPont de Nemours & Co., Waynesboro, Va. H: 1041 Lyndhurst Rd.

14 HARE, Woodrow Wilson. Vegetable diseases and crop breeding (Peas, peppers). b'15. AA '34 (E Miss Jr Coll); BS '37—MS '40 (Miss State Coll); PhD '43 (U Wis). Asso prof plant path Miss State Coll Agrl Expt Station since '48. Am Phytopath Soc —Am Soc Agron—AAAS—Sigma Xi. Box 125, State College, Miss.†

15 HARGER, Rolla Neil. Toxicology (Poisons, alcohol, ether); Forensic chemistry; Chemical tests for alcoholism. b'90. AB '15 (Washburn Coll); AM '17 (Kan U); PhD '22—Nat Research Council fellow '20-22 (Yale). Inventor Drunkometer for testing intoxication '31; consultant and expert witness in many notable cases, including Indianapolis lead epidemic '40-45, mineral oil popcorn '45, Cline wives' ashes '46, Dupont, Indiana mercury cases '46-47, Kaadt diabetic "cure" '48. Chmn enforcement com Indianapolis Safety Council since '41; chmn dept biochem and toxicol Sch Med Ind U since '33; lecturer on chem tests for intoxication before various regional conferences of traffic court judges and prosecutors and at Northwestern U Traffic Inst since '44. Am Chem Soc—Am Soc Biol Chem—Ind Chem Soc—AAAS—Sigma Xi. Indiana University School of Medicine, Indianapolis 7.◎

16 HARGREAVES, Mary Wilma Massey. History of dry farming; Campbell system; Agricultural history of Montana, North Dakota, South Dakota. b'14. AB '35 (Bucknell U); MA '36 (Radcliffe). Author articles in field. Research asst in charge Kress Collection on early econ hist Harvard Business Sch Library '37-39; fellow Brookings Inst Washington '39-40.

Agrl Hist Soc—AHA. 212 W. Maxwell St., Lexington, Ky.†

17 HARING, Douglas G(ilbert). Anthropology of eastern Asia; Japanese civilization, culture and personality patterns; Shinto religion; Racial differences. b'94. BS '14 (Colgate U); BD '23 (Rochester Theological Sem); AM '23 (Columbia); 3 yr diploma '25 (Sch Japanese Lang & Culture Tokyo). Seven years teacher in Japan; relief and reconstruction after earthquake of '23. Author: The Land of Gods and Earthquakes '29; Blood on the Rising Sun '43. Co-author: Order and Possibility in Social Life '40; Editor and Joint author: Japan's Prospect '46. Compiler: Personal Character and Cultural Milieu '49; also articles in field. With Syracuse U since '27, prof anthropology since '46. Asiatic Soc Japan—Am Anthrop Assn(F). Maxwell Hall, Syracuse University, Syracuse 10, N.Y.†

18 HARING, Inez M. Mosses (Arizona, Grand Canyon National Park, water relations of cell walls determining distribution, spore germination). b'75. BL '98—MA '99 (Western Reserve U); MA '34 (Vassar Coll); '30 (Cleveland Sch Art). Collected and started an herbarium of mosses of Grand Canyon Arizona '40, at and for Grand Canyon Museum at Park; collected and started an herbarium of mosses of Arizona for University of Arizona '46; received mosses collected by Robert A Bartlett Greenland Expedition for determination and given to Vassar College '40. Author articles in field. Engaged since '40 in reclassifying entire herbarium around 200,000 specimens for NY Bot Garden NYC; asst hon curator mosses NY Bot Garden. Torrey Bot Club—Am Bryological Soc—Sigma Delta Epsilon. Vassar College, Poughkeepsie, N.Y.

19 HARING, Malcolm Morrison. Electrochemistry; Radiochemistry; Thermodynamics; Powder and explosives. b'94. BA '15 (Franklin & Marshall Coll); MA '16 (Princeton U); PhD '24 (Columbia). Author articles in field. Prof chem Lebanon Valley Coll '19-21; prof phys chem U Md '23-46; lab dir Dayton project US Atomic Energy Commn, Monsanto Chem Co Dayton since '46. Am Chem Soc—Electrochem Soc—Washington Acad Sci—Phi Beta Kappa—Sigma Xi—Phi Lambda Upsilon. Mound Laboratory, Miamisburg, O.†

20 HARK, Ann. Pennsylvania Dutch Custom and Cookery. Grad (Moravian Sem & Coll for Women Pa). Author: Hex Marks the Spot '38; The Story of the Pennsylvania Dutch '43; Blue Hills and Red Barns '52; The Seminary's Secret '36; Sugar Mill House '37; Island Treasure '38; The Phantom of the Forest '39. Co-author: Pennsylvania German Cookery '50. Lecturer since '38. H: 524 Locust Av., Phila. 44.

21 HARKER, David. Crystallography. b'06. BS '28 (U Cal); PhD '36 (Cal Inst Tech). Research on x-ray diffraction and crystal structure; chief Am delegation to International Congress on X-Ray Crystallography London '46. Asso research lab Gen Elec Co Schenectady '41-49, head crystallography div '49-50; dir The Protein Structure Project, Polytech Inst Brooklyn since '50; mem US nat com on crystallography Nat Research Council since '48. Am Soc X-ray and Electron Diffraction (pres '46)—Crystallographic Soc Am—Am Crystallographic Assn—Am Phys Soc—Am Inst ME—Societe Francaise de Mineralogie et de Crystallographie—Sigma Xi—Phi Lambda Upsilon. The Protein Structure Project, 55 Johnston St., Bklyn 1.◎

22 HARKINS, H. Drake. Power engineering (Industrial). b'93. Student ME (U Mo). Studies on co-operation between industrials and public utilities in generation of steam and electricity; developed and applied special techniques for controlling power consumption in large industrial plants thru performance standard system; research of basic economies of large industrial power investment and operating cost control. Author articles in field. Design engr Gulf Refining Co Port Arthur Tex '23-24; power design and application engr Youngstown Sheet and Tube Co '16-23; power design engr, dir consultants, mgr indsl engring div, supervisor engr, power, E I duPont de Nemours and Co Inc since '24. ASME (chmn power div exec com '47). Nemours Building, Wilmington 98, Del.

23 HARLAN, Mabel Margaret. Spanish literature. b'92. AB cum laude '14 (Colo Coll); AM '22—PhD '27 (Ind U); '25-27 (Universidad Central Madrid). Author articles in field. Spanish faculty Ind U since '20. Modern Lang Assn—Hispanic Inst—Internat Inst Girls in Spain—Am Assn Teachers Spanish—Phi Beta Kappa. Indiana University, Bloomington, Ind.†

24 HARLAN, William Robert. Tobacco chemistry and technology; Nicotine. b'04. BS '25 (NM A&M); PhD '29 (Ia State Coll). Author articles in field. Research chem Am Tobacco Co since '30, asst dir research since '36. AAAS(F)—Am Inst Chem(F)—Am Chem Soc (councillor, past chmn Va sect)—Va Acad Sci—So Assn Sci Industry. 400 Petersburg Turnpike, Richmond 24, Va.†

25 HARLAND, James Penrose. Bronze Age of Greece; Aegean archeology; Hellenic alphabet; Sodom and Gomorrah. b'91. AB '13—AM '15—PhD '20, as of '17 (Princeton U); '13-14 (U at Bonn, Am Sch, Athens); Fellow Archeol Inst '20-21, Guggenheim fellow '26-27 (Am Sch, Athens); archeol study '39 (Greece and U Uppsala, Sweden). Excavated at Nemea, Zygouries and other sites. Author: Prehistoric Aigina '25; The Peloponnesos in the Bronze Age '23. Contbg editor Am Jour of Archaeology; author articles in field. Archeol Inst Am (recorder '46-47, lecturer)—Am Schs Oriental Research—Am Philol Assn— Phi Beta Kappa. University of North Carolina, Chapel Hill, N.C.◎

26 HARLEY, Clayton Price. Tree fruits (Apples, pears). b'96. BS '23—MS '24—grad student '24-26, '30-32 (U Md). Research in physiological disorders of apples and pears, blossom-bud initiation in the apple, fruit tree nutrition, and lime-induced chlorosis '26-45, on nutrition of apples trees, hormone sprays to prevent fruit drop since '45. Author articles in field. Physiol Bur Plant Ind US Dept Agr, Wenatchee, Wash '26-45; sr physiol Bur Plant Industry Soils and Agrl Engring US Dept Agr Beltsville Md since '45. Am Soc Plant Physiol—AAAS—Am Soc Hort Sci—Sigma Xi. Bureau of Plant Industry, Beltsville, Md.

27 HARLEY, George Way. Anthropology (Native tribes of Liberia). b'94. AB '16 (Trinity Coll Durham NC); MD '23 (Yale); diploma tropical med and hygiene '25 (London Sch Tropical Med and Hygiene); PhD '38 (Hartford Sem Found). Author: Native African Medicine '41. Editor, contributor: Tribes of the Liberian Hinterland '47. Supt Ganta Mission Ganta Liberia since '26; research asso in anthrop Peabody Mus Harvard U since '32. Royal Soc Tropical Med Hygiene(F)— Royal Geog Soc(F)—Am Geog Soc NY(F)—Phi Beta Kappa. c/o Methodist Board of Missions, 150 Fifth Av., NYC.

10 HARLEY, John Eugene. International organization (League of Nations and United Nations); Motion picture censorship (Worldwide). b'92. AB '17—JD '32 (U So Cal); AM Carnegie fellow '19 (Harvard). Chairman Commission to Study Organization of Peace Southern California Region; director center for International Understanding Los Angeles. Author: The League of Nations and the New International Law '21; International Understanding; Agencies Education for a New World '31; Documentary Textbook on International Relations '34; World-Wide Influences of the Cinema 40; Woodrow Wilson Still Lives: His World Peace Ideals Triumphant '44; The Heritage of Woodrow Wilson '45; Documentary Textbook on the United Nations—Humanity's March Toward Peace (2d edit) '50. Editor: Proceedings of the Institute of International Relations, 2 vols (vol I with K C Leebrick) '27. Prof polit sci U So Cal since '21. H: 1227 W 39th St., LA 37.⊚

11 HARLOW, Victor Emmanuel. Oklahoma history; American realism. b'76. AB '96 (La Grange Mo Coll); AM '99 (Shurtleff Coll Alton Ill); AM '31 (U Okla). Author: A Bibliography and Genetic Study of American Realism '31; Oklahoma, a History '34, and others. Founder, ed Harlow's Weekly since '12. Pres bd Oklahoma City Carnegie Library. 4908 N.W. 23rd St., Oklahoma City.

12 HARLOW, William M(orehouse). Tree identification. b'00. BS '25—MS '26—PhD '28 (NY State U Coll Forestry). Studies on tree identification through their flowers, twigs, buds, fruits; research on microchemistry of cell walls of wood; techniques of outdoor education. Author: Trees of the Eastern United States and Canada: Their Woodcraft and Wildlife Uses '42; Twig Key to the Deciduous Woody Plants of Eastern North America (4th edit) '41; Fruit Key to Northeastern Trees '46. Co-author (with E S Harrar): Textbook of Dendrology (3rd edit) '50. Author articles in field. Contributor: Wood Chemistry '44; New Leica Manual '51. With NY State Coll Forestry since '28, prof wood tech from '49. Sigma Xi—Soc Am Foresters. New York State University College of Forestry, Syracuse 10.

13 HARMAN, Susan Emolyn. Philology; Medieval literature. BEd '16 (Peru State Teachers Coll); AB '17—AM '18 (Neb U); PhD '26 (Johns Hopkins); '23-24 (George Washington U); '25 (Chicago U); '28 (Oxford U). Research in vocabulary study of the Gesta Romanorum. Author: Handbook of Correct English (with H C House) '28; Descriptive English Grammar '35, revised '48; College Rhetoric '38. Asso prof Neb State Teachers Coll '18-19; asst prof Eng Md U '20-26, prof since '42; lecturer Grad Sch US Dept Agr '35-45. Acad Polit Sci—Shakespeare Soc—Medieval Soc Am—Phi Kappa Phi. University of Maryland, College Park, Md. H: 6904 Oakridge Rd., College Heights, Hyattsville.

14 HARMON, Frank Nelson. Grapes (Vegetative propagation, production, breeding). b'95. BS '21—MA '27 (Utah State Agrl Coll). Co-producer two new grape varieties; search for efficient and economical methods for establishment vinifera grape varieties on root stocks resistant to soil pests; development method for increasing production Alexandria grapes by treatment vines with zinc; discovery bud mutations in numerous varieties of fruits. Author articles: Hastening the Production of Fruit in Grape Hybridization Work '37; Some Effects of Zinc Sul-

phate on the Alexandria Grape '42; Some Factors Affecting the Sucess of Green Wood Grafting of Grapes '48; Comparative Value of Thirteen Rootstocks for Ten Vinifera Varieties '49, and others. With USDA since '26, western grape investigations Fresno Cal since '33. Am Soc Hort Sci—Am Genetic Assn—AAAS. Route 3, Boc 307, Fresno, Cal.

15 HARMON, George Dewey. American history (1776-1875, Foreign policy). b'96. AB '21—MA '23 (Trinity Coll); PhD '30 (U Pa). Author articles in field. Prof Am hist Lehigh U since '42, head dept hist and govt since '46. Am Hist Assn—Pa Hist Assn—Phi Beta Kappa. Received the Philadelphia Inquirer Award of $1,000 for an essay on George Washington '36. Department of History and Government, Lehigh University, Bethlehem, Pa.

16 HARMON, Walter S. Radio (Design and engineering). b'04. Exec and design engr various cos '26-36; chief engr Emerson radio and Phonograph Corp '34-36, Mission Bell Radio Mfg Co '36-41; vp in charge engring Hoffman Radio Corp '41-46; pres W S Harmon Co since '46. Inst Radio Engrs (sr)—Radio Old Timers. 4057 McClung Dr., LA 8.

17 HARN, Orlando Clinton. Audits of publications' circulations. b'71. Student (O Wesleyan U); PhB '94 (Cornell U). One of founders Audit Bureau of Circulations including more than 3000 publications of US and Canada, president '20-27, managing director '27-39. With Cleveland Leader '94, later successively telegraph ed Cleveland Press, news ed Scripps-McRae Assn, ed Architect and Builder and Inland Grocer, all of Cleveland; adv mgr H J Heinz Co Pittsburgh '04-05; Nat Lead Co '05-27. Tech Publicity Assn (pres '10-11)—Assn Nat Advertisers (pres '11)—Advt Fedn Am (bd govs '28-38). Awarded Bok gold medal by Harvard Sch Bus Adminstrn for distinguished service to commerce and industry '26. H: 1915 Santa Barbara St., Santa Barbara, Cal.

18 HARNED, Robey Wentworth. Economic entomology (Cotton insects, insecticides for cotton insect control, insects of Mississippi). b'84. Student '01-02 (Franklin Coll); BS '06 (O State U); student (Cornell U, U Chicago). Prin entomol charge div cotton insects Bur Entomol and Plant Quarantine US Dept Agr since '31. AAAS(F)—Entomol Soc Am—Am Assn Econ Entomol (2d vp '22, 4 vp '24, pres '27)—Am Genetic Assn—Entomol Soc Washington (pres '43)—Biol Soc Washington—Sigma Xi. U. S. Department of Agriculture, Washington 25.†⊚

19 HARNWELL, Gaylord Probasco. Atomic physics; Underwater acoustics; Electricity and electromagnetism. b'03. BS '24 (Haverford Coll); Nat Research Council fellow '27-28 (Calif Inst Tech); Nat Research Council fellow '28-29—MA '26—PhD '27 (Princeton). Editor Review of Scientific Instruments since '38. Author: Principles of Electricity and Electromagnetism '39. Co-author: (with John J Livingood) Experimental Atomic Physics '36. Prof physics, chmn dept, dir Randal Morgan Lab U Pa since '38; on leave of absence '42-46 to act as dir U Calif div of war research US Navy Radio and Sound Lab San Diego Calif. Am Phys Soc(F)—Phi Betal Kappa. Medal of Merit div phys sci Nat Research Council '47. Department of Physics, University of Pennsylvania, Phila.⊚

20 HARPER, Floyd A. Price economics. b'05. BS '26 (Mich State Coll); PhD '32 (Cornell U). Author: The Crisis of the Free Market '45; High Prices '48; Freedom and Enter-

prise '45. Co-author: The World's Hunger '45. Author: Liberty—A Path to its Recovery '49; also articles in field. Found for Econ Edn Inc since '46. Am Econ Assn—Am Statis Assn—Am Acad Polit Social Sci—Am Marketing Assn—Am Farm Econ Assn—Acad Polit Sci—Phi Kappa Phi. 30 S. Broadway, Irvington-on-Hudson, N.Y.†⊚

21 HARPER, Francis. Vertebrate fauna of southeastern United States and northwestern Canada; Okefinokee Swamp; Early American natural history; Extinct and vanishing mammals. b'86. AB '14—PhD '25 (Cornell). Zoologist Canadian Geological Survey Expedition to Great Slave Lake '14; US Biological Survey Expedition to Lake Athabaska '20; Arctic Inst Expedition to Nueltin Lake '47. Author: Mammals of the Adirondacks '29; Journals of John and William Bartram '42, 43; Extinct and Vanishing Mammals of the Old World '45. Research asso John Bartram Assn since '39; Penrose Fund grantee Am Philos Soc, ed staff '42-44. Am Ornithol Union—Am Soc Ichthyologists Herpetologists (vp '34-35)—Am Soc Mammalogists (corr sec '31-32)—Biol Soc Washington—Ga Ornithol Soc—Arctic Inst NA (grantee US Office Naval Research '47)—Am Council Learned Societies (grantee)—Phi Beta Kappa—Sigma Xi. R.F.D. 1, Mount Holly, N.J.⊚

22 HARPER, Lawrence A(verell). United States colonial economic history; United States customs law and administration; Utilization of mechanical aids to scholarships. b'01. AB '22—MA '25 (U Calif); PhD '39—U fellow '26-27 (Columbia); Heller Travel fellow '25-26 (U Calif). Author: The English Navigation Laws '39; Charts and Outlines for United States History '43. Editor: (with F F G Harper) Harper's Customs Tariff '30; also articles in field. Instr, later prof US hist U Calif since '28; partner Harper & Harper '28-45, Lawrence, Tuttle and Harper since '45. Am Acad Polit Social Sci—AAAS—AHA—Am Polit Sci Assn—Am Soc Pub Adm—Agrl Hist Soc—Bus Hist Soc—Econ Hist Soc—Phi Beta Kappa. Guggenheim fellow '44-45. 30 Wheeler Hall, University of California, Berkeley 4.†⊚

23 HARRAR, Ellwood Scott. Wood technology; Dendrology. b'05. BS '27—MS '28—PhD '36 (NY State Coll Forestry). Research on wood technology, especially in bonding and anatomy, dendrology, tropical woods, forest products technology. Author: Forest Dendrology '35. Co-author: (with C Hogue) Douglas Fir Use Book '30; (with W M Harlow) Textbook of Dendrology '49; (with A J Panshin, P B Proctor, W Baker) Forest Products '49. Asst prof forests products Coll Forestry U Wash '33-36; asso prof wood tech Duke U '36-42, prof wood tech since '45. Forest Products Research Soc—Soc Am Foresters—Internat Soc Wood Anat (sec-treas '39-44)—Sigma Xi—Phi Kappa Phi. School of Forestry, Duke University, Durham, N.C.†

24 HARRELL, Ruth Flinn. Psychology (Nutritional-mental relations, re-education of aphasic patients). b'00. BS '20 (Wesleyan Coll); MA '24—PhD '42 (Columbia). Research on relation of thiamin to learning. Author articles in field. Research asso Teachers Coll Columbia since '45. Va Acad Sci—AAAS—Am Psychol Assn. Diplomate Counselling and Guidance. Teachers College, Columbia University, NYC. H: 1321 Cornwall Pl., Norfolk 8, Va.

25 HARRELL, William Asa, Jr. Church buildings (Architecture). b'03.

Student '21-23 (Decatur Bapt Coll, Baylor U); '29-30, '37 (George Peabody Coll). Author: Planning Better Church Buildings '47. Compiler and editor: Church Designs, Capacity 100-500 '41; Church Designs Capacity 600-2700 '41; Church Remodeling Designs '42; Modern Homes for Pastors '43; Church Buildings '44. Sec dept ch architecture Baptist Sunday Sch Bd Nashville since '40. North Am Con Ch Architecture. 161 8th Av., Nashville 3, Tenn.

10 HARRELSON, Ottis Miles. Welding; Physical metallurgy. b'03. BS in EE '26 (Clemson Coll); ME '34 (Ga Sch Tech). Special work in welding design and fabrication of electrical machinery; studies on effects of alloying additions, forging processes, heat treating processes of gears and motor parts; directed forging and heat treating of 75MM and 3" HE shells, 81MM trench mortar shells and 75MM AP shells '42-45; research on effect of controlling welding procedure and peening of physical properties and constitutents of metals. Holds patent on special oil burner for tobacco barn furnaces and heating appliances. Author articles in field. In chge welding, heat-treating, metallography, foundry, Ga Sch Tech since '45. Am Welding Soc—Am Soc Metals. Georgia School of Technology, Atlanta. H: 210 North Av., N.W., Apt. 84.

11 HARRINGTON, James Foster. Olericulture. b'16. BS—MS '40 (O State U); PhD '44 (Cornell U); '35-36 (Dartmouth Coll). Author articles: Relation of Soil Pore Space to Growth and Yield of Tomatoes '39; Some Factors Influencing the Reliability of Plant Tissue Testing '44; Trend of Soluble Nitrate, Phosphate and Potassium Concentrate in the Development of the Spinach Petiole '45. Asst prof hort Ia State Coll '44-46; asst prof truck crops U Calif since '46. Am Soc Hort Sci—Am Soc Plant Physiol—Sigma Xi. Division of Truck Crops, University of California, Davis, Calif.†

12 HARRINGTON, Joseph, Jr. Shoe making and leather working machinery (Research and design). b'08. Student (U Ill); SB '30—ScD '32 (MIT). Author: Stresses in a Stretched Plate Containing Two Adjacent Holes '32. With United Shoe Machinery Corp since '32, now asst dir research div. Tau Beta Pi. United Shoe Machinery Corporation, Boston 7.

13 HARRINGTON, Louis Clare. Fuel beneficiation and utilization; Mining valuation; Lignite. b'80. BS in CE '08 (Mich U); EM '09 (Mich Coll Mines). Author articles in field. Prof geol and engring Western Md Coll '09-12; instr U ND '12, asst prof '13-20, asso prof '20-21, prof since '21, dir div mines and mining experiments since '31, dean Coll Engring since '32. Am Inst Mining Metall Engrs—Mining and Metall Soc Am—Am Soc Testing Materials—Am Chem Soc—Am Soc Engring Edn—ND Acad Sci—Sigma Xi. 319 S. 6th St., Grand Forks, N.D.

14 HARRIS, Albert Josiah. Reading (Remedial). b'08. AB '28—MA '29—PhD '30 (Harvard). Research on reading disabilities and their remedies. Author: How to Increase Reading Ability (2d edit revised) '47. Asst psychol Worcester State Hosp '34-35; instr, asst prof edn, supervisor Remedial Reading Service City Coll NY '35-49; dir Queens Coll Ednl Clin and asso prof edn Queens Coll '49-51, prof since '51. Am Psychol Assn(F)—Nat Vocational Guidance Assn—Phi Beta Kappa—NY State Psychol Assn—Am Orthopsychiatric Assn—Am Ednl Research Assn—NEA—Nat Assn Remedial Teachers(mem exec com '50-51)

—Internat Council for Improvement Reading Instruction (v-pres '50-52). Queens College, Flushing, N.Y. H: 345 E. Grand St., Mount Vernon, N.Y.

15 HARRIS, Benjamin Charles. Herbs. b'07. PhG '30 (Mass Coll Pharmacy). Studies of herbs for medicines, foods, dyes, first aid; culinary herbs, superstitions. Author: Better Health with Culinary Herbs '52. Author articles: Eat The Weeds; Foods, Good, bad, and indifferent; Dyeing with native Herbs; The Medicine of Garden Flora; Household Remedies; The Medicines of Our Foods. Curator econ botany Mus Natural History Worcester Mass since '39. Am Inst History Pharmacy—Mass Hort Soc—Natural Hygiene Soc Am—Herb Soc Am. 12 State St., Worcester, Mass.

16 HARRIS, Brice. Literary patronage; Satire; Fable literature. b'00. AB '21 (Erskine Coll); AM '25 (Vanderbilt U); PhD '32 (Harvard); research fellow (Huntington Library). Author: Charles Sackville, Sixth Earl of Dorset, Patron and Poet of the Restoration; also articles in field. Prof and head dept Eng Lit Pa State Coll since '47. Mod Lang Assn Am—Nat Council Teachers of Eng—Coll Eng Assn. Grant-in-aid from Am Council Learned Soc '34. Pennsylvania State College, State College, Pa.

17 HARRIS, Chauncy Dennison. Urban geography. b'14. AB '33 (Brigham Young U); BA '36—MA '43 (Oxford U); PhD '40 (U Chicago). Developed quantitative method of functional classification of cities, contributed to theory of pattern of cities. Author: Salt Lake City: A Regional Capital '40. Co-author: (with Jerome D Fellmann) A Union List of Geographical Serials (2d edit) '50. Editor: (American edit) Economic Geography of the USSR '49. Asst prof U Neb '41-43; with U Chicago since '43, prof geog since '47; with US Dept State '42-43; chief Urban Studies Sect Far E Div OSS '44-45. Assn Am Geog (sec '46-48). Department of Geography, University of Chicago, Chgo 37.☺

18 HARRIS, Cyril Manton. Acoustics (Architectural, physiological); Noise control. b'17. AB '38—Am '40 (U Calif Los Angeles) PhD '45 (MIT). Research on reduction, control and abatement problems of noise, auditorium design for acoustics, measurement of acoustics, acoustical materials. Co-author: (with Dean V O Knudsen) Acoustical Designing in Architecture '50. Author articles in field. With Bemis Found MIT '40, OSRD research '41-44, faculty '43-45; mem tech staff Bell Telephone Lab '45-51; sci cons Office Nav Research '51; vis Fulbright lecturer Tech U Delft '51-52; now dir acoustics lab asso prof engring Columbia. Acoustical Soc Am (F)—Inst Radio Engrs (sr mem)—ASTM (v-chmn com acoustical materials and rep to Am Standards Assn)—Sigma Xi—Phys Soc (London)—Groupement des Acousticiens de Langue Francaise. Acoustics Laboratory, Dept. Electrical Engineering, Columbia University, N.Y.C. 27. H: 315 Riverside Dr., N.Y.C. 25.

19 HARRIS, D. B. Petroleum seismology. b'15. BS (Geol) '37 (U Okla) Geophysicist and seismol interpretation Seismograph Service Corporation Tulsa Okla since '41. Am Assn Petroleum Geol—Soc Exploration Geophysicists—Am Geophys Union. Box 1590, Tulsa 1.

20 HARRIS, Donald Brewer. Design of carrier transmission, data transmission, frequency modulation, and forward transmission radar systems; Linear accelerators (Driver systems); Cyclotrons (Relativistic modifica-

tions). b'01. BA '22 (Yale). Invented product modulation and demodulation systems for multi-channel carrier transmission, invented multi-channel data transmission system eliminating preselection of channel carriers, invented frequency modulation system employing product phase modulation, invented forward transmission radar system in which target lies between transmitter and inert receiver; member three committees of Joint Chiefs of Staff during World War II. Granted patents in field. With Northwestern Bell Telephone Co '24-47, transmission and protection engr 45-47; sci officer in contractual charge Radio Research Lab Harvard (OSRD) '43-45; exec asst to dir research Collins Radio Co '47-50; tech asst to pres Airborne Instruments Lab since '50. Inst Radio Engrs (sr mem, mem bd ed '50)—APS—AAAS—Ia Acad Sci (F)—Telephone Pioneers Am. Awarded War Dept-Navy Dept Certificate Appreciation '48. Airborne Instruments Laboratory, Mineola, L.I., N.Y.

21 HARRIS, Earl Felton. Machine manufacturing. b'21. Student '40 (MIT) '40-41 (Worcester Poly Inst) '41-42 (Babson) (Inst Bus Adminstrn) '42-43 (Lowell Textile Inst) '39-40 (Dartmouth). Vice pres and dir Rodney Hunt Machine Co since '47, gen mgr since '48; vp and dir Rivet-O Mfg Co since '48; dir The Stencil Co since '48. Rodney Hunt Machine Co., 46 Mill St., Orange, Mass. H: Warwick Rd., Orange, Mass.

22 HARRIS, Elwin E(lmer). Forest and cellulose chemistry. b'97. BS '21 (Hamline U); MS '22—PhD '25 (U Minn). In charge of development under Research and Marketing Act of process for production of wood-sugar molasses and fodder yeast from wood residues for stock feed '46-48; modification in wood hydrolysis process and in acclimatization of yeast to simplify process and produce higher yields of alcohol from wood '44-46; investigation Scholler process hydrolysis wood waste Office Production Research Development War Production Board '43-44; technical advisor in preparation TIDC project 30, German Forest Resources and Forest Products Industries '45; research on utilization of lignin and waste products from wood. Author articles in field. Instr chem U ND '23-25, asst prof '25-28, asso prof organic and bio-chem '28-30; asso chem US Forest Products Lab Madison Wis '30-36, chem '36-42, sr chem '42-46, chem specialist since '46. Soc Am Foresters—Am Chem Soc (mem adv com cellulose chem)—Sigma Xi. Forest Products Laboratory, Madison 5, Wis.†

23 HARRIS, Jack Sargent. Nigeria (Anthropology); Ibo (Economics, sociology); Trusteeship (International); Colonial problems (Africa). b'12. BS '36 (Northwestern U); PhD 40 (Columbia). Author articles: Position of women in Nigerian society; Domestic slave trade in Nigeria; Human relationship to land in Ibo society; Economic aspects of life among Ozuitem Ibo; Economics of sixteen Ibo individuals; Education in the Belgian Congo. Asst prof anthrop Ohio State U '40 41; African specialist OSS '41-45; asst prof social sci U Chicago '46-47; sr officer dept trusteeship UN since '47. Internat African Inst—Am Antropol Assn—Am Ethnological Soc—NRC (com on African antrop)—Sigma Xi—Phi Beta Kappa—Social Sci Research Council(F). Department of Trusteeship, United Nations, NYC.

24 HARRIS, Jay C(harles). Surface active agents. b'04. BS '27—MS '30 (Wash State Coll). Holder patents on detergents. Author articles: Annotated Bibliography of Aluminum Cleaning '44; Metal Cleaning I—Indirect Performance Tests '45, II—Soil Removal Performance Methods '44; The Evaluation of Surface-Active Agents '46; and others. Research chem surface active agents Colgate-Palmolive-Peet Co '31-36; group leader surface active agents Monsanto Chem Co since '36. Am Assn Textile Chem and Colorists—Am Electroplaters Soc—Am Chem Soc—Am Oil Chem Soc—Am Soc Testing Materials—Tech Assn Pulp and Paper Industry. Monsanto Chemical Co., Central Research Department, Dayton 7, O.

10 HARRIS, Jesse W. Folklore (Illinois). b'00. BS '27—MA '28—PhD '35 (U Ill). Author: John Bale 1495-1563. Author articles: Dialect of Appalachia in Southern Illinois; German Influences in St Clair County, Illinois; Pioneer Vocabulary Remains in Southern Illinois; Myths and Legends from Southern Illinois; Some Southern Illinois Witch Lore; The Catskin Legend, and others. Faculty So Ill U since '39, now asso prof English; ed Ill Folklore Soc since '46. Am Folklore Soc—Hoosier Folklore Soc—Modern Lang Assn—AAUP. Southern Illinois University, Carbondale, Ill.

11 HARRIS, John Donald. Learning theory; Hearing. b'14. BA '35 (Maryville Coll); MA '36 (Vanderbilt U); '39-40 (U Colo); PhD '40-42 (U Rochester). Research on temporal pattern of stimuli, non-associative factors, anatomy and physiology of learning; research on auditory acuity, sonar personnel selection, group methods of testing hearing, effect of aerotitis media, pitch discrimination, intensity discrimination, speech reception testing, intersensory effects, auditory fatigue. Contributor: Encyclopedia Britannica '48; Encyclopedia of Vocational Guidance '46; Twentieth Century Psychology '46. Faculty U Rochester '40-43; head sound sect Med Research Lab Submarine Base New London since '43. Am Psychol Assn(F)—Acoustical Soc Am(F)—AAAS(F). Medical Research Laboratory, Submarine Base, New London, Conn.

12 HARRIS, John L. Questioned document examination (Handwriting, typewriting, inks, papers). b'94. Testified as an expert witness on subjects relating to handwriting, typewriting, inks, papers and many outstanding trials in civil and criminal courts during past 23 years for US government, state, county and city officials and lawyers representing corporations and individuals. Specialist examination questioned documents Los Angeles since '36; instr on Questioned Documents U So Calif; official handwriting expert for Los Angeles County Sheriff's Office. Am Soc Questioned Document Examiners (sec). 453 S. Spring St., Los Angeles 13.†

13 HARRIS, Kenton L. Microanalysis of foods; Insect and rodent contamination of foods. b'13. BS '35 (U Calif); MS '39 (George Washington U). Author articles in field. Microanalyst US Food and Drug Adminstrn since '37. U.S. Food and Drug Administration, Division of Microbiology, Washington 25.†

14 HARRIS, Loyd E. Oklahoma plants (Chemistry); Microcrystalline waxes (Pharmaceutical use). b'00. PhG '20—PhC '22—BS in Pharm '22—MS '24 (Okla U); Marschall fellow '25-26—PhD '26 (Wis U). Author: Inorganic Pharmaceutical Chemistry (with Parks and Jannke) '49; also articles in field. Asst prof pharmacy U Okla '22-25, prof '26-38, prof chem '38-46; prof pharmacy O State U since '46. Am Pharm Assn—Am Chem Soc—Sigma

Xi. Ohio State University, College of Pharmacy, Columbus 10, O.†

15 HARRIS, Marjorie Silliman. Ibero-American philosophy; Aesthetics. b'90. AB '13 (Mt Holyoke Coll); PhD '21 (Cornell U); Vis PhD '30 (U Chicago). Author: The Positive Philosophy of Auguste Comte '23; also articles in field. Prof philos Randolph-Macon Woman's Coll since '30, head dept since '34. Am Philos Assn—Am Soc Aesthetics—Assn Symbolic Logic —Va Philos Assn (pres '46)—British Inst Philos—So Soc Philos Psychol (mem council '37-41, pres '40)—Phi Beta Kappa. Randolph-Macon Woman's College, Lynchburg, Va.

16 HARRIS, Mary Belle. Penology. AB '94—AM '95—LLD (hon) '27 (Bucknell U); PhD '00 (U Chicago); LLD (hon) '40 (Morris Harvey Coll). Author: I Knew Them in Prison '42; Kalidasa Poet of Nature '36; also articles in field. Supt Fed Indsl Instn for Women Alderson W Va '25-41; retired. Awarded Scroll of Honor for work in penal field from Gen Fed Women's Clubs '41. Lewisburg, Pa.

17 HARRIS, Norman Dwight. International relations; Political science; Negro in America. b'70. PhB '92 (Sheffield Sci Sch Yale); PhD '01 (U Chicago). Research work at Paris, London, Rome '01 and '05; member Colonel House's committee for gathering data for Peace Conference '17-18. Author: History of Negro Servitude in Illinois '04; Intervention and Colonization in Africa '27; Europe and the East '25; Moving On '39; also articles in field. Prof, head dept polit sci Northwestern U '06-29, now emeritus. Am Polit Sci Assn (exec council '13-16)—Am Soc Internat Law—AHA—Am Geog Soc(F)—ALA(F). 1134 Forest Av., Evanston, Ill.

18 HARRIS, Ray Baker. Freemasonry. b'07. Grad (Massanutten Acad); student (George Washington U). Author articles in field. Staff Library Congress '30-39; librarian Supreme Council 33° A&ASR of Freemasonry SJ since '39; 33° Mason. ALA —DC Library Assn—Am Lodge of Research—Bibliog Soc. P.O. Box 3157, Washington 9.

19 HARRIS, Reed. United States foreign relations (History); Public administration; Social geriatrics. b'09. Student (Columbia, George Washington U). Author: King Football '32; Travelers' Windfall '39; How To Get a Job When You're Over 35 '49; also articles in field. Chief communications and records Dept of State '46-48, dir publ '49-50, dep gen mgr internat info and ednl exchange program since '50. Am Acad Polit Social Sci—Am Fgn Service Assn—Soc Advancement Management—Nat Historical Publications Com—Nat Soc Seniors (pres). Department of State, Washington.

20 HARRIS, Samuel W. Asphalts; Drilling muds. b'18. Pet engr '42 (U Okla). Research on soil stabilization, testing and development of asphaltic concrete highways airport runways and parking ramps, plastic remedial work on oil and gas wells. Developed formulation for the emulsion mud now marketed as Jeloil E, developed and wrote specifications for a line of asphalt specialties. Head soils and asphalt lab Anderson Prichard Oil Corp '43-45; development engr Halliburton Oil Well Cementing Co '45-48; chief engr refining div Kerr-McGee Oil Ind Inc since '48. API. Box 125, Wynnewood, Okla.

21 HARRIS, William Pickett, Jr. Mammalogy (Squirrel classification).

b'97. Student '17-21 (Yale Sheffield Sci Sch); MA (hon) '34 (U Mich). Research on descriptions of new squirrels, revision of their classification, and indexing of world species of Sciuridae. Author articles in field. Asso curator mammals U Mich Mus Zool since '28. Sigma Xi—Am Soc Mammalogists—Am Com Internat Protection Wildlife. 1904 Penobscot Building, Detroit. H: 15410 Windmill Point Dr., Grosse Pointe Park, Mich.

22 HARRISON, Arthur E(lliot). Klystron tubes. b'08. BS '36 (U Calif); MS—PhD '36-39 (Calif Inst Tech). Author: Klystron Tubes '47. Engr Sperry Gyroscope Co '40-46; asst prof elec engring Princeton U '46-48; professor elec engring U Washington since '52. Inst Radio Engrs—Sigma Xi. Department of Electrical Engineering, University of Washington, Seattle.

23 HARRISON, Frank. Neurophysiology; Biophysics; Neuroanatomy. b'13. BS '35 (So Meth U); MS '36—PhD '38 (Northwestern U); med br '33-35 (Tex U). Research on determinations of thresholds to stimulation with faradic and direct current in brain stem, activation of heat loss mechanisms by local heating of brain, tongue innervation, Horsley-Clarke stereotaxic instrument, proprioceptive components of cranial nerves, spinal accessory nerve, sensory innervation of spinal accessory and tongue musculature in rabbits, attempt to produce sleep by diencephalic stimulation, function of mesencephalic root of fifth cranial nerve. Author articles in field. Instr anat U Tenn '38-41, asst prof '41-45, asso prof '45-46, prof and chief div anat since '46. Am Assn Anat—Am Physiol Soc. Fellow in neurology, Inst Neurology Northwestern U.'35-38. University of Tennessee, Memphis 3.†

24 HARRISON, George Russell. Instrumentation; Spectroscopy; Atomic physics; Interferometry; Diffraction gratings; Science popularization. b'98. AB '19—AM '20—PhD '22 (Stanford); ScD hon '46 (Northeastern U). Inventor for automatic wavelength comparator; spectroscopic interval sorter and recorder; Echelle spectrograph; interferometric commensurator for screw calibration; Winmac spectrum reducer. Author: Atoms in Action '39, How Things Work '41. Co-author: (with R C Lord and J R Loofbourow) Practical Spectroscopy '48. Editor: MIT Wavelength Tables '39; Journal Optical Soc Am '40-50. Staff Stanford '19-30; NRC Fellow Harvard '23-25; prof physics MIT since '30, dean sci since 42. APS—Optical Soc Am (pres '47 49)—Am Astron Soc—Am Assn Physics Tchrs—AAAS—Am Philos Soc—Am Acad Arts and Scis—Am Inst Physics (chmn since '48)—Sigma Xi—Sigma Pi Sigma. Received Rumford Medal, Ives Medal, Pres Medal of Merit Medal of Freedom. Massachusetts Institute Technology, Cambridge 39, Mass.†©

25 HARRISON, Henry T., Jr. Aviation (Meteorology); Antarctic (Meteorology). b'03. Pioneer in airway weather forecasting; with first Byrd expedition to Antarctic and Little America. Author articles: Flight Planning with Upper Air Charts '47; Some Characteristics of the Upper Level Low and the Jet Stream '50, and others. Co-author articles: (with W K Orendorff) Pre-Coldfrontal Squall Lines '41; (with W B Beckwith) A Reexamination of Hail Patterns Over Western United States '50. Aerological observer US Weather Bur Due West SC '24-28, airway weather forecaster Hadley Field NJ '28, Cleveland '30-35; aerologist-seaman Byrd Antarctic Expedition '28-30; with United Air Lines since '35, airline meteorol since '37, mgr weather service since '48. Tech adv comdg officer AUS Air Force Weather Service '42-46, also staff weather officer Yalta Conf mission, chief Far East Air Forces Weather Central Manila PI, and Hurricane weather officer. Am Meterorol Soc (nat council '49-51)—Air Transport Assn (United Air Lines rep meteorol com since '39). Spl Congressional medal for polar exploration '30. United Air Lines, Operating Base, Stapleton Airfield, Colo.†

10 HARRISON, M a u r i c e Robert. Concrete highways (Expansion and contraction join design). b'01. Student (NYU, Newark U, Rutgers U). Invented form for casting reflectingface curbing, patents pending on highway joints. Dir, sec-treas Behringer Metal Works Inc Newark NJ since '24, corporate and finance officer, mechanical and indsl engr. ASME—Am Soc Metals—Am Ordnance Assn—Am Technion Soc for Haifa, Palestine. 548 Hamilton Rd., South Orange, N.J.

11 HARRISON, Richard Edes. Perspective mapping; Graphic map projections; Cartography (Construction methods). b'01. BA '23 (Yale); BFA '30 (Yale U Sch Fine Arts). Originator of nomographic methods in construction of map projections; cartographer for numerous books in field of geography, politics and military history, and for periodicals. Author: Maps and How to Understand Them '43; Look at the World '44. Co-editor: The New Compass of the World '48; also articles in field. Independent cartographer since '38; map cons to State Dept, OSS, Fortune and Life Mags; lecturer Syracuse U since '45. Royal Geog Soc(F)—Am Geog Soc(F) —AAAS(F)—Am Congress Surveying Mapping—Assn Am Geog—Am Inst Graphic Arts. 22 W. 48th St., NYC 19.

12 HARRISON, Shelby Millard. Social welfare; Philanthropic foundations for public and social welfare; City planning (Social aspects). b'81. AB '06—LLD '32 (Northwestern U); LittD '42 (Boston U); AM '09 (Harvard). Author: City and County Administration in Springfield Ill '17; Public Employment Offices — Their Purpose, Structure and Methods '24. Co-author: (with Allen Easton) Welfare Problems in New York City '26, A Bibliography of Social Surveys '30; (with F Emerson Andrews) American Foundations for Social Welfare '46. Dir dept surveys and exhibits Russell Sage Found '12-42, acting dir dept indsl studies '18-19, vice gen dir '24-31, gen dir '31-37; dir Topeka Improvement Survey '13, Springfield (Ill) Survey '14-15; dir survey social conditions Regional Plan NY and Its Environs '22-31; instr course social surveys NY Sch Social Work '22-32; exec dir Babe Ruth Found since '48; mem President's Research Com on Social Trends '29-33. Mem Child Welfare League Am (mem bd)—Nat Social Welfare Assembly—Survey Assoc Inc—AAAS(F)— Am Social Soc—Am Pub Health Assn —Nat Conf Social Work (pres '41-42) —Social Sci Research Council—YMCA Research Council—Am Assn So Social Workers—Phi Beta Kappa. 30 Jones St., NYC 14.†☺

13 HARRISON, Thomas Randolph. Pyrometry; Electronics; Radiation; Servo-mechanisms; Controllers (Electrical, pneumatic). b'91. BS '18 (George Washington U); student (Va Poly Inst). Author articles in field. Granted over 100 US patents on inventions including inductance bridge flowmeter, electronically operated selfbalancing recorders, radiation pyrometer improvements, automatic con-

trollers. Dir research Brown Instrument Co '24-37, tech adv since '37. Am Phys Soc—Optical Soc Am—Franklin Inst. Certificate of Merit The Franklin Inst '32; Modern Pioneer award NAM. Minneapolis-Honeywell Regulator Co., Brown Instruments Division, Wayne and Roberts Av., Phila. H: 140 Hewett Rd., Wyncote, Pa.

14 HARRISON, Joseph (Whipple Eugene). Food pharmacology; Toxicology. b'96. PD '17—Pharm M '22— ScD (hon) '46 (Phila Coll Pharm and Sci). Co-author: Remington's Practice of Pharmacy; also articles in field. Asst prof pharmacol Phila Coll of Pharmacy and Sci; bd cons chem Bur Foods and Chem Pa Dept Agr since '19, chmn since '37; dir LaWall and Harrison Phila cons in bact, chem, pharmacol, pharmaceutical food industries clinical and toxicological studies. Am Chem Soc—Am Inst Chem (vp '38-40)—Pa Chem Soc (pres '39-42)—Assn Cons Chemists and Chem Engrs—Am Pharm Assn—Pa Pharm Assn—Am Pub Health Assn—Franklin Inst. LaWall and Harrisson, 1921 Walnut St., Phila. 3.

15 HARROLD, Gordon Coleson. Air pollution. b'06. BS '30 (Antioch Coll); AM '31—PhD '34 (U Cincinnati). Expert court witness on air pollution; devised numerous air washing devices for collection gases and submicron particles of metallic fume and organic material to alleviate atmospheric pollution; evaluation health hazards from lead and rare metals, fluorides, welding, fumes and gases, carbonic monoxide; device engineering, corrective measures ranging from exhaust ventilation to wet methods suppression without ventilation; studies in foundry dust conditions and provision economical corrective measures. Chief indsl hygienist Chrysler Corp '35-45; cons to industry, governmental agencies since '45. ACS—Am Indsl Hygiene Assn—Am Heating and Ventilating Soc—Am Pub Health Assn(F)—AA AS(F)—Engring Soc Detroit—Am Soc Safety Engrs—Am Inst Chem(F) —Indsl Ventilating Soc—Am Standards Assn—Sigma Xi. 6432 Cass Av., Det. H 903 E Lincoln Av., Royal Oak, Mich.

16 HARROLD, Orville Goodwin, Jr. Knots (Topology); Applied mathematics. b'09. AB '31—Am '32—PhD '36 (Stanford). Study local knots and relation to isotopy problems; topological characterization of continua admitting a metric of finite length; role of local separating points in problem of continuum structures; certain nonlinear differential equation in applied mathemtics. Nat research fellow math U Va '39-40; prof math U Tenn since '47; cons math Carbon and Carbide Chems Corp Oak Ridge since '49. Am Math Soc—Sigma Xi. Oak Ridge Institute of Nuclear Studies Science Research prize '49. Department of Mathematics, University of Tennessee, Knoxville, Tenn.

17 HARSH, Philip Whaley. Classical drama. b'05. AB '28—AM '30—PhD '33 (U Chicago); '33-34 (Am Acad in Rome, Am Sch Classical Studies Athens). Author: Studies in Dramatic Preparation in Roman Comedy '35. A Handbook of Classical Drama '48; Iambic Words and Regard for Accent In Plautus '49; also articles in field. Asst to asso prof Classics Stanford U since '40. Am Philol Assn (monograph ccm '41-46)—Classical Assn Pacific States (pres '40)—Archeol Inst Am (lecturer '48). Stanford University, Stanford, Calif.†☺

18 HARSHBARGER, Eugene Lee. Structural design; Stress analysis. b'89. Student '09-11 (Washburn Coll

Topeka Kan); BS (CE) '14—CE '28 (U Kan). Stress analysis and structural design of buildings in reinforced concrete and structural steel, including multi-story office buildings, hotels, railway freight and passenger stations, hospitals, schools, and warehouses. Chief engr Truscon Steel Co Dallas '19-20, br mgr Houston '20-24; structural engr Wyatt C Hedrick Ft Worth '25-31 and since '45; architectengr Ft Worth Independent Sch Dist '34-38; engr examiner Pub Works Adminstrn Ft Worth '38-39; private practice structural design Ft Worth '39-40. Structural engr and designer USN '40-43. 5201 Fannin St., Houston 4.

19 HART, Charles William Merton. Ethnology (Pacific Islands). b'05. AM '30 (U Sydney Australia); PhD '32 (U London). Field trips for ethnological research to North Australia— Melville and Bathurst Islands, Alligator River, Daly and Victoria Rivers '28-30, to Northern Canada '35, Windsor Ontario '46-48. Associate editor American Anthropologist since '48. Staff U Toronto '32-47; prof U Wis since '47. Am Anthrop Assn(F)—Am Sociol Soc(F)—Canadian Polit Sci Assn—Soc Applied Athrop—Indsl Relations Research Assn. NRC fellowship N Australia '27-30; Rockefeller fellow U London '30-32. Department of Sociology and Anthropology, University of Wisconsin, Madison, Wis.

20 HART, Frank William. School surveys; Schoolhousing (State and local); Housing (Educational). b'81. AB '08 (Ind U); PhD '20 (Columbia); LLD '38 (U Melbourne Australia). Conducted surveys and issued reports on college and university plant utilization and plant planning; county district and city school surveys. Mem staff Survey Chicago Pub Schs '32; asso prof edn U Cal '20-25, prof '45-49, prof emeritus since '49; lectr edn U Minn '50-51; del Internat Conf Edn (auspices New Edn Fellowship Eng) Australia and New Zealand '37; ednl cons Civil Aeronautics Adminstrn Dept Commerce '42-43. NEA—Phi Delta Kappa. Author: A Standard State Building Code '24; Teachers and Teaching, by 10,000 high school seniors '34. Co-author: (with George D Strayer and N L Engelhardt) Problems in Education Administration '25; (with L H Peterson) Teachers' Salaries in San Francisco. University of California Library Annex, Berkeley, California.†☺

21 HART, Freeman Hansford. American history (Virginia frontier, Confederate Army). b'89. AB '12—AM '17 (Wash and Lee U); MA '22 (Harvard); PhD '42 (Columbia). Research on numerical strength of Confederate Army, history of Virginia frontier, life histories of American historical personages, such as Sam Houston. Author: Valley of Virginia in the American Revolution '42. Contbr to Edward Channings' History of the United States vol VI '26 and to The Dictionary of American Biography; collaborator: Life of Sam Houston (with James) '29; also articles in field. Prof humanities Fla U since '46. AHA— So Hist Soc—Va Hist Soc—Fla Hist Soc—Tau Kappa Alpha Phi Beta Kappa. University of Florida, Gainesville, Fla.

22 HART, George. Electricity (Economics). b'16. Ed pub schs. Research on economic implications of electricity and its applications. Author 5 books, co-author 70 books and author 300 articles in field. Ed Elec Light and power since '50. Electrical Publications, Inc., 22 E. Huron St., Chgo 11. H: 1309 Astor St., Chgo 10.

10 HART, Henry Hersch. Chinese culture, art and history; Marco Polo; Vasco da Gama; Ancient literature; History of Asia; Asiatic and European languages. b'86. AB '07 (U Calif); JD '09 (U Calif); travel and study in East and Europe. Author and translator: A Chinese Market '31; The Hundred Names '33; The West Chamber '36; Seven Hundred Chinese Proverbs '42; A Garden of Peonies '38; What Europe Knew of China Three Hundred Years Ago '36; Venetian Adventurer '42; also articles in field. Lecturer on circuit Associated Executives Clubs Inc '45-46; vis prof 9 midwest colls '49. Royal Geog Soc, London(F)—Societe Asiatique de Paris—Royal Asiatic Soc Gt Britain and Ireland—Japan, China and Hakluyt Soc London—Hawaiian Hist Soc—Am Oriental Soc—Am Council Learned Socs—Sociedade de Geografia, Lisbon. Decorated Chevalier Order White Elephant of Cambodia France '24; Officieg, Order Dragon of Annam '26; collar and gold medal of Instituto de Colmbra Portugal '41. 210 Post St., San Francisco 8.

11 HART, Thomas Arthur. Mosquitoes. b'05. Student '25-27 (U Richmond); BS '30 (Coll William & Mary); MA '33—MS '37 (Emory U); PhD '41 —Rosenwald fellow '38-39 (U Chicago). Research on public health with special reference to malaria control and public health administration. Author articles in field. Prof and head dept biol W Ga Coll '33-42; dir malaria control and asst to chief of party Inst Inter-American Affairs Cochabama Bolivia '46; prof biol and dean sch of arts and sciences Roosevelt Coll Chicago since '47. First lt to lt col San Corps US Army '42-46. Sigma Xi. Roosevelt College, 430 S. Michigan Av., Chicago 5.

12 HARTENBERG, Richard S(cheunemann). Mechanics (Brittle materials, stress, aerial measurements, weapons); Aerodynamics. b'07. BS '28 —MS '33—PhD '41 (U Wis). Author articles in field. Asso prof mechanics Northwestern U since '46. ASME (chairman Chicago sect '50-51, gen com aviation div NY since '47)—Inst Aeronautical Sci—Am Soc Metals—Am Soc Engring Edn—Sigma Xi. Northwestern University, Technological Institute, Evanston, Ill.

13 HARTKEMEIER, Leonard William. Ore analysis; Corrosion chemistry. b'00. BS '21 (U Louisville); MS '24—Shevlin fellow '24-25 (U Minn). Consulting work on various problems of pipe line corrosion, boiler corrosion, industrial water analysis, ore analysis. Author: Quantitative Analysis for Students in Mining, Metallurgy and Geology '40. Asst chem Minn Highway Dept '24-25; Northern Pacific Railroad '25-26; instr Colo Sch Mines '26-27, asst prof analytical chem and ore analysis '27-35, asso prof since '35. Am Chem Soc—ASEE. Colorado School of Mines, Golden, Colo. H: 330 Marion St., Denver 3.†

14 HARTLEY, Carl. Wood deterioration and decay; Tree diseases. b'87. AB '07—MA '09 (U Neb); PhD '20 (U Calif); '16 (Johns Hopkins); '17 (George Washington U). Research on diseases of forest nursery stock; supervision of research on diseases of forest trees, on stains and decays of wood and other forest products. Author articles in field. Sci asst, later path forest path US Bur Plant Ind '09-19, path, prin path since '23; path Inst Plant Diseases Dutch East Indies '20-22. Am Phytopath Soc (vp '36, pres Potomac div '44)—Soc Am Foresters—Forest Products Research Soc—Am Wood Preservers Assn—Am Genetics Assn—Bot Soc Wash. Forest Pathology, Plant Industry Station, Beltsville, Md.†

15 HARTLEY, James C(arl). Steel, magnesium, and aluminum forgings; Beryllium production; Ultrasonic testing. b'06. ME '28 (Polytech Inst Brooklyn). Research and development in tool steels, stainless steels, nitriding and heat treatment, direct reduction of melting stock processes; organized a foundry in New York to make stellite castings '41, ultrasonic reflectoscope; worked with PM Dolan on the development of the Dolan-Hartley beryllium reduction process which is patented. Author articles in field. Constrn design and teaching aerodynamics Fernic Aircraft Corp Am Aeronautical Corp, O'Connor Airways '28-31; metall research asst Crucible Steel Co Am '31-33; metal cons '34-37; dir research United Alloys Inc '37-40, chief metallurgist Minerals & Metals Corp '40-42; Aluminum Forgings Inc '42-45 (chairman post war planning com); chief metall and sales mgr Barium Steel & Forge Inc '46-48, vp and gen mgr '48; staff exec Olin Industries Inc Winchester repeating arms div since '49, asso dir research since '50. ASM—AIME—AISE. Olin Industries, Inc., Winchester Repeating Arms Division, New Haven.

16 HARTMAN, George Bernhardt. Wood preservation. b'94. BS '17—MS '41 (Ia State Coll). Author articles in field. Prof forestry Ia State Coll since '35 head dept since '48. Soc Am Foresters—Am Wood Preservers Assn—Ia Acad Sci—Phi Kappa Phi—Gamma Sigma Delta. Department of Forestry, Iowa State College, Ames, Ia.

17 HARTMAN, Henry. Fruit (Handling and distribution). b'89. BS '17 (Wash State Coll); MS '22 (Ia State Coll). Research fruit maturity, storage, transportation and preservation. Author: The Elements of Horticulture '46. Co-inventor chemically treated paper wraps for preventon of decay in pears '35. Mem faculty Ore State Coll since '19, prof hort since '32, head dept hort since '42; hort USDA '31-32; hort adviser Ore-Wash-Cal Pear Bur since '29. Am Soc Hort Sci (pres Western sect '46)—Ore State Hort Soc—Sigma Xi—Phi Kappa Phi—Alpha Zeta—Gamma Sigma Delta. H: 135 N. 30th St., Corvallis, Ore.†⊙

18 HARTMAN, Olga. Polychaetous Annelids. b'00. AB '26 (U Ill); MA '33 —PhD '36 (U Calif). Author: Marine Annelids of North Carolina '45; Polychaetous Annelids of Alaska '48; also articles in field. Research asso U So Calif since '38. AAAS. Allan Hancock Foundation, University of Southern California, Los Angeles 7.†

19 HARTMAN, Robert S. Ethics; Economics (Profit sharing). b'10. LLB '32 (U Berlin); PhD '46 (Northwestern U). Author articles in field. Asso prof philos O State U since '48; exec sec Council of Profit Sharing Industries since '47. Am Philos Assn—NEA. Ohio State University, Department of Philosophy, Columbus, O.

20 HARTMAN, Edward George. American social history; Americanization; Immigration; Ethnic groups in America; World War II. b'12. AB '37 —MA '38 (Bucknell U); PhD '47 (Columbia). Author: Tough 'Ombres, the Story of the 90th Infantry Division (with Carl Jenkins) '44; The Movement to Americanize the Immigrant '48. Editor: A Short History of the 357th Infantry Regiment (90th Division) '45. Combat historian 90th Infantry Div (Third Army ETO) '43-46; asst prof hist Wilkes Coll Wilkes-Barre Pa '46-47; fellow Modern Hist Library City Coll NY '47-48; dir libraries and asst prof hist Suffolk U Boston since '48. AHA—AAUP—Pa Hist Soc. Suffolk University, Boston. H: 281 S. Welles St., Wilkes-Barre, Pa.†

21 HARTMANN, Hudson T(homas). Olives (Production, culture, California industry); Photoperiodism; Plant propagation. b'14. BS '39—MA '40 (U Mo); PhD '47 (U Calif). Author articles in field. Asst prof pomol U Calif since '48. AAAS—Am Soc Hort Sci—Am Soc Plant Physiol—Sigma Xi —Gamma Sigma Delta. Division of Pomology, University of California, Davis, Calif.†

22 HARTMANN, Irving. Dust explosion research; Coal mine safety. b'05. BS '29—ME '33 (Cooper Union Inst Tech); MA '32 (George Washington U); PhD '35 (Catholic U Am). Research and design on aircraft engines, airship structures, elasticity, prevention of ice formation on airplanes, mine safety problems, coal and metal dust explosibility, physical properties of mine roof rocks, strength of coal, incendiary bombs; member national committee on explosion prevention of NFPA; member President's Conference on Industrial Safety. Author: Coal Mining in Europe; Explosibility of Pulverized Fuel Pitches, of Metal Powders, Plastic Powders, other dusts; Strength of Coal Pillars; Wetting Agents for Coal Dust; Permissible Explosives in Coal Mining, and others. With USN Dept, Nat Bur Standards, US War Dept, US Bur of Mines. AA AS—Am Chem Soc—Coal Mining Inst Am. U.S. Bureau of Mines, Pittsburgh 13.

23 HARTOUGH, Howard Dale. Thiophene chemistry; Petro-chemicals; Mannich reaction. b'13. AB '36 (Hope Coll); MS '38 (George Washington U). Special work in production of chemicals from petroleum sources and synthesis of thiophene and derivatives; research on Mannich reaction, reaction of formaldehyde and ammonium salts with organic compounds such as ketones, phenols, thiophene, articles on aminomethylation of thiophene give first general mechanism proof of reaction. Author articles in field. Holds 40 patents. Research chem Socony-Vacuum Labs since '38. Am Chem Soc—AAAS—Sigma Xi. Socony-Vacuum Laboratories, Paulsboro, N.J. H: 447 W Holly Av., Pitman.†

24 HARTSHORN, Herbert Hadley. Education (Counseling and guidance); Measurements. b'09. BS '30 (Lincoln U Jefferson City Mo); AM '40—PhD '48 (U Minn). Dean St Philip's Jr Coll, San Antonio, '31-32; dir extension schs Samuel Huston Coll Austin '32-33; social worker St Louis '35-36; tchr Lab High Sch Lincoln U '36-40, prin '40-48; asst prof edn Lincoln U '44-48, prof edn '48, dean of students '48-50; dean coll arts and scis Tex So U Houston since '50. AAUP—Am Coll Personnel Assn—State Tchrs Assn—Psi Chi—Phi Delta Kappa. Texas Southern University, Houston 4. H: 2811 Barbee.⊙

25 HARTSTEIN, Jacob Isaac. Jewish Education in the United States; State control of secular education under religious auspices; Higher education in the United States (New York). b'10. BA '32 (Yeshiva Coll NYC); MS '33 (Coll City NY); MA '36 (Columbia); PhD '45 (NYU). Author: A Model Program for the Talmud Torah (with others) '42; Jewish Education in New York City '37; State Regulatory and Supervisory Control of Higher Education in New York '45. Editor: A Guide to General Psychology '47; also articles in field. Prof, head edn and psychol Long Island U since '45 and chmn graduate div since '50; dean Grad Schs Yeshiva U and prof edn since '45, dean Sch Edn and Community Adminstrn since '47; supt schs bd secular edn United Yeshivas since '46. Am Assn Sch Adminstrs—Eastern Psychol Assn—Nat Council Jewish Edn—Am Psychol Assn—Phi Delta Kappa. 380 Pearl St., Brooklyn 1.©

10 HARTZELL, Albert. Insecticides; Contact insecticides (Mode of action); Virus diseases of plants (insect borne). b'91. BS '16—MS '17 (Cornell U); PhD '23 (O State U). Worked out life history of plum leafhopper and confirmed that this species transmits peach yellows; naphthalene as greenhouse fumigant; demonstrated histologically that contact insecticides cause nerve lesions in insects; bioassay insecticide residues in fresh and processed foods. Author: Bionomics and Control of the Potato Leafhopper in Iowa; Naphthalene Fumigation of Greenhouses '26; A Study of Peach Yellows and Its Insect Vector '35; also articles in field. Entomol Boyce Thompson Inst '24-43, head entomol since '43. AAAS—NY Acad Sci—Ia Acad Sci—Am Assn Econ Entomol—Entomol Soc Am—NY Entomol Soc—Am Phytopath Soc—Gamma Sigma Delta—Sigma Xi. Boyce Thompson Institute for Plant Research, Inc., Yonkers 3, N.Y.

11 HARTZOG, Justin R. Planning (State, city, regional). b'92. BS '14 (Denison U); Master Landscape Design '17 (Cornell U). Planning consultant cities states and governmental agencies; chief town planner US Resettlement Adminstrn for Greenhills O '35-37; town planning cons Farm Security Adminstrn '38-40; city planning cons US Housing Authority '38-42; regional coordinator (New Eng) Office Defense Housing Coordinator, adv com Council of Nat Defense '40-41, spl cons for Hampton Roads, New Orleans, Detroit, Los Angeles '41-42; cons Fed Pub Housing Authority '42-43; chief cons city planning Nat Housing Agy '42-43; state planning cons RI State Planning Bd since '43; vis critic in city planning MIT since '38. Officer charge camp planning War Dept and to Constructing QM Camp Travis, Tex '19-20. Am Inst Planners—Am Soc Landscape Architects — Boston Soc Landscape Architects—Am Soc Planning Ofcls—Am Planning and Civic Assn—Cambridge (Mass) Plan Bd. 5 Boylston St., Harvard Square, Cambridge 38, Mass.†©

12 HARVEY, Edmund Newton. Physiology (Cell); Biophysics; Bioluminescence; Marine biology. b'87. BSc '09 (U Pa); PhD '11 (Columbia). Has made special studies in bioluminescence, cell permeability, stimulation and nerve conduction, regulation in plants, ultrasonic radiation, cell surface tension, brain potentials, bubble formation, decompression sickness, mechanism of wounding, etc. Author: The Nature of Animal Light '20; Laboratory Directions in General Physiology '33; Living Light '40. H F Osborn prof biol Princeton U since '33; vp, trustee Marine Biol Lab Woods Hole Mass, Bermula Biol Sta. AAAS—Am Soc Naturalists—Am Soc Biol Chem—Am Physiol Soc—Soc Exptl Biol and Med—Am Soc Zool—Growth Soc—Nat Geog Soc—NY Acad Sci—Am Acad Arts Sci—Soc Gen Physiol—Am Philos Soc—Nat Acad Sci—Nat Research Council—Sigma Xi. Awarded John Price Wetherill medal, Franklin Inst of Pa '34. 48 Cleveland Lane, Princeton, N.J.©

13 HARVEY, Floyd Kallum. Acoustics (Refracting mechanisms). b'13. B Elec Engring '39 (NY U). Investigated Acoustical characteristics of refracting mechanisms or structures originally designed for microwaves. With Bell Telephone Lab since '29, mem tech staff transmission research since '47. Am Inst EE(asso)—Acoustical Soc Am—Inst Radio Engrs(asso)—Eta Kappa Nu. Bell Telephone Laboratories, Murray Hill, N.J.

14 HARVEY, G(eorge) G(raham). Electromagnetic theory (X-rays, theoretical physics). b'08. AB '28—MSc '30—PhD '32 (Washington U); Nat Research Council fellow '32-34 (U Chicago). Author articles in field. Asst prof, asso prof physics MIT since '38, asst dir research lab electronics '50. AAAS—Am Assn Physics Teachers—Am Math Soc—Am Phys Soc—Edinburgh Math Soc—London Math Soc—Math Assn Am—Optical Soc Am—Phys Soc, London—Phi Beta Kappa—Sigma Xi. Department of Physics, Massachusetts Institute of Technology, Cambridge 39, Mass.

15 HARVEY, Lashley Grey. State and local government of New Hampshire and Massachusetts. b'00. AB '25 (William Jewell Coll); AM '30 (Stanford); '36-38, PhD '42 (Harvard). Consultant civic department Boston Chamber of Commerce, consultant to Commission on Structure of Government Massachusetts '50, administration consultant to city of Worcester '50, member of recess commission on Retirement Plans for State Employees (New Hampshire) '41. Exec sec bur govt research U NH '39-45; dir bur pub adminstrn Boston U since '48, chmn dept govt Boston U since '48, Maxwell prof govt Boston U since '49, dir inst pub service Boston U from '50. Am Soc Pub Adminstrn (sec-treas Mass chapter)—Am Polit Sci Assn—NE Polit Sci Assn—Nat Municipal League—Govt Research Assn. Boston University, 236 Bay State Rd., Boston 15.©

16 HARWELL, Richard Barksdale. Confederate and Southern United States History (Bibliography); Confederate music. b'15. BA '37—BALS '38 (Emory U). Author: Confederate Belles-Lettres '41. Editor: King Linkum the First (musical burletta performed 1863) '47; also articles in field. Asst librarian Emory U Library and lecturer hist dept since '48; asso ed Emory Sources and Reprints series since '46. So Hist Assn—Am Library Assn. Emory University Library, Emory University, Ga.†

17 HARWOOD, Edward Crowby. Business analysis. b'00. BS '20 (US Mil Acad); CE '22—MCE '30—MBA '31 (Rensselaer Polytech Inst). Author: Cause and Control of the Business Cycle; Inflation, What Will Devaluation Mean to You?; Insurance and Annuities from the Buyer's Point of View; Where Are We Going?; What Next, and others; also articles in field. Trustee Am Inst Econ Research since '34, dir since '37. Economists Nat Com Monetary Policy—Am Soc Mil Engrs—Sigma Xi. American Institute for Economic Research, Great Barrington, Mass.†©

18 HARWOOD, H(eber) James. Fatty acids and derivatives (Isolation, purification, synthesis). b'05. BS '27—MS '28 (U Utah); PhD '31—Parke Davis and Co research fellow '28-31 (Ia State Coll); E R Squibb and Sons research fellow '31-33 (Yale). Research in guanidine derivatives and polypeptides '28-31; pyrimidines, isoquinoline derivatives '31-33; isolation, purification, synthesis of fatty acids and derivatives since '33. Holder US patents. Author articles in field. With Armour and Co since '33, head fat and oil sect '44-48, asst dir research since '48. Am Chem Soc—Sigma Xi. Chemical Research and Development Department, Armour and Co., Chicago 9.†

19 HARWOOD, Paul D. Parasitology (Taxonomy, therapy); Helminths; Amerindians of southeastern United States. b'06. BS Agr '28 (Cornell U); MA '30—PhD '31 (Rice Inst); '33-34 (U Mich). Research survey of helminths parasitic in amphibia and reptilia in Houston Texas, study of in vitro effect of chemicals against Ascaris lumbricoides v suum, therapeutics of parasitic infections of domestic animals, efficacy of n-butyl chloride in therapy of dogs and horses, phenothiazine as an anthelmintic, and miscellaneous substances against gapeworms, tapeworms and coccidia of chickens. Holds patent for parasiticide. Author article in field. Asst pharmacologist Vanderbilt Med Sch Nashville Tenn '32-34; jr parasitol Vet Sect Drug Div Food and Drug Adminstrn US Dept Agr '34-36; parasitol zool div Bur Animal Industry US Dept Agr Washington '36-40; research dir Dr Hess and Clark Inc since '40. Washington Acad Sci—AAAS(F)—O Acad Sci(F). c/o Dr. Hess and Clark, Inc., Ashland, O.

20 HASCHKE, Theodore Arthur. Industrial chemistry; Agricultural chemistry. b'98. Student '16-17 (Nixon-Clay Coll). With Round Rock White Lime Co '19-26; sales mgr Stauffer Chem Co since '26. Soc Chem Industry. 420 Lexington Av., NYC 17. H: 38 Edgewood Lane, Bronxville, N.Y.

21 HASELTINE, Theodore Raymond. Sewage and industrial waste treatment. b'01. AB '25 (Stanford U); '27-28 (U Ill). Chief designer of grounds utilities and process piping for large shell loading plant and four synthetic rubber plants during '41-44; specialist in food, metallurgical, and tannery wastes. Author articles in field. With Chester Engrs since '40, partner since '46. ASCE—Am Pub Health Assn—Pa Sewage and Industrial Waste Assn—Calif Sewage Works Assn (past pres)—Sigma Xi—Phi Beta Kappa—Tau Beta Pi. 201 E. Parkway, Pittsburgh 12.†

22 HASKINS, Reginald Hinton. Mycology (Physiology of lower fungi); Physiology and taxonomy of Chytridiales; Lower Phycomycetes. b'16. BA '38—MA '40 (U Western Ontario); PhD '48 (Harvard U); '45 (Bot Sch Cambridge U, Eng). Research on culture aquatic phycomycetes, morphology, development, sexuality in chytridiales, pure culture studies of chytridiales, revision taxonomic criteria for chytridiales, nutrition and physiology of chytridiales, and break-down of cellulose, chitin and keratin by chytridiales. Author articles in field. Tutor biol Dunster House Harvard '47-48; asst res officer Prairie Regional Lab Nat Research Council Can '48. Bot Soc Am—Mycol Soc Am—Torrey Bot Club—Brit Mycol Soc—Sigma Xi. c/o Prairie Regional Laboratory, National Research Council, Saskatoon, Saskatchewan, Can.

23 HASLER, Arthur D. Fishery biology; Limnology. b'08. BA '32 (Brigham Young U); PhD '37 (U Wis). Research on fertilization for increasing productivity of inland waters, fish biology and limnology of Crater Lake, Oregon, winter perch population of Lake Mendota eutrophication of lakes by domestic drainage, hastening spawning in trout and salmon with aid of pituitary glands of Carp, use of hormones for conservation of muskellunge, respiratory responses of normal and castrated goldfish to teleost and mammalian hormones. Faculty U Wis since '38. Am Soc Naturalists—Am Soc Limnol Oceanog—Am Soc Zool—Am Soc Ichthyologists—Am Fisheries Soc—Wis Acad Sci—Gamma Alpha—Sigma Xi. Biology Building, University of Wisconsin, Madison, Wis. H: 205 Lathrop St., Madison 5.

10 HASLER, Maurice Fred. Optical and electronic instruments. b'07. BS '29—MS '30—PhD '33 (Calif Inst Tech). Author articles in field. President Applied Research Laboratories Glendale Calif since '50, dir research since '42. ACS—Phys Soc Am—Optical Soc Am—Am Soc Metals—Am Soc Testing Materials—Tau Beta Pi—Sigma Xi. Applied Research Laboratories, 4336 San Fernando Rd., Glendale 4, Calif.

11 HASS, Georg. Evaporated films; Mirrors; Oxidation of aluminum. b'13. PhD '37 (Inst Tech Danziz). Research on structure, properties and applications of thin films produced by high vacuum evaporation; development evaporations methods for producing high reflecting front surface mirrors with good abrasion and corrosion resistance; atmospheric and anodic oxidation of aluminum; new techniques for studying specimens in the electron microscope and by electron diffraction after treatments at high temperatures; methods for study of structure of aluminum oxide and titanium dioxide at various temperatures. Asst prof physics Inst Tech Danzig '38-45, also corp cons; cons Engr Research and Development Labs Ft Belvoir Va '46-51, chief research sect radiation br since '51. 1120-C, Lewis Heights, Ft Belvoir, Va.

12 HASSLER, John Williams. Active carbon; Adsorption. b'93. Student '10-14 (Pratt Inst); '14-15 (U Me). Developed original manufacturing process for production active carbon in America; research on adsorption by active carbon, edible oils, and water purification. Holds patents on manufacture of active carbon. Author: Active Carbon—The Modern Purifier '41; Active Carbon '50, also articles in field. In charge mfr Nuchar Active Carbon '16-36; dir active carbon research WVa Pulp & Paper Co since '36; cons OSRD, WPB, Office Prodn Research and Development '43-45. ACS—Am Water Works Assn—Am Oil Chem Assn—Chem Soc London (F). West Virginia Pulp & Paper Co., Tyrone, Pa.

13 HASSOLD, Ernest Christopher. Culturology; American literature. b'96. Student '09-14 (Concordia Coll); '14-15, '16-18 (Concordia Sem); PhD '34 (U Chicago). Author: American Literary History Before the Civil War '36; also articles in field. Asst prof Eng U Louisville Coll Liberal Arts '27-35, prof and head since '35, chmn div humanities since '39. Modern Lang Assn—Nat Council Teachers Eng—Am Soc Aesthetics. 126 S. Birchwood, Louisville.

14 HASTINGS, Charles Edwin. Navigation (Radio systems); Tracing (Radio systems); Relays (High speed); Air velocity (Measurement); Fluid flow (Measurement). b'14. BS (elec engring) '35 (Johns Hopkins); '28-31 (Baltimore Poly Inst, U Va Ext Div). Raydist navigation and tracking system, measurement velocity flow with improved thermal instruments, radio velocity and position determining system, high speed relays, telemeter, frequency meter, remote control apparatus, magnetic switch, selected by national Junior Chamber of Commerce as one of the ten outstanding young men of the nation during 1949 for "Inventing and developing aeronautical instruments of tremendous military and commercial significance." Holder

patents in above fields. Research phys, sect head instrument development sect, cons instrument engr to flight research div Nat Adv Com for Aeronautics Langley Field '35-45; faculty U Va Ext Div '43-44; pres, chief engr Hastings Instrument Co Inc since '45. Am Inst EE (nat joint sub-committee electronic instruments)—Inst Radio Engrs—Instrument Soc Am—Inst Navigation. Hastings Instrument Co., Inc., Hampton, Va.

15 HATCH, George Bates. High pressure chemistry. b'11. BS '32 (Yale); PhD (chem) '37 (U Wis). Research on high pressure reactors and safety aspects of high pressure operation. Chem Beacon Lab Texas Co since '37. ACS—Am Inst Chem(F)—AAAS.

16 HATCH, John Davis, Jr. Museum administration; History of American and Canadian art; Early American arts and crafts; American artist's drawings; Albany and Hudson river history. Student '26-28 (U Calif); grad Oriental studies '32 (Harvard); grad Near East studies '38 (Princeton); '39-40 (Yale). Studied art museums Mexico '30, '47, France, Holland, and England '31-32, Germany and Italy '35, China and Japan '36; surveyed facilities and materials for Far Eastern Studies in United States and Canada '32-33; founder and adviser Southern Negro Colleges cooperative exhibit group '36-41; founder American Artists Depository '38, American Drawing Annual '40; editor Parnassus '37-39, Early American Industries Chronicle since '42. Co-compiler: Reproductions of Paintings in the I S Gardner Museum '35. Now vis prof U Ore. Am Assn Museums. Norfolk Museum, Norfolk 7, Va.

17 HATCH, Melville Harrison. Beetles (Coleoptera of Pacific Northwest); Sow Bugs (Isopoda). b'98. AB '19—AM '21—PhD '25 (U Mich). Author articles in field. With U Washington since '27, prof zool since '41. AAAS(F)—Entomol Soc Am—Am Soc Zool—Phi Sigma (nat vice-chancellor '33-39). Department of Zoology, University of Washington, Seattle 5. H: 4623 21st Av., N.E.†

18 HATCH, Winslow Roper. Fungi. b'08. AB '30 (Dartmouth Coll); PhD '34 (Johns Hopkins); '35-36 (Harvard). Experimental morphology, and studies sexual phenomena of lower fungi. Aulomyces arbuscula '35; Conjugation and Zygate Germination in Allomyces arbuscula '38; Zoosporogenesis in the Resistant Sporangia of Allomyces arbusculus '44, and others. Instr bot Dartmouth Coll '36-39, asst prof '39; faculty bot Dept State Coll Wash since '39, prof since '45, chmn div biol sci since '49; asso dean Coll Arts and Sci since '53. AAUP—Am Mycol Soc—Bot Soc Am—NW Sci Assn—Sigma Xi—Phi Beta Kappa. State College of Washington, Pullman, Wash.ⓒ

19 HATCHER, Julian Sommerville. Firearms. b'88. BS and honor grad '09 (US Naval Acad). Invented breech mechanism for Army '14; established and headed Army Machine Gun Schools, Mexican Border and Springfield Armory '16-17; lt col, chief machine gun and small arms engring and design Washington '18, later hqrs AEF, Chaumont, France; charge rifle mgr Springfield Armory '19-21, ammunition mfg Frankford Arsenal '23-28, chief small arms div Ordnance '29-33; head ordnance sch and later chief ordnance field service training '37-42, chief ordnance field service '43-45; mgr US Internat Rifle Teams Switzerland '25, Rome '27, Antwerp '30; capt US Internat Rifle Team and winner Webley & Scott Pistol Match with Brit Empire Record of 100x100 Bisley '31;

mem Nat Bd for Promotion of Rifle Practice. Nat Rifle Assn Am (life)—US Revolver Assn—Army Ordnance Assn. Author: Pistols and Revolvers and Their Use '27; Textbook of Pistols and Revolvers '35; Textbooks of Firearms Investigation, Identification and Evidence '35; The Book of the Garand '48. Co-author: Machine Guns '17. Asso ed Arms and the Man '22-23, The American Rifleman '23-31; tech editor The Am Rifleman. H: 6039 Brook Dr.. Falls Church, Va.

20 HATCHER, Robert Dashiell. Radar; Microwaves. b'14. BS '38—'40-44 (Va Poly Inst); '40 (U Cal Los Angeles). Design and installation microwave distribution manifold; development antenna pattern measurement techniques, and microwave power measurement laboratory equipment; research on circuit development for guided missiles, from low frequencies to fractional centimeter wave-lengths; devised method for use of magnetron as oscillator in transmission of music and voice on microwave frequencies; design microwave transmitter. Asst prof graphics Va Poly Inst '39-42, asst prof physics '42-44; now physicist guided missile div Nat Bur Standards. Second lt Corps of Engrs AUS '38-39 lt assigned to electronics lab US Naval Acad USN '44-48. Phi Kappa Phi—Tau Beta Pi. Guided Missile Division, National Bureau of Standards, Washington 25.

21 HATFIELD, Willis Charles. Petroleum geology; Exploration geology; Exploration geophysics; Subsurface geology. b'98. BS '23 (Wesleyan U); PhD '35 (Columbia). Geological exploration and mapping Northern Rhodesia and Colombia; contributed to discovery and development copper deposits and oil fields; planned and directed execution geological and geophysical exploration programs, directed subsurface development oil fields. Field geol Brit S. Africa Co No Rodesia '28-32, Tex Petroleum Co Colombia '37-39, div geol since '40. AIMME—Am Assn Petroleum Geol—Am Geog Soc—Sigma Xi. Texas Petroleum Co., Apartado Aereo 3622, Bogota, Colombia, S.A.

22 HATHAWAY, Ellen Cuthbert (Mrs Roy L Hathaway). Michigan history. Grad '23 (Mich State Normal Coll): BS '40—MS (edn) '49 (Wayne U). Research on history of Michigan, with emphasis on history of Highland Park, state government of Michigan. Author: Good Old Michigan '40; Highland Park History for Children '46; Through the Year in Highland Park '49; Your Capitol and Mine '52; also articles in field. Teacher '23-52. NEA—Mich Edn Assn—Hist Soc Mich (mem bd trustees '48-51)—Nat Council Soc Studies (chmn exhibits '51)—Delta Kappa Gamma. H: 27 Highland Av., Highland Park 3, Mich.†

23 HATT, Robert T. Mammalogy (Life histories); Museum planning. b'02. BSc '23—MA '25—PhD '32 (Columbia). Research on mammals of central Africa and American Midwest, squirrel life-histories, mammals of Yucatan, biological effects of volcanism; expeditions for collecting mammals for University of Michigan to Pacific Northwest '22, southwestern US '24; expeditions to Yucatan '29, '47, to Mexico '44. Asst curator mammals, Am Mus Nat Hist '28-35; dir Cranbrook Inst Sci since '35. NY Zool Soc(F)—Am Soc Naturalists—Am Soc Mammalogists (sec '33-35)—Am Asso Mus (council since '41)—Midwest Mus Conf (pres '43-46)—Am Soc Zool—AAAS(F). Cranbrook Institute of Science, Bloomfield Hills, Mich.†

10 HAUCKE, Oswin. Automobiles (Alignment instruments). b'86. Ed pub schs. Research and development instruments for checking alignment of wheels and chassis simultaneously on automobile vehicles; portable gauge giving angles and right angular positions of all vehicle wheels. Inventor Chass-o-Meter. Automotive engr, wheel alignment equipment specialist Chass-o-Meter Co '33. Soc Automotive Engrs. Chass-o-Meter Co., 736-38 Coney Island Av., Bklyn 18. H: 371 E. 9th St.

11 HAUGE, Sigfred Melanchton. Agricultural biochemistry (Animal nutrition, vitamins). b'95. BA '18 (St Olaf Coll); MS '21—PhD '26 (U Minn). Research on chemistry, distribution, and preservation vitamins, role vitamins and other nutrients in nutrition of poultry and farm anima.s, vitamin retention in dehydrated foods, enzymatic destruction carotene in forage crops, trypsin inhibitor. With Purdue U since '23, asso biochem from '40, asso prof agrl chem from '39. ACS—Am Inst Nutrition—AAAS—Poultry Sci Assn—Sigma Xi—Phi Lambda Upsilon. Department of Agricultural Chemistry, Purdue University, Lafayette, Ind.

12 HAUGEN, Arnold Otto. Wildlife management; Bow and arrow Deer hunting. b'10. BS '35 (Wash State Coll); MS '38—PhD '41 (U Mich). Research on home range, management, and life history of cottontail rabbit; leading publisher data on modern bow and arrow deer hunting; presently engaged studies on improving marshes for muskrat fur production, statistical analysis of bow and arrow deer hunting. Author articles in field. Game area mgr Mich Dept Conservation '40-41, biol in charge Swan Creek Wildlife Exper Sta '42-45, game ext specialist Mich State Coll '45-46, asso prof wildlife management zool dept '47-49; leader Ala coop wild life res unit '49. Am Soc Mammalogists—Wildlife Soc—Sigma Xi. Ala Poly Inst., Auburn, Ala.

13 HAUGEN, Einar Ingvald. Scandinavian languages; Norwegian literature; Linguistics (Bilingualism). b'06. Student '24-27 (Morningside Coll Sioux City Ia); BA '28 (St Olaf Coll Northfield Minn); MA '29—PhD '31 (U Ill). Study Norwegian dialects, standard Norwegian language; clarification of relationship between language, literature, and social life among Scandinavians and Norwegian immigrants; bilingual problems. Author: Beginning Norwegian '37; Reading Norwegian '40; Spoken Norwegian '46; First Grammatical Treatise '50, and others. Author articles: Ibsen in America '34; Phonological Shifting in American Norwegian '38; Georg Brandes and his American Translators '38; On the Stressed Vowel Systems of Norwegian '42; Norwegian Dialect Studies since 1930 '48; A Norwegian-American Pioneer Ballad '49; The Analysis of Linguistic Borrowing '50 and others. Faculty U Wis since '31. Thompson Prof Scandinavian since '38; dir Linguistics Inst '43-44; US cultural relations officer Oslo '45-46; vis prof U Minn '48, U Mich '49. Royal Norwegian Sci Soc—Linguistic Soc Am(pres '50) —Am Council Learned Soc(com on Am speech)—Norwegian-Am Hist Assn (ed bd). Bascom Hall, University of Wisconsin, Madison 6, Wis.

14 HAUGHT, Benjamin Franklin. Mental growth; Intelligence and intelligence testing; Heredity; Learning. b'81. BA '11 (W Va U); MA '14 (Columbia); PhD '21 (George Peabody Coll for Teachers). Author: Interrelation of Higher Learning Processes '21; A Scheme for Combining Incomplete Rankings '23; The Language Difficulty of Spanish-American Children '31; Mental Growth of the Southwestern Indian '34; The Relation of Intelligence of College Freshmen to Paternal Occupation '38. Emeritus prof psychol U NM since '46. AAAS (F)—Am Psychol Assn—So Soc Philos Psychol—NEA (life)—Phi Kappa Phi. P.O. Box 569, Culpeper, Va.⊚

15 HAUPERT, Raymond Samuel. Biblical literature, language and archeology. b'02. AB '22 (Moravian Coll); BD '24 (Moravian Theol Sem); MA '26—PhD '31 (U Pa); Joseph Henry Thayer fellow '30-31 (Am Sch Oriental Research, Jerusalem Palestine). Author: The Transcription Theory of the Septuagint '34; The Lachish Letters '38; The Relation of Codex Vaticanus and the Lucianic Text in the Books of the Kings from the Viewpoint of the Old Latin and the Ethiopic Versions '31. Pres Moravian Coll and Theol Sem since '44. Am Oriental Soc —Archeol Inst Am—Soc of Biblical Lit and Exegesis—Nat Assn Biblical Instructors. Moravian College and Theological Seminary, Bethlehem, Pa.

16 HAUPT, Arthur Wing. Microtechnique. b'94. BS '16—PhD '19 (U Chicago). Original investigations in plant morphology and cytology; member editorial staff Madrono (journal of western botany) '35-40; botanical exploration Costa Rica '40. Author: Fundamentals of Biology; An Introduction to Botany; Plant Morphology. With U Cal at Los Angeles since '24, mem staff extension div since '36, prof botany since '46; prof botany Holmby Coll '28-42. AAAS(F)—Botany Soc Am (pres Pacific sect '38)—Sigma Xi. University of California, Dept of Botany. LA 24.†⊚

17 HAURWITZ, Bernhard. Meteorology; Upper atmosphere; Oceanography. b'05. PhD '27 (Leipzig). Author: Dynamic Meteorology '41; Physical State of the Upper Atmosphere '41; (with J M Austin) Climatology '44; also articles in field. Asst U Leipzig '27-31, lecturer '31-32; research fellow '32-35 Blue Hill Obs Harvard; meteorol Meteorol Service Can '35-41; asso prof MIT '41-47; prof and chmn dept meteorol NYU since '47. Royal Meteorol Soc—Am Meteorol Soc—Am Geophys Union—NY Acad Sci. Department of Meteorology, New York University, NYC 53.

18 HAUSDORFER, Walter. Business and accounting history; Librarianship; Special libraries. b'98. Grad '25 (Temple U); BS '27—MS '30 (Columbia U). Author: Professional School and Departmental Libraries '39; Handbook of Commercial Financial and Information Services '44; also articles in field. Librarian Temple U since '46. ALA—Am Assn State and Local Hist—Bibliog Soc—Econ Hist Assn—Council Nat Library Assns (sec, treas '45-47). 2224 W. Tioga St., Phila. 40.

19 HAUSER, Ernst A. Colloid chemistry; Chemistry of rubber and siliceous matter; Photomicrography. b'96. PhD '21 (U Vienna). Inventor Revertex process '24; Alsifilm '38; Ultramicroscopy of lyogels by incident light '44. Author: Latex '27; The Colloid Chemistry of the Rubber Industry '28; Colloidal Phenomena '39; Experiments in Colloid Chemistry '40; Rationed Rubber '42; Silicie Chemistry '50, and others; also articles in field. Non res asso prof chem engring, later prof colloid chem dept chem engring MIT since '28. Am Chem Soc (past chemn div colloid chem)—Nat Research Council—AICE—AAAS(F)— Am Inst Chem(F)—IRI, London(F)— Sigma Xi. Massachusetts Institute of Technology, Cambridge 39, Mass.⊚

20 HAUSER, George Henry. Aircraft industry (Production). b'96. BS ME '17 —LLD (hon) '50 (NYU). Prodn mgr Curtiss Aeroplane and Motor Corp '18-23; purchasing agt and asst gen mgr Chance-Vought Corp '23-31; v-pres Liberty Aircraft Products Corp since '38. Pi Tau Sigma—Kappa Mu Epsilon— Phi Alpha Theta—Sigma Pi Sigma— Sigma Alpha. Liberty Aircraft Products Corp., Farmingdale, L.I., N.Y.

21 HAUSER, Philip Morris. Demography; Census; Labor force; Social statistics. PhB '29—MA '33—PhD '38 (U Chicago). US representative Population Commission United Nations; chairman Manpower Panel, Committee on Human Resources, Research and Development Board, National Defense Department; associate editor The American Journal of Sociology; Author: Government Statistics for Business Use (with W R Leonard) '46; Workers on Relief in United States (2 vols) '39; Movies, Delinquency and Crime (with Herbert Blumer) '33; also articles in field. Chief, Labor Inventory Works Progress Adminstrn '35-37; asst to dir Study Social Aspects of Depression Social Sci Research Council '37; asst chief statis Nat Unemployment Census '37-38; asst chief statis for population Bur Census '38-42, asst dir '42-47, deputy dir '47-49, acting director '48-49; prof sociol and asso dean div of soc science U Chicago since '47. Social Sci Research Council (rep Am Statis Assn since '48, com on problems and policy and labor market research)—Am Statis Assn (F, vp '44-46)—AAAS(F)— Population Assn Am (sec '42-45, treas since '48, mem bd dir)—Am Econ Assn—Am Sociol Soc—Soc Social Research—Sociol Research Assn—Phi Beta Kappa. University of Chicago, 1126 E. 59th St., Chicago 37.⊚

22 HAUSMAN, Ethel Hinckley (Mrs Leon A. Hausman). American wildflowers. b'91. BS '20 (Cornell U). Author: Illustrated Encyclopedia of American Wild Flowers '46; Beginner's Guide to Wild Flowers '48; also articles in field. Teacher nature study and biol Cornell U '18-22; State Teachers Coll Trenton '23-29. Torrey Bot Club. 259 Harrison Av., New Brunswick, N.J.

23 HAUSMAN, Leon Augustus. Identification of hair; Birds of New Jersey and eastern United States; Methods of attracting birds. b'88. Student '10 (Mt Hermon Sch); AB '14—AM '16 —PhD '19 (Cornell U). Extensive work in identification and comparison of specimens of human and animal hair for detection of criminals and for other purposes; maintains collection of more than 2500 specimens of human and animal hair. Author: Birds of Prey '47; Bird Hiking '48; Fieldbook of Eastern Birds '46; Beginner's Guide to the Seashore '49, to Freshwater Life '50, to Attracting Birds '51, others. Contbr. encys, profl jours. Prof zool NJ Coll for Women (Rutgers) since '25. Am Ornith Union—Am Soc Zool—Phi Beta Kappa—Sigma Xi —Stanton Bird Club. N.J. College for Women, Rutgers U., New Brunswick, N.J.⊚

24 HAUSNER, Henry Herman. Powder metallurgy; Ceramics; Electrical and illumination engineering. b'01. EE '25 (Tech Hochschule, Vienna); DEng '38 (U Vienna). Research on hermetic seals, on sintered semi-conductors, on powder metallurgy processes, high frequency ceramics, electrical contacts; work in development of power plants and substations. Author: Powder Metallurgy '47; Powder Metallurgy (with J Wulff and others) '43; also articles in field. Cons engr since '45; research asso NYU since '46; research cons Rutgers U since '46; adj prof NYU since '47; sect head res and develop labs Sylvania El Prod Inc since '48; chief research engr Gen Ceramics & Steatite Co Keasbey NJ '43-45. NY Acad Sci(F)—Sigma Xi—AIEE—ASM—AIME—Ceramic Assn NJ—Soc Applied Spectroscopy—Ger Soc Met—Swed Powder—Metall Assn Soc Am Mil Engrs. New York University, Research Division, University Heights, NYC 53.

10 HAUT, Irvin Charles. Raspberry, strawberry and peach breeding; Fruit-tree seed germination and after-ripening; Small fruit commercial production; Tree and small fruit nutrition, water relations, cold storage, winter hardiness, root development and measurements of quality. b'06. BS '28 (U Idaho); MS '30 (State Coll Washington); PhD '33 (U Md). Author articles in field. Asso, later head dept hort and horticulturist U Md since '36. Department of Horticulture, University of Maryland, College Park, Md.†

11 HAVENHILL, Robert Samuel. Rubber technology; Zinc pigments. b'03. BS '25 (U Kan). Research on termoplastic rubber adhesives, zinc oxide pigments, heat generation and hysteresis in rubber compounds, anisotropy of rubber compounds, electrostatic properties of rubber, and synthetics and electronics. Holder US patents. Author articles in field. Rubber tech and development metall St Joseph Lead Co since '30. Am Chem Soc—Am Soc Testing Materials—Tau Beta Phi—Sigma Xi. St. Joseph Lead Co., Monaca, Pa.

12 HAVENS, Byron L. High speed electronic digital computing devices. b'14. BS '38 (U Wash); MS '39 (Calif Inst Tech). Development operational studies and assessment of radar search and bombing devices with emphasis on automatic computers; invention and development of high-speed electronic digital computing devices. Research asso and staff Radiation Lab MIT '41-46; sr research engr Watson Sci Computing Lab Columbia Internat Bus Machines Corp since '46. Inst Radio Engrs (tech com on electronic computers). Awarded Presidential certificate of merit for work in World War II. Watson Scientific Computing Laboratory, 612 W. 116th St., NYC 27.

13 HAVENS, George Remington. Eighteenth century French literature (Prévost, Rousseau, Voltaire, English influence). b'90. BA '13 (Amherst); PhD '17 (Johns Hopkins). Author: The Abbé Prévost and English Literature '21. Editor: Selections from Voltaire '25, '30, '40; Voltaire's Marginalia in Rousseau '33; Voltaire's Candide; Rousseau's Discours sur les Sciences et les Arts (critical edition); also articles. Prof French O State U since '21. Modern Lang Assn Am—Phi Beta Kappa. Ohio State University, Columbus 10, O.⊙

14 HAVENS, Ralph John. Upper atmosphere; Infra-red radiation. b'09. PhD '38 (U Wis). Research on infra-red transmission in molten glass, development of infra-red detection devices, pressure, temperature, and composition of upper atmosphere. Author articles in field. Physicist Navy Dept '40-45, Naval Research Lab since '45. Naval Research Laboratory, Washington.

15 HAVENS, Richard Aaron. Technology of tomato products; Mold counting of foods; Frozen foods. b'09. Student '31-33 (Butler U). Special instruction in Howard method mold counting. Granted copyright Havens-Haldeman Canners Slide Rule '47. Au-

thor articles on foods and food processing World Book Encyclopedia, and others. Owner and operator Superior Labs training and supply lab tech. Inst Food Tech—AAAS. 10 W. Ohio St., Indianapolis 4.

16 HAVIGHURST, Walter Edwin. American History (Great Lakes); Mississippi Valley; Northwest Territory); Literary Regionalism (Midwestern United States). b'01. AB '24 (U Denver); AM '28 (Columbia); LittD '47 (Lawrence Coll); LittD '47 (Ohio Wesleyan U). Author: Pier 17 '35; The Quiet Shore '37; Upper Mississippi; A Wilderness Saga '37; The Winds of Spring '40; No Homeward Course '41; The Long Ships Passing '42; Land of Promse '46 (awarded annual prize by Friend of American Writers Award '47); Signature of Time '49; (with Marion Havighurst) High Prairie '44; Song of the Pines. Prof English Miami U Oxford O since '42. Authors League Am—Phi Beta Kappa (hon). Shadowy Hills Drive, Oxford, O.

17 HAVIS, A(ndrew) Leon. Stone fruits (Peaches, plums, cherries); Breeding and anatomy of horticultural crops; Fruit crop soils; Pruning; Thinning. b'08. BS '31 (Tex Tech Coll); MS '32—PhD '35 (O State U). Author articles in field. Asst and asso hort O Agr Expt Sta '32-42; sr hort div fruit and vegetable crops and diseases US Dept Agr since '43. Am Soc Hort Sci—Bot Soc Am—Am Pomol Soc. Plant Industry Station, Beltsville, Md.†

18 HAWK, Philip Bovier. Nutrition; Biochemistry (Foods, metabolism, digestion, vitamins, water, margarine). b'74. BS '98 (Wesleyan U); MS '02 (Yale); PhD '03 (Columbia); ScD (hon) '49 (Wesleyan Univ). Author: Practical Physiological Chemistry '47; What We Eat and What Happens to It '19; Streamline for Health '35; Off the Racket '37; Researches and Writings '42; also articles in field. Pres since '26 Food Research Labs Inc NY, Food Drug and Cosmetic Cons of NY. AMA—AAAS—Am Chem Soc—Am Physiol Soc—Am Soc Biol Chem—Soc Exptl Biol and Med—Am Philos Soc—NY Acad Sci—Soc Med Jurisprudence—Inst Food Tech—Am Inst Chem—Assn Cons Chem and Chem Engrs—Sigma Xi. H:750 West 50th St., Miami Beach, Fla.⊙

19 HAWKES, Alex Drum. Orchids, Palms, Aroids (Taxonomy, cultivation). b'27. AB '47 (U Miami Coral Gables Fla). Orchid research expeditions to South Florida since '43, south central and eastern Cuba '46, '47, '48, '49, '50; studies on world distribution and taxonomy Ordhidaceae, Palmae, Araceae, Malpighiaceae, Velloziaceae and other families; corresponding editor Deutsche Orchideengesellschaft (Germany), Orquidea (Brazil). Author: The Orchids—A Manual for Growers '50; The Orchidaceae of Cuba '50; The Orchids of Florida '50; Genera Palmarum '51; The Major Kinds of Palms '50-51) An Introduction to the Palms '51; The Aroid Family '51, and others. Author articles: The Identity of Grammatophyllum "grandiflorum" '49; The Major Genera of Cultivated Orchids '50-51; The Minor Genera of Cultivated Orchids '50-51; Studies in Florida Botany '49-51; Studies in Antillean Botany '49-51; Studies in Pacific Orchidology '49-51; Studies in Indonesian Orchidology '51; Studies in Brazilian Palms '51; Studies in Brazilian Araceae '51; New or Noteworthy Brazilian Plants '51; Notes on the Palms '50-51, and others. Asst ed Orchid Digest since '45; research asso Fairchild Tropical Garden since '45; fellowship for taxonomic research NY Bot Garden '48. Am Orchid Soc—Or-

chid Soc Cal—S Fla Orchid Soc(Founder, first pres)—Am Soc Plant Taxonomists—Fla Acad Sci—Cal Bot Soc—Deutsche Orchideengesellschaft—Philippine Orchid Soc—Soc Cubana de Botanica—Soc Mexicana de Botanica—Soc Brasileira de Orquidea—Circulo Paulista de Orquidofilos—Am Fern Soc—Nat Hort Soc—Pacific Orchid Soc Hawaii—Hawaii Orchid Soc—Central Fla Orchid Club (Founder). Dept. of Botany, Univ. of California, Berkeley 4, Cal. H: P.O. Box 35, Coconut Grove 33, Fla.

20 HAWKES, Herbert Edwin, Jr. Geology (Chromite, magnetic iron ore); Geochemical prospecting (Ore deposits). b'12. AB '34 (Dartmouth Coll); PhD '40 (MIT). With US Geol Survey since '40. Soc Exploration Geophysicists—Soc Econ Geol—Am Inst Mining Engrs. U.S. Geological Survey, Washington 25.

21 HAWKINS, George Andrew. Ther modynamics (Heat-power apparatus); Heat transmission (Conduction, convection, radiation); Corrosion (High temperature steam); Small arms (Interior ballistics). b'07. Student '26-27, summer '28 (Colo Sch Mines); BS (mech engring) '30—MS (mech engring) '32—PhD '35 (Purdue U); '33 (Univ Denver); '38-39 (Armour Inst Tech). Research on small arms interior ballistics, corrosion of alloys by high temperature steam. Author: Thermodynamics (2d edit) '51. Co-author: (with H L Solberg) Supplementary Notes on Applied Thermodynamics '42; (with Max Jakob) Elements of Heat Transfer and Insulation '50. Author 70 articles in field. Contributor: Corrosion Handbook '48. Prof thermodynamics and Westinghouse research prof heat transfer Purdue U since '44, asso dir Engring Expt Sta since '50, dir small arms ordnance research since '41. Am Soc ME—Am Inst Chem Engrs—Army Ordnance Assn—Nat Rifle Assn—Sigma Xi. Awarded Pi Tau Sigma gold medal '45. Office of Dean of Engineering, Purdue University, Lafayette, Ind.†⊙

22 HAWKINS, Harold Vern. Engineering (Structural, vibration, aeronautical). b'12. BS in CE '34 (U Washington); MCE '35—PhD '37—grad sch scholarship in civil engring '34—Forrest M Towl fellow '35 (Cornell U). Responsible for stress analysis of wing of XP63 pursuit airplane; directed use and development of vibration and electronic equipment for flight test work at Bell Aircraft; supervised structural research on formed steel members and fatigue in welded structural connections Cornell U '36-40. Author articles in field. Prof civil engring Ill Inst Tech Chicago '47-51; now with aircraft div Globe Corp. Inst Aeronautical Sci (asso F)—Am Soc Engring Edn—Nat Soc Profl Engrs—Ill Soc Profl Engrs—ASCE—Tau Beta Pi—Sigma Xi—Phi Kappa Phi. Globe Corp., Box 922, Joliet, Ill.

23 HAWKINS, J(ohn) E(rskine). Thermodynamics; Kinetics; Distillation; Naval stores. b'99. AB '19—BS in chem engring '22—MS '24—PhD '27 (U Pa). Plant supervisor and chief chemist P J Ritter Co Bridgeton NJ '32-33; head chemistry dept U Tampa '33-35; acting head chem engring U Fla '35-36, asst prof chemistry and asso dir naval stores research '36-37, asso prof chemistry '37-45, prof chemistry since '45, dir naval stores since '46. AAAS (R)—Am Inst Chemists(F)—Am Chem Soc (sec-treas Fla sect '38-41, chmn' 43, councillor '45 '46)—Fla Acad Sci(chmn phys sci div '45, pres '49)—AAUP—Alpha Chi Sigma—Gamma Sigma Epsilon—Sigma Xi. Dept of Chemistry, University of Florida, Gainesville, Fla.†⊙

10 HAWKINS, Robert Martyr. New Testament (Language and liteature). b'87. AB '06 (Washington U); MA '07 (Central Coll); BD '10 (Vanderbilt U); PhD '27 (U Edinburgh); DD '23 (Birmingham So Coll); grad study '26-27 (Yale). Author: The Recovery of the Historical Paul '43. Prof philosophy and Bible lit Birmingham (Ala) So Coll '18-23; prof Bibl lit and religious edn Southwestern Coll Winfield Kan '23-28; prof OT Vanderbilt U Nashville '28-32, prof Bibl lit '33-38, prof NT since '39. Soc Bibl Lit and Exegesis. H: S Bellevue Dr., Nashville 5.⊙

11 HAWLEY, Florence. Cultural anthropology. b'06. AB '27—MA '28 (U Ariz); PhD '34 (U Chicago). Author articles in field. Asso prof and research U NM since '34 on southwestern archeol, ethnol, pottery, cultural anthrop of Pueblos; advisor in adult edn to United Pueblos Area Indian Service. Am Anthrop Assn—Sigma Xi —Phi Beta Phi. Department of Anthropology, University of New Mexico, Albuquerque, N.M.†

12 HAWLEY, Willis M(eeker). Development of Chinese writing; Chinese dictionaries; Japanese swords. b'96. Research in the development of Chinese writing arts and culture 20 years; accumulated library of Chinese books numbering 20,000 volumes, several thousand in other languages relating to the subjects; collector Japanese swords, coached by Japanese experts. Author: Oriental Culture Charts since '43. Merchant, Oriental art and antiques since '32, importer since '36; Chinese bookshop since '47; writer and pub since '42. 8200 Gould Av., Hollywood 46, Calif.

13 HAWORTH, Leland J(ohn). Fundamental electronics and thermionocs; Electronic circuits; Radar; Nuclear physics. b'04. Lalor fellow '37-38 (MIT); fellow '29-30—scholar '28-29— PhD '31 (U Wis); AB '25—AM '26 (Ind U). Author articles in field. Various inventions in electronic circuitry, especially radar indicators. Assistant dir Brookhaven Nat Lab '47-48, dir since '48. Staff to group leader div head MIT Radiation Lab '41-46. Sigma Xi—Phi Beta Kappa. Brookhaven National Laboratory, Upton, N.Y.⊙

14 HAWTHORN, Fred William. Farm machinery (Testing); Seeds (Harvesting and processing equipment); Silos (Pit type). b'93. BA (agrl engring) '16 (Ia State Coll). Built first four-row tractor cultivator, operation experimental tractors and power farming equipment, tests on new balloon tractor tires '33, wind electric plant '35, production certified seeds of new farm crop varieties, new harvesting and processing techniques, built new type pit silo '47, perfected new methods unloading forage into silo and hoisting it from pit in feeding operation, using power of an electric chain hoist. Exptl work Minneapolis-Moline Co '29-46; free-lance author. Am Soc Agrl Engrs. Castana, Ia.

15 HAWTHORN, Horace Boies. Rural-urban sociology. b'89. BS '14— MS '15 (Ia State Coll); PhD '21 (U Wis). Author: Outlines of Sociology '24; Sociology of Rural Life '26; Sociology of World Crisis '47; also articles in field. Prof sociol Morningside Coll since '31. Am Sociol Soc—Phi Kappa Phi—Gamma Sigma Delta. Morningside College, Sioux City, Ia†⊙

16 HAWTHORN, Leslie Rushton. Vegetable seed production (Onions). b'02. BS '24—MS '28 (Cornell U). Developed Texas Grano onion, Summerset tomato, Geneva cucumber, and Utah experimental thresher. Author articles in field. Hort US Dept Agr

since '44. AAAS(F)—Am Soc Hort Sci —Genetics Soc Am—Sigma Xi. Box 6, Utah State Agricultural College, Logan, Utah.†

17 HAY, Russell G. Catalysis; Olefin isomerization. b'13. BS '35 (Washington & Jefferson Coll); MS—PhD '46 (U Pittsburgh). Research on hexene isomerization, butene and pentene isomerization, olefin polymerization (particularly isobutene) '41-44, kinetics of butene isomerization, investigation of surface properties and poisoning of catalysts for isomerization '44-46; presently engaged in study of surface and physical properties of catalysts that may contribute to catalytic activity. Author articles in field. With Gulf Research and Development Co since '38. Am Chem Soc—AAAS. Gulf Research and Development Co., P.O. Box 2038, Pittsburgh 30.

18 HAYAKAWA, Samuel Ichiye. Semantics. b'06. BA '27 (U Manitoba); MA '28 (McGill U); PhD '35 (U Wis). Author: Language in Action '41; Oliver Wendell Holmes (with Howard M Jones) '39. Editor: ETC.: A Review of General Semantics since '43. Asst prof Eng Ill Inst Tech '40-42, asso prof '42-47. Soc Gen Semantics (mem gov bd since '42)—Linguistic Soc Am —Modern Lang Assn—AAAS—Am Dialect Soc—Natl Council Teachers Eng. 1356 Hyde Park Blvd., Chicago 15.

19 HAYDAK, Mykola H. Apiculture; Bee and insect nutrition. b'98. '17-19 (U Kiev, Ukraine)—'22 (Charles U, Praha, Czechoslovakia)—'22-26 (Coll Agr and Forestry Poly Inst, Praha)— '27 (Ingeneur of Agr); PhD '33 (U Wis). Research in bee biology, pollen substitutes, food value of honey, vitamins in bee foods, protein starvation in bees, changes in vitamin content in bees, bee management, swarm control, pollination. Author: Pollen and Pollen Substitutes in the Nutrition of the Honeybee '43; Pollen Substitutes '45; Beekeeping in Minnesota '48; also articles in field. Asst entomol Div Entomol and Econ Zool U Minn U Farm St Paul '33-35, instr '35-43, asso prof since '45. AAAS—Am Assn Econ Entomol—Entomol Soc Am—AAUP— Minn Acad Sci—Minn Beekeepers Assn —Nat Fed Beekeepers Assn—Sigma Xi. Award of Merit, Minn Hort Soc. University Farm, University of Minnescta, St. Paul 1.

20 HAYDEN, Arthur Gunderson. Structural engineering; Parkways. b'74. AB '98 (Ripon Coll); BS '01 (MIT). Worked in variety of structures, including simple span, cantilever, lift, bascule and draw bridges, dams, lock-gates and aqueducts; made practical application of Rathbun's theory of skew bridge design; supervised design of over 100 highway and railroad grade separation projects and general plans for several major parkway projects. Developed design and construction of rigid frame bridge, now in general use for short and medium spans; devised method of reinforcing Mohawk River Bridge dams without building falsework. Author: The Rigid Frame Bridge '32; also articles in field. Structural designer and asst engr NY State Barge Canal '04-20; chief designing engr Bronx Parkway Commn '20-26, Westchester County Park Commn '25-37; cons civil engr. ASCE—Nat Soc Profl Engrs—NY State Soc Profl Engrs. Received citation Ripon Coll '48 in recognition of outstanding ability and distinguished accomplishments in engring. 9 Florida Av., Bronxville 8, N.Y.

21 HAYDON, Glen. Musicology (Bibliography, theory of music, history of music, musical aesthetics). b'96. AB '18—MA '21 (U Calif); European stu-

dy private teachers '23-24; PhD '32 (U Vienna). Author: A Graded Course of Clarinet Playing '27; Studies in the Fundamentals of Music '33; The Evolution of the Six-Four Chord '33; Introduction to Musicology '41; and others; also musical compositions. Prof music and head dept music U NC since '34. Am Musicol Soc (pres '42-44)— Coll Music Assn—Music Educators Nat Conf (nat bd '37-41)—Music Teachers Nat Assn (pres '40-42)—NC State Music Teachers Assn (pres '37-40)— Nat Assn Sch Music—Internat Musicol Soc—Music Library Assn—Royal Mus Soc, London—Medieval Acad Am —Phi Mu Alpha—Phi Delta Kappa— Pi Kappa Lambda. Music Department, University of North Carolina, Chapel Hill, N.C.†⊙

22 HAYES, Francis Clement. Spanish drama and proverbs; Folk gestures. b'04. BA '28—PhD '36 (U NC); MA '30 (Columbia). Research on collection of proverbs in Spain and their use as titles and motives in Siglo de Oro drama, sectional speech habits in US. Author: Gesture (in Encyclopaedia Americana) '41; An Elementary Spanish Grammar (with Fernandez) '48; also articles in field. Asso prof Spanish U Fla since '46; asso ed South Atlantic Bulletin; mem ed bd Southern Folklore Quarterly. Am Dialect Soc—NC Dept Edn (com teacher training). Anderson Hall, University of Florida, Gainesville, Fla.

23 HAYES, George Lloyd. Forest fires and meteorology. b'09. Student '27-29 (Brigham Young U); BS '34 (U Ida); MF '40 (Yale); '46-47 (U Calif). Research in topographic variations in forest fire danger; determined that conditions were most favorable for forest fire occurrence and rapid spread at mid-elevations in the thermal belt of mountainous regions; analyses of records demonstrating influence of forest cover on rainfall pattern ground surface and efficiency of various types of rain gage installations, forest fires as a factor in forest ecology. Author articles in field. Forest fire research staff Northern Rocky Mt Forest and Range Expt Sta Missoula Mont '34-41; charge forest fire research Southeastern Forest Expt Sta Asheville NC '41-46; instr and asst prof forest management Ore State Coll '47-48; leader Siskiyou-Cascade Research Center US Forest Service Ore since '49. Soc Am Foresters—Am Geophys Union—Sigma Xi. Siskiyou-Cascade Research Center, Box 389, Roseburg, Ore.

24 HAYES, John Edward. Dams (Earth). b'77. Research on movement of water through earth dams; development method to determine saturation of earth dam; design earth reservoir dams, and diversion dams; devised method for retarding movement in earth dams. Inventor venture flume water measuring device. Author articles: Analysis of and Method of Overcoming Slides in Earth Dams; Pamphlet on Maintenance and Operation of Canal Systems. Chief engr and mgr Farmer's Reservoir & Irrigation Co Colo '11-21; river analysis South Platte Colo, Snake Ida-Wyo; investigation water resources western states US Bur Agrl Econ.; now civil, irrigation and constrn engr. Original Ida Soc Engrs —Colo Soc Engrs (life)—Am Soc CE (life). 147 Seventh Av. E., Twin Falls, Ida.

25 HAYES, Joseph Claude. Language and literature; German language. b'04. BS '28—AM '31 (U Ala); PhD '38 (NYU); student '38-39 (U Heidelberg). Author: Laurence Sterne and Jean Paul '42. Instr German U Ala '28-33 '36-37, asst prof '37-46, asso prof '46-47, prof German since '47, head dept

German since 49. AAUP—Modern Lang Assn Am—S Atlantic Modern Lang Assn—Ala Hist Assn—Gamma Sigma Epsilon—Kappa Delta Pi—Phi Delta Kappa. 812 Seventeenth Av., Tuscaloosa.◉

10 HAYMOND, Frank Cruise. Law. b '87. Graduated '06 (Fairmont State Normal Sch); AB cum laude '10 law student '10-12 (Harvard). Member house of delegates WVa Legislature '16-18, WVa Judicial Council '34-39; apptd judge 16th Judicial Circuit of WVa '39-45; judge Supreme Court of Appeals of WVa since '45; chmn Fed Dist Bd Law Examiners; mem Conf of Chief Justices '49; mem vis com Coll of Law U WVa '50. Am Bar Assn (com elections and privileges house of dels; com on Am citizenship '43; chmn com on membership and program judicial sect '47-48)—WVa Bar Assn (com on refersher courses '45; charter mem WVa Judicial Council '34-39)—Am Judicature Soc (vp) —Am Counsel Assn. State Capitol, Charleston WVa.◉

11 HAYNER, Albert. Syrian Golden Hamster husbandry. b'14. Student (Ill State Normal U). Produced Syrian Golden Hamsters for lab purposes since '46, owner and operator Hayner Hamstery, largest privately-owned colony of hamsters in US '40; editor Hamster Breeder's Research Service since '47. Discovered white faced hamster only known hamster mutant. Author: Successful Hamster Raising '45, and others. West Salem, Ill.†

12 HAYNER, Norman Sylvester. Criminology (Delinquency areas, prison communities, parole). b'96. AB '20 (U Wash); AM '21—PhD '23 (U Chicago). Research on juvenile delinquency, crime prevention, probation and parole, delinquency areas in Pacific Northwest and Mexico City, prisoner community as social group; Washington State administrator Interstate Parole Compact. Jane Addams prof sociol and soc service Rockford Coll '22-25; with U Wash since '25, prof sociol since '37; mem Wash State Bd Prison Terms and Paroles '51. Am Sociol Soc (mem exec com '48-51)—Am Prison Assn—Osborne Assn (nat adv com)—Pacific NW Council Family Relations (founder, first pres)—Nat Council Family Relations—Pacific Sociol Soc. University of Washington, Seattle 5; Washington State Board of Prison Terms and Paroles, 614 County-City Bldg, Seattle 4. H:7566 Roosevelt Way, Seattle 5.

13 HAYNES, Benjamin Rudolph. Business education. b'97. BS in Edn '28—AM '29—PhD '32 (NYU). Co-author: (with Jessie Graham) Research in Business Education '32; (with Graham) Problems in Business Education '33; (with Graham) Study-Guide in Foundations of Business Education '35; (with Clyde W Humphrey) Collegiate Secretarial Training Inventory Test '38; (with John J W Neuner) Office Management and Practices '47; (with Irol Whitmore) Mechanics of Business Letter Writing '42, and others; also articles in field. Pres Wheeler Business Coll Birmingham Ala since '48. NEA (pres bus edn sec '34) —Nat Assn Bus Teacher Training Instns (vp '44-45)—Nat Bus Teachers Assn (2d vp '45, pres '46)—So Bus Edn Assn—Nat Office Mgmt Assn (nat dir '42-44, '46-47, nat chmn ednl and professionalization com '47-48, nat dir and chmn '48-50)—Phi Kappa Phi. 21 Peachtree St., Mountain Brook, Ala.

14 HAYNES, Harry Leonard. Entomology; Insect repellents. b'18. BS '40 (U NH); MS—'42—PhD '47—research fellow '40-41, '42-46 (Rutgers U). Re-

search on certain chemical and physical properties of chemicals and their relationship to mosquito repelling, apparatus used in laboratory insecticide tests, two butoxypolypropylene glycol compounds as fly repellents for livestock, the use of a butoxypolypropylene glycol to control the European red mite on apples. Author articles in field. Research asso entomol Crop Protection Inst, Boyce Thompson Inst Yonkers NY '47-48; entomol biol research div Carbide & Carbon Chemicals Corp Yonkers since '48. Am Assn Econ Entomol—NJ Mosquito Extermination Assn—AAAS—Sigma Xi. Carbide & Carbon Chemicals Corporation Biological Research Division at Boyce Thompson Institute, 1086 N. Broadway, Yonkers 3, N.Y.†

15 HAYNES, Winthrop Perrin. Petroleum geology (Europe, Mexico, Middle East). b'87. AB '11—AM '12—PhD '14 (Harvard). Exploration for petroleum deposits. With exploration div Standard Oil Co of NJ '20-36, geol spl adviser '36-43; vis lectr petroleum geol Harvard since '47. Geol Soc Am (F)—Paleontological Soc Am(F)—Am Geog Soc(F)—Am Assn Petroleum Geol—AAAS—Am Inst Mining Engrs —Sigma Xi. Geological Museum, Oxford St., Cambridge 38, Mass.

16 HAYS, Arthur Alexander. Calvinism. b'75. AB '95—AM '98—DD '14 (Washington and Jefferson Coll); student 00-03 Bernadine Orme Smith fellowship and T B Blackstone fellowship in NT Greek—BD '09 (McCormick Theol Sem); post grad work '03-05 (U Jena Germany). Author: (brochures) How a Medieval Monk Became Martin Luther '15; Pilgrim Puritan, Protestant '20; Tyndale's Ploughboy Opens His Bible. Collaborator: The Handbook to the Hymnal; From the Pyramid to Paul; The Study of the Bible, Today and Tomorrow. Prof Greek lang and lit Washington and Jefferson Coll '05-09; instr history and NT Greek McCormick Theol Sem '09-14, prof ecclesiastical history '14-45, prof emeritus since '45. Soc Bibl Research—Am Soc Church History—Chicago Church History Club—Chicago Cleric—Phi Delta Theta—Phi Beta Kappa. 154 S. Wade Av., Washington, Pa.†◉

17 HAYS, Fred Negley. Furnaces (Design); Fuels (Combustion, steel plant). b'91. BS (Mining engring) '14 (Pa State Coll). Studies in open hearth design; reheating furance design; fuel economics in iron and steel plants; combustion solid, liquid, gaseous fuels; design iron and steel plants. Contributor: Steel Plant Design '49; Making, Shaping and Treating of Steel '49. Fuel and combustion engr Carnegie Steel Co '15-29; fuel and combustion cons Arthur G McKee Co Magnitogorsk Russia '31-32; fuel and power cons Carnegie Ill Steel Co '43-48; vis expert Army of Occupation Japan '49; power planning engr US Steel Co since '48. Am Soc ME—AIMME—Engrs Soc Western Pa—Assn Iron and Steel Engrs—Blast Furance and Coke Works Assn—Iron and Steel Inst Japan (hon). Carnegie Bldg., U.S. Steel Co., Fifth Av., Pitts.

18 HAYS, Norman Pershing. Polar navigation; Navigation (Strategic); Strategic bombing. b'18. BS (engring). '40 (Okla A&M Coll); '41 (Royal Air Force Nav Sch). Intented averager device for aircraft sextants, design precise astrocompass, balance and calibration of directional gyrocompasses, prepared navigation plans for strategic bombing of Japanese cities during World War II and for non-stop distance record-breaking flight of "Dreamboat" from Guam to Washington and for "Dreamboat's"

flight from Honolulu to Cairo via North Pole. Chief nav unit Engring Development Center Wright Field '42-43, '46-48; staff nav officer HG 20th Strategic Air Force '44-45; chief Nav and Bombing Branch HQ US Air Force since '49. Inst Nav (former vp). Strategic Air Division, Director of Requirements, Hdqrs US Air Force, Pentagon, Washington.

19 HAYSTEAD, Ladd. Agricultural public relations; Farm management; Farm news. b'03. Author: Farm for Fortune and vice versa '41; Meet the Farmers '43; If the Prospect Pleases '45; The Squires Can Take It '47. Coauthor: (with Herrell DeGraff) Business of Farming '47. Contbr: Cities Are Abnormal '44. Farm editor Fortune magazine '43-46; has written for over 100 farm magazines. Am Assn Agrl Editors—Am Soc Farm Mgrs—Am Soc Agrl Engrs—Nat Assn Radio Farm Dirs—Soc Mag Writers—Authors League. Room 920, 342 Madison Av., NYC 17.

20 HAYWARD, Herman E. Plant anatomy and physiology; Salinity (West United States agriculture). b'92. AB '17 (U Minn); MS '25—PhD '28 (U Chicago). Research on morphological and physiological responses of plants to saline an alkaline soil conditions, salt problems in western agriculture, characteristics of saline and alkaline soils in relation to their productivity; studies of salt tolerance of plants. Author: The Structure of Economic Plants '38; The Salt Problem in Irrigation Agriculture '46; also articles in field. Prof biol State Teachers Coll River Falls Wis '19-28; asst prof bot U Chicago '28-29, asso prof '29-31, prof '31-39; agent US Regional Salinity Lab '39-40, sr plant anat '40-45, dir since '45. Bot Soc Am(F)—Am Soc Agron—Am Soc Hort Sci—Am Soc Plant Physiol—Soil Sci Soc Am—Sigma Xi. U.S. Regional Salinity Laboratory, Riverside, Calif.

21 HAYWARD, Roger. Optical engineering; Optical instrument design. b'99. BS '22 (MIT). Holds patents on device for grinding and polishing surfaces, apparatus for surface generation, optical system for cameras, means and a method for testing optical surfaces, scanning telescopes; co-holder patent transparent projection screen. Draughtsman and designer Cram and Ferguson Boston '25-29, SE Lunden '29-32, '36-38, since '46; cons optics Nat Tech Labs S Pasadena '40; optical engr Mt Wilson Obs '41-43; cons optics Paramount Pictures Inc '46. Am Inst Architects (medal '22). Lunden, Hayward & O'Connor Architects, 510 S. Spring St., Los Angeles 13. H: 920 Linda Vista Av., Pasadena 3.

22 HAYWOOD, Charles. US Folk songs; US folklore (Musicology and bibliography). b'04. BS '26 (Coll City NY); MA '40—PhD '49 (Columbia); Artist diploma '31—F and diploma '35 (Juilliard Sch Mus). Research on comparative folklore and folk songs. Author: A Bibliography of North American Folklore and Folksong '51; Musical Settings to Cervantes Texts: A Bibliography '48; Life and Work of James A Bland '47. Concert, radio, opera and oratorio performer and soloist radio and symphony orchestras; with Queens Coll since '39, asso prof mus from '50; lectr Juilliard Sch Mus. Am Mus Soc —Am Folklore Soc—NY Folklore Soc —Am Anthrop Soc—AAUP—NY State Singing Tchrs Assn—Phi Beta Kappa. Queens College, Flushing 67, N.Y.

23 HAZARD, James Ovington. Tennessee (Forestry). b'84. PhB '08 (Brown); MF '11 (Yale). Invented and patented forest nursery seeding machine. Cons forester '15-26; asst state forester Va '26-30; state forester Tenn since '30. Soc Am Foresters (chmn Ky-Tenn sect '43)—Nat Assn State Foresters (vp '39). 309 State Office Building, Nashville.

10 HAZARD, John Newbold. Soviet law and government. b'09. BA '30 (Yale U); LLB '34 (Harvard U); Certificate '37 (Moscow Juridical Inst); JSD '39 (U Chicago). Author: Soviet Housing Law '39; also articles in field. Fellow Inst Current World Affairs '34-39 assigned to study of Soviet law (attended Moscow Juridical Inst); lecturer on Soviet form of govt U Chicago '38-39; lecturer on Soviet polit instns Columbia U '40-41; deputy dir USSR br Fgn Econ Adminstrn and predecessor agencies '41-45; adviser on state trading Comml Policy Div Dept State '45-46; adviser on Soviet law to US chief of counsel for Prosecution of Axis Criminality '45; prof pub law and mem staff Russian Inst Columbia U since '46; cons on Soviet law since '39. Am Polit Sci Assn (mem bd ed Am Pol Sci Review '50)—Am Soc Internat Law (mem exec Council '46-49)—Am Bar Assn (chmn com on European law, sec internat and comparative law '45-48)—Am For Law Assn. Columbia University, NYC.⊙

11 HAZLEHURST, Jack Harris. Tests (Psychological); Photography. b '04. BS (EE) '26 (U Ill); MBA '32—PhD (Psychol) '40 (Northwestern U). Development mechanical and sales aptitude tests for industrial use; job studies in field of mechanics; research on fine grain developers and three color processes; organized training programs for portrait photography. Consultant on industrial training and safety '27-50; asst to pres Interstate Elec Co New Orleans since '50. Am Psychol Assn(F)—Royal Photog Soc Gt Brit—Sigma Xi. Interstate Electric Co., S. Peters St., New Orleans 13. H: 1213 Nashville Av., New Orleans 15.

12 HEADINGTON, Clifford E(arl). Petroleum products composition (Applications of mass, infrared, ultraviolet, raman, emission and X-ray spectroscopy). b'05. AB '27 (Upper Ia U); MS '29 (Indsl research fellow '28-29 (Ia State Coll). Author articles in field. Div research dir Atlantic Refining Co since '44. Am Chem Soc—Am Petroleum Inst. Atlantic Refining Co., 3144 Passyunk Av., Phila. 1. H: 525 Country Club Lane, Havertown.†

13 HEADLEE, William Hugh. Parasitology (Medical); Helminthology (Pinworms and Ascaris); Protozoology (Medical); Parasitic infections in humans; Tropical diseases. b'07. AB '29 (Earlham Coll); MS '33—Rockefeller scholar '32-33 (U Ill); PhD '35—Rockefeller fellow '33-34 (Tulane U). Research on the epidemiology of human helminth infections in Egypt, methods for diagnosis of human pinworm infection and other parasitic diseases, epidemiology of Ascariasis in metropolitan New Orleans, human parasite infections in Indiana, incidence of helminth infections in Venezuela. Author articles in field. Asst internat health div Rockefeller Found Cairo '30-32; instr biol Purdue U '35-42, asst prof '42-43; asst prof parasitic diseases Ind U Sch Med '43-46, asso prof since '46; biol and parasitol Nat Ministry Edn Venezuelan Govt '37-38 and head dept biol Nat Pedagogic Inst '37-38; parasitol Ind U Hosps since '43, dept dermato-syphilol Gen Hosp Indianapolis since '47. AAAS(F)—Royal Soc Tropical Med Hygiene(F)—Am Soc Tropical Med—Am Soc Parasitol—Nat Malaria Soc—Ind Acad Sci—Sigma Xi. Markle Found fellow '43, '44. In-diana University School of Medicine, 1040 W. Michigan St., Indianapolis 7.

14 HEADLEY, Leal Aubrey. Mental health. b'84. BS '07 (Carleton Coll Minn); MA '11—PhD '16 (Harvard). Author: How to Study in College '26; Making the Most of Books '32. Instr philosophy Carleton Coll '11-16, prof psychology and edn since '16. AAAS—Am Philos Assn—Minn Psychol Assn NEA—Delta Sigma Rho—Phi Beta Kappa. East Tower, Skinner Memorial Chapel, Carleton College, Northfield, Minn.⊙

15 HEADSTROM, Richard. Bird nests and tracks; Mammal tracks. b'02. Student (MIT) (Harvard). Author: Birds' Nests '49; Whose Track is That? '50; Animal Tracks '51; Birds' Nests of Western United States '51; Knowing the Outdoors '52. Curator entomol Worcester Museum Natural Hist; asso curator bot New Eng Musuem Natural Hist. H: Dover, Mass.

16 HEADY, Harold Franklin. Grassland ecology; Forage utilization by livestock. b'16. BS '38 (U Idaho); MS '40 (NY State Coll Forestry); '40-41 (U Minn); PhD '49 (U Neb). Author articles in field. Asso prof A&M Coll Tex since '47. Ecol Soc Am—Am Soc Range Management (co-organizer, sec-treas '48)—Sigma Xi—Xi Sigma Pi. Range and Forestry Department, Texas Agricultural and Mechanical College, F. E. Box 24, College Station, Tex.†

17 HEALD, Kenneth Conrad. Petroleum geology and exploration. b'88. BS in Engring '12 (Colorado Coll); DSc '28 (U Pittsburgh). With US Geol Survey '14-24, chief sect oil geol '19-24; asso prof petroleum geol Yale '24-25; geol with Gulf Oil Co since '25, vp '45; lecturer on petroleum geol U Chicago and Johns Hopkins '23, '24, U Pittsburgh since '26. Author: Geologic Structure of the Pawhuska Quadrangle Oklahoma '18; Structure and Oil and Gas Resources of Osage Reservation Okla '22; Eldorado Oil Field Ark '25; Geology of Ingomar Anticline Mont '26; also articles in field. Nat Research Council (mem at large '25-26)—Am Assn Petroleum Geol (rep Nat Research Council '21-25)—Soc Econ Geol—Am Inst Mining Metall Engrs—Geol Soc Washington—Geol Soc Am—Am Statis Assn—Am Petroleum Inst—AAAS(F)—Royal Geog Soc. Gulf Oil Corp., Gulf Building, Pittsburg.⊙

18 HEALY, Collins. Irish culture (Analysis, specification); Modern Irish drama. b'07. AB '31 (St John's U); AM '32 (Columbia U); student (Fordham U). Discovered that ancient Irish poetry schools required students of poetry and verse to assume recumbent bodily position while writing or composing verse; first collector and indexer of Irish and Celtic master's essay and doctor's dissertation titles for American eastern universities. Author: Survey of Celtic Offerings in the Colleges and Universities of the United States '38; Decline and Revival of the Irish Language '46; Twenty Centuries of Irish Verse '48, and others; also articles in field. Lecturer Columbia U '38-43, Fordham U since '36. United Irish Counties Assn NY—Folklore Ireland Soc—Irish Texts Soc—Am Irish Hist Assn—Gaelic Musical Soc Am—Irish Cultural Forum Am—Cymric Soc NY Inc (highest Bardic title of Gorsedd '47)—Mod Lang Assn Am—Am Folklore Soc—AAUP—Eastern Psychol Assn—Psi Chi. Fordham Univ, School of Adult Education, 302 Broadway, NYC 7.

19 HEALY, John J., Jr. Sulfuric acid (Catalysts). AB (Chem) '19 (Harvard); BS (Chem engring) '21 (MIT). Development of new catalyst. Is-sued patents in field. Chem Merrimac Chem Co '21-30; with Monsanto Chem Co since '30, asst gen mgr since '47. ACS—AICE—Am Inst Chems(F)—Soc Chem Industry—Comml Chem Development Assn—Chem Market Research Assn—Am Soc Engring Edn—Engring Soc NE. Monsanto Chemical Co., Everett 49, Mass.

20 HEARD, Osborne Overton. Embryos (Reconstruction and modelling); Microtomy. b'90. Diploma (Md Inst Fine Arts). Discovered and invented microtomy with circular reciprocating knife, direct photomicrographic halftone negatives for color reproduction, (with others) tokodynometer and stereo-biological camera. Author articles in field. Dept embryol Carnegie Inst Washington since '13. Department of Embryology, Carnegie Institution of Washington, Wolfe and Madison Sts., Baltimore 5.

21 HEARTMAN, Charles Frederick. North American history and bibliography; Booklore. b'83. Student German Institutions before '05. Author: Checklist of Printers in the US '15; Phillis Wheatley, Critical Attempt and Bibliography '15; Bibliography of Henry H Brackenridge '17; Unpublished Freneauana '18; Checklist of New Jersey Almanacs Prior to 1850 '29; Bibliography of New England Primer '34; John Peter Zenger and His Fight for Freedom of the American Press '34; Bibliography of Non-New England Primer '34; The Blue Book '36; and others. Editor: Americana Collector '25-26; American Collector '26-27; American Book Collector '32-35; Heartman's Historical Series No. 1-75 '13-48. Rare bookdealer since '12. AHA—Conn Hist Soc—Fla Hist Soc—Miss Hist Soc—NH Hist Soc—NJ Hist Soc—NY Hist Soc—So Hist Assn—Texas Hist Assn—Vt Hist Soc—Friends of Bodleian Library (Oxford Eng). Book on John Peter Zenger chosen by Soc Graphic Arts for outstanding typographical excellence as one of fifty best books printed '34. 421 So. Seguin Av., New Braunfels, Texas.

22 HEBERLE, Rudolf. Sociology; Demography; Labor movement; Minorities; Migration; Political parties and elections (Germany). b'96. Student '15-23 (Göttingen U, Freiburg U, Marburg U, Kiel U); Dr Sc Pol '23, Habilitation '29 (Kiel U). Given grants from Social Science Research Council '39-40, Louisiana State University '46-47. Contributed analysis of population mobility in United States and social consequences; studied migration to and from cities, using German data on registration of migrants; studied political movements and elections in region of Germany showing factors contributing to rise of Nazism. Traveled in Germany, Scandinavia, Eastern Europe, France, England and United States; research on Labor movement, migration, national minorities, population, political parties and elections, theoretical sociology. Author: Die Grosstadte im Strome der Binnenwanderung. Wirtschafts-und Bevölkerungs-swissenschaftliche Untersuchungen uber Wanderung und Mobilitat in deutschen Städten (with Meyer) '37; From Democracy to Nazism. A Regional Case Study on Political Parties in Germany '45; also articles in field. Prof sociology La State U since '38; collaborator US Dept Agr; labor market analyst War Manpower Commn La '45. Am Sociol Soc—Rural Sociol Soc—So Sociol Soc—Population Assn Am. Social Science fellowship from Laura Spellman Rockefeller Mem (Rockefeller Found) '26-29. 101 Himes Hall, Louisiana State University, Baton Rouge 15, La.†⊙

10 HECHT, Bernard. Quality control (Radio and electronics industries). b '18. B Elec Engring '40 (Coll City NY); '43 (Newark Coll Engring); '45-48 (U Pa). Research on application of statistics to radio engineering, application of statistical sampling to manufacture and inspection, scientific organization of industrial inspection. With Internat Resistance Co since '45, mgr quality control dept '46-50; mgr assembly control RCA Victor '51; instr fundamentals quality control Temple U since '49. Instr Radio Engrs (v-chmn group on quality control)—Inst Math Statis—Am Soc Quality Control —Tau Beta Pi. RCA Victor Division, Bldg 17-3, Camden, N.J. H: 104 Sunnyhill Lane, Havertown, N.J.†

11 HECHT, Otto Friedrich. Acetylene chemistry; Carbonmonoxide chemistry; Gas reactions; High polymers; Solvents (Plastics); Plasticizers. b'05. BS '27—MA '28—PhD '30 (U Berlin). Research on vinylethers and reactions of acetylene and phenols, aldehydes and ketones; synthesis of acrylic acid and its derivatives and substitution products from acetylene hydrocarbons, carbonmonoxide and reactive components; chemistry of gas reactions and high polymers, molding mixtures from phenol-acetylene resins, adhesives; solvents for plastics, resins and cellulose, internal plasticizers for high molecular plastics and resins, ester plasticizers. Granted patents in field. With Aug Nowack A G '31-35; I G Farbenindustrie A G '35-47; Gen Aniline and Film Corp since '50. ACS—German Bunsen-Gesellschaft. General Aniline and Film Corp., Easton, Pa. H: 230A Rock St.

12 HECK, Arch Oliver. School administration; School records; Pupil personnel; Special education. b'87. BS '13 (Hedding Coll); MS '14 (U Ill); '19-20 (Columbia); PhD '24 (Ohio State U). Member educational commission of fifteen to train School Superintendents Japan '48-49, '49-50. Author: A Study of Child Accounting Records '25; Administration of Pupil Personnel '29; A Study of the Ohio Compulsory Attendance and Child Labor Laws '30; The Education of Exceptional Children '40. Co-author: (with L H Munzenmayer) Handbook of Compulsory Education '31. Editor and writer: Pupil Personnel, Guidance and Counseling '33, Contbr: Nations Schs, Schoolboard Jour, Review of Ednl Research, Ency of Ednl Research, Ency of Modern Edn, Dictionary of Edn. Editorial bd Nations Schools. With Ohio State U since '24, prof edn since '33. 128 E. North Broadway, Columbus 14, O.⊚

13 HECTOR, L(uther) Grant. Electronic tubes (Design, mass production machinery); Rare gases (Magnetic susceptibility, dielectric constants); Hearing (Acoustics); Auditoriums (Acoustics). b'94. BA '20 (Oberlin Coll); MA '22—PhD '24 (Columbia). Granted patents on electronic tubes. Author: Principles of Modern Radio Receivers '27; Introductory Physics '33; Electronic Physics '43; Physics for Arts and Sciences '48. Prof phys Buffalo U, indsl cons '24-41; worked on proximity fuze OSRD, cons WPB '41-45; dir engring Nat Union Radio Corp '43-46; with Sonotone Corp since '46, vp in charge tech operations since '48. Acoustical Soc Am—AAAS—APS— Inst Radio Engrs—Sigma Xi. Sonotone Corp., Box 200, Elmsford, N.Y.

14 HEDGES, Joseph Harold. Gold, silver, copper, lead and zinc mines (US, Mexico, and Canada); Mineral resources of Germany; Copper deposits (Arizona). b'82. BS '03 (Mich State Coll); EM '05 (Mich Coll Mines). Conducted original exploration of San Manuel copper deposit in Arizona.

Contributor: Minerals Yearbook '32-41. Supt Mexico Consol Mining and Smelting Co '06-11; supt Guanajuato Development Co '12; chief engr Moctezuma Copper Co '13-16; mine foreman United Verde Ext Mining Co '17-18; supt Prince Consol Mining and Smelting Co '18-22; field engr Mining Corp Canada '23-25; with US Bur Mines since '26, chief Minerals Div since '49. AIM ME—Tau Beta Pi. US Bureau of Mines, Washington 25. H: 4809 De Russey Parkway, Chevy Chase 15, Md.

15 HEDGPETH, Joel W(alker). Distribution and ecology of marine organisms; Pycnogonida (Taxonomy, evolution, distribution); History of marine biology. b'11. AB '33—MA '39 (U Calif, Berkeley). Research on the evolutionary significance of the pycnogonida, the pycnogonida of western North Atlantic and Caribbean, history of marine biology, evils of progress, aspects of nature, distribution of marine invertebrates of Gulf of Mexico. Author articles in field. Research asso oceanog Inst Marine Sci U Tex since '47 (on leave '49-50), Dept Zool U Calif '49, instr zool Pacific Marine Sta Dillon Beach Calif '48-49. Am Soc Zool—Hist Sci Soc—Am Soc Limnol and Oceanog—Soc Systematic Zool— AAAS. Box 664, Walnut Creek, Calif.†

16 HEER, Clarence. Government (Finance and taxation). b'93. AB '14 (U Rochester); PhD '26 (Columbia). Director Tax Research Foundation and National Bureau of Economic Research Inc. Author: The Post-War Expansion of State Expenditure '26; Income and Wages in the South '30; Recent Social Trends (in collaboration) '33; Federal Aid and the Tax Problem '39. Asso prof pub finance U NC '27-'32, research prof since '32; cons legislative coms and tax dept NY, Va, NJ, NC. Nat Tax Assn—Am Economics Assn—Phi Beta Kappa—Delta Sigma Pi. University of North Carolina, Chapel Hill, N.C.†⊚

17 HEFFELFINGER, Clarence Edgar. Accounting (Teaching); Investments; China, Japan (Geography and history); Business Law for CPA Bus Administration. b'98. AB '20 (Ursinus Coll Pa); MS '31 (Columbia U). Author: Economic Development of the Yangtze Valley in China '31. Prof and bus analyst in Asia '20-29; prof econs Washington and Jefferson Coll '31-39; prof bus adminstrn Centre Coll Ky since '42. Nat Assn Tax Accountants —Am Inst Accountants—Am Geol Soc —AAUP. Awarded Bronze medal for Distinguished Service in China, by Chinese Govt. Centre College of Kentucky, Danville, Ky. H: 226 N. 4th St.

18 HEFFELFINGER, John Brock. Directional antennas; Allocation of television and amplitude and frequency modulation radio frequencies. b'17. BS (Elec engring) '38 (U Kan) MS '40 (O State U). Research on the lower (D) laywer of the ionosphere. Practice before the Federal Communications Commission on frequency allocation matters and design of directional antennas, particularly as they pertain to the broadcasting industry. Design engr Collins Radio Co Cedar Rapids Ia '40-44; sr engr Air Communications Inc Kansas City '45; cons radio engr Kansas City since '46. Am Inst Elec Engrs—Inst Radio Engrs— Sigma Xi—Tau Beta Pi—Eta Kappa Nu—Sigma Tau—Sigma Pi Sigma— Kappa Eta Kappa. 815 E. 83rd St., Kansas City 5, Mo.

19 HEFFERNAN, John Baptist. Naval history. b'94. BS '17 (US Naval Acad); '43 (Naval War Coll); '44 (Army-Navy Staff Coll). Prepared histories of combats in which participated; research and instruction naval and civilian history, archives; director

naval record, history, archives. Commnd ensign '17 advanced through ranks to rear admiral '47; instr history US Naval Acad '32-35, '38-40; dir naval records history Navy Dept since '46. Naval Hist Foundn—US Naval Inst—Am Military Inst—Am Hist Assn—Miss Valley Hist Assn—Ind Hist Soc—Am Cath Hist Assn—Am Irish Hist Soc. Div. Naval Records and History, Op-29, Navy Dept., Washington 25.†

20 HEFFERNAN, Paul Malcolm. Architectural design. b'09. BS (Archtl engring) '29—MS '31 (Ia State Coll); Certificate '35 (Beaux-Arts Inst Design). Asso prof Ga Inst Tech '38-44, prof since '44; partner Bush-Brown, Gailey and Heffernan. AIA— Tau Beta Pi—Phi Kappa Phi. Conde Nast Travelling Fellow in Am Architecture, from Found for Architecture and Landscape Architecture '29-30; Eugene Dodd Medal for freehand drawing and watercolor '34; Julia Amor Appleton Fellow for European travel and study '35; Sheldon Fellow '35; 28th Paris prize of Soc Beaux-Arts Architects '35. School of Architecture, Georgia Inst of Technology, Atlanta, Ga.

21 HEFNER, Robert A(rthur). Distribution and ecology of the Millipedes and Centipedes in North Central United States; Human heredity (Defects in hands). b'92. BS '23 (Ohio Northern U); MS '24—PhD '29 (Ohio State U). Author articles in field. With Miami U since '25, prof and ch dept zool since '40. AAAS(F)—Am Micros Soc—Genetic Soc Am—Human Genetic Soc— Ohio Acad Sci(F). Department of Zoology, Miami University, Oxford, Ohio.

22 HEIBERGER, Charles A(dam). Plasticizers; Synthetic polymers; Benzyl compounds. b'15. BS (chem engring) '35—MS (chem engring) '37— PhD (organic chem) '39 (Lehigh U). Research on chemistry of drying oils, rubber lacquers, resin treatments of textiles, polymerization, alkyd resins, plasticizers, benzyl compounds, esterification, polyesters (alkyds). Research chem US Rubber Co '39-45; dir research Ohio-Apex Inc since '45. ACS— Am Inst Chem(F). Ohio-Apex Inc., Nitro, W.Va. H: 44 21st St.†

23 HEID, John Laurence. Frozen foods. b'00. Student '17-18 (Heidelberg U)—'19-20 (Mo Sch Mines and Engring); BS ChE '23 (George Wash U). Author articles in field. With Skinner Co Omaha Neb '27-29, Fruit and Vegetable Products Research Los Angeles '30-31, in charge Weslaco Tex '32-40; gen mgr Citrus Products Mfg Santa Anna Calif '41-42, Citrus Products Research, in charge US Dept Agr Lab Winter Haven Fla '43; dir research and development Fla Citrus Canners Coop Lake Wales Fla; now gen manager Golden Citrus Juices Inc. AAAS(F)—Am Soc Refrigeration Engrs—Pub Health Assn—Inst Food Technol (1st sect chmn Fla)—Citrus Products Research Council (1st nat chmn, 1st chmn Fla Sect)—Am Chem Soc. Second annual food industries award for achievement in food technol San Francisco '49. Golden Citrus Juices, Inc., Fullerton, Cal.

24 HEIDT, Lawrence Joseph. Photochemistry; Chemical kinetics; Physical and analytical chem of sugars. b'04. BA '27—MS '28—PhD '30 (U Wis). Asso prof phys chem MIT since '46. Am Acad Arts Sci(F)—NY Acad Sci— Am Chem Soc—AAAS(F). Massachusetts Institute of Technology, 77 Mass. Av., Cambridge 38, Mass.

25 HEILBRUNN, Lewis Victor. Viscosity (Protoplasmic); Cell division (Physiology); Anesthesia, Shock

(Theory). b'92. AB '11 (Cornell U); PhD '14 (U Chicago). Author: The Colloid Chemistry of Protoplasm '28; An Outline of General Physiology '37, 2d ed '43. Former mng editor Protoplasm Monographs; mem editorial bd Physiol Zoology; editor biological publs The Dryden Press. With U Pa since '29; prof Zoology since '43; trustee Marine Biol Lab Woods Hole Mass since '31. AAAS (F)—Am Soc Zoologists (vp '32)—Am Soc Naturalists—Am Physiol Soc—Soc for Exptl Biology and Medicine. Guggenheim Memorial Fund fellow '27-28. Add: Zoological Laboratory, University of Pennsylvania, Philadelphia.

10 HEILIGMAN, Harold A. Chromite and magnesia refractories; Dry battery manganese dioxides. b'00. ChE (Lehigh U). Research on manganese ores and ferromanganese, processing firing applications and improvements of chrome and magnesia refractories. development of activated iron oxide for purification of manufactured gas. Author articles in field. Chemist E J Lavino and Co '22, chief chemist '22-26, research engr '26-30, asst technical dir '30-43, gen mgr technical dept since '43. AIC (chmn Pa chap '44)—ACS—Am Ceramic Soc (chmn Phila sect '46)—Am Inst Mining and Metall Engrs—Am Soc Metals—AIChE—Pa Ceramics Assn—Can Ceramic Soc—British Ceramic Soc—Am Soc Testing Materials—Electrochem Soc—Franklin Inst. E. J. Lavino and Co., P.O. Box 29, Norristown, Pa. H: 2203 Coles Blvd.

11 HEIMSATH, Star McDaniel. Philosophy (Whitehead). b'00. Diploma delle Belle Arte '22—Fellow '22 (U of Rome, Italy); BA '23 (Bryn Mawr Coll); PhD '41—Ives fellow '25 (Yale U). Author: Whitehead's Conception of God '41. Author article: Whitehead's Idea of God '43. Asso prof Rockford Coll '43-47, Trinity U since '47. Trinity University, San Antonio, Tex. H: 421 Belknap Pl.

12 HEINES, Neal J. Solar activity; Sunspots. b'92. Student '07-11 (Hope Coll). Dir Solar Div, Pres Am Assn Var Star Observers Harvard Obs for Nat Bur Standards Central Radio Propagation Lab since '44. Internat Astron Union—AAAS(F)—Nat Research Council—Geophys Union—Am Astron Soc—NY Acad Sci. 560 Broadway, Paterson 4, N.J.

13 HEINICKE, Arthur John. Fruit growing; Photosynthesis of fruit trees. b'92. BSA '13—MA '14 (U Mo); PhD '16 (Cornell U). Author articles in field. Prof pomol Cornell U since '20, head dept since '21; dir NY State Agrl Expt Sta Geneva since '42. AAAS (F, counsel sect G '46-50)—Am Soc Hort Sci (pres '37)—Am Bot Soc (chmn physiol sect '38)—Am Soc Plant Physiol—Sigma Xi—Phi Kappa Phi—Gamma Sigma Delta. Cornell University, Ithaca, N.Y.◎

14 HEINICKE, Kurt J. Optical physics (Instruments). b'09. BS '32 (MIT); PhD '35 (U Giessen, Germany). Design high aperture ultraviolet Monochromator. Author articles in field. Optical instrument development Ernst Leitz Wetzlar Germany '32-36, Bausch & Lomb Optical Co Rochester NY '36-48, Ward's Natural Science Establishment '48, Pres Heinicke Instr Corp '49. AAAS. Heinicke Instrument Corp., Rochester 4, N.Y.†

15 HEINLEIN, Oscar Allen. Climatic testing. b'11. BS '32 (US Naval Acad); MS (Meteorol) '42 (Cal Inst Tech); MS (Mech engring) '49 (Stanford). Testing aircraft and ground equipment under extremes of temperature in climatic laboratory at Eglin Air Force Base and American Arctic and tropical regions. Author article: Temperature limitations for design of equipment. From pvt to col USA since '37; spl climatic investigations in Africa and Middle East '45-46, Canada Alaska, Labrador, Greenland, Florida since '46. Am Polar Soc—Am Meteorol Soc—Inst Aeronautical Scis. APO 931 c-o Postmaster, Seattle.

16 HEINRICH, Edward Oscar. Questioned document examination; Authentication (Handwriting, typewriting, mutilated and charred documents, writing materials, cultural objects). b'81. Licientiate in pharmacy Wash '99; BS '08 (U Calif). Expert on questioned documents and other scientific evidence in Hindu-Ghadr revolution plot trials San Francisco '17, in cases US vs William (Jack) Dempsey, US vs Levin (income tax frauds), People vs Roscoe Arbuckle, People vs William Hightower, the d'Autremont train bandits Ore, St Francis Dam failure Los Angeles '28, US vs Germany (Black Tom cases '30-34), US in re Harry Bridges '39, and others. Attended XVth International Criminal Police Commission Conference Berlin '39. Author articles in field. Practice San Francisco since '19; lecturer on criminal investigation U Calif '17-25, '38-39; research asso police sci '30-31; lecturer polit sci '43. Am Inst Criminal Law Criminology—Am Chem Soc—Soc Am Mil Engrs—Soc Pub Analysts Eng—L'Acad Internat de Criminalistique — Internat Medico-Legal Assn (hon F). Marvin Building, 24 California St., San Francisco 11. Laboratory, 1001 Oxford St., Berkeley 7, Calif.

17 HEINRICH, Ross R(aymond). Earthquakes (Central United States); Seismology; Hydrology; Blast and atmosphere vibrations. b'15. BA '36 (U Mo); MS '38—PhD '44—grad fellow '36-38 (U St Louis). Author articles in field. Asso prof geophysics U St Louis since '47, assisting in naval research project on microoscillations in the atmosphere since '47. Am Geophys Union—Seismol Soc Am—Geol Soc Am(F)—Am Meteorol Soc—Am Soc Engring Edn—Sigma Xi. 3621 Olive St., St. Louis 8.

18 HEINRICHS, Walter E(mil), Jr. Mining geophysics. b'19. Diploma geol engring '40 (Colo Sch Mines). Organization, direction, and application of geological and geophysical techniques in mining exploration, for discovery, extension, and development of ore deposits, especially metalliferous. Geophys engr seismic exploration '40-44; geophysicist US Bur Reclamation '46-47; cons geophysicist, geol and engr since '47. Geol officer USN '44-46. Soc Exploration Geophysicists—Airz Geol Soc—Am Geol Soc—Colo Soc Registered Engrs—Am Inst Mining Engrs. H: 2356 S. Campbell Av., Tucson; also 505 21st St., Golden, Colo.†

19 HEINTZELMAN, B. Frank. Alaskan forestry, land use and water power resources. b'88. BF '07 (Pa State Coll); MF '10 (Yale). Co-author: Regional Planning for Alaska—Its Resources and Development '38; also articles in field. Regional forester for Alaska since '37. Soc Am Foresters. U.S. Forest Service, Juneau, Alaska.

20 HEINZ, Winfield Bernard. Operations research; Instrumentation; Automatic controls. b'02. BS '26 (U Wash); GE '31 (Alexander Hamilton Inst). Author articles in field. Asst chief engr Calco Chem Div Am Cyanamid Co '47-49; dep dir Operations Research Office Johns Hopkins U since '49; ind cons development engr '42-47; founded Heinz Eng Co '50, chmn bd dir Gen Engr and Research Corp, Power Generators Ltd. AICE —

ASME—AIEE—Nat Soc Profl Engrs—Assn Phila Sci—Franklin Inst—Tau Beta Pi—Sigma Xi. Heinz Eng Co., 2525 Wilson Blvd., Arlington, Va.†

21 HEISER, Charles B(ixler) Jr. Sunflowers (Taxonomy, evolution, history, uses, Indian varieties); Chili peppers. b'20. AB '43—MS '44 (Washington U); PhD '47 (U Cal). Research on evolution of common sunflower Helianthus annuus, the wild and weed races modified by hybridization and selection. Author: The Sunflower among the North American Indians '51. Faculty Washington U '44-45; herbarium bot U Cal '45-46, asso '46-47; asst prof Ind U '47-51, asso prof since '51. Phi Beta Kappa—Sigma Xi—Bot Soc Am—Soc Study Evolution—Am Soc Plant Taxonomists—Cal Bot Soc—Ind Acad Sci—AAAS—Gamma Alpha. Botany Department, Indiana University, Bloomington, Ind. H: 609½ S. Fess.

22 HEISEY, Paul Harold. Luther and Lutheranism. b'86. AB '07—DD '29 (Midland Coll, Atchison, Kan); BD '10 (Western Theol Sem); AM '11 (State U Ia); PhD (Northwestern U). Author: Psychological Studies in Lutheranism '16; The Lutheran Graded Series, a Study '26; Three Essays on Luther '32, and others; also articles in field. Pastor various churches '10-19; prof philos and psychol U Dubuque '19-21; prof religious edn Wittenberg Coll '21-42; prof Bible and religious edn Newberry Coll Newberry SC since '46. Religious Edn Assn—AAUP. Newberry, S.C.

23 HEIZER, Robert Fleming. California archeology. b'15. AB '36—PhD '41 (U Calif). On Smithsonian Institute expeditions to Kodiak Island Alaska '34, '35; in charge archeology expeditions University California '36-38, '40, '47, '48. Author: Francis Drake and the California Indians '47; An Introduction to the Archeology of Central California '39; Archeological Evidence of Cermeno's California Visit in 1595 '41; Aconite Poison Whaling in Asia and America '41. Asso curator Am Archeol U Calif Mus Anthrop since '47, dir U Calif archeol survey '48, asso prof anthrop. Am Soc Psy Anthrop—Soc Am Archeol (Pacific Coast ed, mem council)—Am Anthrop Assn. University of California, Berkeley 4.

24 HELLAND, Melvin Andreas. Madagascar; Malagasy language. b'96. AB '15 (Augsburg Coll); STM '19—PhD '30 (Hartford Sem Found); Certificate '20 (U Grenoble). Missionary in Madagascar '21-40. Author: Paoly Mpitoriteny '29. Now prof New Testament and comp religion Augsburg Sem. Augsburg College and Theological Seminary, Minneapolis 4.†

25 HELLEBRANDT, Frances Anna. Exercise (Physiology); Posture (Center of gravity); Amputees (Posture mechanics). b'01. BS '28—Md '29 (U Wis); '38-39 (Charles U Prague); '42 (Northwestern U); '43 (Mayo Clinic Rochester Minn). Research on physiology of vertical stance of man, behavior of stomach and kidney during severe exercise, disability evaluation and motor learning; developed electrodynamic brake bicycle ergometer, also series of upper extremity ergographs, and methods for determining location of center of gravity of man. Co-author articles: (with Elizabeth Brogdon, Rubye H Tepper) Posture and its Cost '40; (with Elizabeth Brogdon Franseen) Physiological Study of the Vertical Stance of Man '43; (with EE Mueller, I M Summers, S J Houtz, M F Heap, Rober N Eubank) The Influence of Lower Extremity Amputation on Stance Mechanics '50; (with S J Houtz) Ergographic Study of Hand Dominance '50, and others. Contribuotr: Organizing for Clinical Practice in Physical Therapy '47; Rehabilitation of the Physically Handicapped '50. Faculty U Wis '30-44, asso prof phys med '42-44; prof phys med and dir Baruch Center Phys Med and Rehabilitation Med Coll Va since '44; ed bd Jour Applied Physiol. Am Physiol Soc—AMA—Am Congress Phys Med—Am Acad Cerebral Palsy—Am Acad Phys Edn—Sigma Xi. Am Acad Phys Edn award for research in dynamics and physiol of posture; Am Congress Phys Med gold medal for research in physiol basis of disability evaluation, silver medal for physiol study stance mechanics of lower extremity amputee. Medical College of Virginia, Richmond 19, Va.

10 HELLER, John Roderick, Jr. Public Health and Medical Administration. b'05. BS '25 (Clemson (SC) Coll); MD '29 (Emory U). Co-author: (with R A Vonderlehr) The Control of Venereal Disease. Editor: Journal of Venereal Disease Information; Journal National Cancer Institute. Clinician Ga Dept Health Brunswick '31; acting asst surgeon USPHS '31-34, with regular commd corps since '34; med dir, chief div venereal disease '43; dir Nat Cancer Inst since '48; professorial lectr George Washington U Sch Med since '44. Am Bd Preventive Med and Pub Health (diplomate)—AMA—So Med Assn—Am Pub Health Assn—Am Venereal Disease Assn (pres '48-49)—Phi Chi—Cosmos Club. National Cancer Institute, Bethesda 14, Md.

11 HELLSTROM, Carl Reinhold. Firearms. b'95. CE '14 (Christiania Coll); post grad '15-16 (U Paris); ScD '50 (Lafayette Coll). Member advisory board Springfield Ordnance District; small arms committee American Ordnance Association. French Engring Commn to US '16-17; engr Eastern Coal & Mining Corp '19-20; chief engr Am Rack Co '20-22, pres '22-31; successively research engr, gen supt, works mgr, dir and vp in charge plant operations Smith & Wesson '31-46, pres, chmn bd since '46. Honorable SCD, US Army '18; Citation US Ordnance Dept '47. 2100 Roosevelt Av., Springfield, Mass.©

12 HELM, Everett Burton. Musicology (Comparative). b'13. BA '34 (Carleton Coll); MA '36—PhD '39 (Harvard). Studies of Renaissance music, Latin American music, and contemporary German music; theater and music officer with US Military Government in Germany '48-50. Author articles: Italian Traits in the English Madrigal '46; The Musical Temper of Rio de Janeiro '46; Carl Orff and the Musical Stage '50; Contemporary German Music '50. Contributor: Oxford History of Music. Am Mus Soc—League of Composers (bd dirs). The Harvard Club, 27 W. 44th St., N.Y.C.†

13 HELMERICKS, Harmon Robert. Arctic (Exploration). b'18. Student mech engring (U Ariz). Arctic flight exploration with small aircraft; design of Eskimo-type wearing apparel; field study Arctic survival problems, including living on polar ice, igloo construction, and hunting of polar game; polar photographer and naturalist, also expert on reading polar ice from air for its stability and safety; studies geography of arctic Alaska and Canada. Co-author: (with Constance Helmericks) We Live in the Arctic; Our Summer with the Eskimos; Our Alaskan Winter. Co-author article: (with C Helmericks) Report on the Need for Wildlife and Natural Resource Conservation in Alaska. Arctic Inst NA—Polar Soc—Explorers Club—Aircraft Owners and Pilots Assn. 635 Main St., Montrose, Colo.†

14 HELMREICH, Ernst Christian. Modern European history. b'02. AB '24—AM '25 (Ill U); AM '27—PhD '32 (Harvard). Research in history of the Balkans, diplomacy of World War II. Author: The Diplomacy of the Balkan Wars 1912-13 '38; Central-Eastern Europe (with J S Roucek and others) '46; Contemporary Europe (ed J S Roucek) '47; also articles in field. Prof diplomatic hist Fletcher Sch of Law and Diplomacy '43-44; prof hist and govt Bowdoin Coll since '45. Sheldon Traveling Fellow Harvard '29-30. Bowdoin College, Brunswick, Me.†

15 HELMS, E. Allen. American party and international politics. b'97. AB '22—MA '23—PhD '27 (U Ill). Author: The Eighteenth Amendment '28; co-author: American Politics '47; Democracy in Transition '37; also articles in field. Prof polit sci Ohio State U since '37. Am Polit Sci Assn—Am Acad Polit Social Sci. Ohio State University, Columbus 10, Ohio.†

16 HELTZEL, Virgil Barney. Courtesy (Literature); Literature (Elizabethan); Sir Philip Sidney, Shakespeare, Bacon; Patronage (Literary). b'96. AB '16 (Randolph-Macon Coll); MA '20 (Harvard); PhD '25 (U Chicago). Editor Northwestern University Studies since '48, associate editor Shakespeare Quarterly since '49. Author: Chesterfield and the Tradition of the Ideal Gentleman (dissertation) '25; A Check List of Courtesy Books in the Newberry Library '42; Fair Rosamond '47; English Literary Patronage, 1550-1630. Editor: Richard Earl of Carbery's Letters to his Son '37; Types of English Prose Non-Fiction '41; Of Honour '47; Elizabethan and Stuart Plays '49. Co-editor and translator: (with Hoyt H Hudson) Nobilis, or a View of the Life and Death of a Sidney '40. Prof Eng Northwestern U since '37. Henry E Huntington research F '35-36; John Simon Guggenheim F '49, '50. Northwestern University, Evanston, Ill.

17 HELWIG, Edwin R(oyer). Orthoptera (Cytology; Locusts). b'00. AB '22 (Western Md Coll); PhD '29 (U Pa). Author articles in field. Asst prof U Pa '37-47; Univ of Colorado since '47; research asso Acad Natural Sci Phila since '46. Am Soc Zool—Soc Study Evolution—Sigma Xi. Nat Research Council fellow '29-30. Department of Biology, University of Colorado, Boulder, Colo.†

18 HEM, Halvor Olsen. Weighing scales; Force measuring devices. b'63. CE '00 (Internat Corr Sch Scranton Pa); DSc hon '36 (U Toledo). Design and production weighing scales from 600 lb capacity to railway scales of 300000 lb capacity up to 100 feet in length, also special scales and testing devices; design dynomometer scales up to 500000 feet, integrating scales, scales for wind-tunnels for US and foreign countries, scales to determine center of gravity of airplanes. Holds patents in field. Supt and chief engr Strait Mfg Co & Strait Scale Co Kansas City Kan '90-15; chief engr Toledo Scale Co '15-47. Am Soc CE—ASME (F)—Nat Scale Men's Assn—Am Ry Engring Assn—Norwegian Tech Soc (hon)—Horological Inst Am. Medal of Franklin Inst '36. 3009 Kenwood Blvd., Tol 6.

19 HEMING, Arthur Edward. Drug products (Enzymes, digitalis glucosides, antibiotics). b'13. AB '37—MS '38 (Kalamazoo Coll); PhD '41 (U Wis). Chief chemist Johnson & Johnson de Argentina and Brasil '41-47; research biochemist Smith Kline & French Labs since '48. Am Chem Soc —Assn Study Internal Secretions—AA

AS—Sigma Xi. Smith, Kline & French Laboratories, Phila.

20 HEMINGWAY, Ernest. Cuba (Game fish); Bullfighting (Lore); Spain (Revolution). b'99. Student pub schs. Author: A Farewell to Arms '29; Death in the Afternoon '32; Winner Take Nothing '33; The Fifth Column and the First Forty-Nine '38; Spanish Earth '38; For Whom the Bell Tolls '40; Across the River and Into the Trees '50; The Old Man and The Sea '52. Covered Spanish Civil War for North American Newspaper Alliance '37 '38; war corr China '41, ETO and Western Front '44 '45. H: San Francisco de Pauls, Cuba.

21 HEMKER, Arthur Henry. Agricultural engineering. b'07. BS (elec engring) '29 (Kan State Coll). Studies in application of electricity and electronics to agriculture. Issued patents on special type motor control for farm applications, electrically heated stock watering device. Dist farm electrifcation specialist Gen Elec Co '30-34, rural elec work '40-44, in charge prodn development farm industry div '44-48 mgr farm industry div since '48. Am Soc Agrl Engrs—Sigma Tau—Nat Elec Mfrs Assn. General Electric Co., 1 River Rd., Schenectady 5, N.Y.

22 HEMLEBEN, Sylvester John. History of peace movements; Modern European history. b'02. AB '27—MA '28 (U Ia); '28-30 (Columbia); certificate '29 (Cambridge U Eng); PhD '31 (Fordham U); '35 (Harvard); certificate '36 (Munich U). Author: Outlines of Modern European History 1500-1830 '34; Plans for World Peace Through Six Centuries '43; Guide to European History '48; also articles in field. Prof hist Southwestern La Inst since '47. Royal Hist Soc(F)—AHA. Box 347, Southwestern Station, Lafayette, La.

23 HEMMENDINGER, Henry. Spectroscopy; Astrophysics; Luminescence. b'15. Student '30-32 (Cornell U); '32-33 (U Munich); AB '35—AM '37 (Harvard); PhD '39 (Princeton). Research on interaction of light and matter, organic dyes, inorganic phosphors, physics of solar atmosphere, luminescence. Mem operation research group Office Chief Naval Operations Washington '44-45; physicist General Aniline and Film Corp Easton Pa since '46. Optical Soc Am—Am Astron Soc—Am Phys Soc—Am Inst Phys—Sigma Xi. General Aniline and Film Corp., Central Research Laboratory, Easton, Pa.†

24 HEMPHILL, William Edwin. History of Virginia; Archival science. b'12. BA '32 (Hampden-Sydney Coll); MA '33 (Emory U); PhD '37 (U Va). Asst prof history, archivist of library, Mary Washington Coll, '41-44; asst dir, Va World War II History Commn, Charlottesville Va '44-45, dir since '46. Author: George Wythe the Colonial Briton: a Biographical Study of the Pre-Revolutionary Era in Virginia '37; editor: Gold Star Honor Roll of Virginians in the Second World War '47; Pursuits of War: the People of Charlottesville and Albemarle County, Virginia, in the Second World War '48. AHA—Am Assn State Local Hist—Soc of Am Archivists—AAUP—Miss Valley Hist Assn—So Hist Assn—Va Social Sci Assn—Va Edn Assn—Ga Acad Soc Sci. Virginia World War II History Commission, University of Virginia Library, Charlottesville, Va.†

25 HEMPLE, Henry William. Geodetic engineering. b'92. BS (civil engring) '16 (Ill Inst Tech). Research on geodetic field surveys in US and Alaska, use portable steel towers and making of triangulation and base measurements and precise leveling surveys, in charge trigonometric determination of altitude of stratosphere balloon flight '35. With US Coast and Geodetic Survey since '17, chief Div Geodesy from '45. Am Soc CE (mem exec com div surveying and mapping '47-51, chmn '50)—Soc Am Mil Engrs (dir '49-52)—Am Geophys Union (pres sect geodesy '48-50)—Wash Acid Sci (bd mgrs '48-51)—Am Congress Surveying and Mapping (chmn tech div control surveying '46-49)—AAAS—Washington Soc Engrs (dir '50-51)—Inst Nav—Tau Beta Pi. Exceptional Service (Gold medal) award Dept Commerce '52. US Coast and Geodetic Survey, Washington 15. H: 5712 Nevada Av.†◎

10 HENBEST, Lloyd G(eorge). Fossils; Paleontology (Stratigraphic). b'00. AB '24 (U Ark); AM '27 (U Kan); '28-30 (Yale). Studies and description fossil species protozoan order Foraminifera; historical methods in geology; age determination and correlation rock formations by means fossil Formainifera; development methods in photomicrography. Co-author: Fusulinidae of Illinois; Geology and Biology of the North Atlantic Deep Sea Cores; Pennsylvanian Fusulinidae; Distribution of evolutionary explosions in geologic time. Asst geol Ill State Geol Survey '26-30; geol US Geol Survey since '30. Geol Soc Am(F)—Am Assn Petroleum Geol—AAAS(F)—Wash Acad Sci—Geol Soc Wash—Soc Econ Paleontologists and Mineral—Paleontological Soc Wash. US Geological Survey, Washington 25.

11 HENCH, Atcheson Laughlin. English lexicography and syntax (Middle English period 1100-1500); American English. b'91. AB '12 (Lafayette Coll); MA '17—PhD '21 (Harvard). Adv editor: American Speech '40-41; Funk and Wagnall's College Standard Dictionary '42-45; articles on American Speech; contbr: Dictionary of American English '28-37; Middle English Dictionary '33-34; H L Mencken's American Language Supplement 1 '45; Ency Britannica annual. Asso prof U Va '22-26, prof since '26, Linden Kent Memorial prof English since '40. Modern Lang Assn—Medieval Acad—Southeastern Folklore Soc—Am Dialect Soc (vp '46, pres '47-48)—Phi Beta Kappa. Pavilion IX, West Lawn, University of Va., Charlottesville, Va.◎

12 HENCKEN, Hugh O'Neill. Prehistory and archeology of the old world. b'02. BA '24 (Princeton); BA '26—MA '30—PhD '29 (Cambridge U); hon DLitt '37 (Nat U of Ireland). Carried out archeological excavations in England '28, '30, '31; director Harvard Archeological expedition in Ireland '32-36; excavations in Morocco '47 and Algeria '49. Author: Archeology of Cornwall '32; Cahercommaun '38; contbr tech articles. Curator European Archeol Peabody Mus Harvard since '32; dir Am Sch Prehistoric Research since '45. Soc Antiquaries of London Scotland(F)—Royal Soc Antiquaries of Ireland—Archeol Inst Am—Am Acad Arts Sci—Royal Archeol Inst Gt Brit Royal Irish Acad—Phi Beta Kappa (hon)—Sigma Xi. Peabody Museum, Cambridge, Mass.◎

13 HENDERSHOT, Vernon E(dwards). Seventh-day adventist (Theology and religion); Malay (Language). b'95. Student '13-15 (U Cal); '15-16 (Leland Stanford Jr U); AB '17 (Pacific Union Coll); AM '27—PhD '41 (U So Cal). Author: Malay Language Course (4 vols) '39; First Year of Standard Malay '43; A Historical Critique of the Educational System of British Malaya '41; Dictionary of Standard Malay '45. Pres Malayan Sem Singapore Malaya '20-31; ednl and chaplain work

Penang Malaya '31-33, '36-38; mission dir Sarawak Borneo '35; pastor seventh-day Adventist English Ch Singapore '38-40; dean theology Walla Walla Coll Wash '41-51; pres Seventh-day Adventist Theol Sem Washington since '51. Inst Pacific Relations—Archeol Inst Am—East Indies Inst Am—Phi Kappa Phi—Phi Delta Kappa. 6830 Laurel St., Washington 12.†◎

14 HENDERSON, George Edwin. Rural electrification. b'06. BS '29 (O State U). Research on electric brooding of chicks and electrically heated hotbeds for plant propagation, developed and patented electric stock tank water heater, developed panel covering principles of farm wiring and another on fundamentals of pumps. Rural engr O Edison Co '29-32; Dayton Power and Light Co '32-37; rural engr, asst chief and chief agrl engring div TVA '37-48; coordinator S Assn Agrl Engring and Vocational Agrl Educators U Ga since '49. Delta Theta Sigma—Am Soc Agrl Engrs. Division of Agricultural Engineering, University of Georgia, Athens, Ga.

15 HENDERSON, Harold Gould. Japanese arts and poetry. BA '10—MA Chem E '15 (Columbia). Has the most representative and probably the largest private collection of Japanese paintings in the U. S. Author: Handbook of Japanese Grammar '43; The Bamboo Broom, an Introduction to Haiku '33. Co-author: Illustrated History of Japanese Art '34; The Surviving Works of Sharaku '39. Asst prof Japanese Columbia since '34. Served in World War II as lt col, served on Gen MacArthur's staff as chief of the Religion, education, Arts and Monuments Div '45-46. Soc Japanese Studies (pres)—Japan Soc Am pres). 208 Low Library, Columbia University, NYC.

16 HENDERSON, James H(enry) M(eriwether). Plant physiology and metabolism. b'17. BS '39 (Howard U); MPh '40—PhD '43 (U Wis). Research on mechanisms of respiration and metabolism in higher plants, mineral nutrition and alkaloid content blue lupine. Research asso George W Carver Foundation since '46. AAAS—Bot Soc Am—Nat Inst Sci—Sigma Xi. Tuskegee Institute, Ala.

17 HENDERSON, John Mellish. Malaria and mosquito control; Tropical and municipal sanitation. b'04. CE '27 (Cornell). Author articles in field. Mem ed bds Am Jour Pub Health, Jour Inter-Am Assn San Engring. Prof Sanitary Sci, Sch Pub Health Columbia since '44; consultant USPHS since '47; prin investigator field studies Bionomics of Anopheles Albimanus PR; cons san Kuwait Oil Co, Persian Gulf '48. Am Pub Health Assn—Nat Malaria Soc—Am Mosquito Control Assn—ASCE—Nat Research Council (mem san engr subcom)—Inter-Am Assn San Engring. 600 W. 168th St., NYC 32.

18 HENDERSON, June Rainsford. Garden literature (Eighteenth century). b'95. BA '15 (Coll Women); '17-18 (Columbia); MA '34 (U NC). Research on Pierre Joseph Redoute, Borromean Island gardens, flower prints and flower print makers of the eighteenth century; lecturer 18th century gardens symposium Colonial Williamsburg Va '48. Author: Floralia Garden Paths and By-Paths of the Eighteenth Century '38; Verdant Trails '45; also articles in field. Spl research librarian Library of Congress and others Washington '35-42. Am Bibliog Soc—Am Hort Soc—Garden Club SC (pres '42-44)—Royal Hort Soc—Garden Club Am. 1403 Colleton Av., Aiken, S.C.

19 HENDERSON, Robert Gordon. Tobacco diseases (Virus, downy mildew); Tomato and forage crop diseases. b'03. BS '27 (U Tenn); MS '28 (NC State Coll); PhD '44 (Iowa State Coll). Author articles in field. Plant pathologist Va Agrl Expt Sta since '49. Va Acad Sci—Am Phytopathol Soc—Phi Kappa Phi—Sigma Xi. Received annual award Va Acad Sci for best piece of research '37. Virginia Agricultural Experiment Station, Blacksburg, Va.†

20 HENDERSON, Robert William. Baseball (Origin); Tennis (History); History of ballgames. b'88. Student '11-13 (City Coll NY). Inventor of cubook a unit of measurement of bookstacks. Author: Historical Bibliography in Tennis Origins and Mysteries '32; How Old Is the Game of Racquets '36; Early American Sport '37; Baseball and Rounders '39; Ball, Bat and Bishop '47; The King's Book of Sports in England and America '48; also articles in field. With NY Pub Library since '10, chief main reading room since '45, librarian Racquet and Tennis Club since '19. Biblio Soc Am—ALA. 476 Fifth Av., NYC.

21 HENDREN, Joseph William. Folksong (Verse rhythm); Iconography. b'01. AB '25—PhD '34 (Princeton). Studies in formal interrelationships of verse and melody in folksong; history American graveyard epitaphs. Author: A Study of Ballad Rhythm '36. Author article: Epitaphs from down east. Staff Rice Inst '30-43; asso prof English Western Md Coll since '47. Coll English Assn. Western Maryland College, Westminster, Md.

22 HENDRICK, James Pomeroy. International affairs; Human rights. b'01. AB '23—LLB '27 (Yale). Author: An International Bill of Human Rights '48; The United Nations and Human Rights '48; Progress Report on Human Rights '48; also articles in field. Edited report on plants scheduled for removal as reparations from Germany prepared by ECA Ind Adv Com '49. Office dep adminstrn Econ Cooperation Adminstrn since '48. Asst to Under Sec of War '42-45. Century Assn. Economic Cooperation Administration, 2 Rue St., Florentin, Paris, France. H: Simsbury, Conn.

23 HENDRICKS, James Owen. Adhesives. b'09. AB '31 (Wabash Coll); '31-33 (U Calif); PhD '36 (U Ill). Research in water dispersed adhesives, asphalt adhesives and coatings, rubber adhesives, vinyl polymerizations, organic chemistry. Patents. Author articles in field. Research chem Minn Mining and Mfg Co Adhesives and Coatings Div '36-37, Central Research Dept '37-41, head adhesives sect, colloid sect '41-47, asst dir Central Research Dept since '47. Am Chem Soc. 900 Fauquier St., Minnesota Mining & Mfg Co., St. Paul 6.

24 HENDRICKS, John G(eorge). Rubber (Vulcanization mechanism and agents, reinforcing pigments); Vinyl plastics (Plasticizers, stabilizers, dyes). b'21. BS (Chem E) (Northeastern U); Student (MIT); MS (Chem) (Poly Inst Brooklyn). Formulation of rubber and vinyl plastic compounds; research on mechanism of vulcanization of rubber and stabilization of vinyl plastics; development vulcanizing agents, activators of vulcanization, and reinforcing pigments for rubbers and stabilizers, plasticizers, and dyes for plastics. Author articles: Non-Sulfur Vulcanization '46; Stabilization of Vinyl Plastics Containing Chloroparaffins '50, and others. Co-author article: Degradation and Stabilization of Polyvinyl Chloride '49. Rubber chem Avon Sole Co '40-42;

10 HENDRICKS, Sterling B. Plant biochemistry, biophysics and photoperiodism; Constitution of clays. b'02. BChE '22—hon LLD '46 (U Ark); MS '24 (Kan State Agrl Coll); PhD '26 (Calif Inst Tech). Author articles in field. Scientist US Dept Agr since '28; prin chemist US Bur Plant Industry since '45. Am Chem Soc (Hillebrand prize for work on crystal structure '38)—Am Phys Soc(F)—Am Mineral Soc (vp '46)—Am Soc Agronomy(F). Sci award for work on clays Washington Acad Sci '40. Plant Industry Station, Beltsville, Md.⊙

11 HENDRICKSON, Walter Brookfield. History of science; Intellectual history. b'03. BS '27 (Butler U); AM '36 (Indiana U); PhD '41 (Harvard). Research on natural science academies and museums in Middle West; natural science in nineteenth century, with emphasis on geology and museums; geological surveys of David Dale Owen. Author: David Dale Owen, Pioneer Geologist of the Middle West '43; also articles in field. Prof hist and govt MacMurray Coll since '40. AHA—Miss Valley Hist Assn—Ind Hist Soc—Ill Hist Soc. MacMurray College, Jacksonville, Ill.†

12 HENDY, James Cecil. Hockey (Rules and history). b'06. Ed pub schs. Writer on professional ice hockey since '25. Author 50 articles in field. Ed Ofcl Hockey Guide since '32; Who's Who in Hockey since '32; former dir pub NY Rangers Madison Sq Garden; now mng dir Cleveland Arena, mgr Cleveland Barons Hockey Club. Am Hockey League(dir, dir pub)—Arena Mgrs Assn(dir)—Auditorium Mgrs Assn(dir)—US Hockey League (pres). Named outstanding professional hockey executive by Hockey News '49-50. 3700 Euclid Av., Cleve 15.†

13 HENEL, Heinrich E. K. Literature (German, Old English); Medieval science and folklore. b'05. PhD '27 (Frankfurt am Main); spl Stirling Research Fellow '43-44 (Yale). Author: Die Entwicklung des geschichtlichen deutschen Prosastils bei Johannes von Muller '28; Studien zum altenglischen Computus '34; Aelfric's De Temporibus Anni '42; also articles in field. Prof German U Wis since '48. 86 Bascom Hall, University of Wisconsin, Madison, Wis.

14 HENEMAN, Harlow James. Management; International administration. b'06. BA '28 (U Minn); MA '30 (U Cal); PhD '34 (U London). Consultant on management problems in government organization and economic assistance programs; economic adviser US Political Adviser on German Affairs in Berlin '45; attended London Council of Foreign Ministers Meeting '45. Author: The Growth of Executive Power in Germany '34. Co-author: The Hitler Decrees '33. Asso prof polit sci U Mich '33-45; with Div Adminstr Management US Bur Budget '44-45; spl asst to Asst Sec State for Occupied Areas '46-47; cons Dep US Rep UN Atomic Energy Commn '47; cons Dep Under Sec State '48-49; dir management staff Dept State since '50. Polit Sci Assn—Am Soc Pub Adminstrn—Am Fgn Service Assn—Pi Sigma Alpha. Received Rackham Found grant and Rockefeller Found '41. Department of State, Washington 25.

15 HENION, Henry Mead. Airports; Aviation (Ground facilities). b'98. Student (Armour Inst Tech). Designed and developed underground aircraft servicing ramp facilities, aircraft turntables, passenger loading gangplank and cargo gangplank for horizontal loading of aircraft, incoming and outgoing baggage handling systems and conveyers, wind direction and velocity indicating devices, automatic electric flight information boards for terminal buildings; conducted economic surveys for and established management and operational policies; designed airport and facilities plans for municipalities, Navy and Air Force; supervised construction. Airways engr Civil Aeronautics Administrn '42-43; supt constrn Amazon Div Rubber Development Corp '43; vp and dir engring Airways Engring Corp since '44. Airways Engineering Corp., 1212 18th St., Washington 6. H: 3850 Tunlaw Rd., Washington 7.

16 HENKE, Frederick Goodrish. Psychology of ritualism; Philosophy of Wang Yang-Ming. b'76. AB '97 (Morningside Coll); AM '08 (Northwestern U); PhD '10 (U Chicago). Author: The Psychology of Ritualism '10. Translator: The Philosophy of Wang Yang-Ming '16. Pastor St Paul's Church Kiukiang China '01-04; dist supt Kiukiang '04-07; vp and prof homiletics William Nast Coll Kinkiang '04-07; established first psychol lab in China '10; prof philosophy and psychology U Nanking China '10-13; prof philosophy and edn Willamette U Ore '13-14; acting prof '14-16; Truman D Collins prof philosophy and edn Allegheny Coll Meadville Pa '16-42, prof emeritus since '42. Am Philos Assn—Royal Asiatic Soc—Phi Delta Kappa—Phi Beta Kappa—Pi Gamma Mu—Kappa Phi Kappa. 307 Second Av., Charles City, Ia.†⊙

17 HENKLE, Herman H(enry). Library cataloging; Science bibliography. b'00. AB '28 (Whittier Calif Coll); Certificate in librarianship '31—MA '33 (U Calif); '35-36 (U Chicago). Author: A Survey of the Indiana University Library (with Donald Coney and Flint Purdy) '40; Studies of Descriptive Cataloging '46; also articles in field. Librarian Crerar Library Chicago since '47. Spl Libraries Assn (exec bd '41-47, pres '45-46)—ALA—Hist Sci Soc—AAAS. The John Crerar Library, 86 E. Randolph St., Chicago 1.

18 HENNAN, Clarence W(illiam). Philately. b'94. MD '17 (Loyola U). Formed specialized collection of Chicago Postal History. Author articles in field. Collectors Club NY—Essay Proof Soc—Garfield Perry Stamp Soc (hon)—Royal Philatelic Soc(F)—Am Philatelic Soc (pres '32-34)—Jury Internat Philatelic Exhibitions—Chicago Philatelic Soc (hon)—Sociedade Philatelica Paulista Brazil (hon)—Soc Filatelica de El Salvador—Soc Filatelica de Guatamala—Collectors Club Chicago (pres). 841 E. 63rd St., Chicago 37.

19 HENNING, George F. Agricultural and livestock marketing; Cooperation. b'96. MS '25—PhD '33 (Ohio State U). Author articles in field. Prof agr econ O State U since '34; also agr marketing research Ohio Agrl Expt Sta. Am Farm Econ Assn—Am Marketing Assn—Gamma Sigma Delta—AAUP. Department Agrl Economics, Ohio State University, Columbus, O.

20 HENNING, William Lewis. Animal husbandry, breeding and genetics. b'00. BS '21 (O State U); MS '23 (Pa State Coll); PhD '37 (U Wis). Prof animal husbandry Pa State Coll since '37; sec-treas Am Southdown Breeders Assn since '24. AAAS(F)—Am Genetic Assn—Am Soc Animal Prodn—Gamma Sigma Delta—Phi Kappa Phi —Sigma Xi. Agricultural Building, State College, Pa.

21 HENRY, Berch W(aldo). Tree pathology (Southern pine seedling nursery diseases, diseases of oak trees). b'15. AB '36—MS '38 (W Va U); PhD '41 (U Wis). Research on forest tree diseases, primarily an undescribed dying of oak trees; conducting research on cause and control of an undescribed rootrot of southern pine nursery seedlings. Author articles in field. Path div forest path US Dept Agr since '48. Served as lt '43-46, research work in plant path. Sigma Xi—Phi Beta Kappa. Ashe Nursery, Brooklyn, Miss.

22 HENRY, David W(atters). Education. b'85. Diploma '09 (State Normal Coll Hyannis Mass); AB '11 (State Tchrs Coll Emoria Kan); MA '16 (Columbia U); Diploma '37 (U London Eng). With U Toledo since '14, dean coll edn since '20. AAAS(F)—Coll Tchrs Edn—NEA—Am Acad Polit and Social Sci—AAUP—Am Assn Sch Adminstrs—Ohio Tchrs Assn—Ohio Supts Assn—Acad Polit Sci—Phi Delta Kappa—Kappa Delta Pi. 2538 Goddard Rd.,Tol.⊙

23 HENRY, Edward Carleton. Ceramic engineering. b'05. BSc '26 (Rutgers U); MS '29 (U Nev); PhD '36—Ceramic Engr '41 (Pa State Coll). Research on chemistry of clays and other mineral colloids, flow properties of ceramic bodies, synthesis of industrial minerals. Author articles in field. Prof, chief div ceramics Pa State Coll '45. Am Ceramic Soc(F)—Pa Ceramics Assn (mng dir)—Am Chem Soc—Inst Ceramic Engrs—Ceramic Ednl Council—Pa Acad Sci—Sigma Xi. 214 Mineral Industries Bldg., State College, Pa.

24 HENRY, Jules. Language and culture of Kaingang Indians of Brazil and Pilaga Indians of Argentina; Language of Tarahumara Indians of Chihuahua Mexico; Latin American affairs (Labor conditions). b'04. Student '24-26 (Inst Musical Art NYC); BS '28 (Coll City NY); PhD '36 (Columbia U). Author: Jungle People '41; Doll Play of Pilaga Indian Children '44; also articles in field. Asso prof anthrop Washington U since '47; asso ed Am Journal of Orthopsychiatry since '44. Social sci analyst OWI '42-43. Am Ethnol Soc—Am Anthrop Assn(F)—Am Orthopsychiat Assn (F, chmn com on internat affairs since '44). Honorary prof sociol U Michoacan, Morelia, Mexico. Washington U., St. Louis 5.

25 HENRY, LeRoy K(ershaw). Spermatophytes and fungi (Taxonomy, western Pennsylvania); Mycorrhizae of trees and shrubs. b'05. BS '28—MS '30—PhD '32 (U Pittsburgh). Research in taxonomy of fungi, mycorrhizae of trees and shrubs, fungi of western Pennsylvania, plant ecology and taxonomic botany. Author articles in field. Curator of bot Carnegie Mus since '47. Mycol Soc—Pa Acad Sci—Bot Soc Western Pa—Am Soc Plant Taxonomists. Carnegie Museum, Pittsburgh 13.†

26 HENRY, Merton Thomas. Forest (Timber measurement, appraisal, marketing); Trees (Diseases, diagnosis, and treatment). born '08. BS '29 (NY State Coll Forestry-Syracuse Univ). Author article: How Sound Are Your Trees? '37. Contributor: Forester's Handbook '51. Cons forester and arborist '36-43, and '46-48; prof forestry Rainbow U Zell am See Austria '45-46. Soc Am Foresters—Nat Shade Tree Conf. Atomic Energy Commission Administration Bldg., Oak Ridge, Tenn. H: Old Flatbrook Rd., Bevans, N.J.

10 HENRY, Robert Selph. American history (Railroads, Civil War and reconstruction). b'89. AB '11—LLB '10 (Vanderbilt U); '19 (Queens Coll Cambridge England); LittD (U of Chattanooga). Author: The Story of the Confederacy '31; Trains '34; On the Railroad '36; Portraits of the Iron Horse '37; The Story of Reconstruction '38; This Fascinating Railroad Business '42; "First With the Most" Forrest '44; (with Frank P Donovan Jr) Headlights and Markers '45; The Story of the Mexican War '50. V pres Assn Am R R's since '47; trustee Vanderbilt U. AHA—Miss Valley Hist Assn—So Hist Assn—Soc Am Historians—Phi Beta Kappa. Transportation Bldg., Washington 6.

11 HENSHAW, Francis H(arold). Public library administration and relations; Public and county library extension; State archives. b'03. AB '27 (Occidental Coll); certificate '29 (Library Sch Los Angeles Pub Library); MS '32 (Columbia). Author articles in field. State librarian Tex State Library Austin '46-50; asst chief card div Library of Congress since '50. instr sch library service Columbia '45-46, '47; chmn ex-officio Tex State Bd Library Examiners. ALA—Mass Library Assn (pres '40-42)—Tex Library Assn—Phi Beta Kappa. Awarded Carnegie Fellowship '31. Library of Congress, Washington 25.

12 HENSLEY, James William. Detergent chemistry. b'15. BS '37 (NM State Coll); MS '39 (U Colo); '47-48 (U Wis). Research on application of radioactive tracers to surfaces and detergents. Author articles in field. With Wyandotte Chemicals Corp since '39. Served US Army '42-45, 41st Chem Lab Co, chief chem engr sect. Am Chem Soc—Sigma Xi. Wyandotte Chemicals Corporation, Research Division, Wyandotte, Mich.†

13 HEPBRON, James M(erritt). Criminology. b'91. LLB '13 (U Md); studied penal and police methods and compilation of crime statistics Europe '27-28; LLD '30 (Washington Coll); hon DSc '34 (Temple U); Dr Humane Letters '39 (Md Coll). Author articles in field. Mng dir Baltimore Criminal Justice Commn since '24. 22 Light St., Baltimore 2.

14 HEPBURN, Joseph Samuel. Insectivorous plants; Gastrointestinal temperatures. b'85. AB '03—AM '08 (Central High Sch Phila); BS '07—MS '07 (U Pa); PhD '13 (Columbia); MD '34—ChemD '46 (Hahnemann Med Coll and Hosp Phila). Author articles in field. Asso prof '25-39, professor '39-50, research asso gastroenterology '37-50, registrar '43-50; cons biol chem and physiol. Nat Gastroenterological Assn(F)—Am Inst Homeopathy (hon asso)—ACS (councilor '25)—Am Soc Biol Chem—Pa Chem Soc (gov '38)—Franklin Inst (sec sect phys and chem '09-23, com on sci and arts in charge med awards since '19, mgr '43-44, '48) —Sigma Xi. Received Longstreth Medal '11, Certificate of Merit '21 Franklin Inst. H: 2045 N. Franklin St., Phila 22.ⓒ

15 HEPTING, George H(enry). Tree cankers; Wilts; Littleleaf; Pulpwood stain and decay; Timber and wood aircraft decay; Naval stores production (Fungus use). b'07. BS '29—PhD '33 (Cornell U). Discovered tree diseases known as mimosa wilt, sumac wilt, pitch canker of pine and sapstreak of maple and method of prolonging gum flow in turpentining pines by fungus inoculation, patent granted. Author articles in field. Forest path Div Forest Path US Dept Agr since '31. Am Phytopath Soc—Soc Am Foresters—Nat Shade Tree Conf—Sigma Xi—Phi Kappa Phi. Bureau of Plant Industry, Soils and Agricultural Engineering, 223 Federal Building, Asheville, N.C.†

16 HERBERT, Carl Preston. United States municipal government (Taxation, budgeting). b'93. AB '16 (Miami U). American vice consul Mexico City '17. Author: Twin Cities Postwar Federal Tax Plan (with others) '44; also articles in field. Dir St Paul Bur Municipal Research since '21; vp sec Minn Inst Govt research since '32; sec Twin Cities Research Bur Inc since '44; coordinator of research House Appropriations Com 80th Congress. Am Polit Sci Assn—Governmental Research Assn (pres)—Acad Polit Sci—Am Econ Assn—Am Acad Polit Social Sci—Nat Tax Assn—Minn Tax Assn (past pres). 332 Cedar St., St. Paul 1.

17 HERBERT, Frederick Davis. Aeronautical engineering and design (Navigational instruments and component parts for use in high speed missiles and planes); Ship engineering. b'73. ME '97 (Cornell). Pres Kearfott Engring Co Inc NYC '18-41, sr partner '41-46; pres Kearfott Co Inc since '46. ASME(F)—Soc Naval Archs Marine Engrs—Shipbuilders Council Am—Am Soc Naval Engrs—Instn Naval Arch (London)—NE Coast Engrs Shipbuilders (Newcastle-on-Tyne)—Mfrs Assn US—Maritime Assn NY—Propeller Club US. 1150 McBride Av Little Falls, N.J.ⓒ

18 HERBERT, Jean. Hindu mythology; Mythology (Comparative). b'97. MA '14—LLB '20 (Paris U). Author: Spiritualité Hindoue '46; Wege zum Hinduismus '50; La Sabiduria Hindu '39; Les Adityas '49; La Notion de Vie Future dans L'Hindouisme '44; Indische Mythologie als Geistige Realität '51; Ganesha '46; Narada '49; Agni '49; Le Message de la Mythologie Hindoue '50; The Ten Avatars of Sri Vishnu '48. Vis lecturer various universities. Soc Francaise d'Archeol—Soc Mexicana de Geog y Estadistica. Palais des Nations, Geneva, Switzerland.

19 HERGET, Paul. Computation of orbits; Scientific and large scale computing. b'08. AB '31—MA '33—PhD '35 (U Cincinnati); Morrison Research Fellow Lick Observatory '35-36 (U Calif). Research on computation of orbits of minor planets and comets, recently discovered moons of Jupiter; extensive experience in use standard and special International Business Machine punched card machines for scientific computing, such as Tables of Sunrise and Sunset supplement to 1946 American Ephemeris; prepared operating manual for International Business Machine 601 Multiplying machine. Originated principle Optimum Interval Table '44. Author articles in field. Prof dir Obs U Cincinnati since '43; scientist US Naval Obs Nautical Almanac Office '42-45, asst dir '45-46; cons Manhattan Project '45. Am Astron Soc—AAAS—Sigma Xi—Phi Beta Kappa—Intern Astron Union. Cincinnati Observatory, Cincinnati 8.†ⓒ

20 HERMAN, Edward Pritz. Foreign investment guaranties. b'98. BA '20 (Yale); MBA '22 (Harvard). Interpretation and development of procedures for administration of forward contracting provisions of Foreign Economic Assistance Act of 1950; study and development on policies for administration expropriation and confiscation, also royalty provisions, of 1950 act. Dir projects div Bd Econ Warfare '41-43; chief appeals sect on renegotiations OQMG '43-46; mem Army Price Adjustment Bd on contrast renegotiations '47-48; spl asst to dir indsl div Econ Cooperation Ad-ministrn since '48. 801 Connecticut Av., Washington. H: 302 E. Broad St., Falls Church, Va.

21 HERMAN, John. Gold (Assaying). b'78. BSc '00 (U Neb); DSc '34 (Charles U Prague Czechoslovakia). Developed method for assaying gold with polargraph; research on electrodeposition of gold, tools for use in rock and mineral determination; analysis of procedure for determination of gold in ores, bullion; devised comparator for spectrographic work; manager Western Mineralogical Exposition '40-41. Author articles: Polarographic Studies with the Dropping Mercury Kathode—The Electrodeposition of Gold '34; The Spectrograph and Polarograph '48, and others. Contributor: Gold Assaying in Engineers Handbook '32. Assayer gold in Colo, Ariz, Mexico, Cal; cons gold ore frauds. ACS—AAAS—Am Inst Mining Engrs—So Cal Acad Sci(F)—Mining Assn of SW(F). Licensed chem engr Cal. 920 Santee St., LA 15.

22 HERMAN, Michael. Folk dances. b'10. Student (Western Reserve U). Author: Folk Dances for All '47; folk dance div Music Highways and Byways '36; also articles in field. Ed: The Folk Dancer Mag since '41. Dir Community Folk Dance Center Inc since '40; folk dance dir Internat House NY since '34; arranger of folk dance music for record companies, Sonart, Kismet, Disc, Methodist Bd Edn, Scandinavia. P.O. Box 201, Flushing, L.I., N.Y.

23 HERMANN, Frederick Joseph. Juncaceae of North America; Carex of North America; Lonchocarpus. b'06. AB '28—MA '31—PhD '38 (U Mich). Research on identification of Carex (sedge) and Juncaceae (rushes) for the last 25 years; study of the genus Lonchocarpus. Author articles in field. Asso botanist bur plant industry Beltsville Md '38-43, '44-48; botanist since '48; botanist Foreign Econ Adm Bogota Col '43-44. Am Soc Plant Taxonomists—NE Bot Club—Washington Acad Sci—Phi Beta Kappa—Sigma Xi—Phi Kappa Phi. Plant Industry Station, Beltsville, Md.†

24 HERNANDEZ, J. Eduardo. Military Spanish; Spanish proverbs and psychology. b'08. MA '34—PhD '38 (U Ky). Asso prof Romance Langs U Ky since '36. In military service '41-48, training Latin American students and translating Air Force documents. Am Assn Teachers Spanish—AAUP—Ky Acad Sci. University of Kentucky, Lexington, Ky.†

25 HERNANDEZ MOEDANO, Guillermo. Groundwater; Geophysics; Petroleum exploration. b'13. Elec engr '39 (Escuela Superior de Ingenieria Mecanica y Elec). Operator magnetometer, gravitymeter, seismograph, electrical apparatus '40-44, party chief gravity meter party and seismograph party, '45-46; geophysist (chief) Secretaria de Recursos Hidraulicos '45-50; mgr Servicios Geofisicos, S A de C V since '51. Asociacion Mexicana de Geol Petroleros—Soc Geol Mexicana—Soc Exploration Geophys. Servicios Geofisicos, S.A. de C.V., Balderas Numero 44, Despacho 101-2, Mexico D.F., Mexico.

26 HERON, William Thomas. Hypnosis. b'97. AB '20—MA '21 (U Kan); PhD '24 (U Chicago). Instruction dentists and physicians for use of hypnosis in their practices; study use of hypnosis in training pregnant women for childbirth; research on psychotherapeutic use hypnosis for treatment mental difficulties, and hypnotic relaxation as method self-control. Author: Clinical Applications of Suggestion and Hypnosis '50. Author articles: Hypnosis and Dentistry '49; Some Psychological Aspects of Dentistry '50. Co-author article: (with Milton Abramson) An Objective Evaluation of Hypnosis in Obstetrics '50. Prof psychol U Minn since '43. Am Psychol Assn(F)—Midwest Psychol Assn—Soc Clin and Exptl Hypnosis—Brit Soc Med Hpnotists. Department of Psychology, University of Minnesota, Mpls 14.†

10 HERR, Robert. Recording (Magnetic, tape). b'18. AB (Physics) '39 (Haverford Coll); '39-40 (U Minn); '45-46 (Mass Inst Tech). Research on sound recording tape, basic magnetic recording theory, recording tecnique; discovered contract duplication process for magnetic tapes; development techniques of recording in non-conventional application; technical consultant recording machine manufacturers; research associate acoustics laboratory Massachusetts Institute Technology '45-46. Worker magnetism, magnetic degaussing of ships, magnetic instrumentation Naval Ordnance Lab '40-45; physicist central research dept Minn Mining & Mfg Co St Paul since '46. Acoustical Soc Am—Soc Motion Picture Engrs(sound com). Minnesota Mining & Mfg. Co., St. Paul.

11 HERRICK, Clifford Ernest, Jr. Photochemistry. b'16. ScB '38 (Brown U); PhD '43—fellow Sherman Clarke Fund '40-42 (U Rochester); fellow '38 (Woods Hole Oceanog Inst). Research in photochemistry including photolysis of ammonia, especially interested in the photochemistry and sensitometry of the diazotype process including sensitometric theory of the process. Sci staff War Research Div Columbia '42-44; sect manager SAM Labs Carbide and Carbon Chemicals Co '44-46; group leader Gen Aniline and Film Corp '49. AAAS—Am Inst Phys—Optical Soc Am (asso)—Am Chem Soc—Sigma Xi. Central Research Laboratory, General Aniline and Film Corporation, Easton, Pa. H: R.D. 1.

12 HERRICK, Francis H. British history. b'00. BA '22 (Western Res); MA '23 (Wis); BA '25 (Oxford U, Eng); PhD '35 (Yale). Research on 19th century British political parties. Author articles in field. Translator: Europe Under the Old Regime (by Albert Sorel) '47. Prof Mills Coll since '42, dir of graduate study '40-46. AHA —AAUP—Phi Beta Kappa. Mills College Station, Oakland 13, Calif.†

13 HERRICK, Lee Waldo, Jr. Turkey production. b'13. BSA '36 (Rutgers U); MS (poultry sci) '41 (NC State Coll). Advice on housing, feeding, brooding, growing turkeys on range; growing them in total confinement; grazing crops; dressing, marketing; all phases of management. Author circulars in field. Field mgr SD Poultry Improvement Assn '45; ext turkey specialist Clemson Agrl Ext Service Columbia SC '45-47; ext turkey specialist NC State Coll Raleigh '48-51; asso ext poultry husbandman Va Poly Inst Blacksburg since '51. Va Turkey Fedn —Nat Turkey Fedn—Poultry Sci Assn. Virginia Polytechnic Institute, Blacksburg, Va.

14 HERRICK, Samuel. Celestial mechanics; Rocket navigation. b'11. BA '32 (William Coll); PhD '36 (U Calif). Research on orbits of planets, comets, and rockets. Co-chairman Institute of Navigation committee on upper atmosphere and interplanetary navigation. Author: Grid Navigation; also articles in field. Asst prof U Calif Los Angeles '42-47, chmn Dept of Astronomy '43-45, since '46, asso prof since '47, Inst for Numerical Analysis (Nat Bur Standards) '48-49. Am Astron

Soc—Astron Soc Pacific—Inst Nav (exec secretary since '45)—Internat Astron Union—Brit Inst Nav (F). J. S. Guggenheim fellowship '45-46. Department of Astronomy, University of California, Los Angeles. 24⊚

15 HERRINGTON, Lovic Pierce. Climate (Human reactions). b'07. AB—AM—PhD '30 (Stanford U). Research on thermal physiology, partitional calorimetry, and climatic adaptation; public health applications of psychophysiological techniques; secretary subcommittee on clothing Committee on Medical Research '41-45; consultant Office Quartermaster General and Army Climate Research Lab since '41; panel on psychophysiology Research and Development Board since '47; National Research Council committee on environmental protection since '47; member research committee President's Conference on Industrial Safety since '48 Co-author: (with C E A Windslow) Temperature and Human Life '49. Author articles: The Heat Regulation of Small Laboratory Animals at Various Environmental Temperatures '40; Basic Procedures in the Calculation of the Heat Exchange of the Clothed Human Body '47, and others. Co-author articles: (with I M Moriyama) The Relation of Mortality from Certain Respiratory Diseases to Climatic and Socioeconomic Factors '39; (with A P Gagge) Temperature Regulation '43; (with Gagge) Physiological Effects of Heat and Cold '47, and others. Social Sci Research Council fellow Charite Hosp Berlin Germany, and U Berlin '30-31; faculty Yale since '32, research asso prof pub health Sch Med '40-51, lectr since '51; cons environmental physiol and psychophysiol John B Pierce Found Lab Hygiene '32-33, asso dir '33-34, and dir research since '44. Am Psychol Assn—Am Statis Assn—Am Physiol Soc—Am Pub Health Assn. 290 Congress Av., New Haven 11.

16 HERRO, Alexander Chris. Milk (Concentrated). b'07. BS (Chem Engring) '30 (U Wis). Development concentrated milk with improved keeping qualities and freedom from cooked milk flavor. Acting supt pilot plant research labs Carnation Co '42-45, supt '45-46; dairy tech Nat Dairy Research Labs '46-51, asst to dir of research since '51. Am Dairy Sci Assn—ACS—Inst Food Tech—Metropolitan Dairy Soc NY. National Dairy Research Laboratories, Oakdale, L.I., N.Y.

17 HERROLD, Kenneth Frederick. Group guidance. b'13. AB '36 (Bucknell U); '36-37 (Yale); MS '40 (U Mich); EdD '48 (Columbia). Research on group guidance in student personnel work and administration in secondary schools and colleges, analysis of group behavior, action-research and experimentation in group meetings, human relations in public health, nursing, and educational administration; consultant to American Public Health Association, 1950 White House Conference on Children and Youth, National Organization of Public Health Nursing; consultant and co-director of Conference on Revision of National Curriculum and Training Program for Mental Hygiene Consultants; director Institute Human Relations for Greater New York Dietetic Association and New York League of Nursing; director Institute on Human Relations and Group Process for Public Health Association '50. Author: Conference Planning and Action through Use of Group Process '50. Asst dean and mem faculty Bucknell U '37-42; with Columbia since '46, asst prof dept guidance from '48. AAAS—Am Acad Soc and Polit Sci—Am Guidance and Personnel Assn—Am Psychol Assn—E

Psychol Assn—Soc Psychol Study Soc Issues (mem exec edit com Jour Social Issues since '51)—NY Acad Sci—Phi Sigma—Delta Sigma—Phi Delta Kappa—Kappa Delta Pi. Teachers College, Columbia University, 525 W. 120th St., NYC 27.

18 HERSCHER, Irenaeus. Franciscans (History). b'02. Student '20-24 (St Joseph's Seraphic Sem); BA '29—MA '30 (St Bonaventure Coll); STB '31 (Cath U); BLS '34 (Columbia); '48 (grad library sch U Chicago) Discovered and investigated Franciscan firsts, including first Army chaplain, double-entry booking, printing press in US, library building, union catalog, traveling library, inter-library loan, and other Franciscan contributions to various fields. Dir Franciscan clerics '32-33; prof philos Columbia U '33-34, '42; asst librarian St Bonaventure Coll '34-37, head librarian since '37; treas Franciscan Ednl Conf since '47. Acad Am Franciscan Hist—Cath Hist Soc—US Cath Hist Soc—Am Cath Hist Assn —Cath Library Assn—ALA—NY Library Assn—NY Hist Assn—Cath Philos Assn—Inter-Am Library and Bibliog Assn—Renascence Soc—Inst Internat de Lit Iberoamericano. Friedsam Memorial Library, St. Bonaventure, N.Y.

19 HERSH, Amos Henry. Drosophila genetics: Allometry. b'91. AB '14—hon ScD '46 (Franklin and Marshall Coll); PhD '22 (U Ill). Author articles in field. With Western Reserve U since '23, now prof biol. AAAS—Am Soc Zool—Genetics Soc Am—Soc Study Development Growth—Am Naturalists —Am Soc Human Genetics—O Acad Sci. Western Reserve University, Cleve 6.⊚

20 HERSHBERGER, Guy Franklin. Mennonite history and sociology; Pacifism. b'96. BA '23 (Hesston Coll); MA '25—PhD '35 (U Ia). Author: Can Christians Fight? '40; Christian Relations to State and Community '42; War, Peace, and Nonresistance '44; also articles in field. Prof hist sociol Goshen Coll since '42; exec sec Comm Industrial Relations Mennonite Ch since '39; Grant-in-Aid Social Sci Research Council for study Quaker govt in Colonial Penn '37; sabbatical to write treatise on nonresistance in theory and practise among Mennonites (under sponsorship Peace Problems Comm Mennonite Ch) '43; appt by Comm on Industrial Relations Mennonite Ch to prepare sociol study Mennonite community at Archbold Ohio '47; appt by Mennonite Research Found and Peace Problems Comm Mennonite Ch to write hist Mennonite Ch during World War II '48; sabbatical for study European pacifism '49-50; asso ed Mennonite Quarterly Review since '27; mem bd of ed Studies in Anabaptist and Mennonite Hist since '35; editorial cons Mennonite Ency since '46; sec Mennonite Community Asso since '46. AHA—Mennonite Hist Soc—Rural Sociol Soc. Goshen College, Goshen, Ind. H: 1306 S. 8th St.

21 HERSHEY, Arthur Leroy. Plant morphology; Poisonous plants of New Mexico. b'04. BS '27 (Kan U); MS '30 —PhD '34 (Ia State Coll). Studies on development of vascular system of corn, study of weeds in alfalfa fields, plants of New Mexico, origin and development of the vascular bundle of Zea mays, ontogeny of maize plants (early differentiation of stem and root structures and their morphological relationships); poison plant investigator New Mexico Cattle Sanitary Board '41-44; study of flora of New Mexico '34-48. Author articles in field. Instr biol NM Coll A&MA '34-36, asst prof '36-44, asso prof '44-48; asso prof bot Colo State Coll Edn Greeley '48-49; Ala State

Teachers College since '49. American Assn Plant Taxonomists (charter mem)—Grassland Research Found—Colo-Wyo Acad Sci—Sigma Xi. Alabama State College of Education, Florence, Alabama.

10 HERSHEY, (Howard) Garland. Groundwater; Subsurface geology; Stratigraphy. b'05. AB '29—PhD '36 (Johns Hopkins U). Chairman Coralville '47, Chairton '48, and Red Rock '48 Flood Control Dam Committees, member Iowa Interim Flood Control Committee '48, member Iowa Natural Resources Council since '49 and chairman since '49, member Mississippi River Parkway Planning Commission since '49, Midwestern States Flood Control Conference since '47, chairman '51; member board of directors of National Water Conservation Conference. Author articles in field. With Ia Geol Survey since '36, state geol and dir from '47; dist geol US Geol Survey from '44. Midwest Research Inst (trustee since '47)—Geol Soc Am (F)—Soc Econ Geol—Assn Am State Geol—Am Geophys Union—AAAS—Sigma Xi—Ia Acad Sci (F)—Ia Engring Soc (bd dir '49, v-pres '51, pres '52). Iowa Geological Survey, Geology Annex, Iowa City, Ia.

11 HERSHEY, John W. Tree propagation. b'98. Ed pub schs Specialist in propagation of thick-barked taproot trees as oak, edible nuts, persimmons by grafting and budding; organized world effort to breed trees for timber and crops; organized forest tree crop genetic work for TVA; introduced several new thin-shelled walnut, shagbarks, persimmons, sweet acorns, sweet podded honey locusts; pioneered in planting woody plants, trees, and shrubs for wild life feeding. Author pamphlets: Save America's Nut Heritage '34; Plant America's Nut Heritage '47. Nut Tree Nurseries, Downingtown, Pa.

12 HERSHKOVITZ, Philip. Mammalogy (Neo-tropical mammals, systematics). b'09. BS '38—MS '40 (Mich U). Zoological expedition Ecuador and upper Amazonian region '33-37; zoological expedition Colombia '41-43, '48-50. Author articles in field. Asst curator div mammals Chicago Nat Hist Mus since '47. Am Soc Mammalogists—Biol Soc Washington—Soc Study Evolution. Walter Rathbone Bacon Traveling Scholar, Smithsonian Inst '41-43, '46-47. Chicago Natural History Museum, Chicago 5.

13 HERSHMAN, Joseph Bernard. Radio engineering. b'00. BS (Chem) '22 (Valparaiso U); AM (Phys) '28—PhD '32 (Ind U). Development special courses for civilian and military electronic training on college level; supervision of installation complete laboratories for ultra-high frequencies, broadcasting AM and FM, television, electronics. Author: Laboratory Manual for Radio Measurements '48. Staff Valparaiso U '22-27; asst prof and acting dept head Ind State Teachers Coll '29-31; dir radio dept Dodge Radio Inst '33-41; pres Valparaiso Tech Inst since '41. Inst Radio Engrs—Sigma Xi—A AAS—Soc Motion Picture and Television Engrs. Valparaiso Technical Institute, Box 490, Valparaiso, Ind.

14 HERSKOVITS, Melville Jean. Anthropology; Ethnology (African and New World Negro); Comparative economics; Race-crossing. b'95. PhB '20 (Chicago); AM '21—PhD '23 (Columbia). Leader ethnographic expeditions to Dutch Guiana, W Africa, Haiti, Trinidad, Brazil '28-44. Author: The American Negro, A Study in Racial Crossing '28; Anthropometry of the American Negro '30; (with Frances S Herskovits) Outline of Dahomean Religious Belief '33; (with Frances S

Herskovits) Rebel Destiny, Among the Bush Negroes of Dutch Guiana '34; Dahomey '38; The Myth of the Negro Past '41; Man and His Works '48; and others. Prof anthrop Northwestern U since '35; vis prof anthrop U Ill '48-49; chmn com on African anthrop div anthrop and psychol Nat Research Council; council Internat Anthrop Congress. Royal Anthrop Inst (hon F)—AAAS(F, vp sect H '34)—Soc Research Child Development(F)—Am Anthrop Assn (F, mem exec council '47, ed '49—, pres Central sect '39)—Am Assn Phys Anthrop—Am Folklore Soc (pres '45)—Soc des Africanistes de Paris—Internat African Inst (exec bd)—Internat Inst Afro-Am Studies. Decorated Officer Order of Honor and Merit, Haiti; hon prof anthrop Fac de Filosofia, Bahia, Brazil. Department of Anthropology, Northwestern University, Evanston, Ill.©

15 HERTEL, Kenneth LaDoyt. Textile physics (Cotton). b'98. BE '20 (O State U); PhD '26 (U Chicago). Author articles in field. Prof and head dept physics U Tenn since '35; physicist Agrl Expt Sta since '35. AA AS—Am Phys Soc—Fiber Soc—Sigma Xi. University of Tennessee, Knoxville 16, Tenn.*©

16 HERTIG, Arthur Tremain. Abortion (Pathology of spontaneous); Embryos (Early human). b'04. BS '28 (U Minn); MD '30 (Harvard). Research in human conceptuses (2 to 14 days of age); Spontaneous human abortion (On abnormality of pathological pregnancies, causes); Studies of outer fetal envelope of early human development. Author articles: Abortive Human Ova and Associated Endometria, and others. Co-author articles: (with John Rock) A Series of Potentially Abortive Ova Recovered from Fertile Women Prior to the First Missed Menstrual Period, and others. Contributor: Cancer, Vol II '49. With Boston Lying-in Hosp since '31, senior obstetrician '46-50, pathologist since '38 path Free Hosp for Women since '38; with Harvard Med Sch since '38, prof path since '48, chmn pro tem dept. Am Bd Obstet and Gynec (diplomate)—Am Bd Path (diplomate)—Am Gynecol Soc—Obstetrical Soc Boston—Am Asso Path and Bact—N E Path Soc—N E Obstetrical and Gynecological Soc (pres) —AAAS—AMA—Mass Med Soc—Am Acad Arts and Scis—Sigma Xi. National Research Fellow, Carnegie Institution of Washington; award from American Gynecological Society (with John Rock) for work on early normal and abnormal human development. 221 Longwood Av., Boston 15.

17 HERTZ, David Bendel. Absenteeism. b'19. AB '39—BS '40—PhD '49 (Columbia); '43-44 (USN Postgrad Sch). Exec dir and co-founder National Institute for the Reduction of Industrial Absenteeism. Author: Theory and Practice of Industrial Research '50; Costs, Economics and Budgeting of Industrial Research '51. Asst dir engring research Celanese Corp Am '45-49; asst prof indsl engring Columbia since 49. 409 Engineering Bldg., Columbia University, NYC 27.

18 HERVEY, Ralph Johnston. Soil Microbiology and bacteriology. b'13. AB '37 (Washington U); Fellow '37-38 (Rutgers U); MS '40 (Utah Agr Coll). Author articles in field. Soil microbiologist Tex Agr Expt Sta since '48. Soc Am Bacteriol—Am Soc Profl Biol—AAAS—Internat Soc Study Evolution—Am Soc Protozool—Sigma Xi. Blackland Experiment Station, P.O. Box 414, Temple, Tex.

19 HERZBERG, Max J(ohn). American and English literature; History of American humor; Stephen Crane; Educational methods. b'86. AB '06

(Columbia). Writer of inscriptions on 15 bronze tablets erected by Schoolmen's Club of Newark to mark historical occasions; also tablets at Stephen Crane birthplace. Author: Myths and Their Meaning '35; Off to Arcady, Adventures in Poetry '33; Mark Twain Omnibus '35; Terhune Omnibus '37; Situations in Which Citizenship Can Be Taught '40; Radio and English Teaching '40; Insults: a Practical Anthology '41; English at Command '43; and other books and articles. Editor: Word Study; Photoplay Guides '34-35; Treasure Chest of Sea Stories '48; and others. Prin Weequahie High Sch Newark since '33; lit ed Newark Evening and Sunday News since '20; chmn selection com Teen-Age Book Club since '45; broadcaster over radio stations. Stephen Crane Assn (pres '24-30)—Nat Council Teachers English (pres '42-43)—Secondary Sch Prins Assn NJ (past pres)—Mus Modern Art. 135 Mercer Pl., South Orange, N.J.©

20 HERZOG, George. Folk music; Primitive music; African languages and ethnology. b'01. Student '17-19 (Hungarian Acad Music, Budapest); '20-22 (Hochschule fuer Musik, Berlin); '22-24 (U Berlin); '25-29—PhD '38 (Columbia U). Field survey of Southwestern Indian Music '27, Dakota Indian poetry and music '28, Navajo Indian poetry and music '32; collection of Maine folksongs '28; of Pima Indian poetry, language and music '30-31; Comanche Indian language and music '39; survey of the state of studies and materials in Primitive Music and Folk Music in the US '33; studies of American Indian, Siberian, African and Micronesian music, of Jugoslav and Hungarian folk music; studies of Jewish ritual music; of Jugoslav epic poetry; of W African Pidgin English; of W African drum-signaling '30-31. Author: Research in Primitive and Folk Music in the US '36. Co-author: (with C G Blooah) Jabo Proverbs from Liberia '36; also articles in field. Asst phonograph archives U Berlin '22-24; research asso U Chicago '29-31; in charge U Chicago Expdn to Liberia '30-31; asst prof anthropology Yale U '32-35; Columbia U '36-46, in charge Archives Primitive Music '41-46; cons, research assoc for Expt Div of War Times Communications Research, Library of Congress; prof anthropology, in charge Archives of Folk and Primitive Music Ind U since '48. AAAS(F)—Ethnol Soc Am(F)—Am Anthropol Assn(F)—Am Folklore Soc—Linguistic Soc Am—Linguistic Circle of NY—Am Musicol Soc—Internat Inst African Langs and Cultures, London—Instituto Indigenista Inter-americano, Mexico. Guggenheim Fellow '35-36, '47. Indiana University, Bloomington, Ind.

21 HESLER, Lexemuel Ray. Mycology; Plant pathology; Fruit diseases. b'88. AB '11 (Wabash Coll); PhD '14 (Cornell U). Author: (with others) Laboratory Outlines in Plant Pathology '16; (with H H Whetzel) Manual of Fruit Diseases '17; also articles in field. Prof Bot U Tenn since '19, dean Coll of Liberal Arts since '34. AAAS(F)—Bot Soc Am—Am Phytopathol Soc—Mycol Soc Am—Tenn Acad Sci—Sigma Xi. 1816 Lake Av., Knoxville, Tenn.

22 HESS, Arthur James. Air conditioning (Plant growing research laboratories). b'04. Student '23-26 (U Calif); '26-27 (U Calif Berkeley); '27-28 (U So Calif). Consulting engineer California Institute of Technology various periods '35-40, design and coordinating research of special air-conditioned plant-growing research laboratories to investigate growing plants.

Author articles in field. Chief engr English & Lauer Inc '30-46; pres, chief engr Hess-Greiner & Polland Inc since '46. Am Soc Heating Ventilating Engrs (past pres so Calif chapter)—Am Soc Refrigerating Engrs. 1706 S. Main St., LA 15. H: 897 Linda Vista Av., Pasadena 3, Cal.

10 HESS, David C(larence). Spectroscopy (Mass). b'16. BS '37 (U Denver); PhD '49 (U Chicago). Applications mass spectroscope to study isotopic abundances; radioactive isotopes; chemical analysis. Author articles: The isotopic constitution of Europium, Gadolinium and Terbium. Slow neutron cross sections for neodymium isotopes; and others. Physicist Argonne Nat Lab since '46. Inst Radio Engrs (asso)—APS—Am Inst Physics—AAAS—Sigma Xi. Argonne National Laboratory, P.O. Box 5207, Chgo 80.

11 HESS, Harry Hammond. Mineralogy; Marine geology; Petrology. b'06. BS '27 (Yale); PhD '32 (Princeton). Research on optical properties of rock-forming minerals. Author articles in field. With Princeton U since '34, now prof geol and chmn dept. Nat Acad Sci—Geol Soc Am(F)—Mineral Society America(F)—Am Geophys Union—Soc Econ Geol. Princeton University, Princeton, N.J.

12 HESS, Raymond W. Dyestuff technology; Water pollution; Copper ore flotation. b'89. AB '12 (Morningside Coll); AM '14—PhD '16 (U Ill). Research and development on dyestuffs and their production; methods for diversion industrial wastes from public waters and atmosphere by modification productive processes; recovery of by-products and treatment of wastes; member technical committee NY State Water Pollution Control Board since '49. Holds 11 patents on production of sulfur dyes and intermediates, 20 patents on production and use of copper ore flotation agents. Author articles: Wastes from Chemical Manufacturing '49; Cooperation—Key to Industrial Waste Problems '49, and others. With Nat Aniline Div Allied Chem & Dye Corp since '18, head pollution research since '38, head operating improvements since '41; chmn water pollution adv com Asso Industries NY State Inc since '47. Mfg Chem Assn (water pollution abatement com since '44, chmn '45-48)—ACS—AICE—AAAS—NY Sewage and Indsl Wastes Assn—Fedn Sewage and Indsl Wastes Assns (indsl wastes com since '50—Sigma Xi—Phi Lambda Upsilon—Alpha-Chi Sigma P.O. Box 975, Buffalo 5. H: 171 Linwood Av., Buffalo 9.

13 HESS, Victor Francis. Cosmic rays; Radioactivity; Ionization of the atmosphere; Atmospheric electricity. b'83. Student '01-05 (U Graz), '05-08—PhD '06 (U Graz); ScD '46 (Fordham U NY). Author: Conductivity of the Atmosphere and Its Causes '28; Ionization Balance of the Atmosphere '33; Biological Action of Cosmic Radiation '40. Prof Physics Fordham U since '38; research asso Carnegie Inst Washington since '40. Am Phys Soc (F)—Acad Sci Vienna (life mem)—Am Geophys Union. Awarded Nobel prize in physics for discovery of cosmic rays '36. 20 William St., Mt. Vernon, N.Y.©

14 HESSEL, Frederick A(dam). Petroleum organic chemistry. b'98. MCS '22 (Meurice Inst Chem Brussels); grad '23—ScD '24 (Petroleum Inst U Strasbourg France). Co-author: Chemistry in Warfare '40; Strategic Materials in Hemisphere Defense '42. Pres Montclair Research Corp since '41. Am Inst Chem (treas since '43). 4 Cherry St., Montclair, N.J.

15 HESSELMEYER, Clarence Theodore. Electrical Equipment testing. b '02. AB—EE (Stanford U). General testing of motors, generators, transformers, electrical instruments, protective equipment and relays; dielectric testing of insulation, chiefly by loss or power factor method; development methods for test of high current contacts; field tests of protective relays. Testing Gen Elec Co '25-27, design of generators and power system calculations '27-30; testing elec equipment Chicago Dist Elec Generating Corp since '30. Am Inst EE. Chicago District Electric Generating Corp., P.O. Box 65, Hammond, Ind.†

16 HESSELTINE, William Best. American history (Civil War period, Lincoln); Military prisons; Propaganda and war psychology; Political history. b'02. AB '22—LittD '49 (Wash & Lee U); MA '25 (U Va); PhD '28 (Ohio State U). Lecturer for US Department of State in cultural centers in Costa Rica, Honduras, and Guatemala '47. Author: Civil War Prisons '30; Ulysses S Grant '35; History of the South '36; Syllabus of United States History '40; South in American History '43; Lincoln and the War Governors '48; Rise and Fall of Third Parties '48. Prof hist U Wis since '40. AHA—Miss Valley Hist Assns—Phi Beta Kappa. 4014 Manitou Way, Madison, Wis.

17 HESTER, Edgar Allen. Power system engineering. b'94. BE '16—EE '21 (NC State Coll). Holder various patents covering control and regulation of electrical equipment. Co-author: National Electric Light Association Relay Handbook; articles in field. Cons Duquesne Light Co Pittsburgh since '49. Assn Edison Illuminating Cos—Edison Elec Inst—Engrs Soc Western Pa—Pa Elec Assn—Assn Iron and Steel Engrs—Am Soc Mil Engrs—AIEE—Phi Kappa Phi. 435 Sixth Av., Pittsburgh 19.

18 HESTER, Jackson B(oling). Soil and plant chemistry. b'04. BS (Clemson); MS (U Fla); PhD (Rutgers). Author articles in field. Soil tech Campbell Soup Co since '37. AAAS(F)—Am Assn Hort Sci—Am Soc Agron—Am Soc Soil Sci—Am Chem Soc—Am Inst Chem—Sigma Xi—Phi Kappa Phi. Voted one of the ten most able chemists in field Ohio Section Am Chem Soc. Agricultural Research Department, Campbell Soup Co., Riverton, N.J.

19 HETÉNYI, Miklós. Engineering (Civil and mechanical); Stress analysis; Structural theory. b'06. Engring diploma '31 (U Tech Sci Budapest); PhD '36 (U Mich). Author: Beams on Elastic Foundation '46; also articles in field. Prof theoretical and applied mechanics Northwestern Tech Inst since '46, Walter P. Murphy professor since '50. AAAS—Am Soc Engring Edn—Internat Assn Bridge Structural Engring—ASME (chmn applied mechs div Chicago since '46)—Soc Exptl Stress Analysis (pres '44-45, exec com since '43)—Phi Kappa Phi—Sigma Xi. Northwestern Technological Institute, Evanston, Ill.

20 HETHERINGTON, Charles Ray. Petroleum and gas technology. b'19. BS '40—MS '41 (Univ of Okla); ScD '43 (MIT). Engineering development of chemical system to produce pure oxygen from air, adapted machine to aircraft use; selection and development of processes and preparation of design for new refinery plants; selection of processes and equipment for petroleum and gas refinery, transcontinental gas pipe lines and underground storage. Author: High Pressure Pipe Line Research, 1942; also articles in field. Engr to asso research engr Standard Oil Co of Calif '43-46; div engr Ford Bacon & Davis since '49. Am Gas Assn—Sigma Tau—Sigma Xi—Tau Beta Pi—Am Chem Soc. 39 Broadway, NYC 6.

21 HEUBERGER, J(ohn) W(illiam). Plant pathology; Pest control; Fungicides. b'06. BS '29 (RI State Coll); MS '32—PhD '34 (U Md). Research on plant disease control by fungicides, development of organic chemicals, particularly dithiocarbaniates, as fungicides. Author articles in field. Prof head dept plant path U Del since '47. Am Phytopath Soc (mem fungicide com)—Am Assn Econ Entomol—Sigma Xi—Phi Kappa Phi. University of Delaware, Newark, Del.

22 HEUER, Russell Pearce. Refractory materials (Chemistry). b'96. BS in chem engring '17—Chem E '22—PhD '27 (U Pa). Research on metallurgy, manufacture and use of refractory materials. Holds patents relating to metallurgy of oxygen-free copper, operation of blast furnaces with acid slags, desulfurization of pig iron and the manufacture of refractory materials from diverse raw materials including magnesite, chromite, silica, fire clay, diaspore, etc. Chem engr Gen Chem Co Marcus Hook Pa '17, US Bur of Mines '18, Chase metal Works '19-22; instr chem engring U Pa '22-28; chem engr Gen Refractories Co since '27, now also vp in charge of research and dir. Am Ceramic Soc—AIMME—Am Inst Chem Engrs—Am Soc Testing Matrials—Electrochem Soc—Sigma Xi. 1520 Locust St., Phila.

23 HEWATT, Willis G(illiland). Oyster pollution. b'04. AB '26—MS '29 (Tex Christian U); PhD '34 (Stanford U). Author articles in field. Prof biol Tex Christian U since '33. AAAS—Soc Limnologists Oceanographers—Tex Acad Sci. Biology Department, Texas Christian University, Fort Worth 9, Tex.†

24 HEWES, Charles Kay. Chemistry of gasoline, asphalt and lubricants. b'89. BS '12—MS '14 (U Ill). Research in composition, production and application. Chief chem Gen Pet Corp '16-29, Richfield Oil Corp since '29. Am Chem Soc—Am Soc Testing Materials—Am Ordnance Assn—Am Pet Inst. Box 787, Wilmington, Calif.

25 HEWES, Leslie. Cultural and regional geography; Economic geography (Mexico and central United States). b'06. BA '29 (U Okla); '29-32—PhD '40 (U Calif). Research in progress on drainage of wet prairies as theme in occupancy of central Iowa, occupance forms of Springfield plain of Arkansas. Author articles: Huepac: Agricultural Village Sonora, Mexico '35; Oklahoma Ozarks as Land of Cherokees '42; Indian Land in Cherokee Country of Oklahoma '42; Cultural Fault Line in Cherokee Country '43, and others. Instr geog U Okla '32-39, asst prof '39-43, asso prof '43-45; cons Latin Am sect OSS '42; prof geog U Neb since '45, chmn dept geog since '46. Assn Am Geog—Am Geog Soc—Inter-Am Soc Anthrop Geog. Department of Geography, University of Nebraska, Lincoln, Neb.†

26 HEWETSON, Frank Nutter. Fruit tree culture. b'05. BSA '33 (U BC); MS '36 (Mich State Coll). Author articles in field. Asso prof pomol Pa State Coll since '45. Am Soc Hort Sci—AAAS—Am Soc Plant Physiol—Am Soc Agron—Sigma Xi. Fruit Research Laboratory, Arendtsville, Pa.

27 HEWETT, Donnel Foster. Manganese deposits; Mojave desert. b'81. Metall engr '02—Dr Sci (hon) '42 (Lehigh U); PhD '24 (Yale). Author articles in field. Geol US Geol Survey since '11, charge manganese investigations since '12, chief sect metalliferous deposits '35-44, chief strategic mineral investigations '39-44, staff geol since '44; research asso Calif Inst Tech since '47. Nat Acad Sci—Geol Soc Am (council '31-33, vp '35, '45)—Soc Econ Geol (pres '37)—Mineral Soc Am—AIME—Am Assn Pet Geol—Washington Acad Sci. 1460 Rose Villa St., Pasadena, Cal.†☉

10 HEWITT, Alfred George. Sausage casings (Synthetic); Fabrics (Nonwoven); Unsupported flms (Cellulose, plastic). b'00. Chem E '23 (Lehigh U). Research on manufacture of cellulose sausage casings, granted patents in field; research on manufacture of nonwoven fabrics of cellulose; research on viscose production, cellophane manufacture, cellulose tubing, vinyl and polyethylene tubing, polyethylene sheeting. Chem and supervisor E I Du Pont de Nemours and Co '24-28; with Visking Corp since '28, gen mgr Little Rock div since '47, dir, vp and asst treas since '46. AAAS—ACS—Am Indsl Hygiene Soc—Am Ordnance Soc. Postoffice Box 72, North Little Rock, Ark.

11 HEWITT, Charles A. Soil chemistry (Citrus); Herptology. b'02. BS '25 (Vt U). Research on micro elements in plant nutrition and on soil moisture and fertilization and their control. Chief chem Leffingwell Co Whittier Calif since '25. Am Chem Soc—Am Soc Ichthyologists Herpetologists—Herpetologists League. Leffingwell Co., P.O. Box 191, Whittier, Calif.

12 HEWITT, Harold G. Synthetic drugs; Volatile oils. b'01. BS '23—MS '25—PhD '26 (U Wis). Author articles in field. Dean Coll Pharmacy U Conn since '47. AAAS—Am Chem Soc—Am Pharm Assn—Sigma Xi. University of Connecticut, College of Pharmacy, 150 York St., New Haven.

13 HEWITT, Herbert Henry. Alcoholic abstinence (Among the noteworthy). b'94. student '15-17 (U Chicago). Research among newspapers, books, and periodicals for collection of names of notable persons in the news who abstain from alcoholic drinks. With Chicago Pub Library since '39, chief reference div since '39. ALA—Ill Library Assn—Chicago Library Club—Great Lakes Hist Soc—Ill Hist Soc—Chicago Hist Soc. Chicago Public Library, Michigan Av at Randolph and Washington Sts., Chgo.

14 HEWITT, Joseph Lee. Registry of virus free plants. b'81. BS '05 (Mo U); student (U Calif, U So Calif). Research in development of pest-free sources of fruit tree nursery stock, sources of virus-free fruit tree nursery stock. Author articles in field. Asst in hort U Ark '05, prof plant path '13-18 dist agrl inspector Los Angeles Co Calif '22-26; inspector, later deputy agrl commr Orange Co Calif '27-37; charge statewide nursery inspection Calif since '37. Ark State Hort Soc—Am Phytopath Soc. State Department of Agriculture, 238 Mull Building, Sacramento 14, Cal.†

15 HEWITT, Oliver H(arold). Waterfowl and fur; Marsh management. b'16. BA '39 (McMaster); MSc '41 (Cornell); PhD '44 (Cornell). Research on fur and waterfowl production in marshes, bird distribution, waterfowl damage to grain crops, foods and feeding habits of migratory waterfowl (ducks and geese), populations of migratory game birds. Author articles in field. Dominion wildlife officer Dominion Wildlife Service Ottawa Ont

'44-47, wildlife management officer '47-48; asst prof wildlife management Cornell U since '49. Am Ornithol Union—Wildlife Soc—Am Soc Mammalogists—Wilson Ornithol Club—Sigma Xi. Department of Conservation, Cornell University, Ithaca, N.Y.†

16 HEWITT, William Boright. Diseases of grape. b'08. BS '33—MS '34—PhD '36 (U Calif). Author articles in field. Asso prof plant path and asso plant path expt sta U Calif Coll Agr Davis since '37. Am Phytopath Soc—Am Soc Hort Sci. Division of Plant Pathology, College of Agriculture, University of California, Davis, Calif.

17 HEWSON, Edgar Wendell. Atmospheric pollution; Cloud physics. b'10. BA '32 (Mt Allison U); MA '33 (Dalhousie U); MA '35 (U Toronto); DIC '37 (Imperial Coll Sci & Tech); PhD '37 (U London). Research in meteorological aspects of atmospheric pollution. Co-author: (with R W Longley) Meteorology Theoretical and Applied '44; also articles in field. Research meteorol Meteorol Service Can '38-47, asst controller training and research '47-48; cons meteorol Consol Mining and Smelting Co Can '39-40; US Bur Mines '39-40, '45-46; project dir MIT since '48. Royal Meteorol Soc(F)—Am Meteorol Soc—Royal Soc Canada(F)—Can Assn Physicists (asso)—Am Geophys Union. Received Buchan prize Royal Meteorol Soc '39. Round Hill Field Station, South Dartmouth, Mass.

18 HEXTER, J. H. History of the Reformation; English history. b'10. BA '31 (U Cincinnati); MA '33—PhD '37 (Harvard). Research on political, economic and social traits of the New Monarchy of late fifteenth and early sixteenth century and its impact on the Calvinist revolts. Author: The Reign of King Pym '41; also articles in field. Research in England '36-37; instr, later asst prof history Queens Coll NYC since '39 asso fellow in university seminar on renaissance Columbia Univ '49-53. AHA—Renaissance Club. Bowdoin Prize for best essay in hist Harvard '36; Guggenheim Fellowship '46-47, renewed '47-48. Department of History, Queens College, Flushing, N.Y.†

19 HEXTER, Maurice B. Jewish welfare. b'91. AB '12 (U Cincinnati); AM '24—PhD '25 (Harvard). Author: Social Consequences of Business Cycles '25; Cyclical Fluctuations in the Juvenile Labor Market '26. Supt United Jewish Charities Cincinnati '17-19; exec dir Federated Jewish Charities Boston '19-29; sec Joint Palestine Survey Comm '27-29; exec Jewish Agency for Palestine '29-38; dir Palestine Emergency Fund '29-38; asst exec vp Fedn Jewish Philanthropies NYC '38-41, exec vp since '41; pres Am Jewish Joint Agrl Corp since '41. Dom Rep Settlement Assn (pres since '48). 71 W. 47th St., NYC.

20 HEYDECKER, Wayne Darlington. Marine fisheries. b'91. AB '11 (Columbia). Author articles in field. Sec-treas, exec officer Atlantic States Marine Fisheries embracing 14 states since '42. Am Soc Planning Officials. 11 West Prospect Ave., Mt. Vernon, N.Y.

21 HEYDEN, Francis J. Statistical astronomy; Space densities of stars in southern Milky Way. b'07. AB '30—MA '31—STL '37 (Woodstock Coll); MA '42—PhD '44 (Harvard). Chief astron div Manila Obs PI '31-34; asst dir Georgetown Coll Obs '45-48, dir since '48; participant US Army Air Force-Nat Geog Society eclipse expdn to Brazil May '47 and May '48. Astron

Soc of Pacific—Am Astron Soc—Soc Photographic Engrs. Georgetown University, Washington 7.

22 HIATT, Robert Worth. Coral reefs; Marine ecology. b'13. AB '36 (San Jose State Coll); PhD '41 (U Cal). Studies on racial variation and ecology of Hawaiian anchovy, ecology of coral reefs of mid-Pacific atolls; research on intermolt cycle, ecology, and life history of Pacific Coast crabs; member of US committee on oceanography of Pacific since '47; member US delegation to Seventh Pacific Science Congress New Zealand '49; chairman American Institute of Biological Sciences Committee on Hydrobiology since '51; member of Biological Sciences Panel Office of Naval Research since '51; member Pacific Science Board Invertebrate Consultants Committee for Micronesia since '51. Author articles: Food-Chains and the Food Cycle in Hawaiian Fish Ponds '47; Biotic Interaction in Hawaiian Fish Ponds '47; The Biology of the Lined Shore Crab Pachygrapsus crassipes Randall '48; A Directory to Marine Laboratories of the United States and Canada '50, and others. Instr zool Mont State Coll '41-42, asst prof '42-43; faculty U Hawaii since '42, chmn dept zool and entomol since '46, prof since '50; head upland game bird investigations Mont State Fish and Game Commn '42-43; dir Hawaii Marine Lab since '44; fishery biol Bikini Sci Resurvey '47; marine zool Coral Atoll Project '50; bd ed Pacific Science. AAAS—Am Ornthol Union—Wildlife Soc—Am Fisheries Soc—Am Soc Ichthyologists and Herpetologists—Am Soc Limnol and Oceanog—Am Soc Professional Biol—Ecol Soc Am—Am Soc Zoologists. University of Hawaii, Honolulu, T.H.

23 HIBBARD, Aubrey D. Physiology, nutrition and production of peaches; Breeding watermelons; Nutritive value of fruits and vegetables; Strawberry culture. b'08. BS '31 (Mo State Coll); MA '34—PhD '37 (U Mo). Author articles in field. Asst prof, asso prof hort U Mo since '41. Am Soc Hort Sci—Am Pomol Soc—Sigma Xi—Gamma Sigma Delta. Department of Horticulture, University of Missouri, 202 Whitten Hall, Columbia, Mo.†

24 HIBBARD, Claude W(illiam). Vertebrate paleontology; Recent and fossil mammals. b'05. AB '33—MA '34 (Kans U); PhD '41 (U Mich). Discovered Rexroad fauna '36, Jones fauna '39, Borchers fauna '40, Rezabeck fauna '41, Tobin fauna '42, Wilson Valley fauna '42, Kaintuck fauna '43, Deer Park fauna '42. Author articles in field. Curator vertebrates and asso professor geol U Mich since '46. Am Soc Mammal—Paleontol Soc—Soc Vert Paleontol—Soc Icthyologists Herpetologists—Kansas Academy Science—Mich Acad Sci—Geology Society Am (F)—Sigma Xi. University of Michigan, Museum of Paleontology, Ann Arbor.

25 HIBBEN, Frank Cummings. American Indian anthropology; American mountain lion. b'10. AB '33 (Princeton); MS '36 (U NM); PhD '40 (Harvard). Author: A Preliminary Study of the Mountain Lion '37; Excavation of the Riana Ruin and Chama Valley Survey '37; Tseh Tso A Small House Ruin Chaco Canyon NM '37; The Lost Americans '46; Hunting American Lions '48; also articles in field. Archeol and mammalogist O State Mus '28-29; asst archeol Cleveland Mus '30-33; collector for Am Nature Assn '33-34; instr U NM '34-38, asst prof '39-41, asso prof anthrop since '46. Archeol Soc Am—Am Anthrop Soc—Ecol Soc Am—AAAS—

Sigma Xi — Phi Beta Kappa — Phi Kappa Phi. 3005 Campus Blvd., Albuquerque, N.M.

10 HIBBS, Max L. Alabama political history; China; International relations. b'13. BS '38 (Ala Poly Tech Inst); MA '40 (Duke U). Research history of political parties in Alabama, 1820-1848. Author articles: US Relations with China 1791-1848; International Trade as a Factor of Peace. Graduate Fellow Duke U '40-41; asso prof Georgia Sch of Tech since '49. Am Academy of Political and Social Science — Am Historical Society — Am Economic Asso — Kappa Delta Pi. Department of Economics and Social Science, Georgia School of Technology, Atlanta.

11 HICKEY, Joseph J(ames). Bird-banding statistics; Wildlife ecology, conservation and management (Game). b'07. BS '30 (NYU); MS '42 (U Wis); '43-44 (U Chicago); PhD '49 (U Mich). Author: A Guide to Bird Watching '43. Collaborator US Fish and Wildlife Service since '46; asso prof and chmn dept wildlife management U Wis since '48. AAAS — Am Ornithol Union — Biometric Soc — Ecol Soc Am — Linn Soc NY (pres '39-41, ed '41-42) — Inland Bird-banding Assn — Wildlife Soc — Wis Soc Ornithol (vp '48-49). Guggenheim fellow '46-47. 424 University Farm Pl., Madison 5, Wis.†

12 HICKMAN, Franklin Simpson. Psychology of religion. b'86. AB '17 (De Pauw); STB '20 (Boston U Sch Theol); AM '22 — PhD '23 (Northwestern). Author: Introduction to the Psychology of Religion '26; Christian Vocation '30; The Possible Self '33; Signs of Promise '43; also articles in field. Prof psychology religion Duke U since '27, preacher to U since '32, dean Chapel '38-48. Phi Beta Kappa — Delta Sigma Rho — Phi Delta Kappa — Omicron Delta Kappa. 921 Markham Av., Durham, N.C.◉

13 HICKOK, William Orville, IV. Paper ruling machinery; Economic regional geology. b'05. BS '27 — MS '29 — PhD '33 (Yale); student '29-30 (U Freiburg). With W O Hickok Mfg Co Harrisburg Pa since '36, chmn bd since '45, dir since '34. Nat Assn Mfrs (patents and research com, spl com on distribution knowledge patent system, sub-com atomic energy and research) — Mineral Soc Am. 900 Cumberland St., Harrisburg, Pa.

14 HICKS, John Donald. United States history (Recent and western). b'90. BA '13 — MA '14 (Northwestern); PhD '16 (U Wis). Author: The Constitutions of the Northwest States '25; The Populist Revolt '31; The Federal Union '37; The American Nation '41; A Short History of American Democracy '43; also articles in field. A F and May T Morrison prof hist U Calif since '42, chmn dept '47-50. AHA — Miss Valley Hist Assn — Agrl Hist Soc — Calif Hist Soc — Phi Alpha Theta — Phi Kappa Phi — Phi Beta Kappa (hon). 30 Wheeler Hall, Berkeley 4.◉

15 HICKS, Joseph Skean. Low pressure and molded plastics. b'02. BS '23 (N Tex State Teachers Coll); MS '25 — PhD '27 (U Chicago); LLB '39 (Wayne U). Author: Low Pressure Laminating of Plastics '47. Lecturer in chem U Toledo '47-49; dir chem dept Sam Houston State Teachers Coll since '49; cons. Am Chem Soc — Sigma Xi. Chemistry Department, Sam Houston State Teachers College, Huntsville, Tex.†

16 HICKS, Joseph W. Public relations; Industrial relations. b'99. Student '18 (U So Cal) '19-21 (U Wash); AB '23 (U Okla). Author: Some Techniques of Public Relations; Improving the Stature and Dignity of an Industry; Public Relations, The Glamour Girl of the Professions. Co-author: Pathways to Print. Public relations exec H M Byllesby & Co., Standard Gas & Electric Co, Pub Utility Engring & Service Corp Chicago '25-41; pvt practice pub relations and indsl relations cons since '41; retained by industries and corps in foods, pub utilities, electronics, radio, television, mining, chemicals, finance, confectionery; pub relations counsel Chicago Bd Trade; pres Joseph W Hicks Orgn, T-V Check Inc. Chicago Assn Commerce — Pub Relations Soc Am — Better Bus Bur Chicago — Advt Fedn Am — Nat Soc Advancement Management — Press Club — Federated Advt Club — Publicity Club Chicago. Winner Chicago Federated Advt Club award for best pub relations program conducted in Chicago by Chicago firm '45 and '46; Distinguished Alumni award U Okla for contbn to work in radio industry. Suite 3213, 141 W. Jackson Blvd., Chgo.†

17 HIDY, Ralph Willard. American business (History). b'05. AB '26 (Miami U); MA '28 (Clark U); PhD '35 (Harvard). Author: The House of Baring in American Trade and Finance '49. Editor Business History Series, NYU since '50. Mem faculty Wheaton Coll '32-47, prof '46-47; prof history grad sch arts and sci NYU since '50. Econ History Assn — Am Hist Assn — Econ History Soc(Eng) — Bus History Soc Inc — Phi Beta Kappa. New York University, Washington Square, NYC 3. H: 35 Borage Pl., Forest Hills, N.Y.†◉

18 HIENTON, Truman Edward. Farms (Electrical equipment). b'93. BS '21 — AE(hon) '38 (O State U); BSAE '26 — MSAE '37 (Ia State Coll); DSc '50 (Purdue). Technical research electrically heated chick brooders, pig brooders, poultry water heaters, dairy water heaters, hot beds, livestock drinking tanks; electrically operated threshing machines, feed grinders and hay choppers; electrically refrigerated milk coolers; precooling strawberries, cantaloupes, peaches in refrigerated cars; insect control by electric lamps and traps. With USDA since '46, head div farm electrification. Am Soc Agrl Engrs(F) — Sigma Xi — Alpha Zeta — Gamma Sigma Delta — Phi Kappa Phi. Agricultural Research Center, Beltsville, Md.

19 HIESEY, William McKinley. Plant physiology and taxonomy; Ecology; Environment. b'03. BS '29 — PhD '40 (U Calif). Research on basic biological interrelationships between and within wild species plants using various methods, especialy transplant experiments, varied environments, cytologic and genetic investigations, comparative physiology of ecologically diverse races. Co-author: Experimental Studies on the Nature of Species: I Effect of Varied Environments on Western North American Plants '40, II Plant Evolution Through Amphiploidy and Alloploidy, with Examples from the Madiinae '45, III Environmental Responses of Climatic Races of Achillea '48. Research investigator Carnegie Inst of Washington '29-39, staff mem since '39. Bot Soc Am — Am Soc Plant Physiol — Soc Study Growth — Soc Study Evolution — Calif Acad Sci — Calif Bot Soc — Western Soc Naturalists — AAAS. Carnegie Institution of Washington, Stanford, Calif.†

20 HIESTAND, William Andrew. Vertebrate and invertebrate physiology (Respiration and respiratory mechanisms). BA '25 — AM '28 — PhD '30 — research fellow '29-30 (U Wis). Researches in invertebrate physiology on respiration, Insecta Crustacea, Mollusca, Echinodermata, oxygen tension, hydrogen-ion concentration; in vertebrate physiology on respiration and body temperature regulation in birds and mammals, body temperature limits, blood sugar levels in mice and rats, factors in anoxic resistance; in decompression physiology on simulated high altitudes, primitive respiratory mechanisms. Author articles in field. Asst prof physiol Purdue U '30-38, asso prof '38-46, prof since '46. AAAS — Am Soc Zool — Am Physiol Soc — Soc Exptl Biol and Med — Fed Am Biol Soc — Ind Acad Sci — Wis Acad Sci Arts Letters — Sigma Xi — Phi Sigma — Gamma Alpha. Purdue University, Lafayette, Ind.

21 HIGBEE, Edna. Experimental morphology. BS '21 — MS '27 — PhD '36 (U Pittsburgh). Editor Nature Notes since '43. Author articles in field. Acting editor: The Biologist '42-46. With U Pittsburgh since '34, prin and head biol, dean women U Sch since '44. AAAS — Pa Acad Sci — Am Soc Zool — Am Genetic Assn — Nat Biol Teachers Assn — Phi Sigma — Sigma Xi. University School, 5711 How St., Pittsburgh 32. H: 2845 Broadway Av., Pitts 16.

22 HIGBEE, Edward C. Tropical crops and soils. b'10. BA '36 — MA '38 (U Wis) PhD '49 (Johns Hopkins). Field investigations in P R So and Cent Am Mex. Author articles in field. With US Dept Agr '38-48, senior agron Office Fgn Agrl Relations '44-48; asso prof soils and agr grad school geography Clark U. AAAS — Am Geog Soc — Am Soc Agron — Soil Sci Soc Am. Clark University, Worcester, Mass.

23 HIGBEE, Frederic Goodson. Descriptive geometry; Engineering drawing. b'81. BS in ME '03 — ME '08 (Case Sch Applied Sci). Asst engr Osborn Engring Co and J B Davis & Sons '03-04; instr Case Sch Applied Sci '04-05; asst prof descriptive geometry and drawing State U Iowa '05-08, prof and head dept engring drawing since '08, dir of convocations, chmn Campus Planning Com; Zoning Commn '24-25, Bd of Adjustment Iowa City. Author: Essentials of Descriptive Geometry '15, 4th edit '30; Descriptive Geometry Problems '21; (with H C Thompson, Jr) Engineering Drawing Problems '27; Drawing Board Geometry '37; 101 Problems in Drawing Board Geometry '38; (with J M Russ) Engineering Drawing Problems '40. Editor: T Square Page, Jour Engring Edn '30-36; Jour, Engring Drawing '36-37, Drawing and Drafting Room Practice, ASA Z141 '46. Ia Acad Sci(F) — Am Soc Engring Edn — Sigma Xi — Tau Beta Pi — Pi Tau Sigma. 320 Ronalds St., Iowa City, Ia.

24 HIGGINS, George Clinton. Photographic physics; Visual mechanisms (Function). b'12. BS '34 — PhD '38 (Ia State Coll). Co-author: Fundamentals of Photographic Theory '48; also articles in field. Research physicist Eastman Kodak Co Rochester since '43. Optical Soc Am — Am Phys Soc — Sigma Xi. Research Laboratories, Eastman Kodak Co., Rochester, N.Y.†

25 HIGGINS, George Judson. Airplanes (Performance, control, and stability testing); Wind tunnels (Operation of subsonic); Arrows (Aerodynamics); Clay pigeons (Aerodynamics). b'97. BS '23 — AE '34 (U Mich). Author: A Manual of Experiments in Aerodynamics '30. Co-author: (with Tapy) An Outline for Technical Report Writing. Engr Nat Adv Commn for Aeronautics Langley Field Va '23-28; asso and prof aeronaut engring U Detroit '28-42; prof aeronautics USN Post Grad Sch since '42, Capt S(A) USNR. Inst Aeronautical Sci (asso F)—Soc Automotive Engrs—US Naval Inst. U.S. Naval Postgraduate School, Annapolis, Md.

10 HIGHFILL, Robert David. Shakespeare; Chaucer.·b'89. AB '11 (U Ark); AM '26 (Northwestern U); PhD '27 (U Chicago). Special contributor to Dictionary of American English. Prof and head English dept Ouachita Coll '27-31, Memphis State Coll '31-42; prof English Miss State Coll for Women '46-48; Pollock prof English and head dept Mercer U since '48; vis prof English U Ark '29 '30, Miss State Coll '43-44, Murray State Coll '44-46, Ala State Tchrs Coll '47, Transylvania Coll '48. Modern Lang Assn Am—AAUP.⊙

11 HIGUCHI, Takeru. Physical chemistry (Synthetic rubber, instrumentation analysis); Pharmacy. b'18. AB '39 (U Calif); PhD '43—postdoctorate fellow '43-44 (U Wis). Co-author: Development of Methods of Chemical Analysis of Synthetic Rubber '47; also articles in field. Govt research U Akron '44-47; asso prof pharmacy U Wis since '47. Am Chem Soc—AAAS—Am Pharm Assn—Sigma Xi. Chemistry Building, University of Wisconsin, Madison, Wis. H: 101 W. Lakeside.

12 HILBERT, Frederic L. Chemical engineering; Leather tanning. b'82. BS—ChE '05 (Worcester Polytech Inst). Leather expert in charge production and use of leather for all Army shoe purposes; originator of leather used at present for service and garrison shoes. Author: Technology of Tanning; Use and Manufacture of Leather; Marine Oils and Their Use in the Tanning Industry; also articles in field. Gen mgr Mobile Mills, Am Dyewood Co NY '24-34, dir since '34; pres Hilbert-Topp Tanning Corp; tech dir Shoe and Leather Inst and US Process Corp; tech ed staff Hide and Leather, Shoe and Leather Reporter. Am Leather Chem — Internat Soc Leather Trade Chem—Am Chem Soc—AAAS—Textile Chem and Colorists. 369 Lexington Av., NYC 17.

13 HILBERT, Guido E(dward). Starches; Dextrose; Chemurgy. b'01. ChE '24 (Rensselaer Poly Inst); MS '25 (Lafayette Coll); PhD '28 (Yale). Member committee for surveying field covered by research programs underway in US '38, given task of mapping scientific program of new regional laboratories and assisting in coordination of their programs within broad field of agricultural chemistry; research in field of carbohydrate chemistry, chemistry of cereal grains and other farm commodities. Author articles in field. Research asso Yale '28-30; chief organic research sect Bur Chem and Soils US Dept Agr '30-38, sci advisor to chief of bur '38-40, head starch and dextrose div '40-46, dir No Regional Research Lab Peoria Ill '46-48, chief Bur Agrl and Indsl Chem in Agrl Research Adminstrn since '48. Assn Cereal Chem—Am Soybean Assn—AAAS—Am Chem Soc—Sigma Xi—Gamma Sigma Delta. U.S. Department of Agriculture, Washington.

14 HILBISH, Florence May Anna. Methods of research and bibliographical documentation; Eighteenth century novel. b'92. AB '23 (Dickinson Coll); MA '32 (U Pittsburgh); PhD '36 (U Pa). Author: Charlotte Smith, Poet and Novelist, 1749-1806 '41. Prof Eng, head dept, chmn div lang and lit Taylor U since '46. Coll Eng Assn—Modern Lang Assn. Box 616, Taylor University, Upland, Ind.†

15 HILBORN, Merle Tyson. Wood decay; Plant pathology (Hardwood trees, vegetable crops). b'07. BS '32 —MS '34 (U Maine); vis research sci-

entist '37 (Harvard); PhD '40 (Yale). Research on decay of wood products under natural storage, diseases of hardwood trees, fungicides for apple trees, diseases of vegetable crops, effect of potato diseases on dehydrated potatoes. Author articles in field. Asso plant path Me Agrl Expt Sta since '46. AAAS(F)—Am Phytopath Soc—Mycol Soc Am—Sigma Xi. Maine Agricultural Experiment Station, Orono, Me.†

16 HILDEBRAND, Earl Martin. Plant disease nature and causes (Viruses, bacteria, fungi, physiogens). b'02. BS '28—MS '29—PhD '31 (U Wis). Author articles in field. Plant path Texas A&M College '46-51; professional plant scientist cons. AAAS (F)—Am Phytopath Soc—Bot Soc Am —Am Soc Hort Sci—Soc Am Bact— Am Inst Food Tech. Guggenheim fellow '39-40. 106 Guernsey t., Box 4445, College Station, Tex.

17 HILDEBRAND, Joel Henry. Chemistry (Solubility of non-electrolytes); Skiing; Chemical warfare. b'81. BS '03—PhD '06—DSc (hon) '39 (U Pa). Author: Principles of Chemistry '47; Solubility of Non-electrolytes '36, (with R L Scott) '49; (with W M Latimer) Inorganic Chemistry '40; (with others) Ski Mountaineering; also articles in field. Capt ORC '17, maj Chem Warfare Service '18, lt col '19, dir CWS lab near Paris, later comdt Hanlon Field which included exptl field and AEF Gas Defense Sch; liaison officer OSRD London '43-44 for chem warfare, smokes, incendiaries; expert cons mil planning div QMC '42-45; with U Cal '13-43, prof '18-51, dean Coll Letters Sci '39-43, dean coll chem '49-51; mgr US Olympic ski team '36. AAAS(F)—American Phys Soc—Am Chem Soc—Nat Acad Sci— Royal Soc Edinburgh (hon F)—Phi Beta Kappa—Sigma Xi—Am Philos Society. Awarded Nichols medal '39. 500 Coventry Rd., Berkeley.⊙

18 HILDEBRANDT, Albert C(hristian). Plant pathology, physiology and tissue cultures; Metabolism; Vitamins. b'16. BS '39—MS '41 (Pa State Coll); PhD '45 (U Wis). Research on physiology of normal and pathological growths in plants; crown-gall disease of plants, mineral and carbohydrate metabolism of plant tissue cultures, environmental factors affecting tissue culture growth, vitamins and growth-regulating substances. Author articles in field. Post-doctorate fellow U Wis '45-46, industrial fellow '46-49, assistant professor since '49. AAAS— Am Soc Bact—Am Phytopath Soc— Bot Soc Am—Sigma Xi. Department of Plant Pathology, University of Wisconsin, Madison 6, Wis.

19 HILDRETH, Aubrey Clare. Plant physiology and horticulture. b'93. Research fellow '19-21—'23-25—PhD '26 (U Minn); BS '17 (W Va U); '21-23 (Wash State Coll). Biol '27-30 Me Agr Expt Sta; with US Dept Agr since '30; supt Cheyenne Hort Field Sta and in charge Guayule Research Proj. Author articles in field. AAAS(F)—Sigma Xi—Gamma Sigma Delta—Gamma Alpha. U.S. Department of Agriculture, Cheyenne Horticultural Field Station, Cheyenne, Wyoming.†

20 HILE, Ralph. Aquatic biology; Great Lakes fisheries; Growth of fish. b'04. AB '24 (Ind Central Coll); PhD '30—fellow '28-29 (Ind U). Author articles in field. Aquatic biol Fish and Wildlife Service US Dept Interior since '30; research asso Institute of Human Biology U Mich, honorary appt, since '46, research asso dept zool University Mich, honorary appt, since '48. AA AS(F)—Am Fisheries Soc (chmn ed

bd since '46)—Am Soc Limnol Oceanog —Am Soc Zool—Am Soc Ichthyologists Herpetologists—Ind Acad Sci—Mich Acad Sci Arts Letters (chmn zool sect '46-47)—Wis Acad Sci Arts Letters— Sigma Xi. 1220 East Washington St., Ann Arbor.†

21 HILER, Hilaire. Color (Order systems, psychology); Technique of fine arts painting; Costume (Aesthetics). b'98. Student '16-20 (U Pa); '33-35 (Sorbonne, U Paris). Author: From Nudity to Raiment '29; Notes on the Technique of Painting '33; The Painter's Pocket Book '34-35; (with Meyer Hiler) Bibliography of Costume '39; Color Harmony and Pigments '40. Decorator of clubs and hotels in Paris and US; color consultant for Roos Bros Stores, San Francisco '39; Lab of Anthology, Santa Fe NM '45; paintings exhibited in Paris, NY and San Francisco. Internat Inst Bibliography Belgium—Authors—Soc for General Semantics. 1125 San Acacio, Santa Fe, N.M.†⊙

22 HILGARD, Ernest Ropiequet. Learning (Psychology). b'04. BS '24 (U Ill); PhD '30 (Yale). Experimental investigation within field conditioned response learning, motor skills, level of aspiration. Author: Theories of Learning '48. Co-author: (with Donald G Marquis) Conditioning and learning '40. From asst prof to prof psychol and edn since '33, head dept psychol since '42. Am Psychol Assn— Soc Exptl Psychol—Nat Acad Sci. Received Warren Medal in experimental psychol '40. Department of Psychology, Stanford University, Stanford, Calif.⊙

23 HILGEMAN, Edward Henry. Mechanical engineering. b'11. BS (mech engring) '33 (Rose Poly Inst). Research on industrial plant management, appraisals, and estimates, specification and procurement of process equipment and materials, food processes and production line design, machine design analysis and production machinery economics. Operations engr A & P Tea Co '33-38, engr operations all units '38-42; prin engr Singmaster & Breyer '42-45, partner from '45. Singmaster & Breyer, 420 Lexington Av., NYC 17. H: 47 Riverside Av., Riverside, Conn.

24 HILGER, Mary Inez, Sister. Ethnology (Primitive child life). b'91. BA '23—grad work '31-36 (U Minn); MA '25—PhD '39 (Catholic U Am). Author: Chippewa Child Life and Its Cultural Background; Arapaho Child Life and Its Cultural Background; also articles in field. Am Onthrop Assn (F, council)—Catholic Anthrop Conf (exec bd) —AAAS — Instituto Interamericano. Grants-in-aid Social Sci Research Council '39, '40 for ethnol field work among Chippewa and Northern Arapaho; Am Council Learned Socs '42-43, work among No Arapaho; by Am Philos Soc for work among Araucanians of Chile '46-47. 1406 Sixth Av., N. St. Cloud, Minn. H: St. Benedict's Convent, St. Joseph.

25 HILKEY, Charles Joseph. American Colonial legal history; Legal history (Georgia). b'80. AB '05 (Coll Emporia Kan); AM '07 (U Kan);·U Scholar '08-09—U Fellow '09-10—PhD '10 (Columbia U); JD '15 (U Mich); SJD '24 (Harvard). Author: Legal Development in Colonial Massachusetts '10; History of Supreme Court of Georgia 1858-1870 '44; also articles in field. Prof law '15-18, dean '19-23 Drake U Coll Law; dean Lamar Sch Law Emory U since '25; vis prof Cornell U Law Sch '28, Law Sch U Ga '42; research fellow Harvard Law Sch '28-29. Order of Coif—Phi Beta Kappa—Gamma Eta Gamma—Am Bar Assn—AA UP. 1664 Cornell Rd., Atlanta.

10 HILL, Albert Gordon. Atomic physics. b'10. BS '30—MS '34 (Washington U); PhD '37 (U Rochester). Asso prof to prof physics Mass Inst Tech since '46, asso dir, dir Research Lab of Electronics since '49; cons Fed Tel Labs, Research and Development Bd, Brookhaven Nat Lab Staff Radiation Lab Mass Inst Tech '42-46. Am Phys Soc. Massachusetts Institute of Technology, Cambridge 39, Mass.⊚

11 HILL, A(lfred) Garrett. Dye intermediates. b'06. AB — MA '26 (Baylor U); PhD '32 (Yale). Patents. Author articles in field. Research chemist Am Cyanamid Co Calco Chem Div Bound Brook NJ '32-39, development chemist '39-44, chief chemist Intermediates Dept '44-46, asst mgr process development dept '46-48, tech dir Intermediates Dept since '48. Am Chem Soc—Am Inst Chemists—Am Inst Chem Engrs—AAAS. American Cyanamid Co., Calco Chemical Division, Bound Brook, N.J.

12 HILL, Archibald A. English language (Structure and history); Phonetics and phonemics; Manuscript relationships and descent. b'02. AB '23 (Pomona Coll Cal); AM '24 (Stanford U); PhD '27 (Yale). Author articles: Phonetic and Phonemic Change '36; early Loss of "r" Before Dentals '40; Some Postulates for the Distributional Study of Manuscript Readings '50; Towards a Literary Analysis '51. Prof English and English philology U Va since '39, prof English lang since '50. Modern Lang Assn—Am Dialect Soc—Mediaeval Acad Am—Linguistic Soc Am (sec since '50). Box 1001 University, Charlottesville, Va.†⊚

13 HILL, Bancroft. Engineering and physical aspects of depreciation of property; Rates and effects. b'87. Student '06-07 (Johns Hopkins); BS '11 (Mass Inst Tech). Research in costs, depreciation, valuation, earnings of public utilities. Author articles in field. Draftsman '15; civil engr, harbor engr, pres Harbor Bd of Baltimore, engr Port Development Commn '19-25; valuation engr United Rys and Electric Co '25-35; exec vp Baltimore Transit Co '35-36, pres '36-45. 1812 Sulgrave Av., Baltimore 9.

14 HILL, Bertram Charles, Jr. Quartz crystals; Frequency measuring equipment. b'17. BA (U Tex); grad study (U Md). Invented developed and discovered UHF Harmonic Calibrator for calibration purposes, high precision heterodyne frequency meter for use in micro-wave regions, Naval wide-frequency range primary standard for frequency and frequency measurements, cathode-coupled UHF crystal oscillator, standardized fundamental frequency parallel-resonant oscillator for quartz crystals, a new crystal controlled-continuously variable oscillator, a new crystal mount. Articles in field. Sound engring at B C Hill Jr & Co '39-42; project engr Naval Research Lab '42-47; chief engr Reeves-Hoffman Corp Carlisle Pa '47; pres Hill Electronic Engr & Mfg Co Inc since '51. Inst Radio Engrs (Sr Mem). New Kingston, Pa.†

15 HILL, Carl McClellan. Ketene chemistry. b'08. BS '31 (Hampton Inst); MS '35—PhD '41 (Cornell U); '38-40 (U Pa). Research studies of phenoxy and chlorine substituted phenoxyacetyl chlorides, ketenes and ketene dimers, alpha beta-unsaturated ethers. Author: Experiments in Organic Chemistry '48; General College Chemistry and Laboratory Manual '46; also author in field. Asst prof chem Hampton Inst Va '31-41; asso prof

chem A and T Coll Greensboro NC '41-44; prof chem and head dept Tenn A and I State Coll since '44. ACS—Tenn Acad Sci—AAAS—Nat Inst Sci —Sigma Xi. Tennessee Agricultural and Industrial State College, Nashville, Tenn.

16 HILL, Clyde Milton. Education (School surveys). b'85. AB '10 (Drury Coll Springfield Mo); AM '15—PhD '26 (Columbia U); AM hon '28 (Yale). Administrative survey San Francisco Schools '44, survey Illinois Teacher Training Institutions '44, survey Red Bank, N.J.; dir Cooperative Study Lincoln (Neb) City Schools, Brattleboro (Vt) Schools; adviser to Senate Investigation Committee on Education (Conn); chmn edn com Conn Postwar Planning Bd. Author: The Junior High School Movement '15; Vermont Junior High Schools '18; A Decade of Progress in Teacher Training '26; Editor symposium: Educational Progress and School Administration, Introduction to High School Teaching. President So Mo State Coll '18-26; prof secondary edn Yale since '29. Nat Assn Progressive Edn(dir)—NEA—AAAS —Mo and Conn state tchrs assns—Phi Delta Kappa—Kappa Delta Pi—Delta Pi Epsilon. 105 Mill Rock Rd., New Haven.†⊚

17 HILL, Daniel A. Public utility and industrial economics; Public utility and valuation engineering. b'98. AB—MBA (Western Res U). Indsl engr Ohio Pub Service Co '24-27; comml engr '27-45; gen rate and valuation engr since '45; vice-pres Alliance Pub Service Co '37-43; lecturer Statistics Fenn Coll since '37; cons engr since '24; asso dir research Cooper Metall Lab '42-45; lecturer Indsl Management John Carroll U since '46. Am Econ Assn—Am Statis Assn—Econometric Soc—Am Management Assn—AIEE—Am Electrochem Soc—Nat Soc Profl Engrs. 1633 Compton Road, Cleveland Heights 18, Ohio.

18 HILL, Eldon Cleon. American literature; Hamlin Garland; Social concepts in literature. b'06. AB '27 (DePauw U); MA '30 (U Wis); PhD '40 (Ohio State U). Author: A Biographical Study of Hamlin Garland 1860-1895 '41; also articles in field. Instr to asso prof Miami U since '38. English Assn (London)—Mod Lang Assn—Nat Council Teachers Eng (dir '47-48)—Phi Beta Kappa. English Department, Miami University, Oxford, Ohio.

19 HILL, George William. Rural sociology; Populations; Immigrations; Colonization; Labor relations. b'00. AB '32 (U Minn); PhD '39 (U Wis). Chairman Governor's committee on resettlement of displaced persons in Wisconsin since '48; advisor on economic and social programs Government of Venezuela South America since '45, cons to displaced persons commn. Author articles in field. Prof rural sociol Agrl Coll U Wis since '36. Am Sociol Soc—Rural Sociol Soc—Indsl Relations Research Assn—AAAS. 315 Agricultural Hall, University of Wisconsin, Madison 6, Wis.

20 HILL, Harry. Spectroscopy; Specific heats. b'95. AB '22—MS '24 (W Va U); PhD '35 (U Chicago). Research on hyperfine structure; measurements, and work on specific heats of solids. Co-author articles: (with Bell) A Versatile Calorimeter '48. Asst prof to asso prof physics Tex Tech Coll '26-32 and '34-42; asst prof advancing to asso prof physics Washington and Jefferson Coll since '42. APS—Am Inst Physics—Am Assn Physics Teachers—AAAS—Pa Acad Sci—Optical Soc Am. Department of Physics, Washing-

ton and Jefferson College, Washington, Pa.

21 HILL, Henry Osborne. Soils (Erosion control, water runoff, fertility); Beef cattle (Breeding); Sheep (Breeding). b'09. BS in CE '30 (U NC); post grad work (USDA Grad Sch), (Mary Hardin Baylor) (Tex A&M Coll). Designed terraces, waterways and erosion control works, studied wind erosion and determined evaporation and transpiration in hydrologic cycle; Developed sampling device to determine soil loss in water runoff. With USDA since '30, now supt agrl exptl stations doing research in soil improvement, crop prodn, crop diseases, beef cattle and sheep breed-Am Soc Agrl Engrs(F)—AAAS(F)—Am Soc Civil Engrs. A and M College System, Texas Agricultural Experiment Station, Blue Bonnet Farm, Mc Gregor, Tex.

22 HILL, Herbert Wells. History (United States diplomatic, United States general and New England). b'02. AB '24—AM '26 (Harvard); AM hon '41 (Dartmouth Coll). Author articles in field. Instr to prof Dartmouth Coll since '28, dir Dartmouth Alumni Coll since '36, Dartmouth Speakers' Bur since '44; Democratic candidate for governor '48. AHA—NH Hist Soc (trustee)—Conf of Hist Socs (corr)—Am Assn of State and Local Hist. Reed Hall, Dartmouth College, Hanover, N.H.

23 HILL, Jesse. Geodesist. b'85. Ed pub schs. Topography, including photographic mapping, and municipal engineering. Assisted in preparation reports International Boundary Commission: Source of St Croix River to the St Lawrence River '24; Source of St Croix River to the Atlantic Ocean 34; Northwesternmost point of Lake of the Woods to Lake Superior '31; Gulf of Georgia to Northwesternmost of Lake of the Woods '37; Tongass Passage to Mt St Elias-British Columbia '51. Engr Internat Boundary Commn US-Alaska and Can since '09, chief engr since '29. AM Soc CE—Soc Am Mil Engrs—Washington Soc Engrs. 101 Indiana Av., Washington 25.

24 HILL, Jim Dan. History (Warfare, American, Texas, Naval, recent diplomatic, World War II, Civil War naval). b'97. BA '22 (Baylor U); MA '24 (U Colo); PhD '31 (U Minn). Author: Sea Dogs of the Sixties '35; The Texas Navy '36. Pres State Teachers Coll Superior Wis since '31. Am Hist Assn. Decorations include Air Medal, Legion of Merit, Chevalier Legion d' Honneur. State Teachers College, Superior, Wis.

25 HILL, John A(rthur). Wool production and marketing; Animal husbandry. b'80. BS '07—hon LLD '47 (U Wyo). Co-author: (with F S Hultz) Range Sheep and Wool '31; also articles in field. Wool specialist U Wyo Expt Station since '07; prof textile industry Wyo Agrl Coll since '12, dean Agrl Coll, dir Expt Sta '23-50, dean and dir emeritus since '50, now vp; mem wool adv com Research and Marketing Act USDA since '47. Wyo State Bd Agr—Am Soc Animal Prodn—NEA —Colo Wyo Acad Sci—Wyo Farm Bur —AAAS(F)—Sigma Xi—Phi Beta Kappa—Phi Kappa Phi. Awarded medal for distinguished service to state, Casper Wyo Kiwanis '43. 264 N. 9th St., Laramie, Wyo.

26 HILL, Pope Russell, Sr. Sherlock Holmes; Experimental probability. b'94. BSA '16—MS '26 (Ga U); '22-23 (Emory U); '28-29 (Wis U). Worked in chronology of Sherlock Holmes tales; discovered hidden substructure to Sherlock Holmes stories by Sir Arthur Conan Doyle; experimented in testing fundamental laws of probability by making one hundred thousand separate drawings from can of pennies. Author articles: Dating Sherlock Holmes '47; also articles in field. Asso prof math Ga U since '41. Phi Beta Kappa — Am Statistical Assn — Am Math Assn. Awarded scholarship to Ga U '12-16. H: 190 Morton Av., Athens, Ga.†

10 HILL, Raymond Alva. Irrigation; Flood control. b'92. B Civil Engring '14—CE '22 (U Mich). Research on reclamation projects, developed designs for balanced automatic spillway gates and spiral spillway channels. With Leeds Hill and Jewett since '26. Am Inst Cons Engrs—Am Soc CE (dir '36-38)—Tau Beta Pi. 601 W. Fifth St., LA 17.

11 HILL, Reuben L(orenzo). Milk (Secretion). b'88. Student '08-11 (Brigham Young U); BS '12 (Utah State Agrl Coll); PhD '15 (Cornell). Developed test used and pioneered research on soft curd milk. Holds patent on equipment for curd test. Biochem Bur Chem USDA Washington '16, Md Agrl Expt Sta '16-18; head dept Chem Utah State Coll Agr since '19, human nutritionist expt sta '19-41. Nutritionist US Army World War I and II. ACS—AAAS—Utah Acad Arts, Sci and Letters—Sigma Xi. Chemistry Dept., Utah State Agricultural College, Logan, Utah. H: 645 N. 8th East St.

12 HILL, Reuben Lorenzo, Jr. Family life; Parent education; Social psychology; Marriage. b'12. BS '35 (Utah State Agrl Coll); PhM '36—PhD '38 (U Wis). Author: Love and Marriage in Wartime and After '44. Co-author: (with Howard Becker) Family, Marriage and Parenthood '48; (with E M Duvall) When You Marry '45; (with H Becker) Marriage and the Family '42; also articles in field. Asso prof sociol and home management Ia State Coll '45-49; prof sociol and research prof Inst for Research in Social Sci U NC since '49. Leader family life workshops and institutes in Va, Tenn, Neb, Ia, Utah, Tex, Ill, Colo since '45; bd dir Nat Council on Family Relations since '47. Am Sociol Soc—Rural Sociol Soc—Am Assn Marriage Counselors—Soc Research Child Development(F). 402 Alumni Bldg., University of North Carolina, Chapel Hill, N.C.⊚

13 HILL, Roy William. Paint and varnishes. b'14. Developed fire retardant interior plants, rust-inhibiting enamels, oil type camouflage paints for wood, emulsifiable camouflage paint; inspected European paint and varnish facilities, maintained tropical exposure station in Canal Zone, Arctic exposure station in Canada, and desert exposure station in Arizona; member Committee of Paint Varnish and Related Materials of Federal Specifications Board, member Committee on Equipment and Materials, Panel on Organic and Fibrous Materials, Temporary Working Group, of Research and Development Board. Author articles in field. Paint chem Benjamin Franklin Paint and Varnish Co '37-41; chief Protective Coatings Sect, Material Branch, Engr Research and Development Lab since '42. ACS—Nat Assn Corrosion Engrs—Soc Am Mil Engrs. Engineer Research and Development Laboratories, Fort Belvoir, Va.

14 HILL, Theodore Case. Water supply; Sewage disposal. b'93. Student '11-13 (Allegheny Coll); BSE '17—'17-18 (U Mich). Research on water supply and filtration, dams and reservoirs, sewage disposal and industrial waste treatment. Sr partner Hill and Hill

'45-51; dir Analytical Lab Inc '51. Pa Sewage Works Assn—Prof Engrs NW Pa—NY Sewage Works Assn—Am Soc Prof Engrs. 8 Gibson St., North East, Pa. H: 144 E. Main St.

15 HILLDRUP, Robert Leroy. Early Southern American history; Medieval and modern European history; Political science. b'06. AB '28 (Southwestern Coll); MA '31—PhD '35—seminars in field (Va U); student by correspondence '28 (Chicago U), summer '26 (State Teachs Coll Fredericksburg Va); student '33-34—seminars in field (Johns Hopkins). Extensive research in regulation of corporations with emphasis on Virginia, the Virginia Convention of 1776, Southern agrarianism and the American revolution; studied biography of Edmund Pendleton; did research in Colonial supplies during the American Revolution, marketing laws of the American colonies, government in Colonial Virginia. Author: The Life and Times of Edmund Pendleton '39; also articles in field. Prin Margo High Sch Va '26-29; prin Marye High Sch Va '29-30; teacher Lane High Sch Va '30-33; visiting instr hist King's Coll Tenn summers '35-36; asst prof hist The Citadel SC '35-36; prof hist E Carolina Teachs Coll NC '36-44; visiting prof polit sci Washburn U Kansas summer '46; visiting prof Delaware U summer '47; visiting prof polit sci E Carolina Teachs Coll NC summer '48, '50-52; prof hist Mary Washington Coll since '44. Am Hist Assn—Southern Hist Assn—Virginia Social Sci Assn—Pi Gamma Mu—Am Assn of University Profs. Awarded Society of the Cincinnati prize for doctoral dissertation '35. Mary Washington College, Frederickburg, Va.

16 HILLIER, James. Electron microscopy and diffraction. b'15. BA '37—MA '38—PhD '41 (U Toronto). First to achieve magnifications of 200,000; invented and developed electron microanalyzer for analyzing extremely minute particles of matter; with others developed first successful electron microscope built in North America '37-40; developed a 300,000 volt electron microscope with others '41; scanning microscope '41-42 and invented electron diffraction adapter for electron microscopes '42, small convenient desk type electron microscope, all with others. Author articles in field. Charge electron microscope research RCA Labs; asso Sloan-Kettering Inst Cancer Research. Am Soc Cancer Research—Am Physical Soc(F)—AAAS(F)—Electron Microscope Soc Am (pres '45)—Sigma Xi. R.C.A. Laboratories, Princeton, N.J.†⊚

17 HILLS, George Burkhart. Architectural engineering; Industrial structures; Power plants; River and harbor improvements; Land reclamation. b'90. BS '11—CE '18 (Armour Inst Tech). Member Reynolds Smith and Hills, architects and engineers specializing in industrial structures, power plants, river and harbor improvement. Chief, Price Adjustment Sect, SAD, US Engrs '42-43. ASCE—Newcomen—Soc of N Am—Tau Beta Pi. 227 Park St., Jacksonville 2, Fla.⊚

18 HILLS, Lee. Facsimile newspapers (Editorial aspects). Student '24-25 (Brigham Young U); '27-29 (U Mo); grad '34 (Oklahoma City Law Sch). A pioneer in facsimile newspapers. Author: Facsimile '49; also articles in field. Editorial staff various newspapers '24-41; managing ed Miami Herald since '42, started regular daily electronic newspaper '47. Pan-Am Press Congress—Inter-Am Press Assn US—Am Soc Newspaper Editors—Associated Press Editors Fla (past pres) — Associated Press Managing

Editors Assn (dir and officer). Awarded Maria Moors Cabot Gold Medal Columbia U '46. Miami Herald, Miami, Fla. H: 3811 Segovia St., Coral Gables.

19 HILLWAY, Tyrus. Whales; Herman Melville. b'12. BA '34 (Willamette U); MA '39 (U Calif); PhD '44 (Yale). Collector of Melville first editions and related materials. Author articles in field. Dean evening coll, prof Eng Hillyer Jr Coll Hartford '40-44; prof Eng Jr College Conn '44-46; president Mitchell College Conn since '46. Mod Lang Assn Am—Nat Council Teachers Eng—Melville Soc (co-founder '44, sec since '45, ed Newsletter). Mitchell College, New London, Conn. H: 423 Pequot Av.⊚

20 HILLYER, William Hurd. Banking (Checks); Correspondent Banking; Small Business Financing; Factoring Industry; Mythology (Indians of British Columbia). b'80. Grad '01 (Mercer U). Appeared by invitation '39 before Temporary Nat Econ Com US Senate to describe factoring industry; made presentation of factor's history and functions; correspondent banking specialist American Banker. Author: Songs of the Steel Age '07; The Box of Daylight (Literary Guild Junior selection '31; James Talcott, Merchant '37; The Wall and the Street '41; Keys to Business Cash '42. Contributor: Harvard Q Jour of Economics, Nations Business, Barron's, Banking; contbg editor Forbes Mag Bus; editor Check Clearings. Reporter Atlanta Ga '99-00 news editor '00, editorial writer '01-03; bond broker Atlanta '03-06; sec and treas Hillyer Investment Co '06, vp, treas 10-13, Atlanta Trust Co.; pres Sixth Ward Bank '10-12; organizer Am Bakeries Corp '12, Carolina Pub Service Co '12; co-founder and dir Morris Plan Bank of Atlanta '12; asst vp James Talcott Inc (factors) '33-40. Am Geog Soc. H: 332 E. 84th St., NYC 28.

21 HILSCHER, Herbert Henry. Alaska (Economics, industrial development, aviation, statehood); Arctic (Economics, aviation); Eskimos (Economics). b'02. BBA '24 (U Wash). Author: Alaska Now (revised) '50, '52. Ed Alaska Life Mag '39-42; pub relations counsel since '46; mem Alaska Development Bd. Explorers Club—Royal Geog Soc—Arctic Inst NA. Box 846, Anchorage, Alaska. H: 108 Galewood Dr., Rogers Park, Anchorage.

22 HILTON, Ordway. Questioned document examination (Handwriting, typewriting, anonymous letters, forgeries); Erasures and alterations; Inks; Paper; Scientific Crime Detection. b'13. BS '35—MA '37 (Northwestern U); student '46-48 (NYU)—'48 (Columbia). Author articles in field. Examiner Questioned Documents NYC since '46; editor American Journal Police Science '41-43 and since '47; editorial bd Journal of Criminal Law and Criminology since '41. Document examiner, Chicago police sci crime det lab '38-41. American Society Questioned Document Examiners. 15 Park Row NYC 7. H: 245 Avenue C, NYC 9.

23 HILTON, Wallace Atwood. Acoustical impedance; Absorption coefficients. b'11. AB '33 (William Jewell Coll); AM '39—EdD '41 (Mo U); MS '48 (Ark U). Research acoustical impedance and absorption coefficients of Heerwagen acoustical tiles. Author courses of study and articles in field. Prof Physics William Jewell Coll since '46, dept head since '48. Acoustical Soc Am—AAAS—Sigma Pi Sigma—Ark Acad Sci—Kan Acad Sci. William Jewell College, Liberty, Mo.

10 HILTON, William Atwood. Amphibia (Salamanders). b'78. BS '99—PhD '02—grad scholar '00—fellow '01 (Cornell U). Has collected rare animals new to science such as the Pauropids from Alaska first record above Arctic Circle, first record of Pauropids west of the Mississippi, first record of a whip-scorpion in Cuba, new genus of Salamander from Panama; one of the first to discover sensory terminations in muscle of insects and the first to get an accurate measure of peripheral distribution. Author articles in field. Prof zool and head dept Pomona Coll '12-44, retired '44; dir Laguna Marine Biol Lab '12-46; vis prof zool Mills Coll Calif '49. AA AS(F)—Am Micros Soc—Entomol Soc Am—Herpetological League—Am Assn Anat—Am Soc Zoologists—Western Soc Naturalists—Sigma Xi—Phi Beta Kappa. Crookshank Hall, Room 100, Pomona College, Claremont, Calif.⊙†

11 HINE, Charles Raymond. Production planning; Manufacturing estimates; Materials handling. b'14. EE '36 (Rensselaer Poly Inst); MA (edn) '42 (Columbia). Design and planning of materials handling for mass production. Author: Machine Tools for Engineers '50; Shop Processes Laboratory Manuel '48; Production for Profit '52. Asst prof mfg processes Rensselaer Poly Inst since '43; consultant. Rensselaer Polytechnic Institute, Troy, N.Y.

12 HINER, L. David. Pharmaceutical botany. b'05. PhG '28—PhC '29—BS '29 (SD State Coll); MS '31—PhD '38 (Fla U). Research and writing on cardiac drugs, cultivation of medicinal plants in SD, quality of peppermint and spearmint oils in Fla, domestic ergot of wheat and rye, chimaphila umbellata. Author articles in field. Dean Coll Pharmacy Univ Utah since '47. Sigma Xi—Am Pharmaceutical Assn (chmn Kilmer Research com)—US Pharmacopoeia—Nat Formulary. University of Utah College of Pharmacy, Salt Lake City 1. 949 So. 19th E., Salt Lake City.

13 HINKLE, Samuel Forry. Chemistry and technology of chocolate products. b'00. BS '22 (Pa State Coll). Author articles in field. Chem charge lab Norton Co Ontario '22-23; chief chem Nat Abrasive Co Niagara Falls '23-24; chief chem and dir research Hershey Chocolate Corp '24-47, plant mgr, on bd dirs since '47, director of Hershey Trust Company. Am Chem Soc—Inst Food Technol—Nat Confectioners' Assn (research com)—Am Assn Candy Technol—Phi Kappa Phi. Hershey Chocolate Corporation, Hershey, Pa.

14 HINSHAW, Virgil Goodman, Jr. Epistemology. b'19. BA '41 (Stanford U); MA '42 (State U Ia); MA '43—PhD '45 (Princeton U). Author: A Critical Study of Some Points in Russell's Inquiry into Meaning and Truth '42; An Inquiry into the Factual Basis of Human Knowledge '45; also articles in field. Instr, asst prof philos O State U since '46. Am Philos Assn (Western Div)—AAAS—AAUP—Assn Symbolic Logic—Phi Beta Kappa. Department of Philosophy, Ohio State University, Columbus 10, O.

15 HINTON, William Miller. Vocational guidance. b'07. AB '29—MA '30 (Washington and Lee U); PhD '37 (O State U). Use of psychometric and other tests for determination mental deficiency; administration psychological tests to Armed Services selectees for determination vocational groupings; member Virginia Examining Board for Clinical Psychologists since '48; organization and direction counseling and classification Convalescent Hospital Camp Pickett Virginia. Author articles: A Scale for Rating the Behavior Tendencies of Young Children '38-39; A Study of the Adjustment Behavior of Elementary School Children '39; An Evaluation of the Army Counseling Program in a Separation Center '47-48, and others. Coauthor article: (with J G Matire) Student Beliefs on Certain Selected Social Issues '41. Instr advancing to asst prof psychol and edn Washington and Lee U '30-42, asso prof psychol '46-51, prof since '51, also dir counseling and placement service. Personnel cons AUS '42-44, vocational and ednl guidance officer '44-46. Am Psychol Assn—So Soc Philos and Psychol—Eastern Psychol Assn—Va Acad Sci (sec psychol sect '39-40, chmn '41-42, exec com '47-48)—Am Assn Mental Deficiency—Mental Hygiene Assn—Assn Sch and Coll Placement. Commonwealth of Va mental examiners' certificate '35, certified clin psychol '47. Washington and Lee University, Lexington, Va.

16 HINTZ, Howard William. American literature and philosophy; English literature; International relations. b'03. BA '25 (Coll City NY); MA '28 (Columbia); PhD '37 (NY U); student '25-26 (Yale Divinity Sch). Research and writing on Elizabethan entertainment and the Faery Queene, function of literary studies, study of American democratic thought. Author: Thomas Wentworth Higginson: Apostle of the Newness '39; The Quaker Influence in American Literature '40; Modern American Vistas '41; Basic Necessity for Spiritual Reconstruction '36; Religion and the Crisis of Democracy '39; Adventures in Living: An Introduction to Biography. Asso prof Eng Brooklyn Coll since '46, co-chmn Am Studies div since '40, chmn Dept Curriculum Counseling since '44, chmn speakers Bur since '46; minister Spring St Presbyn Church NY since '45. Modern Language Assn Am—Am Assn United Nations (speakers bur)—United World Federalists (speakers bur). Brooklyn College, Brooklyn.

17 HIRE, Cha(rle)s. Education (Physics teaching). b'87. AB '15—MA '17—PhD '27 (Ind U). Author: Laboratory Studies in College Physics; College Physics for General Education. With Ind U since '15, prof physics since '43; supervisor physics instrn ASTP '43-44, acting chmn dept physics '44-45; head dept phys scis Murray State Coll '25-43. AAAS(F)—Am Phys Soc—Am Assn Physics Tchrs—AAUP—Sigma Xi. Indiana University, Bloomington, Ind. H: 215 E 8th St.⊙

18 HIRES, Clara Sheppard. Sterile culture techniques; Fern and orchid germination. b'97. AB '28 (Cornell U); student (Wellesley Coll); spl courses (Columbia, U Pa, Rutgers U). Has grown many varieties of seedlings plus moss and ferns since '29, sealed completely in glass containers growing well under sterile conditions; research in control seedling environment light experiments; microscopic seed and spore studies with germination, chiefly moss fern and orchids. Developed unique sterile culture room equipment and technique. Sci teacher Edgewood Sch Greenwich Conn '20-25, Shore Road Acad Brooklyn '32-34; owner Mistaire Labs Millburn NJ since '30. AAAS—Bot Soc—Am Soc Plant Physiol—Am Fern Soc—Am Orchid Soc—Torrey Bot Club—NY Microspical Soc—NY Hort Soc. Mistaire Laboratories, Millburn, N.J.

19 HIROSHIGE, Herbert M(asakatus). Agricultural economics (Tropical). b'09. BA '34 (U Cal); MA '50 (U Hawaii). Study of cooperative agricultural accounting based on the Kanai Farmers' Cooperative accounting system. Co-author articles: Farmers' Tax Guide '46; Man Hours Required to Produce Certain Vegetables. Farm supervisor FSA, USDA Kealakekua, Kona, Hawaii '41-43; asst econ U Hawaii '43-45; now partner Hiroshige & Hiroshige, accountants; also exec sec Hawaiian Farm Bureau Fedn. Nat Assn Tax Accountants—Am Soc Hort Sci—Hawaii Farm Bur Fedn. 1180 Alakea St., Honolulu 13, Oahu, T.H.

20 HIRSCH, Harold. Helicopters. b'16. BS in CE '40 (Carnegie Inst Tech); student (U Buffalo, Cornell U). Research on helicopter mechanisms, controls, hubs, rotor blades, rotor dynamics, rotor flutter; co-designer with A F Donovan of Cornell Constant Speed Helicopter Rotor Control and Pitch-Throttle Linkage; responsible for development of Cornell Aeronautical Laboratory glass fiber helicopter tail rotor and main rotor blades for Air Materiel Command, US Air Force. Patents on helicopter rotor pitch control mechanisms. Author articles in field. Stress analyst Curtiss Wright Corp, head helicopter sect research lab '42-46; head helicopter sect Cornell Aeronautical Lab Inc since '46. Inst Aeronautical Sci—Am Helicopter Soc. Cornell Aeronautical Laboratory, Inc., Buffalo.

21 HIRSCHFELDER, Joseph Oakland. Physical chemistry; Theoretical physics. b'11. BS '31 (Yale); PhD '36 (Princeton); grad study '46-47 (Inst Adv Study). Developed theory absolute reaction rates, liquid structure, chemical reactions produced by ionizing radiation; asst prof U Wis '37-42, determination intermolecular forces, gas imperfections, molecular quantum mechanics, semi-empirical theory of activation energies; consultant Div I and III NDRC, developed interior ballistics guns, rockets, recoilless guns, thermodynamics of powder gases and their products. Asst prof U Wis '37-42; group leader Los Alamos Lab atomic bomb development '43-45; dir Theoretical Physics group Inyokern and Pasadena NOTS '45-46; chief phenomenologist Bikini Bomb Test and sci adviser Radiological Safety Com '46; prof chemistry U Wis, dir U Wis Naval Research Laboratory since '47. Chairman board eds United States Atomic Energy Commn treatise: Effects of Atomic Weapons. Author articles in field. AAAS(F)—Am Physics Soc(F)—Am Chem Soc—Am Accous Soc—Sigma Xi—Gamma Alpha. Listed one of ten ablest phys chemists in US, Am Chem Soc, Chicago sect '47. Department of Chemistry, University of Wisconsin, Madison, Wis.⊙

22 HIRSCHLER, Alfred Ernest. Physical measurements; Petroleum chemistry; Adsorption. b'11. AB '33 (Bluffton Coll); MA '36—PhD '37—U scholar '33-34 (O State U). Research in thermodynamics of red and yellow mercuric oxide, oxidation of petroleum fractions, combustion and ignition of hydrocarbons, correlation of physical properties of hydrocarbons, separation of hydrocarbons by adsorption, precise measurement of freezing points, purities and refractive indices of hydrocarbons, solid solution studies in hydrocarbon mixtures. Holder patents on cyclic processes for separation of aromatic hydrocarbons from a mixture of hydrocarbons, purification of paraffinic, naphthenic, olefinic or aromatic hydrocarbons by adsorption. Author articles in field. Research chemist Sun Oil Co since '37. ACS—Sigma Xi—Phi Lambda Upsilon. Sun Oil Co., Research Laboratory, Norwood, Pa. H: 3983 Vernon Road, Drexel Hill.†

10 HIRSH, Frederick Rudolph, Jr. X-ray satellite lines; X-ray photometry. b'05. AB '26—AM '28—PhD '31 (Cornell). Studies on satellite multiple ionization lines accompanying x-ray spectral lines; demonstration aberration in spherical and parabolic mirrors; new method photometry of x-ray spectral lines. Resident doctor physics Cornell U '31-37; research F Cal Inst Tech '37-41; lectr physics U So Cal '42-44, vis asso prof '44-47 APS (F)—Sigma Xi—Optical Soc Am—AA AS(F)—Am Assn Physics Tchrs—NY Acad Scis—Cal Acad Scis—Am Geog Soc(F)—AAUP.

11 HIRSH, Joseph. Alcoholism (Public health and educational aspects). b '15. BS '37 (Coll City NY); AM '39 (Columbia); EdD '49 (NYU). Initating and subventing fundamental research projects on problems alcohol in leading medical schools and research centers; assisting in establishment research and treatment programs of state and local governments; initiated courses on adult education in schools. Author: The Problem Drinker '49; Alcohol Education—A Guide Book for Teachers '52; Public Health and Social Aspects of Alcoholism in Alcoholism '53. Exec dir Research Council on Problems of Alcohol NYC '46-49; prof asso and exec sec com on problems of alcohol Div Med Scis NRC '49-52 cons div med scis since '52; asso Alcoholics Treatment Center NY; mem com tests intoxication Nat Safety Council since '50; mem Alcohol Resch and Rehabilitation Program Va State Dept Public Health since '49; mem NY State Mental Health Com Alcohol Adv Com since '52; Chmn Alcohol Research Sub-com NY Welfare and Health Council since '52. Kappa Delta Pi—Am Pub Assn (Assoc). 145 E. 92 St., NYC 28.

12 HIRST, John Mendel. Limnology of Pennsylvania; Insect and pest control techniques. b'08. BS '32 (Bethany Coll); MS '38—PhD '41 (U Pittsburgh). Author: A Limnological Study of Pike Run Westmoreland County, Pa '38; A Limnological Study of the Streams in the East Tionesta Tract Allegheny National Forest '41; also articles in field. Research entomologist sanitation inspector and malaria control officer US Navy since '42. Pa Acad Sci—Am Soc Limnol and Oceano—Am Mosquito Assn—Fla Anti Mosquito Assn—Sigma Xi—Phi Sigma. Box 8, M-1 United States Naval Air Station, Jacksonville, Fla.

13 HIRST, Lester Larsen. Coal chemistry. b'03. BS (Chem) '25 (Utah State Agrl Coll); PhD '29 (U Cal Berkeley). In charge design, construction and operation experimental coal hydrogenation plant, for coals ranging from lignite through sub-bituminous to high volatile bituminous; study European synthetic fuel plants '45. Author articles: Thermal Efficiency of Coal Hydrogenation '41; Complete Coal to Oil Demonstration Plants '49; Liquid Fuel from Coal '49; Hydrogenation of Petroleum and Lignite Tar Distillates, and others. Phys chem Bur Mines Pittsburgh '29-30, synthetic fuel plant design, constrn, and operation '35-45, chief synthetic fuels demonstration plant Louisiana Mo since '45. ACS. Bureau of Mines, Louisiana, Mo.

14 HIRT, Ray Roland. Tree diseases; Wood decay. b'93. BS '17 (Hamline U); MS '24—PhD '27 (NY State Coll Forestry). Author articles in field. Agt Bur Plant Industry since '27; instr later prof head dept forest bot and pathol NY State Coll Forestry Syracuse U since '21; cons several commercial firms since '39. Soc Am

Foresters — Phytopathol Soc — Nat Shade Tree Conf—Sigma Xi. College of Forestry, Syracuse 10, N.Y.†

15 HITCH, Charles Johnston. Mobilization (Economics). b'10. AA '29 (Kemper Mil Sch); BA '31 (U Ariz); '31-32 (Harvard); MA '38 (Oxford U). Research on material allocations, stabilization policies, feasibility testing, and effects of strategic bombing. Author: America's Economic Strength '41. Author article: Planning War Production '50. Econ Mission for Econ Affairs US Embassy London '41-42; staff econ planning com WPB '42-43; econ OSS Econ Warfare Div US Embassy London and Joint Target Group War Dept '43-45; chief stabilization controls div Office War Mobilization and Reconversion '45-46; chief econ div RAND Corp Santa Monica Calif since '48; vis prof econ U Cal '49-50; cons to spl asst to Pres White House '50, to weapons systems evaluation group Dept Defense '51. Am Econ Assn—Royal Econ Soc—Econometric Soc. RAND Corp., 1500 Fourth St., Santa Monica, Cal. H: 15-410 Albright St., Pacific Palisades.

16 HITCH, Thomas Kemper. Labor economics; Regional economic analysis. b'12. AB '34 (Stanford); AM '46 (Columbia); PhD in econ '37 (U London); student '32 (Nat U Mexico). Special study commodity markets Commodity Exchange Administration, US Dept Agriculture '40; acting head current business research section Dept of Commerce '42-43; head labor dept Naval School Military Government Princeton NJ '44-45; labor officer for assistant chief naval operations for Island Government '45-46; labor adviser Veterans Emergency Housing Program '46-47; economist with special reference to labor economics to the President's Council of Economic Advisers '47-50; dir research Hawaii Employers Council, Honolulu since '50. Am Econ Assn—Indsl Relations Research Assn—Phi Beta Kappa. 1139 Kapiolani Blvd., Honolulu 14, Hawaii.†◉

17 HITCHCOCK, Charles B. South American geography and cartography (Venezuela). b'06. AB '28 (Harvard); AM '33 (Columbia). Engaged field studies in Southern Venezuela, American Museum of Natural History, member of Phelps Expeditions; United States delegate to International Geographical Congress, Amsterdam '38, Pan American Institute of Geography and History, Lima '41, Commission on Cartography meeting in Caracas '46, Buenos Aires '48, Santiago '50, Ciudad Trujillo '52. Editor: Map of Hispanic America (with Raye R Platt) since '38. Associated American Geographical Society since '30, chief Department Hispanic Am Resch since '38, asst director '43-50, executive secretary since '50. Am Assn Photogrammetry — Am Soc Professional Geographers—Assn Am Geographers—AAAS—Arctic Inst NY Acad Sciences. American Geographical Society, Broadway at 156th St., NYC 32.

18 HITCHCOCK, Harold Bradford. Distribution, hibernation and natural history of bats; Homing mechanism pigeons. b'03. AB '26 (Williams Coll); AM '32—PhD '38 (Harvard). Author articles in field. Asst prof biol Middlebury Coll, asso prof since '43. Am Soc Zoologists—Am Soc Mammalogists Am Ornithologists Union—Nat Speleological Soc. Received grant Am Acad Arts Scis '47. Department of Biology, Middlebury College, Middlebury, Vt.

19 HITCHINGS, John Lyman. Exploration (Tropical). b'97. BA '18 (Yale); BS (US Mil Acad West Point NY). Led Bongabong River Expedition

across Mindoro PI '33; discovered and mapped new mountain range in PI; classified and studied clan of natives not previously in contact with white man; study on topography of Mindoro. Served as group comdr antiaircraft New Guinea, New Britain, Luzon World War II. The Explorers Club NYC. Oak Harbor, Southport, Fla.

20 HIXOM, Ephriam. Economic Entomology. b'02. BS '29—MS '30 (Okla A&M); PhD '40 (Ia State Coll). Research on host relation of cotton flea-hopper, and boll weevil control; study livestock parasite control, control of hog mange and corn rootworm, control alfalfa and legume insects. Faculty Okla A&M Coll '30-43, ext specialist '43-46; prof and chmn dept entomol U Neb '46-49, asso dean coll agr since '49. Am Assn Econ Entomol—Alpha Zeta. Agricultural College, University of Nebraska, Lincoln 2, Neb.◉

21 HJORT, Axel Magnus. Relationship chemical constitution drugs to physiological effects. b'89. AB '14—MS '15 (U Ill); PhD '18—MD '21 (Yale); MA '28 (Dartmouth Coll). Studies effects weather on animal responses to drugs, relationship physical properties drugs to physiological effects. Research with Parke Davis & Co '23-26; prof pharmacology Dartmouth Med Sch '26-29; dir med research Chem Warfare Service '29-32; chief physiol and pharmacology Wellcome Lab '32-41; private practice since '41. Alpha Chi Sigma—Gamma Alpha—Nu Sigma Nu—Sigma Xi—Am Med Assn—Am Coll Phys—Am Soc Biol Chem. Research F Internat Coll Anesthetists 39. 14 Fern Way, Postoffice Box 281, Scarsdale, N.Y.

22 HOAD, William Christian. Water supply; Stream control. b'74. BS '96 (Lane U); BS in CE '98 (Kansas U). Consultant in general field of municipal and sanitary engineering since '34; served more than 50 cities and industries in solving problems in field; research in municipal sanitation, drainage, sewage disposal. Author articles in field. Prof Mich U '12-44, prof emeritus since '44; mem engring firm Drury, McNamee and Porter. Maj and lt col engring div Sanitary Corps US Army '18-19. ASCE —Am Water Works Assn—NE Water Works Assn—Sigma Xi. Am Pub Health Assn(F). 2114 Devonshire Rd., Ann Arbor.◉

23 HOAR, Roger Sherman. Psychrometry; Exterior ballistics. b'87. AB '09—LLB '11—MA '21 (Harvard). Discovered that the curvature of the earth is self-correcting in the flight of even the longest range projectiles, first complete theory of effect of rotation of earth on flight of projectiles, extension of the Bliss auxiliary variables to the Franklin variations, derivation of the basic theorem of partial differentiation by use of the undetermined coefficients, complete theory of the psychrometry of dilute liquid water. Invented an attachment for a surveyor's transit for precise location of due north from certain stars without any calculations. Author: A Course in Exterior Ballistics '21; also articles in field. Head legal and patent dept Bucyrus-Erie Co Wis since '21. Capt US Army Aberdeen Proving Ground '19-20, chief Ballistics Div Proof Dept Am Tech Staff War Dept and sr instr advanced math and exterior ballistics. Am Ordnance Assn—Am Soc Heating and Ventilating Engr. 1265 Fairview Av., South Milwaukee, Wis.

24 HOBBS, Cecil (Carlton). Burma (Language, ethnology, history); Buddhism; Bibliographical sources of southeast Asia. b'07. AB '29—'29-30 (U Ill); BD '33—ThM '42 (Colgate-Rochester Div Sch). Member advisory editorial board Far Eastern Quarterly; secured primary source data regarding Burmese language, customs and traditions, Hinayana Buddhism, modern Burmese history; translated Burmese classics Wethandya and Thudamasayi into English. Author: Southeast Asia 1935-1945, '46; Christian Education and The Burmese Family—A Sociological Study. Tchr Burman Theol Sem and Pierce Div Coll under Am Bapt Fgn Mission Soc '35-41; research Colgate-Rochester Div Sch '41-42; reference librarian SE Asia Library Congress since '42, field survey SE Asia '47-48 Burma Research Soc Rangoon—Far Eastern Assn Ithaca—Inst Pacific Relations NY—Nat Geog Soc Washington—Oriental Club Washington. Division of Orientalia, Library of Congress, Washington.

10 HOBBS, Harold Wayne, Sr. Surface runoff; Land use; Water control. b'01. BS (civil engring) '25 (U Wyo); MS (civil engring) '28 (Syracuse U). Hydrologic research on small agricultural watersheds up to 2500 acres under various conditions of soil, topography, climate, and land use; effect of control measures such as strip cropping, contour tillage, ridge rows, diversion and cropland terraces, pasture furrows, mature and cutover woodlands, and prevailing practices on soil and water relationships; design, construction, and maintenance of runoff gaging stations; design of earth dams for flood regulation and farm water supplies and other water control structures; streambank protection by structures and vegetation. Faculty Syracuse U '25-28; asst engr Intercepting Sewer Bd '28-31; resident engr Holmes and O'Brien '31-32; field and office engr Work Relief Bur '33; camp supt NY State Conservation Dept of US Forest Service '33-35; with Soil Conservation Service since '35, project supervisor from '38. Sigma Tau—Phi Kappa Phi—Am Soc CE—Am Soc Agrl Engrs—Am Geophys Union. Soil Conservation Service Research, University of Maryland, College Park, Md.

11 HOBBS, Marvin. Radio sets (Military types); Television receiving sets; Radar. b'12. BS (elec engring) '30 (Tri-State Coll); '31-32 (U Chicago). Research on military type radio sets, low radiation, vhf and uhf communications, mine detectors; large screen type television sets; aircraft control systems and radar search; component parts and materials of radio and radar. Invented low radiation receiver. Government chairman electronics industry advisory committee to Munitions Board and National Security Resources Board. Radio receiver engr '30-40; aircraft radio receiver designer E K Cole Ltd '35-36; radio receiver and television cons '38-39; chief elec branch Radio and Radar Div WPB '42-43, head radio cons Radio and Radar Div WPB '43-44; operations analyst Far E Air Forces '45; cons engr Scott Radio Lab Inc, Radio Corp Am '45-50; dir Elec Div Munitions Bd since '50. Armed Forces Communication Assn—Inst Radio Engrs (sr mem)—Soc Am Mil Engrs—Am Ordnance Assn—Am Rocket Soc. Received Certificate of Appreciation from War Dept '45. Director, Electronics Division, Munitions Board, Pentagon, Washington 25.†◎

12 HOBBS, Robert B(oyd). Leather. BA '35—JD '41 (George Washington U); student (Am U, U Md). Articles in field. Gen technologist org and fibrous materials Nat Bur Standards since '47. Am Chem Soc—Philos Soc Washington—Am Assn Adv Sci—Am Leather Chemists Assn.

13 HOBBS, William Herbert. Glacial and dynamical geology and geography. b'64. BS '83—DE '29 (Worcester Polytech Inst); fellow geol '87-88—AM—PhD '88 (Johns Hopkins U); student '88-89 (Heidelberg U); LLD '39 (Mich U). Worked in field with US Geological Survey '86-06; extended cruises to mandated Pacific Islands '21; directed Greenland expeditions University of Michigan '26-30; designed a transisthmain Canal in Mexico '45; vp of International Glacier Committee '30-36; delegate to International Congresses (Science) Leningrad, Stockholm, Geneva, London (Royal Soc), Toronto, Rome, Paris, Edinburgh, Santiago de Chile, Sydney; research in glaciers and earth features and evolution. Author: Characteristics of Existing Glaciers '11; Earth Features and Their Meaning '12; Earth Evolution and Its Facial Expression '21; Cruises Along By-Ways of the Pacific '23; The Glacial Anticyclones '26; Exploring About the North Pole of the Winds '30; Fortress Islands of the Pacific '45; Glacial Studies of the Pleistocene of North American '47; asso ed Journal of Geology '12-47. Prof and dir geol lab Mich U '06-34, prof emeritus since '34; cons OSS Greeland and Pacific '41-45. Am Philos Soc—Assn Am Geographers—Mich Acad Sci—State Russian Geog Soc (hon) '23—Royal Hungarian Geog Soc (hon) '12. AAAS(F)—Geol Soc Am(F). 1005 Berkshire Rd Ann Arbor.◎†

14 HOBSON, Jesse Edward. Electrical engineering; Power transmission; Industrial research. b'11. BS '32—MS '33 (Purdue U); PhD '35 (Calif Inst Tech). Co-author: Power Transmission and Distribution '41; International Industry Yearbook '48; also articles in field. Exec dir Stanford Research Inst since '48. Am Inst Elect Engrs(F)—Inst Radio Engrs—Western Soc Engrs—AAAS—Am Assn Engring Edn—Nat Research Council (div engring and indsl research). Eta Kappa Nu award as Outstanding Young Electrical Engr '40. Stanford Research Institute, Stanford, Calif.◎

15 HOCHBAUM, Hans Albert. Waterfowl management; Marsh ecology. b'11. BS '33 (Cornell); MS '38 (U Wis). Research on game waterfowl as harvestable natural resource; investigations of life history North American waterfowl on Canadian marshes; director Delta Waterfowl Research Station since '38. Author: The Convasback on a Prairie Marsh '44. Am Ornithologists Union—Wilson Ornithol Club—Wildlife Soc—Sigma Xi. Awarded Brewster medal and wildlife Soc Literary award. Delta Waterfowl Research Station, Delta, Manitoba, Can.

16 HOCHWALD, Werner. Income (Regional); Wages (Economics). b'10. LLB '32(U Berlin); BS (bus adminstrn) '40—AM '42—PhD '44 (Washington U). Research and development new methods to estimate income payments and flows by regions and small areas, economics of guaranteed wages; consultant Federal Reserve Bank St Louis. Contributor: Twentieth Century Economic Thought '50. Prof econ Washington U since '50, acting chmn dept since '49, dir internat econ research since '50. Nat Conf Research in Income and Wealth—Am Econ Assn—Am Statis Assn—Econometric Soc—Midwest Econ Assn—S Econ Assn—Indsl Relations Research Assn—Am Farm Econ Assn—Phi Beta Kappa—Beta Gamma Sigma. Economics Department, Washington University, StL 5.

17 HOCK, Charles William. Cellulose; Fibers; Light and electron mi-

croscopy. b'12. BS '34 (Franklin and Marshall Coll); PhD '38 (U Pa); '37 (State Teachers Coll Pa). Author: Cellulose and Celulose Derivatives '43; The Structure of Protoplasm '42; also articles in field. Research chemist Hercules Powder Co since '44. AAAS (F)—Am Chem Soc—Bot Soc Am—Electron Microscope Soc Am—Phi Beta Kappa—Sigma Xi. Hercules Experiment Station, Hercules Powder Co., Wilmington 99, Del.†

18 HOCKENSMITH, Roy Douglas. Agricultural soil conservation; Land classification. b'05. BS '27—MS '28—'28-29 (U Mo). Author articles in field. Chief soil conservation surveys div Soil Conservation Service US Dept Agr since '46. Soil Conservation Soc Am—Soil Sci Soc Am—Am Soc Agron. Soil Conservation Service, U.S. Department of Agriculture, Washington 25.

19 HOCKETT, Robert Casad. Organic chemistry; Sugar; Carbohydrates; Nutrition. b'06. BA '25—MA '28—PhD '29—Grad asst and analytl chem '25-27—univ scholar organic chemistry '27-28—duPont fellow '28-29 (O State U). Visiting lecturer Switzerland, American-Swiss Foundation for Scientific Exchange '46. Author articles in field. Asso prof Organic Chem MIT since '41; on leave as sci dir Sugar Research Found since '43. Am Acad Arts Sci(F)—Am Chem Soc (chmn div sugar chem and tech '45-46, chmn com on carbohydrate nomenclature)—Inst of Food Technol—AAAS—Sugar Industry Engrs—Amt Inst Chem. 52 Wall St., NYC.◎

20 HOCKETT, Sebern Waldo. Chemistry of coal; Synthetic fuels (Oil). b'83. BS '04—MS '05—'26 (State U Ia); '14-15 (U Mich); '10 (Harvard); '12 (U Chicago); '36-37 (State U Mont). Research in bituminous (high-volatile) coals; synthetic fuels from organic waste, lignite, etc. Author: Economic Calcination Temperatures of Gypsum '05; Industry's Challenge to Coal '47; A New Era in Coal Technology '48. Prof head chem dept Ia Wesleyan Coll Mt Pleasant Ia '42-48; research chem Bonewitz Chemicals Inc since '48. Am Chem Soc—AAAS—Chem Forum—Ia Acad Sci—Schoolmasters' Club—Sigma Xi. Bonewitz Chemicals, Inc., Burlington, Ia.

21 HOCKMAN, James Noah. Petroleum geology. b'98. BS '24—'37-39 (U Okla). Drilling on discovery wells on pool extensions in Illinois Basin. Subsurface and field geol Marland Oil Co '25-27; geol and magnetometer geophys Phillips Petroleum Co '27-31; dist supervisor Okla State Mineral Survey '35-36; Subsurface and dist geol Kingwood Oil Co '39-40; mgr and geol Geophys Cons Service '40-45; dist geol Central Pipe Line Ashland Oil and Refining Co '45-49; independent oil producer since '49. Am Assn Petroleum Geol—AIMME—Soc Econ Paleontologists and Mineral—Ill Geol Soc—Sigma Gamma Epsilon—Independent Petroleum Assn Am. 206A West Main St., P.O. Box 68, Salem, Ill.

22 HODGDON, Albion Reed. Flora of New Hampshire; Taxonomy of Lechea. b'09. BS '30—MS '32 (U NH); PhD '36 (Harvard). Collecting trips for Harvard University to Cuba, Virginia, Florida, Kentucky; independent plant collecting Mexico '38; edited the publications of New Hampshire Academy of Science '42-46; research on flora of Strafford County and New Hampshire, weed control, low-bush blueberry Vaccinium angustifolium, taxonomic studies of Lechea and related genera in the Cistaceae, monographic study of genus Lechea. Author: Protecting Our

Native Plants (with others) '40; Keys to Woody Plants in Winter '43. Asso prof to prof U NH '49, head bot dept Agrl Expt Sta since '41, head U bot dept since '41. AAAS(F)—NH Acad Sci (pres '52-53)—NE Bot Club—Soc Plant Taxonomists—Soc Study Evolution. Botany Department, University of New Hampshire, Durham, N.H.

10 HODGE, Carleton Taylor. Linguistics. b'17. AB '39 (DePauw U); PhD '43 (U Pa); '38-40 (U Mich). Research on spoken Serbo-Croatian and Bulgarian. Author: An Outline of Hausa Grammar '47; also articles in field. Lang instr Fgn Service Inst Dept of State '46-49, asso prof linguistics since '49. Linguistic Soc Am—Am Oriental Soc. Fellow Am Council Learned Socs '42-46. Foreign Service Institute, Department of State, Washington 25.

11 HODGE, Edwin S(tafford). Spectrographic analysis; Photographic MS film. b'11. BS '35 (Davidson Coll); '37 (Syracuse Univ); PhD '40 (O State U). Research and development testing methods for photographic film and methods spectrographic analysis. Spectroscopist U Ky Expt Sta '40-42; cons spectroscopist Harry W Dietert Co '42-46; research asso O State U Research Found '44-45; sr chem Eastman Kodak Co '46-49; F Mellon Inst Indsl Research since '49. ACS—Optical Soc Am—ASTM (mem com E-2 spectrographic analysis)—Alpha Chi Sigma—Sigma Pi Sigma—Sigma Xi. Mellon Institute of Industrial Research, 4400 Fifth Av., Pitts 13.

12 HODGE, Frederick Webb. American Indians. b'64. DSc '33 (Pomona Coll); LLD '34 (U NM); LittD '43 (U So Calif). Editor: Handbook of American Indians, part I '07, part II '10; Curtis's North American Indian (20 vols), and others; also author monographs and articles in field. With Bur Am Ethnol '05-18, Museum Am Indian NY '18-31, now for Southwest Mus Los Angeles; hon prof anthrop and archeol U So Calif. Am Anthrop Assn (founder, mem council, pres)—AAAS (F, vp sect H '16)—Am Antiquarian Soc—Am Folk-Lore Soc—Order of Indian Wars (hon companion), and others. Southwest Museum, Highland Park, Los Angeles 42.

13 HODGES, Fletcher, Jr. Stephen C. Foster. b'06. AB '28 (Harvard Coll); grad study (U Pittsburgh); LLD (hon) '45 (Lincoln Memorial U). Author: A Pittsburgh Composer and His Memorial '38. Editor: Chronicles of Stephen Foster's Family (by Evelyn Foster Morneweck) '44. Co-editor: Foster Hall Reproductions of the Songs, Compositions, and Arrangements by Stephen Collins Foster '33; also articles in field. Curator Foster Hall Collection Indianapolis, U Pittsburgh since '37; mgr Stephen Foster Memorial Bldg U Pittsburgh since '43. Foster Hall Collection, University of Pittsburgh, Pittsburgh 13.

14 HODGES, F(rederick) Allen. Fungi of sugar beets: Molds. b'95. BS '23—MS '25—PhD '32 (Syracuse U). Author articles in field. Microanalyst Food Drug Adm Fed Security Agency since '32. Sigma Xi—Phi Kappa Phi.

15 HODGKISS, Harold Edward. Entomology (Fruit tree insects). b'79. BSc '02 (U Mass); BSc '02 (Boston U). Prof entomol ext and entomol div agr ext Pa State Coll '19-44, prof emeritus entomol ext since '44. AAAS(F)—Am Assn Econ Entomol—Entomol Soc Am—Pa Acad Sci—Sigma Xi. 147 W. Park Av., State College, Pa.

16 HODGSON, Hugh. Music (Education). b'93. BS '15 (U Ga); grad work '15 (Columbia and Guilmant Sch Organ) '36 (U So Cal). Composer: Chamber Music-Trio in G and Quintet in D; Piano Concerto and Solo; Songs; Church Choral Music; Oratorio. Concert pianist debut NYCity; organist and dir Church choirs Athens and Atlanta since '14; dir music dept Lucy Cobb Inst '25; founder and head dept music U Ga since '28, chmn div fine arts since '34, regent's professorship '48. Orignator weekly music and art appreciation programs Ga college centers; vis recitalist Assn Am Colls '40-47; performances with Roth Quartet NY City and Chicago '43-44. University of Georgia, Athens, Ga. H: 570 Springdale.

17 HODGSON, Robert Willard. Subtropical horticulture. b'93. BS '16—MS '17 (U Calif). Advisor to governments of Tunisia, Egypt, India and to citrus and sub-tropical fruit growers in Palestine, Morocco and Central America. Prof subtropical hort U Calif since '34, subtropical hort in expt sta since '29, asst dean Coll Agr U Calif since '43. AAAS(F)—Am Soc Hort Sci—Phi Beta Kappa—Sigma Xi. Decorated Officier du Merite Agricole, France; Nichan Iftikhar, Tunisia; Ouissam Alaouite, Morocco; awarded Aztec emblem Calif Avocado Assn '40. 10958½ Roebling Avenue, Los Angeles 24.

18 HODGSON, Roland. Biochemistry of microorganisms; Bacterial carbohydrates; Wilting factors. b'16. BS '38—MS '41 (Brigham Young U); PhD '46—fellow '46-47 (U Wis). Author articles in field. Research asst plant path and biochem U Wis '41-46, indsl fellow '47-49; now Eli Lilly Co. Am Chem Soc—Sigma Xi. Eli Lilly Co. Indianapolis 6.†

19 HODGSON, Walter Hutchinson. Music (Education). b'04. BS '25 (U Minn); AM '34—PhD '36 (U Ia); student '28-29 (U Berlin). Conductor operas and oratorios; adjudicator band and orchestra contests and festivals. Composer: Symphony in D major '36; chamber music, songs. Supervisor music Austin Minn '25-26; tchr West High Sch Minneapolis '26-31; instr music Cornell Coll '31-36; dir Conservatory Music Mt Union Coll Alliance O '36-41; prof music N Tex State Coll '41-47, dean music since '47. Eastern examiner Nat Assn Schs of Music '41-43; examiner Tex Assn Schs Music '49-51. Music Tchrs Nat Assn—Am Musicol Assn—Music Educators Nat Conf—Tex Music Educators Assn—Tex Assn Music Schs (pres '50-51)—AAUP—Phi Mu Alpha—Pi Kappa Lambda. Henry Hadley medal for conspicous service in the interest of contemporary American music. H: 804 Av D, Denton, Tex.

20 HODSON, Waldo Gee. Radio frequency measuring instruments and signal generators; Radio control systems for airplanes and guided missiles; Radio telemetering. b'10. AB '32—MA '33 (Brigham Young U). Design and development of laboratory standard radio frequency signal generator, wattmeter, noisemeter, device for measuring frequency and impedance, for measuring voltage and power, and radiofrequency millivolt meter; design of radio control system for manned aircraft, and unmanned missiles; research and design of four channel (continuous) telemetering system for measuring and recording acceleration and other data on rocket propelled vehicle. Chief instr Naval Radio Training Sch Logan Utah '42; research engr Stoddart Aircraft Radio Co Hollywood Calif '42-44; asst chief engr Rollin Co Pasadena Calif '44-46; supervisor tele-communications Nor-throp Aircraft Inc Hawthorne Calif '46-50; supervisor elec components unit North Am Aviation Inc since '50. Inst Radio Engrs—Sigma Pi Sigma. North American Aviation, Inc., Downey, Calif.

21 HOEBEL, E(dward) Adamson. American Indian and primitive law; Comanche, Shoshone, Northern Cheyenne, Ute Pueblo Indians. b '06. BA '28 (U Wis); MA '30 (NYU); PhD '34 (Columbia); Am Exchange fellow '28-29 (U Cologne Germany). Research among Comanche Indians '33, Shoshone Indians of Idaho '34, North Cheyenne Indians '35-36, Pueblo Indians '45-46. Author: Man in the Primitive World '49. Co-author: (with K N Lewellyn) The Cheyenne Way: Conflict Case Law in Primitive Jurisprudence '41; The Social Meaning of Legal Concepts: Inheritance '48; Political Organization and Law-ways of the Comanche Indians '40. Translator and editor (with A A Schiller) Adat Law in Indonesia '47; also articles in field. Asst in sociol NYU '29-30, instr '30-36, asst prof sociol and anthropol '36-43, asso prof '43-48; research asso anthrop U Calif '40-41; prof, head anthrop U Utah since '48. AAAS(F)—Am Anthrop Assn(F)—Am Ethnol Soc (past pres)—Am Assn Indian Affairs (dir)—Deutsche Gesellschaft f Socio (corr mem). Fellow Am Council Learned Socs '35, 36; Social Sci Research Council fellow '40-41. Department of Anthropology, University of Utah, Salt Lake City 1.†

22 HOECKER, Frank E(dward). Biophysics; Biological effects of ionizing particles and radiations; Radium poisoning; Distribution and deposition of radium in bone. born '03. AB '30 (Coll of Emporia); MA '32—PhD '35 (U Kan). Inventions and patents: moving phosphorescent screen oscillograph, instantaneous electrocardiogram, a method and apparatus for sectioning undecalcified bone and other hard substances. Author articles in field. Professor physics and astron U Kan since '45; atomic bomb research Manhattan Dist Project Div War Research Columbia U '44-45. Am Phys Soc—Am Assn Physics Teachers—Radiol Soc NA (asso)—Kans Acad Sci—Sigma Xi—Am Coll Radiology(F)—Radiation Research Soc. Department of Physics, University of Kansas, Lawrence, Kan.†

23 HOEFER, George, Jr. Jazz; Jazz recordings. b'09. BS '31 (U NC). Collector rare and out of print jazz and hot music phonograph records since '32; free lance writer for small magazines since '41; member board of experts to select Esquire All-American Jazz Band '44-47. Author articles: Collectors—Personalities and Anecdotes '44; Chicago Jazz History '46, and others. Contributor: Esquire Jazz Books (annual) since '43; Lionel Hampton Swing Book. Chicago music corr Tempo Magazine Los Angeles '38-40; author column on collector's records "Hot Box" Down Beat Chicago since '39; conductor radio record show Jazz in Review WCFL Chicago '40; author column "Collectively Speaking" in Hollywood Note '46; cons RCA-Victor and Hudson-Ross Music Stores Chicago since '46; now mgr record dept Concord Radio Corp; mem bd experts judging new record releases WIND since '46; supervisor recordings Disc Records Inc '46; lecturer jazz U Chicago, Parkway Community Club, and Hot Club of Chicago since '46. Nat Jazz Found—Phi Kappa Sigma. H: 1851 N. Lincoln Av., Chgo 14.

24 HOEFLER, Paul Louis. Education (Audio-visual films); Africa; Asia. b'93. Student (UCLA). Leader African expedition '25-26, found the lost tribe of Kalahari Bushmen, produced adventure film Wild Men of the Kalahari; leader Colorado African expedition '28-29, made first crossing of Africa ever accomplished from Mombasa to Lagos, produced world famous adventure film Africa Speaks; leader Asiatic expedition North and Central India '31-32, produced adventure film Voice of India; photographed first color films in Africa '36-37; produced first educational film, Little Red School House, '19-20; organized first actual production unit to specialize in 16mm color-sound films for educational use. Author: Africa Speaks '31; also articles in field. Producer ednl films in 16mm color and sound; dir pub relations Middle East World War II for USAAF and was directly responsible for establishment 16mm film service in this territory '42-43. NEA—Audio-Visual Edn Assn Calif—Television Film Producers Assn—Television Acad —Allied Independent Producers Assn— Royal Geo Soc(F). 7936 Santa Monica Blvd., Hollywood, Calif. H: 612½ S. Ridgeley Dr., Los Angeles 36.

10 HOEHN, Matthew Anthony. Catholic authors. b'98. AB '21 (St Anselm's Coll Fordham U); BLS '36 (Columbia). Author: Bookplates for Business Firms; Catholic Authors: Contemporary Biographical Sketches 1930-47 '48. Ordained priest Roman Catholic Ch '25; librarian St Benedict's Prep Sch since '27; prior St Mary's Abbey since '46. ALA. 520 High St., Newark, N.J.

11 HOELZER, Charles Fritz. Paintings (Restoration); Ecclesiastical paintings. b'85. Short apprenticeship (A Muller). Own business cleaning paintings since '09, working at major universities and museums and for private individuals. 112 E. 81st St., NYC 28.

12 HOFACKER, Erich Paul. German literature (20th Century). b'98. Grad '18 (Reformrealgymnasium Stuttgart); student (univs Munich, Freiburg); PhD '24 (U Tuebingen). Author: Behold the Man (trans from German by Fr Rittelmeyer, in collaboration with G B Hatfield) '29; Great German Drama Retold '31; German Literature as Reflected in the German Language Press of St Louis Prior to 1898 '46. Co-author: (with Richard Jente) Complete College German '39, German Composition and Conversation '43. Contbr to Columbia Dictionary of Modern European Literature '47. Asst prof German Washington U '29-40, asso prof '40-48, prof German since '48, acting head dept since '50. Modern Lang Assn Am(life)—Assn Am U Profs—Am Assn Tchrs German —Modern Lang Assn Mo(pres '47). Washington University, StL 5. H: 7038 Washington Blvd., University City 5.◎

13 HOFER, Lawrence John Edward. Physical chemistry (Fisher-Tropsch reaction mechanism, thermomagnetic analysis, crystalline structure of catalysts, photochemistry). b'15. BA '37—MA '38 (U Utah); PhD '41— Sherman Clarke fellow '40-41 (U Rochester). Author articles in field. Chief Physical Chem Sect Research and Development Div Office Synthetic Liquid Fuels Bur Mines Pittsburgh since '46. Am Chem Soc—Am Soc X-ray and Electron Diffraction—Phi Beta Kappa —Sigma Xi—Phi Kappa Phi. Bureau of Mines, 4800 Forbes St., Pittsburgh 13.†

14 HOFF, Clarence Clayton. Zoology (Microcrustacea, pseudoscorpions). b'08. BA '30 (Bradley Coll); MS '39—PhD '41 (U Ill). Research in field Isles of Shoals Marine Laboratory '39, Reelfoot Lake Biological Laboratory '42,

Museum Comparative Zoology Harvard '45. Author articles: The Ostracods of Illinois, their Biology and Taxonomy '42; The Subfamily Entocytherinae: A New Subfamily of Freshwater Cytherid Ostracoda '42; and others. Asst prof zool Colo A&M Coll '46-47; associate prof biol U NM. Am Soc Zool—Am Soc Parasitol—Ecol Soc Am—Entomol Soc Am—Phi Beta Kappa—Sigma Xi. Department of Biology, University of New Mexico, Albuquerque, N.M.

15 HOFFER, Clarence Wilfred. Petroleum exploration. b'00. Student '19-21 (NM Sch Mines); '21-22 (U Ariz); '22-23 (U Tex); BS '24—'32-33 (Columbia). Geological and geophysical exploration for oil and gas fields in the United States; development electronic instruments and technique for oil and rare minerals exploration. Petroleum geol and cons '24-41; cons geol since '46. Am Assn Petroleum Geol—Seismol Soc Am—Geol Soc Am—Am Geophys Union—AIMME—Soc Exploration Geophysicists—US Naval Inst— Am Soc Naval Engrs. Licensed profl engr. 532 20th St., Washington 6.

16 HOFFMAN, Daniel Gerard. American Folklore; Paul Bunyan. b'23. AB '47—AM '49 (Columbia). Comprehensive analysis Bunyan legends in oral folk tradition, in various versions popularizers; work creative writers who have used Paul Bunyan as theme or symbol; preparation syllabus for college course in American folklore; study influence folk traditions on American literature. Author: Paul Bunyan, Last of the Frontier Demigods '52 (Chicago Folklore Soc Prize '49). Lectr English Columbia '47-48, Rutgers U '48-50; instr English Temple U since '50; fellow Columbia U '51-52. Am Folklore Soc—NJ Folklore Soc —MLA—Phi Beta Kappa. Poetry Center prize at New York '51. Department of English, Box 264, Temple University, Phila. 22.

17 HOFFMAN, George W. Political geography of Europe, Soviet Russia, near East. b'14. AB '34 (Realgymnasium, Vienna); grad work (U Vienna, Am U, Harvard, U Mich). Research on economic resources and transportation, trade and traderoutes, boundary problems, and political geography of Europe, on indsl development of Soviet Russia, econ developments in Moslem world. Author articles: South Tyrol—Borderland Rights vs World Politics '47; Austria: Her Raw Materials and Industrial Possibilities '48, and others. Editor Wirtschaftlicher Beobachter, Vienna '36-38; research analyst OSS geog div '43-45; research analyst US Dept State '45; asst prof U Vt European study tour '48; fellow U Mich '48-49; asst prof U Tex. Am Assn Geog—Fgn Policy Assn—UN Assn—Am Geog Soc —Vienna Geog Soc. Department of Geography, University of Texas at Austin, Texas.

18 HOFFMAN, James I. Surface, analytical and engineering chemistry. b'93. AB '18—ScD '43 (Franklin and Marshall Coll); MS '21 (George Washington U); PhD '30 (Am U). Research on gallium, aluminum, phosphorus, fluorine, atomic weights of aluminum and gallium, bone char, detergents, aluminum clays, uranium purification. Co-author: Chemical Analysis of Iron and Steel (with G E F Lundell and H A Bright); Outlines of Methods of Chemical Analysis (with G E F Lundell); also articles in field. Chem Nat Bur Standards since '19, chief sect surface chem since '47; teacher grad schs dept agr George Washington U '36-47, Am U '31-36, Washington Acad Sci—Am Chem Soc (councilor)—Sigma Xi—Phi Beta Kappa. Awarded

Hillebrand prize in chem for work on atomic energy and aluminum from clay '47. National Bureau of Standards, Washington 25.†◎

19 HOFFMAN, L. Wallace. Juvenile delinquency; Child welfare. b'03. AB '25—MA '32 (U Mich). Child welfare consultant United Nations Relief and Rehabilitation Administration assigned to Chinese Bureau of Social Affairs '46-47; organized and outlined 10-week training period for teachers, principals, and court workers under sponsorship of Juvenile Court Board of Education and Toledo Police Department '46; conductor training institutes for Indiana, Michigan and Massachusetts State Welfare Conferences, special institute for Federal Probation System. Author articles: Supervision of Federal Probationers '32; Developing Attitudes in Supervision '39, and others. Psychol Psychopathic Clinic Detroit '26-30; chief probation officer US Dist Court Eastern Dist Mich Detroit '30-37, Lucas Co Juvenile Court Toledo '37-46, dir since '47; faculty Grad Sch Social Adminstrn U Mich '36-46. Mich Probation Assn (pres '36-37)—Profl Council of Nat Probation Assn (pres '39-41)—O Probation Assn (exec com '38-39)—Nat Probation and Parole Assn—Am Assn Social Workers. Juvenile Court, Court House, Toledo, O.

20 HOFFMAN, Ross J. S. European history; International relations. b'02. AB '23 (Lafayette Coll); Am '26—PhD '32 (U Penn); four honorary degrees. Special studies on British foreign policy, Mediterranean international relations, political thought of Edmund Burke. Author: The Will to Freedom '35; Tradition and Progress '38; The Organic State '39; The Great Republic '42; Origins of the Second World War (with C G Haines) '43; Durable Peace '44; Burke's Politics (with Paul Levack) '49, and others. Instr hist NYU '26-32, asst prof '32-38; asso prof hist Fordham U Grad Sch '38-44, prof since '44. Phi Beta Kappa—AHA—Am Catholic Hist Assn (pres '38). Winner George Louis Beer Prize. Fordham University, NYC.◎

21 HOFFMEISTER, John Edward. Coral reefs; Corals; Pacific island geology. b'99. AB '20—PhD '23 (Johns Hopkins). B P Bishop Museum fellow '26, '28, investigating general geology and coral reefs of Tonga and Fiji islands; University of Rochester-Bernice B Bishop Museum Eastern Fiji Expedition '34; consultant Army Map Service '42-44; consultant Bikini Bomb Test '46. Author: Some Corals from American Samoa and the Fiji Islands '25; The Geology of Eua, Tonga '32. Co-author: An Orientation in Science '38; Geology of Lau, Fiji '45; also articles in field. With U Rochester since '23, prof soil since '28, dean Coll Arts Sci since '44. Geol Soc Am (F)—Paleontol Soc Am(F)—Phi Beta Kappa—Sigma Xi—Delta Upsilon. Quaker Rd., Scottsville, N.Y.

22 HOFSTADTER, Richard. History; American social thought and political ideologies (Development). b'16. BA '37 (U Buffalo); MA '38—Cutting fellow '41-42—PhD '42 (Columbia). Research in impact of science on Am social thought and development of American political ideologies. Author: Social Darwinism in American Thought, 1860-1915 '44; The American Political Tradition '48; also articles in field. Asst prof hist U Md '42-46; asso prof hist Columbia U since '50. AHA —Soc Am Studies—Phi Beta Kappa. Thesis awarded honorary publn by Beveridge Fund of AHA '44; Alfred A Knopf Fellowship in Hist '45. Columbia University, NYC.†

10 HOGAN, Charles Marshall. Television (Patent law). b'11. AB '30 (Xavier Cincinnati); BS in EE '32 (Purdue); LLB '39 (Franklin Coll Columbus O); '49-51 (Cincinnati Law Sch) '46-47 (De Paul Law Sch) '43 (Columbia U) '45 (George Washington U). Prosecution and investigation radio and television patents. Patent examiner US Patent Office '42; patent lawyer since '43, with Crosley div Avco Mfg Corp since '47. Lt USNR Office Patent Counsel, Bur Ordnance Navy Dept Washington '44-46. Inst Radio Engrs (sr mem)—Cincinnati Patent Law Assn (bd govs)—Am Ohio and Cincinnati bar assns—Phi Alpha Delta. Crosley Division, Avco Mfg. Corp., Cin. 25. H: 31 Meazen Ct., Cin. 17.

11 HOGAN, William Ransom. American social history (Southwestern, Texas, Natchez, ante-bellum Mississippi free Negroes). b'08. BA '29 (Trinity U); MA '33—PhD '37 (U Tex). Author: The Texas Republic: A Social and Economic History '46. Editor: Guide to Manuscript Collections in the Department of Archives Louisiana State University '40; Diary of a Natchez Free Negro, 1835-51 '49; also articles in field. Professor hist Tulane U since '50. Miss Valley Hist Assn—So Hist Assn—SW Hist Assn—La Hist Soc. Received Rosenwald grant, Am Philos Soc grant. Department of History, Tulane University, New Orleans 18.

12 HOGNESS, Thorfin Rusten. Radiobiology; Enzyme chemistry. b'94. BS '18—ChE '19 (U Minn); PhD '21 (U Calif); DSc (hon) '47 (Rockford Coll). Co-author (with W C Johnson) Qualitative Analysis and Chemical Equilibrium '37; (with W C Johnson) Ionic Equilibrium '39; also articles in field. Instr chem U Calif '21-25, asst prof '25-28, asso prof '28-30; asso prof chem U Chicago '30-38, prof since '38, dir phys sci development '47-48, dir Inst Radiobiol and Biophysics since '48, dir chem div Atomic Bomb Project '43-46; sci liaison officer Am Embassy London '42-43; dir Md Research Lab OSS '43. Internat Edn Bd Fellow '26-27, U Gottingen, Germany; spl fellow '37 Rockefeller Found in Europe. Am Chem Soc—Am Biochem Soc—Am Phys Soc—AAAS—Nat Research Council. University of Chicago, Chicago 37.

13 HOGUE, Ernest Newton. Improvement programs (Economic evaluation); Production (Scheduling and Control); Investment programs (Economic evaluation). b'89. BS in elec engring '15 (A and M Coll of Tex). Research on determination production capacity by time studies, analysis past performances; evaluation complete manufacturing costs to determine profits under various operating capacities; analysis production scheduling and control. Chief clk maintenance Westinghouse Electric '19; schedule supervisor Mosher Steel & Machinery Co Dallas '29; asst to supt tin plate dept Jones & Laughlin Steel Aliquippa Pa '37, asst supervisor indsl engring since '51. Assn Iron & Steel Engrs—Am Soc Quality Control. Jones & Laughlin Steel Corp, Aliquippa, Pa.

14 HOHLFELD, John Maurice. Literacy (Foreign adult education); Linguistics (Applied). b'09. Student '39 (U Munich); BS (edn) '40—STB '40 (Temple U); ThM '42 (Princeton Theol Sem); PhD '49 (U Pa). Research on teaching principles of linguistic science, reduction unwritten languages to writing, development scientific orthographies, principles and practices of adult literacy education; language consultant for Committee on World Literacy and Christian Literature of Foreign Missions Conference of North America, literacy consultant on educational mission sponsored by British Guiana colonial government '47, in Africa, sponsored by World Literacy Commission '50. Instr army lang program U Pa '42-44; faculty Ursinus Coll '45-48; with Kennedy Sch Missions since '47, asso prof linguistics from '49; vis prof linguistics Scarritt Coll '49-50. Am Assn Adult Edn—Am Oriental Soc—Linguistic Soc Am—AA UP—Modern Lang Tchrs Assn—Phi Delta Kappa—Kappa Phi Kappa. Kennecy School of Missions, Hartford Seminary Foundation, Hartford 5, Conn.

15 HOHMANN, Walter H(ugo). Mennonite hymnology; Choral music. b'92. BM '22—MM '28 (Bush Conservatory Chicago); student (Westminster Choir Coll Princeton). Editor: Outlines in Hymnology with Emphasis on Mennonite Hymnology '41. Associate editor: Mennonite Hymn Book '27; Treasure Songs for Schools and Churches '37. Co-editor: The Mennonite Hymnary '40; composer original musical compositions. Instr piano and organ Bethel Coll since '23. Music Teachers Nat Assn. Bethel College, North Newton, Kan.†

16 HOIJER, Harry. Anthropology; American Indian languages. b'04. AB '27—AM '29—PhD '31 (U Chicago). Field research on language among Tonkawa, Apache, Navaho, Tewa Indians at intervals since '28. Author: Tonkawa, An American Indian Language of Texas '33; Chiricahua and Mescalero Apache Texts '38. Co-author: Navaho Texts '42; also articles in field. Asst prof, prof anthrop U Calif since '40, chmn dept anthrop and sociol. Linguistic Soc Am—Am Anthrop Assn—Société des Américanistes de Paris—Sigma Xi. Department of Anthropology and Sociology, University of California, Los Angeles 24.†

17 HOKE, Calm Morrison. Metals (Precious). b'87. AB '08 (Hunter Coll NYC); '09 (Wittenberg Coll Springfield O); '10-11 (U Chicago); AM '13—'17-20 (Columbia); '23 (NYU). Development methods for refining precious metal wastes generated in jewelry factories and dental laboratories; design oxy-gas torches for melting and soldering precious metals, especially platinum; identification precious metals and their alloys, especially platinum, and their appraisal. Author: Refining Precious Metal Wastes '40; Testing Precious Metals (3rd edit) '46. Jr chem Harriman Research Lab NYC '11-12; chem Jewelers Tech Adv Co '13-17 and since '19; vp and chem Hoke Inc NYC '26-34. AIMME—ACS—AAA S(F)—Am Inst Chem(F). 123 William St., N.Y.C. 38. H: 1070 Anderson Av., Palisade, N.Y.†

18 HOKE, Roy Edward. Vocational guidance; Personality adjustment; Marriage counsel; Alcoholism. b'96. AB '16—AM '17 (Franklin and Marshall Coll); '17-18 (Theol Sem Lancaster Pa); PhD '22 (Johns Hopkins U). Development methods for correction of speech defects; lecturer educational, psychological, and religious problems; administration and analysis vocational and aptitude tests; writer weekly newspaper column on psychology, weekly radio program on personal problems. Prof psychol and edn Birmingham So Coll '21-28, also dean edn and dir summer sch; prof psychol and religious edn Emory and Henry Coll '28-44; prof edn and psychol Davidson Coll '44-46; founder Psychological Service Center '46. Chaplain AUS World War II. Am Psychol Assn—AA AS—Am Philos Assn—Phi Beta Kappa—Kappa Phi Kappa. The Psychological Service Center, 1717 Cleveland Av., Charlotte 3, N.C.†⊙

19 HOLAND, Hjalmar Rued. Pre-Columbian American history (Kensington rune stone, Newport tower); Runic studies. b'72. AB '98—AM '99 (U Wis). Interpreter Kensington Rune Stone found in Minnesota '98 which tells of journey into mid-America by expedition of 30 Norwegians and Swedes in 1362; presented evidence showing that Newport Tower was built about 1360 as a church and headquarters for royal expedition of 1355-1364. Author: History of the Norwegian Settlements '08; The Last Migration '31; The Kensington Stone '32; Westward From Vinland '40; America: 1355-1364 '46. Editor Peninsula Hist Rev '27-34; curator Wis State Hist Soc since '38. Wis State Hist Soc—Norwegian-Am Hist Soc—Am Hist Soc. Ephraim, Wis.⊙

20 HOLBERT, James Ransom. Corn breeding. b'90. BSA '15—MS (agr) '18 (Purdue U); PhD '26 (U Ill). Research on identification, causes, and effects of corn diseases and their control by breeding, breeding for cold resistance in corn, improvement and maintenance of commercial inbred lines, physiological functions and adaptations of hybrid corn, improvement of strains by selection and breeding for insect resistance in corn, commercial applications of recurrent selection methods in corn breeding, adaptation studies of corn hybrids. Sr agron USDA '18-36; vp, gen mgr, research dir Funk Brothers Seed Co since '36. AAAS—Am Soc Agron—Am Farm Mgrs Assn—Bot Soc Am—Am Seed Trade Assn (pres '47-49)—Alpha Zeta—Alpha Tau Alpha—Sigma Xi. Funk Brothers Seed Co., Bloomington. Ill.

21 HOLDEN, Eugene Davenport. Seed certification. b'93. Student '12-13 (Ia State Coll); BS '15—MS '21 (U Wis). Director of International Crop Improvement Association since '36; production, certification and distribution of certified seeds. Author articles in field. Ext agron U Wis since '17; asst sec Wis Agrl Expt Assn '17-36, sec since '36. Am Soc Agron. Agronomy Building, University of Wisconsin, Madison, Wis.

22 HOLDEN, Francis Richard. Ammonia; Industrial hygiene; Radiation protection. b'07. BS cum laude '30 (Hobart Coll); AM '32—PhD '34 (U Cincinnati). Research reactions in liquid ammonia particularly reductions of inorganic salts by sodium, potassium, calcium; consultant to industry on problems radiation protection. Author articles: A study of the products obtained by reducing action of metals upon salts in liquid ammonia; Prevention of injury from x-radiation. Indsl hygienist Pittsburgh Plate Glass Co '35-40; sr fellow Mellon Institute '40-47; asso chief chem tech div US Naval Radiological Defense Lab since '47. ACS—Am Inst Chems—Am Indsl Hygiene Assn—Alpha Chi Sigma—Phi Beta Kappa—Sigma Xi. US Naval Radiological Defense Laboratory, SF 24. H: 795 Josina Av., Palo Alto, Cal.

23 HOLDEN, Harold Miller. Noses (Plastic surgery). b'99. DDS '21 (Northwestern U); MA—PhD '26 MD '27 (U Berlin). Author: Noses '50. Author article: Recent Advances in Plastic Surgery. Asso prof otolaryngology Cook Co Grad Sch Medicine '32-37; asso attending otolaryngologist Cook County and Mt Sinai Hosps '32-27; attending plastic surgeon Cedars of Lebanon Hosp. Am Bd Otolaryngology

(Diplomate)—Am Acad Ophthalmology and Otolaryngology(F)—Am Otorhinologic Soc for Advancement Plastic and Reconstructive Surgery(F)—AAAS—AMA(F). 520 S San Vicente Blvd., LA 48.

10 HOLDEN, Perry Greeley. Agricultural extension. b'65. BS '89—fellow '89-93—MS '95 (Mich Agrl Coll); BPd '94—MPd '12 (Mich State Normal Coll). Established first agronomy department, University Illinois '96-00; organized Funk Brothers Seed Company for scientific seed corn production '01; originated use of special trains for seed corn improvement campaign, established first agricultural extension department (forerunner of country agents, 4-H Clubs, and others) Iowa State College '02-12; director agricultural extension department International Harvester Company '12-32 for world-wide extension agricultural instruction; conducted agricultural campaigns in South and West for crop diversification, cattle tick eradication, alfalfa production, etc. Awarded medal for distinguished service to agr and agrl edn Panama-Pacific Expn '14, also mem Jury of Awards; diploma for distinguished service to agr U Wis; Mich State Coll distinguished alumni award. Box 263, Charlevoix, Mich.

11 HOLDEN, William Curry. Southwestern United States archeology and ethnology. b'96. AB '23—MA '24—PhD '28 (U Tex). Archeological investigations in Texas Panhandle, New Mexico, and Mexico '32; conducted four ethnological expeditions among Yaqui Indians of Sonora Mexico '34. Author: Alkali Trails '30; Rollie Burns '32; The Spur Ranch '34; Studies of the Yaqui Indians '35; also articles in field. Dean Div Grad Studies Tex Tech Coll since '45; head dept history anthrop sociology, director Coll Museum since '36. Texas State Hist Assn—Tex Archeol Paleontol Soc—Philos Soc Tex—Tex Inst Letters. 3105 20th St., Lubbock, Tex.

12 HOLL, Dio Lewis. Theory of elasticity. b'95. AB '17 (Manchester Coll); MA '20 (O State U); grad fellow dept math '22-23—PhD '25 (U Chicago). Abstractor of papers in applied elasticity for Zentrablatt fur Mechanik '34-39, for Mathematical Reviews since '40. Author articles in field. Prof math Ia State Coll since '34, now head dept, research prof applied math since '37. Am Math Soc—ASME (mechanics sect)—Sigma Xi. Iowa State College, Ames, Iowa.◎

13 HOLLABAUGH, Cleveland Buchanan. Plastic high polymers; Nitrocellulose emulsions; Nitrocellulose lacquer coatings (Chalking); Cellulose derivatives; Synthetic resins. b'08. BS '27 (U Ark); MS '30—PhD '31 (Pa State Coll). Research and development nitrocellulose emulsions, research on causes and mechanism of chalking of pigmented nitrocellulose lacquer coatings. Granted patents in field. With Hercules Powder Co '31-45, dir patents '39-45; patent attorney Dentists Supply Co NY '46-47; patent attorney and chem cons since '47. Sigma Xi—Phi Kappa Phi—Phi Lambda Upsilon—Sigma Pi Sigma—Alpha Chi Sigma—ACS—Am Acad Sci—Tech Assn Pulp and Paper Industry—NY Patent Law Assn. 163 Brompton Rd., Garden City, N.Y.

14 HOLLAENDER, Alexander. Radiation (Effects on biological materials). b'98. AB '29—MA '30—PhD '31(U Wis). Studies on effects of radiation on bacteria, fungi, and viruses; efficiency of different wave lengths of ultraviolet in producing toxic effects, sublethal changes, mutation production, and re-

lated phenomena; relation between effectivity of different wavelengths in the ultraviolet and chemical structure; combined effects of different types of radiation (X rays, infrared and long ultraviolet); control of infectious agents in biological liquids (jaundice factor in blood plasma) and induction of mutation in fungi with increased ability to produce antibiotics (pencillin), etc. Nat Research Council fellow in biol U Wis '30-33, sent abroad, under auspices of Rockefeller Found, to Inst Exptl Med Leningrad 3 mos '34; survey effects electromagnetic radiation on biol materials for Rockefeller Found NY '34; in charge project for Nat Research Council U Wis '34-37; with Washington Biophysical Inst '37-38; joined div phys biol Nat Inst Health of USPHS '38, apptd head biol div Oak Ridge Nat Lab '46. Biology Division, Oak Ridge National Laboratory, Oak Ridge, Tenn.

15 HOLLAND, Daniel John. Trout (Species, life histories, habitant, conservation, angling methods, and tackle). b'14. AB '36 (Dartmouth Coll). Study North American trout and European brown trout in US, Canada, and Alaska. Author: Trout Fishing '49. Contributor: Game Fish of the World. Asso ed Field and Stream '36-41; game-fish specialist Alaska Game Comn '41-42; free lance writer, photog since '45. H: Quechee, Vt.

16 HOLLAND, Laurier Fox-Strangways. Micro-paleontology; Rare metals (Molybdenum, tungsten, vanadium, uranium); Gold and silver mining and metallurgy; Mining and oil geology. b'94. Research work on rare metals, especially molybdenum, on gold and silver amalgamation and flotation processes. Gen mgr and sec Pacific Mines, Oregon Mine, Rose Mine, Texas Hill Placer, Harmon Mine, Excelsior, Epley Mine and the Missouri Flat Placer; sec and treas Placerville Gold Mining Co, all at Placerville, Calif; cons engr; made hundreds of mine evaluations in US, Canada, Mexico. Am Inst Mining Metall Engrs—Am Assn Petroleum Geol—Soc Econ Paleontol Mineral—Legion of Honor. Placerville, California.◎

17 HOLLAND, Leicester Bodine. Architectural archeology; Greek and medieval French architecture; Stained glass. b'82. BS '02—BS in Arch '04—MA '17—PhD '19 (U Pa). Author: Traffic Ways about France in the Dark Ages '19; (with Harry Parker) Ready Written Specifications '25; also articles in field. Teacher archtl design and hist arch U Pa '13-18; asso prof architecture Am Sch Classical Studies at Athens '19-22; prof fine Arts Vassar '25-27, U Pa '29-46; also chief div of fine arts Library Congress '29-43; with OSS '44; arch with Corinth Excavations of Am Sch in Athens '46-47; prof architecture Miami U since '48. AIA(F)—Archeol Inst Am—Am Philos Soc. 415 W. Price St., Phila. 44.

18 HOLLAND, Ray(mond) P(runty). Fish; Game; Hunting dogs; Hunting; Fishing; Wildlife conservation; Sporting firearms. b'84. Was active in promotion of federal legislation for protection of migratory birds, a principal in case of State of Missouri vs Ray P Holland which was carried to US Supreme Court and settled question of jurisdiction of federal government over wild game. Author: My Gun Dogs '29; Nip and Tuck '39; Shotgunning in the Uplands '44; Shotgunning in the Lowlands '45; My Dog Lemon '45; Good Shot! (in collaboration) '45; The Master '46; But Listen, Warden! '46; Bird Dogs '47; also articles in field. Began writing for sportsmen's

mags '03; joined staff US Bur Biol Survey '14; ed Field and Stream '24-41; hunted and fished in all states, Mexico, Can; mem staff Webster's Internat. Am Game Protective Assn (vp '19, now pres, and ed publs)—Internat Assn Game (sec-treas)—Fish and Conservation Commrs.

19 HOLLAND, Raymond Prunty, Jr. Aerodynamics (Popularization, balancing airplane control surface technique); Kites (Theory, development); Flight of birds and insects. b'10. SB '34 (MIT). Inventor stall warning indicator, aircraft engine cowling, windshield air intake, airplane type kite. Author articles in field. Instr coll math NM Mil Inst since '46, part time, also writing and research. Inst Aeronautical Sci. New Mexico Military Institute, Roswell, N.M. H: 421 College Blvd.†

20 HOLLAR, Victor E. Tomatoes (Hybridization); Cucumbers (Hybridization). b'16. BS '40 (Colo State Coll); MS '44 (Ia State Coll). Experiments with commercial growth of hybrid tomato seed produced by use of male sterile parent; production new type hybrid cucumber. Research asst in charge Muscatine field sta Ia State Coll '41-45; in charge production at research farms Burpee Seed Co '46-48; co-owner R H James Co (wholesale seed growers and breeders) since '49. Alpha Zeta—Beta Beta Beta—Gamma Sigma Delta. R. H. James Co., Rocky Ford, Colo.

21 HOLLEMAN, Willard Roy. Paper manufacture literature. b'09. BS '29—MS '43 (Okla Agrl & Mech Coll); BS Library Sci '37 (U Ill). Research and preparation of bibliographies covering paper manufacture; evaluate technical books in field of paper manufacture; developed book collection and guided book selection policies for aeronautical literature; directed reference research compiled indexes bibliographies abstracts in science field. Author: Aeronautical Reference Books '45; Procedures manual at the Boeing Airplane Company Library '47; also articles in field. With Okla A&M College library '37 head rel dept '38-42; instr physics AAF training det '42-44; chief librn Boeing Airplane Co Wichita Kan '44-48; librarian, The Mead Corp research and development div Chillicothe O '48-50; librarian Scripps Inst Oceanog U Calif since 50. Spl Libraries Assn (sci tech group)—Tech Assn of Pulp and Paper Industry. Scripps Institution of Oceanography, Univ of California, La Jolla, Calif.

22 HOLLER, Albert Cochran. Brass; Bronze; Spectrophotometry; Chromatography. b'21. BChem '47—research F chem '47-49 (U Minn). Research on metallurgy and chemical analysis of brass and bronze; visible and ultraviolet spectrophotometry; chromatography of organic compounds. Co-author: (with W T Frier) Introduction to Industrial Chemistry '45. Chief chem and metall US Metal Products Co '41-44; dir chem div Twin City Testing and Engring Lab since '49. ACS—ASTM—Am Inst Chem—Soc Applied Spectroscopy—Minn Indsl Chem Forum—AAAS—Am Foundrymen's Soc—Alpha Chi Sigma—Sigma Xi—Sci Research Soc Am. Thomas F Andrews Prize for undergraduate research U Minn '47. Twin City Testing and Engineering Laboratory, 2440 Franklin Av., St. Paul 4.

23 HOLLEY, Horace. Bahai; Babism. Student '06-09 (Williams Coll). Author: Bahaism; The Modern Social Religion '14; The Social Principle '16; Bahai—The Spirit of the Age '21. Editor: Bahai Scriptures '23; Foundations of World Unity '27; Bahai Administration

'27; Reality of Man '33; Bahai Procedure '42; Bahai World Faith '43; Bahai Centenary '44; What Modern Man Must Know About Religion '48. Sec Nat Spiritual Assembly of Bahais of US and Can '24-30, since '32; sec World Unity Found; ed Bahai World '26-38; co-ed World Order Mag '35-47, Phi Delta Theta. 536 Sheridan Rd., Wilmette, Ill.⊙

10 HOLLEY, Joseph Winthrop. Negro education. b'74. Grad '96 (Revere Say Coll); '96-98 (Phillips Andover); '98-02 (Lincoln U); two hon degrees. Author: You Can't Build Your Chimney from the Top '48; also articles in field. Established '03 Albany Bible and Manual Training Inst, now Ga Normal Coll. Am Geog Soc(F) — Am Acad Polit Social Sci. 270 Holley Highway, Albany, Ga.

11 HOLLINGSWORTH, Richard V(incen). Micropaleontology (Fusulinids, Paleozoic); Stratigraphy (Subsurface); Petroleum geology. b'09. BS '31—MS '33 (U Okla); fellow '33-34—'40-41 (U Chicago). Author: (with R W Harris) New Pennsylvanian Conodonts from Oklahoma '33. Petrographer Shell Oil Co '35-40; asst prof geol U Tulsa '41; regional geol Shell Oil Co '42, sr stratigrapher '42-44; paleontol and owner Paleontological Lab since '44. Am Assn Petroleum Geol—Paleontol Soc—Soc Econ Paleontol Mineral—AAAS—Am Inst Mining Metall Engrs—Tex Acad Sci—Sigma Xi—Phi Beta Kappa. Paleontological Laboratory, P.O. Box 51, Midland, Tex.

12 HOLLOWAY, James K(eever). Biological control of insects and weeds. b'00. BS '26 (Miss State Coll); '26-27 (O State U). Author articles in field. Research on biological control of Japanese beetle '27-31, Oriental fruit moth '31-35, influence of chem sprays on natural control factors of insects in Jones Bankhead Research Project '36-43; studies biological control of weeds by use of insects, first attempt in US, weeds controlled St Johnswort, Gorse. Am Assn Econ Entomol—Calif Entomol Soc—Biometric Soc. University of California, Gill Tract, 1050 San Pablo Av., Albany 6, Calif.

13 HOLMAN, Charles Thomas. Personal counseling. b'82. BA '09—MA '10—DD '46 (McMaster U Toronto); BD '15 (U Chicago) '17 (Ind U); DD hon '44 (Ottawa U). Availability of psychological insights and techniques to the religious counselor. Author: The Cure of Souls; The Church at Work in The Modern World; The Religion of a Healthy Mind (Religious Book Club selection); Getting Down to Cases; Religion and the Present Crisis; Psychology and Religion for Everyday Living. Co-author: (with W C Bower and others) The Church at Work in the Modern World (with John Knox and others) Religion and the Present Crisis; (with Seward Hiltner and others) What the American Family Faces. With Divinity Sch U Chicago since '23, prof '42-47, dean Bapt Div House '42-47, dir vocational training '25-42, emeritus prof and dean since '47; pastor Union Ch Guatemala City CA '47-52; pastor First Baptist Church Albion NY since '52. Am Acad Polit and Social Sci—AAAS—AAUP—Pi Gamma Mu. 106 West Park St., Albion, N.Y.⊙

14 HOLMER, Paul LeRoy. Existentialism. b'16. BA '40—MA '42 (U Minn); Nat Council on Religion in Higher Edn F '44; Rettger F '44-45—PhD '46 (Yale). Research on philosophy of Kierkegaard; history of philosophy of religion; Scandinavian philosophy; secretary Swenson-Kierkegaard Fellowship Committee. Asst prof Gustavus Adolphus Coll '46; with U Minn since '46, asst prof '48-50, asso prof since '50. Am Philos Assn—Am Theol Assn. 110 Westbrook Hall, University of Minnesota, Mpls. H: 101 14th Av. S.E., Mpls. 14.

15 HOLMES, Chauncey Depew. Glacial erosion and sedimentation; Till-fabric technique. b'97. AB '25—AM '27 (Syracuse U); PhD '39 (Yale). Developed till-fabric technique in study of glacial deposits '37-39. Author: Introduction to College Geology '49; also articles in field. Prof geol U Mo '45-51, chmn dept geol and geog since '45. Geol Soc Am(F)—Am Geophys Union—Brit Glaciol Soc—AAAS—Arctic Inst NA (charter asso)—Sigma Xi. Swallow Hall, Columbia, Mo. H: 317 West Parkway Dr.†⊙

16 HOLMES, Donald Carver. Photography (Documentary). b'11. Student '33 (Benjamin Franklin U Washington); '34-36 (George Washington U); '45-46 (Am U Washington). Director of reproduction by microphotography, color photography, photostating, blue printing, and ozalid process; reproduction manuscripts, documents, books, fine arts pieces, photographs, and x-rays; use ultra-violent and infra-red photography for reproduction of faded and hidden writings; design photographic apparatus for special applications. Author articles: Quality in Microphotography '40; Exposure Notes '41; War-Time Photographic Activities and Records Resulting Therefrom '47; The Library of Congress Photoduplication Service '50. Documentary reproduction tech Nat Archives '35-38; head lab photoduplication service Library of Congress '38-42, chief photoduplication service since '45. Photog officer photo-sci lab USN Anacostia DC. NY Acad Sci—Soc Photog Engrs—ALA. Library of Congress, 1 B St. S.E., Washington.

17 HOLMES, Joseph Austin. Petroleum exploration and exploitation. b'95. EM '20 (Lehigh U); Ingeniero de Minas '42 (Universidad Central Venezuela). Dist supt drilling and prodn Midwest Refining Co Rocky Mountain area '24-25; asst chief petroleum engr Pan Am Petroleum & Transport Co NYC '29-30; chief petroleum engr Lago Petroleum Corp Maracaibo Venezuela '31-34; chief petroleum engr advancing to tech asst to pres Standard Oil Co Venezuela '34-42; gen mgr Internat Petroleum Co Ltd Caracas Venezeula since '45. AIMME—Am Petroleum Inst—Colegio de Ingenieros Venezuela—Am Geog Soc. Apartado 1446, Caracas, Venezuela.

18 HOLMES, Kenneth Leeds. History of pre-Revolutionary France and Stuart England; Europe since 1914; Teaching the social studies. b'95. BA '17 (Yale); MA '25 (U Louisville); '35-36 and others (U Minn); '49-50 (Yale). Asst prof hist Macalester Coll '25-30, professor since '38, chairman dept since '32; professorial lecturer U Minn '48-49. AHA—Minn Hist Soc—Nat Council Social Studies. Macalester College, St. Paul 5. H: 1414 Summit Av.†

19 HOLMES, Paul Mordaunt. Swimming pool (Sanitation); Mosquito control; Sand filter (Rural sanitation). b'98. B Civil Engring '25—CE '43 (O State U). Research on malaria and mosquito control in Ohio. Designing engr City Columbus O '28-38; engr Dist Number 2 Mun Water Supplies Pub Works Adminstrn '38-40; chief Environmental San Div O Dept Health '40-46; cons engr since '46. Am Soc CE—ASME—Soc Am Mil Engrs—Nat Soc Prof Engrs. 209 S. High St., Columbus 15, O.

20 HOLMES, Ralph Jerome. Mineralogy; X-ray diffraction; Economic geology; Crystallography; Petrology; Gemology; Clays; Ore deposits. b'06. BS '33—PhD '46 (Columbia). Delegate of New York Academy of Science to International Geological Congress London '48. Author articles in field. Instr, later asst prof geol Columbia U since '43. Geol Soc Am(F)—Mineral Soc Am(F)—Am Inst Mining Metall Engrs—NY Acad Sci—Mineral Soc Gt Brit—Gemological Inst Am (ednl adv bd)—Soc Econ Geologists—Crystallographic Soc—Am Gem Soc (asso)—Sigma Xi. Department of Geology, Columbia University, NYC 27†.

21 HOLMQUIST, Albert Martinius. Hibernation. b'91. AB '14 (St Olaf Coll); MS '17—PhD '25 (U Chicago). Instr St Olaf Coll '17-18, prof biology '20-23 and since '26, chmn dept biology since '49; asst dept zoology U Chicago '23-25; fellow Nat Research Council '25-26; prof zoology Northwestern U summer '32; lectr Biol Sta U Minn summer '36; research fellow U Minn summer '45; prof zoology U SD summer '49. AAAS(F)—Ecol Soc Am—Am Soc Zool—Am Soc Limnology and Oceanography—Minn Acad Sci—Sigma Xi—Gamma Alpha. St Olaf College, Northfield, Minn.⊙

22 HOLSCHER, Harry Heltman. Glass (Technology). b'07. BS (ceramics) '28—Ceramic Engr '45 (U Ill); MS (ceramic engring) '29 — PhD (ceramic engring) '31 (O State U). Research on physical properties of glass as influenced by composition, developed methods and measurements actual temperatures of glass and mold equipment during glass bottle forming operations, temperatures of glass during melting operations. Contributor: Encyclopaedia Britannica (vol III) '44. With engring dept Hot Point Inc '31-37; with Owens-Ill Glass Co since '37, gen research lab '37-45, adminstr research div from '45. Am Ceramic Soc (F, chmn com on classification, nomenclature, and glossary since '48, chmn glass div '50-51)—AS TM—Soc Glass Tech of Eng—Tau Beta Pi—Sigma Xi Owens-Illinois Glass Co., P.O. Box 1035, Tol. 1.

23 HOLSKE, Clifford F(ranklin). Food freezing; Corrosion control; Refrigeration systems (Design). b'01. Ed private schs. Designer large scale refrigeration and air conditioning systems including applications for nitrogen fixation, penicillin manufacture, meat cooling, quick freezing, special applications in chemical and pharmaceutical industries. Test engr Am Ice Co '29-34, research engr '34-40; mgr NY dist Vilter Mfg Co since '41; cons engr. Am Soc Refrigerating Engrs (F, edit bd, standards com '45, pres '48)—Am Standards Assn (refrigerator standards com '39-43)—ASTM—Am Coordinating Com on Corrosion. Professional engr NY. 110 E. 42d St., N.Y.C. 17.

24 HOLT, Grover J(ustin). Iron ore mining and concentration. b'94. BS '16 (U ND)—research fellow '16-17 (U Utah); Engr Mines '42 (U ND). Research iron ore beneficiation, mechanized mining, block caving. Developed ferro-silicon sink-float process for beneficiation of ores. Author articles in field. Supt Basin Metals Mining Corp Utah '17; tunnel contractor Murray Ida '20; mining engr Oliver Iron Mining Co Minn '21-28; chief engr, supt and asst to vp Butler Bros Iron Mining Minn and Mich '28-42; chief engr The Cleveland-Cliffs Iron Co Mich '42-50, mgr Mesaba Range Properties The Cleveland-Cliffs Iron Co since '50. The Cleveland-Cliffs Iron Company, Hibbing, Minn.

10 HOLT, Lucius Hudson. Lexicography. b'81. BA '02—MA '04—PhD '05 (Yale). Author: Leading English Poets '15; Introduction to Ancient History, and others. Asst ed Webster's Internat Dictionary '08-10; prof Eng and hist rank of lt col US Mil Acad '10, rank of col since '20, charge dept econ govt and hist '19-26, prof econ govt and hist '26-30, act dean '26-28; editorial staff Webster's New Internat Dictionary '32-34; mng ed Webster's Dictionaries '34-46, retired '46. Am Geog Soc—Phi Beta Kappa. G. & C. Merriam Co., Springfield, Mass.◎

11 HOLTZ, John C. Gas and explosives engineering. b'04. BS '26—PhD '30 (Johns Hopkins). Author articles in field. Chem diesel fuels Naval Engring Expt Sta Annapolis Md '34-36; gas and explosives engr Bur Mines Pittsburgh '36-48; chem engr fuels Bur Mines Grand Forks ND since '48. Am Chem Soc—ASME—Sigma Xi—Tau Beta Pi. Box LL, University Station, Grand Forks, N.D.

12 HOLZKNECHT, K a r l Julius. Shakespeare; English prose literature (Sixteenth century). b'99. AB '20 (U Louisville); AM '21—PhD '23 (U Pa). Secretary College Conference on English in Central Atlantic States '30-42, pres '45-47, general editor Harper Period Anthologies of English Literature. Author: Literary Patronage in the Middle Ages '23; A Literary Map of the British Isles '34; Outlines of Tudor and Stuart Plays 1497-1642 '47; The Backgrounds of Shakespeare's Plays '49. Editor: A Freshman Miscellany '29; (with Norman E McClure) Selected Plays of Shakespeare '36-41. Co-compiler: (with Homer A Watt) Children's Books of Long Ago '42; also articles in field. Asst prof Eng U Louisville '23-26, asso prof '26-28; instr Eng, later prof Washington Square Coll NYU since '28, head Eng dept NYU since '49. Modern Lang Assn Am—Shakespeare Assn—Modern Humanities Research Assn—Biblio Soc Am—Phi Beta Kappa. 100 Washington Square East, NYC 3.

13 HOLZMANN, Albert William. Teaching methodology (Languages). b'94. LittB '17 (Rutgers U); MA '26 —PhD '35 (Columbia); Grad '27 (Princeton U); '31 (Heidelberg U Germany). Originated competitive declamation of German prose and poetry for high school and college students; research on integration of modern foreign language teaching between high schools and colleges. Author articles: A Decade of Declaration '38; A Method of Teaching German Conversation '43; An Experiment in Methodology '49; The Preparation of Teachers of German in the State of New Jersey '51, and others. Faculty German dept Rutgers U since '23, chmn dept since '34, prof German lang and lit since '47; asst supv fgn area and lang program Army Specialized Training Program '43-44. Modern Lang Assn Am —Am Assn Tchrs German—NJ Modern Lang Tchrs Assn—Assn Modern Lang Tchrs Middle States (vp '41-42, '47-48, '50-51)—Phi Beta Kappa—Delta Phi Alpha. German Department, Rutgers University, New Brunswick, N.J.

14 HOMBERGER, Alfred William. Nutrition; Biochemistry. b'87. AB '05 (U Wis); MS '08—PhD '10 (U Ill). Author articles in field. Prof physiol chem and nutrition, head dept Sch Med U Louisville since '42. AAAS(F)—Am Chem Soc—Ky Acad Sci (pres '39-40) —Sigma Xi. 2368 Carlton Terace, Louisville.

15 HOMSEY, Samuel E. Contemporary architecture (Houses, schools, community buildings). b'04. BS '26— MS '26 (MIT). Author articles in field. Practicing architect since '26. AIA— Am Soc Architects and Planners. Awarded prize for instl bldgs, Pittsburgh Glass Inst '38; Diploma of Merit for Cambridge Yacht Club by Maryland Soc Architects '40. 917 Gilpin Av., Wilmington 12, Del. H: Lancaster Pike, Hockessin.

16 HOMSHER, Lola Mae. Wyoming history. b'13. BS '36 (Colo State Coll Agr Mech Arts); MA '49 (U Wyo). Curator Wyoming Hist Manuscripts Collections and archivist U Wyo since '45. Miss Valley Hist Assn—Am Assn State Local Hist—Soc Am Archivists —Colo-Wyo Acad Sci—Phi Kappa Phi. Library, University of Wyoming, Laramie, Wyo.

17 HONIG, Herbert. Veneers; Rare woods; Wood finishing. b'02. Student Germany, Switzerland. Research on furniture care and revitalizing. Holds US patent on polishing cloth granted '47. Formerly with Veneer and Rare Woods Ind Germany and France; wood finishing expert Premier Crystal Labs Inc NYC; owner Tutch-On Products Co NYC. 570 Ft. Washington Av., NYC 33.†

18 HONIG, Richard E(dward). Molecular and nuclear physics; Radiation chemistry; Mass spectrometry. b'17. BS in EE (Robert Coll, Istanbul Turkey); MS '39—PhD '44 (MIT). Author articles: Gas Flow in the Mass Spectrometer '45; Radiochemical Changes in Some Fatty Acids '46; The Technique of Bombarding Organic Compounds with Deuterons '47; Ionization Potentials of Some Hydrocarbon Series '48, and others. Research asst physics MIT '41-42, exptl work on GSA project on age of earth 42-44, Am Petroleum Institute project on origin of petroleum, work in radiation chemistry, research asso physics '44-46 DTO; sr physicist research labs Socony-Vacuum Paulsboro NJ '46-50; tech staff mem RCA labs since '50. Am Phys Soc—Sigma Xi. RCA Laboratories, Princeton, N.J. H: Franklin Ave., Princeton, N.J.

19 HONIGMANN, John Joseph. Eskimos (Ethnology); North American Indians (Culture and personality). b '14. BA '42 (Brooklyn Coll); MA '43— PhD '47 (Yale U). Field work in northern British Columbia, northern Ontario, and northern Quebec on food consumption of Indians and Eskimos, research on socialization of Eskimo of northern Quebec. Asst prof anthrop Wash State Coll '46-47; research anthrop Nat Com for Community Helath Studies (Can) '47-48; asst prof anthrop NYU '48-51; research asso and asso prof anthrop U NC since '51. Am Antrop Assn—Soc Applied Anthrop. University North Carolina, Chapel Hill, N.C.

20 HONNELL, Pierre Marcel. Seismographs (Testing); Electromechanical newtwork theory. b'08. BS (elec engring) '30—EE '38 (Tex A&M Coll); MS (elec engring) '39 (MIT); MS '40 (Cal Inst Tech); PhD '50 (St Louis Univ). Research on electromechanical transducer for transient testing of seismographs. Mem tech staff Bell Telephone Lab Inc '30-33; geophys The Tex Co '34-38; dir electronics course, US Mil Acad '42-46; asso prof elec engring Washington U '46-50, prof from '50. Am Inst EE—AAAS—Am Soc Engring Edn—Inst Radio Engrs—Soc Exploration Geophys—Seismol Soc Am —Am Geophys Union—Sigma Xi—Tau Beta Pi. Legion of Merit '46. Department of Electrical Engineering, Washington University, StL 5.

21 HONOR, Leo L. Jewish history and education; Assyriology. b'94. BA '14 (Coll City NY); PhD '26 (Colum-bia). Director College Jewish Studies '29-45; executive director Board Jewish Education '34-46; made surveys of Jewish education in Boston, St Louis, Omaha, San Francisco, Indianapolis, Philadelphia. Author: Sennacherib's Invasion of Palestine '26; Survey of Jewish History '32; History of Jewish Eucation in the United States '48; also articles in field. Prof edn and head dept Dropsie Coll Phila since '46. Religion Edn Assn (vp '42)—Nat Council for Jewish Edn (one of organizers, 1st pres)—Jewish Acad Arts Sci— Palestine Hist Ethnog Soc—Jewish Palestine Exploration Soc—Histadrut Ibrit Am (vp '32)—Assn Supervision and Curriculum Development—Am Oriental Soc—NEA—Nat Conf Jewish Social Welfare (vp '46). Dropsie College, Broad and York St., Phila.†

22 HONORE, (Paul) York. Pottery design and glazes; color research. b'12. Student '29-31 (Highland Park Coll); '31-33 (Beaver Edwards Sch Sculpture); '48-49 (Leicester Coll Arts and Sci Eng). Color research, invention of color photo process, development of flame lustre glazes, design in ceramics. Author: Pottery Making From the Ground Up; New Pictorial Use of an Old Medium. Owner Honore Community Pottery since '35; art dir West Nottingham Acad since '37. Am Ceramic Soc—Am Fed Artists. Honore Community, Port Deposit, Md.†

23 HOOD, Elschen. Color development. b'05. Student '23-24 (U Wis); '29, '38 (Louvre). Research on design, color gradation measurement, correlation system of estimating color volume for use in control of commercial production. Author articles in field. With research dept J Walter Thompson Co '26-28, art dept asst T J Erwin '26-28; Marshall Field & Co '29-34; with George B Peck's '34-38; with Spool Cotton Co since '39, dir color research from '47. Inter-Soc Color Council— Fashion Group Inc — Occupational Therapy Assn Am. Spool Cotton Co., 745 Fifth Av., NYC 22.

24 HOOD, George William. Soil and water conservation; Nursery; Horticulture; Forestry. b'88. BSc in hort and forestry '10—MSc '14 (O State U). Auture '29; Viability and Germination of thor: Farm Horticulture '20; Horticul-Tree Seeds '38; Planting of Woody Plants for Erosion Control '39; Seed Collecting of Woody Plants '40; Use of Structures in Gully Control '47; Investigations in Erosion Control and Reclamation of Eroded Land in the Ozark Highlands '48; also articles in field. Forester Soil Conservation Service US Dept Agr '34-36, regional forester '36-43; research specialist in soil and water conservation cooperating with U Ark since '43. Soc Hort Sci— Soc Am Foresters—O Acad Sci—Mich Acad Sci—Neb State Hort Soc—Gamma Sigma Delta—Sigma Kappa Zeta. Experiment Station, Batesville, Arkansas.†◎

25 HOOD, J(oseph) Douglas. Systematic e n t o m o l o g y (Thysanoptera, or thrips, classification); Growth, b'89. AB '10 (U Ill); MA '13 (George Washington U); PhD '32 (Cornell U). Author articles in field. Prof biol Cornell U; collaborator US Bur Entomol since '31. AAAS(F)—Entomol Soc Am (F, charter mem)—Am Assn Econ Entomol—Am Soc Zool—NY Entomol Soc —Entomol Soc Washington—Biol Soc Washington—Entomol Soc Brazil—Natural Hist Soc of Canal Zone (hon)— Sigma Xi—Phi Kappa Phi. Roberts Hall, Cornell Univ., Ithaca, N.Y.◎

26 HOOD, Thurman Losson. Robert Browning. b'88. AB '08—AM '09— PhD '24 (Harvard). Editor: Letters of Robert Browning '33; also articles in field. Asso prof Eng Trinity Coll since '41. Boston Browning Soc (hon life)—Phi Beta Kappa. Guggenheim fellow '32-33. Trinity College, Hartford 6, Conn.

10 HOOK, James William. Machine tools; Electric utilities. b'84. BME '05—ME '12 (Ia State Coll). Research on vacuum steam heating, particularly with thermostatic steam radiator traps, screw threads, machine shop practices. Author articles in field. Pres and dir Allied Machinery Co Am NY '16-23; pres and treas Geometric Tool Co New Haven '23-44; pres and dir United Illuminating Co of New Haven '39-42, chmn bd since '42; dir Acme Wire Co since '27. AAAS—Am Soc ME—Acad Polit Sci. Awarded Marston medal Ia State Coll '40. 80 Temple St., New Haven 6.

11 HOOKER, Edward Niles. Literature and literary criticism (Neo-classical period). b'02. AB '23 (Union Coll); MA '25 (Syracuse U); PhD '32 (Johns Hopkins U). Co-founder Journal of English Literary History '34, co-editor '34-40; co-founder Augustan Reprint Society '46 and co-editor of its publications since '46. Author: The Critical Works of John Dennis (2 vols) '39, '43; also articles in field. Instr U Calif '36-38; asst prof '38-43, asso prof '43-48, prof since '48. Modern Lang Assn—Modern Humanities Research Assn—Phi Beta Kappa. Guggenheim fellow '42-43. University of California, Los Angeles 24.

12 HOOLE, W(illiam) Stanley. Southern United States literary history; Early American humor. b'03. AB '24—AM '31 (Wofford Coll); PhD '34—teaching fellow '31-34 (Duke U); BLS '48 (N Tex State Coll). Author: Charleston Periodicals '36; Sam Slick in Texas '45; The Ante-Bellum Charleston Theatre '46; Let the People Read '46; A Library for Lauderdale '48. Co-author: Mississippi Study of Higher Education '45; Studies of Higher Education in the South '47; A Study of Stillman Institute '47; also articles in field. Asst prof Eng Birmingham-So Coll '34-35, librarian '35-37; librarian Baylor U Waco Tex '37-39; dir libraries N Tex State Coll '39-44; dir libraries U Ala since '44; library cons So Assn Colls and Secondary Schs since '42; mem Commn Instns Higher Edn since '47, chmn Library Com since '47. SE Library Assn—Ala Hist Assn—Ala Library Assn—ALA—So Hist Assn—S Atlantic Modern Lang Assn—Phi Beta Kappa. University of Alabama Library, University, Ala.

13 HOOPER, Bert Leslie. Prosthodontics (Construction artifical teeth, artifical dentures). b'93. DDS '15 (U Neb). Developed method of recording facial features and dimensions by use of photograph and mechanical instruments; method denture construction preserving natural appearance of natural teeth and face; advanced theory of muscular balance and equilibrium for stability of artificial dentures. Author: Prosthodontics as a Fine Art '27; Instructions for the Edentulous Patient '32; A Broader Perspective of Denture Service '33; Denture Esthetics '33; Functional Factors in the Selection and Arrangement of Artificial Teeth '34; Immediate Denture Technique insuring the Preservation of Facial Dimensions '37; others. Prof and chmn dept dental sci, coll dentistry U Neb since '39 (part time), dean coll dentistry since '39 (part time). Am Bd Prosthodontics (diplomate)—Am Dental Assn (chmn prosthetic sect '33 '34)—Internat Coll Dentists(F)—Acad Internat Dentistry(F) —Am Acad Denture Prosthetics(pres '37)—Am Denture Soc(pres '39)—In-

ternat Assn Dental Research—Pierre Fauchard Acad—Omicron Kappa Upsilin—Sigma Xi—Council Dental Edn. 1004 Sharp Bldg., Lincoln 8, Neb.

14 HOOPER, Frank Fincher. Limnology (Plankton). b'18. BA '39 (U Calif); PhD '48 (U Minn); '42-43 (U Chicago Inst Meteorol). Plankton investigation of waters of Yukon Territory and Alaska, limnology and fisheries biology of a northwestern Minnesota Lake, investigation of bottom fauna organisms of Douglas Lake Michigan. Author articles in field. Instr zool U Mich since '48. Ecol Soc Am—Am Soc Limnol and Oceano—Am Soc Zool—Am Micros Soc—Am Soc Ichthyologists Herpetologists—Mich Acad Sci—Minn Acad Sci—Phi Beta Kappa—Sigma Xi. Department of Zoology, University of Michigan, Ann Arbor.

15 HOOPER, Richard H. Television. b'03. AB '28 (Miami U). Producer of television shows in numerous cities of US and abroad. Director television exploitation for Nat Broadcasting Co since '48; television cons to pub relations dir of UN. Am Television Soc —Nat Television Council (founder, first pres)—Radio Mfrs Assn (chmn exhibition com)—Internat Assn Broadcasters (exhibition com). Front and Cooper St., Camden, N. J.

16 HOOPER, William Thomas Francis, Jr. Reinforced concrete (Design); Construction (Earthquake, bomb resistant). b'15. BS (civil engring) '37 (Purdue); MS '41 (U Pittsburgh). Research on admixtures and puzzolans for development lightweight precast reinforced concrete roof slab; developed concrete mix using flyash; designed earthquake resistant buildings Puerto Rican Air Base, bomb-resistant fortifications Chesapeake Bay Harbor defenses; wrote preliminary specifications for permanent earthquake and typhoon resistant structures Okinawa bases. Author: Reinforced Concrete Design and Construction '52. Structural designer, asst chief engr defense projects Graham, Anderson, Probst & White, Chicago and asst chief engr Harbor Defense projects, Greeley & Hansen Norfolk Va '41-42; asst prof civil engring Northwestern Tech Inst '46-50; partner Staben & Hooper & Asso (architects, engrs) Waukegan Ill since '49. Air corps and corps engrs US Army '42-46, in charge air field, bldg constrn islands in Western Pacific. Am Soc CE—Am Concrete Inst —ASTM—Sigma Xi. Registered structural engr Ill, professional engr Ill, Wis. 222 Market St., Waukegan, Ill.

17 HOOPES, Thomas Temple. European and Japanese arms and armor; Firearms prior to 1800. b'98. AB '19 (Harvard); AM '26—research fellow in fine arts '29-30—PhD '31 (NYU). Author articles in field. Asst curator dept arms and armor Met Mus Art NYC '20-27; curator City Art Mus St Louis since '36. Royal Geog Soc(F)— Royal Soc Arts(F)—Verein fur Historische Waffenkunde. Ritterkreuz Verdienst Orden, Austria '36; fellow Carnegie Corp '34-35; fellow Guggenheim Memorial Found '31. City Art Museum, St. Louis 5. H: 48 Washington Terrace, St. Louis 12.

18 HOOTON, Earnest Albert. Physical anthropology (Races, fossil, race mixture, constitutional types, human evolution, criminals, human eugenics, inheritance, craniology); Primates. b'87. BA '07—ScD '33 (Lawrence Coll Appleton Wis); MA '08—PhD '11 (U Wis); Rhodes Scholar '10-13—diploma in anthrop '12—BLitt '13 (Oxford). Author: Ancient Inhabitants of the Canary Islands '25; The Indians of Pecos '30; Up from the Ape '46; Apes, Men

and Morons '37; Crime and the Man, The American Criminal, vol I, Twilight of Man '39; Why Men Behave Like Apes and Vice Versa '40; Man's Poor Relations '42; "Young Man, You Are Normal" '45; also articles in field. Prof anthrop Harvard since '30; curator somatology Peabody Mus since '14. AAAS(F)—Royal Anthrop Inst— Am Acad Arts Sci—Am Anthrop Assn —Am Assn Phys Anthrop—Am Genetic Assn—Am Philos Soc—Am Soc Naturalists—Nat Acad Sci—Phi Beta Kappa. Peabody Museum, Cambridge, Mass.◎

19 HOOVER, C(lifford) Dale. Potash (Fixation, release). b'07. Student '25-27 (Sterling Coll Kan); AB '34—MS '35 (Kan State Tchrs Coll Pittsburg Kan); PhD '39 (Ia State Coll). Member advisory board National Soybean Improvement Council. Research asst Ia Agrl Expt Sta '35-39; asso agron Miss State Coll and Expt Sta '39-46, head dept agron since '46; collaborator southern region soil and fertilizer lab BPISAE USDA '48-50. Nat Phosphate Research Com (chmn sub-com So region on phosphate)—Am Soc Agron (state rep)—Soil Sci Soc Am (co-chmn soil terminology com)—State Farm Bur Fedn.◎

20 HOOVER, Edgar Malone. American economy; Location of industry. b'07. AB '28—AM '30—PhD '32—Shaw travel fellow '28-29 (Harvard). Author: Location of the Shoe Industry in the United States '32; Location Theory and the Shoe and Leather Industries '37; Economia Geografica '43; The Location of Economic Activity '48; also articles in field. Faculty U Mich '36-47, prof econ '46-47; staff econ Council Econ Advisers exec office of the President Washington since '47. Lt USNR assigned to OSS in European theater as econ intelligence analyst '44-45. Am Econ Assn. Recipient of Henry Russel Award '40. Council of Economic Advisers, Executive Office of the President, Washington 25.†

21 HOOVER, Harvey Daniel. Liturgics. b'80. Student '94-96—STD '18 (Gettysburg (Pa) Coll); AB '99—AM '00—BD '02 (Susquehanna U); PhD '07 (Ill Wesleyan U); DD '22 (Wittenberg Coll); LittD '35 (Carthage (Ill) Coll). Author: Master Mind; Lift Up Your Eyes. Editor: Bible Reading Fellowship monthly; Light for Today; Nat Luth Edn Assn (5 vols); Lutheran Church Quarterly. Prof Pastoral Theology and liturgies and dean Sem Chapel Luth Theol Sem Gettesburg since '26; sec common service book com United Luth Ch Am. Religious Edn Assn—Luth Hist Acad—Ch Social Workers—Am Hymn Soc(NY)— Hymn Soc London—Pi Gamma Mu. Lutheran Theological Seminary, Gettysburg, Pa.◎

22 HOOVER, John Edgar. Federal Bureau of Investigation; Criminology. b'95. LLB '16—LLM '17—LLD '35 (George Washington U); 16 honorary degrees US colleges and universities. Director Federal Bureau of Investigation, charged with investigating violations of US laws, collecting evidence in cases in which US is or may be a party in interest, and collecting US criminal statistics; upholding certain criminal laws of US passed by Congress such as Bank Robery Act, Kidnaping Statute, Sabotage and Espionage Acts; directing FBI National Academy; organized a centralized fingerprint collection and built up file to over 125,000,000 sets of prints; established bureau's scientific laboratory. Author: Persons in Hiding '38; also articles in field. Entered US Dept Justice '17, espionage work '17-19, spl asst to atty gen US '19-21, asst dir

Bur Investigation '21-24, dir Fed Bur Investigation since '24; member bars District Ct of US for DC, US Ct of Claims US Supreme Ct; mem nat com pub relations Boy Scouts Am. U.S. Department of Justice Building, Washington.

10 HOOVER, Lyman. Chinese history; Chinese Mohammedanism; YMCA world service (Foreign missions). b'01. BA '22 (Butler U); BD '28—grad study '37, MA '48 (Yale); '30-34 (Col Chin Stud, Peiping). Supervised China YMCA work for soldiers, prisoners of war, internees and repatriates '43-46; assisted in rehabilitation and general relief throughout entire China '45-46; YMCA visits in Asia, Europe, South America, Africa '38-44; member or adviser many China relief committees US and China since '37. Author articles in field. Ordained ministry Ch Disciples Christ '24, pastor Congl Ch Northford Conn '24-28. With YMCA since '28, in China since '30, asso gen sec Nat Com China hdqrs Shanghai '43 to '49; spl lecturer Chinese Mohammedanism Coll Chinese Studies '33-36, '38, W China Lang Sch '41-42. Chinese-Am Inst Cultural Relations—Royal Asiatic Soc—Friends of Moslems Soc (exec com since '32). 420 Lexington Av., NYC 17.†

11 HOPE, Fred J. Chemistry of organic dyestuffs. b'09. BS '36 (Poly Inst Brooklyn). Author articles in field. Chem H Kohnstamm & Co Inc '26-38; chem in charge research since '38. Am Chem Soc—Am Assn Textile Chem and Colorists—AAAS—Am Inst Chem(F)—NY Acad Sci (life). H. Kohnstamm & Co., Inc., 537 Columbia St., Brooklyn 31. H: 93 East Lawn Dr., Teaneck, N.J.

12 HOPKINS, Dwight Lucian. Cytology; Protozoology; Amoebae. b'99. BS —MS '23 (U Va); PhD '26 (Johns Hopkins). Author articles in field. Faculty Duke U '28-38, Mundelein Coll '38-45; asso prof biol and chmn div biol sci U Ill Chicago Undergrad Div since '46; lecturer in parisitol and genetics Northwestern U Coll '45-47; AAAS(F)—Am Soc Zool—Ill Acad Sci —Am Soc Protozool (executive com) '49-50)—Sigma Xi. Received grant Am Phil Soc '37-38. University of Illinois Undergraduate Division, Navy Pier, Chicago 11.

13 HOPKINS, Homer Thawley, Jr. Persistence insecticides in soils and soil aeration on nutrition and growth of plants; Effect of cropping practices on earthworm populations. b'13. BSA '35 (U Del); MS (forest soils) '39 (Cornell). Study action chlorinated hydrocarbon insecticides on growth processes of plants; investigation effect of oxygen supply to roots on rate plant growth, on nutritional content plants; field study three-year crop rotation and sod crops to maintain earthworm populations at high level. Coauthor articles: (with Hopp) Effect of Certain Cropping Systems on Winter Populations of Earthworms '46; (with Specht, Hendricks) Plant Growth and Nutrient Accumulation as Controlled by Oxygen Supply to Plant Roots '50. With USDA since '39, soil sci since '46. Am Soc Agron—Soil Sci Soc Am—Am Soc Plant Physiol— Soil Conservation Soc of Am—AAAS. Plant Industry Station, Beltsville, Md. H: Elmwood Rd.

14 HOPKINS, Leonard O. Bridges (Movable); Foundations; Steel structures. b'79. BS (civil engring) '05 (U Me). Research and patent on Trunnion type of bascule bridge, research on movable spans for bridges. Chief designer, chief mech engr and mng engr Strauss Bascule Bridge Co '12-23; chief engr Nashville Bridge Co

since '26. Am Soc CE—Am Soc ME— Tenn Soc Prof Engrs. Nashville Bridge Co., Nashville, Tenn.

15 HOPKINS, Sewell Hepburn. Fishery biology (Oyster mortality); Parasites of fish and molluscs. b'06. BS '27 (Coll William and Mary); '27-28 (Johns Hopkins); MA '29—PhD '33 (U Ill). Independent investigator U.S. Fisheries Biological Laboratory Beaufort North Carolina summer '39; parasites of fish and molluscs; trematodes; biology of crabs. Author articles in field. Asso prof Tex A&M Coll '41-47, prof since '47; asso biologist Va Fisheries Lab '45-46. Am Micros Soc—Am Soc Zoologists—Am Soc Parasitologists—Am Soc Limnology & Oceanography—AAAS— Sigma Xi—Phi Beta Kappa. Biology Department, Agricultural and Mechanical Arts College, College Station, Tex.

16 HOPKIRK, Howard William. Institutional child welfare and care. b'94. AB '20 (Reed Coll Portland Ore); '20-23 (Union Theol Sem NYC). Author: Institutions Serving Children '44. Cons on child care in institutions Child Welfare League Am '24-34, and since '48, exec dir '40-48; supt Albany (NY) Home for children '35-39. Child Welfare League of America, 24 W. 40th St., NYC 18.

17 HOPP, Henry. Soil conservation and management; Tree selection; Earthworms. b'11. BS '31—MS '33— PhD '36 (NY State Coll Forestry); '32-33 (Forstliche Hochschule Germany, U Berlin, Ecole Nationale Des Eaux et Forets France). Author articles in field. With Dept Agr since '37, biometrician office fgn agrl relations since 49. Ecol Soc Am—Soil Conservation Soc Am—Bot Soc Am—Soc Am Foresters—Am Forestry Assn—Sigma Xi. U.S. Department of Agriculture, Office of Foreign Agricultural Relations, Tech Collaboration Branch, Washington.†

18 HORBALY, William. Slavic geography; Agricultural geography (U.S. S.R., Czechoslovakia). b'20. BS '46 (Kent State U); MA '47—PhD '51 (U Chicago); Inst Internat Edn F '49-50 (Charles U, Prague). Research on Soviet agriculture and collectivization, migration of agriculture in Soviet Union, Sovietizing of Czechoslovak agriculture, Czech collective farms. Author: Agricultural Conditions in Czechoslovakia, 1950. Prof geog US Govt since '51. Assn Am Geog—Nat Council Geog Tchrs. H: 837 S. Frederick St., Arlington 4, Va.

19 HORBERG, Carl Leland. Glacial geology and geomorphology (Wyoming, Illinois, Montana, New Mexico). b'10. AB '32 (Augustana Coll, Rock Island); PhD '38 (U Chicago). Author articles: A Major Buried Valley in East-Central Illinois '45; Preglacial Erosion Surfaces in Illinois '46; and others. With U Ill '38-42, Ill Geol Survey '42-46, U Chicago since '46. Geol Soc Am—AAAS—Am Geophys Union—Ill Acad Sci. Department of Geology, University of Chicago, Chicago 37.

20 HORIAK, Erwin Andreas Victor. Design high-speed and supercharged automotive and marine diesel engines. b'01. Diploma (Engring) '23—DSc '36 (U Vienna). Project leader in development "Mercedes Benz" precombustion diesel '32; designed flat diesel engines suitable for installation in buses and rail cars '39, supercharged marine diesel engines '43; design and test of 8, 16 and 32 cylinder v-type high speed diesel engines '42; developed series of small automotive diesel engines operating at speeds up to 3600 rpm, weighing as little as seven

pounds per brake horse power; first coach installation of turbo-charged diesel engine '50. Author articles: Crankshaft and Big End Bearings for High Speed Compression Ignition Engines; Factors Affecting Fuel Consumption; Cylinder Wear in High Speed Diesel (Engines; Entwicklungsarbeiten An Schnellaufenden Fahrzeug Diesel Motoren. Chief engr Liesinger Motoren Fabrik Austria. '25-27; research engr Daimler Benz Actien Gesellschaft Germany '27-33; dir research J&H McLaren Ltd Eng '33-35; chief engr diesel div Hercules Motors Corp Canton O since '35. Soc Automotive Engrs—Soc Mil Engrs. Hercules Motors Corp., Canton 2, O.

21 HORLACHER, Levi Jackson. Animal husbandry (Beef cattle, sheep). b'96. BS Agr '17 (Purdue U); MS '19 (Kan State Coll); '23-47 (U Ky, U Chicago). Author: Sheep Production '27; Sheep '36; The Golden Hoof '36; author articles in field. Asst dean Coll Agrl and Home Econ, U Ky since '39, prof animal husbandry since '18. Am Soc Animal Prodn—Ky Acad Sci—NEA —Ky Edn Assn—Sigma Xi—Gamma Sigma Delta—Thoroughbred Club Am —Ky Purebred Livestock Assn (dir). University of Kentucky, Lexington, Ky. H: 639 Maxwelton Ct., Lexington 44

22 HORN, Charles Lilley. Ammunition (Small arms). LLB '12 (U Minn). Research on ballistics and small arms ammunition. Pres Fed Cartridge Corp since '22; pres Hoffman Engring Co Anoka Minn since '48. 2700 Foshay Tower, Mpls 2.

23 HORN, Edward C(harles). Life histories of marine Polychaetes; Biological effects of radiation. b'16. BS '38 (Trinity Coll); AM '40—PhD '41 (Princeton U). Author articles in field. Instr, asst prof zool Duke U since '46. AAAS—Am Soc Zool—NC Acad Sci—Sigma Xi. Department of Zoology, Duke University, Durham, N.C. H: 2509 Cascadilla St.†

24 HORNBOSTEL, Lloyd. Papermaking machine. b'00. ME '24 (Lehigh U); EE '25 (Westinghouse). Design construction manufacture operation fourdrinier and cylinder paper-making machines. Issued over 100 patents. With Beloit Iron Works since '26, vp in charge engring since '44. ASME— Tech Assn Pulp and Paper Industry. Beloit Iron Works, Beloit, Wis.

25 HORNER, George Frederick. American literature (Humor, newspapers and periodicals, Benjamin Franklin). b'99. BA '21—MA '24 (Pa State Coll); PhD '38 (U NC); '24 (London U); '25-26 (Harvard). Research at British Museum and Bibliotheque Nationale '24-25; studies on Franklin's Dogood Papers. Author articles in field. Asso prof Eng and chmn freshman-sophomore Eng U NC since '45. So Atlantic Modern Lang Assn (asst ed bull '39-50)—Modern Lang Assn —Modern Humanities Research Assn. Department of English, University of North Carolina, Chapel Hill, N.C.

26 HORNUNG, Clarence P. Trade mark design; Printing and industrial designs. b'99. BS '20 (Coll City NY). Early specialties type design, decorative maps, calligraphy, binding designs for publishers sets. Author: Trademarks of Clarence P. Hornung '30; Handbook of Designs and Devices '32, '46; Lettering from A to Z '46; Handbook of Early American Advertising Art '47; Made in U.S.A.; also articles in field. Editor: Bookplates of Harold Nelson '29. Indsl designer employed various times by Internat Bus Machines, Coca-Cola Co, Chase Nat Bank, Richfield Oil Co, Internat Nickel Co,

NY Times, Longines-Wittnauer Watch Co, Pan-American Airways. Am Designers Inst — Typophiles — Am Inst Graphic Arts. 220 E. 46th St., NYC.

10 HOROVITZ, Samuel Bertram. Workmen's compensation; Personal injury. b'97. AB magna cum laude '19—LLB '22 (Harvard). Author: Practice and Procedure under the Mass. Workmen's Compensation Law '30; Horovitz on Workmen's Compensation '44; Current Trends in Workmen's Compensation '47. Chief of workmen's compensation dept Boston Legal Aid Soc '22-32; specializing workmen's compensations cases since '32; workmen's compensation atty Mass Fedn Labor since '32. Nat Assn Claimant's Compensation Attys (editor in chief NACCA Law Jour since '48——Am Bar Assn —Internat Assn Indsl Accidents Bds and Commns (asso). 6 Beacon St., Boston 8.†◎

11 HORTON, Clarence Reuben, Jr. Inland waterway transportation; Naval architecture; Barge design; Propeller design. b'14. BS '36 (MIT). Naval architect Dravo Corp Pittsburgh '36-51, chief constrn engr '44-45 asst dir research and development since '51. Soc Naval Architects and Marine Engrs—Am Welding Soc. Dravo Corp., Neville Island, Pitts. 25.

12 HORTON, Jerome Sweet. Chaparral ecology. b'10. AB '31 (U Redlands); MS '40 (U Calif). Specializes in chaparral ecology, reforestation, erosion control and hydrology, research in watershed management. Author articles in field. Asst prof, prof forest ecol and range management U Calif '31-33; US Forest Service Calif Forest and Range Expt Sta Berkeley since '33. Soc Am Foresters—Ecol Soc Am—Sigma Xi. U.S. Forest Service, Glendora, Calif.†

13 HORWITT, Benjamin N(orman). Steroid hormones; Enzymes. b'16. BS '37 (Coll City NY); Yale U Scholar '39-40—PhD '41—postdoctoral F '41—Finney-Howell F '42-43 (Yale). Research on purification, isolation and identification of steroids from tissues and urines, metabolism of steroid hormones, bioassay of steroid substances and their physiological activity, effects of steroids on enzyme systems, quantitative differences in oxidative enzyme systems in human cancer tissues. Instr biochem NY Med Coll '46-47; asst prof Princeton '47-48; research chem Arco Co '48-49; asst prof Tulane U and research asso Ochsner Found since '49. Capt (biochem) US Army '43-46. AAAS(F)—ACS—Am Assn Cancer Research—Am Inst Chem (F)—Inst Phys(Soc Rheology)—NY Acad Sci—Endocrine Soc—Assn Study Internal Secretions—Phi Beta Kappa —Sigma Xi—Soc Exptl Biol and Med. Research F Brush Found W Reserve U '42-43. Ochsner Medical Foundation, 3503 Prytania St., New Orleans 15.†

14 HOSKEN, James Cuthbert. Industrial and scientific instruments. b'08. MA '30 (Brasenose Coll Oxford). Survey of US instrument industry '46, Swiss and Czechoslovakian '47. With Arthur D Little Inc since '47. Served Brit Army '39-45; deputy asst dir research and development Brit Supply Mission Washington '43-45; tech liaison army ground radar and other electronic equipment. Arthur D. Little, Inc., 30 Memorial Dr., Cambridge 42, Mass.

15 HOSKINS, Halford Lancaster. Modern Middle Eastern politics and communications. b'91. AB '13 (Earlham Coll); Harrison fellow hist '19-20—AM '21—PhD '24(U Pa); '17-19(U Chicago); '21-24 (Harvard). Research in Egyptian archives and travel in Near East under auspices Social Science Research

Council '30; chairman American delegation to International Studies Conference Prague '38; consultant on Middle Eastern matters Department State '42-44. Author: Preliminaries of the World War '18; An Outline of Modern European History '22; British Routes to India '28; European Imperialism in Africa '30; also articles in field. Co-organizer and dir Sch Advanced Internat Studies '44-49; sr specialist internat relations legis ref library div brary of Congress since '49. Middle East Inst—Am Acad Arts Sci—AHA—Am Polit Sci Assn—Council Fgn Relations—Phi Beta Kappa. Library of Congress, Washington 25.

16 HOSKINS, William Muriece. Insect toxicology and physiology; Insecticides. b'96. AB '19—PhD '22 (U Calif). Research on insect nutrition, insect olfactometers and olfactory responses, deposit of insecticides from sprays, residues important to public health, organic compounds as insecticides. Author: Insects and Other Pests Attacking Agricultural Crops '44; Recent Progress in Insect Physiology '35; Insect Biochemistry '40; Organic Insecticides '46; also articles in field. Instr, later asso prof chem U Nev '23-28; asst prof, prof entomol U Calif since '29; chem agrl expt sta U Calif since '47. Am Chem Soc—Soc Exptl Biol and Med—Am Assn Econ Entomol —Entomol Soc Am—AAAS(F). Agriculture Hall, University of California, Berkeley.

17 HOSKINSON, Albert J. Geodetic gravity and astronomy; Tides and currents. b'95. BS '20 (U Calif). Engaged in re-design and construction of three Brown Gravity instruments '35, experimental work with gravity at sea instruments, crystal chronometers, gravimeters. Invented design of photoelectric and power amplifiers '36, thermostatic temperature control and astronomic amplifier for gravity instruments '38; discovered dynamic temperature correction and new pressure correction equation for gravity instruments. Author: Manual of Geodetic Astronomy (with J A Duerkson) '48; Tides and Currents of Portsmouth Harbor (with E A Lelacheur); also articles in field. Jr officer gravity and astronomic parties US Coast Geodetic Survey '30-31, chief party '32-39, chief astronomic party '39-40, scientist gravity at sea expdn West Indies on submarine Barracuda '37, research and exptl work with gravity and astron instruments since Oct '46; asst chief div geodesy United States Coast and Geodetic Survey since '49. Am Geophys Union—Am Astron Soc—AAAS—Washington Philos Soc. Legion of Merit award for work at Ft Sill '46. U.S. Coast and Geodetic Survey, Washington 25.

18 HOSSFELD, Ralph Lowell. Wood chemistry; Lignin. b'14. BS ChE '37 —MS '39 (U Ida); PhD '42 (U Minn). Research on reaction of wood with pure NaSH at elevated temperature, chemistry of lignin and tree bark, wood pulping processes. Co-holder of patents. Author articles in field. Supervisor organic research Marathon Corp chem div Rothschild Wis '42-46; asso prof wood chem Sch Forestry U Minn St Paul since '46. AAAS—Am Chem Soc—Tech Assn Pulp and Paper Industry—Sigma Xi. School of Forestry, University of Minnesota, St. Paul 1.

19 HOSSFIELD, George Leonard. Typewriting (speed). b'98. Ed pub schs. Holder speed title for many years; demonstrates typing methods and techniques; originator one hand touch typewriting. Author: One Hand Touch Typewriting for the Right Hand

'47; One Hand Touch Typewriting for the Left Hand '47; (monograph) Saving Typing Time. Cons for films: Tips on Typing, Duties of a Secretary. With Underwood Corp since '14, head tchrs adv service. Winner many first places, including World's Profl Championship '18, '20, '21, '22, '26, '27, '29, '30, '36, '37. Am Assn Sch Adminstrs—Assn Sch Bus Ofcls—Nat Bus Tchrs Assn—So Bus Edn Assn—Eastern Bus Tchrs Assn—Tri-State Bus Edn Assn. Underwood Corp., One Park Av., NYC 16.

20 HOSTETTER, John Clyde. Glass (Technology, bibliography). b'86. ScB '08—ScM '09—ChE '30—ScD '36 (Bucknell U); ScD '37 (Alfred U). Author articles in field. Pres Mississippi Glass Co St Louis, chmn bd Walsh Refractories Co since '44. Am Ceramic Soc (F, pres '33-34)—Am Inst Chem—AAAS—Ceramic Assn NY (pres '38)—Am Chem Soc—Am Inst Chem Engrs—Franklin Inst (Howard N Potts medal for part in producing the 200-inch mirror of world's largest telescope Calif Inst Tech Obs)—Soc Heating Ventilating Engrs—Illuminating Engr Soc—Am Soc Test Materials—Washington Acad Sci—NY Acad Sci—Am Soc Mil Engrs—English Soc Glass Tech(F)—Deutsche Glastechischen Gesellschaft. Awarded The Nation's (mag) Roll of Honor '34; Significant Sig medal '37. Main and Angelica Sts., St. Louis.

21 HOTCHKISS, A r l a n d Tillotson. Freshwater algae; Vascular aquatic plants. b'18. Student '36-39 (Cortland State Teachers Coll); BS '44 (Buffalo State Teachers Coll); MS '45—candidate PhD (Cornell U). Asst department biology U Louisville. Bot Soc Am—Phycol Soc Am—Bergen Swamp Preservation Soc. Department of Biology, University of Louisville, Louisville, Ky.

22 HOTCHKISS, Willard Eugene. Education; Labor relations. b'74. PhB '97—Pres Andrew D White fellow '02-03—AM '03—Pres White traveling fellow '03-04—PhD '05 (Cornell U); LLD '27 (Northwestern). Author: Judicial Work of Comptroller of the Treasury '11; Higher Education and Business Standards '18; Business in the New Era '29. Editor and co-author: Stanford Conference on Business Education '27; Mechanization in Bituminous Coal Industry '39; also articles in field. Head econ '09-17 Northwestern U, '17-19 Minnesota U; organized Sch Commerce Northwestern U '08, dean until '17; organized Sch Bus Minn U '19; organized Grad Sch Bus Stanford U '25, dean until '32; pres Armour Inst Tech '32-37; Falk prof social relations, later dir humanistic and social studies Carnegie Inst Tech '38-44; secretary Shipbuilding Labor Adjustment Board World War I; exec director National Ind Fed Clothing Mfrs '20-25; mgt consultant since '24; chmn Calif Econ Research Council '26-29; mem President's Emergency Com for Employment '30-31; referee Nat RR Adjustment Bd '36; mem research staff and chmn Gen Code Authority NRA '34; Chief hearings officer, later public member 10th Region NWLB '43-46. Am Econ Assn (vp '13)—Soc Advancement Management—Indsl Relations Research Assn —Natl Acad Arbitrators. 107 Larkin Pl., Santa Monica, Cal.

23 HOTTENSTEIN, Marcus Stephen. Church incorporation and government. b'76. AB '96—AM '99—LLD '43 (Muhlenberg Coll); LLB cum laude '99 (U Pa). Was instrumental in having amended through the judiciary committee of NY State Senate, Section 15 of Religious Corporations Law of NY, relating to the incorporation of governing bodies having authority over churches '18; secured NY charter for

United Lutheran Church in America, merging the Lutheran General Synod, General Council and United Synod in the South '18; secured NY Charter for the West Indies Mission Board of The United Lutheran Church in America '20. 60 East 42d St., NYC 17. H: 1 W. 72d St., NYC 23.

10 HOTTES, Alfred Carl. Home gardening; Floriculture; Annuals; Perennials; Shrubs; Trees. b'91. BS '13—MSA '14 (Cornell U). Author: Book of Annuals; Book of Perennials; Climbers and Ground Covers; 1001 Garden Questions Answered; Book of Shrubs; The Book of Trees; 1001 Christmas Facts and Fancies; Home Gardener's Pronouncing Dictionary; Garden Facts and Fancies; and others. Prof hort O State U '16-28; asso ed Better Homes & Gardens '28-40. Sigma Delta Chi—Sigma Xi. 481 Rosemont St., La Jolla, Calif.†

11 HOU, T. P. Alkalies; Fertilizers; Leather. b'90. SB in chem engring '17 (MIT); MA '19—PhD '21—DSc '44 (Columbia). Chief engr and prodn mgr Pacific Alkali Co of China 10 yrs; chief engr and works mgr '33-44, later pres Yungli Chem Industries Ltd; cons expert on heavy and light industries to China-Am Council '44. Soc Chem Industry of London (hon mem). Yung-li Chem Industries, Ltd., Room 5105, 233 Broadway, NYC.

12 HOUGH, Lynn Harold. Interpretation of religion (Christian humanism). b'77. AB '98 (Scio Coll); BD '05—ThD '19 (Drew Theol Sem); post-grad work (NYU); DD '12 (Mt Union Scio Coll) '18 (Garrett Bibl Inst); LittD '33 (Allegheny Coll) '47 (Coll Puget Sound); LLD '33 (Albion Coll) '28 (U Detroit) '35 (U Pittsburgh); LHD '32 (U Vt); DD '24 (Wesleyan U Conn); JUD '39 (Boston U). Author: The Theology of a Preacher '12; Living Book in a Living Age '18; The Significance of the Protestant Reformation '18; Evangelical Humanism (Fernley lecture at Lincoln Eng) '25; The Church and Civilization '34; The Christian Criticism of Life '41; Adventures in Understanding '41; Patterns of the Mind '42; Living Democracy '43; The Meaning of Human Experience '45. Mem edit bd Religion in Life. Prof homiletics and Christian criticism of life Drew Theol Sem Drew U '30-47, dean '34-47; vis prof Emmanuel Coll Victoria U Toronto '47; chancellor's lectr Queen's U '47. Soc Bibl Lit and Exegesis. H: 1165 Fifth Av., NYC 29.†☺

13 HOUGHTON, Henry Garrett. Physical meteorology; Fog; Clouds; Spray nozzles. b'05. BS '26—DSc (hon) (Drexel Inst Tech); SM (MIT). Research on physical properties of fog, transmission of light through fog and development of method for the local dissipation of natural fog; research on physics of clouds. US patent on method of dispeling fog and on spray nozzle. Author articles in field. With MIT since '28, prof and head dept meteorol since '45. AAAS(F)—Am Geophys Union—Am Meteorol Soc (pres '46-47). Room 24-514, Massachusetts Institute of Technology, Cambridge 39, Mass.†☺

14 HOUGHTON, Herbert Pierrepont. Languages (Indo-Iranian, Basque, Coptic, Ethiopic). b'80. AB '01—AM '04 (Amherst Coll); fellow in Greek '05-07—PhD '07 (Johns Hopkins); LittD '18 (Waynesburg Coll); LLD '19 (Ripon Coll); student in archeol Athens and Rome '29-30. Author: Moral Significance of Animals as Indicated in Greek Proverbs '15; The Business of the College '16; On Presenting Sanskrit in a Small College '27; Studies in the Languages of the Caucasus '46.

The Basque Verb '44; The Coptic Verb '48; The Amharic Verb '48. Prof and chmn dept classical lang Carleton Coll '23. American Philol Assn—Am Oriental Soc—Finno-Ugric Soc. Helsinki—Indian Philo Soc, Poona—Soc Bibl Lit and Exegesis — Soc d' Archeologie Copte, Cairo—Phi Beta Kappa. 1919 Lewis Mountain Road, Charlottesville, Va.†☺

15 HOUK, Ivan Edgar. Dams; Hydrology; Hydrometeorology; Irrigation. b'88. BE '11 (Ia State U). Research on rainfall, interception, runoff and flood measurements, cloudburst investigations, flood researches and forecasting, channel-flow and soil-moisture; evaporation, transpiration, evapo-transpiration, consumptive use of water, silting of reservoirs, silt control in canals; design of arch and gravity dams including gravity, twist and non-linear stress analyses, trial-load method of stress analyses, foundation and abutment deformations, ice and uplift pressures, temperature control and earthquake effects; member Engineering Foundation Committee on Arch Dam Investigations. Author: Irrigation Engineering (vol 1) '51. Co-author: Engineering Foundation Arch Dam Investigation Reports (vol 2) '34; (and editor) Boulder Canyon Project Final Reports (11 vol) '38-41. Contributor: Engineering Foundation Arch Dam Investigation Reports (vol 1 and 3) '27, '33; Davis Handbook of Applied Hydraulics '42. City engr Dayton O '21-23; with Bur Reclamation '23-45; private practice since '45 as cons engr. Am Soc CE (pres Dayton O sect '23, Colo sect '30, mem com on uplift in masonry dams '51)—Am Geophys Union—AAAS(F) —Am Meteorol Soc—Colo Soc Engrs —Am Standards Assn—Rocky Mt Hydraulic Lab—Am Concrete Inst—Colo-Wyo Acad Sci—W Snow Conf. 2585 Cherry St., Denver 7.

16 HOULGATE, Carroll Deke. History of collegiate football. b'05. Research since '25 on All-American players, complete football records including scores, coaches and game highlights of 278 American Colleges; Compiler: The Football Thesaurus—77 Years On The American Gridiron. Author: Frans Nelson '40. Press Club. 1040 W. Santa Barbara Av., LA.

17 HOUSE, William P. Mountains (Climbing, equipment). b'13. BA '35—MF '37 (Yale). Mountaineering including first ascents and new routes British Columbia, Mexico, American Rocky Mountains and Himalayas; member Karakoram Expedition in western Himalayas which reached height of 26,00 feet on Mountain K2 '38. Co-author: (with R H Bates) Five Miles High '39. Specialist mountain and Arctic equipment and training War Dept World War II. Am Alpine Club (bd dirs)—Appalachian Mountain Club. R.F.D., Chesham, N.H.

18 HOUSLEY, John Elmer. Electrochemical engineering and operation; Oil maintenance; industrial power generation and distribution; Industrial plants. b'93. BS EE '15 (U Tenn). Research on transformer and oil maintenance, electrochemical engineering and operation, power generation and distribution, load control, large industrial substations, reconditioning of insulating oil by activated alumina. Elec engr Aluminum Ore Co East St Louis Ill '15-22; sales engr Aluminum Co Am Kansas City '22-24, asst dist elec supt Alcoa Tenn '24-27, supt power '27-43, dist power mgr since '43. AIEE (chmn Tenn sect '38-39, vp so dist '41-42, pres '46-47, member numerous coms)—Electrochem Soc. Aluminum Company of America, Alcoa, Tenn.†☺

19 HOUTCHENS, H(arold) Max. Child psychology and development (Delinquency); Clinical psychology (Behavior and personality disorders). b'11. BS '33 (U Ida); MA '35—PhD '37 (U Ia). Author articles in field. Br chief clinical psychol VA Seattle '46-50, now asst chief psychologist, Washington; cons several local and state welfare agencies. Am Psychol Assn (F, divs clinical and abnormal psychol, personality and social psychol, cons psychol, counseling and guidance psychol, military psychol)—Am Assn Study Mental Deficiency(F)—AAAS—Sigma Xi. Diplomate Am Bd Examiners Clin Psychol. Exchange Building, Seattle, Wash. H: Apt. 102, 19 Riggs Rd., Washington 11.

20 HOVANITZ, William. Genetics; Cytology; Zoogeography; Environmental physiology. b'15. BS '38 (U Calif); PhD '43 (Calif Inst Tech); fellow zool '43-45 (Nat Research Council); Rackham fellow '45 (U Mich). Research on genetics and environment, colors of insects, genetics of adaptation, chromosome structure, geographical distribution of butterflies. Asst prof biol U Detroit '46; asst prof bot U Mich '46-48, asst biol Lab Vertebrate Biol '46-48, research asso Bot Gardens '46-48, collaborator since '48; asst prof biol Wayne U since '48. Genetics Soc Am —Ecol Soc Am—Entomol Soc Am—Arctic Inst NA (asso)—Calif Acad Sci (life)—Mich Acad Sci Arts Letters—Sigma Xi. University of Michigan, Ann Arbor.

21 HOVDE, Bryn(jolf) J(akob). Adult and international education; Housing; Scandinavia. b'96. AB '16 (Luther Coll, Ia); AM '19—PhD '24 (State U Ia). Author: Diplomatic Relations of the United States with Sweden and Norway '21; The Scandinavian Countries, 1720-1865 '44. Editor: The Evergreen House Report on Urban Planning '44. Acting dir management div US Housing Authority Washington '39-40; chief div cultural cooperation US Dept State '44-45; tech expert on staff Am delegation to UN Conf San Francisco '45; tech sec on staff Am del to London Conf to establish UNESCO '45; chmn bd Nat Public Housing Conf; vp Inst Internat Edn. Dir dept pub welfare City Pittsburgh 36-38; adminstr Housing Authority Pittsburgh '38-44; pres New Sch Social Research NYC '45-50; Fulbright Resrch Scholar Norway '50-51; vis prof U Wis '51-52; now dir Pittsburgh Housing Assn. AHA—Norwegian—Am Hist Assn—Am Soc Pub Adminstrn—Nat Assn Housing Officials. Awarded Guggenheim fellowship '30-31, Am-Scandinavian Found fellowship '32. Room 306, 200 Ross St., Pitts 19.☺

22 HOVEY, Almon Guion. Synthetic resins; Vegetable oils. b'01. BS '23 (Dartmouth Coll); MS '28 (Union Coll). Holds patents on synthetic resins. Author articles in field. Analytical and research chem Remington Arms Co '23-24; research chem Gen Elec Co '24-33; dir research Reichhold Chemicals '33-44; in charge new chemicals dept Gen Mills Inc Min '47-49; research staff Archer-Daniels-Midland Co since '50. Am Oil Chem Soc — AAAS — Am Assn Textile Chem and Colorists — Minn Indsl Chem Forum. Archer-Daniels-Midland Co., Minneapolis, Minn.

23 HOVORKA, Frank. Thermodynamics; Ultrasonics; Electrochemistry. b'97. BA '22 (Ia State Teachers Coll); MS '23—PhD '25 (U Ill). Author articles in field. With Western Reserve U since '25, prof chem since '42, dir U Chem Labs since '42, chmn department of chemistry since '50. Am Chem Soc—AAAS(F)—Electrochem Soc —Soc Chem

Industry Gt Brit—Chem Soc London(F) —Faraday Soc London—Am Electroplaters Soc. Western Reserve University, Cleveland 6. H: 2593 Exeter Rd., Cleveland Heights 18.

10 HOWARD, Arthur David. Geomorphology; Glaciology. b'06. BS '29—MS '31 (NYU); PhD '37 (Columbia). New York University delegate to 17th International Geologic Congress, Moscow '37; geologist with US Navy Antarctic expedition '46-47; research on hurricane damage to New York shorelines, glaciation in eastern Montana and western North Dakota; studies of geologic history of Yellowstone Canyon, terrace studies in US and Hawaii, classification of landforms, origin of pediments; ice investigations in Antarctica. Author books and articles in field. Asso prof geol Stanford U since '48; mem US Geol Survey. Geol Soc Am—Am Geophys Union—AAAS—NY Acad Sci—Washington Geol Soc—Am Geog Soc—Nat Geog Soc—Am Polar Soc—Arctic Inst NA—Sigma Xi. Awarded A Cressy Morrison Prize in natural sci NY Acad Sci '35. Stanford University, Stanford, Calif.

11 HOWARD, August. Antarctic history. b'10. Student '27 (Townsend Harris Hall, City Coll NY); '31 (NYU). Editor and publisher Little America Times for friends and relatives of second Byrd expedition and Lincoln Ellsworth Trans-Antarctic Flight expedition '33-35; Howard Island in Antarctic named in his honor. Editor: The Polar Times since '35. With nat staff Boy Scouts of Am since '28 as pub relations officer. Am Polar Soc (founder '34, sec since '34). Boy Scouts of America, 2 Park Av., NYC.

12 HOWARD, Charles Spaulding. Irrigation water; Dissolved and suspended matter; Chemistry of natural waters. b'96. BS '18 (Worcester Poly Inst); MS—PhD '28 (American U). Author articles in field. Chem US Geol Survey since '20. Am Chem Soc —ASCE—AAAS—Am Water Works Assn—Am Geophys Union. U.S. Geological Survey, Box 2657, Fort Douglas, Salt Lake City.

13 HOWARD, Charles Wilber. Education; College administration; Public school administration. b'49. BS '22—MS '29 (Kan State Coll); EdD '37 (Stanford). Vice chairman committee reorganization school district Walla Walla County Wash '42-44. Prof edn and psychology Whitman Coll '31-44, dir secondary ednl conf '35-42; vis prof edn U Mont summers '38 '39, San Jose State Coll summer '40; prof psychology and dean coll Lewis and Clark Coll Portland Ore '44-50, dean faculty since '50. NEA—Am Coll Personnel Assn (membership com '51-52)—Pacific NW Personnel Assn (sec '46)—Pacific NW Intercollegiate Athletic Conf (bd since '46; sec-treas '49; pres '50)—NW Assn Secondary and High Schs (commn on higher edn '39-44, exec com '42-45)—Pi Kappa Delta—Sigma Delta Chi—Phi Delta Kappa. Lewis and Clark College, Portland, Ore.◎

14 HOWARD, David G. Thermal relay and variable speed induction motors. b'90. BS '13—EE '41 (Worcester Poly Inst). Holder patents in field. Prof elec engring US Naval Acad since '19, lt Naval Reserve '17-19. AIEE—Inst Radio Engrs—AAAS—Nat Geog Soc—Sigma Xi. U.S. Naval Academy, Annapolis, Md.

15 HOWARD, Frank Leland. Minting; Coinage. b'07. BS '30—MS '32 (U Ky); PhD '33 (U Va). Author articles in field. Asst dir Mint since '38. Beta Gamma Sigma. Bureau of the Mint, Treasury Department, Washington.

16 HOWARD, Frank Leslie. Plant pathology; Mycology; Fungicides; Chemotherapeutants. b'03. BS '25 (Ore State); PhD '30 (Ia U); '24 (Calif U); '25-28 (Cornell U); '30-32 res fellow (Harvard U). Author articles in field. Prof plant path RI State Coll '32-45; head dept plant path-entomol RI Agrl Expt Sta since '46. Am Phytopath Soc—Mycol Soc Am—Bot Soc Am—Am Soc Hort Sci. Nat Research Council fellow in biol sci '30-32. Taft Laboratory, Rhode Island State College, Kingston, R.I.

17 HOWARD, Fred Maximilian. Paper board. b'98. BS '20 (U Amsterdam); '22 (Tech Hochschule Berlin, Charlottenburg). Research on sugar chemistry and manufacture of paper board. Comptroller and spl asst to pres Clifton, Whippany, and Durham Paper Bd Co Inc since '43. Tech Assn Pulp and Paper Industry—ACS. 1 Ackerman Av., Clifton, N.J.

18 HOWARD, George Wilberforce. Bridges (Military); Deserts (Environmental effects); Dredging. b'11. BS (CE) '32—CE '38 (Miss State Coll); MS '42 (George Washington U). Study effect of rifling in pipes of hydraulic dredges for transportation sand-water mixtures with minimum power requirements; development optimum design of rifling to provide most material transported per horsepower for various sand and water mixtures; improvement and development fixed and floating military bridges for use by Army; engineering tests on models fixed and floating bridges and auxiliary equipment; studies on effect of environmental factors in desert on equipment used by Engineers Corps; director program of materials, packaging development and climatic research in desert. Author articles: Effects of Rifling on Four-Inch Pipe Transporting Solids '41; Determination of Pipeline Velocities in Brackish Water '49, and others. Co-author: (with John Giliberto) Impact Tests on Military Bridges '48. Project engr and chief hydraulics research center US Waterways Expt Sta '32-39; chief research sect civil works div Office Chief Engrs Washington '39-41; chief bridge br Engr Bd '41-43, with Yuma Test Br '43-49; chief bridge and marine test br Civil and Mil Engring Dept '49-50; chief tech service dept Engr Research and Development Labs Ft Belvoir since '50. Am Soc CE—Soc Am Mil Engrs—Tau Beta Pi. Technical Service Department, Engineer Research and Development Laboratories, Ft. Belvoir, Va. H: Concord Hill Farm, Roseville.

19 HOWARD, Grace Elizabeth. Lichens (Taxonomy, distribution); Fungi. b'86. BA '11—MS '20 (U Wash); PhD '23 (Washington U); Atkinson fellow '31-32 (Wellesley Coll). Identifies, locates lichens for various institutions, companies, private individuals. Author: Lichens of the State of Washington '49; also articles in field. Asso prof bot Wellesley Coll since '38, curator herbarium since '46. Mycol Soc Am —AAAS(F)—Sullivant Moss Soc—Bot Soc Am—Sigma Xi. Department of Botany, Wellesley College, Wellesley 81, Mass.†

20 HOWARD, Harry Nicholas. History, foreign affairs and relations of the Balkans, Near East and Eastern Europe (Turkey, Greece). b'02. AB '24 (William Jewell Coll); Gregory fellow in hist '25-27—AM '27 (U Mo); PhD '30 (U Calif). Adviser US delegate UN Committee on Greece '47, special committee Greece '47-48. Author: The Partition of Turkey; A Diplomatic History '13-23 '31; A Study in the Recent History of the Balkan and Near Eastern Peoples '36; The Problem of the Turkish Straits '47; The United Nations and the Problem of Greece '47; The General Assembly and the Problem of Greece '47; (with R J Kerner) The Balkan Conferences and the Balkan Entente '30-35; also articles in field. Spl asst div Greek, Turkish and Iranian affairs Dept State '47-49; UN advisor Bur Near East, South Asian, African Affairs since '49. AHA—Am Acad Polit Social Sci—Am Soc Internat Law—Middle East Inst—Phi Alpha Theta Department of State, Washington.◎

21 HOWARD, Hildegarde (Mrs. Henry Anson Wylde). Fossil birds; Natural history (United States). b'01. BA '24—MA '26—PhD '28 (U Calif). Author: A Review of the Fossil Bird, Parapavo californicus (Miller) from Pleistocene Asphalt Beds of Rancho La Brea '27; The Avifauna of Emeryville Shellmound '29; Eagles and Eagle-like Vultures of Pleistocene of Rancho La Brea '32; The Rancho La Brea Caracara: A New Species '38; A Review of the American Fossil Storks '42; Fossil Birds '45; A Review of the Pleistocene Birds of Fossil Lake, Oregon '46; New Avian Records of the Pliocene of California '48; also articles in field. Curator avian paleontol Los Angeles Mus since '39. Geol Soc Am(F)—Am Ornithol Union (F, mem com relief European ornithologists)—AAAS(F)—Cooper Ornithol Club (mem bd dirs, sec)—Soc Vertebrate Paleontol—So Calif Acad Sci (mem bd dir)—Soc Study Evolution—Phi Beta Kappa—Sigma Xi. Los Angeles County Museum, Los Angeles 7.◎

22 HOWARD, James Harry. Gem cutting. b'87. Student pub schools. Author: The Working of Semi-precious Stones '31; Handbook for the Amateur Lapidary '35; The Revised Lapidary Handbook '46; also articles in field. Elec engr Huntington and Guerry Inc Greenville SC. 504 Crescent Av., Greenville, S.C.†

23 HOWARD, Richard A(lden). West Indies flora (Investigation); Cuba; Dominican Republic; Survival in tropics (Human). b'17. BA '38 (Miami U, O); MA '40—PhD '42 (Harvard). Monographic studies on Icacinaceae, floristics studies of Caribbean Islands; participated botanical expeditions Adirondacks '36, western US '37, Cuba '40, '41, Puerto Rico and Hispaniola '46, Bahamas '48; organized and conducted jungle survival school for Army; research on problems of surviving in tropics and how to live off land in tropics. Author articles: Comparative Morphology of the Icacinaceae (series) '41-48; Studies of the Icacinaceae (series) '41-48; Notes on the Plants of Cuba (series) '47-48. Asst prof bot Harvard since '48. AAAS —Bot Soc Am—Am Soc Plant Taxonomists—Torrey Bot Club—New Eng Bot Club—Sigma Xi. Awarded Legion of Merit war services. Biological Laboratories, Harvard University, Cambridge, Mass.

24 HOWARD, Richard Foster. History of art; German museums. b'02. BS '24—grad student '29-31 (Harvard). '31 (Inst Human Relations Yale). Dir Dallas Mus Fine Arts '35-42; commd capt field arty US Army '42, lt col '44, chief Monuments Fine Arts and Archives Sect OMGUS '46-48; dir Des Moines Art Center '49-50. Fed Art Washington—Am Assn Mus—Western Assn Art Museum Dirs. Thompson, Conn.

25 HOWARD, Walter Egner. Vertebrate ecology; Mammalogy (Rodents); Ornithology; Economic zoology; Herpetology. b'17. AB '39 (U Calif); MS '41—PhD '48 (U Mich). Research on degree to which rodents compete with livestock for forage on range lands, life history of pocket gopher, protection of broadcast seeds from rodents and birds, dispersal and inbreeding of a population of deermice. Author articles in field. Lect zool, assistant zool in expt sta U Calif since '47. Cooper Ornithol Club—Am Soc Mammalogists Wildlife Soc—Am Soc Range Management—Am Soc Ichthyologists Herpetologists—Ecol Soc Am—Sigma Xi. Department of Zoology, University of California, Davis, Calif.

10 HOWE, Eugene Everett. Amino acids. Biochemistry. b'12. BS '36—MS '37 (Kan State Coll); PhD '40 (U Ill). Author articles in field. Granted patents on synthesis of tryptophane and amino acid solution and process for preparing same. Research chem, later head process development of natural products now head of nutritional laboratory Merck and Co Inc Rahway NJ since '40. Am Chem Soc—NY Acad Sci—AAAS—Sigma Xi. Merck and Co., Inc., Rahway, N.J.

11 HOWE, Henry (Van Wagenen). Micropaleontology; Ostracoda; Gulf Coast stratigraphy; Louisiana geology. b'96. AB '16 (U Ore); '16-17 (Yale); '19-21 (U Calif); PhD '22 (Stanford U). Author articles in field. Dean coll arts and sci La State U '44-49, director school geology since '32. AA AS—Geol Soc Am—Paleontol Soc—Am Assn Petroleum Geol—Soc Econ Paleontol Mineral—Geol and Mining Soc Am Univs—Am Geophys Union—Phi Beta Kappa—Sigma Xi—Phi Kappa Phi. 647 Louisiana State University Av., Baton Rouge, La.

12 HOWE, James Virgil. Ballistics (Small arms). b'89. Student '06-08 (Pratt Inst). Research and development of small arms and ammunition, diesel engines. Holds patents on projectiles and reamers, others pending. Author: The Modern Gunsmith '34; The Amateur Guncraftsman '38; Arms in History '49; also articles in field. Research US Frankford Arsenal Phila '15-23, Ford Motor Co '27-30; ballistic engr Inst Criminal Sci Washington '36-39; research engr Cummins Engine Co Columbus Ind '39-41; lab US Frankford Arsenal Phila '41-43. Archeol Soc Va—Hist Soc Va. Escondido, Ill.

13 HOWE, John Wallace. Tropical animal husbandry. b'01. Diploma '21 (Provincial Sch Agr Olds Alberta); BSc '25 (U Alberta); MSc '28—PhD '46 (Ia State Coll); '35 (U Cambridge). Author articles in field. Dir div agr Tex Coll Arts and Industry since '48. Am Soc Animal Prodn—Am Dairy Sci Assn—AAAS—Agrl Inst Can—Alberta Inst Agrologists—Can Soc Animal Prodn—Gamma Sigma Delta—Sigma Xi. Division of Agriculture, College of Arts and Industries, Kingsville, Tex.

14 HOWE, Laurence Lee. Greek and Roman history (to 500); Near Eastern history (to 1200); Roman coins and political thought; Ancient coin portraiture. b'07. AB '29—LLB '31 (U Louisville); MA '38—PhD '41 in Roman hist (U Chicago). Author: The Pretorian Prefect from Commodus to Diocletian '42; also articles in field. Asst prof hist U Louisville since '42. AHA—Soc Promotion Roman Studies —Am Numismatic Assn—AAUP. Newell scholar Am Numismatic Soc '46. Department of History, University of Louisville, Louisville 8, Ky.†

15 HOWE, Thomas Carr, Jr. Art (Wartime recovery); Museum management. b'04. AB '26—AM '29 (Harvard). Author: Salt Mines and Castles. Dir Calif Palace of The Legion of Honor. Served as lt comdr US Naval Reserve '45-46, monuments fine arts

and archives specialist officer Germany working on recovery and restitution of works of art looted by Nazis. Awards: Chevalier Legion of Honor, France; Officier Order of Orange-Nassau with The Swords Holland. Phi Beta Kappa. California Palace of The Legion of Honor, Lincoln Park, San Francisco 21.

16 HOWELL, Almonte Charles. Education. b'95. AB '17 (Denison U); MA '20 (Columbia); PhD '24 (U NC). Author: Handbook of English in Engineering Usage '40; Military Correspondence and Reports '43; Ensayos sobre Literatura Americana '48. Coauthor: (with R P Baker) The Preparation of Reports '39. With U NC since '20, prof since '38, asst dean coll arts and scis '39-45, sec of gen faculty since '43, in charge English courses sch engring '22-38; vis prof English grad sch NC Coll for Negroes '41-46 (summers); asst dir Wellesley Inst for Fgn Students summer '46; vis prof English U San Carlos de Guatemala '46-48; spl lectr English Inst in San Salvador '46, Tegucigalpa Honduras '47; guest lectr Instituto Guatemalteco-Americano Guatemala '47. Modern Lang Assn—Engring Edn Soc—S Atlantic Modern Lang Assn—Phi Beta Kappa—Phi Mu Alpha Sinfonia. 360 Tenney Circle, Chapel Hill, N.C.◉

17 HOWELL, Benjamin Franklin. Invertebrate zoology; Paleozoic stratigraphy. b'90. BS '13—AM '15—PhD '20 (Princeton). Author articles in field. Prof geol and paleontol Princeton since '47; ed general paleozool Biological Abstracts '26-49. AAAS (F)—Geol Soc Am (vp '45)—Internat Paleontol Union—Soc Econ Paleontol Mineral—Soc Study Evolution—Geol Soc, London. Department of Geology, Princeton University, Princeton, N.J.◉

18 HOWELL, J(esse) V. Petroleum geology; Geological exploration (History). b'91. BS '12 (Penn Coll Oskaloosa Ia); MS '15—PhD '22 (State U Ia). Research on practice and history petroleum geology. Editor: Structure of Typical American Oil Fields, Vol III '48. Geologist Marland Oil Co. US and Can '22-29; cons geologist Tulsa since '29. Geol Soc Am(F)—Am Geog Soc(F)—Am Assn Petroleum Geologists (sec-treas '47-49)—Tulsa Geol Soc (vp '43-44, pres '44-45)—Sigma Xi. 1510 Philtower Bldg., Tulsa 3.◉

19 HOWELL, John Thomas. Taxonomy of flowering plants (Western North America, Galapagos Islands). b'03. BA '26—MA '27 (U Calif). Author articles in field. Asst curator dept bot Calif Acad Sci '30-49; curator since '49. Calif Acad Sci—Calif Bot Soc—AAAS(F)—Sigma Xi—Phi Beta Kappa. California Academy of Sciences, Golden Gate Park, San Francisco 18.†

20 HOWERTON, George. Music (Education); Choral music. b'05. AB '26 (William Jewell Coll); Am '40 (Columbia); grad study (Northwestern U, U So Cal, NY U, Chicago Musical Coll, Harvard); PhD '50 (Northwestern U); studied organ under Marcel Dupre Paris; organ coaching with William Middelschulte, Leo Sowerby, Edwin Arthur Kraft. Adjudicator national competition festivals Los Angeles '40, St Paul '41, Omaha '42; member research council Music Educators National Conference. Author: The Use of Victor Records in the High School Choral Training Program (pamphlet) '44 Co-author: (with Traugott Rohner) Fundamentals of Music Theory '43. Arranger of early music prepared for usage in contemporary choral groups. Mem faculty Northwestern U since '39, dir choral activities '47-51,

dean sch music since '51, organist and dir music chapel services since '47, prof history of music since '50; guest condr and clinic dir univs of Neb, Ky, Ohio, and Ind, DePauw U, Okla A and M Coll, Southwestern Music Educators Conf, So Conf Music Edn, etc. Kappa Alpha, Phi Mu Alpha. H: 1515 Davis St., Evanston, Ill.◉†

21 HOWERTON, Hugh King. Hygrometry. b'21. AB '41 (NE Mo State Coll); MA '47 (George Washington U). Research on methods and apparatus for measuring small quantities of water in gases, determination of water carrying capacity of air at elevated temperatures and pressures, determination of solubility of water in liquefied gases, calibration of hygrometers at low temperatures. Author articles in field. Indsl research F Central Sci Co '41-42; chief atmospheric simulation sect Nav Ordnance Lab '42-47; with Am Instrument Co since '47, chief phys from '49. NY Acad Sci—APS—Optical Soc Am—Sigma Pi Sigma. 8030 Georgia Av., Silver Spring, Md.

22 HOWES, (Benjamin) Durward. Pearl peeling. b'99. Student '16-18 (Stanford U). Research on removing a protuberance or acid stain from pearls, to smooth a surface broken by abrasion or to take off a dead spot caused by one pearl rubbing against another; developed a technique whereby careful peeling, with a slight loss of weight, restores the pearl to its original beauty. Partner B D Howes and Son retail jewelers '19-39, pres since '39. Los Angeles Retail Jewelers Assn (pres '34-35)—Calif Retail Jewelers Assn (pres '36-37)—Am Nat Retail Jewelers Assn (vp '44-46, pres '46-47, chmn nat adv council '48-49). 3059 Wilshire Blvd., Los Angeles 5.

23 HOWLAND, Joe Wiseman. Radiation biology; Ionizing irradiation (Biological effects and treatment); Radio isotopes (Methods preparation and distribution, use in diagnosis and treatment). b'08. BS '28 (Denison U); MSc '29—PhD '31 (Ohio State U); MD '38 (U Rochester). Research on infection in physiologic pathology of radiation syndrome following lethal whole body irradiation and control by specific antibiotics; observations growth factor content of antibiotics in irradiated animals, on mechanism of antibiotic action, on long term affects of acute and chronic irradiation; plan and operation cooperative radio isotope center to supply standardized radio isotopes to participating facilities; use of radio isotopes in clinical medicine, particularly for thyroid diagnosis and treatment and cancer therapy. Mem original US investigating party into Nagasaki and Hiroshima for studying human effects of atomic explosion '45. Chief spl problems Manhattan Engring Dist '44-45, asst chief med research '45-46, chief med research '46-47; cons AEC '47; asst prof radiation biol and chief med div Rochester Atomic Energy Project '48-49, asso prof radiation biology and chief med div '49-50, prof radiation biology and chief med div since '50. ACP—AAAS—Am Bd Internal Med (Diplomate)—Am Indsl Hygiene Assn—Indsl Phys and Surg—Phi Beta Kappa—Sigma Xi—Alpha Omega Alpha. P.O. Box 287, Station 3, Rochester 20, N.Y.

24 HOWLAND, Joseph Emery. Rose culture (Greenhouse); Cut flowers (Keeping quality). b'18. BS '40 (RI State Coll); MS '42 (Mich State Coll); PhD '45 (Cornell U). Made time of day studies on rates of photosynthesis of roses and effects on keeping quality of roses as cut flowers. Discovered with Kenneth Post the usefulness of constant-level watering of commercial florist crops especially roses. Author articles in field. Asso ed Better Homes and Gardens '45-48; garden ed House Beautiful since '48. Am Assn Adv Hort Sci—AAAS—Am Phytopath Soc—Sigma Xi. House Beautiful Magazine, 572 Madison Av., NYC.†

10 HOWLAND, Louis Harold. Elastomers (Rubbers, synthetic rubber); Rubber chemicals. b'02. BS '24—MS '26 (U Louisville, Ky); PhD '28 (State U Ia). US patents on rubber vulcanization accelerators, use of acidylamino diarylamines as antioxidants with rubber, preserving rubber, rubber compositions, treatment of elastic polychloroprene, plasticizing neoprene with amines, Thiazolyl sulfuramides, and others. Author articles in field. Mgr synthetic rubber research and development Synthetic Rubber Div Naugatuck Chemical Div US Rubber Co since '46. Am Chem Soc—Sigma Xi. Synthetic Rubber Plant, Naugatuck Chemical Division of U.S. Rubber Co., Naugatuck, Conn.

11 HOWSON, George William. Power-plants (Hydro-electric). b'83. BS '09 (U Cal). Res engr Strawberry Dam '11-15; engr in charge Phila Dam '15; mem engring commn to Greece on Athens Water Supply '20; res engr Dix River Dam and Power House '22-23; hydraulic engr Fed Power Commn SF '40; coordinator on 24 problem studies Central Valley Project US Bur Reclamation '43-46; hydraulic engr power and irrigation investigations State Cal since '46. Am Soc CE. Dept Public Works, Div of Water Resources, 1120 N St., Sacramento. H: 118 Camino Don Miguel, Orinda, Cal.†

12 HOY, Harry E. Geography of Latin America (Upper Amazon basin). b'08. BS '29—AM '33—PhD '40 (Nebraska U). Exploration on Marañon, Huallaga, Cenipa, Santiago, Nanay and Napo rivers in eastern Andes and basin of Amazon river in eastern Peru. Author articles in field. Asst prof '40-42, asso prof '43-45 Mich State Normal Coll; cartographer OSS '42-43; asso field tech Rubber Development Corp Peru '43; asst prof Western Reserve U '45-46; asso prof, chmn dept geog Oklahoma U since '46. Assn Am Geog —Sigma Xi—AAAS—Am Geog Soc— Am Soc Profl Geog—Council Geog Teachers—Oklahoma Acad Sci — SW Social Sci Council. Department of Geography, University of Oklahoma, Norman, Okla.†

13 HOYMAN, William Greig. Phytopathology (Arizona and New Mexico). b'05. BS '28 (Coe Coll); MS '32—PhD '40 (Ia State Coll). Research on lettuce, alfalfa, small grain, melon, cotton, sugar beet, cereal, winter vegetables, potato, tomato diseases of plants Arizona and New Mexico, and on concentration and characterization of emetic principle in barley infected with Gibberella saubinetii; associate editor Phytopathology '43-47. Author articles: First Report of Colletotrichum Trifolii on Alfalfa in New Mexico '39; Plant Diseases Observed in Arizona and New Mexico 1943 '44; Phymatotrichum on Guar in Arizona '44; Evaluation of Various Spray and Dust Materials in the Control of Insects and the Fungus Causing Early Blight of Potatoes '46; and others. Asst plant path Ariz Agrl Expt Sta '40-43; plant path emergency plant disease prevention project div mycol and plant disease survey US Dept Agr '43-46; agent, plant path div fruit and veg crops and diseases bur plant industry US Dept Agr since '49; asso plant path ND Agrl Expt Sta and plant path ND

State Seed Dept since '45. Am Phytopath Soc—Am Potato Assn—Sigma Xi. Plant Pathology Department, North Dakota State College, Fargo, N.D. H: 1215 14th Av. N.†

14 HOYT, Harrison Val. Industrial relations. b'85. BS '13 (Purdue U); MBA '17 (Harvard); PhD '29 (Stanford). Traveled extensively European, Asiatic, Middle East and Latin American countries; seven summers in Middle America checking for evidence of old Mayan Civilization. Asst engr Ida Power & Light Co Boise '13-15; cons and indsl engr NY City '18-20; prodn mgr J G McDonald Chocolate Co Salt Lake City '20-21; dean sch commerce Brigham Young U '21-31, head dept accounting and bus since '38; prodn mgr J S Ivins Phila '36-38. Telluride Assn—Beta Alpha Psi—Beta Gamma Sigma—Alpha Kappa Psi. H: 74 E Seventh North, Provo, Utah.◎

15 HOYT, Homer. Urban land economics (City growth trends, real estate valuation). b'96. AB '13—AM '13 (Kan U); JD '18—PhD '33 (U Chicago). Made economic surveys of New York, Chicago, Brockton (Massachusetts), Raleigh (North Carolina), Orlando (Florida), and other cities, made reassessment of York (Pennsylvania), and master plan of residential land use of Chicago. Author: One Hundred Years of Land Values in Chicago '33; Principles of Urban Real Estate (with Arthur M Weimer) '48; Structure and Growth of Residential Neighborhood in American Cities '39; Housing Demand of Workers in Manhattan '39; The Economic Status of the New York Metropolitan Region in 1944; also articles in field. Prin housing econ Fed Housing Adminstrn '34-40; cons Urban Land Inst '40-41; dir research Chicago Plan Commn '41-43; asso prof land econ MIT, lecturer in real estate Columbia U '44-46; dir econ studies Regional Plan Assn NYC '43-46; Pres Homer Hoyt Asso since '46. Phi Beta Kappa—Lambda Alpha. 12 West Dr., Larchmont, N.Y.

16 HOYT, Samuel L(eslie). Welding (Low alloys); Carboloy; Smith alloy No 10; Physical metallurgy. b'88. EM '09 (U Minn); PhD '14 (Columbia). Developed carboloy, invented and developed Smith Alloy No 10, heat resistant alloy, other low alloy steels for special uses, particularly welding, general metallurgical research. Author: Principles of Metallography '20; Common Alloys '21; Metals and Metal Data '52. Metall Gen Elec Co '19-30, A O Smith Corp '31-39, dir metall research '34-39, cons '39-41; tech adviser Battelle Meml Inst Columbus O since '39. Battelle Institute, 505 King Av., Columbus 1, O.◎

17 HOYT, William Dana Jr. State and local history; History of Maryland. b'11. BA '32—MA '33 (Washington & Lee U); PhD '40 (Johns Hopkins U); '29 (L'Institut de Tourraine, France). Research for Committee on Publications, Maryland Historical Society '36-37, Committee on Restoration of Old Senate Chamber in State House at Annapolis Maryland '37-38; editor Maryland History Notes '43-47, The State and Local History News '43-49, Between Librarians '46-47. Author articles in field. Asst dir Md Hist Soc '43-47; asso prof hist Loyola Coll since '50. AHA—Am Cath Hist Assn—ALA —Soc Am Archivists—Bibliog Soc Am —Am Geog Soc—Econ Hist Assn—Agrl Hist Soc—Miss Valley Hist Assn—So Hist Assn. Loyola College, 4501 N. Charles St., Baltimore 10. H: 2019 Maryland Av., Baltimore 18.

18 HU, Charles Y. Geography of East Asia (China, Japan, Korea); Map compilation and intelligence; Military and

economic geography. b'09. BA '30 (U Nanking); MS '36—U fellow '34-35 (U Calif); fellow '36-37—PhD '42 (U Chicago). Travel extensively through China, Japan, Korea, and Asiatic Russia. Author: The Frontier Regions of China '35; Notes on a Journey to Japan, Korea, and Asiatic Russia '36; Military Geography of South China Coast '44; Military Geography of South Central China '47, and others; also articles in field. Prof geog U Md since '46; research asso and lecturer dept geog U Chicago '42-44; cons econ geog United Air Lines Corp; research geog and acting chief East Asia Desk Topographic Br US War Dept '44-47 and concurrently prof mil geog Strategic Intelligence Sch US War Dept Gen Staff. Am Soc Profl Geog—Assn Am Geog—Am Geog Soc NY(F)—Am Meteorol Soc—Sigma Xi. Department of Geography, University of Maryland, College Park, Md.

19 HUBBARD, Beverly Raymond. Fog horns; Underwater sound signaling. b'01. BSEE '25 (MIT). Author articles in field. Engr Submarine Signal Co '26-28, dir lab '28-36, sales engr '36-44; tech coordinator Whitney Blake Co since '44. Inst Radio Enrging (asso) —AAAS—Acoustical Soc Am(F)—AI EE. 1565 Dixwell Av., New Haven.

20 HUBBARD, C(larence) Andresen. Siphonaptery. b'97. DSc '19—BE '20 —MSc '22—EdM '24 (U Wash); DSc '38 (Pacific U). American fleas and their hosts, the American mammals and birds; described 20 new species and two new genera western fleas. Author: Fleas of Western North America '47; also articles in field. Prof biol Pacific U Forest Grove Ore '22-44; lecturer premed biol and asst prof Vanport Coll Portland Ore since '46; lecturer biol Portland ext center since '47. Ore Entomol Soc—Pacific NW Bird Mammal Soc—Sigma Xi. Box 109, Route 2, Tigard, Ore.

21 HUBBARD, Donald. Photography (Emulsions); Glass (Optical). b'00. BS (chem engring) '23—MS '24 (U Fla); PhD '32 (Am U). Research on preparation of and chemistry of sensitization and hypersensitization of photographic emulsions, photographic gelatins, research and development optical glass. With Nat Bur Standards since '25. ACS—Am Optical Soc—AAAS— Wash Acad Sci. Medal from Soc Francaise de Photographie '34. National Bureau of Standards, Washington.

22 HUBBARD, Harry Dorris. History (United States). b'89. DC '19—DPA (Am U Chicago); grad '30 (Boeing Sch Aeronautics); '30-31 (U Cal); AB '34 grad work '34-35 (Coll of Pacific). Author historical reference books, historical novels, short stories, novelettes, dramatizations and historical pageants. Author: A History of Money '30) Building the Heart of an Empire '38 (produced at Golden Gate Internat Expn '39-40, Stockton Civic Mem Auditorium '50; radio series KGDM '39-40); Vallejo '41; History of US Army Automotive Schools (published serially in Ordnance Base paper) '43. Cal Hist Soc—Cal Western Folklore Soc— Cal Writers Club—Nat Writers Club. US Post Office, Stockton, Cal.

23 HUBBARD, LaFayette Ronald. Expedition organization and psychology. b'11. BS '34 (George Washington U); Student '45 (Sch Mil Govt, Princeton). Commander Caribbean Motion Picture Expedition and West Indies Minerals Expedition '35, Alaskan Radio Experimental Expedition '40; studies on prevention psychic breakdown and handling of men under stress of expedition conditions. Author: Expedition Personnel; Fear; The Anatomy of Madness; Man Under Stress, and others; also articles in field. Author since '30, explorer since '34; master motor and sailing vessels. Lt USNR '41-46 comdg escort vessels and navigator in all theaters. Box 502, Elizabeth, N.J.

10 HUBBARD, Wynant Davis. Africa (Trade, economic development); Wild animal psychology. b'00. Student '19-21 (Harvard). Explored Kenamou River Labrador making first maps '19; travelled Africa '22-25; director motion picture expedition northern Rhodesia for First National Pictures, returned northern Rhodesia Africa purchased ranch upper Kafue River for wild animal research '30. Author: Wild Animals '26; Bong'kwe '30; Fiasco in Ethiopia '36; The 1000th Frog '35; also articles in field. War correspondent Universal Service Italo-Ethiopian War '35-36; pres Africa Co Inc '38-39; dir livestock development Am Virgin Islands '40-43; prin agr econ Office Fgn Agrl Relations US Dept Agr '43-44; acting dir Agr Div UNRRA Cairo and acting chief UNRRA mission to Ethiopia '44-45; pres Hubbard and Darling Inc Import-Export '47-48; partnership in Hubbard and Kelly. Royal Zool Soc, London(F)—Am Geog Soc(F)—Am Soc Mammalogists—Oologists Soc. c/o L. L. Sanford, 11 W. 28th St., NYC 1.

11 HUBBELL, Donald Sidney. Soil structure (Effects of micro-organisms); Venezuela (Agriculture); Tropics (Erosion control). b'06. BS '29 (Okla A&M); MS '30—PhD '32 (Ia State Coll. Eestablishment of relationship between micro-organisms and soil structure; research on aggregating power of soil fractions and development method for estimating aggregating power of soils; advisor to Venezuelan government on tropical research '41-42; outline current soil conservation laws and action program for Venezuela; technical consultant on erosion control in tropics to foreign laison representative US Soil Conservation Service since '42. Author articles: Land Conditions in Venezuela '42; The Genesis of Soil Structure '46; Relation of Water Stable Aggregation to Soil Texture '50, and others. Chief agrl mission to Venezuela '41-42; supervisor research project soil conservation in NM since '42. Box 56, State College. N.M.

12 HUBBLE, Edwin Powell. Extragalactic nebulae; Cosmology; Exterior ballistics. b'89. BSc '10—PhD '17 (U Chicago); Rhodes scholar from Ill '10-13—BA in Jurisprudence '12—DSc (hon) '34 (Oxford); hon DSc '36 (Princeton); hon DSc '37 (Brussels); LLD '36 (Occidental). Author: The Realm of Nebulae '36; The Observational Approach to Cosmology '37. Astronomer on staff Mt Wilson Obs Pasadena Calif since '19; chief ballistician and dir Supersonic Wind Tunnels Lab, Ballistic Research Lab US War Dept '42-46; hon fellow Queens Coll Oxford. Royal Astron Soc(F, medal '40)—Astron Soc—Astron Soc Pacific—Nat Acad Sci—Am Philos Soc—Sigma Xi. Awarded Barnard medal for scientific service '35, Bruce medal '38, Franklin medal '39, Medal of Merit '46. Mt. Wilson Observatory, Pasadena 4, Calif.⊙

13 HUBER, Miriam Blanton (Mrs Frank S Salisbury). Children's literature. Student (Ward Seminary and Buford Coll Nashville) (Kidd-Key Coll Sherman Tex); BS '25—AM '26—PhD '28 (Columbia). Author: The Influence of Intelligence upon Children's Reading Interests '28; Skags, the Milk Horse '31; Cinder the Cat '31; The

Uncle Remus Book '35; Story and Verse for Children '40 (rev edit) '50. Co-author: (with H B Bruner and C M Curry) The Poetry Book (9 vols) '26; Children's Interests in Poetry '27; (with A L Gates) The Work-Play Books (12 vols) '30 (rev edit) '50; (with F S Salisbury and A L Gates) Core-Vocabulary Readers (4 vols) '43, Todays Work-Play Books (12 vols) '45-46. Mem staff State Dept Pub Instrn Ind '15-23; tchr English pub schs Indianapolis '20-22; mem staff Inst Ednl Research Tchrs Coll Columbia '26-28; editor The Macmillan Co '28-29, Am Book Co '29-32; lectr edn NYU '32-35; prof edn Ariz State Tchrs Coll '35-37. H; 3769 Franklin Ave., Hollywood 27, Cal.⊙

14 HUBER, Wolfgang. Chemical and biological effects of, and sterilization by, high-energy radiation; Ionizing radiation equipment and processes. b'10. BS '32 (U Freiburg); MSc '34 (U Berlin; PhD (chem) '36 (U Gottingen). Research on radiation inactivation of microorganisms and enzymes and destruction of insects in raw and canned foods without heat, deep freezing, or chemical preservatives, sterilization of medicinals with high energy electrons, chemical reactions caused and/or accelerated by high energy electrons such as cracking, polymerization, and halogenation, effect of ionizing radiations on nucleic acids, vitamins, enzymes, antibodies and other nutrients or metabolites, development of generator (capacitron) and auxiliary equipment for industrial use of ionizing radiation, especially electrons. Holder US and foreign patents covering apparatus, methods, and processes in applied ionizing radiation; holder nine patents in medicinal chemistry. Author articles in field. Instr med chem Gottingen '35-37; research F organic chem Gottingen '36-38; chief chem Beta Chem Research Inc. '38-39; research chem Winthrop Chem Co '39-45; with Electronized Chem Corp since '45, v-pres, mem bd from '47; with OSRD '42-45. AAAS—ACS—NY Acad Sci—Soc Chem Industry Gt Brit—Swiss Chem Soc. Electronized Chemicals Corp., 846 Lefferts Av., Bklyn 3.

15 HUCKER, George James. Food technology. b'93. BS '15 (Lenox Coll); AM '16 (Columbia); PhD '24 (Yale); student (Upper Ia U, Cornell U). Member International Education Board Copenhagen, London, Paris '26-27; consultant New Zealand Government '38. Author articles in field. Asst bact, later chief in research NY State Agrl Expt Sta since '18; asst prof, later prof bact Cornell U since '22. Inst Food Technol (sec, pres)—Soc Am Bact—Am Pub Health Assn(F)—Internat Milk Sanitarians. New York State Agricultural Experiment Station, Geneva, N.Y.⊙

16 HUCKINS, Stuart. Timber engineering; Wood properties. b'96. AB '20 (Harvard). Research on modified wood, reinforced and prestressed wood, timber design. Treas P S Huckins Co '25-29; mgr Timber Engring Co NE since '34; dir George McQuesten Co Inc since '41. Forest Products Research Soc—Boston Soc CE. George McQuesten Co., Inc., 422 Border St., East Boston, Mass.

17 HUCUL, Walter Charles. Slavic Europe; History Russian and Soviet Army, Navy, and Air Force. b'22. BA '44—seminars in field '44-45 (U Manitoba); MA '47—Research fellow since '47—PhD '52 (U Cal). Author (Monographs): Russia and the Straits Question 1923-52; The Evolution of Russian Sea Power 1853-1952. Contbr articles and reviews. Contributor articles Collier's Nat Ency. Fellow Inst Slavic

Studies U Cal '48-49, research fellow '49-50, teaching asst '50-51. AHA—Pacific Hist Assn—Phi Alpha Theta. Department of History, 30 Wheeler Hall, University of California, Berkeley 4.

18 HUDDLESTON, Edith Mary. Aptitude and achievement tests. b'18. AB '39—AM '40 (George Washington U). Development scholastic aptitude and achievement tests in English and social studies; devised technique for special English examination for foreign students; research on test development. Asso test development coll entrance examination bd Princton NJ '42-47, Ednl Testing Service since '48. Am Psychol Assn—Nat Council Measurements Used in Edn—Nat Council Social Studies—Am Ednl Research Assn—Phi Beta Kappa. Educational Testing Service, P.O. Box 592, Princeton, N.J.

19 HUDDLESTON, Ora Leonard Physical medicine and rehabilitation. b'03. AB '24—MA '26 (U Cal); MD '31—PhD '35 (U Colo). Research in physiology, endocrinology, physical medicine. Med dir Kabat Kaiser Inst for Neuromuscular Rehabilitation Santa Monica Cal; clin prof phys medicine Med Sch U So Cal. AMA—Am Congress Phys Med (past pres)—Am Bd Phys Med and Rehabilitation (diplomate)—Phi Sigma—Sigma Xi—Alpha Omega Alpha. Kabat Kaiser Inst for Neuromuscular Rehabilitation. 1815 Ocean Front, Santa Monica, Cal.

20 HUDSON, Arthur Palmer. American folksong, folklore, and southern regional literature; English literature (Romantic period). b'92. BS '13—AM '20 (U Miss); AM '25 (U Chicago); PhD '30 (U NC). Author: Specimens of Mississippi Folklore '28; The Singing South '36; Folksongs of Mississippi and Their Background '36. Co-author: Culture of the South (editor W T Couch) '34; A Literary History of the United States '49. Editor: Humor of the Old Deep South '36; (with Edward Wagenknecht and Louis Untermeyer) The College Survey of English Literature (vol II) '42, and others; also articles in field. Prof Eng U NC since '35. Soc Am Historians(F)—Vanderbilt Conf on Humanities (mem exec com)—Am Folklore Soc (exec com)—NC Folklore Council (chmn div oral lit)—NC Folklore Soc (vp, sec-treas)—Se Folklore Soc (exec com)—S Atlantic Modern Lang Assn—Coll Eng Assn (dir)—Phi Beta Kappa. Awarded Smith research prize U NC '30; fellowship in humanities Gen Edn Bd Rockefeller Found '34-35. Greenwood Rd., Chapel Hill, N.C.⊙

21 HUDSON, G(eorge) Donald. Geography (Field methods, land classification, land use planning). b'97. PhB '25—AM '26—fellow dept geog '31-33—PhD '33 (U Chicago). Principal geographer Tennessee Valley Authority '34-37, chief land planning division '37-39; land planning consultant National Resources Planning Board 39-41. Author articles in field. Prof geog Northwestern U '39-51, chmn dept '45-51; prof geog U Wash chmn dept since '51. Geog ed Ency Brit since '42. AAAS(F)—Am Geog Soc—Assn Am Geog—Sigma Xi. Dept of Geography, Smith Hall, Univ. of Washington, Seattle, Wash.⊙

22 HUDSON, Winthrop S. Church and religious history. b'11. AB '33 (Kalamazoo Coll); DB '37 (Colgate Rochester Divinity); PhD '40 (Chicago U). Research in British religious history, Puritanism and mystical groups, including Quakers, Antinomians, Cambridge Platonists, Aberdeen Doctors; study of sixteenth and seventeenth century political thought, and seventeenth century economic thought in England; editorial board Church History. Author: John Ponet, Advocate of Limited Monarchy '42; The Life of God in the Soul of Man '48; also articles in field. Ordained minister '37; instr hist Christianity '42-44, prof and administrative asso Colgate-Rochester Divinity Sch since '47; asst prof Chicago U '44-47. Am Soc Ch Hist (vp)—AHA. Received grant-in-aid Am Council Learned Socs '42. 1100 So. Goodman St., Rochester 7, N.Y.

10 HUELSEN, Walter August. Vegetable crops; Plant breeding; Vegetable crops. b'92. BS '17—grad study '17 (Cornell U); MS '26 (U Ill); '21-30 (U Ill). Breeder and introducer numerous sweet corn hybrids, new varieties of tomatoes, lima beans and mung beans; specialist in agricultural problems relating to vegetable canning and freezing industry and those relating to vegetable seed industry. Author articles in field. Asso olericulture U Ill '21-26, asst prof, asst chief olericulture '26-29, asso prof and asso chief olericulture '29-39, prof and chief olericulture '39-40, prof and chief vegetable crops '40-47, prof and research prof vegetable crops since '47. AAAS (F)—Ill Acad Sci—Bot Soc Am—Am Genetic Assn—Am Statis Assn—Am Soc Plant Physiol—Am Soc Hort Sci—Phi Sigma—Gamma Sigma Delta—Sigma Xi. Department of Horticulture, University of Illinois, Urbana, Ill. H: 508 W. Washington St.†

11 HUETTNER, Alfred Francis. Fruit flies (Embryology); born '82. AB '16 (USD); MA '18—PhD '23 (Columbia). Author: Fundamentals of Comparative Embryology of the Vertebrates '49. Co-author: (with Bruce. T. Kirkpatrick) Fundamentals of Health, '31. Asso advancing to prof NYU '24-37; prof biology Queen's Coll since 38, also chmn dept. AAAS—Am Soc Zoologists—Genetics Assn Genetics Soc—Soc Study Growth and Development—Evolution Soc. Department Biology, Queens College, Flushing, N.Y.

12 HUFF, Clarence Elmer. Agricultural economics (Cooperatives, farm organizations and marketing, insurance). b'82. Student Kan Christian Coll, Lincoln. Comptroller-gen mgr of life, accident and health, and auto ins cos sponsored by Farmers Union since '37. Farmers Union Building, 3501 E. 46th Av., Denver 16.

13 HUFF, Rex L. Medical Physics; Atomic bomb (Bikini tests). b'18. BS '41 (Purdue); MD '44 (Ind U). Research with radio iron in development method to detect small amounts of total body X-irradiation; determination quantity of white blood cells used per day by X-irradiated animals; devised method using radio-iron for immediate determination of effect of radio phosphorous therapy on red cell production in patients with polycythemia; noted epilation in non-irradiated members of parabiotic rats when other member was given large doses X-radiation; observed iron metabolic metapalasia in protected spleens of ir-radiated animals; developed method for use of radio-iron in determination rates, to show location, and failure of marrow red cell production, splenic erythroid metaplasia and hypersplanism; investigation production rates of erythrocytes after radio phosphorous administration to patients with polycythemia vera, and after x-ray radiation; expedition to Peruvian Andes to study iron metabolism of altitude polycythemia. Co-author articles: (with Donald C Van Dyke) Epilation in the Non-Irradiated Member of Parabiotically United Rats '49; (with W F Bethard, J F Garcia, B M Roberts,

L O Jacobson, J H Lawrence) Tracer Iron Distribution Studies in Irradiated Rats with Lead-Shielded Spleens '50; (with Thomas G Hennessy) Depression of Tracer Ion Uptake Curve in Rat Erythrocytes Following Total Body X-Irradiation '50, and others. Asst indsl physician Manhattan Engrs Dist '45-47; radiological safety officer at Bikini; Permanente Found research fellow div med physics U Cal '47-48, Atomic Energy Commn post-doctoral fellow '48-50, research asso since '50, co-dir health physics sect radiation lab since '50. AAAS—Sigma Xi. Division of Medical Physics, Donner Laboratory, University of California, Berkeley 4.

14 HUFF, Wilbert James. Explosives (Research and testing); Fuels (Utilization, conversion). b'90. AB '11—DSc '27 (O Northern U); AB '14—PhD '17 (Yale). Research on rate of hydrolysis of hypophosphoric acid, catalytic air oxidation of benzene to maleic acid, cause of after-corrosion of firearms, and origin of carbon disulfide in gas making; member Mines Safety Board '36-42; chairman board on storage of smokeless powder Army-Navy Bureau of Mines; member major disaster panel, safety and security div Army Ordnance; dir research for explosives div Bur Mines World War II; studies on origin, conversion, distribution, and utilization of fuels, particularly gas. Author articles on explosives and fuels. With research lab Barrett Co NYC '17-18; research chem US Bur Mines '19-20, chief chem explosive div '35-37, cons explosives chem '37-46, con chem engr fuels and explosives div since '46; research chem Koppers Co Pittsburgh '20-24; prof gas engring Johns Hopkins U '24-37; prof chem engring and chmn dept U Md since '37, chmn div phys sci since '38, dir engring Expt Sta since '40. Lt CWS AUS '18-19. AAAS(F)—ACS (chmn gas and fuel div, council '35)—Am Gas Assn (chmn chem com '31—Sigma Xi—Alpha Chi Sigma—Tau Beta Pi. Dept. of Chemical Engineering, University of Maryland, College Park, Md.†ⓒ

15 HUFFAKER, Carl Barton. Biological control; Mosquito control; Bio-ecology. b'14. BA '38—MS '39 (U Tenn); PhD '42 (O State U). Studies on mosquito flights, hibernation, populations, control, physiological effects of variable temperatures '41-43; research in anopheles ecology strengthened evidence against a little-known vector of malaria '43-44; supervision and research malaria studies and control '44-45; since '45 study in biological control of weeds and insects; population studies. Author articles in field. Asst entomol U Del '41-43; entomol Inst Inter-Am Affairs Bogota and West Indies '43-45; asst entomol U Calif since '45. Am Assn Econ Entomol—Ecol Soc Am—Entomol Soc Am. 1050 San Pablo Av., Albany 6, Calif.†

16 HUFFINGTON, Jesse M. Crop production. b'96. BS '22 (U Md). Author articles in field. Vegetable garden ext specialist Pa State Coll '27-46; crop cons Continental Can Co Baltimore since '48. AAAS—Am Soc Hort Sci—Pa Vegetable Growers Assn (sec '41-46)—Am Soc Agron—Am Soc Plant Physiol. 600 DeBaugh Av., Towson 4, Md.

17 HUFFINGTON, Paul. Land Utilization; Glacial geology. b'98. BEd '24 (Ill State Normal U); MA '29 (Clark U); '31 (U Chicago). Research on glacial geology of Bridgewater, Massachusetts, land utilization of New Braintree, Massachusetts; member committee which prepared state

course of study in geography for Massachusetts. High sch tchr '19-28; with State Tchrs Coll, Bridgewater, since '29, prof since '47. Kappa Delta Pi—Gamma Theta Upsilon—Assn Am Geog—Am Geophys Union—Am Geog Soc—NE Geog Conf—AAAS—Nat Council Geog Tchrs. State Teachers College, Bridgewater, Mass.

18 HUFFMAN, Arthur Vincent. Social and governmental structure of modern Afghanistan; Tests for classification and guidance of prison inmates. b'12. Author: Afghanistan—A Pocket Guide '45. Author articles: The Administrative and Social Structure of Afghan Life '51; A Comparative Study of Developmental, Adjustment, and Personality Characteristics of Psychotic, Psychoneurotic, Delinquent and Normally Adjusted Teen Age Youth '45. Supervising officer div supervision delinquents Ill State Tng Sch for Boys '41-42; ednl advisor Royal Afghan Ministry Edn Kabul Afghanistan '42-49; supervising sociologist div criminologist Ill Dept Pub Safety '49-52; asst exec dir Ill Sex Offenders Comm Chgo since '52. 415 Woodruff Rd., Joliet, Ill. H: Oakdale Rd., Cherry Hill, Joliet.

19 HUGANIR, Kathryn. Medieval English language and literature; Ancient books. b'96. BA '21—MA '27—PhD '31 (U Pa); '23-24 (U Pittsburgh); research (U Chicago, Oxford U, Harvard, Columbia). Author articles in field. Asso prof Eng, lecturer in grad dept Am Internat Coll since '47. Medieval Acad Am—Modern Lang Assn Am—Nat Council Teachers Eng. 20 Amaron St., Springfield 9, Mass. H: Box 216 Canaan, N.H.

20 HUGGENVIK, Theodore. Theology and religion. b'89. AB '15 (St Olaf Coll Northfield Minn); AM '16 (U Chicago); student '16 (Chicago Luth Theol Sem) '17-18 (Ltuher Theol Sem St Paul); BTh—STM '22 (Princeton Theol Sem); LLB (corr) '23 (Hamilton Coll Law Chicago); ThD hon '43 (Augustana Coll Sioux Falls SD). Author: Fourteen Men Who Knew Christ '31; The Approach to Jesus '34; An Outline of Church History '35 (rev edit '39); Search the Scriptures '36; Lessons on the Life of Our Saviour '38; Your Key to the Bible '44 (6th printing '47); Martin Luther (narrative poem) '49; We Believe '50. lieve '50. Ordained Luth Ministry '22; Ordained Luth Ministry '22; pastor Westbrook (Minn) Ch '22-26; prof dept religion St Olaf Coll since '26, chmn dept religion and philosophy since '41.ⓒ

21 HUGGINS, Maurice Loyal. Structure of atoms, molecules, crystals, glasses; High polymers; X-ray diffraction. b'97. AB—BS '19—MS '20—PhD '22 (U Calif); Nat Research fellow '22-25 (Harvard, Calif Inst Tech); Johnston scholar '32-33 (Johns Hopkins). Editor Journal of Chemical Physics '41-43. Author articles in field. Instr Stanford U '25-26, asst prof '26-33; asso Johns Hopkins U '33-36; research chem Eastman Kodak Co since '36. Am Soc X-ray and Electron Diffraction (pres '41)—Am Phys Soc(F)—AAAS (F)—Am Chem Soc—Optical Soc Am—Nat Research Council—Internat Union Chem (com on macromolecules)—USA Nat Commn on Crystallography—Sigma Xi. Research Laboratory, Eastman Kodak Co., Rochester 4, N.Y.

22 HUGHES, Elwyn Owen. Fresh water algae. b'16. Student '33-34 (U Manitoba); '35-36 (McGill U); BSc '37 (Dalhousie); MA '39 (U Western Ontario); PhD '42 (O State U). Author articles in field. Asst prof plant sci U Okla since '45. Exec officer Med

Research Subdirectorate Can Army '43-45. Bot Soc Am—Phycol Soc Am—Am Soc Plant Taxonomists—AAAS—Limnol Soc Am—Okla Acad Sci—Sigma Xi. Department of Plant Sciences, University of Oklahoma, Norman, Okla.

10 HUGHES, Everett Clark. Petroleum chemistry. b'04. AB '27 (Carleton Coll); PhD '30 (Cornell U). Holder over 92 patents. Author articles in field. Chief chem and phys research div Standard Oil Co O since '44. Am Chem Soc—Am Petroleum Inst (adv com fund research in composition and properties of petroleum and API Project—AAAS (governing com). Standard Oil Co., 2127 Cornell Rd., Cleveland 6.†☉

11 HUGHES, Ray Osgood. Government; Civics. b'79. AB '00 (Brown U); AM '24 (U Pittsburgh); LHD '41 (Brown). Author: Community Civics '17; Economic Civics '21; Elementary Community Civics '22; Problems of American Democracy '22; Textbook in Citizenship '23; New Community Civics '24; The Making of Our United States '27; American Citizenship Charts '29; Fundamentals of Economics '29; Workbook in Civics '30; Workbook in American History '31; Building Citizenship '33; The Making of Today's World '35; Workbook in World History '36; Building Citizenship Workbook '37; Good Citizenship '40; Today's Problems '42; Pennsylvania, Past and Present '44. Instr Williston Sem Easthampton Mass '00-01; Leland and Gray Sem Townshend Vt '01-02; Wellesley (Mass) Boys Sch '02-03; Keystone Acad Factoryville Pa '03-06; Westbrook Sem Portland Me '06-07; high sch West Chester Pa '07-11; fifth Av High Sch Pittsburgh '11-13; with Peabody High Sch Pittsburgh '13-29, v prin '26-29; dept curriculum study Pittsburgh pub schs '29-39, dir citizenship and social studies '39-45; instr summer sessions Grad Sch Edn Harvard '26-30. AAAS—NEA—Am Hist Assn—Am Polit Science Assn—Nat Council for Social Studies (vp '26-27, '34, '35; pres '36)—Nat Assn Secondary Sch Prins. 5517 Beverly Pl., Pittsburgh 6.

12 HUGHES, Rupert. George Washington and his Times. b'72. AB '92—AM '94 (Adelbert Coll now Western Res U); AM '99 (Yale); LittD '36 (Western Res U). Author: American Composers '00; Love Affairs of Great Musicians '03; Music Lovers' Cyclopedia '14; (biography) George Washington '26 '27 '30. Composed A Riley Album, Cain, and other songs. Asst editor Godey's Mag, Current Lit and The Criterion. Phi Beta Kappa. 204 N Rossmore Av., LA 4†☉

13 HUGHES - SCHRADER, Sally. Chromosome structure and behavior; Neo-tropical insects. b'95. BS '17 (Grinnell Coll); PhD '24 (Columbia). Field work in neo-tropical insects in Mexico, Guatemala, British Honduras, Panama, Costa Rica; research in cytology of coccids and strepsiptera, chromosome studies on mantids and phasmids, cranial nerves of vertebrates. Research asso cytology Columbia since '47. Author articles in field. Am Soc Naturalists—Genetics Soc Am—Am Soc Zool—Phi Beta Kappa—Sigma Xi. Sarah Berliner fellow, Asso Am U Women '29-30. Department of Zoology, Columbia University, NYC 27.†

14 HUGHES, William Hardin. American Negro; Race relations. b'82. PhB '13—MA '15 (U Chicago); EdD '26 (U Calif); fellow by courtesy '32-34 (U So Calif). Associate editor: The Negro Year Book '47. Author articles in field. Am Ednl Research Assn—Am Philos Assn. 1687 Boulevard, N.E., Apartment A-3, Atlanta, Ga.

15 HUIE, William Bradford. World War II history (United States). b'10. AB '30 (U Ala). Author: Mud on the Stars '42; The Fight for Air Power '42; Can Do: The Story of the Seabees '44; From Omaha to Okinawa '45; The Case Against the Admirals '46; also articles in field. Lecturer since '41. Served as lt USN '43-45. Phi Beta Kappa. 8341 Colesville Rd., Silver Spring, Md.†

16 HUKILL, William Virgil. Agricultural products (Storage); Measurement and control of temperature and humidity. b'01. BS '23 (Ore State Agrl Coll). Research '24-40 included studies of refrigerated transport of fruits and vegetables; storage and conditioning of grains; participated in American Institute of Physics symposium on temperature '39; member abstracting staff Refrigeration Abstracts since '45; patent thermocouple anemometer. Articles in field. With US Dept Agrl since '23, now principal engr. Am Soc Agrl Engrs—Am Soc Refrig Engrs—Sigma Xi. Grain Storage Investigations, United States Department of Agriculture, Ames, Ia.

17 HULIN, Carlton D. Mining geology. b'96. BS '20—PhD '24 (U Calif). Author articles in field. With U Calif '21-29 prof geol; consultant in geol since '21, Calif State Div Mines, US Smelting Refining & Min Co, US Bureau Reclamation, Departmento de Fomento y Agricultura of Mexico, East Bay Municipal Utility District, Pan-Am Engring Co, Permanente Cement Co, Bradley Mining Co, Idaho Md Mines Corp, Triumph Mining Co, National Lead Co, Tungsten Mining Corp, and others; cons geol Fgn Econ Adminstrn '44-45, spl mission to India and China, col (assimilated) US Army. Am Inst Mining Metall Engrs (chmn com mining geol '46-48)—Soc Econ Geol (council since '48)—Mining Metall Soc Am—Am Assn Petroleum Geol—Geol Soc Am(F)—AAAS(F)—Sigma Xi—Tau Beta Pi. Shell Building, 100 Bush St., San Francisco 4, Calif. H: 35 Eucalyptus Path, Berkeley 5.

18 HULL, Frank Montgomery. Flies of the world; Animal ecology; Planarian regeneration. b'01. Scholar '24-25—MS '24 (O State U); BS '22 (State Coll Miss); PhD '37—scholar '35-36 (Harvard). Travelled in Europe '36, collecting expedition Cuba '37, Panama '38. Author articles in field. Prof biol and head dept U Miss since '30. AAAS(F)—Am Zool Soc—Am Assn Ecol Entomol—Am Micros Soc—Sigma Xi. University of Mississippi, University P.O., Miss.

19 HULL, Harvard L(eslie). Atomic energy research and development; Remote control development; Isotope separation. b'06. BA '27 (Neb Wesleyan U); PhD '33 (Columbia). Director process improvement electromagnetic process of separation uranium 235. Project engr Sperry Gyroscope Co Brooklyn NY '33-35, research engr '35-40, dir remote control development '40-43; dir process improvement Tenn Eastman Corp Oak Ridge Tenn, Manhattan Project '43-46; asso dir Argonne Nat Lab U Chicago '46-48, dir remote control div since '49. Inst Aeronautical Sci (asso F)—AAAS—Am Phys Soc—Sigma Xi. Argonne National Laboratory, Chicago 80.

20 HULME, Philip M. Molten metals (Impurities in, effect of gases on). b'99. BS '26 (MIT). Investigation effect of impurities and gas metal reactions in copper refining process, also refining of steel. cast iron, brass and bronze, zinc, lead, and aluminum; study methods for removal of sulphur from iron and steel; assisted in introduction use of gaseous oxygen for rapid removal of carbon from steel baths. Holds patents in field. Chem and metall Chile Exploration Co Chuguicamata Chile SA '26-37; metall and test engr Raritan Copper Works Perth Amboy NJ '37-43; metall and project engr Air Reduction Co NYC since '43. AIMME—Am Soc for Metals —Inst Metals (Gt Brit). Air Reduction Co., 60 E. 42nd St., NYC 18†

21 HULPIEU, Harold R(aymond). Pharmacology of alcohol, local anesthetics, and cyanides; Chemical tests for intoxication. b'01. BA '23 (Southwestern Coll); MA '24 (U Okla); Adam T Bruce F '27-28—PhD '28 (Johns Hopkins); student (U Chicago, U Ind). With U Ind Sch Med since '28, prof since '46. AAAS—Am Soc Pharmacology and Exptl Therapeutics—Ind Acad Sci—Am Soc Zool—ACS—Sigma Xi—Soc Exptl Biol and Med. Department of Pharmacology, University of Indiana School of Medicine, Indpls 7. H: 4346 Carrollton Av., Indpls 5.

22 HULTZEN, Lee S(isson). Phonetics; Language communication. b'96. AB '20—PhD '32 (Cornell U); Field worker Linguistic Atlas of New England '31-33; advisory committee on pronunciation Thorndike-Century Dictionaries; editorial board phonetics Quarterly Journal Speech '48-50; managing editor American speech '34-36. Author: Phonetics and Elocution '25; Pronunciation of Form-Words '44; Phonetic Transcription as Communication '48, and others. With Dartmouth Coll '26-33, Columbia '34-36, U Calif Los Angeles '36-40; asso prof and dir speech clinic U Mo '40-43; asso prof speech div gen studies U Ill since '49. Linguistic Soc Am—Internat Phonetic Assn—Am Dialect Soc—Speech Assn Am—Am Speech and Hearing Assn—Nat Council Teachers Eng—Phi Beta Kappa. 335 Illini Hall, University of Illinois, Urbana, Ill.

23 HUMBER, Robert Lee. World federation. b'98. AB '18—LLB '21—LLD '49 (Wake Forest Coll); MA '26 (Harvard); BLitt '23 Rhodes Scholar from NC (Oxford U Eng); Am Field Service Fellow '26-28 (U Paris). Founded '40 at Davis Island NC Movement for World Federation whose principles and objectives were embodied in a resolution approving World Federation, passed by sixteen state legislatures of US; represented Southern Council on International Relations San Francisco Conference '45; vice president United World Federalists '47-50, member national executive council '47-49. Author of resolution: The Declaration of the Federation of the World. Admitted NC bar '20; tutor dept govt, history and economics Harvard '19-20; lawyer and bus exec Paris France '30-40. Phi Beta Kappa. Awarded World Govt News medal for most outstanding service by an individual to World Federation '48; Am War Dads prize for greatest single contbn to World Peace '48. H: 117 W. Fifth St., Greenville, NC.

24 HUMBERD, Charles D(ean). Giants and giantism. b'97. AB '18 (U Mo); BSc '19 (U Minn); MD '23 (George Washington U). Extensive travels in quests of data and to cultivate personal acquaintance of persons of abnormally tall stature (including exhibition giants in particular), leading to physical and clinical examinations and exacting measurements of them, compilations of their biographies and case records; acquisition of a library which attempts to include everything written about giants individually and collectively from all times in all languages, concomitant collection of all available portraits of giants from earliest prints and engravings to latest photographs; museum of memorabilia of all giants including clothing, canes, spectacles, letters, advertising, handbills, and pamphlets, clippings, birth and death certificates, plaster and wax casts and moulages of facial features, hands, and feet; research per feeding experiments and special hormone preparations on rats and goats on problems of growth as related to giantism in its various types and phases, pathological giantism in animals principally mammalia. Author articles in field. Phys and surg gen and family practice since '23. Mo State Med Assn (del)—AMA(F)—Mo Acad Sci. Barnard, Mo.

10 HUME, David Newton. Analytical chemistry; Polarography; Radiochemical analysis; Complex ions. b'17. BA '39—MA '40 (U Calif); DuPont fellow '42-43—PhD '43 (U Minn). Research on an improved salt bridge for polarographic and potentiometric measurement '43, oxidation potential of Chromocyanide-Chromicyanide couple and polarography of complex chromium cyanides '43, iodometric determination of iodate, bromate and permanganate in presence of copper '44, and other studies. Author articles in field. Research asso Oak Ridge Atomic Bomb Project U Chicago '43, group leader Clinton Labs '43-44, sect chief '45-46; asst prof chem U Kan '46-47; asso prof MIT since '50. Am Chem Soc—AAAS—Sigma Xi. Department of Chemistry, Massachusetts Institute of Technology, Cambridge 39, Mass.†

11 HUMES, Arthur Grover. Parasitic Copepoda; Parasitology. b'16. BA '37 (Brown U); MS '39 (La State U); PhD '41 (U Ill). Research on helminth parasites of Amphiuma tridactylum and Siren lacertina from Louisiana, precercarial development of Stichorchis subtriquetrus and its life history, Octolasmis mulleri (Coker) (a barnacle commensal on crabs), male reproductive system in nemertean genus Carcinonemertes, trematode parasites of Louisiana birds, larval Coleoptera and Diptera from marine crustaceans. Author articles in field. Asso prof biol Boston U since '50. Am Soc Parasitol—Am Micros Soc—Am Soc Zool (asso)—AAAS—Sigma Xi—Phi Beta Kappa. Department of Biology, Boston University, 675 Commonwealth Av., Boston 15.†

12 HUMM, Doncaster G(eorge). Temperament; Personnel psychology (Evaluation). b'87. BA '09—ScD '45 (Bucknell U); MA '26—PhD '32 (U So Calif). Author articles in field. Indsl psychol and personnel cons since '29. So Calif Acad Criminology (dir '41-48, pres '46)—Los Angeles Personnel Mgrs Assn (pres '34)—AAAS—Inst Math Statis—Psychometrics Soc—Am Math Soc—Am Statis Assn—Los Angeles Astron Soc—Soc Advancement Management—Nat Inst Indsl Psychol—Am Marketing Assn—Phi Beta Kappa. 1219 W. 12th St., Los Angeles 15.

13 HUMM, Harold J(udson). Agar and related phycocolloids; Marine bacteriology and algae. b'12. BS '34 (U Miami); MA '43—PhD '45 (Duke U). Made survey of Atlantic coast of US for agar-bearing seaweeds for War Production Board '43, directed research agar possibilities of Atlantic coast '44-45. Patent on method of extracting gelose from seawoods such as Hypnea musciformis and other species of genus Hypnea '48. Author articles in field. Dir Duke U Marine Lab '48-49; dir Mar Biol Lab Fla State U since '49. Bot Soc Am—Soc Am Bact—AAAS(F)—Phycol Soc Am—NC Acad Sci—Assn SE Biol—Sigma Xi—Phi Beta Kappa.

Marine Biol Lab., Fla State University, Tallahassee.

14 HUMPHREY, Edward Frank. American history (Revolutionary period, economic, nationalism, diplomacy). b'78. AB '03 (U Minn); AM '09—PhD '12 (Columbia); '10-11 (U Paris). Author: Nationalism and Religion in America, 1774 to 1789 '24; An Economic History of the United States '31. Editor: George Washington on Religious Liberty and Mutual Understanding '32; Liberty Documents '36, and others. Northam prof hist and polit sci Trinity Coll Conn since '15, now emeritus; vis prof Hillyer Coll '48-49. AHA—Am Polit Sci Assn—Acad Polit Sci—Inst Politics—NE Hist Teachers' Assn. 31 Whitney St., Hartford, Conn.ⓒ

15 HUMPHREY, Norman Daymond. Applied anthropology (Negroes, Mexicans and Plains Indians). b'11. Student '30-31 (Detroit Inst Tech); '32 (Mich State Normal Coll); '32-33 (U Tex); AB '35—AM '38—MSW '40—PhD '43—fellow '44 (U Mich). Author: Twentieth Century America '49. Co-author: Race Riot '43; New Outline of the Principles of Sociology '46; also articles in field. Instr, later asso prof social and anthrop Wayne U since '39. Am Anthrop Assn(F) — Sigma Xi. Wayne University, Detroit 1.

16 HUMPHREY, Robert R(egester). Ecology; Range management. b'04. AB '28—AM '29—PhD '33 (U Minn); Carnegie Desert Lab Fellowship '29-30 (U Ariz). Range research on noxious plant control; studies on range management, flood control, range surveys, range condition analyses; use of fire in shrub control. Author articles: Ecology of the burroweed; The use of forage-acre requirements in range surveys; Some fundamentals of the classification of range condition; Fire as a means of controlling velvet mesquite, burroweed, and cholla on southern Arizona ranges, and others. Ecol US Forest Service '33-35, US Soil Conservation Service '35-48; range ecol U Ariz since '48 AAAS(F)—Sigma Xi—Gamma Alpha—Soil Conservation Soc Am—Ecol Soc Am—Range Management Soc Am. College of Agriculture, University of Arizona, Tucson.

17 HUMPHREYS, Adolph Henry. Camouflage. b'18. Student '34-39 (MD Inst Baltimore); '39-41 (Rinehart Sch Sculpture Baltimore). Research and development camouflage for airfields and aircraft, artillery and supporting equipment, armored vehicles, also individual camouflage such as uniforms, face paint, and other personal gear; design, development, and tests on camouflage materiel and technique. Project engr camouflage br Engr Research and Development Labs '42-45, now chief camouflage br. Camoufleur 84th Engrs AUS. Inter-Soc Color Council—Am Soc Mil Engrs. Kiwanis gold medal for sculpture '38; Rinehart European Traveling scholarship '41. Camouflage Branch, Engineer Research and Development Laboratories, Ft. Belvoir, Va.

18 HUMPHREYS, Curtis J(udson). Line, infrared and vacuum spectroscopy; Radiometry; Wavelength standards and Zeeman effect. b'98. AB '18 (O Wesleyan U); MS '21 (U Ky); PhD '28 (U Mich). Author articles in field. Physicist Nat Bur Standards since '35, chief radiometry sect since '44. Am Phys Soc(F)—Optical Soc Am—Washington Acad Sci—Philos Soc Washington—Phi Beta Kappa—Sigma Xi. National Bureau of Standards, Washington 25.

19 HUNT, Edward Eyre. Economics (Stabilization, international). born '85. Student (Harvard U). Delegate Commission for Relief in Belgium '14-16; head economic rehabilitation work of Red Cross in France '17-18, dir gen civilian relief Italy '17; American expert on scientific management World Economic Conference '27. Author: An Audit of America '30; The Power Industry and the Public Interest '44, and others. Co-author: Recent Economic Changes in the United States '29. Chief indsl econ WPB '42-43; asso dir field operations Office Fgn Relief and Rehabilitation US Dept State '43, chief Italian Div Fgn Econ Adminstrn '44, dir '45-46, chief div protective services US Dept State since 47. Federated Am Engring Socs (com on elimination of waste in industry). U.S. Department of State, Washington 7.

20 HUNT, Edward Eyre, Jr. Micronesia (Races and cultures). b'22. AB '42—AM '49—PhD '51 (Harvard). Member Peabody Museum of Harvard Expedition to Yap in western Micronesia. Teaching fellow biol Harvard '47, teaching fellow anthrop '49-50; instr anthrop U Va since '51. Am Anthrop Assn—Am Ethnol Soc—Am Assn Phys Anthrop—AAAS—Sigma Xi. 1243 30th St., Washington 7.

21 HUNT, Franklin Bicknell. Gases (Compressed). b'99. BS '20 (Mass Inst Tech). Research on design and construction carbon dioxide, dry ice plants, oxygen, acetylene and medical gases. Holds patents in field. Author articles in field. With Liquid Carbonic Corp Chicago since '20, exptl refrigeration development '23-29, chief engr carbon dioxide div '35-42, chief engr compressed gas div '42-45, in charge compressed gas div since '47. Am Soc ME—Am Soc Refrigerating Engrs—Compressed Gas Assn. 3100 S Kedzie Av., Chicago 23.

22 HUNT, George M. Wood preservation and utilization; Forest products. b'84. BS '11 (U Calif). Research in wood preservation for 30 years. Co-author: Wood Preservation '38; also articles in field. Dir Forest Products Lab Madison since '46. Am Wood Preservers' Assn—Soc Am Foresters—Forest Products Research Soc—Sigma Xi. Forest Products Laboratory, Madison 5, Wis.

23 HUNT, Lee O. Woody plants of Southern California; Pine beetle control. b'08. BSF '32—MS '34 (Ore State Coll). Directed forestry, woodland, windbreak, and gully planting programs in Southern California including testing and use of native and introduced species of trees and shrubs, organized pine beetle control project to save timber and recreational forest stands of plants. Forester USDA Forest Service '33-36; forester Soil Conservation Service '36-42; soil conservationist Soil Conservation Service since '42; sec Julian Fruit Growers Assn since '43. Soc Am Foresters (sr mem)—Am Forestry Assn—Friends of the Land. Postoffice Box 408, Ramona, Cal. H: Postoffice Box 171, Julian, Cal.

24 HUNT, Lloyd Freeman. Electrical engineering; Synchronous machine operation. BS—EE (U So Cal). Delegate and participant numerous national and regional electrical conventions; delegate and participant Conference Internationale des Grands Reseaux Electriques Paris '48 '50; special tour electrical power systems of Sweden, Germany, Belgium '50. Inventor, holds patents in field. With Westinghouse Co Pittsburgh 3 yrs; now chief elec engr So Cal Edison Co.; spl lectr U So Cal. Am Inst EE(F)—Sigma Xi—

Eta Kappa Nu. Founder Royal W Sorensen Fellows '50. Southern California Edison Co., LA.

10 HUNT, N(icholas) Rex. Foreign plant diseases and quarantines. b'85. BS '07 (State Coll Wash); MS '09—student '19 (U Calif). Determined identity of thousands of specimens of plant diseases found on imported material. Author articles in field. Pathologist fgn plant quarantine work US DA '23-46, retired '46. Felton, Calif.†

11 HUNT, Percival. Humanities. b'78. AB '00—AM '04—fellow in Eng (U Ia). Author: An Outline of Composition, 1930; Student Themes, 1938; also articles in field. Prof and head dept Eng U Pittsburgh '22-41, prof-at-large since '41. Modern Lang Assn Am—Eng-Speaking Union—Phi Beta Kappa. University of Pittsburgh, Pittsburgh. H: Schenley Apartments.

12 HUNT, Rockwell Dennis. California history; Economics of welfare; Political science. b'68. PhB '90—AM '92 (Napa Coll); PhD '95 (Johns Hopkins); LLD '32 (Coll of Pacific); LittD '36 (U So Calif). Author: Genesis of California's First Constitution; California, an American Commonwealth; The First Fifty Years; California—A Little History of a Big State; California—The State Everybody Loves; also articles in field. Prof econs U So Calif '08-20, dean Grad Sch '20-45, dean emeritus since '45; dir Calif Hist Found Coll of Pacific since '47. Pacific Geog Soc—Am Econ Assn—Am Hist Assn—Hist Soc So Calif (pres '17-26)—Calif Acad Social Scis—Calif Hist Soc—Phi Beta Kappa—Sigma Xi—Phi Kappa Phi—Beta Gamma Sigma—Order of Artus—Phi Delta Kappa. 236 West Stadium Drive, Stockton, Calif.

13 HUNTER, Albert Sinclair. Guayule culture; Crop plants (Soil factors affecting nutritive values); Soil moisture relationships; Plant nutrition. b'08. BS '38 (Utah State Agrl Coll); MS '40 (State Coll Wash); PhD '43 (Rutgers U). Author articles in field. Sr agronomist US Nat Rubber Research Station Salinas Calif '48 to '49, prof soils Oregon State Coll and sr soil scicut st USDA (coop) since '49. Am Chem Soc—Am Soc Agronomists—Soil Sci Soc Am—Am Soc Plant Physiologists—Sigma Xi. Now with: Soils Department, Oregon State College, Corvallis, Ore.

14 HUNTER, Charles E(ugene). Economic geology of North Carolina; Mining non-metalic minerals; Mica mining; Industrial minerals (Southern Appalachians). b'11. BS '33 (U NC). Author articles in field. Geologist Tenn Valley Authority since '44. Geologist Bd Econ Warfare '42-43. Geol Soc Am(F)—Am Geo Soc(F)—Am Inst Mining and Metall Engrs—Am Ceramic Soc—AAAS—Pan Am Inst Mining Engring and Geol—Am Geophysical Union—Carolina Geol Soc—Ga Mineral Soc—Tenn Acad Sci—Sigma Xi. Regional Minerals Section, Tennessee Valley Authority, 55 Henrietta St., Asheville, N.C.

15 HUNTER, Dard, Jr. Type and printing ornaments; Hand-made paper. b'17. Student '36-39 (Cleveland Sch Art). Started own typefoundry for the making of type and printing ornaments by using the methods employed in the early centuries of printing; also makes paper by the ancient hand method in the only hand-made paper mill in America located in Lime Rock, Connecticut. Author articles in field. At present makes all the type and ornaments used by the Mountain House Press Chillicothe, O. Mountain House Press, Chillicothe, O. H: Mountain House.†

16 HUNTER, Frederick Lincoln. Metallurgy of tantalum, molybdenum, and tungsten; Thermionic vacuum tubes. b'95. BS '20 (MIT). Consulting engineer on thermionic emission problems, emitters and non-emitters since '28; research on processing and fabrication tantalum and molybdenum, necessary equipment; design, development and operation process equipment using tantalum for heat transfer surfaces together with other materials. Research engr Fansteel Metall Corp N Chicago Ill '28-35, chief engr tantalum '36-46; cons engr since '47. APS—ACS—AICE—Alpha Chi Sigma. Professional engr Ill. 3240 Lake Shore Drive, Chgo 13.

17 HUNTER, George W(illiam), III. Medical zoology; Parasitology; Epidemiology of tropical medicine. b'02. Student '19-20 (Carleton Coll); BS '23 (Knox Coll); MS '24—PhD '27 (U Ill). Morphology and life history studies in helminthology; ecology of protozoan, worm and arthropod fish parasites; epidemiology and control of diseases of fresh-water fishes; studies on the food of fishes; studies on host reactions to larval parasites; studies on stream improvement; diagnosis of trichinosis; epidemiology and control of schistosomiasis; epidemiologic studies on human parasites in the Orient; comparative studies on methods of stool examinations; studies on filariasis. Co-author: Biology—The Story of Living Things '37; Manual of Tropical Medicine '45; College Zoology '49. Mem bd trustees Biol Abstracts '38-47, chmn exec com pres bd '38-42. Asst prof biology Wesleyan U '29-43; research fellow Harvard '40; biologist US Bur Fisheries '27; biologist and parasitologist NY State Conservation Dept '28-34 '36; lectr parasitology Albany Med Coll '29; mem staff Rock Mountain Biol Lab since '32, treas '37-45; biologist Lake and Pond Survey of Conn State Bd Fisheries and Game '39-41; com on Schistosomiasis, Army Epidemiol Bd '45; chief dept parasitology Army Med Dept Res and Grad Sch '46-47; chief dept med zoology 406th Med Gen Lab since '47. Union Am Biol Socs (sec '37-40)—AAAS(F)—Royal Inst Pub Health and Hygiene (F)—Royal Soc Tropical Med and Hygiene(F)—Am Soc Trop Med—Nat Malarial Soc—Am Soc Parasitologists—Soc Am Bacteriologists—Am Pub Health Assn—Am Microscopical Soc—Limnol Soc Am—Am Soc Naturalists—Am Soc Zoologists. General Laboratory, APO 500, SF.†⊙

18 HUNTER, Louis Nathaniel. Heating equipment. b'03. BASc '25 (U Toronto). Research on design and testing of heating equipment made of cast iron, steel, and non-ferrous metals and designed to burn oil, coal, and gas; development codes and standards for heating equipment pertaining to safety, quality, and performance of equipment, improvements in cast iron radiation, development cast iron and non-ferrous convectors, gas burners, oil burners, and emulsion heaters for separating crude oil and salt water emulsions. Contributor: Handbook of Oil Burning '51. Research engr Bryant Heater Co '26-31; research engr, mgr research, and vp charge research Nat Radiator Co since '32. Am Gas Assn—ACS—Am Soc ME—Am Soc Heating and Ventilating Engrs (chmn com research '48-49, mem council since '51)—Air Pollution and Smoke Prevention Assn (bd dirs since '51)—Inst Boiler and Radiator Mfrs (chmn tech com '38-40, chmn research com '40, '47, '48)—Steel Boiler Inst (chmn engring com since '43)—Indoor Climate Inst—Oil-Heat Inst Am (chmn engring com since '49)—Gas Appliance Mfrs Assn. 221 Central Av., Johnstown, Pa.

19 HUNTINGTON, LeRoy Webster. Tropical forestry. b'00. BS (forestry) '24 (U Wash). Research on tropical timber surveys, logging and lumbering. Logging engr Philippines '25-27; resident mgr Dahican Lumber Co '28-32; constrn engr Alaska '32-35; timber surveys and research Ore '35-37; mgr lumbering operations Philippines '37-41; chief forester Pulp and Paper Co '41-43; sr field tch US Govt Amazon River '43-45; consulting since '45. Soc Am Foresters—Am Assn Engrs. 52 Wesley St., Baldwin, N.Y.

20 HUNTOON, Robert DeWitt. Electronic instrumentation and ordnance; Nuclear physics. b'09. BA '32 (Ia State Teachers Coll); MS '35—PhD '38 (U Ia). Staff Nat Research Com Nat Bur of Standards Washington since '41; asst in development radio proximity fuses '41-44; apptd expert cons Office of Sec War '44; European Theatre of Operations '45; sect chief charge basic work all new fuse types '46; asst chief atomic physics div '47, chief since '48, coordinator atomic energy commn projects since '49. Wash Acad Sci—Soc—Inst Radio Engrs (sr)—Sigma Xi—Kappa Delta Pi. Received Naval Ordnance Development award; War Dept Certificate of Appreciation. Division 4, National Bureau of Standards, Washington 25.

21 HURD, Charles Buell. Colloid chemistry; Silicic acid gels. b'94. BS '15—MS '17 (Worcester Poly Inst); AM '20—PhD '21 (Clark U). Asso prof chemistry Union Coll '25-31, prof phys chem since '31. AAAS—Am Chem Soc—AAUP—Sigma Xi—Tau Beta Pi. 1064 University Pl., Schenectady, N.Y.†⊙

22 HURLBUT, Floy. Geography of Far East; Meteorology. b'88. AB '11 (Taylor U); AM '28—PhD '30 (Neb U); student summer '12 (Neb U), '19 (Columbia). Travelled, made field studies in China. Author articles: Climate of Fukien Province '30; The Fukienese, A Study in Human Geography '39. Teacher Am and China '11-26; instr Neb U '30-31; asso prof science Ball State Teachers Coll since '31. AAAS—Sigma Xi—Ind Acad Science (chmn geog and geol sect '48-49)—Nat Council Geography Tchrs—Assn Am Geographers. Ball State Teachers College, 121 W. Tillotson Av., Muncie, Ind.

23 HURLEY, Patrick Mason. Radioactivity of rocks; Radioactivity geochronology. b'12. PhD '40 (Mass Inst Tech). Engaged research in measurement of geologic ages by radioactivity methods, geochemistry of uranium and thorium; studies and writing on helium age measurement. Author articles in field. Asst prof Mass Inst Tech since '46. Royal Soc Canada Research Fellowship '39-41. Massachusetts Institute of Technology, Cambridge, Mass.†

24 HURST, Clarence Thomas. Archeology of southwestern United States. b'95. AB '23—AM '23 (Western State Coll Colo Gunnison); PhD '26 (U Calif). Author: Hegner's Invertebrate Nomenclature—A Dictionary of Zoology '34; Colorado's Old-Timers; The Indians Back to 25,000 Years Ago '46. Editor: Southwestern Lore since '35; also articles in field. Prof zoology and archeology Western State Coll Colo since '28, head dept since '28, chmn div natural sci and mathematics since '37; dir Museum of Archeol Western State Coll since '35; dir field expeditions in archeology Museum of Archeology Western State Coll since '39. AAAS(F)—Am Soc Zoologists—NEA—Am Assn Museums—Am Museum Natural History—Soc for Am Archeology—Colo Archeol Soc (ex sec since '35)—

New Mexico Archeol Soc—Sigma Xi—Am Anthro Assn(F). 420 N. Main St., Gunnison, Colo.

10 HURST, Wilbur Magruder. Crop processing and harvesting. b'98. BS '23 (Miss State Coll); BS '25 (Ia State Coll). Surveys and machinery development rural farm industries, poultry dressing plants, farmers produce markets, freezer locker plants, community canneries and fruit packing houses. Author articles: Flax Machinery and Processing Operations in Oregon '43; Layout and Operation of Cooperative Poultry Dressing Plants '46; Farmers Produce Markets in the United States '47; Farmers Cooperative Feed Mills—Plans and Operations '48; Frozen Food Lockers in Georgia '47. Research farm power and machinery US Dept Agr Washington '26-38, fiber flax machinery development Oregon '38-45; surveys and machinery development Washington since '45. Am Soc Agrl Engrs. Certificate of superior accomplishment US Dept Agr '47. U.S. Department of Agriculture Research Center, Beltsville, Md.†

11 HUSE, Howard Russell. Foreign language learning; French literature; Dante. b'90. Student '09-10 (U Dijon France); PhB '30 (U Chicago). Asst prof Romance langs Newcomb Coll Tulane '16-18; asst US trade commr Athens Greece and Constantinople Turkey '19; asst prof Romance Langs U NC '20, prof since '31, now acting chmn dept gen and comparative literature. Author: Essentials of Written and Spoken French '28; Psychology of Foreign Language Study '31; Illiteracy of the Literate '33; Reading and Speaking Foreign Languages '45. Editor: Contes et Recitis '32; University of North Carolina, Chapel Hill, NC†◉

12 HUSKINS, C(harles) Leonard. Cytology; Genetics; Mutations (Cereals). b'97. Student '15, '20 (Sch Agr Olds Alberta); BSA '23—MSA '25 (U Alberta); PhD '27—DSc '34 (U London). Author articles in field. Asso prof botany McGill U Montreal '30-34, prof genetics '34-45; prof botany U Wis since '45; visiting prof dept botany U Calif '38. Genetics Soc Am—Soc For Study Evolution—Royal Soc Canada (F)—Am Naturalists—Am Soc Human Heredity. Guggenheim fellow Dept Zoology Columbia U '42-43. 108 Biology Bldg., University of Wisconsin, Madison 6, Wis.

13 HUSEBY, Robert Amund. Corrosion; Stainless steels; stress analysis. b'13. Student '38-40 (U Wis); B Metall Engring '43 (Ohio State U). Studies in corrosion mild and alloy steels and welds in paper industry; design refinery and chemical process equipment; studies in metallography of stainless steels; interpretation strain measurements made during operation or test on fabricated metal equipment. Contributor: Book of Stainless Steels (in press). Research tech in metall Battelle Memorial Inst '42-43; research metall and management research engr dept metall research A O Smith Corp since '43. Am Soc Metals—Nat Assn Corrosion Engrs—Soc Exptl Stress Analysis. A. O. Smith Corp., Milw 1.

14 HUSSEY, Russell C. Geology; Ordovician rocks. b'88. AB '11—PhD '22 (U Mich). Research on Ordovician rocks in all parts of the US; European studies in England and France. Author: Historical Geology '44. Co-author: (with Landes) Geology and Man '48; also articles in field. Associated with geol dept U Mich since '21, now prof geol. Paleontol Soc Am—Geol Soc Am—Am Geophys Union—Mich Acad Sci—Mich Geol Soc—Am Assn Pet Geologists—AAAS—Sigma Xi. Department of Geology, University of Michigan, Ann Arbor.

15 HUSTON, Ralph Chase. Organic chemistry. b'85. BS '06 (Parsons Coll Fairfield Ia); MS '08—PhD '14 (Ia U); DSc '41 (Parsons Coll). Asst prof Mich State Coll '11-15, asso '15-25, prof organic chemistry since '25, dean of science '30-44, dean grad studies since '44. Am Inst Chemists (F)—AAAS(F)—Am Chem Soc—Sigma Xi—Phi Kappa Phi. 200A Kedzie Chemical Laboratory, Michigan State College, East Lansing, Mich. H: 4570 Chippewa Dr., Indian Hills, Okemos, Mich.†◉

16 HUTCHESON, Guy Carlton. Radio engineering. b'11. Student '28-29 (N Tex State Teachers Coll); BS (EE) '33 (Tex A&M). Supervision installation of 50,000 watt international broadcast stations for world wide broadcasting Office War Information; radio tech Planning Board '43-46. Author articles in field. Radio engr and operator second Byrd Antarctic Expdn to Little Am '33-35; radio engr gen engring dept CBS NYC '35-41; chief Latin-Am engr '41-42, engr in charge internat broadcasting '42-44, acting engr in charge radio frequency div '44-45; cons radio engr since '45. 1st lt Signal Corps AUS '42. Inst Radio Engrs—Tau Beta Pi. Professional engr Tex. FCC qualified radio expert. 1100 W. Abram St., Arlington, Tex.

17 HUTCHINGS, Imri Joseph. Mushroom production; Mushroom nutrition; Food spoilage organisms; Glass containers; Tin containers; Food processes. b'09. BS '32—MS '33 (Brigham Young U); PhD (microbiol) '36 (Rutgers U). Research on thermal death time determination of heat treatment necessary to sterilize various food products, aseptic filling as related to thermal resistance studies. With Grocery Store Products Co '36-47, tech dir '40-47; with H J Heinz Co since '47, head packaging and sterilizing dept since '50. Sigma Xi—ACS—Soc Am Bact—Assn Cereal Chem—Inst Food Tech. Manager, Food Research, H. J. Heinz Co., Pitts 30.

18 HUTCHINS, Horace William. Fire protection engineer. b'90. Diploma '43 (Mass Inst Tech); diploma (NYU, Boston Fire Coll). Author articles in field. Registered profl engr Mass; with Somerville Mass Fire Dept '16-41, 12 yrs as fire chief; now sr mem firm Hutchins and Tufts cons fire prevention and fire protections engrs since '48; expert examiner for US Civil Service Comm and State of Mass Civil Service Comm for applicants for positions and promotions of fire marshals, fire chiefs and forest wardens since '29. Sr inspector War Dept in war plant protection and security '41-44. Mass Soc Profl Engrs—Nat Soc Registered Profl Engrs—Nat Fire Protection Assn. Received Citation for outstanding war work from the commanding gen of the US AAF. Hutchins and Tufts, 82 Broadway, Cambridge 42, Mass.

19 HUTCHINS, Louis Whiting. Marine biology and zoogeography; Bryozoa; Fouling. b'16. BA '37—PhD '41 (Yale U); Mary S Muellhaupt Scholarship '41-42 (O State U). Research in taxonomy and distribution of American marine bryozoa, antifouling measures, geographical distribution of marine fouling organisms. Author articles in field. Marine biologist Woods Hole Oceanographic Inst since '42; dir Bermuda Biol Sta Research since '49. Biol Soc Wash—Ecol Soc Am—Am Soc Limnology and Oceanography—Am Geog Soc—Soc Systematic Zoologists—Bermuda Biol Sta for Research Inc (mem corp)—Sigma Xi—Phi Beta Kappa—Gamma Alpha. Woods Hole Oceanographic Institution, Woods Hole, Mass.†

20 HUTCHINS, Margaret. Library information services. b'84. AB '06 (Smith Coll); BLS '08 (U Ill); MS '31 (Columbia). Reference materials, methods, and administration; instruction in the use of books and libraries. Author: Introduction to Reference Work '44. Co-author: (with A Johnson and M S Williams) Guide to the Use of Libraries '36; also articles in field. Reference asst U Ill Library '08-14, reference librarian and lecturer '15-27; reference specialist Queens Borough Pub Library NY '27-30; instr sch library service Columbia '31-34, asst prof '34-46, asso prof since '46. ALA—Spl Libraries Assn—Phi Beta Kappa. Recipient fellowship Carnegie Corp NY '30-31. Columbia University, NYC 27.

21 HUTCHINS, Robert Maynard. Higher education (Methods). b'99. LLD (Oberlin Coll); AB '21—hon AM '22—LLB '25 (Yale); LLD '29 (W Va U, Lafayette Coll); LLD '36 (Harvard); hon Dr '46 (U Copenhagen); AM—MA '48 (U Frankfurt); LittD '47 (U Ill). Author: No Friendly Voice '36; The Higher Learning in America '36; Education for Freedom '43; St Thomas and the World State '49; Morals, Religion and Higher Education '50. Chancellor U Chicago '45-51; asso dir Ford Found since '51; dir Ency Britannica Inc since '43. Am and Conn Bar Assns—Order of the Coif—Phi Beta Kappa. 914 E. Green St., Pasadena 1, Cal.

22 HUTCHINS, Wells Aleck. Water laws. b'88. LLB '09 (George Washington U). Research on principles of Western water laws, procedure for acquiring, adjudicating, and exercising water rights for irrigation and other purposes; relation of soil-conserving operations to state water laws and water rights; assistance to legislative bodies in preparing bases for new water laws or improvement existing laws. Author: Selected Problems in the Law of Water Rights in the West '42; The Hawaiian System of Water Rights '46. Irrigation econ USDA since '15; faculty U Cal '50. Commonwealth Club Cal—Nat Reclamation Assn (chmn com desirable principles state water legislation). Received Superior Service award and medal USDA '48 for work on western water rights. Division of Irrigation, SCS, Postoffice Box 180, Berkeley, Cal.

23 HUTCHINSON, Ethel Priscilla. New Hampshire mosses; Mosses, hepatics, ferns and fungi. b'95. Privately educated. Exhibits of mosses, hepatics, ferns and fungi, for educational purposes. Lecturer on mosses, determines mosses and makes microscope slides of the parts; also works in the Hepaticae. Sullivant Moss Soc. Brighthollow, Canaan, N.H.

24 HUTCHINSON, Wesley G(illis). Bacteriology. b'03. AB magna cum laude '25—AM '27 (Brown U); PhD '33 (U Pa). Research worker on deterioration military equipment in tropics. Instr bot Brown U '25-28; instr biol Franklin and Marshall Coll '28-34; asst prof bot U Pa '34-44, asso prof since '44; research asso Office Sci Research and Development '42-45. AAAS(F)—Bot Soc Pa (sec '38-41)—Soc Am Bacteriologists—Mycol Soc Am—Sigma Xi—Phi Beta Kappa. Hygiene Bldg., University of Pennsylvania, Phila.

25 HUTCHISON, Ralph Cooper. Higher education; International affairs (Near East and Iran). b'98. Student '14-16 (Sterling (Kan) Coll); AB '18—DD '30 (Lafayette Coll); AM '19

(Harvard); '19-22 (Princeton Theol Sem); PhD '25 (U Pa); LLD '41 (Otterbein Coll) '42 (U Pittsburgh) '46 (Rutgers); LLD '47 (Jefferson Med Coll); LHD '45 (Lehigh U). Prof philosophy and religion Alborz Coll of Teheran Persia '25-26, dean '26-31; pres Washington and Jefferson Coll '31-45; pres Lafayette Coll since '45. Dir Am Middle East Relief. Pres bd trustees Alborz Coll Teheran. Yorktown medal by Soc of Cincinnati '42, Meritorious Service medal Commonwealth of Pa '46, Certificate of Merit US Govt '47. Home: 515 College Av., Easton, Pa.◎

10 HUTSON, Ray. Economic entomology (Pollination, insecticides, fruit insects, honey bee. b'96. BSA '22 (W Va U); MS '25 (Rutgers U); student '24-25 (Princeton U). Engaged research in insect pollination, laboratory and field studies of insecticides as rotenone and nicotine-bentonite, field performance of insecticides for control of tree, vine and bramble fruit infesting insects, comparison of methods for field application of insecticides as airplane applications to fruit trees, insects infesting blueberries, cutworm control, grasshopper control, control of insects on crops grown on muck land, habits of fruit insects, mosquito faunal and tick faunal surveys, insect control planning, local range of insects and factors in dissemination, surveys of crop insect abundance and control. Discovered better use of honey bees for pollination in eastern orchards, control of cherry case bearer, fruit tree leafroller, red-banded leafroller, strawberry leafroller, tree hopper, codling moth, grapeberry moth, flatheaded apple tree borer and raspberry mites. Author articles: The Cherry Case-Bearer Coleophora pruniella Clemens in Michigan '31; Controlling Diseases and Insects on Ornamental Shrubs (bull with Rasmussen, McDaniel and Strong) '45; DDT Residues on Fruits and Vegetables (with Manalo and Benne) '46. Asst entomologist '22-28; asso entomologist '28-30, NJ Agrl Expt Station; instr entomology Rutgers U '26-30; asso entomologist Mich Agrl Expt Station and asso prof '30-34, entomologist since '34, prof and dept head Mich State Coll since '34; cons entomologist Mich Dept Health since '41. AAAS—Am Assn Econ Entomologists—Entomolog Soc Am—Ontario Entomolog Soc—Sigma Xi—Phi Kappa Phi. Entomology Dept., Michigan State College, Lansing, Mich.†◎

11 HUTT, Frederick Bruce. Genetics (Animal, domestic animals, fowl). b'97. BSA '23 (Ontario Agrl Coll, Guelph, U Toronto); MS '25 (U Wis); MA '27 (U Manitoba); PhD '29—DSc '39 (U Edinburgh). Prof animal genetics Cornell since '40. Nat Research Council (com fellowships in biology and agr '46-49—Poultry Sci Assn (research prize '29, pres '33)—AAAS (F)—Am Soc Zoologists—Genetics Soc Am—Am Genetic Assn—Am Soc Naturalists—Am Ornithol Union—Soc for Study of Evolution—Am Soc Human Genetics—Sigma Xi—Phi Kappa Phi. Borden Award '46. 102 Eastwood Av., Ithaca, N.Y.◎

12 HUTTON, Colin Osborne. Optical, chemical and radioactive mineralogy; Sedimentary petrology; Geology of New Zealand. b'10. BS '33—MS '34 (U New Zealand); PhD '38 (U Cambridge); Sir George Grey and Duffus Lubecki scholar '33-34 (U Otago New Zealand) Shirtcliffe fellow '36-38 (U New Zealand); External Research Studentship '36-38 (Emmanuel College U Cambridge). Author articles in field. Prof mineral Stanford U since '47. Geol Soc London(F)—Mineral Soc

Am(F)—Geol Soc Am(F)—Mineral Soc Gt Britain—Royal Soc New Zealand (asso hon editor, F '43-46)—Cambridge Nat Hist Soc (life)—New Zealand Assn Scientific Workers (hon mem). Recipient of the Hamilton award Royal Soc New Zealand '37. Department of Mineral Sciences, Stanford University, Stanford, Calif.†◎

13 HYATT, James Philip. Old Testament (Bible and Hebrew); Semitics. b'09. AB '29 (Baylor U Waco Tex); AM '30 (Brown U); BD '33—PhD '38 (Yale); student '31-32 (Am Sch Oriental Research Jerusalem); student '32 (U Marburg Germany). Author: Treatment of Final Vowels in Early Neo-Babylonian '41; Prophetic Religion '47; also articles in field. Prof Old Testament and chmn grad dept of religion Vanderbilt U Nashville Tenn since '44; editor Journal of Biblical Literature '48-49. Nat Council on Religion in Higher Edn(F)—Old Testament Sect, Am Standard Bible Com—Am Oriental Soc (vp middle west br '43-44)—Nat Assn Biblical Instrs (vp '41)—Soc Biblical Lit—Phi Beta Kappa. Wesley Hall, Vanderbilt University, Nashville 4, Tenn.◎

14 HYDE, Eber Johnson. Patents (Piezoelectric crystals, magnetic recording and reproducing). b'13. BS in CE '36 (Case Inst Tech); LLB '40 (Cleveland Law Sch). Filing patent applications in field of piezoelectric crystals, microphones, phonograph pickups, magnetic recording and reproducing. Mem patent dept Brush Development Co. Cleveland Engring Soc—Cleveland Patent Law Assn—Theta Tau. The Brush Development Co., 3405 Perkins Av., Cleve 14. H: 2869 Scarborough Rd., Cleveland Heights.

15 HYDE, Howard Kemper. Management engineering; manpower. b'11. AB '34 (Fletcher Coll); AM '35—'36-38 (U Chicago). Director and member executive committee United Seamen's Service '46; member Administrator's Advisory Council US Retraining and Reemployment Administration '46; consultant on government organization Hoover Commission '48; consultant on interdepartmental relationships US Department of State '49; consultant on industrial mobilization Library of Congress '50; member President Truman's committee on Employment of Handicapped. Co-author: Bureaucracy and Trusteeship in Large Corporations. Contributor: Mobilization Planning and the National Security '50. Research analyst and cons US Temporary Nat Econ Com '39-40; asst dir research and edn US Immigration and Naturalization Service '40-42; administr officer, dept dir, dir Recruitment and Manning Organization US War Shipping Adminstrn and Maritime Commn '42-49; Central Intelligence Agency '49-50; management engr US Dept Defense since '50. Soc Advancement Management(nat sec)—Am Soc Pub Administrn—Am Polit Sci Assn—Soc Personnel Adminstrn. Office of Secretary of Defense, US Department of Defense, Washington 25.

16 HYDE, Reed W. Pyrometallurgical engineering; Sintering of ores. b '90. MetE '13 (Columbia). Research on sintering and agglomeration of ores; design and construction of sintering plants. Asst pres Dwight Lloyd Sintering Machinery Corp since '48. Dwight Lloyd Metall Co '35-48; pres SinteringMachin ery Corp since '48. Am Inst Mining Engrs—Mining and Metall Soc—Am Ceramic Soc. Netcong, N.J. H: 84 Mountain Av., Summit.

17 HYDE, Victor A. City planning; Economic geography. b'13. BS '35 (O State U); MS '39 (U Tenn); summer

'40 (U Chicago). Instr Stow O '35-38; teaching fellow geography U Tenn Knoxville '38-39, instr '39-41; project planning div Tenn Valley Authority Knoxville '41-42; sr planning technician Ala State Planning Bd Wilson Dam '42-47; asst prof community planning and community consultant Bur Community Planning Coll Fine and Applied Arts U Ill Urbana since '47. Am Inst Planners (asso mem)—Am Soc Planning Officials—AAG.

18 HYDE, William Humphrey, Jr. Engineering libraries. b'03. BA '25 (Oberlin Coll); BS '29—MS '38 (Columbia U). Author articles in field. Librarian and prof Ill Inst Tech since '45. ALA—Spl Libraries Assn—Am Soc Engring Edn. Illinois Institute of Technology, Chgo 16.†

19 HYDER, Clyde Kenneth. Algernon Charles Swinburne. b'02. AB '24 (Drury Coll); AM '26—PhD '33—Austin travel fellow '30 (Harvard). Author: Swinburne's Literary Career and Fame '33. Co-editor: The Best of Swinburne '37; Selected Nineteenth Century Essays '38; also articles in field. Asst prof Eng U Kan '30-37, asso prof '37-47, prof since '47, gen ed Humanistic Studies since '35, ed U press since '45. Am Folklore Soc—Modern Lang Assn Am. 211 Fraser Hall, Lawrence, Kan.

20 HYLAND, Lawrence A(vison). Engineering administration. b'97. Student Melrose (Mass) High Sch '12-15. With US Navy '20-26, discharged as chief radioman; asst radio engr Naval Research Lab Bellevue DC '26-32; vp Radio Research Co Washington '32-37; vp Bendix Radio Corp Detroit since '37; exec engr Bendix Aviation Corp '43-49, vp for research since '49. Mem guided missile com Research and Development Bd, Nat Mil Establishment since '48. Inst Radio Engrs—Soc Naval Engrs—Soc Automotive Engrs. Fisher Bldg., Det.◎

21 HYMA, Andrew Martin. Vitamins (Chemistry). b'88. AB '39 (Hope Coll); MS '40—PhD '45 (Mich State Coll). With De Pree Co since '12, lab dir since '30. Soc Bact—ACS—Am Pub Health Assn—Am Pharm Soc. The De Pree Co., 130 Central Av., Holland, Mich.

22 HYMAN, Libbie H(enrietta). Lower invertebrates zoology (Physiology, anatomy); Free-living flatworms. b'88. PhD '15—ScD hon '41 (U Chicago). Author: The Invertebrates: Protozoa through Ctenophora '41; also articles in field. Research asso Am Museum Nat Hist NYC since '36. Am Soc Zoologists—Am Microscop Soc—Am Soc Naturalists — Limnol Soc Am — Soc Systematic Zoologists—Phi Beta Kappa—Sigma Xi. American Museum of Natural History, NYC. 24.†◎

23 HYMAN, Stanley Edgar. Folk literature. b'19. AB '40 (Syracuse U). Author: The Armed Vision: A Study in the Methods of Modern Literary Criticism '48; also articles in field. Staff writer New Yorker Magazine since '41; faculty Bennington Coll '45-46. Am Folklore Soc. New Yorker Magazine, 25 W. 43rd St., NYC. H: Saugatuck, Conn.

24 HYNDMAN, Donald E. Photographic engineering. b'04. BSi n CE '26 (U Denver); student '26-27 (U Rochester NY); bus adminstrn '27-29 (Alexander Hamilton Inst). Research in automatic silver recovery from Hypo. Research chem engr Eastman Kodak Co '26-29, Photographic chem engr '29-40, asst engr East Coast div motion picture film dept '40-46, mgr '46-50, mgr Motion Picture Film Dept since '50. Mem motion picture industry adv com WPB '42; cons engr and analyst war activities com Motion Picture Industry '42-43; sub-com adminstr, war com on photography Am Standards Assn '43-46. mem council '47; mem Thomas A Edison Centennial Com '46-47. Soc Motion Picture Engrs (vp '39-45, pres '45-46)—Phi Lambda Upsilon. 343 State St., Rochester 4, N.Y.⊙

10 HYSLOP, Beatrice Fry. European history (French revolution, cahiers de doléances); International relations. b'99. BA '19—Mary E Woolley fellowship '33-34 (Mount Holyoke); MA '24 —PhD '34—grant-in-aid '35-36 (Columbia U). Research France '30-32, summers '35, '38, '46; lecturer United Nations, European history, French history. Author: French nationalism in 1789 '34; A Guide to the General Cahiers of 1789 '36; Repertoire Critique de Cahiers de Doléances en 1789 (in Collections de documents — Révolution française) '33; also articles in field. Instr history Mount Holyoke Coll '26-28, summer '44; instr history Hunter Coll NYC '36-42, asst prof '42-47; assoc prof since '47; lecturer Pontigny-en-Amérique '44. Am Hist Assn—Am Assn United Nations (chmn edn com NY area since '36, judge annual high sch contest since '37, speakers bureau)— Acad Pol Sci—Middle State Council Social Studies—Economic History Assn —Soc d'hist moderne—Soc de Revolution francaise—Soc des Etudes Robespierristes—Phi Beta Kappa. Hunter College, 695 Park Av., NYC 21.

I

11 IDDLES, Alfred. Steam power. b'89. BS in ME '12—ME '17 (Mich State Coll). 35 years in design and construction of power plants for industry and utilities, mostly steam. Specialized in steam generating units and combustion of fuels. In charge of engineering for a widely known manufacturer of such equipment. With Babcock and Wilcox Co since '37, vp '45, dir '47, pres '48. ASME (F vp '39). 85 Liberty St., NYC.

12 IFFT, John Dempster. Vertebrate morphology; Amphibian sex cycles (Salamanders); Sharks (Polyphyodonty). b 14. AB '35 (Whitman Coll); MA '37 (U Calif); PhD '41 (Yale). Author articles in field. Asso prof biol Simmons Coll since '48. Soc Study Development and Growth—Sigma Xi— Phi Beta Kappa. Simmons College, Boston 15.†

13 IIAMS, Thomas Marion. Preservation of paper. b'98. AB '28 (U Calif); MA '39 (U Chicago); fellowship U Chicago Grad Library Sch '38-39. Author: Preservation of Rare Books and Manuscripts '32; (with T D Beckwith) Foxing in Books '37; (with T D Beckwith, W H Swanson) Deterioration of Paper '40; also articles in field. Librarian and prof bibliography Colgate U since '39. Bibliographical Soc Am— ALA (fgn importations com since '40) —NY Library Assn—Early Am Industries Assn—Inter-Am Bibliographical and Library Assn. Colgate University Library, Hamilton, N.Y.

14 IKENBERRY, Oliver Samuel. Teacher education; Higher education; Educational administration; Educational sociology. b'08. AB '29 (McPherson Coll); AM '32—EdD '41 (Colo State Coll Edn); grad study '35-36 (Columbia). Author: Comparative Inequalities in Educational Finance '32; Economic Factors Affecting Education in an Agricultural Community '39; Leisure Activities in a Community '41; Health, Government, Education and Religion in a Community '41. Co-author: The Status of the Elementary School Principal in Colorado '40. Dean

coll, prof edn Salem (WVa) Coll '41-47; prof edn WVa U summers '46 '47; pres Shepherd State Coll Shepherdstown WVa since '47. Pres Colo Assn Classroom Leaders Western Div '38, Colo Assn Secondary Sch Prins '39-40, Coop Research Assn, Colo State Coll '41, Assn Higher Edn WVa '46. NEA—WVa Edn Assn—WVa Council Coll Pres—Phi Delta Kappa—Kappa Delta Pi. Shepherd State College Shepherdstown, W.Va.†⊙

15 IKINS, William Clyde. Petroleum geology. b'16. BS with honors (Geol) '38—AM '38—PhD '41 (U Tex). Author: The Stratigraphy and Paleontology of the Walnut and Comanche Peak Formations in Central Texas. Author article: Some Echinoids from the Cretaceous of Texas. Co-author articles: (with S E Clabaugh) Some Fossils from the Edwards of Texas. With Tide Water Asso Oil Co '41-46; sr geol The Dow Chem Co since '46. Sigma Gamma Epsilon—Sigma Xi—Am Assn Petroleum Geol—Soc Econ Paleontologists and Mineralogists—Am Inst Mining Engrs. 1314 City National Bank Bldg., Houston.

16 ILLICK, John Theron. Cytology (Evening primrose). b'88. AB '10 (Taylor U); AB '12—MA '13 (Syracuse U); PhD '28—Frances Hinton Maule fellow (Princeton U). Research in cytology of the evening primrose, Oenothera, taxonomy of the Hydromedusae from the west coast. Author: Laboratory Experiments for College Zoology '45; A Laboratory Manual for College Biology '25; also articles in field. Asso prof zool Syracuse U since '38. AAAS(F)— Peking Soc Nat Hist(F)—Am Soc Zool—Am Genetics Assn—Sigma Xi. Rockefeller Foundation Nat Sci fellow '23-24. Syracuse University, Syracuse 10, N.Y. H: 105 Kensington Pl.†

17 ILLICK, Joseph S(imon). Forest management; Forest administration; Dendrology: Pennsylvania trees. b'84. AB '07—ScD '27 (Lafayette Coll); BF '11—FE '13 (Biltmore Forest Sch); '10-11 (U Munich); MS '25 (Juniata Coll). Author: Pennsylvania Trees '14; Tree Habits—How to Know the Hardwoods '24; Outline of General Forestry '35; also articles in field. Dean NY State Coll Forestry since '45. Soc Am Foresters(F)—AAAS(F) — Am Forestry Assn—Am Soc Pub Adminstrn. 763 Ostrom Av., Syracuse, N.Y.⊙

18 INBAU, Fred E(dward). Criminology; Lie detection. b'09. BS '30—LLB '32 (Tulane U); LLM '33 (Northwestern U). Author: Lie Detection and Criminal Interrogation '48; also articles in field. Prof law Northwestern U since '45; managing ed Jour Criminal Law and Criminology since '45; dir Chicago Police Scientific Crime Detection Lab '38-41. Chicago Crime Commn (exec com). 357 E. Chicago Av., Chicago 11.†

19 INGALLS, Albert Graham. Telescope making. b'88. AB '15 (Cornell U). Co-leadership in the hobby of amateur telescope making. Co-author and editor: Amateur Telescope Making '26. Editor: Amateur Telescope Making—Advanced '37; also articles in field. Asso editor Scientific American '24-50, contrib ed since '50. Scientific American, 24 W. 40th St., NYC 18. H: 7 Holly St., Cranford, N.J.

20 INGALLS, Walter Renton. Zinc industry; Metallurgy of zinc; Economics and statistics of non-ferrous metals; Systems of weights and measures. b'65. BS '86 (MIT); DE '23 (Mo U). Chief of commission appointed by Canadian government to report on zinc resources of British Columbia '05-06. Author: Production and Properties of Zinc '02; Metallurgy of Zinc

and Cadmium '03; Lead and Zinc in the United States '08; Wealth and Income of the American People '22; Current Economic Affairs '23; World Survey of the Zinc Industry '31; also articles in field. Consulting engr NY '03-47; dir Am Bur Metal Statis '20-47. Am Inst Mining Metall Engrs— Inst Mining and Metall—Mining and Metall Soc Am—Am Inst Weights and Measures (pres)—Soc Chem Industry. Ingaldsby, Boxford, Mass.

21 INGLE, George William. Plastics (Coloring). b'17. AB chem '38 (Colgate U); MS pulp, paper tech '40 (Inst Paper Chem). Research in organic and inorganic colorants by chemistry and physics of color for use in coloring varied plastics especially cellulosics, vinyls, styrenes. Author article: Using Three Dimensions of Color in plastics. Co-author article: (with L Rudick) Control of Small Color Differences in Plastics Manufacture. Contributor: Encyclopedia of Chemical Technology '49. With color lab Monsanto Chem Co since '42, color research group leader since '49. Optical Soc Am—Inter-Soc Color Council—ASTM—Assn Am Textile Chems and Colorists—ACS. Monsanto Chemical Co., Plastics Division, Springfield, Mass.

22 INGLE, Robert Maurice. Oyster biology; Malariology. b'17. BS '39 (U Ill); MS '51 (U Miami). Dir malaria control and tropical diseases prevention Trinidad BWI US Naval Forces '43-45; asst dir Oyster div state bd conservation Fla since '49. Am Micro Soc—Am Soc Limnol and Oceano—AA AS—Fla Acad Sci. State Board of Conservation, Tallahassee, Fla.

23 INGLES, Lloyd Glenn. Mammals of California. b'01. AB '25 (Redlands U); MA '28 (Claremont Coll); PhD '32 (U Calif). Author: Mammals of California '47; Ecology of the Gray Squirrel '47; also articles in field. Prof zool Fresno State Coll since '45. Calif Acad Sci—Am Soc Zool—Am Soc Mammal— Wildlife Soc—Washington Biol Soc— Am Ornithol Union (asso)—Sigma Xi. Fresno State College, Fresno, Calif.†

24 INGLIS, Ruth Ardell. Communication (Mass); Public opinion; Marketing research. b'12. AB—AM (Stanford); PhD '38 (Bryn Mawr Coll). Research in techniques for validating interviewing methods; relationship between fiction and societies. Author article: An Objective Approach to the Relationship between Fiction and Society. Co-author article: (with H C Ludeke) A Technique for Validating Interviewing Methods in Reader Research. Motion picture research project Hollywood '38-39; div pub opinion Curtis Pub Co Phila '40-42; instr sociology Smith Coll '42-44; research asst to dir Commn on Freedom of the Press NYC '44-46; asso prof sociology U Wash '46-48; asst to pres Nat Assn Broadcasters Washington since '49. Am Assn Pub Opinion Research—Am Sociol Soc. Department of Sociology, University of Washington, Seattle. H: 410 W. 24th St., NYC 11.†

25 INGRAM, William Truitt. Public health engineering. b'08. AB '30 (Stanford U); MPH '42 (Johns Hopkins). Research on relationship of training sanitation personnel and environmental control, scope and value of water works schools, pattern of industrial hygiene in the US, public health engineering and sanitation service in a rural-urban area, protection of sewage works in war time, problems of industrial wastes from standpoint of city administration, mosquito control under the health department, the master of public health program for engineers. Author articles in field. Regional surveyor and supervisor Fed and Calif State Mosquito Control '33-34; san engr San Joaquin Local Health Dist Calif '35-41; regional water works adviser Calif State '42; san engr to sr san engr USPHS '42-47; engring field asso Am Pub Health Assn since '47; asso prof pub health engring NYU Coll Engring University Heights. Am Public Health Assn (F)—ASCE (asso)—Nat Soc Profl Engrs—ASEE—Am Indsl Hygiene Assn—Inter-Am Assn San Engrs—Conf Municipal Pub Health Engrs—Am Water Works Assn—Fedr Sewage Works Assn—Calif Sewage Works Assn (sec '39-41, editor jour '39-41, chmn conf '43). NYU College of Engineering, University Heights, N.Y.

10 INKELES, Alex. Social institutions (Comparative); Social structure of Russia. b'20. BA '41—MA '46 (Cornell U); PhD '49 (Columbia); candidate for certificate (Washington Sch Psychiatry). Research on public opinion in the USSR, social organization in Soviet industry and agriculture, the Soviet Communist Party, quantity quality and development; family and church in the Soviet Union. Editor: section on USSR in encyclopedia Lands and Peoples; also author articles in field. Research analyst Div USSR Research Office Strategic Services and Dept of State '43-46; lecturer social relations and regional studies and research asso Russian Research Center Harvard since '48. Am Sociol Soc—Phi Beta Kappa—Phi Kappa Phi. Am Council Learned Socs(F) '41-42; Social Sci Research Council(F) '47-48. Department of Social Relations, Harvard University, Cambridge 38, Mass.

11 INNES, William Thorton. Fish aquariums; Goldfish and tropical fish. b'74. Grad '92 (Friends' Central Sch Phila). Author: Goldfish Varieties and Tropical Aquarium Fishes '17; The Modern Aquarium '29; Exotic Aquarium Fishes '35; The Complete Aquarium Book '36; Goldfish and Water Gardens '47; Your Aquarium '45; editor the Aquarium (monthly mag); contbr to Ency Britannica; also author articles in field. Formed partnership with father in printing business, firm Innes & Son '97, upon retirement of father formed with brother Innes & Sons '10, which still continues; also operates Innes Pub Co. Acad Nat Sci Phila—Am Museum Nat Hist NYC—Pa Hort Soc. 135 N. 12th St., Phila. 7.

12 INSKO, W(yatt) M(arion), Jr. Poultry husbandry (Hatchability, mineral metabolism). b'01. BS '24 (U Ky); MS '27 (W Va U); '27-28 (U Wis). Research on mineral metabolism of laying hens and growing chicks, factors affecting hatchability of chicken eggs, incubation factors affecting hatchability of turkey eggs, studies on causes of hens and growing chicks and value of green pasture of laying hens and growing chicks. Prof charge poultry husbandry Ky Agrl Expt Sta since '41. AAAS—Poultry Sci Assn (pres)—Ky Acad Sci—Sigma Xi (Treas). 730 Rose St., Lexington 29, Ky.

13 INSLEY, Herbert. Petrography of ceramics; Mineralogy. b'93. Student '10-11 (Amherst Coll); BS '14 (Hamilton Coll); PhD '19 (Johns Hopkins). Author: (with F P Hall) Phase Diagrams for Ceramists '46; also articles in field. Chief div mineral products Nat Bur Standards since '47. AAAS—Am Soc Testing Materials—Geol Soc Am(F)—Mineral Soc Am(F)—Am Ceramic Soc(F)—Am Concrete Inst—Geol Soc Wash (pres '43)—Optical Soc Am—Am Geophys Union—Am Soc X-ray and Electron Diffraction—Crystallographical Soc—Electron Microscope Soc

Am—Sigma Xi. National Bureau of Standards, Washington 25.

14 IREDALE, John Rowland. Silvers (Spectrochemical analysis). b'09. BS chem '32 (Hobart Coll); MS edn '36 (Syracuse U). Developed methods and procedures for spectrochemical analysis of silver, sterling silver, silver solders and nickel silvers. With Oneida Ltd since '43, spectrochem from '46. Optical Soc Am—Soc Applied Spectroscopy—Am Inst Phys. Oneida, Ltd., Oneida, N.Y. H: 304 Graley Av.†

15 IREDELL, F(rancis) Raymond. Epistemology; Oriental philosophy (Chinese, Indian). b'94. BA '21 (Pomona Coll); MA '22—PhD '37—James Walker fellow '22-23—Philip H Sears scholar '23-24 (Harvard); CRB fellow '24-25 (U Brussels, Belgium). Member of the panel on The Teaching of Philosophy in Elementary Courses at the Humanities Conference held at Stanford University '45. Prof Philos Robert Denison Found Pomona Coll and prof philos Claremont Grad Sch since '43, head dept Philos Pomona Coll since '38, sec of fac '44-48; dean fac since '48; trustee Claremont Pub Schs since '42. Am Conf Acad Deans—American Philos Assn (exec com Pacific Div '38-40, vp '48)—Symbolic Logic—Soc Oriental Studies (bd dirs since '41, vp '47-48)—Phi Beta Kappa. Pomona College, Claremont, Cal.☺

16 IRELAND, Hubert Andrew. Insoluble residues; Precision tooling; Geologic graphics; Model railroads. b'04. AB '25 (Ohio Wesleyan U); MS '27 (U Okla); PhD '35 (U Chicago). Invented apparatus for automatical recording of data for fundamentals of air currents in lower atmosphere using electrical counters, photography and a bank of anemometers. Author articles in field. Prof geol U Kans since '48. Geol Soc Am—Am Assn Pet Geol. Department of Geology, University of Kansas, Lawrence, Kans.†

17 IRELAND, Joseph C. Plant physiology (Chlorophyll, growth, soil fluorescence). b'93. BS '14 (Wabash Coll); MS '22—PhD '27 (U Chicago). Co-author: three agricultural texts; also articles in field. Prof agronomy Okla A & M Coll Stillwater since '28. Am Soc Plant Physiol—Biol Photographic Assn—Sigma Xi. Oklahoma A & M College, Stillwater, Okla.

18 IRVIN, Robert Roy. Fermentation, cereal and food chemistry. b'87. AB '16—MS '17 (U Kan); student (U Pittsburgh). Research in cereal chemistry, enzyme preparations, certain aspects of coffee as a beverage, certain problems of cheese industry, and especially art of yeast manufacture. Author articles in field. Fellow Mellon Inst '21-32; lab dir Nat Grain Yeast Co '32-41; dir prodn Red Star Yeast and Products Co Milwaukee since '41. Am Chem Soc—Am Assn Cereal Chem—AAAS(F). Red Star Yeast and Products Co., Milwaukee.

19 IRVINE, Paul. Readability. b'91. AB '15 (Willamette U); MA '24—PhD '28 (NYU); student (U Wash, U Ore). Author articles: Educational Levels in the Southern States '46; Sample-Testing a Large Population Group '46; Plain Talk in Government Writing '49; Agricultural Writers' Word List '49. Editor Resource Use Education since '49; The Interpreter since '45. Prof edn Ala Poly Inst since '28, dir research interpretation council since '45; cons on readability Ala State Textbook Com since '46, various pub. Ala Acad Sci. Alabama Polytechnic Institute, Auburn, Ala.

20 IRWIN, (William) David. Arctic exploration; Eskimos; Eskimo husky

dogs. b'10. Student '15-24 (Columbia). Made longest sled trek ever made alone across Alaska to Hudson's Bay taking three years; training Eskimo husky dogs for search and rescue work; lived among primitive Eskimos. Author: Alone Across the Top of the World '36; One Man Against the North '39. Lectr and showing Arctic exhibit. Caribou Lodge, Milford, Pa.

21 IRWIN, Don L(ouis). Alaska (Agriculture, photography). b'88. Student '10-15 (Kan State Agrl Coll); '40 (Minn Agrl Coll). Author: Pasture and Soil Conservation Practices in Alaska '42; Potatoes, their Production Fertilizing and Storage in Alaska '42; Fertilizers, Their Use and Application in Alaska '43; Potatoes, Their Culture and Storage in Alaska '43; Forty-Seven Years of Experimental and Research Work on Grasses and Legumes in Alaska '45; Co-author: Potato Storage in the Matanuska Valley, Alaska '47; also articles in field. Dir Alaska Agrl Expt Sta since '47. AAAS—Soil Conservation Soc Am—Arctic Inst NA. Palmer, Alaska.

22 IRWIN, Emmett MacDonald. Fatigue in metals; Non-destructive testing. b'02. BS in elec engring '24 (Calif Inst Tech). Sole inventor method of non-destructive testing for fatigue in steel, only known method of determining changes produced by fatigue prior to appearance of fatigue cracks, method employs magnetic analysis system and is widely used in oil industry for testing extent of fatigue in sucker rods and drill pipe. Holder several patents. Author articles in field. Owner Induflux Testing Service Los Angeles since '48. Inst Radio Engrs—AIEE—Tau Beta Pi. 1238 S. Gerhart Av., Los Angeles 22. H: 2179 Lorain Road, San Marino 9.

23 IRWIN, Leonard B. New Jersey government and history. b'04. AB '26 (NYU); MA '33—PhD '39 (U Pa); '44-45 (Temple U). Author: New Jersey, The State and Its Government '42; also articles in field. Prin Haddon Heights High Sch since '44; asst ed Social Studies since '45. Haddon Heights High School, Haddon Heights, N.J.†

24 IRWIN, Malcolm Robert. Genetics (Biology). b'97. BS '20—PhD (Genetics) '28 (Ia State Coll); NRC fellow '28-29 (Bussey Inst-Harvard U), '29-30 (Rockefeller Inst Med Research). Research on inheritance of resistance to infections with Salmonella organisms in rodents; genetic studies of antigens of blood cells and serum of various species; studies of nature of natural and acquired resistance of cattle to Bangs disease. Faculty dept genetics U Wis since '30, prof genetics since '39. Nat Acad Sci—AAAS(F)—Am Soc Naturalists—Genetics Soc Am—Am Assn Immunologists—Am Genetic Assn—Soc Exptl Biol and Med—Soc Zool—Soc Study Evolution—Am Soc Animal Prodn. Elliot medal '38 for meritorious work in zoology. Department of Genetics, University of Wisconsin, Madison 6, Wis.☺

25 IRWIN, Robert Benjamin. Blind (Education, relief legislation, sight saving). b'83. Grad '01 (Washington State Sch Blind); BA '06 (U Washington); MA '07 (Harvard); LLD '43 (Western Res U). Chairman sub-committee on visually handicapped White House Conference on Child Health and Protection '30; chairman American Uniform Type Committee which arranged with British authorities for adoption of a uniform braille code for blind of English-speaking world '32; chairman advisory committee on the Blinded Veteran to US Veterans Administration. Exec dir Am Found for Blind NYC since '29. Am Assn Social

Workers—Am Pub Welfare Assn. 15 W. 16th St., NYC 11.

10 ISAAC, Leo A(nthany). Douglas-fir and Ponderosa pine, silviculture, regeneration and management (Seed sources, strains and species improvement, ecology). b'92. BS '20 (U Minn); Agnes Healey Anderson Research fellow '45-46 (U Wash). Author articles in field. Forest examiner to sr silviculturist US Forest Service since '24. Army airplane timber production World War I and II. Soc Am Foresters—Ecol Soc Am—Sigma Xi—Phi Sigma—Xi Sigma Pi. 423 United States Court House, Portland 5, Ore.†

11 ISAACS, John Dove III. Waves and beaches (Types, forecasting, refraction, protection and amphibious operations); Oceanographic research (Instrumentation; Biological adaption in sea). b'13. Student '30, '41 (Ore State Coll); BS '44 (U Cal); '50 (Scripps Inst Oceanog). Developed methods of beach and wave surveys and surveyed Pacific Coast beaches, invented wave measuring instruments, developed method of determining refraction of waves, discovered theory of total of reflection of waves from deep water, consultant in radio-controlled photogrammetry for Operation Crossroads; invented high-speed plankton collectors, deep mid-water trawl, deep filter, automatic titrator, deep bottom detector, depth-flow recorder, high-speed depressor, underwater telescope. Field and project engr, waves investigations U Cal '44-48; asso oceanog Scripps Inst Oceanog '48-51, asst dir since '51. Pi Mu Epsilon—Sigma Xi—Chi Epsilon—Cal Acad Sci—Am Geophys Union—Am Soc Limnology and Oceanography. Scripps Institution of Oceanography, La Jolla, Cal.

12 ISAACS, Moses Legis. Disinfection; Reconstitution of milk. b'99. AB '20—AM '21—PhD '23 (U Cincinnati); '24-26 (Columbia). Author articles in field. Dean and prof Chem Yeshiva Coll since '42. Mordecai Ben David Found (vp)—AAAS—Harvey Soc—Am Chem Soc—APHS—SAB—Internat Asso Milk Food Sanitarians (asso mem)—Société de Chimie Biologique de France—Phi Beta Kappa. Awarded Merrel F U Cincinnati '21-24. Yeshiva College, Amsterdam Av., NYC 33.

13 ISAACS, Raphael. Liver extract (Intravenous forms); Blood diseases (Leukemia, anemia, polycythemia, hematopoiesis). b'91. AB '11—AM '12—MD '18 (U Cincinnati); Marine Biol Lab Woods Hole Mass '11 and '12; '22-23 (Harvard Med Sch). Discovered granule red blood cell '24, effect of X-ray on blood '25, use of desiccated stomach in treatment pernicious anemia '29-30, intravenous form liver extract '32. Co-author: (with C C Sturgis) Diseases of the Blood '37; (with Thos Ordway and L W Gorham) Diagnosis and Treatment of Diseases of the Blood '37. Asso editor Folia Haematologica since '25. Asst dir Simpson Memorial Inst for Med Research U Mich '27-41; attending physician in hematology Michael Reese Hosp Chicago since '40; med bd Hematology Research Found '44, Leukemia Research Found '46; sec US Pharmacopeia Anti Anemia Products Advisory Bd '34-42. Am Coll Physicians(F)—AAAS(F)—AMA(F)—Internat Society Hematology(F)—Assn Am Physicians—Am Soc Clin Investigation—Central Soc Clin Research—Soc Exptl Biol and Med—Am Soc Exptl Path—Soc Francais d'Hematologie—Inst Med—Ill Acad Sci—Gerontol Soc—Phi Beta Kappa—Alpha Omega Alpha—Sigma Xi. Alvarenga prize '25; Bronze medal AMA '30; Maimonides citation Jewish

Theol Sem Am '44. 5052 Marine Drive, Chgo 40.

14 ISANOGLE, Isabel Thompson. Flora of Maryland and Ohio. b'14. AB '36—BE '37—MA '38 (U Cincinnati); PhD '42 (O State U). Author: Geographical Affinities of the Flora of Ohio '39; Effects of Controlled Shading upon the Development of Leaf Structure in Two Deciduous Tree Species '44. Instr Western Md Coll '42-44, asst prof '44-46, asso prof since '46, sabbatical leave for traveling and working on flora of Md '48-49. Ecol Soc Am—Nat Biol Teachers Assn—AAAS—Sigma Xi. Western Maryland College, Westminster, Md.

15 ISELIN, Columbus O'Donnell. Physical oceanography. b'04. AB '26—AM '28 (Harvard U); DS (hon) '47 (Brown U). Member of committee on undersea warfare National Research Council. Research on circulation of North Atlantic ocean, long-period variations in transport of Gulf Stream system, military aspects of oceanography. Author articles in field. Dir Woods Hole Oceanog Inst '40-50, sr physical oceanographer since '50; research oceanog Mus Comparative Zool, Cambridge since '48; pres bd trustees Bermuda Biolog Sta since '36; trustee Marine Biolog Lab since '41. Am Geophys Union—Am Acad Arts Sci—NY Acad Sci. Awarded Agassiz Medal, Nat Acad Sciences '42; Medal for Merit, Pres US '48. Woods Hole Oceanographic Institution, Woods Hole, Mass.

16 ISELY, Jeter Allen. History of United States amphibious warfare in World War II; Horace Greeley and the New York Tribune. b'13. '35-37 (US Naval Acad); BA '37 (U Tenn); MA '39—PhD '41 (Princeton). Author: German Military Power (with J F Meigs) '43; Horace Greeley and the Republican Party 1853-1861, a Study of the New York Tribune '47; An Analytical Account of Amphibious Warfare in World War II '49. Instr his Princeton '41-42, '46-47, asst prof since '47. AHA. History Department, Princeton University, Princeton, N.J. H: 38 Edwards Place.†

17 ISOLA, Henry E. Bicycles. b'14. Student (Columbia). Research on history of cycling, biographies of cyclers, records and statistics; selection annual All-American cycling team; compilation of data for year-end roundups. Contributor: Encyclopedia of Sports '47; Collier's Encyclopedia '50; All Sports Record Book '50; World Almanac '41-52. Correspondent bicycle racing news since '30; asst ed Bicycling '36-38; pub relations dir Amateur Bicycle League Am '37-41, nat sec '38-42, nat legislation bd '40; sports ed Arc Light (ARC pub for China-Burma-India Armed Forces) '43-45; cycling ed Sports Week '45-50. 136 E. 208th St., Bronx 67, N.Y.

18 IVES, Judson Dunbar. Speleology; Cave fauna. b'84. AM '06 (Wake Forest Coll); student (U Chicago, Geo Peabody Coll, Yale U). Author articles in field. Prof biol Carson-Newman Coll since '23. Entomol Soc Am—Ecol Soc Am—Am Eugenics Soc—Am Genetics Assn—Am Forestry Assn—AAAS—Assn So Biol—NY Acad Sci—NC Acad Sci—Tenn Acad Sci—Societe Linneene de Lyon—Sigma Xi. Pinebluff, N.C.

19 IVY, Horace Macaulay. Education (Southern United States; Negro in South; Federal aid). b'84. Student '96-00 (State Normal Cape Girardeau Mo); AB '03—AM '04 (Central Coll Fayette Mo); '04-05 (U Mo); '06 (U Chicago); PhD '22 (George Peabody Coll for Tchrs). Member National Committee on Research in Secondary Education

since '29; member state board of trustees Institutions of Higher Learning in Mississippi since '44. Author: Relation of Certain Factors to the Pay of Teachers '22. State supervisor secondary schs Jackson Miss '20-23; supt schs Meridian Miss since '23. Nat Soc Study Edn—NEA—Am Assn Sch Adminstrs—So Assn Colls and Secondary Schs (pres '28, chmn com on approval Negro schs and colls since '28)—Miss Edn Assn (pres '26)—Phi Delta Kappa. City Hall, Meridian, Miss.†◎

J

20 JACCHIA, Luigi. Variable stars; Meteors. b'10. PhD '32 (U Bologna Italy). Author: Le Stelle Variabili '33. Co-author (with L Campbell) The Story of Variable Stars '41; also articles in field. Astronomer U Bologna Italy Obs '33-38; research asso in astronomy Harvard U '39-41 and since '45. Internat Astron Union (commn 27, variable stars; commn 22, meteors) College Observatory, Cambridge, Mass.—Am Astron Soc—Sigma Xi. Harvard College Observatory, Cambridge, Mass.

21 JACHOWSKI, Leo Albert, Jr. Parasitology; Medical entomology. b'18. Student '37-39 (U Md); BS '41—MS '42 (U Mich). Holds a series of patents on insect repellents. Author articles in field. Teaching asst U Mich '41-43, research asst '42-43; ensign USNR '43-44 as instr malarioi and parasitol, lt '44-47, research in filariasis and insect repellents, Arctic Alaska '46-47 research on Arctic mosquitoes and their control, lt MSC USN American Samoa since '48, research on filariasis and its control. Am Micros Soc—Am Soc Tropical Med—Am Soc Parasitologists—Mich Acad Sci—Biol Soc Wash—AAAS—Royal Soc Trop Med and Hygiene. Awarded Sec of Navy Commendation Ribbon for research on insect repellents. Naval Medical Research Institute, Bethesda 14, Md.†

22 JACKEL, Simon Samuel. Yeast; Vitamin C (Metabolism); Fermentation (Chemistry). b'17. BS '38 (City Coll NY); '42-43 (U Ill); PhD '50 (Columbia). Research on mechanism of biosynthesis of vitamin C by albino rat, changes in nature of starch during staling of bread, prevention or halting of starch retrogradation; metabolism of yeast including sulfur utilization, effect of specific amino acids in glucose utilization, strain differences, aerobic-anaerobic balance, processes in yeast fermentation. Chem Plymouth Lab '38-41; research chem and dept head Fleischmann Lab since '44. ACS—Am Inst Chem—AAAS—NY Acad Sci—Am Assn Cereal Chem—Inst Food Tech—Phi Lambda Upsilon—Sigma Xi. Fleischmann Laboratories, 810 Grand Concourse, NYC 51.

23 JACKSON, Alvin Thomas. Indian pictography in Texas. b'95. Student pub schs, colls. Research in history and prehistory of Texas caves. Author: A Prehistoric Rock Shelter '33; Exploration of Certain Sites in Culbertson County Texas '42; Picture-Writing of Texas Indians '38; also articles in field. Free lance writer, archaeol. Texas Archaeol and Paleontol Soc—Nat Speleological Soc. P.O. Box 370, Austin, Tex. H: 508 East 46th St.

24 JACKSON, Charles H(arold). Radar; Missile guidance. b'15. BS (mech engring) '36—BS (elec engring) '39—MS (engring) '40 (Purdue U); '37-38 (U Mich). Research on electronic identification and ground radar, airborne and shipborne control radars, control of guided missiles. Radio engr office War Dept '41-45; elec engr HQ US Air Force '45-48; electronic engr Navy Bur Ordnance since '48. Inst

Radio Engrs (sr mem)—Am Inst EE (sr mem)—Soc Automotive Engrs (asso mem). Department of the Navy, Bureau of Ordnance, Code Re9a, Washington 25. H: 1203 Radnor Pl., Falls Church, Va.

10 JACKSON, Clarence Evert. Welding metallurgy. b'06. BA '27 (Carleton Coll Northfield Minn); '32 (George Washington U). Research in welding fundamentals of methods, techniques, and materials, particularly with metallic arc and submerged melt processes; development high speed dilatometer for studying continuous transformation. Author articles: Weldability of Cast Steels '45; Summary of Weldability Tests on Carbon and Low Alloy Steels '46; Effect of Welding Technique on Transition Behavior '48; Energy Distribution in Electric Welding '50, and others. Jr metall Nat Bur Standards Washington '30-37; asst metall USN Gun Factory Washington '37-38; metall and head welding sect Naval Research Lab Washington '38-46: research metall and head welding specialties sect Union Carbide & Carbon Research Labs Niagara Falls since '46. Am Welding Soc—Am Soc Metals—AIMME—Brit Inst Welding—Welding Research Council (past chmn weldability com). Award by Sec of Navy with citation for outstanding achievement in field of welding. 4625 Royal Av., Niagara Falls, N.Y.

11 JACKSON, David Houghton. High vacuum processes. b'99. BS '18 (Guilford Coll); MS '20—du Pont fellowship '19-20 (U NC). Research on application of high vacuum to industrial processes such as evaporation, crystallization, drying, deaeration, deodorizing, moisture conditioning and evaporative cooling. Chem gen lab Aluminum Co Am '20-21; asst to research engr Elliott Co '21-26; mgr information and advt dept ACS '26-30; with Croll-Reynolds Co Inc since '31, gen mgr from '49. Am Inst Chemists (F)—Soc Chem Industries—Am Inst Chem Engrs. Croll-Reynolds Co., Inc.. 17 John St., NYC 7.

12 JACKSON, Donald T(ash). Sulfite pulping process; Bleaching processes. b'03. BS '26 (Mont State Coll); PhD '32 (U Pittsburgh). Research in natural fats and synthetic glycerides, pulping processes, pulp bleaching processes and equipment, chlorite and chlorine dioxide pulp bleaching processes, synthetic organic chemistry, safety paper sensitizing chemicals, waste utilization and waste disposal, sulfite waste liquors and sulfite lignin, research management and research personnel. Owner several patents in paper making. Author articles in field. Research chemist Hammermill Paper Co '33-45, asst dir labs '45-48, dir labs since '48. Am Chem Soc—Tech Assn Pulp and Paper Industry—Nat Council for Stream Improvement—Sigma Xi—Forest Products Research Soc. Hammermill Paper Co., East Lake Rd., Erie, Pa. H: 832 E. 30 St.

13 JACKSON, Dugald Caleb, Jr. Electrical and mechanical engineering; Industrial problems World War II. b'95. AB '17 (Harvard); SB '21—SM '22 (MIT). Planning undergraduate curricula; post college in-service training courses. Colonel Ordnance Department, exec officer Instrument Div, Frankford Arsenal, in charge production of fire control equipment and training of personnel; Industrial College of Armed Forces, analyzing indsl problems of World War II with recommendations to War and Navy Depts. Co-author: (with W P Jones) The Profession of Engineering '29; This Scientific Age '30; also articles in field. Cons engr on industrial management and production '47; chief scientific

training Ballistic Research Labs Aberdeen Proving Ground Md since '48. A IEE(F)—ASME(F)—ASCE—Am Soc Engring Edn —Natl Soc Professional Engrs—Inst Aeronautical Sciences—Newcomer Soc—Tau Beba Pi. Ballistic Research Labs., Aberdeen Proving Ground, Md.◎

14 JACKSON, Edith Banfield. Infant welfare (Rooming-in). Grace-New Haven Community Hospital, 789 Howard Av., Room 4084, New Haven 4.

15 JACKSON, Eugene Bernard. Indexing of aeronautical literature. b'15. BS '37 (Purdue U); BS '38—MA '42 (U Ill); '43-44 (Tex Tech Coll); '45 (Sch for Army Librarians). Panel Leader Conference on Problems of Centralized Documentation Wright Field '49. Author: Application of Standard Aeronautical Indexing System and Other Indexing Systems in Central Air Documents '49. Contributing editor: Subject Headings for Aeronautical Engineering Libraries '49; also articles in field. Jr asst in technol Pub Library Detroit '42-43; chief library sect Air Documents Div Air Material Command Wright Field '46-49; chief tech information control sect Research and Development Br OQMG; now chief Office Aeronaut Intell. Inst Aeronautical Sci—Spl Libraries Assn. Office of Aeronautical Intelligence, Nat. Adv. Com. for Aeronautics, Washington 25. H: 3019 Parkway Terrace Dr., Washington 20.

16 JACKSON, Gorham Eddie. Timber estimating, mapping, and surveying; Timber appraisals. b'10. BS (forestry) '35 (NC State Coll). Supervisor Hofmann Forest '35-44; forester '44-45; cons forester since '45. Soc Am Foresters — Assn Cons Foresters — Am Forestry Assn—NC Forestry Assn (vp '49, '50)—NC Forestry Council—NC Forestry Found Inc (dir). 1035 Respass St., Washington, N.C.

17 JACKSON, Herbert William. Limnology; Oceanography; Speleology. b'11. BA '34 (Dartmouth); '34-36 (Harvard); PhD '39 (Cornell). Particularly interested cave ecology, fauna and flora; experimental and investigational work farm fish ponds since '46; general mammalogy research '30-40; extension aromatic (Turkish) Tobacco Specialist '45-46. Collector and instructor U NH summers '27-37; instr vp '39-42, asst prof '42-44, assoc prof since '46, collaborator USDI since '47; Rockefeller Found F Mexico '49-50. Am Fisheries Soc—Am Limnol Soc—Ecological Soc Am—Am Soc Mammalogists—Nat Speleol Soc. Virginia Polytechnic Institute, Biology Department, Blacksburg, Va. H: Box 527.†

18 JACKSON, Marion Leroy. Soil chemistry; Farm runoff chemistry. b '14. BS '36—MS '37 (U Neb); PhD '39 (U Wis). Studies in chemistry of clay fraction of soils; cation exchange mechanism, ionic fixation in soils; physical and chemical properties of soils in relation to crop quality and yield; chemistry of soil phosphates and avilability to plants; soil fertility and crop production; lake pollution from farm runoff. Staff U Wis '41-45, since '46, prof soils since '50; asso prof agron and soil chem Purdue U '45-46. Soil Sci Soc Am—Am Soc Agron—AC S—Sigma Xi—Alpha Zeta, Phi Beta Kappa—Pi Mu Epsilon—Gamma Sigma Delta—Phi Lambda Upsilon. Post doctorate fellow in soils Wis Alumni Research Found U Wis '39-41. Room 104B, Department of Soils, University of Wisconsin, Madison 6, Wis. H: 563 Park Lane, Madison 5.

19 JACKSON, Stuart Wells. French in America; Lafayette; French participation in the American Revolution.

b'75. BA '98 (Yale U); hon D Humane Letters '46 (Lafayette Coll). Book collector, principally concerning Abraham Lincoln and Lafayette; about 2000 items of Lincoln collection given to Yale U Library '44; Lafayette group consists of about 400 autographed letters from 1777-1834, 500 printed vols directly relating to him with extensive collections of Am and French Revolutions; The French in Am with spl emphasis on Lafayette and His Times, French Travellers in Am and French Colonization. Author: Lafayette—A Bibliography '30; also articles in field. Pvt ins bus '14-42; trustee Yale U Library. NY Hist Soc—Conn Hist Soc—Va Hist Soc—Hist Soc of Pa—Am Friends of Lafayette (founder, p pres)—Institut Français de Washington (pres). Chevalier Legion of Honor. H: Gloucester, Va. Also The University Club, 54th St. at Fifth Av., NYC.

20 JACOBS, Melville. Anthropology (Pacific Northwest Indians). b'02. AB '22 (Coll City NY); AM '23—PhD '31 (Columbia). Field researches '26-39 in languages (Sahaptin, Chinook, Tillamook, Salish, Kalapuya, Molale, Galice Athabaskan, Coos, Alsea), folklores, ethnographies, music of Oregon-Washington Indians. Co-author (with B J Stern) Outline of Anthropology '47; also articles in field. Asso anthropol U Wash '28-29, instr '29-37, asst prof '37-45, asso prof since '45. Am Anthropol Assn (council since '30, asso ed American Anthropologist '39-44)—Am Folklore Soc (council since '42)—Am Ethnol Soc—Linguistic Soc Am—Am Anthropol Assn—Interamerican Soc Geog and Ethnography—Sigma Xi. Department Anthropology, University of Washington, Seattle 5.†

21 JACOBSEN, Thorkild. Mesopotamian archeology; Sumerology. b'04. AM '27—Dr Phil '39 (U Copenhagen); PhD '29 (U Chicago). Directed under H Frankfort the excavation of Sennacherib's Aqueduct at Jerwan Iraq '32-34 and excavations at Ishchaly Iraq '34-35. Author: Philological Notes on Eshunna and Its Inscriptions '34; The Sumerian King List '39; Cuneiform Texts in the National Museum of Copenhagen '39. Co-author: (with S Lloyd) Sennacherib's Aqueduct at Jerwan '35; The Gimilsin Temple '35. Participated Nippur expedition University Pa and Oriental Inst, advisor '49. Field assyriologist Iraq expedition Oriental Inst U Chicago '26-37, research asso '37-42, asst prof social instns '42-44, asso prof '44-46, prof since '46, dir Oriental Inst '46-50, dean div humanities since '48. Am Oriental Soc—Archeol Inst Am—Middle East Inst. 5807 Dorchester Ave., Chicago 37.◎

22 JACOBSEN, William Cornelius. Agricultural regulatory procedure; Pest control (Rodents and animals); Interstate cooperation. b'94. In charge rodent, weed and plague control '33-44; collaborated in developing coordinated non-overlapping campaign and practical procedure between official agricultural health and local administration agencies for suppression of field rodents harboring diseases transmissible to humans e.g. plague, relapsing fever, tularemia and spotted fever. AB '16 (U Calif); LLB '37 (McGeorge Coll Law). With Calif State Dept Agr since '19, asst to dir since '49. Am Soc Mammal—Am Wildlife Soc—Am Soc Public Adminstrn. Calif State Dept of Agriculture, State Office Building No. 1, Sacramento 14, Calif. H: 1341 43rd St., Sacramento 19.

23 JACOBUS, David Schenck. Steam engineering; Welding; Construction codes and procedures. b'62. ME '84—Dr Engring '06 (Stevens Inst Tech). Recognized authority on steam engineering. Instr Stevens Inst Tech '84-97, prof exptl mechanics and engring physics '97-06; adv engr The Babcock & Wilcox Co '96-41, now retired; hon mem ASME Boiler Code and chmn '38-42 eds of Am Welding Soc Welding Handbook. ASME (pres '16-17, hon mem)—Soc Naval Architects and Marine Engrs—Am Inst Mining Engrs—Am Math Soc—Soc Promotion Engring Edn—Am Inst Elec Engrs—Am Soc Heating and Ventilating Engrs—Am Soc Refrigerating Engrs (pres '06-07, life mem)—Am Welding Soc (pres '34-35)—Am Petroleum Inst—Am Soc for Metals—Franklin Inst—Holland Soc of NY—AAAA (F). 93 Harrison Av., Montclair, N.J.⊚

10 JAFFE, Bernard. Chemistry (Teaching); Chemistry (History). b '96. Author: Crucibles (concerning lives and achievements of great chemists) '30 (rev edits) '42, '48; Outposts of Science '35; New World of Chemistry '35 (rev edits) '40 '42 '47; Men of Science in America 44. Co-author: (with W Burnett and H Zim) New World of Science '48. Instr chemistry NY City High Schs since '24; head phys sci dept high sch since '31. History of Sci Soc—Am Chem Soc—Phi Beta Kappa. Francis Bacon award for humanizing knowledge (Crucibles) '30. James Madison High School, Bklyn. H: 25 Eastern Parkway.⊚

11 JAFFE, D. Lawrence. Frequency modulation systems. b'13. BS (EE) '35 (Coll City NY); MS '36—PhD '40 (Columbia). Author articles: Wide Band Amplifiers and Frequency Multiplication '42; Modulation Circuit Theory '40; A Theoretical and Experimental Investigation of Tuned Circuit Distortion in Frequency Modulation Systems '45; Intermediate Frequency Amplifier Stability Factors '46, and others. Television development engr CBS '39-42; cons and liaison engr radiation lab MIT and Raytheon Mfg Co '42-44; chief research engr Templeton Radio Mfg Corp '44-45; now pres Polarad Electronics Corp. Inst Radio Engrs. 100 Metropolitan Av., Bklyn 11.

12 JAFFE, Hans. Ceramics; Piezoelectric crystals; Crystallography. b'09. Student '27-29 (U Heidelberg); '29-30 (U Berlin); PhD '34 (U Goettingen). Research on ferro-electricity, crystal light valves, methods of single crystal growth; latter research led to introduction of ammonium dihydrogen phosphate and lithium sulfate crystals in sonic and ultrasonic transducers. Granted patents on single crystals of dihydrogen phosphates. Author articles in field. Head crystal research dept Brush Development Co since '40. AAAS(F) — Am Phys Soc — Crystallographic Soc Am—Inst Radio Engrs (Com on piezoelectric crystals and papers review com). 3405 Perkins Av., Cleveland 14.

13 JAGENDORF, Moritz Adolph. Folklore (United States). b'98. Ed pub schs. Collection folkstories of every state in US. Author: New England Bean Pot '48; Up State Down State '49; The Marvelous Adventures of Johnny Darling '49. NY Folklore Soc (pres)—Am Folklore Soc (exec council) — French Folklore Soc — British Folklore Soc—Acad Polit Sci—Les Amis d'Escoffier Soc. Hotel Dryden, 150 East 39th St., NYC 16.†

14 JAHN, Theodore Louis. Protozoology, taxonomy); Physiology of vision (Photochemistry, electrical aspects in man and animals); Insect physiology (Electrical changes in heart and eye). b'05. AB '27 (Rice Inst); MS '29—teach fellow U Coll '27-31—PhD '31 (NY U); Nat Research Council fellow '31-33 (Yale); research fellow '30 (NY Zool Soc, NY Aquarium); research fel-

low '36 (Cold Spring Harbor Biol Lab). Co-author: (with F F Jahn) How to Know the Protozoa '48; also articles in field. Research asso zool '34-36, asst prof '37-41, asso professor '41-48 (State U Ia); prof zool U Calif since '48, chmn department zoology since '49. AAAS—Am Inst Biol Scis—Am Inst Physics—Am Micro Soc—Am Physiol Soc—Am Soc Naturalists—Am Soc Protozool (sec-treas '47-48)—Am Soc Zoologists—Ia Acad Sci—NY Entomol Soc—Optical Soc Am—Phycol Soc Am—Soc Exptl Biol and Med (pres Ia Br and on Nat Council '42-43)—Sigma Xi. Department of Zoology, University of California, Los Angeles 24.

15 JAHNS, Richard Henry. Geology of non-metalliferous deposits. b'15. BS '35—PhD '43 (Calif Inst Tech); MS '37 (Northwestern U). Research and writing in glacial geology of Massachusetts, New Hampshire and Vermont, geology and engineering aspects of recent floods in New England, graphite in New York, talc in Vermont, refractory materials in Massachusetts, pyrophyllite in California, mica, lithium minerals, gem materials, feldspar and other pegmatite minerals in the southeastern states Rocky Mountain states and southwestern states, tungsten and beryllium minerals in New Mexico. Author articles in field. Jr geologist US Geol Survey '37-41, asst geologist '41-43, asso geologist '43-44, geologist '44-48, sr geologist since '48; asst prof geol Calif Inst Tech '46, asso prof since '46. AA AS(F)—Am Assn Pet Geologists—Geol Soc Am(F)—Am Inst Mining and Metall Engrs—Am Geophys Union—Geol Soc Wash—Soc Econ Geologists—Soc Vertebrate Paleontology. Division of the Geological Sciences, California Institute of Technology, Pasadena 4, Calif.⊚

16 JAHODA, William John. Aquatic biology (Invertebrates, ecology); Limnology; Game management. b'17. BS '41—MS '46 (U NH); PhD '48 (O State U). Distribution of Fresh Water microcrustacea (Lake Erie); ecological influences of beaver flowages. Author: Use of Oaks by Beavers in New Hampshire '46; Survival of Brook Trout in Water of Low Oxygen Content '47; A Contribution to the Ecology of Beaver Flowages '46; The Distribution of Western Lake Erie Diaptomids '48. Research fellow Franz Theodore Stone Lab Ohio State U Put-In-Bay Ohio '46-48, limnology and aquatic research. Am Soc Limnology and Oceanography—Wildlife Soc. Division of Natural Sciences, State Teachers' College, New Paltz, N.Y.

17 JAKKULA, Arne Arthur. Applied and theoretical mechanics; Structural engineering (Bridges, highway). b'04. BS '26—MS '27—CE '37 (U Minn); PhD '33 (U Mich). Author articles in field. Research asst U Mich '26-28, instr civil engring '28-33, asst prof '33-37; asso prof structural engring Agrl and Mech Coll Tex '37-39, prof '39-46, v dir Tex Engring Expt Sta '44-46; exec dir Tex Agrl and Mech Research Found since '46. ASCE (com applied mech of structural div)—Internat Assn Bridge and Structural Engring—ASEE—Tex Acad Sci—Tex Soc Profl Engrs—Nat Soc Profl Engrs—Am Petroleum Institute—Am Geophysical Union—Chi Epsilon—AAAS—Tau Beta Pi—Sigma Xi. Texas Agricultural and Mechanical Research Foundation, Box 44, F.E., College Station Tex.

18 JAKOBSON, Roman. Slavic languages, literatures and folklore; Linguistics; Phonetics; Metrics; Paleosiberian languages. b'96. Grad '14 (Lazarev Inst Oriental Langs Moscow); MA '18 (U Moscow); PhD '30 (U

Prague). Author: Newest Russian Poetry '21; Czech Verse as Compared to Russian '23; The Oldest Czech Spirituals '29; Remarques sur l' evolution phonologique '29; Eurasian Linguistic Affinity '31; Children's Language, Aphasia and General Sound Laws '41; The Wisdom of the Ancient Czechs '43; La Geste du Prince Igor '48; The Vseslav Epos '49; Sound and Meaning '53; also articles in field. Prof Ecole Libre des Hautes Etudes NYC since '42; Columbia U '43-49; SH Cross prof Slavic lang and lit Harvard U since '49. Dan Royal Acad Sci—Norwegian Acad Sci—Internat Phonetic Assn (hon mem)—Linguistic Circle Prague (vp '26-39)—Linguistic Circle New York (vp '43-49) Acta Linguistica (chmn)—Am Anthropol Assn (liaison F)—Chevalier Legion d'Honneur. Harvard University, Cambridge, Mass.⊚

19 JAKOBSON, Svatava Pirkova. Folklore (Moravian); Czech literature. Grad '28 (Prague Classical Gym and of the Coll d'Angouleme France)—PhD (Charles U Prague). Field work in folklore in Czechoslovakia '31-33, Bulgaria '35, '37, America since '41, and in Haiti; research and writing on social functions poetical and musical structure of Moravian folksongs '33, ethnographic sound film The Vanishing World devoted to Moravian popular traditions exhibited in Europe and America produced '32. Author: Questionnaire distributed among American immigrants and natives of Czech and Slovak background published with answers NY. Editor: America since '47. Lecturer Czech lang and lit Ecole Libre des Hautes Etudes '42-46, Columbia '43-49; lecturer Slavic lang and lit Harvard U since '49. Masaryk Social Soc Prague—Am Folklore Soc (editorial com since '46). Harvard University, Cambridge, Mass.

20 JAMES, Alice Galligan. Amazon valley (Social anthropology). b'13. AB '33 (Hunter Coll); AM '39—PhD '45 (Columbia). Author: Village Arrangement and Social Organization Among Some Amazon Tribes '49. Instr anthrop Hunter Coll since '45. AM Anthrop Assn(F)—Am Assn Physical Anthrop—Am Assn U Women. Hunter College, 695 Park Av., NYC.

21 JAMES, Arthur Edwin. Colonial potters, clocks and clockmakers (Chester County Pennsylvania); Medicinal chemicals (Photoelectric colorimetric assay). b'97. BS '21 (Pa State Coll); MA '24 (U Pa); Gen Ednl Bd fellow '29-30—PhD '33 (Cornell). Research in inorganic pharmaceutical assay, liquid ammonia reactions, history of science, Pennsylvania antiques. Author: The Potters and Potteries of Chester County Pennsylvania '45; Chester County Clocks and Their Makers '47; also articles in field. Prof chem sch pharmacy Temple U since '37. AAAS—Am Pharm Assn (pres Phila sect '42)—Am Chem Soc—Pa Acad Sci—Chester Co Hist Soc. Temple University, Phila. 40.†

22 JAMES, Edward M(urdoch). Continuous refining processes for vegetable oils. b'95. AB '16—AM '17 (U Cincinnati). Research on continuous processing for refining cottonseed and soybean oils. Author articles: Centrifugal Force in Chemical Production '29; Now Continuous Process for Refining Vegetable Oils '34, and others. Contributor: chapter in Processing of Cottonseed Oil '48; chapter in Soybeans and Soybean Products '51. Chem Sharples Splty Co Phila (centrifugal engrs) '19-21, chief chem and oil specialist '29-37; development chem edible oil refining Procter & Gamble Co Cincinnati '21-26; chief oil pretreatment sect Lever Brothers Co Cambridge

Mass '37-50, asst to tech advisor since '50. ACS—Am Oil Chem Soc (vp '47-48, '51-52, pres '52-53)—AIChE—Am Soybean Assn (tech com)—Nat Soybean Processors Assn.

10 JAMES, Herman Brooks. Agricultural economics. b'12. BS '32—MS '40 (NC State Coll); PhD '49 (Duke). Farm management specialist NC Agr Extension Service, Raleigh NC '39-42; agr economist Appalachian and Southeast regions USDA '43-44; in charge farm management extension dept NC State Coll '45-46, charge teaching and farm management research dept agrl econs as prof agrl econs '47-49, head dept agrl econs since '49. Am and So econ assns—Am Farm Econ Assn—So Farm Management Research Com(chmn '49-51)—Grange—Farm Bur—Alpha Zeta—Phi Kappa Phi—Kappa Phi Kappa. Dept of Agricultural Economics, NC State College, Raleigh, NC. H: 1323 Lutz Av.†◎

11 JAMES, Herman G(erlach). Public administration; Market research. b '87. AB '06—AM '10 (U Ill); JD '09 (U Chicago); PhD '11 (Columbia); LL D hon '31 (U NM), '36 (Miami U). Author: Principles of Prussian Administration '13; Applied City Government '14; Municipal Functions '17; Local Government in the United States '21; The Constitution System of Brazil '25; The Protection of Public Interests in Public Contracts '46. Teacher pub law U Leipzig, U Tex, U Neb, U Cal, U Chicago, Northwestern '11-29; dean U Neb '25-29; pres U SD '29-35, Ohio U '35-43; with US State Dept '43; dir market research Nat Transitads since '46; pres Inst Transit Advt '43-50. Am Polit Sci Assn—Am Marketing Assn. National Transitads Inc., 400 N. Michigan, Chgo 11.

12 JAMES, John William. Oil burners. b'07. BS in mech engring '28 (Ore State Coll); MS in mech engring '34 (U Wis). Co-author (with Allen and Walker): Heating and Air Conditioning '46. Technical editor: American Society Heating and Ventilating Engineers Guide '36-43; associate editor: Handbook of Oil Burning '51. Contributor Kent's Mechanical Engineers' Handbook (12th edit) '49. Cons engr '28-32; engr Gen Elec Co '34-35; tech sec Am Soc Heating and Ventilating Engrs '35-43; research engr Iron Fireman Mfg Co '43-48; vp research McDonnell & Miller Inc since '48. Am Soc Heating and Ventilating Engrs—ASME—Sigma Xi—Am Soc San Engring. Research F U Wis '32-34. 3500 N. Spaulding Av., Chgo 18.

13 JAMES, Preston Everett. Latin America (Geography). AB '20—AM '21 (Harvard); PhD '23 (Clark U). Appointed by State Department to be US member Commission on Geography of Pan-American Institute Geography and History; research on European colonies in Brazil, research in Brazil for Brazilian Government '49-50. Author: Latin America '42; Brazil '46; Our Earth '47; Using Our Earth '47; Living on our Earth '48; At Home on Our Earth '49; A Geography of Man '49, and others. Editor Brazil geography section Handbook Latin American Studies since '35. With U Mich '23-45, prof '34-45; prof geog Syracuse U since '45; Office Coordinator Information '41-42, chief Latin-Am Div OSS '42-43, asst chief Europe-Africa Div '43-45, lt col since '43. Am Council Learned Socs (joint com Latin-Am studies)—Nat Research Council—Assn Am Geog (sec '36-41)—Am Geog Soc NY—Am Meteorol Soc—Nat Council Geog Teachers—Phi Kappa Phi. Grant-in-aid Nat Research Council '30-31, Harris Found Conf '37,

Social Sci Research Council '38. 220 Standish Dr., Syracuse 3, N.Y.†◎

14 JAMES, Ralph A(rthur). Chemistry; Radioactivity; Transuranium elements. b'20. BS '42—PhD '48 (U Calif). Co-discoverer of the elements americium and curium. Asst prof dept chem U Calif since '48. University of California, Los Angeles 24.

15 JAMES, Reese D(avis). History of the Philadelphia stage. b'89. AB '10—AM '11—PhD '30 (U Pa). Author: Old Drury of Philadelphia '32. Free lance fiction and article writing; with U Pa since '19, asso prof Eng since '37, dir courses in journalism since '21, chmn journalism award com U Pa; trustee Price Sch Advt and Journalism. Pa Hist Soc—Am Assn Teachers of Speech—Phi Beta Kappa. English Department, College Hall, University of Pennsylvania, Phila.

16 JAMES, Robert Frederick. Florida (Resources); Food preservation; Meat preservation and tenderization; Citrus by-products. b'97. Student (Columbia, U Rochester); MS—PhD (U Mich). Author articles in field. Research Detroit Edison Co '28-34, Westinghouse Elec Co '34-36; research cons E I DuPont de Nemours '36-42; defense plant facility US Dept Agr '42-45; The James Found since '45. Shell Mound Experiment Station, Ft. Myers Beach, Fla.

17 JAMES, Thelma Grey. Folklore of ethnic groups in America. '99. AB '20—MA '23 (U Mich); grad study '27-29 (U Chgo). Author: World Neighbors '51. With Wayne U since '23, dir folklore project since '40, prof since '51. Am Folklore Soc (pres '50-51). Wayne U., Detroit 1.

18 JAMES, William Stubbs. Automotive research and engineering; Fuels and lubricants; Fuel economy; Transmissions. b'92. BS in ME (CL) '17 (George Washington U). Author articles in field. Lab aid later physicist in charge power plant sect Bureau of Standards, heat div '11-24; testing engr Hupp Motor Car Co Detroit '24; asst technologist Asso Oil Co San Francisco '24-26; with Studebaker Corp South Bend '26-45, as research engr '36-37, chief engr '37-45; dir research '45-48 Ford Motor Co; vp engring and research Fram Corp since '48. Soc Automotive Engrs (pres '44)—Am Physical Soc(F)—Am Soc Testing Materials—ASME. H: 4805 N. Adams Rd., Birmingham, Mich.◎

19 JAMES, William Thomas. Animal psychology; Inheritance of constitution in dogs. b'03. BS '24 (Furman U); PhD '29 (Cornell U). Research and writing on breeding out of deformities in dogs, Pavlov's theory of internal inhibition, conditioned avoiding response of dog, distemper control, social behavior among dogs, formation of neurosis in dogs by increasing energy requirement of conditioned avoiding response; studies in general relationship between nervous types and adjustment to environment; dominance-submissive differences. Author articles in field. Prof psych Ga U since '46. Am Psycholog Assn—AAAS—Am Genetic Assn—Ga Psycholog Assn—Ga Acad Sci—Sigma Xi. Meigs Hall, Athens, Ga.◎

20 JAMESON, Raymond D. Chinese and comparative folklore; European literature. b'95. BA '16—MA '17 (U Wis). Author: Trails of the Troubadors '27; Short History of European Literature '29; Three Lectures on Chinese Folklore '32; A Comparison of Literatures '35; also articles in field. Research in Europe '23-25; prof comp lit Nat Tsing Hua U Peiping China '25-

38; dir Orthological Inst Peiping China '33-38; cons Library of Congress and adminstr consultant service '38-42; cons historian ANRC '42-48; prof folklore NM Highlands U since '49. 1010 Douglas, Las Vegas, N Mex.†

21 JAMISON, Robert Rosebery. Food (Refrigeration). b'95. BS '19 (Purdue U). Development and design milk cooling and food freezing equipment for farm use. With Esco Cabinet Co since '30. Am Soc Agrl Engrs—Am Soc Refrigerating Engrs—Alpha Zeta. Esco Cabinet Co., West Chester, Pa.

22 JANEWAY, Robert Noah. Vehicle suspension (Railroad car truck design); Internal combustion engine (combustion chamber design). born '02. ME '22 (Cornell). Holds patents on railroad car trucks, and combustion chambers for automotive engines. Author papers, including: Combustion Control by Cylinder Head Design '29; Quantitative Analysis of Heat Transfer in Engines '38; Vehicle Vibration Limits to Fit the Passenger '48; Elimination of Damaging Shock and Vibration in Freight Cars '50. Research engr engine combustion Gen Motors '22-27; cons engr combustion chamber design '27-31; dir dynamics research Chrysler Corp since '31. Soc Automotive Engrs (chmn riding comfort research com). Chrysler Corp., Engineering Division, P.O. Box 1118, Det 31.†

23 JANSE, Olov Robert Ture. European and Far Eastern art and archeology. b'92. AB '16—AM '20—PhD '22 (U Upsala Sweden). Director archeological expeditions sponsored by Paris Museum and Indo China Government General Indo China '34-35, '36-38, Harvard-Yenching Institute to Indo China and Philippine Islands '38-40; vis lect Far East archeol Harvard '40-43; counsellor humanistic studies UNESCO Paris France '46-47; organized numerous exhibitions in museums of Sweden France Indo China United States; classified collections of antiquities in Museums Stockholm and Paris; conducted excavations for Royal Swedish Academy Sweden '12-27, Gen Government Indo China '34-35, '36-38. Author numerous books and articles on archeol of old world. Asst curator French Nat Mus Antiquities '13-30; asso prof nat and prehistoric archeol Ecole du Louvre Paris '25-27; asso prof U Paris '28-36; asst curator Nat Historic Mus Stockholm '26-29; dep chief South East Asia sect Office Stragetic Services Washington '43-45, Dept of State '45-46, with Fgn Service Inst since '48. Awarded Letterstedt fellowship Royal Swedish Acad '30, Vega prize Royal Swedish Anthrop Soc. Foreign Service Institute, Department of State, Washington. H: 2120 16th St NW, Washington 9, D.C.

24 JANSEN, Arthur. Railroad finance and securities. b'04. BSc '27 (Columbia U). Member faculty NYU Grad Sch of Business (courses on analysis of railroad securities); faculty NY chapter Am Inst Banking since '42 (courses on analysis of industrial securities); faculty Columbia U Sch of Gen Studies (courses on corporate finance). Author articles in field. With Wall St houses since '27; mgr statis dept W E Burnet and Co '38, gen partner '43; partner E W Clucas and Co '47-49; partner JR Williston & Co since '49. J. R. Williston & Co., 115 Broadway, NYC 6.

25 JANSEN, William Hugh. Folklore (American, Turkish). b'14. BA '35 (Wesleyan U Conn); PhD '49 (Ind U). Archiving of folklore; field study on "Oregon" Smith; research on tall tale and anecdote in America, and on material transplanted to America; editor in chief Hoosier Folklore '47-49, regional editor Midwest Folklore since '50. Author articles: Changes Suffered by "The Wife Wrapped in Wether's Skin" '45; Lying Abe—A Tale-Teller '48; The Folksinger's Defense '50; From Field to Library '52. Asst prof English and folklore U Ky since '49; vis lectr U Ankara Turkey '51-52. Am Folklore Soc (exec council since '48) —Hoosier Folklore Soc (past pres)— So Folklore Soc (pres since '50)—Folk-Lore Soc Eng—Modern Lang Soc—South Atlantic Modern Lang Soc. Department of English, University of Kentucky, Lexington, Ky.†

10 JANSON, Horst W. Iconology; Italian Renaissance sculpture; Modern art. b'13. Student '32-35 (Hamburg U, Germany); '33-34 (Munich U); Am '38—PhD '42—Charles W Holtzer Fellow '35 (Harvard). Author articles in field. Asso prof dept art and archeology Washington U, St Louis Mo '47-49; prof, chmn fine arts Wash Sq Coll NYU '49. Coll Art Assn Am—Internat Inst (St Louis) (mem bd). Guggenheim Fellow '48-49. Department of Fine Arts, Washington Square College, N.Y. Univ., NYC 3.©

11 JAPS, Archie (B(ernard). Plastics and synthetic rubber; Vinyl chloride and poly vinyl chloride. b'13. BCHE '33 (U Minn). Research in vinyl resin product development, development of processes for producing vinyl chloride and poly vinyl chloride, process development of new plastic products. Holder several US patents. Author: Chemical Engineering Research at the B F Goodrich Company. Control chemist B F Goodrich Co '33-35, research engr '35-37, chem engr '37-40, sr engr '40-42, dir research dept since '42. AICE—ACS.

12 JARDON, Fritz W. Plastic artificial eyes; Movable artificial eyes. b'10. MA '30 (Munich Sch Art and Handwork). Pioneer inventor of all-plastic artificial eye; co-inventor with A D Ruedemann of Ruedemann-Jardon permanent eye implant; co-inventor with William Stone of Stone-Jardon implant. Author: Eyefitting Manual; also articles in field. Owner and mgr Jardon Dental Lab Kansas City '34-40, vp Paul Gougelman Co Chicago '41-43; pres Mono-Plastic Eye Co Inc Evanston Ill '43-44; mfg mgr Monoplex Eye Div Am Optical Co since '44; grad instr Am Acad Ophthalmol since '47; cons Kresge Eye Inst. Owner Fritz Jardon Prosthetic Lab Detroit. Fritz Jardon Prosthetic Laboratories, 112 Madison Av., Det 26.

13 JARECKA, Louise Llewellyn. Polish traditional arts. Class '04 (Kan State U); '04-05 (Chicago Musical Coll); '09, '10 (Schola Cantorum Paris); '11-12 (NE Conservatory Music). Six years study in Poland of weaving, ceramics, folklore, folk music, other ancient skills; American organizer coast-to-coast exhibition Polish Manual Arts opening at Smithsonian Institution '49. Author: Made in Poland, Living Traditions of the Land '49. Author articles: Popular art in Poland; Folk Art in Poland; and others. Dir and script writer Polish Manual Arts film. 897 Second Av., NYC 17.

14 JARNAGIN, Milton Preston. Animal husbandry; Forage crops. b'81. Student '00-03 (U Tenn); '03-04 (U Wis); BSA '05—DSc '21—M Agr '30 (Ia State Coll). Director projects on university experimental farm, and development herds of dairy and farm animals; organization and direction university livestock extension; secretary livestock breeding section Federal Food Administration World War I; chairman Georgia State Swine Com-mittee. Head animal husbandry div U Ga since '07; apptd agrl cons Bd Regents U System of Ga '48. AAAS(F)—Am Soc Animal Prodn—Southeastern Livestock Assn—Am Jersey Cattle Club—Ga Aberdeen-Angus Assn—So Agrl Workers—Ga Acad Sci—Am Assn Advancement Dairy Sci—Ga Dairy and Livestock Assn(past sec) — Swine Growers' Assn—Walking Horse Breeders' Assn Am(bd dirs)—Phi Kappa Phi(sec). Awarded medallion by Assn So Agrl Workers for distinguished service '40, citation from Future Farmers of Am '46. H: 630 Milledge Circle, Athens, Ga.

15 JASKAR, Ade Eugene. Soil mehanics; Engineering geology. b'12. BS '37—'46-47 (U Wash). Research in field and laboratory of compaction, consolidation, permeability, shear, influence of admixtures, relation of geologic occurrence to soil properties; collaborated in design special soil testing equipment; development test procedures and standards. Engring geol Pacific NW and Alaska Corps Engrs '38-47, Bur Reclamation since '48. Am Soc CE—Am Geophy Union—Arctic Inst NA—Nat Geog Soc—Internat Council Soil Mech and Found Engring. H: 321 North E St., Aberdeen, Wash.

16 JASPER, Norman H(ans). Ships (Vibration, strength). b'18. BS (ME) '41 (City Coll NY); MS '50 (U Md). Study strength requirements of ships at sea; research on device for statistical study of strain history of structures, and on automatic statistical instruments for measurement and analysis of strains and motions. Author articles: A Statistical Approach to the Longitudinal Strength Design of Ships '50; On the Vibration of Ships (thesis); Measurement of Hydrodynamic Loads on a High Speed Motor Boat Caused by Wave Impact during Rough Water Trials '51; Instrumentation Problems of the Vibration Field Test Engr '50. Naval architect Puget Sound Naval Shipyard '41-46; mech engr D Taylor Model Basin structural mech lab since '46. Am Soc ME—Am Soc Naval Architects and Marine Engrs—Soc Exptl Stress Analysis. David Taylor Model Basin, Washington 7.

16 JEFFORDS, Russell MacGregor. Paleontology (Corals); Hydrology; Geochemistry. b'18. AB '39 (Syracuse U); AM '41—PhD '46 (U Kan). Research in identification and classification of corals of late Paleozoic age; areal and detailed studies ground-water hydrology in West Virginia, Kansas, New York, Rhode Island, Iowa; research on graphic representation of water analyses; changes in water quality with geologic time. Staff in stratigraphic paleontology Kan Geol Survey '39-42; geol US Geol Survey '42-45, since '48; staff geol Brown '46-47, Tex U '47-48. Am Assn Petroleum Geol—Paleontol Soc—Am Water Works Assn—Soc Econ Paleontology and Mineral—Soc Econ Geol—Am Geophys Union. Geology Annex, Iowa City, Ia.†

18 JEFFRIES, Jasper Brown. Atomic physics. b'12. BS '33 (WVa State Coll); SM '40—'42 (U Chicago). Research on instrumentation, particle counting techniques, and applications of mathematics and physics to nuclear physics, development electronic apparatus for detecting radiations in nuclear research. Staff mem Physics Div Manhattan Project U Chicago '43-46; prof phys and head dept NC Agrl and Tech Coll '46-50; math and physics staff mem RCA Insts NYC since '50. AAAS —Fed Am Sci—APS—Am Math Soc—Math Assn Am—Beta Kappa Chi—Alpha Phi Alpha. RCA Institutes, 350 West 4th St., NYC 14. H: 1142 Union Av., Bronx NYC 59.

19 JEHLE, Ferdinand. Pistons (Aluminum); Heating (Panel). b'88. BS (mech engring) '10—ME '31 (U Ill). Research and development equipment for measuring piston and valve temperature with engine running, development control for hot water and panel or radiant heating systems. With Aluminum Castings Co '16-23; research engr White Motor Co '23-37; with Hoffman Specialty Co '37-51, engring cons '49-51; sec Registration Bd for Profl Engrs & Land Surveyors Ind. Am Society ME(F)—AAAS(F)—Ind Engring Council (boiler code com). 230 State Capitol, Indpls. H: 3055 N. Meridian St., Indpls 8.

20 JEMISON, George Meredith. Silviculture research; Forest fire research; Forest management research. b'08. BS '31 (U Idaho); MF '36 (Yale); PhD '42 (Duke U). Author articles in field. With US Forest Service since '31, chief div forest management research as silviculturist '42-50; dir N Rocky Mountain Forest and Range Expt Sta US Forest Service Missoula since '50. Soc Am Foresters—Sigma Xi—Phi Beta Kappa. N Rocky Mountain Forest and Range Experiment Station, Missoula, Mont.

21 JENKINS, Anna Eliza. Leaf blister fungi of North American maples; Spot Anthracnose fungi; History of mycology and phytopathology (Brazil). b'86. BSA '11—MS '23—PhD '27 (Cornell U); '18-22 (George Washington U). As member of the staff of the US Bur of Plant Industry. Author articles in field. Mycologist US Bur Plant Industry. Washington Acad Sci—AAAS(F) —Phytopath Soc Am—Indian Phytopathol Soc—Mycol Soc Am—British Mycol Soc—Am Soc Agr Sci—Nat Geog Soc—Biol Soc Washington—Bot Soc Washington—Sigma Xi. Bureau Plant Industry Station, Beltsville, Md. H: 2310 Connecticut Av., Washington.†

22 JENKINS, Dale Wilson. Chiggers affecting man (Ecology, epidemiology, rearing methods, taxonomy); Vegetable oil palm production (American hemisphere); Radioactive tracers in insects; Tropical agriculture; Biting insects affecting man (Ecology, Arctic). b'18. Ridgeway fellow '39-40 (U Chicago); BSc '38—MA '39—PhD '47 (O State U). Author articles in field. Entomol Med Div Army Chem Center Md since '46; mem mission to Venezuela for FAO '48; prodn specialist Bd Econ Warfare '42-44. Entomol 1st lt San Corps US Army '44-46. Ecol Soc Am—Entomol Soc Am—Am Assn Econ Entomol—Entomol Soc Washington—Am Mosquito Control Assn—Sigma Xi—Gamma Sigma Delta. Medical Division, Army Chemical Center, Md.†

23 JENKINS, James A(ngus). Genetics, cytogenetics, and evolution in wheat and tomato. b'04. BS '27—MS '29 (U Saskatchewan); PhD '36 (U Calif). Author articles in field. Asso prof genetics U Calif since '49. AAAS —Genetics Soc Am—Am Soc Human Genetics—Soc Study Evolution—Western Soc Naturalists—Am Statis Assn—Sigma Xi—Phi Beta Kappa. Guggenheim fellow '45-46. 314 Hilgard Hall, University of California, Berkeley 4.†

24 JENKINS, Raymond. Edmund Spenser; English poetry of Renaissance. b'97. AB '17 (Cornell U); PhD '21 (Yale). Author articles in field. Head dept Eng Catawba Coll since '25, dean faculty since '47. Modern Lang Assn—So Atlantic Modern Lang Assn. Catawba College, Salisbury, N.C.

25 JENKINS, Raymond Walter. Mining (Methods and equipment). b '14. BS (Mining and metall) '37 (U ND). Standardization development and stoping methods for narrow vein mines; analyses mining and tunneling problems in Europe, Canada, Mexico and US; exploration and development of limestone deposit, and installation trackless and stoping methods. Author articles: Improvements in Mining Methods '48; Advancement in Tunnels '49; A Classification and Application of Drill Jibs '50, and others. Mine engr London Mines & Milling Co Alma Colo '37-39; underground engr engring research dept Anaconda Copper Mining Co Mountain City Nev and Butte Mont '39-45; spl rep Joy Mfg Co Pittsburgh '45-50; asst gen mgr Coplay Cement Mfg Co since '50. AIMME—Am Mining Congress. Coplay Cement Manufacturing Co., Coplay, Pa. H: 3F Linden House, Tremont Apts., Allentown.

10 JENKINS, Wilbert A(rmonde). Plant pathology, anatomy, and breeding; Cytology and sexuality of fungi. b'05. AB '28—MA '29 (Duke U); '29-31 (Cornell U); PhD '34 (Johns Hopkins U). Comparative morphology and cytology of fungi; virus diseases, pathological plant anatomy, tobacco breeding for disease resistance; root rot disease-complexes of tobacco, small grains and other crops. Author articles in field. Bot fellow Johns Hopkins; prof biol Brenau Coll; asst and asso bot Ga Agr Expt Station; now plant path, Va Agr Expt Sta, Tobacco Research Lab, Chatham Va. Am Phytopath Soc—Sigma Xi—Am Men Sci—Am Naturalist. Virginia Agricultural Experiment Station, Tobacco Research Laboratory, Chatham, Va. H: Box 430.

11 JENKS, Albert Ernest. Modern Anthropology, characteristics of American White and Negro, Modern European and Philippine peoples; Prehistory (American Pleistocene man, North African shell-heap culture, European). b'69. BS 96—ScD '24 (Kalamazoo Coll); BS '97 (U Chicago); PhD '99 (U Wis). Author: The Childhood of Jishib, the Ojibwa '00; The Wild Rice Gatherers of the Upper Lakes '01; The Bontoc Igorot '05; Indian-White Amalgamation '16; Chart of Prehistoric Man and Culture '27; Pleistocene Man in Minnesota '36; Minnesota's Browns Valley Man and Associated Yuma-Folsom Artifacts '37, and others. Enthnol, Bur Am Ethnol Smithsonian Instn Washington '01-02; ethnol and asst chief Bur Non-Christian Tribes PI '02-03, chief Ethnol Survey '03-05; prof Anthrop U Minn '06-38, chmn dept sociol and anthop '15-18, dir Americanization training course '18-23, chmn dept anthrop '18-38, dir archeol research fund '29-38, prof anthrop emeritus since '38. Nat Research Council '21-24 (chmn div anthrop and psychol '23-24)—AAAS (F, vp, chmn sect H, anthrop '19-20, '20-21)—Am Anthrop Assn—Am Genetic Assn—Sigma Xi. R.F.D. 1, Linden Shore, Mound, Minn.†☉

12 JENKS, Randolph. Arizona birds. b'12. BA '36 (Princeton); '31-34 (U Ariz); '34, '35 (U Cal). Discovered Arizona golden-crowned kinglet and Arizona pine grosbeak. Curator ornithol Mus N Ariz '31-34. Sigma Xi—Phi Beta Kappa—Am Mus Natural Hist—Am Forestry Assn—Am Nature Assn—Am Geog Soc—Nat Geog Society—Cooper Ornithol Club—Am Ornithol Union—Tucson Nat Hist Soc—Tucson Audubon Soc. H: 2146 E. 4th St., Tucson.

13 JENNER, William Alexander. Birds (Missouri); Weather (Radar). b '15. AB '38 (Central Coll); certificate meteorol '43 (U Chicago); MEd '47 (U Mo); '50-51 (Am U). Research on thunderstorms as disclosed by radar, use of radar in determining amount of rain falling over small area. Weath-

er officer, base weather officer and staff weather officer '43-46; meteorol US Weather Bur '47-49; with Air Weather Service since '49, chief training programs branch since '51. Am Meteorol Soc—Am Geophys Union—Am Statis Assn—Biometric Society—AAAS—Am Ornithol Union—Wilson Ornithol Club—Wildlife Soc—Nat Audubon Soc—Phi Delta Kappa. Headquarters Air Weather Service, Andrews Air Force Base, Washington 25. H: 3426 78th Pl., Washington 19.

14 JENNESS, Leslie George. Hydrogenation; Catalyst production; Oil processing; Fatty acid production. b '98. BS (chem engring) '20 (NH U); MS (chem engring) '24 (U Me); PhD '30 (Columbia). Research in production nickel catalysts and method of variation to control selective hydrogenation of oils, hydrogenation of soya bean oil to produce non-reverting oil; inventor hystrene fatty acids. Granted patents of nickel catalysts, oil hydrogenation, and fatty acid production. Tech dir Intermetal Corp '32-41; dir head Linde Air Products Co '41-47; dir research Humko Co '47-50; asst to pres in charge research Kennecott Copper Corp since '50. Am Oil Chem Soc—Sigma Xi—Alpha Chi Sigma. 135 East 54th St., NYC 22.

15 JENNINGS, Burgess H(ill). Ventilation; Air conditioning; Gas turbines; Refrigeration. b'03. BE '25 (Johns Hopkins); MS '28—MA '35 (Lehigh U). Development work on control of spread of infection by improvement in ventilation and air sterilization; research on absorption type refrigeration, on combustion and heating systems. Author: Internal Combustion Engines '44; Steam and Gas Engineering '47; Air Conditioning and Refrigeration '48. Faculty Northwestern U since '40, now prof and chmn dept mech engring; cons on air conditioning, indsl engring and refrigeration. ASME(F)—Am Soc Refrigerating Engrs(F, pres '49)—Am Soc Heating and Ventilating Engrs. Pi Tau Sigma Richards' memorial award for outstanding accomplishment in mech engring. Northwestern University, Evanston, Ill.; H: 2049 Hawthorne Lane.

16 JENNINGS, Jesse D(avid). Archeology of southeastern United States plains, and Great Basin. b'09. BA '29 (Montezuma Coll NM); PhD '43 (U Chicago). Excavation in several southeastern states '33-37 and of Early Maya archeological site near Gautemala City '37; gathered archeological data through field reconnaissance and excavation for use in parkway motor road location planning '39-42; set up a 20-man research project National Park Service Natchez Trace Parkway Tupelo Miss '45-47. Author: A Variation of Southwestern Pueblo Culture '40; Outline of the Prehistoric and Historic Indian Cultures of Central Nebraska and Kansas '47; Indian History of the Lower Mississippi Valley '48; Plainsmen of the Past '49. Co-author: (with F M Setzler) Peachtree Mound and Village Site, Cherokee County, North Carolina '41; (with A V Kidder and E M Shook) Excavations at Kaminaljuyu, Gautemala '46. Field dir TVA Chickamauga Basin U Tenn '36-37; supervisor Carnegie Institution of Wash '37; acting supt Nat Park Service Macon Ga '38-39; archeologist '39-48; professor anthropol U Utah since '48.

17 JENNISON, Marshall W(alker). Nonmedical bacteriology and microbiology. b'05. BS '27—PhD '32 (Mass Inst Tech). Author articles in field. Prof bacteriol Syracuse U since '46, in charge div bacteriol, dept plant scis. Soc Am Bacteriol (com bacteriol tech-

nic since '34, chmn since '48)—Soc Indsl Microbiology—Am Pub Health Assn(F)—AAAS(F)—Am Soc Limnol and Oceano—Bot Soc Am—Mycol Soc Am—Sigma Xi. Department Plant Sciences, Syracuse University, Syracuse 10, N.Y.†

18 JENS, Stifel William. Hydraulic engineering; Hydrology (Runoff and infiltration); Flood control; Water conservation; Drainage. b'02. BS (CE) '32—MS '33 (Washington U St Louis). Assisted in development technique for determination surface run-off by evaluating overland flow, surface storage or detention, infiltration, channel storage, unit hydrographs; research on hydrologic yield and determination maximum flood spillway quantity; statistical studies available rainfall, resultant runoff, major abstractions from precipitation. Author articles: A State Plan for Missouri—Water Plan '38; Surface Runoff Determination from Rainfall without Using Coefficients '42; Drainage of Airport Surfaces—Some Basic Design Considerations '48. Editor: Section on Infiltration in ASCE Hydrology Handbook '49. Asso water cons Nat Resources Bd '36-37; cons drainage design Washington Nat Airport; cons water supply requirements Houston Tex 43-44; study internal drainage facilities for flood control units Corps Engrs Kansas City; cons urban, airport, expressway storm drainage design, partner Horner & Shifrin St Louis since '38. Am Soc CE—Am Geophys Union—Am Waterworks Assn—Sigma Xi—Tau Beta Pi—Pi Mu Epsilon. Professional engr Mo, Ill, Tex. 803 Shell Bldg., StL 3.

19 JENSEN, Adolph Ladru. Cooperative corporation law. b'96. BA '17 (Brigham Young U); '19 (U Chicago); MA (polit sci) '24—JD '25 (U Cal). Consultant on legal education to American Institute of Cooperation since '45, executive secretary of Committee on Legal Education since '46. Author (with others) Cooperative Corporate Association Law '50. Asso Koford and Woolsey '25-26; prof corp law U Utah since '26; reviewer Law of Cooperative Marketing '37. Am Bar Assn (corp sect, chmn com terminology of coop corp law since '47)—Cal Bar Assn—Utah Bar Assn—AAUP(dir nat council '42-44)—Utah Acad Sci Arts and Letters(F)—Delta Theta Phi—Alpha Phi Zeta. University of Utah College of Law, Salt Lake City.

20 JENSEN, Howard Eikenberry. Social and personal disorganization (Social pathology, criminology) Sociological theory; Sociology and social work; Sociology and Psychiatry. b'89. Student '09-10 (Drake U); AB '14—AM '15 (U Kan); BD '17—PhD '20 (U Chicago); study (Phila Div U Pa). Made social surveys in four republics of Central America '20. Co-author: (with H W Odum and others) Systems of Public Welfare '25; (with W P King and others) Social Progress and Christian Ideals '31; (with C A Ellwood) Methods in Sociology '33; (with J D Kern and others) This America '42. Editor Duke U Sociological series; contbg editor Dictionary of Sociology '44. Dir Latin-Am Survey, Interchurch World Movement '19-20; prof sociology Butler U '20-28; prof sociology and dir social service tng curriculum U Mo '28-31; prof sociology and mental hygiene Duke U Sch Med since '42; lectr sociology Coll of Missions, Normal Coll NA Gymnastic Union, Indianapolis City Hosp. Pres Indianapolis Council Social Agencies '23-25, Durham Council Social Agencies '33-34; chmn exec com NC State Commn for Blind since '35; chmn govs Edgemont Community Center since '43; dir Nat Home Finding Soc '24-30. AAAS

(F)—Am Sociol Soc—Am Assn Social Workers—Am Acad Polit and Social Sci—So Sociol Soc(vp '44-45)—Ind Acad Sci—Institut Internationale de Sociologie—Phi Kappa Phi. 215 E Social Science Bldg., Duke University. Durham, N.C. H: 143 Pinecrest Rd.†⊙

10 JENSEN, John Christian. Thunderstorm phenomena; Lightning (Protection); Precipitation static (Aircraft); Moisture conservation. b'80. BSc '09 (Neb Wesleyan U); AM '16—PhD '39 (U Neb); '16 (U Ia)—'21 (U Chicago). Coordinator Civil Aeronautics Administration, Nebraska Wesleyan University '39-43; research consultant Curtiss-Wright Corporation '43-45. Author articles in field. Prof physics Neb Wesleyan U since '09, dean of men '34-36, '38-46. AAAS(F)—Am Phys Soc(F)—Am Geophys Union—Am Meteorol Soc—Neb Acad Sci (twice pres)—Inst Radio Engrs—Am Optical Soc—Am Interprofl Inst—Sigma Xi—Sigma Pi Sigma—Phi Kappa Phi. 4926 Leighton Av., Lincoln, Neb.⊙

11 JENSEN, Merrill. Early American history (American Revolution, 1763-89); Economic history. b'05. BA '29—MA '31 (U Wash); PhD '34 (U Wis). Author: The Articles of Confederation: An Interpretation of the Social Constitutional History of the American Revolution 1774-1781 '48; also articles in field. Editor: Pacific Northwest Quarterly '35-41. Instr later asso prof U Wash '35-40; asso prof hist U Wis '44-46, prof since '46. Historian Army Air Forces '44. AHA—Miss Valley Hist Assn. Guggenheim fellow '45-46. 193 Bascom Hall, University of Wisconsin, Madison, Wis.

12 JENSEN, Milton B. Military psychology. b'98. BS '24 (Utah State Coll); AM '25—PhD '27 (Stanford U); student (U Chicago). Author: Stanford Educational Aptitudes Test '28; Tests for Color Blindness, Visual Acuity Astigmatism '35; (joint author) Fundamentals of Home Economics '35; also articles in field. Con psychol Louisville '34-42, '45-49; mil psychol Armored Sch US Army Fort Knox '42-44, chief Psychol Services AAF Convalescent Hosp '45, major School Aviation Med Randolph Air Force Base Texas '49-50; cons and dir psychol clinic and service bur Tulane U since '50. Am Psychol Assn(F)—AAAS(F)—Ky Psychol Assn (pres '41-42, '48-49)—Midwestern Psychol Assn. Dept Psychrology, Tulane University, New Orleans 18, La.

13 JENSEN, Peter L. Loudspeakers; Phonograph needles and recordings. b'86. Pioneered in development dynamic loud speaker and public address systems; noise neutralizing microphones. Radio operator for Valdemar Poulsen '04; asst to Valdemar Poulsen Danish radio and wire-recorder inventor '04-09; wireless operator Danish Navy '09; engr Fed Telegraph Co San Francisco '09-10; chief engr Magnavox Co Oakland Calif '11-25; founder Jensen Radio Mfg Co Chicago '27, pres '27-40; vp Utah Radio Products Co Chicago '40-42; pres Jensen Industries Inc Chicago since '42. 329 S. Wood St., Chicago. H: 5025 Grand Av., Western Springs.

14 JENSEN, Vernon Peter. Concrete (Reinforced); Structural engineering. b'04. BS (civil engring) '29—MS (theoretical and applied mechanics) '31 (U Ill); PhD (applied math and mechanics) '36 (Ia State Coll). Developed theory of ultimate strength of reinforced concrete; special analyses on aircraft and vibration problems in engineering mechanics. Author articles: The plasticity ratio of concrete and its effect on the ultimate strength of beams; Some three dimensional aspects of the bridge roller problem; Analyses of skew-slabs; others. Asst prof Ia State Coll '31-36; research asso prof U Ill '36-43; research engr Douglas Aircraft Co '43-45; staff cons C F Braun & Co '45-50, head cons div since '50. Am Soc CE—Am Concrete Inst—Sigma Xi—Phi Kappa Phi—Tau Beta Pi. Awarded Am Concrete Inst Wason Medal for most meritorious paper on research '43. C. F. Braun & Co., Alhambra, Cal.

15 JENTE, Richard. Mythology (Old English; Middle high German folk lore; Proverbs (Medieval, Renaissance). b'88. AB '10—AM '11 (Yale); '13-14 (U Jena); PhD '17 (U Heidelberg). Studies in middle high German folk literature. Author: Die mythologischen Ausdrucke im altenglischen Wortschatz '22; The Proverbs of Shakespeare '26; Proverbia Communia, a 15th Century Collection of Dutch Proverbs '47. At Wash U '22-37, acting head German dept '29, '36-37; prof German and head dept U NC since '37. MLA—Am Assn Tchrs German—Am Folklore Soc—Linguistic Soc—AAUP. Department of German, University of North Carolina, Chapel Hill, N.C.⊙

16 JEPPSON, Lee R. Plant feeding mites. b'10. BS '31 (Brigham Young U); MS '39 (U State Agrl Coll); PhD '43 (Calif U). Research and writing on Lygus bug injury and effect on alfalfa growth, control of mites injurious to citrus. Author articles in field. Asst entomologist Expt Station Calif U since '47. Sigma Xi—Am Assn Econ Entomologists. University of California Citrus Experiment Station, Riverside, Calif.

17 JEPSEN, Glenn Lowell. Fossil mammals; Organic evolution; Vertebrate paleontology; Stratigraphy; Physical anthropology. b'03. '21-22 (U Mich); '22-25 (SD Sch Mines and Tech); BS '27—PhD '30 (Princeton). Research paleontology, anthropology, mammalogy, archeology Canada, Mexico, US various times. Discovered geologically oldest known rodent and tubulidentate (aard vark), many new fossil reptiles and mammals. Author: Stratigraphy and Paleontology of the Paleocene of N W Park Co, Wyo '30; The Mammalian Fauna of the White River Oligocene (with W B Scott) '36; Paleocene Faunas of the Polecat Bench Formation, Park County, Wyoming '40. Dir paleontologic research parties west states since '25; asso editor Biol Abstracts '28-41; dir Wm B Scott research fund expeditions vertebrate paleontol since '35, curator vertebrate paleontol Princeton Mus Natural Hist since '35, dir bicentennial conf genetics, paleontol, evolution Jan '47; chmn sect paleontol Nat Research Council Com on Common Problems Genetics, Paleontol, Systematics since '43; mem Council Soc for study of Evolution '46-47. Instr geology Princeton U '30-34, asst prof '34-40, assoc prof '40-46, Sinclair prof vertebrate paleontology since '46. AAAS(F)—Geol Soc of Amer(F)—Paleontol Soc (F)—Soc Vertebrate Paleontol—Am Soc Mammalogists—NY Acad Sci—Am Philos Soc—Sigma Xi—Phi Beta Kappa. 320 Guyot Hall, Department of Geology, Princeton University, Princeton, N.J. H: 144 Patton Av.⊙

18 JERABEK, Henry S(amuel). Physical metallurgy; Stainless steels; Gun barrels; Corrosion resistant alloys. b'00. BS (Chem E) '26—MS '29—PhD (Metall) '37 (U Minn). Holds patents in field. Co-author: General Metallography '43; Crystallography of the Elements '50. Faculty U Minn '27-42 and since '45, now asso prof metall; research metall USN Research Lab summers '30-31, '34-36; metall cons chem engring div TVA '39-42; metall geophys lab Carnegie Inst Washington '42-45. Am Soc Metals—AIMME—Am Crystallographers Assn—Sigma Xi—Tau Beta Pi—Phi Lambda Upsilon. 304AH, University of Minnesota, Mpls 14.

19 JESSE, William H. Library buildings and architecture. b'08. '29-31 (Transylvania Coll, Ky); AB '33 (U Ky); BS '38 (Columbia U); AM '45 (Brown U). Survey of libraries in State-supported institutions of higher education in South Carolina '45; advisory council southeastern states cooperative library survey, chairman Tennessee State Survey committee '46-48; survey Northwestern State College Library, Natchitoches, Louisiana '47; survey Oklahoma City University Library, Virginia Polytechnic Institute Library (with M Tauber) '49. Author articles in field. Asst dir U Neb Libraries, Lincoln '42; head, readers' and reference div USDA Library, Wash '43; dir libraries U Tenn since '43. ALA (chmn ACRL com on college and univ library buildings '46-47)—Southeastern Library Assn (pres '46-48)—Southern Assn Colls and Secondary Schs. Library, University of Tennessee, Knoxville 16, Tenn.

20 JEWETT, John Mark. Stratigraphic geology of Kansas. b'96. AB '21—MA '30—PhD '43 (U Kans). Experience in ground water geology in eastern Kansas—locating water wells for cities, farms, etc; since '28 research on stratigraphy of Kansas especially of Paleozoic rocks in eastern Kansas and their relationships to oil and gas, coal and other industrial minerals and to engineering operations. Author articles in field. Curator invertebrate fossils U Cincinnati '30-31; instr geol U Wichita '31-37; geol State Geol Survey of Kansas U of Kans since '37. Kans Geol Soc—Kans Acad Sci—Paleontol Soc(F)—Geol Soc Am(F)—Sigma Xi. State Geological Survey, Lawrence, Kans.†

21 JOBES, Frank Watkins. Great Lakes fish (Age and growth, commercial fisheries); Commercial fishing gear and its regulation; Relationship of sea lamprey-lake trout. b'03. AB '26 (Southwestern Coll Kan); MS '27 (Kan State Coll); PhD '40 (U Mich); '27-28 (U Ill). Author articles in field. Aquatic biologist US Fish and Wildlife Service Ann Arbor Mich '30-49; prof biol Yankton College since '49. Am Fisheries Soc—Am Soc Limnol and Oceano—South Dakota Acad Sci. Yankton College, Yankton, S. Dak.

22 JOECKEL, Carleton Bruns. Library government; Library education. b'86. BA '09 (U Wis); BLS '10 (NY State Library Sch); MA '28 (U Mich); PhD '34 (U Chicago). Chairman Librarian's Committee Library of Congress for survey of processing departments '40. Author: The Government of the Am Public Library '35; Library Service '38. Co-author: (with Amy Winslow) A Nat Plan for Public Library Serv '48; (with L Carnovsky) A Metropolitan Library in Action: A Survey of the Chicago Public Library '40. Editor: Current Issues in Library Administration '39; Post-War Standards for Public Libraries '43; Library Extension: Problems and Solutions '44; Reaching Readers '49. Librarian's sec St Louis Pub Library '10-11; asst reference librarian and supt circulation U Calif Library '11-14; librarian Berkeley Pub Library '14-17, '19-27; asso prof library sci U Mich '27-30, prof '30-35; prof library sci U Chicago '35-45, dean Grad Library Sch '42-45; prof Sch Librarianship U Cal '45-50, retired. ALA—Cal Library Assn. 1424 Hawthorne Terr. Berkeley 8.

10 JOFFE, Morris H. Mayonnaise and salad dressing products; Bread and cake baking. b'00. BS '22 (U Ill). Holder patents on cake and method of making same and salad dressing. Author: Bread Baking '27. Editor: Mayonnaise and Salad Dressing Products '42. Vice president in charge of sales and service The Emulsol Corp since '47. Am Soc Bakery Engrs—Am Inst Chem Engrs—Am Inst Chemists—Am Assn Cereal Chemists—Inst Food Technologists—Am Chem Soc—Sigma Xi—Phi Lambda Upsilon. 59 E. Madison St., Chicago 3.

11 JOGLAR-RODRIQUEZ, Francisco. Tobacco agriculture. b'97. BS in agr '19 (Coll Agr and Mech Arts U PR); MS in agr '38 (Pa State Coll). Research tobacco cultivation, seedbeds, selections and conservation seeds, damping-off seedling, soil erosion control, fertilization, control pests, insects and diseases. Author Agricultural Extension Service Bulletins. Supt tobacco or demonstration farm '28-31, citrus and pineapple specialist '31-33, dist supervisor in charge tobacco crop '33-36, extension agronomist, tobacco specialist '38-51; vis prof Coll Agr and Mech Arts U PR '46-47. PR Coll Agronomists—Am Soc Agrl Scis. Extension Agronomist, Agricultural Extension Service, Rio Piedras, P.R. H: Betances St. No. 86, Bayamon, P.R.

12 JOHAN, Howard Ernest. Cotton (Tissue tests). b'19. AB '41 (Santa Barbara Coll); MS '43 (Tex A&M Coll); PhD '50 (Ia State Coll). Research on physiology and nutrition of cotton plant; application of tissue tests. Author articles: Tissue tests as indicators of mineral nutrition of cotton; others. Asst prof plant physiol Tex Agrl Expt Sta and agt physiol BPI SAE div cotton and other fiber crops and diseases since '47. Gamma Sigma Delta—Am Soc Plant Physiols—Sigma Xi. Texas Agricultural Experiment Station, College Station, Tex.

13 JOHL, Janet P(agter). Dolls. b'02. AB '24 (Smith Coll); student (Yale, Columbia). Author: The Fascinating Story of Dolls '41; More About Dolls '46; Still More About Dolls '49; Wilhelmina: A Little Dutch Girl '41; also juvenile stories and articles. Free lance writing. Nat Doll-Toy Collectors Club—Doll Collectors of Am. Trails Corner, Groton, Conn.

14 JOHL, Max G. United States postage stamps (Twentieth century). b'00. BS in econ '22 (U Pa). Member international jury centenary International Philatelic Exhibition '47. Author: The US Postage Stamps of the 20th century '32-37, '39; The United States Commemorative Stamps of the Twentieth Century, 2 vols '47. Treas The Assn for Stamp Exhibitions Inc '46-50; expert The Philatelic Found '46-51. Royal Philatelic Soc London (F)—US 20th Century Postal Cancellation Society (pres since '46). Awarded Crawford Medal of the Royal Philatelic Soc. Trails Corner, Groton, Conn.

15 JOHN, Charles A(lfred). Vegetable breeding (Tomatoes, sweet corn, cucumbers). b'09. BS '30 (State Teachers Coll Pa); MS '33—'39-41 (Cornell). Asst branch mgr Midwest Breeding Station Associated Seed Growers Inc Franklin Ind '47-48; head dept of crop research H J Heinz Co since '48. Am Soc Hort Sci—Am Phytopathological Soc—Am Genetics Soc. H. J. Heinz Company, Bowling Green, Ohio.

16 JOHNSON, Aili Ilona Kolehmainen. Folklore (Finnish, Finnish-American; Kalevala. b'11. AB '32 (Northern Mich Coll Edn); summers '46. '50 (Internat Folklore Inst, Ind U). Collection folklore from various ethnic backgrounds for purposes of comparison with Finnish immigrant folklore; field trips to upper peninsula of Michigan to collect folklore from Finns in rural areas, to midwest cities for urban Finnish folklore; study Finnish folk culture through folklore of Finland and America; Kelvala (translation from Finnish to English; '51. Co-author: (with Bowman and Bianco) Tales from a Finnish Tupa. Author articles: Folklore of the Finnish-American Sauna; and others. Mem bd dirs Flint Internat Inst '47-50; trustee Mich Hist Soc '49-52. Mich Acad Sci Arts and Letters; Mich Folklore Soc—Am Folklore Soc. H: 7711 McClellan St., Utica, Mich.†

17 JOHNSON, Andrew Leigh. Clay and non-metallic minerals. b'12. AB '34 (Bethany Coll); MSc '36 (Rutgers U); ScD '43 (Mass Inst Tech). Author articles in field. Dir research Universal Rundle Corp since '48. Group leader Manhattan Project '45-46, cons Radiation Lab '44-45. Am Ceramic Soc(F)—Am Chem Soc—Sigma Xi. Universal-Rundle Corp., New Castle, Pa.

18 JOHNSON, Bruce Connor. Vitamins; Animal nutrition. b'11. BA '33 —MA '34 (McMaster U Hamilton Ont); PhD '40 (U Wis). Development microbial method for determination of nicotinic acid in presence of its amide; studies on vitamin metabolism; experiments on changes in environmental temperature as related to vitamin requirements; studies on B vitamin nutrition of baby calves, lambs, and pigs; synthetic and artificial milk diets for baby animals. Author: Methods of Vitamin Determination (2d edit) '50. Author or co-author over 80 articles including The Microbiological Determination of Nicotinic Acid, Nicotinamide, and Nicotinuric Acid '45, Thiamine Deficiency in the Lamb '51, The Role of Methionine as a Methyl Donor for Choline Synthesis in the Chick '51. Chem Canadian Canners Hamilton Ont '34-37; research biochem Golden State Co Ltd San Francisco '42-43; faculty U Ill since '43, prof animal nutrition since '51. ACS—Am Soc Biol Chem—Am Inst Nutrition—AAAS—Soc Exptl Biol and Med—Am Soc Animal Prodn—Am Dairy Sci Assn—Assn Vitamin Chem—Sigma Xi—Phi Lambda Upsilon—Phi Sigma—Gamma Alpha. 554 Davenport Hall. University of Illinois. Urbana, Ill.†

19 JOHNSON, Burt (Parker). Cotton (Fiber technology, growing, marketing, utilization). b'05. BA '28 (Park Coll); PhD '31 (U Wis); Nat Research fellow '31-32 (U Calif Citrus Expt Sta). Research in cotton fiber measurements in relation to physiology and genetics of cotton and devising methods of determining properties of cotton fibers '35-38; relation of cotton fiber properties to the quality of tire cords made from those cottons, relation of environment especially fertilizers and variety of cottons to fiber properties '39-45; chemistry and structure of cotton cellulose especially as revealed by microbiological degradation of cotton '45-47; relation of cotton fiber properties to the genetics and growth of the plant, to all phases of the marketing of raw cotton, and its use in the spinning mill since '48. Author articles in field. Asst agronomist Ark Agr Expt Sta '36-38; fiber technologist Goodyear Tire and Rubber Co '39-45; head biol div Inst of Textile Tech '45-47; cotton technologist Nat Cotton Council of America since '48. Fiber Soc. National Cotton Council, Memphis 1.†

20 JOHNSON, Charles Spurgeon. American Negroes; Race relations. b'93. AB '17—Litt D '28 (Va Union U); PhB '18 (U Chicago); LHD '41 (Howard U); Litt D '47 (Columbia); LLD '48 (Harvard U). Delegate to First Assembly of World Council of Churches, Amsterdam Holland '48. Author: The Negro in American Civilization '30; Economic Status of the Negro '33; Shadow of the Plantation '34; Preface to Racial Understanding '36; The Negro College Graduate '36 (Anisfield Award '38); Growing Up in the Black Belt '41; Patterns of Negro Segregation '43, and others. Co-author: The Negro in Chicago '22. Editor: Ebony and Topaz '27; Education and the Cultural Process '44. Pres Fisk U since '46. So Commn Study of Lynching (mem exec com)—So Sociol Soc (mem exec com, pres '45)—Am Social Hygiene Assn (vp)—Nat Commn Children and Youth—Am Missionary Assn (dir relations program '43-48)—Sociol Research Assn (sec-treas '43-46)—Am Sociol Soc (exec com)—Social Sci Research Council—NEA. Awarded Wm E Harmon gold medal for distinguished achievement among Negroes in sci for year '30; cited for distinguished pub service by U Chicago Alumni Assn '45. 1700 Meharry Blvd., Nashville.†⊚

21 JOHNSON, Clarence Nettleton. Sprinkler irrigation (Sprinkler and meter design); Wells (Hydraulics); Pumps (Hydraulics). b'98. BS (engring) '21—ME '37 (U Mich). Research on evaporation losses from sprinkler jets, designed farm irrigation metering devices. Inventor new type rotating sprinkler without water seal stuffing box. Asst supt engring dept Union Oil Co '26-29; with U Cal since '36, asso prof irrigation, asso irrigation engr since '43. Am Soc ME—Am Soc Agrl Engrs—Am Geophys Union (hydrology sect). Division of Irrigation, University of California, Davis, Cal.

22 JOHNSON, Conrad C(lark). Fumigation (Soil); Fumigation (Grain); Fumigation (Industrial). b'01. BA '22 (Wesleyan U); MBA '24 (NY U). Research on use of chemicals in soil to kill nematodes, disease-causing fungi, insects and weedseeds, for grain fumigation and development application equipment; research on pest control in mills and warehouses. Mgr insecticide div Innis Speiden and Co since '33. AAAS—Am Phytopathological Soc—Am Soc Hort Sci—Am Assn Econ Entomol—Nat Pest Control Assn—Assn Operative Millers—Delta Phi Epsilon—Soc Grain Elevator Supts. Innis, Speiden and Co., 117 Liberty St., NYC.

23 JOHNSON, David Horn. Systematic mammalogy. b'12. AB '34—MA '36—PhD '40 (U Calif). Field investigations concerning mammals in western US, islands of south and west Pacific Ocean, Australia, Labrador. Research asst Museum Vertebrate Zool U Calif '40-41; asso curator div mammals US Nat Museum since '41. Mammalogist USN Medical Research Unit No. 2 '43-45. Am Soc Mammalogists—Soc Systematic Zool—Wash Acad Sci —Biol Soc Wash. U.S. National Museum, Washington 25. H: 4604 Calvert Rd., College Park, Md.

24 JOHNSON, E(dward) M(arshall). Tobacco (Diseases); Plants (Virus diseases). b'96. BS '21—MS '23 (U Ky); PhD '30 (U Minn). Specialist tobacco diseases, virus diseases of plants; identification and control of virus diseases of Burley tobacco; control studies of bacterial diseases of Burley tobacco. Agron Ky Agrl Expt Sta Lexington '23-26, asso plant path '26-46, path since '46. Am Phytopath Soc (nat sec '45-47)—Am Soc Agron—AAAS—Alpha Zeta—Sigma Xi. Agricultural

Experiment Station, Lexington 29, Ky.©

10 JOHNSON, Edward W(illiam). Frequency control devices (Precision, military uses); Strategic minerals (Piezo-electric). b'08. BA '31—MA '33 (U Minn). Lt col asst chief crystal sect Office Chief Signal Officer '42-44; crystal coordinator Signal corps '44-45; chief frequency control br Signal Corps Engring Labs Ft Monmouth NJ since '45. Geol Soc Am—Am Assn Pet Geologists—AAAS—Am Inst Mining & Metall Engrs—Am Geographical Soc(F). Squier Signal Laboratory, Ft. Monmouth, N.J.†

11 JOHNSON, Eldridge Reeves Fenimore. Underwater photography. b'99. Student (Haverford Sch, U Pa). Holder five US patents. Author: Helmet Diving '37; also articles in field. Organized Fenimore Johnson Labs '40, specializing in development of submergible equipment. Lt USNR '42, directed underwater camera development, promoted to lt comdr '45. Fenjohn Underwater Photo & Equipment Co since '49. 90 Cricket Av., Admore, Pa.

12 JOHNSON, Frank Harris. Biological reaction rates; Luminous bacteria. b'08. AB '31—PhD '36 (Princeton U.) MA '32 (Duke U). Research and writing on metabolism of micro-organisms, especially bioluminescence in bacteria, kinetics of biological reactions. Author articles in field. Instr biol Princeton '37-41, asst prof '41-46, asso prof since '46. AAAS—Am Soc Zool—Am Physiol Soc—Soc Am Bacteriol—Soc Exptl Biol and Med—Sigma Xi—Phi Beta Kappa. Grad research fellow Woods Hole Oceanographic Inst, Eli Lilly & Co research fellow '37-38, Rockefeller Foundation fellow '39, Guggenheim fellow '44-46; awarded with D E Brown and D A Marsland $1,000 prize of AAAS for '41-42 work on a basic mechanism in biol effects of temperature pressure and narcotics. 11 College Rd., Princeton, N.J.

13 JOHNSON, Fred Elon. Copper ores; Sulfide ores of iron. b'06. BS (mining engring) '31 (U Ariz). Conducted operations of underground extraction, concentration and smelting of sulfide copper-gold ores and iron sulfide ores. Gen supt Lepanto Consol Mining Co '37-41; chief engr quartz crystal program Fgn Econ Adminstrn '43-44; mgr Pigmentos Minerais Ind e Com '45-46; supt Gossan mines, Gen Chem Div, Allied Chem and Dye Corp since '47. Am Inst Mining Engrs., Box 389, Galax, Va.

14 JOHNSON, Frederick. Indians of Central America; Archeology. b'04. BS '29 (Tufts Coll); student (U Pa, Harvard). Ethnological expeditions to Canada Newfoundland '25-32; archeological and ethnological expeditions to Pana '31-33; research on Central American Indians two years; archeological expedition to Alaska and Yukon Territory '44, '48. Author articles in field. Investigation NE archeology R S Peabody Found Phillips Acad Andover Mass since '36. Am Anthrop Assn—Soc Am Archeologists—Geol Soc Am. R. S. Peabody Foundation, Phillips Academy, Andover, Mass.

15 JOHNSON, Gerald Woodrow. Terminal ballistics; Electric discharge; Physics of metals. b'17. BS '37—MS '39 (Wash State Coll); PhD '47 (Calif U). Made experimental investigations of electrical discharge through gases in non-uniform field; research in diffusion in metals, crystal counters; studies and writing on ionization currents in divergent fields. Author: Terminal Ballistics at Naval Proving Ground, Dahlgren Virginia (9 pamphlets) '41-

46; also articles in field. Asst prof physics Wash State Coll now with Brookhaven Nat Lab Upton NY. Am Physical Soc—US Naval Inst—Phi Beta Kappa—Sigma Xi. Research Corp Fellow in physics Calif U '46-47; awarded Bur Ordnance Citation for exptl work, World War II. Physics Dept., Brookhaven Nat Lab., Upton, N.Y.

16 JOHNSON, Harry Prescott. History; Colonial Mexico (Northwest provinces, 17th century); European history (18th century). b'00. AB—AM (U Neb); PhD (U Calif). Research in history of colonial Mexico with particular emphasis on northwest provinces in early 17th century, and 18th century Europe, with specific topic mercantilism. Author: The Bering Sea Controversy '23; Diego Martinez de Hurdaide, Defender of Spain's Pacific Coast Frontier '40; essay in Greater America '45. Chmn dept social sci and prof hist Long Beach City Coll '40-53; Claremont Grad Coll Calif summer '42; prof hist Latin Am hist and culture, U Calif, U Extension Los Angeles. Am Hist Soc—NEA—Calif Teachers Assn—Long Beach City Teachers Club. Long Beach City College, Long Beach 8, Calif. H: 2134 Maine Av., Long Beach 6.

17 JOHNSON, Harvey Leory. Spanish and Portuguese (Language and literature). b'04. AB '25 (Howard Payne Coll Brownwood Tex); summer student '30 (U Mexico) '31 (U Madrid) '35 (Sorbonne Paris). Author: An Edition of Triunfo de los Santos with a Consideration of Jesuit School Plays in Mexico Before 1650 '41; La America Espanola '49. Contributor articles to Rivista Iberoamericana, Hispania, Hispanic Review, Book sect Chicago Tribune. Prof Cedar Crest Coll Allentown Pa '37-40; mem faculty Romance langs Northwestern U '40-50; now prof and chmn dept Spanish and Portuguese Ind U. Modern Lang Assn Am—Sigma Delta Pi—Phi Sigma Iota. Department of Spanish and Portuguese, Indiana University, Bloomington, Ind.†©

18 JOHNSON, Helgi. Stratigraphy; Paleontology; Non-metal economic geology. b'04. BSc '26 (Manitoba U); PhD '29 (Toronto U). Field officer and director of various geological surveys; engaged research and writing on stratigraphy and paleontology of lower Paleozoic gypsum deposits of Newfoundland, strontium deposits of western Newfoundland. Author: Carboniferous Geology of the Bay St George Area '38; also articles in field. Prof geol Rutgers U since '43, chmn dept geol and geog since '45, dir bur mineral research since '46, dir mus geology since '45; geologist USGS Military Geology Branch '49-52. Paleontolog Soc (F)—Geolog Soc Am(F)—AIME—AA AS—Sigma Xi. Rutgers University, New Brunswick, N.J.†

19 JOHNSON, Hildegard Binder. Historical geography (Nineteenth century distribution of settlers in American Midwest); German immigration to United States. b'08. PhD '33 (U Berlin); '28-30 (U Rostock, Marburg, Innsbruck). Geographical excursions in Central Europe and Alpine Mountains. Author articles in field; annual contbr German-American Bibliography. Asst prof geog and head dept Macalester Coll since '47. Hist Soc Minn—Nat Council Geog Teachers—Assn Am Geographers. Grant-in-aid Social Sci Research Council '41-42, '46-47. Department of Geography, Macalester College, St. Paul 5.†

20 JOHNSON, J(ay) Milton. Blindness (Education and orientation adults and youth); Religious education (Training). b'99. Secondary tchr cre-

dential '22 (U Cal at Los Angeles); supervisors credential '25—BS in edn cum laude '34—MS in edn '36—administrative credential secondary grade '36 (U So Cal). Director social welfare and recreation Braille Institute of America Inc; work with Baptist Young Peoples Union in official capacities '25-33; pastor's assistant in personal counseling First Baptist Church of Glendale Cal '42-44; delegate Welfare Council of Metropolitan Los Angeles since '46; president Baptist Mens Council of So Cal '33-35, exec com Nat Council No Bapt Men '29-30, So Cal Interdenom Council Religious Edn (now Cal Ch Council) '28-43. Am Assn Workers for the Blind—Phi Kappa Phi. 741 N Vermont Av., Hollywood 27, Cal.†©

21 JOHNSON, Jerome A(llen). Fire protection engineering. b'96. Student (Harvard, MIT, NYU, U London). Administrative work in Canada between wars on design, manufacturing and installation of coal and ore handling machinery in various ports of world. Author articles in field. Engring and inspection work Factory Ins Assn Hartford Conn since '43. Officer USNR World War I; lt comdr USNR special Naval observer in London, transferred to US Army Ordnance Dept World War II. Am Soc Mech Engrs—Nat Soc Profl Engrs—Harvard Engring Soc. Factory Insurance Association, Hartford, Conn. 37 Kirkland Ave., Cambridge, Mass. or Danvy, Vt.

22 JOHNSON, Jesse Charles. Uranium (Production); Atomic energy (Raw materials). b'94. AB '17 (U Wash Sch Mines). In charge procurement raw materials US and abroad for production atomic energy. Dep dir metals reserve RFC '43-48; dep mgr raw materials operations Atomic Energy Commn '48-50, mgr since '50. AIMME—Sigma Xi. Atomic Energy Commission, Washington.

23 JOHNSON, Jesse Harlan. Stratigraphy; Paleontology; Limestone (Reef, ore deposits); Calcareous algae. b'92. EM (S Dak Sch Mines); Certificate (U Montpellier France); MS (Colo Sch Mines); PhD (U Colo). Author articles in field. Prof geol and curator geol museum Colo Sch Mines since '47; geol US Geol Survey since '47. Am Inst Mining & Metal Engrs (vice-chmn Colo sect '35, sec-treas '40-41, chmn '41-42)—Am Mineral Soc—Am Assn Pet Geologists—Geol Soc Am—Paleontol Soc Am—Societe Geologique de France (vp '34)—Soc Econ Paleontol and Mineral (nat pres '43)—Phycol Soc Am—Colo Sci Soc—Rocky Mountain Assn Geologists (vp '29, pres '30-31, '38, sec '35-36)—Sigma Xi. Department of Geology, Colorado School of Mines, Golden, Colo.

24 JOHNSON, John Kelly. Radio receivers. b'03. BS '23—AB '23 (Penn Coll Oskaloosa Ia); AB '24—BS '26—EE '27 (Columbia). Design radio and communication receivers, filter and circuits, and electronic components; development test equipment and methods; tests on radio signal distribution system. Holds patents on receiver circuits and components. Author articles: Audio Transformer Design '29; High Fidelity Receivers with Expanding Selectors '36. Asst chief engr Silver-Marshall Co Chicago '29-30; development engr Hazeltine Corp NYC '30-34; chief engr Wells Gardner & Co Chicago '34-37; lab engr Hazeltine Service Corp Chicago '37-43; electronics cons Office Sec Navy Washington '43; exec engr Hammarlund Mfg Co NYC '44-45; electronics cons NYC since '45; cons Munitions Bd Washington '51. Inst Radio Engrs(F)—Radio Club Am(F)—Am Inst EE—Sigma Xi—Tau

Beta Pi. 511 Fifth Av., NYC 17. H: 184 South Av., New Canaan, Conn.

10 JOHNSON, J(ohn) Raymond. Heart (Physiology, internal pressures). b'05. BS '26 (Washburn Coll); PhD '34 (Tulane U); F physiol '35-36 (W Reserve U). Developed method of optically recording and measuring pressure alterations in wall of heart. Faculty Long Island Coll Med '36-47; asso prof '45-47; prof, head dept physiol U Ottawa Faculty of Med since '47. Am Physiol Soc—Can Physiol Soc —Soc Exptl Biol and Med—Harvey Soc —AAAS—Sigma Xi. University of Ottawa, Faculty of Medicine, Ottawa, Ontario, Can.

11 JOHNSON, Josef Jerome. Astrophysics; External ballistics of rockets. b'99. BS '30—PhD '35 (Calif Inst Tech); MS '32 (O Wesleyan U). Member Harvard Eclipse Expdn Malaya '29, US Naval Observatory Expdn Niuafou Is '30, Japanese Naval Eclipse Expdn Caroline Is '34, Tokyo Observatory Eclipse Expdn Hokkaido '36, Calif Inst Tech rocket project '43-44. Discovered Supernovae in spiral nebulae NGC 5907 Feb 16 '40, NGC 4545 July 25 '40. Research asst astron Perkins Obs '31-32; teaching fellow astronphysics Calif Inst Tech '32-35, research fellow '35-46, research asso since '46. AAAS—Am Astron Soc—Astron Soc Pacific—Am Geog Soc—Seismol Soc Am—Sigma Xi. Astrophysics Dept., California Institute Technology, Pasadena 4, Calif. H: 1030 San Pasqual St., Pasadena 5.

12 JOHNSON, Jotham. Classical archeology; Primitive time-reckoning. b'05. AB '26 (Princeton); '29-30 (Yale); PhD '31 (Pa U). Field assistant Yale University excavations at Dura-Europos Syria '28-29; field director University of Pennsylvania Museum excavations at Minturnae Italy '31-34; published first complete description of Hellenistic calendar system of Western Asia '32. Ed for Archaeology, Classical Jour since '46. Author: Dura Studies '32; Excavations at Minturnae '33, '35. Editor: Archaeology since '48; Archaeological Newsletter since '46; also articles in field. Asst prof classics U Pittsburgh '37-42, asso prof '45-46; asst prof NY U '46-47, asso prof since '47; chmn classics dept NY U since '48. Archaeol Inst Am—Am Anthropol Assn—Am Philol Assn—Classical Assn Atlantic States. Fellow Am Sch Classical Studies Athens '27-28. Washington Square College, New York University, NYC 3.

13 JOHNSON, Lee H(arnie), Jr. Civil engineering; Slide rule technique. b'09. BA '30—MA '31 (Rice Inst); MS '32— ScD '35 (Harvard). Development of new technique and method of instruction for duplex slide rule operation. Author: The Slide Rule 2nd ed '49; also articles in field. Dean and prof civil engring U Miss '37-50, dean engring and prof civil engring Tulane U since '50. ASCE—AAAS—ASEE—Phi Beta Kappa—Tau Beta Pi. Tulane U., New Orleans 18, La.

14 JOHNSON, Leslie William. Castings (Gray iron). b'10. BS (AE) '32 (SD State Coll); MS '34 (Ia State Coll). Research on principles of gating patterns for gray iron castings, of making sand mold for iron castings. Exptl and design engr John Deere Planter Works Moline Ill '35-41, foundry engr and pattern designer '41-47; plant supt Swanson Foundry Co Moline since '47. Am Foundrymen's Soc—Am Soc Metals—Am Soc AE. Swanson Foundry Co., 2351 23rd Av., Moline, Ill.

15 JOHNSON, Martin Wiggo. Zooplankton; Crustacea (Copepoda); Underwater sound (Animal); Marine wood borers; Echimoderm and Annelid (Life histories). b'93. BS '23—MS '30—PhD '31 (U Washington). Co-author: (with H Sverdrup and R H Fleming) The Oceans, Their Physics, Chemistry and General Biology '46; also articles in field. Prof marine biol Scripps Inst Oceanography since '46. Marine biologist U Calif Div War Research US Navy '42-46. AAAS—Ecol Soc Am— Am Microscopical Soc—Am Soc Limnol and Oceanog—Western Soc Naturalists—San Diego Soc Natural Hist—Sigma Xi. Awarded US Navy certificate of commendation for outstanding service during World War II. Scripps Institution of Oceanography, La Jolla, Calif.†

16 JOHNSON, Maynard S. Rodents (Rats, mice); Aquatic ecology; Fisheries; Periodicities. b'00. AB '21 (Bates Coll); MA '23—PhD '25 (Ill U); '32-34 (Harvard). Research in periodicity of spontaneous activity; tested ability of rats to climb and jump, toxicity and acceptance of 1080 and other rodenticides, programs for rodent control on Midway Islands, American Samoa; research and writing on activity and distribution of certain wild mice in relation to biotic communities, factors affecting productiveness of Minnesota lakes in fish and fish food, midge larvae as fish food; reported on exceptional abundance of midge Chironomus plumosus at Lake Pepin. Author: Common Injurious Mammals of Minnesota '30; Rodent Control on Midway Islands '45; also articles in field. Asst prof zoology, econ zoologist Agr Expt Sta Minn U '25-30; asso prof biology Utah U '30-32; instr histology and embryology Western Reserve U Med Sch '34-35; wildlife technician US Nat Park Service '35-38; refuge mgr Nat Wildlife Refuges, New Holland NC, US Biolog Survey, US Fish and Wildlife Service '38-44; rodent control officer US Naval Reserve since '44. Phi Beta Kappa—Sigma Xi —AAAS(F)—Ecolog Soc Am—Am Soc Mammalogists—Am Fisheries Soc— Wildlife Soc—Audubon Soc. LCDR, HS, USNR, New Holland, N.C.

17 JOHNSON, Melvin Maynard. Freemasonry. b'71. AB—PhB '92 (Tufts); LLB '95 (Boston U Law Sch); LLD '36 (U Vt), '49 (Tufts Coll); DCL '49 (Ill Wesl U); LHD '41 (Marietta Coll). Sovereign Grand Commander of Supreme Council 33° Northern Masonic Jurisdiction US since '33; director Grand Lodge Corp; Board Masonic Relief; trustee Masonic Education and Charity Trust; president Board of Trustees Supreme Council Corp; honorary member many Masonic organizations in US and foreign countries. Author: The Beginnings of Freemasonry in America. Editor: Scribner ed Gould's Revised History of Freemasonry; also author articles in field. Dean emeritus Boston U Law Sch since '43; dir Johnson Automatics Inc. Am Acad Arts Scis—AAAS—Am Law Inst —Am Bar Assn—Phi Beta Kappa. Awarded distinguished service medals of many Grand Lodges in North and South America and Europe; Gourgas Medallist of Supreme Council NMJ, US for notably distinguished service. 1117 Statler Bldg., Boston 16. H: Hotel Statler, Boston 17.†ⓒ

18 JOHNSON, Murray L. Mammals and reptiles of Pacific Northwest; Herpetology. b'14. BA '35—MD '39 (Oregon U); '31-34 (Coll Puget Sound); '39-43 (Union Mem Hosp Baltimore Md). Field work in past 15 years in Pacific Northwest; collection specimens reptiles and mammals; studies of life histories and distribution of subspecies. Described new subspecies Thamnophis elegans nigrescens '41; currently working on mammal collection and life history studies. Coauthor: (with J R Slater) Reptiles of the State of Washington '48. Curator of mammals Nat Hist Museum Coll Puget Sound Tacoma Washington since '46. Pacific Northwest Bird Mammal Soc—Am Soc Mammalogists —AAAS—Am Museum Nat Hist—Am Soc Herpetologists and Ichthyologists —Herpetologists League. 1207 Medical Arts Bldg., Tacoma 2, Wash. H: 3810 N. 35th St., Tacoma 7.

19 JOHNSON, Paul Henry. Synthetic polymeric elastomers; High explosives and pyrotechnique. b'13. Author articles in field. Research chemist Firestone Tire & Rubber Co since '45. Am Chem Soc—AAAS. Firestone Tire and Rubber Co., Research Bldg., Akron, O.

20 JOHNSON, Philip Gustaf. Education (Secondary school science, instructional and visual-auditory teaching aids). b'00. BS '23—MS '31 (Neb U); PhD '33 (Cornell); '25-26 (Minn U). Consultant in instructional aids Am Zone of Germany '46; engaged research in critique for evaluation and development of science courses of study for pre-college years; studies and writing on natural sciences and social life in rural communities. Co-author: (with P B Mann and C Dull) Modern Science in Our Environment '42; Modern Science in Our Daily Life '42; Modern Science in Man's Progress '42; also articles in field. Specialist science div secondary edn US Office Edn since '46. AAAS(F)—NEA—Am Inst Physics— Am Chem Soc (mem div chem ed)— Nat Assn Research Science Teaching. Fellow in nature and science edn, Cornell U '30-33. 406 Holly Av., Takoma Park 12, Md.†

21 JOHNSON, Preston Clarence. Education of American Negroes; Educational measurement. b'94. BS '17 (U Pa); EdM '38—EdD '39 (Temple U). Author articles in field. Prof edn Va State Coll since '39, dir testing since '40. Virginia State College, Petersburg, Va.

22 JOHNSON, Pyke. Highways; Automobile safety. b'88. Student '11 (U Denver). Member board governors DC div AAA; exec sec Highway Edn Bd; exec dir Pan-Am Confederation for Highway Edn; chmn adv com, rep automobile industry Internat Road Congress Seville Spain '23, mem US delegation Milan Italy '26, Washington '30; US mem Permanent Internat Road Commn; exec sec US Delegation at Pan-Am Highway Congress Buenos Aires '25, Rio de Janeiro '29. With Colorado State Highway Dept., '16-18; Washington rep and vp Automobile Mfrs Assn '18-39, exec vp '39-42; pres Automotive Safety Found Washington since '42. Automotive Safety Foundation, Hill Bldg., Washington 6.

23 JOHNSON, Ralph Stevenson. Forest mensuration; Silviculture. b'00. BS '24 (NY State Coll Forestry). Research, cruising, and reconnaisance of forest areas in North and South Carolina, Ontario, Quebec, New Brunswick, Nova Scotia, and Newfoundland; silviculture as applied through cutting methods in forest operations and introduction and carrying out of selection and partial cutting methods in Nova Scotia, forest growth studies and compilation of yield tables for spruce-fir forests in Nova Scotia. Timber estimator W Va Paper Co '24-25; timber estimator James D Lacey & Co '25-28; forester Mersey Paper Co Ltd '28-32; chief forester since '32. Soc Am Foresters—Can Inst Forestry—Forest Products Research Soc—Can Inst Forest Products—Am Soc Photogrammetry—Can Pulp and Paper Assn (Woodlands sect - received J A Bothwell

Award for meritorious achievement in forest conservation). Mersey Paper Co., Ltd., Liverpool, N.S.

10 JOHNSON, Raymond E. Softball. b'04. Vice pres Amateur Softball Assn of the Americas '40-41, president '42-48, chairman of the board, '49, member board of directors '50; vice chairman International Joint Softball Rules Committee '47-48. 1100 Broadway, Nashville 1.

11 JOHNSON, Searcy Lee. Law. b'08. AB '29 (Williams College); LLB '33 (Univ Tex). Legal advisor Gen Hershey on veterans employment '44-45; organizer, special assistant attorney general, chief Veterans Affairs section Dept Justice '45-47. Am Bar Assn. Author: The Loan Shark Fight in Texas. Contbr: Hildebrand's Texas Corporations '42. Mercantile Bank Bldg., Dallas 1.☺

12 JOHNSON, Sherman Wimmer. Perlite (Production, crushing and processing). b'08. Engr Mining Geol '32 (Colo Sch Mines). Specialist in selection and development of perlite deposits, uses and marketing of expanded perlite. With Combined Metals Reduction as mining engr since '39, asst mgr '40, mgr panacalite div since '46; operator perlite expanding business since '50. Perlite Inst (dir). 117 North Britain Rd., Irving, Texas.

13 JOHNSON, Thomas Hope. Wave nature of atoms; Primary cosmic rays; Ballistics. b'99. AB '20—MSc hon '40 (Amherst Coll); PhD '26 (Yale). Research on wave nature of atoms, nature of primary cosmic rays, fundamentals of the interaction of high energy radiations with matter. Author articles in field. Asst dir Bartol Foundation '30-42; research asso Carnegie Inst Wash; chief physicist Ballistic Research Lab Aberdeen Proving Ground '42-47, asso dir '46-47; sr scientist chmn phys dept Brookhaven Nat Lab. Am Phys Soc—Am Geophys Union—Sigma Xi. Fellow Bartol Foundation '27-30. Brookhaven National Laboratory, Upton, N.Y.

14 JOHNSON, Vard Hayes. Economic geology. b'09. BS '32—MS '33 (Brigham Young U); PhD '41 (U Ariz). Studies on maganese, chrome, complex non-ferrous ores, and coal; research on effects of geology on Western coking coal; responsibility of moving ground in oxidation which destroys coking qualities of high-violatile western coal; thermal metamorphism and alternation of coking coals near Paonia, Colo. Author article: Geology and Coal Deposits of Sand and Lookout Mountains, and others. Jr geol and mining engr lead, zinc, and silver ore Park City Utah '36-39; field asst US Geol Survey '40-42, geol since '43; geol Kalunite Co Marysvale Utah '41; asst on chrome US Bur Mines Kenai Peninsula Alaaska '42. Am Inst Mining Engrs—Utah Geol Soc—Geol Soc Am. 506 Federal Bldg., Salt Lake City.

15 JOHNSON, Vivian Annabelle. Solid-state physics; Electrical semiconductors. b'12. BA '32 (Reed Coll); MS '34—PhD '37 (Purdue U). Developed theory of resistivity, thermoelectric power, and thermomagnetic effects in semiconductors. Author articles: Structure of Zinc Oxide '40; (with K Lark-Horovitz) Resistivity of Germanium at Low Temperatures '47. Instr physics Purdue U '38-44, asst prof '44-47, asso prof since '47; research on half-time basis at Purdue U on electrical properties of elementary semiconductors. Am Phys Soc—Am Inst Physics—AAAS (sec B)—Sigma Xi. Physics Dept., Purdue University, Lafayette, Ind. H: 213 Varsity Apts., West Lafayette.

16 JOHNSON, Walter Gilbert. Scandinavian studies. b'05. BA '27 (Augsburg Coll); MA '29 (U Minn); '32 (U Uppsala); PhD '35 (U Ill). Author: James Thomson's Influence on Swedish Literature in the Eighteenth Century '36; Beginning Swedish '47; Continuing Swedish '41; A Handbook of English '46; also articles in field. Instr, later asst prof Eng and Scandinavian U Ill '32-47; prof Eng U SD '47-48; asso prof Scandinavian U Washington since '48. Modern Lang Assn Am—Soc Advancement Scandinavian Study—Swedish Cultural Soc—Phi Beta Kappa—Phi Kappa Phi—Alpha Sigma Phi. 214 Denny Hall, Seattle 5.

17 JOHNSON, Walter H(erbert). Boron hydrides. b'10. BA '33 (Augustana Coll); '36 (U SD)—'38-43 (U Md). Engaged research on thermochemistry of boron and of the hydrides of boron. Author articles in field. With Nat Bur Standards since '38, research in underground corrosion of metals '38, project with ceramics div '41, research on refining and testing of various optical glasses '43, thermochem lab since '43. Am Chem Soc. National Bureau of Standards, Washington. H: 2705 Elnora St., Silver Spring, Md.

18 JOHNSON, Warren C(harles). Physical and Inorganic chemistry (Rare elements, hydrogen compounds, liquid ammonia). b'01. BS '22 (Kalamazoo Coll); AM '23 (Clark U); PhD '25 (Brown U). Author articles in field. Prof chem U Chicago since '43, chmn dept since '45, asso dean div physical scis since '46; cons US Atomic Energy Commn since '46; bd governors Argonne Nat Lab since '48. Dir chem div Clinton Labs Oak Ridge Tenn '43-46. Am Chem Soc—AAAS—Faraday Soc—Sigma Xi. President's Certificate of Award '48. University of Chicago, Chicago 37. H: 5822 Blackstone Av.†☺

19 JOHNSON, William Martin. Soil genesis and classification (North Dakota, Great Plains States, Colombia). b'16. BS '36 (ND Agrl Coll) MS '38 (U Wis); MS '44 (Cal Inst Tech). Research in soil fertility and productivity in North Dakota; studies in fertilizer and irrigation development in Colombia. Asst prof in charge soils ND Agrl Coll '38-43; senior soil correlator Great Plains States Div Soil Survey Bur Plant Industry Soils and Agrl Engring USDA '46-47 and since '49; Soil sci Departamento de Agricultura Ministerio de La Economia Nacional Bogota Colombia '48. Soil Sci Soc Am—Am Soc Agron—Phi Kappa Phi—Sigma Xi. 204 Nebraska Hall, University of Nebraska, Lincoln, Neb.

20 JOHNSON, William Redmond. Technology of coffee, tea, moisture removal and enzymes; Autoxidation. b'07. BS '30 (U Wash); PhD '33 (Johns Hopkins). Processes and technology of green and roasted coffee, soluble coffee production; high vacuum dehydration, spray drying, extraction technology; flash evaporation. Holds patents in field. Co-author articles: (with Joza) Determination of Alpha Anylase) A General Method for Determining the Concentration of Enzyme Preparations, and others. With Fleischmann Labs since '33, now vp in charge research for Standard Brands Inc. A CS—AIC—Am Asso Cereal Chemists—Inst Food Technol—NY Acad Sci—Soc Rheology—Am Inst of City of NY.

21 JOHNSON, William R(ichard). Oils (Hot dip tinning); Cold rolling lubricants. b'21. BS '42 (MIT). Research on fundamental properties of palm oil used in steel mills and developed domestic substitute. Metall Malcomb Steel Div '42-43; metall Metlab Co '43-44; metall and supervisor research information Armour Research

Found since '46. Am Soc Metals—Sigma Xi. Armour Research Foundation, 35 W. 33rd St., Chgo 16.

22 JOHNSON, Willis Hugh. Protozoology; Population ecology. b'02. AB '25 (Wabash Coll); MS '29—PhD '31 (U Chicago). Research in nutrition of ciliates in sterile culture; growth curves in single type and mixed populations. Author articles: Effects of Population Density on Rate of Reproduction in Oxytricha '33; Life History and Morphology of Woodruffia Metabolica '38; Nutrition in the Protozoa '41; Heat Labile Growth Factor for Paramecium '45; also others in field. Instr zoology Wabash Coll '25-29, asso prof '31-35; asst prof biology Stanford U '35-38, asso prof '38-41, prof '41-45; prof zoology and chmn dept Wabash Coll since '45. Am Soc Zoologists—Am Soc Naturalists—Ecological Soc Am—National Research Council (comm Ecology of Animal Populations)—Phi Beta Kappa—Sigma Xi. Wabash College, Crawfordsville, Ind. H: 1003 S. Grant Av.

23 JOHNSTON, Alexander. Wool technology and economics. b'04. BS '33—MS '36 (U Wyo); '22-24 (West of Scotland Agrl Coll Glasgow). Developed method for core testing of domestic grease wools for shrinkage determination. Author articles in field. Wool specialist and prof dept wool tech U Wyo since '48. Rocky Mountain Wool Council (chmn econ and tech research commn)—Phi Kappa Phi—Sigma Xi—Alpha Zeta. Wool Department, University of Wyoming, Laramie, Wyoming.†

24 JOHNSTON, Charles Otis. Plant pathology; Wheat and oat pathology (Rust and smut control); Pathogens. b'93. BS '18—MS '24 (Kan State Coll). Research on nature and control of rusts and smuts of wheat and oats, physiologic specialization of pathogens, source and types of resistance, inheritance of resistance, effect of organisms on yield and physiology of hosts. Author articles: (with Coffman, Heyne, Stevens and Murphy) Improvement and Distribution of Spring-Sown Red Oats '45; (with Quisenberry and Rodenhiser) Bunt Reaction of Hard Red Winter Wheats in 1938-42 '45; (with Reitz and Anderson) A New Combination of Genes in Wheat and Wheatgrass Hybrids '45; also author other articles in field. Pathologist US Dept Agr '20, pathologist since '44. Sigma Xi—Phi Kappa Phi—Gamma Sigma Delta—Kan Acad Sci—Am Phytopath Soc—Am Soc Agronomy. Agricultural Experiment Station, Manhattan, Kansas.†

25 JOHNSTON, Floyd. Dairy husbandry (Jersey cattle). b'99. BS in animal husbandry '24 (Ia State Coll). Field sec Ia State Dairy Assn Waterloo Ia '25-28; in charge dairy extension work Ia Agrl Extension Service Ia State Coll '28-47; exec sec The Am Jersey Cattle Club Columbus O since '47. Am Dairy Sci Assn—Am Soc Animal Prod—Gamma Sigma Delta. The American Jersey Cattle Club, Columbus, O.

26 JOHNSTON, Herrick Lee. Low temperature physics; Thermodynamics; Isotopes; Gases. b'98. AB '22 (Muskingum Coll); BS '22—DSc '43 (Wooster Coll); PhD '28 (U Cal). Member commission on low temperature physics of International Institute of Pure and Applied Physics; member technical committee International Institute of Refrigeration. Asso editor Jour Chem Physics '35-38. Asst prof chemistry Ohio State U '29-33, asso prof '33-38, prof since '38; fellow John Simmons Guggenheim Meml Found,

U Goettingen Germany '33; research engr Gen Electric Research Labs Schenectady NY '37; dir Manhattan Project Research Ohio State U '42-46; dir Cryogenic Lab, Ohio State U. Am Phys Soc(F)—AAAS(F)—Am Chem Soc (past nat sec and nat chmn div phys and inorganic chemistry)—Nat Research Council (com deuterium research '34-37; com termodynamic constants since '40; com on natural and phys constants com on phys chem since '48)—ASME(com properties of gases)—Am Soc Refrigeration engrs (com on low temperature research)—Am Rocket Soc. Ohio State University, Columbus, O. H: 177 Brevoort Rd.†◎

10 JOHNSTON, Ivan Murray. Desert plants; Flora of Mexico, Chile and Argentina. b'98. AB '19—MA '22 (Calif U); PhD '25 (Harvard). Author articles in field. Superv Herbarium and library Arnold Arboretum since '46, asso dir since '48; asso prof Harvard U since '38. Am Acad Arts Scis—Am Bot Soc—Am Soc Plant Taxonomists—Am Soc Naturalists—NE Bot Soc—Sigma Xi. Arnold Arboretum, Jamaica Plan, Mass.◎

11 JOHNSTON, Robert Maurice. Toxicology. b'11. BS '33 (U Notre Dame). Studies on blood groups and identification; expert court testimony on toxicology; chemical and bacteriological study of poisons. Author: Laboratory Methods for Toxicological Problems '52. Toxicologist Bur Foods and Chem Commonwealth of Pa '35-39; cons toxicologist '40-43 and since '46. Lab Officer AUS '43-46. Nat Assn Clin Labs (pres '50-51)—ACS—Am Pub Health Assn—Engrs Soc Pa—Am Soc Professional Biol (vp '49). Certified by Am Bd Clin Chem. Johnston Laboratory, 504 N. Second St., Harrisburg, Pa.

12 JOHNSTON, William Drumm, Jr. Mineral deposits of Brazil and South America; Chromite; Gold veins. b'99. BS '21 (U Chicago); PhD '32 (Geo Washington U). Research in geology, ore deposits. Del 3d reunion Pan-Am Consultation on Cartography Caracas '42, 2d Pan-Am Congress Mining Engring and Geology Rio de Janeiro '46. Author: Ground Water in Northeastern Alabama '33; Gold Quartz Veins of Grass Valley California '40; also author articles in field. Asst prof geology Ky U '23-24; geologist Inst Indsl Research Cincinnati '24-25, hon fellow geology '25-26; asst prof geology N Mex Sch Mines, geologist N Mex Bur Mines '27-28; geologist US Geol Survey '28-41, chief Alaskan and fgn geol br since '49; geol Bd Econ Warfare Brazil '42-45. Geol Soc Am—Mineral Soc Am—Soc Econ Geologists (sec '38-41)—Geol Soc Wash—Am Inst Mining Engrs—Geophys Union—Pan-Am Inst Mining Engring and Geology (chmn US sect '47-49)—Geol Soc Brazil—Geol Soc Argentina—Sigma Xi. U.S. Geological Survey, Washington. H: 1620 Riggs Pl., N.W.

13 JOHNSTONE, Edwin Parker. Textile chemistry; Dyes; Intermediates; Wool shrinkage control; Textiles flammability. b'06. Student '25-29 (Lowell Textile Inst.). Research on melamine resins for textiles, flammability and fire resistance of textiles, reducing wool shrinkage and felting with melamine resins. Granted patents on treatment of Woolen textiles and spinning of lubricated thread. Chief chem Farr Alpaca Co '30-39; tech rep Am Cyanamid Co '40-45; research asso Am Assn Textile Chem and Colorists since '45. Am Assn Textile Chemists and Colorists Research Laboratories, Lowell Textile Institute, Lowell, Mass.†

14 JOHNSTONE, Henry Fraser. Chemical plant design; Waste gases (Treatment). b'02. BS '23 (U South); MS '25—PhD '26 (U Ia). Developed methods treatment waste gases to prevent atmospheric pollution. Author articles in field. Asst prof chem U Miss '26-28; spl research asst engineering expt sta U Ill '26-30, spl research asso '30-32, spl research asst prof '32-35, asst prof chem engring '35-37, asso prof '37-39, prof since '39, head div chem engring since '46. Am Chem Soc —Phi Beta Kappa—Sigma Xi. Awarded Walker Medal Am Inst Chem Engring '43, naval ordnance award '46. 113 Chem. Eng. Bldg. University of Illinois, Urbana, Ill. H: 802 Delaware Av.†

15 JOHNSTONE, Rutherford T(hompson). Occupational diseases. b '03. AB '16 (Geneva Coll); MD '25 (U Pittsburgh). Research and clincial study of workmen suffering from occupational diseases, plant investigations in industrial hygiene, consultation in preventive medicine within industrial medicine, industrial toxicology; consultant on adult health to state of California. Author: Occupational Diseases '41; Occupational Medicine and Industrial Hygiene '48. Co-author: (with Dr Alice Hamilton) Industrial Toxicology '46. Author 75 articles in field. Private practice since '26. W Assn Indsl Phys and Surgeons (past pres, sec)—AMA (mem council indsl health, past sec and now chmn sect indsl med and pub health)—Am Acad Occupational Diseases(dir)—Am Assn Indsl Phys and Surgeons (F, past dir.; winner award for best contbn to indsl med lit '49). 520 W. 7th St., LA 14.

16 JOLEY, Lloyd E(rwin). Propagation and testing of fruits and nuts; Rootstock studies; Pollination studies; Seed germination. b'06. BS '33 —'33-36 (Mich State Coll). Author articles in field. Jr and asst pomologist US Plant Introduction Garden Glenndale Maryland since '36, horticulturist charge introduction propagation and testing of fruits and nuts Chico Calif since '45. Am Soc Hort Sci—AAAS— Sigma Xi. Box 1040, Chico, Calif.†

17 JONASSON, Jonas Adalsteinn. History of the western United States (Pacific Northwest, northwestern railroads); Riel rebellions; US Air Force history World War II. b'03. BA '26 (Linfield Coll); MA '29 (U Wash); PhD '33 (Stanford U); summer '34 (U Calif). Research and writing on the history of logging in douglas fir region and history of Northern Pacific Railway; worked in sawmills and logging camps of Wash. Author: Bricks Without Straw '38. Author articles: Background of the Riel Rebellions '34; The Red River Amnesty Question '37; When the Railroad Titans Battled Portland '38; Portland and the Alaska Trade '39; also others in field. Asso prof hist Linfield Coll '31-34, prof since '34. Ore Hist Soc— Am Hist Assn. Linfield College, McMinnville, Ore. H: 435 S. Cowls St.†

18 JONES, Archie Jeff. Choral music (Conducting techniques); Music education (Curriculum). b'00. BS '29—MA '31 (U Minn); MusD '40 (Mac Phail Coll Music). Author: Techniques in Choral Conducting '49; Jones Music Recognition Test '49. Co-author: (with Floyd Barnard) Introduction to Musical Knowledge '35; (with Matthew I Smith & Robert Wells) Pronouncing Guide to French, German, Italian and Spanish '48. Head music edn dept U Minn '28-35; dir music dept U Ida '35-'40; prof music edn U Tex since '40. Music Tchrs Nat Assn—Music Educators Nat Conf—Tex Music Tchrs Assn(pres)—Phi Mu Alpha(nat pres)

—Tex State Music Council (pres). University of Texas, Austin 12, Tex.

19 JONES, Austin Emery. Geophysics; Seismology; Volcanology; Hydrology. b'98. AB '24—'26-27 (U Cal Berkeley); MS '38 (U Hawaii). Studies of relationship of earthquakes and surface changes to eruptions of Hawaiian volcanoes; investigation mechanism of lava flows; observation earthquakes of Lake Mead area Nevada-Arizona, and of Aleutian Islands; ground water and erosion studies of volcanic areas. Author articles: Classification of Lava Surfaces '43; Earthquake Magnitudes, Efficiency of Stations and Perceptibility of Local Earthquakes in the Lake Mead Area '44, and others. Asst geol US Geol Survey Kilauea Volcano TH '31-35, seismol Aluetian Islands '49-51; instr volcanology U Hawaii summer sch '33-35; asst geol Bd Water Supply Honlulu TH '35-37; asst seismic observer US Coast and Geodetic Survey Boulder City Nev '40-45, Paricutin Mex '45. Seismol Soc Am—Am Geophys Union —AAAS—Arctic Inst NA—Nat Geog Soc—Nat Sci Tchrs Assn. U.S. Geological Survey, 203 Custom House, Balt. 2.

20 JONES, Bassett. Elevators (Illumination, safety); Illumination; Trees (Coastal planting). b'77. Student '96-99 (MIT); ME hon (Stevens Inst Tech). Member sectional committee on elevator safety code American Standards Association '21, past chairman subcommittee on elevator safety research; consultant on illumination New York Worlds Fair, chairman committee on displays; owns experimental nursery on Nantucket Island, developed hardy Nantucket strain Black Japanese Pine (Pinus Thunbergi) now standard for coastal work. Am Standards Assn—ASME—Am Statis Assn— Soc Am Foresters. H: 325 East 79th St., NYC 21.†

21 JONES, Bob, Jr. Education (Language and literature); Shakespeare. b '11. AB '30 (Bob Jones Coll); MA '32 (U Pittsburgh); study (U Ala, Northwestern U, U Chicago); LittD '35 (Asbury Coll); LHD '41 (John Brown U); LLD '43 (Houghton Coll); DD '50 (Northwestern Schs). Shakespearean interpretation. Author: All Fullness Dwells; How to Improve Your Preaching; As the Small Rain; Inspirational and Devotional Verse; Wine of Morning (novel); Showers Upon the Grass. Acting pres Bob Jones Coll '32-47, pres since '47. Shakespeare Assn Am—Am Assn Tchrs Speech. Bob Jones University, Greenville, S.C.◎

22 JONES, Charles W(illiams). Medieval literature and history. b'05. Author: Bedae Pseudepigraha '39; Bedae Opera de Temporibus '43; Saints Lives and Chronicles in Early England '47; Medieval Literature in Translation '50. Contributor to Dictionary of World Literature '45. Member bd editors Cornell U Press '41-45. With Cornell U since '36, prof English since '48, dir summer sessions '46-48, dean grad sch since '48; dir US Mil Acad Preparatory '43-45. Medieval Acad Am (exec com '48-50)—Modern Lang Assn —Phi Beta Kappa. Research fellow Am Council Learned Socs '35-36, Guggenheim Memorial Foundation '39-40. 125 Day Hall, Ithaca.◎

23 JONES, Claude Elbert Edward. Eighteenth century English novel; American poetry and novel. b'07. AB '33 (Syracuse U); PhD '37 (Johns Hopkins U). Author: Smollett Studies '42; Wild Water (poems) '48. Co-author: Concordance of Poetical Works of William Collins '39; Poe '40. Editor Tobias Smollett, Essay on External Use of Water '35; Diaries of Isaac Reed '46 and others. Instr to asso prof U Calif since '37. Mod Lang Assn.

English Department, University of California, Los Angeles 24.†

10 JONES, Edith Carrington. Latin fables. b'94. MA '17 (Washington U); MS '33—PhD '44 (U Ill). Librarian Classics Library and cataloger U Ill since '29. Phi Beta Kappa. University of Illinois Library, Urbana, Ill.

11 JONES, Frances Follin. Archeology (Greek and Roman pottery). b'13. AB '34—MA '36 (Bryn Mawr Coll); '37-38 (Am Sch Classical Studies). Author articles in field. Asst to the dir The Art Museum Princeton U since '46, curator classical art since '45. Archeol Inst Am. The Art Museum, Princeton University, Princeton, N.J.†

12 JONES, Frederick Lafayette. Nineteenth century English literature; P. B. Shelley and his circle; Mary W. Shelley; Romantic movement. b'01. AB '21 (Furman); AM '22—PhD '25 (Cornell). Editor: The Letters of Mary Shelley 2 vols '44; Mary Shelley's Journal '47. Prof Eng U Pa since '47. Modern Lang Assn Am—South Atlantic Modern Lang Assn (vp '41, '46, pres '42-43). Awarded research fellowship abroad by Gen Edn Bd '36-37; postwar fellowship in the humanities by the Rockefeller Found '46. 4537 Pine St., Phila. 43.⊚

13 JONES, George W(illiam). Explosions; Safety engineering. b'91. AB '14 (U Denver). Research on explosibility of gases and vapors, hazardous chemicals, anesthesia, manhole and sewer explosions, ammonium nitrate, explosions in industry. Author 161 articles in field. With US Bur Mines since '15, chief Gaseous Explosions Branch from '51. ACS—Am Fire Protection Assn — AAAS—Phi Lambda Upsilon—Internat Coll Anesthetists (F). Distinguished Service award and Gold Medal US Dept Interior '50. US Bureau of Mines, 800 Forbes St., Pitts 13.

14 JONES, Grover G. Finance (Governmental). b'88. Accountant in charge US Treasury Dept Chicago '35, Phoenix '35-39, Des Moines '39-40; surveyor Treasury field offices New Eng and Southeastern states '40-41, regional accountant in charge Chicago '41-42, fiscal rep for field activities Chicago and elsewhere for fiscal asst sec of Treasury Washington since '42, regional coordinator Interdeptmental Savings Bond Com '43-46, state coordinator since '46; organizer first field organization for promotion sale US Savings Bonds among federal employees Ill, Ind, Ia, and Wis '43; overseas assignment to Eng, France, Switzerland, on loan from US Treasury Dept to foreign Office War Information for purpose of management analysis, and fiscal survey of OWI offices London, Paris and Bierne '45; state chmn also dir for Fed Employees Ill Div Am Cancer Soc Inc since '47. 7149 Merchandise Mart Bldg., Chgo 54.

15 JONES, Harold Charles. Birds of Georgia; Bioecology of northwestern Georgia. b'03. AB '28—AM '30 (Oberlin Coll); PhD '40 (Geo Peabody Coll); student (U Neb). Author articles in field. Associate professor sci E Carolina Coll since '47, field surveys of school resources since '48. AAAS(F)—Ecol Soc Am—Am Ornith Union—Ga Ornithol Soc—NC Acad Sci—So Asso Sci and Ind—Am Nature Study Assn —Nat Wildlife Fed—Wilderness Soc— Am Nature Assn—Carolina Bird Club —Wilson Ornith Soc. Department of Science, East Carolina College, Greenville, N.C.†

16 JONES, Harold Eugene. Soil (Fertility, management); Soil physics; Soil conservation. b'16. BS '40 (Kan State Coll); MS '42—PhD '51 (Purdue U).

Research on influence of boron on crop production, influence of longtime fertility treatments on nitrogen and carbon content of soils, soil aggregation, soil moisture relationships. Asst chem dept agron Purdue U '42-43; asso prof soils Kan State Coll '46-49; ext spl soils Agrl Ext Service U Minn since '49. Am Soc Agron—Soil Sci Soc Am—Soil Conservation Soc Am —Phi Kappa Phi—Sigma Xi—Gamma Sigma Delta—Alpha Zeta. Division of Soils, University of Minnesota, University Farm, St. Paul 4.

17 JONES, Henry A(lbert). Vegetable and onion breeding. b'89. BSA '16 (U Neb); PhD '18 (U Chicago); DSc (U Nebraska) '52. Co-author: Truck Crop Plants '28; The Vegetable Industry '31. Principal olericulturist now head horticulturist US Dept Agr since '36. AAAS—Am Soc Hort Sci— Wash Acad Sci—Sigma Xi. U.S. Department of Agriculture, Plant Industry Station, Beltsville, Md.

18 JONES, Herbert L. Tornadoes (Identification, forecasting). b'04. BA '26 (U Ore); MA '33—PhD '35 (Ore State Coll). Observation and collection of evidence on magnitude of electrical discharges during thunderstorms as compared to tornadoes; test and development electronic equipment to record sferics above pre-set level in forecasting tornadoes. Author articles: Development and Study of a Four-Wire Echo Suppressor Using a Double Audio-Gas Filled Tube '34; An Electron Theory of the Hall Effect and Susceptibility '48; A Sferic Method of Tornado Tracking and Identification '51. Transmission engr Pacific Telephone & Telegraph Co '26-29; radio telephone engr Bell Telephone Labs '29-32; prof elec engring U NM '36-46, Okla A&M Coll since '46. Nat Soc Professional Engrs—Okla Soc Professional Engrs—Am Soc Engring Edn—Am Inst Elec Engrs—Inst Radio Engrs—Sigm Xi—Phi Beta Kappa—Phi Kappa Phi—Sigma Tau— Kappa Mu Epsiilon—Pi Mu Epsilon— Eta Kappa Nu. School of Electrical Engineering. Oklahoma A&M College, Stillwater, Okla.

19 JONES, Hilton Ira. Emulsions; Paper and wood treatments; Textile treatments. b'82. AB '03 (Parker Coll); AM '04 (Drake U); PhD '16 (So Dakota U); '06-08 (Harvard); fellow in chemistry '08-09 (Univ Chicago); ScD '48 (Dakota Wesleyan). Extensive research in industrial chemicals; fire-proofing, moth-proofing, permanent starching, embalming chemicals, polishes and abrasives. Author articles in field. Prof Dak Wesleyan U '12-18; prof Okla Agrl and Mech Coll '18-22; dir scientific research The Redpath Bur '22-29; dir div edn and research Nat Selected Morticians '29-34; mng dir Naselmo Corp Chicago '34-37; mng dir Hizone Products (successor Naselmo Corp) since '37. Am Chem Soc— Am Assn Engrs — AAAS(F) — Am Inst Chemists (F, chmn Chicago chap) —Fellow Chem Soc (London). Hizone Research Laboratory, 1211 Washington Av., Wilmette. H: 1538 Forest Av.⊚

20 JONES, Howard Lewis. Statistics (Order statistics, sequential sampling, multivariate analysis); Quality control; (Clerical work) Stock market (forecasting). born '97. AB '23 (University Illinois). Author articles in field. With Illinois Bell Telephone Co since '23, area supervisor of results since '47. Ill Soc CPA—Am Statis Assn (pres Chicago chap '45-46, dist rep since '47)—Inst Math Statistics— Econometric Soc—Am Soc Quality Control (chmn auditing com since '47, corres sec Chicago sect '46-47). 309 W. Washington St., Chicago 6.

21 JONES, Idwal. California history (Wines and vineyard, Gold Rush period, mines); Gastronomy and culinary history; History of mercury mining; Folklore (Gipsy, western United States, mining). b'91. Privately educated, student engineering. Author: The Splendid Shilling '26; Steel Chips '29; Whistlers' Van '36; Black Bayou '41; The Vineyard '42; High Bonnet '45; The Sierra '47; Vermilion '47; Vines in the Sun '48; Gold Dust Empire '49. Prospector and rancher Calif; teacher, journalist, reviewer and drama critic San Francisco Examiner; editorial writer and columnist NY Am; book critic Life Mag. British Gipsy Lore Soc. 675 Bluebird Canyon, Laguna Beach, Calif.

22 JONES, Jenkin W(illiams). Rice breeding, culture, and processing. b '88. BS '12 (Utah Agrl Coll); MS '24 (U Cal). Expeditions for study rice production and improvement Asia '25-26, '47-49 and '50; experiments in processing, breeding, genetics and cytology of rice; experiments on irrigation, fertilizer, rotation rice crops. Author articles: Rice Culture in the Southern States '38; Rice Culture in California '50, and others. Supt Biggs Rice Field Sta Cal '18-30; in charge rice investigations BPISAE since '31. Am Soc Agron—Am Genetics Assn—AAAS Sigma Xi. Plant Industry Station, Cereal Division, Beltsville, Md.

23 JONES, John Courts. Rodent control; Birds (Food habits). b'13. AB '34 (U Minn); AM '37—'38-'39 (Geo Wash U). Supervision of operations, training, and research for improvements in methods and techniques rodent control; investigations into food habits numerous species birds and mammals for recommendations for management practices. Author bulletins: Manual for rodent control for the pest control operator; Food habits of the American coot, with notes on distribution. Contributor: (with Gardiner Bump) The Ruffed Grouse. Biol-collaborator US Biol Survey '36-39; in charge food habits research lab NY State Conservation Dept '39-43; insect and rodent control US Army '43-46; mammal control supervisor Fish and Wildlife Service US Dept Interior since '46. Am Soc Mammalogists—Am Ornithol Union—Audubon Soc—Cooper Ornithol Club—Wash Pest Control Assn (Hon)—Wildlife Soc—Wilson Ornithol Club. Fish and Wildlife Service, U.S. Department of the Interior, Washington 25.

24 JONES, John McKinley. Sheep (Husbandry, breeding, judging); Goats (Husbandry, breeding, judging). b'86. BS in ME '07 (U Wyo); BS in Agr '11; MA '12 (U Mo). Developed method sampling wool at shearing pens; established research wool scouring plant; livestock judge; agricultural officer (sheep specialist) Ecuador with FAO of UN '51-52, organized Asociacion de Criadores de Ovejas del Ecuador. With Tex A and M Coll '19-47; dir Am Corriedale Assn '38-40; dir Am Angora Goat Breeders Assn '39-40. AA AS(F)—Am Soc Animal Prodn—Nat Geog Soc. 812 Ennis Av., Bryan Tex.

25 JONES, Joyce Hedrick. Lichens. b'97. BS '25—AM '29 (Miami U). Author: Fink's Lichen Flora of the United States '35; also articles in field. Research asst in Herbarium U Mich '29-42, 44-45; asst curator since '46. Mycol Soc Am—Mich Acad Arts Letters Sci. Museums Building, University of Michigan, Ann Arbor.†

26 JONES, Linus H(ale). Plant iron nutrition; Nematodes control; Plant growth (Soil temperature effects). b'93. BSc '16—MSc '19—research fellow '25-26 (U Mass); PhD '22 (Rutgers

U). Trained for research work in plant physiology in experimental station specializing in plant nutrition, water relationships, soil temperature and controlled environment for plants as expressed in greenhouse management; research since '20 on iron nutrition of plants, control of nematodes, plant containers of all types and soil temperature effects on plant growth. Author articles in field. Asst research prof bot Mass Agrl Expt Sta since '26. AAAS(F)—Am Soc Plant Physiologists —Am Soc Hort Sci—Sigma Xi. Department of Botany, University of Massachusetts, Amherst, Mass.

10 JONES, Louis Clark. American folklore (Super-natural). b'08. AB '30 (Hamilton Coll); AM '31—PhD '41 (Columbia). Specialist in American folklore and literature, especially folklore of the supernatural; founder of Jones Folklore Archive, housed in the Farmers' Museum Library, containing thousands of songs, stories, beliefs, etc, of the people of New York collected by State College students. Author: Clubs of the Georgian Rakes '42; Spooks of the Valley '48; The Farmers Museum '48; Cooperstown '49; also articles in field. Editor: New York History: New York Folklore Quarterly. Asst prof NY State Coll for Teachers '34-46; exec dir NY State Hist Assn and of its folk mus, Farmers' Mus, Cooperstown, N.Y. Am Folklore Soc (councillor)—NY Folklore Soc (ed Quarterly since '45)—Am Assn Museums—Soc Am Histories—Am Assn State and Local History—NY Hist Assn—Am, Southern, Hoosier and Western Folklore Assns—NY Hist Soc (hon asso mem)—Council of Historic Sites (asso mem)—Rochester Mus Arts and Scis(F). Guggenheim Fellow '46, study of folklore of supernatural, St Croix, VI '46-47. New York State Historical Association, Fenimore House, Cooperstown, N.Y.☉

11 JONES, Norman R. D. Science teaching (Biology, chemistry). b'99. BS '22 (Eureka Coll); MS '28 (U Ill); '32 (Northwestern U). President American Council of Science Teachers '43-44; vice president, national membership chairman, director '42-48. Instr in sci since '22, St Louis Pub High Schs since '30; dir, organizer St Louis Sci Fair since '48, Sci Summer Sch since '50. AAAS—Nat Sci Tchrs Assn —(pres '48-49)—British Sci Masters Assn—Nat Assn Biol Tchrs—NEA— Central Assn Sci and Math Tchrs. Southwest High School, StL 9. H: 5310 Lindenwood.

12 JONES, Putnam Fennell. English literature; English language (Phonetics, philology). b'02. AB '24—Am '26—PhD '27 (Cornell U). Research in structure of Paradise Lost; word meaning and change of meaning; semantics and semantic change; pronunciation of English in America. Author: A Concordance to the Historia Ecclesiastica of Bede '29. Author articles: Milton and the epic subject from British History: The Gregorian mission and English education; and others. With U Pittsburgh since '27, prof English since '46, chmn dept since '47. Phi Beta Kappa—Nat Council Tchrs English—Coll English Assn—MLA—Medieval Acad Am—AAUP. University of Pittsburgh, Pitts. 13.†☉

13 JONES, Quill. Oriental rugs; Antique fabricated metals of Persia, India and Arabia. b'75. Student in museums of Europe. Visited Oriental countries '05 to study rugs and has since made nine trips to the Orient; was first American archeological collector ever to enter Yemen; has made many trips collecting rugs etc, Sabaean and Himyaritic antiquities, the

later being placed in Pa U Museum; has given addresses before Columbia U, Pratt Inst, NY Sch of Applied Design, etc; has loaned exhibits to various institutions. 711 5th Av., NYC.

14 JONES, Richard Ward. Automatic control and regulation; Electrical machinery. b'04. BS '26 (U Minn); MS '41 (Northwestern U). Design engr Westinghouse Elec and Mfg Co '26-30; design engr Westinghouse Elec Elevator Co '30-37; asst prof engring sci Central YMCA Coll Chicago '37-40; asst prof elect engring Northwestern Tech Inst Evanston '42-46, asso prof since '46. Am Phys Soc—Am Inst Elec Engrs—Am Soc Engring Edn —Sigma Xi. Northwestern Technological Institute, Northwestern University, Evanston, Ill. H: 944 Maple University.

15 JONES, R(obert) Clark. Radiation directors; Light polarization; Thermal diffusion; Sirens. b'16. AB '38—AM '39 —PhD '41 (Harvard). Research on classification radiation detectors; fundamental limits on their sensitivity; sensitivity of existing radiation detectors; minimum energy detectable by photographic materials; general theory of bolometers; research on mathematics of polarized light and on the use of polarizers, on thermal diffusion and its use in separation of isotopes, on hearing by electrical stimulation of the ear, on trapping light within scintillation counters; developed 50 horsepower siren for air-raid protection. Inventor device for automatic elimination of speech in radio reception. Mem tech staff Bell Telephone Labs '41-44; sr physicist Polaroid Corp since '44. Optical Soc Am—Acoustical Soc Am—Phi Beta Kappa—Sigma Xi. Adolph Lomb medal by Optical Soc Am '44. Polaroid Corporation, 730 Main St., Cambridge 39, Mass. H: 1716 Cambridge St., Cambridge 38.

16 JONES, Robert Cuba. Ethnic relations; Inter-American cooperation in the social sciences and social welfare. b'02. AB '23 (Earlham Coll); five years graduate study (Univ Chicago). Research field work Mexicans in the US, study and practice community organization in ethnic communities with particular attention to processes for securing intercultural cooperation. Author: The Mexican in Chicago '31; Directory Inter-American Activities in Chicago Area '42; Mexicans in the United States '43; Mexican War Workers in the United States '45; also articles in field. Consultant Mexican population in Chicago '32-39; dir Pan American Council '40-42; specialist social welfare Pan Am Union since '42. Pan American Union, Washington 6.

17 JONES, Robert E. Concord grape culture. b'12. AB '38 (Miami U); MS '40—PhD '42 (U Md). Author and editor: Growers' Newsletter since '47; also articles in field. Head research dept Church Grape Juice Co Kennewick Wash; now sales mngr agrl products Northwest Chemicals. Wash State Hort Assn—Am Assn Hort Sci—Bot S Am—Inst Food Technologists—Sigma Xi. Northwest Chemicals Inc., Box 701, Yakima, Wash.

18 JONES, Robert Thomas. Airplane aerodynamics and stability; Supersonic aerodynamics. b'10. Student '28-29 (U Mo)—'32-34 (Catholic U Am). Scientific aide National Advisory Committee for Aeronautics '34-39, engaged in research on airplane stability and control, head Stability Analysis Section '39-46, during war assisted Special Weapons Branch Army Air Force in development and testing of automatically controlled aircraft. Author articles in field. Inventions and discov-

eries: Differential linkage for aircraft control surfaces, all-movable tail surface for aircraft, beveled trailing edge form for aircraft control surfaces, design principle of sweepback for supersonic aircraft. Aeronaut research scientist and consultant in supersonic aerodynamics Ames Aeronaut Lab Nat Adv Com for Aeronautics since '46. Fedn Am Scientists. Recipient Sylvanus Albert Reed award of Inst Aeronaut Scis '46 for contributions to understanding of flow phenomena about bodies and wings at speeds below and above the speed of sound. Ames Aeronautical Laboratory, Moffett Field, Calif.†

19 JONES, Susan Wilbur. Russia (Language, translations). b'93. AB '13 (Wellesley Coll); AM '14 (U Chicago); AM '44 (Radcliffe Coll). Rockefeller Foundation fellow on problems of translation Slavic languages and literature; member staff Russian translation project American Council Learned Societies. Translator: History of Early Russian Literature (from 2d Russian edit) '49; Russia in Manchuria; Fallen Family. Staff ed Compton's Encyclopedia since '20. Phi Beta Kappa. H: 12 Traill St., Cambridge 38. Mass.

20 JONES, Thomas Elsa. College administration; Race relations. b'88. AB '12 (Earlham Coll Richmond Ind); BD '15 (Hartford Theol Sem); MA '17 —PhD '26 (Columbia); LLD '28 (Berea Coll); LLD '46 (Wabash). Member international commission studying conditions in South Africa '38; commission on minority groups Assn Am Colls. Author: Mountain Folk in Japan—a Method of Study; Testimony by Work (report of Friends' Civilian Public Service). With Friends' Mission Tokyo Japan '17-24; dir YMCA Vladivostock Siberia '18-19; prof economics Keio U Tokyo '20-24; Friend's reconstruction work Tokyo '23-24; pres Fisk U Nashville '26-46; pres Earlham Coll Richmond Ind since '46. Am Sociol Soc. Earlham College, Richmond, Ind.†☉

21 JONES, Tom Bard. Ancient and Hispanic-American history. b'09. BA '31—MA '32—PhD '34 (U Mich). Author: Introduction to Hispanic American History '39; Short History of Ancient Civilization '41; South America Rediscovered '49; also articles in field. Instr hist U Minn '35-38, asst prof '38-45, asso prof, prof '49. Am Hist Assn—Am Philol Assn. Department of History, University of Minnesota, Minneapolis. H: 1755 Van Buren Av., St. Paul.†

22 JONES, Vincent Starbuck. Readership (Newspaper); Photography (News). b'06. AB '28 (Hamilton Coll); '29-30 (Narvard). Research and application readable writing, and photo journalism. Author articles: By Guess or by Guide '47; Knockouts in Nitrate '48; Bold Experimentation Needed to Improve Newspapers '49. Contributor: The Great Pictures '50. Mng ed Utica Daily Press '30-38, exec ed '42-50; mng ed Utica Observer-Dispatch '38-42, exec ed '42-50; dir news and edit office Gannett Newspapers Rochester since '50. Am Soc Newspaper Ed-- NY State Asso Press Assn (pres '47)— Asso Press Mng Ed Inc (bd dirs). Gannett Newspapers, Times-Union Bldg., Rochester 14, N.Y.

23 JONES, Virgil Carrington. American Confederate history (Colonel John S. Mosby); Hatfield-McCoy feud. b'06. Student '24-26 (Va Poly Inst); AB '30 (Washington and Lee U). Author: Ranger Mosby '44; The Hatfields and the McCoys '48. Mgr Washington office The Curtis Publishing Co since '45. 743 National Press Bldg., Washington.

10 JONES, William H(enry), Jr. Precision heat measurements; Speed of chemical reactions; Solid rocket fuels. b'04. BS '24 (Emory U); MA '25—PhD '29 (Princeton U); research fellow '41-42 (Calif Inst Tech). Author articles in field. Instr chem Emory U '27-30, asst prof '30-36, asso prof '36-48, prof since '48. Lab head with the S-50 (thermal diffusion) plant Oak Ridge World War II. ACS (past chmn Ga sect)—Ga Acad Sci—Am Phys Soc—Phi Beta Kappa—Sigma Xi. Department of Chemistry, Emory University, Emory Univ., Ga.†

11 JONES, William Orville. Tapioca (Production, consumption, and distribution); Black Africa (Agricultural organization). b'10. Student '28 (Tex A&M Coll); '29-30 (S Methodist U); AB '32 (U Neb); '38-39 (U Cal Los Angeles); PhD '47 (Stanford U). Faculty Stanford U '40-41, '44-46, with Food Research Inst Stanford U since '46, asso econ, asso prof since '50. Am Econ Assn—Pacific Coast Econ Assn—Am Farm Econ Assn—W Farm Econ Assn—Am Statis Assn. Food Research Institute, Stanford University, Stanford, Cal.

12 JONES, William Powell. English literature (18th century, Thomas Gray); Relation between folklore and literature in the Middle Ages; Vocabulary building. b'01. AB '21 (Emory U); MA '25—PhD '27 (Harvard). Author: The Pastourelle '31; Thomas Gray, Scholar '37; Practical Word Study '43; also articles in field. Asst prof Western Reserve U '30-38, asso prof '38-47; prof and dean Adelbert Coll since '47. Modern Lang Assn Am—AAUP—Nat Council Teachers of English—Phi Beta Kappa. Western Reserve University, Cleveland 6. H: Gates Mills, O.

13 JONES, Winston William. Citrus physiology; Mineral nutrition of plants. b'10. BS '31 (Ala Poly Inst); MS '33 (Purdue U); PhD '36 (U Chicago). Author articles on Hawaiian fruits and vegetables, especially papaya. Asst plant physiologist U Hawaii '36-41; asso horticulturist U Ariz '42-45, horticulturist and head of dept '45-46; asso horticulturist U Calif since '46. AAAS—Am Soc Hort Sci—Am Soc Plant Physiologists—Sigma Xi. Citrus Experiment Station, Riverside, Calif.†

14 JONTE, John Herbert. Chemistry; Death Valley; Alcoholism. b'85. BS '11 (U Kan); MS '28 (State U Ia); student '38 (U Colo); fellow '45 (Yale). Prof chem Coll of Pacific since '20, Stockton Coll since '35; co-dir Death Valley Expeditions since '33. ACS—AA AS—Calif Acad Scis. College of the Pacific, Stockton 27, Calif.†

15 JOOS, Martin (George). Acoustic phonetics; Index verborum. b'07. Student EE '26-31—MA '36—PhD '41 (U Wis). Research in phonetics and pronunciation, cited as authority on American pronunciation by J S Kenyon in American Pronunciation '35 and later editions; research in acoustic phase of speech, visible speech. Inventor of methods of making an index verborum, Speech Stretcher, and the Flexible Vowel Synthesizer. Author: Acoustic Phonetics '48. Co-author: (with F Whitesell) A Middle High German Courtly Reader '51; Word Index to Joyce's Ulysses '37; Wortindex zu Goethes Faust '40; also articles in field. Editor: Asso ed Studies in Linguistics '42-46, Field worker with Linguistics Atlas of US and Can '31-32; lecturer in German U Toronto '38-42; employee US War Dept '42-46, communications research; asso prof German U Wis '46-49, prof since '49. Lin-

guistic Soc Am. Citation for extraordinarily meritorious civilian service War Dept '45. University of Wisconsin, Madison, Wis.†

16 JOPSON, Harry Gorgas Michener. Herpetology; Ornithology. b'11. BS '32 (Haverford Coll); MA '33—PhD '36 (Cornell). Engaged in research on amphibians and reptiles of southeastern states, and on Triturus of Eastern N Am. Author articles in field. Prof biology Bridgewater Coll since '36. Am Soc Ichthyologists and Herpetologists —Am Soc Mammalogists—AAAS—Virginia Soc Ornithologists—Va Acad Sci. Bridgewater College, Bridgewater, Va.

17 JORDAN, Alvin B. Aircraft lighting. b'21. Student '38-39 (Washington U St Louis); BS '43 (US Coast Guard Acad); '43 (Princeton); '43-44 (MIT). Research and tests on interior and exterior aircraft lighting, and airport and airway lighting systems; development new devices for warning, control, instrument, navigation, formation, and identification lighting. Elec engr photometry and colorimetry Nat Bur Standards '46-47, physicist '49-51; chief engr Sheboygan Machine Co Sheboygan Wis '47-49; elec engr Navy Dept Bur Aeronautics since '51. Am Inst EE—Optical Soc Am—Illuminating Engring Soc—Am Inst Physics. Registered profl engr Washington. Navy Department, Bureau of Aeronautics, Washington 25. H: 4717 Saul Rd., Kensington, Md.

18 JORDAN, Emil Leopold. German civilization; History of American immigration. b'00. PhD '23 (Univ of Konigsberg). Research in geography and geophysics of Germany, origins and results of German culture; research in and recording movements of peoples who came to the US. Author: Kulturgeographie von Deutschland '35; Deutsche Kulturgeschichte '37; Americans: A New History of the Peoples that Settled the Americas '39; From Foreign Lands '49; also articles in field. Mem faculty NJ Coll for Women since '31. N.J. College for Women, Rutgers University, New Brunswick, N.J.

19 JORDAN, Hans. Subway stations; Rectifier (direct current). Waste (Disposal). b'02. MS '23 (Inst Tech Munich Germany); PhD '26 (Inst Tech Hanover Germany); '38 (Inst Tech Zurich Switzerland). Design and construction of subway stations; design and construction of first high voltage direct current recitifier substation and automatic controls; development of food waste disposal. Numerous patents in field. Construction engr European Gen Electric Co '25-31; chief engr Given Machinery Co Los Angeles '40-45; chief engr Given Mfg Co since '45, engring and development div Pasadena Cal since '48; Zenith Die Casting Corp Los Angeles since '49. Am Ordinance Assn—Am Inst EE. 3301 Fruitland Av., LA 58.

20 JORDAN, Howard V. Soil fertility; Cotton; American hemp; Corn. b '96. BS '18 (Mich State Coll); MA '24 (U Mo). Research in soil fertility and soil management practices to obtain higher yields improved quality and disease resistance for cotton, American hemp, and corn. Faculty U Mo '20-24; asst prof agron NM Coll A&MA '24-28; soil sci USDA since '28. Am Soc Agron—Soil Sci Soc Am—AAAS (F)—Biometric Soc—Alpha Zeta—Sigma Xi. Department of Agronomy, Mississippi State College, State College, Miss.

21 JORDAN, Virgil (Dustin). Economics (Statistics, industrial management, agricultural); Social psychology. b'92. BS '12 (Coll City NY); '12-14 (U

Wis, Columbia, European Univs); LLD '39 (Rutgers); LLD '39 (Union Coll). Author: The Kansas Court of Industrial Relations '24; Industrial Progress and Regulatory Legislation in New York State '27; The Agricultural Problem in the United States '27; Manifesto for the Atomic Age '46; also articles in field. Pres Nat Industrial Conf Bd since '32. Phi Beta Kappa. 247 Park Av., NYC.†◎

22 JORGENSON, Theodore. Henrik Ibsen; Ole Edvart Rölvaag; Norwegian literature; Scandinavian unity. b'94. Student '15-18 (Waldorf Luth Coll Forest City Ia); AB '23 (St Olaf Coll Northfield Minn); PhD '35 (U Minn); post grad work '23-24 '33-34 (U Oslo Norway). Author: An Outline of Norwegian Literature '31; History of Norwegian Literature '33; Henrik Ibsen: A Study in Art and Personality '45. Co-author: (with Nora O Solum) Ole Edvart Rolvaag: A Biography '39. Translator and editor: Henrik Ibsen's Epic Brand and Other Poems '50. Contbr Norwegian section in Shipley's Ency of World Lit. With St Olaf Coll since '25, prof and head dept Norwegian since '34, chmn lang and lit div since '50; dir St Olaf Coll Norwegian Inst. Norwegian-Am Cultural League—Norwegian Lang Tchrs Assn —Norwegian-Am Hist Assn—Internat League of Norsemen—Frat Order Sons Norway—Phi Beta Kappa. St Olaf College, Northfield, Minn. H: 815 W. 2d St.◎

23 JOSEPHSON, Bertha Esther. Historical manuscripts; Historical editing and indexing; Archives. BS in Ed '28 —MA '29 (Ohio State U). Compiler: Cumulative Index to Miss Valley Hist Review, Vols. XVI—XXV '40; with C L Weaver Gen Index to Hist of Ohio State Univ, Vols I-V '44. Author: Manual of Style for Publications of the Beveridge Memorial Fund '40; Documentary Data, Manuscript Catalog '46; Indexing '46. Editor and revisor: DD Parker's Local Hist: How to Gather It, Write It, and Publish It '44. Editorial assistant Mississippi Valley Historical Review, Western Reserve Univ Cleveland '30-33, editorial asso '33-41; tech editor Albert J Beveridge Memorial Fund Publs of AHA '39-45; editorial asso O State Archeol and Hist Soc Columbus '41-42; mem bd editors Am Assn for State and Local History '41-44; editorial asso chief dept of documents O State Archeol and Hist Soc '42-45. AHA—Miss Valley Hist Assn—Soc Am Archivists—Am Assn for State and Local Hist—O State Archeol and Hist Soc—O Acad of Hist—Phi Alpha Theta. 218 S. High St., Columbus 15, O. H: 10 Seventeenth Av., Columbus 1.

24 JOSEPHSON, George Wesley. Technology and economics of nonmetallic minerals. b'08. Student '26-29 (Macalester Coll); EMet '33 (U Minn). Research ceramic roofing granules, industrial sand and gravel, mineral pigments, building materials, fertilizers, chemical raw materials, ceramic raw materials and abrasives; scientific consultant with Technical Industrial Intelligence Branch Field Information Agency Technical investigating German nonmetallic mineral technology '45. Co-author: Iron Blast Furnace Slag—Production, Processing, Properties and Uses '49; also articles in field. Inspector Minn Mining and Manufacturing Co '34-35, prodn supt '36-42; asst chief nonmetal econ br US Bur Mines '42-47, chief since '47. Am Inst Mining Metall Engrs. Bureau of Mines, Interior Building, Washington.

25 JOY, Joseph Francis. Mechanical mining of coal. b'83. Self educated mech and elec engring. Design and development of Joy Loader '16-19, special machines for mechanization of coal production '26-30; pioneered mechanical loading of coal; holds US and foreign patents for inventions used throughout coal mining areas of world. Founder and pres Joy Mfg Co Franklin Pa '19-25, Joy Bros Inc Marion O '30-34; gen mgr mining machinery div Sullivan Machinery Co Claremont NH '34-38; cons engr Pittsburgh and Franklin Pa '38-40; sr ordnance engr Office Chief Ordnance War Dept Wash '40-45; cons engr Joy Mfg Co since '45. Recipient NAM Pioneer Scroll '40. Oliver Building, Pittsburgh.†

10 JOYCE, Floyd Edward. Soap. b'89. BA '12 (U Ia); MS '17 (U Minn). With Procter and Gamble '18-20, Haskin Bros and Co '20-39, mgr Nat Soap Refining Co '40-49; supervisor soap mfg Economics Lab Inc since '49. Am Chem Soc—Am Oil Chem Soc—Alpha Chi Sigma—Assn Am Soap and Glycerine Producers. Economics Laboratory Inc., St. Paul.

11 JOYCE, Walter Edward. Suspension bridge cables; Bridges (Long span). b'88. PhB '07—CE '11 (Yale). Originated double-wire spinning parallel wire cables without crossing wires; designed rigid frame hydraulic squeezer for bridge cables. Pres and chief engr W E Joyce Co Inc Kingston NY '21-41; engr in charge Cable Constrn Bear Mt Bridge NY '23-34; cons engr Am Bridge Co Mid-Hudson Bridge '27-29, John A Roebling's and Sons Co on cables for Geo Wash Bridge NY and Golden Gate Bridge Cal '28-38; asso engr D B Steinman since '47. Am Soc CE. Room 1104 117 Liberty St., NYC 6.

12 JOYNER, Leslie Gordon. Adsorption; Catalysis. b'12. BSc (Chem) '37 (Brown U); PhD '41 (Cornell). Extension of theory of heats of adsorption and desorption; collaboration in development technique for determination of pore structure by low temperature gas adsorption; research on hydrocarbon isomerization and cracking catalysis; discovery identical results in isosteric and colorimetric methods for determination heat of adsorption. Author articles: Surface Area Measurements of Activated Carbons, Silica Gels and other Adsorbents '45; Differential Heats of Adsorption of Nitrogen on Carbon Blacks '48; Differential Heats of Adsorption and Desorption of Nitrogen on Porous Glass '48; Determination of Pore Volume and Area Distributions in Porous Substances from Nitrogen Absorption Isotherms '51. Contributor: Scientific and Industrial Glass Blowing and Laboratory Techniques '49. Research catalysis and adsorption Gulf Research & Development Co '41-45; fellow for research catalysis, adsorption, and pore structure of adsorbents Mellon Inst since '45, sr fellow of Bone Products Fellowship since '50. ACS—AAAS—Sigma Xi. 4400 Fifth Av., Pitts. 13.

13 JUDD, Deane Brewster. Colorimetry. b'00. AB-AM '18-23 (O State U); PhD '26 (Cornell). American representative on International Commission on Illumination for colorimetry and artificial daylight '31-35, '39, '47; American representative on International Commission on Optics for colorimetry '48. Author 40 articles in field. Research asso Munsell Research Lab '26-27; asso physicist Nat Bur Standards '27-36, physicist '36-37, sr physicist since '37. Optical Soc (chmn Inter-Soc Color Council '40-44). Jour award for paper on color-blindness Soc Motion Picture Engrs '36. National Bureau of Standards, Washington 25.◎

14 JUDKINS, Wesley Parkhurst. Plant physiology, anatomy, morphology and soils (Fruit crops). b'11. BS '34 (Me U); MS '37—PhD '41 (O State U). Engaged research in cultural problems related to production of apples, peaches and berries, plant hormones, production problems, soil management, fertilization, physiological responses, pruning, irrigation, and variety testing of stone fruits and berries. Author articles in field. Asso hort O Exp Sta, asso prof O State '47-49; prof hort, dept head VPI '49. Sigma Xi—Phi Kappa Phi—Am Soc Horticultural Sci. O Agrl Expt Station Fellowship '36-37; O State U Scholarship '38-39. Va. Agrl Sta, Va Poly Inst., Blacksburg.†

15 JUDSON, Alexander Corbin. Edmund Spenser. b'83. BA '07 (Pomona); MA '08—PhD '11 (Yale). Research on Spenser in England, Ireland, summers '29, '32, '47, at Huntington Library San Marino Calif summers '38-44, '39-40, '42. Author: Spenser in Southern Ireland '33; The Life of Edmund Spenser '45; Notes on the Life of Edmund Spenser '49. Instr English, adjunct prof, asso prof, U Tex '11-23; prof Ind U '23-50, prof emeritus since '50; vis prof Claremont Grad Sch '50-51. Modern Lang Assn Am—Phi Beta Kappa. 452 W Tenth St., Claremont, Cal.

16 JUDSON, James Edward. Cucumber. b'00. BS '22 (U Ill); MS '24—PhD '27 (U Wis). Author: Morphology and Vascular Anatomy of Pistillate Flower of the Cucumber; Floral Development of Staminate Flowers of Cucumber and Muskmelons. Prof biology W Va Wesleyan Coll since '29. AAAS—W Va Acad Sci (sec '36-46, vp '46-47, pres '47-48)—Sigma Xi. West Virginia Wesleyan College, Buckhannon, W.Va.

17 JUDSON, Lewis V(an Hagen). Measurements of lengths and angles; Units of measurement (Foreign, ancient). b'93. AB '16—AM '17 (Clark U) '16 (Harvard)—'22-23 (U Paris)—'18—PhD '25 (Johns Hopkins U). Research in length and angle measurements, history of weights and measures, specialist in units, including foreign, ancient, metric, etc, of weights and measures. Author articles in field. Lab asst Nat Bur Standards '17-18, chief of length sect since '18. AAAS—Am Phys Soc—Optical Soc Am —Washington Acad Sci. National Bureau of Standards, Washington 25. H: 3417 Northampton St. N.W., Washington 15.

18 JUGENHEIMER, Robert William. Corn breeding; Plant genetics. b'04. Diploma '23 (Brown's Bus Coll Davenport Ia); BS '34—MS '36—PhD '40 (Ia State Coll). Author articles in field. Prof plant genetics U Ill since '45. Am Soc Agron—Genetics Soc Am—Am Genetic Assn—AAAS—Am Statist Assn—Ill Seed Producers Assn—Ill Crop Improvement Assn—Internat Crop Improvement Assn—Am Men Sci—Sigma Xi—Gamma Sigma Delta. Department of Agronomy, University of Illinois, Urbana, Ill.

19 JUHREN, Gustaf. Soil conservation (Erosion control, weed and brush control). b'98. MS (Forestry) '23 (Royal Coll Forestry Stockholm). Research in use vegetative measures in control erosion; analysis current methods alleviating soil losses through vegetative control measures; investigations with growing plants to determine possibilities of germination and growth in types soils found within drainage area and response to temperature common to area; research in weed and brush control by use chemical hormone substances. Author articles: Shrubs replace steel and concrete; Ammonium sulfamate as a brush killer. Soil conservationist San Diego County Rd Dept '35-42; forester, silviculturist Los Angeles River flood control project US Forest Service since '45. Soc Am Forresters—AAAS. U.S. Forest Service, Pasadena 3, Cal.

20 JUKES, Thomas H(ughes). Vitamin B complex; Poultry nutrition. b'06. BS '30—PhD '33 (U Toronto); '33-34 (U Calif). Author articles in field. Instr to asst prof U Calif '34-42; head nutrition and physiology research dept Lederle Labs Pearl River specializing in vitamin research. Consultant med research div CWS '44-45. Am Inst Nutrition (council '42-46)—Am Soc Biol Chemists—Soc for Exptl Biology and Medicine—Poultry Sci Assn—Am Soc of Animal Prodn—Animal Nutrition Research Council (treas '48-49)—NY Acad Scis(F)—Sigma Xi. Borden award for research in poultry nutrition '47. c/o Lederle Laboratories, Division American Cyanamid Co., Pearl River, N.Y.

21 JULL, Morley Allan. Poultry husbandry. b'85. BS '08 (U Toronto); MS '14 (McGill U); PhD '21 (U Wis). Representative US government 4th World's Poultry Congress Ottawa Can '27, 5th Congress London Eng '30. Author: Poultry Husbandry '38; Poultry Breeding '40; Successful Poultry Management '43; Raising Turkeys, Ducks, Geese and Game Birds '47. Asst in poultry W Va Expt Sta Morgantown W Va '08-09; poultry commr BC Dept Agr Victoria BC '09-11; head poultry dept Macdonald Coll McGill U Montreal Can '12-23; sr poultry husbandman US Dept Agr Washington DC '23-36; head poultry dept U Md since '36. AAAS(F)—Poultry Sci Assn (past pres)—Sigma Xi. University of Maryland, College Park, Md. H: 6906 Pineway, College Heights, Hyattsville.◎

22 JUNGEBLUT, Claus Washington. Infantile paralysis; Infectious diseases. b'97. MD (U Berne Switzerland); NRC fellow med '27; Fulbright scholarship for study in the Netherlands '51. Studies in poliomyelitis from a clinical, experimental and epidemiological point of view; relation between susceptibility and function of certain vitamins (ascorbic acid) and endocrine substances (anterior pituitary adrenal); relation between suscepibility and blood group factors; extraneural virus distribution and myo-neural lesions in human poliomyelitis (myocardial involvement, skeletal muscle involvement); studies on strains of murine poliomyelitis virus (Col-SK virus, MM virus) and classsification problems; extrahuman rodent reservoirs of virus; chemotherapeutic studies (receptor destroying enzymes; naphthoquinones); mechanism of viral hemagglutination. Mem NY State Bd Med Examiners. Bact NY State Dept Health '23-27; asso prof bact and exptl path Stanford U '27-29; asso prof bact Columbia '29-36, prof bact since '36. Harvey Soc—AMA —Am Assn Immunologists—Am Soc Exptl Path—Am Assn Path and Bact —Soc Exptl Biol and Med—AAAS— NY Acad Med—NY Acad Sci—Soc Am Bact—Am Soc Human Genetics. H: 468 Riverside Drive, NYC

23 JUNGERSEN, Thoger Gronborg, Jr. Casting (Precision). b'20. Ed pub schs. Worked on development of precision casting with father '33-48; holds several patents in field as co-inventor. Sec Arocast Corp Summit NJ '42-44, pres '44-48. Am Soc Metals. 11 Pittsford Way, Summit, N.J.

24 JUREDINE, Gordon Mounier. Inorganic pigments; Driers for paints; Fungicides. b'03. AB—AM '21 (Union Coll); MS '25 (Syracuse U). Research and development to technical coordination and commercial development Harshaw Chem Co since '41. Am Chem Soc—AAAS—Am Oil Chem Soc—Am Soc Testing Materials—AIC—Am Phytopathol Soc—Chem Market Research Assn—Nat Farm Chemurgic Council—Ohio Pesticide Inst. 1945 E. 97th St., Cleveland 6.†

10 **JURJI, Edward J(abra).** Comparative religion; Islamic and Arabic. b'07. BA '28 (Am U Beirut); MA '35—PhD '36 (Princeton); ThB (Princeton Theol Sem). Assistant editor Moslem World Quarterly since '43. Author: Illumination in Islamic Mysticism '38. Editor, co-author: Great Religions of the Modern World '46. Contbr: History of Philos Systems '50. Collaborator: Saudi Arabia '46, and others; also articles in field. Teacher Iraq dept edn '28-30; teacher Am Sch for Boys Baghdad '30-33; mem Inst Advanced Study Princeton '36-38, lecturer semitic languages Princeton U since '43; asso prof Islamics and comparative religion Princeton Thoel Sem since '46; Am Oriental Soc—AAUP—Fellowship Prof Missions. Education Building, 100 Stockton, Princeton, N.J. 34 Hibben Road.†

11 **JUST, Theodor Karl.** Plant morphology and evolution; Taxonomy of Cycadaceae, Gnetaceae and Chenopodium. b'04. PhD '29 (U Vienna). Member editorial board Ecology since '47, assistant editor Chronica Botanica since '40. Editor: Plant and Animal Communities '39; Symposium of Paleobotanical Taxonomy '46. Chief curator dept bot Chicago Natural Hist Mus since '47; research asso dept bot Northwestern U since '47; librarian Lloyd Library and Mus Cincinnati. NE Bot Club(F)—Am Geog Soc—AAAS—Bot Soc Am (chmn paleobot '48)—Torrey Bot Club—Ind Acad Sci (vp '42, pres '43)—Entomol Soc Am—Ecol Soc—Soc Study Evolution—Sullivant Moss Soc—Sigma Xi. Chicago Natural History Museum, Chicago 5. H: 1024 Erie St., Oak Park.◎

12 **JUSTICE, Oren L.** Seed technology. b'07. BS '32—MA '36 (Ohio U); PhD '40—Goldwyn Smith fellow '36-37 (Cornell U). Author: A Study of Dormancy in Seeds of Polygonum '41; Dormancy, Germination and Longevity in Seeds of Cyperus '49. Also author and co-author numerous articles. Chief seed analyst and Director Seed Division Ala Department Agric '40-44; botanist and chief of testing and research sect seed div US Dept Agr since '44. Am Bot Soc—Am Soc Agron—Bot Soc Washington—Assn Official Seed Analysts—Sigma Xi. South Laboratory, Agricultural Research Center, Beltsville, Md.†

K

13 **KAHLENBERG, Herman H(eald).** Medicinal colloids. b'01. BS '22—MS '23—PhD '25 (U Wis); '24 (U Freiburg). Research rexaurom, non-toxic gold colloid for arthritis, colloidal noble metals, silver, gold, platinum, palladium, osmium, iridium, ruthenium, rhodium and their medicinal and toxic properties. Author articles in field. Chem Newport Chem Works '21; chief chem and vp Kahlenberg Labs Inc '25-41, pres '41-44, sci dir and owner since '44. Am Chem Soc—AAAS(F)—Am Inst Chem(F). Main, Higel & Lodge, Sarasota, Fla. H: 175 Clematis St.

14 **KAHN, Reuben L(eon).** Serology (Tests); Immunology. b'87. AB '09—LLD hon '43 (Valparaiso U); MS '13 (Yale); DSc '16 (NYU). Research on science of blood serum reactions, developed Kahn reaction for syphilis and Universl serologic reaction in health and in various diseases; consultant US Public Health Service and US Naval Medical School Bethesda Maryland; participated in conferences of League of Nations Health Committee Copenhagen '28 Montevideo '30, Immunologic Conference of Royal Academy Italy at Rome '33. Author: Serum Diagnosis of Syphilis by Precipitation '25; The Kahn Test—A Practical Guide '28; Tissue Immunity '36; Serology in Syphilis Control '42; Serology with Lipid Antigen, with Special Reference to Kahn and Universal Reactions '50; An Introduction to Universal Serologic Reaction in Health and Disease '51; also more than 180 articles in serology and immunity. Immunologist Mich Dept Health '20-28; dir lab U Hosp, asst prof bact and serology U Mich '28-48, chief serology lab, asso prof serology since '48. AAAS(F, recipient 11th annual award '33)—AMA(asso F)—Soc Am Bact—Soc Exptl Biol and Med—Am Assn Immunologists—Am Assn Path and Bact—Am Pub Health Assn—Mich Acad Sci—Sigma Xi—Pi Lambda Phi—Phi Delta Epsilon—Phi Kappa Phi—Cosmos Club—Asociacion Argentia de Dermatologia y Sifilologia (corr mem)—Soc Chilena Microbiologie e Higene(corr mem)—Med Assn Dominican Rep(hon). Order Carlos J Finley (Cuba); Gold medal Phi Lambda Kappa for contributions to med sci '37. University Hospital, Ann Arbor.◎

15 **KAIN, Richard Morgan.** James Joyce; Modern fiction bibliography. b'08. AB '30 (Swarthmore); MA '31 (U Chicago); '31-32 (Harvard); PhD '34 (U Chicago). Author: Fabulous Voyager: James Joyce's Ulysses '47; also articles in field. Prof Eng U Louisville since '47, act chmn div humanities '48-49; book reviewer Louisville Courier-Journal since '40. Mod Lang Assn (bibliographer for prose fiction group since '47)—Nat Council Teachers Eng—James Joyce Soc. University of Louisville, Louisville.†

16 **KAISER, Elmer Robert.** Coal utilization; Smoke abatement. b'09. BS (ME) '34—MS '34 (U Wis). Research administration, design of smokeless stove, boiler, furnace and stoker for residential heating; coal fired gas producer, automatic coal-fired industrial boiler; research on smoke abatement, and reduction dust and cinder emission. Fuel engr Battelle Memorial Inst Columbus O '35-44; asst dir research Bituminous Coal Research Inc Columbus since '44. Am Soc ME (past chmn fuels div)—Am Inst Mining Engrs (past chmn com on research)—Air Pollution and Smoke Prevention Assn Am—Tau Beta Pi—Pi Tau Sigma. 488 W. Sixth Av., Columbus 1, O. H: 2406 Brixton Rd., Columbus 12.†

17 **KAISER, John Boynton.** Library finance, management, administration and civil service. b'87. BA '08 (Western Res U); BLS '10—MLS '17 (NY State Library Sch). Author: Law Legislative and Municipal Reference Libraries '14. Compiler: Survey of State Supported Library Activities in Washington '17; also articles in field. Dir Newark Pub Library since '43. Am Library Inst (F)—ALA (chmn com on civil service '29-32, chmn com on salaries and employment '32-36, chmn com on library revenues '41-45, mem council '40-45, cons on library finance to Post-war Planning Commn)—Pacific NW Library Assn (pres '17-18)—Calif Library Assn (pres '32-33)—NJ Library Assn (pres '48-49)—Am Soc Pub Adminstrn—Wash State Library (mem adv bd, pres '16-19)—AAAS—Phi Beta Kappa. Public Library, Newark 1, N.J.◎

18 **KALBFELL, David Conrad.** Electronics. b'14. AB '34 (U Cal Los Angeles); AM '36—PhD '39 (U Cal Berkeley). Development special regulated power supplies, wideband amplifiers, capacity maseuring devices, logarithmic attenuators, filters, frequency meters, specialized industrial devices; special purpose frequency modulated receiver and other industrial communication type equipment; design piezoelectric transducers and sonar systems; studies on circuit analysis. Research physicist Standard Oil Co Cal '39-41; physicist and electronics engr Div War Research U Cal '41-45; pres and chief engr Kalbfell Labs Inc since '44; asso prof physics San Deigo State Coll since '48. Inst Radio Engrs—Acoustical Soc—APS—Phi Beta Kappa—Sigma Xi—Pi Mu Epsilon. 1090 Morena Blvd., San Diego 10, Cal.

19 **KALLET, Arthur.** Consumer goods (Testing and rating). b'02. BS '24 (MIT). Research on laboratory test methods for consumer goods; rating of consumer goods by laboratory and use tests. Author: Counterfeit '35. Co-author: (with F J Schlink) 100,000,000 Guinea Pigs '33. Mem staff Am Standards Assn and editor Industrial Standardization '27-34; writer on consumer subjects since '33; dir Consumers Union of US (a non-proit organization which publishes Consumer Reports) since '36. 17 Union Square West, NYC 3.◎

20 **KALLGREN, Carl Alfred.** Student counseling. b'94. AB '17—Am '25 (Colgate U); BD '20 (Rochester Theol Sem); PD hon '40 (Syracuse U). Dean of students Colgate U '33-42, co-ordinator Colgate unit Naval Coll Training Program V-12 '43, dean of college since '43, director student personnel services. Eastern Assn Deans Men—Phi Beta Kappa. Colgate University, Hamilton, N.Y. H: 15 E Kendrick Av.◎

21 **KALOYEREAS, S(ocrates) A(gaesilaos).** Food technology; Greek agriculture. b'02. BS '24 (U Athens); MS '29 — Rockefeller fellow '27-28 (U Calif); British Council fellowship '37 (U Cambridge and Low Temp Inst, Eng); PhD '36 (U Salonica). Research on fats and oils, other aspects food technology and Greek agriculture; made scientific missions to European countries for Greek government visiting various food research institutes '31-37; technical advisor Ministry of Supplies Greece '45; representative Greek government UNRRA Greek Mission '45; participated several international meetings and congresses. Holder six Greek patents, and one American patent. Author: The Fresh Grapes in Greece and Elsewhere '29; Study and Experiments on the Fumigation of Figs '32; Table Olives '32; Contribution to the Study of Technology of Figs '36; Citrus Fruits and Their By-Products '38; Methods for the Production of Early Fruits and Vegetables '38; Practical Guide of Food Preservation '41; Policy of Food Production and Nutrition for Greece '44; and others; also articles in field. Dir research exp sta food technology Athens '33-45, sericulture lab '36-37; now asso prof dept agrl chem and biochem La State U. Am Chem Soc—Am Oil Chem Soc—Inst Food Tech—AAAS—La Acad Sci. Awarded prizes Nat Acad Sci Greece '32, '36-38. Louisiana State University, Baton Rouge, La.

22 **KALTENBORN, Hans V.** Current history; Current events (Radio broadcasting); News reporting. b'78. AB cum laude '09 (Harvard); LLD '39 (U Wis); Dr More Humane Letters '39 (Hamilton Coll); LittD '40 (Miami U). Author: We Look at the World

'30; Kaltenborn Edits The News '37; I Broadcast the Crisis '38; Kaltenborn Edits the War News '42; Europe Now '45. Radio news analyst since '22; corr Russia and Far East '26-27; mem Russian-Am C of C delegation in Russia '29-34 Rep and Dem convs since '32, London Conf '33, League of Nations sessions Geneva '35 '37, Pan-Am Peace Conf Buenos Aires '36, Spanish War Front '36-37, World War II from British Isles, Italy, France, Germany, W Africa, Latin America and SW Pacific '39-45, Inter-Am Conf Mexico City '45, UN Conf San Francisco '45, NY '46-47. Assn Radio News Analysts (founder, 1st pres)—Radio Pioneers (founder, 1st pres)—Phi Beta Kappa Assos (founding mem). Recipient many medals and awards for achievements in news reporting. 167 E 64th St., NYC†◎

10 KAMAN, Charles Huron. Helicopters. b'20. BS (Aeronautical engring) '40 (Catholic U Am). Invention, design, development and production helicopter with aerodynamically controlled rotors, by means of servo-control device; member National Advisory Committee for Aeronautics. Chief aerodynamicist helicopter rotor development, Hamilton Standard Propellers Div United Aircraft Corp '40-45; pres Kaman Aircraft Corp since '45. Inst Aeronautical Sci—Am Helicopter Soc —Helicopter Soc Gt Brit—Wings Club. The Kaman Aircraft Corp., Windsor Locks, Conn.

11 KAMIAT, Arnold Herman. Social psychology (Emotional immaturity and delusion of infallibility). b'97. Student '17-18 (Coll City NY). Author: Social Forces in Personality Stunting '39. Author articles: The Believer's Delusion of Infallibility '25; The Subjectivity of the Believer '29, and others. Ed Thomas Pub Co NYC. Am Philos Assn—NY Conf Method Sci Philos. Thomas Publishing Company, 461 8th Av., NYC 1. H: care Mason, 535 W. 113th St., NYC 25.

12 KAMINSTEIN, Abraham Louis. Copyright law. b'12. BS '32 (Coll City NY); LLB '35—LLM '36 (Harvard Law Sch). Chief exam div Copyright Office Library of Congress since '47. Fed Bar Assn. Research F Harvard Law Sch '36. Copyright Office, Library of Congress, Washington 25. H: 5908 Nevada Av., Washington 15.

13 KAMLET, Jonas. Industrial organic chemistry and microbiology. b'14. PhD (NYU). Research in pharmaceuticals, by-product utilization, cement technology, coal chemicals, industrial catalysis, ferrous and non-ferrous metallurgy, textile and dyestuff chemistry. Holds numerous patents in field. Dir The Kamlet Lab NYC. Am Chem Soc—Am Inst Chem—AAAS. The Kamlet Laboratory, 250 E. 43 St., NYC 17.

14 KAMM, Minnie (Elizabeth) Watson. Glass (Pattern); China (Old); Herbs. b'86. AB '09 (Olivet Coll); MS '13—PhD '15 (U Ill). Research on parasitic Protozoa, garden herbs; domestic pattern glass, old china. Author: Studies on Gregarines (Ill Biological Monographs, Vol II, No 3) '16, Studies on Gregarines II (Vol VII, No. 1) '22. Old-Time Herbs for Northern Gardens '35; Two Hundred Pattern Glass Pitchers '39; A Second Two Hundred Pattern Glass Pitchers '40; A Third Two Hundred Pattern Glass Pitchers '43; A Fourth Pitcher Book '46; A Fifth Pitcher Book '48; A Sixth Pitcher Book '49; Old China '51. Sigma Xi. H: 365 Lake Shore Rd., Grosse Pointe Farms 36, Mich.

15 KAMMER, Edward Joseph. Louisiana shrimp and fur industry. b'08.

BA '33 (St Mary's Sem); MA '39—PhD '41 (Cath U Am). Author: A Socioeconomic Survey of the Marsh Dwellers of Four South Eastern Louisiana Parishes '41. Prof sociol and chmn dept De Paul U '41 to '48; dean Coll Commerce '46-50; dean of faculties '50; vp De Paul U since '44, bd trustees since '44. Am Sociol Soc. 64 E. Lake St., Chicago 1.

16 KAMP, James Richard. Floriculture; Plant physiology. b'07. AB '28 (Wash U); BS '42—MS '43 (Ill U); PhD '47 (O State U). Research on effect of spacing of gardenia plants on yield of flowers, pruning experiments with greenhouse roses, experiments with carnations, selection within a gardenia clon, experiments in handling of old rose plants. Author articles in field. Asso prof floriculture U Ill since '48. Sigma Xi—Am Soc Hort Sci—Am Soc Plant Physiol. University of Illinois, Urbana, Ill.

17 KANE, Harnett Thomas. History of Louisiana and southern United States (Folklore, social customs, politics, plantations, bayous). b'10. BA '31 (Tulane). Author: Louisiana Hayride: The American Rehearsal for Dictatorship '41; Bayous of Louisiana '43; Deep Delta Country '44; Plantation Parade—the Grand Manner in Louisiana '45; New Orleans Woman '46; Natchez on the Mississippi '47; Bride of Fortune '48; Queen New Orleans '49; Pathway to the Stars '50; also articles. Author, critic, lecturer. Lyceum Assn—Authors Guild Am—Soc Midland Authors—Am Newspaper Guild. Guggenheim fellowship for study so problems '43-44, '44-45. 5919 Freret St., New Orleans.◎

18 KANE, John Morris. Industrial ventilation; Dust control. b'08. BS (ME) '33 (U Ky). Design and application local exhaust ventilation to industrial operations; reduction and prevention of air pollution with air cleaning equipment; advisor on industrial hygiene Kentucky Board of Health. Author articles: Design of Exhaust Systems '45; Foundry Ventilation '46; High Temperature Stack Gas Cleaning '50; Air Pollution and the Foundry '51, and others. Engr dust control div Am Air Filter Co '33-44, chief engr '44-50, now mgr. Am Soc Heating and Ventilating Engrs (indsl ventilation adv com)—Indsl Hygiene Found (engring sub-com)—Am Foundrymen's Soc (safety and hygiene com) —Am Standards Assn—Am Indsl Hygiene Assn—Air Pollution and Smoke Prevention Assn. American Air Filter Co., Lsvl 8.

19 KANE, Leslie Joseph. Gas reactions (Catalytic); Fine chemical manufacture; Coal (Gasification); Synthetic rubber. b'07. BS (Chem E) '29 (Armour Inst Tech). Devolatilization of coal by fluidization; manufacture of formaldehyde, benzoic acid, benzaldehyde, and hydroquinone; rubber polymerization (synthetic). Author articles: Partial Devolatilization of Coal by Fluidization; Catalytic Gasification of Higher Hydrocarbons; Investigation of a Photoelectric Cell Device for the Determination of Low Concentrations of Dust in Gas; Determination of Solid and Liquid Impurities in Synthesis Gas; A Moving Bed Filter for the Removal of Dust from Gas. Chem Thiokol Corp Trenton NJ '42-44; asst chem engr Inst Gas Tech Chicago '44-47; now chem engr in charge miscellaneous impurities unit US Bur Mines. ACS—Am Gas Assn. U.S. Bureau of Mines, Mineral Industries Bldg., Morgantown, W.Va. H: 440 Brockway Av.

20 KANTONEN, Taito Almar. Finland (Folklore, language, literature);

Martin Luther and Luteranism. b'00. AB '24 (U Minn); AM '26 (Harvard); STB '28—PhD '31 (Boston U); DD '43 (Augustana Coll). Research and lecturer on origin of Finns, Kalevala, national epic of the Finns, Russo-Finnish wars, the Church of Finland, political and economic life of Finland. Contributor to Finnish-Am jours and newspapers. Guest prof U Helsinki Finland '49; dir Help Finland Inc. Finnish-Am Hist Soc. Wittenberg College, Springfield, O. H: 954 Pythian Av.

21 KAPLAN, Sheldon Z. International law (Public and private); Foreign economic development; Foreign investment; Latin American affairs. b '11. AB '33 (Yale); '33-34 (Harvard Law Sch); BA in jurisprudence '37—MA '45 (Oxford U Eng); internat law student '45 (U Paris and L'Ecole Libre des Sciences Politiques). Assistant legal adviser Dept of State Washington '47-49; staff consultant House Foreign Affairs Committee since '49; mem US Spl Mission to Costa Rica '49, El Salvador '50. Am Bar Assn—UN League of Lawyers—Am Polit Sci Assn—Am Soc Internat Law. House Foreign Affairs Committee, The Capitol, Washington 25. H 2600 36th Place N.W.†◎

22 KAPRELIAN, Edward K(arnig). Optics (Photographic); Optical and photographic instruments and apparatus. b'13. ME '34 (Stevens Inst Tech); '37-38—'43 44 (George Washington U). Research and development lens and mirror systems, variable power telescopes, cameras, shutters, rangefinders, projectors, lenses. Granted patents on optical systems, view and range finders, extreme aperture objectives, variable power view finders. Patent exam US Patent Office '36-42; phys BEW '42-45; patent adv US Army Signal Corps '45-46; chief Photog Branch Signal Corps Engring Lab since '46; cons since '37. Optical Soc Am—ASME—Photog Soc Am (asso 49)—Soc Photog Engrs (pres '49-51) —Soc Motion Picture and Television Engrs—Royal Photog Soc Gt Brit— Phys Soc London(F). Received Meritorious Civilian award '45. Signal Corps Engineering Laboratories, Fort Monmouth, N.J.

23 KARLING, John S. Algae; Fungi; Latex; Gums. b'99. AB—AM '20 (U Tex); fellow '24—PhD '25 (Columbia). Director chicle research Tropical Plant Research Foundation British Honduras '27-32, research fellow Bermuda Biological Station '42; field director exploration department US Government Rubber Development Corp in Brazil '42-43; consulting editor Botanical Reviews. Author: The Plasmodiophorales '42; The Simple Holocarpic Biflagellate Phycomycetes '42; also articles in field. With Columbia U since '28, asso prof Bot '35-48; prof bot and dir dept biol sci Purdue U since '48. Bot Soc Am (sec and mem ed bd)—Am Biol Soc (sec)—Mycol Soc Am—Am Phytopath Soc—AAAS(F)—Sigma Xi. Department of Biological Sciences, Purdue University, Lafayette, Ind.◎

24 KARNES, Houston Thurman. Mathematical education. b'05. Student '24-26 (Lipscomb Coll Nashville); AB '28—Am '29 (Vanderbilt U Nashville); PhD '40 (Peabody Coll). Author articles: Preparation of Teachers of Secondary Mathematics '45; Junior College Mathematics Curriculum Problems in View of the President's Report '50. Co-author article: (W V Parker) The Louisiana-Mississippi Educational Committee '46; Education vs. Legislation '50. Prof math Northwestern Jr Coll Orange City Ia '29-35; prof math and head dept Harding Coll '35-36; faculty dept math La State U since '38, now asso prof and dir Math Inst.

Nat Council Tchrs Math (chmn La-Miss br)—Math State La—Am Math Soc—Math Assn Am—AAUP—Phi Delta Kappa—Kappa Delta Pi—Pi Mu Epsilon—Kappa Mu Epsilon. Department of Mathematics, Louisiana State University, Baton Route 3.†

10 KARPEL, Bernard. Modern art (Bibliography); Motion pictures (Bibliography, classification). b'11. BS '32 (City Coll NY); BLS '38 (Pratt Inst Library Sch); '39-40 (Columbia U Library Sch). Prepared lists of reading materials on modern art, painting, sculpture, photography; supervised purchase, cataloging and organization photographic materials in contemporary arts; administrative head special library with books, slides and photographic collections; organized collections of Museum Modern Art Film Library, established classification and trained personnel for servicing. Exec editor Modern Artists in America since '51; The Arts of the 20th Century: A Bibliography (in progress). Bibliographic contbns to Mus of Modern Art publs since '42. Art librarian 58th St Br NY Pub Library '38-42; chief librarian Mus Modern Art NYC since '42. With Signal Corps photog Center War Dept Film Library '44-45. Carnegie Corp scholar '39-40; Rockefeller Found grant bibliog research '52-53. Spl Libraries Assn (chm mus div NY '48-49)—Archons of Colophon NY. Museum of Modern Art, 11 W. 53d St., NYC 19.

11 KARPER, Robert Earl. Sorghum genetics and breeding; Agronomy (Kafir milo, Sudan grass). b'88. BS '14 (Kan State Coll); MS '28 (Texas Agrl & Mech Coll). Author articles in field. Supt Tex Expt Sta '15-25; asst dir, agron Tex Agr Expt Sta '25-28, v-dir, agron '28-40. AAAS—Am Soc Agron(F)—Am Genetics Assn—Sigma Xi—Phi Kappa Phi. Texas Agricultural Experiment Station, Lubbock, Tex.

12 KARPLUS, Eduard. Variac transformers. b'99. Diplom ingenieur '23 (Inst Tech, Vienna, Austria). Inventor variac transformer, variable ratio auto transformer for regulation of voltage and power, butterfly circuit, wide range tuning unit for high radio frequencies. Author articles in field. Elec measurements General Radio Co Cambridge Mass since '30. AIEE—Inst Radio Engrs (F). General Radio Co., 275 Massachusetts Av., Cambridge 39, Mass.

13 KARR, Charles Lee, Jr. Antique firearms. b'14. BS '35 (NC State Coll). Author: Remington Handgun '47; also articles in field. Partner Engineering Factors Co Avon Conn since '48. Nat Rifle Assn—Conn Gun Guild—O Gun Collectors Assn—US Revolver Assn—Nat Muzzle Loading Rifle Assn. Box 217, Avon, Conn.†

14 KARRER, Sebastian. Properties of solids; Thermoelectricity. b'89. AB—AM '13 (U Wash); PhD '18 (U Ill). Author articles in field. Cons Nat Defense Research Com; chief cons research and development div NM Sch Mines '46-48; chief physics div Fixed Nitrogen Research Lab US Dept Agr '19-26; dir research Consol Gas Elec Light & Power Co Baltimore '26-46; research cons Milwaukee Gas Specialty Co since '46. AAAS—Am Phys Soc—Am Chem Soc—Md Acad Scis (past pres) — Econometric Soc — Newcomen Soc—Sigma Xi—Phi Beta Kappa. Modern Pioneers award; Navy Ordnance award.⊙

15 KARSTAEDT, Clinton Frederick. Publishing (Newspapers, books, periodicals); Dickensiana; Lincolniana. b '88. Ext courses '16 (U Wis). Collaborator in text book Editing the Day's News' 43; colleector of Dickensiana, owns Dickens' works in first editions; collector Dickens Christmas books in first editions; owns large library of books on Lincoln; director Lincoln Fellowship State of Wisconsin. With Daily News Pub Co since '07, dir, sec-treas since '15, co-pub since '40; vp Monroe Times Pub Co. Inland Daily Press Assn(chmn bd) —Wis Daily Newspaper League(sec-treas)—Graphic Arts Industry Inc Minneapolis (dir). Wrote appendix for Newspaper Management (by F Thayer) '26, rev edit '38. 413-15-17 Pleasant St., Beloit, Wis.

16 KARSTEN, Kenneth S(tephen). Lumber (Fungicides for blue stain control); Vegetables (Fungicides for potatoes, tomatoes, celery); Seeds (Fungicides for corn, wheat, peas, beans, sorghum); Clocks (Early American). b'13. AB (Hope Coll Holland Mich); MS (U Nev); PhD (U Wis). Commercial, laboratory and field experience on fungicides for blue stain control; laboratory development, supervision field testing and evaluation vegetables fungicides; chemical development, laboratory and field testing seed fungicides; collector and repair Early American clocks. Author: Clock Collectors Handbook '45. Organic chem Niagara Chem Div Middleport NY '41-45; chem and plant physiol Rohm & Haas Co Bristol Pa '45-47; fungicide development RT Vanderbilt Co Inc NYC since '47. ACS—Am Soc Plant Physiol. R. T. Vanderbilt Co., Inc., 230 Park Av., NYC 17. H: Compo Parkway, Westport, Conn.

17 KARTMAN, Leo. Filariasis: Estoparasites; Plague; Malaria. b'12. BS '36—MS '36 (U Wis); ScD '50 (Johns Hopkins U Sch Hygiene and Pub Health). Research on factors influencing infection of mosquito host with filarial nematodes including index of experimental infection, effects of selection and other genetic factors, effects of passage through mosquito midgut, effects of anticoagulants on fate of parasite in mosquito, effect of filarial periodicity, filarial age, and mosquito feeding mechanism; research on relation of specific host nutritorial deficiencies to ectoparasite economy, relation of host grooming habits to itensity of ectoparasitic infestation, control of ectoparasites, ecology of ecotparasites of rats in relation to plague; malaria in West Africa and Southern United States. bionomics of anopheline malaria vectors and control of anopheline vectors; ecological study of rodents and ectoparasite reservoirs of rural plague in Hawaiian Islands, control methods, possible vectors of plague from man to man in French West Africa. Contributor: Experimental Parasitology '53; Public Health Reports '52. With USPHS since '50. Sigma Xi—Sci Research Soc Am—AAAS—Am Assn Econ Entomol—Am Soc Parasitol—Am Soc Tropical Medicine and Hygiene—Hawaiian Entomol Soc. Division of Commissioned Officers, US Public Health Service, CDCA, San Francisco Field Station, 15th Av. and Lake St., Bldg. 19, San Francisco 18.

18 KASTON, Benjamin Julian. Araneology: Spiders of Connecticut. b'06. BS '30 (NC State Coll); PhD '34—fellow '33-34 (Yale); research fellow '45, '46 (Harvard, Cornell). Author articles in field. Asso prof '46-48, prof biol Teachers Coll Conn since '48. AAAS (F)—Am Soc Zool—Soc Systematic Zool—Sigma Xi—Phi Kappa Phi. Teachers College of Connecticut, New Britain, Conn.†

19 KASZUBA, Frank John. Photography (Chemistry); Polymers; Cellulose esters; Cellulose others; Resins (Synthetic); Gelatin. b'10. BS '32—MS '33 —PhD '37—teaching F '32-37 (Fordham U). Research on high polymers and synthesis and properties of cellulose esters, ethers, and other derivatives, plasticizers for polymers; developed resins with specialized properties 'for specific applications; modification physical and chemical properties of gelatin, gelatin organosols; developed analytical methods for identification resins. Granted patents in field. Asso prof chem Canisius Coll '37-38; with Ansco since '38, mgr chem research lab since '46. NY Acad Sci—ACS—Photog Soc Am. Ansco, Binghamton, N.Y.

20 KATES, Elizabeth Mounce. Penology. b'98. Student '15-17 (Bushnell U). Studies and development modern methods of handling felons and misdemeanant through mediums of medicine, psychiatry, education, religious and vocational training, recreational program to create a community which enables inmates to return to society upon parole. Supt State Prison for Women Va since '30. Am Prison Assn —Osborne Assn. State Industrial Farm for Women, Goochland, Va.

21 KATES, K. C. Parasitology; Cytology. b'10. AB '32 (St Stephens Coll, Columbia U); MA '34—PhD '37 (Duke U). Research on parasites and parasitic diseases of swine and sheep; laboratory diagnosis of parasitological and other diseases, prof lecturer in zool The George Washington U since '46. Author articles in field. Jr parasitol US Dept Agr '38-40, asst zool '40-43, asso zool '46-48, parasitol since '48. AAAS—Am Assn Parasitol. Zoological Division, ARC, Beltsville, Md.

22 KATZ, Donald LaVerne. Petroleum engineering (Petroleum reservoirs); Heat transfer (Finned tubes). b'07. BS '31—MS '32—PhD '33 (U Mich). Holder patent for process for separating oil and gas, with others patents on hydraulic pressure fluid, high pressure separation, patent on absorption process. Co-author: Bibliography for Physical Behavior of Hydrocarbons under Pressure and Related Phenomena '46; Natural Gasoline and Volatile Hydrocarbons '47; The Design and Construction of Pressure Relieving Systems '48; also articles in field. With U Mich since '36, now prof chem engring; cons engr various oil companies, trade assns and govt agencies since '36. Am Inst Chem Engr (chmn student chap com '48)—Am Inst Mining Metal Engrs (petroleum div, chmn papers and program '43, research '39-40, edn '46-47)—Am Soc Refrig Engrs —ASME—Am Chem Soc—Am Petroleum Inst (chmn sub com subsurface sampling '38-42)—Am Gas Assn—Elec Microscope Soc—AAAS—Am Soc Engring Edn. 2028 E. Engineering Building, University of Michigan, Ann Arbor.⊙

23 KATZIN, Leonard Isaac. Chemistry of heavy elements; Nuclear and physical chemistry; Cellular physiology. b'15. AB '35 (U Calif Los Angeles); PhD '38 (U Calif). Research on bioelectric potentials of skin of frogs, distribution of stream plankton in Ohio River system, decimal reduction time concept, effect of environmental temperature on experimental traumatic shock, $4N+1$ radioactive series, decay products of U 233, osmium radioactivities, systems of inorganic salt-water-organic solvent. Author articles in field. Sr chem Argonne Nat Lab since '46. Am Chem Soc—AAAS. Rosenberg research fellow U Calif '37-38, research fellow '38-40; research fellow in radiology Rochester U Med Sch '42-43. Argonne National Laboratory, Box 5207, Chicago 80.

10 KAUPERT, Frank Henry. Wood utilization and preservation; Forest management and pathology. b'05. BS '28—MS '30—PhD '35 (U Minn); '31 (U Halle Germany). Associate editor Journal of Forestry since '46. Coauthor: Wood Aircraft Fabrication and Inspection '44. Prof forestry and chief U Minn since '47. Am Standards Assn (past mem membership com)—Soc Am Foresters—Am Wood Preservers Assn —Bot Soc Am—AAAS—Forest Products Research Assn—Sigma Xi—Gamma Sigma Delta. University Farm, St. Paul.⊙

11 KAUFFELD, Carl Frederick. Reptiles (Behavior, ecology, parasitology, snake venoms and treatment of snake bite). b'11. Student (Brown Prep Sch Phila, Columbia U). Author articles in field. Six-year apprenticeship dept herpetology Am Mus Natural Hist; curator reptiles Staten Island Zoo NY since '36. Am Soc Ichthyologists Herpetologists—Herpetologists League(F). Staten Island Zoo, Staten Island 10, N.Y.†

12 KAUFFMAN, Henry J. Early American handicrafts (Wood, iron, copper, and pewter products). b'08. BS '32 (State Teachers Coll Pa); MS '37 (U Pa). Travelled through southern Canada, Mexico, New England to study weaving and craft work summers '38-41, studied weaving Southern Highlands '40, visited Mexico studying crafts. Author: Pennsylvania Dutch Folk Art '46; Homecraft Course in Pennsylvania German Pewter '47; Homecraft Course in Pennsylvania German Copper and Brass '47; also articles in field. Teacher handicrafts pub schs Pa '30-42; Millersville State Teachers Coll since '42. AAUP—Hist Soc Pa—Conestoga Guild of Handicraftmen. State Teachers College, Millersville, Pa.

13 KAUFFMAN, Treva Erdine. Home economics. b'89. BS '11 (O State U); MA '31 (Columbia U); '16 (U Chicago). Member White House Conference on Child Health and Protection '30, President's Conference on Home Building and Ownership Washington '31; study schools and homes Denmark and Sweden '29. Author: Teaching Problems in Home Economics '30; Young Folks at Home '48; Homemaking Course for Training Girls for Household Service '35; Syllabus on Home Economics; also articles in field. State supervisor home econ edn for NY State Edn Dept since '20; lecturer, cons; adviser to various home econ mags. Nea (com on selection 60 ednl books of year '34-37)—World Assn for Adult Edn—NY Adult Edn Council—Am Home Econ Assn (mem legislative com '37-38)—NY State Home Econ Assn (chmn legislative com '37-51). State Education Department, Albany 1, N.Y.

14 KAUFFMANN-GRINSTEAD, Kurt. Economics (Inflation). b'00. PhD '22 (Heidelberg). Author articles in field. Cons on financial planning since '36; chmn Nat Statis Service Inc; dir or pres various other orgns, 535 Fifth Av., NYC 17.

15 KAUFMAN, Clemens M(arcus). Forest management (Pond pine); Forest grazing (Piedmont forest types). b'09. AB '36 (Bethel Coll Kans); MS '38—PhD '43 (U Minn). Author articles in field. Prof forest management NC State Coll '43-51; dir Sch Forestry U Florida since '51. Soc Am Foresters—Ecol Soc Am. Division of Forestry, North Carolina State College, Raleigh, N.C.†

16 KAUFMAN, Sidney. Radiolocation; Computers (Analog); Seismology. b'08. AB '30—PhD '34 (Cornell U). Research on radiolocation systems of phase comparison type; analog computers for problems in petroleum exploration; study propagation of transient elastic waves. Issued patents in field. Fellow Chas A Coffin Found '34-35; geophys dept Shell Oil Co '36-42, sr physicist since '46. Served as electronics officer First Naval Dist USN '42-45; prin physicist Airborn Radio Div Naval Research Lab '46. APS —Soc Exploration Geophys—Inst Radio Engrs—Sigma Xi. Shell Oil Co., 3737 Bellaire Blvd., Houston 25.

17 KAUFMANN, Godfrey Frensz. Petroleum geology. b'95. EM '21 (Colo Sch Mines). Studies in tectonic geology and interpretation geophysical data in terms of stratigraphy and/or structure; application geophysics to specific problems petroleum exploration in Far East. Author articles: Modern methods in petroleum exploration; The tectonic framework of the Far East and its influence on the origin and accumulation of petroleum; and others. Exploration and exploitation geol Cia Mex de Pet "El Aquila" Tampico Mexico '21-26; asst chief geol subsidiaries Standard Oil NJ in Mexico '26-38, chief geophysicist Venezuela '38-44; research coordinator in geol and geophysics Standard Vacuum Oil Co NYC and foreign since '44. Geol Soc Am—Am Assn Petroleum Geol— Am Geophys Union—Soc Exploration Geophysicists—AIMME—Soc Econ Paleontologists and Mineral—Seismol Soc Am—Tau Beta Pi. Standard Vacuum Oil Co., Room 1562, 26 Broadway, NYC 4.

18 KAUTZ, Karl. Molybdenum compounds (In ceramics); Vitreous enamels (Adherence to metals); Ceramic glazes (Colored). b'98. B Ceramic Engring '23—Ceramic Engr '31—MS '33 (O State U). Research and development on uses of molybdenum compounds in ceramics, especially vitreous enamels; research and development of enameling iron sheets for vitreous enamels; developed special colors and colored glazes in terra cotta and vitreous china sanitary industries. Granted patents in field. Research ceramic engr since '24. Am Ceramic Soc (F)—Inst Ceramic Engrs —Tau Beta Pi—Phi Lambda Upsilon. 713 Ohio Merchants Trust Building, Massillon, O.

19 KAY, (George) Marshall. Geology; Stratigraphy (Ordovician); Paleontology (Ostracodes); Limestone (Chemical); Dolomite (Chemical); Carbonate rocks (Resources). b'04. BA '24—MS '25 (U Ia); '24 (U Chicago); PhD '29 (Columbia). Geologist NY Geological Survey '40-42, US Geological Survey '43-45; delegate International Geological Congress Moscow '37, London '48; member American Commission Stratigraphic Nomenclature '46. Author articles on Paleozoil stratigraphy, chemical limestone and dolomite, continental genesis. With Columbia U since '31, prof geol since '44. Geol Soc Am(F)—AAAS(F)—Paleontol Soc(vp '45)—NY Acad Sci (vp '44-45)—Ia Acad Sci—Am Assn Petroleum Geol— Am Geophys Union—Soc Econ Paleontol and Mineral—Phi Beta Kappa— Sigma Xi. George F Kunz prize NY Acad Sci. '41. Schermerhorn Hall, Columbia University, NYC 27.⊙

20 KAYE, Sidney. Poisons (Isolation, identification). b'12. BS '35 (Washington Square Coll); MSc '39 (NYU). Author articles in field. Toxicologist and dir toxicol labs Office Chief Med Exam Commonwealth of Va since '47; asst prof legal med Med Coll Va since '47. Toxicologist maj US Army Med Dept '41-46. Am Chem Soc—Am Soc Clinical Pathol (asso F)—Va Acad Sci—AAAS—Va Acad Sci—Sigma Xi. Office of Chief Medical Examiner, Commonwealth of Virginia, 404 N. 12th St., Richmond 19, Va.†

21 KAYSER, Elmer Louis. Intellectual history; Nationalism. b'96. AB and Bachelor's Diploma in edn '17— MA '18—LLD '49 (George Washington U); PhD '32 (Columbia); study (Johns Hopkins). Author: The Grand Social Enterprise '32; A Manual of Ancient History '37. Co-author: Contemporary Europe '41. Mem bd editors World Affairs; historian Nat Capital Sesquicentennial Commn '50. With George Washington U since '14, prof since '32, dean since '34; radio commentator on world affairs '40-45. Am Hist Assn —AAUP— Pi Gamma Mu. George Washington University, Washington.⊙

22 KAZMANN, Raphael G(abriel). Water supply; Ground water (Legislation). b'16. BS (civil engring) '39 (Carnegie Inst Tech); '40 (Pa State Coll). Research on ground water supplies, artificial recharge, induced infiltration of river water to wells, underground waste disposal, prevention of dangerous underseepage below dams and levees. With div ground water US Geol Survey '40-45; chief hydrologic engr Ranney Method Water Supplies Inc '46-41; cons since '51. Am Soc CE—Am Geophys Union—AA AS—Am Waterworks Assn. 419 W. Seventh St., Stuttgart, Ark.

23 KEALLY, Francis. Hotel and library architecture. AB '12 (Carnegie Inst Tech); BS in architecture '16 (U Pa). With Alfred Morton Githens designed Brooklyn Public Library, Concord Public Library, Virginia State Library, Joint University Libraries Nashville; with Cass Gilbert Jr developed complete studies for enlarging and modernizing Detroit Public Library; analysed hotel project for Reykjavik Iceland. Practice NYC since '27. Am Hotel Assn (cons architect)—ALA (mem Library Bldgs Com)—ALA(F) —Archtl League NY—Beaux-Arts Inst Design. 17 East 49th St., NYC.†⊙

24 KEAR, Frank Gregg. Electronics; Radio wave propagation. b'03. EE '26 (Lehigh U); SM '28—ScD '33 (MIT). Associated with Vannevar Bush, H L Hazen in development of product integraph and differential analyzer '26-28; developed first combined radio beacon and radio telephone transmitter '31; developed practical means for stabilizing directional pattern of complex antenna array; participated in development of radio beacon system free from night effect; continued development of radio landing systems for aircraft; pioneered in application of directional antennas to broadcasting, participated in development of earth inductor compass as applied to problems in air and water navigation. Holder numerous patents in field of communication in US and England. Author: (with others) Development of a Practical Earth Inductor Compass '39; also articles in field. Chief engr Washington Inst Tech '33-41; lecturer in elec commns U Md '36-41; electronic development cons ABC. Served in World War II as head radio sect Bur Aeronautics US Navy; Navy Dept east coast stations, Eng and France; tech adv at Third CERCA London '45; capt USNR. AAAS—Phi Beta Kappa—Eta Kappa Nu—Tau Beta Pi—Sigma Xi— Inst Radio Engrs. 1703 K St. N.W., Washington 6.

25 KECK, David Daniels. Range grasses. b'03. BA '25 — MA '26 (Pomona Coll); PhD '30 (U Cal Berkeley). Study origin of blue grasses, composition, distribution and relationships to clarify nature of species; research and production new range grasses by breeding. Staff Carnegie Inst of Washington '26-50; head curator NY Botanical Garden since '5!. AAAS—Am Soc Naturalists—Soc Study Evolution—Cal Bot Soc—Bot Soc Am—Soc Plant Taxonomists—Western Soc Naturalists. Awarded Mary Soper Pope medal (with J Clausen and W M Hiesey) by Cranbrook Inst of Sci for research on the nature of species '49. New York Botanical Graden, Bronx Park, NYC 58.⊚

10 KECK, Sheldon. Restoration (Works of art). b'10. AB '32 (Harvard). Author articles: Restoration of an Early American Landscape '35; A Method of Cleaning Prints '36; Craftsmanship in XV Painting '36; Reclaiming an Early Ribera '38; Use of Infrared Photography in the Study of Technique '41, and others. Apprenticed to restorer Fogg Art Mus '32-33; staff restorer Brooklyn Mus since '34; tech cons Am Art Research Council; private restoration work for Mus Modern Art, Whitney Mus, Mus City of NY, Wichita Mus, and others. Brooklyn Museum, Brooklyn, N.Y.†

11 KECK, Walter Edgar. Flotation. gravity, and magnetic separation (Finely divided solids); Industrial by-products as flotation reagents. b'94. BS '27 (Mich Coll Mining and Tech); MS '28 (U Ariz). Research on methods for determination rate of entry of liquids into and volume of voids in porous solids, analytical procedures and processes for volatilization removal of impurities from manganese and zinc ores, sinter agglomeration of lead oxide concentrate and smelter dusts, recovery process for potash from porphyry copper tailing, floatative properties of pyrite, pyrrhotite, chalcopyrite, jarosite, feldspar, quartz, hematite, magnetite, and gypsum; xanthate-soap flotation process, anionic iron oxide and anionic silica flotation process, petroleum sulfonate flotation process developed for iron ores, recovery of tungsten carbide, stainless steel, stellite and high speed tool steel from industrial wastes; chemical compounds from wood wastes. Asst to asso prof U Utah '28-30; metall Pa Salt Mfg Co '31-33; asso prof Mich Coll Mining and Tech since '34. AIMME—ACS—AAAS—Tau Beta Pi—Phi Lambda Upsilon. Michigan College of Mining and Technology, Houghton. Mich.

12 KEEFER, Ralph Ottis. Chemical engineering; Mechanical engineering; Construction engineering; Safety engineering. b'96. Chem E '17 (Syracuse U NY). Supervision construction and operation of company owned plants to '35; supervision purchasing for construction and operation both company owned and government owned aluminum plants World War II; design plants and equipment for manufacture carbon electrodes for aluminum industry, including high temperature furnaces. Author articles: Purchasing for Safety '38; Engineering versus Purchasing '47; Engineers are OK '46, and others. With Aluminum Co Am since '17, chief works mech engr '29-35, asst works mgr '30-35; gen purchasing agt since '37. Nat Assn Purchasing Agents (nat pres '48-49)—Engring Soc Western Pa—Nat Safety Council (chem sect)—Tau Beta Pi—Alpha Chi Sigma. Professional engr Pa. Aluminum Company of America, 2200 Aluminum Bldg., Pitts 19.

13 KEEL, William Arnold. Hebrew syntax (Isaiah). b'94. AB '22 (Miss Coll); ThM '25 — PhD '30 — fellow '25-28 (Southern Baptist Theol Sem). Research on Hebrew Syntax in Isaiah and the problem of authorship '25-30. Head Bible dept Union U Jackson Tenn since '45. Tenn Edn Assn. Union University, Jackson, Tenn.

14 KEELEY, Joseph Charles. Association magazine editor. b'07. LittB '30 (Columbia). Author: Making Inventions Pay '50. Co-author: (with Howard Stephenson) They Sold Themselves '37. Mem pub relations staff N W Ayer & Son NYC '30-38; dir pub relations dept J M Mathes Inc '38-44; editor Am Legion Mag since '49. 580 Fifth Av., NYC 19.

15 KEELING, Harry Walker, Jr. Port facilities; Naval architecture; Marine engineering. b'09. Student '31-32 (U Va); '34 (La Salle U). Research in air and gas cleaning for removal of sub-micron particles using filters, precipitrons and dust collecting apparatus of own design; development shipboard and waterfront fire fighting equipment and programs including all types chemical, fog and water systems; custom designed vessels for specific uses. Nav architect and supervisor US Navy Dept '29-42; nav architect, marine engr, pres Coast Engring Co since '42. Soc Nav Architects and Marine Engrs—NE Coast Instn Engrs and Shipbuilders. 731 W. Princess Anne Rd., Norfolk 7, Va.

16 KEELING, Joe Alfred. Seismic exploration. b'23. Student '38-40 (Ark Poly Coll); BS '43 (Coll Ozarks). Exploration for oil by seismic reflection and refraction methods; party chief seismic field parties in Venezuela '46, '48, Colombia '47, United States '49, Mexico '50, '51. With Seismograph Service Corp since '43, seismol and chief seismic field parties since '45. Soc Eploration Geophys. P.O. Box 1590, Tulsa 1.

17 KEEN, A(ngeline) Myra. Western North American Mollusca (Conchology); Invertebrate paleontology of California. b'05. AB '30 (Colo Coll); MA '31 (Stanford U); PhD '34 (U Calif). Author: An Abridged Check List and Bibliography of West North American Marine Mollusca '37. Co-author: Illustrated Key to West North American Pelecypod Genera '39, and others. Curator paleontol Stanford since '36. Am Malacol Union (pres '47-48)—Geol Soc Am(F)—Paleontol Soc(F). School of Mineral Sciences, Stanford University, Stanford, Calif.

18 KEEN, Frederick Paul. Forest insects; Trees (Rings). b'90. BS (agr) '14 (U Cal). Research and development silvicultural methods of bark beetle control, development classification of Ponderosa pine according to bark beetle susceptibility; study long range tree growth variations and correlation with climatic factors in Pacific Northwest, influence of fire and insects on tree rings. Entomol Forest Insect Investigations Bur Entomol and Plant Quarantine USDA since '14. Soc Am Foresters—Am Assn Econ Entomol—Ecol Soc—AAAS(F). Received USDA Superior Service Award '47. 29 Forestry Building, University of California, Berkeley 4.

19 KEEN, Ray Albert. Horticulture (Ornamental). b'15. BSA '42 (Kan State Coll); MS '47 (Ohio State U). Porpagation use and care lawn and turf grasses, flowers, shrubs in Great Plains Area; studies in identification of Taxus; Central Plains Turf Foundation research project; Juniper propagation. Campus gardener Kan State Coll '38-42, asst prof hort '47-51, asst ornamental hort since '47. Gamma Sigma Delta—Phi Kappa Phi—Sigma Xi—Nat Shade Tree Conf—Kan State Florist's Assn—Assn Kan Landscape Architects—Kan Assn Neurserymen—Kan Hort Soc—Manhattan Garden Club (pres). Department of Horticulture, Kansas State College, Manhattan, Kan.

20 KEESING, Felix Maxwell. Anthropology (Pacific Islands). b'02. AB '24—AM with first class honors '25 (Auckland U Coll); (Laura Spelman Rockefeller Found F) '28-30 (Yale, U Chicago); LittD '33 (U New Zealand); '33-34 (London Sch Econ and Polit Sci). Author: The Changing Maori '28; Maori Progress on the East Coast '29; Dependencies and Native Peoples of the Pacific '31; Modern Saoma '34; Taming Philippine Headhunters, Government and Culture Change in Northern Luzon '34; The Filipinos: A Nation in the Making. '36; Hawaiian Homesteading on Molokai '36; Education in Pacific Countries '37; The South Seas in the Modern World '41; Native Peoples of the Pacific World '45. Co-author: America's Future in the Pacific '47; Specialized Studies in Polynesian Anthropology '47. Editor: Handbook of the Trust Territory of the Pacific Islands '48. Dir research on Pacific dependencies Inst Pacific Relations '30-34; asst prof anthrop U Hawaii '34-35, asso prof '35-37, prof and chmn dept anthrop and sociol '37-43; prof Anthrop Stanford since '43, exec head dept sociol and anthrop since '48; US sr commr S Pacific Commn since '48. AAAS—Am Anthrop Assn—Soc Applied Anthrop. Department of Sociology and Anthropology, Stanford University, Stanford, Cal.†⊚

21 KEHL, George Louis. Metallography; Steel (Fatigue). b'10. BS '34 (U Wis); research fellow '35-37—MS '37 (Lehigh U). Developed thermit welding of main line railroad track to meet AERA specifications; research in X-ray study of preferred orientation in rolled copper, fatigue resistance of steel affected by some cleaning methods, by acid pickling, influence of strain rate on strength and type of failure of C-Mo steel at 850°, 1000°, and 1100°F, room temperature casting resins for metallographic specimens, structure and properties of metals and alloys, uranium and uranium alloy metalography. Author: Principles of Metallographic Laboratory Practice '49; also articles in field. Asst prof metall Lehigh U '37-39; research metall US Steel Corp Research Lab '39-41; cons metallography and phys metall since '41; asso prof metall Columbia U since '47; head metallographic and heat treating div Manhattan Engring Dist Los Alamos Atomic Bomb Project '44-46; research contractor US Atomic Energy Commn NYC since '46; metallography cons Argonne Nat Lab since '48. Am Soc Metals—Am Inst Mining Metall Engrs—Sigma Xi. School of Mines, Columbia University, NYC 27.

22 KEHOE, Arthur Henry. Public utility engineering; Electricity, gas and steam (Design, construction, operation). b'89. BS '11—DEng '44 (U Vt). Engring asst United Electric Light & Power Co NY City '11-14, dist engr '14-19, supt transmission and distbn '19-21, elec engr '21-32, vp United and NY Edison Cos '32-36, dir '35-36, vp merged co Consol Edison Co of NY Inc since '36; dir NY Steam Co. Consol Telegraph & Elec Subway Co, Yonkers Elec Light & Power Co. Am Inst EE (F, Lamme medalist '43)—Nat Fire Protection Assn (dir)—NY Elec Soc (Past pres). 4 Irving Pl., NYC 3.⊚

23 KEILEN, John J(acob), Jr. Lignin chemistry; Compounding of rubber, and of phenolic and vinyl plastics; Utilization pulp mill waste liquors. b '15. BS '36—MS '37 (Carnegie Inst Tech); D Chem Engring '49 (Poly Inst Brooklyn). Developed process for separation of lignin from black liquor, process for reinforcing synthetic rubber, use of cellulose fibers, calcium carbonate and activated carbonin rubber, phenolic and vinyl plastics. Holder patent. Chem engr, project leader, group supervisor WVa Pulp and Paper Co since '37. ACS—AICE—AIMM E—Nat Farm Chem Council—Tau Beta Pi—Phi Kappa Phi—Phi Lambda Upsilon—Sigma Xi. West Virginia Pulp and Paper Co., Charleston, S.C.

10 KEIM, Christopher Peter. Isotopes (Stable, separation, properties). b'06. AB '27 (Neb Wesleyan U); MSc '32—PhD '40—Samuel Avery Fellow '39-40 (U Neb). Engaged in electromagnetic separation natural isotopes of all natural elements, research on development separation process and isotopic properties, and on monomolecular surface films. Engr Lincoln Neb Telephone & Telegraph Co '28-31; prof phys sci York Coll '33-37; chem faculty Tulsa U '40-41; research engr Sylvania Elec Products Corp Salem Mass '41-42; research fellow Mellon Inst Pittsburgh '42-44; sr physicist Tenn Eastman Corp '44-47; sr physicist Carbide & Carbon Chemicals Corp '47. director of isotope research and production division since 1947. AAAS—Am Phys Society—Am Chem Soc—Sigma Xi—Sigma Pi Sigma—Phi Lambda Upsilon. 102 Orchard Lane, Oak Ridge, Tenn.

11 KEISER, George Camp. Architecture (Near and Middle East); Middle East (Modern). b'00. AB '24 (Harvard); BArch '30 (Columbia). Founder The Middle East Inst Washington '46, since served as chairman of board governors; trustee American Research Center in Egypt. Contbr archtl drawings and photographs to Archtl Record; Moore, The Romans World. Research in Islamic architecture and travel in Middle East '38; Registered architect DC Fla Conn Nat Council Archtl Registration Bds. AIA—Fgn Service Ednl Found (trustee)—Fla Assn Architects—Conn Soc Architects. 206 E. Park Av., Winter Park Fla.; also 1306 18th St. N.W., Washington.†◎

12 KEITH, Elmer Davenport. New England antiquities and architecture. b'88. BA '10 (Yale); AB '13 (Oxford U, England). Augmented number of listings in architectural census of Connecticut to around 6,000 houses, with detailed study, both through records and measurements, of some four hundred houses locally dated earlier than 1720, and certain houses of later periods whose date has been in question; has measured houses of 17th century in Massachusetts and Connecticut. Author: Some Notes on Early Connecticut Architecture '39; Connecticut, a Guide to its Roads, Lore and People (architectural introduction) '38. Archtl ed Conn Guide and dir Census of Architecture in state prepared in connection with it '35; archtl advisor to Quinnabaug Village, Sturbridge, Mass '40-41. Soc Preservation NE Antiquities (life)—Conn Hist Soc—Antiquarian and Landmarks Soc Inc of Conn (a founder, trustee)—Early Am Industries Assn. Pond Hill Farm, Clintonville, Conn.

13 KELCEY, Guy. Transportation engineering. b'89. BS '14 (Carnegie Inst Tech). Engaged in engineering and economics of transportation, traffic urban expressways and highways, and studies on methods to control traffic and increase efficiency of vehicular movement on streets and highways. Author articles in field. Mgr traffic engring div Am Gas Accumulator Co Elizabeth NJ '20-41; pres Vehicular Parking Ltd Newark '41-42; regional dir So States Div Local Transport, Office Defense Transportation Atlanta '42-44; highway transport analyst Port NY Authority '44-45; partner Edwards & Kelcey, Engineers NY since '45. Inst Cons Engrs — ASCE — Inst Traffic Engrs—Engring Commn Presidents Safety Conf—Hwy Research Bd—Assn Hwy Officials North Atlantic States. 739 Highland Av., Westfield, N.J.

14 KELEMEN, Pal. American archaeology. b'94. Student (State Latin Sch Budapest) (Univs Munich and Paris); librarian diploma from philosophy faculty (U Budapest). Research in museums Budapest, Vienna, Berlin, Florence, London, Spain; consideration early Christian art, pre-Columbian and Spanish colonial art in Latin America. Author: Medieval American Art 2 vols '43; Baroque and Rococo in Latin America '51. Contbr articles on art and archaeology to Pantheon, L'Art, The Studio, Parnassus, El Palacio, Pan Am Bull, Am Anthropologist, Mag of Art. Royal Anthrop Inst(F). Loon Meadow Dr., Norfolk, Conn.◎

15 KELKER, George Hills. Animal populations (Census methods); Food habits of fur-bearers and birds of prey. b'06. AB '28 (Hiram Coll); BSF '31—MSF '32—Schoene-Rene F conservation '43-44—ScD '46 (U Mich). Research on census methods for animal populations, including total numbers determined from differential loss in sexes, sample obtained from belt transect method, and use of yield table. Tech foreman and jr range examiner US Forest Service '33-35; in charge dept wildlife management Utah State Agrl Coll '37-49, faculty since '37 prof since '48. Wildlife Soc—Am Soc Mammalogists—Wilson Ornithol Club — Soc Am Foresters — AAAS—Utah Acad Arts Sci and Letters—Cal Acad Sci—Am Mus Natural Hist—Nat Audubon Soc—Am Geog Soc—Sigma Xi—Phi Kappa Phi—Xi Sigma Pi (nat sec and fiscal agt '50-52)—Arctic Inst. Utah State Agricultural College, Logan, Utah.

16 KELLAR, Herbert Anthony. Agricultural history; Solon Robinson. b '87. '09 (U Chicago); grad student '09-11 (Leland Stanford U) '11-13 (U Wis). Member board editors Mississippi Valley Historical Review '24-25, Agricultural History since '29. Compiler and editor: Solon Robinson, Pioneer and Agriculturist (2 vols) '36. Contributor to Crusade and to Other Historical Essays '28; Dictionary of American Biography '28-37; also articles, documents, and reviews in hist and library periodicals. Dir McCormick Hist Assn Chicago since '15; in charge McCormick Centennial celebration Va Poly Inst and Washington and Lee U '31; dir hist restoration work period 1800-31 Walnut Grove Plantation, Rockbridge County, Va '37-38; chairman nat adv com hist records survey projects WPA '40-42; mem com on microcopying materials for research Am Council Learned Socs '40-46; member Chicago Metropolitan Library Council '45-46. Am Hist Assn (chmn com on hist source materials '39-46)—Miss Valley Hist Assn—Southern Hist Assn—Agrl Hist Soc (vp '21-22, pres '22-24, sec-treas '24-27)—Soc Am Archivists (vp '40-41, mem council '42-45, vp '48-49)—Council Econ History Soc—Am Assn State and Local History (council since '40)—Am Documentation Inst—Hist Soc Western Pa —Ill La Peoria Augustana and Rockbridge hist socs—Alpha Pi—Phi Gamma Delta—Westerners Club—Civil War Round Table Chicago. 679 Rush St., Chgo 11.

17 KELLER, Dominic Joseph. Gregorian chant: Choral music. b'02. BA '28 (St John's U); MA '34 (U Minn); grad study (Columbia U, Pius X Sch Liturgical Music NYC); choral research (Quarr Abbey Isle of Wight, Solesmes France, Rome Italy). Author: Fundamentals of Gregorian Chant, a Basis for Class Notes and Study '47. Recorded: AD LIBITUM KYRIE Chants for ten-album Kyriale chant collection of Gregorian Institute of America '45; Recorded OCCASIONAL GREGORIAN CHANTS album for Gregorian Institute of America '47. Mem Order St Benedict since '25; choral dir coll and major sem St John's U Collegeville Minn since '40; choir master St John's Abbey Collegeville since '46; prof Gregorian chant U Minn summers '46, '47; instr Gregorian Chant for Gregorian Inst Am Toledo O '47, '48. Nat Cath Music Educators Assn.

18 KELLER, Edward Luther. Industrial engineering; Adult education. b'04. BS '25 (Pa State Coll). Instr engring ext Pa State Coll '26-30, asst prof '30-34, asso prof '34, act head dept '34, dir dept '35, prof engring extra since '37, exec asst Central Ext '42-51, asst dir Gen Ext since '51. Nat University Ext Association (dir '46-49, pres '49-50)—Pa Vocational Assn—Pa Assn Adult Edn—Am Management Assn—ASEE— Assn Land-Grant Colleges and Universities (chmn engring ext sect engring div). 610 N. Burrowes St., State College, Pa.†◎

19 KELLER, George Ernest. Chemistry of coal. b'99. BS (Chem E) '22 (U Ill). Analysis, preparation, and sampling of coal; direction washability tests for cleaning of coal. With Comml Testing & Engring Co since '22, mgr Charleston br since '22, dir labs for analysis coal since '41. Am Inst Mining Engrs—ACS—ASTM—W Va Soc Professional Engrs. Professional engr O, WVa. P.O. Box 898, Charleston 23, W.Va.†

20 KELLER, Henry, Jr. Agricultural and production economics; Farm management. b'95. BS '20 (Pa State Coll); MS '21—PhD '31 (U Wis). Co-author: Shall I Buy a Farm '47. Asst prof Rutgers U '22-27, asso prof '27-28, prof agrl econ since '28. Am Econ Assn—Am Farm Econ Assn—Am Acad Polit Social Sci—Am Statis Soc—Am Geog Soc NY—Econometric Soc. Department of Agricultural Economics, College of Agriculture, Rutgers University, New Brunswick, N.J.†

21 KELLER, John Esten. Spanish philology and Old Spanish literature. b'17. AB '40—MA '42 (U Ky); PhD '46 (U NC). Research on medieval Spanish literature and folklore, classification motifs in early Spanish literature as found in collections of Old Spanish exempla, etymological vocabularies of Old Spanish works. Author: Motif-Index of Mediaeval Spanish Exempla '49. Contribuor: Romance Studies Presented to William Morten Day '50. Faculty U NC '43-46; asst prof U Ky '47; asso prof U Tenn '48-50; asst prof U NC since '50. Medieval Acad Am—Am Assn Tchrs Spanish and Portuguese—MLA—S Atlantic Modern Lang Assn.

22 KELLER, May Lansfield. Anglo-Saxon and German language and literature; Modern drama; Shakespeare; Old and Middle German: Old Norse. b'77. BA '98 (Goucher Coll Baltimore); PhD '04 (Heidelberg); student (U Chicago, U Berlin). Author articles in field. Prof Eng and dean Westhampton Coll, coordinate with Richmond Coll U Richmond since '14. AAAS—Modern Lang Assn Am—Linguistic Soc Am—Phi Beta Kappa. Westhampton College, University of Richmond, Richmond, Va.

23 KELLER, Walter David. Geology; Optical mineralogy; Ceramics; Fire clay; Microscopy and petrography of ice cream. b'00. AB '25 (U Mo); BS '30 (Mo Sch Mines); AM '32 (Harvard); PhD '33 (U Mo). Author: Common Rocks and Minerals of Missouri; also articles in field. Asst prof to prof geol U Mo since '32. Geol teacher US Army Florence Italy '45. Geol Soc Am(F)—Mineral Soc Am(F)—Mineral Soc Eng—Am Ceramic Soc—Am Inst Mining Metall Engrs—Am Assn Petroleum Geol—AAAS—Sigma Xi. 203 Swallow Hall, Columbia, Mo.†☺

10 KELLERMAN, Karl F(rederic). Audio-visual teaching laboratories; Electronic test equipment; Guided missiles. b'08. EE '29 (Cornell) grad study bus law, management; CLU '38 (Am Coll Life Underwirters). Initiated establishment new Radio Frequency Standards lab at Nat Bureau of Standards '44; writer and speaker of airborne electronics, measurements and guided missiles. Communications engr NY Telephone Co '29-36; exec dir com on guided missiles Research and Development Bd Washington '47-49; mgr Washington office Brush Development (electronics) '49-53; president Ednl Labs Inc since '52; head electronics coordination br engring division Bur Aeronautics USNR '42-46. Registered profl engineer DC. Inst Radio Engrs(sr mem)—Cornell Soc Engrs—AAAS—Tau Beta Pi—Eta Kappa Nu. Recipient ofcl Navy commendation for initiation and supervision electronic test equipment standardization program '45. 1625 Connecticut Av., Washington 9.†☺

11 KELLEY, Maurice Joseph. Surface-active chemicals; Synthetic resins; Oil and fat derivatives; Textile processing chemicals; Paper softening agents; Adhesives; Metal working lubricants; Emulsifers. b'16. AB with highest honors '36 (La Salle Coll); MS '41 (Fordham U); PhD '42 (U Pa). Studies in cationics for rayon processing; synthetic detergents, sulfonated oils, esters, amides, aromatics; self-scouring wool oil; emulsion polymers and water-soluble resins; ethylene oxide reactions. Issued eight patents in field. Research chem synthetic development Nopco Chem Co '36-44, chief chem sales development lab '44-48, dir indsl development lab since '48. Am Inst Chem(F)—AAAS(F)—Chem Soc London(F)—ACS—Soc Chem Industry. Industrial Development Laboratory, Nopco Chemical Co., Harrison, N.J. H: 180 Ashland Av., Bloomfield, N.J.

12 KELLEY, Oliver Kenneth. Automotive engineering (Automatic transmissions, hydraulic drives, clutches). b'04. BS in ME '25 (Chicago Tech Coll); '26-27 (MIT). Assisted in development of synchro-mesh transmission at Cadillac Motor Car Company (two patents); directed development of air shift bus transmissions (eight patents); participated in development of Hydra-Matic Drive (patents), Army automatic transmissions for tanks, armored cars and trucks (patents), Dynaflow transmission (patents), fluid drives and hydraulic converters. Invented Polyphase converter, and features of several automatic drives. Author articles in field. Dir transmission development Gen Motors Central Engring since '40. SAE—Engring Soc Detroit. NAM Award of Modern Pioneer '40.

13 KELLOGG, Charles Edward. Fur Farming; Rabbits (Domestic). b'90. AB '12 (Doane Coll Crete Neb); BSA '21 (U Neb); MSA '28 (U Ga). Research on fur animals raised in captivity, also domestic rabbits; supervision feeding, breeding and management research on silver foxes, minks, marten and rabbits at various federal field stations and with cooperating agencies. Prof animal husbandry Ga State Coll Agr '20-32; biol Biol Sur-

vey USDA and Fish and Wildlife Service Washington '32-46, animal husbandman in charge fur farming investigation Bur Animal Industry since '46. Soc Animal Prodn—AAAS—Alpha Zeta—Phi Kappa Phi. Animal Husbandry Division, Agricultural Research Center, Beltsville, Md. H: 323 E. Broad St., Falls Church, Va.☺

14 KELLOGG, Herbert Humphrey. Metallurgical thermodynamics; Surfaces (Adsorption); Flotation; Ores (Dressing). B'20. BS '41—MS '42 (Columbia). Author articles: The use of contact-angle measurements for study of adsorption on glass surfaces; Amine flotation of Sphlaterite-galena ore; Thermodynamic relationships in chlorine metallurgy. Asst prof, chief div mineral preparation Pa State Coll '42-46; asst prof metall Columbia '46-51, asso prof since '51. AIMME—ACS—Electrochem Soc—Sigma Xi—Tau Beta Pi. School of Mines, Columbia University, NYC.

15 KELLOGG, Peter Paul. Natural history photography; Recording bird songs and other natural sounds. b'99. BS '29—PhD '38 (Cornell U). Explorer, lecturer in natural history and ornithology since '29; pioneer in recording bird songs and other natural sounds. Associate editor: American Bird Songs (an album of 72 wild bird songs); Voices of the Night (an album of calls of 26 frogs and toads found in eastern North America). Asst natural hist Cornell '27-29, instr ornithol '29-38, asst prof '38-42; asso dir acoustical research, jungle acoustical studies Rutgers U '44-45; asso prof ornithol Cornell '45-49; dir Albert R Brand Sound Found since '40. Am Ornithol Union—Sigma Xi. Fernow Hall, Cornell University, Ithaca, N.Y.

16 KELLY, Arthur Randolph. Anthropology (Race mixture); Archeology. b'00. BA '21 (U Tex); MA '26—PhD '29 (Harvard). Director Smithsonian Expedition to Ocmulgee '33-34; research assistant to E A Hooton, Harvard, conducted anthropometric field studies on American criminals for Harvard criminal survey '27-29; directed successive archeological expeditions for University of Illinois to Starved Rock, Cahokia, Big Muddy and Fountain Bluff Ill '30-33. Author articles in field. Asst prof anthrop U Ill '30-33; asso archeol Nat Park Service '36, chief archeol sites div '37-41; head dept anthrop and archeol U Ga since '46. AAAS—Am Anthrop Assn(F)—Archeol Inst Am. 203 Le Conte Hall, University of Georgia, Athens, Ga.

17 KELLY, Sherwin Finch. Geophysics (Exploration). b'95. BSc (ME) '17—'22-23 (U Kan); '19-21 (Ecole des Mines Sorbonne U Paris); '23-26 (U Toronto Ont). Assisted in introduction commercial geophysical techniques for mineral exploration and for investigating dam site foundation conditions on power development; investigation ground water studies in Canada, US, Peru, and Chile; experiment with commercial application electrical prospecting techniques; North American representative Societe de Prospection Electrique Procedes Schlumberger Paris '21-27; supervision exploration for mineral deposits, Canada, Newfoundland, Mexico, Ecuador, Peru, Bolivia, Chile, and US. Author articles: Experiments in Electrical Prospecting '22; Geophysical and Geological Approach to Mining Problems '49; Geophysics in the Exploration, Exploitation and Conservation of Water '49; The Rise of Geophysics '50, and others. Contributor: National Encyclopedia since '32; Colliers Encyclopedia '50. Geol Kan Geol Survey '19, Ont Geol Survey '26; asst mgr Schlumberger Elec Prospecting Methods NYC

'27-30; sec and field mgr Combined Geophys Methods Inc NYC '30-37; pres Geophys Explorations Ltd Toronto Ont since '37; pres Sherwin F Keily Geophys Services Inc since '40. Soc Exploration Geophysicists—Am Geophys Union—Am Mining Congress—AIMME (chmn geophys com '37-40, since '51, chmn com geophysics edn '38-41)—Can Inst Mining and Metall (chmn geophys com since '49)—Pan-Am Union Mining Engring and Geol—Am Geog Soc—Sigma Gamma Epsilon. Room 318, 900 Market St., Wilmington, Del. H: Box 23, Amawalk, N.Y.

18 KELLY, William Aultin. Slide rule; Interpretation of aerial photographs. b'96. BA '21—MA '22 (U Alberta); PhD '25 (Princeton). Research in stratigraphy of Michigan, photogeology, Mississippian corals, Upper Devonian brachiopoda. Devised nomograms to be used with slide rule in determining heights of objects from shadows appearing on aerial photographs. Author articles in field. Instr dept geol Mich State Coll '26-30, asst prof '30-37, asso prof '37-44, prof since '44. Paleontol Soc Am—Mich Acad Sci (vp '33)—Mich Geol Soc (vp '47-48, pres '48-49)—Am Soc Photogrammetry—Am Assn Petroleum Geol—Soc Econ Paleontol—Sigma Xi. Department of Geology, Michigan State College, E. Lansing, Mich.

19 KELLY, William Robert. Irrigation law; Probate real estate. b'83. AB '05—LLB '07 (U Colo). Author articles: A River Is a Treasure; Rationing the Rivers; Navigation and Irrigation in the Mountain States. Referee in water adjudication Dists 1 and 2 under Denver and Weld county courts '11-25; atty No Colo Water Conservancy Dist since '35. Am Bar Assn —Colo Bar Assn (pres '40)—Am Judicature Soc—Weld County Bar Assn— Phi Delta Phi. First National Bank Bldg., Greeley, Colo.☺

20 KEMBLE, John Haskell. Maritime and western United States history. b'12. AB '33 (Stanford U); MA '34—PhD '37 (U Calif). Travel and study in eastern US and Isthmus of Panama on Panama route to Pacific Coast; research in Public Record Office, British Museum London on British trans-Atlantic packets in 18th century; research on Pacific shipping. Author: The Panama Route 1848-1869; also articles in field. Instr hist Pomona Coll '36-41, asst prof '41-45, asso prof since '45. Soc Nautical Research —Steamship Hist Soc Am (regional vp)—Naval Hist Found—US Naval Inst—Great Lakes Hist Soc—AHA— Miss Valley Hist Assn—Calif Hist Soc. Huntington Library fellow; grant-in-aid from Pacific Coast Council for Humanities. Department of History, Pomona College, Claremont, Calif.

21 KEMMERER, Donald Lorenzo. American economic and financial history; New Jersey Colonial history. b'05. BA '27—MA '31—PhD '34 (Princeton U); '27 (Lausanne U); '28 (Berlin U); '28-29 (Harvard); '30 (Stanford). Made study on history of industrialization of eastern US for Board of Investigation and Research; technical consultant for platform committee of Republican party on background and issues in international trade, shipping, international finance and air commerce '44; made study on national income trends after major wars in modern times for Pennsylvania Railroad; research on colonial loan office system in New Jersey. Author: Path to Freedom: Struggle for Self-government in Colonial New Jersey, 1703-76 '40; Economic History of the American People (with Bogart) '47; also articles in field. Professor Ill U since '49, in charge courses in Am econ hist since '38. Econ Hist Assn—AHA—Miss Valley Hist Assn—Am Econ Assn—Economists Nat Com Monetary Policy—Am Finance Assn—Phi Beta Kappa. 110 David Kinley Hall, Urbana, Ill. H: 1006 W. Armory Av., Champaign.⊚

10 KEMP, Archie Reed. Rubber technology; Insulations (Wire and cables). b'95. BS '17—MS '18 (Throop Poly Inst, now Calif Inst Tech). Spent several months in Europe introducing paragutta into European submarine cable factories '29-30; research in submarine cable insulation, rubber covered wire insulation development. Thirty-four inventions on paragutta insulation for submarine cables, pressure equalizer material for submarine cable conductors, insulations for continuous vulcanizing process for rubber covered wire and cables, chemical process for manufacturing insulating materials. Author articles in field. Engring dept Western Elec Co NY '18-25; with Bell Telephone Labs Inc NYC '25-48; chem cons Calif since '48. Am Chem Soc (spl US rep at London Rubber Tech Conf '38)—NY Acad Sci—AICE—Inst Rubber Ind Gt Britain(F). Picked by Am Chem Soc as one of best ten rubber chem. 231 Prospect Ave., Long Beach 3, Calif.

11 KEMP, Harold Augustus. Sanitary Engineering; Water supply and distribution; Sewerage and Sewage treatment; Refuse collection and disposal. b'94. BS '17 (Va Poly Inst Blacksburg); short courses '30 (Rutgers U). Prepared book Estimating Data for Bridges and Miscellaneous Engineering Structures for US War Dept Department; also articles on Potomac River. Cons engr for sewage treatment plants, water supply, bridges etc with George C Diehl Inc Buffalo '24-31; sr engr US Engrs Office as chief of design Ill Waterways Chicago '31-33, Upper Miss River Project St Paul '33-34; gen supt design and constrn sewage treatment plant and rebuilding pumping station Washington '34-37; prin engr N Atlantic div office US Army Engrs flood control '37-38; chief engr Dept San Engring Washington '40-44; dir san engring including supervision of water, sewer, refuse, public convenience and sewage treatment divs Dist of Columbia, Washington '40-44; cons engr OCD Planning; US mem Potomac River Basin Commn '41-44, DC mem since '44, chmn '50-51. ASME—ASCE—Am Pub Health Assn—Soc Am Mil Engrs —Am Water Works Assn—Am Pub Works Assn—NY State Sewage Works Assn—Md-Del Water and Sewerage Assn—Engrs Club Washington. Government of the District of Columbia, Washington 4.⊚

12 KEMP, Louis Wiltz. History of Texas. b'81. Student '01-03 (U Tex). Author: Signers of the Texas Declaration of Independence '44. Co-author: The Heroes of San Jacinto '32; Texas Musketeers '35. Co-editor and contributor: Monuments Commemorating the Centenary of Texas '39. With Tex Oil Co since '08; chmn bd Tex State Library since '37; pres San Jacinto Mus Hist since '38. Nat Soc Sons Am Revolution (hist gen '46-48)—Tex State Hist Assn (pres '41-45)—Sons of Republic of Tex (pres state chap '46-49) —Tex State Philos Soc. 214 Westmoreland Av., Houston, Tex.⊚

13 KEMPERS, Garrett B. History of seventeenth century Europe. b'98. AB '21 (Calvin Coll); AM '22—PhD '32 (U Mich). Author articles in field. Prof hist Westmar Coll since '33. AHA. Westmar College, LeMars, Ia.

14 KEMPF, Edward J(ohn). Bisexual differentiation; Psychopathology; Psy-

chotherapy. b'85. AB '07 (Ind U); MD '10 (W Reserve Med Sch). Research on psychopathology and psychotherapy of idea-emotional neuroses and psychoses, holistic organization of mind, physiological and psychological bisexual differentiation and development of man. Author: The Autonomic Functions and the Personality '18; Psychopathology '20. Clin psychiatrist St Elizabeths Hosp Washington '14-20; private practice since '20; cons Veterans Adminstrn '49-50. AMA (F)—A AAS(F)—Am Psychiat Assn—Am Psychopathology Assn (pres '31-33)—NY Acad Med(F)—NY Acad Sci(F)—NY Soc Clin Psychiat—Assn Research Nervous and Mental Disease—Nat Com Mental Hygiene—Cosmos Club— Pi Gamma Mu. Wading River, L.I., N.Y.

15 KEMPNER, Robert Max Wasilii. International penal law and procedure; War Crimes Trials (Nuremberg); European diplomacy and governments; Foreign administration (Political and secret societies); Police and Intelligence systems. b'99. Student law, polit sci, pub adminstrn, criminology—Dr of Law and Pub Adminstrn (univs Berlin, Freiburg, Breslau) (U Pa). Prosecuting, investigative and research activities throughout Europe, Near East, North Africa and US in connection with war crimes trials and prosecution of foreign agents; general counsel to the pre-Hitler centralized German police administration, and advisory post-Hitler Western German and French prosecuting agencies. Author articles: The Enemy Alien Problem in the Present War; The German National Registration System; Impact of Nuremberg on the German Mind; Murder by Government; The Nuremberg Trials as Sources of Recent German Political and Historical Materials. Superior govt counselor Ministry of Interior Berlin and chief legal adviser Prussian police adminstrn, judge civil service tribunal '31-33; lectr German Acad Politics, Sch Social Work and Police Acad Berlin '26-33; counselor in internat law and migration problems '34-35; pres and prof polit sci Fiorenza Coll Florence Italy and Nice France '36-39; research on machinery of European dictatorships under Carnegie and Carl Schurz grants '39-42; expert to Federal courts in espionage and foreign agents trials, expert cons Dept of Justice, OSS and to Sec of War on legal, polit and intelligence techniques of European dictatorships and foreign orgns in US '42-45; US staff prosecutor in Nuremberg trial against Goering, Frick et al, research dir US prosecution '45-46 US dep chief of counsel for War crimes, chief prosecutor German Reich Cabinet members, state secretaries and diplomats, Nuremberg '46-49; vis prof polit sci and law Erlangen U, lectr univs Heidelberg, Tuegingen, Zurich, public forums '46-49; counselor European foreign relations, internat law and administrn ' 50. Am Polit Sci Assn H: 112 Lansdowne Court, Lansdowne, Pa.

16 KEMPNER, Stanley. Television. b '09. BS (journalism) '39 (Northwestern U); '27-29 (Columbia), '38-39 (St Lawrence U) (Brooklym Law Sch). Author: Television Encyclopedia '48. Author articles: Problems and profits for tele retailers; Door to Door or in a Store; How to purchase your new television receiver; The Antenna Problem in set selling. Television editor: Book of the Year, World Scope Encyclopedia '47, Retailing Daily, Fairchild Publications '43-46; television contbg ed, columnist Televiser: Journal of Television '45-46; columnist Tele-Facts TV Guide '49. 129 Pierre-

pont St., Bklyn 2. H: 501 Woodbridge Rd., North Rockville Center, L.I., N.Y.

17 KENDALL, Florence May Peterson (Mrs Henry O Kendall). Muscles (Testing); Posture (Treatment of faulty and painful); Poliomyelitis (Physical therapy care). b'10. BS '30 (U Minn); certificate in phys therapy '32 (Watler Reed Gen Hosp). Co-author: Muscles, Testing and Function '49. Co-producer motion pictures: Moving Picture Demonstration of Examination, Protection and Treatment of Convalescent Poliomyelitis Cases '36; (sound film) Posture Studies '50. Phys therapy aide Walter Reed Gen Hosp '32-33; asst dir phys therapy dept Children's Hosp Sch Baltimore since '33; supervisor phys therapy Md State Dept Health Services for Crippled Children '36-44; instr body mechanics Johns Hopkins Hosp Sch Nursing since '43. Am Phys Therapy Assn— Am Registry of Phys Therapists— Ateneo de Kinesiologia Buenos Aires (hon mem). Children's Hospital School, Greenspring Av., Balt. 11.

18 KENDALL, Henry Otis. Muscles (Testing); Posture (Treatment of faulty and painful); Poliomyelitis (Physical therapy care). b'98. Student '18-20 (Evergreen Sch for the Blind Baltimore). Co-author: Muscles, Testing and Function '49. Co-producer motion pictures: Moving Picture Demonstration of Examination, Protection and Treatment of Convalescent Poliomyelitis Cases '36; (sound film) Posture Studies '50. Dir phys therapy dept Children's Hosp Sch Baltimore since '20; superviser phys therapy Baltimore City Pub Schs since '32; instr body mechanics Johns Hopkins Hosp Sch Nursing since '43. Am Phys Therapy Assn—Am Registry Phys Therapists—Ateneo de Kinesiologia, Buenos Aires (hon mem). Children's Hospital School, Greenspring Av., Balt. 11.

19 KENDEIGH, S. Charles. Ornithology (Ecology, temperature, migration, physiology, nesting behavior). b'04. AB '26—AM '27 (Oberlin Coll); PhD '30 (U Ill). Research on temperature of birds and mammals, nesting behavior of birds, ecological distribution of birds, bird migration, fluctuations in bird abundance, physiological relation of birds to environment. Co-author: Physiology of the Temperature of Birds '32. Author articles: The Role of Environment in the Life of Birds '34; Measurement of Bird Populations, and others. Baldwin Bird Research Lab '25-39; asst prof zool U Ill '36-40, asso prof '41-47, prof since '48. AAAS —Ecol Soc Am—Am Ornithol Union— Ill Acad Sci, and others. Vivarium Building, Wright and Healey Sts., Champaign, Ill.†

20 KENDIG, Isabelle V(irginia). Clinical psychology (Projective techniques). b'89. AB '12 (Oberlin College); AM '30—PhD '33 (Radcliffe Coll); Diploma Clin Psychol '48 (Am Bd Examiners Professional Psychol); Certificate '50 (Washington Sch Psychiat). Co-author: (with Richmond) Psychological Studies in Dementia Praecox '40. Author articles: Studies in Perseveration '36; Projective Techniques as a Psychological Tool in Diagnosis '44; Rorschach Indications for the Diagnosis of Schizophrenia '49, and others. Contributor: Case Histories in Clinical and Abnormal Psychology '47; Handbook of Applied Psychology '50. Instr psychol Pine Manor Jr Coll Wellesley Mass '30-35; psychol Cambridge Sch Cambridge and Kendal Green Mass '32-35; research dementia praecox St Elizabeth's Hosp Washington '36-38, psychol '38-41, chief psychol '41-50; asso clin psy med sch George

Washington U '42-50, instr projective techniques grad sch '47-50; instr projective techniques Catholic U Washington '47-50; asso Washington Sch Psy since '47; chief psychol Veterans Adminstrn Hosp Tomah Wis since '50. Am Psychol Assn(F)—Midwestern Psychol Assn—DC Psychol Assn—Am Psychopath Assn—Phi Beta Kappa—Soc for Projective Techniques and Rorschach Inst (F)—Internat Council Women Psychol—AAAS. Veterans Administration Hospital, Tomah, Wis.

10 KENDRICK, Baynard Hardwick. Blindness (Training, jobs, t a l k i n g books). b'94. Author articles in field. Free lance writer since '32. Consultant to staff, Old Farms Convalescent Hosp for Blinded Vets US Army, Avon, Conn, during World War II. Blinded Vets Assn (sighted adviser and hon life mem). Recipient plaque from Gen Omar N Bradley for service to blinded vets of World War II. Charles Scribners' Sons, NYC.

11 KENKNIGHT, Glenn. Diseases of vegetable crops, peanuts and dates. b'10. BA '34 (Carleton Coll); MS '37 —PhD '39 (Mich State Coll). Author articles in field. Co-inventor a practical hot water seed treater for commercial use; developed Spantex peanut variety. Plant path US Dept Agr Hort Sta Fort Valley Ga since '48. Am Phytopath Soc—Sigma Xi. U.S. Horticultural Field Laboratory, Fort Valley, Ga.

12 KENN, Charles William. Hawaiian language, folklore, ancient sports and chants. Fire walking in Polynesian ceremonies. b'07. AB '31—'32 (U Hawaii). Research on Hawaiian language, customs, and folklore; investigated fire walking demonstrations; historian of Kamehameha I; detailed study of Hawaiian language and variations in means of words; recorded numerous chants and prayers. Author: Fire-Walking From the Inside '49; also articles in field. Vis anthrop U Calif Los Angeles '48; investigations for Huna Research Associates Los Angeles '48; lecturer, feature writer, research for various orgns interested in Hawaiian language and customs. Hawaiian Anthrop Soc—Hawaiian Hist Soc—AAAS—Polynesian Soc—Inst Pacific Relations. 944 20th Av., Honolulu 16, T.H.

13 KENNAMER, Earl Franklin. Fish ponds (Construction and management); Farms (Game improvement); Foxes (Control of rabid). b'18. BS '40 (Ala Polytech Inst). Served as chief forestry, fish and wildlife in Bavaria, Mil Govt '45-46; with Ala Polytech Inst since '40, now fish and wildlife specialist. Wildlife Soc—Gamma Sigma Delta—Phi Kappa Phi.

14 KENNEDY, Clarence Hamilton. Anatomy of insects; Dragonflies; Michigan and Ontario ants. b'79. AB in zool '02—AM '03—DSc hon '50 (Ind U); AM (Entomol) '51 (Stanford); PhD '19 (Cornell). Classification of dragonflies of the World, especially South American; habits, nest structure and distribution of Michigan and Ontario ants; teaching internal anatomy of insects. Faculty dept zool and entomol O State U. Department of Zoology and Entomology, Ohio State University, Columbus 10,©

15 KENNEDY, Daniel. Topographic mapping; Civil engineering; Geodesy; Photogrammetry. b'00. BS (civil engring) '26—CE '35—D Eng (hon) '49 (Mo Sch Mines and Metall). Topographic mapping for US Geological Survey in Missouri, Kansas, Arkansas, Louisiana, Texas, North and South Dakota, Nebraska, Michigan, Minnesota, Wisconsin, Oklahoma, Georgia, Kentucky, Iowa, and Illinois; in charge of surveys and maps for Eniwetok Experiment; made 50 topographic maps. Topog engr US Geol Survey '26-42; chief operations and planning, chief topog engr Army Map Service '46-48 ('47-48 dep engr Task Force Seven Eniwetok A-Bomb Expt); central region engr US Geol Survey since '48. Capt to lt col US Army '42-45, Army Map Service '42, in charge NY office Lake Survey '43, in charge mapping for 3rd Army operations on continent '44-45. Am Soc CE—Am Soc Photogrammetry—Am Mil Engrs—Congress on Surveying and Mapping —Am Geophys Union—Explorers Club —Sigma Xi. US Geological Survey. Box 133, Rolla, Mo.

16 KENNEDY, Harold S(chwinn). Helium production. b'95. Student '14-15. '16-17 (Cornell U); AB '24—MS '26 (George Washington U). Survey for helium bearing natural gas; plan and administration of helium plants; plan and administration of government's helium production. Contributor: Bureau of Mines Minerals Yearbook since '37. Chief helium sect petroleum and natural gas br Bur Mines Washington since '44. AIMME—Am Gas Assn. Bureau of Mines, Washington 25.†

17 KENNEDY, Paul A(lfred). Aviation psychology; Altitude classification. b'87. BS '15—AM '17 (Columbia); PhD '27 (Fordham). Research in aviation psychology and administration altitude classification in tests. Head methods dept Fordham U Grad Sch Edn '27-30; asst supt schs City NY since '35, chmn curriculum com since '47. Lt AS US Army '18-19. NY Acad Pub Edn (chmn bd dirs, past pres), Assn Asst Supts (past pres). Board of Education 110 Livingston St., Bklyn 2.†©

18 KENNEDY, Robert Evan. Earthquake design. (Structural engineering). b'16. BS (CE) '38 (U Colo). Design major structures for seismic conditions; consultant on structural engineering Mayor's Committee on Civil Defense. Author articles: Earthquake Design of a Portland, Oregon Bank Building '50; Surveying Existing Buildings for Shelter '51; Portland Engineers Survey Existing Buildings for Air Raid Use '51. Engr Am Bridge Co Trenton NJ '39-40; engr structural analysis Goodyear Aircraft Corp Akron O '40-45: structural engr since '46. Am Soc CE—Colo Soc Engrs—Structural Engrs Assn Ore (pres '50-51)—Ore Bldg Congress (treas '51). Professional engr Ore, Ariz. 1940 S.W. Fourth, Portland, Ore. H: 7932 S.E. Tibbets, Portland 6.

19 KENNEDY, Ruth Lee. Spanish language and literature. b'95. AB 16 —AM '17 (U Tex); student '24-25 (U Cal); PhD '31 (U Pa). Research on Golden Age of literature of Spain. Author: The Dramatic Art of Moreto '31-32. Teacher Spanish since '17; head Spanish dept SW Tex State Tchrs Coll '22-24 '25-26; head Spanish dept San Antonio Jr Coll '26-28 '29-30; asst prof Smith Coll '30-34, asso prof '35-44, prof Spanish lang and lit since '44; fellowship Am Assn U Women '37-38 '45-46, U Pa '45-46, John S Guggenheim fellow for research on Spanish costume and its importance for literary and artistic chronology. Modern Lang Assn—Am Assn Tchrs Spanish —Hispanic Soc Am—Internat Inst for Girls in Spain—AAUW—Phi Beta Kappa. Smith College, Dept. Spanish, Northampton, Mass.†©

20 KENNEL, Louis. Displays (Stage settings, exhibitions, floats). b'86. Student (Art Students League, Acad Design). E x e c u t e d scenic display Electric Utility Building New York World's Fair; over 500 productions among which are Street Scene, The Storm, Outward Bound; decorations for White Horse Inn, Center Theatre, Latin American Fair; designing and executing floats for R H Macy's & Co and L Bamberger's Thanksgiving Day Parade. Asst scenic artist Ernest Qros Studios '03; mgr head Unett & Weeks Studio '19-17; pres Kennel & Ent Inc since '17; proprietor Louis Kennel Scenic Studios since '19. United Scenic Artists Assn. 1427 44th St., North Bergen, N.J.

21 KENNEY, William Douglas. Peanuts (Production, harvesting, and mechanical drying equipment). b'18. BSAE '42 (U Ga). Research on farm machinery for peanut mechanization: design, construction and field test machines for production and harvesting; improve present methods and develop new methods for drying peanuts, reduce labor requirements, improve quality, improve land fertility; design peanut combine harvester. Co-author articles: (with J L Shepherd) Developing a Peanut Combine Harvester; Peanut Drying. With Bur Plant Industry, USDA since '46, U Ga since '46. Am Soc Agrl Engrs—Ga Soc Agrl Engrs (sec and treas since '48, v chmn '50). Coastal Plain Experiment Station, Tifton, Ga.

22 KENNY, Hamill Thomas. West Virginia and Maryland place names; Maryland Indian place names. b'11. AB '34—AM '35 (Columbia); post-grad study (George Washington U, Cornell, Johns Hopkins); PhD '51 (U Maryland). Author: West Virginia Place Names, Their Origin and Meaning Including Nomenclature of the Streams and Mountains Piedmont, West Virginia '45. Grad asst Eng U Md since '45. W Va Hist Soc. P.O. Box 412, College Park, Md. H: 39 Child Av., Piedmont, W. Va.

23 KENNY, James. Finance (International). b'20. AM with honors '47 (U Glasgow); '47-48 (Princeton U). Research in American investment in Brazil; foreign investment in Brazil, Union of South Africa, and Mexico; policies of far eastern countries regarding foreign investment therein; the European payments union; Colombo plan and point four; foreign investment guarantees; comparison of prewar and postwar structure of international investment. Author: The Mirage of Industralization '50; The Problem of the Sterling Balances—America's Stake '50. Econ UN Secretariat '48-49; econ US Council Internat C of C since '50. Royal Econ Soc (London)—Nat Planning Assn. U.S. Council of the International Chamber of Commerce, 103 Park Av., NYC

24 KENNY, William Vincent. History of street and electric railways (New England). b'15. Student pub schs. Author: The Waterbury and Milldale Tramway '52. Editor and author: 50th Anniversary of the Main Line '51. Editor and co-author: 50th Anniversary of Subway Operation in America '47. Editor Trolley Freight in Massachusetts '48; The Turnout since '39. Motorman Met Transit Authority. Nat Ry Hist Soc Inc—Electric Railroaders' Association. H: 90 Walworth St., Boston 31.

25 KENT, Donald H(arris). Pennsylvania Colonial history, French and Indian War; Pennsylvania maps. b'10. AB '31 (Allegheny Coll). Directed research project which collected sources on western Pennsylvania history in transcript form, surveyed Pennsylvania sources in various depositories. Co-editor: Papers of Henry Bouquet '40-51; Wilderness Chronicles of Northwestern Pennsylvania '41; Travels in

New France by J. C. B. '41; Preliminary List of Maps of Pennsylvania to 1830. Author articles on Pennsylvania History. Historian Frontier Forts and Trails Survey '37-40; asst state historian Pa Hist Commn '40-45; asso state historian Pa Hist and Mus Commn since 1945; asst editor Pa History '49-50, asso editor since '51. Pa Hist Assn—Phi Beta Kappa—Phi Sigma Iota. State Museum Bldg., Harrisburg, Pa.

10 KENT, George Cantine, Jr. Golden hamster (Reproduction). b'14. BA '37 (Maryville Coll); MA '38—PhD '42 (Vanderbilt U). Research on hamster exhibition of heat and the estrous cycle, mating, effects of ovarian hormones on mating and vaginal smears, role of progesterone in reproductive cycle, effects of thiouracil on thyroid gland, effect of X-rays on ovary, pseudopregnancy. Author articles in field. Asso prof zool La State U since '49. Am Soc Zool—Assn SE Biol—Tenn Acad Sci—La Acad Sci (ed proc since '48)—AAAS—Sigma Xi. Department of Zoology, Louisiana State University, Baton Rouge, La.

11 KENT, G(eorge) C(larence). Diseases of corn, potatoes, fruit, cereal and forage crops; Bacteriophages and fungus inhibitors. b'10. Student '27-30 (NM A&M Coll); BA '33 (Oxford U); PhD '36 (Ia State Coll). Author: (with others) Elements of Plant Pathology '39. Prof plant path Cornell U since '45, head department since '50. Am Phytopath Soc—Bot Soc Am—AAS—Phi Kappa Phi—Sigma Xi. Rhodes scholar '30-33. Department of Plant Pathology, New York State College of Agriculture, Cornell University, Ithaca, N.Y.†

12 KENT, John Harvey. Epigraphy; Hellenistic history (Delos, Corinth). b'09. Student '25-26 (Dalhousie U, Halifax Can); BA '30—MA '34 (Queen's U, Can); Ryerson fellow archeol '38-40—PhD '43 (U Chicago); grad student '38-41—Wheeler fellow '40-41—fellow in epigraphy '46, '48 (Am Sch Classical Studies, Athens); summers '46-48 (Inst Advanced Study, Princeton). Research in inscripitons of Delos, commissioned by University of Chicago, by special permission of French School of Archeology in Greece '39-40; excavation at Corinth Greece, commissioned by American School of Classical Studies at Athens '40. Author articles in field. Head Latin dept McCallie Sch Chattanooga Tenn '40-45; prof Latin Southwestern U Memphis '45-50; Roberts prof classics U Vermont since '50; Fulbright Fellow Greece '49-50. AHA—Archeol Inst Am—Am Philol Assn—Classical Assn (Brit)—Classical Assn Can—Soc Promotion Hellenic Studies (Brit)—Soc Promotion Roman Studies (Brit—Middle East Inst—Am Schs Oriental Research. Dept Classics, University of Vermont, Burlington, Vt.†

13 KENT, Norman. Print identification; American drawings (20th Century); American water color (20th Century). b'03. Grad (art) '25 (Rochester Inst Tech); '25-26 (Art Students League of NY). Research on introduction of linoleum cut in America from Europe; private and group instruction on technique and history of xylography; lectures and demonstration on wood cuts and printmaking to museums and art schools; national exhibits and one-man shows since '30. Editor: The Book of Edward A Wilson '48. Co-editor (with Ernest W Watson) The Relief Print '45; Watercolor Demonstrated '45. Editor and compiler: Drawings by American Artists '47. Asst prof advancing to prof art Hobart & William Smith Colls '34-43; mng ed Am Artist '43-48; art dir internat ed Readers Digest since '48. Nat Acad Design—Conn Acad Fine Arts—Audubon Artists—Am Watercolor Soc—Prairie Printmakers—Soc Am Etchers, Gravers, Lithographers and Woodcutters—Soc Am Wood Engravers (co-founder)—Am Inst Graphic Arts—Phila Watercolor Club. H: 437 Carroll Av., Mamaroneck, N.Y.

14 KENT, Olney Brown. Poultry husbandry; Poultry nutrition. b'90. BS '13—MS (agr) '14—PhD '17 (Cornell U). Research on selection of laying hens; US delegate to World's Poultry Congress '33, '36, '48. With Quaker Oats Co since '22, dir feed research from '46. Poultry Sci Assn (pres '20-21, sec-treas '21-22)—World's Poultry Sci Assn (council since '48)—Dairy Sci Assn—Soc Animal Prodn—Sigma Xi. Quaker Oats Co., Merchandise Mart Plaza, Chgo 54.

15 KENYON, Karl Walton. Fur seals (Migration, population); Ornithology (Marine species). b'18. BA '40 (Pomona Coll); MS '41 (Cornell). Research on general biology fur seal habits especially migration, population; study of habits, life history, distribution of marine birds. Author articles: Distribution of Albotrosses in the North Pacific and Adjacent Waters '50; Sea Parrots '50, and others. Instr zool Mills Coll Calif '46-47; wildlife research biol US Fish and Wildlife Service Dept of Interior '47-50. Am Ornithol Union—AAAS—Am Soc Mammals—Pacific Northwest Bird and Mammal Soc—Wilderness Soc—Wildlife Soc—Oceanog Soc of Pacific. 2725 Montlake Blvd., Seattle 2.

16 KEPHART, Calvin Ira. Ethnography; Philology (Word origin); Conflict of laws. BS '13 (U Calif); LLB '22—LLM—DCL '28 (Nat U); BCS '23 (Southeastern U); PhD '33 (Am U). Author articles: Origin of the Name America '38; The Swedes and Swedish Goths '38; Origin of the Conjugal Community and Other Ancient Laws '38; Origin of Armorial Insignia in Europe '38; Origin of the Name Russia '44, and others. Formerly with Interstate Commerce Commission as prin trial examiner; asso prof law Nat U '27-39. Pa Hist Junto Washington (pres '46-47)—Tau Beta Pi—Sigma Xi Box 52, Shady Side, Maryland.

17 KEPPEL, Ruth. History of Holland, Michigan. b'96. Student (Oberlin Conservatory Music); BM—teacher's certificate (Chicago Musical Coll). Author: Trees to Tulips '47; also articles in field. Mich Hist Soc. 85 East Tenth St., Holland, Mich.

18 KEPFER, Raymond John. Galvanizing (Fluxes); Metals (Cleaning, fluxing). b'02. BA '26 (DePauw U); MA '28—PhD '30 (U Wis). Research on metal cleaning, pickling, and fluxing prior to galvanizing or to application of other hot dip metal coatings. Granted patents on galvanizing fluxes. With E I duPont de Nemours & Co since '30, tech service from '42. ACS—Am Wood Preservers Assn—AS TM, E I duPont de Nemours & Co., 2101 Canalport Av., Chgo. 8.

19 KERCHER, Leonard Clayton. Sociology; Consumer cooperatives; Crime and delinquency; Population studies. b'01. Student '22-24 (Western Mich Coll) summer '34 (U London); AB '27—AM '28, PhD '39 (U Mich). Co-author: (with Kebker and Leland) Consumer Cooperatives '41; (with others) Sociological Foundations of Education '42; (with others) Twentieth Century America: Trends in Civilization '51. Prof sociology Western Mich Coll Kalamazoo since '28, head dept sociology since '45, chmn div social scis '48-51; lectr sociology Horace Rackham Sch Grad Studies, U Mich since '39; vis prof summers U Redlands Cal '50. Ashridge Coll Eng '51. Am Sociol Soc—Nat Geog Soc—Am Acad Polit and Social Sci—Mich Sociol Soc—Mich Acad Arts and Scis—Alpha Kappa Delta—Phi Gamma Mu—Kappa Delta Pi. 1451 Maple Street, Kalamazoo 39. Mich.†◎

20 KERCHEVILLE, Francis Monroe. Spain; Spanish language (Pronunciation); Spanish literature. b'01. BA '24 (Abilene Christian Coll); '24 (Nat U Mexico); '26 (U Sorbonne); MA '27—F '29—PhD '30 (U Wis); '35 (U Madrid); Inst Internat Edn F '41 (U Chile). Research on Spain and on Spanish liberal thought, on Larra, Galdos, Ibanez, Azuela; special representative to Spain '35. Author: Handbook of Pronunciation-English and Spanish '34; Practical Spoken Spanish '34. Co-author: Living Spanish '37. Co-editor: Santa Rogelia '41. Asso prof and acting head dept Spanish U SD '30; prof modern lang and head dept U NM since '31; vis prof and lecturer Pan-Am Airways Chile '41. Inst de Lit Ibero-Americana (reorganization com '47-48)—NM Art League (pres '34)—Am Assn Tchrs Spanish and Portuguese (nat pres '40)—MLA—Rocky Mt Modern Lang Assn (co-founder and co-pres '47)—AAUP—Phi Kappa Phi—Phi Sigma Iota. University of New Mexico, Albuquerque, N.M. H: 1819 E. Roma.†◎

21 KERN, Charles James. Nutritional biochemistry; Vitamin technology. b'13. Student '31-33 (U NM); BS '35 (Union Coll); MS '44 (Brooklyn Poly Inst); PhD '49 (NYU). Author articles in field. Vice-pres and tech dir Internat Vitamin Div Ives Cameron Co Inc; now assistant to the president Wyeth Inc. Am Oil Chem Soc—NY Acad Sci—Am Chem Soc—Am Inst Chem—Sigma Xi. 1600 Arch St., Philadelphia, Pennsylvania.

22 KERN, Frank Dunn. Mycology; Uredinales. BS '04 (U Ia); MS '07 (Purdue); PhD '11 (Columbia); DSc '26 (U Puerto Rico). Conducted mycology explorations in Puerto Rico, Dominican Republic and Venezuela; delegate to International Botany Congress Cambridge '30; researches on plant rusts and other fungus diseases in plants. Author books and articles in field. Prof, head dept bot Pa State Coll '13-50, dean Grad School '13-50. AAAS (G, vp, chmn sect bot sci '45)—Ind Acad Sci—Bot Soc Am—Am Phytopath Soc—Pa Acad Sci—Mycol Soc Am (pres '45)—Nat Research Council—Phi Kappa Phi (nat pres since '48)—Sigma Xi—Gamma Sigma Delta. Research scholar NY Bot Garden Jan each yr for 4 yrs. 140 W. Fairmount Av., State College, Pa.◎

23 KERN, Maximilian. Endocrinology; Thyroid and pituitary pathology. b'90. Student Royal Imperial Gymnasium Stanislaw]; MD '11 (LI Coll Hosp Brooklyn); MD '15 (Chicago Coll Med and Surgery (now Med Sch Loyola U). Research in endocrinology, especially thyroid and pituitary pathology. Author monographs: Blindness of Pituitary Origin; Role of Endocrinology in Epilepsy; Endocrines in Ophthalmology and Otolaryngology, Crime and the Endocrines; Les Glandes Endocrines avant la Puberté (Paris); Studies of Endocrine Types; The Sella Turcica in Relation to Endocrinology; Endocrines and Physiotherapy; Relation of the Sella Turcica to Endocrinology; Endocrines and Physiotherapy; Dermagraphia in Relation to Dysthyroidism; The Status of Physical Therapy in the Treatment of Obesity; The Thyroid Gland and Menstrual Disorders; Obesity and the Endocrines; Pituitary Tumors; Hemolytic Streptoccus Bacteremia with Endocarditis and Arthritis Following Scarlet Fever; Clinical Application of Testosterone Propionate; and others. Prof endocrinology Gen Med Foundation Med Coll Chicago since '22; attending internist and sec staff Edgewater Hosp Chicago. AMA—USPH Assn—Soc for Study Goitre—Assn Study Internal Secretions—Am Heart Assn—Phi Gamma Nu. 55 E. Washington St., Chgo 2.

10 KERNER, Robert Joseph. Slavic Europe (Russia, Balkans, Czechoslovakia, Yugoslavia); International relations and foreign affairs(Russia in Asia and on the Pacific, world politics); Modern European history; Northeastern Asia; Alaska. b'87. AB '08—AM '09 (U Chicago); AM'12—PhD'14(Harvard U); LLD '37 (U Omaha); LittD '38 (Park Coll Parkville Mo). Author: The Foundations of Slavic Bibliography '16; The Jugo-Slav Movement '18; Slavic Europe (selected bibliography) '18; Social Sciences in the Balkans and Turkey '30; Bohemia in the Eighteenth Century '32; The Balkan Conferences and the Balkan Entente (with H N Howard) '35; Northeastern Asia (selected bibliography 2 vols) '39; Urge to the Sea (Russia) '42. Editor and co-author: Czechoslovakia '40; Poland '45; Yugoslavia '48; also articles in field. Ed Northeastern Asia Series since '37; gen ed UN Series since '42; Sather prof hist U Calif since '41. AHA—Soc Advancement Slavonic Study—Am Council Inst Pacific Relations—Phi Beta Kappa—Phi Beta Kappa associates. Czechoslovak State Prize for Lit '40; Comdr Order White Lion (Czechoslovakia); Officer, Order of Star (Rumania), Order of Leopold II (Belgium). University of California, Berkeley.⊚

11 KERNKAMP, Milton Frederick. Smut fungi; Forage crops (Diseases). b'11. BS '34—MS '38—PhD '41 (U Minn). Research on growth of types of corn smut fungus Ustilago zeae with relation to genetic and environmental factors; instructor on study ecology of plant pathogens; investigation fundamentals of etiology and epidemiology of diseases of soybeans, alfalfa, and brome grass, and control methods including seed treatment, and breeding for disease resistance. Author articles: Chemical Treatment of Soybean Seed in Relation to Nodulation by Nodule Bacteria '48; Root Rots of Soybeans '49; Seed Treatment of Alfalfa, Red Clover, and Sweet Clover '50; Resistance in Soybeans to Root Rot Caused by Rhizoctonia Solani '50, and others. Co-author articles: Fungi that Poison Soybeans '48; Damping-off of Alfalfa Cuttings Caused by Rhizoctonia solani '49, and others. Asst path div sugar plants USDA Meridian Miss '41-46; asst prof path U Minn '46-49, asso prof since '49. AAAS—Am Phytopath Soc—Sigma Xi—Gamma Alpha. Division of Plant Pathology, University Farm, St. Paul.

12 KERNS, Kenneth Raymond. Morphology, cytology and genetics of pineapple. b'03. BS '26—MS '30 (U Hawaii); '29-32 (U Calif, U Berlin). eticist Pineapple Research Inst since Author articles in field. Asso gen- '26. Genetics Soc Am—AAAS—Sigma Xi. Pineapple Research Institute, P.O. Box 42, Wahiawa, Oahu, T.H.†

13 KERR, Charles, Jr. Transportation; Locomotives. b'99. BS '19 (U Va); BS in EE '22 (MIT). Associated with development of trolley coach for urban transportation '28-30, railway car air conditioning '32-35, electrification of Pennsylvania Railroad '32-39, steam turbine locomotive '40-44, gas turbine locomotive since '45. Author articles in field. With Westinghouse Elec Corp East Pittsburgh since '22,

cons transportation engr since '44. ASME—AIEE. Westinghouse Electric Corp., East Pittsburgh.

14 KERR, John Davidson, Jr. Mineral development (Missouri, Kansas, Oklahoma, and Texas); Industrial site surveys. b'00. Student '22-29 (Washington U St Louis); Grad '43 (Command and Gen Staff Coll). Examination, mapping, and cataloging non-metallic minerals; strategic reconnaissance studies for selection war department ordnance depot sites. Author article: Site for a Tidewater Ammunition Depot to Supply the Canal Zone '40. Co-author article: A Study of the Proposed Louisiana Purchase Exposition in 1953-1954 '47, and others. Prin engr War Dept '40; indsl commr Kansas City Chamber of Commerce '46; dir indsl bur St Louis Chamber of Commerce since '46. AIMME—Am Indsl Council—Mo Resources and Development Commn. 511 Locust St., StL 1.

15 KERR, K(athel) B(edortha). Public health parasitology; Helminthology. b'08. AB '29 (Oberlin Coll); MS '31 (Washington U); ScD '36 (Johns Hopkins U Sch Hygiene and Pub Health); '29 (Marine Biol Sta); '30 (Puget Sound Biol Sta); '31 (U Chicago). Research on immunity to cestode and nematode parasites, public health aspects of trichinosis, made survey of its human incidence, incidence in meat, and serology of clinical cases; consultant laboratory section Rio Doce Project Brazil; work in development anthelmintics for poultry helminths, physiology of poultry helminths. Author articles in field. Jr zool Nat Inst Health '38-40, asst zool '40-42; zool Calif Dept Health '40-41; asso parasitol Inst Inter-Am Affairs '42-43, parasitol '43-45; helminthologist Dr Salsbury's Lab Charles City Ia since '45. Nat Research Council (F, med sci)—Am Soc Parasitol—Am Soc Trop Med—Am Micros Soc—Ia Acad Sci—AAAS—Sigma Xi—Gamma Alpha. Dr. Salsbury's Laboratory, Charles City, Ia.

16 KERR, Ralph Waldo. Starch (Chemistry, manufacture). b'99. AB '21—MA '23—PhD '24 (Columbia U). Holder many patents in field. Author: Chemistry and Industry of Starch; also articles in field. Head Division Starch Research Corn Products Refining Co Argo Ill '29-44, sr chemist Chem Div since '44. Am Chem Soc—AAAS. Corn Products Refining Co., Argo, Ill.

17 KERR, Samuel Logan. Hydraulic engineering (Pipe lines, pumping systems and surge control for water and petroleum). b'99. BS ME '21—ME '24 (U Pa). Author articles in field. Design, constrn and operation of hydroelectric and control equipment I P Morris Corp '21-35; sr engr US Engr Dept '35-36; indsl, hydraulic and chem engring work United Engrs and Constructors Inc Phila '37-45; cons engr gen practice, pres S Logan Kerr & Co Inc Phila since '45; vp, gen mgr Lyophile-Cryochem Corp Baltimore since '46. ASME—ASCE—AWWA—Engring Inst Can. 1528 Walnut St., Phila. 2.

18 KERR, Thomas Jefferson. Vinyl film; Vinyl sheeting (Calendered, cast); Coated fabrics. b'05. BS in chem engring '26—Chem E '32 (Clarkson Coll Tech). Research, development, manufacture, decoration and finishing self-supported films and coatings for fabric an paper; granted patents on coatings and coated fabrics. Chem Dutchess Bleachery Inc '26-31; chem Columbus Coated Fabrics Corp '31-45, supt and asst dir sales calender div '47-48; with Pantasote Co '45-47, dir research '45-47; mgr plastics div Southbridge Finishing Co '48-49; cons

since '49. ACS—Soc Plastics Industry. R.F.D. 1, Gowanda, N.Y.

19 KERR, Willard Augusta. Industrial psychology; Morale; Music in industry. b'18. BEd '39 (So Ill U); MS '40—PhD '42—fellow '41-42 (Purdue). Invented rip method of polling opinion; established Industrial Opinion Institute '44 for standardized measurement of employee job satisfaction with new tear method. Author articles in field. Asso prof psychol Ill Inst Tech since '47; Aviation psychol USN '44-46. Am Psychol Assn—AAAS—Ill Assn Applied Psychol—Ill State Acad Sci—Sigma Xi—Kappa Phi Kappa. Illinois Institute of Technology, Chicago 16.

20 KERRIGAN, (Thomas) Anthony. Spanish-American history; Spanish language; Japanese language. b'18. Student '42 (U Cal); '43-44 (U Mich); '48 (Columbia); '49 (U Havana); '50 (U Fla); '51 (U Barcelona). Translator (Barcia's Chronological History of Continent of Florida '51; Life and Times of Pedro Menendez '52; Lear in the Tropic of Paris '52. Translator Japanese US Army '42-45; ed and pub St Augustine Observer '49-50; translator St Augustine Hist Soc '47-50; translator U Fla since '51. Am Council Learned Soc F '42 for work in Chinese and Japanese. University of Florida Press, Gainesville, Fla.

21 KERSWILL, C(harles) James. Plankton of Great Lakes; Atlantic coast shellfish culture. b'12. BA '35—PhD '41 (U Toronto); MA '37 (U Western Ontario). Author articles in field. Asst prof zool U Western Ontario London Can '46-49; biol charge Atlantic Salmon invest Atlantic Biol Sta St Andrews since '49. Am Soc Limnol Oceanog—Nova Scotian Inst Sci. Atlantic Biological Station, St Andrews, N.B., Can.

22 KESCHNER, Moses. Neuropsychiatry; Medical jurisprudence. b'76. Student (Coll City NY); MD '99 (Columbia); LLB '09 (NY Law Sch). Simulation and study medicolegal aspects of injuries of skull, brain, and spinal cord; delegate to Governor's conference on crime; Dyskinesias, Tice's Practice of Medicine; mental symptoms in cases of brain tumor; the treatment of cerebral vascular lesions; effects of injuries, infections and pregnancy on the course of muliple sclerosis; neuropsychiatric aspects of drug addiction; encephalitic, idiopathic and arteriosclerotic parkinsonism; abnormal mental states encountered in a detention prison. Contributor: Simulation of Nervous and Mental Disease '40. Adjunct neurologist Mt Sinai Hosp NYC '20-31, asso neurologist '32-38; cons neurologist Montefiore Hosp NYC, also Sydenham and Maimonides hosps; med adv bd Nat Jewish Hosp Denver; former clin prof neurol Columbia U. Cons neuropsychiat Induction Sta NYC '44-46. AMA(F)—Am Neurological Assn—NY Acad Med (F, chem neurology and psychiat sect)—Med Soc NY—NY Neurological Soc (past pres)—Assn Research Nervous and Mental Disease—Eastern Med Soc (past pres)—NY Soc Clin Psychiat—Internat League Against Epilepsy—Am Acad Neur(F)—Am Psych Assn. Diplomate Am Bd Psychiat and Neurology. 451 West End Av., NYC 24.

23 KESLER, Carl Chambers. Carbohydrate chemistry; Starch; Paper; Textiles. b'97. AB '20 (Southwestern U); MS '22 (Ia State U); PhD '26 (U Pittsburgh). Holder several US and foreign patents. Author articles in field. With Penick and Ford since '26, research dir since '38. Am Chem Soc—Am Inst Chem—Chem Soc, London—Tech Soc Pulp and Paper Ind—Am Assn Textile Chem and Colorists. Penick and Ford, Inc., Cedar Rapids, Ia.†

10 KESLER, Thomas Lingle. Non-metallic mineral deposits; Appalachian metamorphic geology. b'08. BS '29—MS '30 (U NC). Author articles in field. Geol US Geol Survey Washington '36-46; geol Thompson Weinman & Co since '46. Geol Soc Am(F)—Soc Econ Geol (chief sect nonmetallic products '39-42, subcom for research nonmetallics since '46)—Am Inst Mining Metall Engrs—Am Geophys Union. P.O. Box 367, Cartersville, Ga.†

11 KESLING, Elmer Gilbert. Gear shifting mechanisms. b'81. DDS '03 (Chicago Coll Dental Surgery). Began designing and making gear shifts for automobiles '18, shifts were mechanically operated until '35, vacuum booster after '35. First patent on vacuum shift '36, holds 23 patents on gear shifting mechanisms and related devices. Practice dentistry Bloomfield Mo '05-41, Dexter Mo since '41. Citizens Bank Building, Dexter, Mo.

12 KESO, Edward Elmer. Political geography; Conservation of United States natural resources. b'00. BS '25 (Central Mo State Coll); MA '29—PhD '37 (Peabody Coll). Carrying on continuous series experiments soil conservation; drainage projects, soil improvement. Author: The Senatorial Career of Robert Lathan Owen '39; Conserving Our Resources '46. Author article: The Old and New Oil Field Community '39, and others. Asso prof geog and hist Central State Coll Okla '29-37, prof '37-40; asso prof geog Northeast Mo Teachers Coll '40-42; asst prof geog U Mo, and U Mo dir geog instruction Army AST Air Corps, Engrs, and area and lang programs '42-44; asso prof geog U Okla '44-46; prof geog, head dept geog Okla A&M Coll since '46. Nat Council Geog Teachers—Am Soc Profl Geog—SW Social Sci Assn—Nat Social Sci Council. Oklahoma A&M College, Stillwater, Okla.

13 KESTER, Ernest Bowman. Chemistry and technology of rice, minor vegetable oils, fatty acids, naphthalene, resins, and tar oils. b'97. BA '22—MS '23 (U Minn); PhD '27 (Northwestern U). Stabilization of rice by elimination of extractable oil present with light petroleum solvents; development new food uses for rice; investigation minor sources of vegetable oils in US; degradation cephalin fraction of dried egg powders found to be coincident with deterioration; synthesis of alpha, gamma mixed diglycerides by reacting glycidyl esters of fatty acid with dissimilar acid; devised technique for plasticizing vinyl resins with ether esters of fatty acid to give flexibility at low temperatures; developed method for removal tar acids from alkaline phenate solutions by solvent extraction; discovered means for reacting naphthalene formaldehyde resins with drying oils to give a product with low temperature susceptibility. Holds patents on process for preparation n-acylated derivatives of glutamic acid, extraction of phenols from caustic solutions, modifying naphthalene-formaldehyde resins with fatty oils, stabilizing brown rice by solvent extraction. Author article: Minor Oil Producing Crops of the United States '49. Co-author articles: (with C J Gaiser, M E Lazar) Glycidyl Esters of Aliphatic Acids '43; (with R L Roberts and others) Steam Blanching of Fresh Rough Rice Curbs Spoilage by Fatty Acids '49; (with I R Hunter and R L Roberts) Dimyristo and Eruco-Stearo-cephalin '48, and others. Research chem Sharp & Dohme Baltimore '26-28, Baltimore Gas Engring Corp Charleston WVa '28-30; sr chem in charge organic chem sect US Bur Mines Pittsburgh '30-33; Koppers Co

fellow for research on coal tar oils Mellon Inst Pittsburgh '33-39; in charge oils, fats and waxes sect Western Regional Research Lab '40-47, in charge rice utilization sect since '47. Am Oil Chem Soc—Inst Food Tech—ACS—Phi Beta Kappa—Sigma Xi—Phi Lambda Upsilon—Alpha Chi Sigma. Western Regional Research Laboratory, U.S. Department of Agriculture, Albany, Cal.†

14 KETCHAM, Charles Burgess. Liberal arts education; Education and religion. b'89. AB '13—DD '32 (Ohio Wesleyan U); BD '16 (Drew Theol Sem); AM '16 (Columbia); LLD '44 (Allegheny Coll). Ordained to Methodist Episcopal ministry '16; dir religious edn Trinity Ch Youngstown Ohio '16-17; prof English Bible Mt Union Coll '17-18; instr English Bible Drew Theol Sem '19-20; pastor ME Churches '20-37, dist supt Cleveland Dist ME Ch '37-38; pres Mount Union Coll Alliance O since '38. Chaplain US Army '18-19. Ohio Coll Assn (pres '46)—Nat Assn Schs and Colls Meth Ch (pres '46)—Ohio Edn Assn—Phi Beta Kappa—Pi Gamma Mu. Mount Union College, Alliance, O.©

15 KETCHUM, Bostwick Hawley. Marine microbiology; Oceanography. b'12. BA '34 (Bard Coll, Columbia); PhD '38 (Harvard). Research on nutrient cycles in the sea, marine fouling and antifoulding or ship bottom paints, marine microbiology and pollution. Author articles: (with A C Redfield, H P Smith) The Cycle of Organic Phosphorus in the Gulf of Maine '37; (with A C Redfield) A Method of Maintaining a Continuous Supply of Marine Diatoms by Culture '38; The Absorption of Phosphate and Nitrate by Illuminated Cultures of Nitzschia closterium '39; (with others) The Action of Antifouling Paints '48, and others. Asso marine biol Woods Hole Oceanog Inst '40-46, marine microbiol since '46. AAAS—Ecol Soc Am—Am Soc Limnol Oceanog—NY Acad Sci—Phi Beta Kappa—Sigma Xi. Woods Hole Oceanographic Institution, Woods Hole, Mass.

16 KETTELL, Russell Hawes. Early American furniture and architecture; Historic houses and museums. b'90. AB '14—MArch '19 (Harvard). Author: Pine Furniture of Early New England. Editor: Early American Rooms. Teacher fine arts Middlesex Sch Concord since '21. Soc Preservation NE Antiquities (trustee)—Walpole Soc. Middlesex School, Concord, Mass. H: 10 Eliot Rd., Lexington.

17 KETTERING, Charles Franklin. Automotive engineering; Automotive engine (Combustion, detonation, Starting, lighting, ignition); Industrial research (Administration). b'76. EE in ME '04 (O State U); DSc '28 (U Cincinnati) '32 (Brown U) '34 (Toledo U) '35 (Northwestern U) '36 (Lafayette Coll) '37 (NYU) '39 (Dartmouth Coll) '39 (Harvard); DEng '29 (O State U) '29 (U Mich) '30 (Brooklyn Poly Inst) '34 (U Detroit) '43 (Columbia) '45 (Syracuse U) '47 (Miami U) '47 (Princeton); DEng Research '43 (U Neb); LLD '43 (Antioch Coll) '45 (Temple U); Dr Humanities '46 (Wayne U). Invented automotive starting, lighting and ignitions systems; organized Dayton Engring Labs, Delco, for mfg these inventions; invented, perfected and marketed the Delco-Light for lighting farmhouses, etc.; organizer '14, The Dayton Metal Products Co, Dayton-Wright Airplane Co; former gen mgr research labs, vp Gen Motors Corp, now dir and research cons; chmn Nat Inventors Council, Dept of Commerce, Washington, and Nat Patents Planning Com-

mn. Nat Acad Scis(F)—Soc Automotive Engrs (past pres)—ASME—AIEE—Am Chem Soc—AAAS—Am Acad Scis—Am Soc Testing Materials—Am Soc for Metals—Am Phys Soc—Soc Mil Engrs—Engring Soc Detroit. Awarded Sullivant medal O State U, '29; medal U Cincinnati '30; medal Am Philos Soc '30; Washington award Four Founder Engring Socs and Western Soc Engrs '36; John Scott Memorial award Bd City Trusts of Phila '36; Franklin gold medal Franklin Inst '36; medal Coll of La '36; medal Am Club of Paris '37; French Legion of Honor '37; Order of La Couronne (French) '38; Order of Crown of Belgium '39; Modern Pioneer plaque Nat Assn Mfrs '30; hon F Internat Coll Dentists. H: Rideleigh Terrace, Dayton 9, O

18 KEUR, Dorothy Louise. Navaho Indians (Archaeology). b'04. BA '25 (Hunter Coll); MA '28—PhD '41 (Columbia). Excavations of one hundred house sites, sweat houses, walls, fortifications, and towers, northeastern and northwestern New Mexico. Author article: Big Bead Mesa—An Archeological Study of Navaho Acculturation '41. Contributor: American Antiquity '44. Faculty Hunter Coll since '26, chmn div anthrop '47-50, asso prof dept anthrop since '48. Am Anthrop Assn—Am Ethnol Soc (sectreas '47-49)—Soc Am Archeol. Hunter College, NYC 21.†

19 KEY, David Martin. History (Comedy, Ancient Greece, Rome). b'79. BA '98 (Central Coll Fayette Mo); MA '06 (Vanderbilt U); PhD '16 (U Chicago); LLD '26 (Emory U); teaching fellow Vanderbilt U '05-07. Studies origin and history Greek and and Latin comedy; origin and development literay forms in classical writers. Author: Introduction of Characters by Personal Names in Greek and Roman Comedy '17. Prof classics Pacific Methodist Coll Santa Rosa Cal '00-02, Morrisville Mo Coll '02-05; prof ancient langs Southern U '07-15; Millsaps Coll '15-22, pres '23-38, dean '38-39; prof classics Birmingham-Southern Coll '39-44, chmn humanities div '40-47; vis prof classics Mount Union Coll Alliance O since '47; mem exec com Research Commn State of Miss. Classical Assn—Middle West and South Classical League—Am Archaeol Assn—Am Philological Assn.

20 KEYES, Charles Reuben. Archeology of Iowa. b'71. BPh '94 (Cornell Coll); AM '98—PhD '23 (Harvard); '12-13 (U Munich, U Berlin). Author: Prehistoric Man in Iowa; Antiquities of the Upper Iowa; Minott's Rock Shelter; also articles in field. Lecturer in anthrop Cornell Coll since '41; research asso State Hist Soc Ia since '22; dir Ia State Archeol Survey since '22; visiting research prof anthrop U Ia since '44. Soc Am Archeol(F)—Ia Acad Sci—Central Sect Am Anthrop Assn (pres '26-27)—Wis Archeol Soc—Inter-Am Soc Anthrop Geog—Phi Beta Kappa. 323 10th Av., S., Mt. Vernon, Ia.©

21 KEYES, Donald Babcock. Chemical engineering (Distillation, partial oxidation). b'91. BS '13—DSc (hon) '46 (U NH); MA '14 (Columbia); PhD '17 (U Calif); DEng (hon) '47 (Stevens Inst Tech). Research on column design factors, third component distillation, catalysts for partial oxidation. Co-author: Chemical Engineers' Manual '42; also articles in field. Research chem engr US Indsl Chem Co and US Indsl Alcohol Co NYC '18-24, dir research and patent advice Baltimore '24-26; prof chem engring, head dept, mem exec staff engring expt sta U Ill '26-45; director Am Plastics Corp '46-'48; dir Am Potash and Chem Co '46-50; cons WPB '41-42, chief chem industries br Office Prodn Research and Development '43-44, dir '44-45, mem spl war missions England '43, '45; vp Heyden Chem Corp NYC since '45, dir since '46. AAAS(F)—Am Inst Chem (F)—Am Chem Soc—Am Electrochem Soc—Am Inst Chem Engrs—Ind Research Inst—Chem Warfare Assn—US Army Ordnance Assn—Sigma Xi. Heyden Chemical Corporation, 393 7th Av., NYC 1.⊙

10 KEYES, Harmon Edward. Hydrometallurgy of copper and zinc; Purification of water and sewage with iron salts; Ferric sulphate and sulphuric acid manufacture. b'92. Student '12-13 (MIT); BS '21—MS (chem engring) '22—ChemE '24 (U Wash). Research on overvoltage relations and electrolyte conductivity of electrolytic zinc process; developed, patented and applied improvements in copper recovery from low grade ores including dilute sulphuric acid production by autoxidation; developed and patented improvements in autoxidation process for ferric and ferrous sulphate production using curde sulphur and scrap iron with application to water and sewage purification at Phoenix; developed and applied test procedures for application of iron sulphate and sulphuric acid to correct alkalinity of desert soils; developed and patented process for regenerating steel plant pickling acid. Author article: Innovations in Copper Leaching (US Bur Mines bull Autoxidation Process). Research with Tainton Zinc & Lead Processes '20-24; asso metall US Bur Mines '24-27, cons metall '28; research metall to head research dept Miami Coper Co '30-37; cons on pickle liquor Carnegie-Illinois Steel Corp '39; cons chem and metall engr featuring copper hydromet and autoxidation process developments since '38; designed and placed in practical operation autoxidation plants City of Phoenix '47-50. Maj Chem Warfare Service '41-45; lt col Chem Corps US Army Res '45. Sigma Xi—Phi Lambda Upsilon—Tau Beta Pi—AIMME—Nat Soc Profl Engrs—ACS—Ariz Sewage and Water Works Assn—Am Water Works Assn—Fedn Sewage Works Assn. 2528 E. Monte Vista Dr., Tucson.

11 KEYS, Ancel. Cholesterol (In diet and blood); Obesity evaluation; Physiology (Conditioned reactions of human body); Nutrition (Human). b'04. MA '28—PhD '30 (U Cal); PhD '36 (Cambridge U). Member Food and Nutrition Board of National Research Council, chairman Food and Agriculture Organization Committee on Calories, panel member Research Development Board of Department of Defense, special consultant on foods to Secretary of War '41-44, member special advisory committee of War Claims Commission, expert panel member on nutrition of World Health Organization. Author: Biology of Human Starvation '50; also 200 articles in field. Lecturer Cambridge U '32-33; faculty Harvard '33-36; asst, asso prof biochem Mayo Found '36-37; with U Minn since '37, prof, dir lab physiol hygiene from '46. Am Physiol Soc—Am Pub Health Assn(F)—Am Soc Biol Chem—Soc Exptl Biol and Med—Am Heart Soc—Brit Nutrition Soc—Sigma Xi. Nat Research F '30-32. Received US Army-Navy Award Appreciation '47. Stadium Gate 27, University of Minnesota, Mpls 14.⊙

12 KIBRE, Pearl. Medieval history (Alchemy, medicine, libraries, universities, nations, Albertus Magnus, Pico della Mirandola). b'03. AB '24—MA '25 (Calif U); PhD '36 (Columbia). Research on manuscripts in medieval scientific and pseudo-scientific texts in European libraries, and at Vatican; studied alchemy in Middle Ages with emphasis on works attributed to Albertus Magnus, history of medicine and medieval libraries; member seminars on medieval university of Paris, intellectual history and history of science; studies on intellectual interests reflected in 14th and 15th century libraries, writings of Dominicus de Ragusa. Author: The Library of Pico della Mirandola '36; A Catalogue of Incipits of Medieval Scientific Writings in Latin (with Thorndike) '37; The Nations in the Medieval Universities '48; also articles in field. Research asst to Lynn Thorndike Columbia '29-37; temporary instr Hunter Coll '37-40, instr '39-44, asst prof since '44. Grant Am Council Learned Soc, NY Acad Sci. History Sci Soc—Medieval Acad Am—AHA—Phi Beta Kappa. Hunter College, 695 Park Av., NYC 21.

13 KIDDER, Allan H(ill). Power distribution. b'99. Student '18-20 (U Vt); BS (elec engring) '22— MS (elec engring) '23 (MIT). Research on distribution of electric power, load and construction forecasts, system planning as related to station, substation, and high tension line additions. With Phila Elec Co since '23, asst system development engr since '50. Am Inst EE (insulated conductor com)—Pa Soc Prof Engrs (nat dir)—Assn Edison Illuminating Co (cable engring sect). 900 Sansom St., Phila. 7.

14 KIDDER, George Wallace, Jr. Microbiology; Protozoology; Biochemistry (Tetrahymena). b'02. AB '26 (Ore U); MA '29 (Calif U); PhD '32 (Columbia). Research on morphology and mitosis of Streblomastix strix, conjugation, structure, neuromotor system, binary fission, macronuclear chromatin, and general growth of ciliates; studied nuclear reorganization without cell division in Paraclevelandia simplex, effects of conditioned media upon growth, reactions during feeding, techniques of protozoan culture control, biosynthesis of thiamine, strain differences, biochemistry and other factors in micro-organisms. Author articles: Studies on the Biochemistry of Tetrahymena (with V C Dewey) '47; Dietary Factors in the Utilization of Homocystine (with Dewey) '48, and others. Asst prof Brown U '37-46; asso prof biol Amherst Coll '46-49, now Stone prof biol; Marine Biolog Lab summers '35-40, mem corp. Am Soc Zool—Soc Development and Growth—AAAS—Sigma Xi—Am Soc Biol Chem—Am Acad Arts Sci (F). Biological Laboratory, Amherst College, Amherst, Mass.⊙

15 KIEFFER, Joseph Charles. Ore dressing; Mining of nonferrous metals. b'09. BS '35 (Wash State Coll). Operation ore dressing plants in Peru; management tungsten mine and ore dressing plant Argentina. Foreman Helca Mining Co '45-46; mgr Sunset Minerals Inc '46-48; mgr Spokane-Ida Mining Co, dir Callahan Consol Mines Inc since '48. AIMME—Ida Mining Assn—NW Mining Assn—Colo Mining Assn. Spokane-Idaho Mining Co., Box 930, Kellogg, Ida.

16 KIEKHOFER, William Henry. Economic theory; Finance. b'83. BA '04—LLD '36 (North Central Coll); PhD '13 (U Wis); '09-13 (U London, Berlin, Leipzig, U Wis). Editor: Century Studies in Economics (12 vols). Author: An Outline of Economics '30; Syllabus of Economic Theory '30; Economic Principles, Problems and Policies '36, '46, '51; Problems in Economics '37. Prof econ U Wis since '20; dir First Nat Bank Madison. Am Econ Assn (exec com '24-30)—Econ Nat Com Monetary Policy (exec com)—Am Polit Sci Assn—Am Statis Assn—Wis Acad Sci Arts Letters—Phi Beta Kappa—Phi Kappa Phi (pres Wis Branch '38-39). 1919 Arlington Pl., Madison 5, Wis.⊙

17 KIELY, Edmond R. History of surveying instruments and methods. b'99. BA '24 (St Mary's Coll); MA '26 (Fordham U); PhD '46 (Columbia). Author: Surveying Instruments, Their History and Classroom Use '47. Prof math Iona Coll since '40. Soc Promotion Engring Edn—Nat Council Teachers Math—Math Assn Am. Iona College, New Rochelle, N.Y.†

18 KIERAN, John Francis. American sports; Natural history. b'92. BS '12 (Fordham U). Author: Story of Olympic Games '36; Nature Notes '41. Co-author: We Saw It Happen '38; America Now '38; author articles in field. With NY Times sports dept '15-43; columnist NY Sun '43-44; member bd of experts radio program Information Please. 4506 Riverdale Av., NYC.

19 KIKER, John Ewing, Jr. Sewage (Subsurface disposal). b'06. Student '22-25 (Ga Tech Inst); BS '35 (MIT); M Civil Engring '41 (NYU). Research in economical design water, sewage, industrial waste treatment facilities. Author articles: Sewage treatment research; Subsurface sewage disposal; Rational design criteria for sewage absorption fields; Diatomite filters. Chem engr H C Nutting Co Cincinnati '25-30; san engr Internat Water Co Saigon Indo-China '30-35; dist san engr NY State Dept Health '36-47; asso prof pub health engring U Fla '47-49, prof since '49. Served as chief san engring sect Office Surgeon Gen Hdqrs 7th Service Command Omaha AUS '42-46. Am Soc CE—Nat Soc Profl Engrs—Am Pub Health Assn—Am Water Works Assn—Fedn Sewage and Indsl Wastes Assn—Am Soc Engring Edn. College of Engineering, University of Florida, Gainesville, Fla. H: 1515 N.W. 7th Pl.

20 KILDEE, Henry Herbert. Livestock (Feeding, breeding, judging, management); Land-use (Planning). b'84. BSA '08—MS '17 (Ia State Coll); Dr Agr '40 (ND State Coll). Served as member type and judging committee American Jersey Cattle Club, American Guernsey Cattle Club, Holstein-Friesian Association America; member committee appointed by American Farm Bureau Federation to make recommendations concerning livestock marketing. Author articles in field. Dean div agr Ia State Coll '33-49, dir ext service '46-49, dir agr expt sta '48-49; member board dir Internat Live Stock Exposition, Am Royal Live Stock and Horse Show. AAAS—Am Dairy Sci Assn—Am Soc Animal Prodn—Sigma Xi—Phi Kappa Phi—Gamma Sigma Delta (nat pres '44-46). Awarded gold medal Inter-collegiate Livestock Judging Contest, Internat Livestock Expn '08; gold medal and citation Am Farm Bureau Federation for dist service to Am agriculture '49. Ames, Ia.⊙

21 KILGORE, Lowell Berry. Chemical purification of air; Insecticides and insectifuges. b'01. AB '23—AM '25 (Oberlin Coll); PhD '31 (Johns Hopkins). Inventions include Indalone, synthetic topical anti-malarial; Valone pyrethrum synergist; sun-screens; antioxidants for edible oils; Metazene synthetic organic air deodorant. Author articles in field. Research dir Kilgore Development Corp Washington '35-47; economic analyst Staff War Requirements Com WPB Combined Raw Materials Bd; now chief Chemicals Div Office Domestic Commerce Department of Commerce. Indsl research fellow US Dept Agr '30-33. 3039 Davenport St., N.W., Washington 8.

10 **KILLEFFER, D(avid) H(erbert).** Solid carbon dioxide refrigeration. b'95. BS '15 (U NC). Granted 14 patents on solid carbon dioxide refrigeration. Author articles in field. Market ed Drug and Chemical Markets '20-22; asso ed Industrial and Engineering Chemistry '22-28, contributing ed '31-44; tech dir Dry Ice Corp Am '28-31; cons public relations since '31; contributing ed Scientific American '25-48; cons WPB '43-44. Am Chem Soc—Am Inst Chem Engrs—AAAS. 168 Westchester Av., Crestwood, N.Y.

11 **KILLINGER, Gordon B(everley).** Agronomy (Florida). BS '30—MS '31 —PhD '33 (Ia State Coll). Research on importance of minor elements in growing pasture plants on certain Florida soils, chufas and peanuts in Florida, winter oats as grazing for beef cattle. Soil specialist Soil Conservation Service Kan '34-36; soil scientist Clemson Coll '36-41; agron and prof agron Fla Agrl Expt Sta U Fla since '41. Gamma Sigma Delta— Alpha Zeta—Sigma Xi. Agronomy Department, University of Florida, Gainesville, Fla.†

12 **KILLINGSWORTH, Charles C(linton).** State labor relations (Acts, arbitration). b'17. BA '38 (Mo State Coll); MA '39 (Okla A&M Coll); PhD '47 (U Wis). Author: State Labor Relations Acts '48. Co-author: Trade Union Publications 1851-1941 (3 vols) '44-45; also articles in field. Asso prof econ Mich State Coll '47-49, prof and head dept since '49; arbitrator in approximately 450 labor-management disputes since '43; permanent umpire Bethlehem Steel Co and United Steel Workers Am since '47; panel chmn and spl hearing officer Nat War Labor Bd '43-46. Nat Acad Arbitrators—Indsl Relations Research Assn—Am Econ Assn. Department of Economics, Michigan State College, East Lansing, Mich.†☉

13 **KILLION, Carl Everest.** Bees (Diseases, breeding); Honey (Fancy comb, moisture removal); Nectar (Quality). b'99. Ed pub schs. Research on control of bee diseases, especially American foulbrood, on relation between type of soil and characteristics of nectar secreted by plants grown thereon; specialist in production of fancy comb honey and selective breeding of honeybees for comb building characteristics; developed new process for removal of moisture from comb honey. Author: Honey in the Comb '51. Co-author: Hive and Honey Bee (last edit) '49. Chief apiary insp Ill since '38; mgr Killion & Sons Apiaries since '44. Am Beekeeping Fedn (vp '47-49)—Apiary Insp Am '39-41)—North Central States Apiarists (sec-treas '40-41)—Ill State Beekeepers Assn—Am Honey Inst. 908 Marshall St., Paris, Ill.†

14 **KILPATRICK, William Heard.** Philosophy of education; Education (Process). b'71. AB '91—Am '92—LLD '26 (Mercer U); '91-92 '95-96 (Johns Hopkins); PhD '12—LittD '29 (Columbia); LLD '38 (Bennington Coll). Author: The Montessori System Examined '14; Froebel's Kindergarten Principles Critically Examined '16; Source Book in the Philosophy of Education '23 (rev edit) '34; Foundations of Method '25; Education for a Changing Civilization '26; Our Educational Task '30; Education and the Social Crisis '32; Remaking the Curriculum '36; Group Education for a Democracy '40; La Funcion social, cultural y docente de la escuela '40—Selfhood and Civilization '41. Co-author: (with

Mason Olcott) How We Learn '28. Co-author and editor: The Educational Frontier '33; Intercultural Attitudes in the Making '47; The Teacher and Society '37. Asso prof Tchrs Coll Columbia '15-18, prof philosophy of edn '18-38, emeritus prof since '38. Kappa Delta Pi. 106 Morningside Dr., NYC 27.☉

15 **KILPATRICK, Wylie.** Florida (Government finance); County government). b'96. AB '22 (Stanford); certificate '23 (Inst Pub Administration); MA '24 (Columbia); PhD '27 (Robert Brookings Grad Sch). Reporting procedures and specifications US Census Bureau, Nat Com on Municipal Accounting, Nat Com on Municipal Reporting; surveys of state supervision of local finance, Federal relation to urban government; county government, state and local debt. Author: Problems in Contemporary County Government; Public Reporting; State Supervision of Local budgeting; and others. Asso research prof U Va '27-29; staffs Federal agencies '33-39; '40-47, prof econ U NC '39-40, Duke '47-48, U Fla since '48. University of Florida, Gainesville, Fla. H: 707 Northwest 20th St.

16 **KILZER, Louis Rudolph.** Secondary education; Allied Activities (Extra-curricular). b'94. Student '11-15 (Peru (Neb) Normal Sch); AB '23 (Parsons Coll); AM '26—PhD '28 (U Ia). Chairman for Wyoming of North Central Association since '39, chairman committee on secondary-school relations since '39, member administrative committee '48-51. Author: Supervised Study '31; Standardized Test: The Mathematics Needed in High-School Physics '28. Co-author: High School Administration (with C R Maxwell) '36; (with Helen Carnine) A Book and Magazine List for Small High School Libraries '49. Mem adv bd School Activities mag since '40. University of Wyoming, Laramie, Wyo. H: 515 S. 12th St.☉

17 **KIMBALL, Chase.** International organizations; Human rights. b'02. BA '25—LLB '28—MA '47 (Yale); '49-50 (Fletcher Sch Law and Diplomacy). Study of Universal Declaration of Human Rights, international relations and organization. Planned and collaborated in writing Handbook on International Relations (author Marie J Carroll) '38, supplement editor '39. Law clerk to War Claims Arbiter '28-29; asst prof internat relations U Denver '47; asst prof govt Boston U since '47. Am Soc Internat Law—Am Polit Sci Assn—Internat Law Assn. Department of Government, Boston University, 236 Bay State Rd., Boston.

18 **KIMBALL, Fiske.** History of art and architecture; Restoration of historic American homes. b'88. AB '09—MArch '12 (Harvard); PhD '15 (U Mich); Dr Fine Arts '33 (NYU); Dr Fine Arts '45 (U Pa). Engaged in restoration of important American houses, among them Monticello and home of Robert E Lee, mansions of Fairmount Park Philadelphia; advisory board restoration of Williamsburg; advisory board National Park Service since '35. Author: Domestic Architecture of the American Colonies '22; American Architecture '28; The Creation of the Rococo '43; (with G H Edgell) A History of Architecture '18; (with L Venturi) Great Masterpieces of Painting in America '48. Editor: Foundations of Classic Architecture '19. Asst prof architecture and fine arts U Mich '12-19; prof art and architecture U Va '19-23; Morse prof lit arts of design, in charge dept Fine Arts NYU '23-25; dir Phila Mus Art since '25; served on editorial bds several profl archtl publications; in

charge Amt sect Allgemeines Knustler Lexikon '20-26; chmn Va Art Commn '20-23. Holder Sachs Research Fellowship '16-17. AIA (F, past pres Va chapter)—Am Assn Mus (past pres) —Assn Art Mus Dir—Am Philos Soc— Phi Beta Kappa. Philadelphia Museum of Art, Fairmount, Phila. 30.☉

19 **KIMBALL, James Wilson.** Ringnecked pheasant; Wildlife management. b'12. BS '39 (Minn U). Research on game and habitat development, on small game and fur-bearers, and on pheasant food habits, populations, ecology, life history, census, relationship to agriculture, and management. Author articles in field. Coordinator Pittman Robertson Projects since '47. Wildlife Soc. Department of Game, Fish and Parks, Pierre, S.D. H: 114 S. Jefferson.

20 **KIMBALL, Leo Barnum.** Gas turbines; Jet propulsion. b'96. Student '16-17 (Carnegie Inst Tech). Pres, chief engr Kimball Aircraft Corp '27-30; vp, dir research Fuel Development Corp NYC '31-40; sr engr Nat Bur Standards Washington on NACA Power Plants Subcom Project '40-43; chief engr Spl Projects Div Commonwealth Aviation Inc '44-46. Inst Aeronautical Sci (asso F)—Royal Aeronautical Soc (asso F)—SAE. 286 Pacific St., Stamford, Conn.

21 **KIMBALL, Richard Fuller.** Genetics of the ciliate Protozoa (Radiation effects, mating types, cytoplasmic inheritance); Genetics; Protozoology. b'15. AB '35—PhD '38 (Johns Hopkins U). Author articles: Change of Mating Type During Vegetative Reproduction in Paramecium Aurelia '39; Double Animals and Amicronucleate Animals in Euplotes Patella with Particular Reference to Their Conjugation '41; The Nature and Inheritance of Mating Types in Euplotes Patella '42; Mating Types in the Ciliate Protozoa '43; The Induction of Inheritable Modification in Reaction to Antiserum in Paramecium Aurelia '46, and others. Instr Johns Hopkins U '39-43; asst prof '43-47; si biol Oak Ridge Nat Lab since '47. AAAS—Am Soc Naturalists—Am Soc Zool—Genetics Soc Am—Soc Study Evolution—Phi Beta Kappa—Sigma Xi. Awarded grant-in-aid Cancer Soc Am '46-47; Sterling fellow Yale '38-39. Biology Division, Oak Ridge National Laboratory, Oak Ridge, Tenn.

22 **KIMBERLY, Arthur Evarts.** Paper chemistry; Documents (Preservation). b'05. BS (Chem) '26—MS '28 (George Washington U); '27-28 (NY U). Research on causes of deterioration of paper and methods for preservation paper records; discovery lamination process for reinforcement and preservation fragile or deteriorated records; development methods for reinforcement and preservation of records in quantity; examination questioned and illegible documents; devised equipment for examination of captured enemy documents in combat areas, and developed methods for training of personnel in its use; survey Philippine archives surviving Japanese occupation; design low-cost fire-resistant document container; development standards and criteria for bulk record storage, priority system for rehabilitation of federal archives, supervision security and preservation measures for documents on the Freedom Train. Author articles: The Vacuum Fumigation of Archives '40; Archival Enemies '48; New Developments in Record Containers '50, and others. Co-author article: (with A L Emley) A Study of the Removal of Sulphur Dioxide from Library Air '33, and others. NRC research asso Nat Bur Standards '29-33; chem Dennison Mfg

Co '34-35; chief preservation services br Nat Archieves '35-42, chief archivist since '46. Examination of captured enemy documents Air Force AUS '42-46. Indian Hist Records Commn—Nat Fire Protection Assn. National Archives, Washington.†

10 KIMMERLE, Marjorie M. American dialect and folklore; Norwegian-American surnames. AB '28—MA '31 (Radcliffe Coll); PhD '38 (U Wis). Research in folk sayings, dialect words. Author articles in field. Instr U Colo '39-42, asst professor '42-51, associate professor since '51. Norwegian-American Hist Soc—Linguistic Soc Am—Am Dialect Soc—Am Folklore Soc—Mod Lang Assn—Rocky Mt Mod Lang Assn—Boulder Hist Soc—State Hist Soc Colo. Department of English, University of Colorado, Boulder, Colo.

11 KIMMEY, James William. Forest pathology and management; Forest products deterioration. b'07. BSF '31 —MS '32—McDonald fellow '31-32 (Ore State Coll); PhD '40 (Yale). Research on defects in airplane woods, deterioration of fire-killed timber, white pine blister rust, wood products decay in wooden ships, substructures defense housing, other wood products; presently in charge extended study to determine cull factors for all forest tree species in California. With US Dept Agr since '28, now path. AAAS(F)— Soc Am Foresters—Am Phytopath Soc —AFA. 720 Appraisers Building, San Francisco 11.†

12 KINCAID, Charles Morison. Animal breeding (Genetics); Beef cattle, sheep, swine (Inheritance and production problems); Pasture fertilization. b'02. BS '25—MS '37 (Va Poly Inst); PhD '46 (Ia State Coll). Research on pastures for cattle and sheep, pasture utilization by beef cattle and sheep, production of beef cattle and sheep, inheritance of certain characteristics, particularly vitality and fertility in swine, development of inbred lines of sheep. Author articles in field. Asst animal husbandman Va Poly Inst '37-42; research asso Ia State Coll '43-45; asso animal husbandman Va Poly Inst '46-47, research prof animal husbandry since '48. Am Soc Animal Prodn—Genetics Soc Am—Va Acad Sci—Am Statis Inst—Sigma Xi. Animal Husbandry Department, Virginia Agricultural Experiment Station, Blacksburg, Va.†

13 KINCAID, Randall Rich. Tobacco disease. b'03. BS '25 (Southeast Mo State Teachers Coll); MA '29—PhD '34 (U Mo). Author articles in field. Asst plant path, later plant path N Fla Expt Sta since '29. Am Phytopath Soc (pub relations com)—AAAS(F). North Florida Experiment Station, Quincy, Fla.†

14 KINCHEN, Oscar Arvle. British colonial history; Canadian history; Oklahoma history. b'89. BA '16—MA '20 (U Okla); PhD '34 (U Ia); grad study (Stanford U, U Chicago). Author: Lord Russell's Canadian Policy '45; also articles in field. Asso prof, prof Brit hist Tex Tech Coll since '29. Can Hist Assn—AHA—Okla Hist Assn —West Tex Hist Soc. Department of History, Texas Technological College, Lubbock, Tex.

15 KINDIG, Richard Heath. Locomotive and train photography; Railroad history (Western United States). b'16. Ed public schools. Has collection of locomotive and train photographs including over 6000 negatives with information on each one, has assembled library relating to railroad photography, railroad history and technical information about locomotives and trains; compiling a history and com-

plete roster of all locomotives ever owned by Denver & Rio Grande Western Railroad. Author: My Best Railroad Photographs '48; photographs used by various books and magazines. With Western Elec Co Denver since '36. 3831 Perry St., Denver 12.†

16 KING, Clyde Burdette. US Revolution (North Carolina); Meriwether Lewis (US history); Mound builders (Ohio); Mollusks (Ohio). b'05. BA '30 (N Central Coll); '32 (U NC). Research on Revolutionary War battles in North Carolina, Ohio mound builders and Ohio mollusks as related to mound builders. Supt Moores Creek Nat Mil Park '35-41, Meriwether Lewis Nat Monument '43-46, Mound City Group Nat Monument since '46. Pi Gamma Mu—O State Archeol and Hist Soc. Mound City Group National Monument, Postoffice Box 332, Chillicothe, O.

17 KING, Dale Franklin. Poultry husbandry. b'06. Student '23-25 (U Ida); BS '28 (Ore State Coll); MS '29 (Kan State Coll). Inventor of fertel-egg machine patented '37. Author: Poultry Production in the South; Poultry Handbook For the Southern States; also articles in field. Head dept poultry husbandry Ala Poly Inst since '47. Worlds Poultry Sci Assn—Am Poultry Sci Assn—So Agrl Workers Assn. Alabama Polytechnic Institute, Poultry Department, Auburn, Ala.†

18 KING, John E(thelbert), Jr. Rural education (Undeveloped countries). b '13. AB '32 (Tex State Coll); MS '37 (U Ark); PhD '41 (Cornell). Member 1952 yearbook committee, rural division National Education Association. Research asst rural edn Cornell '37-38; prin Dwight Indian Sch Vian Okla '38-40; sput Tucson Indian Sch '41-43; asst prof rural edn and dir extra mural studies Cornell '45-47; academic dean and prof rural edn U Minn Duluth br since '47, acting provost '50-51, provost since '51. 2007 E. First St., Duluth 5, Minn.†☉

19 KING, Helen Martin (Mrs. Harry King). Hooked rugs. b'95. Student '12-13 (Ark Coll); '15-16 (Cincinnati Conservatory of Music); '15-16 (O Mechanical Inst); '16 (Sophie Newcomb Coll). Private research on hooked rugs and designs '38-49. Author articles: How to Hook Rugs '48; The Art and History of Hooked Rugs '40. Instr rug hooking Ark Coll '48-49. Nat League of American Pen Women. 255 North 8th St., Batesville, Ark.†

20 KING, Herman Lee. Insecticides; Entomology. b'15. BS '39 (Mich State Coll); MS '40—PhD '42 (Pa State Coll). Research on phytocidal effects of certain tar oil fractions, relation between chemical constitution and insecticidal properties in certain N-heterocyclic compounds; studies on toxicology and use of new insecticides, insect control. Author articles: Mercury Substitutes for Cabbage Maggot Control (with Dills and Frear) '44; A New Classification System for Chemical Compounds (with Frear and Seiferle) '46; The Control of Red-Banded Leaf-Roller with Parathion '48, and others. Student asst entomol Mich State Coll '38-39, ext specialist entomol '45-46, asso prof since '50; instr research staff Pa State Coll '43; fruit farm mgr '44. Am Assn Econ Entomol—AAAS—Sigma Xi —Phi Kappa Phi—Mich Insecticide-Fungicide Inst—Mich Hort Soc. Research fellow sponsored by Reilly Tar and Chem Co, in agr and biol chem Pa State Coll '39-42. Department of Entomology, Michigan State College, East Lansing, Mich.†

21 KING, James Ferguson. Latin American history (History of Negro in

Spanish America, Vice-royalty of New Granada). b'13. BA '34 (Minn U); MA '35—PhD '39 (Calif U). Research in archives of Brazil, Venezuela, Colombia; delegate of University of California to first consultative meeting of Commission on History, Pan-American Institute of Geography and History, Mexico City '47; managing editor Hispanic American Historical Review '45-49. Author articles: The Evolution of the Free Slave Trade Principle in Spanish Colonial Administration '42; The Latin American Republics and the Suppression of the Slave Trade '44; The Negro in Continental Spanish America: A Select Bibliography '44, and others. Teaching fellow U Calif '35-37, asst prof '44-47, asso prof since '47; instr Northwestern U '41-43, asst prof '43-44; asso div asst Dept State Div Am Republics '40-41. Phi Beta Kappa—Phi Alpha Theta— AHA—Latin-Am Conf AHA—Rockefeler Found traveling fellow '37-38; Panama Pacific Internat Expn fellow in Pacific coast hist U Calif '38-39. Department of History, University of California, Berkeley 4.

22 KING, John Albert. Organic chemistry (Willgerodt reaction, reaction mechanisms, synthetic medicinals, penicillin, aminoacids). b'16. Student '33-35 (Wabash Coll); AB '38 (Ind U); MS '40—PhD '42—DuPont grad fellow '41-42—Merck post doctorate fellow '42-43 (U Minn). Holder US patents on production and preparation of amides, co-holder US patent on process of making heterocyclic compounds. Author articles in field. Dir organic research Warner Inst Therapeutic Research NYC since '46. Am Chem Soc—NY Acad Sci—Am Inst Chem(F)—Chem Soc, London—Sigma Xi. Warner Institute for Therapeutic Research, 113 W. 18th St., NYC 11. H: 9 Ridge Circle, Manhasset, L.I.

23 KING, John Wesley. Biology; Plant pathology; Genetics. b'14. BS '36 (Tuskegee Inst); MLitt '44—PhD '46 (U Pittsburgh). Research on transmission of asters yellows virus Cuscuta campestris. Author articles in field. Prof biol Morgan State Coll since '46. AAAS—Am Phytopath Soc —Sigma Xi. Morgan State College, Baltimore.

24 KING, Philip Burke. Structural geology. b'03. BA '24—MS '27 (U Ia); PhD '29 (Yale). Delegate representing Geological Society of America on executive board of American Geological Institute '48-50. Author: Permian of West Texas and Southeastern New Mexico '43. Editor: Tectonic Map of the United States '44; also articles in field. Geol US Geol Survey since '30, charge tectonic investigations since '48; rep Am Assn Petroleum Geol on div geol and geog Nat Research Council, mem exec com '46-49; supervised preparation terrain diagrams and physiographic maps Mil Geol Unit Geol Survey for Crops Engrs US Army '43-46. Am Assn Petroleum Geol (research com)—Geol Soc Am—Am Geog Soc—Am Geophys Union—Geol Soc Wash—Tenn Acad Sci. United States Geological Survey, Gatlinburg, Tenn.

25 KING, Ralph T. Vertebrate populations; Wildlife management. b'00. BS '24—MA '25 (U State Agrl Coll); '25-29 (U Minn). Research on cycles in game production, bird banding, essentials of wild life range, upland game. Author: Forest Zoology and Its Relation to a Wildlife Program '42; also articles in field. Dir Roosevelt Wildlife Forest Expt Sta since '37; head dept forest zool NY State Coll Forestry since '37. Wildlife Soc (past pres)—Soc Am Foresters (sr)—AAAS (F)—Wilderness Soc—Phi Kappa Phi

—Sigma Xi—Xi Sigma Pi—Ecol Soc Am. Research fellow econ zool U Minn '29-32. New York State College of Forestry, Syracuse 10, N.Y.†

10 KING, Richard. Acid-proof construction; Industrial floors. b'01. CE '22 (Poly Inst Brooklyn). Chief engr Kayel Engring Co Newark NJ since '38. Nat Assn Profl Engrs. Kayel Engineering Co., 211 Sussex Av., Nwark 4.†

11 KING, Robert Maynard. Ceramic engineering; Porcelain enamels; Refractories. b'93. BA in chem '16 (U Tex); MSc in ceramic engring '23 (O State U). Research on refractories, adherence of porcelain enamels to metals, enamels for heat resisting alloys, architectural application of enamles. Author articles in field. With O State U since '27, prof since '44. Am Ceramic Soc—Am Chem Soc—Sigma Xi. Ohio State University, Columbus 10, O.†

12 KING, Robert Roy. Edible and fatty oils. b'09. BS '31 (Ia State Coll). Study in hydrogenation, deodorization, refining, bleaching oils; engineering administration. Author articles in field. Holds several patents in field. With Procter and Gamble '31-36; Mrs Tucker's Foods Inc Sherman Tex since '36, now tech dir and exec. Am Oil Chem Soc (pres '45)—Tex State Soc Profl Engrs (dir). Mrs. Tucker's Foods, Inc., Sherman, Tex.

13 KING, Willard Leroy. American legal history (Supreme Court, Chief Justice Melville W Fuller). b'93. Student '12-14 (Knox Coll); PhB '16—JD '17 (Chicago U); DCL hon '51 (Bowdoin Coll). Author: (biographies) Melville Weston Fuller '50; Justice David Davis (in prep). Co-author: Law of Opinion Evidence in Illinois; also articles in field. Lawyer Rosenthal, King & Robin Chicago since '26. Am Bar Assn—Ill State Bar Assn—Ill State Hist Soc—Order of Coif. 105 W. Monroe St., Chgo†◎

14 KING, William N(elson). Small arm ammunition. b'07. BS '30 (Hamline U); MS '32 (U Neb). Developed stable non-corrosive primer mixture based on basic lead styphnate for 4.2 chemical mortar and other ammunition, and method of manufacturing steel cases for 30 caliber ammunition for government during World War II. Holder patents in field. Small arms ammunition mfr since '33; tech dir Fed Cartridge Corp Anoka Minn since '44; industry cons Chief Ordnance US Army on small arms ammunition. Small Arms and Ammunition Mfrs Inst (mem tech com). Federal Cartridge Corp., Anoka, Minn.

15 KING, Willis. Fish biology and management; Herpetology. b'08. BS '29 (Wilmington Coll); MA '30 (Haverford Coll); PhD '39 (U Cincinnati). Assisted in supervising wildlife projects throughout southeastern states '34-40; organized and developed freshwater fish program for North Carolina. Author: Important Food and Game Fishes of North Carolina '47; also articles in field. Asst wildlife tech Great Smoky Mt Nat Park '34-40; fish biol NC Div Game and Inland Fisheries '40-44, prin fish biol '46-47; administrative asst NC Wildlife Resources Commn '48 to '49; Tennessee Game and Fish Commn chief of fish management since '50. Internat Association Game Fish and Conservation Commrs—Am Fisheries Soc—Wildlife Soc—Am Soc Ichthyologists Herpetol—Sigma Xi. Commission of Game and Fish, Nashville, Tenn.†

16 KINGMAN, Margaret Mace. Cartography; Speleology. b'12. AB '34—

AM '35—student '37-38 (Radcliffe Coll); '41-42 (O State U); since '47 (Am U, Washington). Constructed Azimuthal Equidistant Projection based on Cambridge (Massachusetts) in collaboration with William Howells, exhibited International Geography Congress, Poland '34; participated in exploration and mapping of Shenandoah Caverns. Collaborator with R Buckminster Fuller on Dymaxion Globe, patented '46. Author articles in field; maps published professional journals. Cartographer map br Geog Div OSS Washington '42-45, Dept State '45-48; detailed to Joint Chiefs Staff '43 as chief cartographer Joint Intelligence Study Pub Bd. AAAS—Am Congress Surveying Mapping—Am Geog Soc—Am Geophys Union—Am Polar Soc—Am Soc Photogrammetry—Am Soc Prof Geog—Internat Geog Cong—Soc Woman Geog—Nat Speoleological Soc. Joint Intelligence Study Publishing Board, Room 2402, Temporary L Building, Washington.†

17 KINGSLAKE, Rudolf. Lenses (Design). b'03. BSc '24—MSc '26—DSc '50 (London U Eng). Research on aberrations and properties of lenses, and on lens testing. Author: Lenses in Photography '51. Author articles: Refractometer for the Near Infrared '37; Design of Wide Aperture Photographic Objectives '40; Classification of Photographic Lens Types '46; Diffraction Study of Elementary Coma Image '48, and others. Optical designer Grubb-Parsons Co Newcastle Eng '27-28; asst prof optics U Rochester NY '27-38; optical designer Eastman Kodak Co since '38, head dept since '39. Optical Soc Am (pres '47-49)—Phys Soc London—Soc Motion Picture and Television Engrs (chmn optics com). Eastman Kodak Co., Hawkeye Works, Rochester, N.Y.†

18 KING-SMITH, August. Vocal development: Singing. b'82. Student '01-03 (U WVa); Artists diploma '05 (U Mich Sch Music). Composer songs and religious music. Tchr organ U Mich Sch Music Ann Arbor '05-07; student and organist Paris France '07-10; tchr and dir music orgns Chattanooga Tenn '10-13; tchr voice Institut Internat des Science des Arts Paris '13-14; organist and choir dir Am Ch Paris '13-14; dir The New King-Smith Sch (profl sch of arts) Washington since '18. Am Guild Organists—Am Nat Music Tchrs Assn. Courtyard 2118 Massachuesetts Av. N.W., Washington. H: Fairfax, Va.†◎

19 KINGSTON, Benson M(edill). Oil and gas wells; Oil and gas (North central Texas). b'09. Student '26-28 (U Tex); '28-30 (U Okla). Invented and developed electrical equipment for surveying oil and gas wells for determining relative permeabilities of rock strata to liquids; invented electrical signaling equipment which aids injection of electrolyte into selected stratum when chemicals are pumped into well; co-inventor of chemical solvent for removal of drilling fluids from permeable rock strata penetrated by oil and gas wells; designed equipment for testing samples of rock strata penetrated by wells to determine capacity to produce oil, gas, or water, and possibility of increasing production by injecting chemicals; well drilling and petroleum production statistics on North central Texas. Author: Acidizing Handbook (2d edit) '46. Treatment engr Oil Well Chem Co '33-38; treatment engr, lab chief Chem Process Co (div Ind E Torpedo Co) '38-46, chief engr since '46. AIM ME—Am Petroleum Inst—Am Assn Petroleum Geol (asso mem). Box 831, Breckenridge, Tex. H: 700 W. Hullum St.

20 KINIERY, Paul. History of early New York state. b'00. BA '24 (St Francis Coll); MA '26—PhD '30 (U Wis). Member editorial board Mid-America. Author article: Efforts of Religious Groups to Maintain Peace in Early New York '34; and others. Asst prof hist Loyola U Chicago '29-32, asso prof '32-35, prof since '35, asst dean grad sch since '31. AHA—Am Cath Hist Assn—So Hist Assn. 820 N. Michigan Av., Chicago 11.◎

21 KINIETZ, W(illiam) Vernon. Ethno-history of Great Lakes Indians. b'07. AB '28 (U Mich); MA '30 (U Chicago). Author: Indians of the Western Great Lakes '40; John Mix Stanley and His Indian Paintings '42; Delaware Culture Chronology '46; Chippewa Village '47. Co-author: Shawnese Traditions '39. Editor: Mearmear Traditions —Account of Delaware Indians '38; also articles in field. With Mus Anthrop U Mich as cataloguer '26-27, asst '27-28, curator '28, research asso '35-44; asst in charge field work Ill archeol explorations U Ill '30-32; office mgr Agrl Lab Anaheim Calif since '44. Box 522, Anaheim, Calif. H: 11552 Orangethorpe, Fullerton.

22 KINNAIRD, Lawrence. Mississippi Valley (Spanish influences). b'93. AB '15 (U Mich); grad student '19 (U Grenoble France); MA '27—PhD '28 (U Cal). Cultural attache US Embassy Santiago Chile '42-45; chairman US delegation Fourth Inter-American Congress of Teachers Santiago '43. Editor: Spain in the Mississippi Valley (3 vol) '45. Asst prof hist San Francisco State Coll '32-34, asso prof '34-36; asst prof Coll Agr U Cal '36-37, asst and asso prof hist '37-48; prof hist U Cal since '48. H: 1541 Hawthorne Terrace, Berkeley 8, Cal.

23 KINNEY, Selwyne Perez. Iron (Metallurgy). b'90. BS (Chem E) '15 —BS '17 (U Utah). Development and application of exploratory field equipment for use in measurement flow of stock, temperature, composition, and velocity of gases in shaft of the iron blast furnaces; consultant design, manufacture, and construction iron blast furnace equipment. Holds patents on blast furnace stoves, gas washers. Author articles: Composition of Materials from Various Elevations in an Iron Blast Furance '26; Relation of Carbon Consumption to Material Smelted in the Blast Furnace '26; Effect of Sized Ore on Blast-Furnace Operation '30, and others. Co-author articles: (with Ralph H Sweetser) Modern Blast Furance Theory and Practice '29; (with A J Boynton) Notes on the Development of the Iron Blast Furnace '35, and others. S. P. Kinney Engineers, Inc., 201 Second Av., Carnegie, Pa. H: 14 Creighton Av., Pitts 5.

24 KINSEY, Alfred Charles. Human sex behavior. b'94. BS '16 (Bowdoin); ScD '20 (Harvard). Author: An Introduction to Biology '26; Field and Laboratory Manual in Biology '27; The Gall Wasp Genus Cynips—A Study in the Origin of Species '30; New Introduction to Biology '38; Workbook in Biology '34; The Origin of Higher Categories in Cynips '36; Methods in Biology '37; Sex Behavior in the Human Male (with W B Pomeroy and C E Martin) '47. Prof zool Ind U since '29, also Waterman research asso; charge study on human sex behavior supported jointly by Ind U, Rockefeller Found and Nat Research Council since '38. AAAS—Am Entomol Soc—Assn Economic Entomol—Am Soc Geneticists—Am Soc Naturalists (sec since '41)—Am Zool Soc—Am Iris Soc—Phi Beta Kappa. 1320 E. First St., Bloomington, Ind.◎

10 KIRALFY, Alexander. Military, air, and naval strategy. b'99. Student various schs and colls, pvt studies. Research on critical analysis of historical and contemporary general and national strategy, also on interrelations of politics, diplomacy, philosophy, and psychology with national strategy; developed theories that pincer movements are basis of success in land warfare, that true sea power consists of major amphibious operation; studied influences of national philosophic and psychological orientations (such as democracy) upon national strategic policies. Author: Victory in the Pacific '42. Contributor to symposiums: Makers of Modern Strategy '43; Brassey's Naval Annual '42; Warships of the World '44, '45; also articles in field. Mil analyst Asia Mag '38-44, Flying Age '44-45; writer. Am Soc Naval Engrs—US Naval Inst—Soc Am Mil Engrs. 1375 Grand Concourse, NYC 52.

11 KIRBY, Chester H. History of nineteenth century England; English social history and game laws. b'99. AB '21—MA '23 (U Ia); MA '24—PhD '29 (Harvard). Research in England '26-27, '32, '38. Author: The English Country Gentleman '37. Author articles: The Attack on the English Game Laws in the Forties '32: The Literary History of English Field Sports, 1671-1850 '41; The English Game Law System '33, and others. With Brown U since '27, asso prof since '45. AHA. Brown University, Providence 12.

12 KIRCHER, Charles E(dmund), Jr. Plant and process development (Animal and vegetable oil extraction, solvents, acetates, alcohols). b'08. BS '31—MS '33 (Calif Inst Tech); PhD '38—'39-40 (Ia State Coll). Research on start-up, initial operation of new process involving catalytic gas phase reactions; experiments on solvent extraction of animal, vegetable oils; work on design, erection, operation solvent extraction plants, and on processes and equipment for production polyvinyl acetates, alcohols, plutonium. Holds patent on equipment and process for solvent extraction pilot plant. With DuPont Co '33-45, tech supervisor '44-45; research engr U Chicago Manhattan Project '43-44; prof, head chem engring dept Rose Poly Inst Terre Haute Ind since '47. Am Inst Chem Engrs—Am Soc Engring Edn—AAAS—AAUP—Tau Beta Pi—Sigma Xi—Phi Lambda Upsilon. Rose Polytechnic Institute, Terre Haute, Ind.†

13 KIRK, Roy Charles. Primary batteries; Electrothermics; Corrosion; Magnesium chemistry. b'08. BS '33—MS '34—PhD '36 (Wash State Coll). Research on electrothermic reduction of magnesium, thermal reduction of sodium, chemical uses of magnesium, corrosion and primary batteries. Holder ten patents relating to thermal methods of producing magnesium and sodium metals. Author articles in field. Research in magnesium labs Dow Chemical Co Midland Mich since '37. Am Chem Soc—Electrochem Soc —Sigma Xi—Phi Beta Kappa—Phi Kappa Phi. Dow Chemical Co., Midland, Mich.†

14 KIRKENDALE, George A(lderson). Structural clay products; Clay brick and tile. b'07. BASc '34 (U Toronto). Author articles in field. Ceramic engr Nat Sewer Pipe Co Ltd Can '36-39; ceramic engr Fed Dept Mines Can '39-47; asso prof ceramic engring NY State Coll Ceramics Alfred U since '47. Am Ceramic Soc—Can Ceramic Soc—Am Soc Engring Edn. New York State College of Ceramics, Alfred, N.Y.†

15 KIRKHAM, Don. Soil physics (Moisture); Drainage of land; Ground water movement. b'08. Student '25-27

(U Utah); BA '33—MA '34—PhD '38 (Columbia). Research on theory of ground water movement and sedimentation in streams, artificial drainage systems for soils, determination of soil permability to water, movement of air in soils. Author articles: Drainage of Land over an Impervious Layer '48; Field Method for Measurement of Water Permeability of Soil Below Water Table '45, and others. Instr, asst prof physics and math Utah State Coll '37-40; asst hydraulic engr Soil Conservation Service US Dept Agr '40; physicist atom bomb Bikini test '46; research prof soil physics Ia State College since '49. Am Phys Soc—Am Geophys Union (mem com physics of soil moisture since '46)—Soil Sci Soc Am—Am Soc Agron—Ia Acad Sci—Sigma Xi. Iowa State College, Ames, Ia.

16 KIRKHAM, Virgil Raymond Drexel. Economic geology: Stratigraphy; Paleography. b'94. BS '20 (U Wash); MS '22 (U Ida); PhD '30 (U Chicago). Discoverer number of oil pools, chiefly in Michigan; technical expert on exploration for war minerals for various government agencies '42; member Michigan State Petroleum Industris Commission; representative to Governors of oil states code hearing '33; chairman Michigan committee for oil control legislation; survey petroleum resources. Author bulletins. articles: Petroleum Possibilities of Certain Anticlines in South East Idaho '22; Geology and Oil Possibilities of Bingham, Bonneville and Caribou Counties Idaho '24; Geology and Ore Deposits of Boundary County, Idaho '24; Snake River Downwarp '31; Phosphate Deposits of Idaho and their Relation to World Supply; Igneous Geology of Southwestern Idaho '31; Revision of the Payette and Idaho Formations '31; Geology of Natural Gas—A Symposium by Am Assn Petroleum Geologists. Contributor: Physiography of Western United States '35. Asst prof geol Sch Mines U Ida '20-29; cons geol oil and mining since '20; chief geol numerous oil and mining companies '29-43; chief geol, pres and dir Geophys Prospecting Corp Detroit '38-41. Hard Rock Drilling Co Grand Rapids since '38. Independent Petroleum Assn (dir, mem constitution and oil control coms)—NY Acad Sci—Am Meteorol Soc—Am Soc Mil Engrs—AI MME——Am Geog Soc—Am Mining Congress—Ill Acad Sci—Mich Acad Sci—Geol Soc Am(F)—AAAS(F) —Internat Geol Congress—Am Assn Petrol Geol—Northwest Sci Assn (past sec)—Oil and Gas Assn Mich (dir and vp)—Sigma Zi. H: S. 148 Coeur d'Alene, Spokane 43, Wash.

17 KIRKLAND, Edwin Capers. Tennessee folklore and folksongs. b'02. BA '22 (Wofford Coll); MA '24 (Vanderbilt U); PhD '34 (Northwestern U). Collected American folksongs in Tennessee '36-40; attended Folklore Institute America '46; research on effect of oral tradition of Robin Hood and Little John; compiled check-list of Tennessee folksongs. Author articles in field. Professor Eng U Fla since '51. Modern Lang Assn (chmn popular lit sect)—Am Folklore Soc (council)—SE Folklore Soc (mnging ed Southern Folklore Quarterly, past pres)—Tenn Folklore Soc (past pres)—S Atlantic Modern Lang Assn. Department of English, University of Florida, Gainesville, Fla.

18 KIRKMAN, Robert A(keridge). Radar (Meteorological, missiles); Direction-finders; Radiosonde; Cavities (Resonant). b'14. Development various microwave radar sets and direction-finders; equipment for meteorological purposes; direction-finder

which employs a loop and very low frequency used for storm detecting; radiosondes which constitute airborne transmitting link used with direction-finder class equipment; research and design data recording systems for guided missile and jet plane instrumentation; to determine physical and mathematical nature of oscillation modes in resonant cavities field. Patents issued in resonant cavities field. Jr engr Gen Elec Co '37-39; engr MBS '39-41; sect engr US Signal Corps Engring Labs '41-48; supervising engr Cook Elec Co '48-50; sr engr Consol-Vultee Aircraft Corp since '50. Inst Radio Engrs (sr mem)—Am Radio Relay League (dir '40-46). Consolidated Vultee Aircraft Corp., San Diego, Cal.

19 KIRKPATRICK, Charles Milton. Wildlife management (Physiology and anatomy of ring-necked pheasant and other game birds); Ornithology. b'15. BS '38 (Purdue U); MA '40—PhD '43 (U Wis). Author articles: Body Weights and Organ Measurements in Relation to Age and Season in Ring-necked Pheasants '44; Development of the Testis in the Ring-necked Pheasant (with F N Andrews) '44; The Winter Foods of Some Indiana Owls (with Clinton H Conaway) '47, and others. Faculty Purdue U since '41, now asst prof. Ind Audubon Soc—Ky Ornithol Soc—Limnol Soc—Sigma Xi —Wildlife Soc—Wilson Ornithol Soc —Wis Ornithol Soc. Department of Forestry, Purdue University, Lafayette, Ind.†

20 KIRKPATRICK, Sidney Dale. Chemical engineering and economics. BSc in Chem E '16—grad study '16-17 (U Ill); ScD '46 (Clarkson); D Engring '48 (Polytechnic, Brooklyn). Editor: Twenty Five Years of Engineering Progress '33; also articles in field. With McGraw-Hill Pub Co NYC since '21, ed Chemical Engineering since '28, con ed chem engring series of text and reference books (25 titles) since '28; dir McGraw-Hill Book Co; investigator German chem industry '45. Am Inst Chem Engrs (dir '32-39, since '47, vp '40-41, pres '42)—Am Electrochem Soc (dir '33-35, vp '31-35, pres '44-45)—Am Chem Soc (councillor '49)—Soc Chem Industry Gt Brit (dir 42-44, chmn '46) —AAAS—Am Soc Engring Edn—Sigma Xi. Awarded silver anniversary medal Am Inst Chem Engring '33; Chem Industry Medalist '45. 330 W. 42nd St., NYC 36.☉

21 KIRKPATRICK, William John. Catalysis (Preparation and characteristics of nickel and palladium catalysts). b'08. BS '35—PhD '39 (Johns Hopkins). Study effect of small additions of various elements on nickel catalysts prepared from aluminum-nickel alloys; preparation of pure nickel hydroxide for use in producing catalysts; determination of relationship between wetting of supports by nickel or nickel subsulfide and properties of such catalysts; dehydrogenation of hydroaromatic compounds to aromatic compounds over palladium catalysts; adaptation of platinum dioxide catalysts to large-scale reactions. Holds nine patents in field. Contributor: Advances in Catalysis (Vol 3); Encyclopedia Americana. Research chem expt sta Hercules Powder Co '39-45; sr fellow in research Mellon Inst since '46. AAAS—ACS—Am Crystallographic Assn—Pa Soc Profl Engrs. Mellon Institute, 4400 Fifth Av., Pitts 13.

22 KIRNER, Walter Raymond. Organic chemistry. b'95. BS '18—MS '20 (U Ill); Austin teaching fellow '20-21 —DuPont research fellow '22—PhD '24 (Harvard); '29 (U Graz Austria);

'29-30 (U Munich Germany); '29-30 (University Coll London Eng). Correlation of effect of structure of chemicals on their biological activity; development new microanalytical equipment and techniques for use in industrial laboratories; study effect of structure of organic halides on rate of reaction with inorganic halides; synthesis of furfuryl chloride and its derivatives; chemical warfare agents, organic microanalyses of coal; direct micro determination of oxygen in organic compounds. Co-author: Coal Utilization '45. Contributor: Science in World War II '48. Faculty dept organic chem Rice Inst '24-30, asst prof '26-30; organic research chem Coal Research Lab Carnegie Inst Tech '31-40; with Nat Defense Research Com '40-46, chief div chem '42-46; chief chemical research branch Chem Warfare Service, US Army '43-45; dir Chem Biol Coordination Center NRC since '46. ACS—AAAS—NY Acad Sci—Sigma Xi—Gamma Alpha—Phi Lambda Upsilon—Alpha Chi Sigma. National Research Council, 2101 Constitution Av., Washington 25.

10 KISCH, Guido. History of law (Medieval, modern); History of Jews (Medieval, modern, American); Sachsenspiegel; Numismatics (Medals). Student '07-11, '11-12 (Prague U); '12-13 (Leipzig U); JUD '13—Sc Pol D '13 (Prague U). Research on source history of Sachsenspiegel and influence of Bible on medieval law, medieval law of fisheries, collections of magistrates verdicts of Magdeburg and Leipzig, laws affecting status of Jews in medieval Germany, the University of Prague and the Jews; studied legal and constitutional history, civil, exchange and miners law; editor Historia Judaica. Author: Leipziger Schoeffenspruchsammlung '19; Zur Saechsischen Rechtsliteratur der Rezeptionszeit '23; The Jews in Medieval Germany: A Study of Their Legal and Social Status '49; Jewry-Law in Medieval Germany '49 In Search of Freedom: A History of American Jews from Czechoslovakia '49; Pseudo-Philo's Liber Antiquitatum Biblicarum '48; and others. Prof ordinarius and law librarian Koenigsberg U '20-22, Halle U '22-33, dean faculty law polit sci Halle U '25-26, Prague U '24-25; visiting prof Jewish Inst Religion NY since '37; research asso medieval studies Notre Dame U '42-47; prof German lang and lit NY Coll Music since '46; vis prof law U Lund Sweden '49. Jewish Acad Arts Sci (hon F)—Am Acad Jewish Research(F) — AHA—Medieval Acad Am—Am Numismatic Soc—Am Numismatic Assn, and fgn societies. Research fellow Am Acad Jewish Research '35-37; Saxony State Award for most outstanding work in legal hist '19. 40 W. 68th St., NYC 23. H: 415 W. 115th St., NYC 25.

11 KISER, Clyde Vernon. Population (Factors affecting family size, migration, aging). b'04. AB '25—AM '27 (UNC); PhD '32—Richard Watson Gilder fellow '30-31 (Columbia). Research study of 300 Negro migrants from St Helena Island to Harlem and other cities; early trends of occupational differences in fertility, an analysis of the fertility data collected in the National Health Survey of '35 from some 700,000 families in 83 cities of 18 states; participating in a cooperative study of social and psychological factors affecting fertility since '39. Author: Sea Island To City: A Study of St Helena Islanders in Harlem and Other Urban Areas '32; Group Differences In Urban Fertility '42; Social and Psychological Factors Affecting Fertility '46, '50, '52; also articles. Research asso and tech staff

Milbank Memorial Fund since '34; adjunct prof sociol Grad Sch Arts and Sci NYU since '45; research asso Office Population Research Princeton U since '42. Am Acad Polit Social Sci—Am Statis Assn—Am Sociol Soc—Eastern Sociol Soc—Population Assn Am (bd dirs and pres—Internat Union Science Study Population (adm bd US Nat Com). Received Grant Squires prize Columbia '40; research fellow Milbank Memorial Fund '31-33. Milbank Memorial Fund, 40 Wall St., NYC 5.

12 KISH, George Political and historical geography (Europe, Russia); History of geography and cartography. b'14. AB '35 (Ecole des Sci Pol, Paris); AM '37 (U Paris); MS—DSc '39 (U Budapest); PhD '45 (U Mich). Author: Le Probleme de la Population au Japon '36. Teaching fellow geog U Mich '40-43, instr hist '42, asst prof geog since '46; cons and research analyst OSS '43-45; curator maps W L Clements Library U Mich '45-46. Hungarian Geog Soc—Assn Am Geog—Am Soc Profl Geog—Am Geophys Union—Mich Acad—Am Council Inst Pacific Relations. University of Michigan, Ann Arbor.†

13 KISKER, George Wolfgang. Psychopathology. b'12. AB '38—MA '39—PhD '43 (O State U). Author articles in field. Asso prof psychol U Fla '46-47, Grad Sch Arts Sci U Cincinnati since '47. Psychol US Army '42-46. Am Psychol Assn—AAAS—O Acad Sci—Soc Psychol Study Soc Issues—Am Acad Polit Social Sci—Internat Com Mental Hygiene—Ohio Psychological Assn—Sigma Xi. University of Cincinnati, Cincinnati.

14 KISSAM, Philip. Methodology and instrumentation for surveying and photogrammetry. b'96. CE (Princeton). Established principles of describing land boundaries by state plane coordinate systems; author first legislative act legalizing state systems of plane coordinates; tests of new type phototheodolites by astronomical observation; development special plotter for rectified high oblique air photographs that give orthogonal projection. Author: Surveying, Instruments and Methods '47. Co-author: (with Searles Ives) Field Engineering (22nd edit) '49. Co-author manual: Horizontal Control Surveys to Supplement the Fundamental Net. Faculty Princeton U since '21, now prof civil engring; profl civil engr specializing in photogrammetry and surveying since '26; research with Nat Defense Research Council and OSRD '41-45. Am Soc CE—Am Geophys Union—Am Soc Photogrammetry—Am Congress Surveying and Mapping. Princeton University, Princeton, N.J.

15 KISSIN, Gerald Harvey. Electrochemistry; Electrometallurgy. b'14. BS '35 (City Coll NY); MS '36—PhD '44 (U Mich). Research and process development in electrochemistry and metallurgy of non-ferrous metals, especially zinc, copper, lead, indium; research on manganese metallurgy. Developed process for electrochemical production battery-active manganese dioxide from low-grade domestic ores. Author articles: Improvements in the Potentiometric Titration of Chlorides (with R P Yeck) '45; Electron Emission and the Photovoltaic Effect (with A L Ferguson) '46; The Electrochemical Production of Battery Active Manganese Dioxide (with J S Carruthers) '48, and others. Research asso Nat Defense Research Com Cornell U '42; research engr central research lab Am Smelting Refining Co Barber NJ '42-47; research asst prof chem engring and supervisor metall and electrochem state engring expt sta Ga Inst Tech '47-48, research asso prof '48-49; cons

Berkeley '49-50; research engr Kaiser Aluminum and Chem Corp since '50. Am Chem Soc—Electrochem Soc—AA AS—Sigma Xi—Phi Lambda Upsilon. Div of Metallurgical Research, Kaiser Alum and Chemical Corp., P.O. Box 1451, Spokane, Wash.

16 KISSNER, Jacob. Boats (Small craft); Water sports. b'03. Ed pub schs. Design and construction boats for paddling, sailing, and water sports; development folding boat; sport and recreation. Author article: Foldboat Holidays '40, '45, and others. Founder and pres Folbot Corp since '33. Winner Nat White Water championship '41. 42-09 Hunter St., Long Island City 1, N.Y.

17 KITE, Walter Edwin. Wine and brandy (Production). b'10. AB '34—'34-36 (Stanford). Research on the production of wine brandy and byproducts. Chief plant chem Roma Wine Co Inc Fresno Calif '37-38, chief chem '38-43; gen chem Calif Vineyards Assn '43-47; prodn control mgr Schenley Industries Inc wine div since '47. Am Chem Soc—Wine Inst (chmn com tech advise '48-49). Roma Wine Co., P.O. Box 1592, Fresno, Calif.

18 KITTEL, Charles. Magnetism; Operational research. b'16. Student '34-36 (MIT); BA '38 (Cambridge U); PhD '41 (U Wis). Research on radioactivity, nature and development of operations research, theory of ferromagnetic resonance, interpretation of thermal conductivity of glasses. Author articles in field. Theoretical physicist Naval Ordnance Lab '40-42, supervisor submarine operations research groups Hdqrs Commander-in-Chief US Fleet '42-45; research asso Research Lab Electronics MIT '45-46; research physicist Bell Telephone Labs '47-51; asso prof physics U Calif since '51. Am Phys Soc(F). Guggenheim fellow '46-47. Dept. of Physics, University of California, Berkeley.

19 KITTREDGE, Henry Crocker. Cape Cod, Massachusetts. b'90. AB '12 (Harvard); MA (hon) '38 (Trinity Coll). Author: Cape Cod, Its People and Their History '30; Shipmasters of Cape Cod '35; Mooncussers of Cape Cod '37. Rector St Paul's Sch Concord NH since '47. NH Hist Soc—Am Antiquarian Soc—Phi Beta Kappa. St. Paul's School, Concord, N.H.☺

20 KITZINGER, Charlotte. Calorimetry. b'17. Physician's license '43 (U Freiburg Germany); MD '43 (U Berlin). Development of continuously recording methods for physiological and clinical research of human heat exchange. Co-author article: (with Dr T Benzinger) Direct Calorimetry by Means of the Gradient Principle '49. Research staff calorimetry and radiometry Naval Med Research Inst Bethesda since '47. Naval Medical Research Institute, Bethesda 14, Md.

21 KITZINGER, Ernst. History of medieval and Byzantine art. b'12. PhD '34 (U Munich). Author: Early Medieval Art in the British Museum; in addition to many articles in field. Asst prof Byzantine art and archeol Dumbarton Oaks (Harvard U) since '46. Dumbarton Oaks Research Library and Collection, 3101 R St., N.W., Washington 7.†

22 KLAER, Fred Harlen, Jr. Ground water geology and hydrology. b'14. BA '35 (Amherst Coll); MS '37 (Northwestern U). Research on artificial recharge of ground water. Author bulletin: Ground Water Resources of St Joseph County, Indiana '48. Co-author: Groundwater Resources of Cincinnati Area, Butler and Hamilton Counties, Ohio '48; also articles in field. Dist geol US Geol Survey Ind since '46. Sigma Xi—Am Geophys Union—Am Water Works Assn—Ind Acad Sci—Am Assn Petroleum Geol. U.S. Geological Survey, 311 W. Washington St., Indianapolis 4.

10 KLAGSBRUNN, Hans A(lexander). Law. b'09. Student '22-25 (Vienna Gymnasium); AB '29—LLB '32 (Yale U); '32-33 (Harvard Law Sch). Executive vp, gen counsel, director and mem exec com Defense Plant Corp; surplus property dir and asst gen counsel RFC; RFC mem Hancock Contract Settlement Bd and Clayton Surplus Property Bd in Office War Mobilization; dep dir Office War Mobilization and Reconversion The White House '45-46. Am Bar Assn—Am Judicature Soc—Phi Beta Kappa—Order of Coif—Phi Beta Kappa Assos. Ring Bldg., Washington 6.

11 KLAK, George Edward. Limnology (Plankton, trout, minnows). AB '23 (Ripon Coll); MA '30 (U Minn). Author articles in field. Aquatic biol Fish and Wildlife Service Dept Interior '37-39; asso prof Coll William and Mary since '47. Am Fisheries Soc—Am Micros Soc—Wis Acad Sci Arts Letters—Am Phycol Soc—Am Soc Limnol Oceanog. College of William and Mary, Virginia Polytechnic Institute, Norfolk 8, Va. H: 8246 McCloy Rd., Norfolk 5.

12 KLARMANN, Emil G. Disinfectants (Antiseptics, medicinals, cosmetics). b'00. Chem Eng '22 (Tech Inst Bruenn); DSc '23 (U Halle). Holder numerous patents on new germicidal compositions. Author articles in field. Vice-pres charge research Lehn and Fink Inc since '45. Am Chem Soc—Am Inst Chem—Am Inst Chem Engrs—Pub Health Assn—Soc Am Bact—Soc Cosmetic Chem. c/o Lehn and Fink, Inc., Bloomfield, N.J.†

13 KLAUBER, Laurence Monroe. Rattlesnakes; Reptiles of the Southwest; Reptile literature and folklore. b'83. AB '08 (Stanford); LLD (hon) '41 (U Calif); grad apprenticeship course '10 (Westinghouse). Curator of reptiles San Diego Zoological Society, curator of herpetology San Diego Society Natural History; research on life histories and taxonomy of southwestern reptiles, especially rattlesnakes, and on application of statistical methods to reptile taxonomy. Discoverer new species and subspecies. Author: A Key to the Rattlesnakes '36; Reptile Life in Arid Southwest '39, and others. With San Diego Gas and Elec Co since '11, pres '46-49, chmn of board since '49; lecturer in herpetology Stanford U. Am Mus Natural Hist (corr mem)—Am Soc Icthyologists Herpetologists (pres '38-40)—Am Ecol Soc—Western Soc Naturalists (pres '46)—Sigma Xi—AAAS(F)—Calif Acad Sci(F) — Herpetologists League(F). 233 W. Juniper St., San Diego 12, Cal.†◎

14 KLAUS, Hellmut. Petroleum (Exploration, gravimetric); Sulphur (Exploration). b'02. Student '20-22 (Georgia-Augusta U, Goettingen, Germany); Dipl Ing '25 (Berlin Inst Tech and Mining Acad). Research and exploration structural and stratigraphic conditions essential to accumulation of oil, gas and sulphur by gravimetric methods, using gravimeter and torsion balance. Torsion balance party chief and supt torsion balance Gypsy Oil Co '25-32; geophys Gulf Research and Development Co '32-36; pres, geophys and geol Klaus Exploration Co since '36. Am Assn Petroleum Geol—Soc Exploration Geophys—AIMME—Tex Acad Sci (F). P.O. Box 1617, Lubbock, Tex.

15 KLEBBA, Arthur Anthony. Oceanography (Instrumentation); Waves and currents (Measurements); Underwater exploration (Instrumentation). b'16. BS '41 (Mont State Coll). Author article: Shore Based Wave Recorder and Ocean Wave Analyzer. Research asst Sylvania Elec Products Inc '41-42; development engr Baird Assos Inc '42-44; research engr Woods Hole Oceanographic Inst '44-51. Am Phys Soc—Optical Soc Am —Am Assn Physics Tchrs—AAAS. 76 Grove St., North Brookfield, Mass.

16 KLEIBER, Max. Energy metabolism; Food utilization; Metabolic tracers (Isotope uses). b'93. DSc '24 (Inst Tech Zurich). Research on relation between body size and metabolic rate, effect of climate, age, pregnancy, lactation, and growth hormones on metabolic rate and food utilization, effect of body size on rate of tissue metabolism in vitro, fetal metabolism, casein and glucose utilization by lactating cows, composition and origin of rumen gases, tympanometer for measuring rumen gas pressure from outside. Author articles in field. Prof animal husbandry U Calif since '38. Soc Exptl Biol and Med—Am Chem Soc—Am Physiol Soc—Am Inst Nutrition—Am Soc Animal Prodn—Sigma Xi—Phi Beta Kappa. Borden Award for Nutrn '52. College of Agriculture, University of California, Davis, Calif.

17 KLEIN, Arthur Jay. Higher education (United States). b'84. BA '06 —LLD '32 (Wabash Coll); BD '09 (Union Theol Sem); MA '09—PhD '16 (Columbia). Director Survey of Land Grant Colleges and Universities authorized by Congress, survey higher institutions Oregon, survey public higher education Arkansas for US Office Education, survey Ohio Wesleyan University '47, survey University of Wyoming '47-48; associate director or member staff other surveys West Virginia, Washington, California, District of Columbia. Editor: Adventures in The Reconstruction of Education '41; also articles in field. Dean emeritus O State U since '45. Phi Beta Kappa. 6064 Olentangy River Rd., Worthington, O.

18 KLEIN, Frederic Shriver. Historical research methods; Pennsylvania local history. b'04. AB '23 (Franklin & Marshall Coll); AM '27 (Columbia). Author: An Introduction to Historical Method '31; Research Methods in History '39; Publications Lancaster County 1841-1941 '41; Two Hundred Years of Hardware History '44; also articles in field. Instr hist Franklin and Marshall Coll Lancaster Pa '29-37, prof since '46. AHA—Pa Hist Assn —Hist Soc Pa—Phi Alpha Theta. 1050 Maple Av., Lancaster, Pa.

19 KLEIN, Otto C. Zinc sulfate Barium sulfide; Lithopone chemistry; Paint pigments. b'16. Research fellow '37-39—MS '39 (Pa State Coll); BS '37 (U Ill). Holder US patents and one patent pending. Author articles in field. With Glidden Co since '39, lab dir chem and pigment div Collinsville plant since '45. Chemical and Pigment Company, Collinsville, Ill.

20 KLEIN, Philip Shriver. American history (Pennsylvania, President James Buchanan). b'09. BA '29 (Franklin & Marshall Coll); MA '32 (U Chicago); Harrison fellow hist '36—PhD '38 (U Pa). Research on Pennsylvania history, Lancaster county political history and politics, John Binns, John Andrew Shulze, Senator William Maclay. Author: The Story of Wheatland '36; (co-author) Checklist of Pennsylvania Newspapers '44; Pennsylvania Politics, 1817-1832 '41; (co-author) Lancaster County 1841-1941 '42; also articles in field. Asst prof Am hist Franklin & Marshall Coll '38-41; asso prof Am hist Pa State Coll '41-42, since

'46. AHA—Pa Hist Assn (sec since '46)—Hist Soc Pa—Am Assn State Local Hist—Phi Beta Kappa. Department of History, Pennsylvania State College, State College, Pa.

21 KLEINHANS, Robert Burton. Greek elections. b'07. Student '26-27 (Cleveland Coll); AB '31—MA '33— teaching certificate '37 (W Reserve U); '47 (U Fla). Executive secretary for Allied Mission for Observing Greek Elections on Island of Crete '46. With Xavier U Dept Biol since '48. ACS —Fla Entomol Soc—Near E Coll Assn —AAAS—Nav Inst. Xavier Downtown College, Cincinnati. H 3535 Evanston Av., Cin 7.

22 KLEINHOLZ, Lewis Hermann. Comparative invertebrate physiology; Animal color changes. b'10. BSc '30 (Colby Coll); MA—PhD '37—Sheldon Travel fellow '37-38 (Harvard). Research on hormonal control of retinal pigment migration in crustaceans, diurnal rhythms in activity of crustacean chromatophores, color changes in echinoderms, relation between light-intensity and retinal adaptation, hormonal factors in reptilian color changes, nervous and hormonal regulation of teleost chromatophores, calcium deposition and molting and regulation of blood-sugar concentration in crustaceans, assay method for detection of relaxin. Author: Selected Invertebrate Types (with others) '49; also articles in field. Asso prof biol Reed Coll since '46; instructional staff Marine Biol Lab Woods Hole since '48. Ore Acad Sci—Am Soc Zool—Phi Beta Kappa—Sigma Xi. Guggenheim fellow '45-46. Reed College, Portland, Ore.†

23 KLEINHOLZ, Milton Paul. Petroleum chemistry (Lubricating oil). b'14. BS '35 (Colby Coll); '36-38 (Harvard); student (U Chicago). Holder patents on detergents, rust-inhibitors, oxidation-inhibitors for lubricating oils. Group leader lubricating oil additives Sinclair Refining Co since '46. Am Chem Soc.

24 KLEINSCHMIDT, Robert Baumgartner. Bells; Carillons; Chains (Stresses). b'10. BS (Civil engring) '31—MS '32—AM (Math) '40 (U Pa). Research in production synthetic bell-tones; relation shape and sound of traditional bells; wire-sections and link-shapes of specialized chain, stud-link chain; impact effects on chain. Author bulletin: The Mechanics of the Carillon; 101 Arrangements for the Carillon '50. Carillonneur First Methodist Church Germantown Phila since '31, Rainbow Tower Niagara Falls Ont; vp Liberty Carillons Inc '47; asst prof mech Lehigh U since '47; cons on acoustics Stromberg-Carlson Co since '48. Am Soc CE (Asso)—Soc Exptl Stress Analysis—Acoustical Soc Am— Guild Carillonniers NA—Nat Soc Profl Engrs. Lehigh University, Bethlehem, Pa. H: 247 East Market St.

25 KLENKE, William Walter. Woodcraft (Fine furniture); Colonial Churches of New Jersey. b'88. Scholarship in art '13 (Pratt Inst). Put out set of church commemorative service plates, showing old Episcopal churches of New Jersey, plates made by Wedgwood '34. Author: Art and Education in Wood Turning '21; The Home Workshop '35; Odd Pieces in Wood '38; Furniture Joinery '43; Klenke's Furniture Book '48; and others. Instr tech dept Central Comml and Tech High Sch Newark NJ since '13; designer and builder of fine furniture since '13. 111 Mercer Place, South Orange, N.J.◎

26 KLIEVER, Waldo Harold. Temperature controls; Humidity measurements. b'07. BS '29 (Bethel Coll); PhD '39 (U Chicago). Research on electronic temperature controls with resistance bridges, methods for relative and absolute humidity measurements. With Gaertner Sci Corp '30-38, USDA '38-40; research Minneapolis-Honeywell Regulation Co since '40, now dir research. APS—Am Optical Soc—Am Soc Agrl Engrs—Sigma Xi —Soc Automotive Engrs—Am Soc Heating and Ventilating Engrs. Minneapolis-Honeywell Regulator Co., 2753 Fourth Av. S., Mpls 8.

10 KLINE, Gordon Mabey. Plastics; Adhesives; Airplane dopes. b'03. BA '25 (Colgate U); MS '26 (George Washington U); PhD '34 (U Md). Editor: Modern Plastics Encyclopedia also articles in field. Research chem Nat Bur Standards Washington since '29, chief organic plastics sect since '35, asst chief organic and fibrous materials div since '47; tech ed Modern Plastics Mag NY since '36; ed dir Modern Plastics Encyclopedia since '36; tech investigator plastics Office Chief Ordnance War Dept in European Theater Operation '45. Am Chem Soc —Am Inst Chem—ASME (adv com rubber and plastics div)—Am Soc Testing Materials (chmn com D-20 on plastics, com D-14 on adhesives)—Soc Plastics Engrs—Soc Plastics Industry—Washington Acad Sci—Phi Beta Kappa—Sigma Xi. National Bureau of Standards, Washington 25.†

11 KLINE, Hibberd Van Buren, Jr. African and Mediterranean geography; Cartography. b'13. AB '36 (Syracuse U); MA '38—PhD '41 (Wis U). Research on geography of Union of South Africa, the Rhodesias, East Africa, Congo, and northwest Africa, related particularly to geography of settlements, resources, economic activities, development of cartographical presentation of such data. Co-author: (with P E James) A Geography of Man '49; also articles in field. With OSS '41-45, chief cartography sect '43, chief map div Algiers '43-44, European Theatre Operations London '44-45, spl asst to chief of map div Washington '44; chief map intelligence sect Interim Research and Intelligence Service Dept State '45, chief cartographic br Dept State '46, spl map procurement officer Africa '46; asso prof geog Syracuse U since '49. Phi Beta Kappa—Phi Kappa Phi—Sigma Xi—Assn Am Geog—Am Soc Profl Geog—NY State Geog Soc—S African Geog Soc—Royal African Soc, London—Am Cong Surveying Mapping —Am Acad Polit Social Sci. U scholar dept geog U Wis '40-41. Department of Geography, Syracuse University, Syracuse 10, N.Y.†⊙

12 KLINE, Nathan Schellenberg. Psychiatry (Methodological problems of research in); Catatonia (Mechanisms); Schizophrenia (Physiological responses in); Somatotypes (Correlation with mental illness); Brain (Neurophysiological changes following operations on); Race (Correlation with types of mental illness). b'16. BA '38 (Swarthmore Coll); '38 (U Pa); '38-39 (Harvard); MD '43 (NYU); '41-42 (New Sch Soc Research); '46 (Rutgers U); '47-48 (Princeton); '50-51 (Clark). Contributor: Ships Medicine Chest '47; The Psychobiological Program of The War Shipping Administration '47; Rehabilitation of the Handicapped '49; Selective Partial Ablation of the Frontal Cortex: A Correlative Study of its Effects on Human Psychotic Subjects '49; Problems of the Human Frontal Lobe. Research psychiat US PHS '44-46; exec sec research com Veterans Administrn '46-50; Columbia-Greystone asso '46-49; NY State brain research asso '48-50; research asst Columbia '48-50; dir research Worcester State Hosp. Diplomate Am Bd Psychiat Neurology. Am Psychiat Assn

(F)—NY Acad Med(F)—Am Psychol Assn(asso)—Assn Research in Nervous and Mental Diseases—Sigma Xi— NJ Neuropsychiat Soc—Inst Soc Psychiat(London)—Am Assn Hist Med— Am Coll Phys(asso)—AAAS. Research Service, Worcester State Hospital, Worcester 1, Mass.

13 KLINEFELTER, Theron Albert. Clays (Ceramic engineering). b'85. BS '08—B Ceramic Eng '15—Profl Ceramic Engr '37 (Ohio State U). Engineer plants manufacturing electrical porcelain, sainitaryware, terra cotta, faience tile, sewer pipe, refractories; Research clays for ceramic and non-ceramic uses. Author: Syllabus of Clay Testing '43. Research engr Westinghouse Elec & Mfg Co Pittsburgh '15-20; supt Atlantic Terra Cotta Co NYC '20-22; supt pottery dept J L Mott Iron Works Trenton NJ '22-24; ceramic engr Gladding McBean & Co Lincoln Calif '24-26; supt Columbus (Ohio) br Nat Bur Standards '27-33, ceramic tech Washington '33-41; mineral tech US Bur Mines Tuscaloosa Ala '41-51, Raleigh NC since '51. ACS(F)—Inst Ceramic Engrs—AIMME. U.S. Bureau of Mines, Box 471, Norris, Tenn.

14 KLIPSCH, Paul Wilbur. Loudspeakers; Dynamic acoustics; Vibration mechanics; Filter networks. b'04. BS (EE) '26 (NM Coll A&M); EE '34 (Stanford). Design, development, and manufacture of loudspeakers. Holds patents in field. Author article: A Low Frequency Horn of Small Dimensions '41, and others. Mgr and engr loudspeaker systems Klipsch & Asso since '46. Am Inst EE—Inst Radio Engrs—Acoustical Soc Am—Tau Beta Pi—Sigma Xi. Klipsch & Associates, Hope, Ark.

15 KLIPSTEIN, Kenneth Hampton. Industrial chemistry; Synthetic organic chemicals. b'00. AB '21—MA '24 (Princeton). Patents in field of industrial chemistry. Author articles in field. With Calco Chem Div Am Cyanamid Co since '33, now asst gen mgr. Am Inst Chem Engrs—Am Chem Soc—Am Inst Chem. Calco Chemical Division, American Cyanamid Company, Bound Brook, N.J.

16 KLOEPFER H(enry) Warner. Human genetics; Mapping of human chromosomes. b'13. PhD '42—MA '38 —BS '34 (O State U); AB '35 (Muskingum Coll). Author article: An Investigation of 171 Possible Linkage Relationships in Man '46, and others. Academic dean, prof biol Coll of Ozarks since '47. AAAS—Ark Acad Sci—Sigma Xi. College of the Ozarks, Clarksville, Ark.

17 KLOETZEL, Milton Carl. Organic chemical synthesis (Diels-Alder reaction, polymethyl aromatic hydrocarbons, potential antimalarial drugs, nitroparaffins reactions). b'13. BS '34—PhD '37 (U Mich). Author articles in field. Asst prof, asso prof U So Calif since '45; responsible investigator OSRD '43-45. Am Chem Soc. University of Southern California, Los Angeles 7.†

18 KLOSTERMAN, E(arle) W(ayne). Animal nutrition. b'19. BS '42 (SD State Coll); MS '43—PhD '46 (Cornell). Protein requirements of lambs and breeding sheep, effect methionine and minerals on protein utilization; vitamin A studies with beef cattle and rats; study vitamin needs of swine. Co-author articles: (with Willam and Morrison) Lamb Feeding Experiments '46; (with Bolin and Buchanan) The Blood Proteins of Pregnant Ewes and How The are Affected by Protein in the Ration '50; (with Dinusson, Lasley and Buchanan) Effect of Trace Minerals on Growth and Fattening of Swine '50 and others. Asst

animal husbandry Cornell '42-46; asst prof animal husbandry SD State Coll '46-47; asso prof nutrition, asso animal nutritionist ND Agrl Coll since '47. Am Soc Animal Prodn—AAAS(F) —Sigma Xi—Alpha Zeta. Department of Animal Husbandry, North Dakota Agricultural College, State College Station, Fargo, N.D.

19 KLOTS, Alexander Barrett. Falconry; Butterfly and moth Taxonomy and ecology; Mosquitoes; Animal distribution, ecology and evolution; Butterflies of eastern United States. b'03. BS—MS—PhD (Cornell). Entomological collecting and field work in all parts of North America, West Indies, Brazil, and West Africa. Author: Field Guide to Eastern Butterflies '51; also articles in field. Asst prof Coll City NY since '45; research asso Am Mus Nat Hist since '46. Maj San Corps US Army '43-46. NY Entomol Soc (pres '40)—Entomol Soc Am(F)—Soc Study Evolution—Am Mus Nat Hist (hon life)—Am Falconer's Assn—Sigma Xi —Phi Kappa Phi. 17 Lexington Av., NYC 10.†

20 KLOTZ, Irving M. Chemistry (Proteins, thermodynamics, spectra). b'16. SB '37—U fellow '39-40—PhD '40 (U Chicago). Author articles: The Application of the Law of Mass Action to Binding by Proteins, Interactions with Calcium '46; The Antibacterial Activity of p-Aminobenzenephosphonous Acid (with R T Morrison) '47; The Adsorption Wave '46, and others. Research asso Northwestern U '40-42, instr chem '42-46, asst prof '46-47, asso prof since '47. Phi Beta Kappa—Sigma Xi—AAAS—Am Chem Soc—Am Soc Biol Chem. Department of Chemistry, Northwestern University, Evanston, Ill.⊙

21 KLUCKHOHN, Clyde Kay Maben. Anthropology; Navajo Indians; Child psychology (Primitive). b'05. '22 (Princeton); AB '28 (U Wis); '31-32 (U Vienna); MA '32 (Oxford U); PhD '36 (Harvard; LHD '49 (U NM). Author: To the Foot of the Rainbow '27; Beyond the Rainbow '33; The Navajo (with D Leighton) '46; Children of the People (with D Leighton) '47; Personality in Nature, Society and Culture (with H A Murray) '48; Mirror for Man '49. Asst prof anthrop U NM, research asso in archeol Sch Am Research '32-34; instr anthrop Harvard '35-37, asst prof '37-40, asso prof '40-46, prof since '46, dir Russian Research Center since '47; cons US Indian Service since '42; dir Verde Valley Sch. Am Anthrop Assn (pres '47)—Am Acad Arts Sci—Phi Beta Kappa. Awards: Rhodes scholarship, Guggenheim fellowship. Peabody Museum, Cambridge 38, Mass.⊙

22 KLUG, Clarence. Glass fabrics; Plastic foams. b'01. Ed pub schs. Research in textile dyes for glass fabrics, textile processing equipment; designer continuous processing of glass fabrics. Issued patents in both fields; trademarks. Author articles: Rapid Process for finishing glass fabrics; continuous dyeing of glass fabrics, and others. Research dir Waterway Projects Inc Los Angeles '46-49; gen mgr Soft-Flex Glass Fabrics Los Angeles since '49. ACS—Franklin Inst— Am Assn Textile Chem and Colorists— Textile Color Card Assn of US.

23 KLUVER, Heinrich. Psychology (Brain mechanisms and behavior, vision, eidetic imagery, hallucinations, personality types); Porphyrins and the nervous system; Fluorescence spectra (biological materials). b'97. Student '20-23 (U Hamburg Germany and U Berlin); PhD '24 (Stanford U); Fellow Social Sci Research Council '26-28; research psychol behavior research fund

'28-33; mem Otho S A Sprague Memorial Inst '38-46, prof exptl psychol since '38. Am Psychol Assn—AAAS—Am Physiol Soc—Am Neurological Assn—Soc Exptl Psychol—Optical Soc Am—Soc Exptl Biol and Med—Nat Inst Psychol—Soc Biol Psychiat—Human Genetics Soc Am. Culver Hall, University of Chicago, Chicago 37.©

10 KNAPP, John Oliver. Agriculture (Extensions). b'93. BSA '16 (WVa U). Advisor national rural youth committee American Farm Bureau Federation; chairman of committee on extension organization and policy Association Land Grant Colleges and Universities; visiting expert on agriculture Office Military Government in Germany '49. Dist agt agrl ext service W Va U '23-33, dir since '33. West Virginia University, Morgan, W.Va.

11 KNAPP, Lewis Mansfield. Novelists (Eighteenth century); Tobias Smollett. b'94. BA '16 (Amherst); MA '20 (Columbia); PhD '28 (Yale); '19 (U Clemont - Ferrand France). Author: Tobias Smollett, Doctor of Men and Manners '49; also articles in field. Asst prof Eng Williams Coll '29-38; asso prof Eng Colo Coll '39-40, prof since '40, chmn dept since '47. Modern Lang Assn Am—Colo-Wyo Acad Letters—Phi Beta Kappa. Research grants Am Council Learned Soc '30, Williams Coll '37. Colorado College, Colorado Springs, Colo.©

12 KNEBEL, George M. Exploration for petroleum. b'99. BA '22 (U Tex). Research on transformation of organic material into petroleum. Co-author: (with E A Wendlandt) Lower Claiborne of East Tex '29; Mount Sylvan Dome. Smith Co, Texas: Gulf Coast Oil Fields '36. Charge surface geol and core drilling East Tex Humble Oil & Refining Co '24-30; chief geol Standard Oil Co of Venezuela '30-35, asst mgr '35-38, mgr '38-39, exec staff charge exploration work for Venezuela '39, exec staff NY office '39-44, head exploration div NY since '44. Geol Soc Am—AAPG—Am Geophys Union—Am Geog Soc—AIME — PAIMEG. Room 2150, 30 Rockefeller Plaza, NYC 20. H: 10 Paddington Rd., Scarsdale.

13 KNEBERG, Madeline. Southeastern United States archeology (Tennessee); Prehistory of Creek, Cherokee, Yuchi and other Indian cultures (Tennessee). b'03. AB '33—MA '47 (U Chicago). Co-author: Hiwassee Island '46; also articles in field. Full prof anthrop U Tenn since '49. Am Anthrop Assn(F)—Soc Am Archeol—Tenn Archeol Soc—Tenn Acad Sci—Sigma Xi—Phi Beta Kappa. Biology Building, University of Tennessee, Knoxville, Tenn.†

14 KNEEN, Eric. Enzymes; Amylases; Malt. b'09. BSc '31 (U Alberta); MS '33—PhD '42 (U Minn). Author articles in field. Dir research Kurth Malting Co Milwaukee since '46. Am Chem Soc—AAAS—Am Assn Cereal Chem—Am Soc Brewing Chem—Masters Brewers Assn Am—Inst Food Technol—Sigma Xi. Co-recipient of Chemurgic award Omaha C of C '45; voted by Chem Bull readers as one of ten leading agrl and food chem in US '47. Kurth Malting Co., P.O. Box 1146, Milwaukee 1.

15 KNEER, Vernon Ralph. Water supply. b'02. BS '25 (U Wis). Author articles: Saginaw Midland Water Supply; The Need for Increased Water Rates; Des Moines Softens and Increases Supply; Construction Trends in the Water Works Field. Resident engr Saginaw-Midland Water Supply '47-48, Des Moines Water Softening Plant '49, Bedford Park Ill Water Supply Project '50, Dayton O Water Soft-

ening Plant '51. Am Soc CE—Western Soc Engrs—Am Water Works Assn. 1401 Civic Opera Bldg., Chgo 6.

16 KNEISS, Gilbert Harold. United States history (Railroad, western); Outdoor Dramatic Producing. b'99. BS '23 (U Nev); grad work (U Calif). Technical director Cavalcade, Golden Gate International Exposition and Railroads on Parade New York World's Fair '38-40. Author: Bonanza Railroads '41; Between Train '36; The Iron Horse and The Days of Gold '37; The Locomotives of the Union Iron Works '46, and others. Now asst to pres Western Pacific RR Co San Francisco. Ry and Locomotive Hist Soc (res vp). 18 Forest Lane, Berkeley 8.©

17 KNEPLER, Abraham Eleazar. Cherokee Indians (Education); Intergroup relations. b'11. BS '32 (Rutgers U); PhD '39 (Yale). Research on methods of teaching secondary school, college, and informal adult groups, also of marriage and family on college and informal adult levels. Author articles: Eighteenth Century Cherokee Educational Efforts '42; Education in the Cherokee Nation '43, and others. Research asst advancing to asso ed democracy series Am Council on Edn Commn on Motion Pictures '44-47; asst prof sociol U Bridgeport since '47, dir Inst on Race Relations '48, '49, dir Workshop on Intergroup Relations '51. Am Acad Polit and Social-Sci—Am Anthrop Assn—AAAS—Am Sociometric Assn—Am Sociol Soc—Autonomous Groups—Eastern Sociol Soc—NEA—Nat Council on Family Relations — Soc Applied Anthrop — Soc Psychol Study Social Issues — Soc Group Psychotherapy and Psychodrama—Phi Delta Kappa. University of Bridgeport, 301 Park Pl., Bridgeport 4, Conn.

18 KNICKERBOCKER, William Skinkle. Victorian literature and science; British education; Contemporary American literature. b'92. AB '17—AM '18—PhD '25—Proudfit fellow '18-20 (Columbia). Editor Sewanee Review '26-42. Author: Creative Oxford '25. Editor: Culture and Anarchy by Matthew Arnold '25; Classics of Modern Science '27. Prof Eng Emerson Coll since '48. Modern Lang Assn Am—Phi Beta Kappa. 33 Clark St., Newton Centre, Mass.©

19 KNIFFEN, Fred Bowerman. Folk house types; Indian geography; American costumes. b'00. AB '22 (Mich U); PhD '29—U and teaching fellow '25-29 (Calif U); '17-20 (Superior Teachers Coll); '38-39 (Munich U). Research on historic Indian tribes of Louisiana, Walapai ethnography, Louisiana house types, mounds and middens of Plaquemines and St Bernard parishes, Louisiana, Indian mounds of Louisiana. Author: Achomawi Geography '28; The Primitive Cultural Landscape of the Colorado Delta '31; Pomo Geography '39; also articles in field. Asst prof, later prof La State U since '29. Phi Beta Kappa—Sigma Xi—Assn Am Geog—Am Anthrop Assn. Rosenwald fellow Munich U '38; scholar Southwest Lab Anthrop '29. School of Geology, Louisiana State University, Baton Rouge 3, La.†©

20 KNIFFIN, Herbert Reynolds. Fine arts (Masks). Student (Cooper Union Sch NYC, Nat Acad Design NYC, Art Student's League NYC); diploma '09 (Columbia); '11 (Munich, Germany)—'19-25 (Academie de LaCluse and Academie Mont Parnasse, Paris). Exhibited at National Academy Design, American Water Color Society, New York Color Society, Architectural League, Salon D'Automn Paris, Carnegie Institute Pittsburgh; chairman

New Jersey State Art Commission. Author: Masks '31; also articles in field. Prof fine arts NJ Coll for Women, Rutgers U since '30. Chi Psi Lodge, Rutgers University, New Brunswick, N.J.

21 KNIGHT, J. Brookes. Paleontology (Paleozoic gastropoda); Zoological nomenclature. b'88. AB '11 (Princeton); MA '28 (Columbia); PhD '31—research asso '32-33—Sterling Fellow '33 (Yale). Author articles in field. Research in Europe under Geol Soc Grant '34-35; lecturer and curator paleontol Princeton '36-45; curator invertebrate peleontol and palebot US Nat Mus Washington '45; research asso in paleontol Smithsonian Instn Washington since '45; research asso in fossil invertebrates Am Mus Natural Hist NYC since '41; chmn com on zool nomenclature for Paleontol in Am '45-47, '48-49. Geol Soc Am (vp '47)—Soc Econ Paleontol Mineral (vp '45)—Paleontol Soc (pres '46, councilor '46-49—Am Assn Petroleum Geol—Malacol Soc of London—Society Study Evolution—Am Malacol Union—Soc Systematic Zool (councilor '48-49)—Nat Research Council (exec com div geol and geog '47). Smithsonian Institution, Washington 25.

22 KNIGHT, Odon Stahlhut. Chemical engineering design and unit operations. b'07. BS '28—MS '32—PhD '33—ChE '35 (U Colo); student (U Mich). Author articles in field. Supervising chem engr Commercial Solvents Corp since '43. Am Inst Chem Engrs—Am Chem Soc—Am Soc Engring Edn—Sigma Xi—Tau Beta Phi. Commercial Solvents Corporation, Terre Haute, Ind. H: 1000 S. Center.

23 KNIPLING, Edward F(red). Biology and chemical control of lice, mosquitoes, mites, ticks, and fleas, affecting man and animals. b'09. BS (entomol) '30 (Tex A&M); MS (entomol, zool) '32—PhD (entomol, zool) '47 (Ia State Coll). Research on DDT leading to adoption of insecticide by Army and Navy for insect control. developed other insecticides and repellents for Armed Services. Author 100 articles on medical and venterinary entomology. With Bur Entomol and Plant Quarantine USDA since '30, prin entomol in charge Div Insects Affecting Man and Animals since '46. Am Assn Econ Entomol—AAAS—Am Mosquito Control Assn—Nat Malaria Soc—Wash Entomol Soc—Sigma Xi—Gamma Sigma Delta. Awarded Medal for Merit for research on control of arthropods of medical importance, King's Medal for Services in Cause of Freedom, US Am Typhus Commn Medal for contributions to control of lice, mites, flies, mosquitoes and fleas, vectors of human diseases. Bureau of Entomology and Plant Quarantine, Washington.

24 KNOBLOCH, Irving William. Agrostology; Pteridology; Brome grass. b'07. BA '30—MA '32 (U Buffalo); teach fellow '30-31 (Harvard); PhD '42 (Ia State Coll). Author: Readings in Biological Science '48; also articles in field. Asso prof biol sci Mich State Coll since '47. Bot Soc Am—Mich Acad Sci—Am Fern Soc—Sigma Xi. Department of Biological Science, Michigan State College, East Lansing, Mich.†

25 KNODT, Cloy Bernard. Cattle (Dairy); Pasture management; Physiology and nutrition of dairy cattle. b'17. BS '40—PhD '44 (U Minn); MS '42 (U Conn). Research on physiology of ketosis in dairy cattle, physiology of lactation, development use of antibiotics in semen diluters, milk replacement for dairy calves, development calf starters. Author 41 articles in field. Faculty Cornell '44-45; prof dairy husbandry Pa State Coll since '46. Sigma Xi—ACS—Am Genetics Assn—Am Dairy Sci Assn—Am Soc Animal Prodn—AAAS—Soc Exptl Biol and Med. Department of Animal Husbandry, Pennsylvania State College, State College, Pa.

10 KNOLES, George Harmon. Social and intellectual history of the United States; Foreign and domestic criticism of United States civilization. b'07. AB '28—MA '30 (Coll of the Pacific); PhD '39 (Stanford U). Author: The Presidential Campaign and Election of 1892. Article: The Religious Ideas of Thomas Jefferson, and others. Asst hist Stanford U '35-36, instr '37-41, asst prof '42-46, asso prof since '47; prof hist Colorado State Coll Edn '41-42. AHA—So Hist Assn—Miss Valley Hist Assn. Department of History, Stanford University, Stanford, Calif.☉

11 KNOLLENBERG, Bernhard. History of the American Revolution; American biographies of the eighteenth century; Federal and state income tax. b'92. AB '12—LLD '44 (Earlham Coll, Ind); AM '14—LLB '16 (Harvard); AM (hon) '38 (Yale). Author: Washington and the Revolution: A Re-appraisal '40; Whitewater Valley '46; also articles in fields. Cons expert US Treasury '39-40; senior deputy adminstr Lend-Lease Adminstrn '43-44; divisional deputy OSS '44-45. Mass Hist Soc—Am Antiquarian Soc. Parker's Point, Chester, Conn.☉

12 KNORR, L. Carl. Plant diseases (Potatoes, citrus). b'14. AB '40 (U Ill); MS '42 (Mich State Coll); PhD '45 (Cornell U). Author articles in field. Asso plant path Citrus Expt Sta U Fla since '48; editor Phytopathological Classics. AAAS(asso)—Am Phytopath Soc—Sigma Xi—Phi Kappa Phi. Citrus Experiment Station, University of Florida, Lake Alfred, Fla.†

13 KNOTT, Emmet Kennard. Ultraviolet irradiation of blood. b'97. DSc '40 (Hahnemann Med Coll). Research and development of method for exposing circulating or auto-transfused human blood to selected wave lengths and intensities of ultraviolet rays for treatment of disease, designed precision machine used in process of blood irradiation, performed first successful irradiation on human being in '28. Author article: Development of Ultraviolet Blood Irradiation. Co-author article: (with Virgil K Hancock) Irradiated Blood Transfusion in the Treatment of Infections; (with G J P Barger MD) Blood: Ultraviolet Irradiation (Knott Technic). Contributor: Medical Physics (vol 2) '50. In research since '25. Am Blood Irradiation Soc (dir). 110 Prefontaine Place, Seattle, 4.†☉

14 KNOTT, James Edward. Plant physiology; Vegetable production (Ecological factors). b'97. BS '20—DSc (hon) '42 (RI State Coll); MS '24—PhD '26 (Cornell U). Author: Vegetable Growing '41. Author articles: Effect of Localized Photoperiod on Spinach '34; The Effect of Temperature on the Photoperiodic Response of Spinach '39, and others. Instr plant physiol Cornell '23-25, instr vegetable gardening '25-26, asst res prof veg crops '29-32, res prof veg crops '32-40; asso prof, head div veg gardening Pa State Coll '26-27, prof '27-29; prof, head dept veg crops U Calif since '40; prin prodn specialist Australian mission Bd Econ Warfare '42-43. AAAS (F)—Calif Seed Council (pres '47, '48) —Am Soc Plant Physiol—Am Soc Hort Sci (vp '46, '47, pres '48)—Am Soc Agron—Soil Sci Soc Am—Sigma Xi—Phi Kappa Phi—Gamma Sigma Delta.

Awarded Vaughan research award Am Soc Hort Sci '42. Department of Vegetable Crops, University of California, Davis, Calif.

15 KNOWER, Franklin Hayward. Speech education; Psychology of speech, the audience, and communication. b'01. BA '25 (Northwestern U); MA '28 (Syracuse U); PhD '33 (U Minn). Chairman of committee of Speech Association of America which prepared two bulletins on speech for National Association of Secondary School Principles; developed graduate examinations and program in communication; past associate editor Quarterly Journal Speech and Speech Monographs, editor Speech Monographs '51; editor research studies published by National Society for Study of Communication. Author: Speech Education in Ohio '50; A Speech Attitude Scale, A Speech Experience Inventory '38. Coauthor: (with A C Baird) General Speech '49. With U Minn '28-39; with Ia State U '39-46; with O State U since '46. Speech Assn Am(exec council '39-42, '46-49)—Am Psychol Assn(F)—AA AS(F)—Am Speech and Hearing Assn (F)—Nat Soc Study Edn—Am Ednl Research Assn—Am Ednl Theatre Assn—Am Assn Pub Opinion Research —Nat Soc Study Communication—Central States Speech Assn (pres '39)—Sigma Xi—Delta Sigma Rho—Pi Kappa Delta. Department of Speech, Ohio State University, Columbus 10, O.

16 KNOWLES, Edwin Blackwell. Cervantes (In English literature, bibliography). b'03. BA '24—MA '29 —PhD '38 (NYU). Author articles: Don Quixote through English Eyes '40; Allusions to "Don Quixote" before 1660 '41; Notes on the Madrid, 1605, Editions of "Don Quixote" '46, and others. Asso prof Eng Pratt Inst since '48. Modern Lang Assn—Bibliog Soc Am—NC Teachers Eng—Phi Beta Kappa. Pratt Institute, Brooklyn 5, N.Y.

17 KNOWLES, Hugh Shaler. Acoustics (Loudspeakers, sound recording and reproduction, electroacoustic devices, microphones, electromechanical traducers). b'04. AB '27 (Columbia); '30-34 (U Chicago). Inventor in field of acoustics and electronics; chairman acoustics panel Research and Development Bd '48-50; member National Research Council '49, executive committee, physical science division '50-51; chairman acoustics panel Research and Development Board, Office of Secretary of Defense '48-50. Author: Acoustics, Loudspeakers, Telephone Receivers and Microphones '50. Inst Radio Engrs (F, chmn standards com electroacoustics '38-41)—Acoustical Soc Am (exec council '42-44, pres '45-47). 350 Forest Av., Glen Ellyn, Ill.†☉

18 KNOWLTON, George F(ranklin). Economic entomology (Aphid taxonomy, insect ecology, biological control of insects); Food of lizards and birds. b'01. BS '23—MA '25 (Utah State Agrl Coll); PhD '32 (O State U). Author articles in field. Collaborator entomol US Dept Agr since '27; Utah state leader in grasshopper control since '36; Utah state ext entomol since '43; prof zool and entomol Utah State Agrl Coll since '45. Rocky Mt Entomol Conf (vice chmn '39-40)—Am Assn Econ Entomol (vp '41-42, chmn Pacific slope br '41-42)—Utah Acad Sci Arts Letter (F, chmn biol sect '42-44)—Entomol Soc Washington—Utazoa Soc—AAAS (F)—Entomol Soc Am(F)—Herpetologists League(F)—Pacific Coast Entomol Soc—Northwest Vegetable Insect Control Conf (chmn '48-49)—Northwest Fruit Spray Conf. Utah State Agricultural College, Logan, Utah.☉

19 KNOX, Arthur Stewart. Pollen (Analysis, fossil); Photogrammetry; Wilson Photoalidade; Peat technology. b'03. BS '28—MEd '39—Olmstead fellow '27-28—scholar '38-39 (Tufts Coll); AM '30 (Harvard). First to outline a late glacial and postglacial pollen chronology for eastern New England, and to describe bromoform method of separating pollen and other microfossils from sediments; discovered fossil pollen in Cretaceous Tertiary and Pleistocene deposits of Atlantic coastal plain. Author articles in jours. Topographic engr US Geol Survey since '44. AAAS(F)—Am Geog Soc—Bot Soc Am—Paleontol Soc—Am Geophys Union—Geol Soc Washington—Am Soc Photogrammetry. U.S. Geological Survey, Department of the Interior, Washington 25.†

20 KNUDSON, Albert Cornelius. Systematic theology. b'73. AB '93—STB '96—PhD '00 (Boston U); '97-98 (U Jena and Berlin); DD '06 (Allegheny Coll); Theol D '23 (U Berlin); LLD '26 (Lawrence U). Author: The Doctrine of God '30; The Validity of Religious Experience '37; The Principles of Christian Ethics '43; The Philosophy of War and Peace '47; Basic Issues in Christian Thought '50; and others. With Boston U since '06, prof systematic theology '21-43, dean '26-38, emer since '38. Am Acad Arts Sci(F)—Am Theol Soc—Am Philos Assn—Phi Beta Kappa. 18 Forest St., Cambridge, Mass.☉

21 KNUDSON, Lewis. Plant physiology. BSA '08 (U Mo); PhD '11 (Cornell). Invited to establish plant physiology in Spain, lecturer on subject at Museo Nacional de Ciencias Naturales Madrid and at Barcelona '20-21; research on cambial activity, mycorrhiza, effects of X-rays on plants, culture and ripening of bananas, vanilla seed germination and culture, fermentation, enzyme production, organic nutrition of plants, germination of orchid seeds, symbiosis, wilt disease of banana, chloroplasts, native plants as sources of rubber. Prof plant physiol, head dept bot Cornell U. AAAS(F)—Bot Soc Am—Am Soc Naturalists—Real Socieded Espanola de Historia Natural—Sigma Xi—Phi Kappa Phi. Cayuga Heights Rd., Ithaca, N.Y.†

22 KNULL, Dorothy Johnson. Leafhopper identification. b'08. BS '31 (Ia State Coll); MS '32 (U Neb); PhD '35 (O State U). Author: (with D M De Long) A Check List of Leafhoppers of the Cicadellidae (Homoptera) North of Mexico '45; also articles in field. Asst O Biol Survey '32-35, '42-45. Entomol Soc Am(F)—Sigma Xi. 330 E. Dunedin Rd., Columbus 2, O.

23 KNULL, Josef Nissley. Forest insects. b'91. BSc '15 (Pa State Coll); MSc '24 (O State U). Author articles in field. Entomol Pa Bur Plant Industry '16-30; research entomol Pa Forest Research Inst '30-33; curator insects O State U since '34. Soc Econ Entomol—Entomol Soc Am(F)—O Acad Sci(F)—Gamma Sigma Delta—Sigma Xi. Department Zoology and Entomology, Ohio State University, Columbus 10, O.†

24 KNUTSON, Herbert Claus. Mosquitoes; Orthoptera; Cutworms; Armyworms. AB '36 (Ia Wesleyan Coll); MS '37 (So Meth U); PhD '41 (U Minn). Author articles in field. Asso prof and head dept zool RI State Coll since '48. 1st lt to capt USPHS '43-46. Am Assn Econ Entomol—Entomol Soc Am—Nat Malaria Soc—Am Soc Profl Biol(treas) —NE Forest Disease and Insect Pest Control Com (sec)—Am Mosquito Control Assn—Sigma Xi—Phi Kappa Phi. Department of Zoology, Rhode Island State College, Kingston, R.I.†

10 KOCH, G(eorge) David. Regional geography; Political geography; Soil conservation. b'01. AB '29 (State Tchrs Coll Wayne Neb); MA '34—PhD '38 (U Neb). Research on Nebraska geography. Prof geog Kearney State Tchrs Coll '34; soil tech US Bur Soils '35-36; prof geog Miami (Ohio) U '36, '37, '39; prof geog State Coll Charleston Ill '38-39; prof geog Ind State Tchrs Coll since '39. Ind Acad Sci(F) —AAAAS—Sigma Xi—Am Geog Soc —Assn Am Geog—Nat Council Geog Tchrs (F)—Audubon Soc—Am Nature Assn. Department of Science, Indiana State Teachers College, Terre Haute, Ind.

11 KOCH, Peter. Dutch Guiana: Art (Primitive); Florida birds; Wildfowl (Sanctuaries). b'04. Student '25-27 (evening coll U Cincinnati). Research on rare Florida birds, effect sanctuaries on wildfowl, exploration upper Surinam River in Dutch Guiana with studies of Pagan primitive art, rituals and customs of primitive Djuka tribes and secret voodoo burial rituals. Chief photog Cincinnati Times Star '29-44; dir visual edn Cincinnati Mus '46-48; producer travel films since '44; proprietor Koch Camera Shop since '48. Photog Soc Am—Am Ornithol Unnion—Cooper Ornithol Club. Postoffice Box 37, Big Bend National Park, Tex.†

12 KOCH, Ralph Henry. Pyrometry; Casting (Centrifugal). b'14. BS (chem engring) '39 (Clarkson Coll Tech). Research on pyrometry as applied to cast iron field in melting and heat treating, developed radiation pyrometer for molten iron, developed machines for applying concrete linings to cast iron pipe fittings. Research engr US Pipe and Foundry Co '39-48, plant development engr from '48. Am Foundryman's Soc—Am Ceramic Soc—Am Welding Soc. US Pipe and Foundry Co., Burlington, N.J.

13 KOCH, Thomas Warman. Petroleum exploration. b'02. BS '24—'26-28 (U Calif). Field work in San Joaquin Valley California, Arabia, Java, Sumatra. Author articles in field. Field geol Standard Oil Co Calif '28-33, '33-35, field and dist geol '35-39, dist geol '39-41; subsurface geol Standard Oil of Tex '41-43; asst chief geol Superior Oil Co '43-44, chief geol midcontinent dist since '44. Am Assn Petroleum Geol—Sigma Xi. Box 510, Midland, Texas.

14 KOCK, Winston E(dward). Acoustics; Microwaves; Electronic Organs. b'09. EE '32—MS '33—DSc hon '52 (U Cincinnati); Internat Exchange F '33-34—MA '34—PhD (U Berlin); '36-37 (Inst for Advanced Study Princeton); '37 (Indian Inst Sci Bangalore India). Director projects on speech analysis, speech transmission, speech-operated devices, speech synthesis; telephone instruments, hearing analysis, sound transmission, microwave, acoustic analogues, underwater sound; inventor microwave lens; development special radar equipment; developed pipeless pipe organ. Holds patent on electronic organ. Dir electronic research Baldwin Piano Co Cincinnati '35-42; research physicist Bell Telephone Labs '42-48; dir acoustics since '50. Acoustical Soc Am (F, mem exec council)—Am Phys Soc(F)—Inst Radio Engrs(F)—American Guild Organists—Tau Beta Pi—Eta Kappa Nu—Sigma Xi. Outstanding Young Elec Engr award Eta Kappa Nu; Naval Ordnance award '46. Bell Telephone Laboratories, Murray Hill, N.J.

15 KOEHL, George Martin. Gun erosion; Thermoelectricity. b'09. AB '31 (U NC); AM '33 (George Washington U). Author articles in field. Physicist Carnegie Inst of Washington '43-45; asst prof physics George Washington U '46-47, asso prof since '47; asst dean Jr Coll George Washington U since '47. Am Assn Physics Teachers (pres DC sect '48-49)—Am Phys Soc. Received Naval Ordnance Development Award for work on gun erosion. George Washington University, Washington 6.

16 KOEHLER, Walter Allos. Chemical engineering; Ceramics; Electrochemistry; Industrial corrosion. b'93. BS in Chem Engring '19—ChE '20—PhD '23 (U Wis); MS '22 (U Ill). Author: Applications of Electrochemistry '44; also articles in field. Instr chem engring W Va U '24, asst prof '24-29, prof and head dept chem and ceramic engring since '45, acting dir engring expt sta. Am Inst Chem Engrs—Am Ceramic Soc—Electrochem Soc—Am Chem Soc—W Va Acad Sci—Tau Beta Pi—Sigma Xi. 412 Linden St., Morgantown, W.Va.†

17 KOEHN, George Willis. Industrial adhesives; Metal cleaning. b'17. BA '38 (Coe Coll); MA '41 (U Kan). Research and development of adhesives for specific industrial application. Chem Cycle-Weld Div Chrysler Corp '40-43, asst chief chem '43-46; sect head charge development indsl adhesives and coatings Armstrong Cork Co since '46. Am Chem Soc—ASTM (sec com on adhesives since '48). Armstrong Cork Co., Lancaster, Pa.

18 KOEHNKE, Marx Frederick. Potato inspection and certification. b'03. BSc Agrl '25—grad study '27, '32 (U Neb). Author articles in field. Inspector certified seed potatoes U Neb Coll Agr '27, certification mgr in charge potato certification in Neb since '30. Potato Assn Am (pres '47) —Am Phytopath Soc. c/o Nebraska Certified Potato Growers, Certification Department, Alliance, Neb.

19 KOELLEIN, Charles Lumsden, Jr. River towboats. b'10. BS (elec engring) '34 (U Tenn). Research on design and construction river towboats and barges for petroleum products and dry cargo in bulk; member of Western Rivers Technical Committee of American Bureau of Shipping. Marine engr in charge marine engring dept Nashville Bridge Co since '47. Am Inst EE—Nat Soc Profl Engrs. Nashville Bridge Co., Nashville 1.

20 KOENIG, Charles Jacob. Ceramics (Whitewares, glass, enamels); Nepheline syenite in ceramic wares. b'11. B Cer E '32—MS '33—PhD '35— Cer E '48 (O State U). Author: Use of Syenites in Semi-vitreous Ware '37; Nepheline Syenite in Ceramic Ware '39; Literature Abstracts Pertaining to Nepheline Syenites '47; also articles in field. Ceramic research O State U '35-41; dir research Am Nepheline Corp NY and Great Lakes Foundry Sand Co Detroit under auspices of O State U Research Found since '45. Am Ceramic Soc(F)—Can Ceramic Soc—Inst Ceramic Engrs (chmn publ com)—Sigma Xi. Engineering Experiment Station, Ohio State University, Columbus 10, O.†

21 KOENIG, John Henry. Dielectrics; Refractories; Whitewares (Ceramics). b'09. BS (Chem engring) '31—ChemE '35—MSc '35—PhD '38 (Ohio State U). Author: Ceramic Glazes '41. Issued patents in field. Research chem dielectrics Gen Elec Co '31-35; engring exptl sta whitewares ceramics Ohio State U '35-38; research ceramist whitewares and porcelain Hall China Co '38-42; Bur Ships Dielectrics USN '42-45; dir sch ceramics NJ Ceramic Research Sta Rutgers U since '45. Am Ceramic Soc (F)—Inst Ceramic Engrs—Engrs Council for Profl Development—Ceramic Assn NJ—Sigma Xi—Tau Beta Pi—Keramos. School of Ceramics, Rutgers University, New Brunswick, N.J.

22 KOEPSELL, Harold J(ohn). Fermentation biochemistry. b'15. BS '40 —MS '41—PhD '44 (U Wis). Author articles in field. Fermentation div No Regional Research Lab US Dept Agr since '46. Am Chem Soc—Sigma Xi. U.S. Department of Agriculture, Northern Research Laboratory, Peoria, Ill.

23 KOERNER, Harold Elton. Vertebrate paleontology (Colorado, Montana). b'05. BA '29—MA '30 (U Colo); PhD '39 (Yale). Author articles in field. Asso prof geol U Colo since '47. AAAS—Paleontol Soc—Soc Vertebrate Paleontol—Sigma Xi—Phi Beta Kappa. Department of Geology, University of Colorado, Boulder, Colo.†

24 KOFFLER, Henry. Microbial physiology and comparative biochemistry (Mold metabolism and penicillin). b '22. BS '43 (University Ariz); MS '44—PhD '47—Wis Alumni Research Found fellow '43-46 (U Wis). Author articles in field. Asst prof bact Purdue U '47-49, asso prof since '49. Soc Am Bact—Am Chem Soc—AAAS—Ind Acad Sci—Phi Kappa Phi—Sigma Xi. Nat Research Council predoctoral fellow '46-47, Internat scholar '40-43; Purdue Research Foundation Coordinator for Biol Sciences since '49. Laboratories of Bacteriology, Department of Biological Sciences, Purdue University, Lafayette, Ind.†

25 KOHLS, Glen Milton. Ectoparasites (Ticks, fleas, mites). b'05. BS '29 (Montana State Coll); MS '37 (U Minn). Has studied ticks of world, with special emphasis on North American species, with regard to taxonomy, biology, and role as transmitting agents of such diseases of man as Rocky Mountain spotted fever, tularemia, and Q fever; also research in taxonomy and geographical distribution of North American rabbit fleas. Author articles in field. Sr entomol USPHS Rocky Mountain Lab Hamilton Mont. Lt col US Army Sanitary Corps '43-46 as instr in course in tropical and mil med, field parties engaged in research on tsutsugamushi disease in New Guinea and India, Burma and China. AAAS—Am Soc Parasitol—Am Assn Econ Entomol—Sigma Xi. Recipient USA Typhus Comm Medal. Rocky Mountain Laboratory, Hamilton, Mont.†

26 KOHMAN, Girard Theodore. Physical chemistry; Insulation engineering. b'97. BS '20 (Kan U); PhD '23 (Yale U). Author articles in field. Research chem Bell Telephone Labs since '23. Am Chem Soc—Am Ceramic Soc—Sigma Xi—Tau Beta Pi—Sigma Tau. Bell Telephone Laboratories, Murray Hill, N.J.†

27 KOHNKE, Helmut. Soil physics and conservation (Hydropedology, mulch tillage, run-off, infiltration, reclamation of strip mine spoil banks. b'01. Diplom-Landwirt '24—Doktor der Landwirtschaft '26 (U Berlin); MSc '32 (U Alberta); PhD '34 (O State U). Author articles in field. Soil scientist and asso prof agron Purdue U since '43. Soil Sci Soc Am—Am Soc Agron—Am Geophys Union—Ind Acad Sci. Agronomy Department, Purdue University, Lafayette, Ind.†

28 KOKATNUR, Vaman Ramachandra. Chemical engineering; Industrial planning. b'86. BS '11 (Bombay U); '12-13 (U Cal); MS '14—Shevlin fellow '14-15—PhD '15 (U Minn). Inventor war gases, jelled gasoline for M-59 bomb and flame thrower; development aeroplane dope solvent and vat dyes. Holds over 40 chem patents. Chief research dept Niagara Alkali Co '18-20; asst chief vat dye group Nat Aniline & Chem Co '20-21; spl chem By-Products Steel Corp and duPont Co '21-22; cons since '22; cons regular chlorine and caustic soda Russia Five Year plan '28; faculty mem Inst Chem Northwestern U '28; tech adv and cons mgr Sri Shakti Alkali Works Dhrangadhra India '30-31; hon tech adv Am Trade Commn India '30-33; chmn cons USN '38-47; dir research Antoxygen Inc since '34. AAAS(F)—Am Inst Chem(F)—ACS—Hist Sci Soc—Am Electrochem Soc—Soc Am Mil Engrs—Indian Sci Congress—Sigma Xi. Honored as outstanding inventor US Patent Office Sesquicentennial celebration '40. 114 E. 32d St., NYC.

10 KÖKERITZ, K(arl) A(ugust) Helge. English philology (Chaucer, medieval drama, Shakespeare's pronunciation, language, history. English dialects, place-names); History of shorthand: Swedish language. b'02. MA '24—PhD '32 (Uppsala U Sweden); AM (hon) '44 (Yale). Author: Stenografi (Melins system) '28; Tysk Stenografi '29; The Suffolk Dialect '32; Engelsk Stenografi '35; The Place-Names of the Isle of Wight '41; Mather Flint on Early Eighteenth Century English Pronunciation '44; This Is America '46; Learning Swedish. Books I-IV '46-49, and others; also articles in field. Prof Eng Yale since '44; mem ed staff Hermod Corr Coll Malmö Sweden since '28. English Place-Name Soc—Medieval Acad Am—Modern Lang Assn—Linguistic Soc Am—Internat Phonetic Assn. Davenport College, Yale University, New Haven.☺

11 KOKOMOOR, Franklin Wesley. History of mathematics. b'90. BS '15 (Valparaiso); MA '24—PhD '26 (U Mich). Author: Mathematics in Human Affairs '42. Author articles: Checklist of Seventeenth Century Geometries '28; The Distinctive Features of Seventeenth Century Geometry '28; The Status of Mathematics in India and Arabia During the Dark Ages of Europe '36, and others. Asst prof math U Fla '27-29, asso prof '29-31, prof since '31, chmn genl math since '35. Am Math Soc—Math Assn Am (past chmn SE sect)—Nat Council Teach Math (state rep)—Hist Sci Soc—Fla Edn Assn (past ed math page)—Phi Kappa Phi (past pres, vp, sec). WA 205 University of Florida, Gainesville Fla.☺

12 KOLEHMAINEN, John Ilmari. Finnish-American history. b'10. AB '33—MA '34—PhD '37 (Western Reserve U). Author articles in field. Asst prof Suomi Coll Hancock Mich to direct reorganization of Finnish-Am historical library '46; U Wis Commn on studies in Wis Economy and Culture to prepare study on Finns of Wis '47; prof polit sci Heidelberg Coll since '38. Social Sci Research Council grant-in-aid for research in Finnish-Am hist '45-46; Am Philos Soc grant '48. Heidelberg College, Tiffin O.†

13 KOLESNIKOFF, Vladimir Stephan. Industrial and commodity classification. b'86. MS '29—grad work '29-31 (Columbia); '06-10 (St Petersburg U Russia). Consultant to United Nations Secretary-General '48, United Nations Statistical Office '47-50. Author articles in field. Chief econ Div Statis Standards Bur Budget Executive Office of President since '39. Am Statis Assn—Beta Gamma Sigma. Bureau of the Budget, Washington 25.†

14 KOLLMORGEN, Walter Martin. Agricultural and cultural geography; Agricultural history. b'07. BSc '31—

MA '33 (U Neb); PhD '40 (Columbia). Research on agricultural islands in South, dairy industry of Nebraska, land reclamation in Alluvial valley of lower Mississippi River. Author articles: The German-Swiss in Franklin County, Tennessee '40; The Old Order Amish of Lancaster County Pennsylvania '42; Immigrant Settlements in Southern Agriculture '45; The Search for the Rural Community '46. Co-author: Past and Prospective Drainage Reclamation in the Coastal Marshlands of the Mississippi River Delta '47, and others. Agr Econ Bur Agr Econ US Dept Agr '39-42, '43-46; research dir Tenn State Planning Commn Nashville '43; asso prof geog dept geol U Kan '46-47, prof geog, chmn dept geol since '47. Am Assn Geog—Agrl Hist Soc. Grant Social Sci Research Council '37-38. Department of Geography, University of Kan., Lawrence, Kan.†

15 KOLLROS, Catharine Lutherman. Flour beetles: Behavior of chickens. b'17. SB '38—PhD '44 (U Chicago). Co-author articles: (with W C Allee and N E Collias) Modification of the Social Order in Flocks of Hens by the Injection of Testosterone Propionate '39; (with W C Allee) An Experimental Study of Certain Effects of Temperature on Differential Growth of Pullets '40; (with T Park and E V Gregg) Interspecific Competition in Populations of Granary Beetles '41, and others. Research and teaching asst U Chicago '38-40, '42-45; instr State U Ia since '46. Ecol Soc Am—Sigma Xi—Phi Beta Kappa. 331 Melrose Ct., Iowa City, Ia.

16 KOMAREK, Edwin Vaclay. Mammalogy (Game management, ecology): Hybrid corn. b'09. Student '29-33 (U Chicago). Author articles in field. Agrl and wildlife cons. Am Soc Mammalogists—Ecol Soc—Wildlife Soc—Am Soc Agron—Soil Sci Soc Am—Nat Speol Soc—Fla Acad Sci. Birdsong Plantation, Thomasville, Ga.

17 KONIUSZY, Frank Robert. Alkaloids: Anti-biotics: Vitamins. b'13. BS '36—MS '37 (U Ill). Holder five US patents, others pending. Author articles in field. Research chem Merck & Co Inc since '37. Research Division. Merck & Company., Inc., Rahway, N.J.†

18 KONZO, Seichi. Air conditioning: Combustion; Fluid flow. b'05. BS '27 (U Wash); MS '29 (U Ill). Research on warm air heating, summer air conditioning, flow of air, combustion of fuels, winter air conditioning. Author: Winter Air Conditioning, '39; also articles in field. Spl research asst U Ill '29-32, research asso '32-35, asst prof '35-37, asso prof '37-40, prof since '40; cons in fuels with Ill Geol Survey. Am Soc Heating Ventilating Engrs—Tau Beta Pi—Sigma Xi. 126 Mechanical Engineering Building, University of Illinois, Urbana, Ill. H: 510 S. McKinley Av., Champaign.†

19 KOOKEN, Don Leo. Criminology (Police, lie detection, criminal investigation and detection, cryptography). b'91. Worked in field for US Treasury Dept and Chicago Assn of Commerce; engaged research and writing on post war influence on criminal investigation, ethics in police service. Associate editor American Journal Police Science since '45. Author: Crime Control: Black and Blue Jay '33; also articles in field. With US Treasury Intelligence Unit and Bur Prohibition Criminal Investigation '27-31; asst dir Secret Six of Chicago C of C '31-33; mem faculty Traffic Inst Northwestern U since '39; mem Ind State Police Bd since '45; acting dir Inst Criminal Law Adminstrn Ind U and dir safety

since '46. Internat Assn Chiefs Police—Ind Social Hygiene Assn (dir, exec com). Institute of Criminal Law Administration, Indiana University, Bloomington, Ind.

20 KOOKER, Arthur Raymond. American history (Anti-slavery movements, social, military). b'07. AB '32—Am '33—PhD '41 (U Mich). Author articles in field. Asso prof hist U So Calif since '47. Officer AAF '42-46, historical officer '43-46. AHA—Miss Valley Hist Assn—So Hist Assn—Soc Am Archivists—Abraham Lincoln Assn. University of Southern California, University Park, Los Angeles 7. H: 3830 West Blvd., Los Angeles 8.†

21 KOONZ, Carl H(enry). Food preservation, manufacture, and processing (Poultry, eggs, meat): Industrial microscopy; Animal cytology. b'07. BA '31 (Carroll Coll); MA '34—PhD '37 (Northwestern U). Research on spermatogenesis in haploid parthenogenetic hymenopteran, low-temperature preservation of meats, relation of ante-mortem and post-mortem factors to quality of meats, methods of handling poultry and poultry products to improve and maintain quality, microscopy of foods including changes during processing and manufacture. Author articles: A Method for Studying the Histological Structure of Frozen Products '39; A Rapid and Simplified Method for Revealing the Surface Pattern of Hair '45; Influence of Freezing on Color of Bones and Adjacent Tissues '47, and others. Research biol Swift & Co since '37, head poultry research and egg research divs, head div histology and micros. Am Soc Parasitol—Am Micros Soc—Ill State Acad Sci—AAAS—World Poultry Sci Assn—Biol Photographic Assn—Inst Food Technol—Sigma Xi. Swift & Company Research Laboratories, Union Stock Yards, Chicago 9.

22 KOOPMANS, Tjalling Charles. Econometrics; Mathematical economics; Economics of transportation; Statistics. b'10. MA '33 (U Utrecht); PhD '36 (U Leiden). Research on application of mathematical and statistical methods to economic problems, particularly economic fluctuations and welfare economics. Author: Tanker Freight Rates and Tankship Building '39. Editor: Statistical Inference in Dynamic Economic Models; also articles in field. Specialist financial section League Nations '38-40; lecturer statis NYU '40-41; statis combined Shipping Adjustment Bd and Brit Merchant Shipping Mission Washington '42-44; professor econ U Chicago '45-48, research asso Cowles Commn Research Econ since '44, and director of research since '48. Am Statis Assn—Am Econ Assn—Econometric Soc (F)—Inst Math Statis(F). University of Chicago, Chicago 37.

23 KOOS, Earl Lomon. Family sociology. b'05. ScB '31 (O State U); MA '44—PhD '46 (Columbia). Research on relation of family problems to community resources, family interpersonal relationships to effect of problems on family, middleclass family's relation to problems and community resources, relation of family structure and social position in community to health attitudes and behavior, effect of movement of people to suburban communities upon communities and people themselves. Author: Families in Trouble '46; Sociology of the Patient '50; Middle-Class Family and its Problems '51; Suburbanization in Webster, N.Y. '46. Dir research Rochester Council Soc Agencies '42-44; lecturer Smith Coll, Sarah Lawrence Coll, U Tex '46-50; prof and chmn dept sociol U Rochester since '48, dir Study Community Health since '46, vis cons Hogg Found Mental Hygiene since '49. Am Sociol Soc—Nat Council Family Relations. Research F Clark Fund '32-39, research F Josiah Macy Jr Found '40-42. University of Rochester, Rochester 3, N.Y.†

10 KOPAC, M(ilan) J(ames). Microsurgery; Physical properties of protoplasm; Enzymatic cytochemistry; Cancer research. b'05. BS '27—MS '29 (U Neb); PhD '34 (U Cal). Investigator Trotugas Laboratory Carnegie Institution summers '33-37; civilian investigator OSRD US Army and US Navy '40-43; consultant national Cancer Institute USPHS '47-48; principle investigator cancer research grants USPHS since '47; member panel cell physiology com on growth National Research Council since '49. Marine Biol Lab Corp—Woods Hole—Bermuda Biol Sta Inc—NY Acad Sci(F)—Soc Zoologists —Soc Gen Physiology—Soc Cell Biol —Assn Cancer Research Inc—Soc Exptl Biol—Harvey Soc. 100 Washington Square E., NYC 3.⊚

11 KOPP, Paul Joseph. Chemical patent literature. BA '32 (Lehigh U); MA '33 (Duke U); LLB '49 (George Washington U). Analytical chem jr exec research and development dept Colgate-Palmolive-Peet Co '35-41; asst patent dept Gulf Oil Corp Washington '46-48; member prof staff research and develop bd dept defense since '48; registered patent lawyer. First lt to lt colonel chem warfare service US Army '41-46. Am Chem Soc—Am Phys Soc—Am Math Soc—AAAS—ASME— Am Statis Assn—Am Petroleum Inst— Am Soc Testing Materials—ALA— Franklin Inst. Hollygate Farm, RFD 1, Manassas, Va.

12 KOPPLIN, Karl. Thermoset synthetics; Laminates; thermoplastic synthetic resin plastics. b'05. BS (Beloit Coll); grad work (Northwestern U) (U Chicago). Holder three process patents in plastics industry. Plastics research especially in thero-set synthetics, laminates and injection molding of thermoplastic resins. Author article: Liquid Resins as Plywood Adhesives. With indsl research div Western Elec '29-36; chief engr Roddis Veneer Co '36-38; in charge liquid resin adhesive development Catalin Corp '38-40; set up plant for processing sisal fibre and synthetic resins for F Burkart Mfg '40-42; cons in laminated plastics for various indsl firms '42-45; vp Plastics Molding Co '45-48; pres Kopplin Molding Corp since '48. Soc Plastics Industry—Soc Plastics Engrs (dir). Kopplin Molding Corp., 1440 Blair, StL 6.

13 KOREE, Jean Ulyxes. Industrial engineering (Automatic mechanical equipment). b'94. Pvt tutors (Bucharest and Berlin). Invented many mechanical devices on razors, blades and automatic production of safety razor blades; since '35 many improvements on automatic firearms, airplanes, airplane equipment, and other mechanical devices. Indsl engr. Bar Building, 36 W. 44th St., NYC.⊚

14 KORFF, Serge Alexander. Nuclear and upper atmosphere physics; Cosmic rays; Geiger counters; Balloon techniques. b'06. AB '28—MA '29—PhD '31 (Princeton U). Research fellow California Institute of Technology and leader cosmic-ray expeditions to Mexico and Peru '34-35. Author: Counters '45. Prof physics NYU since '47. Am Phys Soc(F)—Am Astron Soc—Royal Geog Soc—Sigma Xi. New York University, NYC 53.⊚

15 KORSON, George. Pennsylvania and American folklore and folksongs. b'99. Collector of indigenous folklore

and folksongs of miners since '25 beginning search among a n t h r a c i t e miners of Pennsylvania; founded and directed Pennsylvania Folk Festival first held at Allentown '35, Bucknell U '36, '37, Beaver Coll '38; toured bituminous coal regions recording ballads as miners sang, collecting stories and legends '38-41, directed Library of Congress ballad-recording field expedition in anthracite region '46. Author: Songs and Ballads of the Anthracite Miner '27; Minstrels of the Mine Patch '38; Black Land '41; Coal Dust on the Fiddle '43. Editor: P e n n s y l v a n i a Songs and Legends '49; Albums of Anthracite Songs '48. Co-editor: The Child's Book of Folklore '47. Reporter various papers '17-34; devoted entire time to folklore '35-42; writer news editor and fgn editor ARC Nat Hdqrs Washington '42-46; editor The Red Cross Courier '47-50. Pa Folklore Soc (vp) —Pa Hist Assn—Poetry Soc Am— Am Folklore Soc (councillor). 1301 15th St. N.W., Washington.

16 KOSANKE, Robert M. Paleozoic spores and pollens; Pennsylvanian stratigraphy; Coal botany; Illinois coal beds. b'17. BA '40 (Coe Coll); MA '42—student '42-43 (U Cincinnati); '44-45 (U Ill). Author articles in field. Asso geol Ill Geol Survey since '47. AAAS(F)—Am Bot Soc — Paleontol Soc—la Sci Acad(F)—Ill Acad Sci—Ill Mining Inst—Soc Econ Geol (com coal research)—Nat Research Council (com interrelations of paleobot)—Sigma Xi. Illinois Geological Survey, Urbana, Ill.

17 KOSCO, George Francis. Antarctic geography; Arctic geography. b'08. BS '30 (USN Acad); '37-39 (Post grad Sch Annapolis Md); MS '40 (MIT). In charge collection of meteorological data scientific expedition to Arctic; meteorological studies Antarctic, Alaska and Aleutian areas. With USNs ince '30. Explorer's Club—Propeller Club. Navy Weather Central, Seattle 5.

18 K O S H U B A, Walter (Joseph). High temperature metallurgy. b'17. BMetE '40 (U Minn). Research in heavy forgings, technology of processing, turbine castings for elevated temperature service, forging of hi-temperature steels, X-ray and metallographic studies of welds for elevated temperature application, p r e c i s i o n casting technology (refractories, waxes and binders), creep studies of hi-temperature materials, elevated temperature materials for atomic power. Author articles in field. Student engr Allis-Chalmers Mfg Co '40-42, asst research engr '42-43, asst supt research engring '43-46; cons Bergen Precision Castings Corp '46; gen supt and expt engr Solar Aircraft Co '46; sr metallurgist NEPA Div Fairchild Engine and Airplane Corp '47, principal metallurgist and head materials sect since '47. Am Inst Mining and Metal Engrs—Am Soc Metals—Am Ceramic Soc—AAAS. NEPA Division, Box 415, Oak Ridge, Tenn.†

19 KOSIKOWSKY, Frank Vincent. Fermented milks; Cheese (Chemistry, bacteriology, manufacture); Milk pasteurization (Phosphatase methods). b '16. BS '39 (U Conn); MS '41—PhD '44 (Cornell). Dairy Industries Supply Association fellowship for study of gradying dairy products '39; National Cheese Institute research project on Cheddar and foreign types cheese relative decomposition products formed in cheese during ripening, effect of introduction special type bacteria to cheese; development phosphatase methods pasteurization of milk '48, phosphatase test for effect pasteurization on cheese, chocolate milk, ice

cream; study of factors affecting quality of buttermilk, isolation special bacteria to produce cheese from fermented milk. Author articles: Filter Paper Chromatography as a Means to Determine the Amino Acids and Amines Developed in Cheddar Cheese during Ripening '49; A Smiple Universal Dairy Products Phosphatase Test '49, Co-author articles: (with A C Dahlberg) The Tyramine Content of Cheese '48; (with A C Dahlberg) The Development of Flavor in American Cheddar Cheese made from Pasteurized Milk with Streptococcus faecalis Starter '48; (with H J Brueckner) A Study of Factors Influencing the Quality of Buttermilk '41; (with E S Guthrie) The Manufacture of Cultured Buttermilk '47. Research asso Cornell '44, asst prof dairy sci '45-47, asso prof since '47. Am Dairy Sci Assn—AAAS —Inst Food Tech—Sigma Xi. Department of Dairy Industry, Cornell University, Ithaca. H: 116 Delaware Av.

20 KOSKI, Walter S. Physical chemistry; Explosives; Nuclear chemistry. b'13. PhD '42 (Johns Hopkins U). Author articles in field. Asso prof chem Johns Hopkins since '47, on leave to Brookhaven Nat Lab '48; Los Alamos Sci Lab '44-47. Am Chem Soc—Am Phys Soc—Sigma Xi—Phi Beta Kappa. Johns Hopkins University, Department of Chemistry, Baltimore 18.

21 KOSOLAPOFF, Gennady Michael. Phosphorus (Chemistry). b'09. BS (Chem E) '32 (Cooper Union); MS '33 —ScD '36 (U Mich). Research on chemistry of organic phosphorus compounds and application to biochemistry; development new synthetic methods, investigation chemical properties, and application organic phosphorus compounds to medicinal agents, insecticides, plasticizers and flame proofing agents. Holds 21 patents in field. Author: Organophosphorus Compounds '50. Contributor: Organic Reactions (Vol 6) '51. Research Monsanto Chem Co '38-48, Ala Poly Inst since '48. ACS—Chem Soc London— Phi Lambda Upsilon—Phi Kappa Phi. Alabama Polytechnic Institute, Auburn, Ala. H: P.O. Box 830.†

22 KOSTER, William Jacob. Sculpins of New York; Distribution of fishes, amphibians and reptiles of New Mexico. Grad scholar '32-34—BS—PhD '36 (Cornell U). Author articles in field. Asst, asso, to prof biol U NM since '38. Am Soc Ichthyologists Herpetologists—Am Soc Limnol Oceanog—Am Fisheries Soc—Ecol Soc Am—AAAS— NM Acad Sci—Sigma Xi—Phi Kappa Phi—Phi Sigma. University of New Mexico, Albuquerque, N.M.

23 KOSTING, Peter Robert. Guns (Erosion); Steel (Fatigue). b'03. BS '25 (Cooper Union); MChE '26—PhD '28 (Rensselaer Poly Inst). Research in fatigue of steel and in erosion of guns. Author article: Progressive Stress Damage in Surface Stressing of Metals. Metall Nat Bur Standards Washington '31-32, Watertown Arsenal Lab Mass since '32. AIME—ASTM— Am Soc Metals. Watertown Arsenal, Watertown 72, Mass.

24 KOTTAS, Harry. Machine design; Plant engineering; Air handling plants; Turbo-expanders; Bearings; Dynamometers; Gas turbines. b'10. BS (ME) '32—MS '33 (U Neb). Engineering and layout air handling plants and equipment, including compressors, exhausters, refrigeration, dehumidification, heat exchange, and piping; development refrigeration turbines for production extremely low temperatures in a flowing gas stream; design high speed, journal and thrust, hydrodynamic and anti-friction bearings; also high speed dynamometers; design of gas turbines and components. Mech design engr Roberts Dairy Co Lincoln Neb '35-36; mech engr Swift & Co Omaha Neb '36-37; with Nat Adv Com Aeronautics since '37, now chief mech engring div. ASME—Soc Automotive Engrs—Inst Aeronautical Sci. Lewis Flight Propulsion Laboratory, National Advisory Committee for Aeronautics, Cleveland Airport, Cleve 11. H: R.F.D. 4, Box 194½, Huntsville, Ala.

10 KOUCHAKJI, Fahim Joseph. Art, glass and pottery (Greek, Roman, Syrian, Persian, Egyptian, Arabic). b'86. Student (Ecole Grecque Episcopal St Nicholas Aleppo); '04-09 (Credit Lyonnaise Cairo Egypt). Author: The Great Chalice of Antioch '25. Co-author: Glass '27. Collaborator: (with G A Eisen) Portraits of Washington (3 vols) '33; Ancient Oriental Cylinder and other Seals '40. Pres Kouchakji Freres NY '24-25. Met Mus Art—Iranian Inst Art and Archeology. 32 E. 57th St., NYC.⊙

11 KOULOMZINE, Theodore. Magnetic and electrical prospecting; Magnetometers; Mining geology (Northwest Quebec and Algeria). b'06. Licencie es Sciences '28 (U Paris France Sorbonne); Ingenieur ENSP '29 (U Strasbourg France). Supervized and interpreted results of over 275 geophysical surveys in Canada; invented improvements in magnetometers, new methods geophysical prospecting, designed new instruments; chairman geophysical committee Can Inst Mining and Metallurgy '46-47; member associal committee on geodesy and geophysics National Research Council of Canada '46-48. Engr research dept Ste Mines de Fer de Rouina, Algeria and Morocco '29-33; tech mgr Ardoises and Crayons, Paris '33-34; staff engr then pres Techni-Counsel Ltd, cons geophysics firm, NW Queber '37-42; mgr Central Cadillac Mines Ltd '42-43; partner Koulomzine Geoffray & Co cons since '43. Corp Profl Engrs Que Can—Inst Mining and Metall—AIMM E—Engring Inst Can—Geol Assn Can —Soc Exploration Geophysicists—Am Geophys Union—AAAS. 1263 7th St., Val d'or, P.Q., Can.

12 KOUWENHOVEN, John Atlee. Interrelationships between the arts and technology in America. b'09. AB '31 (Wesleyan U); AM '33—PhD '48—President's U scholar '36-37 (Columbia). Author: Adventures of America 1857-1900 '38; Made in America—The Arts in Modern Civilization '48; also articles in field. Mem lit faculty Bennington Coll '38-41; asst ed Harper's Mag '41-44, asso ed '44-46, contbg ed since '46; asso in Eng and Am studies Barnard Coll '46-48, asso prof Eng since '48. Barnard College, Columbia University, NYC 27.†⊙

13 KOVARIK, Alois Francis. Radioactivity. b'80. AB '04—AM '07—PhD '09 (U Minn); John Harling research fellow in physics and research in radioactivity '09-11—DSc '16 (Victoria U Eng); MA hon '25 (Yale); Doktor Rerum Naturalium hon '32 (Karlova U Prague). Researches in radioactivity, ionization of gases, statistical methods in studying Alpha, Beta Gamma and X-rays and first automatic registration of rays, problem of age of the earth, nuclear physics. With Yale since '16, prof physics '25-48, emeritus since '48. Mem Radioactivity Congress Brussels '10. AAAS(F)—Am Phys Soc(F)—Natural History Mus (F)—Am Math Soc—Math Assn Am —Am Meteorol Soc—Société des Mathématiciens et des Physiciens of Czechoslovakia (hon)—Société Francaise de Physique—Phi Beta Kappa—Sigma Xi —Pi Gamma Mu. Sloan Physics Laboratory, Yale University, New Haven.⊙

14 KRAEMER, Albert J. Oil shale utilization. b'92. BS '15 (U Ky). Technical advisor Petroleum Administrative Board '34; secretary technical committee on lubricants and liquid fuels Federal Specifications Board since '26. Author articles in field. Asso with Union Oil Co Calif '16-17, Standard Oil Co Ky '19-23; asst chem to asst chief Bur Mines US Dept Interior Washington since '23. Am Soc Testing Materials (com D-2 since '26)—Am Standards Assn (com Z-11)—Nat Fire Protection Assn (flammable liquids com)—Am Chem Soc—Am Petroleum Inst. Bureau of Mines, U.S. Department of Interior, Washington 25.

15 KRAEMER, J(ohn) Hugo. Forestry (Forest resources, management, silviculture, timber mechanics, economics, wood waste utilization, relations of growth and quality, relations between influencing factors and mech properties of red pine and central hardwoods). b'09. Graduate '28 (NY State Ranger Sch, Syracuse U); BSF '34 (U Ida); MF '35 (Harvard); PhD '43—research fellow '41-43 (Yale U). Author: Native Woods for Construction Purposes in the Western Pacific Region '44; Native Woods for Construction Purposes in the South China Sea Region '44. Co-author: They Need Not Vanish '43; also articles in field. Asso in forestry dept forestry and agrl expt sta Purdue U since '47. Soc Am Foresters—Ecol Soc Am—Forest Products Research Soc—Sigma Xi—Xi Sigma Pi. Department of Forestry, Purdue University, Lafayette, Ind.†

16 KRAFT, Ferdinand. Wood pulp. '24 (Tech U Darmstadt). Preparation b'99. Diploma in engring '23—D Eng wood pulp by acid and alkaline processes; multistage and continuous bleaching all types wood pulp; chemical refining wood cellulose for rayon, transparent films and manufacture of high alpha cellulose for high tenacity yarns; research on use wood cellulose for explosives, wood pulp for all types paper products, and refined wood cellulose for plastics. Author articles: Pulp Bleaching in America '38; Sulfate and Sulfite Bleaching '46. Contributor: Pulp and Paper Manufacture '50. Cons wood pulp and rayon industry Am and Europe '29-45; asst to tech dir Can Internat Paper Co Temiskaming Que Can '35-44; tech dir Marathon Paper Mills of Can Martahon Ont since '45. AICE—Engring Inst Can— Tech Assn Pulp and Paper Industries —Can Pulp and Paper Assn—Corp Professional Engrs Que. Marathon Paper Mills of Canada, Marathon, Ont. H: 6 Drake St.

17 KRAMER, Amihud. Agricultural chemistry; Quality control of foods; color measurement. b'13. BS '38—MS '39—PhD '42 (U Md). Research on nutritive value raw, canned, frozen and dehydrated foods, relation nutritive values to consumer acceptance of foods. Developed rapid fiber test for determining toughness of asparagus, photoelectric methods for determining ripeness and color in fruits and vegetables, rapid blendor method for determining fibrousness green and wax beans, objective methods for testing maturity and color lima beans, succulometer for measuring succulence sweet corn, application alcohol insoluble solids test to maturity measurement sweet corn, test for determining pericarp toughness and quality in sweet corn, standardization of tenderometers for measuring quality peas, test for grittiness of pears. Author articles in field. Cooperative agt Soil Conservation Service '39-40; food chem Nat Canners Assn '41-43; research asso U Md dept hort since '44. Am Soc Hort Sci—Am Soc Plant Physiol—

Inst Food Technol—Am Statis Assn. Department of Horticulture, University of Maryland, College Park, Md.†

18 KRAMER, Fred Siegfried. Aviation gas turbines; Aerodynamics; Jet propulsion. b'06. Student '25-27 (Institute of Technology Berlin Germany); Graduate (ME) '27 (Goetze School Berlin). Member editorial board and screening committee for captured documents on jet propulsion US Air Force '45. Holds patents on aviation gas turbine design and application. Independent aeronautical cons Union S Africa '39-40; Am factory rep airplanes and equipment S Africa '39-40; instr engring dept Spartan Sch Aero Tulsa Okla, and ground sch classes AAF and Brit Royal Air Force; flight test engr Consol-Vultee Corp San Diego Calif '42-43, preliminary design group '42-43; engineer service department Convair '44; preliminary design section aviation gas turbine division Westinghouse Phila '45; bus engring and investigation since '47. Inst Aeronaut Sci (asso F)—Royal Aeronaut Soc Gt Brit (asso F)—Soc Automotive Engrs. Holds pvt pilot licenses. Box 6092, Arlington 6, Va.

19 KRAMER, Hans. Flood control and navigation; Dams; Foundations; Hydraulic structures. b'94. Student '12-13 (Mich U); BS '18 (US Mil Acad); grad Engr Sch '29; MS '28 (Pa U); DE '32 (Dresden Tech U Germany). Acted as consultant for Panama Canal sea-level studies; represented US on Colorado-Kansas-Arkansas River Compact Commission; supervising engineer Panama Canal Third Locks Project. Author: Modellgeschiebe und Schleppkraft '32. Commd 2d lt Corps Engrs US Army '18, advancing to brig gen '42, retired '45. Am Inst Cons Engrs— Soc Am Mil Engrs—ASCE—Permanent Internat Assn Nav Congs—Am Geophys Union—Internat Assn Hydraulic Research. Awarded Freeman Traveling Scholarship ASCE '30-31. 462 Nevada Av., San Mateo, Calif.

20 KRAMER, Herbert Harvey. Forage crop breeding. b'16. BS '39 (Colo A&M); MS '41—PhD '46 (U Minn). Research on selection, evaluation, and testing forage crops, calculation of linkage intensities and combining linkages. Author articles in field. Prof agron Purdue U since '51. Am Society Agron—Alpha Zeta Phi Kappa Phi— Sigma Xi. Agronomy Department, Purdue University, Lafayette, Ind.

21 KRAMER, Paul Jackson. Botany; Plant physiology (Tree). b'04. AB '26 (Miami U); MSc '29—PhD '31 (O State U). Research on plant and soil water relations, physiology of woody plants, photosynthesis of trees, photoperiodism in woody species, length of growing season, absorption of water by plants. Author articles in field. With Duke U since '31, prof bot since '45; dir Sarah P Duke Garden since '45. Bot Soc Am—Am Soc Plant Physiol (sec-treas '41-43, vp '43-44, pres '45-46) —AAAS—NC Acad Sci—Phi Beta Kappa—Sigma Xi. Department of Botany, Duke University, Durham, N.C.

22 KRAMER, Samuel Noah. Sumerology; Cuneiform studies; Near Eastern studies. b'97. BS '21 (Temple U); '26-27 (Dropsie Coll); PhD archeol and Semitics '26-29 (U Pa). Laid foundations of, made first beginning in, scientific restorations and trustworthy translation of Sumerian literature; member University Pennsylvania's excavating expeditions to Billah, Gawra, and Fara in Iraq '30-31, research elsewhere in Near East. Author: Gilgamesh and the Huluppu Tree '38; Lamentation Over the Destruction of Ur '40; Sumerian Mythology: A Study of Spiritual and Literary Achievement in the

Third Millenium B C; Sumerian Literary Texts from Nippur '44. Editor: Sumerian Epics and Myths; Sumerian Texts of Varied Contents; also articles in field. Research asst Oriental Inst U Chicago '32-35, research asso '36-42, work at Mus Ancient Orient '39; annual prof Am Schs Oriental Research Instanbul and Bagdad '46-47; studying and copying Sumerian lit tablets in U Mus U Pa since '39, research fellow U Mus, asso curator, Clark research prof Assyriology, curator tablet collections. Fellow '30-31 Am Council Learned Soc, Am Sch Oriental Research at Bagdad; Guggenheim fellow '37-39. Am Philos Soc—Am Oriental Soc—Am Anthrop Assn—AAAS—Archeol Inst Am—Soc Biblical Lit. 33rd and Spruce Sts., Phila.

10 KRAMISH, Arnold. Nuclear weapons (Effects). b'23. BS '45 (U Denver); MA '47 (Harvard); '47-48 (Stanford). Experience on classified and non classified work on Nuclear weapons and their effects. Co-editor: Effects of Atomic Weapons '50. Mass spectrometer maintenance supervisor Fercleve Corp Oak Ridge '44-45; quality control Los Alamos Lab '45-46; declassification MED '46; declassification cons AEC '47-49, physicist since '49. APS—AAAS—Washington Philos Soc. 1901 Constitution Av, Washington 25.†

11 KRANER, Hobart McKinley. Refractories; Steel furnaces; Ceramics; Electrical porcelain; Fused minerals. b'96. BCerE '21—MSc '22 (O State U). Author articles in field. Research Engr Bethlehem Steel Co since '35. AIME—Am Iron and Steel Inst—Am Ceramic Soc (pres '49-50)—Inst Ceramic Engrs. Bethlehem Steel Company, Bethlehem, Pa.⊚

12 KRANTZ, Fred A. Potato breeding and production. b'90. BS '18—MS '21—PhD '24 (U Minn). Research on inheritance in potato, methods of breeding. Developed and introduced Warba, Red Warba, Mesaba, Kasota, Waseca, Chisago and Satapa varieties of potatoes. Author: Potato Breeding Methods I, II, III—'24, '29, 46; also articles in field. Instr hort U Minn '19-24, asst prof '24-35, asso prof '35-37, prof, head sect vegetable gardening div hort since '37. Potato Assn Am (pres '38)—Am Soc Hort Sci—Gamma Sigma Delta—Sigma Xi. Awarded bronze medal for contributions to sci of breeding potatoes and development new varieties of merit Minn State Hort Soc '43. University Farm, St. Paul 1.⊚

13 KRAPPE, Alexander Haggerty. Folklore and mythology. b'94. MA '17 (U Ia); PhD '19 (U Chicago). Research on folklore, philology, literature. US delegate Jubilee Cong of Folklore Society. Author: Balor with the Evil Eye '27; Etudes de mythologie et de folklors germaniques '28; The Science of Folklore '30; Mythologie Universelle '30; La Genese des Mythes '38; also articles in field. Instr romance langs Ind U '19-22; asst prof Romance lang U Minn '24-28; grad lecturer Romance lang Columbia U summers '26, '28; asst prof Romance lang Geo Washington U '31-33; charge de cours Ecole Libre des Hautes Etudes NYC since '43. Am Folklore Soc — Brit Folklore Soc — Inst de Philologie et d'Histoire Orientales et Slaves Belgium. Awarded Medal of Arts and Literature Hispanic Soc Am. P.O. Box 221, Princeton, N.J.

14 KRASKA, E(ugene) J(ames). Canneries. b'21. BS (chem) '41 (St Olaf Coll); '41-43 (U Minn). Research on grading canned goods, inplant chlorination in relation to spoilage and spoilage control, adaptability of refractometer in determining maturity of fresh fruits and vegetables, agitated heat processing, steam blanching, bacteriological control, production creamogenized corn, cannery operations and damage control, sanitary can construction, packaging. With Fresh Fruit and Vegetable Branch USDA '43-45; chief chem Lakeside Packing Co Manitowoc Wis '45; owner Kraska Food Lab since '46; canned goods spl Assn Am RR since '50. Inst Food Tech. Kraska Food Laboratory and Association American Railroads, 720 Oak St., Manitowoc, Wis.

15 KRAUS, Bertram S. Physical anthropology; Archeology (Japanese). b'13. AB '34 (Western Reserve U); MA '46 (U Chicago); PhD '49 (U Chicago). Editor: Prehistory of Japan '49; also articles in field. Asst prof dept anthrop U Ariz since '47. Am Anthrop Assn(F)—Am Assn Phys Anthrop—Am Soc Human Genetics—Sigma Xi. Department of Anthropology, University of Arizona, Tucson, Ariz.

16 KRAUS, Edward Henry. Mineralogy; Gems and gem materials. b'75. BS '96—MS '97—ScD (hon) '20—LLD '34 (Syracuse); PhD '01 (U Munich). Author: Essentials of Crystallography '06; Descriptive Mineralogy '11. Co-author: Mineral Tables '30; Mineralogy '36; Gems and Gem Materials '47; also articles in field. Dean U Mich, emeritus since '45. Geol Soc Am(F)—AA AS(F)—Mineral Soc Am (pres '20)—Am Chem Soc—Optical Soc Am—Am Inst Mining Metall Engrs—Gemological Inst Am (pres '46)—Phi Beta Kappa —Sigma Xi—Phi Kappa Phi. Awarded Roebling medal Mineral Soc Am '45. 1155 Arlington Blvd., Ann Arbor.⊚

17 KRAUS, E(zra) J(acob). Ornamental plants (Hybridizing and selection for improved varieties). b'85. BS '07—(Mich State Agrl Coll); PhD '17 (U Chicago); DSc '38 (Ore State Coll) '49 (Mich State Coll). Researches in reproduction and metabolism, effect of growth regulating substances and nutrition on plants of economic importance. Prof hort research Ore Agr Coll '09-18, dean coll letters and sci '18-19; prof applied botany U Wis '19-27; prof botany U Chicago '27-50, emeritus, distinguished service prof '43-50, chmn dept botany '34-47; prin plant physiologist USDA '38-51. Am Soc Hort Sci(pres '27)—Bot Soc Am(pres '33)— Ecol Soc Am—Entomol Soc Washington—Am Soc Plant Physiol(pres '28) —Am Soc Naturalists (vp '31)—Phi Beta Kappa—AAAS (F, vp and chmn sect G '30). Horticulture Dept., Oregon State College, Corvallis, Ore. H: Hotel Benton.†⊚

18 KRAUS, James E. Vegetable crop physiology and culture; Vegetable breeding (Onions); Canning and freezing crops. b'09. BS '32 (Colo A&M Coll); MS '34 (U Wis); PhD '40 (Cornell U). Author articles in field. Head dept hort, prof and horticulturist U Ida, Ida Agrl Expt Sta since '48 asso dir Ida Agrl Expt Sta since '49. Am Soc Hort Sci—NW Assn Hort Entomol Plant Path—Sigma Xi. Morrell Hall, University of Idaho, Moscow, Ida.†

19 KRAUS, John Daniel. Antennas. b'10. BS '30—MS '31—PhD '33 (U Mich). Originator corner reflector antenna, flat-top beam (W8JK type), helical beam antenna, T-match antenna, twin-3 antenna, several multi-wire doublets, and a number of specialized antenna types. Author: Elements of Electromagnetics '49. Co-author: Very High Frequency Techniques '47; also articles in field. Div head Naval Ordnance Lab '40-43; group leader Radio Research Lab Harvard U '43-46; asso prof elec engring O State U since '46. Inst Radio Engrs—Phys Soc— Acoustical Soc—AAAS—Sigma Xi. Department of Electrical Engineering, Ohio State Univ., Columbus 10. O.⊚

20 KRAUS, Robert A(nthony). Lubrication; Welding. b'20. BS (ME) '42— MS '47 (Ill Inst Tech). Lubricant applications for all types industrial equipment; study methods and installation automatic lubrication equipment; design automatic application systems; research on additives for improved lubricant performance; hard surfacing by welding; maintenance equipment using submerged arc welding methods. Author articles: Lubrication Equipment Maintenance '48; Modern Sealing Devices for the Steel Industry '49, and others. Lubrication engr Republic Steel Corp Chicago '42-48, asst supt mech maintenance since '48. Am Soc Lubrication Engrs (chmn bd dirs)—Assn Iron and Steel Engrs (bd dirs, exec com, lubrication com)— Am Welding Soc—ASME—Blast Furnace & Coke Assn—Chicago Tech Soc Council. Republic Steel Corp., 116th and Burley, Chgo 17. H: 8543 S. Elizabeth St., Chgo 20.

21 KRAUSE, Arthur Herman. Rubber chemistry; Synthetic resins. b'02. BSc (U Chicago). Developed purification method for succinic acid, developed and improved microanalytical methods of toxic substances, research on plastics and rubber derivatives. Holder US patent. Author articles in field. With research and development dept Monsanto Chem Co St Louis '27-32; with Miner Labs cons chem Chicago '36-38, Interlake Iron Corp '39-40; research and prodn Motloid Co Inc Chicago '41; div indsl hygiene Dept Pub Health State Ill '41-45; research chem Marbon Corp Gary Ind since '45. Am Chem Soc. Marbon Corporation, 1926 W. 10 St., Gary, Ind. H: R.R. 1, Niemeyer Rd., Crown Point.

22 KRAUSE, Ernst Henry Upper atmosphere; Guided missiles; Nuclear physics; Cosmic rays. b'13. BS '34— MS '35—PhD '38 (U Wis). Member National Advisory Committee for Aeronautics, special sub-committee on upper atmosphere; consultant Joint Research and Development Board panel on upper atmosphere '46-48; cons Atomic Energy Commission since '47. Author articles in field. With communication security sect Naval Research Lab '38-43, head sect '43-45, head guided missile subdiv '45-46, head rocket sonde research sect '46-47, head nuclear physics spl research sect '47-48, head accelerator sect nucleonics div since '48, head, chmn V-2 upper atmosphere research panel '46-48. Inst Radio Engrs—Am Phys Soc—Tau Beta Pi—Sigma Xi. Naval Research Laboratory, Washington 20.

23 KRAUSE, Herbert. Social history; Folklore and literature of Upper Midwest; Social history, folklore and writings of Red River Valley (North); Ornithology (Upper Midwest); Creative expression (Laboratory method) b'05. AB cum laude '33 (St Olaf Coll Northfield Minn); AM '35—grad work '35-38 (U Ia); student summer '35 (Bread Loaf Sch English). Author: Wind Without Rain '39; Neighbor Boy (verse) '39; The Thresher '46; Oxcart Trail '49. Head dept English Augustana Coll Sioux Falls SD since '38; member staff Writers Conf U Ia summers '39 '41. $1000 prize for novel Wind Without Rain from Friends Am Writers '39. Authors' Guild Authors League Am—League Minn Writers— SD Hist Soc—State Hist Soc Ia—Minn Hist Soc — Hist Soc Wis — Norwegian-Am Hist Soc—SD Endl Assn— Modern Lang Assn. Augustana College, Sioux Falls, S.D. H: RFC 3, Fergus Falls, Minn.†⊚

10 KRAUSE, William Frederick. Chemistry of refining sour crude oils. b'08. BA '30 (Macalester Coll St Paul); MA '32—PhD '34 (U Wis). Supervision catalytic desulfurization of petroleum, catalytic polymerization and catalytic cracking in processing sour crude oils; director research on problems of corrosion, waste disposal and water chemistry. Research chem Globe Oil & Refining Co '34-38, chief chem and director research '38-52, technical manager since 1952. ACS—Inst Petroleum Technology. Globe Oil & Refining Co., Lemont, Ill. H: 10 Logan St.†

11 KRAUSS, Beatrice H(ilmer). Pineapples (Anatomy and water relations); Anatomy of Bromeliaceae. b'03. BS '26—MS '30 (U Hawaii); '27-28 (U Berlin); research '39 '41 (Cornell). Pineapple investigations Canary and Azores Islands '39; extensive travel to visit biological research institutions Asia, Philippines, Europe, Great Britain, Near East since '27. Asst plant physiol Pineapple Research Inst U Hawaii since '26. Am Bot Soc—AAAS(F)—Hawaiian Bot Soc (sec '32)—Hawaiian Acad Sci (sec-treas '35). Pineapple Research Institute, University of Hawaii, P.O. Box 3166, Honolulu 2, Hawaii. H: 2437 Parker Pl., Honolulu 5.

12 KRAUT, Ralph John. Machine tools (Manufacturing). b'08. BS '30 (U Wis). Asst Works Mgr and asst to pres Giddings & Lewis Machine Tool Co Fond du Lac Wis '35-39, dir and exec vp '39-42, pres gen mgr and dir since '45; pres and dir Kaukauna (Wis) Machine Corp '39-45, vp treas and dir since '45, now chmn bd and dir. Nat Machine Tool Builders Assn (dir)—ASME—Am Soc Tool Engrs—Am Foundrymen's Assn—Am Management Assn—Tau Beta Pi. Giddings & Lewis Machine Tool Co., Fond du Lac, Wis.◎

13 KRAUTHEIMER, Richard. Florentine sculpture; Early Christian architecture. b'97. PhD '23 (U Halle Wittenberg). Research on Florentine sculpture of 15th century, especially Ghiberti; survey Early Christian basilicas in Rome; excavations in Saint Domitilla and Saint Lorenzo. Author: Corpus Basilicarum Christianarum Romae '37; Lorenzo Ghiberti and the Early Renaissance. Author article: Ghibertiana '37. Asst prof art U Louisville '35-37; adjunct prof Inst Fine Arts NYU '47-49; now prof art Vassar Coll; Guggenheim fellow '50-51. Corpus Basilicarum Christianarum Romae (dir). Vassar College, Poughkeepsie, N.Y.

14 KREBS, Robert William. Petroleum refining; Hydrocarbon synthesis. b'12. BS '33—MS '35—PhD '37 (Ill U). Research on liquid film gas absorption coefficients, applications of fluid catalyst technique to catalytic cracking and hydrocarbon synthesis. Holds patents on catalytic cracking, both fixed and fluid bed, and on application of fluid catalyst technique to other chemical processes. Author articles in field. Asst dir Esso Standard Oil Co Lab since '47. Am Chem Soc—Am Inst Chem Engrs—Sigma Xi. Esso Laboratories, Esso Standard Oil Co., Louisiana Division, P.O. Box 551, Baton Rouge 1, La.†

15 KREBS, William Samuel. Public utility regulation. b'89. AB '13 (U Ill); AM '14 (U Wis); Nathaniel Currier fellow '14-16 (Yale). Author: Outlines of Accounting (vol 2) '27; Accounting Laboratory Manual '24; Types of Utility Rates Bases '45. Asst prof econ U Me '16-17, U Mich '17-18; asso prof accounting Washington U '18-19, prof since '19; dir Teachers Nat Loan Assn '25-40; official cons accountant City of St Louis; mem staff The Accountants Handbook. Am Accounting Assn (vp '24-26, pres '27)—Beta Gamma Sigma. Washington University, St. Louis 5.

16 KREDEL, Fritz. Military and civilian costumes. b'00. Grad '18 (Realgynmansium Darmstadt); '20 (Kunstgewerbeschule Offenbach). Author and illustrator: Die Uniformen der Landgraeflich-Hessen-Darmstaedtischem Infanterie 1788 '38. Co-author: Das Barock, Rockoko, Empire und Biedermeier in den Uniformen der Europaeischen Armeen '35. Illustrator: Soldiers of the American Army 1775-1941 '42, and others. Faculty Technische Lehranstalton, Offenbach Germany, instr mil and civilian costumes '27-33; illustrator. Am Mil Inst—Am Inst Graphic Arts. Awarded gold medal for illustration Paris Exhbn '37. 175 Pinehurst Av., NYC.

17 KREGER, Clarence William. Sanitary chemistry. b'96. AB '19 (Miami U); MA '22 (U Ill); PhD '25 (O State U). Author: The Structure of Disalicyl Aldehyde '22. Prof chem Miami U since '37, administrative asst to pres '46-48, vp since '48; coll and U examiner North Central Assn Colls and Secondary Schs since '38. AAAS—Phi Beta Kappa—Sigma Xi. Miami University, Oxford, O.†◎

18 KREIDL, Norbert J(oachim). Glass technology; Ceramics. b'04. PhD '27 (U Vienna). Author articles in field. Research asst Kaiser Wilhelm Inst '27-28; dir research mgr glass works Schreiber and Nephews Czechoslovakia '28-38; asst prof glass technol Sch Mineral Inds Pa State Coll '39-43; head glass lab chem research labs Bausch and Lomb Optical Co Rochester '43-48, dir chem research since '48. ACS—Am Ceramic Soc—Optical Soc Am—Brit Soc Glass Tech—Sigma Xi. Bausch and Lomb Optical Co., Rochester 2, N.Y.

19 KREITLOW, Kermit William. Fungi, bacteria and virus causing diseases of forage grasses and legumes (Identification and control). b'13. BS '36 (U Minn); MS '38—PhD '40 (La State U). Associate editor Phytopathology '48-50. Author articles in field. Fellow Rockefeller Inst for Med Research Princeton NJ '40-41; asso path US Regional Pasture Research Lab State Coll Pa '41-50; sr path div forage crops and diseases plant ind sta Beltsville. Am Phytopath Soc—AAAS—Sigma Xi—Phi Kappa Phi—Bot Soc Wash—NY Acad Sci. U.S. Plant Industry Station, Beltsville, Md.

20 KREMER, Alvin W(ebster). Library collections (Preservation). b'04. AB '28—'28-29 (George Washington U). Research on protection preservation and custody of diverse collections including books and pamphlets, manuscripts, maps and views, microfilms, motion pictures, music phonograph recordings, photographic negatives prints and slides, fine prints and other library materials in non-book formats. Bookstack attendant Library of Congress Wash '23-28, charge inventorial project '28-30, research asst '30-39, spl asst to supt of reading rooms '39-40, keeper of the Collections since '40. The Library of Congress, Washington 25.

21 KREMERS, Howard Earl. Rare earths. b'17. AB '39 (Western Reserve U); MS '41 (Syracuse U); PhD '44 (U Ill). Research on separation of rare earth elements. Author articles in field. Research chem Lindsay Chemical Company West Chicago '44-46, director research since '46. Am Chem Soc—Am Inst Chem (F)—Sigma X., Lindsay Chemical Co., West Chicago, Ill. H: 461 Church St.

22 KREML, Franklin Martin. Traffic engineering (Traffic control, accident prevention). b'07. Student'23-24(U Wis); '25-29 (Northwestern U); LLB '32 (John Marshall Law Sch Chicago). Author: Traffic Safety '36; Public Safety '37; Traffic Engineering and the Police '38; Accident Investigation '40; Evidence Handbook '43; also articles in field. Dir Traffic Officers Training Sch Northwestern U since '32; dir traffic div Internat Assn Chiefs Police since '36. Entered US Army '42, maj, later lt col overseas as transportation officer '43-45; chief planning and logistics br Highway Div Office Chief Transportation War Dept '45-46. Internat Assn Chiefs Police—Inst Traffic Engrs. 1704 Judson Av., Evanston, Ill.◎

23 KRENKEL, John Henry. Port of Los Angeles (History); Internal Improvements in Illinois (History). Arizona State College, Tempe, Ariz.

24 KREPS, Theodore John. Price and chemical Economics; Cartels and monopolies; Full employment; International economic policy. AB '20 (U Colo); AM '24—PhD '28 (Harvard). Representative US Government to prepare technical tripartite conference on reduction of hours in chemical industry Geneva '36; adviser to American delegate to 23d Conference of International Labor Office Geneva '37; delegate 4th Biennial Conference of Institute of Pacific Relations Shanghai '31, round table secretary to 5th Biennial Conference Banff Canada '33, deput rapporteur 6th Conference Yosemite California '36. Author: Business and Government under the National Recovery Administration '36; Economics of the Sulphuric Acid Industry '38; Measurement of the Social Performance of Business '41; also articles in field. Prof bus econ Stanford U since '40. Royal Econ Soc(F)—Am Econ Assn—Am Acad Polit Social Sci. 2335 Waverly St., Palo Alto, Calif.◎

25 KRIES, David Alson. Wood (Commercial tropical, molded, laminated). b'96. BS—MS (U Minn); PhD (Yale); NRC fellow (Harvard). Study of structure, identification, properties, uses, and distribution of commercial tropical woods; collector wood samples; research on molded and laminated woods for aircraft, wood impregnation with resins, moisture-excluding coatings for wood. Author: Commercial Foreign Woods on the American Market '50. Author articles: Comparative Anatomy of the Woods of the Meliaceae '30; Salient Lines of Structural Specialization in the Wood Rays of Dicotyledons '35; Salient Lines of Structural Specialization in the Wood Parenchyma of Dicotyledons '37, and others. Dir research woods process div Fairchild Aricraft Corp '43-44; chief wood tech Timber Engring Co Washington '44-45; now prof plant anatomy and wood tech Pa State Coll. Sigma Xi. Tropical Woods Laboratory, Department of Botany, Pennsylvania State College, State College, Pa.†

26 KRIDER, Harry Read. Tools (Portable power). b'10. Student (Pa State Coll); BS (ME) '33 (Carnegie Inst Tech). Application and demonstration of drills, saws, chain saws, concrete vibrators, and flexible shaft equipment, including electric, pneumatic, and gasoline driven. Br mgr western NY area Mall Tool Co of Chicago since '46. Pi Tau Sigma—Theta Tau. Mall Tool Co., 3212 Union Rd., Buffalo 25. H: 40 Brantwood Rd., Snyder 21, N.Y.

10 KRIDER, Jake Luther. Swine husbandry (Nutrition). b'13. BS '39—MS '41 (U Ill); PhD '42 (Cornell U). Research on value of certain protein and vitamin supplements, vitamin requirements of young pigs fed synthetic diets, heritability of growth rate, importance of nutrition of sow upon mortality and growth of her pigs, nature of deficiencies of cornbelt rations for young pigs and brood sows. Author articles in field. Asso in animal husbandry U Ill '42-43, asst prof '43-46, asso prof '46-47, prof animal sci dir research and edn McMillen Feed Mills Div Central Soya Co Inc Decatur. American Soc Animal Prodn—AAAS—Sigma Xi—Phi Kappa Phi—Gamma Sigma Delta. McMillen Feed Mills Division, Central Soya Co., Inc., Decatur, Ind.

11 KRIEBEL, Warren Walter, Jr. Law of evidence; State and federal taxation. b'05. AB '27—LLB '29 (U Ill). Attorney Berwyn Park District since '31; instructor in evidence John Marshall Law School since '40. Am Bar Assn—Am Judicature Soc—Chicago Law Inst—Phi Beta Kappa—Order of Coif—Phi Delta Phi—Pi Mu Epsilon. 1 N. LaSalle St., Chgo 2.⊚

12 KRIEG, Abraham. Physical chemistry (Catalysis, lubrication). b'17. BA '38 (Brooklyn Coll); MS '48 (U Pittsburgh). Research on problems concerning lubricating oils, engine sludges and deposits, diesel fuels, battery waters, etc, and on life and performance of naval aircraft and marine engines, corrosion problems in bearings and Diesel injection systems, mechanism of Fischer-Tropsch synthesis. Author articles in field. Chem US Naval Engring Expt Sta Annapolis Md '41-44; phys chem US dept Interior '45-48; leader research sect Gen Am Transportation Co East Chicago since '48. AAAS—Am Chem Soc. c/o Research Laboratories, General American Transportation Corp., 4405 Euclid Av., East Chicago, Ind.†

13 KRIEG, Edwin Holmes. Power plant economics and design (High pressure and temperature). b'00. ME '22 (Cornell U). In charge design of high-pressure, high-temperature steam-electric power plants. Author articles: Economics in Power Station Design '48; Progressive Engineering Offsets Increased Costs of Steam-Electric Power Generation '48, and others. Mech engr Sanderson & Porter NYC '22-25; project engr Elec Bond & Share Co NYC '25-33; chief design engr and cons engr Am Gas & Elec Service Corp NYC '33-48; cons engr Stone & Webster Engring Corp since '48. Am Soc ME (F)—Am Inst EE—Nat Soc Professional Engrs—Edison Elec Inst —Mass Soc Professional Engrs—Cornell Soc Engrs—Am Standards Assn. Professional engr NY, Mass. Stone & Webster Engineering Corp., 49 Federal St., Boston 7.

14 KRIEG, Wendell Jordan. Human brain; Anatomical illustration. b'06. BS in medicine '28 (U Neb); MS '31—PhD '35 (NYU). Author and illustrator: Atlas of Reconstructions of Human Brain '41; Functional Neuroanatomy '42; also articles. Prof neurology and dir Inst Neurology U Med Sch Chicago '46-48, prof anatomy since '48. Am Assn Anatomists. 303 E. Chicago Av., Chgo.⊚

15 KRIEGE, Herbert Frick. Mineral aggregates. b'95. BS '16 (Central Wesleyan Coll); MS '20—scholar '19-20 (U Mo); PhD '26—Nat Agstone Assn research fellow '24-26 (O State U). Research in flint fireclays and other silicates, chert, cement content of concrete, dissolution rates of limestones, mineral aggregates, stone and blast furnace slag; development of various test methods and equipment such as method of determining cement content of hardened concrete, minitrack for fabricating and testing bituminous mixes under moving wheel loads; development of limestone fine aggregates for concrete and bituminous uses. Author articles in field. Research chem Mo State Highway Dept '23-24; tech dir The France Stone Co since '26. Am Soc Testing Materials—ACS—O Acad Sci—Asphalt Paving Tech Assn—Nat Research Council (highway research bd)—Nat Slag Assn (problems com). 110 W. Second St., Perrysburg, O.†

16 KRIEGER, Charles John. Spectrophotometry; Engineering (Aircraft acoustics and passenger comfort). b'98. EE '22 (Inst Tech Munich); PhD '29 (U Calif). Author articles: A Determination of Magnitudes, Spectral Types and Color Indices in the Scutum Cloud, with a Statistical Discussion '29; Elements of Minor Planet 1930 VE '31, and others. Lick Obs fellow Mt Hamilton '28-29; instr math and physics St Louis U '29-31, asst prof astron '31-40; asst prof astron San Diego State Coll '41-43; group engr Consol Vultee Aircraft Corp '43-44, research engr since '44. Am Astron Soc—AAAS(F)—Sigma Xi. Consolidated Vultee Aircraft Corp., Engineering Test Laboratory, San Diego, Calif.†

17 KRIEGER, E. C. Football (Rules). Former editor football rules book; editor question and answer booklet on grid rules for 19 years. 127 S. Dawson Av., Columbus, O.

18 KRIEGER, Herbert William. Caribbean cultures; Philippine Islands. b'89. MA '08 (U Ia). Author: Material Culture of the People of Southeastern Panama '26; The Collection of Weapons and Armor of the Philippine Islands '26; Aborigines of the Ancient Island of Hispaniola '30; Island Peoples of the Western Pacific '43. Curator ethnol US Nat Mus Washington since '25. Am Anthrop Assn—Anthrop Assn Washington—Washington Acad Sci. U.S. National Museum, Washington.⊚

19 KRIEK, Peter Paul. Viscose rayon manufacturing. b'95. Mech Engring C L '19 (Delft Tech Univ Netherlands). Research on design and development special machinery for rayon manufacture. Granted patents in field. With Enka since '26, dir engring since '46. ASME. American Enka Corp., Enka, N.C.

20 KRINITSKY, Ellis Louis. Soils (Arctic); Permafrost; Engineering geology. b'24. BS '45 (Va Poly Inst); MS '47 (U NC); PhD '50 (La State U). Studies of permafrost conditions; construction problems in permafrost; interpretation of geology and soils from airphotos; studies on traffic-ability of soils; problems in engineering geology. Asst prof geol Southwestern La Inst '46-47; geol Waterways Expt Sta Corps Engrs '48-50, soils engr Permafrost div Corps Engrs since '50 Geol Soc Am—Am Assn Petroleum Geol—Am Geophys Union. Permafrost Division, Corps of Engineers, St. Paul.

21 KRISHNAMURTHI, Sundaram. Plant growth regulators; Tropical fruits and vegetables; Citrus; Papaya; Banana; Ornamental gardening; Silk industry; Indian agriculture; History and culture of peoples of India. b'11. BSc '32 (Madras Agrl Coll); spl training '41 (Fruit Research Sta Kodur Madras India); MS '47 (U Calif Los Angeles); post grad student since '47 —PhD '49 (Mich State Coll). Board editors Madras Agricultural Journal '40-41, '45-46. Author articles in field. With Madras Sericulture Dept '32-33; staff Imperial Council Agrl Research New Delhi India '33-35; staff Madras Agrl Coll and Research Inst '35-40, '42-45; specially deputed by Govt Madras India for studies in hort in US since '46. AAAS—Bot Soc Am—Am Soc Hort Sci—Am Soc Plant Physiol—Sigma Xi. Horticulture Department, Michigan State College, East Lansing, Mich.

22 KRISHNAYYA, Pasupuleti Gopala. India (Ghandi). b'02. AB '26 (Madras U India); AM '32—MS '33 (Columbia); '34-38 (NYU). Author: India, the War and the Crips Mission '42; Mahatma Gandhi and the U.S.A. '49. Pres Hindustan Assn '35-36; gen ed The Orient and World Press since '43; managing ed The India and USA News Service since '43; pres PG Krishnayya's Newsreel Service. Fgn Press Assn. Room 373, Press Section, United Nations, N.Y.

23 KRIZ, A. Anthony. Electron mulipliers; Phosphorescence. b'14. BS in phys '38 (U Chicago); '41-42 (Ill Inst Tech); LLB '49—JD '50 (Blackstone Coll Law). Research on determination of low energy levels of phosphorescent light, design and construction equipment for use with electron multipliers and nuclear scintillation counters, research with radio-active isotopes to find method of standardizing electron multipliers and scintillation counters. Supervising metall Rheem Mfg Co '41-43; chief design engr Solar Capacitor Co '43-46; research engr Ill Inst Tech '46-48; chief engr W M Welch Mfg Co '48-49; elec engr Testing Div City of Chicago since '49. Am Inst EE—Am Polar Exploration Soc—Am Soc Mil Engrs. Testing Division, City of Chicago, 3100 S. Sacramento, Chgo 23.†

24 KROBER, Orland Alvin. Soybeans (Chemical analysis); Protein; Amino acids. b'08. BS '31 (Greenville Coll); MA '37—grad study (U Kan); '46 (U Ill). Author articles: Effect of Relative Humidity on the Determination of Oil in Soybeans (with F I Collins) '44; Some Factors Which Affect the Determination of Oil in Soybeans (with others) '45; Sampling Soybeans for Analysis (with others) '45; Mobility of Food Reserves in Soybean Cotyledons and Their Influence on the Development of the Plant (with D F McAlister) '50; The Effect of Weather Damage on Chemical Composition of Soybeans '48, and others. Head sci dept Central Coll McPherson Kan '37-41; asso chem US Regional Soybean Lab Urbana Ill since '41. Am Chem Soc. U.S. Regional Soybean Laboratory, Urbana, Ill.†

25 KROEGER, William J(ohn). Military weapons and ammunition (Development); Recoilless rifles; Emergency escape catapults for aircraft; Rocket fuels and propellants. b'06. BS '27(Carnegie Inst Tech); MS '34—PhD '37 (U Pittsburgh). Research effects of lightning on transmission lines; development of microphotometer for recording optical density of spectrograms; calculation of binding energy of O^{16}; experimental study of forces resisting projectile penetration of armor, interior ballistics of small arms weapons, visibility of glare of gun flash, interior ballistics of recoilless rifles; catapult ejection of human body from military aircraft. Co-holder patent recoilless infantry weapon. Author articles in field. Field engr transmission engring dept Westinghouse Elec Co '27-31; tech asst Fed Bur Investigation '36; physicist Putman-Dunn Lab Frankford Arsenal Phila since '40, br head phys br since '48. Am Phys Soc. Pitman-Dunn Laboratory, Frankford Arsenal, Phila 37. H: 5935 Frontenac St.

10 KROGMAN, Wilton Marion. Physical anthropology; Child growth and development; Medico-legal aspects of the human skeleton. b'03. PhB '26—MA '27—PhD '29 (U Chicago); Nat Research Council fellow '30-31 (Royal Coll Surgeons, Eng). Consultant law enforcement agencies and expert in crime detection in determining probable physical characteristics of unknown persons from portions of skeleton. Author: Growth of Man '41; Bibliography of Human Morphology '41; Physical Anthropology of the Seminole Indians of Oklahoma '35; also articles in field. Asso prof anat and phys anthrop Western Reserve U '31-38, U Chgo '38-47: prof phys anthrop, dir Phila Center Resrch Child Growth since '47. AAAS (F, chmn and vp section H '48)—Am Assn Phys Anthrop (pres '45-49). Graduate School of Medicine, University of Pennsylvania, Philadelphia.†©

11 KROHN, Ernst Christopher. Music bibliography; Musicology. b'88. Ed pvt teachers. Author articles: The Bibliography of Music '19, and others. Lecturer music U Coll Washington Univ since '38 and City Art Museum since '43. Am Musicol Soc—Music Library Assn—Medieval Acad Am—Internat Soc Musicol—Music Teachers Nat Assn. 388A North Euclid Av., St. Louis 8. H: 3806 Juniata St.

12 KROLL, Harry Harrison. American folk speech; Southern United States folklore. b'88. BS '23—MA '25 (Peabody Coll for Teachers). Author: Comparative Study Southern Folk Speech '25; The Mountainy Singer '28; I Was a Share-Cropper '37; The Usurper '41; Waters Over the Dam '44; Their Ancient Grudge '46; Darker Grows the Valley, and others. Asso prof and head dept Eng U Tenn Jr Coll. Am Dialect Soc. Martin, Tenn.©

13 KROMBEIN, Karl V. Wasps; Bees. b'12. BS '34—MA '35—grad study '37-39 (Cornell U); '31-32 (Canisius Coll); '29-31 (Carnegie Inst Tech). Author articles in field. Entomol US Dept Agr since '41. Entomol Soc Am (F)—Entomol Society Washington—Am Entomol Soc—Sigma Xi. Division of Insects, U.S. National Museum, Washington.

14 KROMER, Clarence Herbert. Concrete aggregates. b'82. BS (CE) (U Cal Berkeley). Scientific proportioning of concrete mixes; supervision construction; foundation engineering; analysis and design of buildings, bridges and high masonry dams; specialization in aseismatic and rigid frame structural design and construction; member disaster code committee California Chamber Commerce; member code changes committee Pacific Coast Buildings Conference '34-40. Author article: Earthquake Resistant Design for School Buildings '34, and others. Contributor: Earthquake Resistant Buildings. Insp advancing to structural engr Cal State Dept Engring '11-18, asst state architect '19-21; chief structral engr Cal State Dept Pub Works '21-40; cons engr City of Sacramento '24-25, City of Long Beach '33; cons civil structural engr since '47. Corps Engrs AUS '18-19, archtl and structural engr '44-47. Am Soc CE—Structrual Engrs Assn Cal—Seismol Soc Am—Am Geophys Union—Nat Acad Sci. Registered civil and structural engr Cal. 2633 Fifth Av., Sacramento 18.

15 KRONENBERG, Max. Metal cutting; Machine tools design and testing; Vibration, deflection and stress; European industry. born '94. ME '20—Dr Engring '27—Dr Habil '27 (U Berlin). Holds US patent on thermally controlled machine tool, Germany and Austria patent on instrument for selection of machine tools, France and Belgium patent logarithmic progression of speeds and feeds in machine tools. Author: Grundzuege der Zerspanungslehre '27; also articles in field. Management engr Nema Works Machine Tool Mfr Neisse Germany '20-23; sales engr machine tools Berlin '23-25; cons engr machine tools metal cutting and prodn improvements '25-36; judge international courts arbitration machine tools and prodn problems '32-36; prof engring coll U Berlin '27-34; research engr Cincinnati Milling Machine Co Cincinnati '36-48; cons to Sec of War Washington '45; cons engr since '48. Am Soc Tool Engrs—Sigma Xi. 15 E. 8th St., Cincinnati 2. H: 945 Marion Av., Cincinnati 29.†

16 KROPA, Edward L(ewis). Resins and plastics. b'07. BS '29—MA '30 (Wesleyan U Conn); PhD '32 (NYU). Holder numerous US patents in field of resins and plastics, high polymers, low pressure molding, coatings, laminating. Author articles in field. Research chem Am Cyanamid Co since '37-49; chem dir Chem Div Borden Co since '49; vp Chem Div since '51; adj prof chem engring NYU since '46. Am Chem Soc —Am Mus Nat Hist—NY Acad Sci—Sigma Xi—Phi Beta Kappa—Commercial Chem Develmt Assn—Am Ordnance Assn. Chemical Division, Borden Co., 350 Madison Av., NYC 17.

17 KROPF, Richard Thomas. Fiber yarns and threads. b'09. BS '31 (MIT). Research on natural and synthetic fiber yarns and threads, mechanical applications of textiles and the development and design of sewing threads and yarns for specific mechanical and chemical applications. Developed the Monocord a non-twisted yarn and sewing thread. Co-author: Textile Testing in Germany; also articles in field. Textile research engr Belding Heminway Co '31-32, lab dir '32-38, tech dir and merchandise mgr NYC '38-43, dir research '43-49, vp and dir research since '49. AAAS—Am Assn Textile Technol—Am Chem Soc—Am Phys Soc—Am Soc Testing Materials—NY Acad Sci—Fiber Soc. Belding Heminway Co., Inc., 119 W. 40 St., NYC 18.

18 KROUSE, F. Michael. John Milton. b'16. BA '39—MA '41 (Oberlin Coll); PhD '46 (Johns Hopkins). Historical study of growth of Christian conception of Samson of Judges, its place in Christian tradition and bearing on criticism of John Milton's Samson Agonistes; research on Milton and tragic Agon. Author: Milton's Samson and the Christian Tradition '49; also articles in field. Asso prof Eng U Cincinnati since '46. Phi Beta Kappa—Modern Lang Assn. McMicken College of Liberal Arts, University of Cincinnati, Cincinnati 21. H: 2725 Hyde Park Av., Cin. 9.

19 KRUEGER, Albert Paul. Bacteriology (Airborne infections). b'02. AB '25—MD '28 (Stanford U). Research on airborne infections and preparation of undenatured bacterial antigens, biological warfare; bacteriophages. Author 125 articles in field. Faculty Stanford U '28-29; asso gen physiol Rockefeller Inst '29-31; with U Cal since '31, prof bact since '38, chmn dept bact since '46. AAAS(F)—Am Pub Health Assn(F)—AMA(F)—Soc Exptl Biol and Med—Am Assn Immunologists—Soc Am Bact—Am Soc Exptl Path—Assn Mil Surgeons. Department of Bacteriology, University of California, Berkeley 4.

20 KRUEGER, Hilmar Carl. Medieval economic history. b'04. BA '25 (Northwestern Coll); PhD '32 (U Wis). Research on Genoese trade with northwest Africa, routine of their commerce and wares of exchange in twelfth century, early Genoese trade with Atlantic Morocco, reactions to first missionaries in northwest Africa. Co-editor: Notai Liguri del Sec XII: Guglielmo Cassinese (2 vol) '38, Bonvillano '39, Giovanni de Guiberto (2 vol) '40; also articles in field. Asso prof hist U Cincinnati since '46; asso ed Medievalia et Humanistica since '41. AHA—Medieval Acad Am—Econ Hist Assn. Fellow U Wis '26-27; Charles K Adams Scholar U Wis '28-29; grants-in-aid, Social Sci Research Council '39, U Wis Alumni Research Found '39, U Cincinnati '49. Department of History, University of Cincinnati, Cincinnati 21.†

21 KRUGER, Frederick Konrad. Diplomatic history (Recent European, United States-German). b'87. Student '07 '08 (U Berlin Germany); AM '08 (U Neb); PhD '10 (U Tubingen Germany); grad study '12 (Columbia). Author: Brannkohlenindustrie der Niederlausitz '11; Government and Politics of the German Empire '15. Editor: An Undiplomatic Dairy (The Bandholtz Diary) '33. Contbr articles on German govt to Ency Americana. Prof polit sci Midland Coll Fremont Neb '15-16, U Omaha '19-23; asso prof polit sci Wittenberg Coll Springfield O '23-25, prof '25-43; Am exchange prof U Gottingen Germany '27-38; Am guest prof in Berlin winter semester '34-35; prof sociology Valparaiso (Ind) U since '45. Valparaiso University, Valparaiso, Ind.†©

22 KRUGMAN, Morris. Clinical psychology; Vocational guidance. b'99. BS '19 (Brooklyn Poly Inst); MA '25—PhD '28 (NYU). Development projective techniques; analysis Rorschach test results; research in clinical psychology, psychometrics, guidance techniques, education. Author articles: The Rorschach in Child Guidance '43; Psychosomatic Study of Fifty Stuttering Children—Rorschach Study '46; The Preparation of Psychiatrists for Practice, Teaching, and Research '46, and others. With Bd Edn NYC '24-49, chief psychol Bur Child Guidance '32-47, asst supt schs in charge guidance since '47. AAAS—Am Acad Polit and Social Sci—NY Acad Pub Edn—NY Acad Sci—Am Psychol Assn(F, pres div sch psychol)—NY State Psychol Assn (past pres)—Rorschach Inst (F, past pres) — Am Orthopsychiatric Assn (F, pres-elect)—NEA. 110 Livingston St., Bklyn 2.

23 KRUMBEIN, William Christian. Beach erosion; Sedimentary rocks; Petroleum geology (Sedimentary aspects). b'02. PhB '26—MS '20—PhD '32 (U Chicago). Co-author: (with Carey G Groneis) Down to Earth '36; (with F J Pettijohn) Manual of Sedimentary Petrography '38; (with L L Sloss) Stratigraphy and Sedimentation '51. Research geologist Gulf Research & Development Co Pittsburgh '45-46; mem geology faculty U Chicago '32-45, asso prof '44-45; prof geology Northwestern U since '46; John Simon Guggenheim fellow '41-42. Geol Soc Am—Am Geophys Union—Am Assn Petroleum Geol—Soc Econ Paleontol and Mineralogists (pres '50-51)—Sigma Xi—Phi Beta Kappa. Department of Geology, Northwestern University, Evanston, Ill. H: 1725 Orrington Av.†©

24 KRUSCHKE, Emil Paul. Wisconsin (Hawthorns, borage plants, conservation); Herbarium plant specimen (Preparation method). b'07. BS '33—MS '35 (U Wis). Twelve years intensive collecting of Wisconsin hawthorn specimens, both flowering and fruiting and with accompanying complete ecological data; also black and white and colored photographs of hawthorn trees and shrubs; developed new method for preparing and mounting herbarium plant specimens. Author articles: Boraginaceae of Wisconsin '44; Hawthorns of Wisconsin '53. Asso curator bot Milwaukee Pub Museum since 38. Am Soc Plant Taxonomists—Wis Hort Soc—Wis Acad Sci—Phi Sigma—Midwest Museums Conf—Citizens Natural Resources Assn of Wis—Wilderness Soc—Wildflower Preservation Soc. Milwaukee Public Museum, Milw 3.

10 KRUSE, Cornelius Wolfram. Public health engineering; Aircraft insecticide application. b'13. BS '34—CE '39 (Mo Sch Mines Metall); MS '40 (Harvard); spl student (Johns Hopkins). Author articles in field. Sanitary engr TVA '35-46 working on water supplies, sewage disposal, malaria control, airplane distribution aerosols and sprays, other aspects environmental sanitation; teaching and research san engring Johns Hopkins U Sch Hygiene and Pub Health since '46. ASCE—Nat Malaria Soc—Am Pub Health Assn—AAAS—Am Water Works Assn. Johns Hopkins University, School Hygiene and Public Health, 615 N. Wolfe St., Baltimore 5.

11 KRUTCH, Joseph Wood. Arizona desert. b'93. AB '15 (U Tenn); MA '16—PhD '23 (Columbia). Philosophy Hall, Columbia University, NYC.⊚

12 KRYN, Jeannette Miriam. Wood anatomy; Tropical woods. b'13. BA '34—BE '35—MA '44 (U Cincinnati); PhD (U Mich). Research on the preparation of slides of tropical woods; study of the Anomalous wood structure Pisonia grandis from Bikini, stem anatomy of non-American members of the Anacardiaceae. Asst prof bot dept biol U Buffalo since '47. Mich Acad Sci—Bot Soc Am—AAAS—Sigma Xi. Department of Biology, University of Buffalo, Buffalo 14.

13 KRZYWOBLOCKI, Maria Zbigniew. Gas dynamics; Theoretical aerodynamics. Student '22-30—Diploma Ingenieur '36 (Lwow Inst Tech), '38-39 (Warsaw U); M Ae E '43—Dr Ae E '45 (PolyTech Inst Brooklyn); MS '46 (Brown U); MA '46 (Stanford U). Author: Wood in Glider Construction; Plywood in Glider Construction; Glues in Glider Construction; Auxiliary Materials in Glider Construction; also articles in field. Asso prof dept aeronaut Eng '46-49, prof since '49. Con Naval Ordnance Lab since '48. Royal Aeronautical Soc, London (asso F)—Inst Aeronautical Sci NY (asso F)—Am Math Soc—Sigma Xi. Department of Aeronautical Engineering, College of Engineering, University of Illinois, Urbana, Ill.†

14 KUBIS, Joseph Francis. Deception detection (Lie detector). b'11. BA '32 (St John's U); MA '35—PhD '37—research since '33 (Fordham U). Research in the development of the Fordham pathometer. Author: Electronic Methods of Detecting Deception; Medicine and Lie Detection. Asso prof psychol Fordham U Grad Sch since '41; cons CYO and Archdiocesan Vocational Service since '40; cons to city, co, state and fed police authorities in criminal investigations, also to Armed Forces. Fordham University, NYC 58.

15 KUBLER, George Alexander. History of art (Medieval European); Latin American pre-Conquest archeology; History of Indians in Latin America (Colonial regime). b'12. BA '34—MA '36—PhD '40 (Yale U); grad fellow '36-38 (Inst Fine Arts NYU). Author: The Quechua in the Colonial World '46; Religious Architecture of New Mexico '40; Mexican Architecture in the Sixteenth Century '48; also articles in field. Lecturer Wesleyan U '43-44; ed Art Bulletin '45-47; faculty Yale U since '38, prof hist art since '47; anthrop Inst Soc Anthrop (Smithsonian Instn) Lima Peru '48-49. Travel grant Am Council Learned Soc '41, Guggenheim fellow '43-44; '52-53. Sch of Fine Arts, Yale University, New Haven.†⊚

16 KUCHLER, August Wilhelm. Vegetation (Geographic distribution, maps physiognomy). b'07. PhD '35 (Munchen U). Research on vegetation maps of world and North America, broadleaf deciduous forests of Pacific Northwest, geographic system of vegetation, biogeography, vegetation of Manchuria (map), physiognomic classification of vegetation. Author articles in field. Asst prog geog Rochester U '45-50; asso prof geog Kansas U since '50. Sigma Xi—Assn Am Geog. University of Kansas, Lawrence, Kansas.

17 KUDER, G(eorge) Frederic. Personnel and industrial psychology; Test theory and construction; Psychometrics. b'03. AB '25 (U Ariz); MA '29 (U Mich); PhD '37 (O State U). Editor Educational and Psychological Measurement since '41, Personnel Psychology since '48. Author: Kuder Preference Record; also articles in field. Research asso Personnel Research Dept Procter and Gamble Co '29-32; examiner U Chicago '36-40; personnel methods cons Social Security Bd '40-42; chief test construction and review unit US Civil Service Commn '42-43; chief civilian studies sect information and Edn Div War Dept '43-45, cons '46-47; prof psychol Duke U since '48. Am Psychol Assn (F, council '46-47, since '48, pres div counseling and guidance '47-48)—Am Coll Personnel Assn (exec council '48-49)—AAAS(F)—Psychometrics Soc—Sigma Xi—Phi Kappa Phi. Diplomate in indsl psychol Am Bd Examiners in Psychol. Department of Psychology, Duke University, Durham, N.C.

18 KUDO, Richard Roksabro. Protozoology; Protozoa (Parasitic, Cnidosporidia). b'86. D Ag Sc '10—DSc '24 (Tokio). Author: Protozoology; Manual of Human Protozoa; also articles in field. Instr in zool U Ill '18-21, asso '21-25, asst prof '25-36, asso prof '36-44, prof since '44. AAAS(F)—Am Soc Naturalists—Am Soc Zool—Am Soc Protozool (exec com)—Am Soc Parasitol—Am Soc Limnol Oceanog—Soc Systematic Zool—Biol Stain Commn—Sigma Xi—Phi Sigma Soc (hon). Department of Zoology, University of Illinois, Urbana, Ill.

19 KUEBLER, John R(alph) Chemistry (Fraternities). b'90. AB '12—Fellowship '14-15—AM '15 (Ind U). Dist officer Alpha Chi Sigma '17-22, asst editor The Hexagon '20-22, editor since '22, mem nat bd officers since '20, sec-treas and editor since '26. Research div CWS, US Army '17-19. Am Chem Soc (pres Ind sect '44-45)—Ind Chem Soc (pres '45-46)—Profl Interfrat Conf (sec-treas since '48)—AA AS—Ind Acad Sci. 5503 E Washington St., Indpls. 19.†⊚

20 KUENZLI, Irvin R. International labor education. b'97. AB '21—AM '23 (Wittenburg Coll Springfield O). Member International Committee Public School Education Paris Exposition '37; fraternal delegate National Union of Teachers of England, Margate England in '38; with wife represented American Federation of Teachers on first 'round-the-world educational flight in history of aviation for promoting international friendship and world peace '48. Author articles in field, also large part of edn program of Am Fed of Labor since '40, and articles to mag.; With Am Fed Teachers since '36, sec-treas since '36. 28 E. Jackson Blvd., Chicago.⊚

21 KUGELMASS, I(saac) Newton. Children (Exceptional); Blood (Nutrition). b'96. BS '16—F '17 (Coll City of NY); MA '17 (Columbia); PhD '21 (Johns Hopkins); Docteur Special in Sciences Physiologiques '22 (U Brussels); MD '25 (Yale); grad study '20-21 (Sorbonne Paris, U Zurich, U Gottingen, U Leipzig, Pasteur Inst, Paris and Brussels). Determination of secondary blood phosphates; blood equilibria involving inorganic ions; buffer mechanisms for inorganic ions in the blood; prenatal prevention of potential hemorrhagic disease of the newborn; role of blood clotting factors in thrombosis and embolism; role of nutrients in blood clotting function; buffer values of foods; bleeding and clotting diets; first sign of infant allergy; developed relationship between essential nutrients and child development) electronic medication; basic feeding in tuberculosis; mechanism of callus formation and calcification; phosolipid determinations in the blood; mechanism of anemias of childhood; mechanism of hemophilia in childhood; acid-base values of nutrients; nutritional therapy of dental caries; nutritional improvement of child mentality; androgenic arrest of familial enuresis. Author: Growing Superior Children '34; Pediatric Nutrition '37; The Newer Nutrition in Pediatric Practice '39; Blood Disorders in Children '41; Superior Children through Modern Children '43; Management of Everyday Problems of Infants and Children '45; How to Raise a Normal Child '49. Contributor on infant and child nutrition accelerating child growth and development, management nervous and mental disorders in children to professional journals. Dir Heckscher Inst for Child Health; pediatrist and chief children's clinic for immunology French Hosp; cons nutritionist Dept Health and Dept Hosps City of NY. AMA(F)—Soc Exptl Med and Biol(F)—AAAS (F)—Am Acad Applied Nutrition—Soc Research Child Development—NY Acad Sci—Am Assn Mental Deficiency —Am Pub Health Assn—Nat Tb Assn —Am Therapeutic Soc—NY Endocrinological Soc—Assn Am Tchrs Diseases Children—Alpha Mu Sigma. 1060 Park Av., NYC 28.

22 KUHN, Harry A. Industrial chemistry; Military industrial planning. b'95. PhB—MS '25 (U Wis); '33-35 (U Ill). Has five inventions on improvements of military gas masks and for civilian dust respirator. Author articles in field. Col US Army ret; indsl chem cons since '46. NY Acad Sci—Am Chem Soc—AMA—Am Soc Pharmacol Exptl Therapeutics—Armed Forces Chem Assn (pres). 3915 Fulton St., N.W., Washington 7.

23 KUHN, Wayne E(dward). Petroleum products. b'03. BA '25 (Reed Coll); PhD '30 (Cornell U). Holds 10 patents in field. Author articles: Inhibitors in Action of and on Steel '29; Improvement in Effusion Method of Determining Sp-Gr Gases '35; Petroleum Industry and Jet Propulsion '48; Plane Crash Fire Studies '48. Various positions with Texas Co since '29, mgr tech and research div since '39. Am Petroleum Inst—Am Soc Testing Materials—SAE—Am Chem Soc—IPT—AAAS—Am Rocket Soc—Inst Chem Soc—Chem Ind—Com Chem Dev Assn

—Army Ordnance Assn—Chem Corp Assn—Am Geog Soc—Am Forestry. 135 E. 42nd St., NYC 17.

10 KUIPER, Gerard Peter. Planets; White dwarf and double stars; Stellar statistics. b'05. BSc '27—PhD '33 (U Leyden, Netherlands); Resrch fellow Lick Obs U Calif '33-35. Discovered new satellite Miranda to plant Uranus '48, Nereid to planet Neptune '49, presence of carbon dioxide and water on Mars '48, only satellite atmosphere (Titan) of planet Saturn '44; first to find densities of stars up to 100,000,000 times water (white dwarfs) '35. Editor: Planetary Atmospheres '48; also articles in field. Mem Dutch Eclipse Expdn to sumatra '29; research asso Lick Obs U Calif '35; lecturer Harvard '35-36; asst prof astron U Chicago '36-37, prof since '43; with Yerkes Obs Williams Bay Wis since '36, dir since '47; with McDonald Obs Fort Davis Tex since '39, dir since '47; research asso Radio Research Lab Harvard '43-45; cons operational analysis sect Eighth Air Force Eng '44; mem War Dept (ALSOS) mission to Europe '45. Internat Astron Union—Am Astron Soc—Astron Soc Pacific—Royal Astron Soc. Yerkes Observatory, Williams Bay, Wis.⊚

11 KUKACHKA, Bohumil Francis. Wood indentification, structure and microtechnique. b'15. BS '37—PhD '42 (U Minn). Author articles in field. Specialist wood structure and identification US Forest Products Lab Madison Wis since '45. Soc Am Foresters—Sigma Xi—Xi Sigma Pi. U.S. Forest Products Laboratory, Madison 5, Wis.†

12 KULJIAN, Harry A. Hydro-electric and steam power generation; Power transmission; Rayon spinning and processing. b'93. SB '19 (MIT). Patents on new machine continuous rayon spinning and processing, boiler feed level recorder and controller, density recorder and indicator; designer numerous time-saving devices and equipment chemical, textile, petroleum plants and public utilities. Established H A Kuljian & Co cons engrs Phila '31; organizer and pres Kuljian Corp, engrs and constructors since '41. Am Soc EE—Franklin Inst—Tech Assn Pulp and Paper Industry. Awarded Army and Navy E for outstanding engring service to Chem Warfare Dept; Meritorious award (Navy). 1200 N. Broad St., Phila. H: 131 Raynham Rd., Merion, Pa.†⊚

13 KUMMER, Theodore Herman. Automatic food and dairy machine design. b'00. BS '31—MS '33 (Ala Polytechnic Inst); '37-38 (Armour Inst Technol). Designer several patents in connection with milk bottle filler designs. Draftsman and machine designer Continental Can Co Inc '33-40; machine designer Cherry-Burrell Corp Milwaukee '40-41, exec engr '41-43, chief engr since '44. Am Soc Metals—Am Soc Agrl Engrs. 3002 W. Burleigh St., Milwaukee 10.

14 KUNZE, Walter Gustav. Starch chemistry; Rubber lubricants. b'04. Student (Darmstadt U Germany, Danzig U, U Graz, Dresden U); Dr Engring Chem '33 (Darmstadt Tech U). Holds US patents on various subjects. Engineering chem Knabe & Co Germany '33-35; chief chem Victor G Bloede Co Baltimore since '36; sci cons Office Mil Govt for Germany '46-47; cons indsl chem since '44. Am Chem Soc. 14 Dunmore Road, Catonsville 28, Md.†

15 KUO, Ping-chia. China; Far East. b '08. AM '30—PhD '33 (Harvard). Counsellor of Ministry of Foreign Affairs, China '43-46, participated in Cairo Conf as special political assistant to Generalissimo Chiang Kai-shek, Nov.

'43; during war years in Chungking also served Chinese Govt concurrently as member foreign affairs com National Supreme Defense Council '39-46, chief of editorial and publications department Ministry of Information '40-42, member central planning board '41-45, technical expert to Chinese delegation San Francisco Conf '45; chief trusteeship section in secretariat of UN London '45-46. Prof modern History and Far Eastern Internat relations Nat Wuhan U Wuchang China '33-38, editor China Forum Hankow and Chungking '38-40; counsellor Nat Mil Council Chungking China '40-46; apptd top-ranking dir Dept Security Council Affairs UN NY '46-48. Author: A Critical Study of the First Anglo-Chinese War, with Documents '35; Modern Far Eastern Diplomatic History (in Chinese) '37. Decorated Kwany Hua medal Nat Mil Council Chungking '41; medal of Auspicious Star, Nat Govt Chungking '44; Victory medal Nat Govt '45. H: Palm Acres, 2403 Graton-Occidental Rd., Sebastopol, Cal.⊚

16 KURATH, Gertrude Prokosch (Tula). American and Mexican Indian dances; Iroquois musicology. b'03. BA '22—MA '28 (Bryn Mawr Coll); '29-30 (Yale Sch Drama) '37. '17-19 (U Tex); '19-20 (U Chicago). Field research Mexico especially Otomi and Yaqui ceremonials '46, Sauk and Fox Indians '45 and '47, Iroquois Seneca of Allegany Reservation and Cayuga and Onondaga of Six Nations Reserve Canada '48-49, Cherokee of Qualla Reservation '49; pioneer methods of dance ethnology and comparative choreography; inventions of special dance notation for recording dances. Author articles and books. Engaged in resch at present. Am Anthrop Assn—Am Folklore Soc (edn and membership coms) — Mich Folklore Soc (treas). Viking Fund grant '49. East and West Association, 62 W. 45th St., NYC. H: 1125 Spring St., Ann Arbor.⊚

17 KURATH, Hans. Linguistics (Middle and American English); Linguistic geography. b'91. AB '14 (U Tex); fellow '16-17, '19-20—PhD '20 (U Chicago). Author: American Pronunciation '28; Handbook of the Linguistic Geography of New England '39; Linguistic Atlas of New England (3 vols) '39-43; A Word Geography of the Eastern United States '49; also articles in field. Prof Eng, ed The Middle English Dictionary U Mich '46, dir Linguistic Inst since '47; dir Linguistic Atlas of the US and Can sponsored by Am Council Learned Socs Washington. Linguistic Soc Am—Modern Lang Assn Am—Am Acad Arts Sci. Awarded Guggenheim Memorial fellowship '44, Loubat Prize Columbia U '48. Angell Hall, University of Michigan, Ann Arbor.⊚

18 KURDIAN, Harry (Haroutiun). History of silver and porcelain; Armenian manuscripts, art, and history. b'01. Contb editor The Armenian Review, Boston; free-lance writer for Armenian and English periodicals on Armenian manuscripts, art, history, economy, lit; lecturer on English silver, porcelain; teacher '46-48 U Kan Extension Wichita on history of silver and porcelain. Royal Asiatic Soc Gt Brit and Ireland—Am Oriental Soc Am. 1321 E. Douglas, Wichita 7, Kan.

19 KURSHAN, Daniel Lubell. City government (New York City); Municipal finance. b'13. BA '34—LLB '36 (Cornell); M Pub Adminstrn '40—'36-38 (NY Sch Social Work). Made and published numerous studies concerning finances and administration of New York City; organized and reorganized agencies of state and local gov-

ernment; established training programs governmental research; served on numerous committees for civic betterment. Author pubs for citizen's budget commn and other articles in field. Asso counsel State (NY) Commn on administrative agencies; spl cons NY State Commn Against Discrimination; dir div coordination and research NYC Dept Investigation; chief administrative management unit Div Analysis NYC Bur Budget; exec dir Citizens Budget Commn. Am Soc Pub Administrn (sec NY chpt)—Governmental Research Assn (chmn program com). 51 E. 42d St., NYC 17.

20 KURTZ, Lester Touby. Soil chemistry and fertility; Soil testing; Nutrient deficiencies of plants. b'14. BS '38 (Purdue U); MS '40—PhD '43 (Ill U). Research on determination of total, organic and available forms of phosphorus in soils, apparatus for microevaporations, corn-nitrate, simplified technique in use of liquid amalgam reductors. Author articles in field. Asso prof agron dept and Ill Agrl Expt Sta Ill U since '38. Am Soc Agron—Am Soil Sci Soc—Am Chem Soc—AAAS—Sigma Xi—Gamma Sigma Delta—Phi Kappa Phi. Agronomy Department University of Illinois, Urbana, Ill.†

21 KURTZWORTH, Harry Muir. Industrial art (Product design); Consumer education (Motion pictures). b'87. Student (Detroit Acad Fine Arts, Art Mus Sch, and in Paris, Munich, Rome, Phila); grad fine arts '11 (Columbia U); AFD '37 (Andhra U, Brit S India). Delegate Fourth International Art Congress Dresden; devised Lucideum consumer movie '39; consultant Shaw-Walker, Sears, Roebuck and Company, Boeing, Convair, Lockheed, Paramount Studios, and others; industrial arts director Academy Fine Arts Chicago and Kansas City Art Inst '21-26. Author: Industrial Art—A National Asset '18; International Art '36, and others; also articles in field. Adv art dir Woodbury Coll. Eastern Arts Assn—Western Arts Assn—Am Fedn Arts—AIA—Art Mus Dirs Assn—Am Assn Mus—Western Assn Art Mus Dirs Delta Phi Delta—Am Art Soc (dir). Awarded Order of Merit France '39. 810 S. Lucerne Blvd., Los Angeles.⊚

22 KUSSEROW, Gerhard William. Oils; Alkaloids; Solutions (Intravenous); Canning (Bacteriology, sanitation). b'14. AB '36 (Stanford); PhD '41 (Eidgen, Tech Hochschule Zurich Switzerland). Research on structure elucidation sesquiterpenes, manufacture and control problems of intravenous solutions; study of canning bacteriology, sanitation, qualitative container requirements for canning foods; isolation, evaluation and manufacture of hypotensive ester alkaloids from Veratrum viride. Dir prodn research intravenous solutions Cutter Labs '42-44; asst lab dir canning Gerber Products Co '44-47; vp in charge research Veratrum alkaloids Rexall Drug Co and Riker Labs Inc Los Angeles since '47. AAAS—Inst Food Tech—ACS—Alpha Chi Sigma. Registered chem engr Cal. 8480 Beverly Blvd., LA 48.

23 KUTNEWSKY, Fremont Coates. Minerals of New Mexico (Nonmetallic); New Mexico (Industry). Freelance writer for trade press since '22, specializing in the non-metallics of New Mexico since '28; articles on desert plants of the Southwest having industrial possibilities, salt potash pumice perlite fluorspar, coal clays, cotton and others. Author articles: Albuquerque Atom Boom Town; Los Alamos City; What Makes Albuquerque Tick. Advt mgr NM (State) Mag since '42; mgr Albuquerque Mfrs Assn '50-51; corr Business Week, Baker's Helper, McGraw Hill Publs. NM Miners and Prospectors Assn—Southwest Bakers Assn(historian)—NM Press Assn—Albuquerque Pub Relations Assn. P.O. Box 1023, Albuquerque, N.M.

10 KUTTNER, Stephan George. History of canon law; Medieval manuscripts (Legal, canonical). b'07. JUD '30 (U Berlin). Research in Italy, survey and analysis manuscripts. Author: Kanonistische Schuldlehre '35; Repertorium der Kanonistik '37; Decreta septem priorum sessionum concilii Tridentini '45; also articles in field. Research asso Vatican Library '34-40; asso prof hist canon law Pontifical Inst Canon and Civil Law Rome '37-40; prof hist canon law Cath U since '42; hon cons Library of Congress since '43. Société d'Histoire du Droit Paris; Riccobono Seminar Roman Law in America (pres '42-43). Fellow German Council Sci Investigations '30-31, '33. Catholic University, Washington 17.

11 KUYKENDALL, Ralph Simpson. History of the Hawaiian Islands. b'85. AB '10 (Coll Pacific San Jose Calif); MA '18 (U Calif). Author: The Hawaiian Kingdom (1778-1854) '38; Constitutions of the Hawaiian Kingdom '40; (with H E Gregory) A History of Hawaii '26; (with L T Gill) Hawaii in the World War '28; (with A G Day) Hawaii: A History '48; also articles in field. Mem bd editors Pacific Hist Rev '35-37; with U Hawaii since '32, asso prof hist since '38. AHA—Am Assn State Local Hist—Hawaiian Hist Soc (trustee '26-38, pres '40-43)—Inst Pacific Relations—Phi Kappa Phi. Univ. of Hawaii, Honolulu, T.H.†◎

12 KYLE, Robert Petroleum chemistry. b'10. B Engring '31 (Johns Hopkins). Research in production of gases and by-products of petroleum. Br mgr Gen Controls Co '47-48; gas sales engr Gas Machinery Co since '48. Am Gas Assn—Instrument Soc Am—ACS. 16100 Waterloo Rd., Cleve 10. H: 577 Quilliams Rd., Cleve 21.

13 KYLLINGSTAD, Henry C(arrel). Bird life; Bird banding; Bird photography. b'14. BA '39 (State Teachers Coll ND). Collected botanical specimens in Alaska also banded and collected birds; co-discoverer with David Allen of nest of bristle-thighed curlew on expedition of Arctic Inst North America, National Geographical Society and Cornell University '48; owns still and motion pictures of birds never before photographed, including several Alaskan species. Author: The Secret of the Bristle-thighed Curlew '48; also articles in field. With US Indian Service Mt Village Alaska '41-48, Ft Yates ND '48-49, information and editorial specialist ednl film lab since '49. Am Ornithologists Union (asso)—Arctic Inst NA—Cooper Ornithol Club—Wilson Ornithol Club—Eastern Bird Banding Assn—Inland Bird Banding Assn —Western Bird Banding Assn—Nat Audubon Soc. Educational Film Laboratory, United States Indian School, Santa Fe, N.M.†

L

14 LAANES, Theophil. Translating technical and scientific Estonian, Russian, French, German. b'98. PharmG '25 —MPharm '26 (Tartu U, Estonia). Abstractor for biological Abstracts '34. for Chemical Abstracts '37 from foreign language literature; represented Estonia at International Congress of Eugenics NY '32. Instr pharmacognosy, pharm chem and legal chem Estonian State U '25-28; research asst

dept genetics Carnegie Inst Washington '29-45; lit research chem Rumford Chem Works, sci lit researcher Heyden Chem Corp since '46. Estonian Pharm Soc—Genetics Soc Am—ACS-AAAS. Heyden Chemical Corporation, Garfield, N.J.

15 La BARRE, Weston. Peyote; Culture and personality studies. b'11. AB summa cum laude '33 (Princeton U); PhD '37 (Yale). Research Kiowa Indians '35, Peyote cult '36, Aymara Indians, Uru Indians Lake Titicaca Plateau Bolivia '37-38. Author articles in field. Teacher Family Welfare Assn Am Inst '39, Rutgers U '39-43; asst to asso prof anthropol Duke U since '46. Intelligence parachutist ONI India China '43, OSS-CBI India '44, OSS-SEAC Ceylon '44-45; att staff ComDesLant '45, CinClant '45. Am Anthropol Assn(F)—Am Folklore Soc—Soc Applied Anthropol—Nat Research Council (com So Am studies '48, Orient '49) —Phi Beta Kappa—Sigma Xi. Guggenheim fellow '46, summer '48; Social Sci Research Council fellow '38-39. 215C Soc Scis Bldg, Duke Univ, Durham, N.C.†

16 LABES, Willis George. Fire protection engineering. b'15. BS '38 (Ill Inst Tech). Tests of tempered polished plate glass doors to determine fracture characteristics and safety for the Chicago Fire Department; consulting engineer specializing in explosions and fire protection engineering. Author: Safe Mounting and Clearances for Heating Equipment '48. Asst prof Fire Protection Engring Ill Inst Tech. 14th Naval Dist Fire Fighters Sch '44-45; Fire Marshal USS Intrepid '45-46. Nat Fire Protection Assn—Western Soc Fire Protection Engrs —Soc Fire Protection Engrs —Am Soc Safety Engrs. Illinois Institute of Technology, Chicago.

17 LACH, Donald Frederick. History of Germany and the Far East. b'17. AB '37 (W Va U); PhD '41 (U Chicago). Research asst in hist U Chi '40-42, instr '42; asst prof hist Elmira Coll '42-43, asso prof '43-45, prof '45-48; asst prof modern hist U of Chicago since '48. Author: Contributions of China to German Civilization '41; China and the Era of the Enlightenment '42. Co-author: (with H F MacNair) Modern Far Eastern International relations '50 (with Louis Gottschalk) Europe and the Modern World '51. Far Eastern Assn—Phi Beta Kappa —AHA. Department of History, University of Chicago, Chicago 37.

18 LACKEY, Charles F(ranklin). Virus diseases of plants; Tissue relationships of dodders. b'99. BS '24 (Washington State Coll); MS '34 (U Calif). Author articles in field. With US Dept Agr since '22, plant pathol div sugar plant investigations since '24. Am Phytopathol Soc—Am Bot Soc— Biol Photog Soc(F)—AAAS—So Calif Bot Soc. Box 31, 3949 Lime, Riverside, Calif.†

19 LACKEY, James Bridges. Microbiology (Water, sewage); Marine ecology (Protozoa, algae). b'93. AB '15— MA '22 (Miss Coll); Certificate '19 (Montpellier U); PhD '30 (Columbia). Research and writing on taxonomy, cytology and life histories of protozoa and algae, pollution and purification of streams and lakes. Teacher '15-18; research zool Sewage Investigations Lab NJ State Expt Station '24-26; instr biol Washington Sq Coll NYU '25-28; prof and head dept biol Southwestern Coll '28-32, Seton Hall Coll '32-35; asso aquatic biol Tenn Valley Authority '34-36; sr biol USPHS '36-45; editor Blakiston Co '45-52; prof sanitary science U Fla since '52. Tenn Acad Sci—O Acad Sci(F)—AAAS—Am Microbiol

Soc—Phycological Soc—Limnolog Soc (past vp)—Sigma Xi. University of Florida, Gainesville, Fla.

20 LACY, George John. Questioned Document Examination; Handwriting identification. b'95. Grad (Northwestern U Sci Crime Detection Lab). Author articles: Questioned Documents— Genuine or Fraudulent? '41; How the Questioned Document Examiner Proves the Facts '43; Handwriting and Forgery Under Hypnosis '45; Documents and the Legal Profession '48. Examiner of questioned documents operating own office and lab since '28. Am Soc Questioned Document Examiners (charter mem and dir)—Internat Assn Identification (past pres Tex div). Esperson Bldg., Houston 2.

21 LACY, Raymond Elmer. Radio engineering. b'16. BS in elec engring '38 (Drexel Inst Tech); MS in elec engring '40—'50 (NYU); '40-41 '48 (Poly Inst Brooklyn). Design, development, installation radio communication systems; development, design portable frequency modulation military radio sets and radio relay communication sets; in charge research and development vehicular and portable sets, microwave relay equipment, and long range equipment. Author: Table of Operational Transforms. Author articles: Two Multichannel Microwave Relay Equipments for the United States Army Communication Network '47; A Portable Microwave Communication Set '48. Cadre engr Potomac Elec Power Co Washington '34-36; radio cons engr Philco Corp and Chubbuck & Patrick Phila '37-38; faculty elec engring dept. NYU '38-40; engr Coles Signal Lab since '40, now exec engr. Inst Radio Engrs—Armed Forces Communication Assn. Coles Signal Laboratory, Signal Corps Engineering Laboratories, Ft. Monmouth, N.J. H: Box 42, RFD 1, Red Bank.

22 LADD, Harry S. Geology (Coral reefs origin, paleoecology, Pacific island, Tertiary paleontology, marine ecology). b'99. AB '22 (Washington U); MS '24—PhD '25 (Ia U). Author articles in field. Principal geol US Geol Survey since '45. Geol Soc Am (F)—AAAS—Paleontol Soc—Geol Soc Washington—Am Assn Petroleum Geol —Am Geophys Union—Sigma Xi. Fellow Bishop Museum '26, '28. United States Geological Survey, Washington 25.◎

23 LADERMAN, Jack. Mathematical statistics; Mathematics (Numerical methods, mass computation, probability, computing machines, finance, quality control). b'14. BS '34 (CCNY); MA '35 (Columbia). Conducts research and prepares procedures for the numerical solution of mathematical problems and for the large scale computation of mathematical functions. Author articles in field. Mathematician Computation Lab Nat Bur Standards '46-49; served as statis, chief statis sect Chem Corps War Dept '40-46 meritorious civilian award); now with Columbia University. Sigma Xi—Am Math Soc—Inst Math Statis—Am Statis Assn—AAAS. Recipient meritorious award from NYC Bd Edn. Computation Laboratory, Columbia University, 116th Street & Broadway, NYC 27. H: 1705 Andrews Av., Bronx 53.

24 La DUE, Harry Jay. Fur farming; Mink nutrition and breeding. b'86. Ed pub schs. With Arthur Schleicher, built first large mink ranch in US; internationally-known judge of live fur animals; with James Freer made mink industry's first investigations in nutrition and physiology of breeding. Co-inventor with Freer of open-face

Freer Animal Exercise Wheel, co-developer animal restraint cage and other devices. Author articles in field. Asst commr State Game and Fish Dept St Paul Minn '18-24; ed American Fox & Fur Farmer '24-29; ed and owner American Fur Breeder since '29. Nat Bd Fur Farm Orgns (a founder, dir nat bd) — Am Soc Mammalogists — Wildlife Inst — Am Genetic Assn — Izaak Walton League, and others. 405 E. Superior St., Duluth 2, Minn.

10 LA FARGE, Oliver. American Indian ethnology (Mayan); Acculturation of United States Indians; Aviation (Military transport). b'01. AB '24 — Hewenway fellow '24-26 — AM '29 (Harvard); MA (hon) '32 (Brown U). Made three archeology expeditions to Arizona and three archeology and ethnology expeditions to Mexico and Guatemala. Author: Laughing Boy (Pulitzer prize for best novel of year) '29; The Year Bearer's People '31; All the Young Men '35; As Long as the Grass Shall Grow '40; The Copper Pot '42; Raw Material '45; Santa Eulalia '46. Editor: The Changing Indian '42; also articles in field. Research asso ethnol Mus U Pa since '47; advisory bd Lab Anthrop Santa Fe since '46. AAAS(F) — Am Anthrop Assn. 647 College St., Santa Fe, N.M.©

11 LAFFERTY, Robert H(ervey), Jr. Uranium and fluoride analysis. b'16. BS '37 (Davidson Coll); PhD '41 (Cornell U). Research in the development of methods for the determination of Uranium and Fluorine. Article in field: (with J C Barton and J A Westbrook) Liquid Flourine-Cotton Explosion '48. Research chemist The Kellex Corp '43-45; research analysis Carbide and Carbon Chem Corp since '45. Am Chem Soc — Phi Beta Kappa — Sigma Xi. Carbide and Carbon Chemicals Co., P.O. Box P, Oak Ridge, Tenn.†

12 LAFLEUR, Laurence J(ulien). Jeremy Bentham; René Descartes; Ant behavior. b'07. BA '28 (Princeton U); '28 (U Grenoble); '28-29 (Edinburgh U, U Berlin); PhD '31 (Cornell U). Author: Descartes' Discourse on Method '50; Descartes' Meditations '51; Bentham's Principles of Morals and Legislation '48; also articles in field. Asso prof Fla State U since '48. Am Philos Assn — AAAS. University of Akron, Akron, O.

13 LaFUZE, Henry Harvey. Trees of Kentucky; General education (Science methods). b'08. AB '29 (DePauw U); MS '30 — PhD '36 (State U Ia); '41 (Northwestern). Author: Biology of Plants: Laboratory Outlines '48; Biology and Man '48; also articles in field. Prof, head dept biol Eastern Ky State Coll since '46. Ky Acad Sci — Bot Soc Am — Nat Assn Biol Teachers. Department of Biology, Eastern Kentucky State College, Richmond, Ky.†

14 LAGEMANN, Robert Theodore. Ultrasonics; Infra-red; The Faraday effect. b'12. Research fellow '39-40 — PhD '40 (O State U); AB '34 (Baldwin-Wallace Coll); MS '35 (Vanderbilt U). Author articles in field. Prof Emory U since '48. Research in isotope separation Manhattan Project '43-44. Am Phys Soc — Am Assn Physics Teachers — Ga Acad Sci — Sigma Xi. Research award Ga Acad Sci '45, W Va Acad Sci '41; grant-in-aid Sigma Xi '47, The Research Corp '47-48. Department of Physics, Emory University, Ga.†

15 LAIDACKER, Samuel H. American historical glass; Anglo-American historical Staffordshire. b'04. Student '24-27 (Pa State Coll). Collected and published cumulative auction records for historical Staffordshire, publica-tion work resulted in becoming a specialist cataloger for Parke-Bernet Galleries NY in the field of American glass and decorative as well as historical pottery; edited compiled and published The Standard Catalogue of Anglo-American China '38. Author articles in field. Newportville Road, Bristol, Pa.†

16 LAIDLAW, Harry Hyde, Jr. Apiculture; Honeybee genetics and breeding (Artificial insemination of queens). b'07. BS '33 — MS '34 (La State U); PhD '39 (U Wis). Designed instrument for the artificial insemination of queen bees and developed a technique of insemination. Author articles in field. Asst prof entomol U Calif since '47. Capt entomol San Corps US Army '43-46. Am Assn Econ Entomol — AAAS — Am Soc Zool — Entomol Soc Am — Genetics Soc Am. Department of Entomology and Parasitology, University of California, Davis, Calif.†

17 LAIDLER, Harry Wellington. Socialism; Labor; Industrial democracy. b'84. AB '07 — AM (hon) '33 (Wesleyan U); LLB '10 (Brooklyn Law Sch); PhD '14 (Columbia). Author: Boycotts and the Labor Struggle '14; Socialism in Thought and Action '20; A History of Socialist Thought '27; Concentration of Control in American Industry '31; Socializing Our Democracy '35; A Program for Modern America '36; Social-Economic Movements '44. Exec dir League for Indusl Democracy since '21; dir Nat Bureau Econ Research since '20; mem Indsl Div Fed Council of Churches '24-51; dir Nat Pub Housing Conf since '31. Phi Beta Kappa. 112 E. 19th St., NYC 3.©

18 LAING, James Tamplin. Race relations; Sociological theory. b'99. AB '24 (WVa U); MA '29 — PhD '33 (Ohio State Univ). Co-author: Sociological Foundations of Education '42; also articles and monographs. Prof sociology Holbrook Coll '33-34; asso prof W Va Inst Tech '34-35; asso prof sociology Kent (O) State U '35-37 prof and head dept since '37; pres Kent Welfare Bd '44-45 '45-46. Am Sociol Soc — WVa Acad Sci — AAUP — Ohio Valoey Sociol Soc — Alpha Kappa Delta — Pi Gamma Mu. 304 Kent Hall, Kent State University, Kent, O.†©

19 LAIRD, Alton Wilson. Hydraulic controls engineering. b'00. ME '22 (Rensselaer Poly Inst). Engaged design motorized fire fighting equipment, development automobile brake design. Machinist apprentice, spl duty apprentice, repair foreman Pa RR '22-26; engr Am LaFrance Foamite Corp Elmira NY '26-29; engr asst to pres, hydraulic controls engring div NY Air Brake Co since '29. SAE — Am Soc M E — Aircraft Industries Assn — AOA — Soc Am Mil Engrs. New York Air Brake Co., 420 Lexington Av., NYC 17.

20 LAIRD, Wilson Morrow. Devonian and Mississippian stratigraphy; North Dakota geology (Ground water). b'15. BA cum laude '36 (Muskingum Coll); MA '38 (U NC); PhD '40 (U Cincinnati). Author articles in field. Prof geol U ND since '40; State geol ND since '41; cons geol since '48. Geol Soc Am — Am Assn Pet Geol — Am Inst Mining and Metall Engrs — Paleontol Soc — Am Assn State Geol (vp '48) — ND Acad Sci — Sigma Xi. Recipient with L L Sloss of pres award of Am Assn Pet Geol '48. Department of Geology, University of North Dakota, Grand Forks, N.D.©

21 LAITINEN, Herbert August. Electrochemistry; Polarography; Amperometric titrations. b'15. BCh '36 — PhD '40 — Shevlin fellow (U Minn). Research on polarography, amperometric titrations and other analytical chemical subjects. Author: Ph and Electro-titrations '41; also articles in field. U Ill since '40, prof chem since '47. Am Chem Soc — The Electrochem Soc — Sigma Xi. Dept. of Chemistry, University of Illinois, Urbana, Ill.†

22 LAKELA, Olga. Taxonomy of flowering plants; Flora of Minnesota. b'90. BS '21 — MS '24 — PhD '32 (U Minn). Author articles in field. Prof bot Duluth Br U Minn since '46; head dept biol '46-49; herbarium curator since '50. Minn Acad Sci — Am Bot Soc — Am Ecol Soc — Soc Plant Taxonomists. University of Minnesota, Duluth 5, Minn.

23 LA LANCE, Saens Wirt. Highway bridge design and material handling. b'93. Ed (Chicago Acad, Pa Acad, Marshall Coll); ME '29 — CE '38 (W Va State Bd). Special engineer design section Blue Stone Dam War Department US Engineers Office; special city engineer in charge of flood wall work Huntington West Virginia; devised system of storing coal in 200,000 ton piles without fire danger; developed a formula for the computation of railroad rail as reinforcement and a type of pier and formula for bridges using corrugated culvert pipe, 100 pound rail and vibrated concrete. Author: Book of Lyrics. Dist engr Barber-Green Co Aurora Ill 10 yrs; cons engr P C Thomas; vp and gen mgr mines Koopers Coal and Coke Co; civil engr W Va State Rd Commn Dist 2. Soc Am Mil Engrs — ASME — ASCE. State Road Commn, 2224 5th Av., Huntington 12, W. Va.

24 LAMAR, John Everts. Geology of industrial minerals. b'97. BS '20 (U Chicago). Author articles in field. Asst to geol and head indsl minerals div Ill State Geol Survey since '20. Geol Soc Am(F) — Soc Econ Geol — Am Inst Mining and Metall Engrs — Ill Acad Sci — Sigma Xi. 309 Natural Resources Bldg., Urbana, Ill.

25 LAMAR, William Luther. Water chemistry. b'05. BS '29 (U Md); AM '32 (George Washington U). Research on quality of water investigations, chemical and physical properties of surface and ground waters, salinity, measurement and evaluation of suspended sediment carried by streams, analytical methods for analysis of water, stream pollution, industrial utility of water supplies. Author articles: The Chemical Character of Natural Waters; Determination of Fluoride in Water: a modified zirconiumalizarin method; Chemical Character of Surface Waters of North Carolina; and others. With US Geol Survey since '29, dist chem O Basin Regional Lab since '48. ACS — Am Water Works Assn. US Geological Survey, 2822 E. Main St., Columbus 9, O. H: 2595 Brentwood Rd., Bexley, Columbus 9.†

26 LAMB, Alvin Romaine. Nutrition. b'90. BS in chem '13 — MS '15 — PhD '30 (U Wis). Research in vitamins, acid-base balance and physiological effects of fluorine; Hawaiian sugar by-products in livestock feeding; relative nutritional efficiency glucose and sucrose; influence microorganisms and plant enzymes on corn silage fermentation; military sanitation. Chief in nutrition Ia Agr Expt Sta '19-25; biochemist USPHS '31-33; research asso Expt Sta Hawaiian Sugar Planters Assn since '35; mem Territorial nutrition Com '37-42. AAAS(F) — Am Soc Biol Chem — Am Inst Nutrition — Hawaiian Sugar Tech — Phi Lambda Upsilon — Sigma Xi. Exec officer food control Office Mil Gov Hawaii '42. Experiment Station, H.S.P.A., Honolulu, Hawaii.

10 LAMB, Cecil Alexander. Small grain breeding (Wheat). b'00. BSA '21 (U Brit Columbia); MSA '24 (Mc Gill U); PhD '35 (Cornell U). Introduced Thorne wheat '37, Butler wheat '47. Author articles in field. Asso agronomist O Agrl Expt Sta since '35; prof agronomy O State U '48-50; asso chmn dept agron O Agrl Expt Sta since '50. AAAS(F)—Am Soc Agronomy—Am Assn Cereal Chem—Am Genetics Assn. Dept of Agronomy, Ohio Agrl Expt Station, Wooster, O.†

11 LAMB, George A. Mineral economics (Coal, fuel); Coal industry (Statistics, markets, prices, distribution). b'06. AB '29 (U Portland); Strathcona Fellowship '31-32—MS '32 (Yale). Author articles in field. Mgr bus surveys Pittsburgh Consol Coal Co since '46. Am Statis Assn—Am Econ Assn—Am Inst Mining and Metall Engrs. 746 9th St., Oakmont, Pa.†⊙

12 LAMB, George Goodrich. Aviation fuels and lubricants. b'06. BSE '27—MS '28 (U Mich); PhD '35 NYU). Exploratory research in petroleum refining; group leader research developing new catalytic petroleum refining and synthesis processes; section leader two groups research on lubricants, waxes and specialty products from petroleum. Patents granted (with B L Evering) on hydrocarbon conversions to produce high anti-knock motor fuels. Author articles in field. Lt to capt USNR '41-46, head fuels and lubricants sect, power plant div, Bur Aeronautics Navy Dept Washington. Prof chem engring Northwestern Tech Inst Evanston Ill since '46; Ill profl engrs examining com '46-52, chmn '50-52. Am Inst Chem Engrs—Am Soc Testing Materials—Am Chem Soc—SAE—Am Ordnance Assn—Phi Kappa Phi—Sigma Xi. Northwestern Technological Institute, Evanston, Ill.†

13 LAMB, George Newton. Mahogany; Walnut; Tropical woods. b'87. BSc '09—MA '11 (U Neb). Research and work mahogany, walnut, tropical woods and veneers, cabinet-work and furniture produced, technical director motion picture mahogany-wood of the ages '47. Author: Logging American Walnut '27; The Story of American Walnut (1st to 7th edns) '20-29; The Mahogany Book (1st to 6th edns) '34-47; How to Identify Mahogany and Avoid Substitutes '36; How to Select Walnut Stumps '24; Willows, Their Growth, Use and Importance '25; Why Wood is Beautiful '38. Co-author: Characteristics of Modern Woods '39; also articles in field. Forest exam US Forest Service '11-18; mng dir Walnut Export Sales Co '19-30; sec-treas Flexwood Co and US Plywood Co '24-26; sec, mng Mahogany Assn Inc; sec, mng Am Walnut Mfgrs Assn '18-30; commr Nat Woodwork Inst '24-26. 75 E. Wacker Drive, Chicago 1.

14 LAMBERT, Edmund Bryan. Mushroom culture; Antibiotics; Cereal pathology. b'97. BS '20—MS '22—PhD '27 (U Minn). Author articles in field. Sr mycologist div fruit and vegetable crops and diseases US Dept Agri Plant Industry Sta Beltsville Md since '48. AAAS—Am Phytopathol Soc—Mycol Soc—Wash Acad Sci—Wash Bot Soc—Mushroom Growers Assn England—Sigma Xi—Gamma Sigma Delta. Plant Industry Station, Beltsville, Md.

15 LAMBERT, Jean William. Barley breeding and genetics; Soybean breeding. b'14. BS '40 (Neb U); MS '42 —PhD '45 (Ohio.) Research in culture and adaptation of Brome Grass. Asso prof U Minn since '49. Am Soc Agron —Genetics Soc Am—Sigma Xi—Gamma Sigma Delta. Department of Agron-omy and Plant Genetics, University Farm, St. Paul.†

16 LAMBERT, John Ralph, Jr. Maryland history; American political history (1865-1912). b'16. AB '37 (Western Maryland Coll); MA '40—PhD '47 (Princeton U). Author articles in field. Instr to asst prof hist Carnegie Inst Tech since '46. Am Hist Assn—Maryland Hist Soc—So Hist Assn—Miss Valley Hist Assn. Carnegie Institute of Technology, Pittsburgh 13.

17 LAMBERT, William Vincent. Animal genetics research administration. b'97. BS '21 (U Neb); MS '23 (Kan State Coll); Rosenberg Scholar '29-30 —PhD '31 (U Calif). Research on genetics of disease resistance in animals and poultry, physiology of reproduction. Author articles in field. Inst genetics Iowa State Coll '23-29, asst prof '30-36; sr animal husbandman charge genetics investigations US Dept Agr '36-40; asso dir Ind Exp Sta '40-45; asst research adminstr US Dept Agr '45-46, research adminstr '46-48; dean Coll of Agr U Neb '48. Mem US delegations FAO of United Nations Copenhagen '46, Geneva '47; member US Mexican Agrl Commn '46-48; bd alternates Pres' Sci Research Bd '47; US Govt Interdepartmental Com on Sci '48. AAAS(F)—Am Soc Naturalists—Am Soc Zool—Genetics Soc Am —Poultry Sci Assn—Am Soc Animal Prodn—Sigma Xi. Dean, College of Agriculture, University of Nebraska, Lincoln 1, Nebraska.⊙

18 LAMBOU, (Mrs.) Madeline G(omila). Seed storage and viability. BA '28—MS '29 (Tulane U). Author articles in field. Chem So Regional Research Lab New Orleans since '42. Am Soc Plant Physiol—Am Chem Soc—Am Oil Chem Soc—Sigma Xi. Southern Regional Research Laboratory, 2100 Robert E. Lee Blvd., New Orleans 19.

19 La MER, Victor Kuhn. Physical chemistry; Colloids; Thermodynamics and kinetics of electrolytes; Light scattering. b'95. AB '15 (U Kan); PhD '21 (Columbia U); '16 (U Chicago); '22-23 (Cambridge); '23 (Copenhagen). Translator and editor (with Eric Jette) of Fundamentals of Physical Chemistry by Arnold Eucken '25. Asso editor: Jour of Chem Physics '33-36; editor-in-chief Jour of Colloid Sci. Prof chem Columbia U since '35. Nat Acad Sci—NY Acad Sci (F, vp '39-41, treas '43)—Am Chem Soc—Am Phys Soc—Faraday Soc (Eng) — Sigma Xi. 353 Moore Av., Leonia, N.J.⊙

20 La MERI (Russell Meriwether Hughes). Hindu and Spanish dances. Specialist in interpretation native dances of India and Spain; world-wide performances since '23. Author: Principles of the Dance Art '33; Dance as an Art-Form '33; Gesture Language of the Hindu Dance '41; Spanish Dancing '48; also articles in field. Dir Ethnologic Dance Center New York. Teacher; mem bd directors Jacob's Pillow U of Dance. Am Soc Aesthetics—Assn Am Indian Affairs, and others. 110 E. 59th St., NYC 22.†

21 LAMEY, Carl Arthur Pre-Cambrian geology; Metamorphism; Ore deposits (Iron). b'92. BS '25 (Mich Coll Mines); fellow '25-26—MS '27—PhD '33 (Northwestern U). Research Michigan and California geology, Pre-Cambrian geology of Lake Superior region, igneous intrusions, metamorphism, Michigan copper district and Menominee iron range. Author articles in field. With O State U since '35, prof geol since '46; mem staff US Geol Survey since '42. Geol Soc Am—Sec Econ Geol—AIME—Am Geophy Union—AA AS—O Acad Sci—Mich Acad Sci—Tau Beta Pi—Phi Beta Kappa—Sigma Xi. Geology Department, Ohio State University, Columbus 10, O.

22 LAMLEIN, Harold Arthur. Coating, combining and finishing fabrics. b'11. BS '33 (Worcester Polytechnic Inst). Research and manufacturing rubber and synthetic resin coated fabrics, raincoats, imitation leather upholstery fabrics, calendered and spreader coated fabrics and impregnated fabrics, automobile fabrics, shoes; commercial dyeing and finishing cotton fabrics. Chem Am Rubber Co Cambrige Mass '33, US Rubber Co fabric div Mishawaka Ind '33-35; chief chem The Landers Corp Toledo Ohio '35-44, tech controller since '44. Am Chem Soc—Sigma Xi. The Landers Corp., Box 911, Toledo 1, Ohio.

23 LAMMERTS, Walter E(dward). Plant genetics and evolution; Taxonomy (Ornamental plants); Embryo culture and plant physiology. b'04. BS '27 —PhD '30 (U Calif). Research plant breeding, roses, peaches; problems relating to growth hybrid seedlings of peaches; camellias, peaches and other fruits; originated Robin, Redwing, Meadowlark, Flamingo, and Daily News Star series flowering and fruiting peaches. Nat research fellow Cal Inst Tech '30-32; research asso Univ Cal '32-34; asso nursery business Temple City Calif '34-36; plant breeder Armstrong Nurseries Ont Cal '35-40; hort and geneticist U Calif LA '40-45; hort cons and plant breeder Descano Gardens La Canada California since '45. Am Soc Hort Sci—Am Soc Bot—Am Sci Affiliation—Am Rose Soc—Am Hort Council—Phi Beta Kappa—Sigma Xi—Phi Sigma—Alpha Zeta. Awarded gold medal best new rose in Am for 5 years Am Rose Soc '45, gold medal most important rose in Am regarding breeding of future roses Charlotte Armstrong '45, Fuerstenberg prize '44, John Cooke medal '41, Gertrude Hubbard gold medal '44. Descano Gardens, La Canada, Cal.

24 La MOTTE, Ellen Newbold International opium traffic. b'73. Grad '02 (Training School Johns Hopkins Hosp). Travel and observation in Far East '16-17. Author: The Tuberculosis Nurse '14; Pekin Dust '19; The Opium Monopoly '20; The Ethics of Opium '24; Snuffs and Butters '25; also articles in field. Johns Hopkins Hosp Alumnae Assn—The Huguenot Soc of Am—Soc of Women Geog. Decorated medal of spl membership and Order of Merit by Japanese Red Cross; Lin Tse Hsu memorial medal for work against opium by Chinese Nat Govt '30. 3115 O St. N.W., Washington.

25 LAMPE, John Harold. Electrical engineering (Liquid insulation); Magnetism; Magnetic analysis. b'96. BS in Engring '18—MS '25—Dr EE '31 (Johns Hopkins U). Author articles in field. Contbr editor to Internat Critical Tables on liquid insulation. Dean engring NC State Coll since '45. AIEE (F)—Am Soc for Testing Materials—Conn Soc CE—Am Soc Engring Edn—Nat Roster Sci and Specialized Personnel—Am Assn U Prof—Asso Land Grant Coll and U—NC Soc of Engrs—Sigma Xi—Tau Beta Pi—Eta Kappa Nu. 305 Forest Rd., Raleigh, N.C.

26 LAMPERT, Lincoln Maximilian. Dairy chemistry; Sanitary chemicals; Detergents. b'97. BS '22 (U Cal Berkeley). Developed method for determination quantity of egg yolk in ice cream and other foods; devised accurate procedure for testing homogenized milk; development of single-stain solution for bacteriological examination of milk; studied effect of preservatives on milk samples and formulated mercury-free preservative tablet; devised simple, direct tablet procedure for phosphatase tests on milk and other biological substances; method for rapid means to measure exact concentration of quaternary ammonium compounds in sanitizing solutions; consultant food chemistry and plant sanitation procedures. Author: Milk and Dairy Products '47. Chem in charge QMC Lab AUS '22-23; research chem and asst research dir Golden State Co Ltd '26-37; sr chem Cal Dept Agr. Am Inst Chem(F)—ACS—Am Dairy Sci Assn (com standardization of Babcock tests). P.O. Box 1266, Sacramento.

10 LANCASTER, Clay American architecture; Buddhist and Oriental art. b'17. BA '38—MA '39 (Ky U). Research and writing on work of John McMurtry, Oriental forms in Am architecture 1800-70, architecture of Sunnyside, builders' guide and plan books, origin of Chinese architecture, European palaces of Yuan Ming Yuan, octagonal forms in Southern architecture, Cambodian architecture and sculpture. Author articles in field. Ware librarian Avery Arch Library, Columbia '46-50, lecturer Dept Fine Arts since '48, lecturer art dept Vassar since '50. Phi Beta Kappa—Soc Archt Hist (sec-treas '48). 623 West 113 St., NYC 25.

11 LANCASTER, Talbot Augustin. Plastic films and coatings. b'15. BS '36 (U Mich). Research on practical application of principles of organosol techniques to casting of thin vinyl films, transfer printing techniques, specialized coatings having controlled moisture vapor transmission rates, blocking surface slip, adhesion of printing inks, seam strength. Author articles in field. Plant chem Plastic Film Corp since '44. Am Chem Soc—Soc Plastics Industry (com on plastic films). Box 166, Canterbury, Conn. H: Talamac, Westminster Rd.

12 LANCOUR, Adlore Harold. Colonial immigration; Heraldry; Auction sales. b'08. AB '32 (U Wash); '30-31 (Inst Univ de Hautes Etudes Internat, Geneva Switzerland); BS '36—MS '42 (Columbia Library Sch); EdD '47 (Columbia Teachers Coll). Compiler: Passenger Lists of Ships Coming to North America, 1607-1825 '38; Heraldry: A Guide to Reference Books '40; American Art Auction Catalogues, 1785-1942 '44. Asst dir Library School and prof library sci U Ill since '47. ALA—Assn of Coll and Reference Libraries (bd dirs '46-49)—Am Soc for Engring Edn—Bibliog Soc Am—Am Antiquarian Soc—Am Assn U Prof—Assn of Am Library Sch. Library School, University of Illinois, Urbana, Ill.

13 LAND, Edwin Herbert. Polarized light; Synthetic polarizing sheet; Photographic (One step, three dimensional, vectographs); Optical filters and instruments. b'09. Class '30 (Harvard); hon ScD '47 (Tufts Coll). During college years began development of means for polarization of light as an applied science; invented polarizer used as camera filter; established business with George W Wheelwright 3rd Boston Mass '35; organized Polaroid Corp Cambridge Mass '37 becoming pres, chmn of board and dir of research; invented camera that delivers finished photograph immediately after exposure is made '47; present research includes automobile headlight system and three-dimensional pictures; during World War II conducted research leading to development of new weapons and war materials including plastic optical lenses for devices for seeing at night, filters for pre-adapting eyes of personnel for night duty, new

types of light-weight stereoscopic rangefinders and an infinity optical ring sight used on anti-aircraft guns and bazookas. Sigma Xi. Recipient of Hood medal of Royal Photographic Soc, Cresson medal of Franklin Inst, Rumford medal Am Acad Arts and Sci. 730 Main St., Cambridge, Mass.☺

14 LAND, Frank Sherman. Boys work; Order of DeMolay. b'90. Founder '19 and since secretary general Grand Council Order of DeMolay, boy's organization of Masonic Order; president board trustees DeMolay Dormitory Association of University of Missouri; past potentate Ararat Temple Kansas City Mo; imperial second ceremonial master Shrine for North America '48; founder '27 Young Men's Civic Forum International; co-founder '30 Metro Clubs; mem Nat Youth Week Com for US; life mem Kansas City Conf of Social Work. Mason (33°, Shriner). Achievement medal City of Toledo '32. 201 East Armour Blvd, KC 2, Mo†☺

15 LANDAU, Ralph. Chemical plant design; Fluorine; Corrosion. b'16. BS '37 (U Pa); ScD '41 (Mass Inst Tech). author articles in field. Nine patents pending. Exec vp Sci Design Co, charge design various chem plants since '46. Am Chem Soc—Asso Cons Chem and Chem Engrs—Am Inst Chem Engrs—Electrochem Soc—Tau Beta Pi (F). ASTM prize, Kellex Key award. 2 Park Av., NYC 16.†

16 LANDECKER, Fred K(laus). Shot peening; Flame hardening. b'19. Student '36-38 (Poly Inst London); '40 (Wayne U); '46-47 (U Cal Los Angeles). Research and development controlled shot peening process and its application to products of aircraft, automobile and oil tool industries. Mgr Metal Improvement Co since '46. Am Soc Metals—Soc Non-Destructive Testing—Soc Exptl Stress Analysis—Technion. Metal Improvement Co., 1721 East 47th St., LA 58.

17 LANDEN, David. Photogrammetry. b'08. Student '26-29 (MIT). Charge of aerial mapping program in Maine '37-40; research and development Trimetrogon Mapping System for World Aeronautical Charting '41-44; organized and directed US Air Force School of Photo-Topography Lowry Field, Denver '43; originated and developed photogrammetric methods, directed topographic mapping 10 million square miles Aeronautical Charting from Trimetrogon Photography '44-49. Invented principal plane photoalidade, February '45; vertical photoalidade, October '43. Author articles: Tri-Metrogon Mapping '43; A Principal Plane Photoalidade for Oblique Photographs '45; Reconnaissance Mapping with Photoalidade '48; Photo-Topography '49. Asst cartographic engr Agrl Adjustment Adminstrn US Dept Agr '37-40; topographic field mapping US Geol Survey '40-41, asst to asso topographic engr Alaskan Br '41-44, chief Photo-Topographic Mapping Unit since '44; chief research and develop unit since '49. Am Soc Photogrammetry—Am Congress Surveying and Mapping—Wash Soc Engrs. US Dept Interior Award of Merit outstanding service development Trimetrogon System '43. U.S. Geological Survey, Washington 25. H: 313 N George Mason Drive, Arlington, Va.

18 LANDIS, Carney Abnormal, clinical and physiological psychology; Psychopathology; Personality; Emotion; Sex adjustments; Brain physiology. b'97. AB '21 (O State U); MA '22 (Dartmouth); PhD '24 (U Minn);

Nat Research Council fellow '24-25 (U Minn); '25-26 (U London). Author: Studies in the Dynamics of Behavior '32; Modern Soc and Mental Disease '38; The Startle Pattern '39; Sex in Development '40; Personality of the Physically Handicapped Woman '42; Textbook of Abnormal Psychology '46; Problems of the Human Brain '49; also articles in field. Prof psychol Columbia U since '43; prin research psychol NYS Psychiatric Inst since '38. AAAS(F)—Am Assn Applied Psychol (council clin sect '39-41)—NY Acad Med (asso F)—Am Psychol Assn—Am Physiol Soc—NY Assn Applied Psychol—Nat Inst Psychol—Soc Exptl Psychol—Com for Study of Sex Variants (treas since '36)—Soc for Exptl Biol and Med—Nat Research Council (div anthropol and psychol '38-41, '48-51)—Phi Beta Kappa—Sigma Xi. 722 W. 168th St., NYC 32.☺

19 LANDOLT, Percy Edward. Electrical precipitation; Industrial gas purification; Iron alloys, heat treatment; Lithium metals and alloys; Smoke nuisance. b'91. ChemE '12 (Columbia). Research on fractional precipitation, recovery of potash from cement kiln operations, volatilization of lithium from cement kilns; chemical reactions using electrical precipitation, recovery of ammonium bromide; improvement of pearlitic irons, spheroidized types of pearlitic malleable iron, production of nodular iron structures; court testimony on atmospheric pollution and abatement of smoke nuisance; work on occupational hazards in production of chemical and metallurgical products; administration of patent research operations. Author articles: Eliminating Waste and Nuisance in Smoke, Fume and Gas '21; Electrical Precipitation in the Chemical Industry '22; Use of Lithium Cartridges in Treating High Conductivity Copper and Copper-Base Alloys '49, and others. Contributor: Handbook of Non-Ferrous Metallurgy '26; Chemical Engineering—Unit Processes and Principles '32. Mgr comml dept Research Corp NYC '19-24; eastern mgr Western Precipitation Corp Los Angeles '24-32; with Allied Process Corp since '29, cons engr since '33, pres since '35; chief engr C S Sale & Co indsl engrs '37-38; pres Lithaloys Corp '40-46; exec vp Lithium Corp Am Inc since '46; chmn bd Am Metallic Chems Corp since '51. Assn Cons Chem and Chem Engrs (past pres)—ACS—Electrochem Soc—Am Inst Chem Engrs—AAAS(F)—Am Inst Chem(F)—Am Soc for Metals—AIMME—Phi Lambda Upsilon—Tau Beta Pi—Sigma Xi. Profl engr NY. 36 W. 44th St., NYC 36.

20 LANDON, Charles Earl. Transportation economics (Railroad, iron, steel); Industrial geography. b'95. AB '20—MA '21—fellow '20-21 (U Kan); PhD '26 (U Ill). Senior economist Board of Investigation and Research Transportation Act of '40; senior economist OPA '45; economic consultant State Planning Board of North Carolina '45, report on the advisability of improving the Port of Wilmington; economic consultant to State Utilities Commission of North Carolina in Carolina Coal Cases before Interstate Commerce Commission. Author: Industrial Geography '39. Co-author: (with E L Bogart) Modern Industry '26; (with I Wright) Readings in Marketing '26; also articles in field. Asso prof econ Duke U since '45. Am Econ Assn. Duke Station, Durham, N.C.†

21 LANDROCK, Arthur Harold. Food (Packaging materials). b'19. BS in biol '41 (Queens Coll); AM in biol '50 (Boston U); '45-49 (MIT). Water vapor permeability measurements at 100° F. and 0° F., development new method gas permeability measurements, new test method for flavor and odor transfer through packaging materials; insect resistance of packaging materials, insects attacking food in general especially stored food products, shelf life measurements stored food products in packages, development new test method for moisture or humidity equilibria of food products; development method measuring free oil in foods. Chem Continental Can Co Inc '45-47; tech asst, cons packaging MIT Dept Food Tech since '47. Tech Assn Pulp and Paper Industry (mem packaging materials testing com, chmn subcom flavor and odor)—Packaging Inst (acting ofcl rep for MIT Dept Food Tech, mem food com)—Soc Plastics Industry—Inst Food Tech—Sigma Xi. Department of Food Technology, Massachusetts Institute of Technology, Cambridge 39, Mass.†

10 LANDSBERG, Helmut (Erich). Physical climatology; Atmospheric suspensions. b'06. PhD '30 (U Frankfurt). Author: Physical Climatology '41; also articles in field. Exec dir Com on Geophysics and Geog Research and Development Bd Washington since '48. Special cons and operations analyst US Army Air Force '43-45. Am Meteorol Soc. Research and Development Board, Washington 25.†

11 LANDWEBER, Louis. Potential flow; Frictional resistance; Directional stability. b'12. BS '32 (NYC); MA '35 (George Washington U); PhD '51 (U Md). Physicist David Taylor Model Basin since '32, now chief hydrodynamic div. Soc Naval Architects and Marine Engrs—Assn Technique Maritime et Aeronautique—Schiffbau Technischen Gesellschaft—Am Phys Society —Washington Philos Society—Phi Beta Kappa. Meritorious service award from the Navy Dept. David Taylor Model Basin, Washington 7.†

12 LANE, George Sherman. Indo-European linguistics. b'02. BA '26— MA '27 (U Ia); PhD '30 (U Chicago); '27-28 (U Reykjavik, Island); '28-29 (U Paris); '32 (U Freiburg). Engaged work and research Indo-European linguistics especially Celtic, Germanic, Tocharian; comparative philology and linguistics. Author: The Tocharian Punjavantajataka: Text and Translation '47. Research asst comparative philology U Chicago '30-34; asst prof Sanskrit, comparative philology Cath U Am '34-37; asso prof germanic, comparative linguistics UNC '37-42, prof since '42; visiting prof linguistic inst U Mich summer '47, '48. Linguistic Soc Am—Am Philol Assn—Modern Lang Assn—Am Oriental Soc—Soc de linguistique de Paris. University of North Carolina, Chapel Hill, N.C.◎

13 LANE, John Clyde. Petroleum refining (Technical literature and information); Synthetic petroleum. b'19. BS '42—scholar '38-42 (U Rochester). Experimental research on catalytic cracking and hydroforming, literature and patent research on petroleum refining and allied subjects, collection classification and dissemination technical information through information service methods. Co-author: (with B H Weil) Synthetic Petroleum from the Synthine Process '48; also articles in field. Research process engr Gulf Research and Development Co '42-43, tech information specialist '43-45, head information service '45-48; head information service Inst Gas Tech since '48. Am Chem Soc—AAAS—Am Gas Assn. 17 W. 34th St., Chgo 16.†

14 LANE, Merton Chesleigh. Wireworms (control and taxonomy). b'93.

BS '15 (U Mass). Author articles in field. Sci asst Bur Entomol and Plant Quarantine to sr entomol US Dept Agr since '17. AAAS(F)—Am Assn Econ Entomol—Ore Entomol Soc—Puget Sound Entomol Soc—Washington Entomol Soc. P.O. Box 616, Walla Walla, Wash.

15 LANE, Richard Oscar. Ceramics. (Whiteware and crystalline glasses). b'05. BCE '30—Prof Degree CE '40 (O State U); SM '36 (MIT). Research on whiteware and crystalline glasses; abrasives, refractories. Research ceramist Norton Co Worcester Mass '30-33; asst foreman Am Steel & Wire Co New Haven '33-35; asst research engr Macklin Co Jackson Mich since '36, chief sales engr since '44, now vp charge sales engineering. Am Ceramic Soc—Inst Ceramic Engrs. The Macklin Company, 2914 Wildwood Av., Jackson, Mich. H: 878 White Lake Road, R.F.D. 1, Munith.†

16 LANE, Wheaton Joshua. Transportation. b'02. AB '25—PhD '35 (Princeton); AM '26 (Yale). Author: From Indian Trail to Iron Horse '30; Commodore Vanderbilt '42. Co-editor: The Highway in Our National Life '48. Received Lloyd Smith award Princeton Grad Sch to write first vol in Princeton History of NJ; first Knopf fellowship in biography to write life of Commodore Vanderbilt. AHA—Econ Hist Assn—NJ Hist Soc—NY State Hist Assn—NH Hist Soc—Phi Beta Kappa. Nassau Club, Princeton, N.J.

17 LANFEAR, Leslie Hofer. Hepatics of western Pennsylvania; Liverworts. b'96. BA '18 (Tex U); MA '22 —Curtis scholar '21-22 (Columbia); PhD '33 (U Pittsburgh). Author articles: A Manual of the Hepatics of Western Pennsylvania '33. Independent research on Bryology Carnegie Mus Pittsburgh. Pa Acad Sci—Bot Soc Western Pa—Sullivant Moss Soc—Sigma Xi—Phi Beta Kappa. 4360 Centre Av., Pitts 13.

18 LANG, Aldon Socrates. History of Texas public lands. b'97. AB '22 (Baylor U); AM '25 (State U Ia); PhD '31 (U Tex). Author: Financial History of Public Lands in Texas; also articles in field. Dean sch bus and prof econ Baylor U since '48. Am Econ Assn—Am Assn U Profs—Southwestern Social Sci Assn (gen program chmn, exec council '47)—Tex State Teachers Assn. Box 111, Baylor University, Waco, Tex.◎

19 LANG, Oscar Theodore. Horology. b'88. Student '11-15 (U Fa). Extensive collection of watches and clocks which contains over seventy variations of watch and clock escapements and is generally acknowledged to be the most complete in America; has made numerous detailed drawings of rare and unusual watch escapement variations. Author articles in field. Architect Minneapolis since '22. Nat Assn Watch and Clock Collectors (council dir)—Horological Inst Am. 802 Wesley Temple Bldg., Minneapolis 3.

20 LANG, Walter Barnes. Potash; Saline geology. b'90. AB '15—MS '16 (U Minn); '16-17—'20-22 (Yale); '21 (Columbia). Authority on potash in the Permian of the southwest; research on formation marine saline deposits. Author bulletins: Permian formations of the Pecos Valley of New Mexico and Texas; Salado formation of the Permian Basin; Basal beds of Salado formation—Fletcher core test; and others. Geol US Geol Survey since '22, reconniasance search for potash in Permian of SW '22-32. Geol Soc Am (F)—Am Geog Soc(F)—Am Geophys Union—AAAS(F)—Am Assn Petrol-

eum Geol—Am Soc Photogrammetry —Instrument Soc Am—Seismol Soc Am —AIMME—Pan-Am Inst Mining Engs and Geol—Wash Acad Sci—Geol Soc Wash. U.S. Geological Survey, Washington 25.

21 LANGER, Paul Fritz. Communism (Japan); Soviet-Japanese relations. b'15. Eleve Diplome '36 (Ecole Nat); Diplom '37 (U Berlin); AM '51—certificate '51 (Columbia and E Asian Inst). Research on background, origin, development and potential of Communism in Japan. Co-author: Red Flag in Japan '52; Bibliography on Japanese Communism '50; An Annotated Bibliography of Japanese Communism '51. Asst chief civil censorship dept SCAP '45-47; lectr Claremont Coll '48, U Cal Los Angeles '48-49; fellow Social Sci Research Council '51-52. Far E Assn. Received grants from Rockefeller Found, USo Cal, Inst Pacific Relations NY, Cal Coll in China, Russian Inst, Columbia, East Asian Institute, Columbia University, 433 W. 117th St., NYC 27.†

22 LANGER, Theodore William. Lubricants (Synthetic); Oils (Metal working); Electrolytic solutions. b'06. AB '28 (Johns Hopkins); PhD '31 (Yale). Investigation properties of polyalkylene glycol type synthetic lubricants especially applicable to industrial utilization; development additive combinations to extend use of lubricants, or to remove limitations, including products such as heat transfer media, gear lubricants, cutting compounds, greases, and non-flammable water base hydraulic fluids; product development petroleum base soluble oils, gear lubricants, waxes, and greases; commercial process development using electrolytic solutions for pure and attractive salt crystals. Holds six patents in field, including process for producing uniform epsom salt crystals, and process for crystallizing salt. Author articles: Some Industrial Experiences with Synthetic Lubricants '51, and others. Chem Tex Co '31-42, project leader '42-46; research chem Linde Air Products Co div Union Carbide & Carbon Corp since '47. ACS— Am Soc Lubrication Engrs—Am Inst Chem—NY Acad Sci—Sigma Xi.

23 LANGFORD, George Shealy. Insect control; Insecticides. b'01. BS '21 (Clemson Agrl Coll); MS '24 (U Md); PhD '29 (O State U). Author articles in field. Editor: Entoma, a directory of insect and plant pest control. Deputy State Entomol Colo '24-27; research O Expr Sta '28-29; specialist insect control U Md since '29. Entomol Soc Am —Am Assn Econ Entomol—Washington Entomol Soc—Insect Soc Washington—Sigma Xi. Entomology Department, University of Maryland, College Park, Md.

24 LANGFORD, Michael Hendrix. Hevea rubber tree diseases. b'15. BS '36 (Clemson Coll); PhD '40 (U Wis). Author articles in field. Agt US Dept Agr '40-45, sr pathol since '46. Am Phytopathol Soc—Washington Bot Soc—Washington Rubber Group. Office of Rubber Investigations, Plant Industry Station, Beltsville, Md.

25 LANGFORD, Russell Raymond. Archeology (Plains Stone Age); Yuma and Folsom complexes; Texas Long Horns; Navajo rugs and saddle blankets. b'00. AB '23 (Stanford U). Nonprofessional archeologist since '25, personal collection contains 30,000 specimens of Plains Stone Age, 300 specimens of Yuma and Folsom (Momnoth Hunter) complexes; small collection well matched horns of Texas Long Horns including vari-colored specimens; Navajo rugs and saddle blankets dating from 1890. Campbell AAA Court, 1400 West 12th St., North Platte, Neb.

10 LANGLOIS, Thomas Huxley. Island sociology; Ichthyology and limnology (Aquatic productivity, fish behavior, habits, life histories). b'98. BS '24—MS '25 (U Mich); PhD '35 (O State U). Devised methods of handling pike-perch eggs to prevent clumping by use of chalk; devised methods of rearing smallmouth bass with minimal cannibalism by use of narrow ponds, vegetation control, acceptable foods, and feeding techniques to prevent or destroy territorialism; discovered and formulated sociological succession; discovered that the biological productivity of water impoundments depends upon the initiation of the process in limited parts, or key areas, and that the occurence of dominant year classes within fish stocks is due to seasons of successful initiation of the process, while the failure of year classes is the result of the abortion of the process at its beginning. Author articles in field. Dir F T Stone Lab and prof zool O State U since '38. O Acad Sci (F in sect of zool)—AAAS(F)—Am Soc Zool —Am Soc Ichthyologists and Herpetologists—Am Soc Limnologists and Oceanographers—Am Fisheries Soc (pres '39-40)—Wildlife Soc (vp '41)—Toledo Zool Soc (bd dirs since '39)—Isaac Walton League Am (nat bd dirs '47-48, pres Buckeye Chapter '47-48). P.O. Box C, Put-in-Bay, O.

11 LANGSAM, Walter C(onsuelo). Modern European history; Austriaca; Christian education. born '06. BS '25 (City College NY); MA '26—PhD '30 (Columbia); LLD '50 (Gettysburg College). Author: The Napoleonic Wars and German Nationalism in Austria '30; The World since 1914 '33, sixth edit '48; Major European and Asiatic Developments since 1935 '39; In Quest of Empire: The Problem of Colonies '39; Documents and Readings in the History of Europe Since 1918 '39; Since 1939: A Narrative of War '41; Francis the Good: The Education of an Emperor 1768-1792 '49. Pres Wagner Coll since '45. Am Geog Soc(F)—AHA —Fgn Policy Assn—Am Mil Inst—Council on Fgn Relations—NY Acad Pub Edn—Soc Am Historians—Phi Beta Kappa. Wagner College, Staten Island 1, NY.†◎

12 LANGSNER, George. Freeway design. b'08. BS '31 (Cal Inst Tech). Planning and design major arterial highways (expressways) in urban areas. With Cal Div Highways since '31, asst dist engr since '49. Am Soc CE. 120 South Spring St., LA 12.

13 LANGTON, Clair Van Norman. Higher education administration. (Health and physical education); Public health. b'95. Life certificate '16 (Mich State Normal Coll); BS '23—MS '25—DrPH '28 (U Mich); EdD '38 (U Ore). Organizer one of first schools coordinating health contributing services in institutions of higher learning, including health service, department of hygiene, physical education for men and women, intramural sports and campus sanitation. Author: Orientation in School Health '41. Co-author: The Practice of Personal Hygiene '33) Hygiene Guide-Book, Books I, II, III '34 '35 '38. Asst dir intramural athletics and asst prof hygiene U Mich '26-28 also in charge pub health lab '27-28; developed program for san survey of resorts, camps, hotels and inns Mich State Health Dept '28; dean and dir health and phys edn Ore State Coll since '28, tech counselor san engring Engring Expt Station since '29; work with State Basic Science Examining

Com (hygiene) since '38, coordinating health programs with State Joint Staff Com (represents State Bd Health, State Office Pub Instruction, State System Higher Edn) since '41, chmn '50-51; leader sch health workshop U Hawaii summer '46, cons on sch health orgn and adminstrn to Territorial Health Dept and Dept Pub Instrn TH. Am Student Health Assn—Nat Conf Coll Hygiene—Am Pub Health Assn (F)—Am Assn Health Phys Edn and Recreation(F)—Pre Acad Sci—Am Sch Health Assn(F)—Delta Omega. Division of Physical Education, Oregon State College, Corvallis, Ore.

14 LANTZ, Harvey L(ee). Pomology (Fruit breeding). b'88. BS '16 (Ore State Coll); MS '19 (Ia State Coll). Research in variety trials, orchard soil management, fine turf, breeding of hardy apples pears plums peaches and small fruits; the experiment station as a result of the breeding work has named and introduced 12 varieties of apples, one pear, one peach and one plum. Author articles in field. Asst fruit breeding pomology sect Ia Agr Expt Sta '17, research asst prof '28, research asso prof'45, head pomol subsect since '47. Am Soc Hort Sci—Am Pomol Soc (sec '30-46, bd mgrs '46)—Ia State Hort Soc (pres '46-47)—Gamma Sigma Delta—Sigma Xi. Horticulture Department, Station A, Ames, Ia.

15 LaPAZ, Lincoln. Meteoritics (Meteors, meteorites); Mathematics (Inverse variation problems, military, ballistics); Mathematical astronomy. b'97. AB '20 (Fairmont Coll); MA '22 —U scholar '20-21 (Harvard); PhD '28 —Nat Research Council fellow '28-29 (U Chicago). Director of first and second Ohio State University Meteorite Expedition to the Canyon Diablo and Odessa meteorite craters '39, '41; dir Institute of Meteoritic survey leading to the location of the strewn field of the great meteoritics shower of February 18, '48 and to the subsequent location and recovery of the Furnas County Nebraska achondrite, the largest stony meteorite so far recovered anywhere in the world. Author: The Calculus (with others) '38; also articles in field. Inst math U Chicago '29-30; asst prof to prof math O State U '30-45; head dept math and astron, dir Inst Meteoritics U N Mex since '45. With Office Sci Research and Development '43-44, tech dir operations analysis sect Hdqrs Second Air Force '44-45. AAAS(F)—Am Math Soc —Math Assn Am—Internat Astron Union (commn on meteors)—Am Astron Soc—Royal Astron Soc Can—Astron Soc Pacific—Meteoritical Soc (F, past pres, vice pres since '50)—Phi Kappa Phi—Kappa Mu Epsilon—American Meteor Soc (director Southwest sect —O Acad Sci(F)—NM Acad Sci—Sigma Xi. Letters of commendation from Secretary of War Patterson and Gen H H Arnold, Major Gen Robert Williams, Brig Gen J K Lacey and Col W B Leach all of the AAF. Box 190, University of New Mexico, Albuquerque, N.M.◎

16 La PLANTE, Clarence A. Industrial electricity; Electric welding; Automatic handling equipment. b'95. Application electricity to industrial needs, electric welding arc and resistance applications; automatic presenting of work to metal stamping and forming presses and resistance welders. Holds patent in field. Chief elec USN '18-20; elec repair field '20-35; elec engr in charge Clark Grave Vault Co since '35. Am Welding Soc. Clark Grave Vault Co., 375 E. Fifth Av., Columbus, O. H: 2349 Brandon Rd., Columbus 12.

17 LAPORT, Edmund Abner. Radio transmission. b'02. Student (McGill U, Morrill Sch Mechanic Arts NH). Went to Peking China to supervise construction three short-wave radio communication stations for Ministry of Communications '28, to Rome and Milan Italy to supervise building of high power broadcasting stations for Italian Government '29, '32; to Moscow USSR as part of tech liaison group '45. Author articles in field. Radio Corp of Am since '36, chief engineer RCA International Division NYC since '44. Inst Radio Engr—UN Ednl Sci and Cultural Orgn (del to com on Mass Communication Tech Needs radio sect '47-48, pres radio sect '48). RCA International Division, 30 Rockefeller Plaza, NYC 20.

18 LAPP, Philip Alexander. Aircraft instrumentation; Airborne geophysics. b'28. BASc '50 (U Toronto); SM '51 (MIT). Research and development airborne magnetometry technique; design automatic control systems, servomechanisms, and closed loop systems on airborne equipment and wind tunnel controls; investigation positional and time variations of earth's magnetic field in Canada. Research, design and instr instrumentation MIT since '50. Assn Profl Engrs Ont—Optical Soc Am—Gamma Alpha Rho. Graduate House, Massachusetts Institute of Technology, Cambridge 39, Mass. H: 2 Beaufort Rd., Toronto 8, Ont., Can.

19 LAPP, R(alph) E(ugene). Nuclear radiation (Physics); Cosmic rays (Physics); Atomic bomb (Physics, civilian defense); Hydrogen bomb (Physics, civilian defense). b'17. Student (Canisius Coll Buffalo); BS '40 —PhD '46 (U Chicago). Research on nuclear physics Manhattan Project '43-45; consultant scientist Bikini bomb tests '46. Author: Nuclear Radiation Physics '48; Must We Hide? '49; Nuclear Science Data '51. Asso physicist and asst lab dir Metall Lab Chicago '43-45; asst dir Argonne Nat Lab Chicago '45-46; sci adv atomic energy War Dept Gen Staff '46-47; exec dir Research and Development Bd Com on Atomic Energy '47-48; head nuclear physics br Office Naval Research '49; cons physicist Nuclear Sci Service Washington since '50. AAAS—Am Inst Physics—Inst Radio Engrs—Sigma Xi —Phi Beta Kappa. Nuclear Science Service, Carillon House, 2500 Wisconsin Av., Washington 7.

20 LAPP, Walter S(wartz). Turf development (Lawn and golf). b'93. AB '18—AM '26—PhD '42 (U Pa); '26-29 (Columbia). Invented the Rollosprayer '46. Author articles: Factors Affecting the Growth of Lawn Grasses '43. Teacher soils and lawns course Pa Sch Hort Ambler Pa '47-49; teacher chem Northeast High Sch Philadelphia '20-51; head science dept Overbrook High School Philadelphia since '51; hort cons Agrl Chem Div Am Chem Paint Co Ambler Pa '43-49. ACS—Bot Soc Am—Pa Acad Sci (vp '41, '46, president '51-52)—Acad Nat Sci—Pa Hort Society—Franklin Inst—Phila Sci Tchrs Assn (pres '45-46)—AAAS(F)—Nat Science Teachers Assn (vp '48-50)—NEA—Sigma Xi. 724 Derstine Av., Lansdale, Pa.

21 LAPRADE, William Thomas. History of England in the eighteenth century; Education (Academic freedom and tenure). b'83. AB '06 (Washington Christian Coll); PhD '09 (Johns Hopkins). Author: England and the French Revolution '09; British History for American Students '26; Public Opinion and Politics in 18th Century England '36. Editor: Parliamentary Papers of John Robinson '22. Prof hist Trinity College, now Duke Univ since '09. AHA—Royal Hist Soc(F)—Phi Beta Kappa—NC State Lit and Hist Assn (pres)—NC Dept Archives and Hist (exec bd since '41). Duke University, Durham, N.C.◉

10 LaQUE, Francis L(aurence). Practical aspects of corrosion; Properties of corrosion resisting metals and alloys. b'04. BS '27 (Queen's U). Author articles in field. With Internat Nickel Co since '27, charge corrosion engring sect development and research div since '45. Am Chem Soc—Am Soc Metals—Am Soc Testing Materials—Nat Assn Corrosion Engrs (pres '48-49)—Soc Naval Architects and Marine Engrs—Electrochem Soc—Tech Assn Pulp and Paper Ind—British Iron and Steel Inst—Inst Metals—AAAS. 67 Wall Street, NYC 5.

11 LARGE, John Runyon. Pecan and tung diseases. b'01. BS '26 (Wash State Coll); MS '28—fellow cotton wilt investigations (U Ark); '28-29 (Ia State Coll). Research on storage molds of pecans, injurious effects of bordeaux mixture on pecan tree, methods of meeting menace of premature defoliation in pecan orchards, pecan scab, insects and diseases of the pecan and their control, root knot of tung, canker and tung diseases. Jr plant path pecan disease lab US Dept Agr Albany Ga '31-41, asst plant path US Tung Field Sta La '42-48, asso plant path Fla Pecan Investigations U Fla since '49. Phytopath Soc Am—Am Soc Hort Sci. Pecan Investigations, Monticello, Fla.

12 La RIVERS, Ira. Taxonomic entomology (Coleoptera, Hemiptera); Great Basin zoogeography. b'15. BS '37 (U Nev); '37-38 (NC State Coll); PhD '48 (U Calif). Field agent US Bureau of Biological Survey '36, Bureau of plant Industry '37, Bureau of Entomology and Plant Quarantine '39; University of California associates in tropical biogeography expedition to lower California '47; research biologic control of the Mormon cricket, taxonomy of Tenebrionidae, Naucoridae, faunal endemism in western Great Basin, aquatic entomology. Author articles: The wasp Chlorion laeviventris as a natural control of the Mormon cricket '45; other articles in field. Field agt US Dept Agr '42; agrl insp Calif Dept Agr '42; asst prof biol U Nev since '48. Nev Acad Nat Scis (pres '41)—Nev Wildlife Conservation Soc (exec com since '48)—Entomol Soc Am—Entomol Soc Washington—Oahu Micros Soc (pres '44)—Soc Vertebrate Paleontol—Am Soc Ichthyologists and Herpetologists—Nev Audubon Soc (pres '41). Department of Biology, University of Nevada, Reno, Nev.†

13 LARREMORE, Thomas Armitage. Social hygiene (Law enforcement); Choral music; Press books; Law teaching. b'89. AB '11 (Yale); LLB '16—MA in pub law '22 (Columbia); MusB '31 (Syracuse); MusM Sacred '32 (Union Theol Sem); student summers Westminster Choir Sch. Author: Portland and Legal Aid '21; Cases on the Law of Personal Property '28; The Duodecimos '37; An American Typographic Tragedy '49. Co-author: (with Amy H. Larremore) The Marion Press '43. Author articles and compositions in fields. Ed Ore Law Rev '28-'29; The Sinfonian '38-40. Prof law Ore '19-21, Tulane '21-22, Kansas '22-28, Washburn Coll '32-33; dean and prof law Hartford Law College '33-34; vis prof law Columbia, Colo, Pa, Ohio State and George Washington U. Dir glee clubs, choirs Washburn Coll, Stanford, Tulane, Kan U and Am

Legion posts and auxiliaries. Legal cons Am Soc Hygiene Assn '43 and since '48. Collector press books esp imprints modern private presses England and US. AAUP—Phi Beta Kappa—Phi Mu Alpha-Sinfonia (supreme historian '38-40)—Order of the Coif—Phi Delta Phi—Grolier Club—Am Soc Hygiene Assn (hon life mem '50)—Conductors Club NY (treas since '44)—Intercoll Mus Council (bd dirs since '26). Sand Brook, Hunterdon Co., N.J.

14 LARRIMER, Walter Harrison. Research organization, administration and statistical methods. b'89. BS in forestry '13—PhD '25 (O State U); MS in Biol '21 (Purdue). Has made special researches on application of statistical methods to biological research; research on insect pests of cereal and forage crops. Research staff asst US Forest Service since '35. AAAS(F)—Am Assn Econ Entomol—Entomol Soc Am—Sigma Xi. Forest service, U.S. Department of Agriculture, Washington.†◉

15 LARSELL, Olof. Medical history of the Pacific Northwest. b'86. BS '10—ScD (Linfield Coll); MA '14—PhD '18 (Northwestern U). Author: (translator) Autobiographical Notes of Jons Jacob Berzelius; Neuro-Anatomy and Sense Organs; Anatomy of the Nervous System; The Doctor in Oregon, a Medical History; also articles in field. Prof anat U Ore Med Sch since '21. AAAS(F)—Am Acad Ophthalmology and Otolaryngology(F)—Am Assn Anat—Soc Exptl Biol and Med—Hist of Sci Soc—Sigma Xi. 4100 Dosch Rd., Portland 1, Ore.◉

16 LARSEN, Delmar H. Colloid chemistry (Drilling muds); Clay chemistry; Patents (Petroleum engineering, absorption refrigeration, treatment of nonmetallic minerals, colloidal clays, oxygen analysis, pharmaceuticals). b '11. BS '33—MS '36 (Cal Inst Tech). Research on colloid chemistry of nonmetallic minerals, drilling muds, well treatments, bentonite compounds. Research chem, research dir, mgr patent dept Baroid Sales Div Nat Lead Co since '36; lectr USo Cal since '40. ACS—AIMME—Am Petroleum Inst—AAA S. Baroid Sales Division, National Lead Co., 830 Ducommun St., LA 12.

17 LARSEN, Esper Signius, Jr. Mineralogy; Petrology; Geologic ages. b '79. BS '06—PhD '18 (U Cal). Author: The Misroscopic Determination of the Nonopaque Minerals '21. Co-author: (with S F Emmons) Geology and Ore Deposits of the Creede District, Colorado '28; (with Whitman Cross) A Brief Review of the Geology of the San Juan Mountains of Southwestern Colorado; (with others) Igneous Rocks of the Highwood Mountains, Montana; (with W Cross) Batholith of South California, The Geology of the San Juan Mountains Colorado. Asst petrographer Geophys Lab '07-09, asst geol US Geol Survey '09-14, geol since '14, in charge sect petrology '18-23; acting prof geol U Cal '15-16; prof petrography Harvard '23-49. Nat Acad Sci—Geol Soc Am—Mineral Soc Am—Mineral Soc Great Britain—Am Acad Arts and Scis—AIMME—Soc Econ Geol. Section Geochemistry and Petrology, U.S. Geological Survey, Washington 25.◉

18 LARSEN, Henning. Old English; Old Norse; Norwegian folk-tale. b'89. AB '08 (Luther Coll); AM '11 (U Ia); PhD '15 (Princeton). Author: An Old Icelandic Medical Miscellany '31; also articles in field. Prof Eng U Ill since '45, head dept since '46, dean coll of liberal arts since '47; asso editor Jour of Eng and Germanic Philol '41-42, since '46. Modern Lang Assn Am

(mem edit com)—Linguistic Soc Am—Medieval Acad Am—Soc for Advancement of Scandinavian Study—Norwegian Am Hist Soc. 807 W. Oregon St., Urbana, Ill.◉

19 LARSEN, Spencer Allen. Airfreight (Economics, packaging). b'03. BS in commerce '25 (Brigham Young U); MS in retailing '26—DCS '33 (NYU). Directed Wayne University's air cargo research studies, served '43-45 as chief regional research consultant to the War Production Board, developed packages for eggs, fresh produce, and fresh seafoods for air freight shipments, director Detroit Business Communications Conference. Holder patents in field. Author: Air Cargo Potential in Fresh Fruits and Vegetables '44; Outlook for Air Cargo in Fresh Produce '44; Air Cargo Potential in Drugs and Pharmaceuticals '45; Markets for Airborne Seafoods '48. Editor: Effective Business Communications '50. Prof, chmn dept marketing and management U ND '27-38; dir ND Tax Survey '35-37; with Wayne U since '38, prof since '44, chmn dept marketing and gen business since '46, dir air cargo research '43-48. Am Marketing Assn (vp '36, meritorious service citation from NY chapter '48 for outstanding accomplishment in marketing, especially effective use of research techniques in evaluating market potentials for a new industry service)—Soc Indsl Packaging and Materials Handling Engrs—Engring Soc Detroit—AAUP—Alpha Kappa Psi—Beta Gamma Sigma—Eta Mu Pi. First place Trans-World Airline's 11th Annual Aviation Writing award '47-48. Wayne University, Det 1.

20 LARSON, Agnes Mathilda. History of the Minnesota lumber industry. b'92. AB '16 (St Olaf Coll Northfield Minn); MA '21 (Columbia); PhD '38 (Harvard). Research on development and growth of lumber industry, operation of state and national laws in acquisition of timber lands and stumpage in Minnesota area, importance of lumber industry in building of Minnesota. Author: History of the White Pine of Minnesota '49. With St Olaf Coll since '25, prof Am hist dept since '38, chmn dept since '42. Am Hist Assn—Minn Hist Assn—Norwegian Am Hist Assn—Phi Beta Kappa. St. Olaf College, Northfield, Minn.

21 LARSON, Cedric Arthur. War propaganda; Swedish-American relations. b'08. AB '35 (Stanford U); AM '38 (George Washington U). Research on psychological warfare. Author: Office of War Information (in preparation). Co-author: Words That Won the War '39. Free-lance author. Am Assn Pub Opinion Research—Acad Polit Sci—Nat Vocational Guidance Assn—Am Sociol Soc—AHA—Internat Soc Gen Semantics—Phi Beta Kappa. H: 53 Arch Lane, Hicksville, L.I., N.Y.

22 LARSON, Harold American history (United States Army transportation); Virgin Islands; Björnstjerne Björnson; United States Army in Korea; Alexander Hamilton. b'01. BA '27 (Morningside Coll Ia); MA '28—PhD '43 (Columbia); '29-30 (U Oslo). Author: Björnstjerne Björnson '44. Author articles: Björnson and America, a Critical Review, with E Haugen, '34; Some Recent Books on the Virgin Islands '39; The Birth and Parentage of Alexander Hamilton '45. Instr hist and polit sci McKendree Coll Lebanon Ill '31-32; instr hist Municipal U Omaha Neb '35-36; archivist Nat Archives Washington '36-43; spl asst Fed Archives St Thomas VI '36 -37; lecturer polit sci '38, '42-43 U Md; hist Army Transportation Corps Washington '43

46; chief hist XXIV Corps US Army in Korea '46-47; hist Hist Div Spl Staff Dept of Army Washington '47-52; Air U Hist Liaison Office USAF Washington since '52. AHA—Norwegian-Am Hist Assn—Soc Am Archvsts. Roberts fellow in hist Columbia U '27-29, '32-33; Roberts Traveling fellow Norway '29-30. Air University Hist Liaison Office, USAF, Washington. Washington 25. H: 4827 Yorktown Blvd., Arlington 7, Va.

10 LARSON, Harry. Hydrology; Hydraulics. b'95. BS '24 (Ia State Coll); MS '30 (U Mich); '31-32 (U Wis). Studies of surface and underground water as source of supply for domestic consumption, for industrial uses and for irrigation; analyses of stream flow; location of suitable controls for establishment of stream gauging stations, frequency and intensity of rainfall, run-off relations, and evaporation; investigations rate and quantity of water occuring in various geologic formations; studies underground water Atlas Mountain area N Africa, sources of water in Afghanistan and Iran; examination methods for collection underground water, such as use of interception galleries, types of storage, and distribution of water for domestic consumption in Italy; analyses hydrological data for flood control and power projects; hydraulic investigations and analyses channels and stream flow, and of hydraulic structures for control of maximum discharges; research on flow of water over broad-crested weirs. Author articles on: Rainflow and runoff of Mississippi River Basin; Allegheny, Beaver and Monongahela Rivers; flood control on Potomac River. Asso engr US Engr Dept '30-31 and '36-40; cons engr since '48. Am Geophys Union—AAAS—Am Soc CE—Am Geog Soc. 725 Cooper Bldg., 1009 17th St., Denver 2. H: 1440 Columbine St., Denver 6.

11 LARSON, Henrietta Melia. Business history (US). b'94. AB '18—LittD hon '43 (St Olaf Coll Northfield Minn); MA '21—PhD '26 (Columbia); '22-24 (Minn U). Author: The Farmer and the Wheat Market in Minnesota 1858-1900 '26; Jay Cooke, Private Banker '36; Guide to Business History '47. Co-author (with N S B Gras) Casebook in American Business History '39. Editor Business Historical Society Bulletin; co-editor Harvard Studies in Business History. Research and faculty grad sch bus adminstrn Harvard since '28, asso prof since '42; vp and spl dir research Bus Hist Found Inc '47-50. Bus Hist Assn—Econ Hist Assn—Econ Hist Soc—AHA—Am Econ Assn—AAAS—Phi Beta Kappa. 296 Merriam St., Weston 93, Mass.

12 LARSON, Leslie Lundegren. Pulp and paper technology. b'10. BS '34—MS 36 (U Idaho); PhD '40 (Inst Paper Chem, Wis). Research in experimental paper machine coating of paper, groundwood pulp bleaching. Author articles in field. Research chem Kimberly Clark Corp Neenah Wis '39-42; tech dir Detroit Sulphite Pulp and Paper Co since '45. Chem US Govt on impermeable p r o t e c t i v e clothing against war gases '42-45. Tech Assn Pulp and Paper Industries—Am Chem Soc—Sigma Xi. 9125 W. Jefferson St., Detroit 17. H: 19179 Montrose.

13 LARSON, Paul Stanley. Metabolism; Toxicology; Biologic effects of tobacco. b'07. Student '26-28 (Modesto Jr Coll Cal); AB in chem '30—PhD in physiol '34 (U Cal). Research on protein and purine metabolism, water and salt metabolism, potassium metabolism, toxicology of pesticides, and

biologic effects of nicotine and tobacco. Co-author articles: (with I L Chaikoff) The Influence of Insulin and Epinephrine on Purine Metabolism '35, The Influence of Carbohydrates on Nitrogen Metabolism in the Normal Nutritional State '37; (with R A Cutting and A M Lands) Cause of Death Resulting from Massive Infusion of Isotonic Solutions '39; (with G Brewer) Relation of Blood Pressure to the Plasma Potassium Level '38; (with H B Haag) Studies on the Fate of Nicotine in the Body '42 '43; (with H B Haag and J K Finnegan) Factors Influencing Toxicity of Nicotine '45, Studies on the Fate of Nicotine in the Body '46 '47 '49, Tissue Distribution and Elimination of DDD and DDT Following Oral Administration to Dogs and Rats '49; (with C B Van Slyke) Role of the Adrenal Medulla in the Blood Pressure Response to Nicotine '50. Instr physiol Georgetown Sch Med '34-39; asso in physiol Med Coll Va '39-40, research prof pharm since '41; pharmacol Frederick Stearns & Co Detroit '40-41. Am Soc Pharmacol and Exptl Therap—Am Physiol Soc—Soc Exptl Biol and Med—NY Acad Sci—AAAS—Va Acad Sci. Department of Pharmacology, Medical College of Virginia, Richmond 19.

14 LARSON, T. Alfred. The History of Wyoming. born '10. AB '32—MA '33 (U Colo); PhD '37 (U Ill); '37-38 (U London). Author articles in field. Instr hist U Wyo '36-37; research Pub Record Office London Eng '37-38, U London '37-38; instr to asst prof hist U Wyo '38-43, asso prof, acting head dept hist '46-48, prof and head dept since '48; dir study Hist Wyo in World War II since '47. AHA—Miss Valley Hist Assn. Department of History, University of Wyoming, Laramie, Wyo.†⊙

15 La RUE, Carl Downey. Plant tissue culture and morphology; Rubber plants. b'88. BS '10—AB '11 (Valparaiso U); AB '14—AM '16—PhD '21 (U Mich). Rubber investigations in Brazil, Bolivia, Nicaragua, and Mexico; specialist rubber production and co-director Ford Motor Co Amazon Expedition '27; lecturer and writer on plant tissue culture. Author article: Estate Rubber Its Properties and Testing. Instr bot Syracuse U '16-17; research bot sumatra '17-20; instr bot U Mich '20-23, asst prof '24-34, asso prof '34-44, prof since '44, staff Biol Sta since '25; prin rubber spl US Dept Agr '43-44. AAAS(F)—Bot Soc Am—Mich Acad Sci—Am Soc Naturalists—Sigma Xi. Department of Botany, University of Michigan, Ann Arbor.†

16 La RUE, Daniel Wolford. Emotions; Mental hygiene; Character education. b'78. Grad '98 (State Normal Sch E Stroudsburg Pa); AB '04—AM '05 (Dickinson Coll); AM '07—PhD '11 (Harvard); grad work '08 (Columbia) '13 (Cold Spring Harbor NY). Author: Psychology for Teachers '20; The Childs' Mind and the Common Branches '24; Mental Hygiene '27; Educational Psychology '39. Co-author: (with R M Yerkes) Outline of a Study of the Self '14. Research worker on value phonetic alphabet AAAS '19; member educational survey Honesdale Pa '21; chief psychological examiner Camp Meade Maryland. Supt schs Augusta Me '07-10; prof psychol and edn, head dept State Tchrs Coll E Stroudsburg '11-49, acting pres '39; lectr Harvard Grad Sch Edn. NEA—Am Eugenics Soc Inc—Pa State Ednl Assn—Am Genetic Soc—AAAS(F)—Nat Com Mental Hygiene — Phi Beta Kappa. Awarded prize for best statement of principles of Am democracy as basis for world govt in contest sponsored

by Fed Union Inc '43; Medal of Liberation King Christian X of Denmark 46.⊙

17 LA RUE, Mervin Worthington, Sr. Motion pictures (Microscopic, medical). b'92. Student US univs and aboard. Engineered and developed special equipment for making microscopic and macroscopic motion pictures, production medical and scientific films as visual aids to medical teaching. Cinematographer Pathe '18-26; sales engr Bell and Howell Co '26-31; with Burton Holmes Films '31, '36-37; Mervin W La Rue Inc since '37. Biol Photog Assn(F)—Soc Motion Picture and Television Engrs—Internat Photog. Mervin W. La Rue, Inc., 159 E. Chicago Av., Chgo 11.

18 LASLET, Herbert Reynolds. Educational psychology. b'91. AB '18 (U Kan); AM '22—PhD '26 (Stanford U). Co-author articles: (with H A Cooprider) Predictive Values of the Stanford Scientific and Engineering and Scientific Aptitude Tests '48; (with Walter Tyszkowski) Some Characteristics of Physically Defective Students '48, and others. Prof edn and psychol Whitman Coll Walla Walla Wash '26-28; prof ednl psychol Ore State Coll since '28. AAAS(F)—Am Psychol Assn (F, also F mil psychol div)—Sigma Xi—Phi Kappa Phi. Oregon State College, Corvallis, Ore.

19 LASLETT, (Lawrence) Jackson. Nuclear physics; Particle accelerators. b'13. PhD '37 (U Calif); BS '33 (Calif Inst Tech); Rockefeller and H C Oersted fellow '37-38 (Inst Theoretical Physics, Copenhagen); Rackham research fellow '38 (U Mich). Participated in construction or operation of cyclotron at University of California, Copenhagen, University of Michigan and Indiana University; Iowa State College synchrotron. Author articles in field. Instr Ind U '38-41; research asso MIT radiation lab '41-45; prof department physics and physicist Inst for Atomic Resch Ia State Coll since '46; head nuclear physics br Office Naval Research '52-53. Am Phys Soc—AAAS—Tau Beta Pi—Sigma Xi. Department of Physics, Iowa State College, Ames, Ia.†

20 LASSETER, Dillard Brown. Agricultural credit. b'94. AB '13 (Emory U); MA '14 (NYU). Author articles in field. Am Fgn Service 15-24; state compliance officer NRA Ga '33-35; state and regional dir deputy nat adminstr Nat Youth Adminstrn '35-43; regional dir Southeastern States War Manpower Commn '43-45; nat adminstr Farm Security Adminstrn and adminstr Farmers Home Adminstrn since '46. Ga Bar Assn—Am Soc Pub Adminstrn. Room 5020, South Agriculture Building, United States Department of Agriculture, Washington 25. H: Chevy Chase Club, Chevy Chase 15, Md.

21 LASSETTER, James G(reen). Soil conservation; Land use; Pastures; Terracing; Cover crops. b'16. Student '36-37 (W Ga Jr Coll); BS in agrl engring '40 (U Ga). Research on requirements, needs, and utilization of Pensacola bahia grass for pasture and seed production and selection of new strain. Author article: Bahia Fights for Itself '50. Supervisor Farm Security Adminstrn '40-41; soil conservationist Soil Conservation Service since '41. Soil Conservation Soc Am—Am Soc Agrl Engrs. Soil Conservation Service, Chipley, Fla.†

22 LATHAM, Allen. Queen bees; Crystallized honey. b'68. AB '92 (Harvard). Raiser of queen bees since '20; development method for production of honey in crystallized state with fine grain. Author: Allen Latham's Bee Book '49. Conn Beekeepers Assn (pres '04-10). H: RFD 8, Norwichtown, Conn.

10 LATIMER, Claiborne Green. Algebra; Numbers theory. b'93. BS '20—MS '21—PhD '24 (U Chicago). Author articles in field. Asso editor: Duke Mathematical Journal '38-41. Prof Math Emory U since '47, chmn dept since '48. Am Math Soc (mem council '30-31 and '40-42)—Math Assn of Am (mem bd govs '42-45)—Sigma Xi. 39 Princton Way, N.E., Atlanta 6⊚

11 LATIMER, John Francis. Greek epic poetry. b'03. BA '22 (Miss Coll); MA '26 (Chicago U); PhD '29 (Yale). Studies in field in Athens, Greece and Naples, Italy; research and writing on Hesiodic society, Hesiod and Perses, Vergilian society, Aeneas and Cumaean Sibyl. Author articles in field. Chm dept classics, George Washington U since '36. Am Philol Assn—Classical Assn Middle Atlantic States. George Washington University, Washington.†

12 LATIMER, Murray Webb. Social and unemployment insurance; Old age pensions; Guaranteed wages. b'01. AB '19 (Miss Coll); MBA '24 (Harvard). Participated in formulation of Railroad Retirement Act of '37, Carriers Taxing Act of '37 and Railroad Unemployment Insurance Act. Author: Trade Union Pension Systems in U.S. and Canada '32; Industrial Pension Systems in U. S. and Canada '33. Coauthor: (with K S Boardman) Distribution of Textiles '26; (with K Tufel) Trends in Industrial Pensions '40; (with others) Guaranteed Wages '47; also articles in field. Mem bus research staff Harvard '23, supervisor and instr in finance '24-25; econ and old age ins expert Indus Relations Counselors Inc NYC '26-33; mem adv com US Dept Labor '33-35; dir Fed Bur Old Age Benefits US Social Security Bd '36; lecturer econ Wharton Sch Commerce and Finance U Pa '36-37; chief exec officer Office Fgn Relief and mem Am delegation UNRRA Atlantic City '43; cons econ since '47. Am Econ Assn—Am Statis Assn—Am Management Assn. 1625 K St. N.W., Washington.†

13 LATTA, Frank Forrest. History of California and the San Joaquin valley. b'92. '15, '17 (U Calif); summers '22-28 (Santa Barbara State Teachers Coll); '31 (Fresno State Teachers Coll); '33 (San Diego State Coll). Began interviewing California pioneers '06, since then has interviewed more than 10,000; Kern Co committee California Centennials Commission; citizens committee California division of beaches and parks, restoration of Fort Tejon. Author volumes: Uncle Jeff's Story; California Indian Folklore; Handbook of Yokuts Indians; Black Gold in the Joaquin. Teacher San Joaquin Valley High Schs '15-44; dir Kern Co Hist Mus since '44. So Calif Archeol Assn—Kern Co Hist Soc (sec '34-38, pres '38-40). Kern County Museum, Bakersfield, Calif. H: 2104 B St.

14 LATTA, Randall Kirk. Agricultural fumigation; Insecticidal aerosols. b'05. AB '27 (Ia Wesleyan Coll); MS '28 (Ia State Coll). Research in bulb insects, commodity treatments. Author articles in field. Jr entomol Calif Bur Entomol and Plant Quarantine US Dept Agr '28-29, asst entomol Washington and NY '30-37, asso and entomol Washington '38-43, sr entomol '43-46, El Paso '46-48, Beltsville since '48. Am Assn Econ Entomol—Entomol Soc Am—Washington Entomol Soc—Washington Insecticide Soc. Agricultural Research Center, Beltsville, Md.

15 LAUCK, C(harles) Harold. Use of Baskerville type; Fine printing typography and design; History of printing; Graphic arts education. b'96. AB '18 (Roanoke Coll); '21 (Washington U). Author: A Short History of Printing '32; also articles in field. Supt Journalism Lab Press Washington and Lee U since '32; lab instr in journalism since '32. Printer to the Army Sch for Personnel Services '42-45. Nat Graphic Arts Edn Assn (sec '36-37, treas '37-38, vp '38-39, pres '39-40)—Internat Benjamin Franklin Soc—Bibliog Soc London—Bibliog Soc Am—Chicago Soc Typog Arts-Typocrafters—Am Assn Teachers Journalism. Awarded Harry J Friedman Gold medal for distinguished service in the cause of Graphic Arts Edn '44. 6 Houston St., Lexington, Va.

16 LAUDON, Lowell Robert. Mississippian paleontology and stratigraphy; Crinoidea (Evolution, classification). b'05. BA '28—MA '29—PhD '30 (Ia U). Research and writing on evolution and classification of fossil Crinoidea; travel and geologic research in Alaska, Yukon, Northwest Territory and Canadian Rockies; director of University of Kansas expedition by amphibious plane to Wapiti Lake area in British Columbia summer '47; directed University of Tulsa gold exploration in Patuca River area Honduras '38. Author articles in field. Asst prof geol Tulsa U '30-32, asst registrar '32-34, dean of men '34-36, asso prof '36-38, prof '38-39; prof geol Kan U '39-40, chmn dept '40-48; exploration geol Imperial Oil Co Can summer '44; prof geol Wis U since '48. Geol Soc Am—Paleontol Soc Am—Am Assn Petroleum Geol—Sigma Xi. Dept. of Geology, University of Wisconsin, Madison, Wis.

17 LAUFER, Stephen. Brewing and fermentation chemistry. b'94. Dr Eng '22 (Hochschule fur Bodenkultur in Vienna, Coll for Agr Vienna). Coauthor: Yeast Fermentation and Pure Culture Systems '36; also articles in field. Research biochemist Schwarz Labs Inc NYC '29-32, dir research '33-37, dir labs '37-46, tech dir in charge brewing technol since '46; tech editor Am Brewer. Am Soc Brewing Chemists (sec, vp since '48)—AAAS—Am Chem Soc—Am Oil Chem Soc—Am Assn Cereal Chem—Inst Food Technol—Assn Consulting Chem and Chem Engrs—Chemist Club. Received Cincinnati Achievement Award for '36 presented by Dist Cincinnati Master Brewers Assn of Am for Outstanding and Conspicuous Research Work on Current Brewing Problems. Schwarz Laboratories, Inc., 202 East 44th St., NYC 17.

18 LAUFFER, Paul G. Cosmetic chemistry; Perfume chemistry. b'00. BS '21—MS '23 (Washington and Jefferson Coll); MA '24—PhD '26—Fritzsche F perfume chem '26-27 (Columbia). Research on theory of odor, pharmacological action and chemical structure; odor and chemical structure. Contributor: Colloid Chemistry (vol VII) '50. Chief chem Pinaud Inc '27-33; chief chem George W Luft Co since '33. Phi Lambda Upsilon—Sigma Xi—ACS—Am Inst Chem(F)—Soc Cosmetic Chem (dir since '49, pres '52)—Toilet Goods Assn (chmn sci sect '50-51). 34-12 36th Av., Long Island City 1, N.Y. H: 9 Ashley Rd., Hastings-on-Hudson, N.Y.

19 LAUGHLIN, John Edward, Jr. Law. AB '27 (Georgetown University); LLB '30—LLM '31 (Harvard); LLD (St Vincent College). Editor: Harvard Law Review '30. Practice of law Pittsburgh since '34; director and president St. Vincent College Educational Found Incorporated. American, Pennsylvania, Allegheny County bar assns—Am Law Inst—Lawyers Club NYC. 2812 Grant Bldg., Pitts 19.⊚

20 LAURENCE, Robert Abraham. Dam foundations; Barite Deposits; Geology of Tennessee. b'08. AB '29—MA '31 (U Cincinnati); '32-34 (U Minn). Dam and tunnel exploration in Tennessee '36-43, in Puerto Rico '47. Author articles in field. Asst geol to geol TVA '34-43; jr geol to regional geol US Geol Survey since '34. Geol Soc Am—Soc Econ Geol—Am Inst Mining and Metal Engrs—Geol Soc Philippines—AAAS(F)—Tenn Acad Sci—Sigma Xi. Room 13, Post Office Bldg., Knoxville 2, Tenn.

21 LAURIE, Alex. Floriculture. b'92. BS '14 (Cornell U); MA '17 (Washington U). Originated shading of plants, prepackaging of flowers, flower preservatives; research on commercialized soil-less culture, exact methods of growing greenhouse crops. Author: Flower Shop '30; Chrysanthemums '46; Soils and Fertilizers '46; Co-author: (with D C Kiplinger) Commercial Flower Forcing '34, five revisions '48; (with L E Chadwick) Modern Nursery '30; Floriculture '42. Also articles in field. Prof floriculture Ohio State U since '29, hort Ohio Agrl Expt Sta since '29. O Acad Sci—Am Soc Hort Sci (pres '36)—Roses Inc (sec-treas)—Royal Hort Soc (Eng)—Ohio Florists Assn (sec-treas)—Gamma Sigma Delta—Sigma Xi. Ohio State University, Columbus, Ohio.†⊚

22 LAWLER, Lillian Beatrice Brady. Greek dance; Mediterranean archeology. b'98. BA '19 (U Pittsburgh); MA '21—PhD '25 (U Ia); FAAR '26—Prix de Rome fellow '25-26 (Am Acad in Rome). Delegate American Classical League to UNESCO Conference Philadelphia '47; lecturer on Mediterranean archeology and the Greek dance. Author articles in field. Asst prof classics Hunter Coll since '29, asso prof since '43; asso editor Auxilium Latinum since '30; editor in chief The Classical Outlook since '36; mem exec council Am Classical League since '36. Am Philol Assn—Archeol Inst Am—Class Assn Atlantic States (pres '47-49)—Am Class League—NY Class Club —Assn Pvt Sch Teachers of NY and Vicinity—Class Soc of Am Acad in Rome (vp '46, '48). Chosen to U Pittsburgh's Women's Hall of Fame. Hunter College, 695 Park Av., NYC 21.

23 LAWRENCE, Joseph Douglas, Jr. Caves. b'24. Student '46 (Washington and Lee U); BS (EE) '51 (Va Poly Inst). Development methods for organizing and executing exploration expeditions; preparation cave maps; studies on rescue procedures and techniques of cave rigging. Author articles: A Report on Some Fluorescein Tests at Starnes' Cave '49; Elementary Cave Rigging '50. Nat Speleological Soc—Am Inst EE—Inst Radio Engrs—Tau Beta Pi—Eta Kappa Nu. H: RFD 2, Columbia, S.C.

24 LAWRENCE, Marion. Early Christian and medieval art. b'01. Student '13-15 (Paris and Eng); AB '23 (Bryn Mawr Coll); AM '24—PhD '32 (Radcliffe Coll); fellow '41-42 (Inst for Advanced Study Princeton). Research early Christian sculpture, Italian Romanesque art. Author: The Sarcophagi of Ravenna '45; also articles in field. Asst in art Wellesley Coll '24, Radcliffe Coll; instr hist of art Bryn Mawr Coll '27-28; instr to profesor fine arts Barnard Coll Columbia since '29, chmn dept since '38. Coll Art Assn (dir '39-45)—Archeol Inst Am—Medieval Acad —Phi Beta Kappa. Carnegie fellow '25-27; Fulbright research grant Italy '49-50. 812 Schermerhorn Hall, Columbia University, NYC.*

10 LAWRENCE, Samuel Eugene. River and harbor engineering; Hydraulic dredges; Sea wall. b'82. BS '07 —ME '27 (Purdue U). Charge dredges Atlantic City Port of Wilmington Del '20-24, rock removal East River and Hell Gate New York Harbor '24-25. Invented and patented mechanical lubricator scale conversion instrument; precast sea wall. Author articles in field. Spl field training dredging fleet Corps Engrs Tex '07-10; jr mech engr operation and maintenance dredges lock and dam constrn '10-13; supt machinery and floating plant River '13-16; rock removal Del River '16; cons engr and pres East Coast Stone & Constrn Co Ft Lauderdale Fla '25-33; harbor and drainage engr Port Everglades Fla '31-32; flood control engr Miss River '33-40; prof hydraulic engring and asst in orgn spl course river and harbor engring La State U since '46. Capt 57th engrs U S Army operating on French Rivers and Harbors and the Rhine '17-19, coll engr and transportation corps rep U S Army on Combined Chiefs of Staff com for stabilization marine design '43-46, assigned to marine plant constrn program CofE '46-47, research com Transportation Corps on floating derricks water jet-propelled boats tugs. ASME—La State Engring Soc—Soc Am Mil Engrs—Tau Beta Pi. Faculty Club, Louisiana State University, Baton Rouge, La.

11 LAWRENCE, Thomas Gordon. Plant geography. AB '25 (La State U); MA '32—'42-45 (Columbia). Research on wild plants which grow in cities. Contributor: Book of Knowledge '44-50. Ed Teaching Biol '41-44; ed Teaching Sci '44-47; chmn phys sci Walton High Sch '46-49; chmn biol Erasmus Hall High Sch since '49. Nat Sci Tchrs Assn—Nat Biol Tchrs Assn. Erasmus Hall High School, Bklyn 26.

12 LAWRENCE, William Mason. Aquatic biology (Fish resources); Fresh-water game fishes (Life history, ecology, managment). b'18. BS '38—Schuyler fellow '40-41—PhD '41 (Cornell U). Author articles in field. Sr aquatic biol NY State Conservation Dept since '46. Am Fisheries Soc—Am Soc Ichthyologist and Herpetologists—Am Soc Limnology and Oceanography—Atlantic Fisheries Biol—Sigma Xi. 30 Main Street, Saranac Lake, N.Y.

13 LAWS, G(eorge) Malcolm, Jr. Ballads; Folksongs. b'19. Student '37-40 (Princeton); AB '42—AM '46—PhD '49 (U Pa). Comprehensive survey all traditional ballads which originated in US; British broadside ballads. Author: Native American Balladry: A Descriptive Study and a Bibliographical Syllabus '50. Staff English U Pa since '42. MLA—Am Folklore Soc. 314 Bennett Hall, University of Pennsylvania, Phila 4.†

14 LAWSHE, C(harles) H(ubert). Industrial psychology. b'08. BS '29—PhD '40 (Purdue U); AM '35 (U Mich). Author: Principles of Personnel Testing '48. Co-author: (with Joseph Tiffin and E J Asher) Workbook for Psychology of Normal People. Faculty Purdue U since '41, prof psychol div edn and applied psychol since '47, research asso Statis Lab since '48; diplomate indsl psychol Am Bd Examiners Profl Psychol. Am Psychol Assn(F)—AAAS(F) — Sigma Xi. Occupational Research Center, Purdue University, Lafayette, Ind.

15 LAWSON, Chester Alvin. Biological patterns of development; Differential regeneration in plants (Chicory roots); Embryology of aphids. b'08. BS '30 (Thiel Coll); MS '31—PhD '34 (U Mich). Author articles in field. Prof and head dept biol sci Mich State Coll since '44. Mich Acad Sci Arts Letters—AAAS(F)—Am Soc Zool—Genetics Soc Am—Sigma Xi—Phi Kappa Phi. Department of Biological Science, Michigan State College, East Lansing, Mich.†⊙

16 LAWSON, Francis Raymond. Insects (Ecology, plant resistance). b'06. AB '29 (U Ill); '30-31 (U Calif). Research on the abundance and distribution of the host plants of the beet leafhopper and on the migrations of that insect, resistance of vegetable crops to insects. Author articles in field. Research Bur Entomol and Plant Quarantine US Dept Agr since '29. Research and writing on survival in tropical countries, on the deterioration of materiel in the tropics US Air Forces '42-45. Ecol Soc Am—AAAS—Am Assn Econ Entomol—Wildlife Soc Box 1011, Oxford, N.C.

17 LAWSON, Fred A. Dock leaf beetle; Entomology-insect biology, morphology and control. b'19. BS '43 (U Ark); MSc '48—PhD '49 (Ohio State U). Biology of dock leaf beetle and others; morphology and classification cockroach egg capsules; internal morphology stored grain insects; insecticide testing household and stored grain insects. Asst prof entomology U Tenn '49-52; asst prof entomol Kan State Coll since '52. Entomology Department, Kansas State College, Manhattan.

18 LAWSON, Murray Grant. American colonial economic history; Canadian history; Research techniques. b'15. BA '36 (U Toronto); Teaching Certificate '37 (Ontario Coll Edn); MA '38 (U Toronto); PhD '42 (U Calif). Research on economic history of colonial Boston 1630-1765, American-Canadian-English trade relations 1875-1914. Author: A Study in English Mercantilism 1700-1775 '43. Author articles: Thirty Dollars Every Thursday '38; Canada's Trade Relations with Soviet Russia 1920-1939 '39; An Act for the Better Regulation of the Indian Trade, 1713 '47; The Machine Age in Historical Research '48; The Worshipful Company of Feltmakers: An Episode in the History of the Hudson's Bay Company '48; The Boston Fleet of 1753 '48; The Trade Routes of Boston, 1752-1765 '48. Archbishop Riordan Scholar Am Hist U Calif '38-39, teaching asst hist '39-40, research asst Colonial Am Econ Hist '40-42, research asso summer '46; instr hist NYC '46-48; asst prof Syracuse U since '48, served as chief research asst London Eng office of Ofcl Hist Royal Canadian Army Med Corps '44-46. Am Acad Polit and Social Sci—AHA—Canadian Hist Assn—Canadian Polit Sci Assn—Econ Hist Assn—Hist Assn of Eng—Phi Alpha Theta—Phi Beta Kappa. History Department, Syracuse University, Syracuse 10, N.Y.†

19 LAWTON, George. Gerontology; Old age: Aging (Psychology). born 1900. BA '22—MA '26—PhD '32 (Columbia). Research and work aging, old age, mental hygiene, psychology; private practice as psychological consultant to older persons and to organizations in connection with problems of older persons; popular lecturer aging; radio speaker on America's Town Meeting, We, the People, Life Begins at 80, and others. Author: The Drama of Life After Death, A Psychological Study of the Spiritualist Religion '32; Prophet and Pilgrim (with H W Schneider) '42; New Goals for Old Age '43; Aging Successfully '46; How to be Happy Though Young. Research associate Council of Humanities Columbia '28-29; psychiat social worker Jew Board Guardians '28-29; teacher English, director psychol Bur Tests and Measurements Evander Childs High Sch Bronx NY '30-43; instr dept psychol and philos NYC evenings '32-36, summers '36-39; cons Andrew Freedman Home for Aged '38-40; cons sect on care of aged Welfare Council NY '40-41; staff mem Psychol Corp '43-44; cons Fashion Inst Tech and Design NY '44-45; cons Moosehaven Home for Aged of Loyal Order of Moose '45; attending psychol older patients dept psychiat Vanderbilt Clinic Columbia Med Center '46-47; cons Stamford (Conn) Home for Aged '47; cons Shell Oil Co on retirement problems; lectr NYU since '47; lectr Yeshiva U since '50. Am Psychol Assn(F), pres div maturity and old age '49-50)—Am Orthopsychiatric Assn (F)—NYAcad Sci(F)—NY Assn Applied Psychol (president)—AAAS—NY State Assn Applied Psychol—Am Gerontology Soc. 7 W. 96th St., NYC 25.

20 LAZAR, Irving. Group behavior (Prediction); Child development (Infant and preschool personality growth); Interpersonal relations (Research design and application); Diagnosis and Counseling (Clinical psychology). b'26. BSS '48 (City Coll NYC); MA '48—PhD '51 (Tchrs Coll Columbia). Research and development methodologies for study in interpersonal perceptions and individual value structures and their effects upon social behaviour, in social and perceptual development of young children; application of developmental principles to curriculum organization; development methodologies and instruments for study and control social phenomenon; projective techniques, counselling. Instr child development Bard Coll '49-50; instr child development and cons U Ill since '50. Am Psychol Assn —Soc Research in Child Development —Soc Psychol Study Social Issues (chmn com on community consultation)—AAAS—AAUP—SCA. College of Education, University of Illinois, Urbana, Ill.

21 LEACH, Clayton Blaine. Automobiles (Engine design); Torpedoes (Design). b'12. AB '34 (Park Coll). Original work in casting design; automotive engines (valve gear, manifolds); pressure regulator for torpedo. Holds patents in field. With Pontiac Motor Div since '36, motor development engr since '50. Soc Automotive Engrs. Naval Ordnance Development award for Torpedo design and 20mm gun design. Pontiac Motor Div., General Motors Corp., Pontiac 11, Mich. H: 7899 Cooley Lake Rd.

22 LEACH, Julian Gilbert. Plant pathology and diseases (Insect relations). b'94. BSA '17 (U Tenn); MS '18—PhD '22 (U Minn); Fellow study in Europe '27-28 (Internat Edn Bd). Research physiology specialization of fungi, bacterial diseases of plants, insects in relation to plant diseases, seed treatment. Author: Insect Transmission of Plant Diseases '40; also articles in field. Agent US Dept Agr '18-19; asst plant pathol U Minn '18-19, instr '20-22, asst prof '22-27, asso prof '29-37, prof '37-38; asso prof plant pathol and bot Colo Agrl Coll '19-20; prof plant pathol, head dept W Va U since '38. Am Phytopathol Soc (vp '40, pres '41)—AAAS—Potato Assn Am—Sigma Xi—Phi Kappa Phi—Gamma Sigma Delta. Department of Plant Pathology, Bacteriology, and Entomology, West Virginia University, Morgantown, W. Va. H: 106 Kenmore St.⊙

23 LEACH, MacEdward. Medieval literature, folklore, and manuscripts. b'96. AB '16—MA '17 (U Ill); PhD '30 (U Pa). Author: Amis and Amiloun, A Study of the Folk Backgrounds of the Story '32; Methods of Editing Medieval Manuscripts. With U Pa since '22, now asso prof. Modern Lang Assn—Am Anthrop Assn(F)—Am Folklore Soc (sec-treas). University of Pa., Phila.†

10 LEACH, Maria. Folklore (American, Irish, French). BA '14 (Earlham Coll); MA '17 (U Ill); fellow '19-20 (Johns Hopkins U). Research also in American English and slang. Am Eng editor Funk and Wagnalls New College Standard Dictionary '41-47, editor Dictionary of Folklore Mythology and Legend since '47. Am Anthrop Assn—Am Folklore Soc—French Folklore Soc—Mod Humanities Research Assn. Funk and Wagnalls, 153 E. 24 St., NYC 10.

11 LEAR, Bert. Soil fumigation; Nematology. b'17. BS '41 (Utah State Agrl Coll); PhD '47 (Cornell U). Author articles in field. Asst prof plant pathol Cornell U '48-52; nematologist New Mexico A. and M.A. since '52. Am Phytopathol Soc—Phi Kappa Phi—Sigma Xi. Fellow Dow Chem Co '43-47. Department of Biology, New Mexico A. and M.A., State College, New Mexico.†

12 LEAR, Floyd Seyward. Medieval and legal history; Political theory. b'95. AB '17 (U Rochester); AM '20—PhD '25 (Harvard). Author articles: The Medieval Attitude Toward History '33; St Isidore and Medieval Science '36; The Idea of Majesty in Roman Political Thought '36; other articles in field. Head hist dept DuPont Manual Training high sch Louisville Ky '20-22; asst in hist Harvard U '22-23, Austin teaching fellow '23-24, instr '24-25; instr hist The Rice Institute '25-27, asst prof '27-45, prof since '45, chmn dept hist since '35. Am Geog Soc(F)—Medieval Acad Am—AHA—Classical Assn of Middle W and S—Am Assn U Profs—Phi Beta Kappa. 211 Anderson Hall, The Rice Institute, Houston 1, Tex.

13 LEARNED, Henry Dexter. French elements in English to 1400; Old French language; Anglo-Norman; Phonetics; Metrics; Orthography; Vulgar Latin. b'93. AB '12—PhD '17 (U Pa); Rosengarten traveling scholarship '14; spl research fellow '38 (Belgian-Am Ednl Found); research grant Am Philos Soc '39. Author: Syntax of Brant's Narrenschiff '17; Modern Introductory French Book '32. Assistant editor: Websters New Internat Dictionary, Second Edition; also articles in field. Prof and head dept of French Temple U since '30. Modern Lang Assn—Medieval Acad Am—Anglo-Norman Text Soc—Linguistic Soc Am—Phi Beta Kappa. 333 W. Schoolhouse Lane, Germantown, Phila 44.©

14 LEARY, Lewis. Philip Freneau; American literature (Bibliography, eighteenth century). b'06. BS '28 (U Vt); AM '31—PhD '40 (Columbia). Author: That Rascal Freneau: A Study in Literary Failure '41; The Last Poems of Philip Freneau '45; also articles in field. Professor Am lit Duke U since '50. Mod Lang Assn Am (bibliog Am lit group since '47, chmn com bibliog '42-47)—So Atlantic Mod Lang Assn—Coll Eng Assn—Soc Am Hist. Box 4633, Duke Station, Durham, N. Carolina.†©

15 LEAS, A. Robert. Petroleum exploration (North America, South America, Central America, Mexico); Petroleum engineering, economics, management problems). born '05. Research, exploratory expeditions and tests for oil in South America, Central America, United States and Mexico. Pres and gen mgr Leas and English '32-41, Leas & Howe Royalties '33-41,

Leas Exploration Trust '34-41; spl petroleum cons US Navy in charge fuel oil facilities '41-47; independent cons since '47. AIMME—Nat Assn Corrosion Engrs—Soc Am Mil Engrs—Explorers Club (dir). 1026 17th St., Washington 6.

16 LEASURE, John Hicks. Cacti. b'89. Student '17-18 (Sch Cinematography Columbia); student '20 (Brunel Sch Photography NYC); '21-22 (El Paso Jr Coll); '23 (U So Calif). Author articles: Story Cactus, with 100 photographs and drawings '39; The Effect of Rontgens' X-rays on the Seed Genes in the Reproduction of Cacti as to Shape Size and Spines. Lecturer on Texas Cacti, Preparation Chihuahua Cacti, Big Bend Cacti; cactus grower. Tex Acad Sci—AAAS—Cactus and Succulent Soc Am. 4431 Montana St., El Paso, Tex.†

17 LEAVELL, Charles. Vibration elimination. b'06. Research in theory of equations, various thermodynamic and mechanical topics, defining principles and corresponding mechanical means for prevention and isolation of linear, torsional, unbalance vibrations in operating machines, especially pneumatic percussive tools, reciprocating engines and compressors, high speed rotors, and centrifuges. Pres Mech Research Corp since '41. 2200 Girard Trust Bldg., Phila. 2.

18 LEAVITT, Charles Townsend. United States agricultural history before 1860; Money and banking. b'02. BA '25 (Beloit Coll); MA '28—PhD '31 (U Chicago). Author articles: Attempts to Improve Cattle Breeds in the United States 1790-1860 '33; The Western Meat Packing Industry, 1830-1860 '31; Transportation and the Livestock Industry of the Middle West to 1860 '34. Teacher hist and speech Wausau Wis High Sch '25-27; prof hist Dakota Wesleyan U '31-32; instr social sci Milwaukee Vocational Jr Coll '34-46; asst prof Am hist and econ Ia State Teachers Coll since '46. Iowa State Teachers College, Cedar Falls, Ia.

19 LEAVITT, Floyd Haven. Ammonia as a fertilizer; Soils and fertilizers. b'03. BA '26 (Pomona Coll). Discovered nitrojection, a method of injecting ammonia directly into soil for fertilization purposes. Chem to managing dir chem Assn Lab Anaheim Calif '26-39; agr tech to sr tech western div Shell Chem Corp since '39. Calif Fertilizer Assn—Nat Fert Assn. Shell Chemical Corporation, 100 Bush Street, San Francisco 6.

20 LEBACQZ, Jean Victor. Pulse generation; Cathode-ray oscillography; Gaseous breakdown phenomena. b'11. PhD '35 (Stanford U). Author: Pulse Generators '48; also articles in field. Asst prof elec engring Johns Hopkins since '46. Staff Radiation Lab MIT '43-46. Am Inst Elec Engrs—Inst Radio Engr—Sigma Xi. Johns Hopkins University, Baltimore 18.

21 LeBARRON, Russell K(enneth). Harvesting, regeneration and care of jack pine and black spruce; Forest growth and artificial reforestation; Management and silviculture of western white, ponderosa and lodgepole pines, larch, Douglas fir and Engelmann spruce. b'07. BS '31 (U Idaho); '40 (U Minn). Author articles in field. Chief forest mgt research Cal Forest and Range Exptl Sta since '52. Ecol Soc Am—AAAS—NW Sci Assn—Mont Acad Sci—Soc Am Foresters. Cal Forest and Range Exptl Sta, Berkeley, California.†

22 le BEAU, Désirée S. Colloids; Rubbers; Clays. b'07. Degree '31—PhD (U Graz, Austria). Co-author:

Silicic Chemistry; also articles in field. Holder two patents on the reclaiming of natural and synthetic rubber in the US '48. Dir research Midwest Rubber Reclaiming Co since '45. ACS (chmn colloid div)—AAAS—NY Acad Sci—British Inst Rubber Ind—Sigma Xi. Midwest Rubber Reclaiming Co., East St. Louis, Ill.†

23 LEBEDEFF, Gabriel A. Corn breeding and genetics; Genetics of Drosophila and beans. b'94. Student '14-15 (Poly Inst Kiev Russia); '21-23 (Zagreb U Yugoslavia); BS '28 (U Conn); MS '31—PhD '38 (Cornell U). Genetic research with Drosophila, beans, corn. Author articles in field. Research asso dept of genetics Carnegie Inst '31-35; research dept of plant breeding Cornell U '35-40; plant breeder Agr Expt Sta U Puerto Rico '40-43; asso agronomist Ga Agrl Expt Sta since '43. Genetics Soc Am—Am Soc Agron—Sigma Xi—Phi Kappa Phi. Georgia Agricultural Experiment Station, Experiment, Ga.

24 LEBEDEFF, Yurii E(ugene). Extractive metallurgy (Non-ferrous). BS in mining engring '27—MetE '37 (SD Sch Mines). Research in extractive metallurgy lead, zinc, tin, antimony, arsenic, indium, selenium, bismuth, tellurium, copper, thallium, cadmium. Issued 35 US and 20 fgn patents in field. Author article: De-bismuthizing lead with alkaline earth metals including magnesium, and with antimony. With Am Smelting and Refining Co since '27, supt chem metall Central Research dept since '45. AIMME—ACS—AAAS—NY Acad Sci—Sigma Xi. Central Research Dept., American Smelting and Refining Co., Barber, N.J. H: 195 Woodbridge Av., Metuchen, N.J.

25 LeBEL, Clarence Joseph. Sound measurement and recording; Electronic circuits; Electronic measuring instruments and measurements. b'05. SB '26 (EE)—SM '27 (MIT); '39-40 (Columbia). Designed variety of electronic and sound measurement and recording equipment, including minature preamplifiers, wide-range logarithmic voltmeters, equalizers and wave filters, magnetic recording tape, and disc recording machines, amplifiers, mixers, and accessories; also designed large anechoic chamber, and equipment for measuring characteristics of headphones, loudspeakers, microphones, phonographs and phonograph records; research on, design of instruments for, fitting hearing aids and testing hearing; designed subminiature electronic stethoscope and supervised development of surgeon's metal locator; member board of editorial consultants of Audio Engineering. Consultant since '32; chief engr Audio Devices Inc '37-42, vp since '40; chief engr The Maico Co Inc '42-45, Audio Instrument Co since '47. Audio Engring Soc (pres '48-49, bd govs '49-51)—Acoustical Soc Am—Soc Motion Picture Engrs—Inst Radio Engrs. Audio Engring Soc award '49. 133 W. 14th St., NYC 11.

26 Le BOEUF, Randall James, Jr. Public utility law (State vs Federal); Constitutional law. b'97. LLB '20 (Cornell U). Deputy assistant atty general State of New York '25-27, special counsel '27 and '28, commissioner census investigation '27-28; director National Information Bureau. Contbr to law and public utility jours. Sr partner law firm Le Boeuf, Lamb & Leiby NYC. Am, NY State bar assns—NY County Lawyers Assn—Assn Bar City NY—Fed Power Bar Assn—Cornell Law Assn—Delta Chi—Sigma Delta Chi. Office: 14 B 15 Broad St., NYC 5.©

10 LEBOWICH, Richard Jacob. Instruments (Medical). b'98. MD '22 (Harvard Med Sch). Developed soapwax tissue technique, quadruple pipetting machine for use in quantitative Wasserman test, vacuum dehydration method for permanent preservation of heart, method for determination of formaldehyde in air. Author articles in field. Asst path Cleveland City Hosp '27-30; path and dir lab Eugene Littauer Memorial Lab and Fulton Co Lab Littauer Hosp since '30. AAAS—Am Assn Path and Bact—ACS—Soc Am Bact—NY State Assn Pub Health Labs (vp '48-49, pres '49-50). Fulton County Laboratory, Littauer Pl., Gloversville, N.Y.

11 LECHER, Hans Z(acharias). Synthetic dyes, pigments, rubbers. b'87. PhD '13 (U Munich). Directed early work on Buna rubbers. Holds numerous patents in the field of intermediates, dyes, pigments. Author articles in field. Head rubber dept I G Leverkusen works '27-32, dir research '29-32; dir organic research Calco Chem Co '34-38; asso dir research Calco Chem div Am Cyanamid Co '38-49, dir research since 49. Am Inst Chem(F)—Am Chem Soc—Soc Chem Ind—AAAS. Calco Chemical Division, American Cyanamid Co., Bound Brook, N.J. H: 1049 Kenyon Av., Plainfield.

12 Le CLERC, Helen G. Food chemistry. b'97. Student '13-15 (Winthrop Coll); '15-17 (Chicora Coll Women); summer '19 (Columbia); AB and certificate in science '17 (Va U). Research in elimination of toxemia from human body by means of fasts, specialized raw foods; teacher, lecturer 15 years in dietetics, food chemistry, biochemistry. Author: Feeding the Family '34; Health Cook Book '35; The Proper Diet for Every Case of Impaired Health '35; Health and How to Keep It '34. Internat Soc Biochem—Italian Chem Soc. Kingsley Lake, Starke, Fla.

13 LeCOMPTE, Stuart B(urnette), Jr. Plant physiology; Glass technology. b'13. AB '34—PhD '39 (Johns Hopkins). Research in chemistry of soils, tobacco leaves and plant pigments. Author articles in field. Plant physiol Conn Agrl Expt Sta '40-44; asso prof and asso research specialist vegetable crops dept hort Rutgers U and NJ Agrl Expt Sta since '47. AAAS(F)—Am Soc Plant Physiol—Am Chem Soc—NJ State Hort Soc—Bot Soc Am—Sigma Xi. Department of Horticulture, Rutgers University, New Brunswick, N.J. H: 1408 Chetwynd Av., Plainfield.†

14 LE CONEY, Horace Morgan, Jr. Petroleum products (Testings and applications). b'16. BS '37 (NC State Coll); MS '38 (Va Poly Inst). Research and interpretation tests on petroleum products with respect to condition for further use and freedom from contamination, recommendation proper fuels and lubricants for industrial, automotive, marine, truck and bus and aviation applications. With Esso Standard Oil Co '38-41, since '45, indsl sales mgr from '49; petroleum sect Bur Ships USN '41-45. ASME. Esso Standard Oil Co., Broad and Hamilton Sts., Richmond, Va.

15 LE COQ, John Peter. France (Literature); Spain (Literature). b'83. AB —APh—Lic-es-Lettres '05—Lic in Phil '06—D '12 (U Paris Sorbonne). Author: Understanding South America; French Life and Ideals. Co-author: (with Churchman and Young) Manuel de la Litterature Francaise '36. With Drake U since '18, now prof and head dept. Phi Beta Kappa—Phi Sigma Iota — MLA — AAUP — Am Assn Tchrs

French. Drake University, Des Moines, Ia.

16 LeCRONE, Fred. Vegetable production; Fruit and nut tree culture; Market outlet expansion (Fruit, vegetable, pecans). b'08. BS Agr '30 (Okla A&M Coll); MS '31—grad fellow '30-31 (Ia State Coll). Research in tomato pectins as related to storage of fruit, marketing practices as related to quality fruits and vegetables, irrigated vegetable producing areas, marketing methods of expanding market outlets for fruit, vegetables and pecans. Co-author: General Text in Horticulture '49; also articles in field. Asso prof hort Okla A&M Coll since '46, gen hort, pomology, pruning, spraying. Am Soc Hort Sci—Am Pomology Soc—Okla Pecan Growers Assn. Horticulture Department, Oklahoma A&M College, Stillwater, Okla.†

17 LEDNICKI, Waclaw. Slavic and comparative literature; Pushkin Mickiewicz, Tolstoy, Dostoevsky; Russian-Polish relations. b'91. Student '10-11 —PhD '22 (U Cracow); diploma 1st degree '15 (U Moscow). Chmn founder Polish Soc Study Eastern Europe and Near East Cracow; vp Polish Commn Polish-Belgian Intellectual Exchange '36; vice chairman of Society for Protection Polish Monuments Moscow '15-18. Author: Alfred de Vigny '23; Eugeniusz Oniegin Aleksandra Puszkina '25; Aleksander Puszkin '26; Jules Slovacki '27; Pouchkine et la Pologne '28; Jezdziec Miedziany Aleksandra Puszkina '32; Quelques Aspects du Nationalisme et du Christianisme chez Tolstoi '35; Przyjaciele Moskale '35; Puszkin (1827-1937) '37; Moj Puszkinowski Table Talk '39; Poland and the World '43; Russian-Polish Relations '44; Life and Culture of Poland '44; Henry K Sienkiewicz '47; Panslavism '48; editor pubs Polish Soc; also articles in field. Prof Russian lit U Cracow since '28; prof Slavic lit U Brussels '33-47, hon prof since '47; prof slavic langs U Calif since '45. Oriental, Slavonic Inst (Brussels, NYC)—Polish Inst Arts Sci (chmn sect lit, arts, mem bd '42)—Slavonic Inst Prague (fgn mem '38—Polish Acad Arts Letters (corr '37). Decorated Cross Valour, comdr Belgian Order Leopold I.©

18 LEE, Alan Porter. Oils (Edible, deodorizing, hydrogenation); Fats (Shortening); Soaps (Spray process). b'89. BS '08 (Washington and Lee U). Design, development and construction oil refining and deodorizing plants, shortening and margarine, soap and soap powder, acid distillation and hydrolysis, stearic and oleic acid manufacturing plants US and abroad; developed continuous fatty acid distillation. Holds patent on process for fatty acid distillation and others in field. Design engr, cons since '26; ed tech journs in field ACS—Am Inst Chem(F)—Am Inst Chem Engrs—Am Oil Chem Soc—Assn Cons Chem and Chem Engrs—ASTM. Licensed profl engr NY, NJ. Miller Rd., Morristown, N.J.†

19 LEE, Arthur Bennett. Typography; Copy-fitting. b'00. Student (U Cincinnati, Northwestern U). Invented Lee Streamlined copy-fitting system. Author articles: Streamlined Copy-Fitting Index Chart and Gauge '40. Prodn mgr and typographical dir The B D Iola Co Inc NYC since '31. Assn Advt Men—Type Dir Club. Awards by NY Employing Printers Assn in annual exhibits '40, '43. 551 Fifth Av., NYC 17.†

20 LEE, Carl. Hoists (Mine). b'91. EE U (Tex). Installation, maintenance, and remodeling of mine hoists, up to 1300 horsepower; engineering design

of hoist drums, mechanical layout, redesign electrical equipment for faster electrical hoists. Test engr Gen Elec Co Schenectady NY '11-13; elec engr Peabody Coal Co Chicago '13-41, chief engr since '41. Am Inst EE—Ill Mining Inst. Room 2000, 231 S. La Salle, Chgo 4.

21 LEE, Charles Foster. Fishery and food technology; Composition of fishery products (Starfish, oysters); Ambergris; Seaweed gums. b'06. BS '28 (Case Inst Tech); '36-37 (U Md). Co-author: Pacific Salmon Oils '39; also articles in field. Biochem Bur Fisheries since '31, fish and Wildlife Service Coll Park Md since '39. Am Chem Soc—AAAS. Fisheries Technological Laboratory, College Park, Md.

22 LEE, Clarence E(dgar). Poultry and small animal nutrition. b'93. BS '16 (Conn Agr Coll, U Conn); '21-23 (Cornell U). Investigations in various phases of poultry nutrition, feeding of dogs and rabbits, poultry housing and management. Granted US and Canadian patents on improved pelleted feeds and others. Author articles in field. Head dept poultry husbandry State NY Inst Agr '23-27; lecturer Columbia U '25-27; poultry specialist Beacon Milling Co Inc '27-35, vp, dir poultry, game bird and small animal research since '35. AAAS(F)—Poultry Sci Assn NA—World's Poultry Sci Assn —Am Soc Animal Prodn—Nutrition Council of Am Feed Mfrs Assn (chmn '42)—Animal Nutrition Research Council—NY Acad Sci. c/o Beacon Milling Co., Inc., Cayuga, N.Y. H: RD 4 East Genesee Rd., Auburn.

23 LEE, Dorothy (Mrs. Otis H.). Conceptual implications of language; Social anthropology. b'05. AB '27 (Vassar Coll); PhD '31 (Calif U); '33-34 (Kiel U). Intensive study of primitive cultures for the discovery of their codification of experienced reality; main emphasis on linguistic analysis for the discovery of basis of classification. Author articles: A Primitive System of Values '40; Linguistic Reflection of Wintu Thought '44. Instr anthropol Washington U '31-32, Sarah Lawrence Coll '32-33; lecturer Pomona Coll '36-37; Vassar Coll since '39, asso prof anthropol since '47. Am Anthropolog Assn(F)—Am Folklore Assn—Inst Ethnic Affairs—Am Ethnolog Soc. Vassar College, Poughkeepsie, N.Y.†

24 LEE, Douglas Harry Kedgwin. Human and animal climatology (Reactions); Physiology of settlement and community development. b'05. BSc '24 —MSc '27 (U Queensland); MB '29— BS '29—DTM '33—MD '40 (Sydney); Fellow (Royal Australasian Coll of Physicians); Sharpey scholar '34-35 (U Coll London). Consultant Climatology and Environmental Protection Section, US Quartermaster Corps, Dept Defense, Food and Agriculture orgn UN; research, lectr and tchr in field. Author articles in field. Prof physiol climatology and lecturer in physiol hygiene Johns Hopkins U since '48. Am Soc Heating and Ventilating Engrs (physiol research com)—Royal Soc Tropical Medicine, Hygiene—Physiol Soc of Gt Britain—Poultry Sci Assn— Am Soc Animal Prodn—Am Geog Soc —Arctic Inst N Am. Sydney U medal '29; Schaefer Prize, U Coll London '35. Johns Hopkins University, Baltimore 18.†

25 LEE, George Hamor. Experimental stress analysis; Theory of elasticity; Mechanics of rigid bodies. b'08. BS '36 (U Pittsburgh); MS '37—PhD '40—McMullen research scholar (Cornell U). Research on expansion of boiler tubes; extensive work on extension of photoelastic method of stress analysis to plates under transverse flexure. Author articles in field. With Aluminum Research Labs New Kensington Pa and Massena NY '27-33; instr mech Cornell U '37-40; Carnegie Inst Tech '40-41; asst prof mech Cornell U '41-45, asso prof '45, coordinator and supervisor math and mech engring sci and management war training program '41-45; research Babcock and Wilcox Co '42; asso prof mech engring US Naval Postgrad Sch since '45. AAAS—ASME (sec biblio and translations com, indsl instruments and regulators div)—Am Soc Testing Materials—Sigma Xi. U.S. Naval Postgraduate School, Annapolis, Md.†

10 LEE, George Joseph. Chinese ceramics, Early Chinese jade. b'19. AB cum laude '40—AM '47—Chinese Govt cultural fellow '45-48 (Harvard). Autor articles in field. Asst curator Oriental Art Fogg Museum Harvard '48-49; editor Far Eastern Ceramic Bull '48-49. Curator Oriental Art Brooklyn Museum since '49. Oriental Ceramic Soc (London)—Chinese Art Soc NY. Brooklyn Museum, Eastern Parkway, Brooklyn 38.†

11 LEE, Gordon M(elvin). High-speed oscillography; Dielectrics; Fast transients. b'17. BEE '38 (U Minn); MS '39 (U Mo); DSc '44 (MIT). Research on failure of porcelain insulators, magnetron starting time, dielectric breakdown in sodium chloride; developed high-speed microoscillograph, improved '46. Author articles in field. Research asst Lab for Insulation Research MIT '39-44, DIC staff '44-45; tech dir elec engring Central Research Labs Inc Red Wing Minn since '45. AIEE—Inst Radio Engrs—Am Phys Soc—Sigma Xi—Tau Beta Pi. Received Thompson memorial prize IRE '46. Central Research Laboratories, Inc., Red Wing, Minn.†

12 LEE, J. Murray. Education (Curriculum, elementary). b'04. AB '26 (Occidental Coll); AM '28—PhD '34 (Columbia). Tchr city schs Burbank Cal '26-29, dir research '29-36, dir curriculum and research '36-37; asst prof edn U Wis '37-41; dean sch edn, dir summer sessions, prof edn State Coll Wash since '41; vis prof summers Tchrs Coll Columbia '32, Coll William and Mary '35, Columbia '32, U Tex '36 '37; cons on curriculum Beloit and Wauwatosa Wis. NEA(dept secondary sch prins, dept elementary sch prins, dept social studies)—AAAS—Council Tchrs Math—Edn Research Assn—Phi Delta Kappa. State College of Washington, Pullman, Wash.†⊚

13 LEE, James Augustine. Telephone transmission. b'19. BE '41—ME '46 (Yale). With Am Telephone and Telegraph Co since '46. Served as radioradar officer USN '41-45. 195 Broadway, NYC 7.

14 LEE, James Augustine. Corrosion control. b'94. AB '17—BS '17 (Washington and Lee U); '18 (MIT); MS '23 (Columbia). Studies on corrosion of metals used in construction of chemical processing equipment; research on effects of high temperatures and abrasion of metals and nonmetallic materials; selection of material for construction of equipment used in production, handling, or packaging of commercial chemicals. Author: Materials of Construction for Chemical Process Industry '50. Contributor: Chemical Engineers Handbook '50; Corrosion Handbook '48; Book of Stainless Steel. Chem engr Fed Dyestuff & Chem Co '17, Indianapolis Gas Co '18; mng ed Chemical Engineering (formerly Chem and Metall Engring) '28-49, southwestern ed since '49. AICE—ACS—Royal Soc Arts Brit—Tech Assn Pulp and Pa-

per Industry—Nat Assn Corrosion Engrs—Electrochem Soc (pres '48-49). McGraw-Hill Publishing Co., 566 M & M Bldg., Houston 2.

15 LEE, LeFever Mackey. Furnace brazing; Metal joining. b'08. BA '31—MSc '32—Fellow '32-33 (O State U). Specialized in soft solder metal joining, soft solder dipping, silver soldering, torch brazing, furnace brazing; consultant to other industries in furnace brazing problems. Engr and foreman Box Anneal dept Bethlehem Steel Corp '35-41; design and production engr Fedders-Quigan Corp Buffalo NY since '41. Nat Soc Professional Engr. 57 Tonawanda St., Buffalo 7, N.Y. H: 23 Darlick St., Hamburg.†

16 LEE, Linwood Lawrence. Soil classification; Soils and geography of New Jersey. b'94. BS '16 (Rutgers U); '24-25 (Princeton); DSc '31 (U London Eng). Author USDA soil survey reports of New Jersey '16-31. Author articles: Norway Spruce as a Christmas Tree Crop in New Jersey '31; The Possibilities of an International System for the Classification of Soils '31, '32; The Land Resources of New Jersey '33; The Soil Erosion Problem '33; Soil Erosion a National and State Menace '33; The Principal Soils of New Jersey and their Utilization for Agriculture '34; others. Asst to State Geol of NJ in charge soil survey '16-25; asst prof soils Rutgers U Coll Agr '25-29; research specialist land utilization NJ Agr Expt Sta, fellow Rockefeller Found Internat Edn Bd Europe '29-31; Research fellow National Research Council Europe '31; member staff Rothamsted Experimental Station Harpenden Eng '29-31; asst prof soils Rutgers U '31-34; research specialist land utilization NJ Agrl Expt Sta with AAA '34; with US Dept Interior '35; state conservationist Soil Conservation Service USDA since '35. Internat Soc Soil Sci—Soil Conservation Soc Am—Am Soc Agronomy—Sigma Xi—Soil Sci Soc Am—New Brunswick Sci Soc—NJ Agrl Soc—NJ State Soil Conservation Com. Post Office Bldg., New Brunswick, N.J.⊚

17 LEE, Milton Oliver. Physiology (Nutrition and foods); Scientific journals (Publication). b'01. AB '22—AM '23—PhD '26 (Ohio State U); grad work '23 '27 (Marine Biol Lab). Managing editor Endocrinology and Journal of Clinical Endocrinology '35-42, American Journal Physiology and Physiological Reviews, Journal Applied Physiology, Federation Proceedings. Exec sec div biol and agr Nat Research Council; exec dir Fedn Am Socs for Exptl Biol. Research fellow in physiol, asso and physiol Memorial Found Neuro-Endocrine Research Harvard '27-47. Am Physiol Soc(exec sec)—Am Inst Nutrition—Soc Exptl Biol and Med—Assn Study Internal Secretions (vp '29)—Gamma Alpha—Phi Beta Kappa —Sigma Xi. 2101 Constitution Av., Washington 25.⊚

18 LEE, Rensselaer Wright. French art (17th and 18th centuries); Italain art (16th to 18th centuries); Theory of art. b'98. AB '20—PhD '26 (Princeton). Author: Ut pictura poesis, The Humanistic Theory of Painting '40. Editor-in-chief The Art Bull '42-44, editorial board since '45; chmn editorial com for articles on art and architecture Ency Brit since '46. Asso prof history of art and chmn dept Northwestern U '31-34, prof '34-40; prof art Smith Coll '41-48, Columbia since '48; vis prof Princeton '48; vp Am Com for Restoration of Italain Monuments since '47. Am Council Learned Socs (F 30-31, chmn com research and publ in the Fine Arts '42-44, exec sec com on protection cultural treasures in war

areas '44-45)—Archeol Inst Am—Coll Art Assn Am(sec '39-42, pres '45-46) —Mediaeval Acad Am. Schermerhorn Hall, Columbia University, Morningside Heights, NYC.⊚

19 LEE, Ronald Freeman. Preservation of American historic sites and buildings. b'05. BA '27—'31-33 (Minn U); MA '29 (Chicago U). Directs historical and archeological research relating to acquisition, planning, development and public use of all areas in National Park System including prehistoric antiquities, sites of colonial settlements, battlefields, houses. Chief hist Nat Park Service '38-51; asst dir in charge research and interpretation since '51. Nat Trust for Hist Preservation (sec)—Am Assn State and Local Hist—Internat Council Mus—Am Assn Mus—AHA—Miss Valley Hist Assn—Am Pioneer Trails Assn—Assn Preservation Va Antiquities—Phi Beta Kappa. National Park Service, Dept. of Interior, Washington.†

20 LEE, Rose Hum. Chinese-Americans in US (Community life and family). b'04. BS '42 (Carnegie Inst Tech); AM '43—PhD '47 (U Chicago). Research on Chinese communities of Rocky Mountain region, cultural and psychological adjustment of war wives of San Francisco Bay region, Chinese culture, urban society, and social institutions. Contributor: One America '51. Lecturer Adult Edn Council '44-50; acting chmn sociol dept Roosevelt Coll '50-51, asso prof sociol since '50. Am Sociol Soc—Chinese Sociol Club (past chmn)—Phi Delta Gamma(founder, past chmn)—Phi Delta Alpha—A AUP—Am Acad Polit Soc Sci—Am Assn U Women—E-W Fellowship (chmn scholarship fund). Received Soc Sci Research Grant '49. Roosevelt College of Chicago, 430 S. Michigan Av., Chgo 5.

21 LEE, Sherman E. Art (Far Eastern). b'18. AB '38—MA '39 (Am U); PhD '41 (W Reserve U). Research on art of India, Indonesia, China, Korea and Japan, with emphasis of Chinese art and ceramics and Japanese painting and sculpture and arts of Kamakura Period 1186-1333 A. D. Curator Oriental art Detroit Inst Arts '41-46; adv free arts GHQ SCAP '46-48; asso dir Seattle Art Mus and lectr U Wash since '48. Far E Assn—Am Oriental Soc — Soc Japanese Studies — Far E Ceramic Group—Coll Art Assn. Seattle Art Museum, Seattle 2.

22 LEE, Shu-Hsien. Horticultural botany (China, vegetable crops). b'17. BAgr '40 (Nat Central U); MS '47—PhD '48 (Mich State Coll). Research horticulture, fruit trees vegetable crops China; taxonomy of Asiatic species of beans, citrus fruits, and oriental pears; first to use phytogeograph method to divide China into six fruit regions and eight subregions; vegetable crops combining physiolog ical and morphological methods to study effect of growth hormones on foliar abscission of cabbage and cauliflower in storage. Author articles: The Culture and Classification of Jute Plants in China, with Special References to a New Cultigen Species of Corchorus '42; A Preliminary Study of Chinese Cultivated Brassicas '42. Co-author: The Fruit Regions of China '44; A Taxonomic Survey of the Oriental Pears '48; The Effects of Bud Pollination on Fertility and Fruit Characters of Some Chinese Brassicas '48. Research asst Nat Central U China '40-45; selected by Agrl Assn of China as a hort to pursue advanced study in hort sci at Mich State Coll '45. Agrl Assn China—Am Soc Hort Sci—AAAS —Sigma Xi—Am Plant Life Soc. Department of Horticulture, **Michigan State College**, East Lansing, Mich.

10 LEE, William Arthur. Cryptanalysis; Theatrical hair and beards. b'90. Student W Acad Dramatic Art, Hunter Coll. Devised simplified method of determining "period" of bifid and trifid ciphers and of layout for easier visualization of part values of clear letters, inventor bifid and trifid slide rule, work on Phillips cipher and theory of substitutions; perfected method of construction permanent, beards, mustaches, sideburns, from crepe hair. Free-lance actor. Am Cryptogram Assn. Hotel Endicott, 440 Columbus Av., NYC 24.

11 LEEDY, Daniel Loney. Wildlife research (Pheasants); Land use in relation to wildlife. b'12. AB '34—BSc '35 (Miami U); MSc '38—PhD '40—wildlife research fellow '36-40 (O State U). Research and writing on pheasants, wildlife economics, wildlife land use relationships; charge cooperative wildlife research unit program in which 17 land grant colleges or universities, 17 state game departments, the wildlife management institute and the fish and wildlife service cooperate in a program of wildlife research and training personnel for conservation positions. Co-author: (with W L McAtee) The Ring-necked Pheasant '45; also articles in field. Instr wildlife management O State U '40-42; biol US Fish and Wildlife Service '45-48, charge cooperative wildlife research unit program since '48. AAAS—Wilson Ornithol Club—Am Soc Mammalogists—Am Ornithol Union—Wildlife Soc—O Acad Sci—Sigma Xi. United States Fish and Wildlife Service, Washington 25.†

12 LEEDY, Halden A. Architectural acoustics; Acoustical materials (Testing). b'10. AB '33 (N Central Coll Naperville Ill); MA '35—PhD '38 (U Ill). Research in sound and noise measurements, magnetic recording; administration of research. Physicist Armour Research Found Chicago '38-44, chmn physics research '45-48, dir Armour Research Found of Ill Inst Tech since '48; pres Greater Noise Reduction Council Chicago '45-48, bd dirs since '48. Acoustical Soc Am(F)—APS—Inst Radio Engrs—Am Inst Physics—Ill Acad Sci—Am Inst Elec Engrs—AAAS—Nat Electronics Conf—Am Standards Assn—ASTM(chmn com acoustical materials since '49)—Sigma Xi—Sigma Pi Sigma. 35 W. 33rd St., Chgo 16.

13 LEEDY, Paul Francis. Alexander Pope; Eighteenth century English literature. b'03. AB '30—AM '31—PhD '40—ABLS '46 (U Mich). Author articles in field. Instr Eng to prof Eng and librarian Bowling Green State U since '38. Mod Lang Assn Am—Am Library Assn—Phi Kappa Phi. Bowling Green State University, Bowling Green, O.

14 LEEDS, Charles Tileston. Flood control; Water supply; Seacoast protection. b'79. Grad '03 (US Mil Acad); BS '06 (MIT). Member board of engineers for flood control Los Angeles County California '14-15; engineer Orange County Harbor Commission '16-23; consulting harbor engineer cities Los Angeles, Santa Barbara, Long Beach, Oakland, Richmond, San Diego, Coronado, Counties of Orange and Ventura, and Oxnard Harbor dist California; consulting engineer on water supply Division of Public Works California '30-31, on seacoast protection since '31; consulting engineer Los Angeles County Sanitation Districts '32-38. Mem firm Leeds, Hill & Jewett,

cons engrs since '46. Served in CE US Army '17-19, Engr RC '25-30; dist engr charge fortification constrn and maintenance Los Angeles and San Diego Cal, also all river and harbor improvement between Monterey Cal and Mexico World War I; engr various contonments and nat def projects World War II. ASCE—Soc Am Mil Engrs —Am Geophys Union—Seismol Soc Am—Am Assn Port Authorities—Soc Terminal Engrs—Am Water Works Assn—Am Shore and Beach Preservation Assn—Am Inst Cons Engrs—Sigma Xi—Tau Beta Pi. Edison Bldg., LA 13.☉

15 LEET, Lewis Don. Vibrations (Measurements and effects); Industrial blasting (Vibrations); Seismic prospecting; Microseisms (Earth waves). b'01. Student '19-20 (Columbia); BS '23 (Denison U); MA '30 (Harvard). Study of vibrations from earthquakes, dynamite blasts and industrial sources; applied seismological techniques to geological prospecting problems for oil and bauxite; developed Leet 3-component portable seismograph for recording vibrations from explosions and industrial sources. Author: Practical Seismology and Seismic Prospecting; Vibrations From Blasting (manual); Causes of Catastrophe; (monograph) Earth Waves '50. Author articles: Vibrations from Delay Blasting; Microseisms in New England—Case History of a Storm; others. With Harvard since '27, in charge seismograph station since '31, head tech services div Underwater Sound Lab '44; cons transition office Radiation Lab MIT, Office Sci Research and Development Washington; head spl project Office Field Service; '45; cons on measurement ground motion Atomic Bomb test NM '45; cons Isthmian Canal Studies for Panama Canal '46-47, Office Chief Engrs US Army '47-48, The Texas Co '47, TVA '49. Am Geophys Union—Soc Exploration Geophysicists—Geol Soc Am—Seismol Soc Am—Sigma Xi—Phi Mu Alpha. Harvard University, Cambridge 38, Mass.†☉

16 LEFEVER, D(avid) Welty. Educational tests; Personality tests. b'01. AB '21 (La Verne Coll); AM '22—PhD '27 (U So Cal). Assisted in construction job knowledge and job performance tests for Air Technical Service Command covering 60 trades related to airplane maintenance World War II; survey of construction of civil service examinations for California; statistical analysis of Rorschach test data for several hundred psychiatrically defined cases; assisted in devising standardized summary score for Rorschach test. Co-author: (with Turrell, Weitzel) Principles and Techniques of Guidance (rev edit) '50. Instr advancing to prof edn U So Cal since '26; cons testing Air Tech Service Command San Bernardino Cal '43-45, Inglewood City Schs since '47. Am Ednl Research Assn—Psychometric Soc—Am Statis Assn—Phi Delta Kappa. University of Southern California, University Park, LA 7.†

17 LEFFLER, George Leland. Furniture industry (Economics); Pennsylvania (Textile industry); Stock market (Economics). b'99. AB '27 (U Kan); MA '30—PhD '32 (U Wis). Author: The Stock Market '51. Author article: The Pennsylvania Textile Industry '48. Contributor: Americana Encyclopedia Annual '47-50. Prof finance and ed Toledo Business Survey U Toledo '32-37; prof econ Pa State Coll since '37; asst dir Bur Bus Research and ed Pa Bus Survey since '38. Am Econ Assn —Phi Beta Kappa. Bureau of Business

Research, Pennsylvania State College, State College, Pa.

18 LE GALLEY, Donald Paul. Guided missiles; Naval ordnance; Nuclear energy. b'01. BSc '25 (Heidelberg Coll); MSc '30—PhD '35 (Pa State Coll). In charge of special research projects in Guided Missile Branch Research Division of Bureau of Ordnance '46-50; Naval Ordnance CNO US Navy since '50. Author: Lab Manual of Physics '28; also articles in field. Instr phys Capitol U '26-28, Pa State Coll '28-37; head phys dept Phila Coll Pharmacy and Sci '37-46; asso prof phys Haverford Coll '43-44; cons research for OSRD and NDRC '44-46; Research Div Bur Ordnance Navy Dept '46-50; Naval Ordnance CNO US Navy since '50. Am Phys Soc—Am Assn Phys Teachers—Sigma Xi—Sigma Pi Sigma. 4611 49th St. N.W., Washington.

19 LEGGETTE, Ralph Maxwell. Ground water geology. b'99. SB '23—'25-28 (U Chicago). Author articles in field. Geologist US Geol Survey '28-42; cons ground water geol since '44. Maj Corps of Engrs US Army '42-44. Geol Soc Am—Geol Soc Washington—Am Geophys Union—ASCE—Am Water Works Assn—New Eng Water Works Assn—Inst Ground Water Research (chmn). 551 Fifth Av., NYC 17.

20 LeGEYS, Herbert James. Graphite; Carbon. b'01. Chem Engr '24 (Rensselaer Poly Inst). Reg profl engr (Pa, Mass). Development engr Stackpole Carbon Co St Marys Pa '25-29, chief chem since '29. Am Chem Soc —Electrochem Soc—AAAS—ASTM—Am Inst Chemists(F). Stackpole Carbon Co., St. Marys, Pa.†

21 LEGSDIN, Adolph. Mineral dressing; Industrial plant design; Metallurgical slimes (Beneficiation). b'99. Engr of Mines '23 (Freiberg); MS '33 (Columbia); '40 (MIT). Author articles in field. Prof mineral dressing Mo Sch Mines since '40. Am Inst Mining and Metall Engr. Missouri School of Mines and Metallurgy, Rolla, Mo.†

22 LEHMANN, Emil Wilhelm. Rural electrification; Soil conservation; Farm drainage; Isolated homes (Water supply, sewage disposal). b'87. BS '10 (Miss A&M Coll); EE '13 (Tex A&M Coll); BS '14—AE '19 (Ia State Coll). President Hoover's Conference on Home Building and Home Ownership Committee on Farm and Village Housing '31. Author: (with F D Crawshaw) Farm Mechanics '22; also articles in field. Prof agrl engring and head dept U Ill since '21; State Rural Electrification Com, Nat Safety Council Occupational Advisory Com; childrens Bur US Dept Labor. Am Soc Agrl Engrs (past officer)—Ill Soc Profl Engrs (past officer)—Am Soc Engring Edn—Am Farm Bur Federation—Asso U Profs—Am Forestry Assn—Ill Agrl Assn—Nat Soc Profl Engrs—Sigma Xi—Phi Kappa Phi—Gamma Sigma Delta. The Pines, R.R. 2, Urbana, Ill.

23 LEHMANN, Heinz Edgar. Nitrous oxide (Psychiatric therapy); Afterimages (Objective measurement); Nicotinic acid (Psychiatric therapy); Iron in cerebro-spinal fluid (Brain metabolism). b'11. MD '35 (U Berlin). Development therapeutic administration nitrous oxide in psychiatric disorders until ensueing anoxia produces unconsciousness followed by period of mental facilitation which may be utilized in psychotherapy; discovery method of obtaining objective measurement of some properties of negative afterimage phenomenon through device permitting study of afterimages in small children and uncooperative subjects; demonstration therapeutic effectiveness of massive doses of nicotinic acid in cerebral concussion (traumatic); study of iron content of cerebral spinal fluid and relation to metaboliam of brain cells. Psychiatrist staff Verdun Protestant Hosp Montreal since '37, now clin dir; demonstrator psychiatry McGill U '45-48, lectr psychiatry since '48. Am Psychiatric Assn—Psychol Assn PQ—Montreal Psychoa Soc—Soc for Projective Techniques and Rorschach Inst (F). Verdun Protestant Hospital, Verdun, Can.

10 LEHMANN, Valgene William. Wildlife management (Bobwhite quail, prairie chicken, predation). b'13. BA '35 (U Tex); MS '40 (Tex A&M Coll). Engaged research management, life history and ecology quail and Attwater's prairie chicken, coyote food habits and control methods, relation rainfall upland game increase. Discovered ward drive quail trap, rope census method prairie chickens, truck drag bar for locating bobwhite nests, night poisoning technique coyotes, headquarters cover concept quail management. Author articles in field. Wildlife mgr King Ranch since '46. Am Soc Mammalogists—Wildlife Soc—Tex Acad Sci. King Ranch, Kingsville, Tex.†

11 LEHMANN-HAUPT, Hellmut E. Book arts; Graphic art. b'03. PhD '27 (Frankfort U). Author: Seventy Books About Bookmaking '41; The Terrible Gustave Doré '41. Co-author: The Book in America '39; Bookbinding in America '41; also articles in field. Curator rare books Columbia U '30-37; asst prof books Columbia since '37; publ control officer SHAEF '45; civil arts adm officer Monuments Fine Arts and Archives Sect OMCUS Berlin '46-48. Gutenberg Soc—Grolier Club—Am Inst Graphic Arts—Bibliog Soc Am. 2728 Henry Hudson Parkway, NYC 63.†

12 LEIBLE, Arthur Blank. English literature (Animal symbolism, sixteenth century satire, emblem, Spenser's satire, Milton, sixteenth and seventeenth century animal lore). b'92. BA '15—MA Chem '16—MA Eng '24 (Ind U); PhD '30 (Chicago U). Research and writing on conventions of animal symbolism and satire in Spenser's Mother Hubberd's Tale. Asst dean arts and sci Ind U '41-49, asso prof Eng since '50. Phi Beta Kappa. Indiana University, Bloomington, Ind. H: 515 Hawthorne Drive.

13 LEICESTER, Henry Marshall. Biochemistry of teeth and dental caries; Russia (History of chemistry). b'06. AB '27—MA '28—PhD '30 (Stanford). Research on mechanism of dental caries with special attention to action of phosphatase inhibitors; compilation and evaluation of biochemical data relating to formation and reactions of the teeth; history of chemistry with special attention to history of chemistry in Russia and in California. Co-author: (with Klickstein) A Source Book in Chemistry '52. Editor-in-chief Chymia, vol III '50, vol IV '53. Asst prof biochem Coll Physicians and Surg SF '38-46, asso prof '46-48, prof and head dept physiol scis since '48; adv bd Smith Collection in History of Chem U Pa since '46. ACS—AAAS—Internat Assn Dental Research—Sigma Xi—Alpha Chi Sigma—Phi Lambda Upsilon—Hist Sci Soc. College of Physicians and Surgeons, 344 14th St., SF 3.

14 LEIDECKER, Kurt Friedrich. Oriental philosophy; Scientific German. b'02. Fellow '25-27—PhD '27 (U Chgo); BA '24—MA '25 (Oberlin Coll). Author: Josiah Royce and Indian Thought '31; Pragmatic Approach to Scientific German '41; Yankee Teacher, The Life of William Torrey Harris '46; Volumen Medicinae Paramirum '49; German-English Technical Dictionary of Aeronautics '49; also articles in field. Asst prof philos Mary Washington Coll U Va since '48. Am Philos Assn—Am Oriental Soc. Mary Washington College of the University of Virginia, Fredericksburg, Va.

15 LEIFFER, Murray Howard. Sociology of religion; Community research. b'02. Student '18-19 (Coll City NY); AB '23 (U So Cal); BD '25 (Garrett Bibl Inst); AM '28 (U Chicago); PhD '32 (Northwestern U). Author: City and Church in Transition '38; Manual for Study of the City Church '39; Retirement and Recruitment in Methodist Ministry '44; The Layman Looks at the Minister '47; The Effective City church '49; Methodist Student Work at Colleges and Universities '51; The Methodist Ministry in 1952 '52. With Garrett Bibl Inst Evanston Ill since '29, prof sociology and social ethics since '35, dir bur of social and religious research; ordained to ministry of Methodist Church '27, mem So Cal Conference. Am Sociol Soc —Am Acad Polit and Social Sci—Phi Beta Kappa—Pi Gamma Mu—Alpha Kappa Delta—AAUP. 721 Foster St., Evanston, Ill.☉

16 LEIFSON, Gunnar. Hydrographic surveying; Geodesy. b'00. BS—PG '25 (U Washington). Chief survey sect US Navy Hydrographic Office since '46. Am Geog Soc(F)—Am Geophys Union —Am Congress of Surveying and Mapping—Union Geodesique et Geophysique Internationale (affiliated with research and development bd com on geophysical scis). Hydrographic Office, Navy Department, Washington 25.

17 LEIGH, William Colston. American and English antiques; Sandwich glass. b'01. Ed pub and parochial schools NYC and Portsmouth Virginia; student Columbia University Extension. Author articles in field. Collector and authority on Am and Eng antiques and Sandwich glass; pres W Colston Leigh Inc since '29. 521 Fifth Av., NYC 17.

18 LEIGHTON, Morris Morgan. Geology (Industrial minerals, reservoir and dam sites, glacial deposits). b'87. AB '12—MS '13 (State Univ Ia) PhD '16 (University Chicago). Member Illinois State Planning Commission '35-45; Illinois Postwar Planning Commission '45-47; Advisory Committee to United States Geological Survey. Author: Roadbuilding Sands and Gravels of Washington '19; A Model State Resource Survey '36; Geology of Soil Drifting on the Great Plains '38; Atlas of Illinois Resources '44. Chief Ill Geol Survey since '23; bus editor Econ Geol; mem State Mus Bd; editor State Geol Jour since '49; dir Am Geol Inst '50-51. Chgo Geog Soc(F)—Geol Soc Am(F)—AAAS (F, vice pres)—Am Ceramic Soc(F) — American Assn State Geols—Soc Econ Geols (pres '50) —Chicago Acad Sci—Am Assn Petroleum Geols—Am Inst Mining and Metall Engrs—Am Mining Congress—Ill Soc Engrs—Ill State Acad Sci (pres '30)— Ill Mining Inst (pres '41)—Western Soc Engrs—Royal Soc Arts(F)—US Office Prodn Management (com on metals and minerals '46-46)—Sigma Xi. Frank O Lowden prize in geol; Ia Citation as Distinguished Alumnus '47. 121 Natural Resources Bldg., University of Illinois, Urbana, Ill.☉

19 LEINBACH, Frederick Harold. Animal nutrition and physiology (Beef cattle, sheep). b'01. BS '26 (Ia State Coll); MS '27 (Colo State and A&M Coll); PhD '40 (Cornell U). Director National Livestock Conservation Program Headquarters Chicago '43-44. Pres SD State Coll Brookings since '47. AAAS(F)—Am Soc Animal Prodn—US Livestock Sanitary Assn—Gamma Sigma Delta—Phi Kappa Phi—Sigma Xi. 929 Tenth St., Brookings, S.D.

20 LEITCH, Richard Duddleston. Acid mine waters (Chemistry and occurrence); Safety engineering; Sealing abandoned mines; Warning agents for manufactured gases. b'94. BS '16—ChE '21—MS '22 (Rose Poly Inst). Author articles in field. Chem Terre Haute Ind Water Co '12-16; research chem Rubber Regenerating Co '16-17, E I DuPont de Nemours '17-18, Ia Light Heat & Power Co '19-20; vp Cellulo Co '20-21; US Bur Mines since '22, chief explosives control div '42-45, bur safety engr since '45. Second lt US Army World War I. Nat Research Council—Nat Mine Rescue Assn —Coal Mining Inst Am—Nat Rifle Assn—Pittsburgh Coal Mining Inst— Fed Interdep Safety Council—Fed Fire Council—Am Soc Safety Engrs. 307 Bureau of Mines, College Park, Md.

21 LELAND, Simeon Elbridge. Government finance (Taxation, public debts); Higher education (Administration). born '97 AB '18—LLD '47 (De Pauw U); AM '19 (U Ky); PhD '26 (U Chicago). Author: Taxation in Kentucky '20; The Classified Property Tax in the United States '28; also articles in field. Prof econ and dean coll liberal arts Northwestern U since '46. Am Econ Assn—Nat Tax Assn— Royal Econ Soc—Acad of Polit Sci— Phi Beta Kappa. Awarded Hart Schaffner & Marx Econ Prize (second prize) 1926. Northwestern University, Pearsons Hall, Evanston, Ill. H: 2702 Sheridan Rd.☉

22 LEMBERGER, W(illia)m A. Biological specimens. b'14. Specializing in production of frogs, turtles and biological specimens for educational and research establishments. AAAS—Am Soc Ichthologists and Herpetologists. The Lemberger Co., 1436 S. Park Av., Oshkosh, Wis.

23 LEMCKE, Karl Wolfgang. Bridges. b'86. ME '08 (Stevens Inst). Design suspension bridges, bascule bridges, vertical lift bridges, fixed arch bridges; most retaining walls for Cross Bronx Express Way NYC; Manasquan River Bridge New Jersey; four highway bridges for Virginia; Hanover skew bascule bridges over Miami Canal Fla. Detailer and shop insp Am Bridge Co '08-12; engr erection dept and asst sales engr Bethlehem Steel Bridge Corp '12-18; designer Hardesty and Hanover since '38, asso engr since '49. Profl engr NY. Am Soc CE—Am Concrete Inst—Am Welding Soc. Hardesty and Hanover, 101 Park Av., NYC 17.

24 LEMKE, Arthur Athniel. Sewage (Activated sludge). b'13. BS (CE) '34 —MS '35—CE '46 (U Wis). Design activated sludge plants; study hydraulics of activated sludge sewage treatment plants and air lift pumps; development method for selection air main sizes based on allowable pressure drop in the main. Author article: Flow of Air in Pipes (thesis) '46. Mgr hydraulic and equipment engring dept sewage equipment div Chicago Pump Co since '46. Am Soc CE—Central States Sewage and Indsl Wastes Assn. Profl engr Ill, Wis. Chicago Pump Co., 622 W. Diversey, Chgo 14. H: 529 W. Belden Av.

25 LEMMON, Allen B. Fertilizing materials; Economic poisons; Spray residue. b'08. AB '30—EP '32 (Stanford U). Author articles in field. With Calif Dept Agr since '33 as inspector, senior inspector and district inspector of economic poisons and fertilizers, chief bur chem since '46. Assn Econ Entomol—Assn Official Agrl Chems—Assn Econ Poisons Control Officials (exec com '48)—Assn Am Fertilizer Control Ofcls (vp '47, pres '48). 243 Mull Building, 1125 10th St., Sacramento 14, Calif.†

10 LEMMON, Dwight M(oulton). Geology and economics of tungsten deposits. b'12. AB '32—AM '35—PhD '37 (Stanford U). Author articles in field. Geol US Geol Survey since '39, sr geol since '48. Eighteenth Internat Geol Congress London '48. Colo Sci Soc—Am Inst Mining Engrs—Geol Soc Wash—Soc Econ Geols—Geol Soc Am (F)—Mineral Soc Am—AAAS—Sigma Xi. United States Geological Survey, Geologic Branch, Federal Center, Denver 14.

11 LEMON, Paul C(lipfell). Forests of northeastern United States (Ecology, classification, management); Native pine woods (Georgia coastal plain); Forestry and wildlife management; Ponderosa pine. b'12. AB '35 (U Neb); MSc '36 (U Ill); PhD '43 (U Minn). Holds commercial airplane pilot's license. Author articles in field. Asst prof biol NY State Coll since '48. Soc Am Foresters (jr)—Ecol Soc Am—Sigma Xi. Biology Department, New York State College, Albany, N.Y.†

12 LENDRUM, James Thoburn. Architectural housing; Early architecture of southeastern Michigan. b'07. Student '25-26 (O Wesleyan U); BS '30 (U Mich); MS '46 (U Ill). Special study in early architecture of southeastern Michigan. Co-author: (with F M Porter) Architectural Projection; also articles in field. Teacher in general engring dept U Ill '30-44; asso coordinator small homes council and asso prof dept gen engring and drawing '44-49. Acting dir Small Homes Council since '49. Small Homes Council, Mumford House, Urbana, Ill.

13 LENEL, Fritz Victor. Powder metallurgy. b'07. Student '25-26 (U Breslau); '26-27 (U Munich); PhD '31 (U Heidelberg); '31-33 (U Goettingen). Research in development of powder metallurgy as applied to the production of structural parts from iron powder. Author articles in field. Metall Charles Hardy Inc NYC '33-37, Moraine Products div Gen Motors '37-47; asso prof metall engring Rensselaer Poly Inst since '49. Am Inst Mining & Metall Engrs—Am Soc Metals. Rensselaer Polytechnic Institute, Troy, N.Y.†

14 LENEY, Lawrence. Wood technology, anatomy and utilization; Photomicrography and microtechnique of woody materials. b'17. MS '48 (NY State Coll Forestry). Research on surface-active agents and detergents for softening wood preparatory to sectioning '48. Instr wood tech NY State Coll Forestry since '46. Forest Products Research Soc—Bot Soc Am—Soc Am Foresters. Wood Technology Department, New York State College of Forestry, Syracuse 10, N.Y.†

15 LENGYEL, Emil. Southeastern Europe (History and economics); Middle East (History and economics). b '95. Student '01-13 (Budapest Secondary Schs); LLD '18 (Royal Hungarian U). Author: Cattle Car Express '31; Hitler '32; The Cauldron Boils '32; The New Deal in Europe '34; Millions of Dictators '36; The Danube '39; Turkey '41; Dakar: Outpost of Two Hemispheres '41; Siberia '43; America's Role in World Affairs '45;

They Came from Hungary '47; (film scenario) World in Revolt. Co-author: Eye Witness; Nazism: An Assault on Civilization; Modern World Politics; Origin and Consequences of World War II; As We See Russia. With NYU Sch Edn since '39, asso prof since '47. Served in Austro-Hungarian Army, World War I; prisoner in Siberia 20 months. Acad Polit Sci—Authors League Am—AAUP—NEA—Fgn Policy Assn—PEN Club—Overseas Press Club. New York University, Washington Square, NYC 3.†⊚

16 LENON, Robert. Mining methods (Management). b'08. BS (Mining engr) '30 (U Ariz). Management and operation prospects and mines; surveys of claims and mines; examinations, reports, and valuation of prospects and mines. Author article: Discussion of Mineral Land Surveys in Western States '49. Contributor: Peele's Mining Engineers Handbook '41. Mineral surveyor Gen Land Office '32-40 and '46-49; supervision and development heavy-mining methods for copper in large ore bodies Phelps Dodge Corp Bisbee Ariz '35-40; supervision gold mining in small veins Long Valley Mines & Mill Pine Valley Cal '40; regional mineral surveyor Bur Land Management Ariz, NM, Okla, and Tex since '50. AIMME—Nat Soc Profl Engrs. Profl mining engr Ariz. 325 McKeown Av., Patagonia, Ariz.

17 LENT, Constantin Paul. Research engineer; Rockets and jets. b'08. Grad engr '27 (U Mittweida, Germany); '28-29 (NYC). Holder seven US Patents. Author: True Democracy '39; Rocket Research '44; Rocketry '47; Food Enough For All '47; Atom '48; The Art of Drafting and Machine Design '49; of War and Revolt '49; The Tarpon '49. Editor: Quarterly Rocket-Jet Flying; New Stand; Democracy In Action; also articles in field. Pres Nat Design and Drafting Co, Pen-Ink Pub Co, Photofilm Co, Pan-Electric Co; self employed since '42. Am Rocket Soc (vp '44). 156 West 105 St., NYC.

18 LENZEN, Victor F. Philosophy of science; Scientific methodology; Theory of knowledge; History of physics; Analytical dynamics; Statistical mechanics. b'90. BS '13 (U Calif); PhD '16 (Harvard); Harvard Sheldon fellow '16-17 (Cambridge, Eng, and Paris). Author: The Nature of Physical Theory '31; Procedures of Empirical Science '38; The Figure of Dionysos on the Siphnian Frieze '46; also articles in field. Instr to asst prof '21-39, prof physics U Calif since '39. Am Phys Soc(F) — Am Math Soc — Am Philos Assn (pres Pacific div '44) — History of Sci Soc — Am Assn Physics Teachers—Archeol Inst Am—Phi Beta Kappa. Guggenheim fellow, Goettingen Germany '27-28. Physics Department, University of California, Berkeley 4.⊚

19 LEONARD, Frederick Charles. Meteorites (Meteorites); Astronomy (Visual double stars). b'96. SB '18—SM '19 (U Chicago); PhD '21 (U Calif). On Expedition of Meteoritical Society which recovered the 1¼-ton Goose Lake Modoc County California siderite or nickel-iron meteorite '39; was first person to announce and describe that specimen; owner of a representative collection of meteorites; has pioneered in the establishment of the science of meteoritics and has contributed ideas and terms to that science. Author: An Investigation of the Spectra of Visual Double Stars '23; A Catalog of Provisional Coördinate Numbers for the Meteoritic Falls of the World '46; also articles in field. Prof astron U Calif (Los Angeles) since '44, organizer

dept astron '31, chmn dept '31-39, '40-43, '45-46; research associate Inst Meteoritics U NM since '46. Royal Astron Soc Eng—AAAS—Meteoritical Soc (organizer '33, pres '33-37, editor since '33, councilor '37-41)—Am Astron Soc—Astron Soc Pacific—Brit Astron Assn—Internat Astron Union (com on meteors)—Am Meteor Soc—Phi Beta Kappa—Sigma Xi. Department of Astronomy, University of California, LA 24.†⊚

20 LEONARD, Oliver Andrew. Nut grass; Weed control in cotton. b'11. BS '33—MS '35 (Washington State Coll); PhD '37 (Ia State Coll). Research on root development of cotton, sweet potatoes, mineral nutrition of sweet potatoes; studies on the control of nut grass since '39; first to show annual weeds could be controlled in cotton using the dinitro herbicides applied to the soil right after planting. Author articles in field. Instr bot, gen biol, plant pathol Tex A&M Coll '37-39; with Miss Agrl Expt Sta State Coll '39-50; botany div Calif Agrl Expt sta since '50. American Soc Agronomy—Bot Soc Am—Am Soc Hort Sci. Agricultural Experiment Station, State College, Miss.†

21 LEONARD, Reid Hayward. Wood sugars; Fermentation chemistry. b'18. BSA '40 (U Vt); MS '42 (W Va U); PhD '47—fellow '42-44, '45-46 (U Wis). Author articles in field. Asso chem US Forest Products Lab '43-45; research chem Salvo Chem Corp '47; research chem Newport Inds Inc since '47. Am Chem Soc—AAAS—Phi Beta Kappa—Sigma Xi. Newport Industries, Inc., Pensacola, Fla.†

22 LEONARD, V. A. Police organization and administration. b'98. BS '38 (Tex Wesleyan Coll Ft Worth); AM '39 (Tex Christian Coll); PhD '49 (O State U). Studied police systems in Eng, France, Italy, Switzerland, Belgium, and Holland, summer '47. Author: Police Communication Systems '38; Survey and Reorganization of Police Department Seattle '48. Editor: Police Science Series; asso editor Jour Criminal Law and Criminology since '44. Entered police service Police Dept City of Berkeley Cal as patrolman '25, follow-up officer '27-29, identification expert '30-32, supt records and identification '32-33, Ft Worth, Tex '34-39; prof and chmn dept police sci and adminstrn State Coll Wash Pullman since '41. Internat Assn Chiefs of Police—Internat Assn for Identification (past pres Tex div)—Alpha Phi Sigma—Pi Sigma Alpha. H: 16 Harvey Rd., Pullman, Wash.†⊚

23 LEONARD, Warren Henry. Field crops (Cereals); Barley genetics; Applied statistics; Japanese agriculture. b'00. BS '26 (Colo A&M Coll); MS '30 (U Neb); PhD '40 (U Minn). Research on cultural methods of corn, effect of foreign pollen, and breeding; research on inheritance of fertility in barley; research on sampling and statistical treatment of percentage data; formulated policies for Japanese agriculture for Supreme Commander Allied Powers Tokyo. Co-author: (with Andrew Clark) Field Plot Technique '39; (with John H Martin) Principles of Field Crop Production '49; (with Robert S Whitney) Field Crops in Colorado '50. With Colo A&M Coll '26-28, '29-42, '46-48, since '49, prof agron since '46; chief agr div Natural Resources Sect SCAP '45-46, '48-49. AA AS(F)—Am Soc Agron—Bot Soc Am—Am Genetics Assn—Am Statis Assn—Biometrics Soc—Genetics Soc Japan—Sigma Xi. Department of Agronomy, Colorado A&M College, Fort Collins, Colo.

10 LEOPOLD, Charles S. Electrical engineering; Air conditioning; Refrigeration; Ventilating; Heating. b'96. BS in EE '17—EE '47 (U Pa). Designed air conditioning for US Capitol and (old) House Office Building, Palmer House Chicago, Pennsylvania State Capitol, House and Senate Chambers, Madison Square Garden and Bankers Life Building Des Moines; also designed air conditioning and electricity Pentagon Building. Author articles: Mechanism of Heat Transfer, Panel Cooling, Heat Storage; Hydraulic Analogue for the Solution of Problems of Thermal Storage, Radiation, Convection and Conduction. Cons engr in office under own name Phila since '22. Am Soc Refrigerating Engrs (Pres '46) —Am Soc Heating Ventilating Engrs (mem council)—Sigma Xi—Eta Kappa Nu. 213 S. Broad St., Phila 7⊙

11 LEOPOLD, Richard William. American diplomatic history. b'12. AB '33 (Princeton U); AM '34—PhD '38 (Harvard). Robert Dale Owen: A Biography (awarded John H Dunning Prize, Am Historical Assn for best manuscript in field of Am history of '40) '40; annual article on history in American Year Book '41, '46-50; articles in field. Inst to asst prof hist Harvard U '37-48; asso prof Am hist Northwestern U since '48. Phi Beta Kappa—Am Hist Assn—Miss Valley Hist Assn—So Hist Assn—Naval Hist Found. Pre-doctoral field fellow, Social Science Research Council '35-36; Princeton fellowship Harvard '33-34; Edward Austin fellow '34-35; Coolidge fellow '36-37. Department of History, Northwestern University, Evanston, Ill.

12 LeROY, Leslie W. Stratigraphic geology. b'09. Geol E '33—Dr Geol E '45 (Colo Sch Mines). Author articles in field. Stratigraphic geol Standard Oil Co '34-37, '46-48; Nederlandsche Pacific Petroleum Maatschapij Dutch East Indies '37-42; instr to professor geol Colo Sch Mines since '42. Am Assn Pet Geol—Geol Soc Am(F)—Soc Econ Paleontologists and Mineralogists —AAAS. Colorado School of Mines, Golden, Colo.

13 LESLAU, Wolf. Ethiopic studies. b'06. Licencié-ès-lettres (Sorbonne Paris); élève diplomé de l'Ecole des Hautes Etudes (Paris); élève diplomé de l'école Nationale des langues Orientales (Paris). Field trip to Ethiopia '46-47. Author articles: Records of a South Ethiopic Language '45; Bibliography of the Semitic Languages of Ethiopia '45; Short Grammer of Tigre '45; other articles in field. Asso prof Semitic The Asia Inst NY since '46. Am Oriental Soc—Linguistic Soc Am —Linguistic Circle NY—Societe Asiatique Paris—Societe de Linguistique de Paris. Guggenheim fellow '46-48; fellow Am Philos Soc '43, '48-49. The Asia Institute, 7 East 70th St., NYC 21.†

14 LESSELLS, John Moyes. Applied mechanics; Materials. b'88. Student '04-10 (Lauder Tech Sch); '11-12 (Heriot-Watt Coll); BS '15 (Glasgow U). Research in fatigue of materials. Author: Applied Elasticity (with S Timoshenko) '25. Editor: Stephen Timoshenko 60th Anniversary Volume '38; Jour Applied Mechanics; editorial bd Quarterly of Applied Mechanics. Apprentice Dunfermline '04-10; insp aircraft materials Brit War Office London '15-17; spl engr Rolls-Royce Ltd '17-19; mgr mech div research labs Westinghouse Elec and Mfg Co '20-31, mgr engring '31-35; asso prof mech engring MIT since '36; president Lessells and Assos Boston since '46. ASME—SAE—Am Soc Testing Materials—Instn Mech Engrs London—Iron

and Steel Inst London. Fellow Acad Arts and Sciences—Awarded Lauder (Carnegie) Scholarship '12—Bernard Hall prize Inst Mech Engrs London '26—Levy medal (with Dr C W MacGregor) Franklin Inst '41. 984 Memorial Drive, Cambridge 38, Mass.⊙

15 LESSENBERRY, D. D. Business education; Typewriting. b'96. BS '23 (Duquesne U); AM '34 (NYU); LLD '43 (Westminster Coll). Author: 20th Century Typewriting (coll edit) '30 '42 (4th edit with S J Wanous) '47; 20th Century Typewriting (complete) '27 '33 (4th edit) '42 (5th edit with T J Crawford). Director of courses in comml edn and prof edn U Pittsburgh since '30. Nat Comml Tchrs Fedn(nat pres '35)—Eastern Comml Tchrs Assn (pres '44)—NEA—Tri-State Bus Edn Assn(pres '42)—Phi Delta Kappa— Kappa Phi Kappa—Delta Delta Lambda—Delta Pi Epsilon (nat pres '41-42). University of Pittsburgh, Pitts 13. H: 1027 Morewood Av.⊙

16 LESSER, Alexander. American Indians; Intergroup relations. b'02. AB '23—PhD work completed '29 (Columbia); '20-25 (New Sch for Social Research). Field research among American Indians on social life and conditions, religion, linguistics and problems of assimilation and readjustment to national culture. Author: Pawnee Ghost Dance Hand Game '32. Co-author: Social Anthropolgy '31; also articles in field. Social sci analyst Office Coordinator Inter-American Affairs '43-44; chief Econ Studies Sec, Latin Am Div OSS '45; chief North and West Coast Countries Latin Am Div Office Research Intelligence U S Dept State '45-47; exec dir Assn Am Indian Affairs Inc; mng editor The American Indian. Am Anthrop Assn (council since '31, rep to Nat Research Council since '47) — Am Ethnol Soc (sec-treas '33-38, vp '39-41, editor '37-40, dir '42-44)—Soc Applied Anthrop—Am Folklore Soc (council '33-40)—Sigma Xi. Fellow Social Sci Research Council '29-30, Am Council Learned Socs '31-32. Association on American Indian Affairs, 48 E. 86 St., NYC.†

17 LESSER, Milton Albert. Glycerine and soap; Drugs and pharmaceuticals; Sanitary supplies; Sanitation. b'07. BS '31 (NYC). Author: Glycerine, Its Role in Medicine '36; Glycerine, Its Industrial and Commercial Applications '45; Soap in Industry '46; also articles in field. Tech writer and chem consultant since '39; tech editor Drug and Cosmetic Industry since '43; contbg asso Soap and San Chems since '44. Am Chem Soc—AAAS—Am Pharm Assn. Drug and Cosmetic Industry, 101 W. 31st St., NYC 1.

18 LESSING, Ferdinand D. Cult and iconography of Tibetan Buddhism. b '82. Student '02-05—PhD '46 (U Berlin). Studied Tibetan Buddhism with native priests in temples of North China and Inner Mongolia '30-32, in West China Cheng-tu '47. Author: Yung-ho-Kung, an Iconography of the Lamaist Cathedral in Peking (with notes on Lamaist iconography and cult) '42. U Cal Berkeley. Am Oriental Soc—Far Eastern Assn—Gesellschaft fur Natur-und Volkerkunde Ostasiens. Lowell lectr Lamaism '46-51; Knight comdr North Star (Sweden). University of California, Berkeley 4, Cal. H: 660 Euclid Av., Berkeley 8.

19 LESTER, Bernard. Marketing (Distribution and sale of machinery and equipment for industrial purposes). b'81. BS '04—MS '07 (Haverford Coll); '10 (U Pittsburgh). Author: Marketing Industrial Equipment '35; Applied Economics for Engineers '39;

Sales Engineering '40, rev '49; also articles in field. With Westinghouse Elec & Mfg Co becoming comml engr, mgr small motor dept, asst indsl sales mgr, mgr resale dept, spl rep, mgr indsl dept East Pittsburgh Pa '05-47; lecturer grad sch U Pittsburgh '35-39, Stevens Inst NYU, Brooklyn Poly Inst; cons on machinery and equipment marketing and sales training since '47. ASME—AIEE—Am Marketing Soc— ASEE—Am Management Assn (planning com marketing div)—Newcomen Soc Am. 140 Cedar St., NYC 6.†

20 LESTER, Charles Turner. Organic chemistry (Abnormal Grignard reactions, indigosols production, carbonyl compounds). b'11. AB '32—MA '34 (Emory U); PhD '41 (Pa State Coll). Author articles in field. Holder US patents assigned Am Cyanamid Co. Prof chem Emory U since '50. Am Chem Soc(chmn Ga sect '48)—NY Acad Scis—Sigma Xi—Phi Beta Kappa— Phi Kappa Phi. Chemistry Department, Emory University, Georgia.†

21 LESTER, James George. Petrography; Mineralogy; Geology of Georgia; Volcanoes. b'97. BS '18—MS '23 (Emory U); MS '26 (Ga Inst Tech); PhD '38 (U Colo). Author articles in field. With Emory U since '19, prof geol and chmn dept since '38. Ga Mineral Soc—Ga Soc Naturalists—Ga Acad Sci(F)—SE Geol Soc—Carolina Geol Soc—Sigma Xi—Phi Beta Kappa—Geol Soc Am—Soc Engring Geol —Geophysical Union. Emory University, Ga.

22 LETICHE, J. M. International trade; Trade agreements. b'18. Allen Oliver fellow '40-41—BA '40—MA '41 (McGill U); PhD candidate '43—Marshall Field fellow '41-43, Hillman Foundation fellow '43-44 (U Chicago). Author: Reciprocal Trade Agreements in the World Economy '48; also articles in field. Council on Foreign Relations '45-46; lecturer dept econs U Calif since '47, Faculty Institute Slavic Studies since '48. Am Econ Assn— Econometrica Soc — World Affairs Council Calif—Commonwealth Club. Department of Economics, 119 South Hall, University of California, Berkeley.

23 LEUTERMAN, Theodore, O. S. B. Cassinese liturgy (Eleventh century). b'12. BA magna cum laude (St Benedict's Coll); BTh '37—Licentiate Theol '39—STD '41 (Internat Benedictine Coll Pontifical U Sant Anselmo Rome). Research study '39-41 in manuscripts pertaining to the eleventh century Cassinese liturgy in Archives of Montecassino Abbey, Italy, and Vatican Library. Author articles in field. Prof St Benedict's Abbey Sch Theol since '41, instr St Benedict's Coll since '41, dir divinity students since '45, dir retreats for laymen since '47. Am Benedictine Acad. St. Benedict's Abbey, Atchison, Kan.

24 LEUTGOEB, Rosalia Aloisia. Chemistry (Glucuronic acid, dried yeast, synthetic rubber). b'01. BS '35 —MS '36—PhD '38 (Marquette U). Author articles in field. Red Star Yeast Co '42-44; research chem synthetic rubber Govt Labs Akron O '44-45; asso prof chem Mundelein Coll since '45. Am Chem Soc.

25 LEVENSON, Harold Samuel. Coffee technology. b'16. BS in chem engring '37—MS '39—PhD '41 (Lehigh U). Research on physical chemistry of coffee roasting and staling, manufacture soluble coffee, quality control coffee roasting plant. Granted patent in field. With Gen Foods Corp since '41, plant chem Maxwell House Coffee Div '47-52, research mgr Maxwell House div Hoboken NJ since '52. Inst

Food Tech—ACS—Am Soc Quality Control. Maxwell House Div., General Foods Corp., Hoboken, N.J.

10 LEVENTHAL, Harold. Law (Trade regulation; Administrative law); Government (Administrative management). b'15. AB '34—LLB '36 (Columbia). Editor-in-chief Columbia Law Review '35-36; admitted NY bar '36, DC '46; law sec Justice Harlan F Stone Supreme Ct US '36-37, Justice Stanley Reed '38; staff Office of Solicitor Gen '38-39; chief litigation Bituminous Coal Div, US Dept Interior '39-40; asst gen counsel OPA '40-43; staff Justice Jackson, Nuernberg Trials '45-46; exec officer task force on ind regulatory commns Hoover Commn '48; pvt practice law Washington '46-51, since '52; chief counsel OPS '51-52. Fed Bar Assn (nat council)— DC Bar Assn—Phi Beta Kappa. 1632 K St., Washington 6.⊙

11 LEVER, Chauncey Waldo. Public relations (Community); Chamber of Commerce (Administration). b'25. Student '42-43 '46-48—BS (Wofford Coll); '43-44 (The Citadel). Originator The Greenwood Plan for piercing the Iron Curtain and promoting permanent peace; study of Chamber of Commerce administration and public relations, search for plan for organizations and groups on local level to survey citizenry, screen ideas, and transmit through some medium such as Voice of America and Radio Free Europe to other sections of world. Editor: The Cracker Barrel (ofcl publ Ga State C of C Execs Assn) '49-50. Exec dir Jesup and Wayne County Ga Chamber of Commerce '48-50; vp Ga C of C Execs Assn '49-50; exec sec US 25 Highway Assn Inc '49-50; exec dir Greenwood SC C of C since '50. Greenwood Chamber of Commerce, Suite 200, The Grier Bldg., Greenwood Chamber of Commerce, Suite 200, The Grier Bldg., Greenwood, S.C. H: 145 Bailey Circle.

12 LEVERING, Samuel Ralph. World federalism. b'08. BS '30—PhD Candidate (Cornell U). Original member and joint founder World Federalists USA Inc '45, United World Federalists USA Inc '47, executive council since origin, chmn committee on organization and field work '47-50, executive director '47, chairman Virginia section '47-48; chairman Peace Board five years meeting of Friends since '45, vice-chairman Friends committee on National Legislation '47-50, regional director American Friends Service Committee '45-46. Author: World Government, the Path to Peace '46; also articles in field. Orchardist since '39. Am Soc Hort Sci —United World Federalists—Am Assn for United Nations—Soc of Friends. R. 2, Ararat, Va.

13 LEVERONE, Louis Edward. Vocational guidance. b'80. BS '04 (Dartmouth Coll); '12 (John Marshall Law Sch); LLD '51 (Bradley U). Founder vocational guidance committee Dartmouth College '37; chairman Illinois Development Council since '43; board chairman Illinois Citizenship Conference since '38; board of managers National Air Council since '48; member Council of Social Agencies Chicago, and Illinois Post War Planning Committee; honorary chairman Illinois Council Managers Committee. Dir Northwestern U Settlement '36-43, pres '40-43. Phi Gamma Delta (founder vocational bureau '23, bd govs since '36, pres '43-46)—Nat Aero Assn (pres since '48). 1430 Merchandise Mart, Chgo 54.

14 LEVESQUE, Lucien. Biogeography; Ecology. b'02. LicSc Nat '40— MSc '43—DSc '49 (Univ Montreal Que). Investigation on flora of Lake Nominingue region Quebec; studies Hepatica acutiloba; pollen analyses of Quebec bogs. Author articles: Biological Spectrum of Lake Nominingue Region Quebec '47; Geographical Relations in the Floristical Elements of the Lake Nominingue Region Quebec '47; Distribution of Hepatica acutiloba '49, and others. Research asst Service de Biogeographie U Montreal since'44, asst dir since '49, lectr biogeography U Montreal since '47. Soc Natural Hist Can—Soc Geog Montreal—Bot Soc Am —Am Soc Plant Taxonomists—AAAS —Ecol Soc Am—Internat Assn Plant Taxonomy. Service de Biogeographie, Universite de Montreal, 2900 Boulevard du Mont-Royal, Montreal 26, Can.

15 LEVI, Wendell Mitchell. Pigeons. b'91. AB '12 (Coll Charleston); PhB '15—JD cum laude '15 (U Chicago). Discovery and creation, with others, auto-sexing of pigeons; studies in history, breeds, anatomy, physiology, genetics, behavior, diseases, feeding, housing, commercial production, racing, exhibiting all types pigeons. Author: The Pigeon '41; Making Pigeons Pay '46. Editor: Question and Answer Dept American Pigeon Journal since '27. Pres Palmetto Pigeon Plant since '23. Served in AUS in charge pigeon sect SE Dept Signal Corps '17-18. Nat Pigeon Assn—Am Pigeon Club—Am Carneau Assn—Poultry Sci Assn— World's Poultry Sci Assn—Am Genetic Assn. P.O. Drawer 751, Sumter, S.C.

16 LEVINE, Harold. Nutrition; Biochemistry (Vitamins, yeast, inorganic elements). b'00. BS '22 (Wesleyan U); PhD '26 (Yale). Author articles in field. Holder US patent 1741194 '29, co-holder patent 2295036 '42. With Pabst Brewing Co '34-49. Inst Food Tech—Assn Vitamin Chems—Am Chem Soc—Am Assn Biol Chems—Am Inst Nutrition—Sigma Xi. 941 E. Sylvan Ave., Milwaukee, Wis.†

17 LEVINE, Morris. Natural gas (Chemistry). b'98. BS '22—PhD '25 (U Chicago); MS '23 (U Ill). Research on preparation iron carbonyl and its possibilities as antiknock agent, conversion natural gas to acetylene, concentration and purification acetylene, development dorcol as solvent for acetylene, conversion petroleum to aromatic hydrocarbons. Granted patents on gasoline refining, gas polymerization and acetylene. Research chem Universal Oil Products Co '26-31; research chem Mariner and Hoskins '31-32; research chem Tex Pacific Coal and Oil Co '32-33; dir research and chief chem S Prodn Co Inc since '33. Sigma Xi—ACS—Am Inst Chem(F). P.O. Box 670, Ft. Worth.

18 LEVITT, I(srael) M(onroe). Applied optics; Photoelectric photometry; Popularization of science; Electronic simulation systems. b'08. BS '32 (Drexel Inst); AM '37—PhD '48 (U Pa). Author: Precision Laboratory Manual '32. Co-author: Star Maps for Beginner's (with R K Marshall) '40. Invented emergency oxygen breather; co-invented multiplier shield for reducing signal to noise ratio in photometers, pulse counting photoelectric photometer. Associate dir in charge astron, photography, seismology Franklin Inst since '49; director Fels Planetarium since '49; research asst Cook observatory '35-41; research asst U Pa '41-42; physicist Franklin Inst Lab for research and develop '42-48. AAAS —Rittenhouse Astron Soc—Am Astron Soc—Pa Acad Scis—British Astron Soc —British Interplanetary Soc—American Rocket Soc. The Franklin Inst., Phila. 3.

19 LEVORSEN, Arville Irving. Petroleum geology. b'94. EM '17—DS (hon) '47 (Minn U); DE (hon) '42 (Colo Sch Mines). Representative of American Association Petroleum Geologists on National Research Council. Editor: Possible Future Oil Provinces of US and Canada '41; Statigraphic Type Oil Fields '41. Geologist Greenwood Co, Getzandaner and Johnston, and Gypsy Oil Co '1726; chief geologist Philmack Co and Independent Oil Co '26-30; cons geologist '30-34, '36-45; chief geologist Tidewater Oil Co '34-36; prof and dean sch mineral sciences Stanford U '45-49. 27th Engrs (mining) US Army '18-19. Am Assn Petroleum Geol—Soc Belgium—Geol Soc Am(F)—Am Geog Soc(F). 164 Encinal Av., Menlo Park, Atherton, Cal.⊙

20 LEVOWITZ, David. Dairy products; Food technology. b'08. BS '27 (Coll City NY); MS '29—PhD '36 (Rutgers U). Research in standardization of analytical methods for control of fluid milk products; development dairy products control systems for governmental agencies; continuous process for conversion cream to butter without churning; calibration of potencies of disinfectants of various types; development food processing systems and equipment, particularly packaging specialties. Dir NJ Dairy Labs since '36; analyst dairy products NJ State Dept Agr since '31; dairy products control officer various NJ municipalities since '29. Sigma Xi— Phi Lambda Upsilon—Am Dairy Sci Assn—Soc Am Bact—Inst Food Tech —Internat Assn Milk and Food San— ACS—NY, Vt, Conn, Pa milk sans. 222-26 Easton Av., New Brunswick, N.J.

21 LEVY, Maurice Lewis. Radio receiver circuits; Frequency modulation circuit development; High fidelity audio and frequency modulation radio receivers. b'02. BS in elec engring '24 (Union Coll). Development overload limiter for audio circuits, high power audio output circuits for radio receivers, and electronic applications to infra-red circuits; experiment, measurement, and field test of narrow and wide band frequency modulation; research and development high fidelity radio receivers using overcoupled circuits; design audio circuits for high fidelity receivers; director television receiver circuit design. Author articles: Automatic Volume Control Circuits; Automatic Frequency Compensation Circuits; Wide Band and Narrow Band Frequency Modulation Studies and Measurements '43; Audio Amplifier Limiter Circuits to Prevent Overload. Engr Stromberg Carlson Co '24-43, asst chief radio engr '36-43; chief engr spl products Emerson Radio & Phonograph Corp '43-49; staff cons television Philco Co Phila '49; dir spl engring Teletone Radio NYC '49-50, dir engring '50-52; dir engring Video Products Corp since '52. Inst Radio Engrs—Radio Television Mfg Assn. Video Products Corp., 42 West St., Red Bank, N.J.

22 LEWENTHAL, Reeves. Art; Crystal. b'09. Student '28 (Slade Sch London Eng); ext course '26-27 (U Mich). Member New York City Commission for Adult Education '35-37; member art advisory committee War Department '42; expert consultant for art to Chief of Engrs US Army '42. Dir pub relations Nat Acad '29-34, Beaux Arts Inst '30-31; Municipal Art Soc NY '30-33, Soc Am Etchers '29-34, Allied Artists of Am '29-34; pres Asso Am Artists '34-44, chmn bd since '44. Crystal Collectors' Soc-(sec)—Am Inst Graphic Art—Acad Polit Sci. Gold medal for contribution to Am art from Nat Commn to Advance Am Art '32. 711 Fifth Av., NYC.†Ⓖ

10 LEWINSKI, Robert John. Psychometric screening tests; Utilization of psychological testing methods; Selection of personnel; Psychological aspects of migraine. b'12. PhB '34 (U Toledo); AM '36—PhD '39 (State U Ia). Research on differential diagnosis by psychometric tests in epilepsy, anxiety neurosis, and migraine, use psychological testing methods in personnel selection. Contributor: Case Histories in Clinical and Abnormal Psychology '47. Dir, chief clin psychol Juvenile Court Psychol Clin '39-41; with The Great Atlantic & Pacific Tea Co since '46, personnel mgr from '48. Am Psychol Assn(F)—Midwestern Psychol Assn—Assn Mil Surgeons US—Sigma Xi—Gamma Alpha (pres Ia chpt '38). Personnel Department, Great Atlantic & Pacific Tea Co., 51 S. State St., Indpls 1. H: 819 Oaklawn St. N.E., Grand Rapids, Mich.

11 LEWIS, Alberta Anne Lochman. Colonial heraldry. Student '96-97 (Moravian Coll); '99-00 (Moore Inst Art Phila); '00 (U Pa.) Author articles in field. Heraldic artist since '20; writer, lecturer heraldry and related subjects. Pa Acad Fine Arts —DAR—Daughters of 1812 (hon pres) —Daughters Colonial Wars (hon state pres) — Pa Soc Colonial Dames Am. Langdon Manor, 8250 Crittenden St., Chestnut Hill, Phila. 18.†

12 LEWIS, Arthur Walther. Lubricating oils. b'05. BS '27—PhD '34 (Cornell U). Research catalytic cracking and refining of naphthas, lubricating oil processing. Holds 15 patents in field of lubricating oil additives and preservative lubricating oils. Author articles in field. Development engr lubricating oil Tide Water Associated Oil Co Bayonne NJ '34-36, research chem '36-44, research supervisor since '44. Am Chem Soc—SAE—Electrochem Soc—Sigma Xi. Tide Water Associated Oil Company, East 22 St., Bayonne, N.J.

13 LEWIS, Cleona. Economics (International trade and finance). b'85. PhB '17—AM '21 (U Chicago); PhD '30 (Brookings Instn). Author: The International Accounts '27; America's Stake in International Investments '38; Nazi Europe and World Trade '41; Debtor and Creditor Countries '38; The United States and Foreign Investment Problems '49. Co-author: (with H G Moulton) The French Debt Problem '26; (with E G Nourse and others) America's Capacity to Consume '34; (with H G Moulton et al) Capital Expansion, Employment and Economic Stability '40; (with C K Leith and J W Furness) World Minerals and World Peace '43. Mem staff Inst of Economics (now Brookings Instn) '22-50. Am Statis Assn. 220 Orchard St., Danville, Ill.Ⓖ

14 LEWIS, Edward Shakespear. American Negro (Problems); Housing and employment problems (Minority groups); Human relations (Education problems). born '01. PhB '25 (University Chicago); Am '39 (U Pa). Board of directors Welfare Council of New York City, Citizens Housing Council of New York City Harlem Defense Recreation Center and other similar organizations; adviser to superintendent of New York City Schools; committee on Planned Parenthood of America; committee on race relations Uptown Chamber of Commerce; secretary Governor's Committee on Problems of Negro Population of Maryland '42; National Labor Relations Board Region four '40. Author articles in field. Exec dir Urban League of Greater NY since '43. Am Assn Social Work—Nat Assn for the Advancement of Colored People—Ply Sch Assn of Am (adv com)—Nat Conf Social Work (nominations com and social action com). On Afro-Am Newspaper Honor Roll awarded to outstanding leaders in Baltimore '41. 202-6 W. 136th St., NYC 30.Ⓖ

15 LEWIS, Fred Herbert. Fruit diseases (Apple, sour cherry); Fungicides. b'13. BS '37 (Clemson A&M Coll); PhD '43 (Cornell U). Author articles in field. Research asst plant path Cornell U '37-43; asst prof '43-47, asso prof plant pathol Pa State Coll since '47. Am Phytopathol Soc—Am Soc Hort Sci—AAAS—Sigma Xi—Phi Kappa Phi. Fruit Research Laboratory, Arendtsville, Pa.

16 LEWIS, Harold MacLean. City planning. b'89. AB '09 (Williams Coll); CE '12 (Rensselear Polytechnic Inst). Engineer planning officer regional and local planning associations; preliminary designs of public works; consultant municipalities preparation comprehensive plans, zoning, rezoning, studies traffic parking; population land values studies, population movements, facilities needed. Author: City Planning—Why and How '39; Planning the Modern City '49; also articles in field. Exec engr Com Regional Plan NY and environs '21-32; chief engr, planning officer '32-42; cons Nat Resources Planning Bd Washington '35-39; cons engr Office Pres Borough Manhattan '42-45; cons engr city planner since '29. ASCE—Am Inst Cons Engrs—Am Inst Planners—Am Society Planning Officials—Sigma Xi—Phi Beta Kappa—Tau Beta Pi. 15 Park Row, NYC 7. H: 1511 Albemarle Rd., Brooklyn 26.

17 LEWIS, Harry Fletcher. Wood chemistry and utilization; Lignin and paper chemistry. b'91. BS '12—MS '13 (Wesleyan U Conn); PhD '16 (U Ill); DSc '44 Cornell Coll Ia); DSc '48 (O Wesleyan U). Author articles in field. Dean Inst Paper Chemistry Appleton Wis since '36. Am Chem Soc (chmn Ia sect '24, NE Wis sect '30; counsilor '31, '39-44; v chmn cellulose div '33-34, chmn '34-35)—Tech Assn Pulp and Paper Industry—Sigma Xi. 903 E. Alton St., Appleton, Wis.†

18 LEWIS, Isabel Eleanor Martin (Mrs. Clifford S. Lewis). Sun and moon eclipses; Moon occultations. b'81. AB '03—AM '05 (Cornell U). Author: Splendors of the Sky '19; Astronomy for Young Folks '22; A Handbook of Solar Eclipses '24; also articles in field. Connected with US Naval Obs '09-51, ret. Expeditions for observation total eclipses of sun Russia '36, Peru '37. AAAS(F)—Am Astron Soc. 6515 16th St. N.W., Washington 12.†Ⓖ

19 LEWIS, Jessamine DeHaven. Scientific technology (History); American history. b'89. AB '10 (Allegheny Coll); '23-46 (Pittsburgh U). Engaged research in Congressional Record, 1789-1900. Pittsburgh Post Gazette, 1787-1820, transportation technology as clipper ships, ocean steamers, railroads, telegraph, highways; technology of aluminum, building, electricity, food preservation, iron and steel, petroleum, rubber, printing press, paper, typesetting, illustration, newsgathering; biographical research on James Finley, bridge builder, and William Bullock, inventor of webb perfecting press. Hist research asst in sci and tech Pittsburgh U since '38. Am Hist Soc—Hist Soc W Pa—Phi Alpha Theta. University of Pittsburgh, Pittsburgh 13.

20 LEWIS, John Roberts. Physical metallurgy and chemistry. b'95. AB '19 (Brigham Young U); MS '20 (Utah U); PhD '24 (Wisc U); student '36-37 (Princeton). Extensive research in non ferrous and ferrous metallurgy as adsorption of gasses on metal, oxidation of metallic surfaces, ignition of magnesium and alloys, preparation of alkali metal peroxides. Author: An Outline of First Year College Chemistry '32, 6th edition '45; also articles in field. Instr in chem Wis U '24-29; asso prof Utah U '30-41, prof '41-42, prof and head dept metallurgy since '42. Lieut Chem Warfare Res US Army '27-32. Am Chem Soc—Am Inst Mining and Metall Engrs—Utah Acad Scis—Am Soc for Metals—Utah Soc Professional Engrs—Sigma Xi. University of Utah, Salt Lake City.

21 LEWIS, Kenneth Burnham. Wire and wire products. b'82. AB '04 (Harvard). Research design and marketing wire mill equipment. Holds patents in field. Co-author: The ABC of Iron and Steel. Translator: Le Trefilage de L'Acier. Asso editor: Wire and Wire Products. Research Am Steel & Wire Co '07-09; with Morgan Construction Co '09-32; cons since '32. Wire Assn. 43 Midland St., Worchester 2, Mass.

22 LEWIS, Millard. Aeronautical engineering. Brig. general US Air Force; director Intelligence, hdqrs USAFE. Hdqrs US U.S.A.F.E. APO 633, care P.M., NYC.Ⓖ

23 LEWIS, Montgomery Smith. Abraham Lincoln (Legends). b'87. AB '11 (Harvard). Author: Legends That Libel Lincoln '46. Pres State Nat Securities Corp since '32. Ind Hist Soc. Brendonwood, Indpls. 44.†

24 LEWIS, Naphtali. Antiquity (Classical). b'11. AB '30 (NYC); AM '32 (Columbia); PhD '34 (U Paris). Author: L'industrie du papyrus dans l'Egypte greco-romaine '34; A Hoard of Folles from Seltz '37. Co-editor: Les Papyrus Fouad I '39. Asst prof classical langs Brooklyn Coll since '47. Translator US War Dept '43-44; research dir Columbia U Div War Research '45. Am Philol Assn—Int Assn Papyrologists—Phi Beta Kappa. Am Field Service fellow for study in France '33-34, fellow Am Acad in Rome '34-36. Brooklyn College, Brooklyn 10.

25 LEWIS, Robert Compton. Vibration control. b'12. BS '36 (U Ill). Acoustic research and noise reduction University of Michigan physics department '37; founder and partner The Calidyne Company, Winchester, Massachusetts; consultant on patents; survey on passenger seating; vibration Isolaters and isolating suspensions; instruments for vibration measurement. Author articles: A Simplified Method for the Design of Vibration Isolating Suspensions '47. Research engr Crane Co, Chicago '36-40; vibration engr, head vibration dept engring div Vega Aircraft Co and Lockheed Aircraft Co '40-44; chief engr The M B Mfg Co New Haven Conn '44-46; research engr, project supervisor Guggenheim Aeronautical Lab MIT '46-50; The Calidyne Company since '48. Am Inst Physics—ASME—Inst Aeronautical Sci —Soc for Exptl Stress Analysis. The Calidyne Company, 751 Main St., Winchester, Mass. H: 165 Cambridge St.†

26 LEWIS, Robert Edward. Motion picture engineering; Furniture development. b'17. BS (U Chicago); student (Inst Design Chicago). Research and development on profile comparator directly adaptable to polar, metric, log, or other coordinates, on graphic methods of geometrical optics applicable to aspheric systems, on parabolic mirror curve generator; studies on theory of internally reflecting light guides; design motion picture and slide projector condensor; examination reduction of waveform distortion due to motion picture sound slits, box camera tolerances, and large tube color or television systems; synthesis of motion picture sound; mathematical studies efficient storage of furniture; development piezometric blanket to measure seating comfort, warmth of touch, economics of seating. Holds patent on reticle comparator. Author articles: Use of G-3 Film Processing Tank '48; Graphical Ray-Trace and Surface Generation Methods for Aspheric Surfaces '51, and others. Instr Inst Design Chicago '40, '48-49; asst optical engr Bell & Howell Chicago '41-42; optical engr DeVry Corp Chicago '43-45; asso physicist Armour Research Found Ill Inst Tech since '45. Soc Motion Picture and Television Engrs—Illuminating Engring Soc—Soc Photog Engrs—Optical Soc Am—Sigma Xi. Armour Research Foundation, Illinois Institute of Technology, 35 W. 33rd, Chgo 16. H: 10230 S. May, Chgo 43.

10 LEWIS, Thomas M. Nelson. American archeology (Tennessee). b'96. AB '19 (Princeton); '20 (U Wis). Directed state-wide archeological investigations in Tennessee '34-41; archeological field and laboratory techniques; southeastern US archeology. Co-author: (with M Kneberg) Hiwassee Island '46, The Archaic Horizon in Western Tennessee '47; also articles in field. Tenn state archeol since '39; head dept anthropol U Tenn since '34. Tenn Acad Sci—Fort Loudoun Assn—Am Anthropol Assn—Soc Am Archeol—Tenn Archeol Soc—Wis Archeol Soc. Awarded Lapham Medal for anthropol research. University of Tennessee, Knoxville 16, Tenn.†

11 LEWIS, William Abbett, Jr. Transmission and protection of electric power systems. b'04. BS '26—MS '27—PhD '29 (Calif Inst Tech). Research on electric power transmission, electric power system analysis and stability, analysis of electric machinery, relay protection of power systems. Research prof Ill Inst Tech and cons engr Armour Research Foundation since '44, dean grad sch Ill Inst Tech since '46. Am Inst Elec Engrs(F)—Sigma Xi. Illinois Institute of Technology, 3300 Federal St., Chgo 16.†

12 LEWIS, Wilmarth Sheldon. Horace Walpole. b'95. BA '18—MA (hon) '37 (Yale); Litt D '45 (Brown U); Litt D '46 (Rochester U). Author: Editor: A Selection of the Letters of Horace Walpole '26; Horace Walpole's Fugitive Verse '31; Yale Edition of Horace Walpole's Correspondence, 14 vols, '37-48. Trustee Redwood Library Newport RI, Miss Porter's Sch, Inst for Advanced Study, Watkinson Library. Farmington, Conn.

13 LEWY, Hildegard. History of ancient Oriental religions and science. b'03. PhD '26 (U Giessen Germany). Research on Assyro-Babyl, history of ancient Oriental calendars, judicial texts from the Arrapkha-Nuzi region. Author: Uber den Zerfall einiger Metallhalogenide im Licht '26; Le Calendrier Perse '41; The Nuzian Feudal System '41; The Origin of the Week and the Oldest West Asiatic Calendar '43; also articles in field. Asst in phys dept U Giessen '26-28; independent research since '28. Am Oriental Soc. 543 Glenwood Av., Cincinnati 29.†

14 LEWY, Julius. Assyriology; History of the ancient Near East; Semitic languages. b'95. PhD (Berlin U). Author: Untersuchungen zur akkadischen Grammatik '21; Die Kultepetexte der

Sammlung Blanckertz '29; Die altasyrischen Rechtsurkunden vom Kultepe, two vols '30-35. Co-author: (with H Lewy) The Oldest West Asiatic Calendar and the Origin of the Week '48; also articles in field. Prof Semitic Langs and Bibl hist Hebrew Union Coll Cincinnati since '40. Soc Bibl Lit and Exegesis—Am Oriental Soc—Am Schs Oriental Research (asso)—Internat Soc Oriental Research—Groupe Linguistique d'Etudes Chamito-Semitiques. Hebrew Union College, Cincinnati '20. H: 543 Glenwood Av., Cincinnati 29.†

15 LEY, Willy. Rockets; History of science. b'06. Student '27 (U Berlin). Free lance science writer since '27; information specialist, consultant office tech services US Dept Commerce since '47. Author: Die Moeglichkeit der Weltraumfahrt '28; Konrad Gesner, Leben und Werk '30; Grundriss einer Geschichte der Rakete '31; The Lungfish and the Unicorn '48; Bombs and Bombing '41; Shells and Shooting '42; The Days of Creation '42; Rockets '44; Rockets and Space Travel '47; also articles in field. Science editor PM NYC '40-44; research engr Washington Inst Tech College Park Md since '44. German Rocket Soc (one of founding mems '27, vp '28-33)—Brit Interplanetary Soc(F)—Inst Aeronaut Sci—Am Rocket Soc—Pacific Rocket Soc—Royal Astron Soc Canada—Soc Am Mil Engrs. Pine Manor, Montvale, N.J.

16 LEYBURN, James Graham. Social anthropology; Haiti; South Africa. b'02. AB '20—AM '21 (Duke U); AM '22 (Princeton); PhD '27 (Yale). Field work on anthropology and sociology in Haiti; economic, social investigations in South Africa. Author: Handbook of Ethnography '31; Frontier Folkway '35; The Haitian People '41 (awarded John Anisfield prize $1000 for best work in racial relations); Pierson College, The First Decade '44; contbr: The Fields and Problems of Cultural and Folk Sociology in The Field and Problems of Sociology '33; The Making of a Black Nation in Essays in the Science of Society '37; The Sociological Point of View in Foreign Influences in American Life. Instr econs, sociol Hollins Coll Va '22-24; instr social, econs Princeton U '24-25; instr in sociology Yale '27-29, prof '29-47; dean Washington and Lee U since '47; lend-lease Mission Officer to South Africa '43-44. Am Anthropol Assn—Am Sociol Society—Phi Beta Kappa—Sigm Xi. Lexington, Va.

17 LI, K(uo) C(hing). Tungsten; Antimony; Tin; Bismuth. b'92. Asso '15 (Royal Sch Mines London); ME (Hunan Tech Inst China). Discoverer first tungsten deposits in China; pioneer Chinese tungsten industry; expert in mining, metallurgy, chemistry, economic and trade of tungsten, antimony, tin, bismuth. Co-author: Tungsten: Its History, Geology, Ore-Dressing, Metallurgy, Chemistry, Analysis, Applications and Economics '47. Gen mgr Shukuoshan Mining and Smelting Co; pres Hunan Govt Lead Smelting Works; chief engr Hunan Mining Bd; pres and chmn bd Wah Chang Corp; chief engr and chmn bd Wah Chang Smelting and Refining Co Am Inc. AIMME—Mining and Metall Soc Am—Chinese Inst Engrs—Sci Soc China—Am Geog Soc. Wah Chang Corp., 233 Broadway, NYC 7.†◎

18 LIBBY, Willard Frank. Age determination by testing natural radioactive carbon content; Radiochemistry (Nuclear physics applications). b'08. BS '31—PhD '33 (U Calif). Research on natural radioactivity since '31, on application nuclear physics to physical chemistry including use of tracers and study of chemistry of energetic atoms

produced by nuclear processes since '34; recent studies include testing carbon ashes of wrappings for radioactivity to determine age of Peruvian mummy. Author articles in field. With U Calif '33-45, asso prof '42-45; chem war research div Columbia U '42-45; prof chem U Chicago since '45. Am Chem Soc—Am Phys Soc—Sigma Xi—Phi Beta Kappa. Awarded Guggenheim fellowship Princeton and Columbia '41-42, U Chgo '51-52. Institute for Nuclear Studies, University of Chicago, Chgo 37.

19 LICHTEN, Frances. Pennsylvania-German folk art. b'89. Grad (Pa Museum's Sch Indsl Art). Author: Folk Art of Rural Pennsylvania '46; Pennsylvania German Chests. Portfolio: Folk Art of Rural Pennsylvania '39. Free lance designer and artist; supervisor Fed Art Project '36-41. 1709 Sansom St., Phila 3.†

20 LICHTENSTEIN, Joseph. Cooling towers. b'92. ME '18 (Poly Inst Zurich Switzerland). Design of towers and fans used in power, oil, and chemical industries for re-use and for preservation of water; design modern cooling towers and cooling tower fans; study economics of application of cooling tower equipment to various industries. Author articles: Performance and Selection of Mechanical Draft Cooling Towers '43; Cooling Tower Analysis '48; Recirculation in Cooling Towers '52, and others. Mech engr and mgr Foster Wheeler Corp NYC '28-47, cons engr since '47. AS ME. Foster-Wheeler Corp., 165 Broadway, NYC 6.

21 LIDDEL, Urner. Nuclear physics; Cosmic rays; Spectroscopy (Infrared). b'05. AB '26 (Central Coll Fayette Mo); '28 (U Chicago); PhD '41 (George Washington U). Extensive research in physical optics, cosmic radiation and nuclear physics. Co-author: Infra-red Spectroscopy '44. Author articles on Flying Saucers. Phys chem Fixed Nitrogen Research Lab USDA Washington '29-36; physicist in charge optics and spectroscopy Stamford Labs Am Cyanamid Co '36-42. With US Navy Office Research and Inventions '45-46, head physics br Office Naval Research '46-48, head nuclear physics br '46-49 and since '49, dir phys sci div '49. APS(F)—NY Acad Sci(F)—Inst Radio Engrs—Optical Soc Am—ACS—Sigma Xi. Office Naval Research, Navy Dept., Washington 25.◎

22 LIDDELL, Anna Forbes. Nicholas of Cusa. b'91. AB '18—PhD '24—Keenan fellow '32 (UNC); MA '22—scholar (Cornell U). Study of the philosophy of Nicholas of Cusa, translation from Latin of his De Docta Ignorantia now in final revision. Author: Alexander's Space, Time and Deity, A Critical Consideration '25; also articles in field. Prof hist and sociol Chowan Coll NC '25-26; asso prof philos Fla State Coll for Women '26-30, prof '30-47, since '47 known as Fla State U. Am Philos Assn—So Soc Philos and Psychol (pres '32-33)—So Soc Philos Religion (vp '40-41, '46-47, pres '47-48)—Am Soc Aesthetics—Medieval Acad Am—AAUP—Am Association U Women—Horace Williams Philos Assn—Internat Congress Philos—Audubon Soc. Florida State University, Tallahassee.

23 LIDDICOAT, Richard Thomas, Jr. Gemology; Mineralogy. b'18. BS '39—MS '40 (U Mich); MS '44 (Calif Inst Tech); '41 (Gemological Inst Am). Author: Handbook of Gem Identification '47, '48; also articles in field. Asst dir Gemological Inst Am since '48, dir eastern headquarters '49, '50. Am

Gem Soc (hon certified gemologist)—Australian Gemmological Assn (hon vp)—Sigma Xi. 541 South Alexandria Av., Los Angeles 5.†

10 LIEB, Frederick George. Baseball (History). b'88. Ed pub schs. Baseball writer and historian since '10; research on national game. Author: The Boston Red Sox '47; The Pittsburgh Pirates '48; Story of the World Series '49; The Baseball Story '50; and others. Baseball ed NY Evening Telegram '20-27, NY Post '27-33; feature writer Sporting News '42-47; free-lance sports writer since '47. 136 Seventh Av.N.E., St. Petersburg 2, Fla.

11 LIEBER, Eugene. Organic chemistry (Petroleum, nitrogen compounds). b'07. BS Chem '30 (Pa U); MS '34—PhD '37 (Brooklyn Poly Inst). Engaged research and writing on reduction of nitroguandine by catalytic hydrogenation, application of Xanthate reaction to identification of certain solvents, low temperature fractionation of hydrocarbon gases, catalytic conversion of organic sulfur compounds, Paraflow Process improvement and development, reduction of alpha-Alkyl-gamma-nitroguanidines, high molecular weight hydrocarbons and hydrocarbon intermediates. Holds 82 patents in field including condensation product and method of preparing and using same, mineral oil lubricating composition. Author articles in field. Asst prof chem Ill Inst Tech since '44. Am Chem Soc—Am Inst Chem—Am Soc Lubrication Engrs—Am Soc Testing Materials—Electrochem Soc —Am Inst Chem(F)—Sigma Xi—SAE—Tau Beta Pi—Indusl Packaging Engrs Assn Am. Illinois Institute of Technology, Technology Center, Chicago 16.

12 LIEBERMANN, Leonard N(orman). Ultrasonics. b'15. PhD '40 (U Chicago). Research on underwater sound, echo ranging, acoustic streaming, second viscosity, acoustic absorption. Author articles in field. Asst prof physics U Kan '41-43; prin physicist Woods Hole Oceanog Inst and Bur Ships USN '43-46; asso prof physics U Calif Marine Phys Lab since '46. Am Phys Soc—Acoustical Soc Am. Marine Physical Laboratory, University of California, San Diego 52, Calif.

13 LIEBERSON, Goddard. History of music; Music recording. b'11. Student '33-37 (Eastman Sch Music). Lecturer on music history and contemporary music; also composer. Author: Three for Bedroom C '47; Columbia Book of Musical Masterworks '47. Contbg editor: International Cyclopedia of Music and Musicians. Exec vp Columbia Records. Columbia Records, Inc., 799 Seventh Av., NYC 19.

14 LIEBMAN, Emil. Oceanography and biology of East Mediterranean coastal waters (Nile flow); Economically important sea and fresh-water fishes and animals (Occurrence, migrations, spawning seasons); Leucocytes (Growth, dependence). b'00. PhD '25 (U Vienna); student (British Museum, Naples, Woods Hole). Discovered that certain leucocytes whose nature and function were unknown for nearly one hundred years carry and supply nutritive and growth substances to various regions of the body especially where growth takes place. Author: Theory of Trephocytosis. Head Labs, adv Fisheries Service, Palestine Govt '28-38; research asso Tulane U, Duke U, Princeton U '40-47; aquatic biol and hematologist The Aquarium NY Zool Soc since '47. NC Acad Scis—AAAS—Am Soc Zools—Soc Exptl Biol and Med—Sigma Xi. New York Zoological Society, Bronx Park, NYC 60.

15 LIEBMANN, Alfred J. Microbiology; Fermentation chemistry; Alcohol. b'85. CE '07 (Fed Polytech Zurich); PhD '09 (U Zurich). Author articles: Alcohol for War Purposes '43; Butanediol—A New Polyhydric Alcohol '45; Penicillin—History, Scientific Development and Production '44; Changes in Whisky While Maturing, '49. Gen Elec Research Labs '09-10; Munich Lamp Works '11; chief chem Watt Elec Lamp Works Vienna '12; vp dir mgr Independent Lamp and Wire Co NJ '12-20; mgr Elkon Works Gen Elec Co NJ '20-26; indsl cons '26-33; tech and research dir Schenley Distillers Corp NYC since '33. Am Chem Soc—Oil Chem Soc—AAAS—NY Acad Sci—Sigma Xi. Schenley Industries Inc., 350 Fifth Av., NYC 1.

16 LIEFF, Morris. Technology and chemistry of wood and plastics. b'15. BA '34—MA '35 (Queen's Coll, Kingston); PhD '38 (McGill U). Research on structure of lignin, its relation to other plant constituents, development of plastics from wastes, controlling wood shrinkage, expansion, impregnating with resins. Author: Chapter in Engineering Laminates. Author articles: Studies on Lignin and Related Compounds '39; The Extraction of Birch Lignin with Formic Acid '39; Modification of the Micromethoxyl Apparatus to the Viebock Procedure '37; Wood Plastics and Synthetic Hardboard '41; Need of Research for the Furniture Industry '46. Sessional chem Forest Products Labs Ottawa '36; research chem Elemendorf Corp Chicago '38-43, dir research '43-47; teacher wood tech war training program Ill Inst Tech '43-45; lecturer tech wood, plastic materials indsl design dept Art Inst Chicago '45-47, Inst Design '47; vp and tech director SK Insulrock Corp since '50. American Chem Soc—AAAS—Sigma Xi—Forest Products Research Soc (charter mem). Awarded medal in chem Queens U '34, recipient two Nat Research Council of Can awards '36-37. Smith & Kanzler Corp., East Linden Av., Linden, N.J.†

17 LIEN, Arnold Johnson. Political ideologies (Democracy, communism, socialism, fascism, anarchism); American and foreign government; International law and organization. b'86. AB '08—AM '09 (U Minn); PhD '13—Richard Watson Glider fellow '12-13 (Columbia). Author: Privileges and Immunities of Citizens of the United States '13; Outline of American Government '21; Citizenship of the American Indians '25. Co-author: The American People and Their Government '34; also articles in field. Head dept polit sci Washington U since '24. Am Soc Internat Law—Am Polit Sci Assn—Internat Law Assn—Am Acad Polit and Social Sci—Phi Beta Kappa. Washington University, StL 5.☺

18 LIEN, Arthur P. Petroleum chemistry. b'14. AB '37 (Ottawa U); MS '39—PhD '41 (O State U). Engaged research and writing on methods of synthesis of di and trialkylbenzenes, hydrocarbon conversion reactions, solvent extraction, reactions of sulfur compounds, petroleum refining processes, isomerization of paraffin hydrocarbons: nature and control of side reactions, isomerization of naphthenes: rate studies. Holds patents for conversion of naphthenes to paraffins, catalytic alkylation of aromatic hydrocarbons with paraffins, catalytic isomerization of hydrocarbons, catalytic cracking of hydrocarbons with fluoride catalysts, selective extraction of aromatic hydrocarbons, desulfurization of oils, desalting of oils, production of ethers from alcohols and olefins. Author articles in field. Group leader, exploratory research on petroleum pro-

cesses Standard Oil Co since '46. Am Chem Soc—Sigma Xi. Standard Oil Co Research Laboratory, Whiting, Ind.

19 LIEN, Carl Bernt. Pest control; Sanitation. b'06. Specialist washroom sanitation, pest control work, industrial safety, sanitary maintenance procedures, sewage disposal work. Pres Lien Chem Co since '29. Nat San Supply Assn—Nat Pest Control Assn—Am Pub Health Assn—Nat Safety Council —Am Soc Safety Engrs—Am Chem Soc—Am Indsl Hygiene Assn—Central States Sewage Works Assn. 9229 W. Grand Av., Franklin Park, Ill. H: 5813 N. Nicolet Av., Chicago 31.

20 LIEVENSE, Stanley James. Fisheries biology; Trout lakes. b'18. BS '43 (U Mich). Conducted a series of water analysis at ten day intervals throughout the season on three depressions; detailed observations of spawning activities of the fish found in that lake; discovered lakes suited for trout '47 and observed new trout lakes for their success '48. Asst on lake survey party Mich by Inst for Fisheries Research Mich Dept of Conservation '41, '42, part time '43; creel census clerk on a lake in Mich Inst for Fisheries Research Mich Dept Conservation '46, dist biologist northern Mich '47, dist fisheries supervisor upper peninsula since '49. Am Fisheries Soc—Limnology Soc Am—Am Soc Ichthyologists and Herpetologists. Department of Conservation, Baldwin, Mich.†

21 LIGHTBODY, Howard D. Biochemical food technology (Metabolism of amino acids, proteins and carbohydrates, toxicity, antibiotics, food stability). b'91. BE '14 (Ill State Normal Coll); MS '17 (Chicago U); PhD '30 (Mich U). Engaged research and writing on toxicity of isopropanol, rotenone, derris and cube, subtilin production in surface and submerged cultures, effect of bacteria on quality of stored lyophilized egg powders. Author articles in field. Dir Food Labs, QM Food and Container Inst for Armed Forces since '47. Am Chem Soc —Am Soc Biolog Chems—AAAS—Soc Exptl Biol and Med—Inst Food Tech—Sigma Xi. QM Food and Container Institute for the Armed Forces, 1849 W. Pershing Rd., Chicago 9.

22 LIGHTFOOT, Thomas Culver. Alcohol plants; Grain processing plants; Chemical plants. b'06. BS '27—EE '36 (Swarthmore Coll Pa). Electrical design of industrial alcohol plant using by-product molasses from sugar cane; design and construction of grain processing plant for production of industrial alcohol. Switchgear application engr chem plants Gen Elec Co NYC '37-42; chief elec engr Publicker Industries Inc Phila '42-44; cons engr Jenkintown Pa '44-50; project engr chem and pharm plant work Stewart A Jellett Co since '50. Am Inst EE—Nat Soc Profl Engrs—Pa Soc Profl Engrs—Soc Am Mil Engrs. Stewart A. Jellett Co., 1200 Locust St., Phila 7. H: 214 Runnymede Av., Jenkintown, Pa.

23 LIGON, William Scherffius. Soil classification and mapping. b'03. BS Agr '25 (Ky U); MS '30 (W Va U); PhD '34 (Mich State Coll). Directed reconnaissance soil survey of Japan '46-47; engaged research and writing on influence of soil type on success of tree plantings for erosion control. Author articles: The Solubility of Applied Nutrients in Muck Soils '35; Soil Classification and Soil Maps: Original Field Surveys '49; A Key to Kentucky Soils; other articles in field. Asso prof soils U of Ky '43-47; soils sci

Div Soil Survey Bur Plant Industry US Dept Agr since '47. Soil Sci Soc Am—Sigma Xi. Potash fellow Mich State Coll '31-34. 509 New Sprankle Bldg., Knoxville, Tenn.†

10 LILIEN, Ernest. Polish language. b'72. Author: Wydawnictwo Slownika Liliena.

11 LILJEBLAD, Sven Samuel. Folklore; Ethnology. b'99. PhD '27 (Lund U); research fellow '44-48 (Harvard). Research in Scandinavian and comparative folklore, folkloristic fieldrecording. Author: Die Tobiasgeschichte und andere Marchen mit toten Helfern '27; En slavo-keltisk folksaga '28; Swedish Folktale Collections '38. Co-editor: (with J Sahlgren) Svenska sagor och sagner '37-40. Docent Lund U '29-46; asst archivist Dialect and Folklore Archives of Uppsala U '33-38; asst teacher Uppsala U '38-39; prof Ind U '43-44. Royal Gustavus Adolphus Acad—Am Anthropol Assn(F)—Internat Comm Folk Arts and Folklore. Fellow Am-Scandinavian Foundation '39-42. 48 Brattle St., Cambridge 38, Mass.

12 LILLARD, Richard Gordon. History of Nevada; American fiction (Realism); American forests (History). b'09. BA '30 (Stanford); MA '31 (Mont State U); PhD '43 (Ia State U); '26-28 (Sacramento Jr Coll); '34-35 (Harvard). Engaged research and writing on realistic fiction in America since 1860, Washoe journalism and humor, factors that enabled Europeans to settle successfully in American forests; worked in Sierra Nevada Range. Author: Desert Challenge: An Interpretation of Nevada '42; The Great Forest '47. Co-author: (with Coan) America in Fiction '41; also articles in field. Instr Mont State U summer '31; Valley Ranch Sch '31-32; Marysville High Sch Calif '32-33; Los Angeles City Coll '33-42; Ind U '43-45, asst prof '45-47; Calif U '47-49; Los Angeles City College since '49. editorial assistant of Miss Valley Hist Review, Ia State U '42-43. Guggenheim fellow '45-46. Los Angeles City College, 855 N. Vermont Av., LA 29.

13 LILLY, Daniel M(cQuillan). Ciliate protozoa (Nutrition, physiology). b '10. AB '31—MSc '36 (Providence Coll); PhD '40 (Brown U). Research articles on nutrition and growth of ciliates. Author articles in field. Instructor and asst prof biol Providence Coll '32-42; asst prof to prof biol St John's U since '46. Served US Army '42-46, statis and lab work Station Hosp England, instr Shrivenham Am U England. AAAS—Am Soc Zool—Am Soc Protozool—Sigma Xi. Biology Department, St. John's University, 75 Lewis Av., Brooklyn 6.†

14 LILLY, John Henry. Entomology (Orchard and field crop insects); Insect physiology and ecology; Insecticides. b'07. BS '31—PhD '39 (U Wis). Author articles: Influence of Certain Factors on the Oviposition Responses of the Cherry Case Bearer '36; A Method for Measuring Effects of Dormant Sprays upon Apple Tree Growth '38; The Effect of Arsenical Grasshopper Poisons upon Pheasants '40; A History of Entomological Teachering and Research at the University of Wisconsin '40; Combination Rotenone-Nicotine Blends for Pea Aphid Control '43; Fight the Corn Borer Now '45. Research asst Econ Entomol U Wis '31-37, instr '37-42, asst prof econ entomol and zool '42-46, asso prof '46-48; prof entomol Iowa State Coll '48. Phi Kappa Phi—Sigma Xi. Insectary Bldg., Ames, Ia.

15 LIN YUTANG. Chinese history and philosophy. b'95. BA '16 (St John's Coll Shanghai); MA '22 (Harvard Grad Sch); PhD '23 Leipzig U Germany); DLitt '41 (Elmira Coll); DLitt '42 (Rutgers). Author: Letters of A Chinese Amazon '27; My Country and My People '35; A History of the Press and Public Opinion in China '36; The Importance of Living '37; Wisdom of Confucius '38; The Gay Genius '47. Editorial bd China Critic (English weekly of Chinese opinion) since '27, T'ien Hsia Monthly (English) since '36; Chief Arts and Letters Section, UNESCO '48. John Day Co., 62 W. 45th St., NYC 17.☉

16 LINCICOME, David Richard. Tropical parasites; Parasitic helminths. b'14. BS '37—MS '37—scholar '36-37 (U Ill); PhD '41 (Tulane U Med Sch). Studies on taxonomy of Cestoda and Acanthocephala, chemotherapy and host-parasite relationships. Author articles in field. Asst med inspector New Orleans Port of Embarkation '43-44; asst prof zool U Ky '46; asst prof parasitol U Wis Med Sch '47-49; sr research parasitol E I du Pont de Nemours Co since '49. Parasitol, cmdg officer 22nd Malaria Survey Unit US Army '44-45, chief parasitol service and cmdg officer 14th Med Lab '45. Royal Soc Tropical Med(F)—Am Soc Tropical Med—Nat Malaria Soc—Ky Acad Sci (co-ed Transactions '48-48) Midwest Conf Parasitol (sec '48-49)—Ny Acad Sci—Am Soc Protozool—Am Soc Parasitol—Wis Acad Sci Arts Letters—AAAS—Am Micros Soc—Soc Systematic Zool—Sigma Xi—Phi Beta Kappa. E. I. du Pont de Nemours and Co., Veterinary Chemicals Laboratories, Newark, Del. H: 53 Kells Av.

17 LINCOLN, Bert Hartzell. Chemistry (Petroleum); Lubricating oils. born '00. BS '23 (Univ Ark); graduate study '23-26 (Univ Colo). Studied the uses of crude oil, gasoline, kerosene, diesel fuel, gas oil, wax, coke, lubricating oil, and grease pertinent to Petroleum Chemistry; also the effects of prepared lubricants on rubbing surfaces of engines rotated with metal and alloy bearings. One hundred and eight US Patents as Inventor or Co-inventor and Fifty-three Foreign Country Patents as Inventor or Co-inventor. Contbr: The Science of Petroleum. Research chem Continental Oil Co '26-30, asst to mfg mgr '30-33, chief chemist '33-48, patent adviser since '48; sec Lubrizol Development Corp since '35. Am Chem Soc—Am Inst Chem(F)—Sigma Xi. Continental Oil Co., Ponca City, Okla.☉

18 LINCOLN, Frederick Charles. North American birds (Distribution, migration); Wildlife conservation; Small arms markmanship. b'92. Student in basic biology '11-12 (U Denver). Director of bird banding activities in America '20-46; president Cuban-American Ornithological Commission '48-49; research in distribution and migration of North American birds; discoverer of flyway concept '35 of migratory bird populations now used in administration of game species. Author: American Waterfowl '30; Bird Banding '32; Our Greatest Travelers '38; The Migration of American Birds '39; The Waterfowl Flyways '41; Migration Routes and Flyways '42; The Future of American Wildfowl '47; also articles in field. Chief sect distbn and migration of birds '35-46, asst to the dir Fish and Wildlife Service since '46. Am Ornithol Union (F, treas, bus mgr '44-48)—Wilson Ornithol Club—Cooper Ornithol Club—Biol Soc Washington (treas '20-45, vp '45-48, pres '49-50)—Baird Ornithol Club (sec '23-38, pres '38-41)—Cosmos Club—Explorers Club—Arctic Inst NA. US Fish and Wildlife Service, Washington 25.☉

19 LIND, Levi Robert. Roman ideas; Nonnos of Panopolis; Reginald of Canterbury; Medieval Latin rhymed Saints lives; Latin poetry (Verse translations). b'06. AB '29—MA '32—PhD '36 (U Ill). Author: Medieval Latin Studies: Their Nature and Possibilities '41; Reginald of Canterbury, Vita Sancti Malchi '42; The Epitome of Andreas Vesalius '49; also articles in field. Asst to asso prof Latin and Greek U Kans since '40, chmn dept since '45. Classical Assn Middle W and S—Am Philol Assn—Am Classical League—Am Council Learned Socs (sec Am Com Dictionary Medieval Latin since '37)—AAUP—Phi Beta Kappa. Department of Latin and Greek, Fraser Hall, University of Kansas, Lawrence, Kans.

20 LINDAHL, Eric J. Hydraulic and power plant engineering; Mechanical equipment for buildings. b'05. BS '32 —MS '33 (U Wyo). Engaged research on efects of pulsation on flow meter accuracy, heating and ventilating, plumbing and electrical designs for buildings; studies and writing on reading wide line charts, loss of heat from underground pipe, elementary gas laws and relation to displacement and orifice meters. Co-author: (with Beitler) Hyraulic Machinery '47; also articles in field. Cons engr, prof and head mechanical engring dept Wyo U since '47. Sigma Tau—Tau Beta Pi—ASME—Am Soc Engring Edn—Am Soc Heating and Ventilating Engrs. Mechanical Engineering Dept., University of Wyoming, Laramie, Wyo.

21 LINDBECK, John M(atthew) H(enry). Modern Chinese and Japanese history. b'15. BA '37 (Gustavus Adolphus Coll); (U Minn); BD '40—PhD '48—fellow (Calhoun Coll, Yale); '44 (Columbia); Rockefeller fellow '46-48 (Harvard Yenching Inst). Author articles on Chinese Communism, Moslems and other subjects in field. Lecturer Sch Mil Govt Planning Bd '41-45; with OSS '45; asst prof Far Eastern studies Yale '48-52, Humanities Research fellow '51-52; head China sect Office Pub Affairs Dept State since '52. AHA—Far Eastern Assn. H: 3216 Klingle Rd., Washington 8.

22 LINDBERG, David Oscar Nathaniel. Institution administration (Tuberculosis); Fluorophotography. b '91. Student '03-07 (Adams Acad Quincy Mass); MD '15 (Boston U). Special research and study Stockholm, Leysin and Schatzalp Switzerland, Copenhagen, Hamburg, Paris, Oslo, Lisbon, Rio de Janeiro; invitational studies Tokyo and Moscow authorities; introduced fluorophotography to US '37. Clin dir USPHS '21-28; sanatorium directorships since '28, now supt, med supt and med dir Utah State Tuberculosis San; asst clin prof med U Utah Sch Med; tuberculosis cons Utah State Dept Health. Am Coll Physicians(F)—Am Coll Chest Physicians(F)—Nat Tb Assn(past vp)—AMA—Am Trudeau Soc—Phi Alpha Gamma—Sociedade Brasileira de Tuberculose(corr mem) —Internat Union Against Tb (titulaire mem). American Trust Co., SF.

23 LINDEGREN, Carl C(larence). Yeast (Genetics, cytology); Neurospora genetics. b'96. BS '22—MS '23 (U Wis); PhD '31 (Calif Inst Tech). Author: The Yeast Cell '49; also articles in field. Prof So Ill U since '48. AAAS(F)—Am Soc Bot—Genetic Soc Am—Am Soc Naturalists—Soc Am Bacteriol. South Illinois University, Carbondale, Ill.

24 LINDELL, Karl Victor. Asbestos (Mining). b'05. BS '28 (Mich Coll Mines). Research on mining, milling and exploration of asbestos. Mining engr Royal Tiger Mines '28; mining engr and underground supt Internat Nickel Co Can Ltd '29-45; underground supt, mine mgr Can Johns-Manville Co Ltd since '45. AIMME—Can Inst Mining and Metall—Tau Beta Pi. Canadian Johns-Manville Co., Ltd., Box 1500, Asbestos, Que., Can.

10 LINDGREN, Ralph Melvin. Pathology (Plant, forest tree and products). b'04. BS '26—MS '28—PhD '37 (U Minn). Author articles in field. Public use and private patent applications for several materials used in preventing fungal defects in various wood products. Sr pathol US Dept Agr charge forest tree and products diseases in Gulf States since '47. Soc Am Foresters—Am Phytopathol Soc—Am Wood Preservers Assn—Forest Products Research Soc—Sigma Xi—Gamma Sigma Delta. 1008 Federal Building, New Orleans.†

11 LINDGREN, Raymond E(lmer). History of Scandinavia. b'13. AB '35—MA '40—PhD '43 (U Cal Los Angeles). Research on history of immigration to southwestern US from 1848-1900; study early modern and contemporary periods; Fulbright scholar to Norway and Gustav V fellow to Sweden '49-51. Author article: A Projected Invasion of Sweden 1716 '44. Contributor: Collier's Encyclopedia; American Swedish Yearbook '49. Faculty hist dept Occidental Coll Los Angeles '42-45; asst prof hist dept Vanderbilt U '45-49, now asso prof; lectr in Scandinavian hist U Minn '49-50. AHA—Am Scandinavian Found. Social Sci Research grant from Vanderbilt U and grant from Huntington Library for study immigration of Scandinavians into US. History Department, Vanderbilt University, Nashville.†

12 LINDMARK, John. Bibliography; Early American fiction; Appraiser (Books, manuscripts). b'89. Ed by private tutors. Work devoted entirely to preservation valuable historical data and research in early American fiction (1789-1850). 55 and 57 Church St., Poughkeepsie, N.Y.

13 LINDNER, Robert C. Plant physiology (Tropical fruits and flowers); Plant virus diseases and nutrition. b'14. Student '31-35 (Fresno State Coll); AB '36 (U Calif); PhD '39 (U Chicago). Author articles in field. US Dept Agr Fresno Calif '29-39, Wenatchee Wash '39-45; State Coll Washington since '47. AAAS—Am Soc Plant Physiol—Am Soc Hort Sci—Am Phytopathol Soc. Tree Fruit Experiment Station, Wenatchee, Wash.

14 LINDOW, Carl Warning. Agricultural and food chemistry; Composition and processing of foods and feeds; Nutrition; Feeds and feeding. b'99. BS '22—MS '27—PhD '29 (U Wis). Engaged research and writing on manganese and copper content of plant and animal materials, antioxidants, vitamins, proteins and amino acids, byproduct utilization. Author articles. The Determination of Copper in Biological Materials (with Elvehjem) '29; The Copper Content of Plant and Animal Materials (with Elvehjem and Peterson) '29; The Copper Metabolism of the Rat (with Peterson and Steenbock) '29; other articles in field. Chmn dept chem W Ky State Teachers Coll '22-26; asst instr agr chem Wis U '26-29; chmn dept chem Central State Teachers Coll Wis '29-30; research chem Kellogg Co '30-36, dir research since '36. Am Inst Chem(F)—Am Chem Soc—Am Soc Testing Materials—Sigma Xi—Cereal Inst (tech advisory com)—Nutrition Found (food industries advisory com). Selected as one of ten ablest chemists or chem engrs working in agrl and food chem in US, Chem and Engring News '47. Kellogg Co., Battle Creek, Mich. H: 2550 W. Michigan Av.

15 LINDOW, (John) Wesley. Business conditions; Money and banking; US Government (Finances and dept management). b'10. AB '31 (Wayne U); MA '40 (George Washington U). Economist Farm Credit Adminstrn Washington '34; economist US Treasury Dept Washington '34-37, asst dir research and statistics '44-47; economist Irving Trust Co NY City since '47, vp since '48. Am Econ Assn—Am Finance Assn—Am Statis Assn. Irving Trust Company, 1 Wall St., NYC 15.◎

16 LINDQUIST, Arthur W. Entomology (Livestock insects). b'03. BS '26 (Bethany Coll); MS '31 (Kan State Coll). Research on livestock insect pests such as myiasis producing Diptera, hornflies, blowflies, ticks and botflies; development of uses of DDT and other new compounds; improved chemicals and methods for mosquitoes, deer flies, sheep tick, cattle grubs and black flies. Author articles in field. Entomol Bur Entomol and Plant Quarantine Tex and Calif '31-41, Orlando Fla '41-46, charge Bur Entomol and Plant Quarantine Corvallis Ore since '46. AAAS—Am Assn Econ Entomol—Entomol Soc Am—Kan Entomol Soc—Fla Entomol Soc—Sigma Xi. Bureau of Entomology and Plant Quarantine, P.O. Box 332, Corvallis, Ore.

17 LINDQUIST, H. L. Philately. b'86. Spl study in accounting and journalism). Stamps (Guatemala, Norway, War Savings). Author articles in field. Owner and publisher of community newspapers Chicago '07-17; western mgr group trade papers Chicago '18-21; gen mgr Gehring Pub Co NY '21; promotion mgr Geyer Pub Co NY '22-32; owner Asso Etchers NYC since '22; owner Stamps, weekly pubn since '32. Nat Fed Stamps Clubs (nat chmn)—Assn for Stamp Exhibitions (pres) — New York Athletic Club (pres). 2 W. 46th St., NYC.

18 LINDSAY, George Clayton. Coal mine mechanization and modernization. b'12. BS (U Ill). Studies of modern coal-mine installations, newest methods, and application of all types of machinery to coal mining; mechanical analyses to determine probable future trends in mechanization and production of coal mines. Recipient award of Merit for editorial excellence from Industrial Marketing in 1951. Author articles: Continuous Mining Grows Up '51; Mine Costs and Realization '52, others. Asst mining engr Rex Coal Co '34-39; asst editor Mechanization—The Magazine of Modern Coal '39-43, asso editor '43-46, editorial bd '46-47, editor since '48; co-editor Mechannual —The Book of Mechanization Progress '39-46, editor since '47; editorial bd Utilization—The Magazine of Modern Coal Uses since '47. Soc Bus Mag Editors—White House Corrs Assn—AI MME—Coal Mining Inst Am—Rocky Mt Coal Miing Inst—Ill WVa coal mining insts—Open Pit Mining Assn—Ill Soc Coal Prep Engrs and Chem—Nat Press Club. 1120 Munsey Bldg., Washington 4.

19 LINDSAY, James Armour. Teacher education; Community leadership (Training programs). b'97. BS '19—MS '30—(Colo U); PhD '33 (Columbia). Supervising prin schs N Arlington NJ '33-35; supt schs Johnstown Colo '25-29, Bloomington Ill '35-38; asso prof U Ala '38-41, Miss State Coll '41-44; ednl div The Berry Schs Mount Berry Ga '44-45, pres 46-51. Am Soc Study Edn—Am Acad Polit and Social Sci—State and Nat edn assns—Kappa Delta Pi—Phi Delta Kappa—Acacia. 210 S. 1st St., San Jose. H: 1127 Delynn Way, San Jose 25, Cal.†◎

20 LINDSAY, Robert Bruce. Ultrasonic transmission (Solids, gases, liquids); Physics (Theoretical, philosophy, methodology); Acoustics; History of physics. b'00. AB '20—MS '20 (Brown U); PhD '24 (Mass Inst Tech). Author: Physical Mechanics '33; General Physics for Students of Science '40; Physical Statistics '41; Handbook of Elementary Physics '43. Co-author: (with G W Stewart) Acoustics '30; (with H Margenau) Foundations of Physics '36; also articles in field. Hazard prof physics Brown U since '36, dir Ultrasonics Lab since '46, dir Research Analysis Group of Com on Undersea Warfare Nat Research Council since '48. AAAS(F)—Am Math Soc—Am Phys Soc (F, council '43-47)—Acoustical Soc Am (F, exec council '42-45)—Am Acad Arts Sci(F)—Philos Sci Assn—Hist Sci Soc—Am Assn Physics Teachers (exec com '46-48, bd editors '45-47. Am - Scandinavian Foundation fellow '22. Department of Physics, Brown University, Providence 12.†◎

21 LINDSAY, William W(ilson), Jr. Radar; Electronics. b'99. Student Tech Sch Hannover, Göttingen U, Germany, '12-16, spl courses Columbia '20-21, MIT '43-'45. Research covering airborne radar, radio communications and electronic countermeasures; collaborated in development variable width wave-guide scanners, GCA talk-down principles and electronic circuits associated with atom bomb. With Gilfillan Bros Inc Los Angeles since '24, asst chief engr and chief design in active charge electronic and mech engring, research and design '44-49; staff electronic engr, mil operations research div Lockheed Aircraft Corp Burbank Cal since '49; independent cons electronics and mechanics since '28. Inst Radio Engrs(F)—Soc Motion Picture Engrs(F)—Radio Club Am(F)—Acoustical Soc Am—Am Inst Physics. Lockheed Aircraft Corp., Burbank, Cal.

22 LINDSEY, Almont. American labor history (Pullman strike); Recent American history. b'06. BS '28 (Knox Coll); MA '30—PhD '36 (U Ill). Author: The Pullman Strike: the Story of a Unique Experiment and of a Great Labor Upheaval '42; also articles in field. Prof hist Mary Washington Coll U Va since '37. AHA—Nat Geo Soc. Mary Washington College, University of Virginia, Fredericksburg, Va.

23 LINDSEY, Alton Anthony. Plant ecology; Antarctic biology. b'07. BS '29 (Allegheny Coll); PhD '37 (Cornell U). Biol Byrd Antarctic expdn II, research in Antarctic biology '33-35; instr Cornell U Botany Dept '29-33, '36-37; instr Am U, Washington, Botany Dept '37-40; asst prof biol U of Redlands, research in plant ecol, Colorado Desert, Cal '40-42; asst prof U of NM, research in plant ecol of southwestern lava beds '42-47; asst prof biol Purdue U, teaching and research in plant ecol since '47. Ecol Soc of Am—Bot Soc of Am—Am Polar Soc—Sigma Xi—Phi Beta Kappa. Spl Congl Medal. Biology Dept., Purdue University, Lafayette, Ind.

24 LINDSEY, Arthur Ward. Lepidoptera (Hesperioidea); Evolution; Genetics. b'94. AB '15—ScD '46 (Morningside Coll); MS '17—PhD '19 (State U of Ia). Author: Textbook of Evolution and Genetics '29; The Problems of Evolution '31; A Textbook of Genetics '32; The Science of Animal Life '37. Co-author: Van Nostrand Scientific Encyclopedia '38; also articles in field. Prof biol sci and head of dept

Denison U since '40. AAAS(F)—Ia Acad Sci—Ohio Acad Sci (sec '41-46, pres '47-48)—Entomol Soc Am (editor Annals '45-48)—Am Genetic Assn—Sigma Xi. Denison University, Granville, O.⊚

10 LINDSEY, Loyd Putnam. African violets. b'91. CSB '31 (Mass Metaphys Coll); '42 (Plonk Sch Creative Arts). Research on care and culture of African violets. Author: Care and Culture of African Violets (4th edit) '49. African Violet Soc Am—Men's Garden Club Am. P.O. Box 1262, Asheville, N.C.

11 LINDUSKA, Joseph Paul. Wildlife management; Medical entomology. b'13. BA '36—MA '38 (U Mont); PhD prep '39-41, '47 (Mich State Coll). Engaged research economic entomology, farm game and rodent ecology, insects involving medical importance in charge state-wide (Mich) pheasant survey, chemical control agents as they effect wildlife; repellents and insecticides for medical insects. Author articles in field. Entomol Bur Entomol and Plant Quarantine Moscow, Ida '37-40, Orlando, Fla '43-46; game biol game div Mich Conservation Dept '40-43, '46-47; biol US Fish and Wildlife Service since '47. Am Assn Econ Entomol—Wildlife Soc—Am Soc Mammalogists—Am Mosquito Control Assn—Soc Exptl Biol and Med. Patuxent Research Refuge, Laurel, Md.†

12 LINEBARGER, Paul Myron Anthony. Chinese politics and communism; Kuomintang; Sunyatsenism; Psychological warfare; Military propaganda. b'13. AB '33 (Geo Washington U); PhD '36 (Johns Hopkins); '20-24 (Brit Cathedral Sch, Shanghai; Oberrealschule, Baden-Baden); '26 (Kaiser Wilhelm Sch, Shanghai); '30 (U Nanking); '30 (N China Union Lang Sch). Participated in formation of Office War Information as Far Eastern specialist, Operation Planning and Intelligence Board '42. Author: The Political Doctrines of Sun Yat-sen: An Exposition of the San Min Chu I '37; Government in Republican China '38; The China of Chiang K'aishek: A Political Study '41; Psychological Warfare '48; ROTC Textbook on Psychological Warfare '48. Editor: The Gospel of Sun Chungshan '32; also articles in field. Prof Asiatic polit Sch Advanced Internat Studies Johns Hopkins Washington since '46; lecturer on Chinese polit in US, China, Philippines, Malaya, France and Japan; cons to G-3 div War Dept Gen Staff since '46. Commd 2d lt US Army '42 and advanced through grades to maj on duty with gen staff corps '45; assigned to MIS; transferred to China-Burma-India Theater Forward Echelon G-2, preparing reports and performing liaison and other functions with Chinese Communist and Kuomintang intelligence systems; assigned to propaganda br War Dept Gen Staff '45. Am Polit Sci Assn—Am Soc Internat Law—So Polit Sci Assn (recording sec '41)—Am Acad Polit and Social Sci—Inf Assn—Reserve Officers Assn US—Phi Beta Kappa. Awarded Bronze Star medal in China Theater '45; War Dept Commendation ribbon '46. 1906 Florida Av., Washington 9.⊚

13 LINEHAN, Urban J(oseph). Physical geography; Air-mass and synoptic climatology. b'11. BS '33 (Bridgewater Mass State Teach Coll); MA '40 (Clark U). Research on type of air mass and certain features of the associated weather at each synoptic hour at Pittsburgh for selected months. Co-author: Geography: Army Training Programs (with J L Rich, DP Bergsmark) '44. Instr geog U Cincinn '40-45, asst coordinator geog Army Training Prog '43-44; instr geog U Pittsburgh '45-47,

asst prof '47-48; asst prof geog Cath U since '48. Am Soc Profl Geographers—Am Geog Soc—Royal Geog Soc—AAAS—Nat Council Geog Teach—Am Meteorol Soc—Sigma Xi. Catholic University of America, Washington 17.†

14 LININGER, Frederick Fouse. Milk marketing; Agricultural economics; Farm management. b'92. BS '17 (Pa State Coll); MS '26—PhD '28 (Cornell U). Author: Dairy Products Under the Agricultural Adjustment Act '34; Consumer Cooperation Here and Abroad '39; also articles in field. Supervisor agr Morrison Cove Vocational Sch '20-23, dir '23-25; asst prof agrl econs Pa State Coll '26-28, prof '29-41, head dept '38-41, v dean Sch Agr and v dir Pa Agrl Expt Sta '40, dir since '42; on leave of absence engaged in research at Brookings Instn '33-34. NEA—Am Acad Polit and Social Sci—Pa State Edn Assn—Am Farm Econ Assn—Internat Conf of Agrl Econ—Gamma Sigma Delta—Phi Kappa Phi—Sigma Xi. 159 W. Park Av., State College, Pa.⊚

15 LINK, Conrad Barnett. Greenhouse flower crops; Roses; Chrysanthemums; Cut flowers. b'12. BS '33—MS '34—PhD '40 (O State U). Author articles in field. Prof floriculture U Md since '48. Am Soc Hort Sci—AAAS—Bot Soc Am—Am Genetic Assn—Sigma Xi. Department of Horticulture, University of Maryland, College Park, Md.

16 LINK, Karl Paul. Agricultural chemistry (Sugars); Disease resistance in plants; Blood coagulation. b'01. BS '22—MS '23—PhD '25 (U Wis); microanalyst's certificate '26 (U Graz Austria). Headed team of scientists that developed the drug Dicumarol, a blood anticoagulant used to combat intravascular clotting, thrombosis and pulmonary embolism. Author articles in field. Prof biochem U Wis since '31; consultant to Clinton Foods Inc since '38, Pabst Brewing Company since '44. Nat Acad Sci (hon)—AAAS—Am Chem Soc—Fedn Am Socs for Exptl Biology (biol chemists sect)—Sigma Xi—Phi Kappa Phi. Biochemistry Dept,. University of Wisconsin, Madison 6, Wis.*

17 LINKER, Robert White. Romance philology (Old French and Italian); Provencal literature; Francois Villon; Paleography. b'05. AB '25—MA '28—PhD '33 (UNC). Author: A Provencal Anthology '40; Aucassin et Nicolete '48. Co-author: The Works of Guillaume de Salluste Sieur du Bartas, 3 vols, '35-40; also articles in field. Asso prof UNC since '46. Modern Lang Assn Am—South Atlantic Modern Lang Assn—Mediaeval Acad Am. University of North Carolina, Chapel Hill, N.C.†

18 LINSCOTT, Eloise Hubbard (Mrs). Folksongs of old New England. b'97. AB '20 (Radcliffe Coll). Research on sea chanteys, lumbermen's songs, Indian, Shaker, British ballads through Yankee tradition, dances, fiddle tunes, singing games, kissing party songs and craft songs. Author: Folksongs of Old New England '39. 36 Mayo Av., Needham 92, Mass.†

19 LINSDALE, Jean M(yron). Birds and mammals of western United States (California); Ground squirrel; Magpies. b'02. AB '24—AM '25—fellow '25 (U Kan); PhD '27 (U Calif). Author: The Birds of Nevada '36; The Natural History of Magpies '37; The California Ground Squirrel '46. Co-author: Fur-bearing Mammals of California, 2 vols '37. Asso editor: The Condor since '28; The American Midland Naturalist since '42; edit bd: Au-

dubon Field Notes since '47; also articles in field. Research asso Mus Vertebrate Zool U Calif since '27. AAAS(F)—Am Ornithol Union—Herpetologists League—Calif Acad Sci—Am Soc Zool—Am Soc Mammalogists—Am Soc Ichthyologists and Herpetologists—The Wildlife Soc—Ecol Soc Am—Soc Study Evolution—Sigma Xi. Museum Vertebrate Zoology, University of California, Berkeley 4.

20 LINSLEY, Earle Gorton. Entomology (Systematic, bionomic); Coleoptera; Apoidea. b'10. BS '32—MS '33—PhD '38 (U Calif). Editor: Pan-Pacific Entomologist '43-50. Instr to associate prof U Calif since '39; jr entomol Agrl Expt Sta Calif '39-43, asso entomol since '49; chmn dept entomol and parasitol since '51; resch asso Coleoptera Calif Acad Sci since '39. AAAS(F)—Entomol Soc Am (vp '48)—Calif Acad Scis—Am Assn Econ Entomol—Pacific Coast Entomol Soc (sec '34-38, '40-42, pres '38-40)—Southern Calif Acad Sci—Western Soc Naturalists—Soc Study Evoln—Sigma Xi—Am Soc Naturalists—Society Systematic Zool—Colepterists Soc. Guggenheim fellow '47-48. 112 Agriculture Hall, University of California, Berkeley 4.

21 LINTON, Calvin Darlington. Shakespearean staging. b'14. BA '35 (George Washington U); MA '39—PhD '40 (Johns Hopkins). Engaged research staging of Shakespeare in London 1893 to 1940, listing of all productions, relationship between acting technique and scholarly criticism of plays, influence of "New Movement" in staging; research brings up to date Odell's Shakespeare from Betterton to Irving. Author articles: Some Recent Trends in Shakespearean Staging '40. Instr eng Johns Hopkins '39-40; asso prof Eng, chmn dept Queens Coll Charlotte NC '40-41; asso prof Eng George Washington U since '45. Modern Lang Assn. Department of English, George Washington University, Washington 6.†

22 LINTON, Ralph. Personality and culture; Primitive art; Anthropology (Marquesas Islands, Madagascar). b'93. BA '15 (Swarthmore Coll); MA '16 (U Pa); PhD '25 (Harvard). Author: The Material Culture of the Marquesas Islands '24; Use of Tobacco Among North American Indians '24; The Archeology of the Marquesas Islands '25; Guide to the Polynesian and Micronesian Collections, Field Museum '25; The Tanala, A Hill-Tribe of Madagascar '32; The Study of Man, An Introduction '36; Acculturation in Seven American Indian Tribes '40; Cultural Background of Personality '45. Sterling prof anthropology Yale U since '46. Am Anthrop Assn (pres '46)—AAAS—Nat Acad Scis—Academie Malgache (hon mem)—Royal Anthrop Inst Gt Britain (hon F)—Phi Beta Kappa—Sigma Xi. Dept. of Anthropology, Yale University, New Haven.⊚

23 LION, Kurt S. Instrumentation; Physical and technical measurements; Research methods (Physical). b'04. DEng '33 (Darmstadt, Germany). Author articles in field. Holder several US patents. Dept biophysics U Instanbul, Turkey '35-37; dept physics U Fribourg, Switzerland '37-41; with Mass Inst Tech since '41. Am Inst Physics—Sigma Xi. Massachusetts Institute Technology, Cambridge 39, Mass.†

24 LIPKIND, William. Primitive linguistics; South American Indian; Siouan language. b'04. BA '27 (NYC); PhD '45 (Columbia). Research on Caraja Indians Brazil, Bovarion Culture. Author: Winnebago Grammar '45; also articles in field. Viking postdoctoral fellow, The Viking Fund since '47. Asst prof anthropol O State U

'42-44; anthropologist Am Mil Govt in Germany '45-46. Am Anthropol Assn (F). 3 E. 10 St., NYC 3.

10 LIPPINCOTT, Benjamin Evans. Political science; Government control; Theory of socialism; History of political ideas; Air force history. b'02. BS '25 (Yale); '26 (Oxford Eng); PhD '30 (U London). Author: Victorian Critics of Democracy '38. Editor: Government Control and the Economic Order '35; Lange and Taylor On the Economic Theory of Socialism '38; History Thirteenth Air Force '44-45, '46; From Fiji Through the Philippines with the Thirteenth Air Force '48, Prof polit sci U Minn since '46. Commd first lt AC US Army '42, historian 13th Air Force '44-45, disch 1t col '46. Am Polit Sci Assn (chmn research com polit theory '41-42)—Social Sci Resch Council (civil liberties com '41-43)—Air Force Assn—Air Reserve Assn. Awarded Legion of Merit. Dept Political Science, University of Minnesota, Mpls.

11 LIPPINCOTT, Horace Mather. Philadelphia history; Quakerism. b'77. PhB '97—hon MA '40 (U Pa). Author: Mather Family of Cheltenham, Pennsylvania '10; The Colonial Homes of Philadelphia and Its Neighborhood '12; A Portraiture of the People Called Quakers '15; Early Philadelphia, Its People, Life and Progress '17. The University of Pennsylvania; Franklin's College '19; An Account of the People Called Quakers in Germantown, Philadelphia '23; A Searching Time for Quakers '45; Chestnut Hill, Springfield, Whitemarsh and Cheltenham '48; Abington Friends Meeting and School '49; Quaker Meeting Houses '52. Pa Hist Soc—Friends Hist Soc (vp)—Old York Road Hist Soc (past pres). East Lane, Chestnut Hill, Pa.

12 LIPPINCOTT, Isaac. Economic and social history of the United States; World commerce. b'81. AB '02 (Harvard); AM '08 (Washington U); PhD '12 (U Chicago). Author: A History of Manufacturers in the Ohio Valley '14; Problems of Reconstruction '19; Economic Development of the United States '21; Economic and Social History of the United States (with H R Tucker) '27; What the Farmer Needs '28; Economic Resources and Industries of the World '29; The Development of Modern World Commerce '35; Sold Out '36; (with Orval Bennet) Public Finance '49. Prof econ resources Washington U since '18, now acting dean sch of bus and pub administrn, head dept of econ. Am Econ Assn. 5470 Clemens Av., StL.

13 LIPPITT, Ronald. Social and group psychology; Human relations; Group action; Social therapy. b'14. BS '36 (Springfield Coll); Certificate '34-35 (U Geneva Switzerland, Jean Jacques Rousseau Inst); AM '38—PhD '40 (U Ia). Author: Training for Community Relations; also articles in field. Research asst Child Welfare Research Sta U Ia '38-40; asst prof ednl psychol and child development Southern Ill State Normal U '40-41; asst dir research and statis service Boy Scouts of Am '41-43; asso prof psychol and dir research Research Center for Group Dynamics Mass Inst of Tech '46-48; program dir, professor psychology and sociol Research Center for Group Dynamics U Mich since '48; cons Nat Inst of Mental Health, USPHS. Served as Lt JG USPHS assigned to psychol unit of US Maritime Training Stations, later to Office of Strategic Services World War II '43-45. Soc for Research Child Development(F)—Am Psychol Assn—AAAS—Sociometric Soc (exec com)—American Sociological Society—Nat Commn Children and Youth—Am Assn Social Group Workers—Soc Psychol Study of Social Issues (pres, '48-

49)—Sigma Xi. Research Center for Group Dynamics, University of Michigan, Ann Arbor.

14 LIPPMANN, Walter. Political philosophy; Political science; Public opinion. b'89. AB '09—grad study philosophy '09-10 (Harvard). Author: A Preface to Politics '13; Drift and Mastery '14; The Stakes of Diplomacy '15; The Political Scene '19; Liberty and the News '20; Public Opinion '22; The Phantom Public '25; Men of Destiny '27; American Inquisitors '28; A Preface to Morals '29; The Method of Freedom '34; The New Imperative '35; The Good Society '37; Some Notes on War and Peace '40, US Foreign Policy: Shield of the Republic '43; US War Aims '44; The Cold War '47. Editor: The Poems of Paul Mariett '13. Special writer NY Herald-Tribune and other newspapers; asst to sec of war '17; sec of orgn directed by EM House to prepare data for Peace Conf; capt US Army Mil Intelligence, attached to 2d sect Gen Staff, Gen Hdqrs AEF and Am Commn to Negotiate Peace. Phi Beta Kappa (senator '34-40)—Nat Inst Arts and Letters—Am Acad Arts and Letters. Herald-Tribune, 230 W. 41st St., NYC.©

15 LIPSCOMB, Edward Lowndes. Public relations (Agriculture). b'06. AB '27 (U Miss). Author: Grassroots Public Relations for Agriculture '50; Personal Practice of Freedom '52. Reporter, newscaster Gulf Coast Guide Gullport Miss '27-31; mng editor '31-36; dir Miss Advt Commn Jackson '36-39; dir pub relations Nat Cotton Council since '39; speaker before nat agrl and profl groups. Pub Relations Soc Am(pres '52)—Textile Bag Mfrs Assn (advt adv com since '44)—Gulf Coast Press—Assn—Miss Press Assn—Beta Theta Pi. Pub Relations News ann achievement award '50, Freedoms Found Honor medal for pub addresses '50. 162 Madison Av., Memphis 1.

16 LIPSEY, George Cherry. Mine management. b'02. BASc '24 (U BC). Author article: Mine Cars of Canada '44. With Britannia Mines BC '24-45, mine supt '39-45; gen supt Howe Sound Co Holden Wash '37-38; mgr and dir Howe Sound Exploration Co Ltd Snow Lake Manitoba Can since '45. Can Inst Mining and Metall—Mining and Metall Soc Am—AIMME—BC Profl Engrs Assn—Manitoba Profl Engrs Assn—Can Standards Assn—Midwest Mining Assn(pres '50). Howe Sound Exploration Co., Ltd., Snow Lake, Manitoba, Can. H: Lakeshore Drive.

17 LIPSON, Goldie Sylvia. Art (Education); Water color. b'05. Studied with Carl Nelson. One man shows Uptown Gallery NYC '42, Charles Barzansky Gallery NYC '46, '47, '49; gave demonstrations Nat Acad Art '45, '46, '47, '48; exhibits in traveling shows US and Can; exhibited Aquarelles Gallery Paris '49, nat juried shows of Am Water Color Soc, Audubon Soc, Allied Artists Am, Nat Acad Art. Dir and tchr Mt Vernon Sch Fine Arts since '47. Nat Assn Women Artists—Artists Equity—Mt Vernon Art Assn(exec bd)—New Rochelle Art Assn—Westchester Arts Assn. Mt Vernon Art Assn, 1st prize oil '47 '49, 1st prize water color '48; New Rochelle Art Assn, 1st prize water color '49, 3d prize water color '49; top prize oil Westchester Co Center '49. 17 E. Prospect Av., Mt. Vernon, N.Y.

18 LIPTZIN, Sol. Comparative literature (English, German Yiddish Israel). b'01. BA '21 (NYC); MA '22—PhD '24 (Columbia); student (U Berlin). Author: Shelley in Germany '24; The Weavers in German Literature '26;

Lyric Pioneers of Modern Germany '28; From Novalis to Nietzsche '29; Arthur Schnitzler '32; Richard Beer-Hofmann '36; Historical Survey of German Literature '36; Germany's Stepchildren '44; Peretz '47; Eliakum Zunser '49. Tutor Coll City NY '24, instr '26, asst prof '33, asso prof '40, prof '48, chmn dept Germanic and Slavic since '43. College of the City of New York, NYC.©

19 LISTER, Charles Baynard. Firearms (History, training, legislation); Ballistics. b'98. Student pub schs and high schs Wilmington Del. Author tech and instrn manuals pertaining to small arms, ballistics and training methods. Writer for Nat Rifle Assn of Am since '21, now ex dir. Editor: The American Rifleman; editorial consultant several pub of shooting books. Army Ordnance Assn—US Olympic Assn—US Naval Inst—Am Mus Natural Hist—Nat Geog Soc. 1600 Rhode Island Av N.W., Washington 6.

20 LITKENHOUS, Edward Earl. Bagasse (Separation, utilization); Cellulose (Continuous nitration); Sports and Football statistics (National ratings). b'07. BS in chem engring '30—MS '31 (U Louisville); PhD '34 (U Minn). Granted patent on continuous nitration of cellulose. Author: Bagasse as a Source of Pulp '44. Asst and asso prof chem engring U Louisville '36-41; prof and head dept chem engring Vanderbilt U since '41; cons. Am Inst Chem Engr—ACS—Am Soc Engring Edn—AAAS—Tech Assn Pulp and Paper Industry—Sigma Xi—Tau Beta Pi—Phi Lambda Upsilon—Alpha Chi Sigma. Vanderbilt University, Nashville 4.

21 LITTAUER, Sebastian Barkann. Quality control. b'00. ChE '20 (Rensselaer Poly Inst); AM '28 (Columbia); ScD '30 (MIT); Nat Research Fellow '30-32 (Harvard). Engr NYC '20-22; research asso in chem engring, math instr Mass Inst Tech '28-30; asst prof math US Naval Acad '35-42; cons nav Weems System of Nav Annapolis '40-42; Office of Civilian Supply WPB Washington '42-43; Bendix Radio Div Bendix Aviation Corp Baltimore '43-45; research math applied physics lab Johns Hopkins U Silver Spring Md '45-46; head math dept Newark Coll Engring; professor indsl engring Columbia U. Department of Industrial Engineering, Columbia University, NYC 27.†

22 LITTLE, Elbert L(uther), Jr. Dendrology (Nomenclature); Trees of the United States (Native, naturalized). b'07. BA '27—BS '32 (U Okla); MS '29—PhD '29 (U Chicago). Author: A Collection of Tree Specimens From Western Ecuador '48; Important Forest Trees of the United States '49; also articles in field. Asst Forest ecol, '34-39, asso '39-42; dendrologist Forest Service US Dept Agr '42-43 and since '46. Washington Acad Sci—Soc Am Foresters—Bot Soc Am—Am Soc Plant Taxonomists—Ecol Soc Am—Bot Soc Washington—Biol Soc Washington—Calif Bot Soc—Sociedad Botanica de México—Am Fern Soc—Am Bryological Soc—Okla Acad Sci—Sigma Xi—Phi Beta Kappa. United States Forest Service, Washington 25.†

23 LITTLETON, Leonidas Rosser. Explosives; Dyes. b'89. AB '07 (Birmingham-Southern Coll); AM '10—teaching fellow mathematics '08-10 (Tulane U); PhD '12—fellow organic chemistry '10-12 (U Ill). Consulting chemist on high explosives, filtration. Asst chem Ordnance Dept US Army Picatiny Arsenal Dover NJ '17-18; prin chem engr Research Engring Office QM Gen '41, prin chem Ordnance Dept '41-43, head engr since '43; mem spl com on high explosive storage Va '28. AAAS (F)—Am Chem Soc—Va Acad Sci—Sigma Xi. 1611 N. Greenbriar St., Arlington, Va.☺

10 LITTLEWOOD, William Herbert. Oceanography (Physical, biological). b'24. BS '48 (U Fla); MS in zool '49 (U Mich). Research on oceanography of Caribbean, Arctic, Africa and Europe. Oceanog US Navy Hydrog Office since '50, now head operations section div oceanography; Fulbright grant for rsearch in Denmark '53-54. Phi Sigma—Am Society Ichthyologists and Herpetologists—Am Soc Oceanog and Limnol. Division of Oceanography, US Navy Hydrographic Office, Washington 25. H: 314 Poplar St., Wyandotte, Mich.

11 LITZENBERGER, Samuel Cameron. Small grain breeding, pathology and genetics. b'14. BS '37 (Colo State Coll); MS '39 (Mont State Coll); PhD '48 (Ia State Coll). Research in small grain improvement, weed control, pasture crops, crop breeding, crop identification, perennial weeds. Author articles in field. Asso prof and agron Mont State Coll '43-46; asso agron U Fla '48-49; agron ARA Alaska Agrl Expt Sta since '49. Am Soc Agron—Am Phytopath Assn—Am Statis Assn—AAAS—So Agrl Workers—Sigma Xi—Gamma Sigma Delta—Phi Sigma. Alaska Agricultural Experiment Station, Palmer, Alaska.

12 LIVERMORE, Josiah Randall. Potato breeding; Statistical analysis. b'90. BS '13—PhD '27 (Cornell). Author articles in field. Instr dept plant breeding, Cornell U '21-31, asst prof '31-39, asso prof since '39. AAAS(F)—Am Soc Agronomy—Potato Assn Am (past pres)—Phi Kappa Phi—Sigma Xi. Cornell University, Ithaca, N.Y.

13 LIVESAY, Thayne M(iller). Counseling and guidance. b'94. AB '17 (Pacific U Forest Grove Ore); AM '21—PhD '31 (U Wash); part time student '21-24 (Stanford). Member National Commission on International Educational Cooperation. Author: Public Education in Hawaii '32. Prof psychol and edn U Hawaii '24-39, dir summer sessions '27-39, dir admissions '31-39, dean coll arts and scis and prof psychol '39-51, dean grad sch and sr prof psychol since '51; vis prof psychol various univs summers since '35. AAAS—Hawaiian Acad Sci—Am Psychol Assn—Phi Beta Kappa—Phi Kappa Phi—Pi Gamma Mu. 2206 University Av., Honolulu 5, Hawaii.☺

14 LIVINGSTON, Milton Stanley. Nuclear physics (Cyclotron design). b'05. BA '26 (Pomona Coll); MA '28 (Dartmouth Coll); PhD '31 (U Calif). Aided development first cyclotron; chairman, accelerator project, Brookhaven National Laboratory, design of 3 Bev proton synchrotron '46-48. Author articles in field. Instr, research asso U Calif '31-34; asst prof physics Cornell U '34-38; research asso MIT '38-39, asst prof physics '39-44, asso prof since '44. Am Phys Soc(F)—Sigma Xi. Massachusetts Institute of Technology, Cambridge, Mass.☺

15 LIVINGSTON, Robert Greig. Photogrammetry. b'14. BS in civil engring '39—MS '47—CE '50 (Mo Sch Mines); '47-48 (Ia State Coll); '51 (Ohio State U). Investigation techniques and equipment for making maps from aerial photographs; analyses of tilt in aerial photographs; distortions in aerial camera lenses; camera calibration procedures; effect equipment errors on mapping accuracy. Research photogrammetrist Aerial Photographic Br ERDL Wright-Patterson Air Force

Base since '48. Am Soc Photogrammetry—Am Soc CE—Soc Am Mil Engrs—Ohio Profl Engrs Soc—Theta Tau. Aerial Photographic Branch, ER DL, Wright-Patterson Air Force Base, Dayton, O. H: 2104 California Av., Dayton 9.

16 LIVINGSTON, Robert (Stanley). Physical chemistry; Photochemistry; Reaction kinetics; Photosynthesis. b '98. BS '22—MS '23—PhD '25 (U Cal Berkeley). Author: Physico Chemical Experiments '39 (revised edit) '48. Contributor scientific papers to Journal Am Chem Soc and Journal Physical Chemistry. Asst prof phys chemistry U Minn '27-37, asso prof '37-43, prof since '43; with Nat Defense Research Corp U Chicago '42-43, Md Research Labs '43-45. ACS—AAAS—Minn Acad Sci—Sigma Xi. Recipient Army Navy Certificate of Appreciation '48. University of Minnesota, Mpls 14. H: P.O. Box 72, Excelsior, Minn.☺

17 LLEWELLYN, Leonard Meese. Wildlife conservation and management (Game bird, wild fur animals). b'07. BS '36 (Frostburg State Teachers Coll); MS '41 (Va Poly Inst); student '26-28 (WV Univ). Engaged research and writing on molting pattern in adult foxes, muskrat investigations, cottontail rabbits of Va, polygamous mating of bobwhite quail in captivity, timing fox matings for maximum production, population and production studies of fur animals, effect of increased or decreased length of daylight on pelt primeness in adult silver foxes. Author articles in field. Investigator, US Fish and Wildlife Service, Dept Interior since '41. Am Soc Mammalogists—Wildlife Soc—Md Ornithol Soc. Patuxent Research Refuge, Laurel, Md.

18 LLOYD, E(dwin) Russell. Stratigraphy. b'82. Grad '01 (WVa Conf Sem); AB '05—Rhodes scholar '05—BA '08—Burdett Coutts scholar '08-09 (Oxford U); grad work and Fell '09-11 (U Chicago). Asst and asso geol US Geol Survey Washington '11-17, in charge coal land classification '15-16, asso geol '18-19; geol Sinclair-Central Am Oil Co '17-18; chief geol Sinclair-Wyo Oil Co Casper '19-21, Mid-Kan Oil & Gas Co Mineral Wells Tex '21-23, Argo Oil Co Denver '23-24; cons practice, also chief geol NY Oil Co Denver '24-26; dist geol Roxana Petroleum Corp Roswell NM '27; cons practice Denver and Midland Tex '28-32; dist geol Superior Oil Co Midland '32-36; cons practice since '36. Geol Soc Am (F)—Am Assn Petroleum Geol (hon)—Am Geophys Union—Sigma Xi—Gamma Alpha. P.O. Box 1026, Midland, Tex.†☺

19 LLOYD, Trevor. Geography of Arctic, Greenland, northern Canada and northern Scandinavia. b'06. BS '29—DSc '49 (U Bristol); PhD '40 (Clark U); MA hon '44 (Dartmouth Coll). Research on Far North, Arctic, Russian Northern Sea route, Mackenzie Waterway, Greenland, Lapland. Author: Geography and Administration of Northern Canada '51; Sky Highways. Co-author: Canada and her Neighbours '47. Prof geog Dartmouth Coll since '42. Arctic Inst NA(F)—Royal Geog Soc(London)—Am Geog Soc—Assn Am Geog—Greenland Soc—Can Inst Internat Affairs. Department of Geography, Dartmouth College, Hanover, N.H.

20 LOBECK, Armin Kohl. Geographic illustration; Geomorphology. b'86. AB '11—MA '13—PhD '17 (Columbia). Developed techniques of geographic illustration, particularly Block Diagrams and Field Sketching; analysis of physiographic regions of the different

continents. Author: Block Diagrams '24; Geomorphology '39; Airways of America (guidebook) '34; Physiographic Diagrams, with text of United States, Europe, Asia, Africa, Australia, others, 1921-52. Cartographer Department State, attached Am Com to Negotiate Peace, Paris '18-19; asst and asso prof physiography U Wis '19-29; prof geology Columbia since '29; cons to War and State depts since '42. Geol Soc Am(F)—Assn Am Geographers(F)—Sigma Xi. Columbia U., NYC 27.

21 LOCHHEAD, John Hutchison. Physiology of crustacea. b'09. BA '32—PhD '37 (Cambridge U); MA '30 (St Andrews U). Engaged research various aspects Crustacea, feeding mechanisms, blood and related tissues, swimming mechanisms. Author articles in field. Asso prof zool Vt U since '49; instr invertebrate zool Marine Biol Lab Woods Hole Mass since '43. Am Soc Zool—Sigma Xi. Department of Zoology, University of Vermont, Burlington, Vt.

22 LOCKE, Arthur Preston. Common cold; Bacterial toxins; Nonspecific factors in resistance to infection. b'97. AB '18 (Morningside Coll); PhD '22—Coman fellow '24-34 (U Chicago). Research on applications of chemistry to medicine, purification of immune serums, nature of bacterial toxins, common cold. Author articles in field. Research staff Inst of Path West Penn Hosp Pittsburgh '34-44; asst prof chem Morningside Coll '20-21; research dir Zonite Products Corp since '44. AAAS—Am Chem Soc—Am Assn Immunol (ed bd Journal '36-49)—Soc Exptl Biol and Med—Am Inst Chem. Zonite Products Corporation, New Brunswick, N.J.

23 LOCKHART, Ernest Earl. Food chemistry; Flavor; Food acceptance. b'12. BS '34—MS '35—PhD '38 (MIT); American Scandinavian Foundation fellow '38-39 (U Stockholm). Research in cold weather metabolism, nutrition with US Antarctic Service '39-41. Author articles in field. Asst prof food chem dept food tech Mass Inst Tech since '45. Am Chem Soc—AAAS—Inst Food Technologists—Boston Bacteriol Soc—Mass Hort Soc—Sigma Xi—Alpha Chi Sigma. Congressional Medal US Antarctic Service. Department Food Technology, Massachusetts Institute Technology, Cambridge, Mass.†

24 LOCKMILLER, David Alexander. History and political science (United States, Latin America); History of the University of North Carolina; William Blackstone. b'06. BPh '27—AM '28 (Emory U); LLB '29—LLD '40 (Cumberland U); PhD '35 (UNC). Research in social science; teacher and writer. Author: Magoon in Cuba, A History of the Second Intervention 1906-09 '38; Sir William Blackstone '38; History of North Carolina State College of Agriculture and Engineering 1889-1939 '39; The Consolidation of the University of North Carolina '42; also articles in field. Pres U Chattanooga since '42. AHA—Am Polit Sci Assn—So Hist Assn—So Polit Sci Assn—Am Mil Inst—Conf on Latin Am Studies—State Literary Assn of NC—State Hist Assn of NC—Phi Beta Kappa—Phi Kappa Phi—Tau Kappa Alpha. University of Chattanooga, Chattanooga 3, Tenn.†☺

25 LOCKWOOD, Maurice Herbert. High analysis fertilizers. b'99. BS '21 (U Conn). Research on formulation, processing, distribution of high analysis fertilizers. Author: Trends in the Use of the Major Plant Foods '46; Higher Analysis Fertilizers '47. Field man Maine and NH Eastern States Farmers Exchange '24-26, mgr fertilizer div West Springfield Mass '26-46; pres Nat Fertilizer Assn Inc Washington '46-48; vp charge plant food div Internat Minerals and Chem Corp Chicago since '48. ACS—Am Soc Agron—Soil Sci Soc Am—Internat Soil Sci Soc —AAAS—Soil Conservation Soc Am—Nat Fertilizer Assn (dir). 20 N. Wacker Drive, Chicago 6. H: 745 Sheridan Road, Winnetka.

10 **LOEB, Edwin Meyer.** Anthropology. b'94. PhB '16—PhD '22 (Yale). Research in Polynesia, California Indians, Dutch East Indies, Europe, Africa. Author: Pomo Folkways '26; Traditions and History of Niue '26; Sumatra: Its History and People '35; also articles in field. Lecturer in anthropol U Calif since '22. Am Anthropol Assn (F). Guggenheim fellow '28-29. Department of Anthropology, University of California, Berkeley.†

11 **LOEHR, Rodney C.** Forest industry; Military history of World War II. BA magna cum laude '30—MA '31—PhD '38 (U Minn). b'07. Author articles in field. Editor: Minnesota Farmers Diaries '38; Forest Products History Foundation Publication Series '47-48. Asso prof hist dept U Minn since '48, dir Forest Products Hist Foundation since '46. Served US Army '42-45; historical officer Joint Chiefs of Staff '43-45. AHA—Econ Hist Assn—Miss Valley Hist Assn—Agrl Hist Assn—Mil Hist Soc—Minn Hist Soc—US Infantry Assn. History Department, University of Minnesota, Minneapolis 14.†

12 **LOEHWING, Walter Ferdinand.** Plant physiology (Nutrition, growth, development, sex); Biochemistry (Agricultural). b'96. BS '20—MA '21—PhD '25 (Chicago U); Certificat Superieur '19 (Alliance Francaise); '19 (Pasteur Inst). Research in mineral nutrition and physiology of reproduction as related to growth and development in plants, physiology of sex and sex differentiation; delegate to US Government sixth Botanical Congress, Amsterdam '35; engaged research and writing on effects of mineral fertilizers, amino acid synthesis in plants, effects of light and soil characteristics on balance of mineral nutrients, heteroauxin applied to soil and plants, photoperiod as factor in sex organ inception in flowers, sex reversal in dioecious plants, photoperiodic aspects of plant development. Author articles: Recent Advances in the Plant Sciences '45; The Developmental Physiology of Seed Plants '48. Editor: Plant Physiology. Prof, head chem, dean State Sch Mines Okla '20-23; asst prof bot Ia U '25-28, asso prof '29-30, prof since '31, dept head since '40; dean graduate college since '50; civilian cons Chem Corps US Army. Ia Academy Science (F, past treas)—Am Soc Plant Physiol (past sec, past vp, past pres)—AAAS (F, past vp)—Bot Soc Am (past vp)—Soc Exptl Boil and Med—Am Soc Agronomy—Am Soc Hort Sci—Am Genetics Soc—Am Soc Naturalists—Am Chem Soc. Dept. of Botany, State University of Iowa, Iowa City, Ia.†◎

13 **LOESCHER, Frank Samuel.** Race relations in industry; Fair employment and educational practices; Church and the American Negro and other minority groups. b'11. AB '32—MS '35—PhD '46 (U Pa); student (U Chicago, Harvard). Director of special staff of representatives of agencies which co-operated to promote a successful campaign for a local ordinance establishing a Philadelphia Fair Employment Practices Commission, ordinance passed '48. Author: The Protestant Church and the Negro '48; also articles in field. Dir Placement Service for Minority Groups, Am Friends Service Com '45-48; exec dir Phila Fair Employment

Practice Commn since '48. Asst prof sociol Temple U '48-49; vis prof sociol Haverford Coll '49-50. Am Sociol Soc—Am Acad Polit and Social Sci—Nat Council Religion in Higher Edn (F). Fair Employment Practice Commission, Room '395A, City Hall, Phila 7.†

14 **LOETSCHER, Lefferts A(ugustine).** Presbyterian church history. b '04. Student '18-21 (Lawrenceville Sch); AB '25 (Princeton); ThB '28—ThM '29 (Princeton Theol Sem); AM '32—PhD '43 (U Pa); DD '40 (U Dubuque). Research on history of Presbyterian church in US. Author: A Brief History of the Presbyterians (2d edit) '44. With Princeton Theol Sem since '41, asso prof church hist since '48; bd dirs dept hist Presbyterian Church in US since '47. AHA—Am Soc Church Hist. H: 43 Hibben Rd., Princeton, N.J.

15 **LOEVINGER, Lee.** Trade regulation law; Scientific investigation of legal problems. b'13. BA '33—LLB '36 (U Minn). Suggested new discipline of jurimetrics, scientific investigation of legal problems to replace jurisprudence, the philosophical contemplation of legal problems; jurimetrics purports to be fusion of law and science. Author volumes: The Law of Free Enterprise: How to Recognize and Maintain the American Economic System '49; Jurimetrics '49. Asso Watson, Ess, Groner, Barnett, Whittaker, Kansas City Mo, specializing in corp and trade regulation law; atty with Nat Labor Relations Bd '37-41; spl atty Antitrust Div US Dept of Justice '41-46; partner Larson, Loevinger, Lindquist, Freeman Minneapolis since '46, specializing in trade regulation law. Minn Bar Assn—Mo Bar Assn—Phi Beta Kappa—Sigma Xi. 334 Midland Bank Bldg., Minneapolis 1.

16 **LOEWEN, Solomon Leppke.** Flukes; Tapeworms. b'98. AB '23 (Tabor Coll); MA '28 (U Minn). Engaged research in parasitology, described several new species of flukes and tapeworms. Author articles in field. Prof zool since '42 Tabor Coll. AAAS(F)—Am Soc Parasitologists—Am Micros Soc—Kans Acad Sci. AAAS research award. 517 S. Lincoln Street, Hillsboro, Kans.

17 **LOFTON, William M(ilford), Jr.** Coal tar chemicals and intermediates; Chemical warfare agents; Thermosetting resins and adhesives. b'04. Ba '25 (Miss Coll); MA—PhD '28 (UNC); spl research '32-33 (U Pittsburgh). Holder several patents. Asst dir U Louisville Inst Indsl Research '46-49; dir research and devel div Gloss-Sheffield Steel and Iron Co since '49. Am Chem Soc — AAAS(F) — Sigma Xi. Gloss-Sheffield Steel and Iron Co., 3131 First Av. N., Birmingham 2, Ala.

18 **LOFTUS, Donald Laurence.** Economics (Transportation). b'21. BS '48 (Northwestern U). Studies on possibilities of self-propelled railway cars. Co-author: (with Stanley Berge) Diesel Motor Trains. Research asst transportation dept Northwestern U '48-49, lectr since '49; research analyst Pullman-Standard Car Mfg Co since '49. 11001 S. Cottage Grove Av., Chgo. H: 3436 Western Av., Park Forest, Chicago Heights, Ill.

19 **LOGAN, Henry Leon.** Lighting (Commercial). b'96. BS (EE) '15 (Poly Inst Birmingham Eng). Correlation visual stimulus with sensation through measurement of natural lighting distribution accompanying optimum climatic conditions; development technique for use of color to permit or assist proper distribution of bright-

ness throughout visual field on quantitative engineering basis; brightness level correlation with accident rate to eliminate accidents depending on visual stimuli for occurrence; inventor apparatus for pre-determination of mixtures of colored light, for measurement distribution of light in field of view, for determination of illumination levels. Author articles: Artifical Light as an Aid to Surgery '28; Role of Lighting in Accident Prevention '43; Practical Mechanics of Designing Optimum Lighting Patterns '48, and others. Contributor: Motion Picture Theatre '49. With Holophane Co Inc since '19, mgr dept of applied research '46-49, vp in charge research since '49. Am Inst EE(F)—Illuminating Engrs Soc(F)—Mexican Inst Illumination—Da Vinci Sci Soc—Inter-Soc Color Council. 342 Madison Av., NYC 17.

20 **LOGAN, Herschel C.** Antique arms; small arms and ammunition. b'01. Student '20-21 (Chicago Acad Fine Arts). Author and illustrator: Hand Cannon to Automatic, A Pictorial Parade of Hand Arms '44; Cartridges, A Pictorial Digest of Small Arms Ammunition '48. Arms cons Kan State Hist Soc; commercial artist since '21; art dir Consol Printing & Stationery Co Salina Kan since '31. Nat Rifle Assn (life)—Nat Muzzle Loading Rifle Assn (life). 400 S. 9th St., Salina, Kan.

21 **LOGAN, John A.** Food distribution. b'96. PhB '21 (U Chicago). Developed nationwide program to market farm surpluses; aided in development and establishment of Food Stamp Plan; member Famine Emergency Council, President's Citizens Food Committee, Nat Nutrition Com; cons OPA, WFA, Qtrmstr Corps, OPM; mem advisory com Sec Agriculture. Author articles in field. Exec vp Food and Grocery Chain Stores Am '34, now pres and dir Nat Assn Food Chains, successor orgn. Nat Consumer-Retailer Council—Am Trade Assn Execs (dir). 726 Jackson Pl., Washington 6.

22 **LOGAN, Rayford W.** Trusteeships and mandates. b'97. AB '17—AM '29 (Wiliams Coll); AM '32—PhD '36 (Harvard). United States National Commission for UNESCO '47-50; advisory committee Coordinator of Inter-American Affairs '41-43. Author: The Diplomatic Relations of the United States with Haiti 1776-1891 '41; The Operation of the Mandate System in Africa, with an Introduction on the Problem of the Mandates in the Post-War World '42; The Senate and the Versailles Mandate System '45; The Negro and the Postwar World: A Primer '45; The African Mandates in World Politics '48. Editor: What the Negro Wants '44. Bd editors: Hispanic American Historical Review since '49. Prof hist Va Union U '25-30; asst to editor Journ of Negro History '30-32; head dept hist Atlanta U '33-38; prof dept hist Howard U since '38, head dept hist since '42, act dean Grad Sch '42-44; fgn affairs editor Pittsburgh Courier since '45; Fulbright fellow France to study adminstrn overseas tys '51-52; cons Problems of Parliamentary Government in Colonies (pub Hansard Soc) '53. Phi Beta Kappa. 1519 Jackson St., Washington 17.

23 **LOGAN, Robert Archibald.** Cree language. b'92. Dominion land surveyor Canadian Govt '14; study Cree language 40 years; correspondence with Indian informants in Cree language and Cree syllabic writing; engaged in writing grammar and dictionary. Contributor: The Viking and the Red Man (vol 6). The Explorers Club, 10 West 72d St., NYC.

10 LOGGINS, Vernon. Literature (American, Negro, modern provencal). b'93. AB '14 (U Tex); AM '17 (U Chicago); PhD '31 (Columbia). Author: Chansons du Midi '24; The Negro Author '31; American Literature '33 (reprinted '47); I Hear America '37; Two Romantics '46; also articles in field. Teacher Eng U Chicago '16-17, U Minn '17-18, Ala Poly Inst '19-20, NYU '20-25, Columbia U since '25; sometime lecturer Am lit Brooklyn Coll Grad Sch and Rand Sch Social Sci. Soc Felibrige Provence—Authors League Am—Poetry Soc Am—AAUP. Columbia University, NYC 27.◉

11 LOGRASSO, Angeline Helen. Italy (Intellectual and cultural relations with United States); Early Italian Risorgimento. b'96. AB '17—AM '18 (U Rochester); PhD '27—Rebecca Greene fellow '25-26—Augustus Anson Whitney traveling fellow '27-28 (Radcliffe Coll); grad study (Columbia U, Sorbonne Paris, U Rome, U Florence Italy, College de France). Author articles in field. Instr, asst prof French, Spanish and Italian U Rochester NY '17-25. With Bryn Mawr Coll since '30, asso prof Italian lang and lit, head dept since '30; sec-treas Luigi Sturzo Sociol Found Inc. Modern Lang Assn Am—Am Assn Teachers Italian—Phi Beta Kappa—Medieval Acad Am. College Inn, Bryn Mawr, Pa.

12 LOHMANN, Melvin Rudolph. Education (Industrial engineering). b'14. BS '37 (U Minn); MS '41 (U Pittsburgh); post grad '46-47 (Okla A and M Coll) '51 (State U Ia). Indsl engr Aluminum Cooking Utensil Co and Aluminum Co of Am Pittsburgh '37-41; prof indsl engring Okla A and M Coll and vice dean Okla Inst Tech since '41; asso dir Ia Summer Management Conf since '50; management cons to bd govs Fed Reserve System '47-48, to Dept of Defense '50, to industry since '42; cons Fedn Norwegian Industries and Fedn Swedish Industries Oslo and Stockholm summer '50. Registered profl engr Okla. Nat and Okla socs profl engrs—Am Soc Engring Edn—Am Inst Indsl Engrs—Soc for Advancement Management(nat dir)—Indsl Relations Research Assn—Sigma Tau. H: 1810 West Admiral Road, Stillwater, Okla.†◉

13 LOKEN, Robert DeLong. Psychology (Industrial); Management training. b'12. AB (Psychol) '38 (San Jose State Coll); PhD '41 (U Cal Los Angeles). Development and application of wage and incentive plants, of selection programs for industry and cities; development new test of color vision; revision color test and installation testing program for AAF; development Army-Navy management training programs. Author: Supervision in Business and Industry '49. Author articles: The colormeter—a new test of color vision; "ABC" of supervision. Instr psychol dept U Cal Los Angeles '38-41; supervisor trade testing Cal State Dept Edn '41-42; training dir Neisman-Marcus Co Dallas '46-48; prof management U Ill since '48. AAAS—Am Psychol Assn—Am Vocational Assn—Sigma Xi. University of Illinois, Urbana, Ill.

14 LOKKE, Carl Ludwig. French Revolution; G o v e r n m e n t records (United States); Klondike gold rush. b'97. Student '17-18 (Wash U); AB '22—AM '23 (Calif U); PhD '32 (Columbia). Research on Jefferson and Leclerc expedition, reasons why Talleyrand was not envoy to Constantinople, London merchant interest in St Domingue plantations of émigrés, French foreign office records under Third Republic, food administration papers for Virginia in National Archives, secret negotiations for maintaining Peace of Amiens, the Trumbull episode. Author: France and the Colonial Question: A Study of Contemporary French Opinion, 1763-1801 '32. Co-editor: Handbook of Federal World War Agencies and their Records 1917-1921 '43; also articles in field. Instr Columbia '25-29, lecturer '32-33; asst prof Smith Coll '30-31; archivist on staff Nat Archives since '35, chief foreign affairs sect since '49. AHA (life)—Soc Am Archivists (asso ed Am Archivist '49-52) —Assn Study Negro Life and Hist. Awarded Columbia U fellowship in modern European hist '24-25. The National Archives, Washington 9. H: 1801 16th St., N.W.

15 LOLLAR, Robert M(iller). Leather chemistry; Biochemistry. b'15. MS '38 —PhD '40 (U Cincinnati). Author articles in field. Research supervisor dept applied sci in tanning research U Cincinnati since '41. Am Chem Soc—Am Leather Chem Assn—Sigma Xi—Tau Beta Pi. Department of Applied Science in Tanning Research, University of Cincinnati, Cincinnati 21.†

16 LOMAX, Alan. American folklore. b'15. AB '36 (U Tex); '31-32 (Harvard). Radio writer producer American School of the Air '39-41; writer Back Where I Came From '41; writer-producer Library of Congress '41; writer producer narrator Transatlantic Call '42; writer Cavalcade of America, Eternal Light, CBS WorkShop, This Land is Bright and others. Edited: record albums, Dust Bowl Ballads, The Midnight Special, The Wayfaring Stranger, Josh White, Roll the Union On, Songs for Victory, Folk Music of the USA, American Folk Music Series. Co-editor: (with John A Lomax) American Ballads and Folk Songs; Negro Songs as Sung by Lead Belly; Cowboy Songs; Our Singing Country; Folksong: USA, Mister Jelly Roll. Asst in charge Archives Am Folklore Library of Congress '37-42; dir folk music Decca Recording '45-49; writer narrator Your Ballad Man Mutual Broadcasting System '47-49; bd dirs People Songs Inc. Am Folklore Soc—NY Folklore Soc—Tex Folklore Soc—Phi Beta Kappa. Fellow Council Learned Socs '41; Guggenheim fellow '47. 405 E. 55th St., NYC.

17 LOMBARDO, Josef Vincent. Creative art; Art education; Art history; Creative writing. b'08. Diploma '24 (Asso Art Studios) '26 (Cooper Union Sch); BFA '31 — BA '39 — Carnegie scholarship '36-39 (NYU); MA '32— PhD '49—Profl diploma '50—vis scholar '50—post-doctoral scholarship '50-51 (Columbia); LittD '34—grad fellow '33—Gold medalist '34—U medal '50 (U Florence); Am fellow '33 (Royal Acad Fine Arts Florence); fgn study '29, '32-24 (France and Italy); LLD '51 (Villanova). Special assistant examiner fine arts Board of Education NYC '44. Author: Santa Maria del Fiore: Arnolfo di Cambio '34; Attilio Piccirilli (1866-1945): Life of an American Sculptor '44; Chaim Gross, Sculptor '49. Mem dept art Brooklyn Coll '37-38, NYU '44, Columbia '46-49; chmn dept art Queens Coll '33-42, mem instrn staff since '38; dir fine arts Columbia '50; chmn adv com fine arts Carlton Pub Corp NYC '45-49; art cons Prang Co pubs NYC since '51. Mus Modern Art—NEA—Eastern Arts Assn—AAUP—Nat Art Edn Assn— Queens College, Flushing 67, N.Y.†◉

18 LONG, Chester H. Physics (Education). b'98. AB '22—MA '23—PhD '47 (U Kan). In charge mathematics Clifton College '24-26, in charge science '26-32 (responsible for getting school accredited for science courses); in charge testing beginning science courses Northwest Missouri State Teachers College '35-36. Part time instr physics U Kan '37-40, instr physics '43-44, elec engring '44-45; in charge physics dept Southwestern Coll '41-43; in charge physics dept Ill Wesleyan U since '47. Am Inst Physics—Am Physics Soc—Am Assn Physics Tchrs —AAAS—AAUP—Phi Beta Kappa— Sigma Xi. 101 E. Division St., Bloomington, Ill.◉

19 LONG, Clarence D(ickinson), Jr. Economics; Building cycles. b'08. AB '32—AM '33 (Washington and Jefferson Coll); AM '35—PhD '38 (Princeton). Author: Building Cycles and the Theory of Investment '40; The Labor Force in Wartime America '44. Co-author: (with Frederick C Mills) Task Force Report on Statistical Agencies, Appendix D (Commn on Orgn Exec Br of Govt); The Statistical Agencies of the Federal Government (Nat Bur Econ Research) '49; Labor Force and Full Employment '50. With Wesleyan U Conn '36-39, '40-45, asso prof '41-45; econ surveyor Montmorency Paper Co Ltd Can '39; lectr Hartford Coll '40-41; asso prof Johns Hopkins U '46, prof since '47; sr labor specialist WPB '42; mem research staff Nat Bur Econ Research since '46; mem Inst for Advanced Study Princeton '41-46. Am Econ Assn—Am Statis Assn—Econometric Soc—Acad Polit Sci—Phi Beta Kappa—Alpha Tau Omega. Johns Hopkins University, Balt 18.◉

20 LONG, Clarence Edward. Industry management (Iron and steel); Industry improvement commissions (Chambers of Commerce). b'88. Student '07 (Purdue U); BS in civil engring '08 (Bucknell U). Analyses of plant layouts, equipment and facilities for use executives, appraisers and financiers; regional area surveys and reports for attraction of new industries and additional transportation via rail, water, motor truck. Office engr Jones & Laughlin Steel Corp '09-11, Carnegie-Ill Steel Corp '11-13; cons engr since '13. Am Soc CE—Soc Am Mil Engrs. P.O. Box 1922, Pitts 30.

21 LONG, E(ugene) Hudson. American literature and social history; Mark Twain; O. Henry; American drama. b '08. AB '31—MA '31 (Baylor U); PhD '42 (U Pa); grad work '33-34 (U Va) '35 (Oxford U). Author: O. Henry, the Man and his Work '49; Mark Twain Handbook (in preparation). Faculty English Ala Polytech Inst '37-41. U Del '41-42, U Pa '45-46; asst prof Ohio State U '46-47, Vanderbilt U '47-49; prof Am lit Baylor U and co-chmn Am Civilization Program since '49; asst historian Combined Chiefs of Staff Washington '43-45. Modern Lang Assn Am—Modern Humanities Research Assn—S Central Modern Lang Assn—Sigma Tau Delta. Baylor University, Waco, Tex.◉

22 LONG, James Dewey. Agricultural engineering; Adobe construction. b'99. Student '17-18 (Upper Ia U); BS Agr Engring '22 (Ia State Coll); MS Agr Engring '28 (U Calif). Author articles in field. Asst prof, asst agrl engr agrl expt sta U Calif Davis '22-40; field agr engr Douglas Fir Plywood Assn Tacoma Wash '40-47, dir research, dir market research and edn; cons agrl engr Instituto Nacional de Abastecimiento Bogota Colombia SA '47-48; spl asst agrl engring research adminstrn US Dept Agr Beltsville Md since '48; adv council Wash State Coll Inst Tech '45-47, Am Soc Agrl Engrs (F, pres '45 council '46-48, chmn farm structures div '38, rep US C of C Constrn Industry Adv Council '45-47)—AAAS—ASEE—Forest

Products Research Soc—Inst Food Technol. U. S. Department of Agriculture, Agricultural Research Center, Beltsville, Md.

10 LONG, James Scott. Chemistry (Paint, drying oils). b'92. Chem E '13—MS '15 (Lehigh U); grad study '16 (Columbia); PhD '22 (Johns Hopkins U). Co-author: Chemical Calculations; Qualitative Analysis '27; also many articles in field. Chem dir Devoe & Raynolds Co Inc since '34, mem bd dirs since '35. Am Soc Chem(F)—Textile Chem Assn—Am Chem Soc—Tau Beta Pi—Sigma Xi. 2620 Dundee Rd., Lsvl.

11 LONG, Mary McDonald (Mrs. Percy W. Long). English literature (Medieval). BS '30 (State Teachers Coll Worcester Mass); MA—PhD '43 (NYU). Author: The English Strong Verb from Chaucer to Caxton '44. Instr Eng Hunter Coll '47-49, asso prof '49; asst prof Catholic Univ Am since '49. Received Carleton Brown Memorial award '43. Mod Lang Assn Am—Med Acad. 3829 Veazey St., Washington 15.

12 LONG, Robert Grant. Brazil (Regional geography). b'18. AB '41 (U Mich); AM '43 (Syracuse U); PhD '49 (Northwestern U). Studies in land use in Paraiba Valley, Brazil; research on regional geography Brazil. Author article: Volta Redonda: Symbol of maturity in industrial progress of Brazil. Geog US Bd on Geog Names US Dept Interior '43-44; asst prof geog U Tenn since '49. Served as cartographic officer lt (jg) USNR '44-46. Assn Am Geog—Associacao dos Geografos Brasileiras. Department of Geology-Geography, University of Tennessee, Knoxville.

13 LONGENECKER, Herbert Eugene. Biochemistry. b'12. BS '33—MS '34—PhD '36 (Pa State Coll). Member food and nutrition board National Research Council; member committee on food research office of QMG; biochemistry and nutrition study sect US Public Health Service; associate member panel on programs, committee on chemical warfare Research and Development Board since '49; member research council Chemical Corps Advistory Board since '49. Scientific editor: Fats, Oils and Detergents. Sr research fellow and lectr chem U Pittsburgh '38-41, asst research prof chem '41-42; prof chem and dir Buhl Found Research Project '42-44; dean of research in natural sciences U Pittsburgh since '44, dean grad sch since '46. Am Chem Soc—Am Soc Biol Chem—Biochem Soc London—Am Oil Chemists Soc (vp '46-47)—Am Inst Food Technol—Am Inst Nutrition—Am Pub Health Soc—Sigma Xi—Phi Delta Kappa—Alpha Zeta—Phi Kappa Phi—Phi Lambda Upsilon. H: Elmhurst Pl., Pitts 15.☺

14 LONGLEY, Lewis Edward. Apple and chrysanthemum breeding. b'80. BS '04 (Coe Coll); MS '17 (Wash State Coll); PhD '32 (Cornell). Author articles in field. Asst prof hort U Minn since '29. Am Soc Hort Sci—Minn Hort Soc (life)—Phi Kappa Phi. Horticulture Division, University Farm, St. Paul 1.

15 LONGLEY, W(illiam) Warren. Economic and Pre-Cambrian geology; Petrology. b'09. BS '31—MS—PhD '37 (U Minn). Geologist charge exploration expeditions in Pre-Cambrian of Quebec; directed much of early discovery and exploration work of Allard Lake Titanium deposit, described as one of most outstanding mineral discoveries in North America of last decade; directed discovery prospector to discovery location of Bachelor Lake Mineral District; geologist Kennco explorations '45. Author articles in field. Asso prof geol U Colo since '40; geol Quebec Dept Mines since '36, Kennecott Copper Corp '44. Geol Soc Am—Geol Assn Can—Soc Econ Geol—Soc Exploration Geophysicists—Am Assn Petroleum Geol—Am Inst Mining Metal Engrs — Am Soc Photogrammetry—Sigma Xi. Department of Geology, University of Colorado, Boulder, Colo.

16 LONGYEAR, John Munro, III. Maya archeology. b'14. AB '36 (Cornell U); PhD '40 (Harvard); '31 (No State Teachers Coll). Archeological expeditions to Copan Honduras '38, '39, '46, El Salvador '41-42; reconnaissance expedition to Chiriqui Panama '41. Author articles in field. Asst prof anthrop and sociol Colgate U since '48. Am Anthrop Assn(F)—Soc Am Archeol—Inter-Am Soc Anthrop and Geog—Sociedad Mexicana de Antropologia—Sociedad de Antropologia y Arqueologia de Honduras. Colgate University, Hamilton, N.Y.†

17 LONGYEAR, Robert Davis. Diamond core drilling; Mineral exploration. b'92. AB '14 (Williams Coll); MA '15 (U Wis); '15-16 (Stanford U) '33 (U Minn). Research on exploration for nickel, oil, copper, gold and other minerals with emphasis on diamond drilling. Pres E J Longyear Co since '24. AIMME—Soc Econ Geol—Diamond Core Drill Mfrs Assn (pres '30-45)—Can Inst Mining and Metall Engrs—Minn Soc Profl Engrs. E. J. Longyear Co., 1700 Foshay Tower, Mpls 2.

18 LONSDALE, John Tipton. Petrography; Igneous rocks; Mineralogy; Meteorites; Ground water; Mineral resources of Texas. b'95. AB '17—MS '21 (U Ia); PhD '24 (U Va). Author articles in field. Dir Bur Econ Geol, prof geol, U Tex since '45. Geol Soc Am(F)—Mineral Soc Am(F)—Am Assn Petroleum Geol—Am Inst Mining Metall Engrs—Am Geophys Union—AAAS. Research grants from Geol Soc Am '37, '40. Bureau of Economic Geology, University of Texas, University Station, Austin, Tex.†

19 LOOMIS, Arthur Kirkwood. Education (Curriculum, public school, finance). b'88. AB '09—LHD '44 (Baker U); AM '17 (Kan U); PhD '26 (Columbia). Chief specialist for curriculum National Survey of Secondary Education, Office of Education '30-31; editor Denver courses of study series '25-31. Author: Estimating School Equipment Costs '26; The Program of Studies (with Lide) '32. Dir curriculum Denver Pub Schs '25-31; prin U High Sch, asso prof edn, asso dean Coll U Chicago '31-36; supt schs Shaker Heights O '36-44; dir sch edn and prof edn Denver U '44-47; spl adviser ednl reorganization GHQ SCAP Tokyo '47-49; chief edn div CIE, GHQ, SCAP since '49. American Ednl Research Assn—Am Edn Fellowship—Nat Soc Study Edn—NEA—Colo Ednl Assn—Kappa Delta Pi—Phi Delta Kappa. CI and E, GHQ, SCAP, APO 500, c/o Postmaster SF.

20 LOOMIS, C(harles) Grant. Folklore; Germanic languages and literature. b'01. AB '23 (Hamilton Coll); '25-26 (Columbia); '26-28 (U Munich); AM '29—PhD '33 (Harvard). Research on growth of Saint Edmund Legend, Saint Edmund and the Lodbrok, legend and folklore. Author: White Magic: An Introduction to the Folklore of Christian Legend '48; also articles in field. Asst prof German U Calif '41-47, asso prof since '47. Modern Lang Assn Am—Medieval Acad Am (councillor '46-49)—Am Folklore Soc (second vp '46-47, councillor '47-50)—Calif Folklore Soc. Guggenheim fellow '45-46. University of California, Berkeley.

21 LOOMIS, Charles Price. Rural sociology; Applied anthropology. born '05. BS '28 (New Mexico State College); MS '29 (NC State Coll); PhD '33 (Harvard); '33-34 (Heidelberg and Koenigsberg U); summer '42 (Nat U Mexico). War department employee and participant in activities of Strategic Bombing Survey in Germany. Author: Studies of Rural Social Organization in the U S, Latin America and Germany '45. Translated and elaborated: Fundamentals Concepts of Sociology — Gemeinschaft and Gesellschaft by F. Toennies '40. Editor Journal Rural Sociology. Head dept sociol and anthrop Mich State Coll, dir Social Research Service. Rural Sociol Soc (pres '48)—Am Sociol Soc—Am Sociometric Soc—Soc Applied Anthrop—(Pres)—Soc for the Psychol Study of Social Issues—Am Anthrop Soc—AAUP—Mission for Inter-governmental Com on Refugees to Andean Countries (head '47)—Phi Kappa Phi. Department of Sociology and Anthropology, Michigan State College, East Lansing, Mich.☺

22 LOOMIS, Nathaniel Horace. Grape breeding (Southern United States conditions). b'07. BS '30—grad study '32 (Ia State Coll); '38 (U Minn). Author articles in field. With US Dept Agr since '31. Am Soc Hort Sci—Am Genetic Assn. U.S. Horticultural Field Station, Rt. 6, Meridian, Miss.†

23 LOOMIS, Richard Biggar. Chiggers; Amphibians and reptiles of Nebraska; King snakes. BSc '48 (U Neb). Phi Sigma—Sigma Xi—Kan Acad Sci—Am Soc Icth and Herpet—Herpet League—Am Soc Mammal. Department of Zoology. University of Kansas, Lawrence, Kan.

24 LOOMIS, Roger Sherman. Arthurian romance. b'87. BA '09 (Williams Coll); MA '10 (Harvard); BLitt '13 (Oxford U). Author: Celtic Myth and Arthurian Romance '27; Thomas of Britain, Romance of Tristram and Ysolt '31; Arthurian Tradition and Chrétien de Troyes '49. Co-author: Arthurian Legends in Medieval Art '38; also articles in field. Prof Eng Columbia U since '47. Modern Lang Assn Am (chmn Arthurian group, chmn medieval sect)—Medieval Acad Am. Rhodes Scholar '10-13. Philosophy Hall, Columbia University, NYC 27.†☺

25 LOPEZ, Robert Sabatino. Trade (Genoese, Byzantine). b'10. LittD '32 (U Milan); PhD '42 (U Wis). Research on commerce of Middle Ages and Renaissance, and agriculture, industry, economic thought, literature, and arts as connected with trade development, social classes, town institutions and development, commercial law, and history of technology. Author: Genova marinara nel Duecento '33; Studi sull'economia genovese nel Medioevo '36; Storia delle colonie geneovesi nel Mediterraneo '38. Co-author: (with I Raymond) Medieval Trade in the Mediterranean World '52. Contributor: Cambridge Economic History (vol II) '51; Enciclopedia Italiana 1929-1948. Asso prof, prof hist Tchrs Coll Cagliari, Pavia, and Genoa '33-36; asst prof hist U Genoa '36-38; research asst U Wis '39-42; script ed Italian sect OWI '42-43; faculty Brooklyn Coll '43-44; news ed CBS Listening Sta '44-45; faculty Columbia U '45-46; with Yale U since '46, asso prof hist since '50. Soc Ligure di Storia Patria(F)—Soc di Storia Arte Archeol di Alessandria(F)—AHA—Medieval Acad—Econ Hist Assn—Conn Acad. Received Lattes prize U Milan '33, Gautieri prize Acad Turin '34. Guggenheim F

'48-49, '51-52. 107 Harkness Hall, Yale University, New Haven.†

10 LORCH, Fred W. American literature (Mark Twain, Thoreau); California gold rush. b'93. AB '18 (Knox Coll); AM '28—PhD '36 (U Ia). Author articles in field. Prof Eng since '21, prof and head dept Eng and speech since '42, adviser to coll Eng '38. Nat Council Teachers Eng—Mark Twain Assn Am—Ia Colls Conf Eng—Nat Eng Assn—Phi Kappa Phi. 618 Stanton Av., Ames, Ia.⊙

11 LORD, Richard Collins. Spectroscopy (Infrared, Raman effect). b'10. BSc '31 (Kenyon Coll); PhD '36 (Johns Hopkins); Nat Research Council fellow '36-37 (U Mich); Rockefeller fellow '37-38 (U Copenhagen). Author: (with others) Practical Spectroscopy '48. Dir spectroscopy lab and asso prof chem MIT since '46. Tech aide and deputy chief optics div Nat Defense Research Com Washington '42-46. Am Phys Soc—Am Chem Soc—Optical Soc Am. Massachusetts Institute of Technology, Cambridge 39, Mass.†

12 LORD, Royal Bertram. Heavy construction; River works; Locks and dams. b'99. BS '19 (Brown U); BS '23 (US Mil Acad); grad '24 (Engring Sch Ft Belvoir Va); MS in E '27 (Calif U); LLD (hon) Brown U '46. In charge construction and operations Passamaquoddy Tidal Bay power project Eastport Maine '35-36; coordinator of Resettlement Administration and chief engineer and coordinator of Farm Security Administration in charge design and construction 100,000 housing and farm structures '36-38. Invented Lord portable steel emplacement and Lord portable military cableway used by US Army. Author articles in field. USN World War I; commd 2d lt US Army '23, advancing to maj gen '44; chief operations Bd Econ Warfare '41-42, asst dir since '42; comdg gen assembly area command France redeployment of troops and materiel since '45; Theatre Gen Bd Versailles since '45. Lighter Than Air Transportation Com—Am Soc Engrs. Holder US and fgn decorations. 8 Dunham Rd., Scarsdale, N.Y.⊙

13 LORENZ, Anthony Joseph. Nutrition; Food technology; Vitamin C; Food habits; Flavonoid pigments. b '92. Student (Josephinum Coll Columbus O). Research on dietary and pharmacological effects of vitamins D, C, and flavonoid pigments; studies on history of food processing, dietetic background of citrus fruits, their metabolism, and pharmacological effects of products of citrus fruits; examination data on history of feeding wounded and relation to wound healing, effects of external stresses on creation vitamin C deficiencies, and relationship between food and medicine; delegate White House Conference on Nutrition '41; technical consultant Quartermaster Research Laboratory; board of directors Associates Food and Container Institute of Armed Services; member committee on industrial feeding plans War Food Administration. Author articles: Army Hospital Diets '44; Scurvy in Parry Expedition of 1819 '45; Dual Nature of Vitamin C '49, and others. Co-author article: (with Arnold) Preparation and Estimation of Crude Citrin Solutions (Vitamin P) '41. Food and nutrition cons Lord & Thomas; pres Biol Engring Lab (cons) Chicago '28-34; dir nutrition research Cal Fruit Growers Exchange Los Angeles since '34; chmn state food and nutrition com Cal State War Council '42-46. ACS (chmn flavonoid symposium Chicago '49)—Inst Food Tech (nat counsellor and first chmn So Cal sect)—AAAS—NY Acad Sci—Barlow Soc Med Hist. 707 W. Fifth St., LA 14. H: 1610 Comstock Av., LA 24.

14 LORING, Rosamond B. (Mrs.). Design and making of colored book papers. b'89. Student (Haskell's Sch, Boston). Author: Marbled Papers '33; Decorative Book Papers '42; also articles in field. Hon curator exhibits Peabody Mus Salem Mass since '45, trustee since '46; hon curator paper collections graphic arts dept Harvard since '48. Arts and Crafts—Am Inst Graphic Arts—Bibliog Soc Am. 2 Gloucester St., Boston 16. H: 573 Hale St., Prides Crossing.

15 LORRAINE, Helen. Medical illustration. b'92. Student '09-13 (Art Club, Richmond, Va); '13-15 (Johns Hopkins Med Sch). Illustration of anatomy, pathology and surgery; editor Graphics '45-50, editorial board member since '50. Illustrator: Operative Surgery (6th edit) '51; Urological Surgery (2nd edit) '50; Surgery of the Stomach and Duodenum '33. Co-illustrator: Surgical Operations '49; Emergency Surgery '48. Head dept med illustration St Elizabeth's Hosp Richmond '15-45, free lance med illustrator and staff cons since '45. Assn Med Illustrators (charger mem)—Med Artists Assn Gt Brit (hon). 5212 Sylvan Rd., Richmond 25, Va.

16 LOSCO, Ezekiel. Alloys. b'16. BS in phys metall (MIT); MS (Met E) (Carnegie Inst Tech). Research and development improved special purpose alloys, and improved methods for melting, casting, fabrication, heat treating, and testing; development new compositions for applications requiring resistance to high temperatures and stresses, including critical gas turbine components, high temperature springs, wear-resistant dies, corrosion and weak resistant bearings, steam tubing, and hardfacing materials; production of precipitation-hardened alloys with high strength, corrosion resistance, and non-magnetic for electric equipment, also low expansion and magnetic alloys. Holds patents on heat resisting alloys, and on procedures for casting and fabrication. Author article: Iron Base Alloy has Good High Temperature Strength '50. With Westinghouse Elec Corp since '46, supervisor spl alloy development materials engring dept since '48. AIMME —Am Soc Metals—Sigma Xi. Profl metall engr Pa. Westinghouse Electric Corp., Materials Engineering Department, East Pittsburgh, Pa. H: 4764 Rolling Hills Rd., Whitehall Boro, Pitts.

17 LOTHROP, Warren Craig. High explosives; Aromatic chemistry; Hand weapons. b'12. AB '33—MA '35—PhD '37 (Harvard). Author articles: Diazotization of Picramid '38; The Structure of Fluorene '39; Biphenylene '41, and others. Co-author articles: (with L F Fieser) Structure of Naphthalene '35; (with Fieser) Structure of Anthracene '36; and others. Contributor: Science in World War II '48. Tech aide OSRD-Nat Defense Research Com Washington '42-46; asst ed Journ Am Chem Soc Cambridge Mass '47-49; staff Arthur D Little Inc since '46. ACS—Am Inst Chem—Soc Chem Industry—Am Ordnance Assn. Arthur D. Little, Inc., 30 Memorial Drive, Cambridge 42, Mass.

18 LOTTICK, Kenneth Verne. Education (Principles, methods). b'04. Student '25-27 (U Louisville); AB '28 (Hanover Coll Ind); MA '33 (O State U); '44-46 (Columbia); '47-49 (Harvard). Development procedure for determination of value of merit system in small schools; studies on progress in educational methods. Author articles: Evaluation of Ethical Discrimination '48; Higher Education and Religious Guidance '48; Professional Education and Civic Responsibility '49; Why and How to Teach a Unity in Geopolitcal Understanding '49, and others. Asso prof hist and geog Elon Coll NC '43-44; asst prof social studies State Tchrs Coll Fredonia NY '44-48; asst in Social and Philos Foundations of Edn Tchrs Coll Columbia summers '45-46; asso prof edn Willamette U since '48. AHA-AAUP—NY State Council Social Studies—NY Assn State Tchrs Coll Faculties—NEA—Ore Edn Assn. Willamette University, Salem, Ore.

19 LOTZ, John. Linguistics; Phonetics; Finno-Ugric languages. b'13. Eotvos Collegium '31-35 (U Budapest); dr phil sub auspicus Gub Hung '35; docent '39 (Stockholm U). Author: Das ungarische Sprachsystem '39; also articles. Vis asso prof Hungarian studies Columbia U '47-49, asso prof gen and compar linguistics Columbia U since '49; vis asso prof Linguistics U Chgo '49. Finnougric Soc—Hungarian Linguistic Assn. Columbia University, NYC 27.†

20 LOUDERBACK, George Davis. Geology (Physical, stratigraphic, structural, sediments, earthquakes and faults, engineering). b'74. AB '96—PhD '99—LLD '46 (U Calif). Author articles in field. Prof emeritus U Calif since '44; geol cons on various engring projects since '20. AAAS(F)—Geol Soc Am (past sec, chmn '19-22, Cordilleran sect, vp '36)—Seismol Soc Am (sec '07-10, pres '14, '29-35, ed since '35)—Am Inst Mining Metall Engrs—Am Geog Soc—Mineral Soc Am—Soc Econ Geol (vp '39)—Am Petroleum Geol—Phi Beta Kappa—Sigma Xi—Tau Beta Pi. 107 Ardmore Rd., Berkeley 7.⊙

21 LOUGEE, Richard Jewett. Physiography; Geology of Alaska. b'05. BS '27 (Dartmouth Coll); MA '29 (U Mich); PhD '38—fellow '32-33 (Columbia U). Delegate 17th International Geology Congress, Russia '37. Author: Reports on Physiography of New England; Geology of the Connecticut Valley; Floods, Earthquakes, Glacial History of New England; Geology of Alaska. Research Am Geog Soc '29-32; asst prof geol U Vt '35; asst soil conservationist US Dept Agr '35-36; chmn dept geol Colby Coll '36-47, asst prof geol '36-37, asso prof '37-46, prof '46-47; research analyst OSS '45; professor physiography Clark U since '50. Me Mineral Geol Soc (pres '38-40)—Geol Soc Finland (corr). Clark University, Worcester 3, Mass.†

22 LOUGHEAD, Harvey John. Watershed management; Forest harvesting; Management hardwood and pine forests. b'07. BS in forestry '31 (NC State Coll); MS in forestry '37 (U Cal). Research on management of Southern Pines, studies damage caused by fires to Appalachian hardwoods; design experiments and equipment to evaluate influence of forests on streamflow, ground water, interception and other components of hydrology on forested watersheds; examinations and surveys on major streams in Southeastern US to evaluate frequency, magnitude and damages caused by floods and to design and evaluate watershed measures for alleviation of floods and resulting damage; operation and applied management to Southern Pine forests for timber production and naval stores; harvesting of sawtimber, pulpwood, poles and other products from Southern Pines and Appalachian Hardwoods; in charge personnel management for largest forest products research laboratory in the world. With Appalachian Forest Expt Sta US Forest Service '31-41, in charge flood control '37-41, asst to dir forest products research Forest Products Lab '42-46, cons forester since '46. Soc Am Foresters(sr mem)—Forest Products Research Soc —NC Forestry Assn—Fla Forest and Park Assn—Am Geophys Union—Am Forestry Assn—Soc Am Mil Engrs. 15 E. Forest Rd., Biltmore Station, Asheville, N.C.

10 LOUGHRIDGE, Donald Holt. Physics; Nuclear reactors (Design); Cyclotron design; Cosmic ray measurements. b'99. BS '23—PhD '27 (Cal Inst Tech). Supervised construction of cyclotrons. Author 40-50 articles in field. Research phys US Steel Corp '28-29; asst, asso and prof phys U Wash '31-41; prin phys Nat Bur Standards '41-42; research phys U Cal '41-43; sr sci adv to sec army '48-51; dep dir Reactor Div Atomic Energy Commn since '51. APS(F)—Inst Aeronautical Sci(asso F)—Inst Radio Engrs(sr mem)—Sigma Xi—Tau Beta Pi. Atomic Energy Commission, 1901 Constitution Av., Washington. H: 3465 N. Edison St., Arlington, Va.†⊙

11 LOUGOVOY, Boris Nicholas. Chewing gum base; Synthetic resins; Flashless, smokeless powder. b'88. MS '08-13 (L' Academie d'Artillerie Michel); PhD '13 (U St Petersburg, Russia); '14-15 (U Sorbonne, Paris); '15 (U du Toulouse, France). Inventor flashless, smokeless powder in Russia; holder numerous patents. Author articles in field. Chief research chem Ellis-Foster Co Montclair NJ '22-28, Am Chicle Co LI City since '28. Am Chem Soc—Am Inst Chem(F)—Nat Geog Soc(F). American Chicle Co., 30-30 Thompson Av., Long Island City, N.Y. H.: 86-10 34th Av., Jackson Heights.†

12 LOUIE, Man Goo. Civil engineering; Structural design. b'14. BS in civil engring '41 (U Cal Berkeley). Design schools, commercial, light and heavy industrial buildings and plants. Structural designer Fluor Corp '42-43; stress analyst Douglas Aircraft Co '43-45; sr structural design engr Kaiser Engrs Inc '45-47, '48-49; structural engr Austin Co '47-48, E G Bangs since '49. Registered civil engr Cal. Am Soc CE —Am Concrete Inst. 605 Market St., SF 5.

13 LOUNSBURY, Floyd Glenn. In- '46 (U Wis); PhD '49 (Yale). Research on Oneida, Cherokee, Tuscarora, Onondians (Language). b'14. BA '41—MA dada, Seneca, and Cayuga languages. Author: Comparative Iroquoian Morphology '53. Asst prof anthrop Yale since '49. Linguistic Soc Am—Am Anthrop Assn(F). Department of Anthropology, Yale University, New Haven.

14 LOUSTALOT, Arnaud J(oseph). Photosynthesis; Mineral nutrition; Physiology and evaluation of cinchona and derris plants; Chemical weed control. b'13. BS '35—MS '36 (La State U); PhD '39 (Cornell U). Author articles in field. Asso chem, asst dir and sr plant physiol US Dept Agr Fed Expt Sta Mayaguez Puerto Rico since '45. Am Soc Hort Sci—Am Soc Plant Physiol—Am Soc Agron—Sociedad Americana de Ciencias Agricolas—Sigma Xi— Gamma Sigma Delta. Federal Experiment Station, Mayaguez, Puerto Rico.†

15 LOVE, J(ohn) David. Stratigraphy; Petroleum geology; Geology of Wyoming. b'13. BA '33—MA '34 (U Wyo); PhD '38 (Yale). Author articles in field. Geol Shell Oil Co '38-42; geol US Geol Survey since '42, geol charge Wyo Basins Projects for Fuels Sect

since '43. Geol Soc Am—Am Assn Petroleum Geol—Paleontol Society— Wyoming Geol Association—Sigma Xi —Phi Beta Kappa. U.S. Geological Survey, Geology Hall, University of Wyoming, Laramie, Wyo.

16 LOVE, Katharine Stith. Ammonia (Catalytic synthesis); Fertilizers (Synthesis of nitrogenous); Surface area measurements. b'95. AB '17 (U Richmond); '19-20 (U Chicago); MS '25 (George Washington U). Research on kinetics of ammonia decomposition over various catalysts, adsorptions on such catalysts, and thermal decomposition and reduction by hydrogen of iron nitrides made from such catalysts; collaborator in development synthetic nitrogenous fertilizer of low solubility composed of polymers of urea and formaldehyde. Co-author articles: (with P H Emmett) The Catalytic Decomposition of Ammonia over Iron Synthetic Ammonia Catalysts '41; (with Stephen Brunauer) The Effect of Alkali Promoter Concentration on the Decomposition of Ammonia over Doubly Promoted Iron Catalysts '42; (with Robert G Keenan, Brunauer) Adsorption of Nitrogen and the Mechanism of Ammonia Decomposition over Iron Catalysts '42, and others. Chem USDA since '21, chem BPISAE since '41. ACS—AAAS. Bureau of Plant Industry, Soils, and Agricultural Engineering, U.S. Department of Agriculture, Beltsville, Md.

17 LOVE, Samuel Kenneth. Chemical quality of natural waters; Fluvial sediments. b'03. BS '27—MS '30 (U Fla). Measurement of sediment discharge of San Juan River '29, Little Colorado River '31, Boise River Basin '39-40; supervision of investigation of chemical quality of natural waters in southeastern Florida '40-44. Co-author: (with W D Collins, C S Howard) Quality of Surface Waters of the United States '41, (with Collins) '42, (with Howard) '43; also articles in field. With US Geol Survey since '28, chief quality of water br since '46. Am Chem Soc (exec com div water sewage and sanitation '47-48, chairman '49—Am Geophys Union—Am Water Works Assn. Water Resources Division, U.S. Geological Survey, Washington 25.

18 LOVEJOY, James Donovan. Marine engineering. b'02. BS '24 (US Naval Acad); '27 (US Naval Submarine Sch). Direction procurement and scheduling all materials required for construction major naval and maritime shipbuilding programs during World War II. Marine engr Westinghouse Elec Corp '29-36; marine engr and dir procurement and prodn Gibbs and Cox Inc since '36. Lt (jg) USN '24-29. Soc Naval Architects and Marine Engrs— Am Soc Naval Engrs. Gibbs and Cox Inc, 21 West St., NYC 6.

19 LOVELL, Harvey Bulfinch. Ornithology (Kentucky); Bird nesting and breeding habits; Plant ecology. b'03. BA '24 (Bowdoin); MA '27—PhD '33 (Harvard). Author articles: Unusual Behavior in the Chimney Swift '39; The Nesting of the Starling in Kentucky '42; Gambles Sparrow in Kentucky '43; Observations of the Breeding Habits of the Prairie Horned Lark '47; Ovenbird Parasitized by Cowbird in Southern Kentucky '47; Bibliography of Kentucky Ornithology '48, and others. Asst prof biol U Louisville '29-36, asso prof since '36; asso ed transactions Ky Acad Sci '41-44; ed Kentucky Warbler since '45. Wilson Ornithol Club—Assn Am Ornithol Union— Ky Ornithol Soc (pres '42-44)—Ky Soc Natural Hist (a founder, pres '37)—Inland Bird-Banding Assn—Am Soc Zool —Soc Mammalogists—Am Ecol Soc. University of Louisville, Louisville.

20 LOVERING, Thomas Seward. Economic geology; Geochemistry; Petrology; Heat conduction; Mineral economics. b'96. ME '22 (Minn Sch Mines); MS '23—PhD '24 (U Minn). Research on relation of rock alteration to blind ore deposits; experimental and mathematical studies of geologic thermal models. Author: Minerals in World Affairs '43; Rock Alteration in East Tintic District Utah '48; also articles in field. Geol US Geol Survey Washington '25-26, Golden Colo '26-34, investigator mineral deposits for prodn program Eureka Utah '42-46, research geol metals sect since '46; asso prof econ geol U Mich '34-38, prof 38-47. AAAS—Am Inst Mining Metall Engrs —AAPG—GSA—GU—SEG—PAIME— Sigma Xi—Tau Beta Pi. U.S. Geological Survey, Washington 25.⊙

21 LOVING, Alvin DeMar. Secondary school curriculum (Development); Human relations; Home and family living education; Guidance and counseling; Workshop techniques and procedures. AB '31 (Western Mich Coll); ME '40—Doctoral candidate (Wayne U). Co-author: (with Eleanor Wolf and Donald C Marsh) Some Aspects of Negro-Jewish Relations in Detroit. Consultant for Michigan Schools in Human relations; directed summer educational workshop Oklahoma City Public Schools '47 '48; directed Michigan August Curriculum Conference '49 '50 '51; graduate fellowship Wayne University to study Negro-Jewish relations in Detroit '42. Tchr English and speech Miller High Sch Detroit '35-48; administrative counselor Northwestern High Sch Detroit '48-51; instr coll edn Wayne U '47-51. Northwestern High School, 6300 Grand River, Det 8. H: 591 Josephine, Det 2.

22 LOW, Frank Norman. Peripheral vision; Visual acuity; Form perception. b'11. BA '32—PhD '36 (Cornell U). '32-33 (Buffalo U). Investigated projects in field for Office of Scientific Research and Development '43-45, Civil Aeronautics Administration '43-45, Office of Naval Research '46 49. Author articles: Effect of Training on Acuity of Peripheral Vision '46; Some Characteristics of Peripheral Visual Performance '46, and others. Instr anat UNC '37-39, asst prof '39-45; asso anat U Md '45; asso prof anat U W Va '46; asst prof anat Johns Hopkins '46-49; asso prof anat LSU Med Sch since '49. Am Assn Anat— Sigma Xi. Anatomy Department, LSU Med Sch, New Orleans.

23 LOW, Jessop Budge. Wildlife and waterfowl management. b'14. BS '37 (Utah State Agrl Coll); MS—PhD '41 (Ia State Coll). Research in waterfowl management, big game and pheasant management. Author articles in field. Game technician Ill State Nat Hist Survey '41-43; asst prof Utah State Agrl Coll charge wildlife management '43-44, hon prof since '45; wildlife biologist Utah Fish and Game Dept '44-45; biologist and leader Utah Coop Wildlife Research Unit since '45. Wildlife Soc—Phi Kappa Phi—Sigma Xi. Utah Cooperative Wildlife Research Unit, Utah State Agricultural College, Logan, Utah.

24 LOW, Julian William. Geology. b '04. AB '34 (U Colo). Devised new table techniques for geologic investigations in laboratory and field. Author: Plane Table Mapping '52; Manual for Microscopic Examination of Well Cuttings '52. Tech illus Carnegie Instn Wash '32-34; sr topog engr US Geol Survey '36-37; div stratigrapher Cal Standard Oil Co since '37. Am Assn Petroleum Geol—Sigma Xi. 1002 US National Bank Building, Denver.

10 LOWE, Boutelle Ellsworth. Labor (International relations). b'90. AB '11 (Dension U); AM '12 (U Rochester); PhD '18 (Columbia). Author: Representative Industry and Trade Unionism of an American City '12; International Aspects of the Labor Problem '18; The International Protection of Labor '21; International Education for Peace '29. Co-author: (with others) Historical Survey of International Action Affecting Labor '20. Tchr Hackensack High Sch since '20, head dept social sciences '29-37, prin since '37; prin Hackensack Summer Sch '33-36; pres Language Inst Inc NY City '18-34; prof econ Jr Coll Bergen County Teaneck NJ '33-42. H: 125 Lawrence Av., Hasbrouck Heights, N.J.†⊙

11 LOWE, Edmund Waring. Photographs (Developing). b'05. SB '26 (Hamline U); MS '29—PhD '30—Julius Steiglitz F med chem '30-34 (U Chicago); '48-50 (Purdue U). Research and development various photo developing and fixing agents, photographic preparations for fine grain development, high-speed fixing, paper development, and film processing operations. Author: Modern Developing Methods '39; What You Want to Know About Developers '40. Co-founder and pres Edwal Lab Inc '34-47, chmn bd since '47; founder and pres Edwal Sci Products Inc since '50. ACS—Sigma Xi—Photog Soc Am(asso). Edwal Scientific Products Corp., Ringwood, Ill.

12 LOWENFELD, Berthold. Psychology and education of the blind. b'01. PhD '27 (U Vienna). Introduced talking books as an educational medium in schools for blind '39-41; organized first National Conference on blind preschool child '47. Author: The Blind Preschool Child '47; Braille and Talking Book Reading: A Comparative Study '45; Teachers of the Blind: Their Status and Salaries '41; also articles in field. Head teacher Sch of Blind Vienna '22-33; dir Children's Inst Vienna '33-38; lecturer spl edn Teachers Coll Columbia '44-49; dir Ednl Research Am Found Blind NYC '38-49; supt Calif Sch for Blind Berkeley since '49; vis prof U Wash summer sessions since '44; grad faculty Inst Social Work U Mich summer sessions '45-49. Am Assn Workers for Blind (bd dirs '41-47, sec bd certification home teachers '45-51)—Am Psychol Assn—International Council Exceptional Children (ed bd). Rockefeller research fellow '30-31. 2927 Derby St., Berkeley 5.

13 LOWENHAUPT, Abraham. Corporate reorganization (Taxes). b'78. PhB '00 (U Mich); LLB '02 (Lake Forest U). Author articles in field. Am Bar Assn (tax com). 408 Olive St., St. Louis.

14 LOWINSKY, Edward Elias. Renaissance (Music). b'08. Student '17-26 (Humanistisches Gymnasium Stuttgart); '23-28 (Hochschule fur Musik Stuttgart); PhD '33 (U Heidelberg Germany). Author: Orlando di Lasso's Antwerp Motetbook (in German) '37; Secret Chromatic Art in the Netherlands Motet '46 (2d edit) '52. Author articles: The Goddess Fortuna in Music '43; The Function of Conflicting Signatures in Early Polyphonic Music '45; The Concept of Physical and Musical Space in the Renaissance '46; Music History and its Relation to the History of Ideas '46; The Use of Scores by 16th Century Musicians '48; On the Tabula Compositoria of Lampadius '49; A Newly Discovered 16th Century Motet Manuscript at the Biblioteca Vallicelliana in Rome '50. Asst prof mus Black Mountain Coll NC '42-47; asso prof mus Queens Coll Flushing NY since '49; vis asso prof mus U Chicago summer '49. Am Musi-

col Soc—Dutch Musicol Soc—Belgian Musicol Soc—Internat Soc Musicol. Guggenheim fellow '46. Department of Music, Queens College, Flushing, N.Y.

15 LOWRIE, Donald Charles. Spiders. b'10. BSc '32—PhD '42 (U Chicago). Author articles in field. Asso prof zool U of Ida since '49. Am Soc Zool—Ecol Soc Am—Soc Study Evolution—Sigma Xi. University of Idaho, Moscow, Ida.†

16 LOWRIE, Samuel Harman. Dating and courtship in America; culture of Brazil and Latin America. b'94. BA '17 (Rice Inst); MA '22—PhD '32 (Columbia). Author: Culture Conflict in Texas 1821-1835 '32; Immigraçao e Crescimento da Populaçao no Estado de Sao Paulo '38; also articles in field. Prof sociol Bowling Green State U since '39.

17 LOWRY, H(omer) H(iram). Coal chemistry. b'98. AB '18 (O Wesleyan U); MA '19—PhD '20—DuPont F '18-20 (Princeton). Research on chemistry of utilization of coal and derived products. Author 50 articles in field. Editor: Chemistry of Coal Utilization (2 vols) '45 for National Research Council. Research chem W Elec Co '20-25; with Bell Telephone Lab '25-30; dir Coal Research Lab Carnegie Inst Tech since '30. ACS—AAAS—Am Gas Assn—E States Blast Furnace and Coke Oven Assn—AIMME—Inst Fuel(F)—Am Coke and Coal Chem Inst (hon)—Phi Beta Kappa—Sigma Xi—Phi Kappa Phi. Carnegie Institute of Technology, Pitts. 13.⊙

18 LOWRY, Robert Lee, Jr. Irrigation; Flood control; Power distribution. b'00. AB '22 (Trinity U); BS in civil engring '29 (U Tex). Research irrigation water requirements various crops in various places; hydrologic and hydraulic studies for storage as silt control, conservation storage, flood control, power, spillway capacity requirements. Author articles: Excessive rainfall in Texas; others. Co-author: (with Arthur F Johnson) Consumptive use of water for irrigation. Hydraulic engr Denver US Bur Reclamation '35-39, Pecos River Joint Investigation Nat Resources Planning Bd '39-42, Internat Boundary and Water Commn US and Mexico '42-49; cons hydrologist R J Tipton and Assos in S Am '50; cons engr, mem neutral internat commn Helmand River Delta Commn for Iran and Afghanistan '50. Am Soc CE—Am Geophys Union—Sigma Xi—Tau Beta Pi. 324 W. Missouri St., El Paso, Tex.

19 LOWRY, W(elles) Norwood. Photovoltaic effect; Electrical measurements; Education (Demonstration lectures). b'00. BS cum laude '22—MS '23 (Bucknell U); PhD '29 (Cornell U). Author: Laboratory Manual of Physics. With physics dept Bucknell U since '20, prof and chmn dept since '42, chmn sci group since '46. AAAS(F)—Am Phys Soc—Am Assn Physics Tchrs—Sigma Xi—Pi Mu Epsilon—Sigma Pi Sigma. H: 206 S. 13th St., Lewisburg, Pa.⊙

20 LOWRY, William Leonard. Country newspapers (United States). b'98. BA in Journalism '28 (Wis U); '34 (U Fla); '37-38 (U So Calif). Research on consumer evaluation of advertising, mechanical practices of weekly newspapers. Author articles in field. Asso prof journalism U Fla since '41. Sigma Delta Chi. 106 E Building, University of Florida, Gainesville, Fla.†

21 LOWTHER, Conley Vernon. Wheat pathology (Powdery mildew, stinking smut). b'18. BS '40 (W Va Wesleyan Coll); MS '43 (W Va U); PhD '48 (Wash State Coll). Author articles in field. Plant path US Dept

Agr Plant Ind Sta since '48. Am Phytopath Soc—Sigma Xi. U.S. Department of Agriculture, Plant Industry Station, Division of Cereal Crops and Diseases, Beltsville, Md.†

22 LOWTHER, Hugh Sears. Philology; Classical and Romance languages. b'77. State-scholar '95 (Cornell U); AB '99 (Syracuse U); Harrison fellow '02-04—PhD '04 (U Pa); '01, '08 (Alliance Française, Paris). Travel and research in archeology and philology in Europe various periods '01-28; travel in Hawaii and South Seas '34, Mexico '37. Author: The Historical Brutus '99; The Problem of Evil in Dante, Milton and Goethe '00; Notes on Syntax of Martial '04; also articles in field. Prof classical langs and chmn div foreign langs Occidental Coll '24-42, emeritus since '42. Classical Assn Pacific States (pres '26-28)—So Calif Modern Lang Assn (vp '29-30)—Phi Beta Kappa—Phi Kappa Phi. 330 S. Santa Anita St., San Gabriel, Cal.†⊙

23 LUBKIN, Samuel. Digital Electronic computers (Logical and engineering design, coding); Measurement (Design of special instruments, calibration of instruments). b'06. BS (EE) '27—EE '44 (Cooper Union Inst Tech); MS '28 (U Chicago); PhD '39 (NYU). Design automatic sequence all-electronic computer; developed optimum measuring technique for determination photoflash lamp characteristics, characteristics of co-axial cable, and properties of textile fibers; consultant on design and construction of electronic test equipment; devised equipment for automatic measurement of sound transmission to elevator cars, determination source of radio interference caused by elevators; test and analysis of design elevator control systems. Author articles: Bimodal Oscillator '46; Decimal Point Location in Computing Machines '48; A Digital Computer for Solution of Simultaneous Linear Equations '50; A General Purpose Digital Computer of Moderate Cost '50, and others. Engr Otis Elevator Co '28-39; civilian dir insp lab Signal Corps '40-46; engr in charge computing machines Ballistics Research Lab Aberdeen Proving Grounds Md '46-47; engr in charge digital computer sect Reeves Instrument Corp '47-48; cons electronic computers Nat Bur Standards '48-49; pres and chief engr Electronic Computer Corp since '49. Inst Radio Engrs—AAAS—Assn Computing Machinery. Prol engr NY. Electronic Computer Corp., 265 Butler St., Bklyn 17. H: 2942 Nostrand Av., Bklyn 29.

24 LUBY, Sylvester Daniel. History of the South; Civil War military history; History of Missions in the Middle West; Railroad history. b'02. AB '24 (Loras Coll); STB '27—Am '28 (Sulpician Sem Cath U); grad work '30 (Columbia U) '42-44 '45-46—Charles Kendall Adams fellow in history '45 (U Wis). Ordained priest '28; examiner of jr clergy since '44; archdiocesan consultor since '47; appointed domestic prelate with title of Right Rev Monsignor by Pope Pius XII '48; instr history Loras Coll '28-32, asst prof '32-36, asso prof '36-38, prof '38-47, chmn dept '41-47, pres since '47; vis prof history Cath U summers '41 44. Nat Cath Ednl Assn—Am Hist Assn—Miss Valley Hist Assn—Am Cath Hist Assn—Cath Assn Internat Peace—State Hist Soc Ia—Va Hist Soc—Ia Coll Pres Assn—Delta Epsilon Sigma. Keane Hall, Loras College, Dubuque, Ia.†⊙

25 LUCAS, George Michael Cohan. Construction organization. b'04. CE (Union Coll). Specialist in organization construction projects; speed and economy through proper organization. Construction engr. Fla Soc Engrs—Assn Am Engrs—Am Soc CE—Am Mil Engrs. H: 1301 18th St. West, Bradenton, Fla.

10 LUCAS, Isaac Brock. Dwarf fruit trees. b'97. Imported, propagated, and tested with cooperation of research stations in Canada and US dwarf fruit trees of every kind except citrus; designed a model dwarf fruit tree garden for Montreal Botanical Gardens '48; studied European fruit growing methods. Author: Dwarf Fruit Trees for Home Gardens '46; also articles in field. Lawyer since '23, now practicing in Toronto and Markdale. Am Soc Hort Sci. Markdale, Ontario, Can.

11 LUCAS, Walter Arndt. Railroad history. b'94. Student pub schs, YMCA Night Sch Easton Pa, ICS. Researches in history and development of railroad car building and locomotive manufacturing. Author: History of the New York, Susquehanna and Western Railroad '39; From the Hills to the Hudson '44; Popular Picture and Plan Book of Railroad Cars and Locomotives '51; Pocket Guide to American Locomotives '53. Author articles: Freaks and Oddities in Locomotives '46; Lafayette at Wagaraw '51, others. Engring drafting, research, inventing and shop work various railroads and euipment cos '12-31; writing railroad history '13-33; corr Paterson Morning Call '34-36; writer, service dept Simmons-Boardman Pub Corp NY '36-45; asso editor Car Builders Cyclopedia and Locomotive Cyclopedia since '45. Railroadiana of Am NY—Passaic Co Hist Soc NJ—NY Railroad Club—NJ Hist Soc—Eastern Car Foremans Assn NY. 30 Church St., NYC 7.

12 LUCE, Alexander Walker. Voting machines; High-ash combustion. b'99. BS '21—ME '23 (U Minn); '22 (U Chicago). Author: Machine Design (editions since '33); Engineering Standards (editions since '39). Co-author: (with T E Butterfield and B H Jenning) Steam and Gas Engineering '47. Asst prof machine design Lehigh U '30-33, asso prof '33-40; prof and head dept mech engring U Conn '40-42; mech engr Fellows Gear Shaper Co Vt '42-46, advisor since '46; chmn curriculum and head dept mech engring Pratt Inst since '46; expert cons voting machines for Commonwealth Pa and others '31-46; cons Lehigh Navigation Coal Co on development pilot plant for burning 75%-ash mine waste '40. ASME (rep on Am Standards Assn, sect com A-11, chmn sect com B-6 gears, safety code correlating com)—Am Gear Mfgrs Assn—ASEE. Pratt Institute, Brooklyn 5. H: Sunny Mowings, Springfield, Vt.

13 LUCKE, Elmina R. Social service training in India, Burma and Ceylon. b'89. BA (Oberlin Coll); MA (Columbia U); student (U Chicago, U Mich, U Berlin, U Tokyo). Studied needs for welfare training in India, Pakistan, Burma, Ceylon, Malaya, Siam. Author: Teaching of the Far East in American Schools; also articles in field. Founded Delhi Sch Social Work granting first MA degree in social work in Asia under University Delhi, under auspices YWCA of India, Burma, and Ceylon with cooperation of foreign division National Board YWCA's of US '46-48, acting dir until Indian staff was formed and installed '48. Inst Pacific Relations—Am Fed Internat Insts—Am Assn Social Workers—AHA—Internat Assn Social Workers—NEA—Phi Beta Kappa. 3755 Sulphur Spring Rd., Ottawa Hills, Toledo, O.

14 LUCKE, John B(ecker). Geomorphology (Shorelines); Interpretation of aerial photographs. b'08. BS '29—AM '32—PHD '33 (Princeton U); '32-33 (Columbia). Author chapter on shorelines in Book of Science, and section in Aerial Photographs: Their Use and Interpretation; also articles in field. Asst prof geol U W Va '36-40; prof and head dept geol Conn U since '40. Lt photographic interpretation officer charge all beach and terrain studies at Joint Intelligence Center Pacific Ocean Areas US Navy '44-45. Sigma Xi (pres Conn chap '47-48). University of Connecticut, Storrs, Conn.

15 LUCKEY, Bertha Musson. Clinical psychology (Handicapped children). b '90. AB '10—Am '12—PhD '16 (U Neb); '12-14 (U Göttingen). Specialist in problems handicapped children and educational adjustments. Chief psychol Bd Edn Cleveland since '17. Iota Sigma Pi—Phi Beta Kappa—AAAS(F)—Am Orthopsychiatric Assn(F)—Internat Council Exceptional Children—Am Assn Mental Deficiency(F, vp)—Ohio Assn Applied Psychol—Am Psychol Assn(pres div sch psychol '50, pres elect div cons psychol '50). Received U Neb Alumni Assn Distinguished Service award for work in field of youth and handicapped children '48. 1380 East 6th St., Cleve 14.

16 LUCKHARDT, Arno Benedict. Anesthesia; History of physiology and medicine. b'85. Student '97-03—LLD '33 (Conception Mo Coll); BS '06—MS '08—PhD '11 (U Chicago); MD '12 (Rush Med Coll); ScD '34 (Northwestern U). Discoverer with J Bailey Carter of ethylene gas as an anesthetic agent with properties superior to nitrous oxide, commonly known as "laughing gas"; research in physiology of parathyroid glands, gastric and pancreatic secretion, and in history of physiology, dentistry and medicine. With U Chicago '08-50, prof '23-41, chmn dept physiology '41-50, Dr William Beaumont Distinguished Service prof in Physiology '47-50; mem bd dirs Dr William Beaumont Found Inc Prairie du Chien Wis. AMA(F)—Soc Exptl Biol and Med(F)—Internat Coll Anesthetists(F)—Internat Soc Dental Research(F)—Am Coll Dentists(hon F)—Internat Anesthesia Research Soc—Am Physiol Soc(past pres)—Inst Traumatic Surgery—Fedn Am Soc Exptl Biol(pres '33-35)—Am Physiol Soc—A AAS—Ill State Med Soc—Phi Beta Pi—Sigma Xi—Phi Beta Kappa—Gamma Alpha—Alpha Omega Alpha. Alpha Omega medal '38; certificate of award Walter Reed Soc '52; Callahan Mem Award medal Ohio Dental Soc; Phi Beta Pi Man of the Year Citation '48.ⓒ

17 LUCKIESH, Matthew. Physics (Seeing, light, lighting, vision, radiant energy, ultraviolet). b'89. BS in EE '09—DE '35 (Purdue); MS '11 (State U Ia); EE '12—DSc '26 (Ia State Coll). Author: Color and Its Applications '15; Lighting Art '17; Artificial Light '20; Visual Illusions '22; Ultraviolet Radiation '22; Light and Color in Advertising and Merchandising '23; Light and Health '26; Seeing '31; The Science of Seeing '37; Reading as a Visual Task '42; Applications of Germicidal, Erythemal and Infrared Energy '46, and others; also articles in field. Dir Lighting Research Lab Lamp Dept Gen Elec Co since '24. Edison Elec Inst—Illuminating Engring Soc—AIEE—Am Phys Soc—Franklin Inst—Optical Soc Am—Am Acad Optometry—Sigma Xi—Tau Beta Pi. Awarded Longstreth medal and certificate for work on visibility of airplanes, Franklin Inst; Gold medal by Distinguished Service Found of Optometry for researches in seeing; medalist Illuminating Engring Soc. Nela Park, Cleve.ⓒ

18 LUCY, Frank Allen. Optical design; Light; Chemistry and physics of interfaces; Chemistry and physics of textiles. b'07. PhD '33 (Stanford U). General lens design, design complete optical instruments for special purposes; chemical and physical studies of surfaces and other interfaces, particularly by optical methods; mathematical studies of forces between and within molecules. Author articles: The Photoismerization of the o-Nitrobenzaldehydes; Laboratory Detergency Tests; Studies of Surface Films by Reflection of Polarized Light; others. Staff Los Alamos Sci Lab U Cal since '47. Am Chem Soc—Sigma Xi. Box 1663, Los Alamos, N.M. H: 1472-A 40th St.

19 LUDINGTON, Flora B(elle). Libraries (College); International cultural relations. b'98. BA '20 (U Wash); BLS '25 (NY State Library Sch); MA '25 (Mills Coll). Author articles: Books and the Sword—Symbols of our Time '43; Evaluating the Adequacy of the Book Collection '40; others. Reference librarian Mills Coll '22-36; librarian Mt Holyoke Coll since '36; dir US Information Library Bombay India '44-46; vis expert SCAP '48. ALA (chmn internat relations bd '42-44, since '50). Mount Holyoke College, South Hadley, Mass.

20 LUDINGTON, John Robert. Educational philosophy; Education (elementary, secondary); Industrial arts (Education). b'09. BS '31 (Ball State Tchrs Coll Muncie Ind); MA '34—PhD '40 (O State U). Author articles: Industrial Arts Curriculum Construction in the Secondary School '34; Industry and Education—A Study of Certain Policies and Practices of Organized Industry with Implications for Public Schools '40; Industrial Arts Teaching as a Career, and others. Asst prof indsl arts Ball State Tchrs Coll '35-38; prof and head dept indsl arts edn U NC '40-48; spl indsl arts edn div state and local sch systems FSA Office of Edn since '48; ed adv bd Tchrs Digest, and School Shop Magazine. Am Ednl Research Assn—Am Indsl Arts Assn—Am Vocational Assn—Nat Assn Secondary Sch Prins—NEA—Nat Soc Study Edn—Phi Delta Kappa—Phi Kappa Phi—Kappa Delta Pi. Federal Security Agency, Office of Education, Washington 25.

21 LUDLUM, John Charles. Structural and economic geology; Soil trafficability. b'13. BS '35 (Lafayette Coll); MS '39—PhD '42 (Cornell U). Author articles in field. Asso prof structural and econ geol W Va U since '50. Major AUS, research on effects weather and soil conditions on movement mil vehicles, USAAF Air Weather Service '42-46. Geol Soc AM(F)—Am Inst Mining Metall Engrs—Soc Econ Geol—Sigma Xi—Phi Kappa Phi—Phi Beta Kappa. 313 Mineral Industries Building, West Virginia University, Morgantown, W. Va.†

22 LUDLUM, Robert Phillips. American history (Anti-slavery movement, Joshua R. Giddings). b'09. AB '30—MA '32—PhD '35 (Cornell U). Author: This is America's Story (with Howard B Wilder and Harriett M Brown) '48. Author articles: The Anti-Slavery Gag Rule '41; Joshua R. Giddings, Radical '36, and others. Instr hist A&M Coll Tex '35-37, asst prof '37-40; asst prof '37-40; asst prof hist and polit sci Hofstra Coll '40-42; asso social sci analyst OWI '42; asso sec AAUP '42-47; vp Antioch Coll '47-49; president Blackburn Coll since '49. Research asso General Edn Bd project Methods of Teaching High School Students to think Critically about Social Issues in Ithaca NY. AHA—Miss Valley Hist Assn—AAUP. Antioch College, Yellow Springs, O.

10 LUDWICK, Thomas Murrell. Cattle (Dairy). b'15. BS '36 (Eastern Ky State Tchrs Coll); MS (in agr) '39 (U Ky); PhD '42 (U Minn); '43 (U Chicago); '43-44 (U Va) (U Mich). Derivation of formula for measurement persistency of lactation in dairy cattle; development method of artificial insemination for difficult breeding cows; devised technique for measurement of semen quality by incubation. Co-author articles: (with Petersen, Boyd) The Effect of Stilbestrol upon Mammary Development and Lactation in the Cow '42; (with Petersen) A Measure of Persistency of Lactation in Dairy Cattle '43; (with Petersen, Fitch) Some Genetic Aspects of Persistency in Dairy Cattle '43; and others. Contributor: Dairy Cattle Breeding '51. Research and teaching dairy cattle U Ky '46-48; research dairy cattle breeding with Bur Dairy dairy cattle breeding with Bur Dairy Industry O State U since '48. Sigma Xi —Gamma Alpha—Gamma Sigma Delta. Dairy Department, Ohio State University, Columbus 10, O.

11 LUDWIG, Daniel. Insect physiology (Japanese beetle). b'02. AB '23 (Ursinus Coll); PhD '28 (U Pa). Research on effects of DDT on metabolism of Japanese beetle, effects of temperature and humidity on development and metamorphosis and biochemistry of metamorphosis. Author articles in field. Asst prof entomol Okla A&M Coll '28-29; asst prof biol NYU '29-37, asso prof since '38. AAAS(F)— NY Acad Sci(F)—Am Soc Zool—Entomol Soc Am—Sigma Xi. Department of Biology, New York University, 181st St. and University Av., NYC.

12 LUDWIG, Louis Edward. Chemistry (Paints, varnish, pigments, vinyl resins, synthetic rubber). b'06. BS '28 —MS '36 (U Chicago). Author articles: Metallic Phthalates as Paint Pigments '37; Extenders for GRS Synthetic Rubber '45; Softeners for GRS Synthetic Rubber '44; Investigation of Aqueous Dispersions of Vinyl Polymers '48. Chem research and development div Devoe and Raynolds Co Chicago '28-37, chief chem Chicago and Louisville plants '37-41; research chem synthetic rubber B F Goodrich Co Akron O '43-45; research Montgomery Ward Paint Works Chicago Heights Ill '41-43, in charge since '45. Am Chem Soc—Fedn Paint Varnish Prodn Clubs—Sigma Xi. Awarded three first prizes nat competition of Fedn Paint Varnish Clubs '37, '46, '48. Montgomery Ward Paint Works, Chicago Heights, Ill.†

13 LUEBCKE, Henry N. Irrigation (Supplemental); Drainage (Open ditches, tile, mole). b'10. BS in agrl engring '34 (Kan State Coll). Research, design, and installation tile drainage systems, developed grading device for tile ditching machine, design and construction supplemental irrigation systems. Cons irrigation engr '35-36; with Bur Agrl Engring and Soil Conservation Service USDA since '36, on loan to Brit govt '41-45. Am Soc Agrl Engrs (com on depth and spacing of drain tile)—Soil Conservation Soc Am. Soil Conservation Service, Wapakoneta, O.

14 LUECK, Roger Hawks. Corrosion; Food technolgoy; Packaging technology. b'96. BS '19—DSc '43 (Carroll Coll Waukesha Wis); MS '22 (U Wis). With Am Can Co since '22, research chemist '22-26, mgr San Francisco Lab '26-34, mgr Hawaiian factories '34-36, mgr Maywood lab '36-41, dir research '41-44, sales mgr Pacific div '44-50, gen mgr research and tech dept since '50; cons OQMG USA '42-44; chmn Nat Prodn Authority task group

on tin conservation '51. Am Chem Soc —Inst Chemists—Inst Food Tech—AA AS—Sigma Xi—Tau Kappa Epsilon. American Can Co., 100 Park Av., NYC.◎

15 LUEDY, Arthur Ernst. Horticulture. b'94. Student '13-15 (Central Inst Cleveland); '20-22 (Cleveland Sch Art); '29-35 (John Huntington Poly Cleveland). Improvement by cross pollination strain of Christmas Rose (Helleborus niger altifolius), also hybrids of Lenten Rose (Helleborus orientalis); development new seedling plant Rhamnus frangula Luedy (Column Buckthorn); hybridizing of poppies (Papaver orientale). Author: The Christmas Rose '48. Nurseryman since '21. O Assn Nurserymen. Hathaway Rd., Bedford, O.

16 LUEHRING, Frederick William. Swimming pools; Swimming rules. b '82. PhB '05 (North Central College Naperville Ill); PhM '06 (U Chgo); PhD '39 (Columbia). Author of Swimming Pool Standards, various pamphlets on swimming, life-saving. Contbr to phys edn jours. Mem Nat Collegiate Swimming Rules Com since found '13, chmn '14-35; mem Am Olympic Com, X and XI Olympiads; chmn Olympic men's swimming com '34-36. Am Assn Health Phys Edn and Recreation(life mem, F)—Coll Phys Edn Assn(past pres)—Am Assn Sch Adminstrs—AAUP—Nat Collegiate Life Saving Soc—Am Acad Phys Edn—Am Camping Assn—Am Pub Health Assn —Nat Workshop on Facilities for Athletics Phys Edn and Recreation—Pa Acad Sci—Phi Delta Kappa—Kappa Delta Pi. H: Swarthmore, Pa.

17 LUFKIN, Garland. Glass and glass container engineering and application. b'96. BS '20 (MIT). Draftsman, furnace foreman, chief draftsman, chief engr Ill Glass Co Alton Ill '21-29; chief engr Owens Ill Glass Co '29-31, plant mgr '31-37, gen mgr Closure div '37-41, vp and gen mgr Glass Container Div '41-43, vp gen mgr Packaging and Process Research Dept since '43. ASME. Owens Illinois Glass Company, Tol.

18 LUHRS, Henry Ernst. American toys; Musical boxes and novelties; Lincolniana; Pennsylvania history. b'01. BS '23 — MS '25 (Cornell U). Author: The True Story of the Liberty Bell '25; Our Friend Mr. Lincoln '36; Why Honor Lincoln? He Went About Doing Good '39, and others; also articles in field. Pres dir gen mgr the Beistle Co since '28; pres and gen mgr The Lincoln Publishers; founder and mng dir The Lincoln Library, Shippensburg Pa since '29. Toy Mfgs of USA Inc—Pa State, NY State, Miss Valley, So and Am hist assns—Bibliog Soc Am—Lincoln Fellowship of Pa— Am Numismatic Assn—Acad Polit Sci —Phi Kappa Phi. 200 Fifth Av., NYC 10.

19 LUKACS, Eugene. Mathematical statistics; Descriptive and projective geometry; Actuarial mathematics. b'06. PhD '30—Actuary '31 (U Vienna). Author articles in field. Prof, chmn dept math Our Lady of Cincinnati '45-48; statis USNOTS Inyokern Calif '48-50; statis engring lab Nat Bureau Standards Washington since '50, also parttime tchr Am U; reviewer for Math Reviews since '40. Am Math Soc—Inst Math Statis—Am Statis Assn (reviewer for Journal since '47)—Actuarial Soc Switzerland—Internat Congresses Actuaries (permanent com). Statistical Engineering Laboratory, National Bureau of Standards, Washington 25. H: 3727 Van Nesse St., Washington 16.†

20 LUKENS, Alan R., III. Calcium carbonate pigments (Technology);

Non-metallic mineral processing (Chemistry); Yacht racing. born '93. ChemE '15 (Pratt Inst Brooklyn); ScD '23 (U Cincinnati); '33-39 (Mass Inst Tech). Specialized in manufacture and use of calcium carbonate powders since '33. Holds patents in field including process for mfg colored asphalt floor tile, asphalt battery container. Author article: A Basic Compounding Study of Carbon and Non-Carbon Pigments '44. Co-author article: (with C G Landes and T G Rochow) Comparison of Waterground Natural and Precipitated Calcium Carbonates for Paper Coating '45, and others. Chem, chief chem Baltimore Roofing & Mfg Co Asbestos Md '15-18; chief chem and dir research The Richardson Co Lockland O and Melrose Park Ill '18-26; mgr bituminous products development Hood Rubber Co Watertown Mass '26-33; research dir Thompson Weinman & Co Inc Cambridge Mass '33-43; vp Pigment Research Labs Cambridge '43-45; pres Powdered Material Research Labs since '45; vp Wingdale Chem Corp Wingdale NY since '47, Laminar Calcium Corp Morgan City La since '49. ASTM—Am Ceramic Soc—ACS (rubber div)—Tech Assn Pulp and Paper Industry—Fedn Production Clubs Paint Varnish and Laquer Assn. 11 Windsor St., Cambridge 39, Mass. H: 100 Memorial Dr., Cambridge.

21 LUM, Paul (Poy). China (Genealogical history). b'23. BA '45—'45-46 (U Ore). Research on general genealogy of China and its problems, systematic genealogy of China, problems criticisms findings and applications; comparative genealogies between some families of China and US and Europe. Author articles in field. Grad asst Far Eastern Dept U Washington since '46. AHA—Nat Reconstruction Forum. 317 N.W. 4th Av., Portland 9, Ore.

22 LUMIANSKY, Robert Mayer. Chaucer; Old English. b'13. AB '33 (Citadel); MA '35 (U SC); PhD '42 (U NC). Author: Chaucer's Canterbury Tales in Modern English Prose '48; also articles in field. Head dept Eng Coll Arts Sci Tulane U since '48; Modern Lang Assn Am—Medieval Acad Am —Linguistic Soc Am—Am Dialect Soc —Nat Council Teachers Eng—S-Central Modern Lang Assn—AAUP. Department of English, Tulane University, New Orleans 18. H: 1314 Audubon St., New Orleans 15.

23 LUND, Clarence Edward. Refrigeration (Home freezers, ice cube machines); Heating, ventilating and air conditioning. b'06. B Mech Engring '33 —MS in mech engring '34 (U Minn). Research in technical phases of home freezer development; heat transmission through insulation; condensation; vapor transmission; air filtration; built-up roofing. Heating ventilating air conditioning insp City Minneapolis '35-37; research engr Engring Expt Sta U Minn '37-41, asst prof and asst dir '41-42, asso prof, asst dir and asst head mech engring dept '42-44, prof and asst dir since '47; dir research Seeger Refrigerator Corp St Paul '44-47. Am Soc Refrigerating Engrs—Am Soc Heating and Ventilating Engrs— AAAS—Am Soc Engring Edn—Nat Assn Profl Engrs—Sigma Xi—Pi Tau Sigma. Wolverine award '46; Am Soc Refrigerating Engrs Outstanding Publication award for tech publ in field of refrigeration '46. Engineering Experiment Station, University of Minnesota, Mpls 14.

24 LUND, Everett Eugene. Diseases of domestic rabbits; Ciliate protozoa; Enterozoa of man in Near East. b'07

BS '29 (Ia State Coll); MA—PhD '32 (U Calif). Author articles in field. Parasitol US Dept Agr since '46; instr U Calif Ext Div since '45. AAAS—Am Soc Zool—Am Soc Parasitol—Am Soc Tropical Med—Soc Am Bact—Am Soc Mammal—Phi Kappa Phi—Sigma Xi—Phi Sigma—Gamma Sigma Delta. U.S. Rabbit Experiment Station, 210 N. Cypress, Fontana, Calif.

10 LUND, F. Edward. British Empire history. b'09. BA '33—MA '34 (Washington & Lee U); PhD '44 (U Wis). Research on British chartered companies 1870-1900, North Borneo, East and West Africa, Rhodesia. Prof hist Wis State Coll Superior Wis '38-45, fellow in European hist '38-39, fellow in Brit Empire hist '44-45 U Wis; research fellow Yale U '45-46; dean and prof hist State Teachers Coll Florence Ala since '46. Phi Beta Kappa—AHA—So Hist Assn. State Teachers College, Florence, Ala.

11 LUNDBERG, Walter O(scar). Chemistry of fats and oils. b'10. PhD '34—fellow '38-39 (U Minn); fellow '30-34—PhD '34 (Johns Hopkins U). Research on chemistry fats and oils especially oxidation fats and oils in relation to rancidity and to drying of protective coatings, biochemistry of fats in relation to metabolism of fats in man and animals; discoverer methods for prevention of rancidity in edible fats and oils. Author: A Survey of Present Knowledge, Researches and Practices in the United States concerning the Stabilization of Fats '47; also articles in field. Asst prof physiol chem U Minn '44-45, asso prof '45-47, prof since '47, resident dir Hormel Inst '44-49, exec dir since '49. Am Chem Soc—Am Oil Chemists Soc—AAAS—Soc Exptl Biol and Med—Am Soc Biol Chem—NY Acad Sci—Phi Beta Kappa—Sigma Xi. Hormel Institute, Austin, Minn.

12 LUNDELL, Cyrus Longworth. Economic and systematic botany; Flora of Texas, Mexico, and Central American Plant geography; Maya civilization (Environmental background). born '07. AB '32 (So Meth Univ); AM '34—PhD '36 (U Mich). Director and botanist University of Michigan-Carnegie Institution of Washington expeditions to Mexico and Central America '33-38; discoverer and explorer of Maya cities of Calakmul '31, Polol '33. Author articles in field. Head bot and dir Texas Research Found since '46. Tex Chemurgic Council (dir)—AA AS(F)—Am Soc Plant Taxonomists—Calif Bot Soc—Tex Acad Sci—Tex Geog Soc—Sigma Xi—Phi Kappa Phi. Texas Research Foundation, Box 43, Renner, Tex.†◎

13 LUNDGREN, Harold P(almer). Chemistry of proteins and synthetic protein figers; Chemistry of keratin protein; Chemistry of wool. b'11. BS '32 (ND State Coll); PhD '35 (U Minn); '35-37 (U Uppsala Sweden); '37-41 (U Wis). Study unfolding corpuscular protein molecules to fibrous forms; discovery method for preparing synthetic fibers from unfolded corpuscular proteins; examination structure and chemical modification of wool and mohair fibers. Holds patents on solubilizing proteins, process for scouring wool. Author articles: Proteins and Amino Acids '49; Synthetic Fibers Made from Proteins '49. With Western Regional Research Lab US DA since '41, chief chem since '49. Am Soc Biol Chem—ACS—Soc of Rheology—Sigma Xi—Gamma Alpha—Phi Kappa Phi—Phi Lambda Upsilon. Western Regional Research Laboratory, US Department of Agriculture, Albany 6, Cal.

14 LUNDIN, Charles Leonard. Baltic German history; History of the American Revolution. b'07. AB '29—MA '31 (Harvard); '29-30 (U Berlin); PhD '36—Proctor fellow '35-36 (Princeton). Author: Cockpit of the Revolution '40; also articles in field. Instr and asst prof hist Ind U since '37. AHA. Social Sci Research Council grant '48-49. Department of History, Indiana University, Bloomington, Ind.

15 LUNDQUIST, William Emil. Pressure sensitive adhesive tapes; Plastics; Resins. b'12. BCE '34 (U Minn); MS '36—PhD '38 (U Ill). Granted patents on copolymerizing maleic anhydride and polymerizable vinyl compounds, tanning skins, maleic anhydride-terpene condensation products, vinyl acetate copolymers. With E I duPont de Nemours Expt Sta '38-42; research chem Minn Mining & Mfg Co St Paul '42-45, dir research and development Scotch Tape div since '45. Am Chem Soc—Sigma Xi—Tau Beta Pi—Phi Beta Kappa. Minnesota Mining and Manufacturing Company, St. Paul 6.

16 LUNGSTROM, Leon George. Mosquitoes. b'15. BS '40 (Bethany Coll); MS '46—PhD '50 (Kan State Coll). Research on virus encephalitis and especially on arthropods which may be possible vectors. Entomol USPHS '45-46, med entomol since '49. Kan Acad Sci—Kan Entomol Soc—Tex Acad Sci—Am Assn Econ Entomol—Soc Am Bact—Sigma Xi. US Public Health Service, Box 1132, Greeley, Colo.

17 LUNZ, G(eorge) Robert. Oyster culture; Marine fouling organisms; Taxonomy of stomatopod and decapod Crustacea. b'09. BS '30—MS '32 (Coll Charleston). Author: Report on Oyster Cultivation '38; also articles in field. Curator Crustacea Charleston Mus '32-48, dir com '42-46; biol charge oyster investigations US Engr Office '36-37; spl investigator Bur Const & Repair USN '39-40; cons biol Fla Inland Navigation Dist '40-41, Corps Engrs War Dept '42-43, SC State Planning Bd '43-44; commr SC to Atlantic States Marine Fisheries Commn since '49; dir Bears Bluff Labs since '46. SC Acad Sci (pres '50)—AAAS (life) Biol—Soc System Zool—So Assn Sci and Ind—Nat Shellfisheries Assn. AA AS research grant '40, '41, '47; Charleston Ednl Sci Found grant '46; Jefferson award for research on oysters '41; Guggenheim fellow '49. Bears Bluff Laboratories, Wadmalaw Island, S.C.

18 LUNZ, Henry. Germination and purity of clover and alfalfa seeds; Control by chemicals and cultivation of weeds affecting agricultural crops; Poisonous and medicinal plants of Wisconsin. b'80. AB '13—MS '21 (U Wis). Author articles: Value of Hard Seeds in Certain Legumes '32; How to Reduce Weed Loses '46; Seed Certification in Relation to Seed Control '48. With Wis Dept Agr since '17, agron in charge seed and weed div since '47. Seed Analysis Assn NA—N Central States Seed Control Ofcls(pres '49)—N Central States Weed Conf—Am Soc Agron. Agronomy Bldg., University of Wisconsin, Madison.

19 LUOMA, John Walter. Iron and steel roll metallurgy. b'04. BS '29 (Carnegie Inst Tech). Investigations and research study on iron and steel roll manufacture; phases planning, molding, melting, pouring, heat treating, physical testing; metallographic investigations, specifications. Iron roll metall Hubbard Steel Foundry Co '29-34; supt roll foundry Continental Roll & Steel Foundry Co '34-47; roll research metall Continental Foundry & Machine Co since '48. AIMME—Roll Mfrs Inst—ASTM. Continental Foun-

dry & Machine Co., Box 299, East Chicago, Ind.

20 LURIE, Eli Moses. Centralized radio; Electronic fire control and detection systems; Electronic sirens and emergency power systems. BEE '29 (Northeastern U). Developed internal fire detectors for hotel room radios to give both rate of rise and smoldering fire alarm with location indicator. Granted patents on combination multichannel radio receiving and signaling systems, volume control arrangements, alarm systems for hotels. Elec engr RCA 29-30; Hotel New Yorker and Nat Hotel Management '30-36; pres, chief engr Am Communications Corp since '36. Inst Radio Engrs (asso). American Communications Corp., 306 Broadway, NYC. H: 226-38 Mentone Av., Laurelton, Long Island, N.Y.

21 LURTON, Douglas Ellsworth. Human relations; Publications (Management). b'97. Student '16-18 (U ND). Author: Make the Most of Your Life '45. Collator: Roosevelt's Foreign Policy 1933-41 '42. Mng editor Literary Digest '36-37; vp and bus mgr Kingsway Press Inc, Your Health Publs Inc since '37, Yourself Publs Inc since '39, Publs Management Inc since '41, Womans Life Publs Inc since '42,Wilfred Funk Inc since '42; pubs cons since '41; pres and bus mgr Basic Publs Inc since '45; originator, pub and editor Your Life since '37, Your Personality since '39, Your Health since '39, Woman's Life since '42, Success Today since '46. Phi Delta Phi. 227 E. 44th St., NYC 17.†◎

22 LUSINK, Clarence Irving. Design and testing of railway car trucks, couplers, and draft attachments. b'96. BS (ME) '20 (U Rochester NY). Chief mech engr Symington-Gould Corp since '37. ASME. 2 Main St., Depew, N.Y.

23 LUSK, Harold F. Consumer financing. b'93. Student '11-14 (Central Mich Normal Coll); AB '21—JD '25—SJD '41 (U Mich). Research on legal aspects of consumer financing. Author: Business Law Principles and Cases '46; also articles in field. Law practice Grand Rapids '25-31; asst prof bus law Ind U '31-36, asso prof '36-39, prof since '39. Am Bus Law Assn (Sec-treas '34-38, vp '38-40, pres '40-41) — NEA — Ind Acad Social Sci — Am Acad Polit Social Sci—Mich and Ind State Bars. School of Business, Indiana University, Bloomington, Ind.

24 LUSZKI, Margaret Barron. Employee relations; Group dynamics. b '07. AB '28—PhD '51 (U Mich); MA '30 (U Md); '39-40 (Sch Social Work Cath U Am); '45-47 (Washington Sch Psychiat); '46 (Psychodramatic Inst Beecon NY); '47-48 (MIT). Research and training on dynamics of role playing, social psychology, group dynamics, mental health; consultant on human relations problems in work setting and on human relations training; development and direction employee counseling program of Social Security Board. Author articles: Welfare Programs for Federal Employees '40; Employee Counseling in a Federal Agency '42; Employee Relations Functions of a Central Personnel Agency '45, and others. Co-author article: (with Gilbert K Krulee) Case Study of a Basic Skill Training Group '48, and others. Chief employee counseling sect FSA '39-43, chief employee relations sect '44-47; staff Nat Training Lab in Group Development summers '47-49; plan and conduct of research project on emphatic ability and social perception '50; project coordinator Work Conferences in Mental Health Research since '51. Am Psychol Assn—NEA—Soc Psychol Study Social Issues—Am Sociol Soc—Soc Applied Anthrop—AAAS—Am Sociometric Assn—Phi Kappa Phi. 1201 16th St., Washington 6. H: Box 33, Seabrook, Md.

10 LUTHIN, Reinhard Henry. Abraham Lincoln (Politics, Civil War period, Lincolniana). b'05. AB '33—AM '34—PhD '44 (Columbia); U fellow '34-35 (Duke U). Author: The First Lincoln Campaign '44. Co-author: Lincoln and the Patronage '43. Lecturer in contemporary civilization Columbia U '37-43; lecturer in hist Barnard Coll '44-46; asso in hist and bibliographer in Am hist Columbia since '46. AHA. 35 Claremont Av., NYC.

11 LUTTRINGER, Leo A., Jr. Pennsylvania mammalogy and ornithology; Wildlife conservation. b'01. Grad '21 (Harrisburg Business Coll). Author: Mammals of Pennsylvania '31; Pennsylvania Birdlife '39; Pennsylvania Wildlife '38; Pennsylvania Birdlife '48; also articles in field. Editor Pennsylvania Game News since '30; mem Pa Game Commn staff since '22. Nat Wildlife Soc—Am Ornithol Union—Am Soc Mammalogists—Nat Assn Conservation Edn and Publicity. Pennsylvania Game Commission, Harrisburg, Pa.

12 LUTZ, Alma. Emma Willard; Woman suffrage; American history (Woman's role). b'90. AB '12 (Vassar Coll); (Boston U Sch Bus Adminstrn). Research on subject of women's role in American history and the woman's rights movement; writer column A Feminst Thinks It Over in Equal Rights '38-46. Author: Emma Willard, Daughter of Democracy '29; Created Equal, The Biography of Elizabeth Cady Stanton '40; Challenging Years, Memoirs of Harriot Stanton Blatch '40; With Love, Jane; Letters from American Women on the War Fronts '45. Writer for National Woman's Party and Longyear Foundation. Nat Woman's Party (nat council '31-46, nat council Conn Com for the Equal Rights Amendment)—Am Hist Assn. 22 River St., Boston 8.

13 LUTZ, Caroline Stookey. Puppetry (illustration of literature by); Nineteenth century English literature (American correlations). b'89. BA '11 (Goucher Coll); MA '15 (Columbia). Special study in field of English literature of nineteenth century and its American correlations; taught class for ten years at Westhampton College on problems in American literature in its world relations; developed marionette repertory theatre correlated with world literature; research on writings of Clyde Fitch, biography of F. Hopkinson Smith. Author articles in field. With Westhampton College since '19, elected chmn faculty cooperative world literature class '49. Westhampton College, University of Richmond, Richmond, Va. H: 5816 York Road.

14 LUTZ, Samuel Gross. Electronic and communication engineering. b'07. BSEE '29—EE '33—MS '34—PhD '38 (Purdue U). Developed time lapse equipment and filmed The Heavens Declare the Glory of God, an accelerated motion study of cloud dynamics '44; developed gas discharge electron tube for viewing magnetic fields. Prof and chmn elec engring dept NYU since '46. Naval Research Lab '40-46, head measurement and direction finding sect '44-46; developed early broad-band panoramic receivers, panoramic recorder and other analysis equipment. AIEE—IRE—ASEE—SMPE. New York University, University Heights, NYC 53.©

15 LUZZATTO, Jack. Crossword puzzles (Construction). b'09. Ed pub schs. Co-author: Doubletalk Crossword Puzzles '42. Co-cartoonist: Laughs From the Saturday Review '46. Edited prize crosswords for Fawcett Publications '42, edited New Crosswords '49; contributed to Simon and Schuster puzzle books, NY Herald Tribune, NY Times, many puzzles and quizzes to a variety of popular magazines. Cartoonist for Saturday Review of Lit, Collier's, Judge, King Features '34-42; constructor crosswords since '27. 3108 Wilkinson Av., Bronx 61, NYC.

16 LYCAN, Gilbert Lester. American history (Diplomatic, early national period); International relations. b'09. AB '34 (Berea Coll); MA '36—PhD '42 (Yale); '39 (Carnegie Endowment summer session Montreal). Co-author: Bases of World Order '45. Author article: Alexander Hamilton and the North Carolina Federalists '47. Spl div Dept State Washington '42-43; head dept hist Queens Coll Charlotte NC '43-45, asso prof '43-44, prof '44-45; head dept hist and social sci State Teachers Coll Maryville Mo '45-46; head dept hist and chmn div social sci John B Stetson U since '46. AHA—Am Soc Internat Law—Am Acad Polit Social Sci—So Hist Assn—Fla Hist Soc—N C State Lit and Hist Assn—So Polit Sci Assn—AA UP. Awards: fellowship Carnegie Endowment for Internat Peace '34-35 grad work Yale; grants-in-aid Carnegie Found and John B Stetson U summer '47, summer '48, research on Hamilton. John B. Stetson University, DeLand, Fla. H: 119 S. Lakeview Av., Lake Helen.

17 LYCAN, William H(iram). Drying oils; Synthetic resins; Surface coating; Surgical dressings. b'03. BS '24—MS '26—PhD '29 (U Ill). Group leader to exec dir research plant div Pittsburgh Plate Glass Co '38-49; dir research Johnson & Johnson, New Brunswick NJ since '49, co dir since '50, vp since '51. Am Chem Soc—Am Oil Chem Soc—AAAS. Johnson & Johnson, New Brunswick, N.J.©

18 LYDENBERG, John. American political and social novel. b'13. AB '34 (Oberlin Coll); MA '38—fellow Am civilization '39-40—PhD '46 (Harvard); grad study (Downing Coll, Cambridge U, Eng; Phillips-Universitaet, Marburg, Germany). Faculty Bennington Coll '42-44, research on Am polit novel 1865-1901; asso prof Eng Hobart and William Smith Colls since '46; book reviews NY Times, Saturday Review Literature, others. AHA. Hobart College, Geneva, N.Y.

19 LYLE, Eldon W(ood). Roses (Diseases). b'08. BS '30 (Ore State Coll); PhD '37—fellow '31-37 (Cornell U). Research on white pine blister rust control, hop mildew, diseases of greenhouse roses and field grown roses, diseases and problems connected with commercial production of roses including storage. Author articles in field. Agt US Dept Agr '27-31; plant path Tex Agrl Expt Sta '37-42, '42-46; plant path Tex Rose Research Found Inc since '46. Am Phytopath Soc—AAAS—Sigma Xi—Phi Kappa Phi—Gamma Sigma Delta—Alpha Zeta. Award East Tex Rose Growers and Expt Sta '42. Texas Rose Research Foundation, Inc., Rt. 9, Box 159, Tyler, Tex.†

20 LYLE, (Eu)gene P(erry), III. Photography (Advertising illustration, industrial, physical, chemical treatment). b'08. Student '29-32 (San Diego State Coll) summer sessions '50-51 (U Cal at Los Angeles). Research in dyeing localized areas of negatives to locally alter contrast when using bluesensitive paper, chemical and abrasive

treatment print surfaces to alter detail and contrast; design of junction box for photographic use. Free-lance photog '36-40; photog Convair '43-44; newspaper, magazine and advt illus photog since '46; prof still photog San Diego Vocational High Sch and Jr Coll since '47. Photog AUS '41-43. Photog Assn Am. 5348 Valle Vista, La Mesa, Cal.

21 LYLE, Florence L. Antarctic place names; Place name history. BA '24 (Ill Wesleyan U). Cooperated preparation special publication Board Geographic Names Geographic Names of Antarctica '47. Ed George F Cram Co map pub Indianapolis '29-42; historian bd Geographic Names US Dept Interior since '45. AHA—Am Assn State Local Hist—Arctic Inst NA. U.S. Department of Interior, Washington 25.

22 LYLES, Victoria. Curricula and organization of elementary education. AB '26 (Northeastern State Teachers Coll Okla); MA '28—EdD '44 (Columbia). Research on children's studying whole problems or units of work; supervised first detention school used in connection with probation work and courts; organized the curricula for the School in Detention Home; helped organize and conduct wartime child-centers and nursery schools for children of war-working parents; delegate to first educational conference at Lake Success by United Nations and New York University '48; helped organize a branch of Association for Childhood Education in Korea '47-48. Dir elementary edn York Pa pub schs since '30; dir curriculum for pupils held in detention by court since '46. Pa State Assn for Childhood (pres '44-46)—Pa State Edn Assn (pres primary kindergarten sect '39, elementary sect Southern Conv Dist pres '40)—NEA—Assn for Children Edn. Board of Education, 329 S. Lindbergh Av., York, Pa.

23 LYMAN, John. Sailing ships (Pacific coast); Chemical oceanography. b'15. BS '36 (U Cal); MS '51 (UCLA). Editor for oceanography Transactions of American Geophysical Union; mem editorial advis board The American Neptune. Director division oceanog U SN Hydrographic Office ed and pub Log Chips (periodical publication of recent maritime hist) since '48. Ensign USNR '41-42, lt comdr '45, participated Bikini atom bomb tests. Soc Naut Research—Steamship Hist Soc Am—Nautical Research Guild. 7801 Gateway Blvd., Washington 28.†

24 LYNCH, J(ohn) Joseph. Seismology. b'94. Student '05-11 (St Ignatius Coll London) '13-14 (St Joseph's Coll Phila) '14-16 (St Andrew-on-Hudson); AB—AM '20 (Woodstock Coll Md); '23-27 (St Ignatius Coll Holland); summers '23-27 (U Observatory Oxford Eng); PhD '39 (NYU). Author: General Physics '33; Our Trembling Earth '40; The Effect of Occluded Hydrogen on the Rigidity of Palladium '40. Asso prof physics and dir observatory Fordham U since '28. Royal Astron Soc(F)—Am Geog Soc(F)—AAAS(F)—New York Acad Scis(F)—APS—Am Geophys Union—Seismol Soc Am (chmn Eastern sect '31-32)—Soc Exploration Geophysicists—Franklin Inst—AAUP—Am Association Physics Tchrs—Sigma Xi. Fordham University, NYC.

25 LYNCH, Kenneth Merrill. Asbestos (Pathological effects); Dust hazards, industrial (Pathological effects). 16 Lucal St., Charleston 16, S.C.

26 LYNIP, Benjamin Franklin, Jr. Sugar (Marketing, economics, prices). b'06. BS '28 (U Cal); MBA '32 (Harvard). Research on factors affecting general wholesale price changes; production planning of sugar refining, and marketing conditions. Contributor: Encyclopedia Britannica '45. Valuation engr Cal State Bd Equilization Sacramento '34-35; statis in charge market analysis and production budgeting '35-50; now dir planning and statis Cal & Hawaiian Sugar Refining Corp Ltd. Am Marketing Assn (N Cal chpt) Am Statis Assn—Econometric Soc—Farm Econ Assn—Population Assn. Am Marketing Assn (N Cal chapt) award for outstanding contribution to development of marketing '50. 215 Market St., SF 5. H: 6 Hillcrest Ct., Berkeley 5.

10 LYNN, William Gardner. Embryology; Reptiles and amphibians (Taxonomy). b'05. AB '28—PhD '31 (Johns Hopkins). Member Johns Hopkins University expeditions to Jamaica, British West Indies '32, '36, '41; research on thyroid function in amphibian metamorphosis, sense organs of snakes, taxonomy of living and fossil; reptiles and amphibians; studies on structure and function of facial pit of pit-vipers, fossil turtles of Maryland, embryology of Eleutherodactylus nubicola (an anuran having no tadpole stage), oxygen consumption and water metabolism of turtle embryos. Author articles in field. Prof biol Cath U since '46. Phi Beta Kappa—Sigma Xi—AAAS—Washington Acad Sci—Am Soc Zool—Am Soc Ichthyologists Herpetologists—Herpetologists League—Natural Hist Soc Jamaica—Natural Hist Soc Md. Rockefeller Found fellow Yale '39-40; Fulbright fellow University College of the West Indies Jamaica BWI '52-53. Department of Biology, Catholic University of America, Washington 17.†

11 LYON, Channing Bruce. Plant nutrition; Tomatoes; Pineapple. b'15. SB '38 (U Neb); SM '39—PhD '41 (U Chicago); '32-34 (U Rochester); '39-40 (Calif Inst Tech). Research on cultivation and pruning of trees and ornamentals, propagation of seedling nursery stock, breeding of lettuce and cantaloupe for disease resistance, studies on germination of native grass seeds, supervision of large-scale grass seed collection, and germination and purity tests; selection breeding and propagation of fruits and vegetables; research on interaction of environment and heredity in relation to response of plants to toxic salt concentrations, nutrition of soils plants and animals, nutrition of pineapple plant and its response to various growth substances, tomato development. Author articles in field. Soil Conservation Service US Dept Agr '35-38, sci aide US Hort Field Sta Cheyenne Wyo '38-39, jr physiol US Regional Salinity Lab Riverside Calif '40; asst and asso physiol and plant physiol US Nutrition Lab Ithaca '41-44; physiol Hawaiian Pineapple Co Honolulu since '44. Hawaiian Pineapple Co., Honolulu, Hawaii.

12 LYON, Charles Julius. Plant physiology (Respiration, osmosis); New England tree rings. b'96. BS '18 (Middlebury Coll); AM '20—PhD '26 (Harvard). Botany editor Tree Ring Bulletin since '40. Author: Flowering Plants and Vegetation '38; translator and editor: Kostychev's Plant Respiration '27, Chemical Plant Physiology '31; also articles in field. Instr, later prof bot Dartmouth Coll since '20. Am Soc Plant Physiol—Ecol Soc Am. Dartmouth College, Hanover, N.H.

13 LYON, Elmer Bernhard. Diplomatic history of the United States; History of the American frontier. b'91. BS '14 (Northwestern U); AM '23 (Columbia U). Research on diplomacy of American Civil War, American neutrality, 1914-1917; US boundary con-

troversies and adjustments. Head hist dept Fort Dodge Iowa Jr Coll '23-24; asst prof hist Mich State Coll '24-31, asso prof since '31. AHA—Miss Valley Hist Assn—Phi Alpha Theta. 434 Morrill Hall, Michigan State College, East Lansing, Mich. H: 821 Snyder Rd.

14 LYON, James. Poultry (Beak cauterization, electric equipment); Beekeeping (Electric hive warming). b '07. BS '32 (U Ariz). Invented vibration-proof incubator thermostat without magnetic or snap action, low wattage egg candler, electric bee hive warmer, glass display and laboratory fan incubators, attachable brooder heaters. Granted patents on air filters and medicators for poultry hovers, infra-red brooder, beak cauterizers for fowl, beak and wing trimmers and beak burners for fowl. Research engr Lyon Elec Co '32-38, gen mgr since '38. Am Soc Agrl Engrs—Alpha Kappa Psi—Phi Kappa Phi. 2075 Moore St., Box 30, San Diego 12, Cal.

15 LYON, Leverett Samuel. Government's relation to industry; Price policies; Marketing; Business education. b'85. PhB '10—AM '19—PhD '21 (U Chicago); LLB '15 (Chicago-Kent Coll Law). Author books and articles. Formerly faculty mem U Chicago; dean Sch Bus Washington U; exec vp Brookings Instn; chief exec officer Chicago Assn Commerce and Industry since '29. Chicago Bar Assn—Am Econ Assn—Acad Polit Sci—Am Statis Assn—Am Marketing Assn (pres '33). 1 N. La Salle St., Chgo.ⓒ

16 LYONS, Clifford Pierson. English literary history and criticism; English literature (Renaissance). b'04. AB '25 (Cornell Coll); PhD '32 (Johns Hopkins); grad work (U Chicago). Cofounder and asso editor: ELH a journal of Eng Lit Hist '34. Asso editor: South Atlantic Bulletin '39-48; also articles in field. Prof Eng, head dept UNC '46-52 dean Coll Art and Scis since '52. Mod Lang Assn America—Medieval Acad Am—Coll Eng Assn (dir '38-40)—So Atlantic Mod Lang Assn (pres '39)—Phi Beta Kappa. Chapel Hill, N.C.

17 LYONS, Sanford Carlisle. Clay technology; Papermaking clays. b'97. Student '21-24 (MIT). Research on, developments of industrial particle size control of finely divided pigments, mining refining and processing of clays, kaolin, papermaking clays, pigments. Holds patents in field. Author: Clays as Papercoating Pigments; also articles in field. Pres Vermont Kaolin Corp since '23; tech dir Georgia Kaolin Co since '35. Tech Assn Pulp & Paper Ind—Am Ceramic Soc—Am Chem Soc—Soc Rheology. Georgia Kaolin Co., Dry Branch, Ga.

18 LYTLE, Charles Augustus, Jr. Automobile racing (History). b'06. AB '29 (Yale). Assembled comprehensive file on motor racing, including 11,000 microfilmed pages of contemporary race reports. Author articles in race supplements. Contributor: Grand Prix Racing '50; Life of Ted Horn '49; Austin Records '49; World's Land Speed Record '51. Am Automobile Assn—Automobile Mfrs Assn—Sports Car Club Am. 159 Pitt St., Sharon, Pa.

19 LYTLE, W(ilbert) Vernon. Abnormal and developmental psychology; Personality. b'89. AB '15 (Bethany Coll); PhD '27 (Yale). Author articles in field. Prof psychol, head dept edn Doan Coll Crete Neb '25-26; prof psychol, head dept De Pauw U '27-31; pres, trustee Defiance (O) Coll '31-33; founder Woman's Coll New Haven, pres, trustee '33-39; organizer and pres W

Vernon Lytle and Co counselors NYC since '39; vis prof psychol Bradley U '47-48, Ida State Coll since '49. AAAS (F)—Nat Geog Soc—Tau Kappa Alpha—AAUP. 135 E. 50th St., NYC 22.†ⓒ

20 LYTLE, William Orland. Research engineering; Glass products development. b'94. AB '16—AM '17 (U Kan). Developed transparent conductor of electricity called NESA electric glass; research on electrostatically coupled circuits, glasses for lighting. Author articles in field. Asst physicist Nat Bur Standards 3 yrs; now with Pittsburgh Plate Glass Co., successively asst mgr new process dept, chief engr and tech dir Duplate Div, sec Central Research Dept, research engr at Research Lab. ASME—IES—Am Ceramics Soc—AAAS—SAE. Pittsburgh Plate Glass Co., Creighton, Pa.

M

21 MABRY, William Alexander. Negro suffrage in the South; Early industries in Ohio. b'06. BA '27—PhD '33 (Duke U); MA '29—Watauga fellow history '28-29 (Harvard); '28 (U Chicago). Editor: Branch Historical Papers published periodically Randolph-Macon Coll. Author: The Negro in North Carolina Politics Since Reconstruction '40; also articles in field. Vaughan prof hist govt chmn social sci div Randolph-Macon Coll Ashland Va since '46. AHA—So Hist Assn—Va Social Sci Assn—Phi Beta Kappa. Randolph-Macon College, Ashland, Va.

22 MacADAM, David L(ewis). Optics (Color vision and measurement). b'10. BS '32 (Lehigh U); PhD '36—teaching fellow '32-36 (MIT). Research in color measurement and application to color photography; Optical Society representative on US National Committee US technical representative on colorimetry International Commission on Illumination; participant International Conference on Color Vision Cambridge England '47. Co-author: Handbook of Colorimetry '36; also articles in field. Eastman Kodak Co Research Lab since '36. Optical Soc Am — Am Standards Assn (chmn subcom color measurement) — Inter-Soc Color Council (councillor)—Munsell Color Found (trustee)—Phi Beta Kappa—Sigma Xi. First recipient Adolph Lomb medal for noteworthy contbns to optics by Optical Soc Am '40. Research Laboratories, Kodak Park, Rochester 4, N.Y.

23 MacCARDLE, Ross Clayton. Cytology; Anatomy; Aviation physiology. b'01. BS '27 (U Mich); PhD '32 (Brown U); student '36 (Columbia). Research in histochemistry by microincineration, ultra-centrifugation, phase-contrast, frozen-drying; effects of mitotic poisons on tumor and nerve cells; mechanism of cell division; cellular fats and calcium; temperature on mitochondria of liver cells; physiological aspects of high altitude parachute escape; explosive decompression in pressurized aircraft; accomplished eight high altitude experimental parachute jumps; intracellular minerals. Discovered human cutaneous magnesium deficiency; cell mixochondriome. Author: Physiological Anatomy of the Head and Neck '49; also numerous articles in field. Editor: Journal Nat Cancer Inst. Asst prof Wash U Sch Med '38-46; research asso Barnard Free Skin and Cancer Hosp '38-46; sr cytologist Nat Cancer Inst since '46; lecturer anatomy Johns Hopkins U Med Sch and George Wash Univ Med. School. Maj Air Corps US Army Air Forces; student Sch Aviation Med Randolph Field Tex; assigned to Aero Med Lab Wright Field O '42-45. Sigma Xi — Am Assn Anatomists—Am Assn Cancer Research—Am Soc Exptl Path—Am Soc Zool. National Cancer Institute, Bethesda 14 Md.

10 MacCARTHY, Gerald R(aleigh). Geophysics; Permanently frozen ground. b'97. Student '15-17 (Colby Coll); '19 (Universite de Poiters France); AB '21 (Cornell U); AM '24 —PhD '26 (NC U). Geophysical work in Northern Canada, the Aleutians and Alaska '47-48, geophysical investigations of ground water in Hawaiian Islands '37-40; supervising geophysicist charge field investigations east of Mississippi River for US Bureau of Mines during war; now engaged in investigation on frozen ground in northern Alaska. Author articles in field. Prof geol and geophys U NC '25-37, '40-42, since '45; geophysicist US Dept Interior, '37-40, '42-45, part time since '45. Geol Soc AM(F) — AAAS(F) — Am Geophys Union—NC Acad Sci—Sigma Xi. University of North Carolina, Chapel Hill, N.C.

11 MacCORMICK, Austin Harbutt. Penology; Parole; Juvenile delinquency; Crime prevention; Military offenders. b'93. BA '15—ScD (hon) '34 (Bowdoin Coll); MA '16 (Columbia); LLD (hon) '37 (St Lawrence U). Administration and research American prisons, reformatories and training schools, penology, parole, juvenile delinquency, crime prevention, military offenders, mental hygiene, problems of alcoholism, adult and child education in correctional institutions; member National Conference Juvenile Agencies (president '43-44); Columbia University Forum Study and Prevention Crime (executive committee); Citizens Committee on Children of NYC; member board directors Madison Square Boys Club, Children's Village, Wiltwyck School for Boys; chairman NY State Committee Youth Correction Authority Plan; member executive committee International Committee Mental Hygiene, council of National Committee Mental Hygiene; member executive committee National Committee Education on Alcoholism, Research Council on Problems of Alcohol; expert consultant US secretary of War since '42; chairman War Dept board consultants on correctional problems, vice chairman advisory board clemency, chairman advisory board parole; member US Navy committee consultants on confinement policies. Author: Handbook of American Prisons (with P W Garrett) '26; Handbook of American Prisons and Reformatories (with P W Garrett) '29; The Education of Adult Prisoners '31. Editor: Handbook of American Institutions for Delinquent Juveniles '43; co-editor The Prison World; member adv com Fed Prob Qtrly; also articles in field. Asst dir US Bur Prisons '29-33; exec dir Osborne Assn Inc NYC since '40; Prof criminology U Cal since '51. War Dept exceptional civilian service award '46, Pres medal for merit '47. Am Prison Assn (pres '38-39, bd dir)—Nat Prisoners Aid Assn (pres '41-42)—Soc Prevention Crime (exec bd)—Am Assn Adult Edn (pres '43-44, mem council)—Phi Beta Kappa. School of Criminology Berkeley 4, Cal. H: 894 Regal Rd., Berkeley 8.

12 MacDANIELS, Laurence Howland. Plant anatomy; Plant propagation; Orchard pollination; Northern nut bearing trees; Banana distribution in the Pacific Isles. b'88. AB '12 (Oberlin Coll); PhD '17 (Cornell U); fellow '26-27 (Bishop Mus Honolulu). Botanist Botanical Raw Products Committee, National Research Council '18; worked on problem of Polynesian migrations as related to plant distribution, traveling to Fiji, Tonga, Samoa and Tahiti; director of agriculture for Near East Foundation program in Syria, Lebanon '44; acting director agriculture, United Nations Relief and Rehabilitation Administration, Albania '44-45. Author: (with A J Eames) An Introduction to Plant Anatomy '47; also articles in field. Prof hort and head dept floriculture and ornamental hort Cornell U since '40. AAAS(F)—Am Soc Hort Sci (pres '40)—Am Hort Soc (chmn Lily com '38-47)—Mass Hort Soc—Bot Soc Am—Am Soc Naturalists —Northern Nut Growers Assn—N Am Lily Soc (pres '47)—Sigma Xi—Phi Kappa Phi. 422 Chestnut Station, Ithaca.†⊚

13 MACDONALD, Gordon Andrew. Ground water of Hawaiian Islands; Geology of western Sierra Nevada; Petrology of Pacific volcanoes; Volcanology. b'11. AB '33—MA '34— PhD '38 (U Calif). Author articles in field. Asst prof geol U So Cal '47-49; geol Hawaiian Volcano Obs of US Geol Survey '48-51, volcanologist in charge since '51. Geol Soc Am(F)— Mineral Soc Am(F)—Seismol Soc Am —Am Geophys Union—Am Assoc Petrol Geol—Hawaiian Vol Rsrch Assn— Hawaiian Acad Sci—Sigma Xi. United States Geological Survey, Hawaiian Volcano Observatory, Hawaii National Park, T.H.†

14 MACDONALD, H(enry) Malcolm. Marxian socialism. b'14. AB'35 (U San Francisco); AM '37—PhD '39 (Harvard). Research in 20th century political theory with emphasis on Marxian movement. Author articles: Karl Marx: Friedrich Engels and the Southern Slavic problem; Marx: Engels and the Polish national movement. With U Tex since '38, asso prof since '47; vis lectr U San Francisco '40; instr USN Acad '45-46. Am Polit Sci Assn— Southwestern Social Sci Assn—Royal Econ Soc London (F). Department of Government, University of Texas, Austin 12.

15 MACDONALD, Ronald G(ordon). Manufacture and technology of pulp, paper, and converted products. b'99. SB (Chem E) '22 (MIT); MBA '26 (NYU). Engineering and chemistry of suphite, sulphate, soda, ground wood, semi-chemical wood pulp, fine and coarse papers, and paperboard; tests of all pulps, papers, and converted products, including fibrous agricultural wastes, for paper making. Engr Pejepscot Paper Co Brunswick Me '22-24; chem engr Oxford Paper Co Brooklyn '24-26; sec-treas and ed Tech Assn Pulp and Paper Industry since '27. ACS—Am Inst Chem Engrs—Am Soc ME—ASTM—Brit Paper and Board Makers' Assn—Can Pulp and Paper Assn—Assn Printing House Craftsmen—Am Inst Graphic Arts—Am Pulp and Paper Mill Supts Assn—Am Assn Textile Chem and Colorists—Swedish Assn Pulp and Paper Engrs. Technical Association Pulp and Paper Industry, 122 E. 42d St., N.Y.C. 17.

16 MacDONALD, William Alexander. Electronics (Military). b'95. Ed pub. schs.; '18-19 U Paris. Assisted in establishing first laboratory of Division of research and inspection at Paris, '17; participated in trials of first airborne radio-telephone equipment; pioneered in design and development complex military electronics equipment using radar, including identification friend or foe and distance measuring equipment. Vice pres, chief engr and dir Hazeltine Corp since '34; dir Hazeltine Electronics Corp since '39, pres since '42; pres, dir Hazeltine Research Inc Cal since '46; vp, dir Latour Corp since '35; Am Soc Naval Engrs— Armed Forces Communications Assn —Nat Security Indsl Assn—Radio Television Mfrs Assn (dir)—Inst Radio Engrs (sr mem)—Am Ordnance Assn, Electronics Equipment Industry Adv Com Munitions Board—Joint Electronics Equipment Industry Adv Com. Certificate of Merit for outstanding contributions and service to US during World War II in field of electronics '46. Hazeltine Electronics Corp., 58-25 Little Neck Parkway, Little Neck, L.I., N.Y.

17 MacDOUGALL, Curtis Daniel. Hoaxes; Public opinion. b'03. BA '23 (Ripon Coll Wis); MS '26 (Northwestern U); PhD '33 (W Wis). Effect of media of communication upon public opinion and especially effect of public opinion upon the media of communication. Author: Hoaxes '40; Newsroom Problems and Policies '41; Covering the Courts '46; Interpretative Reporting (last edit) '48; Understanding Public Opinion '51. Ed Evanston News Index Ill '34-37, Nat Almanac and Year Book '37-40; state supervisor writers project Ill '40-42; ed writer Chicago Sun '42; prof journalism Northwestern U since '42. Am Assn for Pub Opinion Research—Am Assn Tchrs Journalism (past pres). Northwestern University, Evanston, Ill.

18 MacDOUGALL, Mary Stuart. Protozoology (Cytology. genetics); Chilodonella (Polyploids); Malaria (Chromosemes). b'85. AB '12 (Randolph-Macon Coll); MS '17 (U Chicago); PhD '25 (Columbia); ScD '35 (Université de Montpellier). Author: Biology, The Science of Life '43; also articles in field. Prof zool head dept biol Agnes Scott College '20-52. Southeastern Biol (pres '42-46)—Am Soc Zool—AAAS—Ga Acad Sci (pres '27)—Phi Beta Kappa—Sigma Xi. Guggenheim fellow for study abroad '31-32. 423 Clairemont Av., Decatur, Ga.†

19 MACELWANE, James Bernard. Geophysics; Seismology. b'83. Student '07 (St Stanislaus Coll, John Carroll U); AB '10—AM '11—MS '12 (St Louis U); PhD '23 (Calif U). Research on discontinuities and other details of interior structure of earth, causal connection between ocean storms and a certain type of microseisms; micro-oscillations of the atmosphere, short period microseisms, crustal structure, seismicity of the Mississippi Valley. Author: Loose Leaf Manual of Laboratory Experiments in College Physics (with J I Shannon) '14; Theoretical Seismology Vol I Geodynamics '36; When the Earth Quakes '47; also articles in field. Editor and joint author Bull of Nat Research Council on Seismology '33. Prof geophysics and dir dept St Louis U since '25, dean grad sch '27-33, dean Inst Geophys Tech, trustee since '33. AAAS(F, past pres)—Nat Acad Sci— Geol Soc Am—Am Geog Soc—Am Phys Soc—Seismol Soc Am (past pres) —Jesuit Seismol Assn (pres)—Am Meteorol Soc—Am Geophys Union (past pres seismol sec)—Am Inst Mining Metall Engrs—St Louis Acad Sci (past pres)—Optical Soc Am (asso)—Societa Sismologica Italiana— Societa Meteorologica Italiana — Soc Exploration Geophys—Sigma Xi. 221 N. Grand Blvd., St.L.3.†⊚

20 Mac FADDEN, Frederick Alexander Ray. Accounting, auditing and finance (Municipal, public utility and governmental). b'98. BCS—MCS (NY U.); PhD '23 (Oskulousa Coll Ia); student (U Toronto) (Queen's Univ)

(London Sch Econ Eng). Member reorganization committees of Dominion Manufacturers Investment Assn.; municipal auditor numerous municipalities, public utilities, public hospitals, etc; consultant to public commissions and governmental bodies. Public utility auditing Price Waterhouse & Co. '20-25, Barrow Wade & Guthrie '25-28; public utility management Electric Bond & Share Corp & Affiliates '28-33; public practice on own account in municipal and public utility auditing, finance, consultations (45 municipal corporations) since '33. Inst. Chartered Accountants Ont—Royal Econ Soc(F)—Municipal Finance Officers Assn—Canadian Tax Foundations—Inst Pub Adminstrn Can (council '49-51). 22 College St., Toronto; also 46 Second St. W., Cornwall, Ont., Can.

10 MacGEE, Alfred Ernest. Petroleum solvents (Chemistry); Industrial solvents (Handling); Fats and oils (Solvent extraction); Abrasives (Aluminous bonds); Refractories and clays (Physical characteristics). b'99. Student '15-18 (Southwestern La Inst); BS '21—MS '22 (La State U); PhD '25 (O State U). Developed procedures for safe handling of industrial solvents from standpoint of fire and health hazards; devised special hydrocarbon fractions for use in manufacture fats and oils by solvent extraction process, in compounding quick-setting rubber cements, in formulating quick-drying inks; design high-strength, low expansion glass-type bonds for aluminous grinding wheels; determined specific heat and drying characteristics of refractories and heavy clays. Author articles: Vegetable Oil Extraction Solvents '47; Handling Industrial Solvents with Safety '48; Some Physical and Chemical Properties of Extraction Naphthas '49; Paint, Varnish and Lacquer Naphthas-General Chemical Composition '50, and others. Research engr Abrasive Research Assn Columbus O '25-26; asso ceramic chem Bur Standards Washington '27-29; plant mgr Viking Gasoline Corp Charleston W Va '29-30; mgr. solvents div Skelly Oil Co Kansas City since '30. Am Inst Chem(F)—ACS—Am Oil Chem Soc—Tri-States Oil Mill Supts Assn—Nat Paint Varnish Lacquer Assn—Independent Petroleum Assn Am—Sigma Xi—Alpha Chi Sigma—Phi Lambda Upsilon—Gamma Alpha. 605 W. 47th St., KC 10, Mo.

11 MacGILLIVRAY, John Henry. Tomato color; Vegetable irrigation, production, food value. b'99. BS '21—MS '22 (U Ill); '22-23 (Cornell U); PhD '25 (U Wis). Research on effect of phosphorous on composition of the tomato plant, tomato quality and particularly tomato color in connection with the canning industry, estimates of food value of vegetables per pound, acre and man hour, effect of irrigation on vegetable production under arid conditions, storage in transit of cantaloupes and white potatoes. Author articles in field. Olericulturist and prof U Cal since '49. AAAS(F)—Am Soc Hort Sci—Am Soc Plant Physiol—Inst Food Tech—Potato Assn Am. Vegetable Crops Division, Davis, Cal.†

12 MACHIN, James Stewart. Chemistry of high temperature silicate slags and glasses; Mineral wool; Surface of finely divided solids; Measurement of physical properties. b'93. AB '21 (Westminster Coll); MS '22 (U Ill); PhD '32 (U Chicago). Author articles in field. Chem and head indsl minerals div Ill State Geol Survey since '36. Am Chem Soc—Am Inst Mining Metall Engrs—AAAS—Sigma Xi. Natural Resources Building, Urbana, Ill.†

13 MacINTIRE, Walter Hoge. Chemistry of liming materials; Phosphatic fertilizers, slags, and fluorine; Lysimetry (Calcium, magnesium, potassium, sulfur, nitrogen, phosphorus, fluorine). b'85. BS '05 (NC State Coll); MS '09 (Pa State Coll); PhD (Cornell U) DSc '37 (Clemson Coll). Originated the theory of reciprocal repression exerted by alkaline-earth incorporations in soils; fathered the practice of inclusions of raw dolomite and of selectively calcined dolomite in superphosphate, patent assigned to University of Tennessee; holder series of patents on the production of phosphates of calcium, magnesium and manganese and process for the removal of fluorine from potable waters. Author articles in field. Soil chemist chemist and head dept chem U Tenn Agr Expt Sta since '12. Am Chem Soc (sect chmn, councilor)—Am Soc Agron—Soil Sci Soc Am—Internat Soc Soil Sci—Assn Ofcl Agr Chem (vp and pres '27)—AAAS(F)—Sigma Xi—Phi Kappa Phi. Herty medalist through Ga sect Am Chem Soc '36; designated as one of 10 ablest fertilizer chemists US by Am Chem Soc. Morgan Hall, University of Tennessee, Knoxville 16, Tenn.†

14 MacIVER, Robert Morrison. Social theory; Social phenomena (Causation); Political theory (History); United States racial and ethnic groups (Sociology of control of discrimination). b'82. MA '03—DPh '15 (Edinburgh U); BA '07 (Oxford U); LittD '29 (Columbia); LittD '36 (Harvard). Author: Community — A Sociological Study '17; Labor in the Changing World '19; The Modern State '26; Society—Its Structure and Changes '31; Society—A Textbook of Sociology '37; Toward an Abiding Peace '43; The Web of Government '47; The More Perfect Union '48. Lieber prof polit philos and sociol Columbia University since '29, emeritus since '51. V chmn Canada War Labor Board '17-18. Royal Soc Canada(F)—Am Acad Arts Sci—Am Philos Soc—Am Sociol Soc—Inst Internationale de Sociologie—Phi Beta Kappa. Palisades, N.Y.☉

15 MACK, Carl Theodore. Patent law; Electrical engineering. b'96. EE '17 (Lafayette Coll); LLB '24 (George Washington U). Trustee Lafayette College Research Foundation. Engr Henry L Doherty and Co '17-21; asst in patent lawyers office '21-28; mem patent law firm Stone Boyden & Mack since '28. Am Patent Law Assn (treas '44-46, sec '46-48, bd mgrs since '48)—DC Bar Assn—Am Bar Assn—Phi Beta Kappa—Tau Beta Pi. 866 National Press Bldg., Washington 4.†☉

16 MACK, Pauline Beery. Human nutrition; Textile chemistry. b'91. AB '13 (Mo State U); AM '19 (Columbia); PhD '32 (Pa State Coll). Author: Chemistry Applied to Home and Community; Stuff—The Science of Materials in the Service of Man; also articles in field. Staff department chem Pa State Coll since '19, prof household chem since '32, dir Ellen H Richards Inst since '40. Am Inst Chem(F)—AAAS(F)—Soc Research Child Development(F) — Am Pub Health Assn(F)—Am Acad Polit Social Sci—Am Assn Adult Edn—Am Assn Phys Anthrop—Am Assn Textile Chem and Colorists—Am Assn Textile Technol—Am Chem Soc—Am Congress Obstetrics and Gynecol—Am Dietetics Assn—Am Home Econ Assn—Am Soc Testing Materials—Textile Research Inst—Phi Beta Kappa—Sigma Xi—Phi Kappa Phi. Ellen H. Richards Institute, School of Chemistry and Physics, Pennsylvania State College, State College, Pa.

17 MACK, Warren Bryan. Horticulture; Vegetable gardening; Plant nutrition; Wood engraving. b'96. PhB '15—ScD hon '46 (Lafayette Coll Easton Pa); BSc '21 (Pa State Coll); MSc '24 (Mass Agrl Coll); PhD '29 (Johns Hopkins). Mineral nutrition and fertilization of vegetable crops; soil management horticultural crops; foliar diagnosis (leaf analysis) for nutrient requirements of horticultural crops; physiology horticultural crop plants. Contbr papers and articles to profi and tech jours since '22. With Pa State Coll since '23, head dept horticulture since '37, prof since '30. AAAS(F)—Am. Soc Hort Sci(pres '44-46, dir Am Hort council since '46)—Am Soc Plant Physiologers—Bot Soc Am—Pa Hort Soc—Audubon Artists—Soc Am Etchers—Gravers Lithographers & Wood cutters—Phi Beta Kappa—Phi Beta Kappa Assos—Sigma Xi—Nat Acad Design (asso graphic sect)—Phi Kappa Phi. Warren H Manning Purchase Prize '38, Appalachian Mus Purchase prize '40, 2d prize Nat Exhbn prints '43, 3d prize '46; Dr Marvin F Jones purchase prize Salmagundi Club NY '48. 245 E Hamilton Av., State College, Pa.☉

18 MACKAY, Thomas Raymond. Deepwell turbine pumps; Propeller pumps. b'13. BS (ME) '35 (U Utah). Design and application of deepwell turbine and propeller type pumping equipment for domestic, agricultural reclamation, industrial, and municipal liquid supply and liquid transfer. Design engr Pomona Pump Co. '36-38, field application engr '39-40, application and sales engr '40-41; supervisor application engring western states area Joshua Hendy Iron Works Pomona Pump Div '42-44; supervisor application engring Fairbanks Morse & Co '44-48, mgr engring since '48. ASME. Fairbanks, Morse & Co., Pomona, Cal.

19 MACKENSEN, Otto. Honey bee breeding; Queen bee artificial insemination. b'04. BS (Tex A & M Coll); MA '33—PhD '35 (Tex U). Author articles in field. Apiculturist Bur Entomol and Plant Quarantine US Dept Agr since '35. Southern States Beeculture Laboratory, Baton Rouge 3, La.†

20 MacKENZIE, Barbara Kruger. Social psychology; Minority placement problems; Educational and personnel psychology. b'03. AB '24 (Barnard Coll); AM '30—PhD '48 (Columbia); '30 (U Vienna); '37-38 (U So Calif). Author articles in field. Dir placement Brooklyn Coll '40-48, dept edn since '48. Am Psychol Assn (Diplomate in counseling guidance)—Am Coll Personnel Assn. George Davis Bivin Foundation fellow '38-39. Brooklyn College, Bedford Av. & Av. H, Brooklyn 10.

21 MacKENZIE, James Tucker. Gray iron (Centrifugal casting, metallurgy, and cupola melting). b'91. BCE '12—MA '12—DSc '30 (University South); DSc '48 (U Ala). Studied German centrifugal casting methods on mission for Federal Foreign Economic Administration '45. With Am Cast Iron Pipe Co since '12, tech dir since '48. Am Welding Soc—Iron and Steel Inst Gt Brit—Assn Foundry Tech France —Am Foundrymen's Soc (chmn. gray iron div '36-37, John H Whiting gold medal '38, 1st Hoyt lectr '47)—AI MME (chmn iron and steel div '37-38, dir '39-42, Howe memorial lectr '44)—ACS (sec, counselor Ala sect) —ASTM (dir, past chmn com A-3 on cast iron)—Electrochem Soc—Am Soc Metals—Soc Automotive Engrs—Am Ceramic Soc—Am Petroleum Inst—Soc Exptl Stress Analysis—Am Water Works Assn—Am Gas Assn. American Cast Iron Pipe Co., Birmingham 2, Ala.

10 MACKIN, John Gilman Sr. Limnology; Marine shell fisheries; Parasitology. b'03. BS '24 (East Central State Coll); MS '27—PhD '33 (U Ill). Research in productivity of lakes and ponds, problems of turbidity in ponds, causes of mortality of oysters on Louisiana and Texas coasts. Author articles in field. Prof biol oceanog Texas A&M Coll College Station, dir. Tex A&M Research Found Marine Lab Grand Isle La. Okla Acad Sci(F)—Limnol Soc Am—Am Microscopical Soc—AAUP—Am Soc Zool—AAAS—Sigma Xi. Dept. of Oceanography, Texas A&M College, College Station, Tex.

11 MACKINNEY, Gordon. Plant coloring matters (Chlorophylls, carotenoids); Stability of pigments in food processing; Dehydration (Fruits and vegetables, biochemical deterioration in storage). b'05. BSA '26 (U Toronto); PhD '33 (U Calif). Author articles in field. Full prof U Calif since '49. Am Chem Soc—Am Soc Plant Physiol — AAAS — Inst Food Technol. Guggenheim fellow '47.

12 MacKINNEY, Loren Carey. Medieval medicine; Medieval France; History of pharmacy and drugs; Animal substances in pharmacy. b'91. AB '13 (Lawrence Coll); AM '16 (U Wis); PhD '25 (U Chicago). Author: Early Medieval Medicine; with Special Reference to France and Chartres '37; The Medieval World '38; also articles in field. Prof medieval hist U NC since '30. AHA—Medieval Acad Am—Hist Sci Soc—Am Assn Hist Med—So Hist Assn. Chapel Hill, NC.

13 MACKLIN, Charles. Concrete pressure. b'04. BS in civil engring '27 (Case Inst Tech). Study concrete pressures in connection with form design; evaluation variables affecting pressure. Field engr Hunkin-Conkey Constrn Co Cleveland '27-32, Hecker Moon Co '33; structural designer James Stewart & Co Inc Chicago '42. Am Concrete Inst (Job Problems and Practice award '44-45)—Soc Exptl Stress Analysis. Old Jacksonville Rd., Springfield, Ill.

14 MACKLIN, Justin Wilford. Patents and industry; Inventions; Machine-made jobs; Patent system (Value). b'89. LLB '16 (Baldwin-Wallace Y, Berea O). Author articles in field. Law practice Cleveland since '16. Am Patent Law Assn—Am Bar Assn. Leader Bldg., Cleveland.

15 MACKWORTH, Gordon D(otter). Forest education; Administration. b'95. BS '16 (Ohio State U); MF '17 (Yale); '19 (U Edinburgh); '32 (U Ga). Research in and analysis of requirements for proper administration of forest areas; legal requirements; administrative regulations; administrative organization; fire protection; civilian education for good forestry practice. Asso prof to head dept forestry La State U '25-31; prof and head div forestry U Ga '31-35, prof and dir sch forestry '35-39; prof forestry management U Wash since '39, dean since '45. Soc Am Forestry—Council Forestry Sch Execs—Forest Products Research Soc—Sigma Xi—Phi Kappa Phi—Phi Sigma—Xi Sigma Pi. College of Forestry, University of Washington, Seattle 5.☺

16 MacLANE, John Fisher. Jurisprudence; Military and naval science. b'78. AB '99—LLD '38 (Westminster Coll); LLD '49 (U Idaho); AB '00 (Yale); LLB '02 (U Minn). Editor: Revised Code of Idaho '08. Practice of law since '02; asst atty gen Idaho '09;

code commr Idaho '07-08; acting dean coll law U Ida '09-11; judge Dist. Court 3rd Dist Idaho '11-12; justice pro tem Supreme Court of Idaho '11. Am Bar Assn—NY Ba State Bar Assn—Bar Assn City of NY—Phi Beta Kappa Assos. 120 Boradway, NYC.☺

17 MacLEAN, Basil Clarendon. Hospitals (Construction); Public health. b'95. MD, CM '27 (McGill U); Master Public Health '42 (Johns Hopkins U). Author articles in field. Hosp cons and surveyor; dir Strong Memorial Hospital and professor hosp adminstrn U Rochester NY since '35. Am Hospital Assn (chmn Commn Hosp Service '36-41, pres '41-42)—NY State Hosp Assn—Rochester Visiting Nurse Assn—Am Coll Hosp Adm—Am Pub Health Assn—Rochester Acad Medicine—AMA. Diplomate American Board Preventive Medicine. 260 Crittenden Blvd., Rochester 20, N.Y.

18 MacLEOD, Malcolm Lorimer. Robert Herrick (Diction, sematology); Marine shells of Southwestern Florida Coast. b'01. BS '27—MS '29—PhD '36 (U Va). Author: A Concordance to the Poems of Robert Herrick '36; An Analysis of Herrick's Vocabulary '36. Asso prof Eng U Fla since '47. 301 Anderson Hall, University of Florida, Gainesville, Fla.

19 MacMAHON, Andrew Merritt. Photo-conductivity (Selenium, sulfur, tellurium). b'93. Student '12-14 (Drake U Des Moines Ia); AB '16—MS '17 (U Ia); PhD '27 (U Chicago); '27-28 (U Göttingen Germany). Author articles: Action of Roentgen and Gamma Radiations on Electrical Conductivity '20; Light-Sensitiveness of Crystalline Selenium (Thesis) '27, and others. Co-author articles: Two New Selenium Crystal Bridges '25; Light Sensitiveness of Selenium, Tellurium, and Sulphur, and others. Fellow physics U Chicago '25-27; asso physics U Gottingen Germany '27-28; curator div phys sci Mus Sci and Industry Chicago '28-37; cons physicist since '37. APS—Am Optical Soc—AAAS—Soc Exploration Geophysicists—Hist Sci Soc—Phi Beta Kappa—Sigma Xi—Phi Delta Kappa—Gamma Alpha. Southwestern Physical Laboratories, 2301 W. Alabama Av., Houston. H: 2501 Southmore Blvd., Houston 4.

20 MacMASTERS, Majel Margaret. Starch (Production, properties); Cereal grains (Structure, chemistry); Rhythmic crystallization. b'05. BSc '26 (Mass Agrl Coll); MSc '28—PhD '34 (Mass State Coll). Author articles in field. Co-holder US Patents. Asso to sr chem Northern Regional Research Lab US Dept Agr since '40, charge starch granule sect since '44. AAAS — Am Chem Soc — Am Assn Cereal Chem—Am Soc Plant Physiol—Phi Kappa Phi—Sigma Xi. Selected as one of 10 ablest in starch field by Chicago sect Am Chem Soc '47. Northern Regional Research Laboratory, 825 North University St., Peoria 5, Ill.

21 MacMILLAN Charles Wight. Automobiles (Maintenance and safety testing equipment). b'02. BS '25 (Dartmouth); SB in mech engring '33 (MIT). Designed and developed photo-electric headlight testers, wheel aligners, brake equipment, engine testing guages and tools. Granted 18 patents. Engr Kent Moore Orgn Inc. '36-40; engr Hinckley-Myers Co '40-41; free-lance engr '46-50; chief engr Bear Mfg Co since '50. Soc Automotive Engrs. Award Elec Engring mag '38. Bear Manufacturing Co., Rock Island, Ill.

22 MacMILLAN, Howard Gove. Plant pathology (Potatoes, truck crops); Economic development of the Pacific area. b'90. PhB '12 (Brown U);

MS '13 — PhD '19 (U Wis). Plant explorer Peru, Chile, Bolivia, potato improvement research, leader expedition to Manchuria, Gobi Desert on soil conservation and grass introduction '34. Author articles in field. Sci asst, later sr path US Dept Agr '15-30, sr path '30-42; cons Bd Econ Warfare Pacific Area '43; deputy spl rep Fgn Econ Adminstrn '44-45; field dir US Commercial Co Econ Survey '46; econ development Research Council South Pacific Commn since '48. AAAS(F)—Am Phytopath Soc—Am Meteorol Soc—Soc Patholog de Vegetal de France. South Pacific Commission, Pentagone Noumea, New Caledonia. H: 1725 Fifth Av., Los Angeles 6.

23 MacMILLIN, Howard Francis. Hydraulics. b'97. Student '15-16 (Coll of Wooster); SB '21 (MIT). Research and design hydraulic machinery and applications of hydraulic power and control equipment. Holds 21 US Patents on hydraulic machinery and systems; co-inventor of 22 other patents. Author articles in field. Application engr, later vp and asst gen mgr The Hydraulic Press Mfg Co O '21-38, pres and gen mgr '38-44; with Arthur D Little Inc Cambridge since '45; pres MacMillin Engring Corp Chicago since '46; affiliated with Towler Brothers Limited of Rodley Eng since '48. ASME—Western Soc Engrs—Soc Plastics Ind. MacMillin Engineering Corporation, 6806 North Clark St., Chicago 26.†

24 MACMULLEN, Clinton William. Detergents; Surface active agents. b'09. BChE '30—PhD '35 (U Minn). Research in textile chemicals, resins, synthetic detergents, wetting agents, bactericides; developed detergents for laundry, metal cleaning, food sanitation, paper and allied trades; sodium metasilicate manufacture. Holds 20 patents in field. Author articles in field. Research chem Rohm & Haas Co Phila '35-43; tech dir Cowles Chem Co '43-52; chief new products sect and fats and oils sect Olin Industries since '52. Am Chem Soc—American Institute Chem(F) — AAAS — Tech Assn Pulp Paper Industry — Am Assn Textile Chem Colorists — Am Soc Testing Materials — Sigma Xi — Phi Lambda Upsilon. Olin Industries, Inc., 275 Winchester Av., New Haven, Conn. H: 73 Jesswig Dr., Hamden, Conn.

25 MACY, C(harles) Ward. Finance (Public); Taxation; Fiscal policy. b'99. AB '20 (Grinnell Coll Ia); AM '23 (U Ia). Royall Victor fellow econ '28-29—PhD '32 (Stanford U). Research on incidence and effects of taxes; study effect of property tax exemptions, relationship between cost-price structure and net income tax of corporations. Author articles: Financing National Defense '40; A Program for Preventing Inflation '41; Social Security Taxes in the War Finance Program '43; Economy in Postwar Federal Taxation '45; Sources of Revenue for Public Education '45; Incidence or Effects of Taxes? '46, and others. Co-editor: Public Finance '34. Contibutor: New Peoples Encyclopedia '48. Faculty econ dept Coe Coll '23-50, prof '32-50; prof econ and head dept U Ore since '50. Tax Inst (adv council)—Nat Tax Assn—Am Econ Assn—Midwest Econ Assn (pres '48-49)—Pacific Coast Econ Assn—Phi Beta Kappa—Phi Kappa Phi. Department of Economics, University of Oregon, Eugene, Ore.†☺

26 MACY, Ralph W(illiam). Parasites; Trematodes; Cestodes; Butterflies. b'05. BA '29 (Linfield Coll); MA '31—PhD '34 (U Minn); '28-29 (U Wash). Co-author: Butterflies '41; also articles in field. Prof biol Reed

Coll since '42, head dept since '43. AAAS—Am Soc Parasitol—Am Micros Soc—Ore Entomol Soc (past pres)—Ore Soc Microbiol (vp)—Ore Acad Sci. Reed College, Portland 2, Ore.†

10 MADER, William John. Analytical chemistry; Antibiotics; Synthetic rubbers; Pharmaceuticals; Chemical munitions. b'11. BA '32 (Western Res U); MS '34 (O State U). Author articles in field. Chief analytical research Merck and Co since '46. Chem Warfare Service Huntsville Arsenal production officer '42-44. Am Chem Soc—Am Soc Applied Spectroscopy—Chem Warfare Assn—Am Assn Advancement Sci. Merck and Company, Rahway, N.J.

11 MADIGAN, Marian East. Educational measurements; Guidance; Youth surveys. b'98. AB '24 (U Neb); MA '27 (Columbia); PhD '36 (U Chicago). Research on mental growth, aptitude testing, use of tests in guidance of student nurses. Author: Psychology: Principles and Applications '50. Psychol and spl Milwaukee Vocational and Adult Schs since '41; instr Stout Inst summer '45, '47; vis prof U Ariz summer '48-49. Phi Beta Kappa—Nat Vocational Guidance Assn—Internat Council Women Psychol(F)—Am Psysh Assn(asso). 1015 N. Sixth St., Milw 3.

12 MADSEN, Herbert Stanford. Food processing (Pacific Northwest fruits, citrus fruits, wines); Tapioca starch. b'09. BS '33 (U Wash); MS '44 (Ore State Coll). Research on improvement alcoholic beverages, dehydration and other preservation of native small fruits, tapioca starch technology, development of frozen concentrated citrus juices by freezing and separating ice from concentrated juice and by low temperature evaporation; studies on food materials considered as colloid systems and development of processing and preservation approach on this basis; pectin technology. Author articles in field. Chief chem Ore Liquor Control Commn and asst chem and asst food technol Ore State Expt Sta '41-44; Research chem sect head Central Labs Research and Dev Dept Gen Foods Corp '44-48; mgr Citro-Mat dept Bireley's Div Gen Foods Corp Hollywood '48-50; mgr citrus prodn Birds Eye-Snider Div Gen Foods Corp Lakeland since '50. Am Chem Soc—Inst Food Technol—Sigma Xi. Birds Eye-Snider Division, General Foods Corporation, Lakeland, Fla. H: Lake Morton Dr.

13 MAGALHAES, Hulda. Golden hamsters; Marine snails. b'14. BS '35 (NJ Coll Women); MA '37 (Mt Holyoke Coll); PhD '44 (Duke U). Author articles in field. Asso prof physiol and hygiene Bucknell U since '48. AAAS—Am Zool Soc—Biol Photog Assn—Royal Photog Assn Gt Brit—Sigma Xi—Phi Beta Kappa. Box 496, Bucknell University, Lewisburg, Pa.

14 MAGAW, Elden Samuel. Contracts; Insurance and administrative law; Life and fire insurance. b'06. AB '28—LL B '31 (U Okla); '37-39—SJD '39 (Georgetown U Sch Law). Author: Legal Aspects of Administrative Hearings and Findings '39; also articles in field. Arbitrator in labor relations cases; prof law Temple U Sch Law since '33, asst dean since '47. Okla State Bar Assn—Pa Bar Assn. 7259 Spruce St., Upper Darby, Pa.

15 MAGEE, Warren Egbert. Medical law, b'08. LLB '30—LLM '31 (Am U). Extensive studies in medical law as gen counsel for medical societies; trial counsel in case of USA vs AMA et al. Author articles: Expert Med-

ical Testimony '39; Adoption Law Needs Clarification '45; The Corporate Practice of Medicine '47; Privileged Communications '50. Cons Med Soc DC, Med Service DC, AAAS, Med Service Bur, Am Psychiatric Assn, Am Diabetes Assn; DC counsel Nat Physicians Com, AMA, Blue Shield. Bar Assn DC—Am Bar Assn—Am Judicature Soc—AAAS. 745 Shoreham Bldg., Washington 5.

16 MAGIE, Robert Ogden. Gladiolus diseases; Fungicides. b'06. BS '29 (Rutgers U); MS '30—PhD '34 (U Wis). Author articles in field. Path Gladiolus investigations Fla Expt Sta Bradenton Fla since '45. Am Phytopath Soc—Fla Hort Soc. Gulf Coast Experiment Station, Bradenton, Fla.

17 MAGILL, Mary Annetta. Organic chemistry nomenclature; Absorption spectroscopy. b'09. BA '30—MA '31—PhD '33 (O State U). Author articles in field. Asso ed Chem Abstracts O State U since '39. Am Chem Soc (com nomenclature spelling pronunciation since '43)—AAAS—Phi Beta Kappa—Sigma Xi. Chemical Abstracts, Ohio State University, Columbus 10, O.†

18 MAGISTAD, Oscar Conrad. Pineapple culture; Alkali soils. b'00. BS '22—MS '23—PhD '24 (U Wis). Research on pineapple production and canning, chemistry alkali soils and reclamation, crop tolerance to alkali soils. Author articles in field. Dir research Libby McNeill & Libby Hawaii since '45. Am Chem Soc—AAAS—Am Soc Plant Physiol—Am Soc Hort—Am Soc Agron—Am Soc Soil Sci — Geophys Union — Hawaiian Bot Soc (pres '38)—Western Soc Soil Sci (vp '42-43)—Hawaiian Acad Sci (pres '38)—Phi Kappa Phi—Sigma Xi. 2721 Puuhonua St., Honolulu 54, Hawaii.☺

19 MAGLIO, M. Martin. Plasticizers; Stabilizers; Soap; Organic synthetics; Surface active agents. b'14. BS '37 (Manhattan Coll); MS '39 — fellow '37-39 (Catholic U); '43-44 (Brooklyn Poly); '42-43 (NYU); '47-48 (St Louis U). Research on plasticizers, organic nitrogen compounds, sulfa analogs, surface active agents, paint driers, resin stabilizers, rubber chemicals, germicides, detergents, soaps, emulsion waxes, resins, varnishes. Author articles in field. Formerly chem director Vestal Labs Inc St Louis; sec-treas Worth Labs and Worth Chem and Paint Co. NY Acad Sci—Cath Round Table Sci—Am Chem Soc—Am Soc Testing Materials—AAAS—Drug Chem Allied Trades Assn—Metropolitan—L I Chem Assn. 1800-1816 Tenth Av. N., Lake Worth, Fla. H: 225 So. K St., Lake Worth.

20 MAGNITZKY, Albert Wayne. Sea water (Chemistry); Wastes (Industrial, chemistry); Oceanography. b'18. BS '46 (Tulane U). Analysis sea water for crude oil, oil fractions, sulfur, oil bleedwater, dairy and brewery wastes, and acid mine drainage; deionization of sea water; study action of crude oil and oil fractions upon oyster activity and production; determination degree of pollution of streams; compilation of data on ocean tides and currents; preparation charts and tables of tides and currents, swell, temperature, geomagnetism, salinity of shallow waters, harbors, bays, channels, etc. for military operations. Author article: A Preliminary Note on a Naturally Occurring Organic Substance in Sea Water Affecting the Feeding of Oysters. Sea water chem Gulf Refining Co Pensacola Fla '47-50; sanitary chem Water Conservation Bd State of Vt Montpelier '50; now chem oceanographer USN Hydrog Office. ACS—Arctic Inst NA—Nat Shell

Fisheries Assn. US Navy Hydrographic Office, Suitland, Md.

21 MAGON, Jero. Puppetry; Marionettes. b'00. Graduate Pratt Inst Sch Fine Applied Arts; BS '41 (NYU); Master Puppeteer '37 (awarded by Puppeteers Am). Author: Staging the Puppet Play. Instr fine arts, puppetry and stagecraft NYC high schs since '24; producer, dir, designer puppet plays: The Emperor Jones, Marco Millions by Eugene O'Neill; The Porcelain God; Punch and Judy; Somebody-Nothing; Man Who Married a Dumb Wife; In Henry's Back-yard; Arabian Nights; Aladdin and His Wonderful Lamp; lecturer on masks and puppetry Sch Art League, Am Lecturers Assn; dir radio broadcasts on puppetry over WEVD, WNYC; examples of work in leading books on puppetry. 135 MacDougal St., NYC 12.

22 MAGOUN, Francis Peabody, Jr. Germanic antiquities; Anglo-Saxon language and literature. b'95. AB '16—PhD '23 (Harvard); '19 (Trinity Coll, Cambridge, Eng). Managing editor: Speculum a Journal of Medieval Studies 1926-30; editor: Harvard Studies and Notes in Philology and Literature '34-35. Co-author: An Old-English Anthology (with J A Walker) '50. With Harvard University since '19, prof comparative literature '37-51, professor English since '51; Harvard exchange professor to U Paris and U Strassbourg '31-32. Medieval Acad Am(F)—Modern Lang Assn Am —English Place-Name Soc—Soc Advancement Scandinavian Study—American Name Soc—Soc Neophilologique. Medaille de l'Universite de Strasbourg '32. 29 Reservoir St., Cambridge 38, Mass.☺

23 MAGOUN, Herbert William. Prosody (English, Latin, Greek, Sanskrit, Hebrew); Biblical geology. b'56. AB '79 (Ia Coll); PhD '90 (Johns Hopkins). Research on metrical, philological, Oriental, religious, critical, scientific, psychological and other subjects including Biblical exegesis. Author: Volts from a Layman's Dynamo (series beginning '27); also articles in field. Redactor: Mexican Linguistics and the Asuri-Kalpa, a Sanskrit witchcraft text. Pres Mass Coll Osteopathy '21-26; literary work since '27. Am Oriental Soc (life)—Am Philol Assn (life)—Phi Beta Kappa. 89 Hillcrest Rd., Belmont 78, Mass.☺

24 MAGOWAN, David. Advertising (Rural market). b'87. AB '11 (Cornell). Author trade paper articles on advertising to the rural market; addresses on same subject before state and sectional press assn meetings. Adv dir Western Newspaper Union since '25, vp since '38. V chmn Com Econ Development, Information Com since '45. 310 E. 45th St., NYC.†

25 MAGRUDER, Roy. Olericulture; Vegetable gardening plant breeding (Principal American varieties of vegetables, lima bean, vegetable seed production). b'00. BSA '22 (Purdue U); PhD '31 (Cornell U). Cultural and breeding research with vegetables. With Bur Plant Industry US Dept Agr Washington since '31, prin hort since '46, asst to adminstr Research and Marketing Admin since '48, research coordinator since '49. American Soc Hort Sci—AAAS—Genetics Soc Am. US Department of Agriculture, Agricultural Research Administration, Washington 25.†

26 MAHAN, Bruce Ellis. Radio and audio-visual education; Midwestern United States and Iowa history. b'90. BA '14—MA '20—PhD '27 (U Ia). Collaborator: Dictionary of American

Biography '28. Author: Old Fort Crawford and the Frontier '26; Stories of Iowa for Boys and Girls (with R A Gallaher) '29; also articles in field. Prof dir ext div U Ia '29-47, dean ext div since '47. NEA—AHA—Miss Valley Hist Assn—Ia State Hist Soc—Ia State Edn Assn—Nat Univ Ext Assn (pres '38-39). 303 Melrose Av., Iowa City, Ia.

10 MAHLER, Ernst. Paper cellulose wadding. b'87. Grad Chem Engr (Tech U Darmstadt Germany); DSc(hon) '37 (Brown U). American Delegate to the Allied Commission on Reparations. With Kimberly-Clark Corp papers mfrs Neenah Wis since '14; chmn bd Internat Cellucotton Products Co; trustee Lawrence Coll and Inst Paper Chemistry; director of Allis-Chalmers Mfg Co; director First Wis Nat Bank Milwaukee, First Nat Bank Neenah Wis; vp Spruce Falls Power and Paper Co Kapuskasing Can. Awarded gold medal of Tech Assn of Pulp and Paper Industry '32; Army Medal of Freedom. Box 524, Neenah, Wis.

11 MAHLER, Joseph. Stereoscopy; Polarizing materials. b'99. Student '15-19 (Comml Coll Vienna). Research and invention in three-dimensional presentations (stereoscopy); polarizing films and pictures. Inventor of Photoplastikon, Vectographs, Polarizer, Vectoscope. Amateur work in stereoscopy since '16; research and development Vectographs and Polarizers Polaroid Corp Cambridge Mass '38-46; research polarizers and stereoscopy Am Optical Co since '46. Tech Soc Southbridge (Mass)—Boston Camera Club. American Optical Co. Research Laboratory, Box 137, Stamford, Conn.

12 MAHOOD, Harry Samuel. Ammunition depots (Design). b'94. BS in civil engring '16 (U Ill). Dir tech div Nav Ammunition Depot since '50. Am Soc CE—Ark Engrs Club. Naval Ammunition Depot, Shumaker (Camden), Ark. H: Post Office Box 204, Camden, Ark.

13 MAHR, August Carl. Drama and theatre (Forms); Folk art and customs; Moravian Indian missions (Ohio). b'86. Student '05-11 (U Heidelberg Germany, Caen France, London); PhD '11 (U Heidelberg); state high sch teacher's diploma '12 (Karlsruhe Germany). Author: Dramatische Situationsbilder '26; The Visit of the Rurik to San Francisco in 1816 '32; The Origin of the Greek Tragic Form '38; Relations of Passion Plays to St Ephrem the Syrian '42; The Cyprus Passion Cycle '47; also articles in field. Prof German O State U since '30, dir publ and research project Grad Sch and O State Archaol and Hist Soc '48. O Acad Sci(F)—Medieval Acad Am—Modern Lang Assn Am—Am Council Coll Studies Switzerland. Department of German, Ohio State University, Columbus 10, O. H: 2079 W. 5th Av., Columbus 12.†

14 MAI, William Frederick. Plant pathology (Potatoes). b'16. BS '39 (U Del); PhD '45 (Cornell U). Author: Studies on the X Virus of Potatoes '47. Author and co-author bulletins and papers on Golden Nematode Disease of Potato. Research asst plant pathol Cornell U '39-45, asso prof since '49, prof since '52. Am Phytopath Soc—AAAS—Phi Kappa Phi. Department of Plant Pathology, Cornell University, Ithaca, N.Y.

15 MAIER, Eugene. Viruses; Zootoxins; Venoms; Immunology; Malariology. b'96. Student '18-20 (U Tubingen); '20-21 (U Marburg); PhD '22 (U Erlangen, Germany). Research on bacteriophage, rabies, reptile venoms, Vitamin A, amino acids. Author articles in field. Dir of labs Fla Med Center Venice Fla since '37; abstractor Chem Abstracts. Am Soc Bact—AAAS. P.O. Box 2, Winter Park, Fla.†◎

16 MAIER, Norman Raymond Frederick. Comparative and industrial psychology; Frustration. b'00. AB '23—MA '25—PhD '28 (U Mich). Author: The Psychological Approach to Literary Criticism (with H W Reninger) '33; Principles of Animal Psychology (with T C Schneirla) '35; Studies of Abnormal Behavior in the Rat '39; Psychology in Industry '46; Frustration: the Study of Behavior Without a Goal '49; Principles of Human Relations: Applications to Management '52; also articles. With Univ. Mich since '31, prof psychology since '46; cons (human relations) Mich Bell Telephone Co since '45, Detroit Edison Co since '47; staff Survey Research Center, U Mich since '48. AAAS—Am Psychol Assn—Midwestern Psychol Assn—Soc Psychol Study Social Issues. Department of Psychology, University of Michigan, Ann Arbor. H: 1111 Fair Oaks Pkwy.†◎

17 MAINA, Barth(olomew) (Anthony). Breeding and behavior of goldfish; Biology and systematics of the Bombidae (Apoidea). b'16. BS '39. Grad honor scholar '39-40—U fellow '40-42, '46-47—(U Chicago). Research asst in zool U Chicago '47-49; instr biol Chgo City Jr Coll since '49. Ecol Soc Am—AAAS—Entomol Soc Am—Ill State Acad Sci—Royal Entomol Soc London—Soc Study Evolution—Soc Systematic Zool-Am Assn Econ Entomol—Ill State Beekeepers Assn. Department of Biological Sciences, Chicago City Junior College, Herzl Branch, 3711 Douglas Blvd., Chgo. 23. H: 10623 Church St., Chgo. 43.†

18 MAINS, Edwin Butterworth. Mycology (Entomogenous fungi, physiologic specialization of fungi); Inheritance of disease resistance in plants. AB '13—PhD '16 (U Mich). Scientific expedition British Honduras '36. Author articles in field. Dir Herbarium U Mich since '31. AAAS(F)—Ind Acad Sci—Bot Soc Am—Am Phytopath Soc—Am Mycol Soc (pres '42)—Am Soc Naturalists—Mich Acad Sci—Sigma Xi. 1911 Lorraine Pl., Ann Arbor.

19 MAIR, Alexander. Naval architecture. b'08. Certificate in naval archt '29 (Royal Tech Coll). Research on hull design, design cargo and all refrigerated ships, ship conversion, floating drydocks. In charge hull sci sect United Shipyards Inc '33-38, Geo G Sharp, naval archt '38-40; hull supervisor Gulf Shipbldg Corp '40-50; in charge hull sci sect Ingalls Shipbldg Corp '50; naval archt Palmer & Baker Inc since '50. Soc Naval Archts and Marine Engrs—Am Welding Society (asso). Palmer & Baker Inc., Staples Pake Bldg., Mobile, Ala.

20 MAIZEL, Benjamin L(eo). Yeast derivatives and extracts; Vitamin B complex; Ergosterol (Extraction, activation); Wood pulp (Bleaching). b'07. BS '28—PhD '32 (U Chicago). Research dir and vp Vi-Co Products Co since '35. Am Chem Soc—Chem Arts Forum—NY Acad Sci—Assn Vitamin Chem. Vi-Co Products Co., 2817 N. Oakley Blvd., Chicago.

21 MAJOR, Hoguet Alexander. Dialect (French Creole); Louisiana Fr speech. b'87. AB '08 (La State U); '22-23 (U Chicago); '30-31, '34-35 (John Hopkins). Study of French Creole dialect of Louisiana and its development; comparison with development of other French Creole dialects; study of Louisiana French vocabulary and syntax; tracing of sources from French dialects, African languages, Indian languages, Spanish and other foreign sources. Faculty dept romance langs La State U since '17, now prof and head dept. Modern Lang Assn—Am Assn Tchrs French—South Central Modern Lang Assn. Louisiana State University, Baton Rouge.†

22 MAJOR, Mabel. Southwestern American literature and folklore (Texas). b'93. AB '14—BS '16—MA '17 (U Mo); student (U Chicago, Columbia, U Calif). Author: Browning and the Florentine Renaissance '24. Co-author: My Foot's in the Stirrup '37; Southwest Heritage, A Literary History '48. Co-editor: The Southwest in Literature '29; Duval's Early Times in Texas '36; Duval's Adventures of Big Foot Wallace '36; Signature of the Sun: Southwest Verse 1900-1950 '50 Professor English Texas Christian U. Mod Lang Assn—S Central Mod Lang Assn—Tex Inst Letters (vp '47-48, '48-49)—Tex Folklore Soc (pres '37)—Tex Poetry Soc. Texas Christian University, Fort Worth, Tex.†

23 MAKEMSON, Maud Worcester. Mayan and Polynesian astronomy; Orbits of asteroids and comets; History of astronomy. b'91. AB '25—AM '27—PhD '30 (U Calif). Author: The Morning Star Rises: An Account of Polynesian Astronomy '41; The Maya Correlation Problem '46; The Book of the Jaguar Priest '51; also articles in field. Asst prof astron Vassar Coll '32-36, prof since '44, chmn dept and dir Vassar Coll Obs since '36. Am Geog Soc(F)—Am Astron Soc—Phi Beta Kappa—Sigma Xi. Awarded Guggenheim fellowship to study Maya astronomy '41-42. Vassar College, Poughkeepsie, N.Y.

24 MALCOLM, Ola Powell. Home economics (Demonstration, food preservation). b'89. Student (State Coll Columbus); grad '13 (Drexel Inst Phila). Sent to France summer '21 to direct unit of workers on food preservation under auspices French minister agriculture and American Committee for devastated France; sent by US Dept Agriculture to Spain and Italy to study methods used in preserving and utilizing Spanish pimentos and other fruits and vegetable products and to secure other information to use in home demonstration work; in France '22 for purpose of organizing and establishing home demonstration work in France. Author: Successful Canning and Preserving '17; also articles in field for US Dept Agr. With US Dept Agr since '14, home demonstration work 15 So states; Puerto Rico as sr home econ; head food prodn food conservation program since '43. 5511 Oak Pl., Alta Vista, Bethesda, Md.*

25 MALCOLM, Roy. American democracy and citizenship; Japanese problems in the United States; American efforts toward world peace. b'81. AB '06 (So Calif); AM '09 (Harvard); PhD '10 (Boston U). Author: The Spirit of American Democracy '28; American Democracy Unafraid '38, also articles in field. Prof pol sci U So Calif since '16-48, chmn div econ polit sci U So Calif '29. AAAS—Am Polit Sci Assn—Am Acad Polit Social Sci—UN Assn (exec com)—AAUP—Japan Soc So Calif (pres)—China Soc So Calif—Phi Beta Kappa. 867 Muirfield Rd., Los Angeles.◎

26 MALETZ, Michael. Gear geometry and design; Engineering mathematics; Stress analysis (Analytical, experimental); Diesel engines (Analytical design). b'97. BS '26—ME '42 (U Ill);

'44 (Marquette U); '42 (MIT); '18-'21 (Inst Mines). Research work in analytical determination of strength form factor in a tooth; combined stresses in gear teeth; designer medium and heavy special machinery. Designer medium and heavy machinery A O Smith Corp '27-'29; mech designer Wis Steel Works '30-'31; gear engr Perfection Gear Co '32-'36; diesel engine designer Fairbanks Morse & Co '36-'38; dynamicist Allis-Chalmers Mfg Co '38-'39. Gear specialist and stress analyst Kearney & Trecker Corp Milwaukee since '39. ASME—AAAS—Inst Aeronautical Sci—SESA—ACMA. 9030 Kittyhawk, LA 45.

10 MALIN, James Claude. Agricultural history, human ecology of American grasslands region; Kansas history; John Brown. b'93. AB '14 (Baker U); AM '16—PhD '21 (U Kan). Author: The Grassland of North America: Prolegomena to its History '47; Essays on Historiography '46; Winter Wheat in the Golden Belt of Kansas '44; John Brown and the Legend of Fifty-Six '42; also articles in field. Prof hist U Kan since '38. Kan State Hist Soc (pres '40-41)—Agrl Hist Soc (pres '43-44)—Assn Am Geog. History Department, University of Kansas, Lawrence, Kan. H: 1541 University Dr.

11 MALKIEL, Maria-Rosa Lida. Old Spanish literature. PhD '47 (U Buenos Aires). Author: El cuento popular hispanoamericano y la literatura '41; Selección del Libro de buen amor de Juan Ruiz: Introducción y notas '41; Dido y su defensa en la literatura española '43; Introducción al teatro de Sófocles '44; Juan de Mena, poeta del prerrenacimiento espanol '50; La idea de la fama en la Edad Media castellana '52. Asso editor: Nueva Revista de Filologia Hispanica since '47, Hispanic Review since '51. Rockefeller Foundation research fellow '47-48. University Medal Facultad de Filosofia y Letras U Buenos Aires '33; laureate Club del Libro Buenos Aires '44; Guggenheim Found research fellow '49-51. 4333 Dwinelle Hall, University of California, Berkeley.†

12 MALKIEL, Yakov. Comparative romance linguistics. b'14. AB '33 (Werner Siemens Realgymnasium Berlin-Schöneberg); PhD '38 (Friedrich-Wilhelm U Berlin). Author articles in field. Professor Romance philol U Calif since '52; founder and editor-in-chief Romance Philology pub by U Calif. Linguistic Soc Am—Linguistic Circle NY—Philol Assn Pacific Coast —Modern Lang Assn (one of two founders group comparative romance linguistics '46)—Medieval Acad Am. 4333 Dwinelle Hall, University of California, Berkeley 4.†

13 MALKUS, Alida Sims. Pre-Columbian civilization. b'97. Student (Mark Hopkins Art Sch San Francisco) (U Mich) (U Pa) (U Colo). Went to Mexico and Yucatan to study ruins '30; visited the ruins of Inca and Pre-Incaic civilizations '37. Author: Raquel of the Ranch Country '27; The Dragon Fly of Zuni '28; Caravans to Santa Fe '28; Pirates' Port '29; The Dark Star of Itza '30; Eastward Sweeps the Current '37; The Citadel of a Hundred Stairways '41; Along the Inca Highway '41; The Magic Islands, Constancia Lona '47; Colt of Denting '52; Little Giant of the North '52; The Story of Pasteur '52; The Story of Good Queen Bess '53. Reporter on Albuquerque Morning Jour; editorial staff McClure's Mag and Success '22; author and illustrator. Soc Women Geographers—Authors League —Women's Nat Book Assn. John C. Winston Co., Phila.

14 MALLACH, Lawrence Walton. Pulse transformers. b'14. BS in elec engring '38—EE '48 (Wash State Coll); '50 (U Cal Los Angeles). Research and design of pulse transformers for radar systems. Research asso MIT '42-43; engr Raytheon Mfg Co '43-47; chief engr Houston Corp '46-.48; pres and chief engr Canoga Corp '48-51; mgr and chief engr Century Electronics division Century Metalcraft Corp '51. Inst Radio Engrs (sr mem)— Tau Beta Pi. Box 2098, Van Nuys, Cal. H: 6826 Chisholm Av., Van Nuys, Cal.

15 MALLON, Marguerite Genevieve. Food chemistry and nutrition. BS '15 (Illinois Inst Tech); MS '15—PhD '25 (U Chicago). Research on calcium retention as affected by high and low fat, chlorophyll (a plus b), lemon juice, grapefruit juice, and canned tomato juice; the distribution of calcium in vegetables; comparison of calcium retention of milk with American cheese and lettuce. Author articles in field. Asso prof U Calif since '36. AAAS(F) —Sigma Xi. University of California, Los Angeles 24.

16 MALLORY, Lester De Witt. United States foreign affairs; Pomology; Foreign agriculture. b'04. BS '27— MS '29 (Brit Columbia U); PhD '35 (Calif U). Advisor to US delegation and alternate member on permanent commission, 2d Inter-American Conference on Agriculture, Mexico City '42. Author articles in field. Agrl attache Paris '39, Mex City '39-45; fgn service officer US Dept State '39; mem Mex US Agrl Commn '44; agrl attache Paris '45; agrl liaison officer Wash DC '46-47; counselor of Embassy Havana since '47. Am Farm Econ Assn—AAAS—Am Soc Plant Tax— Commn Merite Agricole. Mail Room U. S. Department of State, Washington.

17 MALLORY, Louis Arthur. Speech; Psychology of communication; Theatre; Semantics. b'96. BA '25— MA '29—PhD '38 (U Wis). Author: History and Criticism of American Public Address '43; also articles in field. Asso prof speech Brooklyn Coll since '40. Research asso OSRD '43, dir voice communications project '44. Speech Assn Am—Am Ednl Theatre Assn—AAUP. Brooklyn College, Bedford Av. and Av. H, Brooklyn 10.†

18 MALLORY, Virgil S(ampson). Mathematics education (Curriculum). b'88. AB '14—AM '19—PhD '39 (Columbia U). Member of Council of Education Survey Committee New Jersey high schools '24; reader College Entrance Examination Board '25-28; made survey of Rahway New Jersey public schools '31 Critic US Armed Forces Institute Mathematics Examinations '42-45; chairman committee on essential mathematics for minimum Army use '41; member reviewing committee Educational Dictionary '42. Author: Modern Plane and Solid Geometry '29-30; First and Second Course in Algebra '36; Achievement Tests in First Year Algebra '39; Using Arithmetic '41; Arithmetic Refresher '43; Plane Trigonometry '46; First Albegra '50. Co-author other textbooks and arithmetic workbooks. Prof math head math dept State Teachers Coll Montclair NJ since '34. AAAS(F)—NEA—Math Soc Am— Am Math Assn—Nat Council Tchrs Math (policy commn since '44)—Brit Math Soc. State Teachers College, Montclair, N.J.☉

19 MALLORY, Walter Hampton. Am foreign policy; International relations; Far Eastern questions; China. b'92. Student (Troy Conf Acad); '13-15 (Columbia U). Delegate to International Studies Conference Paris '34; member advisory committee on foreign participation New York World's Fair '39; trustee China Institute in America (president '43-47); member China Medical Board since '47; member Allied Mission to Observe the Elections in Greece with rank US minister '46. Author: China, Land of Famine '26. Editor: Political Handbook of the World (with Malcolm W Davis) '29-29, (alone) since '30. Contbr. to mags on Far Eastern affairs and internat relations. Leader Columbia Relief Expdn to Serbia '15; first exec officer Near East Relief '15-16; spl asst to Am ambassador at Petrograd '16-17; fgn rep US Shipping Bd '19; exec sec China Internat Famine Relief Commn Peking '22-26; exec dir Council Fgn Relations since '27. Am Asiatic Assn—Am Geog Soc—Acad Polit Sci—Acad Polit and Social Sci— Council on Fgn Relations. Order of Pure Gold (China). 32 E. 64th St., NYC 21.☉

20 MALM, Carl J. Cellulose chemistry. b'99. Diplom Chem Engr '23 (Abo Akademie, Finland). Chemist, inventor, and co-inventor 160 US patents. Author articles in field. Eastman Kodak Co '23-35, asst supt chem plant '35-47, supt cellulose acetate development dept since '47. Am Chem Soc—AAAS. Received Nat Assn Mfrs Modern Pioneer Award '40. Kodak Park, Eastman Kodak Co., Rochester 4, N.Y.

21 MALONE, Dumas. Thomas Jefferson; History of the United States and Southern United States; American biography. b'92. AB '10—LittD '36 (Emory U); BD '16—AM '21—PhD '23 (Yale); LLD '35 (Northwestern U); LittD '36 (U Rochester); LittD '37 (Dartmouth Coll); sr Sterling traveling fellow Yale '27; Guggenheim fellow '51-52. Author: The Public Life of Thomas Cooper '26; Edwin A Alderman '40. Co-author: The Interpretation of History '43; Jefferson the Virginian '48, Jefferson and the Rights of Man '51 (Vols I and II of a five volume work entitled Jefferson and His Time). Editor: Correspondence between Thomas Jefferson and P S du Pont de Nemours '30; (with Allen Johnson) Dictionary of American Biography vols IV to VII '29-31; editor in chief vols VIII to XX '31-36; also articles in field. Prof hist Columbia University since '45; mng ed Political Science Quarterly since '53. AHA—Am Antiquarian Soc—Am Acad Arts Sci—Mass Hist Soc—Phi Beta Kappa. Winner of John Addison Porter prize Yale '23. Fayerweather Hall, Columbia University, NYC.☉

22 MALONE, J(ohn) Walter, Jr. Christian education. b'88. AB '09 (Western Res U)—BD '19 (McCormick Theol. Sem Chicago); F '20-21 (U Edinburgh Scotland); DD hon '29 (Blackburn Coll Carlinville Ill). Recorded minister Society of Friends '14; transferred to ministry of Presbyterian Church '20; pastor Homewood Ill '17-22, McKinley Memorial Church and Foundation University of Illinois Champaign '22-41; moderator Presbyterian Church Synod of Illinois '27-28; vice president McCormick Theological Seminary 41-46; president James Millikin Univ Decatur Ill since '46; dir. McCormick Theol Sem, McKinley Foundation. Phi Beta Kappa—Phi Kappa Phi. James Millikin University, Decatur, Ill.☉

23 MALONE, Kemp. Old and Middle English language and literature; History of English language; English lexicography, etymology, semantics, grammar; Icelanic language and literature.

b'89. AB '07—LittD '36 (Emory U); PhD '19 (U Chicago). Author: The Literary History of Hamlet '23; The Phonology of Modern Icelandic '23; Dodo and the Camel '38; Ten Old English Poems '41; also articles and verses. Co-author: Literary History of England '48. Editor: Studies in English Philology '29; Deor '33; Widsith '36; Hesperia Erganzungsreihe; managing editor and founder with Louise Pound: American Speech. Prof Eng Johns Hopkins since '26. Medieval Acad Am(F, councillor '34-37)—Am Geog Soc(F)—Soc Am Hist(F)—AAAS(F)—Am Scandinavian Found (asso)—Am Philos Soc—Am Soc Aesthetics—Coll English Assn—Am Dialect Soc (vp '42-43, pres '44-46)—Soc Study Medieval Lang Lit—Am Philol Assn—Soc Advancement Scandinavian Study (vp '23-24)—Nat Council Teachers Eng—Linguistic Soc Am (vp '38, pres '44)—Modern Lang Assn Am—Shakespeare Assn Am—Am Iona Soc—Irish Texts Soc (mem cons com)—English-Speaking Union US—Sogufjelag Islands—Islenzkt Bokmentafjelag (hon '37)—Vereinigung der Islandfreunde—Viking Soc—Internat Council Eng—Am Folklore Soc—Grundtvig Selskab—Phi Beta Kappa. Decorated with King Christian X Freedom Medal Denmark '46. 2710 Maryland Ave., Balt. 18.◎

10 MALONE, Miles Sturdivant. Southern United States colonial history. b'97. BS '27 (U Va); AM '28—PhD '35 (Princeton U). Research in Southern colonial history two decades preceding Revolution in 1775 and the Revolutionary period and intensive study of nationalities in the Shenandoah and colonial South Carolina during that time. Author articles in field. Instr Am hist Phillips Acad since '37. AHA. 193 Main St., Andover, Mass.

11 MALONE, Rose Mary. Wyoming (History). AB '24 (Coll St Catherine); MA '25 (U Minn); MA '49 (U Denver). Research on pioneer history of Wyoming. Author: Wyomingana: Two Bibliographies '50. Asst librarian Natrona County High Sch since '47. Natrona High School Library, Casper, Wyo.

12 MALONE, Thomas Francis. Atmospheric pressure changes. b'17. SB '40 (SD State Sch Mines and Technol); ScD '46 (MIT). Research on the mechanism of pressure changes in the atmosphere, dynamic and synoptic meteorology. Author: Interdiurnal Pressure and Temperature Variations in the Free Atmosphere over North America '46; also articles in field. Research asst MIT '41-42, instr '42-43, asso prof meteorology since '51; editor Compendium of Meteorology since '49. Am Meteorol Soc. Department of Meteorology, Massachusetts Institute of Technology, Cambridge 39, Mass.

13 MALONEY, John Ransom. Water (Chemistry, bacteriology, purification). b'08. BS in chem tech '30 (Ia State Coll). Cultivation of iron bacservance factors affecting their teria in laboratory cultures and obgrowth especially pH dissolved oxygen and free carbon dioxide; studies of methods of controlling growth of iron bacteria in plant installations; iron removal by treatment and sedimentation without filtration; stabilization of lime softened water; research in establishing correlation between presence of certain biological life and odors in water with ultimate aim of isolating odor-producing substance and determining its composition and properties. Chem, chief chem Des Moines Water Works since '30. Am Water Works Assn. Des Moines Water Works, 1003 Locust St., Des Moines, Ia.

14 MALONY, Harry James. Current European affairs (Greece); Current Asiatic affairs (India). b'89. BS '12 (US Mil Acad); grad '22 (Field Arty Sch); '26 (Command and Gen Staff Sch); '36 (Army War Coll). Author: (with J S Hatcher, G P Wilhelm) Machine Guns '16. Chief Hist Div War Dept '46-49; dep administr Khashmir Plebiscite '49; cons Dept Defense on SE Asian affairs '51-52. Commd 2d lt inf US Army '12, transferred to field arty '16, advanced through grades to maj gen '42. Decorated DSM with oak leaf cluster, Silver Star, Bronze Star; Officer Legion d'Honneur, Croix de Guerre, Ordre d'Etoile Noire (France). 1020 26th St. S., Arlington, Va.◎

15 MALOTT, Clyde Arnett. Speleology (Cavern development); Indiana geology (Underground drainage, stratigraphy, petroleum); Geomorphology. b'87. AB '13—AM '15—PhD '19 (Ind U). Author articles in field. Prof geol Ind U '24-47, retired '47. Ind Acad Sci (F, vp '37, pres '44, E R Cummings award '48)—Geol Soc Am—Ind-Ky Geol Soc—AAAS—Nat Speleol Soc—Sigma Xi—Phi Beta Kappa. Department of Geology, Indiana University, Bloomington, Ind.

16 MALPHURS, Ojus. Power plants (Hydroelectric). b'03. BS in chem engring '24—BS in civil engring '32 (U Fla). Construction and structural design dams and powerhouses for Tennessee Valley Authority and Corps Engrs. With US Coast and Geodetic Survey and Corps of Engrs '32-36, TVA '36-39, '40-45; structural designer Panama Canal '39-40; with Corps Engrs since '45, chief design branch '49-51. Phi Kappa Phi —Sigma Tau—Am Soc CE. Corps of Engineers, US Army, Norfolk District, Norfolk, Va.

17 MALPICA, Jose Mireles. Transformers (Electrical). b'05. MS in physics '32 (Union Coll Schenectady NY). Research on electrical transformation; development electrostatic transformer of direct current. Author article: Electrostatic Direct Current Transformer of 300 Kilovolts. Co-author article: A New Light-Beam Electrostatis Voltmeter, and others. Development engr Gen Engring Lab Gen Elec Co Schenectady NY '32-42; dir research lab Fabrica Nacional de Polvora Santa Fe Mexico '43-45; sci investigator Instituto since '47; now cons physicist. Am Inst EE—Optical Soc Am—APS—AA AS—Am Soc Metals—Mex Assn ME and EE. Fellowship Comision Impulsora y Coordinadora de la Investigacion Cientifica '50, Instituto Nacional de la Investigacion Cientifica '51. Escuela Superior de Ingenieria Mecanica y Electrica, I.P.N., Allen de No. 38, Mexico, D.F., Mexico.

18 MALTBY, Lucy Mary. Cookery (Home equipment). b'00. BS '21 (Cornell U); MS '27 (Ia State Coll); PhD '45 (Syracuse U). Author: It's Fun to Cook. Dir home econ Corning Glass Works Corning NY. Am Home Econ Assn — Am Dietetic Assn. Corning Glass Works, Corning N.Y.

19 MANCHA, Raymond. Mine ventilation. b'02. BS '26 (MIT). Research on use of fans for mine ventilation. Mgr mine ventilation dept Jeffrey Mfg Co '35-46; vp ventilation Joy Mfg Co since '46. AIMME (chmn mine ventilation com '44-46)—AAAS—Am Soc Heating and Ventilating Engrs—Am Soc Nav Engrs Ill Mining Inst—Coal Mining Inst Am. 318 Henry Oliver Building, Pitts. 22.

20 MANCHESTER, Alan Krebs. Brazil and the Portuguese Empire; European expansion overseas; Imperialism. b'97. AB '22 (Vanderbilt U); MA '22 (Columbia U); PhD '30 (Duke U). Research on expansion of European institutions, culture, economics and political control overseas; the Portuguese Empire and rise of Brazil, the British Empire and British activity in non-empire areas, sea power, imperialism. Author: British Preeminence in Brazil: Its Rise and Decline '33; Descriptive Bibliography of the Brazilian Section of the Duke University Library '33; Economic Literature of Latin America, A Tentative Bibliography '35; South American Dictators, During the Century of Independence '37; Brazil '47; also articles in field. With Duke U since '29, asso prof since '42, dean undergraduate studies since '49; cultural affairs officer Am Embassy Rio de Janeiro '51-52. Duke University, Durham, N.C. H: 2016 Myrtle Dr.†◎

21 MANDELBAUM, David G(oodman). Culture of India and Southeastern Asia. b'11. AB '32 (Northwestern U); PhD '36 (Yale). Author articles in field. Asso prof to prof U Calif since '45. Am Oriental Soc—Am Anthrop Assn—Soc Applied Anthrop—Sigma Xi. Nat Research Council fellow '37-38. Guggenheim Fellow '49. University of California, Berkeley 4.

22 MANDERFELD, Emanuel C(arl). Film equipment b'99. BS '21—EE '23 (U Minn). Design film recording and reproducing equipment. Issued about 12 patents on parts. Author articles: A light weight sound recording system; Permanent-Magnet Four ribbon light-valve for portable push-pull recording; and others. Development recording and reproducing equipment Western Elec Co '30-42; motion picture camera and projector development Mitchell Camera Corp since '45. Am Inst EE—Inst Radio Engrs—Sigma Xi—Eta Kappa Nu—Soc Motion Picture Engrs—Instrument Soc. Mitchell Camera Corp., 666 W Harvard, Glendale 4, Cal.

23 MANDRAGOS, Nicholas Constantine. Photoelastic engineering; Structural engineering. b'96. BS in civil engring '34 (NYU); '35-36 (Poly Inst Brooklyn). Research on stress analysis by means of polarized light, determination of stress distribution by direct measurements and testing of parts in transparent models, determination of stresses in statically indeterminate structures, applications of principles of photoelasticity to structures such as continuous girder, rigid frame and arch; design of buildings of steel and reinforced concrete, minimum requirements for protection of munitions plants against air attacks, design of building for human occupancy for exposure to high explosive, incendiary or gas bombs. Engring draftsman and structural engr NY Central RR Co '26-37; asso structural engr, research structural engr and sr structural engr Constrn Div Office QM Gen '38-42; with Bur Yards and Docks Navy Dept. '42-47, asst div head research and records div and head tech and research sect '44-47; vis asso prof George Washington U '47-49; cons engr since '50. Army Ordnance Assn—Soc Am Mil Engrs—Nat. Soc Profl Engrs—Wash Soc Engrs. 1420 New York Av., Washington 5. H: RFD 1, Box 40, Brandywine, Md.

24 MANGELSDORF, Albert John. Sugar cane agriculture. b'96. BS '16 (Kans State Coll); MS '25—ScD '27 (Harvard). Author articles in field. Geneticist Expt Sta Hawaiian Sugar Planters Assn Honolulu since '26. Genetics Soc Am—Hawaiian Bot Soc—Hawaiian Acad Sci—Hawaiian Sugar Technol—Internat Soc Sugarcane Tech

—AAAS. Experiment Station, Hawaiian Sugar Planters Association, Honolulu 14, T.H.†

10 MANGELSDORF, Paul Christoph. Indian corn; Plant genetics and breeding. b'99. BS '21 (Kan State Coll); Sm—ScD '25 (Harvard). Co-author: (with R G Reeves) The Origin of Indian Corn and its Relatives '39; also articles in field. Prof bot Harvard since '40, dir Bot Mus since '45. Am Soc Agron(F)—Am Soc Naturalists—AAAS—Am Bot Soc—NE Bot soc—Genetics Soc Am—Am Acad Arts Sci—Nat Acad Sci—Gamma Sigma Delta—Sigma Xi. Harvard University, Cambridge, Mass.◎

11 MANN, Arvin William. Nutritional deficiency diseases (Oral phases); Periodontology; Prosthondontia; Restorative dentistry. b'08. Student '26-28 (Oberlin Coll); BS '30—DDS '32 (Western Res U). Research in oral phases of nutritional deficiency diseases; found decreased incidence of dental caries in Pellagrins and others suffering from water soluble deficiency disease; established importance of mechanical factors (decreased vertical dimension and failure to restore facial contours in constructing artificial dentures) in the etiology and treatment of Angular Cheilosis in addition to nutrient therapy in malnourished edentulous patients; tests on malnourished children who were later given milk supplements and changes in both growth and development noted; established in collaboration with J S McKenzie method treatment of sensitive necks of teeth especially post gingivectomy; invented instrument to center and parallel Dowel pins while pouring a hydrocollois impression for fixed prosthesis. Author article: A Critical Appraisal of the Hydrocolloid Technique Its Advantages and Disadvantages. Contbr. chapter to American Textbook of Prosthetic Dentistry. Research asso nutrition clinic Hillman Hosp Birmingham. Am Acad Restorative Dentistry—Am Acad Denture Prosthetics—Am Acad Periodontology—Southern Acad Periodontology—Am Acad Applied Nutrition—Pierre Fauchard Acad—Omicron Kappa Upsilon—Internat Coll Dentists(F)—Delta Sigma Delta—Internat Assn Dental Research. 430 E. Las Olas Blvd., Ft. Lauderdale, Fla.

12 MANN, Clair Victor. Engineering psychology and aptitude tests; Missouri railroad history (Frisco Road); History of Phelps County and South Central Missouri (Industrial); Personographs. b'84. BS in Civil Engring '14—CE '21 (Coll Engring U Colo); PhD '29 (U Ia). Research in field of tests of aptitude in engineering, construction and use of such tests; research and design of classroom tests in engineering drawing, graphics, descriptive geometry, aided Colonel Bukema of US Army in revisions of such tests for ASTP program during World War II; designing of personographs, charts or maps of personality that exhibit instantly all measured traits in an individual, also wall maps in which the chart for each student appears, showing unique make-up of student groups. Author: Objective Type Tests in Engineering Education '30; Source Materials History Frisco Railroad (5 vols) '47; Archives of History Phelps County Missouri vols 1-22; History of Missouri School of Mines and Metallurgy '39-41; Proceedings of Phelps County Historical Society, vols 1-6, '38-43; and others; also articles in field. Successively asst prof, asso prof, prof Engring Drawing and head dept Mo Sch Mines '20-46; historian

Frisco Railroad '45-46. ASCE—Soc Promotion Engring Edn (vp Mo branch '35-36, mem com tests since '31)—Mo, Kan, Okla state hist socs—Phelps Co Hist Soc (historian).   210 E. 8th St., Rolla, Mo.◎

13 MANN, Edward Beverly. Guns; American history (Western and Southwestern, Western gunmen). b'02. Student '23-27 (U Fla). Author: Man From Texas '31; Blue-Eyed Kid '32; Valley of Wanted Men '32; Killers' Range '33; Stampede '34; Gamblin' Man '34; Rustlers' Round-up '35; Thirsty Range '35; El Sombra '36; Boss of the Lazy 9 '36; Comanche Kid '36; With Spurs '37; Shootin' Melody '38; Gun Feud '39; Mesa Gang '39; Troubled Range '40; Gunsmoke Trail '41; The Whistler '53. MNG ED: American Rifleman '43-46. Asso editor gun books Military Service Pub Co '45-48. Guns and gunning editor: Sun Trails. Free lance writer fiction and articles since '28; dir University New Mexico Press since '49. Nat Rifle Association (life mem, instr rifle and pistol, referee). 1020 Parkland Pl., Albuquerque, N.M.

14 MANN, Eric. International travel; International affairs (Current); Educational policies. b'02. PhD '26 (U Vienna). Pioneer in field of education for travel; courses introducing prospective travelers to countries to be visited and for travel officials to increase their knowledge and efficiency; attendance all significant national and international music and art festivals in America and Europe in development plans for international festivals. Author pamphlet: Germany Prepares for War '44. Contbr. articles for papers in Argentina, Austria, US and other countries. Actor Vienna, Berlin, New York '22-30, singer with German opera company '27-30; Tchr various univs since '36; world traveller collecting for material for lectures; lectr on internat affairs Town Halls, scientific and service orgns. and schools since '34; asst prof history and German Grinnell Coll Ia '43-44; exec dir Inst for Intercontinental Studies NYC since for Intercontinental Studies NYC '49-50; lectr N.Y.U. Div Gen Edn since 1950. 340 W. 86th St., N.Y.C. 24.

15 MANN, Harvey Blount. Soil chemistry; Plant nutrition. Potash fertilizing. born '98. BS '20 (NC State Coll); MS '25—PhD '29 (Cornell U). International Soil Congress Oxford England '35. Author articles in field. Asst agronomist NC State Coll '20-29, agronomist '29-36; asst so mgr Am Potash Inst Atlanta Ga '36, so mgr '37-48, vp '48-49, pres and chmn bd dirs Washington since '49. AAAS(F)—Am Soc Agron—Soil Sci Soc Am—Internat Soil Sci Soc—So Agrl Workers—Soil Sci Soc Fla. 1155-16th St., Washington.◎

16 MANNING, Clarence A(ugustus). Slavic languages, literature and archeology; Orthodox Church. b'93. AB '12—AM '13—PhD '15 (Columbia); PhD '48 (hon) (Ukrainian Free U Prague). Author: A Study of Archaism in Euripides '16; Ukrainian Literature—Studies of the Leading Authors '44; Soldier of Liberty, Casimir Pulaski '45; Taras Shevchenko Poet of Ukraine '45; The Story of Ukraine '47; (with O M Fuller) Marko The King's Son, Hero of the Serbs '32; also articles in field. Asst prof Slavic lang Columbia U since '47; mem adv bd Slavic archeol Am Jour Archeol, mem ed bd Review of Religion. Polish Inst Arts Sci in Am—Modern Lang Assn—Linguistic Soc Am Station, College Station, Tex.†

17 MANNING, Cleo Willard. Cotton genetics and breeding. b'15. BS '40

(Ill Wesleyan U); MS '42 (Tex A&M Coll); '46-47 (Ia State Coll). Cotton exploration trip to Mexico and Guatemala '46, 48. Asso prof Tex Agrl Exp Sta since '48. Agricultural Experiment Staton, College Station, Tex.†

18 MANNING, George Charles. Naval architecture (Ship construction, design and stability). b'92. BS '14 (US Naval Acad); SM '20 (MIT). Author: Manual of Naval Architecture '29; Manual of Naval Architecture '42; Basic Design of Ships '45; Fundamentals of Naval Architecture '48; also articles in field. Head department naval architecture and marine Engring. MIT since '50. Soc Naval Architects Marine Engrs—Am Soc Naval Engrs—Instn Naval Architects—US Naval Inst. 28 Symmes Rd., Winchester, Mass.†◎

19 MANNING, John Walker. Government in Kentucky; American politics and government; Public administration. b'99. AB '21 (Georgetown Coll); MA '26 (U Louisville); PhD '30 (U Ia); '25-27 (U Chicago). Author: The Woman Citizen '32; The Government of Kentucky '37. Co-author Government of the American People '40; Introduction to Politics '41; also articles in field. now Commr finance Ky. Officer charge occupational analysis, later pub relations officer for Adj Gen US Army '41-46, released as Col. Am Polit Sci Assn—Soc Pub Adminstrn. Department of Finance, Frankfort, Ky.

20 MANNING, Melvin Lane. Silicone insulation application (Transformers); Power and distribution transformers; Power systems; High voltage testing. b'00. BS '27 (SD State Coll); MS '32—Coll teachers cert '35 (U Pittsburgh); '28 (Westinghouse Elect Corp). Author articles in field. Chief engr Kuhlman Electric Co Bay City Mich '45 to '49. Am Soc Engring Edn—AIEE (F, bd dirs Mich '48)—Nat Elect Mfgrs Assn. Now charge develpt, Pa Transformer Co, Canonsburg, Pa.

21 MANNING, Thomas Henry. Artic mammalogy, ornithology, geography and surveying; Eskimo anthropology. b'11. Student '30-32 (Jesus Coll Cambridge). Field work: Southampton Island '33-35, Southampton Island, Baffin Island, Melville Peninsula '36-41, Southampton Island '42-43, Ungava '44, '46, Manitoba and Keewatin '45, west coast James Bay and south coast Hudson Bay '47. Cons Arctic Div Defense Research Bd since '48. Am Soc Mammalog—Am Ornithol Union—Brit Ornithol Union—Am Anthrop Assn—Soc Am Archeol—Royal Geog Soc(F)—Can Geog Soc(F)—Can Field-Naturalists' Club. Bruce Memorial Medal for Arctic exploration '46, Patron's Gold medal Royal Geog Soc '48 for Artic survey and adaptation of Eskimo methods. 37 Linden Terrace, Ottawa, Ont, Can.†

22 MANNING, Wayne E(yer). Walnuts; Taxonomy of flowering plants. b'99. AB '20 (Oberlin Coll); PhD '26 (Cornell U). Engaged research on walnut family of world since '22; taxonomy of flowering plants of central Pennsylvania since '45. Author articles in field. Asst botany Cornell U '21-24, instr '24-27; instr botany U Ill '27-28; asst prof botany Smith Coll '28-34, asso prof '34-42; asst prof botany Bucknell U '45-47, asso prof since '47. Bot Soc Am—AAAS(F)—Torrey Bot Club—Pa Acad Sci—New Eng Bot Club. Botanical Laboratory, Bucknell University, Lewisburg, Pa.; H: 27 Brown St.†

23 MANOIL, Adolph. Psychology; Rumanian language. b'06. BS '26 (Lyceum Roman Rumania); MA '29—PhD '32 (U Bucharest); diploma of Corsodi Orientamento Professionale '34 (Torino Italy); diploma '40 (Inst Nat d'Etude du Travail et d'Orientation Professionnelle Paris). Author: Psihotehnica '30; La Psychologie Experimentale en Italie '38; Rumanian Sociology in the Twentieth Century '45 and others; also articles in field. Prof psychol, head dept, dir bur tests measurements Park Coll since '46. Head Rumanian desk War Dept ASF Information and Edn Div Lang Sect '43-45. Am Psychol Assn (asso) —AAAS—AAUP—Am Assn Mental Deficiency—Linguistic Soc Am. Park College, Parkville, Mo.†

10 MANOV, George Gregory. Radioactivity (Standardization of measurements, radiological safety, laboratory design). b'09. BS '33—MS '34—PhD '37 (U Cal). Supervises and coordinates work of assisting isotope users in laboratory design, health protection, isotope disposal, and radiation shielding, standards of radio activity; consultant in applying radio-active tracer techniques to analytical, engineering and special research problems. Faculty U Cal '34-37; with phys chem sect Nat Bur Standards '37-48, with radioactivity sect '48-49; chief adv field service br Isotopes div Atomic Energy Commn since '49. ACS (div phys and inorganic chem)—ASTM (com on determination of hydrogen ions, subcom electrometric methods analysis com on radiostopes)—Wash-Acad Sci. Advisory Field Service Br, Isotopes Division, US Atomic Energy Commission, Oak Ridge, Tenn. H: 109 Olney Lane.

11 MANSFIELD, Ralph. Differential systems (K-point boundary conditions); Mathematics of population; Automotive electrical engineering; Electrical test equipment. b'12. SB '35—SM '37—PhD '42 (U Chicago); '44 (Ill Inst Tech). Author articles in field. Vice Pres charge research and development Auto-Test Inc since '47. Am Math Soc—Math Assn Am—Math Assn Gt Brit—Am Assn Advancement Sci—Inst Radio Engrs—Inst Math Statis—Sigma Xi. 1452 S. Michigan Av., Chicago 5.

12 MANSHARDT, Clifford. India (Social conditions); Mohandas K Gandhi. b'97. Student '14-15 (Bradley Poly Inst Peoria Ill); PhB '18—AM '21—PhD '24 (U Chicago); BD '22—DD '32 (Chicago Theol Sem); '22-23 (Union Theol Sem). As official various dia, studied welfare of infants, children, the blind, released prisoners; local and national organizations in In-also studies on prisons, venereal disease conditions, public health, adult education; mem committee on social studies Central Advisory Board of Education, Government of India '40-41. Author: The Social Settlement as an Educational Factor in India '31; Christianity in a Changing India '33; The Hindu-Muslim Problem in India '36; The Delinquent Child (in India) '39; Freedom Without Violence '46; The Terrible Meek—An Appreciation of Mohandas K Gandhi '48. Editor: The Mahatma and the Missionary '49, and others. Contributor some 200 articles to Indian magazines, and Indian and American professional jours. Dir Nagpada Neighbourhood House Bombay India '25-41, Sir Dorabji Tata Trust Bombay '32-41, Sir Dorabji Tata Grad Sch Social Work Bombay '36-41; chmn adult edn com Bombay govt '38; ed quarterly Indian Jour Social Work '40-41; lectr world problems of christianity Chicago Theol Sem '42-43. Listed in Who's Who in India '35-41. 13862 E. Orangethorpe. RD 1, Fullerton, Cal.

13 MANSON, Byrne C(oghill). Lumber seasoning. b'14. AB '35 (Stanford U); '35-36 (U Cal). Developed method of controlling drying schedule of lumber by use of internal board temperature, developed mathematical equation to represent drying rate and method of controlling schedule by use of drying rate. Author: Kiln Operator's Manual '49. Dry kiln supt Alexander-Yawkey Lumber Co '38-39; field engr Herbert Fryer '39-41; with Cal Redwood Assn since '45, dir research '49-52, dir advt since '53. ASME—Forest Products Research Soc. California Redwood Association, 576 Sacramento St., San Francisco 11.

14 MANTELL, Charles L. Chemical engr (Electro-chemistry); Adsorption; Non-ferrous metallurgy. b'97. Student '14-16 (McGill U Montreal); AB '18—BS '18 (Coll City NY); AM '24—ChemE '24—PhD '27 (Columbia. Author: Industrial Carbon '28, '46; Tin '29, '49; Industrial Electrochemistry '31, '40, '50; Sparks from Electrode '32; Technology of Natural Resins '42; Adsorption '45; Calcium Metallurgy and Technology '45; Water Soluble Gums '50. Chem engr Aluminum Co Am '18-21, Celluloid Corp '21-22; prof chem engring Pratt Inst Brooklyn '22-37; cons engr since '24; dir research Am Gum Importers Assn '34-39; tech adviser Netherlands Indies Govt since '34; tech dir W B Driver Co Newark '34-39; tech dir United Mchts and Mfrs Management Corp '40-47; vp United Mchts Labs Inc '45; prof and chmn dept chem engring Newark Coll Engring since '48; cons various govts and agencies. AIMME—Am Chem Soc—Am Inst Chem Engrs—Electrochem Soc—Am Soc Metals—Phi Lambda Upsilon—Sigma Xi. 457 Washington St., NYC 13.©

15 MANTELL, Murray Irwin. Concrete building construction; Ship stability and stern launching; Naval ordnance alignment. b'17. Student '35-38 (U Miami); BME '40—ME '48 (U Fla); MSCE '45 (U So Calif); diploma Naval Arch '43 (The Citadel); PhD '52 (University of Texas). Prof civil engring U Miami Fla since '46. Naval arch US Navy Yard Charleston '41-43; ordnance engr US Naval Drydocks Terminal Island Calif '45. Fla Engring Soc—Am Soc Engring Educ—Am Soc Civil Engrs—Phi Kappa Phi. University of Miami, Coral Gables, Fla.†

16 MANTER, Harold Winfred. Helminthology; Parasitology; Trematoda; Platyhelminthes. b'98. BA '22 (Bates Coll; MA '23—PhD '25 (U Ill). Member Third Allan Hancock Expedition to Galapagos Islands '34; guest investigator Biological Laboratory Carnegie Institution at Tortugas, Florida '30, '31, '32. Author: Some North American Fish Trematodes '26; Some Digenetic Trematodes from Deepwater Fish of Tortugas, Florida '34; also articles in field. Prof zool U Neb since '35. AAAS(F)—Am Soc Parasitol—Am Micros Soc—Soc Systematic Zool—Am Soc Zool—Sigma Xi—Phi Beta Kappa. 204 Bessey Hall University of Nebraska, Lincoln 8, Neb.†

17 MANVILLE, Richard H(yde). North American mammals (Mt Desert Island, Maine; Huron Mountains, Michigan); Small mammal populations (Northern Michigan); Vertebrate ecology. b'10. AB '32 (Dartmouth Coll); MA '35 (U Calif); PhD '47 (U Mich). Author articles in field. Asst prof dept zool Mich State Coll since '47. AAAS—Am Soc Mammalog—Am Soc Ichthyolog and Herpetolog—Wilson Ornithol Club—Arctic Inst NA—Wil-

derness Soc—Sigma Xi. Department of Zoology, Michigan State College, East Lansing, Mich.†

18 MANWARING, Wilfred Hamilton. Immunology; Experimental pathology. b'71. MD '04 (Johns Hopkins); '07-10 (U Berlin, U Leipzig, Frankfort-on-Main, U Vienna, U London). Research in theoretical immunology and experimental pathology. Prof bacteriol exptl pathol Stanford U '13-37, emeritus since '37. Soc Exptl Pathol—Am Assn Pathol Bacteriol—Am Assn Immunolog (pres '26)—Soc Exptl Biol Med — Soc Am Bacteriol—AMA—AAAS(F)—Sigma Xi. Palo Alto, Calif.

19 MAPES, Carl Herbert. Maps (Historical). b'00. AB '22—MS '31—PhD '43 (U Wash). Author historical maps Historic Oregon Country '43. Contbg author: Geography of the Pacific Northwest (ed O F Freeman and H H Martin) '43; chpt 3 Physical Geography (ed A L Seeman) '42. With Rand McNally & Co since '24, chief map editor since '48; instr aerology Naval Flight Prep Sch Seattle '43. Nat Council Geog Tchrs(F)—Assn Am Geographers—Am Geog Soc—Alpha Delta Phi. 536 S. Clark St., Chgo 5.

20 MARBAKER, Edward Ellsworth. Chemical Engineering; Match, cast iron and porcelain enamel manufacturing. b'88. BS '10—PhD '14—Chem E '30 (U Pa). Research on zirconia and titania-opacified porcelain enamels. Editor: Handbook on Cupola Operation '46; Mellon Institute News since '40; Journal American Ceramic Society '47-50; also articles in field. Investigator coatings for wire-wound resistors; Office Production Research Development WPB '43-45; senior fellow Mellon Inst since '43. Am Ceramic Soc (mem com pubs since '46). Mellon Institute, 4400 5th Av., Pittsburgh 13, Pa.

21 MARBERG, Carl Mauritz. Biochemistry; Pharmaceuticals; Textile printing; High polymers. b'02. BS '27—PhD '30—Sch Bus '48-49 (U Chicago). Holder patents on textile printing with pigments. Author articles in field. Chmn organic chem research Midwest Research Inst Kansas City Mo '45-47; research asso Standard Oil Co Whiting Ind '47-49; research chem Gustin-Bacon Mfg Co Kansas City since '49. AAAS—Am Assn Textile Chem Colorists — Sigma Xi. Gustin-Bacon Manufacturing Co., 1412 W. 12th St., KC 7, Mo.

22 MARBLE, John Putnam. Geochemistry (Geologic time measurement); Meteorites; Adirondacks. b'97. BA '18 (Williams Coll); MA '28—PhD '32 (Harvard); student (Clark U, George Washington U). Author articles in field. Research asso com measurement geologic time div geol and geog Nat Research Council '31-34, vice-chmn '34-46, chmn since '46. Am Chem Soc — Electrochem Soc — Am Geophy Union—Washington Acad Sci —NY Acad Sci—Adirondack Trail Improvement Soc—Am Assn Adv Sci(F) — Mineral Soc Am — Geol Soc Am—Meteoritical Soc. 321 US National Museum, Washington 25.†

23 MARBURG, Theodore Francis. History of manufacturing; Brass (History); History of marketing. b'14. BA '36 (Antioch Coll); MA '37—PhD '42 (Clark U). Research on history of business management and innovation in non-ferrous metals fabrication. Author: Management Problems and Procedures of a Manufacturing Enterprise 1802-1852; A Case Study of the Origin of the Scovill Manufacturing Company; also articles in field. Instr econ Princeton U '46, asst prof '47-50;

prof econ Hamline U since '50, head dept econ and bus adm since '52. Econ Historical Assn—Econ Historical Soc —Bus Hist Soc—Am Econ Assn— AHA. Department of Economics, Hamline University, St. Paul.

10 MARCH, Herman William. Theory of elasticity (Applied to plywood and sandwich structures used in aircraft). b'78. AB '04—AM '05 (U Mich); PhD '11 (U Munich). Author articles in field. Prof math U Wis since '29; cons math US Forest Products Lab Forest Service since '28, math on leave for war work '41-46. AAAS— Am Math Soc—Am Math Assn—Phi Beta Kappa—Sigma Xi. Forest Products Laboratory, Madison, Wis.†⊙

11 MARCHAND, George. Museum preparations; (Dioramas, models, animations). b'02. Created series of wild flower models Buffalo Museum of Science '24-45; four undersea dioramas depicting prehistoric life of Rochester New York area Rochester Museum '45-46. With Springfield Ill Mus '18; NY State Mus '22-23; Buffalo Mus Sci '24-45; opened own studio '46. Am Assn Mus. George Marchand Studio, Transit Rd., Ebenezer, N.Y.

12 MARCHMAN, Watt Pearson. American history (1865-1900); Rutherford B Hayes; History of Ohio and Florida. b'11. AB '33—AM '37 (Rollins Coll); '36 (Duke U). Investigations in American biography, American military history and local history of the US; research director for the papers and library of President Rutherford B Hayes. Author: A History of the Florida Historical Society. '40; also articles in field. Archivist Rollins Coll '34-39; librarian and corres sec Fla Hist Soc '39-42; dir research Rutherford B Hayes and Lucy Webb Hayes Found Fremont O and dir Hayes Memorial Library since '46. AHA—Soc Am Archivists—Am Assn State Local Hist—O State Archaeol and Hist Soc —Nat Soc Autograph Collectors—Fla Hist Soc—O Acad Hist. Hayes Memorial Library, Fremont, O.

13 MARCOVITCH, Simon. Insecticides; Strawberry insects. b'90. BS '14 (Cornell U); PhD '27 (U Minn). Developed use of cryolite and sodium fluosilicate as insecticides. Author: Cryolite Spray Residues and Human Health; Fluorine Compounds as Insecticides. Asst entomol U Minn '14-18; entomol U Tenn since '18. Am Assn Econ Entomol—Sigma Xi. University Farm, Knoxville, Tenn.†

14 MARCSON, Simon. Race relations; Intergroup relations; Intercultural relations. b'10. AB '36—AM '41—PhD '50 (U Chicago). Studies of the Negro in America; research on racial problems in education and communication; comparative studies race and culture. Co-author: Intergroup Relations in Teaching Materials '49. Contributor: An American Dilemma '44; Perspectives of a Troubled Decade—Science, Philosophy, and Religion '50. Asst prof sociol Pa State Coll '42-46; lectr anthrop and sociol Queen's Coll '46-51; lectr anthrop and sociol Brooklyn Coll since '51; social affairs officer population div United Nations '51; cons Am Council on Edn '45, Bur for Applied Research Columbia '48-49, Am Jewish Com '51, Flushing Community Audit '49-51; vis prof anthrop and sociol Temple U '49, Wayne U '50. Am Sociol Soc—Am Applied Anthrop Soc—AAAS—AAUP—E Sociol Soc—Soc Psychol Study Social Issues. Dept of Sociology, Brooklyn College, Bklyn.

15 MARCUS, Jacob Rader. American Jewish history. b'96. Student '14 (Lane Theol Sem) '15 (U Chgo); AB '17 (U Cin); Rabbi '20 (Hebrew Union Coll); '23 (U Kiel); PhD '25 (U Berlin). Research in history of American Jew from earliest times to present day. Author: Israel Jacobson '28; A Brief Introduction to the Bibliography of Modern Jewish History '35; Jewish Festschriften '37; The Rise and Destiny of the German Jew '34; Jew in the Medieval World '38; Early American Jewry, Vol I '51, Vol II '53. Adolph S Ochs prof Jewish history Hebrew Union Coll Jewish Inst Religion Cin, dir Am Jewish Archives and editor Am Jewish Archives. Central Conf Am Rabbis(past pres)—Am Jewish Hist Soc(vp)—Jewish Pub Soc (chmn pub com)—Union Am Hebrew Congregations—Jewish Acad Arts and Scis—Acad Jewish Research. Hebrew Union College, Clifton Av., Cin 20. H: 401 McAlpin Av.⊙

16 MARCUS, Joseph Anthony. American foreign trade; Russia; Russian psychology (Communist, noncommunist). b'94. Student '17-18 (Geo Wash U); '18 (Catholic U Am); '19 (NYU). Author: Labor Conditions in Puerto Rico; Foreign Trade is Not For Amateurs; The Real Russian Challenge; What Became of Lenin's Dream?; Soviet Trade Piracy in the US; Soviet Industrial Espionage in America; The Reds Reach for Your Wallet; Russia—Stalin's Guinea Pig. Foreign trade cons; with E A Filene as financial adviser Consumer Distribution Corp NYC since '35; dir Russian Dept Am Radiator and Standard San Corp NYC; adv US Senate Com Chmn; pres Inst Fgn Trade, Standard Petroleum Corp Del since '52. 60 E. 42 St., NYC 17.

17 MARDEN, John W(esley). Rare metals. b'87. BS '09—DSc '47 (Ill Wesleyan U); '09-10 (U Ill)—'12-13 (U Minn); MS '10—DSc '12—fellow '10-12 (NYU). Research on cadmium and zinc vapor lamps, effects of temperature on fluorescent lamps, brightness of mercury arcs, effects of impurities on fluorescent compounds, ultra-violet excitation of fluorescent compounds, chemicals in fluorescent compounds. Author articles in field. Instr chem U Mo '14-16, asst prof '16-18; metall US Bur Mines Golden Colo '18-19; asso prof U Mo '19-20; research engr. Westinghouse Lamp Div Pittsburgh '20-22, asst dir Bloomfield NJ '22-47, mgr molybdenum development since '47. Am Chem Soc— AAAS — Franklin Inst — Ill Engring Soc—Electrochem Soc (hon life mem '47) — Tau Beta Pi. Westinghouse Order of Merit '44, Presidential citation '48. Westinghouse Lamp Division, Bloomfield, N.J.

18 MARDER, Arthur Jacob. British naval history. b'10. AB '31—AM '34 —PhD '36 (Harvard). Author: The Anatomy of British Sea Power: a History of British Naval Policy in the Pre-Dreadnought Era 1880-1905 '41; also articles in field. Asso prof U Hawwaii since '44; vis prof U Calif Santa Barbara Coll summer '47, Harvard '48 '49. AHA—US Naval Inst. Winner George Louis Beer Prize AHA '41; Coolidge traveling fellow Harvard '35-36, Guggenheim fellow '41, 45-46. Department of History, University of Hawaii, Honolulu, T.H.

19 MARESH, Charles. Chemical microscopy; Textile microscopy; Pigments; Petrographic methods. b'13. BA '35—MS '37 (Western Reserve U); PhD '40 (Pa State Coll). Author articles in field. Chief micros Calco Chem Div Am Cyanamid Co since '43. NY Micros Soc—Am Chem Soc—Crystallographic Soc Am—Electron Micros Soc Am—Sigma Xi—Phi Beta Kappa. Calco Chemical Division, American

Cyanamid Company, Bound Brook, N.J.†

20 MARGENAU, Henry. Epistemology of physics; Intermolecular forces; Nuclear moments. b'01. MSc— PhD '29 (Yale); Sterling Research fellow '29-30 (Munich and Berlin). Author: Foundations of Physics '36; Mathematics of Physics and Chemistry '43; The Nature of Reality '50. With Yale U since '28, prof physics and natural philos Yale since '45; cons Argonne Nat Lab; staff Radiation Lab MIT '45. Am Phys Soc—Sigma Xi (governing com Assn Philos Sci). Sloane Physics Laboratory, Yale University, New Haven.†

21 MARION, Claud Collier. Vocational agriculture (Study construction); Negro land grant colleges (Instructional programs). b'13. BS '36 (Fla A&M Coll); MS '41 (U Minn); PhD '48 (Cornell). Author: A Qualitative and Quantitative Study of the Effectiveness of Instructional Programs in Technical Agriculture in Negro Land Grant Colleges (in process). Teacher-trainer and in charge instruction Div Agr Md State Coll since '48. Am Vocational Assn—AAUP—Am Edn Assn —Agrl Research Assn—Phi Delta Kappa. Maryland State College, Princess Anne, Md.

22 MARK, Herman Francis. Polymerization of synthetic rubber and plastics. b'95. PhD '21 (U Vienna). Research on natural and synthetic fibers, rubbers and plastics; mechanism of polymerization reactions, properties of macromolecules in solution. Author books and articles in field. Prof organic chem Poly Inst Brooklyn since '40, dir. Inst Polymer Research since '45. AAAS—APS—ACS. 99 Livingston St., Bklyn. 2.

23 MARK, Mary Louise. Social sciences (Research methods); Population; Standards and costs of living. b'78. AB '03 (Ohio State U); AM '07 (Columbia). Co-author: Immigrants in Cities (Vols 26 and 27 of Report of Immigration Commn) '11; Law and Order on Indian Reservations of the Northwest '32; Leisure in the Lives of Our Neighbors '41. With Ohio State U since '14, prof sociology '23-32, prof social adminstrn '32-43, emeritus prof since '43; mem staff Survey of Indian affairs Inst for Govt Research Washington '27. Royal Statis Soc London(F)—Am Statis Assn—AA UP—Am Sociol Soc—Population Assn Am—Am Acad Polit and Social Sci— Am Soc Pub Adminstrn—Nat Conf Social Work—Phi Beta Kappa—Alpha Kappa Delta. H: 270 S. State St., Westerville, O.⊙

24 MARKOWITZ, William. Time; Variation of latitude and longitude; Proper and stellar motions. b'07. BS '27—MS '28—PhD '31 (U Chicago). Author articles in field. Astronomer US Naval Obs since '36, now dir Time Service Division; lecturer mathematics Cath Univ since '47. Am Astron Soc— Internat Astron Union. US Naval Observatory, Washington, 25.

25 MARKS, Alvin Melville. Polarizing materials; Polarized illumination; Optical laminated filters; Third dimension television system; Electronic power generators. b'10. Emil Schweinberg scholarship—BS '32 (Cooper Union Inst Tech); '35-36 (Brooklyn Poly Inst); '44 (Harvard); '45 (MIT); '46-47 (NYU). Invented and developed supported continuous crystalline polarizer, intensification process, cross-linked polarizer, modern polarizers; discovered iodoalkanesilicate and manufacturing process; invented radial non-glare polarizer, invented micro-lamination used for polarizers for general illumination, color filters, and shatterproof safety lenses; invented electric generator having no moving parts except in auxiliaries for direct conversion of heat from atomic reactors or combustion to electric power, also basic new system of third dimension television. Granted 40 patents in fields. Chief research engr Elec Development Corp '34-35; vp charge research and development Polarized Products Corp '36-44; cons WPB '43, Office Nav Research '49; pres Polalite Corp since '47. Am Inst Phys—Optical Soc Am. Polalite Corp., 153-16 Tenth Av., Whitestone, L.I., N.Y.

10 MARKS, Henry Clay. Water treatment; Disinfection; Chlorine. b'09. AB '30 (U Pa); PhD '40 (Columbia U). US patents on process of manufacturing N-chloro-azo-dicarbonamidines; solutions of organic chlorine compounds; chlorine detection by electrode depolarization; electrical determination or control of chlorine in liquids; electrical cell apparatus; detection of oxidizing or reducing substances by electrode depolarization; procedure for disinfecting aqueous liquid. Author articles in field. Dir chem research Wallace & Tiernan Co since '47. Am Chem Soc—AAAS—Am Water Works Assn—NY Acad Sci—Sigma Xi. Wallace & Tiernan Company, Inc., 11 Mill St., Belleville, N.J.

11 MARKWARDT, L(orraine) J(oseph). Timber engineering. b'89. BS '12—CE '22 (U Wis). Invented hand hardness tool; cleated fiber box. Co-author: Descriptive Geometry; also articles in field. Research engr Forest Products Lab '12-14, '17-38, chief div timber mechanics '38-43, asst dir since '43. Soc Am Foresters—ASCE—Am Soc Testing Materials—Forest Products Research Soc—Am Ry Engring Assn—Internat Union Forest Research Orgn (FAO sub-com mech wood tech, NACA sub com aircraft structural materials). Forest Products Laboratory, Madison 5, Wis.

12 MARKWOOD, L(ouis) N(ewman). Insecticides; Nicotine and tobacco; Industrial chemicals. b'96. BS Chem Engring '17 (Case Inst Tech). Holds five patents. Author articles in field. Chem econ Bur Fgn Domestic Commerce Washington '42-51; dir chem div Office Internat Trade Dept Commerce since '51. Am Inst Chem—Am Chem Soc. 5420 Connecticut Av., Washington 15.

13 MARLATT, Charles Lester. Systematic and economic entomology; Plant quarantine. b'63. BS '84—MS '86—DSc '21 (Kan State Coll). Directed effort to secure a national law to prevent importation of infested and diseased plants into US, resulting in the Plant Quarantine Act '12, chairman Federal Horticultural Board to supervise enforcement of this act '12-28; responsible for reorganization and assembling from other bureaus of the Department of Agriculture of all plant quarantine and regulatory work under a new office, created by the secretary of agriculture of Plant Quarantine and Control Administration, was chief of this office '28-29. Author articles in field. Engaged in hist and geneal work since '33. AAAS(F)—Entomol Soc Washington (pres '97-98)—Assn Econ Entomol (pres '99)—Washington Acad Sci—Biol Soc—Archeol Soc—Geog Soc—Phi Kappa Phi. 1521 16th St., Washington 6.*

14 MARLING, John Bertram. Spectrographic analysis. b'15. Student '33-35, '38-39, '42 (U Cincinnati); '35-36 (Rollins Coll); AB '37 (O State U); '50-51 (Los Alamos ext U NM). Research on chem analysis by means of emission spectrograph including analysis of aluminum, magnesium, copper, low alloy steels, stainless steels, analysis of residuals, inclusions, spectrographic tracer techniques, uranium, transuranic elements; research on spl techniques of spectrographic analysis using emission spectrograph, multiple exposure and instrument combinations and cathode layer. Instrumental phys Champion Paper Co '37-41; spectroscopist Wright Aeronautical Co '42-45; cons spectroscopist Diakel Corp and William Powell Valve Co '43-45; emission spectroscopist Celanese Corp '45-46; acting leader Los Alamos '47-51; with Jarrell-Ash Co since '51. Am Optical Soc—Am Inst Phys—ACS. H: 1344 Devonshire Dr., El Cerrito, Cal.

15 MARMOR, Ralph A(nton). Chemistry of fats and oils. b'09. Student '27-29 (Tex A&M Coll). Research in inhibiting reversion in oils, phosphatides. Granted patents in field. Control chem A E Staley Mfg Co '30-40, research chem fats and oils '40-48; fats and oils sect head Pillsbury Mills Inc Minneapolis since '48. Am Chem Soc—Am Oil Chem Soc—(inter-soc color com '48-49, soap stock analysis com '40, bleaching methods com '42-46, chmn '47-49, oil color com '46-48). 208 3rd Av., S.E. Minneapolis 14.

16 MARON, Samuel Herbert. Physical chemistry; Rubber; Latex. b'08. BS '31—MS '33 (Case Inst Tech); PhD '38 (Columbia). Co-author: Fundamental Principles of Physical Chemistry '44; also articles in field. Prof phys chem Case Inst Tech since '45; dir research project on synthetic rubber and latex for Office of Synthetic Rubber since '43; cons pvt companies. Am Chem Soc—AAAS—Am Inst Chem Engrs—Am Soc Testing Materials (sub-com specifications and test methods)—Sigma Xi—Tau Beta Pi. Case Institute of Technology, Cleveland 6.

17 MARQUART, Linford Allen. History of United States (Middle period); Holiness movement. b'03. AB '28 (Olivet Nazarene Coll); AM '29 (Boston U); '30 (Western Reserve U); '43-49 (U Chicago). Head dept history Olivet Nazarene Coll Kankakee Ill '40-49, acting dean '44-45, dir summer sch '43-45; seminar middle period US hist Chgo U '43; registrar Nat Coll Edn Evanston since '49. Author: Let Us Look at India; Study Book of American Missions in India '46. NEA—AHA—Am Assn Coll Registrars—Ill Assn Coll Registrars. National College of Education, Evanston, Ill. H: 6 Main St., Bourbonnais, Ill.†

18 MARQUETTE, Bleecker. Housing and city planning; Public health; Community organization. b'92. AB '15 (Cornell); '12 (Sorbonne Paris). Co-author: A Housing Manual for Teachers; Postwar Housing in the U. S.; also articles in field. Exec sec Better Housing League Cincinnati since '18; Pub Health Fed Cincinnati since '21; dir health survey Detroit '48; cons Cinn Metrop Housing Authority. Am Pub Health Assn(F)—Nat Com Housing Assns—O Housing Council (pres)—Mental Hygiene Assn (past pres)—O Welfare Conf (past pres)—Am Assn Social Workers—Am Inst City Planning—Am Soc Planning Officials—Nat Health Council (mem bd)—Phi Beta Kappa and others. Received award for Distinguished Health Service to Cincinnati '47. 312 W 9th St., Cin 2.

19 MARQUETTE, Clare Leslie. History (Wisconsin); History of flour milling in Northwest. b'04. MA '37—PhD '40 (U Wis). Author articles in field. Prof Am hist U Miss since '46. State Hist Soc Wis—Econ Hist Assn—Miss Valley Hist Soc—So Hist Assn—Miss Hist Assn. Department of History, University of Mississippi, University, Miss.†

20 MARR, John Winton. Plant ecology (Arctic region). b'14. BS '36 (Tex Tech Coll); PhD '42 (U Minn). Research on ecology of vegetation transition areas, ecology of trees, tree-ring analysis, character of and plant reaction to winter environment in Colorado Rockies. Member botanical expedition to East coast Hudson Bay '39; organizer and leader of University of Colorado '48 Botanical Expedition to Ungava Bay, Canada. Instr biol U Colo '44-46, asst prof since '46. Served as artic region specialist US Army Air Force '42-44, '49. AAAS—Ecol Soc Am—Sigma Xi. Department of Biology, University of Colorado, Boulder, Colo.

21 MARRARO, Howard Rosario. Italian culture and Italians in America; Italo-American relations; Italy (Language, literature, education, history). b'97. AB '23—AM '25—PhD '32—U Scholar '25-26—Cutting Traveling Fellow '30-31 (Columbia). Educational adviser to Italian Consulate New York since '33; director Italian Interuniversity Bureau '35-38. Author: American Opinion on the Unification of Italy, 1846-1861 '32; Nationalism in Italian Education '25; Contemporary Italian Short Stories '27; Philip Mazzei: Virginia's Agent in Europe 34; The New Education in Italy '36; Memoirs of Philip Mazzei '42; also articles in field. Professor Italian Columbia U since '53. Modern Lang Assn—Am Assn Teachers Italian; Am Cath Hist Soc—NY State Hist Assn—Italian Hist Soc. Awarded Grant-in-aid Council for Research in Social Scis '34, '45, '47; Chevalier of the Crown of Italy; Fulbright fellow '53. Columbia University, NYC 27. H: 600 W. 116th St.†

22 MARRINER, John Edward. Marine power plant design; Ship repair. b'14. Student '33-35 (Long Beach City Coll); '36-37 (U Mich). Design diesel, steam and electric power plant for ships; direction repairs and alterations to hull, accomodations and machinery of steel and wood-hulled ocean-going vessels. Naval arch and marine engr Craig Shipbldg Co '37-46, sales engr '46-48, sales mgr since '48. Am Assn Engrs—Soc Naval Architects and Marine Engrs. Craig Shipbuilding Co., Long Beach 2, Cal.

23 MARRIOTT, Ross W. Solar eclipses. b'82. BS '04 (Valparaiso U); AB '06 (Ind U); AM '07 (Swarthmore); PhD '11 (U Pa). Swarthmore College eclipse expeditions Mexico '23, New England '25, Sumatra '26, 29, New England '32; US Naval Observatory Eclipse Expedition '30. Author articles in field. Prof math Swarthmore since '27. AAAS(F)—Royal Astron Soc—Am Astron Soc—Am Math Soc—Math Assn Am—Sigma Xi. 213 Lafayette Av., Swarthmore, Pa.

24 MARRON, Thomas Urban. Analytical chemistry; Product quality and process control; Clinical methods; Instrumental analysis. b'14. BS '36 (St Ambrose Coll); MS '37—PhD '42 (State U Ia). Development and modification of methods in clinical chemistry; blood alcohol testing program State of Iowa; cellular enzyme systems in plants; enzymic steak tenderizing process; physico-chem investigations of keratins; analytical research on dyes, intermediates and detergents; development of analytical techniques into full-scale industrial processes; theoretical and applied chemistry in various branches of graphic arts; laboratory planning, design and administration. Chem Ia Lutheran Hosp '38-41; analytical research Nat Aniline div Allied Chem & Dye Corp '42-46; research supervisor A B Dick Co since '46. ACS—Optical Soc Am—Sigma Xi—Alpha Chi Sigma. A.B. Dick Co., 5700 W. Toughy Av., Chgo 31

10 MARRS, Garland John. Archeology (Canada, Tunisia, US Southwest, Mexico); Weapons (Primitive); Knife throwing. b'16. AB '46 (U Mich); MA '49 (U NM); '50 (Yale); '50-52 (U Ariz). Research on test effectiveness of Indian bows including weight, range, penetration, rapidity of fire, etc.; knife fighting and throwing; archeological expeditions. Faculty U NM '46-49. Soc Am Archeol—Am Anthrop Assn. Department of Anthropology, University of Arizona, Tucson, Ariz. H: 301 West 28th St.

11 MARSCHAK, Jacob. Econometrics (Mathematical economics, economic and National income statistics, business cycles). b'98. PhD '22 (U Heidelberg); MA '35 (U Oxford). Author: Elasticity of Demand '31. Co-author Capital Formation '36; Economic Aspects of Atomic Power '50; Statistical Inference in Dynamic Economic Models '50; Studies in Econometric Method '53. Prof econ U Chgo since '43; research dir Cowles Commn Research in Econs '43 to '48. Econometric Soc (pres '46)—Am Statis Assn (vp '47)—Internat Statis Inst. University of Chicago, Chicago 37.©

12 MARSH, Albert Franklin. Hamsters. b'11. Student '40 (U Fla). Author: The Hamster Manual. Author articles and booklets in field. Started with hamsters in '45. 1514 Basil St., Mobile 17, Ala.

13 MARSH, Benjamin Clarke. Lobbying; Taxation. b'77. BA '98 (Grinnell Coll); '99-00 (U Chicago); '02-05 (U Pa). Author: Taxation of Land Values in American Cities '10; (with G B Ford) An Introduction to City Planning '09. Spl agt Phila Soc for Organizing Charity '02-03; sec Pa Soc Protect Children from Cruelty '03-07; exec sec Com Congestion Population NY '07-18; sec NYC Commn Congestion Population and NY State Commn Distribution Population '10-11; managing dir Farmers' Nat Council and exec sec People's Reconstruction League '18-25; sec The People's Lobby; ed People's Lobby Bulletin. Phi Beta Kappa—Nat Press Club. 810 F St., Washington 4.

14 MARSH, Burton Wallace. Traffic engineering. b'98. BS '20 (Worcester Poly Inst); '20-21 (Yale). Pioneer municipal traffic engineer in US; aided in development of traffic engineering principles and techniques; member executive committee and past chairman Highway Research Board National Research Council. Traffic planning in various cities '21-24; city traffic engr Pittsburgh '24-30, Phila '30-33; dir traffic engring and safety dept Am Auto Assn since '33; lecturer, instr, dean in traffic courses and schs including Traffic Engring and Traffic Officer Training Schs at Harvard, Northwestern U, Pa State Coll, U Md. Inst Traffic Engrs (past pres)—Nat Com for Traffic Training—Eno Found for Hwy Traffic Control Inc (bd cons)—Am Pub Works Assn—ASCE—Sigma Xi. Penn Av and 17th St., Washington 6.

15 MARSH, Daniel L. American higher education. b'80. AB '06—AM '07—LittD '27 (Northwestern U); STB '08 (Boston U); DD '13 (Grove City Coll); LLD '26 (U Pittsburgh); LLD '38 (Simpson Coll); LLD '41 (U So Calif);

LLD '43 (Dickinson Coll); LLD '45 (R I State Coll); LLD '48 (U Chattanooga); LittD '39 (Portia Law Sch); LHD '29 (Cornell); PhD '31 (U Bologna Italy); ScD in Edn '34 (Ia Wesleyan Coll); JUD '36 (Ill Wesleyan U); DCL '37 (O Northern U); NPhD '41 (Neb Wesleyan U). Author: The Faith of the People's Poet '20; Higher Education Plus the Highest Education '27; The Art of Fine Living '29; The Quest of a Better Tomorrow '33; Can Education's Virtue Counteract War's Vice '47; The American Canon '39; The Charm of the Chapel '50; and many others. Pres Boston U '26-51; chancellor of Boston U since '51. One of the founders and incorporators of NE Deposit Library. Historic Winslow House Assn (board governors, vice pres)——Am Acad Arts Sci(F)—Am Geog Soc—Am Council Edn—Assn Am Colls—AAAS—NEA (life)—National Econ League (nat council)—Nat Fedn Commerce Industry of France—Am Council African Edn (adv bd)—Phi Beta Kappa—Beta Gamma Sigma. Recipient of Northwestern U Alumni Award for distinguished service to edn '33; Nat Book Week Award for The American Canon '40; Mass Girls' State Gold Medal Americanism Award for greatest contribution to patriotism '47. 226 Bay State Road, Boston.

16 MARSH, Frank Edward. Housing. b'01. BS '23 (Knox Coll). Author: Forty Profitable Years of Limited Dividend Housing '39; also articles in field. Administrative officer Fed Housing Adminstrn '34-41; regional adminstrator W Coast region OPA '41-43. dep adminstr charge all field operations '43-46; mgr Washington office San Francisco C of C; exec vp gen mgr San Francisco Bay Area Council. 315 Montgomery St., San Francisco 4.

17 MARSH, Frank Lewis. Speciation: Theories of origins; Theory of special creation: Animal and plant ecology. b'99. AB '27—BS '29 (Emmanuel Miss Coll Mich); MS '35 (Northwestern U); PhD '40 (U Neb). Author: Water Content and Osmotic Pressure of Certain Prairie Plants In Relation to Environment '40; Evolution, Creation and Science '44; Studies in Creationism '49; also articles in field. Prof biol. head dept Union Coll Neb '41-50; prof biol. head dept Emmanuel Missionary Coll Berrien Springs since '50, Am Soc Mammal—AAAS—Ecol Soc Am—Sigma Xi. Emmanuel Missionary College, Berrien Springs, Mich.

18 MARSH, Homer Ellsworth. Cooperatives; Income taxation; Social security; Job insurance; Federal expenditures. b'12. BS '35—'35-36 (Ind U). Author: Bibliography of Public Employment Offices (with Thomas W Rogers) '35; Solvency of Indiana Unemployment Compensation Fund '43; Cooperative Expansion in the Petroleum Industry '44; Cooperative Competition in New England '46; The Other Tax Exempts '47: Facts in the Matter '47; Facts and Figures on Tax Exempts '50. Dir research Nat Tax Euality Assn. Govtl Research Assn—Beta Gamma Sigma—Nat Tax Assn—Internat Finance Assn. 231 S La Salle St., Chgo. 4. H: 916 Michigan St., Wheaton, Ill.

19 MARSHALL, Charles Edmund. membranes (Electrochemical properties; Clays (Mechanical analysis); Soils (Mineralogy): Silicates (Colloid chemistry). b'03. BS in chem '24—MS '25 (U Manchester); PhD in agrl chem '27 (U London); '27-28 (Poly Inst Zurich). Research on colloid chemistry of silicates, especially clays; mineralogy of sands, silts and clays; research on membrane electrodes

with cation-selective properties. Author: Colloids in Agriculture '35; The Colloid Chemistry of the Silicate Minerals '48; also 60 articles in field. Asst. lectr agrl chem U Leeds '28-36; with U Mo since '36, prof soils since '42. ACS—Soil Sci Soc Am(pres '46)—Am Soc Agron—Mineral Soc Am(F)—AAAS(F). Mercer Research scholar U Manchester '24-25; min agr research scholar '25-28; Hoblizelle Nat Award agrl sci '51. Department of Soils, University of Missouri, Columbia, Mo.

20 MARSHALL, Housden Lane. Fertilizers; Phosphate rock; Analytical and Inorganic Chemistry. b'02. BS '25—MS '26 (U Md); '32-34 (US Dept Agr Grad Sch). Author articles in field. Research chem So Acid and Sulphur Co; now chief chemist Baltimore Plant Mathieson Corp. Assn. Official Agrl Chem—Am Chemical Society. Mathieson Chemical Co., Mathieson Bldg., Balt. 3.

21 MARSHALL, John Sedberry, Philosophy (Theological, civilization, Anglo-Saxon thought; Richard Hooker, Aristotle). b'98. AB '21 (Pomona Coll); PhD '26 (Boston U); '23-25 (Harvard, U Basel Switzerland); '28 (U Calif); (U Prague). Author: Hooker's Polity in Modern English '48. Co-author: Value and Existence '35; also articles in field. Prof U of South since '46. Am Philos Assn—AAAS—British Inst Philos—So Soc Philos Religion. University of the South, Sewanee, Tenn.©

22 MARSHALL, John S(idney). Anthracite mining. b'02. BS '22 (Va Poly Inst). Research on development, design, and management anthracite coal mining; served on North African Economic Board and coal committee Supreme Headquarters, Allied Expeditionary Force; international coal mine consultant. Mine supt Wyoming Valley Colliers Co '32-37; partner Greenwood Mining Co since '38; vp Raleigh Mining Co since '47; exec vp Pierce Management Inc since '51. AI MME—Nat Soc Profl Engrs—Am Mining Congress. Pierce Management, Inc., Scranton Electrical Building, Scranton, Pa.

23 MARSHALL, Lauriston C. Physics (Resrch); Accelerator (Particle); Tubes (Vacuum, microwave, resnatron, very high power); Radar; Microwaves. b'02. AB '23 (Park Coll); PhD '29 (U Cal); Nat Research Council F physics '29-31 (Princeton). Research in high voltage phenomena; development resnatron and tubes for production high power at high frequencies; development, construction linear accelerator; supervision and direction radar development and design, operational research and analysis. Author articles; Recombination of Ions and of Ions and Electrons in Gases '29: The Theory of Recombination of Gaseous Ions '29. Co-author: (with D H Sloan) (Ultra-High Frequency Power '40; others. Physicist USDA '31-37; faculty dept elec engring U Cal since '37, prof, staff radiation lab and dir microwave lab, on leave since '52: now dir research Link-Belt Co.; staff radiation lab MIT '40-46; chief operational research Hdqrs US Air Force Pacific Ocean area '44-45. APS—Am Inst EE—Inst Radio Engrs—Eta Kappa Nu—Gamma Alpha. 220 S. Belmont Av., Indpls.

24 MARSHALL, Leon Soutierre. Economic history of the Nineteenth Century; English Social and economic history (Manchester). b'04. BA '23 (Coll Emporia); MA '28 (U Colo); PhD '37 (U Pittsburgh); Research scholarship Manchester English-speaking Union '33-34 (Manchester U). Research on basic tendencies in contemporary industrial society as they appeared in first industrial city, Manchester, England. Author: The Development of Public Opinion in Manchester, 1780-1820 '46; The Emergence of the First Industrial City: Manchester: 1780-1850 (in The Cultural Approach to History) '40; also articles in field. Prof hist Kent State U since '48. AHA—Econ Hist Assn. Kent State University, Kent, O.

10 MARSHALL, Nelson. Fisheries biology; Marine ecology; Oceanography. b'14. BS '37 (Rollins Coll); MS 38 (O State U); PhD '41 (U Fla); resch fellow summers '43-44 (Woods Hole Oceanog Inst). Author articles in field. Dir Va Fisheries Lab, prof biol, dean Coll William and Mary '47-52; asso dir Oceanographic Inst Fla State U since '52. AAAS—Fla Acad Sci—Ecol Soc Am—Am Fish Soc—Am Soc Ichthyol and Herpetol—Am Society Limnology and Oceanography—Sigma Xi. Oceanographic Institute, Florida State Univ., Tallahassee, Fla.†

11 MARSHALL, Samuel Lyman Atwood. Tactics (Armored, amphibious combined arms, airborne); Logistics (Airborne, infantry forces, combat); Strategy (History, theory); Psychology (Combat, military leadership); Military orientation; Combat nature of morale; Military history (United States Army: World War II, methodology in combat). b'00. Student '20-22 (Tex Coll Mines). Established The Army News Service; wrote basic national policy on Americans of Japanese blood, army policy on indoctrination of enemy prisoners of war; developed historical combat coverage in US army '43-44. Author: Blitzkrieg '40; Armies on Wheels '41; Island Victory '44; Bastogne '46; Makin '46; Men Against Fire '47; Toward Greater Mobility '48; Leadership in the Armed Forces '50; The Armed Forces Officer '50; also articles Guide to Information Materials, Guide to Occupation of Enemy Territory, and other official manuals. Editorial writer, fgn corr and mil critic Detroit News since '26. Enlisted in Engr Corps US Army '17 advancing to 1st lt inf '19; re-entered mil service as civilian experts cons to Sec War '42; Comm maj inf, and assigned as chief of orientation US Army '42; assigned hist div WDGS '43; comm col GSC '44; apptd chief historian ETO '45; hon disch May '46; operations analyst 8th Army combat forces Korea '50-51. Appointed Historical Advisory Comm WD '46. Decorated Legion of Merit, Bronze Star with cluster, citation ribbon with clusters; C de G with palms, Comm Ordre de Leopold (Bel); Croix de Guerre with palm; Ordre d'Armee (Fr); C di G, F di G (Italy); Korean medal. 16861 Gilchrist Av., Det.☺

12 MARSHALL, Thurgood. Civil rights (Negro). b'08. BA (Lincoln U); LLB '33 (Howard U Law Sch) LLB (hon) '48 (Va State Coll). Active charge all legal cases National Association for Advancement of Colored People to secure and protect civil rights for Negroes, has appeared before Supreme Court of United States and federal and state courts for most states of South; author briefs and other legal documents in connection with civil rights cases. Pvt practice law Baltimore '33-37; counsel Baltimore City Br NAACP '34-36, apptd asst special counsel '36, spl counsel since '38. Md State Bar—Nat Bar Assn—Nat Lawyers Guild. Awarded Spingarn medal NAACP '46. 20 W. 40th St., NYC 18.

13 MAR SHIMUN XXIII MAR ESHAI SHIMUN. History and problems of Assyria; Aramaic language. b'08. Ed tutors, Iraq; St Augustine's Coll, Canterbury, Eng; Westcott House, Cambridge, Eng, '25-27, Consecrated Catholicos Patriarch CXIX of Church of the East '20, succeeding uncle; appeared for Assyrians, League of Nations '33-37; represents Church of the East on World Council of Churches; presented Assyrian cause at World Security Council San Francisco '45, UN '46; presented question of Assyrians of Azerbaijan Iran, Iraq and Syria UN '47. Translator Aramaic liturgy; lecturer on Christianity and current events in Middle and Far East; came to US '40 to supervise Church of East. Am Soc Ch Hist—AHA. The Patriarchate, 6346 N. Sheridan Rd., Chicago.

14 MARSTON, Anson. Civil engineering (Hydraulic); Engineering valuation; Depreciation accountancy. b'64. CE '89 (Cornell); Dr Engring '25 (U Neb), '27 (Mich State Coll). Author: Sewers and Drains '07; Engineering Valuation (with T R Agg) '36; also articles in field. Prof civ engring Ia State Coll '92-20, dean emeritus since '37. Commissioned maj engrs '17; lieut col engrs '18; comd 97th Engrs till demobilization '18. ASCE (dir '20-22, vp '23-24, pres '29)—Am Soc Testing Materials—Soc Promotion Engring Edn (treas '06-07, pres '14-15) —Am Assn Land Grant Coll and U (pres '29). Chanute medal Western Soc Engrs '03; Fuertes medal Cornell U '04; Lamme medal '41. Soc Promotion Engrng Edn, Ames, Ia.*

15 MARSTON, Frank Alwyn. Sewage treatment. b'85. BS in civil engring '07 (Worcester Poly Inst). Research and design water works water filter plants, sewers and drains, sewage disposal plants, aeration process, disposal turbid drainage waters. Partner Metcalf & Eddy since '19. Am Soc CE—Am Water Works Assn—Boston Soc CE (past pres)—NE Water Works Assn—Am Pub Works Assn—ASTM—NE Sewage Works Assn—Nat Com Soil Mech (exec com). 1300 Statler Building, Boston 16.

16 MARSTON, Otis. American rivers history (Colorado); Fast water navigation. b'94. BS '16 (U Calif); ME '17 (Cornell U). Head investment dept E F Hutton & Co San Francisco until '47. Submarine comdr US Navy '18-19. 2333 Vine St., Berkeley 8.

17 MARSTON, Philip Mason. New England and New Hampshire history. b'02. BA '24—MA '27 (U NH); (Harvard). Editor, co-author: History of the University of New Hampshire 1866-1941 '41; also articles in field. with U NH since '24, asso prof hist, head dept since '44. AHA—N E Assn Social Studies Teach—Hakluyt Soc—Am Assn State Local Hist—NH Hist Soc (trustee)—Phi Kappa Phi—Kappa Delta Pi. Department of History, University of New Hampshire, Durham, N.H.

18 MARTH, Paul C(harles). Plant growth, dormancy and propagation; Abscission of fruits and flowers (Regulating substances); Parthenocarpy; Fruit ripening; Selective weed control. b'09. BS '30—MS '33—PhD '42 (U Md). Co-author: Growth Regulators '47; also articles in field. With Bur Plant Ind US Dept Agr since '33. Am Soc Hort Sci—Washington Acad Sci—Sigma Xi. Plant Industry Station, Beltsville, Md.

19 MARTIN, Albert Jr. Genetics. b'16. BS '42—MS '46—PhD '47 (Pittsburgh U). Made genetic studies of parasitic wasp Habrobracon juglandis Ashmead or Microbracon hebeter Say; research on new linkage group, genetic evidence of catenation and speciation, and present dynamics of linkage groups in Habrobracon juglandis. Author articles in field. Prof biol Mt Mercy Coll '46-53; associate member of the graduate school faculty and lecturer biol dir genetic research Pittsburgh U since '45. Sigma Xi—Pa Acad Sci—Genetics Soc Am—Am Genetic Assn—AAUP—Soc Systematic Zoology—Phi Sigma—Kappa Phi Kappa—AA AS. University of Pittsburgh, Pitts. 13.†

20 MARTIN, A(lexander) C(ampbell). Seed morphology; Wildlife foods. b'97. AB '20 (Oberlin Coll); MS '24 (NC State Coll); PhD '44 (George Washington U). Research on wildlife foods, morphology of seeds, quail-food plants of southeastern states, food of game ducks in US and Canada, comparative internal morphology of seeds. Author articles in field. Biol US Fish Wildlife Service since '29. Patuxent Research Refuge, Laurel, Md.

21 MARTIN, Alfred Edward. Colorimetry; Luminescence; Radiometry; Television optics. b'11. BS in phys '32—U State NY scholarship '28-32 (Coll City NY); MS in phys '33—Gen Edn Bd F in phys '38-40 (U Mich). Research on principles, construction and application of filter-photocell combinations to tristimulus colorimetry, studies of basic colorimetric aspects of monochrome and color television; research and instrumentation for studies of phosphor emission, absorption, excitation spectra, and thermoluminescence glow; design and construction automatic recording spectroradiometers, absolute measurement of radiant energy; study and design optical systems for projection television receivers, study surround lighting as applied to television receivers; member Jetec subcommittee on cathode-ray tube screens and phosphor characteristics for standardization purposes, member American Standards Association sectional com on photographic sensitometry. Asst project engr Allen D Cardwell Mfg Corp '44-46; head photonics sect Sylvania Elec Products Inc since '46. APS—Am Assn Phys Tchrs —Optical Soc Am—Inst Radio Engrs —Electrochem Soc—Kappa Delta Pi. Physics Laboratories, Sylvania Electric Products Inc., Bayside, N.Y.

22 MARTIN, Boyd Archer. American government (Local government); Political parties and politics; Public administration; International relations. b'11. BS '36 (U Ida); AM '36—PhD '43—John M Switzer fellowship summer '39-40 (Stanford U). Attended UN Conference San Francisco, Great Plains, UNESCO Conference Denver '47; member Idaho State Council on UNESCO '47 and '48. Author: The Direct Primary in Idaho '47; also articles in field. Prof head dept social sci, asst dean Coll Letters and Sci U Ida since '47. Am Polit Sci Assn—Nat Municipal League—Am Soc Pub Administrn—Inst Pacific Relations—Inland Empire Br Inst Pacific Relations (pres '47)—Foreign Policy Assn —UN Assn—Phi Beta Kappa—Kappa Delta Pi. University of Idaho, Moscow, Ida.☺

23 MARTIN, Edward Burns. Shakespeare; Ireland. b'84. AB '20—AM '21 (U Denver); grad study (Garrett Bibl Inst Evanston Ill) (Chgo Theol Sem) (U Chicago); DD (O Northern U). Study on Shakespeare follow by teaching and lecturing in colleges, summer assemblies, clubs and churches, in effort to polularize and presenting him primarily as ethical teacher and artist; travel and study of Ireland, it's people and literature. 219 Russell St., Hammond, Ind.

10 MARTIN, Foster Newton Jr. Pharmacology of sympathomimetic amines and potassium; Poisonous plants. b'07. BS '37 (Newberry Coll); '36 (U SC); MD '32 (Med Coll State Sc); PhD '45 (U Mich). Research on comparison of changes in serum glucose, serum potassium and blood pressure after epinephrine, chemotherapy of plasmodium knowlesi infections in Macaca mulatta monkeys, distribution of potassium and sodium in cells and body fluids. Author articles in field. Asso prof pharm Tulane U Sch Med since '49. Am Soc Pharm Exptl Therapeutics—Soc Exptl Biology Med—SC Acad Sci—AAAS—Bot Soc Am—Sigma Xi. Department of Pharmacology, Tulane Medical School, PO Station 20, New Orleans.†

11 MARTIN, F(rederick) O(skar). Geography and geology of Columbia South America. b'71. DC '02 (Columbian U); (Harvard, Catholic U). Honorary counsul for Austria at Los Angeles '32-33; Delegate to International Geology Congress Madrid, International Congress de Forage Paris '29, World Engineering and Power Congress Tokio '29. Author: Explorations in Columbia, South America. Pvt practice since '41. Royal Geog Soc—Am Geog Soc—Pacific Geog Soc—Am Inst Mining Metall Engrs—Am Assn Petroleum Geol. 2038 Pine St., South Pasadena, Calif.

12 MARTIN, Fredericka. Aleut language, sociology and history; History of fur sealing. b'05. Student pub schools. Translator Aleut poems in Aleutian Manuscript Collection by A Yarmolinsky NY Pub Library '44; consultant on Aleut affairs to National Congress of American Indians; consultant on colonial women to the Congress of American Women. Author: Hunting of the Silver Fleece: Epic of the Fur Seal '46; also articles in field. Editor: The Aleut Language; dictionary and grammar pub by US Dept of Interior '46. Soc Women Geog—Inst Ethnic Affairs—Assn Am Indian Affairs. 480 Central Park West, NYC 25.

13 MARTIN, Gustav Julius. Graying hair; Brain Chemistry. b'10. BS '32 (U Washington); ScD '35 — fellow '32-35 (Johns Hopkins); fellow '35-36 (U Chicago). Research brain chemistry, detoxication, gray hair, amino acid nutrition, application of exchange resins to field of medicine ulcers and hypertension. Author articles in field. Prof chem Coll St Teresa Minn '36-37; asst dir Warner Inst NYC '37-44; dir research Nat Drug Co Phila since '44. ACS—AAAS—Soc Exptl Biol and Med —Soc Investigative Dermatol—NY Acad Sci—Soc Bacteriol. Research Laboratories, The National Drug Company, Phila.

14 MARTIN, Helen M. Glacial geology; Hydrology; Stratigraphy of Michigan; Water supplies. b'89. AB '08—MS '17 (U Mich). Author: Ne-Saw-Je-Won Story of the Great Lakes '39. Co-author: Rocks and Minerals of Michigan '38; They Need Not Vanish '42; also articles in field. Research geol ed lecturer Geol Survey Div Mich Dept Conservation since '35, teacher and condr field trips in training sch. Geol Soc Am(F)—AAAS(F)—Am Assn Petroleum Geol—Mich Acad Sci Arts —Am Mus Natural Hist—Nat Geog Soc—Am Forestry Assn. Geological Survey Division, Michigan Department of Conservation, Lansing, Mich.

15 MARTIN, James Wellford. Carbon dioxide (Production uses); Explosives; Chemical warfare material. b'91.

Grad in chem '11 (U Va). Member of Interallied Commission to Inspect Enemy Chemical Plants World War I; in charge engineering and construction chemical warfare manufacturing arsenal World War II; production of first commercial dry ice; application carbon dioxide to oil recovery; design and construction carbon dioxide plants. Holds patents on manufacture carbon black, and on manufacture and use carbon dioxide. Co-author: Chemistry in Warfare. Chem and supt prodn acids DuPont Co; asst supt TNT plant Tenn Copper Co; research supr Union Carbide & Carbon Corp; chief engr Dry Ice Corp '25-29; cons engr carbon dioxide '29-42 and since '44; engring mgr constrn Pine Bluff Arsenal Ark World War II. AICE—Am Inst Chem(F)—Am Soc Refrigerating Engrs. Profl. engr NY, Fla. Room 3300. 405 Lexington Av., NYC 17.†

16 MARTIN Joh Allen Jr. Sweet potato, pepper and sesame breeding; Sweet potato seed scarification; Condiment crop culture; Aromatic tobacco. b'12. (Clemson Agrl Coll); (Tex A&M); (Purdue U). Author articles in field. Research asst to asso hort SC Expt Sta since '42. Am Soc Hort Sci—Am Genetics Assn. SC scholar '32-33. Clemson Agricultural College, Horticulture Department, Clemson, S.C.

17 MARTIN, John Rogers. Asphalts. b.'09. BS ChemE '35 (Tex U); CE '49 (Okla A. and M). Research on asphaltic materials and asphalt pavements; developed curing index for cutback asphalts; collaborated in development effective specific gravity for paving aggregates; hygrometric method for determining saturated surface-dry point for fine aggregates. With Tex Highway Dept '35-47, chief lab engr 44-47; research prof civil engring Okla A & M Coll '47-51; chief engr Hot Mix Asphaltic Concrete Assn of Okla Inc. Sigma Xi—Chi Epsilon— Am Inst Physics—Highway Research Bd—Assn Asphalt Paving Tech—Soc Profl Engrs. 424 Cravens Bldg., Oklahoma City.

18 MARTIN, J(oseph) Holmes. Poultry genetics and husbandry. b'95. BS '17 (Purdue U); MS '24 (U Ky); PhD '29 (U Wis). Co-author: Turkey Management; also articles in field. Head poultry dept Purdue U since '40; coordinator poultry breeding research North Central stations '45-47. Quartermaster Subsistance Lab US Army. AAAS(F)—Poultry Sci Assn—Worlds Poultry Sci Assn (mem exec council '38-39)—Nat Turkey Fed (hon life) —Genetic Soc Am—Sigma Xi. 501 Carrolton Blvd., W. Lafayette, Ind.

19 MARTIN, Paul Sidney. Archeology of Southwestern United States; Southwestern archeology and ethnology. b'98. PhB '23—PhD '29 (U Chicago). Archeology field work in Wisconsin, Illinois, Yucatan, Colorado and New Mexico; director of Chicago Natural History Museum expeditions in American Southwest '30, '48. Author: Handbook of North American Archeology '33; Lowry Ruin in Southwestern Colorado '36; Archeological Work in Ackmen-Lowry Area Southwestern Colorado '38; The SU Site—Excavations at a Mogollon Village New Mexico '40, '43, '47; Anasazi Painted Pottery '40; History of Pine Lawn Valley, New Mexico, '48; Indians before Columbus (with Quimby and Collier) '47; also articles in field. Head curator anthrop Chicago Natural Hist Mus since '35; prof Anthrop U Chicago since '42. Am Anthrop Assn—Soc Am Archeol. Chicago Natural History Museum, Chgo. 5.◉

20 MARTIN, Robert Earl. Agricultural politics. b'14. AB '36—AM '38 (Howard U); PhD '47 (U Chicago). Research on referenda program under Agricultural Adjustment Act, "white primary", poll tax, and Virginia politics. Julius Rosenwald fellow '40-42; with A & T Coll '39-47, prof soc sci '46-47; asso field rep OWI '42-43; Social Sci Research Council fellow '45-46; asst prof govt Howard U since '47; vis asst prof govt Columbia '49-50. Am Polit Sci Assn—Soc Advancement Edn—Assn Soc Sci Tchrs. Department of Government, Howard University, Washington 1.

21 MARTIN, Robert Ray. Sociology (Community organization, human ecology, marriage). b'93. AB '28—AM '29 —PhD '35 (U Wash). Co-author: Society Under Analysis; Youth Faces It's Problems '50; also articles in field. Prof sociol head dept Hamline U St Paul since '38; organized Hamline-Asbury Sch Nursing, dean '40-44. Am Sociol Soc—Rural Sociol Soc— Am Inst Family Relations. Hamline University, St. Paul 4.

22 MARTIN, Samuel William. Coal (Technology); Petroleum (Technology). b'10. BA '32 (Williams Coll); PhD '35 (Yale). Study coal carbonization, and activated carbon and carbon black; city gas production and purification; thermal cracking residuum oils to aromatic light oil, tars, and lamp black; distillation of tar. Author articles: The Determination of Subsieve Particle Size Distributions by Sedimentation Methods '42; Characterization of Creosole Oils '49, and others. Phys chem Nat Lead Co Titanium Div, '35-42; supervisor Inst Gas Tech '42-45; dir research and development Portland Gas & Coke Co '46-50; gen mgr engring and development Great Lakes Carbon Corp since '50. ACS— Am Inst Chem—Am Petroleum Inst —Am Wood Preservers Assn—Phi Beta Kappa—Sigma Xi—Gamma Alpha. Great Lakes Carbon Corp., 333 N. Michigan Av., Chgo.

23 MARTIN, Thomas Powderly. Business and economic history; Cotton textile history; International business history; Archives and research libraries. b'87. AB '13 (Stanford U); MA '14 (U Calif); PhD '22 (Harvard). Author articles in field. Asst chief div manuscripts Library Congress '28-48; unofficial adv and cons Gregg Found Graniteville Co since '43; Ind U. Library since '48; vis prof hist World Politics O U, WVa U '48-49; Indiana U '50-52. Agr Hist Soc—Econ Hist Assn — So Hist Assn — AHA — Miss Valley Hist Assn—Am Mil Hist—Royal Hist Soc(F)—Phi Beta Kappa. Bloomington, Ind.; also Dunn Loring, Va.†

24 MARTIN, Weston Joseph. Plant pathology (vegetable crops, rubber trees, smut fungi). b'17. BS '37 (Southwestern La Inst); MS '39 (La State U); PhD '42 (U Minn). Author articles in field. Asso path La Agr Expt Sta since '47. AAAS — Am Phytopath Soc—La Acad Scis—Sigma Xi.

25 MARTIN, William McKinley. Food preservation; Aseptic canning methods. b'97. BSA '24—MS '26—Scholar Nat Research Council of Can '24-26—Fellow '26-27 (U Alberta); PhD '29— Caleb Dorr Fellow '28-29 (U Minn). Research in uses of superheated steam in processing foods and sterilization; canning technology; can manufacture; methods and apparatus for extraction, clarification, flash-sterilization and packing; formulation of ingredients as to balanced nutrients, palatability, freedom from coagulation during thermal sterilization process;

machine for evaluating consistency of canned products; tenderometer for measuring tenderness; formulation and thermal processing related to curdling; deaerator of special design for viscous liquids, semifluids; high temperature flash-sterilization of evaporated milk, involving stabilization of milk proteins and butter fat during thermal sterilization and storage; handling and filling homogenized whole milk in dairy; electrochemical nature of corrosion of steel and corrosion resistance of tinplate; method and equipment for commercial manufacture of solderless can embodying compound-lined double-lock side seam construction; plastics containers; quick-freezing methods and practical problems involved in packaging and merchandising; developmental work on container construction, manufacturing and packaging problems. Holds 32 patents. Author articles in field. American Chem Soc—Inst Food Technol—Gamma Alpha—Sigma Xi—Phi Kappa Phi. Vice president James Dole Engineering Co. 58 Sutter Street, San Francisco. H: 457 Virginia Av., San Mateo.†

10 MARTINDALE, Earl Henry. Electric motor maintenance; Small business (Problems). b'85. BS '08—EE '12 (Case Sch Applied Sci). Author: Who Really Owns My Business; also articles in field. Pres and gen mgr Martindale Electric Co Cleveland. AIEE (former chmn indsl and domestic power com, chmn membership com, mgr and vp)—Assn Iron Steel Elec Engrs—Elec League—Smaller Businesses Am (dir, chmn com Nat Coordination)—NAM—O Mfrs Assn—Tau Beta Pi. Martindale Electric Co., Cleveland 7.

11 MARTINSON, Earl Pehr. Industrial engineering. b'97. AB '21 (Augustana Coll); AM '24 (U Neb). Research into costs of production and reasons therefor; physical factors which make for smooth operation; qualifications of supervisory personnel; employee morale. Employment mgr, costs mgr, div sales mgr Consol Industries Rockford Ill '28-'35; works mgr, purchasing agt The Weiman Co '35-38; mgr, supt The Mengel Co Baton Rouge '38-42; asst exec engr Fairchild Aircraft Hagerstown Md '42-47; head prof indsl engring U Fla since '48. Am Inst Indsl Engrs—Soc Advancement Management—Am Soc Engring Edn—Fla Engring Soc—Sigma Xi. College of Engineering, University of Florida, Gainesville.

12 MARTON, Ladislaus L(aszlo). Electron physics (Optics and microscopy). b'01. PhD '24 (U Zurich Switzerland). Pioneer work in electron microscopy. Holder numerous patents. Author: Le Microscope Electronique et ses Application '35; Electron Optics and Electron Microscopy; also articles in field. Research physicist Tungsram Research Lab Hungry '25-28; instr and asst prof U Brussels '28-38; research physicist RCA Mfg Co NJ '38-41; asso prof and head div electron optics Stanford '41-46; physicist Nat Bur Standards Washington since '46, chief electron physics sect since '48. Electron Microscope Soc Am (vp '46)—Philos Soc Washington—Washington Acad Sci—Am Assn Physics Teachers—Am Phys Soc (vice chmn div electron and ion optics '44, chmn '45, program com '45. Editor-in-chief Advances in Electronics. National Bureau of Standards, Washington 25.

13 MARTORELL, Luis Felipe. Forest and sugar cane insects; Insects of Venezuela and Puerto Rico. b'09. BS Agr '32 (Coll Agr Mayaguez PR); MS '34—PhD '43—fellow entomol '42-43

(Ohio State U). Research on parasites in Venezuela, Brazil, Trinidad, Virgin Islands, Lesser Antilles; control of sugar cane moth borer by means of parasitic flies. Author articles in field. Asso entomol Agr Expt Sta U Puerto Rico Rio Piedras PR. Entomol Soc Am(F)—Am Assn Econ Entomol—Entomol Soc Washington—Entomol Soc P R—Sociedad Americana de Ciencias Agricolas—Gamma Sigma Delta—Sigma Xi. Agricultural Experiment Station, Rio Piedras, P R.†

14 MARTZ, Charles S. Photo engraving; Photography. b'03. Student comml art sch. Established Aurora Missouri School of Photo Engraving; designed process cameras, vacuum printing units, routers, etching machines and plate whirlers; originator and designer of first one-man photo engraving plant and training course '31, first packaged photo engraving plant '46; developed Tasope automatic aperture '36; established Tasope School Modern Photography '38; Salon exhibitor since '38, salon judge since '41; recent oil accepted by jury and hung in City Art Museum St Louis Mo. Author: Modern Photo-Engraving and Allied Graphic Arts Processes '46; also articles in field. Royal Photog Soc Gt Brit (F)—Photog Soc Am (asso). Tasope Building, Aurora, Mo.

15 MARTZ, Velorus. History of education in Indiana; Philosophy of education. b'80. AB '01—AM '05—PhD '27 (Ohio State U). Co-author: Introduction to Education '41; also articles in field. Prof edn Ind U since '29, emeritus since '50. Phi Delta Kappa—Phi Beta Kappa. RFD, Unionville, Ind.©

16 MARX, Alexander. Jewish history and literature of the Middle Ages; Hebrew printing and bibliography. b'78. PhD '03 (Koenigsberg); DHL '38 (Inst Religion), '45 (Hebrew Union Coll); DL '48 (Dropsie Coll). Author: Untersuchungen zum Siddur des Gaon R Amram '08; The Correspondence between the Rabbis of Southern France and Maimonides about Astrology '26; Zunz's Letters to Steinschneider '34; The Scientific Work of Some Outstanding Medieval Jewish Scholars '38; Studies in Jewish History and Booklore '44; Studies in Jewish Biography '47; and others. Editor (with A Freimann and M Hildesheimer) Berliner Gesammelte Schriften I '13; (with H Malter) M Steinschneider, Gesammelte Schriften I; (with S Baron) Jewish Studies in Memory of George Alexander Kohut; and others; also articles in field. Came to US '03; prof hist, librarian Jewish Theol Sem since '03; director of libraries since '50. Jewish Publications Socety Am (mem Publ Publishers Soc America (member Publ Com)—Kohut Memorial fund (pres)—Am Acad Jewish Research '50—Medieval Acad Am(F)—Am Jewish Hist Soc—Jewish Hist Soc Eng (corr mem). 3080 Broadway, NYC 27.

17 MARX, Frank. Radio engineering; Design, construction and installation of broadcast plants. b'10. Student (Shreveport Coll, U Va, William and Mary Coll, Columbia U). Responsible for design construction and installation of several complete broadcast plants. Dir gen engring Am Broadcasting Co '45-47, vp charge engring since '48; cons to WMCA Inc. Mem com on sabotage radio stations World War II. Inst Radio Engrs—Wash Engr Club—Fed Communications Cons Engrs Assn—Radio Pioneers. American Broadcasting Company, 7 West 66th St., NYC 23.

18 MARZOLO, Leo A. Paintings (Restoration). b'87. Student (Hopkins

Inst Art San Francisco). Relining, retouching, revarnishing, cleaning and general repair bruised areas old master paintings; transposition art surface from canvas to panel or viceversa; removal painted surfaces to reveal true painting. Restorer Art Inst Chicago, other museums of Middle West since '28. Palette and Chisel Acad Arts (past pres; awarded Gold medal '32) 1012 N. Dearborn St., Chgo.

19 MASHBIR, Sidney Forrester. Japanese language and psychology; Scientific concrete; Aeronautics (Radio landing systems); Meteorology (Radio sondes). b'91. Student '14 (U Ariz). Japanese language expert Manila surrender USS Missouri; pres and inventor process Scientific Concrete Service Corp and Intercontinental Service Corp. Exec officer, Office Adj Gen Washington since '48. Lt col Mil Intelligence Res '27-39; chief Intelligence Br, Office Chief Signal Officer '42; col comdg Allied Translator and Interpreter Sect GHQ '42-45. 4934 Indian Lane, N.W., Washington.

20 MASLENIKOV, Oleg A(lexander). Russian language and literature; Slavic philology. b'07. AB '34—PhD '42 (U Calif); fellow '35-36 (Inst Internat Edn Charles U Prague). Gave spot translation ABC radio of speech of USSR Foreign Commissar V M Molotov at first plenary session of United Nations Conference San Francisco '45. Editor: Slavia '42; Elementary Russian Reader '46; co-editor: Advanced Russian Readers I-IV '43-44; also articles in field. Asso prof Slavic Langs U Calif since '48, chmn dept since '44; faculty adv Russian program Far Eastern and Russian Lang Sch. Modern Lang Assn (chmn Slavic sect '47)—Am Assn Teachers Slavic East European Lang (president '49, president California chap)—Philol Assn Pacific Coast—Linguistic Soc Am—Cercle Linguistique—Soc Promotion Byzantine Studies—Soc Advancement Edn. Slavic Department, University of California, Berkeley 4.

21 MASLIN, T(homas) Paul. Herpetology (Phylogeny, amphibians and reptile anatomy and taxonomy). b'09. BA '33—MA '39 (U Calif); PhD '45 (Stanford). Author articles in field. Asso prof biol U Colo since '47. Am Soc Ichthyol Herpetol—Calif Acad Sci—Colo-Wyo Acad Sci—AAAS—Soc Study Evolution. Department of Biology, University of Colorado, Boulder, Colo.

22 MASON, A. Hughlett. Applied mathematics (Structural and vibration mechanics); Astronomy (Celestial mechanics); Geophysics. Born 1905. BS in CE '29 (U SC); MS '31—PhD '53 (U Pa). Developed interpolative method of determining natural frequency of torsional vibration of diesel engine crankshafts; devel nomographic method of solving Kepler's equation; torsiograph engr on largest single acting diesel engine ever built US. Author: Polar Moments of Inertia of Circles. Co-author: 1414 Observations of 1033 Double and Multiple Stars made with Eighteen Inch Refracting Telescope of the Flower Astronomical Observatory. Sr physicist General Staff US Army. AA AS—Am Astron Society—Am Geophys Union—Philos Soc Washington. General Staff, Dept. of the Army, Pentagon Bldg., Washington.

23 MASON, Clarence Tyler. Halogenated ethers; Vegetable mucilages. b'08. BS '31 (Northwestern U); MSc '33—PhD '35 (McGill U). Research on dialysis speed of electrolytes, constituents persimmon fruit, paper pulp from southern agricultural wastes, organic inhibitors oxidation in inks, fungicides for ink, brominated ethers, vegetable mucilage from linseed oil meal. Patent application (with LA Hall) Linseed Meal Gum. Author articles in field. Asst prof, prof head Dept Sci Dillard U '35-44; research dir GW Carver Found Tuskegee Inst since '44. Am Chem Soc—Am Inst Chem(F)—Sigma Xi. G. W. Carver Foundation, Tuskegee Institute, Ala.

10 MASON, E. Gilbert. Industrial design and architecture; Design (Product, furniture package, materials); Transportation interior engineering designing (Airplanes, trains, buses, automobiles, boats). b'09. Student '27-28 (Columbia); '28-29 (Grand Central Art Sch, Beaux Arts Inst Design). Designed six special deluxe interiors of airplanes for army and navy at Consolidated Aircraft Co., Ft Worth, Texas '42-43; designed special deluxe interior furnishings of planes for President Roosevelt, Secretary Knox, General MacArthur, General Eisenhower, General Sumerville, General DeGaulle, Douglas Aircraft Co '43-44; designed interiors for Douglas DC-6, President Truman Special DC-6 Independence and 27 executive DC-3's '44-47. Opened own office NYC designing homes, furnishings, industrial products '31; in Los Angeles '35 designing motion picture sets for MGM and Universal, homes, furnishings, industrial products; in Ft. Worth and Houston '39; closed all offices '42 due to war; since war has opened new offices in Los Angeles and Hurst Tex practicing industrial design and architecture; opened Masonbilt Mfg Co Wood Products and Furniture Factory Hurst '50. SAE—Inst Aeronautical Sci —Soc Indsl Designers. 827 Moraga Dr., Bel-Air, LA 24. Hi Yellow Head Ranch, Smithfield, Tex.

11 MASON, Edward Charles. Physiology. b'91. AB '14 (Drury Coll); MD '20—PhD '21 (U Cincinnati). Introduced use of heparin in transfusions, and for prevention thrombosis and embolism; demonstrated that insulin produced initial rise in blood sugar, and acted after destruction of central nervous system, parasympathetic and sympathetic systems; development theory that water mobilization in body is related to carbon dioxide exchange; devised technique for use of tannic acid in treatment of burns. Author articles in: Acid-Base-Water Balance '47; Shock Resulting from Autolysis and Traumatized Tissues '47; Blood Coagulation, Thrombosis and Embolism '49, and others. Asst prof pharm U Cincinnati '19-21; sr fellow Mayo Clinic Rochester Minn '21-22, staff '22-23; asso path Henry Ford Hosp Detroit '23-25; prof physiol med sch U Okla since '28. Am Coll Physicians(F)—Am Physiol Soc—Soc Exptl Biol and Med—AAAS—Sigma Xi. University of Oklahoma School of Medicine, 801 N.E. 13th St., Oklahoma City 4.

12 MASON, Gregory. Cultural, physical and archeological anthropology; American history (Pre-Columbian); Spanish-American War; Alcoholism (Psychological aspects); Newspaper psychology; Law and cultural functions of the press. b'89. AB '11 (Williams Coll); PhD '38 (U So Calif). Organizer (with Dr Herbert J Spinden and Ludlow Griscom) and leader archeological and ornithological expedition to Eastern Yucatan in collaboration with Peabody Museum of Harvard and American Museum of Natural History '26; field leader aerial and archeological expedition Museum of University of Pennsylvania to Central America '30; and other expeditions. Author: September Remember (with R F Mason under pen-name Eliot Taintor); Green Gold of Yucatan; Mexican Gallop (with R Carroll); Silver Cities of Yucatan; Remember the Maine; The Culture of the Taironas; South of Yesterday; Columbus Came Late; and others; also articles in field. With NYU since '37, chmn dept journalism since '41, lecturer cultural functions of press grad sch since '48. Am Anthrop Assn—Am Ethnol Soc — Newspaper Guild — Authors League. Department of Journalism, New York University, Washington Square, NYC 3.

13 MASON, Leonard Edward. Micronesian anthropology. b'13. AB '35—MA '41 (U Minn); '41-44 (Yale). Anthropological field work among Swampy Cree Indians Canada '38, '40; anthropologist economic survey of Micronesia US Commercial Co '46; investigation of Bikini Islanders at Rongerik Atoll Marshall Islands Navy Department '48. Author articles in field. Asso prof anthrop U Hawaii since '47; operational cons Pacific Sci Bd since '47. Am Anthrop Assn(F)—Am Geog Soc(F) — Anthrop Soc Hawaii — Hawaiian Acad Sci. University of Hawaii, Honolulu 14, T.H.†

14 MASON, Lester B. German problem (nineteenth and twentieth Centuries); European history since 1789 (Germany); European conservatism. b'05. AB '29 (Dartmouth Coll); AM '30 (Columbia); PhD '40 (Cornell U); '30-31 (Berlin U, Bonn U); '31-32 (Aix-en-Provence U). Research on German class structure, institutional basis of German conservatism, nineteenth century German political thought, German foreign policy since 1870, political institutions since 1860, economic development, general developments in Germany since 1871; studied American and French conservatism. Author articles in field. With NY State Coll Teachers Buffalo '40-43, asst prof '43-48, prof since '48. Am Polit Sci Assn—Econ Hist Assn—AHA—Foreign Policy Assn. New York State College for Teachers, Buffalo 9.

15 MASON, Mary Gertrude. Far Eastern (China) and modern European history. b'00. PhB '23 (U Chicago); AM '27—PhD '33 (Columbia). Research on European opinion of China during second half of nineteenth century. Author: Western Concepts of China and the Chinese, 1840-1876 '39. Asst prof hist Vassar Coll Poughkeepsie NY since '47. AHA—Am Geog Soc — Inst Pacific Relations — Acad Polit Sci—Far Eastern Assn. Vassar College, Poughkeepsie, N.Y.

16 MASON, Warren P(erry). Ultrasonics; Piezoelectricity; Mechanics; Electrical networks; Dielectrics; Acoustics. b'00. BS '21 (U Kan); MA '24—PhD '28 (Columbia). Research on carrier current telephony, mechanical and acoustical wave propagation, filters, piezoelectric crystals, ultrasonics, electrical filters and networks, dielectrics and acoustics. 120 issued patents dealing with electric wave filters piezoelectric crystals, filters and oscillators and various ultrasonic processes. Author: Electromechanical Transducers and Wave Filters '48; Piezoelectric Crystals and Their Applications to Ultrasonics '49; also articles in field. With Bell Labs since '21, head mechanics research group since '45. Am Phys Soc(F)—Inst Radio Engrs(F)—Acoustical Soc Am(F). Bell Telephone Laboratories, Murray Hill, N.J.

17 MASON, W(illiam) Clark. Copper ores. b'07. BS '29—EM '29 (Mich Coll Mining and Tech). Design and operation of small pilot leaching plants; discovery method for retarding growth of sprouts (trees) on copper cathodes; development laboratory scale model of continuous operating electrolytic cells for accurate prediction of large electrolytic plant capacity to recover copper from leaching solutions. Holds patent in field. Engr Inspiration Consol Copper Co Inspiration Ariz '29-48, metall '40-48; metall engr Merrill Co San Francisco '49-50; cons metall engr since '50. Am Inst Mining Engrs. H: 220 Mountain Av., Piedmont 11, Cal.†

18 MASSA, Frank. Electro-acoustics; Sonar; Acoustics, ultrasonics. b'06. BS '27—MS '28 (MIT). Developed numerous electro-acoustic apparatus including loud speakers, microphones, sound-powered telephones, special instruments; originated more than 100 types of underwater sound transmitters and receivers for use in submarine warfare; designed and constructed hydrophones, underwater transducers and special ultrasonic and other equipment. Holds 50 patents in field of electro-acoustics. Author: Acoustic Design Charts '42. Co-author: Applied Acoustics '34. Research engr Radio Corp Am Camden NJ '28-40; dir acoustical engring div Brush Development Co '40-45; electro-acoustic cons and dir Massa Labs Inc since '45. Acoustical Soc Am(F)), past mem exec council—Inst Radio Engrs. 5 Fottler Rd., Hingham, Mass.

19 MASSER, Harry L. Public utilities (natural gas); Gas manufacture; Synthetic rubber; Mechanical computing instruments. b'90. BS in Chem Engring '14 (U Calif). Gas engr Los Angeles Gas and Elec Corp '24-28, vp and exec engr since '28; exec vp dir So Calif Gas Co since '37; in charge constrn and operation of Govt Synthetic Rubber Plant SR No 44; dir Los Angeles Gas and Electric Corp, Los Angeles Lighting Co, Jas H Knapp Co., indsl gas furnaces. Pacific Coast Gas Assn (pres '45). 810 S. Flower St., Los Angeles.

20 MASSEY, Mark F(uller). Horology; Mechanical engineering (Ordnance). b'89. Student '09-12, '14-15 (U Kan); '19 (George Washington U). Ordnance engr Office Chief Ordnance Research and Development Div Dept of Army Washington since '42. Am Ordnance Assn — Horol Inst Am — Horol Guild Greater Washington—Nat Assn Watch Clock Collectors (chmn membership com)—British Horol Inst.

21 MASSEY, William Clifford. Lower California (Linguistics, archaeology, ethnology and history). b'17. AB '40 —grad work (U Calif). Field work in archeology California '37-39, Baja Calif '41, '46-49. Author articles in field. Teaching asst dept geog U Calif '46, dept anthrop '47-49; instr anthropology U Wash since '50; dir North Mexican Center for Anthropology since '53. Soc Am Archeol—Sigma Xi. Department of Anthropology, University of Washington, Seattle 5.

22 MASTERS, Charles Otto. Mosquito control. b'13. AB '38—MS '40 (Western Reserve U). Author: The Selective Breeding Habits of Mosquitoes as Correlated with Specific Gravity, The Military Surgeon '43; Some Notes on the Ability of Mosquito Pupae to Survive Exposure to Air, Mosquito News (vol 8) '48. Ohio Acad Sci—Nat Malaria Soc—Am Mosquito Control Assn. 4357 Jennings Road, Cleveland 9.

23 MASUR, Gerhard. Simon Bolivar; History of modern Europe; Latin American history; History of ideas. Studies of 19th Century Germany, history of ideas and historiography; late 18th and early 19th centuries, Independence movement, contemporary

Latin America, particularly Colombia, Venezuela, Peru and Ecuador. b'01. Student '19-25 (U Berlin, U Marburg); PhD summa cum laude '25 (U Berlin). Author: Rankes Begriff der Weltgeschichte '26; Friedrich Julius Stahl '30; Goethe '39; Simon Bolivar '48. Privat-dozent U Berlin '30-35; tech adv to Minister Edn, Bogota, Colombia '36-38; head lang dept Escuela Normal Superior, Bogota '38-45; prof hist Sweet Briar Coll since '47. Ateneo de Bogota—AHA-AAUP. Sweet Briar College, Va.

10 MATEER, Florence (Edna). Psychosomatic medicine (Psychological factors); Endocrinology (Behavior aspects); Child psychology. b'87. AM '14—PhD '16 (Clark U); '11-14 (Vineland NJ Training Sch). Author: Child Behavior '18; The Unstable Child '24; Just Normal Children '29; Glands and Efficient Behavior '35; also articles in field. Private practice as cons psychol with assos Psychological Service and Merryheart Sch since '21; vis prof in clin psychol Grad Sch of Associated Claremont Colls Claremont Cal '47-50 prof since 50; vis prof Pomona Coll '48-50; clin psychol Pub Schs Pomona Cal since '47. AAAS(F)—O Acad Sci (F)—Am Psychol Assn—Assn Consulting Psychol—NEA—O Ednl Research Assn. P.O Box 429, Claremont, Cal.

11 MATENKO, Percy. German-American literary relations; Ludwig Tieck; Old Yiddish. b'01. BA '24—MA '25 (Toronto U); PhD '33 (Columbia). Worked on unpublished correspondence of German romanticist Ludwig Tieck, and topics connected with him and other German romanticists; studying influence of Tieck on America and opposite phase; completed a study of poetic paraphrase in old Yiddish of Abraham-Isaac sacrifice story (with Sloan); research on Goethe, Schiller, and Byron translations of Saaling album, Tieck's diary fragment of 1803 and his novelle Eine Sommerreise, his relations with Russia and Austria. Author: Ludwig Tieck-Friedrich von Raumer Letters (with Zeydel) '30; Tieck and Solger '33; Letters of Ludwig Tieck Hitherto Unpublished 1792-1853 (with Zeydel and Fife) '37; also articles in field. Instr to asso prof German Bklyn Coll since '30. Mod Lang Assn—Yiddish Sci Inst. Fellowship in German Columbia '26-27. Brooklyn College, Bedford Av. and Av. H, Brooklyn.†

12 MATHER, Deane Winslow. Wildlife. b'10. BS '32 (NY State Coll Forestry); '39 (U Mich). Author articles in field. With US Forest Service since '33, wildlife specialist regional office Fla Nat Forests adjacent states since '47. Am Soc Mammologists—Wildlife Soc—Soc Am Foresters—Am Museum Nat Hist. U.S. Forest Service, Box 739, Ocala, Fla.†

13 MATHER, Eugene. Beef-cattle production (Geographic aspects); Nebraska Sandhills Region (Geography). b'18. AB '40—MS '41 (U Ill); '35-38 (U Ia); PhD '51 (U Wis). Asso prof dept geo and geol U Ga since '51. Assn Am Geog—Sigma Xi. Department of Geography and Geology, University of Georgia, Athens, Ga.†

14 MATHERS, Frank C(urry). Electrochemistry (Addition agents in electroplating, metal refining); Rarer elements (Tellurium, selenium). b'81. AB—AM '05 (Ind U); PhD '07 (Cornell U). Author articles in field. Holder US Patents. Prof Ind U since '23. Am Electrochem Soc (past pres). Chemistry Department, Indiana University, Bloomington, Ind.

15 MATHESON, George Wilson. Law of agency and damages. b'94. AB '14

(Columbia); LLB '17 (St Lawrence U); LLD '26 (St John's U). Author: Principles of Law of Agency '21; Cases on Law of Agency '22; Cases on Law of Damages '22. Dean St John's U Sch of Law since '25. Am Arbitration Assn (arbitrator)—Am Bar Assn —Brooklyn Bar Assn (chmn com legal edn; mem com coop with young lawyers, post admission legal edn, post war readjustments)—Nassau Bar Assn (chmn com vet adjustment; mem membership com)—NY State Bar Assn (mem com legal edn; mem membership com)—Joint Conf Legal Edn NY State (mem exec com; chmn arbitration com)—Am Law Inst—NEA. 96 Schermerhorn St., Brooklyn 2.

16 MATHESON, Robert. Entomology (Medical); Mosquitoes. b'81. BS '06 —MS '07—PhD '11 (Cornell U). Author: Handbook of the Mosquitoes of North America '45; Medical Entomology '32; Laboratory Guide in Entomology '39; Entomology '44; also articles in field. Prof entomol Cornell U since '14; cons health sec TVA. AAAS(F)—Entomol Soc Am—Am Soc Parasitol—Am Assn Econ Entomol— Am Soc Tropical Med—Washington Acad Sci—Phi Kappa Phi—Sigma Xi. 204 Parkway, Cayuga Heights, Ithaca, N.Y.

17 MATHEWS, John Joseph. Indians (Osage). b'95. AB '20 (U Okla); BA '23 (Oxford U); '23 (U Geneva). Research on assumption of duality of Osage Indian, effect of this assumption upon struggle with European culture and Christianity. Author: Wah-Kon-Tah, The Osage and the White Man's Road '32; Talking to the Moon '45. Phi Beta Kappa. Guggenheim F '39-40, The Blackjacks, Pawhuska, Okla.

18 MATHEWS, Joseph Howard. Scientific crime detection. b'81. BS '03—AM '05 (U Wis); AM '06—PhD '08 (Harvard). Author articles in field. Prof chem U Wis, chmn dept, dir course in chemistry '19-52; prof emeritus since '52. Commd capt Ordnance Dept US Army '17, maj '18. AAAS(F)—Am Chem Soc—Sigma Xi— Phi Kappa Phi. 128 Lathrop St., Madison, Wis.©

19 MATHEWS, Joseph J(ames). Modern European diplomatic history; History of journalism (Gathering and distribution of foreign news, war news and censorship). b'08. AB '30—AM '31 (Duke U); PhD '35 (U Pa). Author: Egypt and the Formation of the Anglo-French Entente of 1904 '39; also articles in field. Prof hist Emory U since '46, chmn hist dept since '48. Commd lt jg, advanced to lt comdr, US Naval Reserve; research historian Office Quartermaster Gen US War Dept '42-43; on active duty '43-46 US Navy Dept in charge of hist program Naval Bur of Ordnance and ordnance activities; for Office Quartermaster Gen War Dept made studies of training and officer procurement problems, and study of development of quartermaster replacement training centers '42. AHA—So Hist Assn—Soc Am Hist—Phi Beta Kappa. Department of History, Emory University, Ga.

20 MATHEWS, Ted Corbet. Mining (Sub-arctic, arctic); permafrost. b'10. BS (U Wash); B Mining Engring (U Alaska). Research on sub-arctic and arctic exploration for minerals and petroleum; research on permanently frozen ground and its effect on mining and exploration. Mgr Am Creek Exploration Co '38-40; mgr Gold Mines Ltd '40-42; engr Northwest Service Command and Fairbanks dist engr US Engrs Dept '43-45; supt and asst project mgr Arctic Contractors since

'46. AIMME—Arctic Inst NA—Am Geophys Union. Box 2061, Fairbanks, Alaska.

21 MATHIEU, Rosella Feher, (Mrs. Aron M). Herbs (Fragrant-leaved plants). b'06. Student (O State U, U Cincinnati). Work on fragrant leaved plants which hold their odor when dry and which may suitably be added to various formulae for sachets and pot-pourris; experiment and research in finding unusual herbs of this type which may be grown in Ohio. Author: The Herb Grower's Complete Guide; articles in field. Lecturer on herbs. Herb Soc Am. Fragrant Herb Farm, 3744 Section Rd., Silverton 36, O.†

22 MATSON, Gustave Albin. Blood banks. b'99. AB '27 (U Utah); MA '29 (U Kan); PhD '35 (Wash U St Louis). Author article: Blood Grouping of Mummies '36. Co-author articles: (with H F Schrader) Blood Grouping Among the Blackfeet and Blood Tribes of American Indians '33; (with Schrader) The Distribution of the Four Blood Groups Among the Ute Indians of Utah '41; (with K Landsteiner, A S Wiener) Distribution of Rh Factor in American Indians 42, and others. Cons blood bank Latter-Day Saints Hosp '45-48, dir '48-49; cons blood bank Salt Lake Co Gen Hosp Salt Lake City '45-48; now dir Minneapolis War Memorial Blood Bank. Soc Am Bact—Am Pub Health Assn—Utah Acad Sci—Am Assn Phys Anthrop—Am Assn Immunologists—Am Assn Blood Banks (pres '48-49)—AAAS—Internat Soc Hematology—Sigma Xi. War Memorial Blood Bank, 1914 La Salle Av., Mpls 3.

23 MATSON, Howard Oren. Flood control; Irrigation (Gravity and sprinkler); Drainage (Surface). b'02. AB '24 (Cotner Coll Lincoln Neb); BS in AE '27 (U Neb); MS '29 (U Cal). Irrigation and drainage investigations, flood control surveys, studies rainfall-runoff relationships as affected by soil and cover characteristics; sedimentation investigations, planning systems of small detention reservoirs and sediment control structures to reduce agricultural flood damages. Author articles: More Production from Improved Irrigation Practices '43; Benefits of Water Retardation Structures '49; Making a Creek Flow Gently '51. Contributor: US Department of Agriculture Yearbook '48. Erosion control engr Civilian Conservation Corps Ky '33-34; project engr erosion control demonstration Lindale Tex '34-36; regional engr Soil Conservation Service USDA Tex, Okla, Ark, and La '36-45, now acting assistant regional director engring and planning water conservation div. Am Soc AE—Am Geophys Union—Soil Conservation Soc Am—Sigma Tau. Soil Conservation Service, U.S. Department of Agriculture, Box 1898, Ft. Worth 1.

24 MATSON, Theodore M. Traffic engineering. b'03. AB ChE '23—ME '24—EE '25 (Stanford U). Author articles in field. Research asst, asst prof Bur St Traffic Research Yale U '38-43; prof, dir Bur Hwy Traffic Yale since '43; lecturer Traffic Engring Training Sch Harvard U '37, So Traffic Officers Training Sch U Ala '39, Rutgers U '39; instr Nat Inst Traffic Safety Training U Calif '41, Yale U '42, Ohio State U '43, Northwestern U '44-49, Ore State Coll '46; dir Inst Traffic Engrs; mem commn Nat Safety Council, Hwy Research Bd, Am Soc Municipal Engrs, Inst Traffic Engrs. Am Road Builders Assn—Am Pub Works Assn—Sigma Xi. 315 Strathcona Hall, Yale University, New Haven.

10 MATTES, Merrill John. Conservation of historic sites; Early history of western United States. b'10. AB '31 (U Mo); MA '33 (U Kan). Research in historic sites particularly relating to Oregon and California Trail, exploration, western fur trade, Indian wars, railroads, military posts, and homesteading. Author articles in field. Regional historian for Region Two Office Nat Park Service Omaha since '49, hist Mo River Basin Surveys '46-49. Neb State Hist Soc—American Pioneer Trails Assn—Oregon Trail Memorial Assn—SD Hist Soc—Westerners. National Park Service, 307 Federal Building, Omaha, Neb.

11 MATTHEWS, H(arry) Alexander. Music. b'79. Studied music with father; MusD hon '20 (Muhlenberg Coll); MusD hon '24 (U Pa). Wrote over 200 compositions in music, including sacred and secular contatas, anthems, duets, solos, secular songs, piano and organ pieces. Principal works: (cantatas) Life Everlasting; The Conversion; The Story of Christmas; The Triumph of the Cross; The City of God; (hist pageants) The Song of America; Easter Pageant; (opera) Hades, Inc.; (operetta) Play the Game. Tchr in Phila since '00; organist and choirmaster St Stephen's Ch Phila; condr Phila Music Club Chorus; head theoretical dept Clarke Conservatory of Music. Am Guild Organists (asso) —Am Soc Composers Authors and Pubs. 20 S.18th St., Phila. ©

12 MATTHEWS, John L(arkin). Ophthalmology (Aviation) (Sunglasses). b'08. AB '29—MD '33 (U Tex). Author articles: Use of Goggles and protective lenses by flying personnel; Use of Absorptive lenses: Facts for the profession; Some considerations in the selection of flying sun glasses; and others. Dept Ophthal A̅A̅F Sch Aviation Med Randolph Field Tex '42-45, chief dept '43-45; ophthal cons Brooke Army Hosp Fort Sam Houston since '46; asso prof clin ophthal grad sch med Baylor U since '49; asso. prof ophthal clin faculty San Antonio br U Tex since '50. Am Bd Ophthal(Diplomate)—Am Acad Ophthal and Otolaryngology(F)—Assn Research Ophthal—Aero Med Assn—Armed Forces -NRC Vision Com—Nat Soc Prevention Blindness. 414 Navarro St., San Antonio 5.

13 MATTHEWS, Joseph Brown. Communism; Oriental languages. b'94. AB; MA; BD; STM; PhD. Author: Hymnal in Malay language '21; Partners in Plunder '35; and others; also articles in field. Dir research spl com Un-American Activities '38-45; pvt research on Communism since '45; Chief Investigator Ill Legislature Subversive Activities Investigation Commn '49; Research on Communism Wash State Legislature '48; Research on Communism Mass Legislature '49; Research on Communism in labor unions US House of Representatives '48; Lecturer on Communism American Legion '47-49. Royal Geog Soc. 311 W. 56th St., NYC.

14 MATTHEWS, Samuel A. Physiology (Endocrinology-respiration, thyroid, sex cycles). b'02. BS '23—MA '24 (Boston U); MA—PhD '25-28 (Harvard U). Special research projects Scripps Institute La Jolla California on endocrines and respiratory metabolism in fishes '41, thyroid gland of fishes Bermuda Biological Station '47. Author articles in field. Asst prof biol Williams Coll '37-43, prof since '43; instr Marine Biol Lab Woods Hole '32-40. Am Assn Anat—Am Soc Zool—Am Physiol Soc—Marine Biol Lab Corp—Bermuda Biol Assn—Sigma Xi. Williams College, Williamstown, Mass.

15 MATTHEWS, Velma Dare. Mycology; Camellias. b'04. AB '25—AM '27—PhD '30—research '32-34 (U NC); research '36 (U Va). Author: Studies on the Genus Pythium '31; Saprolegniales, North American Flora, Vol II '37; also articles in field. Prof biol head dept Coker Coll Hartsville S.C. since '35. SC Acad Sci (vp '41-45, pres '46-47)—NC Acad Sci—Bot Soc Am—AAAS—Mycol Soc—Am Fern Soc —Sigma Xi. Coker College, Hartsville, S.C.

16 MATTHEWS, William. English and American speech, dialects and slang; History of shorthand. b'05. BA '29—MA '31—PhD '34 (U London). Author: Cockney, Past and Present '38; Diary of Dudley Ryder '39; English Pronunciation and Shorthand '43; Our Soldiers Speak '43; American Diaries '45; British Diaries '49. Asst prof U Calif '39, asso prof '43, prof since '48. Modern Lang Assn—Linguistic Soc—Am Dialect Soc (adv bd '39-40, western sec '46). Guggenheim fellow '46-47. English Department, University California, Los Angeles 24.

17 MATTIMORE, John Dalton. Piping engineering. b'99. ME '22 (Stevens Inst Tech). Research on welding pipe fittings and flanges, design test and application of valves and fittings for severe or unusual service. Invented anti-freeze draw off valve for liquid storage tanks, streamlined reciprocating plug type stop valve, large capacity valve for ultra-high temperature service; co-inventor pipe welding back-up ring. Author articles in field. Project engr Thomas E Murray Inc '22-27; Hedges Walsh Weidner Boiler Co '28; engring econ Combustion Engring Corp '29; asst mgr engring products div Walworth Co '30-32, asst to chief engr '33-37, works engr '37-42; dir research Tube Turns Inc '42-46, chief engr since '46. ASME —Am Welding Soc—Soc Exptl Stress Analysis—Am Petroleum Inst—Am Soc Heat and Ventilating Engrs — Am Standards Assn (sect com B16) — Mfgrs Standardization Soc Valve and Fittings Industry. Tube Turns, Inc., 224 E. Broadway, Louisville 1, Ky.

18 MATTINGLY, John W(aller). Steel (Tubular); Pipes (Cutting); Tubing (Fabrication). b'20. BS (AE) '48 (U Ill). Design and production planning of machines and structures for use of tubular materials, resulting in weight reduction, low equipment and tooling costs, high rate of production and simplified materials handling. Pres Heath Engring Co since '50. Am Soc AE. Heath Engineering Co., P.O. Box 69, Fort Collins, Colo. H: 503 S. Grant.

19 MATZ, Kenneth Rule. Carbon processing; Molding (Metal powder). b'07. Student '25-26 (Heidelberg U); '26-28 (Pharm) (O Northern U); '42-43 (Toledo U). Development analytical techniques for adaptation to new products and raw materials; application photomicrography and chemical microscopy to study of carbon products; quality control graphite and metal graphite brush; product control lampblack, tar, and pitch production. With Nat Carbon Co Fostoria O'29-49, head of brush development engring Cleveland Works since '49. Nat Soc Profl Engrs—O Soc Profl Engrs—O State Pharm Assn. Profl chem engr O., Am Soc Metals—Am Inst Mining and Metall Engrs. National Carbon Co., Inc., W. 117th St. and Madison Av., Lakewood 7. O.

20 MAUCHLY, John W(illiam). Electrical and electronic computers; Geophysical statistics. b'07. Pioneered with J P Eckert Jr in development of first electronic integrator and computer, Eniac; developed initial plans for Edvac, an improved electronic computer; co-designer of Binac and Univac, the latter a simplified standard general-purpose electronic computer for commercial and scientific use. Inventor devices for electric and electronic computing. Author articles in field. Partner Electronic Control Co since '46; pres Eckert-Mauchly Computer Corp since '47. Cons Naval Ordnance Lab White Oaks Md '44-46. Am Phys Soc—Franklin Inst Phila—Am Geophys Union—Inst Radio Engrs — AIEE — Inst Math Statis — Am Meteorol Soc—Am Statis Assn—Assn Computing Machinery (vp '47, pres '48) —Phi Beta Kappa—Sigma Xi. 219 St. Marks St., Phila 4.

21 MAUDLIN, C(ecil) V(earl). Economics; Anthracite; Import tariffs; Matches; Wood pulp; Electric power; Industrial management. b'95. BS in CE '17 (Purdue). In charge coordination and operations US Forest Products Laboratory '19-22; business manager American Forestry Association and American Forests and Forest Life Magazine '22-28; managing director and treas Bureau Applied Economics '28-38; in charge US Senate Investigation of Food Products '31; special expert Anthracite Coal Industry Commission Commonwealth of Pennsylvania '37. Sigma Xi. Mills Bldg., Washington 6.†©

22 MAUGHAN, William. Forest management; Forestry (Timber and timberland appraisals, forest valuation and surveying, southern lumber production). b'00. BS '25 (U Minn); MF '29 (Yale); (U Mich). Author articles in field. Forester Cary Lumber Co Durham NC since '48; ind cons forester companies and individual timberland owners in Carolina since '39. Soc Am Foresters—NC Forestry Assn—Sigma Xi—Gamma Sigma Delta. Cary Lumber Company, Durham, N.C.

23 MAURER, David W. Argot and slang (Chiefly criminal); Linguistics. b'06. BA '28—MA '29—PhD '35 (O State U). Author: The Technical Argot of the Pickpocket and Its Relation to the Culture Pattern '47; The Big Con—The Story of the Confidence Man and the Confidence Game '40; The Dictionary of American Criminal Argots '39; Narcotics and Narcotic Addiction '53; and others; Prof lang lit U Lsvl since '37; staff cons specialist indsl edn Joseph E Seagram & Sons Inc '42-52. Mod Lang Assn Am—Am Dialect Soc—Phi Beta Kappa. The University of Louisville, Lsvl. 8.†

24 MAUTNER, Franz Heinrich. German literature since 1750; Aesthetics and philosophy of language. b'02. PhD '26 (U Vienna); '23-25 (U Heidelberg). Research on history and aesthetic meaning of plays on words as a stylistic device, the aphorism as a literary genre, German writers G Chr Lichtenberg and Ed Moerike, the science of physiognomics in 18th and 19th centuries, history and semantics of the English and German words Nazi, Sozi, Sudetens, Yugos; Biedermeier as a literary period; problems of translating from and into German. Author: Johann Nestroy Und Seine Kunst '38; also articles in field. Lecturer and Chargé du Cours in German Classicism U Besançon France '29-30; asst prof Ind U '39-40, Hobart Coll '41-44, O Wesleyan U '44-48; asso prof German and comparative lit Kenyon Coll since '48. Modern Lang Assn—Am Assn Teachers German — Mod Humanities Research Assn.

25 MAUTNER, Leonard. Television (Transmitters); Radar (IFF, display methods; Electronics (Circuits). b'17. BS in elec engring '39 (MIT); '41-42 (Stevens Inst Tech). Developed improved portable television camera equipment for broadcasting use, use of automatic electronic fade and lap dissolve techniques, research in improved and new display methods for IFF (identification, friend or foe) radar, analysis of video amplifiers for transient response; vice-chairman panel 8 National Television Systems Committee. Granted patents on television and radar. Author: Mathematics for Radio Engineers '47. Television engr NBC '42; staff mem Radiation Lab MIT '42-45; head display sect Combined Research Group NRL (Naval Research Lab) '44-45; mgr television transmitter div A B DuMont Lab '45-48; pres Television Equipment Corp '48-50; cons Hughes Aircraft Co since '50. Inst Radio Engrs (sr mem, mem tech com television—Eta Kappa Nu—Radio Mfrs Assn (chmn studio facilities, television transmitters com '47-50). Research and Development Laboratories, Hughes Aircraft Co., Culver City, Cal.

10 MAUTNER, Steven Etienne. Vibration (Supersonic, mechanical); Aeronautics (Sandwich-type construction). b'95. Student '14 (Polytech Inst Berlin); DS '26 (U Sorbonne). Pioneer in sandwich construction; designed and built sandwich-type wing surface used in US '39; pioneer designer of all-metal pursuit plane '22-25, semi-rigid dirigible '25-26; inventor artificial horizon '26-34; co-designer and builder helicopter with autorotation '36-38. Author articles: Sandwich Construction '44; Sandwich Construction in Gliders; Buckling of Sandwich Type Panels; Bending and Buckling of Sandwich Type Beams '46; Bending and Buckling of Sandwich Beams '48. Chief designer Pioneer Airplane Factory Budapest '17-20; research engr Soc Des Avions Borel France '22-25; chief research lab Societe Zodiac Paris '25-26; tech dir, adminstr Societe La Forge Testard '26-34; constrn engr Rep Compagnie Francaise de Levant of France, Moscow '34-36; tech dir Societe Des Etude et Avions Paris '36-38; vp, chief engr Skydyne Inc Port Jervis since '38. Inst Aeronautical Sci (asso F)—Soc Exptl Stress Analysis—Soaring Soc Am—Am Soc Testing Materials. 170 E. Main St., Port Jervis, N.Y.

11 MAVERICK, Lewis Adams. China (Ancient, economics). b'91. BS '13 (Wash U); EdD '25 (Harvard); PhD '31 (U Cal). Author: China, a Model for Europe '46; Kuan-tzu (in process). Author articles: Chinese influences upon the physiocrats; Hsu Kuang-ch'i, Chinese authority on agriculture; Pierre Poivre, eighteenth century explorer of southeast Asia; (pamphlet) Chinese influences upon Quesnay and Turgot. Instr to asso prof U Cal Los Angeles '21-35; prof econ So Ill U since '46. Am Econ Assn—Midwest Econ Assn—Royal Econ Soc—Am Statis Assn—Econometric Soc—Far Eastern Assn—Am Econ Hist Assn—St Louis Soc Financial Analysts. Southern Illinois University, Carbondale, Ill.⊙

12 MAVIS, Frederic Theodore. Civil, hydraulic and structural engineering. b'01. BS in CE '22—MS '26—CE '32 —PhD '35 (U Ill); '27-28 (Technische Hochschule Karlsruhe, Baden, Germany). Author: The Construction of Nomographic Charts '39; also articles in field. Successively asst prof mechanics and hydraulics, to head of dept, State U Ia, asso dir in charge lab to cons engr, Ia Inst of Hydraulic Research, '28-39; prof and head dept Civ Engring, Pa State Coll, '39-44; prof, head dept Civil Engring Carnegie Inst Tech Pittsburgh since '44. AAAS—ASCE—ASME—Am Soc Testing Materials—Am Soc Engring Edn—Soc Am Mil Engrs—Am Water Works Assn—Am Geophys Union—Newcomen Soc—Tau Beta Pi—Phi Kappa Phi—Sigma Xi. 5816 Elmer St., Pitts 6.†⊙

13 MAVRIS, Nicholas George. Dodecanese Islands (Political history, diplomatic history, folklore); Egyptian folklore; Greece (Modern, folklore, literature). b'99. MD '22 (U Athens Greece); '23-24 (U Paris France); '35-36 (Sorbonne Paris); '37 (Institut de Phonetique Paris). Investigation public records of Paris, Washington, Venice, and Athens for historical documents concerning Dodecanese Islands; compilation and publishing melodies and folk songs of Dodecanese Islands; president Dodecanesian National Council. Author: Historical Archieves of Kassos, Dodecanese (3 vols in Greek) '37-38; The Dodecanesians are not Enemy Aliens '42; The Legal Status of the Dodecanese (in Philellene) '43. Co-author: Dodecanesian Lyre (in Greek) '28. Author article: Certain Misconceptions in Relation to the Eastern Mediterranean and Greece '46, and others. Edieor: The Greek Dodecanese '44. Contributor: Encyclopedia Americana; Encyclopedia Britannica; Great Greek Encyclopedia; Dutch Encyclopedia. Visiting prof hist U Wyo '45; prof modern Greek folklore Ecole Libre des Hautes Etudes (Franco-Belgian U) NYC '46; editor Byzantina-Metabyzantina NYC since '46; lectr modern Greek lit Columbia U '47-48; gov-gen Dodecanese Islands '48-50; mem Greek Parliament '51. Dodecanesian League Am(hon pres)—Soc Byzantine and Modern Greek Studies(founder, sec gen)—Soc Hist Studies Greece(founder)—Am Acad Polit Sci—Am Folklore Soc—Soc Greek Hist Studies NY—Hist and Ethnol Soc Greece—Greek Folklore Soc—Soc Acad d'Hist Internationale —Lit Soc Parnassos of Greece. Hotel Grande Bretaque, Athens, Greece.

14 MAXFIELD, Frederick Austin. Torpedoes. b'08. BS in EE '29—PhD '38 (U Wis); MS (in physics) '34 (U Pittsburgh). Development electrical and electronic components of torpedoes; in charge research and development torpedoes and torpedo launchers; studies on underwater acoustics, controls, propulsion and hydrodynamics. Author article: Propulsion Systems '49. Engr Bur Ordnance Navy Dept Washington '43-46, tech head torpedo br, responsible for all research and development of torpedoes and launchers '46-52; mgr research Given Mfg Co since '52. Am Inst EE—APS—Tau Beta Pi—Sigma Xi. 1523 L St. N.W., Washington 5. H: 36 E Woodbine St., Chevy Chase 15, Md.

15 MAXFIELD, Joseph Pease. Acoustics; Sound recording and reproduction. b'87. SB '10 (MIT). Research and development in sounds, auditorium acoustics, microphone techniques, sound recording, transmission, and reproduction, and military sound triangulation; credited with major developments of Orthophonic Victrola and electric sound recording systems for phonograph, motion picture and radio industries. Author: The Voice, Its Production and Reproduction (with Douglas Stanley) '33; also articles in field. Cons engr Elec Research Products Inc '29-33, staff engr '33-36, dir comml engring '36-41; supt comml engring Western Electric Co Inc '41-42; prof and dir div phys war research Duke Univ '42-46; Bell Tel Lab Inc '46-47 engring cons, ind cons '47-48;

supt scientist US Navy Electronic Lab San Diego Cal since '48. Sigma Xi—Am Phys Soc(F)—Acoustical Soc Am(F)—AIEE(F)—Soc Motion Picture Engrs (F)—Am Geog Soc(F)—Inst Radio Engrs (sr mem). 665 Catalina Blvd., San Diego, Cal.

16 MAXFIELD, Kathryn Erroll. Psychology of blindness; Visually handicapped children (Developmental problems, vocational guidance). b'95. BA '18 (Mt Holyoke Coll); MA '23—PhD '36 (Columbia). Author: The Blind Child and his Reading; also articles in field. Dir research and personnel Perkins Inst '32-34; dir Arthur Sunshine Home and Nursery Sch for Blind '34-38; psychol cons agencies for blind; cons psychol Student Life Dept City Coll. Am Psychol Assn(F) — AAAS(F) — NYAS(F) — Metropolitan NY Assn Applied Psychol —Eastern Psychol Assn—NY State Psychol Assn—Am Assn Workers Blind. Dept. Student Life, City College, 139th St. and Convent Av., NYC 31.

17 MAXFIELD, Myles. Physical chemistry (Nerve proteins). b'21. AB '42—MD '45 (Harvard); PhD '50 (MIT). Research in isolation and physico chemical study of proteins of nerve; isolation and study of axon filaments (the protein of neurofibrils). Author: Studies of Nerve Proteins: Isolation and Physico-chemical characterization of a Protein from Lobster Nerve '51. Postdoctoral fellow Nat Inst Health '48-50; research asso biol MIT '50-52, asst prof biophysics since '52, advisor to premed students since '52. Sigma Xi—AAAS—Electron Microscope Soc Am—Am Crystallographic Soc. Biology Department 16-509, Massachusetts Institute of Technology, Cambridge.

18 MAXON, Marcus Arthur. Ornamental horticulture (Plant materials); Native wild flowers (Propagation, life cycles, culture). b'10. BS '37—MS '39—research fellow '37-39 (Ia State Coll); '46-48 (Mich State). Author articles in field. Asst prof hort SD State Coll '48-52. 903 Boone St., Webster City, Ia.

19 MAXSON, John H(aviland). Petroleum geology; Geomorphology. b'06. BS '28—MS—PhD '31 (Calif Inst Tech). Seventeenth International Geological Congress Moscow USSR '37. Author articles in field. Instr Geol Calif Inst Tech '31-35; pet geol Govt Turkey '36-37; asst prof geol Calif Inst Tech '38-46 mil leave '41-45; Rocky Mt Div geol The Bay Petroleum Corp '47-48; mgr Rocky Mt Div Andersen-Prichard Oil Corp '48-50; pres Aerial Exploration Company since '50. Second lt corps engrs res '35, air corps res '38, asst G-2 4th Air Force '41, class dir AAF Intelligence Sch '42, chief training br asst chief Air Staff Intelligence War Dept '43, European and North African Theater '44-45, lt col air res '44. Geol Soc Am(F)—Paleontol Soc Am—Am Geog Soc—Soc Econ Geol—Am Assn Pet Geol—Rocky Mt Assn Geol—Am Inst Mining Metall Engrs—Am Geophy Union—Soc Vertebrate Paleontol—Geol Soc Turkey—Sigma Xi. 1585 Kearney St., Denver 7.†

20 MAY, Luke S. Crime (Detection). b'86. Student (pub schs, bus coll and Gordon Acad Salt Lake City). Inventor system identification by fingernails, system bullet classification, system handwriting identification; president Northwest International Anticrime Conference '21-25. Author: Scientific Murder Investigation '33; Crime's Nemesis '35; Field Manual of Detective Science '39. Editor Luke May's dept in True Detective Mysteries. Criminologist since '10; pres Revelare Internat Secret Service '14-32; dir Scientific Detective Labs since '22; pres Inst Sci Criminology since '28; adviser to faculty com Northwestern U Law Sch '29; instr criminal investigation, examination questioned documents U Wash '22-24, U Ore '27, Willamette U '30-31; mem commn which organized Ore State Police '31; as acting chief of detectives reorganized Seattle Detective Dept '33-34. Pacific Coast Internat Assn Law Enforcement Ofcls (pres emeritus, life mem, chmn com criminal investigation and evidence)—Internat Assn Chiefs Police (asso)—World Assn Detectives (asso) —Ore Dist Attys Assn(hon life)—Pros Atty Assn Wash(hon life). Henry Bldg Seattle 1.

10 MAY, Orville Edward. Agricultural and food chemistry; Fermentation. b'01. AB '24—MS '26—PhD '29 (George Washington U). Research chem fermentation US Dept Agr Washington '23-36; direction administrn research on utilization agrl products US Dept Agr Urbana, Ill, Peroia, Ill, Washington '36-46; vicepres Coca-Cola Co Atlanta Ga since '48. Am Inst Chem (F)—Am Chem Soc—Am Oil Chem Soc—Inst Food Technol—Am Pub Health Assn—AAAS —Sigma Xi. 310 North Av. N.W., Atlanta.

11 MAY, Samuel Chester. Public administration; Resource planning; Civilian defense; War mobilization; Health insurance; Municipal government. b'87. LLB '12 (Yale U Law Sch); MA '20 (Columbia U). US delegate to Union of Cities Paris France '25; US delegate to International Congress of Local Authorities London '32, Berlin '34, 36; US delegate International Institute Administrative Sciences Warsaw '36, Bucharest '38; State representative to San Francisco Bay Region Metropolitan Defense Council since '41. Author articles in field. Prof polit sci U Calif since '30, dir Bur Pub Adminstrn since '30; exec com Calif State Council Defense since '40. Am Soc Pub Adminstrn— Am Polit Sci Assn—Calif Acad Sci— Western Govt Research Assn (pres since '47)—Social Sci Research Council—Internat City Mgrs Assn (research com)—Institut Internat des Sciences Administratives. 2330 Vine St., Berkeley.

12 MAY, Stacy. International trade and development; War and defense planning and economics; Public control of business (Antitrust, public utilities). b'96. PhD '25 (Brookings Grad Sch Econ and Govt Washington). Director Bureau Research and Statistics of Advisory Commission to the Council of National Defense, Office of Production Management and Statistics Division War Production Board '40-43; director Bureau Planning and Statistics War Production Board '43-44; special representative of War Department to combine US and United Kingdom war procurement data '41; joint economic analyst Combined Shipping Adjustment Boards '42-43; member consumers advisory board NRA '34-35; Business Advisory Council for Department Commerce '40-42. Author or co-author: Control of Wages '23; Public Control of Business '30. Economist for the Rockefeller office and the Internat Basic Economy Corp since '47; dir research Internat Development Adv Bd '50-51; cons The President's Com on Govt Reorgn '53. Am Econ Assn (ex com '41-43)—Nat Planning Assn (chmn Internat com '44-47)— Am Statis Assn (vp '47) — Council Foreign Relations (com on studies) Room 5600, 30 Rockefeller Plaza, NYC 20.

13 MAYCEN, Rudolph Frank. Liquified petroleum gases. b'08. BS in civil engring '35—'41-42 (Ill Inst Tech); Certificate Gas Engring '38 (Columbia); MBA (Northwestern U); since '50 (LaSalle U). Studies in combustion liquified petroleum gases; utilization; industrial applications of gases; research on reformation of natural gases. Author manual in field. Plant engr Peoples Gas Light & Coke Co Chicago '38-45; engring cons liquified petroleum gas div Shell Oil Co Inc NYC '45-47; lectr liquified petroleum gas short course U Minn '49-50; gen mgr, sec Blue Star Gas & Appliance Co since '47; cons engr since 43. Am Gas Assn—Liquified Petroleum Gas Assn—Western Soc Engrs— Am Soc CE. 290 Harding Av., Des Plaines, Ill.

14 MAYER, Charles A(lbert). Asphalt (Paving engineering). b'96. Ed pvt schooling. Inspector and field engr, paving constrn in eastern and so states Dow & Smith '19-35; mem firm A W Dow Inc bituminous paving cons '35-46; adminstrv engring asst to gen mgr The Asphalt Inst since '46; paving engr for Shreve Lamb & Harmon and Fay, Spofford & Thorndike on 8 off-continent US Army air bases, designing bases, directing field work and writing completion reports '43-44. Am Soc Testing Materials— ASCE—Asphalt Paving Technol Assn —Nat Hwy Research Bd (asso). 801 2nd Av, NYC 17.

15 MAYER, Claudius Francis. Medicine (Nomenclature, Renaissance, history); Medical incunabula, lexicography, and bibliography. b'99. BA '17 (High Gymnasium, Eger, Hungary); '14-17 (Coll Cistercian Sem)— '17-18 (U Innsbruck); MD '25 (U Budapest); '25-28 (Pathol Inst Budapest, Urological Clinic, Budapest)— '28 (Karl-Sudhof Institut, Leipzig); scholarship '28 (Hungarian Govt for study abroad); certificate biochem '31 (NY Post grad Med Sch). Assistant in organization of International Health Exhibit Budapest '27; consultant in medical history and literature for Public Health Museum Budapest '28-30; research on 16th century medicine and its literature '41, on medical nomenclature '40; compilation of an encyclopedic terminology of medicine '40. Author articles in field. Ed Index-Catalogue Surgeon-General's Library, Army Med Library, since '32. AAAS—Hist Sci Soc—Assn Hist Med —Med Library Assn. Awarded prize for essay on respiration of skin Budapest '23. Army Medical Library, 7th & Independence Av., S.W., Washington. H: 5513 39th St. N.W.†

16 MAYER, Harold M(elvin). Urban and transportation geography; City planning research. b'16. BS '36 (Northwestern); MS '37 (Washington U); PhD '43 (U Chicago). Author: Railway Pattern of Metropolitan Chicago '43. Co-author: Master Plan of Residential Land Use of Chicago '43; also articles in field. Zoning specialist Chicago Land Use Survey '40-41; research planner Chicago Plan Commn '41-45; geog OSS '43; chief Div Planning Analysis Phila City Planning Commn '45-48; lecturer Geog U Pa '47-48; dir research Chicago Plan Commn '48-50; lectr geog Northwestern U '49-50; asst prof geog U Chicago since '50. Am Inst Planners—Am Soc Planning Officials—Assn Am Geog— Am Soc Profl Geog—Am Geog Soc— Sigma Xi—Phi Beta Kappa. department of Geography, University of Chicago, Chgo. 37.†

17 MAYER, Joseph E. Statistical mechanics; Ballistics (Interior, terminal); Theories of liquids; Phase transitions; Electron affinities; Ionic crystals. b'04. BS '24 (Calif Inst Tech); PhD '27 (U Calif); Internat Edn Bd Research fellow '29-30 (U Gottingen Germany). Author: Statistical Mechanics (with Maria Goeppert Mayer) '40. Prof Inst Nuclear Studies dept chem U Chicago since '45; cons Ballistic Research Lab Aberdeen Proving Ground Ordnance Dept US Army since '42; ed Jour Chem Physics '40-52. Am Chem Soc—NY Acad Scis—Nat Acad Scis—Tau Beta Pi—Sigma Xi. Department of Chemistry, University of Chicago, Chicago 37.⊚

18 MAYER, Leo Kenneth. Labor economics; Transportation. b'97. LLB '18 (NY Law Sch). Author: The Receivership Plan for Labor '46; History of Municipal Railways '25; Savings Bank Life Insurance '35; The Enigma of the Rail Rate '37; Depressions Since the Civil War. Comptroller dir indsl relations Manufacturers Machine & Tool Co '42-49; executive coordinator De Jur-Amsco Corp Long Island City NY since '49. Royal Econ Soc(F) —Royal Statis Soc(F)—Am Econ Assn —Econometric Soc—Nat Assn Cost Accountants—Inst Internal Auditors— Tax Exec Inst—Am Accounting Assn —NY Indsl Relations Club—Am Management Assn—Soc Advan Mgfr—Nat Panel Arbitrators. De Jur-Amsco Corp., Long Island City, N.Y. H: 6 Polo Road, Great Neck, N.Y.†

19 MAYER, Walter Edwin. educational psychology; Social psychology; Psychological theory; Attitudes. b'95. AB '20 (Ohio No U); MEd '34—PhD '39 (U Pittsburgh). Author: Study of Attitudes (doctoral dissertation). Faculty Youngstown College Ohio since '47, professor and head department of psychology since '48. Doctoral Assn Educators H: 372 Fairgreen Av., Youngstown, O.†⊚

20 MAYERS, Martin A. Mechanical engineering; Combustion; Gas turbine; Rocket motor. b'06. BS '27—MS in ME '30 (Yale). Research on combustion of solid fuel, reactivity of coke, carbonization of coal, properties blast furnace coke, combustion underfeed stokers, high intensity oil-fired combustor for gas turbine set, heat transfer design, thermodynamic cycle analysis of gas turbine, oxygen plant cycles, elbow combustion chamber, mechanical design of rocket thrust cylinders. Author articles in field. Mem staff Coal Research Lab Carnegie Inst Tech Pittsburgh '30-42; development engr Engring Research and Development Dept Elliott Co Jeannette Pa '42-45; engr Spl Projects Dept M W Kellogg Co '45-51; chief engr Spl Projects Burns and Roe since '51. Am Soc Testing Materials—Eastern States Blast Furnace Coke Oven Assn —Am Inst Mining Metall Engrs—Am Chem Soc—ASME—Yale Engring Assn. Listed as one of ten ablest chemists or chem engrs in field of Gas & Fuel Chemistry, Chicago Sect., Am Chem Soc '47. 50 Parker Av., Maplewood, N.J.

21 MAYERS, May R. Industrial health (Administration); Occupational diseases and industrial toxicology (Diagnosis and prevention). b'90. AB '11 (Barnard Coll Columbia); AM '13 (Columbia) MD '21 (Coll Phys and Surg Columbia). Assistant director and chief medical unit Division of Industrial Hygiene New York State Department of Labor; research studies in occupational disease diagnosis and prevention, especially lead poisoning, carbon monoxide poisoning, industrial solvents, occupational causes of cancer; consultant in occupational diseases; lecturer on occupational diseases and industrial toxicology to medical students and others. Author articles: Lean Anemia '26; Lead Poisoning and Compensation '46; Diagnostic Problems in Occupational Diseases '47; Occupational Causes of Cancer '50; and others. Co-author reports and bulletins of NY State Dept Labor. Contbr: chapter on Lead Poisoning to Oxford Medicine (in press). With div indsl hygiene NY State Dept Labor since '23; asst in indsl medicine Harvard Sch Pub Health '31-33. AMA—NY County Med Soc—Am Pub Health Assn(F)—Am Indsl Hygiene Assn—Conf Govtl Indsl Hygienists. Division of Industrial Hygiene, N.Y. State Dept. of Labor, 80 Centre St., NYC 13. H: 214 E. 18th St., NYC 3.

10 MAYHAM, Stephen Lorenzo. Perfumes and cosmetics. b'92. PhB '13 (Union Coll); student (Brooklyn Poly Inst, Albany Law Sch). Author: Marketing Cosmetics '38; also articles in field. With Toilet Goods Assn Inc since '39, exec vp since '42. Perfumery Importers Assn (exec sec)—Soc Cosmetic Chem. 9 Rockefeller Plaza, NYC 20.

11 MAYNARD, Charles Addison. Magnets (Permanent). b'01. Student '20-23 (U Kan); BS '26 (Taylor U). Design and application permanent magnets to meters, motors, generators, magnetos, loudspeakers, electronic focusing, microphones, phonograph recording and pick-up heads, magnetic separators, holding magnets, and polarized relays. Author articles: Permanent Magnets Have Four Major Jobs '44; Pertinent Facts About Permanent Magnets '49. Co-author article: (with J E Mitch) Permanent Magnet Test Methods and their Validity in Determining Product Performance. Chief engr Ind Steel Products Co '32-47, dir research and engring since '47. Am Inst EE—Instrument Soc Am—Inst Radio Engrs—ASTM. 700 Valparaiso St., Valparaiso, Ind.

12 MAYNARD, Harold Bright. Methods and management engineering (Time and motion, wage incentives, scientific management). b'02. ME '23 (Cornell). Represented Society for Advancement of Management at 8th International Management Congress Stockholm Sweden '47; represented National Management Council at CIOS Executive committee Paris '47, Basel '48. Co-author: (with Lowry, Stegemerten) Time and Motion Study and Formulas for Wage Incentives '27; Effective Foremanship '41; (with Stegemerten) Guide to Methods Improvement '44; (with Stegemerten, Schwab) Methods—Time Measurement '48; also articles in field. Founded Methods Engineering Council Pittsburgh '34, pres since '34, offices also in Kansas City, Bridgeport, Conn. Soc Advancement Mgmt (nat dir '38-44, chmn gen research com '44, exec vp '44-46, pres '46-47)—ASME (mem com standardization of therbligs, process charts and their symbols, chmn work standardization com '48, mgmt com, exec com mgmt div)—Assn Cons Mgmt Engrs (chmn research com since '45) —Nat Mgmt Council (pres '48)—Am Mgmt Assn—Am Arbitration Assn. Awarded Gilbreth Medal '46. 718 Wallace Av., Pitts. 21.†

13 MAYNARD, John Earl. Radio (AM, FM); Radar pulse; Receivers; Television; Electronic computers. b'06. BS in elec engring '29 (U Wash); MS '32 (Union Coll). Granted patents on signal transmission system, resistance network for amplifiers, frequency variation response network, voltage indicating circuit, radio receiver, and calibrating device. Development engr Gen Elec Co '30-47; research engr

Boeing Airplane Co since '47. Inst Radio Engrs(sr mem). H: 3465 W. Mercer Way, Mercer Island, Wash.

14 MAYO, Evans Blakemore. Mining geology; Granite tectonics; Volcanology. b'02. AB '27 (U SD); MA '29 (Stanford); PhD '32 (Cornell). Research in granite tectonics '33-38; mining geology since '38. Author articles in field. Kelowna Exploration Co '40-41, since '46; resident geol Catopaxi Exploration Co '42-46. Mineral Soc Am—Geol Soc Am(F)—AAAS—Am Geophys Union. Kelowna Exploration Company, Hedley, B.C., Can.

15 MAYO, Margot. Folklore. Student pvt schs. Inst Musical Art, Martha Graham Sch. Founder American Folk Group in New York City '33-34, later became American Square Dance Group; released five albums of records of American square dances; collector folklore privately since '30, for Library of Congress during recording trip through Tennessee, Kentucky, North Carolina summer '46; radio guest appearances. Author: The American Square Dance '43; The Margot Mayo Collection of Early American Choral Pieces '49; also articles in field. Editor: Promenade. Teacher folklore, music, dramatics since '35. Mills College of Education since '46, New Sch '49, Henry St Music Sch '49, die folklore Shaker Village Work Camp New Lebanon, N.Y. '47-49. Served in W A C '43-45. Am Folklore Soc—NY State Folklore Soc—Tenn Folklore Soc. 550 Riverside Dr., NYC 27.

16 MAYO, Robert Sprague. Tunnel construction. b'00. BS (Ill Inst Tech); student (Mich Coll Mines). Design steel forms for concrete lining of tunnels and main haulageways of mines; shields and air lock for constructing sub-aqueous tunnels; skips and headframes for hoisting rock or ore from tunnels or mines. Co-author: Practical Tunnel Driving '41. Designer special equipment 15 yrs. Am Soc CE—Western Soc Engrs—Assn Marine Corps Officers. Lancaster, Pa.

17 MAYR, Ernst. Birds of the Southwest Pacific and Philippines; Evolution; Pacific area zoology. b'04. PhD '26 (U Berlin). Expeditions to Dutch New Guinea '28, '29; Whitney South Sea Expedition Solomon Islands '29-30; chmn committee on terrestrial faunas of Pacific, Pacific Science Congress '47. Author: Systematics and the Origin of Species '42; Birds of the Southwest Pacific '45; co-author: Birds of the Philippines '46; Methods and Principles of Systematic Zoology '53. Chairman Sanford Hall Am Mus Nat Hist since '44. Leidy medal Philadelphia Acad '46. Museum of Comparative Zool, Harvard University, Cambridge 38, Mass.

18 MAYS, Benjamin Elijah. American Negro religious history. b'95. AB '20—DD '47 (Bates Coll); MA '25—PhD '35 (U Chicago); LLD '45 (Denison U); DD '45 (Howard U); LittD '46 (SC State Coll). Representative US at Oxford Conference on Church Community and State Oxford University '37, YMCA of US at Plenary Session of World Committee Stockholm '39, Youth Conference Amsterdam '37; World Council of Churches Amsterdam '48. Author: The Negro's God '38; Seeking to be Christians in Race Relations '46; also articles in field. Pres Morehouse Coll since '40. So Edn Found—Nat YMCA (mem bd)—Academic Council Nat Fdn Constl Liberties—Assn Ch Social Workers—Am Assn Coll (mem com Academic Freedom Tenure)—World Student Service Fund (vp)—World Council Ch (mem

Central Com)—Inst Internat Edn (bd mem)—Phi Beta Kappa. Schomberg Honor Roll of Race Relations '44 as one of the twelve negroes who have done outstanding work in better race relations in America. 820 Fair St., Atlanta.◎

19 MAZOUR, Anatole G. Russian Revolution (Social forces). Research on history of Decembrist movement and revolt of December 14, 1825; interpretive analysis Russia's past and present-day role in post-war crisis. Author: The First Russian Revolution, 1825 '37; An Outline of Modern Russian Historiography '38; Russia—Past and Present '51. Asst prof dept hist Miami U Oxford O '35-36; asso advancing to prof dept hist U Nev '37-46; asso prof Russian hist Stanford U '46-52 prof since '52. AHA—Phi Beta Kappa—Phi Kappa Phi—Phi Alpha Theta. Stanford University, Stanford, Cal. H: 781 Frenchman's Rd.

20 MAZZETTI, Maurice Jean. Textile industry (Mechanical engineering); Export (Machinery). b'14. Textile Engr '37 (Institut Technique Roubaisien Roubaix France). Technical and engineering department S A Industrias Reunidas F Matarazzo Sao Paulo Brazil '39-42, general purchasing agent '42-44, special purchasing agent since '44. Brazil Export Corporation, 50 Broadway, NYC.

21 McAFEE, Almer McDuffie. Petroleum refining (Aluminum chloride catalysis). b'86. BA '08 (U Tex); PhD '11 (Columbia). Discovered catalytic cracking and refining action of aluminum chloride on petroleum hydrocarbons '12; introduced Alchlor process into petroleum industry; began manufacture of aluminum chloride from bauxite on large scale. Holds 45 US patents. Engaged in petroleum refining since '11; with Gulf Oil Corp since '13. Am Chem Soc—Sigma Xi—Am Inst Chem Engrs. Listed in Industrial and Engineering Chemistry as one of 38 notable American chemical inventors '35. P. O. Box 109, Port Arthur, Tex.

22 McALISTER, Dean F(erdinand). Physiology of soybean and grass. b'10. BS '31—MS '32 (Utah State Agrl Coll); PhD '36 (U Wis). Research on plant viruses, physiology of range and pasture grasses with particular emphasis on water relations, effect of environmental factors on the growth and chemical composition of soybeans. Author articles in field. Asso physiol US Regional Soybean Lab Urbana Ill '46-48, physiol since '48. Am Soc Plant Physiol—AAAS(F)—Am Soc Agron—Am Soybean Assn—Phi Kappa Phi—Sigma Xi. 205 Davenport Hall, Urbana, Ill.

23 McALISTER, Samuel Bertram. Texas (Public school law, financing of higher education). b'98. AB '26—MA '26—PhD '31 (U Tex). College representative on college budgets before Legislature since '33; director of research financial and public relations for institutions higher education since '46. Author: The Government and Law of the Texas Public School System '34; State and Local Government in Texas '48. Prof govt N Tex State Coll Denton '26-50; first asst state supt edn Tex '38; legal interpreter Tex State Dept Edn '38. NEA—Tex State Tchrs Assn—SW Polit Sci Assn. N. T. Station, Denton, Tex.

24 McALLISTER, Sumner Hatch. Petroleum refining; Petrochemicals and by-products. b'07. AB '29—MA '30 (Stanford U). Research on chemicals from petroleum, particularly ketones, alcohols, and on isooctane, alkylation of isoparaffins, isomerization of paraffines and naphthenes, lubes, fuels, greases, waxes. Holds more than 43 patents. Author articles: The Catalytic Polymerization of Butylenes by Sulfuric Acid; Processes for the Conversion of Light Hydrocarbons to High Anti-Knock Aviation Fuel, and others. Asst chem Shell Development Co Emeryville Cal '30-34, chem '34-37, dept head applications '37-40, process development '40-42, asso dir research '42-46, asso dir research charge petroleum tech since '46. Am Inst Chem Engrs—Am Chem Soc—Am Petroleum Inst—Sigma Xi. Shell Development Company, 4560 Horton St., Emeryville 8, Cal. H: Las Huertas Road, Lafayette.

10 McANDREW, John. Mexican art; Modern architecture. b'04. BS '24—M Arch '41 (Harvard). Organizer numerous exhibitions of modern art NY Museum Modern Art, Musee du Jeu de Paume Paris, Sociedad de Arte Moderno Mexico, Farnsworth Art Museum. Author: Guide to Modern Architecture in the Northeast States '40. Editor: Alvar Aalto '38; A New House by Frank Lloyd Wright '38; also articles in field. Asso prof Wellesley Coll since '45, dir Farnsworth Mus Art since '47; Sociedad de Arquitectos Mexicanos (hon and corr)—Sociedad de Arte Moderno Mex—Mus Modern Art—Am Soc Archtl Hist — The Atheneum. Wellesley College, Wellesley, Mass.

11 McARTHUR, Richard Norment. Printer-advertising typographer; Book and type designing; Calligraphy. b'82. Member graphic arts seminar, Europe under Prof Fuhrmann of NYU '32; Grad '39 (Dale Carnegie Inst Pub Speaking). Research on type faces and relation to advertising; introduced advertising types: Cooper faces, Ransom's Parsons faces, Trenholm faces, Munder faces; designed McArthur's Old Dutch decorative capitals, Foster Italic for Hart Schaffner & Marx advertising; owns collection of type specimen books US and foreign. Author and designer: Specimen Book of Barnhart Brothers and Spindler type foundry '25; also articles in field. Writer-designer PIA national assn Certificate and Grayda-Barnum type specimen in Eastern Corp series; editor house mag Sez Higgins - McArthur. Half-owner Higgins-McArthur Co, creative printers and advertising typographers since '25; staff cons typography, Emory U Div Journalism since '43. Am Institute Graphic Arts (past regional vp)—Printing Industry Am (past dir). 302 Hayden St., N.W., Atlanta.

12 McBEE, Earl Thurston. Organic chemistry (Halogination). b'06. BA '29 (William Jewell Coll); MS '31—PhD '36 (Purdue U). Research on chlorination of organic compounds including paraffin hydrocarbons and partially chlorinated derivatives, fluorination of organic compounds, analysis of organic compounds containing fluorine and other halogens, preparation of organic fluoro compounds including ethers of trifluoromethyl-substituted phenols, of fused ring fluorocarbons, aliphatic and aromatic derivatives generally heterocyclic derivatives. Holds patents (US and Canada) for chlorination process and products thereof, process of chlorinating propane and partially chlorinated derivatives, chlorination process, process of chlorinating propane and isobutane, halogenation of nitro compounds, fluorination process perfluorocyclohexadiene. Author articles in field. Prof, head dept chem Purdue U. Alt. mem Council Reps Participating Insts, Argonne Nat Lab since '48. Am Chem Soc (chmn Symposium on Fluorine Chem)—Sigma Xi—Am Assn Sci

Workers—Ind Chem Soc—AAAS. Modern Pioneer Award NAM '40; Certificate Effective Service in Prodn of Atomic Bomb War Dept '45; Certificate Effective Service in Prosecution of Second World War OSRD '45; Annual Sigma Xi Research Award '46. Department of Chemistry, Purdue University, Lafayette, Ind.

13 McBIRNEY, Stanley Ward. Sugar beet production machinery. b'01. BS '23 (Ia State Coll). Author articles in field. Farm machinery research engr US Dept Agr since '27. Am Soc Agrl Engrs—Am Soc Sugar Beet Technol—Tau Beta Pi—Gamma Sigma Delta. Colorado A&M College, Fort Collins, Colo.†

14 McBRIDE, Gordon W(illiams). Fats (Continuous processing); Federal research; Food standards. b'10. BS '31—Chem E '34 (Yale). Assisted in development first commercially successful continuous hydrolysis and saponification of fats; study new technology in fats and oils processing; study Federal research programs particularly with reference to chemical process industries, food standardization programs of Food and Drug Administration and US Department of Agriculture. Author articles: Continuous Process for Soap '47; Progress in Fats and Oils Field '48, and others. Chem engr Proctor & Gamble Co Ivorydale O '34-38; cons chem engr Washington since '39; prin chem engr USDA '43-45. ACS—Am Oil Chem Soc AICE—AAAS—Washington Acad Sci—Alpha Chi Sigma—Sigma Xi. 1518 K St., Washington 5.

15 McBRYDE, Felix Webster. Latin-American native cultures (Guatemalan, Mexican, Peruvian); Climatology; Physiography; Geography (Ethnogeography); Ethnobotany; Cartography. b'08. BA '30 (Tulane U); geog and geol fellow '30-31 (U Colo); geog fellow '31-32 (Clark U); PhD '40 (U Calif). Field work in Latin-America especially Maya area; devised graphic map representations for physical and cultural data; system relief representation for military interpretation, climatic classification; type detailed relief representation based aerial mosaic photographs; discovered large group early pre-Inca petroglyphs Viru Valley Peru. Author: Cultural and Historical Geography of Southwestern Guatemala '47; also articles in field. Sr geog in charge Lat-Am region topographic br Mil Intell Div US War Dept '42-44, head geog '44-45; cultural geog, dir Peruvian Office Inst Social Anthrop Smithsonian Inst Lima '45-47; cons geog 1950 census of Americas US Bur Census since '48. Am Anthrop Assn—AAAS—Am Geog Soc—Am Geophys Union—Am Soc Profl Geog (founding pres '43-45, sec-treas '43-44) —Assn Am Geog—Lima Geog Soc—Soc Am Archeol — Inter-Am Soc Anthrop and Geog — Nat Research Council (F '40-41, chmn subcom census '44)—Phi Beta Kappa. c/o U.S. Embassy, Quito, Ecuador.†

16 McBURNEY, John White. Masonry materials (Brick, concrete, mortar); Flooring (Asphalt tile). b'90. AB '13 (O State U). Author articles in field. Sr technol Nat Bur Standards since '35; liaison Nat Bur Standards and Office Technical Service also Nat Housing Authority since '46. AAAS(F) —Am Inst Chem—Am Ceramic Soc—Brit Ceramic Soc—Rheological Soc—ASME—Am Concrete Inst—Soc Chem Industry — Washington Acad Sci — Washington Philos Soc—Am Soc Testing Materials (chmn com mortar '37-44, chmn sub-com building brick of com on Masonry units '37-49)—Am Standards Assn (sec com masonry

since '34, sec com plastering since '35). National Bureau of Standards, Washington 25.

17 McCABE, Leo Orvine. Domestic relations. b'99. BA cum '20 (Columbia Coll Dubuque Ia); '20-21 (U Minn); LLB '23 (Yale); (State U Ia, Ia State Coll). Author: Cases on Persons and Domestic Relations; also articles in field. Prof law De Paul U Chicago '29-43, '46-48; atty Securities Exchange Commn Pub Utilities Div Phila '43-46. Nat Conf Family Relations — Am Bar Assn — Chicago Bar Assn. 2325 Asbury Av., Evanston, Ill.

18 McCABE, Louis C(ordell). Fuels technology; Air pollution control. b'04. BS '31—MS '33—PhD '37 (U Ill). Author articles in field. Dir Los Angeles Co Air Pollution Control Dist '47-49; chief office air and stream pollution Research US Bureau Mines '49-51; chief fuels and explosives div US Bureau Mines since '51. Capt and chief fuel and heating sect OQMG US Army '41; capt to lt col Office Chief of Engineers '41-44, chief utilities sect office Chief of Engineers '41-44, chief Belgian solid fuels SHAEF '44, German solid fuels '45, Col GSC '45. Geol Society America(F)—Am Inst Mining Metall Engrs—Am Soc Mil Engrs—AAAS—Sigma Xi. Received Legion of Merit, OBE Brit, Order of the Crown Belgium. Chief, Fuels and Explosives Division, U.S. Bureau of Mines, Washington 25.

19 McCABE, Warren Lee. Chemical engineering (Distillation, crystallization, thermodynamics, heat transmission). b'99. BS '22—MS '23—PhD '28 (U Mich). Director American Institute Chemical Engineers '42-44 and since '46; director Central Engineering Laboratory University of Pennsylvania '44-45. Co-author: (with W L Badger) Elements of Chemical Engineering '30-36; also articles in field. Prof Carnegie Inst Tech '36-47, head dept. Chem Engring '37-47; dir research Flintkote Co. since '47, vice pres since '49. Am Chem Soc—Am Inst Chem Engrs (dir '46-48, vp '49, pres '50)—ASME-Tau Beta Pi—Sigma Xi. Am Inst Chem Engrs Walker award '38. The Flintkote Co., Whippany, N.J.☉

20 McCAHAN, David. Insurance. b'97. BS Econ '20—MA '22—PhD '28 (U Pa); '22-26 (George Washington U); CLU '29 (Am Coll Life Underwriters). Author: State Insurance in the United States '29. Co-author (with S S Huebner) Life Insurance as Investment '33. Editor: Life Insurance: Trends and Problems '43; The Beneficiary in Life Insurance '48; Investment of Life Insurance Funds '53; Significant Developments of War Period in Life Insurance '45; also articles in field. Prof ins Wharton Sch U Pa since '36; dean and trustee Am Coll Life Underwriters '34-52, pres since '52; executive director S S Huebner Foundation for Ins Edn; past pres Swarthmore Bd of Sch Dirs; trustee Am Inst for Property and Liability Underwriters Inc. Teachers Ins and Annuity Assn Am (former trustee, executive com)—Coll Retirement Equities Fund (trustee)—C of C of US (ins com)—Am Acad Polit Social Sci—Am Assn U Teachers Ins (pres '40, 41) — Am Econ Assn — Am Soc Chartered Life Underwriters (sec '30-45)—Beta Gamma Sigma. Dietrich Hall, University of Pennsylvania, Phila.

21 McCAIN, William David. Mississippi history and archives. b'07. BS '30 (Delta State Teachers Coll); teaching fellow in history '30-31—AM '31 (U Miss); fellow in history '33-35—PhD '35 (Duke U). Author: The

United States and the Republic of Panama '37; also articles in field. Dir Miss Dept Archives and History since '38; prof hist U Miss since '47; lecturer in hist Millsaps Coll '41-42, '46-48; hist Dept Am Legion since '46; hist Miss Res Officers Assn '47-48. US archivist in Italy, '44-45; editor Journal Miss Hist since '39. Soc Am Archivists (founding mem, vp since '46)—AHA—Miss Valley Hist Assn—So Hist Assn—Miss Hist Assn—Miss Library Assn (pres '41-44). Department of Archives and History, Jackson, Miss.

10 McCALL, Charlie Campbell. Municipal bonds. b'95. LLB '21—LLM '22 MPL '22 (Georgetown University); LL M '22—MPL '22—SJD '36 (National University); LLM '23 (American U); studied (U Ala) (US Mil Acad); grad '44 (Sch Mil Govt) '45 (AAF Sch Applied Tactics and Sch Applied Personnel Management). Chief counsel pub bodies sect, legal div Fed Emergency Adminstrn Pub Works '33-34; chief legal adviser NY State Office Fed Emergency Adminstrn Pub Works '34-35; counsel Pub Works Adminstrn '35-38; acting gen counsel PR Reconstruction Adminstrn San Juan '37; asst gen counsel Pub Works Adminstrn Washington '38—39, acting gen counsel '39-40, gen counsel '40-41; spl asso gen counsel Fed Works Agency '41-42, asst gen counsel '45-48; chief financing atty div of law, slum clearance staff Housing and Home Finance Agency Washington since '49. Am Bar Assn—Fed Bar Assn—Am Acad Polit and Social Sci—Nat Assn Attys Gen (pres '30)—Sigma Nu Phi—Chi Psi Omega. Housing and Home Finance Agency, 1626 K St. N.W., Washington.©

11 McCALL, Herbert Max. Heating. b'16. Student '36-37 (Coyne Elec Sch Chicago), '42 (Pa State); grad '35 (Internat Corr Sch, Scranton); LLB '49 (Blackstone Coll). Compiler: Manual Outlining the Design, Installation and Engineering of Gravity Warm Air Heating, Forced Warm Air Heating, Gravity Hot Water Heating, Forced Hot Water Heating and Steam Heating '46. Organized McCall's Plumbing-Heating-Electrical '37; formed Ind Wholesale Plumbing and Heating '46. Am Soc Heating Ventilating Engrs. 1142-1146 Philadelphia St., Indiana, Pa.

12 McCALLA, Thomas Mark. Soil microbiology and conservation; Mulch. b'09. BS '34 (Miss State Coll); MA '35—PhD '37 (U Mo). Author articles in field. Bact soil conservation service research US Dept Agr and prof Agron Neb Agrl Expt Sta Lincoln since '41. Soc Am Bact—Am Soc Agron—Soil Sci Soc Am—Neb Acad Sci—Kan Acad Sci—Am Geophy Union—AAAS(F)—Sigma Xi—Gamma Sigma Delta. College of Agriculture, Lincoln, Neb.†

13 McCALLAN, Samuel Eugene Alan. Fungicides. b'02. BSA '23 (U Toronto); PhD '29 (Cornell U). Author articles in field. Head plant path fungicide project Boyce Thompson Inst since '43. AAAS—Am Phytopath Soc (pres NE Div '47)—Am Statis Assn—Crop Protection Inst (bd gov since '43, v chmn '43-44)—Sigma Xi—Phi Kappa Phi. Naval Ordnance development award tropical deterioration project of Nat Defense Research Com '45. Boyce Thompson Institute of Plant Research, Inc., Yonkers 3, N.Y.†

14 McCAMMON, G(eorge) A. Marine foundations (Design, construction); Pile drivers (Design). b'05. BS in gen engring '26 (U Ill). Design Marine foundations including worldwide patents on caisson foundations used extensively for oil field foundations in

deep water marine fields; planning research projects such as field studies of unconventional new type structures and soils studies to develop access and foundations for inaccessible swamp areas; design heavy marine pile drivers; construction marine foundations. Author: Prefabricated Caisson Foundations for Submarine Oil Wells '46. Holds patents in field. With Creole Petroleum Corp Venezuela since '27, now chief of gen engring. Am Soc CE—ASTM—Am Concrete Inst—Am Waterworks Soc. Creole Petroleum Corp., Apartado 889, Caracas, Venezuela.

15 McCANTS, E(lliott) Crayton. South Carolina history and traditions. b'65. BS '86 (SC Mil Acad); LittD '27 (U SC). Author: In the Red Hills '04; One of the Gray Jackets '09; Stories and Legends of South Carolina '27; White Oak Farm '28; Ninety Six '30; also articles in field. Supt emeritus city schs Anderson SC since '45; instr state and co summer normal schs for teachers since '00. State Teachers Assn SC. Anderson, S.C.

16 McCARTHY, Henry Francis. Railroad management; Freight and passenger traffic. b'06. BS '27 (Harvard); MS '30 (Yale). Asso dir Office Defense Transportation '42, dir div traffic movement '42-44, dir ry transport dept '44; dir Nat Ry Publs Co '44, exec asst pres NY, NH and Hartford RR '45, vp '48. Am Assn Passenger Traffic Officers (pres '44-45). Awarded Presidential Certificate of Merit '46. 494 S. Station, Boston.

17 McCARTY, Kenneth Scott. Electron microscopy; Milk factor (Cancer); Cell (Biochemistry). b'22. BS '44 (Georgetown U); PhD candidate '52 (Columbia). Research on use electron microscope as aid to study of cell in cancer research, designed and built ultracentrifuge for use in electron microscopy, developed method segregation for nuclei and other cell components, designed high speed homogenizer for tissue fragmentation, effect high frequency radiation on spontaneous mouse tumors, developed method of tumor impressions to determine relative volume of tumor at various stages of growth. Research biochem Food and Drug Adminstrn '45; electron micros Interchem Research Lab '45-46; first asst. to dir cancer research Lillia Babbit Hyde Found '46-52; cons electron micros Bronx Veterans Adminstrn Hosp since '50. ACS —NY Micros Soc—NY Acad Sci—Electron Micros Soc Am—Soc de Chimie Industrielle—AAAS—Histochem Soc—NY Soc Electron Micros. Electron Microscopy, Cancer Research Division, Bronx Veterans Administration Hospital, 130 W. Kingsbridge, Bronx, N.Y.

18 McCARY, Ben Clyde. American Revolution (French role); French travelers in America 18th century; Virginia (Indians). b'01. AB '23 (U Richmond); Dr Universite '28 (U Toulouse). Research on role of Charles Gravier, Comte de Vergennes and secretary of state for foreign affairs under Louis XVI, in American Revolution; research on travels of Ferdinand-M Bayard, French traveler in America 1791-92; research on Rappahannock and Chickahominy Indians of Virginia and location of Indian sites described by Captain John Smith in Tidewater Virginia. Editor and translator: Ferdinand-M. Bayard's Travels of a Frenchman in Maryland and Virginia, or Travels in the Interior of the United States 1791 '50. Asso prof French U Richmond '28-30; with Coll William and Mary since '30. AAUP—Am Assn Tchrs French—Soc

Am Archeol—Va Hist Soc—Soc Preservation Va Antiquities—Archeol Soc Va (pres since '49)—Sigma Pi. Box 123, Williamsburg, Va.

19 McCAUGHEY, William John. Mineral composition of ceramic products, metallurgical slags and refractories. b'82. BS '06 (Pa U); PhD '12 (George Washington U); '10 (Johns Hopkins). Research on phase equilibrium in high temperature systems, mineral technology, microscopic petrography. Author articles in field. Asst prof metall and mineral O State U '11, prof and chmn dept since '16; mem US Assay Commn '09. Am Mineral Soc — Am Geol Soc — Am Geophys Union — Am Inst Mining Engrs—Am Chem Soc—AAAS—German Mineral Soc—Sigma Xi. 2375 Andover Rd., Columbus 12, O.

20 McCLELLAN, Oliver. Seismology (Interpretation). b'08. BS '34 (U Tex). Computer and seismol Petty Geophys Enring Co since '34. Soc Exploration Geophys. P.O. Box 2061, San Antonio.

21 McCLELLAN, Wilbur Dwight. Plant pathology (Garden flowers). b'14. BS '36 (Calif U); PhD '41 (Cornell U). Research on control of powdery mildew of roses, use of fungicides and growth substances in control of Fusarium scale rot of lilies, effects and influences of various fertilizers and nutrient solutions on growth. Author articles in field. Path Bur Plant Industry, Soils Agrl Engring US Dept Agr since '41. Sigma Xi—Phi Kappa Phi—AAAS—Am Phytopath Soc—Bot Soc Washington—Washington Acad Sci. Plant Industry Station, Beltsville, Md.

22 McCLELLAND, Nancy Vincent. Old wall papers; Eighteenth century interior decoration (French and American styles). AB '97 (Vassar). Author: Historic Wall-Papers '24; Decorative Wall Treatments '25; The Young Decorator '27; Furnishing the Colonial and Federal House '36; Duncan Phyfe and the English Regency '39. Pres and treas Nancy McClelland Inc, antiques and mural decorations. Am Inst Decorators (pres '41-43)—Royal Soc Arts London(F)—Mark Twain Internat Soc (hon). Decorated Chevalier Legion of Honor France '30; received the first Justice P Ahman award from the Nat Wallpaper Assn '46; awarded the Friedsam medal by the Arch League NY '48. 15 E. 57th St., NYC.

23 McCLESKEY, Charles Shelton. Bacteriology of foods; Sanitary bacteriology; Diagnostic bacteriology; Teaching of bacteriology. b'97. BS '24 (Tex A&M Coll); MS '26—PhD '30 (Ia State Coll). Research on characteristics of Leuconostoc mesenteroides, survival of pathogenic bacteria in frozen foods, physiology of Shigella sonnei, bacteriology of crabmeat, enterococci and coliform bacteria in water and seafoods. Co-author: (with W N Christopher) Laboratory Manual and Workbook for Elementary Bacteriology '47. Asso prof biol John Tarleton Coll '24-27; with Ia State Coll '27-37, asst prof bact '34-37; with La State U since '37, prof bact since '46. Soc Am Bact—AAAS—La Acad Sci—Am Pub Health Assn. Department of Botany, Bacteriology, and Plant Pathology, Louisiana State University, Baton Rouge.†©

24 McCLINTOCK, Miller. Traffic and transportation engineering; Advertising; Education (Radio, motion pictures). b'94. AB '18—AM '20 (Stanford); AM '22—PhD '24 (Harvard); DSc (hon) '38 (Tufts). Consultant on traffic and transportation to various cities, states and Federal Government

'25-32; chief executive Traffic Audit Bureau Inc '33-42; director Advertising Research Foundation '39-41; advisor to Canadian Manufacturers Institute '41-42; executive director Advertising Council, Inc. '42; president Mutual Broadcasting System '43-44; president Instructional Films, Inc; president of Sound Book Press Society, Inc since '49; Senior Consultant to Rural Radio Network Incorporated; on board and consultant to Encyclopaedia Britannica Films Incorporated '45-46. Author: Street Traffic Control; Traffic and Trade; Circulation Values of Window Display Advertising; A Limited Way Plan for the Greater Chicago Traffic Area. Dir Bur St Traffic Research and dir Bur Municipal Research Harvard '25-38; dir Bur for St Traffic Research Yale '38-42; mem bd Asso Musak '45-46. Inst Traffic Engrs— Am Polit Sci Assn—SAE—AAUP. 6 Heathcote Rd., Scarsdale, N.Y.

10 McCLOY, Charles Harold. Physical education (Biometry, anthrometry, body build, motor skill, psychology, tests). PhB '07—MA '10—ScD '47 (Marietta Coll); PhD '32 (Columbia U); '11-12 (Johns Hopkins Med Sch); '19-20 (O State U). Author: The Physiology of Exercise '15; An Outline of Kinesiology '17; Soccer Football '18; A Textbook of Physical Examinations '23; The Measurement of Athletic Power '32; Appraising Physical Status: The Selection of Measurements '36; Appraising Physical Status: Methods and Norms '38; Tests and Measurements in Health and Physical Education '39. General editor: Appleton-Century Crofts physical edn series, also articles in field. Prof phys edn State U Ia since '30; expert cons US War Dept since '41. Am Acad Phys Edn(F), sec treas '41-46, pres '47-49) —Am Assn Health, Phys Edn Recreation—Pan-Am Inst Phys Edn (pres '46-49)—Phi Beta Kappa—Sigma Xi. Recipient Research Award Am Acad Phys Edn '38; Gulick Medal '44. 1 Oak Ridge, Iowa City, Ia.

11 McCLOY, Shelby Thomas. Social and cultural history of Eighteenth century France; French inventions (Eighteenth century). b'98. BA '18— MA '19 (Davidson Coll); '19-20, '22-23 (Union Theol Sem); BLitt '22—BA '24—Rhodes Scholar '20-22, '23-24 (U Oxford, Eng); '26-27—Jacob H Schiff fellow '29-30—PhD '33 (Columbia). Research on eighteenth century French charities, housing projects, government aid, flood control and relief, rationalists and religion, other social and cultural phases history; e x t e n s i v e travel Europe and Near East '20-24. Author: Gibbon's Antagonism to Christianity '33; Government Assistance in Eighteenth-Century France '46; French Inventions of the Eighteenth Century '52; also articles. Instr hist Duke U '27-41, asst prof '41-45; vis prof hist U Ky '44-45, prof since '45. AHA— So Hist Assn—Soc Am Hist—Phi Beta Kappa. Social Science Research Council grants-in-aid '37, '39, '46; Frederic Bancroft History Prize 2nd award from Assn Study Negro Life Hist '45. Department of History, University of Kentucky, Lexington 29, Ky.†

12 McCLUER, Samuel Campbell. Dams (Concrete, structural behavior). b'04. AB '30 (Berea Coll); MS '32 (U Ky). Studies by electrical resistance thermometers, strain meters, stress meters, hydrostatic pore pressure cells, and deflection lines of data on various dams. Concrete engring work TVA '34-45; materials engr structural research lab Bur Reclamation '45-47, concrete dam constrn Corps Engrs US Army since '48, Chief Joseph Dam, Bridgeport Wash since '51. Am Con-

crete Inst. Bridgeport, Wash. H: RFD 3, Concord, Tenn.

13 McCLUNG, Leland S(wint). Bacteriology (Anaerobic); Microbiology. b'10. AB '31—AM '32 (U Tex); PhD '34—research fellow '30-34—Nat Research Council fellow '34 (U Wis); John Simon Guggenheim Memorial Fund fellow '39 (Harvard Med Sch). Co-author: The Anaerobic Bacteria and their Activities in Nature and Disease '39; and Supplement I '41; General Bacteriology Laboratory Manual '46; also articles in field. Prof bact Ind U since '48, chmn dept since '47. AAAS(F) — Am Assn Immunol — Am Chem Soc—Am Pub Health Assn(F)— Ind Acad Sci(F, chmn bact sect '43) —Soc Am Bact (chmn program Com '43-46, council '43-48)—Soc Gen Microbiol—Soc Exptl Biol Med—Sigma Xi. Indiana University, B a c t e r i o l o g y Office, Bloomington, Ind.☉

14 McCLURE, Frank James. Fluorine (Physiological effects). b'96. BS '19—MS '26 (Purdue U); PhD '30 U Ill). Research on effects fluorine on calcium metabolism, retention fluorine in bones and teeth, inhibitory effects fluorine on induced rat caries, presence of fluorine in human sweat, correlation of urinary excretion of fluorine with fluorine in drinking water. Contributor: Annual Review of Biochemistry '49. Research asso U Ill '26-30; research asso Pa State Coll '30-36; biochem Nat Inst Health and Nat Inst Dental Research since '36. Sigma Xi—Internat Assn Dental Research—Am Pub Health Assn—AAAS—Wash Acad Sci—ACS— Am Dental Soc Europe(hon.). National Institute of Dental Research, Bethesda, Md.

15 McCLURE, James Gore King. Rural economics and rural Church; Co-operative dairies; Forestry. b'84. BA '06—MA (hon) '39 (Yale); DSc (hon) '29 (Berea Coll); MA (hon) '41 (Harvard); LLD (hon) '42 (U NC). Engaged in farming in NC since '16; first pres since '20 Farmers' Federation Inc organized to develop markets and stimulate production of farmers in Western NC and sponsor the Lord's Acre movement; pres Skyline Cooperative Dairies; pres Treasure Chest Cooperative; pres Farmers Loan Corp; ed Farmers Fedn News; pres Appalachian Mutual Inc; mem NC Bd Conservation and Development. Am Forestry Assn (past pres)—NC Forestry Assn (dir). Awarded gold medal Inst Social Scis '44. Asheville, NC.☉

16 McCLURKIN, William Dean. Education (Administration, school buildings and finance). b'10. AB '29 (Hendrix Coll); MA '34 (U Ark); PhD '40 (George Peabody Coll). Author articles in field. Prof sch adminstrn George Peabody Coll for Teachers since '46, dir Division Surveys and Field Services. Naval officer '42-45. NEA— Ark Edn Assn (pres '43)—Tenn Edn Assn—Am Assn Sch Adminstrs ('49 yr-bk com)—Nat Council Schoolhouse Construction (sec-treas)—Assn Sch Bus Officials. George Peabody College, Nashville 4, Tenn.

17 McCOLLAM, Millard E(arl). Fertilizers; Agrostology. b'94. BS '17 (U Calif). Leaf analysis used as diagnostic aid in study of plant nutrition. Author: Profitable Fertilization —Choosing a Fertilizer '21; Fertilizer Trials on Common Soil Types '22; Reinforcement of Farmyard Manure '22; The Spring Catch of Clover and Grass '23; Fertilizers for Lawn and Garden Use '23; The Possibilities of Creeping Bent Grass '24; A Guide for Fertilizer Users '25; Permanent Pastures '27. Western States mgr Am Potash Inst

since '35. Am Soc Agron—Soil Sci Soc Am—Am Soc Hort Sci—Western Soil Sci Soc—Calif Fertilizer Assn. 314 First National Bank Building, San Jose 15, Calif.†

18 McCOLLUM, John Paschal. Quality constituents in vegetables. b'05. BS '27 (Okla A&M Coll); PhD '32 (Cornell U). With U Ill since '31, now asso prof veg crops. Am Soc Hort Sci — Am Soc Plant Physiol— Sigma Xi—Gamma Sigma Delta. Department of Horticulture, University of Illinois, Urbana, Ill.†

19 McCOLLUM, Otis Harry. Tire and tube compounding. b'16. BS '39 (Cornell U). Author articles in field. Chemist sales and service Rubber Lab E I DuPont de Nemours Inc Wilmington Del since '47. ACS. Rubber Laboratory, E. I. DuPont de Nemours Inc., 40 E. Buchtel Ave., Akron 8, O.†

20 McCONAGHA, Glenn Lowery. Correspondence e d u c a t i o n (Adult); Curriculum development. b'10. AB '32 (Muskingum Coll); MA '34—PhD '42 (O State U); '36-37 (U Pittsburgh). Author articles in field. Exec officer US Armed Forces Inst Madison Wis '44-45, director since '50. NEA— British Royal Army Ednl Corps (honorary) —Phi Delta Kappa. 102 N. Hamilton St., Madison 3, Wis.

21 McCONNELL, Duncan. Applied petrography and geochemistry; Minerals; Physical chemistry of concrete, cement and aggregate; Sedimentary rocks (Clays). b'09. BS '31 (Washington & Lee U); MS '32 (Cornell U); '32-33 (U Chicago); fellow '34-35 (Stanford U); PhD '37 (U Minn). Articles in field. Prof Mineralogy Ohio State U since '50, chmn dept since '52. Geol Soc Am(F)—Mineral Soc Am(F) —Soc Econ Geol—Mineral Soc Gt Brit Ireland—Am Crystallographic Assn— Am Chem Soc—Mineral Soc France— Sigma Xi. Dept. of Mineralogy, Ohio State University, Columbus 10.†

22 McCONNELL, Robert A. Parapsychology. b'14. BS in physics '35 (Carnegie Inst Tech); PhD '47 (U Pittsburgh). Scientific study psychic phenomena, including extrasensory perception and psychokinesis. Author articles in field. Group leader engaged in work on pulsed Doppler radar Radiation Lab, MIT '41-46. Am Soc Psychical Research—Soc for Psychical Research (London)—Sigma Xi. Department of Physics, University of Pittsburgh, Pitts. 13.†

23 McCONNELL, Wallace Robert. Human geography. b'81. AB '12 (U Ill); AM '17 (U Wis); PhD '25—fellow '23-24, '24-25 (Clark U). Author: Problems in the Geography of Europe '25; Geography of Ohio '29; Geography of World Peoples '52. The United States in the Modern World '39; Living in the Americas '34; Living Across the Seas '39; Living in Different Lands '36; Living in Country and City '37; and others. Prof geog Miami U since '18. AAAS — Nat Council Geog Teachers (pres '24-25)—Kappa Delta Pi. 402 E. Withrow Av., Oxford, O.*

24 McCORD, Carey Pratt. Control of odors; Occupational skin diseases; Metallic poisoning; Industrial fatigue; Air Conditioning; Tropics (Occupational diseases); Occupational Medicine (History). Author: A Blind Hog's Acorns—Vignettes of the Maladies of Workers '45; also 700 articles in field. Co-author: (with Floyd P Allen) Industrial Hygiene for Engineers and Managers '31; (with Wm N Witheridge) Odors—Physiology and Control '47. Contributor: Medical Uses of Soap '45; Industrial Hygiene and Toxicology Vol I, II '48. Cons editor Indsl

Medicine and Surgery '50. Dir research Mich State Hosp '14-16; asso prof preventive medicine U Cincinnati '19-35; med dir The Indsl Health Conservancy Lab since '20; med cons occupational diseases Chrysler Corp since '34; prof occupational diseases Wayne U '35-39; dir Div Indsl Health Detroit '35-39; non-resident lectr indsl hygiene U Mich Sch Pub Health since '43. Diplomate Am Bd Preventive Medicine Pub Health. AMA—Am Assn Indsl Physicians and Surgeons—Am Public Health Assn—Am Acoustical Soc—Mich State Med Assn—Delta Omega—Phi Chi—Ramazzini Soc. William S Knudsen award for most outstanding contbn to indsl medicine '46-47. 10 Peterboro St., Det. 1. H: 120 East Fountain St., Glendale, O.

10 McCORD, (William) Fletcher. Clinical psychology; Personality (Structure and dynamics); Perception; Memory; Motivation; Meaning and symbolism (Psychology); Social ideologies; Propaganda. b'02. AB '30 (Mercer U); PhD '38 (Duke U). Member panel of consulting psychologists for Veterans Administration 9th branch since '46; director board of family and child welfare service Tulsa since '47; research associate on joint program of Tulane-Office of Naval Research '50-51. Teaching fellow and research asst Duke U '33-36; instr psychology U Kan '36-38, asst prof '39-45; prof psychology U Tulsa since '48; vis prof psychology Tulane U '50-51; clin psychologist. AAUP—AAAS—Am Psychol Assn—Okla State Psychol Assn(exec com)—Okla Acad Sci—Kan Acad Sci—Sigma Xi—Psi Chi. Diplomate psychology Am Bd Examiners in Profl Psychology. Psychiology Dept., Tulsa University, Tulsa 4.⊙

11 McCORMICK, Charles Perry. Human relations; Management. b'96. Grad Baltimore City Coll '15; '19 (Johns Hopkins U). Author: Multiple Management '38; Sparks '41; The McCormick System of Management; also articles in field. Pres, chmn bd McCormick & Co Inc Baltimore since '32; chmn bd McCormick Overseas Trading Inc; pres, chmn bd McCormick de Mexico SA; chmn bd A Schilling & Co San Francisco. Soc Advancement Mgmt (human relations award com chmn)—Am Mgmt Assn. Awarded Soc Advancement Mgmt Citation and Medal for Human Relation '46. McCormick Bldg., Baltimore 2.

12 McCORMICK, Richard Patrick. New Jersey history; Political machinery in the United States. b'16. AB '38—MA '40 (Rutgers U); PhD '48 (U Pa. Author: Experiment in Independence: New Jersey in the Crtical Period 1781-1790 '49; also articles in field. Asst prof hist Rutgers U since '48, U hist since '48, asso ed Journal Rutgers U Library since '48. AHA—Am Assn State Local Hist—NJ Hist Soc—Mid States Council Social Studies—Phi Beta Kappa—Tau Kappa Alpha. History Department, Rutgers University, New Brunswick, N.J.†

13 McCORMICK, William Thomas. Occupational hygiene engineering; Safety engineering (Iron ore and fluorspar mines, limestone quarrying). b'08. BS '30—EM '30 (Mich Coll Mining and Tech). Evaluation of environmental health exposures, including temperature, humidity, illumination, dusts, radiant energy, repeated motion, poisons, and noise, and recommendation for their control; appraisal accident and health hazards and recommendation for prevention industrial injuries. With Inland Steel Co since '35, supervisor occupational hy-

giene since '47. AIMME—Am Soc Safety Engrs—Illuminating Engring Soc—Am Indsl Hygiene Assn. 3210 Watling St., East Chicago, Ind.

14 McCOWN, Chester Charlton. New Testament interpretation; Hellenistic history and Greek; Palestinian archeology and geography. b'77. BA '98—LLD '48 (DePauw U); BD '02—DD '19 (Garrett Bibl Inst); '06-08 (Heidelberg and Berlin); PhD '14 (U Chicago); DD '47 (Pacific Sch Religion). Director American School Oriental Research Jerusalem '29-31, annual professor and acting director '35-36; joint director Yale University-American School Expedition at Jerash (Gerasa) '30-31; member Archeological Advisory Board of Palestine Government '29-31, '35-36; member 19th International Congress of Orientalists Rome '35. Author: The Promise of His Coming '21; The Testament of Solomon '22; Genesis of the Social Gospel '29; The Search for the Real Jesus '40; Ladder of Progress in Palestine '43; Tell en-Nasbeh Excavations '47; also articles in field. Prof NT lit and interpretation Pacific Sch Religion since '14, dean '28-36, '45-46, emeritus since '47; dir Palestinian Archeol Inst '36-47. Archeol Inst Am (vp 48)—Soc Bibl Lit Exegesis (vp '39, pres '40)—Am Philol Assn—Philol Assn Pacific Coast (treas '25-28, vp '35, pres '40)—Am Oriental Soc—Palestine Oriental Soc—Palestine Exploration Fund (hon sec). Award: Thayer fellowship Am Sch Oriental Research Jerusalm '20-21. 1611 Scenic Av., Berkeley 9.⊙

15 McCOWN, Donald Eugene. Archeology (Iranian; prehistoric Indian); Ancient Oriental history. b'10. AB '32 (U Calif); PhD '41 (U Chicago). Archeological assistant excavations at Jericho Palestine '30-31, Wadi Mughara Athlit Palestine '30; Persepolis expedition Iran '33-38. Author: The Comparative Stratigraphy of Early Iran '42. Co-author: Tall-i-Bakun A, Season of '32 '42; also articles in field. Also prof arch Oriental Inst U Chicago, field dir the Iranian Project excavating at Tall-i-Ghasir, Khuzistan Iran '48-49; field dir Joint Expdn Nippur since '48. Oriental Institute, University of Chicago, Chicago 37.†

16 McCOWN, Theodore D(oney). Fossil man; Osteology. b'08. Taussig Travel fellow '33-34—Bowles Johnson Travel fellow '34-35—AB '30—PhD '40 (U Calif); research fellow '32, '35-37 (Am Sch Prehistoric Research). Archeological assistant joint expedition American School Prehistoric Research and British School Archeology in Jerusalem Mt Carmel Palestine '30-31, field director '32; supervisor project 9 Institute Andean Research North Peru '41-42; discovery Neanderthal cemetery Mt. Carmel Palestine '31-32. Co-author: The Stone Age of Mt Carmel, Vol II '39. Professor and curator Anthrop Mus U Calif since '51. Am Anthrop Assn(F)—Royal Anthrop Inst Gt Brit Ireland—AAAS—Am Geog Soc—Soc Study Evolution—Soc Am Archeol—Sigma Xi—Phi Beta Kappa—Am Assn Phys Anthrop—NY Acad Sci(F). Department of Anthropology, University of California, Berkeley 4.†

17 McCOY, William John, Jr. Refrigeration. b'06. Student '23-24 (U Tenn). Research in application of refrigeration to foods, cooling and freezing problems, functional design of food processing and freezing plants, application of refrigeration to chemical manufacture and storage, design of refrigerated and pressure storage facilities for anhydrous ammonia used in direct fertilization of soil, air conditioning systems. Holds patents on

refrigeration electrical control systems and special instruments. Refrigeration engr W J Savage Co Knoxville '35-36; erecting engr Worthington Pump and Machinery Corp '36-39, asst to chief engr '39-40, application engr refrigeration div Holyoke Mass '40-45; spl application refrigeration engr and regional mgr Burge Ice Machine Co Inc Chicago since '45, on loan to U Tenn as chief engr design refrigeration Agrl Coll Food Processing Lab since '48. Refrigeration Service Engrs—Am Soc Refrigeration Engrs. Burge Ice Machine Co., Inc., 302 W. Church Av., Knoxville, Tenn.

18 McCRACKEN, Harlan Linneus. Business cycles; Economic theory (Economics of J M Keynes and Austrian school); Monopolistic Competition; Technological unemployment. b'89. BS '14—AM '16 (Penn Coll, Ia); BS '15 (Haverford Coll); PhD '23 (U Wis). Research on ways and means of providing full employment, capacity production, high national income and general prosperity by reducing the amplitude of the business cycle. Author: Secular Trends and Business Cycles '22; Value Theory and Business Cycles '36; An Appraisal of the Possibility of Plenty '35; The Corporation Surplus Tax in Its Relation to the Business Cycle '37; Monopolistic Competition and Business Fluctuations '38; Technological Unemployment; Possibilities of Reabsorption '37; Why Wars Produce Post-war Depressions '42; Economic Contradictions '47. Prof econ La State U since '34, head dept since '37; ed Southern Economic Jour; econ adv problems industry div Gen Fedn Women's Clubs '24-26; panel mem War Labor Bd. Am Econ Assn—So Econ Assn (vp '45, pres '46)—SW Social Sci Assn—AAUP—Phi Kappa Phi (pres '41-42)—Beta Gamma Sigma (pres '44-45). 2348 Myrtle Av., Baton Rouge, La.⊙

19 McCRADY, Edward. Opossum (Embryology; Fossil cats; Cave salamanders; Radiobiology. b'06. AB '27 (Coll of Charleston); MS '30 (U Pittsburgh); PhD '33 (U Pa). Research on respiratory, auditory, circulatory mechanisms of opossum; discovered a new species of fossil cat and troglodytic salamanders from caves of Tennessee. Author articles in field. Research scientist Wistar Inst of Anatomy U Pa '30-37; head biol dept U of South since '37; biol Atomic Energy Commission Oak Ridge Tenn since '48, chief biol div '49; president University of the South since 1951. AAAS—Am Soc Zoölogists—Am Assn Anatomists—Acoustical Soc Am—Nat Speleological Soc—Tenn Acad Sci (pres '44) — Assn Southeastern Biologists—Sigma Xi. Invited speaker in symposium on hearing Am Otolog Soc U Toronto '35, XI Congres International de Psychologie Sorbonne U Paris '37; research awards Tenn Acad Sci '40; Mt Lake Biol Sta '41, Carnegie Foundation '42, '47, '48. University of the South, Sewanee, Tenn.

20 McCRADY, John, Jr. Sewer systems (Design). b'21. BS (CE) '43 (The Citadel). Resident engr John McCrady Co since '46, design sewer systems since '48. SC Acad Sci—SC Soc CE—SC Soc Profl Engrs (ethics com). 9 State St., Charleston, S.C.

21 McCRADY, Mac Harvey. Water (Bacteriology); Milk (Bacteriology). b'95. BS '06 (Beloit Coll Wis); '06 (U Chicago); '08-09 (U Wis); '09-10 (MIT). Studies on quality control milk and water supplies; development tables for rapid interpretation of fermentation-tube results. Co-author: (with S C Prescott, C E A Winslow) Water Bacteriology (6th edit) '46. Author article: A Practical Study of Procedures for the Detection of the Presence of Coliform Organisms in Water '37. Co-author article: (with E M Langevin) The Coli-aerogenes Determination in Pasteurization Control '32, and others. Engring asst Mass State Bd Health Boston '10-11; chem and asst bact Que Provincial Bd Health Montreal '11-28; dir Div Labs Que Ministry of Health since '28. Am Pub Health Assn (F, com on standard methods analysis for water and dairy products)—Am Water Works Assn—Internat Assn Milk and Food Sanitarians—Fedn Sewage and Indsl Wastes Assn—Can Pub Health Assn (chmn com bact examination of water and sewage)—Corp Profl Engrs Que. Am Water Works Fuller award '47. 1570 St. Hubert St., Montreal 24, Que., Can.†

10 McCREERY, Donald Chalmers. Constitutional law. b'86. Grad '04 (Cutler Acad Colorado Springs Colo); AB '08 (Colo Coll); LLB '11 (Harvard). Research on constitutional law particularly the lawful scope and permitted manner of administration of governmental functions under the Constitution and statutes. Practice of law Denver since '19, mem firm Lee Shaw & McCreery. Capt Judge Advocate Gen Dept USA '18-19. Am Bar Assn(chmn sect on mineral law 47-48)—Colo State Bar Assn (pres '27-28)—Denver Bar Assn. First National Bank Bldg. Denver.†◎

11 McCULLOCH, Warren Sturgis. Neurophysiology. b'98. AB '21 (Yale); AM '23—MD '27 (Columbia); Hon research F '34-35, Sterling F '35-36 (Yale). Studies on activity central nervous system; physiological processes underlying psychoneuroses; mechanisms for spread of epileptic activation of brain; somatic functions of central nervous system. Staff lab neurphysiol Yale '34-41; dir labs Ill Neuropsychiatric Inst '41-51; asso prof psychiatry U Ill '41-45, prof '45-52; research central nervous system Dept Indsl Cooperation Mass Inst Tech since '52. AAAS(F)—Alpha Omega Alpha—Am Anatomical Soc—Am Inst EE—Am League Against Epilepsy—Am Neurol Assn—Am Physiol Soc—Assn Computing Machinery—Assn Research in Nervous and Mental Diseases(vp)—Biometric Soc—Chicago Neurol Soc—Inst Med Chicago—NY Acad Sci—Sigma Xi—Soc Biol Psychiatry—Soc Exptl Biol and Med. Massachusetts Institute Technology, Cambridge 39, Mass.

12 McCULLOUGH, C(ampbell) Rogers. Power from nuclear energy; Rocket fuels. b'00. AB '21 (Swarthmore Coll); MS '22—PhD '28 (MIT). Research and preparation of alkyl bromides and diphenyl derivatives; manufacture of phosphates, rocket propellants and rocket motors; design of nuclear power reactors. Fully or mainly responsible for patents on inhibiting the corrosive action of phosphoric acid on steel, transformer oil; biphenylmonosulfonic acid, mononitrobiphenyl, halogenating biphenyl, acid sodium pyrophosphate, water treating composition, production of phosphates, process for producing styrene. Author articles in field. Project mgr dev and mfg rocket propellants NDRC '44-46, dir power pile div Clinton Lab '46-48, gen development dept '48-51; asst dir gen dev dept since '53. Am Inst Min & Metal Engrs—Electrochem Soc—Am Chem Soc—Am Inst Chem Engrs—Phi Beta Kappa—Sigma Xi. Awarded President's Certificate of Merit '49. Monsanto Chemical Co., 1700 S. Second St., St. Louis.

13 McCULLOUGH, Herbert Alfred. Plant ecology (Violets); Succession;

Alabama flora. b'14. BS '35—MS '37 PhD '39 (U Pittsburgh). Research on Violets, plant succession on fallen logs, local Alabama flora. Author: Laboratory Outline for General Biology '45; also articles in field. Prof biology Howard College Birmingham Ala since '50; dep dir Far East Program Division ECA '50-51. AAAS—Ala Acad Sci—Ecol Soc Am—Torrey Bot Soc—Ecol Union. Department of Biology, Howard College, Birmingham 6, Ala.†

14 McCUNE, Joseph C. Brakes: Friction materials. b'90. ME '11 (Cornell Univ). Research in compressed air, pneumatic machinery, air compressors, friction materials, retardation of single vehicles and trains, anti-wheel slip devices, retardation regulating devices, shock in trains, types of brakes. Holds over 200 patents in brakes and related equipment. Author articles in field. Asst to chief engr Westinghouse Air Brake Co '13-15, mech expert '15-20, asst to dist engr '20-21, asst dist engr '21, dist engr '23-26, asst dir engring '26-38, dir research '38-53. AAAS—AS ME—SAE—Am Welding Society—Air Brake Assn.

15 McCUNE, Shannon. Geography of Korea and Far East. b'13. BA '35 (Wooster Coll); MA '37 (Syracuse U); PhD '39 (Clark U). Research on geography of Monsoon Asia, especially Korea, in various aspects; in charge of economic intelligence work in New Delhi, India, Kandy, Ceylon, Chungking, China, head economic intelligence officer, Foreign Economic Administration '42-45; travelled in Japan, Korea and China. Author articles in field. Professor, chmn dept geog Colgate U since '50. Assn Am Geog. William Libbey travelling fellow Clark U '38-39. Chairman, Department of Geography, Colgate University, Hamilton NY.†

16 McCURDY, John Lloyd. Plastics production and processing; Petroleum processing; Petrochemical production. b'16. BS '39 (Grove City Coll); MS '41—PhD '43 (U Mich). Author articles in field. Research and development phys research lab Dow Chem Co Midland Mich '46-51; plant mgr Torrance Plant Western Div Dow Chem Co since '51. Am Chem Soc—Am Inst Chem Engrs (jr). Dow Chemical Co., Torrance, Cal.†

17 McCUTCHAN, Robert Guy. American hymnology and church music. b'77. MusB '04—MusD '27 (Simpson Coll); D Sacred Music '35 (Sou Meth U); DLitt '43 (Southwestern U). Organizer many schools of music; composer of many hymn tunes. Author: Our Hymnody '42; Hymns in the Lives of Men '45; (with others) Better Music in Our Churches '25; Music in Worship '27; (monographs) Early American Composers of Church Music '32; the Congregation's Part in the Order of Music Worship '34; and others; also articles in field. Dean Sch Music De Pauw U '11-37, emeritus since '37; spl lecturer religious music Claremont Grad Sch since '39; dir choirs festival orgns. Music Teachers Nat Assn—Am Musical Soc—Nat Assn Ch Choir Dirs—Methodist Hist Soc. 790 Mayflower Rd., Claremont, Calif.*

18 McCUTCHEON, William Andrew. Motor equipment management; Transportation Engineering (Motor vehicle). b'98. Student '19-21 (Carnegie Inst Tech Pittsburgh); '33-34 (U Cincinnati). Analysis movement of persons and property by motor vehicle to obtain efficient vehicle utilization; plan and execution of program for effective motor equipment management in Federal government; operation and

maintenance motor vehicle fleets; establishment and operation oversea shops for vehicle assembly, maintenance and tire rebuilding. Author article: A Preventive Maintenance Plan for Government Motor Vehicles '48. Supt automotive dept West Penn Power Co. Pittsburgh '23-29; pres, gen mgr White Swan Lines Columbus O '30-31; gen mgr Harmony Short Line Motor Transportation Co Pittsburgh '31-32; asst transportation engr Kroger Co Cincinnati '32-33; supt transportation (military leave '42-44) Washington Gas Light Co Washington '37-45; staff mem motor equipment management and chmn Interdepartmental Motor Equipment Bur Budget Washington '46-51; now lt col Gen Staff Corps US Army Washington (military leave Bur Budget). Soc Automotive Engrs (vice chmn transportation and maintenance Washington '50-51)—Am Soc Mil Engrs (military engr mem). US Army, The Pentagon, Washington 25. H: 4879 Potomac Av., Washington 7.

19 McDADE, Clint. Orchids; Camellias. b'92. Grad (Valparaiso U). Author articles in field. Owner Armstrong & Brown orchid growers Tunbridge Wells; chmn bd Clint McDade & Sons orchid growers Signal Mountain Tenn since '40; partner Goetz Parry and McDade florists Chattanooga since '46; managing partner Semmes Nurseries camellia growers Mobile Ala. Am Orchid Soc (trustee)—Am Camellia Soc—Royal Hort Soc London(F). Southland News Company, 1501 McCallie Av., Chattanooga, Tenn.

20 McDANIEL, Allen Boyer. Structural engineering (Building design and construction); Water supply, sewerage and drainage; Excavating machinery; Personnel classification. b'79. BS arch engring '01 (MIT). Author: Excavating machinery '13; Excavation '15; Excavation, Machinery Methods and Costs '19; Structural Engineers' Handbook Library '23. Sec-treas Research Service Inc, and cons engr Washington '24-32, dir '33-39; chief engr Arlington Co Sanitary Dist '33-34; supervising and mng engr Bahai Temple '30-43; cons engr Nat Resources Com '36-40; professional lecturer civil engring George Washington U '39-41, lecturer defense engring training courses '41-44; asso with Griffenhagen; exec asso Va and War Dept Manpower Bd surveys; cons agrl and engring products '44, bldg constrn projects since '46. AAAS(F)—Am Geog Soc; Am Inst Cons Engrs—ASCE—Washington Soc Engrs (vp '31, pres '32)—Am Assn Engrs (vp '21)—Am Concrete Inst—DC Council Engring Archtl Soc—Waterford Found—Sigma Xi—Sigma Tau. Awarded first Wason medal Am Concrete Inst. 324 Bowen Bldg., 821 15th St. N.W., Washington.†◎

21 McDANIEL, W(alton) B(rooks), II. Medical libraries, history and bibliography. b'97. AB '20 (Harvard Coll); AB '28 — PhD '32 (NYU). Author articles in field. Librarian Coll Phys of Phila '33-53, curator historical collections since '53, editor Transactions and Studies since '37, cons editor Journal of History of Med since '46. Med Library Assn (pres '46-47)—Am Assn Hist Med (sec '44-46)—Hist Sci Soc (delegate to Am Council Learned Socs '44-48) — Spl Libraries Assn. College of Physicians of Philadelphia, 19 S. 22 St., Phila 3.

22 McDAVID, Elizabeth Harris. Murals in medieval literature. b'07. Diploma in piano '26 (Cumberland U); BA '27—MA '28—PhD '35 (Vanderbilt U). Master's thesis on comparative literature, Vergil and Milton; doctoral dissertation concerned with backgrounds in Greek and Latin literature and ancient and medieval art for decorative literary murals in medieval French and Latin as well as Italian and Middle English. Author: The Mural as a Decorative Device in Medieval Literature '35. Asst prof Latin and Eng, Lincoln Memorial U '28-30; teaching fellow Vanderbilt U '30-32; prof Eng Grenada Coll '32-34; prof Eng·Coll of the Ozarks '34-37; asst prof Eng Winthrop Coll '37-41; asst prof Eng Southern Ill Normal U '41-43; head of dept Eng Coll of the Ozarks '46-50. 313 West Main St., Lebanon, Tenn.

10 McDAVID, Raven Ioor, Jr. American dialect geography; Burmese; Phonemics. b'11. BA '31 (Furman U); MA '33—PhD '35 (Duke U); research fellow '42-44, '45 (ACLS Nat Sch Mod Oriental Langs and Civilizations). Field investigator Linguistic Atlas US and Canada since '46; linguist US Board on Geographical Names '47. Author: Some Principles of American Dialect Study '43; Dialect Geography and Social Science Problems '46; Burmese Phonemics '45. Asst prof Eng SW La Inst '40-42; visiting asst. prof Eng U Ill '49-50; vis asst prof Mod Lang Cornell U '50-51; asst prof Eng Western Reserve U since '52. Lang technician Lang Sect War Dept '44-45. Mod Lang Assn Am (life)—S Atlantic Mod Lang Assn—S-Central Mod Lang Assn—Linguistic Soc Am (life)—Am Oriental Soc (life)—Am Anthrop Assn (F)—Am Dialect Soc—AAAS (life). Rosenwald fellow '41. Department of English, Western Reserve U., Cleveland 6, O.

11 McDERMOTT, John Francis. Intellectual and social history of the Mississippi valley; Franco-American relations; Art in the early Middle West. b'02. AB '23—AM '24 (Washington U). Author: Private Libraries in Creole Saint Louis '38. A Glossary of Mississippi Valley French 1673-1850 '41. Editor: Tixier's Travels on the Osage Prairies '40; The Western Journals of Washington Irving '44; also articles in field. Asso prof Eng Washington U since '49. Mo Hist Soc—Biblio Society Am—Institut Francais de Washington—Miss Valley Hist Assn—Soc Am Hist—Modern Lang Assn—Modern Humanities Research Assn—St. Louis Hist Documents Found. Newberry Library fellow '47. Department of English, Washington University, StL 5.†

12 McDERMOTT, John P. Cartography; Entomology Africa; Tsetse fly; Geographical cartography and exploration; Natural history; Big-game hunting. b'98. Student '14-15, '19-22 (Gordon's Coll, Aberdeen, Scot). Spent over 32 years traveling, exploring, hunting, mapping, organizing expeditions in Africa; prepared and completed first African map Cape Town to London Motor Road (12,127 mi), first African map showing Tsetse fly areas (4½ million sq mi); made map showing every motor road throughout African continent, only all-African road map in existence; listed scientific data dealing with every big-game animal in Africa; collected scientific data for various institutions from Africa's mineral, agricultural, forest wealth, flora, fauna; made films African tribal and animal life; studies Tsetse fly habits; speaks Swahili, Mashona, Matabele, Zulu; mapped route through jungle for Armand Denis and Leila Roosevelt to film Dark Rapture '36-37; participated expeditions Ituri Forest to study pygmy customs, Orinoco River Venezuela, Amazonas country Brazil mapping and collecting rare orchid specimens of region '42. Author: Big Game Hunt-

ing in Africa '46; also articles in field. Chief cartographer Govt Expdns Africa '22-41. Explorers Club—NYC Zool Soc—Arctic Inst NA (charter asso)—Big Game Hunters Assn (Nairobi, Kenya Colony, E Africa)—Nat Audubon Soc—Am-Irish Hist Soc. Explorers Club, 10 W. 72nd St, NYC 23.

13 McDERMOTT, William C(offman). Classical and Medieval Latin literature; Suetonius; Cicero; Roman history; Latin epigraphy; Gregory of Tours. b'07. AB '28 (Dickinson Coll); AM '30—PhD '34 (Johns Hopkins). Author: The Ape in Antiquity '38; The Minor Writings of Gregory of Tours '49. Asso editor: The Classical Weekly '45-49; editor U Pa translations and reprints from orig sources history since '49; also articles in field. Asso prof classical studies U Pa since '48. Am Philol Assn (auditor '44, '46-48)—Archaeol Inst Am (officer Phila Soc '42, '44-47)—Classical Assn Atlantic States (exec com '45-48)—L'Association Guillaume Budé (Am Com: sec '45-47, chmn since '47). Department of Classical Studies, University of Pennsylvania, Phila 4.

14 McDIARMID, Orville John. International trade and finance; Commercial policy. b'09. MA '33 (U Toronto); PhD '36 (Harvard). Author: Commercial Policy in the Canadian Economy '46; also articles in field. chief financial sect occupied areas econ affairs div US Dept State '46-47; chief Financial Affairs Div US Dept State '49-51; dir Fiscal and Trade Policy Div Mutual Security Agency Manila Philippines. Am Econ Assn—Can Pol Sci Assn—Royal Soc Can(F). MSA APO 928 c-o P.M. SF.†◎

15 McDONALD, Frederick Honour. Industrial engineering; Industrial and community development; Geodetic surveys (Georgia). b'92. BS in Elec and Mech Engring '14 (Clemson Coll, SC); '15-16 (U Pittsburgh). Author: How to Promote Community and Industrial Development '38; Geodetic Survey of Georgia '30; Manual for the Business Aid Clinic '40. Pres McDonald & Co engrs and architects '24-32; private practice as cons engr Atlanta '32-39; founder Community Research Inst dir since '39; development and indsl engr SC Pub Service Authority '39-41; cons mngmnt and indsl engr Charleston SC specializing in tax planning, plant location, power and community developments etc since '41; pres, cons engr So Research Corp; dir Ga Geodetic Control Surveys '34-39. Am Inst Cons Engrs—ASCE (nat dir '34-36)—Am Inst Mining Metall Engrs—SC Soc Engrs. Peoples Building, Charleston, S.C.

16 McDONALD, William Andrew. Greek archeology; Classical languages. b'13. BA '35—MA '36 (Toronto U); PhD '40 (Johns Hopkins); '38-39 (Am Sch Classical Studies Athens). Staff member of Johns Hopkins excavation at Olynthus, Greece '38, University of Cincinnati excavation at Messenian Pylos, Greece '39, '53. Author: The Political Meeting Places of the Greeks '43; also articles in field. Faculty mem U Minn since '48. Archeol Inst Am—Am Philol Assn. Royal Soc of Canada fellow '38-39; Regents' scholarship, Victoria Coll, Toronto U '34; Vogeler fellow in classical archeology Johns Hopkins '36-38. 115 Folwell Hall, University of Minnesota, Minneapolis 14.†

17 McDONOUGH, E(ugene) S(towell). Genetics; Mycology; Plant pathology; Cytology. b'05. BS '28—MS '31 (Marquette U); PhD '36 (Ia State Coll). Research on cytolgy fungi, fungus-host relations, diseases flower-

ing plants, polyploidy, human heredity. Author articles in field. Asso prof bot Marquette U since '40; co-dir H V Hunkel Research award since '44. AAAS(F)—Am Bot Soc—Am Phytopath Soc—Am Genetic Assn—Genetics Soc Am—Am Mycol Soc—Soc Study Evolution—Wis Acad Arts Sci Letters. Recipient Wis Acad Sci Arts and Letters research award '44. Biology Department, Marquette University, Milwaukee 3. H: 253 N. Pinecrest, Milwaukee 13.

18 McDOUGAL, Taine Gilbert. Mechanical and chemical engineering (Ceramic insulators, semi-conductors, refractories and kiln design, spark plugs); Overhead irrigation. b'89. Ceramic Engr '11 (Ohio State U). Dir research spark plug engring A C Spark Plug Co, Flint, vp since '28; dir Renown Stove Co Owosso, Mich; dir Rain Guns Inc, Flint, Mich. Tech rep attached to US 8th Air Force '44. Awarded Lamme medal '45 by Ohio State U. Am Ceramic Soc(F)—Sigma Xi. 1117 South Dr., Flint 3, Mich.

19 McDOUGALL, Alexander Miller. Food packaging and quick freezing; Warehousing. b'84. Student (U Minn). Pioneered in hermetically sealing and subjecting food products to quick freezing; patents issued on ship designs. Organizer former pres Terminals & Transportation Corp of Am and Minn Atlantic Transit Co; pres Lake Railways Inc; builder ships for US World War. 3260 Gough St., San Francisco.*

20 McDOUGALL, John Edward. Petroleum exploration; Shock (Dynamite); Geophysics. b'14. BS '37—MS '39 (La State U). Experiments to determine and measure effects of seismograph shock waves on marine life. Co-author articles: (with J N Gowanloch) Shrimp Don't Mind Dynamite '45; Exploration Can be Harmless to Aquatic Life '45; Effects of Seismographic Dynamite Underwater Explosions on Marine Aquatic Life '46; Effects of Underwater Dynamite Explosions on Oysters '46, and others. Geophysicist La Dept Conservation '41-45; now dist geol So Prodn Co. Soc Exploration Geophysicists—SW La Geol Soc—Am Assn Petroleum Geol. Southern Production Co., Box 1268, Baton Rouge.

21 McDOWELL, Samuel John. Ceramic engineering. b'94. B Ceramic Engring '17—Ceramic Engr '33 (O State U). Research and development ceramic whiteware bodies for electronic, electric, and textile fields. Ceramic engr A C Spark Plug Co '19-25, '33-35; supt Columbus O Sta Nat Bur Standards '26-27; plant mgr Gen Ceramics & Steatite Corp '35-41; works mgr Am Lava Corp '41-46, development and sales engr since '46. Sigma Xi—Am Ceramic Soc (F)—Inst Ceramic Engrs—Ceramic Assn NJ (pres '49)—Am Inst EE(Asso). 671 Broad St., Newark 2. H: 52 Elm St., Metuchen, N.J.

22 McEACHRON, Karl Boyer. Lightning; High voltage phenomena; Atmospheric electricity. b'89. ME '13—DE '35 (O Northern U); MS in EE '20—DS '41 (Purdue U). Research on nitrogen fixation, lightning protection of ordnance plants and dead storage; developed thyrite; studied lightning hazards. Author: Magnetic Flux Distribution in Transformers '22; Lightning to the Empire State Building '39; Playing with Lightning (with K Patrick '40); also articles in field. Head research engr high voltage engring lab Gen Elec Co '33-45, designing engr power transformer engring div '40-45, asst mgr engring '45-49, mgr engr '49-51, cons professional employee relations since '53; mem National Advisory Commission Aeronautics (lightning hazards subcomm) '37-46; mem bd Mass State Bd Registration Professional Engrs and Land Surveyors '42-52. Ind Acad Sci — AIEE(F). Awarded Coffin prize '31, Edward Longstreth medal Franklin Inst '35 Edison Medal AIEE '49; Eminent Engineer Membership by Eta Kappa Nu '52; New England Award ESNE '52. General Electric Co., 100 Woodlawn Av., Pittsfield, Mass.

10 McELROY, Paul Kinney. Attenuators (Resistive); Ferromagnetism; Coils (Iron-cored); Transformers (Iron-cored). b'99. AB '20—AM '21 (Harvard). Research on early faders for sound movies; research and design coils and winding machinery, behavior iron-cored inductors carrying direct current, behavior ferromagnetic materials. Engr Gen Radio Co since '21. Phi Beta Kappa—Inst Radio Engrs(F). General Radio Co., 275 Massachusetts Av., Cambridge 39, Mass. H: 58 Douglas Rd., Belmont 78.

11 McELROY, Roy Hardin. Brick, tile, and pottery machinery; Air movement. Ceramic engr '09 (O State U). Design pottery extrusion machines permitting evacuation of air from prepared pottery body; construction and design axial fans and blowers for movement of high temperature and corrosive gases, particularly stacks, duct systems, and high temperature fumes. Holds patents in field. Ceramic engr C W Raymond Co '09-15; with Internat Clay Machinery Co since '17, pres and treas since '23; pres Internat Engring since '32. Am Ceramic Soc. International Clay Machinery Co., 1145 Bolander Av., Dayton, O.

12 McELVARE, Rowland Robbins. Moths (Heliothid). b'93. AB '13—MA '14 (Columbia). Research on ecology, morphology, and taxonomy of Heliothid moths with emphasis on host plants and distribution. Lepidopterists Soc—Cal Acad Sci—Soc Systematic Zool—Brooklyn Entomol Soc. The Bank for Savings, 280 4th Av., NYC 10.

13 McELWEE, Edgar Warren. Floriculture. b'07. BS '30 (Miss State Coll); MS '32 (Ala Poly Inst); '33-35 (O State U). Author articles in field. Prof floriculture Miss State Coll and Miss Argl Expt Sta since '47. Am Soc Hort Sci—Sigma Xi—Gamma Sigma Delta. Department of Horticulture, Mississippi State College, Box 1449, State College, Miss.†

14 McEWEN, George Francis. Physical oceanography; Applied mathematics and statistical methods. b'82. AB '08—PhD '11 (Stanford); '01-05 (Ia State Coll). Delegate to 1st Pan-Pacific Science Congress Honolulu '20, International Mathematics Congress Toronto '24, 3d Pan-Pacific Science Congress Tokyo '26; chairman national sub-committee for US, Physical and Chemical Oceanography of Pacific '27; research on oceanic circulation, turbulence, evaporation, heat exchange problems of dispersal of floating material, eddy diffusion. With Scripps Instn Calif U since '12, prof since '28, mem faculty extension div San Diego dist since '24. AAAS(F)—Nat Research Council—Am Com Oceanog Pacific—Internat Com Unification Methods Instruments Phys Oceanog—Am Acad Arts Sci—Math Assn Am—Am Meteorol Soc—Calif Acad Sci—Am Phys Soc—Am Math Soc—Inst Math Statis—Am Geophys Union (pres sect oceanog '47)—Am Statis Assn—Am Geog Soc—Am Assn Engrs—Polish Inst Arts Sci Am—Sigma Xi—Phi Beta Kappa. Award of merit Am Assn

Engrs '27. Scripps Institution of Oceanography, La Jolla, Calif.*

15 McEWEN, Robert Jardine. Quicksilver. b'08. AB '31 (U Cal). Research on mining, marketing, chemistry, statistics and history of mercury. Mine mgr '32-41; chief mercury sect WPB '41-44; pres Metalsalts Corp since '45. AIMME—Mfg Chem Assn. Metalsalts Corp., 200 Wagaraw Rd., Hawthorne, N.J.

16 McEWEN, Robert Stanley. Vertebrate embryology and genetics. b'88. AB '11—MA '12 (Western Reserve U); PhD '17 (Columbia). Research on various aspects fish embryology. Author: A Text Book of Vertebrate Embryology '49; also articles in field. With Oberlin Coll since '17, to prof and head dept, prof emeritus since '54. AAAS—Am Genetic Assn—Am Soc Zool—O Acad Sci—Phi Beta Kappa—Sigma Xi. Oberlin College, Oberlin, Ohio.†

17 McFADDEN, Edgar Sharp. Wheat and other small grains (Evolution, origin, breeding and genetics, diseases). b'91. BS—DSc '50 (SD State Coll). Synthesized common wheat from cross between two wild grasses; instrumental developing winter flax in Texas; developed disease resistant varieties of wheat, oats, barley and flax, including Hope wheat which was first transfer of disease resistance of emmer to common wheat, Hope wheat is parent of numerous disease resistant varieties now widely grown from Canada to the tropics. Author articles in field. Agronomist United States Dept Agr Coll Station Tex since '35. Am Soc Agron(F)—Am Genetic Assn—Am Phytopath Soc—AAAS. Readers Digest '46 award of $2,500 for exceptionally meritorious contribution to public welfare; Texas Chemurgic Council in '47 for distinguished service to American agriculture; monument to commemorate development of Hope wheat erected by old neighbors at birthplace, Webster, SD '47; Am Agr Ed Assn '48 award for outstanding service rendered American agriculture and country life; USDA '50 distinguished servic award. Agronomy Department, Texas Agricultural Experiment Station, College Station, Tex.

18 McFARLAN, Arthur Crane. Stratigraphy; Stratigraphic paleontology; Geology (Structural, Kentucky). b'97. BA '19 (Cincinnati U); PhD '24 (Chicago U). Research on unexposed silurian section Irvine field Kentucky; made county geological maps. Author: Geology of Kentucky '43; also articles in field. Faculty mem Ky U since '23, dept head since '27; cons in charge Natural Resources Com for Ky '46-48; dir Kentucky Geological Survey '48. National Research Council (subcom Ordovician Stratigraphy)—Geol Soc Am(F)—Paleontolog Soc Am(F)—Am Assn Petroleum Geol—Am Geophys Union—Appalachian Geol Soc—Ky Geol Soc—Sigma Xi. Department of Geology, University of Kentucky, Lexington, Ky.◎

19 McFARLAND, Carl. Administrative and federal law; Legislation. b'04. AB '28—AM '30—LLB '30 (U Mont); SJD '32 (Harvard Law Sch). Co-editor revised statutes of Montana by appointment of Supreme Court '33-36; asst Atty Gen '37-39. Author: Judicial Control of the Federal Trade Commission and the Interstate Commerce Commission '33; (with Arthur T Vanderbilt) Cases and Materials on Administrative Law; also articles in field. Practiced in law firms of Toomey & McFarland Helena Mont and Cummings & Stanley Washington '39-44; mem com apptd at direction Pres to study and make recommendations

on fed administr procedure '39-41. Am Bar Assn (chmn com and later sect administrative law '41-43, '44-46)—Am Acad Polit Soc Sci—Am Polit Sci Assn—Am Soc Internat Law. Received in '34 first Ross award and in '46 thirteenth gold medallion of Am Bar Assn. One of twelve which received first award Henderson Memorial Prize by Law Sch Harvard U. McFarland & Sellers, Suite 502, 1302 Eighteenth St., N.W., Washington.

20 MC FARLAND, Forest Rees. Automobiles (Conventional and automatic transmissions); Airplanes (Engines). b'99. BSME '21 (Mich State Coll); grad (Mich State Auto Sch). Design and research work on automobile front and rear suspensions, engine components including vibration dampers, crankshafts, connecting rods and balancing, standard transmission components, overdrive controls, rear axles, automatic transmissions including torque converters; designer highly stressed gearing and driving mechanisms of aircraft engines. Holds 20 patents in field. Author articles: Tooth Deflection and Scuffing in Design of Highly Loaded Gears; Packard Automatic Transmission, and others. With Packard Motor Car Co since '24, chief engr research div since '44. Soc Automotive Engrs—Engring Soc Detroit—Soc Exptl Stress Analysis—Indsl Math Soc—Tau Beta Pi. Packard Motor Car Co., 1580 E. Grand Blvd., Det 32.

21 McFARLAND, Ross Armstrong. Air transportation (Occupational health & safety); Industrial hygiene. b'01. AB '23 (U Mich); PhD '28 (Harvard); ScD hon '42 (Park Coll); research F '27-28 (Trinity Coll Cambridge Eng). Directed flight fatigue studies of air crews on initial transpacific & transatlantic air transport routes; studied effects high altitude and human aspects on air transport design and operation. Author: The Psychological Effects of Oxygen Deprivation on Human Behavior '32; Studies at High Altitudes in the Andes '36; Studies of Visual Fatigue '42; Keeping Fit for Flying '43; Human Factors in Air Transportation—Occupational Health and Safety '53. Med coordinator Pan Am Airways System '36-51; cons United Air Lines Inc '36-40 USPHS '37-40, Lockheed Aircraft Corp '42-45; cons to the Surgeon Gen since '51; dir commn on accidental trauma Armed Forces Epidemiol Bd since '50. NY Acad Scis(F, vp '35-36)—Am Geog Soc(F)—NY Acad Med(associate F)—Aero Med Assn(hon F)—Am Psychol Assn—Airlines Med Dirs Assn(hon)—Inst Aero Sci—AAAS—Am Physiol Soc—Am Soc Research in Psychosomatic Problems—Optical Soc Am—Sigma Xi—Theta Chi. Harvard Sch Public Health, 695 Huntington Av., Boston 15.◎

22 McFAYDEN, Donald. Ancient Greek, Roman, and Hebrew history. b'76. BA '97 (U Toronto); MA '01 (Harvard); '01-02 (Harvard Div Sch); STB '04 (Andover Theol Sem); PhD '17 (U Chicago); '04-06 (U Marburg Germany, U Cambridge Eng). Author: History of the Title Imperator under the Roman Empire '20; Understanding the Apostles' Creed '27. Editor: chapter on Greek History in AHA Guide to Historical Literature. Prof hist Washington U '22-44, emeritus since '44. Clayton, Mo.

23 McFERRIN, John Berry. American financial history (Corporation, southern). b'10. BA '32 (Southwestern Memphis); MA '33—PhD '37 (U NC). Author: Caldwell & Company: A Southern Financial Empire '39; also articles in field. Head prof bus orgn and operation U Fla since '48. Lt USNR

'43-46. Am Fin Assn—So Econ Assn—Am Econ Assn. College of Business Administration, University of Florida, Gainesville, Fla.†

10 McGAUGH, Maurice E(dron). Settlement (Geography of) Great Plains (Geography); Saginaw Basin (Geography). b'06. BS in edn '39—MA in geog '41 (U Kan); PhD in geog '50 (U Chicago). Research on methodology for study geography of settlement of Saginaw Basin, settlement of Great Plains demonstrating application of studies of climate, agriculture and human use in region. With Central Mich Coll Edn since '45, asso prof geog since '51. Assn Am Geog—Nat Council Geog Tchrs—Mich Acad Sci—Sigma Xi—Mich Ednl Assn—Phi Delta Kappa. Central Michigan College of Education, Mount Pleasant, Mich.

11 McGAUHEY, Percy Harold. Hydrology; Stream pollution; Sewage treatment; Water supply. b'04. BS '27 (Ore State Coll); CE '29 (Va Poly Inst); MS '41 (U Wis). Author articles in field. With Va Poly Inst since '27, prof san engring '42-48; vis prof civil engr U So Calif since '48; Va State Bd Engr examiners. Am Water Works Assn (past chmn Va sect)—ASCE (vp Va sect)—Va Acad Sci—Va Indsl Wastes Sewage Works Assn—Tau Beta Pi—Phi Kappa Phi—Sigma Tau—Omicron Delta Kappa. University of Southern California, University Park, Los Angeles.†

12 McGAUGHY, John Bell. Airfield (Design); Industrial plant (Design). b'14. BS in civil engring '38 (Duke U). Research and design airfields and structural design of factories, terminal garages, etc. Chief design sect US Engrs Office '41-43; cons engr and sr partner John B McGaughy Asso since '43. Am Soc CE—Nat Soc Profl Engrs(dir)—Va Soc Profl Engrs(past pres). 21st at Llewellyn Av., Norfolk 10, Va.

13 McGAVOCK, Ina Beth Sessions. Dramatic monologue (In literature). b'03. BA '22—MA '23 (Southwestern U); MA '24 (Vanderbilt U); BM '28 (Kidd-Key Coll & Conservatory). Author: The Dramatic Monologue in American and Continental Literature '33; The Dramatic Monologue '47. Head Eng dept Westmoorland Coll San Antonio '28-33; head Eng dept U San Antonio '33-38, prof '39-42; asso prof Eng Trinity U San Antonio since '42. Modern Lang Assn—Eng Inst—Coll Teachers Eng—AAAS. Trinity University, San Antonio 1, Tex. H: 1702 Waverly Av.

14 McGEE, John Edwin. History of Great Britain (Ethical movements). b'93. BA '17—MA '20 (U Tenn); PhD '31 (Columbia U). Author: A Crusade for Humanity; The History of Organized Positivism in England '31; A Syllabus in the Teaching of History '34; An Outline of English History '36; A History of the British Secular Movement '48; also articles in field. Asso prof social sci La Poly Inst '31-42, prof since '42. AHA. Louisiana Polytechnic Institute, Ruston, La.

15 McGHEE, Dorothy Madeleine. French and Spanish literature (Eighteenth century); Phonology for drama (American and foreign intonations); Philosophic tale (Literary genre). b'01. AB '22—AM '23 (U Minn); Certificat '26 (U Paris); PhD '30—all U scholar and fellow '28-30 (O State U). Author: Voltairian Narrative Devices '33; Comparative Phonology for Drama '42; also articles in field. Prof and head Romance Langs Hamline U since '31. Modern Lang Assn Am—Am Assn Teachers French—Am Assn Teachers Spanish — Modern Humanities Research Assn—AAUP—Phi Beta Kappa. Hamline University, St. Paul 4.

16 McGINNIES, William G(rovenor). Range and forestry management; Plant ecology. b'99. BSA '22 (U Ariz); PhD '32 (U Chicago). Author articles in field. Dir US Forest Service Rocky Mountain Forest and Range Expt Sta Fort Collins Colo since '45. AAAS—Ecol Society Am—Colo-Wyo Acad Sci—Soc Am Foresters—Sigma Xi—Phi Kappa Phi. Rocky Mountain Forest and Range Experiment Station, Forestry Building, Ft. Collins, Colo.†

17 McGLOTHLIN, John Thomas. Petroleum geology; Gulf Coast stratigraphy. b'06. BS '28 (Okla U). Author articles in field. Associate editor: American Association of Petroleum Geologists Bulletin. Zone geol So Ark and N La '37-39, Miss and Ala since '39. Miss Geol Soc (first sec-treas '40, vp '41, pres '42)—Am Assn Pet Geol (Southeastern US Dist rep '43-45)—Am Geophys Union—Mid-Continent Oil Gas Assn. Room 4, Fuller Building, Laurel, Miss.

18 McGOWAN, Harry James, Jr. Plastics (Metal plating, tolerances in molded parts). b'11. BS '34 (U Pittsburgh). Design, material selection and fabrication of plastics, engineering and development electro-plated plastic parts. With Bakelite Div Union Carbide & Chem Co, sr tech rep since '36. Soc Plastics Industry (mem subcom standards for tolerances on molded plastic parts)—Soc Plastics Engrs (vp '46, pres Detroit sect '49). 807 Stephenson Building, Det 2.

19 McGRATH, Mary Alice. Wyoming history. b'04. Spl instrn in library (U Wyo). Author articles in field. State librarian and ex-officio state historian '43-50; ed Annals of Wyo state historical magazine '43-50. Bibliog Center Research Denver—Wyo State Library Assn (sec '44-45)—Am Assn Law Libraries. 2601 16th St. N.W., Meridian Hill Hotel, Washington.

20 McGRATH, Ralph Martin. Industrial noise; Psycho-acoustics. b'02. PhB '31—MS '36 (U Chicago); '38-42 (Northwestern U, U Pa, U Chicago). Research on measurement of noise environment and standards of injury, discomfort and annoyance and their relationship to field of communication engineering. Author articles: Some of the Practical Problems Involved in a Study of Industrial Noise '49; An Objective Method of Classifying Industrial Noise '52; Current Trends in Research in Industrial Noise '51. With Bell System '20-26; W Elec since '45. Acoustical Soc Am—Am Psychol Assn—Am Indsl Hygiene Assn—AAAS(F)—Psi Chi—Phi Beta Kappa. Western Electric Co, Chgo. H: 400 S. Leitch Av., La Grange, Ill.

21 McGREAL, Martin Edward. Organic chemistry (Detergents, germicides, hormones). b'01. BS '23 (U NH); MS '24—PhD '28 (NYU); '29 (U Graz, Austria). Research on quaternary, compounds, betaine homologs, phenolic condensates. Holds patents pertaining to detergents. Author articles in field. Prof St John's U since '37; cons, part owner corp holding patents. Served in US Navy '42-46, advancing from 1t to 1t comdr. Am Chem Soc. St. John's University, 75 Lewis Av., Brooklyn.†

22 McGREGOR, Douglas. Human relations in industry; Industrial relations (Morale, group relations, management philosophy); Social psychology. b'06. AB '32 (Wayne U); MA '33—PhD '35 (Harvard). Author articles in field. Pres Antioch Coll since '48; cons in human relations various companies. Am Arbitration Assn (panel of arbitrators since '44)—Am Mgmt Assn—Labor Relations Research Assn—Sigma Xi. Antioch College, Yellow Springs O.†

23 McGREGOR, Malcolm Francis. Greek history; Attic epigraphy. b'10. BA '30—MA '31 (Univ BC); PhD '37 (Cincinnati U); Univ fellow '31-33 (Mich U). Author: The Athenian Tribute Lists, vols I to IV, '39-53; also articles in field. Professor Classics and ancient history Cincinnati University since '52, acting dean Grad Sch Arts Sci '41-42; mem Inst Advanced Study Princeton '37-38, 48. Am Philol Assn—Archaeol Inst Am—Hellenic Soc. John Simon Guggenheim Memorial Fellow '48. Department of Classics, University of Cincinnati, Cincinnati 21.†

24 McGREGOR, Rob Roy. Silicone chemistry; Chemistry of fur felting. b'92. BA '16—MA '22 (McMaster U Toronto); PhD '26 (U Ill). Author articles in field. Holds patents. Fellow Mellon Inst '27-31, sr fellow since '31. AAAS(F)—Am Chem Soc—Sigma Xi. Mellon Institute, Pittsburgh.†

25 McGREGOR, Ronald Leighton. Taxonomy and ecology of Kansas plants. b'19. AB—MA (U Kan). Author articles in field. Asst instr bot U Kan '40-42, instr since '46. Bot Soc Am—Am Soc Plant Taxonomists—Sullivant Moss Soc—Am Fern Soc—Sigma Xi—Kan Acad Sci. Department of Botany, University of Kansas, Lawrence, Kan.

26 McGREGOR, Samuel Emmett. Apiculture. b'06. BS in Agr '31 (Tex A and M Coll); MS '36 (La State U). Research on honeybee losses in relation to crop dusting with arsenicals, environmental factors and size variations in honeybee appendages, nutritional value of certain foods for adult honeybee. Author: Beekeeping Near Cotton Fields Dusted with DDT (with Vorhies) '47; also articles in field. With US Dept Agr Entomol Plant Quar Div Bee Culture Coll Sta Tex '48 to '49. Sigma Chi. Division of Bee Culture, University of Arizona, Tucson, Ariz.

27 McGUINNESS, William James. Structural design and construction of buildings. b'02. ME '24 (Stevens). Co-author: Camouflage Manual '43; also articles in field. Prof architecture Pratt Inst; lecturer in arch Sch Gen Studies Columbia U; partner McGuinness & Duncan, Engrs, ASCE. Department of Architecture, Pratt Institute, 215 Ryerson St., Brooklyn 5.†

28 McGUIRE, Martin R(awson P(atrick). Christian antiquity; Medieval Latin language and literature. b'97. AB '21 (Holy Cross Coll); AM '25—PhD '27 (Catholic U. Am). Member President's commission on higher education '47-48, Author: S Ambrosii de Nabuthae: A Commentary with Introduction and Translation '27. Co-author: The Confessions of St Augustine books I to IX '31; A Concordance of Ovid '39; St Basil's Address to Young Men on Reading Greek Literature '34; also articles in field. With Catholic U Am since '27 prof Greek and Latin since '46; US Adv Commn Ednl Exchange since '48. Am Philol Assn—Medieval Acad Am—Am Catholic Hist Assn—AHA—Catholic Biblical Assn—Catholic Anthrop Conf. Catholic University of America, Washington 17.†

29 McGUIRE, Ollie Roscoe. Constitutional, governmental and international law. b'92. AB '17—LLD '38 (La State U); AM '19—LLB '21 (George Washington U); SJD '23 (Am U). Sometime special assistant to various attorney generals of US, special assistant to various US attorneys, for trial of special cases in many courts; speaker before many state and city bar associations and business organizations. Author: The Vanishing Rights of the States (with James M. Beck) '26; Our Wonderland of Bureaucracy '32; Americans on Guard '42; Manual of Procedure Under Government Contracts '45; also articles in field. Lawyer, author, lecturer. Am Bar Assn (mem spl com administrative law, chmn '35-36, 38-41)—Bar Supreme Court US—Fed Bar Assn—Va State Bar Assn—DC Bar Assn—Acad Social Polit Sci—Am Acad Polit Sci—Am Writers Asso. Southern Building, Washington.

10 McHALE, Kathryn. Educational psychology. BS '19—AM '20—PhD '26 (Columbia); LHD(hon) '41 (Brown U); LHD(hon) '42 (Russell Sage Coll); LHD(hon) '46 (MacMurray Coll). Author: Comparative Psychology and Hygiene of the Overweight Child '26; Current Changes and Experiments in Liberal Arts Education '32; Housing College Students '34; also articles in field. Non-resident prof of edn Goucher Coll Baltimore since '35; dir gen Am Assn U Women since '29; chmn citizens' fed com on edn US Office Edn; mem Commn Internat Ednl Reconstrn; mem bd ednl advisers Nat Found Edn Am citizenship; mem exec council Am Assn for Adult Edn; mem exec com US Nat Commn for UNESCO. AAAS(F)—Am Psychol Assn—Nat Soc Sci Study Edn—Kappa Delta Pi. 1634 I St., N.W., Washington 6.☺

11 McHATTON, Thomas Hubbard. Southern (United States) pomology and gardening; Horticulture (Pecans, peaches); Chemical warfare. b'83. BS '03—Sc D '07 (Springhill Coll Mobile Ala); BS '07—M of Hort '21 (Mich Coll Agr). Author: Armchair Gardening '47. Co-author: Land Teaching '10; also articles in field. Professor emeritus div hort U Ga. Capt Air Service Prodn US Army '18; col CO 301st Chem Regt to '41; col Chem Warfare Service; dir War Dept Civilian Protection Schs, Edgewood Arsenal Md, U Fla, Stanford U '42-43, since retired. Am Soc Hort Sci—Am Pomol Soc—Hort Sect So Agrl Workers—Nat Pecan Growers' Assn—AAAS(F)—Phi Kappa Phi. 847 Milledge Av., Athens, Ga.☺

12 McINNIS, Charles Ballard. Law (Federal income taxation). b'99. Accounting '21 (Benjamin Franklin U); LLB '24—AB '27 (George Washington U). Collaborator: (with Randolph E Paul and Jacob Mertens Jr) Law of Federal Income Taxation '34, (with Jacob Mertens Jr) revised edit '42. Practice law Washington and NYC since '26; auditor and atty US Bur Internal Revenue '20-25; sr partner Roberts & McInnis Washington since '36. Am Bar Assn—DC Bar Assn—Sigma Phi Epsilon—Phi Alpha Delta. De Sales Bldg., Washington 6.☺

13 McINTIRE, Floyd Cottam. Histamine determinations; Chem of allergy and microorganisms. b'14. AB '36—MA '37 (Brigham Young U); PhD '40 (U Wis). Research on histamine in anaphylaxis and allergy, the mechanism of histamine release in tissues, antihistaminics and pollen allergens. Author articles in field. Research biochem Abbott Labs N Chicago Ill since '42. Am Chem Soc—AAAS—Sigma Xi. Abbott Laboratories, North Chicago, Ill.†

14 McINTYRE, Arthur Clifton. Conservation (Forest, soil, water). b'94. BS in forestry '24 (Mich State Coll); MS in soils '29 (Pa State Coll). Studies on influence of land use and forests on water; use of wood fragments in soil and water conservation. Author articles: Why waste wood?; Humus from wood; Wood chips for conservation farming; Wood chips, water and soil. Editor: Pennsylvania Forests. Research forester Pa State Coll '27-35; regional forester Soil Conservation Service Region 1 USDA since '35. Soc Am Foresters—Soil Conservation Soc Am—Pa Forestry Assn—Friends of Land. Soil Conservation Service, U.S. Department of Agriculture. Center Bldg., Upper Darby, Pa. H: 1710 Lynnewood Dr., Havertown, Pa.

15 McINTYRE, Glenn Hazel. Porcelain enamels. b'02. AB (Stanford U); MA '27—PhD '39—Cushman Research fellow '25-28 (Western Reserve U). Author articles in field. Vice pres and dir research Ferro Enamel Corp since '47. Am Ceramic Soc(F)—Porcelain Enamel Inst—Sigma Xi—Am Chem Soc. 4150 E. 56th St., Cleveland 5.

16 McINTYRE, Lewis Wedsel. Traffic engineering. b'91. BS '12—CE '27 (U Pittsburgh). City Planning Commission Pittsburgh '35-41, Better Traffic Committee '25-35. Author: Economics of Highway Transport. Asst engr City of Pittsburgh '12-17; chief engr Bur Traffic Planning and traffic engr City of Pittsburgh '30-35; faculty U Pittsburgh since '17. Served as 2d lt CAC World War I, 1t col World War II. ASCE—Inst Traffic Engrs (pres '35-36)—Am Rd Builders Assn—Western Pa Safety Council (dir). Blvd. of Allies at Wood St., Pittsburgh.

17 McKAY, Francis. Parasitology (Chemotherapeutic agents); Aviation (Spraying herbicides and insecticides). b'17. BS '40 (Ia State Coll). Mgr and tech supervisor Safe-Way Crop Dusting Co. Decatur Ill since '48. Am Soc Parasitol—Am Soc Econ Entomol—Ia Acad Sci. Safe-Way Crop Dusting Co., Decatur, Ill.

18 McKAY, George Leslie. Bibliography (Sir Rider Haggard, Robert Bridges). b'95. AB '20 (U Chicago); '19 (U Paris); '22-23 (Columbia Sch Library Service). Author: A Bibliography of the Writings of Sir Rider Haggard '30; A Bibliography of Robert Bridges '33; American Book Auction Catalogues 1713-1934 '37; A Register of Artists, Engravers, Booksellers, Bookbinders, Printers & Publishers in New York City, 1633-1820 '42. Curator The Grolier Club since '23, curator and librarian since '44. Am Antiquarian Soc—Am Inst Graphic Arts—Biblio Soc (London)—Biblio Soc Am (permanent sec '40-44)—NY Hist Soc. 47 East 60 St., NYC 22.

19 McKAY, Herbert Couchman. Stereoscopy; Stereoscopic photography; Photomicrography; Photographic technique and optics. b'95. Student (Ind State Normal Sch). Author: Motion Picture Photography for the Amateur '24; Professional Cinematography '24; Photographic Technique '27; Handbook of Motion Picture Photography '27; Amateur Movie Making '27; McKay Photographic Test Chart; The Photographic Negative '41; Principles of Stereoscopy '47. Ed Stereoscopic and lab dept Am Photography; tech dir Radio Camera Club, NBC camera program; dir McKay Research Lab; founder and dir Stereo Guild; ed and pub The Third Dimension; Stereo columnist U.S. Camera. Royal Photographic Society Gt Brit(F)—Oval Table Soc—Stereoscopic Soc. Eustis, Fla.

20 McKAY, Kenneth Gardiner. Electronics (Secondary electron emission); Electron bombardment conductivity. b'17. BS '38—MS '39 (McGill U); ScD '41 (MIT). Author articles in field. Research physicist dept phys electronics Bell Telephone Labs since '46. Am Phys Soc—Inst Radio Engrs—Sigma Xi. Awarded Anne Molson Gold Medal '38; Moyse Travelling fellow '39. Bell Telephone Laboratories, Murray Hill, N.J.

21 McKAY, Robert James. Corrosion (Electrochemistry, Nickel and nickel alloys); Nickel (Electrodeposition). b'87. AB '10 (Butler Coll); BS '13 (U Cal). Research on action electrochemical concentration cells and differential solution effects as major cause local corrosion of Monel and nickel alloys; air content as controlling factor in immersed corrosion of metals and need of aeration control in corrosion testing; studies in improvement nickel plating. Issued patent in field; others applied for. Author: Corrosion resistance of metals and alloys '36. Author articles: Corrosion by electrolyte concentration cells; Common occurrence of corrosion by electrolyte concentration cells; Properties and uses of Inconel; History of nickel plating in U.S.A.; and others. Refinery research supt Internat Nickel Co Inc '16-20; Nickell fellowship Mellon Inst Indsl Research '21-22; supt tech service on nickel alloys Internat Nickel Co Inc '23-34, development and research '34-37, sect head sales and tech development nickel plating since '38. ACS—Electrochem Soc(vp)—ASTM—Soc Chem Industry. care International Nickel Co., 67 Wall St., N.Y.C. 5.

22 McKEAN, Herbert Baldwin. Wood technology and products. b'11. BS '33—MF '34 (Syracuse U); PhD '41 (U Mich). Author articles in field. Asso dir research Timber Engring Co and Nat Lumber Mfrs Assn Washington since '50; asso ed Journal of Forestry since '46. Soc Am Foresters (chmn div forest products '48-49, sec '46-47, vice-chairman '47-48)—Forest Products Research Soc—Am Wood Preservers Assn. Timber Engineering Company, 1319 18th St. N.W., Washington 6.†

23 McKEARIN, Helen. Glass (American antique). b'98. Grad '21 (Wellesley Coll). Compiler of catalogues featuring Maclay, Fish, and Gaston collections of American glass. Co-author: (with George S McKearin) American Glass '41; also articles in field. Collector and dealer McKearin's Antiques Inc '23-33; supervisor glass and ceramic div NYC unit Index American Design WPA art project '36-39; research and writing since '39. Phi Beta Kappa.

24 McKEE, Edwin D(inwiddie). Sedimentary stratigraphy; Geology of Arizona. b'06. AB '28 (Cornell U); student (U Calif, Yale). Author: Cambrian History of the Grand Canyon Region '45; also articles in field. Asst dir and geol research Mus Ariz Flagstaff since '41; prof geol U Ariz since '42; research asso Carnegie Inst Washington since '34. Geol Soc Am(F), v-chmn Cordilleran sect '48)—Paleontol Soc Am. Department Geology, University of Arizona, Tucson, Ariz.†

25 McKEE, Paul Gordon. Elementary education (Reading, language and spelling teaching methods). b'97. AB '20 (Monmouth Coll); AM '21—fellow '23-24—PhD '24 (U Ia). Author: Reading and Literature in the Elementary School '34; Language in the Elementary School '39; How to Speak and Write (with Harriet Peet and George F Nardin) '40; The Teaching of Reading in the Elementary School '47; and others. Editor: English for Meaning '43; also articles in field. Prof elementary edn State Coll Edn

Greeley Colo since '26, dir dept since '42; instrn cons to state depts edn, city school systems; ed Riverside Textbooks in Education Houghton Mifflin since '42. Nat Soc study Edn (contbr chapters to yearbooks)—Tau Kappa Alpha—Kappa Delta Pi. 1215 Nineteenth St., Greeley, Colo.

10 McKENNA, Philip Mowry. Cemented carbides. b'97. AB '21 (George Washington U). Evolved processes of extracting and refining metals particularly tungsten; discovered new inter-metallic compound, tungsten-titanium-carbide; developed new tool compositions using this ingredient; invented and patented method of separating nickel and cobalt. Author articles in field. Pres Kennametal of Can Ltd since '40; pres Kennametal Inc., Latrobe. AAAS(F)—Am Inst Mining Metall Engrs—Am Soc Metals—Am Chem Soc—Am Soc Tool Engrs—Engrs Soc Western Pa. 1 Lloyd Av., Latrobe, Pa.

11 McKENNAN, Robert Addison. Indians, Northern Athapaskan; Arctic and sub-arctic geography and living; Interior Alaska. b'03. AB '25 (Dartmouth Coll); PhD '33 (Harvard). Anthropological field work Arizona '29, Alaska '29-30, '33. Articles in field. With Dartmouth Coll since '30, prof sociol since '38, chmn dept '37-41, chmn social sci div '47-51, dir Northern Studies Program since '52. With AAF in Alaska '42-44; field test of AAF search and rescue equipment on Mt. McKinley '45. Am Anthrop Assn—Soc Applied Anthrop—Arctic Inst NA—Phi Beta Kappa. Dartmouth College, Hanover, N.H.†

12 McKENZIE, Frederick Francis. Artificial insemination; Reproduction; Livestock fertility. b'00. BSA '21 (U BC Can); AM '23—PhD '25 (U Mo); '31 (Mich State Coll); '37 (Roy Vet Coll Stockholm, Cambridge U Eng). Designed instruments for collecting semen for artificial insemination from swine and horses; research work directed toward increasing efficiency in livestock breeding. Author articles in field. Cooperative appointment with US Dept Agr; collaborator US West Sheep Breeding Lab since '41. AAAS(F)—Am Assn Anat—Am Soc Animal Prodn—Soc Expt Biol Med—Am Soc Study Sterility—Am Dairy Sci Assn—Societe de Sexologie Paris—Sigma Xi. Medal Soc Nac de Agricultura Chile '41. Animal Husbandry Department, Oregon State College, Corvallis, Ore.†☉

13 McKERN, Will Carleton. Archeology (Northern Mississippi valley); Ethnology (Western Great Lakes Indians); Museology (Methods). b'92. AB '17—field fellow in anthropology '17 (U Calif). Editor: American Antiquity '34-38; also articles in field. Dir Milwaukee Pub Mus since '43. Am Anthrop Assn (central sect, pres '33)—Soc Am Archeol (pres '40)—AAAS(F)—Am Assn Mus—Midwest Mus Conf (pres '47). Milwaukee Public Museum, Milw.

14 McKIBBEN, Eugene George. Agricultural engineering; Farm power and machinery. b'95. BS '22—PhD '36 (Ia State Coll); MS '27 (U Calif). Agricultural engineer National Research Project WPA Washington '36; Farm Machinery consultant War Production Board '44; consultant automotive division Aberdeen Proving Ground '45. Co-author: (with L K Macy and L E Arnold) Changes in Technology and Labor Requirements in Crop Production, Corn '38; (with R A Griffin) Changes in Farm Power and Equipment, Tractors, Trucks, and Automobiles '38; (with R B Elwood,

L E Arnold, and D C Schmutz) Changes in Technology and Labor Requirements in Crop Production, Wheat and Oats '39; also articles in field. Prof, dept head agrl engring Mich State Coll '42-45; agrl engr, dept head Pineapple Research Inst Honolulu Hawaii '45-50; charge USDA Till Mach Lab '50-52; dir agrl engring research Bureau Plant Industry Soils and Agrl Engring US DA since '52. Am Soc Agrl Engrs—SAE—Engring Assn Hawaii—Tau Beta Pi. Paper award Am Soc Agrl Engrs '40; Awarded Cyrus Hall McCormick Medal by Am Soc Agrl Engrs '49. 4226 Longfellow St., Hyattsville, Md.

15 McKINLAY, Arthur Patch. Arator; Drinking problem in classical times. b'71. AB '93 (U Ore); AM '04—PhD '06 (Harvard). Author: Studies in Arator I, the Manuscript Tradition of the Capitula and Tituli '32; Studies in Arator II, The Classification of the Manuscripts of Arator '43; The Indulgent Dionysius '39; How the Athenians Handled the Drink Problem Among Their Slaves '44; The Wine Element in Horace, Classical Journal '46; Christian Appraisal of Pagan Temperance '47. Editor: Arator; the Codices '42. Translator: The Passing Show '43; also articles in field. Prof emeritus Latin U Calif since '41. Am Philol Assn—Philol Assn Pacific Coast (pres '24)—Classical Assn Pacific States (pres '21)—Medieval Acad Am —Phi Beta Kappa. 769 Glenmont Av., Los Angeles 24.

16 McKINLEY, Charles Wesley. Automotive design. b'88. ME (Cornell U). Research and design inventions covering automobile engines, transmissions, axles, brakes, bodies and accessories such as carburetors, speedometers, tachometers, gasoline and pressure gauges, air cleaners, oil filters. Chief engr and sales engr Tillotson Carburetor Co '20-25; with AC Spark Plug div Gen Motors Corp since '25, chief engr automotive products from '31. Soc Automotive Engrs. AC Spark Plug Division, General Motors Corp., Flint, Mich.

17 McKINNEY, Fred. Psychological counseling. b'08. AB '28—MA '29 (Tulane U); PhD '31 (U Chicago). Studies in retroactive inhibition, learning under stress, factors emphasizing the development of personality and counseling; studies in free writing as a personal adjustment technique; originated the Pre-Interview Blank, autobiographical case hist blank. Author: Psychology of Personal Adjustment '49. Editor: Personnel-O-Gram '47-49. Associate-editor: Educational and Psychological Measurement '46-49; Journal of Consulting Psychology since '48; also articles in field. Instr psychol U Mo '31-34, asst prof '35-38, asso prof '39-43, prof since '44, psychol student health service '38, chmn dept since '45. Midwestern Psychol Assn(council '45-49)—Am Psychol Assn(F)—Midwestern Assn Coll Psychiat and Clinical Psychol (sec-treas '45-46, pres '46-47)—Mo Psychol Assn (vp '47-48, pres '48-49)—Sigma Xi. University of Missouri, Columbia, Mo.

18 McKINNEY, Harold Hall. Plant viruses; Virus diseases, preservation and classification. b'89. BSA '18 (Mich State Coll); MS '20 (U Wis); '24 (Johns Hopkins U Sch Hygiene). Made first systematic approach to use of quantitative biological assay methods in virology; effected control of mosaics caused by soil-borne viruses in wheat and oats through use of resistant varieties; on basis of experimental work on virus mutation and work with pure-lined virus mutants, developed concept that viruses represent essentially simple gene systems

that are alive; developed rapid methods for testing tobacco and pepper plants for resistance to tobacco-mosaic virus; proposed system for classifying plant viruses in two families and 18 genera; developed basis for virus type-culture system, whereby mutation and contamination will be held to minimum, cultures exchanged among workers throughout world. Author articles in field. Agt, path US Bur Plant Industry Wis Agrl Expt Sta Madison '19-26, path sr path Arlington Farm Va '26-41, Plant Industry Sta Beltsville Md since '41; mem Allison V Armour Plant Collecting Expdn Canary Islands W Africa and Fernando Po '26-27. Am Phytopath Soc (mem com Classification Nomenclature Plant Viruses, chmn '43, mem sub-com virus preservation and type-culture procedure, chmn '48—Nat Research Council (mem com Genetics Microorganisma since '41)—AAAS(F)—Washington Acad Sci—Bot Soc Am—Soc Plant Physiol—Soc Am Bact — Bot Soc Washington — Phi Sigma. Plant Industry Station. Beltsville, Md. H: 1620 N. Edgewood St., Arlington, Va.

19 McKINNEY, Leonard Laurence. Industrial utilization of corn and soybeans; Flame throwers and flame warfare. b'08. BS '31 (U Ark); MS '50 (Bradley U); student (George Washington U) (U Ill). Industrial utilization of proteinaceous materials from soybeans and corn-studies on use as adhesives, plastics, synthetic fibers, water paints; chemical modification of amino acids, proteins to enhance industrial properties; research on manufacturing of table salt, Epsom salt, calcium chloride, magnesium hydroxide, bromine and ethylene dibromide from oil-well brines. Holder patents. Author: Portable Flame Throwers Operations in World War II '50. With Texaco Salt Products Co '31-34, US Food and Drug Adminstrn '35-37, US Soybean Indsl Products Lab '37-42, Northern Regional Research Lab since '46. Lt col Chem Corps US Sixth Army Pacific '42-46. ACS—AAAS—Peoria Acad Sci—Armed Forces Chem Assn —Sigma Xi—Alpha Chi Sigma—Phi Lambda Upsilon. Legion of Merit and Bronze Star medal. Northern Regional Research Laboratory, 815 N. University, Peoria 5, Ill.

20 McKOWN, Harry Charles. Education (Extracurricular, student council, home room guidance, character, youth activities). b'92. BS '13 (Knox Coll); MA '17 (U Ill); MA '22—PhD '23 (Columbia). Author: Trend of College Entrance Requirements '24; Extracurricular Activities '27, revised edit '37, '51; School Clubs '29; Assembly and Auditorium Activities '30; Commencement Activities '31; Home Room Guidance '46, also Spanish edit; Character Education '35, also Spanish edit; Activities in the Elementary School '38; A Boy Grows Up '46; How to Pass a Written Examination '43; The Student Council '44, also Japanese edit; and others. US Dept Edn specialist to Germany '50, '51. NEA—Kappa Delta Pi. Gilson, Knox County, Ill.†☉

21 McLAUGHLIN, Donald Hamilton. Mining geology and engineering (Ore deposits in United States and Latin America, mine valuation). b'91. BS '14 (U Calif); AM '15—PhD '17 (Harvard). Chairman advisory committee on Exploration and Mining Atomic Energy Commission '47-52; Chairman National Minerals Advisory Council '47-49; member Committee on Public Domain (Hoover) Commission on Organization of Executive Function since '47; member National Sci Bd since '50. Dean Coll Mining U Cal '41-42, prof mining engring '41-43; dean College

Engring '42-43; vp Cerro de Pasco Copper Corp '43-46, gen mgr in Peru '44-45; dir Internat Nickel Co since '48; dir Bunker Hill and Sullivan since '49; dir San Luis Min Co since '46, vp since '49; dir Triumph Min Co since '46; dir Cerro de Pasco Corp since '43, Empire Trust Co since '44, Am Trust Co since '47, The Dorr Co since '47; dir '43 Homestake Mining Co pres since '44. Geol Soc Am(F)—Am Acad Arts Sci—Soc Econ Geol (sec '33-37, pres '38)—Mining Metall Soc Am—Am Inst Mining Metall Engrs (vp, dir '44-47, '48-50)—Mineral Soc Am—Seismol Soc Am—Sociedad Geologica del Peru (hon)—Soc de Ingenieros del Peru (corr mem)—Newcomen Soc—Phi Beta Kappa—Sigma Xi—Tau Beta Pi. Boston Jubilee award '50. 100 Bush St., SF.☉

10 McLAUGHLIN, Glenn E(verett). Industrial location; Economics (Resources and regional). b'04. AB '25 (Colo Coll); MS '26 (Columbia); MA '28—PhD '33 (Harvard); '31-32 (Germany). Co-author: Factors Influencing the Location of Recent Manufacturing Plants in the South '49; Industrial Location and National Resources '43. Author: Growth of American Manufacturing Areas '38; also articles in field. Chief econ Nat Security Resources Bd since '48. Am Econ Assn—Am Statis Assn (rev ed Jour '38-45)—Royal Econ Soc—Nat Planning Assn (aircraft ind com)—Am Farm Econ Assn—Phi Beta Kappa. National Security Resources Board, Washington.

11 McLAUGHLIN, James Francis. Public utility economics. b'95. Student (Brown U). Author articles in field. Pres, dir Puget Sound Power and Light Co Seattle Wash since '31; pres, dir Diamond Ice and Storage Co. 860 Stuart Building, Seattle 1.*

12 McLEAN, Forman T(aylor). Gladiolus; Lilies; Plant genetics and chemical nutrition. b'85. PhB '07—MF '08 (Yale); PhD '15 (Johns Hopkins). Discovered manganese deficiency of crops on overlimed soil. Author: The Gladiolus '46. Co-author: The Gladiolus Book '27; also articles in field. Vegetable genetics Va Truck Expt Sta since '47. NE Gladiolus Soc. Virginia Truck Experiment Station, Norfolk, Va.

13 McLEAN, James Douglas, Jr. Micropaleontology; Sedimentary analysis; Stratigraphic correlation. b'19. AB '44 (Washington and Lee U); '45 (Bryn Mawr Coll, Acad Nat Sci); MS '47 (La State U). Research and development specific faunas and stratigraphically important Foraminiferal groups used in stratigraphic correlation; analysis minerals and sedimentary constituents of samples from oil and water wells to determine formations; correlation geologic formations of Atlantic and Gulf Coastal plains. Author: The McLean Card Catalogue of American Foraminifera (annually since '50); Later Tertiary Foraminiferal Zones of Gulf Coast '50; Forminiferal Guide Fossils of Atlantic Coastal Plains Region Between New Jersey and Georgia '49. Contributor: Contributions from Cushman Foundation for Foraminiferal Research '51. Research and cons geol since '47; acting head dept geol Va Mil Inst '48-49. Am Assn Petroleum Geol (subcom on geol names and correlations)—Soc Econ Paleontologists and Mineral—Paleontol Soc—Geol and Mining Soc Am U—Nat Oil Scouts and Landmen's Assn. P.O. Box 916, Alexandria, Va. H: 4 Summit Pl., Belle Haven, Alexandria.

14 McLEAN, Max C. Physical oceanography; Navigation; Nautical astronomy. b'23. Student (US Merchant Marine Acad) (George Washington U) (A&M Coll Tex). Development new methods of obtaining oceanographic data, and new instruments for use in gathering data at sea; analysis physical and chemical properties of sea water samples and preparation reports for ocean area surveyed; tests on new oceanographic instruments. Chief officer Pacific Tanker's Inc '47-48; oceanog tech Woods Hole Oceanog Inst '48; with USN Hydrog Office since '48, now oceanog. Am Soc Limnol and Oceanog—Am Geophys Union—Am Polar Soc—USN Inst. US Navy Hydrographic Office, Division of Oceanography, Washington 25; also Department of Oceanography, A.& M. College of Texas, College Station, Tex.

15 McLEAN, Ross Hanlin. Contemporary English and European history. b'88. AB '11 (Cornell U); AM '20—PhD '25 (Mich U). Member of Carnegie Party of professors of history and international relations, sponsored by Carnegie Endowment for International Peace, for study of workings of League of Nations and other international organizations in Paris, The Hague, Delft, Leyden, Geneva, summer '26; seminar in international law, University of Michigan summer '36. Author articles in field. With Emory U since '19, prof since '25, dept chmn '41-48. AHA—So Hist Assn (founder)—Miss Valley Hist Assn—Acad Polit Sci—Phi Beta Kappa. Department of History, Emory University. H: 1088 Clifton Rd., N.E., Atlanta 6.

16 MC LEMORE, Nannie Pitts. Mississippi history. b'00. AB '21 (Athens Coll); MA '27 (George Peabody Coll); '30-31 (Vanderbilt U). Research in Archives du Ministere des Affaires Etangeres, Library of Congress, Mississippi Department of Archives and History. Co-author: (with R A McLemore) Mississippi Through Four Centuries (2d edit) '50. Tchr pub schs of Ala and Miss. Am Assn U Women (pres Miss div '50-52). 109 31st Av. South, Hattiesburg, Miss.

17 McLEMORE, Richard Aubrey. History of The Mississippi Valley; Franco-American relations (Jacksonian period). b'03. AB '23 (Miss Coll); MA '26 (George Peabody Coll); PhD '33 (Vanderbilt U). Author: Franco-American Diplomatic Relations 1816-1836 '40; Mississippi Through Four Centuries '45; also articles in field. Prof Miss So Coll since '38, dean since '45. AHA—So Hist Assn—Miss Hist Soc—NEA. Mississippi Southern College, Hattiesburg, Miss.

18 McMAHON, Howard Oldford. Very low temperatures; Liquified gases. b'14. BA '35—MA '37 (U British Columbia); PhD '41 (MIT). Research and development of special equipment for liquefaction of air and separation of oxygen, commercial machine for liquefaction of helium (Collins Helium Cryostat), fundamental developments in gas to gas heat exchangers. Five patents pending field of oxygen production apparatus. Science dir Arthur D Little Inc. Am Acad Arts Sci(F)—Am Chem Soc—AAAS—Sigma Xi. Winner Longstretch Medal Franklin Inst '51; Frank Forrest Award American Ceramic Soc '52. Arthur D. Little, Inc., Cambridge, Mass. H: 45 Spring Street, Lexington

19 McMAHON, John Francis. Ceramics (Brick and tile). b'00. BS (Alfred U NY). Research on Canadian slip clay, production low-fire whiteware bodies, silica from quartz sand; development insulating refractories, adaptation of clays for dry pressing, development craft pottery, use Canadian kyanite, influence compositions underslips glazes bodies on blistering other glaze defects. Author articles in field. With NY State Coll Ceramics since '36, prof '44-47, acting head dept ceramic research '47-48, dean since '49. Am Ceramic Soc(F)—Inst Ceramic Engrs—AAAS—Keramos. New York State College of Ceramics, Alfred, N.Y.

20 McMAHON, John Robert. History of aviation; Wright Brothers; Agricultural economics. b'75. Author: Toilers and Idlers '07; The House That Junk Built '15; Success in the Suburbs '17; Your House '27; The Wright Brothers — Fathers of Flight '30. Editor and co-author: How These Farmers Succeeded '19. Writer; traveled Europe '19, USSR '33. Little Falls, N.J.

21 McMANUS, Joseph Forde Anthony. Carbohydrates (Histochemistry). b'11. BS '33 (Fordham U); MD '38 (Queens U); '45-46 (Oxford). Research includes introduction of periodic acid as histochemical reagent for carbohydrates. Author articles in field. Asst prof path Med Coll Ala '46-48; asso prof path U Va Sch Med '50-53; prof and chmn path Med Coll Ala since '53. Am Assn Path and Bact—Internat Assn Med Mus—Soc Exptl Path. Medical College of Alabama, Birmingham 5, Alabama.†

22 McMATH, Robert R(aynolds). Civil engineering; Astronomical observatory and telescope design and construction; Time lapse photography of celestial phenomena; Infrared spectroscopy. b'91. BCE '13—hon AM '33 (U Mich); DSc '38 (Wayne U), '41 (Penn Mill Coll). Member advisory committee 200-inch Astrophysical Project, California Institute of Technology; chairman board of trustees Cranbrook Inst. Science 46-50; vp and trustee Rackham Engineering Foundation; director Cranbrook School '29-46, chairman of board '41-42; member Section 16.1, National Defense Research Committee and consultant to several divisions '42-46; official investigator Office of Scientific Research and Development '42-44, member engineering panel '44-46; consultant to Office of Army Surgeon General '45-46. Asst mgr, later vp and gen mgr Motors Metal Mfg Co '22-25, pres '25-38, chmn bd since '38; prof of astronomy U Mich '51, co-donor McMath-Hulbert Observatory to U Michigan '31, dir since '31. AAAS(F)—Royal Astron Soc—Soc Research Meteorites—Am Geog Soc — Photographic Soc Am(F) — American Astronomical Society (pres '52-54)—Optical Soc Am—Astron Soc Pacific—ASCE—Washington Academy Sci—Am Geophys Union—Am Philos Soc—Internat Astron Union (Paris)—Franklin Inst Sci—Newcomen—Am Phys Soc—Tau Beta Pi—Sigma Xi—Rittenhouse Astron Soc. Awarded John Price Wetherill medal Franklin Inst '33; Soc Motion Picture Engrs Jour award '40; elected to Cuadro de Honor of Astron Soc Mex. University of Michigan, McMath-Hulbert Observatory, RFD 4, Pontiac 4, Mich.☉

23 McMILLAN, Edward Bellamy. Biphysics; Geophysics; Instrumentation; Radomes; Radar; Microwave optics; Antennas (Recessed). b'10. BS '33 (US Naval Acad); '42-46 (MIT). Research on microwave diffraction, radomes, refraction, reflection, recessed antennas; studies on electrical potting compositions, radome sandwich-constructions, special radomes, speical dielectrics, radio teletypes, voice reproduction devices, adhesives, plasticizers, special polymers, propellants. Co-author: (with an MIT group Radar Scanners and Radomes '48. Reseach engr Dow Phys Research Lab '40-42; in charge radome research sect radiation lab MIT '42-46; cons SPB '43-45; in charge chem research United Shoe Machinery Corp '46-50; dir research McMillan Lab Inc since '50. ACS—APS—Inst Radio Engrs—AAAS. McMillan Laboratory, Inc., Ipswich, Mass.

10 McMILLAN, Fred Orville. Electrical engineering (High-voltage phenomena and measurements). b'90. BS '12 (Ore State Coll); MS '19 (Union Coll). Specialist in electrical engineering to Chinese Government in China '43-44. With testing dept Gen Elec Co Schenectady NY '12-14, designing engring '14-20; asst prof elec engring Ore State Coll '20-23, asso prof '23-30, research prof '30-37, prof and head dept since '37. Am Inst EE (F, vp '34-36, dir '48-51, pres '51-52)—AAAS(F)—Inst Radio Engrs(sr mem)—Am Soc Engring Edn—Nat Soc Profl Engrs—Profl Engrs Ore (pres Mid-Willamette sec '48-49)—Corvallis Engrs—Phi Kappa Phi—Eta Kappa Nu—Sigma Tau—Sigma Xi—Tau Beta Pi. Oregon State College, Corvallis, Ore.†◎

11 McMILLAN, James Benjamin. Linguistics (American dialects); English phonetics, grammar, place names. b'07. BS '29 (Ala Poly Inst); MA '30 (U NC); PhD '41 (U Chicago). Author articles in field. Prof linguistics U Ala since '31; dir U Ala Press since '45. Am Dialect Soc—Linguistic Soc Am—Modern Lang Assn Am—Nat Council Teachers Eng—So Atlantic Mod Lang Assn. Drawer 2877, University, Ala.†

12 McMILLIN, Frederick Anston. Geology; Dam foundations; Roads; Quarries. b'91. AB '16—MS '17—'21-23 Teaching fellow (U Wash). Research in manganese ores of western Washington; seven trips to Alaska. Co-author: Tacoma the City We Build; also articles in field. Prof geol Coll Puget Sound since '24; geologist Am Manganese Corp since '33, geologist in charge City of Tacoma sec Nisqually Project '39-44; cons practice AIME, USGS '44-46. College Puget Sound. Tacoma 6, Washington.

13 McMILLION, Ovid Miller. Alaskan geography. b'05. AB '30 (U Ohio); MA '34 (Peabody Coll); '37 (Cambridge U Eng)—'38 (U Chicago)—'40 (Clark U)—'41 (U Pa). Checked measurements flow speed Yukon River over great length Dawson to Tanana in floating rowboat '32. Author: New Alaska '39; also articles in field. Asst prof geog Wilson Teach Coll since '39; vis inst geog Johns Hopkins U '48-49. Second lt later lt col mil intelligence service US Army during World War II in Alaska, NA, Pacific theaters. Nat Council Geog Teach—Nat Geog Soc—Assn Am Geographers. Wilson Teachers Coll, 11th and Harvard Sts N.W., Washington.

14 McMINN, Howard Earnest. Botany of California and the Pacific Coast (Trees, shrubs, hayfever plants). b'91. BS '14 (Earlham Coll, Richmond); MA '16 (U Calif). Author: A Manual of Trees, Shrubs and Vines '19; The Genus Ceanothus in California '30; An Illustrated Manual of Pacific Coast Trees '35; An Illustrated Manual of California Shrubs '39; Ornamental Shrubs and Woody Vines of the Pacific Coast (co-author) '41; Part II of the Genus Ceanothus '42; also articles in field. Prof bot Mills Coll since '18. AAAS(F)—Calif Bot Soc (past pres)—Am Soc Plant Taxonomists—So African Bot Soc—Forest Genetics Found—Calif Acad Sci—Sigma Xi. Mills College, Oakland 13, Cal.

15 McMURRAY, Howard Johnstone. Political parties (Legislation); Public administration; International rela-

tions. b'01. AB—AM '36—PhD '40 (U Wis). Author: American Politics in Transition '50. With dept polit sci U Wis '36-42; mem 78th Congress from 5th Wis Dist and mem fgn affairs com '43-45; lectr polit sci U Wis '45-46; prof polit sci Occidental Coll '47-49; prof govt and head dept govt and citizenship U NM since '49. Am Acad Polit and Social Sci—Acad Polit Sci—Western Govtl Research Assn—Western Polit Sci Assn—Govt Adminstrn Group—Town Hall Los Angeles. University of New Mexico, Albuquerque.†◎

16 McMURRY, Robert N. Industrial psychology (Employee relations). b'01. PhD '25—MA '32 (U Chicago); PhD '34 (U Vienna). Development non-verbal test of intelligence, techniques for employee selection, merit rating, participative job evaluation, employee training, executive development, counseling, employee-management communication, market research. Author: Handling Personality Adjustment in Industry '44; How To Select Employees '51. Asso dir Psychol Corp Chicago '35-43; propr Robert N McMurry & Co Chicago personnel management, indsl relations, market research, since '43. Am Psychol Assn—Ill Soc Cons Psychol—Am Assn Applied Psychol—Am Marketing Assn—Am Statis Assn—Am Sociol Assn. Diplomate in industrial psychology Am Bd Examiners in Profl Psychology. 332 S. Michigan Av., Chgo 4.

17 McNAIR, James Birtley. Chemical and economic botany; Ethno botany; Fermentation; Poison ivy; Wine analysis and chemistry. b'89. AB '16—AM '17 (U Calif); '18 (U Pa); '22-25 (U Chicago); '29, 43 (Chem Warfare Sch Edgewood Md). Research in economic botany, analysis of acids, inter-relation between chemical substances in plants, taxonomic and climatic distribution of chemical products in plants, chemical products in forms, habits and habitats, law of mass action and production of alkaloids. Author: McNair, McNear and McNeir Genealogies '23; Rhus Dermatitis, Its Pathology and Chemotherapy '23; Citrus Products Part I '26, Part II '27 Analysis of Fermentation Acids '47. Cons in Ethnobot Southwest Museum Los Angeles since '29; asst wine maker chem Pacific Wines Inc Los Angeles since '45. Pvt Med Enlisted Res Corps US Army '18, 1t '19; capt CWORC '23, maj '28; chief information intelligence sect '35; chem warfare officer '42; post chem officer '42-44. Awarded Certificate of Merit by Inst Am Genealogy '39. AAAS(F)—Am Bot Soc—Am Chem Soc—Sigma Xi. 818 S. Ardmore Av., LA 5.

18 McNAMARA, Edward P. Ceramic engineering; Glass technology. b'10. Student (Rensselaer Polytech Inst); BS '35 (Alfred U); MS '36 (Pa State Coll). Research work ceramics '35-36; designed and wrote courses of study Pennsylvania State College. Author: Ceramics 3 vol; Refractories for Iron and Steel Industry; also articles in field. Prof, dir dept ceramics and NJ Ceramic Research Sta Rutgers U '42-44; pres, gen mgr Pfaltzgraff Pottery Co York Pa '44-46; head control Shenango Pottery Co New Castle Pa '46-53; tech dir Cambridge Tile Mfg Co Cincinnati since '53. Am Ceramic Soc—Inst Ceramic Engrs—Sigma Xi. Cambridge Tile Mfg Co., Cin.

19 McNAUGHT, James Bernard. Proteins; Nicotine toxicity; Poison (Derris). born '94. AB '16—AM '17 (Kan U); MD '31 (Stanford). Research on botany (algae) and bacteriology, cerebrospinal fluid protein,

blood plasma protein regeneration, trichinosis, chronic toxicity of phenothiazine, nicotine, and derris. Author articles in field. Bact and clin path Grant Hosp Columbus O '22-23; dir clin path Burnett Sanitatium Fresno Calif '23-27; instr path Stanford '31-34, asst prof '35-40, asso prof '40-45; path Bur Chem and Soils US Dept Agr San Francisco '35-37; dir lab Palo Alto Hosp and PH Dept Calif '37-45; prof and head path Colo U since '45. Am Assn Path and Bacteriologists—AMA—Am Soc Tropical Med—Am Soc Parasitologists—Am Soc Clinical Path—Am Soc Exptl Path—Calif Acad Sci—Fedn Am Soc Exptl Biol—Soc Exptl Biol and Med—Am Bd Path (bd trustees)—Sigma Xi—Alpha Omega Alpha. 4200 E 9th Av., Denver 7.

20 McNEILL, E(llis) Meade. Taxonomy of algae; Algae of West Virginia. b'01. AB '27 (Concord Coll); MS '30 (U WVa); PhD '46 (Duke U). Author articles in field. Prof Concord Coll since '32, head dept biol since '44. W Va Acad Sci (past pres)—AAAS(F)—Am Soc Plant Taxonomists—Bot Soc Am—So Appalachian Bot Soc—Phycol Soc Am. Athens, West Va.†

21 McNEW, George Lee. Nursery, orchard and vegetable crop diseases (Nature, causes); Parasitism in phytopathogenic bacteria; Organic fungicides. b'08. BS '30 (NM State Coll); MS '31—PhD '35 (Ia State Coll). Prof, head bot dept Ia State Coll '47-49; dir Boyce Thompson Inst since '49. AAAS—Ia Acad Sci—Bot Soc Am—Am Phytopath Soc—Sigma Xi—Phi Kappa Phi. Boyce Thompson Institute for Plant Research, Yonkers 3, N.Y.

22 McNISH, Alvin Greene. Radio propagation; Terrestrial magnetism; Atmospheric electricity; Upper atmosphere; Aurora; Ionosphere. b'03. AB '24—MS '31 (George Washington U). Research on de-gaussing of ships; developed navigational instruments for World War II including odograph with another person. Author articles in field. Physicist, chief basic ionospheric research Central Radio Propagation Lab Nat Bur Standards '46-49; asst chief of laboratory since '49. Spl. investigator Nat Defense Research Com '39, '41-45. Am Geophys Union—Wash Acad Sci—Philos Soc Washington—Inst Navigation. National Bureau of Standards, Washington 25.

23 McNOWN, John Stephenson. Hydraulic engineering. b'16. BS '36 (U Kan); MS '37 (U Ia); PhD '42 (U Minn). Investigations of turbulence, pressure distribution, sedimentation, manifold flow, cavitation and waterhammer. Author articles: Pressure Distribution and Cavitation on Submerged Boundaries '47; Research in Turbulent Flow; Influence of Boundary Proximity on the Drag of Spheres '48. Asst prof mech and hydraulics State U Ia '43-47, professor since '52, in charge Ia Inst Hydraulic Research '52-53; hydraulic research cons Bureau Public Roads since '49, expert cons Corps Engineers US Army since '52. ASCE—Am Geophys Union—ASEE—Ia Engring Soc—Sigma Xi. Received J C Stevens prize Am Soc Civil Engrs '47, special research prize '49; Fulbright scholar to Grenoble France '50-51. Iowa Institute of Hydraulic Research, State University of Iowa, Iowa City, Ia.

24 McPHEE, Hugh Curtis. Sex in plants (Genetics, length of day effects); Breeding improvement of livestock. b'96. BS '18—MS '21 (U Maine); MS '22—DSc '23 (Harvard). Delegate to World's Poultry Congress Germany '36; charge American delegation World's Genetics Congress Scotland

'39; scientific advisor 4th Inter-American Congress of Agriculture Venezuela '45. Asso geneticist later asst chief charge research Bur Animal Ind US Dept Agr since '23. AAAS(F)—Wash Acad Sci—Am Genetic Assn—Genetic Soc Am—Am Soc Animal Prodn. Bureau of Animal Industry, US Department of Agriculture, Washington 25.

10 McPHERSON, Archibald Turner. High polymers; Rubber technology; Dielectrics; Reclaimed rubber. b'95. AB '14 (Trinity U Waxahachie Tex); AM '17 (U Texas); PhD '23 (U Chicago). Author articles in field. Chem, technol Nat Bur of Standards Washington since '23, chief rubber sect '30-43, asso dir div organic fibrous materials since '51. Am Phys Soc—Am Chem Soc—Philos Soc Washington—Washington Acad Sci—Sigma Xi. National Bureau of Standards, Washington 25.

11 McPHERSON, William Heston. Labor relations (Japanese); Collective bargaining; Labor dispute settlement. b'02. AB '23 (Harvard); MA '24 (O State U); '24-26 (U Calif); diplome '27 (U Paris); PhD '35 (U Chicago). Author. Labor Relations in the Automobile Industry '40. Co-author; How Collective Bargaining Works '42; Labor Policies and Programs in Japan '46; also articles in field. Prof econ Inst Labor and Indsl Relations U Ill since '46. Indsl Relations Research Assn (sec-treas '48-50). Institute of Labor and Industrial Relations, University of Ill., Urbana, Ill.†◎

12 McQUAID, Harry W(inchester). Metallurgy for automotive, farm machinery, drill and drilling equipment applications. b'92. ME '13 (Stevens Inst Tech). Research on electric furnace steel melting, developed direct method hydrogen reduction of iron ore at low temperature, developed applications of continuous casting to flat products, designed billet type ingots for direct conversion, developed different types steel for automotive and farm implements fields, introduced different type steel for oil drills. Granted patents on burners, refractories, steel types, furnace controls, case hardening, high temperature alloy containers, ore reduction, mold design. Chief metall Timken Roller Bearing Co '18-22; with Precision Gear Blank Co '22-24; chief metall Timken Roller Bearing Co, Timken Detroit Axle Co '24-34; asst chief metall Rep. Steel Corp '34-46; WPB '41-43; cons metall engr since '46. Am Soc Metals (Souveur award '38, Campbell lectr, Woodside lectr)—AIMME. (Chmn elec furnace steel com; Statuette award '47)—Soc Automotive Engrs—Brit Iron and Steel Inst—Soc Exptl Stress Analysis—Assn Iron and Steel Engrs—Am Ordnance Assn. 1241 Union Commerce Building, Cleve. 14.

13 McQUARRIE, Irvine. Metabolism (Water, electrolytes, lipids, carbohydrates, proteins). b'91. AB '15 (U Utah); PhD '19 (U Calif); MD '21 (Johns Hopkins). Consultant to Rockefeller Foundation for survey of medical education and research in Japan '47. Author: Experiments of Nature and Other Essays. Asso editor: Pediatrics. Editor-in-chief: Brennemann's Practice of Pediatrics; also articles in field. Prof pediatrics U Minn since '30. AAAS(F)—AMA(F)—Soc Exptl Biol Med—Am Pediatric Soc—Am Physiol Soc—Am Soc Clin Investigation—Am Soc Exptl Path—Am Inst Nutrition—Soc Pediatric Research—Am Acad Pediatrics—Cuban Pediatric Soc (hon)—Mexican Pediatric Soc (hon)—Minn Pathol Soc—Minn State Med Assn—Central Interurban Clin

Club—Sigma Xi. 2615 Park Av., Mpls 7.

14 McSHANE, Edward James. Mathematics (Calculus of variations, Integration theory. b'04. BE '25—BS '25—MS '27 (Tulane U); PhD '30 (U Chicago); student (Princeton, Harvard, Ohio State, U Gottingen); ScD (hon) '47 (Tulane U). Author: Integration '45; also articles in field. Prof U Va since '35. Math Ballistic Research Lab Aberdeen Proving Ground '42-45. Am Math Soc—Math Assn Am—Assn Symbolic Logic—AAAS—Va Acad Sci —Nat Acad Sci. Nat Research Council Fell '30-32. University of Virginia, Charlottesville, Va.†◎

15 McVICKAR, Malcolm Hedley. Agronomy; Fertilizer usage. b'13. BS '36 (U Ill); PhD '39 (O State U); '47 (Va Poly Inst). Author articles in field. Chief agron Nat Fertilizer Assn since '48. Am Soc Agron—Am Soc Soil Conservation—Soil Sci Soc Am—Gamma Sigma Delta—Sigma Xi—Phi Kappa Phi. National Fertilizer Association, 616 Investment Building, Washington 5.

16 McWHORTER, John Francis. Rubber (Finishes, plasticizers, fillers, bonding to metal). b'00. BS '21—MS '22 (U Del); Firestone fellowship '23 (U Akron). Application of paint to rubber engine mounts and steering wheels; development method for baking finish on hard rubber steering wheels, technique for bonding rubber to metal with cement; specification development for reclaims, plasticizers, and inorganic fillers for economical, large volume processing of automotive running boards and steering wheels; chairman material section Society Automotive Engineers-American Society for Testing Materials Technical Convention on automotive products. Holds 8 patents in field. Author articles: Mechanical Rubber '44; Comparing Rubber '48; Materials —Rubber '49. Research engr Inland Mfg Co '28-36; research engr Ohio Rubber Co since '36. ACS—ASTM (chmn vibrator insulator sect)—Soc Automotive Engrs—Rubber Mfrs Assn (chmn molded, extruded, lathe-cut, and sponge tech com). Naval ordnance award for rubber developments in World War II. Ohio Rubber Co., Willoughby, O.

17 MEACHAM, William Shands. Parole and penology. b'00. Student pub sch. Member White House Conference on Parole '39. Author articles in field. Parole commr Va '42-47; dir Va Council on health and med care since '47; mem bd dirs Richmond Div Coll of William and Mary. Va Cancer Found (mdm bd trustees) — Mental Hygiene Soc Va (pres '46)—Richmond Chapter Va Cancer Found (hon pres)—Va Edn Commn (chmn research com '44)—Va Social Sci Assn (pres '41)—Va Conf Social Work (pres '39-40)—Nat Commn Alcohol Hygiene, Inc (mem exec com)—Am Parole Assn (treas)—Am Prison Assn (vp). Received Lee Editorial award for distinguished editorial writing '38. 1 W. Main St., Richmond, Va.

18 MEAD, Leo Roy. Receivers (Radio, television). b'03. Student '21-23 (Knox Coll); '23-25 (U Ill). Research on circuit analysis pertaining to radio, television, electronics; colored television development; portable radio design and development; closed line transmitters for colored television; pulse and sync generator development. Project engr Sentinel Radio Corp '25-35, jr project engr '36-40, elec engr '41-50, alternate chief engr '48-50; elec engr Hallicrafters Co since '50. Ill Soc Engrs—Inst Radio Engrs. 4401

West 5th Av., Chgo 24. H: 200 North Knight Av., Park Ridge, Ill.

19 MEAD, Warren Judson. Mining and engineering; geology. b'83. BS '06—MA '08—PhD '26 (U Wis). Co-author: Metamorphic Geology (with C K Leith) '15. Head dept geol MIT since '34; cons econ engring geol. Geol Soc Am —AAAS—Soc Econ Geol—Am Acad Arts Sci—Am Inst Mining Metall Engr—Nat Acad Sci—Sigma Xi. 88 Rutledge Rd., Belmont, Mass.

20 MEADE, Elizabeth Winston (Mrs. Roger Thomas). Maryland history; Archives; Calendaring. b'04. BA '26 (Wellesley Coll); MA '35 (Johns Hopkins); '26-27 (U Berlin); '43-44 (Am U). Author articles in field. Now records cons AAUP. AHA—Soc Am Archivists. American Association of Univ Women, 1634 I St., N.W., Washington, H: 239 Prince George St., Annapolis, Md.†

21 MEADE, Francis Louis. Philosophy of education; Thomistic philosophy; Modern European history. b'94. MA '28 (St Joseph's Coll); MA '32 —PhD '34 (Niagara U). Ordained Roman Catholic priest Vincentian Fathers '20; prof edn and philosophy Niagara U '28-32, dean coll arts sci since '32, vp '39-47, pres since '47; dir engring sci management war training '42-45; dir Army Coll training programs '43-45; ednl adv second Service Command army specialized training programs '43-45. Nat Cath Ednl Assn (bd dir)—Assn Deans NY State—Delta Epsilon Sigma (exec com since '44). Faculty House, Niagara University, N.Y.

22 MEADE, George Peterkin. Sugar refining and technology. b'83. BS '05 —Chem E '21 (NYU); '14 (U Mich). Research in methods of sugar analysis manufacture and refining for sugar committee 8th International Congress of Applied Chemistry New York '12, International Commission Uniform Methods of Sugar Analysis '36, and technical advisory committee Sugar Research Foundation; studied chemistry and technology of sugar, particularly cane sugar. Author: Cane Sugar Handbook (with G L Spencer) '45; also articles in field. Gen supt Colonial Sugars Co '23-28, mgr since '28. AAAS(F) Herpetologists League —Am Inst Chem(F)—Am Chem Soc— Am Inst Chem Engrs—Internat Soc Sugar Cane Tech—Am Soc Ichthyologists Herpetologists—NY Zool Soc—SCV—Phi Beta Kappa. Gramercy, La.

23 MEADE, Robert Douthat. History of South; Patrick Henry; Judah P Benjamin. b'03. AB '24 (Va Mil Inst); MA '26 (U Va); asst '26-27 (U Ill); PhD '35 (U Chicago). Research for authoritative biography of Patrick Henry. Author: Judah P. Benjamin, Confederate Statesman '43 Contributor: Dictionary of American Biography. Hist asst Dept Interior '33-35; asso prof hist Randolph-Macon Woman's Coll '36-40, prof and head dept since '40. So Hist Assn—Nat Civil Service League (adv council)—Va Social Sci Assn(pres '52-53). Grants-in-aid for historical writing Rosenwald Found, Library of Congress, Am Philos Soc, Carnegie Found, Guggenheim Found; So Author's award by jury '43. Randolph-Macon Woman's College, Lynchburg, Va.

24 MEANS, Ralph Kingsley. Naval engineering. b'16. BS in archtl engring '38 (U Kan). Studies of specialized ship construction problems; development ship calculation, ordnance alignment, measurement of hull deformation procedures; variety ship launching devices. Naval architect Charleston Naval Shipyard '38-47, supervisor scientific section '42-47; naval architect Pearl Harbor Naval Shipyard since '47, chief hull engr '47-49 and since '50. Soc Naval Architects and Marine Engrs—Soc Naval Engrs—Nat Assn Naval Tech Supervisors—Tau Beta Pi. Awarded Bur Ordnance Development emblem. 214 Kailna Rd., Lanikai, Oahu, T.H.

10 MEANEY, Cornelius Daniel. Tide and current phenomena. b'96. Student '14-15 (U Maine); BS '18 (Dartmouth Coll). Hydrographic wire drag topographic and geodetic surveys along Atlantic Pacific and Gulf coasts of United States, southeast southwest and Aleutian coasts of Alaska, Philippine Islands; wire dray survey of one hundred square mile submarine trial course in depths from 225 to 350 feet in open sea forty-five to sixty miles from nearest land. Entered duty US Coast and Geodetic Survey '18, now capt and chief div tides and currents. Am Soc Mil Engrs — Am Geophys Union. United States Coast and Geodetic Survey, Washington 25.

11 MEARNS, David Chambers. Library of Congress (History); Reference library administration; Lincolniana; Constitution (Manuscript history). b'99. Student (St Albans The Nat Cathedral Sch, George Washington U, U Va). Author: The Story Up to Now '47 (history of the Library of Congress); The Lincoln Papers (two vols) '48; Co-author: (with V P Clapp) The Constitution of the United States, an Account of Its Travels '37; Lincoln and the Image of America '53; also articles in field. With Library of Congress since '18, supt reading rms '39-41, chief reference librarian '41-43, dir reference dept '43-49, asst librarian '49-51; asst librarian Am Collections, chief Manuscripts Div and incumbent Chair Am History since '51. ALA—Spl Libraries Assn DC Library Assn— Bibliog Soc Am—Manuscripts Soc—A HA—Am Friends Lafayette—Am Studies Assn—Soc Am Archivists. The Library of Congress, Washington 25.

12 MEARS, Robert Bruce. Corrosion; Cathodic protection; Inhibitors of corrosion; Passivity; Stress corrosion. b'07. BS '28 (Penn State); PhD '35 (Cambridge U). Author article: Mechanism of Cathodic Protection '47. Coauthor articles: (with R H Brown and E H Dix) A Generalized Theory of Stress Corrosion '44; (with R H Brown) Causes of Corrosion Currents '41; A Theory of Cathodic Protection '38; others. Mgr research lab Carnegie-Ill Steel Corp Pittsburgh since '46. Electrochem Soc—AIMME—Am Inst Chem Engrs—Am Soc Metals— Nat Assn Corrosion Engrs (pres '49-50). Carnegie and British Iron & Steel Inst scholar '32-35; W R Whitney award in the Science of Corrosion '49. Research Laboratory, Carnegie-Illinois Steel Corp., 234 Atwood St., Pitts 13.

13 MEBANE, William Marion. Jet propulsion; Solid propellant rocket powders. b'03. BS in chem '25—MS in chem '26—PhD in chem '29 (U NC). Research in jet propulsion, consultant jet propulsion US Naval Post-graduate School '46-49. Prof chem Tenn State Coll '30-41; asso prof chem US Naval Postgraduate Sch '46-49; mgr, tech dir Redstone Div Thiokol Chem Corp since '49. Am Rocket Soc—ACS —Sigma Xi—Alpha Chi Sigma—Am Ord Assn. Redstone Division, Thiokol Chemical Corp., Huntsville, Ala.

14 MEDLIN, Calvin J. School yearbooks (Editing, management, cost). b'95. BS (Journ) '20—MS '38 (Kan State Coll). Author textbook and articles on editing and management

school yearbooks; conducted short summer school courses for school yearbook advisers '47-50. Author: Hints for Yearbook Editors '46; School Yearbook Editing and Management '49. Ed Yearbook Kan State Coll '20; sales mgr sch yearbook dept Burger-Baird Engraving Co Kansas City Mo '21-34, pres '30-34; faculty dept journ Kan State Coll '38-50, prof journ since '48 Am Assn Tchrs Journ. Kansas State College, Manhattan, Kan.

15 MEDULPHA, Sister Mary S.S.N.D. Mexican immigrants in Illinois; Cairo during the Civil War. b'08. BA '39 (Ark State Teachers Coll); MA '44 (St Louis U). Head hist dept LeClerc Coll Belleville Ill '44-46, head sociol dept since '46. AHA—Cath Hist Soc—Ill State Hist Soc—Miss Valley Hist Soc. LeClerc College, Belleville, Ill.

16 MEEK, Frederick J. Mining and metallurgical engineering; Zinc. b'97. Student '15-17 and '20 (U Ill). Improvement design of various units extractive metallurgical equipment for zinc; assisted in design method and equipment for continuous production zinc oxide; in charge exploration and development mining. Engr Egyptian Coal & Mining Co Marissa Ill '17-24; plant engr Eagle Picher Lead Co Hillsboro Ill '32-38; chief engr Eagle Picher Mining & Smelting Co Marion Ky '39-41; plant engr and supt power and mech dept Fairmount City Plant Am Zinc Co of Ill since '41. AIMME— Am Soc Profl Engrs. Profl engr Ill, Ky, mine engr Ill. American Zinc Co. of Ill., Box 495, E. St. Louis, Ill.

17 MEEK, Wilbur Thornton. Finance (Mexican). b'00. AB '22 (Princeton); AM '30—PhD '47 (Columbia). Research in the money, banking, and public finance of Mexico. Author: The Exchange Media of Colonial Mexico '48. Author article: Algunas Consideraciones de Post-guerra. Prof banking and finance Nat U Panama '42-44; asso prof econ U Fla '47-49; prof econ La Poly Inst since '49. Am Econ Assn. Louisiana Polytechnic Institute, Ruston, La.

18 MEEK, William G. Book design; Modern British books; Printing. b'08. Student (London U). Work exhibited Friedman Gallery New York City October '46; represented in American Institute Graphic Arts exhibitions. Author articles in field. Art dir pharm div Doherty, Clifford and Shenfield 47; free lance designer advt art, books, textiles and publs NYC. Am Inst Graphic Arts — Typophiles (NY) — Societe des Arts Graphiques (Cairo Egypt). 45 Astor Pl., NYC 3.

19 MEEKER, Royal. Cost of living indexes; Unemployment; Labor (Wages, earnings, hours). b'73. BSc '98 (Ia State Coll); '99-03—PhD '06 (Columbia). LLD '24 (Ursinus Coll, Collegeville, Pa). Established US Bureau of Labor Statistics Monthly Labor Review, the International Labor Review and other publications of International Labor Office. Author: History and Theory of Shipping Subsidies '05; Directory of Connecticut Manufacturing and Mechanical Establishments '39, '42, '43; also articles in field. Press Index Number Inst, New Haven, Conn '30-36; Spl agent Conn Dept Labor since '35, administrative asst '42-46. 625 Whitney Av., New Haven.

20 MEEKS, Carroll Louis Vanderslice. History of architecture since 1400 (Evolution of building types); Railroad architecture. b'07. PhB '28 —BFA Architecture '31 — MA '34 (Yale); PhD '48 (Harvard). Author articles in field. Asso prof architecture art hist Yale since '45; archtl practice

offices Leonard Asheim and Voorhees, Gmelin and Walker. Coll Art Assn— Railroad Locomotive Hist Soc—AIA— Soc Archtl Hist (pres). Guggenheim fellow '47. Yale University Art Gallery, New Haven.†

21 MEGLITSCH, Paul Allen. Protozoology; Myxosporidia; Systematic zoology. b'14. BS '35—MS '36—PhD '38 (Ill U); '32 (Ill Coll). Made cytological observations on Endamoeba blattae, taxonomy of Illinois and Atlantic Coast Myxosporidia. Author articles in field. Faculty mem Chicago City Jr Coll since '38. Am Soc Zool —Am Soc Parasitol—Am Soc Protozool —Am Micros Soc—Soc Systematic Zool. Drake University, Des Moines, Ia.

22 MEHL, Joseph Martin. Commodity futures; Futures trading; Speculation; Hedging. b'86. B Accounts '05 (Jewell Lutheran Coll); LLM '19— MPL '19 (Georgetown U). Author articles in field. Adminstr Commodity Exchange Authority US Dept Agr Washington since '47. U.S. Department of Agriculture, Washington.

23 MEHREN, Edward J. Civil engineering (Highways and motor transport). b'81. AB '99 (Loyola U); BS in CE '06 (U Ill). Director American Road Builders Association '23-25; chairman Paving Brick Varieties Committee, US Department of Commerce '22-29; member executive committee Construction League of US '32-34; member executive commitee National Safety Council '35-37. With engring party locating Milwaukee and Puget Sound Ry '06; asso editor Engring Record NY '07-11; sec, manager Emerson Co, efficiency engrs '11-12; editor Engineering Record '12-17; editor Engineering-News Record '18-23; vp Mc-Graw-Hill Pub Co, Inc '21-31; pres Portland Cement Assn '31-37. ASCE— Ariz Civilian Defense Bd—Tau Beta Pi—NJ Soc Professional Engr Land Surveyors (hon mem). 536 Arenas St., La Jolla, Calif.

24 MEHRHOF, Norman Ripley. Agricultural economics; Poultry husbandry. b'99. BS '21 (Rutgers U); Mgr '25 (NC State Coll); '32-33 (Fla U). Research on culling for egg production, elimination of slacker hens, poultry raising in South Carolina, methods of feeding grain to laying pullets, Florida calcareous supplements for egg production, suggested war-time feeds for chickens, shark liver oil as source of Vitamins A and D, defluorinated superphosphate, utilization of citrus meal, feeding experiments with solvent extracted tung oil meal, comparison of purebred and crossbred cockerels with respect to fattening and dressing qualities, dehydrated vegetable products, protein supplements, shark meal, sweet potato meal, grazing trials with poultry, breeding meat types birds, broiler studies (floor space requirements, protein levels), egg processing. Author articles in field. Extension poultryman Fla U '24-35, and head poultry dept since '49. Poultry Sci Assn—Am Poultry Assn—Assn So Agrl Workers—World's Poultry Sci Assn— Fla Poultry Council (sec). University of Florida, Gainesville Fla.

25 MEHRING, Arnon Lewis. Agricultural chemistry (Fertilizer, plant-food consumption). b'92. BS '22 (George Washington U); '28-29 (U Md). Research on chemical composition spices, placement of fertilizers to crops, drillability of fertilizers, economics of fertilizer usage, chemical composition of fertilizers, planning for adequate supplies fertilizers during war, elimination of unnecessary filler in fertilizers, standardization of fertilizer grades to save materials and labor. Chemist US Bur Plant Industry '43-46, sr chem '46-53. Member US subcom Fertilizer Com of Internat Emergency Food Council; mem interdept chem statis com Fed Govt; Chem Statis Reference Service; abstractor on fertilizers Chem Abstracts '23-40. Am Inst Chem(F)—Am Chem Soc—Am Soc Agronomy—Assn Official Agrl Chem. Selected one of ten outstanding chemists in field of fertilizer in US, Chem Bulletin. U.S. Bureau of Plant Industry, Soils and Agricultural Engineering, Beltsville, Md.

10 MEHRLICH, Ferdinand Paul. Pineapple research. b'05. AB '27 (Butler U); PhD '30 (U Wis). Holds three US Patents directed to control of fruiting in pineapple plants. Dir research Hawaiian Pineapple Co Ltd '43-49, asst vp '45-49; asst to vp charge research Internat Basic Econ Corp '49-50; vice president Ibec Research Institute since 1950. Am Society Plant Pathl—Am Soc Plant Physiol—Inst Food Tech—AAAS(F)—Phi Kappa Phi—Sigma Xi. Ibec Research Institute, 30 Rockefeller Plaza, NYC 20.

11 MEHTA, Abdul Khaliq. oil (Geology); Chrome ore (Geology). born '18. Faculties of Sci '35-37 (Aligarh Muslim U) '37-39 (Forman Christian Coll) (Lahore and Indian Sch Mines Dhanbad); '39-42 (Colo Sch Mines) U Tex); BS in geol '42 (Tex Tech Coll). Delegate to Pakistan First Industries Conference Karachi '47; adviser to Bahawalpur State, East Pakistan Government and West Punjab Government on oil resources and possibilities of petroleum development; organized department geology and mines Pakistan Industries Ltd, discovered new chrome and other mineral deposits; mineral prospecting carried out throughout West Pakistan. Author articles: Petroleum Resources of India '45; Mineral Resources of Pakistan '45. Mng dir Marks Bros Ltd Calcutta '45-47; state geol and development officer Pakistan '47-48; cons geol and mgr Mining & Indsl Cons Quetta '48-49; chief geol Pakistan Industries Ltd since '49. AIMME—Am Assn Petroleum Geol—Soc Exploration Geophysicists—Nat Geol Soc—Pakistan Assn Advancement Sci—Sigma Gamma Epsilon—Internat Muslin Acad Scis and Letters (organizing com). Pakistan Industries Ltd., West Wharf Rd., Karachi 2, Pakistan.

12 MEHURIN, Roger Melville. Meat food products Federal approval new materials, Analytical methods. b'88. Student '08-09 (Washington and Lee U); BS in chem '15—'22-23 (George Washington U). Examination materials used by and products produced by meat packing industry for acceptability under regulations Meat Inspection Act; AOAC referee on analysis meat food products. Chem meat inspection service USDA '14-45, chief lab sect since '45. Am Inst Chem(F)—Assn Ofcl Agrl Chem. Meat Inspection Service, US Department of Agriculture, Washington 25.

13 MEIERHENRY, Wesley C. Motion pictures (Educational uses, school libraries of); Audio-visual education. b '15. Student '32 (Western Union Coll LeMars Ia); BS '36 (Midland College Fremont Neb); MA '41—PhD '46 (U Neb). Experimental study of motion pictures in certain selected secondary school subjects; study appropriate methods of providing experiences to teachers in audio-visual field; organization motion picture libraries. Author: Enriching the Curriculum Through Motion Pictures '52. Author articles: See and Hear '47; Movies Enrich the Curriculum '47; Enrichment Through Motion Pictures '47. Co-au-

thor articles: A Convocation Film Program That Works '46; How I Introduced a A-V Program '52. Mem edit bd Audio-Visual Communication Review. Dir Neb Program of Ednl Enrichment Through the Use of Motion Pictures '46-50; asst prof edn U Neb '46-52, asso prof edn since '52. NEA (dept audio-visual instrn, resch com, county and rural program com). 312 Teachers College, University of Neb., Lincoln.

14 MEIGS, Joe V. Gynecology. b'92. AB '15 (Princeton); MD '19 (Harvard). Research on tumors of female pelvic organs, excision of superior hypogastric plexus (presacral nerve) for primary dysmenorrhea, endometriosis, syndrome of fibroma of ovary, carcinoma of cervix and other cancers. Author articles in field. Editor: Progress in Gynecology (with Sturgis) '46. Chief gynecol Mass Gen Hosp since '41; surgeon Pondville Hosp Walpole Mass since '27; chief Vincent Mem Hosp Boston since '30; gynecol Palmer Mem Hosp Boston since '45; clin prof gynecol Harvard Med Sch since '42. Am Surgical Assn—Am Gynecol Soc—Am Soc Obstet, Gynecol Abdominal Surgeons—NE Surgical Soc—NE Obstet Gynecol Soc. Diplomate Am Bd Surgery, Am Bd Gynecology and Obstetrics. Vincent Memorial Hospital, Fruit St., Boston.

15 MEIGS, Peveril. Geography (Historical, regional, economic); Anthropogeography; Regional editing. b'03. AB '25—PhD '32 (U Calif). Field work in northeast California '24, Baja California, Mexico summer '25-29, 36. Author: The Dominican Mission Frontier of Lower California '35; The Kiliwa Indians of Lower California '39. Prof geog Calif State Coll '29-42; research and analysis OSS '42-45; ed in chief Jt Intelligence Study Pub Bd (State Dept rep) '45-47; Arctic Inst N Am '48-49; research and develop OQMG since '49. Association American Geographers—American Geographical Society—American Anthrop Association—Washington Anthrop Society—Assn Pacific Coast Geog—Nat Council Geog Teach—Inter-Am Soc Geog Anthrop—Am Geophys Union—Phi Beta Kappa—Sigma Xi (asso). Vienna, Va.†

16 MEIN, William Wallace. Portland cement (Production); Lime (Production); Petroleum (Production); Metal mines (Production). b'73. BS '00 (U Cal). Dir Internat Nickel Co Inc '19-39; pres Bishop Oil Co since '20; pres Calaveras Cement Co '25-51, chmn bd since '51; dir Bank Am N T & S A since '38. Inst Mining and Metall (London)—Can Inst Metall—S African Inst Engrs—AIMME—Mining and Metall Soc. 315 Montgomery St., SF 4.

17 MEINE, Franklin J. American humor and folklore (Mark Twain). b'96. PhB '17 (U Chicago); MA '19 (Carnegie Inst Tech); '20-22 (Harvard); fellow '38-40 (Northwestern U). Author: Tall Tales of the Southwest '30; American Humor '39; Stories of the Streets and of the Town, Chicago '40; John McCutcheon's Book '48. Co-author: (with Walter Blair) Mike Fink, King of the Keelboatmen '33. Editor Consolidated Book Publishers '38-48; editor-in-chief American Peoples Encyclopedia '48. Soc Midland Authors (treas since '45)—Am Folklore Soc (dir '48)—Cliff Dwellers (dir '44-46). 153 N. Michigan Av., Chicago 1.

18 MEINECKE, Emilio Pepe Michael. Forest pathology and forest hygiene; Uredineae (Rusts). b'69. Student (U Freiburg, Leipzig, Bonn); PhD '93 (U Heidelberg). Author: Die Hefe (transl) '98; Allgemeine Botanik (transl) '09;

Forest Tree Diseases Common in California and Nevada '14; Forest Pathology in Forest Regulation '16; Les Vanillieres de Tahiti and Moorea '16 (Tahitian transl '17); also articles in field. Principal path in charge research planning and criticism US Dept Agr '29-39, retired since '39. AAAS(F)—Calif Acad Sci(F)—Mycol Soc Am—Bot Soc Am—Bot Soc Calif—Am Naturalists—Soc Am Foresters—Am Phytopath Soc—Sigma Xi. 3157 Jackson St., San Francisco 15.

19 MEINEKE, Ellsworth. Honey candies. b'98. Began as honey producer '19; developed and began mfg honey candies '29. Ill State Beekeeper's Assn (pres '45-48)—Ill Beekeeping Com (chmn '45-48)—Cook-DuPage Beekeepers Assn—Am Beekeeping Fedn. R. R. 1, Arlington Heights, Ill.

20 MELCHER, Daniel. Book publishing; Libraries; Printing; Communication techniques. b'12. AB '34 (Harvard). Author: Young Mr Stone, Book Publisher '39; The Printing and Promotion Handbook '49. With R R Bowker Co Publishers since '46. Publs cons War Finance Div US Treasury Dept Washington '42-43, nat dir edn sect '43-45, dir Nat Com Atomic Information Washington '46. Am Inst Graphic Arts. R. R. Bowker Co., Publishers, 62 W. 45th St., NYC 19.

21 MELCHER, Frederic Gershom. Publishing; Bookselling. b'79. Ed (pub sch Newton Mass). Founder of Children's Book Week '19; lecturer and writer on publishing and bookselling; established John Newbery medal awarded each year by American Library Association to the most distinguished contributor to American literature for children and Caldecott medal for the best. American picture book for children. Co-editor: The Publishers' Weekly since '18; pres R R Bowker & Co. Am Booksellers' Assn (hon F, sec '18-20)—NY Library Assn (pres '35-36)—Nat Assn Book Pub (exec sec '20-24)—Am Inst Graphic Arts (pres '27)—Am Library Inst—ALA (hon life). Awarded gold medal Am Inst Graphic Arts '45. 62 W 45th St., NYC 19.

22 MELHUS, Irving E. Corn; Latin American agriculture. b'81. BS '06 (Ia State Coll); PhD '12 (U Wis). Co-author: (With Dr. G C Kent) Plant Pathology '39. Prof plant path Ia State Coll since '17, head dept bot '30-46, dir Ia State Coll Guatemala Tropical Research Center. Am Soc Naturalists—Bot Soc Am—Am Phytopath Soc—Crop Protection Inst—Torrey Bot Club—Sigma Xi—Phi Kappa Phi—Gamma Sigma Delta. Iowa State College, Ames, Ia.

23 MELLEN, Frederic Francis. Oil geology; Stratigraphy; Mississippi mineral resources. b'11. BSc '34 (Miss State Coll); MSc '37 (U Miss). Discovered extensive commercial bentonite deposits in Mississippi; discovered the Tinsley Dome Yazoo County Mississippi '38-39. Author articles in field. Cons geol since '40. Am Assn Pet Geol—Paleontol Soc—Miss Geol Soc (pres '46-47). 113½ W. Capitol St., Jackson, Miss.

24 MELLEN, Ida M. Ichthyology (Aquariums); Felinology; Roof gardening. b'77. Student '08-10 (Marine Biol Lab Woods Hole Mass)—'12 (Eugenics Research Assn Cold Spring Harbor NY); hon DSc '21 (Coll Sciences). Pioneer in aquatic-animal therapy. Author: Fishes in the Home '27; Young Folks' Book of Fishes '27; Roof Gardening '29; A Practical Cat Book '39; The Science and the Mystery of the Cat '40; The Wonder World of

Fishes '51; The Natural History of the Pig '52. Co-author: 1001 Questions Answered About Your Aquarium (with R J Lanier) '35. Aquarist NY Aquarium '16-29, care and feeding aquatic animals in captivity; research and writing since '29. 547 E. 4th St., Brooklyn 18.

10 MELLON, Melvin Guy, Chemistry (Analytical); Colorimetry; Spectrophotometry. b'93. BS '15—ScD '70 (Allegheny Coll); MS '17—PhD '19 (O State U). Author: Chemical Publications '28; Methods of Quantitative Chemical Analysis '37; Quantitative Analysis Record Book '44; Colorimetry for Chemists '45; Absorptimetry and Colorimetry '49; Quantitative Analysis '51. Editor: Absorptimetry and Colorimetry '49; also articles in field. With Purdue U since '19, prof analytical chem since '31. Am Chem Soc—Am Soc Testing Materials—AAAS(F)—Optical Soc Am—Ind Acad Sci (pres '42)—Inter-Soc Color Council. Fisher award analytical chem '50. Department of Chemistry, Purdue University, Lafayette, Ind.⊙

11 MELLON, Ralph Robertson, Bacterial variation; Chemotherapy. b'83. BS '01—hon DSc '36 (Grove City Pa Coll); MD '09—MS '12 (U Mich); DrPH '16 (Harvard Med Sch). Pioneered in the experimental development of bacterial variation; one of earliest experimenters with sulfa drugs in America, his laboratory pioneered in application of sulfathiazole to pneumonia. Author articles in field. Successively instr in med, asst and asso prof and dir Lab of Clin Pathol U Mich '09-15; dir lab Highland Hosp Rochester '16-27; dir Mellon Inst Med Research Fund in Inst Pathol The Western Pa Hosp, dir Inst Path. Soc Am Bacteriologists—Am Soc Immunologists—AMA—Assn Path. Western Pennsylvania Hospital, Pitts.

12 MELNICK, Daniel. Food technology. b'10. PhB '31 (Yale Coll); PhD '36—Coxe fellow '36-37 (Yale). Research on Proteins, blood transfusions, vitamins, enzymes, food preparations and stabilization, nutrition. Author articles in field. Chief vitamin research lab U Mich '37-40; chief chem and supervisor of research Food Research Lab Long Island City NY '40-47; chief food development div QM Food and Container Inst for Armed Forces Chicago '47-49; chief tech The Best Foods Inc since '49. Am Chem Soc—Biol Chem—Am Inst Nutrition—Sigma Xi—Am Assn Vitamin Chem—Inst Food Tech. Research Laboratories, The Best Foods Inc., Bayonne, N.J.

13 MELOCHE, Villiers Willson. Chemistry Analytical, inorganic, selenium, tellurium, rhenium, trace elements; Instrumental analysis, hydroanalysis. b'95. BS '21—MS '23—PhD '25 (U Wis). Co-author: (with Town, Hall) Manual of Quantitative Analysis; also articles in field. With dept analytical chem U Wis since '25, prof since '38. Wis Acad Sci—AAAS—Am Chem Soc—Sigma Xi. Department of Chemistry, University of Wisconsin, Madison 6, Wis.

14 MELONEY, Henry Mitchell. Forestry and forest products. b'96. BS '19—MF '22 (NY State Coll Forestry); fellow '20 (Royal Swedish Inst Forestry); student (Columbia U). Exec sec Business Forms Inst since '44. Am Trade Assn Execs—Trade Assn Execs NY—Soc Am Foresters—For Products Research Soc. Business Forms Institute, 220 E. 42d St., NYC 17.

15 MELSTED, Sigurd W(alter). Soil chemistry (Fertilizers; base-exchange equilibria reactions, colloids, nutrient levels, analysis). b'11. BS '38 (ND Agrl Coll); MS '40 (Rutgers U); PhD '43 (U Ill). Engaged research soil analysis and new techniques including X-ray, spectroscopic analysis, infra red, radio active isotope work. Author articles in field. Chem Soil Testing Lab Rutgers U '38-40; first asst Soil Survey Analysis U Ill '40-43, asso prof soil analysis research since '46. AAAS—Am Chem Soc—Am Soc Agronomy—Soil Sci Am—Sigma Xi—Gamma Sigma Delta—Phi Kappa Phi. 316 Davenport Hall, University of Illinois, Urbana, Ill.†

16 MELTON, Frank Armon. Aerial photographic geology; Geomorphology; Structural geology. b'96. BS '15 (Okla A & M Coll); PhD '24 (U Chicago); post doctoral study (Columbia U, U Bonn Germany; Technische Hochschule Zurich). Author articles in field. Asso prof geol U Okla '26-48, prof since '39; cons geol for aerial-photo discovery of oil and gas structures. Geol Soc Am(F)—AAAS(F)—Am Geophys Union—NY Acad Sci—Okla Acad Sci—Am Assn Pet Geol. Geology Department, University of Oklahoma, Norman, Okla.†

17 MELVILLE, Donald Burton. Chemical structure of biotin. b'14. BS '36—MS '37—PhD '39 (U Ill). Special work in determination of chemical structure of biotin, a vitamin of the B-complex; work on the chemical structure of penicillin, organic syntheses with radioactive isotopes. Research asso dept biochem Cornell U Med Coll '39-46, asst prof '46-47, asso prof since '47. Am Chem Soc—Harvey Soc—NY Acad Sci—Am Soc Biol Chem—Sigma Xi—Phi Kappa Phi. Cornell University Medical College, 1300 York Av., NYC 21.

18 MELZER, John Henry. Functional logic; Critical monism; Philosophy of DC Macintosh. b'08. AM '34—PhD '37 (Vanderbilt U); '35 (Yale). Author: An Examination of Critical Monism '37; a Guide to Philosophical Terminology '37; Functional Logic '51. Asso prof philos U Ky since '51. Am Philos Assn—So Soc Philos & Psychol. Department of Philosophy, University of Kentucky, Lexington, Ky.

19 MENAUL, Paul Lynn. Corrosion (Subsurface); Oil well cementing and acidizing. b'01. AB '15—MS '17 (U NM). Research on methods of inhibitary sub-surface corrosion in oil wells. Holds three patents in field. Author articles in field. Senior chem Stanolind Oil and Gas Co since '42. Stanolind Oil and Gas Co., Tulsa, Okla. H: 1308 S. Marion.

20 MENCKEN, Henry Louis. American language. b'80. Student (Baltimore Polytechnic). Author: Ventures Into Verse '03; A Book of Prefaces '17; In Defense of Women '17; The American Language '18, 4th revision '36, Supplement I '45, Supplement II '48; Prejudices—First Series '19, Second Series '20, Third Series '22, Fourth Series '24, Fifth Series '26, Sixth Series '27; Treatise on the Gods '30; Treatise on Right and Wrong '36; Christmas Story '46; The Days of H L Mencken '47. Dir Alfred A Knopf Inc. Modern Lang Assn—Linguistic Soc—Am Dialect Soc. 1524 Hollins St., Baltimore 23.⊙

21 MENDELL, Clarence Whittlesey. Latin literature. b'83. AB '04—MA '05—PhD '10—LLD '53 (Yale). Author: Sentence Connection in Tacitus '11; Latin Sentence Connection '17; Prometheus '26; Jeanne d'Arc '31; Or Seneca '41. With Yale U since '07, asst prof Greek and Latin '11-19, Dunham prof Latin language and literature '19, dean coll '26-37, master Branford coll '32-43,

Sterling prof since '47, pub orator '47-50; Annual prof Am Acad Rome '32-33, now trustee. Am Philol Assn—Classical Assn Gt Brit—Phi Beta Kappa. 72 Yale Station, New Haven.⊙

22 MENDEZ PEREIRA, Octavio. Education; History. b'87. Grad '08 (Normal Sch Panama); '13 (U Chile); Dr honoris causa (U San Marcos Lima) (Faculty Law and Polit Sci Panama) (U Havana) (U So Cal) (Nat U Colombia); certificate (U London). Author: Higiene del Estudiante '12; Elementos de Instruccion Cívica (5th edt); Parnaso Panameno '16; Ejercicios de Lenguaje (New York); Dante '22; El Canal de Panamá; En el Surco '25; Emociones y Evocaciones (Paris) '28; El Tesoro del Dabaibe '33; Historia de Ibero-America '36; Tierra Firme '40; other hist works. Founder, now pres U Panama. Panamanian del League of Nations, Internat Labor Conf, San Francisco Conf 1st Gen Assembly United Nations NY; dir Regional Center of UNESCO in Western Hemisphere '50. Acad Panamena de la Lengua, Acad Panamena de la Historia—Union Iber-Americana of Panamá—Sociedad Bolivariana—Sociedad Panamena de Derecho Internacional—Asociacion de Maestros(hon)—Comité France-Amérique. Medal Pub Instrn Chile. Universidad de Panama, Panama.⊙

23 MENEFEE, Ferdinand Northrup. Mechanics of materials; Reinforced concrete; Hydraulic structures. b'86. BS in CE '08—CE '32 (Nebraska U); CE '10 (Cornell); DE '37 (Lawrence Inst Tech). Research in properties of materials; precast and prestressed reinforced concrete, vibration problems, expert testimony patent and damage case USPHS overall problems in river engineering. Author: Materials Testing Manual '32; St Lawrence Seaway '40; Structural Members and Connections (co-reviser with R R Zipprodt) '43; also articles in field. Instr Mich U '10-13, asst prof drawing '14, asst prof engring, mechanics '15-16, prof since '19; sec United Engring Corp Detroit '19-20, v pres '20-29; Menefee and Dodge '25-35; pres Bd Pub Works Ann Arbor '35-40; pres Oak Park Land Co since '25; treas Dana Fiduciary; dir Peerless Cement Corp; pres Lus-Trus Extruded Plastics Inc. ASCE—Am Soc Testing Materials—Am Concrete Inst—Mich Engring Soc—Mich Patent Law Assn—Engring Soc Detroit—Sigma Xi. 104 W. Engineering Building, University of Michigan, Ann Arbor.

24 MENEFEE, Selden Cowles. American folkways; Mexican immigrants in the United States; Attitude measurement; Public opinion. b'09. AB Magna cum laude '33—AM '35—fellow psychol '33-34 (U Wash). Author: Pecan Shellers of San Antonio '40; Mexican Migratory Workers of South Texas '41; Vocational Training and Employment of Youth '42; Assignment: U.S.A., Am edit '43, Brit edit '44; also articles in field. Editor and publisher San Juan Record, Fair Oaks Calif since '48. Am Geog Soc(F)—Am Sociol Soc—Phi Beta Kappa. P.O. Box 38, Fair Oaks, Calif.

25 MENGES, Karl Heinrich. Slavic and Altaic Languages (Turkic, Mongol, Manchu-Tungus). b'08. PhD '32 (U Berlin). Research and field work Soviet-Union including Turkistan and Caucasus, Yugoslavia '31, Syria and Lebanon '38; Persia '48. Author: Qaraqalpaq Grammar, I: Phonology '47; also articles in field. Asso prof Slavic and Altaic Langs Columbia U since '47. Linguistic Soc Am—Am Oriental Soc—Am Geo Soc—Societe Finno-Ougrienne—Societe d'Iranologie

—NY Linguistic Cercle. Columbia University, NYC 27.†

10 MENKE, Warren Wells. Tubes (Electronic); Illumination. b'20. SB '42 (MIT); MS '49 (Purdue U). Research on reflex klystron. Chief engr reflex klystron Sylvania Elec Products Inc '43-46; supervisor illumination courses Purdue U since '46. Eta Kappa Nu—Sigma Xi—Sigma Pi Sigma—Optical Soc Am—Illuminating Engring Soc. Room 332, Electrical Engineering Bldg., Purdue University, West Lafayette, Ind.

11 MENNINGER, Edwin Arnold. Flowering tropical trees. b'96. AB '16 (Washburn U); '16-19 (Columbia). Research in showy-flowered trees of the tropics since 33. Author Catalog of Flowering Tropical Trees '46. Co-author: (with David Sturrock) Shade and Ornamental Trees for South Florida and Cuba '47; also articles in field. Owner and publisher South Florida Developer '23-28, Stuart Daily News Stuart Fla '28-34, Stuart News since '34. Royal Hort Soc(F)—Fairchild Tropical Garden—NY Bot Garden—Am Forestry Assn—Am Hort Soc—Bot Soc South Africa—Fla State Hort Soc. Bin 1, Stuart, Fla.

12 MENZEL, Donald H(oward). Flying saucers; Eclipses; Spectroscopy; Solar atmosphere. b'01. AB '20—AM '21 (U Denver); AM '23—PhD '24 (Princeton); AM hon '42 (Harvard). Research in fields astrophysics, solar atmosphere, eclipses, planetary temperature, absorption and emission lines, theory of gaseous nebulae, wave mechanics, spectroscopy, ionosphere, radio propagation. Author: A Study of the Solar Chromosphere '31; Star and Planets '31; Story of the Starry Universe '41; Manual of Radio Propagation '47; Our Sun '49. Editor The Telescope '36-40; bd editors Sky and Telescope since '40; editor Prentice Hall Physics Series since '47. Asst astronomer Lick Observatory '26-32; asst prof astronomy Harvard '32-35, asso prof astrophysics '35-38, prof astrophysics since '38, chmn dept astronomy '46-49, asso dir Harvard Observatory for solar research since '47; mem Lick Obs-Crocker eclipse expdns '30-32; dir Harvard-Mass Inst Tech eclipse expdn USSR '36; dir US-Brit eclipse expdn Can '45. Am Philos Soc—AAAS —Am Astron Soc(councillor '38-41, vp '46-48)—Am Assn Variable Star Observers—Astron Soc Pacific—Am Acad Arts and Scis—Nat Acad—Royal Astron Soc—Am Phys Soc—Internat Astron Union—Internat Radio Union—Sigma Xi. A Cressy Morrison award NY Acad Sci '26 '28. H: 32 Hubbard Park, Cambridge 38, Mass.☺

13 MERCER, Samuel Alfred Browne. Religion (Ancient Egyptian, Semitic, Babylonian, Assyrian, Old Testament); Egyptian archeology; Ethiopic and Old Testament language and literature; Ancient Near Orient (History, civilization). b'80. BSc '00 (St John's Newfoundland); BD '04 (Nashotah House Wis); BA '08 (Harvard); Semitic studies (Göttingen; Heidelberg; the Sorbonne; Munich); PhD '10 (U Munich); ThD '38 (Paris); DSLitt '39 (Kenyon Coll). Founder Anglican Theol Review; founder and editor of the Jr Society of Oriental Research. Author: Extra-Biblical Sources for Hebrew History '13; The Ethiopic Liturgy '15; Sumers-Babylonian Sign List '18; Ethiopic Grammar '19; Assyrian Grammar '21; Egyptian Grammar '27; Ethiopic Text of Ecclesiastes '31; The Tell el-Amarna Tablets '39, Horus, Royal God of Egypt '42; Sumers-Babylonian Year Formulae '46; Religion of Ancient Egypt '48. Editor: Egyptology in Webster's New

Internat Dictionary; also articles in field. Prof Semitic lang and Egyptology Trinity Coll Toronto '23-46, prof emeritus since '46. Am Oriental Soc—Internat Soc Apocrypha (vp)—Royal Asiatic Soc — Royal Geog Soc(F). Retired.☺

14 MERCHANT, Mylon Eugene. Machinability of metals; Mechanics of cutting metals; Cutting fluids. b'13. BS '36 (U Vt); '32-33 (US Naval Acad); DSc '41 (U Cincinnati). Research on machinability of metals, mechanics of metal cutting and fundamentals of cutting fluid action and boundary lubrication, fundamentals of friction, lubrication and the metal cutting process; developed theory of dry friction and basic metal cutting theory, details of mechanics of metal cutting. Author articles in field. Grad coop fellow sponsored by the Cincinnati Milling Machine Co at the Basic Sci Lab U Cincinnati '36-40; assistant director of research The Cincinnati Milling Machine Co. American Physics Soc — ASME — AM Soc Lubrication Engrs—Am Soc Metals—Am Chem Soc —Engring Soc Cincinnati. Research Department, The Cincinnati Milling Machine Company, Cincinnati 9. H: 3709 Center St., Mariemont.

15 MERCIER, Vincent James. Well logging. b'14. Student '31-33 (U Mo); '34-35 (First Nat Television Inc). Research on interpretation and application radioactive measurements applied to oil wells, recording natural gamma ray emanations from geologic formation and recording induced radiation by neutron bombardment of formation. Chief observer Nat Geophys Co '36-42; div engr Lane Wells Co '42-50; div mgr Perforating Guns Atlas Corp since '50. Am Assn Petroleum Geol—AIMME—Am Petroleum Inst—Ind Petroleum Assn Am—Kan Geol Soc—Kan Ind Oil and Gas Assn—Soc Exploration Geophys. 203 Insurance Bldg., Wichita 2, Kan. H: 1570 Gentry Dr., Wichita 14.

16 MEREDITH, Howard V(oas). Physical growth of child; Human physical development. b'03. AA '29 (Graceland Coll); BA '31—MA '32—PhD '35 (U Ia). Author: The Rhythm of Physical Growth '35; Physical Growth of White Children '36; Physical Growth from Birth to Two Years '43; also articles in field. Research asso '35-39, asst prof '39-42, asso prof '42-48, prof phys growth Ia Child Welfare Research Sta State U Ia '48-49; prof and cons in phys growth and dental research U Ia since '52. Am Assn for Health, Phys Edn, and Recreation—AAUP—Soc Research Child Development—Am Assn Phys Anthrop—Sigma Xi. W-510 East Hall, Iowa City, Ia.†

17 MEREDITH, Mamie Jane. American language research. b'88. AB '13 —AM '29 (U Neb); '21, '23 (U Wis); '35 (U Chicago). Collector of neologisms (coinages) in the American language; advisory board American Speech magazine '39, '40. Author articles in field. Teacher Eng and supervisor student publications Neb Secondary Schs '14-22; teacher Eng U Neb Ext Div '23-28; teacher bus Eng U Neb since '29. Am Bus Writing Assn (vp Mid-West '47-49)—Coll Eng Assn —Am Dialect Soc—Mod Lang Assn —Nat Council Teachers Eng. 116 Andrews Hall, University of Nebraska, Lincoln 8, Neb.

18 MERILH, Edmond L(ouis). Bacteriology (Pathologic). b'98. BS '17 (Spring Hill Coll); MS '23—certificate of merit '44 (Loyola U); '17-19 (Tulane U Med Sch). Author: Bacteriology Guide for Dental Students '41, rev '45. Asso prof bot, zool, bacteriology, his-

tology, serology Loyola U '22-43, prof since '43. La Acad Sci—Am Pharm Soc—AAAS—NCEA—Am Micros Soc. Department of Biology, Loyola University, 6363 St. Charles Av., New Orleans 15. H: 2219 Pine St.

19 MERILLAT, Louis Adolph. History of veterinary medicine (Military). b'68. DVS '88 (Ontario Vet Coll U Toronto). Author: Veterinary-Military History of the United States (vols I and II) '35. Editor: Jour Am Veterinary Assn and Am Jour Veterinary Research. Exec sec Am Vet Med Assn; Maj Vet Corps US Army '17, lt col '19; lt col Vet ORC, served as div vet 41st Div US Army; chief vet first Army AEF during St Mihiel and Meuse-Argonne operations. Am Vet Med Assn. 600 S. Michigan Av., Chicago.*

20 MERIWETHER, Robert Lee. South Carolina history. b'90. AB '12 —LittD '38 (Wofford Coll); AM '14 —PhD '39 (Columbia). Engaged collecting, preserving articles, documents concerning South Carolina history. Author: Expansion of South Carolina, 1729-1765 '40; also articles in field. Dir SC Library '41; mem Hist Commn SC '29-49. AHA—So Hist Assn—SC Hist Soc—SC Hist Assn—US Caroliniana Soc—Phi Beta Kappa. University of South Carolina, Columbia, S.C.

21 MERK, Frederick. United States history (Westward movement, agricultural, fur trade, Oregon boundary negotiation). b'87. AB '11 (U Wis); Edward Austin fellow '16-18—PhD '20 — Sheldon travelling fellow '20-21 (Harvard). Author: Economic History of Wisconsin during the Civil War Decade '16; Albert Gallatin and the Oregon Problem '50. Co-author: (with Frederick J Turner) List of References on the History of the West '22; also articles. With Harvard U since '18, prof Am hist since '36, head dept '41-46, Gurney prof hist, polit sci since '46. AHA—Miss Valley Hist Assn—Mass Hist Soc—Agrl Hist Soc—Phi Beta Kappa. Harvard University, Cambridge, Mass.☺

22 MERLE, James Joseph. Coal beneficiation; Coal chemistry. b'11. BS '33 (Pa State Coll); research F US Bur Mines and MS '34 (U Wash). Research on vacuum flotation of fine sizes of coal, coal analysis with relation to product control, dewatering and thermal drying of coal. Preparation engr and asst chief chem Island Creek Coal Co '34-40; chief chem Ayrshire Collieries Corp and Mining Subsidiaries '40-48, asst preparation mgr since '48. AIMME(chmn com on drying methods Coal Div)—ACS—Ill Mining Inst—Ind Coal Preparation and Utilization Society(dir '46-48)—Sigma Gamma Epsilon—Am Mining Congress(coal preparation com). Ayrshire Collieries Corp., Box 86, Danville, Ill.

23 MERONEY, Howard. Old and Middle Irish and English; History of philology (Vernacular grammatical writings). b'06. BA '26 (Baylor U); MA '28 (U Tex); PhD '43 (U Chicago). Editor: Journal of Celtic Studies; also articles in field. Asso prof Eng Temple U since '47. Mod Lang Assn Am—Mediaeval Acad Am. Temple University, Phila 22.

24 MERONI, Charles F. patent law; Postal history. b'05. LLB '24 (Chicago Kent Coll Law); LLM '27 (De Paul U); student grad sch bus adminstrn '30 (Northwestern U). Practice patent law Chicago since '24, partner Hill Sherman Meroni Gross and Simpson since '32; patent law lecturer DePaul University and John Marshall Law

School. Chicago Patent Law Assn—Am Bar Assn—Ill Soc Profl Engrs—Nat Soc Profl Engrs—Postal History Soc of The Americas—Royal Philatelic Soc—Am Philatelic Soc—Soc Philatelic Americans—Postal History Soc London—Soc Postal Historians London—Chicago Philatelic Soc—Phi Alpha Delta—New York and Chicago collectors clubs. Gold award on origin of posts in London Internat Exhibn '50, Canadian Internat Exhibn '51. 53 Jackson Blvd., Chgo 4.☉

10 MERRIAM, Lawrence Campbell. National parks; Forestry. b'98. AB '20—BS '21 (U Calif). Administrator of National Park Service areas and cooperative work with other park agencies. Logging engr and timber cruiser Madera (Calif) Sugar Pine Co '21-22; forest engr David T Mason and Mason and Stevens Portland and San Francisco '22-31; cons forest engr San Francisco '31-33; dist officer and regional officer charge Emergency Conservation Work in western park areas US Dept Interior Nat Park Service '33-37, supt Yosemite Nat Park '37-41, regional dir Nat Park Service Region Four since '50. Soc Am Foresters—Save the Redwoods League (councillor). National Park Service, 180 New Montgomery St., SF 5.

11 MERRILL, Grant. Peach varieties (Breeding). b'99. BS '23 (U Calif). Started peach variety breeding program '32, introduced to trade the following varieties: Merrill June, Merrill Gem, Merrill Beauty, Merrill Delicious, Merrill Goldenrose and numerous others. Farming and peach growing, shipping and breeding since '28. Nat Peach Council (director)—American Pomol Soc (exec com). P.O. Box 877, Red Bluff, Calif.

12 MERRILL, John Ellsworth. Double stars; Variable stars; Visual aids in teaching astronomy. b'02. AB '23 (Boston); MS '27 (Case Inst); MA '29 —PhD '31 (Princeton). Research on eclipsing variable stars; observations with visual polarizing photometer; methods for more efficient analysis of light curves by tabular methods; determination of diameters, brightness (and distribution over disk), masses, densities, of components; fast graphical solutions of light curves; designed models showing spatial and physical relationships of stars exhibited at Harvard Tercentenary and 1936 meeting of AAAS, other astronomical models and charts for museum and classroom use. Author: revision of Starry Heavens of Collier's Popular Science Library '38 section on astronomy for Collier's National Atlas '39; articles on astronomical progress for American Year Book; Nomographic Solution for Eclipsing Binaries '46; Tables for Solution of Light Curves of Eclipsing Binaries '50. Buck Scholar and F Boston and Harvard '24; Thaw F Princeton '30-31; grants for research Am Philos Soc '41,'42; instr math Case Inst '24-28; asst prof astron, acting head dept U Ill '31-32; curator astronomy and physics Buffalo Mus Sci '32-36; instr math Princeton '29-30, research asst astron '36-37, resident dir Princeton Pilot Training Program Orwigsburg Pa '42-43, vis asst prof physics '43-44, vis asst prof astron '44-45, research asso since '45; instr astron Hunter Coll '37-39, asst prof '39-47, asso prof since '48. AAAS —Am Astron Soc—NY Acad Scis—Internat Astron Union—Sigma Xi—Phi Beta Kappa. Department of Physics and Astronomy, Hunter College, 695 Park Av., NYC 21; also Princeton University Observatory, Princeton, N.J. H: 324 Magnolia Pl., Leonia, N.J.

13 MERRILL, John Espy. Far Eastern History. b'11. AB '33—'34-35, '38-40 (Stanford); AM '34 (Harvard); '40-41 (U Calif, U Hawaii). Part time research on Japanese continental policy from '05-14, '38-40 and other scattered times. Author articles in field. Private study of Japanese language, Tambaichi, Japan '35-38. asst prof Far Eastern hist and others San Diego State Coll since '46. Japanese Lang Officer USMC '41-46. Asiatic Soc Japan—Am Inst Pacific Relations—Far Eastern Assn—AHA—Phi Alpha Theta. San Diego State College, San Diego 5, Calif.

14 MERRILL, Joseph Francis. Mormonism. b'68. Grad Normal Sch '89—hon DSc '20 (U Utah); BS '93 (U Mich); PhD '99 (Johns Hopkins U). Author: Descendants of Marriner W Merrill '38; The Truth-Seeker and Mormonism '45. Prof physics and elec engring U Utah '99-28; mem bd trustees and of exec com Brigham Young U and Church Bd of Edn since '39. AAAS(F) — Utah Acad Sci(F) — NEA —Utah Teachers Assn. 47 E. S. Temple St., Salt Lake City 1.†☉

15 MERRILL, Marcellus S. Measurement of vibration and electronic balancing. b'00. BS '23 (U Colo). Developed methods and instruments for measuring vibrations and balance in automotive, aircraft and industrial field; invented automotive and ski equipment. Patents in field. Organizer Merrill Engr Labs Colo and NJ, Merrill Axle-Wheel Service, Colo, Neb, Ia, Cal. Soc Automotive Engrs—Colo Soc Engrs. 1240 Lincoln St., Denver 3. H: 335 Colorado Blvd., Denver 7.

16 MERRILL, Maud Amanda. Psychology (Mental tests, delinquency, personality). b'88. AB '11 (Oberlin Coll); AM '20—PhD '23 (Stanford U). Author: Problems of Child Delinquency '47. Co-author: Measuring Intelligence '37; Studies in Personality '42. With Stanford U since '21, now prof emeritus. AAAS(F)—Am Psychol Assn—Sigma Xi. Psychology Department, Stanford University, Stanford, Cal.

17 MERRILL, Maurice Hitchcock. United States law (Constitutional, oil and gas, public utility, administrative, municipal, labor); Government of Oklahoma. b'97. AB '19—LLB '22 (U Okla); SJD '25 (Harvard). Author: Covenants Implied in Oil and Gas Leases '26; Oklahoma Annotations to Restatement of Agency '40; Cases and Materials on Administrative Law '50; Law of Notice '52. Co-author: The Government of Oklahoma '24; also articles in field. Atty U Okla Research Inst since '41; on labor panel Am Arbitration Assn since '44; on Okla Nat Conf Commrs on Uniform State Laws since '44; on Judicial Council of Okla since '47. Am, Okla bar assn —SW Social Sci Assn—Okla Hist Soc—Am Judicature Soc—Phi Beta Kappa. Monnet Hall, University of Oklahoma, Norman, Okla.☉

18 MERRILL, Robert Hall. Archaeological measurements; Mayan archaeology. b'81. BS in CE '02 U Mich; student (Am Sch Prehistoric Research, Europe). Surveyor Tulane expedition to Uxmal for reproduction of Maya temple, Chicago World's Fair '30; mapped Folsom (New Mexico) site for Laboratory of Anthropology and American Museum Natural History, San Jon (New Mexico) site for Roberts' expedition, Smithsonian Institution; accompanied Hrdlicka's expedition, excavation of midden Kodiak Island, Alaska '35; located prehistoric sites Durango, Mexico for University Museum, Philadelphia '36; developed surveying technique, ancient cemetery excavation, Cocle, Panama; research

on mapping Maya cities in Yucatan, photographic surveying, calendar stick of Winnebago Indian. Author articles: Maya Sun Calendar Dictum Disproved '45; A Graphical Approach: Maya Astronomy '46; A Note on the Maya Venus Table '47, and others. Asst engr NY barge canal '06-18; prin asst Grand Canal Improvement Bd China '18-21; mem Spooner and Merrill cons engr '21-48. ASCE. 1111 Jefferson, S.E., Grand Rapids 7, Mich.†

19 MERRILL, Samuel Jr. Pomology; Vegetative propagation; Bud selection; Plant breeding; Tung and pecan production. b'02. BS '25 (Ore State Agr Coll); MS '27 (Ia State Coll); seminar '47 (Va Poly Inst). Research on vigor of apple seedlings, pecan leaf scorch, burrknot, effect of time of planting and stratification on germination, nursery fertilizers, budding. Author articles in field. Mem Bud Selection Dept Calif Fruit Growers US Dept Agr since '34 asso hortic Bur Plant Industry, Soils and Agrl Engring. Am Soc Hort Sci. U.S. Laboratory for Tung Investigations, Bogalusa, La. H: 621 St. Augustine St.†

20 MERRILL, T. A. Fruit orchard (Fertilization). b'08. BS '31 (Utah State Coll); MS '33—PhD '42 (Mich State Coll). Research on fertilization fruit orchard, orchard soil management and cover cropping on varieties of apples, pears, stone fruits. Author articles: Effects of Soil Treatments on the Growth of Highbush Blueberry '44; Diagnosing Nutritional Needs in the Orchard '44; Soil Management Practices in the Orchard '46; others. Chmn dept horticulture State Coll Washington since '46. AAAS—Mich Hort Soc—Sigma Xi. Department of Horticulture, State College of Washington, Pullman.

21 MERRIMAN, Daniel. Oceanography; Marine biology; Ichthyology. b'08. BS '33—MS '34 (U Wash); PhD '39 (Yale); '27-30 (Harvard). Research on haddock, striped bass, prime-fishing, effect of temperature on development of eggs and larvae of cut-throat trout, spawning habits; marine resources, methods of measuring fish; morphological and embryological studies of marine catfish Bagre marinus and Galeichthys felis, and on distribution, morphology and relationships of Trachurus lathami. Author articles: The Biology and Economic Importance of the Ocean Pout, Macrozoarces americanus (with Olsen) '46; Notes on the Midsummer Ichthyofauna of a Connecticut Beach at Different Tide Levels '47; The Conservation of Marine Fish with Special Reference to Striped Bass '48, and others. Conn State Bd Fisheries and Game, Am Wildlife Inst, US Bur Fisheries '36-38; instr biol Yale '38-42, asst prof '42-46, asso prof since '46; dir Bingham Oceanog Lab since '42; mem adv com Mar Lab Miami U since '46; spl cons Survey Marine Fisheries U NC '46-48. Sigma Xi—Conn Acad Arts Sci—Nat Research Council (chmn com food resources coastal waters) — NY Zool Soc(F) — Woods Hole Oceanog Inst (trustee, mem corp)—Am Mus Natural Hist (research asso dept fishes and aquatic biol). Master Davenport Coll since '46 Bingham Oceanographic Laboratory, Box 2025, Yale Station, New Haven.

22 MERRY, Glenn Newton. Marketing. b'86. AB '10—diploma Sch Speech '11 (Northwestern U); AM '15—PhD '21 (U Ia); MBA '25 (Harvard). Author: Investigation of Markets '42; Handbook for Marketing Research '48; Supervision of Salesmen '48; also articles in field. With State U Ia '12-24, prof speech and head dept '21-24; lecturer on psychol applied to bus Mass U Ext Div '24-25; prof marketing NYU since '37; treas Marine Fuels Inc NJ and exec various coal companies; chmn bd dirs Ednl Pub Co Darien Conn since '38; chmn Anthracite Credit Assn '44-45, Am Econ Assn—Am Statis Assn—Am Marketing Assn. 180 Cabrini Blvd., NYC 33.

10 MERTIE, John Beaver, Jr. Economic geology; Structural geology; Petrology. b'88. AB '08—PhD '11 (Johns Hopkins U). Author articles in field. Geol mapping and exploration Alaska US Geol Survey '11-42, aerial photogrammetry '18; geol investigations, western and southeastern states since '43; oil exploration for Standard Oil Co NJ, Bolivia, Argentina '20-21. Geol Soc Am—Mineral Soc Am—Soc Econ Geol—AAAS—Am Geophys Union —Geol Soc Washington (past pres)— Phi Beta Kappa. U.S. Geological Survey, Washington 25.

11 MERTLE, Joseph Stephen. Phototechnology; Photomechanics. b'99. Pioneered '30-33 with Ellis Bassist in practical introduction of dot etching and deep etch platemaking to American lithographers; research on suitability of plastic substances as substitute for zinc and copper plates in photoengraving relief etching '42. Author: Process Photography and Plate Making '35; Principles of Dot Etching '37; Direct Halftone Color Photography '40; Historic Events in Photoengraving '44; Modern Photoengraving '48, and others. Tech dir G Cramer Dry Plate Co St Louis since '34, Internat Photo-Engravers' Union '37-44, Chemco Photoproducts Co Glen Cove NY '44-47, G C Dom Supply Co Cincinnati since '45, Kemart Corp San Francisco since '47; asso ed Graphic Arts Monthly, Printing News, Production Yearbook; photomech ed National Lithographer; hist ed PSA Journal. Royal Photog Soc Gt Brit(F)—Photog Soc Am(F)—Am Mus Photography (charter and life mem) — Soc Photog Engr — Internat Photo-Engravers Union NA—Franklin Inst. 7 Lake Boulevard, Oshkosh, Wis.

12 MERTON, Robert K. Social aspects of science; Sociology of occupations. Mass communications (Propaganda and content analysis). b'10. AB '31 (Temple U); MA '32—PhD '36 (Harvard). Author: Science, Technology and Society in 17th Century England '38; Mass Persuasion '46; Social Theory and Social Structure '49; Elements de Methode Sociologique '53. Co-author: The Focused Interview '52. Also articles in field. Asso prof Tulane U '39-40, prof and chmn dept '40-41; asst prof Columbia '41-44, asso prof '44-'47, prof since '47; asso dir Bur Applied Social Research since '42; member bd dirs Center for Advanced Study in the Behavioral Sciences; adv ed sociol Harcourt Brace & Co. Am Sociol Soc—Hist Sci Soc—E Sociol Soc. Fayerweather Hall, Columbia University, NYC.☺

13 MERTZ, Edwin Theodore. Agricultural chemistry; Amino acids; Proteins; Hemostasis. b'09. BS '31 (U Mont); MS '33—PhD '35 (U Ill). Research on isolation and reactions of blood-clotting proteins, hemostatic mechanism in swine suffering from inherited bleeding disease, amino acid requirements of swine, rats, and humans, proteins and amino acids of alfalfa and corn. Co-author: Laboratory Experiments in Biochemistry '48; Plant and Animal Biochemistry '48; also articles in field. Asso prof biochem Purdue since '50. Am Chem Soc—AAAS— Soc Biol Chem. Department of Biochemistry, Purdue University, Lafayette, Ind.

14 MERWIN, Bruce Welch. School buildings and surveys; Training school custodians. b'89. AB '11—BS in edn '11—AM '24—PhD '29 (U Kan). Author article: Training Custodians '49; and others. With So Ill U since '27, dir training schools '29-46, acting pres '44, prof emeritus since '46. Ill Edn Assn(1st vp)—AAAS—Am Assn Sch Adminstrs—Soc Coll Tchrs Edn—NEA—Nat Council Schoolhouse Constrn—So Ill Custodian Engr Assn (chmn bd dirs since '38)—Ill Schoolmasters Club—Kappa Phi Kappa (past pres)—Phi Delta Kappa. 601 W. Walnut St., Carbondale, Ill.

15 MERWIN, Herbert Eugene. Mineralogy; Petrology; Color. b'78. Student '98-01 (NY State Normal and Training Sch Oneonta); BS '07—PhD '11 (Harvard). Assistant petrologist geophysics laboratory Carnegie Institution '09-17, petrologist '17-45, acting director '40, technical representative on war contract '45, research associate '46-48. Chemist-at-large Ordnance Dept US Army World War I. Am Phys Soc—Am Geophys Union—Geol Soc Am(vp '30)—Mineral Soc Am (past pres).☺

16 MESAVAGE, Clement. Forests (Measurements, surveys). b'11. BS in forestry '36 (Pa State Coll). Constructed tables for estimating cubic and board-foot volume in standing timber eastern US; designed procedure for sampling area occupied by forests, amounts of standing timber, growth of timber on state-wide basis. Holds patent on tree volume calculator. Author article: Tables for Estimating Cubic-foot Volume of Timber '47. Co-author articles: (with James W Girard) Tables for Estimating Board-foot Volume of Timber '46; (with William A Duerr) Timber Resources of the Lower South '46. Resident in charge anthracite region econ survey Allegheny Forest Expt Sta Wilkes Barre Pa '39-42; in charge forest inventory sect So Forest Expt Sta New Orleans '45-47, officer in charge Central Ozarks Br Harrison Ark since '47. Soc Am Foresters—Xi Sigma Pi. Southern Forest Experiment Station, Harrison, Ark.

17 MESERVE, W(ilbur) E(rnest). Electrical engineering; Servo-mechanisms; Control engineering. b'01. BS '23—MS '26 (U Me); MEE '29—PhD '33 (Cornell). Research on photo-electric effect, electrolytic effect. Author articles in field. With Cornell U since '26, now prof elec engring; engr Gen Elec Co '38-39, '48, RCA Victor Co Camden NJ '30-31. AAAS—Am Soc Engring Edn—AIEE—Tau Beta Pi— Eta Kappa Nu—Sigma Xi—Phi Kappa Phi. 103 Franklin Hall, Cornell University, Ithaca, N.Y.☺

18 MESSAMORE, Ford. History of Civil War and Reconstruction; Technical aids in historical research. b'99. AB '33—MA '35—PhD '39 (U Ky). Author: Alta Vela, A Forgotten Isle of the Caribbean '43; also articles in field. Prof hist, polit sci Culver-Stockton Coll since '44, head dept hist and polit sci, chmn div social sci since '47. Ark State Hist Assn—Ill State Hist Soc—So Hist Assn—AHA—NEA—Nat Council Social Studies—Ry and Locomotive Hist Soc—Am Soc Internat Law—Am Polit Sci Assn—Am Geog Soc—Am Acad Polit Social Sci—Phi Alpha Theta—Phi Delta Kappa. Culver-Stockton College, Canton, Mo.

19 MESSINA, Angelina Rose Foraminifera; Micropaleontology. b'10. BA '32 (NYU); MA '35 (Columbia). Associate editor The Micropaleontologist. Co-author: Catalogue of Foraminifera (30 volumes, and supple-

ments) '40-48. Asso curator dept micropaleontol Am Mus Nat Hist since '41. Paleontol Soc—AAAS—NY Acad Sci— Am Assn Petroleum Geol—Soc Econ Paleontol Mineral—Soc Study Evolution—Sigma Xi.

20 MESSINGER, Bernard. Air conditioning and refrigeration; Heat transfer; Thermodynamics; Aircraft thermal anti-icing; Pressurization; Heating; Ventilation. b'12. BS '35 (Armour Inst Tech). Author articles in field. Head thermodynamics group, engring dept, Lockheed Aircraft Corp since '43. ASME (aviation heat transfer com '43-46)—SAE (aircraft airconditioning com A-9 since '47)—Inst Aeronautical Scis. Lockheed Aircraft Corp., Burbank, Cal.

21 METCALF, George J(oseph). Modern and Older Germanic philology b'08. AB '28 (Wabash Coll); AM '31— PhD '35 (Harvard); student (U Munich). Author: Forms of Address in German 1500-1800 '38; also articles in field. Asst prof, asso prof Germanic philol U Chicago since '41. Modern Lang Assn Am—Linguistic Soc Am. University of Chicago, Chicago 37.†

22 METCALF, Woodbridge. Sequoia; Eucalyptus; Cork (Bark recovery). b'88. AB '11—MS in Forestry '12 (U Mich). Research on seed production, planting, and growth of young stands of Sequoia gigantea; studies adaptability of various species of Eucalyptus for windbreaks, fuel, and ornamental uses; propagation, planting, and growth of cork oak Quercus suber, and experimental stripping of cork from tree. Asst advancing to asso prof forestry U Cal since '14, extension forester since '26. Soc Am Foresters —Sigma Xi—Xi Sigma Pi. University of California, Berkeley 4.

23 METCALF, Zeno Payne. Morphology and taxonomy of Homoptera. b'85. AB '07 (O State U); DSc '25 (Harvard). Author: Introduction to Zoology '32; A Text Book of Economic Zoology '30; Bibliography of the Homoptera of the World (2 vol); General Catalogue of the Hemiptera (10 parts); also articles in field. Asso dean Grad Sch UNC since '43; dir grad studies NC State Coll since '40, prof zool since '12. Micros Soc (vp '22, pres '27)—NC Acad Sci (vp '14, pres '21)—Assn Econ Entomol (chmn Cotton States br '40)— Entomol Soc (pres '47)—Ecol Soc Am (pres '49). Box 5215, State College Station, Raleigh, N.C.†☺

24 METCALFE, June M. Metal, mineral, and mining popularizations; History of copper and aluminum. Student (U Alaska, U Calif, U Colo, U Utah, NYU). Author: Copper, the Red Metal '44; Aluminum from Mine to Sky '47. Co-author: The Story of Mountain City Copper Company '38; also articles in field. Now cons editor; lecturer metals and Alaskan ivory since '44. Authors' League—Women's Nat Book Assn—Soc Woman Geog— Am Inst Mining Metal Engr (asso). Book Clinic selection Copper, The Red Metal '44; scholarship MacDowell Colony summer '46. 88 Morningside Dr., NYC 27.†

25 METZLER, Lloyd A. International trade and economic relations; Business cycles. b'13. AB '35—MBA '38 (U Kan); MA '41—PhD '42 (Harvard). Author: Employment and International Trade; also articles in field. Econ adviser tax problems to law firms Washington '42-44; econ OSS Washington '43-44; mem tech staff Pres Com to Investigate Cost of Living '44; econ cons spl com on post-war econ policy and planning Ho of Reps Washington '45; econ bd gov Fed Reserve System

'44-46; asst prof dept econ Yale '46-47; asso prof dept econ U Chicago since '47. Econometric Soc. Guggenheim Found fellow '42-43; David A Wells prize book '45. Department of Economics, University of Chicago, Chicago 37.☉

10 MEULI, Lloyd Joseph. Plant disease control by chemicals. b'10. BS '32—MS '34—PhD '40 (U Wis); '37-38 (U Minn). Research on taxonomy and morphology of timber blue-stain fungi, on drought resistance of forest species, chemical control of plant diseases with foliage sprays and dusts, soil fumigants for nematode and fungus plant parasites. Developed Dow 9B seed protectant for cotton seed and peanut seed treatment. Author articles in field. Forest Products Lab Madison Wis '32-34; US Forest Service St Paul '34-39; Dow Chem Co Midland Mich '40-46, Great Western Div Seal Beach Calif since '46. Am Phytopath Soc. Dow Chemical Co., Box 245, Seal Beach, Calif. H: 2120 Maine Av., Long Beach 6, Calif.

11 MEYER, Alvin Felix, Jr. Radiation protection; Water supply. b'20. BS in civil engring '41 (Va Mil Inst). Studies on preventive medical phases of radiation protection; evaluate, design water supply facilities ETO. Author articles: Sanitary engineering in the occupied zone of Germany; Interim precautionary measures, radiological health hazards; and others. Asst to surgeon, officer in charge sanitation AAF Overseas Replacement Depot Kerns Utah '43-46; chief san engr Office Air Surgeon USAAF Wiesbaden Germany '46-48, dep chief preventive and indsl med div and chief san engring sect Office Air Surgeon Hdqrs Air Materiel Command since '48. Am Pub Health Assn—Am Soc CE(asso) —Assn Mil Surgeons—Am Assn Mil Engrs—Am Conf Governmental Indsl Hygienists—Inter-Am Assn San Engrs. Box 486, Area A, Hdqrs. Air Material Command, Wright-Patterson Air Force Base, Dayton, O.

12 MEYER, Garson. Industrial chemistry; Plastics. b'96. BS '19 (U Rochester). Author articles in field. Chief chem, dir Camera Works Labs Eastman Kodak Co since '20; tech and adv com Naval Aircraft Army and Navy on plastics standardization and engring data World War II. AAAS(F) —Soc Plastics Industry (chmn tech com since '43)—Soc Plastics Engr (chmn consumers' view of plastics since '46)—Plastics Pioneers Assn (bd govs '48)—Am Chem Soc—Am Soc Testing Materials. 333 State St., Camera Works, Eastman Kodak Co., Rochester, N.Y.

13 MEYER, George Wilbur. Wordsworth; Naturalistic novel. b'12. AB '32—PhD '41 (U Mich); '33-34 (U Paris). Author: Wordsworth's Formative Years '43; also articles in field. Prof Eng, head dept Newcomb Coll Tulane U since '46. Modern Lang Assn Am. Guggenheim fellow '43.

14 MEYER, H(ans) Arthur. Forest mensuration and management; Forestry (Mexico, Venezuela, Costa Rica). b'08. FE '30—Dr tech sci '34 (Fed Inst Tech, Switzerland). Research on forest growth determination, application of statistical methods in forest mensuration, methods and accuracy of forest cruising, structure and growth of forests, bark determination of trees, accuracy of growth determinations made from increment cores and based on repeated inventories of stands; delegate from Switzerland to United Nations Scientific Conference on Conservation and Utilization of Resources '49. Co-author: (with A B Recknagel

and D D Stevenson) Forest Management '52. Asst dept forestry Fed Inst Tech '32-34; collaborator USDA '34-35; spl insp prof forestry Mexico '35-37; faculty Pa State Coll since '37, prof forestry since '49; with Fgn Econ Adminstrn '43-46 (US govt cinchona survey Venezuela, plantation mgr Am Cinchona Plantation, Costa Rica). Soc Swiss Foresters—Soc Natural Hist (Mexico)—Soc Am Foresters—Sigma Xi—Alpha Zeta—Xi Sigma Pi. Department of Forestry, Pennsylviania State College, State College, Pa.

15 MEYER, Harvey Kessler. Industrial arts and design; Navigation. b'14. BA '36 (Berea Coll Ky); MA '42 (Eastern Ky State Coll); EdD '51 (U Fla). Studies architecture and building construction, naval architecture, aeronautical engineering and design, mathematics. Author article: Application of Classic Motifs to a Series of Designs for Industrial Arts (thesis); Curriculum Design in Technics (dissertation); and others. Furniture designer Berea Student Industries '32-35; shop supervisor Nat Youth Adminstrn Jacksonville Fla '37-38; asst prof indsl arts Eastern Ky State Coll '41-43; navigation officer, staff Chief Naval Air Training USNR '43-46; faculty U Fla since '46, asso prof indsl arts since '48. Am Indsl Arts Assn (chmn small schs programs and exhibits '47-50)— Am Council Indsl Arts Tchr Edn—Am Vocational Assn—Fla Indsl Arts Assn (chmn exhibits '47-51)—Ky State Indsl Arts Assn (bd dirs '40-41)—So Highland Handicraft Guild—Inst Navigation—Phi Kappa Phi—Phi Delta Kappa—Kappa Delta Pi. Department Industrial Arts, University of Florida, Gainesville, Fla.

16 MEYER, Heinrich Karl. Goethe; Botany (History); Cosmology (History). b'04. PhD '27 (U Freiburg). Research on scientific history of 16th to 18th centuries. Author: Goethe—Das Leben im Werk '51; The Age of the World: History of an Idea '51. Mem faculty German Rice Inst '30-43; asso prof German Muhlenberg Coll '47-51, prof German since '52; co-ed Philosophia '36-37. Prize award Kantgesellschaft '30, Guggenheim '53. Muhlenberg College, Allentown, Pa.

17 MEYER, Jacob C. American history (Contemporary, foreign relations, Colonial and Federal period); International relations. b'88. AB '16 (Goshen Coll); AM '17 (Ind State U); AM '18—PhD '24 (Harvard); '20, '21 (U Chicago); '29. Research in Europe, Scandinavia, England, Switzerland; studies on Autonomist Movement in Alsace-Lorraine; Federalist period of American history, colonial administration. Author: Church and State in Massachusetts from 1740 to 1833 '30. Author articles: Alsace-Lorraine (Encyclopedia Britannica), and others. Faculty mem Goshen Coll '19-21, Simmons Coll '22-23, Western Reserve U since '23, now asso prof; mem Inst Politics Williamstown Mass '25, '26, '31, '32; lecturer US and abroad. AHA —Am Acad Polit Social Sci—O Acad Hist—Am Soc Ch Hist—Nat Council Social Studies—Mennonite Hist Soc— Miss Valley Hist Assn — Phi Beta Kappa. Western Reserve University, Cleveland 6.

18 MEYER, Louis H. Plywood. b'88. Ed pub sch. Pioneer advocate and promoter use of plywood in small boat construction. Co-author: Plywood Handbook of Residential Construction. Author: Plywood—What It Is; What It Does; also articles in field. Successively newspaper reporter and ed, advtg agency sales counsel; advtg mgr, field research dir United States Plywood Corp NYC '37-43; now adv

agency principal. 1457 Broadway, NYC 18.

19 MEYER, Martin. Organic and physical chemistry (Compounds, explosives); History of chemistry. b'99. BS '18 (Coll City NY); MA '20—PhD '21 (Columbia). Research on organic sulfur and organo-metallic compounds, lead tetraethyl, perfumes, dehydrothiotoluidin, industrial toxicology, mathematical chemistry, catalysis, explosives, mathematical theory of rockets, isotopic separation, corrosion. Author: Science of Explosives '43; also articles in field. Cons chem since '21; asst prof chem Brooklyn Coll '27-35, asso prof '36-37, prof since '37, acting chmn dept '35-37, '38, '41-44, chmn since '44, prof chem Biarritz Am U '45-46. Am Inst Chem(F)— AAAS(F)—Am Chem Soc—Sigma Xi— Phi Beta Kappa Associates. Department of Chemistry, Brooklyn College, Bklyn 10.

20 MEYER, Max F(riedrich). Psychology (Brain functioning, eye, hearing); Cochlea; Music (Theory, history). b'73. Grad '92 (Municipal Gym, Danzig); PhD '96—post-doctoral research '96-98 (U Berlin). Research on accommodation and mechanism of eye, acoustics (difference-tones), synaptic theory brain functioning, Chinese music, mechanical functioning of cochlea, theory of hearing, growth and future musical keyboard, musical typewriter and staff writing, musical scales (theory and practice), history of quartertone music. Constructed hydraulic models cochlea and internal accommodation of eye, quartertone keyboard (24 tones per octave). Author: The Musician's Arithmetic '29; Introduction to the Mechanics of the Inner Ear '07; Abnormal Psychology '27, and others; also articles in field. Prof psychol U Mo since '00; vis prof U Miami Fla since '32 (leave of absence). AAAS(F) —Am Psychol Assn—Acoustical Soc Am—Sigma Xi—Phi Beta Kappa. University of Miami, Coral Gables, Fla.

21 MEYER, Robert T. Indo-European and Celtic philology; Greek and Latin linguistics. b'11. AB '33 (John Carroll U); MA '35 (Western Reserve U); PhD '43 (U Mich); '41-42 (UNC); '39-40, '45-46 (U Mich); fellow '47-48, '48-49 (Johns Hopkins U). Author articles in field. Asso professor Celtic and comparative philology Cath U Am Washington since '53. Linguistic Soc Am—Modern Lang Assn—Class Assn Middle West and South—Mich Acad Arts Sci—Am Philol Assn—Am Oriental Soc—Am Council Learned Societies (F)—Irish Texts Soc—Pali Text Soc. Catholic University of America, Washington 17.

22 MEYER, Samuel L. Plant physiology (Mosses); Ascomycetes (Taxonomy and genetics); Biological effects of heavy water. b'06. AB '30 (Central Coll); MS '32 — teaching fellow in biol '31-32 (Vanderbilt U); PhD '40 (U Va); Gen Edn Bd scholar summers '34-38—Gen Edn Bd research fellow summer '42—Philip Francis duPont research fellow in biol '36-37 (Mountain Lake Biol Sta U Va). Author articles in field. Prof and head dept bot U Tenn since '46. AAAS(F)—Ga Acad Sci(F)—Bot Soc Am—Sullivant Moss Soc—Assn SE Biol (mem exec com '42-46, sec-treas '46-47, pres '48-49) —Tenn Acad Sci—Sigma Xi—Phi Kappa Phi—Phi Beta Kappa. 3828 Sequoyah Av., Knoxville 16, Tenn.

23 MEYER, Walter H. Forest management and mensuration; Statistical methods. b'96. AB '19—MF '22—PhD '29 (Yale); '22-23 (Royal Inst Forestry Stockholm Sweden). Co-author: (with H H Chapman) Forest Valuation; Forest Mensuration also articles in field. Researcher in forest mensuration NE and Pacific NW US Forest Service '23-35; prof forest management Coll Forestry U Wash '36-39; asso prof forestry '39-45, Harriman prof forest management Sch Forestry Yale U since '45; cons forestry practice in S and Pacific NW since '39. Am Forestry Assn—Soc Am Foresters (senior mem)—Phi Beta Kappa—Sigma Xi—Am Statis Soc—Biometric Soc. Yale School of Forestry, New Haven.☉

10 **MEYER, Willis George.** Petroleum geologist. b'06. AB '30 (U Neb); MA '32—PhD '40 (U Cincinnati). Specialist in estimation of oil and gas reserves, their development, management, and appraisal. Author articles in stratigraphy and structural Subsurface and exploration geol Amerada Petroleum Corp '34-37; geol DeGolyer and MacNaughton '37-42, partner '42-47; partner Meyer and Achtschin since '47. Geol Soc Am—Am Assn Petroleum Geol—AIMME—AAAS—Am Geog Soc(F)—Am Geophys Union—Sigma Xi. 1600 M & W Tower Bldg., Dallas 1.

11 **MEYER, Wolfgang E(berhard).** Combustion research on, and fuel injection systems for diesel and gasoline engines and gas turbines. b'10. BS in mech engring '33 (Tech Hochschule, Stuttgart, Germany); Dipl Ing '35 (Tech Hochschule, Hannover, Germany); '37-38 (Pa State Coll). Developed fuel injection pump, mechanical governor, gasoline injection pump for aircraft engines and associated master control. Co-author: (with K J DeJuhasz) Bibliography on Sprays, with Supplement '48-49. Research engr Daimler-Benz A G '35-37; lab engr Am Bosch Corp '38-40; research engr Yale '41-43; development engr fuel injection div Bulova Watch Co '44-45; chief engr Research Engring Corp '45-47; asso prof engring research expt sta Pa State Coll since '47. Soc Automotive Engrs. Engineering Experiment Station, Pennsylvania State College, State College, Pa.†

12 **MEYERHOFF, Howard Augustus.** Geomorphology (North America); Mineral raw materials; Antillean geology. b'99. AB '20 (U Ill); MA '22—PhD '35 (Columbia). Author: Geology of Puerto Rico; Flow of Time in the Connecticut Valley. Curator paleontology Columbia '21-24; prof geology Smith Coll '24-49; geol Sci Survey Puerto Rico and Virgin Islands '24-43; cons geologist PR Bur Mines '32-43; tech advisor subsurface survey City of Springfield Mass '40-42; cons geol Dominican Govt '37, '38, '42-49; vis prof Yale '43. Am Inst Mining and Metall Engrs—Engring Soc NE—Geol Soc Am—Asso Am Geographers—AAUP—Am Geophys Union—AAAS(exec sec '45-46, adminstrv sec since '49), NY Acad Sci—Paleontol Soc—Soc Research on Meteorites—Soc Econ Geol—Am Assn Petroleum Geol—Phi Beta Kappa—Sigma Xi—Cosmos Club. H: 5417 Mohican Road, Washington 16.†☉

13 **MEYERS, T(heodore) Ralph.** Geology and mineralogy of New Hampshire. b'02. AB '26—'26-27 (O State U); '31-32 '44 (Harvard). Author articles in field. With dept geol U New Hampshire since '27, now prof; state geol New Hampshire State Planning and Development Commn since '42. Am Inst Mining and Metall Engr—Assn Am State Geol—Geol Soc Am—Mineral Soc Am—Am Geophy Union. Department of Geology, University of New Hampshire, Durham, N. H.†

14 **MEYKAR, Orest Albert.** Machine design; Production tooling; Induction heating. b'02. Student '25-28 (U Minn);

'29-30 (U Mich). Research and design automatic production machinery involving electrical, hydraulic and pneumatic controls. Granted patents on applications of induction heating and mechanical auxiliary devices. Project engr Machine and Tool Designing Co NY '44-46; design engr US Rubber Co '46-48; project engr Devenco Inc '48-50; mech engr Am Smelting & Refining Co '50; design engr Westinghouse Elec Corp since '51. ASME—Nat Soc Profl Engrs—Am Soc Tool Engrs—Am Ordnance Assn. Profl engr N.Y. Westinghouse Electric Corp., Balt 2. H: 1101 N. Calvert St.

15 **MICHAEL, Franz Henry.** Chinese history (19th and 20th centuries); Manchu dynasty (Origins). b'07. Student '28-30 (U Berlin); Dipl Sin '30 (Orientalische Seminar); Referendar '31—Dr Jur '33 (U Freiburg). Research on Chinese history and political science of 19th and 20th centuries and origin of Manchu dynasty. Author: Der Streit um die Mandschurei '33; The Origin of Manchu Rule in China '42. Contributor: China '46; China Land and People '52; World Scope Encyclopedia Book of Year '51. Prof Nat Chekiang U '34-38; Guggenheim F '39-42, research asso and Charles Lathrope F Walter Hines Page Sch Internat Relations Johns Hopkins U '39-42; with U Wash since '42, prof Chinese hist and asst dir Far E and Russian Inst since '48. Far E Assn—Inst Pacific Relations. Far Eastern and Russian Institute, University of Washington, Seattle 5.

16 **MICHAEL, Robert Warren.** Diamonds (Alluvial); Diamond washing. b'88. Studies on improvement mining methods and diamond washing processes, design of improved equipment, design grease table for recovery alluvial diamonds. Chief exptl dept Companhia de Diamantes de Angola Dundo Angola Portuguese West Africa '27-41; field mgr exploration and sampling diamond alluvials Compania Anonima Minera Gran Sabana Caracas Venezuela '46-47; cons on design diamond washing equipment NY Engring Co since '49. Am Inst Mining Engrs. 66 Park Av., 16A, NYC 16.

17 **MICHAL, Aristotle D(emetrius).** Mathematical, tensor and functional analysis; Differential geometry; Abstract spaces; Mechanics; Topology; Integral equations. b'99. AB '20—AM '21 (Clark U); PhD '24 (Rice Inst); Nat Research fellow '25-27 (U Chicago, Harvard, Princeton). Author: Matrix and Tensor Calculus with Applications to Mechanics, Elasticity and Aeronautics '47. Editor: Mathematics Mag since '47; also articles in field. Prof math Calif Inst Tech since '38, dir research in math analysis, geometry and applied math, also dir engring, sci; management War Training program in advanced training math and mech '42-45. AAAS(F)—Am Math Soc (council '38-40, sec '42-44) — Math Assn Am — Assn Symbolic Logic — Sigma Xi. 2028 Amherst Drive, South Pasadena, Cal.

18 **MICHAUD, Howard Henry.** American natural resources conservation. b'02. AB '25 (Bluffton Coll); MA '30 (Ind U); '43-44 (Purdue U). Author articles in field. Asso prof conservation Purdue U since '45; (dir conservation education camp since '46). Ind Acad Sci(F, biol survey com)—Wilson's Ornithol Club—Nat Assn Biol Teachers (pres '48)—Am Nature Study Soc—Ind Audubon Soc (pres '48)—Wildlife Soc—AAAS (Acad Conf, chmn '47). Department Forestry, Purdue University, Lafayette, Ind.†

19 **MICHEL, Earl R.** Refrigeration and and air conditioning engineering. b'10. BS '31 (U Ky). Application engr diesel and gas engines Worthington Pump and Machinery Corp Buffalo '32-35, application engr Harrison NJ plant '35-36, Chicago Dist Office '36-41, dist rep air conditioning and refrigeration div Cleveland Dist Offices '41-45 asst mgr air conditioning and refrigeration div Harrison NJ since '46. Am Soc Refrig Engrs — Tau Beta Pi. Worthington Pump and Machinery Corporation, Harrison, N.J.

20 **MICHEL, Rudolph.** Marine engineering; Marine power plant design; Mechanical vibrations. b'94. BS '16 (U Wis); MS '28 (U Ill); '39-40 (Johns Hopkins). Author articles in field. Marine engr Bur Ships Navy Dept Washington since '34; lecturer in mech engring George Washington U since '40. Mech engr War Dept '17-18. ASME (past chmn Wash sect '45-46, chmn Nat Agenda com '48-49, chmn student activities com region III '48-49)—Am Soc Naval Engrs. Bureau of Ships, Navy Department, Washington.

21 **MICHELMAN, Joseph.** Violin varnish. b'96. BS cum laude '23 (Harvard). Research in violin varnish used by old Italian makers since '35. Discovered plausible recreation of varnish used by Stradivarius, the Amati, Guarneri. Author: Violin Varnish '46; also articles in field. 6316 Wiehe Rd., Cin 13. H: 5050 Oberlin Blvd.

22 **MICHELS, Walter Christian.** Electrical measurements; Psycophysics. b'06. EE '27 (Renselaer Poly Inst); PhD '30 (Calif Inst Tech); fellow Nat Research Council '30-32 (Princeton). Author: Advanced Electrical Measurements '41; also articles in field. Test engr Utica Gas and Electric Co '26; asso in physics Bryn Mawr Coll '32-34, asso prof '34-46, head dept physics since '36, prof since '46, Marion Reilly prof since '48. Physicist Bu Ord USN '41-43, Lt comdr USNR and officer in charge Mine Warfare Operational Research Group '43-44, comdr USNR '44-46. Am Phys Soc — Am Assn Physics Teachers—NY Acad Sci—Assn Phila Sci (pres '46-47)—Sigma Xi. Bryn Mawr College, Bryn Mawr, Pa.

23 **MICHENER, Charles Duncan.** Entomology (Wild bees, evolution, social insects, ants, moths, chiggers). b'18. BS '39—PhD '41 (U Calif). Professor U Kan since '50, chmn dept entomol since '49. Capt Army Sanitary Corps '43-46, research on chiggers in Panama. Entomol Soc Am(F)—N Y Entomol Soc—Pacific-Coast Entomol Soc—Soc Study Evolution. Department of Entomology, University of Kansas, Lawrence, Kan.†

24 **MICHENER, H(arold) David.** Food microbiology; Antibiotics; Production of ergot; Dormancy in plants. b'12. BS '34—PhD '37 (Calif Inst Tech). Author articles in field. Chem Western Regional Research Lab Bur Agr, Ind Chem US Dept Agr, Albany Cal since '42. Am Chem Soc—Soc Am Bacteriologists. Western Regional Research Laboratory, U. S. Department of Agriculture, Albany 6, Cal.†

25 **MICHENER, John W(atson) Sr.** Ion exchange. b'16. BS '38 (Va Poly Inst). Author articles: Some Applications of Ion Exchange in Beet Sugar Factories '48. Research and development dept Allied Chem and Dye Corp Barrett Div '38-44; with the Dorr Co Denver, NY since '44 specializing in ion exchange all fields of commercial application. Chem sect Industry Br Econ Div Office Mil Govt for Germany '46-47. AICE—Tau Beta Pi. The Dorr Company, Cooper Bldg., Denver 2.

10 MICHIE, James Newton. Math analysis (Differential equations, differential geometry, vector analysis). b'79. BS '08 (U Va); AM '19 (U Mich). Author: Differential and Integral Calculus, '47. Author articles: Modifications of Graeffe's Method in the Solution of Numerical Equations of Higher Degree than Six; also other articles in field. Instr math U Va '06-09, asst prof summer sch '09-18, asso prof '19-25, prof '25-29; asst prof math Tex A&M Coll '09-18; asst prof math U Mich '18-19; asso prof Tex A&M Coll '19-20; U Tex '20-25; prof and head dept math Tex Tech Coll since '25, prof math emeritus since '51. Fellow Tex Acad Sci—AAAS—Am Math Soc—Math Assn of Am Inc—Kappa Mu Epsilon. 2110 17th St., Lubbock, Tex.

11 MICKEL, Clarence Eugene. Taxonomy of the Mutillidae (Hymenoptera). b'92. BSc '17 (U Neb); MS '23—PhD '25 (U Minn). Author articles in field. Extension entomol U Neb '17-20; research entomol Am Beet Sugar Co Rocky Ford Colo '20-22; extension entomol U Minn '22-25, asst prof zool and entomol '25-31, advanced to prof '41-44, acting chief div entomol and econ zool '44-45, head dept since '45; fellow John Simon Guggenheim Memorial Foundation '30-31. Am Assn Econ Entomol—Royal Entomol Soc London—Entomol Soc Am (sec-treas '36-43, pres '44)—Sigma Xi. Awarded grant for research Elizabeth Thompson Sci Fund '26. Department of Entomology and Economic Zool, University of Minnesota, St. Paul 1.◎

12 MICKEY, George H(enry). Cytogenetics. b'10. AB '31 (Baylor U); MS '34 (U Okla); PhD '38 (U Tex). Attended Eighth International Congress of Genetics Stockholm '48; Thirteenth International Congress of Zoology Paris '48. Author articles in field. Asso prof zool Northwestern U since '49. AAAS—Am Soc Zool—Genetics Soc Am—Am Genetic Assn—Soc Study Evolution—La Acad Sci (pres '47-48)—Sigma Xi. Guggenheim fellow '48 Department of Biological Sciences, Northwestern University, Evanston, Ill.†

13 MICKLE, David Grant. Traffic engineering. b'08. BS in civil engring '30 (U Mich); MS in civil engring '31 (Harvard). Research on traffic control measures such as one-way streets, left turn prohibitions, rush hour parking prohibitions; driver behavior, accident analysis, municipal street transportation, street traffic management, financing off-street parking, effect of parking on land values and retail trade; chairman Highway Research Board Committee on Origin and Destination Survey Techniques. Contributor: Traffic Engineer's Handbook '41-50. Dir Mass Highway Accident Survey '33-34; traffic and transportation cons '35-39; planning engr Mich State Highway Dept '35-39, traffic and safety engr '39-40; Detroit city traffic engr '40-43; dir Traffic Engring Div Automotive Safety Found since '43. Am Soc CE—Inst Traffic Engrs (past pres)—Am Pub Works Assn Am Soc Planning Ofcls—Cosmos Club. 700 Hill Bldg., Washington 6.

14 MIDDLETON, Arthur Pierce. Early American and Maritime History. b'16. MA Summa cum laude '37 (U Edinburgh); MA '38—PhD '47 (Harvard). Conducted investigation resulting in exposure of Horn Papers as spurious. '46-47; mem editorial advisory board The American Neptune since '47. Author: Tobacco Coast: The Maritime History of Chesapeake Bay, Colonial Period '49. Author articles: Chesapeake Convoy System, 1662-1763

'46; The Mystery of the Horn Papers (with D Adair) '47; The Strange Story of Job Ben Solomon '48; The Struggle for the Cape Henry Lighthouse, 1721-1791 '48; New Light on the Evolution of the Chesapeake Clipper-Schooner '49; Yachting in Chesapeake Bay 1676-1783 '49. Fellow hist Colonial Williamsburg Inc '40-41, research asso '42-46; research asso Inst Early Am History and Culture Williamsburg '46'-48; lecturer hist Coll Wm and Mary '47-48; dir research dept, Colonial Williamsburg '48; vicar Blisland Parish James City Co. Am Hist Assn—Soc Am Hist—Va Hist Soc—Md Hist Soc. Colonial Williamsburg, Williamsburg, Va.

15 MIDDLETON, John Tylor. Vegetable crop diseases; Root rot fungi; air pollution injury agricultural crops. b'12. BS '35 (U Calif); PhD '40 (U Mo). Research on Pythium root rots of ornamental and vegetable table crops; the taxonomy of Phytophthora and Pythium species; fungicidal control of vegetable diseases; identification of air pollutants responsible for crop damage; methods for protecting plants from injury by olefinic peroxides. Author articles in field. Asso in expt sta to asso plant pathol U Calif since '39. Am Phytopathol Soc—Mycol Soc Am—Torrey Bot Culb—Sigma Xi. University of California, Riverside, Calif.

16 MIDDLETON, Robert Hunter. Type design and calligraphy; Thomas Bewick. b'98. Student '23 (Art Inst Chicago); student (Northwestern U). Author: Making Printers Typefaces '38; Chicago Letter Founding '37; Thomas Bewick Portfolio '45; also articles in field. Dir dept typeface design Ludlow Typograph Co Chicago since '34; owns and operates pvt The Cherryburn Press. Am Inst Graphic Arts—Soc Typographic Arts. 2032 Clybourn Av., Chicago 14, Ill.†

17 MIELENZ, Richard Childs. Petrography; Clays (Processing, treatment); Concrete technology. b'13. AA '33 (Marin Jr Coll Kentfield Cal); AB '37—PhD '40 (U Cal Berkeley). Field examination, laboratory testing, analysis and research engineering sites, construction materials; determination of geologic structure, stratigraphy, petrography; correlation geologic and petrographic characteristics rocks and formations to engineering properties; study mineralogy of clays, analysis and testing of clays, processing and treatment for engineering properties, application of microscopy, staining tests, x-ray diffraction, differential thermal analysis, chemical analysis to clays for engineering purposes; selection, testing, analysis and research on aggregates, portland cement, pozzolans, admixtures and agents; microscopic study of concrete for improvement durability and strength and control adverse chemical reactions; development chemical test for alkiali reactivity of aggregates, pozzolans, methods for processing and treating pozzolans, petrographic analysis of aggregates. Author articles: Petrographic Examination of Concrete Aggregates '46; Materials for Pozzolan '49; Petrography and Engineering Properties of Igneous Rocks, and others. Geol Standard Oil Co Taft Cal '39-41; petrographer Bur Reclamation Denver '41-47, head petrographic lab since '47. Geol Soc Am(F)—Mineral Soc Am—ASTM—Am Concrete Inst—Soc Econ Paleontol and Mineral—Sigma Xi—Phi Beta Kappa—Theta Tau. Am Concrete Inst Leonard C Wason research medal '48; ASTM Sanford E Thompson award '49. Petrographic Labora-

tory, Bureau of Reclamation, Denver Federal Center, Denver.

18 MIEROW, Charles Christopher. Classical philology; Medieval Latin; Jordanes; Otto of Freising; Tacitus; St. Jerome. b'83. AB (Latin salutatorian) '05 (Princeton); AM '06—PhD '08—LLD '27 (U Colo); LHD '33 (U Denver); '33-34 (Am Sch of Classical Studies in Rome); EdD '34 (Colo Coll). Author: The Essentials of Latin Syntax '11, 2nd edit '17; The Essentials of Greek Syntax '11; The Gothic History of Jordanes '15; Hugo de sancto Victore '17; translator of The Two Cities—A Chronicle of Universal History to the Year 1146 AD by Otto, Bishop of Freising '28; The Classics; Medieval Latin Literature; also articles in field. Prof biog Carleton Coll since '34, on Ambrose White Vernon Found since '45. Am Philol Assn—Classical Assn Middle West and S (pres '36-37)—Am Classical League—Archeol Inst Am (lecturer '35-37)—Cliosophic Soc—Med Acad Am—British Classical Assn—Classical Soc of Am Acad in Rome—Phi Beta Kappa. 205 E. 2d St., Northfield, Minn.◎

19 MIESSNER, Benjamin Franklin. Radio engineering; Electronic-musical instruments; Electro-acoustics. b'90. Grad '09 (US Navy Elec Sch, Brooklyn); student '13-16 (Purdue). Pioneer in aircraft radio, electric phonography, radio dynamics, electric radio receivers, electric musical instruments, directional microphones for aircraft or submarine location. Granted more than 100 patents in US and fgn countries. Author: Radio Dynamics '16; Hum in All-Electric Radio Receivers '29. Wireless operator, US Navy '09-11; in charge radio torpedo control invention and development with John Hays Hammons Jr and Dr Fritz Lowenstein '11-13; expert radio aide for aviation US Navy in charge development of radio for aircraft Pensacola Fla '16-18; radio engr Emil J Simon NY in charge aircraft radio and transoceanic receiver developments '18-20; dir acoustical research lab Brunswick, Balke, Collender Co Chicago '21-22; cons engr Wired Radio Inc '22-25; pres Miessner Radio Corp '25; chief engr Garod Corp, Belleville NJ '26-27; pres, Miessner Inventions Inc. Radio Club of Am(F)—Inst of Radio Engrs(F)—Acoustical Soc Am(F)—Am Phys Soc—AAAS—Veterans Wireless Operators Assn. Sundown, Van Buren Rd., Morristown, N.J.◎

20 MIESSNER, W(illiam) Otto. Music (Composer, editor, lecturer); Musical Instruments. b'80. STD music (Cinn Coll Music); under pvt tutors in piano, voice, composition (Chicago, NYC and Berlin); Dr Ped hon (Cinn Conservatory Music); MusD (Chicago Musical Coll). Composer of many children's songs and other music; organized the first high school Band in America in '07. Developed the first successful miniature upright piano in '18, invented melody bells, the bandello, the rhythophone and the phonoscope. Author: Melody Way to Play the Piano; Progressive Music Series '15; Music Hour Series '27; New Music Horizons '42-49; Guide to Symphonic Music; An Absolute Tonal System. Dir Sch Music, Milwaukee '14-22; chmn dept music edn U Kansas '36-45; dir Miessner Inst of Music, Chicago '24-'48. Pi Kappa Lambda. Deefield, Ill.

21 MILAM, Paul W(illiam). Southwestern states (Industrial development). b'03. BA '23—MBA '26 (U Tex); DSC '33 (NYU). Author articles: Industrialization of the Southwest '42. Contributor articles: Arkansas Business Bulletin '31-43; Arkansas Valley

Study of National Resources Planning Board '42. With U Ark since '30, dean coll bus adminstrn from '44; indsl cons Nat Resources Planning Bd '41. Am Econ Assn—So Econ Assn—SW Soc Sci Assn—Beta Gamma Sigma—Alpha Kappa Psi. Business Administration Bldg., University of Arkansas, Fayetteville, Ark.

10 **MILAS, Nicholas Athanasius.** Synthesis of vitamins. b'97. BS '22 (Coe Coll); MS '23—PhD '26 (U Chicago); Nat Research fellow '26-28 (Princeton). Inventor of several processes in the synthesis of vitamins, organic peroxides. Author articles in field. Asso prof chem MIT since '41. Am Acad Arts Sci(F)—Am Chem Soc—Sci Hist Soc—NY Acad Sci(F)—AAAS—Sigma Xi. 34 Payson Terrace, Belmont, Mass.

11 **MILES, Catharine Cox (Mrs. W. R. Miles).** Psychology (Sex, personality). b'90. AB '12—AM '13—PhD '25 (Stanford U); student (U Calif, U Jena, U Berlin). In charge child feeding American Friends Service Committee Berlin District '19-20. Author: Early Mental Traits of Three Hundred Geniuses '26; Sex in Social Psychology '35. Co-author: Sex and Personality '36; also articles in field. Clin prof psychol Yale since '31; attending psychol New Haven Hosp and Dispensary since '32; cons clin psychol Vet Adminstrn since '46. AAAS(F)—Am Psychol Assn—Phi Beta Kappa—Sigma Xi. 333 Cedar St., New Haven.

12 **MILES, Charles.** Washington State history; North American aboriginal artifacts. b'94. AB '20 (U Cal). Research on history of western Washington state; aboriginal artifacts of North American Indians and Eskimos. Co-editor: Building A State '39. News staff Oakland Post and San Francisco Chronicle '20-32; tchr Oakland pub schs since '32. Wash State Hist Soc—Soc Am Archeol—The Late Watch. H: 5070 Cochrane Av., Oakland 18.

13 **MILES, George Carpenter.** Islamic archaeology, numismatics and epigraphy. b'04. AB '26—MA '30—PhD '37 (Princeton); '28 (Perugia); '29 (Heidelberg); '30 (Columbia). Epigraphist and assistant field director Joint Expedition to Persia, University Museum, Philadelphia, and Museum of Fine Arts, Boston, '34-37. Author articles in field. Acting chief curator Museum Am Numismatic Soc of NYC since '53. Am Numismatic Soc of NY (F)—Royal Asiatic Soc London(F)—Royal Numismatic Soc London(F)—Am Geog Soc NY(F)—Am Oriental Soc—Archeol Inst Am—Hispanic Soc Am—Council for Old World Archeology. Museum of the American Numismatic Society, Broadway at 155th St., NYC 32.†

14 **MILES, Ivan E(rnest).** Southern United States soil conditions. b'04. BS '30 (Miss State Coll); MSA '31 (U Fla); PhD '38 (U Md). Research on methods of soil testing to determine lime, fertilizer requirements of soil. Author articles: Rapid Testing of Soils for Plant Food Deficiencies Under Southern Conditions. Leader Ext Agron and charge soil testing service Miss since '48. Army engr US Army '42-44 assigned to Jacksonville Fla dist office with function of establishing natural vegetation necessary to control erosion and camouflage army camps airports and secret coastal military installations. Am Soc Agron—Am Soc Soil Sci—AAAS(F)—Am Assn Plant Physiol (chmn So sect)—Assn Officials of Agrl Chem (asso referee in soils). Leader, Extension Agronomy, State College, Miss.

15 **MILES, John Richards.** Optical instrument (Mechanical engineering and design); Astronomical instruments. b'11. AB '34 (Kalamazoo Coll Mich); student (U Rochester N Y). Design telescopes, spectrographs colorimeters, microscopes, cameras, ophthalmic instruments, projectors, spotting scopes, camera objectives and afocal camera attachments, periscopes, glossmeters, and industrial inspection apparatus; engineer and supervisor of inspection military optical instruments; in charge design and engineering sextants, driftmeters, rifle sights, gunsights, and bombsights; development compact binocular with wide field view and high light gathering power. Holds 17 patents on optical instruments. Optical instrument design Bausch & Lomb Optical Co; dir research and development Argus Inc; in charge optical instrument design Pioneer Instrument Div Bendix Aviation Corp; chief engr Swain Nelson Co '45-47; designer and cons since '47. Optical Soc Am—Soc Motion Picture and Television Engrs. 4821 N. Sheridan Rd., Chgo 40. H: 9411 Greenwood Dr., Des Plaines, Ill.

16 **MILES, Walter Richard.** Vision; Olfaction; Aviation psychology. b'85. AB '08 (Earlham Coll); MA '10—PhD '13 (Ia State U). Author: Alcohol and Human Efficiency '42; Efficiency Under Prolonged Restricted Diet '19; Age in Human Society '35. Editor: Psychological Studies of Human Variability '36. Prof exptl psychol Stanford '22-32; prof psychol Yale since '31; asso psychol Grace-New Haven Hosp since '32; chmn bd dir The Psychol Corp NY since '45; Am Inst for Research Pittsburgh since '46. Nat Acad Sci (exec com and council '43-49, chmn sect '38-41)—Am Philos Soc—Optical Soc Am—Am Psychol Assn (pres '32)—Soc Exptl Psychol—Am Physiol Soc. Received the Pres Certificate of Merit '48; Howard Crosby Warren medal and award '49. Psychology Department, Yale University, New Haven.©

17 **MILEWSKI, Chester Anthony.** Communications (Equipment procurement). b'15. BS in elec engring '38 (Northeastern U); courses (U Conn) (Yale) (Temple) (U Pa). Research, procurement and inspection of communications equipment. Inspr communications equipment, contracting officers engr Dept of Army Signal Corps '41-42, procurement equipment '46-50, chief tube, crystal, resistor, capacitor, transformer and coil sect '50-51, investigation procurement Europe '51; contract spl since '51. Signal Corps Procurement Agency, 225 S. 18th St., Phila.

18 **MILEY, Henry Artis.** Metal oxidation, tarnishing, resistivities and temperature coefficients; Upper air physics; High altitude sky brightness; Radar; Oxide coated cathodes. b'02. AB '24—AM '25—fellow '23-24 (Miss Coll); MS '27—PhD '29—research fellow '26-27, '28-29 (U Colo); summer '28 (U Chicago); PhD '37—Carnegie research scholar '36, '37 (Cambridge U, Eng). With W B Pietenpol developed new method of measuring elec resistivities and temperature coefficients of lead, tin, zinc and bismuth in solid and liquid states; determined the function of oxide films in supporting molten wires of these metals when freely suspended. Author articles in field. Physicist Camp Evans Signal Laboratory Belmar NJ '42-43; staff mem Radiation Lab MIT '43-46. Physicist Air Materiel Comd Research Lab Cambridge Mass since '46. AAAS(F)—Okla Acad Sci(F)—Optical

Soc Am—Sigma Xi. Received Okla Research award from AAAS through Okla Acad Sci '38. 440 Weston Rd., Wellesley, Mass.

19 **MILFORD, John Warren.** Public relations. b'03. Student '22-26 (NYU). Developed Christmas outdoor lighting program '26; publicity representative Light's Golden Jubilee '29; founder and editor Revenue, Magazine of Light; originated Better-Light-Better Sight program '33, Buy American campaign '33; promoted New American Demonstration Home Building Program '35; established public relations bureau New York City '36. Successively handled direct mail, trade publicity advertising, splty promotion, and orgn publicity Edison Lamp Works Gen Elec Co Harrison NJ '26-29, estab G-E ed service bur Nela Park Cleveland '30; founder and pres pub relations firm J W Milford & Co Inc NYC since '39. Pub Relations Soc Am—Sales Exec Club NY. 55 W. 42d St., NYC 36.

20 **MILL, Edward W.** Far Eastern government (Philippines). b'16. BA '40 (U Wis); MA '41 (U Mich). Author articles in field. Second sec and chief polit sect U S Embassy Manila Philippines '48-49; principal officer and American Consul Sorabaya Indonesia since '50. Office Strategic Services '43-45, Asst Chief, Div Philippine Affairs, Dept State, '45-48. Am Polit Sci Assn. Department of State, Washington.

21 **MILLARD, Laurance Oscar.** Materials handling equipment; Conveyors. b'97. Student '21-23 (U Ill). Research and development bulk handling, conveyors and conveyor problems, developments in coil conveyor equipment design, materials handling in steel industry. With Link-Belt Co since '13, asst gen sales mgr since '48. AIMME—Am Mining Congress—Assn Iron and Steel Engrs—E States Blast Furnace and Coke Oven Assn—Tech Assn Pulp and Paper Industry. 307 N. Michigan Av., Chgo 1.

22 **MILLER, Agnes Roman.** China (Economics); International finance. b '07. Student (Brookings Instn) (U Chicago) (Northwestern U); PhD '28 (Royal Hungarian U Budapest). Development program for collecting and evaluating financial information throughout China; background studies of economics of China proper, Manchuria, Mongolia, Formosa to indicate relief requirements and rehabilitation needs; research on economic and business conditions in Shanghai; analysis methods financial administration Japan, China and other countries occupied by Japan, Japan's pattern of economic exploitation, financial aspects of economic potential of Japan; problems of public finance, money and banking, industrial banking during war and price control in countries under Japanese occupation; study economic activities in Nazi Germany, France, Argentina, Brazil, Chile, Mexico; research in international investments during interwar period. Author articles: American investments in the Far East; UNRRA in China: Factory Workers in China; Public Finance in Postwar China. Head research dept Chinese Postal Remittances and Savings Banks Shanghai '34-37; econ Temp Nat Econ Com '40; asst to cons Nat Resources Planning Bd '40-41; econ anlyst Fgn Econ Adminstrn '42-44; econ analyst UNRRA's China Office '44-45, financial advisor '46-47, chief reports div '47-48. Far Eastern Assn—Inst Pacific Relations—Am Econ Assn.

23 **MILLER, Arild J.** Physical and radiation chemistry; Photosynthesis;

Radiochemistry. b'18. BA '39 (Carleton Coll); PhD '43 (Purdue U). Research on leaf pigments and catalysis, heats of combustion of polynitroparaffins, radiation chemistry and radiochemistry, photosynthesis and chlorophyll, role of iron in chlorophyll formation and possible substitutes for iron in process of photosynthesis. Author articles: The Solubility of Anthracene and Phenanthrene in Various Solvents '39; The Heats of Combustion of Some Polynitroparaffins '45; The Role of Iron in Chlorophyll Formation '47. Research chem Metall Lab U Chicago '43-45; research chem Clinton Labs Monsanto Chem Co Oak Ridge Tenn '45-46; asst prof chem Antioch Coll, research chem Charles F. Kettering Found '46-49; asso prof chem, chmn dept Carleton Coll since '49. Am Chem Soc—Am Phys Soc—Sigma Xi—Sigma Pi Sigma. Chemistry Department, Carleton College, Northfield, Minn.†

10 MILLER, Arthur K. Fossil cephalopods; Paleontology. b'02. AB '24—MA '25 (U Mo); PhD '30 (Yale). Official delegate 17th Internat Geol Congress Soviet Russia '37; member Princeton University Bicentennial Conference Genetics Paleontology and Evolution '47; geological field work in northern Mexico '36, Mexican-Guatemalan border '40, west-central shore Hudson Bay '46, Baffin Island '47. Author articles: Devonian Ammonoids of America '38; Permian Ammonoids of the Guadalupe Mountain Region and Adjacent Areas '40; Ozarkian and Canadian Cephalopods '42-44. Instr geol U Mo '27-29; instr geol Yale U '29-31; asst prof geol State U Ia '31-35, prof since '40. Geol Soc Am(F)—Am Assn Petroleum Geol—Paleontol Soc(F)—Soc Econ Paleontol and Mineral—AAAS—Ia Acad Sci—Soc for Study Evolution. Geology Department, State University of Iowa, Iowa City, Ia.☉

11 MILLER, C. Blackburn. Dogs (Hunting). b'85. Student '09 (Columbia U). Author: Ballyhoo; Hudson Valley Squire '41. Dog ed Outdoor Life Magazine since '45; salt water fishing ed Adventure Magazine '42. 1360 Midland Av., Bronxville 8, N.Y.

12 MILLER, Carl Frederick. Archeology of Southeastern United States; Dendrochronology. b'06. BS '28—MA '29 (U Ariz). Completed an archeological survey of Savannah River above Augusta Georgia, the basin of Clark Hill dam locating Stalling's Island site which is contemplated for excavation; located number of Folsom camp sites in Buggs Island dam reservoir on Roanoke River, the first noted east of Mississippi River. Author articles. With Bur Am Ethnology Smithsonian Inst Washington since '46. Am Anthropol Assn—AAAS. Bureau of American Ethnology, Smithsonian Institution, Washington 25.

13 MILLER, Carl Wallace. Color photography; Optics. b'93. AB '15—AM '22—PhD '23 (Harvard); '15-16 (U Zurich); '16 (U Paris); '29-30 (U Leipzig). Discovered rectifying action of selenium while at University of Zurich; pioneer work on the impedance bridge, thermionic voltage stabilizers and utilization of non-linear vacuum tube characteristics; director of OSRD research project at Brown University dealing with binoculars as an aid to night vision '43-45; National Geographic Society Eclipse Expedition to Siam '48; director of research project at Brown University dealing with the photographic reproduction in color of art objects '41-42; continuous research on topics related to color printing methods, particularly pigment and dye transfer processes and mask-

ing techniques for improvement of color rendition since '30; developed a mathematical theory of masking making use of the matrix algebra '41. Author: Principles of Photographic Reproduction '42. Author articles: A Linear Photoelectric Densitometer '35; New Filter Technique in Miniature Photography '45. Asst prof phys Brown U '24-29, asso prof '29, prof since '45. Royal Photographic Soc Gt Brit(F)—Am Phys Soc(F)—AAAS(F)—Photographic Soc Am (asso). Franklin L Burr prize Nat Geo Soc '48. Brown University, Providence.

14 MILLER, Cecil Hale. Applied logic; Dialectic; Social ethics; Materialism. b'06. AB '30 (U Kan); MA '33—fellow '33-38 (U Calif); scholar '30-31 (U Wis). Co-author: (with L E Hahn) The Elements of Logic '46; also articles in field. Asso prof Kan State Coll since '45. Am Philos Assn—SW Philos Conf (exec comm '47)—AAAS—Kan Acad Sci—Am Assn U Prof. Philosophy Department, Kansas State College, Manhattan, Kan.

15 MILLER, Christine Jane. Ceramics; Pottery design. b'15. Student '33-35 (Ashland Coll); '38-39 (Western Reserve U and Cleveland Sch Art); '45-47 (Cranbrook Acad Art); AB '38—AM '41 (Oberlin Coll); MFA '47 (Cranbrook Acad Art); '49 (Ohio State U). Exhibited ceramics Oberlin Museum, Syracuse Museum, Wichita Kansas, Louisville, Smithsonian Inst; permanent collections Cranbrook Museum, Syracuse Museum. Asst to head art dept Oberlin Coll and teacher Oriental Art seminar '39-41; teacher head art dept Ashland Coll '41-44; teacher Kingswood Sch for Girls Bloomfield Hills Mich '46-47; teacher design painting ceramics Berea Coll '47-53. Phi Beta Kappa. One of four winners of the Richard B Gump award for best pottery designs for mass production at 12th Annual Ceramic Exhibition at Syracuse NY '47. 617 Grant St., Ashland, O.

16 MILLER, Clyde Raymond. Academic freedom (Civil liberties). Propaganda (Analysis); Intergroup education (Prejudice prevention). b'88. AB '11 (O State U); ED '37 (Am Internat Coll). Founder with E A Filene Inst for Propaganda Analysis Inc NYC '37; in '39 proposed type of education known as The Springfield Plan to prevent racial religious and related prejudices. Author: How to Detect and Analyze Propaganda '39; The Process of Persuasion; How to Prevent Prejudice '47; What Everybody Should Know About Propaganda—How and Why It Works. Co-author: (with Fred Charles) Publicity and the Public School '24. Mem staff and faculty Teachers Coll Columbia U '28-48; chmn Commn for Propaganda Analysis Methodist Fedn for Social Action since '47; cons on prevention of racial religious and related prejudices to League of Fair Play since '42; dir Commn for Acad Freedom, Nat Council Arts Sci Professions since '48. Received spl award from Nat Conf of Christians and Jews for contbrns to intercultural edn '47. Room 785, 11 W. 42nd St., NYC 18.

17 MILLER, David Hewitt. Physical and regional climatology; Snow hydrology; Meteorology. b'18. BA '39—MA '44 (U Calif). Research maximum storms and floods, regional climatology, airways forecasting, effects weather army clothing and equipment under development, factors meteorology and hydrology related mountain snowpacks, snow investigations particularly melting at rapid rates; influence topography and vegetation atmospheric processes, stream

flow in dependence on melting factors, heat-transfer processes, precipitation in relation to topographic factors, integration meteorological elements various regions of world. Author articles: Temperature and Humidity Conditions Encountered in Exposure of Tents '46; Hydrometeorological Log of the Central Sierra Snow Laboratory 1945-46 '47; The Central Sierra Snow Laboratory: Its Physical Geography and Instrumentation '49. Co-author articles: Reports of Field Study of Quartermaster Clothing and Equipment for the Tropics '44; Report on Wet-Cold Field Trials of Clothing, Equipment, and Tentage '45. Meteorol corps engrs US Army San Francisco, Salt Lake '41-43. Meteorol, geog office QM gen Washington '44-46; asst chief analysis unit coop snow investigations Corps Engrs South Pacific div Oakland (Calif) Army Base since '46; forecaster Transcontinental Western Air Lines '43-44. Am Meteorol Soc—AAAS—Asso Am Geog—Soc Pacific Coast Geog—Am Geophys Union—Phi Beta Kappa—Sigma Xi. Cooperative Snow Investigations, Corps of Engineers, South Pacific Division, Oakland Army Base, Oakland 14, Calif.

18 MILLER, Donald Elbert. Limnology; Freshwater hydras. b'06. AB '25 (Thiel Coll); MS '29—PhD '35 (U Mich); five summer sessions (U Mich Biol Station). Author articles: A Limnological Study of Pelmatohydra With Special Reference to Their Quantitative Seasonal Distribution '36. Asst and asso prof sci Ball State Teachers Coll since '36. Am Soc Limnology and Oceanography—Ind Acad Sci—Central Assn Sci and Math Teachers—Nat Assn Biol Teachers—Sigma Xi. Ball State Teachers College, Muncie, Ind.†

19 MILLER, Edmund Thornton. State finances (Texas); Paper money (Texas issues). b'78. AB '97 (Weatherford Coll); AB '00—AM '01 (U Tex); AM '03—PhD '09 (Harvard). Texas Tax Survey Committee '27. Author: A Financial History of Texas '16. Prof econ U Tex since '17. Am Econ Assn—Nat Tax Assn—Am Numismatic Assn—Tax Research Found—Phi Beta Kappa — Tex State Hist Assn(F). Henry Lee Memorial fellow '08-09. 910 Poplar St., Austin, Tex.

20 MILLER, Edwin Lynn. Zoology (Glyphelmines quieta, North American cercaria). b'06. BS '28 (Ia Wesleyan Coll); '26 (U Ia Biol Sta); MS '30—grad fellow '31-32—PhD '32 (U Ill); '31 (U Washington Biol Sta); '34 (U Minn Phys Med Sch). Research on biological effects DDT and other chemicals on insects destructive to paper; studies of premedical and higher education, Korea '46-48. Author articles: Preliminary Notes on Louisiana Mollusca, Amphibia and Reptiles of the Baton Rouge Area '36; Studies on North American Cercaria '33; other articles in field. Inst, later asso prof La State U '32-42; asso prof biol Lawrence Coll '42-46; spl zool research specialist Inst Paper Chemistry Appleton Wis '45; advisor premed edn and higher edn Korea US Mil Govt '46-48; head dept biol Stephen Austin Coll Nacogdoches, Tex since '48. Ia Acad Sci—Am Soc Zool—Soc Ichthyologists Herpetologists—AAAS—Am Biol Teach Assn—Am Soc Parasitol—Washington Helminthol Soc—Sigma Xi—Phi Sigma. Department of Biology, Stephen Austin College, Nacogdoches, Tex.†

21 MILLER, Elizabeth Maxfield (Mrs John Alexander). Romansh language and literature; Raeto-Romance languages. b'10. Inst Internat Edn scholarship (U Paris); AB '31 (Swarthmore Coll); AM '36—PhD '38 (Radcliffe Coll); John Lockwood and Anne Radcliffe fellowships (U Zurich, U Munich, Institut de Phonetique Paris). Author: Studies in Modern Romansh Poetry in the Engadine with Special Consideration of Zaccaria Pallioppi 1820-1873, Gian Fadri Caderas 1830-1891, and Peider Lansel 1863 '38; also articles in field. Asst prof French Wheaton Coll since '48. Stipend from Anton Cadonau Found Zurich for work on Romansh '36-37. Wheaton College, Norton, Mass.

10 MILLER, Elroy John. Wax emulsions; Colloidal iodine; Charcoal. b '91. BS '14—MS '15—PhD '23 (U Mich). Development activated sugar charcoal, and method production ash-free adsorbent charcoal from commercial impure materials; studies on adsorption from solution by activated ash-free charcoals; development wax emulsions for prevention desiccation nursery stock and plant materials, of colloidal iodine for antibiotic uses. Hold patents in field. Faculty Mich State Coll since '15, research asso expt sta '24-30, head dept agrl chem since '31. ACS—AAS—Mich Acad Sci. Sigma Xi award for meritorious research in fundamental and applied colloid chemistry. Department of Agricultural Chemistry, Michigan State College, East Lansing, Mich. H: 262 Cedar St.

11 MILLER, Elwood Morton. Termite biology. b'07. BS '29 (Bethany Coll); MS '30—PhD '41 (U Chicago). Author articles in field. Instr, later prof and chmn zool U Miami since '30. Officer in charge entomol unit 52 US Navy '43-45. Fla Acad Sci (treas '38, pres '47)—Sigma Xi. Department of Zoology, University of Miami, Coral Gables (University Branch), Fla.

12 MILLER, Ernest C. History of early Pennsylvania (Oil industry). b'12. BA '34—grad student '35 (Pa State Coll). Research on John Brown's ten years in northwestern Pennsylvania, Fountain and Hequembourg flowing oil wells, oil mining in Pennsylvania. Author: Oil Mania '41; John Wilkes Booth: Oilman '47. Editor: The History of Pithole '45; also articles in field. Spl investigator West Penn Oil Co since '40. West Penn Oil Co., Warren, Pa. H: 10 Hertzel St.†

13 MILLER, Erston Vinton. Fruit biochemistry and physiology (Physiology of stored fruits, citrus fruits). b'98. BS '19—MS '21 (U Md); PhD '26 (Mich State Coll). Author articles: Physiology of Citrus Fruits in Storage '46; Specific Effects of Certain Temperatures on Stored Fruits, Vegetables, and Flower Bulbs '46, and others. Asst physiologist Orlando Fla US Dept Agr '28-47; prof biol U Pittsburgh since '47. AAAS(F)—Am Soc Plant Physiol—Sigma Xi. Department of Biological Sciences, University of Pittsburgh, Pittsburgh 13.†

14 MILLER, E(ugene) Willard. Economics of minerals; Economic and physical geography; Geography of manufacturing. b'15. BS '37 (Clarion State Teachers Coll); MA '39 (U Neb); PhD '42 (O State U). Asst prof Western Reserve U '43-44; geog OSS '44-45; chief div geog Pa State Coll since '45; specialized geographic research for OQMG since '47. Am Soc Profl Geog (a founder)—Assn Am Geog—Am Geophys Union—AAAS. Division of Geography, Pennsylvania State College, State College, Pa.†◎

15 MILLER, Francis Trevelyan. American military history (Civil War, World War II); American social and economic history; World history. b'77. LittD '13 (Washington Coll); LLD '13 (U Ky). Engaged in historical research throughout world, headquarters in London, Paris; founder and president Historical Foundations for research; organized Brady Secret Service negatives, authorized by President Lincoln, with board of 45 military authorities into Photographic History of the Civil War (10 vol); with board of 50 authorities History of World War I (8 vol); True Stories of Great War (6 vol). Author: Martyrs on Altar of Civilization '07; Portrait Life of Lincoln '10; America's Greatest Battleground—Gettysburg '13; America—the Land We Love '15; The World's Great Adventure: History of 1000 Years of Polar Exploration '29; Biography General Douglas MacArthur—Fighter for Freedom '42; Biography General Dwight D. Eisenhower '44; History of World War II '46; and others. Historian, author; now conducting research for history of the world with bd of eminent scientists. Phi Beta Kappa. 15 W. 68th St., NYC.

16 MILLER, Fred Mathias. Document examination. b'05. AB '29—MA '33—PhD '35 (Ind U). Examiner of questioned documents, side-by-side comparison of physical evidence recovered as instruments of crime such as handwriting, typewriting, forgeries for purpose of establishing identity of writer; examinations of other evidence such as inks, pencils, papers, obliterated or eradicated writing, true age, seeking to prove or disprove genuineness of documents; expert witness on such testimony in state and federal courts; research on related matters, particularly age of ink on paper. Spl agt FBI since '35, instr on document examination and related matters. Sigma Xi. Federal Bureau of Investigation, Washington 25.

17 MILLER, F(rederick) DeWolfe. Ralph Waldo Emerson; US literature (Nineteenth century). b'07. AB '30 (Davidson Coll); '32-33 (Union Theol Sem); MA '35—PhD '42 (U Va). Research on literary caricatures in America and caricatures of Ralph Waldo Emerson; research on James Russell Lowell and American anthologies to 1900. Author: Christopher Pearse Cranch and his Caricatures of New England Transcendentalism '51. Contbr: American Literature '42; Studies in Bibliography (vol IV) '51; Studies in Honor of James Southall Wilson '51. Faculty U Va '40-42, Bucknell U '45-46; assistant professor U Tenn '46-52, now associate professor since '52. Phi Beta Kappa—MLA—S Atlantic MLA (chmn Am lit '50, chmn com status and promotion of humanities since '50). Department of English, University of Tennessee, Knoxville 16.

18 MILLER, George J. Economic geography; Geography of North America; Drainage. b'80. Student '02-03 (U Mich); '98-00—D Edn '48 (Mich Normal Coll); SB—SM '13 (U Chicago). Field studies western US, England, Europe, Canada various periods '04-41; editor Journal of Geography since '20. Author: Geography of North America '28; Geography of Minnesota '22; Essentials of Geography '24. Co-author: Our Natural Resources and Their Conservation; also articles in field. Prof Mankato State Teachers Coll Minn '13-48, Ind U since '48. AAAS(F)—Minn Acad Sci (pres '46-47)—Minn Edn Assn—Nat Soc Study Edn—Assn Am Geog—Nat Council Geog Teachers (founder and past pres). Received Distinguished Service Award in recognition of contributions to advancement geog edn '38; citation by Chicago Geog Soc for distinguished editorial service. Indiana University, Social Science Hall 404, Bloomington, Ind.◎

19 MILLER, Harold Chalmers. Weapons (Interior ballistics); High pressure (Physics). b'16. BS in elec engring '39 (Mo Sch Mines and Metall). Research on interior ballistics of major caliber weapons. Chief engr and vp Charles Hardy Inc '47-49; asst chmn phys research dept Armour Research Found since '49. Am Ordnance Assn—Armed Forces Communications Assn—Am Inst EE. Armour Research Foundation, 35 W. 33rd St., Chgo. 16.

20 MILLER, Harold James. Fungicides. b'11. BA '33 (O State U); '34-37 (Cornell U); PhD '42 (Pa State Coll). Author articles in field. Sr plant path Pa Salt Mfg Co since '48. AAAS(F)—Am Phytopath Soc. Pennsylvania Salt Manufacturing Company, Chestnut Hill, P.O. Box 4388, Phila. 18.†

21 MILLER, Harold Vincent. State planning; Regional and applied geography. b'09. BS '32 (Ball State [Ind] Teach Coll); MS '34 (U Chicago). Editor The Professional Geographer '46-48. Geog TVA '34-37, asso regional planner '37-42, community planner '42-44; dir east Tenn office Tenn State Planning Commn '44-48, exec dir Commn since '48. Am Inst Planners—Am Soc Planning Officials—Am Soc Profl Geogr—Assn Am Geog—Sigma Xi. 517 Commerce, Nashville 3, Tenn.

22 MILLER, Henry. Power plants. b'96. CE '17 (Valparaiso U Ind). Design engineer on hydroelectric plants; consultant on construction power plants. Author article: Fort Peck Hydro Plant Provides for Three Power Units '48. Designer advancing to chief designing engr Harza Engring Co '20-42. Am Soc CE—Am Mil Engrs—Ill Soc Profl Engrs. 8 S. Dearborn St., Chgo. H: 7616 Rogers Av., Chgo 26.

23 MILLER, James Grier. Psychology (Unconsciousness); Personnel (Selection, psychology). b'16. Student '33-34 (Columbia Bible Coll SC); '33-34 (U SC); '34-35 (U Mich); AB summa cum laude '37—MD cum laude '42—PhD '43 (Harvard). Author: Unconsciousness '42. Co-author: Assessment of Men '48. Member editorial committee Annual Review of Psychology. Asst and tutor psychol Harvard '37-38, asst prof clin psychol '46-47, asst psychiatry med sch '43-44; intern medicine and resident in psychiatry Mass Gen Hosp '42-43, asst resident and resident in psychiatry '43-44; Lowell lectr Boston '44; mem assessment program OSS '44-46; chief clin psychology sect Veterans Adminstrn '46-47; prof psychology, dept psychology and div psychiatry, chmn dept psychol U Chicago since '48; resident psychiatry U Ill Med Sch since '51; cons Research and Development Bd, Nat. Mil Esbablishment, Office Surgeon Gen, Veterans Adminstrn. Am Psychol Assn(F)—Soc Fellows Harvard—Am Psychiatric Assn—Group for Advancement Psychiatry—Phi Beta Kappa—Sigma Xi. Dept. of Psychology, University of Chicago, Chgo 37.◎

24 MILLER, John Allen. Animal behavior and neuroanatomy (Neuromuscular mechanism-behavior). b'05. BA '26 (Ashland Coll); MS '27—PhD '32 (O State U); '26-29, '35 (Franz Theodore Stone Lab). Research on production of balanced square waves for electronic stimulation, galvanotropic responses of paramecium to balanced square waves, nerve regeneration, neuron polarity. Author: General Zoology Work Book '49; The Leeches of Ohio '29. Prof and supervisor zool O

State U since '48. AAAS—Am Soc Zool—O Acad Sci—Sigma Xi. Department of Zoology, Ohio State University, Columbus 10, O.†

10 MILLER, Julian Creighton. Horticulture (Potatoes). b'95. BS '21 (Clemson Coll); MS '26—PhD '28 (Cornell U). Research on breeding and production of sweet potatoes for food and industrial uses, relation of some growth characters of stoloniferous condition in seedling Irish potatoes, carotene content of sweet potatoes. Author: Eight-Year Summary of Horticultural Investigations (with Kimbrough) '37, and others; also articles in field. Prof and head dept hort La State U since '29; collaborator Regional Vegetable Breeding Sta US Dept Agr. Am Soc Hort Sci (past pres)—Genetic Assn Am—Potato Assn (past pres)—Phi Kappa Phi—Sigma Xi. Man of Year, Progressive Farmer mag '47. Agriculture Center, University Station, Baton Rouge 3, La.⊙

11 MILLER, Julian Howell. Mycology; Plant pathology. b'90. BSA '11—MS '24 (U Ga); PhD '28 (Cornell). Author articles in field. Prof plant path and head dept U Ga since '36; collaborator US Dept Agr Plant Disease Survey for Ga since '24. AAAS(F)—Am Mycol Soc—Am Phytopath Soc—Brit Mycol Soc—Ga Acad Sci—Ga Naturalists—Phi Beta Kappa—Phi Kappa Phi—Sigma Xi. 458 Dearing St., Athens, Ga.†⊙

12 MILLER, Lawrence Frederick. Fisheries biology; Fish management. b'10. BA '33—MA '35 (U Ill). Studies on spring and yearly creel census, fish harvesting, fish migration, depth distribution, fish population, tree and brush shelter, effects of pollution. Author articles in field. Aquatic biol Fish and Game Branch TVA since '37. AAAS—Am Fisheries Soc—Ecol Soc Am—Wildlife Soc—Am Soc Limnol Oceanog—Am Soc Ichthyologists Herpetologists—Tenn Acad Sci. Fish and Game Branch, Tennessee Valley Authority, Decatur, Ala.

13 MILLER, Lawrence Peter. Agricultural biochemistry; Glycosides; Herbicides. b'01. BS '23 (Penn State Coll); MS '25 (U Wis); PhD '33 (Purdue U). Research on effect of stimulative chemicals on bud development and composition of potato tubers and woody plants with special reference to enzyme activity and carbohydrate content, effect of manganese deficiency on plant composition, sulfur metabolism in higher plants, physiology of sulfate reducing bacteria; studies on methods for improving flavor and color of chocolate and cocoa products; determination of particle size distribution in cocoa powders. Induced formation of beta-glycosides in higher plants through addition to nutrient medium of chemicals which can serve as aglycons; studies on the mechanics of plant protection from fungi using radioactive tracers. Abstractor Chemical Abstracts since '25; asst biochemist and biochemist Boyce Thompson Inst Plant Research Inc since '29. AAAS(F)—Am Inst Chem(F)—Am Chem Soc—Bot Soc Am—Am Soc Plant Physiol—NY Acad Sci—Sigma Xi Boyce Thompson Institute for Plant Research, Inc., 1086 North Broadway, Yonkers 3, N.Y.

14 MILLER, Maynard Malcolm. Geomorphology; Glaciology; Glacial geology; Geology. b'21. BS '43 (Harvard); MA '48—PhD '52 (Columbia); Fulbright fellow '51-52 (Cambridge U Eng). Participant and director fourteen arctic and sub-arctic projects involving geology and field research and development expeditionary operation and administrative techniques; in charge several glacier survey expeditions on fiorded Alaskan coast; photography and mapping current positions and studies of regimen and structures of existing ice masses; mapping survey and glaciological studies Glacier Bay and Forest Fiords Southeastern Alaska and also numerous remnant glaciers in western mountains of US; leader first American ascent of Mt St Elias in Alaska; aerial survey 400 Alaskan glaciers along coast; glaciologist Arctic Inst of North America expedition to Seward Glacier in Yukon Territory; field explorations and glaciologic studies Chile, Peru and Greenland, Ellsmore Land (air) and Canadaia Arctic Archipeago (air); first exploration and mapping of Brady ice field via Glacier Bay and first ascent of Mt Bertha, Alaska. Author articles: The Vanishing Glaciers '49; Glacial Geology of the Ameghino Valley, Argentina '51; Englacial Investigations of the Taku Glacier, Alaska '51; Intercalated Lava Beds and Glacial Tills, Mesta de Charillo Malo, Patogonia '52; Glaciological Research on the Juneau Ice Field, Alaska '51; The Juneau Ice Field Research Project '50; Ice Islands in the Polar Sea '51; Recent Variations in the Glaciers of Icy Bay and Yakutat Bay, Alaska '52; others. Summit guide on Mt Rainier '40; mem New Eng Mus Natural Hist and Harvard Inst Geog Exploration expdn Fairweather Range Alaska '40; Am Geog Soc Expdn SE Alaska '41, Aleutian Islands '42; aerial survey Alaskan glaciers '46 and '47, SA glacier studies '49, dir Juneau Ice Field Research Project '48, '49 '50, winter and summer '51, research asso Am Geog Soc since '48, dir Greenland glaciologic project '52. Geol Soc Am—Brit Glaciological Soc—Arctic Inst NA—AIMME—Am Assn Petroleum Geol—Am Geophys Union (sub-com glaciers)—Royal Geog Soc—Am Alpine Club(bd dirs, chmn nat safety com)—Explorers Club—Mountaineers Inc—Sigma Xi—Phi Beta Kappa. Department of Exploration and Field Research, American Geographical Society, Broadway and 156th St., NYC 32.

15 MILLER, Milton A(lbert). Rodent control; Isopod Crustacea (Systematics, ecology); Biology and control of marine fouling organisms and the pocket gopher. b'07. AB '29 (U Ill); PhD '34 (U Calif). Author: Laboratory Manual for Vertebrate Anatomy '48; also articles in field. Asso prof zool and asso zool expt sta U Calif since '49. Ecol Soc Am—Am Soc Mammalogists—Western Soc Naturalists—AAAS—Soc Systematic Zool—Sigma Xi. Department of Zoology, University of California, Davis, Cal.†

16 MILLER, Muriel McLatchie (Mrs Floyd Miller). Medical illustration. b'00. Student '26-28 (Max Brödel Sch Art Baltimore); '32-34 (Butera Sch Art Boston). Author article: Medical Illustration '46. Department of art as applied to medicine Johns Hopkins Medical School '27-29; illus med jours; head med illus dept Mass Gen Hosp dir Sch Med Illus. Assn Med Illus (bd govs '45-51, corr sec '45-48, vp '48-49). Massachusetts General Hospital, Boston 14.

17 MILLER, Neal E(lgar). Psychology (Learning, aggression, fear, conflict, aviation). b'09. BS '31 (U Wash); MA '32 (Stanford); PhD '35 (Yale); Social Sci research fellow '35-36 (Vienna Psychoanalytic Inst). Co-author: Frustration and Aggression '39; Social Learning and Imitation '41; Personality and Psychotherapy '50. Editor: Psychological Research on Pilot Training. James Rowland Angell prof of psychology Yale since '52; expert consultant American Institute Resch (personnel selection) since '46. Officer charge research psychological research unit Number 1 AAF Nashville '42-44, director psychol research project Randolph Field '44-46. AAAS—Soc Exptl Psychol(F)—Am Psychol Assn(F)—Eastern Psychol Assn—Sigma Xi—Phi Beta Kappa. Department of Psychology, Yale University, 333 Cedar St., New Haven 11.

18 MILLER, Norman Christian. Engineering (Executive training); Adult education; Labor relations. b'90. BS '12 (U Mich); MS '16 (Pa State Coll). Editor: Foreman Training '22; Engineering for Apprentices '24. With Pa State Coll '13-25, head dept engring ext '18-25; dir U ext Rutgers U since 25, dean U Coll since '40; mem pub panel 2d region Nat War Labor Bd '43-45; dir Inst Management and Labor Relations since '47. Am Assn Adult Edn—Deans and Dirs Evening Colls—Nat U Ext Assn (past pres)—Am Arbitration (mem panel)—Tau Kappa Alpha—Delta Sigma Pi. 135 N. 7th Av., New Brunswick, N.J.

19 MILLER, Paul Gerard. Puerto Rico (Government, education). b'75. BA '10—MA '11—PhD '14 (U Wis); Dr edn honoris causa '40 (U Porto Rico). Participated in Puerto Rican expedition '98 executive council of Puerto Rico '15-21; delegate from Porto Rico to 2nd Pan-American Scientific Congress Washington '15-16. Author: Civil Government of Porto Rico; Spanish-American Readers; Education in Porto Rico (six annual reports); Historia de Puerto Rico '49. Editor: Spanish-American edits of Hale's A Man Without a Country and Shakespear's Julius Caesar; Linares Rivas' El Abolengo y La Cizaña; Manual para Globos Terrestres; also articles in field. Supervisor schs San German PR '99-02, supt schs San Juan '02; chief div supervision Dept Edn PR '02-03; prin Insular Normal Sch '03-08; commr edn PR '15-21; with Rand McNally & Co '21-48. Nat Geog Soc—Am Geog Soc(F)—Comite Cultural Argentino. Winneconne, Wis.

20 MILLER, Paul William. Plant pathology. b'01. BS '23—MS '24 (U Ky); PhD '29 (U Wis). Research on filbert and walnut tree diseases and control, causes Strawberry root rot, Strawberry virus diseases. Plant path Bur Plant Industry US Dept Agr since '30. Phytopath Soc—Sigma Xi. Room 138, Agriculture Building, Oregon State College, Corvallis, Ore.†

21 MILLER, Perry Gilbert Eddy. Puritanism. b'05. PhB '28—PhD '31 (U Chicago); '30-31 (Harvard). Author: Orthodoxy in Massachusetts '33; The Puritans '38; The New England Mind '39; Jonathan Edwards '49. Prof Harvard. Colonial Soc Mass—Mass Hist Soc—Am Antiquarian Soc—Modern Lang Assn—AHA. Guggenheim fellowship '37-38. Widener 16, Harvard University, Cambridge 38, Mass.

22 MILLER, Pierre A. Plant pathology (Subtropical fruit and landscape plant diseases). b'97. BS '24 (Ore State Coll); MS '25 (Kan State Agr Coll). Author articles in field. Asso prof plant path U Calif Los Angeles since '43. Bot Soc Am—Nat Shade Tree Conf—So Calif Hort Inst (mem bd dirs '45-48)—AAAS(F)—Am Phytopath Soc—Mycol Soc Am—Sigma Xi—Phi Kappa Phi—Gamma Sigma Delta. University of California, 405 Hilgard Av., Los Angeles 24.

23 MILLER, Ralph L. Stratigraphy and structure of Appalachians; Petroleum geology. b'09. BS '39 (Haverford Coll); PhD '37 (Columbia). Author articles in field. Geol US Geol Survey since '42; chief Navy Oil Unit directing geol exploration Naval Petroleum Reserve No 4 Arctic Alaska '48-51; chief fuels branch since '51. Geol Soc Am(F) —Am Assn Petroleum Geol—Am Inst Mining Metall Engrs. U. S. Geological Survey, Department of Interior, Washington 25.†

10 MILLER, Raymond Wiley. Public relations research; Trade relations. b'95. Student '14-16 (San Jose State Coll); '15 (U Calif); LLB '43 (LaSalle Ext U); LLD(hon) '42 (St John's U, Minn). Member World Conference on Democracy Columbia University '39, White House Conference on Rural Education Washington '44, National Conference on Juvenile Delinquency Washington '46; consultant Food and Agriculture Organization of United Nations; cons tech coop adminstrn State Dept '52. Author: Keepers of the Corporate Conscience '46; The Corporation, A Brotherhood of Service '47; Take Time for Human Engineering '47; The Farm Cooperative Corporate Association '48; Humanizing the Corporate Person '49. Co-author: Business Administration '47; The Place of Public Relations in Business '47; Marketing Handbook '48; Our Economic Policy in Asia '51; also articles in field. Pres Argl Trade Relations Inc since '36; president World Trade Relations Ltd since '40, Pub Relations Research Corp since '48; pres, gen counsel Am Inst Corporation '45-48, dean pub relations '48; pub relations cons since '30; lecturer on pub relations since '39; vis lecturer Harvard U Grad Sch Bus Adminstrn since '48. Am Council Pub Relations (award '45)—Am Farm Econ Assn. Linden, Cal.

11 MILLER, Rene Harcourt. Helicopters (Design). b'16. BA '37 (Cambridge U, Eng). Author articles: A Method for Improving the Inherent Stability and Control Characteristics of Helicopter '49; Jet Propulsion Applied to Helicopters '46, and others. Chief aerodynamics and development McDonnell Aircraft Corp St Louis '39-44; formerly asso prof aero engring MIT; vp engineering Kaman Aircraft Corp. Nat Adv Com Aeronautics (helicopter subcom). Kaman Aircraft Corp., Bradley Field, Windsor Locks, Conn.

12 MILLER, Richard Franklin. Properties of metals at elevated temperatures. b'08. BA '30 (Williams Coll); ScD '34 (MIT). Designed and constructed improved apparatus for studying creep of metals at elevated temperature; consultant on design of pressure vessels for operation at elevated temperature, on selection of materials for use in construction of oil-cracking stills, and on strength and operation of alloy steels at elevated temperature; member War Metallurgy Committee's project committee on heat-resisting metals for gas turbine parts; patents in field. Author articles in field. Research metall US Steel Corp Research Lab Kearny NJ '36-43; development engr Carnegie-Illinois Steel Corp '43-48, asst to vp since '48. ASME (mem subcom on ferrous materials of Boiler Code Com, mem joint com on effect of temperature on properties of metals with Am Soc Testing Materials—Am Soc Metals—Am Inst Mining Metall Engrs—Iron and Steel Inst, Brit— Sigma Xi. United States Steel Corp., 525 Wm. Penn Place, Research and Technology Department, Pittsburgh 30. H: 21 Zama Dr., Mt. Lebanon 16.

13 MILLER, Robert Rush. Ichthyology (Classification, zoology); Natural history. b'16. AB '39 (U Calif); MA '44 —PhD '44 (U Mich). Personal field work in California, Nevada, Oregon '36-39, '47, northwestern Mexico '39, Arizona '47; field assistant ichthyological survey of Nevada U Michigan '38; expeditions to western US University Michigan Museum Zoology '39, 40, '42; Smithsonian expedition Guatemala '46-47; survey of Arnhem Land Australia for Australian Government-Smithsonian Institution-National Geographic Society '48. Author articles in field. Asso curator fishes US Nat Mus Smithsonian Instn; now with Museum Zoology University Mich. AAAS —Am Soc Ichthyologists Herpetologists—Mich Acad Sci—Am Fisheries Soc —Soc for Freedom in Sci—Washington Acad Sci—Limnol Oceanog Soc Am— Sigma Xi. Museum of Zoology, University of Michigan, Ann Arbor.

14 MILLER, Samuel Charles. Periodontia and oral diseases; Oral diagnosis; Diseases of the temporomandibular joints; Rampant caries (Control). b'03. Student '19-20 (Coll City of NY); DDS '25 (NYU). Original classification causes of periodontal disease, of alveolar bone types. Author and editor: Textbook of Periodontia (with members of NYU Periodonita staff) '38,'43, '50; Oral Diagnosis and Treatment (with 26 contributors) '36, '46. Prof periodontia NYU Coll Dentistry; cons and tchr USN Dental Corps; cons VA; attending in oral med NY Polyclinic Hosp and Med Sch. 57 W. 57th St., NYC 19.

15 MILLER, Sydney Lincoln. Transportation and public utilities; Economics. b'90. AB '12 (Kan State Teachers Coll); AM '16—PhD '20 (U Wis). Author: Railway Transportation, Principles and Point of View '24; Inland Transportation '33; also articles in field. Prof and head dept transportation and pub utilities U Pittsburgh since '46. Am Econ Assn—Mid-West Econ Soc (pres '34-35)—Am Soc Traffic and Transportation — Beta Gamma Sigma. 44 Altadena Dr., Pittsburgh 16.

16 MILLER, Warren Widmer. Radioactive tracers and carbon fourteen. b'15. BS '41 (O State U); PhD in chem '44 (U Calif Berkeley). Author articles in field. Research asso NDRC research Washington '43-44; dept chem Harvard U, '44-45; Mem Radio Activity Center MIT '45-47; dept chem Brookhaven Nat Lab Upton LI NY '47-50; dept chem Pa State Coll since '50. Department of Chemistry, Pennsylvania State Coll, State College, Pa.†

17 MILLER, William Timothy. American constitutional history; Theory of history; Historiography. b'02. BS '26 (Central Mo State Teachers Coll); MA '27 (U Mo); PhD '33—U fellow '31-32— (O State U). Studies on liberalism in Supreme Court, thought of recent and contemporary American historians on writing of history, with emphasis on history as a science. Author articles: The Progressive Movement in Missouri '28; Nullification in Georgia and in South Carolina as Viewed by the New West '30, and others. Asso prof hist Peru State Teachers Coll Neb '33-44; prof hist, head dept Jamestown Coll ND '44-45; prof hist, chmn div social sci Neb State Teachers Coll Chadron since 45. AHA—Miss Valley Hist Assn —NEA—Neb State Edn Assn. Nebraska State Teachers College, Chadron, Neb.

18 MILLER, Willis Hamilton. Planning (State, national and regional); Geography (economic and political). b'06. AB '29 (U Calif Los Angeles); PhD '33—SM '31 (U Chicago). Author articles in field. Asst research tech Nat Resources Planning Bd Washington '34-35; asso cons Nat Resources Planning Bd Los Angeles '37; chief planning tech, sec, co-author and ed reports Calif State Planning Bd '37-42; chief research and asst chief coordination Vets Administrn Br Office 12 San Francisco since '46. Am Inst Planners (asso)—Assn Am Geog—Assn Pacific Coast Geog (sec-treas '41-42)—Calif Planners Inst—Sigma Xi.

19 MILLER, Woodrow Alma. Honey production; Bee keeping. b'13. Student '32-33 (Brigham Young U); '35-36 (George Washington U). Author articles in field. Engaged in large scale honey prodn and packing since '36. Nat Fed Beekeepers Assn Am (pres '47-48)—Am Honey Inst (bd dirs '45-48)—Sioux Honey Assn (bd dirs '34-38). 125 Laurel St., Colton, Cal.

20 MILLETT, John David. Public administration; Educational finance. b '12. AB '33 (De Pauw U); AM '35— PhD '38 (Columbia). Member President's Committee on Administrative Management '36, member Committee on Public Administration of Social Science Research Council '39-41, staff National Resources Planning Board '41-42, assistant to executive director Hoover Commission on Organiation of Executive Branch of Government '48-49, executive director Commission on Financing Higher Education '49-52. Author: The Works Progress Administration in New York City '37; The British Unemployment Assistance Board '39; The Process and Organization of Government Planning '47. Co-author: (with A W Macmahon) Federal Administrators '39, The Administration of Federal Work Relief '41. Asso prof Columbia '45-48, prof since '48. Am Polit Sci Assn—Am Soc Pub Adminstrn. Fagerweather Hall, Columbia University, NYC 27.†◎

21 MILLIGAN, Winfred Oliver. Colloids; Oxides (Inorganic). b'08. AB '30—ScD hon '46 (Ill Coll); MA '32 —PhD '34 (Rice Inst). Research on x-ray and electron diffraction examination of inorganic oxides, dehydration studies on colloidal gels, adsorption studies such as water vapor and hydrocarbon gases on oxides; member National Research Council committee on application of x-ray and electron diffraction to chemistry '38-41; associate editor Journal of Physical and Colloid Chemistry since 50. Author 75 articles in field. Contributor: Advances in Colloid Science '42. Prof chem Rice Inst since '34; cons catalysis since '36. ACS (div colloid chem —chmn '43, v-chmn '42, sec '41, since '47)—APS—Am Crystallographic Assn —Phi Beta Kappa—Sigma Xi—Phi Lambda Upsilon—Alpha Chi Sigma. Rice Institute, P.O. Box 1892, Houston 1.

22 MILLIKEN, Henry Augustus. Maine (Hunting, logging, lumbering and pulpwood industries); Whitetailed deer (Habits, hunting methods). b'07. Author: Hunting in Maine '47; also articles in field. 43 Main St., Freeport, Me. H: 4 Cottage St.

23 MILLS, Harlow Burgess. Entomology; Wildlife management. b'06. BS 29'—MS '30 (ND '34 (Ia State Coll). Editor Journal of Wildlife Management. Author: Monograph of the Collembola '34; Bugs, Birds, and Blizzards in the Yellowstone '37; also articles in field. Asst prof Tex A&M '30-31; Ia and Tex Agrl Expt Sta '32-34; ranger, naturalist, wildlife tech Yelowstone Nat Park '34-35; asst state entomol Mont '35-37; state entomol Mont, head dept zool and entomol Mont State Coll '37-47; chief Natural Hist Survey Div of Ill since '47. Entomol Soc Am(F) —Am Assn Econ Entomol—AAAS— Wildlife Soc Am—Sigma Xi—Phi Kappa Phi. Illinois State Natural History Survey, Urbana, Ill.†

10 **MILLS, Lloyd Clarence.** Micropaleontology. b'09. AB '32—AM '36 (U Neb). Author: Development in West Texas and Southeastern New Mexico '47. Paleontol and geol Pure Oil Co '36-47; oil geol Southland Royalty Co since '47. Am Assn Petroleum Geol—Soc Econ Mineral Paleontol—AAAS. P.O. Box 773, Midland, Tex.

11 **MILLS, Marion Elbert.** Tall buildings (Wind stresses); Bridges (Elastic arch, rigid frame); Continuous girders; Continuous trusses. b'82. BS in civil engring '08—CE '27 (Purdue U). Research on wind stresses in tall building frames, continuous girders and frames of variable moment of inertia, various phases of statistically indeterminate stress. Chief engr Truscon Steel Co '20-25; structural engr and designer Wyatt C Headrick Inc '25-27; prof civil engring U Okla since '27. AAUP—Am Soc CE. University of Oklahoma, Norman, Okla.

12 **MILLS, Wilford R(ichard).** Potatoes (Disease resistance breeding); Phytophthora infestans (Biological races). b'09. BS '31—PhD '39 (Cornell U). Author articles in field. Asst prof plant path research Pa State Coll '41-49, now asso prof. Am Phytopath Soc—AAAS—Am Potato Assn—Sigma Xi. Department of Botany, Pennsylvania State College, State College, Pa.

13 **MILLS, William Hayne.** Soil stabilization; Paving design. b'03. BS, CE (Clemson A&M Coll SC); (U SC). Development soil cement; research on soil stabilization with tar and asphalt materials; investigation thickness design of flexible base pavements through study of subgrade soils and base course materials; highway engineering. Material engr SC State Highway Dept '29-42; chief airport engring div Civil Aeronautics Adminstrn '46-49; dist engr Asphalt Inst '49—. ASTM—Am Soc CE—Highway Research Bd—Ga Engring Soc—SC Soc Engrs (past pres)—Tau Beta Pi. 305 Mortgage Guarantee Bldg., Atlanta 3.

14 **MILLSPAUGH, William Hulse.** Paper production machines; Centrifugal casting of metals. b'68. Student '87-90 (Keuka NY Coll). Patented and developed suction rolls and paper-making devices, established new world records for speed and production of paper; also patented and developed centrifugal casting of metals. Organizer Sandusky Foundry & Machine Co, pres until '29; organized Millspaugh Ltd Sheffield Eng '33, sold '46; pres Centrifugal Steel Inc Sandusky O. ASME—Tech Assn Am Pulp & Paper Assn (gold medalist)—US Mil Engrs—Instn Mech Engrs, London—Army Ordnance Assn. —P.O. Box 547, Sandusky, O. H: 805 Idlewyld Dr., Ft. Lauderdale, Fla.☺

15 **MILNE, Lorus Johnson.** Insect vision; Invertebrate behavior; Biophotography. b'10. BA '33 (U Toronto); MA '34—research fellow '34-36—PhD '36 (Harvard); '26-29 (Humberside Collegiate Inst); '34, '41 (Woods Hole Marine Biol Lab). Author: A Multitude of Living Things (with Margery Milne) '47; also articles in field. Asso prof zool U NH since '48; lecturer. AAAS(F)—Entomol Soc Am(F)—Sigma Xi—Limnol Soc Am—Zool Soc Am. George Westinghouse Sci Writing Award '47; grant from Carnegie Corp '40; research grant U Va Biol Sta summers '38-40, Woods Hole Biol Sta summer '41. University of New Hampshire, Durham, N.H.

16 **MILNE, Robert Bruce.** Forests (Management). b'13. BS in forestry '37 (Syracuse U). Consultant timber and lumber acquisition programs, management forest land property, and sale of timber. Forester Southern Johns-Manville Jarratt Va '37-41, lumber div Am Hardware Co Inc Petersburg Va '41-46; cons forester since '46. Soc Am Foresters—Am Forestry Assn—Va Forests Inc. P.O. Box 371, Petersburg, Va. H: 515 Riverview Rd., Colonial Heights.

17 **MILOVSOROFF, Basil.** Puppetry. b'06. AB '32—AM '34 (Oberlin Coll). Puppet maker and stylist; experimentation in non-imitative imaginative aspects of the Puppet theater. Author articles: The Artist in Puppet Theatre '47; Synthesis '49; Puppets and Robots '51; Showmanship '52; Reality with Strings Attached '53. Program chmn Nat Festival Puppeteers America Dartmouth College '54. Creation and production puppet plays based on folktales, exhbns and plays art mus and children's theaters since '34. Puppeteers Am Assn. Folktale Puppet Studio, Norwich, Vt.

18 **MINARIK, Charles Edwin.** Plant physiology (Growth regulators, nutrition, weed control). b'11. BS '33—MS '35 (Mass U); PhD '39 (Rutgers U). Research in mineral nutrition of plants, role of trace elements, hydroponics, physiological disorders of rice including straighthead and white tip, black kernel disease, rice nutrition, use of plant growth regulators as herbicides; studies and writing on effects of herbicides on beneficial insects and animals, absorption and movement of 2, 4-D and role of onion juice in enhancing activity of 2, 4-D, effect of boron in substrate on calcium accumulation in soybean plants, effect of vitamin B on growth of rice plants. Author articles: The Control of Aquatic Plants with Phenoxyacetic Compounds (with Surber and Ennis) '47; Tests for Evaluating Potential Herbicides '48 and others. Plant physiol Tex Agrl Expt Sta '39-42; lab officer Chem Warfare Service Camp Detrick '45, plant physiol and br chief Chem Corps Camp Detrick since '46. Am Soc Plant Physiol—Bot Soc Am—AAAS—Sigma Xi—Am Soc Hort Sci—NY Acad Sci—Soc Research Soc Am. Camp Detrick, Frederick, Md.

19 **MINEKA, Francis Edward.** English periodicals; English literature (Victorian). b'07. AB '29—AM '31 (Hamilton Coll); U F '41-42—PhD '43 (Columbia). Research on inter-relations Victorian period of literature with social, economic, political and philosophic background; research on English religious periodicals 1700-1825 and of liberal English periodical The Monthly Repository 1806-1838. Author: The Dissidence of Dissent: The Monthly Repository, 1806-1838 '44. Faculty Hamilton Coll '29-32, '34-35, asst prof '35-42; asst prof Eng U Tex '42-46; with Cornell U since '46, prof Eng since '51, chmn dept since '48; Ford Found F '52-53. Phi Beta Kappa—Modern Lang Assn—Coll Eng Assn. Goldwin Smith Hall, Cornell University, Ithaca.

20 **MINER, Dwight Carroll.** History of the Panama Canal; History of Columbia University. b'04. AB '26—AM '27—PhD '40—William Mitchell fellow '26-27—U fellow '28 (Columbia). Author: The Fight for the Panama Route '40. Co-editor: Contemporary Civilization in the West. Instr hist Columbia '27-42, asso prof '45-48, prof since '48, historian Columbia Univ since '46. Acad Polit Sci—AHA—Fgn Policy Assn—Phi Beta Kappa. Hamilton Hall, Columbia University, NYC 27.☺

21 **MINER, Roy Waldo.** Marine zoology; Phylogeny. b'75. AB '97—ScD '27 (Williams Coll); grad '00 (Gen Theol Sem); PhD '23 (Columbia). Submarine studies of coral reefs from sea bottom with submarine tube and diving helmet Bahamas '23, '24, '26, '30, '33; to Christmas Island, Tongareva and Samoa for submarine studies of pearl beds and Pacific corals '36; studies sponge reefs and fisheries west coast Fla '39 '41 '42. Author: Animals of the Wharf Piles '12; The Pectoral Limb Musculature of Eryops and other Primitive Vetebrates '25; Diving in Coral Gardens '33; The Kingdom of the Tides '34; A Transplanted Coral Reef '35; Field Book of Sea Shore Life '50. Asst curator invertebrate zoology Am Mus Natural History '05-16, asso curator 17-21, curator marine life '22-43, curator emeritus since '43. Nat Research Council—NY Acad Scis(F, pres, editor)—AAAS(F)—Am Ecol Soc—Am Mus Assn—Am Geophys Union—Marine Hist Soc—Phi Beta Kappa—Sigma Xi. New York Academy of Sciences, 2 East 63rd St., NYC 21.

22 **MINGINS, Charles Robert.** Electromagnetic waves; Electromechanical filters; Crystals (Oscillations); Microwaves. b'99. Fisk scholar '24-25—AB '25 (Wesleyan U); PhD '35 (Cornell U). Research on electromagnetic wave propagation. Author articles: Electromagnetic Wave Fields Near the Earth's Surface '37; The Rotating Field '37; others. Head dept phys and math Green Mt Jr Coll '37-43; with Tufts Coll since '43, prof since '51, dir Research Lab Phys Electronics since '47. Inst Radio Engrs(sr mem)—APS—Am Assn Phys Tchrs—Am Soc Engring Edn—Am Inst Phys—AAUP—Sigma Xi—Phi Beta Kappa—Sigma Pi Sigma. Research Laboratory of Physical Electronics, Department of Physics, Tufts College, Medford 55, Mass.

23 **MINICH, Arthur.** Metallic soaps; Varnish driers; Microbicides. b'07. BS '26 (Vienna Inst Chem Tech). Author articles in field. Asst chief chem research in protective coatings Rinshed-Mason Co Detroit '28-31, Ault & Wiborg Co Cincinnati '31-32; vp Nuodex Products Co Inc Elizabeth NJ since '32, direction of research in metallic soaps, paint and varnish driers, microbicides. Patents. Am Soc for Testing Materials—Am Wood Preservers Assn—Soc Rheology—Textile Research Inst—Am Oil Chem Soc. Certificate of Merit from WPB protective coatings br; from War Dept and Navy Dept for outstanding contribution to the work of Office of Scientific Research and Development during World War II. Nuodex Products Co., Inc., 830 Magnolia Av., Elizabeth, N.J.

24 **MINOGUE, James Alexander.** Records administration (Official maps); Land planning; Cartography. b'12. BE '34 (State Teach Coll Minn); MA '36 (Clark U). Research on land utilization in Dublin (New Hampshire), administration federal map collections, official American cartography, military geography. Research cons NH Found Concord '36-37; geog, cartographer Miss State Plan Commn '37-38; map curator Nat Archives Wash '38-42; geog Dept Army Wash since '46. Lt Comdr USNR hydrographic office Div Air Navigation '42-46. Am Geog Soc(F)—Asso Am Geog—Am Geophys Union—Am Soc Photogrammetrists. 704 S. Overlook Dr., Alexandria, Va.†

25 **MINOR, Wine Thomas, Jr.** Colonial American handicrafts and tools. b '17. BS '38 (College William and Mary). Research, development and equipping operating shops to perform work in colonial manner. Editor The Chronicle of the Early American Industries Association. Dir archaeol lab

Colonial Williamsburg since '38. Colonial Williamsburg, Inc., Williamsburg, Va.

10 MINOT, George Richards. Blood disorders; Curative effect of liver on pernicious anemia. b'85. AB '08—MD '12—SD(hon) '28 (Harvard). Research work on liver treatment of anemia; pathological physiology and clinical description of anemia; several studies on curative effects of anemia. Prof medicine Harvard since '28. ACP(F)—Royal Coll Physicians—Royal Soc Medicine—Am Soc Clin Investigations—Am Clin and Climatol Assn—Phi Beta Kappa. Awarded jointly with William P Murphy and George H Whipple Nobel prize for medicine '34, work on liver treatment of the anemias. Thorndike Memorial Laboratory, Boston City Hospital, Boston.◎

11 MISCH, Peter. Structural and metamorphic geology; Origin of granite. b'09. PhD '32 (U Goettingen, Germany); '30 (U Graz, Austria). Research in Spanish Pyranees structure '30-32, N.W. Himalayas as member of Nanga Parbat Expedition, metamorphism '34, Kwangtung Province, general and structural geology '36-38, Yunnan Province, stratigraphy, structure, metamorphism, discovery of bauxite and phosphate deposits '39-46, Yunnan Triassic '47, northernmost Cascades Wash, structure and metamorphism '49-53, structure E Nevada '51-52. Author articles in field. Teaching asst Univ Goettingen, geol mapping, gen geol '32-33, research fellowship for petrologic work on rocks collected in NW Himalayas '35-36; prof structural and field geol Nat Sun Yat-sen U Canton '36-38, Chengkiang, Yunnan '39-40; adv to Geol Survey of Kwangtung and Kwangsi '36-40; prof structural geol and petrology U Peking '40-46 (Nat Southwestern Asso U Kunming Yunnan until '46); adv to Geol Survey of Yunnan '42-45; research on Yunnan Triassic, Stanford U '47; asst prof geol U Washington '47-48, asso prof '48-50, professor since '50, advanced and regional structure, metamorphic petrology. Am Assn Petroleum Geol—Geol Society London(F)—Geol Soc Am (F)—Am Geophys Union—Resch Soc U Wash—Am Alpine Club—Geol Vereinigung. Department of Geology, Univ of Washington, Seattle 5. H: 5726 E. 60th St.†

12 MISHOFF, Willard Oral. American Colonial history; Library statistics. b'96. BA '19 (Carroll Coll); MA '23—PhD '33 (Ia State U); student '14-16 (Wis State Normal Sch), summer '20 (Wis U), '27-28 (Columbia), '36-37 (Chicago U); AB Library Sci '31 (Mich U). Research on Indian policy of Sir William Johnson, school library furniture and equipment, what federal government offers to elementary school library. Author: A Guide to Thesis Writing (with Morrow) '32; Public Library Statistics (with Foster) '47; also articles in field. Specialist for coll and research libraries, Fed Security Agency, Office Edn since '46. Am Assn Adult Edn—AHA—ALA—Nat Edn Assn US. Scholar in library sci, Carnegie Corp NY '30-31; fellow in edn, Library of Congress '45. Federal Security Agency, Office of Education, Washington 25.

13 MISRAHI, Jean P. Old French literature; Medieval culture. b'10. AB '29—PhD '33 (Columbia); Diplome d'Etudes francaises '27 (U Nancy France); Certificat d'Etudes Superieures de Civilization francaise '28 (U Paris). Author: Le Roman Des Sept Sages '33; editorial bd: Thought; also articles in field. Asst to asso prof and chem dept Romance Langs and Lit Grad Sch Fordham U since '38. Modern Lang Assn Am—Societe des Anciens Textes Francais—Phi Beta Kappa—Medieval Academy of America. Guggenheim Fellowship in France '36-37. Fordham University, NYC 58.

14 MITCHELL, A r t h u r E(dwin). Fruit production (Spraying, dusting, growth regulators). b'09. BS '36 (U NH); MS '37—student '41-42 (O State U). Author articles in field. Asso prof hort Mich State Coll Agr and Expt Sta since '47. Am Soc Hort Sci—Sigma Xi—Gamma Sigma Delta. Department of Horticulture, Michigan State College, East Lansing, Mich.

15 MITCHELL, D o n a l d William. United States Naval history; History of World War II. b'11. AM '32—MA '35—PhD '39 (U So Calif). Author: History of the Modern American Navy; 1883 through Pearl Harbor '46; also articles in field. Asst prof govt Sam Houston State Coll '41-43, prof '43-47; asst prof govt Newark Coll Arts & Sci Rutgers U since '47. AHA—Am Mil Inst—US Naval Inst. Hdqrs, Continental Air Command, Mitchel Air Force Base, N.Y. H: 33 Brookdale Av., Verona, N.J.

16 MITCHELL, Elmer Dayton. Physical education (Intramural sports). b'89. AB '12—AM '19—PhD '38 (U Mich). Consultant on physical education National Congress Parents and Teachers '35; special consultant education policies commission National Education Association '36; Joint Army and Navy Committee on Welfare and Recreation '41. Inventor game of speedball '21. Author: Intramural Athletics '25; Social Games for Recreation '35; Active Games and Contests '35; Sports for Recreation '36; Intramural Sports 39; Sports Officiating '49. Editor: Journal of Health and Physical Education '30-43; Research Quarterly '30-43; also articles in field. Varsity athletic coaching staff U Mich '17-19, dir intramural athletics since '19, asst prof phys edn '21-26, asso prof '26-38, prof since '38. Lt comdr USNR '43, comdr '45, officer charge phys training 8th Naval Dist. Am Acad Phys Edn(F)—Am Phys Edn Assn (hon) Middle W Soc Phys Edn (ex-sec)—Intramural Dirs Assn—Am Assn Health Phys Edn and Recreation (past sec)—Mich State Phys Edn Assn—Coll Phys Edn Assn—Nat Collegiate Athletic Assn. Received Gulick award for distinguished service in phys edn '49. 1425 Cambridge Rd., Ann Arbor.

17 MITCHELL, E n o c h Lockwood. History (Tennessee and Old South). b'03. BS '29 (Memphis State Coll): MA '38 (George Peabody Coll). Author articles in field. Prof hist Memphis State Coll since '39. Tenn Hist Soc (sec since '45)—So Hist Assn—West Tenn Hist Soc (sec since '41), ed papers since '47. Memphis State College, Memphis 11.

18 MITCHELL, George Frederick. Tea (Procurement, blending, processing, packaging); Cassina; Food processing (Flavor balancing). b'81. BS '02 (Clemson Coll). Studied in Far East cultivation, manufacture, and commercial handling of tea for US government '17-18. Patentee machine for pruning tea, processes for manufacture of beverages for cassina (an American plant containing caffeine). Sci asst US Dept Agr experiments in growing and mfg tea in Am '03-12; supervising tea examiner to adminstr Tea Act '12-29; plant mgr Maxwell House Tea Div Gen Food Corp '29-48; independent tea cons; mem US Bd Tea Experts. Tea Assn USA (past pres). 3913 Second Av., Brooklyn.

19 MITCHELL, Harold Hanson. Nutrition (Protein and energy metabol- ism, mineral requirements). b'86. AB '09—MS '13—PhD '15 (U Ill). Editorial board Journal of Nutrition. Co-author: Studies in Nutrition (Vol I) '17; Biochemistry of the Amino Acids '29; Nutrition and Climatic Stress '51; also articles in field. Prof and chief div animal nutrition U Ill since '25. AAAS—Am Chem Soc—Am Soc Animal Prodn—Am Soc Biol Chem—Am Inst Nutrition—Am Dietetic Assn—Soc Exptl Biol and Med—QM Food and Container Inst (liason and sci adv bd Armed Forces). Recipient Bordon Award from Am Inst Nutrition '45; Morrison Award from Am Soc Animal Production '50. 909 W. Nevada St., Urbana, Ill.◎

20 MITCHELL, Harold Loren. Southern States forest region: Forest management; Naval stores pine; Trees of northeastern United States; Tree physiology; Forest soils; Mycorrhizae; Solar radiation; Shade trees. BS '30 (U Minn); MF '32 (Harvard). Author articles in field. Dir Southern Forest Expt Station US Forest Service since '51. Am Soc Plant Physiol—Soil Sci Soc Am—Soc Am Foresters—Sigma Xi. Southern Forest Experiment Station, U.S. Forest Service, Lowich Building, New Orleans, La.

21 MITCHELL, John W. Plant growth (Regulating substances). b'05. BS '28—MS '29 (Ida U); PhD '32 (U Chicago). In charge research in US Department Agriculture on plant growth regulating substances and uses in agricultural practice; developed 2, 4-D as herbicide; studies on sensitivity of grasses and crop plants to growth regulators, chemical composition of plants. Co-author: Plant Growth Regulators; also articles in field. Research asso US Dept Agr since '38. Am Soc Plant Physiol—AAAS—Washington Acad Sci—Sigma Xi. U.S. Department of Agriculture, Bureau of Plant Industry, Beltsville, Md.

22 MITCHELL, Lane. Clay; Ceramics and minerals of Georgia. b'07. BS '29 (Ga Sch Tech); MS '31 (U Ill); '32 (Rutgers U); PhD '41 (Pa State Coll); '43-44 (Harvard, Mass Inst Tech). Author: Classification of the Clays of Georgia '48; also articles in field. Dir and prof ceramic engring Ga Inst Tech since '41. Am Ceramic Soc—Inst Ceramic Engrs—Am Inst Mining and Metall Engr—Am Soc Test Metals—Georgia Mineral Soc—Ga Acad Science—Ga Engring Soc—Sigma Xi—Phi Kappa Phi—Tau Beta Pi. School of Ceramic Engineering, Georgia Institute of Technology, Atlanta.†

23 MITCHELL, Robert Buchanan. Urban land use and redevelopment; City planning; Planning administration; Neighborhood planning and conservation; Housing. b'06. BS '28 (U Ill). Co-author: Action for Cities '43; Systems and Structures of Urban Traffic '50; also articles. Research prof urban land use and housing Columbia since '48; lecturer in polit sci U Pa '44-49; chmn dept land and city planning, dir Inst for Urban Studies U Pa. Am Inst Planners (bd govrs)—Am Soc Planning Ofcls—Nat Assn Housing Officials. Institute for Urban Studies, University of Pennsylvania.

24 MITCHELL, Thomas E d w a r d. Mining engineering. Mine development and operation. b'74. Privately tutored; student (U Calif, U So Calif). Granted patents on several mechanical devices. Author articles in field. Successively miner, shift-boss, foreman and supt mines Anaconda Copper Mining Co, Butte Mont '97-13; asst gen mgr, directing development of one of the greatest silver, lead, zinc ore deposits ever discovered, also driving two-mile double track tunnel Burma Mines Ltd Burma India '14-15, gen mgr '15-18; gen mgr, Burma Corp, Ltd, '15-18; gen mgr, chief engr, cons engr various companies '20-29, gen cons practice since '29. Am Inst Mining Metall Engrs. 12745 Hanover St., Brentwood Park, Los Angeles 24.

10 MITCHELL, Will, Jr. Mineral beneficiation. b'14. BS '39—MS '42 (Mont Sch Mines); '45 (MIT). Research on combination of unit opeations to develop flow-sheets for concentration or upgrading of ores such as gold, silver, lead, zinc, iron, tungsten, bismuth, feldspar, titanium, coal, sulfur, cobalt, copper, zirconium, radio-active ores, cement raw materials, mica, abrasives, and rock products; research and testing, solvent oil extraction, milling, and wood and paper pulp processing. Research engr MIT '44, '45; adminstrv asst Manhattan Project '46 '47; dir processing research lab Allis-Chalmers Mfg Co '47-51, asst dir research since '51. Registered profl engr Wis. AIMME —Theta Tau. Research Laboratories, Allis-Chalmers Mfg Co., Milw.†

11 MITTLER, Sidney. Genetics; Nutrition; Tumors. b'17. BS '38—MS '39 (Wayne University); PhD '44(U Mich). Engaged research influence high temperature upon sex ratio Whitefly, genes interaction, expressivity, penetrance in Drosophila, Drosophila population genetics. Iodine and cobalt nutrition in mammals. Author articles: Production of Females by Virgin Females in Green House Whitefly, Trialeurodes vaporariorum, Under Influence of High Temperature '46; Brilliant Cresyl Blue as Stain for Chromosome Smear Preparation '48; Influence of Genetic Environment on Reduction of Bristles by Dichaete Gene in Drosophila Melanogaster '48. Instr zool Bowling Green State U '45-46; instructor zool Ill Inst Tech '46-47, asst prof '47-52; research biol Armour Research Found of Ill Inst Tech since '52. Genetics Soc Am—AAAS—Ill Acad Science—Soc Study Evolution—American Genetics Assn—Sigma Xi. Armour Research Foundation, Illinois Institute of Technology, Chicago 16.

12 MIZE, John Townsend Hinton. Musicology. b'10. MB-BA '34 (Baylor U); MS '38 (Tex A&M); MA '39 (Columbia); EdD '41 (NYU); '39-41 (U Sorbonne, Julliard Inst, U South Calif, SW Tex Teach Coll, Wofford Coll, Tex U). Consultant music NYC since '40, American music OWI '43-44, sacred music Sacred Songs Inc since '47; author programme notes phonograph record albums Mary Lou in Recital, Hymnody; author weekly syndicated newspaper column Record Review Music News Syndicate; composed Pensive, Consolation, Tone Poem. Author: Thesaurus of the Clarinet '41; Bing-Crosbyana Through Biography-Photography-Discography '46; Panorama of All-American Music '47; The Duke: Ellingtonia Thru Biography-Photography-Discography '48; also articles in field. Dir music Allen Mil Acad '34-37; instr wood-winds Paris '37, Rome '38, NYC '38-41; dir mus orgns Gen Motors '41-42; head dept music Ellisville (Miss) Coll '38-40; chmn all-Am music expts Rye NY High Sch '42-44; pub Monograph Publs since '39. Music Educators Nat Conf—Esquire Mag Bd Jazz Experts—Asso Am Musicology (pres '46-47). Suite 301, 1650 Broadway, NYC 19.

13 MOCKMORE, Charles Arthur. Civil engineering; Hydraulic Machinery. b'91. BEng '20—CE '26—MS '32— PhD '35 (State U Ia). Asst supt grounds and bldgs U Ia, '20-21; instr civil engring Ore State Coll '21-31, advancing to prof and head dept

civil engring since '34; research asso U Ia '31-32; mem Ore State Bd of Engring Examiners. Author: Hydraulic Machinery, Estimating and Cost Analyses '35. ASCE—Am Asso for Engring Edn—Tau Beta Pi—Sigma Xi. Big Ten medal U Ia in dual field of scholarship and athletics, '20; Croes medal, ASCE '39. 962 Van Buren St., Corvallis, Ore.◎

14 MODLIN, George Matthews. American economics (Business regulation, transportation, utilities, economic history, labor relations). b'03. AB '24 —LLD '47 (Wake Forest N C Coll); MA '25—PhD '32 (Princeton). Co-author: (with F T de Vyver) Development of Economic Society '36, rev '46; (with A M McIsaac) Social Control of Industry '38. Pres U Richmond since '46. Am Econ Assn—So Econ Assn —Va Social Sci Assn—Phi Beta Kappa. 2 Bostwick Lane, University of Richmond, Va.

15 MOE, Carl. Kraft pulp; paper mill chemistry; Pulp (Fiber losses). b'74. Grad '93 (Tech Sch Oslo). Research on chemical control of mill processes, determination losses of fibers and chemicals, production phenal-formaldehyde resins and laminated plastics from spent liquor solids. Formerly chief chem Minn & Ont Paper Co and Stevens Point Pulp & Paper Co; now chief chem Jay Pulp & Paper Corp. ACS—AAAS—Tech Assn Pulp and Paper Industry. Jay Pulp & Paper Corp., Stevens Point, Wis.

16 MOE, Owen A(rnold). Organic chemistry. b'13. AB '36 (St Olaf Coll); PhD '42 (U Minn)—F '41-43 (Northwestern U). Research on rearrangement of phenyl allyl ethers, synthesis and properties of war gases, structure of polymeric carbohydrates, syntheses of amino acids and organic amines. Granted patents in fields. Research with Gen Mills since '43. Sigma Xi—Phi Lamba Upsilon—ACS— AAAS. General Mills, 2010 E. Henn Av., Mpls. 13.

17 MOEHLMAN, Arthur B. American education (School administration, public school finance and plants, Michigan). b'89. BA '12—MA '21—PhD '23 (U Mich); '12-13 (Cornell U Grad Sch). Chairman Michigan State Committee on Child Accounting and Uniform Finance System '22-25; consultant New Jersey State School Survey '28, Military Academy '30-40, President's Advisory Committee on Education '36-38, Michigan Public Education Study Commission '42-45; director finance, organization, personnel, plant surveys in many schools. Author: Survey of Michigan State Normal Schools '22; Child Accounting, '23; Public Education in Detroit '25; Public School Relations '27; Public School Finance '27; (with Keyworth) Hamtramck School Code '27; Public School Plant Program '29; Finance Procedures for Hammtramck '29; Public School Budget Procedure '29; Public Elementary School Plant (with Spain and Frostic) '30; Social Interpretation '38; School Administration '40; Improvement of Public Education in Michigan '45. Prof adminstrn and supervision Sch Edn U Mich since '23; editor The Nations Schools since '32. AAAS(F)—Am Edn Fellowship—NEA—Am Assn Sch Adminstrns—Am Assn Adult Edn—Am Acad Polit and Social Sci—Mich Edn Assn—Am Ednl Research Assn (pres '29)—Coll Teachers of Edn—Nat Council on Schoolhouse Constrn (pres '39)— Mich Acad Sci—Mich Authors League —Nat Advisory Council on Sch Bldg Problems (pres '35, '36)—Phi Delta Kappa—Phi Kappa Phi. University High School Bldg., Ann Arbor.◎

18 MOEHLMAN, Arthur Henry. History and philosophy of education in the Americas; International education (Mexico, Canada, England, Germany, France, Italy, Russia, Scandinavia, India, China, Japan, Egypt); Pioneer settlements in America; Frontier populations in relation to landscape; Military history and geography of Russia; Central and western European powers. b'07. AB '28 (U Rochester); AM—PhD '32 (U Mich); internat fellow '29 (U Basle Switzerland); grad '46 (Command and Gen Staff Sch U S Army). Population Research Consultant Planning Committee State of Ohio '34-35; delegate to International Town and Regional Planning Meeting London '35; surveys of English, Scandinavian, German and French Education '35; survey of Mexican Education '36; served with United States Army '41-46, chief German section Military Intelligence Division G-2, assisted plans for demobilization, laws for prohibition and elimination military training in Germany, United States Group Control Council for Germany; demobilization representative at Potsdam Conference Member Commission in International Education '46. Author articles in field. Prof hist and philoso of edn U Ia since '46. Am Geog So NY(F)—AHA—AAAS —Phi Beta Kappa. College of Education, State University of Iowa, Iowa City.†◎

19 MOEHLMAN, Conrad Henry. American church history; Christian-Jewish relations; History of Christianity. b'79. MA '17—DD '29 (Rochester U); BA '02—PhD '18 (U Mich); '05 (Rochester Theol Sem); DD '29 (Hillsdale Coll). Author: Topics in Church History; Getting Acquainted with the Bible; The Story of the Ten Commandments; What is Protestantism?; The Unknown Bible; The Story of Christianity; The Christian-Jewish Tragedy; Christianity and War; Understanding the Contemporary World Crisis; The Church as Educator; The Wall of Separation between Church and State. James B. Colgate prof his Christianity Colgate-Rochester Div Sch '28-44, prof emeritus since '44. Soc Biblical Lit and Exegesis—Am Ch Hist Soc (pres '33); Am Geog Soc—Phi Beta Kappa. 3416 Haymie Av., Dallas.

20 MOFFAT, James Ernest. Economic theory (History, contemporary); American economic thought. b'83. AB '14 (McMaster U); AM '16—PhD '24 (U Chicago); '23-24 (London Sch Econs). Co-author: Economic Problems of War '42; Economics: Principles and Problems '47; also articles in field. Instr to prof Ind U since '16, head dept econ '35-45; spl administrative asst to President since '38. Am Econ Assn—Royal Econ Soc—Midwest Econ Assn—Ind Acad Social Sci—Phi Beta Kappa—Beta Gamma Sigma—Delta Sigma Pi. Department of Economics, Indiana University, Bloomington, Indiana.◎

21 MOFFETT, Ernest Cutter. Liquid bath hardening of steel. b'88. BS '10 —MS '31 (Rutgers U). Manufacture and operation of liquid baths for case hardening steel. Author articles: New Carburizing Bath Affords Increase in Depth of Case. Holds six US Patents. Chemist US Metals Ref Co '10-11, NY '11-16; sec-treas dir Stillwell Lab Inc '16-20, cons chemist '20-22; charge exptl lab Am Cyanamid Co '22-26, asst tech '26-33, asst to vp charge development work '33; Woodbridge Township Com '25; chmn Woodbridge Indsl Com since '46. ACS—Phi Beta Kappa, 582 Barron Ave., Woodbridge, N.J.

22 MOFFETT, James W(illiam). Limnology; Production and protection of fishery resources. b'08. AB '33—MA '35 (U Utah); PhD '39 (U Mich). Research in the management control and production of fresh water fishes, production and protection of fishery resources affected by water development projects under Federal Government sponsorship. Author articls in field. Teaching fellow dept zool U Mich '35-39; aquatic biol Mich Conservation Dept Ann Arbor '39-41, US Fish and Wildlife Service Stanford U '41-49, chief Great Lakes Fishery Investigations Ann Arbor since '50. Am Micros Soc—Ecol Soc Am—Am Fisheries Soc—Am Soc Limnology and Oceanography — Wildlife Soc — Sigma Xi (commendation for research)—Phi Kappa Phi. U. S. Fish and Wildlife Service, 1220 E. Washington St., Ann Arbor.

10 MOFFIT, Fred Howard. Alaska (Geology). b'74. AB '95 (Williams Coll); AM '99 (Lafayette Coll); F in geol '02-03 (Columbia). Investigation geology and mineral resources Seward Peninsula, Copper River, Upper Tanana River, Prince William Sound, Cook Inlet areas Alaska. With US Geol Survey part-time '95-02, full-time '02-45, Alaskan br '03-45. AAAS—Geol Soc Am(F)—Soc Econ Geols—Wash Soc Engrs—Wash Acad Sci(F) — H: Cosmos Club, Washington 5.©

11 MOFFITT, George Wilber. Physics (Optical and instrument design and development; Astronomical instruments; Photographic apparatus and equipment). b'87. BA '10 (State U Ia); PhD '13 (Stanford U). Patents include refractometer for liquids, coincidence prism for range finders and range finder compensated for flexure. Author articles in field. Independent consultant to manufacturers of a great variety of optical instruments and associated devices for naval, military and civilian use. 157 Melrose Place, Ridgewood, N.J.†

12 MOFFITT, James William. Southern Indian history. b'98. Student '16-19 (U Ark); ThG '22 (So Bapt Theol Sem); BS '27 (E Tenn State Tchrs Coll); BA '52 (E Tenn State Coll); MA '31 (Duke University); PhD '47 (University Oklahoma). Secretary Oklahoma Historical Society, editor The Chronicles of Oklahoma '36-44; lecturer on history, army training detachment (air crew) Oklahoma City University '42-44; associate professor history Furman University '47-50; research under Carnegie grant '50; High Point Coll since '51. Am Bapt Hist Soc (F)—Am Assn State and Local History (Council '40-45)—So Bapt Hist Soc (exec com '37-47)—So Historial Assn—Miss Valley Hist Assn(com on territorial papers)—Nat Council for Social Studies—NEA—State hist socs Arkansas, Ga, Mo, Okla, NC, Tenn—Pi Gamma Mu—Kappa Delta Pi. Box 216 High Point College, High Point, N.C.†©

13 MOGER, Allen Wesley. History and government of Virginia since 1880. b'05. AB '27 (Randolph-Macon Coll); MA '35—PhD '40—fellow '36-37 (Columbia U); '27-28 (Johns Hopkins). Author: The Rebuilding of the Old Dominion: A Study in Economic Social and Political Transition from 1880 to 1902 '40; also articles in field. Professor hist Washington and Lee U since '51. Chief research dept sch personnel services Army Service Forces Lexington Va '44-46. So Hist Assn—Va Social Sci Assn (pres '48-49)—Phi Beta Kappa. Washington and Lee University, Lexington, Va.†

14 MOHL, Ruth. Estates (Literature); Milton; Spencer; Theory of monarchy. b'91. BA '13—MA '14 (U Minn); PhD '33 (Columbia). Author: The Three Estates in Medieval and Renaissance Literature '33; Studies Spencer, Milton and Theory of Monarchy. With Brooklyn Coll since '42, Asst prof since '48. Mod Lang Assn Am—AAUP—Milton Soc Am—Nat Council Tchrs Eng—Medieval Club NY—Renaissance Club NY—Phi Beta Kappa. Brooklyn College, Brooklyn 10.

15 MOHLMAN, Floyd William. Chemical, industrial a n d Packinghouse wastes; Stream pollution; Sewage treatment. b'90. BS '12—MS '14—PhD '16 (U Ill). Author articles in field. Chief chem and dir labs San Dist Chicago since '19; editor Sewage Works Jour '28-43, now adv editor; chmn sub-com Nat Research Council '44-48; cons on stream pollution and disposal of industrial wastes including chem industry, steel industry, munitions plants and packinghouses. Am Chem Soc—Am Inst Chem Engrs—Am Water Works Assn — Am Pub Health Assn—Sigma Xi. 910 S. Michigan Av., Chgo.

16 MOHR, Charles Edward. Caves; Bats and vampires; Nature photography. b'07. AB '30—AM '31 (Bucknell U); Rockefeller Fellow in Mus Training '38-39 (Buffalo Mus Sci). Carried on studies of cave life, particularly of bats, including vampires, since '30, banded bats since '32; wrote chapter on cave fauna in Pennsylvania Caves by Ralph W Stone Pa Geol Survey '32; editor The Caves of Texas '48; also articles in field. Asst zool Bucknell U '29-31; naturalist and librarian Reading Pub Mus and Art Gallery '31-33, '33-38; biol instr high sch Reading '33-38; dir edn Acad Natural Sci Phila '39-47; dir Audubon Nature Centre Greenwich Conn since '47. Pa Acad Sci (pres)—Am Nature Study Soc (pres '43-46)—Am Ornithol Union—Am Soc Mammalogists—Speleological Soc (vp)—Sigma Xi. Audubon Nature Center, Greenwich, Conn.

17 MOLDENKE, Alma Lance. Plants of the Bible; Shamrock. b'08. BA '31 (Hunter Coll); '31-39 (Columbia). Research associate with husband in fields of taxonomic botany Bible plants nature study since '42; delegate to Second South American Botanical Congress Tucuman Argentina '48. Co-author: (with H N Moldenke) Plants of the Bible '49; also articles in field. Critic teacher sci Hunter Coll Model Sch '31-34; nature councillor and dir Northrop Camp for Nature Study '36-42; biology teacher and guidance councillor Evander Childs High Sch since '34. AAAS—Torrey Bot Club—Nat Sci Teachers Assn—Sch Nature League Assn. Evander Childs High School, 800 East Gun Hill Rd., NYC 67.

18 MOLDENKE, Harold Norman. Taxonomic botany; Botanical nomenclature. b'09. BS '29 (Susquehanna U); MA '32—PhD '34 (Columbia); scholar '29 (NY Bot Garden). Collected and distributed 125,000 plant specimens in United States, Canada, Europe, Central America, South America; specialist on the Verbenaceae, Avicenniaceas, Stilbaceae, Symphoremaceae and Eriocaulaceae of the world; resch in plant taxonomy and nomenclature, tautonyms, cultivated plants, flora of the Watchung Mountains in New Jersey, flora of southern Florida, vernacular plant names, plants of the Bible. Co-editor: Phytologia Asso editor: Plant Life, Herbertia; also articles in field. Part time asst NY Bot Garden '29-32, asst curator '32-37, asso curator '37-48, curator and administrator of the herbarium '48-52; supervisor Nature Activities Union County NJ Park Commn and dir Trailside Mus Watching Reservation since '52. AAAS(F)—NY Acad Sci(F)—Bot Soc Am—Am Soc Plant Taxonomists — NY Mycol Soc — Assn Study of Speciation—Assn Sudamericana de Fitotaxonomistas—Soc Bot de Mexico—Soc Cubana de Bot—Sigma Xi. Nat Research fellow '35-36, fellow AAAS '38, NY Acad Sci '39, Am Geog Soc '41. 15 Glenbrook Av., Yonkers 5, N.Y.

19 MOLITOR, Hans. Pharmacology; Toxicology; Physiology (Metabolism). b'95. MD '22 (U Vienna). Studied nervous and hormonal regulation of water metabolism, physiology and pharmacology of sleep, liver hormones, preanesthetic medication, water soluble vitamins, bioassay techniques, chemotherapy, antibiotics; investigated the safety of new drugs; engaged research and writing on pharmacological properties of bulbocapnine, vinyl ether, trichlor-ethanol, sulfanilamide and benzylsulfanilamide, sodium sulfapyridine, iontophoresis, anti-malarials, influence of inhalation anesthetics on liver. Author articles: Ueber die Serumreaktionen bei einem Fall von X 19-Infection (Mischinfektion mit Paratyphus A) in ihrer Beziehung zur Weil-Felixschen Fleckfieber-Reaktion (with Weltmann) '19; Ueber die Einwirkung kortikaler Erregungen auf die Wasserdiurese bei Tieren '26; Hormone und Wasserhaushalt '30; A Comparative study of the effects of five choline compounds used in therapeutics '36; Bacterial Chemotherapy '46; (with O E Graessle) Pharmacology and toxicology of antibiotics '50. Asst Prof Pharmacol Vienna U '23-26, privatedocent '27, asso prof pharmacol and therapeutics '27-32; director Merck Inst Therapeutic Research since '33; mem Pharmacology Study Sect USPHS '47-50. Am Physiol Soc—Soc Exptl Biol and Med—Am Soc Tropical Med—Am Pharmacol Soc—AAAS—Nat Malaria Soc—So Med Assn—AMA—Phila Physiol Soc—NY Acad Sci(F, councilor, vp). Rockefeller fellow Edinburgh U '24 Merck Institute for Therapeutic Research, 141 E Lincoln Ave., Rahway, N.J. H: Box 304 W Pt. Pleasant.©

20 MOLLER, Herbert. History of population; Social history of Europe. b'09. '29 (U Heidelberg); '30 (U Berlin); '31-33 (U Frankfort-am-Main); PhD '42 (Boston U). Research on effects of population changes on (European) society, 1500 to 1800 '42. Author articles: Sex Composition and Correlated Culture Patterns of Colonial America '45. Asst prof European hist coll liberal arts Boston U since '46. Am Hist Assn—Population Assn Am. Boston University, College of Liberal Arts, 725 Commonwealth Ave., Boston 15.

21 MONAGHAN, James (Jay) IV. Lincolniana; History of western United States. b'91. AB '13—Hannah A. Leedom fellowship '17 (Swarthmore Coll); MA '18 (U Pa); DLitt '47 Monmouth Coll). Discovered cliffhouse village in extreme north periphery of culture and helped secure Interior Department legislation to set it aside as Yampa National Monument; located early trapper forts and interviewed Indians for Colorado Historical Society '35. Author: Bibliography of Lincolniana 1839-1939; Diplomat in Carpet Slippers-Lincoln Deals with Foreign Affairs '45; The Legend of Tom Horn '46; The Overland Trail '47; This is Illinois '49; The Great Rascal '52. Ill state historian in charge of library '46-51; sec Ill State Hist Soc and editor Journal '46-50; fellow Huntington Library '51-52; spl cons Wyles Library Lincolniana since '52; editor American Trails Series since '47. AHA—Miss Valley Hist Assn—Illinois State Hist Soc—Abraham Lincoln Assn. Awarded Rockefeller Foundation fellowship by Newberry Library Chicago '44-45; Diploma of honor by Lincoln Memorial U '44. Phi Beta Kappa. University of California at Santa Barbara, Santa Barbara, Cal.

10 MONDOLFO, Lucio Fausto. Light alloys; Aluminum; Magnesium. b'10. BE '29 (Bologna U); PhD '33 (Milano Poly Inst). Research on refining heat treatment, casting, fabrication, electroplating. Author: Metallography of Aluminum Alloys '43. Research metallurgist Isotta Fraschini, Milano Italy '35-38, US Reduction Co E Chicago '39-40, Reynolds Metals Co Ky '40-41; chief metallurgist Howard Foundries Inc Chicago '42-43; asst chief metallurgist Reynolds Metals Co NY '44-46; professor metallurgy Ill Inst Technol since '51. ASM—Inst Metals London—AAAS—AIME. Illinois Institute of Technology, 10 W. 33d St., Chgo 16.†

11 MONEYMAKER, Berlen Clifford. Engineering and economic geology; Caves; Earthquakes. b'04. BS '28—MS '29—fellow in geology '28-29 (U Tenn). Asso geol with the Puerto Rico Reconstruction Administration '36-37, cons geol '39. Prin geol (chief) Tenn Valley Authority since '41. Geol Soc Am(F)—ASCE (asso mem)—Soc Econ Geol—AAAS—Tenn Acad Sci—NC Acad Sci—Am Assn Petroleum Geologists—Carolina Geol Soc—Mineral Soc Am—Seismol Soc Am—NY Acad Sci—Soc Am Mil Engrs—Knoxville Tech Soc—Am Geophys Union—Nat Speleol Soc—Phi Kappa Phi. Tennessee Valley Authority, 510 Union Building, Knoxville, Tenn.†◉

12 MONFORT, R(aymond) A. Television engineering (Administration); Color television engineering. b'08. Student '25-28 (Kan U); '32-34 (NYU). Supervision and administration television broadcasting facilities for individual station and network type operations; development work on color television. Holds patents on synchronizing generators and video switching apparatus. Author article: Measurement of the Slope and Duration of Television Synchronizing Impulses '42, and others. Engring dept and television development lab NBC '32-46, in charge color television engring NY '50; chief engr television sta Los Angeles Times '46-50; cons Color Television Inc San Francisco '50; television administrative capacities since '40. Inst Radio Engrs—Soc Motion Picture and Television Engrs—Acad Television Arts and Sci—Acoustical Soc Am. Profl engr. National Broadcasting Co., Radio City, NYC 20.

13 MONROE, Robert Ansley. Power plants (Hydroelectric and steam). b'89 BS in civil engring '12 (U Cal). Planning and design multi-purpose river control projects, dams, hydroelectric projects, and steam generating stations; vibration studies on overhead transmission lines. Author articles: Baffle Bar Experiments on Models of Pit River Dams; Vibration of Overhead Transmission Lines. With Pacific Gas and Elec Co '12-29; Aluminum Co Am '29-33; US Bur Reclamation '33-37; TVA since '37, chief design engr since '45. Am Soc CE—Am Inst EE. 305 Union Building, Tennessee Valley Authority, Knoxville, Tenn.◉

14 MONROE, Wendell Potter. Electric power engineering. BS '17—EE '25 (Washington U St Louis); MS '18 (MIT); SM '18 (Harvard). Plan and design large electric power systems for public utilities, railroads, industrial plants, and municipalities. Asst engr electrification of Chicago terminals Ill Central RR '21-28; traction engr Jackson & Moreland '28-

31; cons elec engr San Francisco-Oakland Bay Bridge '36-38; with Chicago Dept Subways and Superhighways '39-43; sr elec engr Sargent & Lundy since 43. Am Inst EE—Nat Soc Profl Engrs—ATA—Am Assn RR. Sargent & Lundy, 140 S. Dearborn St., Chicago 3. H: 8456 S. Rhodes Av., Chgo. 19.†

15 MONSAROFF, Boris. Textile chemistry (Cellulose); Leather chemistry (Synthetic tanning materials, leather finishes); Paints (Textile and emulsions); Pigment dyeing; Plastics (Cellulose acetate); Plant design. b'87. Candidate Econ Sci '14—ChemE '21 (Kiev Russia). Research and development work waterproofing and fireproofing; improvement heat and acid resistance of cellulose fabrics and yarn; processes for waterproofing, fireproofing and mildew-resistance of fabrics; economics and estimates; cost accounting for process and chemical industries, synthetic resins, printing inks, paints and varnishes. Chem Edwards & Edward Leather Mfrs Ont Can '27-32; cons practice since '32. Assn Profl Engrs Ont—Chem Inst Can (F)—ACS—Am Leather Chem Assn—AAAS. 83 Hillcrest Av., Hamilton, Can.

16 MONSON, Louis Travis. Emulsions; Demulsification. b'03. BS '24—MS '26 (Washington U). Research and development in fields of chemical demulsifying agents for crude petroleum emulsions, anti-foamers, wax-and mudremoving reagents for use in oil wells and crude oil lines, scale-removers, corrosion preventives, chemical demulsifiers for oil-in-water emulsions, mineral flotation agents. Holds 30 patents in field. Author articles in field. Chem The Tretolite Company, St Louis, Mo '26-31; chief chem Tretolite Company of Calif, Los Angeles since '31. Am Chem Soc—Tau Beta Pi—Sigma Xi. 5515 Telegraph Rd., Los Angeles 22.

17 MONTAGU, Montague Francis Ashley. Physical and cultural anthropology; Anatomy; Child growth and development; Social biology. b'05. PhD '37 (Columbia). Engaged research and work human and non-human primate anatomy, culture and personality, social biology, history of science; expert legal trials identification body or bones, matters of heredity; expert on racial problems; produced, wrote screw cured financing movie One World or None for Amer Fed Scientists and Nat Com on Atomic Information. Devised new anthropometric instruments, new methods locating certain landmarks on body, developed theory adolescent sterility; first suggested rooming-in of babies and mothers in maternity hosp. Author: Coming into Being Among the Australian Aborigines '37; Man's Most Dangerous Myth: The Fallacy of Race '42 (2nd ed '45); How to Happiness and Keep It '42; Edward Tyson, FRS, MD 1650-1708; and the Rise of Human and Comparative Anatomy '43; Introduction to Physical Anthropology '45; Adolescent Sterility '46. Research asso zool Brit Mus Natural Hist '26-27; curator phys anthropol Wellcome Hist Med Mus London '29; lecturer child growth and develop New Sch Social Research NYC '31, '49; anthropol div child growth and develop NYU '31-34, asst prof anatomy '31-38; asso prof anatomy, Hahnemann Medical Coll and Hosp, Phila '38-49; lecturer postgraduate training program in psychiatry, Veteran's Adminstrn Phil '46-'49, NYC '48. AAAS(F)—Royal Anthropol Inst (Gt Brit, Ire)—Am Anthrop Assn(F)—Am Assn Anatomy—Am Assn Phys Anthrop—Am Soc Genet—Soc Study Evolution—Soc Child Growth and

Develop—Hist Sci Soc—Sigma Xi. Morris Chaim Prize and Medal, First District Dental Soc NY '34; Chicago Forum Literary Contest, first prize; Honorary Corr Mem Anthropol Soc Florence '29; Honorary Corr Mem Anthrop Soc Paris '46. Rutgers University, Box 621, New Brunswick, New Jersey.◉

18 MONTEITH, Lloyd George. Host preferences of entomophagous insects (Biological control). b'19. BSA (Ont Agrl Coll); MSA (U Tronto); grad work 2 yrs (U Minn). Research on preferences of entomophagous insects for certain hosts with emphasis on roll of olfactory senses, conditioning of parasites to certain hosts, influence of environment; factors which influence the efficiency of sawfly parasites; in charge mass production certain sawfly parasites, devised methods increased production to increased survival of parasites. Agrl scientist, unit of biol control Div of Entomol Can Dept Agr. Ont Entomol Soc—Ecol Soc Am—Entomol Soc Can. Dominion Parasite Laboratory, Box 179, Belleville, Ont., Can.

19 MONTERMOSO, Juan C. Chemistry (Rubber, technology, high polymer); Physiology (Plant). b'09. AB '35—MS '37—PhD '42 (U Calif). Author articles in field. Research Office Naval Intelligence '42; Rubber tech Mare Island Lab '42-48; chief rubber chem Office Quartermaster Gen Washsinton since '49. Am Chem Soc—AAAS—Rubber Chem and Tech—Sigma Xi. Research and Development Division, Office of the Quartermaster General, Washington.

20 MONTGOMERY, Edwin Jones, Sr. Alaskan helicopter operations; Tropical helicopter operations; Helicopter insurance. b'12. BS '34—BS '36 (U Ariz); '42-43 (U Cal Los Angeles); '43-44 (Cal Tech); '45 (U So Cal). Research on structural analysis and design of helicopters; headed mapping expedition in Alaska and railroad location expedition in tropical Mexico using helicopters; research on unusual aspects of helicopter insurance. Aeronautical engr Douglas Aircraft Co '41-43, Hughes Aircraft Co. '43-45; chief executive Arizona Helicopter Service since '43. Inst Aeronautical Science—Soc Exptl Stress Analysis—Nat Soc Profl Engrs—Am Helicopter Soc—Aircraft Owners and Pilots Assn—Phi Delta Kappa—Theta Chi. P.O. Box 1181, Tucson.†

21 MONTGOMERY, James McKee. Water supply and treatment; Wastes and waste disposal. b'96. BChemE '20 (O State U). Holds patents on loss-in-weight type gravimetric chemical feeder, sludge blanket filtration, and variable-throat venturi meter. Engr and partner Hoover & Montgomery Columbus O '30-41; cons engr Los Angeles '41-45, Pasadena since '45. Am Soc CE—ACS—Am Water Works Assn—AAAS—Am Pub Health Assn—Tau Beta Pi. 15 N. Oakland Av., Pasadena 1, Cal.

22 MONTGOMERY, Royal Ewert. Labor economics and relations; Wage and price policies. b'96. PHB '21—Ma '23—PhD '25 (U Chicago). Author: Industrial Relations in the Building Trades '27. Co-author: (with H A Millis) Labor's Progress and Problems '38, Labors Risks and Social Insurance '38, Organized Labor '45. Mem editorial bd Am Econ Review '38-41. Asst prof economics Cornell '29-37, prof since '37, Staff Brookings Inst '38; pub rep and chmn various industry coms Wage and Hour div US Dept Labor '40-45; arbitrator and publicity panel mem Nat War Labor

Bd '42-45; arbitrator Fed Mediation and Conciliation Service since '47. Am Econ Assn (rep on Social Sci Research Council '41-44)—Am Statis Assn—Am Arbitration Assn—AAUP. Dept. of Economics, Cornell University, Ithaca.©

10 MOOD, Fulmer. American colonial and intellectual history; American archives (California). b'98. AB '21—Am '25—PhD '29 (Harvard U). Research English history, Tudor and Stuart periods, American colonial period, American nineteenth century; conducted survey library resources University Calif (2,250,000 vols) on eight campuses, archival and record resources. Editor: The Early Writing of Frederick Jackson Turner '38; The Development of F J Turner as an Historical Thinker '43; The English Geographers and the Anglo-American Frontier in the Seventeenth Century '44; also articles in field. Instr hist and polit sci Beloit Coll '22-23, Simmons Coll '26-27, Harvard '27-32; Guggenheim Memorial Fellow '32-35; research fellow Huntington Library '35-36; instr hist Harvard '36-37; asst prof hist Redlands '39-41; asst prof librarianship U Calif Berkeley '41-44; spl asst to pres. U Calif '44-48; professor history U Texas since '50. Served as chief archives sect Hist Div Army Air Forces Hdqrs Washington '43-44. AHA—Colonial Soc Mass (corr mem). 116 Garrison Hall, University of Texas, Austin 12, Tex.

11 MOODY, Alton B. Marine navigation. b'11. BSc '35 (US Naval Acad); '35 (US Army Primary Flying Sch). Patents pending: Star finder '45; great circle course and distance finder '45. Author: Navigation and Nautical Astronomy '48; American Practical Navigator; also articles in field. Deputy director Division Navigational Sci US Navy Hydrographic office since '50. Inst Navigation (editorial com)—Naval Inst—Arctic Inst NA—Am Polar Soc. United States Navy Hydrographic Office, Washington 25.

12 MOODY, V. Alton. American history (Slavery in the old South); European economics (Agrarian reform). b'88. AB '12 (Meridian); MA '13 (Tulane U); PhD '17 (U Mich). Studied negro slave labor, food, clothes, homes, health, marriage, discipline; European land problem, overpopulation, estates, constitutions, distribution. Author articles: Ante-Bellum Trade between the North and South '32; The Ante-Bellum Plantation Sustenance in the Lower Mississippi Valley '34; The Spanish Land Problem '35; Slavery on Louisiana Sugar Plantations '24; Early Missionary Efforts in the Lower Mississippi Valley in Miss Valley '35; Agrarian Reform before Post-War European Constituent Assemblies '33; Europe's Recurrent Land Problem '48. Head dept English, Latin, Rugby Acad, New Orleans '13-14, '15-16; asst Am hist U Mich '16-17; head dept hist, econ, State Coll, Murfreesboro, Tenn; dept history and econ, Albion Coll, Mich, '22-25; dept hist and govt Ia State Coll since '25. AHA—Miss Valley Hist Assn—So Hist Assn—Agrl Hist Soc. Dept History, Iowa State College, Ames, Ia. H: 427 Hawthorne.

13 MOOG, Florence. Biochemical embryology; Enzymology. b'16. AB '36 (NYU); AM '38—PhD '44 (Columbia). Research on enzymogenesis in chick and frog embryos, metabolism of embryos and regenerating tissues, histochemical methods, developmental endocrinology. Author: A Manual for Comparative Anatomy and Embryology of Vertebrates '49; also articles. Asso prof zool Washington U since '51.

AAAS—Am Soc Zool—Soc Study Development and Growth—Sigma Xi. Department of Zoology, Washington University, St. Louis 5.†

14 MOOK, Paul V(incent). Tree diseases. b'01. BSc '23 (Allegheny Coll), MSc '26 (U Md). Research on shade tree diseases, rot and decay of trees in northeast, decay of wooden buildings, causes of stain and discoloration lumber and forest products. Forest path USDA since '33. Tech USN testing mil equipment deterioration Panama Canal Zone '45-46. Am Phytopath Soc—Soc Am Foresters—Phi Kappa Phi. Allegheny Coll Heckel prize in sci '23. U.S. Department of Agriculture, 360 Prospect St., New Haven.

15 MOON, Hubert Hill. Pear breeding; Apple production. b'93. BS (Cornell U). Author articles in field. With US Dept Agr since '26, asso pomol and hort fruit since '40. Am Soc Hort Sci. U.S. Department of Agriculture, Plant Industry Station, Beltsville, Md.†

16 MOOR, Arthur Prichard. Asia (Culture); Music (Oriental); Library and museum education. b'99. BS '19 (John B Stetson Univ); AM '21 (Princeton); AB '23—'23-24 (Oxford U Eng); PhD '38 (Columbia). Research in and compilation of Oriental music; integration Oriental material in college curriculum; building libraries, bibliographies, Asiatic cultures. Author: The Library—Museum of Music and Dance. Author article: Oriental Color in Western Music. Contributor: International Cyclopedia of Music and Musicians; Grove's Dictionary Music and Musicians. Research library, museum edn, Oriental music, lecturing, writing '34-40; dir arts div Adelphi Coll '40-45; curator edn Brooklyn Mus '45-46, supervisor music and radio '46-47; head sch fine arts Olivet Coll '47-49; spl programs The Voice of America, State Dept '51; edn div Field Enterprises Inc since '51. Am Assn Mus—Asia Inst—Tibetan Library and Mus—Phi Mu Alpha, Sinfonia. H: 126 Salisbury Av., Garden City, N.Y.

17 MOORE, Albert Burton. Alabama (History); Confederacy (Conscription and conflict). b'87. BS '11—MS '12 (Ala Poly Inst); MA '15—PhD magna cum laude '21 (U Chicago); LLD '42 (U Ala). Author: Conscription and Conflict in the Confederacy '24; History of Alabama and Its People '27; History of Alabama '35. Contributor to Dictionary of American Biography, National Educator Encyclopedia, Britannica Year Book, Dictionary of American History. Prof history U Ala since '23, dean grad sch since '25; regional dir Survey of Federal Archives '36. Am Council Edn(pres '51) —Am Hist Assn—Ala Hist Assn— (pres '51)—Ala Edn Assn—Miss Valley Hist Assn—So Hist Assn(pres '42) —Conf So Grad Deans (pres '36)— Phi Beta Kappa—Kappa Delta Pi. H: Riverside Dr., University, Ala.©

18 MOORE, Alfred Douglass. Literacy. b'86. BA '10—MA '30 (Wesleyan U); grad '16 (Union Theol Sem); '16, '36 (Columbia). Author: Literacy Unlocking the Bible '48. Collaborator: Fundamental Education '47; Stream-Lined English Lessons '50. Sec World Literacy Com Fgn Mission Conf since '44; specialist on Laubach literacy system UNESCO Mexico City '47; fgn mission conf rep UNESCO since '48. 156 5th Av., NYC. H: Box 524 Chappaqua, N.Y.

19 MOORE, Carl Richard. Sex differentiation; Internal secretions; Hormones; Reproduction. b'92. AB '13—MS '14—ScD '48 (Drury Coll); PhD '16 (U Chicago). Prof zool U Chicago

since '28. Am Soc Zool (vp '26)—Am Soc Naturalists—AAAS (vp, sect, F '43)—Marine Biol Lab Corp—Assn Study Internal Secretions (pres '44-46) —Soc Exptl Biol and Med—Nat Acad Sci—Sigma Xi—Am Acad Arts Sci. Received first Francis Amory Award '41; Fourth Award Am Urological Assn '50. H: 5702 Blackstone Av., Chicago.©

20 MOORE, Charles Alexander. Oriental and Indian philosophy. b'01. AB '26—PhD '32 (Yale); '36-41 (Oriental Inst U Hawaii); '47-48 (Benares Hindu U). Chmn East-West Philosophers Conferences University Hawaii '39, '49. Editor and co-author: Philosophy-East and West '44; Essays in East-West Philosophy: An Attempt at World Philosophical Synthesis '51. Co-editor: Junjiro Takakusu's The Essentials of Buddhist Philosophy '47; also articles in field. Prof phil U Hawaii since '47. Am Oriental Soc—Indian Philos Congress Assn—Inst Pacific Relations—Am Philos Assn. Guggenheim fellow '47-48. University of Hawaii, Honolulu, Hawaii.

21 MOORE, Charles H., Jr. Petrology; Geochemistry; Crystal chemistry; Synthetic gems; High temperature physical reactions; Titanium metal and compounds. b'15. BS '36—MS '37 (U Va); PhD '40 (Cornell). Holds eight patents. Author articles in field. Head geochem and metall dept Research Lab Titanium Div Nat Lead Co '48-49; asst to exec research dir '49-51; research cons and vis prof ceramics dept Rutgers U '46-50; div mgr metals and ceramics div P R Mallory and Co since '51. American Inst Mining Metall Engineers—Am Ceramic Soc—American Crystallographic Soc—Sigma Xi— Phi Kappa Phi. P. R. Mallory & Co., Indianapolis, Ind.

22 MOORE, Clyde B. Educational supervision; Boards of education. b'86. Grad '09—BEd '13 (Neb State Tchrs Coll); AB '12 (Neb Wesleyan); AM '16 (Clark U); PhD '20 (Columbia). Author: Civic Education '24; Citizenship Through Education '29; Case Studies in the Supervision of Village Schools '30; Our American Citizenship '36; others. Co-atuhor: (with G A Lundquist) Rural Social Science '29; (with W E Cole) Sociology in Educational Practice '52. Prof edn Cornell U since '25, dir extra-mural courses '35-45; editor and dir Ithaca Course of Study '30; studied educational systems in Europe '32-33, '39, Mexico '46; mem NY State Commn on Social Studies Curriculum since '36. AAAS (F)—Am Ednl Research Assn—NY State Edn Research Assn—Nat Soc Study Edn—NEA—Nat Soc Coll Tchrs Edn—Nat Council Social Studies— Dept Supervisors and Dirs Instrn— Am Assn Sch Adminstrs—NY State Sch Bd Assn(pres)—NY State Ednl Conf Bd(chmn since '40)—AAUP— Phi Delta Kappa—Kappa Phi Kappa —Alpha Kappa Delta—Phi Kappa Phi. School of Education, Cornell University, Ithaca.†©

23 MOORE, Coyle E. Family life education; Social work education. b'00. BS '20 (The Citadel); MS '25 (U NC); PhD '28—research fellow '25-28 (U Chicago). Governor's commission on social legislation '37; president Florida State Conference on Social Work '37. Prof social work Fla State U since '41, chmn div applied social sci since '47, dean sch social welfare since '49. Am Sociol Soc—So Sociol Society— Nat Conf Social Work—Fla State Conf Social Work—Fla Acad Sci—AAAS— Am Assn Social Workers—Nat Conf Family Relations—Nat Probation Assn —Nat Assn Schs Social Adminstrn (exec com since '45). Florida State University, Tallahassee, Fla.©

10 MOORE, Dwight Muson. Arkansas flora (Ferns, orchids, grasses, ligneous plant, spermatophy. b'91. BS '14—MS '21 (Denison U); PhD '24 (Ohio State U); spring '19 (U Montpellier France). Author: Trees of Arkansas. Editor: Proceeding Ark Acad Sci since '41. Asst prof botany U Ark '24-26, prof and head dept since '26, prof plant ecology Ohio Conservation Lab summers '40-42; regional supervisor Milkweed Floss Div War Hemp Industries '44. AAAS—Bot Soc Am—Am Soc Plant Physiol—Plant Taxonomists—Ecol Soc Am—Am Fern Soc—Ohio Acad Sci—Ark Acad Sci(pres '32-34)—Lambda Chi Alpha. 506 Vandeventer Av., Fayetteville, Ark.⊙

11 MOORE, Emmett Burris. Steel structures; Timber structures. b'00. BS '24—CE '28 (Mont State Coll); MS '33 (State Coll Wash). Structural engineer for wood and steel framing; structural designing buildings and bridges. Author: A Manual of Structural Design in Steel '40; Advisory Committee on Effective Teaching '50. From instr to prof dept civil engring State Coll Wash since 1929, chmn dept since '45. Am Soc CE(pres Spokane sect '52)—Am Soc Engring Edn—Am Water Works Assn—Fedn Sewage Works Assn—Phi Kappa Phi—Tau Beta Pi—Sigma Tau. Department of Civil Engineering, State College of Washington, Pullman, Wash.⊙

12 MOORE, Ermer Leon. Tobacco and corn breeding and pathology. b'15. BSA '40—MSA '41 (U Ga); PhD '47 (U Wis). Conducted survey to determine prevalence and cause of corn ear rots and extent of weevil damage in corn stored on farms in Georgia; research in development of disease resistant inbred lines for the purpose of crossing to produce high yielding hybrids in corn '40-41; tested corn inbreds and hybrids for silage production, reaction of corn inbreds and hybrids to low temperature and soil fungi for purpose of developing cold tolerant inbreds and hybrids '41-43, '46-47; research development of disease resistant tobacco varieties with improved production of cigarette tobacco since '47. Author articles in field. Asst in plant pathol U Ga '39-41; research asst agron U Wis '41-43, '46-47; asso pathologist '47-50, agron since '50 US Dept Agr Research Adm Bur Plant Industry Div Tobacco Medicinal and Spl Crops and jointly asst pathologist N C Agrl Expt Sta since '47. Am Phytopathol Soc—Am Genetic Assn—Sigma Xi. Tobacco Experiment Station, Oxford, N.C.†

13 MOORE, Ernest Carroll. History of education; American education. b'71. AB '92—LLB '94 (O Normal U); AM '96 (Columbia)—'10 (Yale); fellow in edn '97-98—PhD '98 (U Chicago); four honorary degrees. Author: How New York City Administers Its Schools; What Is Education?; Fifty Years of Education in America; What the War Teaches About Education; The Story of Instruction, the Beginnings '36; The Story of Instruction, The Church, The Renaissances, The Reformations. Editor: Minimum Course of Study; Thomas Starr King's Socrates; Thomas Davison's Education as World-building; The Story of the United States by Those Who Made It. Prof philosophy and edn '36-41, prof edn and dir '19-29, vp and provost '31-36, retired '41, U Calif at Los Angeles. Calif Teachers Assn, Southern Sect—N E Assn Colls and Secondary Schs (pres '14)—Western Assn Colls and Secondary Schs—AAAS(F)—Hellenic Soc Gt Brit—Phi Beta Kappa (hon, Stanford). 516 Woodruff Av., Los Angeles.⊙

14 MOORE, George A(ndrew). Gases in metals; Metals (Mechanical failures); Metallaography (Experimental methods). b'13. BS '34 (Union Coll); MS '35 (Harvard); PhD '39 (Princeton). Analysis, mode of entry, methods of removal, effect on structure of metal, effects on mechanical properties, failures due to presence of gases; abnormal properties of metals leading to mechanical failure, effects unusual conditions of service, low temperature service, failures of welded structures, flaws due to non-metallic inclusions and gasses; design experimental methods, especially fractographic examinations, special measuring devices, mechanical properties, gas analysis, vacuum technique and vacuum melting of metals; photographic methods for investigative and industrial purposes, color photography. Asst prof metall U Pa since '48. AIMME—Electrochem Soc—Sigma Xi. University of Pennsylvania, Phila 4.

15 MOORE, George M(itchell). Limnology; Microscopic bottom fauna. b'06. AS '26 (U City Toledo); BS '28 (Otterbein Coll); MS '32—PhD '38—teach fellow '37-38 (U Mich). Author articles in field. Professor zool U New Hampshire since '44-48, head zool dept since '47. AAAS(F)—Limnol and Oceanog Soc Am—Ecol Soc Am—Mar Biol Lab—NH Acad Sci—Sigma Xi. Zoology Department, University of New Hampshire, Durham, N.H.†

16 MOORE, Harry Hill. Ordnance; Ballistics; Strength of materials; Fuse development. b'89. BS '14—ME '20 (Purdue U). Research on interior and exterior ballistics, strength of materials and structures for Department of Navy; collaborator in development and compilation National Electrical Safety Code; developed special apparatus and instruments for studies and researches in ballistics; developed special fuses and pyrotechnic devices for Naval Service. Inventor of apparatus and method for hydrodynamic shock test for testing hollow articles, steam condenser tubes or other heat exchange devices. Nat Bur Standards Washington '15, physicist '23; charge ordnance div Naval Research Lab Bellevue DC '23-32, charge fuse research and development Naval Ordnance Lab Navy Yard Washington '32-45; cons Naval Ordnance since '45. Am Soc Testing Materials—Washington Soc Engrs—Engrs Club Washington. Naval Ordnance Laboratory, Silver Spring 19, Md.†

17 MOORE, Howard Roswald. Plastics and paint; Surface and colloid chemistry; Physico-chemical instruments & devices. b'01. BS '21—MS '22—PhD '24 (U Chicago). Heat resistant glass laminates, foaming polyester resins; surface treatment of paint pigments; application plastics and thermodynamics in construction of compressed gas bombs, to electromagnetic and acoustic location devices. Colloid chemist Celanese Corp Am '30-33; resin and paint chemist Am Cyanamid Co '35-36, Ault & Wiborg Corp '36; tech dir Kay & Ess Co '36-37; paint tech Phila Naval Shipyard '38-44; phys chemist, metal surface treatments '44-48; sect head and chem cons Naval Air Development Center Johnsville Pa since '48. Sigma Xi—Am Inst Chemists(F)—Soc Plastics Industry—Am Soc Testing Materials. Aeronautical Electronic Electrical Laboratory, US Naval Air Development Center, Johnsville, Pa.

18 MOORE, Jack Wiles. Gas (Drying agents); Adsorbents (Manufacture and use); Insecticides; Fungicides; Paint (Pigment processing). b'17. BS in chem engring '39 (Mo Sch Mines). Research on development solid desiccant for dehydration of natural gas for pipeline transmission and dehydration of air, liquid hydrocarbon and other gases; development base for pesticide concentrates using dust base concentrates and wetable powders; research on white pigments. Author articles: Design and Use of Adsorptive Drying Units '47; New Data on Activated Bauxite Desiccants '43; Granular Desiccants '47. With Ozark Smelting & Mining '39-41; with Floridin Co since '41. Tau Beta Pi—Alpha Chi Sigma—ACS—Am Inst Chem Engrs—Am Gas Assn—Nat Agrl Chem Assn—Entomol Soc Am. Floridin Co., 220 Liberty, Warren. Pa.

19 MOORE, John Alexander. Evolution; Embryology; Effects of temperature on organism. b'15 AB '36—MA '39—PhD '40 (Columbia). Research on development of hybrid frogs and embryonic temperature tolerance of amphibia. Author articles: Embryonic Temperature Tolerance and Rate of Development in Rana Catesbeiana '42; An Embryological and Genetical Study of Rana Burnsi Weed '42; Geographic Variation in Rana pipiens Schreiber of Eastern North America '44. Exec off Dept Zool Columbia U since '49; asst professor Barnard College '43-47, associate professor since '47, executive officer Zoology Department since '48; instr embryology Marine Biol Lab Woods Hole Mass '46-47; research asso herpetology Am Mus Natural Hist. NY Acad Sci(F)—Am Soc Zool—Am Soc Ichthyologists and Herpetologists—Evolution Soc—Am Soc Ecologists—Sigma Xi. Dept of Zoology, Barnard College, Columbia University, NYC.

20 MOORE, John Robert. English literature (Daniel Defoe, William Shakespeare, Sir Walter Scott, English and Scottish popular ballads). b'90. AB '10—AM '14 (U Mo); PhD '17 (Harvard); '26-27, '30, '45-46 (Europe). Author: Daniel Defoe and Modern Economic Theory 35; Defoe in the Pillory and Other Studies '39; Defoe's Sources for Robert Drury's Journal '43, and others. Editor: Representative English Dramas '29; Defoe's An Essay on the Regulation of the Press '48; also articles in field. Prof Eng and speech Shrivenham Am U England '45; prof Eng and library cons in Augustan lit Ind U. Modern Lang Assn Am—Bibliog Soc London—Bibliog Soc Am—Modern Humanities Research Assn—Facsimile Text Soc. 611 S. Jordan Av., Bloomington, Ind.†⊙

21 MOORE, Junius Teetzel. Heavy industrial structures. b'95. BS '17 (Va Polytechnic Inst). Designed approximately 5000 structures since '21 including bridges, mill buildings, crane runways, mine structures. Author: The Modern Industrial Structure. Chief designing bridge engr W Va Road Commn, '21-25; pres Fireproof Products Co since '26; pres Ferroseal Waterproofing Co, '30-40; pres Indsl Engrs since '38; vp Jefferds and Moore Mech Engrs since '47. ASCE—W Va Soc Profl Engrs. 422 Professional Bldg., Charleston 28, W. Va.

22 MOORE, Raymond Cecil. Petroleum geology; Regional and structural geology; Stratigraphy; Invertebrate paleontology. b'92. AB '13—ScD '35 (Denison U); PhD '16 (U Chicago). Geologist on government expedition which made trip by boat through Grand Canyon of the Colorado, Arizona 1923. Author: Historical Geology; also articles in field. Prof geol U Kan since '19; state geol of Kan since '17. Geol Soc Am(F)—Paleontol Soc(F), pres '47)—Am Assn Petroleum Geol—Kan Geol Soc — Soc Econ Paleontol and Mineralogy (pres '28)—Am Comm on Stratigraphic Nomenclature (c h m n

'47-51)—Sigma Xi—Phi Beta Kappa. University of Kansas, Lawrence, Kan.◎

10 MOORE, Raymond Lee. Vegetable tanning of leathers; Soil analysis for improvement of crop production. b'88. BS '12 (Wesleyan U); degree '13 (Tanners Council Leather Sch Brooklyn). Author articles in field. Tanning cons chem A W Hoppenstedt Lab Buffalo '14-15; chief chem Proctor Ellison Co Ekland Pa '16-17; cons chem A W Hoppenstedt Lab '18-33; dir and owner The Moore Lab Buffalo since '34. Am Leather Chem Assn—Soc Leather Trades Chem Eng—Am Chem Soc—Nat Research Council—Chemergic Council. 64 South Division St., Buffalo, 3.†

11 MOORE, Robert. Forest management; Stripmine spoilbank reclamation. b'00. BSF '22 (Pa State Coll); '31-34 (La State U). Author articles in field. Lumber man and forester '17-29; extension forester La '29-34; sr agrl econ US Dept Agr '34; forester Northeastern Lumber Mfrs Assn NYC '34-35; chief forest management Pa Dept Forests and Waters Harrisburg Pa '35-39; cons forester '35; cons on stripmine spoilbank reclamation to Atty Gen of Pa '47. Assn Cons Foresters (pres '51)—Soc Am Foresters. 110 W. Market, Danville, Pa.

12 MOORE, Robert Catchings. Fruit breeding. b'98. BS '22—MS '32 (Va Poly Inst). Studies breeding problems of grape, raspberry, peach, and apple; production studies of blueberry, strawberry, black walnut and chestnut. Asst hort Va Agrl Expt Sta since '22. AA AS—Am Soc Hort Sci—Am Genetic Assn—Va State Hort Soc—Va Acad Sci—AAUP. Virginia Agricultural Experiment Station, Blacksburg, Va.

13 MOORE, Theodore Lynn. Water works design. b'07. BSc '30 (Neb Central Coll); '32-33 (U Neb). Research and design of water supply, treating and pumping stations. Civil engr US Nat Park Service '34-42; civil engr Atchinson Topeka and Santa Fe Ry '42-44; civil engr Synthetic Fuel Div US Bur Mines since '44. Am Water Works Assn—Fed Sewage Works Assn—Inter-Am Assn San Engrs—Am Pub Health Assn—Am Assn Engrs. H: Lake Hiawatha, N.J.

14 MOORE, Walter G. Limnology; Aquatic ecology. b'13. BA '34 (Wayne U); MA '38—PhD '40 (Minn U). Field work in lake and stream surveys, limnological studies of Louisiana lakes; consultant on biological problems pertaining to Louisiana State Parks; research and writing on feeding habits of fishes and oxygen requirements of some fresh water fishes. Author articles in field. Asso prof biol Loyola U since '46; mem Biol Advisory Council, La State Parks Commn since '46. New Orleans Bot Soc (past pres)—New Orleans Acad Sci (sec)—Am Soc Limnology and Oceanog—Ecolog Soc Am—Am Soc Ichthyologists and Herpetologists—AAAS—Am Micros Soc—Sigma Xi. Awarded research grant, Carnegie Found since '46. Dept of Biology, Loyola University, New Orleans 18.†

15 MOORE, Wilbert Ellis. Demography; Industrial sociology. b'14. BA '35 (Linfield Coll); MA '37 (U Oregon); Edward Austin Fellow in sociology '37-38—PhD '40 (Harvard). Research associate Office of Population Research, Princeton University since '43; research on economic and demographic problems of Eastern and Southern Europe, prospects for international migration, institutional and demographic characteristics of southern Africa and modes of labor recruitment

and utilization in newly developing areas. Author: Economic Demography of Eastern and Southern Europe '45; Industrial Relations and the Social Order '46. Co-editor: Twentieth Century Sociology '45; also articles in field. Asst prof sociol Pa State Coll '41-43; asst prof Princeton U '45-48, professor sociology since '51. Am Sociol Soc—Population Assn Am—Union Internationale pour l'Etude Scientifique de la Population—Indsl Relations Research Assn—Sigma Xi. Office of Population Research, Princeton University, Princeton, N.J.

16 MOORE, William Cullen. Ionosphere (Radio propagation); Rockets (Television and radio instrumentation); Radio receiving sets (Design of small portable). b'12. AB '36 (Reed Coll); AM '49 (Boston U). Research, design, construction and testing of V-2 rocket electronic instrumentation; circuit research and atmosphere and missile instrumentation; circuit research and production design of frequency modulation set, research on standard and color television; military pack and aircraft radio design, microwave propagation and microwave relay systems, supervised design of rocket-borne radio receivers, transmitters, power supplies, television cameras and antennas. Granted patents on radio frequency transformer design, frequency modulation detector, and radio range indicator system. Communications engr United Airlines Communication Lab '37-38; with Galvin Mfg Corp '38-47, sr project engr '41-47; project supervisor Boston U Upper Atmosphere Research Lab '47-51; chief engr Tracerlab Inc Boston since '51. Inst Radio Engrs (sr mem)—Nat Elec Conf (bd dir '45)—Am Assn Phys Tchrs. Tracerlab Inc., 130 High St., Boston 10. H: 186 Pleasant St., Newton Centre 59, Mass.

17 MOORHEAD, Dudley Thomas. National history; California history; Military history. b'13. AB '34 (San Jose State Coll); MA '38—PhD '42 (Stanford U). Editor: California, a Study in Population '46; also articles in field. Asso prof hist San Jose State Coll since '46. Capt hist officer XIII Bomber Command 13 Air Force '43-45. AHA — Phi Alpha Theta. San Jose State College, San Jose 14, Calif.†

18 MOORMAN, Mildred Prinzing. Geographical nomenclature. b'04. BS '27 (U Minn). Research on geography and place names of British Isles, Balkan States, Baltic States, USSR, Iran; Russian transliteration: writing and editing with Columbia U and Columbia Ency '30-42; asso geog US Bd Geog Names since '43. Soc Women Geog—Am Soc Profl Geog (asso edit '46-47); Am Geog Soc(F). Board on Geographic Names, Interior Dept, Washington.

19 MOOSE, Joe Eugene. Phosphorus; Phosphates; Bone ash; Lampblack; Detergents; Carolimetry. b'95. AB '17 (So Methodist U); MS '22—PhD '24 (U Ill). Author articles: A Re-determination of the Heats of Oxidation of Certain Metals '24; A Chemical Study of Oklahoma Coals. Issued patents in field. Asst prof chem U Okla '24-26, asso prof chem engring '26-29; research chem Swann Research Corp Anniston (Ala) '29-35; research chem engring Monsanto Chem Co '35-45; prof chem U Nev since '45, director research and graduate studies since '53. ACS—Am Inst Chem Engrs—AAAS—AAUP—Sigma Xi—Phi Kappa Phi—Phi Lambda Upsilon—Alpha Chi Sigma—Gamma Alpha. University of Nevada, Reno. H: 721 Arlington Av.

20 MORAN, Robert Breck, Jr. Radar surveying. b'13. AB '36 (Stanford).

Inventor and designer portable radar surveying system in use in Arabia. Contributor: Exploration Geophysics. Electronic research engr Cal Inst Tech '43-45; instrument designer and sr cons US Naval Ordnance Test Sta '45-48; electronic instrument designer William Miller Corp '48-50; cons Moran Instrument Corp since '50. Soc Exploration Geophysicists—Inst Radio Engrs—Tau Beta Pi. Moran Instrument Corp., 170 E. Orange Grove Av., Pasadena 3, Cal.

21 MORAN, William Thomas. Advertising (Psychology, research); Communications (Psychological research); Attitudes (Measurements, research, surveys); Marketing (consumer, economics industrial, methods, research); Product design (Consumer satisfaction, research); Product (Development, testing techniques). b'23. Student AS TP '43 (Harvard Grad Sch); AB '47 (Princeton). Development new advertising and psychological research techniques, and cooperation in development consumer product test technique; creation, administration, and analysis of opinion, attitude and morale studies among consumers, employees, and trade; psychological research of advertising, promotion, and communications; determination market and economic potentials of new and existing products. Author articles: Reliability of the Question in Public Opinion Polling (unpub thesis) '47; Measuring Exposure to Advertisements '51. Co-author article: Product Testing: A Study of Comparative Test Design and Theoretical Implications (Am Marketing Assn nat award) '49. Research analyst comml research dept Pillsbury Mills Inc since '47; marketing cons jewelry Gordon Erickson Co Minneapolis since '48; dir cons service marketing and product development Bus Cons Clinic Minneapolis since '49. Am Marketing Assn (exec ed Market News, dir Minn chpt '50-51)—Psychometric Soc—Sigma Xi. Pillsbury Mills, Inc., Pillsbury Bldg., Mpls 2. H: 2825 Yosemite Av., Mpls 16.

22 MORCH, Ernst Trier. Anesthesia; Dwarfism; Respirators: Laryngoscopes; Endotracheal catheters; Anesthetic machines. b'08. MD '35—PhD '42 (U Copenhagen Denmark). Study heredity of dwarfism in Denmark; design automatic device which gives artificial respiration inside chest cavity when open during surgical operations, illuminated spatula for examination and treatment inside throat and larynx, and for induction of rubber tube in airways during certain types surgical operations, special rubber tube to be inserted in airways during certain surg procedures, and machine to produce analgesia by means of nitrous oxide for self-administration by patient during deliveries. Author: Anesthesia (Danish) '49. Author article: Chondrodystrophia Dwarfs in Denmark (thesis) '41, and others. Postgrad surgical training Denmark '35-46; Brit Council Scholar Anesthesiology U Oxford Eng; faculty anes dept U Copenhagen '43-49; asst prof anesthesiology U Kan '50-52; prof and dir anesthesia U Chicago since 1953. Scandinavian Anes Soc—Danish Anes Soc—Danish Surgical Soc—Scandinavian Surgical Soc—Royal Soc Med Eng(F)—Assn Anesthetists Great Britain and Ireland(F)—Royal College Surgeons of England—American Society Anesthesiologists—Internat Anesthesia Research Soc—Internat Coll Anesthetists(F)—Kan Soc Anesthesiologists—Soc d'Anesthésie et d'Analgesie de France (fgn corr)—Soc Cubana de Anestesiologia (hon). University of Chicago, Chgo 37.

10 MORDEN, William J(ames). Exploration (Central Asia, Africa). b'86. PhB '08 (Yale). Explorer and field collector since '22, expeditions '22-23 Africa, '23-24 Asia, '26 central Asia, '29-30 central Asia and Siberia, '47 Africa. Author: Across Asia's Snows and Deserts '27; By Coolie and Caravan Across Central Asia '27; also articles in field. Field asso dept mammals Am Mus Natural Hist NYC '27-40; chief desert and tropic sect Arctic, Desert, and Tropic Information Center AAF '44-45. Royal Geog Soc, Eng (life F)—Am Mus Natural Hist (hon F)—East African Profl Hunters Assn, Kenya Colony (hon). c/o Bronxville Trust Co., Bronxville, N.Y. H: Campfire Rd., Chappaqua.

11 MORE, Robert Elmer. Evergreens. b'92. AB '13 (Dartmouth Coll); LLB '16 (Harvard). Experiment vegetative propagation of outstanding types evergreens for horticultural use; discovery and introduction new types juniper, spruce, pine, and falsecypress. Author: Evergreens for Colorado Landscaping '41; Colorado Evergreens '43. Operation Glenmore Arboretum since '33. Holme, Roberts, More, Owen & Keegan, First National Bank Bldg., Denver 2.

12 MOREE, Ray. Genetics. b'13. BS '37 (State Coll Washington); MS '39—PhD '45 (U Mich). Research spermatogenesis; hybrid sterility; population genetics. Author articles: Genic Sterility in Interspecific Male Hybrids of Peromyscus '46; A Confirmation of Rafalko's Feulgen Method '47; The Normal Spermatogenetic Wave-Cycle in Peromyscus '47; Heterozygosity Measurements in Experimental Populations of Drosophila '47. Asst prof Washington State Coll since '46. Am Genetic Assn—Soc for Study Evolution—AAAS—Genetics Soc Am—Sigma Xi. Awarded Sigma Xi grant '47, Washington State Coll Research Fund grant '47. Zoology Department, State College of Washington, Pullman, Wash.†

13 MOREHOUSE, Clarence K. Dry cell batteries. b'17. BS '39 (Tufts Coll); MS '40 (McGill U, Can); PhD '47 (MIT). Co-author: (with E M Otto, G W Vinal) Low Temperature Dry Cells; (with W J Hamer, G W Vinal) Effect of Inhibitors on the Corrosion of Zinc in Dry Cell Electrolytes; (with W C Schumb) Anhydrous Lower Bromides of Hafnium '47. Research chem Naval Ordnance Lab, Washington '42-43; research chem Nat Bur Standards '43-45; research and development chemist research and development div, Olin Industries, East Alton, Ill '47-49; research chemist RCA Laboratories Division, Princeton, NJ since '53. Am Chem Society—Electrochem Society—AAAS—Sigma Xi. Jefferson Road, Princeton, N.J.

14 MOREHOUSE, Neal F. Parasitology; Protozoology; Poultry (Chemotherapy). b'08. BS '33 (Kans State Coll); MS '35—PhD '36 (Ia State Coll). Chemotherapeutic studies on coccidiosis and histomoniasis in poultry, control of cecal coccidiosis due to Eimeria tenella; discovered a product to cause earlier maturity, faster growth and earlier egg production. Author articles in field. Scientist in protozool Dr Salsbury's Labs Charles City since '37, mgr research farm since '45. Am Soc Parasitologists—AAAS—Am Micros Soc — Ia Acad Sci — Phi Kappa Phi. Dr. Salsbury's Laboratories, 500 Gilbert St., Charles City, Ia.

15 MORELAND, Geo(rge) E(dward). Helminthology; Medical entomology; Trematoda (Larvae, adult and life cycle). b'95. BS '21 (Greenville Coll); MS '29 (U Mich); PhD '38 (Cornell U). Author: Laboratory Manual in General Zoology '34. Prof biol, chmn div sci Greenville Coll '22-41; prof zool Houghton Coll since '41, chmn div sci and math since '41. Am Micro Soc—Am Soc Zool—Am Ornithol Union—Sigma Xi. Zoology Department, Houghton College, Houghton, N.Y.

16 MORELL, William Nelson. Insurance law; International law; American Federal government; American colonial history. b'98. Student (Macalester Coll) (U Minn) (Southeastern U Law Sch); LLB '22—LLM '23 (Nat U Law Sch). Author: Government Insurance Claims and Actions Thereon. Atty Compensation and Ins Div Vets Bur '22-24; asso counsel Solicitor's Office '24-29; chief legal adviser Ins Claims Council Veterans Adminstrn '29-33; mem US Bd Vets Appeals since '34. Fed Bar Assn—Am Soc Internat Law—Am Bar Assn—Am Judicature Soc—Am Acad Polit and Social Sci—Sigma Delta Kappa.

17 MORETTI, Louis R. Economic geology; Talc; Barytes; Clay; Fluorspar. b'97. AB '23—EM '25 (Stanford U). General manager, president Industrial Minerals and Chemical Co Berkeley since '35; owner operator Spanish Mine Nevada County California since '45. Author articles in field. Mining engr Minas Del Tajo Bolanos Mexico '26-27; chief engr Cia Minas del Oro '27-28; gen supt Non Metallic Mineral Ind Death Valley region '28-29; cons mining engr San Rafael Calif., since '30; sec-treas Heckathorn & Co. 6th and Gilman Sts., Berkeley 10.†

18 MOREY, Albert Anderson. Insurance engineering. b'03. BBA in bus adminstrn and indsl engring '25 (Boston U). Development pressure inspection for oil refineries to prevent explosions; all phases of engineering as applies to insurance, safety, industrial, mechanical, etc. Author: Rehabilitation '45; Forty-Plus '44; It Happened At Home '46. Author articles: Safety Rides the Rails '49. Co-author: Women at work '50. With Employers Liability Assurance Corp Boston '25-29, Marsh & McLennan Inc since '29, partner '46, vp since '47. Safety code Chem Warfare Div USA World War II. ASME—Ill State C of C(aviaton com)—Inst ME London Eng—Am Soc CE—Am Inst Mining Engrs—Am Soc Heating and Ventilating Engrs—Soc Automotive Engrs—Am Petroleum Inst—Am Soc Mil Engrs—Am Soc Safety Engrs—Am Ordnance Assn—Western Soc Engrs—Vets of Safety—Nat Aeronaut Assn—Nat Soc Profl Engrs. Profl engr Ill, Mo. 231 S. La Salle St., Chgo 4. H: 815-A Forest Av., Evanston, Ill.

19 MORGAN, Agnes Fay. Food chemistry and nutrition (Heat effects on protein value, anti-grey hair vitamins, vitamin D, dehydrated fruit and food nutritive values). b'84. BS '04—MS '05—PhD '14 (U Chicago). Co-author: Experimental Food Study '38; also articles in field. Prof household sci since '23, prof home econ, chmn dept and biochem in agrl exptl sta since '38 U Calif. AAAS(F)—Am Soc Biol Chem—Am Inst Nutrition—Soc Exptl Biol and Med—Am Home Econ Assn—Am Pub Health Assn — Am Chem Soc (garvan medallist '49) Sigma Xi—Phi Beta Kappa. University of California, Berkeley 4.

20 MORGAN, Ann Haven. Fresh water biology; Conservation; Hibernation. b'82. AB '06—PhD '12 (Cornell U); '26 (Tropical Lab British Guiana). Author: Fieldbook of Ponds and Streams '30; Animals in Winter '39; also articles in field. Prof zool Mt Holyoke Coll since '18. AAAS(F)—Am Soc Zool — Am Soc Naturalists — Am Assn Museums—Entomol Soc Am—Am Limnol Soc—Ecol Soc—NY Herpetol Soc—Nat Com on Policies in Conservation Edn. Research grants Sigma Xi '26, '30, AAAS '26, '30. South Hadley, Mass.†⊙

21 MORGAN, Barton, Education (Rural, vocational, teacher, adult). b'89. Student '15 (U Washington); BS '19 (Northeast Mo State Teachers Coll); MS '22 (Ia State Coll); PhD '34 (U Ia). President's Committee on Vocational Education '37; White House Conference on Rural Education '44. Author: History of the Extension Service in Agriculture and Home Economics of Iowa State College '34; A Possible Intermediate Step in the Reorganization of Rural Elementary Education in Iowa '36; Uniform County School Maps for Iowa '40. Head dept and dir teacher edn Ia State Coll since '36, head vocation edn section Iowa Agrl expt sta. Am Assn Sch Adminstrs — Nat Soc Coll Teachers Edn — Am Ednl Research Assn—Am and Ia Vocational Assns—Nat Soc Study Edn—Gamma Sigma Delta. 220 Curtiss Hall, Iowa State College, Ames. Ia.†⊙

22 MORGAN, Charles Stillman. Transportation economics. b'91. AB '14 (U Mich); PhD '20 (Yale U). Author: Regulation and the Management of Public Utilities (Hart Schaffner & Marx prize essay) '23; Public Aids to Transportation (4 vol) '40; Problems in Regulation of Domestic Transportation by Water '46. Co-author: with H G Moulton, A L Lee) The St Lawrence Navigation and Power Project (Inst of Economics Series) '29. Dir and co-author: Comparative Labor Standards in Transportation (4 parts) '36-37; also articles in field. Chief carrier research analyst Interstate Commerce Commn since '42. Am Econ Assn—Am Statis Assn. Interstate Commerce Commission, Washington 25.⊙

23 MORGAN, Clifford T(homas). Psychology (Hoarding, audiogenic seizures, neuro-psychology, hunger, psycho acoustics). b'15. AB '36 (Maryville Coll); AM '37—PhD '39—fellow '38-39 (U Rochester). Author articles in field. Prof, chmn dept, dir psychol lab Johns Hopkins U since '48. Tech aide div physics Nat Defense Research Com '43-46. AAAS—Am Psychol Assn (div physiol and comparative psychol) — Am Physiol Soc — Eastern Psychol Assn—Acoustical Soc Am—Soc Exptl Psychol. Recipient War-Navy Certificate of Appreciation. Department of Psychology, Johns Hopkins University. Baltimore.⊙

24 MORGAN, Frank. Oil production; Lubrication. b'02. BS '27 (Ohio U); MS '30 (Purdue U); PhD '36 (Ohio State U). Research in oil production aimed at increasing efficiency of recovery of oil from a reservoir; investigations in flow of fluids through porous media; development x-ray technique for measuring saturations of sands; use radioactive tracers in flow studies; development flowmeter for measuring injection or production profiles in wells; lubrication bearings and plane sliders; friction studies and stick-slip phenomena. Research physicist Gulf Research and Development Co '36-50, dir physics div since '50. APS—Pittsburgh Phys Soc—AAAS—Am Petroleum Inst—Sigma Xi—Sigma Pi Sigma. Gulf Research and Development Co., P.O. Drawer 2038, Pitts. 30.

25 MORGAN, George David. Marine and desert flora and fauna. b'92. BS '24 (Denison U); MS '26 (U Pittsburgh); PhD '36 (O State U). With an expedition to the Jungles of British Guiana to study its fauna and flora '25. Author articles in field. Asst prof biol Denison U '27-37, asso prof since '37. AAAS—O Acad Sci—Denison Sci Assn—Sigma Xi. Denison University, Granville, O.†

10 MORGAN, Sister M(ary) Sylvia. Analysis of various types of oranges. BS '16—AB '17 (Coll of New Rochelle); MS '20 (Fordham U); DSc '25 (U Calif); student (U Notre Dame, Columbia). Author: Analysis of Various Types of Oranges; Surface Tension in Detoxication Productions. Pres Marywood Coll Scranton Pa '43-49; dir science Marywood College since '49. AAAS(F) — Am Chem Soc Audubon Soc—NY and Pa Acad Sci. Marywood College, Scranton 9, Pa.

11 MORGAN, Newlin Dolbey. Buildings. b'88. BS '10—CE '25 (U Colo); MS '28 (U Ill). Structural and architectural engineering. Co-author: (with Hardy Cross) Statically Indeterminate Structures '26, Continuous Frames of Reinforced Concrete '32. Detailing Am Bridge Co '10-13; design bridge and bldg structures Chicago Milwaukee & St Paul Ry Chicago '13-18; bridge engr Colo State Highway Dept and US Bur Pub Rds Denver '19-22; asso to prof U Ill since '24, now prof archtl engring. Am Soc CE—Am Concrete Inst—Am Inst Architects—AAUP—Am Assn Engring Edn—Sigma Xi—Tau Beta Pi—Alpha Rho Chi—Scarab. Licensed profl engr Ill. 306 Architecture Bldg., Urbana, Ill.

12 MORGAN, Ora Sherman. Agriculture (International, Near and Far East, economics, philanthropy). b'77. AB '05 (U Ill); MSA '07—PhD '09 (Cornell U). Made agricultural studies in Japan, China and India '34; made agricultural survey of Near Eastern countries as collaborator of Bd of Econ warfare and surveyor for Near East Found '42-43. Editor and part-author: Agricultural Systems of Middle Europe '33. Prof agrl econ, head dept Columbia since '11, prof emeritus '43; a dir Near East Found since '30; lecturer on China and the Near East. Sigma Xi. Rt 1, Box 454, Beaumont, Cal.

13 MORGAN, Ralph. Basketball. b'84. BS '06 (U Pa). Founder College Basketball Rules Committee '05, now National Basketball Rules Committee; founder '11 Eastern Inter-Collegiate Basketball League, secretary and treasurer '11-20, statistician and recorder since '11. Contbr annually to Nat Basketball Guide since '05. Pres Morgan Rogers and Roberts Inc; trustee U Pa; commr Cheltenham Twp Pa since '23, vp since '34. 64 Wall St., NYC.

14 MORGAN, William James. Psychology (Aptitude and proficiency tests). b'10. BA '33 (U Rochester); PhD '37 (Yale). Specialist construction aptitude tests for vocation guidance in schools and colleges and for personnel selection and placement in business and industry. Author: Principles of Conditioning in Human Goal Behavior '39; also articles in field. Dir Aptitude Assos Washington since '47; cons psychologist Inst Languages and Linguistics Sch Fgn Service Georgetown U since '51; cons Research and Development Bd Dept Defense since '52; cons and evaluations officer Psychol Strategy Bd Exec Offices White House since '52. Am Psychol—Eastern Psychol Assn—British Inst Indsl Psychol—Sigma Xi. Box 1128, Washington.

15 MORGEN, Ralph Alexander. Chemical industrial engineering; Thermodynamics. b'03. BS '23—PhD '26 (Calif U). Research in lead and alloys, industrial diamonds for wire drawing,

gas purification, oil field corrosion, detergent specialties for laundry and dry cleaning industries, water softening and use of sodium hexametaphosphate removal of poisonous spray residue from agricultural products, concentration of orange, lemon and lime oils, development of improved oil seal of leather impregnated with synthetic resins, oil and water proofing of leather and textiles, development of cosmetics. Holds patents on gas purification, clarification by absorption, dry cleaning apparatus, treating dry cleaning fluids, filtering apparatus, solvent recovery process. Author: CECO Clarifications '32; also articles in field. Formerly dir Fla Engring and Industrial Expt Sta Fla U; program dir for engring Nat Sci Found. Am Inst Chem Engrs—Am Chem Soc (chmn Fla sect '48)—Sigma Xi—Tau Beta Pi—Am Soc Engring Edn (past chm Chem Engring div)—Fla Acad Sci—Fla Engring Soc (sr)—Tech Assn Paper and Pulp Industry. Program Director for Engineering, National Science Foundation, Washington 25.

16 MORIARTY, John H. University libraries (Methods). b'03. AB '26—BS in LS '34—MS '38 (Columbia); '45 (Chicago U). Research on essentials in organization of acquisition work in university libraries, special librarians, microprint, agricultural libraries, national libraries. Author: Directory Information Material (Printed) for New York City Residents, 1626-1786 '42; Non-Technical Aspects of Engineering Education '38; also articles in field. Prof and dir Purdue U Libraries since '44. Phi Beta Kappa—ALA—Assn Coll and Research Libraries—Spl Libraries Assn (pres Ind chapt)—Ind Library Assn—Ind Sch Librarians Assn. Pudue University Libraries, LaFayette, Ind.

17 MORISON, Elting Elmore. Naval administration; Logistics; American history (1890-1914). b'09. AB '32—MA '37 (Harvard). Author: Admiral Sims and Modern American Navy '42; Selected Documents on Naval Administration 1915-1940 '44; also articles in field. Asst prof Mass Inst Tech since '46; dir Theodore Roosevelt Research Project since '46; cons Research and Development since '46. Dir hist sect Office Chief Naval Operations '44-46. Massachusetts Institute of Technology, Cambridge, Mass.

18 MORLEY, Sylvanus Griswold. Middle American archeology; Maya hieroglyphic writings. b'83. CE '04—hon PhD '21 (Pa Mil Coll); AB '07—AM '08—research fellow in Central Am Archeology '07-08 (Harvard). In charge Carnegie Institution archeological expeditions to Central America; director Chichen Itza Project '24-40. Author: Introduction to Study of Maya Hieroglyphs '15; Guide Book to the Ruins of Quirigua '35; The Inscriptions of Peten '37, '38; The Ancient Maya '46; Guide Book to the Ruins of Chichen Itza '48. Co-author: (with Alfredo Barrera Vasquez) The Maya Chronicles '48; also articles in field. Dir of combined Sch of Am Research, Mus of NM and Lab of Anthrop at Santa Fe NM since '47. Royal Anthrop Inst (hon F, Great Britain)—Order of Quetzal (hon F, Guatemala '39)—Soc Am Archeology—Am Philos Soc. Museum of New Mexico, Santa Fe, N.M.☉

19 MORRELL, Fred. Forestry. b'80. BSC '02—grad work '04-06 (U Neb); MF '20 (Ia State Coll). Junior forester '06, forest inspector '07-08, assistant regional forester '09-19, regional forester '20-29, asst chief Forest Service '30-33; chief Office Civilian Conservation Corps Activities,

US Department of Agriculture '34-43; now Washington representative American Paper and Pulp Association. Soc Am Foresters(sr mem). 711 14th St. N.W., Washington.☉

20 MORRELL, Joseph Alan. Pharmacology. b'97. BA (Chem) '21—MA '22—PhD '24 (U Toronto Ont Can). Manufacture of tablets, liquids, ointments and parenterals; production and assay of endocrine products; development and direction clinical evaluation tests of new drugs and their application. Head glandular products div E R Squibb & Sons New Brunswick NJ '24-41; research dir and plant mgr Laboratorios Lex Havana Cuba '42-46; tech dir R J Strasenburgh Co Rochester since '46. ACS—Soc Exptl Biol and Med—Assn Study Internal Secretions. R. J. Strasenburgh Co., Rochester 14, N.Y.

21 MORRICAL, Keron C. Acoustics; Sound. b'08. BS '29—MS '33—PhD '36 (U Ill). Author articles: Sound Absorbing Values of Portland Cement Concretes '36; A Modified Tube Method for the measurement of Sound Absorption '37; Fundamentals of Theater Acoustics 40; Interactions Between Microphones, Couplers, and Earphones '49, and others. Engr and supervising engr RCA Victor Camden NJ '36-47; research asso Underwater Sound Lab Harvard U '42-44; proof elec engring Washington U St Louis, and research asso Central Inst for Deaf St Louis since '47. Acoustical Soc Am(F)—Inst Radio Engrs (sr mem)—Sigma Xi—Tau Beta Pi. Washington University, St Louis.

22 MORRIS, Alton Chester. Southern folklore; Florida folklore and folksongs; Place names of Florida and their background; William Cullen Bryant (Florida visits). b'03. ABE '27—MA '28 (U Fla); PhD '40 (U NC). Counsellor for the folksong div of Library of Congress '38-39. Author: The Folksongs of Florida and Their Cultural Background '40. Editor: Southern Folklore Quarterly since '36; also author articles in field. Prof Eng U Fla. SE Folklore Soc (pres '40-41)—Am Folklore Soc (councilman '45-48)—Am Dialect (chmn Fla com proverb collecting Com)—Modern Lang Assn (chmn Folksong Com Popular Lit Sect)—Gen Edn Bd fellow '37-39. Language Hall, University of Florida, Gainesville, Fla.†

23 MORRIS, Charles (William). Semantics. b'01. BS '22 (Northwestern U); PhD '25 (U Chicago). Guest lecturer philosophy Harvard '40, Institute Design Chicago New School for Social Research, visiting lecturer Harvard '50-53. Author: Six Theories of Mind '32; Logical Positivism, Pragmatism and Scientific Empiricism '37; Foundations of the Theory of Signs '38; Paths of Life '42; Signs, Language, and Behavior '46; The Open Self '48. Editor: Works of George H. Mead. Asso editor: Internat Ency of Unified Science. Lecturer philos U Chicago. Am Philos Assn—Hist Sci Soc. Guggenheim fellow '42; Rockefeller fellow '43. University of Chicago, Chgo 37.

24 MORRIS, Leonard Leslie. Physiology of vegetables (Relating to storage, transit and marketing). b'14. BS '37 (Purdue U); MS '39—PhD '41 (Cornell U). Faculty mem staff department vegetable crops U Cal since '41. Am Soc Hort Sci—Am Soc Plant Physiol—Sigma Xi—Phi Kappa Phi. University of California, Department of Vegetable Crops, Davis, Cal.†

25 MORRIS, Melvin S. Range management and ecology (Northern Rocky Mountain region). b'07. BS '30—MS

'32 (Colo Agrl Coll); '40 (U Chicago). Author articles in field. Asst to asso prof forestry Mont State U '36-48, prof since '49. Colo-Wyo Acad Sci (chmn plant sci div '32)—Am Soc Range Management (treas '49) — Soc Am Foresters (chmn Northern Rocky Mountain sect '45)—Mont Acad Sci (vp and chmn biol sci sect '41, sec-treas '42-46, pres '47). School of Forestry, Montana State University, Missoula, Mont.†

10 MORRIS, Morgain James Reginald. Steel (Alloy, hardenability). b'93. Student '15-17, '19-20 (Imperial Coll Sci and Tech, London); Asso (Royal Sch Mines London); '20-22 Freechville scholarship (Columbia). Research on flaking and gas control for alloy steels, factors affecting hardenability and its control for heat treating steels. With Central Alloy Steel Co Div Rep Steel since '22, chief metall since '26, dir research since '44. Am Soc Metals—Iron and Steel Inst (Brit)—Inst Metals(Brit.). Republic Steel Corp., Central Alloy Div., Massillon, O.

11 MORRIS, Percy Amos. Conchology. b'99. Spl studies (Yale). Author: Nature Photography Around the Year '38; What Shell is That? '39; They Hop and Crawl '44; A Field Guide to the Shells '47; The Boy's Book of Snakes '48; also articles in field. Lecturer photography and natural history, radio broadcasting Sta WOR. Am Malacol Union. Peabody Museum, Yale University, New Haven.

12 MORRIS, Richard Brandon. American history (Labor, legal, economic, colonial, bibliography, archives). b'04. AB '24 (Coll City NY); AM '25—PhD '30 (Columbia U). Author: Studies in the History of American Law '30; Government and Labor in Early America '46; Fair Trial '52. Co-author: Guide to the Principal Sources for Early American History (with E. B. Greene) '29; (with J S Schapiro) Civilization in Europe '29; (with L L Snyder and J E Wisan) Handbook of Civilian Protection '42. Editor: Era of the American Revolution: Studies Inscribed to Evarts Boutell Greene '39; Encyclopedia of American History '53; New American Nation Series, 40 vol (with Henry Steele Commager) in progress. Instr hist Coll City of NY '27-32, asst and asso prof hist '32-47, prof '47-48; visiting prof hist Columbia U '46-49; visiting prof hist Princeton U '48-49; mem Inst Advanced Study, '48; prof hist Columbia U since '49. AHA (life mem)—Soc Am Archivists —Econ Hist Assn—Am Arbitration Assn. Fayerweather Hall, Columbia University, NYC 27. H: 151 Ridgeway, Mt. Vernon, N.Y.⊚

13 MORRIS, Ross Elliott. Rubber (Technology). b'10. BS '31—MS '32 (Cal Inst Tech). Research on compounding guayule rubber and its blending with synthetic rubbers, properties of natural and synthetic rubbers at low temperatures particularly from standpoint of gasket service, role stearic acids in dispersion of carbon black in rubber, sound transmission through natural and synthetic vulcanizates at audio frequencies. Author 41 articles in field. Research chem and compounder Goodyear Tire & Rubber Co '33-35, chief compounder '35-38; chief chem Kelly Springfield Tire Co '38; rubber tech in charge rubber lab Mare Island Nav Shipyard since '39. Tau Beta Pi—ACS—N Cal Rubber Group. Registered chem engr Cal. Rubber Laboratory, Mare Island Naval Shipyard, Vallejo, Cal.†

14 MORRIS, Samuel Brooks. Water and power resources; Hydraulic en-

gineering; Geophysics; Seismology. b'90. AB '11 (Stanford); LLD '53 (U Calif). US Com Internat Commission on Large Dams of World Power Conference since '38; designed and built Morris Dam 328 feet high, San Gabriel Canyon for City of Pasadena '32-34. Chief engr Pasadena Water Dept '13-35; gen mgr chief engr Dept Water and Power City of Los Angeles since '44; cons civil and hydraulic engr since '35; com on geophys sci Research and Development Bd Nat Mil Establishment since '46; com on engring seismol US Coast and Geodetic Survey since '47. AAAS—Am Concrete Inst— Am Geophys Union—ASCE (pres Los Angeles sect '25, pres San Francisco sect '43)—AIEE—Am Water Works Assn (dir '31-33, vp '42-43, pres '43-44; pres Calif sect '27-28)—Seismol Soc Am (dir '36-41, vp '38-40)—Am Soc Engring Edn—Sigma Xi—Tau Beta Pi. Awarded John M Diven medal by Am Water Works Assn '33. Department of Water and Power, 207 S. Broadway, Los Angeles.†

15 MORRIS, Vlon Neilan. Adhesive tapes. b'01. BS—MS '24 (Purdue U). PhD '26 (U Minn); student (Mass Inst Tech, Rutgers U). Research on latex compositions and the colloid chemistry of rubber, alkyd resins and resin emulsions, pressure-sensitive tapes, thermoplastic tapes, themosetting films and tapes, various adhesive cements. Holds patents and patent applications on adhesives, impregnated paper backings for tapes and primer coating for tapes. Co-editor: Science of Rubber '34; also articles in field. Research chem and group leader Firestone Tire & Rubber Co '27-35; research supervisor Resinous Products & Chemical Co Phila '35-39; tech dir supervisor research and development labs Industrial Tape Corp New Brunswick '40-51; coordinator research Johnson & Johnson since '53; chmn indsl pressure-sensitive tape cons tech adv com for War Prodn Bd and govt agencies '42-51. Johnson & Johnson, New Brunswick, N.J.

16 MORRISETT, Lloyd N. School administration (Housing, salaries, curriculum and surveys). b'93. Member national advisory committee on secondary education to US Office of Education; director educational surveys Montana and California public school districts '40-47; educational consultant to county departments of education; served as deputy chief Civilian Training Branch and chief training program section Army Service Forces, War Department Washington '44; consultant Industrial Personnel Division '46; public panel member National War Labor Board 10th Regional Office '45-46. Prof edn U Cal since '41. Cal Council Tchr Edn—NEA—Am Assn Sch Adminstrs—Nat Assn Secondary Sch Prins—Kappa Delta Pi. University of California, LA 24.⊚

17 MORRISON, Deming W. Dam design; Flood control; Hydraulic engineering. b'03. AB '25 (Stanford). Hydraulic engr dam dept state engr's office State of Calif '30-34; hydraulic engr Bur Agrl Engring US Govt '34-35; head dam design US Engrs War Dept Los Angeles Dist '35-41, maj and lt col Corps of Engrs US Army '42-46, head engring design US Engrs War Dept Sacramento Dist Calif Central Valley Projects '46-47; cons engr Cheyenne Wyo since '47. ASCE. 420 Hynds Bldg., Cheyenne, Wyo. H: 820 East 17th St.†

18 MORRISON, Edward Bondurant. Manuscripts. b'04. AB '29 (George Washington U); student summer '24 (Columbia). Engaged research in and

processing of manuscripts. Author articles. First asst Manuscript Div NY Pub Library since '49. New York Public Library, 476 5th Av., Room 319 NYC 18.†

19 MORRISON, Edward Lester. American farming; Sugar cane; Farm irrigation. b'00. BS '25 — MS '30 (Okla A & M Coll). Mem region 12 Farm Security Advisory Com '39-44, mem St Mary Soil Conservation Dist since '46; mem bd dir St Mary Sugar Cane Cooperative Mill; contact com mem Am Sugar Cane League since '46; agrl coordinator Okla A and M Coll since '48; dir of housing Okla A & M since '48, dir auxiliary enterprises since '53. Stillwater, Okla.

20 MORRISON, Frank Barron. Animal husbandry (Nutrition, livestock feeding). b'87. BS '11—DSc '50 (U Wis); DSc '47 (U Vt). On American Commission to Study Live Stock Industry in Germany '28; conducted survey of live stock industry of Philippine Islands for Philippine Government '37. Author: Feeds and Feeding '36; Feeds and Feeding Manual '15; Feeds and Feeding Abridged '37. Prof animal husbandry and animal nutrition Cornell U since '28. AAAS(F)—Am Chem Soc—Am Soc Animal Production—Am Dairy Sci Assn—Nutrion Soc (Gt Brit) —Sigma Xi—Phi Kappa Phi. 409 Highland Av., Ithaca.⊚

21 MORRISON, Gordon. Plant genetics; Vegetable seed breeding and production (Gardening, industrial). b'95. BS '23 (Mich State Coll). Organized Detroit victory garden program '43. Author articles in field. Dir seed breeding and research Burgess Seed and Plant Co Galesburg Mich since '43. AAAS(F)—Genetics Soc Am. Burgess Seed and Plant Co., Galesburg, Mich.

22 MORRISON, Paul Cross. Economic geography; Geography of Great Lakes area; Central American geography. b'06. BS '28—MA '33 (O State U); PhD '41 (Clark U). Research in industrial and agricultural geography as phases of economic geography. Teaching asst O State U '30-31; fellow Clark U '37-38; instr geog Mich State Coll '31-38, asst prof '38-42, professor since '50, asst Dean Sch Sci and Arts since '44, guest scientist Inter-Am Inst Agrl Scis, Turrialba district, Costa Rica '47-48. Assn Am Geographers— Nat. Council Geog Teach—Mich Acad Science Arts and Letters—Sigma Xi. Department of Geography, Michigan State College, East Lansing, Mich.†

23 MORRISON, Paul Leslie. Finance. b'99. BA '21 (DePauw U); MBA '22; PhD '27 (Northwestern U). Co-author: Principles of Accounting '26, 2d edit '31; also articles in field. Faculty Northwestern U since '23, now prof finance, chmn finance dept, dir grad div Sch of Commerce; pres Owen L Coon Found; dir Chicago Nat Bank, Gen Finance Corp Chicago, Wacker Corp Chicago. Commd capt to lt col finance dept US Army '42-46. Am Finance Assn — Am Econ Assn — Phi Beta Kappa. Northwestern University, School of Commerce, Evanston, Ill.

24 MORRISON, Robert. Dismal swamp. b'27. Student '44 (Davidson Coll); AB—AM '47 (UNC); '47-48 (U Ill); '48-51 (U Kansas). Exploration and photography of the Great Dismal Swamp '47, research on literature biology and history, geography and mineralogy of Great Dismal Swamp since '46. Author: The Literature and Legends of the Great Dismal Swamp '47. Editor The Eagle Hickory NC '42-44; columnist The Hickory Daily Record '41-43; feature writer various papers '46; counselor UNC '45-47; ext speaker U Ill '48-49; ed and pub Daily Catawba News-Enterprise, Newton N C since '52. Am Bus Writing Assn—Phi Beta Kappa. West Lake Hills, Newton, N.C.

10 MORRISON, Roger Leroy. Highway and traffic engineering. b'83. AB '11 BS '12 CE '17 (U of Ill); AM '14 (Columbia). Co-author (with A H Blanchard) Elements of Highway Engineering '28; also author articles in field. Engr with SP Co and WP RR Co '05-09; instr civil engring U Tenn '11-12; jr engr Ill Highway Dept '12; supt road constrn then sales engr United Gas Imp Co '13-14; prof highway engring Tex A and M Coll '14-19; engr tests Pittsburgh Testing Lab '19-21; treas and gen mgr Concrete Products Co Birmingham Ala '21-24; dir Mich State Highway Lab '24-27; asso prof, later prof highway engring and highway transport since '24, curator Transportation Library since '45 U Mich; cons engr since '16. ASCE (past chmn highway division)—Army Transportation Assn—Assn Asphalt Paving Tech (past pres)—Inst Traffic Engrs (past pres)—Internat Assn Road Congresses—Am Soc Engring Edn—Highway Research Bd of Nat Research Council (past chmn)—Nat Safety Council (past gen chmn street and highway traffic sect)—Eno Foundation Highway Traffic Control (mem bd cons)—Engring Soc Detroit Mich—Engring Soc—Sigma Xi. 1928 Lorraine Pl., Ann Arbor.☺

11 MORRISON, Willard Langdon. Refrigeration and food preservation; Liquefaction of methane; composting apparatus. b'92. Student '09-10 (Chandler Business College); '11-14 (Boston University); '15-17 (Babson School Business Administration). Produced and marketed first—120 degree cascade steel chillers for steel treatment completing conversion of austenite to martensite after heat treatment, stabilizing, shrinking for assembly as automobile, valve seat inserts, bushings during war; produced blood plasma desiccators for Duetch Serum Center project, Parke-Davis, US Navy; pioneer frozen cooked food research; produced super chilling device for shipping frozen food, Electrocellar for storing fresh foods, clothes dryer appliance using refrigeration cycle. Invented Deepfreeze and Deepfreeze principle of refrigeration. White Motor Truck Boston '15-17; Dole Valve Co Chicago '21-23; Clark Equipment Co Buchanan Mich '33-35; Pines Winterfront Chicago '35-36; mgr Deepfreeze div Motor Products Corp Chicago '36-44; Gen Am Transportation Corp and Lab Highland Pk Ill since '44. Am Soc Refrigeration Engrs. 470 King Muir Rd., Lake Forest, Ill.†☺

12 MORRISS, Elizabeth Cleveland (Mrs John). Adult elementary education. b'77. AB '95 (Judson Coll); LI '98 (Peabody Coll for Teachers); BSc '32—MA '33 (Columbia). Began organizing community schools for adult illiterates in Buncombe County '19; developed plans for standardizing schools for native illiterates; member National Committee of nine that outlined courses of study for these schools; made film for depicting problems of adult illiteracy. Author: Writing and Composition Book for Adult Beginners '21; Citizen's Reference Book '22; Adult Adventures in Reading '39. Chmn State Literacy Commn since '28; dir Adult Edn Div State Dept Pub Instrn '40-41, ret '41. NEA (life mem, exec dir dept adult edn '29-31, vp '38-40) NC Ednl Assn—Kappa Delta Pi. 514 19th St., N.W., Washington.

13 MORRISSEY, James H(ildebrand). Metrology; Colorimetry; Calculations with numerical matrices. b'13. BS '40—MS in math '41—MA in phys '48 (U Mich). Research on precise calibration of physical standards of length, angle, and area; determination of ICI co-ordinates of color areas. Phys Nat Bur Standards '42-45; phys Kodak Research Lab since '48. APS—Optical Soc Am. Kodak Park Works, Rochester, N.Y.

14 MORRO, William Charles. Methane (Oxidation); Gas purification. b'13. BS '35 (Tex Christian U); MA '37 (Ia State U); '38-41 (Harvard). Research and development pyrolysis and catalytic cracking of low molecular weight hydrocarbon, oxidation low molecular weight hydrocarbon, especially methane; design gas purification units related to solvent extraction methods. With Carbide and Carbon Chem Co since '41. ACS—Alpha Chi Sigma. Carbide and Carbon Chemical Co., 437 MacCorkle Av., South Charleston, WVa.

15 MORROW, Glenn D(avis). Tax research; Taxes (Kentucky). b'11. AB '33 (Murray State Teachers Coll); MA '40 (George Peabody Coll for Teachers); '41-44 (U Ky). Author: Kentucky City Finances '46; Taxation of Manufacturing in the South '48. Co-author: (with W Martin) Organization for Kentucky Local Tax Assessments. Research asst Bur Bus Research U Ky '41-44; field rep Ky Dept Revenue '43; asst administr gen Internal Revenue Adminstrn Am Finance Mission Iran '45; research asso Bur Bus Research U Ky '46; cons and dir div research and statis Ky Dept Revenue '48; now Internal Revenue specialist Japan. So Econ Assn—Am Econ Assn—Am Soc Pub Adminstrn—Nat Tax Assn. ESS-IR GHQ SCAP APO 500 c/o PM SF.

16 MORSE, Dorothy Clum. Plankton; Oysters. b'17. BA '39—MSc '41 (O State U). Author: Some Observations on Seasonal Variations in Plankton Population Patuxent River Md '47; also articles in field. Asst prof biol and chem Alfred U Jamestown NY '42-43; asst chem and research in Plankton Md Dept research and edn Solomons Md '43-45; instr biol and research in plankton U Miami '45-46; instructor biol U Dayton '47. AAAS—O Acad Sci—Am Micros Soc—Sigma Xi—Phi Beta Kappa. 1027 Hampshire Road, Dayton 9, O.†

17 MORSE, Frederick Tracy. Applied energy. b'02. EE '24—ME '24 (U Va). Author: Power Plant Engineering and Design '32, revised '42; Elements of Applied Energy '47. Engineering editor and contributor to Van Nostrand's Scientific Encyclopaedia '38, revised '47. With U Va since '33, prof mech engring since '46, dir spl on-campus aviation training for mil services '41-44; practicing engr in field of heat power plants since '38; mem Miller & Morse cons engrs Charlottesville since '38. Soc Automotive Engrs—Am Soc Engring Edn—Tau Beta Pi—Sigma Xi—Theta Tau. Dept. of Engineering, University of Virginia, Charlottesville.†☺

18 MORSE, Glenn Tilley. Silhouettes; Wax portraits; Silver; Seals; Medallion portraits; Wedgwood; Shells. b'70. BA '98 (Harvard); BD '01 (Episcopal Theol Sch Cambridge). Lecturer on historic and antiquarian subjects and art; has the largest collection of silhouettes in the world, also large collection of wax portraits, seals medallions and Wedgwood; painter of landscapes and portraits. Author: Old Newbury Initiatives; Twenty-five Years of All Saints Church; Silhou-ette A Fine Art. Founder '10 and rector All Saints Ch West Newbury '10-38, retired '38; founder and rector All Saints Ch Georgetown '16-38. Soc Preservation New Eng Antiquities (trustee)—Am Antiquarian Soc—Arts Crafts Soc Jeweller Craftsmen, Boston—Wedgwood Club (1st vp). 186 High St., Newburyport, Mass.

19 MORSE, Horace Taylor. Philosophy of general education; Tests and measurements; Teaching methods. b'05. AB '28—AM '30—PhD '39 (U Minn). Co-author: Selected Items for the Testing of Study Skills '40. Co-editor: The Gopher Historian; also articles in field. Dean U Minn since '46. AHA—Nat Council for Social Studies (chmn com publs '41-45)—Am Assn for State and Local Hist—Minn Edn Assn—Minn Hist Soc (chmn sch com). 1933 James Av. S., Minneapolis 5.

20 MORSE, Jarvis M(eans). New England history. b'99. BA '22—MA '23—PhD '30 (Yale). Author: American Beginnings '53; A Neglected Period of Connecticut's History 1818-1850 '33; Under the Constitution of 1818 '33; The Rise of Liberalism in Connecticut '33; Connecticut Newspapers in the Eighteenth Century '35. Editor: Rhode Island: A Guide to the Smallest State '37; also articles in field. Asst prof hist Brown U '33-41; asst to the field dir War Finance Drive Treasury Dept Washington '41-45, ednl dir US Savings Bonds Div since '46. AHA—Am Acad Polit and Social Sci—Soc Mayflower Descendants—RI Hist Soc. United States Savings Bonds Division, Treasury Department, Washington 25.

21 MORSE, Richard Stetson. High vacuum. b'11. SB '33 (MIT); '34 (Tech Hochschule Munich). Research in sound reproduction, color photography; development high vacuum pumps, gauges, vacuum processes; low temperature dehydration; vacuum metallurgy; vacuum distillation. Author articles in field. Sci staff Eastman Kodak and Distillation Products Inc '35-40; dir research Nat Research Corp '40-49, dir, pres since '40; dir New Enterprises Inc, Boston; pres and dir Vacuum Metals Corp; dir Hydrofoil Corp. Am Chem Soc—Am Optical Soc—Am Inst Physics—Engrs Club (Boston, NY). 70 Memorial Dr., Cambridge 42, Mass.

22 MORSE, Roy R(obert). Oil exploration; Geology of China. b'90. BS '13—PhD '22 (U Calif). Geological exploration China and Philippine Islands '14-16, California and mid-continent '18, southwestern Alaska summer '22. Author articles in field. Dir exploration Shell Oil Co Inc Houston Tex since '46. Geol and mining engr manganese and chrome War Minerals Investigation US Bur Mines US Geol Survey and Calif Council for Defense '17-18. Geol Soc Am(F)—Am Assn Pet Geol—Econ Geol Soc—Am Inst Mining and Metall Engrs—Am Geophy Union—AAAS—Houston Geol Soc—Texas Acad Sci—Seismol Soc Am—Sigma Xi. 2229 Shell Building, Houston.†

23 MORSE, William Clifford. Stratigraphical geology. b'74. AB '06—AM '08 (O State U); PhD '27 (MIT). Author articles in field. Prof and head dept geol U Miss since '34; dir Miss Geol Survey since '34. O Acad Sci(F)—AAAS(F)—Geol Soc Am(F)—Paleontological Soc—Sigma Xi. 520 S. Mississippi Geological Survey, University, Miss.☺

24 MORSER, Roy Christian, Jr. US jazz music (History); Discography; Mason and Dixon Line (History). b'26. Asso arts '48 (Norfolk Va Div Coll William and Mary - Va Poly Inst);

BA '50 (Coll William and Mary); MA '51 (U Miami). Research on jazz musicians, history of jazz music, jazz phonograph recordings. Co-author article: (with C R Henderson) Southeastern Corner of Pennsylvania Essence of Mason and Dixon Line History '51. Contributor: New Hot Discography '48; Jazz Directory (in press); New Index to Jazz (in press). Co-editor: The Disc-Counter Jazz Magazine '48-51. AHA—Phi Alpha Theta. H: 203 W. 35th St., Norfolk 4, Va.

10 MORT, Paul R. American public education (Finance methods, law, principles). b'94. AB '16 (Ind U); AM '22—PhD '24 (Teachers Coll Columbia); LittD '40 (Rutgers). Author: The Measurement of Educational Need '24; State Support for Public Schools '26; State Support for Public Education '33; Federal Support for Public Education '36; Principles of School Administra-F W Cyr and A J Burke) Paying for Our Public Schools '38; (with W C Reusser) Public School Finance '41; (with Hamilton) The Law and Public Education '41. Teacher elementary and high schs, elementary prin, sch supt Ind and Ariz '11-22; Teachers Coll Columbia '22, dir Sch of Edn '29-35, dir Advanced Sch of Edn '35-40, research in edn finance since '24; mem commns NY, W Va, Ala, Pa, Kan, Fla. Neb, Colo, Mo, Mich, Okla, Ohio, NJ, Me, RI and Nat Finance Surveys '31-33; cons Adv Commn on Ed '37-38. NEA—Am Statis Assn—Nat Soc Study Edn—Soc Coll Teachers Edn—Kappa Delta Pi. Awarded Butler silver Medal '33. 4662 Iselin Av., Riverdale, NYC.☺

11 MORTENSEN, E(rnest). Agriculture (Southwestern Texas, Greece, subtropical fruits). b'02. BS '21 (Tex A&M Coll). Horticulture specialist Am Mission Aid to Greece '48. Author: Factors in Insect and Disease Control of Prickly Pear in Texas '33; Citrus Growing in Texas Winter Garden '45; Date Palm Culture in Texas Winter Garden '46; Ornamentals for S W Texas '47; also articles in field. Entomologist Prickly Pear Bd Australia '21-29; supt Expt Sta A&M Coll Winter Haven Tex '29-47; horticulturist Tex Agrl Expt Sta Winter Haven Tex since '47 horticulturist Point Four Program Kingdom of Jordan '52-54. Tex Acad Sci—AAAS—Am Genetic Assn—Am Soc Hort Sci. 3312 Merrie Lynn, Austin 2, Tex. †

12 MORTENSON, Everett N. Grease. b'11. BS in chem engring '34 (Ia State Coll). Research in grease recovery and grease loss surveying. Author: Grease Losses in the Meat Packing Industry. Div head chem engring, research lab Swift & Co '42-46, chief research engr plant food div since '48. Am Inst Chem Engrs—Am Chem Soc. Swift & Company, Plant Food Division, 150 Marble St., Calumet City, Ill.

13 MORTIMER, John William. Metals (Non-destructive testing); Pressure vessels (Design); Welding (Nonferrous). b'12. BS in mech engring '35 (Pa State Coll); metall '39 (Poly Inst Brooklyn). Research on use of X-ray, magnaflux, zyglo, and supersonic non-destructive tests of metals, welding brass and aluminum with inert arcs, welding pure copper to asme code with inert arc, structural design pressure vessels including high pressure and vacuum service, high and low temperature service, heat exchangers and coils, pressure, pipe work. With M W Kellogg Co '35-41; welding insp and cons Union Carbide & Carbon Corp '41-43; welding engr and cons Whitlock Mfg Co since '43. Am Welding Soc. Whitlock Manufacturing Co., Hartford 10, Conn.

14 MORTON, Conrad Vernon. Ferns; Fern allies; Gesneriaceae; Flora of West Indies and Mexico. b'05. AB '28 (U Calif). Editor: American Fern Journal. With Smithsonian Inst since '28, curator div ferns since '48. Smithsonian Institution, Washington 25.†☺

15 MORTON, Harry E. Medical bacteriology. b'06. Grad '25 (Mich Normal Coll); BS '30—MS '31—DSc '36 (U Mich). Research and writing on correlation of recorded variations and observations and dissociative studies of potentialities of species Corynebacterium diphtheriae, bacterial filters and filtration technics, new style assembly for fritted filters, improved technic for growing microorganisms under anaerobic conditions, bacteriostatic and bactericidal actions of some mercurial compounds on hemolytic streptococci in vivo and vitro studies. Author articles in field. Asso prof bacteriology Pa U Med Sch since '42. Sigma Xi—Electron Microscope Soc Am (charter)—Soc Am Bacteriologists. University of Pennsylvania, School of Medicine, Phila. 4. H: 4114 School Lane, Drexel Hill, Pa.†

16 MORTON, Hudson T. Bearings (Anti-friction). b'02. BS in chem engring '24 (U Mich); BBA '27 (La Salle Ext U). Research on testing and design anti-friction bearings, manufacture, application, load characteristics, and lubrication. Author: Anti-friction Bearings. Author articles: Balls for Bearings '39; others. Chem, metall, sales engr Hoover Ball & Bearing Co '24-25; standards engr The Fafnir Bearing Co '45-50; pres and gen mgr Morton Bearing Co since '50. Soc Automotive Engrs—Am Soc Metals—Engring Soc Detroit—Am Standards Assn(committeeman). Morton Bearing Co., 815 Wildt St. H: 2708 Brockman Blvd., Ann Arbor, Mich.

17 MORTON, Joseph Edward. Economic statistics; Sampling; Business cycles and time series. b'07. JD '30 (U Paris, U Prague); '31-32 (U Frankfurt); DSc '35 (U Geneva). Research in labor, sampling designs applied to human population, analysis of economic time series, inter-area comparisons of statistical nature; development and role of quantitative methods in social sciences. Author: L'Employé Privé '35. Research asst labor statis, law and econ Internat Labor Office Geneva '33; lecturer math econ and statis U Geneva '35-36; sec market research Czechoslovah Pulp and Paper Mfg Assn '36-38; prof statis and econ Knox Coll '39-45; research asso econ, statis, price analysis, sampling Nat Bur Econ Research NYC since '42; prof statis Cornell U since '46; cons housing statis Nat Housing Adminstrn since '47; chief statis research and development staff housing and house finance agency Washington since '50. Am Statis Assn—Am Econ Assn—Am Mathematics Society—Inst Math Statistics—Soc Quality Control Engrs—Econometric Soc — Royal Econ Soc — Royal Statis Soc(F). Housing and House Finance Agency, Rochambeau Bldg., Washington 25.

18 MORTON, Ohland. Texas-Mexican relations; Creek Indians. b'02. AB '25 (Southeastern Okla Teachers Coll); MA '29 (U Okla); PhD '39 (U Tex). Author: Teran and Texas '48; also articles in field. Okla Hist Soc (life mem)—Southwestern Hist Assn—NEA. Edinburg Junior College, Edinburg, Tex.

19 MORTON, Robert Lee. Mathematics (Arithmetic teaching methods, curricula, learning and textbooks). b'89. BS in edn '13 (Ohio U); grad study summers '14, '15 (Tchrs Coll Colum-

bia); AM '19—PhD '25 (Ohio State U). Member technical advisory group and special investigator Ohio School Finance Survey '32; consultant Educational Policies Commission; member Ohio Committee of National Survey of School Finance; member advisory board, education department Films Inc. Author: Teaching Arithmetic in the Intermediate Grades '27; Teaching Arithmetic in the Primary Grades '27; Laboratory Exercises in Educational Statistics '28; Statistical Tables '28; Teaching Arithmetic in the Elementary School, vol I Primary Grades '37, vol II Intermediate Grades '38, vol III Upper Grades '39. Co-author: Ohio Curriculum Guides in Arithmetic; Mathematics Through Experience, vols 1-3 '37; Making Sure of Arithmetic, Grades 1-8 '46-48; 10th Yearbook, National Council of Teachers of Mathematics '35, and 16th Yearbook '41. Prof edn Ohio U since '36. AAAS (F)—NEA—Ohio Edn Assn—Ednl Research Assn—Nat Soc for Study Edn—Nat Soc Coll Tchrs Edn—Nat Council Tchrs Math—Sigma Xi—Phi Beta Kappa.☺

20 MORTON, Stratford Lee. American antiques (Lamps, early lighting devices). b'87. Student '10 (Washington U). Has collected and studied American antiques 30 years and has a museum containing early examples of such things as early maps, prints, kitchen utensils, butter molds, churns, farm implements, boot jacks, paperweight-China-axes, early lighting fixtures from 1000 BC to kerosene in 1859, comprising some 850 different items. Large library early Western Americana. Gen agt emeritus Conn Mutual Life Ins Co. Acad Sci St Louis (chmn bd, pres)—Rush Light Soc New Eng. 1825 Boatmens Bonds Bldg.

21 MORTON, Walter Albert. Money; Banking; Utility rates of return. b'99. AB—MA '24 (U Michigan); fellow '24-25 (Robert Brookings Graduate Sch); PhD '27 (Univ Wis). Author: Outline of Money and Banking '37; British Finance 1930-1940 '43; also articles in field. Asst prof econ U Wis '27-31, asso prof '31-37, prof since '37. Social Sci Research Council Fellow '34-35 (U Chicago and London Sch Econ). Am Econ Assn—Mid West Econ Assn—Econometric Soc. Sterling Hall, University of Wisconsin, Madison, Wis. H: 108 N. Spooner St.☺

22 MORTON, William Markham. Charrs; Salmon and trout; Helminth parasites of salmon. b'05. BA '33 (Ia U); '35 (U Minn); MS '42 (Wash U). Columbia River surveys US Bur Fisheries Seattle '38-39; detailed study of charrs red salmon investigations at Karluk Alaska '39-42; pilchard studies US Fish and Wildlife Service '42-43; office Coordinator Fisheries Calif '43-46; US Fish and Wildlife Service Alaska Salmon Stream investigations '46-49, with River Basin Studies since '49. Am Fisheries Soc—Am Micros Soc—Soc Ichthyologists and Herpetologists—Am Soc Parasitol—Wildlife Soc. Fish and Wildlife Service, Swan Island, Portland 18, Ore.

23 MOSBY, Henry Sackett. Wildlife management; Wild turkey management; Forestry. b'13. BS '35 (Hampden Sydney); BSF and MF '37—PhD '41 (U Mich Sch Forestry and Conservation). Developed method of making large area wild turkey census. Co-author: (with C O Handley). The Wild Turkey in Virginia. Its Status, Life History and Management '43. Research fellow Va coop Wildlife Research Sta June-Dec '38; field biologist Commn Game and Inland Fisheries '39-42, acting supt '42-43, district game tech '46-47; dir Va coop Wildlife sta since Sep '47. Wildlife Soc—Soc British Foresters — Soc Mammalogist — Asso Am Ornithol Union—Va Council Wildlife Tech. Va Coop Wildlife Unit, Dept biology, Blacksburg, Va. H: Turner St.

10 MOSELEY, John Ohleyer. Christian antiquities (The Chalice of Antioch); College fraternities. b'93. Student '08-10 (Southwestern Presbyn U Clarksville Tenn); '29-30 (Grad Sch Stanford) summer '20 (Columbia); '25 (So br U Cal); AB '12—LLD '36 (Austin Coll Sherman Tex); grad '13 Southeastern Tchrs Coll Durant Okla); AM '16 (U Okla); BS '22—MA Rhodes Scholar '28 (Oxford Eng). Originator leadership training schools for national social fraternities; member permanent committee National Interfraternity Conference; province recorder Sigma Alpha Epsilon '23-24, archon '24-31, supreme herald '31-32, supreme dep archon '32-34, supreme archon '34-37, honorary supreme archon '37-39, director leadership training since '37. Pres U Nev since '44. Classical Assn Middle West and South—Am Philol Assn—Okla State Council Christian Edn(pres '39)—Phi Delta Phi—Eta Sigma Phi—Sigma Tau Delta—Alpha Phi Sigma—Pi Kappa Delta—Kappa Delta Pi—Phi Delta Kappa—Phi Eta Sigma—Phi Kappa Phi. P.O. Box 1856, Evanston. Ill.†◉

11 MOSER, Reuben Allyn. Birds of Nebraska. b'90. Student '08-10 (U Utah); AB '12—MD '15 (U Neb). Author articles in field. Asso prof medicine and dir med clinic at dispensary U Neb Coll Medicine since 1941; asst supt U Neb Coll Medicine Hosp since '42; staff mem Methodist, Clarkson and Immanuel Hosp Omaha; surgeon Reserve U S Pub Health Service since '43; med staff Union Pacific R R Employes Hosp Assn since '37; med dir Am Reserve Ins Co Omaha since '20. Omaha Midwest Clinic—Omaha Douglas Co Med Soc—Neb State Med Soc —AMA—Med Sect Am Life Assn— Assn Life Ins Med Dirs—Neb Ornithologists' Union—Ia Ornithologists' Union—Wilson Ornithol Club—Cooper Ornithol Club — Am Ornithologists' Union (treas and bus mgr). 1407 Medical Arts Bldg., Omaha 2, Neb. H: RFD No. 1, Omaha 4.†

12 MOSHER, Robert H. Chemistry and technology of coated and treated papers. b'19. BS (U Mass); MSc (Inst Paper Chem) (Lawrence Coll). Co-author and editor: Specialty Papers '50; Technology of Coated and Processed Papers '51. Contributor: Plastics Year Book '46-48; The Encyclopedia of Plastics '50. Research and development dept plastic div Monsanto Chem Co '42-45; tech dir Marvellum Co '45-48; indsl cons paper chem since '47; mgr mfg Holyoke Card & Paper Co '48-49; mgr Miami Valley Coated Paper Co since '50. Am Management Assn—ACS —Tech Assn Pulp and Paper Industry. Miami Valley Coated Paper Co., Franklin, O.

13 MOSKOVICS, Fredrick Ewan. Automobiles (Design, technological history); Power plants (aircraft). b'79. Student (Armour Inst Tech) (Poly Zurich). Designed and built Allen-Kingston car, Haupt-Rockwell; designed first taxicab in America; studies in technological history of the motor car; design aircraft power plants, propellers, gun turrets and collateral equipment. Issued patents relating to motor cars and equipment. Partner Brandenbury Bros & Co '04-08; vp, gen mgr, organizer Bristol Engring Corp '09-13; vp, comml mgr Nordyke & Marmon Mfg Co Indianapolis '13-23; pres, gen mgr Stutz Motor Car Co '23-29; pres Improved Products Corp '29-31; chmn exec com Dictograph Products Corp NYC '36-40; tech adv USAF '41-44; indsl cons A O Smith Corp since '44. Soc Automotive Engrs—Inst Aeronautical Scis. Received Meritorious Civilian Service Commendation with citation from US AF for work during World War II; Distinguished Service citation Automobile Old Timers '50.

14 MOSS, Fred August. Psychology (Endocrinology, psychiatry, automobile accidents). b'93. AB '13 (Mercer U); MA '20 (Columbia); PhD '22—MD '27 (George Washington U). Devised first objective method for measuring strength of emotional drives '22. Secretary Hoover Committee on Causes of Automobile Accidents, '25-26; director physiological studies for Society Automotive Engineers since '29. Author: Applications of Psychology '29; Psychology for Nurses '31; Comparative Psychology '34. Co-author: (with T Hunt) Foundations of Abnormal Psychology '32. Supt pub sch Alma Ga '13-17; dir standards and tests 1st Div US Army '19-21; prof psychol, George Washington U, '21-36; prof psychol Columbia, summer '31; visiting prof psychol Grad Sch US Naval Acad, Annapolis, summers '32-37; staff psychol Bur Pub Personnel '24-25; asst alienist DC '29-35; dir aptitude test Assn Am Med Colls since '29; dir Doctors Hosp. Washington Med Bldg Corp, Columbia Med Bldg Corp, Columbia Operating Co. AAAS(F)—AMA—Am Psychol Assn—Med Soc DC—George Washington U Med Soc — Am Med Editors' and Authors' Assn—Nat Soc Promotion Biol and Physiol Psychiatry —Southern Assn Philosophy and Psychol. Awarded Baylock sci medal Mercer U '13. Columbia Medical Bldg., 1835 I St. N.W., Washington. H: Seminary Hill, Alexandria, Va.◉

15 MOSSE, George L. Development of English sovereignty. b'18. Student '37-39 (U Cambridge, Historical Tripos); BS '41 (Haverford Coll); MA '41—PhD '47 (Harvard U). Research in development of the idea of sovereignty in England, 16th and 17th centuries; influence of French idea of sovereignty in England. Author: The Struggle for Sovereignty in England '50; The Reformation '53. Author articles: Thomas Hobbes: Jurisprudence at the Crossroads '46; Change and Continuity in the Tudor Constitution '47; The Anti-League '48; The Influence of Jean Bodin's Republique on English Political Thought '48. Asso prof hist State U Ia since '49. Medieval Acad Am—AHA—Econ Hist Assn, Eng. Department of History, University of Iowa, Iowa City, Ia.

16 MOSSER, Sawyer McArthur. Numismatics (Bibliography, ancient). b'05. AB '27 (Gettysburg Coll); AM '30 (Princeton). Author: A Bibliography of Byzantine Coin Hoards '35; The Endicott Gift of Greek and Roman Coins '41. Editor: Numismatic Notes and Monographs, The American Numismatic Society Museum Notes and Numismatic Literature since '47. Asst librarian Am Numismatic Soc '30-38, librarian '38-47, sec since '47. Am Numismatic Soc(F). American Numismatic Society, Broadway at 156th St., NYC 32.

17 MOSTELLER, (Charles) Frederick. Mathematical statistics; Public opinion. b'16. BSc '39—MSC '39 (Carnegie Inst Tech); AM '41—PhD '46 (Princeton U). Co-author: Gauging Public Opinion '43; Sampling Inspection '48; also articles in field. Asso prof Math statistics dept social relations Harvard since '48. Inst Math Statistics(F)—Am Statis Assn — Math Assn Am — Am Math Soc—AAAS—Am Soc Quality Control—Biometric Soc. Emerson Hall, Harvard University, Cambridge, Mass.

18 MOSTHAF, Edwin F. Ceramic powders; Metal powders. b'03. ME (Mich State Coll). Forming of ceramic and metal powders into tools, dies, special machinery, furnaces, and tunnel kilns; design first high temperature tunnel kilns for firing aircraft spark plug insulators and ignition terminals. Holds patents in field. Author articles: Precision Grinding or Fired Ceramics Using Metal Working Equipment; Tools and Dies for Powdered Metal Parts; Small Heat Treating Furnace, and others. Gen mgr B G Corp (mfr aircraft accessories) NYC '41-43; asst gen mgr H L Crowley Corp (mfrs ceramic and powdered metal parts) '43-47 asst gen mgr Gen Ceramic Corp '47-49; gen mgr Jeffry-Dewitt Corp (mfrs ceramic elec porcelain) '49-51. Am Ceramic Soc—Brit Ceramic Soc—Royal Soc Arts and Sci —Am Soc Tool Engrs. Registered profl engr 10 states.

19 MOTT, Frederick Dodge. Rural areas (Medical facilities, quality of medical care); Rural health; Health insurance (Compulsory, voluntary). b'04. AB '27 (Princeton); MD '32 (McGill U). Responsible for organization and administration first compulsory hospital care insurance program in North America; supervised pilot plan of compulsory medical care insurance in Saskatchewan; dealt with problems of public health, health facilities, personnel and training, research, quality of health care, and both voluntary and compulsory health insurance. Author: Rural Health and Medical Care '48. In field voluntary health insurance '37-46; chief med officer FSA '42-46; chief health services br Office Labor, War Food Adminstrn '43-45; chmn Saskatchewan Health Services Planning Commn since '46; acting dep minister Dept Pub Health Govt Saskatchewan since '49. Am Bd Preventive Med and Pub Health(founders group)—Am Pub Health Assn(F)— Can Pub Health Assn—Can Med Assn. See Latest Listings and Sketch Additions on page 601.

20 MOTT, Seward Hamilton. Site planning. b'88. Ed pub schs. Research on selection and planning of land for residential, commercial and industrial use, research on city planning problems. Co-author: Shopping Centers, an Analysis '49; (and editor) Community Builders' Handbook (3rd edit) '50. Mem Pitkin and Mott '14-35; dir Land Planning Div Fed Housing Adminstrn '35-42; exec dir Urban Land Inst '42-50; land planning engr and cons since '45. Am Inst Planners(bd gov '47-49) —Lambda Alpha—Urban Land Inst— Am Soc Planning Ofcls. 2151 K St., Washington 7.

21 MOULTON, William G(amwell). Linguistics (Germanic); Swiss German dialect and Romance patois. b'14. Student '33 (U Nancy); AB '35 (Princeton); '35-36 (U Berlin); PhD '41 (Yale). Consultant to State Department on teaching of German. Frankfurt, Germany, '50. Co-author: (with Jenni Karding Moulton) Spoken German '44. Faculty, instr, asst prof German Yale '37-47; asso prof, prof Germanic linguistics Cornell since '47; lang suervisor Office Provost Marshal Gen '44-45. Modern Lang Assn—Linguistic Soc Am. Division of Modern Languages, Cornell University, Ithaca.◉

22 MOUNTENEY, Leonard. Books (Binding, design). b'88. Student (Sch Art Nottingham Eng); '03-04 (Leicester Sch Art); 04-08 (Battersea Poly

London Eng). Bookbinder since '98, specialiing in hand binding since '05. Asst tchr bookbinding Sch Art Leicester Eng '10-12; master binder, designer, hand gold tooler Robert Riviere & Son London (book binders by appointment to royal family '13-24; controller fine hand binding Cuneo Press Inc Chicago since '26; work on permanent exhbn Cincinnati Inst Fine Arts. Awarded grand prix Empire Exhbn '11. The Cuneo Press, Inc., 2242 Grove St., Chgo.

10 MOUZON, James Carlisle. Electronics; Industrial instruments and automatic controls. b'07. AB '27 (Southern Methodist U); PhD '32 (Calif Inst Tech). Research in ionization of gases by positive ions, electronics, nuclear physics, submarine detection, temperature measurement, radiation pyrometry, nuclear instruments, automatic control. Holder various patent applications on amplifier design, industrial instruments and automatic controls. Author: Characteristics of Conversion Amplifiers and Self-Balancing Potentiometers '48; also articles in field. Instr and asst prof phys Duke U '32-41; physicist Naval Ordnance Lab Wash '41-42; asso prof phys Duke U '42-44; engring dept Brown Instrument Co '44-48, dir research '48-49; research and development bd Office Sec of Defense Wash '49-50; operations analysis Div Atomic Air Warfare. Am Phys Soc—AAAS—Sigma Xi. Hdqrs. U.S. Air Force, Assistant for Operations Analysis, Washington 25.†

11 MOVIUS, Hallam Leonard, Jr. Palaeolithic archeology (Old world); Pleistocene geology. b'07. BS '30—MA '32—PhD '37 (Harvard). Research in stone age archeology eastern hemisphere; contributed articles Britannica Book of the Year '40-42; field assistant Harvard-U Pa Expedition Central Europe Czech '30, Joint British-American Archeol Expedition Palestine '32; assistant director in charge stone age excavations Harvard Archeol Expedition Ireland '32-36; archeologist and assistant director American Southeast Asiatic Expedition Burma and Java '37-38; director Peabody Museum Expedition Eastern France '48. Author: The Irish Stone Age '42; two other books, also articles in field. With Peabody Mus since '36, curator palaeolithic archeol since '48. Soc Antiquaries of Lond(F)—Royal Archeol Inst Gt Brit and Ire—Royal Irish Acad—Geol Soc Am(F)—Am Anthropolog Assn(F)—Prehistoric Soc. Fellowship Am Sch Prehistoric Research western and central Europe '31. Peabody Museum, Harvard University, Cambridge '38, Mass.

12 MOWRER, O(rval) Hobart. Behavior (Learning, therapy). b'07. AB '29 (U Mo); PhD '32 (Johns Hopkins); NRC fellow '32-33 (Northwestern U) '33-34 (Princeton); Sterling fellow '34-36 (Yale); MA hon '48 (Harvard). Research on dynamics of personality, psychotheraphy, learning theory, psychology of language; consultant Community Service Society New York '43-44; clinical psychologist Office of Strategic Services Washington '44-45. Author: Learning Theory and Personality Dynamics '50. Co-author: Frustration and Aggression '39; Patterns for Modern Living '49. Contributor: Personality and Behavior Disorders '44; The Field of Clinical Psychology '48. Mem research staff Inst Human Relations and instr psychol Yale U '36-40; asst prof edn Harvard '40-43, asso prof '43-48, ed Harvard Edn Review '45-48; research prof psychol U Ill since '48. Am Psychol Assn(F, com on training in clin psychol, chmn '50 51) —AAAS(F)—AAUP— Midwestern Psychol Assn—Am Orthopsychiatric

Assn(F). Diplomate in clin psychol Am Bd Examiners Profl Psychol. 445 Gregory Hall, University of Illinois, Urbana, Ill.ⓖ

13 MOWRY, George Edwin. American political and social history (Progressive movement, liberalism, Theodore Roosevelt, twentieth century). b'09. AB '33 (Miami U); AM '34—PhD '38 (U Wis). Author: Theodore Roosevelt and the Progressive Movement '46. Co-author: American Society and the Changing World '42. Contbr: War as a Social Institution — T h e Historian's Perspective '41; also author articles in field. Instr hist U NC '38-40, asst prof '40-42; analyst QMC '42-43; policy analyst WPB '43-44; May Treat Morrison prof Am hist Mills Coll '44-47; prof Am hist U Ia '47-50; prof Am hist U Cal LA since '50. AHA—Miss Valley Hist Assn—AAUP—Railway and Locomotive Hist Soc Inc—Soc Am Historians. Department of History, University of California, LA. H: 3033 Roscomare Rd.

14 MOWRY, Harold. Subtropical horticulture; Subtropical ornamentals; Plant nutrition (Minor elements); Tung tree; Symbiotic nitrogen fixation (Casuarina). b'94. BSA '29—MSA '34 (U Fla). Author articles in field. Asst and horticulturist Fla Agrl Expt Sta U Fla '22-33, asst and asso dir '33-43, dir '43-50, ret.; agriculturist office fgn agricultural relations USDA since '50. AAAS(F)—Am Soc Hort Sci—Bot Soc Am—Fla Soc Hort—Fla Acad Sci—Sigma Xi—Phi Kappa Phi. Distinguished Service Award Fla Vegetable Com '47. 203 North West 15th Terrace, Gainesville, Fla.

15 MOYER, Andrew Jackson. Penicillin and organic acid production; Industrial fermentation; Fungus physiology. b'99. AB '22 (Wabash Coll); MS '25 (ND Agrl Coll); PhD '29 (U Md). Devised the lactose-corn steep liquor medium which is now used in the large scale production of penicillin in both surface and submerged (deep tank) cultures. Holder of US and foreign fermentation patents; US Patents on penicillin production. Author articles in field. With US Dept of Agr since '29, now research at Northern Regional Research Lab. Bur. of Agrl and Indsl Chem Peoria Ill. Bot Soc Am—Ill Acad Sci—Phi Kappa Phi—Sigma Xi. Lasker group award '46. Northern Regional Research Lab., Bureau of Agrl and Indsl Chemistry, Peoria, Ill.†

16 MOYER, Joseph Kearney. Federal and state taxation; Education for business. b'90. BCS cum laude '17 (NYU); LLB '26—LLD hon '47 (Southeastern U Washington); spl course '12 (Cornell U). With US Treasury, Bureau Internal Revenue '19-34; private law practice since '34; dean Southeastern U. Am Bar Assn—Am Inst Accountants—Beta Gamma Sigma. Author articles on federal taxation. 1343 H St., Washington 5.ⓖ

17 MOYER, Wendell William. Starch and lignin chemistry. b'03. BS '24 (Findlay Coll O); AB '26—MS '27—PhD '29 (U Ill). Research on the structure of chlorophyll, strychnos alkaloids, chemiluminescence and molecular rearrangements, synthesis of phenol and detergents, reactions of nitrosyl chloride, products derived from corn and soybeans, structure of starch, composition of corn syrups, monosodium glutamate and amino acids, nutrients for antibiotics, levulinic acid, refining of soybean oil, paper pulp and wood. Patents on dyes, reactions of nitrosyl chloride, phenol, sulfonated fatty acids, levulinic acid, refining soybean oil, nutrients for penicillin and streptomycin production. Author articles in field.

Research asst to Prof J B Conant Harvard '29-30; research asso Princeton '31-33; project leader nitrogen div Solvay Process Co Syracuse '33-37; dir research A E Staley Mfg Co Decatur Ill '37-47; dir research Central Research Department Crown Zellerbach Corp Camas Wash since '47. ACS (chmn div sugar chem and technol '47)—AAAS—Tech Assn Pulp and Paper Ind—Sigma Xi—Starch Round Table. Nat Research Council fellow '30-31. Central Research Department, Crown Zellerbach Corporation, Camas, Wash.

18 MOYLE, John B. Aquatic chemical biology (Seed plants); Production of waters. b'09. BA '33—PhD '38 (U Minn). Research in chemical factors affecting distribution of larger aquatic plants '34-38, biological survey of streams of north shore of Lake Superior '40-42, wild rice in Minn '40-44, factors influencing pike-perch production in ponds '39-44, aquatic and marsh vegetation in Minn '44-45, chemistry of Minn lakes and streams '40-48, surveys of St. Louis River, Root River and upper Mississippi River watershed in Minn '39-48, algal control with copper sulphate at AAAS symposium '47. Co-author: (with N Hotchkiss) The Aquatic and Marsh Vegetation of Minnesota and Its Value to Waterfowl '45; (with L L Smith Jr) A Biological Survey and Fishery Management Plan for the Streams of the Lake Superior North Shore Watershed '44; (with L L Smith Jr) Factors Influencing Production of Yellow Pike-Perch in Minnesota Rearing Ponds '45; also author articles in field. Teaching asst U Minn '33-38; aquatic biologist Minn Dept Conservation '38-48. Wildlife Soc—Limnological soc—Phycological Soc—Am Fisheries Soc—Minn Acad Sci—Phi Beta Kappa —Sigma Xi. 355 Shubert Bldg., St. Paul.

19 MRAK, Emil M(arcel). Food technology; Yeast taxonomy and ecology; Fruit dehydration. b'01. BS '26—MA '28 —PhD '37 (U Calif). Co-author: (with G F Stewart) Advances in Food Research; also author articles in field. Prof and mycologist head div food tech U Calif since '48. Food technologist chmn food research War Dept QMC '44-45. Soc Am Bacteriologists—Inst Food Technologists—Am Mycol Soc—Calif Bot Soc—Soc Gen Microbiol (England)—Sigma Xi. Division of Food Technology, University of California, Berkeley 4.†ⓖ

20 MRGUDICH, John Neil. Instrumentation; X-ray diffraction; Electron miscroscopy; Dry cells. b'07. BS '29—MS '30 (U Ariz); PhD '33 (U Ill). Teaching asst U Ariz '29-30, U Ill '30-33; spl lecturer physics Marquette U '33-34; research asso U Ill '34-40; research dir asso chief engr Burgess Battery Co '40-46; electron microscopist Signal Corps Engring Labs '46; chief photog br Signal Corps '47; research dir elec div Winchester Repeating Arms Co since '47. Am Electrochem Soc—Am Chem Soc—Army Signal Assn. Winchester Repeating Arms Co., New Haven, Conn. H: 47 Homelands Terrace, Hamden.

21 MUCHNIC, Helen. Russian literature. b'03. AB '25 (Vasaar Coll); '28-29 (London U); PhD '37 (Bryn Mawr Coll). Author: Dostoevsky's English Reputation '39; Thomas Hardy and Thomas Mann in Essays in Honor of W A Neilson '46; An Introduction to Russian Literature '47; also articles in field. Instr English Lit Smith Coll '30, prof Russian and comparative Lit since '47; lecturer ASTP Program Yale '43-44; vis lecturer Harvard '48. 69 Belmont Av., Northampton, Mass.

10 **MUDD, Harvey Seeley.** Mining Engineering, exploration, development and management. b'88. EM '12—ScD '47 (Columbia); LLD '41 (U Cal), '43 (Loyola U). Mining engr Bisbee Ariz '12; pres and mng dir Cyprus Mines Corp since '28; dir So Pacific Com since '40, Texas Gulf Sulphur Com since '36; trustee Rand Corp; voting trustee Pacific Mutual Life Ins Co since '38; engr US Bur of Mines '17-18; sec War Minerals Comm '17-18; dir Founders Ins Co since '46; dir Mesabi Iron Co trustee S W Museum since '28; Cal Inst Tech since '29; chmn bd fellows Claremont Coll since '35. AI MME(past pres)—Mining and Metall Soc—Sigma Xi—Tau Beta Pi. Pacific Mutual Bldg., Los Angeles. H: 1240 Benedict Canyon Dr., Beverly Hills.◎

11 **MUDD, Richard Dyer.** Industrial hygiene. b'01. AB '21—MA '22—PhD '25—MD '26 (Georgetown U). Organizer first symposium on industrial health sponsored by a county medical society '39; organized first American Medical Association approved residency training program in industrial health '49; former medical director several divisions General Motors Corporation; organized industrial medical services various Air Forces Bases during World War II. Author articles: Potential Inguinal Hernia '34; Prevention of Colds by Vaccinotherapy '36; Relation of Accidents to Day of Week '37; Cleanliness in Industry '41; Tuberculosis in Industry '38; Disabling Sickness among Industrial Workers '41; Absenteeism in Industry '41; A Cooperative effort in the Control of Tuberculosis '38; Influenza Epidemic at Chevrolet-Grey Iron Foundry '47. Intern Tuberculosis Hosp Washington '25-26; intern, resident Henry Ford Hosp Detroit '26-28; med dir several divisions Gen Motors Corp; instr indsl health Sch Aviation Med San Antonio '43-46; dir, residency indsl health Saginaw Gen Hosp '49; surgeon 10th Air Force Hdqrs Selfridge AFB Mich since '50. Am Bd Preventive Med and Pub Health—Am Indsl Hygiene Assn—Am Pub Health Assn—AMA (F) —Nat. Rehabilitation Assn—Am Assn Indsl Physicians. 10th Air Force, Selfridge Air Force Base, Mich.

12 **MUEHLBERGER, Clarence Weinert.** Toxicology; Scientific criminal investigations; Alcoholic intoxication; Bombs and explosions. b'96. BS in Chem Engring '20 (Armour Inst Tech); MS '22—PhD '23 (U Wis). Author articles in field. Lecturer in toxicology U Mich since '41; Mich State toxicologist and dir Mich Crime Detection Lab since '41. AMA(F)—Am Chem Soc—Soc for Pharmacology and Exptl Therapeutics—Soc Exptl Biology and Medicine—AAAS—Soc Med Jurisprudence—Am Indsl Hygiene Assn—Mich Path Soc—Am Pub Health Assn—Tau Beta Pi—Sigma Xi. Michigan Department of Health Laboratories, Lansing, Mich.†◎

13 **MUELDER, Milton E.** Military government (Administration). b'08. AB '30 (Knox Coll); '30-31 fellowship Inst Internat Edn (Freiburg U Germany); AM '32—PhD '39 (U Mich); AM '43 (Columbia). Served as lieutenant US Navy '43-45; chief program branch control office Office Military Government US '45-47; deputy director educational and cultural affairs div '48-49. Faculty Mich State Coll since '35, head dept polit sci and pub adminstrn since '49, dir office research development and co-ordinator program for adoption U Ryukus at Okinawa, Office of President since '51, dean sch sci and arts since 1952. Internat City Mgrs Assn—Am Polit Sci Assn—Am Soc Pub Adminstrn—Am Hist Assn—Nat Municipal League—Phi Beta Kappa. Michigan State College, East Lansing.◎

14 **MUELLER, Alexander.** Chemical spectrophotometry; Vitamin technology. b'13. BSc '37—MSc '39 (Mich State Coll); advanced study (Wayne U). Research in biophysical chemistry and instrumentation. Author articles: Absorption Spectrum of the Antimony Trichloride-Ergosterol Reaction '46; Absorption Spectra of Steroid-Antimony Trichloride Reaction Products '49. Co-author: (with S H Fox) Chemical Determination of Niacin '47; (with F W Lamb and G W Beach) Quantitative Determination of Ergosterol Cholesterol and 7-Dehydrocholestrol '46. Spectrochemist Gelatin Products Corp Detroit '39-42; vitamin research chemist R P Scherer Corp Detroit '42-46, research cons vitamin technol since '46. Optical Soc Am—Am Chem Soc—AAAS—Am Phamaceutical Assn—Nat Farm Chemurgic Council. 9425 Grinnell Av., Detroit 13. H: 682 Thayer Blvd., Northville.

15 **MUELLER, Alfred Don.** Clinical psychology (Rorschach and other projective techniques); Psychotherapy; Child guidance; Adult education; Educational psychology. b'93. PhB '18—PhM '19 (U Wis); AM '26—PhD '27 (Yale). Clinical study and evaluation of personality and its dynamic operation, analysis and treatment of personality and education of the maladjusted personality; psychological adjustment of neuro-psychiatric and paraplegic veterans. Author: Progressive Trends in Rural Education '26; Teaching in Secondary Schools '26; Principles and Methods in Adult Education '37. Contributor to Encyclopedia of Child Guidance '43; also author articles in field. Teach pub schs Osaukee County Wis '12-14: supervising prin pub schs Cashton Wis '18-21; prof edn and psychology Mass State Normal Sch '23-29; lecturer Fitchburg Normal Sch summers '27-28; U extension div Mass State Dept Edn '25-29, Grad Sch of Edn Yale '28-29; asso prof secondary edn U Tenn '29-38, dir student teaching '34-38; dir Psychol Service Center Knoxville; dir psychologist Knoxville Child Guidance and Adult Adjustment Clinic '38-47; Am Red Cross '43-37; prof psychol Ft Sanders Hosp Nurses Training Sch '45-47; clin psychol Veterans Administrn med teaching group Kennedy Hosp Memphis since '47; chief clinical psychologist since '50; director curriculum studies Tenn high schs '29-34; mem Curriculum Com of Tenn Ednl Survey '34; mem Commn of Assn Colls and Secondary Schs of So States '29-35. Am Psychol Assn—Clin Psychology (F)—Acad Polit and Social Sci—Nat Soc Coll Teachers of Edn—Nat Soc Study of Edn—AAAS—AAUP—Tenn State Teachers Assn—Phi Kappa Phi. Diplomate in clin psychol. VA Med Group, Box 130, Kennedy Hospital, Memphis 15. H: 4035 Tutwiler Rd., Memphis 12.†◎

16 **MUELLER, Hans Alexander.** Woodcuts; Woodengraving. b'88. Ed in Germany. Author: Woodcuts and Woodengraving, How I Make Them '38; How I Make Woodcuts and Woodengraving '45; Woodcuts of New York '38. Teacher graphic arts Columbia U since '38; illustrator books for Limited Edition Club NY, Random House, Doubleday-Doran, Viking Press, Peter Pauper Press and others. Columbia University, Art School, NYC.

17 **MUELLER, John Henry.** Musicology; History of symphony orchestra; Sociology of art. b'95. AB '20—MA '21 (U Mo); PhD '28 (U Chicago); '19 (U de Montpellier France). Author: Theories of Aesthetic Appreciation '34; Is Art the Product of Its Age? '35; Deutsche Musik in USA '38; The Folklore of Art '38; Some Sociological Reflections on the Dance '39. Co-author: (with K Hevner) Trends in Musical Taste '42; The American Symphony Orchestra '51; also author articles in field. Asst prof sociol U Mo '25-26; asso prof sociol U Ore '26-33; Ind U '35-46, prof since '46. Am Sociol Soc—Am Musicol Soc—Am Statis Assn—Population Assn Am—Phi Beta Kappa. Indiana University, Bloomington, Ind.†

18 **MUELLER, Oswald.** Lepidoptera, flora and fauna of Texas; Texas history. b'89. Student summers '36-37 (U Houston). Translator: Roemer's Texas '36; also articles in field. Teacher Lutheran Sch Houston '10-43; lecturer on nature subjects. Tex Acad Sci—Houston Outdoor Nature Club. 746 E. 6½ St., Houston 7, Tex.

19 **MUELLER, William A(nton).** Cellulose chemistry; High polymers. b'11. BS '33—PhD '38 (U Wis). Study structure and processing cotton linters and wood pulp in relation to utilization for rayon yarns, films, manufacture derivatives. Issued patents in field. Asst prof chem SE MO State Coll '38-43, asso prof chem and physics Southwestern U '43-44; research chem Buckeye Cotton Oil Co since '44, head research dept since '50. ACS—Tech Assn Pulp and Paper Industry—Sigma Xi—Phi Beta Kappa. Buckeye Cotton Oil Co., Memphis 8.

20 **MUENSCHER, Walter Conrad.** Aquatic plants; Weeds; Algae; Myxomycetes; Poisonous plants of the United States. b'91. AB '14 (State Coll Washington); AM '15 (U Neb); PhD '21 (Cornell U). Author: Keys to Woody Plants, sixth edit '46; Keys to Spring Plants, sixth edit '46; Aquatic Plants of the United States '44; Poisonous Plants of the United States '39; Weeds '42. Asst in bot Cornell U '16-17, instr '17-23, asst prof '23-37, prof since '37. Bot Soc Am—Am Soc Plant Taxonomists. Department of Botany, Cornell University, Ithaca, N.Y.

21 **MUENSTERBERGER,** **Warner.** Human relations (Far East and Southeast Asia); Psychodynamics; Pomo Indians (California); Indonesian personality and culture. b'13. Student '33 (U Heidelberg); '33-36 (U Berlin); '36 (U Leyden Holland); PhD '38 (U Basle Switzerland). Study of culture and personality; research in human relations, especially in the Far East and Southeast Asia; field studies among the Pomo Indians California. Author several books and articles on Indonesian personality and culture (in Dutch). Contributor: Psychoanalysis and the Social Sciences '50, '51; Beitraege zur Gesellungs und Voelkerwissenschaft '50. Editor of Psychoanalysis and Culture '51. Research asso and cons Royal Inst for Tropics Amsterdam '39-47; lectr Columbia U dept anthrop '47-48, cons research project in contemporary cultures '47-49; lectr NY State U Med Center dept psychiatry since '50. Am Psychol Assn—NY State Psychol Assn—Am Orthopsychiatric Assn—Am Ethnol Soc—Am Soc Applied Anthrop—Royal Anthrop Inst Gt Brit and Ireland(F)—Netherlands Royal Inst for Indies(F). 50 East 72d St., NYC 21.

22 **MUHLENBRUCH, Carl William.** Engineering materials (Strength, properties). b'15. BS '37 (U Ill); MS '43 (Carnegie Inst Tech). Holder several US patents. Author: Testing of Engineering Materials '44; also articles in field. Asso prof civil engring Northwestern Tech Inst since '48. Am Soc Testing Materials (com D-7 on wood) —Research Council on Riveted and Bolted Structural Joints—ASCE—Am Soc Engring Edn—Sigma Xi. Received Sanford E Thompson award of Am Soc Testing Materials '45. Department of Civil Engineering, Northwestrn Technological Institute, Evanston, Ill.†

10 MUIR, J Lawrence. Petroleum geology. b'03. BS in geol '30—MS '30 (U Okla). Sub-surface interpretation of stratigraphy by detailed studies of well cuttings. Author article: Methods in the Examination and Logging of Well Cuttings '51; Gypsum-Anhydrite Problem of the Blaine Formation, Oklahoma. Surface geol Gulf Refining Co of La '30; sub-surface geol Amerada Petroleum Corp Okla '33-48; chief geol Champlin Refining Co '48-51, now vp in charge exploration and development. Am Assn Petroleum Geol—Am Inst Mining Engrs—Soc Econ Paleontol and Mineral—Geol Soc Am—Phi Beta Kappa—Sigma Gamma Epsilon. Champlin Refining Co., Enid, Okla.

11 MULAIK, Stanley B. Isopods; Reptiles; Spiders; Mites. b'02. BS '28 (Pa Teachers Coll); MS '31 (Cornell U); summer '29 (Mich U); '44-48 (Utah U). Co-author: (with Dorothea Mulaik) New Species and Records of American Terrestrial Isopods '42. Author: New Mites in the Caeculidae '44; also articles in field. Instr biol Utah U since '39. Tex Acad Sci(F)—U Acad Sci—Sigma Xi—AAAS—Soc Systematic Zool—Am Nature Study Soc (past vp) —Am Soc Herpetologists and Ichthiologists—Herpetologists League. Biology Department, University of Utah, Salt Lake City.

12 MULLEN, Buell (Mrs. J. Bernard Mullen). Murals (Metallurigcal). b'01. Grad (Miss Spence's Sch NY) (U Sch for Girls Chicago); student (Brit Acad Rome); private study. Research, experimentation, development technique of painting on stainless steel and other metals, to provide permance, texture, and express technological development; experimented with heat-treating of stainless steel to produce color or tone; works with gold, stainless steel, monel, aluminum, copper, chromium, etc.; first mural on stainless steel in world placed in Hispanic Room Library of Congress '40; two murals US Naval Academy '41; mural for Ministry of War Buenos Aires '42, Great Lakes Naval Station '43, Ministry of Communications Rio de Janerio '45, Dun & Bradstreet '51, others; panels on steel for US Steel '49-50; 2 panels Searle Found.; 2 murals for Armco Steel, 1 mural Dorland Steel; panel Carbide & Carbon Corp. Author: (movie short) Painting on Metals. Gold medal All-Ill Soc Fine Arts. Exhibns Feragil, Findlay, Smithsonian Nat Collection, Dayton Art Inst, Architectural League NY, Nat Mural Painters, Art Inst Chicago, Salon Paris, Gruppo Moderno Rome. 222 Central Park South, NYC.†◎

13 MULLEN, Cronan. Theology and religion. b'05. EE '30 (Polytech Inst Brooklyn); certificate '31 (Gen Electric Test Course); AB '35 (St Bonaventure Coll NY); student '36-40 (Holy Name Coll Washington). Instr math and physics St Bonaventure Coll '33-35; joined Franciscan Order '35, ordained priest Roman Catholic Church '39; asst professor physics Siena Coll Loudonville NY '40-44; prof physics, head physics dept, chmn science div, mem bd instruction since '44. Am Inst EE—Am Assn Physics Tchrs—Am Soc Engring Edn—AAAS —Theta Kappa Nu. Siena College, Loudonville, N.Y.◎

14 MULLER, Cornelius Herman. American oaks (Taxonomy, southwestern United States, Mexican, Central American); Vegetation of Mexico; Plant root development; Taxonomy of tomato; Plants of southwestern United States. b'09. BA '32—MA '33 (U Tex); PhD '38 (U Ill). Expeditions to Mexico to collect plants and study vegetation. Author articles in field. Asso prof bot U Calif since '50; research asso and adv council Santa Barbara Bot Garden since '48. Ecol Soc Am—Am Soc Plant Taxonomists—Calif Bot Soc—Western Soc Naturalists—Sigma Xi. University of California, Santa Barbara College, Santa Barbara, Calif.

15 MULLIN, Charles Earl. Textile chemistry (Rayon wool anti-shrink processes, depainting wool and noils). b'90. (Juniata Coll); MSc (National U); DSc (U de Nancy, France); (Phila Textile Sch). Consulting chemist textile, rayon and related industries since '17; research on acetate silk and its dyes. Author: Acetate Silk and Its Dyes '27; also articles in field. Abstractor Chem Abstracts since '20. Traveling chem Marshall and Co Chicago '10-12; chief chem, asst supt Chem Pigments Corp St Helena Md '13-14; chief chem Eavenson and Levering Co Camden '14-27; prof chem head div chem Clemson Coll SC '27-33; cons chem since '17. Textile Inst Eng(F)— Am Inst Chem(F)—Am Chem Soc—Am Assn Textile Chem and Colorists—Soc Dyers Colourists (Eng)—Soc Chem Industry (Eng)—Chem Soc Eng(F). 111 Fourth St., Huntington, Pa.

16 MULLIN, Francis Joseph. Physiology. b'06. AB '29 (U Mo); SM '33— PhD '36 (U Chicago). Research in physiology of sleep, effect of drugs on peripheral sensitivity, and ionic changes in the cerebro spinal fluid affecting circulation and respiration. Author articles in field. Adjunct prof physiol U Tex Med Sch '35-38; instr physiol U Chicago '38-43, asst prof '43-47, asso prof since '47, asst dean students biol sci div including Med Sch '44-46, dean of students since '46, sec of faculties since '47. Am Physiol Soc —Assn Am Med Colls (com on personnel practices)—Soc Exptl Biol and Med—Sigma Xi. Award for excellence in undergrad teaching U Chicago '46. University of Chicago, Chicago 37.

17 MULLIN, Robert Spencer. Plant pathology. b'12. BS '34 Hampden-Sydney Coll); MS '36 (Va Poly Inst); PhD '50 (U Minn). Research in entomology and plant quarantine, plant disease control, barberry eradication, Blacksburg Va '36-37. Asst state leader barberry eradication in Blacksburg Va '37-41, state leader '41-44; work in plant path, plant breeding Va Truck Expt Sta '45-46; asso prof biol Va Poly Inst Blacksburg '46-48; plant path Va Truck Experiment Sta Norfolk since '48, head department plant pathology. AAAS—Bot Soc Am—Am Phytopath Soc—Va Acad Sci. Virginia Truck Experiment Station, P.O. Box 2160, Norfolk, Va.

18 MULLISON, Wendell Roxby. Plant physiology; Plant hormones; Weed killers. b'13. BA '34 (U NM); PhD '38 (U Chicago). Author articles in field. Plant physiologist Dow Chem Co since '46. Am Bot Soc—Am Soc Hort Sci—Am Soc Plant Physiol—Am Agron Soc Am Soc Soil Sci—Sigma Xi. Asst tech dir Dow Inter-American and Dow International Dow Chemical Company, Midland, Mich.†

19 MUMAW, Everett Elliott. Calendar reform. b'87. Student '05-06 (Hiram Coll); '07-09 (U Wash); BS in CE '15—CE '20 (Case Inst). Research and compilation tables of dates dividing the year into 13 equal months starting with the Vernal Equinox. Author Spectrum calendar. AAAS—Sigma Xi. H: P.O. Box 214, Kingsville, O.

20 MUNCH, James Clyde. Pharmacology; Bioassays; Toxicology; Statistics. b'96. BS '15—MS '16 (Ill Wesleyan U); PhD '24 (George Washington U). Revision committees United States Pharmacopoeia X, XI, XII; National Formulary VI; Recipe Book III. Author: Bio-assays—A Handbook of Quantitative Pharmacology '31; Manual of Biological Assaying '37; Elementary Pharmacology '45; also articles in field. Prof pharmacol and dir research pharmacy sch Temple U since '31, prof pharmacol Dental Sch since '44; lecturer pharmacol Hahnemann Med Coll and Hosp since '40; cons lab service in pharmacol and bio-assays since '38. Served as lt San Corps US Army '18-19. AAAS(F)—ACS (life mem)—Am Pharm Assn (vp)—Assn Mil Surgeons —Internat Physiol Soc—Physiol Soc— Md and Pa Acad Sci—Am Statis Assn (life mem)—Sigma Xi—Phi Kappa Phi. 306 S. 69 St., Upper Darby, Pa.†◎

21 MUNCIE, Curtis Hamilton. Instruments (Medical); History of medicine Deafness. Diagnosis and correction deformities of Eustachian tubes by digital reconstruction; research, cause and corrective treatment deafness. 515 Park Av., NYC.

22 MUNCY, Lysbeth Walker. History of modern Germany; Junkers. b'10. AB '31 (Vassar Coll); MA '38—PhD '43 (Brown U); Resident fellow '42-43 (Mt Holyoke Coll); Exchange fellowship for Berlin from Inst of Internat End '34-35; Miss Abbott's Sch Alumnae Fellowship '40-41 (Brown U). Special study of political and sociological influence of Junkers in modern Prussia carried on since 1941. Author: The Junker in the Prussian Administration under William II, 1888-1914; also articles in field. Instr in hist and govt Sweet Briar Coll '43-47, asst prof '47-53; asst dean '47-51; asso prof since '53. AHA—Va Soc Sci Assn—Am Assn U Profs—So Hist Assn. Sweet Briar College, Sweet Briar, Va.

23 MUNDAL, Torald. Power plants; Flood control. b'97. CE '23 (Tech U Norway). Design hydro-electric, flood control, navigation, irrigation projects in separate or combined developments both foreign and US. Designer hydroelec and steam power plants Duke Power Co Charlotte NC '25-29, W S Lee Engring Corp '29-34; project design engr TVA '34-45; engr in charge Clark Hill Design and Constrn US Corps Engrs '45-47; hydro-elec engr Interam Constrn Corp Buenos Aires '47-48; chief design engr Internat Engring Co Inc since '48. Am Soc CE. 74 New Montgomery St., SF 5.

24 MUNDAY, Daniel Peter. Medieval philosophy. b'07. AB '29 (St. Joseph's Coll); MA '35 (Niagara U); PhD '38 (U Toronto). Prof philos Niagara U '38-50, dean Sch Edn and Grad Sch '48-50. Pres St Joseph's College Princeton NJ since '50. Chaplain US Navy '43-46. Medieval Acad Am. St. Joseph's College, Princeton, N.J.

25 MUNGER, Hamnett Pitzer. Air pollution; Strip steel finishing. b'03. BS in chem engring '25 (Georgia Inst Tech); MA in chem engring '28 (Columbia); PhD in phys chem '29 (U Pittsburgh). Research on methods of reducing contaminant concentration from air in industrial plants, invented directional dirt-fall collector for correlating wind direction and dirt fall; research and development, installation and operation in final commercial form sheet electro-galvanizing equipment and strip electrolytic tin-plate equipment. Granted patents in field. Indsl research F Mellon Inst '26-28; in charge metall research lab Armco Steel Corp Research Lab '29-36; asst chief metall and supt elecfroplating Rep Steel Corp '36-43; supt tin finishing Youngstown Sheet and Tube Co '45-48; research air pollution Battelle Memorial Inst since '48. Sigma Xi—Phi Kappa Phi—Alpha Chi Sigma—Phi Lambda Upsilon—ACS—Am Inst Chem Engrs—Am Meteorol Soc—Air Pollution and Smoke Prevention Assn Am—Am Iron and Steel Inst—Assn Iron and Steel Engrs—Am Indsl Hygiene Assn—ASME (mem air pollution com). Battelle Memorial Institute, 505 King Av., Columbus 1, O.

10 MUNHALL, Burton David. Firearms and ammunition. b'10. Spl student (Cleveland Coll, Penn Coll, Case Sch Applied Sci). Research and development of new types of arms and ammunition, identification of old arms and amunition, physical testing of arms and ammunition as to velocity, pressure, function; consultant in crimes or civil cases; has access to one of largest accumulations of arms and ammunition data in US with full testing facilities, extensive ammunition reference collection and large comprehensive arms collection. Author: Metric Pistol and Revolver Cartridges '48. Co-author: (with H P White) Catalog of Cartridge Manufacturers and Base Markings '44; also author articles in field. With H P White Co ordnance engrs since '36, mgr since '39. Nat Rifle Assn—Army Ordnance Assn—Cleveland Engring Soc—Internat Assn for Identification. H. P. White Lab., Box 331, Bel Air, Md. H: 700 Ridgewood Rd., Bel Air.

11 MUNN, Norman Leslie. Animal psychology; Human adjustment. b'02. AB '27 (Springfield Mass Coll); AM '28—Fellow '28-29—PhD '30 (Clark U). Author: An Introduction to Animal Psychology '33; Psychological Developent '38; A Laboratory Manual in Experimental Psychology '38-48; Psychology—The Fundamentals of Human Adjustment '46; A Student's Manual to Accompany Psychology '46. Prof and head dept psychol Bowdoin Coll since '46. AAAS(F)—Am Psychol Assn—Australasian Soc for Psychol and Philos—So Soc for Philos and Psychol—E Psychol Assn—Sigma Xi. 17 Belmont St., Brunswick, Me.

12 MUNNS, Edward Norfolk. Shelterbelts; Watershed management; Reforestation. b'89. MS '11 (U Mich). Field investigations of shelterbelts since '35; participated in International Union of Forest Research Organizations and investigation of forest research methods throughout western Europe '29. Author articles in field. Dir Converse Forest Experiment Sta San Bernardino Calif '12-17; forest examiner Forest Service Washington detailed to War Inds Bd on wood prodn problems '17-19; research asst Forest Service San Francisco '19-21, asst state forester Sacramento Calif '21-23, charge office of forest expt stas Washington '23-38, chief Div Forest Influences Research Washington since '38. AAAS(F)—Soc Am Foresters—Am Meteorol Soc—Soil Sci Assn—Am Geophys Union—Internat Union Forest Research Organizations (vp, exec council for US). United States Forest Service, Department of Agriculture, Washington 25.†

13 MUNRO, Jonathan Alexander. Economic entomology; Beekeeping. b'96. BSA '22 (Ontario Agrl Coll); MS '25 (Kan State Coll); '34-35 (U Minn); PhD '42 (Cornell). Author articles in field. Chmn dept entomology, state entomologist ND Agrl Coll since '26. Entomol Soc Am—AAAS(F)—Am Assn Econ Entomol(F, vp '44)—ND Hist Assn—Apiary Inspectors Am (pres since '47)—Central States Plant Bd (sec-treas since '45)—Sigma Xi—Phi Kappa Phi. Department of Entomology, North Dakota Agricultural College, Fargo, ND.

14 MUNRO, Thomas. Art (Philosophy, psychology, education, museums, primitive); Aesthetics (comparative); Cultural history. b'97. AB '16—AM '17—PhD '20 (Columbia). Author: Scientific Method in Aesthetics '28; Great Pictures of Europe '30; Educational Work at the Cleveland Museum of Art '40; The Arts and Their Interrelations '49. Co-author: An Introduction to Reflective Thinking '23; American Economic Life '25; Primitive Negro Sculpture '26; Art and Education '29; Methods of Teaching the Fine Arts '35; Art in American Life and Education '41; The Future of Aesthetics '42. Editor: Journal of Aesthetics; also author articles in field. Prof art Western Reserve U since '31; curator of edn Cleveland Museum of Art since '31. Am Philos Assn—Coll Art Assn—Nat Art Edn Assn—Am Assn Museums—AAAS—Am Society for Aesthetics (pres '42-44)—Am Head Arts Sci(F). Cleveland Museum of Art, Cleve. 6.†☉

15 MUNSON, William Bruce. Near Eastern history (Ottoman Empire, Turkey); Eighteenth century intellectual history. b'13. AB '36—AM '37—PhD '40 (U Ill). Author: Guide to the Study of the History of Western Civilization '47; The Peace of Karlowitz '40. Asso prof hist U Miami since '46. Received grant-in-aid Am Council Learned Socs for study Turkish and Arabic langs '38. University of Miami, Miami, University Branch, Fla.†

16 MUNTWYLER, Edward. Biochemistry (Blood and tissues). b'03. AB '24 (Denver U); MS '27—PhD '28 (State U Ia). Research on hydrogen ion concentration of blood, acid-base balance of blood in normal and pathological conditions, electrolyte and water equilibria of blood and issues, and tissue enzymes and proteins. Faculty sch med Western Reserve U '27-44, prof exptl biochem '43-44; prof biochem LI Coll Med '44-50, med Center NYU since '50. Am Soc Biol Chem—Soc Exptl Biol and Med—ACS—AAAS—Sigma Xi. 350 Henry St., Bklyn 2.

17 MUNYAN, Arthur Claude. Stratigraphy; Non-metallic geology; Geomorphology; Economic geology of Georgia. b'08. BS '30 (U Ky); MA '31 (U Cincinnati); '41, '47 (U Chicago), '48 (U Cincinnati). Author: Econ Geology of Ga '42-45; also articles in field. Asst state geol Ky '36-37; asst state geol Ga '37-41; Asst prof geol Emory U '41-45, asso prof since '45. Am Assn Pet Geol—Am Geophys Union—Ga Mineral Soc—Sigma Xi. Department of Geology, Emory University, Ga.

18 MURAKISHI, Harry Haruo. Plant diseases (Soybeans, cotton, vegetable, carnation and orchid viruses, other ornamentals). b'17. Dow Chem Co resch fellow '44-45—MS '45 (UNC); BS '40 (U Calif); PhD '48 (U Minn). Author articles in field. Asso plant path Hawaii Agrl Expt Sta Honolulu since '52. Am Phytopath Soc—AAAS—Sigma Xi. Department of Plant Pathology, University of Hawaii Agricultural Experiment Station, Honolulu 10, T.H.

19 MURCHISON, Carl. Criminal intelligence; Publicaton (Compilation, editing). born '87. AB '09—ScD '30 (Wake Forest Coll); Rumrill fellow '09-10 (Harvard); Johnstone Scholar '22-23—PhD '23 (Johns Hopkins); hon Dr '37 (U Athens). Author: American White Criminal Intelligence '24. Asst Prof psychol Miami U '16-17; asso prof '19-22; prof Clark U '23-36. Instr Army Sch Mil Psychology '18; psychol examiner and morale officer Camp Sherman '18-19. Am Psychol Assn—AAAS(F)—Phi Beta Kappa. 2 Commercial St., Provincetown, Mass.†☉

20 MURDOCH, Joseph. Opaque minerals. b'90. BA '11—MS '12—PhD '15 (Harvard). Author: Microscopical Determination of the Opaque Minerals '15; also articles in field. With Russell and Co mfrs Cambridge Mass '15-28; instr geol U Calif LA '28, asst prof '32-39, professor since '49; Geol Soc Am (F)—Mineral Soc Am(F)—Sigma Xi. H: 630 23rd St., Santa Monica, Calif.

21 MURDOCH, Richard Kenneth. History (Latin-American, Florida and colonial). b'13. Student '26-32 (Roxbury Latin Sch); '32-33 (Amherst Coll); AB '36 (Harvard Coll); MA '40—PhD '47 (U California). Research in Florida history in late Spanish colonial period, 1783-1821. Author: The Georgia-Florida Frontier, 1793-1796 '51. Asso prof hist dept Carnegie Inst Tech since '53. AHA—Miss Valley Hist Assn—Hispanic Am Hist Soc—Pacific Hist Soc—Fla Hist Soc—Ga Hist Soc—So Hist Soc. History Department, Carnegie Institute of Technology, Pittsburgh 13.

22 MURDOCK, John Robert. Constitutional history of Arizona. b'85. AB '12 (Kirksville Mo State Teachers Coll); AM '25 (U Ia); '23 (U Ariz); '29 (U Calif). Author: Constitution of Arizona '29; Constitutional Development of Arizona '33. Instr Tempe Teachers Coll Tempe Ariz '14-32, on leave; Dean Ariz State Teachers Coll '33-37; mem 75th to 82d Congress '37-53. Tempe, Ariz.

23 MURDOCK, Kenneth Ballard. American and English literature (Seventeenth century); Seventeenth century English and American history (Intellectual, religious thought). b'95. AB '16—AM '21—PhD '23 (Harvard); LittD '30 (Middlebury Coll Vt); LHD '32 (Trinity Coll); LLD '33 (Bucknell U) LHD '38 (U Vt). Author: Portraits of Increase Mather '24; Increase Mather, The Foremost American Puritan '25; The Sun at Noon, Three Biographical Sketches, '39. Editor: Publs Colonial Soc Mass '25-30, New England Quarterly '28-38 and '39-49; American Literature '29-38 and since '39; also author articles in field. Prof English Harvard since '32. Am Acad Arts and Scis—Am Antiquarian Soc—AHA—Mass Hist Soc. 53 Chestnut St., Boston 8.☉

24 MURIE, Adolph. American mammals (Moose, fox, coyote, wolf). b'99. PhD '29 (U Mich). Author: The Moose of Isle Royale '34; Following Fox Trails '36; Ecology of the Coyote in the Yellowstone '40; The Wolves of Mount McKinley '44. Biologist Nat Park Service Fish and Wildlife Service since '34. McKinley Park, Alaska. H: Moose, Wyo.

25 MURIE, Olaus Johan. Mammalogy (Big game species of Alaska, Western Canada and United States); National Parks and wilderness areas (Conservation, social importance). b'89. BA '12 (Pacific U); MS '26 (Mich U). Field naturalist on expeditions to Labrador and Hudson Bay for Carnegie Museum '14-17; field biol US Fish and Wildlife Service '20-45. Author: Alaska-Yukon Caribou '35; Food Habits of the Coyote in Jackson Hole, Wyoming '35; The Elk of North America '51; also articles in field. Director Wilderness Society sinc '46. AAAS—Am Soc Mammalogists—Ecolog Soc Am—Am Ornithologists Union—Cooper Ornitholog Club—Wilson Ornitholog Club—Nat Audubon Soc—Wildlife Soc—Am Forestry Assn. Moose, Wyo.†◉

10 **MURPHEY, Bradford.** Marriage counseling; Child guidance; Community psychiatry; Industrial counseling. b'91. AB '18—MD '20 (U Neb); DSc hon '39 (Colo Coll). Chairman Colorado White House Conference on Children in a Democracy '42; chairman Colorado White House Conference on Children and Youth '50; vice president Denver Area Welfare Council; member executive committee Denver Council of Social Agencies. Chief cons psychiatrist New Eng Home for Little Wanderers Boston '26-27; dir Bemis-Taylor Found Child Guidance Clinic Colorado Springs Colo '27-38; dir Children's Service Center Child Guidance Clinic Wilkes-Barre Pa '38-40; prof mental hygiene Colo Coll '28-38; lectr psychiatry Pa Sch Social Work and U Pa Coll Med '38-40; asst prof psychiatry U Coll Colo Coll Med '28-38 since '40; lectr ednl psychiatry U Denver since '41; asso clin prof psychiatry U Coll Sch Med; active staff Denver Children's Hosp; cons psychiatrist Denver Pub Schs, Nat Luth Sanitarium, Denver Orphans Home, Nat Swedish Sanitarium, Nat Jewish Hosp, others. AMA(F)—Am Coll Phys(F)—Am Psychiatric Assn(F)—Am Orthopsychiatric Assn(F)—Colo Neuropsychiatric Soc—Rocky Mountain Pediatric Soc—Central Neuropsychiatric Soc—Colo-Wyo Acad Sci—Colo Conf Social Work—Nat Com Mental Hygiene—AAAS. Diplomate Am Bd Psychiatry and Neurology. 1612 Tremont Pl., Denver.

11 **MURPHY, Arthur Edward.** Ethics; American philosophy. b'01. AB '23—PhD '25 (U Cal). Author: The Uses of Reason '43; Philosophy of Alfred North Whitehead '41; The Philosophy of G. E. Moore '42. Editor: The Philosophy of the Present (G H Mead) '32; Prentice-Hall Philosophy Series. Coeditor: Essays in Political Theory '48. Prof philosophy Brown U '31-39; prof and head dept philosophy U Ill '39-45; prof Sage sch philosophy Cornell U '45-50, Susan Linn Sage prof philosophy since '50; vis prof U Wash '49. Am Acad Arts and Scis(F)—Am Philos Assn—Phi Beta Kappa. Cornell University, Ithaca.◉

12 **MURPHY, Glenn.** Theoretical and applied mechanics; Mechanics of fluids; Stress analysis. b'08. BS in CE '29—MS '30—CE '37 (U Colo); MS in CE '32 (U Ill); PhD '35 (Ia State Coll). Author: Properties of Engineering Materials '47; Mechanics of Fluids '42; Advanced Mechanics of Materials '46. Asso editor: General Engineering Handbook '40; also articles in field. Instr civil engring U Colo '29-30; special research grad asst in civil engring Eng Exp Sta U Ill '30-32; instr theoretical and applied mechanics Ia State Coll '32-34, advanced to prof since '41. ASCE—ASME—Inst Aeronautical Sciences—Am Soc Engr Edn—Soc for Exptl Stress Analysis—Am Concrete Inst—ASTM—Sigma Xi—Tau Beta Pi—Phi Kappa Phi. Iowa State College, Ames Ia. H: 2054 Cessna St.

13 **MURPHY, Hickman Charles.** Disease resistant small grain breeding; Oat diseases. b'02. BS '26 (WVa U); MS '27—PhD '30—research fellow '26-28 (Ia State Coll). Discovered important new Helminthosporium disease of oats which caused an almost complete changeover of oat varieties grown in the United States; developed many important disease resistant oat varieties. Author articles in field. Asst plant pathologist USDA Ames Ia '29-36, asso '36-39, plant pathologist '39-45, principal plant pathologist in charge oat investigations USDA since '52. AAAS—Am Phytopathol Soc—Am Soc Agron—Ia Acad Sci—Sigma Xi—Phi Kappa Phi—Gamma Sigma Delta. Botany Hall, Iowa State College, Ames, Ia.†

14 **MURPHY, James Raymond.** Casualty insurance and suretyship. b'87. LLB '12 (State U Ia). Author articles in field. Gen counsel Assn Casualty & Surety Companies since '44. Am, Ia State and Polk County bar assns. 60 John St., NYC 38.

15 **MURPHY, John E.** Gaelic literature. b'01. AB '28—AM '29 (Boston Coll); '35-39 (U Wales and Ireland); PhD '39 (Nat U Ireland). Author articles in field. Faculty Boston Coll since '39, prof since '39, chmn dept Gaelic Lit since '39; lecturer on Irish lit lang and hist Boston Coll Adult Edn and before Irish socs. Eire Soc Boston. Boston College, Chestnut Hill, Mass.

16 **MURPHY, Nelson Francis.** Metal finishing and corrosion prevention. b'06. ChE '29 (U Cincinnati); PhD '34 (Cornell). Research in electroplating, chemical surfaces, corrosion protection. Author articles in field. Chemist Procter & Gamble Co '24-29; grad instr chem Cornell U '30-34; research chemist head of explorator dept Gen Chem Co '34-39; asst prof chem engr and cons Syracuse U '39-45; head engring and development div Bristol Labs '45-47; prof chem engring Va Poly Inst since '47. Am Inst Chem Engr—ACS—Am Electroplater Soc—Soc Engring Edn—Sigma Xi. Virginia Polytechnic Institute, Blacksburg, Va.

17 **MURPHY, Walter J.** Chemical engineering. b'99. BS '21 (Polytechnic Inst of Brooklyn); DSc(hon) '47 (Centre Coll). Co-author: Strategic Materials in Hemisphere Defense '41; (published privately): I Did Leave Home; The Lagoon of Decision; author articles in field. Began as research chemist and chem engr '21; research and plant operation Air Reduction Co '21-22; tech service and development Am Cyanamid Co '22-25; market research Naugatuck chem div US Rubber Co '26; vp in charge operations George Chem Co and Seaboard Crystal Co '25-28; asst to pres Mutual Chem Co of Am '28-30; mng ed Chemical Industries '30-39, ed and gen mgr '39-43; ed Industrial and Engineering Chemistry, Analytical Chemistry, Chemical and Engineering News since '43; dir Am Soc News Service; mem corp Poly Inst of Brooklyn; mem bd trustees Midwest Research Inst; mem Tech Indsl Intelligence Com of Fgn Econ Administrn '45. Am Inst Chemists(F)—Am Inst Chem Engrs (Bikini Atom Bomb tests '46)—Soc Chem Industry (Am sect)—Salesmen's Assn of Chem Industry—Sigma Xi—Wash Acad Sci. Gold Medal Am Inst Chemists '50. 1155 16th St., Washington 6. H: 1825 Parkside Dr. NW, Washington 12.◉

18 **MURRAY, Albert Nelson.** Structural and petroleum geology; Limestone; Stratigraphy. b'94. AB '22—MS '24 (U Colo); PhD '28 (U Ill). Author articles in field. Field asst Colorado Geol Survey '20, '21; asst geol U Colo '21-22; jr geol Standard Ind Casper Wyo '22; grad asst U Colo '22-23; jr geol Colo Geol Survey '23-25; asst geol U Ill '25-26; field asst Ga Geol Survey '26; prof geol head dept U Tulsa since '28; geol oil cos summers. AAAS(F)—Mineral Soc Am—Am Geophy Union—Am Assn Petroleum Geologists—Okla Acad Sci(F)—Tulsa Geol Soc. University of Tulsa, Tulsa 4, Okla. H: 1211 South College.†

19 **MURRAY, Elwood.** Communication in human relations; Public speaking; Speech correction; Semantics. b'97. BA '22—LLD '49 (Hastings Coll); MA '24—PhD '31 (U Ia); student (Columbia, Colo U). Author: The Speech Personality '37, rev '44; also articles in field. Prof and dir Sch Speech U Denver since '31. Am Soc Speech and Hearing Disorders(F)—Inst Gen Semantics(F)—Western Speech Assn (pres '37-38)—Speech Assn Am (vp '41-42)—Internat Soc Gen Semantics (vp '48-49)—Colo-Wyo Acad Sci—Inst Gen Semantics. University of Denver, Denver.†

20 **MURRAY, Everitt George Dunne.** Bacteriology. b'90. BA '12—Ma '18 (U Cambridge); LMSSA '16 (London). Research on serological typing of bacteria, quantitative agglutination reactions, biology of Neisseria meningitidis, virulence and pathogenicity of bacteria, techniques of diagnostic bacteriology and immunology, bacteriological taxonomy and nomenclature; recorder bacteriology section 5th International Botanical Congress '30, vice-president section VII Third Congress '39 International Association Microbiologists, also vice-president section I Fifth International Congress, Canadian representative on Permanent International Commission '38; member committee Bergey's Manual Determinative Bacteriology '33-36; member National Research Council subcommittees on infections, shock and blood substitutes, and scientific advisory subcommittee of Institute of Parasitology '47; chairman biological warfare committee Directorate of Chemical Warfare and Smoke and superintendent research National Defense Headquarters, Canadian chairman joint US-Canadian Commission during World War II; member trustee board of editors Bergey's Manual Determinative Bacteriology since '36; chairman Special Conference on Gas Gangrene in US '42; associate editor American Journal Medical Sciences since '40. Co-editor: (with prof R S Breed and prof A P Hitchens) Bergey's Manual of Determinative Bacteriology (6th edit) '48. Contributor: Practice of Medicine in the Tropics; Bergey's Manual of Determinative Bacteriology; Dubo's Bacterial and Mycotic Infections of Man; others. Med Research Council research bact '20-26; with U Cambridge '23-31, dir med studies Christ's Coll '24-30; prof bact and immunology and chmn dept McGill U since '30; cons to various hosp. Internat Assn Microbiol (com bact nomenclature, chmn '39, mem jud commn permanent com on nomenclature)—Am-Can Com Bact Nomenclature—Soc Am Bact (council '40-42, com Inter-Am Soc Microbiol '40, com teaching bact '44, nominating com '47)—Can Pub Health Assn (chmn lab sect '37-38, chmn program com '46)—Montreal Med-Chirurgical Soc (vp, chmn finance com '40-41, pres '42, council and trustee '46)—Arctic Inst NA—Internat Fed Culture Collections Microorganisms—Path Soc G N and Ireland—Am Assn Path and Bact—Sigma Xi—AAAS—Am Assn Immunologists—Montreal Physiol Soc—Biol Photog Assn—Can Med Assn—Can Physiol Soc—Royal Soc Can(F)—Inst Food Tech—Soc Biol de Montreal—Osler Soc. Department of Bacteriology and Immunology, McGill University, Montreal, Que., Can.

21 **MURRAY, Florence.** American Negro. b'00. AB (Howard U); spl courses (Columbia U, Chicago U). Editor: The Negro Handbook '42, '44, '46-47, '49; also articles in field. Proofreader Howard U Press Washington

29-33; news reporter Afro-American Newspaper Washington '34-37; city editor Washington Tribune '38-40; Washington corres Chicago Defender '40-41; sec to the curator Schomburg Collection of Negro Lit NY Pub Library '42; copy editor the People's Voice NY '44-48. Julius Rosenwald fellow '43. Macmillon Company, 60 5th Av., NYC.

10 MURRAY, Grover E(lmer). Cenozoic and Gulf coast stratigraphy; Petroleum and surface geology. b'16. BS '37 (U NC); MS '39—PhD '42 (La State U). Author articles in field. Prof stratigraphy Louisiana State Univ. Geol Soc Am—Am Assn Petroleum Geologists (chmn Cenozoic sub-com, geologic names and correlations com)—AAAS—Am Geophy Union—Soc Econ Paleontol and Mineral—Geol and Mining Soc Am Universities—Miss Geol Soc—Shreveport Geol Soc—New Orleans Geol Soc—So La Geol Soc—Sigma Xi. School of Geology, Louisiana State University, Baton Rouge 3, La.†

11 MURRAY, John Courtney. Church and state relations (United States). b'04. MA '27 (Boston Coll); STD '37 (Gregorian U Rome). Author: Government and Religious Freedom '49; also articles in field. Prof theol Woodstock Coll since '37; editor Theological Studies since '41. Catholic Theol Soc Am. Received the Cardinal Spellman Award '47. Woodstock College, Woodstock, Md.©

12 MURRAY, John Joseph. English and European diplomatic history (Anglo-Baltic relations); Scandinavian history (Foreign policy); Trade and commerce (Eighteenth century). b'15. AB '37 (U Me); MA '38 (Ind U); PhD '42—teaching fellow '38-41 (U Calif). Research on England's diplomatic relations with Baltic countries during early eighteenth century, during later Stuart period; pamphlet warfare, astute use of propaganda by Whig Hanoverian government to stir up anti-Swedish sentiment; Scandinavian history, Swedish medieval history, foreign policy of Charles XII and his minister Baron Georg von Goertz; influence of trade and commerce on foreign policy early eighteenth century. Author: A Student Guidebook to English History '48; Baltic Trade and Power Politics in the Early Eighteenth Century '45; Robert Jackson's Memorial on the Swedish Tar Company, Dec. 29, 1709 '47; Scania and the End of the Northern Alliance '44; The Peasant Revolt of Engelbrekt Englebrektsson and the Birth of Modern Sweden '48; Daniel Defoe, News Analyst and the Commentator on Northern Affairs '47; British Public Opinion and the Rupture of Anglo-Swedish Relations in 1717 '48. Instr European History O State U '44-45; instr and asst prof European History Northwestern U '45-46; asso prof English History Ind U since '49. AHA—Am Scandinavian Found Karolenska Förbundet. Awarded grad asst Ind U, three teaching fellowships U Calif Los Angeles; Fulbright grant for study in Netherlands '51-52. History Department, Indiana University, Bloomington, Indiana.†

13 MURRAY, Joseph James. Virginia and Southern Appalachian ornithology. b'90. BA '09 (Davidson Coll); BD '13 (Union Theolog Sem Va); '14-15 (United Free Church Coll Glasgow), '34 (Oxford U). Research and writing on history of Virginian ornithology, topographic survey of Virginian ornithology, birds of Rockbridge County Va, altitudinal distribution of birds in Virginian Mountains. Author: Wild Wings '47; also articles in field. Editor: The Raven since '30. Minister 1st

Presbyn Church, Lexington Va since '24. Am Ornithologists Union—Wilson Ornitholog Club—Nat Aubudon Soc—Va Soc Ornithology—Va Acad Scis. 6 White St., Lexington Va.†

14 MURRAY, Leo T. Vertebrate ecology; Ichthyology; Herpetology. b'02. BA '27 (Sul Ross State Teachers Coll); MS '31—PhD '35 (Cornell U); '31 (W Va U). Leader, project investigations, Missouri River Basin studies, US Fish and Wildlife Service. Asst prof biology Ball State Teachers Coll '35-36; asso prof and dir museum Baylor U '36-44, physics teacher ASTP World War II; asso prof zoology Tex A and M Coll '44-46; visiting prof zool Southern Calif U summer '47; aquatic biol US Fish and Wildlife Service since '46. Am Soc Ichthyology and Herpetology —Am Fishery Soc—Am Soc Mammalogists—Ecolog Soc Am—Am Ornithology Union—Wilson Soc—Wildlife Soc—Tex Acad Sci—Ind Acad Sci—AAAS. Box 1381, Fish and Wildlife Service. H: Box 138, Billings, Mont.

15 MURRAY, Mary Elizabeth. Journalism (Scholastic publications). BA '29—MA '30—fellow '30 (Univ Md). Conducted clinics at the annual Columbia Scholastic Press Association Convention NY since '38. Author: The History of the Columbia Scholastic Press Association '49; also articles in field. Mem coms which compiled: The Journalism Syllabus '45; school Newspaper Fundamentals '48; Fundamentals in Yearbook Production, in press. Instr hist and journalism Allegany High Sch Cumberland Md since '30; organized and dir Maryland Scholastic Press Assn for secondary sch publ U Md since '46; bd judges Columbia Scholastic Press Assn since '40; Allegany Co reporter for The Maryland Teacher '48-50; writer script daily Editorial Page WCUM. Nat Assn Journalism Dirs—Columbia Scholastic Press Advs Assn (pres '48-50) — Nat Scholastic Press Assn—So Interscholastic Press Assn—Phi Kappa Phi. Awarded Gold Key by Columbia Scholastic Press Assn for outstanding work in the field of scholastic publs '43. Allegany High School, Cumberland, Md.

16 MURRAY, Maurice Allen, Ceramic engineering. b'19. BS '41 (Va Poly Inst); '50 (MIT). Research and development in zircon and alumina procelains; stabilization zirconia and alumina ceramics for high temperature and high frequency electrical insulation; development and methods of polishing alumina ceramics for textile thread guides; development ceramic cores for carbon coated resistors. Research ceramic engr Am Lava Corp since '41. Am Cermaic Soc—Inst Ceramic Engrs. American Lava Corporation, Chattanooga 5, Tenn.

17 MURRAY, Ray M(essinger). Structural engineering; Bridge design and construction. b'76. CE (Ohio Northern U). Chief design and construction of Hansen Suspension Bridge Hansen Idaho, Rock Creek Canyon Bridge Twin Falls Idaho; designer and in charge construction Bridge of the Gods Cascade Locks Oregon, Snake River Canyon Bridge, Twin Falls Idaho, Aurora Bridge project Seattle and others. Author articles in field. Structural engr Am Steel and Wire Co Pittsburgh '02-04; chief engr Winona Interurban Ry Co Warsaw Ind '04-10; contracting engr on structural work '10-13; cons bridge and structural engr '13-22; chief engr Union Bridge Co Portland '26-29; with Wash State Dept Highways '29-33; bridge engr for State Toll Bridge Authority, Lake Washington Floating Bridge '38-40; design engr Spokane St Viaduct Seattle

'40-42; miscellaneous constrn projects '42-46; cons engr on design Alaskan Way Viaduct Seattle '46-50; cons and design engineer Waterfront Arterial Ketchikan Alaska since '50. ASCE(life mem)—Engrs Club Seattle—Prof Engineers Ore. 1031 Securities Bldg., Seattle 1.

18 MURRAY, Raymond William. Religion and sociology; Prehistoric man. b'93. LLB '18 (U Notre Dame); PhD '26 (Catholic U). Organized first curriculum in correctional administration U Notre Dame '29; member University of Alaska-American Museum of Natural History expedition to St Lawrence Island '37. Author: Juvenile Court of the District of Columbia '27; Introductory Sociology '35, 2d edit '46; Study Guide for Introductory Sociol '37; Man's Unknown Ancestors '43. Coauthor: (with F T Flynn) Social Problems '38; Sociology for a Democratic Society '50. Prof and head dept sociol U Notre Dame since '28; ed bd Am Cath Sociol Review since '45. Am Sociol Soc—Am Cath Sociol Soc (pres '39)—Cath Anthrop Conf (mem exec council). University of Notre Dame, Notre Dame Ind.

19 MURRAY, William MacGregor. Experimental stress analysis (Photoelasticity, stresscoat, wire strain gages); Properties of materials and testing. b'10. BS '32 (McGill U); SM '33—ScD '36 (Mass Inst Tech). Research in various aspects of experimental stress analysis including photoelasticity, stresscoat, wire strain gages and as allied subjects testing materials, properties of materials and certain phases of theoretical stress analysis. Author articles: Heat Dissipation Through an Annualr Disk or Fin of Uniform Thickness '38; New Developments in Seamless Steel Tubing '38; Visible Stress '40; An Adjunct to the Strain Rosette '43; Stress Analysis Methods '46. Instr mech engring MIT '35-40, asst prof '40-45, asso prof since '45, charge courses in photoelasticity since '37, exptl stress analysis since '45. ASME (past chmn applied mechs div) —Soc Exptl Stress Analysis (past pres, now sec-treas)—Am Soc Testing Materials—Corp Profl Engrs Quebec. Massachusetts Institute of Technology, Cambridge 39, Mass.†

20 MURSELL, James Lockhart. Music education; Educational psychology. b'93. BA '15 (U Queensland Australia); PhD '18 (Harvard); grad study (Union Theol Sem) (Columbia). Author: Principles of Musical Education '27; Psychology of Secondary School Teaching '32; Principles of Education '34; Human Values in Music Education '34; Workbook in Principles of Education '34; Streamline Your Mind '36; Psychology of Music '37; Educational Psychology '39; A Personal Philosophy for Wartime '42; Music in American Schools '43; Education for American Democracy '43; Successful Teaching '46; Psychological Testing '47; Education for Musical Growth '48; Development of Teaching '49; Music and the Classroom Teacher '51; Using Your Mind Effectively '51. With Tchrs Coll Columbia since '35, prof edn since '39. Music Educators Nat Assn (research council). Teachers College, Columbia University, NYC.©

21 MUSCHAMP, George M(orris). Industrial instrumentation and automatic control. b'08. Student '31-35 (Mech Engring Drexel Inst). Attorney of record in approximately 160 patents in the field of scientific and industrial measuring and control appartus. Vice pres charge engring Brown Instrument Co since '43; chmn engring execs group Recorder-Controller Sect Sci Apparatus

Makers of Am. ASME—Phila Patent Law Assn—Soc Advancement Management—Chem Warfare Assn. Brown Instrument Company, Wayne & Roberts Avs., Phila.

10 MUSGRAVE, John Reichert. Thermal insulation (Mineral wool, diatomaceous earth); Germanium (Extraction); Gallium (Extraction); Particle size (Analysis). b'06. BS in chem engring '27 (Lafayette Coll Easton Pa); PhD '33 (U Toronto Can). Studies on sources, concentration, extraction, and purification of germanium and gallium; photoelectric sedimentation of sub-sieve sizes, and studies on general particle size methods. Holds patent on insulating cement. Author articles: A New Method for Particle Size Determination in the Sub-sieve Range '47; Developments of Germanium and Gallium During '1949 '50. Co-author article: (with Harner) Turbimetric Particle Size Analysis '47. Asst dept mgr and chem H K Mulford Co Phila '28-29; asst and demonstrator U Toronto '29-33; chief phys research labs Eagle-Picher Co since '35. ACS—Electrochem Soc (sec-treas electronics div since '49)—Alpha Chi Sigma. The Eagle-Picher Co., P.O. Box 290, Joplin, Mo. H: 518 N. Pearl.

11 MUSHAM, Harry Albert. Navy architecture; Great Lakes; Chicago (History, fire). b'86. BS in marine engring '10 (U Mich). Ship design, calculations, and form analysis; application study of rhythmic fluctuations of levels of Great Lakes to long range weather forecasting. Author: Maritime History of The Great Lakes. Author articles: Fire Boat Fuel Costs; The Location of the First Fort Dearborn '39; The Great Chicago Fire '40; Rhythmic Fluctuation of the Levels of the Great Lakes '43, and others. Draftsman Exptl Model Basin Navy Yard Washington '08-12; cons naval architect and mech engr since '22. Soc Naval Architects and Marine Engrs—Steamship Hist Soc NA—Great Lakes Hist Soc—Chicago Hist Soc—Ill State Hist Soc. 741 N. Rush St., Chgo 11.

12 MUSHER, Joseph. Actuarial aspects of pension plans in the railroad and steel industries. b'12. BS '32—MS '33 (Coll City of NY); '40-42 (George Washington U). Development appropriate rates of mortality, withdrawal, disability, retirement, remarriage; graduation such rates; development basic service tables and monetary values on basis of these rates, construction salary and benefit scales, and appropriate employee and annuitant censuses; determination required tax cost of benefit structure. Author reports of RR Retirement Bd; papers in field. With US Railroad Retirement Bd since '36, actuarial cons on indsl pension plans for steel industry '50. Soc Actuaries—Phi Beta Kappa. U.S. Railroad Retirement Board, 844 Rush St., Chgo 11.

13 MUSKAT, Morris. Oil recovery. b'06. BA '26—MA '27 (O State U); PhD '29 (Cal Inst Tech). Resch in investigating mechanics of oil recovery and developing methods for increasing efficiency of oil recovery. Holds ten patents in field. Author: Flow of Homogeneous Fluids Through Porous Media '37; Physical Principles of Oil Production '49; also articles in field. Research physicist Gulf Research and Development Co, Pittsburgh for 6 yrs, later dir physics div tech asst to vp charge prodn since '50. Am Phys Soc(F)—AAAS(F)—Am Petroleum Inst—Am Inst Mining and Metall Engrs—Soc Exploration Geophysicists—Am Geophys Union—Pittsburgh Phys Soc (past pres)—Phi Beta Kappa—Sigma Xi. Gulf Oil Corporation, Pitts.

14 MUSSELMAN, George Abraham. Petroleum exploration. b'14. BA '38—MA '40 (U Tex); '29-31 (Victoria Jr Coll); '31-32 (Bluffton Coll). Jr geologist Carter Oil Co Tulsa Okla '39-40, office geologist '41-42, sr geologist '42-43, dist geologist Miss-Ala Dist '43-45, asst div geol So Div Shreveport '45-46, asst to vp charge exploration and research Tulsa '46-48, chief geol since '48. Am Assn Pet Geol—Tulsa Geol Soc—Am Inst Mining and Metall Engr—Sigma Gamma Epsilon—Sigma Xi. 238 Parklane Dr., San Antonio.

15 MUSSELMAN, John Rogers. Geometry (Analytic); Statistics (Mathematical). b'90. AB '10—MA '13 (Gettysburg Coll); PhD '16 (Johns Hopkins); '25 (U London). Research on hexagons, circles connected with three and four lines, equation of motion of equal maps, line of images. Author articles: On An Imprimitive Group of Order 5184 '27; Some Loci Connected With a Triangle '40; others. Asso editor: Am Math Monthly '28-43. Faculty Johns Hopkins '20-25, asso prof '25-28; prof math W Reserve U since '28, chmn dept since '36. Math Assn Am—Am Math Soc—AAAS(F, council '50-52)—Phi Beta Kappa—Sigma Xi. Western Reserve University, Cleve 6.†☉

16 MUSSELMAN, Thomas Edgar. Illinois and American ornithology; Hole-nesting birds; Bluebird box routes. b'87. AB '10—AM '13 (U Ill); ScD '34 (Carthage Coll). Author: history of the Birds of Illinois '23; One Grand Year in Nature '36, and others; also articles in field. Sec Gem City Bus Coll since '10; researcher in ornithol since '06; state lecturer Aububon Soc; dir Wild Life Sch McGregor Ia. Nat Commercial Teachers Feds (pres private schs dept '35)—Kappa Delta Pi (founder). Hornaday award for conservation and service to wildlife 50.☉

17 MUSSER, Ralph Hershey. Erosion. b'90. BS '14 (Kansas State Coll). Administrator of program of soil and water conservation in Upper Mississippi Region of Soil Conservation Service (eight states). Author: articles in field. Erosion specialist project mgr and asst regional dir Soil Conservation Service Colo Springs '35-36; asst chief Erosion Control Practices Div Washington '36-37; regional director Upper Miss Region Soil Conservation Service since '37. Soil Conservation Soc Am—Friends of the Land. 434 N. Plankinton, Milwaukee 1. H: 926 E. Lexington Blvd., Milwaukee 11.

18 MUTZIGER, John George. Geographical names (Linguistic aspects). b'10. MA '32—'33-42 (George Washington U); '37-38 (U Tubingen). Author articles in field. Chief linguistics sect div geo Interior Dept Washington. Linguistic Soc Am. Division of Geography, Room 7134, Department of Interior, Washington 25.

19 MUZIK, Thomas J. Tropical plants. born '19. AB '42—MS '42—PhD '49 (University Michigan); '37-39 (Morton Junior College). Research morphogenesis '42, growth physiology and yield in Hevea brasiliensis, also on developmental anatomy and regeneration. Author articles in field. Research bot Firestone Plantations Co Harbel Liberia West Africa '42-47; teaching fellow dept bot U Mich, Newcomb fellow '49; now plant physiologist Fed Expt Sta Mayaguez. Michigan Acad Sci Arts Letters—AAAS—Bot Soc Am—Phi Sigma—Phi Kappa Phi—Sigma Xi. Federal Experiment Station, Mayaguez, P.R.†

20 MYATT, DeWitt O'Kelly. Chemical technology; Technical expression and editing. b'15. BChE '37—MChE '38 (U Louisville). Author articles in field. Managing editor Industrial and Engineering Chemistry '46-53; mgr development Atlantic Research Corp since '53. Am Chem Soc—Am Inst Chem Engrs—Sigma Tau. 1 Bolling Rd., Alexandria, Va.

21 MYER, Walter Evert. Political science (United States). b'89. AB '10—LLD '34 (Southwestern Coll); AM '13 (U Chicago). Writer, publisher and teacher. Co-author: (with Clay Coss) The Promise of Tomorrow '38; (with Clay Coss) Education for Democratic Survival '42; (with B Brown and Maxwell Stewart) America in a World at War '42; (with Clay Coss) America's Greatest Challenge '52. Owner and editor Civic Edn Service, publs of Am Observer, Weekly News Rev, Junior Rev, The Young Citizen and The Civic Leader Washington since '25. Am Sociol Soc. 1733 K St. N.W., Washington.

22 MYERS, Edward DeLos. Philosophy of history; Philosophy of religion. b'07. AB '27 (Roanoke Coll); MA '28—PhD '31 (Princeton); student '33-35 (Gen Theol Sem NY); summer seminar in arabic and Islamic studies '35 (Princeton); summer sch '39 (Denmark). Author: The Foundations of English '49. Author articles: Toynbee's Study of History '44; Soviet Challenge to Christianity '46; Note on Collingwood '47. Asst prof linguistics Trinity Coll Hartford '37-45, sec admissions '42, dean freshmen '43-45, dean and prof humanities Roanoke Coll '45-49; prof philosophy Washington and Lee U since '49; Taft lectr U Cincinnati '46. AAAS—Va Acad Sci—Linguistic Soc Am—Soc Bibl Lit and Exegesis—So Soc Philosophy of Religion—Am Philos Assn—Guild Scholars in Episcopal Ch (past pres)—AAUP—So Humanities Conf(sec)—Va Philos Assn (past pres). Department of philosophy, Washington and Lee University, Lexington, Va.†☉

23 MYERS, Frank E(vans). Electron scattering and polarization; High voltage generators; Nuclear physics; Small arms ballistics. b'06. BA '27 (Reed Coll); MS '30—PhD '34 (NYU). Author articles in field. Prof physics since '46, head dept and dir curriculum engring physics Lehigh U since '47. Am Phys Soc—AAAS(F)—Am Assn Physics Teachers—Am Soc Engring Edn—Sigma Xi. Lehigh University, Bethlehem, Pa.☉

24 MYERS, Fred P. American foreign and diplomatic relations. b'85. BA '13 (Bridgewater Coll); MA '20 (Va U); LLB '22 (Nat U); LLM '25 (Am U); PhD candidate '26 (Johns Hopkins). Research on constitutional opinions of chief justice Taft, legislative control of foreign affairs. Author articles: Wars and Rumors of Wars '13; The Latin-American Policy of Woodrow Wilson '20; England's Attitude toward the Monroe Doctrine '41; Robert E Lee, the American '46. Practicing lawyer since '22. Polit Sci Assn—Am Bar Assn—AHA—Acad Polit Sci—Columbia Hist Soc—Am Judicature Soc. Fellowship Am U '20-22; Johns Hopkins scholarship '22-23. 1324 18ɑ St. N.W., Washington 6.

25 MYERS, Garry Cleveland. Mental health; Child development and psychology; Parent and character education; Family life; Children's literature. b'84. AB '09 (Ursinus Coll); PhD '13 (Columbia). For thirty years has been an exponent of the return of folk lore and fairy tales and fables to young childen; also of possibilities of teaching ideals through words; receives about 15,000 letters a year from readers of daily syndicated newspaper column. Author: A Study in Incidental Memory '13; Myers Mental Measure '20; Pantomime Group Intelligence Test '22; The Learner and His Attitude '25; Letters to Parents '29-30; The Modern Parent '30; Developing Personality in Child at School '30; Building Personality in Children '31; The Modern Family '34; (with Mrs. Myers) Homes Build Persons '50; and others; also articles in field. Head department parent education W Reserve University '27-40; tchr training NYC, Cleveland '14-27; lectr on child psychology; certified cons psychology; founder '46, editor Highlights. AAAS(F)—Am Psychol Assn (F)—Am Assn Applied Psychol(F)—Nat Ednl Research Assn(F). Boyds Mills, Pa.©

10 MYERS, George Sprague. Fishes; Amphibians and reptiles; Zoogeography; Aquariums; Fauna of South America. b'05. AB '30—AM '31—PhD '33 (Stanford U). Study habits and classification small aquarium fishes; secretary or judge numerous aquarium and fish exhibitions; expeditions Mexican Border, West E Texas, Death Valley, Panama, Colombia, Peru, Ecuador, Galapagos Islands; leader Crocker-Stanford Deep-Sea Expedition '38; delegate and member fisheries organization committee 6th Pacific Science Congress '39; ichthyological consultant and lecturer in ichthyology and fisheries biology Museum Nacional do Brazil, Brazilian Div Fish and Game '42-44; director survey Brazilian marine fishes of commercial importance '43-44; fishery work in Brazil '50. Editor: Stanford Ichthyological Bull since '38. Asso editor: The Aquarium Phila since '32. Asst curator in charge div fishes US Nat Museum '33-36; asso prof biol and curator zool collections Stanford U '36-38, prof biol and head curator zool collections since '38. Cal Acad Scis(F, 2d vp since '45)—AAAS (F)—Herpetologists League(F)— Am Soc Ichthyol and Herpetol (pres '50-52)—Am Fisheries Soc—Biol Soc Washington—Wildlife Soc—San Francisco Aquarium Soc—Western Soc Naturalists—Soc Study Evolution—Soc Systematic Zoologists—Sigma Xi —Washington Biol Field Club. Medalist Société Nationale d'Acclimatation de France '36. Natural History Museum, Stanford University, Cal.†©

11 MYERS, Jack (Edgar). Physiology (Algae); Photosynthesis; Plant pigments. b'13. BS '34 (Juniata Coll); MS '35 (Mont State Coll); PhD '39 (U Minn). Botanical research plant pigments, photosynthesis, physiology of the algae, time course of photosynthesis and fluorescence, effects of light of high intensity on Chlorella. Author articles: A Study of the Pigments Produced in Darkness by Certain Green Algae '40; Studies on the Spirilleae: Methods of Isolation and Identification '40; Comparative Rates of Oxidation of Isomeric Linolenic Acids and Their Esters '41; Culture Conditions and the Development of the Photosynthetic Mechanism, I: The Growth of Chlorella Pyrenoidosa Under Various Culture Conditions, II: An Apparatus for the Continuous Culture of Chlorella '44. Fellow Nat Research Council Smithsonian Inst '40-42; asst prof zool U Tex '42-46, asso prof '46-48, prof since '48. Bot Soc Am—Am Soc Plant Physiol. Department of Zoology, University of Texas, Austin, Tex.

12 MYERS, Henry Alonzo. American civilization. b'06. AB '29 (Niagara U); PhD '33 (Cornell U). Author: Short History of English Literature '38; The Spinoza-Hegel Paradox '44; Are Men Equal: an inquiry into the meaning of American Democracy '45. Member faculty Cornell U since '35, prof English since '47, acting chmn dept '52-53, chmn com Am studies since '50; vis prof dramatic lit Stanford '45-46; vis prof Am lit and philosophy Salzburg Seminar in Am studies Austria '50; first vis prof Am lit U London King's Coll '51-52; research fellow Am Council Learned Socs and vis scholar Harvard '34-35. Coll Conf on English—Phi Beta Kappa—Phi Kappa Phi. H: Ellis Hollow Rd., Ithaca.©

13 MYERS, John Dashiell. Patent, trademark and copyright law. b'88. BL '11 (George Washington U). Writer on patent, copyright and general law topics. Lawyer private practice of patent, trade mark and copyright law since '24; mem Sec of Commerce's patent office adv com since '37, chmn '48. Am Bar Assn (chmn sect of Patent, Trade Mark and Copyright Law '43-44, v chmn '42-43; patent law rev com '41-43; spl com on custody and mgmt of alien property '43-47; spl com on Procedure in US Court of Claims '46-48. American Patent Law Assn — Nat Council of Patent Law Assns (v chmn '43-44)—Phila Patent Law Assn—NY Patent Law Assn—Am Group of Internat Assn for Protection of Indsl Property—Pa Bar Assn—Phila Bar Assn. 1420 Walnut St., Phila 2.

14 MYERS, Latimer D. Fatty acids; Mineral oil sulfonates. b'03. BChem—'23—PhD '27 (U Pittsburgh). Holds patents on mineral oil sulfonates, surface active agents, fatty acids. Research chem Emery Industries '27-31, research dir '31-44, chem dir '44-48, now tech asst to exec com. 4300 Carew Tower, Cincinnati.

15 MYERS, Leroy O. Economic and urban geography; Geography of Europe; Mineral economics (Coal stripping). b'13. BA '37 (Pa State Coll); MA '38 (Mich U). Research on land use damage in a bombed German city, bituminous coal stripping in U.S., state taxation as a factor in plant location. Author: Geographic Technique for Urban Planning '45 also articles in field. Asst prof geog WVa U since '48. Assn Am Geog—O Acad Sci—Mich Acad Sci, Arts Letters—Sigma Xi—Sigma Gamma Epsilon. Department of Geology and Geography, West Virginia University, Morgantown, W.Va. H: 1328 College Av.†

16 MYERS, Otto Jay. Core binders. b'15. AB '37 (Princeton U); MS (Geol engring) '42—EM '42 (Colo Sch Mines). In charge development new binders derived from vegetable and marine oils for core sand mixtures; research on foundry cereal binders, including corn and wheat starches, on clays and base sand for manufacture of cores. Asst geol Am Smelting & Refining Co '38; dir foundry practice Wright Aeronautical Corp '42-45; dir foundry research Archer-Daniels-Midland Co since '45. AIMME—Am Foundrymens Soc—Assn Tech de Fonderie —Sigma Xi. P.O. Box 839, Mpls 2. H: 4140 W. 44th St., Mpls 16.

17 MYERS, Robert Page. Dairy bacteriology. b'00. BS '23 (U Calif); MS '26—PhD '28 (Cornell U). Research in chemical sterilizers for dairy use, fermented milk products, acidophilus milk, pasteurization and sterilization of milk and milk products, fermentation of whey and drying of lactic cultures. Five patents relating to milk and milk products. Author articles in field. Bacteriol Mead Johnson & Co '28-29; chief bacteriol research labs Nat Dairy Products Corp '29-48, dir microbiol research '48-50; bact Environ Health Center since '50. Soc Am Bacteriol (councilor '46-47)—Am Pub Health Assn(F)—Am Dairy Sci Assn—AAAS(F)—Sigma Xi. Environmental Health Center, 1014 Broadway, Cin 2. H: 6924 Miami Bluff Drive, Mariemont, Cincinnati 27.

18 MYERS, R(oy) Maurice. Physiology and anatomy of leaf abscission; Prairie vegetation of west-central Illinois; Vegetation of Idaho. b'11. BS Edn '34—MA '37—PhD '40 (O State U); '38-40 (Northwestern U). Research in relationship to plant hormones to abscission of leaves. Author articles in field. Asst prof biol Western Ill State Coll Macomb Ill '45-49, asso prof since '49. O Acad Sci(F)—Ecol Soc Am—Am Soc Plant Physiol—Torry Bot Club—Ill Acad Sci—Sigma Xi.†

19 MYERS, Will Martin. Cytogenetics; Plant breeding. b'11. BS '32 (Kan State Coll); MS '34—PhD '36 (U Minn). Research in polyploidy, chromosomal behavior in meiosis, interspecific hybridization, and inheritance in forage grasses and legumes; improvement of Dactylis glomerata, Bromus inermis, Trifolium repens and Medicago sativa by breeding; methods of breeding across pollinated forage crops. Author articles in field. Asso agronomist US Regional Pasture Research Lab State Coll Pa '37-40, geneticist '40-46, sr geneticist '47-49; prof cytogenetics Pa State Coll '46-49; head agrl research br Natural Resources Sect SCAP Tokyo Japan '46-47; head agron in charge div forage crops and diseases BPISAE, ARA, USDA '49-51; head dept agron and plant genetics U Minn since '52. Am Soc Agronomy—Bot Soc Am—Genetics Soc Am—Am Genetic Assn—Am Soc Naturalists. Department of Agronomy and Plant Genetics, University Farm, St. Paul, Minn.

20 MYERS, William Graydon. Radiological safety. b'08. AB '33—MSc '37—PhD '39—MD '41 (O State U). Author articles in field. Research asso Ohio State University Research Foundation '42-45, Julius F Stone research associate professor med biophysics since '49. monitor radiological safety sect Operation Crossroad, Bikini, '46. Am Chem Soc—AMA—O State Med Assn—AAAS—Am Fedn Clin Research —Am Assn Cancer Research—Sigma Xi. Ohio State University, Columbus 10, O.

21 MYERS, William Irving. Agricultural economics; Farm finance; American agriculture. b'91. BS '14—PhD '18 (Cornell U). Assistant to chairman Federal Farm Bd '33; deputy governor Farm Credit Adminstrn '33, governor '33-38 absent on leave from Cornell U; president Federal Farm Mortgage Corporation '34-38; dir Federal Surplus Relief Corporation '34-38; mem President's Committee on Farm Tenancy '37; chairman Land Committee of National Resources Planning Board '38-43. Author articles in field. Instr in farm mgmt Cornell U '14-18, asst prof '18-20, prof farm finance since '20, head dept agrl econs '38-43, dean coll agr since '43; mem Agrl bd Nat Research Council; mem NY State Commn on Agr since '45. Am Farm Econ Assn (sectreas '27-31; pres '34)—Internat Conf of Agrl Econ—Sigma Xi—Phi Kappa Phi. Received Am Farm Bur Fedn award for distinguished service to organized agr '38. R.F.D. 1, Ithaca, N.Y.©

22 MYERS, William Starr. Comparative government; Political parties; American military and political history; Civil War and reconstrucion. b'77. BA '97 (U NC); PhD '00 (Johns Hopkins). Author: Socialism and American Ideals '19; American Democracy Today

'24; Fifty Years of the Prudential '26; The Republican Party, a History '28; American Government of Today '31; General George B McClellan '34; The Foreign Policies of Herbert Hoover '40; Co-author: Story of New Jersey '45; (with W H Newton) The Hoover Adminstration '36; Woodrow Wilson: some Princeton Memories, '46; also author articles in field. Prof politics Princeton '18-43, emeritus '43. Phi Beta Kappa. 104 Bayard Lane, Princeton, N.J.*

10 MYLCHREEST,. George. Lewis. Industrial plant design. b'84. BS '07 (Wesleyan U), '10 (MIT). Development new details construction to improve safety and reduce construction costs and operation costs industrial plants. With firm engrs '10-24; own bus engring and architecture since '24. Am Soc CE—Conn Soc CE—Nat Soc Profl Engrs—Conn Soc Profl Engrs —AAAS—Am Concrete Inst. 238 Palm St., Hartford 12, Conn.

11 MYLONAS, George Emmanuel. Greek archeology. b'98. BA '18 (Internat Coll Smyrna); PhD '27 (U Athens); PhD '29 (Johns Hopkins U). Field director excavations at Olynthus Greece '38; director excavations at Haghios Kosmas Greece '30, 31, at Eleusis '30-31, summers '32-34, at Akropotamos '38; managing committee American School of Classical Studies Athens '37-39 and since '45; national committee for Restoration of Greece. Author articles in field. Asso prof history of art Washington U St Louis '35-38, chmn dept since '37, prof, head dept art and archaeology '38-39 and since '40. Soc for Byzantine Studies (vp)—Archeol Inst Am—Am Acad Polit and Social Sci—Archaeol Soc Greece—Anthrop Soc Greece—Assn des Etudes Grecques, Paris—Phi Beta Kappa—Phi Kappa Phi. Washington University, StL 5.†☉

12 MYRES, Samuel Dale, Jr. United States government (Texas); International relations (Mexico, Palestine); Southern United States politics; Argentine beef. b'99. AB '20—AM'25—Arnold fellow in govt '24-25 (So Meth U Dallas); PhD '29 (U Tex); Diplôme Inst de Hautes Etudes Geneva '21; LLD '37 (Trinity U). Editor: The Government of Texas—A Survey '34; The Cotton Crisis '35; The Southwest in International Affairs '36; The United States and Mexico '38; After the War What? '43; Toward International Order '44; also articles in field. Prin Sweetwater Tex Schl '21-23; instr Dallas pub schs '23-24; mem bar of Tex since '24; asst prof So Meth U '25-28, prof since '35; instr in govt U Tex '28-29; dir Arnold Foundation in Pub Affairs since '33; dir Inst of Pub Affairs since '34; mem So Regional Com of Social Sci Research Council '34-38; mem nat com Internat Labor Orgn; mem Carnegie Endowment group investigating conditions in SA '41. Am Polit Sci Assn—Am Soc Internat Law—SW Social Sci Assn—Tau Kappa Alpha. Fellow of Social Sci Research Council for investigation at Geneva and in Palestine '30-31. 6607 Hillcrest Av., Dallas.

13 MYSELS, Karol J(oseph). Colloids; Complex salts; Conductivity of electrolytes. b'14. Ingenieur Chimiste '37 (U Lyon); PhD '41 (Harvard); '37-38 (U Paris). Author articles in field. Holder French patent on improvement in tanning drums, US patent on use of radioactive tracers in leak detection. Asso prof U So Calif since '50. Am Chem Soc—AAAS—Faraday Soc—Sigma Xi. First prize and Placide Peltereaux prize Lyon '37. Chemistry Department, University of Southern California, Los Angeles 7.

N

14 NAAMANI, Israel Tarkow. Recent English history; Jewish education in America. b'12. PhB '35 (Marquette U); MA '42—PhD '45 (Ind U). Author articles: The Significance of the Act of Settlement in the Evolution of English Democracy '43; The Abandonment of "Splendid Esolation" by Great Britain '46; Hebrew Schools in American culture '46, and others. Asso dir Humboldt Inst Jew Studies Chicago '35-36; prin Rodfei Zedek Schs Chicago '36-41; dir edn B'nai Israel Schs Chicago '42-45; exec dir Bur Jew Edn San Francisco '46-48; exec dir Bur Jewish Edn Louisville since '48; lectr on Am Assn Jewish Edn—AHA—Am Polit Sci Acad—Nat Council Jewish Edn.

15 NABOKOV, Vladimir Vladmiriovich. (pen name Vladimir Nabokov-Sirin. Butterflies; European fiction. b'99. LittB '22 (Trinity Coll Cambridge U Eng). Fellow in Lepidoptera Museum of Comparative Zoology Harvard '42-48; travel in search of butterflies Europe and North America, and description several new species and subspecies. Author: The Real Life of Sebastian Knight '42; Nikolai Gogol '44; Three Russian Poets '44; Bend Sinister '47; Nine Stories; Conclusive Evidence (memoir) '51. Lectr Russian lit and art of writing Stanford U summer '41; in charge Russian dept Wellesley Coll '41-48; faculty Cornell U since '48, now asso prof Russian lit; vis lectr Harvard '52. Guggenheim fellow '43-'52.

16 NABRIT, Samuel Milton. Biological regeneration. b'05. BS '25 (Morehouse Coll); MS '28—PhD '32 (Brown U). Research on the role of the basal plate of the tail in regeneration of fish, experimental regeneration in central nervous system of embryo fishes. Author articles in field. Prof Atlanta U since '32, dean grad sch arts and sci since '47. AAAS—Am Soc Zool—Soc Study Growth and Development—NY Acad Sci—Nat Inst Sci. Atlanta University, Atlanta.†

17 NADEAU, Betty Kellett (Mrs. Edouard Hollis Nadeau). Micropaleontology (Fossil Ostracoda). b'05. AB '27—'27-28 (U Kan). Research fossil Ostracoda since '27. Author articles in field. Formaniniferal research Cushman lab '28-29; subsurface stratigrapher Amerada Pet Corp '29-34; Phillips Petroleum Co '36-37; research asso micropaleontology since '47. Geol Soc Am(F)—Paleontol Soc—Soc Econ Paleontol and Mineralogists—Am Assn Petroleum Geol—Sigma Xi. Department of Geology, Washington University, St. Louis 5. 1018 Bompart Av., Webster Groves 19.

18 NADEAU, Gale Francis. Manufacture of photographic film; Cellulose chemistry; Synthetic resins; Plastics. b'05. BS '27—MS '28 (U Toledo); PhD '31 (Ohio State U). Author articles in field. Holder of over 100 patents and pending applications. Teaching fellow chem U Toledo '27-28; grad asst chem O State U '28-29, spl asst in chem '29-31; research chem Eastman Kodak Co Rochester NY since '31, supervisor of development film base dept since '35. Am Chem Soc—Photog Soc Am—NY Acad Sci—Nat Geog Soc—Sigma Xi—Phi Lambda Upsilon—Soc Textile Chem and Colorists—Soc Rheology. Eastman Kodak Co., Rochester, NY.

19 NAESER, Charles Rudolph. Rare element chemistry. b'10. BS '31 (Wis U); MS '33—PhD '35 (Ill U). Engaged research on beryllium, uranium, rhenium, rare earths; studies and writing on electrolytic reduction of ytterbium;

field sampling methods for gasses, smokes, and insecticides. Author: Laboratory Manual, Experiments in General Chemistry '42; also articles in field. Exec officer dept chem George Washington U since '47. Am Chem Soc —AAAS—Sigma Xi. George Washington University, Washington 6.†

20 NAESETH, Henriette Christiane Koren. Swedish theatre in Chicago; American literature and theatre; Scandinavian literature. AB '22 (Grinnell Coll); AM '24 (U Minn); PhD '31 (U Chicago). Author articles: Early Norwegian Drama in Chicago '38; Drama in Swedish in Chicago '48. Translator: Sigrid Undset's Return to the Future '42. Instr Eng U Chicago '28-31; asst prof Eng Goucher Coll '31-32; prof Eng Neb State Teachers Coll '32-34; prof Eng Augustana Coll since '34, head dept since '35, chmn div humanities since '45. Norwegian-Am Hist Soc—Augustana Hist Soc—Phi Beta Kappa. Grant Council Social Studies '42. Augustana College, Rock Island, Ill.†

21 NAGEL, Charles. Early American rooms (Architecture). b'99. BA '23—BFA '26—MFA '28 (Yale); student '26 (Ecole des Beaux Arts Fontainebleau). Co-author: Early American Rooms '36; Editor: Bulletin Associate in Fine Arts '36. Curator decorative arts, asst prof hist art Yale U '30-36; acting dir City Art Museum, St Louis '43-45; dir Brooklyn Museum since '46; bd Textile Museum. Am Assn Mus—Asn Mus Dirs—Mus Council NYC—Jefferson Nat Expansion Memorial Assn—AIA—Mo Assn Architects. Brooklyn Museum, Eastern Parkway, Brooklyn 38.

22 NAGLER, Alois. Theatre (History); Drama (History); Germanic literature. b'07. Student '26-30 (U Graz and Vienna); PhD '30 (U Graz). Research on comparative scale of theatrical and dramatic history, research on theater audiences and staging of opera, University theaters. Author: Hebbel und die Musik '28; Ferdinand von Saar als Novellist '30; Sources of Theatrical History '52. Drama critic and lit ed Vienna '32-38; asst prof Germanic lang and lit Pa State Coll '46-46; with Yale since '46, asso prof dramatic hist and criticism from '48. Conn Acad Arts and Sci—Soc D'Hist du Theatre—Am Ednl Theatre Assn. Yale University Theater, New Haven 11.

23 NAIR, John H(enry). Dehydration (Foods); Food (Preservation); Dairy (Products, processing). b'93. BS cum laude '15 (Beloit Coll Wis); grad study chem '16-17 (Syracuse U). Research on dried whole milk, skim milk, modified milks, dehydrated fruit juices, fluid cream, lecithin, emulsions, butterfat, ice cream, evaporated milk, condensed milk, cured and processed cheese, mincemeat, dessert mixes, dehydrated soups, dehydrated vegetables, processes for dehydration of foods. Holder patents on processing dairy products. Author articles: Drying Materials by the Film and Spray Systems '28; Lipase in Raw, Heated and Desicated Milk '30; British Food Processors Make Best of Bad Situation '49, and others. Teaching fellow chem Syracuse U '16-17; research chem Merrell-Soule Co Syracuse NY '19-28; asst dir research Borden Co Syracuse '28-38; tech adv dry milk sales Borden Co NYC '38-42; asst dir research Continental Foods Inc and Thomas J Lipton Inc Hoboken NJ since '42. Am Chem Soc—Inst Food Technol—Soc Chem Industry—Am Inst Chem—Sigma Xi—Alpha Chi Sigma. Thomas J. Lipton, Inc., Hoboken, N.J.

10 NAJARIAN, Herand Kalost. Zinc smelting. b'89. Mining Eng '14 (Yale). Developed and patented vacuum condensation process for zinc smelting with George F Weaton; other mechanical patents vacuum filter, vibrating screen, flexible coupling. Author articles in field. Designed and built metallurgical plants Northern NY, Mont, Utah, Mo and Argentina '15-30; mech supt Josephtown Electrothermic Zinc Smelter St Joseph Lead Co '30-40, gen supt operations since '40. Am Inst Mining and Metal Engrs. St. Joseph Lead Co., Monaca, Pa.

11 NAKARAI, Toyozo W(ada). Biblical Hebrew; Shintoism; Buddhism. b'98. AB '20 (Kokugakuin U Tokyo); '20-21 (Nippon U Tokyo); AB '24—AM '25 (Butler U); PhD '30 (U Mich); '24, '25, '30 (U Chicago); '34 (Linguistic Inst Am); '48 (Rabbinical Inst Hebrew Union Coll). Author: A Study of the Kokin-shu '31. American School Oriental Research (asso)—Am Oriental Soc—Soc Biblical Exegesis—Nat Assn Biblical Instrs—AAAS—Phi Kappa Phi—Theta Phi. Butler University, Indianapolis 7.

12 NASATIR, Abraham. Latin American history; American history (Western, Anglo-Spanish rivalry in Mississippi Valley; French in California). b'04. AB '21—MA '22—PhD '26 (U Calif). Author: The French in the California Gold Rush '34; Inside Story of the Gold Rush '35; French Activities in California: An Archival Calendar-Guide '45; also articles in field. Prof San Diego State Coll since '28; v consul of Paraguay since '36, Ecuador since '44. AHA—Hispanic Am Hist Assn—Mo Hist Soc—State Hist Soc Mo—La, Tex, and Calif Hist Soc —Miss Valley Hist Assn—San Diego Hist Soc. San Diego State College, San Diego 5, Calif.†

13 NASH, Harold Siegrist. Ceramic art (Greek glaze and pottery); Glass decoration. b'94. BS '19 (NY State Coll Ceramics). Developed bridged metal stencils for airbrush decoration on glass. Prof ceramics and head dept U Cincinnati since '27. Am Ceramic Soc(F)—Ceramic Guild Cincinnati(F). Charles Fergus Binns Medal. Department of Ceramics, University of Cincinnati, Cincinnati.

14 NASH, Nat H. Food stabilizers, emulsifiers, and flavors. b'14. BS (City Coll NY); war training course (Manhattan Coll). Research and development new stabilizers and emulsifiers for ice cream, emulsifiers for cake, icings and bread, softeners for bread, flavors and stabilizers for frozen confections, development food flavors. Patents pending in field. Chem M B Picker Corp NYC '39-42; chief food chem Joe Lowe Corp NYC '42-47; chief chemist and tech dir Lanco Products Corp NYC since '47. ACS—Am Inst Chem—Am Assn Cereal Chem—Am Oil Chem Assn—Inst Food Tech—Met Dairy Tech Soc—Met Bakery Prodn Mens Club. Lanco Products Corp., 601 W. 26th St., NYC 1. H: 3444 Knox Pl., NYC 67.

15 NASH, Ray. Calligraphy (American); Prints and printing (History); Typography. b'05. BA '28 (U Ore); MA (Harvard); AM (Hon) Dartmouth Coll). Organization first comprehensive exhibition on American handwriting development; compilation history and bibliography American handwriting from colonial beginnings to Spencerian; editorial consultant on graphic arts; improvement design of transportation typography; lectr Société Plantin; adviser Plantin Moretus Mus. Lecturer on Book of the Renaissance U Ore Renaissance Inst '51; editor Renaissance News. Author: An Account of Calligraphy and Printing in the Sixteenth Century '40; Some Early American Writing Books and Masters '43; Durer's 1511 Drawing of a Press and Printer '47; Preliminary Checklist of American Writing Manuals and Copybooks to 1850 '50. Faculty art dept Dartmouth since '37, printing adviser to coll since '38, prof since '49; typog cons Boston & Me RR '40-45. Soc Printers Boston—Bibliog Soc Am—Coll Art Assn Am. Dartmouth College, Hanover, N.H.

16 NASON, Howard King. Plastics; Plasticizers; Physical testing; Rheology; Water treatment; Industrial microbiology; Applications for chemicals. b'13. AA '32 (Kans City Jr Coll); AB '34 (U Kans); '38 (Wash U). Holder US patents on silicon-modified phenolic resins, safety glass, plastic polyvinyl acetal compositions, algicides, molding cellulose ester compositions. Author articles in field. Asso with Monsanto Co since '36, now asst to vp. Am Chem Soc—Soc Rheology—AAAS —Am Soc Testing Materials (com D-20 on plastics, D-9 elect insulating materials, D-14 adhesives, ordnance adv com, bd dirs). Recipient certificate of commendation Am Standards Assn in recognition of contribution to development of standards for Army and Navy electronic equipment and of work done as mem Assn War Com on radio. Monsanto Chemical Company, 1700 S. 2nd St., StL 4.

17 NASSET, Edmund S(igurd). Digestion; Biological value of protein. b'00. BA '25 (St Olaf Coll); MS '27 (Pa State Coll); PhD '31 (U Rochester). Author articles in field. Instr physiol U Rochester '31, prof physiol since '48. Nutrition officer Lt Col with US Ninth Air Force Europe '44-45. Am Physiol Soc—Am Inst Nutrition—Soc Exptl Biol and Med—Sigma Xi. Bronze Star US Army in France '45. Department Physiology and Vital Economics, University of Rochester, Rochester 20, N.Y.†

18 NAUDAIN, Glenn Garnet. Food chemistry; Chemical warfare. b'94. BS '17—MS '22—PhD '23 (Ia State Coll); '15-16 (Occidental Coll); '23-25 (Mellon Inst U Pittsburgh); BEd '26 (Kan State Coll); MA '39 (NYU); DSc '37 (Academia de Sciencias E Arts of Rio de Janerio). Author: Food and Physiological Chemistry '28. Author articles: A Survey on Teaching of Chemistry in the Secondary Schools of South Carolina; A Survey of the Chloride Production in the US for Chemical Warfare Serv. Prof chem head dept Winthrop Coll SC '26-50; cons chem since '50. Served World War I; served lt col and col World War II CWS US Army. AAAS(F)—Royal Soc Arts London—Am Chem Soc (ex-pres SC sect)— SC Acad Sci (exec council, pres '38-39, sec-treas '40-41)—SC Edn Assn. 919 Charlotte Av., Rock Hill, S.C.†⊙

19 NAUTH, Raymond. Plastics; Coal tar products; Electro-biology. b'97. BS '14 (U Tech Sch. Buffalo); '25-28 (U Buffalo); Licentiate '29 (Coll Phys and Surg Ont); MD '29 (U Mannheim); PhD '34 (U Freiberg, Germany). Designed and supervised construction of coal (lignite) distillation and tar by-products plant at Minot ND for Western Carbon & Chemical Corp to produce coal briquettes, phenol, cresolic acid, ammonium nitrate and other tar fractions for plastics industry; also similar plants for other firms; research on plastics and cutting tools, supervised plastics tooling for aircraft manufacture, also for Norden bombsight and Sperry gyroscope; appointed by President to National Health Conference '38; instrumental in New York Blue Cross bill and other health bills. Author: Chemistry and Technology of Plastics '47; Fundamentals of Electronics and Television '52; also articles in field. Granted about 30 patents relating to ignition systems, armature winding, fluorescent lighting, artificial fever, and plastics. Engr and electro-biol research various firms '15-28; practiced med in Canada '28-31; chief engr Flexlume Corp Buffalo '34-36; cons engr specializing in plastics '36-44; factory mgr Am Electric Heater Co '42-44; gen mgr Ray-Metal Co since '44; director edn Radio-Electronics-Television Sch Detroit since '48. Engring Soc Detroit —Am Soc Tool Engrs—Soc Plastic Engrs. 3330 Taylor Av., Det 6.

20 NAWIASKY, Paul. Vat dyes; Acetate silk dyes. b'83. PhD '04 (U Berlin). Research and development vat and acetate silk dyes. Granted more than 100 US and foreign patents in field. Research and development I G Farbenindustry A G '07-36; research and development Gen Aniline & Film Corp '36-51. ACS—AAAS—Am Assn Textile Chem and Colorists. H: 206 Springfield Av., Summit, N.J.

21 NAYLOR, E(still) E(ss). Federal budget system; Federal accounting. b'97. Student '16-17 (U Mo); AB '21— AM '22 (George Washington U); LLB '25—BCS '36 (Southeastern U); M Fiscal Adminstrn '48 (Columbus U). Author: The Federal Budget System in Operation '41; Federal Contracts and Procurement Procedures '46; Federal Accounting '49. In govt service since '19, clerk of Treas Dept '19; office of auditor for war '19-21; gen accounting office '21-25; asst budget officer and asst auditor (DC) Dist Govt '25-29; investigator Bur Efficiency '29-33; asst auditor and chmn legal adv com Agr Adjustment Adminstrn '33-35; asst to commr accounts and deposits and chief of voucher procedure and review div Treas Dept '35-41; deputy dir and adminstrv officer contract distbn War Prodn Bd '41-42; spl asst to fiscal dir Army Service Forces, spl asst to Chief of Finance War Dept since '45; War Dept '42-45, dir studies Grad Accounting Sch; prof fed accounting, the federal budget system and related subjects Columbus U Washington. Awarded commendation for Exceptional Civilian Service by Sec of War '44. Asst Director of Finance, Department of the Air Force, Pentagon Building, Washington.

22 NEALE, M(ervin) Gordon. Educational administration; School building programs, surveys. b'87. BS in edn '11 (U Mo); AM '17—PhD '20 (Teachers College Columbia). Author: (brochures) Great Neck (Long Island) School Survey (with George D. Strayer) '17; School Reports '20; Duluth School Building Survey '22; A School Building Program for Winona, Minn. '22; Studies of Instruction in Public Schools of Austin, Minn. '23; Sch Bldg Program for Columbia Mo '24, Joplin Mo '25, Mexico Mo '25, Sedalia Mo '27, Springfield Mo '28, Moberly Mo '29, Duluth Minn '45. Dir edn Maryville State Tchrs Coll Mo '14-15; tchr-training high sch insp Mo State Dept Edn '15-16; asso ednl adminstrn Tchrs Coll Columbia '19-20; prof sch adminstrn U Mo '20-21, dean sch edn '23-30; prof sch adminstrn U Minn '21-23, prof ednl adminstrn since '37, dir field studies and surveys since '48; pres U Idaho '30-37; dir 19 ednl and sch bldg surveys in pub sch systems '49-52, including Minn cities of Faribault, Hastings, Fergus Falls, Winona, White Bear Lake, Hibbing, St Paul; coll Surveys including Augsburg '45, Wartburg '45, Ark Agrl,

Mech and Normal '47, Concordia Tchrs (River Forest, Ill.) '48, Ark Poly '48, Dana '49, Bethany-Peneil '50, Concordia Tchrs (Seward, Neb) '51, Mission House '52, U New Mexico '52; coll examiner for North Central Assn Colls and Secondary Schs since '38, participating in 76 official surveys; dir. survey relating to establishment Municipal Univ, Canton (O) in '59. Association Heads of Depts in Edn State Univs(pres '24-25)—NEA—Nat Council Edn—Mo State Tchrs Assn (pres '29-30)—Inland Empire Edn Assn(pres '34-35)—Phi Delta Kappa. H: 1101 E. River Rd., Mpls 14.☉

10 NEARING, George Guy. Rhododendrons; Hollies; Lichens; Fungi. b'90. BS '11 (U Pa); grad work (Harvard, U Pa, Columbia). Devised the Nearing method of propagating rhododendrons. Author: The Lichen Book '41-47; also articles in field. Resident naturalist Greenbrook Sanctuary '47-49. Mass Hort Soc (hon)—Am Rhododendron Soc—Torrey Bot Club—Sullivant Moss Soc. Jackson Dawson Memorial medal '40. R.F.D. Box 216, Ramsey, N.J.

11 NEEDHAM, Paul Robert. Fisheries research, management and conservation. b'02. BS '24—MS '26—PhD '28 (Cornell U). Author: Trout Streams '39. Co-author: (with J G Needham) Fresh Water Biology; also articles in field. Dir Fisheries for Ore State Game Commn '45-48; fishery mng biol US Fish and Wildlife Service since '48. Am Fisheries Soc (Western Div pres '48)—Wildlife Soc (pres '42)—Am Soc Ichthyologists and Herpetologists—Am Forestry Assn—Pacific Fishery Biol—Sigma Xi—Phi Kappa Phi. Route 16, Box 710, Portland 2, Ore.†

12 NEEDHAM, Wesley Eugene. Tibet. b'03. Student '23-25 (U Conn). Translation Tibetan books and manuscripts into English; inscriptions on objects in Tibetan collections at museums; studies religion, art, culture of Tibet. Collaborator: catalogue of Tibetan Collection Newark Museum. Am Oriental Soc-New Haven Oriental Club. H. M. Bullard Co., Elm St. at Orange, New Haven. H: 462 Second Av., West Haven 16, Conn.

13 NEEDLE, Haskell Cahn. Fermentation; Foods (Dehydration); Acids (Lactic). b'06. BS '29—MS '33 (MIT). Research on keeping quality refrigerated and quick-frozen foods; studies of fermentation methods for production alcohol, acids, problems related to fermentation and production of syrups from cereal grains by enzyme conversion; investigation of development new food products such as dehydrated soup mixes, sauces, desserts. Holds patents on process for production lactic acid fermentation, fermentation process white calcium lactate, process for syrup manufacture. Research asso MIT '29-34; head biochem and bact div Am Maize Products '34-38, Clinton Industries '38-42; dir research in charge prodn Waverly Sugar Co '43-44; in charge biochem and bact research Apex Chem Co '44-46; cons United Distillers of Am '46-48; dir research and development new food items Wyler & Co since '48. ACS—Inst Food Tech. R. S. Aries & Associates, 26 Court St., Bklyn 2. H: 4944 N. Harding Av., Chgo 25.

14 NEELY, James Winston. Cotton (Genetics, breeding); Weed control (Cotton); Crop improvement by breeding. b'06. BSA '28 (U Ark); PhD '35 (Cornell U). Research on order and regularity of blooming in cotton plant, effect genetic factors and environmental influences on characteristics of upland cotton, inheritance of characters and linkage in cotton, varietal and strains tests with cotton, control of weeds in cotton by flaming. Asst plant breeding U Ark '28-30; asst agron Cornell U '30-34; asst agron soil conservation '34-35; sr geneticist USDA '35-46; plant breeder Stoneville Pedigreed Seed Co '46-50; vp and dir plant breeding and agrl research Coker Pedigreed Seed Co since '51. Sigma Xi—Phi Kappa Phi—AAAS. Coker Pedigreed Seed Co., Hartsville, S.C.

15 NEFF, Carroll Forsyth(e). Denicotinization; Yeasts. b'08. AB '29—'31, '38 (Washington U St Louis); AM '30 (U Calif Berkeley). Research on chemotherapy of coccidiosis chickens, product development and nutritional studies yeasts and yeast extracts and derivatives (plant production); denicotinization of tobacco (dry process); chemotherapy, nutrition. Author articles in field. Research dept chemotherapy and nutrition Ralston-Purina Co St Louis '26-31; head biol lab nutrition Anheuser-Busch Inc St Louis '31-38; Vitamin B-1 adv com USP '34-40; mgr The Centaur-Caldwell div Sterling Drug Inc Atlanta '38-51, Sterling Internat '50-51; asso Law & Co since '51. Inst Food Tech—Ga Acad Sci—Am Marketing Assn—AAAS—Am Chem Soc—Sigma Xi—Phi Sigma. Teaching fellow zool U Cal '29-30. 193 Princeton Way N.E., Atlanta 6.

16 NEFF, Marshall Snow. Tung culture. b'08. BS '35 (U Utah); MS '37 (Ia State Coll); PhD '43 (U Chicago). Author articles in field. Asst plant physiol US Dept Agr lab and field investigations in tung culture '42-47, asso physiol '47-48; head US Dept Agr Lab for Tung Investigations Cairo Ga since '48. U.S. Department of Agriculture, Laboratory for Tung Investigation, Cairo, Ga.

17 NEGADO, Susano R. Real estate (Evaluation); Housing (Planning, construction); Architectural engineering. b'08. BSc in civil engring '33 (U Philippines); BSc in arch '37 (Mapua Inst Tech Manila); seminar courses arch engring and housing NY and S Am schs. Observations and studies on recent trends in architecture, engineering and sanitary engineering in Europe, US, West Indies and South America; studied and observed housing, town planning, architectural and engineering trends in England, Europe and US under auspices of Department of State; member board of examiners for architects '50. Author article: Economical Housing Design from Locally Produced Materials '50. Prof drawing engring, practical constrn and estimates Mapua Inst Tech '31-36; structural, estimating and constrn engr Pedro Siochi & Co Manila '36-37; architect and design engr charge Metropolitan Water Dist '37-44; chief evaluation expert and chief planning Manila Real Estate br Office of Chief Engr AFWESPAC, US Army '45-46; chief architect and civil engr housing projects US Embassy Manila '46-48; former gen mgr and vp Internat Constrn Corp Inc Manila; $1-a-year tech cons Metropolitan Water Dist Bd, Dept Pub Works and Communications; cons on arch and engring ECA, US Embassy. Philippine Inst Arch—Philippine Soc CE—Philippine Soc San Engrs—Nat Mater Plumbers Assn Philippines—Elec Contractors Assn Philippines—Am Soc CE—Town and Country Planning Assn Eng—Inter-Am Assn San Engring. P.O. Box 80, Manila, P.I.

18 NEGLEY, Glenn. Political and legal philosophy; Utopian thought. b'07. AB '30—MA '34 (Butler U); PhD '39 (U Chicago). Author: The Categories of Political Analysis '42; The Organization of Knowledge '42. Co-author: (with T V Smith) Democracy vs Dictatorship '42; also articles in field. Prof Philos Duke U since '46, chairman department since '49. Am Phil Assn—Am Polit Sci Assn. Rockefeller Foundation research fellow '46. Duke University, Durham, N.C.

19 NEGUS, Sidney Stevens. Chemistry; Nutrition; Science popularization. b'92. AB '13 (Clark U); MA '17 (Harvard); PhD '23 (Johns Hopkins). Author articles in field. Head dept chem Med Coll of Va since '27. AAAS (F, dir press relations)—Am Chem Soc—So Assn Sci and Industry—Nat Assn Sci Writers (hon) — Va Acad Sci (pres) — Add: 4102 Wythe Av., Richmond, Va.☉

20 NEHRLING, Arno Herbert. Flower shows; Roses and tropical plants. b'86. Grad '05-09 (Shaw Sch Bot); (Washington U). Author rule book for flower show judges; also articles in field. Prof floriculture and head dept Mass Agrl Coll '14-17; pres McDonald Floral Co Crawfordsville Ind '17-21; prof floriculture Cornell U '21-27; sales mgr Hill Floral Products Co Richmond '27-33; dir exhbns '33-36, exec sec since '47, dir publs since '47 Mass Hort Soc Boston. Am Hort Council (trustee)—Nat Garden Inst (trustee)—Am Rose Soc—Soc Am Florists (past pres) — Chrysanthemum Soc Am (past pres)—Northeastern Florists Assn (regional dir)—Mass Arborists Assn—Mass Gladiolus Soc—Mens Garden Clubs Am(sec dir). 300 Massachusetts Av., Boston.

21 NEIBURGER, Morris. Physics of cloud and fog; Atmospheric pollution. b'10. BS '36—PhD '45 (U Chicago); '38-39, '40-41 (MIT). Research forecasting of maximum temperature, reflection and transmission of solar radiation by clouds and by the sea surface, use of potential vorticity in meteorology, air pollution. Author articles in field. Instr meteorol dept U Calif '41-43, asst prof '43-48, asso prof since '48; project dir Calif Stratus Investigation '43-48; cons Los Angeles Co Air Poll Control Dist since '48. Am Meteorol Soc—Am Geophys Union—AAAS—Sigma Xi. Meisinger award Am Meteorol Soc '46. University of California, Los Angeles 24.

22 NEILL, James Maffett. Microbiology (Bacteriology); Immunology. b'94. BS '17—DSc '40 (Allegheny Coll Meadville Pa); PhD '20 (Mass Agrl Coll). Conducted research in oxidation and reduction of blood pigments and of bacterial hemotoxins; hypersensitiveness and anaphylaxis to diptheria toxin and bacterial products; serologically reactive substances in sugars and other foods; serological properties of dextrans and levans of microbiological origin; immunological relationships between bacteria and fungi; general microbiology. Prof bact and immunol Cornell Med Coll since '31. Am Assn Immunol—Am Assn Path and Bact—Soc Am Bact—Am Pub Health Assn—Soc Exptl Biol and Med—Harvey Soc—AAAS—NY Acad Sci—Sigma Xi—Phi Delta Theta. 1300 York Av., NYC 21☉

23 NEISWANDER, Claud Revere. Insects affecting corn, greenhouse vegetables, and ornamental plants; Biology, ecology, and control of white grubs. b'93. AB '22—MSc '23—PhD '26 (O State U). Assited in European cornborer investigations '23-32; study control of white gurbs in lawns, pastures and field corps; evaluation corn strains for resistance or suceptibility to corn insect infestation and injury. Author article: The Sources of American Corn Insects '31. Co-author article: (with L L Huber, R M Salter) The European Corn Borer and its Environment '28; others. Asst entomol O Agrl Expt Sta '23-27, asso entomol '27-48, asso chmn dept entomol since '48; asso prof zool and entomol dept O State U '47-50, prof since '50. Am Assn Econ Entomol—Entomol Soc Am—O Acad Sci—Phi Beta Kappa—Sigma Xi. Ohio Agricultural Experiment Station, Wooster, O.

10 **NEISWANDER, Ralph Blosser.** Agricultural entomology (Peach, apple, strawberry, hothouse vegetable insects). b'98. Student '16 (O No U); BSc '27—MS '28—PhD '34 (O State U). Research in developing control measures for tomato pinworm, strawberry leaf roller, apple flea weevil, and plum curculio. Author articles: The Alimentary Canal of the Oriental Fruit Moth '35; Oriental Fruit Moth Investigations in Ohio '36; Insect Pests of Strawberries in Ohio '44; The Tomato Pinworm '45; DDT and Its Use in Control of Greenhouse Insects '46. Asst entomologist O Agrl Expt Sta '28-44, asso entomologist since '44; asso prof entomology O State U since '46. Am Assn Econ Entomol—Entomol Soc Am—O Acad Sci—Sigma Xi—Gamma Sigma Delta. Ohio Agricultural Experimental Station, Wooster, O.

11 **NELLER, Joseph R.** Soil fertility, chemistry and biology. b'91. BS (Macalester Coll); MS (U Minn); PhD (Rutgers U). Research on nutrition of sulfur in plants of western soils, physiology of herbicides and sprays on crops and fruits, conservation organic soils, phosphates in soils, use of radioactive phosphorus in soil fertility, soil fumigants. Patent on removal of color in oil. Author articles in field. Research asst soils dept Minn Agrl Expt Sta '15, NJ Expt Sta '16-20; research chem The Tex Co '20-21; agrl chem Washington Agrl Expt Sta '21-30; research chem Everglades Expt Sta '30-44; soil chem Fla Agrl Expt Sta since '44, chmn publications com. Northwest Sci Assn (chmn chem sect '35)—Soil Sci Soc Am—Fla Soil Sci Soc (pres '43)—AAAS(F)—Am Soc Agronomy—Phi Kappa Phi—Sigma Xi. University of Florida Agricultural Experiment Station, Gainesville, Fla.†

12 **NELSON, Arnold L(ars).** Wildlife biology; Economic zoology; Animal ecology. b'07. BS '28 (U Mich). Research and investigations in wildlife biology with emphasis on development of a foundation of practical information relating wildlife, the positive and negative relationships of wildlife and agriculture forestry and horticulture; methods for controlling injurious wildlife; management of wild fur animals; wildlife diseases and methods for their control. Co-author: Wildlife and Plants '49; also articles in field. Jr biol US Biol Survey Washington '31-35, asst biol '35-37, asso biol '37-40; biol US Fish and Wildlife Service Washington '40-45, sr biol Md '45-49, dir wildlife research station since '49. Am Ornithol Union—Wildlife Soc—Am Soc Mammalogists—Cooper Ornithol Club—Wilson Ornithol Club—Wash Biol Soc—Am Soc Ichthyologists and Herpetologists. Patuxent Research Refuge, Laurel, Md.

13 **NELSON, Bernard Anton.** Wildlife management; Ringnecked pheasant. b'18. BS '42—'42-43 (U Minn). Engaged in research and study general wildlife; ecology, life history, management, population, census techniques Ring-necked Pheasant. Game biol Minn Dept Conservation '43-46; game tech SD Dept Game, Fish, Parks '46-47; leader SD Small Game and Fur-bearers Study '47-51, Federal Aid co-ordinator since '51. Wildlife Society. Dept. of Game, Fish and Parks, Pierre, S.D.†

14 **NELSON, DeWitt.** Forestry (Fire protection, timber harvesting, range improvement, control of forest killing insects). b'01. Student '19-20 (U Ia); BS '25 (Ia State Coll). Worked on forest practice rules for timber harvesting on private lands, range improvement of low value brush covered lands, cooperative control of forest killing insects, adequate fire protection for forest, watershed, and range lands. State forester Calif Div Forestry since '45. Soc Am Foresters. 301 State Office Building No. 1, Sacramento, Calif.

15 **NELSON, (Mrs.) Dorothy Middleton.** Archeology; Ethnology; Indians. b'03. Grad '21 (Moorestown Friends Sch). Researched with Dr Warren King Moorehead; special studies on the reservations of the habits, crafts and symbolism of most major tribes of the US and Canada, made member of Stoney Indian family in western Canada '37. Author articles in field. Indian adv council State NJ '27-31; exec bd Archeol Soc NJ since '31; founder and dir Thunderbird Indian Museum since '26. Archeol Soc NJ—Archeol Soc Del—Pa Society for Archaeology—NJ State Museum Assn. Thunderbird Museum, Mt. Laurel Rd., Moorestown, N.J.†

16 **NELSON, Everett John.** Metaphysics; Epistemology; Logic (Symbolic); Philosophy of science. b'00. AB magna cum laude '23—AM '25 (U Washington); AM '28—PhD '29—U scholar '27-28—James Walker Fellow —Philip H Sears scholar '28-29—Frederick Sheldon Travel fellow '29-30 (Harvard); '29-30 (U Göttingen, U Freiburg Germany, Sorbonne Paris). Author articles in field. Cons editor: Journal of Symbolic Logic since '36. Prof philos U Washington, exec officer dept philos. Am Philos Assn (Pacific Div exec com '35-37, '45-47, vp '40, pres '46)—Am Philos Assn (Nat Assn organizing com for first Inter-Am Congress, also the second, chmn Nat Bd officers '46)—Assn Symbolic Logic (exec com '40-43—council '40-43)—Phi Beta Kappa. Guggenheim fellow '39-40. Department of Philosophy, Ohio State University, Columbus 10.†⊚

17 **NELSON, Frank Eugene.** Dairy bacteriology (Cheese, ice cream, methods of bacteria count, bacteriophage, microbial enzymes). b'09. BS '32—MS '34 (U Minn); PhD '36 (Ia State Coll). Research in bacteriology of ice cream, methods of enumerating bacteria in dairy products, molds in cream; research in yeast classification, manufacture of Blue and Cheddar cheeses from pasteurized milk, enzyme production by microorganisms and bacteriophage active against Streptococcus lactis. Author articles in field. Quality control Franklin Coop Creamery Assn Minneapolis summers '34-35; instr dairy bacteriology and mfg U Minn '36-37; asst prof Kan State Coll '37-41, asso prof '41-43; prof and research prof Ia State Coll since '43; editor Jour Dairy Sci '47-52. Am Dairy Sci Assn—Soc Am Bact—Am Chem Soc—Internat Assn Milk and Food Sanitarians—Phi Lambda Upsilon—Sigma Xi—Phi Kappa Phi—Gamma Sigma Delta—Alpha Zeta. Dairy Industry Department, Iowa State College, Ames, Ia.†

18 **NELSON, George Carl Edward.** History of biological sciences. b'00. BS '25—MS '26—fellow '20 (Coll City NY); PhD '31 (Columbia). Author: Introductory Biological Sciences in Liberal Arts College; History of Bio-logical Sciences in Secondary Schools of United States; Test in Educational Biology. Prof and librarian Fairleigh Dickinson Coll since '52. ALA—Bibliog Soc Am. Fairleigh Dickinson College, Rutherford, N.J. H: 401 Wearimus Rd., Westwood. 31.†

19 **NELSON, George H.** American history (Asiento of 1713, Negro slavery, civil liberties). b'02. AB '26 (Northern Mich Coll Edn); AM '29—PhD '33 (U Mich). Author articles: Contraband Trading Under the Asiento, 1730-1739 '45; What of the Bill of Rights? '44; Responsibility in the Bill of Rights '44; Landholding and Democracy '45; The Demilitarized Border '44; Peaceful International Cooperation '46 (with R L Wysong). Instr hist Central Mich Coll Edn '35-38, advanced to prof since '44, asst dir grad studies '46-47, dir since '47. Mich Acad Sci, Arts and Letters—AHA—Soc Advancement Edn. Central Michigan College of Education, Mt. Pleasant, Mich.

20 **NELSON, John A(lbert).** Dairy technology (Products, manufacturing). b'90. BS '22—MS '23—PhD '32 (Ia State Coll). Official judge of dairy products; licensed government grader for butter and cheese. Co-author: Judging Dairy Products '34, 2nd edit '48; also articles in field. Prof dairy Mont State Coll since '29; supt Advanced Registry Testing for Mont '22-50; dairy products ext specialist '25-50; advisor for Mont Dairy Plants since '25; spl lecturer on dairy manufacturing problems and dairy products. Am Dairy Sci Assn (chmn West Sect '34-36, dir '37-39, vp '44-45, pres '45-46)—Gamma Sigma Delta—Phi Kappa Phi —Sigma Xi. Department of Dairy Industry, Montana State College, Bozeman, Mont.†⊚

21 **NELSON, Leonard Edwin.** Waste disposal (Cannery). b'11. B Agrl Engineering '34 (U Minn). Designed, developed, supervised construction cannery waste disposal system consisting of collection system, wet well, pumping station, portable sprinkler irrigation system utilizing waste for irrigation farm crops. Patent applied for. Partner Nelson and Gray. Am Soc Agrl Engrs—Minn Soc Agrl Engrs. Plainview, Minn.

22 **NELSON, Roger James.** Log loads (Rate of hauling). b'09 BS in civil engring '32 (SD State Sch Mines and Tech). Research on rate of travel and costs of hauling log loads of various weights as affected by surface type, gradient, road curvature, width, size of load and horsepower of hauling unit; economics of log hauling. Preconstrn engr US Forest Service '40-50, highway engr since '50. Am Soc CE. 402 Bankers Security Building, Phila. 7.

23 **NELSON, Thurlow C(hristian).** Marine biology (Oysters and other molluscs); Limnology (Water supply). b'90. BS '13—DSc (hon) '39 (Rutgers U); PhD '17—fellow zool '13-17 (U Wis); '31 (London Sch Trop Medicine). Author articles in field. Biol Oyster Research Lab NJ Agrl Expt Sta since '19; prof zool Rutgers U since '26; biol NJ State Div Shellfisheries Trenton since '20; in charge NJ Oyster Research Lab since '16; chmn Div Water Policy and Supply of NJ since '45, commr since '29. Am Soc Zool (treas '39-41, vp '47-48)—Am Micros Soc—Soc Parasitologists—Ecol Soc Am—Limnology Soc Am—Am Soc Naturalists—Soc Exptl Biol and Med—Nat Shellfisheries Assn (pres '31-33) —Am Geophys Union—Phi Beta Kappa—Gamma Alpha—Sigma Xi. Received Rutgers award and medal Distinguished Scientist and Gifted Teacher. Rutgers University, New Brunswick, N.J. H: 77 Adelaide Av., Highland Park.◎

10 NELSON, Vincent Edward. Structural geology (Middle Rocky Mountains); Ore Deposits. b'13. AB '35 (Augustana Coll); PhD '42 (U Chicago). Author articles in field. Asso prof geol U Ky '45-49, prof since '49. Geol Soc Am(F). Department of Geology, University of Kentucky, Lexington, Ky.†

11 NELSON, William K(enneth). Asphalt; Lubricants. b'01. AB '24—Chem E '25 (Stanford U). Synthesis of superior asphalt products (paving materials, binders, roofing materials) from waste by-products of petroleum refining; exhaustive investigations into the physical and chemical constitution of natural and manufactured asphaltic materials as a basis for synthesis; research and process engineering in connection with development of improved methods of lubricating oil manufacture. Holds patent on process for preparation high grade asphalts. Exptl and asphalt chem Pan Am Petroleum Co '25-29; asst chief chem Shell Petroleum Corp '30-33, sr research chem '33-39; now chief chem Golden Bear Oil Co. ACS—AS TM—Am Petroleum Inst—Phi Lambda Upsilon—Alpha Chi Sigma—Sigma Xi. Professional chem engr Cal. Golden Bear Oil Co., Oildale, Cal.

12 NESS, Fred C. Firearms; Applied small arms ballistics. b'96. Camping, fishing, hunting, shooting, and nature study; writer on outdoor magazine subjects. Author: Practical Dope on the Big Bores '49; American Sighting Scopes; also articles in field. Chief technician Nat Rifle Assn '30-46. Associate editor: The American Rifleman. Nat Rifle Assn—Am Acad Arms —Am Gunsmith's Guild (hon). Box 59, Red Wing, Minn.

13 NETHERCOT, Arthur Hobart. The Metaphysical poets; Drama (British and American); S T Coleridge; Bernard Shaw. b'95. AB '15—MA '16 (Northwestern U); student '19 (Oxford U); PhD '22 (U Chicago). Author: Abraham Cowley '31; Sir William D'avenant '38; The Road to Tryermaine '39. Editor: A Book of Long Stories. Co-editor: Elizabethan and Stuart Plays. With Northwestern U since '19, prof English since '39. Modern Lang Assn Am (sec drama group '42-43)—Modern Humanities Research Assn—Shakespeare Assn—AAUP (pres local chpt '48-49)—Phi Beta Kappa. H: 811 Ridge Terrace, Evanston, Ill.†◎

14 NETTELS, Curtis Putnam. America (Colonial history, economic history); American Revolution. b'98. AB '21 (U Kan). AM '22—PhD '25 (U Wis). Author: The Money Supply of the American Colonies '34; The Roots of American Civilization '38. Member editorial board A History of American Economic Life (9 vols) since '45, Journal of Economic History since '41, American Historical Review '43-49. With U Wis '21-44, prof history '33-44, chmn dept '39-40; prof Am history Cornell U since '44; lectr Harvard '37-38, Columbia '38, Johns Hopkins '41; Guggenheim Meml Found fellow '28; research grant Social Service Research Council '33. Am Hist Assn(nominating com '39-40, program com '41)—Miss Valley Hist Assn— Econ Hist Soc—Colonial Soc Mass— Soc Am Historians—Am Econ Hist Assn—Mass Hist Soc—Phi Beta Kappa. 227 Boardman Hall, Cornell University, Ithaca.◎

15 NETTING, M. Graham. Conservation; economic herpetology; Museum administration; Zoogeography. b'04. BS '26 (U Pittsburgh); AM '29 (U Mich); ScD '50 (Waynesburg). Author articles in field. Asst Carnegie Mus '26-28, asst curator herpetology '28-32, curator since '32, assistant director '49, acting director since '53; lecturer biol geog U Pittsburgh since '36, asst prof geog since '44. AAAS(F)—Am Asso Museum—Am Geog Soc—Nat Speleolog Soc—Am Soc Ichthyologists and Herpetologists (sec '31-48, pres '48-50) —Am Soc Mammalogists—Ecol Soc Am—Pa Acad Sci—Sigma Xi—Soil Cons Soc Am. Carnegie Museum, Pittsburgh 13.†

16 NETTLETON, Lewis Lomax. Geophysical exploration; Structural geology; Gravity (Methods and techniques for analysis and interpretation); Interpretation of aeromagnetic surveys; Salt domes. b'96. BS '18 (U Idaho); PhD '23 (U Wis). Author articles in field. Partner Gravity Meter Exploration Co Houston Tex since '46. AAAS— Am Geophy Union—Am Physical Soc— Am Assn Pet Geologists—Geol Soc Am —Soc Exploration Geophysicists (editor '45-47, vp '47-48, pres '48-49)— Houston Geol Soc. Gravity Meter Exploration Co., 340 Esperson Bldg., Houston 2, Texas.†◎

17 NEUBAUER, Emil Theodore Paul. Applied mechanics; Thermodynamics. b'05. ME '31 (U Mich); MS '33 (MIT). Engaged developing and designing air-conditioners, high speed refrigerating compressors, special atomic equipment; research thermodynamics; torsional stress analysis by membrane analogy, vibration control problems, shaft seals to meet special conditions. Author articles in field. Holds patents three inventions of special valves and refrigerating machinery. Engr Gen Electric Co Lynn Mass '31-32; engr York Pa Ice Machinery Corp '33-43; in charge lab mech research Columbia U '43-44; engr in charge engring prodn spl equipment for Manhattan Project Allis-Chalmers '44-45, engr blower-comp dept '45-47; chief engring and design Kellex Corp NYC '47-48; engr charge reciprocating compressor development and design Trane Co since '48. ASME— AAAS—Am Soc Refrigerating Engrs. The Trane Co., La Crosse, Wis.

18 NEUBAUER, Loren Wenzel. Wood preservation; Adobe; Farm structures. b'04. BS in civil engring '26—MS '32 —PhD '48 (U Minn). Research on wood and fence-post durability treatment; stream-bed erosion; adobe brick construction and stabilization; effect of admixtures, waterproofing, strengthening; potato storehouse design; automatic feeders for poultry. Asst prof agrl engring U Cal '40-48, asso prof since '48. Am Soc Agrl Engrs —Sigma Xi—Tau Beta Pi—Chi Epsilon —Am Geophys Union—Theta Tau. Div of Agricultural Engineering, University of California, Davis.

19 NEUBERT, Alfred M(ax). Processing fruits and vegetables. b'12. BS—MS '35—PhD '41 (State Coll Washington). Co-author: (with R M Smock) Apples—Their Chemistry, Physiology, and Technology '49; also articles in field. Asst state chemist Washington State Dept Agr '35-37; chem US Fruit and Veg Prod Lab Bur of Agr and Ind Chem, US Dept Agr, Pullman Wash since '37; chemist in charge US Fruit and Veg Prod Lab since '44; chem Agr Expt Sta State Coll Wash '37-52, charge fruit and vegetable investigations of Pacific Northwest since '52. ACS—Inst Food Tech—Sigma Xi. Superior Service award US Dept Agr '48. U.S. Fruit and Vegetable Products Laboratory, Prosser, Wash.†

20 NEUBURGER, Rudolf. Education (Installment financing of tuition). Instrumental in introducing installment plan of financing school and college tuition fees as vice-president of Tuition Plan Inc. New York City. b'89. BA '11 (Cornell). Author articles in field. President Tuition Plan Inc, NYC since '38. 424 Madison Av., NYC 19.

21 NEUDA, Paul Maria. Human blood (Immunological role in diseases). b'87. MD '12 (U Vienna). Arterial blood in veins; spontaneous thrombosis and embolism; origin of human cancer through immunization; blood group enzyme as a pathological agent. Issued patent in field. Med cons Robinson Found Inc and dir Lab for Study of Human Blood since '48. AMA —AAAS—Soc Physicians Vienna (corr). 254 W. 31st St., NYC 1; also 177 E. 79th St., NYC 21.

22 NEUMAN, Abraham A. Spanish and Jewish history. b'90. BS '09—MA '12 (Columbia); Rabbi '12—HLD '14 —LittD '47 (Jewish Theol Sem); LLD '45 (U Pa); HLD '45 (Hebrew Union Coll). Author: Cyrus Adler: A Biographical Sketch '42; Jews in Spain: Their Social, Political and Cultural Life During the Middle Ages (2 vols) '42; Saadia Studies (edited with Solomon Zeitlin) '43; Relation of the Hebrew Scriptures to American Institutions; Judaism (The Great Religions of the Modern World) '46; Samuel Usque: Marrano Historian of the 16th Century '46. Chairman editorial board for Jewish Apocryphal Literature; editor Jewish Quarterly Review; member publ com Jewish Publ Soc Am; revising editor Universal Jewish Ency. With Dropsie Coll for Hebrew and Cognate Learning since '13, prof '34-41, pres since '41; hon rabbi Congregational Mikveh Israel Phila. Am Jewish Hist Soc(vp)—Am Hist Soc—Am Oriental Soc—Hist Soc Pa—Jewish Acad Arts and Scis (hon F)—Am Acad Jewish Research(hon)—Jewish Hist Soc Eng (Corr). Dropsie College, Broad and Yorks sts., Phila 32.◎

23 NEVITT, Henry John Barrington. Communications (Longdistance). b'08. BA Sc in applied sci '34 (U Toronto); MEngr '45 (McGill U). Manufacture and development telephone, telegraph, carrier and radio equipment, frequency-shift radio teleprinter receiving systems; planning and design long distance electrical communicaton systems, especially Venezuelan long distance national and international telephone and telegraph services. Radio work Rogers Batteryless Radio Co and Marconi Co '26-28; development engr Zavod Electropribor '32-33; mfg engr N Elec Co '34-39; equipment engr Can Pacific Ry '39-44; equipment engr Defense Communications Ltd '43-44; staff engr RCA Internat Div '44-47; chief engr and cons engr Ericsson Telephone Sales Corp and Telefonaktiebolaget L M Ericsson since '47. Inst Radio Engrs (sr mem)—Inst Elec Engrs Gt Brit—Am Inst EE—AAAS— Sigma Xi. Ericsson Telephone Sales Corp., 100 Park Av., NYC; Telefonaktiebolaget L. M. Ericsson, Stockholm, Sweden.

24 NEW, James Richard. Photogrammetry; Geophysical exploration. b'15. Student '33-35 (Tex A&M); '43 (Harvard). Designed topographic camera and conversion projector for photographic surveying and geometrigraph, a traverse and elevation plotting instrument. Geophys engr Petty Geophys Engring Co '39-42; div engr Rep Exploration Co since '47; partner Geophotometric Engring Co since '47; partner Imperial Instrument Co since '49. Capt CE US Army '42-46. Soc Exploration Geophys—Am Soc Photogrammetry—Am Geophys Union. Box 2208; Tulsa. H: 3217 E. 28th St.

10 NEWCOMBE, Curtis L(akeman). Shell fish; Water Pollution. b'05. BA '26—MA '27 (Acadia U); MS '29 (W Va U); '30 (Puget Sound Biol Sta U Wash); '30-31 Bursary Award NRC —PhD in marine biol '33 (U Toronto). Provided proof of annual ring method of age determination in soft shell clams of North Atlantic waters, research on growth characteristics of Molluscs; member Chesapeake Bay Fishery Commission of Rockefeller Foundation '41-45, member Advisory Committee on Natural Resources for State of Virginia '45-46, member of Fishery Advisory Committee of Atlantic States Marine Fisheries Commission '43-46, member Scientific Advisory Committee Natural Resources Council of America '47-50. Author: Laboratory Directions for an Elementary Course in General Zoology '38; 63 articles in field. Contributor: Year Book American Philosophical Society '40. Mem faculty and asst prof zool U Md '33-40; in charge research Chesapeake Biol Lab '37-39; asso prof biol Coll William and Mary and dir and biol Va Fisheries Lab '40-46; zool Cranbrook Inst Sci, lectr Wayne U and collaborator lab vertebrate biol U Mich '46-49; biol Div Water Pollution Control USPHS since '49; research asso bot U Cal since '51. Va Acad Sci (co-chmn com natural resources '44-45, chm biol sect '44-46, mem long-range planning com '45-46) —Ecol Soc Am (chmn com preservation natural conditions '38-45, mem com applied ecol '38-52, com study plant and animal communities '46-49, chmn com resolutions since '50)—Nat Park Assn (bd trustees '39-48)—Ecol Union (v-chmn '45-46, chmn com preservation natural conditions '45-49)— Detroit Acad Natural Scis (pres '49) —Grassland Research Found (sec since '50)—The Nature Conservancy (vp '51-52). US Public Health Service, 441 Federal Office Bldg., SF 2. H: 8 Middle Rd., Hidden Valley, Lafayette, Cal.

11 NEWELL, Earl Lester. Ocean telegraph cables. b'96. BS '21 (Union Coll); EE '22 (Columbia). Made lab studies necessary to pioneer design of high-speed loaded ocean cables, supervised first loaded cable duplexed, developed methods for improving duplex balances, frequency modulated carrier system for cables, networks for suppression of radio interference originating in telegraph equipment. Holder US patent automatic plotting relative humidity. Engineer research and development eng dept Western Union Telegraph Co since '22. Am Inst Elect Engrs—Tau Beta Pi—Sigma Xi. Western Union Telegraph Company, 60 Hudson St., NYC 13.

12 NEWELL, Irwin M(ayer). Ecology; Arctic biology; Mites; Marine biology. b'16. BS '39—MS '41 (State Coll Wash); MS '42—PhD '45 (Yale). Biological studies on orchard mites in central Washington; studies on ecology and systematics of the Halacaridae (marine mites) of eastern North America; studies on ecology of spruce budworm moth in Quebec and New York, biology of marine fouling organisms; distribution of marine organisms, especially the mites, of the Pacific coast; studies on the marine mites of the world. Asst prof biol U Ore '46-48; asso entomol U Hawaii since '49. Am Micros Soc—Arctic Inst NA—Soc Systematic Zoologists—Phi Beta Kappa—Phi Kappa Phi—Sigma Xi. Department of Entomology, University of Hawaii, Honolulu 14.

13 NEWELL, William B. Iroquoian societal evolution and history. b'92. AB '24 (Syracuse U); MA '34 (Penn U); Rank I Teaching Certificate '50 (State Fla); spl studies field edn leading to doctorate '49-51 (U Fla). Leader in drive to secure adequate schools for New York State Indian reservations '20-24; founder Six Nations Association Indian Welfare Society of New York State '26; missionary to the Seneca Indians Cattaraugas Reservation NY '24-28; founder Society Neighborhood Indians Phila '33; director educational projects, recreational council Delaware County Pa '34-35; founder Big Soldier Playgrounds Mayette Kan '36. Editor: The Quipu (museum publ); The Six Nations (NY State Indian Welfare Soc Pub). Dir Am Indian Museum Arts and Scis '38-43; asso prof sociol U Fla '47, vis asso prof and acting head dept summer '48, spl studies, '49-51; chmn dept sociol and anthropol U Conn '46-49, chmn dept sociol and anthropol Trumbull bd New London. Am Acad Polit and Social Sci—Am Anthropol Assn—AAAS—NEA—Fla Edn Assn— Am Assn Museums—AAUP—Phi Delta Kappa. H: 2508 Kathleen St., Tampa, Fla.†⊙

14 NEWHALL, Allan Goodrich. Diseases of vegetables and cacao; Control of nematodes; Soil fumigation. b'94. BS '19 (U Minn); PhD '29 (Cornell U). Research on fungus diseases of vegetables, control of nematodes, soil sterilization by means of steam, electrical, or chemical treatments, seed treatments of vegetables; cold storage diseases of carrots; research on cacao diseases Inter-American Institute of Agricultural Sciences Costa Rica '47. Assistant path Ohio Agrl Expt Station '25-29; asso prof plant path Cornell U '39, prof since '44. AAAS(F)—Am Phytopathy Soc (patron)—Sigma Xi— Phi Kappa Phi—Gamma Sigma Delta. Plant Science Building, College of Agriculture, Ithaca, N.Y.†

15 NEWHALL, Sidney M. Color (Measurement. vision, psychology, systems). b'96. BS '19—MA '21 (Wesleyan U); PhD '23 (Columbia U). Research on visual instruments, methods for measuring perceived colors, color terms and definitions. Author articles in field. Asso in psychol Johns Hopkins '37-42; tech dir Foxboro Fire-Control Lab '44-45; supervisor psychol research Eastman Kodak Co since '46. Phi Beta Kappa—Sigma Xi—Am Psychol Assn(F)—Optical Soc Am (colorimetry com, chmn subcom on color spacing '37-43, com on uniform color scales)—Inter-Soc Color Council (chmn com on color terms since '44)—Am Standards Assn—Am Soc Testing Materials—NY State Psychol Assn. Color Control Department, Kodak Park, Rochester 4, N.Y.

16 NEWITT, John Henry. Electronics; Radio direction finding; Anti radar devices; Electronic remote controls; electronic digital computers and business machines. b'17. Student '37-40 (Newark Coll Engring); '40-42 (Johns Hopkins); BS '42 (McKinley-Roosevelt Found); '43-46 (Stevens Inst Tech). Automatic radio direction finding devices; automatic and remote controlled accounting equipment; electrical recording equipment, tabulating, totalizing and computing machines. Author: High Fidelity Techniques '53. Co-author (with J R Johnson) Practical, Television Servicing '48. Author articles: RC Oscillator performance; Wide band television antenna considerations; others. Issued patents in field. Production engr Electron Tubes '36-40; tech writer Aircraft Radio Manuals '40-42; project engr Fed Tele-

communications Labs '42-46; asst to pres Hillyer Instrument Co '47-48; vp Electronic Management Control Inc '48-50; chief engr. Central Records Inc '46-51; now with Digital Computer Lab, MIT. War Manpower Commn and OSRD awards for engring contbns to prosecution World War II. H: 58 Hollett St., North Scituate, Mass.

17 NEWKIRK, Burt Leroy. Vibration; Shaft behavior; Lubrication. b'76. AB—MA (U Minn); PhD (U Munich, Germany). Inventions and studies on process for dynamic balancing, critical speeds and behavior of rotating shafts, oil film whirl and cramped shaft whirl of rotating shafts, mercury boiler for power generation. Author articles: Shaft Whipping due to Oil Action '25; Whirling Balanced Shafts '30; Oil Film Whirl '34; Instability of Oil Films and More Stable Bearings '37, and others. Asst prof math and mechanics Coll Minn '07-20; research engr Gen Elec Co '20-36; prof vibration theory and practice Rensselaer Poly Inst since '37. AAAS(F)—ASME —Inst Aero Sci. Rensselaer Polytechnical Institute, Troy, N.Y. H: 17 Rosa Rd., Schenectady 8.†

18 NEWMAN, Arthur Stanley. Plant growth regulators; Soil microbiology. b'16. BS '38 (ND Agrl Coll); MS '40 —PhD '42 (Ia State Coll). Research on effect plant growth regulators on soil microorganisms and effects soil microflora on growth regulators, evaluation of plant growth regulators when applied to soil. Author articles in field. Jr soil scientist Spokane Wash Soil Conservation Service US Dept Agr '39-40; US Army plant growth regulator investigations Camp Detrick Md '44-46, agron Chem Corps since '46. Am Soc Agron—Soil Sci Soc Am—Sigma Xi—Phi Kappa Phi. Camp Detrick, Frederick, Md.†

19 NEWMAN, Edwin Stanley. Civil rights; Civil liberties; Race relations. b'22. AB '40 (Coll City NY); LLB '43 (Columbia). Research on anti-discrimination legislation and constitutional protection for fundamental freedoms, on interaction of law and education in problems of equality of citizenship for all Americans, on techniques for utilizing community resources to develop better intergroup understanding; chairman Committee on Community Organization of NY State Committee on Discrimination in Housing. Author: The Law of Civil Rights and Civil Liberties '49. Editor: Tools for Human Relations. Asso dir NY chpt Am Jewish Com '46-50, finance sec '50-51; exec ed Oceana Publications since '49; lectr New Sch Soc Research. Phi Beta Kappa—Assn Jewish Community Relations Workers —Am Civil Liberties Union.

20 NEWMAN, Harold B. English parliamentary history (Seventeenth Century). b'09. BA '29 (Amherst); MA '31 (Oxford U); MA '36 (Harvard); Simpson F '29-30 (Amherst Coll at Oxford U); PhD '49 (Harvard). Policy Eng parliament toward the royalists during civil wars and interregnum of seventeenth century. Asst dept hist Harvard '36; with Brooklyn Coll since '37, asst prof history since '50 AHA— AAUP. Brooklyn College, Bedford Av., Brooklyn. H: 209 Lincoln Place, Brooklyn 17.

21 NEWMAN, Harry. Buttons (Plastic); Plastics (Thermosetting, decoration). b'04. BS '25 (MIT). Developed mottled urea buttons in US, developed process for decorating thermosetting plastics. In charge research Rochester Button Co '29-37; vp and research head Button Corp Am '37-49; partner Riverdale Lab since '49. Soc Plastics Engrs.

Riverdale Laboratories, 9 Webster St., Newark 4.

10 NEWMAN, Harry Shaw. Old prints; Americana; Maps (Old American). b'96. BS '19 (Columbia). Research on pictorial Americana in old prints and maps. Pres Old Print Shop Inc since '28. Century Assn—Grolier Club. Old Print Shop, Inc., 150 Lexington Av., NYC 16.

11 NEWMAN, Marshall Thornton. American Indian (Physical anthropology); Anthropology of the Ryukyu Islands. b'11. Student '29-31 (Dartmouth Coll); PhB '33—MA '35 (U Chicago); PhD '41 (Harvard); Bolton fellow '35-36 (Western Reserve U). Field trips in archeology '32, '33, '34; excavations in Florida '33-34. Author articles: A Metric Study of Underformed Indian Crania from Peru '43; Indian Skeletal Material from the Central Coast of Peru '47. Co-author: (with R L Eng) The Ryukyu People: A Biological Appraisal '47, and others. Cons phys anthrop TVA '38-40; supervisor project 8 Inst Andean Research Peru '41-42; asso curator phys anthrop US Nat Mus since '42 . Am Anthrop Assn(F)— Am Assn Phys Anthrop—Soc Applied Anthrop — Anthrop Soc Washington (sec)—Sigma Xi. U.S. National Museum, Washington.†⊚

12 NEWMAN, Ralph Geoffrey. History, bibliography and manuscripts (Lincoln period); Americana. b'11. Discovered Leland-Baker trial printing of Lincoln's Emancipation Proclamation, Lincoln's autobiographical letter to John Coulter in 1860, Ward Hill Lemon's letter to General Gridley in 1865, other documents. Co-author: The American Iliad (with O Eisenschiml) '47. Editor: The Diary of a Public Man '45; also articles in field. Owner Abraham Lincoln Book Shop since '33; partner Americana House Pub since '46; mem advisory com Ill State Hist Lib since '42. Ill State Hist Soc—AHA —Bibliog Soc Am—Ind Hist Soc—Ia Hist Soc—Abraham Lincoln Assn— Lincoln Group Wis—Miss Valley Hist Soc. 18 E. Chestnut St., Chicago 11.

13 NEWMAN, Russell Wallace. Anthropometry. b'19. AB '41—PhD '49 (U Cal). Research on skeletal analysis of prehistoric populations especially American Indians; research on military and civilian applications of body measurement data with reference to fitting clothing and equipment to man and fitting man to job on basis of physique. Co-author: A Manual of Archeological Field Method '49. Head anthrop unit QM Climatic Research Lab since '50. Am Assn Phys Anthrop—Am Anthrop Assn—Soc Am Archeol—Am Soc Human Genetics— Phi Beta Kappa—Sigma Xi—Phi Sigma. Quartermaster Climatic Research Laboratory, Lawrence, Mass.

14 NEWMAN, Samuel Clayton. Marriage statistics; Divorce statistics. b'10. AB in sociol '31 (U Pittsburgh); AM '34 (Oberlin Coll); PhD '39 (O State U). In charge development federal program for collecting vital staistics on marriages and divorces through cooperation with state vital statistics offices. Author articles: Needs and Future Prospects for Integrating Marriage and Divorce Data with other Vital Statistics '49; The Development and Status of Vital Statistics on Marriage and Divorce '50; Trends in Vital Statistics of Marriages and Divorces in the United States '50, and others. Formerly sociology faculty Oberlin Coll, O State U, U Louisville; with Nat Office Vital Statistics Pub Health Service FSA since '45, chief marriage and divorce analysis br since '47; also lectr sociol

Am U Washington. Am Sociol Soc— Eastern Sociol Soc—So Sociol Soc— Am Acad Polit and Social Sci—Am Statis Assn—Am Pub Health Assn— Population Assn Am—Nat Council Family Relations—AAUP. National Office of Vital Statistics, Public Health Service, Federal Security Agency, Washington 25.

15 NEWMAN, Stanley Stewart. Linguistics; Anthropology. b'05. .PhB '27 —AM '28 (U Chicago); PhD '32 (Yale). Field work among Indians California '30-31, British Columbia '32. Author: Yokuts Language of California. Coauthor: Language in General Education; Language, Culture and Personality; Yokuts and Western Mono Myths; also articles in field. Cons instr on personality development Progressive Edn Assn '39-41; research asso dept anthrop Columbia '41-43; Unit War Dept '43-45; anthrop Smithsonian Instn '45-49; asso prof anthrop U NM '49-53, professor since '53. AAAS—American Anthropological Association—Linguistic Society Am—Phi Beta Kappa—Sigma Xi. Research fellow Social Sci Research Council '32-34, Am Council Learned Socs '34-36. Department of Anthropology, University of New Mexico, Albuquerque, N.M.

16 NEWMARK, Nathan M. Structural and applied mechanics (Numerical methods, stress analysis, elasticity, buckling, effects of impact and explosion on structures and reinforced concrete slabs). Born '10. BS in CE '30 (Rutgers Univ); MS '32—PhD '34 (Ill U). Research on reinforced concrete highway bridge floors, impact on reinforced concrete beams, numerical and approximate methods of analysis of structural and machine elements, analysis of stresses in notched bars subjected to tension, development of simple means of analysis of beamcolumns and other structures when stressed beyond elastic limit, determination of stresses in plates or slabs, stresses in foundations. Author articles in field. Research prof structural and civil engring Ill U since '43; chmn Digital Computer Lab since '51. Mem Scientific Advisory Bd US Air Forces since '45, bd cons Underground Explosion Test Program Office Chief Engrs War Dept since '47. Phi Beta Kappa—Tau Beta Pi—Sigma Xi—AS CE (Croes Medal '45)—ASME—Phi Kappa Phi—Am Concrete Inst—Am Soc Testing Materials—Soc Exptl Stress Analysis — Inst Aeronautical Sci—Internat Assn Bridge and Structural Engring. 111 Talbot Laboratory, University of Illinois, Urbana, Ill.

17 NEWTON, Earle Williams. History of Vermont and New England. AB '38 (Amherst); AM '39—student '39-40 (Columbia). Editor Vermont Quarterly '43-50, Vermont Life '46-50, American Heritage since '49; managing editor History News '47-49. General editor: Growth of Vermont (10 vol) '45-; American States Series (48 vol) '49; also articles in field. Dir historical research Webster Pub Co '40-42; exec officer Vt Evacuation Authority '43-44; field historian USN Pacific area '44-46; exec sec Am Assn State and Local Hist '46-52. Society Am Historians (sec)—AHA—Vt Hist Soc—Am Assn Mus—Newcomen Soc. Old Sturbridge Village, Sturbridge, Mass.

18 NEYHART, Amos Earl. Automobiles (Driving skill tests, driver training). b'98. BS '21—MS '34 (Pa State Coll). Developed system for driver training based on educational principals; developed driving skill tests for commercial fleets; pioneer teacher-training courses in driving. Head nat driver training program Am Automo-

bile Assn '36-38, road training cons since '38; adminstr head inst pub safety Pa State Coll since '38; trainer instrs in emergency driving Office Civilian Defense, ARC. Soc Automoive Engrs—NEA—Nat Safety Council (com on comml vehicles, driver-training)—Phi Delta Kappa—Kappa Phi Kappa—Sigma Tau. Pennsylvania State College, State College, Pa. and American Automobile Association, Washington.

19 NICHOL, Andrew A. Guayule; Plants (Desert). b'95. BSA '25 (U Minn); '20-32 (U Ariz). Research in culture production and ecology of guayule, distribution, native uses, commerical potentials desert plants; effects flouride on vegetation and livestock. Author articles: The Olive Parlatoria in Arizona; The natural vegetation of Arizona; The cacti of Arizona; also mimeographed publication on guayule. Entomol and ecol U Ariz '26-37; ecol US Dept Interior '38-39; State of Ariz '40-42; ecol USDA '42-46, '47-49; charge guayule research Stanford Research Inst '47-49, Fluoride investigations and research since '49. AAAS—Am Wildlife Soc—Ecol Am—Sigma Xi—Alpha Zeta. 840 S.E. Washington St., Portland 14, Ore.

20 NICHOLS, James B(ryant). Seismic interpretations; Seismic velocities. b'13. Student '32-36 (Tex A&M Coll). Research on seismic interpretation leading to discovery petroleum reserves; designed slide rule for velocity functions and migrations. Geophys Rogers-Ray Inc since '41. Soc Exploration Geophys—AIMME. Postoffice Box 6557, Houston 5.

21 NICHOLS, Jeannette Paddock (Mrs Roy F Nichols). History of Alaska; American political and economic history; International monetary relations. AB '13—LLD '51 (Knox College); AM '19—PhD '23 (Columbia University). Author: History of Alaska '24; Twentieth Century United States '43; (with Roy F Nichols) Growth of American Democracy '39; (with Roy F Nichols) The Republic of the United States '42; (with Roy F Nichols) A Short History of American Democracy '43. Co-editor: Democracy in the Middle West '41; History in the High School and Social Studies in the Elementary School '44; also articles in field. Vis prof U Birmingham Eng '48. Middle States Council Social Studies (pres '43-44)—AHA (chmn com govt publs)—Miss Valley Hist Assn—Am Assn U Women (V J Hill fellow '44)— League Women Voters—Nat Council Soc Studies—Phi Beta Kappa—Phi Alpha Theta—Internat Fedn U Women (leader in internat econ relations Toronto '47, Zurich '50). 438 Riverview Rd., Swarthmore, Pa.†⊚

22 NICHOLS, Madaline Wallis. Latin American history, literature and bibliography; Inter-American relations. b'98. AB '18 (Mount Holyoke Coll); AM '22 (Cornell); PhD '37 (U Cal): '19-20 (Columbia); '26 (Harvard) '23, '27 (Sorbonne); '30, '31, '34 (Stanford U); '37 (University Chile). Author: Cuentos y leyendas de Espana '30; Sarmiento: A Chronicle of Inter-American Friendship '40; Bibliographical Guide to Materials on American Spanish '41; The Gaucho: Cattle Hunter, Cavalryman, Ideal of Romance '42, and others; also articles in field. Asso prof history Florida State University '48-50; vis prof Lat Am hist U NM '50-51. Hispanic Soc Am (corr)—Am Geog Society—Nat Soc Women Geog— AHA—Modern Lang Assn—Sociedad de geografia e historia de Guatemala (corr). Travel grant from Carnegie Endowment for Internat Peace. 1028 Ann Av. S.W., Albuquerque.⊚

10 NICHOLS, Robert Leslie. Vulcanology; Glaciology; Polar geology. b'04. BS '26 (Tufts Coll); MA '30—PhD '40 (Harvard). Geologist Ronne Antarctic Research Expedition '47-48; geologist US Navy Task Force to Greenland and Ellesmere Island '48. Author articles in field. Instr, later prof geol Tufts Coll since '29, head geol dept since '40; mem US Geol Survey since '40. Geol Soc Am(F)—Am Geog Soc (F)—AAAS (F)—Am Geophys Union—Arctic Inst NA—Am Polar Soc—Sigma Xi. Department Geology, Tufts College, Medford, Mass.†

11 NICHOLS, Roy Franklin. American political history (Parties, federalism). b'96. AB '18—AM '19—LHD '41 (Rutgers); PhD '23—fellow '20-21 (Columbia U); LittD '37 (Franklin and Marshall Coll)—MA '48 (Cambridge U England); LLD '53 (Moravian University). Author: The Democratic Machine '50-54 '23; Franklin Pierce '31; Disruption of American Democracy '48. Co-author: America Yesterday and Today '38; Growth of American Democracy '39; The Republic of the United States: A History '42; A Short History of American Democracy '43. Assistant Professor history U Pa '25-30, professor since '30, dean graduate sch since '52; visiting professor Am history Cambridge U '48-49. Social Sci Research Council—Am Philos Soc—AHA (mem council '43-47, exec com '45-47)—Middle States Assn Hist Teachers (pres '32-33)—Pa Hist Assn (pres '36-39)—Pa Fedn Hist Socs (pres '40-42)—Hist Soc Pa (vp)—AAUP—Am Assn State Local Hist (mem council)—Phi Beta Kappa—Phi Alpha Theta. 101 Bennett Hall, University of Pennsylvania, Phila 4.☉

12 NICHOLS, Rudolph Henry, Jr. Acoustics; Communications; Noise reduction. b'11. AB '32 (Hope Coll); AM '33—PhD '39 (U Mich). Lecturer Northwestern University Symposium on Hearing '44, '46; discussion chairman US Navy Sound Conference New London, Connecticut '45. Author articles in field. Physicist Owens Ill Glass Co Alton '39-41; spl research asso Cruft Lab Harvard '41-44, asst and asso dir Electro-Acoustic Lab '45-46; mem tech staff Bell Telephone Lab Murray Hill NJ since '46. Acoustical Soc Am(F)—Am Standards Assn (sub-group chmn, sub-com on audiometry and hearing aids)—Sigma Xi—Gamma Alpha. c/o Bell Telephone Laboratories, Murray Hill, N.J.

13 NICHOLSON, A(rnold) J(oseph). Wildlife management; Mammalogy; Ecology. b'12. BS '34 (Mich State Coll); PhD '38 (U Mich). Research breeding and food habits fox squirrel; home life of peromyscus; wildlife survey and restoration areas north central Tex; investigations wildlife resources in connection water development program; project leader basin-wide survey fish and wildlife resources Mo River Basin. Author: A Hibernating Jumping Mouse '37; The Homes and Social Habits of the Wood-Mouse in Southern Michigan '41; Conservation of Megapods by Solomon Island Natives '46; Bats from New Caledonia, New Hebrides, and Solomon Islands '48. Co-author: Parasitism and Malnutrition of Deer in Tex '43. Service with US Army '43-46, on New Caledonia in malaria and epidemic control unit with rodent control team; made collection rodents for Nat Mus, bats for Chicago Mus, amphibians and reptiles for U Mich Mus, birds, mammals, reptiles and snails on Solomon Islands for Nat Mus; conducted ecol investigation of rodents. Research asst Lab Vertebrate Genetics U Mich '34-38; Fed aid div **Tex game fish** and oyster commn '38-

46; game mgr '38-42; leader wildlife trapping and transplanting project '42-46; US Fish and Wildlife Service Mo River Basin Studies Billings Mont since '46. Mich Acad Sci—Tex Acad Sci—Wildlife Soc—Am Soc Mammalogists—Sigma Xi. Box 1381, Billings, Mont. H: 1201 Yale.

14 NICHOLSON, John Elliot. Stone preservation (Chemical treatment of stone decay); Exterior waterproofing of buildings; Restoration of historic buildings. b'99. Student '22 (Princeton). President Nicholson and Galloway Inc since '32, founded by grandfather 1849; asso Larsen & Rostrop Copenhagen Denmark in uses of Decksoit in Am in restoration natural building stone. National Assn Insul-Mastic Licensees (pres). 426-428 East 110th St., NYC 29.

15 NICHOLSON, Madison G(artrell), Jr. Radio (Frequency modulation, patents, tubes). b'06. Grad student in physics, communication engring '27-29 (Columbia); BS '28 (U Ga). Research circuit development, frequency modulation, radio tube development. Holds 20 patents in field. Author articles: A Simple Harmonic Analyzer '32; A Noise Reducing Circuit '36; Comparison of Amplitude and Frequency Modulation '47; New Circuit Design for "Wow" Tester '48. Research physicist Westinghouse Electric Corp Bloomfield NJ '29-30; circuit development Nat Union Radio Corp Newark '30-39, chief comml engr '39-41; research and tech cons Sylvania Electric Products Inc Buffalo since '41. Co-winner outstanding development award radio tube and lamp div Westinghouse Electric Corp '29-33. Colonial Radio and Television Div., Sylvania Electric Products, Inc., 1280 Main St., Buffalo 9.

16 NICKELL, Frank Andrew. Geology (Engineering). b'06. BS '27—MS '28—PhD '31 (Cal Inst Tech). Investigations dam and reservoir sites; studies hydro-electric and irrigation projects; study geological features of engineering projects. Author article: Development and Use of Engineering Geology '42. Geol US Bur Reclamation '31-39, head geol '39-43; geol Shell Oil Co '43; cons Mexico '44; geol Stanolind Oil & Gas '44; cons geol Argentina, Venezuela, Colombia, India, Israel, Nepal, and Afghanistan since '45. AIMME. H: 2312 Dudley St., Pasadena 7, Cal.

17 NICKELS, Clarence B(obo). Chemical control of casebearers, borers, weevils and mites affecting pecan trees. b'97. BS '17 (Miss State Coll); MS '20 (U Md). Development method collection and examination of eggs of first brood of nut casebearer in timing of spray treatments for control Texas and Oklahoma '36-38; experimentation with lead arsenate-nicotine sulfate spray for pecan trees in control casebearers '41; devised method for coorelation figures overwintering population pecan nut casebearer and injury to next nut crop; study control of borers on pecan trees, types of pecan mites, effect lead arsenate sprays on the pecan weevil. Author articles: DDT and Lead Arsenate Compared for the Control of the Pecan Nut Casebearer '45; Experiments in the Control of the Pecan Weevil; Some Minor Insect Pests of Pecan in Tex, and others. Co-author articles: (with W C Pierce) Control of Borers on Recently Top-Worked Pecan Trees; (With W C Pierce) Control of the Pecan Nut Casebearer with Lead Arsenate, Nicotine Sulfate, Summer Oil; (with W C Pierce) Effect of Lead Arsenate Sprays on the Pecan Weevil and other Pecan Insects), and others. Entomol US Bur Entomol since '26,

asso entomol Brownwoood Tex since '29. Am Assn Econ Entomol—Entomol Soc Am. U.S. Bureau of Entomology, Box 209, Brownwood, Tex.

18 NICKERSON, Dorothy. Color technology. b'00. Spl courses various institutions. Research on color measurement in grading and standardization of agricultural and other products, disk colorimetry, artificial daylighting, use of psychological scales in color measurement. Author articles in field. Color technol US Dept Agr since '27. Optical Soc Am—Inter-Soc Color Council (sec '38-52)—AAAS—Assn Textile Chemists and Colorists—Illuminating Engring Soc—Washington Acad Sci. Cotton Branch, U.S. Department of Agriculture, Washington.

19 NICKERSON, Walter John. Physiological mycology (Yeasts); Mycopathology. b'15. BS '37 (Westchester State Coll Pa); MA '40—PhD '42 (Harvard). Author: Biology of Pathogenic Fungi '47; also articles in field. Asso prof, head bot dept Wheaton Coll '48-50; lecturer med mycol Tufts Med Sch Boston '47-50; asso prof microbiol Rutgers U since '50. Mycol Society America—Bot Soc Am—Soc Am Bact—Danish Bot Society—Netherlands Soc Microbiol—Internat Assn Microbiol (chmn com med mycol). Guggenheim Memorial fellow '47-48. Department of Microbiology, Rutgers University, New Brunswick, N.J.†

20 NICOL, David. Fossil pelecypoda; Evolution and geographic distribution. b'15. AB '37—MS '39 (Texas Christian University); '39-40 (University Tex); AM '43—PhD '47 (Stanford). Asso curator Cenozoic and Mesozoic invertebrates US Nat Mus since '48. Paleontol Soc—Geol Soc Am—Malacol Soc London—Palaontol Gesellschaft—Soc Systematic Zool—Soc Study Evolution —Am Malacol Union—Paleontol Soc—Soc Econ Paleontol Mineral—Washington Acad Sci—Sigma Xi. Room 303, U.S. National Museum, Washington 25.

21 NIDA, Eugene Albert. Linguistics (New Testament Greek); Languages (Northern Mexican Tarahumara, Mexican and Guatemalan Mayan, Sudanic, Bantu). b'14. AB '36 (U Calif); MA '39 (U So Calif); PhD '43 (U Mich). Author: Morphology: The Descriptive Analysis of Words '46; Bible Translating '47; Translator's Commentary of Selected Passages '47, and others; also articles in field. Prof linguistics Summer Inst Linguistics U Okla since '37; sec Versions Am Bible Soc since '43. Linguistic Soc Am. 450 Park Av., NYC 22.†

22 NIELSEN, Erik R. Vapor phase oxidation; Furan chemistry; Coffee; Soybeans. b'97. Student '17 (U Copenhagen); '17-19—'24 (Polytechnical Inst Copenhagen). Holder US patents on tanning of glue, improved restaurant coffee, vapor phase oxidation of furfural. Author articles in field. Supervisor plastics research Armour Research Found since '44, now sr sci and gen cons chem and chem engring dept. Am Chem Soc—Soc Plastics Engrs. Received prize from Assn Danish Mfrs for ideas on mfr pectin from Danish waste materials '36. Armour Research Foundation, 35 W. 33rd St., Chicago 16.†

23 NIELSEN, Etlar L(ester). Forage grass cytology and breeding (Poa, Bromus); Taxonomy and cytology of Amelanchier (Minnesota); Interglacial peat deposits in southern Minnesota. b'05. BS '28—PhD '36 (U Minn). Author articles in field. Agron Ark Agrl Expt Sta '36-41; agron US Dept Agr Div Forage Crops and Diseases since '41. Bot Soc Am—Am Soc Agron—Sigma Xi. Department of **Agronomy**,

University of Wisconsin, Madison 6, Wis.†

10 NIER, Alfred O. Physics (Isotope measurement and separation). b'11. BEE '31—MS in EE '33—PhD '36 (U Minn). Research on existence and separation of isotopes, and in developing mass spectrometer as tool for use in other fields of research such as measurement of geological age and application of separated stable isotopes as tracers in chemistry and biology. Author articles in field. Prof physics U Minn since '45. Am Phys Soc(F)—AAAS—Minn Acad Sci—Sigma Xi. Nat Research fellow Harvard '36-38. University of Minnesota, Minneapolis 14.☉

11 NIETZ, John Alfred. History of American education; History of adult education; School textbooks (Old). b'88. AB '14—BPd '14 (O No U); MA '19 (O State U); '24-26—PhD '33 (U Chicago). Collector school textbooks over 50 years old; over 5500 copies of such books in collection. Author articles in field. With Sch Edn U Pittsburgh since '26, asso prof edn '29-39, prof since '39. NEA—Pa Edn Assn—Nat Soc Study Edn—Nat Soc Coll Teachers Edn—AAUP—Am Assn Adult Edn. 526 Hillcrest Pl., Pittsburgh.

12 NIGHTINGALE, William Thomas. Petroleum and natural gas geology of Wyoming and Colorado. b'97. BSc '19—MSc '24 (U Washington). Author articles in field. Vice-pres Mt Fuel Supply Co since '41, vp and dir charge exploration prodn and transmission since '45, discovery geol Powder Washington field northwest Colo '36, Church Buttes field southwest Wyo '46. AAAS(F)—Am Assn Petroleum Geol—Am Geog Soc—Am Inst Mining Metall Engrs—Am Gas Assn—Geol Soc Am (life F)—Am Geophys Union(F)—Am Petroleum Inst. P.O. Box 1129, Rock Springs, Wyo.

13 NIGRELLI, Ross F(ranco). Fish parasites, diseases and pathology; Aquatic biology. b'03. BSc '27 (Pa State Coll); MSc '29—PhD '36 (NYU). Engaged research aquatic biology, fish parasites and diseases especially those producing human and other mammalian diseases, occurrence, treatment, prevention; experimental ichthyology; fish pathology especially cancer and other neoplastic diseases; consultant Fish and Wildlife Service US Dept Interior '43-48; fish diseases Bingham Oceanographic Lab Yale since '43. Author articles: Causes of Diseases and Death of Fishes in Captivity '43; other articles in field. Instr microbiol '43-45, vis asst prof '45-49; adjunct asso prof since '48; research fellow NY aquarium NY Zool Soc '31-32, pathol since '34; cons fed security agency US Pure Food and Drug Adminstrn since '45; tech advs com fish disease, marine ecol Atlantic States Marine Fisheries Commn since '46. Am Soc Zool—Am Soc Parasitologists—Am Microscop Soc — Am Soc Bacteriologists—Soc Exptl Biol and Med—Am Assn Cancer Research—Am Soc Protozool (pres '48-49)—Bermuda Biol Sta Research. New York Aquarium, New York Zoological Society, NYC 60.☉

14 NIKHILANDANDA, Swami. Hindu religion and philosophy; Advaita (non-dualistic) Vedanta philosophy. b'95. Student '13-16 (Dacca Coll, U Calcutta). Research in comparative religions and philosophies Advaita Ashrama, Himalayan monastery of Ramakrishna Order '21-27, in non-dualistic Vedanta philosophy, Mysore, India '30-31; lecturer Hindu religious and philosophical thought, translations of Hindu scriptures and religious books '31-50; collaborator inter-faith and inter-cultural discussions. Translat-

or: The Gospel of Sri Ramakrishna (Bengali) '42; Bhagavad Gita, Upanishads, and other works (from the Sanskrit). Founder Ramakrishna-Vivekananda Center of NY '33, leader since '33. Am Philos Assn. 17 E. 94th St., NYC 28.

15 NIKITIN, Alexander Alexis. Chemistry (Agricultural and colloid). b'94. CheE '15 (Moscow Imperial Tech Inst); BS '20 (MIT); PhD '37 (Columbia); fellow '32-37 (U Del). Holder 17 US Patents, one British Patent and one Canadian Patent. Research on zealitic copper compounds as fungicides '37; also articles in field. Dir agrl research Tenn Corp Copperhill Tenn and College Park Ga since '37. AAAS—ACS—Am Phytopath Soc—Am Assn Econ Entomol—Tenn Acad Sci—Sigma Xi. Tennessee Corporation Research Laboratories, 900 Roosevelt Highway, College Park, Ga.

16 NILES, (Edward) Abbe. Blues music (History); American popular and folk song; Jazz. b'94. Ab '16 (Trinity Coll Hartford Conn); '19-20 (Oxford); LLB '23 (Harvard). Reviewed New York musical comedy stage for New Republic '27-28, Boston Transcript '29; study and collection American popular and folk songs, jazz. Co-author: (with W C Handy) Blues: An Anthology '26 (with Frank Butcher) The Hoosac Boar's Head and Yule Log '30; (with W C Handy) Treasury of the Blues '49. Contributor: article on Jazz to Encyclopedia Britannica '29. Conducted dept Ballads, Songs and Snatches, Bookman '28. 14 Wall St., NYC 5.

17 NILES, Blair (Mrs. Robert Niles). Latin American countries (History); Virginia (History). Member expeditions to Mexico, Venezuela, British Guiana, The Orient; lived among headhunting Dyaks in interior of Borneo and among Kachin tribes on the Burma-Yuman frontier; visited and studied natives in Ecuador, Colombia, Haiti, French and Dutch Guianas, Guatemala, Peru and Mexico. Author: Casual Wanderings in Ecuador '23; Colombia, Land of Miracles '24; Black Haiti '26; Condemned to Devil's Island (presented as moving picture Condemned) '28; Free (novel) '30; Peruvian Pageant (awarded gold medal City of Lima) '37; Passengers to Mexico; The Last Invasion of the Americas '43; The James: From Iron Gate to the Sea '45; Martha's Husband: An Informal Portrait of George Washington '51. Constance Lindsay Skinner medal achievement '41; Gold medal Soc Woman Geographers '44. 59 E. 54th St., NYC 22.☉

18 NILES, John Jacob. Folk songs (US, Appalachian). b'92. Student (Universite de Lyon) (Schola Cantorum Paris); MusD hon '49 (Cincinnati Conservatory). Original compositions, folk song adaptations and arrangements. Lectr Julliard Sch Mus '45, U Kansas City '48,'50, Cincinnati Conservatory Mus '49; Boston U '51; concert singer US and Can. H: Boot Hill, R.F.D. 7, Lexington, Ky.

19 NININGER, Harvey Harlow. Meteorites (Surface features, terrestrialization, tektites and lunar craters origin, geographical and minerological distribution, geological significance, ballistics and aerodynamics bearing, dust). b'87. AB '14—DSc '37 (McPherson (Kan) Coll); AM '16 (Pomona Coll, Claremont Calif); '15-18 (U Calif). Reported to have made largest private collection of meteorites in world; discoverer meteorodes, metallic spheroids and dolomite silica-glass in association with meteorite craters. Author: Our Stone-Pelted Planet '33; A Comet Strikes the Earth '42; Chips

from the Moon '47; Out of the Sky. Co-author: Nininger Collection of Meteorites; also articles in field. Founded Nininger Laboratory for Research on Meteorites, Denver, director since '30 (became Am Meteorite Laboratory '37); curator of meteorites Colo Mus Natural Hist; established Am Meteorite Mus '46; dir Meteorite Inst Inc since '45. AAAS(F)—Kan Acad Sci(F)—Am Astron Union. Sedona, Ariz.☉

20 NITSCH, Jean Paul. Tomatoes (Soil-less culture); Fruits (Culture in test-tubes). b'21. Student '43-44 (U Grenoble France); '46 (Sorbonne U Paris); Ingénieur Agronome '47 (Inst Nat Agronomique Paris); '48 (U Mich) PhD (Plant physiol) '50 (Cal Inst Tech). Research on hormonal action pollen and fertilized ovules in fruit growth, obtention of fruit from flower ovaries excised from palnts and planted on sterile synthetic media. Research fellow plant physiology Centre National des Recherches Agronomiques Versailles France '47; study plant tissue culture Dr Gautheret's laboratory Paris '47-48; French relations culturelles fellow to American laboratoires for study plant growth hormones '48; Lucy Mason Clark fellow plant physiology California Instiute Technology '49; research fellow in plant physiology Harvard '50. Author articles: Growth and Morphogenesis of the Strawberry as Related to Auxin '50; Culutre of Excised Fruits in vitro '50. Bost Soc Am—Am Soc Plant Physiol—Sigma Xi.

21 NITZSCHE, George E. Pennsylvania history (Philadelphia, University of Pennsylvania); Moving Picture history (Muybridge); Unitarians; Joseph Priestley. b'74. LLB '98 (U Pa); LittD '37 (Ursinus Coll). Founder of Pennsylvania Gazette, official weekly of the University, editor '02-16; president Priestly Conference Unitarian Churches '29-31; organizer Priestley Home for Unitarians '31, president until '37, now honorary president. Author: Philadelphia (10 edits); University of Pennsylvania (3 edits); University of Pennsylvania—Its Traditions, Memorials, etc (9 edit); Philadelphia and Her Great University; The Christmas Putz of the Penn-Germans '41. Editor: University of Lectures (7 vols); Historical Sketch of University of Pennsylvania, 1740-1929; also articles in field. Recorder of U Pa '01-44, ret as emeritus. Pa Hist Soc—Phila City Hist Soc (vp since '44)—Moravian Hist Soc—Layman's League Germantown (pres '21-23)—Anthropol Soc (vp '12-13, pres '29-31)—Pa German Folklore Soc (dir since '35). 1024 Westview Av., Germantown, Phila.

22 NIXON, Roy W(esley). Dates. b'95. Student '13-14 (Emory Coll, Ga); BSA '22 (U Ariz). Studied taxonomy and ecology of date varieties in Iraq and west Persia '28-29, in French No Africa '48-49 (Guggenheim fellow); investigations in culture, varieties, metaxenia, fruit thinning, leaf pruning. Hort US Dept Agr since '23. AAAS(F)—Am Soc Hort Sci. U.S. Date Garden, Indio, Cal.

23 NIXON, Stuart. Piston rings (Automotive); Pistons (Automotive). b'97. SB '21 (MIT). Research and development piston rings, ring coatings, treatment of surfaces, ring set-ups for applications to compressors, gasoline, gas and diesel engines. Metall and mech engr Continental Motors Corp '22-33; with Sealed Power Corp since '34, research engr since '47. Soc Automotive Engrs—Am Soc ME—Theta Tau. Sealed Power Corp., Muskegon, Mich.

24 NOBLE, Charles MacIntosh. Highway engineering; Hard rock tunnelling.

b'96. Student (Columbia U). Author: The Modern Express Highway '36; The Factor of Safety in Highway Design '37; Design Features of the Pennsylvania Turnpike '40; Engineering Design of Superhighways '41. Registered profl engr NY, NJ, Pa; practiced hwy engring Fla, Ala, Ky, NJ; engr for Port of NY '25-38; engr on design of Goethals Bridge, Outerbridge Crossing, George Washington Bridge, Bayonne Bridge, Lincoln Tunnel; hwy engr Pentagon Bldg Washington; NJ State Hwy Engr, chief engr NJ Turnpike Authority since '49; lecturer on hwy design and safety. ASCE (Arthur Wellington prize '38)—Boston Soc CE (Clemens Herschel Prize '38)—Hwy Research Bd—Am Road Builders Assn. New Jersey Turnpike Authority, New Brunswick, N.J.

10 NOBLE, Elmer Ray. Nuclear structure of Protozoa; Trypanosomes (Cytology, nutrition); Amoebae (Life cycle). AB '31—MA '33—PhD '36 (U Calif). Research on cytology and life history of Myxosporidia. Co-author: A Brief Anatomy of the Turtle (with G A Noble) '40; also articles in field. Asso prof zool U Calif, Santa Barbara Coll, '43-48, prof zool since '48, chmn dept biol sci '47-51, dean div liberal arts since '51. AAAS—Am Soc Zool—Am Soc Parasitol—Am Micros Soc—Soc Protozool—Sigma Xi. Dept. Biological Science, University California, Santa Barbara College, Santa Barbara, Cal.†

11 NOEL, Edward B. Mercury lamps; Germicidal lamps. b'07. BS '28—MS '29—EE '40—fellow '28-29 (U Ill). Research on development and production of high pressure mercury lamps in glass and quartz, on germicidal and bactericidal lamps, glass and quartz flashtubes for single flash and stroboscopic multiple flash and for durations from 1-300 ms, photo-flash lamps. Author articles in field. Gen engring dept Gen Elec Co '29-33; lamp development engr, Lamp Development Lab Gen Elec Co Cleveland since '33. AIEE—Illuminating Engring Soc—Photographic Soc Am (tech div)—Tau Beta Pi—Sigma Xi. General Electric Company, Lamp Development Laboratory, Nela Park, Cleveland 12.†

12 NOEL, Francis W(right). Audiovisual education. b'01. AB '32 (U Calif); MS '35 (U Southern Calif); summer '37 (Progressive Edn Workshop Mills Coll). Author: The Navy Turns to Training Aids '44; Looking Ahead Twenty-five Years in Audio-Visual Education '46. Co-author: Teachers Relationship to the Administration and Use of Audio-Visual Materials '47; articles in field. Dir audio visual edn Santa Barbara Calif city schs '35-42, dir audio visual edn Santa Barbara Co Schs '39-42; lecturer audiovisual edn U Calif Santa Barbara Branch '39-40; audio visual edn consultant US Dept of State to Conf of Allied Ministers of Edn '44-45; chief Bur Audio Visual Edn Calif State Dept Edn since '45; mem adv bd Nat Audio Visual Edn Stephens Coll Columbia Mo since '46. Audio Visual Edn Assn of Southern Calif (past pres)—Nat Edn Assn—Calif Audio-Visual Edn Assn—Kappa Delta Pi. State Department of Education, Library and Courts Bldg., Sacramento 14.†

13 NOETZEL, Grover A. J. International political and economic affairs. b'08. AB '29—PhD '34—fellow '32-34 (U Wis); certificate '30 (U London); certificate '36 (Inst Universilaires de Houtes Etudes Internationales Geneva). Author: Recent Theories of Foreign Exchange '34; also articles in field. Prof econ U Miami '46-48, dean sch bus admnstrn since '48. Am Econ Assn—So Econ Assn—Am Acad Polit and Social Sci. University of Miami, University Branch, Coral Gables, Fla.

14 NOLAND, Lowell Evan. Protozoa. b'96. BA '17 (DePauw U); '19 (U Montpellier, France); MA '21—PhD '24 (U Wis). Research on invertebrate zool, protozoa, ciliates; ecology and physiology of snails. Author articles in field. Prof zool U Wis since '35. AAAS—Am Soc Zool—Ecol Soc Am—Am Soc Protozool—Limnology Soc Am—Biol Stain Commn—Am Soc Naturalists—Entomol Soc Am—Am Micros Soc (pres '39)—Wis Acad Sci Arts and Letters (sec-treas '30-33, pres '46-48)—Am Inst Biol Sci—Phi Beta Kappa—Sigma Xi—Gamma Alpha—Phi Sigma. Biology Bldg., University of Wisconsin, Madison 6, Wis.☉

15 NOLL, George Carl. Metals (Strength, fatigue); Stress (Concentrations, residual). b'18. BS in mech engring '43 (Ind Tech Coll); MS in automotive engring '45 (Chrysler Inst Engring). Stress analysis by calculation and measurement with electrical and mechanical strain gages and photoeleastically of elements of aircraft engines, tanks, automotive equipment; evaluation strength of metal specimens and actual parts to resist static and fatigue loading. Co-author: (with C Lipson, L S Clock) Stress and Strength of Manufactured Parts '50. Project engineer Chrysler Corp '43-48, Thew Shovel Co since 48. ASME—Soc Exptl Stress Analysis. Thew Shovel Co., Lorain, O. H: 7272 Avon Belden Rd., North Ridgeville, O.

16 NOLLA, José A(ntonio) B(ernabé). Phytopathology and plant breeding (Sugar-cane, tobacco, vegetables). b'02. BS '23 (U Puerto Rico); MS '26—PhD '32 (Cornell U); '32-33 (U Wis). Member agricultural mission Cauca Valley Columbia summer '29; special adviser Ministry of Agriculture of Venezuela summer '36; vice chairman section agriculture and conservation eighth American Science Congress Washington '40, Inter-American Conference Agriculture Mexico City '42. Author articles in field. Founder and dir Tobacco Inst of PR '36-38; dir Agrl Expt Sta Mayaguez '38-43. AAAS(F)—Am Phytopathol Soc—Genetical Soc Am—Torrey Bot Club—Am Soc Natural History—Agrl Hist Soc—Sugar Tech Assn of PR (pres '38-40)—Am Soc Agrl Sci—Britton-Stahl Bot Club—Washington Acad Sci—Gamma Sigma Delta—Sigma Xi. Awarded Guggenheim fellowship '32-33. Mayaguez, P.R.

17 NOMEJKO, Charles A. Oyster culture. b'14. Student '32-34 (Catholic U); '34-37 (Georgetown U fgn service sch). Co-author: (with V L Loosanoff) Feeding of Oysters in Relation to Tidal Stages and to Periods of Light and Darkness '46; (with same) On the Growth of Oysters During Hibernation '46. Oyster culturist Milford (Conn) Fishery Biol Lab since '44. Milford Fishery Biological Laboratory, Milford, Conn.

18 NOON, Paul A. T. Libraries (Extension, state aid, regional, county). b'01. AB '30 (O State U); BLS '32 (Columbia U); MA '33 (NYU). Author articles in field. Asso librarian Jacksonville Pub Library since '47. ALA—Fla Library Assn—Nat Assn State Librarians (vp '35, pres '37-39)—League Library Commns. Jacksonville Public Library, Jacksonville, Fla.

19 NORDIN, Vidar John. Hardwoods (Decay); Conifers (Gall, canker, decay). b'24. BA botany '46—BS in forestry '47 (U BC); PhD '51 (U Toronto). Research on decay in sugar maple, yellow birch, western hemlocks and fir, gall and canker diseases of conifers. Asst forest path BC and Ontario '45-49; officer-in-charge Lab Forest Path Maritime Provinces '49-51, Alberta since '51. Can Inst Forestry—Am Soc Foresters—Mycol Soc Am—Can Phytopath Soc. Laboratory of Forest Pathology, 102 11th Av E., Calgary, Alberta, Can.

20 NORDLINGER, Ernest William. Vegetable growing and processing; Tomato culture. b'19. BS '42 (Purdue U); '37-40 (North Park Coll). Research on canning crops mainly with growing tomatoes, spraying tomatoes to control diseases, how to pick tomatoes. Author articles in field. Hort research staff Purdue U '42-44, managing editor Purdue Agriculturist '41-42; crops editor Food Packer mag '44-51; now asst editor Food Processing mag. Am Phytopathol Soc—Am Soc Hort Sci—Chgo Hort Soc—Inst Food Tech. 111 E. Delaware Pl., Chgo 11. H: 5324 N. Bernard St., Chgo 25.

21 NORDMEYER, Henry W(aldemar). German literature (Middle High, Goethe, Heinrich von Kleist). b'91. Grad '10 (Gymnasium, Braunschweig, Germany); '10-13 (U Leipzig); PhD '14 (U Wis). Author: Introduction to Commercial German (with K E Richter) '31; translator into German verse Edward Fitzgerald's Rubaiyat des Omar Khayyam, Letzte Fassung deutsch '26. Prof German and chmn dept U Mich since '35. Modern Lang Assn Am—Soc for Advancement Scandinavian Study—Am Assn Teachers of German—Phi Kappa Phi. 2303 Lenawee Dr., Ann Arbor.☉

22 NORDSIEK, Frederick William. Foods (Technology, microbiology, sanitation, nutrition). b'09. BS '31 (MIT). Establishment and administration food quality control testing programs; technical management food manufacture, distribution, and promotion; administration food product design and development; organization courses instruction on sanitation of foods. Contributor: Encyclopedia Americana; Britannica Books of the Year since '45. Research bact Borden Co NYC '31-34, Dr L K Mobley NYC '34-35; exec sec NY Diabetes Assn '35-38; asso dir nutrition dept Am Inst Banking '38-43; instr sch for inspectors City Dept Health NYC '41; asst dir research service dept Standard Brands Inc '43-51; asst sec research com Am Cancer Soc Inc since '51. Am Pub Health Assn(F)—Inst Food Tech—Soc Am Bact—Delta Omega. Standard Brands, Inc., 595 Madison Av., NYC 22. H: 29 W. 64th St., NYC 23.

23 NORDSTROM, Carl Julius. Naval architecture, engineering. b'94. Student '12-14 (U Wash). Design merchant vessels and special ships for special jobs, such as newsprint carriers, railway and highway ferries; shop and yard layouts for maintenance and construction; evaluation of seaworthiness; industrial management of shipyards. Cons naval arch '28-30, '31-41, since '45. US Naval Inst—Soc Naval Architects and Marine Engrs—Structural Engrs Assn Wash. 534 Exchange Bldg., Seattle 4.

24 NORLIE, Olaf Morgan. Norwegian-American history. b'76. BS—MAccts '97—PdD '10 (Dixon Coll); AB '98 (St Olaf Coll); AM '01 (U Wis); CT '07 (United Ch Sem); PhD '08 (U Minn); STD '17 (Augustana Sem); LittD '17 (Wittenberg Coll); MusD '32 (Chicago Coll Music). Founder of the Norlie Library (Norwegian Americana and American-Lutherana). Author: Norsk - Engelsk Sondagsskolesangbog (with N B Thvedt) '11; Alterbogen '12; Norsk Lutherske Prester i Amerika

'14, '15; Norsk Lutherske Menigheter i Amerika '18; History of the Norwegian People in America '25, '26; Who's Who Among Norwegian Lutheran Pastors '27; Fra Pionerpresternes Saga '32; Norwegian-American Doctors '33; Eielsen Was First '42; English Bibles '44; Ho Ga Te Me '46; Antiquarian Books '46; Norwegian-American Papers 1847-1946 '46; also other books in field. Archivist and classifier St Olaf Coll Library since '41. Slooper Soc Am (sec '27-42)—Am Lutheran Statis Assn (pres '17-33, hon pres for life since '33)—AAAS(F)—Am Math Soc—Am Philol Assn—Am Psychol Assn—Midwestern Psychol Assn—Soc for Advancement of Scandinavian Studies—Namdalslaget — Nordmannsforbundet Trönderlaget. 818 Forest Av., Northfield, Minn.

10 NORMAN, Arthur Geoffrey. Plant biochemistry, nutrition and hormones; Soil microbiology. b'05. BSc '25—PhD '28 (U Birmingham, Eng); MS '32 (U Wis); DSc '33 (U London). Research on biochemistry and decomposition of plant cell-wall polysaccharides, soil organic matter and soil nitrogen transformations, nitrogen nutrition of soybeans, growth regulating substances. Author: The Biochemistry of Cellulose, the Polyuronides, Lignin '37; chapters in Wise's Wood Chemistry '44, Ott's Cellulose and its Derivative '42; Editor: Advances in Agronomy; also articles in field. Biochemist in charge biochem sect Rothamsted Exptl Sta Eng '33-37; prof soils Ia State Coll '37-46, research prof Ia Agrl Exptl Sta '37-46; division chief biological department Chem Corps Camp Detrick Frederick Md '46-52; prof bot, research biochem U Mich since '52; biochem cons Chem Warfare Service Camp Detrick '43-45. Royal Inst Chem Gt Brit (F)—Biochem Soc—Am Soc Agronomy —Soil Sci Soc Am—Am Society Plant Physiol—Soc Am Bact—Sigma Xi. Radiation Laboratory, Univ. of Michigan, Ann Arbor.

11 NORMAND, Charles Ernest. Slow electrons in gases (Absorption coefficients); High vacuum equipment, systems and measuring devices. b'97. BA—MA '20 (U Tex); PhD '30 (U Calif). Engaged research absorption coefficients for slow electrons in gases; development and testing of large scale, high vacuum equipment and systems; high vacuum measuring devices. Author articles in field. Prof physics Harrisonburg State Teachers Coll '30-37; prof physics Texas State Coll Women '37-42; physicist charge vacuum development Rad Lab Berkeley Calif '42-43; physicist charge vacuum development Tenn Eastman Corp Oak Ridge Tenn '43-46; prof physics Tex State Coll Women '46-47; physicist Carbide and Carbon Chemicals Corp Oak Ridge Tenn since '47. Sigma Xi. Carbide and Carbon Chemicals Corporation, Oak Ridge, Tenn.†

12 NORMAN-WILCOX, Gregor. English and early American silver; Early American furniture; Antiques (Ceramics, glass); Folk arts. b'05. Author articles in field. Curator decorative arts, Los Angeles Co Mus since '31. St Dunstan Soc. Los Angeles County Museum, Exposition Park, Los Angeles 7.

13 NORONA, Delf. History and cartography of colonial Northwestern Virginia; Military postal history (Spanish-American, World War). b'95. Engaged research and writing on Pacific coast postal service before the Gold Rush, US domestic postage rates, genesis of registration system, express-mail of 1837-39, early postal service in western Virginia, cartography of West Virginia, Joshua Fry's report on back settlements of Virginia. Invented American system for classifying military postmarks. Editor: Cyclopedia of US Postmarks and Postal History '33, '35; General Catalog of US Postmarks '35; War Cover Philatelist '38; also articles in field. Editor and publisher Upper Ohio Valley Pioneer since '46. Am Philatelic Soc —Upper O Valley Hist Soc (past pres) —WV Hist Soc (past pres)—Va Hist Soc. Award of Honor, first Am Philatelic Cong '35. 315 7th St., Moundsville, W.Va.†

14 NORRIS, Charles B(razer). Plywood; Sandwich construction. b'94. BS '17 (U Wis). Author: The Technique of Plywood '42. Mech engineer charge engineering, research Haske lite Manufacturing Corp, Grand Rapids Mich '20-36; cons engr Am Boxboard Co '36-38; tech dir Lauxite Inc, Merritt Engring and Sales Co NY '38-42; engr Forest Products Lab US Forest Service, Madison, Wis since '42. ASME— Soc Experimental Stress Analysis— Forest Products Research Soc. Forest Products Laboratory, Madison 5, Wis.†

15 NORRIS, Ferris Waldo. Electrical engineering (Transmission lines); Clock mechanisms (Electric-synchronous). b'94. BSc '16—MSc '25—profl engr '27 (U Neb). Designed the football and basketball clock mechanism now used by the University of Nebraska Athletic Department, which was probably the first electric synchronous clock that was built in the US for the use of the official timekeeper as well as spectators. Co-author: (with Edison) Electrical Engineering Laboratory Practice '28; (with Bingham) Introductory Study of Electrical Characteristics of Power and Telephone Transmission Lines '36. With dept elec engring U Neb since '20, prof since '43, chmn dept elec engring since '49. AIEE (F, chmn Neb sect '37-38)— Inst Radio Engr—Am Soc Engring Edn —Nebraska Engring Soc. Sigma Xi. Department of Electrical Engineering, University of Nebraska, Lincoln, Neb.†

16 NORRIS, Frank Giles. Steel manufacture (Open hearth). b'05. BS in chem engring '26—ChemE '34 (Purdue U); MS in chem engring '28 (Carnegie Inst Tech). Research on viscosity of open hearth slag, relation of composition to red-shortness; work on special deoxidizers including patent on deoxidation of liquid steel with metallic sodium; correlation studies of factors affecting open hearth production. Author: Iron and Steel Production (in press). Co-author: statistical sect Am Soc Metals Handbook '48; Am Inst Mining Engrs book Basic Opean Heatlh Steelmaking '46. Various jobs on open hearth furnace Ill Steel Corp Gary '25-27; research engr Am Rolling Mill Co Middletown O '28-37; open hearth metall, asst metall engr and metall engr (statistics) Steubenville plant Wheeling Steel Corp since '37. Am Soc Metals—AIMME— Iron and Steel Inst—Am Soc Quality Control—Ohio Assn Profl Engrs—Sigma Xi. Wheeling Steel Corp., Steubenville, O.

17 NORRIS, Leo Chandler. Nutrition; Biochemistry. b'93. BS '20—PhD '24 (Cornell U). Author articles in field. Asst, instr, asst prof, prof nutrition Cornell U since '20; mem edit bd Soc for Exptl Biol and Med NYC; Agrl Bd and chmn com on animal nutrition Nat Research Council, Washington. AAAS—Am Chem Soc—Am Soc Biol Chem—Am Inst Nutrition— Soc Exptl Biol and Med—Am Soc Animal Production—Am Dairy Sci Assn—Poultry Sci Assn—Phi Kappa Phi —Sigma Xi. Rice Hall, Cornell University, Ithaca, N.Y.

18 NORRIS, Louis William. Metaphysics; Theory of value; Philosophy of history. b'06. Roswell R Robinson fellow '31-32—Borden Parker Bowne fellow '34-35—STB magna cum laude '31—PhD '37 (Boston U); AB '28 (Otterbein Coll); student '30-31, '36-37 (Harvard), '31-32 (U Berlin). Polarity in metaphysics, the theory that the universe is throughout a balance of opposites, applying to forces in nature, theory of value and methods of throught; traveled extensively in Europe, participated Ninth and Tenth Conferences on Science Philosophy and Religion. Author articles: Teaching and the Philosophy of History '49; The Teacher as Prophet '50; Values and the Non-Spiritual '50; Existence and Its Polarities '50. Prof philos DePauw U since '46, chmn dept philos and religion since '47, dean '50-52; pres MacMurray Coll since '52. Am Philos Assn—Nat Assn Biblical Instrs (treas since '47). Mac Murray College, Jacksonville, Ill.

19 NORRIS, Russell Taplin. Ornithology (Passerine birds, woodcock); Wildlife management and research. b'16. BS '38 (U Me); MS '41 (Pa State Coll). Engaged in biological investigations of proposed flood control dams and their resevoir areas; experience and research largely in ornithology. Author articles: Banding Woodcocks on Pennsylvania Singing Grounds '40; Coopers Hawk Takes Crippled Coot '42; Cottontail Rabbit Suckling Young '43; Notes on a Cowbird Parasitizing a Song Sparrow '44; The Cowbirds of Preston Frith '47; Nesting Heights of Breeding Birds '47. Tech Lake and Stream Survey Me Dept Inland Fisheries and Game summer '37, '38; grad asst wildlife research Pa State Coll '38-40; spl investigator woodcock wintering grounds US Fish and Wildlife Service '40-42; biol ornithol research Preston Lab Butler Pa '41-46; biol River Basin studies US Fish and Wildlife Service Boston since '46. Wildlife Soc—Am Ornithol Union—Wilson Ornithol Club —Cooper Ornithol Club—Am Soc Mammalogists—Am Fisheries Soc. 59 Temple Pl., Boston 11.

20 NORTHEN, Henry Theodore. Protoplasm; Orchids (Physiology). b'08. BS '32—MS '34 (State Coll Wash); PhD '36 (U Calif). Research on relationship of protoplasmic structure to physiological processes. Author articles: Effects of Various Agents on the Structural Viscosity of Elodea Protoplasm '46; Relationship of Dissociation of Cellular Proteins by Incipient Drought to Physiological Processes '43; Relationship of Dissociation of Cellular Proteins by Auxins to Growth '42; Studies on the Protoplasmic Nature of Stimulation and Anesthesia '39, and others. With U Wyoming since '36, prof since '47. AAAS(F) —Bot Soc Am—Am Soc Plant Physiol —Colo-Wyo Acad Sci — AAUP—Phi Beta Kappa—Sigma Xi. Department of Botany, University of Wyoming, Laramie, Wyo.

21 NORTHEY, Elmore Hathaway. Chemotherapy; Sulfa drugs. b'05. BA '27—PhD '30—duPont fellow '29-30 (U Minn). Holder several patents. Author: The Sulfonamides and Allied Compounds '48; also articles in field. Administrative dir Stamford research labs American Cyanamid Co '45-50; asst to vp charge research, NYC since '50. AAAS—AIC—Am Inst Chem Engrs— NY Acad Sci—Sigma Xi. American Cyanamid Company, 30 Rockefeller Plaza, NYC 20.

22 NORTHROP, Stuart A(lvord). Stratigraphy and paleontology (Gaspé); Stratigraphy and minerals of New Mexico. b'04. '21-23 (Robert Coll

Constantinople); BS '25—PhD '29—Binney fellow '25-28 (Yale). Field work in Gaspé '27, '28. Author: Paleontology and Stratigraphy of the Silurian Rocks of the Port Daniel-Black Cape Region, Gaspé '39; Minerals of New Mexico '44; also articles in field. Asst prof and act head dept geol U NM '28-29, asso prof '29-30, head dept geol since '29, prof geol since '30, curator geol mus since '40; collaborator seismol US Coast and Geodetic Survey since '41; geol fuels sect US Geol Survey since '43. Geol Soc Am(F)—Paleontol Soc Am(F)—Seismol Soc Am—Am Assn Petroleum Geol—Geol Soc NM—Sigma Xi. University of New Mexico, Albuquerque, N.M.

10 NORTON, Clarence Clifford. Family; Race and race relations; Economic adjustments; Political parties. b'96. BS '19 (Millsaps Coll); MA '20 (Emory U); PhD '27 (U NC). Research on native life, marriage, race relations, economic adjustments in Union South Africa '39. Author: The Democratic Party in Anti-Bellum North Carolina; Enriching Family Life '45; also articles in field. Prof polit sci and sociol Wofford Coll since '25, dean '42-49; dean of administration since '49. Phi Beta Kappa. 526 Gadsden Ct., Spartanburg, S.C.

11 NORTON, Clark Frederic. State government; American national government; Michigan courts. b'12. BA '35—MA '36—Rackham pre-doctoral fellowship '38-40—PhD '40 (U Mich). Author articles in field. Asso prof polit sci DePauw U since '48. Am Polit Sci Assn—AHA—Mich Hist Soc—Mich Acad Sci Arts Letters—Phi Kappa Phi. DePauw University, Greencastle, Ind.

12 NORTON, Frederick Harwood. Ceramics; Refractories; Aeronautical instrument design. b'96. BS '18 (MIT)—PhD '49 (Alfred). Author: The Creep of Steel at High Temperatures; Refractories; Elements of Ceramics. Prof ceramics MIT since '26. Am Ceramic Soc. Massachusetts Institute of Technology, Cambridge, Mass.†

13 NORTON, Grady. Hurricane warnings; Weather forecasting. b'94. Author: Weather Forecasting in Southeastern United States '43. Co-author: Florida Hurricanes '49; also articles in field. Supervising forecaster Hurricane Warning Service US Weather Bur since '35, prin meteorol charge Miami Hurricane Warning Center. Am Meteorol Soc—Nat Assn Weather Forecasters. Meritorious service award US Dept Commerce '49. U.S. Weather Bureau, Miami 32, Fla.

14 NORTON, Horace Wakeman. Holstein-Friesian cattle (Breeding); Pedigrees and breed records (Cattle). b'83. BS '03 (Mich State Coll). Dir Bur Animal Industry Mich '21-27; with Holstein-Friesian Assn Am since '28, exec sec and treas since '47. Purebred Dairy Cattle Assn(sec '41-45)—Am Dairy Sci Assn. Holstein-Friesian Association of America, Brattleboro, Vt.

15 NORTON, Horace Wakeman. Mathematical statistics. b'14. BS Chem Engring '35 (U Wis); MS '37 (Ia State Coll); PhD '40 (U London). Research on general formulae for homozygosis, effects selection of dams may have on sire indexes, potential usefulness of pressure patterns for weather forecasting, calculation of chi-square for complex contingency tables, orthogonal squares. Author articles in field. Statis US Atomic Energy Commn since '47. Am Statis Assn—Inst Math Statis—Biometric Soc—Sigma Xi. U.S. Atomic Energy Commission, Box E, Oak Ridge, Tenn.†

16 NORTON, James Jennings. Pegmatites; Economic geology; Geology of Black Hills (South Dakota). b'18. AB '40 (Princeton U); MS '42 (Northwestern U); '47-48 (Columbia). Geol Geol Survey US Dept Interior '42-44, since '46. Geol Soc Am—Phi Beta Kappa. Geological Survey, U.S. Department of the Interior, Washington 25. H: 53 Mackey Av., Port Washington, N.Y.

17 NORTON, Karl B. Food chemistry (Frozen fruits and vegetables). b'90. Student '12 (Syracuse U NY). Prodn mgr frozen fruits and vegetables Frosted Foods Sales Corp (Birds Eye) '30-44; Standard Brands Inc NY since '44; food cons since '48. 11 Park Pl., NYC.

18 NORTON, Leland Bernard. Insecticide chemistry. b'10. BS '28 (Hamilton Coll); PhD '34 (Cornell U). Research on spray residues of arsenical and organic insecticides, composition of arsenicals, lead contamination in maple food products, chemistry and insect toxicology of nicotine and its derivatives, composition of rotenone-bearing plants, properties of inert diluents and carriers for insecticides, chemistry and insect toxicology of chlorinated hydrocarbons and organic phosphates used as insecticides. Author articles in field. Asst chem Cornell U '28-34, asso in research expt sta, asst prof entomol dept '38-46, asso prof insecticidal chem entomol dept since '46. Am Chem Soc—Am Assn Econ Entomol. Department of Entomology, Cornell University, Ithaca, N.Y.

19 NORTON, Leland Davis. Dictating machines. b'94. BSEE '16 (U Neb); '17 (Union Coll); '42, '49 (U Bridgeport). Research in sound recording in business, designing to new requirements in electronic dictation. Holds 25 patents on dictation machines and accessories. Author articles in field. Supervisor communication Pa Power and Light Co '26-29; dir research Dictaphone Corp '29-47, research cons since '47. Acoustical Soc Am. Dictaphone Corporation, 375 Howard Av., Bridgeport 5, Conn.

20 NORTON, Margaret Cross. Illinois history and archives. b'91. PhB '13—MA '14 (U Chicago); BLS '15 (NY State Library Sch). Managing editor The American Archivist '46-49. Author: Illinois State Census Returns, 1810, 1818, 1820; also articles in field. Archivist Ill State Library since '22. Soc Am Archivists (pres '44-45)—AHA—Miss Valley Hist Assn—Abraham Lincoln Assn—Ill State Hist Soc—ALA. Illinois State Library, Springfield, Ill.

21 NOTT, Stanley Charles. Jade (Chinese); Oriental and Chinese culture; Chinese art; Gemmology; Mineralogist (Nephrites, jasiites and chloromelanites). b'02. Student Westminster; Epsom; Oxford. Founder, national president The Chinese Culture Study Group of America; conducted five years of active mineralogical research in the interior of China '32-37; geographically located and recorded extant Oriental jade workings '38; formulated the historic Chinese Jade Collections for various individuals and also for the Norton Gallery Collection of Florida. Present owner of reputedly the most valuable collection of Ritualistic Chinese jades in the New World; created the only existing comprehensive photographic record of the famous Chinese ritual jades in the Imperial collections of China, India, England, France, Norway, Sweden and the Museums of Europe and America; formulated for educational purposes thousands of stereopticon slides recording all known ritual creations in jadeites, nephrites and chlormelanites in private collections; assembled many thousands of microscopical slides tabulating and categorizing fine jade minings in all parts of the world including the recent finds in America and the Orient; lectured on Chinese life and culture in universities and colleges; directed and produced for the CCSGA the first technicolor film made to demonstrate the cultural background of the Chinese through the medium of their arts; formulated the first methods used in microscopical photographic analysis to determine the date and method of cutting of any given type of jade creation; originated the International scale of values used in assessing the commercial worth of gem jade; consultant assessor to Lloyds and other insurance companies upon the subject of jade values; compiled the comparative scale of color values for jadeites, nephrites and chloromelanites contained under the amphibole and pyroxene groups of nephritoids; internationally consulted by the offices of Customs and Excise on the commercial worth of jade objects; compiled the mineralogical classification of Chinese jade from data accumulated from scientific, optical, microscopical and refractive index methods of research; translated rare Oriental writing refering to the symbology of ritual objects created in jade. Author: The Catalogue of Ch'ien Lung Jades '27; Chinese Hardstone Carvings '30; Imperial Jades in the Summer Palace Collection '31; Chinese Jade Carvings on Exhibition London, Paris and Berlin (4 vols) '32-35; Chinese Jade Throughout the Ages '37; Chinese Jade Carvings XVI-XIX Century (3 vols) '38-40; Catalogue of Rare Chinese Jade Carvings '40-41; The Symbolic Importance of Chinese Jade '41; The Geographical Locations of Chinese Jade '41; One Hundred and One Famous Chinese Jades '41; Chinese Jades in the Stanley Charles Nott collection '42; Chinese Art of World Renown '44; The Charm '44; Chinese Civilization, Past, Present and Future '45; Chinese Culture in the Arts '46; Voices from the Flowery Kingdom '47; Personalities in Chinese Art '48; also articles in field. Dir Charles Nott Ltd London '36-39, pres Stanley Charles Nott, New York '40-46; pres the House of Jade, Ltd New York '46; dir and curator for Life Oriental Art The Norton Gallery West Palm Beach Fla. Chinese Culture Study Group Am(F)—Chinese Art Soc Am—AAAS—Coll Art Assn Am—Am Fed Arts. Westchester Country Club, Rye, N.Y.†◉

22 NOWAK, Frank Thaddeus. History (Polish, Russian, Bohemian, Balkans). b'95. AB '17 (U Rochester); AM '20—PhD '24 (Harvard). Author: Medieval Slavdom and the Rise of Russia '30; also articles in field. Prof hist Boston U since '30; prof diplomatic hist Fletcher Sch Law and Diplomacy since '44. AHA—Phi Beta Kappa (pres Mass Epsilon since '33). Medal for work on Am Relief Assn Poland '19. 725 Commonwealth Av., Boston.◉

23 NOWLIN, William David. Concrete production and control. b'98. Student '19-21 (U Ky); '21-24 (U Tenn). Development concrete mix designs for use low cement content concrete; procedures to reduce heat rise and maximum temperature in mass structures to reduce tendency to crack. Co-author: (with W R Johnson and W R Waugh) Concrete Production and Control '47. Materials engr VA '34-44, Corps Engrs '44-46; asst resident engr Buggs Island Dam Project '47-49; resident engr Philpott Dam Project since '49. Am Concrete Inst. Philpott Project, P.O. Box 72, Bassett, Va. H: Delray Beach, Fla.

10 NOYCE, William K(night). Organic chemistry of synthetic sweetening materials. b'11. AB '33 (Doane Coll); MSc '35—PhD '38 (U Neb). Research in the preparation of certain synthetic sweet materials related to some of the sweetening agents now in use, vinylogs of dulcin and related compounds are being prepared as a means of testing the principle of vinylogy in connection with physiological reaction. Developed a modified Dumas nitrogen apparatus. Author articles in field. Asst prof chem '37-41, asso prof chem '41-46 U Omaha; asso prof chem U Ark '46-51, prof chem since '51. ACS, University of Arkansas, Fayetteville, Ark.

11 NOYES, Robert Gale. Eighteenth century English novel. b'98. AB '21—AM '21 (Brown U); AM '23—PhD '29 (Harvard). Research on the drama and stage as reflected by the English novelists 1740-1780. Author: Ben Jonson on the English Stage, 1660-1776 '35; The Thespian Mirror: Shakespeare in the Eighteenth-Century Novel, 1953. Asst prof English Harvard '36-37; asso prof English Brown U '37-51, prof English since '51. Phi Beta Kappa. Brown University, Providence 12.

12 NOYES, Russell. English literature (Romantic movement, William Wordsworth). b'01. BS '24 (U Mass); AM '28—PhD '32 (Harvard). Author: Drayton's Literary Vogue since 1631 '35; Wordsworth and Jeffrey in Controversy '41; also articles in field. Professor Ind U since '32, chairman dept Eng since '41. Modern Lang Assn Am—Coll Eng Assn—Modern Humanities Research Assn. Indiana University, Bloomington, Ind.†◉

13 NUCKOLS, Samuel B. Sugar beets (Breeding). b'87. BS '11—MA '12 (U Mo). Research on methods and cost of growing sugar beets from breeding plants to utilization of by-products, improvements in planting date, spacing, irrigation, manuring, rotations. Author 58 articles in field. Agron USDA '14-49. AAAS—Am Soc Agron—Am Soc Sugar Beet Tech (meritorious service award '50). 11 E. 17th, Scottsbluff, Neb.

14 NUESSLE, Albert Christian. Cellulose chemistry; Synthetic resins. b'15. BS '36 (U Pa). Research on flame-proofing of textiles; textile finishing with starches, gums and resins; textile auxiliaries such as detergents, penetrants, enzymes and stripping agents; stabilization, creaseproofing, glazing and embossing, durable bodying and stiffening effects on textiles. With Joseph Brancroft & Sons '36-46; head textile applications lab Rohm & Haas Co since '47. ACS—ASTM—Am Assn Textile Chem and Colorists. Rohm & Haas, Phila.

15 NUGENT, Robert Logan. Colloid chemistry. b'02. BS in chem '23—MS '25 (U Ariz); BA Rhodes scholar '27 (Oxford U); PhD '28 (Cornell). Member Arizona State Board of Examiners in Basic Sciences '36, secretary-treasurer '36-40, '42; state gas consultant Arizona Civilian Defense Council '43; president Arizona College Association '50. Research fellow US Bur Mines '24, jr chem summer '25; Heckscher research asst Cornell '27-28; physical chem Gladwyne Research Lab Pa '28-32; instr biochem Grad Sch Med U Pa '30-32; asst prof U Ariz '32, asso prof '35, prof, dean grad coll '40, prof, dean coll liberal arts '44, prof, vp since '47. AAAS(F)—ACS—Phi Beta Kappa—Phi Kappa Phi—Phi Lambda Upsilon—Sigma Xi—Phi Delta Chi. 1946 E. Speedway, Tucson.◉

16 NUGENT, Thomas John. Plant pathology (Tomatoes, potatoes, water-melons, spinach). b'10. BSA '33—MS '37 (Purdue U). Author articles in field. Asso plant path Va Truck Expt Sta Norfolk Va since '46. Am Phytopath Soc—Va Acad Sci—Sigma Xi. Virginia Truck Experiment Station, P.O. Box 2160, Norfolk 1, Va.

17 NUNN, William Curtis. Texas history. b'08. BA '28 (Southwestern U); MA '31—PhD '38 (U Tex). Co-author: Texas, The Story of the Lone Star State '48. Asso prof hist Tex Christian U '46-51, professor of history since '51. History Dept., Texas Christian University, Fort Worth, Texas.

18 NUTT, David C. Arctic exploration and navigation. b'19. AB '41 (Dartmouth Coll). Seaman R A Bartlett Greenland Expedition '35, ornithologist '37, curator '38, navigator and curator '39-40. Author articles in field. Arctic specialist Dartmouth Coll since '47. Exec officer USS Bowdoin (IX-50) US Navy hydrographic survey of Greenland '42-43; exec and comdg officer Pacific Fleet Survey Ship USS Sumner '44-46; comdg officer Task Group in North China and Yangtze River operation '45; naval observer and rep Smithsonian Inst Second Antarctic Development Project US Navy '47, '48; served as comdr USNR since '46; master US Merchant Marine since '46; master sch "Blue Dolphin," engaged in Arctic Research since '48. Arctic Inst NA—Am Geog Soc(F)—NH Acad Scis—Nat Geog Soc—Am Ornithologists Union—Am Polar Soc—AAAS. Dartmouth College, Hanover, N.H.

19 NUTTALL, Edwin De Witt. Communications engineering; Telemetering; Natural gas sytems (Control); Electric power systems (Control). b'03. Ext work (Tex A&M Coll) (Kilgore Coll). Research on remote control and supervisory control applications to natural gas and electric power systems by means of microwave or wire line carrier. Asst chief elec Cuyamel Fruit Co '21-23; supt telephone and telegraph Internat Ry Central Am '26-34; supt heavy constrn various co '29-34; supt transmission and distbn Ark-Mo Power Corp '34-38; chief load dispatcher SW Gas and Elec Co '39-41, communications engr '41-47; electronic engr United Gas Corp since '47. Am Inst EE—Inst Radio Engrs—Am Radio Relay League—Audio Engring Soc—Petroleum Industry Elec Assn. Registered profl elec engr La. Box 1407, Shreveport, La. H: 5511 Sussex St.†

20 NYE, William Preston. Apiculture. b'17. Research on extent and causes of heavy losses of adult honey bees in Utah, relationship between arsenic in Blossoms of white sweet clover and in the soil. Apiculturist US Dept Agr Div Bee Culture Logan Utah since '47. Entomol Soc Am—Am Assn Econ Entomol. U.S. Legume Seed Research Laboratory, Utah State Agricultural College, Campus Box 80, Logan, Utah.

21 NYLUND, Robert Einar. Horticulture; Olericulture. b'16. BS '38—MS '42—PhD '45 (U Minn). Research in mineral nutrition of vegetable crops and potatoes, growth regulators and their effects on growth and fruiting of vegetable crops, chemical weed control in vegetable crops, storage of vegetables and potatoes. Author articles in field. Instr hort div hort U Minn '41-45, asst prof '45-51, associate professor since '51. AAAS(F)—American Soc Hort Science—Am Soc Plant Physiol—Potato Assn Am—AAUP—Gamma Sigma Delta—Gamma Alpha—Sigma Xi. Department of Horticulture, University Farm, St. Paul 1.†

22 NYSTROM, John Warren. Geography of Caribbean; Political geography.

b'13. AB '36—MA '37—PhD '42 (Clark U). Author: Surinam, A Geographical Study '43. Instr geog RI Coll Edn '37-39, asst prof '40-43; asso prof, head dept geog U Pittsburgh '43-48, prof and head dept since '48; dir Pittsburgh Regional Inter-Am Center '43-45; exec dir Fgn Policy Assn '45-53; head fgn policy dept C of C of US since '53. Nat Fgn Policy Assn (dir)—Assn Am Geog—National Council Geog Teach—AAUP—Am Geog Soc—Sigma Xi. University of Pittsburgh, Pittsburgh.†

23 NYSTROM, Paul Henry. Retailing; Marketing; Consumer and fashion economics. b'78. PhB '09—PhM '10—PhD '14 (U Wis). Vice-chmn, chmn National Retail Code Authority under National Recovery Authority; editor American Marketing Journal '35-36; member Federal Board Vocational Education '36-45, com. education Chamber Commerce US '42-49. Author: Economics of Retailing '30, and others. Editor: Marketing Handbook '48. Prof marketing Columbia since '26; bus and marketing cons since '27; pres Limited Price Variety Stores Assn since '34. Am Vocational Assn (vp '38-44)—Nat Retail Assns (chmn Central Council since '42. 25 W. 43rd St., NYC 18.◉

O

24 OAK, Vishnu Vitthal. Negro businesses and newspapers. b'00. AB '20 (U Bombay); MA '23 (U Cal); BSJ '24 (U Ore); '31-32 (U Chicago); MBA '32 (U Ia); PhD '37 (Clark U). Author: The Negro Newspaper '48; Negro's Adventure in General Business '49. Faculty Howard U '26; prof Wiley Coll '26-27, Wilberforce U '27-30, Lincoln U '30-32; prof, dir social studies Langston U '32-33; prof, dean of men Cheyney Training Sch for Tchrs '33-35; prof Samuel Houston Coll '36-37; prof NC Coll Negroes '37-39; prof, dir pub relations, editor Negro Coll Quarterly, Wilberforce U '39-48; dean adminstrn, asst to pres Alcorn A&M Coll '48-49; prof Stowe Tchrs Coll '49. 4968 Highland Av., StL 13.

25 OAKHILL, Frederic Emery. Plant engineering and maintenance; Industrial management. b'03. Student '28-31 (Northwestern U); BS '47 (Ill Inst Tech). Author: Plant Engineering and Maintenance '36 (four revised edits); over 50 articles in tech publs. Plant engr Bauer & Black '28-39; chief mech engr United Wallpaper Inc '39-40; staff prodn engr US Gypsum Co '40-41; staff cons engr Bus Research Corp '41-42; vp in charge mfg O-Cedar Co Corp Chicago '42-45, vp and asst mgr '45-47; vp in charge engring Nat Research Bur '47-48; cons engr, pres Prismacolor Pictures Inc Chicago since '48; spl lectr plant engring and maintenance and indsl management eve div Ill Inst Tech; spl design cons and mfg advisor serveral mfg firms; spl mfg cons US Govt '41. Soc Advancement Management(charter mem)—ASME—Am Inst EE—Soc Motion Picture and Television Engrs—Chicago Tech Soc Council (exec vp)—Delta Sigma Pi. 661 N. LSalle St., Chgo 10. H: 711 Linden Av., Wilmette, Ill.

26 OATES, Whitney J. Ancient philosophy and classics (Greek, Roman, St Augustine). b'04. AB '26—AM '27—PhD '31 (Princeton U). Broadcast on Invitation to Learning Program CBS '40-52. Author: The Influence of Simonides of Ceos upon Horace '32. Editor: The Stoic and Epicurean Philosophers '40; Basic Writings of St Augustine '48; also articles in field. Prof classics Princeton U since '45, chmn dept Classics, chmn spl program

See pages 801 and 831 for additional knowers; page 851 for information sources.

505

in the Humanities. Am Philol Assn—Classical Assn Atlantic States—Phi Beta Kappa. Rockefeller post war fellow '48. Department of Classics, Princeton Univ., Princeton, N.J.†☺

10 OBERBILLIG, Ernest. Ore concentration (Tin, tungsten, antimony). b'15. BS '37—MS in metall engring '38 (U Ida). Specialist in gravity methods and flotation non-metallics; operation tin, tungsten, antimony, quicksilver concentration and refining plants; design new-type concentration jig. Mill supt and metall Sociedad Minera Pirquitas Jujuy Argentina '39-41; metall US Bur Mines LaPaz Bolivia '41-45; mgr Hermes Mine Yellow Pine Ida '45-47; owner and operator Hermada Mine since '47. Am Inst Mining Engrs—Am Ordnance Assn. Twin Springs, Ida.

11 OBERG, Kalervo. Ethnology; Economics; Archeology. b'01. BA '28 (U BC); MA '30 (U Pittsburgh); PhD '33 (U Chicago); Post-doctoral '33 (London Sch Econ). Ethnology with particular emphasis on primitive economics and law of Indian tribes of North West Coast of North America, native tribes of Uganda Africa, Indian tribes of Mato Grosso Brazil, five expeditions '46-50; land use economics of New Mexico, Rio Grande Valley, food production economics of Ecuador and Peru; reports of Burnt Rock mounds in Central Texas. Author: The Social Economy of the Tlingit Indians '33; Banyankole Kinship Organization '38; The Kingdom of Ankole '40; Crime and Punishment in Tlingit Society '34; Land Use Planning in Cuba Valley, New Mexico '41; The Bacairi of Northern Mato Grosso '49; others. Ethnology Alaska '31-32, Uganda '34-36; archaeology Texas '38; econ analyst USDA '39-42; econ analyst coordinators office Inter-Am Affairs, Ecuador and Peru '42-43; econ analyst Fgn Econ Adminstrn Washington '43-45; anthropologist Smithsonian Instn Sao Paulo Brazil since '46. Sigma Xi—Am Anthropol Assn—Royal Anthropol Inst—Internat African Inst. Escola de Sociologia e Politica, Largo Sao Francisoc 19, Sao Paulo, Brazil.

12 OBERLE, George David. Fruit breeding and genetics; Pomology (Deciduous fruits); Oenology. b'07. BS '31—MS '36 (Kan State Coll); PhD '38 (Cornell U). Engaged research in photosynthesis of apple trees, grape floral morphology and function, breeding types of cucurbits resistant to virus diseases and improved varieties of fruits resistant to diseases, insects and other adverse agencies by hybridizing and other means, effects produced on yields of American grape varieties through grafting them on hybrid rootstocks, physiological response of fruit trees receiving applications of petroleum oil sprays and other insecticides and fungicides; worked in breeding programs devoted to peaches, pears, strawberries, red raspberries, black raspberries, blackberries, blueberries, apples, grapes; named and introduced three new varieties of grapes; in charge of developing fruit breeding program to produce varieties adapted for culture under environmental conditions in Virginia. Author articles: A Genetic Study of Variations in Floral Morphology and Function in Cultivated Forms of Vitis '38: An Evaluation of the Use of French Hybrid Wine Grapes in Breeding Hardy Grapes for the Eastern United States '43; Some Physiological Responses of Fruit Trees to Petroleum Oil Sprays (with Chapman, Pearce and Avens) '44; Three New Grapes Developed by the New York State Agricultural Experi-

ment Station Which Show Promise '47; Grafting American Grapes on Vigorous Rootstocks '45. Asso prof agr Ark State Teachers Coll '36: research asst Div Pomology NY State Agrl Expt Sta '37; agent US Dept Agr '38-39; asst prof and asso in research NY State Agrl Expt Station and Cornell U '39-44, asso prof '44-48; hort Va Agrl Expt Sta since '48. AAAS—Am Soc Hort Sci—Am Genetic Assn—Va Acad Sci—Sigma Xi. Recipient of award for outstanding piece of grad research, Kan State Coll chapt of Sigma Xi '36. Virginia Agricultural Experiment Station, Blacksburg, Va.†

13 OBRECHT, Carl Bernard. Mosquitoes; Great Lakes biology. b'16. BS '39 (Central Mich Coll Edn); MS '42-50 (U Mich). Research on systematics and distribution mosquitoes of Northeastern US, James Bay Region Ontario; investigations aquatic biology throughout Great Lakes Region; cold-blooded vertebrates; aquatic invertebrates. Instr biol U Detroit since '46. Med entomol and malaria control AUS '45. Soc Systematic Zool—Am Soc Limnol and Oceanog—AAUP—Phi Sigma—Gamma Alpha—Alpha Epsilon Delta. Department of Biology, University of Detroit, Det 21. H: 19700 Bentler, Det 19.

14 O'BRIEN, Brian. Optical physics; Solar radiation; Photometry; High speed photography; Ultra violet and infrared devices; Vision and illuminating engineering. b'98. PhB '18—PhD '22 (Yale); grad study (MIT, Harvard). Research on solar radiation, solar ultra violet spectrum, energy distribution in spectra, solar radiation in upper atmosphere and atmospheric ozone, optical properties of materials; infra red sensitive phosphorus, infra red telescope systems, flicker phenomena in binocular vision, high speed photographic photometry, ultra high speed motion photography, effect of radiation on micro organisms, irradiation induced vitamin D, methods of bioassay for vitamin D, radiographic effects of vitamin D and phosphorus deficiency. Author articles in field. Prof physiol optics U Rochester since '30, dir Inst Optics since '38, research prof physics and optics since '46. Am Phys Soc(F)—AAAS(F)—AIEE(F)—Optical Soc Am—Am Geophys Union. University of Rochester, Rochester, N.Y.☺

15 O'BRIEN, Brian, Jr. Optics (Applied); Missile guidance (Optical-electronic); Camouflage; Photography (High speed); Graphic arts (Photomechanical processes). b'23. BS in optics '44 (U Rochester); SM in phys '49 (MIT). Research, design and development optical-electronic missile guidance systems, camouflage and visibilty studies, ultra-high speed photography, application photomechanical processes to graphic arts, research on photoengraving and printing processes, development equipment. Research phys Am Newspaper Pub Assn Lab. Optical Soc Am—APS—Am Inst EE—Aircraft Owners and Pilots Assn. American Newspaper Publishers Association Laboratory, R.F.D. 2, Easton, Pa. H: 154 Lincoln St.

16 O'BRIEN, Cyril Cornelius. Alcoholism (Industry); Music aptitude; Music esthetics; Palestrina. b'06. BA '26 (U St Mary's Coll Halifax NS); MusL '31 (McGill U Montreal Que Can); MA '32 (Mt Allison U Sackville NB); BPaed '34 (U Toronto Ont); MusB '37 (Laval U Quebec City Que); DPaed '37—MusD '50 (U Montreal Que); PhD '44 (U Ottawa Ont). Devised technique for test of harmonic esthetic judgment. Author articles: Part and Whole Methods in the Memorization of Music '43; Tone Color

Discrimination '45; Alcoholism as a Diciplinary Problem in Industry '49; Alcoholism in Industry, and others. Organist various churches '29-47; head dept psychol Maritime Acad Mus Halifax NS '35-47; asst prof edn Marquette U since '47, lectr indsl psychol Labor Coll since '50; cons psychol Allis-Chalmers Mfg Co since '48. AAAS(F)—Am Psychol Assn(F)—Royal Statis Soc(F)—Royal Econ Soc (F)—AAUP—NEA—Am Ednl Research Assn—Nat Soc Study Edn—Royal Soc Tchrs—Am Sociol Soc—Acoustical Soc Am—Am Inst Physics Can Coll Organists (vp '46-47) (NS Music Tchrs Assn—Wis Acad Sci Arts and Letters—Midwest Psychol Assn—Wis Psychol Assn—Econometrica—Midwest Social Soc (exec '51-53). AAAS research grant in aid on alcoholism '50. Marquette University, Milw 3. H: 2531 N. Oakland Av., Milw 11.

17 O'BRIEN, Harold Charles, Jr. Electron microscopy; Microtomy. b'14. BS '35 (Geneva Coll); MS '41 (Duquesne U); PhD '45 (U Pittsburgh). Research on pigment dispersion methods and thin undistorted sections for electron microscopy, invented ultramicrotome thin sections for electron microscopy. Metall Jones & Laughlin Steel Co '36; research chem St Joseph Lead Co '37-46; with Royston Lab since '46, pres and dir rsrch since '49; cons Nat Assn Corrosion Engrs—Pa Acad Sci—AAAS—APS—Am Ceramic Soc—AmSocMetalls—ACS—Electron Micros SocAm—ASTM—Phi Sigma—Sigma Xi. Sr research fellow U Pittsburgh '45-49. Royston Laboratories Inc., 128 First St., Blawnox, Pa.

18 O'BRIEN, Ruth. Standards, grade labeling, and specifications for clothing and household textiles; Uniform sizing of women's and children's clothing. b'92. BS '14—MA '15—DSc '52 (U Neb); LLB '31 (George Washington Univ). Development consumer specifications for cotton sheeting, broadcloth for men's shirts, terry cloth, upholstery fabrics and blankets; director large-scale scientific measurement of women and children to provide data for uniform sizing of clothes and patterns. Head textiles and clothing division Bureau Human Nutrition and Home Econ USDA '24-44, asst chief of bur since '44. ACS—Am Assn Textile Chem and Colorists—Am Home Econ Assn—Textile Research Inst—Phi Beta Kappa—Sigma Xi—Omicron Nu—Order of the Coif—Phi Delta Delta—Iota Sigma Pi. George Washington U alumni achievement award '44; USDA Distinguished Service Award '51. Bureau of Human Nutrition and Home Economics, US. Department of Agriculture, Washington 25.

19 O'BRIEN, William J(ames). Pigments; Soya protein; Vegetable oils; Paints; Metal powders. b'88. BChem '11 (Cornell U). Research and writing on analysis of phosphorus in acetylene, new method of producing photogenic effects, study of lithopone, process for treating garbage, conversion of ammonia to nitric acid. cadmium reds, industrial uses of the soybean. Author articles in field. Scientist US Dept Agr '14-18; charge research Grasselli Chem Co '18-22; gen mgr chemical and pigment div Glidden Co '22-30, dir and vp in charge mfg '30-48, research and sales of processes '48-53; exec vp Gen Bio Chem Corp since '53. The General Bio Chem Corporation, Chagrin Falls, Ohio.

20 O'BRYAN, Deric. Archeology, (No Mexico, Southwest United States, Arctic Canada). b'13. SB '36 (Harvard); DPhil '39 (Oxford U). Research in Southwest United States, Mexico,

Northwest Territories of Canada. Author articles in field. Research archeologist to asst dir Gila Pueblo Archeological Found '39-49; chief arctic sect Arctic Desert Tropic Information Center, Air U since '49. AAAS—Am Anthropol Assn—Royal Anthropol Inst. Research Studies Institute, Maxwell Air Force Base, Ala.

10 O'CONNOR, John Woolf (Jack). Southwestern birds and mammals; Sporting arms. b'02. Student '21-23 (Ariz State Tchrs Coll) '23-24 (U Ariz); AB '25 (U Ark); AM '27 (U Mo). Former pres Tucson Game Protective Association. Author: Conquest '30; Game in the Desert '39; Hunting in the Southwest '45; Your Sporting Gun '46; Hunting in the Rockies '47; The Rifle Book '49. Editor: Arms and Amunition dept Outdoor Life mag since '39. Outdoor Life, 353 th Av., NYC.

11 O'CONNOR, Leslie Michael. Professional baseball (History, regulations). b'89. LLB '16 (Chicago-Kent Coll Law). Editor: Professional Baseball in America (6 edits) '21-36; 1943 Baseball: Official Baseball (record books) 1944, 1945 '46. Sec-treas Baseball '21-44; chmn adv council Major & Minor Leagues '45; spl asst to Commissioner '45; gen mgr Chicago Am League Baseball Club '46-48; mem Major League Exec Council '47-48; atty specializing in profl baseball '49-50. 150 N. Wacker Dr., Chgo 6. H: Leonard Manor, Crystal Lake, Ill.†

12 O'CONNOR, Patrick Andrew. Art (Pre-Christian, Medieval Irish). b'09. Student (Prado, Madrid, Paris Louvre, Nat Mus Dublin). Exhibited: Paris Salon, Royal Hibernian Academy, Dublin, Royal Scottish Academy, Museum Modern Art Amsterdam; represented permanent collection Dublin Municipal Gallery Art; one man shows Paris, London, New York, Reinhardt Gallery. Dir O'Connor Gallery NY; collaborator with Metropolitan Mus in exhibition of ancient Irish Art at Irish Acad. Irish Acad (pres). Awarded bronze medal Mus Modern Art Amsterdam '28. 180 Bleecker St., NYC 12.†

13 O'CONNOR, Robert Barnard. Architecture of libraries, museums, institutional buildings. b'95. AB '16 (Trinity Coll); MFA '20 (Princeton). Contributor chapter on Museums to Forms and Functions of 20th Century Architecture '52. Member committee of review on Planning the University Library Building '49. In arch practice NYC since '21; partner R B O'Connor & W H Kilham Jr since '43; vp, dir Architects' Offices Inc since '45; supervising arch Princeton U; works include Firestone Library Princeton U, Met Mus Art NYC (A Embury II asso), Avery Mus, Co Home for Aged, others. AIA(F), pres NY chpt '43-44, Medal of Honor NY chpt '46)—Beaux Art Inst Design (trustee)—NY Bldg Congress —Phi Beta Kappa—Delta Psi. 101 Park Av., NYC 17.†⊙

14 O'CONNOR, William F. Chemical, safety, fire protection engineering. b'10. BS '31—MS '32 (Manhattan Coll); MA '33—PhD '35 (Columbia). Prof chem Manhattan Coll NYC '31-42; dir Fire and Safety Dept Koppers Co Pittsburgh '42-45, cons since '39; cons chem Westchester Co, White Plains NY since '39; prof safety engrng NYU '45-47; tech dir Jasper Chem Co, Yonkers NY since '45; asso prof chem Fordham U since '47; cons Atomic Energy Commn since '48. Am Chem Soc—Electrochem Soc—Am Soc Safety Engr—ASME— Am Pub Health Assn—NY State Sewage Works Assn—Nat Fire Protection Assn. Fordham University, NYC.

15 ODELL, Theodore Tellefsen. Ecology of freshwater fishes. b'96. BS '20

(Hobart Coll); MA '27—PhD '34 (Cornell U). Author articles in field. Instr biol Hobart and William Smith Coll '21-28, asst prof '28-34, prof since '35; biol NY State Conservation Dept summers '27-39, Vt Fish and Game Service summers '40-41. AAAS(F)—Am Fish Soc—Ecol Soc Am—Limnolog Soc Am—Am Soc Ichthyology and Herpetology—Sigma Xi—Phi Beta Kappa. Hobart and William Smith Colleges, Geneva, N.Y.

16 ODGERS, Ira Douglas. Exploration (Diamond drill). b'08. BS in geol '32 (Mich Coll Mining and Tech). Exploration for commercial minerals from surface or underground, including iron ore; use of churn or rotary drilling through overburden. Mining engr and asst supt NJ Div Alan Wood Steel Co '37-46; diamond drill contracting Odgers Drilling Co since '46. Am Inst Mining Engrs—Mich Soc Profl Engrs—Nat Soc Profl Engrs. Profl mining engr Mich, N.J. Odgers Drilling Co., Crystal Falls, Mich.

17 ODIORNE, Joseph Milton. Physiology of pigment cells; Polydactylism (Human). b'04. BS '25 (Bowdoin Coll); MA '31—PhD '34 (Harvard). Research on aspects of physiology of pigment cells in fishes and resulting color changes, comparative physiology of pigmentation in vertebrates, inheritance of polydactylism in related New England families; one of first to emphasize variable responses of pigmentary systems of different animals to same hormone; described occurrence of leucophores (guanophores) in Fundulus; made quantitative study of effect of surroundings on pigmentation of fishes; member of Conf on Biol of Normal and Atypical Pigment Cell Growth, Section of Biology, NY Academy Sciences '46. Author articles in field. Asst prof zool Fla State U '47-50; asst prof anatomy NYU Coll Med since '50. NYU-Bellevue Medical Center, 477 1st Av., NYC 16.

18 ODOM, Charles L(eonard). Vocational guidance. b'94. BS '25 (Centenary Coll La); AM '27 (U Chicago); '38-39 (Columbia). PhD '40 (NYU); spl training in counseling and psychotherapy, projective techniques '47 (La-State U Law Sch). Author articles: The Mental Growth Curve, with Special Reference to the Results of Group Intelligence Tests '29; Closing the Gap Between School and College '41; The Undergraduate Program in Psychology '50; The Time Required to Do a Rorschach Examination '50, others. Personal counselor to veterans on personal problems VA '46-47, chief clinical psychologist VA Hosp New Orleans '47-48, chief clinical psychol VA Regional office since '48; asso prof med pshycol La State U Sch Med since '48; pvt practice clinical and cons psychol since '49. Am Psychol Assn(F)—Am Coll Personnel Assn— Nat Council Family Relations—Southern Soc Philos and Psychol—La Psychol Assn—La Soc Mental Health (mem state bd)—Nat Vocational Guidance Assn(profl mem)—Alpha Chi (co-founder, pres '38-39). 602 Carondelet Bldg., New Orleans 12.

19 O'DONNELL, Thomas J(ohn). Geophysical prospecting; Circuit theory; Tapered transmission structures; Guided missiles. b'12. BS in phys '33 —DSc '51 (Carnegie Inst Tech). Research on seismic geophysical prospecting for oil; circuit theory research on tapered transmission structures, chiefly lumped circuit analogs; helped develop AZON and RAZON radio-guided high-angle bombs. With Gulf Research & Development Co since '33, asst dir geophys operations since '51. Soc Exploration Geophys—Am Geophys

Union—APS—Inst Radio Engrs—Tau Beta Pi—Sigma Xi—Phi Kappa Phi— Eta Kappa Nu. Gulf Research & Development Co., P.O. Box 2038, Pitts 30.

20 ODORFER, Adolf. Ceramic sculpture and plastermolds; Pottery; Earthenware; Engobes. b'02. Student (Wilnerberger Werkstatten Schule Fuer Keramik Vienna, Prof Friedrich Thetter and Prof Robert Obsieger). Author articles in journals. Work with Ceramica Jundiakyense, San Paulo Brazil '23-26; pottery in Tlaquepaque, Jalisco, Mexico '27-35; own workshop for ceramics Fresno Cal since '35; ceramics instr Fresno State Coll since '48. Awarded several prizes and several hon mentions Nat Ceramic Exhibition Syracuse Mus Fine Arts. 4715 North Thorne Av., Fresno 4, Cal.

21 ODUM, Eugene P(leasants). Ornithology (Georgia); Vertebrate ecology; Mammalogy; Cardio-vascular system (Comparative physiology). b'13. AB '34—AM '36 (U NC); PhD '39 (U Ill). Co-author: Birds of Georgia '45, also articles in field. Asso prof zool U Ga since '45. Am Ornithol Union— Eastern Bird Banding Assn—Ga Ornithol Soc (pres '42-45)—AAAS—Ecol Soc Am—Wildlife Soc—Am Soc Mammalogists—SE Biol (vp '48)—Sigma Xi. Department of Biology, University of Georgia, Athens, Ga.

22 OEHSER, Paul Henry. History of American science. b'04. AB '25 (Greenville Coll); '24 (U Ia); '25-30 (Am U). Author: Sons of Science (the story of the Smithsonian Institution and its leaders); also articles in field. Asst editor Bur Biol Survey, US Dept Agr '25-31; editor US Nat Mus '31-50, asst chief editorial div Smithsonian Institution '46-50, chief editorial division since '50; editorial exec Journal of the Washington Academy Science since '39. Wash Biol Field Club—Wash Acad Sci —Biol Soc Wash—Am Ornithol Union. Smithsonian Institution, Washington 25.†

23 OELKE, William Christoff. Physical chemistry; Semi-micro analysis. b'06. AB '28 (Grinnell Coll); MS '29 (Holy Cross Coll); PhD '35 (State U Ia). Research on utilization of sulfite waste liquor '42; investigation of oxidation-reduction potentials of photographic developers '40; corrosion inhibition on graphited surfaces; determination of solubilities and activity coefficients of lanthanun iodate '31-35, activity coefficients of Cd $(IO_3)_2$ '38-39. Author: Semimicro Qualitative Analysis '49; also articles in field. Instr chem Holy Cross Coll '29-30, lecturer '30-31; instr chem Grinnell Coll '31-41, asst prof '41-44, asso prof '44-49, prof since '49, chmn chem dept since '48. Am Chem Soc—Ia Acad Sci— Sigma Xi. Grinnell College, Park St., Grinnell, Ia.†

24 OFFORD, Harold Reginald. Weed control; Forest protection. b'03. BA '24—MA '25 (Brit Columbia); '25-26 (Imperial Coll Sci, London); '26 (College de France U Paris). Research on blister rust control methods, toxic action of chemicals on plants, tannins, starches; new herbicides; methods for chemical control noxious plants; fireproofing textiles; propagation woody plants in nutrient solutions; use of chemicals in brush burning. Author articles in field. Agt, chem, Bur Plant Industry US Dept Agr '27-33, pathol in charge blister rust control investigations, Bur Entomol and Plant Quarantine since '34. AAAS—Soc Am Foresters—Am Forestry Assn—Sigma Xi. 4 Forestry Bldg., University of California, Berkeley 4.

25 OGBURN, Sihon Cicero, Jr. Chemical industrial research. b'00. BS '21

—PhD '26 (U NC); MS '23 (Washington & Lee U). Policies, objectives, functions and management of industrial research and development activities; appraisal technological projects and evaluation of research results. Several patents covering industrial chemical processes relating to phosphates and fluorine materials. Author articles in field. Cons to chem ind '26-36; tech supervisor and research mgr Gen Chem Co NYC '36-43; mgr research and develpt Pa Salt Mfg Co Phila '43-48; mgr research and develpt Foote Mineral Co Phila since '48, dir since '49. Indsl Research Inst—Research Management Group Phila—ACS —AIChE—ASEE — Electrochem Soc—Chem Soc London—Sigma Xi. Awarded Smith research prize in applied sci U NC '26. P.O. Box 576, Berwyn, Pa. H: 618 Woodleave Road, Bryn Mawr, Pa.

10 OGBURN, Vincent Holland. Thomas Percy. b'87. PhB '10 (Drake U); AM '11—fellow '10-11 (U Pittsburgh); '13-14, '23 (U Chicago); PhD '36 (Stanford U). Research on Bishop Thomas Percy and his relation to the romantic revival, particularly the ballad revival. Author: New Light on the Life and Works of Bishop Thomas Percy '35; also articles in field. Asst prof Eng Utah Agrl Coll '14-20, Colo Coll '20-22; prof Eng Coe Coll '23-36; prof Eng head div lang lit and fine arts Eastern NM U '37-52, emeritus '52. 134 Lyell St., Los Altos, Cal.

11 OGDEN, Bryan Kneass. Marine insurance; Workmen's compensation and liability insurance. b'83. AB '05 (Princeton U). Worked with US Maritime Commission in wartime shipbuilding program in connection with workmen's compensation and liability insurance; examines and approves all insurance submitted by mortgagors, charterers and other contractors. Jobs with brokerage house, railroad, and travel '05-08; entered marine ins bus '09, assisted with ins problems of US Shipping Bd Merchant Fleet Corp Washington '17-46; instr Marine Ins Sch of Fgn Service Georgetown U. retired Mar '53. H: 3518 Newark St., Washington 16.

12 OGDEN, Eugene Cecil. Phytotaxonomy; Potamogeton; Pollen. b'05. BS '32 (Mich State Coll); MS '34 (U Me); AM '36—PhD '39 (Harvard). State bot NY since '52. Eastern NY Bot Soc—Am Bryol Soc—Bot Soc Mexico—Am Soc Plant Tax—Sigma Xi—New Eng Bot Club—Josselyn Bot Soc—Am Bot Soc—Am Moss Soc—Phycol Soc Am. New York State Museum, Albany 1, N.Y.

13 OGDEN, John Trecartin. Glass; Packaging. b'92. AB (Yale). Twenty five years experience specialized publishing in field of glass and packaging. Am Ceramic Soc(F)—Soc Glass Tech England. Ogden Publishing Co., 55 W. 42d St., NYC 18.

14 OGDEN, Laurence Armstead. Petroleum (Development and production). b'92. Student '11-15 (Stanford); '18-19 (USN Acad Annapolis Md). Development efficient production methods for oil and gas wells primary and secondary production, by means of gas, air, and water drive. Asst petroleum engr US Bur Mines '23-24; petroleum engr Empire Companies '24-33; div petroleum engr Pure Oil Co since '33. AIMME—Am Petroleum Inst. The Pure Oil Co., Box 271, Tulsa 2.

15 OGDEN, William Frederick. Codes (Electric). b'04. AB—BS in elec engring '26 (Swarthmore Coll). Member advisory committees to National Production Authority and Office Price Stabilization. Central station engr

Gen Elec Co '27; with Ga Power Co '28-36; with Edison Gen Elec Appliance Co '36-47, asst chief engr '46-47; mgr products Hotpoint Inc since '47. Nat Elec Mfrs Assn (exec mem, voting rep, mem codes and standards com, article com Nat Elec Code, chmn elec range tech com, chmn elec water heater tech com, chmn elec range sect and mem gen engring, refrigerator and freezer com, chmn com standards color white for kitchen and laundry appliances, major appliance div, v-chmn refrigeration sect, mem defense activities and pub com)—Am Standards Assn(Nat Elec Mfrs Assn rep com 62 coordination of dimensions for equipment and building materials, mem com elec range standards, com on water heater standards)—Joint Nat Elec Mfrs Assn—Edison Elec Inst Com Preferred Voltages Ratings—Am Inst EE(mem standards com, chmn domestic and comml applications com) —Underwriters Labs (mem industry adv conf on ranges, water and thermostats)—Soc Am Mil Engrs. Registered profl engr Ill. General Electric Co., 570 Lexington Av., NYC 22.

16 OGG, Oscar. Calligraphy; Book design. b'08. BS Arch '31 (U Ill). Author: An Alphabet Source Book '40; The 26 Letters '48; Lettering As a Book Art '49; also articles in field. Asst to art dir Huxley House NYC '32-34; art dir Swafford & Koehl '35-36; free lance designer NYC '35-48; asst to Boardman Robinson Colo Springs Fine Arts Center '38-39; design consultant Book-of-the-Month Club NYC '45-48, art dir '48-49, director of advertising since '49; design consultant Wm Sloane Asso New York City '46-48; consulting editor Am Artist NYC since '46; lecturer calligraphy Columbia U since '46. Am Inst Graphic Arts—Typophiles. H: Westover Rd. at Long Close Rd., Stamford, Conn.

17 OGILVIE, Ida H(elen). Glaciers (British Columbia); Volcanic rocks (Maine); Geology (Adirondack Mountains, New Mexico Ortiz Mountains, California San Gabriel Mountains). BA '00 (Bryn Mawr Coll); PhD '03 (Columbia U); student (U Chicago). Geological explorations and investigations California, New Mexico, Mexico. Author articles in field. Lecturer to prof geol Barnard Coll Columbia U '03-41, retired prof emeritus '41. Geol Soc Am(F)—AAAS(F)—NY Acad Sci (F)—Seismol Soc Am—Sigma Xi—Phi Beta Kappa. 39 Claremont Av., NYC 27.

18 OGILVIE, John William Greene. Aviation (International cargo); International broadcasting. b'02. Grad '24 (Hamilton Coll); (Queens Coll Oxford U). Assignments Cuba, Chile, Argentina, Puerto Rico and Spain during Civil War there. With Internat Telephone and Telegraph Corp '27-41, charge radio operations NY office '38; with Office Coordinator Inter-Am Affairs '41-45; dir radio div Dept of State, chief Internat Broadcasting Div '45-46; pres Radio Corp Puerto Rico '35; vp and gen mgr Puerto Rico Telephone Co; cargo sales mgr Pan American World Airways. Chrysler Bldg., NYC 17.

19 O'HARA, Charles Edward. Criminology (Scientific crime detection); Criminalistics. b'12. BA '34—MS '36 (St Peter's Coll Jersey City); '37-41 (NYU). Development of new techniques of scientific crime detection, investigation of new types of clue materials and improvement of existing methods of examination of evidence. Co-author: (with James Osterburg) An Introduction To Criminalistics '49. Staff Police Lab NYC Police Dept since '41. Police Laboratory, 400

Broome St., NYC 13. H: 5312 Thomas Rd., Washington 22.

20 O'HARE, George Alfred. Drying oil technology; Linoleum (Manufacture). b'12. AB '34 (Harvard); PhD '39 (U Pa). Research on mechanism of drying oil oxidation (linseed, soybean, manhedan), manufacture of linoleum; application of dielectric properties to study of drying oil oxidation. Mgr tech service Congoleum-Nairn Inc Kearny N.J. ACS—Am Oil Chem Soc—ASTM. 195 Belgrove Drive, Kearny, N.J.

21 O'KELLY, Arlington Adrian. Petroleum chemistry and technology (Alkylation and polymerization). b'04. AB '26 (Univ of Ark); PhD '29 (Univ of Colo). Research chemist and director research and development oil producing companies; catalytic alkylation of paraffins with olefins; catalyst for polymerizing unsaturated hydrocarbons; polymerization inhibitors. Inventor and co-inventor 17 patents on motor fuels. Prof chem Union Coll Barboursville Ky '29-30; asso prof chem, physics Middle Tenn Coll Murfreesboro '30-35; research chem Socony Vacuum Oil Co Inc NJ '35-42, supervising chem '42-47, asso dir research and development since '47; tech dir Alox Corp Niagara Falls. Am Chem Society —Sigma Xi. Socony-Vacuum Oil Co., Inc., Paulsboro, N.J.

22 OKIMOTO, Marion Chiyoko. Pineapple fruit diseases and anatomy. b'13. BS '34 (U Hawaii); MS '43 (Cornell U). Author articles in field. Sci aide to asst pathol Pineapple Research Inst since '34. Soc Am Bacteriologists—Bot Soc Am—AAAS—Hawaiian Acad Sci—Hawaiian Bot Soc. Pineapple Research Institute, P.O. Box 3166, Honolulu 2, T.H.

23 OKRESS, Ernest Carl. Magnetron design and development; Vacuum tube and microwave circuit design. b'10. BEE '35 (U Detroit); MS '40 (U Mich); '46-49 (NYU). Bactericidal lamp development, klystron development, microwave circuit and magnetron development, magnetron and microwave gas switching tube design and development and consultation on microwave problems; patents; nationally registered professional engineer. Author articles in field. Lecturer on ultra-high frequency radio Rutgers U '42; grad student Westinghouse Elec Corp Bloomfield NJ '40-41, jr engr '41, lab and materials engr '41-43, research engr '43-46, engr since '46. Am Phys Soc—Inst Radio Engrs—Sigma Xi. Westinghouse Electric Corp., Bloomfield, N.J.†

24 OKULITCH, Vladimir Joseph. Palaeozoic corals and sponges. b'06. BASc '31—MASc '32 (U British Columbia); PhD '34 (McGill U); research fellow '36 (Harvard). Collected fossils in the Cordileran region of Southeast British Columbia. Author articles: Some Black River Corals '38; Evolutionary Trends of Some Ordovician Corals '39. Asst to asso prof geol and geog U Brit Columbia since '44. Paleontol Soc(F)—Geol Soc Am(F)—Royal Soc Can(F)—Brit Columbia Acad Sci—Assn Profl Engrs Brit Columbia. Research fellow Royal Soc Can '34-36. Department of Geology, University of British Columbia, Vancouver, British Columbia, Can.†

25 OLBERG, Ralph Charles. Petroleum chemistry; Catalysis; Terpene chemistry. b'14. BA '37 (Cornell Coll Ia); MS '43—PhD '47 (Northwestern U). Am Chem Soc—Sigma Xi. Shell Development Co., Emerville, Cal.

26 OLCOTT, Irwin. Vitamins. b'11. BS '32 (U Denver); MS '33 (U Ia); '33-35 (Pa State Coll). Synthesis of vitamin D2, vitamin D3, choline, and calcium pantothenate; vitamin stability, and blending. Exec chem and engr, supervising production, research, pilot plant and engring Dawe's Vitamins Inc since '36. ACS—AAAS—Assn Vitamin Chem—Animal Nutrition Research Council—Inst Food Tech—Am Assn Cereal Chem—Am Oil Chem Soc. 4800 S. Richmond St., Chgo 32.

10 OLCOTT, Perry. Oil and gas reserve estimates and appraisals; Subsurface and surface geology. b'96. Student '26-27 (U Chicago). Oil scout Empire Gas & Fuel Co Shreveport La '20; surveyor and recorder, oil scout, plane table geological assistant Standard Oil Co New Jersey, Venezuela '20-26; secretary Petroleum Administration for War committee on oil reserves district three '43-45, chairman gas reserves '43-45. Author articles: History of Reserves and Production of Natural Gas and Natural Gas Liquids in Texas '46. Associate editor: Stratigraphic Type Oil Fields '41. Head statis and evaluation sect Humble Oil & Refining Co Houston '36-52, ret now cons. Houston Geol Soc (pres '38)—Am Assn Petroleum Geol (vp '46)—Am Gas Assn (com on gas reserves '44-52)—Am Petroleum Inst (sub-com on oil reserves '38-52). 2609 Sunset Blvd., Houston 5.

11 OLD, Bruce Scott. Ferrous and process metallurgy; Pig iron blast furnace (High top pressure); Open hearth and rolling mills; Sulfur in coke tracers; Nuclear reactors. b'13. Fellow—ScD (MIT); BS (U NC). Author articles in field. Metallurgist Arthur D Little Inc '46-50, dir '49-52, vp '50-52; chief metall and materials br div research AEC '47-49; pres and director Cambridge Corp since '51; office Coordinator of research and development Office Sec Navy, Navy Dept '41-46. Am Soc Metals—Am Inst Mining and Metall Engrs—Eastern States Blast Furnace and Coke Plant Assn—AAAS. Cambridge Corporation, 119 Windsor St., Cambridge, Mass.

12 OLD, Marcus Calvin. Zoology (Marine and freshwater); Sponges. b'97. BA '23—MA '25 (Lehigh U); PhD '30 (U Mich). Author articles in field. Asst prof, later prof biol Hofstra Coll since '30, dean faculty since '48. AAAS—Am Assn Limnol Oceanog—NY Acad Sci—Am Micros Soc—Am Soc Zool—NY Zool Soc—Sigma Xi. Hofstra College, Hempstead, N.Y.†

13 OLDEN, Roger George. Electromechanical devices; Scanners and recorders (Radio facsimile). b'02. BS '21 (Real-Gymnasium Wien XVII); ME '28 (Tech U Vienna). Research and design radio facsimile scanners and recorders. Holds patents in field. Research engr RCA Labs since '42 Received RCA Labs award for outstanding work in research '50. RCA Laboratories, Princeton, N.J.

14 O'LEARY, Willaim J. Ceramics; High temperature chemistry. b'02. AB '23 (Laval U); '24-26 (U Dayton); AM '30—PhD '33 (Cornell). Research with refractory metals, oxides, enamels; refractory borides, carbides, nitrides; metal-ceramics (cermets). Editor: Hydrides of Silicon and Boron '33; Applied Radiochemistry '36. Contributor: Scotts Standard Methods of Chemical Analysis '39; Advanced Quantitative Analysis '43. Ceramic engr Fairchild Engine & Airplane Corp NEPA Div '47-51; with materials br US AEC Savanah River Operations. Office Wilmington Del since '51. ACS—Am Ceramic Soc—Am Soc Metals—Am Mineral Soc—AAAS—Optical Soc Am—Crystallographic Soc—Am Inst Physics—Sigma Xi—Phi Kappa Phi—Sigma Gamma Epsilon.

15 OLECK, Howard L. Bankruptcy; Debtor-creditor law; Corporate reorganization; World War II (History). b'11. Grad '28 (Townsend Harris Hall Prep Sch); AB '33 (U Ia); LLB '38 (NY Law Sch). Author: Creditors' Rights '47; Creditors' Rights and Remedies '49; Debtor-Creditor Law '53; Corporate Officers Encyclopedia '53; Organizing Corporations '52. Author War Department Historical Div publications: The Roer-Rhine Drive, The Occupation of Germany, History of the XXII Corps in the Rhineland, History of 15th Army (collaboration), Chronology of Allied Planning of Operations, E.T.O., 1939-45, History of Allied Planning of Operations, E.T.O., 1939-45 (all published '45). Practice of law since '38; assistant professor NY Law Sch since '47; pres, chmn bd dirs Able Pub Co Inc since '49; spl dep atty gen NY State '48, '50. Pvt to maj US Army '42-45; War Dept hist reprtr, historian and editor. Am Arbitration Assn (nat panel)—Am Bar Assn—NY C Bar Assn—Societe de Legislation Comparee—US Res Officers Assn. New York Law School, 244 William St., NYC 38.†Ⓞ

16 OLESON, Calvin Carl. Portland cement. b'01. BS in civil engring '25 (SD State Coll); MS in civil engring '28 (Ia State Coll). Survey and analysis of concrete serviceability in field use; observation and report characteristics of fresh concrete in field test projects; study new developments in Portland cement concrete by users. Project engr Mo Highway Dept '29-36; prof civil engring SD State Coll '36-46; dist concrete engr Pa Turnpike Commn '39-40; prin research engr Portland Cement Assn since '46. Am Soc CE—Am Concrete Inst. Profl engr and land surveyor SD. Portland Cement Association, 5420 Harrison St., Skokie, Ill.

17 OLIPHANT, Abner Chambers. Coal storage; Street and road signs (Standardization); Utility engineering. b'92. Grad '12 (Mercersberg Acad); EE '15 (Drexel Inst); grad work (Columbia). National committee work on storage of coal and national standardization of street signs, signals and markings. Engr joint com of Nat Utility Assns '28-31; operator Oliphant Washington Service for electric, gas and natural gas industries; exec sec Storage of Coals Com and Nat Standard Street Signs, Signals and Markings Com of Am Engring Cluncil. ASME—Am Inst EE—Washington Soc Engrs—Washington Acad Sci—Acad Polit Sci—Army Ordnance Assn—AAAS—Tau Rho Delta. 729 15th St., Washington.Ⓞ

18 OLIPHANT, J(ames) Orin. Cattle industry (History); Pacific Northwest (History); Missions (Home, US). b'94. AB '16—Denny F '23-24—AM '24 (U Wash); Austin scholar '29-30—PhD '30 (Harvard). Research on relationship between range cattle industries of Pacific Northwest and Great Plains and similarity of eastward cattle drives from Pacific Northwest to northward cattle drives from Texas; historical background of missions in Pacific Northwest dating from 1790's; member board of editors Washington Historical Quarterly '25-30, book review editor Pennsylvania History '46-50, editor Bucknell University Studies since '49. Co-author: (with C S Kingston) An Outline of the History of the Pacific Northwest, with Special Reference to Washington '26. Faculty E Wash Coll Edn '24-30; with Bucknell U since '33, prof hist since '42. AHA —Am Geog Soc—Am Soc Church Hist —Miss Valley Hist Assn—Hudson's Bay Record Soc—Ore Hist Soc—Phi Beta Kappa. Bucknell University, Lewisburg, Pa.

19 OLIVE, Lindsay Shepherd. Mycology. b'17. AB '38—AM '40—PhD '42 (U NC). Research on cytology, morphology, parasitism of rust fungi; Uredinales, Septobasidium, Aspergillus, and Glomerella, meiosis in fungi Tremellales (jelly fungi). Author articles in field. Mycol and plant disease diagnostician Emergency Plant Disease Prevention Project US Dept Agr Beltsville Md '44-45; asst prof bot div biol sci U Ga Athens Ga '45-46; asso prof bot La State U Baton Rouge La since '46; research scholarships Highland NC Biol Lab summers '39, '41, '43. Am Bot Soc—AAAS—Mycol Soc Am—Sigma Xi—Phi Beta Kappa. Department of Botany, Plant Pathology and Bacteriology, Louisiana State University, Baton Rouge, La.†

20 OLIVE, William John. Elizabethan and Early English drama; Shakespeare; Dramatic burlesque. b'07. AB '29—PhD '37 (U NC); grad work '30 (U Chicago). Faculty Eng dept La State U since '29. Department of English, Louisiana State University, Baton Rouge.†

21 OLIVER, Douglas Llewellyn. Oceanic anthropology; Dependent peoples. b'13. AB (Harvard); PhD (U Vienna). Anthropological research in Melanesia '37-40. Author books in field. Research asso Peabody Mus Harvard since '48; asso prof anthrop Harvard since '50; mem Pacific Sci Board Nat Research Council since '46; cons Dept State Office Far Eastern Affairs '48-51; area econ analyst Board Econ Warfare '42-43. Soc Applied Anthrop— Am Anthrop Assn. Peabody Museum, Cambridge, Mass.†

22 OLIVER, James Arthur. Systematics, distribution and relationships of neotropical amphibians and reptiles; Distribution of venomous snakes. b'14. Student '32-34 (U Tex); '34-41, AB— AM—PhD '41 (U Mich). Has made two expeditions to southern Mexico; two field trips to Bahamas, British West Indies. Author articles in field. Asst. curator Am Mus Natural Hist '42-48, research asso since '48; asst prof biol U Fla '48-51; curator reptiles NY Zool Soc since '51. Am Soc Ichthyologists Herpetologists (gov since '46, vp '47-48)—Herpetologists League (F)—Soc Vertebrate Paleontol—Soc Study Evolution—Fla Acad Sci—NY Zool Soc(F)—Sigma Xi. New York Zoological Park, NYC.†

23 OLIVER, James Henry. Greek and Roman epigraphy. b'05. BA '26—PhD '31 (Yale); '27-28 (Bonn U), '28-30 (Am Acad Rome). Excavator and epigraphist with American Archeological Mission for excavation of ancient Athenian Agora '32-36. Co-author: (with H G Evelyn White) Metropolitan Museum of Art Egyptian Expedition (vol XIV) '38. Author: The Sacred Gerusia '41; The Athenian Expounders '50, also articles in field. Instr Latin Yale '30-32; asst prof hist Columbia '36-42; prof Greek Johns Hopkins since '46. Archeol Inst Am—Am Philol Assn. Soldiers and Sailors Meml Fellowship for classical philol Yale '26-28; Jesse Benedict Carter Fellowship, Am Acad Rome '28-30; post-service fellowship, John Simon Guggenheim Found '46. John Hopkins University, Baltimore 18.Ⓞ

24 OLIVER, Smith Hempstone. History of automobiles. b'12. Student '29-31 (Worcester Poly Inst); '31-32 (Geo Washington U). Author (bulls on collections of Div Engring of US Nat Museum) Catalog of the Automobile and Motorcycle collection '50, Catalog of the Cycle collection '53. Editor: Sports Car Mag '47; Mercedes, Pioneer of an Industry '48. Asso curator sect land transportation US Nat Mus Smithsonian Inst Washington since '46. U.S. National Museum, Washington 25.†

10 OLMSTED, Charles Edward. Physiological ecology (Grasses); Plant geography, physiology and ecology; Range ecology. b'08. AB '29 (U Neb), MSc '31 (U Okla); PhD '36 (Yale U); '33-34 (U Chicago). Botanical editor Ecology '42-46; editor Botanical Gazette since '46. Author: Vegetation of Certain Sand Plains of Connecticut '37; Early Development of Bouteloua Curtipendula in Relation to Water Supply '41; Photoperiodic Responses in the Genus Bouteloua '43; Photoperiodic Responses in Twelve Geographic Strains of Sideoats Grama '44, and others. With U Chicago since '34, prof since '48. AAAS(F)—Bot Soc Am—Ecol Soc Am—Am Soc Plant Physiol—Ill State Acad Sci—Am Soc Naturalists—Phi Beta Kappa—Sigma Xi. Department of Botany, University of Chicago, Chicago 37.†◎

11 OLMSTED, John Whipple. History of scientific expeditions (1600-1815); Seventeenth century scientific institutions and astronomy. b'03. BA '25 (U Calif); BA '28 (U Oxford); PhD '44 (Cornell U). Author articles in field. Asso hist U Calif '28-31, asst prof '31-44, asso prof '44-52, prof '51-52, prof hist and chmn div humanities since '52. Rhodes scholar Oxford U '25-28. AHA—Hist Sci Soc (council '46-48). University of California, Riverside, Cal.†

12 OLNEY, Albert Jackson. Kentucky horticulture and pomology (Methods). b'88. BS '13—M Hort (hon) '20 (Mich State Coll); MS '25 (U Chicago). Research on pruning fruit trees, preparation from tobacco of spraying solution, response of peaches to cultivation, cover crops, sod culture. Author articles in field. Asst prof hort U Ky since '16, head dept since '30. Sigma Xi—Ky Acad Sc—AAAS(F)—Am Soc Hort Sci—Am Pomol Soc. University of Kentucky, Lexington 29, Ky.

13 OLNEY, Marguerite. Folk songs; Folk music. b'07. MusB '29 (U Rochester); '29 (Wash U); '30-31 (Columbia); '35-36 (Dalcroze Sch Music). Research and collecting New England folk songs and music; cut 2700 mechanical recordings. Dir ext Wilmington Music Sch since '31; curator Flanders ballad collection Middlebury Coll since '41. Middlebury College Library, Middlebury, Vt.

14 OLSEN, Aksel G(ilkrog). Pectin; Food technology. b'93. AB '22 (Neb Wesleyan U); MS '23—PhD '28 (U Minn). Research in gelatins, pectins, flavoring materials, emulsifiers, enzymes, hydrogen ion concentration temperature relationships, rancidity; loss of flavor, food values, therapeutic uses for pectin. Owns several patents, mainly on pectin and gelatin. Author articles in field. Research chem Battle Creek Research Lab '23-33; dir research, chief chem Walter Baker Chocolate Co Dorchester Mass '34-36; research chem Battle Creek Found, Gen Foods Corp Battle Creek Mich '36-39, div head colloidal div Hoboken NJ '39-41, dir food labs '41-43, mgr central laboratories '43-48, manager applied research '48-50, director project planning since '50, tech dir applied research since '51. American Chemical Society—AAAS—American Assn Cereal Chem—Inst Food Tech (nat councilor '47-49). 1125 Hudson St., Hoboken, N.J.

15 OLSEN, Charles W. John Brown. b'91. BS '15 (Valparaiso U); MD '19 (Loyola U Sch Med); post grad study (Paris, Vienna). Owner of John Brown homestead and farm, as well as the old John Brown Tannery, at New Richmond, Pennsylvania. Author articles in field. Ill Hist Soc—Utah Hist Soc—Pa Hist Soc—Abraham Lincoln Assn Ill. 6558 S. Halsted St., Chicago.

16 OLSEN, John T. Drainage engineering. b'98. Profl Civil Engr—BS Agrl Engring (Ia State Coll). Author articles in field. With US Dept Agr since '36, asst chief water conservation div Soil Conservation Service since '44. ASCE—Am Soc Agrl Engrs—Soil Conservation Soc Am. Water Conservation Division, Soil Conservation Service, U.S. Department of Agriculture, Washington.

17 OLSEN, Marlow William. Poultry embryology and physiology. b'06. BS '29—MS '30 (Ia State Coll); PhD '41 (U Md). Author articles in field. Poultry physiol Agrl Research Center Beltsville Md since '46. Veterinary Corps Chicago QM Depot US Army '42-45. Poultry Sci Assn—Sigma Xi. Beltsville, Md.

18 OLSEN, O(liver) Wilford. Parasitology of cattle and wildlife. b'01. BA '29 (Brigham Young U); MA '31—PhD '36 (U Minn); '32-33 (Harvard). Developed and perfected treatment for controling liver flukes in cattle. Author articles in field. Parasitologist US Bur Animal Ind '39-48; prof and head zool dept Colo A&M Coll; pathologist Colorado A&M Experiment Sta. American Society Parasitologists—Am Micros Soc—Sigma Xi. Colorado Agricultural & Mechanical College, Fort Collins, Colo.◎

19 OLSON, Birger Henry. Fermentation microbiology (Antibiotics, yeast, penicillin). b'17. BS '42 (Bethany Coll); MS '45—PhD '49 (U Wis). Author articles in field. Research microbiol Rohm and Haas Co '48-51. Am Chem Soc—Soc Am Bact—Sigma Xi. Division of Laboratories, Michigan Department of Health, DeWitt Rd., Lansing, Mich.†

20 OLSON, Clair Colby. Chaucer. b'01. AB '23 (Oberlin Coll); AM '26—PhD '38 (U Chicago). Author articles: The Minstrels at the Court of Edward III; Chaucer and the Music of the Fourteenth Century. Co-editor: Chaucer's World '48. Prof Eng Coll of the Pacific since '43, chmn dept since '50. Mod Lang Assn Am—Mediaeval Acad Am—Am Musical Soc. Office: College of the Pacific, Stockton 4, Cal.

21 OLSON, Franklyn C(arl) W(ester). Lake currents; Inshore oceanography; Thermal processing of canned foods. b'10. BS '33 (U Chicago); PhD '50 (O State U). Research on currents of western Lake Erie, currents in Wanaque Reservoir to determine minimum storage time of reservoir waters, coastal and bay currents in Gulf of Mexico. Co-author: (with C O Ball) Sterilization by Heat '51. Asst prof phys, head dept U Ill Chicago br '46-47; research asso Franz Theodore Stone Inst Hydrobiology '47-50; research asso oceanog Oceanog Inst Fla State U since '50. Am Soc Limnol and Oceanog—Am Micros Soc—Sigma Xi. Oceanographic Institute, Florida State University, Tallahassee.

22 OLSON, Raymond Verlin. Soil boron and iron. b'19. BS '41 (ND State Agrl Coll); MS '42—PhD '47 (U Wis); '37-39 (ND Sch Forestry). Author articles in field. Asso prof soils Kan State Coll '47-50, prof soils '50-52, head dept agron since '52. Agronomy Department, Kansas State College, Manhattan, Kan.

23 OLSON, Sigurd F. Wilderness preservation, conservation and ecology; Quetico-Superior wilderness. b'99. BS '20—post grad work '23 (U Wis); MS '31 (U Ill). Wilderness guide for expeditions into Superior National Forest of Minnesota, Quetico Provincial Park of Ontario and waters of Rainy Lake watershed and lower Hudson's Bay watershed since '20. Author articles in field. Head zool and bot dept Ely Jr Coll '23-35, dean '36-45; wilderness ecol Izaak Walter League of Am since '47; cons Pres Truman's Quetico-Superior Com; cons Wilderness Soc since '47; free lance writer since '26. Wilderness Soc—AFA—Am Ecol Union—Ecol Soc—Nat Parks Assn—Am Camping Assn—Outdoor Writers Assn—Izaak Walton League—Sigma Xi—Wildlife Management Institute—AAAS. Izaak Walton League of America, 31 N. State St., Chgo. H: Ely, Minn.

24 OLSON, Walter Sigfrid. Petroleum geology (Colombia, Venezuela). b'04. EM '25 (U Minn). Special studies geophysical methods for locating oil-bearing structures; results of lateral gradients of seismic velocities. Chief geol Colombian Petroleum Co '33-36; with Texas Co since '37, dir geol and geophys exploration in SA since '41. Sigma Xi—Tau Beta Pi—Am Assn Petroleum Geol—AIMME—Soc Exploration Geophysicists—Am Geophys Union—Instituto Colombiano de Petroleo—Instituto Sude Americano de Petroleo—Seismol Soc Am—Swiss Geol Soc—Am Petroleum Inst. 135 East 42d St., NYC 17.

25 O'MALLEY, Charles D. History of science (Sixteenth century). b'07. BA '28—MA '29—PhD '45 (Stanford). Author articles in field. Now prof hist Stanford University. Lecturer med hist U Calif Med Sch since '46; dir hist collections Lane Med Library, San Francisco since '48. History of Sci Soc—Am Assn Hist of Med. Dept. of History, Stanford University, Stanford, Calif.

26 OMAN, Paul Wilson. Taxonomy of Auchenorhynchous Homoptera (Nearctic fauna). b'08. AB '30—MA '35 (U Kans); PhD '41 (Geo Washington U). Author articles in field. Jr entomol to asst leader Div Insect Identification Bur Entomol and Plant Quarantine US Dept Agr since '30. Officer US Army San Corps '42-46; asst leader div insect identification, Bur Entomol and Plant Quarantine '46-50; officer US Army Med Service Corps '50-53. Wash Acad Science—Entomol Soc Am Wash Entomol Soc—Am Assn Econ Entomol—Sigma Xi—Phi Beta Kappa. 5215 11th Rd. South, Arlington 4, Va.

27 OMANSKY, Morris. Rubber chemistry and technology (Natural and synthetic rubber); Naval stores industry (Rosin, pine tars and oils). b'89. BS '11 (MIT). Inventor of processes and products in rubber, leather, textile and plastic industries. Chemist Boston Woven Hose & Rubber Co '11-17; chief chemist Plymouth Rubber Co '17-20, '22-24; cons chemist since '20; chief chemist Needham Tire Co '20-22; cons litigations and research; civilian cons US Army '17-20, '41-45; Naval stores Ind since '28. ACS—AICE. 238 Main St., Cambridge 42, Mass.

28 OMOHUNDRO, Allen Llewellyn. Pharmaceutical chemistry. b'03. BS '25 (U Pa); MS '26—PhD '28 (U Paris); PhD (hon) '40 (Conn Coll Pharmacy). Research and development of methods of manufacture and purification of insulin and penicillin, synthesis of sympathomimetic amines, extraction purification and biological investigation of vitamins, development of special processes for biochemical and general pharmaceutical manufacture; War Production Board committee on penicillin manufacture. Nine

United States patents and numerous foreign patents. Author articles in field. Asst to pres in charge labs and mfgr Frederick Stearns Co '28-34; vp and tech dir plant and labs McKesson and Robbins Inc since '34. AIC(F)—Am Pharm Assn—Conn Pharm Assn—AAAS(F)—Soc Chem Ind—NY Acad Scis. McKesson and Robbins, Inc., Bridgeport, Conn. H: Whitestone, Chestnut Hill, Wilton.

10 O'NEIL, Frederic Wallin. Pulp and paper manufacturing. b'11. BS—MS '35 (NY State Coll Forestry). Co-author articles: Lime Chlorine System in the Manufacture of Bleach Liquor; Accelerated Corrosion of Tin Cans in Various Containers; Properties of Flexible Impregnated Sheets; The Manufacture of Chemigroundwood Pulps from Hardwoods. Professor of pulp and paper mfg State University of New York College of Forestry since '37. Tech Assn Pulp and Paper Ind—Can Pulp and Paper Assn—Sigma Xi. State University of New York, College of Forestry, Syracuse 10, N.Y.†

11 O'NEILL, John (Joseph). Popularization of science and engineering; Constructive applications of atomic energy; Structure of solar atmosphere; Personality (Seasonal effects of birth); Moon (Surface markings); Meteors. Student pub schs and night sch (NY and Internat Corr Sch). Author: Enter Atomic Energy '40; Prodigal Genius, The Life of Nikola Tesla '44; Almighty Atom, The Real Story of Atomic Energy '45; You and the Universe '45; Engineering the New Age '48; also articles in field. Sci editor NY Herald Tribune since '33. Am Geog Soc—Am Geophysical Union—Amateur Astronomers Assn—AAAS—Am Genetic Assn—Am Inst City NY (chmn bd mng '33-37)—Am Soc Psychical Research (chmn research com and trustee '33-37)—Am Acad Polit and Social Sci—Am Rocket Soc—Nat Assn Sci Writers (charter, vp '39 pres '40)—Royal Astron Soc—Am Meteorol Soc—Am Arctic Soc—Nat Geographic Soc. Recipient Pulitzer Award in Journalism Columbia U '37; Best Science Story of Year U Kan '38; Westinghouse Distinguished Science Writing Medal from AAAS '46. 230 W. 41st St., NYC.

12 ONISHI, George Eric. Automobile (Testing instruments, carburetion, cooling systems). b'05. BS '27 (MIT). Development instruments for road and laboratory automotive testing; testing car carburetion and automatic choke operation; study and development car heating and ventilating system; member equipment survey group motor fuel div Coordinating Research Council. With Studebaker Corp since '27, test engr since '45. Soc Automotive Engrs. Profl engr Ind. Studebaker Corp., Engineering Division, South Bend 27, Ind.

13 OOSTING, Henry J(ohn). Piedmont forest and coastal dune ecology; Vegetation (Piedmont, North Carolina, rock outcrops); Virgin forest (Phytosociology); Aquatic flowering plants; Pulpwood forests of Maine. b'03. AB '25 (Hope Coll); MA '27 (Mich State Coll); PhD '31 (U Minn). On Boyd expedition to Greenland '37. Author: The Study of Plant Communities—An Introduction to Plant Ecology '48; also articles in field. Professor bot Duke U since '49. AAAS—Ecol Soc Am—Torrey Bot Club—NC Acad Sci—Sigma Xi. Department of Botany, Duke University, Durham, N.C.†

14 OPLER, Marvin K(aufmann). Cultural anthropology and sociology (Ute Indians, Japanese-Americans). b'14. Student '31-34 (U Buffalo); AB '35

(U Mich); PhD '38—Stefansson research fellow '38—U fellow '36-37—Social Sci Research Council fellow '46 (Columbia). Co-author: Acculturation in Seven American Indian Tribes '41; Impounded People '46; Twentieth Century Social Sciences '49; also articles in field. Chmn dept sociol and anthropol Occidental Coll '46-49; asso prof anthrop Stanford U '49-51; asso prof social relations dept Harvard '51-52; vis prof anthrop dept psychiatry Cornell U Med Coll since '52. Am Anthropol Assn—Am Ethnol Soc—Southwestern Anthropol Soc (exec bd). Department of Psychiatry, Cornell Univ Medical College, Payne Whitney Clinic, New York Hospital, NYC.†

15 OPLER, Morris Edward. American Indian (Southwestern regions); Cultural and applied anthropology; Japanese culture; Culture India. b'07. AB '29 (U Buffalo); BA '30—PhD '33 (U Chicago). Author: Myths and Tales of the Jicarilla Apache Indians '38, of the Lipan Apache Indians '40, of the Chiricahua Apache Indians '42; An Apache Life-Way '41; Character and Derivation of Jicarilla Holiness Rite '43; Childhood and Youth in Jicarilla Apache Society '46; Caste and Village Organization in Northern India '48. Prof anthrop Cornell U since '48. Am Anthrop Assn—Am Folklore Soc—Soc for Applied Anthrop—Phi Beta Kappa—Sigma Xi. Fellow Social Sci Research Council '32-33, '46-47; John Simon Guggenheim Memorial Foundation '42. Morrill Hall, Cornell University, Ithaca, N.Y.

16 OPPENHEIMER, Fritz Ernest. International and foreign law. b'98. Student '08-15 (Coll Royal Français Berlin) '19-20 (Berlin U) '20-21 (Freiburg U); LLD '22 (Breslau U); '24-25 (Paris U); '25 (London U). Legal adviser to Secretary of State at conferences Council of Foreign Ministers Moscow '47, London '47, Paris '49; US dep fgn minister on treaty for Austria '47; legal adviser to US ambassador at 6-Power Conference on Germany, London '48. Asso solicitors London Eng '25-35; counselor in chambers of atty gen for Eng and to Brit Treasury '36-40; mem Soc Inner Temple London '38; Eng barrister-at-law '46; practiced law as mem German bar, also Paris France, The Hague Holland; chief analyst Bd Econ Warfare Washington '45; spl asst US Mil Govt for Germany Berlin '46; spl asst for German-Austrian affairs, office of legal adviser Dept of State '46-48; pvt practice NYC since '48. Pvt to lt col US Army '43-45, legal staff officer SHAEF London, Versailles, Rheims, Frankfurt, in charge reform German law and court system '44-45; contbd to preparation of documents and plans in connection with Germany's mil. surrender at Rheims and Berlin '45; participated in draftsing mil govt and control council legislation for Germany. NY City Bar Assn—Am Soc Internat Law—Internat Law Assn London—Société de Legislation Comparée Paris. 20 Exchange Pl., NYC 5.☉

17 OPPENHEIMER, Jane Marion. Anatomy (Embryology); History of biology. b'11. BA '32 (Bryn Mawr Coll); PhD '35 (Yale), Sterling fellow biol '35-36. Demonstration of organizers in fish eggs; demonstration of regulation in developing brain of fishes; studies on fish embryology, organization of teleost blastoderm, development of structure and function in central nervous system of teleosts; studies in history of biology, history of embryology, studies of John and William Hunter in relation to their contemporaries. Instr biol Bryn Mawr Coll '38-42, asst prof '43-47, asso prof

'47-53, professor since '53. American Society Zool—Am Association Anat—AAAS(F)—Marine Biol Laboratory—Am Assn Hist Med—History Sci Soc—Soc for Study of Development and Growth—Sigma Xi. Yale U Scholarship '32-33; Susan Rhoda Cutler Fellow '34-35; Guggenheim fellow '42-43, '52-53, Rockefeller fellow '50-51. Bryn Mawr College, Bryn Mawr, Pa.

18 ORCHIN, Milton. Fuel technology (Synthetic liquid fuels). BA '36—MA '37—PhD '39 (O State U). Research in polynuclear syntheses, carcinogenic compounds, coal chemistry, distillation, composition of synthetic liquid fuels. Holder five patents. Author articles in field. Chem US Food Drug Adminstrn '39-42, US Dept Agr '42-43; chief organic chem sect research and development br synthetic liquid fuels office US Bur Mines '43-53; asso prof applied sci U Cin since '53. ACS—Phi Beta Kappa—Sigma Xi. Guggenheim fellow '47-48. University of Cincinnati, Cin. 21.

19 ORCUTT, Reginald. Foreign paper markets; Expeditions; Travel films; Iceland; Greenland. AB '15 (Harvard). b'94. Director International Business Conference Rye NY, 52 nations attending under sponsorship of National Association of Manufacturers, US Chamber of Commerce, International Chamber of Commerce, National Foreign Trade Council '44; field surveys of markets for paper Japan, China, Philippines, for paper and graphic machines Brazil, Uruguay, Argentina, Chile '15-17. Author: Merchant of Alphabets '45, '46. Co-author: Explorers Club Tales '34; also articles in field. Expeditions, color films, East Greenland and Iceland '31, Spitzbergen 32, Iceland '33, with Can East Arctic Patrol Hudson's Bay, Baffia, Devon, Ellesmere Islands '34, W Greenland '35, second circumnavigation Australasia, Indonesia, India, Pakistan, Iraq '46, Africa Union S Africa, Rhodesias, Gold Coast '47; with Mergenthaler Linotype Co Brooklyn NY '20-49, since '36 vp for overseas. Royal Geograph Soc London(F)—Societe de Geographie Paris(F)—Greenland Soc (Copenhagen)—India House (NY)—Explorers Club—Circumnavigators Club (NY, gov). Order of the Icelandic Falcon by King Christian X of Denmark and Iceland '33, Order of Merit from King Carol of Romania '33. Mergenthaler Linotype Co., Bklyn 5. H: 36 Catherine St., Newport, R.I.†

20 ORIANS, George Harrison. American literature (Nineteenth century fiction, romanticism); Hawthorne (Tale sources). b'00. AB '22 (North Central Coll); AM '23—PhD '26 (U Ill); '37 (Library of Congress); '36 (Yale). Author: Short History of American Literature '40; The Indian in the Metrical Romance '29; Sources of Hawthorne's Tales '34-45. Co-author: (with Warfel) American Local Color Stories '41; (with Richardson, Brown) The American Heritage '49. Editor: The Souvenir of the Lakes '39. Asst prof Eng U Idaho '28-29; lecturer Am Lit U Toledo '30-34, prof Eng since '34, dir summer session since '34, chmn Eng dept since '38; lecturer Nat Audubon Soc since '48. University of Toledo, Toledo 6, O.

21 ORLANSKY, Jesse. Aircraft lighting; Industrial psychology. b'14. BSS '35 (CCNY); MA '37—PhD '40 (Columbia). Author articles: Psychological Aspects of Stick and Rudder Controls in Aircraft '49; The Effect of Similarity in Form on Apparent Visual Movement '40. Co-author articles: (with M Hertzman) Personality Organization and Anoxia Tolerance '44; (with C P Seitz) A Study in Cockpit

Illumination '40. Vision and aircraft lighting research US Navy '43-46; staff mem, indsl psychology, Psychol Corp, NYC '46-48; vp indsl psychol Dunlap and Asso Inc since '48. Am Psychol Assn(F)—Eastern Psychol Assn—NY State Assn Applied Psychol—Armed Forces—Nat Research Council (asso member, vision committee)—Sigma Xi. 429 Atlantic St., Stamford, Conn.†

10 ORMOND, Willard Clyde. Photography (Wildlife); Wildlife (Conservation). b'06. Student '24-26 (Brigham Young U); '30 (Chicago Art Inst). Research on US and Canadian wildlife such as grizzly and black bears, mountain goats, deer, elk, antelope, moose, coyotes and sheep, and sport fish. Patent pending on improved film-developing tank. Author: Hunting in the Northwest '48. Contributor: Anthology of Fishing Adventures '45; The Hunter's Encyclopedia '49. Free-lance author since '38; columnist Ida Falls Post-Register since '46. Outdoor Photog League—W States Fed Sportsmen(dir)—Ida Wildlife Fedn(chmn big-game). RFD 2, Rigby, Ida.

11 ORMSBEE, Thomas Hamilton. Early American and American Victorian furniture. b'90. AB '15 (Middlebury Coll Vt). Author: Early American Furniture Makers '30; The Story of American Furniture '34; Collecting Antiques in America '40; Prime Antiques and Their Current Prices '47; A Field Guide to American Furniture '51; A Field Guide of Victorian Furniture '52; others. Founded Am Collector '33, editor to '46; author weekly syndicated newspaper feature Know Your Heirlooms since '46; lectr on antiques. Chi Psi. H: Red Shingles, New Canaan, Conn.

12 O'ROKE, Earl C(leveland). Forest (Zoology); Wildlife (Conservation); Michigan grouse; Waterfowl (Conservation); Deer (Lungworms). b'87. AB '12—MA '16 (U Kan); PhD in protozool '29 (U Cal). Investigations, research on parasitic protozoa causing disease in upland game birds and waterfowl, lungworms of deer; collaborator division wildlife research, Fish and Wildlife Service US Department of Interior since '32; grouse investigations State Dept Conservation Mich. With U Mich since '29, asso prof forest zool since '37. Soc Am Foresters—U Mich Sci Research Club (past pres)—Wildlife Soc—Am Soc Zool—Am Soc Parasitol(councilor). School of Forestry and Conservation, University of Michigan, Ann Arbor.

13 O'ROURKE, Francis Leonard. Plant propagation (Blueberries, holly); Hort ecology; Nursery management. b'98. BS '19 (Delaware U); MS '51 (Md U), '46-52 (Mich State Coll). Research on physiological aspects of blueberry propagation; effects of humidification and other environmental influences on propagation by cuttings. Public Service Patent with others for propagation under fluorescent lights '45. Author articles in field. Faculty mem dept hort Mich State Coll since '45, dir Hidden Lake Gardens '50-52; research on cocao, point four program US Dept Agriculture. Am Soc Horticultural Science—Northern Nut Growers Assn—Am Holly Society—Nat Shade Tree Conf—Landscape Assn Mich—Mich Hort Soc. USDA Tropical Experiment Station, care US Consulate General, Guayaguil, Ecuador.†

14 ORR, Kenneth Gordon. Eastern United States and North American archeology. b'16. BA '37 (Columbia); MA '42—PhD '44 (U Chicago). Assistant archeologist and cartographer, Smithsonian Institution Eastern Plains Expedition '37. Author articles: Field

Report on the Excavations of Indian Villages in the Vicinity of the Spiro Mounds, Leflore County, Oklahoma '39; The Eufaula Mound: Contributions to the Spiro Focus '41; The Archeological Situation at Spiro, Oklahoma: A Preliminary Report '46. Archeol in charge Spiro Mounds Excavation, U Okla '38-39, Cherokee Co Archeol Project '39; research archeol lab anthrop '39-40, archeol in charge The Eufaula Mound site, Okla, Okmulgee Creek Hist Soc U Okla '40; archeol supr, The Kincaid Site Ill, U Chicago '41, asst in charge Mus Anthrop '42-43; asst prof dept anthrop U Okla, acting chmn dept '46; asst prof curator mus dept anthrop U Chicago since '46. Soc for Am Archeol—Am Anthrop Assn—Ill Archeol Soc—Caddoan Archeol Area Com—Linguistic Soc Am—Sigma Xi. Dept. of Anthropology, University of Chicago, Chicago.

15 ORR, Phil C(ummings). Paleontology; Anthropology. b'03. Student '23 (U Mont), '24-25 (U Wash), '25-27 (U Neb). Exploration of caverns Hawaii, United States, Mexico; exploration Channel Islands, California and Mexico. Author articles in field. Curator paleontol and anthropol Santa Barbara Mus Natural Hist since '38. —Archeol Survey Assn S Cal—SW Anthropol Assn—Am Anthropol Assn—Nat Speleol Soc—Soc Vert Paleont. Museum of Natural History, Santa Barbara, Calif.†

16 ORR, Robert Thomas. Systematics and natural history of North American birds and mammals; Life histories of North American bats; Mammals and birds of Lake Tahoe California; Bird and mammal distribution in Western North America. b'08. BS '29 (U San Francisco); MA '31—PhD '37 (U Calif). Author articles in field. Curator birds and mammals Calif Acad Scis since '45; asso prof biol U San Francisco since '49. Am Soc Mammalogists (recording sec '38-42, '47-52)—Am Ornithol Union—Biol Soc Washington—Calif Acad Sci (F, asso editor Pacific Discovery)—Cooper Ornithol Club—Ecol Union—Nat Geo Soc—Sigma Xi. California Academy of Sciences, Golden Gate Park, San Francisco 18.†

17 ORT, John M(ouk). Drugs; Cosmetics. b'96. BChemE '18—MS '19—PhD '24 (O State U). Animal and human evaluation of drugs; research on membrane potentials and oxidation-reduction potentials; pharmaceutical compounding and manufacturing. Holds dive patents on manufacture of cyclopropane. Co-author articles: (with Clifton) Active Glucose '30; (with Roepke) Rates of Formation of Active Reductants of Several Sugars '31; (with Power, Markowitz) Studies in Cardiac Permeability '31, and others. Asst prof biophysics Mayo Found U Minn '24-32; operating head development dept E R Squibb & Sons '33-44; dir labs Am Pharm Co '44-46; dir research Smith Pharm Co '46-50; research dept Colgate-Palmolive Peet Co since '50. ACS—Am Soc Biochem—Am Pharm Soc—Am Inst Chem—AAAS—NY Acad Sci—Sigma Xi, Colgate-Palmolive Peet Co., Jersey City.

18 ORTEGA, Joaquin. Spanish language and literature (Editing). b'92. Spanish govt grad fellowship in econ in US '15-17; MA '17—'17-22 (U Wis); research '26-28, '29-30 (Archivo Historico and Biblioteca Nacional, Madrid Spain); LittD '41 (U NM). Prehistoric studies La Pileta Cave, La Tomo, Spain. Author articles in field. Editor: The New Mexico Quarterly Review since '48. Prof, chmn dept Spanish, Portuguese '30-41 U Wis; dir sch inter-Am affairs U NM '41-48, prof Spanish since '41. Wis Soc of Archeol Inst Am

(hon mem)—Phi Kappa Phi. 611 N. Girard Av., Albuquerque, N.M.

19 ORTHMANN, August Caesar. Leather chemistry; Tanning industry. b'88. Student pub schs, spl tutoring math and chem. International authority on tanning processes; developed vegetable tanning process that reduced time from three months to seven hours for type of leather used for baggage case and strap; research in new methods for mineral tanngaes. Holds several patents. Author: Tanning Processes '45. Co-author: Laboratory Manual '18; also articles in field. Pres, dir, prin owner Orthmann Labs Inc since '29. Am Leather Chem Assn (pres '37-38)—Am Chem Soc—Am Oil Chemists' Soc—Forest Products Research Soc—Am Assn Textile Chem and Colorists—Tech Assn of Pulp and Paper Industry. 922 North 4th St., Milwaukee 3.

20 ORVILLE, Howard Thomas. Meteorology; Aeronautics. b'01. BS '25 (US Naval Acad); SM '30 (MIT); '26 (Naval Torpedo Sch Newport RI). Conducted research in micrometeorology and atmospherics '31-33, exhaustive research of upper atmosphere '34, organized Navy's global wartime aerological organization, originated Navy plan for aircraft tracking of hurricanes and typhoons, microseismic methods for locating storms, organized weather network in China, Navy representative to International Allied Conferences Washington '44, Manila '45, London '46, Stockholm and London '48, Navy subcommittee Air Coordinating conference '45-49, US technical adviser to Conference of directors of International Meteorological Organization Washington. Officer US Navy since '25, various executive and administrative positions specifically the Naval Aeronautical Organization, head Naval Aerology Flight Div Bur Aeronautics Washington and under Dep Chief of Naval Air Operations since '43, rank of capt. Am Meteorol Soc (councilor '44-46, pres '48-49)—Inst Aeronautical Sci—Am Geophys Union—AAAS. Awarded Legion of Merit. Friez Instrument Division, Towson 4, Md. H: Long Green, Md.†◎

21 OSBORG, Hans. Lithium technology; High energy fuels (Chemistry, manufacture, derivatives); Titanium metallurgy; Electrolysis (Fused); Gas-metal reactions; Manufacturing techniques (Chemical and metallic). Candidate in chemistry '24—Diplomate in physical chemistry '25—D Eng '27 (Tech U Braunschweig Germany). Pioneering research on lithium metallurgy, chemistry, manufacturing methods, economics, markets and applications: (inorganic and organic syntheses, condensation, alkylation, hydrogenation, through use of lithium-alkyls, -aryls, -hydrides, -amide; "solid" hydrogen for immediate conversion into gaseous hydrogen at point of use through special utilization of lithium-hydride, lithium-borohydride, calcium-hydride; nitrogen fixation in the recovery and purification of helium; low melting fluxes and slags in metal refining and welding through application of lithium compounds and master alloys); manufacturing methods for hydrides of boron, diborane and derivatives, hydride of nitrogen, applications and derivatives, lithium-hydride, calcium-hydride; collaborator in development and design continuous commercial production method titanium metal and its alloys; investigation phys chemistry of degasification oxidation molten metal and application to super-refined ductivity bronze for electric

development of methods for electroplating of zinc, copper, nickel and other metals especially on magnesium alloys; detailed study of production non-ferrous metals especially light metals by metallurgical and electrochemical methods, melting, refining, casting and working ferrous and nonferrous metals and alloys. Holds 50 patents on inorganic chem compounds, processes for mfr, application to field of chem and metall, on melting, refining and casting metals and alloys. Author: monograph on Lithium '35. Author articles: Mining and Metallurgy '37; Metal Progress '38, and others. Dir research and prodn metal dept Maywood Chem Works NJ '30-34; cons phys chem and metall Cooperative In Research and Development since '34; vp, gen mgr Lithaloys Corp NYC '40-46; vp, gen mgr Metalec Corp Bladensburg Md since '50. ACS—AIMME—Am Soc Metals P.O. Box 152, 80 Longview Rd., Port Washington, N.Y.

10 OSBORN, Albert D(unbar). Questioned documents examination (Handwriting, typewriting, inks, paper, ultraviolet light uses). b'96. Certificate Dartmouth Coll). Used ultra violet light in court for the first time '32; testified in many cases including the State of New Jersey versus Hauptmann for the Prosecution. Co-author: Questioned Document Problems '44, second edit '46. Asso with Albert S Osborn '18-46. Am Soc Questioned Document Examiners (bd dirs). 233 Broadway, NYC 7.

11 OSBORN, Byrle Jacob. Human ecology and conservation; Labor and industrial ecology. b'88. STB '17 (Episcopal Theol Sch, Cambridge, Mass); '07-08 (U Minn); '09 (Ind U); '14-15 (Seabury Div Sch); '15-17 (Harvard. Research on various forms socialism, social and political trends; practical ecology experiment in development of planned community in abandoned northeast rural neighborhood, studying process of human conservation by use of creative reasoning by design. Author: Christian Education '20; Cotton Mather versus Gregory of Nazianzen '20; A Forgotten 17th Century Man '34; The Stuttering Vox Populi '36; Character as a Banking Asset '36; Measure of Man '45; The Science of Creative Reasoning '46; The Science of Human Ecology '47; The Science of Science '47. Various bus positions Wis, Mont, Minn '08-14; chaplain Episcopal students Harvard '19-21; rector St James Ch Bozeman Mont '21-23; prop Byrle J Osborn Co indsl engrs Minneapolis Boston '23-33; asst to chmn adminstr labor adjuster Mass NRA '33-35; dir Mass WPA Dist 2 '35-37; research ecol expt '37-47. AA AS—Ecol Soc Am. 22 Lyman St., Waltham 54, Mass.

12 OSBORN, Chase Salmon. Michigan; Lake Superior; United States-Canada boundary; Areas of the Great Lakes states; Chippewa Indians; Timber; Outdoor life; Economic and cosmic geology. b'60. BS '80 (Purdue U); MD '09 (Detroit Coll Medicine); LLD '11 (U Mich), '11 (Olivet Coll), '12 (Alma Coll Mich), '22 (Northwestern U), '35 (Atlanta Law Sch); ScD in Natural Sci '44 (Wayne U). Discoverer of source of firefly's light, Moose Mountain iron range (Canada) and Ndanga iron range (S E Africa); persuaded US Government to add 40,000 square miles to official area of Michigan, 21,000 to other Great Lakes States; postmaster Sault Sainte Marie Michigan '89-93; state game and fish warden Michigan '95-99; commissioner of railroads for Michigan '99-03; regent University of Michigan '08-11; governor of Michigan '11-

12; member Michigan Unemployment Commission '32; member advisory committee Detroit and Michigan Exposition '35, Michigan Works Project Administration '41; vice chairman Michigan State Chamber of Commerce. Author: Short History of Michigan '26; The Earth Upsets '27; Northwoods Sketches '48; The Iron Hunter '19. Co-author: (with S B Osborn) The Conquest of a Continent '39; Schoolcraft-Longfellow-Hiawatha '42; Errors in Official US Area Figures '45. AAAS(F)—Lake Superior Mining Inst—Am Ornithol Union—Am Inst Mining and Metall Engrs—Seismol Soc Am—Am Geog Soc—Am Mus Natural Hist—Am Forestry Assn—Archeol Inst Am—Outdoor Writers Assn—Great Lakes Hist Soc (trustee)—State Hist Soc of Mich—Northern Mich Sportsmen's Assn—Am Pioneer Trails Assn (charter). Sault Sainte Marie, Mich. Deceased.

13 OSBORN, George Coleman. Southern and recent United States history. b'04. BA '27 (Miss Coll); MA '32—PhD '38 (Ind U); summer '43 (Harvard). Author: John Sharp Williams—Planter Statesman of the Deep South '43. Editor: Papers of General John Campbell '49; also articles in field. Head dept social sci Berry Coll Mt Berry Ga '35-41; majority research expert finance com US Senate '37-38; prof, head hist dept Bob Jones Coll Cleveland Tenn '41-43; acting asso prof hist U Miss '43-44; prof hist Memphis State Coll '44-47; asso prof social sci U Fla since '47. AHA—Miss Valley Hist Assn—So Hist Assn—Miss Hist Soc—Am Acad Polit Social Sci—So Polit Sci Assn. Peabody Hall, University of Florida, Gainesville.

14 OSBORN, James Marshall. John Dryden; Shakespeare's editors; Edmond Malone. b'06. BA '28 (Wesleyan U); MA '34 (Columbia); BLitt '37 (Oxford U). Author: John Dryden: Biographical Facts and Problems '40. Editor: Work in Progress in the Modern Humanities '38-42; Seventeenth century Newsletter '42-46; also articles in field. Research asso eng Yale since '38. Modern Lang Assn—Modern Humanities Res Assn—Eng Inst—Index Soc (edit bd)—Bibliog Soc (Lond)—Oxford Bibliog Soc—Bibliog Soc Am. Yale University, New Haven.

15 OSBORN, Lawton Earl. Photography. b'01. Student (Dickinson State Tchrs Coll). Photographer since '22. Received second and third place awards Little International Conv '48, Minn '48, first and third awards at Minnesota Photographers Association Conv '49; 17 merit awards for photographs selected for hanging by jury Photographers Assn Am; 37 merit awards for services rendered photographic profession. Cameracraftsmen Am—Photographers Assn Am (mem bd dir—Photographic Craftsmen Award '50—Master of Photography Award '53)—ND Photographers Assn. Osborn's Studio, 17 Second Av., West Dickinson, N.D.

16 OSBORN, Robert Henry. Photometry; Colorimetry; Instrumentation; Pyrometry. b'07. BS '29 (SD Sch Mines and Tech); MS '36—PhD '38 (U Pittsburgh). Research and determination of thermal conductivities of tungsten and molybdenum by optical pyrometer method, instrumental methods of color grading, effect of light scattering on color, methods determining particle size by light scattering measurements, use solutions of inorganic salts as color standards, spectrophotometry of naval stores products and cellulose plastics, development analytical and process instrumentation in chemical industry, especially optical instruments. Contributor: Cellulose and Cel-

lulose Products '43. Research phys and supervisor phys Div Hercules Expt Sta Hercules Powder Co since '37. Sigma Xi—Optical Soc Am—Intersoc Color Council—Instrument Soc Am—Sigma Tau. Hercules Experiment Station, Hercules Powder Co., Wilmington, Del.

17 OSBORN, Robert Randolph. Aeronautical engineering (Civilian and fighting plane design, helicopters, jet engines). b'00. BS '25 (U Pa). Designed Curtiss "Tanager" winner $100,000 first prize Guggenheim Safe-Aircraft competition '29; made basic designs fighter, scouting, observation and dive-bombing airplanes for US Navy, single and twin-engined attack airplanes for US Army; in charge organizations designing accepted standard fighter, attack, scouting, observation and liaison airplanes for US Army and Navy, US Navy twin-engine, twinrotor helicopter, US Air Force ram-jet powered helicopter, pulse and ramjets. Author articles in field. Cons engr Helicopter and Propulsion div, McDonnell Aircraft Corp, St Louis since '43. Inst Aeronautical Sci(F)—Royal Aeronautical Soc (asso F)—Sigma Tau—Eta Kappa Nu. Awarded A Atwater Kent and Merrick memorial prizes. McDonnell Aircraft Corp., Lambert-St. Louis Airport, StL 21.⊙

18 OSBORN, Stellanova. Chippewa Indian; Henry Rowe Schoolcraft; Hiawatha; United States-Canada International Boundary; Areas of Great Lakes states. b'94. AB summa cum laude '22—AM '30 (U Mich). Author: Eighty and On '41; A Tale of Possum Poke in Possum Lane '46; Balsam Boughs (verse) '48; Jasmine Springs (book of verse) '53. Co-author (with Chase S Osborn) The Conquest of a Continent '39, Schoolcraft-Longfellow-Hiawatha '42, Hiawatha With Its Original Indian Legends '44; Errors in Official U.S. Area Figures '45; Northwoods Sketches '49. Engaged as writer, editor, and speaker. Chippewa Co Hist Soc—Detroit Hist Soc—Tippecanoe Co Hist Soc—Head-of-the-Lake Hist Soc—Great Lakes Hist Soc—Northwestern O Hist Soc—Ga Hist Soc—Mich Hist Soc—Ont Hist Soc—Mich Acad Sci Arts Letters—Mich Authors Assn—Mich League—Ga Authors Assn—Nat Arts Club—Am Geog Soc—Phi Beta Kappa. Sault Sainte Marie, Mich.

19 OSBORNE, Douglas. Inland Empire archeology; Western Arctic archeology; Micronesia archeology; Primitive technologies (Basketry, stone working, skin working); Michoacan archeology. b'12. AB '38 (U NM); MA '42—PhD '51 (U Cal). Research on Inland Empire of Washington and Oregon; archeology of Marianas Islands, primitive technology of non-ceramic types, such as basketry, stone-working, skin-working; chairman Northwest Anthropological Conference '52, member National Research Council's Committee for Pacific Archeology '53. Expdn mem Archeol Surveys '38-39; archeol TVA-U Tenn '40-41; acting field dir Smithsonian Instn River Basin surveys Pacific Coast Area '48-49; faculty dept anthrop U Wash, curator anthrop Wash State Mus since '49. Am Anthrop Assn (F, editor New Bulletin)—Soc Am Archeol—AAAS—Sigma Xi. Department of Anthropology, Washington State Museum, University of Washington, Seattle 5.

20 OSCARSON, Roger Oswald. Mineral economics. b'99. Student '15-17 (Carleton Coll); AB '19 (U Minn); MBA '21 (Harvard). Research, exploration, and development of metal mining properties; consultant on mine appraisal and mineral resource development studies to Washington State

Planning Council, National Resources Planning Board, Defense Plant Corporation, and Bonneville Power Administration; editor Modern Prospector '48-50. Owner and mgr Arlington Mine Lease '33-42; prodn spl Spokane Dist Office WPB '43-45; asst dist mgr Civilian Prodn Adminstrn '46-47; sec NW Mining Assn '47-50; mgr Spokane Dist Office Nat Prodn Authority since '50. AIMME—Am Mining Congress(bd gov W div). National Production Authority, 107 S. Howard St., Spokane 8, Wash.

10 OSER, Bernard L(evussove). Biochemistry of vitamins and foods; Labeling and advertising of foods and drugs. b'99. BS '20—MS '25 (U Pa); PhD '27 (Fordham U). Research on physiological availability of vitamins, biological value of proteins; assay of vitamins by biological, chemical and physical methods; member committees on revision standard procedures for US Pharmacopoeia and similar agencies; expert chemical testimony in federal, state and municipal court cases, before Federal Trade Commission, Food and Drug Administration. Co-author: (with Hawk and Summerson) Practical Physiological Chemistry (12th edit) (Blakiston) '47. With Food Research Labs since '26, dir since '34. AAAS(F)—Am Inst Chem(F)—NY Acad Sci(F)—Assn Cons Chem and Chem Engrs—ACS—Inst Food Tech—Am Council Comml Labs—Am Assn Clin Chem—Am Inst Nutrition—Soc Am Bact. 48-14 33rd St., Long Island City 1, N.Y.

11 OSGOOD, Robert Lewis. Square dances and round dances (American). b'18. BBA '39 (Santa Monica Jr Coll Cal); Grad '41 (Woodbury Coll Los Angeles). Caller and instructor American and American-Western square and round dances; producer dance sequences and shows for recreation, television, and motion pictures. Editor: Sets in Order (nat sq dancing pub). Now owner splty store for square and round dance records, books, and supplies. 462 N. Robertson Blvd., LA 48.

12 OSMAR, John Joseph. Ramie (Processing); Paper (Sizing). b'25. BS in chem '46 (St Vincent Coll Latrobe Pa); '46-50 (grad sch U Pittsburgh). Research on history, agriculture, decortication, processing and complete chemical treatment ramie fiber from plant to finished yarns and materials; research paper on ultraviolet colorimeter, paper sizings, paper size additives Mellon Institute Industrial Research Pittsburgh. Research chem RFC, Office Rubber Reserve, and Strathmore Paper Co Pittsburgh '47-49; tech dir Ramie Products Corp Pittsburgh '50-51; pres Osmar Chem Processes Inc Lantana Fla since '51. ACS—Am Assn Textile Chem and Colorists—Tech Assn Pulp and Paper Industry—Nat Farm Chemurgic Council—Phi Lambda Upsilon. Osmar Chemical Processes, Inc., Lantana, Fla.

13 OSTERBERG, Arnold Erwin. Clinical toxicology; Clinical investigation of drugs. b'94. BS in chem engring '16 (U Wash); MS '21—PhD '25 (U Minn). Research on chemistry of analgesics and general anesthetics. Author 200 articles in field. With Mayo Clin '17-46, clin biochem '30-46; with U Minn '24-26, prof biochem '44-46; asso clin investigator Abbott Lab since '46. ACS—Soc Biol Chem—AAAS—Soc Exptl Biol and Med—Am Bd Clin Chem—Phi Lambda Upsilon—Sigma Xi. Received Certificates of Merit from AMA '41 and Am Acad Dermatology and Syphilology '48. Abbott Laboratories, N. Chicago, Ill.

14 OSTERBURG, James W(illiam). Criminology (Scientific crime detection). b'17. BA '38—'38-40 (Brooklyn Coll). Examines physical evidence and clue materials found at the scene of the crime in over three hundred cases a year. Co-author: (with Charles E O'Hara) An Introduction to Criminalistics '49; also articles in field. Staff police lab NYC Police Dept since '42; cons police depts. Police Laboratory, 72 Poplar St., Bklyn.

15 OSTERWEIS, Rollin Gustav. Southern history (Romanticism 1815-1861); New Haven Connecticut (History). b'07. BA '30—MA '43—PhD '46 (Yale U); '29, '31 (Oxford U); 31-32 (Georgetown Fgn Service Sch); '30-31 (Geneva Sch Internat Studies, Yale Law Sch). Instr Am hist Yale U '43-46, research asst hist '46-48, asst dir debating and pub speaking '46-48, dir, asst prof since '48. Author: Romanticism and Nationalism in the Old South '49; Sesquicentennial History of the Connecticut Academy of Arts and Sciences '49; Three Centuries of New Haven, 1638-1938 '53. AHA—Conn Acad Arts Sci. Department of History, Yale University, New Haven.

16 OSTROM, Carl E(ric). Gum naval stores (Production); Silviculture. b'12. BS '33 (Pennsylvania State Coll); MF '41—PhD '44 (Yale University). Author articles in field. With United States Forest Service since '34, now research forester Asheville NC. Soc Am Foresters—AAAS—Sigma Xi. Southeastern Forest Experiment Station, Box 2570, Asheville, N.C.

17 OSTROW, Albert A. Parlor and card games. b'09. Stu '29-31 (U Tex). Author: The Complete Card Player '45; Modern Basics of Contract Bridge '48; Take a Card '47; also articles in field. Games authority Esquire, Coronet '43-44; cons Pastimes, Inc NYC '44; games lecturer Am Theatre Wing '44-45; cons expert Assn Am Playing Card Mfrs since '45; instr, lecturer contract bridge Brooklyn Coll Div Adult Edn since '47; pub dir Am Contract Bridge League '48; cons expert Am Coll Dictionary '48. 995 President St., Brooklyn 25.

18 O'SULLIVAN, Jeremiah F. Monasticism. b'03. AB '27—AM '28 (Villanova Coll); PhD '33 (U Pa). Research in monasticism in Europe; gathering large collection sources for library. Author: Cistercian Settlements in Wales and Monmouthshire 1140-1540 '47. Staff Villanova Coll '27-36 asso prof Fordham U '36-46, prof since '36. Mediaeval Acad Am (exec council since '49)—AHA—Cath Hist Assn. Department of History, Fordham University Graduate School, NYC. 58.

19 OSWALD, John Wieland. Plant pathology; Potato disease (Virus); Cereal diseases (Root rots). b'17. AB '38 (DePauw U); PhD '42 (U Calif). Author articles: Fungi Causing Root Rots of Cereals in California '47; A Virus Causing Internal Necrosis in White Rose Potato '48, and others. Asst prof plant path U Calif Davis Calif since '46. Sigma Xi—Phi Beta Kappa. University of California, Davis, Calif.

20 OSWALT, Wendell Hillman. Eskimo archeology (Alaska); Tree-ring dating. b'27. Student '46-52 (U Alaska). Research on dendrochronology and archeology in relation to Alaskan Arctic, establishment tree-ring sequences for Lower Yukon and Copper River regions. Mus asst U Alaska Mus since 147. Soc Am Archeol. Received grants-in-aid from Arctic Inst NA '50, U Alaska '51. H: Box 83, College, Alaska.

21 OTHMER, Donald Frederick. Chemical egineering, Industrial engineering; Chemistry (Indsl); Sugar refining; Wood waste (Utilization); Wood distillation; Wood hydrolysis; Wallboard manufacture; Solvent manufacture; Plastics manufacture; Petrochemical manufacturing; Refrigeration of railroad cars; Fermentation; Pulp and paper manufacturing; Cellulose; Lignin; Tannin; Economics of chemical industry; Chemical Plant design; Industrial equipment for distillation, evaporation, and extraction; Acetic acid manufacture; Alcohol manufacture; Pharmaceutical manufacturing; Rayon manufacture. b'04. Student '21-23 (Armour Inst); BS '24 (U Neb); MS '25—PhD '27 (U Mich). Co-invent- or wallboard made from wood and other cellulosic wastes, research on refrigeration and heat transfer, penicillin, synthetic rubber, plastics, rayon, sugar; consultant Chemical Corps and Ordnance Corps US Army, US Navy, Department of State, and War Production Board, also foreign governments. Granted 75 US patents and foreign patents on methods, processes, and engineering equipment in manufacturing of rayon, plastics, wood distillation, refrigeration, etc. Author 150 articles in field. Co-editor: (with Kirk) Encyclopedia of Chemical Technology (14 vols) '47-53. Development engineer Eastman Kodak Co and Tenn Eastman Corp '27-31; with Poly Inst Bklyn since '32, prof since '33, head dept chem engring since '37; cons chem engr; spl lecturer in US and many other countries. Licensed profl engr NY, NJ, Pa, Ohio. AAAS(F)—Am Inst Chem(dir '50)—Am Inst Chem Engrs (chmn NY sect '44)—ACS(mem council '45)—Soc Chem Industry(exec com '47-50)—ASME (chmn process industries div '49;—Am Soc Engring Edn —Sigma Xi—Tau Beta Pi—Phi Lambda Upsilon—Iota Alpha—Alpha Chi Sigma, 99 Livingston St., Bklyn 2.©

22 OTIS, Jay Lester. Industrial psychology (Job evaluation, wage administration, vocational guidance, employee selection, labor relations). b'07. AB '29—AM '31—PhD '36 (U Pa). Author: Handbook of Job Evaluation for Factory Jobs '46; Handbook of Job Evaluation for Clerical Jobs '48. Co-author: Occupational Counseling Techniques '40; Job Evaluation '48; also articles in field. Asst prof, later prof psychol Cleveland Coll Western Reserve U since '38, dir research and service center for bus and ind Western Reserve since '50. American Psychol Assn(F)—Soc Advancement Management—Nat Vocational Guidance Assn —Am Management Assn—O Psychol Assn. Western Reserve University, 314 Superior Av., Cleve. 14.

23 OTT, Ellis R(aymond). Statistical quality control. b'06. AB '28 (SW Coll Kan); MA '29 (U Kan); PhD '33 (U Ill). Research on sampling procedure for design tests of electron tubes '46; indirect calibration of electronic test-set '47, difference equations in average value problems '44. Instr, asst prof, asso prof math U Buffalo '33-44, prof math, asst dean '46; exec engr charge statis quality control Nat Union Radio Corp Newark '44-46; asso prof math and chmn dept U Coll Rutgers U since '46, organizer and leader conference series in quality control since '47, profl cons quality control since '46. Am Soc Quality Control(F). 77 Hamilton St., New Brunswick, N.J.

24 OTT, Emil. Cellulose and cellulose derivatives; Resins and terpenes. b'02. Maturitaet '21 (Oberrealschule, Zurick); Diploma Physioochem '25— DSc Nat '27 (Swiss Inst Tech). Research on cellulose and cellulose derivatives, synthetic resins, terpene and rosin chemistry, papermaking, chlorinated rubber and paraffin, plasticizers, explosives, X-ray studies organic and inorganic compounds; member Food and Agriculture sub-committee on chemistry of wood United Nations; member advisory board Industrial and Engineering Chemistry since '48. Holds 26 patents in field. Editor: Cellulose and Cellulose Derivatives '43; also articles in field. Chem Hercules Powder Co Wilmington Del since '33, research dir since '39. Internat Union Chem (mem com macromolecules)—Nat Research Council (com macromolecules) —AAAS (F, v-chmn research conf organic high polymers '44, chmn '45, v-chmn advs bd Gordon research confs) —Am Chem Soc—Am Inst Chem(F)— Am Phys Soc(F)—Am Inst Chem Engrs—Soc Chem Industry (mem exec com Am sect since '47)—Sigma Xi. Hercules Powder Company, Wilmington, Del.

10 OTT, Walther H(enry). Poultry nutrition; Biometrics of bioassays. b'11. BS '34—MS '36 (Ore State Coll); PhD '42 (Pa State Coll); '45 (Yale). Research on nutritional requirements of growing chicks, vitamin assays with chicks, development of quantitative procedures for biological assays. Author articles: Effect of Deficiencies in Vitamins and in Protein on Avian Malaria '46; Antipyridoxine Activity of Desoxypyridoxine in the Chick '46; A Quantitative Assay Method for Pyrogens '49, and others. Research fellow poultry husbandry Penn State Coll '37-39, biol chemistry '39-41; research asso charge poultry nutrition Merck Inst Therapeutic Research since '42, head dept biol control '45-52. Am Chem Soc (div biol chem, div agrl and food chem)—Poultry Sci Assn—Am Statis Assn (biometrics sect)—Biometrics Soc—AAAS —NY Acad Sci—American Institute of Nutrition. Merck Institute for Therapeutic Research, Rahway, N.J. H: 1874 Quimby Lane, Westfield.

11 OUKRAINSKY, Serge (Leonide Orlay de Carva). Ballet (Choreography and design); Costume and stage design (Ballet). Student '96-01 (Lycee Condorcet, Lycee Carnot, Acad Julian Paris). Creator first original American ballet; work includes choreography to twenty ballets, four motion picture sequences and forty-seven operatic ballets, many ballet scenarios; designed costumes and scenery for Anna Pavlowa, the Chicago and San Francisco operas, and his own ballet company. Author: My Two Years with Anna Pavlowa '40. Choreographer and ballet master; toured US and South America, Mexico and Havana with his company the Pavley-Oukrainsky Ballet, presented to Paris Grand Opera '32; asso nine years with Chicago Grand Opera; dir Serge Oukransky Ballet since '31; ballet instr and dance dir Perry's Theatre Studio Hollywood since '34; ballet master Nat Grand Opera '44; founder and artistic dir Am Nat Ballet '48. Melrose Academy, 1001 Melrose Av., Hollywood, Cal.

12 OUSDAL, Asbjorn P(ederson). Fossils (Microscopic); Meteorites (Photomicrographs, plant fossil remains, microfossil materials earth and meteorites). b'79. DO (Coll Osteopathic Phys & Surg LA); MD (U Cal LA); grad study '40-51 (U So Cal). Research in origin and continuity of life since '05, evolution of form (fossils) since '16, a continuous creation since '36, microfossils in meteorites '40, colors in meteoritical fossil material '45; deductive and speculative observation in fossil material on earth compared with microfossil material from meteorites,

that a pre-purposive factor is present in the nucleous of the Atomic structure, that life is without beginning or ending and observable by the corelation evidenced in these fossils, demonstrating continuous creation. Lectures with lantern slides on microscopic-fossils; pvt research Micro-Fossil Lab. 431 Calle Alamo, Rutherford Park, Santa Barbara, Cal.

13 OVERCASH, Jean Parks. Horticulture; Pomology (Small fruits). b'17. BS '38 (NC State Coll); MS '39— Alumni Research Found scholar '38-40 —PhD '41 (U Wis). Research on breeding strawberries and raspberries; cultural studies with grapes, dewberries, raspberries and strawberries; research on peach fertilizers and physiology. Author articles. Asso prof hort Miss State Coll since '45. Am Soc Hort Sci— Am Pomological Soc—Sigma Xi. Dept. of Horticulture, State College, Mississippi.

14 OVERHOLT, John A. Personnel administration; Civil service (Merit ratings). b'95. LLB '25 (Columbus U). Author: Management-Employee Boards as Judicial Bodies; Appraising Employee Performance; Efficiency Ratings in a Trustee-Management System; Efficiency Rating Manual. Specialized in fields of position classification, merit ratings and employee relations fed civil service since '22; Civil Service Commn since '32; chmn adv council to staff of Senate Civil Service Comm '47-49; cons to Fed Personnel Council; atty Md and DC Bars. Soc for Personnel Adminstrn—Civil Service Assembly — Civil Service Commn Club (pres). Civil Service Commission, Washington 25.†

15 OVERMAN, James Robert. Educational administration (College and university); Mathematics (Principles and methods of teaching); Transfer of training. b'88. AB '09 (Ind U); AM '14 (Columbia); PhD '30 (U Mich). Author: Principles and Methods of Teaching Arithmetic '20, '25; A Course in Arithmetic for Teachers and Teacher Training Classes '23; An Experimental Study of Certain Factors Affecting Transfer of Training in Arithmetic '31; Junior-Life Mathematic (books 1, 2, 3) '38; Algebra, The Language of Mathematics '40. Co-author: (with C Woody, F S Breed) Child-Life Arithmetics (grades 3-8) '36, Arithmetic for You (grades 3-8) 45. Professor mathematics Bowling Green State U since '14, dean coll liberal arts '30-48, dean of faculties since '51. AAAS(F)—Am Math Soc—Math Assn Am—Nat Council Tchrs Math-NEA—AAUP—Phi Beta Kappa—Phi Delta Kappa. Bowling Green State University, Bowling Green, O.◎

16 OVERMAN, William D. History and archives of Ohio. b'01. BS '25— MA '26—PhD '31 (O State U). Author articles: Israel D Andrews and Reciprocity in 1854 '34; Ohio Archives '42; and others. Prof hist Waynesburg Coll '31-34; curator hist and archivist O State Archeol and Hist Soc '34-43; exec sec O War Hist Commn '42-44; head dept Firestone library and archives since '43. Phi Alpha Theta—AHA —Miss Valley Hist Assn—Soc Am Archivists—Am Assn State and Local Hist—O Acad Hist (sec '36-48). 1200 Firestone Parkway, Akron 17, O. 31 Mull Av., Akron 3, O.

17 OVERTON, Richard C(leghorn). United States railroad history. b'07. BA '29—MA '34 (Williams Coll); MA '36—PhD '44 (Harvard U). Rsrch on railroad and business history of US, Chicago, Burlington and Quincy Railroad, Charles E Perkins, Chicago railways, bibliography of secondary works in railroad history, railway builders.

Author: Burlington West '41; Milepost 100 '49; Gulf-to-Rockies '53. Author of articles in field: Scholars Get Access to the Burlington Records '44; Problems of Writing the History of Large Business Unit with Special Reference to Railroads '48; Good and Useful Railroad History '48, and others. Asst hist dept Harvard '35-36, counsellor '38-39; investigator old records CB&Q RR '36, exec asst '39-42, research dir '42-43, supt relief dept '43-45; prof bus hist Sch Commerce Northwestern U since '45. AHA—Miss Valley Hist Assn—Am Econ Assn—Econ Hist Assn —Newcomen Soc Eng—Vt Hist Soc— Ry and Locomotive Hist Soc—Phi Beta Kappa. Commerce Building, Northwestern University, Evanston, Ill.†

18 OWEN, David Edward. English hist (19th-20th Century). b'98, PhB '20 (Denison U); PhD '27 (Yale); fellow Social Sci Research Council '32-33. Author: Imperialism and Nationalism in the Far East '29; British Opium Policy in China and India '34. Instr History Yale '23-27, asst prof '27-38; vis lecturer Harvard '37-38, asso prof '38-46, prof since '46. 27 Everett St., Cambridge 38, Mass.

19 OWEN, Edgar Wesley. Petroleum geology (Texas, New Mexico). b'96. BS in geol '15 (Denison U); AM '16 (U Mo). Active exploration as petroleum geologist in Texas and New Mexico; study petroleum reserves in area; discovery several oil fields. Geol L H Wentz Oil Div San Antonio '27-42, since '45. Am Assn Petroleum Geol—Geol Soc Am(F)—Am Geophys Union—AA AS—Sigma Gamma Epsilon. 532 Milam Bldg., San Antonio 5.

20 OWEN, Gwilym Emyr. Physics (Quartz growth, critical conditions for water). b'97. PhB '19 (Lafayette Coll); PhD '28 (U Pa). Author articles in field. Prof physics and director quartz research project Antioch Coll since '29; asst ed Webster's New International Dictionary since '34; exchange lecturer U Wales '39-40. Am Phys Soc—AAAS(F)—Am Association Physics Tchrs—Phi Beta Kappa—Sigma Xi. Antioch Coll., Yellow Springs, O.†

21 OWEN, Howard Malcolm. Oysters (Cytology, ecology); Marine ecology; Invertebrate zoology. b'13. AB '35 (Hampden-Sydney Coll); MA—PhD '45 (U Va). Author: Guide to the Study of Marine Biology '46; also articles in field. Dir oyster research State of La '47-50. AAAS—Am Micros Soc—American Soc Protozool—Tenn Acad Sci— SC Acad Sci—Nat Shellfisheries Assn —Sigma Xi. Department of Biology, University of the South, Sewanee, Tennessee.†

22 OWEN, (Edgar) Lyle. Economics of taxation (Balanced systems); Ozarks region (People, politics); American race relations (Negro, Jewish). b'06. AB '27 (Southwest Mo State Coll); MA '28—PhD '37 (U Wis). Author articles: Why Tax Business '42; Should State and Local Taxes be Cut '42; Your Million Fathers '44; An Ozarker and the Jews '45; A White Man looks at the Negro '45; A Professor Runs for Office '45. Prof econs, head dept U Tulsa since '47. Am Econ Assn—AAUP— Ozark Folklore Soc. University of Tulsa, Tulsa 4. H: Branson, Mo.

23 OWEN, Ray David. Animal blood group inheritance; Serological genetics. b'15. BSc '37 (Carroll Coll); PhM— PhD '41—research fellow '41-43 (U Wis); Gosney fellow '46-47 (Calif Inst Tech). Research on dairy cattle blood test for parentage determination, animal immunogenetics, parabiosis, animal and plant serological genetics. Author articles. Asso prof Cal Inst

Tech '47-53, prof '53. Genetics Soc Am —Am Society Zool—American Soc Naturalists—Soc Study Evolution—Am Genetics Assn—AAAS—Am Soc Animal Prodn—Sigma Xi. California Institute of Technology, Pasadena 4, Calif.†

10 OWEN, Robert P(aul). Micronesia (Entomology). b'16. BS '48 (U Wash Seattle). Studies on agricultural pests, public health pests, beneficial insects, biological control of insects, and administration of quarantine; collection and identification of insects from islands of American Micronesia. With Bur Entomol and Plant Quarantine '46-48; entomol Govt of Guam and Trust Ter '49-50; chief entomol Trust Ter of Pacific Islands since '50. Entomol Soc Am—Hawaiian Entomol Soc. Trust Territory of the Pacific Islands. Office of the Entomologist, care District Administrator, Koror, Caroline Islands.

11 OWEN, William Bert. Mosquitoes. b'03. AB '27 (U Ky); AM '29—PhD '36 (U Minn). Taxonomy and biology of mosquitoes of Minnesota including a list of species, larval habitats, seasonal cycles, habits and importance of each species; described new species of anophiline mosquito (Anopheles koliensis) from Guadalcanal, British Solomon Islands; established a laboratory colony of Theobaldia inornata successful for first time. Prof zool U Wyo since '31. Served as capt to maj san corps AUS as commanding officer malaria survey detachment PTO '43-45. Am Soc Parasitol—Am Assn Econ Entomol—Am Mosquito Control Assn—Entomol Soc Am. Department of Zoology, University of Wyoming, Laramie, Wyo.

12 OWENS, James Samuel. Light; Optics; Spectroscopy; Spectrophotometry; Spectrographic analysis; Glass technology; Infrared radiation sources and detectors. b'08. BS '28 (U Chattanooga); MS '30—PhD '32 (U Mich). Author articles in field. Exec dir O State U Research Found and prof O State U since '46. Am Phys Soc—Am Chem Soc—Am Ceramic Soc—Phi Beta Kappa—Sigma Xi. Ohio State University Research Foundation, Columbus 10, O.

13 OWENS, (Arthur) Neal. Burns. b '99. Student U '18-19 (U Chicago); BS in med '24 (U Ala); MD '26 (Emory U). Original work in tissue transplanting, treatment of burns, use of celluloid in correction of defects of contour, use of periosteal grafts, development and treatment of burns; developed surgical tub for treatment of burns and infected wounds, also a protective occlusive pressure dressing for wound treatment. With Tulane U New Orleans since '33, prof clin surgery (plastic surgery) since '43; head dept plastic surgery Eye Ear Nose and Throat Hosp New Orleans since '33 sr vis surgeon Touro Infirmary; vis surgeon Charity Hosp New Orleans; lectr plastic surgery and burns. Am Bd Plastic Surgery (Founders group, dir, chmn bd)—ACS(F)—Am Assn Plastic Surgeons—Am Assn Plastic and Reconstructive Surgery (pres)—So Surg Assn—Am Assn Surgery Trauma —New Orleans Acad Scis—Sigma Xi. 1515 American Bank Bldg., New Orleans 12.

14 OWENS, William A. American balladry and folklore. b'05. AB—MA '33 (So Meth U); PhD '41 (U Ia). Recorded folk music in Southwest, has 1000 items in private collection. Author: Swing and Turn: Texas Play-Party Games '36; Texas Folk Songs '50; Slave Mutiny '53. Asst professor Eng Columbia U since '48. Am Folklore Soc—Modern Lang Assn—Texas Folklore Society. Columbia University, NYC.†

15 OWINGS, Donnell MacClure. Colonial history of Maryland; Heraldry. b'12. AB '34 (DePauw U); MA '37—PhD '42 (Harvard). Author: His Lordships Patronage: Offices of Profit in Colonial Maryland; also edited list of private manors. Asso prof hist U Okla Norman Okla since '52, asso dean grad coll since '51. Md Hist Soc—Am Assn State Local Hist—AHA—Miss Valley Hist Assn—So Hist Assn—Phi Beta Kappa. Faculty Exchange, University of Oklahoma, Norman, Okla.

16 OWNBEY, (Francis) Marion. Liliaceae (Allium, Calochortus); Cytotaxonomy; Hybridization. b'10. BA '35—MA '36 (U Wyo); PhD '39 (Washington U). Biosystematic research on genus Calochortus since '37, genus Allium since '40; maintains large garden collection of both genera for experimental purposes; participant Princeton Bicentennial Conference Genetics, Paleontology and Evolution '47; member board editors Madrono since '41. Author articles: A Monograph of the Genus Calochortus '40; Natural Hybridization in the Genus Balsamorhiza '43; Cytological Studies in Relation to the Classification of the Genus Calochortus '43. Instr bot, curator herbarium State Coll Wash '39-42, asst prof '42-46, asso prof since '46; bot cinchona mission Fgn Econ Adminstrn '43-44. AAAS(F)—Bot Soc Am—Am Soc Plant Taxonomists—Soc Study Evolution—Torrey Bot Club—Calif Bot Soc—Sigma Xi—Phi Kappa Phi. Department of Botany, State College, Pullman, Wash.

17 OWSLEY, William D(avid). Oil well cementing and oil field service equipment design. b'10. Student '27-29 (Ga Sch Tech); BS '31 (Okla U). Inventor and co-inventor of various oil well service equipment and processes, designer of high pressure portable equipment for oil well cementing and related oil well service processes, six patents. Author: Drilling Practice '37; Pump Equipment for Oil Well Cementing '42; also articles in field. Drafting and field work Halliburton Oil Well Cementing Co '29-31, engr dept '32, dist engr Tex '32, Calif '34, div engr Tex '35, design engr Duncan Okla headquarters '36, supervisor mech research and development '40, chief engr war products div '42, chief engr for co '43, tech advisor to management '43-48; in charge engineering, production and materials '49, vp and technical adviser since '50. American Inst Mining and Metal Engrs—ASME. Halliburton Oil Well Cementing Company, P.O. Drawer 1120 Duncan, Okla.

18 OXTOBY, Gurdon Corning. Theological education; Old Testament interpretation; Palestine (Topography); Semitic languages. b'02. AB '23 (U Cal); MA '29 (Columbia); BD '27—ThD '38 (San Francisco Theol Sem); DD '38 (Albany Coll); San Francisco Theol Sem Alumni fellow '27-28 '31 (U Berlin), '28-29 (American Sch Oriental Research Jerusalem). Instructor leadership training schools and summer conferences under Board of Christian Education of Presbyterian Church in USA and International Council of Religious Education '29-51; member Presbyterian Council on Theological Education, chairman curriculum committee '48-51; secretary committee on Christian Education Synod of California '36-51; secretary Pacific regional conference American Association Theological Schools '37-51, Westminster Foundation of Northern California '39-45; member editorial council Theology Today. Ordained ministry Presbyn Ch USA '27; instr Semitics San Francisco Theol Sem '29-30, Gray prof Hebrew Exegesis and OT lit since '30, dean since '37; vis prof OT Berkeley Bapt Div Sch since '37. Archaeol Inst Am—Soc Bibl Lit and Exegesis—Phi Beta Kappa. H: 26 Kensington Court, San Anselmo, Cal.†⊚

19 OYLER, James Russell. Food processing (Thermal). b'15. BS '37 (Mt St Mary's Coll); '37-38 (U Pa); MS '40 —Gen Mills Inc F '41-42—PhD '42 (Pa State Coll), Nutrition Found F '42-45 (Columbia). Research and development new procedures for processing apple, cherry, peach and tomato products, research on suitable fruit varieties for processing, proper handling and storage of fruits, plant equipment and design for processing. Dir research Knouse Corp '45-47, tech dir since '49; tech dir Nat Fruit Products Co '47-49. Nat Research Soc—Sigma Xi—Phi Lambda Upsilon — Phi Kappa Phi—Gamma Sigma Delta—Alpha Chi Sigma —ACS—Inst Food Tech—Am Inst Chem—AAAS—Pa Acad Sci. Knouse Foods, Peach Glen, Pa.

P

20 PABST, Adolf. Mineralogy; Crystallography; Crystal structure; Petrography. b'99. AB '25 (U Ill); PhD '28 (U Cal). Author: Minerals of California '38; Mineral Tables '38; also articles in field. Lecturer, later professor mineral U Calif since '27. Mineral Soc Am(F, councilor '42-45, vp '48, pres '51)—Geol Soc Am(F, vice pres '52)—Crystallographic Society America (vp '47-48, president '48-49). Fellow American Scandinavian Found '27-28; fellow Guggenheim Found '38-39. Dept. of Geological Sciences, University of California, Berkeley 4.†⊚

21 PABST, Charles Frederick. Sunburn; Athlete's foot (Prevention); Fireproofing (Ships, clothing, fabrics). b'87. MD '09 (LI Coll Hosp). Study skin diseases Puerto Rico and Venezuela; investigated prevalance ringworm infection of feet, originated term "athlete's foot", started health campaign against bare feet; pointed out dangers of over exposure to summer sun, gave term "heliophobe" to individuals whose skin will not tan; gave US Government forumla for fireproofing ships, clothing, and fabrics. Attending dermatologist, chief clinic for skin diseases Greenpoint Hosp since '15. AMA(F)—Am Acad Dermatology and Syphilology(F)—NY State Med Soc —King Co Med Soc. 15 Clark St., Bklyn 2.

22 PACE, Donald Metcalfe. Cell physiology (Growth). b'06. BA '28 (Susquehanna U); MA '29—PhD '31 (Duke U); '24-26 (Temple U). Research on effects of vitamins and growth-promoting substances on growth in Chilomonas paramecium, relation between concentration of growth-promoting substance and effect on growth in same, relation between metabolic activity and cyanide inhibition in Pelomyxa carolinensis Wilson. Author: Laboratory Outlines for Vertebrate Physiology '47; Elements of Physiology '49; also articles in field. Prof physiol U Neb since '48, chmn dept physiol and pharmacology since '46. AAAS—Am Physiol Soc—Am Soc Protozool—Am Soc Zool—Neb Acad Sci—Soc Exptl Biol and Med—Soc Gen Physiol—Sigma Xi. Department of Physiology, University of Nebraska, Lincoln 8, Neb. H: 2030 Sumner St., Lincoln 2.

23 PACKARD, Fred Mallery. Conservation of natural resources; Ornithology; Wildlife management. b'13. BA '36 (Harvard); MA '42 (U Colo). Field research on birds, wildlife problems of national parks, other conservation activities. Author articles in field. Austin Ornithol Research Sta N Eastham Mass in charge banding land birds '34-36; Pan Am Union Washington '36, '37; sec Emergency Conservation Committee NY; wildlife tech Nat Park Service '38-40; executive sec Nat Parks Assn Washington since '50; in charge administrn National Parks Association. Am Ornithol Union—Am Soc Mammalogists—Wilderness Society—Defenders of Fur-bearers (dir). Rsrch fellow biology University Colorado '42. National Parks Association, 1840 Mintwood Pl. N.W., Washington.†

10 PACKARD, Sidney Raymond. Medieval history. b'93. BA '15 (Amherst Coll); MA '16—PhD '21—Bayard Cutting traveling fellow '19-20 (Harvard). Author: Europe and the Church Under Innocent III '27. Ed Berkshire series in European History since '27; spl cons medieval hist Am Coll Dictionary Random House '47; prof hist Smith Coll since '30, chmn dept '38-43, '48-51. AHA—Medieval Acad Am—Royal Hist Soc—Phi Beta Kappa. Awarded Guggenheim fellowship '29-30. Smith Coll, Northampton, Mass.†⊙

11 PADDOCK, F(loyd) B. Apiculture. b'88. BSE '11 (Colo A&M Coll); MS '15 (O State U). Author articles in field. Asso prof, prof apiculture Ia State Coll since '19; Ia State apiast since '19. AAEE—AAAS(F)—Ia Acad Sci—Ia Beekeepers Assn (sec since '19)—Apiary Inspectors Am (sec '28-32). Zoology and Entomology Department, Morrill Hall, Iowa State College, Ames, Ia.†

12 PAGE, Ben(jamin) M(arkham). Structural geology (California coastal ranges, Nevada); Mineral deposits (California, Nevada, Utah, New Mexico). b'11. AB '33—MA '34—PhD '40 (Stanford U). Author articles and maps in field. Asso prof geol Stanford U '43-52, professor since '52. Geol Soc Am(F)—Soc Econ Geol—Am Geophys Union—Sigma Xi. School of Mineral Sciences, Stanford University, Cal.†

13 PAGE, David Perkins. Government (Military); Foreign government. b'02. Student '20 (MIT); grad '24 (US Mil Acad); AM '35 (Columbia). Observation and research in Austria, Czechoslovakia, Hungary and Germany during and following the period of Anschluss '38. Commd 2d lt ORC '24 advancing to col '43, active duty '41-49, with War Dept Gen Staff '41-43, exec officer Civil Affairs, Hdqrs ETO '43; mem staff Gen Omar Bradley as chief publicity and psychol warfare sect Hdqrs 1st Army, and deputy civil affairs and military government officer Hdqrs 12th Army Group '44-45; deputy administr Veterans Affairs, NY, PR and Virigin Islands '46-49. 139 E. 36th St., NYC 16.⊙

14 PAGE, John Orion. Pharmaceuticals (Analysis); Foods (Analystical chemistry). b'06. BS in chem '27 (U Rochester NY); PhD '33 (U Ill). Author article: Extraction and Purification of Nordihydroguaiaretic Acid '51. Chief chem Hosp Liquids Inc Ill '35-36; research chem The Upjohn Co Mich '36-38; chem Anheuser Busch Co Mo '39; development chem Kroger Grocery & Baking Co O '41-42; research chem Shell Chem Co Cactus Ordnance Works Tex '43-44; research chem Eldorado Oil Works Cal '44-45; asst prof and asst chem A&M Coll NM '46-47; asst prof chem U Ida '47-48; chem Casner Candelilla Co Tex '47-50; asst prof chem A&M Coll Tex '48-51; asso prof chem since '51. ACS—Sigma Xi. A&M College of Texas, College Station, Tex.

15 PAGE, Lincoln Ridler. Geology; Pegmetites. b'10. AB 31 (Dartmouth) —MA '32—PhD '37 (U Minn). Known as authority on pegmatites, particularly on the economic aspects of pegmatite work. Instr geol Dartmouth Coll '32-35, U Minn '35-37; field asst Minn geol sur '36; asst geol Standard Oil Co of Tex '37-38; asst prof geol U Colo '38-39; with US geol sur since '39, geologist since '44, supervisor pegmatite group since '47. AAPG—AAAS —Geophys Union. Geological Survey, Washington 25.

16 PAGE, Ralph George. Dancing (Square). b'03. Ed pub schs. Teacher American and international folk dances since '32; originated four New England Contra dances, also wrote music; recorded album of New England squares '46, four albums New England quadrilles and contra dances '49; associate editor American Squares Magazine; editor Northern Junket. Co-author: (with Beth Tolman) The Country Dance Book '37. Teacher square and folk dances YWCA Boston since '43, Putney Sch Vt '43-46, Carnegie Inst Tech '46, Oglebay Folk Dance Camp '48, NYU '48, Me Folk Dance Camps since '49, Cal Folk Dance Camp '50, Dixie Folk and Square Dance Inst '50. NH Folk Fedn—NY Folklore Soc—Am Folklore Soc—Eire Soc of Boston—Cal Folklore Soc—NJ Square Dance Callers and Tchrs Assn—NE Folk Festival Assn. 182 Pearl St., Keene, N.Y.

17 PAGE, Stanley Henry. Engines (Internal combustion); Organs. b'85. Student '06-08 (MIT). Design and development carburetors, induction systems and fuel spray systems; engine design and development on gasoline, distillate and Diesel engines; design and development expression-control device for pipe organs. Issued patents on constructions used on aircraft engines. Author instruction manuals on engines. In charge exptl design and development light-oil engines Union Gas Engine Co '10-16; in charge design and development first aircraft engine to pass govt endurance tests at Wash Navy Yard '14-21; vp Union Gas Engine Co '16-21; own dynamometer lab '30-40; Union Diesel Engine Co '40-43; charge Diesel development Hendy Iron Works '44-46; own lab since '46. Soc Automotive Engs—ASME. P.O. Box 404, Los Gatos, Cal.

18 PAINE, Clarence Sibley. Great Plains and Rocky Mountain West 1840-1900; Calamity Jane and Wild Bill Hickok. b'08. AB '36—AM '37 (U Neb); BS '37 (U Ill). Author: Calamity Jane and Wild Bill Hickok '49. Editor: The Diaries of a Nebraska Farmer '47; The Black Hills (with others) '52; also articles in field. Dir Okla City libraries since '48. Utah Hist Soc—Wis State Hist Soc—Okla Hist Soc—Am Assn State and Local Hist—Miss Valley Hist Assn—Westerners (Chicago chap). Hist research fellow Rockefeller Found '44. Oklahoma City Libraries, Oklahoma City 2.†

19 PAINE, Harry W(arren). Vocational education (Trade analysis, teacher training). b'90. BS '12—ME '28 (Ia State Coll); MS '27 (U Wis); EdD '43 (U Mich). Inventions include automotive tools, devices, chain locks, smoking pipes. Co-author: Milling Machine Indexing '42; Helical Milling '43; Aviation Mathematics '44; Shop Sketching and Blue Print Reading Made Easy '47; also articles in field. Prof vocational edn and dir vocational teacher improvement service U Cincinnati since '42. NEA—O Vocational Assn—O Soc Profl Engrs—O Ednl Assn—Am Vocational Assn—Nat Assn Indsl Teacher Trainers—Phi Kappa Phi. Department of Vocational Education, Teachers College, University of Cincinnati, Cincinnati 21.

20 PAINE, Robert Treat, Jr. Japanese art. b'00. AB '22—AM '28 (Harvard). Specialist in Japanese screen paintings and prints. Author: Japanese Screen Paintings—Birds, Flowers and Animals '35; Japanese Screen Paintings—Landscapes and Figures '38; Ten Japanese Paintings '39. Co-author: (with Harold G. Henderson) Japanese Art. Asst curator Dept Asiatic Art Mus Fine Arts since '45. Museum of Fine Arts, Boston.

21 PALICKAR, Stephen Joseph. Slovakia. b'96. Ed parochial and pub schs. Research on historical, political, social, and economic life of Slovakia. Author: Slovakia of Today '33; Slovakia, from Hungarian Despotisim to Atheistic Czech Communism '48; Rev. Joseph Murgas, Priest-Scientist, His Musical Wireless Telegraphy and the First Radio '50; Slovakian Culture, In the Light of History (in press). With Am Newspaper Pub Assn '27-37; Am News Co '42-46; lectr Slovak history, politics, and social science Columbia. 632 W. End Av., NYC 24.

22 PAINTER, Reginald Henry. Entomology (Insect resistance in crop plants, taxonomy of Diptera, corn ear worm, hessian fly). b'01. BA '21—MA '24 (U Tex); PhD (O State U). Author articles in field. Prof Kan State Coll since '41. Entomol Soc Am(F)—Am Assn Econ Entomol—Am Soc Agron—Kan Entomol Soc—AAAS(F)—Am Soc Naturalists—Sigma Xi. Post-doctoral fellow O State U '48-49. Department of Entomology, Kansas State College, Manhattan, Kan.†

23 PAINTER, Sidney. History of medieval France and England. b'02. AB '25—PhD '30 (Yale U). Research on reign of King John in England, English feudal baronies, English castles, Magna Carta and its background, ideas of chivalry in France, French chivalric literature, life of nobles in France and England in Middle Ages, French feudal politics 1200-1250. Author: William Marshal: Knight-errant, Baron, and Regent of England '33; The Scourge of the Clergy: Peter of Dreux, Duke of Brittany '37; French Chivalry: Chivalric Ideas and Practices in Medieval France '40; Studies in the History of the English Feudal Barony '44; The Reign of King John '49. Instructor hist Yale U '27-30, asst prof '30-31; with Johns Hopkins U since '31, prof since '45. AHA—Medieval Acad Am—Medievalia et Humanistica (editorial bd since '43)—Speculum (editorial bd '43-46). Johns Hopkins University, Balt 18.⊙

24 PAIT, James Albert. Seventeenth century philosophy (Descartes); Cambridge Platonism; Existentialism. b'14. BA '37 (Duke U); MA '39—PhD '41—Francis duPont fellow '40-41 (U Va); '39-40 (Columbia, Union Theol Sem). Author: The Influence of Descartes on Seventeenth Century English Philosophy '41. Prof humanities Stephens Coll '48-49; chairman department philosophy and theology Ripon College since '50. So Soc Philos and Psychol—Am Soc Aesthetics—Phi Beta Kappa. Bennett Wood Green travel fellow '39-40; Carnegie grant-in-aid '47. Department of Philosophy, Ripon College, Ripon, Wis.†

25 PALEY, Charles. Dairy and food technology. b'97. Student '15-17 (Brooklyn Polytech Inst); BS '19—MS '38 (Columbia Univ); LLB '28 (St Johns U); PhD '39 (Temple Bar Coll); '18 (Cornell U). Chemical research on food sanitation, devices for bottle washers, control of diseases and germs in milk production, milk and butter fat testing, pasteurization and controls. Co-developed Broadhurst-Paley bacteriology stain; invented Paley test bottle, Paley drip tube. Author articles in field. Chem Bur Food and Drugs NYC '20-22, inspector of foods '23-26; chem Certified Labs Inc '26-30, dir since '30. Am Inst Chem(F)—Am Chem Soc—Inst Food Tech—Am Pub Health Assn—Dairy Sci Assn—Soc Am Bact—Internat Assn Milk and Food Sanitarians. 19 Hudson St., NYC 13.

10 PALLETT, Earl Manley. College administration; Teacher placement. b '92. Student '12-14 (Wis State Normal Sch Platteville); '19 (Univ Toulouse France); BS '21—MS '22 (U Wis); summer '23 (U Chicago); PhD '31 (U Ore). Author: (monograph) Studies in Student Mortality at University of Oregon '33. Registrar U Ore '27-48, prof edn, sch edn since '49, acting dean of men '29-30, exec sec and asst to pres '30-49, dir tchr placement service since '49. Am Assn Collegiate Registrars—Nat Instnl Tchr Placement Assn—Pacific Coast Assn Collegiate Registrars (pres '37-33)—NW Assn Coll Placement Ofcls (pres '51-51)—Ore Assn Instnl Placement Ofcls(pres '50-51)—Phi Delta Kappa—Alpha Zeta. 814 Lorane Highway, Eugene, Ore.†◎

11 PALLISTER, Hugh Davidson. Industrial mineral reserves (Iron ore, tin, coal, mercury, graphite, and mica); Alabama geology (Minerals and ores). b'83. BS '06—EM '14 (Case Inst Tech). Study mercury deposits in Texas and California; calculation quantity, quality, and recovery of graphite, mica, copper, lignite, and pyrite in Albama; geological study reserves of iron ore, coal, and limestone in southeastern US; economic study ores and minerals in Alabama. Author article: Mineral Resources of Albama and Her Economic Position Among the States '48. Co-author articles: (with R W Smith) Alabama Flake Graphite in World War II '45; (with J R Thoenen) Albama Copper Bearing Pyrites '48, and others. Prof and head depts geol and mining engring U Tex '15-19; cons oil, ores, minerals and geol '15-19; dir sch mines and state mine expt sta U Ala '21-29, research prof mining engring on reserves and geol raw materials '45-47; vp Mech Development Co '29-42; mining engr strategic ores in Ala US Bur Mines '42-45; sr geol Geol Survey of Ala since '47. AIMME—AAAS—Ala Acad Sci—Tau Beta Pi—Sigma Xi—Theta Tau. Geological Survey of Alabama, University, Ala.

12 PALLISTER, John C(lare). Insects of Central and South America and the Pacific Islands; Beetles (Taxonomy and geographical distribution). b '91. Student (Cleveland College Western Reserve U). Entomological expedition to Central and South America and Pacific Islands '30-31, Florida '36, Mexico '45, Peru and headwaters of Amazon River '46-47; research on distribution, habits of beetles, classification, photography, especially leaf beetles (family Chrysomelidae) and click beetles (family Elateridae). Co-author: (with C. H. Curran) Insects of Pacific World '44. Head dept entomol and invertebrate zool Cleveland Museum Natural Hist '22-32; pub lectr natural hist and travel '32-38; dept insects and spiders Am Museum Natural Hist since '39. Entomol Soc Am—Soc Systematic Zool. American Museum of Natural History, NYC 24. H: Yacht Marion II, 2501 Knapp St., Bklyn 35.

13 PALMER, Brooks. Horology (American clocks). b'00. BS '23 (Dartmouth Coll). Research on, classification and correlation of information pertaining to, American clocks and watches and their makers; collection of data includes over 6,000 names; Associate editor American Antiques Journal. Author: Book of American

Clocks '50; also section Clocks and Watches and 29 biographies Colliers Ency '49-50. Life ins business NY since '30. United Horological Assn Am—Nat Assn Watch and Clock Collectors(pres) —Horological Inst Am. 295 Madison Av., NYC 17. H: 1235 Park Av., NYC 28.

14 PALMER, Charles Forrest. Housing and town planning; Traffic control; Slum clearance; Satellite towns. b'92. Represented US at Congress of International Federation for Housing and Town Planning Mexico City '38, England '46; defense housing coordinator National Defense Commission and Executive Office of the President '40-42; chairman Atlanta Techwood Homes '33, first US Slum Clearance Housing Authority '38-40. Author articles in field. Pres Palmer Inc Atlanta since '21. Nat Planning Assn—Am Soc Planning Officials — Internat Fedn Housing and Town Planning—Nat Assn Housing Officials (pres '40)—Urban Land Inst, and others. Palmer Building, Atlanta 3.†

15 PALMER, Charles Walter. Radar testing; Radar noise. b'07. Student (Cornell U) (Cooper Union) (Columbia) (NYU) (Stanford). Design electronic equipment for testing radar systems, radar components, and microwave radio equipment; study noise measurements, including radiation, conduction, and susceptibility, and their correction; research on effects high frequency currents on human and animal nerve systems. Author series articles: Microwaves '50. Co-author article: Calculation and Design of Resistance-Coupled Amplifiers Using Pentode Tubes '40, and others. Tech ed Radio News Magazine '25-26; chief engr Dressner Mfg Co '29; engr and chief test set design dept Western Elec Co '29-32 and since '36; tech ed Radio-Craft Magazine '32-36, Inst Radio Engrs—Radio Club Am Inc (F). Western Electric Co., Inc., Chatham Rd., Winston-Salem, N.C.

16 PALMER, Ernest Jesse. Hawthorn oak (Taxonomy); Walnut (Taxonomy). b'75. Student '98-00 (Webb City Baptist Coll). Research on geographical distribution of North American trees and shrubs. Author: Catalogue of Plants of Jasper County, Missouri '16. Co-author: (with Julien A Steymermark) An Annotated Catalogue of the Flowering Plants of Missouri '35. Collector and research asst Arnold Arboretum Harvard '21-48. AA AS(F)—NE Bot Club (pres '44-46)—Am Fern Soc—Am Soc Plant Taxonomists. H: 321 S. Main St., Webb City, Mo.

17 PALMER, George David, Jr. Sulphur (Organic compounds); Lignin. b'97. BS '19 (Clemson Coll); MA '21—PhD '24 (Johns Hopkins U). Research on direct sulfuration of organic compounds, organic chemistry of molten sulphur, chemistry and by-products of lignin, chemistry of sulfur dyes, plastics, and rubbers. Author: Plastic and Allotropic Forms of Sulphur '42; Introduction to Organic Chemistry '34; Introduction to Formula System of Organic Chemistry '40, and others; also articles in field. Head dept chem Guilford Coll '21-22; asst prof Kan Agrl Coll '24-27; prof organic chem U Ala since '27, head dept organic chem since '48. Am Chem Soc—AAAS—Am Inst Chem—Ala Acad Sci—So Assn Sci and Industry—So Research Inst—Ala Edn Assn—Sigma Xi. Received So Assn Sci and Industry Award '47. School of Chemistry, University, Ala.

18 PALMER, Harold King. Water surges; Density currents; Water measurements. b'78. BS '98—PhD '03 (Univ Cal). Development elimination of check

valve slam and dangerous surges in force mains; density currents in ocean disposal of sewage; sedimentation of sand in irrigation lines, sludges in sewage disposal plants; invented Palmer-Bowlus Flume for sewage measurements. From jr engr to engr US Indian Irrigation Service '09-25; from design engr to cons engr Los Angeles County San Dist '25-48; investigating hydraulic problems since '48. Am Soc CE—Cal Sewage Works Assn.

19 PALMER, Harold Schjoeth. Geology (Ground waters, Hawaiian areal). b'90. BA '12—PhD '23 (Yale). Asst prof, later prof geol U Hawaii since '20. Geol Soc Am—Seismol Soc Am—Hawaiian Acad Sci (pres '29-30)—Sigma Xi. Department of Geology, University of Hawaii, Honolulu 14, T.H.†

20 PALMER, Henry Francis. Rubber (Reclaimed, synthetic). b'99. AB '21 (Dartmouth Coll); MS '22—U scholarship '23-24—Grasselli F '24-25—PhD '25—ChemE '38 (O State U). Research on manufacture and use reclaimed rubber, developed high pressure reclaiming method; research on operation and production synthetic rubber plants. Granted patents in field. With Firestone Tire & Rubber Co '25-46, asst dir chem lab '44-46; cons rubber tech '46-50; gen mgr Ky Synthetic Rubber Corp since '50. ACS(dir rubber div)—AICE—Am Inst Chem(F)—Soc Profl Engrs—Chem Club NY—Alpha Chi Sigma—Gamma Alpha—Phi Lambda Upsilon—Sigma Xi. Kentucky Synthetic Rubber Corp., P.O. Box 360, Lsvl 1. H: 2419 Brighton Dr., Lsvl 5.

21 PALMER, Lawrence Alfred. Masonry (Efflorescence, water retention and transmittion); Pavements Flexible, load bearing capacities); Soils (Consolidation); Piles (Soil, mechanics); Landslides (Control). b'93. BS '17 (U Neb); MS '28 (George Washington U). Research in causes and means of prevention of efflorescence on brick masonry, essential properties of masonry mortars, water retentivity and plasticity of masonry mortars, causes and means of prevention of water transmission through walls of unit masonry; developed new method design flexible type pavements, original and new approach to evaluating load carrying capacities of flexible type pavements; research in the control of landslides, additions to theory of soil consolidation, new expressions for computing earth stresses produced by various type surface loads; analysis problem of earth pressure and deflections of foundation piles subjected to lateral thrust. With Nat Bur Standards '21-35; soil mechanics and paving US Bur Pub Roads '35-41; Bur Yards and Docks USN Dept since '41. ASTM—Highway Research Bd—AAAS—Research and Development Bd Panels (US Dept Defense—Washington Soc Engrs — Soc Mil Engrs. Bureau of Yards and Docks, Navy Dept., Washington 25.

22 PALMER, Martin Franklin. Speech correction; Logopedics. b'05. AB '27 (Olivet Coll Mich); AM '31—ScD '37 (U Mich). Author articles in field. Prof, head dept logopedics Municipal U of Wichita since '34; dir Inst Logopedics Wichita since '34; abstracting ed all articles dealing with speech, hearing and related topics for Biol Abstract and other jours. Am Speech and Hearing Assn(F, chmn com on edn since '40, pres '48)—AAAS—Nat Forum Deafness and Speech Path—Am Hearing Soc—Am Assn to Promote Teaching of Speech to Deaf—Speech Assn Am—Kan Acad Sci—Central States Speech Assn—Am Dialect Soc. Institute of Logopedics, 2400 Jardine Dr., Wichita 14, Kan.

10 PALMER, Mary Leigh. Visual education; Religious education. AB (Fla So Coll); '30-36 (U Chicago); AM—PhD '38 (Northwestern U). Organizer, director Annual International Workshop in Visual Education, and Visual Education Fellowship '44-47; consultant and member faculty visual education various institutions '45-47; chairman vacation church school committee Chicago Church Federation '38-40, chairman leadership education committee '40-41; member board annual conference on childhood education National College Education Evanston; member curriculum committee, committee on weekday schools North Side Council of Religious Education Chicago; executive secretary leadership education, professional advisory section International Council Religious Education '40-44, director religious education, professional advisory section committee on Curriculum Guide for Local Church '44-47, committee on visual education '44-47, chairman vacation church school committee. Author: Curriculum Guide for the Local Church '46; Bring New Life Into Leadership Education '44; Visual Method in Vacation Religious Education '44; Visual Method in Weekday Religious Education '44; Picture Guides for International Lessons '44-48; Picture Guides for Vacation Religious Education Courses (series of 8) '44-45. Author syndicated articles in religious education press '43-47. Editor program resources, asso and acting dir visual edn Internat Council Religious Edn Chicago '43-47; vis prof audio-visual education Columbia U, Union Theol Sem summer '47; asso prof social scis John B Stetson U '48-49, prof psychol and audio-visual edn since '49. AAUW—Pi Lambda Theta. John B Stetson University, DeLand, Fla.◉

11 PALMER, Norman Dunbar. Modern Irish history; American diplomacy; International politics. b'09. AB '30 (Colby Coll); MA '32—PhD '36 (Yale). Author: The Irish Land League Crisis '40. Co-author: An Introduction to Political Science '48. Author articles: Makers of Modern China (series) '48-49, and others. Faculty Colby Coll '33-47, chmn dept hist and govt '46-47; asso prof polit sci Wharton Sch Finance and Commerce U Pa '47-51, prof since '51, chmn polit sci dept since '49. AHA—Am Polit Sci Assn—Fgn Policy Assn—Irish Hist Soc—AmAcad Polit Social Sci—Phi Beta Kappa. Fellow Newberry Library Chicago '47. Political Science Department, Wharton School of Finance and Commerce, University of Pennsylvania, Phila.†

12 PALMER, Ralph Simon. Behavior, ecology, and life history of North Am birds and mammals. b'14. BA '37 (U Maine); PhD '40 (Cornell). Author: A Behavior Study of the Common Tern '41; Maine Birds '49; also articles in field. Assistant prof zoology Vassar '47-49; state zoologist NY State Museum and State Science Service since '49. Am Soc Mammalogists—Am Ornithol Union—Wilson Ornithol Club—Linnaean Soc NY—Sigma Xi. N.Y. State Museum, Albany 1, N.Y.

13 PALMER, Richard William. Figs; Avocado. b'18. BSA '42 (U Cal Los Angeles). Author: Home Avocado Production in Los Angeles County. Co-author: (with Ira J Condit) The Dooryard Fig Tree in Southern California; (with Wallace Sullivan) Planning a Small Farm Home. Hort and farm adv Los Angeles Co for U Cal Agrl Ext Service since '46; specialist in home food production. Am Soc Hort Sci—Cal Avocado Soc—Am Orchid Soc. 511 East Aliso St., LA 12.

14 PALMER, Theodore Paine. Engineering mathematics. b'06. BA '28 (Amherst Coll); AM '31—grad work '34-36 (Harvard). Instr, asso prof math Rose Polytechnic Inst Terre Haute Ind since '49. Am Soc Engring Edn—AAAS —Am Math Soc—Am Geog Soc—AHA —AAUP—Assn for Symbolic Logic. Rose Polytechnic Institute, Terre Haute, Ind.

15 PALMER, Thomas Waverly. Oil laws of Argentina, Bolivia, Brazil, and Peru; Laws of Spain and Curacao. b '91. AB '10 (U Ala); LLB '13 (Harvard). Sheldon traveling fellow for legal research in Spain '13-14; president and director Venezuelan Chamber of Commerce of US Inc '42-45; counsel Petroleum Supply Commission for Latin America under Petroleum Administration for World War II. Author: Guide to the Law and Legal Literature of Spain '15; Digest of the Laws and Regulations of Argentina, Applicable to Petroleum, Peru '30; Oil Laws of Argentina, Bolivia, Brazil and Peru '30. Co-author: (with others) The Law and Legal Literature of Curacao '34. Atty Chile Exploration Co, and US counsular agt Chuquicamata Chile '19-21; atty Standard Oil Co NJ '21-26, '29-50; exec rep and counsel Tropical Oil Co Colombia SA '27-29; pres and dir Ancon Ins Co, Balboa-Ins Co. Am Geog Soc(councilor, dir)—Instituto da Ordem dos Advogados Brasilerios (corr and hon mem)—Am Bar Assn—Assn Bar City NY—Phi Beta Kappa—Pi Gamma Mu. Radiocentre 909, Havana, Cuba.◉

16 PALMER, Wayne St. Clair. Techniques for weather forecasting research; Weather map analysis. b'15. AB '39 (Neb Wesleyan U); '41-42 (U Chicago). Engaged in development of techniques for systematically forecasting behavior of cyclones. Author article: On Forecasting the Direction of Movement of Winter Cyclones '48. Weather observer with US Weather Bureau at Lincoln Neb '37-40, Chicago Ill '40-41, spl asst to chief Division Special Scientific Services US Weather Bur '44-45; No Hemisphere weather map analyst at spl project NYU-US Weather Bur '42-43, supervising No Hemisphere weather map analyst '43-44, supervising SW Pacific weather map analyst at NYU '44, research meteorol in Short Range Forecast Development Sect Washington since '45. U.S. Weather Bureau, Washington 25.†

17 PALMITER, DeForest Harold. Plant pathology (Fruit diseases) Fungicides. b'04. BS '27 (Ore State Coll); MS '29—PhD '32 (U Wis). Author articles: Ground Treatments as an Aid in Apple Scab Control '46; Experience with Dithiocarbamate Fungicides in the Northeastern States; Relation of Spray Materials to Russeting of Delicious and Golden Delicious Apples '45, and others. Grad asst plant path U Wis '28-32, research asso '32-37; asso in research NY State Agr Expt Sta Geneva '37-41, asst prof plant pat '41-45, asso prof '45-49, prof since '49. Am Phytopath Soc—AAAS—Phi Kappa Phi —Sigma Xi. Cottage Rd., Poughkeepsie, N.Y.

18 PALSER, Barbara F. Angiosperm morphology. b'16. AB '38—AM '40 (Mt Holyoke Coll); PhD '42—fellow '40-42 (U Chicago). Research on morphology of pteridophytes and angiosperms, especially floral morphology in Ericaceae. Author articles: Studies of floral morphology in the Ericaceae I; Organography and vascular anatomy in the Andromedeae II. Megasporgenesis and megagametoplyte development in the Andromedeae; Early endosperm development and embryozing in Cassiope hypnoides. U Chicago since '42, asso prof since '51. Internat Soc Plant Morphology—Bot Soc Am—AAAS—Torrey Bot Club—Ill State Acad Sci—Phi Beta Kappa—Sigma Xi. Department of Botany, University of Chicago, Chicago 37.†

19 PALSGROVE, Grant Knauer. Hydraulic power and machinery. b'88. ME '11 (Rensselaer Poly Inst). Author: Solution of Special Problems in Pipe Flow by Graphical Analysis '43; Variable Flow of Fluids '34; also articles in field. Asst mech engring Rensselaer Poly Inst '11-13, instr '13-17, asst prof '17-20, prof hydraulic engring '20-45, prof mech and hydraulic engring since '45; cons and tech expert So States Power Co NC '38-43; cons W and L E Gurley Co since '38; cons and tech expert for Doehler-Jarvis Die Casting Corp since '48.; secretary faculty Rensselaer Poly Inst '20-43. ASME —AAAS(F)—Am Soc Engring Edn— Soc Am Mil Engrs—Internat Assn Hydraulic Research—Sigma Xi—Tau Beta Pi—Pi Tau Sigma. 1514 Sage Av., Troy, N.Y.

20 PAMPLIN, John William. Phosphate rock. b'08. BS '28 (Va Poly Inst); MS '29 (U Ala). Research on ore dressing equipment, planning and layout of phosophate washers and recovery plants. Metall S Phosphate Corp '29-40; metall engr Davison Chem Corp '46-50, chief engr since '50. Am Inst Mining Engrs.

21 PANTZER, Kurt Friedrich. Jurisprudence (Techniques of practice, office management, draftsmanship, negotiation and trial advocacy). b'92. Student '09-11 (Wabash Coll); AB '14 —LLB '17—SJD '20 (Harvard). Author: Preliminary Treatise on the Principles Underlying Collective Bargaining Agreement '47; Idea Draft of a Collective Bargaining Agreement '47; Preliminary Lectures and Forms in Support of a Plea for a Uniform System of Draftsmanship: (a) Techniques and and Principles of the Science of Draftsmanship (b) Bilateral Agreements for Acquisition of Capital Assets and the Financing of such Acquisition; (c) Corporate Forms and Practice; (d) Divorce Forms and Practice; (e) Partnership Forms and Practice; (f) Commercial Forms and Practice under the Proposed Uniform Commercial Code '49-50. Co-author: (with F Hodge O'Neal) The Drafting of Corporate Charters and By-Laws '51. Practice of law since '20; mem Winthrop & Stimson NYC '20-22; mem Barnes, Hckam, Pantzer & Boyd Indianapolis since '40. Internat Law Assn —Am Law Inst(edit bd for uniform comml code, com on continuing legal edn)—Am Bar Assn(council sect corp banking and business law, com on corp laws)—Bar Assns 7th Fed Circuit (pres '51-52)—Am Judicature Soc—Nat Conf Commrs Uniform State Laws(chmn spl com on uniform acts to prevent organized crime)—Phi Delta Phi. 1313 Merchants Bank Bldg., Indpls.◉

22 PAPENFUSS, George Frederik. Algology; Marine algae (structure, reproduction, classification). b'03. BS '29 (NC State Coll); PhD '33—Slack scholar '31-32—U scholar '32-33—Johnston scholar '34-36 (Johns Hopkins U); fellow by courtesy '34-40 (U Lund and Uppsala, U Cape Town). Author articles in field. Asso prof bot U Calif since '48. Bot Soc Am—Calif Bot Soc— Phycological Soc Am—Western Soc Naturalists — Phi Beta Kappa — Phi Kappa Phi—Sigma Xi.

23 PAPERNO, Albert Jacob. Fruit (Processing, preserves); Citrus fruits (Chemistry, products); Beverages (Carbonated, still). b'12. BE '34 (State Tchrs Coll Milwaukee); MS '39 (Marquette U). Consultant in production of preserves US and abroad; developed system quality-control insuring uniform quality preserves, process for utilizing over-ripe fruit in products for human consumption; developed formulae for new citrus products; consultant citrus products, by-products; designed citrus by-products plant for production cattle-feed, citrus-molasses, yeast production citrus peels after extraction of oils; developed formulae for still and carbonated soft-drink beverages, fresh fruit concentrated bases for bottlers, alcoholic extracts. Chem in charge prodn Mission Dry Corp '42-45; establisher-operator Foods Service Labs Los Angeles since '45. ACS—Inst Food Tech. 4917 Huntington Dr., LA 32.

10 PARENT, Joseph Dominic. Fluid flow; Thermodynamics, Natural gas. b'10. BS in chem engring '29 (Cath U Am); MS in chem '31 (Rensselaer Poly Inst); '31-32 (U Md); PhD in chem engring '33 (O State U). Research fluidization and thermodynamic properties of natural gas. Author bulletins: The Storage of Natural Gas as Hydrate; Equilibrium Calculations for the Carbon-Oxygen-Steam System. Faculty Loyola U '35-42; asso prof chem engring Kan State Coll '42-44; with Inst Gas Tech since '44, ednl dir since '47. Am Chem Soc—Am Inst Chem Engrs—Am Gas Assn—Sigma Xi—Phi Lambda Upsilon—Alpha Chi Sigma. Institute of Gas Technology, 17 W. 34th St., Chgo 16.

11 PARENTON, Vernon Joseph. Culture of Louisiana. b'08. BA '36—MA '38 (La State U); PhD '48 (Harvard). Studies on acculturation and race relations among French-speaking peoples of Louisiana. Author articles in field. Instr dept sociol La State U '40-42, '44-46, asso prof since '49. Am Sociol So Sociol Soc—Rural Sociol Soc—Am Acad Polit Social Sci—AAUP—Phi Kappa Phi. Department of Sociology, Louisiana State University, Baton Rouge, La.

12 PARK, Charles F(rederick), Jr. Mining geology (Ore deposits). b'03. BS '26 (NM Sch Mines); MS '29 (U Ariz); PhD '31 (U Minn). Author articles in field. Prof geol Stanford since '46, dean sch mineral sciences since '50. Geol Soc Am—Am Mineral Soc—Soc Econ Geol—Am Inst Mining Metall Engrs—Geol Soc Washington. School of Mineral Sciences, Stanford University, Cal.†◎

13 PARK, James Grant. Petroleum (Solvent). b'96. BS '19—MS '28 (Brooklyn Poly Inst). Original market research and development for petrochemicals; inter-relationships organic chemicals and their interrelationships regarding end uses; original research on use secondary alcohols, solvents, ketones derived from petroleum. With Standard Oil Co NJ since 1921, vp and gen sales mgr all divs Enjay Co Inc since 1938. Salesmen's Assn Am Chem Industry—Am Inst Chems—Soc Chem Industries—Comml Chem Development Assn. Enjay Company, Inc., 15 West 51st St., NYC 19.

14 PARK, Jay Boardman. Field crop breeding (Sweet corn, soybeans, sweet clover, oats). b'84. Student '04-06 (De Pauw U); AB '08—MS '12 (U Ill); ScD '16 (Harvard). Author articles in field. Prof agron O State U since '33. AAAS—O Acad Sci—Genetics Soc Am—Am Soc Agron—Soc Study Evolution—Am Soybean Assn (pres '38)—Sigma Xi. Received J Clarence Sullivan award '45. Ohio State University, Columbus, O.

15 PARK, John Howard. Electrical generation and measurement (High voltage surge). b'06. BS '28 (U Wash).

Research and development special high precision electrical measurement and improved methods of measurements, current transformers, AC-DC transfer instruments, generation and measurement of high voltage and high current surges. Co-author: Section I, The Standard Handbook for Electrical Engineers; also articles in field. Elec instrument sect Nat Bur Standards since '30. AIEE—Wash Acad Sci. National Bureau of Standards, Washington 25. H: 7815 Custer Rd., Bethesda 14, Md.

16 PARK, Joseph Dal. Fluorine (Chemistry); Sugar (Chemistry); Calorimetry (Chemistry). Born '06. BS in ChemE '29 (U Dayton O); PhD '37 (O State U). Synthesis and correlation physical and chemical properties fluorinated organic compounds; study of heats of reactions of organic halogen compounds; optical studies on arabinose and derivatives. Holds 20 patents in field, including process for preparation of fluorine compounds, and pyrolysis of polytetrafluoroethylene. Author articles: Synthesis of Tetrafluoroethylene '47. Co-author article: (with J R Lacher) Reaction Heats of Organic Fluorine Compounds '49. Contributor: Fluorine Chemistry '50. Research engr Frigidaire Corp Dayton O '29-33; research chem Jackson Lab DuPont & Co Wilmington Del '37-43, group leader fluorine research '43-47; asst prof chem U Colo '48, asso prof since '49. Colo-Wyo Acad Sci(chmn chem division '50)—AAAS—ACS—Sigma Xi—AAUP. Department of Chemistry, University of Colorado, Boulder.

17 PARK, Orlando. Animals (Ecology); Beetles (Pselaphidae). b'01. BS '25—PhD '29 (U Chicago). Author: Laboratory Manual of Animal Ecology and Taxonomy '39; A Study in Neotropical Pselaphidae '42. Co-author: Principles of Animal Ecology '49. Asst prof zool Kent Coll O '29-30; asst prof zool Northwestern U '34-37, prof since '42; sec and ed Biol Abstracts; hon curator zool Chicago Acad Sci. AAAS(F)—Entomol Soc Am(F)—Brit Ecol Soc—Am Soc Zool—Ecol Soc Am(pres '43)—Am Soc Naturalists—Panama Canal Zone Natural Hist Soc—Biol Soc Wash.H: 2201 Sherman Av., Evanston, Ill.†◎

18 PARK, Oscar Wallace. Honey bees; Floral nectars. b'89. '10-12 (Coll of Emporia); BS '17 (Kan State Coll); MS '20—PhD '(Ia State Coll). Developed technique for simple and rapid determination of sugar content of floral nectars; demonstrated with others existence of resistance to American foulbrood disease in honey bees, developed and made available to beekeeping industry strains of honey bees highly resistant to American foulbrood. Author articles: Studies on the Sugar Concentration of the Nectar of Various Plants '29; Variation in the Concentration of Floral Nectars '30; The Honeybee Colony—Life History '46; Activities of Honeybees '46, and others. Asso prof apiculture Ia State Coll and research asso prof apiculture Ia Agrl Expt Sta '25-48, research prof apiculture since '48. AAAS(F)—Am Assn Econ Entomol—Ia Acad Sci(F)—Am Beekeeping Fed—Iowa Beekeeper's Assn—Ia State Hort Soc—Phi Kappa Phi—Gamma Sigma Delta—Sigma Xi. Department of Zoology and Entomology, Iowa State College, Ames, Ia.

19 PARK, Richard Leonard. India (Modern history). b'20. SB '42 (Northwestern U); MA '48—PhD '51 (Harvard). Research on Indian nationalism in Bengal, growth of Pakistan, labor and politics and Indian trades unionism. Teaching fellow in govt Harvard '47-48, '49-50; fellow Social Sci Research Council '48-49; Middle E Inst

fellow '51-52; free-lance writer since '50. Am Polit Sci Assn—Royal Asiatic Soc Bengal—Hansard Soc(London)—Inst Pacific Relations—Middle E Inst. 11859 Edgewater Dr., Lakewood 7, O.

20 PARKE, Nathan Grier, III. Applied theoretical physics, mathematics and statistics (Electromagnetic theory, mechanics, optics, aeronautical theory). b'12. AB '34 (Princeton U); '40-41 (U Md Grad Sch); '41-42 (Johns Hopkins Sch Higher Studies); PhD '48 (MIT). Author: Guide to the Literature of Mathematics and Physics '47. Cons physicist pvt practice since '48; head applied math sect engring div aviation design research br Bur Aeronautics Navy Dept Washington '42-45. Inst Aeronautical Sci (asso F)—Am Math Soc—Am Phys Soc—Inst Math Statis—Am Statis Assn—AAAS—Optical Soc Am (asso)—Sigma Xi. 39 Main St., Concord, Mass.

21 PARKER, Alfred Browning. American architecture; Slum clearance (Florida). b'16. BS cum laude '39 (Fla U); student '39 (Royal Acad Stockholm). Author articles in field. Asso prof arch U Fla '40-47. Fla Arch and Allied Arts (dir)—AIA—Phi Kappa Phi. Awarded Fine Arts Society Gold Medal, Soc Four Arts Show first prize arch '38-39; Am-Scandinavian Found Exchange Scholar to Sweden '39; Pan-Am Airways Fellow to Mex '40-41. 2921 S. W. 27th Av., Miami 33, Fla.

22 PARKER, Dean Roberts. Genetics (Induced crossing over). b'13. BA '33—PhD '39 (U Tex). Author articles in field. Asst prof, asso prof biol dept U Miss since '47. Genetics Soc Am—Am Genetic Assn—Soc Study Evolution. Box 202, University, Miss.

23 PARKER, Garald Gordon. Ground-water hydrology; Salt-water encroachment; Geology of Florida. b'05. AB '35 (Central Wash Coll Edn); MS '40 (U Wash). Author articles in field. With US Geol Survey since '40, US Dist Geol So Fla Dist '46-48; field research geol US Geol Survey assigned to Atomic Energy Commn Hanford Engineer Works '48-49; sr geol '48; asst chief sect ground water geology US Geological Survey Wash since '49, principal geologist since '53. AAAS—Am Assn Petroleum Geol—Am Geophys Union—American Water Works Assn—Fla Acad Sci—Fla Engring Soc—Soc Econ Geol—Soil Sci Soc Fla. Awarded Gold Achievement Medal Fla Acad Sci '45. U.S. Geological Survey, Washington 25.

24 PARKER, Graham Woodward. Factory location; American manufacturing methods (Industrial decentralization, branch factories, United States regional industries). b'09. BA '29 (Yale); MBA '31—Sheldon Fellow '32 (Harvard). Has installed American manufacturing methods in more than forty overseas factories during the past fifteen years. Author surveys, articles and reports in field. Professional consultant to private industry on factory location and br plant prodn methods. ASME. 100 Park Av., NYC 17.

25 PARKER, Harry Clarence. Museology; Nature interpretation. b'06. Student '23-24 (Kan State Coll); '24-25 (Kenyon Coll); AB in zool '30 (U Kan); AM in geog '38 (Clark U). Member faculty Yosemite Field School for training interpretive naturalist; planning, adminstration natural history programs. Contributor articles to museum surveys and periodicals. Asso editor: Yosemite Nature Notes (monthly). Curator mammals U Kan '29-30; dir Mus Natural Hist Worcester Mass '30-40; from jr park naturalist to asso park naturalist Yosemite Nat Park '40-42, since '46. Am Orinthol Union(asso)—Am Soc Mammalogists—Am Nature Study Soc. Yosemite Museum, Yosemite National Park, Cal. H: Box 546.

10 PARKER, Ivy May. Cerrosion (Petroleum industry, fresh water). b'07. BA '28 (West Tex State Coll); MA '31—PhD '35 (U Tex). Author articles. Field technician Plantation Pipe Line Co Bremen Ga since '45. Nat Assn Corrosion Engrs (ed Corrosion since '45)—Am Inst Chem—Am Chem Soc—Electrochem Soc. Plantation Pipe Line Co., Box 423, Bremen, Ga.

11 PARKER, James Strong. Social security finance. b'00. AB '22 (Beloit Coll); MBA '28 (Northwestern U); PhD '41 (U Wis). Research and analysis financial principles, policies and problems associated with reserve accumulation for old-age and survivors' insurance programs and for retirement systems, analysis financial policy for comprehensive social security systems in US and foreign countries and issue of government contributions to social security programs. Author: Social Security Reserves '42. Asst prof econ U Wis Ext Div '35-43; econ Bur Research and Statis Soc Security Adminstrn '43-47, econ Bur Old-Age and Survivors Insurance since '47. Am Econ Assn—Am Finance Assn—Indsl Relations Research Assn—Am Soc Pub Adminstrn. Bureau of Old-Age and Survivors Insurance, Equitable Bldg., Balt 2. H: 107 Kent Rd., Glen Burnie 9, Md.

12 PARKER, John Albert. City and regional planning. b'09. Student '27-28 (U BC); SB '31—MArch '33—Master City Plan '45—student '45 (MIT). Author articles in field. Founder and head dept city and regional planning, research prof Inst Research Social Sci U NC since '46; planning cons. Am Soc Planning Officials—Am Planning and Civic Assn—Am Inst Planners (asso). Department of City and Regional Planning, University of North Carolina, Chapel Hill, N.C.†

13 PARKER, John Dyas. Marine snails (Fossil); Cave exploration (Safety). b'15. BS '39 (Rutgers U). Research on Florida Tertiary fossils; chairman National Shell Show '40-48; member editorial committees of Nautilus Magazine; research on safety and rescue work in cave exploration. Author articles: A New Cassis and other Mollucks from the Chipola Formation '48; Ostraea on Nassa '49; Safety Rules for Cave Exploration (pamphlet); How to Collect Shells '50. Contributor: Handbook of Speleology '52. Asst dept Mollusks Acad Nat Sci Phila since '46. Am Malacological Union—Nat Speleological Soc(chmn safety and equipment com, chmn Phila grotto—mem ed com)—AAAS.

14 PARKER, John Huntington. Plant breeding; Disease resistance in crop plants. b'91. BS '13 (U Minn); MS '16 (Cornell U); PhD '28 (Sch Agr Cambridge U Eng). Author articles in field. Plant breeder Kan State Coll '17-39; vis prof plant breeding Cornell U '31-32; dir Kan Wheat Improvement Assn '39-45; dir Midwest Barley Improvement Assn Milwaukee since '45. AAAS—Am Genetic Assn—Am Soc Agron—Sigma Xi. 828 N. Broadway, Milwaukee.†

15 PARKER, Johnson. Trees (Physiology, ecology). b'17. AB '41 (Harvard); MF '47 (Yale); Dr Forestry '50 (Duke Sch Forestry). Studies in transpiration and photosynthesis in tree seedlings; leaf structure, physical and chemical aspects; activity of de-

hydrogenases and other systems associated with normal cellular activity in tree leaves; on ecological factors affecting the natural range of various tree species. Staff botany U Ida since '49. Soc Am Foresters—Am Soc Plant Physiol—Ecol Soc Am—Sigma Xi—NW Sci Assn. Department of Biological Sciences, University of Idaho, Moscow.

16 PARKER, Kenneth G. Plant pathology; Fruit tree and virus diseases; Dutch elm disease (Epiphytology and control). b'06. AB '28 (De Pauw); PhD '34 (Cornell U); '40-41 (U Wis). Author articles in field. Asst prof dept plant path Cornell U '34-46, asso prof '46-51, prof since '51. Am Phytopath Soc—AAAS(F)—Sigma Xi. Dept Plant Pathology, Cornell University, Ithaca, N.Y.

17 PARKER, Malcolm Vernon. Ecology (Reptiles and amphibians); Worms (Parasitic); Reptiles and amphibians (Parasites). b'13. Student '32-33 (U Mich); BS '36 (Southwestern U); MS '39 (U Ga); '40-42 (Northwestern U). Research on natural history of amphibians and reptiles of midsouth, taxonomy and life cycles of trematode parasites of amphibians and reptiles. Author article: Notes on the Bird-voiced Tree Frog '50; others. Faculty S Coll Optometry '47-50; research herpetology since '51. Am Soc Ichthyologists and Herpetologists—Herpetologists League—Xi Phi Xi—AAAS—Soc Systematic Zool—Tenn Acad Sci. H: 683 N. Berclair Rd., Memphis 12.

18 PARKER, M a r g a r e t T(errell). European and Asian geography. b'92. BS '16—PhD '39 (U Chicago); MA '21 (Wellesley Coll); '21-22 (U Coll of Wales). Author: Lowell: A Study of Industrial Development '40. Co-author: Europe and Asia '27. Prof geol and geog Wellesley Coll. Soc Woman Geog—Assn Profl Geog—Am Geog Soc—Nat Council Geog Teachers. Department of Geography, Wellesley College, Wellesley, Mass.†

19 PARKER, Marion Wesley. Plant physiology; Photoperiodism. b'07. BS '28 (Hampden-Sydney Coll); MS '29—PhD '31 (Md U). Research on influence of photoperiods on differentiation of meristems and blossoming of biloxi soy beans, effectiveness of photoperiodic treatments of plants of different age, effect of variation in temperature during photoperiodic induction on initiation of flower primordia in biloxi soy bean, relationship between day length and crop yields, environmental factors and control in plant experiments, action spectrum for photoperiodic control of floral initiation of long- and short-day plants; physiology of Hevea, biosynthesis of rubber in Hevea. Author articles in field. Sr plant physiol US Dept Agr Bur Plant Industry '48-53; head dir rubber plant investigations since '53. Sigma Xi—Phi Kappa Phi—Am Soc Plant Physiol—Washington Bot Soc—Biol Soc Wash—Washington Acad Sci. Plant Industry Station, Beltsville, Md.

20 PARKER, Milton E(llsworth). Food engineering elements. b'99. SB '23 (MIT). Holder 13 US patents, one Canadian patent on food processing apparatus and methods, chem products. Author: Food Plant Sanitation '48; Elements of Food Engineering '52. Consultant food engineer Chicago since '44; dir and professor Illinois Food Engring Inst Tech since '48. Inst Food Tech (councilor)—Am Inst Chem(F)—Sigma Xi—Am Pub Health Assn(F)—American Chem Society—ASME—Internat Assn Milk and Food Sanitarians—Am Dairy Sci Assn (dir). 3300 S. Federal St., Chgo 16.

21 PARKER, Ralph Halstead. Tabulating machines (Library usage). b'09.

BA '29—MA '30—PhD '35 (Tex U); '36-37 (U Chicago). Introduced punched card methods into libraries, assisted in developing equipment for this purpose, developed records procedures for libraries utilizing tabulating equipment. Dir libraries U Ga '40-47; librarian U Mo since '47. ALA (library adminstrn com '36-41, library equipment com '41-43, '46-51, chairman '42-43, '46-48)—Mo Library Assn. 616 S. Glenwood, Columbia, Mo.

22 PARKER, Richard Anthony. Ancient Egypt (History, language and science). b'05. AB '30 (Dartmouth Coll); PhD '38 (U Chicago). Field director epigraphic and architectural survey Luxor Egypt '47-48. Author: The Calendars of Ancient Egypt '49. Co-author: Medinet Habu IV, Festival Scenes of Ramses III '40; Babylonian Chronology 626 BC-AD 45 '46. Wilbour prof Egyptology Brown U since '48. Am Oriental Soc—Egypt Exploration Soc—Internat Assn Egyptologists—Societé française d' Egyptologie. Brown University, Providence 12.☉

23 PARKER, William Riley. English literature (Milton, seventeenth century); Scriveners; English booksellers and printers (1557-1700). b'06. AB '27 (Roanoke Coll); MA '28 (Princeton); BLitt '34 (Oxford U). Author: Milton's Debt to Greek Tragedy in Samson Agonistes '37; Milton's Contemporary Reputation '40. Editor: The Dignity of Kingship Asserted '42; The MLA Style Sheet '51. Professor English NYU since '46. Modern Lang Assn (asso sec '46-47, exec sec since '47)—Bibliog Soc (London)—Bibliog Soc Am—Phi Beta Kappa. 6 Washington Square No., NYC 3.☉

24 PARKHURST, Charles Percy. Early Christian art; Medieval art; Color theories (History). b'13. AB '35 (Williams Coll); MA '37 (Oberlin Coll); MFA '41 (Princeton). Research on history of early Christian and medieval art. Author: Good Design Is Your Business '46. Asst curator and registrar Nat Gallery Art '41-43; asst curator Albright Art Gallery '46-47; asst dir art mus and asst prof art hist Princeton '47-49; chmn dept fine arts, dir mus and prof hist and appreciation fine arts Oberlin Coll since '49 Coll Art Assn Am—Archeol Inst Am—Am Soc Aesthetics—Am Assn Mus—Mus Dir Assn. Department of Fine Arts, Oberlin College, Oberlin, O.

25 PARKHURST, Douglas Llewellyn. Surveying and scientific instruments. b'93. BS '15—ME '26 (Worcester Poly Inst). Invention and development of scientific and surveying instruments for trigonometric surveys, earthquake recording, hydrographic and tidal surveys, precision levels and level rods. Was granted patents on time clocks, marine water samplers, grenade fuses, artillery bore sight. Author articles in field. Designer Ordnance Department Washington '17-21; associate engineer Bur Standards '21-23; gen engr US Coast & Geodetic Survey Washington since '23. Washington Soc Engrs—Washington Philos Soc. 1810 Commerce Bldg., Washington.

26 PARKHURST, Raymond Thurston. Poultry (Nutrition, husbandry). b'98. BSc '19 (U Mass); MSc '26 (U Ida); PhD '32 (U Edinburgh Scotland). Research on vitamin factors and protein sources for egg production and hatchability U Ida '20-27, vitamin A and D needs of poultry '32-38; investigation distillers' by-products, crab meal, fish meal, manganese, and excess calcium in laying and breeding rations; study of broiler feeds '43. Author articles: The Anti-Sterility Vitamin E and Poultry '27; Corn Dstillers' By-Products in

Poultry Rations '44. Co-author articles: (with Marie S Gutowska) Studies in Mineral Nutrition of Laying Hens '42; (with John W Kuzmeski) Supplements for Distillers' By-Products in Poultry Breeding Diets '46, and others. Head dept poultry husbandry U Ida '21-27; dir Nat Inst Poultry Husbandry Harper Adams Agr Coll Newport Eng '27-32; head dept poultry husbandry U Mass '38-44; dir research and nutritional service Flory Milling Co '44-49. Brit Poultry Edn Assn (1st pres)—World Poultry Sci Assn—Am Poultry Sci Assn—Am Dairy Sci Assn—Soc Animal Prodn—AAAS—Animal Nutrition Research Council—Sigma Xi—Phi Kappa Phi. Lindsey-Robinson & Co., Inc., Roanoke, Va. H: 2502 Wycliffe Av.

10 PARNELL, John Vaze, Jr. Embryology (Frog); Neural anatomy. b'15. BS '38—MA '40 (Boston U); AM '46—PhD '48 (Harvard). Neuroembryology. Prof zool Bennett Coll '43-44; inst zool Va State Coll '40-43, assoc prof '44-49, prof since '49. Va Acad Sci—AAAS—Sigma Xi. Virginia State College, Petersburg, Va.

11 PARRETT, Arthur Newton. Cellulose. b'96. BS (Chem E) '22 (U Minn); PhD '24 (U Pittsburgh). Research and development on manufacture purified forms of wood cellulose for chemical conversion processes used in production of rayon, cellulose acetate fiber, plastics, photographic paper, and film. Holds patents on manufacture wood cellulose and cellulose acetate. Contributor: Rayon Handbook '50. Research chem E I duPont de Nemours & Co '25-30; asst dir chem research A O Smith Corp Milwaukee '30-32; chem dir Rayonier Inc since '32. AICE—ACS—AAAS—Tech Assn Pulp and Paper Industry—Phi Lambda Upsilon—Tau Beta Pi. Rayonier, Inc., Shelton. Wash.

12 PARRISH, Charles Ithamer. Petroleum derivatives; Synthetic rubbers and resins. b'07. BS '30 (U Ill); MS '31 (U Va); PhD '33 (Northwestern U). Study on theory and mechanisms of reactions; applications of products. Author articles in field. Chief chem Pacini Cons Lab '33-34; publicity dept and research dept Universal Oil Co '35-36; research group leader Penn Salt Mfg Co '37-43; research supervisor B F Goodrich Co '43-50; U of Akron government labs since '50; patent law La Salle Ext U since '47. Am Chem Soc—AAAS—Sigma Xi. Univ of Akron, Government Labs., 351 W. Wilbeth Rd., Akron, O.

13 PARRISH, Fred Louis. History of religions and cultures. b'93. AB '17—MA '22 (Northwestern U); BD '20—seminar in Hebrew lit '20 (Garrett Bibl Inst); PhD '38 (Yale U). Introduced courses in ethics and religion in the public high school; also introduced upper division college courses in the history of religions, cultural history of Asia and courses in world cultures; research in history of religion. Author: The Classification of Religions '41. Co-author: (Syllabi) Man and the Cultural World I '45; Man and the Cultural World II '46. Co-editor: An Encyclopedia of Religion '45. Prof and head dept hist, govt Kan State Coll since '42. Nat Council on Religion in Higher Edn(F)—Hazen Found—Phi Kappa Phi (hon to faculty mem by faculty chapter of Soc). Kansas State College, Manhattan, Kan.

14 PARRISH, Mary Alice. International relations; Modern history and economics. b'86. AB '09—BS '11 (U Mo); summer '10 (U Chicago, '13 (U of Jena, Germany); '13-14 (U of London, London Sch of Econ, and Oxford U); '11-15—PhD '17 (Bryn Mawr Coll).

Lecturer on international relations for various organizations '38-48; participated in panel discussion at Inter-American Conference, Houston '48; at present preparing paper on the critical moment in American Revolution from world point of view, using manuscripts in Library of Congress. Author: Trade of the Delaware District Before the American Revolution '17; also articles in field. AHA—Am Geog Assn (F)—Polit Sci Assn—The Arctic Inst of N. A. Awarded European fellowship, Byrn Mawr Coll, 206 West State St., Vandalia, Mo.

15 PARRISH, Philip Hammon. Oregon history. b'96. Student '13-16 (Ore State Coll); '16-17 (U Wis). Chairman Old Oregon Trail Centennial Commission '42-43; toured occupation of Europe fall '46 and '47. Author: Before the Covered Wagon '31; Historic Oregon '37. Editor editorial page The Oregonian Portland since '39. Ore Hist Soc (dir). The Oregonian, Portland, Ore.

16 PARRY, Albert. Russia (Language, civilization). b'01. AB '35—PhD '38 (U Chicago). Author: Whistler's Father '39; Russian Cavalcade, a Military Record '44; also articles in field. Professor Russian civilization and lang Colgate U since '47. Am Assn Teachers Slavonic and East European Langs. Colgate University, Hamilton, N.Y.†

17 PARRY, John Jay. Arthurian romance; Welsh and Cornish literature; Geoffrey of Monmouth; Andreas Capellanus and courtly love. b'89. BA '12—MA '14—PhD '15 (Yale). Author: A Bibliography of Critical Arthurian Literature (vol I) '30, (vol II) '36; Vito Merlini '25; Brut y Brenhinedd '37; Andreas Capellanus, the Art of Courtly Love '41; The Welsh Texts of Geoffrey of Monmouth's Historia, Speculum V '30. Editor: The Poems and Amyntas of Thomas Randolph '17. Contbr to Ency Lit '46 and to Critical Bibliography of French Literature '47; prof English U Ill since '39. Modern Lang Assn—Medieval Acad (councillor '37-40)—Linguistic Soc—AAAS—Soc for Study Medieval Langs and Lit—Modern Humanities Research Assn—Internat Arthurian Soc—Hon Soc of Cymmrodorion. 216 Gregory Hall, University of Illinois, Urbana, Ill.◉

18 PARSONS, Coleman Oscar. Demonology and witchcraft; Misers; Folklore (Scotland); Scottish literature. b'05. Student '23-25 (U Cal Los Angeles); '25-27 (U Chicago); '28 (Columbia); PhD '31 (Yale). Studies on eccentrics and their money; interrelations folklore and literature; Scottish literature, the use of the supernatural in works by Scott, Stevenson, etc.; research projects in Scotland, England. US; papers on Twain, Coleridge, miser lore. Author 30 articles on Sir Walter Scott's use of the supernatural in fiction and poetry. Asst prof City Coll NY since '48. Modern Lang Assn. Internat Research fellow Huntington Library '35-36. City College of New York, Convent Av. and 139th St., NYC 31. H: 14 Grange Lane, Levittown, N.Y.

19 PARSONS, Douglas Eugene. Reinforced concrete; Masonry. b'94. AB '17—Civil Engr '22 (Cornell Coll). Author articles in field. Engr Nat Bur Standards Washington '23-30, chief masonry constrn sect '30-45, mineral products div '45-46, bldg tech div since '47. Am Concrete Inst (dir '41-49, vp '43-44, pres '45-46)—Am Soc Testing Materials—Bldg Res Advisory Bd of Natl Res Council—Am Ceramic Soc—Soc Exptl Stress Analysis—Am Assn Sci—Washington Acad Sci—ASCE—Am Standards Assn (chmn A-41 on

masonry). National Bureau of Standards, Washington.◉

20 PARSONS, Rhey Boyd. Educational teaching methods (Army, adult illiterates); Psychology of learning. b'92. BS '17—MA '23—PhD '35 (U Chicago). Civilian employee of War Department in Europe, branch chief in charge of German Elementary, Secondary, Vocational and Special Schools, Military Government Wurttemberg-Baden. Author articles in field. Prof edn Murray State Coll since '48. Am Ednl Research Assn—NEA(F)—AAAS (F)—Phi Delta Kappa—Kappa Delta Pi. Murray State College, Murray, Ky.

21 PARSONS, Willard Hall. Mineralogy; Petrography; Aggregates. b'11. BS '33 (Hamilton Coll); MA '35—PhD '36 (Princeton U). Author articles: Aggregate Reaction with Cement Alkalies '48; Some Properties of Materials Used for Jewel Instrument Bearings '47. Research on mineral products at Nat Bur Standards '41-46; professor Wayne U since '46, chmn dept geol since '48. Mineral Soc Am(F)—Geol Soc Am(F)—Am Geophy Union—Yellowstone-Bighorn Research Assn (pres '52-53)—Mich Geol Soc—Mich Mineral Soc (vice pres '48-49; pres '50-51)—Geol Soc Washington—Mich Acad Science—Sigma Xi—Phi Beta Kappa. Department of Geology, Wayne University, Detroit 1.

22 PARSONS, William Sterling. Atomic energy (Military applications); Atomic bomb. b'01. BS '22 (US Naval Acad). Commd ensign USN '22, advanced through grades to rear admiral '46; special asst to director OSRD for development radio proximity fuse '42-43; ordnance division leader, later asso director Atomic Bomb Project Los Alamos NM '43-45; flew with first atomic bomb to Hiroshima Japan '45; asst chief Naval Operations (spl weapons) '45-46; deputy for tech direction to Comdr Joint Task Force One (Operation Crossroads, Bikini tests of atomic bomb) '46; dir atomic defense Office Chief of Naval Operations, mem military liaison com to Atomic Energy Commn '46-49; deputy comdr Joint Task Force Seven (atomic tests at Eniwetok Atoll) '48; with weapons systems evaluations group of Joint Chiefs of Staff and Research and Development Bd '49-51; comdr cruiser div six Atlantic Fleet '51-52; dep chief Bur Ordnance since '52. Legion of Merit, Silver Star, Distinguished Service Med. US Naval Inst—Cosmos Club. Bureau of Ordnance, Navy Department, Washington.◉

23 PARTAIN, Lloyd Elmer. Soil conservation; Farm marketing. b'06. BS '32 (Okla A&M Coll); '39-41 (US Dept Agr Grad Sch). National planning committee and delegate to American Forest Congress '46; planning committee and editorial committee National Land Policy Conference '48. Author articles in field. Asst state coordinator Soil Conserv Service US Dept Agr Stillwater Okla '35-37; states relations officer Soil Conserv Service US Dept Agr '37-42; dir agrl div and asso field dir War Finance Div US Treasury Dept Washington '42-43; cons expert War Finance Div US Treasury '43-46; Country Gentleman research The Curtis Publishing Co Phila '43-45, mgr comml research div research dept '45-52, farm market dir Country Gentleman mag since '52. Soil Conserv Soc Am (first vp '47-48, nat pres '48-49)—Am Forestry Assn (bd dirs, exec com, vp)—Pa Forestry Assn—Farm Film Foundn—American Marketing Assn—Friends of the Land—NAM (vice chmn comm on timber, soil, water). The Curtis Publishing Co., Independence Square, Phila.

10 PARTRIDGE, Edward G(raffam). Latex technology. b'02. AB '24 (Oberlin Coll); PhD '27 (U Ill). Holder of patents in field of latex and dispersions. Author articles: Latex Compounds for the Paper Industry '48. Co-author articles: (with M E Hansen) Drying of Latex Rubber Deposits '48. Research chem B F Goodrich Co '27-41; research and development chem American Anode Inc '41-44, dir research '44-50, tech supervisor since '50. Am Chem Society—Am Society for Testing Materials—Phi Beta Kappa—Sigma Xi. 60 Cherry St., Akron 8, O.

11 PATAI, Raphael. Anthropology (Jewish and Near Eastern). b'10. PhD '33 (U Budapest); PhD '36 (Hebrew U Jerusalem); '30-31 (U Breslau). Author: Water: A Study in Palestinian Folklore '36; Man and Earth in Hebrew Custom Belief and Legend '42-43; The Science of Man: An Introduction to Anthropology (two vols) '47; Man and Temple in Ancient Jewish Myth and Ritual '47; On Culture Contact and Its Working in Modern Palestine '47; Israel Between East and West: A Study in Human Relations '53. Jerusalem science director Anthropol Inst of Israel since '44; vis prof anthrop U Pa '48-49; prof anthrop Dropsie Coll Phila since '48. Royal Anthrop Inst (Gt Br and Ireland)—Folk-Lore Soc (London)—Am Anthrop Assn(F)—Am Folklore Soc. Dropsie College, Phila.†

12 PATCH, Roland Harrison. Floriculture (Dahlia, iris, gladiolus, rose, tropical plants). b'88. BS '11 (Mass Agrl Coll); BS '11 (Boston U); MS '16 (Cornell). Superintendent Storrs American Dahlia Society Trial Garden 23 years; conducted trial gardens for Connecticut Gladiolus Society and American Iris Society. Chief gardner Nat Home Disabled Volunteer Soldiers '16-17; instr floriculture W Va U '17-18, asst prof '19-22; asst prof floriculture U Conn '22-29; asso prof '28-45; asso prof emeritus since '45; asso prof floriculture Hampton Inst '46-47; garden cons since '47. Dahlia Soc (life mem)—Conn Florists Assn—Mass Hort Soc—Am Soc Hort Sci. R.F.D. 2, Storrs, Conn.

13 PATE, William Wesley. Soils (Classification, chemistry, base exchange); Bananas (Soils, production). b'98. BS '24—MS '26 (Ala Poly Inst). Soil chemistry analysis classification Mexico Central America Jamaica Colombia; soil erosion management midwest states. Soil chemist United Fruit Co. Honduras '27-35; soil technologist conservation service USDA '35-38 sr soil scientist '38-46; prin soil scientist BPISAE since '46. Am Soc Agronomy—Soil Conservation Society Am—Soil Sci Soc Am. BPISAE Beltsville, Md. H: 4605 Harvard Rd., College Park, Md.

14 PATRICK, Austin L(athrop). Soil science, conservation and survey. b'89. Grad '09 (East Stroudsburg State Normal Sch); BS '13—MS '25 (Pa State Coll); PhD '31 (Cornell U). Research in soil erosion '34-37; in charge development of Soil Erosion Experiment Station Pennsylvania State College; served as regional conservator for Soil Conservation Service in Northeastern Region composed of twelve states '35-37. Co-author: Soil and Soil Fertility '24; also articles in field. Sci in soil surveys US Dept Agr '13-19; asst prof, asso prof, prof soil tech Pa State Coll '19-37; chief Div Watershed and Conservation Surveys Washington, Soil Conservation Service '37-39, asst chief in charge of phys surveys, econ surveys, project plans, cartographic, land management, instn adjustment '39-42, regional conservator for Region I directing activities of Service in twelve Northeastern States, hdqrs Upper Darby, Pa since '42. Am Soc Agronomy(F)—Soil Sci Soc Am—Friends of the Land—Soil Conservation Soc Am(F)—Sigma Xi—Phi Kappa Phi—Gamma Sigma Delta. Soil Conservation Service, 6816 Market St., Upper Darby, Pa.

15 PATRICK, John Max. Utopias; Utopianism. b'11. BA (U Toronto); BLitt—DPhil (Oxford U). Conducted research on utopian thought in the seventeenth century England, France, Canada and US '37-46. Author articles in field. Prof English University Fla '48-51, Queens Coll since '51. Queens College, Flushing 67, N.Y.†

16 PATRICK, Rembert Wallace. History of Florida and Southern United States. b'09. AB '30 (Guilford Coll); AM '34—PhD '40 (U NC); '26-27 (Maryville Coll); '30-31 (Harvard). Research collecting of historical material '44-45; studies of acquisition of Florida by US. Author: Jefferson Davis and His Cabinet '44 (Bohnenberger Award for best first book by Southern author '46); Florida Under Five Flags '45; also articles in field. Asst prof hist Meredith Coll '39-40; asst prof social sci Fla U '40-43, asso prof '43-45, prof since '45, prof hist since '48. So Hist Assn—Southern Polit Sci Assn (past sec-treas)—Fla Hist Soc (past dir, sec)—AHA. Award $500 PhD dissertation UNC '41. Faculty Bldg., University of Florida, Gainesville, Fla.

17 PATRICK, Ruth. Diatoms. b'07. BS '29 (Coker Coll); MS '31—PhD '34 (U Va). Research on ecology, taxonomy, nutrition and geological relationship of diatoms, on biological measurement of stream conditions. Prof bot Pa Sch Hort '35-46; curator limnol Acad Nat Sci Phila since '47. AA AS(F)—Bot Soc Am—Am Soc Plant Taxonomists—Am Limnol Soc—Sigma Xi—Internat Limnol Soc—Acad Natural Sci Phila. Academy of Natural Sciences, Phila 3.

18 PATTEN, Bradley Merrill. Embryology; Microscopical anatomy. b'89. AB summa cum laude '11—Chamberlin fellow '11-12 (Dartmouth); AM '12—PhD '14 (Harvard). Investigations in development of the heart, congenital defects of the heart; micromoving picture studies of first heart beats and beginning of the embryonic circulation. Author: The Early Embryology of the Chick '20; The Embryology of the Pig '27; Human Embryology '46. Author articles: The Changes in Circulation Following Birth '30; The Closure of the Foramen Ovale '44; Changes in Fetal Circulation Following Birth; Initiation and Early Changes in the Character of the Heart Beat in Vertebrate Embryos; others. Asso editor Am Jour Anat since '41. With Western Res U Med Sch '14-34, asso prof histology and embryology '21-34; asst dir for med scis Rockefeller Found '34-36; prof, head dept anatomy U Mich Med Sch since '36; vis investigator Carnegie Embryological Inst Baltimore '25, Path Inst Vienna '27; Nat Sigma Xi lectr '49-50. AAAS(F)—Am Naturalists—Am Soc Zool—Am Assn Anat(2d vp '34-36)—Marine Biol Lab—Phi Beta Kappa (hon)—Sigma Xi—Alpha Omega Alpha. H: 2126 Highland Rd., Ann Arbor.

19 PATTERSON, Bryan. Vertebrate paleontology (Fossil mammals). b'09. Student '23-26 (Malvern Coll, Eng). Expeditionary work collecting fossil animals in Colorado, Nebraska, Texas since '30. Research on the earlier tertiary mammals of North America, especially the orders Pantodonta, Dinocerata, Taeniodonta and Insectivora, and on the Tertiary mammals of South America. Author articles in field. Preparator paleontol Chicago Natural Hist Mus '26-30, asst '30-35, asst curator '35-42, curator since '42; lectr geol U Chgo since '45; John Simon Guggenheim Meml Found F '51-52. Goel Soc Am—Soc Vertebrate Paleontol (sectreas '46-48, pres '48-49)—Soc Study of Evolution—Sigma Xi. Chicago Natural History Museum, Chicago 5.

20 PATTERSON, George William. Calculating machines; Computers (Digital, large-scale, electronic logical, syntactical, data-handling); Machine languages. b'12. BS in elec engring '34 (U Vt); MA '36 (Columbia); '37-38 (Harvard); '44-46 (Am U); '46-51 (U Pa). Planning and design arithmetic circuits for electronic discrete variable computer; research on mathematical and logical theory of digital computers, and of analysis of calculation, control and switching networks and their relations to transformations in machine languages; developed principle permitting direct subtraction and addition to be combined in one circuit. Phys Nat Bur Standards '39-46; asst prof Moore Sch Elec Engring and head math engring sect Research Div U Pa '47-51; sr research engr and head analysis sect Burroughs Adding Machine Co since '51. Inst Radio Engrs (tech com on electronic computers)—Am Math Soc—Math Assn Am—Assn Symbolic Logic—Assn Computing Machinery—Franklin Inst (com sci and arts)—Sigma Xi—Phi Beta Kappa—Tau Kappa Alpha. Burroughs Adding Machine Co., 511 N. Broad St., Phila 23.

21 PATTERSON, Paul Morrison. Bryology (Bryophytes). b'02. AB '25 (Davidson Coll); AM '27 (U NC); PhD '33 (Johns Hopkins). Research on morphology and ecology of bryophytes. Presently engaged in a study of the bryophyte flora of Virginia. Author articles in field. Prof biol, dept head, chmn Div Natural Sci and Math, Hollins College since '34. Am Bryological Soc (pres)—Bot Soc Am—Ecol Soc Am—So Appalachian Bot Soc—AAAS—Va Acad Sci—Sigma Xi. Hollins College, Va.

22 PATTERSON, Richard Sharpe. Treaties of US; Seal of US; Unperfected treaties of US. b'08. AB '29—'29-31 (George Washington U). Research in records of Federal Government on treaties executive agreements international acts. Author articles: Seal of the United States '41; The Old Treaty Seal of the United States '49; The First Seal of the Department of State '49; The Seal of the Department of State '49. Prin asst to editor treaties US Dept State '29-44, acting editor treaties '44-48; historian Dept State since '48. AHA. Division of Historical Policy Research, Department of State, Washington 25.

23 PATTERSON, Samuel White. American revolution; Life and speech of Jesus; Education (Literature and reading). b'83. AB '03 (Coll City NY); MA '06—PhD '13 (NYU); AM '10 (Columbia U). Research on American Revolution, in lives of members of Continental Congress, life of Gen Horatio Gates and life of Gen Charles Lee; American literature; religion in first century of Christian Era, lives of Jesus Christ from John Mark to present day, study of possible speech-ways of Jesus; on education in reading as basic subject in our schools. Author: The Spirit of the American Revolution as Revealed in the Poetry of the Period, 1760-1783, '15; Famous Men and Places in the History of New York City '23; Old Chelsea and St Peter's Church '35; Horatio Gates, Defender of American Liberties '41; Junior High School Literature Series '28; **Teaching**

the Child to Read '30; Etchings in Verse '39; Centerless Education '24; What Language Did Jesus Speak? '46; also articles in field. Lecturer Am hist (1760-1875) NYC Bd Edn and elsewhere '09-25; head dept Eng NY Teacher Training Coll '20-30; asso prof '30-48; prof edn Hunter Coll since '48, spl lecturer Am history '43-44, acting dir evening and extension sessions '41-42. Mem ednl staff US Surgeon Gen '18. Schoolmasters Assn NY and Vicinity (pres '20-21)—NY State Hist Assn—AHA—Soc for Advancement Edn. Hunter College, 695 Park Av., NYC 21.◉

10 PATTERSON, Thomas L(eon). Physiology; Oro-physiology; Dental research. b'84. AB '09—AM '11 (Kansas City U); grad study '10-11 (Yale); MS '15—PhD cum laude '20 (U Chicago); ScD honoris causa '44 (Clark U). Asso prof biol and physiol U Md '12-15; asst prof physiol Queen's U Can '15-17, exptl physiol '17-19; asst prof physiol U Ia '19-21; prof and dir dept physiol Detroit Coll Med and Surgery (now Wayne U) '21-34, '34-41, research prof physiol since '41; prof physiol U Detroit '41-47, prof oro-physiol since '47, dir dental research since '48. AAAS (F)—Royal Soc Arts London(F)—Ia Acad Scis(F)—Am Physiol Soc—Can Physiol Soc—Detroit Physiol Soc(treas '37-39, councilor '37-42, pres '40-41)—Am Physiol Congress—Soc Exptl Biol and Med—Am Soc Zool—NY Acad Scis—Mich Acad Sci and Arts—Kingston Med Soc—Kingston and Frontenac Med Soc Can—Wayne Med Soc—Dr William Beaumont Meml Found Inc—Internat Assn Dental Research—Sigma Xi. A Cressy Morrison prize NY Acad Sics '31. 1512 St. Antoine St., Det. 26.†◉

11 PATTON, Francis Lester. Diminishing returns; Economics (General). b'91. AB '13 (O State U); BA '16—MA '19 (Oxford U Eng); PhD '20 (Columbia). Thirty years collection data on diminishing returns. Author: Diminishing Returns in Agriculture '26. Asso prof advancing to prof econ Hamilton Coll Clinton NY '20-51. Am Econ Assn—AAAS(F)—Royal Econ Soc(F). 2051 Iuka Av., Columbus 1, O.

12 PATTON, Odis Knight. Legislative procedure (Iowa). b'89. BA '12—MA '13—PhD '16—LLB '17 (U Ia); SJD '23 (Harvard). Editor: (with U G Whitney) Code of Iowa '24; Legislative Procedure and Practice in Iowa '40; also books and articles in field. With U Ia since '23, prof law since '27. Am and Ia State bar assns—State Hist Assn Ia—Order of Coif. 524 W. Park Rd., Iowa City, Ia.

13 PATTY, Ernest Newton. Placer mining; Gold dredging; Arctic mining geology. BS '19—EM '25 (U Wash). Research on stripping frozen muck, thawing gold bearing gravels; Mining engr Wash State Geol Survey '19-20; engr in charge Black Rock Mine Northport Wash '21; prof geol and mineral U Alaska '22-25, head sch mines '25-35; pres and gen mgr Gold Placers Inc and Alluvial Golds Inc Fairbanks Alaska since '35; pres and gen mgr Clear Creek Placers Ltd since '40, Yukon Gold Placers Ltd Yukon Ter Can since '46. AIMME—Am Mining Congress—NW Mining Congress—Alaska Miners Assn (past pres, dir)—Can Metal Mining Assn (dir)—Explorers Club NYC. College Center Bldg., 4556 University Way, Seattle 5.

14 PAUL, Benjamin D(avid). Ethnology. b'11. PhD '42 (U Chicago). Field research in San Pedro la Laguna Guatemala '40-41 and '46. Asst prof social anthropol dept social relations Harvard '48-51, lectr social anthrop sch pub health since '51. School of Public Health, Harvard University, Boston.†

15 PAUL, Rodman Wilson. Western American history; Economic and social history of United States. b'12. AB '36—AM '37—PhD '43 (Harvard). Research and writing on economic and social development of California. Author: The Abrogation of the Gentlemen's Agreement '36; California Gold: The Beginning of Mining in the Far West '47. Asso prof hist Calif Inst Tech '47-51, professor since '51. AHA—Miss Valley Historical Assn. Dabney Hall of Humanities, California Institute of Technology, Pasadena 4, Calif.†

16 PAUTZKE, Clarence Frederick. Life history of fresh water fish; Radio biology. b'07. BS '32 (U Washington). Co-author: (with R C Meigs) Studies on the Life History of the Puget Sound Steelhead '40, Additional Notes on the Life History of the Puget Sound Steelhead '41. With Game Dept State of Washington since '33, now chief fisheries biol; lecturer U Washington Fisheries Sch; Radiological Safety Sect, applied Fisheries Group, Bikini '46-47. Am Fisheries Soc—Limnol Soc Am—Pacific Fishery Biol. 509 Fairview Avenue N., Seattle 9.

17 PAWLOWSKA, Harriet. Polish-American folklore and folksongs. BS '39—MA '44 (Wayne U); summer '41 (U Ind). Author articles in field. Collected and recorded Polish folksongs, Detroit '40-43, Polish proverbs, legends and tales; Am Folklore Inst and seminar U Ind '41; translated Yakut riddles from Polish into English U Calif Berkeley '42; compiled bibliography of Polish folklore available in US for Am Library Assn, Am Assn Colleges joint study of comparative lit of world '43; community research work for U Wis Studies in Am Culture, Rockefeller Foundation, collected hist data on immigration into community from a Polish community in Upper Silesia '46-47; recorded Polish folksongs, folkways, religious songs in Lib of Congress and U Wis. Am Folklore Soc—Mich Folklore Soc—Badger Folklore Soc—Polish Am Hist Studies. Pershing High School, Ryan and Seven Mile Roads, Detroit 12. H: 951 Whitmore Rd., Detroit 3.

18 PAXSON, Alfred Moore. Industrial economics. b'02. Grad '21 (Staunton Mil Acad); '21-23 (Franklin and Marshall Coll); AB '27—MA '28 (Pa State Coll); PhD '33 (Cornell). Co-organizer Pennsylvania Rural Rehabilitation Corporation '34-35; professor business administration Tulsa U '35-36, organized college business administration and served as dean '36-44; director conference division National Industrial Conference Board '44-45; now administrative director Economic and Business Foundation; consultant National Resources Planning Board '42. Southwestern Social Science Association—Pi Gamma Mu—Gamma Sigma Delta. Economic and Business Foundation, New Wilmington, Pa.†◉

19 PAXTON, Avis Meigs. Hartley Burr Alexander; Henry Purmort Eames. b'95. Library science '16 (Carnegie Inst Tech); PhB '21 (U Chicago); Nature Guide '26 (Yosemite Field Sch); AM in arts '51 (Claremont Grad Sch Cal). Research on life of Hartley Burr Alexander from point of view of spiritual progress and development, achievements in fields of philsophy, mythology, anthropology, education, literature, and architectural symbolism; research in fine arts. Author: Hartley Burr Alexander, Architect and Builder of the Life of the Mind; Hans Sachs and the Nuremberg of His Day; Henry Purmort Eames. Editor:

Our Book Friends in Child Life Mag '22-28. Library Detroit Pub Library, Long Beach Cal Sch System Cal '22-50. Am Aesthetics Soc—Southwestern Archaeol Fedn—Am Anthropol Assn—ALA. P.O. Box 923, Long Beach, Cal.

20 PAYNE, Ben Iden. Shakespeare Memorial Theatre. b'81. Directed Stratford-on-Avon Festival Company at Shakespeare Memorial Theatre, England, '35-42. Guest prof drama various schs and at U Tex since '47. University of Texas, Austin 12.

21 PAYNE, Florence King. Tropical medicine and public health (West Indies). b'84. MD '09 (Syracuse U); Dr Sci in hygiene '23 (John Hopkins U). Research and writing on relative effectiveness of iron and anthelmintics in treatment usage; expeditions to Trinidad and Puerto Rico '21, '22; medical survey of Haiti '24-25; hookworm epidemiology and control Puerto Rico '26-40; volunteer investigator associated with projects supported by Internat Health Div Rockefeller Foundation in West Indies '21-40, volunteer investigator '49. Am Micros Soc. Room 5500, 49 W. 49th St., NYC 20.

22 PAYNE, Wilfred. Humanities (Logic); Pipe organ design. b'97. BA '22—MS '23—PhD '30 (U Wis); '23-25 (U Calif). Research on humanism logic and architectural design of organs. Author: Problems in Logic '26; New Problems in Logic '29; Examples of Architectural Style '48. Co-author: (with Margaret Stacy) A Study of Fallacies '25; also articles in field. Prof philos U Omaha since '31, head dept humanities since '32. Am Philos Assn. University of Omaha, Omaha 1, Neb. H: 5510 Howard St.†

23 PEABODY, Ernest H. Combustion engineering; Gas treatment. b'69. ME '90—DE honorary '48 (Stevens Institute Technology). Work in the combustion of fuels especially in burning oil fuel; expert in combustion problems. Developed and patented one of the first mechanical atomizers for oil fuel in America, which was widely used and adopted as standard by the US Navy; later first and original wide range Mechanical Atomizer; other inventions include combined oil and gas burners, air registers, combined burners for three fuels (simultaneously or singly). Author articles in field. Formed Peabody Engring Corp '20, pres NY, dir Peabody Ltd London. ASME—Soc Naval Architects and Marine Engr—Am Naval Engr. 580 Fifth Av., NYC 19.

24 PEABODY, William Alden. Liver and meat extracts; Commercial bile salt derivatives; Creatine. b'00. Student '18-19 (US Naval Acad); '19-20 (MIT); ChE '23 (Colo Sch Mines); MS '26—PhD '29 (U Colo). Author articles in field. Metallurg chemist Denver Rock-Drill Mfg Co '23-24; assoc in chem Med Coll Va '29-32; chemist tech dir, vp, to chem dir Valentine's Meat-Juice Co and Valentine Co Inc Richmond Va since '32. ACS—Va Acad Sci—Am Inst Chemists(F)—AAAS—Sigma Xi. Valentine Co., Inc., Box 1214, Richmond 9, Va.

25 PEACOCK, William Henry. Coloring agents (Dyes, pigments, stains, lacquers); Employee recreational activities; Social geriatrics. b'94. BS '20 (Cooper Union); '20-21 (Brooklyn Poly Inst); '21-22 (Columbia); '31-32 (Rutgers U). Development of industrial employee recreational activities and pre-retirement training programs 15 years. Author articles in field. Chemist Read Holliday and Sons Ltd NYC '13-15; asst supt dye prodn Holliday Kamp Co '15-21; dye chemist Sandoz Chem Co '22; tech ser application chemist and lab superv Calco Chem Div Am Cyanamid Co '23-42, asst lab mgr since '42. Am Assn Textile Chem and Colorists—Am Soc Cosmetic Chemists—Soc Plastics Engrs—Soc Plastics Ind—ACS. Calco Chemical Division, American Cyanamid Co., Bound Brook, N.J.

10 PEAK, J(ohn) Elmer. Judicial administration. b'88. Student '07-09 (U Chicago); AB '11 (Ind State U); LLB '12 (U Notre Dame). Studied judicial administration in all parts of the world, made more than twelve round trips to Europe, South America, The Far East and British Isles; originated and conducts a clinical method of training trial lawyers at Notre Dame. Author: The Tide of World Affairs '37, '38, '39. Jud Superior Ct South Bend Ind since '31; prof law U Notre Dame since '42. Am Bar Assn—Am Judicature Soc—Ind State Bar Assn. Decorated with Polish order of Haller's Swords. College of Law, University of Notre Dame, Notre Dame, Ind.⊚

11 PEARCE, George Whitenack. Insecticidal properties of petroleum oils, chemistry of arsenical insecticides; analysis of insecticides and spray residues, and animal tissues for presence of organic insecticides; synthesis of radioactive isotope labeled organic insecticides. b'07. BS '29—MS '30—PhD '46 (Pa State Coll). Research on chemical constitution of petroleum fractions and synthetic hydrocarbons to their insecticidal properties; study of chemistry calcium and other arsenates especially in relation to safety to host plants; analysis of insecticides, spray residues on fruits and vegetables, animal tissues for organic insecticide deposits; radioactive isotope labeling of DDT, parathion; studies of insect toxicology of organic insecticides including insect resistance to insecticides. Div chem NY State Agrl Expt Station, Cornell U '30-51, asso prof chem '45-51; chief chem sect, tech development br Communicable Disease Center USPHS since '51. ACS—AAAS—Am Assn Econ Entomol (Gold medal award '40, '42, 48)—Sigma Xi—Phi Lambda Upsilon—Gamma Sigma Delta. Technical Development Branch, Communicable Disease Center, P.O. Box 769, Savannah, Ga. H: Box 282, Savannah Beach, Ga.

12 PEARCE, Thomas Matthews. Folklore (Southwestern US); Vocabulary, pronunciation (Southwestern US); English Renaissance, Christopher Marlowe. b'02. AB '23 (U Mont); AM '25—PhD '30 (U Pittsburgh); '28 (U Cal); '29 (U Chicago); '42 (U Pa). Studies in regional American English vocabulary and pronunciation of Southwest; literature, fiction, poetry of Southwest. Author: America in the Southwest '33; Lane of Llano '36; Southwesterners Write '47; Southwest Heritage, a Literary History with Bibliography '48; Signature of the Sun, Southwest Verse '50; and others. Author articles: The English language in the southwest; Christopher Marlowe, Figure of the Renaissance; and others. Editor: New Mexico Folklore Record since '47; New Mexico Place Name Dictionary since '48; (contributing) Western Folklore. With U NM since '27, prof since '40, head English dept '40-51. Am Dialect Soc—Modern Humanities Research Assn—MLA—Rocky Mountain Modern Lang Assn—Coll English Assn—AAUP—Phi Kappa Phi—Am Folklore Soc—NM Folklore Soc. Department of English, University of New Mexico, Albuquerque.

13 PEARDON, Thomas Preston. British Empire governments; History of political thought. b'99. BA '21 (U British Columbia); MA '22 (Clark U); '22-23 (Cornell); PhD '33 (Columbia). Author: The Transition in English Historical Writing 1760-1830 '33. Co-author: Modern World Politics '45. With dept govt Barnard Coll since '23, prof since '45. Canadian Hist Assn—Am Polit Sci Assn—AHA—Canadian Polit Sci Assn—Acad Polit Sci. William Bayard Cutting fellow in England '29-30. Barnard College, Columbia University, NYC 27.

14 PEARL, Irwin A(lbert). Sulfite waste liquor; Lignin; Vanillin chemistry; Vanillic acid. b'13. BS '34—MS '35—PhD '37 (U Washington). Research on rapid method for the determination of sulfite waste liquor in sea water '40; vanillin from lignin materials by oxidation with copper oxide '41, vanillic acid esters as food preservatives '45, conidendrin from western hemlock sulfite waste liquor '45, slime control with mercurated vanillin and lignin derivatives '46-48. Author articles in field. Research Asso Inst Paper Chem since '41. Am Chem Soc—AAAS—Sigma Xi. The Institute of Paper Chemistry, Appleton, Wis.†

15 PEARL, Richard Maxwell. Gemology; Mineralogy; Geology of Colorado. b'13. BA '39—MA '40 (U Colo); AM '46 (Harvard). Author: Nature As Sculptor: A Geologic Interpretation of Colorado Scenery '48; The Art of Gem Cutting '45; Mineral Collectors Handbook '47; Popular Gemology '48; also articles in field. Asst prof geol Colo Coll since '46. Am Gem Soc (certified gemologist)—Colo Mineral Soc (co-founder '36, sec-treas '36-42, pres since '48)—Rocky Mt Fed Mineral Socs (founder '41, pres '41-42)—Gem Assn Gt Brit(F)—AAAS—Mineral Soc Am—Colo-Wyo Acad Sci—Am Geo Soc(F)—Gem Assn Australia (hon vp since '46)—Am Crystallographic Assn—Am Fed Mineral Soc (co-founder '47, vp '47-48, pres since '48)—Phi Beta Kappa—Sigma Xi. Colorado College, Colorado Springs, Colo.

16 PEARSALL, David Edelblute. Blasting fuses; Thermal aerosols; Chemistry of explosives; Plastic waterproofings and insulations. b'99. BS '22—Chem E '30 (U Pa). Research on burning mechanisms in small trains; modification and control of powder burning speeds by metalic oxides, polyvinyl alcohols; developed, patented clover fuses, petrolatum wax-ester gum moistureproofings; vaporization and dispersal of aerosols by thermal methods. Author articles in field. Invented Cordacide method DDT dispersion by controlled heat, holds US and foreign patents. Research chem engr Atlas Powder Co Tamaqua Pa '22-23; research chem engr, plant foreman Vulcan Detinning Co Pittsburgh '23-26, Western Elec Co Chicago '26-30; Ensign-Bickford Co indsl fellow Mellon Inst Pittsburgh '30-41, dir and treas Bickford research labs Avon Conn since '41. Am Chem Soc—Am Inst Chem Engrs—Textile Research Inst—Conn Nat Soc Profl Engrs—Am Soc Testing Materials—NY Acad Sci—Sigma Xi. Avon, Conn.

17 PEARSE, C(harles) Kenneth. Grazing management; Range reseeding and ecology. b'07. BS '30—MS '32—'32-34 (U Chicago). Author articles in field. Chief div range research Southwestern Forest and Range Expt Sta Tucson Ariz since '48. AAAS—Ecol Soc Am—Am Soc Agron—Soc Am Foresters—Am Soc Range Management. Southwestern Forest and Range Experiment Station, Box 951, Tucson, Ariz.†

18 PEARSON, Allen Mobley. Game management. b'09. BS '31 (Ala Poly Inst); MS '32—PhD '36 (Ia State). Research on life history and foods of mourning dove, management and foods in southeast of bobwhite quail, foods in southeast US for red and grey fox, white-tailed deer, wild turkey. Author articles in field. Asso biol US Fish and Wildlife Service '36-43; specialist Ala Ext Service '43-47; asso prof Ala Poly Tech since '47. Wildlife Soc Am—Am Soc Mammalogists—Am Ornithol Union—Sigma Xi. Department of Zoology, Alabama Polytechnic Institute, Auburn, Ala.

19 PEARSON, Anthony A(ugustus), Jr. Anatomy of nervous system; Embryology. b'06. BS '28 (Furman U); AM '30—PhD '33 (U Mich). Research on functional components of the cranial nerves, comparative anatomy of nervous system of man and other animals. Author articles in field. Asso, asst prof anat Loyola U '37-43; vis asst prof anat U Tenn '41; asso prof anat Baylor U Coll Med '43-46; prof anat U Ore Med School since '46, head dept anatomy since '52. AAAS(F)—American Assn Anat—Sigma Xi. Univ of Oregon Medical School, Portland, Ore.

20 PEARSON, Harold Earl. Ornamental plants (Soil salinity); Ion exchange; Water treatment (Softening). b'14. BS '35 (U NM); PhD '51 (U Cal). Research on effects of water spreading on rangeland soils, effects of irrigation water quality on soil salinity, growth of ornamental plants (azaleas, begonias, camellias) effects of sodium on citrus, use of zeolites and other ion exchanges for water treatment, especially water softening. Author articles in field. Research agrl chem Metropolitan Water So Calif since '42. Am Chem Soc—Am Soc Hort Sci—Am Soc Agronomy—Soil Sci Soc Am. Metropolitan Water District, Box 38, La Verne, Calif.†

21 PEARSON, Jay Frederick Wesley. Apidae; Marine zoology; Biological exhibits. b'01. BS '25—MS '26 (U Pittsburgh); PhD '32 (U Chicago). Member Arcturus expedition '25, Guiana Expedition '24; in charge biological exhibits Century of Progress, Chicago '31-33; in charge biological exhibits of University of California at Golden Gate Exposition '38-39. Author articles in field. Prof zool U Miami since '33, vp since '47. AAAS(F)—Am Soc Zool (asso mem)—Fla Acad Sci (pres '41-42)—Fla Basic Sci Bd—Sigma Xi. 1329 Alhambra Circle, Coral Gables, Fla.⊚

22 PEARSON, Oliver Payne. Mammalogy (Taxonomy, ecology and anatomy). b'15. AB '37 (Swarthmore Coll); MA '40—PhD '47 (Harvard). Research on habits and reproduction of Peruvian mammals, metabolism of small mammals, reproduction of furbearing mammals; associate expeditions Panama Academy Natural Science Philadelphia '37, '38; expedition to Peru for Harvard Museum Comparative Zoology '39-40, '46. Author articles in field. Research Civilian Pub Service '41-45; instr zool U Calif since '47. Am Soc Mammalogists. Museum of Vertebrate Zoology, University of California, Berkeley.†

23 PEARSON, Paul Brown. Animal nutrition and biochemistry (Mineral metabolism, vitamins, fat relation to protein and amino acid metabolism). b'05. BS '28 (Brigham Young U); MS '30 (Mont State Coll); PhD '37 (U Wis). Author articles in field. Prof animal nutrition Agr and Mech Coll Tex since '37, grad prof since '41, head dept biochem and nutrition and dean Graduate School since '47; chief biology branch US Atomic Energy Commission since '49. AAAS(F)—Soc Animal Production—Soc Exptl Biol and

Med—Biochem Soc, London—Am Chem Soc—Inst Nutrition—Soc Biol Chem. Division of Biology and Medicine, Atomic Energy Commission, Washington 25.

10 PEARY, Joseph Ygor. Water buffaloes (Biology and husbandry); Bioeconomic problems (Agriculture, conservation and medical hygiene). Author: Les Buffles. Alderson-Broaddus College, Philippi, W.Va.

11 PEASE, Clarke Demorest. Farms (Mechanized operation); Roadside markets (Farm produce distribution). b'95. AB '11 (Lewis Inst); BS '15 (Yale); grad modern prodn '44 (MIT). Developed mechanization farm operations, processing raw material at farm into retail form, distribution through organized roadside markets; member President Roosevelt's commitee on Decentralization; governor Agricultural Industrial Marketing Foundation. Author: Creating Jobs Through a More Efficient System of Distribution. Chief engr for conversion WPB '42-43; head indsl engr Bur Econ Warfare '43-44. ASME—Soc Advancement Management—Am Soc Agrl Engrs—Am Acad Polit and Social Sci—Alpha Delta Phi. See Latest Listings and Sketch Additions.

12 PEASE, Murray. Art conservation; Treatment of paintings. b'03. AB '26 (Harvard). Author articles in field. Curator tech lab Metropol Mus Art since '41. NY Acad Sci—Am Assn Mus—NY Athenaeum. Fellow in conservation Fogg Art Mus Harvard '36-41. Metropolitan Museum of Art, Fifth Av. and 82nd St., NYC 28.†

13 PEATMAN, John Gray. Psychology in radio; Psychometric methods. b'04. BA '27—MA '28—PhD '31 (Columbia). Research on application of psychology of attitude and opinion to analysis and improvement of radio and television programs. Author: Descriptive and Sampling Statistics '47; Listener Attitudes Towards Radio Broadcasts (with T Hallonquist) '45; Diagnosing Your Radio Program (with Hallonquist) '47. Editor: Radio and Business; also articles in field. Tutor psychol CCNY '29-31, instr '31-35, asst prof '36-42, asso prof '42-47, prof since '48, asso dean since '44; chmn com Nat Radio Awards '45-47; pres Office of Research Inc NYC since '41. Am Psychol Assn (F, chmn, com student affiliates '45-46, chmn conf State Psychol Assn '47-48)—Am Assn Applied Psychol (bd affiliates '41-45)—NY State Assn Applied Psychol (pres '46-47, bd dir '41-49)—Eastern Psychol Association—Am Statis Assn—Phi Beta Kappa—Sigma Xi. City College of New York, NYC 31.

14 PECHUMAN, L(aVerne) L(eRoy). Tabanidae (Horseflies). b'13. BS '35—MS '37—PhD '39 (Cornell U). Author articles in field. Dist mgr Calif Spray Chem Corp for western NY, Ontario, Quebec since '47. Am Assn Econ Entomol—Entomol Soc Am—Entomol Soc Canada—Sigma Xi. California Spray Chemical Corporation, Medina, N.Y. H: 7 Davison Rd., Lockport, N.Y.†

15 PECK, David Cameron. Antique automobiles; Automobile history. b'12. BS '35 (Northwestern U). Restoration and research all types self-propelled road vehicles, steam, electric, gasoline. Curator transportation Mus Sci and Industry Chicago since '42; trustee Larz Anderson Mus Brookline Mass since '49. Antique Automobile Club Am (pres)—Sports Car Club Am (pres)—Veteran Motor Car Club Am—Horseless Carriage Club—Veteran Car Club of Great Britain—Vintage Sports Car Club of Great Britain—Sports Car Club of Australia. 140 W. Ontario St., Chgo 10.

16 PECK, Ralph Brazelton. Soil mechanics. b'12. CE '34—DCE '37 (Rensselaer Poly Inst). Research on measurements of pressures and movements in connection with foundations, tunnels, retaining walls and other structures resting on or in earth materials. Co-author: Soil Mechanics in Engineering Practice '48; Foundation Engineering '53. Rsrch prof soil mech U Ill since '42. ASCE (recip Norman Medal '44)—Am Railway Engring Assn—Am Institute Consulting Engineers—Nat Soc Profl Engrs—Highway Research Bd—Sigma Xi—Tau Beta Pi—Phi Kappa Phi. 113 Talbot Laboratory, University of Illinois, Urbana, Ill.†

17 PECK, Raymond E(lliott). Stratigraphy and micropaleontology of nonmarine formations (Charophyta, Ostracods); Paleozoic and Mesozoic Crinoidea. b'04. AB '26 (Park Coll); PhD '32 (U Mo). Author articles in field. With U Mo since '30, now prof geol. Geol Soc Am(F)—Paleontol Soc Am(F)—Am Assn Petroleum Geol. 208 Swallow Hall, Columbia, Mo.†☺

18 PECK, William Fuller. Microscopes; Ordnance instruments; Projection instruments; Measurements (Opthalmic, optical). b'08. AB '32 (Dartmouth Coll). Design, development, production engineering, and application of scientific optical instruments. Holds 45 patents in field. Development engr optical instruments Am Optical Co (formerly Spencer Lens Co) '36-40, chief development engr '40-43, mgr development sci instrument div '43-48, mgr mfg instrument div since '45. Optical Soc Am—Am Ordnance Assn—Am Soc Metals. American Optical Co., Instrument Division, Box A, Buffalo 15.

19 PECKHAM, George Taylor, Jr. Corn; Cornstarch (Derivatives); Lactic acid. b'06. BS in agr '27 (U Mo). Associate referee Association Official Agricultural Chemists; corn collaborator US Northern Regional Laboratory. Granted patents on manufacture of sirups. Contributor: Chemistry and Industry of Starch '44. With Clinton Foods Inc since '30, research dir since '46. ACS—AAAS—Am Leather Chem Assn—Inst Food Tech—Soc Chem Industry Brit—Am Assn Cereal Chem. Clinton Foods, Inc., Clinton, Ia.

20 PECKHAM, Robert H(amilton). Blindness (Color); Vision (Night); Sun Glasses (Visual acuity); Physiological optics. b'08. BA '30 (U Rochester NY); PhD '33 (Johns Hopkins). Research on night vision, color blindness, visual acuity through sun glasses; phosphors for television and fluorscopy; visual aspects of automobile driving. Author articles: Report of a Case of Total Color Blindness '32; Binocular Vision '36; Protection of Night Vision '49; Visual Acuity Thru Sun Glass Lenses '49, and others. Fellow Nat Research Council '33-34; asso prof research ophthal sch med Temple U '34-40 and since 46. lectr biostatistics since '46. Comdr USNR, OSRD vision com Bur Med and Surgery '40-45. Optical Soc Am—Sigma Xi—Phi Beta Pi. Temple University School of Medicine, Phila. 40.

21 PECORA, William Thomas. Geology (Petrology). b'13. BS '33 (Princeton); PhD '40 (Harvard). Field and laboratory investigations of the petrology, mineralogy, economic geology and general geology in areas in Montana, Washington, Oregon, Alaska and Brazil. Author articles in field. Geologist US Geol Survey Washington since '39. Geol Soc Am(F)—Mineral Soc Am(F)—Sigma Xi. U.S. Geological Survey, Washington 25.

22 PEDERSEN, Marion Walter. Alfalfa (Breeding, seed production, nectar production, pollination). b'16. BSc '41—MSc '42 (U Neb); PhD '52 (U Minn). Assisted development large portable cages for use in studying alfalfa pollination; assisted in formulation alfalfa seed production recommendations; investigation processes for examining and breeding alfalfa for seed production; also in development use of bumble bee colonies for controlled pollination. Co-author articles: (with F E Todd) Pollinating the Alfalfa Seed Crop '48; (with F E Todd) Selection and Tripping in Alfalfa Clones by nNectar-Collecting Honey Bees '49 (with staff) Growing Alfalfa for Seed in Utah '50. Forage crop research USDA since '46. AAAS—Am Soc Agron—Sigma Xi. US. Legume Seed Research Laboratory, Logan, Utah.†

23 PEDERSEN, Tage Viggo. Diesel engines (Opposed piston). b'02. Student '20-23 (Tech Coll Copenhagen). Co-designer opposed piston diesel engine, research on installation, operation and maintenance diesel engines, invented variable beginning fuel injection pump and car engine heater. Development engr spl projects Fairbanks Morse & Co; gen partner Roscoe (Ill) Industries. Soc Automotive Engrs. Fairbanks, Morse & Co., Beloit, Wis. H: Chestnut St., Rocie, Ill.

24 PEEBLES, Bernard Mann. Latin literature (Fourth to sixth centuries AD); Latin paleography. b'06. Student '21-22 (Hampden-Sydney Coll); BA '26 (U Va); AM '28—PhD '40 (Harvard); Diploma '34 (Am Acad in Rome). Author: The poet Prudentius '51. Co-editor: Servianorum in Vergilii carmina commentariorum volumen II. Asso prof Greek and Latin Catholic U since '48. Served US Army '42-45, chief clerk subcommn for monuments fine arts and archives Allied Commn Italy. Am Philol Assn—Medieval Acad Am. Box 206, Catholic University, Washington 17.†

25 PEEBLES, Robert Hibbs. Cotton (Breeding); Arizona (Plants). b'00. Assisted in production two new varieties long staple cotton. Co-author: (with Thomas H Kearney and collaborators) Flowering Plants and Ferns of Arizona '42. Author articles: Preservation of Cactus Material '42; Pureseed Production of Egyptian-type Cotton '42. Co-author articles: (with Thomas H Kearney) Arizona Plants: New Species, Varieties and Combinations '39; (with H J Fulton) Ratooned SxP Cotton '44, and others. With Bur Plant Industry USDA since '20, supt field sta Sacaton Ariz since '45. Cactus and Succulent Soc Am(F)—Am Soc Agron—Bot Soc Am. US Field Station, U.S. Department of Agriculture, Sacaton, Ariz.

26 PEERY, Paul Denver. Carillons (Electronic). b'06. Student '23-24 (Lenoir-Rhyne Coll Hickory NC); BS '28 (US Mil Acad). Research on history and types of electronic carillons, their use, methods of playing electronic instruments, and musical acoustics. Author: Chimes and Electronic Carillons '48. Cons electronic carilloneur Maas Cathedral Chimes Co Los Angeles; carilloneur San Diego Calif. Tchr creative writing Coronado Cal '37-52; lectr U Cal Writing Conf since '52. H: 1414 Tenth St., Coronado, Cal.†

27 PEET, Louise J. Household appliances; Kitchen planning; Home Lighting. b'85. AB '08—MA '11 (Wellesley Coll); PhD '29 (Ia State Coll). Research on selection, cost of operation of household appliances, research on remodeling kitchens and improving home lighting. Co-author: (with Lenore Sater Thye) Household Equipment (3rd edit) '49. Prof, head household equipment dept Ia State Coll since '30. Phi Beta Kappa—Sigma Xi—Sigma Delta Epsilon—Omicron Nu. Home Economics, Iowa State College, Ames, Ia.†

10 PEEVY, Fred Alton. Range conservation. b'17. BS '40—'43-44 (La State U). Research on grazing values on southern pine lands, weed control, poisoning undesirable hardwoods. Author articles in field. Mem research and expt div US Dept Agr Forestry Service since '45. Am Soc Agron—La Forestry Assn. P.O. Box 1192, Alexandria, La.†

11 PEI, Mario Andrew. Old French literature (Religious and Epic works of ninth to thirteenth centuries); Romance philology; Italian language (History); International languages; Comparative linguistics. b'01. AB '25 (Coll City of NY); PhD '32 (Columbia). Associate editor of Symposium, Romanic Review, Modern Langauge Journal. Author: The Language of the Eighth-Century Texts in Northern France '32; The Italian Language '41; Languages for War and Peace '44; The World's Chief Languages '48; French Precursors of the Chanson de Roland '48; The Story of Language '49; The Story of Eng Swords of Anjou '53. Asst prof romance langs Columbia '37-47, asso prof romance philol '47-53 prof romance philol since 53. Modern Language Assn—NY State Fedn Modern Lang Tchrs—Am Assn Tchrs French—Am Assn Tchrs Italian—Linguistic Circle NY—Phi Beta Kappa. Columbia University, NYC 27.

12 PEIKER, Alfred Louis. Colloids; Dyes, pigments. b'03. BS '25—MS '27 (Trinity Coll Hartford Conn); PhD '30 (McGill U). Research on colloidal aspects of dyes, pigments, dyeing procedure and theory; surface area of pigments in relation to pigment properties and performance. With Calco Chem Div Am Cyanamic Co Bound Brook NJ since '34, mgr dyes tech service lab '45-48, asso dir application research dept since '48. Am Assn Textile Colorists and Chemists—Tech Assn Pulp and Paper Industry—ACS—Comml Chem Developments Assn—Soc Dyers and Colourists Eng. Calco Chemical Division, American Cyanamid Company, Bound Brook, N.J.

13 PEIRCE, Josephine Halvorson (Mrs Frank D Peirce). Antique stoves and cooking utensils. b'88. Student (Mass Art Sch, Eric Pape Art Sch). Studies on evolution and history from earliest stove types, patents, manufacturing, design, ingenuity. Author: Fire on the Hearth '49; also articles in field. Free lance feature writer subjects pertaining to general antiques; food ed Worcester Telegram-Gazette since '31; mgr Worcester Better Bus Bur Inc since '40. Early Am Inds Assn (apptd ed The Chronicle '49). 32 Franklin St., Worcester 8, Mass. H: 51 Paxton St., Leicester.

14 PEITHMANN, Irvin Milton. US archeology (Southern Illinois). b'04. Ed pub schs. Research on archeological mounds, village sites of southern Illinois, mapping and photography of sites. Author articles: Evidences of Early Woodland Culture at Chalk Bluff Rock Shelter '38; Some Recent Hopewell finds in Southern Illinois '47; others. Curator archeol S Ill U Mus since '49. Ill State Acad Sci—S Ill Hist Soc—Ill State Archeol Soc (sec, dir; Gold award and citation '40). Research Ill State Archeol Soc. Midwest Mus Assn. Southern Illinois University Museum, Carbondale, Ill.

15 PELL, John Howland Gibbs. Ticonderoga and Lake Champlain history.

b'04. Student '22-26 (Harvard). Author: Life of Ethan Allen '29; also articles in field. Director of Fort Ticonderoga Museum since '26; investment counsel John H G Pell & Co Inc since '32; exec other orgns. Am Antiquarian Assn—NY Hist Soc—NY State Hist Soc—Vt Hist Soc. Soc Colonial Dames Am award work in Colonial hist '30. 1 Wall St., NYC.

16 PELZER, Karl J(osef). Economic and regional geography (Southeast Asia, tropics, Pacific area); Pioneer settlement; Tropical land utilization. b'09. PhD '35 (U Bonn). Member economic survey of former Japanese mandated islands '46. Author: Arbeiterwanderungen in Sudostasien '35; Economic Survey of the Pacific Area, Part I, Population and Land Utilization '41; Pioneer Settlement in the Asiatic Tropics '45. Research asst Inst Pacific Relations '38, research asso PI and Netherlands Indies '40-41; sr regional specialist Far Eastern Br OWI '44-45; agrl econ Office Fgn Agrl Relations US Dept Agr '45-47; professor geog Yale U. Am Geog Soc—Assn Am Geography—Inst Pacific Relations—Far Eastern Assn. 29 Cooper Road, North Haven, Conn.

17 PENDELL, Elmer. Population. b'94. BS '21 (U Ore); MA '23 (U Chicago); PhD '29 (Cornell U). Research on diminishing returns from land, differential birth rate, displacement theory of population, marriage laws as tools for social control of reproduction. Author: Population on the Loose '51. Co-author: (With G I Burch) Population Roads to Peace or War '45; Human Breeding and Survival '47. Contributor: Society Under Analysis '43. With Baldwin-Wallace College since '46. American Econ Assn—Am Soc Human Genetics —Human Betterment Assn Am—Population Assn Am. Department of Economics, Baldwin-Wallace College, Berea, O.©

18 PENDLETON, Robert Larimore. Tropical soils; Laterite; Siam (Agriculture). b'90. BS '14—PhD '17 (Calif U). Member soil surveys Mindanao Exploration Commission, Philippines, to locate refugee colonies for displaced persons, commission to locate cinchona plantations in Costa Rica; represented Gwalior State on Indian Board Agriculture and Indian Central Cotton Committee; research on ravine reclamation in Gwalior State, Central India, soils of Siam, results of termite activity in Siamese soils, laterite and uses as structural material in Siam and Cambodia; reforestation in Philippines with Ipilipil; soils of Central America, Ecuador, Peru and Brazil, field work '43-49. Soil scientist Office Fgn Agrl Relations US Dept Agr since '42; prof tropical soils and agr Isaiah Bowman Sch Geog, Johns Hopkins U since '47; adviser in agr FAO mission to Siam '48, head of mission '50-52. Am Chem Soc—Am Soc Agron—Am Soc Soil Sci—Am Geog Soc (hon)—Am Geophys Union—Siam Soc Bangkok—Sigma Xi. Department of Geography, Johns Hopkins University, Balg. 18.†©

19 PENFOUND, William T(heodore). Plant ecology; Aquatic plants; Malaria control. b'97. AB '22 (Oberlin Coll); AM '24—PhD '31 (U Ill). Author articles in field. Prof Tulane U '27-47; prof plant sci U Okla since '47; malaria cons TVA. AAAS—Bot Soc Am (chmn sect G '46)—Ecol Soc Am —La Acad Sci—Okla Acad Sci. Dept. Plant Sciences, University of Oklahoma, Norman, Okla.†

20 PENN, Dorothy. Medieval French drama; American history (Early French settlers in Missouri). b'99. BS

'19—AB '20 (U Mo); MA '28 (Columbia); PhD '32 (U Wis). Author: Staging of the Miracles de Nostre Dame par personnages '33; also articles in field. Head modern lang dept Mary Baldwin Coll Staunton Va since '46. Modern Lang Assn Am—Am Assn Teachers French—Am Assn Teachers Spanish—Modern Lang Assn Va (ed bull '47-48). Mary Baldwin College, Staunton, Va.†

21 PENN, William Y. Petroleum geology. b'08. AB '29—MA '31 (Stanford U). Petroleum exploration; evaluation of oil and gas producing properties. Cons geol since '35. Am Assn Petroleum Geol—Mid-Continent Oil and Gas Assn—Tex Independent Producers and Royalty Owners Assn—AIMME—Sigma Xi. 21 Permian Bldg., Midland, Tex.

22 PENNAK, Robert William. Lake and stream biology; Limnology (Colorado); Rotatoria; Fresh-water invertebrates. b'12. BS '34—MS '35—PhD '38 (U Wis). Author articles in field. Professor biol U Colo since '49; vis investigator Woods Hole Oceanog Inst Woods Hole Mass '39. Am Soc Limnol Oceanog. Biology Department, University of Colorado, Boulder, Colo.†

23 PENNEBAKER, Edwin Noel. Geology of copper deposits in western United States, Cuba, and South Africa; Exploration for copper ore bodies. b'02. BS '24 (U Cal). Interpretation of leached outcrops of copper mineralization; studies of relations of ore bodies to geologic structure; outline exploration programs in search of copper ores. Chief geol and cons geol Consol Coppermines Corp since '28; cons geol Minas de Matahambre SA '38-43, O'okiep Coppper Co Ltd Union of South Africa since '46. AIMME—Mining and Metall Soc Am—Can Inst Mining and Metall—Soc Econ Geol—Geol Soc S Africa. Scottsdale, Ariz.†

24 PENNEY, Clara L(ouisa). Incunabula; Rare Spanish books and manuscripts. BS '12 (Simmons Coll). Author: Luis de Gongora y Argote '26; List of Books Printed Before 1601 in the Library of the Hispanic Society of America '29; List of Books Printed 1601-1700 in the Library of the Hispanic Society of America '38; Catalogue of Publications of the Hispanic Society of America '43. Bibliog Hispanic Soc Am since '19. AHA—AAAS —Hispanic Soc Am. Recipient Mitre Medal Hispanic Soc Am '37. 788 Riverside Dr., NYC 32.

25 PENNINGTON, Roy Platt. Soil fertility; Clay minerals. b'18. BSA '42 (Ont Agrl Coll) PhD '49 (U Wis). Research on fertilization for establishment and maintenance forage and pasture crops; study preparation soil clays for quantitative analysis by x-ray diffraction. Co-author articles: (with A L Willis, M L Jackson) Mineral Standards for Quantitative X-Ray Diffraction Analysis of Soil Clays '47; (with M L Jackson) Segregation of the Clay Minerals of Polycomponent Soil Clays '47; (with M L Jackson, W Z Mackie) Crystal Chemistry of Soils '48; (with M L Jackson, S A Tyler, A L Willis, G A Bourbeau) Weathering Sequence of Clay-Size Minerals in Soils and Sediments '48. Research asst soils dept U Wis '46-49; asst prof soils Pa State Coll since '49. Am Soc Agron —Soil Sci Soc Am—Sigma Xi. Agronomy Department, Pennsylvania State College, State College, Pa.

26 PENNINGTON, William Alvin. Steel (Decarburization, alloys); Refrigerants (Purification, azeotropes, thermodynamic properties); Refrigeration (Dehydration of systems). b'04. BS in chem '25 (Union U); PhD '33 (Ia

State Coll). Discovered mechanism of decarburization of solid steel, developed extra-soft corrosion-resistant alloy, invented new refrigerant, research on various means of dehydration including chemical desiccants. Research engr Armco Steel Co '35-40; indsl F Mellon Inst Indsl Research '40-44; chief chem and metall Carrier Corp since '44. Alpha Chi Sigma—Phi Lambda Upsilon—Sigma Xi—ACS—Am Soc Refrigerating Engrs—Electrochemical Soc—Am Soc Metals (Howe Medal '47) —AAAS(F)—Am Inst Chem—Am Inst Chem Engrs. Carrier Corp., Syracuse 1, N.Y.

10 PENNOYER, Charles Huntington. Community planning; Intergroup relations. b'78. Student '93-96 (St Francis Coll); grad '99—DD '37 (Tufts Div Sch); spl studies '00-03 (Harvard and Columbia); summer study '26 '28 (Britain and Continent); LittD '44 (U Vt). Author: Engineering for Brotherhood '17; The Spiritual Laboratory '19; Confession of Social Faith '29; The American Code of Nobility '30; The Traveler's Goodwill Code '37; Teaching and Technique of Liberalism '38; The Cure and Prevention of Prejudice '39; The U.F. and the U.N. '47; One World and You '49; O Ye of Great Faith '50; and others. Exec sec Universal Fellowship, interpersonal movement for interfaith and intercultural unity and informal fellowship, since '46. Am Geol Soc(F)—Royal Econ Soc(F)—Royal Soc Arts Ft Brit(F)—AAAS—Am Acad Polit and Social Sci—Am Sociol Soc—Ethical Soc—others. 14 John St., Valley Falls, R.I.

11 PENQUITE, Robert. Poultry nutrition (Minerals and hormones); Poultry genetics. b'97. BS '22—MS '28 (Okla A&M Coll); PhD '36 (Ia State Coll). Co-author: (with others) Laboratory Exercises in Poultry Husbandry; also articles in field. Prof poultry husbandry Ia State Coll, Ames, Ia since '48. Poultry Sci Assn—Okla Acad Sci—Louis Research Soc—Sigma Xi.

12 PENROD, E(stel) B(urdell). Refrigeration; Heat transfer; Heat pumps; Soils (Thermal properties). b '90. BS in mech engring '15—MS in phys '20 (Purdue U); MME '23 (Cornell U). Research on discoloration of meat while in storage, research on measurements of thermal diffusivity in soils by use of heat pump. Research engr Armour Research Found '42-46; head dept mech engring U Ky since '46. Am Soc ME—Am Inst Phys—Sigma Xi—Ky Acad Sci(pres '50-51)—Ky Soc Profl Engrs. University of Kentucky, Lexington 29.

13 PENTLER, Charles Frederic. Food yeast; Food problems of densely populated areas. b'10. BS in food tech '34 (MIT); PhD in microbiol '40 (U Cal Berkeley). Chairman regional foreign service committee Am Friends Service Committee(Quakers) since '46, special studies food problems of Japan in effort to solve these problems in interest of promoting peace. Food tech Golden State Co Ltd '41-44, Lyons-Magnus Inc '45-49; cons chem since '50. Am Acad Polit and Social Sci—Am Beekeeping Fedn—ACS—Am Dairy Goat Register—Am Inst Pacific Relations—Am Pub Health Assn—Apis Club England—Inst Food Tech—Northern Nut Growers Assn—Population Assn Am—Rural Life Assn—Soc Am Bact. H: 1322 Martin Av., Palo Alto, Cal.

14 PEPINSKY, Abe. Psycho-acoustics; Music in industry. b'89. BA '31—MA '32 (U Minn); PhD '39 (U Ia). Author articles: Contributions of Science to an Appreciation of Music

'43; Physical Dynamics in Music '44; The Growing Appreciation of Music and Its Effect Upon the Choice of Music in Industry '44, and others. Guest conductor Minneapolis Symphony Orchestra '13-40, and others; prof psychol and head dept Haverford Coll since '45; cons psychol USN Electronics Lab. Acoustical Soc Am—Acad Sci Minn and Ia—Am Musicol Soc—Sigma Xi. Haverford College, Haverford, Pa.

15 PERETTI, Ettore Alex James. Non-ferrous extractive and physical metallurgy. b'13. BS—MS '35 (Mont Sch Mines); ScD '36 (Wuerttemberg Inst Tech); '35 (U Hamburg). Author: A New Method for Studying Mechanism of Roasting '48; An Analysis of Copper Converting '48. Prof metall and head dept Metall Univ Notre Dame since '51. AAUP—AIME—ASM—ASTM —ASEE—Sigma Xi—Tau Beta Pi. Internat exchange fellow to Germany '35-36. Box 145, University of Notre Dame, Notre Dame, Ind.†

16 PERKINS, Clarence Basil. Herpetology (Breeding, rearing). b'88. Student '07-13 (Princeton U). Author articles: The Snakes of San Diego County with Descriptions and Key '38; A Key to the Snakes of the United States '40; Notes on Captive-bred Snakes in Copeia '43. Herpetologist Zool Soc San Diego since '32. Am Soc Ichthyologists and Herpetologists — Herpetologist's League(F)—San Diego Soc Nat Hist (F, past pres)—AAAS. Zoological Society of San Diego, Box 551, San Diego 12, Calif.†

17 PERKINS, Ernest Ralph. International relations and diplomatic history of the United States. b'93. AB '17 (Wesleyan); AM '21—PhD '30 (Clark). Author chapter on The Nonapplication of Sanctions Against Japan 1931-32, in Essays in History and International Relations '49. Associate professor history Norwich University '22-30; asso in hist research US Dept State '30-36; ed Foreign Relations of the United States since '36; detached to Am Embassy London '44-45; attache office US polit adviser on German affairs SHAEF '45. American Historical Assn—Am Soc Internat Law. Div. Hist Policy Research, U.S. Department of State, Washington 25.†

18 PERKINS, G(eorge) Holmes. Town and country planning in Great Britain; Planning of new towns. b'04. AB '26—MArch '29 (Harvard). Editor of Journal of American Institute of Planners since '49. Author articles: Britain's New Towns; New Towns for America; Britian Plans; Theory and Reality (Framingham Study); Our Future Cities, and others. Contributor: Form and Functions of 20th Century Architecture '51. Asso prof architecture Harvard '40-45, Norton prof regional planning '45-51; acting dir div urban development Nat Housing Agency '44-45; cons to Ministry of Town and Country Planning Gt Brit '46; dean sch fine arts U Pa since '51. AIA—Am Inst Planners—Am Soc Planning Ofcls. School of Fine Arts, University of Pennsylvania, Phila. 4.

19 PERKINS, John Sheperd. New England industrial history. b'11. AB '32 (Mt Union Coll, Alliance O); MBA '34 (Boston U). Author: (with Ralph G Wells) Trends in New England Industries '35; New England Community Statistical Abstracts '37, '39, '42; also articles in field. Controller, asst treas and sec Wm Filene's Sons Co since '46. Am Statis Assn—Am Econ Assn—Nat Assn Cost Accountants—Am Management Assn. 426 Washington St., Boston.

20 PERKINS, Milo Randolph. Foreign investment; Point Four program. b'00. Ed pub schs. Committee work in foreign investment and Point Four Program, International Chamber of Commerce, New York and Paris. Author article: What We Can Now Do Under Point Four '50. Asso adminstr AAA and pres Fed Surplus Commodities Corp since '39; dir marketing USDA since '50, adminstr Surplus Marketing Adminstrn 'r0; chmn US sect Joint War Prodn Com, US and Can '41-42; exec head Econ Defense Bd '41; exec dir Bd Econ Warfare '41; fgn trade cons since '44. 1200 18th St NW, Washington.†◎

21 PERKINS, R. Marlin. Herpetology; Venoms b'05. Student (U Mo). Research on herpetology of Arkansas, venomous and harmless snake bites, intelligence of gorillas and their growth rates. Author: Animal Faces '44. Author articles: (with Clifford Pope) Differences in the Patterns of Bites of Venomous and Harmless Snakes '44, and others. Curator reptiles St Louis Zoo '26-38; gen curator Buffalo NY Zoo '38-44; dir Lincoln Park Zoo Chicago since '44. Am Soc Icthyologists Herpetologists. Lincoln Park Zoo, Chicago 14. H: 519 W. Barry Av.

22 PERKINS, Ralph Newton. Swimming pools (Design, water filtration systems). b'83. Ed pub schs. Design and construction diatomaceous earth filtering system for swimming pools employing vacuum principle; improvement pressure type diatomaceous earth filtering system. Holds patent on vacuum sand filter system for swimming pools. Author: Swimming Pool Operators Manual '50. Author articles: Sediment Removal from Swimming Pools '46; The Municipal Swimming Pool '47; Some Aspects of Diatomite Filter Design '49, and others. Nat Soc Profl Engrs—Neb Soc Engrs—Omaha Engrs Club. Registered profl engr Neb. 2884 Newport Av., Omaha.

23 PERKINS, Rollin Morris. Criminal law and procedure; Police science. b'89. AB '10 (U Kan); JD '12—SJD '16 (Harvard). Author: Cases on Criminal Procedure '29; Iowa Criminal Justice '32; Manual for Iowa Peace Officers '39; Elements of Police Science '42; Police Examinations '47; Criminal Law Enforcement '48, and others; also articles in field. Frank C Rand prof law Vanderbilt U '46-49; prof law U Cal Los Angeles since '49. Am Law Inst—Inst Criminal Law and Criminology—State Bar Tenn—State Bar Calif —Am Acad Polit Social Sci—Phi Beta Kappa—Order of Coif. University of California School of Law, LA 24.

24 PERRETEN, Paul H(arrison). Taxes; Legislation. b'00. AB '22—LLB '26 (U Mo). Research on taxation and corporation law. Law practice and lectr on law '26-36; atty Farm Credit Adminstrn '33-36; vp managing ed Found Press Inc '37-38; exec dir Citizens Pub Expenditure Survey Ill '39-40; Tax Found '40-44, dir research '42-44; legislative analysis Am Enterprise Assn '44-49, exec vp since '49; law practice since '47. 475 Fifth Av., NYC 17.

25 PERRY, Ben Edwin. Ancient fiction and folklore; Aesopic fable. b'92. AB '15—AM '16 (U Mich); PhD '19 (Princeton). Author: The Metamorphoses Ascribed to Lucius of Patrae '20; Studies in the Text History of the Life and Fables of Aesop '36; Aesopica '52; and articles. Co-author: Index Apuleianus '34. Asst prof classics U Ill '24-28, asso prof '28-41, prof since '41. Am Philol Assn—Am Oriental Society. Guggenheim fellow '30-31. 126 Lincoln Hall, Urbana, Ill. H: 504 **Vermont** Av.

10 PERRY, Bruce A(llen). Vegetable breeding for increased production, quality, disease and insect resistance (Onions, spinach, tomatoes). b'09. BS '30—MA '36 (Wake Forest); '37-38 (Duke U); PhD '42—rsrch fellow '38-42 (U Va). Author articles in field. Hort vegetable breeding Tex Agrl Expt Sta since '46. Bot Soc Am —Genetics Soc Am—Am Genetics Assn —Am Soc Hort Sci—Sigma Xi. Texas Agricultural Experiment Station, Winter Haven, Tex.

11 PERRY, Clay. Speleology (New England, New York, Virginia, West Virginia); Roleo (Log birling). b'87. Student '08-11 (Lawrence Coll). Explorer of over 200 caverns and caves in New England, New York State, Virginia and West Virginia. Author: Underground New England—Tall Tales of Small Caves '39; New England's Buried Treasure '46; Underground Empire '48; also articles in field. Freelance writer since '18. Outdoor Writers' Assn Am—West Va Hist Soc— Nat Spelol Soc (chmn folklore com, organizer and first pres NE Grotto '40) Nat Roleo Assn (dir). 109 Wendell Av., Pittsfield, Mass.†

12 PERRY, E. J. Artificial insemination of dairy cattle. b'91. BS '16 (Pa State Coll; MA '28 (Columbia). Study artificial insemination experiments in Denmark; pioneered organization first artifical breeding association in America '38, assisted organization in Puerto Rico; assisted in formulation of rules governing artificial insemination of purebred, registered dairy cows, and establishment system of record-keeping to safeguard artificial breeding of both grade and purebred cattle. Author: Among the Danish Farmers. Editor: The Artificial Insemination of Farm Animals. Dairy specialist WVa U '20-23; ext specialist diary husbandry Rutgers U and U NJ since '23. Am Dairy Sci Assn (chmn breeding com)—Am Soc Animal Prodn. USDA superior service award '49; DeLaval award ($1000 and scroll) for achievements in dairy hsubandry extension. Dairy Department, Rutgers University, New Brunswick, N.J.

13 PERRY, (Lorin) Edward. Aquatic and fishery biology; Impounded waters; Limnology; Salmon; Malaria control. b'14. Student '32-34 (U Utah); '37-38 (Brigham Young U); BS '39 (Utah State Agrl Coll); PhD '43 (U Mich). Author articles in field. Aquatic biol US Fish and Wildlife Service Portland since '46. Am Fisheries Soc —Am Soc Limnol Oceanog—Am Society Ichthyol-Herpetol—AAAS—Sigma Xi— Phi Kappa Phi—Pacific Fishery Biol. U.S. Fish and Wildlife Service, Swan Island, Portland 18, Ore.

14 PERRY, James Whitney. Surface active agents (Detergents, synthetic soaps, washing agents); Russian technical language (Chemical nomenclature); Chemical information methods. b'07. Student '23-24 (USC); BS— MS '28 (NC State Coll); SM '32 (MIT); '32-33 (Technische Hochschulen Stuttgart and Berlin). Author: Chemical Russian, Self-Taugh '48; An Introduction to Scientific Russian '49. Co-author: Surface Active Agents, Their Chemistry and Technology '49. Co-editor: Punched Cards and Scientific Information Problems '49; also articles in field. Library fellow chem dept MIT '45-49, asso prof modern lang dept since '49; ballistician Ballistic Rsrch Lab Aberdeen Proving Ground '42-45; research chem Nat Aniline Div Allied Chem and Dye Corp '33-42. Am Chem Soc (abstractor for Chem Abstracts since '32, chmn punched card com since '46, program chmn chem lit group and Chem Lit Div since '45).

Consultant member Gmelin Institut fur anorganische Chemie und Grenzgebiete since '48. Room 14 S 312 Massachusetts Institute of Technology, Cambridge 39, Mass.†

15 PERRY, Thomas Doane. Plywood and veneer; Woodwork adhesives; Woodworking machinery; United States stamped envelopes. b'77. AB '97 (Doane Coll); BS '00 (MIT). National Wood Utilization Committee '26-33. Author: Guide to US Stamped Envelopes '40; Modern Plywood '42, '48; Modern Wood Adhesives '44. Tech editor: Veneers and Plywood '26; also articles in field. Vice-pres, mgr Grand Rapids Veneer Works '11-24; cons engr Bigelow Kent Willard Co Boston '25-29; works mgr engr New Albany Ind Veneering Co '29-34; engr housing projects New Albany and Jasper Ind '34-36; development and sales engr Resinous Products and Chem Co Phila '36-47; now with Rohm & Haas Company Phila; chmn glue com, Central Com on Lumber Standards since '45. Am Philatelic Soc—Philatelic Library Assn— US Envelope Soc—ASME(F)—United Postal Stationery Soc. 301 E. Main St., Moorestown, N.J.

16 PERRYMAN, James Dale. Petroleum exploration. b'11. Student '28-29 (Colo Coll); geol engr '35 (Colo Sch Mines). Research on interpretation of seismic data from steep dip and fault problems. Seismic observer and computer Ark-La Gas Co '35-37; with Geotech Corp since '37, vp since '50, bd dir Geotech Fgn Corp. Am Assn Petroleum Geol—Soc Exploration Geophys. 3712 Haggar Dr., Box 7166, Dallas 9. H: 6414 Lake Hurst, Dallas 5.

17 PERSHING, Benjamin Harrison. American history (Revolutionary, Confederation, westward movement, Ohio). b'88. AB '12 (Wittenberg Coll); AM '21 (U Pittsburgh); PhD '27 (U Chicago); '47 (U Minn). Author: The Ordinance of 1787 '49; also articles in field. Prof hist Wittenberg Coll since '39, dean of men '26-39, dean of students '39-45. AHA—Miss Valley Hist Assn—So Hist Assn—O State Archeol and Hist Assn—Archeol Inst Am—Fgn Policy Assn—Academico Correspondiente de la Academia de la Historia de Cuba. Awarded cash prize $1,000 by Fed Commn for Sequicentennial of settlement of the Old Northwest for manuscript The Ordinance of 1787 '38. Wittenberg College, Springfield, O.

18 PERSING, Ellis Clyde. Forest conservation; Science education (Tchr training); Photography (High school and college). AB '11 (Bucknell U); MS '26 (U Chicago); '31-32 (Columbia). Author: Elementary Science by Grades (6 vols) '32. Co-author: Work Book in General Science '27. Editor-in-chief: The Classroom Guide '29. Contributor: Childcraft (vol 9) '46. Asst prof natural sci W Reserve U '21-36, lectr sci edn Cleveland Coll since '36; with sci dept W Tech High Sch since '36. Ohio Acad Sci—Nat Sci Tchrs Assn—Nat Assn Research in Sci Teaching—NEA—Central Assn Sci and Math Tchrs—Photog Assn Am—Photog Soc Am. H: 3316 Warrington Rd., Cleve. 20.

19 PERSONS, C(hristopher) E(dgar). Public relations (College and university). b'82. BL '01 (O Wesleyan U). Author: Public Relations for Colleges and Universities—A Manual of Practical Procedure '45. Director pub relations San Francisco Employers Council since '36, Stanford U since '36. 114 Sansome St., San Francisco 4. H: Route 1, Box 724, Los Altos, Calif.

20 PETER, Alfred Meredith. Soil technology. b'57. Student '72-78 (Ky U); BS '80—MS '85 (Agrl and Mech Coll Ky); ScD hon '13 (State Coll Ky).

Author articles in field. Asst chem and chem Ky Agrl Expt Sta '86-08, chief chemist '09-11, head chem dept '12-27, acting dir '16-17; supervising chem Ky Geol Survey '04-12; prof soil tech State U Ky '10-27, prof emeritus since '27. AAAS(F)—Am Inst Chemists(F). Experiment Station, Lexington 29, Ky.

21 PETERING, Harold G(eorge). Pterines; Antimetabolites; Plant lipids. b'10. BS '34—grad study (U Chicago); PhD '38 (U Wis). Research on experimental tumor chemotherapy, biochemistry of animal tumors, tumor-host interaction; biochemistry of folic acid and animal protein factor B12, chemistry of pteridines; xanthine oxidase, biochemistry of enzyme antegonists, anti-metabolites; stabilization of carotene and vitamin D$_3$. Isolated new provitamin and vitamin D from modiolus demissus Dillwyn; plant lipids. Granted patents on recovery and separation of carotene and plant lipids, stabilization of carotene in plant tissue and feedstuffs. Author articles in field. Asst prof agrl chem Mich State Coll '38-41; research chem Biol Lab duPont Co '41-45; group leader biochemistry Upjohn Co since '45. Am Chem Soc— AAAS—Sigma Xi—Phi Beta Kappa— Gamma Alpha—NY Acad Sci. Upjohn Company Research Laboratory, Kalamazoo, Mich.

22 PETERS, Frazier Forman. Low cost stone and concrete masonry. b'93. ChemE '16 (Columbia). Research in improving Flagg method of stone construction, concrete integrally faced with stone. Patent applied for on improved method of integrally insulating and waterproofing masonry walls. Author: Houses of Stone '33; Without Benefit of Architect '37; Pour Yourself a House '49; also articles in field. Pres Peters-Violet Builders '20-31; supervising architect Glen Goin Development Alpine NJ '32-49; pres Tensit Houses Inc Warwick NY since '47; owner dir Points of View a farm colony in Warwick since '36. Points of View, Warwick, N.Y.

23 PETERS, Harold Seymour. Birds of Newfoundland; Mourning dove; Ectoparasites of wild birds. b'02. BS '25—MS '26 (O State U). Adviser to Newfoundland government on wildlife problems, study of mourning dove in eastern US, research on Mallophaga of birds. Co-author: (with T D Burleigh) Birds of Newfoundland '51. Asst entomol Va Truck Expt Sta '26-27; asst entomol US Bur Entomol '28-35; in charge Ala Coop Wildlife Research Unit '35-37; Atlantic Flyway biol Fish and Wildlife Service '37-48, research biol from '48. Am Ornithol Union—Wilson Ornithol Soc—Ga Ornithol Soc—Arctic Inst—Wildlife Soc— Sigma Xi. Fish and Wildlife Service, Peachtree & Seventh Bldg., Atlanta 5.

24 PETERS, Isaac Isaac. Blue cheese; Microbial lipase; Homogenized milk. b'10. BSA '42 (U Manitoba Winnipeg Can); MS '44 (Mich State Coll); PhD '47 (Ia State Coll). Manufacture of blue cheese from pasteurized, homogenized milk, and ripened with aid of microbial lipase produced by Candida lipolytica; discovery electric attraction between fat globules and leucocytes in milk. Author articles: The Role of Leucocytes in the Sediment Formation in Homogenized Milk (thesis) '44; The Lipolytic Enzyme System of Mycotorula lipolytica (thesis) '47. Co-author articles: (with G M Trout) The Attraction Between the Fat Globules and the Leucocytes of Milk '45; (with F E Nelson) The Influence of Mycotorula lipolytica Lipase upon the Ripening of Blue Cheese made from Pasteurized Homogenized

Milk '48. Research asst prof dairy industry Ia State Coll '48-50; now asst prof dairy husbandry dept A&M Coll Tex. Am Dairy Sci Assn—Soc Am Bact—Inst Food Tech—Sigma Xi. Dairy Husbandry Department, A&M College of Texas, College Station, Tex.

10 PETERS, Theodore Frank. Farm equipment (Rototiller). b'10. BS '33 (Valpariso U); diploma '37 (Refrigeration Air Conditioning Inst, Chicago). Re-designed and adapted to mass production original Swiss-made Rototiller, machine for preparing aerated seed bed ready for immediate planting in one operation. With Graham-Paige Motors Corp '35-46, engr charge farm equipment div '45-46; lab supervisor, test and exptl engr Gen Motors Diesel Research '37-44; with Gar Wood Industries Inc since '46, tech asst to vp engring since '47. SAE—Am Ordnance Assn. Gar Wood Industries, Inc., Wayne, Mich.

11 PETERSEN, Frederick Adolph. Porcelain enamels. b'13. BS '37 (U Ill); MSc '39 (O State U). Author articles in field. Setting up process control Florence Stove Co '41-42; research U Ill '42-51. Am Ceramic Soc(F)—Inst Ceramic Engring—Sigma Xi. Hunter-Thomas Associates, Keith Bldg., Cleve.

12 PETERSEN, George E. Museum exhibits (preparation of); Air Force emergency survival equipment. b'05. Student '23-24 (Chicago Art Inst); '28-29 (U Chicago). Expedition to South America '26-27 to collect plant specimens for reproduction, various other expeditions in US; constructed carboniferous forest group at Field Museum Natural History, groups for North American Hall, South Sea Groups for Whitney Hall and others, American Museum Natural History; during World War II designed kits for emergency survival during forced landings, bail-outs, and rescue work, and directed training film on proper use of equipment. With Field Mus Natural Hist Chicago '24-33, Am Mus Natural Hist NYC since '33, chief dept preparation since '49; civilian specialist Army Air Force Wright Field Dayton O '43-45. American Museum of Natural History, Central Park West at 79th St., NYC 24.

13 PETERSEN, William John. American history (Steamboating, the West, Mississippi River, Iowa). b'01. BA '26 (U Dubuque); MA '27—grad fellow '26-30—PhD '30 (U Ia). Author: Two Hundred Topics in Iowa History '32; Steamboating on the Upper Mississippi '37; Iowa: The Rivers of Her Valleys '41; A Reference Guide to Iowa History '42. Co-author: (with Edith Rule) True Tales of Iowa '32; The Story of Iowa (2 vols) '52; Iowa History Reference Guide '52; also articles in field. Lecturer history Univ Iowa since '36; research asso State Hist Soc of Ia '30-47, supt since '47. AHA—Am Acad Polit and Social Sci—Miss Valley Hist Assn—So Hist Assn—Minn Hist Assn —Mo Hist Soc—State Hist Soc Ia. Received Ia Library Assn award for best contribution to Am lit by an Iowan in '37. State Historical Society of Iowa, Iowa City, Ia.

14 PETERSON, Allan George. Potato insects; Mosquitoes. b'14. BS '37—MS '39 (SD State Coll); '39-42—research fellow, PhD '49 (U Minn). Author articles in field. Jr entomol to sr asst sanitarian Reserve Corps US Pub Health Service malaria control in war areas '42-47; research fellow U Minn since '47. Am Assn Econ Entomol— Entomol Soc Am—Potato Assn Am— Am Phytopath Soc. Division of Entomology, University Farm, St. Paul 1.†

15 PETERSON, Alvah. Entomology; Insect larvae and biological control. b'88. BS '11 (Knox Coll); MA '13—PhD '16 (U Ill). Asso prof entomol Rutgers U '16-25; sr entomol research US Dept Agr Bur Entomol and Plant Quarantine '25-28; prof entomol O State U '28-48; research prof O Agrl Expt Sta '43-45; prof entomol U Minn summer '48. Author: Manual of Entomological Techniques '53; Larvae of Insects, part I '49, and part II '51. AAAS—Am Assn Economic Entomol—Entomol Soc Am—O Acad Sci—Phi Beta Kappa— Sigma Xi—Gamma Alpha. Ohio State University, Columbus, O.

16 PETERSON, Enoch Ernest. Egypt (Graeco-Roman archeology). b'91. AB '12—LittD hon '41 (Luther Coll); MA '22 (U Mich). Member University of Michigan excavation staff on expeditions to Antioch '24, Carthage '25, Karanis '25-26; director University of Michigan excavations in Egypt at Karanis '26-35, Dimay '31-32, and Terenouthis '34-35; member board trustees American Research Center in Egypt. Author: Dimay: Soknopaiou Nesos '31. Co-author: (with A E R Boals) Karanis Topographical Report '24-28. With U Mich since '24, curator Mus Archeol '35-50, dir since '50. Am Archeol Assn. Museum of Archeology, University of Michigan, Ann Arbor.

17 PETERSON, Floyd Charles. Cellulose chemistry (Pulp, paper): Cellulose derivatives. b'02. BS '24—MS '25— PhD '36 (NY State Coll Forestry). Research cellulose derivatives, development cellulose ethers. Author articles in field. Asst prof pulp and paper mfg NY State Coll Forestry '32-37; research chem The Dow Chem Co Midland Mich '38-40, dir research and development cellulose products div '43-48, mgr '48-50, asst to the general mgr since '50. Am Inst Chem Engineers—Midland Engring Soc—Sigma Xi. The Dow Chemical Company, Midland, Mich.

18 PETERSON, Horace C(ornelius). Propaganda (War); History of World War I. b'02. BA cum laude '31 (Pomona Coll); MA '32—PhD '35 (Cornell U). Author: Propaganda For War '39 (chosen by Current Hist Mag as one of ten most significant books of '39). Prof hist U Okla since '36; asst mil attache Am Embassy Dio de Janeiro Brazil. Miss Valley Hist Soc. History Department, University of Oklahoma, Norman, Okla.†

19 PETERSON, John Booth. Soil science (Fertility, petrography, morphology, structure formation, erosion and control). b'05. BS '28 (Ore State Coll); MS '29—PhD '36 (Ia State Coll); Nat Research fellow '39-40 (U Calif). Author articles in field. Prof and head dept agron Purdue U since '48. Am Soc Agron—Soil Sci Soc Am. Received W H Stevenson award for outstanding research in field of soils '48. Agronomy Department, Purdue University, Lafayette, Ind.†©

20 PETERSON, Joseph S. Mining engineering. b'84. EM '08 (Minn U). Design and construction cyanide mill, mining and gold milling plant; design construction and operation mining and milling plants, flotation, cyanidation and gravity concentration milling, and underground metal mining. Metall and supt cyanide plant SA Development Co '12-14; gen supt Ophir Gold Mines '14; cyanide plant design and constrn Tomby Gold Mines '14-16, asst gen mgr '16-25; supt mines Cia de Real del Monte Y Pachuca '25-37; supt advancing to gen mgr Balatoc Mining Co PI since '37. Am Inst Mining Engrs. Benguet Consolidated Mining Co., Baguio, Mt. Prov, P.I.

21 PETERSON, Lawrence Eugene. Engineering (Consulting); Astronomy. b'97. BSc '20—CE '27 (U Ill). Engaged preparation design and plans industrial plants, emphasis on malting plants including breweries, tanneries, factories, cold storage plants, power houses, warehouses, commercial buildings, public buildings; furnished professional structural, mechanical, electrical, sanitary, air conditioning engineering, architectural services world's largest malt houses (Fleischmann Malting Co, Schlitz Brewing Co, Kurth Malting Co, Bavaria Co in Colombia South America, storage, bottle, brew houses, office and lab buildings for numerous plants; consulting services Milwaukee County Court House, schools, churches, stadiums; led expedition to study sun's eclipse God's Lake Manitoba Can Jul '45. Cons engr Milwaukee, Wis since '27. Am Inst Cons Engr—ASCE—Nat Soc Profl Engr (vp) —Soc Am Mil Engr—Am Concrete Inst—Am Astron Soc—Milwaukee Astron Soc (dir, pres '43-44, '45). 601 E. Ogden Av., Milw 2; also 52 Wall St., NYC 5.†©

22 PETERSON, Mendel Lazear. Military and naval history, insignia and uniforms; Numismatics. b'18. BS '38 (Miss So Coll); MA '40 (Vanderbilt U); '45-47 (Lowell Textile Inst); '43 (Harvard). Research on the historical significance of early British and Anglo-Saxon coinage. Author articles: Jungle Mints '46; Emergency Currency of Leyte '47. Recorder Naval Uniform Bd US Navy '43-48; act curator Naval and Mil Hist US Nat Museum since '48. Am Numismatic Soc—Am Numismatic Assn—Washington Numismatic Soc. U.S. National Museum, Washington 25.†

23 PETERSON, Roald Arnold. Range and grassland ecology; Range management. b'13. BS—MS '39 (ND Agrl Coll); grad work (U Minn). Author articles in field. With US Forest Service since '37, range conservationist Northern Rocky Mountain Forest and Range Experiment Station. Ecol Soc Am—Am Soc Range Mgt. Northern Rocky Mountain Forest and Range Expt. Station, Missoula, Mont.

24 PETERSON, Roger Tory. Bird art and identifications. b'08. Student '27-28 (Art Students League NYC)—'29-31 (Nat Acad Design NYC); DSc '52 (Franklin and Marshall Coll). Author: A Field Guide to the Birds '34, '39, '47 (Brewster Medal '44, Am Ornithologists Union); The Junior Book of Birds '39; A Field Guide to Western Birds '41; Birds Over America '48; How to Know the Birds '49; Field Guide to Birds of Europe. Lecturer on birds, illustrator of bird books; bird painting exhibited; ednl asso Nat Audubon Soc '34-49; editor Houghton-Mifflin Co Nature Field Guide Series since '46; invented system field identif birds. Cosmos Club—Cooper Ornith Soc—Wilson Ornith Club—Baird Club —Nuttall Ornith Club—Linnaean Soc —Washington Biologists Field Club— Am Ornithologists Union(F). Box 7, Glen Echo, Md.

25 PETERSON, Rowena Beryl. US folklore (New York, religion, industry education, transportation); Canadian folklore. b'16. AB '38 (Houghton Coll); BS '41 (Geneseo State Tchrs Colo); AM '46 (Cornell U). Research on relation of industry and transportation to folklore, folklore of Northern New York State, particularly Jefferson County, Canadian folklore; associate editor North Country Life. Tchr, librarian and research analyst since '38. NY Folklore Soc—NY State Hist Assn —Nat Council Tchrs Eng—Am Folklore Soc. Holland Patent Central School and Mappa Hall, Barneveld, N.Y. H: 130 Stuart St., Watertown, N.Y.

10 **PETERSON, Shailer Alvarey.** Aptitude tests; Test scoring machines. b'08. BA '30—MA '32 (U Ore); PhD '44 (U Minn). Developed scoring machines and statistical calculating equipment. Author articles in field. Head sci dept U Minn High Sch and instr spl methods Coll Edn U Minn '36-42; asso prof dir ednl research and measurements SD A and M State Coll '42-43; inst exam staff U Chicago '43-44, vis asst prof phys sci '44-45, research asso and asst prof edn '44-46, dept ed Sch Sci and Math '45-49; dir ednl measurements council dental edn Am Dental Association '45, secretary council since '48. AAAS—Nat Assn Research Sci Teaching—Central Assn Sci and Math Teachers—Biometric Soc —Psychometric Soc—Am Statis Assn —Sigma Xi. American Dental Association, 222 E. Superior St., Chicago 11.

11 **PETERSON, Walter John.** Chemical methods for analysis of carotene and riboflavin; effect of soils, weather, cooking processes on nutritive value of plants; mineral requirements of livestock. b'09. BS '30—MS '33 (Mich State Coll); PhD '35 (U Ia). Research on spectrophotometric techniques for assay of carotene in foods and feeds, photofluorometric analysis for riboflavin in foods and feeds, influence of soils, weather and cooking processes on composition and nutritive values of plants. Contributor: Biological Symposia (vol 12) '47. Asst prof chem Kan State Coll '35-42; prof, head nutrition sect animal industry dept NC State Coll '42-49, prof and head chem dept since '49. Alpha Chi Sigma—Phi Lambda Upsilon—Sigma Xi—AAAS— ACS. Chemistry Dept, North Carolina State College, Raleigh, N.C.

12 **PETRIDES, George A(than).** Wildlife ecolog (Population dynamics of game and fur animals). b'16. BS '38 (George Washington U); MS '40 (Cornell); PhD '48 (O State). Author articles: Observations on the Relative Importance of Winter Deer Browse Species in Central New York; Age Determination in American Gallinaceous Game Birds '42; Naturalist Publications for Parks '43; Sex Ratios in Ducks '44; The Ohio Game Hearing System '46; Sex and Age Ratios in Fur Animals. Game tech Conservation Com W Va '41; jr and asst park naturalist Nat Park Service Washington '41-43; asst leader wildlife research unit O State U '46-48; leader wildlife research unit and asso prof Tex A&M since '48. Wildlife Soc—Am Soc Mammalogists—Am Ornithol Union—Wilson Ornithol Club—Cooper Ornithol Club—Wilderness Soc—Sigma Xi. Texas Cooperative Wildlife Research Unit, Texas Agricultural & Mechanical College, College Station, Tex.⊚

13 **PETROCELLI, Joseph Vincent.** Electrodeposition; Corrosion; Metal finishing. b'10. BA '34—MA '36 (Wesleyan U); PhD '43 (Yale). Research on fundamentals of electrode reactions, electron theory of metals. Author articles: The Electrochemical Behavior of Aluminum '51; The Kinetics of Oxidation-Reduction Electrode Reactions '51, others. Dir research Patent Button Co since '50. Am Electroplaters Soc— Electrochem Soc—ACS—AIMME—Sigma Xi—AAAS. 41 Brown St., Waterbury 88, Conn.

14 **PETTIJOHN, Francis John.** Geology (Petrology, sedimentation). b'04. BA '24—MA '25—PhD '30 (U Minn); '27-28 (U Calif). Author: Sedimentary Rocks '49. Co-author: (with W C Krumbein) Manual of Sedimentary Petrography '38. Asst prof geol U

Chicago '31-39, asso prof '39-46, prof '46-52; prof geol Johns Hopkins since '52; geol US Geol Survey since '43; editor Journal Geol '47-52. AAAS(F)— Geol Soc Am(F)—Am Assn Pet Geol— Soc Econ Paleontol and Mineralogists. Department Geology, Johns Hopkins University, Balt. 18.⊚

15 **PETTINGILL, Olin Sewall, Jr.** Ornithology; Life histories, distribution, behavior and ecology of birds in the United States, Canada and Mexico; Wildlife photography. b'07. BA '30 (Bowdoin Coll); PhD '33 (Cornell). Research on birds and other wildlife subjects; member Carnegie Museum Zoological expedition to Hudson Bay '31; conducted expeditions to study sea bird populations Great Duck Island Maine '29, Grand Manan Archipelago New Brunswick '32, '35, '37, Cobb Island Va '33; research asso Cranbrook Inst Sci '40-45; lecturer Nat Audobon Soc since '43; editor section on Aves Biological Abstracts since '42; author-photographer eight motion picture films bird life Coronet Instructional Films '41; co-leader Cornell U-Carleton Coll Ornithol Expdn Mexico '41; commissioned to photograph wildlife Texas wildlife sanctuaries '44; lead expdn northwest Canada sponsored Nat Audobon Soc and US Fish and Wildlife Service in search Whooping Cranes '46. Author: The American Woodcock '36; A Laboratory and Field Manual of Ornithology '46; The Bird Life of the Grand Manan Archipelago '39; A Guide to Bird Finding East of the Mississippi '51; A Guide to Bird Finding West of the Mississippi '53; also articles in field. Associate prof zool Carleton College since '46; member staff Univ Mich biol sta Cheboygan summers '38-45, since '47. Am Ornithol Union (F, sec '46-51)—Wildlife Society—Northeast Bird-banding Assn—Pacific Northwest Bird and Mammal Soc—Am Soc Mammalogists—Am Soc Ichthyol and Herpetol—Sigma Xi. Carleton College, Northfield, Minn.†

16 **PETTIS, Charles Emerson.** Waterworks; Water treatment; Sewage treatment. b'01. B Civil Engring '23—CE '33 (O State U). Research on design and operation locomotive water stations; design and supervision construction municipal and industrial waterworks systems, water treatment plants, sewer systems and sewage treatment plants. Asst supervisor bldgs NY Central RR '27-31; cons engr Finkbeiner Pettis & Strout since '33. Am Soc CE—Nat Soc Profl Engrs—Ohio Soc Profl Engrs—Mich Engring Soc. 518 Jefferson Av., Tol 4.

17 **PETTITT, George A.** Anthropology (Primitive education). b'01. AB '26—PhD '40 (U Calif). Author: Primitive Education '46; The Quileute of La Push, 1775-1945. Asst to pres U Calif charge pub relations on eight campuses since '36, lecturer in anthrop since '40. Am Anthrop Assn—Ethnol Soc Am—Phi Beta Kappa—Sigma Xi. 225 Administration Bldg., University of California, Berkeley 4.†

18 **PETTY, Benjamin Harrison.** Highway engineering. b'88. BSCE '13 (Purdue U). Author articles in field. Instr highway engring Purdue '20-22, asst prof '22-29, asso prof '29-33, prof since '33; planning and supervising Annual Purdue Road Sch '24-43, since '46; cons jobs highways. ASCE—Hwy Research Bd—Am Soc Mil Engrs—Soc Profl Engrs—Tau Beta Pi. Civil Engineering Bldg., Purdue University, Lafayette, Ind. H: 707 Crestview Place, W. Lafayette.

19 **PETTY, Julian Jay.** Economic geography; Demography. b'01. BS '24 (Denison U); MA '29 (Harvard); PhD

'43 (O State U). Work on regional, economic geography of South Carolina and US; growth, distribution and characteristics of the population of South Carolina; population problems. Author articles: Physical Characteristics of the State, The People of South Carolina '38; The Growth and Distribution of Population in South Carolina '43; Population (in South Carolina, Economic and Social) '45. Asso prof geog U SC '29-44, prof since '44, population cons SC State Planning Bd '38-44. Assn Am Geog—Nat Council Geog Teach— Am Geog Soc—AAAS—Population Assn Am. Department of Geology and Geography, University of South Carolina, Columbia, S.C.†

20 **PETTY, Milton Andrew, Jr.** Diseases of potatoes, tomatoes and soybeans; Fungi (Genetics, physiology); Microflora of feedstuffs and other natural materials; Development of processes and industrial fermentations of antibiotics and vitamins. b'15. BS '35 (Southwestern La Inst); MS '37 (La State U); PhD '40 (U Minn). Author articles in field. Mycol Lederle Labs Div Am Cyanamid Co Pearl River NY since '44. Am Phytopath Soc—Bot Soc Am—Mycol Soc Am—Soc Am Bacteriologists—Bot Soc Washington—Sigma Xi. Lederle Laboratories Division, American Cyanamid Co., Pearl River, N.Y.†

21 **PETTY, Olive Scott.** Geophysical prospecting, instruments and designs; Seismology. b'95. BS '17—CE '20 (U Tex). Pioneer in geophysical research as applied to geology and exploration for petroleum. Inventor seismograph and gravity measuring instruments used in explorations for petroleum. Pres Petty Geophys Engring Co San Antonio Tex since '25, Petty Labs Inc, Petty Geophys Co, Petty Geophys Personnel Co, Petty Geophys Engring Co of Fla; dir Tex Mid-Continent Oil and Gas Assn. ASCE—Am Inst Mining and Metall Engr—Am Assn Petroleum Geol —Soc Exploration Geophys—Am Geophys Union—AAAS. 317 6th St., San Antonio.

22 **PETTYJOHN, Elmore Shaw.** Production, distribution and utilization of fuel gases and production of synthesis gas. b'97. AB '18—BSE, MSE '22—ChE '30 (U Mich). Location of oil shale mines and Demonstration Plant Naval oil shale reserve No 1. Shale oil refining, production of synthesis gas and synthetic liquid fuels. Author articles in field. Asso prof chem engring U Mich '37-45; special fuels sect Bureau Ships '44-45 US Navy, in charge Oil Section US Naval Tech Mission in Europe '45; dir inst gas tech Chicago since '45. AAAS—AAUP—ACS—ACC CI—AGA—AIChE—AIME — ASEE — ASTM—NACE—WSE — Blast Furnace and Coke Assn—Sigma Xi—Tau Beta Pi. Institute of Gas Technology, 3300 S. Federal St., Chicago 16.⊚

23 **PEYSER, Julius I.** Banking legislation. LLB '99 (Georgetown U); LLM '00 (Columbian (now George Washington U); DCL '01 (George Washington Sch Diplomacy and Comparative Jurisprudence). Financial advisor Children's Art Center. Admitted DC bar '99 since practiced in Washington; chairman Security Savings & Commercial Bank since '15; former vice president Traders National Bank and Merchants and Mechanics Bank; professor equity practice National University Law School. Bar Assn DC(pres '29)— Am Bar Assn(vp for DC '29, com on current banking decisions and legislation '46-47)—UN League of Lawyers (charter mem)—Board Trade—Mchts and Mfrs Assn. Investment Bldg., 15th and K Sts N.W., Washington.⊚

10 PEYTON, Green. Texas (History); Southwestern United States (Culture). b'07. Student '24-25, '27-29 (U Va). Author: San Antonio—City in the Sun '46; America's Heartland: The Southwest '48; For God and Texas '47; also articles in field. Texas Inst Letters. Awarded annual prize of Tex Inst Letters for best writing about Tex '46; fellow Rockefeller Foundation to gather material for a book about culture of US Southwest '47. 1101 Garrity Road, San Antonio 9, Tex.

11 PFADT, Robert Edward. Grasshoppers (Biology and control); Insect pests of livestock. b'15. BA '38—MA '40 (U Wyo); PhD '47 (U Minn). Research on distribution, and importance of food plants as factors in ecology of grasshoppers; influence temperature and humidity on development common cattle grub. Author articles: Effects of Temperature and Humidity on Larval and Pupal Stages of the Common Cattle Grub '47; Food-plants, Distribution and Abundance of the Bigheaded Grasshopper Aulocara elliotti 49; Food-plants as Factors in the Ecology of the Lesser Migratory Grasshopper Melanoplus mexicanus '49. Research on Mormon crickets US Bur Entomol and Plant Quarantine USDA '39; head entomol dept Wyo Agrl Expt Sta since '43. Am Assn Econ Entomol—Entomol Soc Am—Sigma Xi. Entomology Department, University of Wyoming, Laramie.

12 PFEIFFER, Ehrenfried Erwin. Crystallization (Blood); Humus research of soils, compost and manures; Soil conservation; Industrial waste (Humus from garbage). b'99. Student '20-25 (U Basel); MD hon '39 (Hahnemann Med Coll Phila). Experiment and development sensitive crystallization method to test small amounts of human capillary blood for early diagnosis of disease; introduction food health program to Holland; research on soil conservation and relationship of humus to health; microbiology and chemistry of soils, humus, compost, and manure; development process for production of compost from city and industrial waste on commercial scale. Author: Sensitive Crystallization Processes '36; Formative Forces in Crystallization '36; Bio-Dynamic Farming and Gardening '38; Soil Fertility, Renewal and Preservation '47; The Earth's Face and Human Destiny '47, and others; also articles in field. Dir Biochem Research Lab Free Acad Spiritual Sci Dornach Switzerland '27-40; dir N V Cultuur Maatschappy Loverendale Serooskerke Holland '28-39; agrl cons Europe and Middle East '30-39, US since '33; dir Kimberton Farms and Agrl Sch '40-44, Biochem Research Lab Spring Valley NY since '45. English Biodynamic Assn Soil and Crop Improvement (pres since '45)—NY Acad Science—Bio-Dynamic Farming and Gardening Assn US (sci adv)—AAAS—ACS—Soil Conservation Soc Am—Am Soc Agron—Soil Sci Soc. Biochemical Research Laboratory, Threefold Farm, Spring Valley, N.Y.†

13 PFEIFFER, Robert Henry. Semitic languages; Ancient history of the Near East. b'92. BD '14-15 (U Geneva); '13-14 (U Berlin and Tubingen); AM '20—PhD '22—STM '23 (Harvard). Author: The Archives of Shilwateshub '32; State Letters of Assyria '35; One Hundred New Selected Nuzi Texts (with A E Speiser) '37; Introduction to the Old Testament '41; History of New Testament Times '49; also articles in field. With Harvard U since '22, asst prof Semitic langs and history '30-36, lecturer '36-53, Hancock professor of Hebrew and other Oriental languages since '53; curator Sem-

itic Museum, Harvard since '31; with Boston U '23-29, lecturer '36-47, prof since '48. Am Acad Arts Sci—Archeol Inst—Soc Bibl Lit—Am Oriental Soc—Nat Assn Bibl Instr. 57 Francis Av., Cambridge 38, Mass.☉

14 PFEILER, William Karl. Modern German novel; German literature (Nineteenth century, Goethe). b'97. Certificate of Maturity '20 (Realgymnasium Cologne); PhD '24 (Cologne U); '21-22 (Bonn U), summer '25 (Stanborough Coll), summer '28 (Mich U). Studied in Germany on German war novel, working in libraries and interviewing authors; research on German refugee literature. Author: War and the German Mind '41. Co-author: In Deutschland (with Alexis) '30; Uncle Sam and His English (with Wittmann) '32; also articles in field. Prof German lang and lit Neb U since '43, chairman of department since '50. Modern Language Assn Am—Humanities Research Assn—Gesellschaft der Freunde Wilhelm Raabes Germany. University of Nebraska, Lincoln 2, Neb. H: 1627 Woodsview.

15 PFIFFNER, John McDonald. Municipal administration; Personnel management; Public administration; Supervisory training; Human relations; Organization and management. b'93. AB '16—AM '17—PhD '27 (State U Ia); student '17-18 (Columbia). Author: Public Administration '35 (revised edit) '46; Municipal Administration '40; Research Methods Pub Adminstrn '40; The Supervision of Personnel '51. Prof polit sci Municipal U Wichita Kan '27-29; with U So Cal since '29, now prof pub adminstrn; personnel commr Los Angeles School Dist; personnel cons War Dept '45; pres Cal Merit System League. Am Polit Sci Assn—Civil Service Assembly—Am Soc Pub Adminstrn—Am Acad Polit and Social Sci—Western Governmental Research Assn—Pacific SW Acad(pres). H: 3948 S. Bronson Av., LA 8.

16 PFIRMAN, Kenneth Robert. Indian (Arts); Firearms (History); Northeast US (Archeology); Southwest US (Archeology). b'09. Ed pub schs. Research on American Indian ethnology with emphasis on arts and crafts, history and development of firearms, their manufacture and use. Am Anthrop Assn—AAAS—Archeol Inst Am—Soc Am Archeol—Nat Geog Soc—Am Mil Inst—Am Ordnance Assn—Nat Rifle Assn—Nat Muzzle-Loading Rifle Assn. H: 347 E. 17th St., Erie 5, Pa.

17 PFISTER, C(arl) Eugene. Rose culture. b'96. Developed test rose garden for hardiness in mid-west; private research on cultural practices, breeding, new variety introductions. Author articles in field. Vice-pres Magill-Weinsheimer Co since '34; commr park dist Highland Park Ill '41-44, mem city plan commn '39-44. Men's Garden Clubs Am (pres '45-47, pres Ill sect '42)—Men's Garden Club of Chicago Region (dir, pres '45, '46)—Chicago Hort Soc and Garden Center (pres since '45)—Am Rose Soc (dir)—Am Hort Council Inc (dir)—Chicago Plant, Flower and Fruit Guild (hon v-pres). 1322 S. Wabash Av., Chicago 5.

18 PHELAN, Robert K(imball). Food preservation; Sarawak; Mice (Albino Swiss). b'09. BS '31 (MIT). Development improved methods for manufacture baby food, chewing gum, coffee, peanut butter, and gelatin; survey coastal jungle areas of Sarawak for latex bearing trees '38-39; maintenance inbred colony Albino Swiss Mice. Chem Atlantic Gelatin Co Mass '31-35; research asst MIT '35-36; chem Beech-Nut Packing Co '36-37, tech supt gum mfg '41-45, asst research dir since

'45; gen mgr Chicle Development Co Singapore '37-40. ACS—Am Geog Soc—Inst Food Tech—AAAS. Beech-Nut Packing Co., Canajoharie, N.Y.

19 PHELPS, Doris Hawkins. Anatomy and physiology of reproduction. b'98. BA '24—MA '25—PhD '37 (Vanderbilt U). Research and writing on effects upon uterine motility of urine from dysmenorrheic and normal individuals, endometrial vascular reactions and mechanism of nidation. Author articles in field. Research asst obstetrics and gynecology Vanderbilt U Sch Med '33-40, research asso since '40. Am Assn Anatomists—Am Study Internal Secretions—AAAS—Sigma Xi. Guggenheim fellow '48-49. Vanderbilt U School of Medicine, Nashville 4.

20 PHELPS, Everett Russell. Physics; Television (Science presentation); Mathematics (Practical shop). b'94. AB '14 (Clark U); AM '17—PhD (Physics) '23 (U Mich). Active in presenting science on television; programs include Magic of Science series, 3 mos '49; Mr Weather spring '50; Science Shorts '50-51; producer weekly science programs by Wayne U 3 mos '50; The Taystee Weatherman since '51. Co-author: (with John H Wolfe) Practical Shop Mathematics (3rd edit) '43; Mechanics Vest Pocket Reference Book (5th edit) '45. Faculty dept physics and astron Wayne U since '25, prof since '44, now acting chmn physics, supervisor courses in phys sci. APS—Am Assn Physics Tchrs—Am Inst Physics—Indsl Math Soc—NEA—Mich Edn Assn—Sigma Xi. Department of Physics, Wayne University, Det.

21 PHILBRICK, George A(rthur). Computers (Analog). b'13. BS '35 (Harvard); '46 (MIT). Development high-speed all-electronic analog computer and techniques for its application; series analog computer components. Inventor automatic control mechanisms. Author articles: Unified symbolism for regulatory controls; Automatic control and the high-speed analog. Research engr Fuxboro Co '36-42, research cons since '45; tech aide and cons OSRD '42-45; pres and chmn bd G A Philbrick Research Inc since '46. ASME. Received Naval Ordnance Development award for aiming controls '45, Presidential Certificate Merit '48, 230 Congress St., Boston 10.

22 PHILHOWER, Charles Alpaugh. New Jersey Indians, flora, fauna. b'78. BS '09—MA '12 (Dickinson Coll); MA '14 (Columbia U). Field work on Indians of New Jersey since '00; has collection of artifacts of Lenapes, about 50,000 items; library of books maps and articles relating to Lenape or Delaware Indians; one of three persons on Indian Sites Survey of New Jersey '36-41. Author articles in field. Lecturer on Indians of NJ Newark State Normal Coll '37-39; pub lectr on Delaware or Lenape Indians since '28. NJ Archeol Soc (chmn orgn com '31, ed '31-36)—Eastern States Archeol Fedn (one of organizers)—Soc Am Archeol Am Anthrop Assn. 303 Mountain Av., Westfield, N.J.

23 PHILIP, William Booth. Illinois history (Sectionalism). b'84. Diploma '21—BAS '23 (George Williams Coll); PhB '24—AM '26—PhD '40—Spellman Fellow '24-27 (U Chicago). Author: Chicago and the Down State—A Study of Their Conflicts 1870-1934 44; also articles in field. Prof hist and polit sci Bradley U since '43, dir admissions since '47. Am Hist Assn—Miss Valley Hist Assn—Ill State Hist Soc—Peoria Hist Soc—Am Acad Polit Social Sci—Am Polit Sci Assn—Ill State Acad Sci—Nat Edn Assn—Kappa Delta Pi. Bradley University, Peoria 5, Ill.

10 PHILIPPI, Olof Ahlen. Concrete (Bituminous). b'09. Student '29-30 (Tex A & M Coll). Co-designer gyratory molding machine for molding specimens bituminous concrete; design photoronic-bituometer, minor testing equipment, methods relative to design and control bituminous paving mixtures; general supervision on construction bituminous concrete pavements. With Tex Highway Dept since '31, lab research on bituminous concrete mixtures '39-45, supervising bituminous constrn engr '47-50, asst constrn engr since '50. Nat Sor Profl Engrs—Assn Asphalt Paving Tech—High Research Bd (asso). Texas Highway Department, Highway Bldg., Austin 14.

11 PHILLIPS, Albert J(ohn). Gases in metals. b'02. BS '23—MS '25—PhD '28 (Yale). Author articles: Melting Practice for Lead and Lead Alloys '46; The Separation of Gases from Molten Metals '47. Co-author: (with J S Smart Jr and A A Smith Jr) Preparation and Some Properties of High-purity Copper '41, and others. Research metall Scovill Mfg Co Waterbury Conn '25-31; supt research American Smelting Refining Co Barber NJ '31-40, mgr research '40-49, dir research '49-53, vp since '53. Inst Metals, Eng—ASTM—Am Soc Metals—Am Inst Mining Metall Engrs (dir '48, Inst Metals div chmn '37, lectr '47)—Sigma Xi. American Smelting & Refining Co., South Plainfield, N.J.

12 PHILLIPS, Allan R(obert). Birds (Distribution, taxonomy, classification, migration). b'14. MS '39 (U Ariz); PhD '46 (Cornell). Studies in distribution and migration of birds in western US and Mexico; also Okinawa, Riu Kiu Islands. Author article: Complexities of Migration; also papers on several individual species. Co-author article: (with George M Sutton) June bird life of the Papago Indian Reservation, Arizona. Curator ornithol Mus Northern Ariz Flagstaff since '40. Am. Ornithol Union—Cooper Ornithol Club —Wilson Ornithol Club. H: 113 Olive Rd., N., Tucson.

13 PHILLIPS, Arthur William. Food processing; Frozen foods. b'15. BS '39—MS '41 (U Notre Dame); ScD '47 (MIT). Aided in pioneering studies on germ-free life at Lobund; conducted research on filtration of microorganisms from air and on experimental air-borne infections, microbiology of frozen foods and related food poisoning problems, effects of industrial processing conditions on amino acids and vitamin B_{12} in food products, basic research in borderline fields of biology with their applied aspects to foods pharmaceuticals fermentation products. Author articles in field. Charge spl bacteriological research Notre Dame '43-45; research asso MIT '47-49, prof; now head biol engring div Lobund Institute. AAAS —Soc Am Bacteriologists—Inst Food Technol—Sigma Xi. c/o Lobund, University Notre Dame, Notre Dame, Ind.

14 PHILLIPS, Charles John. Glass (Manufacture, tempering); Glass (Double glazing units); Glass beads. b'08. BS in phys '30 (U Pittsburgh); AM in phys '31 (Oberlin Coll). Research on glass tempering theory relating kind and amount of permanent stress with physical properties of glass and thermal history, design self-desiccated double-glazing units, methods manufacture glass beads in large quantities. Granted patents on tempering means and media. Author: Glass: The Miracle Maker (2d edit) '48. Co-author: (with D J Duffin) Get Acquainted with Glass '50. Contributor: Ency Britannica '42; Collier's Ency '48. With

Corning Glass Works '31-47; cons and project dir Pittsburgh Plate Glass Co '47-50; sales mgr and project dir Pittsburgh Plate Glass Co '47-50; sales mgr and project dir Pittsburgh Corning Corp '50-52; vp Dunbar Glass Corp since '52; cons. Omicron Delta Kappa —Sigma Delta Chi. Dunbar Glass Corp., Dunbar, W.Va.

15 PHILLIPS, George Lewis. Chimney sweeping (Hist). b'09 AB '31 (Dartmouth); MA '32 (Harvard); PhD '37 (Boston). Research on habits and customs of chimney sweeps; study of the trade of chimney-sweeping in the United States 1650-1850; compilation material on life of Edward Wortley. Author monograph: England's Climbing-Boys. A History of the Long Struggle to Abolish Child Labor in Chimney-Sweeping '49. Author articles: May-Day is Sweeps' Day '49; Women Chimney-Sweepers '49; Sweeps' Luck, and others. Asst prof comparative lit Hofstra Coll '40-43; asst prof Eng San Diego State Coll since '47. Modern Lang Assn—Philol Assn Pacific Coast—Folk Lore Soc Eng. San Diego State College, San Diego 15, Cal.

16 PHILLIPS, Howard Mitchell. Cytogenetics. b'10. BS '32—MA '34—ScD '53 (Wake Forest); PhD '38—Blandy Resch fellow '34-38 (U Va). Resch on cytogenetical investigations of the Plumbaginaceae, karyology and cytogenetics of Erythronium, cytological study of Macrostomum tuba, Epilachna corrupta, karyology and phyletic relationships of salamanders. Author articles in field. Instr biol Emory U '38-40, asst prof '40-43, asso prof '43-45, prof since '45, chmn div nat sci and math '45-46, chmn dept biol '48-52, dean grad sch since '53; mem council Oak Ridge Inst Nuclear Studies since '53. AAAS(F)—Genetics Soc Am—Am Genetics Assn—Human Genetics Soc—Bot Soc Am (chmn southeastern sect '47-48)—Nat Soc Sci Teachers—Am Assn Anat—Soc Study Evolution—Am Soc Mammalogists—Assn SE Biol (vp '46-47, pres '48-49)—Sigma Xi. Department of Biology, Emory University, Emory University, Ga.

17 PHILLIPS, Josephine Elvira Frye. Ohio (Early history and development); Old Northwest Territory (Early development). b'96. Student '13-16 (Oberlin Coll); AB '34 (Marietta Coll). Author: Wagons Away '41. Contributor: Real People Biographies '50. Freelance author and research worker. Ohio Archeol & Hist Soc—Miss Valley Hist Soc—Essex Inst—Am Assn State and Local Hist—Nat Soc Autograph Collectors. 309 Fort St., Marietta, O.

18 PHILLIPS, Percy Wilson. Federal taxation; Federal fiscal policies and spending; Government control of business (Federal). b'92. LLB '15 (Cornell U). Joint author: The Federal Gift tax, and Taxation Under the A.A.A. Member US Board Tax Appeals '25-31; private practice specializing in federal tax law and procedure; lectr U NC '29-31, Cornell U '37. Am Bar Assn (sect taxation sec '41-42, vice chmn '42-44, chmn '44-46, sect del to ho of dels of assn '46-48, chmn com on appointments to Tax Court since '48; rep to Nat Conf Lawyers and CPAs '43-48)—DC Bar Assn (chmn rep assn at DC Conf Lawyers and CPAs) —NY State Bar Assn—City NY Bar Assn—Cornell Law Assn (vp). Southern Bldg., Washingtn.⊚

19 PHILLIPS, Ralph Wesley. Sheep and swine husbandry; Animal breeding; Animal husbandry (China, India); Genetics and physiology of reproduction; Internation cooperation in agricultural improvements. b'09. BS '30

(Berea Coll); MA '31—PhD '34 (U Mo). Author articles in field. With US Bur Animal Ind since '41, chief animal ind br FAO since '46, dep dir agr div since '49. Am Soc Animal Prodn (past ed Journal Animal Sci)—Am Genetics Assn (ed bd Journ Heredity)—AAAS —Sigma Xi—Gamma Sigma Delta. Agriculture Division, Food and Agriculture Organization of the United Nations, Viole delle Terme di Caraculla, Rome, Italy.

20 PHILLIPS, Rufus Colfax, Jr. Airport design; Aircraft (Loading equipment). b'98. BS '18 (Trinity Coll); PhB '21 (Columbia). Research and design airports and airport facilities, design passenger and cargo loading equipment for aircraft. Vice pres Bennett Converse and Schwab '24-26; pres Colfax Phillips Inc '26-30; vp and dir Aviation Engring Inc '30-41; pres Airways Engring Inc since '43. Delta Psi —Nat Aeronautic Assn—Am Road Builders Assn. Airways Engineering Corp., 1212 18th St., Washington.

21 PHILLIPS, T(homas) D(avid). Heat transfer. b'91. Student '10-11 (Rollins Coll Winter Park Fla); AB '16 (Oberlin Coll); ScM '23 (U Mich); PhD '34 (Boston U). Research on heat transfer through clothing. Asst prof physics Marietta Coll O '23-24 and '27-32, prof '33-42 and since '45; research in physics US Nat Bur Standards Washington '37-38 and '39. AAAS—APS—Am Soc Rheology—Am Assn Physics Tchrs —Ohio Acad Sci—Phi Beta Kappa. H: 309 Fort St., Marietta, O.†⊚

22 PHILLIPS, Walter Sargeant. Ferns of Arizona; Morphology of desert plants. b'05. AB '29 (Oberlin); PhD '35 (Chicago). Author article: Check-list of the Ferns of Arizona (serial) '46-47. Prof bot and head dept bot and range ecol Coll Agr U Ariz since '40. Am Fern Soc. College of Agriculture, University of Arizona, Tucson, Ariz.⊚

23 PHILLIPS, Wendell. Human paleontology; African exploration. b'21. AB '43 (U Calif). University of California Museum of Paleontology Expedition to Northern Arizona '40, to Monument Valley southern Utah and Grand Canyon Arizona '42; now organizer and leader University of California African Expedition, largest American scientific expedition to explore continent of Africa; organizer Am Found Mt Sinai Expdn '49-50; organizer and leader American Foundation Arabian expedition '49. Author articles in field. Royal Anthrop Inst Gt Brit and Irland(F)—Nat Geog Soc(F) —Royal Archeol Inst Gt Brit and Ireland—NY Acad Sci—Soc. Vertebrate Paleontol—Soc Study Evolution—Am Anthrop Assn—Soc Am Archeol—AAAS. Concord, Cal.

24 PHILLIPS, William John. Fiction (Modern British); Drama (Modern British); Folklore (Pennsylvania Dutch). b'95. BA '20—MA '24—PhD '30 (U Pa). Contributor: Standard Dictionary of Folklore '50. Instr advancing to asst prof English U Pa '21-46; asso prof advancing to prof English Ursinus Coll since '46. Modern Lang Assn Am—Am Folklore Soc. Ursinus College, Collegeville, Pa.

25 PHINNEY, Harry Kenyon. Taxonomy of Algae (Cladophorales, phytoplanktonology); Algae of southern Illinois. b'18. BA '41 (U Cincinnati); MA '43 (Albion Coll); PhD '45—Wade Fetzer fellow '43-45 (Northwestern '?); Theresa Seessel fellow '45-46 (Yale). Author articles in field. Asst prof bot Ore State Coll '47-49, asso professor botany since '49; associate prof bot Ore Inst Marine Biol since '49. Phycol

Soc Am—Am Micros Soc—Bot Soc Am—Limnol Soc Am—Sigma Xi. Department of Botany, Oregon State College, Corvallis, Ore.

10 PHIPPS, Cecil G(lenn). Approximation; Mathematical economics. b'95. BA '21 (Mont State U); MA '24—PhD '28 (U Minn). Author articles in field. With U Fla since '24, now prof. Math Assn Am—Econometric Soc—Fla Acad Sci—AAAS—Phi Kappa Phi. Box 2514, University Station, Gainesville, Fla.†☺

11 PICHEL, Charles Louis Thourot. Heraldry; Coats-of-arms. b'90. PhD '25 (Universal Coll Sci). Founder, dir Am Heraldry Soc since '28. Imperial and Military Order Yellow Rose Am—Royal Order of Bourbon France (dir in Am)—Herald-Marshal Coll of Arms, Canada—Chevalier Order St Lazare of Jerusalem—Grand-Cordon Order Crown of Stuart, England—Imperial Order St Stanislaus, Russia. Shickshinny, Pa.

12 PICKENS, A(ndrew) L(ee). Symbiosis (Termite castes; pollinators). b '90. MS '24 (U Va); PhD '32 (U Cal). Originated inhibition or ectohormonal theory of termites and their caste control, originated observation culture method. Co-Author: Termites and Termite Control (2d edit) '34. Compiler: Semi-decadal Lists of Bird-visited Flowers in Nearctic Region. Field biol Termite Investigations Com U Cal '28-32; biol prof Queens Coll since '50. AAAS. Queens College, Charlotte 7, N.C.

13 PICKENS, Claude Leon, Jr. Chinese Islam. b'00. AB '23 (U Mich); BD (Va Theol Sem); MA '45 (Columbia). Research on Chinese Islam in Shensi, Kansu, Ningsia, Suyuan and Chahar; associate editor Friends of Moslems since '27, associate editor Muslim World since '38. Author: Annotated Bibliography of Literature on Islam in China '50; Islam in China (in preparation). Soc Friends of Moslems(sec since '26)—Royal Geog Soc(F)—Royal Asiatic Soc(N China br)—Religious Tract Soc. 281 Fourth Av., NYC 10.

14 PICKENS, William. History of the Negro in America; American Negro in World War II. b'81. AB '02 (Talladega Coll); AB '04 (Yale); AM '08 (Fisk U); LittD '15 (Selma U); LLD '18 (Wiley U). Author: Abraham Lincoln, Man and Statesman '09; The Heir of Slaves '10; Frederick Douglass and the Spirit of Freedom '12; Fifty Years of Emancipation '13; The Ultimate Effects of Segregation and Discrimination '15; The New Negro '16; The Negro in the Light of the Great War '19; American Aesop '26. Instr Latin and German Talledega Coll '04-09, prof Greek, Latin, German '09-14; prof Greek and sociol Wiley U '14-15; dean Morgan Coll '15-18, vp '18-20; field sec NAACP Colored People '20; chief interracial sect nat orgns subdiv war savings staff US Treas Dept since '42. Am Negro Acad—Phi Beta Kappa. Savings Bonds Division, U.S. Treasury Department, Washington.

15 PICKETT, Allison DeForest. Orchard insects (Biology, ecology, control). b'00. BSc '29—MSc '36 (McGill U). Studies on long-time effects of spray chemicals on populations of orchard insects. Author articles in field. Provincial entomol NS Can '29-39; officer-in-charge Entomol Lab Annapolis Royal '39-51, Kentville since '52. Entomol Soc Can—AAAS—Am Soc Hort Sci—Am Genetic Assn—Agrl Inst Can—Acadian Entomol Soc. Kentville, Nova Scotia, Can.†

16 PICKETT, Gerald. Concrete pavements. b'01. BS in elec engring '27 (Okla A&M); MS '31 (Kan State Coll);

PhD in mechanics '38 (U Mich). Studies of stresses in concrete; vibration of elastic bodies; moments and deflections airport pavements. Author articles: Application of Fourier Method to the Solution of Certain Boundary Problems in the Theory of Elasticity; Equations for computing elastic constants from flexural and resonant frequencies; and others. Research physicist Portland Cement Association '40-45; prof applied mechanics Kan State Coll '45-51; prof mechanics U Wis since '51. ASME—ASTM—Am Concrete Inst (Wason medal '46) Soc Exptl Stress Analysis—Sigma Xi—Pi Tau Sigma. Department of Mechanics, University of Wisconsin, Madison.☺

17 PICKFORD, Jerome Michael. Gas mixing; Gas systems (Design); Gas measurement (Large volume); Gas losses (Reduction); Gas conversion; Gas purification. b'99. BS in chem engring '35 (U Wis). Research and design gas distribution systems and gas transmission lines, conversion gas properties from one gas to another gas, such as manufactured gas to natural gas; engineering and operation involved in mixing various combustible gases, purification, compressing and storage of gas. With N Ind Pub Service Co since '23, mgr gas and water engring since '50. Am Gas Assn (chmn com unaccounted-for gas, distribution, distribution design, consumer's service, pub, mem gas mixing and prodn com)—Ind Gas Assn (chmn tech and operation com, appliance service com, distribution com, research com). Northern Indiana Public Service Co., Hammond, Ind.

18 PIEMEISEL, Robert Louis. Plant communities (Semi-desert); Semi-desert vegetation (Ecology). b'89. AB '12 (U Minn). Author articles in field. Sci asst, later sr plant physiol Plant Ind Bur US Dept Agr since '12. AAAS—Ecol Soc—British Ecol Soc—Washington Acad Sci. P.O. Box 826, Twin Falls, Ida.†

19 PIERCE, James Gray. Animal by-products (Fats and oils); Photography of unusual cloud formations. b'15. BA '37 (Ia Wesleyan Coll); '35 (Ia State Coll); certificate '43 (U Chicago). Research on animal fats and oils, animal feeds, soaps, fertilizers and other related products, bleaching and deodorization of fats and oils, feeding swine with dried whey and other condensed products. Operated feeding research sta Western Condensing Co '37-38; asst state chem Ia Dept Agr '39-41; chem Nat By Products since '41. Am Chem Soc—Am Oil Chem Soc. National By Products, Box 615, Des Moines, Ia.

20 PIERCE, Jerry Albert. Inorganic gel adsorbents (Silica gel); Inorganic gel catalysts (Silica gel). b'86. AB '09 (U Ia); MS '23 (U Denver); PhD '28 (Johns Hopkins). Pioneer in production extruded gel catalyst, spherical gels; work on metal coated silica gel for catalysis; production gel films for structural study; work on substitute gel catalysts from bentonite clay. Co-author: (with Dr G C Connolly) The Inorganic Oxide Gels, their Manufacture and Uses. Research chem Silica Gel Corp (now Davison Chem Corp) Baltimore '29-32; research chem (exploratory) Esso Standard Oil Co Baton Rouge since '39. Am Chem Soc—Am Inst Chem(F)—Sigma Xi. H: 1785 Country Club Drive, Baton Rouge 12.

21 PIERCE, John Alvin. Electronics (Sound reproductions, radio aids to navigation, radio wave propagation). b'07. BA '28 (U Me). Theoretical and experimental studies of sources of distortion in sound reproduction from

phonograph records; research in physics of upper atmosphere, including ionospheric observations during solar eclipses in Kazakstan USSR '36 and Union South Africa '40; also work in development of Loran navigation and research in radio transmission in connection with it. Co-author and co-editor: Loran '48; also articles in field. Research fellow Harvard '34-41, since '46; div head Radiation Lab MIT '41-45. Inst Radio Engrs(F)—Inst Navigation—AAAS(F)—Sigma Xi. Cruft Laboratory, Harvard University, Cambridge 38, Mass.†

22 PIERCE, John Robinson. Microwave electron tubes; Electron optics. b'10. BS '33—MS '34—PhD '36 (Calif Inst Tech). Research on reflex oscillators, traveling-wave tubes, electron guns, double-stream amplifiers, pulse code modulation. Holds 20 patents. Author articles in field. Tech staff Bell Telephone Labs since '36. Inst Radio Engrs(F)—Am Phys Soc(F)—AIEE. Morris Liebman Memorial prize '47; Eta Kappa Nu's Outstanding Young Elec Engr '42. Bell Telephone Laboratories Inc., Murray Hill, N.J. H: 275 McMane Av., Berkeley Heights, N.J.

23 PIERCE, Walter Howard. Breeding of disease resistant plants (Peas, beans). b'02. MS Agr '26 (U Ida); PhD '33 (U Wis). Developed varieties of Great Northern beans resistant to mosaic, Idaho Refugee resistant to common bean mosaic; identified many viruses affecting leguminous plants. Author articles in field. Geneticist and plant path Associated Seed Growers Inc since '37. Sigma Xi. Twin Falls, Ida.†

24 PIERCE, Watson O'Dell. Industrial psychology; League of Nations; Irish prehistoric archeology; Chinese jades. b'04. BS in chem engring '28—MSc in psychol '30 (Manchester U Eng); '30 (Vienna U); '41 (Columbia). Measurement individual differences in normal color discrimination; intercultural studies on vocational groups; job choice and vocational adjustment studies; Bronze and Iron Man Age excavations for National Museum Dublin; studies archaic Chinese jades; member bd editors Personality Symposia. Author: The Selection of Colour Workers '34; Air War: Its Psychological, Technical and Social Implications '39. Research staff Nat Inst Indsl Psychol '29-34; indsl research vocational psychol 15 occupations, for govt agencies '35-38; cons NYC '39-41; prof psychol Chaffey Jr Coll Calif '41-43; with War Dept '43-47, survey Air Service Command War Dept Manpower Bd '43, with civilian personnel div Office Sec War '43-44; research analyst Indsl War Coll of Armed Forces Washington '44-47; vp Nejelski & Co Inc management counsels NYC '47-48; dir Center for Psychol Services '48-49; tech cons Employment Asso Inc since '49. Brit Psychol Soc—Am Psychol Soc—Scottish Child Guidance Council—Phi Delta Kappa. Employment Associates, Inc., 18 John St., NYC.

25 PIERCY, Paul LaVerne. Cattle (Anaplasmosis, toxicology, hematology). b'03. Student '22-23 (Des Moines U); DVM '33—research fellow '33 (Ia State Coll). Research anaplasmosis in cattle with special emphasis on entomological vectors, practical diagnosis and control, certain Louisiana plants with relation to livestock toxicology, blood studies of normal and mineral deficient dairy cattle in Louisiana. Author articles in field. Ext veterinarian U Mo '34-37; veterinarian Tex Agrl Sta '37-43; asso veterinarian and asso prof La State U '43-48; prof and head dept physiol and pharmacol Sch Veterinary Med U Ga since '48. Am Vet Med Assn—Research Workers Animal Diseases NA—Animal Disease Research Workers SE States—Phi Kappa Phi—Gamma Sigma Delta. School of Veterinary Medicine, University of Georgia, Athens, Ga.

10 PIERRE, Dorathi Bock. History and evolution of the dance and drama. Ed private tutor; '30-33 (U Ore). Directed Gay's Beggars Opera University of Oregon '33; lectures and radio programs for Hollywood Bowl dance programs '37-38; ed-public Educational Dance '38-42; director Folk Festival Hollywood Bowl '46. Co-author: Only a Few Can Tell '44; also articles in field. Edn and research edit Dance Magazine since '47; lecturer; profl theatrical press agent with musical plays and legitimate drama since '42. Nat Coll Players—Assn Theatrical Press Agents and Mgrs—Las Fiestas de las Americas (pres '46-49)—Nat Assn Music and Related Arts (adv bd since '48). 8148 Mannix Drive, Hollywood 46, Calif.

11 PIERSOL, Robert James. Coal and industrial physics. b'90. AB '12 (Allegheny Coll); AM '13 (Tulane U); Tyndale research fellow '13-15 (U Pa); PhD '16 (U Calif). Holds 15 patents in industrial physics. Developed new flotation machine, machine for concentration of radium and uranium ores, process for copper plating iron in a vacuum, flectural piezo-electricity, and others. Author articles in field. Research physicist and head physics div III State Geol Survey '31-46, physicist emeritus since '46. Am Physical Soc—Am Inst Mining and Metall Engrs—Am Math Soc—Am Electrochem Soc—British Assn Advancement Sci—Am Optical Soc—Ill Profl Engrs—Am Profl Engrs—Ill Acad Sci. 213 Natural Resources Bldg., Urbana, Ill.

12 PIERSON, Donald. Brazil (Sociology, anthropology). b'00. AB '27 (Coll Emporia Kan); AM '33—PhD '39 (U Chicago). Author: Negroes in Brazil: A Study of Race Contact at Bahia (Anisfield award '42) '42; Teoria e pesquisa em Sociolga '45; Survey of the Literature on Brazil of Sociological Significance '45; Cruz das Almas: A Brazilian Village '51. Editor: Biblioteca de Ciencias Sociais (book series) since '42; asso editor Acta Americana since '45. Co-editor: Sociologia Sao Paulo since '51. Prof sociol and sociol anthrop Escola Livre de Sociologia e Politica of Sao Paulo Brazil since '39, chmn dept sociol and anthrop '41-43, dir grad div since '43; Inter-Am exchange prof US State Dept '44-46; anthrop Inst Social Anthrop Smithsonian Instn in charge Brazilian program of research and research training in cooperation with Escola Livre de Sociologia e Politica of Sao Paulo since '46. Am Anthrop Assn—Am Sociol Soc—Sociedade Brasileira De Sociologia—Inter-Am Soc Anthrop and Geog. Escola Livre de Sociologia e Politica, Largo de Sao Francisco 19, Sao Paulo, Brazil.◎

13 PIERSON, George Wilson. History of Yale; American history (Frontier theory, relationship of American and European civilization); Alexis de Tocqueville. b'04. BA '26—PhD '33 (Yale). Author: Tocqueville and Beaumont in America '38; Yale College: an educational history, 1871-1921 '52. Contbr: American Universities in the Nineteenth Century: The Formative Period to the Modern University (ed Margaret Clapp) '50. With Yale University since '26, Larned professor history since '46. Davenport College, Yale U (F)—AHA—Miss Valley Hist Assn.

1321 Davenport College, Yale University, New Haven.◎

14 PIERSON, Warner N. Refrigeration. b'00. BChE '30—MS '44 (U Detroit). Research engr Norge engring dept Borg Warner Detroit '44-46, head dept since '46. Am Soc Metals—Am Soc Refrig Engrs. Norge Division, Borg Warner, Chattanooga, Tenn.

15 PIERSON, William Haskell. Regional and physical geography; Cartography; Regional and economic geography of Latin America. b'02. BA '25 (U Tex); MS '34 (U Washington); grad study Europe Near East and N Africa '25-26—PhD '53 (U Chgo). Author articles in field. Pvt bus '25-32; U fellow U Chicago '35-36; mem faculty dept geog U Washington '37-46, mem Puget Sound Regional Planning Commn '43-46; asso prof dept geography U Fla since '46; cartographer Dept State Washington '42. Assn Am Geog—American Geog Society—Am Geophys Union—Am Polar Soc—Assn Pacific Coast Geog—Soc Am Mil Engrs—Sigma Xi—AAAS—Am Assn U Profs. Department of Geography, University of Florida, Gainesville, Fla.

16 PIGMAN, William Ward. Chemistry (Carbohydrate; enzyme, wood, paper). b'10. BS '32—MS '33 (George Washington U); PhD '36 (U Md). Co-author: Chemistry of the Carbohydrates '48. Co-editor: (with M L Wolfrom) Advances in Carbohydrate Chemistry (vols 1-4); also articles in field. Organic group leader, Inst Paper Chem Appleton Wis '46-49; asso prof biochem U Ala Medical-Dental Sch since '49. Am Soc Biochem—American Chem Soc—Washington Acad Sci—Tech Assn Paper and Pulp Ind—Swiss Chem Soc—Sigma Xi. Lalor fellow '38-39. Institute of Paper Chemistry, Appleton, Wis.†

17 PIKE, Kenneth Lee. Linguistics (Phonetics, phonemics, intonation, tone language). b'12. ThB '33 (Gordon College Theology and Missions); PhD '42 (University Mich). Special linguistic consultant American Bible Society field trip to Ecuador Peru Bolivia for research on Quechua and Aymara orthographical problems '43-44. Author: Phonetics: A Critical Analysis of Phonetic Theory and a Technic for the Practical Description of Sounds '43; The Intonation of American English '45; Phonemics: A Technique for Reducing Language to Writing '47; Tone Languages: The Nature of Tonemic Systems with a Technique for Analysis of Their Significant Pitch Contrasts '48 and others; also articles in field. Linguistic worker for the Wycliffe Bible Translators Inc Glendale Cal since '35; prof, co-dir since '42; asso prof linguistics English and anthrop U Mich since '48. Linguistic Soc Am—Acoustical Soc Am—Internat Phonetic Assn—Am Anthrop Assn (liaison F). Box 870, Glendale 5, Cal.

18 PIKE, Robert Dickson. Mineral processing; Soda ash; Concentrated fertilizer; Light weight concrete. b'85. BS '07 (U Calif). Manufacture of periclase (dead burned magnesia) from dolomite of northwestern Ohio. Holds patents on cement and lime manufacture, periclase, potash, phosphate, engine bearings, refrigerator cars, reduction of iron oxide to iron by gaseous reduction, electrolytic iron, fixation of atmospheric nitrogen and manufacture of soda ash. Author articles: Volatilization of Phosophorus from Phosphate Rock '30; Proposed Manufacture of Monopotassium Phosphate at Green River Wyoming '33; Recent Developments in Light Weight Burned-Clay for Concrete Aggregates-Gravelite '38; Process for Manufacture of

Dead-burned Magnesite and Precipitated Calcium Carbonate from Dolomite '47, and others. ACS—Am Inst Chem Engrs—Am Ceramic Soc—Am Inst Mining and Metall Engrs. Profl engr Pa, Conn. Gurley Bldg., Stamford, Conn. H: Brook Lane, Greenwich.

19 PILANT, Elizabeth Carter. US folklore. AB '28 (U Wash); MA '31 (U Hawaii); '31 (Northwestern U); EdD '39 (U Cal); '42 (U Colo). Organized National Conference on American Folklore for Youth to further integration of folklore materials into existing subject fields in public schools, instituted course on teaching methods for presenting US folklore materials in elementary and secondary schools. Author: Sky Bears (verse) '52. Contributor: Dictionary of Folklore (vol II) '50; Child's World (Volume VI) '51. Asso prof English Ball State Coll since '47. Am Folklore Soc—Hoosier Folklore Soc—So Folklore Soc—W Folklore Soc—Folklore Soc United Kingdom—Am Folk Music Research (Ind State chmn). Ball State Teachers College, Muncie, Ind.

20 PILGRIM, Mariette Shaw. Alaska history. b'98. Student (Ore Coll Edn, U Wash). Author: Alaska, Its History, Resources, Geography and Government '45; Oogaruk, The Aleut '48. Supt schs Fairbanks Alaska since '48. Box 1896, Fairbanks, Alaska.

21 PILLEMER, Louis. Protein and immunochemistry; Immunology; Bacteriology. b'08. BS '32 (Duke U); PhD '38 (Western Reserve U). Author articles in field. Professor biochemistry Inst Path Western Reserve U since '42. NY Acad Sci(F)—Am Assn Immunologists—Am Chem Soc—Soc Exptl Biol and Med—Sigma Xi—AAAS (F)—Am Soc Biol Chem. Institute of Pathology, Cleve. 6.

22 PINCUS, Gregory Goodwin. Reproduction (Physiology); Steroid hormones. b'03. BS '24 (Cornell U); MS '27—ScD '27 (Harvard). Research on ovum development in mammals and effects of hormones, research on ovulation, ovum development in vitro and in vivo, steroid hormone metabolism in normal, cancerous, and arthritic men and women, relation of steroid metabolism and adrenal function to stress and schizophrenia in man and steroid hormone biogenesis in animals and man; member endocrinology study section and also on panel of appraisers National Research Council, chairman Laurentian Hormone Conference, chairman committee on assay of chorionic gonadotrophin, member committee on steroid standards of US Pharmacopoeia. Author: Eggs of Mammals '36. Editor: Experimental Biol Monographs since '36; Recent Progress in Hormone Research since '46; The Hormones '49-50. Asst prof gen physiol Harvard '31-38; vis investigator Cambridge U '37-38; research prof exptl zool Clark U '38-45; dir lab Worcester Found Exptl Biol since '44; research prof physiol Tufts Coll Med Sch '47-51; research prof biol Boston U since '51. Am Soc Naturalists—Am Soc Zool—Am Assn Anatomists—Am Genetics Soc—Am Physiol Soc—Assn Study Internal Secretions (pres '51-52)—Soc Endocrinology (Gt Brit)—Soc d'Endocrinologie (France)—Soc Gen Physiol—Am Assn Cancer Research—NY Acad Sci—Soc Human Genetics—Soc Study Growth and Development—Sigma Xi—Am Acad Arts and Sci—AAAS. NRC F '27-30; Guggenheim F '39-41. Worcester Foundation for Experimental Biology, 222 Maple Av., Shrewsbury, Mass. H: 68 S. Lenox St., Worcester 2, Mass.

10 PINES, Herman. Organic chemistry (Catalysis applied to hydrocarbons and petroleum). b'02. Certificate of Higher Studies in Indusl Chem '26—CE '27 (Lyons U); PhD '35 (Chicago U). Engaged research in alkylation of aromatics, naphthenes and paraffins, polymerization, isomerization of naphthenes, paraffins and olefins, alkylation of aromatics accompanied by hydrogen transfer, isomerization accompanying alkylation, catalytic reactions applied to terpenes, reaction of phenols and thiophenol, mechanism of isomerization of saturated hydrocarbons. Holds 109 patents in field including basic patents on alkylation and isomerization of paraffins. Author 90 articles in field. Vladimir Ipatieff Research prof organic chem Northwestern U since '53, dir Ipatieff High Pressure and Catalytic Lab since '53. Am Chem Soc—Sigma Xi—Phi Lambda Upsilon. Dept. Chemistry, Northwestern University, Evanston, Ill.

11 PINKNEY, David Henry, Jr. Economic and social history of France (Nineteenth and twentieth centuries). b'14. AB '36 (Oberlin Coll); AM '37—PhD '41 (Harvard). Research in France on growth of Paris under the Second Empire. Author articles in field. Associate professor hist U Mo since '46. AHA—Econ Hist Assn—Societe d' Histoire moderne (France). Department of History, University of Missouri, Columbia, Mo.†

12 PINSON, Koppel Shub. History of Germany; Problems of nationalism. b'04. BA '25 (U Pa); PhD '34 (Columbia U). Author: Pietism and the Rise of German Nationalism '34; A Bibliographical Introduction to Nationalism '35. Co-author: (with H Lichtenberger) The Third Reich '37. Ed: Essays on Antisemitism '46; also articles in field. Hist ed Ency of the Social Sciences '29-35; lecturer on nationalism New Sch Social Research '34-36; dept hist Queens Coll since '37; study and research in Germany '32-33, '35, '45-46; ednl dir for Jewish Displaced Persons in Germany and Austria '45-46; mng ed Social Research '35; exec ed Jewish Social Studies since '37; vp Conference Jewish Relations since '51; research commn Yiddish Sci Inst since '50. AHA—NY State Hist Soc—Conf Jewish Relations—Yiddish Sci Inst. Queens College, Flushing, N.Y.

13 PIORE, Emanuel Ruben. Electronics; Surface physics; Color television. b'08. BA '30—PhD in physics '35 (Wis U). Research on vapor pressure of metals, work functions, surface physics and mechanisms involved in operation of iconoscope and similar devices, physical aspects of color television, surface field emission, willenite, secondary electron emission. Author articles in field. Mem bd editors Reviews of Modern Physics and Advances in Electronics. Research engineer RCA Mfg Co '35-38; engr in chge Television Labs CBS '38-42; in chge Guided Missiles Sect Electronics Div Bur of Ships Navy Dept '42-44; head Electronics Bur dir Phys Sci Div, Office Naval Research '46-51, chief sci since '51. Am Soc Naval Engrs—Nat Research Council (div phys sci)—Cosmos Club—Am Phys Soc—Inst Radio Engrs—Sigma Xi. 1812 Office Naval Research, Navy Department, Washington.

14 PIPKIN, Marvin. Electric lamp technology. b'89. BS '13—MS '15 (Ala Polytechnic Inst). Research on inside frosting of incandescent lamps, pebble phosphate field. Engr lamp dept Gen Elec Co Cleveland since '19. Am Chem Soc—AAAS. Nela Park, Cleveland 14. H: 3815 Parkdale Rd.

15 PIRKEY, Jane Sedgwick (Mrs Frank Z Pirkey). Mass feeding; Food allowances. b'02. BS '23 (U Minn); '24-26 (U Cal Los Angeles and ext div); '26-27 (U So Cal); '42-43 (U Chicago). Research on mass feeding with emphasis on successful use of food and cost of feeding operations, nutritional adequacy and acceptability of dietaries provided for those for whom governments assume full or partial responsibility, development and adjustment of food allowances according to populations served. Nutritionist Los Angeles City Pub Health and Corrective Phys Edn Dept '24-27; nutritionist Los Angeles Co Pub Health Assn '28-29; nutrition expert Cal State Tuberculosis Assn '29-30; nutrition adv Cal State Dept Pub Health, '30-32 nutrition cons '40-44; food adminstr Cal State Dept Instn '32-40; food adminstr Cal Youth Authority since '44. Cal Probation and Parole Assn—Inst Food Tech—Am Home Econ Assn—Am Dietetics Assn —Am Pub Health Assn(F)—Assn W Hosp. 401 State Office Building 1, Sacramento 14.

16 PIRNIE, Miles David. Wildlife management; Waterfowl; Marsh management. b'98. BS '23—PhD '28 (Cornell U). Consultant duck club marshes Ohio and Ontario; collector data on wet lands management for waterfowl and muskrats; study Canada Goose in Gull Lake area of Michigan; advisor Delta Duck Station Manitoba Canada '38-42. Author: Michigan Waterfowl Management '35. Ornithol Mich Dept Conservation Lansing '28-31; dir W K Kellogg Bird Sanctuary Mich State Coll '31-48, prof wildlife since '48. Wildlife Soc—Am Ornithol Union—Sigma Xi. Conservation Bldg., Michigan State College, East Lansing, Mich.†

17 PIROK, John Nicholas. Concrete (Reinforced); Water purification; Penstocks. b'04. Student '26 (Ill Coll); BS '31—MS '33 (U Ill); '35 (U Colo). Research on theoretical behavior of reinforced concrete arch bridges and comparison measurements with calculated values; research, development and design water purification plants; design steel penstocks with attendant supports, self-supporting tees and wyes, surge tanks, anchors expansion joints. Chief engr Soil Conservation State of Ill '33-35; asst engr US Bur Reclamation '35-36; development engr water purification plants '36-40; engr-designer Chicago Bridge & Iron Co '40-42, prin designer since '45. Tau Beta Pi—Sigma Tau—Sigma Xi—Am Soc CE. Registered structural engr. 1305 W. 105th St., Chgo 43.

18 PIRONE, Pascal Pompey. Plant diseases (Ornamental); Air pollution. b'07. BS '29—PhD '33 (Cornell U). Discovered three new species of bacteria attacking ornamental plants; inventor Rutgers aero-plant propagator for rooting plants without soil or other solid media. Author: Maintenance of Shade and Ornamental Trees '48. Co-author: Grounds for Living '46; The home Owners Guide to Lawns, Trees, and Gardens '48. Plant path NY Bot Garden since '47. Nat Shade Tree Con (bd gov and exec com)—Am Phytopath Soc—AAAS(F)—Sigma Xi —Phi Kappa Phi. New York Botanical Garden, Bronx Park, NYC 58. H: 1522 Dwight Pl., NYC 61.

19 PIRTLE, George William. Petroleum geology. b'02. BS '24—MS '25 (U Ky); '25 (U Chicago). Research on Michigan structural basin and its relationship to surrounding areas '32, petroleum and gas developments in East Texas '38. Co-author: Geology of Jessamine County, Kentucky '25; Geologic Maps Coleman and Brown Counties, Texas '29. With Ky Geol Survey '25-26; partner firm Hudnall and Pirtle specializing in exploration and appraisal of oil producing properties since '26. Am Assn Petroleum Geol—Geol Soc Am—Mich Acad Sci—AIME—Sigma Xi. Peoples National Bank Building, Tyler, Tex.

20 PITELKA, Frank Alois. Bird ecology, behavior and taxonomy; Terrestrial biotic communities; American jays. b'16. AB '39 (U Ill); PhD '46 (U Calif). Author articles in field. Asst prof zool U California '47-52 associate professor since '52, curator of birds Museum of Vertebrate Zoology since '46. AAAS—Ecol Soc Am—Brit Ecol Soc—Am Soc Zool—Soc Study Evolution—Western Soc Naturalists—Am Ornithol Union—Cooper Ornithol Club (asso edit Arctic Institute NA Condor since '46)—Phi Beta Kappa—Sigma Xi. Museum of Vertebrate Zoology, University of California, Berkeley 4.†

21 PITKIN, William A(sbury). American history (Progressive movement: 1896-1917, Republican insurgency). b'98. BA '22 (DePauw U); MA '27 (U Colo); PhD '40 (U Tex). Research on insurgency within Republican Party, Muckrackers, Roosevelt-Taft fued 1909-13, Bull Moose party, Theodore Roosevelt and judicial recall, Wilson's new freedom, Taft administration. Instr hist Superior (Wis) State Teach Coll '31-36, asst prof '37-45; asso prof history South Illinois U since '45. AHA—Miss Valley Hist Assn—Am Econ Assn—Midwest Econ Assn. Southern Illinois University, Carbondale, Ill.

22 PITMAN, Earle Carver. Nitrocellulose lacquers; Lamination (High frequency); Shoe cementing; Fluorescent tubes. b'93. AB in chem '14 (Harvard); BS in chem engring '16 (MIT). Developed many Duco lacquers. Issued patents in specialisms. Chem duPont Co Arlington and Parlin NJ '19-43; cons since '43. ACS—Soc Chem Industry—Electrochem Soc—AAAS—Am Inst Chem(F)—Nat Paint Varnish and Lacquer Assn—Phi Beta Kappa. Modern Pioneer award Nat Assn Mfrs '40. Norumbega, High St., Camden, Me.

23 PITTMAN, Richard Saunders. Nahuatl language. b'15. AB '35 (Asbury Coll); '45 (U Mich); MA '48—PhD '53 (U Pa); grad fellow '38-40 (Wheaton Coll). Resch on Nahuatl language since '40. Author: La Historia de Pedro Sa-kinemilea '45; Nahuatl Honorifics '48; Nuclear Structures in Linguistics '48; A Grammar of Tetelcingo (Morelos) Nahnatl '53. Director Mex br Summer Inst Linguistics '47-51, Pacific br since '52. Linguistic Soc Am—Am Anthropol Assn—Linguistic Circle NY—Consejo de Lenguas Indigenas Mexico. Box 1488, Manila, P.I. H: Box 123, Sulphur Springs, Ark.

24 PITTS, Thomas Jefferson. Public law. b'95. Student asst govt and hist (Northeastern State Coll); LLB—grad research fellow pub law—LLM '30 (Chicago Law Sch); LLD hon '47 (Howard Payne Coll). Chairman advisory board for registrants Selective Service '40-47; US attorney American Mexican Claims Commission, delegate International Bar Association Conference '45; special civilian judge US Court in Germany '47. Author monographs in American, Latin-American and Roman law. Master in chancery state and US courts; practice of law since '22; special judge, county and dist cts. Am Bar Assn—Ector County Bar Assn(pres '46-47)—State Bar Tex (pres President's Club '44-46, chmn com on legal edn '40-42, com on criminal law and procedure since '47)—Am Judicature Soc—Acad Polit Sci Columbia—Law Soc U Paris(hon)—Council for Research in Am Legal Hist—Order of Coif—Phi Delta Phi. Congressional medal and Presidential certificate for meritorious service in administrn Selective Service law '47. Henderson Bldg., Odessa, Tex.†◎

10 PITZ, Henry Clarence. American illustration; History of costumes; Art criticism; Art education. b'95. Student '14-17 (Pa Mus Sch Indsl Art); '19-20 (Spring Garden Inst). Executed three murals for US Government Building in Century of Progress Chicago '33, mural for Franklin Institute Philadelphia presentation; represented in permanent exhibitions various art collections. Author: The practice of Illustration '47; A Treasury of American Book Illustration '47. Co-author: Early American Costume '29. Illustrator of books and mags since '20; dir illustration and decoration Pa Mus Sch Indsl Art since '32. Am Water Color Soc—Southern Printmakers—Am Fedn Arts — Soc of Illustrators—Graphic Arts Forum—Am Inst Graphic Arts. 320 S. Broad St., Phila.

11 PIZZUTO, Frank Laurel. Italian language and literature. b'96. BA '23 (Boston U); '23-25—MA '40 (Harvard); '26-27 (Drew Theol Sem); MA '28 (Webster U); ThB '38—DD '42 (Milton Coll). Research on St Thomas Aquinas and Dante's Divine Comedy; Italian Literature in Spain; Don Quijote and Orlando Furioso. Author: La Religione di Dante '27; Catechismo Cristiano '32; also articles in field. Instr Italian Suffolk U Boston since '38, asst prof Italian and Spanish since '40, prof Romance lang '44. Modern Lang Assn—East Mass Assn Teachers Italian (pres '46-47)—Nat Ed Assn US —Phi Beta Kappa. Suffolk University, Boston.

12 PLACE, Ian Cameron Munro. Forestry (Silviculture, eastern region); Eastern spruces (Regeneration); Balsam fir regeneration. b'17. BSc '40 (U NB Fredericton NB); MF '47 (Yale). Regeneration survey cut-over pulpwood lands Maritime Provinces of Canada; detailed study influence of seedbeds on growth and incidence of spruce and fir seedlings. Author articles: A Discussion of Techniques in the Study of Natural Forest Tree Reproduction (thesis) '47; Origin of Reproduction on Black Spruce Swamps '50; The Identification of Spruce Seedlings '50, and others. Forest engr research div forestry br Can Dept Resources and Development '45-49, silviculturist Maritimes Dist since '49. Can Inst Forestry—Soc Am Foresters. P.O. Box 843, Fredericton, N.B., Can.

13 PLACE, Ruth Mosher. Horticulture (Delphinium, phlox). b'83. AB (Oberlin). Research in control of diseases affecting Phlox (pathology); Phlox species and nomenclature; description and selection garden hybrids; experimentation in media for propagation of Delphiniums from seed. Author articles: Delphinium for fun; Horticultural Help for city gardeners; Gardening is healthful; and others. Garden ed The Detroit News '34-48; instr hort U Mich since '41. Am Soc Hort Sci—AAAS—Mich Acad Sci Arts and Letters—Phi Beta Kappa—Am Rose Soc—Am Iris Soc—Am Delphinium Soc. Minnie A Robinson gold medal for hort achievement '41; Setigera gold medal for services to the rose '46. University of Michigan, Extension Service, Ann Arbor.

14 PLAKIDAS, Antonios George. Plant pathology. b'95. BS '24—PhD '27 (U Calif); Gen Edn Bd Scholar '40-41 (Cornell). Author articles in field. Asst plant path La Agr Expt Sta '27-31, asso '31-43; plant path and

prof bot La State U since '43; agrl officer UNRRA Egypt and Greece '44-46; mem commn FAO Greece to study agr conditions and recommend changes. AAAS(F)—Am Phytopath Soc—Mycol Soc Am—Sigma Xi. Botany Department, Louisiana State University, Baton Rouge, La.

15 PLATH, Karl. Ornithology; Bird art. b'93. Chicago Acad Fine Arts '25-27 (Art Inst Chicago). Specializes in painting birds; studied habits and painted birds West Indies, Bermuda, Florida, Alaska; lecturer, using for illustrations his paintings and skins of rare birds; one man shows in various cities; exhibits in Art Institute Chicago; maintained aviary in garden with over 100 species. Contbd black and white bird illus World Book '45-46; color illus for Nelson Ency '47-48; also articles in field. Curator of birds Chicago Zool Park Brookfield Ill since '35. Brit Aviculture Soc—Am Aviculture Soc (vp)—Am Ornithol Union. Chicago Zoological Park, Brookfield, Ill.

16 PLATT, Haviland Hull. Helicopters (Convertible, twin rotor); Automotive engines and parts. b'89. BS in elec engring '09—ME '30 (U Pa). Design and development twin rotor helicopter for Army Air Corps; design convertible airplane. Holds patents in field. Author articles: Important Factors in Piston Ring Design '27; The Case for Vertical Flight '34; The Helicopter—Propulsion and Torque '36. Chief engr Wilkening Mfg Phila '17-45; vp in charge research and development Platt-LePage Aircraft Co '38-45; engring cons and patent expert since '45. Soc Automotive Engrs—Inst Aeronautical Sci—Am Helicopter Soc—AAAS—Sigma Xi. 19 E. 53rd St., NYC 22.

17 PLATT, Raye Roberts. Political geography and cartography of Latin America. b'91. AB '21—MEd (hon) '33 (Mich State Normal Coll). Author articles in field. Head dept hispanic Am Research Am Geog Soc '23-37, research asso since '37; ed Millionth Map Hispanic Am '23-37; mem edv com US Bd Geog Names '32-47. Assn Am Geog—Geog Soc Lima, Peru (hon mem). American Geographical Society, Broadway at 156th St., NYC.†

18 PLATT, Robert Swanton. Geography (Latin American, political, air transport). b'91. AB '14 (Yale); PhD '20 (U Chicago). Author: Latin America, Countrysides and United Regions '42. Prof geog U Chicago since '39. Assn Am Geog (treas '29-34, vp '43, pres '45)—Sigma Xi—Phi Beta Kappa. Department of Geography, University of Chicago, Chgo 37.

19 PLETTA, Dan Henry. Statically indeterminate structures and rigid frames; Engineering materials; Materials testing; Theory of elasticity and plasticity. b'03. BS '27—MS '31—CE '38 (U Ill). Author articles in field. Asst prof later prof and head applied mech dept Va Poly Inst since '32; cons engr and stress analyst. Maj. Ordnance Dept US Army '42-46. ASCE—Am Concrete Inst—Soc Exptl Stress Analysis —Tau Beta Pi—Sigma Xi. Applied Mechanics Dept., Virginia Polytechnical Inst., Blacksburg, Va.†

20 PLOCHERE, Gustave. Color classification. b'88. Ed pub schs. Devised with Gladys Plochere color system giving mixing formulas and two, three, and four split complementary colors. Color cons; bd cons Color Research Inst Am since '45. Inter-Soc Color Council—Cal Color Soc. 1820 Hyperion Av., LA 27.

21 PLOUGH, Harold Henry. Genetics; Mutations in bacteria; Biology; Effect of temperature on genetic processes

and on evolution. b'92. BA '13 (Amherst); MA '15—PhD '17 (Columbia); research (Marine Biol Lab, Carnegie Marine Lab, Dry Tortugas Fla, Stazione Zoologica Naples). Delegate to 5th International Congress of Genetics Berlin '27, 6th at Ithaca '32, 7th at Edinburgh '39, 8th at Stockholm '48; research on effect of temperature on genetic processes and on evolution as shown by the fly Drosophila; developments of Ascidians; bacteriological assay of penicillin; radiation-induced mutations in bacteria. Author articles in field. With Amherst Coll since '17, prof biol since '24, Rufus T Lincoln prof biol since '33, Edward S Harkness prof since '49, curator zool Nat Hist Mus since '32. Maj US Army '45 serving as bact Lovell Gen Hosp Fort Devens '42-44. AAAS(F)—Am Soc Zool—Am Soc Naturalists (treas '39-42)—Soc Am Bact—Genetics Soc Am—Am Soc Phys Anthrop—Mass Archeol Soc—Sigma Xi. Biological Laboratory, Amherst College, Amherst, Mass.

22 PLUM, Svend Munk. Plumbing; Sanitary engineering (Installations); Miniature theatres. b'95. Architect '17 (Royal Acad Fine Arts Copenhagen); '18 (MIT). Author: Plumbing Practice and Design '43; also articles in field. Cons engr Detroit since '38, sanitary installations for numerous large factories; founded Theater Model Co for miniature stage productions and artistic effects '47. Am Pub Health Assn—ASCE—Mich Sewage Works Assn. 3629 Dudley, Dearborn, Mich.†

23 PLUMLEY, Harold Jamison. Guided missiles; Conductivities in dielectrics. b'12. BS '33—PhD '37 (U Chicago). Holder eight US patents in electronics and naval ordnance. Author articles in field. With Naval Ordnance Lab since '41, chief guided missile div since '49. AIEE—Phi Beta Kappa—Sigma Xi. Naval Ordnance Laboratory, White Oak, Md.†

24 PLUMMER, Carlyle J(unker). Canal, narrow channel and harbor piloting; Ship handling. b'95. Grad '15 (Culver Summer Naval Sch); '09-11 (Allen Acad); '11-13 (Columbia Mil Acad). Author: Use of Anchors in Maneuvering '42; Adapting Ocean Steamers to Inland Waters '42; Ship Handling in Narrow Channels '45. Began career as seaman quartermaster '08, mate on ocean steamers master harbor and coastwise tugs '16, dep pilot '20, br pilot since '21; with Sabine Pilots since '21. Lt comdr US Coast Guard '43-45, comdr '45. Sabine Pilots, Port Arthur, Tex.

25 PLUMMER, Fred Leroy. Volatile liquids (Conservation); Welding. b'00. AB '20 (Ohio U Athens); BS '22—MS '24 (Case Inst Tech Cleveland). Analysis and design bridges, storage and process vessels, including special conservation tanks for storing volatile liquids. Holds patents on conservation tanks, including floating roofs, gas holders, and flexible diaphragm pressure tanks, foundations, welding. Author articles: Field Erected Pressure Vessels '46; Design of Low Pressure Vapor Conservation Tanks '47; Use of Aluminum in the Petroleum Industry '49, and others. Chief design engr Main Av Bridge Projects Cleveland '37-40; dir engring Hammond Iron Works Warren Pa since '40; head AUS Corps Engrs mission to Japan for manufacture of steel, fabrication of bridges '50. Am Soc CE—Am Soc ME—Am Soc Metals—American Petroleum Isnt—Am Welding Soc(president '52-54)—Am Concrete Inst—Am Soc Engring Edn—ASTM—Welding Research Council—Nat Research Council—Phi Beta Kappa—Sigma Xi—Tau Beta Pi. Profl engr. Ohio, NY, NJ. Box 629, Warren, Pa.

10 PLUMMER, Helen Jeanne. Micropaleontology; Stratigraphy; Subsurface and Texas geology. b'91. AB '13—AM '25 (Northwestern U); '24 (U Chicago). Author articles in field. Research scientist Bur Econ Geol Austin Tex since '48. Bureau of Economic Geology, Austin, Tex.

11 PLUMMER, Norman. Ceramics; Geology of clays. b'01. AB '25 (U Kan). Research on clays of Kansas and to a limited extent of other states, ceramic uses of other mineral resources such as volcanic ash chalk and sand, work on ceramic glazes and bodies; developed use of semi-fused clays and silts for railroad ballast and concrete aggregates. Author articles in field. Instr techniques ceramics dept design U Kan '34-35; head ceramics div State Geol Survey Kan since '36. Am Ceramic Soc—Sigma Xi. State Geological Survey of Kansas, University of Kansas, Lawrence, Kan.†

12 PLUMMER, William Edwin. Frequency allocation; Directive antenna. b'05. BE in elec engring '29 (Johns Hopkins). Research on frequency utilization by all US agencies, frequency allocation studies for standard broadcast, high frequency, frequency modulation, television, very high and ultra high frequency and microwave; design and adjustment of directive antennas for standard broadcast stations up to eight towers; past War Department representative Interdepartment Radio Advisory Committee, member Frequency Allocation Committee Joint and Combined Communications Board, alternate War Department representative Central Radio Progation Laboratory Executive Council. Cons radio engr Glenn D Gillett & Asso '33-41, partner '46-50; asst chief, chief communication liaison br. Office Chief Signal Officer War Dept '41-46; staff Pres Communication Policy Bd '50-51; telecommunications specialist Staff, Telecommunications Advisor to the President since '51. Inst Radio Engrs (sr mem)—Assn Fed Communications Cons Engrs (charter mem). Office, Executive Office of the President, Washington 25.

13 PLUNGUIAN, Mark. Cellulose chemistry. b'04. BS '30 (NY State Coll Forestry); MS '31 (U Ida); PhD '34 (McGill U). Author: Cellulose Chemistry '42; also articles in field. Indsl chem Celanese Corp of Am Summit NJ '46-53; dir research So Chem Cotton Co Chattanooga. Am Chem Soc—Sigma Xi. Souther Chemical Cotton Co., Chattanooga, Tenn.

14 PLYMALE, Edward Lewis. Plant morphology (Leaves); Vascular plant (West Virginia). b'14. AB '35 (Marshall Coll); MS '39 (U Ky); PhD '42 (State U Ia); certificate in meteorology '43 (U Chicago). Author articles in field. Asso prof bot head dept Marshall Coll since '46. Bot Soc Am—So Appalachian Bot Assn—Sigma Xi. Department of Botany, Marshall College, Huntington 1, W. Va.†

15 POGO, Alexander. History of astronomy; Egyptian astronomy; Maya chronology. b'93. BS '13—EE—ME '20 (U Liége); AM '26 (Columbia U); PhD '28 (U Chicago). Research on diagonal calendars from Asyut, prismatic clepsydrae, eclipse cycles Dresden Codex, penumbral lunar eclipses, Easter dates, cylindrical diagrams of saros series and golden numbers. Carnegie Inst Wash. AAAS(F)—Am Astron Society —Hist Sci Soc—Netherland Soc Hist Sci (corr mem). Mount Wilson Observatory Library, 813 Santa Barbara St., Pasadena 4, Cal.

16 POHL, John Florian. Cerebral palsy; Infantile paralysis (Kenny treatment). b'03. BS '26—MB '28—MD '29 (U Minn); '22-23 (Harvard); '35-36 (U Manchester Eng). Author: The Kenny Concept of Infantile Paralysis and Its Treatment '43; Cerebral Palsy '50. Orthopedic surg Minneapolis since '37; dir research and med supervisor Elizabeth Kenney Inst '40-48; clin asst prof orthopedic surgery U Minn '37-48; orthopedic surg Michael Dowling School for Crippled Children since '37; research on treatment of poliomyelitis with special reference to deformities, treatment of cerebral palsy. Nu Sigma Nu—Am Acad Orthopedic Surgs—Am Acad Cerebral Palsy—AMA—Minn-Dakota Orthopedic Soc—Twin City Orthopedic Club. 1945 Medical Arts Bldg., Mpls.

17 POHL, Richard W(alter). Agrostology; Angiosperms. b'16. BS '39 (Marquette U); PhD '47 (U Pa). Author articles in field. Asst prof bot Ia State Coll since '47. Wis Acad Arts Sci Letters—Bot Soc Am—Am Soc Plant Taxonomists — Grassland Research Found—Gamma Sigma Delta—Sigma Xi. Department of Botany, Iowa State College, Ames, Ia.†

18 POINDEXTER, Hildrus Augustus. Tropical diseases. b'01. AB '24 (Lincoln U Pa); MD '29 (Harvard); AM '30 —PhD '32 (Columbia) MS in pub health '37 (Delmar Inst Pub Health of Columbia and U PR). Studies on cultivation and physiological requirements of Endameba histolytica, Trypanosoma equiperdum and gambiense; epidemiological studies of syphilis, malaria, filariasis, and hookworm infections; cultivation studies on human schistosomiasis Philippine Islands and Africa; research on immunology to parasitic infections. Author articles: Cultivation of Intestinal Protozoa '32; Epidemiological Studies in Liberia '49; Filaria bancrofti '50; Tropical Ulcers '50, and others. Rockefeller Found fellow microbiol and pub health Med Center NYC '29-31; asst prof advancing to prof and administrative head dept bact, preventive med and pub health Howard U Washington '31-47; chief lab and med research and dir USPHS mission in Liberia since '47. Tropical med specialist AUS '43-47. AMA(F)—Am Pub Health Assn(F)—AAAS(F)—American Found Tropical Med—Soc Am Bact —Am Soc Parasitol—Assn Mil Surgeons US—Nat Med Assn(vp)—Internat Congress Microbiol—Am Society Tropical Med—NY Acad Sci—AAUP—Am Soc Protozool. U.S. Public Health Service, Monrovia Station, c/o American Embassy, Monrovia, Liberia.

19 POLAND, Frank F. Copper coating; Furnace (Design for high temperature). b'95. Developed improved electrical contacts for electrolytic copper refining, high temperature distillation of zinc from copper base alloys for US Navy and adapted this to use for scrap brass and galvanizer dross; invented first commercial continuous casting process in US; patents on continuous casting process, recovery of selenium and tellurium, coloring copper, electrical contacts and methods of casting copper shapes. Metall research and jr exec Am Smelting & Refining Co to '23, chief metallurgist Baltimore plant '23-33, research and consulting metallurgist on copper NYC '33-40; research metallurgist, administrv asst to vp in charge research and development Revere Copper & Brass Inc since '40. Am Soc for Metals. Revere Copper & Brass Inc., Rome, N.Y. H: 910 N. George St.

20 POLAND, Reginald. Art museum directorate; Spanish arts. b'93. AB

'14 (Brown U); MA '15—fellowship early Christ Archeology Am Sch Rome '17 (Princeton); MA '17 (Harvard). Opened Fine Arts Gallery San Diego built up collection from valuation $50,000 to $2,250,000; worked especially in field Spanish Arts, French Arts, Decorative Arts, contemporary American painting; member National Jury Ceramic Arts Annual '38-41, chairman National Jury '41; chairman Southern California regional committee '46, '47; member National Committee Pepsi Cola's Pictures of the Year Annual '46-47. Author: Apse Mosaic of Old St Peter's '16. Dir Fine Arts Gallery San Diego '26-50. Art Mus Dir Assn —West Assn Art Mus Dirs (pres '37-41)—Am Fed Arts—Coll Art Assn (exec council '30)—Globe Theatre (pres '41-46). Fellowship Carl Schurz Found spl travel study Europe '36.

21 POLEMAN, Horace Irvin. Indolog. b'05. BA '27—MA '30—PhD '33 (U Pa); research fellow Sanskrit '34-35 (U Pa)—Hindu rituals '37-38 (Yale). Author: Indic manuscripts and paintings '39, America and Indic studies '40, The Indic manuscripts '42; also articles in field. Cataloger of Indic manuscripts in US and Can, Am Council of Learned Societies '33-38; instr Sanskrit U Pa '34-35; chief South Asia Sect Oriental Div Ref Dept Library of Congress since '38. Am Council of Learned Socs—Social Sci Research Council—Am Oriental Society— Phi Beta Kappa. Library of Congress, Washington 25.

22 POLETIKA, Nicholas Vladimir. Glues and plywoods. b'18. BS '41 (U Conn); research fellowship '46-48—MF '46—DF '48 (Yale). Research in adhesives, plywood, laminated wood, sandwich construction, wood anatomy and identification, lumber utilization. Author articles in field. Wood tech Research Lab Timber Engring Co '48-49, lab supt since '49. Soc Am Forestry—Forest Products Research Soc—Sigma Xi. Wood award '48 for outstanding paper on Forest Products Research. 4812 Minnesota Av., N.E., Washington 2.

23 POLFUS, William Frederick. Paper coating and flame proofing. b'13. Student '34 (Western State Teachers Coll, Mich); ChE '39 (Ind Tech Coll); '42, '49 (U Cincinnati). Research on paper coating, purchasing pigments and chemicals, administration, paper flame proofing, pigments application. Asst tech dir research and control Clopay Corp. Clopay Corporation, Clopay Square, Cincinnati 14.

24 POLIAKOFF, Rouvime. Mechanic engineering. b'80. ME '02 (Tech Inst Moscow Russia); Spl student '07 (Municipal Sch Tech Manchester Eng). Research on twist drills and other metal cutting tools; equipment of machine shops and factories for production of metal products; inventor milling machine dynamometer, lead cable covering press and machine shop rule; chief consultant engineering branch Foreign Economic Development, Office International Trade Department Commerce Washington; chief consultant engineering service Foreign Economics Administration World War II. Author articles: Metal Cutting Tools '23; Design of Milling Cutters '23; Torque and Twist for Twist Drillls '26; Hot Spot Machining '50, and others. Editor: Complete German-Russian Technical Dictionary 1907-08. Cons engr mfg and engring firms Russia; chief machine and tool dept Russian Govt Supply Com '15-17; commr Russian Govt War Industries Bd Washington '17. Am Ordnance Assn—Am Rocket Soc—ASME—AIMME—AAAS. 126-11th Av.,

NYC 11. H: 276 Riverside Drive, NYC 25.

10 POLIVKA, Jaro Joseph. Concrete (Shell structures). b'86. BS '06—MS '09—D Engring Sci '17 (Tech U Prague); '10-12 (Confed Inst Tech); spl research '19 (Ecole des Ponts et Chaussées). Concrete shell structures; research and application precast and prestressed concrete structures; solidification of soils and foundations. Issued patents in field. Author articles in field in 5 langs. Designer navigation locks for Austrian Govt '07-09; design Belvedere Tunnel Prague (winner internat competition) '09; design and supervision concrete bridge over Ohre River Bohemia '09-10; cons engineer Italy '11, Zurich '11-16; partner Dr Emperger Vienna '16-17; cons engineer Central Europe '18-38, Czechoslovakia '39; research asso Engring Materials Lab U Cal, also structural engr Bethlehem Alameda Shipyards, Kaiser Shipyards '39-44; cons engineer Berkeley-San Francisco since '45; lectr Stanford U since '50; West Coast editor Architecture d'Aujourd'hui. Am Soc CE—ASTM—Am Chem Inst—ASME—Soc French Civil Engrs—Internat Association Bridge Structural Engring—Swiss Assn Testing Materials—Sigma Xi. Received French Soc Civil Engrs Colombet award '36; 4 diplomas and medals Paris Internat Expn. 1150 Arch St., Berkeley 8, Cal.

11 POLLACK, Philip. Optometry. b '01. Student (Sch of Optometry Columbia U). Author: Careers in Science '45; Opportunities in Optometry and Optics '53. Contribr: Optometric World (asso ed), Optical Jour and Review, Optometric Weekly, Am Jour Optometry, Am Jour Psychology, Plastics. Practice optometry NYC since '24. Fellowship for analysis of optometric theory Distinguished Service Found in Optometry '42. 1400 Broadway, NYC 18. H: 107 W. 74th St., NYC 23.

12 POLLAK, Arthur. Tall oil, lignin, turpentine, and pulp processes; Terpenes. b'02. BS '27 (City Coll NY); AM '29 — PhD '41 (Columbia). Specializes in wood pulp and related processes and their secondary products such as lignin, terpenes, tall oil. Holds ten patents. Author articles in field. Past dir development dept WVa Pulp & Paper Co Charleston SC; consulting chem engr, NYC. Am Chem Soc—Am Soc for Testing Materials—AICE—Soc for Chem Industry—Tech Assn Pulp & Paper Industry—Am Oil Chemists Soc—Am Forestry Assn—Nat Farm Chemurgic Council—Sigma Xi. 1718 Grand Av., NYC 53.

13 POLLARD, Cash Blair. Organic chemistry; Toxicology; Scientific crime detection. b'00. AB '21 (William Jewell Coll); MS '23—PhD '30 (Purdue); '24 (U Wis). Consulting chemist to Florida state attorneys on scientific crime detection since '30; expert witness Florida and Federal courts on toxicology, blood stains and powder marks; consultant to Gainesville Police Department since '31, Alachua County Sheriff's Office since '30. Coauthor: Laboratory Manual and Study Outline of General Chemistry (with L A Test) '37; Bibliography of Animal Venoms (with R W Harmon) '48. Asst editor: Outline of Organic Chemistry '37. Asso editor: Quadri-Service Manual of Organic Chemistry '38. Collaborator: Fundamental Organic Chemistry '40; The Work Book of Fundamental Organic Chemistry '41; also articles in field. Asst prof chem U Fla '30-35, prof since '37; cons practice since '27. Am Inst Chem(F)—Am Chem Soc—Fla Acad Sci—Sigma Xi—Phi Kappa Phi. USPHS research

grant '47. Chemistry Building, University of Florida, Gainesville, Fla.†◎

14 POLLARD, E(lisha) F(red). Vegetable oilseeds (Solvent extraction); Rubber (Extraction from domestic plants). b'97. BS in chem engring '19—MS in chem engring '20 (Ala Poly Inst); grad study '23-25 (Ia State Coll); Jeavon F '31-32—PhD in inorganic chem '34 (Western Res U). Research upon reactions in molten state; industrial utilization of cotton, cottonseed, sweet-potatoes and peanuts; solvent extraction of vegetable oilseeds; fractionation of cottonseed meals; extraction rubber from domestic plants. Author: Solvent Extraction of Cottonseed and Peanut Oils; Reactions in Inert Fused Substances; Pilot Plant Fractionation of Cottonseed; Instrumentation for Pilot Plants; The Nutritive Value of Cotton seed for Chicks as Affected by Methods of Processing and Content of Pigment Glands; Holds patents on procedure for obtaining rubber from Goldenrod; fractionation of cottonseed. With chem dept Tulane U '26-42, prof '27-42; chem tech So Regional Research Lab bur agrl and indsl chem US Dept Agr '42-46, chem engr since '46. Am Chem Soc—(pres '43-44, exec com '45-48)—Am Inst Chem Engrs—La Engring Soc—Am Oil Chemists Soc—So Assn Sci and Industry—New Orleans Acad Sci—Alpha Chi Sigma—Phi Lambda Upsilon—Kappa Psi—Phi Delta Chi. 2100 Robert E. Lee Blvd., New Orleans 19.

15 POLLARD, Herschel Newton. Entomology (Insecticides, biological control, economic). b'13. Student '32-33 (Austin Peay State Coll Tenn)—'39-40 (Coll William and Mary); '45-46 (U Va). Research on insects affecting dark-fired and burley tobacco, insects affecting cabbage and strawberries, laboratory toxicity tests, stored-tobacco insects, principally fumigation experiments and rearing insects, insects affecting flue-cured tobacco, biological control, mass production, liberation, and recovery of Comstock mealybug parasites, effect of insecticides on orchard pests and their parasites. Author articles in field. With US Dept Agr Bur Entomol Plant Quarantine truck crop garden insect investigations Clarksville Tenn '31-37, Chadbourn NC '37-39, Richmond Va '39-41, Florence SC '41-43, fruit insect investigations Charlottesville Va '43-49, Fort Valley Ga since '49. Am Assn Econ Entomol—AAAS. Fort Valley, Ga.

16 POLLARD, James E(dward). Newspaper law; History of Ohio; History of the United States Presidency. b'94. BA '16—MA '17—PhD '39 (O State U). Author: History 47th US Infantry '20; The Journal of Jay Cooke '35; Principles of Newspaper Management '37; The Newspaper as Defined by Law '40; The Presidents and the Press '47. Prof dir sch journalism O State U since '38; ed Ohio Newspaper since '34. Am Assn Teachers Journalism—O Archeol Hist Soc. Winner Sigma Delta Chi distinguished service award for journalism research '47. 2033 Bedford Rd., Columbus, O.

17 POLLARD, James Joseph. Architectural engineering. b'07. BS in engring '29 (Emory U); Diplome '39 (Fontainebleau Ecole des Beaux Arts); BA in architecture '41 (Harvard Univ Grad Sch Design); MS '48 (Ga Sch Tech). Research on concrete structural framing systems for sports stadia '44-45. Author article: Stadium Press Box on Stilts '48, and others. Civil and archtl engr '44-47; asso prof archtl engring Ga Sch Tech '44-47; prof archtl engring and chmn dept U Tex since '48. AIA—Am Soc CE—Am Concrete

Inst—Am Soc Engring Edn (chmn div archtl engrs)—Soc Exptl Stress Analysis—Nat Soc Profl Engrs—Phi Beta Kappa—Tau Beta Pi—Chi Epsilon. Department of Architectural Engineering, University of Texas, Austin.

18 POLLARD, Lancaster. History of the Pacific Northwestern United States. b'01. AB '22 (U Mo). Author: History of the State of Washington '37; Building a State (contbr) '40; Oregon and the Pacific Northwest '46; Northwest Harvest (contbr) '48; also articles in field. Supt Ore Hist Soc since '43; research asso U Ore since '43; ed Ore Hist Quar since '43. AHA—American Association State Local History. 235 S.W. Market St., Portland 1, Ore.

19 POLLOCK, Chauncey Lloyd. International relations. b'86. AB '08 (Franklin Coll); BD '11 (Xenia Theol Sem); AM '26—'27-29 (Columbia). Fgn tchr English Am Boys High Sch Cairo Egypt, Japanese Imperial Govt Schs and Mission Coll '16-20; staff dept head hist dept. Tarko Coll '45-48. Am head hist dept Tarko Coll '45-48. Am Assn Geo—Acad Polit Sci—Am Assn Internat Law. H: P. O. Box 73, St. Clarisville, O.

20 POLLOCK, Harry Evelyn Dorr. Maya archeology. b'00. AB '23—MA '30—PhD '36 (Harvard). Author: Sources and methods in the study of Maya Architecture '40; The Casa Redonda at Chichen Itza, Yucatan '37; Round Structures of Aboriginal Middle America '36; A Preliminary Study of the Ruins of Coba, Quintana Roo, Mexico '32. Archeologist Carnegie Instn Washington since '30, dir dept archaeology since '50 research fellow Harvard '53-56. Am Anthropol Assn—Soc Am Archeol—AAAS. 10 Frisbie Place, Cambridge, Mass.

21 POLLOCK, Harvey C(arlyle). neering. b'94. BS in mech engring (Ill Coll); DDS '07 (U Mich); '11 (Angle Sch Orthodontia). Editor American Journal Orthodontics fifteen years, now editor-in-chief. Formerly prof orthodontics St Louis U Sch Dentistry and Washington U Sch Dentistry. 8015 Maryland, StL.

22 POLLOCK, Herbert Chermside. Particle accelerators; Uranium isotope separation; Radar. b'13. BA '33 (U Va); PhD '37—Rhodes Scholar (Oxford U Eng). Research on X-ray tube design for high voltage equipment; gaseous insulation problems of high voltage X-ray equipment; uranium isotope separation; anti-submarine weapon development; synchrotron and development. Author articles in field. Research lab General Electric Co Schenectady since '37. Radio research lab Eglin Field Fla Div 15 OSRD '43-44, radiation lab Berkeley '44-45. Am Phys Soc. Research Laboratory, General Electric Co., Schenectady, N.Y. H: 2147 Union St., Schenectady 9.†

23 POLYAK, Stephen. Neuroanatomy; Visual organs and nerve centers; Optics (History); Neuroanatomy of eye; Civilization (History of). b'89. Student '01-09 (Classical Gymnasium Zagreb Crotia); '09-14 (Med Sch Graz Austria) '20 (Zagreb Yugoslavia); special studies (London, Madrid, Chicago). Anatomical studies of neuroanatomy especially of visual organs and nerve centers, including structure and function. Asst prof neurol U Chicago '30-32, asso prof '32-42, prof anatomy since '42. Am Assn Anatomists—Am Neurol Assn.◎

24 POMERANTZ, Sidney I. History of American journalism; Business history; New York history. b'09. BSS '30 (City Coll NY); MA '32—PhD '38 (Columbia U). Asst prof hist City Coll NY since '49. Author: New York: An American City, 1783-1803 '38. Co-author: The Era of the American Revolution '39; also articles in field. AHA —Am Polit Sci Assn—Am Econ Assn —Bus Hist Soc—Am Assn State Local Hist—NY State Hist Assn—AAUP— Econ Hist Assn—Bibliog Soc Am—Phi Beta Kappa. Research grant '48 Am Philos Soc. City College School of Business & Civic Adminstration, 17 Lexington Av., NYC 10.

10 POMEROY, Charles Ross. Mechanical engineering; Power press engineering. b'94. BS in mech engring (Ill Inst Tech). Design single and double crank power presses, single, double, and triple action power presses, four-point mechanical single, double, and triple action presses, also dial, roll, and transfer feeds for presses; large iron and steel castings design, and steel weldments. Contributor: Power Press Handbook '50. Sr design engr E W Bliss Co '24-45 and '49, asst chief engr '45-48 and since '50. ASME—Am Soc Quality Control—Ohio Soc Profl Engrs—Tau Beta Pi. Profl engr Ohio. E. W. Bliss Co., 1420 Hastings St., Tol 7.

11 POMEROY, Hugh Reynolds. County and municipal planning; Zoning; Housing. b'99. Student (Occidental Coll). Author: A Planning Manual for Zoning; also articles in field. Dir Westchester NY Co Dept Planning since '46; lecturer in planning Columbia U, NY Sch Social Work. Am Inst Planners (pres '43)—Nat Assn Housing Ofcls (bd govrs '46-47)—Am Planning Civic Assn—Citizens Housing Council NY. 914 County Office Building, White Plains, N.Y.

12 POMEROY, Kenneth Brownridge. Natural regeneration of Loblolly pine; Planting and cultivation of Guayule. b'07. BS '28 (Mich State Coll); MF '48 (Duke U). Study seed production and dispersal Loblolly pine; investigation importance of seedbed preparation and selection of seed trees; germination and initial survival surveys; land acquisition and ground preparation for Guayule crops. Author articles: Germination and Initial Establishment of Loblolly Pine under Various Surface Soil Conditions '49; Bugs in Loblolly Pine Cones '50; Twenty Years without Fire Protection '50, and others. Co-author articles: (with F K Green, L B Burkett) Importance of Stock Quality in Survival and Growth of Planted Trees '49; (with C F Korstian) Further Results on Loblolly Pine seed Production and Dispersal '49. Foreman Mich Shade Tree Co Battle Creek; dist ranger Nicolet Nat Forest Rhinelander Wis; management asst Mainstee Nat Forest Muskegon Mich; plantation mgr Emergency Rubber Project Salinas Cal '42-43; asst area supervisor Timber Prodn War Project Winchester Ky '43-45; silviculturist Southeastern Forest Expt Sta Franklin Va '45-50, now forester, Lake City Fla. Soc Am Foresters—Sigma Xi. Lake City, Fla.

13 POMEROY, Richard Durant. Industrial waste; Water (Chemistry). b '04. BS '26—MS '27 —PhD '31 (Cal Inst Tech). Consultant engineer on sewage treatment plant design; studies on control of hydrogen sulfide and other odors in sewage; development standard method of analysis for sulfides; research on problems of water quality; investigation of ground water pollution by rubbish dumps. Holds six patents in field. Author articles: Multiple Stage Sewage Sludge Digestion; Progress Report on Sulfide Control Research, and others. Research chem Los Angeles Co Sanitation Dists '32-40;

cons water, sewage, and indsl waste problems since '40. ACS—Am Soc CE— Am Water Works Assn—Sewage and Indsl Wastes Fedn. Am Soc CE James Laurie prize for research on multiple stage sewage sludge digestion; Sewage Works Fedn Harrison Eddy award for research on sulfide control. 660 S. Fair Oaks Av., Pasadena 2, Cal.

14 POND, Samuel Ernst. Aviation power plants. b'90. BH '12 (Springfield Coll); AM '17—PhD '21 (Clark U). Developed gear and lubricant tester; research and analysis of state of mixture for internal combustions, hazards controls in handling aviation fuels, micro-bore calibration methods for submerged manometers, reclamation mercury for instrumentation, flame propagation velocity measurements of safety fuels, portable electro-static precipitator for measurement of dessicant dusts, precision air pressure regulator for VDI orifice calibrator, back pressure regulation schema for fuel flow control in flow-meter calibrations by standpipe manometer methods, embolism-like injection methods for engine testing in analysis of erratic performance of radial piston aviation engines, comparison of fuel/air ratio indicator analyzers, performance improvements in tri-rotor pumps with remote variable delivery controls. Radiations research Gen Elec Co Nela Research Lab '21-24; faculty Washington U '24-25; asst prof U Pa and work with NRC Lab '25-33; tech mgr Marine Biol Lab Woods Hole '33-41; with Nav Research Lab '42; with Pratt & Whitney Div United Aircraft Corp since '42. AAAS—Am Physiol Soc—Optical Soc Am—Franklin Inst—Sigma Xi. 400 S. Main St., East Hartford 8, Conn.

15 POOL, Raymond John. Plant ecology, taxonomy, mycology and pathology; Vegetation and crops (Sulphur dioxide relations). b'82. AB '07—AM '08—PhD '13 (U Neb); '08 (U Chicago). Author: Vegetation of Nebraska Sand Dunes; Experiments in Plant Physiology; Handbook of Nebraska Trees; Flowers and Flowering Plants; Marching with the Grasses; Basic Botany for Colleges; also articles in field. Prof bot U Neb since '07, head bot dept '15-48. AAAS(F)—Bot Soc Am (pres syst sect '24)—Am Mus Natural Hist —Am Soc Plant Taxonomists—Phi Beta Kappa—Sigma Xi. 2845 S. 27th St., Lincoln 2, Neb.☉

16 POOLE, Earl Lincoln. Mammals of Eastern Pennsylvania and North America; Birds of eastern North America; Indian sites in eastern Pennsylvania; Folk arts. b'91. Jessup Scholar '13-15 (Acad Nat Sci Phila); '12-13, '22-23 (U Pa); ScD '48 (Franklin and Marshall Coll). Expedition to Guatemala and Honduras '15, Arizona desert '31; studied installations in European museums '34. Author articles in field. Dir Reading Pub Mus Art Gallery since '39. Reading Public Museum and Art Gallery, Reading, Pa.

17 POOLE, Fenn Eugene. Medicine (Industrial). b'06. BS '29 (Emmanuel Missionary Coll); MD '32 (Coll Med Evangelists). Research in high altitude physiological effect of training program of flight personnel in pressure chamber; in detection industrial health hazards and protection of employees in aircraft industry; study and development efficient medical record systems to utilize machine methods and prepare statistical analyses of medical functions for management. Med dir Lockheed Aircraft Corp since '38; med dir Rexall Drug Co since '46. Am Assn Indsl Physicians and Surgeons (dir '42-47)—AMA(F)—Aero Med Assn (F)—Western Assn Indsl Physicians

and Surgeons(dir). 660 W. Broadway, Glendale 4, Cal.

18 POOLE, H(enry) Gordon. Mineral dressing. b'09. BS (Case Inst Tech); MS (U Idaho); student (MIT). Research on oxide, sulfide and non-metallic hydro- and pyro-metallurgical extraction processes. Patent applications on extraction process for silicate nickel ores and beryl and chromite flotation. Author articles in field. Asso prof sch mineral engring U Washington '47-48, on leave absence as metall US Bur Mines tech mission attached to Am Embassy Mexico City since '48. Am Inst Mining Metall Engrs (mineral dressing com, edn com)—Colo Utah Northwest Mining Assns—Sigma Xi—Tau Beta Pi. 2114 E. 61 Street, Seattle.†

19 POOLE, Robert Franklin. Economic plant pathology (Disease control). b'93. BS '16—DSc '37 (Clemson SC Agrl Coll); MS '17—PhD '21 (Rutgers U); LLD '42 (U SC); LittD '50 (Furman University). Research on control disease causative agents Bacterium pruni, Bacterium solanacearum, Fusarium batatis, Monilochaetes infuscans, Pythium ultimum, Phytophora nicotinia, Corticium vagum, and arsenical injury on peaches; discovered and perfected economic control measures for diseases of the sweet potato. Author articles in field. Pres Clemson Agrl Coll since '40; prof plant path NC State Coll '28-40. AAAS(F)—Am Phytopath Soc—So Phytopath Soc— Am Mycol Soc—AAUP—Am Hort Soc —NC Acad Sci—Assn So Agrl Workers—So Assn Coll Secondary Schs—SC Assn Colls—Phi Kappa Phi—Sigma Xi. Clemson College, Clemson, S.C.☉

20 POOR, Russell Spurgeon. Economic geology. b'99. BS '23—MS '25—PhD '27 (U Ill). Specialist in sedimentary iron ores, coal and certain non-metallics. Editor: Proceedings of the Auburn Conference on the Use of Radioactive Isotopes in Agricultural Research '47. Asso prof geol Birmingham-Southern Coll '27-28, prof geol and head geol dept '28-44, dir ext dept '36-40, chmn div nat scis '37-44, admin asst to the pres '43-44; dean grad studies dir Auburn Research Found Inc Ala Poly Inst '44-48; chmn U Rel Div Oak Ridge Inst Nuclear Studies since '49. Ala Acad Sci (chmn research com, pres '35)—Am Inst Mining and Metal Engrs (chmn SE sect '42-43)— ASEE (research br)—So Assn Sci and Ind—Phi Beta Kappa—Phi Kappa Phi —Soc Eco Geol(F)—Geol Soc Amer (F)—Sigma Xi. Oak Ridge Institute of Nuclear Studies, Oak Ridge, Tenn.

21 POPE, Clifford Hillhouse. Herpetology of China and the Appalachian regions; Turtles of the United States; Snake bite treatment; Care of captive reptiles. b'99. Student '16-18 (U Ga). BA '21 (U Va). Herpetologist Chinese division Central Asiatic Expeditions American Museum Natural History '21-26, assistant division Asiatic Exploration and Research. Author: The Reptiles of China '35; Snakes Alive and How They Live '37; Turtles of the United States and Canada '39; China's Animal Frontier '40; The Reptiles and Amphibians of the Chicago Region '44; also articles in field. Curator div reptiles and amphibians Chicago Natural Hist Mus since '41. NY Zool Soc(F)—Am Soc Ichthyologists Herpetologists (past pres). Chicago Natural History Museum, Chicago 5.

22 POPE, John Alexander. Chinese ceramics and bronzes. b'06. AB '30 (Yale Coll); MA '40 (Harvard); '38 (U London). Co-author: China '44; A Descriptive and Illustrative Catalogue of Chinese Bronzes '46; Fourteenth Century Blue-and-White '52; also articles in field. Asst dir Freer Gallery Art Smithsonian Inst since '46. Am Oriental Soc—Oriental Ceramic Society (London)—College Art Assn—Archeol Inst Am (bd govrs Wash Soc)—Far Eastern Assn (bd dirs '48-50)—Far Eastern Ceramic Group (pres). Harvard-Yenching Inst fellow '38. Freer Gallery of Art, Washington 25.†

10 POPENOE, Paul. Marriage and family life; Human heredity and eugenics; Population problems: Sterilization. Social biology and hygiene; Techniques of counseling. b'88. Student '05-07—hon DSc '29 (Occidental Coll, Calif); '07-08 (Stanford U). Author: Modern Marriage '40; The Conservation of the Family '26; The Child's Heredity '29; Practical Applications of Heredity '30; Marriage, Before and After '43; and others. Dir Am Inst Family Relations since '30. Am Genetic Assn—Genetic Soc Am—Am Social Hygiene Assn (exec sec '19-20) —Assn Study Human Heredity—AAAS —Am Eugenics Soc—Population Assn Am. 5287 Sunset Blvd., LA 27.☉

11 POPENOE, Willis Parkison. Upper Cretaceous invertebrate faunas (Pacific Coast). b'99. BS '30—MS '33—PhD '36 (Calif Inst Tech); student (Johns Hopkins). Author articles in field. Asso prof geol UCLA Since '48. Geol Soc Am(F)—Paleontol Soc(F)—Sigma Xi. Department of Geology, University of California, Los Angeles 24.†

12 POPOFF, Constantine Constantinovich. Minerals (Russia); Minerals (Northwestern US). b'97. ME '26 (Leningrad Inst Geol and Prospecting USSR); MS in geol '41 (U Ariz). Examination, geologic mapping, sampling and reserves estimates; analysis, interpretation, and appraisal exploration data. In charge field parties Central Geol and Prospecting Inst Leningrad USSR '27-30, Geol and Prospecting Trust Tiflis USSR '30-33; in charge field parties Leningrad region and Ural Mountains '33-36; mining engr in charge project investigations lead-zinc, antimony, limestone, silica, high-alumina clays of northwest US Bur Mines since '42. AIMME—Sigma Xi. Profl engr Wash. U.S. Bureau of Mines, Region II, Mining Division, 1201 N. Division Spokane 2, Wash.

13 POPP, Henry William. Plant physiology (Radiation). b'92. Student '12-14 (Carnegie Inst Tech); BS '17— MS '22 (Pa State Coll); PhD '26 (U Chicago). Biochemist '23-25 Boyce Thompson Institute Plant Research, Yonkers. Co-author: Chemistry in Agriculture '26; Botany, a Textbook for Colleges '36. Co-author and asso editor: Biological Effects of Radiation '36; also articles in field. Prof bot Pa State Coll and Agrl Expt Sta since '37, head department botany since '50, com mem '24-29 Natl Res Council. Bot Soc Am (v chmn physiol sect '38, chmn com sect structure '39-40, chmn physiol sect '43)—Pa Acad Sci—Am Soc Plant Physiol—Wildlife Assn AS(F)—Gamma Sigma Delta—Sigma Xi—Phi Kappa Phi. John W White Medal Pa State Coll '17. Department of Botany, Pennsylvania State College, State College, Pa.†

14 PORRATA, Oscar E. Puerto Rico (Education). b'98. BE '29 (Poly Inst PR); MA '34 (U Chicago); EdD '47 (Pa State Coll). Research on progress and promotions of public schools of Puerto Rico. Author monographs: Retardation in the Elementary Public Schools of Puerto Rico '34; Suggested Policy for the Administration and Control of Public Education in Puerto Rico '49. Advanced from asst supt to supt pub schs PR '21-34; gen supervisor dept edn PR '34-37; prof edn U PR since '37, now

dir practicing teaching and acting dean coll edn. AAUP—NEA—PR Tchrs Assn —Phi Delta Kappa. University of Puerto Rico, Rio Piedras, P.R.

15 PORTER, Alton M. Tomatoes; Seeds; Vegetable varieties and rotations; Electricity on the farm. b'94. Student (U Me, Ia State U); BS '17 —MS '32—PhD '37 (Michigan State College). Author articles on field and vegetable seeds. Chief seeds fruit and vegetables Foreign Export and Fgn Trade Promotion of Commodities Dept of Commerce Washington since '45. Veg Growers Assn Am—Am Soc Hort Sci—Am Statis Assn—Am Soc Plant Physiol—Am Assn Adv Sci— Sigma Xi. Chief of Seeds, Fruit and Vegetables, Food Branch, Office of International Trade, Department of Commerce, Washington 25.†

16 PORTER, Cedric Lambert. Stockpoisoning plants; Rocky Mountain flora. b'05. BS '28—MS '29 (U Mich); PhD '37 (U Wash). Research on flora Wyoming, leguminous genera Astragalus and Oxytropis in North America; also aquatic seed plants Western North America. Author 52 articles in field. With Rocky Mountain Herbarium U Wyo since '36; prof bot and curator since '42. Sigma Xi—Torrey Bot Club —Am Soc Plant Taxonomists—International Assn Plant Taxonomy—Cal Bot Club—AAAS. University of Wyoming, Laramie.

17 PORTER, Charles Wesley III. American history (Conservation of historical sites and buildings; French diplomatic history. b'04. BA '26—MA '27 (U Va); PhD '32 (U Pa). Concerned with the preservation, restoration, historical interpretation and public use of 100 national historic sites, buildings, and battlefield parks in the US National Park System. Author: The Career of Theophile Delcasse '36; Perry at Put-in-Bay; Echoes of the War of 1812 (National Park Service Popular Study Series No 8) '41; also articles in field. Chief planning and interpretive sect br hist Nat Park Service Washington '38-43, asst chief hist '43-46, hist '46-47, chief br preservation and use history div since '37. Phi Beta Kappa—AHA—Am Assn State Local Hist—Va Hist Soc. National Park Service, Department of the Interior, Washington.

18 PORTER, Dale Albert. Internal parasites of cattle. b'09. AB '30 (Kalamazoo Coll); MS '32 (Kan State Coll); ScD '35 (Johns Hopkins). Author articles in field. Parasitol US Dept Agr since '35; director Regional Animal Disease Research Lab BAI Auburn Ala since '50. First lt to maj San Corps US Army '43-46. Am Soc Parasitol—Am Soc Zool—Am Micros Soc—Helminthol Soc Wash—Sigma Xi —Gamma Sigma Delta. U.S. Regional Animal Disease Research Laboratory, Auburn, Ala.†

19 PORTER, Francis Marion. Descriptive geometry. 512 W Nevada St., Urbana, Ill.

20 PORTER, Kenneth W. Early American commerce; Negroes on the American frontier; The Southwestern oil industry; Fur trade; Minorities. b'05. AB '26 (Sterling Coll); AM '27 (U Minn); PhD '36 (Harvard). Author: John Jacob Astor, Business Man (2 vols) '31; Relations Between Negroes and Indians within the present limits of the United States '32; Christ in the Breadline: a book of poems for holy days '33; Pilate before Jesus: Biblical and Legendary Poems '36; The Jacksons and the Lees: Two Generations of Massachusetts Merchants 1765-1844 (2 vols) '37; The High Plains '38; No Rain from These Clouds '46. Sr asso,

Bus Hist Found Inc since '48. AHA. Awarded first prize Am Assn Study Negro Life Hist '32. 601 Lane Tower, Eugene, Ore.

21 PORTNOFF, George. Russian and Spanish language and literature. b'92. AB '10 (Kiev Gymnasium Kiev Russia); AM '28—PhD '32 (Columbia). Author: Sol de La Aldea '19; Divine Treasure '36; La Literatura Rusa en Espana '32. Co-author: The Forgotten Song. Translator Russian novels and dramas into Spanish; also original poems and articles in field. Prof, head Fgn Lang Dept Ariz State Coll since '45. Sociedad de Autores Espanoles—Am Assn Teachers Slavic East European Langs —Am Assn Teachers Spanish—Hispanic Inst. Arizona State College, Tempe, Ariz.

22 PORTNOY, Louis. Fertility (Human). b'06. AB '27 (Columbia); MD '31 (LI Coll Med). Research human sterility and reproductive disorders; analysis and evaluation human seminal fluid and spermatozooa; utilization artificial insemination; effects endocrine disturbances. Co-author: (with Jules Saltman) Fertility in Marriage '50. Author article: Diagnosis and Prognosis of Male Infertility '42. Sterility Clin gynecol dept Mt Sinai Hosp NYC since '40, chief male sterility clinic since '50; staff fertility service Margaret Sanger Research Bur NYC since '46. NY Acad Med(F)—Am Soc Study Sterility—Endocrine Soc—AMA. 23 West 11th St., NYC 11.

23 PORTOR, Laura Spencer (Mrs. Francis Pope). Human relations; Parent-child psychology; American cultural education (Home, school); Shakespeare. Author: The Larger Vision (under pen name Anne Bryan McCall); You, Yourself, An Introduction to General Psychology also Psychology Work Book and Note Book (under pen name) '37; Shakespeare Is Yours '47; Craftsmanship of Shakespeare '47; Music ticles in field. Editorial staff Woman's Shakespeare Loved '48; Places Shakespeare Loved '48, and others; also articles in field. Editorial staff Woman's Home Companion, conducted human relations dept under pen name. The Francis Pope Shakespeare Center and Library of Remembrance, Garrison-on-Hudson, N.Y.

24 POSEY, Chesley J(ohnston), Jr. Hydraulics of open channel flow; Design and testing reinforcing bars for concrete. b'06. BS '26—CE '33 (Kan U); MS '27 (U Ill). Author: Tests of Anchorages for Reinforcing Bars '33; Hydraulics of Steady Flow in Open Channels (with Sherman M Woodward) '41; also articles in field. With State U Iowa since '29, head civil engineering since '50. ASCE (vp Ia sect '48-49)—Ia Engring Soc (employer-employee relations com since '44, state bldg code com since '48)—Am Geophys Union—Am Concrete Inst (com 115 Research since '38)—ASEE (chmn North Mid-West sect '48-49)—AAAS— Rocky Mt Hydraulic Lab (treas and dir since '45)—AAUP (mem nat council '48-51)—Sigma Xi—Tau Beta Pi. Engineering Building, State University of Iowa, Iowa City, Ia.☉

25 POSEY, Rollin Bennett. American government; Public administration. b '07. AB '27 (U Kan); MBA with distinction '30 (Harvard); PhD '42 (U Pa). Author: The Significance to Private Industry of Personnel Administration in the City of Cincinnati '42; Outline of American Government '52; Our American Democracy '52. Editor: Basic Police Patrolling '38; Advanced Police Patrolling '39. Executive secretary Philadelphia Charter Commission '37-38; director Public Service Institute Pennsylvania '38-39; member bd directors Illinois Civil Service Association since '43, Chicago Crime Commission since '51; member 7th US Regional Loyalty Board since '48. Asst dir Cincinnati Bur Govtl Research '33-'34; dir dept municipal research City Hartford '34-35; cons US Bur Budget '36; research asso Inst Local and State Govt U Pa '37-40; asst to dean of faculties Northwestern U '40-42 dir summer session '42-43, dir civil affairs training sch '43-45; asso prof polit sci '40-47, prof since '47, dean univ coll '43-48, chmn dept polit sci, coll liberal arts since '48. Am Polit Sci Assn—Am Soc Pub Adminstrn—Indsl Relations Research Assn—Alpha Sigma Lambda (founder, nat chmn.). Northwestern University, Evanston, Ill.☉

10 POSNER, Ernst Maximilian. Archives; History of administrative institutions. b'92. PhD '20 (Berlin Germany). Author: Ubersicht uber die Bestande des Geheimen Staatsarchivs in Berlin-Dahlem (with Muller) '34; Zum Archivwesen der Gegenwart '40; also articles in field. Prof hist archives adminstrn, dean Sch Social Sci Pub Affairs Am U since '48. Am Hist Assn—Soc Am Archivists (council)—Am Assn State Local Hist. 1901 F St., N.W., Washington 6.†

11 POST, Emily (Mrs. Price Post). American manners and social customs; Home arts. Ed pvt Sch. Author: The Flight of a Moth '04; Purple and Fine Linen '06; Woven in the Tapestry '08; The Title Market '09; The Eagle's Feather '10; By Motor to the Golden Gate '15; Etiquette '46; Parade '24; How to Behave Though a Debutante '28; The Personality of a House '48; Children Are People '40; Emily Post Inst Cook Book (collaboration with Edwin M Post Jr) '50; also articles in field. Contbr daily column on good taste in 171 newspapers (Bell Syndicate) since '32; pres Emily Post Inst Inc '46; radio speaker since '31. 39 E. 79th St., NYC.

12 POST, Gaines. Thirteenth Century history (Universities, Latin and Roman influence). b'02. BA '24 (U Tex); MA '25—PhD '31 (Harvard). Author numerous articles in field. Asst to prof U Wis since '35. Am Hist Assn—Medieval Acad Am. Guggenheim fellow '39-40. University of Wisconsin, Madison, Wis.

13 POST, Kenneth. Floriculture; Ornamental horticulture. b'04. BS '27 (Mich State Coll); MS '28 (Ia State Coll); PhD '36 (Cornell U). Research in day length, temperature, soils, fertilizer practices, water and methods of watering of florist crops. Research teaching and extension in floriculture Cornell U since '30, now prof floriculture. Sigma Xi. Department of Floriculture, Cornell University, Ithaca, N.Y.

14 POST, Levi Arnold. Ancient Greek literature (Drama, Menander, philosophy, Plato, dramatic theory, Aristotle, feminism); Greek language. b'89. AB —AM '11 (Haverford Coll); AM '12 (Harvard); AB '16—AM '22—Rhodes Scholar (New Coll Oxford U Eng); '19 (U Caen, France); Guggenheim fellow '32. Author: The Vatican Plato and Its Relations '34; From Homer to Menander '51. Editor: Loeb Classical Library since '40. Translator: Thirteen Epistles of Plato '25; Menander, Three Plays '29; also articles in field. Sather prof classics U Calif '47-48. Am Philol Assn (sec-treas '35-39, vp '44-45, pres '45-46)—Archeol Inst Am—Phi Beta Kappa. Haverford College, Haverford, Pa.

15 POST, Richard Lewis. Thysanoptera (Thrips) of Oregon and the Pacific Northwest; Preservation, preparation and display of insects. b'10. BS '32 (Mich State Coll); PhD '47 (Ore State Coll). Invented Wards Display Mount and Explano Mount for insect material. Author articles in field. Asso entomol ND Agrl Expt Sta, State Seed Dept and asso prof entomol ND Agrl Coll since '46. Specialist in pest control US Coast Guard '42-45. Entomol Soc Am—Am Assn Econ Entomol—Entomol Soc Manitoba—Entomol Soc Ore (one of organizers, sec '39-46)—Entomol Soc Ontario—Sigma Xi—Gamma Sigma Delta—Phi Sigma. North Dakota Agricultural College, Department of Entomology, Fargo, N.D.

16 POSTE, Emerson Peck. Vitreous enamels; Industrial chemistry. b'88. BS '10—CE '18 (Carnegie Inst Tech). Author articles in field. Dir labs Elyria Enameled Products Co and Elyria div Pfaudler Co '12-25; chem engr Chattanooga Stamping and Enameling Co '25-29, factory mgr and asst sec '29-30; cons chem engring and owner comml chem lab '30; dir bur air pollution control, boiler insp. City of Chattanooga since '42. Am Ceramic Soc (past dean of fellows)—Inst Ceramic Engrs—Am Chem Soc—Am Inst Chem Engrs—Am Soc Testing Materials—Tau Peta Pi. 309 McCallie Av., Chattanooga 3, Tenn.

17 POTTER, George Frederick. Tung culture; Horticulture (Deciduous fruit trees); Plant physiology. b'91. BS '13 —MS '16 (Wis U); PhD '30 (Cornell U). Research on cold injury to woody plants, blossom bud differentiation in fruit trees, culture and nutrition of deciduous fruit trees, culture, nutrition and improvement of tung trees; investigated production problems in tung orchards, breeding improved varieties. Author articles in field. Prin physiol Bur Plant Industry, Soils and Agrl Engring, Agrl Research Administn US Dept Agr since '38. Am Soc Hort Sci (past pres)—Am Soc Plant Physiol—AAAS(F)—Sigma Xi — Phi Kappa Phi. Post Office Building, Bogalusa, La.†

18 POTTER, Ralph Kimball. Visible speech and music. b'94. BS '17 (Whitman Coll); EE '23 (Columbia). Research speech and other sounds and their visible representation. Numerous inventions in field of communications. Sr author: Visible Speech '47; also articles in field. Development and research dept Am Tele and Telegraph Co '23-34; Bell Tel Labs Inc since '34, dir trans eng '43-44, trans research since '44. ASA(F)—IRE(F)—AAAS. Bell Telephone Laboratories, Murray Hill, N.J.

19 POTTINGER, Samuel Remey. Fishery technology (Amino acid content fish proteins, production of crab meat and oysters); Product containers, packaging, freezing and storage. b'04. BS '28 (George Wash U); '36-37 (U Md). Research on production methods, and chemical and physical properties of fish oils. Author articles in field. With US Bur Fisheries since '29, chem US Fish Wildlife Service College Park Md since '35. Am Chem Soc—AAAS— Inst Food Technol—Sigma Xi. U.S. Fish and Wildlife Service, College Park, Md.†

20 POTTS, James Manning. Methodist history. b'95. BA '17—MA '20— DD '35 (Randolph Macon Coll); ThB '24—ThM '25 (Princeton Theol Sem); student (U Va, Chicago U, Union Theol Sem). Research on Methodist beginnings in Virginia and Richmond, Francis Asburg, historical effects of Christianity to 300 AD. Author articles in field. Editor of The Upper Room and The Upper Room Pulpit since '48. Tau Kappa Alpha—Omicron Delta Kappa—

Fed Council Ch Christ—Assn Meth Hist Soc (mem exec com)—Hist Soc of Southwestern Jurisdictional Conf (sec treas). Fellow in apologetics and Christian ethics, Princeton Theol sem '25. Deer Park Circle, Nashville.

21 POTTS, Robert William Latelle. Quarantine entomology; Butterflies (Nymphalidae); Biological dioramas and scale models. b'11. Student '29-31 (Colo Agrl Coll); BA '34 (U Denver); MSc '43 (U Calif). Mexico entomological expedition '41; developed a series of 11 1/5th scale dioramas of Cambrian through late Pleistocene animals and plants considered the best prehistoric reproductions in America. Co-author: (with M A Stewart) Laboratory Manual of Medical Entomology '43, '49; also articles in field. Act curator entomol Colo Mus Nat Hist '36-38; head curator Cheyenne Mt Mus '38-41; systematic entomol Calif State Dept Agr since '45; asso in entomol Nat Research Council '49. Pacific Coast Entomol Soc—Entomol Soc Am —Calif Acad Scis—Phi Sigma—Sigma Xi. Agricultural Bldg., Embarcadero at Mission, San Francisco 5.

22 POTTS, Samuel Frederick. Insecticides (Aerial spraying); Insect toxicology. b'00. BSc '21 (Miss State Coll); exp fellow—MSc '24 (U Md); '24-25 (O State U). Research on insect toxicology, physiology; development new insecticides mixtures and ground and aerial equipment, sex attractants for the male gypsy moth; with R R Whitten conducted basic research leading to development of revolutionary improvements in sprays and in ground and aerial spraying equipment which make it possible to apply insecticides, fungicides, hormones, and herbicides at rate of one to six gallons per acre. Holds patent on mist blowers. Jr entomol div insect investigations Bur Entomol and Plant Quarantine US Dept Mgr Melrose Mass '26-27, asst entomol '27-40, asso entomol New Haven '40-45, entomol since '45. AAAS—Am Assn Econ Entomol (life)—Entomol Soc Am—Nat Shade Tree Conf—Am Soc Foresters—Cambridge Entomol Soc — Conn Tree Protective Assn—Entomol Soc Washington. 335 Prospect St., New Haven 11. H: 60 Jaenicke Lane, Hamden, Conn.

23 POUGH, Frederick Harvey. Mineralogy, vulcanology, gems. b'06. SB '28 (Harvard); MS '32 (Washington U); '32-33 (Heidelberg U Germany); PhD '35 (Harvard). Author: Field Guide to Rocks & Minerals '53; All About Volcanoes and Earthquakes '53. Curator phys geol mineral Am Mus Natural Hist '45-52; gem cons Jewelers Circular. Min Soc Am(F)—Geol Soc Am— Mineral Soc Gt Brit—NY Mineral Club —NJ Mineral Club (hon). 4680 Independence Av., NYC 71.☉

24 POUGH, Richard Hooper. Wildlife (Conservation, management); Birds (Effects of insecticides and weedicides). b'04. BS '26 (MIT); '26-27 (Harvard Grad Sch). Additional research on census methods, millinery plumage, ecology, conservation and banding of hawks, owls, and fish-eating birds. Author: Audubon Bird Guide '46; also articles in field. Research asso Nat Audubon Soc '36-48; chmn Dept Conservation Am Mus Nat Hist since '48. Ecol Soc Am—Wildlife Soc—Am Ornithol Union—Linnaean Soc NY (pres '43-45)—AAAS. American Museum of Natural History, NYC 24.☉

25 POUND, Glenn Simpson. Plant pathology and virology. b'14. BA '40 (U Ark); PhD '43 (U Wis). Research in diseases of vegetable plants grown for seed. Author articles in field. Asst plant path U Wis '40-43, asso prof since '49; asso plant path Bur Plant Industry US Dept Agr '43-46. Am Phytopath Soc—Sigma Xi—Phi Beta Kappa. Department of Plant Pathology, University of Wisconsin, Madison 5, Wis.†

10 POWELL, Alfred Richard. Fuel chemistry (Coal, gas, synthetic liquid fuel). b'91. BS '14 (U Kans); AM '15 (U Neb); PhD '18 (U Ill). Research on military poison gases, sulphur in coal, coke and gas, coal chemicals, synthetic liquid fuels; consultant Army Air Force '43; member Technical Oil Mission Technical Industrial Intelligence Committee Joint Chiefs of Staff '44-45. Holds 15 US and foreign patents. Author articles in field. Asso dir research Koppers Co Inc since '32. Served as 2d lt Chem Warfare Service US Army '18-19. Am Chem Soc—Am Inst Mining Metall Engrs—Am Gas Assn—Soc Chem Industry—Engrs Soc Western Pa—Am Coke Coal Chem Inst—Eastern States Blast Furnace Coke Oven Assn. Koppers Co., Inc., Koppers Building, Pittsburgh 19. H: 57 Sunnyhill Dr.

11 POWELL, Herbert James. Educational buildings (Architecture). b'98. AB '20 (U Redlands); AM in architecture '24—Sheldon traveling scholarship '24-25 (Harvard). Practice of architecture since '25, emphasis on educational buildings; member firm Marsh, Smith & Powell architects for elementary and high school buildings, University of Southern California Founder's Hall, chapel and commons U Redlands, and others. AIA (F, dir So Cal chpt '41-42, vp '43, pres '44), Cal Bd Archtl Examiners (pres '47). 208 W. 8th St., LA 14.⊚

12 POWELL, Knox Archibald. Industry; engineering, b'94. BS '20—ME '31—MS '32 (U Minn). Tool design, steam turbine, tractor; plant layout research; coordination design engineering and foundry and machine shop. Research engr Minneapolis-Moline Co Minneapolis since '34. ASME—Am Soc Metals—Am Foundry Soc—Soc Exptl Stress Analysis—Minn Assn Profl Engrs—Twin City Soc Indsl Engrs—Sigma Xi. care Minneapolis-Moline Company, Box 1050, Mpls.

13 POWELL, Louis Harvey. Spherical maps; Minnesota paleontology. b'04. BS '24—PhD '33 (U Minn). Author: A Study of the Ozarkian Faunas of Southeastern Minnesota; The Giant Beaver, Castoroides, in Minnesota; New Uses for Globes and Spherical Maps. Dir, Science Museum St Paul since '31. The Science Museum, St. Paul 3.

14 POWELL, Ralph Waterbury. Hydraulics; Hydrology; Mechanics; Flood frequency estimation (Plotting). b'89. BS '11 (Mich State Coll); CE '14 (Cornell U); PhB '16 (Yale); '18-19 (Peking Lang Sch); '27-29 (O State U). Invented a plotting paper for estimating flood frequency '43. Author: Mechanics of Liquids '40; Hydraulics and Fluid Mechanics '51; also articles in field. Prof mechanics O State U since '45; sec Rocky Mt Hydraulic Lab Allenspark Colo since '46. ASCE—Am Soc Engring Edn—Am Geophy Union—AA AS—Internat Assn Hydraulic Structures Research—Tau Beta Pi—Sigma Xi. Industrial Engineering Building, Ohio State University, Columbus 10, O.†

15 POWELL, Wilfred E(vans). Religious Education (Principles, methods, church leadership). b'93. AB '19 (Phillips U); BD '21—MA '22—PhD '29 (Yale). Member executive committee Research Section of International Council of Religious Education '48-49; member Committee on Church School

Administration; member Adult Education Section of Curriculum Committee, Disciples of Christ, for evaluation of programs and materials and research. Author: Vacation School Manual for Intermediates '24; The Growth of Christian Personality '29; Education for Life with God '34; The Understanding of Adult Ways '41. Ordained to ministry Disciples of Christ '19; prof religious edn Phillips U Enid Okla since '22, vis prof Yale '25-26, '28-29. 2001 E. Cypress St., Enid, Okla.*

16 POWELSON, John Maureese. Mining geology; Economic geology. b'10. Student '28-29 (U Alberta Can); '29-31 (U Utah); AB '41 (U Minn). Consultant in economic and administrative phases of mining geology, special stress on base metals in Canadian fields. Gen engr and geol Nev, Utah, Que '31-33; jr engr Internat Nickel Co Ltd '34-37, chief geol Levack Mine '37-39; with Consol Mining and Smelting Co of Can '41-49, exploration supt Eastern Dist '47-49; cons mining geol since '50. Am Inst Mining Engrs—Can Inst Mining and Metall—Geol Assn Can—Profl Engrs Province of Ont. Haileybury, Ont., Can.

17 POWER, Donald Clinton. Public utility law and rate procedures. b'99. Student '18-20 (Denson U); summer '24 (Cornell); BS '22—LLB '26—AM '27 (Ohio State U). Vice chairman Ohio Administrative Law Commission '42-46. Author: The Law of Contracts Condensed '33. Admitted to Ohio bar '26—since practiced in Columbus; mem firm Power & Griffith since '43; asst atty gen Ohio, atty for Pub Utilities Comn Ohio '33-36; with Ohio U part time '22-39; sec to gov Ohio '39-43; dir Gen Telephone Corp. Central Ohio Light & Power Co, Ohio Asso Telephone Co. Am Bar Assn—Ohio State Bar Assn—Columbus Bar Assn—Beta Gamma Sigma—Phi Delta Phi—Sigma Chi. 50 W. Broad St., Columbus 15, O.⊚

18 POWER, Eugene Barnum. Documentary reproduction (Microfilm). b'05. AB '27—MBA '30 (U Mich). Research on methods and uses of microfilm technique for reproduction materials for research; founder University Microfilms '38; organized Microfilms Inc as distribution agency using microfilm as reproduction medium for scientific and technical materials '42; organized Projected Books Inc a nonprofit corp for distribution of reading and educational materials in photographic form to physically incapacitated '44; delegate International Federation of Documentation Conference Zurich '39, Paris '46, Berne '47; special representative Coordinator of Information and Library of Congress London '42. Author articles in field. Engaged in work U Microfilms since '38. ALA—Bibliog Soc Am—Am Documentation Inst—Photog Soc Am—Royal Photog Soc. 313 N. First St., Ann Arbor.

19 POWER, Maxwell Elliott. Insect neurology; Invertebrate zoology; Parasitology; Fly populations. b'13. AB '36 (Ind U); MS '38 (U Okla); PhD '42 (Yale); '41 (Woods Hole). Author articles in field. Asso prof biol Kenyon Coll '50-53, professor of biology since '53. Am Soc Zool—Genetics Soc Am—American Society Parasitol—AAAS—Sigma Xi. Kenyon College, Gambier, O.

20 POWER, Roy Burton. Electrical engineering (Arcs, elements, power cable). b'11. BSEE '33 (U Kan); MS '35—ScD '37 (Harvard). Research on the design and construction of a water tunnel, the hydrodynamic counter-part of a wind tunnel to be used for development of superior underwater devices such as propellers. Author:

Notes on Elements of Electrical Engineering '44; also articles in field. Prof engring research Ordnance Research Lab Pa State Coll '45-50; sci advisor to chief research and development div Office of Chief of Ordnance. AIEE—AAAS—Sigma Xi—Tau Beta Pi. Room 2E 358, Pentagon, Washington.†

21 POWERS, Alfred. Pacific northwest history (Orgeon, northern California); Pacific coast literature. Student (U Okla, U Ore). Author: Marooned in Crater Lake '30; History of Oregon Literature '35; Early Printing in the Oregon Country '41; Legends of the Four High Mountains '44; Prisoners of the Redwoods '48; Redwoods and Lava Country '49; and others. Prof creative writing Ore State System Higher Edn; ed Binfords & Mort book pub Portland. Ore Hist Soc—Pioneer Trails Assn—Phi Beta Kappa. Binfords and Mort, Portland, Ore.

22 POWERS, Donald Howard. Textile chemicals and plastics. b'01. BA '21 (Boston U); MA '23—PhD '24 (Princeton). Research on hydroxamic acids, rubber accelerators, antioxidants, colors and synthetic rubber, textile resins for anticrease, shrinkage control, textile sizing agents, wetting agents, textile enzymes; director Textile Research Institute '40-54; advisor Textile Foundation since '46. Author articles in field. Dir textile dept Monsanto Chem Co Boston '43-49, dir research Warner-Hudnut since '49. AA AS—Am Soc Testing Materials—Am Chem Soc—Am Assn Textile Chem Colorists—Am Assn Textile Tech. Warner-Hudnut Co. Inc., 111 West 18th St., NYC.

23 POWERS, Felix William. Industrial refrigeration. b'87. Ed pub schs. Assisted development of first refrigerated show windows for meat markets; development and design refrigerating machinery, enclosed and horizontal types; design concentric combined valves for refrigeration compressors, special steam driven compressor, ice cream and quick freezing plants, ice-making and cold storage plants, and electric defrost system for large plants; expert court testimony on refrigeration; consultant on air circulation in refrigeration; devised methods and equipment for refrigeration and freezing of fish aboard ships and boats; studies on banana cooling, ripening, and storage, on fish storing and freezing, and orange and other citrus fruit precooling. Holds patents in field. Engr and cons '22-26, application and design refrigeration equipment '26-49; mgr Felix W Powers (indsl refrigeration) Pasadena since '49. Nat Assn Practical Refrigerating Engrs—ASME—Am Soc Refrigerating Engrs. Profl engr Cal. 1732 E. Mountain St., Pasadena 7, Cal.

24 POWERS, Howard Adorno. Volcanology. b'04. BS '24 (SD State Coll); MA '26 (U Ore); PhD '29 (Harvard). Research on petrology and field geology of volcanics of Hawaii, ground water investigations of Island of Maui; coordination of volcanic studies of Hawaii, Aleutian Islands, Alaska, and continental US. Author articles in field. Geol US Geol Survey, Volcano Investigations Section of Gen Geol Branch since '48. Geol Soc Am (F)—AAAS—Am Geophys Union—Seismol Soc Am—Hawaiian Acad Sci. U.S. Geological Survey, Denver Federal Center, Denver 14.†

25 POWERS, John Joseph. Community canneries (Operation and layout); Processing of pimientos; Microbial food spoilage; Food processing (Oxidation-reduction reactions). b'18. BS '40—PhD '45 (U Mass). Development top-

steam method of heating retorts and atmospheric cookers for community canneries, improvement safety and quality; diagnosis spoilage and prevention of spoilage in processing pimentos, developed method improving texture with calcium salts, thermal death time determinations on spoilage organisms and derivation adequate processing times; research on spoilage and processing pickles, wines, frozen sea foods and canned foods, research on mold and slime formation on country cured hams and bacon; use ascorbic acid as food antioxidant, effects light and reactions induced by container on chemical deterioration of foods during processing and storage; abstractor for Chemical Abstracts since '44. Cons since '42; faculty U Mass '42-46; asst prof food tech O Agrl Expt Sta, O State U '46-47; asso prof food tech U Ga, Ga Agrl Expt Sta '47-52, prof and head dept since '52. Sigma Xi—Phi Kappa Phi—Inst Food Tech(chem '50-51 Dixie Regional sect —Councillor '52-54)—ACS—AAUP. Research F U Mass '40-42. Department of Food Technology, College of Agriculture, University of Georgia, Athens, Ga.

10 POWERS, John Robert. Models (Training); Model agencies. b'96. Student (Easton Acad) (Lafayette Coll). Author syndicated column Secrets of Charm. Formed first model agency in the world, now president Powers Schools in New York, Philadelphia, Pittsburgh, Detroit, Boston, Buffalo; creator of the Powers Girls; lectr ednl subjects. 247 Park Av., NYC.

11 POWERS, Paul O(dell). Plastics; Synthetic rubber; Resins. b'97. AB '19 (Boston U); MS '22—PhD '24 (U Pittsburgh). Research and development on terpenes and rosin derivatives, synthetic resins rubbers and drying oils. Holds several U S patents. Author: Synthetic Resins and Rubbers '43; Plastics Chart, Plastics Ency '47, '48, '49. Research chemist Mellon Inst '24-26; Calco Chem Co NJ '26-28; Newport Inds Inc Fla '28-36; chief chem Armstrong Cork Co Lancaster Pa '36-46; lecturer plastics Franklin and Marshall Coll '42-46; tech advisor Battelle Memorial Inst Columbus O since '46. ACS (chmn paint varnish and plastic div '48)—Am Oil Chem Soc (Columbus section '49). Battelle Memorial Institute, Columbus 1, O.

12 POWERS, Treval Clifford. Technology of cement and concrete. b'00. BA '25 (Willamette U); '36 (MIT). Research on properties of concrete, mixformulation, pozzolanic materials, physical and colloid chemistry of portland cement and physics of concrete. Author: The Bleeding of Portland Cement Paste, Mortar and Concrete '39; Workability of Concrete '43; A Working Hypothesis for Further Studies of Frost Resistance of Concrete '45; Studies of the Physical Properties of Hardened Portland Cement Paste '48; The Nonevaporable Water Content of Hardened Portland Cement Paste—Its Significance for Concrete Research and Its Method of Determination '49. Concrete technician Bull Run Dam Ore '27-28; research chemist Beaver Portland Cement Co '29; asso engr Portland Cement Assn Research Labs Chicago '30-39, asst dir research '36-44, mgr basic research since '44. Am Concrete Inst—Nat Acad Sci (highway research bd)—Am Chem Soc—AAAS. Wasonmedals '32, '34, '47. Portland Cement Association, 33 W. Grand Av., Chicago 10.

13 POWERS, Wilbur Louis. Irrigation requirements; Drainage; Alkali land reclamation; Plant nutrition (Minor elements); Soil (Organic colloids, sulfur usage). b'87. BS '08 (U Ill); MSc '09 (N Mex Coll); PhD '26 (U Calif). Research on irrigation, drainage, minor elements in plant nutrition, and organic colloids in soils, soil-plant science particularly sulfur and boron contents of Oregon soils and need to supply those elements for the optimum yields of alfalfa and such crops as have high requirements; land classification, soil survey. Author: Irrigation Practice '12; Land Drainage '32; The Use of Sulfur in Soils '39; also articles in field. Prof soils drainage and irrigation Ore State Coll since '18; cons US Bur Reclamation. Internat Soc Soil Sci (rep Ore first, second congresses, mem organizing com first congress)—Soil Sci Soc Am—Am Soc Agron(F)—Am Chem Soc—Am Soc Plant Physiol—AAAS—Nat Geog Soc —Am Soc Agrl Engrs—ASCE (asso)— Northwest Sci Assn—Western Irrigation Drainage Research Assn—Oregon Reclamation Congress (sec '25-42, sec drainage sect since '15)—Willamette Basin Project Com—Sigma Xi—Gamma Sigma Delta. Soils Department, Oregon State College, Corvallis, Ore.

14 PRAEGER, Emil Hugh. Civil engineering (Foundations and superstructures, buildings, bridges and waterfront structures). b'92. CE '15 (Rensselaer Poly Inst); D Eng (hon) (Manhattan Coll). Consulting engineer for United Nations permanent headquarters New York City. Cons engr since '30; partner, chief engr Madigan-Hyland since '34; head dept civil engring Rensselaer Poly Inst '39-46. Served as lt sr grade Corps CE US Navy World War I; capt US Naval Reserve World War II. Newcomen Soc Am—ASCE—Am Inst Cons Engrs— Tau Beta Pi—Sigma Xi. 66 Rugby Rd., Bklyn.

15 PRANGE, Gordon W. German history (German-Russian relations, Bismarck period, World War I and II); History of World War II (Allied operations in Southwest Pacific and other Pacific areas, Japanese grand strategy and military operations); Russian-Japanese relations. b'10. BA '32—MA '34—PhD '37 (U Ia); '35-36 (U Berlin); student (Columbia, U Calif). Author: Hitler's Words, Two Decades of National Socialism '44; also articles in field. With U Md since '37, prof European hist since '46. Served lt, lt comdr US Navy '43-46, now chief Pacific Theater Hist Div G-2 Hist Sect GHQ FEC Tokyo Japan as war dept civilian on leave from U Md. AHA— Asiatic Soc Japan—Infantry Journ Assn—AAUP. Scholar Inst Pacific Relations for Russian study '37. History Department, University of Maryland, College Park, Md.

16 PRAT, Henri. Grasses (Histology, taxonomy, ecology); Plant gradients (Histo-physiology); Micro-calorimetry (Biological applications). b'02. BS '20 —License phys chem sci '22 (Paris U); License natural sci '24—Agregation '26—DS '31 (Ecole Normale Supérieure, Paris U). Rsrch in grass epidermis, laws of repartition of epidermic cells, methods description; dermograms, dermotypes; application to taxonomy, histol relationships between wheat and species of Agropyrum; notion of epidermic gradation; studied interdependance of physiological and histological gradients, gradients of resistance of plant tissues to physical, chemical and biotic agents as heat, mechanical actions, toxics and fungi; microcalorimetry, thermogenesis of seed germinations, bacterial cultures, insects; bionomic levels on intertidal zone on shores of France, Can, Bermuda; evolution peat bogs; mycorrhizae of Taxus; experimental cancer of Crysanthemum; regeneration in pine trees; made observations on erosion on rocky coasts, evolution of reefs. Author articles in field. Prof plant biol Montreal U '31-35 and since '45. Bot Soc Am—Société Canadienne d'Histoire Naturelle (past pres)—Société Botanique de France. Doctor honoris causa Montreal U '45; Guggenheim Found Fellow '48. Director Institute of Biology, University of Montreal, Montreal 26.

17 PRATHER, Charles Lee. Money and banking; Finance. b'90. EdB '22 PhD '49 (Eastern Ill State Coll); AM '23—PhD '27 (U Ill); student '43 (Mil Govt Sch) '43 (Brit Civil Affairs Staff Centre); '44 (Royal Inst Internat Affairs). Author: Money and Banking (3rd edit) '46; Gold Policy of the Federal Reserve System '27; Manual of Objective Tests '47; Solutions Manual '47. Prof finance and chmn dept finance, ins and real estate U Tex since '46. With US Army '43-45, specialist in economics and finance Gen Staff Corps. Am Finance Assn(pres '41-42) —Am Econ Assn—Beta Gamma Sigma —Phi Kappa Phi. 2200 Parkway, Austin 3, Tex.©

18 PRATT, Carl Davis. Explosives (Hexitols, emulsifiers). b'97. BA '18 (Swarthmore Coll). Patents on blasting powder, dynamite and blasting explosive assemblies. Author articles in field. Atlas Powder Co Wilmington Del since '18. Armed Forces Chem Assn—Franklin Inst—Comml Chem Development Assn—Am Inst Chem Engrs —ACS—Sigma Xi. Atlas Powder Company, Wilmington, Del.

19 PRATT, Harold Parker. Trout; Soil Conservation. b'06. AB '31—AM '33 (Western State Coll); PhD '38 (U Colo). Research on food habits, life histories of insects used as food, food chains, habits, environment of Western trout; studies on irrigated lands of the West for soil conservation. Author articles: Population studies of the trout of the Gunnison River; Ecology of the trout of the Gunnison River, Colorado. Wildlife biol Nat Park Service Mesa Verde Nat Park Colo '35; area biol Soil Conservation Service Grand Junction Colo '39-42; soil conservationist Montrose since '42. Ecol Soc Am—Colo-Wyo Acad Sci—Wildlife Soc—Soc Icthyologists and Herpetologists—Soc Mammalogists—Sigma Xi. Received cash grant for research from Colo-Wyo Acad Sci and AAAS '35. Soil Conservation Service, 242 Main St., Montrose, Colo. H: 1133 East Main St.

20 PRATT, Harry Edward. Abraham Lincoln; Illinois history; Stephen A Douglas. 'b01. BS '23—MS '26—PhD '30 (U Ill). Editor Journal of Illinois State Historical Society. Author: Lincoln 1840-1846 '39; Lincoln, 1809-1829 '41; The Personal Finances of Abraham Lincoln '43; Concerning Mr. Lincoln '44. Author 60 articles in field. Ill state historian since '50. Abraham Lincoln Assn (exec sec '36-43). Illinois State Historical Library, Centennial Building, Springfield, Ill.

21 PRATT, Ivan. Pacific marine invertebrates; Trematode parasites. b '08. AB '32 (Coll Emporia); MS '35 (Kan S Coll); PhD '38 (U Wis). Asso prof zool Ore State Coll since '47; resident mgr and prof Ore Inst Marine Biol since '46. Ore Acad Sci—Sigma Xi. Department of Zoology, Oregon State College, Corvallis, Ore.†

22 PRATT, Jabez H. Carbon dioxide. b'90. SB '12—MS '13 (MIT). Research on the production of carbon dioxide. Author articles in field. Jr engr Liquid Carbonic Corp '13-16, gen supt '16-20, asst vp '20-30, vp and in charge mfg and engring '30-42, exec vp since '42. 3100 S. Kedzie Av., Chgo.

10 PRATT, Robert Armstrong. Chaucer; Medieval schoolbooks; Boccaccio; Sercambi; Walter Map. b'07. AB '29—PhD '33 (Yale); '31-32 (U Florence). Author articles in field. Asso prof Eng Queens Coll '48-51; professor English U NC since '51. Modern Lang Assn (chmn Biblio research com Chaucer Group '37-44; sec Chaucer Group '45, chmn '46; Chaucer Library com since '47)—Medieval Acad (com research activities '47-50)—Am Assn Teachers Italian—NY Medieval Club (pres '48-49). Guggenheim fellow '46-47. Department of English, University of North Carolina, Chapel Hill, N.C.

11 PRAY, George Emerson. Electronics (Television, radar, ultrasonics, loran direction finders, sono-radio equipment). b'03. EE '28 (Rensselaer Poly Inst); student (Rutgers U). Holder numerous patents; responsible for development or manufacture of Signal Corps BC-189 first Army superheterodyne receiver, BS-197C, Air Force TS-251, Navy XAQ first radar receiver, DAG, DBA, DBN, JM-1, RBF-1 and others. President Radio Sonic Corp; vp General Electrosonics, Inc. Institute Radio Engrs (sr)—Nat Soc Profl Engrs—NY State Soc Profl Engrs—NJ State Soc Profl Engrs. Radio Sonic Corporation, 186 Union Av., New Rochelle, N.Y.

12 PREBLE, Edward Alexander. Ornithology; Mammalogy and plants (Distribution, life habits, ecology). b'71. Ed high schs Mass. Established Ossipee Wildlife Sanctuary Ossipee New Hampshire '39; specialized in geographical distribution, life habits, ecology and protection of birds, mammals, fishes, reptiles, amphibians and plants. Author: A Biological Investigation of the Hudson Bay Region '02; A Biological Investigation of the Athabaska-Mackenzie Region '08; The Fur Seals and Other Life of the Pribilof Islands, Alaska, in 1914 '15, Birds and Mammals of the Pribilof Islands, Alaska '23 (with others). With Biol Survey US Dept Agr '92-35, retired; asso ed Nature Mag Washington. Am Ornithol Union—Biol Soc Washington—Am Soc Mammalogists—Am Soc Ichthyologists Herpetologists. 3027 Newark St., Washington.

13 PREBLE, Norman Alexander. Ornithology, mammalogy. b'11. AB '36 (U Kan); MS '40—PhD '42 (O State U). Author articles in field. Asso prof biol and chmn dept biol Northeastern U since '48. Am Soc Mammalogists—Am Assn Adv Sci—O Acad Sci—Am Nature Assn—Am Micros Soc—Wilson Ornithol Club—Am Ornithol Union—Am Soc Zool—Sigma Xi. Department of Biology, Northeastern University, Boston.

14 PREISMAN, Louis. Inorganic chemistry (Research). b'02. BS '23—ChE '24 (Coll City NY). Patents on phosphate of soda manufacture, hydrofluoric acid and hydrogen sulfide and carbon disulfide manufacture. Chem research Gen Chem Co '26-32, plant supervisor '35-41, asst prodn mgr '41-44; tech dir Barium Reduction Corp since '44. ACS—AAAS—Phi Beta Kappa. Barium Reduction Corporation, P.O. Box 8097, South Charleston 3, W. Va.

15 PRENTICE, John Rockefeller. Dairy cattle breeding (Artificial insemination). b'02. BA '28 (Yale Coll); LLB '31 (Yale Law Sch). Pres Wis Scientific Breeding Inst Madison Wis and chmn bd of predecessor organizations since '41; owner and operator Ind Artificial Breeding Assn Indianapolis, Northwestern Artificial Breeding Assn Duluth, Southeastern Artificial Breeding Assn Asheville NC. Am Dairy Sci

Assn—Am Soc Animal Prodn—Nat Assn Artificial Breeders—Am Found Study Genetics (pres). 325 North Wells St., Chgo.

16 PRESCOTT, Frank Howard. Automobiles (Generators, starting motors, ignition systems, shock absorbers); Locomotives (Diesel electric). b'92. BS in elec engring '15 (Mich State Coll). With Gen Motors Corp '26-43; chief engr Delco-Remy Div '26-32, gen mgr Guide Lamp Div '33-34, gen mgr Delco Products Div '34-36, gen mgr Electro-Motive Div '36-43. Soc Automotive Engrs. Received Certificate of Commendation US Navy Bur Ships. H: Austinburg, O.

17 PRESCOTT, G(erald) W(ebber). Algal cultures; Algae (Control); Fish (Food problems). b'01. AB '23 (U Ore); AM '26—PhD '28 (U Ia). Research on fresh water biology, algae control, feeding problems of fish. Author: Algae of the Central Great Lakes Region '49; How to Know the Freshwater Algae '50. Asso prof bot Albion Coll Mich '29-46; investigator Ia State Fish and Game Commn '31-32; field survey Ore and Ida USDA '35; investigator Wis Geol and Natural Hist Survey '36-38; asso prof bot U Mich Biol Sta '40-48; field bot US Fgn Econ Adminstrn '44; prof bot U Mont Biol Sta '50; prof bot and plant path Mich State Coll since '46. Am Micros Soc—Limnol Soc Am—Am Soc Taxonomists—Phycology Soc Am—NE Bot Soc—Mich Acad Sci—O Acad Sci—Sigma Xi—Gamma Alpha. H: 352 Marshall St., E. Lansing, Mich.†◎

18 PRESLEY, John T(homas). Cotton diseases. b'06. Student '27-29 (U Fla); BS '35 (U Md); PhD '47 (U Minn). US Dept Agr Bur Plant Ind Office cotton, other fiber crops, diseases since '29; head dept plant pathol, physiol Miss Agrl Expt Sta and US Dept Agr; head Botany Dept Miss State Coll; now prin path USDA Plant Industry Station Beltsville. Am Phytopath Soc—Torrey Bot Club—Am Genetic Assn—Mycol Soc Am—Minn Acad Sci—Miss Acad Sci—AAAS. Plant Industry Station, Beltsville, Md.

19 PRESNALL, Clifford Charles. Mammalogy (Predation, ecology); Wildlife management (Conservation and recreation, predator and rodent control). b'98. BS '23 (Ore State Coll). Explored wilderness areas in United States, Mexico and Canada; examined areas proposed for National Park status in Florida, Utah, Oregon, Mexico; studied ecology of big game ranges in National Parks and Indian Reservations throughout the West; investigated game-livestock-predator relationships on ranges in California, Arizona, Utah; surveyed fur resources of Indian lands in all northern states; made ecological survey of Wind River Indian Reservation, Wyoming; studied range management of buffalo herds in Wyoming, Montana, S. Dakota, and Manitoba; directed national rat control program. Author articles in field. Asst chief Wildlife Div Wash DC '38-41; in chge Wildlife on Pub Lands Fish and Wildlife Service Wash DC '41-46, asst chief Br Predator Rodent Control since '46. Am Soc Mammalogists—Soc Am Foresters—Wildlife Soc—Wildlife Soc. Fish and Wildlife Service, Washington 25.†

20 PRESTINI, James. Design research; Industrial design. b'08. BS '30 (Yale U); '38 (U Stockholm); '39 (Inst of Design). Design work exhibited at various universities and museums. Coauthor: The Place of Scientific Research in Design '48. Research engr Armour Research of Ill Found Inst Tech Chicago '43-53; design consultant

Midwest Research Inst Kansas City since '46, Museum of Modern Art NY since '46; adv bd Inst Contemporary Art Washington '48. One of six designers given grants by the Museum of Modern Art NY to do research in low cost furniture '48; co-winner best research report Internat competition for low-cost furniture design. 329 Winchester Av., Glendale 1, Cal.

21 PRESTON, Dudley A. Legumes (Diseases); Plant rust (Malvaceae). b'10. BS '33 (Wash State Coll); MS '40—PhD '47 (U Minn). Research of rusts of malvaceae; host indexes of plant diseases in Oklahoma and Minnesota. Author articles in field. Instr dept botany and plant path Ala Poly Inst '42-43; asso mycol Emergency Plant Disease Prev US Dept Agr '43-45; asso prof and plant pathol dept bot and plant pathol and plant pathol Expt Sta Okla A&M Coll '45-48; asst prof Div Life Scis San Diego State Coll since '48; cons air pollution damage to crop plants. Am Phytopath Soc—Mycol Soc Am—Soc for Study Evolution—Okla Acad Sci—AAAS—Gamma Alpha—Phi Sigma. Division of Life Sciences, San Diego State College, San Diego 5, Calif.

22 PRESTON, Richard J(oseph), Jr. Forestry education; Silviculture; North American trees; Wood technology. b'05. BA '27—MSF '28—PhD '41 (U Mich); '30-32 (Stanford U); '32-33 (U Chicago). Research on wood products, preservation and gluing. Author: Rocky Mountain Trees '47; North American Trees '48; also articles in field. Dean Sch Forestry NC State Coll since '48. Soc Am Foresters—Forest Products Research Soc—Sigma Xi. School of Forestry, North Carolina State College, Raleigh, N.C.†

23 PRESTON, Walter Bonham. Sulphur mining plants. b'04. BS in mech engring '26 (U Tex). With Tex Gulf Sulphur Co since '28, mgr mech and municipal dept '44-52. Tau Beta Pi—Pi Tau Sigma—ASME. Registered profl engr Tex. Box 385, Newgulf, Tex.

24 PRETTYMAN, Irven Bernhard. High polymer physics; Elastic and plastic deformation (Theories); Textiles and elastomers (Physical properties); Tirecord research and development. b'11. BS '33—MS '35 (Case Inst Tech); LLB '40 (Akron Law Sch). Research on Joule effect in rubber, X-ray study of rubber, thermal decomposition, tread cracking and stress relaxation of natural and synthetic rubber stocks, hysteretic and elastic properties of rubberlike materials under dynamic shear stresses, effects of temperature and humidity on physical properties of tire cords, measurement of thermal conductivity of non-metallic solids. Author articles in field. Research physicist Firestone Tire and Rubber Co since '35; admitted O State Bar '40. Am Phys Soc (div high polymer physics)—Am Chem Soc (rubber div)—AAAS(F)—Sigma Xi. The Firestone Tire and Rubber Co., Akron 17, O. H: 210 Crescent Dr.

25 PRICE, Don Krasher. Federal government organization; American presidency; Legislative-executive relations; Local government (City manager plan); British government; Organization of scientific research. b'10. BA '31 (Vanderbilt U); BA '34—B Litt '35 (Oxford U). Field survey of 18 cities in US having council-manager form of government '37-39. Author articles in field. Asso dir Pub Adminstrn Clearing House since '45; lecturer polit sci U Chicago; asst former Pres Hoover on study US Presidency under auspices commn orgn Exec Br Govt; dep chmn Research and Development Bd

US Dept Def '52-53; staff dir Com on Dept Def Orgn '53; cons to Pres Adv Com Govt Orgn since '53. Am Soc Pub Adminstrn—Am Polit Sci Assn—Internat City Managers' Assn—Nat Municipal League—Phi Beta Kappa. Public Administration Clearing House, 815 17th St., Washington 6.†

10 PRICE, Edward Thomas, Jr. US populations (Mixed-blood, racial strains); Racial segregation (US). b '15. BS '37 (Cal Inst Tech); PhD '50 (U Cal). Research on culture, status, demography, and origin of Melungeons of eastern Tennessee, Cajans of Alabama, Redbones of southwest Louisiana, Guineas of West Virginia, and Jackson Whites of northern New Jersey. Group supervisor Cal Inst Tech '42-45; instr and asst prof geog U Cincinnati '46-51; asst prof Los Angeles State Coll '51-53, head dept '52, asso prof since '53. Tau Beta Pi—Assn Am Geog—Ohio Acad Sci(F)—Am Geog Soc(F)—Nat Council Geog Tchrs—Sigma Xi(asso). Geography Department, Los Angeles State College, 855 N. Vermont Av., LA 29.

11 PRICE, Erwin Hugh. French literature (Eighteenth century). b'94. LLB '17—MA '27—PhD '35 (O State U); '18-19 (U Toulouse France). Author articles in field. Prof French, head mod lang dept Miss State Coll since '37. Mod Lang Assn Am—Am Assn Teachers French—S Central Mod Lang Assn —O Archeol Hist Soc. Box 554, State College, Miss.

12 PRICE, Francis. American-Spanish history and folklore; Water law of California. b'90. AB '14—JD '15 (Stanford U). Chief counsel in case of Gin S Chow vs City Santa Barbara et al which resulted in modification of riparian water rights doctrine; compiled from oral sources ancient pastoral play Los Pastores; translated from original Spanish manuscripts records of early California history. Admitted to Calif bar '15, began practice Santa Barbara firm Heaney Price Postel and Parma; spl counsel various California public bodies in connection water supply problems. Am Judicature Soc—Am Bar Assn—Soc Mexican Pilgrims. 21 E. Canon Perdido St., Santa Barbara, Cal.

13 PRICE, Harold Charles. Pipe line construction (Oil, natural gas). b'88. EM '13 (Colo Sch Mines). Pioneered electric welding of oil and gas pipelines; developed internal line-up clamp to facilitate welding of pipe joints; contributed to technique of applying seamless mastic coating to pipelines for corrosion protection; responsible for research and development Hevicote process for adding weight to oil and gas lines being laid at river corssings and in marshy country; responsible for numerous other improvements in pipeline construction equipment and technique. Author articles: Improvements in the Electric Welding of Gas Transmission Lines '38; Arc Welding of Pipe Lines '39; Electric Welding of Mene Grande Pipe Line in Venezuela '39; Electric-Arc Roll-Welding and Stove-Pipe Welding in Pipe Line Construction '40, and others. Contributor: American Welding Society Handbook (rev edit) '42. Pres H C Price Co., Bartlesville Okla since '21. AIMME— Am Petroleum Inst—Am Gas Assn— Ind Natural Gas Assn—Am Welding Soc—Pipe Line Contractors Assn of Asso General Contractors Am. Colo Sch Mines distinguished achievement medal for distinction in the fields of pipeline engineering and construction and business management. Union National Bank Bldg., Bartlesville, Okla. H: Star View Farm.

14 PRICE, Leslie D(aniel). Electrical engineering (Standardization, legislation). b'01. BS '22 (MIT). Elec equipment design, economics; miscellaneous articles on electrical measurements, standardization in the electrical industry, and effects of legislation on electrical industry. Meter and wiring engr Pub Service Elec and Gas Co Newark '38-45; mgr engring and safety regulations dept Nat Elec Mfrs Assn since '45. Am Inst EE(F). Received Public Service Elec and Gas Co Thomas N McCarter medal for development electrical metering methods, and devices resulting in economies in operation '44. 155 E. 44th St., NYC 17.

15 PRICE, Paul Hurvey. Rural sociology; Latin America (Peoples and institutions). b'19. AB '40 (SE La Coll); MA '47 (La State U); Cordell Hull F Inst Brazilian Studies—PhD '51 (Vanderbilt U). Research on immigration, assimilation and acculturation of Poles in Brazil, distribution medical personnel and health problems of rural population in Louisiana. Asst prof and asst rural sociol La State U since '49. Am Sociol Soc—So Sociol Soc— Rural Sociol Soc—La Acad Sci—AA UP—Phi Kappa Phi. Department of Sociology, Louisiana State University, Baton Rouge.

16 PRICE, Percival. Bells; Carillons. b'01. BMus '27 (U Toronto); diplome '27 (Beiaardschool te Mechelen (Belgium); pvt composition (Arthur Willner Vienna); Basler Hochschule fur Musik Graduate (Basle Switzerland and Vienna). Research carillons in Europe and North America both ancient and modern, carillon design mechanism keyboards practice keyboards and installation, harmonics of bells and bell tuning, archeological aspects of bells, sequestration and destruction of bells in Europe as result of recent war; developed musical script conventions for writing carillon music, theory of carillon harmony and technique. Author: The Carillon '33; Campanology-Europe '48; also articles in field. Composer about 50 compositions for carillon including one concerto, a symphony, several chamber works and songs, arrangements of carillon music. Massey Memorial carillonneur Toronto Can '22-25; carillonneur Rockefeller Memorial Carillon NY '25-27; Dominion carillonneur House of Parliament Ottawa '27-39; prof composition and U carillonneur U Mich '39-49, prof campanology and U carillonneur since '49. Guild of Carrillonneurs in No Am (past pres). Awarded Pulitzer prize in music '34; Coronation Medal '38. Burton Tower, Ann Arbor.

17 PRICE, Robert. Middle Western literature and folklore. b'00. PhB '28 (Denison U); MA '30—PhD '43 (O State U). Author: John Chapman: A Bibliography of Johnny Appleseed '44; also articles in field. Co-author: (with S A Harbarger and A B Whitmer) English for Engineers '43; Johnny Appleseed: A Voice in the Wilderness '45. Asso prof dept Eng Otterbein Coll '46-47, prof since '48. Am Folklore Soc —Coll Eng Assn—Eng Speaking Union —Am Dialect Soc—Am Council Teaching Eng—Melville Soc—Phi Beta Kappa. Library of Congress grant-in-aid '45-46. Otterbein College, Westerville, O.

18 PRICE, Thomas Moore. Concrete aggregate production; General construction. b'91. AB '12—BS in civil engring '15 (U NC). Designed and constructed plants to produce aggregates for Henry J Kaiser Pacific Coast, Hoover Dam Bonneville Dam Grand Coulee Dam, Washington, Detroit Dam,

Oregon; heavy construction on these dams and management section Deleware Aqueduct, Fontana Steel Plant Cal, 3d Locks Panama Canal. Am Soc CE—Am Inst Mining Engrs—Am Assn Indsl and Structural Engrs. 1924 Broadway, Oakland 12, Cal.⊚

19 PRICE, W(illiam) Armstrong, Jr. Geomorphology of arid regions; Quaternary diastrophism (Gulf Coast); Origin of caliche; origin of mima mounds; Sand and clay dunes; Deltaic coastal plains (Louisiana; Texas; Tamaulipas). b'89. AB '09 (Davidson Coll); PhD '13 (Johns Hopkins U). Discovered oil and gas fields Texas '28-45; organized and led field conference on Ogallala and Quaternary of Llano Estacado Plateau Texas and New Mexico '45. Author articles in field. Geol and cons work. Geol Soc Am—AAAS—Tex Acad Sci (vp '35, pres '36, dir '39-41, ed Handbook)—Am Assn Petroleum Geol—American Geophys Union. Dept. Oceanography, A.&M. College of Texas, College Station, Tex.

20 PRICE, William Conway. Plant pathology and virology. b'06. BS '27 (Va Poly Inst); PhD '32 (Columbia). Research on purification of viruses, properties of viruses, acquired immunity in plants, classification of viruses. Author articles in field. Asso research prof U Pittsburgh '45-47, research prof since '47, dir Plant Virus Lab since '49; editor-in-chief Phytopathology since '52. AAAS(F)—Am Phytopath Soc—Bot Soc Am—Am Soc Naturalists—Biometric Soc—Soc Exptl Biology and Med—Sigma Xi. R.D. 7, Pitts. 29.

21 PRICHARD, Arthur Carlton. Precise frequency control. b'04. BS '26 (U Ky); MS '28 (Pa State Coll). Design of communication receivers, radiosonde equipment, radar countermeasures equipment and receivers; development of crystal units of greater frequency stability, overtone crystal units, crystal oscillator and test circuits; research in crystal filters and quartz crystal resonators having characteristics necessary for use in filters. Joint patent on DC restorer, for radar applications. With Signal Corps engring lab Ft Monmouth NJ since '35, frequency control br since '44. Inst Radio Engrs (sr mem)—Test Equipment Panel and Frequency Control Devices Subpanel RDB (dep mem) —Pi Mu Epsilon—Sigma Pi Sigma. Frequency Control Branch, Signal Corps Engineering Laboratories, Fort Monmouth, N.J.

22 PRIEN, Charles Henry. Oil shale and shale oil. b'16. BS '38—PhD '48 (Purdue). Project head research on hydrogenation of Colorado coal, Colorado State Industrial Research Board '45-46, project head basic studies on hydrogenation, oxidation, extraction Colorado oil shale '46-48. Author articles in field. Asst prof, chem engr, research engr Engring Exptl Station U Colo '44-48; asso prof chem and project engr Indsl Research Inst U Denver since '48. Am Chme Soc—Am Inst Chem Engrs—Am Soc Engring Edn— AAAS—Sigma Xi—Sigma Tau—Phi Lambda Upsilon. Department of Chemical Engineering, University of Denver, Denver 10.†

23 PRIEST, Alan. Art (Far East). b'98. AB '20—'21-24 (Harvard). Author: Chinese Sculpture in the Metropolitan Museum of Art '43; Costumes from the Forbidden City (monograph) '45; various other monographs and catalogues. Contributor to Bulletin of the Metropolitan Museum of Art. Asst in fine art Harvard '21, assistant and tutor '22-23; member second Fogg expedition to China '24-25; Carnegie fellow China '25; Sachs fellow China '26-27; curator dept Far Eastern Art, Metropolitan Museum of Art since '28. Metropolitan Museum of Art, NYC.◎

10 PRIEST, Loring Bensen. United States Indian relations since 1865. b'09. LittB '30—Student '44 (Rutgers U); AM '31—PhD '37 (Harvard). Author: Uncle Sam's Stepchildren '42; The Reformation of United States Indian Policy 1865-1887; also articles in field. Mem hist staff Biarritz Am U '45; asst prof U Coll Rutgers '46-48; asso prof Gannon Coll '48-49; dir soc studies Lycoming Coll since '49. AHA—Miss Valley Hist Assn—Pa Hist Assn—Phi Beta Kappa Lycoming College, Williamsport, Pa. H: 215 Eldred St.

11 PRIMOFF, Ernest S. Development trade tests and aptitude tests. b'13. AB '34—MA '37 (NYU). Development numerous written, oral, and performance tests for selection of workers in specific trades positions, including chauffeurs, truck drivers, apprentices, and mechanic helpers; validated interest inventory to determine which trade most suitable to applicant according to his interests; field research on tests requiring minimum of administration time; director preparation of written examinations for public service psychologists. Author articles: Correlations and Factor Analysis of the Abilities of the Single Individual '43; Job Analysis for Constructing Written Tests '47; Special Problems in the Development of Performance Tests '47; Machine-Scored Civil Service Tests of Dexterity and Perception '49; Use of Job Analysis in Developing a Differential Battery '50, and others. Examining asst NYC Civil Service Commn '39-40; occupational psychol and chief trade tests and worker evaluation div occupational analysis War Manpower Commn '40-44; chief trade testing unit test development sect US Civil Service Commn since '45. Am Psychol Assn—Phi Beta Kappa. Test Development Section, U.S. Civil Service Commission, Washington 25.

12 PRIOR, Granville Torrey. History of southern United States (South Carolina); Newspaper history. b'09. BA '31 (Amherst); MA '32 (Brown U); MA '34—PhD '47 (Harvard). Research history antebellum South Carolina, history Charleston Mercury. Author articles: Charleston Pastime and Culture During the Nullification Decade, 1822-1832 '40; Huguenot Descendants in Ante-bellum South Carolina '47; Henry L Pinckney's Editorship of the Charleston Mercury '40. Prof hist Elon Coll NC '34-36; asst prof hist Citadel '36-46, prof, chmn dept since '46. AHA—So Hist Assn—SC Hist Soc—SC Hist Assn. The Citadel, Charleston, S.C.†

13 PRITCHARD, Earl Hampton. Far eastern history; Chinese history; Sino-foreign relations since 1514. b'07. BA '28 (State Coll Wash); AM '29—Scholar '28-29 (U Ill); Rhodes Scholar '30-33—DPhil '33 (Oxford U Eng); '37-39 (Columbia U). Author articles in field. Asso prof far eastern hist U Chicago since '47; ed Far Eastern Quarterly '41-51. AHA—Am Oriental Society—Far Eastern Assn (founder, officer). Rockefeller Found Postwar Fellow and Fulbright Scholar for research on Sino-Foreign Relations '48-49. Department of History, University of Chicago, Chgo 37.

14 PRITCHARD, James Bennett. Palestine (Archeology); Near Eastern literature (Ancient). b'09. AB '30 (Asbury Coll); BD '35 (Drew U); PhD '42 (U Pa). Director American School of Oriental Research expedition to Herodian Jericho, Hashemite Kingdom of Jordan, which discovered ruins of Herodian building '51; associate edi-

tor Near East Journal of American Oriental Society since '48. Author: Palestinian Figurines '43. Editor: Ancient Near Eastern Texts '50. Prof OT lit Crozer Theol Sem since '42; annual prof Am Sch Oriental Research '50-51; research asso U Mus U Pa since '50. Am Oriental Soc—Soc Bibl Lit and Exegesis. Received grant from Am Philos Soc '49. Crozer Theological Seminary, Chester, Pa.

15 PRITCHETT, William Kendrick. Greek inscriptions; Ancient Greek chronology and history. b'09. BA '29 (Davidson Coll); MA '31 (Duke U); PhD '42 (Johns Hopkins). Author: Chronology of Hellenistic Athens (with Meritt) '40; Five Attic Tribes after Kleisthenes '43; Calendars of Athens (with Neugebauer) '47; The Attic Stelai '53. Asso prof dept classics Cal U since '48; Guggenheim fellow '51; senior research Fulbright fellow Greece '51-52. AHA—Am Philol Assn—Archeol Inst Am. Research fellow Am Sch Classical Studies Athens '45-46. Department of Classics, University of California, Berkeley 4.†

16 PRITHAM, Carroll F(red). Waterworks. b'07. BS in elec engring '29 (U Me). Research, development and operation rapid sand filter plants for municipal water supplies, development engineering and design sewage treatment plants. Supervisor Me Water Dist '47-49; asst supervisor W Springfield Water Dept since '49. NE Water Works Assn—Am Inst EE. 126 Park St., West Springfield, Mass.

17 PROCTOR, Arthur Marcus. Education (County school reorganization and consolidation, school building plans). b'86. AB '10 (Trinity Coll); AM '22—PhD '30 (Columbia); hon fellow '37 (U So Calif). Author: Principles of School Administration '38; also articles in field. Prof sch administrn Duke U since '23, dir summer sessions since '47; cons on co sch reorgn and consolidation and bldg programs State Dept Edn Raleigh NC. Nat Soc Study Edn—Nat Council Schoolhouse Constrn—Am Soc Pub Adminstrn—Am Assn Sch Adminstrs —Assn Deans Dirs Summer Sessions. College Station, Duke University, Durham, N.C.

18 PROCTOR, Bernard E(merson). Food preservation and processing. b'01. SB '23—PhD '27 (MIT). Civilian consultant on research and development on foods and packaging for Office of Quartermaster General, US Army Washington '42-43, director subsistence and packaging research '43-44. Coauthor: Food Technology '37; also articles in field. Prof food tech MIT since '43, dir Samuel Cate Prescott Labs Food Tech since '45. Inst Food Tech—Refrigeration Research Found— Nat Assn Refrigerated Warehousemen —Am Chem Soc—Am Pub Health Assn —Am Soc Refrigerating Engrs—Soc Am Bacteriol—Nat Research Council (com on foods)—AAAS—Sigma Xi. Director, Food Technology Laboratories, Massachusetts Institute of Technology, Cambridge 39, Mass. H: 100 Memorial Dr., Cambridge 42, Mass.◎

19 PROCTER, William. Marine and insect life of Mount Desert region; Marine biology; Entomology. b'72. PhB '94 (Yale); DSc '36 (U Montreal). Established laboratory on Mount Desert Island Me '21; established Biological Survey of Mount Desert region '26; has contributed to curricula of universities and state biological departments. Author articles in field. Mem bd mgrs Wistar Inst Anat Biol Phila '28-36; mem adv bd dept zool Columbia U Entomol Soc Am(F)—AAAS

(F)—Acad Natural Sci—Boston Soc Natural Hist—Entomol Soc Am (mem ed bd '40-48)—Am Micros Soc— Ornithol Union—Genetic Soc—Ray Soc London Eng—Plymouth Marine Assn Eng—So Calif Acad Sci—Ecol Soc Am —Royal Can Inst—Sigma Xi. Bar Harbor, Me.

20 PROEBSTING, Edward Louis. Mineral nutrition of fruit trees; Orchard soil management. b'97. BS '18 (U Calif); MSA '21—PhD '24 (Cornell). Author articles in field. Prof pomology U Calif since '43. AAAS— Am Soc Hort Sci—Bot Soc Am—Western Soc Soil Sci. Nat Research Council fellow '31-32. Division of Pomology, University of California, Davis, Calif.†

21 PROELL, Wayne Arthur. Alkanesulfonic acids; Sulphur chemistry; Fuel oils. b'15. BS '37—'38-40, '47-48 (U Chicago). Research on fuel oils, diesel fuels, sulphur chemistry particularly low molecular weight alkanesulfonic acids (manufacturing methods, properties, utilization); research and patents include fuel oil stabilization, diesel fuels, naptha additives, synthesis of alkanesulfonic acids, synthesis of sulfur compounds. Author articles in field. Chem Standard Oil Co Ind since '38. AAAS—Am Chem Soc—Phi Beta Kappa. Standard Oil Company (Ind.), Whiting, Ind.

22 PROJECTOR, Theodore Hertzel. Searchlights; Aircraft lighting; Photometry. b'14. BS '34 (City Coll NY). Test and development airway beacons and aircraft lighting equipment; research and tests on photographic discharge lamps; in charge test and development anti-submarine searchlights, aircraft position lights and flashing systems, instrument and panel lighting systems, and signal lights; development apparatus and technique for testing searchlight and projection photometry equipment; chairman technical committee on calculation projector systems US national committee International Commission on Illumination. Physicist photometry sect Nat Bur Standards since '38, now in charge naval aircraft lighting project. AAAS— Illuminating Engrs Soc(mem aviation lighting com, chmn searchlight com)— Optical Soc Am. National Bureau of Standards, Washington 25. H: 2904 Stanton Av., Forest Glen, Md.

23 PROSKOURIAKOFF, Tatiana, Maya architecture; Pre-Columbian art. b'10. BS '30 (Pa State Coll); '29-31-32 (U Pa). Research architecture of Maya sites, history pre-Columbian art styles in Middle America. Author: An Album of Maya Architecture '46; A Study of Classic Maya Sculpture '50. Archtl draftsman U Pa Mus '37-38; archtl draftsman and archeol Carnegie Instn Wash since '39. Soc Am Archeol —Am Anthropol Assn—AAAS. Carnegie Institution of Washington, 10 Frisbie Place, Cambridge 38, Mass.

24 PROUDFOOT, Lewis C. Coats-of-arms and crests. b'05. Students (Arts Students League NYC). Painted presidential seals, US seal for foreign ambassadors and ministers, and official coats of arms for South American presidents as well as maharajahs, rulers and diplomats in America and foreign countries. Artist L Proudfoot & Son since '73. 1819 Broadway, NYC 23.

25 PUCKETT, Newbell Niles. Negro folklore and religion. b'97. BS '18 (Miss Coll); PhB '20—AM '21—PhD '25 (Yale). Research in South collecting Negro folklore, folk songs, superstitions, and making studies of Negro churches and religious beliefs; collected Negro names from slave records, college catalogs, city directories, school census lists, social agencies and through field interviews. Author: Folk-Beliefs of the Southern Negro '26; also articles in field. With Western Res U since '22, prof sociol since '38. Am Sociol Soc—O Valley Sociol Soc—Rural Sociol Soc. Western Reserve University, Cleveland 6. H: 2629 Wellington Rd., Cleveland Heights 18.⊙

10 PUCKETT, W(illiam) O(lin). Zoology (Embrology, anatomy). b'06. AB '27 (Davidson Coll); AM '31 (NC U); PhD '34 (Princeton). Research on regeneration in amphibians, sex differentiation in amphibians, biological effect of X-radiations, plastics in biological works. Author articles in field. Prof biol Davidson (NC) Coll since '46. Am Soc Zool—Am Assn Anat—Sigma Xi. Davidson, N.C.

11 PUFFER, Ruth Rice. Public health (Statistics). b'07. AB '29 (Smith Coll); '37-38 (Johns Hopkins Sch Hygiene); DrPH '43 (Harvard). Application statistical method in field public health with development method analysis of longitudinal data in studies of tuberculosis and careful studies of prevalence and incidence of tuberculosis in a population group under observation for many years, the significance of exposure to tubercle bacilli and susceptibility to the disease; development teaching of practical statistics in public health to doctors, nurses, statisticians and students; analyses and research in tuberculosis, syphilis, industrial hygiene, cancer, vital statistics, morbidity statistics, others. Author: Familial Susceptibility to Tuberculosis '44; Practical Statistics in Health and Medical Work '50. Dir statis service Tenn Dept Pub Health Nashville since '33; vis prof Sch Pub Health U Chile '46; cons UN for teaching in Inter-Am Seminar of Biostatistics '50; lectr Meharry Sch Nursing since '49; instr Vanderbilt Sch Med since '47. Am Statis Assn—AAAS—Population Assn Am—Am Pub Health Assn—Delta Omega—Sigma Xi. Award of Tenn State Nursing Assn as lay person contributing most to nursing '50. Tennessee Department of Public Health, Nashville 3.

12 PULS, Edwin E(rnest). Lubrication (Industrial machinery and automotive engines). b'99. SB '23 (Neb State Tchrs Coll); BS '24 (U Ill). Research in metal cutting fluids and coolants; conducted original field work in application heavy duty soluble oils in grinding, milling, drilling operations; practical expert on correct usage of core oils as binders in cores in ferrous and non-ferrous foundries. Lubrication engr and combustion cons Cities Service Oil Co since '30. Soc Automotive Engrs—Am Soc Lubrication Engrs.

13 PURYEAR, Vernon John. History (International relations, Napoleon, Near East); American institutions. b'01. AB '21 (Baylor U); AM '25 (U Mo); teaching fellow in European history '28-29—PhD '29 (U Calif); research fellow '30-31 (Social Sci Research Council). Author: England, Russia and the Straits Question (1844-56) '31; International Economics and Diplomacy in the Near East '35; France and the Levant '41; Napoleon and the Dardanelles '51; also articles in field. Professor history U Cal since '48. AHA—Am Acad Polit Social Sci—Econ Hist Assn—Fgn Policy Assn. 647 D St., Davis—Cal.

14 PUTNAM, Alfred. Dogs; Dog breeding (Boxers, Weimaraners). b'95. Student '08-12 (St Pauls Sch Concord NY); '12-14 (Phillips Exeter Acad); AB '17 (Harvard). Has served as an American Kennel Club licensed judge, officiating at shows in several states. Author articles in field. Owner Puttenham Kennels specializing in breeding boxers; gen partner Auchincloss, Parker and Redpath, brokers, since '33; vp, dir Investment Corp of Phila; pres White Williams Found. Land Title Bldg., S.W. corner Broad and Chestnut sts., Phila. 10.

15 PUTNAM, John Alfred. Technical quality and utility of hardwood timber; Nature and identification of hardwood timber defects; Silviculture and management of hardwood forests; Dendrology and silvics. b'01. BS in forestry '48 (U Mich). Definition standards of quality and utility for grading timber in forest surveys; research on nature and identification log defects, significance all recognizable blemishes and abnormalities of hardwood logs; study of stocking and stand condition relative to growth and yield prospects in hardwood forest management; investigation taxonomic composition, economic utility and silvicultural properties various hardwood types. Author articles: A Tentative Report on the Probable Yield From an Area of Second Growth Hardwood in the Mississippi Delta '32; Management of Southern Hardwood Forests '50. Co-author articles: (with Henry Bull); The Trees of the Bottomlands of the Mississippi River Delta Region '32; (with R K Winters) Forest Resources of the North-Louisiana Delta '38; (with Henry Bull) Improvement Cuttings in the Bottomland Hardwood Forests of Mississippi '40; (with C R Lockard and R D Carpenter) Log Defects in Southern Hardwood '50; others. Assisted and collaborated in first profl investigation of forestry situation in southern bottomland hardwoods Louisiana Delta '28; with So Forest Expt Sta US Forest Service '31-37, in charge survey Miss River Delta Region forests '31-37; expt and demonstration hardwood forest management Delta Expt Sta Stoneville Miss '40-41 and since '45; Soc Am Foresters—Phi Sigma. Delta Experiment Station, Stoneville, Miss.

16 PUTNAM, Roger Lowell. Package machinery. b'93. AB '15 (Harvard); '15-16 (MIT). Vice-pres Package Machinery Co '21-27, pres '27-42, chairman board since '48; director Van Norman Machine Tool Co, Perkins Machine & Gear Co, Am Bosch Corp. Dir research development Amphibious Force US Atlantic Fleet; deputy dir Office Contract Settlement Washington '44-46. Sole trustee Lowell Observatory. AAAS(F)—Am Astron Assn—Astron Soc Pacific. Package Machinery Co., East Longmeadow, Mass.

17 PYATT, Charles Lynn. Old Testament. b'86. AB '11—AM '12 (Transylvania Coll); Diploma '12 (Coll of the Bible Lexington Ky); Bd '13 (Yale Div Sch); ThD '16 (Harvard Div Sch); Post-doctoral study '42-43 (Johns Hopkins). Editor and contributor The College of the Bible Quarterly. Prof OT Coll of the Bible since '20, chmn faculty '28-37, dean since '38. Dir bd higher edn Disciples of Christ since '34, vp '36-38; asso in council Council for Clin Training of Theol Students since '36; mem Commission Religion and Health of Federal Council of Churches of Christ; chmn Southeastern Regional Conf '40-42; mem Commn on Clin Training Am Assn Theol Schs '40-42, exec sec since '46. Am Oriental Soc—Soc Bible Lit and Exegesis—Nat Assn Bible Instrs—Phi Kappa Tau—Theta Phi. The College of the Bible, Lexington, Ky.†⊙

18 PYENSON, Louis L. Entomology; Insect control. b'09. BS '31 (U Mass); MS '32 (Rutgers U); PhD '35 (Cornell U). Author: Pest Control in the Home Garden '44; Elements of Plant Protection '49; also articles in field. Sr instr plant protection LI Agrl & Tech Inst since '38. Am Assn Econ Entomol—AAAS—Sigma Xi. Long Island Agricultural and Technical Institute, Farmingdale, L.I., N.Y.†

19 PYKE, Wesley Emerson. Food (Chemistry, processing, technology); Cooking (High altitude). b'96. AB '14 (Baker U); PhD '40 (U Cal Berkeley). Research on high altitude baking and cookery, dehydration foods and feeds, freezing and frozen storage of foods, composition and quality of foods, processing methods, development industrial uses for agricultural products, nature of effect of plant hormones. Author article: No Tenderometer? Determine Quality from Pea Solid Readings '45. Co-author articles: (with Gestur Johnson) Relationships Between Certain Physical Measurements upon Fresh and Stored Eggs and their Behavior in the Preparation and Baking of Cake '41; (with A M Binkley) Freezing Vegetables and Fruits '43; (with L W Charkey) Making and Using a Food Dehydrator '43, and others. Asso in food research Colo Agrl Expt Sta '38-43, prof and chief chem sect since '45; prof food research Colo A&M Coll '43-45, prof chem and head dept since '45. ACS —Swiss Chem Soc—Inst Food Tech—AAAS—Soc Exptl Biol and Med—Sigma Xi—Colo-Wyo Acad Sci—Gamma Sigma Delta. Chemistry Dept., Colorado A&M College, Ft Collins, Colo.⊙

20 PYM, Michael. Islamic culture and affairs; Revolutions (Techniques); International politics and economics. b'89. Ed in Eng, pensionnat de Melsele and Sorbonne, Paris. Author: The Power of India '30; also articles in field. Mem staff La Reina de la Moda SA, Milwaukee Jour, Pittsburgh Pa Dispatch until '22; spl corr NY Annalist '35; NY Herald-Tribune India '26-30, at Round Table Conf London '30-31. Soc Woman Geog. Decorated Officer d'Academic (France). 4230 Douglas Rd., Miami 33, Fla.

Q

21 QUAIFE, Mary Louise. Biochemistry; Vitamin E research. AB '38—MS '39—Lucy Elliot Memorial fellow '41-42 (U Mich); PhD '42 (U Ill). Author articles in field. Sr research chemist Distillation Products Inc Rochester NY since '43. Am Soc Biol Chemists—Soc Exptl Biol and Med—Am Chem Soc —Am Inst Nutrition—Sigma Xi—Phi Beta Kappa. Distillation Products Industries, Division Eastman Kodak Co., 755 Ridge Road West, Rochester 13, N.Y.

22 QUALEY, Carlton Chester. American immigration; History of American foreign policy; Norwegian-American history (Immigration). b'04. BA '29 (St Olaf Coll); MA '30—Shevlin fellow '31-32 (U Minn); PhD '38—U fellow '32-33 (Columbia). Author: Norwegian Settlement in the United States '38; also articles in field. Prof Am hist Carleton Coll since '46. AHA—Miss Valley Hist Assn—Norwegian-American Hist Assn—Minn Hist Soc (sec-supt '47-48)—Soc Am Archivists—Fgn Policy Assn. Carleton College, Northfield, Minn.†

23 QUALIA, Charles Blaise. Spanish and French language and literature. b'92. BA '16—MA '21—PhD '32 (Tex U); '19 (Lyon U); '29 (Paris U). Research in libraries of Paris, Madrid and Mexico City; studies and writing on French neo-classical tragedy in

Spain in eighteenth century, Voltaire's tragic art in Spain, vogue of decadent French tragedies in Spain, 1762-1800. Author articles in field. Head dept fgn lang Tex Tech Coll since '37. Modern Lang Assn Am—S Central Modern Language Assn (pres '47-48). Texas Technological College, Lubbock.

10 QUALLEY, Orlando W. Classical languages (Archeology). b'97. AB '18 (Luther Coll); AM '23—PhD '31—Buhl Classical fellow '22-23, '30-31 (U Mich); student (Columbia). Prof classical lang Luther Coll since '25, dean of coll since '46. Am Philol Assn—Classical Assn Middlewest and S—NEA—Phi Beta Kappa. Luther College, Decorah, Ia.†

11 QUAM, Louis Otto. Rocky Mountains (Physiography, geomorphology); Military geography. b'06. AB '31—MS '32 (U Colo); PhD '38 (Clark U). Research on Front Range of Rocky Mountains and Great Plains areas; observer and adviser to Juneau Icefield Project of American Geographical Society '50; consultant and panel chairman for Research and Development Board of Department of Defense '46-50. Co-author: (with E J Foscue) Estes Park, Resort in the Rockies '49. Asst prof geol U Colo '38-42; research geog Office Qm Gen '42-43; dir Joint Intelligence Study Bd '46-47; asso prof geog U Va '47-50; sci head Geog Branch Office Nav Research since '50. Sigma Xi—Assn Am Geog (sec adv ed Annals)—Am Geog Soc (F)—Am Geophys Union. Office of Naval Research, Navy Department, Washington 25.

12 QUARLES, Benjamin. American Negro history; Abolition movement; Frederick Douglass. b'04. BA '31 (Shaw U); MA '33—PhD '40—Pres Adams fellowship modern history '37 (U Wis). Study of philosophy, technique, influence of moral suasion Garrisonian abolitionists and political action non-Garrisonian abolitionists. Author: Frederick Douglass '48; The Negro in the Civil War '53; also articles in field. Prof hist Dillard U '42-53, Morgan State Coll since '53; asso editor Journal Negro History. Julius Rosenwald Fellowship '37, '45; grant-in-aid Com on So Fellowships, Social Sci Research Council '41. Morgan State College, Balt 18.

13 QUARLES, Richard Wingfield. Chemistry of vinyl resins. b'11. BS in chem engring '31—PhD '35 (U Va); '36 (U Mich). Use of vinyl resins in protective coatings, adhesives and in films, solvents, plasticizers and stabilizers for these and related resins, development vinyl resin dispersions (organosols and plastisols) and their formulation and resulting effects on flow properties and film formation, development new epoxide resins for low pressure laminating and molding especially for use in orthopedic braces. Holder patents for resin stabilizers, new vinyl resins and method of production, cloth coating, dispersions of vinyl chloride resin (with C I Spessard), method moistureproofing paper (with A K Doolittle), method insolubilizing polyvinyl butyral (with H D Cogan). Research asst U Va '35-37; research chem Carbide & Carbon Chem Corp '37-39; Carbide & Carbon fellow Mellon Inst since '39. ACS—Am Inst Chem Engrs—Tau Beta Pi—Alpha Chi Sigma—Sigma Xi. Mellon Institute, Pitts 13.

14 QUARTERMAN, Elsie. Plant ecology (Cedar glades, mosses). b'10. AB '32 (Ga State Woman's Coll); AM '41—PhD '49 (Duke U); Vanderbilt scholar summer '43, '44 (Highlands Lab). Ecological investigations of plant communities of cedar glades of middle Tennessee at intervals '45-49. Author articles in field. Instr biol dept Vanderbilt U '43-48, asst prof biol '48-52, associate professor since '52. Tenn Academy Science—SE Biol—Ecol Soc Am—Am Bryology Society—Sigma Xi. Box 62, Vanderbilt University, Nashville 4, Tenn.†

15 QUEEN, William Albert. Analytical chemistry (Foods, drugs, cosmetics). b'97. AB '19 (Wake Forest Coll). Food and drug chem NC Dept Agr '20-37, asso state chem and administrative officer '37-42; chief div state cooperation and chmn food standards com Food and Drug Adminstrn FSA since '42. Assn Food and Drug Ofcls US (pres '40-41, exec com '40-51)—Assn Ofcl Agrl Chems NA (pres '50, exec com '45-51)—Am Pub Health Assn—Assn Am Feed Control Ofcls. Food and Drug Administration, Federal Security Agency, Washington 25.

16 QUEER, Elmer Roy. Heat transfer and insulation; Dehumidification; Long-term preservation of materials in storage). b'04. BS '26—MS '28 (Pa State Coll). Heat transmission and water vapor transmission research in low temperature insulation; condensation problems in housing; heat transmission research and measurement of heat transfer coefficients of warship constructions for US Navy and merchant ship constructions for US Maritime Commission. Author articles in field. Instr engring research engring expt sta Pa State Coll '28-34, asst prof engring research '34-41, prof since '46, charge Thermal Test Plant, dir engring research since '52; consultant Reynolds Metals Corporation, Pittsburgh Lectrodryer Corp, Pittsburgh Corning Corporation, Insulmastic Corporation of America. Comdr USNR active duty Bur Ships Air Conditioning Sect, exec officer charge ship board ventilation and air conditioning investigations. Am Soc Heat and Ventilating Engrs—Soc Naval Architects and Marine Engrs—ASTM. Engineering Experiment Station, State College, Pa. H: 338 Arbor Way.†

17 QUENEAU, Bernard Russell. Ferrous metallurgy; Temper brittleness; Stainless steels. b'12. BS '32—MetE '33 (Columbia University NYC); PhD '36 (University Minn) X-ray studies of solid-solubility limits in nickel-chromium alloys, austempering of case carburized parts, hardenability line, temper brittleness. Author articles in field. Charge metall lab Duquesne Works Car Ill Steel Pa '36-38; asst prof metall Columbia '38-41; chief development metall South Works Carnegie-Ill Steel Corp '46-50; now chief metall Duquesne works US Steel Co Duquesne Pa. Comdr USNR '41-46, charge armor and projectile lab Dahlgren Va. AIMME—Am Society Metals—Am Iron and Steel Inst—ASTM—British Iron and Steel Institute—Sigma Xi. Duquesne Works U.S. Steel Co., Duquesne, Pa.

18 QUENEAU, Paul. Extractive metallurgy; Beneficiation. b'11. BA—BSc—EM '33 (Columbia); Evans fellow '33-34 (Cambridge U Eng); grad '43 (Army Engr Sch) (Command and Gen Staff Coll). Beneficiation, smelting and refining of nickel and copper; beneficiation and agglomeration of iron ores; participated in invention and development various processes for recovery of nickel and associated metals from ores. With Internat Nickel Co since '34, research engr Copper Cliff Ont '37-41, dir research '41-42 and '45-48, exec group NY since '48. With Corps Engrs AUS World War II, chief of staff task force Army Engrs Ruhr Mines '45. AIMME—Can Inst Mining and Metall—Brit Instn Mining and Metall—Arc-

tic Inst NA—Tau Beta Pi—Sigma Xi. The International Nickel Co. of Canada, Ltd., 67 Wall St., NYC 5. H: Old Academy Rd., Fairfield, Conn.

19 QUICK, Clarence R(oy). Autecology (Habitat analysis); Native seed germination (Forcing methods). b'02. AB '28 (Coll of Pacific) MA '30 (U Calif); '22-23 (Fresno State Coll). Author articles in field. Microanalyst US Dept Agr '31-35, plant path '35-41, forest ecol since '41. AAAS—Soc Am Foresters—Cal Bot Soc (sec '42-43)—Sigma Xi. 6 Forestry Building, University of California, Berkeley 4.†

20 QUIGLEY, Tho(ma)s H. Vocational education (Philosophy, tchr training, trade and industrial, plant training, textile manufacturing). b'96. Student '11-18 (Ind U, U Wis). Research various aspects vocational education; agriculture and economic problems of the cotton belt; consultant and lecturer vocational education private employers, local and state educational authorities, federal bureaus, local, state and national associations and colleges since '24; dir US Employment Service and War Manpower Commn Ga '42-46; chmn com Standard Textile Courses of state depts edn so textile mfg states '28-36; chmn Ga Cotton Textile Indsl Relations Bd '33-35; moderator-sec management-labor Ga State Adv Com Indsl Edn and War Prodn Training '37-42; mem staffs surveying pub edn Boston '44, W Va '45, Mobile '47; appt by Secs War and Navy to Com US Armed Forces Inst '46-48. Author: Cotton Mill Mathematics (with W S Smith, 10 edns) '27-47; In the Sweat of Thy Face '42; Vocational Education in a Democracy (with C A Prosser) '48; also articles in field. Head indsl edn dept, Georgia Institute of Tech since '26. NEA (chmn subcom edn for vocational effectiveness '46-47)—Am Vocational Assn (vp, pres '31-39). Georgia Institute of Technology, Atlanta.

21 QUIMBY, George Irving. North American Indians and Eskimos (Archeology and ethnology). b'13. BA '36—MA '37 (U Mich); '38-39 (U Chicago). Research archeology and ethnology of eastern North America from Arctic to Gulf of Mexico; expeditions to Michigan, Wisconsin, Hudson Bay, Louisiana, and New Mexico. Author: The Goodall Focus (Hopewell Indian Culture in Michigan and Indiana) '41; Aleutian Islands '44. Co-author: Indians before Columbus '47. State supervisor fed archeol project La '39-41; dir Muskegon Mus Mich '41-42; asst curator NA archeol and ethnol Field Museum Chicago '42-43; curator exhibits anthrop Chicago Natural Hist Mus since '43. Soc Am Archeol(sec '48-52)—Mich Acad Sci Arts and Letters—Am Anthrop Assn(F)—Arctic Inst NA—Sigma Xi—Phi Sigma. Chicago Natural History Museum, Chgo 5.

22 QUINN, Alfred Stafford. Airport electrical distribution systems; High intensity runway lighting systems; Aircraft navigational aids. b'10. EE '33 (Columbia). Development lower cost power and more efficient operation of electrical systems for airports, economical and efficient lighting systems for civil airport control towers and administration buildings; proper lighting and coding of hazards and obstructions to aircraft; improvement and installation low cost high intensity runway marker light systems permitting operation of civil aircraft on lower weather minimums in adverse weather. Author articles: Lightning and Underground Cable; Modern Airport Maintenance; Aircraft Fueling and Schedules. Distribution engr NY & Queens Elec Light & Power Co

NYC '32-36; pres Radiolite Mfg Co Jackson Miss '36-40; chief elec engr US Engring Dept Mobile Ala; chief elec and lighting div Civil Aeronautics Authority Atlanta since '45. Ga Engring Soc—Illuminating Engring Soc—Soc Mil Engrs—Nat Flying Farmers. 50 Seventh St. N.E., Atlanta.

10 QUINN, Howard Walter. Vessels (Design, construction, maintenance, repair); Ocean shipping (Terminal operation, modern materials handling methods). b'06. BS '30 (US Mil Acad West Point); grad '47 (Indsl Coll Armed Forces). Transportation officer Corregidor '37-39; asst planning officer, hull and machinery Navy Yard Norfolk '39-40; supt constructor new ship constrn War Dept Washington '40-41; presidential advisor, landing craft and amphibious equipment '42; chief marine design, Army Transport Service, also chief engring div, dep supt NY '42-44; dep port comdr, port comdr SW Pacific '44-45; supply officer Transportation Corps San Francisco '46; port comdr Inchon Korea '47-48; supt water div and harbormaster Yokohama and Tokyo ports '48-49; chief transportation survey mission from Washington to Far East '50; expert cons ECA Washington '50-51; advisor to the President of Peru on seaports and merchant shipping '51. Soc Naval Architects and Marine Engrs—Nat Defense Transportation Assn—Propeller Club of US. Care The Klein Mission, 514 Avenida Uruguay, Lima, Peru.

11 QUINN, James Alfred. Human ecology (Urban); Urban sociology; delinquency. b'95. Fellow '27-28—PhD '31 (U Chicago); AB '17—AM '21 (U Mo). Author: Human Ecology and Its Relation to Areal Planning; also articles in field. Instr to prof sociol U Cincinnati since '22, head dept since '46. Am Sociol Soc—O Sociol Soc (sec, vp, pres)—Royal Geo Soc(F)—Population Assn Am. University of Cincinnati, Cincinnati 21.

12 QUINN, James Harrison. Museum exhibition and arrangement (Fossil skeleton preparation and mounting). b'06. BS in stratigraphy and paleontology '51 (U Ariz). Author: Rubber Molds and Plaster Casts '40. Chief preparator Chicago Natural History Museum '37-47. 3001 Windsor Rd., Austin, Tex.†

13 QUINN, Robert Gerard. Asbestos. b'01. ChemE '23 (U Notre Dame). Research on sheet products and processes based upon asbestos, such as electrical and heat insulating materials, roofings, asbestos tissues, papers and boards. Granted patents in field. With Am Cyanamid Co '23-26; research div Internat Paper Co '26-36; with Johns Manville since '36. Tech Assn Pulp and Paper Industry—Am Inst Chem Engrs. Johns Manville Research Center, Manville, N.J.

14 QUINSEY, William Edgar. Corrosion (Atmospheric). b'13. BS (CE) '37—MS '49 (U Mich). Studies on methods for protection of steel surfaces from corrosion; tests on use of copper to combat atmospheric corrosion of steel. Co-author: (book or article) (with J H Cissel) Durability of Lightweight Steel Construction. Structural draftsman Am Bridge Co Gary Ind '37-38; engr Consoer, Townsend & Quinlan Chicago '38-42; research engr and instr U Mich '42-45, asst to dir Engring Research Inst and half-time asst prof dept civil engring '45-47, asst to dir Engring Research Inst since '47. ASTM—Soc Exptl Stress Analysis—Nat Soc Profl Engrs—Engring Soc Detroit—Soc Am Mil Engrs. 2038 E. Engineering Bldg., University of Michigan, Ann Arbor.

15 QUISENBERRY, John Henry. Poultry genetics and breeding. b'07. BS '31 (Tex A&M Coll); MS—PhD '36 (U Ill). Research in breeding for disease resistance in animals, inheritance of hairlessness, genetic differences in vitamin A requirements of mammals and resistance to coccidiosis of chickens, use of Koa Haole in improving hatchability of chicken eggs, efficacy of various insecticides for control of poultry parasites, breeding for improved meat type of poultry, use of hormones in poultry production, simplified rations for laying hens. Author articles in field. Asso prof genetics Agrl and Mech Coll Tex '36-44; head dept poultry husbandry U Hawaii '45-46; prof and head dept poultry husbandry Tex A&M Coll since '46. Hawaii Acad Sci—Tex Acad Sci—AAAS—Poultry Sci Assn—Worlds Poultry Sci Assn—Genetics Soc Am—Am Genetic Assn—Am Soc Animal Prodn—Sigma Xi—Gamma Sigma Delta. Poultry Department, A&M College of Texas, College Station, Tex.

R

16 RABBITT, James A. Industrial engineering in Asia; Metals and alloys in Asia; Nickel alloys. b'77. Study on industrial potential Philippine Islands and China '47; compiled economic surveys on Japan, Manchuria, Siberia, China, Philippines, Java, Malaya, and Siam last forty years; member committee on mineral resources for compilation of report on industrial disarmament of Japan submitted to Secretaries of State, War, and Navy by National Engineers Committee of Engineers Joint Council '47. Author: Elementary Foundry Practice for Plain and Nickel Alloy Cast Irons; Nickel Alloys in Machine Tools and Related Equipment; Nickel Alloys in Railway Engineering; Nickel Alloys in the Mining and Metallurgical Industry; Nickel Alloys in the Chemical Industry; also articles in field. Chief engr and gen mgr F W Horne Co and Nipponophone Co Ltd '02-17; spl asst Dept of State Wash '18-19; pres The James A Rabbitt Engring Corp '20-24; practicing cons engr NY '25-29; cons engr The International Nickel Co Inc, Far Eastern Rep '30-41, since '45; civilian volunteer tech cons MISNY '42-44. Am Chem Soc—Am Inst Mining Metall Engrs—Iron and Steel Inst—Mining and Metall Soc Am—ASME(F). c/o International Nickel Co., Inc., 67 Wall St., NYC 5.

17 RABBITT, John Charles. Uranium (Geochemistry); Petrology (Metamorphic). b'07. BS '35—MS '37 (Mont Sch Mines); MA '41—PhD '46 (Harvard). Investigation radioactive raw material for Atomic Energy Commission. Author articles: A New Study of the Anthophyllite System '48, and others. Geol US Geol Survey since '42, now chief Trace Elements Sect. Mineral Soc Am (F)—Am Geophys Union—AAAS(F)—Sigma Xi. U.S. Geological Survey, Washington 25.

18 RABIDEAU, Glenn Sylvester. Plant metabolism (Stable and radioactive isotope); Photosynthesis. b'12. BA '38—MA '39 (U Wis); PhD '43 (U Minn). Author articles in field. Asso prof bot U Tex since '48; research asso Plant Research Inst since '47. AAAS (F)—Am Chem Soc—Am Soc Plant Physiol—Bot Soc Am—Minn Acad Sci—Tex Acad Sci—Sigma Xi. Botany Department, The University of Texas, Austin 12, Tex.

19 RABOLD, C(harles) Norris. Cotton (Bleaching, dyeing, finishing). b'03. BS '25 (Dickinson Coll); '25-28 (Pa State Coll). Consulting editor Textile World since '44. Chem and sect lab chief Pacific Mills '28-33; mem research service Corn Products Refining Co '33-36; chief chem Union Bleachery '36-45, research dir '45-48; dir research and development Erwin Mills Co Inc since '48. Am Assn Textile Chem and Colorists (pres '50, vp '47-49, councilor '44, chmn Piedmont sect '42, treas '41)—ACS(charter mem W Carolina sect)—Quartermaster Assn—Soc Dyers and Colourists Eng—Textile Inst Eng). Erwin Mills Co., Inc., Coolemee, N.C.

20 RADASCH, Arthur H(itchcock). Coal-tar and tar products refining; Distillation. b'98. SB '20 (MIT). US and Canadian patents. Head dept chem engring Cooper Union since '38; cons coal tar and tar products refining since '38. Am Inst Chem Engr—Am Chem Soc. Cooper Union, Cooper Square, NYC 3.†

21 RADCLIFFE, Donald Hewson. Oil geology. b'89. BS '13—EM '18 (Mo Sch Mines Rolla). Discoverer new oil pools including Josey Pool in Oklahoma. Instructor minerology and lithology Mo Cch Mines'13-16; geol Gypsy Oil Co Tulsa '16; mem Cox & Radcliffe cons geol Tulsa '17-19; chief geol Josey Oil Co '19-26; investor and oil producer since '26. AIMME—Am Assn Petroleum Geol—Am Geog Soc—AAAS. Box 298, Palos Verder Estates, Cal.

22 RADCLIFFE, Milton Ray. Vinyl plastics; Chlorinated rubber. b'13. BSc '34—'35-37 (Rutgers U). Holder US Patents on formulation and stablization of chlorinated rubber and polyvinyl chloride. Author articles in field. Tech dir plastics div O'Sullivan Rubber Co since '46. Am Chem Soc—SPI (com chmn film div). O'Sullivan Rubber Corporation, Winchester, Va.†

23 RADFORD, William Henry. Electrical communications. b'09. BS '31 (Drexel Inst); SM '32—Tau Beta Pi fellow (MIT). Author articles in field. With MIT since '32, asso dir Radar Sch since '41; engring cons radio systems and electronic applications since '38. Inst Radio Engrs—AIEE—Am Soc Engring Edn—AAAS—Sigma Xi—Tau Beta Pi. Massachusetts Institute of Technology, Cambridge, Mass.†

24 RADMACHER, Donald Stelling. Radio interference; Field intensity meters. b'15. BS in elec engring '39 (Wash State Coll). Research on development radio interference and field intensity meters in 15-1000 megacycle range. Jr and asst elec engr Bonneville Power Adminstrn '40-42; elec and project engr div war research Columbia '42-44; radio and project engr Stoddart Aircraft Radio Co since '45. Inst Radio Engrs—Am Inst EE—Sigma Tau—Tau Beta Pi. 6644 Santa Monica Blvd., Hollywood 38, Cal. H: 14709 Plummer St., Van Nuys, Cal.

25 RADOFF, Morris Leon. Maryland and colonial American history; Government archives. b'05. Student '22-24 (U Tex); '24-25 (U of Paris, and Florence); AB '26—AM '27 (U N Carolina); PhD '32 (Johns Hopkins Univ). Author numerous articles in field. Archivist Hall of Records Annapolis Md since '39. Soc Am Archivists—AHA—So Hist Assn—Md Hist Soc. Hall of Records, Annapolis, Md.

26 RAE, John Bell. History of United States transportation; Rhode Island history. b'11. AB '32—AM '34—PhD '36 (Brown U). Author: The Development of Railway Land Subsidy Policy in the United States '39. Co-author: (with T H D Mahoney) The United States in World History '49; also articles in field. With MIT since '39, asso prof hist since '47. AHA—Econ Hist Assn. Massachusetts Institute of Technology, Cambridge 39, Mass.†

10 RAEDER, J(ohn) Milford. Potatoes (Diseases and growth). b'92. BS '15—MS '20 (Ia State Coll); (U Calif). Author articles in field. With Ida Agr Expt Sta since '21, asso plant pathologist and asso prof path since '36. Am Phytopath Soc—AAAS(F)—Northwest Assn Hort Entomol Plant Pathol—Sigma Xi—Gamma Sigma Delta. Department of Plant Pathology, University of Idaho, Moscow, Idaho.†

11 RAEDER, Warren. Concrete (Reinforced); Steel (Structures). b'91. BS in civil engring '16 (U Cal); MS '26 (U Colo). Research and design reinforced concrete and steel structures. Author: Principles of Reinforced Concrete '38. With Am Bridge Co '17, Stupp Brothers Bridge and Iron Co '21-25; with U Colo since '26, prof and head dept civil engring since '43. Am Soc CE—Am Concrete Inst—Am Soc Engring Edn—Tau Beta Pi—Sigma Tau—Chi Epsilon. Department of Civil Engineering, University of Colorado, Boulder.

12 RAFTON, Harold Robert. Paper manufacture (Chemistry); Calcium carbonate; Coated paper. b'90. AB '10 (Harvard). Research in utilizing waste calcium carbonate from causticizing process and other forms of calcium carbonate as pigment in coated paper and filler in magazine paper, sizing paper filled with calcium carbonate, methods manufacturing finely divided calcium carbonate and calcium carbonate magnesium hydroxide, methods for treatment of pigments to modify their properties, and chemical engineering machinery, valve, fine screens, colloid mill, Rafton mill. Holder numerous patents. Author articles in field. Pres and chem dir Raffold Co of Am since '16; pres Raffold Process Corp, Raffold Internat Corp, Rafton Labs Inc, Rafton Engring Corp since '28. Am Chem Soc—Soc Chem Ind (British)—NY Acad Sci—Tech Assn Pulp Paper Industry—AAAS(F). 16 Haverhill St., Andover, Mass. H: Alden Road.†

13 RAGSDALE, A(rthur) C(hester). Dairy husbandry; Animal breeding and nutrition. b'90. BS '12 (U Mo); scholar '24-25—MS '25 (U Wis). Author: Dairy Laboratory Manual and Outline '48; also articles in field. Ext asst prof diary husbandry U Mo '16-19, prof and chmn dept diary husbandry since '19. Am Dairy Sci Assn (pres '44-45)—Dairy Industry Council Mo (exec sec since '26)—AAAS—Am Soc Animal Prodn—Am Pub Health Assn—Am Assn Milk and Food Sanitarians—Gamma Sigma Delta. 103 Eckles Hall, University of Missouri, Columbia, Mo.

14 RAHDER, Johannes. Comparative linguistics; Buddhist philosophy; Asiatic languages (Japanese). b'98. BA '20—MA '22—DLitt '26 (Utrecht); BA '26 (Leiden). Author articles in field. Prof Japanese Yale since '47. Am Oriental Soc—Linguistic Soc Am—Far Eastern Assn—Conn Acad Arts Sci. Hall Graduate Studies, Yale University, New Haven.†

15 RAHMEL, Henry A. Radio advertising and research (Disc recording). b'10. Student '29-30 (Armour Inst Tech); BS '33—MS '34 (MIT). Inventor curvilinear diaphragm for dynamic loudspeakers. Vp radio field mng and gen engring Nielsen Co since '46. A. C. Nielsen Company, 2101 Howard St., Chicago 45.

16 RAHN, Elisha Miller. Vegetable crop culture. b'13. BS '33 (Pa State Coll); MS '37 (O State U). Research on culture of vegetable crops, especially use of weed killers, fertilizers, growth regulators to improve fruit-setting variety testing. Author: Getting the Most from Fertilizers for Vegetable Crops '43; The Effect of Various Fertilizer and Manure Treatments on the Yield, Size, Stand, and Disease Resistance of Cantaloupes '45; also articles in field. Associate professor Delaware U since '44. Am Society Hort Sci—Peninsula Hort Soc. Department of Horticulture, University of Delaware, Newark, Del.†

17 RAHN, Otto. Bacteriology; Disinfectants; Food preservation; Dairy physics; Biological radiations. b'81. PhD '02 (Göttingen U). Co-author: Physik der Milchwirtschaft (with P F Sharp) '28; Handbuch der Milchwirtschaft (with others) '31; Physiology of Bacteria '32; Invisible Radiations of Organisms '35; Mathematics in Bacteriology '39; Injury and Death of Bacteria by Chemical Agents '45; Microbes of Merit '45; also articles in field. Prof bact Cornell U '27-49, Ida State Coll since '49; research on biochem of old age, using bacteria for expts. Pharmacy Bldg., Idaho State College, Pocatello.

18 RAILSBACK, Howard Marion. Farm implement industry. b'85. AB '11 (U Ill). Member advisory committee of industrial management University of Illinois. Writer and co-writer various farm and business articles pertaining to farm implement industry. Editor Hustling for Business '16-31; editor The Furrow, a publ for farmers produced by Deere & Co '17-51, editor-in-chief since '51. Am Soc Agrl Engrs—Assn Nat Advertisers. Hon Am Farmer. Deere & Company, Moline, Ill.

19 RAINEY, Froelich Gladstone. Arctic ethnology and archeology; International transport. b'07. PhB '29 (U Chicago); PhD '35 (Yale); '30 (Am Sch in France). Research and survey in West Indies, Bahama Islands, Haiti, San Domingo and excavations in Puerto Rico for Peabody Museum Yale; research for American Museum of Natural History in Alaska and on St Lawrence Island '35-42; chairman organizing committee for 29th International Congress of Americanists '49. Author articles in field. Dir U Mus Phila since '47; cons to Dept State since '48. Am Anthropol Assn—Soc Applied Anthropol—Am Archeol Soc—Internat Congress Anthropol and Ethnol Sci. University Museum, 33rd and Spruce Sts., Phila 4.

20 RAISZ, Erwin. Cartography (Land-type mapping); Physiography. b'93. AM '24—PhD '29 (Columbia); diploma '14 (Royal Polytechnicum). Two summers in Yellowstone National Park preparing geological museum exhibits; four summers studying and sketching physiography and geology of Western United States and Mexico chiefly for landform maps; two seasons in Cuba for land-type mapping; one summer land-type mapping in Northern Canada and Alaska. Invented dovetailed globe gores, patented. Author: General Cartography '48; Atlas of Global Geography '44; landform maps US, Alaska, Can, Near East; articles in field. Lectr in cartography and map curator Inst Geog Exploration Harvard since '31; acting prof U Va since '52. Assn Am Geog (chmn cartog com)—Royal Geog Soc(F)—Sigma Xi—Soc Geog Mexico—Am Geog Soc—Nat Council Geog Teachers—Cartophile Soc—Geog Soc Cuba—AAAS(F). Paul Goode Prize Nat Council Geography Tchrs '47. 107 Washington Av., Cambridge 40, Mass.†

21 RAITT, George Henry. Business management; Plant and business appraisal; Plant layout. b'91. BS '14 (Queen's U). Cons Santa Monica Land & Water Co '23-45; cons and mgr liquidations Pensacola Co '24-46; cons Herrick Iron Works '49-51; cons. ASME Newcomen Society Eng—ASTM—Am Welding Soc. 44 El Camino Real, Berkeley 5, Cal.

22 RALEIGH, Walter P. Potato diseases; Seed disinfectants. b'01. BS '23 (Kan State Coll); PhD '28 (Ia State Coll). Author articles in field. Grower certified seeds of small grains sweet clover and brome grass; developing new varieties potatoes, hybrid corn and wheat since '37. AAAS(F)—Am Phytopath Soc—Phi Kappa Phi—Sigma Xi. Clyde, Kan.†

23 RAMAGE, William Haig. Iron and steel technology and manufacturing; Ingot moulds. Grad (Phillips Exeter Acad); CE (Cornell U). Pres Valley Mould and Iron Corp since '29. Am Iron Steel Inst—Am Iron Steel Engrs. Valley Mould and Iron Corporation, Hubbard, O.☺

24 RAMALEY, Edward Jackson. Selenium rectifiers; Magnetic tape; Electropolish; Electrophotography; Gun erosion. b'07. MS in elec engring '35 (U Colo). Research and development manufacturing details on selenium rectifiers; magnetic coatings for magnetic tape, electropolishing methods. Granted patent on erosion testing device. Research engr Battelle Memorial Inst '37-48; mfg methods research engr Lockheed Aircraft Corp since '49. AI MME—Am Inst EE—Am Soc Metals. Department 37-07, Plant A-1, Lockheed Aircraft Corp., Burbank, Cal.

25 RAMBERG, Walter Gustave Charles. Mechanics of solids. b'04. AB '26 (Cornell U); Dr sc Tech '30 (Tech Hochschule Munich). Research on flashover in insulators, nature of aircraft propeller vibration. Brinnel hardness number, ballast requirements for balloons, strength of tubing, strength of reinforced channels for aircraft, strength of box beams, tensile and compressive stress strain curves, normal pressure tests of flat plates, instability of extrusions, vacuum tube acceleration pickup, landing impact of aircraft, and resistance wire strain gages. Asst physicist Nat Bur Standards '31-36, physicist '36-46, chief engr mechs sect '46-48, chief mechs div since '47. Am Soc Testing Materials—ASME—Column Research Council Engring Found—Inst Aero Sci—Philos Soc Washington (past pres)—Soc Exptl Stress Analysis—Washington Acad Sci—Washington Audio Soc—Sigma Xi. Recipient award Washington Acad Sci '42. National Bureau of Standards, Washington. H: 7000 Rolling Rd., Chevy Chase 15, Md.

26 RAMO, Simon. Electronics; Microwaves; Guided missiles. b'13. BS '33 (U Utah); PhD '36 (Calif Inst Tech). Development of high speed cathode ray oscillography '37; pioneer in microwaves, numerous patents in microwave generation amplification and electron optics; co-developer of General Electric's Electron Microscope '42. Author: Introduction to Microwaves '45. Co-author: (with John R Whinnery) Fields and Waves in Modern Radio '44; also articles in field. Supervisor advanced engring course, head phys sect electronics lab research lab Gen Elec Co '36-46; research asso Calif Inst Tech since '46; dir research electronics dept Hughes Aircraft Co '46-48, dir guided missile research development '48-49; co-dir research devel labs '49-51, vice pres operations since 1951. Am Phys Soc—Institute Radio Engineers (board ed since '41)—AIEE—Eta Kappa Nu (outstanding young elec engr award '41)—Sigma Xi—Tau Beta Pi—Phi Kappa Phi. Hughes Aircraft Company, Culver City, Calif.

10 RAMSER, Charles Ernest. Soil conservation; Drainage; Flood control; Hydrology; Farm terracing. b'85. BS in CE '09 (U Ill). In charge planning and directing engineering experiments on first ten soil erosion experiment stations of US Department Agriculture, later in charge hydraulic and hydrologic investigations throughout US; devised and developed first scientific method terracing farm lands to prevent soil erosion; actual measurements to determine roughness coefficients and discharge through wooded floodways during '27 Mississippi Flood have become principal factors in design of lateral floodways in Mississippi River Flood Control plan. Author USDA bulletins. Sr drainage engr US Bur Pub Roads '17-35; head div watershed studies Soil Conservation Service '35-37, chief hydrologic div '37-42, research specialist in hydraulics hydrology '42-47; cons agrl engr drainage soil conservation since '47. Am Soc Agrl Engrs—ASCE—Soil Conservation Soc Am—Am Geophys Union—Friends of Land—AAAS—Tau Beta Pi—Sigma Xi. Recipient John Deere gold medal from Am Soc Agrl Engrs '44. 4615 Kenmore Drive, N.W., Washington 7.†◎

11 RAMSEY, Ernest Glen. Rectifiers; Porous tantalum condensers. b'07. EE '36 (Lewis Inst); '33 (Chicago U), '37-39 (Northwestern U). Research of porous tantalum electrolytic condenser, selenium rectifiers; studies and writing on applications for selenium rectifiers, selenium rectifiers in signal and communication service. Author articles in field. Mgr Rectifier Div Fansteel Metallurg Corp '42, now vp. Assn Am Railroads (Signal and Communications sects) — AIEE — Railway Bus Assn. Fansteel Metallurgical Corp., N. Chicago. H: 4841 N. Wolcott Av., Chicago 40.†

12 RAND, A(ustin) L(oomer). Birds. b'05. BSc '27 (Acadia U); PhD '31 (Cornell U). Exploration and research in Madagascar, Dutch New Guinea, Papua, North and Central America; adv board Archbold Expeditions; ornithological editor Candian Field Naturalist '42-47. Author: Distribution and Habits of Madagascar Birds '36; Mammals of Yukon Canada '45; Mammals of Eastern Rockies and Western Plains of Canada; Development and Enemy Recognition of the Curve-billed Thrasher '41. Co-author: (with R. Archbold) New Guinea Expedition '39. With Am Mus Natural History '29-42, research asso '37-41; with Nat Mus Can '42-47, acting chief div biology '45-47; curator birds Chicago Natural History Mus since '47. Am Ornithol Union(F)—Am Soc Mammalogists—Chicago Natural History Museum, Chgo.

13 RAND, Paul. Contemporary art; Advertising and industrial design (Typography). b'14. Grad '32 (Pratt Inst); '32 (Parsons and Art Students League). Designed booklets and posters for US Government, Washington; pioneer in modern art in advertising and industrial designing. Author: Thoughts on Design '46; also articles in field. Art dir Weintraub Advt Agency; rep in all exhbns Art Dirs Club (except '42) since '36; lecturer on contemporary art and arch. Received Alexander and Saint Gaudens medals and Sch Art League scholarship '32; hon mention Am Inst Graphic Arts '38; first award for distinctive merit on Coronet advt campaign Art Dirs Club '43; distinctive merit award on Airwick Advt campaign '44; Dubonnet '45; Double medal for best designed advt in Art Dirs Club Show (Jacqueline Cochran) '45; Direct Mail award '46; among 50 best books award '48; distinctive merit award '47 Art Dirs Club for Ohrbach's news-

paper campaign; Soc Typographic Artists Chicago award '47. 30 Rockefeller Plaza, NYC.

14 RANDALL, Glenn O(rvice). Floriculture (Roses and other floral crops). b'98. BS '22 (U Ark); MS '23 (Ia State Agrl Coll); (U Ill, Cornell U). Author articles in field. With NC State Agrl Coll since '24, prof hort since '46. Am Soc Hort Sci—Am Rose Soc (dir '48-50)—Men's Garden Clubs Southeast (vp). North Carolina State Agricultural College, Raleigh, N.C.†

15 RANDALL, Robert Henry. Cartography (Surveying, mapping); City, regional, national and international planning. b'90. Student '11-12 (O Wesleyan U). US representative International Public Works Committee International Labor Office Geneva '38; US member, and chairman Commission on Cartography Pan-American Institute Geography and History Mexico City since '42, 1st vp and chmn Exec Com '46-50, pres since '50; chmn first second third and fourth Pan-Am cons on cartography Wash '43, Rio de Janeiro '44, Caracas '46, Buenos Aires '48. Co-author: Manual 10, Technical Procedure for City Surveys; also articles in field. Chief examiner charge programming, coordinating fed surveying mapping Bur Budget since '41. ASCE—Am Inst Planners—Am Soc Planning Ofcl—Am Planning Civic Assn—Am Congress Surveying Mapping (first pres)—Am Geophys Union—Am Soc Photogrammetry—Geog Soc Lima—Nat Inst Geog Investigations Uruguay—Assn Am Geog. Executive Office of the President, Bureau of the Budget, Washington. H: 4009 East-West Highway, Chevy Chase, Md.

16 RANDLE, Stacy Boyce. Agricultural biochemistry (Nutrition). b'05. BA '30—MS '35 (Miss U); PhD '39 (Wis U). Research on distribution of grass juice factor in plant and animal material, effect of vitamin K content of hen's ration on clotting ability of chick blood, agricultural insecticides and fungicides, commercial feeds. Author articles in field. State chem NJ Agrl Expt Sta Rutgers U since '46. Sigma Xi—Am Chem Soc—AAAS. Post doctorate fellow Wis U '39-40. Rutgers University, New Jersey Agricultural Experiment Station, New Brunswick, N.J.†

17 RANDOLPH, Corliss Fitz. Seventh Day Baptists (History). b'63. AB—AM '88—LHD hon '03 (Alfred U NY); grad study classical philol '96-99 (Columbia); PhD '04—LLD '13 (Salem Coll WVa). Author: History of Seventh Day Baptists in West Virginia '05; History of German Seventh Day Baptists '10; Rogerines '10; The Sabbath and Seventh Day Baptists (5th revision '45); A Century's Progress: A History of the First Seventh Day Baptist Church of New York City '48. Joint author: A Manual of Seventh Day Baptist Procedure '23, '26; Manual of Information Concerning Seventh Day Baptists '48. Editor: Seventh Day Baptist Year Book '14-28. Editor and contbr to Seventh Day Baptists in Europe and America '10. Pres Am Sabbath Tract Soc '14-41, pres emeritus since '41; pres and librarian Seventh Day Bapt Hist Soc since '16; pres Seventh Day Bapt Gen Conf '31-32. NJ Hist Soc—Am Soc Ch Hist—Am Hist Soc—Société Academique et Historique Internationale Paris—Congl Hist Soc Eng. H: 83 Jefferson Av., Maplewood, N.J.◎

18 RANDOLPH, Lowell Fitz. Cytology, cytogenetics and morphology of maize and iris; Chromosome numbers; Induced polyoloidy; Embryo culture; Cytogenetic effects of radiation. b'94.

PhB '16 (Alfred U); PhD '21 (Cornell U). Author articles in field. Prof bot Cornell U since '39; agt, sr cytologist US Dept Agr since '47. Am Iris Soc (chmn sci com since '46)—Bot Soc Am—Genetics Soc Am—Am Soc Naturalists—Soc Study of Evolution—AAAS—Sigma Xi—Phi Kappa Phi. Fellow Internat Edn Bd Nat Research Council '26-27; recipient Vaughn award '43 for experiments on plant embryo culture. Department of Botany, College of Agriculture, Ithaca, N.Y.

19 RANDS, Robert Delafield Sr. Plant pathology; Production of natural rubber; Sugar cane and Irish potatoes. b'90. BS '13 (U Neb); MS '15—PhD '17 (U Wis). Extensive travel and prolonged residence in Indonesia, study trips to Egypt, India, Malaya and the Philippines; twelve years cooperative rubber research and development in 11 tropical American republics. Author articles in field. With US Dept Agr since '17, head agr charge div rubber plant investigations '48-52, now collaborator. AAAS(F)—Washington Acad Science—Washington Botanical Society—American Phytopath Society—International Soc Sugarcane Tech. Lake of the Hills, Lake Wales, Fla.

20 RANKAMA, Kalervo. Geochemistry (Upper lithosphere). b'13. MA '38—PhD '44 (U Helsinki). Research on the geochemistry of tantalum and niobium. Author articles in field. Research in geochem at geochem lab inst geol U Helsinki Finland '36-46; research asso geochem U Chicago since '47. Department of Geology, University of Chicago, Chgo 37†

21 RANKIN, A(lexander) Donald. Ruminants. b'16. DVM '39—MS '40—Doctoral work '41-42—'46-47 (Cornell). Author: A Study of Absorption from the Rumen of Sheep '42. Asso prof dept physiol Colo A&M Coll since '47, head dept since '48. US Army '42-46, maj Res '46, exec officer 5568th Research and Development Group since '49. AAAS—AAUP—Am Vet Med Assn—No Colo Vet Med Soc—Sigma Xi—Phi Kappa Phi. 911 Woodford Av., Ft. Collins, Colo.

22 RANKIN, Carl Emmet. Deaf (Education). b'92. Student '11-13 (Elon Coll NC); AB '17 (Davidson Coll NC); AM '20—Naomi Norsworthy grad fellow Tchrs Coll— '32-33—PhD '36 (Columbia); grad work (U NC). Member North Carolina Governor's Commission of Education '47-48; advisory council special education North Carolina Department of Education since '48. Asst supt NC Sch for Deaf Morganton NC '35-37, supt since '37. Conf Execs Am Schs for Deaf—Conv Am Instrs of Deaf (bd dirs)—Phi Delta Kappa—Kappa Delta Pi. North Carolina School for Deaf, Morganton, N.C.◎

23 RANKIN, Charles Waldron. Spectroscopy (Criminal investigation). b'08. SB '31 (MIT); MA '33 (NY State Coll for Teachers Albany). Author articles: Application of the Spectograph to Criminal Investigation '39; Applications of the Spectograph to Toxicological Investigations '41. Physicist NY State Police Lab Albany '37-41 and since '45, Army Air Force Wright Field Dayton '42-45. Optical Soc Am 545 Broadway, Albany 7, NY.

24 RAPER, John R(obert). Sexual hormones in Plants; Biological effects of beta rays. b'11. AB '33—MA '36 (U NC); MA and PhD '36-39 (Harvard). Research on biological effects of beta rays on various biological materials, acute and chronic effects of total surface and partial surface irradiation with beta rays on various laboratory mammals, development of beta and gamma ray sources for radiobiology use. Author articles: Sexual Hormones in Achlya I-VI '39-42, and others. Asso prof bot U Chicago since '49. Bot Soc Am—Sigma Xi. Austin teaching fellow Harvard '36-39; nat research fellowship Calif Inst Tech '39-41. Department of Botany, University of Chicago, Chicago 37.†

10 RAPER, Kenneth Bryan. Mycology; Micro-biology. b'08. BA '29 (U NC); MA '31 (Geo Washington U); PhD '36 (Harvard). Research on penicillin, taxonomy of saprophytic molds, morphogenesis in slime molds, mold fermentations. Co-author: Manual of the Aspergilli (with C Thom) '45; Manual of the Penicillia (with C Thom) '49; articles in field. Sr microbiol No Regional Research Lab Peoria Ill '41-47, prin microbiol '47-52; vis professor bot U Ill '46-52; prof bact U Wis since '53. Nat Acad Sci—Am Acad Arts and Sci—Nat Research Council—Am Soc Naturalists—Soc Ind Microbiol (pres 1953)—AAAS—Am Bot Soc (sec microbiol sect '46-49, (chmn 1950)—Society Am Bacteriol—Mycol Soc Am (pres 1951)—Sigma Xi—Phi Beta Kappa. Department Bacteriology, University of Wisconsin, Madison.☺

11 RAPP, Janet Lorraine Cooper. Insect and invertebrate physiology. b'21. BSc '43 (NJ Coll for Women); MSc '45—PhD '48—fellow '47-48 (U Ill); research fellow '43-44 (Rutgers U). Research in insect physiology, studies on insect blood, structure of insect fats; development of special chemical analytical methods for use in insect physiology, especially single drop methods. Author articles in field. Instr biol Doane Coll '48-49; dir research Archem Corp '49-52; asso prof chem Doane Coll '51-52; dir J-B Labs Lincoln Neb since '52. Am Chem Soc—Entomol Soc Ontario—Sigma Xi. J-B Laboratories, Lincoln, Neb. H: 2759 F St., Lincoln 8.†

12 RAPP, William Frederick, Jr. Psychodidae (Systera); Equisetum (Taxonomy). b'18. BSA '44 (Rutgers U); MS '45 (U Ill). Research on morophology, immature and adult taxonomy, ecology, and distribution of Psychodidate; living species, taxonomy of group of genus Equisetum. Author articles in field. Instr dept biol Doane Coll since '47; ecol survey Great Swamp Chatham Twp Morris Co NJ since '44. Am Entomol Soc—Entomol Soc Am—Am Fern Soc—Neb Acad Sci—Soc Systematic Zool. Department of Biology, Doane College, Crete, Neb. H: Gaylord Hall.†

13 RASMUSSEN, Daniel Irvin. Wildlife management (Big game); Mule deer; Sage Grouse; Beaver. b'03. BS '28 (Brigham Young U); MS '30—PhD '32 (U Ill); '30 (Scripps Inst Oceano). Author articles in field. Author articles: Mule Deer Range and Population Studies in Utah '39; Beaver-Trout Relationships in the Rocky Mountain Region '40; (with Nolan West) Experimental Beaver Transplanting in Utah '43, and others. Leader Utah Coop Wildlife Research Unit US Fish and Wildlife Service '35-45; charge wildlife management Intermountain Region US Forest Service since '45. Wildlife Soc—Am Soc Mammalogists—Sigma Xi—Phi Kappa Phi. U.S. Forest Service, Ogden, Utah.†

14 RASMUSSEN, Lowell. Weed control; Plant physiology; Soil, water and crop management; Effects of herbicides on plants. b'10. BS '40—MS '41 (Utah State Agrl Coll); PhD '47—research fellow '45-47 (Ia State Coll). Author articles in field. Asso prof and asso agron Wash State Coll and Expt Sta since '47. Am Soc Plant Physiol—Am Soc Agron—Sigma Xi—Phi Kappa Phi. Agronomy Department, Washington State College, Pullman, Wash.†

15 RASMUSSEN, Marius Peter. Economics and marketing of fruits and vegetables. b'93. BS '19—PhD '24 (Cornell U). Research and writing on efficient and improved methods of marketing and handling products from farm to consumer; special study on prepackaging fruits and vegetables, and improving shipping, wholesaling and retailing operations. Author articles in field. Prof marketing Cornell U since '24; investigator in marketing NY State Agrl Expt Sta since '24; expert marketing specialist Farm Credit Adminstrn Washington '34-41; chief cons WPB '42-43; head cons War Food Adminstrn '43-44; advisor and cons Am Nat Coop Exchange Inc NY since '33; econ cons United Fresh Fruit and Vegetable Assn since '35; adviser and cons econ Farm Credit Adminstrn since '49. Am Marketing Assn—Am Farm Econ Assn—Internat Conf Agrl Econ—Alpha Zeta—Phi Kappa Phi—Sigma Xi. 28 Cornell St., Ithaca, N.Y.

16 RASMUSSEN, Wayne David. American agricultural history (Indian, World War II); History of agricultural settlements in Latin America; United States Department of Agriculture. b'15. BA '37 (Mont State U); MA '39 (George Washington U); '32-33 (Eastern Mont Normal Sch); '38 (U Mich); PhD '50 (George Washington U). Research on farm labor supply program during World War II; US plant explorers in South America during 19th century; history of American Indian agriculture; history of agricultural colonization in Latin America. Author articles in field. US Dept of Agr since '37; hist work Bur of Agrl Econ since '40. AHA—Agrl Hist Soc. Bureau of Agricultural Economics, U.S. Department of Agriculture, Washington 25.

17 RASQUIN, Priscilla. Fishers (Endocrinology, pigmentation). b'09. AB '31 (Mount Holyoke Coll); '42-43 (NYU). Research on progressive pigmentary regression in fishes associated with cave environments; the reappearance of melanophores in blind goldfish, light sensitivity of blind characins from a series of Mexican caves; effects of carp pituitary, ACTH and cortisone on endocrine and lymphoid systems in characins; hormonal imbalance in fishes kept in darkness. Author articles in field. Department fishes aquatic biol Am Mus Natural Hist since '45. NY Acad Sci—Am Soc Ichthyol Herpetol—Soc Study Evolution. American Museum of Natural History, Central Park and 79th St., NYC 24.†

18 RATCHFORD, Fannie Elizabeth. Bronte; Nineteenth century forgeries; Thomas J Wise; Texas history and folklore. b'87. BA '19—MA '21 (U Tex). Author: The Brontes Web of Childhood '41. Editor: (with A W Terrell) From Texas to Mexico and the Court of Maximilian, 1865 '33; (with William C DeVane) Legends of Angria '33; The Story of Champ d'Asile '37; Between the Lines, letter and memoranda interchanged by H Buxton Forman and Thomas J Wise; Letters of Thomas J Wise to John Henry Wrenn; A Further Inquiry into the Guilt of Certain Nineteenth Century Forgers '44. Librarian rare book collections U Tex since '19. Guggenheim Fellow '29-30, '39-40; Rockefeller Fellow '34-35, '35-36. Rare Book Collections, University of Texas, Austin, Tex.

19 RATH, Frederick Louis, Jr. Historic sites and buildings (Preservation). b'13. BA '34 (Dartmouth Coll); MA '36 (Harvard). Co-author: Franklin D Roosevelt's Hyde Park '47. Historian Morristown Nat Hist Park NJ '37-38, Revolutionary War research, Fort Pulaski Nat Monument Savannah Ga '39-40; Civil War research, Vicksburg Nat Mil Park Miss '40-42, Civil War research, Home of Franklin D Roosevelt Nat Historic Site Hyde Park NY '46-48; dir Nat Trust for Historic Preservation since '49. AHA—Society Archtl Historians—Nat Parks Assn—Assn State Local Hist. National Trust for Historic Preservation, 712 Jackson Pl., Washington 6.

20 RATH, R. John. Austrian, German and Italian history (19th Century). b'10. AB '32 (U Kan); AM '34 (U Calif); PhD '41 (Columbia U). Author: The Fall of the Napoleonic Kingdom of Italy '41; also articles in field. Assoc editor: Journal of Central European Affairs '47-51. Asso prof hist U Colo Boulder Colo '47-51; professor hist U Texas since '51. AHA (member Austro-Hungarian microfilming committee since '47)—Phi Beta Kappa. Department of History, University of Texas, Austin.

21 RATHKEY, Arnold Chester. Gas (production, distribution). b'97. BS in chem engring '20 (U Neb). Author articles: Leakage survey; Metering industrial gas; Progress summary on production substitute gas; Substituting butane and propane for manufactured gas. Gas engr United Gas Improvement Co and successors since '20; div gas engr Ia Pub Service Co '27-45, gas engr since '45. Am Gas Assn—Midwest Gas Assn—Waterloo Tech Soc—Alpha Chi Sigma Sigma Tau. Iowa Public Service Company, Waterloo, Ia.

22 RATHMANN, Heinrich Wilhelm. Ferro-alloys; Vanadium; Uranium. b'08. MetE '31 (U Minn); '38-40 (Carnegie Inst Tech); '41-42 (Washington and Jefferson). Research on ferro-alloys, production of ferro-chromium and ferro-vanadium, extraction of vanadium and uranium from ores and other materials, refining crude vanadium and uranium products. Research metall Vanadium Corp Am Bridgeville Pa '37-44, asst mgr research development dept '44-49, chief metall western div since '49. Am Chem Soc—Am Inst Mining Metall Engrs—Am Soc Metals—Tau Beta Pi. Jarrett Dr., Lewiston, N.Y.

23 RAUBITSCHEK, Antony Erich. Attic epigraphy and history; Greek literature. b'12. PhD '35 (U Vienna). Field work in Greece '35-38. Author articles in field. Mem Inst Advanced Study Princeton '38-42, '44-45; asso prof classics Princeton since '47. Am Philol Assn—Archeol Inst Am. Department of Classics, Princeton University, Princeton, N.J.

24 RAUTENSTRAUCH, Walter. Machine design; Machine drafting; Manufacturing enterprises (Design). b'80. BS '02—LLD '32 (U Mo); MS '03 (U Me); '03-04 (Cornell). Industrial and engineering design of machines, tools and manufacturing enterprises; studies of industrial economics; principals of modern industrial organizations. Author: Syllabus of Lectures on Machine Design '06; Machine Drafting '08; The Economics of Business Enterprise '39; Who Gets the Money? '39. Co-author: Mechanical Engineers Handbook '16; The Successful Control of Profits '30; Tomorrow in the Making '39; Industrial Surveys and Reports '40; The Design of Manufacturing Enterprises '41; Principals of Modern Industrial Organization '44; Economics of Industrial Management '49. Prof indsl engineering Columbia '06-46, emeritus prof since '46; cons indsl econs Bank of Mexico. Nat Research Council—NY Acad Scis(F)—AAAS(F)—Am Soc Refrigerating Engrs—ASME—Franklin Inst—Am Acad Polit and Social Sci—Tau Beta Pi—Sigma Xi. 235 Dorin Court Rd., Palisades, N.J.◉

10 RAWLINS, Thomas Elsworth. Plant pathology (Virus diseases). b'95. BS '21—PhD '26 (U Calif); MS '23 (U Wis). Studies on nature of viruses and histochemistry of plants. Author: Phytopathological and Botanical Research Methods '33; also articles in field. Prof plant path U Calif Berkeley since '45. AAAS—Bot Soc Am—Am Phytopath Soc—Am Soc Naturalists—Sigma Xi. University of California, Berkeley.†

11 RAY, Charles, Jr. Flax genetics, breeding and diseases; Plant cytogenetics; Botany of vegetable fiber plants. b'11. AB '37 (Lafayette Coll); PhD '41 —research fellow '37-41 (U Va). Author articles in field. Geneticist Plant Research Dept Calif Central Fibre Corp '41-52; staff dept biol Emory U since '52. AAAS(F)—Bot Society America—Am Soc Agron-Genetic Soc Am-Am Genetic Assn—Phytopath Soc—Sigma Xi. Annual research award Va Acad Sci '41; Walker prize '41. Dept. Biology, Emory University, Emory, Ga.

12 RAY, Francis Earl. Radiochemistry (Cancer research). b'98. BSc '21—DSc '31 (Oxford U); MA '26 (U Ill). Synthesis of first radioiodo compounds for cancer research; synthesis of organic compounds for synthesis of the radioactive carcinogen, acetylaminofluorene; study of metabolism of radioactive p-tolvenesulfonamidofluorene; study chemical carcinogensis and gastric cancer; relation between carcinogenicity and physical chemical properties of compounds. Author: Experimental Chemistry (last edit) '37; Organic Chemistry '41 (2d edit) '47; Experimental General Chemistry '47; and others. Author articles: Organic Radioiodo Compounds for Cancer Research '46; Compounds for Cancer Research—Further Bifluoryl and Bifluorylidene Derivatives '49; Metabolism of radioactive carcinogens, and others. Asst prof advancing to asso prof and dir lab radiochem U Cincinnati '30-49; dir Cancer Research Lab U Fla since '49. ACS(councilor '35 and '41)—Am Assn Cancer Research—Ohio Acad Sci(F, vp '40-41, administrative bd '41-43)—Ia Acad Sci(F)—Fla Acad Sci—Soc Exptl Biol Med Cancer Research Laboratory, University of Florida, Gainesville.

13 RAY, Joseph James. Industrial psychology. b'94. Student '14-15 (O Wesleyan U); BD '24 (Yale); AB '31 (YMCA Grad Sch); MA—PhD '36 (Peabody Coll). Invented and patented multitester, electric testing device '34; designed portable polygraph used with above instrument '34, multiple choice reaction machine. Author: Generalizing Ability of Dull, Bright and Superior Children '36; also articles in field. Recruiting representative and supervisory training Work Improvement Program US Civil Service Commn Washington '42-44; dir supervisory development Gen Shoe Corp, Nashville, since '44. Am Psychol Assn—So Soc Philos Psychol—Am Training Dirs Assn (board mgrs)—Kappa Delta Pi. Diplomate in Industrial Psychology. General Shoe Corp., Nashville, Tenn.

14 RAY, Louis Lamy. Geomorphology (Physiography); Glacial (Pleistocene) and military geology. b'09. AB '30—MS '32 (Washington U); MA '37—PhD '38 (Harvard). US delegate to 18th session International Geological Congress '48; special field work Alaska Colorado and New Mexico, Scandanavia, Georgia, Kentucky. Author articles in field. Geol US Geol Survey since '42. Geol Soc Am(F)—Am Geog

Soc(F)—Am Assn Geo(F)—AAAS(F) —Am Soc Photogrammetry—Am Geophys Union—Brit Glaciol Soc—Geol Soc Washington—Soc Econ Geol—Arctic Inst NA—Sigma Xi. U.S. Geological Survey, Washington 25.†

15 RAY, W(illiam) Winfield. Leaf-curl fungi; Leaf parasites; Cotton, nut and crop diseases. b'09. Student '27-29 (Haverford Coll); BS '31—MS '33 (Northwestern U); PhD '38 (Cornell U). Research on leaf-curl fungi, leaf parasites, and cotton, nut and crop diseases: fungus diseases of grasses. Dir identification lab emergency plant disease survey Stillwater Okla '43-45; prof bot U Neb since '47, chmn dept since '48; mycol Agr Expt Sta Lincoln since '47. Am Phytopath Soc—Mycol Soc Am —Bot Society of America—Nebraska Acad Sci—AAAS(F). Department of Botany, University of Nebraska, Lincoln 8, Neb.†

16 RAYBURN, Otto Ernest. Folklore. b'91. Student '14-16 (Baker U Baldwin City Kan); '33-35 (E Tex State Tchrs Coll Commerce Tex). Research and study of folklore in Ozarks '21-53, also lecturer on folklore. Author: (poetry) The Inward Real '27; Dream Dust '34; (essays) Roadside Chats '39; Ozark Country (4th vol Am Folkway Series) '41—Ark Folklore Soc(pres '52-54). Ed Ozark Guide Magazine. 77 Spring St., Eureka Springs, Ark.

17 RAYNER, H(edley) John. Trout; Fishery management. b'11. BS '35—MS '36 (U Calif); PhD '41 (Cornell U). Research on the food of trout of Yosemite National Park, the determination of the food grade of streams, the experimental stream a method for study of trout planting problems, planting fish in lakes. Author articles in field. Chief of operations div fisheries Ore State Game Commn. Sigma Xi. State Game Commission, Box 4136, Portland, Ore.

18 READ, Allen Walker. English usage. b'06. BA '25 (Ia State Tchr Coll); MA '26 (State U Ia); Rhodes scholar LittB '33 (Oxford); student '27, '32-34 (U Chicago), '46-47 (New Sch Social Research). Author: A Semantic Guide to Current English. Collaborator: Dictionary of American English on Historical Principles '34-38; (with C L Barnhart) Dictionary of United States Army Terms '44; American College Dictionary '47. With English dept Columbia since '45, asst prof since '48; editorial asst Am Speech mag '42-47, mng editor since '48; lectr Brooklyn Coll '46, U Denver '46; lectr, cons Inst Gen Semantics Lakeville Conn since '45. Lexicographical adv mil intelligence div, information and edn div US Army '42-45. Modern Lang Assn (see present day English group '38-40, chmn '40-41)—Am Dialect Soc (exec com '40-42; sec '42-43, vp '47-48, pres'49-50; mem dialect dictionary com since '46)—Linguistic Soc Am (exec com '50-51)—Nat Council Tchrs English (com linguistic resources)— Am Folklore Soc (council '47-48)— Nat Soc Study Communication (com propaganda)—Inst Gen Semantics(F) —NY Soc Gen Semantics(pres '49-51)—Philol Soc Eng—Speech Assn Am —AAAS. Fellow Guggenheim Memorial Found to compile Briticisms: a Dictionary of the Speech of England (in preparation) '38-41. Business Bldg, Room 301, Columbia University, NYC 27. H: 38 W 12th St, NYC 11.

19 READ, Gladwin A(dolph). Feed (Defluorinated phosphate). b'04. BS '25 (Kan State Coll); MS '31 (U Cal). Development phosphorus supplement suitable for all livestock and poultry feeds; standardization processes for commercial production defluorinated phosphorus. Mgr poultry service Pio-

neer Hatchery Petaluma Cal '26-33; mgr feed dept Internat Minerals & Chem Corp Chicago since '42. Gamma Sigma Delta—Alpha Zeta. 20 N. Wacker Drive, Chgo. 6.

20 READ, Lloyd C. Housing construction; Prefabrication. b'05. CE '28 (Rensselaer Poly Institute); '28 (Alexander Hamilton Institute). Research, design, and testing light framing systems, foundations, coverings, coatings of any material for conventional and prefabricated structures; development widely-spaced light-gage steel and glued wood trusses, integral panel constructions, prefabricated flooring. In charge housing research Ingalls Iron Works '42-43; in charge structural research John B Pierce Found since '43. Nat Soc Profl Engrs—Soc Exptl Stress Analysis—Am Soc CE. John B Pierce Foundation, Raritan, N.J.

21 READ, William Thornton. Industrial chem; Organic chemistry; Applications of chemistry to military problems. b'86. AB '05—AM '08 (Austin Coll Sherman Tex); AM '15 (U Tex); student '15-16 (Harvard); PhD '21 (Yale). Author: Industrial Chemistry '43. Head dept chemistry Tex Tech College Lubbock '25-30; dean school chemistry Rutgers U '30-43; section chief National Roster '43-46; chemistry adviser War Dept Gen Staff since '46. 1st lt CWS US Army '18. ACS—Am Inst Chem Engrs—Am Inst Chemists —Soc Chem Industry Eng—Sigma Xi —Alpha Chi Sigma—Phi Lambda Upsilon—Chemists Club New NY. General Staff, Department of Army, Pentagon Bldg., Washington 5.◉

22 READING, Douglas K(ugler). Eighteenth Century Russia; Mercantilism. b'12. AB '33 (Colgate U); PhD '37 (Yale). Author: The Anglo-Russian Commercial Treaty of 1734 '38. Asso prof European hist Colgate U since '46. OSS research and analysis br Russian Div Washington '43-45, assignment in Berlin office '45. Colgate University, Hamilton, N.Y.†

23 READING, Thomas James. Concrete (Aggregates, cracking, construction). b'15. BS in civil engring '36 (Ohio U); SM '39 (MIT). Investigation strains, stresses and cracking in concrete walls due to drying shrinkage and temperature change; design, control and testing concrete mixes: testing concrete ship compartments to determine seaworthiness and locate imperfections; production aggregates and field operations connected with concrete construction. Research MIT '39-43; head Corps Engrs Dist Lab '46-49, concrete engr Ft Randall Dam project since '49. Am SocCE—Am Concrete Inst. Corps of Engineers, Ft. Randall Dam Project, Pickstown, S.D.

24 REBER, Grote. Radio physics and astronomy. b'11. BS in EE '33 (Ill Inst Tech). Research on radio waves from sky, sun and milkyway. Author articles in field. Radio eng Stewart Warner '33-46; radio physicist Bur Standards radio astron since '46. National Bureau of Standards, Washington.

25 RECKNAGEL, Arthur Bernard. Forest management. b'83. AB '04—MF magna cum laude '06 (Yale); '11-12 (Eberswalde Forst Akademie Germany). Forest adviser Northeastern Lumber Manufacturers Association under Lumber Code; member Joint Committee of ten to carry on work of Conservation Conference '34-37. Author: Forest working plans '13, 17; The Forests of New York State '23; Syllabus—Introduction to Forestry '27. Co-author: (with John Bentley Jr and C H Guise) Forest Management

'19; (with S N Spring) Forestry '29; (with C B Pond) Forest and Woodland Taxation in New York State '46. Collaborator: Forstliche Rundschau. Editor bull Empire State Forest Products Assn. Chief of reconnaissance US Forest Service '06-13, area forester, timber prodn War project '43-45; spl lectr forestry U BC '38; prof forestry Cornell U '13-43, head forestry dept '42-43, acting head dept forestry '47-48; forester and sec Empire State Forest Products Assn '17-47; tech dir forestry St Regis Paper Co. St. Regis Paper Co., 230 Park Av., NYC 17.†◎

10 RECORDS, Ralph Hyden. American history (Western Oklahoma, colonial New England). b'89. BA '22—MA '23 (U Okla); PhD '36 (U Chicago). Research on history of commerce on Great Lakes, land as a basis social discontent in Massachusetts and Maine 1660-1776, colonial New Hampshire. Author articles in field. With U Okla since '26, prof since '44. AHA—Miss Valley Hist Assn—Southwestern Social Sci Assn—Okla Hist Soc—Soc Am Hist —Phi Beta Kappa. Faculty Exchange, University of Oklahoma, Norman, Okla.

11 RECTOR, Nelson H. Mosquito control (Drainage); Fire protection equipment. b'99. BS in civil engring '21 (Johns Hopkins). Research in methods mosquito control by drainage, filling, larviciding, screening, use of predators, all phases mosquito control work on impounded water; promotion, organization, execution special type concretelined ditch with sodded banks as permanent type drainage. Inventor rolling fire escape and fall proof scaffold. Malaria control Ala State Bd Health '22-25; in Italy with Rockefeller Found '25-27, Miss State Bd Heatlh '28-42; malaria control in war areas USPHS '42-46, Communicable Disease Center Atlanta since '46. Am Pub Health Assn (F)—Am Soc CE—Nat Soc Profl Engrs—Nat Malaria Soc—Sci Research Soc Am. Communicable Disease Center, 50 Seventh St. N.E., Atlanta. H: 230 Bolling Rd. N.E.

12 REDD, Oliver Franklin. Grinding in ball mills (Methods and equipment); Mixing (Methods and equipment). b'04. EdB '26 (So Ill U); BS '29 (U Ill); (U Chicago). Patent for process preparation of calcined gypsum. Author articles in field. Tech dir Patterson Foundry and Machine Co since '35. Engr Signal Corps US Army '42-45. H: 437 Thompson Av., East Liverpool, O.†

13 REDDING, Jay Saunders. Negro literature. b'06. PhB '28—MA '32—U scholar '32-33 (Brown U); '33-34 (Columbia). Research on American Negro thought from 1650, early American Negro writers, collection of Southern folk material. Author: To Make a Poet Black '39; No Day of Triumph (Mayflower award) '42; Stranger and Alone '50; They Came in Chains '50; On Being Negro in America '51. Mem editorial bd Am Scholar. Prof Eng Hampton Inst since '43; Guggenheim fellow '44-45; vis prof English Brown '49-50; vis lectr Am Friends Con since '50. Assn Study Negro Life Hist—Am Folklore Soc—Eng Assn—Phi Beta Kappa. Recipient Mayflower award NC Hist Soc '44; Nat Urban League award for distinguished service '50.†◎

14 REDDISH, George Fults. Industrial bacteriology; Antiseptics; Disinfectants; Fungicides. b'94. BS '19 (U Ky); PhD '22 (Yale). Author articles in field. Bact Lambert Pharmacal Co St Louis since '29; prof bact St Louis Coll Pharmacy Allied Sci since '32. AA AS—Soc Am Bact—Am Pub Health Assn—Nat Assn Insecticide Disinfectant Mgrs. 2117 Franklin Av., StL 6.

15 REDDY, Charles S. Seed protectants. b'87. BS '15—MS '16—PhD '22 (U Wis). Research in cereal crop diseases, onions, flax, and sugar beets; first in successful corn seed treatment, flax seed treatment. Patent on sterocide, corn seed treatment. Author articles in field. Ia Agrl Expt Sta bot plant path sect since '27. Phytopath Soc—Phi Kappa Phi—Sigma Xi. Botany Hall, Iowa State College, Ames, Ia.

16 REDFORD, Emmette S. Governmental controls (Field adminstration); Rationing (Wartime); Price control. b'04. AB '27—AM '28 (U Tex); PhD '33 (Harvard). Author: Field Administration of Wartime Rationing '47. Author articles: Security to Aged, Dependent Children and the Blind with Particular Reference to the Southern States '36; Trends in Banking Control '40; The Value of the Hoover Commission Reports to the Educator '50. Contbr chpter State Regulation of Business to the Government of Texas: A Survey '34. With U Tex since '33, prof pub adminstrn since '39 (leave of absence '42-45), pres Univ Cooperative Soc (retail store) since '46; asst dep adminstr for rationing OPA '44-45, with price div regional office '42-44; cons on field adminstrn NSRB and ESA '50-51. Am Polit Sci Assn—Am Soc Pub Adminstrn—Southwestern Social Sci Assn—So Polit Sci Assn. University of Texas, Austin.

17 REDMOND, W(illiam) B(rinson). Malariology (Immunity); Electrophoresis. b'01. AB '27—MS '28 (Emory U); PhD '37 (Chicago U). Research on cross-immune relationship of strains of plasmodium cathemerium and plasmodium relictum, characteristics of immunity to human malaria; devised method of vaccination of birds against malaria; perfected circulator for aerating whole blood used for culturing malaria parasite; discovered that blood cells infected with malaria parasite have reduced electrical charge. Author articles in field. With Veterans Administration since '50. Sigma Xi—Phi Beta Kappa—Am Society Bact—Am Society Parasitol—Soc Exptl Biol Med—Assn Southeastern Biol—AAAS(F)—Ga Acad Sci(F), past pres). Rsrch grants Penrose Fund of Am Philos Soc, Permanent Sci Fund Am Acad Arts Sci, Woodruff Malaria Research Fund Emory U, USPHS. Emory University, Box 534, Atlanta.†

18 REED, Carroll Edward. Pennsylvania German dialects; Linguistic geography. b'14. BA '36—MA '37 (U Wash); PhD '41 (Brown U). Engaged in preparing a dialect atlas of Pennsylvania German. Author: The Pennsylvania German Dialect Spoken in the Counties of Lehigh and Berks '49; also articles in field. Asst in German Brown U '38-41, instr '41-42; asst prof German U Ga '46; U Washington since '46, asso prof since '52. Mod Lang Assn —Linguistic Soc Am—Am Dialect Soc —Pa German Folklore Soc—Internat Phonetic Assn. Received Carl Schurz grants for research in Pa German '40, '42. University of Washington, Seattle 5.

19 REED, Clyde Franklin. Ferns. b'18. AB '38 (Loyola Coll); MA '40 (Johns Hopkins); PhD '42 (Harvard). Author articles. Am Soc Plant Taxonomy—Internat Soc Plant Morphologists —Am Fern Assn—Sullivant Moss Soc— Am Bot Soc—So Appalachian Bot Soc— NE Bot Soc—Bot Soc So Cal—AAAS— Sigma Xi. Baltimore Junior College, Balt.

20 REED, David E. Structural geology. b'15. BS '38 (U Okla). Analysis and interpretation data resulting from air-borne and ground magnetic surveys. Magnetometer party chief Stano-

ind Oil & Gas Co '41-45; supervisor magnetics dept Frost Geophys Corp '45-46; owner Reed Magnetic Surveys since '46. Soc Exploration Geophysicists—Am Assn Petroleum Geol—Am Geophys Union—Tulsa Geol Soc—Geophys Soc Tulsa. 323 Ritz Bldg., Tulsa 3 H: 1123 E. 36th Pl., Tulsa 5.

21 REED, Erik Kellerman. Archeology of Southwestern United States (Arizona; New Mexico); Archeology of Micronesia (Marianas); History of Guam; The Galapagos Islands; Early hist of So western United States (New Mexico). b'14. AB '32 (George Washington U); AM '34—PhD '44 (Harvard). Author articles in field. Regional Archeol Nat Park Service since '35. Am Anthrop Assn—Soc Am Archeol— AAAS. National Park Service, Santa Fe, N.M. H: 238 Griffin St.†

22 REED, Eugene Clifton. Subsurface geology; Stratigraphy; Ground water; Geology of Nebraska. b'01. AB '23—MSc '33 (U Nebr). Author numerous articles in field. Nebr Geol Survey since '33, asso state geol since '44. Am Assn Pet Geol—Geol Soc Am(F)— Nebr Assn Adv Sci—Soc Econ Geol and Paleontol—Nebr Well Drillers Assn (sec '35-48)—Sigma Xi. Conservation and Survey Division, University of Nebraska, Lincoln.

23 REED, Frank Hynes. Coal chemistry. b'90. AB '11 (Wabash Coll); PhD '17 (U Chicago). Chief chem Ill Geol Survey Urbana since '31. AAAS (F)—Am Chem Soc (chmn gas fuel div '39, chmn U Ill sect '46-47)—Am Inst Mining Metall Engrs (sec-treas indsl minerals div '39-40, chmn chem raw materials com '37-38, mem sect com classification NAm coals since '33)— Nat Research Council (mem com chem utilization coal since '38)—Sigma Xi— Phi Lambda Upsilon. Natural Resources Building, Urbana, Ill.◎

24 REED, Henry Clay. History of Delaware; American penal history. b'99. AB '22 (Bucknell U); AM '29 (Pa State Coll); PhD '39 (Princeton). Research in history of crime and punishment in the US. Author articles in field. Editor: Delaware, A History of the First State, 3 vols '47. Instr to prof hist U Delaware since '24. AHA— Archaeol Soc Del—Hist Soc Del—Inst Del Hist Culture—Phi Kappa Phi—AA UP—Am Assn State and Local Hist— Natural Hist Soc Del. University of Delaware, Newark, Del.

25 REED, Irvin F(ay). Tillage machinery; Production and harvesting machinery for oil bearing crops. b'03. BS '26 (U Neb); MS '28 (O State U); AE '41 (U Neb). Author articles in field. US Dept Agr since '28, sr agrl engr charge tillage machinery lab '42-50; in charge research on peanut and tung production and harvesting machinery. Am Soc Agr Engrs—Soil Sci Soc Am. Box 792, Tillage Machinery Laboratory, Auburn, Ala.†

26 REED, Marion C(apps). Vinyl plastics; Vinyl resin plasticizers; Vinyl resin stabilizers. b'98. BS '21 (Kan State Coll); MS '22—PhD '25 (Ohio State U); '23 (U Ill). Author articles: Behavior of Plasticizers in Vinyl Chloride—Acetate Resins '43; Survey of Plasticizers for Vinyl Resins '47; Nitrile Rnbbers as Plasticizers in Vinyl Resins '49, others. Patents in field. Chem development dept Bakelite Co since '41. ACS. Bakelite Co., Bound Brook, N.J.

27 REED, Merton J(ay). Range management; Northern great plains. b'16. BA '39 (Mont State U); MS '42 (U Notre Dame). Range conservationist Northern Rock Mt Forest Range Expt Sta US Forest Service since '42. Northwest Acad Sci—Mont Acad Sci—AAAS—Am Ecol Soc—Am Soc Range Management. Northern Rocky Mountain Experiment Station, Missoula, Mont.†

10 **REED, Raymond Edward.** Hair (Waving chemistry); Keratin chemistry; Textile chemistry. b'08. Grad '27 (Crane Coll); student (Harvard, U Chicago, MIT). Patents on surgical bandage, heat producing compositions, padding material, textile fabrics, hair waving. Author articles in field. Research chem Kendall Co '29-41; vp Raymond Labs Inc '41-46; dir cosmetic research Warner-Hudnut NYC '46-47; vp Toni Co Chicago since '47; pres Reed Chem Corp Chicago since '47. Soc Cosmetic Chem (pres '49)—Am Chem Soc—AAAS—Minn Fedn Engring Soc. 456 Merchandise Mart, Chicago. H: 743 N. Belmont Av., Arlington Heights, Ill.

11 **REED, Robert F(indley).** Lithography; Printing papers and inks (Processes). b'90. Chem E '14 (U Cincinnati). Research on science and technology of the lithographic processes; development and introduction of improved processes and materials. Patents on the dampening system for planographic press, planographic printing surface, improved lithographic solvent, device for measuring moisture content of paper, deep-etched lithographic plates, clearing deep-etched plates, device for measurement of ink consistency. Author articles in field. Research dir Lithog Tech Found '25-46; lithog cons Armour Research Found '46-47; Lithog Tech Found since '47. Am Chem Soc—Am Inst Chem Engrs—AAAS—Tech Assn Pulp Paper Industry—Tech Assn Lithog Ind—Soc Rheology. 1800 S. Prairie Av., Chgo 16.

12 **REED, Stanley F(oster).** Strain gages. b'17. Student '41-42 (Johns Hopkins U); '42-44 (George Washington U). Developed strain gage dynamometers for study of full scale resistances of air-towed and underwater towed objects for US Navy '46; developed strain gage torquemeter for Army Engineers '47; invented variable capacitance dynamic strain gage '47; developed strain gage ballistocardiograph for USPHS '47; developed other instruments utilizing strain gages as measuring elements for shock, pressure, vibration, temperature and load. Dir Reed Research Inc Washington since '44. Soc Naval Architects Marine Engrs—Am Soc Heat Ventilating Engrs—Inst Radio Engrs—Quartermaster Assn—AAAS. 1048 Potomac St., Washington 7.

13 **REED, Stephen Winsor.** Primitive societies; Cultural contacts in colonial areas; Cultural demography. b'12. BA '34—PhD '39 (Yale). Sociological field research in mandated territory of New Guinea, Kwoma culture, acculturation in New Guinea. Author: Making of Modern New Guinea '43; also articles in field. Asso prof sociol Yale since '50, also dir Southeast Asia studies. Sigma Xi—Am Sociol Soc—American Population Assn—Soc Applied Anthrop. Yale University, New Haven.†

14 **REEDER, John Raymond.** Taxonomy and phylogeny of grasses; Grasses of New Guinea. b'14. BS '39 (Mich St); MS '40 (Northwestern U); '40-42 (Ore State Coll); MA '46—PhD '47—Sheldon Travel fellow '46-47 (Harvard). Author articles in field. Instr bot curator Eaton Herbarium other bot collections Yale '47-51, asst prof bot, curator herbarium since '51. Internat Assn Plant Taxonomists—Am Soc Plant Taxonomists—Bot Soc Am—AFA—Torrey Bot Club—NE Bot Club—Sigma Xi. Osborn Botanical Laboratory, Yale University, New Haven.†

15 **REEDER, Ward Glen.** School administration. b'91. AB '14 (Ind U); AM '18—PhD '21 (U Chicago). Author: The Chief State School Official '23; Two Thousand Spelling Demons '25; How to Write a Thesis '25 (rev '30); The Business Administration of a School System '30 (rev '41); Fundamentals of Public School Administration; A First Course in Education '37 (rev '43); An Introduction to Public School Relations '37; The Administration of Pupil Transportation '39; A Manual for the School Bus Driver '39; The State Board and State Department of Education '39; The School Board Member and His Work '40; Outlines and Exercises for First Course in Education '43; School Boards and Superintendents '44; Campaigns for School Taxes '45. Participated in school surveys Ohio, Mich, WVa, Pa, Ind. With Ohio State U since '22, prof edn since '33. Am Ednl Research Assn—Phi Delta Kappa—Phi Sigma Pi. Ohio State University, Columbus.†©

16 **REES, Don M(errill).** Mosquitoes; Medical entomology; Invertebrate zoology. b'01. BS '26—MS '29 (U Utah); PhD '36 (Stanford). Engineer and supervisor of Salt Lake City mosquito abatement district '30-37; virus and rickettsial disease commission of Army Epidemiological Board in Japan and Orient '47. Author articles in field. With U Utah since '29, head dept invertebrate zool and entomol since '48. AAUP—Entomol Soc Am—AAAS—Am Pub Health Assn—Am Mosquito Control Assn—Utah Acad Sci—Sigma Xi—Phi Sigma. University of Utah, Salt Lake City 1.

17 **REES, Orin W(ainwright).** Analytical chemistry; Fuel chemistry and analysis (Coal); Illinois coal. b'98. BS '22 (Earlham Coll); MS '25—PhD '31 (U Ill). Author articles in field. Chem, head analytical div Ill State Geol Survey since '39. Am Chem Soc—AAAS (F)—Am Soc Testing Materials—Am Gas Assn—Ill Acad Sci—Ill Mining Inst. State Geological Survey, Natural Resources Building, Urbana, Ill.†

18 **REESE, Elwyn Thomas.** Mushroom production; Penicillin; Cellulose decomposition. b'12. PhD '46—research fellow '42-43, '45-46 (Penn State Coll). Research in mushroom production, penicillin and cellulose decomposition. Mycologist Knaust Bros Mushroom Co '41-42, Philadelphia Q M Depot Biol Lab since '48. Soc Am Bacteriol—Mycol Soc Am—Am Chem Soc—Sigma Xi. Philadelphia Q.M. Depot, Biological Laboratory, Phila 45.†

19 **REESE, Gustave.** Medieval and Renaissance music; Music publishing. b'99. LLB '21—Mus B '30 (NYU); Dr Mus hon '47 (Chicago Musical Coll). Author: Music in the Middle Ages with an introduction on Music of Ancient Times '40. Editor: A Birthday Offering to Carl Engel '43; also articles in field. With NYU since '27, adjunct prof grad sch since '48. Asso ed Musical Quarterly '33-44, ed '44-45; dir pub Carl Fischer, Inc since '45. Internat Soc Mus Research (bd dirs since '48)—Am Musicol Soc (sec '34-46, vp since '46)—Medieval Acad Am—Renaissance Club—Royal Mus Assn—Vereeniging voor Nederlands Muziekgeschiedenis. Music Department, New York University, Washington Square, NYC.

20 **REESE, Montana Lisle.** South Dakota (History, Indians, place names). b'10. Student '28-32 (U SD) (No State Tchrs Coll). Research on Black Hills, other areas of South Dakota. Author: Legends of the Mighty Sioux '41; South Dakota: A State Guide Book '51. Editor: South Dakota Place-Names; Vacation Guide to Custer State Park;

Fifty Million Pheasants; Aberdeen, A Middle Border City; Hamlin Garland: A Biography. Contributing editor: The American Guide '49. State dir, ed SD Fed Writers' Project '35-41; free lance author. 1723 S. Minnesota Av., Sioux Falls, S.D.

21 **REESE, Raymond C.** Structures; Rigid frames. b'93. BS '20 (MIT); '17-20 (Harvard). Designed rigid frame warehouse US Ordnance Erie Proving Ground, depots at Rossford and Marion O, reinforced concrete grain elevators, schools, department stores, hotels, low cost housing, Toledo Public Library involving 3-story rigid frames. Author: Reinforced Concrete Design (with Sutherland) '39; also articles in field. Chief engr Bldg Products Co (later Hausman Steel Co) Toledo O since '22; cons engr since '22; lecturer structural subjects U Toledo since '24. ASCE—Internat Soc Bridge Structural Engrs—Nat Soc Profl Engrs—Am Concrete Inst—Am Soc Engring Edn. 300 Sandusky St., P.O. Box 58, Toledo 1, O.

22 **REESIDE, John Bernard, Jr.** Mesozoic paleontology and stratigraphy; Cretaceous Ammonites; Stratigraphy (Western United States). b'89. AB '11—PhD '15 (Johns Hopkins). Geologist US Geological Survey since '15. AAAS(F)—Geol Soc American—Nat Acad Sci—Paleontology Soc (pres '43)—Am Assn Petroleum Geol—Washington Acad Sci—Washington Geol Soc (pres '41)—Biol Soc—Geol Soc Peru—Phi Beta Kappa—Sigma Xi. Mary Clark Thompson Medal '46. U.S. National Museum, Washington 25.†©

23 **REEVE, Eldrow.** Soil chemistry; Mushroom nutrition and culture; Tomato diseases. b'17. BS '39—MS '41 (Utah State Agrl Coll); PhD '44 (Rutgers U). Author articles in field. Div mgr agrl research Campbell Soup Co since '45. Am Soc Plant Physiol—Am Chem Soc—Am Soc Agron—Am Soil Sci Soc—Sigma Xi. Box 215, West Chicago, Ill.†

24 **REEVE, Frank Driver.** Indians (Federal policy, Navaho, Apache); New Mexican history. b'99. AB '25—MA '28 (U NM); PhD '37 (U Tex). Author articles: The Government and the Navaho '39, '43, and others. Prof hist U NM since '47. NM Hist Soc(F)—AHA—Southwestern Social Sci Assn. University of New Mexico, Albuquerque, N.M.

25 **REEVE, William Alexander.** Tramways (Aerial rope). b'87. Diploma ME '07 (U London Eng). Design and erection tramways for mines and other industries, in Europe, US, and Latin America; studies availability of construction materials and labor costs in foreign countries. Author articles: Speedy Erection of a Suspension Bridge '35; Transporter Bridge in Bolivia '43, and others. Prof engring London U Eng '05-10; with John A Roebling's Sons Co Trenton NJ since '31, now cons and sr engr bridge div and all fgn operations. ASME—Am Soc CE—AIMME—Am Concrete Inst—Internat Assn Navigation Control—Internat Assn Bridge and Structural Engrs—Inst ME London—Soc des Ingenieurs Civils de France. John A. Roebling's Sons Co., Trenton 2, N.J.

26 **REEVES, James Russell.** Petroleum seismology; Airborne magnetometry. b'03. AB '24 (Phillips U); MS '26 (U Okla). Applied seismic interpretation as related to petroleum geology; development of airborne magnetometer techniques. Seismic party chief Barnsdall Oil Co '40; contract physicist Naval Ordnance Lab '41-43; seismic party chief Nat Geol Co '43-46; chief geophysicist Lee Geophys Corp since '46. Soc Exploration Geophysicists—Am

Assn Petroleum Geol. 504 Reynolds Bldg., Cisco, Tex.

10 **REGAN, Lewis M(artin).** Applied mathematics (Aerodynamics, aircraft design); Numismatics. b'04. AB '24 (Mo Valley Coll Marshall); AM '28 (U Kan); student '28-30 (U Ill), '32-45 (NYU). Co-author: College Algebra '40, '48. Asst prof math Polytech Inst Brooklyn '30-46; asso prof math U Wichita since '46. Am Numismatic Soc (F)—Royal Numismatic Soc Eng(F)—Am Numismatic Assn(gen sec, comptroller since '44)—AAUP—Am Math Soc—Math Assn Am—Sigma Xi—Pi Mu Epsilon. University of Wichita, Wichita 6, Kan.⊙

11 **REHBERG, Chessie Elmer.** Chemistry of lactic acid. b'11. BS '33 (Ga State Coll for Men); MS '37 (Emory U); PhD '41 (U Tex). Holder 23 US patents, about 25 pending. Author articles in field. Chem US Dept Agr E regional research lab since '42. Am Chem Soc—Sigma Xi. Eastern Regional Research Laboratory, Phila 18.†

12 **REHDER, Harald Alfred.** Mollusks. b'07. AB '29 (Bowdoin Coll); AM '32 (Harvard); PhD '34 (George Washington U). Author articles in field. With Div Mollusks US Nat Mus Washington since '32, curator since '46. Am Malacol Union (pres '40)—Malacol Soc London—Conchol Soc Gt Brit Ireland—AAAS—Am Geo Soc—Washington Acad Sci—Biol Soc Wash. U.S. National Museum, Washington 25.†

13 **REICH, Nathan.** Labor relations; Comparative economic systems. b'00. AB '25—AM '26—fellow econ '25-26 (McGill U); '26-27 (U Montreal); fellow econ '27-28 (U Chicago)—fellow '29-30 (Brookings Inst Econ Research); PhD '37 (Columbia U). Author: Pulp and Paper Industry in Canada '27; Labor Relations in Republican Germany '38. Co-author: The American Jew '43. With Hunter Coll NYC since '34, asso prof '47, chmn dept econ since '47-52; lecturer Columbia U Sch Gen Studies since '45-52. Am Econ Assn. ERA Seligman prize for distinguished scholarship Columbia U '38; Guggenheim fellowship '40-41. Hunter College, 695 Park Av., NYC.

14 **REICHERT, Robert J.** Binoculars (Design, uses). b'93. Math scholar '12-14 (Cambridge U). Designer and manufacturer of the mirocular binocular. Author articles in field. Binocular designer and computer; founder Mirakel Optical Co and Mirakel Repair Co since '23. 14 West First St., Mount Vernon, N.Y.

15 **REICHLEY, Marlin S(herwood).** Economic mobilization for war. b'15. BS '35—MS '36—PhD '39 (Georgetown U). General editor: Applied Military Economics, A Case Study of the American War Economy '47. Asst prof polit sci Sch Fgn Service Georgetown U since '35; deputy dir and act dir dept research on economic mobilization and demobilization Indsl Coll Armed Forces '45-47, dir tech analysis '47-48, dir instrn since '48. Acad World Econ (bd dirs)—AHA—Am Geog Soc—Am Mil Inst. Industrial College of The Armed Forces, Washington 25.

16 **REID, Cecil Warren.** Lake improvement; Ichthyology; Limnology; Fishes of Texas. b'13. BS '42—'42-43, '47 (Tex A&M Coll). Author: The Fishes of Texas. Asst prof A & M Coll Texas '48; founded the Lake Improvement Company '47. Am Soc Ichthyologists Herpetologists—Wildlife Soc—Am Fisheries Soc. 104 East 13th St., Austin, Tex.†

17 **REID, Charles Frederick.** United States territories and outlying possessions (Education, colonial administra-

tion and government, Alaska, Hawaii, Puerto Rico, Guam, American Samoa, Canal Zone, Panama Canal Zone, Virgin and Philippine Islands). b'98. AB '23 (Colgate U); AM '29—PhD '40 (Columbia). On Educational survey commission Holyoke Mass '29, Panama Canal Zone '30; National Advisory Committee on Education '30-31, '37. Author: Education in the Territories and Outlying Possessions of the United States '41; Overseas America '42. Editor: Bibliography of the Island of Guam '39; Bibliography of the Virgin Islands of the United States '41; also articles in field. Asst prof dept edn Coll City NY since '31. AAAS(F)—Am Geog Soc—Am Assn Sch Adminstr (life)—Bibliog Soc Am—Am Geog Soc (F). College of the City of New York, NYC.

18 **REID, Dudley Alver.** History of Northwestern Missouri. b'72. Ed pub sch Mo. Author numerous articles in field. Pub West Des Moines Express la since '31. West Des Moines Express, West Des Moines, Ia.

19 **REID, Elbert Hann.** Range management (Reseeding, ecology, forestry, wildlife). b'12. Student '30-31 (Visalia Jr Coll Calif); '32 (Fresno State Teachers Coll); BS '34 (U Washington); '34-35 (U Calif). Author articles: Important Plants on National Forest Ranges of Eastern Oregon and Eastern Washington '42; Plant Succession on Subalpine Grasslands as Affected by Livestock Management '41; Guides to Determine Range Condition and Proper Use of Mountain Meadows in Eastern Oregon '42; Forage Utilization on Summer Cattle Ranges in Eastern Oregon '48. Forest ecologist and research center leader Blue Mountain Research Center Pacific Northwest Forest and Range Expt Sta '46-48; range conservationist '48-51, asst chief div range research US Forest Service Wash since '51. Soc Am Foresters—Ecol Soc Am—Am Soc Range Management—Soil Conservation Soc Am—Northwest Sci Assn—Sigma Xi. U.S. Forest Service, Washington 25.

20 **REID, Elliott Gray.** Aerodynamics. b'00. BS '22—MS '23—Aero Engr '38 (U Mich). Research on stability and performance of airplanes, aircraft propellers, aerodynamics of internal flow, streamlining of motor cars. Author: Applied Wing Theory '32; also tech reports and articles. Jr aeronautical engr Nat Adv Commn for Aeronautics Langley Field Va '22, asst '24, asso '27, wind tunnel and flight research in aerodynamics; professor aerodynamics Stanford U and cons engr since '27. Inst Aeronautical Scis(F)—Sigma Xi—Tau Beta Pi.⊙

21 **REID, George Graham.** Sewage disposal. b'95. Design and supervision building projects, waterworks, sewerage, incinerators, dams, drainage projects. Contributor articles on sewage disposal to Consulting Engineering. Assn Profl Engrs Ont—Inst Sewage and San Can—Am Waterworks Assn. Licensed in Que, Manitoba and Alberta. 264 Avenue Road, Toronto, Ont, Can.

22 **REID, George W.** Industrial hygiene; Sanitary engineering; Industrial wastes. b'17. BS '42 (Purdue); SM '43 (Harvard); '48-49 (Johns Hopkins). Author articles in field. Asso prof Ga Tech; now asso prof pub health and san engring U Okla; cons USPHS '47; partner Reid & Ingols, cons on water, sewage, wastes and sanitation. Tau Beta Pi. University of Oklahoma, Norman.

23 **REID, John Edward.** Lie detection; Criminal interrogation. b'10. Student '30-31 (Loyola U); LLB '35 (DePaul U); '44 (Northwestern U). De-

veloped new manner and methods of criminal interrogation with the aim of obtaining confessions '41-44; discovered hitherto unknown methods in lie detection to simulate without apparent movement blood pressure changes in the records; invented new attachment for the lie-detector; devised a new questioning technique incorporating control lies in each record and guilt complex questions. Author articles in field. Dir John E Reid and Asso Scientific Personnel Investigations Chicago since '47. 910 South Michigan Av., Chicago 5.

24 **REID, John Gilbert.** China (History); China's pre-war diplomacy; Career of P'u-yi (Manchu emperor). b'99. AB '21 (Hamilton Coll); MA '31—PhD '34 (U Calif); seminar on Far East '34 (U Calif); Penfield scholar in diplomacy, internat affairs and belles-lettres '35-36 (U Pa). Newspaper man and writer in China for many years in research in Chinese history; with State Dept as expert on foreign relations in Far East. Author: The Manchu abdication and the Powers '35; also articles in field. Newspaper reporter, editor, writer in China '22-28; research at U Calif '30-34; asst prof History State Coll Wash '37-39; with State Dept Washington, research asso in internat relations (Far East) '39-46, head Far East Sect Foreign Relations Br since '46. AHA. Division of Historical Policy Research, U.S. Department of State, Washington 25.

25 **REID, Loren Dudley.** Speech (18th Century). b'05. AB '27 (Grinnell Coll); AM '30—PhD '32 (State U Ia). Author: Charles James Fox: An Eighteenth Century Parliamentary Speaker '32. Author articles: Speaking in the Eighteenth Century House of Commons '49; Sheridan's Speech on Mrs. Fitzherbert '47. Prof speech U Mo since '44, chmn dept speech since '45; vis prof speech U So Cal summer '47; vis lectr speech confs La State U '49, U Mich '50. Eastern Pub Speaking Conf(exec council)—Speech Assn Am(exec sec since '45)—Am Speech Correction Assn—NY State Speech Assn(pres '42-44)—Central States Speech Assn(exec sec '37-39)—AAUP—Mo State Tchrs Assn (pres '47)—The Hansard Soc London. 111 Switzler Hall, University of Missouri, Columbia.

26 **REID, (Willard) Malcolm.** Physiology of helminth parasites; Poultry parasites. b'10. BS '32 (Monmouth Coll); MS '37—PhD '41 (Kan State Coll); '33 (Heidelberg U); '37-38 (Brown U), '38 (Cold Spring Harbor Biol Lab), '29 (Mich Biol Sta). Research on life history, biology, cysticercoid of fowl tapeworm, Raillietina cesticillus, its nutritional requirements and methods of removal as host starvation for brief periods, Choanotaenia infundibulum and its host, the housefly, and echinodermata. Author articles in field. Head dept biol Monmouth Coll since '38, prof since '47; instr invertebrate zool Marine Biol Lab Mass since '44. Am Soc Zool—Am Soc Parasitol—Sigma Xi—Am Soc Limnol Oceanog. Monmouth College, Monmouth, Ill.†

27 **REID, W(alter) Spencer.** Sintering; Lead (Metallurgy). b'94. BS '18—MS '19 (U Utah). Granted patent on improved method of sintering; lead metallurgy. Mining engr Haynes Stellite Co Leesburg Ida '19; mill foreman Mineral Products Corp Marysvale Utah '20-22; with Am Smelting & Refining Co since '22, gen mgr since '49. AIMME. 405 Montgomery St., SF 4.

28 **REID, William Stabler, Jr.** Cables (High tension); Networks (Secondary); Power equipment (Installation). b'12. BS '33 (Johns Hopkins). Research and installation high tension oil-filled cables and secondary networks; design, installation and testing central station equipment for large power plants; balancing large rotating equipment. Elec engr. Potomac Elec Power Co '33-36, Gen Elec Co '36-40, Consol Elec Light & Power Co '40-41; pres Imagineering Asso Inc '46-48; cons and project engr Gen Tire & Rubber Co '48; project engr Ralph M Parsons Co '49-50; vp, gen mgr and chief elec engr Am Archtl Engrs Inc since '50. Am Inst EE—Nat Soc Profl Engrs—Omicron Delta Kappa. P. O. Box 326, Balboa Island, Cal.

10 REIF, Charles Braddock. Limnology; Minnesota birds. b'12. BA '35—MA '38—PhD '41 (U Minn). Author articles: Minnesota Nesting Record '41; Winter Bird Census '41, and others. Prof biol Wilkes Coll since '42. Limnol Soc Am—Micros Soc Am—Phytology Soc Am—Minn Ornithol Union — AAAS — Sigma Xi. 184 S. River St., Wilkes-Barre, Pa.

11 REIGNER, Charles Gottshall. Business (Education). b'88. AB '15— EdB '15 (U Pitts); student (Princeton, U Pa, N.Y.U.); LittD '50 (Hampden-Sydney Coll); LLD '52 (Waynesburg (Pa) College). Author numerous textbooks in field of business edn. Tchr successively Strayer Sch, Wanamaker Inst Industries Phila, Business and Westinghouse high schs Pittsburgh; mem teaching staff summer sessions Bowling Green Coll Commerce Ky, Syracuse U, U Cal Berkeley and Los Angeles, U Wash; became editor H M Rowe Co Baltimore '19, pres since '26. NEA(life)—Nat Assn Secondary Sch Prins—Nat Bus Tchrs Assn(pres Nat Shorthand Tchrs Assn '14)—Eastern Bus Tchrs Assn—So Bus Edn Assn— Nat Shorthand Reporters Assn—Phi Delta Kappa—Delta Pi Epsilon. H. M. Rowe Co., 624 N. Gilmor St., Balt 17.

12 REIMANN, Irving G(eorge). Devonian and Silurian blastoids; Fossils; Museum exhibits. b'09. Student '26-29 (Harvard). Research on western New York paleontology; planned fossil dioramas made by Marchand for the Rochester Museum of Arts and Sciences, the Royal Ontario Museum, Chicago Natural History Museum, Buffalo Museum and others; collected fossils and minerals in many parts of North America for the Buffalo Museum. Author articles in field. Curator geol paleontol and mineral Buffalo NY Mus Sci '31-46; research cons George Marchand Studio since '46; prefect of exhibits U Mus U Mich since '47. Paleontol Soc Am—Mich Acad Sci Arts Letters. University Museums, Ann Arbor.†

13 REIMER, John Joseph. Refractories; Floor tile. b'10. BS in ceramics engring '35 (NY Coll Ceramics). Developed first airsetting plastic refractory; developed formulae and equipment to produce vitreous ceramic floor tile at a fast firing cycle. Issued patent in field. Chief ceramic engr Penn Tile Works Co '26-42; pres Keystone Ceramic Corp since '46. Am Ceramic Soc—Brit Ceramic Soc—Inst Ceramic Engrs—Keramos. Keystone Ceramic Corp., Bendersville, Pa. H: 86 Springs Av., Gettysburg, Pa.

14 REIN, Charles Robert. Serology; Syphilis (Serodiagnosis tests). b'08. BS '24 (U Toledo); MD '28 (U Mich). Co-author tests for serodiagnosis of syphilis; special consultant to US Public Health Service and United Nations World Health Organization. Author article: The Value of the Kline Exclusion Test in the Serodiagnosis of Syphilis '36; others. Contributor: Laboratory Methods of the U.S. Army

'44; Diseases of the Skin '39; others. Asso clin prof dermatology and syphilology, post grad div NYU; attending dermatologist and syphilologist NYU-Bellevue Med Center and mem med bd; asso vis dermatologist and syphilologist Bellevue Hosp; pvt practice NYC since '33. Chief div serology Army Med Center World War II. Diplomate Am Bd Dermatology and Syphilology. Am Acad Dermatol and Syphilol—Soc Investigative Dermatol—Am Pub Health Assn(F)—AMA—Am Soc Path and Bact—Am Venereal Disease Assn—Am Dermatol Assn—Am Acad Compensation Med(F)—Assn Mil Surgeons US—US-Mexico Border Pub Health Assn—Phi Delta Epsilon, others. 580 Fifth Av., NYC 19.

15 REINHARD, Frederick Peter. Coal Mining. b'14. BS in mining (Va Poly Inst). Management and operation coal mines Empire Coal & Coke Co Landgraff WVa '37-39, Tioga Coal Corp W Va '39-42, Lillybrook Coal Co Berkley WVa '42-50. AIMME—WVa Soc Profl Engrs. Virginia Wood Preserving Co. Batesville, Va.

16 REINHARDT, Guenther. Investigations; International intelligence; Propaganda; European politics. b'04. AB '22 (Royal Coll Mannheim Germany); BS '25 (State U Econ Mannheim); AM '25 (Heidelberg); '25-27 (Columbia U). Political commentator radio station WINS New York '43-45; consultant US House of Representatives special committee on Un-American activities '34-35, Office of US Co-ordinator of Inter-American Affairs '44-45; special consultant on enemy propaganda Writers' War Board '43-45, with Counter Intelligence Corps US Forces ETO '46-47; expert consultant to Assistant Secretary of Army '47-48. Author: The Organization of the German Steel Trust (German) '25; The Jews in Nazi Germany '33; Fish and Torpedoes (Jap espionage) '38; The Psychology of German Espionage '43; and others; also articles in field. 95 Christopher St., NYC 14.†

17 REINHART, Frank Walter. Plastics technology; Adhesives; Organic coatings. b'07. BS '30 (Juniata Coll); '30 (Columbia); '37-42 (U Md); '37-45 (Grad Sch Nat Bur Standards). Author articles in field. Chem plastics coatings adhesives Nat Bur Standards '37-48, now chief organic plastics section Am Chem Soc—Am Soc Testing Materials—Washington Acad Sci—Am Phys Soc (Div High Polymer Physics) —Soc Plastics Engrs. National Bureau of Standards, Washington 25. H: 9918 Sutherland Rd., Silver Spring, Md.†

18 REINHART, Warren Harry. Health and safety (Industrial). b'03. BS '24 (Pa State Coll); MS '26 (U Cincinnati). Development urine sulfate test for measuring workers' exposure to benzene, research on hazards of manganese, lead, mercury and lead arsenate in various industries, possible factors in etiology of baggassosis; prepared sections on sampling and analysis of carbon monoxide, hydrogen sulfide, benzene, and carbon bisulfide for American Standard Association Codes and prepared industrial health regulation for Louisiana. Research US Bur Mines '30-35; indsl. health research USPHS '36-41; with La State Health Dept since '44, chief indsl hygiene since '43. ACS—Am Indsl Hygiene Assn—AAAS—Am Conf Govt Indsl Hygienists—Am Soc Safety Engrs—Am Pub Health Assn(F) —Sigma Xi. Industrial Hygiene Section, Louisiana State Department of Health, New Orleans 7.

19 REINHOLT, Oscar Halvorsen. Mining engineering (Oil, mineral ex-

ploration and valuation); Natural resources conservation. b'76. BS (St Olaf Coll Minn); Student (U Minn, Wis). Made first extensive map of the 150-mile Mesabi belt for Minnesota Geological Survey; surveyed first Philippine forest reserve '03; examined mining prospects Colorado, Idaho, Utah '05-06; field work in oil and gas in a dozen states at various times '13-39; pioneered in West Texas Oil development '15-20; gold mining, mine examinations, manganese ore producer, valuation engineer etc in different states. Author: Oildom, Its Treasures and Tragedies '24; Geographical Handbook on Natural Resources (for teachers) '01; 90 Noteworthy Counties in Natural Wealth '45; (with H H Helble) Waste of Wealth '41; also articles in field. Miner brown ore US Steel subsidiary Ala '48-49, broadcasting, lecturing writing on mineral econ since '31. Am Acad Polit Social Sci—AFA—Internat Adventurers (hon life)—Geol Soc Washington—NC Acad Sci—and others. Medalist War Dept and Panama-Calif Expn. 1143 E. Howard St., Pasadena 6, Cal.

20 REINKING, Otto August. Plant pathology. b'90. BA '12—MS '15—PhD '22 (U Wis). Research in soil fungi in relation to disease, disease resistance in plants, diseases of tropical plants, fusaria and phytophthoras in relation to plant diseases. Author: Die Fusarien (with Wollenweber) '35. Head div plant path NY State Agr Expt Sta Geneva, prof plant path Cornell U '36-50, prof emer since '50; fgn agrl adviser research adminstrn office fgn agrl relations USDA since '50. AAAS— Am Phytopath Soc—Bot Soc Am—Am Genetic Assn—NY State Acad Sci— Corp Protection Inst. American Embassy, Manila, P.I.†

21 REISCHAUER, Edwin Oldfather. History of China and Japan. b'10. AB '31 (Oberlin Coll); MA '32—PhD '39 (Harvard); Harvard travel fellow '33-38 (France Japan Korea China). Member Army Department Cultural and Social Science Mission to Japan '48-49. Author: Japan Past and Present '47. Co-author: Elementary Japanese for University Students '41; Elementary Japanese for College Students '44; The United States and Japan '50. Co-compiler: Selected Japanese Texts '43; also articles in field. Professor Harvard since '51; sr research analyst Office Far Eastern Affairs State Dept '41, spl asst to Asst Sec State and chmn Japan-Korea secretaiat '45-46. Maj to lt col US Army '43-45. Far Eastern Assn—Am Oriental Soc—AHA—Phi Beta Kappa. Received Legion of Merit. Harvard-Yenching, Institute, Boylston Hall, Cambridge 38, Mass.○

22 REISER, Allan Rawlings. Mining geology; Mining properties (examinations, evaluation). b'12. BS '33—MS '34 (U Utah). Supervision mine development procedures, planning, and operations. Chief geol Park City Consol Mines Co '38-41, gen supt '41-47; gen supt MacIntyre Development titanium div Nat Lead Co and asst plant mgr '47-48, asst. mgr St Louis Smelting & Refining Div since '48, also asst mgr mining d pt and asst chmn mining com. AIMME—Sigma Gamma Epsilon. U Utah research fellowship award in ore dressing microscopy '33-34. National Lead Co., 111 Broadway, NYC 6.

23 REISTLE, Carl Ernest, Jr. Crude oil (Production). b'01. BS'22 (U Okla); '48 (Harvard Sch Bus Adminstrn). Engineer in charge Humble Oil & Refining Company '36-40, chief petroleum engineer '40-45, general superintendent production '45-46, manager production department '46-48, director, manager production department since '48. Am Petroleum Inst—AIMME— Sigma Xi—Sigma Tau—Alpha Chi Sigma—Houston Engineers Club. L 1200 S. Main, P.O. Box 2180, Houston.◎

10 REITER, Paul David. Archeology; Anthropology. b'09. BA '31—MA '33 (U NM); '39-40 (U Calif); PhD '45—Thaw fellow '44 (Harvard). Two archeological expeditions to Southeastern Chihuahua Mexico; excavations in New Mexico since '30. *Author articles in field.* Asso prof anthropol U NM since '48. Am Anthrop Assn(F)—Am Assn Phys Anthrop—Soc Am Archeol—NM Archeol Soc—Sigma Xi—Phi Kappa Phi. Department of Anthropology, University of New Mexico, Albuquerque, N.M.†

11 REITH, John William. Economic geography. b'14. Student '31-34 (Franklin and Marshall Coll); BS in econ '38 (Millersville State Tchrs Coll); MA '41 (Clark U); PhD '49 (Northwestern U). Research on industrial locations, geography of manufacturing and minerals. Head geog dept U So Cal since '48. Assn Am Geog—Nat Council Geog Tchrs—Cal Council Geog Tchrs—Sigma Xi—Assn Pacific Coast Geog—Am Geog Soc (F). Department of Geography, University of Southern California, LA 7.

12 REITZEL, Albert Emmet. American law (Immigration, nationality, administration); International law. LLB—LLM '15 (Nat U Washington); AB '21 (George Washington U). Draftsman of US prevailing rate of wage law '31, present law on immigration and alien laborers Dominican Republic '38, and Air Commerce Regulations of US '41; member President's Interdepartmental Radio Advisory Committee '26-40; US representative Conference of International Civilian Aviation Organization (on facilation International air transport) Geneva '48. Author: Immigration Laws of the United States—An Outline; Alien Seamen and Airmen under the Immigration Laws of the United States. Prin atty US Immigration and Naturalization Service Dept Justice '40-41, acting gen counsel '42-45, asst gen counsel since '45. Inter-Am Bar Assn(com on immigration and nationality)—Am Bar Assn—Am Soc Internat Law—Fed Bar Assn—NC Bar Assn. Department of Justice, Washington.

13 RELYEA, Kenneth Elam. Hybrid tomato; Hybrid and midget vegetables; Vine crop breeding; Trout fishing (Angling). b'13. BA '37 (Colgate U); student (New Paltz Teachers Coll); '41-42 (U Minn). With Farmer Seed and Nursery Co since '43; bd dirs since '48, vp ser dir gladiolus breeding program. Am Soc Hort Sci—Minn Hort Soc—Am Seed Trade Assn—So Seed Trade Assn—Minn Crop Improvement Assn. Faribault, Minn.†

14 REMP, George Edward. Power plants. b'16. BS '39—MSE '46—ME '48 (U Fla). Research in industrial water treatment, power plant betterment. Author: Fundamentals of Power Plant Engineering '49. Plant betterment engr Fla Power & Light Co '39-45; asst prof mech engring U Fla since '47. ASME—Nat Soc Profl Engrs—Am Soc Engring Edn—AAUP—Sigma Tau—Phi Kappa Phi. Engineering Building, University of Florida, Gainesville.

15 RENZETTI, Nicholas A(ugustus). Ballistics (Exterior, physical measurements). b'14. AM '36—PhD '40 (Columbia). Research on physical measurements, electricity and magnetism, atomic physics, hyperfine structure, electron and nuclear moments, ballis-

tics, free flight aerodynamics, rocket and guided missile systems. Author articles in field. Naval countermine warfare research '40-44, atomic physics '36-40; physicist '44-45, Michelson Labs USNOTS Inyokern, chief physicist, head exterior and terminal ballistics '45-47, head measurements div, asso head development dept since '47. NY Acad Sci—Am Phys Soc—Am Math Soc—Am Inst Physics—AAAS(F). Michelson Laboratory, USNOTS, Inyokern P.O., China Lake, Calif.

16 RETTALIATA, J(ohn) T(heodore). Gas and steam turbines; Jet propulsion; Education. b'11. BE '32—D Engring '36 (Johns Hopkins U). Holder several patents on steam and gas turbines and jet propulsion; sent to England by US Navy Bureau of Aeronautics on mission involving jet propelled aircraft '43, sent to Germany US Navy Bureau ships to investigate enemy technical developments '45. Author articles in field. Mgr gas turbine div Allis-Chalmers '42-45; dir dept mech engring Ill Inst Tech '45-48, dean engring '48-50, vice pres '50-52, pres since '52, also president Armour Research Found of Ill Inst Tech and Inst Gas Tech. ASME (chmn gas turbine power div '48, spl gas turbine award '52, vp '50-52) American Society Naval Engrs—AAAS(F)—ASEE (adm council exec com)—Western Soc Engrs—Sigma Xi—Tau Beta Pi. Received jr award ASME '41, Pi Tau Sigma Gold Medal award '42; certificate of commendation US Navy World War II. 3300 S. Federal St., Chicago 16.†

17 RETTEW, Granville Raymond. Cultivated mushrooms; Penicillin production. b'03. Student '22-23 (U Del); '23-26 (Swarthmore Coll); '26-27 (U Pa); '35-36 (Phila Sch Pharmacy Sci). Patents on improved methods of production of mushroom spawn; developed methods of production and purification of penicillin. Author: Manual of Mushroom Culture '48. Dir penicillin prodn Wyeth Inc West Chester Pa since '42. Am Chem Soc—Soc Am Bact—Inst Food Technol—Am Phytopath Soc—NY Acad Sci—Torrey Bot Club—AAAS(F). Presented scroll by the Cultivated Mushroom Inst Am '44. Wyeth, Inc., West Chester, Pa.

18 RETTGER, Theodore Levin. Cotton linters. b'98. Student '24-25 (Ga Inst Tech). Invented lint brushing machine; developed quantitative analysis of lint on cottonseed. Author articles in field. Chem DuPont Co '16-19, So Cotton Oil Co '19-24; div chem Buckeye Cotton Oil Co since '24. Am Chem Soc—Am Oil Chem Soc (winner Smalley Found cup '42-43). Buckeye Cotton Oil Co., Chelsea Av., Memphis.

19 RETZER, John Leonard. Soil surveying; Aerial photography. b'10. BS '34 (U Ill); MS '40 (Ia State Coll); '32 (Blackburn Coll): PhD '50 (U Wis). Spl assignment during war Guayule Rubber Project in charge of soil investigations to select and classify land suitable for guayule culture; research on relation of soils and physical landscape factors to forest, range, and watershed management problems in mountainous areas, geology, geomorphology in relation to land management, aerial photography. Soil Sci Rocky Mt Forest and Range Exptl Sta since '45. Soil Sci Soc Am—Western Soc Soil Sci—Am Soc Agron—Ecol Soc Am—AAAS. Rocky Mountain Forest and Range Experiment Station, Ft. Collins, Colo.

20 REUSZER, Herbert William. Soil microbiology. b'03. BS '25 (U Mo); MS '30—PhD '32 (Rutgers U). Author articles in field. Asso bact Colo Agr Expt Sta '33-40; soil scientist Soil Conservation Service US Dept Agr '40-47; asso microbiol Purdue U Agrl Expt

Sta since '47. AAAS—Biochem Soc—Soc Am Bact—Am Soc Agron—Soil Sci Soc Am (sec '42, chmn soil microbiol sect '43)—Sigma Xi. Purdue University Agricultural Experiment Station, Lafayette, Ind.†

21 REUTHER, Walter. Sub-tropical horticulture; Plants (Mineral nutrition, irrigation, water relations). b'11. BS '33 (U Fla); PhD '40 (Cornell U). Research on trace elements in mineral nutrition of citrus and tung, isolated and described manganese deficiency symptoms in field for citrus tung and certain ornamentals, role of potassium in fertilization of deciduous fruits in NY State, relation of manganese deficiency to photosynthetic activity of tung leaves, relation of irrigation practice to production dates and citrus in desert regions, pollination of dates, citrus chlorosis in desert soils, relation of temperature to fruit set of dates. Author articles in field. Asso plant physiologist US Dept Agr '41; sr horticulturist in charge US Date Gardens Indio Calif '41-46; prin horticulturist USDA Horticultural Field Sta Orlando Fla since '46, supervise research, mineral nutrition and soil fertility investigations of citrus and other subtropical fruit plants. AAAS—Soil Sci Soc Am—Am Soc Hort Sci (chmn ed com)—Am Soc Plant Physiol—Am Geophys Union—Fla State Hort Soc—Soil Sci Soc Fla—Date Grower's Inst—Sigma Xi. U.S. D.A. Horticultural Field Station, 2300 Camden Rd., Orlando, Fla.

22 REY, Agapito. Medieval Spanish literature; Spanish exploration and colonization of the southwestern United States. b'92. BS '21—MA '22 (U Mich); PhD '29 (U Wis). Author: (with G P Hammond) The Rodriguez Relation of the Chamuscado Expedition '27; also articles in field. Prof Spanish Ind U since '44. Modern Lang Assn Am—Am Folklore Soc—Sociedad Folklorica de Mexico. Indiana University, Bloomington, Inc.◎

23 REYERSON, Lloyd Hilton. Colloid chemistry adsorption; Catalysis; Gasification of solid fuels; Isotopic exchange reactions; Cellulosic materials (Chemical preparation). b'93. AB '15 (Carleton Coll); AM '17 (U Ill); PhD '20 (Johns Hopkins U). Member Colloid Committee National Research Council; US delegate to International Union of Pure and Applied Chemistry Warsaw Poland '27, The Hague, The Netherlands '28; scientific consultant Royal Norwegian government summer '46. Author articles in field. Prof chem U Minn since '30, dir Northwest Research Inst since '34, asst dean since '45. Served as 2d lt Chem Warfare Service '18-19. AAAS(F)—Am Chem Soc—Am Phys Soc—Minn Acad Sci—Sigma Xi—Phi Beta Kappa. 2280 Folwell St., St. Paul 8.◎

24 REYNOLDS, Blake. Internal combustion engines; Fuel injection; Auxiliary power plants (Aircraft); Controls (Engine). b'14. BA '36 (Wesleyan U); MS '38 (MIT). Engaged in the development of the "Texaco Combustion Process" for reciprocating engines. Author articles: The Charging Process in a High-Speed, Single-Cylinder, Four-Stroke Engine (with H Schecter, E S Taylor) '39. Test engr Lawrance Aeronautical Corp Linden NJ '40-41, project engr '41, chief exptl engr '41, exec engr '42-45; tech asst Texaco Development Corp since '45. Inst Aeronautical Sci—SAE—Sigma Xi—Phi Beta Kappa. Texaco Development Corp., 135 E. 42nd St., NYC 17.

25 REYNOLDS, Bruce Dodson. Protozoology; Parasitology. b'94. BS '20 (U Va); '20-21 (U Ia); DSc '23—research fellow '21-23 (Johns Hopkins). Author articles in field. Prof biol U Va since

'38, organized Blandy Exptl Farm and chmn com since '27; dir Mountain Lake Biol Sta '30-33 and since '46. AAAS(F) —Am Soc Zool—Am Soc Parasitol— Assn Southeastern Biol—Va Acad Sci —Sigma Xi. Biology Building, University of Virginia, Charlottesville, Va.⊙

10 REYNOLDS, Harold Culvin. Mammalogy (Life history and ecology of opossum). b'17. BS '39 (Drury Coll); MA '42 (U Mo); '46-47 (U Calif). Research on habits of opossum in the wild, rearing opossums for laboratory experimentation, growth of young opossums, physiological problems relating to the ecology of the opossum, development of the skeleton of the opossum. Edward K Love research fellow U Mo ecology of opossum in central Missouri '40-42; asst curator zoology U Neb State Mus '43-45; lecturer zool, asst curator mammals U Calif since '46. Am Soc Mammalogists—Wildlife Soc— West Soc Naturalists—Am Ornithol Union—Cooper Ornithol Club. Museum of Vertebrate Zoology, University of California, Berkeley.†

11 REYNOLDS, Horace (Mason). Anglo-Irish literature (Yeats); American folksongs, riverways and language. b'96. AB '19—AM '23—'31-34 (Harvard). Discovered and edited Yeats's Letters to the New Island '34. Author: A Providence Episode in the Irish Literary Renaissance '29; also articles in field. Teacher eng Brown, Harvard etc '19-42; free lance writer since '43. 322 Harvard St., Cambridge, Mass.

12 REYNOLDS, Ralph Arthur. Public health in Soviet Russia and England. b'94. AB '21—MD '25 (U Calif); Zeugnis and Gold Key '29 (U Vienna Med Sch). Studied health program and health facilities in Soviet Russia by invitation Minister of Health Soviet Russia '29, '36, '38; studied England's National Health Act '49. Author: American Medicine (Voks), Moscow, USSR '29; also articles in field. San Francisco Co Med Soc—Calif State Med Assn—AMA—AMA Vienna (pres '28-29)—Am Pub Health Assn—Assn Study Internal Secretions—Calif Heart Assn. 490 Post St., San Francisco.

13 REYNOLDS, Stephen Edward. Thunderstorms. b'16. BS '39 (U NM). Co-author: (with E J Workman) A Suggested Mechanism for the Generation of Thunderstorm Electricity '48; Electrical Activity as Related to Thunderstorm Cell Growth '48; Electrical Charge Separation Produced by Rapid Freezing of Rainwater '48; Electrical Phenomena Resulting from the Freezing of Dilute Aqueous Solutions '48; also other articles in field. Process engr Phillips Pet Co '39-42; asst prof mech engring U NM '42-43; thunderstorm project supervisor research development div NM Sch Mines since '46. Am Phys Soc—Am Meteorol Soc—Nat Soc Profl Engrs. New Mexico Institute of Technology, Box 52, Campus Station, Socorro, N.M.†

14 REZNECK, Samuel. American economic history; American depressions; Samuel A Law. b'97. AB '19— AM '21—PhD '25 (Harvard); Sheldon Travelling Fellowship '19-20 (Harvard). Author articles: The Depression of 1819-22 '33; Panic of 1819 '40; The Social History of an American Depression 1837 '35; The Influence of Depression Upon American Opinion, 1857-59 '42; The Rise and Early Development of Industrial Consciousness in the United States '32; Mass Production Since the Civil War '44; Coal and Oil in the American Economy in the Tasks of Economic History '47; Outline of Economic History '41; Samuel A Law, Entrepreneur '33. Prof hist Rensselaer Poly Inst Troy NY since '25. AHA—

Econ Hist Assn. Rensselaer Polytechnic Institute, Troy, N.Y.

15 RHOADES, Rendell. Crayfishes; Picture post cards. b'14. BSc '36 (Wilmington Coll); MSc '37—'38-39—'43-44 (O State U). Research on medieval crayfish literature, papers describe 17 new species and subspecies, collected about 100,000 specimens many of which are in US National Museum; developed systematic classification of post cards based upon printers and serial numbers and suggested the name "deltiology" for the collecting and study of picture post cards. Author articles in field. Biol on Goss-King-Scott Tierra del Fuegan Expdn '53. Curator of Collections, Cleveland Museum Natural Hist., Cleve.

16 RHOADS, Arthur Stevens. Diseases of woody plants (Forest and deciduous fruit trees, grapes, citrus); Wood decay and preservation; Wood-rotting fungi; Marine borers. b'93. BS '14—MS '15 (Pa State Coll); PhD '17 (NY State Coll Forestry). Author articles in field. Plant path since '30. Am Phytopath Soc—Mycol Soc Am—Sigma Xi. Mycology and Disease Survey, Plant Industry Station, Beltsville, Md. H: 29 West 21 St., Jacksonville 6, Fla.†

17 RHOADS, Cornelius Packard. Research administration; Public health; Institution management; Disaster relief; Atomic bomb (Casualty administration). b'98. AB '20—DSc hon '44 (Bowdoin Coll); MD cum laude '24 (Harvard). Special consultant US Public Health Service, National Advisory Cancer Council since '47; consultant medical division Chemical Corps, Army Chemical Center Md '48-50; mem disaster relief advisory committee Am Red Cross; mem sub com on blood substitutes National Research Council '40-42, com on war gas casualties '41-43, on veterans medical problems '45-47, chmn com on growth '45-48 (exec com '46-47), on atomic bomb casualties '46, advisory com of chem biol coordination center '46-47, mem at large div med sciences '46-49. Asso Rockefeller Inst for Med Resch '28-33, asso mem in charge service for study hematologic disorders '33-39, pathologist hosp '31-39; dir Memorial Center for Cancer and Allied Diseases NYC '50-52, sci dir since '53; Memorial Hosp for Treatment Cancer and Allied Diseases NYC '40-50; dir The Sloan-Kettering Inst for Cancer Research since '45; mem med bd James Ewing Hosp since '50; prof path dept Cornell U Med College '40-52, dept biology and growth, Sloan-Kettering Div, since '52. Mem com to visit Dept Chemistry, Harvard; trustee Charles F Kettering Found since '51. Am Coll Physicians (F)—NY Acad Med(F, mem com pub health Relations '42-43, vp '43-45, com on hon fellowship since '52)—Am Cancer Soc (bd dirs '41-46, exec com '44-46)—Blood Transfusion Assn (med bd '40-50)—Harvey Soc—Soc Exptl Biol and Med—Soc Med Jurisprudence—Am Assn Path and Bact—AAAS—Am Assn Cancer Research—Am Indsl Hygiene Assn—AMA—Am Radium Soc—Am Soc Clin Investigation—Am Soc Exptl Path —Assn Am Physicians—Med Soc Co NY (spl com on cancer control)— NY Acad Scis—Interurban Path Club —Interurban Clin Club. Col MC AUS, chief med div CWS '43-45. Memorial Hospital for Cancer and Allied Diseases, 444 E. 68th St., NYC 21.⊙

18 RHOADS, Philip Garrett. Mechanical engineering (Leather belting). b'02. BS '24 (Haverford Coll); BS '27 (MIT). Author articles in field. With J E Rhoads & Sons since '27, factory mgr since '37. Am Leather Belting Assn (engr com)—ASME. Box 71, Wilmington, Del.†

19 RHODE, Robert David. American local color fiction; American poetry. b'11. BA '33—MA '35—PhD '40 (U Tex). Author articles in field. Prof English and dir div grad studies Tex Coll Arts and Industries since '51. Tex Conf Coll Tchrs Eng—Border Poets Tex (pres since '45). Texas Coll of Arts and Industries, Kingsville, Tex.†

20 RHODES, Arnold Densmore. Forest ecology; Silviculture; Dendrology. b'12. BS '34 (U NH); MF '37 (Yale). With U Mass since '39, prof dendrology forest ecol silviculture and forest soils since '47. Soc Am Foresters—Bot Soc Am—Ecol Soc Am—British Ecol Soc. Forestry Department, University of Massachusetts, Amherst, Mass.†

21 RHODES, Benjamin Franklin, Jr. Irrigation history in California. b'14. BA '35 (Harding Coll); MA '37 (Peabody Coll); PhD '43 (U Calif). Research on The Modesto Irrigation District. Prof hist head dept social sci Harding Coll '43-50; asso prof dept social sci Abilene Christian College since '50. AHA—Miss Valley Historical Assn. Abilene Christian College, Abilene, Texas.

22 RHODES, Fred H(offman). Chemical engineering (Coal tar products); Chemical plant design. b'89. AB '10 (Wabash Coll); PhD '14 (Cornell). Holder of several patents covering improvements refining coal tar products. Author: Elements of Patent Law '49; Technical Report Writing '41. Dir research chem dept, Barret Co, mfrs coal tar products, Frankford, Pa, '17-20; prof indsl chemistry, Cornell U, '20, now dir Sch Chem Engring and Herbert Fisk Johnson prof indsl chem; mem bd of review, cons ed Paint and Varnish Production Manager Record; dir Gen Aniline & Film Corp. Am Chem Soc—Am Inst Chem Engrs—Soc Promotion Engring Edn—Phi Beta Kappa—Sigma Xi—Tau Beta Pi—Phi Kappa Phi. Bellayre Apts, Ithaca.⊙

23 RHODES, Willard. Indian music (Sioux, Navajo). b'01. AB—BMus '22 (Heidelberg Coll); diploma music (Wittenberg Coll); MA '25 (Columbia); (David Mannes Music Sch, Ecole Normale de Musique Paris). Research and field trips in the collecting of North American Indian music since '39. Author: La Opera en Los Estados Unidos '41; On the War Path '42; Music of the Sioux and Navajo. Conductor and chorus master Am Opera Co '27-30; asst conductor Cincinnati Summer Opera Co '28-33; producer-dir Rhodes Chamber Opera Co '32-35; concert pianist and accompanist '30-35; dir music Bronxville Pub Schs NY '35-37; asso to asst prof music Columbia since '37, dir Opera Workshop since '44; edn specialist US Office Indian Affairs since '38. Am Musicol Soc—Am Anthropol Assn—Am Ethnol Soc—Am Folklore Soc—Music Library Assn—ALA NY Fed Music Clubs (opera chmn). Department of Music, Columbia University, NYC 27.

24 RHYNE, Charles Sylvanus. Aviation (Law); Unionization of governmental employees. b'12. Student '28-29, '32-34 (Duke U)—'34-35 (Duke U Law Sch); LLB '37 (George Washington U Law Sch). Author: Civil Aeronautics Act Annotated '38; Airports and the Courts '44; Labor Unions and Municipal Employee Law '46; Aviation Accident Law '47; Cases on Aviation Law '50. Counsel many court cases. Special lecturer aviation law George Washington U Law Sch; counsel Nat Inst Municipal Law Officers. Am Bar Assn (chmn com on aero law '46-48, chmn sect Internat and Comparative Law '48-49)—Nat Aeronautics Assn (bd dirs '45-48)—Aero Club Washington (chmn aviation planning com). 730 Jackson Pl., N.W., Washington 6.⊚

10 RICE, Arthur Henry. Public relations (School). b'00. Teachers Certificate '25—AB '26 (Central State Teachers Coll Mt Pleasant Mich); MA '34—PhD '47 (U Mich); LLD hon '50 (Central Mich Coll Edn). Co-editor: Today's Techniques—Successful Practices in School Public Relations; Ninety Guides to Better Public Relations; Public Relations for Rural and Village Teachers; also articles in field. Mng ed Mich Edn Jour '29-34, ed '34-37; dir publicity pub relations Mich Edn Assn '37-47; mng ed Nation's Schs since '47. Ednl Press Assn Am (pres, vp)—NEA—Am Assn Sch Adminstrs—Sch Pub Relations Assn—Am Ednl Research Assn—Am Assn Adult Edn—AAAS—Am Acad Polit Social Sci—Phi Kappa Phi and others. Received Burke Aaron Hinsdale Scholar award U Mich '45-46. The Nation's Schools, 919 N. Michigan Av., Chgo 11.

11 RICE, Harvey Mitchell. History of the United States; Aerial and Celestial navigation. b'07. AB '29 (Concord State Coll W Va); MA '33 (W Va U); PhD '38 (O State U). Author: Life of Jonathan M Bennett: A Study of the Virginias in Transition '43; Study Outline History of the US, 1492-1865 '45, 1865-1947 '47. Prof hist NY State Coll Teachers Albany '43-47; pres Oswego State Tchrs Coll '45-51; pres NY State Coll for Tchrs Buffalo since '51. Served head adminstrn br Spl Devices Div Office Research Invention Exec Office Sec Navy '45-46. AHA—NY State Hist Assn—NY State Tchrs Assn—Special Devices Assn. N.Y State College for Teachers, Buffalo 22, N.Y. H: 1320 Elmwood Av., Buffalo 22.

12 RICE, Heber Holbrook. Government claims; Litigation. b'82. BS '04 (U Ky); LLB '07 (Harvard); LLD '44 (Athens Coll). Organizer of legal, civic and patriotic bodies; successfully defended the governor in martial law litigation while practicing law in Huntington West Virginia; defended government suits in Court of Claims, US District Courts and Supreme Court while special assistant to US Attorney General; supervised 150,000 land law suits and procedings in all 48 states while attorney with HOLC Washington. Author: Collected Speeches '47; US Land Litigation Map Charts '38; also articles in field. On gen counsel staff comptroller gen office Washington since '44. Lt col judge advocate gen Dept Res War Dept World War II '40-42; asst chief legal div office Chief Chem Warfare Washington '42; staff judge advocate and chief legal div Huntsville Ala Arsenal '42-43; inactive status since '43, promoted to col Inactive Res '45. Am Law Inst—Am Soc Internat Law—Inter Am Bar Assn (del to Havana conf '41)—Am Bar Assn (chmn com pvt claims, former chmn com comparative land laws, mem house delegates '48)—Fed Bar Assn (chmn adm com, past nat president)—UN League of Lawyers (hon pres, original sec gen '46)—and others. General Accounting Office, 5th and F Sts., N.W., Washington. H: 5 Taylor St., Chevy Chase, Md.⊚

13 RICE, John Winter. Bacteriology (Paper food containers and closures, counter contamination of meat and meat products). b'91. BS '14—MS '15 (Bucknell U); PhD '22 (Columbia). Special investigator on bacteriology of paper milk containers NY State Agricultural Experimental Station at Geneva summers '38 and '39; for Pennsylvania Association of Dairy Sanitarians '32-39. With Bucknell U since '16, prof bact since '24, chmn dept biol '39-42 and since '44; cons bact Geisinger

Memorial Hosp; pres Lewisburg Bd Health '24-48; pres Milk Control Dist 4 Pa since '27; pres Pa Assn Dairy and Milk Insps '27-28; chmn com Pa Dept Health '31; chmn Union Co Nutrition Council '42-43. Served as 2d lt San Corps US Army during World War I. Am Pub Health Assn—Am Social Hygiene Assn—AAAS—Soc Am Bact (pres Central Pa Br '35-36). 610 St. George St., Lewisburg, Pa.⊚

14 RICE, Theodore D(avenport). Education (Curricula). b'04. AB '27—MA '32 (U Denver); PhD '43 (Northwestern); '36 (Colo State Coll Edn); '37 (Ohio State U). Member Oklahoma State Commission on Teacher Education and Certification '46-47; coordinator, professional staff Governor's Fact-Finding Commission on Education Connecticut '49-50. Co-author: (with J C Parker and J W Menge) First Five Years of the Michigan Secondary School Study '42. Editor series: Leads to Better Secondary Schools in Michigan, 44-45. Chmn social studies curriculum com Denver Pub Schs '32-37, chmn planning com '36-39, supervising tchr '37-39; faculty Northwestern '39-41; cons Mich Secondary Curriculum Study '41-43, dir '43-45; dir instruction Okla City Pub Schs '45-47; prof edn Okla A&M Coll '45-47; prof edn NYU since '47, asso and dir Center for Field Services '48-51. Assn Supervision and Curriculum Development—Nat and Secondary Prin Assn—Nat and State Edn Assn. School of Education, New York University, NY C 3.

15 RICH, George R. Hydroelectric engineering. b'96. BS in civil engring '9—DEng hon '48 (Worcester Poly Inst). Research and design hydraulic and hydroelectric projects on Tennessee Valley Authority to '45. Author: Hydraulic Transients '51. Contributor: Handbook of Hydraulics '52. Structural engr Jackson & Moreland '28-29; hydraulic engr Stone & Webster Engring Corp '29-31; hydraulic engr US Army Corps Engrs '31-37; chief design engr TVA '37-45; partner Charles T Main Inc since '45. Am Soc CE—ASME—Am Math Soc—Sigma Xi—Tau Beta Pi. Charles T. Main, Inc., 80 Federal St., Boston 10.⊚

16 RICH, J(oseph) Harry. Wood utilization and technology. b'88. BS '13—MF '37 (NY State Coll Forestry); '41 (U Wis). Research in veneer production yields and pulp wood production, proper uses of wood especially in field of seasoning, adhesives, and fabrication. Engaged in mfr and distribution of forest products '17-33; staff U Mass since '33. With Army Air Forces in field of wood tech '42-45. Soc Am Foresters—Tech Assn Pulp Paper Inst—Forest Products Research Soc—Sigma Xi. Conservation Bldg., University of Massachusetts, Amherst, Mass.†

17 RICH, Lorimer. Architecture (Schools, colleges, memorials). b'91. BArch—DFA hon '40 (Syracuse U); study '21 '22 (Am Acad in Rome). Architect Tomb of Unknown Soldier Arlington National Cemetery (winner nation-wide competition), also approaches to Tomb and Amphitheatre; improvement Herald Square NYC (winner competition); spclizng school buildings, colleges and memorials. Critic in design, sch architecture Columbia; critic in archtl and city planning Pratt Inst since '44; cons architect US Treasury Dept; mem board archtl examiners NY State. AIA(F, chairman competition com)—Architectural League NY—Municipal Art Soc—Cosmos Club. 215 Montague St., Brooklyn.†⊚

18 RICH, Raymond Thomas. Public relations and opinion; Community relations; American foundations, nonprofit organizations and educational institutions; Medical economics. b'99. Student Phillips Acad Andover Mass '17; Amherst '17-19; AB '22 (Brown U). Dir World Peace Found '27-36; chmn Raymond Rich Asso counselors public relations mgmt ednl promotion for pub interest orgns found since '36; chief Div Organized Groups US Office Facts and Figures '42; prin civilian mobilization adv US OCD '42-43; with Office Coordinator Inter-Am Affairs '42-44 as dir Inter-Am Centers in US; asso dir dept US activities and spl services; dir Council for Inter-Am Cooperation Inc '44-46; pub affairs asso for Twentieth Century Fund '36-40; spl cons Am Council Edn, Am Law Inst, Nat Information Bur, Colo State Med Soc, Lingnan U, Colo Sch Mines, Am Pub Health Assn and others. Council Fgn Relations—Pub Relations Assn Am—Phi Beta Kappa. 860 Broadway, NYC.†

19 RICH, Saul. Fungicides; Virus diseases of leguminous plants. b'17. BS '38—MS '39 (Calif U); PhD '42 (Ore State Coll). Research on sweet clover ring spot, mosaic viri of celery, yellow bean, pea, alfalfa, antisporulants, methods of assaying pesticides, natures and origins of viri. Author articles: A Rapid Stain Method for Detecting Certain Plant Virus Inclusions '48; The Chemical Nature and Origin of Phaseolus Virus 2 Crystalline Inclusions '48; Progress in Fungicides '48; also other articles in field. Research asst plant pathology Ore State Coll '39-42; asso plant path Wyo Agrl Expt Sta '50. Conn Agrl Expt Station since '47. Sigma Xi—Am Phytopathalog Soc. Connecticut Agricultural Experiment Station, P.O. Box 1106, New Haven.†

20 RICH, Stephen Gottheil. Philately (Polish, South African); United States telegraph stamps. b'90. BS '14—PhD '23 (NYU); MA '15 (Cornell). Chairman mounting and demounting Centenary International Philatelic Exhibition NY '47. Author: Philately of the Anglo-Boer War 1899-1902 '42; A Highway into Stamp Collecting '23. Co-author: US Telegraph Issues '47; Poland. The Stampless Period '42; Poland to 1870 '43. Publisher: Bureau Print Catalog '33-53; The Precancel Bee '33-41; Postal Markings '33-37; Handbook of US Postage Meters '38-45; Canada and Newfoundland Stampless Cover Catalog '46; also articles in field. Pub philatelic books & jour since '33. Assn Stamp Exhbn (dir '31-47)—Soc Philatelic Am (sec '39-40, treas '44-48, '50-53)—Collectors Club NY (bd govs '51-53)—Essay-Proof Soc (sec '43-48)—Phi Beta Kappa. P.O. Box B, Verona, N.J.

21 RICHARDS, A(lbert) Glenn. Physiology and cuticle of insects: Electron microscopy (Biological application). b'09. BA '29 (U Ga); PhD '32 (Cornell U). Research on taxonomy of moths, descriptive and experimental embryology, insecticide action and histopathology of insects, permeability insect cuticle, electron microscope studies of cuticle structure, mosquito control. Author articles: Electron Microscope Studies Insect Cuticle '42; Correlation Chitinous Cuticle and DDT Action '45; Studies on Arthropod Cuticle I-X '47-53; The Integument of Arthropods '51; also many others in field. Biologist Nassau County Mosquito extermination com summer '37; instr biology CCNY '37-39; instr zoology U Pa '39-44, asst prof '44-45; investigator physiology insecticide action com med research Office Scientific Research & Develop '42-45; asso prof insect physiology U Minn '45-49, prof since '49.

Soc Gen Physiol—Am Soc Zoologists— Am Entomol Soc—Entomol Soc Am— NY Entomol Soc—Marine Biol Lab— Electron Microscope Soc Am—Sigma Xi. Department of Entomology, University of Minnesota, St. Paul 1.

10 RICHARDS, Alfred Newton. Kidneys (Function, physiology); Histamine (Effects on circulatory system). b'76. AB '97—MA '99 (Yale); PhD '01 (Columbia). With H H Dale demonstrated capillary action of histamine '18; with Plant showed dominating influence of renal blood pressure on urine formation '16-24; with Schmidt '20-24 demonstrated accessibility of circulation in amphibian kidney to direct microscopic study during life; with Wearn '21-22 collected fluid from glomerulus and showed qualitative identity with plasma filtrate; with succession of collaborators developed refined methods for collection fluid from different parts of amphibian nephron and ultramicromethods for their quantitative analysis providing evidence in support of the filtration reabsorption concept of kidney function; utilized insulin clearance as measure of glomerular filtration in mammals; by study of action of mercury on frog's kidney contributed to understanding of toxic anuria. Prof pharm Northwestern U '08-10; prof pharm U Pa '10-26, vp in charge med affairs '39-48; chmn com med research Office Sci Research and Development '41-46; mem com on fed med services Hoover Commn '48. Nat Acad Sci(pres '47-50)—Royal Soc London (foreign) —Royal Soc Edinburgh(fgn)—Royal Danish Acad Sci—NY Acad Med(hon F')—Phila Coll Physicians (hon F)— Brit Med Assn(hon fgn)—Am Assn Physicians—Am Physiol Soc—Brit Physiol Soc—Am Soc Biol Chem—Am Pharm Soc—Soc Exptl Biol and Med —Harvey Soc—Am Urological Soc— Royal Soc Med—AAAS(F)—Am Acad Arts and Sci(F)—Sigma Xi—Phi Beta Kappa—Alpha Omega Alpha. University of Pennsylvania, Phila 4.☺

11 RICHARDS, Cyril Fuller. American higher education (Function of independent college of liberal arts). b'94. BS '18—LHD hon '47 (Linfield Coll McMinnville Ore); BD '24 (Colgate-Rochester Theol Sem); AM '35 (U Manitoba). Author: Denison—A Small College Studies Its Program. Prof philosophy Brandon Coll Manitoba Can '24-37, coll dean '35-37; dean of men Denison U Granville O '37-42, dean of coll since '43. Am Conf Acad Deans—Am Psychol Assn—Omicron Delta Kappa. Denison University, Granville, O.☺

12 RICHARDS, Dorothy Burney. Beavers. b'94. Ed pub sch. Extensive study of beavers since '41 through observation in natural habitat; in '43 was issued first permit given by New York State Conservation Department to keep beavers in captivity; kept beavers in own home in order to study more closely their lives and habits; discovered that many accepted facts concerning their habits are untrue. Author articles in field and has been subject of many published articles, particularly in book The Lost Woods (Edwin Way Teale). Defenders of Furbearers (Dir '49). Beaversprite Sanctuary, R.D. 1, Dolgeville, N.Y.

13 RICHARDS, Hans Kohn. Nucleonics; Radioactivity; Electronics: Quartz crystals. b'02. PhD '30 (U Hamburg). Research on interaction of nuclear radiation with matter; radioactivity short waves, FM dimensioning of quartz crystals; design electrometers and instrumentation for nucleonics; shortwave equipment for dielectric

heating, quartz crystals for industrial application; shortwave and FM equipment; equipment for solution of radon in fluids. Patents on crystal controlled FM and thermostatic controlled quartz crystals. Author: Radioactivity, Nucleonics, Electronics. Chief rsrch engineer Russel Elec Chgo '45-47; sr engr Motorola Chgo '47-49; principal physicist Oak Ridge Nat Lab since '49. Health Physics Div., Oak Ridge National Laboratory, Oak Ridge, Tenn.

14 RICHARDS, Horace G(ardiner). Paleontology (Pleistocene, Tertiary); History of New Jersey. b'06. AB '27— MS '29—PhD '32 (U Pa). Expeditions to Mexico and Central America, Arctic Canada, Caribbean Islands, Venezuela. Author: Animals of the Seashore '38; Record of the Rocks '53; also articles. Staff Acad Nat Sci Phila since '40; lecturer geology Univ Pa since '49. Assn Geol Tchrs—AAAS—Am Assn Pet Geol (co-chmn com correlation)—Am Malacol Union—Geol Soc Am(F)—Pa Acad Sci—Arctic Inst—Paleontology Society—N J Folklore Soc—Sigma Xi. Received president's award from Am Assn Pet Geol for work on geol of Atlantic Coastal Plain '45. Academy of Natural Sciences, 19th & Parkway, Phila 3.†

15 RICHARDS, Lorenzo Adolph. Physics (Soil moisture); Electrical control circuits. b'04. BS '26—MA '27 (Utah Coll); PhD '31 (Cornell); Nat Defense Research fellow '42-45 (Calif Inst Tech). Research on electric control circuits, measurement and control soil moisture, rocket launchers. Holds patents in field. Editor: Diagnosis and improvement of Saline and Alkali Soils '47; author articles in field. With USDA since '39, prin soil physicist US Salinity Labs since '45. Am Society Agron—Soil Sci Soc Am—Am Geophys Union—Sigma Xi—Phi Kappa Phi. Awarded Presidential Certificate Merit for work Calif Inst Tech '42-45. U.S. Salinity Laboratories, Riverside, Cal.†

16 RICHARDS, Oscar W(hite). Biology; Microscopy; Growth of organisms (Yeast, Mytilus); Pedagogy of biology; Biomathematics: Cinephotomicrography. b'02. BA '23—MA '25 (U Ore); Ralph Sanger scholar '26-27 (Harvard); PhD '31 (Yale). Research on effect of changing environment on yeast population growth, transformed coordinate analysis of growth, flourscence, phase microscopy. Author: Exploring the World With the Microscope '37; Formulae and Methods '36; Effective Use and Proper Care of the Microscope '41; also articles in field. Research supervisor biology Am Optical Co since '50. Am Zool Soc—Soc Exptl Biology—Biol Photog Assn (dir '33-47, vp '47-49, pres '49-51)—Am Micros Soc (vp '46-47)—Am Physiol Soc—Am Assn Anat—Am Statis Assn—Am Stand Assn (chmn sub-com photog). Rsrch Laboratory, American Optical Co, Research Center, Southbridge, Mass.

17 RICHARDS, Richard K(ohn). Pharmacology; Anesthetic and circulatory drugs; Anticonvulsants; Blood coagulation; Toxicology. b'04. MD '31 (U Hamburg); student (U Berlin); vis fellow '35 (U Amsterdam); research fellow physiology '35-36 (Michael Reese Hosp Chicago). Discoverer of anticonvulsive action of Tridione, only presently known effective drug treatment of certain forms of epilepsy '43; first to describe the occurrence of competitive inhibition as mode of action of certain drug on brain '46. Author articles in field. Pharmacologist Abbott Labs North Chicago Ill '36, dir pharmacologic research since '44; spl lecturer and faculty mem Northwestern U Med Sch Chicago since '46. ACP(F)—International Coll Anesthetists(F)—AMA(F)—

Am Pharmacol Soc—Am Physiol Soc— Am Soc Anesthesiologists—Am Soc Exptl Biol Med—Central Soc Clin Research—Swiss Soc Physiologists and Pharmacologists (fgn mem). Abbott Laboratories, North Chicago, Ill.

18 RICHARDSON, Chester Northup. Mercury cathode electrolytic cells. b'95. BS '16 (MIT). Research and Pilot-plant work on development of Matheson stationary cell, mercury-cell processes for making sodium sulfide, hydrogen peroxide and sodium alcoholates, processes for making dichlorstyrene ditolylethane, ethylbenzene and hydrazine, high-tension electric discharge processes for hydrogen peroxide, high pressure ammonia synthesis, developed method making NH_3 catalysts. Research engr Matheson Chem Corp Niagara Falls '24-38, supt pilot plants '38-45, mgr research engring '45-48; cons since '48. Electrochem Soc—AIEE—NY State Soc Profl Engrs. R.F.D. 1, Youngstown, N.Y.

19 RICHARDSON, Edgar Preston. American paintings. b'02. Student '25 (Williams Coll, Pennsylvania Acad Fine Arts). Author: Washington Allston '48; American Romantic Painting '44; The Way of Western Art 1776-1914 '39; also articles in field. Dir Detroit Inst Arts since '45; ed Art Quarterly since '38. The Detroit Institute of Arts, Detroit 2.†☺

20 RICHARDSON, Eugene Stanley, Jr. Invertebrate paleontology. b'16. AB '38 (Williams Coll); MS '42 (Pa State Coll). Author articles in field. Instr geol Bryn Mawr Coll '44-46; curator invertebrate fossils Chicago Nat Hist Mus since '46. Paleontol Soc— Pa Acad Sci—Soc Study Evolution— Ill Acad Sci—Sigma Xi. Chicago Natural History Museum, Chicago 5.

21 RICHARDSON, Frank Edison. Pipe lines (Gas transportation, oil transportation, petroleum products transportation). b'91. Student '08-11 (O Wesleyan U). Author papers on hydraulics and construction practices of pipe lines. Chief engr Gt Lakes Pipe Line Co '30-41; mgr Pan Am Pipe Line '41-45; cons engr since '45. Am Soc CE. P.O. Box 1612, Shreveport, La.

22 RICHARDSON, George Arthur. Milk (properties). b'93. BSc in agr '20 (U Toronto Ont Can); MS '25— PhD '27 (U Minn). Tests of food value of milk from standpoint of nutrient energy, quality of milk and milk products, and value of carotene as a butter color; studies on variation in composition of milk, including natural variations and those due to environment and disease; research on rennin coagulation and foaming properties of milk. Co-author articles: Vitamin A in Butter; Composition of Milk, Effect of Environmental Temperature and Effect of Breed, and others. Faculty U Cal '26-48, asso prof dairy industry and asso dairy chem '36-48; prof dairy husbandry and dairy chem Ore State Coll since '48. ACS—Am Dairy Sci Assn—Inst Food Tech—AAAS—Ore Acad Sci—Phi Lambda Upsilon—Sigma Xi—Alpha Zeta. Borden award in dairy chem '50. Oregon State College, Corvallis, Ore.

23 RICHARDSON, George Oliver. Synthetic organic detergents. b'92. B textile chem and dyeing '16 (Lowell Textile Inst). With Nat Aniline Div Allied Chem and Dye Corp since '18, mgr spl products div since '35. Am Chem Soc. Special Products Department, National Aniline Division, Allied Chemical and Dye Corporation, NYC 6.

24 RICHARDSON, Howard Lockhart. Pathology (Anatomical, clinical);

Cancer research; Forensic science. b'15. BS '36 (Coll of Puget Sound); MA in biochem '40—MD '40 (U Ore). Studies in cell cytology, morphological aspects of a cancer cell in various sites of the body, studies in animal experimental pathology, relating to the formation of tumors by use of carcinogenic agents; cytological application to the study of liver cell change, anticarcinogenic study of carcinogens, and inhibitory action of such carcinogens on the induction of liver tumors. With U Ore Med Sch since '46, asst prof path since '48, dir crime lab '46-51. Asst chief lab service US Army Barnes Hosp '41, chief lab service 166th Station Hosp '42-44, med lab officer overseas '44-45. Am Soc Clin Path (counselor Ore '50-51)—Am Coll Path—AMA—Am Assn Path and Bact—NW Soc Path—Am Bd Path—Am Acad Forensic Sci—m Bd Legal Med—AAAS—Sigma Xi. Pathology Department, University of Oregon Medical School, Portland 1.

10 RICHARDSON, Leon Josiah. Latin literature; Adult education. b'68. AB '90 (University of Michigan); LLD '39 (Univ Calif); '95-97 (Univ Berlin). Author: Helps to the Reading of Classical Latin Poetry '07 (with Fairclough); The Phormio of Terence '09; Arrows and Driftwood, Essays in Lifelong Learning '35; Quintus Horatius Flaccus '35. Prof Latin emeritus U Calif since '38. Am Philol Assn—Am Assn Adult Edn—Phi Beta Kappa. 2335 Pacific Av., SF 15.⊙

11 RICHARDSON, Rupert Norval. History of Texas and the Southwestern United States; Indians of the Southwest; Baptist history. b'91. AB '12 (Simmons Coll); PhB '14 (U Chicago); AM '22—PhD '28 (U Tex). Author: The Comanche Barrier to the South Plains Settlement '33; The Lone Star State '43. Co-author: The Greater Southwest; also articles in field. Prof hist Hardin Simmons U since '17, dean students '26-28, vp '28-38 exec vp '38-40, acting pres '43-45, pres since '45. Tex State Hist Assn(F)—AHA—Miss Valley Hist Assn—Southwestern Social Sci Assn (adv ed '29, '31, pres '36-37)—Tex Philos Soc. 2210 Hickory St., Abilene, Tex.⊙

12 RICHARDSON-KUNTZ, Pedro. Sugar cane. b'92. BSA (U PR). Determination soil capability, fertilizer requirements, breeding methods, varietal adaptability and rendiments; study diseases, pest control, and cultural improvements; expeditions for study sugar cane agriculture St Domingo, Cuba, Mexico, Venezuela, and Panama; consultant on production problems. Author articles: Historical Sketch of Sugar Cane Varieties in Puerto Rico; Comparative Study of Uba, Kavangerie and Cayenne Sugar Cane Varieties; Oustanding Problems of the Sugar Cane Industry of Puerto Rico; Study of the Sugar Cane Industry of the El Tocuyo Valley of Venezuela, and others. Agron in charge sugar cane field expt Insular Agrl Expt Sta PR 36-42; chief agron and sugar cane expt Agrl Expt Sta USDA U PR '43-45; now cons sugar cane PR, Mexico, Panama, Venezuela. Sociedad Americana de Ciencias Agricolas—PR Assn Sugar Cane Tech—Internat Soc Sugar Cane Tech—PR Soc Agron. College Station 448, Mayaguez, P.R.

13 RICHINS, Calvin A(lexander). Autonomic nervous system. b'13. BA in zool '35—MA '37—teachers diploma '40 (U Utah); '37-38 (U So Cal); PhD '46 (St Louis U). Development freezing technique for study of vasomotor activity; innervation of bone marrow.

Author article: The Innervation of the Pancreas '45, and others. Co-author articles: (with Albert Kuntz) Reflex Pupillodilator Mechanisms—An Experimental Analysis '46; (with Kuntz) Components and Distribution of the Nerves of the Parotid and Submandibular Glands '46; (with Kuntz, Edwin Casey) Reflex Control of the Ciliary Muscle '46. Faculty St Louis U since '44, asso prof anatomy since '51. Sigma Xi—Am Assn Anatomists—Phi Sigma. St. Louis University, 1402 S. Grand, StL 4.

14 RICHLIN, Isadore M. Organic biochemistry (Endocrine, preparative, estrogen production). b'16. BS '35—PhD '40—Eli Lilly fellow '39-40 (U Chicago). Patent application for estrogen production with A W Turner and E C Elliott. Author articles in field. Dir control development Bedwell Labs '46-48; pres Crowne Chemicals of California Los Angeles. Am Chem Soc—Assn Study Internal Secretions. 715 Lindaraxa Park, Alhambra, Calif.†

15 RICHMOND, Henry Hugh. Intermediates; Agricultural chemicals; Coal chemicals; Explosives. b'16. BA '39—MA '41—'41-43 (U Toronto). Developed manufacturing processes for sulfa drugs, dyestuff intermediates, explosives such as RDX, coal tar by-product derivatives. Granted 10 patents in field. Research chem Dominion Rubber Co '43-48; with Pittsburgh Coke & Chem Co since '48, asso dir research fine chem div since '51. ACS, NRC, fellow U Toronto '42-43. Pittsburgh Coke & Chemical Co., Pitts 25. H: 256 Catalpa Pl., Pitts 34.

16 RICHTER, Charles Francis. Seismology. b'00. Student '16-17 (U So Calif); AB '20 (Stanford); PhD '28 (Calif Inst Tech). Introduced instrumental scale for earthquake magnitudes '32. Co-author: Seismicity of the earth and associated phenomena '49. Co-author: Internal Constitution of the Earth '39; also articles in field. Asst prof seismol Calif Inst Tech '37-47, asso prof since '47. Seismol Soc Am—Am Geophys Union—AAAS—Sigma Xi. Seismological Laboratory, 220 North San Rafael Av., Pasadena 2, Calif.

17 RICHTER, Conrad Michael. Early American life and speech (Pennsylvania, Southwest). b'90. LittD '44 (Susquehanna U). Author: Early Americana and Other Stories '37; Sea of Grass '37, The Trees '40 (gold medal for lit from Soc Libraries NYU '42); Tacey Cromwell '42; The Free Man '43 (hon award from Pa German Soc Juniata Coll '47); The Fields '46 (medal Ohioana Library Assn Columbus '47, also for The Trees); Always Young and Fair '47; also articles in field. PEN—Authors' League. c/o Paul R. Renolds, 599 Fifth Av., NYC.

18 RICHTER, George Holmes. Colloidal mechanisms of anesthesia, disinfectants, and drug action; Furane compounds; Barbituric and naphthenic acids; Pyridine derivatives; Hydrocarbons; Stereochemistry. b'04. BA '26—MA '27—PhD '29 (Rice Inst); Nat research fellow '29-31 (Cornell U). Author: Textbook of Organic Chemistry '38; Laboratory Manual of Elementary Organic Chemistry '40. With Rice Inst since '31, prof and chmn dept chem since '47. Am Chem Soc—German Chem Soc—Sigma Xi—Phi Beta Kappa. Department of Chemistry, The Rice Institute, Houston, Tex.†

19 RICHTMYER, Nelson Kellogg. Chemistry of sugars. b'01. AB '23—AM '25—PhD '27 (Harvard). Research on d-altrose and derivatives, degradation of sugars and glycosides, enzymatic hydrolyses with invertase and

beta-d-glucosidase; oxidation of polyols by Acetobacter suboxydans anhydrosugars. Editor: (with R M Hann) The Collected Papers of C S Hudson 2 vol '46-48. Research in chem lab Nat Inst Health since '34. Am Chem Soc. National Institutes of Health, Bethesda 14, Md.

20 RICKER, Norman Hurd. Loudspeaker (Paper cone); Seismic prospecting; Wavelet theory of seismogram structure. b'96. AB '16—AM '17—PhD '20 (Rice Inst). Inventor papercone type loud speaker; pioneer in seismic prospecting; organizer geophysical work of first American oil company to do its own geophysical work; basic research in propagation of transient elastic disturbances in solid bodies. Issued about 50 patents. Research worker Western Elec Co '21-23; head geophysics dept Humble Oil & Refining Co Houston '23-25; sr research physicist Carter Oil Co since '38. AAAS—APS—Am Math Soc—Acoustical Soc Am—Am Inst Physics—Seismol Soc Am—Am Geophys Union—Soc Exploration Geophysicists. The Carter Oil Co. Research Laboratory, P.O. Box 801, Tulsa.

21 RICKER, William Edwin. Fishery biology; Stoneflies; Salmon. b'08. BA—MA '31—PhD '35 (U Toronto). Research on the sockeye salmon of the Fraser River, warm-water fish populations in Indiana including their abundance, total mortality rates at successive ages, rates of exploitation and rates of growth, stoneflies. Author: Stoneflies of Southwestern British Columbia '43; Methods of Estimating Vital Statistics of Fish Populations '48; also articles in field. Asst prof, later prof zool Ind U '39-50; dir Ind Lake and Stream Survey; ed Fisheries Research Board of Canada. Pacific Biological Station, Nanaimo, B.C., Can.†

22 RICKETT, Harold William. History of botany; Biography of botanists; Inflorescence; Plant nomenclature; Gardens (History); Dogwoods (Taxonomy). AB '17—MA '20—PhD '22 (U Wis). Co-author: Botany, a Textbook for College and University Students (with W J Robbins) '29; (with W J Robbins) Laboratory Directions for General Botany '29; (with E Naylow) Instructions for Laboratory in General Botany '35; (with B O Dodge) Diseases and Pests of Ornamental Plants '42; also articles in field. Bibliographer NY Bot Garden since '42. AAAS—Am Soc Plant Taxonomists—Bot Soc Am—Sigma Xi—Phi Beta Kappa. The New York Botanical Garden, NYC.⊙

23 RIDDELL, Guy C(rosby). Mining, metallurgy, processing, and economics of non-ferrous minerals. b'82. BS '04 (MIT). Exploration and consultation on mineral resources in Russia, Canada, Alaska, Australia, South Korea, China, Mexico, Germany, Poland, Venezuela, Honduras, and Panama; specialist in processing and economics of mica, antimony, lead, copper, tin, tungsten, manganese, chromite, mercury, graphite, zinc, helium, oil shale, and oil sands; survey existing oil and mining facilities Soviet government '30-33; consultant development of new rare metal industries throughout US SR '30-33; contracting engineer for creation of Russian helium industry '33-34; American sponsored survey Russian potash, sulphur, nickel and petroleum industries and resources '35-41; consultant on beryllium and potash industries for New York banks; consulting engineer for gold, mercury, antimony, and mica mines in Mexico, Alaska, California, Arizona, Colorado, Montana, and Porcupine,

Ontario. Author: Industrial Readjustments of Mineral Industries Affected by the War '20. Author articles: Fundamentals of Mineral Property Valuation '40; Enginers Should Lead in Planning a World Federation for Peace '45, and others. Contributor: Handbook of Non-Ferrous Metallurgy '26, '45. Chief minerals and petroleum div Bur Fgn and Domestic Commerce '24-25; Dept Commerce tech rep on Fed Oil Conservation Bd '25; chief mining projects sect Bd Econ Warfare '42-43; cons Fgn Econ Adminstrn '43-46; adv Chinese govt and Fgn Econ Adminstrn on five-year plan for mining and metall industry '44-45; research adminstr indsl research and development div Dept Commerce '46-47; chief mining adv Nat Econ Bd US Mil Govt South Korea '47-48; cons mining engr NYC and Washington since '48. Brit Inst Mining and Metall —AIMME—Mining and Metall Soc Am—Pan Am Inst Mining Engring and Geol. Engineers Club, 32 W. 40th St., NYC 18. H: Little Plaindealing Farm, Royal Oak, Md.†⊚

10 RIDENOUR, Louis N(icot), Jr. Design electronic digital computers, and television and radar equipment. b'11. BS '32 (U Chgo); PhD '36 (Cal Inst Tech). Holds basic patent on radar automatic tracking; co-inventor Telemeter system of pay-as-you-see television; inaugurated work at University of Illinois leading to design and construction of Ordvac and U Ill machine. Author: Radar System Engineering '47. Through grades to prof physics U Pa '38-47 (on leave '40-46); staff mem and asst dir radiation lab MIT, editor radiation lab series of 28 tech vols '40-46; prof physics, dean grad coll U Ill '47-51; vp engring Internat Telemeter Corp LA since '51. Chief sci US Air Force '50-51; awarded Bronze Star and Medal for Merit for war-time work on radar. APS(F)—AAAS(F)—IRE(sr mem)—Assn for Computing Machinery—Operations Resch Soc Am—Phi Beta Kappa—Sigma Xi. 2000 Stoner, LA 25.

11 RIDER, (Arthur) Fremont. Library science (Microcards, equipment). b'85. PhB '05—LHD '37 (Syracuse U); MA '34 (Wesleyan U). Inventor of book truck stack shelving and other library equipment. Author: A Study of Library Policy '43; Melvil Dewey, a Biography '44; The Scholar and the Future of the Research Library '44; Compact Book Storage '49, and others. Librarian Wesleyan U since '33. Am Geneal Index (chmn since '34) —Nat Microcard (chmn since '44)— Conn Library Assn (ex pres)—ALA— Phi Beta Kappa. Arawana, Middletown, Conn.

12 RIEDEL, Frederick Carl. Medieval romances and criminal law. b'02. BS '24 (Hamilton Coll); MA '27—PhD '38 (Columbia). Author: Crime and Punishment in the Old French Romances '38; also articles in field. With City Coll NY since '32, asso prof Dept Eng since '53, dept supervisor summer session since '45. Mod Lang Assn—Medieval Club. The City College of New York, 139 St. and Convent Av., NYC 31.

13 RIEGER, Wray Montgomery. Dahlias (Inulin); Missouri (Northeast geology). b'02. BS '27 (U Mo); MS '28 (U Chicago); PhD '34 (U So Cal). Research in preparation inulin and levulose from dahlia tuber with view toward commercial production; artificial selection seedling dahlias with analysis various types for maximum inulin yield and maximum freedom from impurities; geology Northeast Missouri, particularly, oil, coal and water reserves. Prof chem Northeastern Mo State Tchrs Coll '34-42,

head dept sci and math since '46. Phi Kappa Phi—Phi Lambda Upsilon— Sigma Xi — AAAS — AAUP — ACS. Northeastern Missouri State Teachers College, Kirksville.

14 RIEHL, Merrill Landis. Water (Softening, purification); Wastes (Treatment, disposal). b'09. B Chem Engring '39—'49-50 (O State U); '40-41 (Case Inst Tech). Research on chemical and physical analyses water supplies, purification and softening of water. Civil engr Columbus Ohio Water Dept '42; san engr US Engr Corps '42-45; chief chem Ohio Dept Health Lab '45-51; supt purification Mahoning Valley San Dist since '51. Am Water Works Assn—Sewage Works Fedn—ACS—Soc Am Bact—Tau Beta Pi—Sigma Xi—Phi Lambda Upsilon —Alpha Chi Sigma. Mahoning Valley Sanitary District, Box 298, Youngstown 1, O.

15 RIEMAN, Gustav Herman. Disease resistance in plants. b'02. BS '25 (Ia State Coll); MS—PhD '30 (U Wis). Research on disease resistance in plants and its application to agriculture; development of disease resistant varieties of vegetables especially onions, peas and potatoes; production of disease-free vegetable seed in the US. Author articles in field. Asso prof genetics plant path and hort U Wis '36-41, prof since '41. AAAS—Genetics Soc —Genetic Assn Am—Phytopath Soc— Soc Hort Sci—Soc Study Evolution. Department of Genetics, University of Wisconsin, Madison 6, Wis.†

16 RIENOW, Robert. Government (Comparative); International law; Citizenship training. b'07. AB'30 (Carthage Coll Ill); MA '33—Glider fellow internat law '33-34—PhD '37 (Columbia); fellow govt '35-36 (Ohio State U). Research on political problems of French government, and use of colonial power; political affairs of England and France; nature of law establishing relation of vessels to countries whose flags they fly; investigation presidential power of concluding executive agreement, excepting formal treaties. Author: The Test of the Nationality of a Merchant Vessel '37; Calling All Citizens '43, '48; American Problems Today '51; Introduction to Government '51. Instr advancing to asst prof govt NY State Coll for Tchrs '36-43, prof since '46; ext instr NY Sch Labor and Indsl Relations Cornell since '46. Am Polit Sci Assn—Nat Council Social Studies —Pi Gamma Nu. New York State College for Teachers, Albany.

17 RIESER, Max. Epistemology of poetry; Foreign language groups in the United States. b'93. Dr Law '20 (U Vienna). Author articles in field. With Common Council for American Unity NY since '43; contbr editor. Am Philos Assn—Am Soc Aesthetics. 519 West 121 St., NYC 27.

18 RIFE, Clarence White. Vermont history (Separatist movement, diplomatic history of the Republic). b'88. BA '14 (U Saskatchewan); MA '18— Western fellow '17-18 (U Toronto); Bulkley fellow '19-22—PhD '22 (Yale). Author articles in field. Prof head hist dept Hamline U since '27, head dept hist polit sci since '29. AHA— Can Hist Assn—Am Polit Sci Assn— Minn Hist Soc—Vt Hist Soc. Hamline University, St. Paul 4.

19 RIFE, David C. Human heredity; Genetics of Coleus. b'01. BS '22 (Cedarville Coll); BSc '23—MA '31—PhD '33 (O State U). Author: Dice of Destiny '45; also articles in field. Geneticist dept zool O State U since '34. Genetics Soc Am—O Acad Sci—Human Genetics Soc Am—Sigma Xi—Gamma

Sigma Delta. Department of Zoology, Ohio State University, Columbus, O.

20 RIFE, John Merle. Post-classical Greek. b'95. AB '16 (Cedarville Coll); '21 (Xenia Theol Sem); '21-22 (Miami U); MA '27 (Ind U); PhD '31 (U Chicago). Research on Papyrus words and their relation to other Greek; translation phenomena in the Greek versions of Daniel, dextrality. Author: A Beginning Greek Book '48; also articles in field. Prof classical lang Muskingum Coll New Concord O since '36. Soc Biblical Lit and Exegesis— Linguistic Soc Am. Muskingum College, New Concord, O.†

21 RIFENBURGH, Sumner Adam. Drosophila genetics (Effects of ultraviolet radiation). b'96. BS '15—AB '16—AM '21 (Valparaiso U); MS '22 (U Chicago); PhD '35 (Purdue U). Author articles in field. With Valparaiso U '14-23, prof and head dept zool '22-23; with Purdue U since '23, asso prof since '46. Ind Acad Sci—Nat Assn Biol Teachers—Am Genetic Assn—Human Genetics Soc Am (charter mem)— Sigma Xi—AAAS(F). Biology Annex, Purdue University, West Lafayette, Ind. H: 246 Marstellar St.

22 RIGG, George Burton. Peat and Sphagnum bogs of North America; Washington (Peat resources). b'72. BS '96 (State U Ia); MA '09 (U Wash); PhD '14 (U Chicago). Author: The Pharmacists Botany '24; College Botany '30. Co-author: (with T C Frye) Northwest Flora '12, Elementary Flora of the Northwest '14. Author articles: The Development of Sphagnum Bogs in North America, 40; others. With U Wash since '09, prof botany since '28, head dept '40-42, mem univ com in charge lignin and cellulose research since '40; mem staff Oceanographic Labs since '30; scientist in charge expdns for investigations of kelp as source of potash US Bur Soils, Puget Sound region '11, '12, Western Alaska '13; dir biol survey Wash State Dept Fisheries '22; field work on peat bogs Eastern US '35, '41; now spl cons on peat Wash State Div Mines and Geology. Bot Soc Am (pres Pacific sect '40)—Am Soc Plant Physiol—Ecol Soc Am—Western Soc Naturalists(past pres)—Wash Acad Sci—NY Acad Sci—AAAS—AAUP— Gamma Alpha—Sigma Xi—Phi Sigma. Botany Department, University of Washington, Seattle 5.†⊚

23 RIGGS, Frederick W(arren). Far East (China and Indonesia, international relations); France (Politics, foreign policy); Italy (Foreign policy); Pressure (Groups). b'17. AB '38 (U Ill); MA '41 (Fletcher Sch Law and Diplomacy); PhD '48 (Columbia). Study international relations and politics France and Italy for Foreign Policy Association; research on pressure groups, analysis legislative process in Congress including public pressure, administration, intralegislative force interaction; analysis strategy and tactics pressure groups. Author: Pressures on Congress '50. Author articles: Italy's Road Back '49; Role of France and Italy on the World Stage '49; Self Government in Dependent Territories and the United Nations '50; World Refugee Problems '51; and others. Research asso Fgn Policy Assn since '48. Am Polit Sci Assn—Far Eastern Assn—Inst Pacific Relations—Am Acad Polit and Social Sci. Foreign Policy Association, 22 E. 38th, N.Y.C. 16.

24 RIGGS, William Adams. Mineral valuation; Industrial engineering. b'14. Special evaluations of mineral properties, geologic mapping for such evaluations; economic studies of mining and industrial ventures. Mining engr Pittsburgh Limestone Corp '39-41, Republic Mining & Mfg Co '41-42; supervising engr RFC '42-43; indsl geol Atlantic Coast Line RR '46-48; indsl engr Gulf Mobile & Ohio RR since '48. Am Gas Assn—Am Assn Petroleum Geol(asso)—Am Geophys Union—AIMME—Am Mining Congress—ASME—Am Soc Photogrammetry—Forest Products Research Soc—Geol Soc Am. Gulf Mobile & Ohio Railroad, Mobile, Ala. H: 1623 Lamar Av.

10 **RIGHTER, Francis Irving.** Forest tree breeding; Experimental thinnings in forestry. b'97. BS '23—MF '28 (Cornell U). Author articles: New Perspectives in Forest Tree Breeding '46; and others. Asst prof forest management Cornell U '29-31; geneticist Eddy Tree Breeding Sta Placerville Calif '31-32, Inst Forest Genetics Placerville '32-35, Calif Forest and Range Expt Sta US Forest Service Berkeley Calif since '35. Am Genetic Assn—AAAS—Soc Am Foresters—Soc Study Evolution—Calif Bot Soc—Sigma Xi—Phi Kappa Phi. California Forest and Range Experiment Station, 329 Forestry Hall, University of California, Berkeley.

11 **RIGHTS, Douglas LeTell.** History of American Indian in North Carolina. b'91. AB '13 (U NC); BD '15—DD '47 (Moravian Theol Sem); STB '16 (Harvard). Editor Bulletin of Archeological Society of North Carolina '48. Author: A Voyage Down the Yadkin-Great Peedee River '28; The American Indian in North Carolina '47. Archivist So province Moravian Church in Am since '49; mem adv ed bd NC Hist Review since '50. Wachovia Hist Soc(pres since '28)—Archeol Soc NC(first pres '33)—Eastern States Archeol Fedn(vp '36-40)—NC State Lit and Hist Assn(vp '35)—NC Soc for Preservation Antiquities (vp '40) —Hist Soc NC—Am Assn Museums —Soc Am Archivists—Soc Am Archeol. Box 68, Salem Station, Winston-Salem, N.C.

12 **RIIS, Sergius Martin.** Russian revolution. b'83. Student '03 (NY State Nautical Coll); '07 (US Marine Sch Application Annapolis); '08 (Columbia U). Research on activities of Karl Heinrich Marx and the Soviet leaders in relation to fallacies of so-called Marx-Engels ideologies as to economics. Author: Yankee Komisar (2d edit) '39. USN attache to Am Embassy in Russia '18-39; spl agt Dept State to South Russia; with Intelligence Service Russia and Far East. Am Soc Naval Engrs Washington— USN Inst—Explorers Club. US Navy Cross, Brit Distinguished Service Order, French Legion of Honor and six Imperial Russian decorations for intelligence work in Russia. Columbia University Club, 4 W. 43rd St., NYC.

13 **RILEY, Arthur Joseph.** Church history (New England Catholics); Anti-Semitism (to 1500); Knights of Columbus. b'05. AB '25 (Boston College); MA—PhD '35 (Catholic University Am). Drew up plans for reorganization of Archdiocesan Archives; prepared only extant guide to organization of seminary libraries. Author: Catholicism in New England to 1788 '36; History of St. John's Seminary, Brighton, Mass (with John E Sexton) '45; Anti-Semitism to 1500 '44; also articles in field. Prof librarian St. John's Seminary Brighton Mass since '37, registrar '41-50; historian Supreme Council of Knights of Columbus since '50; archivist archdiocese of Boston '44-47. Colonial Soc Mass—Cath Library Assn—ALA—Cath Hist Assn—A

HA—Miss Valley Hist Assn—Biog Soc Am—Spl Libraries Assn. P.O. Drawer 1670 New Haven 7. H: St. Raphael's Hospital, 1450 Chapel St., New Haven 11.

14 **RILEY, John Winchell, Jr.** Surveys (Sociology). b'08. AB '30 (Bowdoin Coll); MA '33—PhD '36 (Harvard). Survey methods and techniques for research on communications, the impact of television, inter-group relations, and alcoholism. Co-author: The Student Looks at his Teacher '50; The Status of the Social Sciences (in preparation). Study dir div program surveys USDA '42; asso dir domestic surveys OWI '43; prof and chmn dept sociol Rutgers U since '45; cons to Operations Research Office Air Force CBS. Overseas service Psychol Warfare Div AUS '44, Air Force mission to Korea '50-51. Am Sociol Soc (sec since '49)—Am Assn Pub Opinion Research—Am Econ Assn—Eastern Sociol Soc. Department of Sociology, Rutgers University, New Brunswick, N.J.

15 **RINALDO, John B(each).** Mogollon archeology. b'12. AB '34 (Carleton Coll); MA '38—PhD '41 (U Chicago). Co-author: Prehistory of the Pine Lawn Valley Western New Mexico '49; also articles. Asst curator archeol Chicago Nat Hist Mus since '50. Soc Am Archeol—Am Anthrop Assn(F)—Sigma Xi. Chicago Natural History Museum, Roosevelt Road and Lake Shore Drive, Chicago 5, Ill.

16 **RINE, Josephine Zeh.** Dogs (All breeds; Boston terries). b'01. Student (Columbia Sch Journalism). Author: Care and Feeding of Dogs '36; The Ideal Boston Terrier '47; Toy Dogs '35; Your Dog From Puppyhood to Old Age '48; Dog Owners Manual '44; also articles in field. Book ed Series on Pure-bred Dogs Orange Judd Pub Co since '32. Medal awarded by the Dog Writers Assn Am for most outstanding work in the field of dogs for year '40. 15 Arlington Av., Caldwell, N.J.

17 **RING, Elizabeth.** Maine history. b'02. AB '23—AM '26 (U Me); fellow '30-31 (Bryn Mawr Coll); '29 (Oxford U); '33-35 (Columbia U). Author: The Progressive Party of 1912 and the Third Party of 1924 in Maine '33; A Reference List of Manuscripts Relating to the History of Maine. Dir research hist records survey Me '38-41; instr Maine hist Bates Coll summers '39-41; instr hist Deering High School Portland Me since '41; dir Me travel course State Dept Edn '48-53. AHA— Maine Hist Soc—NEA—Maine Teachers' Assn. 193 Clark St., Portland 4, Me.

18 **RINGER, Ferdinand.** Organic chemistry (Plastics, solid fuel). b'87. Student '98-07 (Gym Austria); PhD '12 (U Vienna). Holder various patents; inventor so called Everlasting Match. Author articles in field. Research and cons chem labs in Vienna, Paris, NY since '40. Am Chem Soc—Assn Cons Chem Chem Engrs—Am Soc European Chem Pharm. 114 E. 32nd St., NYC 16.

19 **RINGQUIST, Clarence LaVerne.** Heating; Ventilating; Air conditioning; Refrigeration. b'05. BS (U Ill); study (Ill Wesleyan U). Research and systems and defrosting cycles. Granted patents on air conditioning systems and units and defrosting cycles. Author articles: Regulation of Air Temperature and Humidity '39; Human Side of Comfort '50; others. With Trane Co since '31, mgr air conditioning div from '46. Am Soc Heating and Ventilating Engrs. Registered profl engr Wis. Trane Co., La Crosse, Wis. H: 724 S. 20th St.

20 **RINKER, Royden C(arrington).** Thermosetting adhesives; Resorcinol resins. b'15. BS '39—'39-42 (George Washington U). Research on adhesives, catalysts for adhesives and their effect on wood, development of coatings, resin research and development, control of plant products, silk screen processing of textiles with coatings of own development. Author articles in field. Organic plastics sect Nat Bur Standards '40-45; dir resin research development chem Pa Coal Products Co '45-47; chief chem Koppers Co '47-48; owner gen mgr Plas-Tex Shop since '48; materials engr army ordnance since '50. AS TM (com D-14, rep Nat Bur Standards '43-45, Pa Coal Products Co '45-47, Koppers Co '47-48)—Plastics Materials Mfgrs Assn—Am Chem Soc. Plas-Tex Shop, 1229 L St., N.W., Washington.†

21 **RIOCH, David McKenzie.** Nervous system (Anatomy, physiology); Research administration. b'00. Student '13-15 (Philander-Smith Naini Tal UP India); AB '20 (Butler U); MD '24 (Johns Hopkins). Research on nervous system, anatomy and physiology of the basal ganglia. Author articles on neuroanatomy and neurophysiology of the thalamus, hypothalamus and striatum. Medical fellow Nat Research Council, U Mich, dep Anatomy and Central Inst for Brain Research Amsterdam Holland '28-29, Laboratories of Physiol Oxford England '29-30; asso in psychol Johns Hopkins '30-31; asst prof anatomy Harvard Med Sch '31-38; prof neurology Washington U St Louis '38-43; dir research Chestnut Lodge Sanitarium since '43. Chestnut Lodge Sanitarium, Rockville, Md.

22 **RIORDAN, John Lancaster.** Arthurian literature (German); Middle High German (Language and literature. b'13. AB '38—MA '41—PhD '44 (U Calif); '38-39 (U Heidelberg). Read paper at Second International Arthurian Congress Quimper France '48. Author articles in field. Asst prof Germanic Langs U Va since '47. Mod Lang Assn Am—AAUP—Internat Arthurian Orgn. Department of Germanic Languages, Minor Hall 7, University of Virginia, Charlottesville, Va.†

23 **RIPLEY, Dillon Sidney II.** Ornithology. b'13. BA '36—PhD '43 (Harvard). Author: Trail of the Money Bird '43; Search for the Spiny Babbler '52; also articles in field. Associate curator, asst prof zool Peabody Mus Natural Hist Yale since '45. Intelligence Officer OSS '42-45, collected for US Nat Mus while in southeastern Asia '43-45. Siam Soc(F)—Am Ornithol Union—Brit Ornithol Union— Bombay Natural Hist Soc. Fellow Jonathan Edwards Coll Yale '46. Peabody Museum of Natural History, Yale University, New Haven.

24 **RIPPIN, Jane Deeter (Mrs. James Yardley Rippin).** Girl Scouts of America; Probation. b'82. BS '02—MA '14 (Irving Coll Mechanicsburg Pa). Organized probation work of Municipal Court of Philadelphia; in charge organization first Woman's Court Building Philadelphia where social, mental and physical diagnoses are presented before presiding judge at time of hearing; made special study of women camp followers World War I; worked to develop Girl Scout movement into nation-wide organization. Chief probation officer Phila '14-17; dir sect women and girls Commn on Training Camp Activities of War and Navy Depts '17-19; nat dir Girl Scouts Inc '19-31; woman's ed Westchester Co Pub. Nat Information Bur (bd dirs)— Nat Inst Social Sci—Nat Council Social Agencies—Nat Conf Social Work— Nat Council Out-door Activities. Westchester County Publishers, 8 Church St., White Plains, N.Y.

10 RISLEY, Paul L(emuel). Reptiles and amphibia; Turtles; Sex differentiation in vertebrates; Cytology; Embryology. b'06. AB '27 (Albion Coll); MS '29—PhD '31 (U Mich). Research in germ cell history in reptiles, reproduction and hormones in reptiles and amphibia, induction in embryogeny, regeneration and embryogeny, chromosomes and centrioles in turtles and sex differentiation in vertebrates. Author articles in field. Professor biological dept U Ore since '45. AAAS—Am Soc Zool—Am Soc Anat—Am Soc Naturalists—Ore Acad Sci—Sigma Xi. Received Walker prize '44. Biology Department, University of Oregon, Eugene, Ore. H: 2728 Baker Blvd.

11 RISTER, Carl Coke. History of the frontier and western United States. b'89. BA '15—D Litt '42 (Hardin-Simmons U Abilene Tex); MA '19—PhD '25 (George Washington U). Two research grants from Social Science Research Council New York for studies of southern plains frontier social and military history; grant from American Philosophical Society at Philadelphia for study of dust bowl; grant from Standard Oil Company for the compilation of materials and writing of a history of Southwestern Oil. Author: The Southwestern Frontier 1865-1881 '28; Border Captives '40; Land Hunger '42; Border Command '44; Robert E Lee in Texas '46; No Man's Land '48; Oil! Titan of the Southwest; (with L R Hagen) Western America. U Okla '29-51, prof hist '35-45, chmn dept '44-45, research professor '45-51, Texas Technical College Lubbock since '51. AHA—Miss Valley Historical Assn (exec com)—So Hist Assn—Soc Am Historians—Tex Hist Soc—Westerners —Okla Hist Soc—West Tex Hist Assn —Phi Beta Kappa. Texas Technological College, Lubbock.◎

12 RITCHIE, Andrew C. Art (British medieval, eighteenth century and contemporary). b'07. BA '32—MA '33 (U Pittsburgh); PhD '35 (U London, Eng). Author: English Painters, Hogarth to Constable '42; Sculpture of the Twentieth Century '53; also articles in field. Dir Albright Art Gallery Buffalo '42-49; dir dept painting and sculpture Museum of Modern Art New York since '49. College Art Assn Am. Awarded Cross Legion of Honor for work in returning looted art objects '46; awarded the Order of Nassau with rank of Officer by Netherlands government for merits as an organizer of exhibitions of Dutch paintings which toured US and Canada '48. Museum of Modern Art, 11 W. 53d St., NYC 19.

13 RITCHIE, William Ludlow. Politics (Military). b'02. BS '25 (US Mil Acad); '29-30 (Air Corps Primary and Advanced Flying Schs); '32-33(Air Corps Tech Sch); '38-39 (Air Corps Tactical Sch); '39-40 (Command and Gen Staff Sch). Commd 2d lt US Army '25, advanced through grades to brig gen; chief SW Pacific Theatre sect, dep chief strategy and policy group, operations div War Dept Gen Staff, and dep army planner Joint and Combined Staff Planners '42-44; chief of staff and chief air div US mission to USSR, also mil attache Moscow '44-45; became chief war plans div Hdqrs AAF Washington '46; participated in internat confs Quebec '42, '44, Cairo '43, Yalta and Potsdam '45; assigned dep chief of staff to comdr-in-chief Naval Forces Eastern Atlantic and Mediterranean '49. H: 34 Kalorama Circle, Washington 8.◎

14 RITER, William Emerson. Wildlife management. b'01. BS '22 (Utah State Agrl Coll). Research on stock poisoning plants of range; predatory animal and rodent control work, rodent control in relation to plague suppression; study in perfecting field organizations to most effectively and efficiently conduct organized control operations against predatory animals and injurious rodents. Biol Fish and Wildlife Service US Dept Interior '29-47, district agent '36-39, asst div chief since '39; lectured Army Sch Tropical Mil Med Washington '43-45. Am Soc Mammalogists—Am Wildlife Soc. 2001 N.E. 70th Av., Portland 4, Ore.

15 RITTENHOUSE, Gordon. Geology (Petroleum); Sedimentary petrology. b'10. SB '32—SM '33—PhD '35 (U Chicago); '34-35 (U Minn). Author ar-Cincinnati since '46; cons geol '47-51; geol Shell Oil Co Tulsa since '51. Am Assn Pet Geol—Society Econ Paleontology Mineralogy—Geol Soc Am (F)—Appalachian Geol Soc—O Acad Sci(F). Shell Oil Co., Tulsa.

16 RITTER, Cassandra. Water bacteriology. b'98. AB '21 (U Kan); AM '28 (U Kan); '41-42 (U Mich). Author articles in field. Bacteriologist div san Kan State Bd Health since '22. Soc Am Bacteriologists—Am Pub Health Assn(F)—Am Soc Limnol Oceano— Kan Acad Sci—Sigma Xi. State Water Laboratory, University of Kansas, Lawrence, Kan.†

17 RITTMAN, Walter Frank. Physical chemistry (Industrial processes, fuel, oil and gas). b'83. CE '05 (O Northern U); AB '08—MA '09—ME '11 —ChE '16 (Swarthmore Coll); PhD '14 (Columbia U). Author articles in field. Prof engring Carnegie Inst Tech '21-33; cons engr State Pa '23-24; cons engr US Dept Agr '25-37. AAAS(F)— Am Chem Soc—Am Inst Chem Engr— Franklin Inst—ASME—Am Inst Mining Metall Engrs—Soc Indsl Engrs (nat pres '25-30)—Am Engring Council (administr bd '25-30)—Tau Beta Pi. 6112 Alder St., Pitts 6.◎

18 ROACH, William J(oseph). Old French (Textual criticism, continuators of Chretien de Troyes); Arthurian literature; Holy Grail; Twelfth and Thirteenth Century French authors (Robert de Boron, Chretien de Troyes, Wauchier, Pseudo-Wauchier, Manessier, Gerbert de Montreuil); Thirteenth Century French grail romances (Perlesvaus, Didot-Perceval). b'07. Student '25-28 (Univ Notre Dame); PhB '29 —PhD '35 (U Chicago); '30-31 (Ecole des Hautes Etudes Paris, Sorbonne U Paris). Author: The Didot-Perceval according to the MSS of Modena and Paris '41; The Continuations of the Perceval of Chretien de Troyes '49; also articles in field. Prof romance langs U Pa since '47. Modern Lang Assn Am—Medieval Acad Am—Societe des Anciens Textes Francais—Anglo-Norman Text Soc. Bennett Hall, University of Pennsylvania, Phila. 4.†

19 ROARK, Raymond Jefferson. Engineering (Stress analysis, dynamics, structures); Big game hunting. b'90. BS '11—MS '12 (U Ill); '13-14 (U Wis). Botanical and big game collecting expedition Tanganyka East Africa '27; hunting expedition French Indo-China '29, Mexico '37. Author: Formulas for Stress and Strain '38. Co-author: Mechanics for Engineers '45; also articles in field. Prof mechanics U Wis since '37. Soc Exptl Stress Analysis—Soc Engring Edn—Sigma Xi—Tau Beta Pi. Univ. of Wisconsin, Madison, Wis.†

20 ROBB, Jane Sands. Electrocardiographic studies; Heart. b'93. AB '15 (Syracuse U NY); MD '18—DSc hon '50 (Woman's Med Coll Pa); ScD '24 (U Pa). Studies on dissection of muscle bundles composing heart, blood supply to these muscles, function of muscle bundles; identification and reconstructions of connecting tissues in the heart; papers relating electrocardiography to cardiac anatomy and physiology. Contributor: Annual Review of Physiology '49. NRC fellow for study of cardiac physiol '23-25; prof physiol Woman's Med Coll Pa '25-29; asso prof pharm Syracuse U since '29. Am Physiol Soc(F)—Am Heart Assn—Soc Exptl Biol and Med—NY Acad Sci —Sigma Xi—Alpha Omega Alpha— Sigma Delta Epsilon. NY State Med Soc first prize for original work cardiac anatomy and physiol '35, also AMA bronze medal '35. Medical Center, Syracuse University, Syracuse 10, NY.

21 ROBB, Walter Johnson. Philippine Islands (American and foreign capital, Chinese, overseas commerce). b'80. Author: The Khaki Cabinet and Old Manila '26; Romance and Adventure in Old Manila '28; Filipinos '39. Author articles: The Philippine Mission Trail; Galleon Commerce; Americans in the Philippines; Man Tracks on Luzon 10,000 Years Old. Newspaper work and foreign news correspondence Manila '18-41; writing and lecturing since '41. 464 42d Av., SF 21.

22 ROBBINS, Frank Mix. Foundry practice. b'86. BS '07 (Denison U Granville O); '08-09 (Colo Sch Mines). Operation and management of foundries for iron, steel, and malleable metal; metallurgist ferrous products. Holds patents in field. Plant engr advancing to asst gen mgr Marion Malleable Iron Ind '11-18; vp and gen mgr Positive Rail Anchor Co Marion Ind '12-18; vp and asst gen mgr Ross-Meehan Foundries Chattanooga '18-33, pres and gen mgr since '33; vp Meehanite Metal Corp Chattanooga since '24. Am Acad Sci—So Assn Sci and Industry—Tenn Acad Sci—Am Iron and Steel Inst—ASTM—Steel Foundries Soc Am. Steel Founders Soc Am Lorenz award for meritorious service to steel castings industry. Ross-Meehan Foundries, 1601 Carter St., Chattanooga 1.

23 ROBBINS, Ray Nichols. Textiles (Styling); Yarn blendings; Piece goods (Designing). b'91. Ed pub pvt and spl schs. Research on fabrication, coloring, patterning and market consultation on woven piece goods fabrics, research on yarns and weaves of wool, cotton, and synthetic mixtures. Patents in field. Pres Robbins Styling Service since '26. Phi Psi. Received award from Am Woolen Co for drafting and weaving seven separate and different color fabrics on one loom at same time. 288 Montgomery St., Bloomfield, N.J.†

24 ROBBINS, Samuel Tubbe. Family life education; Sex education; Social hygiene. b'05. Grad '25 (Savage Sch Phys Edn); BS '42—MA '43—EdD '48 (NYU). Research on strategies for improving, strengthening and enriching family living through education; consultant American Social Hygiene Association. Author: The Case for Sex Education '49; Family Living: Our First Line of Defense '51. Co-author: (with William G. Hollister and Eva F Dodge) Education for Responsible Parenthood '50. Asst prof Miss So Coll '46-48; free-lance lecturer and author since '48. Phi Delta Kappa—Nat Council Family Relations (former v-chmn com family life edn secondary schs)—So Council Family Relations(former exec com mem)— Miss Soc Hygiene Assn(exec dir '46-48)—Edn Responsible Parenthood (Miss state dir '46-48). Box 53, Warren, Pa.

10 ROBBINS, William Jacob. Vitamins; Antibiotic substances; Plant tissue and culture; Physiology of fungi; Growth. b'90. AB '10—DSc '37 (Lehigh U); PhD '15 (Cornell); DSc '45 (Fordham U). Co-author: Textbook on Botany (with others) '39; also articles in field. Prof Columbia U and dir NY Bot Garden since '37. AAAS(F)—Nat Acad Sci—Am Philos Soc—Bot Soc Am—Phi Beta Kappa—Sigma Xi—Phi Kappa Phi. New York Botanical Garden, NYC 58.†◎

11 ROBERT, John. Tar distillation; Roofing machinery. b'89. Student '00-08 (Akademisches Gymnasium); ME '14 (Tech Hochschule Vienna). Research and design of roofing machinery and equipment for tar distillation. Granted patents in field. Plant engr Barrett Co '19-44; chief engr Globe Roofing Products Co Inc since '44, vp in charge engring since '52. ASME—Tech Assn Pulp and Paper Industry. Globe Roofing Products Co., Inc., Whiting, Ind. H: 2516 E. 76th St., Chgo 49.

12 ROBERT, Joseph Clarke. American history (Tobacco, slavery controversy). b'06. BA '27 (Furman U); AM '29—PhD '33 (Duke U); '29-30 (Harvard). Author: The Tobacco Kingdom '38; The Road from Monticello: A Study of the Virginia Slavery Debate of 1832 '41; The Story of Tobacco in America '49. Asst prof hist Duke U '38-44, asso prof '44-49, prof '49-52, asso dean grad sch '48-52; pres Coker Coll since '52. AHA—Miss Valley Hist Assn—So Hist Assn—Agrl Historical Soc. Coker College, Hartsville, S.C.†

13 ROBERTS, Carl Leonard. Explosives; Chemical safety. b'10. Student (Internat Correspondence Sch, Alexander Hamilton Inst). Co-inventor of process for manufacture of Trinitroresorcinol '43. With Olin Industries Inc since '31, exec asst to dir research and development since '48. Olin Industries, Inc., East Alton, Ill.†

14 ROBERTS, Cecil Andrew. Poultry. b'04. BS '28—MS '36 (Okla A&M Coll); '40-41 (Miss State Coll). Research on egg preservation, egg coolers, turkey grading, operation and use of electric brooders. Author article: A Study of the Deposition of Fat in Broilers as Influenced by Different Cereal Grains '36. Co-author articles: A Home Made Egg Cooler for Farm Use '40; Construction and Operation of the Summer Egg Cooler 43; Slaughtering Poultry '44. Contributor: Mississippi Poultry Improvement Association Year Book '43-46. Foreman poultry farm and expt sta Okla A&M Coll '30-36, faculty poultry husbandry dept '36-43 and since '47, now asso prof; field rep Nat Poultry Improvement Plan Miss '43-44; asst ext poultryman Miss '43-44, ext poultry marketing specialist '45, ext poultryman '45-47. Poultry Sci Assn. Poultry Department, Oklahoma A&M College, Stillwater.

15 ROBERTS, Frank Harold Hanna. American archeology (Early man in New World). b'97. AB '19—AM '21 (U Denver); AM '26—PhD '27 (Harvard). Member National Geographic Society's Pueblo Bonito Expedition '25-26; in charge of Smithsonian Institution field parties in Southwest US, Canada, Mexico during last 23 years, excavated numerous Basket Maker and Pueblo ruins, worked in sites attributable to Early Man in America, particularly those of Folsom Man; vice-chairman Division of Anthropology and Psychology National Research Council '46, executive committee '48; sent to International Congress of Archeologists Cairo, Egypt '37 as one of two Amer-

ican experts; US representative on International Commission for Historic Monuments '39. Author articles in field. Archeol Bur Am Ethnol Smithsonian Instn Washington '26-44, asst chief '44-46, asso chief '46-48, asso dir since '48; dir River Basin archeol surveys since '46. Am Anthrop Assn—Soc Am Archeol—Washington Acad Sci (pres '49). Smithsonian Institution, Washington 25.◎

16 ROBERTS, George, Jr. Petrochemicals. b'11. BS '32 (U Ky); '33 (U Mich). Holder several patents, principally on catalytic processes for hydrocarbon synthesis and conversion of hydrocarbons. Author articles in field. Chem engr Kellogg Co '33-43; mgr research dept Stanolind Oil and Gas Co since '43. Am Petroleum Inst—Am Chem Soc—Am Inst Chem Engr. Box 591, Tulsa Okla.

17 ROBERTS, H(oward) Radclyffe. Grasshoppers (Taxonomy); Mosquitoes (Taxonomy and control). b'06. BS '29 (Princeton U); PhD '41 (U Pa). Research taxonomy and biology of grasshoppers and their allies. Co-author: Mosquito Atlas '43; also articles in field. Director Academy Natural Sci Phila since '47. Am Soc Zool—Sigma Xi. Academy of Natural Sciences of Philadelphia, 19th St. and Parkway, Phila 3.

18 ROBERTS, Jean M(orris). Electrical engineering (Servomechanisms, automatic controls, power systems). b'02. EE '26 (U Va); MS '28 (MIT). Asst prof elec engring La Poly Inst '28-30; asst prof elec engring U L '30-35, asso prof '35-42; elec engr special products development dept Eclipse-Pioneer Div Bendix Aviation Corp '46-47; elec engr design engring and constrn dept, Ebasco Services Inc (NY) since '47. Inst Radio Engrs (sr mem) —AIEE—Nat Soc Professional Engrs —NY State Soc Professional Engrs— Tau Beta Pi. Ebasco Services Inc., 2 Rector St., NYC 6.†

19 ROBERTS, Joseph Kent. Virginia (Geology, paleontology). b'89. AB '10 (Emory and Henry Coll); MA '15— PhD '22 (Johns Hopkins). Author reports on Virginia Triassic, Cretaceous and Tertiary of Upper Gulf Embayment of Tennessee and Kentucky, Virginia Tertiary, and Virginia geology; Catalogue of Topographic and Geologic Maps of Virginia; Annoted Bibliography of Virginia Geology; Laboratory Manual for General Geology. Prof geol U Va since '26; asst. geol survey Va '20-23, '27, '31, '40, '41, Tenn summers '24, '25, Ky '26, '29, '44; Mt Lake Va Biol Sta summers '38, '42. AAAS(F)—Geol Soc Am(F)—Paleontol Soc Am(F)—Geol Soc Washington(F)—Am Geog Soc(F)—Va Acad Sci(F)—AAUP—Seismol Soc Am(E div)—Gamma Alpha—Sigma Xi (vp '31-32 pres '32-33). Box 1471, University Station, Charlottesville, Va.†◎

20 ROBERTS, Katharine Eggleston. Language and literature. b'95. AB '17 —AM '18 (State U Ia). Author: Divorce Me, Dear (play) '31; Center of the Web (novel) '42; Private Report (novel) '43; And The Bravest of These (non-fiction on post war reconstruction) '46. European corr Belgium, France, Holland, Gt Britain '19-20; editorial asst Reilly & Le Pub Co Chicago '20-22; writer, lecturer, broadcaster on internat topics; European corr '45. Care of B. Livingstone 52 West 58th St., NYC 19.†◎

21 ROBERTS, Kenneth. Water dowsing. AB '08 (Cornell U); LittD '34 (Dartmouth); LittD '35 (Colby); Litt D '38 (Bowdoin); LittD '38 (Middlebury); LittD '45 (Northeastern U).

Author: Henry Gross and his Dowsing Rod '51. Kennebunkport, Me.

22 ROBERTS, Kenneth (Lewis). Early American, Haitian and North African hist.; Antiques; Water Dowsing. born '85. AB '08 (Cornell Univ) five hon degrees. Author: The Collector's Whatnot (with Booth Tarkington and Hugh McNair Kahler) '23; Black Magic '24; Concentrated New England '24; Antiquamania '28; Rabble in Arms '33; Northwest Passage '37; Trending into Maine, March to Quebec '38; Good Maine Food (with Marjorie Mosser) '39; Moreau de St Mery's American Journey (with Anna M Roberts) '47, and others. Newspaper and magazine writer '09-37. Nat Inst Arts Letters—Phi Beta Kappa. Kennebunkport, Me.

23 ROBERTS, Marguerite. English literature in the drama and novel (Thomas Hardy). b'04. AB '24 (Evansville Coll); AM '28—PhD '43 (Radcliffe Coll); research in Mrs Thomas Hardy's home '34-35; in England '48. Author: Hardy and the Theatre '43; Tess in the Theatre '50. Author article: Dramatic element in Thomas Hardy's Poetry, and others. Asst prof English lit and dean of women McMaster U '37-46; lecturer English U Toronto '46-47; prof English and dean of Westhampton Coll U Richmond since 1947. AAUP—Nat Assn Deans— AAUW—Va Writers—Phi Beta Kappa. Westhampton College, University of Richmond, Va.

24 ROBERTS, Merritt E(lisha). Antibiotics (Fungal); Toxins; Fungicides; Bactericides; Soluble antigens; Mass production of bacteria. b'07. AB '30—MS '31—PhD '37 (University of Kansas). Resch on the alkyl derivs of isomeric ortho and para phenoxy phenyl thiazolidones, pertussis toxin-antitoxin neutralization technic, pertussis antitoxin and its relationship to protection in actively and passively immunized mice and rabbits. One patent pending and one granted on production of whooping cough toxin and whooping cough anti-toxin. Author articles in field. Dept head Lederle Labs Inc NY '37-43; research asso Nat Research Council Washington '46-49; chem biol research dept Cutter Labs Calif since '49. Lab officer US Army Med Center Walter Reed Hosp '43-46. NY Acad Sci—Am Chem Soc—Sigma Xi; Biological Research Department, Cutter Laboratories, 4th and Parker Street, Berkeley 1.

25 ROBERTS, Patricia Easterbrook. Flower Craft; Floristry (Technical). b'10. Ed private schs. Study of floristry US and abroad since '29. Author: Technical Floristry '45; Flower Craft '49. Rep Florists Telegraph Delivery Fleurop Conv Luxembourg '37, toured 12 European countries studying telegraph delivery methods; weekly radio program on flowers since '40; opened Roberts Sch Dramatic Floriculture '40; mgr and dir publicity organized orchid growers East Coast. H: 11 Cresthill Pl., Shippan Point, Stamford, Conn.

26 ROBERTSON, Constance Noyes. Oneida community; Underground railroad; Copperheads; Vallandigham. b'97. Student '16-18 (U Wis). Research on 16th century religious communistic experiments, especially Oneida Community; underground railroad activities in central New York state, activities of Copperheads, especially Knights of the Golden Circle, during Civil War; life of Clement L Vallandigham. Author: Seek-No-Further '38; Salute to the Hero '42; Fire Bell in the Night '44; The Unterrified '46; The Golden Circle '51. Staff mem

Seminars on Am culture, '48-51. NY State Hist Assn—Authors League—PEN. Struan House, Kenwood, Oneida, NY.

10 ROBERTSON, Edwin J(acob). Cooking and packaging of meats. b'05. BS '34 (Ia State Coll); 43-46 (Inst Am Econ). Research and new product development in meat cooking, meat curing, meat freezing, meat packaging. Am Soc Refrig Engrs. Research and Technical Division, Wilson & Co., 4100 S. Ashland Av., Chicago 9.

11 ROBERTSON, Florence. Geophysics; Seismology; Geomagnetism; Physics; Mathematics. b'09. AB '35—AM '36 (Tex Tech Coll); PhD '45 (St Louis U); fellow in Physics '35-36 (Tex Tech Coll); fellow in Geophysics '36-39 (St Louis U). Research on earthquakes and seismographic disturbances, selection of a seismograph, variability of vibrations from quarry blasts. Author articles in field. With St Louis U since '39, professor of geophysics and geophysical engineering since '51. Seismol Soc America (chmn Eastern Sect '46)—Am Geophy Union (sec sect seis '47)—Am Phys Soc(F)—Soc Exploration Geophys—Am Soc Engring Edn—Sigma Xi—Geol Soc Am(F)—AIME. 3621 Olive St., St. Louis 8.†

12 ROBERTSON, Joseph Henry. Range revegetation and ecology. b'06. AB '28 (Peru Neb State Teachers Coll); MS '32—PhD '39 (U Neb). Author articles: How to Reseed Nevada Range Lands '43, and others. Asso prof range management and agron U Nev since '47, also head dept range management. Ecol Soc Am—Am Soc Range Management—Sigma Xi. College of Agriculture, University P.O., Reno, Nev.†

13 ROBERTSON, Percival. Pleistocene geology; Geodes; Glacial phenomena in Illinois and Missouri. b'89. PhB '15 (Yale U); MS '24—PhD '36 (Washington U). With Principia Coll since '15, prof geol since '30. Geol Soc Am(F)—Assn Geol Teachers (pres '42-45)—Ill State Acad Sci—Sigma Xi. The Principia College, Elsah, Ill.

14 ROBERTSON, William Fenton. Food technology. b'97. BS '20—MS '36 (U Mass); grad study (Mich State Coll). Research on canning and freezing of cherries, preserves, jelly, jam, pickles, kraut, confections; introduced refractometer in confectionery business, introduced infra-red blanch, research on effect of delays between harvest and canning on vitamins in canned food and delays between blanching and processing on vitamins in canned vegetables, frozen fruit juice concentrates, method to return condensable esters to preserves. Faculty U Mass '20-27; with ZaRex Co '27-29; chief chem and plant supt ZaRex Co Boston '27-29, Pfaudler Research & Tilford '31-33; with Dutchland Farms '35-37; chem and factory supt Trufruit Syrups Corp '40-43; asso prof hort Mich State Coll since '43. Am Soc Hort Sci—AAAS—Inst Food Tech (charter mem). 110 Horticultural Building, Michigan State College, East Lansing.

15 ROBINETTE, Hillary, Jr. Textile chemistry; Embalming chemistry. b'13. AB '34 (Temple U). Research on resins, surface active agents, textile finishes and wet processing agents; development embalming agents. Granted seven US patents on surface active agents, mercerizing assistant, water repellent treatment for textiles, and hydantrin derivative textile lubricants. Organic research chem Rohm & Haas Co '33-39; pres W H and F Jordan Jr Mfg Co '39-40; market

development Comml Solvents Corp '40-42; research Publicker Industries '45-48; research dir Amalgamated Chem Corp since '48. ACS—Am Inst Chem—Am Assn Textile Chem and Colorists—Soc Chem Industry—Soc Mil Engrs. Amalgamated Chemical Corp., Rorer and Ontario sts., Phila 34. H: 1007 Remington Rd., Phila 31.

16 ROBINSON, Clarence C(ramer). Voice; Choral composition and arranging. b'79. Student part-time '20-22 (Pa State Coll); MMus hon '27 (Cincinnati Conservatory); pvt instrn NY and Chicago. Dir sch music Ohio U '22-47, prof since '47; composer choral music, sacred and secular; adjudicator Welsh eisteddvods, and sch contests. Army song leader Camp Upton World War I; former music adminstr War Camp Community Service San Francisco. Nat Music Tchrs Assn—Phi Mu Alpha. Ohio University, Athens.†©

17 ROBINSON, David M(oore). Greek and Roman art, archeology and literature; Classical studies. b'80. AB '98—PhD '04 (U Chicago); '01-03 (Am Sch Classical Studies Athens); '03-04 (U Berlin, U Halle); '09 (U Bonn); PhD hon '51 (Univ Thessalonia). Directed excavations at Pisidian Antioch and Sizma '24, Olynthus '28-38; has excavated at Sinope, Corinth and Sardis. Author: Ancient Sinope '06; The Songs of Sappho '25; Sappho and Her Influence '24; The Greek Idylls '26; Greek and Latin Inscriptions from Asia Minor '26; Deeds of Augustus '26; Roman Sculptures from Pisidian Antioch '26; Greek and Latin Inscriptions of Sardis '32; Greek Vases at Toronto, 2 vols '30; Excavations at Olynthus, 13 vols '30-49; Corpus Vasorum, the Robinson Collection 3 vols '33-38; Inscriptions from Macedonia '38; A History of Greece '36; Pindar '36; Prehistoric and Greek Houses '39; The Glory and Glamour of the Dodecanese '44; Baalbek Palmyra '46; America in Greece '48 and others; also articles in field. Prof archeol epigraphy and Greek Johns Hopkins '05-46, research prof '46-'47, prof emeritus of art and archeol '47-48; prof classics and archeol U Miss since '48. Am Acad Arts Sci—Am Philos Soc—Archeol Inst Am—Archeol Soc Greece—Royal Numismatic Soc Eng—Am Geog Soc—Am Classical League (vp)—Coll Art Assn (pres '19-23, dir since '23, ed in chief art bull '19-38)—Am Philol Assn—Assn Promotion Byzantine Meta-Byzantine Studies (pres)—AHA—NEA—Classical Assn Middle West S—Archtl Hist—Phi Beta Kappa. University of Mississippi, Oxford, Miss.†©

18 ROBINSON, Edgar Eugene. American politics and political parties; Presidential vote in the United States. b'87. AB '08—AM '10—LLD '42 (U Wis). Author: Evolution of American Political Parties '24; The Presidential Vote (1896-1932) '34; American Democracy in Time of Crisis '34; The Presidential Vote (1936) '40; The New United States '46; They Voted for Roosevelt '47 and others. Prof Am hist Stanford U since '23, dir Inst Am Hist since '43. AHA (pres Pacific Coast br '29)—Royal Hist Soc(F)—Phi Beta Kappa. Stanford University, Stanford, Cal.©

19 ROBINSON, Edwin Allin. Synthetic fiber. b'07. AB '28—MS '29 (U Denver); PhD '33 (Columbia U). Holds 21 patents on preparation of surface active chemicals, textile processing operations, application of surface active chemicals to textile fibers and yarns. Author: Machine Measures Knitting Factor of Synthetic Yarns '45. Tech dir Nopco Chem Co Harrison NJ

'36-48, asst vp '48-53, vp since '53. Am Chem Soc. Nopco Chemical Co., Harrison, N.J. H: 99 Fairmount Av., Chatham, N.J.

20 ROBINSON, Howard Addison. Physics of cork and glass; Ultra-violet spectroscopy. b'09. BS '30—PhD '35 (MIT); Am German exchange student '30-31 (U Munich); Langmuir fellow '36-37 (U Uppsala, Sweden). Editor: High-Polymer Physics: A Symposium '48; also articles in field. Chief physicist and mgr phys research Armstrong Cork Co Lancaster Pa '42-48, '50-52; 1st sec of Embassy, Paris, France since '52. Am Phys Soc(F)—Optical Soc Am ASME—AAAS(F). American Embassy, 2 Av Gabriel, Paris, France.

21 ROBINSON, Hoyt Ellsworth. Children (Exceptional, education). b'01. BS '31—MS '36 (N Tex State Coll); EdD '48 (U Tex). Author: Teachers Guide for Special Education '46. Supt sch '18-37, dep state supt schs Tex '37-39, dir equalization '39-45, dir spl edn since '45. Tex State Tchrs Assn—Internat Council for Exceptional Children. Texas Education Agency, Austin.

22 ROBINSON, Joseph L(ee). Crop production. b'93. BS '16 (Okla A&M Coll); MS '18—PhD '33—fellow '16-17 (Ia State Coll). Conducted Iowa corn yield test '20, '53; responsible for field crop seed certification in Iowa '20-53; managed Iowa State corn and seed show '21-41. Author articles in field. Research and ext prof agrl Ia State Coll since '46. Ia Corn Small Grain Growers Assn (sec, trea)—Internat Crop Improvement Assn (dir)—Commn Agr Development (prod mgr). Farm Crop Department, Iowa State College, Ames, Ia.†

23 ROBINSON, Karl Davis. Printing (Gelatin); Lithography (Desensitizing agents); Colloidal acid resists. b'84. BS '12 (Columbia). Study of gelatin as amphoteric electrolyte, and printing characteristics of gelatinates in collotype process; investigation colloidal acid resists in dry offset; hydrophilic colloids as desensitizing agents in lithography, and especially carboxymethyl cellulose and other cellulose compounds. Author: Line Photography for the Lithographic Process '48; What the Lithographer Should Know About Air Conditioning '50. Editor: The American Go Journal. Staff McClure's Magazine and Harper's Weekly '12-15; promotion mgr NY Eve Post and Literary Review '20; cons research and development div Mergenthaler Linotype Co since '50. Tech Assn for Graphic Arts—Lithographic Tech Found (research com). Mergenthaler Linotype Co., 29 Ryerson St., Bklyn 5.

24 ROBINSON, L. V(ernon). Variable stars; Differential equations. b'98. BA '21—MA '22 (U Tex); PhD '31 (Harvard); Vanderbilt fellow '23-24 (U Va). Recent discoveries generalized differential operators, operator methods in solving partial differential equations. Author: Variable Stars '32; also articles in field. Asst prof math Okla City U '24-25; adjunct prof math Tex Tech Coll '26-30; instr astron Radcliffe Coll '30-31; astron Harvard Coll Obs '31-32; asst soil conservationist US Dept Agr '34-37; instr math Amarillo Coll '37-40, asst prof math U Miss '40-43; asst prof phys Marshall Coll '43-44; asso prof math Emory U '44-45; asso prof math and astron USC '45-50; math Ball Research Lab since '50. American Astron Society—Royal Astron Soc (London)—Astron Soc Pacific—AAAS(F)—Am Math Soc—Math Assn Am. Ballistics Research Laboratory, Aberdeen, Md.

10 ROBINSON, Leigh Fowler. Santo Domingo. b'87. Student (Ind U); MD '12 (Jefferson Med Coll). Lieutenant Medical Corps US Navy '17-20, surgeon Santo Domingo under US Military Government '20-25. ACS(F)—Southeastern Surg Congress—Am Protologic Soc—Fla Med Assn—AMA. Sweet Bldg., Ft. Lauderdale, Fla.

11 ROBINSON, Leland Rex. Investment management; International economics (Middle East); Political economy. born '93. Student '11-12 (Hillsdale College Michigan); AB '15—PhD '23 (Columbia). Author: Foreign Credit Facilities in the United Kingdom '23; Economic and Spiritual Forces in the Development of the U.S. 25; Investment Trust Organization and Management '29; also articles in field. Mem Am Persian Relief Commn '18-19, dir Am Relief Persia '19; asst dir US Bur Fgn Domestic Commerce '21-22; Am Financial trade commr London '22-23; pres 2nd Internat Securities Corp, Internat Securities Corp Am. US and British Internat Co Ltd '25-35; chmn investment adv com Am Gen Corp '36-37; adv Higher Edn NY State Dept Edn '41-42; chmn Bishops Service '46; lecturer Columbia '42; adjunct prof polit econ NYU; mem Dept Internat Justice Goodwill; mem exec com, chmn com Displaced Persons; mem com Study Orgn Peace, Alien Enemy Hearing Bd NY; vp Iron Found; dir Republic Investors Fund, Sovereign Investors. Econ Nat Com Monetary Policy (vp)—Am Fedn Internat Inst—Royal Econ Soc (F)—AAAS—Am Econ Assn—Acad Polit Sci—Am Statis Soc—Council Fgn Relations—Fed Grand Jury Assn—Phi Beta Kappa. Recipient special rosette star order of China. 76 Beaver St., NYC 5 & 1 Madison Av., NYC.†◉

12 ROBINSON, Mark. Beetles (Coleoptera and Scarabaeidae of the United States). b'06. Student (Williamson). Research of Canthon, Phanaeus, and Choeridium inhabiting US. Author articles in field. Research asso dept insects Acad Nat Sci Phila. Am Entomol Soc (pres '47-48)—Acad Nat Sci—Am Mus Nat Hist. Academy of Natural Sciences, Phila. 3.

13 ROBINSON, Otto Louis. Fire protection engineering. b'93. BS '16 (Purdue U). Research in design, construction and operation of automatic sprinkler equipment, extinguishers, fire alarm equipment, gas and oil fired burners, boilers and furnaces. Author articles in field. Engr Underwriters Labs Inc since '17; instr later asso prof dept fire protection engring Ill Inst Tech since '20. Am Soc Engring Edn. 207 E. Ohio St., Chicago 11.

14 ROBINSON, Robert Ross. Soil aspects of pasture production; (Pasture management, soil fertility). b'09. BS '31—MS '33—PhD '36 (W Va U). Author articles in field. Agron US Regional Pasture Research Lab and Div Soil Management and Irrigation BPI SAE since '47. Am Soc Agron—Soil Sci Soc Am—Sigma Xi. U.S. Regional Pasture Research Laboratory, State College, Pa.†

15 ROBINSON, William Morrison, Jr. History of the South and the United States; Confederate history (Administrative, Naval, judicial). b'91. BS in CE '11—CE '24 (Ga Sch Tech). Author: The Alabama-Kearsarge Battle, a Study in Original Sources '24; The Confederate Privateers '28; Justice in Grey, a History of the Judicial System of the Confederate States '41; also articles in field. Civil engring practice in corp and pub positions and as private cons in civil and valuation engring '11-41; Army '17-19 and '41-50, retired; now engaged on a history of confederate seapower. AHA—So Hist Assn—Naval Hist Found—Am Mil Institute—Soc Am Mil Engrs—Am Soc CE. P.O. Box 507, Quincy, Fla.

16 ROBINTON, Madeline Russell. Modern English history; United States prize court (Procedure, history). b'09. BA '29—Internat fellow for Study Abroad '29-30 (Barnard Coll); MA '31 —PhD '44 (Columbia U); '29-30 (U London, U Heidelberg). Author: An Introduction to the Papers of the New York Prize Court (1861-1865) '45. Editor: Microfilm of Files of New York Prize Court Papers 1861-1865 '46. Asst prof hist Brooklyn Coll since '46. AHA—Econ Hist Assn—Econ Hist Soc Gr Brit—Phi Beta Kappa. Department of History, Brooklyn College, Brooklyn 10, N.Y.

17 ROBISON, Daniel Merritt. History (Tennessee and Southern). b'93. AB '20—MA '30—PhD '32 (Vanderbilt U). Author: Bob Taylor and the Agrarian Revolt in Tennessee '35. Editor: Tennessee Historical Quarterly since '43. Vanderbilt U '36-50; Tenn State librarian and archivist since '49. Miss Valley Hist Assn—So Hist Assn (exec council '46-48)—Tenn Hist Soc—East Tenn Hist Soc—West Tenn Hist Soc. Tennessee State Library, Nashville 4.

18 ROBOTTI, Frances Diane. Nathaniel Hawthorne: History of Salem; Witchcraft: Massachusetts (Seventeenth, eighteenth, nineteenth centuries). b'17. AB '40 (Hunter Coll); (Columbia U). Research on Salem and Massachusetts history: houses, furnishings, architecture, location of historical sites such as churches, meeting houses, lanes and streets, mills, changes in topography, wharves, shipbuilding yards, Puritanism, Quakers, Indian and other wars, Federalism, Salem's literary and scientific men. Author: Chronicles of Old Salem: A History in Miniature '48; Whaling in Old Salem '50. Research at Essex Inst, NY Pub Library '45-47, Mass Hist Soc Boston since '47. Essex Inst—Am Assn U Women. 2109 Gleason Av., NYC 61.

19 ROCHEDIEU, Charles Alfred. Anglo-French relations (18th century); Rousseau. b'92. BA '24 (U Manitoba); MA '28—PhD '34 (Peabody Coll); '27-28 (Vanderbilt U); '36 (Universite de Dijon). Director French Institute Emory University summer '34; director French School Oglethorpe University summers '47, '48. Author: Bibliography of French Translations of Works in English, 1700-1800 '48; also articles in field. Asso prof French Vanderbilt U since '24. Modern Lang Assn—S Atlantic Modern Lang Assn—Tenn Philol Soc—Am Assn Teachers French—Bibliographic Soc Am. Vanderbilt University, Nashville 4, Tenn. H: 211-24th Av., S., Nashville 4.

20 ROCHOW, Eugene George. Silicones. b'09. BChem '31—PhD '35 (Cornell U). Author: Introduction to Chemistry of the Silicones '45; also articles in field. Asso prof chem Harvard '48-52, professor of chemistry since '52. Am Chem Society—AAAS—Tau Beta Pi—Phi Kappa Phi. Lovenberg prize '31, Baekeland award '49. 12 Oxford St., Cambridge 38, Mass.†

21 ROCHOW, Theodore George. Metallography; Microscopy (Electron microscopy); Resinography. b'07. B Chem '29—PhD '34 (Cornell U). Worked on Manhattan Proj, smoke filters for Chem War Service, anti-fog and anti-rain agents for Naval Bureau of Ordnance, metallurgical and crystallographic problems in production of military propellants. Co-author articles in field. Am Cyanamid Co since '34, initiated organized microscopical analysis of materials in the Exptl Lab Linden NJ, transferred with latter to Stamford Comm '37. Am Soc Metals—Am Soc Testing Materials—Electron Microscope Soc Am—AAAS—ACS—Sigma Xi. Rsrch Laboratories, American Cyanamid Co., 1937 W. Main St., Stamford, Conn.

22 ROCKIE, William Allan. Soil conservation, agricultural geography, physiography, climatology, land use and glaciation in Pacific Northwest, Palouse, Alaska and Nebraska. b'90. BS in agrl geog '14 (U Neb); grad work (U Neb, Ore State Coll, Wash State Coll). Mapped and studied soils and soil problems in above regions, studies in applied plant ecology, planned, initiated and directed erosion control and other soil conservation work in Pacific Northwest, Alaska and Pacific region. Contributor: The Pacific Northwest '42; Conservation of Natural Resources '50. Ecol BPISAE USDA '22-30; supt Pacific NW Soil Conservation Expt Sta '30-33; with Soil Conservation Service since '33 as regional dir Pacific NW region, chief Alaska studies and chief of planning. AAAS—Assn Am Geog(F)—Am Geog Soc(F)—SOil Conservation Soc Am—Friends of the Land—Arctic Inst Am —Polar Soc—Asso Pacific Coast Geog —NW Sci Assn (pres '35, trustee '36-47)—Ore Acad Sci c/o Soil Conservation Service, Swan Island, Portland 18, Ore.

23 ROCKWELL, Harvard Seldon. Grain elevators (Terminal, cribbed wall). b'91. BS in engring '14 (U Minn). Research on structural design for reinforced concrete terminal grain elevators and cribbed wall country grain elevators. Structural engr Fegles Constrn Co '23-25; Rockwell Engring Co '25-42; Austin Co '42-45; chief engr McKenzie-Hague-Simmons Co '45-47; structural engr T E Ibberson Co since '47. Am Soc CE (asso) —Theta Tau. T. E. Ibberson Co., 300 Corn Exchange, Mpls.

24 ROCKWELL, William Walker. Church history. b'74. AB '95 (Harvard); STB '00 (Andover Theol Sem); '00-02 (U Berlin); STL '03—ThD '30 (Marburg U); AM—PhD '14 (U Gottingen Germany). Chairman commission on international relations Nat Council Congregational Churches '29-31) research on Papacy, and Protestant Reformation; studies on history and policy of Congregational Churches in England, and in New England since 1620; served as expert witness on rights of Ruthenian Uniates; reader of wills and parish registers in Southern England. Author: Rival Presuppositions in the Writing of Church History '35. Editor: Papers of American Society Church History (3 vols) '12, '14, '17. Contributor: Encyclopedia Britannica '10-11, Dictionary of Religion and Ethics. Ordained to Congl ministry '05; asst prof church hist advancing to librarian Union Theol Sem '05-42, librarian emeritus since '42; faculty Polit Sci Columbia '12-42, philos '35-37; sec bd eds Am Ency of Christianity '20-26; vis prof Div Sch U Chicago '25-31. Am Society Church Hist(pres '26)—Medieval Acad Am—NY Medieval Club—Spl Libraries Assn—Bibliog Soc Am—Bibliog Soc London—Soc Genealogists London—New Eng Hist Genealogical Soc —Hymn Soc Am(F, librarian)—NY Geneaological and Biog Soc—NY Hist Soc—Conn Hist Soc—Educators Congl Commn on Free Church Policy and Unity. 39 Claremont Av., NYC 27.

25 ROCKWOOD, Raymond Oxley. Eighteenth Century French history (Enlightenment, Voltaire). b'07. BS '29 (Boston U); AM '31—PhD '35 (Chicago U); '25-27 (Antioch Coll). Research in Paris; studied cult of Voltaire to 1791. Author articles in field. Colgate U since '34, now prof hist, dir summer session '48-49. AHA—Foreign Policy Assn—Soc Histoire Révolution Française. Catherine Cleveland fellow, Chicago U, Paris '32-33, Chicago U Social Science Research fellow '33-34; Augustus Howe Buck Scholar, Boston U '27-29, Univ fellow at Chicago U '29-32. Colgate University, Hamilton, N.Y.†

10 RODABAUGH, James H(oward). Ohio history and personalities. b'10. BA '32—MA '33 (Miami U Oxford O); PhD '37 (O State U). Author: Robert Hamilton Bishop '35; Bibliography of Ohio Archeology (with R G Morgan) '47; Nursing in Ohio: A History (with Mary Jane Rodebaugh) '51. Asst dir O Hist Records Survey Project '38-40; asst dir Hayes Memorial '40-44; dir Ohio War Hist Commn '44-49; research asso O State Archeol Hist Soc since '44, ed since '46, head div hist and science since '52; spl feature ed History-News '48-49. O Acad Science (F)—O State Archeol Hist Soc—Miss Valley Hist Assn—Am Assn State Local Hist—American Historical Assn—Phi Beta Kappa. Ohio State Museum, Columbus 10. H: 510 Selby Blvd., So., Worthington, O.†

11 RODECK, Hugo George. The inquiline bee genus Nomada in North America. b'02. AB '28—MA '29 (U Colo); PhD '44 (U Minn). Author articles in field. Professor nat hist, dir U Colo Mus since '33. Entomol Soc Am—Am Soc Mammalogists—Colo-Wyo Acad Sci (exec sec since '47)—Sigma Xi. University of Colorado Museum, Boulder, Colo.†

12 RODENHOUSE, Irma Zintheo. Marine zoology; Litoral ecology; Seashore animals. b'07. BS '30—MS '39 (U Wash). Research on Puget Sound animal life; ecology of shore life Puget Sound area; morphology and behaviour Cushion Star Fish. Tchr Seattle Pub Schs. Sigma Xi(asso)—Phi Sigma—Am Pub Health Assn—Wash Edn Assn—Wash Assn Health Phys Edn and Recreation. Ballard High School, Seattle.

13 RODGERS, Andrew Denny, III. Ohio (History); American forestry (History); Plant sciences (History); American plant pathology (History). b'00. AB '22—LittD '46 (Ohio Wesleyan U); LLB '25 (Ohio State U); grad study '33-35 (Northwestern U). Research, author on persons historically active some field of North American biological sciences: Liberty Hyde Bailey, Bernard E. Fernow, Erwin F. Smith. AAAS—Hist Sci Soc—Sigma Alpha Epsilon—Delta Sigma Rho—Phi Delta Phi. 30 S. Dawson Av., Bexley, Columbus, O.

14 RODGERS, Edith C(ooperrider). Military history (United States Air Force); History of the Middle Ages. b'93. AB '16 (Ohio State U); MA '32—PhD '40 (Columbia). Author: Discussion of Holidays in the Later Middle Ages '40; also articles in field Historian hist div US Air Force since '43, chief research sect since '46. AHA—Medieval Acad Am—So Hist Assn—Phi Beta Kappa. Historical Division, U.S. Air Force, Air University, Maxwell Air Force Base, Ala.

15 RODGERS, John. Geology of Appalachians Eastern Tennessee, Western New England and adjacent New York (Geologic stratigraphy and structure, soils). b'14. BA '36—MS '37 (Cornell U); PhD '44 (Yale U). Field geologist US Geological Survey '38-46, summers since '46. Author articles in field. Asso prof geol Yale since '52. Geol Soc Am(F)—Am Assn Petroleum Geol. Department of Geology, Yale University, New Haven.†

16 RODKEY, Fred Stanley. Eastern Europe (History and Culture); Near East (Modern history and culture); Ottoman Empire (Nineteenth Century); Russian Revolution (Background). b '96. AB '17—AM '18 (U Kan); PhD '21 (U Ill); '27 (U London, Eng). Author: The Turco-Egyptian Question in the Relations of England, France, and Russia, 1832-41, '24; An Historical Approach to the World Problems of Today '34; also articles in field. Asso prof hist Miami U Oxford O '22-29; asso prof hist U Ill '29-39, prof since '39. Fellow Social Sci Research Council for study in Europe '27-28, awarded Herbert Baxter Adams Prize of Am Hist Soc '25; Alexander Prize medal of Royal Hist Soc of Gt Brit '29. AHA—Royal Hist Soc of Gt Brit(F). 327 Lincoln Hall, University of Illinois, Urbana, Ill. H: 201 South Busey Av.

17 ROEDEL, Phil M(organ). Biology of Pacific Coast mackerel, sardines, and tuna. b'13. AB '35 (Stanford). Research on distribution, migration, populations, age, maturity, and spawning of Pacific and jack mackerel; exploratory work at sea off California and Baja California, Mexico, on mackerel, sardines, and tuna; editor California Fish and Game since '50. With Cal Div Fish and Game since '36, marine biol in charge Pacific and jack Mackerel investigations since '46. Am Soc Ichthyologists and Herpetologists—Am Soc Limnol and Oceanog. California State Fisheries Laboratory, Terminal Island Station, San Pedro.

18 ROEDER, Elwood Shoenly. Theoretical music (Twelve-degree mode, physical basis of music scales and modes, sixteenth century counterpoint). b'88. Diploma '16 (NE Conservatory Music, Boston); BMus '37—MMus '38—research fellowship in 16th century counterpoint '37-38 — George Eastman Scholarship '36-37 (Eastman Sch Music, U Rochester). Private research in the physical basis of music scales and modes against a common microtonal background; discovered 12-degree mode, mode of perfect fifth. Author articles in field. Asso prof theoretical music and composition depts Wesleyan Coll since '38, Wesleyan Conservatory and Sch Fine Arts Macon Ga. Acoustical Soc Am—Am Inst Physics—Nat Assn Am Composers and Conductors — AAUP — Music Teachers Nat Assn—Music Library Assn. 2264 Kingsley Av., Macon, Ga.

19 ROEDIGER, Virginia More (Mrs. Carl S. Johnson). Costumes of North American Indians. b'08. AB '28 (U So Calif); MFA '31—PhD '37 (Yale). Architectural tour Europe '27; photographed and sketched Pueblo Indian ceremonial costumes '36; studied costumes and theater Mexico '39. Author: Ceremonial Costumes of the Pueblo Indians '41. Scene and costume designer Goodman Theater and lecturer art sch Art Inst Chicago '31-34; research asso in anthrop U Calif since '42; illustrator for Museum Leaflet and Museum Talk Santa Barbara Mus Nat Hist '44-46; Arts Club Chicago—Cal Arts Club—Am Anthropol Assn (liaison F). Box 68, Fort Morgan, Colo.

20 ROETZEL, Frank J. Paint (color standardization). b'85. Student (Mendota Coll). Research and development on application of McCorquadale method of paint color standardization in connection with such industries as paint, tile, rubber, chemicals, ceramics where a true duplication of color is desired; development of T-T-C-595 Federal specifications for ready-mixed paint. With Magill-Weisnhei-

mer Co since '37, now vp, sales mgr color marketing div. Soc Color Council—Nat Paint Varnish and Lacquer Assn. 1814 E. 40th St., Cleve. 3. H: 1210 Chase Av., Lakewood, O.

21 ROGERS, Albert Alan. History (Civilization, American, European, cultural, social). b'04. BA '26 (U Richmond); BS '37—MA '37—PhD '39 (U Va). Prof hist and social sci Middlesex U '41-46; head dept history Richmond Division Coll William and Mary since '46. AHA—Am Sociol Soc—Miss Valley Hist Assn. Box 2072, Richmond, Va.

22 ROGERS, Carl R(ansom). Psychotherapy; Personality theory. b'02. AB '24 (U Wis); MA '28—PhD '31 (Columbia). Author: Measuring Personality Adjustment in Children '31; Clinical Treatment of the Problem Child '39; Counseling and Psychotherapy '42; Client-Centered Therapy '51. Coauthor: (with J Wallen) Counseling with Returned Servicemen '46. Research in psychotherapy (client-centered) and counseling (client-centered). Prof psychol and exec sec counseling center U Chicago since '45. Am Orthopsychiatric Assn(vp '41-42)—Am Assn Applied Psychol (pres '44-45)—Phi Beta Kappa. University of Chicago, Chgo 37.©

23 ROGERS, Charles H. Ornithology. b'88. LittB '09 (Princeton). Built Princeton ornithological collection into one most representative of birds of world in US; gives course in birds of the world; studied birds afield on all continents and on many islands, excepting Antarctic. Author articles in field. Asst ornithol Am Mus Natural Hist '12-20; curator Princeton Mus Zool since '20; lecturer ornithology Linnaean Society NY, Delaware Valley Ornithology Club; head Elk-Lake (summer) Nature-Study Camp for ten yrs; led PMZ expedition to Panama '23. American Ornithology Union—Linnaean Society NY (secretary five years) —Delaware Valley Ornithology Club—Wilson Ornithol Club—NJ Field Ornithologists—NJ Audubon Soc (pres six yrs). E. Guyot Hall, Princeton, N.J. H: 20 Haslet Av.†

24 ROGERS, Colonel Hoyt. Cotton diseases (Root rot); Plant disease resistance breeding (Cotton, tobacco). b'06. BS '26 (Clemson A&M Coll); MS '27 (U Ky); PhD '31 (Rutgers U). Author articles in field. Plant pathologist Coker's Pedigreed Seed Co since '42. Am Soc Agron—Am Phytopathol Soc—Bot Soc Am—SC Acad Sci—SC Seedsmen Assn—Assn So Agrl Workers—Sigma Xi. Coker's Pedigreed Seed Company, Hartsville, S.C.

25 ROGERS, Cornwell Burnham. French Revolution; Public opinion. b'98. AB '20 (Princeton); MA '25—PhD '43 (Columbia U). Collector of documentary materials—songs, hymns, ceremonies, dramas—relating to the cultural and social history of the French Revolution. Author: The Spirit of Revolution in 1789—A Study of Public Opinion As Revealed in Political Songs and Other Popular Literature at the Beginning of the French Revolution '49. Editor: Key to Contemporary Affairs '40-41. Author article: Songs-Colorful Propaganda of the French Revolution '47. Instr hist Yale U Freshman Faculty 26-28; research hist of French Revolution since '28; teacher Millbrook Sch NY '31-32, '35-40; lecturer in hist Columbia U '43-46; Am Red Cross Hist Div '48-49. American Field Service(F)—AHA. H: Wiscasset, Maine.

26 ROGERS, Donald Atwater. Chemical plant design. b'99. ME '24 (Cornell U). Economics and design of chemical manufacturing plants. With Allied Chem & Dye Corp since '24, mgr Central Engring since '51. Tau Beta Pi—Phi Kappa Phi—ASME—ACS—Am Inst Chem Engrs—Va Acad Sci. Allied Chemical & Dye Corp., Morristown, N.J.

10 ROGERS, Donald Philip. Mycology (Basidiomycetes). b'08. BA '29 (Oberlin Coll); PhD '35 (U Ia). Phylogeny, cytology, and taxonomy of lower Basidiomycetes. Author: The Basidium '34. Nat research fellow Harvard '35-36; instr bot Ore State Coll '36-40; research Harvard '40-41; instr bot Brown U '41-42; asso prof biol Am Internat Coll '42-45; asst prof bot U Hawaii '46-47; curator NY Bot Garden since '47. Mycological Soc Am—Brit Mycological Soc—Bot Soc Am—Torrey Bot Club—Am Soc Plant Taxonomists. New York Bot Garden, NYC 58. H: Scarsdale.

11 ROGERS, (Harry) Barrett. Wage incentives; Motion and time study; Standard time data; Job evaluation; Merit rating. b'03. BS in EE '27 (U Minn). Management consultant. Author articles in field. Prof indsl management Sch Commerce Northwestern U since '42, head management dept since '48. Indsl Management Soc (chmn job evaluation research com '35-37, program vp '45-47, dir '47-48, exec vp '48-49)—Am Soc Engring Edn—Am Management Assn—Soc Advancement of Management—Acad of Management —Am Soc for Qual Control—Chicago Soc for Qual Control—Am Econ Assn. Northwestern University, Evanston, Ill.†

12 ROGERS, Lewis Henry. Analytical chemistry; Spectrochemistry (Uranium, agriculture). b'10. BS chem engring '32—MS '34 (Fla U); PhD '41 (Cornell U). Research in development of spectrochemical procedures for agricultural research, role of trace elements, analytical and spectrochemical studies of uranium; studies and writing on microdetermination of zinc, infrared absorption spectra of vitamins C and D, and some sugars and furans, distribution of macro and micro elements in soils of penisular Florida, determination of exchangeable bases with air-acetylene flame and quartz photoelectric spectrophotometer. Author articles in field. Research chemist, Carbide and Carbon Chem Corp Oak Ridge Tenn since '48. Am Chem Soc—AAAS—Optical Soc Am—Sigma Xi. P.O. Box P, Carbide and Carbon Chemical Corp., Oak Ridge, Tenn. H: 187 California Av.†

13 ROGERS, Linwood Nicholas. Cellulose acetate (Manufacture); Cotton linter pulp (Cellulose derivatives); Wood pulp; Protein research. b'01. BS in chem '25 (U Va). Research on digestion and bleaching of cotton linter pulp and its uses for cellulose derivatives; cotton linter pulp and wood pulp using soda, sulfite, sulfate, and prehydrolyzed sulfate processes; granted patents on cellulose acetate and carboxymethylcellulose. With Celanese Corp '25-29, Buckeye Cotton Oil Co since '29, tech dir '34-48, dir research since '48. ACS —Am Oil Chem Soc—Tech Inst Pulp and Paper Industry—ASTM—Alpha Chi Sigma—AAAS. Buckeye Cotton Oil Co., 2899 Jackson Av., Memphis.

14 ROGERS, Paul. Structural engring (Power stations, Turbine supports). b'09. BS '34—CE '37 (Ecole du Genie Civil Paris); '41 (Ill Inst Tech). Research on structural aspects of power plant design, design of turbine foundations. With Pub Utility Engring & Service Corp '41-42; A J Boynton & Co Inc '42-44; Hiram Walker & Sons Inc '44-45; Roberts & Schae-

fer Co '45-46; cons engr '46-47; Ralph H Burke '47-49; Sargent & Lundy since '49, also cons practice. Am Soc CE—W Soc Engrs (award '50)—Am Concrete Inst—Am Soc Engring Edn —Internat Assn Bridge and Structural Engring—French Civil Engring Soc. H: 5108 N. Avers Av., Chgo 25.

15 ROGERS, Paul Patrick. Spanish literature and drama (Eighteenth and nineteenth centuries). b'00. BSc '21 (U Miss); MA '25 (Acadia U); PhD '28 (Cornell U). Author: Pre-Romantic Drama of Spain '28; Goldoni in Spain '41; Catalog of the Oberlin College Spanish Drama Collection '40, '46. Asst prof Spanish Oberlin Coll '29-31, asso prof '31-45, prof romance langs since '45. Mod Lang Assn Am—Am Assn Teachers Spanish and Portuguese—Internat Mark Twain Soc (hon). Decorated by Spanish Govt with Cross of the Royal Order of Isabel la Catolica '27. Department of Romance Languages, Oberlin College, Oberlin, O.

16 ROGERS, Spencer Lee. Physical anthropology; Medical folklore; Weapon culture. b'05. BA '27 (San Diego State Coll); MA '30 (Claremont Colleges); PhD '37 (U So Calif). Research and writing on the healing of trephine wounds in skulls from Pre-Columbian Peru, aboriginal bow and arrow of North America and Eastern Asia; physical anthropology of Southwestern Indians. Author articles. Instr anthrop San Diego State Coll '30, asst prof '35, asso prof '40, now prof. Am Anthrop Assn(F) — Am Assn Phys Anthrop—Soc Am Archaeol—Archaeol Inst Am (bd govs Sch Am Research). Science director San Diego Museum of Man. San Diego State College, San Diego 15, Cal.

17 ROGERS, Thomas Henry. X-ray tubes and apparatus. b'06. AB '28 (Miss State Coll); BS '28—MEE '33 (Polytechnic Inst Brooklyn). Research on physiological effects of electric shock; effect of cable length on radiation output of shock proof X-ray tubes; intensity radiation of various X-rays and X-ray tubes. Has several patents on X-ray tubes and apparatus. Author articles in field. Field engr Machlett Labs Inc '34-44, mgr engring since '44. AIEE—Tau Beta Pi. Machlett Laboratories, Inc., Springdale, Conn.

18 ROGERS, Tyler Stewart. Buildings (Materials, equipment, thermal insulation). b'95. BSc '16 (U Mass); grad sch landscape arch city planning '17 (Harvard). Research on economic factors, technological developments, proper use building materials and equipment; studies on insulation products and practices, on vapor transmission, condensation, ventilation, economic factors; member Building Research Advisory Board, National Research Council. Author: Plan Your House to Suit Yourself (last edit) '50. Co-author and editor: Reference Manual of American Architect '35. Vp Taylor, Rogers & Bliss Inc (merchandise cons), Wells & Rogers Inc (market research) '29-32; tech ed Am Architect & Architecture '32-38, originator and pub Time Saver Standards for architects; cons merchandising '38-39; dir tech pub Owens-Corning Fiberglas Corp since '39. Owens-Corning Fiberglas Corp., Tol.

19 ROGICK, Mary Dora. Bryozoa (Fresh-water, marine); Biology (Educational methods and techniques); Fish digestive tract histology. b'06. AB '29 —AM '30 (U Neb); PhD '34 (Ohio State U). Author: General Zoology Laboratory Manual '47; also articles in field. Prof biol Coll of New Rochelle since '35. Am Micro Soc—Am Soc Zoologists —Am Soc Limnol & Oceanography—

Nat Assn Biol Teachers—Marine Biol Assn—Phi Beta Kappa—Sigma Xi. College of New Rochelle, New Rochelle, N.Y. H: 25 Prospect St., Apt. 1-K.†

20 ROHEIM, Geza. Psychoanalysis (Application to anthropological data). b'91. Student '09-14 (Leipsig, Berlin, Budapest); PhD '14 (U Budapest). Interpretation of dreams, sublimation, symbolism; anthropology, mythology, religion, personality and culture, folklore Australia, Melanesia, Hungary, North American Indian; first application of psychoanalysis to anthropological data. Author: Australian Totemism '25; Animism, Magic and the Divine King '30; The Riddle of the Sphinx '34; The Origin and Function of Culture '43; The Eternal Ones of the Dream '45; Psychoanalysis and Anthropology '50. Staff Hungarian Nat Mus '17—20; field work in anthrop '28-31; teaching psychoanalyst Budapest Psychoanalytic Inst '32-38, Worcester State Hosp '38, '39; lecturer NY Psychoanalytic Inst '40-50. NY Psychoanalytic Soc(hon)—Am Anthrop Assn(F)—Royal Anthrop Inst Great Britain. 1 West 85th St, NYC 24.

21 ROHLICH, Gerard Addison. Water treatment; Sewage treatment. b'10. BS '34 (Cooper Union Sch Engring); BS '36—MS '37—PhD '41—research fellow '39-40 (U Wis). Author articles in field. Prof hydraulic and sanitary engring lab U Wis since '46. Sr san engr Office Chief Engrs War Dept Washington '42-44. ASCE—Am Water Works Assn—Fed Sewage Works Assn —AAAS—Interamerican Assn San Engring—Am Pub Health Assn—Sigma Xi. Hydraulic and Sanitary Engineering Laboratory, University of Wisconsin, Madison 6, Wis.†

22 ROLAND, Mary C(atherine). Child guidance; Child psychology; Psychotherapy. b'14. AB '36 (Seton Hill Coll Greensburg Pa); MA '37 (Columbia). Secretary American Association Psychiatric Clinics for Children since '51. Author articles: The Psychological Examination as a Beginning in Therapy '45; Help for Problem Children '45; Behavior Deviates —The Emotionally Maladjusted Child '45; The Use of Therapy as an Experience in Growth Within the Structure of a Child Guidance Clinic '49, and others. Co-author article: (with Marjorie R Landis) Some Factors that Affect the Emotional Development of Institutionalized Children '41. Contributor: Readings in the Clinical Method in Psychology '49. Psychol Children's Inst Allentown State Hosp Pa '37-41, Lehigh Valley Child Guidance Clinic Bethlehem Pa '37-41; psychol Child Guidance Center of Harrisburg '41-46, psychotherapist since '46. Am Psychol Assn—Eastern Psychol Assn—Pa Psychol Assn—Am Orthopsychiat Assn. Care of Child Guidance Center of Harrisburg, 107 Boas St., Harrisburg, Pa.

23 ROLBIECKI, John J(oseph). History of ancient and medieval philosophy; Dante's political doctrines. b'89. AM '19—PhD '21 (Catholic U Am); student (Laval U Montreal, U Mich). Author: The Political Philosophy of Dante Alighieri '21; The Prospects of Philosophy '39; also articles in field. Instr philos Catholic U Am Washington '21-25, asso prof '26-39, prof since '40. AAAS(F)—Am Philos Assn—So Soc Philos and Psychol—Am Catholic Philos Assn—British Inst Philos—Polish Inst Arts Scis in Am (corres). Catholic University, Washington 17.⊙

24 ROLFE, Franlin P. Prose fiction (17th Century); English literature (Victorian period); Publications (Motion picture and radio). b'02. BS '24

—MA '25 (Dartmouth); PhD '31 Harvard). Member board of editors The Hollywood Quarterly. Sheldon travelling fellow Harvard '31-32; with U Cal since '32, chmn dept English '44-48, prof English since '48, dean div humanities. 310 Royce Hall, University of California, LA 24.

10 ROLLER, Duane (Emerson). Metallic conduction; Language of physical science. b'94. AB '23—MS '25 (U Okla); PhD '28 (Calif Inst Tech); '14-15 (U Wis); '15-17 (Ohio State U). Co-author: (with R A Millikan and E C Watson) Mechanics, Molecular Physics, Heat and Sound '37; (with H L Dodge) Laboratory Manual of Physics '26; also author articles in field. Prof physics Wabash Coll '44-52; asst dir Hughes Research & Development Labs since '53; vis lecturer Harvard U '48-49. Am Phys Soc(F)—Am Assn Physics Tchrs—AAAS(F)—Sigma Xi—Phi Beta Kappa. Hughes Aircraft Co., Culver City, Cal.

11 ROLLINS, Fitzhugh S. Aircraft and heavy duty lubricants. b'06. BS '30 (U Calif). Co-inventor foam inhibited oils US patent 2402487 '46. Research in fundamental factors affecting lubrication in the internal combustion engine; development of lubricants suitable for aircraft service, including supervision of laboratory and airline fleet tests. Author articles in field. Research engr Calif Research Corp since '44. ASME. California Research Corporation, Richmond, Calif.

12 ROLLINS, Howard Arthur. Pomology. b'99. BS Agr '23—MS Horticulture '25 (U NH). Research work in fruit thinning and soil management for tree fruits and small fruits. Author articles: A New Method For Use in Apple Thinning Experiments '27; The Value of Thinning Baldwin Apples '30. Co-author articles: Nitrates and Tree Growth in a Young Peach Orchard '43; Toxic Sprays for Apple Blossom Thinning '45; The Effect of Planting Treatment and Soil Management System on the Production of Cultivated Blueberries '47; also author numerous service bulls on phases tree and small fruit prodn. Extension horticulturist U NH '25-30; extension fruit specialist U Conn '30-45, head Plant Sci Dept since '45; visited 36 US Dept Agr and State Expt Stas in 32 states where fruit research was being conducted '37. Am Soc Horticultural Sci—Am Pomol Soc—Am Hort Soc. Plant Science Department, University of Connecticut, Storrs, Conn. H: 17 Willowbrook Rd.

13 ROLLINS, Hyder Edward. English literature (Elizabethan, romantic); Shakespeare; Ballads. b'89. BA '10—LLD '33 (Southwestern U); MA '12—fellow in English '11-12 (U Tex); '14-15 (Johns Hopkins U); MA '16—PhD '17—Sheldon traveling fellow '19-20 (Harvard); '26-27 Guggenheim memorial fellow (Eng and France). Editor or author: Shakespeare's Poems '38; The Passionate Pilgrim by Shakespeare '40; Shakespeare's Sonnets '44; Keats' Reputation in America to 1848 '46; The Keats Circle, 2 vols '48; and others. Compiler: An Analytical Index to the Ballad-Entries in the Stationers' Registers '24; also author articles in field. Gurney prof Harvard U since '39; gen ed Harvard Studies in English since '33; ed A New Variorum Shakespeare since '47. Am Acad Arts and Scis(F). 1 Waterhouse St., Cambridge, Mass.

14 ROLLINS, Reed Clark. Plant taxonomy and genetics (Cruciferae, guayule rubber plant, Parthenium). b'11. BA '33 (U Wyo); MS '36 (State Coll Washington); PhD '40 (Harvard). Author articles in field. Asso prof bot and dir Gray Herbarium Harvard U since '48. Am Soc Naturalists—Bot Soc Am—Genetics Soc Am—Western Soc Naturalists—Calif Bot Soc—New Eng Bot Club—Soc Study Evolution—Am Soc Plant Taxonomists—Sigma Xi. Gray Herbarium, Harvard University, Cambridge 38, Mass.†

15 ROLSHAUSEN, F. W. Micropaleontology; Foraminifera (Photomicrography); Brines (Oil Field). b'94. BS '20 (Rose Poly Inst). Co-inventor: (with S L Bishkin) Oil base drilling fluid; (with S E Swain) Sidewall coring and sampling device; Bottom hole fluid sampling device. Design laboratory equipment for processing, testing, filing and examining cores and cutting samples obtained from wells in search of oil; design photographic equipment especially for foraminifera and similar objects. Author article: The Occurence of Siderite in Cap Rock at Carlos Dome, Grimes Co., Texas. Co-author article: (with Frank Jessen) Waters of the Frio Formation Texas Gulf Coast '44. Paleontologist Humble Oil & Refining Co since '24, now research paleontologist. Am Assn Petroleum Geol—Soc Econ Paleontologists and Mineral (pres '46-47)—Soc Exploration Geophysicists—Am Geol Inst (dir '49-50, chmn geol information com)—Am Geophys Union—Am Inst Mining and Metall. P.O. Box 2180, Houston 1.

16 ROMAN, Herschel Lewis. Genetics; Chromosomal behavior; Cytogenetics of maize. b'14. AB '36—PhD '42 (U Mo); Gosney fellow summers '46, '47, '48 (Calif Inst Tech). Author articles in field. With dept botany U Wash '42-44 and since '46. Genetics Soc Am—AAAS—Sigma Xi. Dept. of Botany, University of Washington, Seattle 5.†

17 ROMANELL, Patrick. Contemporary Italian and Mexican philosophy; G Gentile; B Croce; A Caso; J Vasconcelos; W P Montague; Neo-naturalism; John Locke; Ethical Methodology; Italian Existentialism. born '12. BA '34 (Brooklyn College); MA '36—PhD '37 (Columbia). Author: The Philosophy of Giovanni Gentile '38; Croce Versus Gentile. A Dialogue on Contemporary Italian Philosophy '46; Making of the Mexican Mind: A Study in Recent Mexican Thought. Co-author: Homenaje a Antonio Caso '47; Can We Agree? A Scientist and a Philosopher Argue About Ethics '50. also author articles in field. Asso prof med philos and ethics U Tex (Med br) since '52. Am Philos Assn—AAAS—Internat Phenomenol Soc—Phi Beta Kappa—Carnegie Endowment fellow to Mexico '45-46. Medical Branch, University of Texas, Galveston.†

18 ROMANOFF, Alexis Lawrence. Chemical and avian embryology b'92. BS '25—MS '26—PhD '28 (Cornell U); student (Tomsk U, Vladivostok Poly Inst). Discovered method for cultivation for the avian embryo in an opened egg; beneficial effect of lowering the temperature in the latter part of incubation of eggs; invented gas conditioning apparatus and egg sorting method and mechanism. Co-author: (with A J Romanoff) The Avian Egg '49; also author articles in field. Asso prof Cornell U '43-48, prof chem embryol since '48. AAAS(F)—Am Chem Soc—Soc Exptl Biol and Med—Am Soc Zool—Am Soc Genetics—Poultry Sci Assn—Sigma Xi. Rice Hall, Cornell University, Ithaca, N: 700 Stewart Av.©

19 ROMANOWITZ, Harry Alexander. Electronics; Electrical communications. b'01. EE '24—MS '39 (Cincinnati U); PhD '47 (U Mich). Member Ultra-High Frequency Techniques Conference Massachusetts Institute Technology '42; Servomechanisms Conference '43; research on measurement, analysis and statistical nature of deionization time in a mercury vapor thyraton. Author: Laboratory Manuals in Physics and Electricity '37; Principles of Electronics '49. Asst prof elec engring U Ky '42, asso prof '43, prof '46, chairman dept of elec engring since '52. Tau Beta Pi—Sigma Xi—AAUP—AIEE—Am Soc Engring Edn —Ky Soc Profl Engrs—Ky Acad Sci. University of Kentucky, Lexington 29.†

20 ROMBERG, Frederick Ernst. Geophysical prospecting; Gravity meters; Gravity prospecting. b'10. BA '29 (U Tex); AM '32 (Harvard). Research in seismograph, design and application of gravity meter, first application of gravity meter to estimating ore masses '43. Co-author articles: (with V E Barnes) Gravity and Magnetic Observations on Iron Mountain Magnetite Deposit Llano County Texas '43; Observations of Relative Gravity at Paricutin Volcano '48; other articles in field. Geophysical observer and computer Humble Oil and Refining Co '29-30; asst in physics Harvard '32-33; seismograph party chief Geophysical Service Inc Dallas '33-41; geophysicist LaCoste and Romberg Austin Tex since '41. Soc Exploration Geophysicists—Am Geophys Union—Phi Beta Kappa—Sigma Xi. 3810 Speedway, Austin, Tex.

21 ROMER, Margaret H. History of southwestern United States (Lower Colorado River region, California). b'89. AB '19—MA '23 (U Southern Calif). Research on history of Imperial Valley and the entire region around the lower Colorado River from the point of Nevada to the Gulf of Calif. Author: A History of Calexico '22. Co-author: (with A Ralph Romer) Sky Travel '30. Instr hist Calexico High Sch Calexico Calif '20-22; instr Burbank High Sch Burbank Calif '22-23; high sch San Diego '23-53, La-Jolla High School '33-53. AHA—San Diego Hist Soc. P.O. Box 417, Pacific Beach Station, San Diego 9, Calif. H: 2176 Garnet Av.

22 ROMIG, Orlando Elliott. Steel (Flat rolled); Steel (Metal coatings); Technical photography. b'98. AB '20 (Pacific U Forest Grove Ore); BS (Chem E) '22 (Ore State Coll); AM '24 (Harvard). Preparation of metallic single crystals; studies on mechanical properties, structure, and corrosion resistance of tin-plate and flat rolled steel products; technical photography of metals and alloys; development processes for coating steel with tin and zinc. Holds patent on process for manufacture of silicon steel sheets. Author article: Constitution of Iron-Tin Alloys '42 and others. Co-author article: Metallography of Tin and Tin Coatings on Steel Metals and Alloys '41. Contributor: Am Soc Metals Handbook '48. Chem research asst Gen Elec Co Research Lab Schenectady NY '23; metall research lab Am Sheet & Tin Plate Co Pittsburgh '24-26, asst chief metall Vandergrift Works Vandergrift Pa '26-29; chief metall Gary Sheet Mill Gary Ind '29-35; with US Steel Co Pittsburgh since '35, now asst mgr research lab. Am Soc Metals—Nat Assn Corrosion Engrs—AIMME—Assn Iron and Steel Eng—ASTM—Photog Soc Am(asso)—Royal Photog Soc Gt Brit(asso)—Tau Beta Pi—Sigma Xi—Phi Lambda Upsilon—Alpha Chi Sigma. U.S. Steel Research Laboratory, 234 Atwood St, Pitts 13. H: 425 Olympia Rd., Pitts 11.

23 RONAN, Wilbert Cathmor. Design of stained glass. b'87. CE '10 (O State U); BS '13 (U Pa). Co-author: Architectural Shades and Shadows '30. Prof architecture O State U since '13; practicing architect, designer stained glass. AIA. Ohio State University, Columbus 10, O.

10 RONNE, Finn. Polar navigation, flying, living, and surface transportation; Trimetrogon photography. b'99. Degree '22 (Horten Tech Coll). Was first to discover that Alexander I Land was an island, on 1264 mile sledge-journey in 84 days, 450 miles of new Antarctic coastline discovered; accompanied Admiral Byrd's second expedition to Antarctica '33-35; head Ronne Antarctic research expedition conducting research in geology, meteorology, tidal and salinity recordings, terrestrial magnetism, cosmic ray and atmospheric refraction measurements, solar radiation, climatology, seismology, and geology exploration using trimetrogon aerial photography; proved Antarctica to be one continent with no connection between Ross and Weddell Seas. Author: Antarctic Conquest; also articles in field. Mech engr Westinghouse Elec Corp Pittsburgh '24-33, '35-39; chief of staff and 2d in command East Base Palmer Land US Antarctic Service expdn '39-41. Am Geog Soc(F)—Arctic Inst NA(F)—Am Polar Soc (vp)—Geophys Union—Am Photogrammetry Engring Soc. Awarded spl Congressional medals for participation in second Byrd and US Antarctic Service expedition. 6323 Wiscassett Rd., Washington 16.†☉

11 ROOD, Paul. Physics (Education). b'94. AB '16 (Albion Coll Mich); AM '21—PhD '38 (U Mich); '33 (Cal Inst Tech). Research on photoelectric effect Research Laboratory General Electric Company Schenectady NY '26-27. With faculty physics dept Western Mich Coll Edn Kalamazoo since '16, prof physics since '37, head physics dept since '44. Am Assn Physics Tchrs—AAAS—Am Physics Soc—Am Optical Soc—NEA—Mich Edn Assn—Assn Coll Physics Tchrs Mich—Sigma Xi. Western Michigan College of Education, Kalamazoo.☉

12 ROOFE, Paul G(ibbons). Endocrinology; Neurology. b'99. BS '24 (Kan State Coll); BD '29 (Meadville Theol Sch); Wm Wilder Jr fellow '32-34—PhD '34 (U Chicago). Research and writing endocranial blood vessels, histology, morphology of hypophysis and blood vascular system of Amblystoma tigrinum; genesis of vertebrate behavior, effect of radium chloride and protein deficiency upon hemopoiesis. Author articles: The Endocranial Blood Vessels of Amblystoma tigrinum '35; Innervation of Annulus Fibrosus and Posterior Longitudinal Ligament '40; Role of the Axis Cylinder in Transport of Tetanus Toxin '47, and others. Dir Thessilonica Agrl and Indsl Inst Salonica Greece '24-25; instr chem Haskell Inst '25-27; dairy chem Sidney Wanzer and Sons Chicago '30-34; asst anat U Louisville '34-35, instr '35-41, asst prof '41-45; prof anat, chmn dept U Kan med sch since '45. AAAS—Am Assn Anat—Am Soc Zool—Kan Acad Sci—Kan City Acad Med—Sigma Xi. Department of Anatomy, University of Kansas, Lawrence, Kan. H: 1318 Louisiana St.

13 ROOP, Wendell P(rescott). Watercraft (Primitive); Steel structures (Brittleness). b'87. AB '07 (Stanford). Research on design of steel structures for ductility, work for Welding Research Council, member National Research Council and original Ship Structure Committee for Navy Department; research on Amazonian and Eskimo boats. With Constrn Corps US Navy '17-46; in charge applied mech David Taylor Model Basin '39-46; with

Structural Research Lab Swarthmore Coll since '46. Phi Beta Kappa—Sigma Xi. Structural Research Laboratory, Swarthmore College, Swarthmore, Pa. H: Anchorage Farm, Sewell, N.J.

14 ROOS, Charles Frederick. Dynamic economics (Statistical technique and analysis, mathematical theories). b'01. BA '21—MA '24—PhD '26 (Rice Inst); Nat Research Council fellow '26-28, '26-27 (U Chicago); '27-28 (Princeton). Research concerned chiefly with statistical technique and analysis and development of mathematical theories of dynamic economics. Author: Dynamic Economics '34; NRA Economic Planning '37; Charting Your Business. Coauthor: Economic Measures '38; Dynamics of Automobile Demand '39. Editor and contbr: Stabilization of Employment '33; also author articles in field. Teaching asst math Rice Inst '20, teaching fellow '24-26; asst prof math Cornell U '28-31; sec sect K (econ, sociol, statis) AAAS '28-31, permanent sec and mem exec com '31-33; prin econ and dir of research NRA '33-34; dir research Cowles Com Research econ '34-37; prof econometrics Colo U '34-37; now pres Econometric Inst; mem adv editorial bd Econometrica. Econometric Soc (pres and F, joint founder, sec treas '31-32)—Am Math Soc—Math Assn Am—Am Statis Assn(F)—Inst of Math Statis(F)—Nat Research Council (commn on applied Math Statis)—Sigma Xi—International Statis Inst. Fellow John Simon Guggenheim Memorial Found. 230 Park Av., NYC 17.☉

15 ROOS, Frank John, Jr. History of American architecture; History of art. b'03. PhB (Chicago U); PhD '37 (O State U); '27-28, '31 (Harvard). Research on origin, restoration and design of colonial, early republican architecture, use of color on early American architecture; made index of examples of early American architecture of eastern US and photographic collection; studied influence of Builders Handbooks on early Am architectural design. Author: An Illustrated Handbook of Art History '37; Writings on Early American Architecture '43; Sources of Early Architectural Design in Ohio '38; also articles in field. Professor Dept Art Ill Univ since '46. O Acad Sci(F)—O Valley Fine Arts Conf (past pres)—Am Soc Archtl Hist (past sec)—Coll Art Assn—Am Soc Aesthetics. Carnegie fellow Harvard '27-28, Carnegie scholar '31. 115 Architecture Building, University of Illinois, Urbana, Ill.

16 ROOSEBOOM, Auguste. Petrochemical and related processes; Foreign chemical processes applicable to American industry; Urea manufacture; Patent commercialization. b'01. Chem engr (U Delft Netherlands). Royal Dutch Shell Co, Netherlands '34-38; Shell Union Oil Co NY '38-44; vp R W Greeff and Co '44-46; pres Fulton Internat Co NY. Am Chem Soc. 10 Rockefeller Plaza, NYC 20.†

17 ROOT, Raymond Willard. Fish respiration. b'05. AB '26 (Milton Coll); AM '29—PhD '31—fellow zoology '28-31 (Duke U). Research on respiratory function of the blood of fishes and the effect of thyroid and thyroxin on oxygen consumption in fishes. Co-author: (with P L Bailey Jr) A Laboratory Manual In General Physiology '38, '40, '46; also articles in field. Instr gen physiol Coll City NY since '33, head div since '36. Soc Gen Physiol. College City of New York, 139 St. and Convent Av., NYC 31.

18 ROOT, Robert Walter. Church (International affairs). b'14. BS in

econ '36 (Ia State Coll); Lydia Roberts F '36-37—MS in journ '37—Pulitzer traveling scholarship '37-38 (Columbia). Member ecumenical press committee World Council of Churches '45-47 and secretary preparatory publicity committee of first assembly; director public relations first international conference of Churches on International Affairs England '46; director public relations second World Conference of Christian Youth Norway '47; secretary Iowa Civil Liberties Union '43-45. Contbr to Church Sci Monthly, Highroad. Reporter, ed writer Des Moines Register and Tribune '38-45; faculty Drake U '39-44, U Bridgeport since '50; corr reconstruction dept World Council of Churches '45-47; free-lance author on church in Asia '47-48; lecturer internat affairs '48-49; exec ed Worldover press and World Interpreter since '49; asst in pub relations Internat Com of YMCA NY since 50. Sigma Delta Chi—Phi Kappa Phi. Worldover Press, Wilton, Conn. H: Brookside Place.

19 ROPER, Elmo Burns, Jr. Public opinion analysis. b'00. Student '19-20 (U Minn); '20-21 (U Edinburgh); AM hon '43 (Williams Coll); LLD hon '47 (U Louisville). Research on techniques for discovering what public thinks and why, also extent employee dissatisfaction and why. Marketing cons and pub opinion analyst since '33; dir Fortune Survey Pub Opinion '35-50; asso prof Columbia '43-49; columnist '44-49; commentator CBS since '48. Market Research Council(pres '42-43)—Am Assn Pub Opinion Research—World Assn Pub Opinion Research—Am Marketing Assn—Am Statis Assn—Am Econ Assn. 30 Rockefeller Plaza, NYC 20.

20 ROPER, John Caswell. Methodism. (Historical). b'73. AB '96—AM '04 (Wofford Coll); BS '04 (Coll Charleston); PhD '29 (U SC). Delegate at large from Methodist Episcopal Church South to Federal Council of Churches '30-34. Author: Religious Aspects of Education '26; The Supreme Law '32; The Historical Basis for a Methodist Theodicy '32; also articles in field. Pres Inter-Ch Movement in SC in interest of temperance, social service, civic righteousness, prohibition and church cooperation since '31; mem Internat Relations Com since '32. Clover, S.C.

21 RORABAUGH, Matthew Irvin. Ground water hydraulics; Stream flow. b'16. BS in CE '37 (Pa State Coll); '41 (Colo State Coll). Rainfall-runoff studies of stream basins Sesquehanna River Basins; collection and analysis stream flow data; correlation of stream-flow records for Ohio River Basin; statistical analysis hydrologic data studies relationships of precipitation, temperature, basin storage, and run-off; studies of quantity, quality, temperature of ground-water resources Louisville Kentucky area; research on problem of induced infiltration from river; analysis of effects of river elevation and river temperature, and barometric pressure on discharge, discharge temperature and water levels in production wells. Author articles: Forecasting Stream-Flow of the Salt River Arizona '46; The Induced Infiltration of River Water to Wells '48. Structural drafting Am Bridge Co Ambridge Pa '37-38; jr hydraulic engr advanced to dist engr Water Resources Br US Geol Survey since '38, surface water div Harrisburg Pa '38-39, Louisville Ky '39-44, div water utilization Washington '44-45, groundwater div Ky since '45. Am Geophys Union—ASCE. 209 Commerce Bldg., Lsvl 2. H: 5018 South Side Dr., Lsvl 14.

10 RORIMER, James J. Tapestries and sculpture of the Middle Ages; Scientific examination of works of art. b'05. Student '21 (Ecole Gory Paris France); AB '27 (Harvard). Introduction new methods for restoration of sculpture, washing of tapestries, lacquering metalwork, and fumigation art objects; development use of ultra violet rays for examination works of art. Author: Ultra-violet Rays and their Use in the Examination of Works of Art '31; The Cloisters—the Building and the Collection of Mediaeval Art '38, '51; Medieval Monuments at The Cloisters—as They Were and as They Are '41; Metropolitan Museum of Art, A Guide to the Collections (Mediaeval Section) '35; Medieval Tapestries '47; Survival—the Salvage and Protection of Art in War '50. Staff Metropolitan Museum of Art NYC since '27, curator dept medieval art since '34, dir The Cloisters since '49. Am Fedn Arts—Am Geog Soc—Am Inst Decorators—Am Mus Assn(chmn art tech sect '48)—Coll Art Assn—France-Am Soc —Medieval Acad Am—Soc Francaise d'Archeologie. Metropolitan Museum of Art, Fifth Av. and 82d St., NYC 28.⊙

11 ROSAHN, Paul Dolin. Syphilis. (Experimental); Human cancer; Biostatistical methods. b'03. Author monograph: Autopsy Studies in Syphilis '47; more than 80 papers in field. Tech aide in charge contracts on venereal diseases OSRD '44-45; research grants for investigation of experimental syphilis from Nat Insts Health since '45; special consultant venereal disease division USPHS since '40. Teaching staff dept path Yale U Sch Med since '38, now asso clin prof path; path and dir tumor clinic New Britain Gen Hosp since '37. Am Bd Path (Diplomate)—Coll Am Path(F)—AA AS—Am Assn Path and Bact—Am Soc Exptl Biol—Am Soc Cancer Research —Soc Exptl Biol and Medicine—Am Pub Health Assn—Harvey Soc—Am Venereal Disease Assn—New Eng Path Soc. New Britain General Hospital, 92 Grand St., New Britain, Conn.

12 ROSAIRE, Esme Eugene. Petroleum prospecting; Four handed chess. b'97. BS '20—MS '21—PhD '26 (U Chicago). Research in development and application of seismic methods of petroleum prospecting, geochemical and geoelectrical methods; active in introduction of reflection seismograph to Gulf Coast prospecting. First American seismologist to discover salt dome with refraction seismograph; invented method of logging crooked bore hole with refraction seismograph; invented geochemical well logging; contributed to the discovery of several oil fields by geochemical prospecting. Author articles in field. Owner and gen mgr Subterrex since '36; sr partner, Geochem Surveys since '41. Soc Exploration Geophysicists (charter mem, past pres)—Am Assn Petroleum Geol —Am Inst Mining and Metall Engrs— AAAS(F)—Soc Am Mil Engrs—Am Phys Soc—Am Geophys Union—Sigma Xi. Route 7, Box 412-D, Dallas 6, Tex.

13 ROSANDER, Arlyn Custer. Sampling; Statistical inquiry design. b'03. BS '25 (U Mich); MA '28 (U Wis); PhD '33 (U Chicago). Statistician Bureau of Labor Statistics urban study of consumer purchases, War Production Board. Statis Bur Internal Revenue Washington since '45. Inst Math Statis —Am Statis Assn—Am Soc Quality Control. Awarded research fellowship Gen Edn Bd '35-36. Statistical Division, Bureau of Internal Revenue, Washington 25.†

14 ROSBOROUGH, Melanie Rohrer. Germanic civilization. AB (Hunter Coll); AM (Columbia). Prof German U Miami Fla since '27. Translator US Govt '41-42. Mod Lang Assn—So Atlantic Mod Lang Assn—Am Assn Teachers German—Phi Beta Kappa. University of Miami, Miami 46, Fla.

15 ROSCOE, Theodore. World War II (Naval history, submarine warfare and destroyer operations). b'06. Student '25-26 (Columbia). Author: This is Your Navy '50; United States Submarine Operations '49; United States Destroyer Operations '53; Picture History of the Navy '54. Free-lance writer since '26. Tech writer USN publications '43-45. Box 43, Main Post Office, Arlington, Va.

16 ROSE, E(rnest) H(erbert). Ores (Beneficiation of low grade). b'97. BS in chem engring '20 (U Kan). Participated in development selective flotation between copper and iron sulphides, copper and nickel sulphides; developed and patented use of sodium hexametaphosphate and metallic salts as selectivity modifiers and activators for flotation non-sulphide minerals; method for separation choorophyll and keratin; separation lump ores according to their dielectric properties; member raw materials advisory committee Atomic Energy Commission. Author about 25 papers on various phases of ore-dressing. Mill supt Patino Mines & Enterprises, Inc. Llallagua Bolivia '25-27, Moctezuma Copper Co Nacozari Sonora Mexico '28-30; asst mill supt Internat Nickel Co of Can Copper Cliff Ont '30-36; mill supt Internat Nickel Co '36-46; cons metall Copper Range Co Painesdale Mich '46; research engr Tenn Coal Iron & RR Co Birmingham Ala since '46. ACS— AIMME—Canadian Inst Mining and Metall—Can Inst Chem(F)—Mining and Metall Soc Am—AAAS—Tau Beta Pi. Tennessee Coal, Iron & R.R. Co., 424 Brown Marx Bldg., Birmingham, Ala.

17 ROSE, H(arold) Wickliffe. Rayon and synthetic fiber industry; Textile (Research, education); Tariff (Protective). b'96. AB '19 (Harvard). Author: Story of Rayon '37; Rayon and Synthetic Fiber Industry of Japan '46. Director and past chmn bd Textile Research Inst; mem bd trustees, past chmn bd govs Phila Textile Inst; pres Am Tariff League; chmn tariff com Rayon Yarn Producers Group; adv com Textile research QMC; nat edn com Soc Plastic Engrs; internat relations com Nat Assn Mfrs. With Am Viscose Corp NYC since '24, gen asst to pres since '47; mem State Dept and Army Textile Mission to Japan '46; lecturer on research and patents Practising Law Inst. Am Council on Japan—Franklin Inst—Friends Hist Assn—Phi Psi(hon). See Latest Listings and Sketch Additions on page 801.

18 ROSE, Lisle Abbott. Technical communication, American literature (Economic, political, technical). b'04. PhB '25—MA '28—PhD '35 (U Chicago); '21-24 (U Mich). Research and writing on English poets of social protest, 1830-60, American economic and political documents of '65-17, engineering education, history of engineering, reports. Author: Modern American Novel '30; Technical Communication '49; Preparing Technical Material for Publication '51; also articles in field. Prof engring coll Ill U, editor Ill Engring Expt Sta, sec Sta staff, exec com Coll Engring, dir engring information and publs since '47. Am Society Engring Edn—Roy Soc Arts Mfrs and Commerce(F)—Am Acad Polit and Soc Sci—Acad Polit Sci—Assn US Army. Scholar and fellow U Chicago '26-28.

Engineering Hall, University of Ill., Urbana.†*

19 ROSE, William Clayton. National manpower (Resources, uses); Amateur Athletics (National, international). b'90. BS '10 (Miss A&M Coll); '28-29 (Command and Gen Staff Sch); '35-36 (Army War Coll); grad (Nat War Coll). Commissioned 2d lieutenant US Army '11, advanced through grades to Major general (temporary) '45; with War Manpower Commission as chief of military division, chief of executive services, and vice chairman successively '42-45; chief of staff and military advisor to US High Commissioner to Philippine Islands '45-46; retired from Army '46; manpower consultant Office Secretary of Defense '50-51. Mem Am Olympic Committee '22-40, '50. 3333 Connecticut Av., Washington 8.⊙

20 ROSEBOOM, Eugene Holloway. American and Ohio history. b'92. BA '14—MA '16 (O State U); PhD '32 (Harvard). Author: The Civil War Era, 1850-1873 '44. Co-author: (with F P Weisenburger) A History of Ohio '34; also articles in field. Instr hist O State U '23-29, asst prof '29-39, asso prof '39-46, prof since '46. AHA—Miss Valley Hist Assn—Agrl Hist Soc—O State Archeol and Hist Soc—AAUP— Phi Beta Kappa. 211 University Hall, Ohio State University, Columbus 10, O. H: 2610 Henthorn Rd.

21 ROSEN, Carl George Arthur. Engines (Diesel). b'91. BS '14—ME '25 (U Cal). Development heavy duty engine lubricants and fuels; research on combustion phenomena in diesel engines; field studies on piston and piston ring development; material studies on liner, piston and piston ring design, and performance. Holds patents on precombustion chamber high-spectrum automotive type diesel engines, fuel injection equipment for diesel engines, and combustion systems for diesel engines. Diesel and chief engr Dow Pump & Diesel Engine Co San Francisco '15-22; cons engr '22-28; with Caterpillar Tractor Co since '28, dir research '42-49, now cons engr administrative dept. ASME —Soc Automotive Engrs—ASTM— Sigma Xi—Pi Tau Sigma. Caterpillar Tractor Co, Peoria 8, Ill.

22 ROSEN, Harold. Lubricants (Stick). b' 92. Ed pub schs. Research and development in compounding and molding stick lubricants; research formation, structure, oil retaining properties various wax blends; perfection technique of molding composition into predetermined sizes and shapes; design and development special equipment for process. Issued patents in field. Founder Am Grease Stick Co '31, chief engr and gen mgr since '31. Soc Automotive Engrs. American Grease Stick Co., 1146 Hoyt St., Muskegon, Mich.

23 ROSEN, Harry Robert. Roses; Flora of District of Columbia; Plant pathology (Insect galls, rusts, small grains and grasses bacterial disease, sweet potato mosaic disease, pear and apple fire blight); Breeding for disease resistance in small grains and roses. b'89. BS '13 (Penn State Coll); MS '15 (U Wis); PhD '22—Rufus J Lackland fellow '21-22 (Washington U). Bred the oat varieties Traveler and Arkwin, the climbing roses Stephen Foster and Miriam's Climber. Author articles. Prof plant path, plant path Agrl Expt Sta Ark U since '18. Am Rose Soc (cons)—Bot Soc Am— Am Phytopath Soc—Mycol Soc Am— Am Soc Agron—AAAS(F)—AAUP— Sigma Xi—Phi Kappa Phi. University of Arkansas, Fayetteville, Ark.

10 ROSENBACH, Joseph Bernhardt. Tests (Placement and achievement). b'97. Student '14-15 (Brooklyn Poly Inst); AB '17 (U NM); '17 (U Colo); MS '19 (U Ill). Development battery of placement tests for pre-engineering and pre-science students and achievement tests for engineering and science students. Author: Mathematical Tables '37; Plane and Spherical Trigonometry with and without Four Place and Five Place Tables '43; College Algebra (3rd edit) '49; Essentials of Plane Trigonometry with and without Tables '50; Essentials of College Algebra '51; Intermediate Algebra for Colleges '51; and others. Coauthor: Pre-Engineering Inventory; Achievement Tests in Mathematics. Faculty Carnegie Inst Tech since '20, prof and head dept math since '35, in charge evening math classes Coll Engring and Sci '33-45, sec div of humanistic and social studies '44-46. Am Assn Engring Edn—AAAS(F)—Am Math Soc—Math Assn Am—Circolo Matematico di Palermo—AAUP—Phi Kappa Phi—Sigma Xi—Pi Mu Epsilon—Tau Beta Pi. Carnegie Institute of Technology, Pitts 13. H: 2550 Beechwood Blvd., Squirrel Hill, Pitts 17.

11 ROSENBERG, Hans W. Modern German history; History of business cycles. b'04. Student '22-27 (U of Cologne, Freiburg, Berlin); PhD '27 (U Berlin). Author: Deutsche Geschichtquellen des 19 Tahrhunderts, vol 28, '30; Rudolph Haym und die Anfange des klassischen Liberalismus '33; Die Nationalpolitische Publizistik Deutschlands, 2 vols, '35; Die Weltwirtschaftskrisis Von 1857-59 '34; Political and Social Consequences of the Great Depression of 1873-96 in Central Europe '43; The Rise of the Junkers, 1410-1653 '43-44. Research fellow Bavarian Acad Sci '27-28; research asso Historische Reichskommission, Germany '28-34; privatdozent of hist U Cologne '32-33; research fellow Inst of Hist Research, U London '34-35; asst prof hist and polit sci Ill Coll '36-38; asst prof Bklyn Coll '39, asso prof '48, prof '52; vis prof Free U Berlin '49-50; specialist in hist Dept of State '50. AHA—Econ Hist Assn—AAUP. Guggenheim fellow '45-47, Brooklyn College, Brooklyn 10. H: 1969 E. 28th St.

12 ROSENBERG, Jakob. Renaissance and Baroque paintings in Northern Europe; Old master drawings and prints. b'93. PhD '22 (Munich). Author: Die Handzeichnungen von Martin Schongauer '22; Jacob von Ruisdael '28; Rembrandt '48 and others. Coauthor: (with E Bock) Die niederlandischen Handzeichnungen im staatlichen Kupferstichkabinett Berlin '30; Lucas Cranach (with M J Friedlander) '32. Resident fellow and lecturer Fogg Art Mus Harvard '37-39, curator prints since '39, asso prof '40-47, prof fine arts since '48. Fogg Art Museum, Harvard University, Cambridge, Mass.⊚

13 ROSENBERG, Louis James. Foreign affairs. b'76. LLB '00 (Detroit Coll Law); studied fgn langs various countries. Attorney and counsel foreign diplomatic and consular officers in Michigan, also in extradition cases for Dominion of Canada; American consul at Seville Spain '06-09, Pernambuco Brazil '09-10; agent in Michigan for International Bureau of International Exposition Turin Italy '10; delegate Pan-American Commercial Conference '19. Hon consul of Panama at Detroit since '23; legal adv Mich State Bd Escheats. Am Bar Assn—Mich State Bar Assn—Mich Acad Sci Arts and Letters—Fgn Policy Assn—Pi Gamma Mu. Decorated Knight of the Order of Isabella the Catholic (Spain); Knight of the Order of Vasco Nunez de Balboa (Panama). 2017 Dime Bldg., Detroit 26.

14 ROSENBERG, Paul. Ultrasonics; Supersonics; Radar; Navigation; Potentiometers; Space travel (Interplanetary). b'10. AB '30—MA '33—PhD '41 (Columbia). Developed ultrasonic components for radar and loran trainers, invented sine-cosine potentiometers; granted patents in fields; general chairman joint meeting of Radio Technical Commission for Aeronautics, Radio Technical Commission for Marine Services and Institute of Navigation '50, co-chairman National Committee for Upper Atmosphere and Interplanetary Navigation '47-50. Lectr physics Columbia '34-41; research asso MIT '41; staff mem Radiation Lab Nat Defense Research Com '41-45; pres Paul Rosenberg Asso since '45. Inst Nav (pres '50-51)—AA AS(F)—Sigma Xi—Epsilon Xi—APS—Inst Radio Engrs—Inst Aeronautical Sci—Acoustical Soc Am—ACS. Paul Rosenberg Associates, 100 Stevens Av., Mt Vernon, NY.⊚

15 ROSENBERGER, Homer Tope. American history (Pennsylvania, Pennsylvania-Germans); Educational administration (Adult education, employee training). b'08. Grad '29 (Albright Coll); MA '30—PhD '32 (Cornell U). Research on visual education and vocational guidance, employee training, occupational tests; extensive collection of material on Pennsylvania history and Pennsylvania Germans; organized Pennsylvania Historical Junto '42, president '42-46, member executive committee since '42, chairman program com '46-49; chmn Training Officers Conference US Government since '49, steering com since '48 (chmn com on preparation of training specialists directory). Author articles: Early Maps of Pennsylvania '44; William Penn—Criminologist and Penologist '46; Teaching and the Ideal Teacher '47; Testing Occupational Training and Experience '48; Lucretia Mott '48; In-service Tng of Prison Employees '51; Pre-Service Edn and In-Service Tng; Parallels and Contrasts '52. Ednl research and adminstrn US Office Edn Fed Security Agency US Govt '35-42, supervisor training US Bur Prisons US Dept Justice since '42. Pa Hist Assn—Penn-German Soc—Pa Prison Soc (mem acting com). U.S. Department of Justice, Washington 7. H: 2229 40th Pl., Washington 7.⊚

16 ROSENTHAL, Franz. Medieval philosophy (Arabic); Arabic literature; Graeco-Arabic relations; Aramaic. b'14. PhD '35 (U Berlin). Author: The Technique and Approach of Muslim Scholarship '47; Die aramaistische Forschung '39; Ahmad b. at-Tayyib as-Sarakhsi '43; A History of Muslim Historiography '52; and others. Asso prof Arabic University Pa '48-51, professor since '51. Army OSS Dept State '43-46. Am Oriental Soc—Soc Biblical Lit. Internat Lidzbarski prize Brussels '38; Guggenheim fellow '47-48. University of Pennsylvania, Phila. 4.†

17 ROSIN, Seymour. Optics (Instruments, design). b'10. AB '30—MA '32—PhD '35 (Columbia). Arrangement of optical systems, and correction of their aberrations; application optical design to military instruments, including telescopes, rangefinders, bombsights, and gunsights; design precision instruments such as spectrometers, spectrophotometers, and optical measuring devices. Holds patents in field. Columbia U '31-41; in charge optical design Farrand Optical Co NYC since '42. Optical Soc Am—AA AS—Phi Beta Kappa—Sigma Xi. Farrand Optical Co., Inc., 4401 Bronx Blvd., NYC 70. H: 4445 Post Rd., NYC 71.

18 ROSINGER, Lawrence K. Modern Chinese history and society; Far Eastern history and current developments; Modern India. b'15. AB '35 (Coll City NY); MA '36 (Columbia); Am Council Learned Socs; grant for study of Chinese lang and Far Eastern history '38-39 (Columbia); Rockefeller Found Fellow '39-40 (staff Inst Pacific Relations). Author: China's Wartime Politics '37-44 '44; China's Crisis '45; Restless India '46; Det urolige Indien (Danish translation) '47; also articles in field. Research asso on Far East, Fgn Policy Assn NYC '42-48; research asso and asso ed Far Eastern Survey, American Institute of Pacific Relations '48-50. Phi Beta Kappa 2775 Morris Av., NYC 58.

19 ROSLEY, Howard A(dolphus). Thermoplastics. b'08. BS in chem engring '33—MS '36 (NYU). Development and technical service on fabrication, injection, and compression molding of thermoplastics; production control on cellulose nitrate and acetate sheets, rods, tubes, and molding powder. With E I du Pont de Nemours & Co since '34, dist engr since '48. Soc Plastic Engrs. E. I. du Pont de Nemours & Co., Inc., Polychemicals Department, 7 S. Dearborn St., Chgo. 3. H: 2107 Oak St., Northbrook, Ill.

20 ROSS, Douglas Hull. Rockets (Propellants); Explosives (Liquid). b'10. AB '32 (Yale); '32-33 (Tchrs Coll Columbia). Research on rocket propellants especially nitrogen componds, rocket fuel oxidizers, liquid explosives containing nitrogen tetroxide, production and use lithium compounds including lithium metal, lithium hypochlorite, hydroxide and carbonate. Asst mgr product development Solvay Process Div Allied Chem & Dye Corp NYC since '34. Am Chem Soc—Am Rocket Soc—AAAS—ASME—Am Oil Chem Soc. Allied Chemical & Dye Corp., 40 Rector St., NYC 6. H: 558 Lotus Rd., Ridgewood, N.J.

21 ROSS, Herbert H. Taxonomy; Zoogeography; Caddis flies. b'08. BSA; MS; PhD. Author: A Textbook of Entomology '48. Author articles: How to Collect and Preserve Insects '41; The Mosquitos of Illinois '47. Asst entomol Dominion Entomol Br Can '26-27; asst entomol Ill Natural Hist Survey '27-31; systematic entomol since '31, prof entomol U Ill since '48. Entomol Soc Am (pres '53-54)—Entomol Soc Washington—Wash Academy Sci—Limnol Soc Am—Soc Study Evolution—Soc Systematic Zool—Pan Pacific Entomol Soc—AAAS—Ill State Acad Sci—Sigma Xi. Nat History Survey, Natural Resources Building, Urbana, Ill.

22 ROSS, James Alexander. International economic affairs (British commercial and financial); Security markets (Stock). b'99. BS '22 (Princeton U); BA '25 (Oxford U); MA '33—PhD '34 (Harvard). Member US delegation to United Nations Economic Commission for Asia and the Far East Shanghai China and Ootocamund India '47-48. Author: Speculation, Stock Prices and Industrial Fluctuations '38. Co-author: Introduction to Responsible Citizenship '41. With Dept of State '42-49; adviser on British Commonwealth commercial affairs economic commr ECA London '49; Directorate of Intelligence US Air Force since '51. 1641 35 St., Washington 7.

23 ROSS, James George. Economic breeding of grasses (Cytology, genetics). b'16. BS Agr '41—MS '42 (Alberta U); PhD '47 (Wis U); '42-43 (McGill U). Research in barley breeding, cytology of flax, cytological study of Russian rubber-bearing dandelion and native dandelions, native Wisconsin plants, cytological evidence for hybridization between Juniperus horizontalis and J virginiana, selection and breeding of grasses adapted to sub-humid and semi-arid environments. Asst agronomist, asst prof SD State Coll since '47. Sigma Xi—Soc Study Evolution. Nat Research Council of Can Scholar, McGill U '42-43. Agronomy Department, South Dakota State College, Brookings, S.D.†

10 ROSS, Marvin Chauncey. Medieval and Renaissance art; European art protection during World War II. b'04. BA '28—MA '30 (Harvard); '27 (U Berlin); '29 (Centro de Estud Historicos Madrid); '33 (NYU). Research and work medieval, renaissance, Byvantine art, medieval limoges enamels; organized exhibition early Christian and Byzantine art Baltimore '47; research and study history of ivory, Coptic bronze flasks, European art protection during World War II; member visiting com Dumbarton Oaks Research Lib and Collection and Hammond - Harwood House Annapolis. Author articles: French Protection of Their Historical Monuments '45; A Faience Head of a Byzantine Emperor '45; A Fourth Century Ivory Statuette in the Walters Art Gallery '45; War Damages in Chartres '46; also others in field. Instr fine arts U Pittsburgh '28-29; curator medieval art Brooklyn Mus '34; curator medieval and subsequent decorative arts Walters Art Gallery '34; now chief curator of art LA Co Museum. Capt USMC Gen Eisenhower's adminstrv staff, deputy advisor monuments, fine arts and archives, participated policy-making and planning for protection monuments in Northwestern Europe '42-45. Hispanic Soc Am (corr)—Am Archeol Assn—Medieval Acad Am—Am Oriental Soc—Coll Art Assn. Received Carnegie Resident fellowship '27-28, travelling fellow '29-30, '30-31; received Guggenheim fellowship '38, '39. Los Angeles County Museum. H: 4069 Eighth Av., LA 8.

11 ROSS, Sydney. Foams. b'15. BSc '36 (McGill U); PhD '40 (U Ill). Research on foaming of aircraft engine lubricating oils for NACA, on adsorption of gases by solids for Atomic Energy Commission. Author: (with others) Foaming of Aircraft-Engine Oils as a Problem in Colloid Chemistry; (with others) X-Ray Diffraction by Aluminum Soaps; Chemical Antifoaming Agents; and others. Instr chem Monmouth Coll Ill '40-41; research asso Stanford U Calif '41-45; asso prof U Ala '45-46; sr chem Oak Ridge Nat Lab Oak Ridge Tenn '46-48; asso prof colloid sci Rensselaer Poly Inst '48-50, prof since '50; vis asso prof U Ore '49. ACS (chmn colloid div). Rensselaer Polytechnic Institute, Troy, N.Y.

12 ROSS, Thurston Howard. Economic valuation (Industrial, real estate, land); Industrial management. b'94. BS '17 (Otterbein Coll); MBA '22—PhD '24 (U Southern Calif). Appraisals for financial purposes and economic surveys. Author: Real Estate Appraisal '27; Some Economic Aspects of Urban Land Valuation; Mathematical Approach to Industrial Valuation. Editor: Southern California Business Review; also author articles in field. Asso prof U Southern Calif '26-28, prof and chmn dept management since '28, dir Bur Bus Research, dir Sch Merchandising U Southern Calif '30-42. ASME—Am Inst Real Estate Appraisers (governing council)—Am Management Assn (councilor)—Phi Beta Kappa—Phi Kappa Phi. 9229 Wilshire Blvd., Beverly Hills, Cal.

13 ROSSINI, Frederick D. Physical petroleum chemistry; Thermochemistry; Chemical thermodynamics; Hydrocarbons. b'99. BS '25—MS '26 (Carnegie Inst Tech); PhD '28 (U Calif). Author: Thermochemistry of the Chemical Substances '36; Selected Values of Properties of Hydrocarbons '47; and others; also articles. Mem staff Nat Bur Standards '28, asst sci phys chem Thermochem Lab, chief sect thermochem and hydrocarbons '36-50; professor and head department chem and dir petroleum research laboratory Carnegie Inst Technology since '50; dir Am Petroleum Inst Research Project 6 on analysis purification and properties hydrocarbons since '34, Project 44 on data on properties hydrocarbons and related compounds since '42; dir coop program on standard samples of hydrocarbons since '44; US mem com on thermochem Internat Union of Chemistry, chmn since '45. ASTM—Am Chem Soc—Am Phys Soc—Am Institute Chem Engrs—Am Petroleum Inst—AAAS—Tau Beta Pi—Sigma Xi. Carnegie Inst of Technology, Pitts 13.©

14 ROSSMAN, Joseph. Patent law (Chemical); Inventions (History, psychology). b'99. BS in chem engring '22 (U Pa); AM '27—LLB '27 (George Washington U); MPL '27 (Washington Coll Law); PhD '30 (Am U). Author: The Psychology of the Inventor '31 (Swedish translation) '35; The Law of Patents for Chemists '32; The Protection by Patents of Scientific Discoveries '34. Editor Journal of Patent Office Society '31-35. Patent examiner US Patent Office '23-25; patent counsel Marathon Corp since '35; lectr patent Law Grad Sch US Dept Agr '34-35. Am Inst Chem(F)—Franklin Inst(F)—AAAS(F; chmn com patents, trademarks)—Am Chem Soc—Tech Assn Pulp and Paper Industry—Am Inst(F)—AAAS(F); (chmn com pats, Electrochem Soc—Nat Mfrs Assn (patent com)—Patent Office Soc. Dupont Circle Bldg, Washington 6.†©

15 ROSSMAN, Kenneth R(aitz). American Colonial history; United States civil service. b'11. BA '33 (U Toledo); MA '36—scholarship '35 (O State U); scholarship '37-40—PhD '40 (State U Ia). Research various phases colonial history, development American civil service, political conventions, Thomas Mifflin, immigration. Author: Chester A Arthur and the Civil Service Reform '36. Author articles: Thomas Mifflin '40; The Conway Cabal '42; Thomas Mifflin, the Revolutionary Patriot from Pennsylvania '43; Thomas Mifflin-Revolutionary Patriot '48; Development of the Civil Service '39; also others in field. Grad asst hist State U Ia '38-40, research fellow '40; teacher hist Toledo high schs '33; instr hist Ferris Inst Big Rapids Mich '41; prof hist, chmn dept Doane Coll Crete Nebr since '46. AHA—Miss Valley Hist Assn—Nat Council Social Studies—Phi Alpha Theta. Recipient grant Penrose fund Am Philos Soc '40. Doane College, Crete, Neb. H: 2048 Cummings Av., Toledo 9, O.

16 ROSTLER, Fritz S. Rubber compounding; Petroleum by-products. b'06. PhD '34 (U Vienna). Inventor of Naftolen internationally used rubber compounding ingredient produced from petroleum; holder 12 US patents. Author numerous articles in field. Dir research and development Golden Bear Oil Co Oildale Calif since '47. Am Chem Soc—AAAS—Inst Rubber Industry (London). Golden Bear Oil Co., P.O. Box 846, Oildale, Calif.

17 ROTH, Elmer Rudolph. Tree diseases (Rots, cankers, little leaf). b'08. AB '31—MS '32—'32-33 (W Va U). Author articles in field. Pathologist Div Forest Pathol Bur Plant Ind Soils and Agrl Engring US Dept Agr since '34. Am Phytopathol Soc—Soc Am Foresters—Sigma Xi. 223 Federal Bldg., Asheville, N.C.†

18 ROTH, Herman Moe. Stars (Equilibria, atmospheres); Atomic energy. b'07. BS '27—MS in phys '28 (U Va); PhD in phys '32 (Ohio State U). Asst prof, asso prof, prof phys Okla A&M Coll '35-41; chief rsearch div Oak Ridge Operations Office Atomic Energy Commn since '47. APS—Tenn Acad Sci—AAAS—Sigma Xi—Pi Mu Epsilon. P.O. Box E, Atomic Energy Commission, Oak Ridge, Tenn.

19 ROTHAN, Martin. Baseball (Rules, decisions). b'81. Research on complicated and example plays, correct decisions for umpires; readily understood interpretations and explanations of official rules of baseball for players and fans. Author: Baseball Rules and Decisions Book (annually since '47). Semi-profl baseball player, mgr, and umpire. Baseball Decisions Co., Box 517, Lexington, Ky.

20 ROTHEMUND, Paul Wilhelm Karl. Chemistry of pyrrole, porphyrins, hemin, chlorophyll and photosynthesis; Micro and radiochemistry; German colonies (History, status, economy). b'04. Diploma '27—D Eng (chem) '30 (Tech Hochschule Munchen Germany). Author articles in field. Asso prof chem Ohio State U since '37 and Ohio State U Grad Center USAF Inst Tech Wright Field since '47; prof chem Antioch Coll since '47; cons chem engineer, research chem Charles F Kettering Found for the Study of Chlorophyll and Photosynthesis since '30. AAAS—Am Soc Biol Chemists—Am Chem Soc—Ohio Acad Sci(F)—Optical Soc Am (O Valley sect)—Schweizerische Chemische Gesellschaft. Charles F. Kettering Foundation, Antioch College, Yellow Springs, O.†

21 ROTHROCK E(dgar) P(aul). Geology of South Dakota. b'89. AB '12—AM '14 (Oberlin Coll); PhD '22 (U Chicago). Author articles in field. Comml petroleum geol '14-17, '18-21; prof geol U SD since '22; state geologist SD since '26. Am Assn Pet Geologists — Geol Soc Am(F) — AAAS(F). State Geological Survey, Vermillion, S.D.†

22 ROTHSCHILD, V. Henry, II. Law (Tax, corporate, general business); Compensation of executives. b'08. Student '23-25 (Phillips Exeter Acad); AB with honors '29 (Cornell); LLB with honors '32 (Yale). Co-author: (with Judge George Thomas Washington) Compensating the Corporate Executive '51. Editor Yale Law Sch Jour '30-32. Practice law NYC since '32; specializing in corporate and tax work since '40; mem (formerly chief counsel and thereafter vice chmn) Salary Stabilization Bd since '51. Am Bar Assn—Inst for Practical Politics—Phi Beta Kappa—Phi Kappa Phi. 50 Broadway, NYC.©

23 ROUDYBUSH, Franklin. United States diplomatic foreign service (Training, administration). b'06. BFS '30 (Georgetown U); MA '44 (George Washington U). Author: An Analysis of the Administration of the Department of State and the Foreign Service in Relation to the Background and Experience of Ambassadors; Ministers and Professional Personnel; An Analysis of the Educational Background and Experience of 828 US Foreign Service Officers; Evaluative Criteria for Foreign Service Schools and Foreign Service Training. Editor: Affairs Mag '38-42. Dean Roudybush Fgn Service Sch

'31-42; prof Internat Econ Relations Southeastern U '38-45; dir Pan-Am Inst Washington. Am Soc Internal Law, 3034 P St., Washington 7.

10 ROUSE, Charles H. Range management (Big game, livestock, reindeer); Alaska (Tundra ecology, muskoxen). b'05. Student '24-25 (Mont State Coll); BS '29 (U Mont). Co-author: (with L J Palmer) Alaska Tundra '45. Biologist US Fish and Wildlife Service. Soc Am Foresters—Am Soc Mammologists—Wildlife Soc. 365 S. F St., Lakeview, Ore.

11 ROUSE, Irving. Anthropology; Archeology (West Indies). b'13. BS '34—PhD '38 (Yale). Field trips Haiti '35, Puerto Rico '36-38, Cuba '41, Fla '44, Trinidad '46, Connecticut '48. Author articles in field. Asst curator anthropol Yale '38-45, asso curator since '45, instr anthropol '39-43, asst prof '43-48, asso prof since '48. Eastern States Archeol Fed (pres)—Archeol Soc Conn (ed)—Soc Am Archeol (pres). Awarded Medalla Commemorativa del Vuelo Panamericano pro Faro Colon by Cuban Govt '45, A Cressy Morrison prize in nat sci by NY Acad Sci '48. Peabody Museum Laboratories, Yale University, New Haven.†

12 ROUSE, John Thomas. Petroleum geology; Volcanic rocks; Physiography; Stratigraphy. b'06. BA '29—MA '30 (U Cincinnati); PhD '32 (Princeton U). Author articles in field. Staff geologist Magnolia Pet Co Dallas since '50. Geol Soc Am(F)—Am Assn Pet Geologists (chmn research com '48)—Am Geophy Union—AAAS(F)—Soc Exploration Geophysicists—Sigma Xi. Magnolia Petroleum Co., Box 900, Dallas 1.

13 ROUSSEL, David Murray. Forest mensuration; Logging costs. b'20. B Commerce '43—BSF '44 (U BC). Research on logging costs, growth and yield studies of timber. Logging bookkeeper and accountant since '48. Can Inst Forestry. Box 116, Agassiz, B.C., Can.

14 ROUTH, Joseph I(saac). Electrophoresis; Keratin (Chemistry); Wool and hair (Chemical composition). b'10. BS '33—MS '34 (Purdue U); PhD '37 (U Mich). Research and writing on the chemistry of keratin of wool and its reduction products, the kerateines, the enzymatic digestion of wool, powdered wool, composition of human hair; physico chemical studies on the water-soluble fraction of powdered wool, powdered keratins '44. Author articles in field. Asst in chem Purdue U '34; asst in biochem U Mich '34-37; instr biochem State U Ia '37-42, asst prof '42-46, asso prof '46-51, prof since '51. ACS—Soc Exptl Biol and Med—Am Soc Biol Chem—Sigma Xi. Clinical Biochemistry Laboratory, University Hospital, State University of Iowa, Iowa City, Ia.†

15 ROUTIEN, John B(roderick). Mushrooms; Soil fungi. b'13. AB '34 (DePauw U); MA '36 (Northwestern U); PhD '39 (Mich State Coll). Author articles in field. Mycologist Charles Pfizer & Co Inc since '46. Lab tech then officer charge sections in Army Hosp Lab '42-46. Ind Acad Scis—Bot Soc Am—Mycol Soc Am—Torrey Bot Club—AIBS—Sigma Xi. Charles Pfizer & Co., Inc., 11 Bartlett St., Brooklyn 6.†

16 ROVE, Olaf N(orberg). Mining geology; Mineral economics; Iron ores; Ferro alloy ores; Base metals. b'98. BS '22—MS '25 (U Wis); PhD '39 (Mass Inst Tech). Geologist chief br mineral deposits US Geol Survey Washington since '47. Am Inst Mining and Metal Engrs—Geol Soc Am—Soc Econ Geologists (sec since '46). U.S. Geological Survey, Washington 25. H: Annandale Rd., Falls Church, Va.⊙

17 ROVELSTAD, A(dolph) M(arius). Classical languages; Etomology (English words derived from Latin). b'81. AB '03 (St Olaf Coll); AM '06—Buhl Classical fellow '06-07 and '20 —University fellow '14-15—PhD '21 (U Mich). Etymological studies of Latin and Greek words in English; comparative philology and Sanskrit; study of Greek and Roman historians. Author: The Indebtedness of Valerius Maximus to Livy and the Lost Epitome of Livy (unpublished doctoral dissertation); Latin and Greek Words in English (in preparation). Head Greek dept Luther Coll Decorah Ia '07-10, head Latin dept '10-27; head Latin dept St Olaf Coll '27-30; prof Latin U ND '30-45, prof classical langs and head dept since '45. Am Philol Assn—Archeol Inst Am—Am Classical League—Classical Assn Middle West and South (exec com '27-31, chmn state ND since '32). Department of Classical Languages, University of North Dakota, Grand Forks.⊙

18 ROWAN, Hugh Williamson. Chemical warfare; Military chemicals; Industrial mobilization. b'94. PhB '15 (Yale); '15-17 (Harvard); grad Chem Warfare Sch '21 (Army Industrial Coll). Government procurement of chemicals; effect and distribution of war load on the chemical industry; tactics and technique of chemical warfare. Author: Textbooks of Chemical Corps Sch on chemical agents and weapons '21, many later revisions. 2d lt US Army '17 advancing to brig gen '44; div chem officer '18-19, mem Chem Corps since '20, pres Chem Corps Bd, Army Chemical Center, Md since '46; chemist Tide Water Oil Co '19-20. Am Chem Soc. H: 30 Quincy St., Chevy Chase 15, Md.

19 ROWE, Arthur Eugene. Material handling; Industrial construction. b'01. Student '23, '27(Cleveland Coll); '28, '31 (Case Inst Tech); '35, '36 (John Huntington Inst). Research on electric hydraulic material handling devices, material handling in paint, chemical, assembling, fabricating and warehousing operations. Contributor: American Welding Society Handbook. Designing and project engr Austin Co '25-31, '36-40; cons '32-35; with Arthur E Rowe & Asso since '41; pres Rowe Methods Inc since '47. Am Soc CE—Am Soc Profl Engrs—Am Welding Soc—Am Concrete Inst—Nat Bur Engring Exam. 1743 E. 25th St., Cleve 14.

20 ROWE, Margaret Talbot Jackson. Museum curator; Ancient textiles (Care and preservation, history, techniques of weaving and dyeing in Near and Far East). b'88. AB '10 (Radcliffe Coll); '10-13 (Am Sch Classical Studies Rome)—'38-47 (Asia Inst, NY). Care and exhibition of collections; research in techniques of weaving and dyeing and history of textiles in Near and Far East. Author: The Museum '17. Voluntar Assistentin, Kaiser Friederich Mus, Berlin, Germany, '12; volunteer assistant, Fogg Art Mus, Harvard U, '13-14; asst to dir, Minneapolis Inst of Arts, '14-15, asst dir, '16; curator, Hobart Moore Memorial Collection, textiles, since '38, Yale U Art Gallery. Am Assn Museums—British Museums Assn—Am Oriental Soc—Needle and Bobbin Club—Asia Inst. Yale University Art Gallery, New Haven. H: 298 Lawrence St., New Haven 11.

21 ROWE, R(aphael) Robinson. Puzzles; Culverts; Bank protection. b'96. AB in math '16—SV in civil architecture '18 (Harvard); BS in civil engring '18 (MIT). Research on mathematical and engineering puzzles and contributor (nom de plume N G Neare) to monthly magazine column Civil Engineering since '40; protection river banks along highways and at bridges. Cons engr Allen & Rowe '26-33; asso bridge engr San Francisco-Oakland Bay Bridge '33-37; with US Forest Service and Fed Power Commn '37-38; supervising bridge engr Cal Div Highways since '38. Box 1499, Sacramento 7.

22 ROWELL, Henry Thompson. Latin literature; Imperial Roman army; Roman daily life. b'04. AB '26—PhD '33 (Yale). Author articles in field. Editor: Daily Life in Ancient Rome '40; American Journal of Philology since '46. Prof Latin Johns Hopkins U since '40, chmn dept classics since '46; dir summer sch Am Acad in Rome '47-51. Archeological Institute America (pres '52)—Am Philol Assn—Classical Assn Atlantic States (exec com '48). Cavaliere Ufficiale della Corona D'Italia '45. The Johns Hopkins University, Baltimore 18.⊙

23 ROWLAND, Mrs. Dunbar (Eron Rowland). American history (British Colonial Florida). Litt D '32 (U South). Author: Andrew Jackson's Campaign Against the British '26, and others; also articles in field. Cons, librarian Rowland Hist and Research Library Jackson Miss; for 37 years assisted husband in creating and establishing State Dept Archives and Hist of Miss. Dunbar Rowland Historical Research Library, 429 Capital Sq., Mississippi St., Jackson, Miss.

24 ROY, Ram Sagar. Plant breeding and genetics; Fruit and vegetable crops (Manurial requirements, pests). b'12. BSc '35 (Banaras Hindu U India); MSc '48 (U Cal Coll Agr Davis). Evolution of new variety of brinjal as a mutant, of hybrid cliilies and inheritance studies of their fruit position, of three eggplant types from selection, of five early and prolific bearing hybrid cowpeas and their inheritance studies of several characters; control measures of litchi mite and mango hopper; fixation of manurial doses in mango, litchi, cauliflower, cabbage, tomato and onion crops; botanical studies of the fruit varieties grown in Bihar; finding chromosome numbers of Bihar bananas for evolution of disease resistant varieties. Former fruit prodn officer Bihar Sabour India; now hort Bihar and prof hort Bihar Agrl Coll Sabour, Bhagalpur India; mem editorial board publ Indian Jour Hort New Delhi. Am Soc Hort Sci—Sigma Xi(asso)—Hort Soc India—Soc Plant Breeding and Genetics New Delhi—Bihar Hort Soc Sabour(sec; chief editor Bagwan mag). Bihar Agricultural College, Sabour, Bhagalpur, India.

25 ROY, Robert Hall. Industrial engineering; Printing. b'06. BE '28 (Johns Hopkins). Research on time standards for hand composition, precision printing, printing plant air conditioning, press packing and engineering. Author articles in field. Apprentice engr to vp engring Waverly Press Inc Baltimore since '28; prof indsl engineering Johns Hopkins since '49, dean school of engineering since '53. ASME—Soc Adv Management. The Johns Hopkins University, Baltimore 18.†⊙

26 ROY, Sharat Kumar. Meteoritics. b'97. ISc '15 (U Calcutta); AB '22—MS '24 (U Ill); '25-37—PhD '41 (U Chicago). Leader Capt Marshall Field Geol and Paleontol Expedition to Newfoundland '28; geology expedition to the Salt Range Punjab India '45; geologist Rawson MacMillan Arctic expedition of Chicago Natural History Museum '27-28; conducted expeditions in many parts of US. Author articles in field. Chief curator geol Chicago Natural Hist Mus since '47. AFA—Royal Geog Soc(F)—Geol Soc London—AAAS—Paleontol Soc—Polar Soc (bd mem)—Mineral Soc—Soc Research in Meteorites—NY Acad Sci—Sigma Xi—Arctic Inst NA (charter mem). Chicago Natural History Museum, Chgo 5.

10 ROYER, George Lewis. Dye application (Chemical microscopy, microchemistry, spectrophotometry, physical chemistry). b'08. BS '29 (Akron U); PhD '32 (Cornell U). Research on wool, nylon, rayon, and leather. Author articles in field. Holder several patents in the field of dye application. Director of analytical chemistry Calco Chem Div Am Cyanamid Company since '42. American Assn Textile Chem and Colorists—Am Assn Textile Tech—Textile Inst Eng—Soc Dyers and Colourists Eng—Photog Soc Am—Metro Microchem Soc—NY Micros Soc—Biol Photog Assn—Am Inst Chem(F)—Optical Soc Am—Am Chem Soc. American Cyanamid Company, Calco Division, Bound Brook, N.J.

11 ROZEBOOM, Lloyd Eugene. Mosquitoes; Phlebotomus. b'08. BS '31 (Ia State Coll); DS '34 (Johns Hopkins); '27-29 (Morningside Coll). Research on transmission of malaria in Panama, taxonomy and biology of mosquitoes, transmission of anaplasmosis, malaria transmission in Trinidad, taxonomy of Phlebotomus. Author articles in field. Asso prof parasitol Johns Hopkins Sch Hygiene and Pub Health since '46. AAAS—Am Soc Parasitol—Am Soc Tropical Med—Entomol Soc Am—Entomol Soc Washington—Nat Malaria Soc—Phi Kappa Phi—Sigma Xi. Bailey K Ashford Award in Tropical Med '41. 615 North Wolfe St., Baltimore 5.

12 RUBEL, Veré L(aura). Non-dramatic Tudor literature; Bible as literature. b'93. BA '16 (U Cincinnati); diploma '18 (Nurses Training Course Vassar); MA '28 (U Wis); PhD '38 (NYU). Courier-instructor of groups travelling in Europe '20-26. Author: A Study of Poetic Diction in the English Renaissance '40; also articles in field. With Hunter Coll since '29, now asso prof Eng; cons PMLA on rhetoric since '43. Modern Lang Assn—Nat Council Teachers Eng—Coll Eng Assn—AAAS—Phi Beta Kappa. Hunter College, 695 Park Av., NYC 21.

13 RUBINSTEIN, Hyman Solomon. Neuroanatomy. b'04. PhG '24—MD '28—BS '32—PhD '34 (U Md); psychiatry '32-35 (Johns Hopkins); neuropath '34-36 (Geo Wash U); psychoanalysis '45-50 (Wash-Baltimore Psychoanalytic Inst). Research in structure, function, pathology of nervous system; endocrine effects on growth and sex; use of trichlorethylene in migraine; treatment of morbid sex craving; endocrine therapy in neuropsychiatric disorders; effect of electric shock on the electroencephalogram; sleep electroshock therapy in psychoses; use and limitations of hypnosis in diagnosis and treatment. Author: Laboratory Manual of Neuroanatomy '32. Co-author: (with C L Davis) Stereoscopic Atlas of Neuroanatomy '47. Contributor: The Pituitary Gland. Asso neuroanatomy and chief neurological clin U Md '33-35; dir lab for neuroendocrine research Sinai Hosp '35-45; dir Alfred Ullman lab for neuropsychiatric research Sinai Hosp Baltimore '45-51. Am Bd Psychiatry and Neurology (Diplomate)—AMA(F)—Assn Research Nervous and Mental Disease—Am Psychiatric Assn(F)—AAAS(F)—Am Psychoso-

matic Soc—Am Assn Anatomists—Am Acad Neurology—Phi Alpha—Phi Lambda Kappa. 2349 Eutaw Pl., Balt 17. H: 7808 Crossland Rd., Pikesville 8, Md.

14 RUBLY, Grant Russell. Copper mining. b'06. BS in mining '28—EM '39 (Case Inst Tech). Studies in use of block caving mining methods; studies geological data, ore deposit estimates; evaluation tonnage and value deposit; development production underground barite mine; exploration Castle Dome copper deposit, San Manuel Copper deposit. With Miami Copper Co '28-44, chief mining engr '37-44; in charge exploration San Manuel Copper Corp '44-47; mine supt and chief mine engr Magnet Cove Barium Corp '48-50; mine engr US Bur Mines since '51. AIMME—Theta Tau—Sigma Xi. H: P.O. Box 154, Malvern, Ark.

15 RUBY, Glen Matthew. Oil exploration (Geology). b'89. BSc '16 (U Neb). Managed geological exploration for Argentine Government '39-40, discovered several fields in Argnetina; directed exploration for Chile Government five years, found the two existing fields in Tierra del Fuego; also worked in Bolivia, Brazil and Uruguay; assisted in drawing petroleum code for Uruguay and Canada. Author articles in field. Dir exploration in Portugal; dir Navy exploration in Alaska Navy Petroleum Bd. Geol Soc Am(F)—Am Assn Petroleum Geol—Am Inst Mining and Metall Engrs.

16 RUDERT, Frank Joseph. Chemistry and bacteriology of yeast and fermentation. b'17. AB '37—PhD '40 (Cornell). Research on production bakers' and nutritional yeast, production riboflavin and other vitamins and butylene glycol by fermentation, production antibiotics, particularly penicillin and streptomycin. Faculty Ore State Coll '40-41; research bact Comml Solvents Corp '41-45; research bact William S Merrell Co '45-47; dir research and development Red Star Yeast & Products Co since '47. ACS—Soc Am Bact—AAAS—Inst Food Tech—Sigma Xi. Red Star Yeast, 325 N. 27th St., Milw. 8.

17 RUDINGER, George. Fluid mechanics; Scientific instrumentation; X-ray and radium physics. b'11. Ing applied physics '35 (Vienna Inst Tech). Research on evaporation of metals in vacuum and use of thin layers produced in this way for vacuum thermocouples, X-ray photography, X-ray and radium dosimetry, blurring of fluorescent intensifying screens, jet propulsion particularly pulse jets, non-steady flow phenomena in ducts, heat addition to flows. Invented a special slide rule for radium dosage calculations, automatic filter control and dosage rate indicator for X-ray therapy machine, and an automatic level control for glass furnaces; co-inventor of a new method and measuring instrument to determine definition of fluorescent intensifying screens, self-illuminating reflector sight, ordnance device involving automatic calculating mechanisms and servo-systems. Author articles in field. Research physicist Austrian X-Ray Standards Lab Vienna Gen Hosp '35-38; physicist Sydney Hosp Australia '39-46; with Australian Ministry of Munitions '44-45; physicist Australian Glass Mfrs Pty Ltd '45-46; sr research physicist Cornell Aero Lab Inc Buffalo '46, now prin physicist. Sigma Xi—American Phys Soc—F Institute Phys, London—AAAS. Cornell Aeronautical Laboratory, Inc., 4455 Genesee St., Buffalo 21.

18 RUDOLF, Paul O. Reforestation; Silviculture; Forest ecology. b'06. BS

'28 (U Minn); MF '29 (Cornell U). Research on best species, classes of stock, mixtures, and methods of planting trees on different sites, racial variation in red and Scotch pines, white and Norway spruces, research on tree seeds for improved quick methods of overcoming seed dormancy, effects of pelletting on tree seed germination, sowing densities and watering practices in forest nurseries, factors affecting early survival and growth of planted pines, chemical control of woody plants. Jr forester S Forest Expt Sta '29-30; with Lake States Forest Expt Sta since '30, forester and asst to chief of forest management research div since '46. AAAS—Minn Acad Sci—Minn Hort Soc—Gamma Sigma Delta—Alpha Zeta—Xi Sigma Pi. Lake States Forest Experiment Station, University Farm, St. Paul 1.

19 RUEHE, Harrison August. Foods (Bacteriology, chemistry); Dairy products (Production, processing, distribution). b'88. BS '14—MS '16 (U Ill); PhD '21 (Cornell U). Devised method of inverting sugar for ice-cream making widely used during war; developed method for standardizing intensity of flavor in butter; appointed official state delegate to World's Dairy Congress Washington '23, International Dairy Congress Copenhagen '31; chairman Commission to Study Milk Markets '39. Asso editor Jour Dairy Sci. Contbr to dairy journs, also World Book Ency, Ency Brit. With U Ill since '12, prof dairy mfg coll agr, and chief dairy mfg Ill Agrl Exptl Sta since '45; sec Am Butter Inst Chicago '43-45. Am Dairy Sci Assn(pres '35-36)—Alpha Zeta—Phi Kappa Phi—Gamma Sigma Delta—Sigma Xi. Department of Dairy Science, University of Illinois, Urbana.†☉

20 RUEHLE, Geo(rge) D(ewey). Plant diseases (Potatoes, tropical and citrus fruits). b'98. BS '23—PhD '30—fellow '26-30 (State Coll Wash). Author articles in field. Vice-dir charge Sub-tropical Expt Sta Fla since '42. AAAS(F)—Am Phytopath Soc—Mycol Soc Am—Torrey Bot Club—Potato Assn Am—Fla State Hort Soc (vp '46-48)—Sigma Xi. University of Florida Sub-Tropical Experiment Station, Rt. 2, Box 508, Homestead, Fla.†

21 RUHLE, George Cornelius. National Parks (American); Natural history; Magnetic compass; Oregon (Conservation and natural resources). b'00. BS in chem engring '21 (U Ill); PhD in phys chem '25 (U Cal Berkeley); grad study '30, '31 (U Mont) '40-41 (Yale) '43-44 (Va Poly Inst) '45-46 (U Panama). Research on extraction of radium from ores, disintegration of nitrogen atoms, thermodynamic treatment of fused salt solutions; bird studies in Glacier, Crater Lake, other national parks; geology Yosemite, Yellowstone, Glacier, Crater Lake, and Hawaii National Parks; ethnology in the Arctic, Montana, and South Pacific regions; mammology in Glacier National Park and South Africa; botany in South and Middle Americas, South Africa, and the Klamath-Siskiyou mountains; museum studies and work in Glacier National Park, Yale University, Hawaii National Park; travel expeditions in Latin America, 6 major trips, since 1934, in South and Central Africa, 1949-50. Author: Guide to Glacier National Park, 1949; Guide to Roads of Crater Lake National Park, 1953. Metall Sears Roebuck & Co '17-18; instr U Cal Berkeley '25-26; ranger naturalist Yosemite National Park '26, '27, prof phys and math chem U Okla '26-28; park ranger Yellowstone Nat Park '28-29; park naturalist Glacier Nat Park '29-40, Great Smoky Mts '33-34; spl scholarship Yale '40-41; park naturalist Crater Lake Nat Park '42, '46-52; Hawaii Nat Park since '52. Sigma Xi—Am Nature Study Soc—Am Mus Natural Hist—Glacier Natural Hist Assn—Crater Lake Natural Hist Assn—Hawaii Natural Hist Assn (exec sec)—Explorers Club NYC—Club de exploraciones de Mexico—Am Polar Soc—Phi Lambda Upsilon—Alpha Chi Sigma—Phi Delta Chi—Gamma Omega—Ore Acad Sci—Bot Soc S Africa—Wildlife Protection Soc S Africa—Am Ornithologists Union—Hawaii National Park, Hawaii; also 503 S West Av., Kankakee, Ill.

10 RUKEYSER, Merryle Stanley. Finance; Investments; Trade. b'97. LitB '17 (Sch Journalism Columbia U); MA '25 (Columbia). Author: The Common Sense of Money and Investments '24; Financial Advice to a Young Man '27; Investment and Speculation '30; The Doctor and His Investments '31; The Diary of a Prudent Investor '37; Financial Security in a Changing World '40; also articles in field. Edit writer for Hearst Newspapers since '31. Acad Polit Sci—Alumni Asso Sch of Journalism of Columbia U (pres '24-27). 150 W. Pine Brook Drive, New Rochelle, N.Y.

11 RULKOETTER, Aubrey Henry. School administration. b'91. Student '29-32 (Macalester Coll St Paul); AB '36 (Union Coll Lincoln Neb); AM '39—PhD '48 (U Neb). Educational secretary Central Union Conference '35-38; president Union College Lincoln Neb '38-42; dean school theology Washington Missionary College Washington '42-46; academic dean Emmanuel Missionary College Berrien Springs Mich since '46. Phi Delta Kappa.⊚

12 RUMBALL-PETRE, Edwin Alfred Robert. Bibles (Rare). b'80. Student '99 (City of London Coll); '01-03 (Harley Coll). Research on rare editions of Bible, importation of rare Bibles in ancient and modern languages for public and private libraries including American Bible Society, Rosenbach Company, San Francisco Theological Seminary; appraisal biblical manuscripts, rare Bible collections, and miscellaneous family Bibles. Author: Rare Bibles: An Introduction for Collectors '38; America's First Bibles '40. Founder and proprietor Bibles of Yore since '30. 3201 Malcolm Av., Los Angeles 34.

13 RUMBERGER, George Glen. Petroleum waxes. b'12. BS '33 (Allegheny Coll). Holds 8 patents. Research chemist Quaker State Oil Ref Co '33-36, process engr '36-39, dir labs '39-41; Wax research Marathon Corp '41-46, project supervisor '46-50, asst director research since '50. American Chem Soc. Marathon Corporation, Menasha, Wis.

14 RUNNER, Meredith N. Mammalian embryology; Reproduction; Genetics. b'14. AB '37—PhD '42 (Ind U). Research on physiology of reproduction, maternal influences on development, transplantation of mamamalian embryos. Author: Devlpmt Mouse Eggs in the Anterior Chamber of the Eye '47; Transplantability of skin, Ovary and Tumor in Mice, 1950; Comparison of Immature and Pregnant Mice for Estimation of Gonadotrophin, 1951; Differentiation of Intrinsic and Maternal Factors Governing Prenatal Survival, 1951. Faculty Instr U Conn '42-47, asst prof zoology '46-47; Finney-Howell fellow Roscoe B Jackson Memorial Lab '46-48, rsrch asso since '48. AAAS—Am Genetics Association—Am Assn Cancer Research—Sigma Xi. Roscoe B. Jackson Memorial Laboratory, Bar Harbor, Me.

15 RUNNER, Waldo Arthur. Gas turbine engineering. b'15. Student '33-35 (U Mich). With Gen Electric Co since '36, gas turbine field engr supervisor since '43. SAE—Am Ordnance Assn. General Electric Company, Edwards Air Force Base, Muroc, Calif.

16 RUNYAN, Damon Ogden. Water (Supply, treatment); Sewage (Treatment); Structures (Steel, concrete, timber); City planning. b'13. BS in archtl engring '35 (U Colo). With Horner & Wyatt '36-37, Harrington & Cortelyou '37-41, Smith Hinchman & Grylls '41-42, G Meredith Musick '42-43; partner Runyan & Slee '43-47; cons engr since '43. Am Soc CE—Am Chem Inst—Am Water Works Assn—Rocky Mt Sewage Works Assn. Licensed architect and engr. 8592 W. Colfax Av., Denver 15.

17 RUNYON, Robert. Plants (Texas). b'81. Ed pub schs. Discoverer following undescribed species: Acaulon Runyoni Grout, Meliola condaliae Stevenson, Digitaria Runyoni Hitch, Runyonia tubiflora Rose, Cooperia Smallii Alexander, Selenia grandis Martin, Rubus riograndis Bailey, Esenbeckia Runyoni Morton, Euphorbia innocua Wheeler, Coryphantha Runyonii Britton and Ros, Escobaria Runyonii Britton and Rose, Cuscuta Runyoni Yuncker, Verbena Runyoni Moldenke, Justicia Runyoni Small, Grindelia oolepsis Blake, Cyperus aristatus Runyoni, and others. Author: Vernacular Names of Plants Indigenous to the Lower Rio Grande Valley of Texas '47. Co-author: Texas Cacti '30. Am Brylogical Soc—Bot Soc Am—Am Soc Plant Taxonomist—Cactus and Succulent Soc Am(F)—Phi Sigma. H: 812 E. St. Charles St., Brownsville, Tex.

18 RUNZHEIMER, Rufus E. Auto allowance engineering; Salesmen's compensation. b'99. AB '19 (Ripon Coll); '23 (U Chicago); '23-28 (La Salle Ext U). Research on the compensation of salesmen for the use of cars. Author articles in field. Propr Runzheimer and Company, Cost Research Engrs since '35. 221 North LaSalle St., Chicago 1.

19 RUPEL, I(saac) Walker. Dairy husbandry (Dairy cattle nutrition; artificial insemination). b'00. BS '23 (U Ill); MS '24—PhD '32 (U Wis). Research on vitamin D for dairy calves; milk substitute rations for calves; protein level and quality for dairy cattle including urea as a protein substitute; mineral needs of dairy cattle, cobalt deficiency in dairy cattle; artificial insemination, mechanics and techniques. Author articles in field. Prof and head dairy husbandry dept Tex A & M Coll since '45. Am Dairy Sci Assn—Am Soc Animal Prodn—Sigma Xi—Alpha Zeta—Phi Sigma. Dairy Husbandry Department, 229 Faculty Exchange, College Station, Tex.

20 RUPERT, Laurence R(emington). Moths. b'02. BS '24—MA '33 (NY State College Teachers); '33-34 (Cornell U). Research on moths of northeastern North America, with emphasis on geometers, and including life history, distribution, specific differences, group relationships, and seasonal variation. Entomol Soc Wash—Lepidopterists Soc. Sardinia, N.Y.

21 RUPNIK, John Joseph. Petroleum exploration (Seismographic method). b'10. MS '41 (Calif Inst Tech); Geol Engr '43 (Colo Sch Mines). Geophysical exploration in California, Louisiana, Mississippi, Oklahoma, Wyoming and Texas; research on velocity studies San Joaquin Valley; explored continental shelf off southern California and south Louisiana; research on reflection seismograph interpretation method. Author articles in field. Geophys div The Texas Co '33-39; research United Geophys Co Pasadena '42-46; research computer Sun Oil Co '46; geophys Sinclair Oil and Gas Co Tulsa Okla since '46. Am Assn Petroleum Geol—Soc Exploration Geophys—Sigma Xi. P.O. Box 521, Tulsa 2, Okla.

22 RUPP, William James. Pennsylvania-German folklore; Birds of Pennsylvania. b'11. AB '33 (Franklin and Marshall Coll); BD '36 (Lancaster Theol Sem). Author: History of Chestnut Hill Union Church '38; History of Great Swamp Reformed Sunday School '40; Bird Names and Bird Lore Among the Pennsylvania Germans '46. Pastor Great Swamp and Chestnut Hill Evang Ref Chs Spinnerstown Pa since '36. Pa German Soc—Pa German Folklore Soc—Phi Beta Kappa. Spinnerstown, Pa.†

23 RUPPENTHAL, Jacob Christian. International language; Universal alphabet; Phonetic alphabet; Phonetics (Acoustic). b'69. AB '95—LLB '95 (U Kan) summers '88-91 (Salina Normal U). Developed universal scientific phonetic alphabet to serve as conveyance of every language, and dialect, each symbol to have only one sound; phonetic acoustics; international alphabets; international languages. Pub sch tchr '88-96, law sch tchr U Kan '19-20. Mem Kan State Library Survey Commn; Kansas chpt of Commn for UNESCO; Pres bd dirs Pub Library Russell Kan since '01; Interna Phonetic Assn—ALA—Kan Libr Assn—American Bar Assn—Internat Bar Association. 714½ Main St., Russell, Kan.†⊚

24 RUSCH, Hugh Leonard. Industrial surveys; Opinion surveys. b'02. SB in elec engring '23 (U Wis). Inventor patented devices as hydraulic transmission, electrohydraulic motor. Eastern dist mgr A C Nielsen Co Chicago '24-28, exec vp '38-46; supervisor tech data Johns-Manville Corp NYC '28-32; vp and eastern mgr No Pump Co Minneapolis '32-37; vp Opinion Research Corp Princeton NJ since '46. Am Inst EE—Am Marketing Assn—Tau Beta Pi—Phi Kappa Phi—Eta Kappa Nu. 44 Nassau St., Princeton, N.J.†⊚

25 RUSH, Kenneth. Chemicals (Manufacturing). b'10. AB '30 (U Tenn); LLB '32 (Yale). With Union Carbide & Carbon Corporation since '36, member operating committee since '45, vice president since '49; director Linde Air Products Co, Niacet Chemicals Corp., Bakelite, Ltd (Eng), Canadian Resins & Chemicals, Ltd. Mem bd govs Northeastern Dispensary NYC.⊚

26 RUSH, Richard H(enry). Industrial management. b'15. BA '37—MCS '38 (Dartmouth); MBA '41—DCS '42 (Harvard). Advisor to aviation industry on war preparedness, including aircraft, engine and propeller production, air transportation, airports, airways, fixed base operations, and private and corporate flying; business consultant on governmental relations, mobilization problems, and governmental sales. Author articles: Trade Barriers in the Food Industry '43; Opportunities for Establishing New Businesses in Aviation '47, and others. Spl asst to pres All Am Aviation Wilmington Del '43-45; chief aviation Bur Fgn and Domestic Commerce '45-46; bus cons aviation problems since '45; staff head Super Market Inst Boston '47-48; dir aircraft div Nat Security Resources Bd since '48. Am Marketing Assn (chmn aviation com '46-48). Aircraft Div., National Security Resources Board, Washington 25.

10 RUSHTON, John Henry. Oxygen production; Low temperature operations; Petroleum processing; Mixing. b'05. BS '26—PhD '33 (U Pa). Consultant chemical engineering specializing petroleum processing, oxygen production, mixing operations, to equipment manufacturers and process industries since '33. Co-author: (with H McCormack) Applications of Chemical Engineering '38; (with H C Hesse) Process Equipment Design '46; also articles in field. Chem engr Royal Electrotype Co Phila '26-28; chem engr Kieckheffer Container Co Delaware NJ '28-29; asst prof Drexel Inst Tech Phila '29-36; asst prof U Mich '36-37; prof, chmn sch chem engring U Va '37-46; dir thermodynamics research lab U Pa '45-46; tech aide and sect chief office sci research and development Nat Defense Research Com '42-46; prof, dir chem engring dept Ill Inst Tech Chicago since '46. Am Chem Soc—Am Inst Chem Engrs (Wm H Walker award '52)—ASME—Am Soc Engring Edn—Soc Chem Industry—Sigma Xi. Technology Center, Chicago 16. H: 5128 Hyde Park Blvd.

11 RUSINOFF, Samuel Eugene. Mechanical engineering (High speed drilling); Tool design; Manufacturing methods. b'94. BS '21—ME '24 (Cooper Union Inst Tech). Research in high speed drilling of stainless steel, monel metal and aluminum alloys. Author: Practical Descriptive Geometry '47; Mathematics for Industry '49; Manufacturing Processes '49. Prof mech engring Ill Inst Tech Chgo since '40. ASME—SAE—Army Ordn Assn—Am Soc Engring Edn—Sigma Xi. Illinois Institute of Technology, Chgo.†

12 RUSKA, Walter Ernst Adalbert. Instruments (Magnetic). b'04. ME '27 (Poly Inst Oldenburg Germany). Development, design and manufacture of magnetic observatory, surveying, and prospecting instruments. Asst prodn engr Askania Werke Berlin Germany '28-29; supt research shop Humble Oil & Refining Co Houston '29-35; pres and gen mgr Walter Ruska & Co Inc Houston '35-42, Ruska Instrument Corp since '43. Am Geophys Union—Soc Exploration Geophysicists. 4607 Montrose Blvd., Houston 6.

13 RUSOFF, Louis Leon. Animal nutrition. b'10. BS '31 (Rutgers U); MS '32 (Pa State Coll); '32-34 (U Fla); PhD '39 (U Minn). Author articles: The Distribution and Concentration of Copper in the Newborn Calf as Influenced by the Nutrition of the Dam '41; Alyce Clover Hay vs Lespedeza Hay for Milking Cows '43; Blood Studies of Louisiana Dairy Cows '47; Utilizing Sweet Potatoes as Feed for Dairy Cattle '47; Antibiotics for Milking Cows and Breeding Bulls '52; Blood Studies of Red Sindhi-Jersey Crosses '52. Asst Nutrition Lab Fla Agrl Expt Station '32-35, lab asst animal nutrition '35-37, instructor animal nutrition Univ Fla '35-37, asst prof '38-42, asst animal nutrition '38-42; asso dairy nutritionist La State U '42-50, asso prof dairy nutrition '48-50, nutritionist and prof dairy nutrition '50. AAAS(F)—Biology Sect Fla Acad Sci (chmn '41)—Am Inst Nutrition—Am Chem Soc (radio chmn '49)—La Acad Sci—Soil Sci Soc of Fla—Am Dairy Sci Assn—La Jersey Cattle Club—Sigma Xi—Gamma Sigma Delta. Dairy Department, 204 Creamery Building, Louisiana State University, Baton Rouge 3, La. H: 3281 Carlotta St.

14 RUSS, William Adam, Jr. History of the Civil War and Reconstruction; Hawaiian annexation; Pennsylvania history. b'03. BA '24 (O Wesleyan U); MA '26 (U Cincinnati); PhD '33 (U Chicago); '27 (U Wis). Author articles: Registration and Disfranchisement under Radical Reconstruction '34; Hawaiian Immigration and Labor Problems before Annexation '43; The Role of Sugar in Hawaiian Annexation '43; The Origin of the Ban on Special Legislation in the Constitution of 1873 '44; What is the Central Theme of Pennsylvania History '46; The Price Paid for Disfranchising Southerners in 1867 '45. Instr hist De Pauw U '27-30, asst prof '30-33; prof hist and polit sci Susquehanna U since '33. Susquehanna University, Selinsgrove, Pa.

15 RUSSELL, Andrew George Alexander. Canadian game fish and big game; Trout fly fishing; Big game hunting and photography. b'15. Discovered and invented several new types of flies especially suited for use on western Canadian trout. Author articles in field. Photographer and writer for outdoor publications on wildlife subjects. Outdoor Writers Assn Am—Alberta Fish and Game Assn. Twin Butte, Alberta, Can.

16 RUSSELL, Carl Parcher. National parks administration; Nature protection; American history (Sierra Nevada, especially Yosemite; Fur trade, sources, interpretation). b'94. AB '15 (Ripon Wis Coll); MA '17—PhD '31 (U Mich). Oberlaender fellowship, studied museums of Germany and Austria, investigated program of national parks in Germany '36. Author: One Hundred Years in Yosemite '47; also articles in field. US Nat Park Service since '23, now supt Yosemite Nat Park; (on leave) Guggenheim fellowship (writing western fur trade history) '53, '54. AAAS(F)—Am Soc Mammalogists—Am Assn Mus—Am Planning and Civic Assn—Soc for State and Local Hist—Ecol Soc Am—Sierra Club (hon life)—Sigma Xi. National Parks Service, Yosemite National Park, Cal. H: Genoa, Nev.

17 RUSSELL, Don(ald Bert). American frontier history (Indian wars, Cody, Custer); American military history since the Civil War (Organizational, tactics). b'99. Student '16-17, '19 (Northwestern U); BA '21 (U Mich). Research on American western frontier history and the Indian Wars. Editor: The Westerners Brand Book since '46. Articles in field. Newspaperman '22-50; asst editor American Peoples Ency. Am Hist Association—Am Mil Hist Soc—Ill State Hist Soc—Kan State Hist Soc—Civil War Round Table. 179 W. Mich. Av., Chgo 1. H: 191 Clinton Av., Elmhurst, Ill.

18 RUSSELL, Earl A. Vulcanized fibre; Laminated plastics. b'95. BS '19 (Syracuse U). Spaulding Fibre Co since '29, now chief engr. NEMA (adv com vulcanized fibre and laminated products sect)—Am Soc Testing Materials (com D 9, D 20)—Soc Plastics Engrs (nat dir). Spaulding Fibre Company, Tonawanda, N.Y.

19 RUSSELL, Elizabeth Buckley Shull. Physiological genetics. b'13. BA '33 (U Mich); MA '34 (Columbia); PhD '37 (U Chicago). Research on variable attributes of pigment granules, estimates of total amount of pigment, problems in biochemistry and physiological genetics of pigmentation mammals, inheritance of tumors; inheritance and development of anemias in mice. Author articles: A Quantitative Study of Genic Effects on Guinea-Pig Coat Colors '39; The Inheritance of Tumors in Drosphila Melanogaster, with Especial Reference to an Isogenic Strain of St Sr tu 36a '42; A Quantitative Histological Study of Pigment Found in the Coat-Color Mutants of the House Mouse '49. Investigator Jackson Lab Bar Harbor Me '37-46, research asso since '46. Genetics Soc Am—Am Soc Zool—Human Genetics Soc Am—Am Assn Cancer Research. Finney-Howell fellow Jackson Lab '46-47. Jackson Laboratory, Bar Harbor, Me.

20 RUSSELL, Fred McFerrin. Football. b'06. Student (Vanderbilt U). Author: I'll Go Quietly; I'll Try Anything Twice; Funny Thing About Sports; Fifty Years of Vanderbilt Football. Contributor: Pigskin Preview in Saturday Evening Post. Sports ed and columnist Nashville Banner since '30. Nat Headliners Club award for best newspaper feature of year '36. Nashville Banner, 1100 Broadway, Nashville. H: 3804 Brighton Rd., Nashville 5.

21 RUSSELL, George Franklin, Jr. Natural gas processing. b'13. BS in ChE '43—ME '44 (Oklahoma University); '33-34 (Southeastern State Tchrs College), '37-39 (Houston University). Research in vapor-liquid equilibria between natural gas and diethylene glycol at high pressure, hydrocarbon fractionation and absorption, adsorption of water vapor and hydrocarbons by activated alumina and other aluminum oxide desiccants, water vapor contents of saturated natural gas at high pressure, retrograde behavior of high molecular weight absorption oils. Invented method for prevention of tubing corrosion in high pressure gas distillate wells, and automatic recording water vapor analyzer for natural gases. Author articles in field. Instr and research asso chem engring Okla U '43, asst prof '44; chem engr Esso Standard Oil Co La div '45; asso prof La State U '46; process design engr Hudson Engring Corp Tex '47; mgr Natural Gas and Gasoline Div Consolidated Western Constructors Inc '48-50; pres Russell Engring Corp (Tex) since '50. Am Chem Soc—AIMME—Sigma Xi—Tau Beta Pi—AAAS—Am Gas Assn(F, Okla U '42). 2609 Sunset Blvd., Houston 5.†

22 RUSSELL, I(saac) Willis. English usage; New words. b'03. AB '24—MA '29—PhD '31 (Johns Hopkins). Author articles in field. Asst prof Eng Birmingham-Southern Coll '29-30; asso prof Eng Shorter Coll '31-35; asst prof Eng U Ala '35-44, asso prof '44-47, prof since '47. Mod Lang Assn Am—South Atlantic Mod Lang Assn—Am Dialect Soc—Nat Council Teachers Eng—Coll Eng Assn. University, Ala.

23 RUSSELL, John Dale. Higher education (Administration, finance). b'85. AB '17—AM '24—PhD '31 (Ind U); '27-29 (U Ky); '28 (U Chicago). Sec sch edn Ind U '22-25; dir research Ind State Dept Pub Instrn '25-27, Ball State Tchrs Coll Muncie Ind '27; asso prof edn K U Ky '27-29; asst dir surveys Meth Ednl Instns '29-31; asso prof edn U Chicago '31-38, prof '38-46, sec dept edn '34-42, asso dean div social sci '39-44, dean of students '39-45; sec Commn on Colls and Univs, N Central Assn Coll and Secondary Schs '44-46; dir div higher edn US Office of Edn '46-51, asst commr for higher edn '51-52; exec sec NM Bd Ednl Finance since '52. American Ednl Research Assn—Nat Soc Coll Tchrs Edn—Phi Beta Kappa—Phi Delta Kappa. Board of Educational Finance, Box 528, Santa Fe, NM.†

24 RUSSELL, John William. Lanolin (Wool-grease). b'96. B Textile Ch '20 (Lowell Textile Inst). Research in utilization of wool grease or lanolin, by-products obtained from the scouring or cleansing of wool. Chief chem and cons US Worsted Corp '22-29; chief chem E Frank Lewis Co Wool Scouring since '29; gen mgr and dir Am Lanolin Corp Lawrence Mass since '29. Am

Assn Textile Chem and Colorists—Am Oil Chem Soc—Am Soc for Metals. Box 1078, Lawrence, Mass.

10 RUSSELL, Josiah Cox. Population history; History of medieval England and Spain. b'00. AB '22 (Earlham Coll); MA '23—PhD '26 (Harvard U); '20-21 (U Rome, Italy). Author: Dictionary of Writers of Thirteenth Century England '36; British Medieval Population '48. Co-author: (with J P Heironimus) The Shorter Latin Poems of Master Henry of Avranches relating to England '35; also author articles in field. Royal Hist Soc of London(F)—Population Assn of Am—AHA—Medieval Acad Am. Guggenheim Fellow '30-31; ACLS grants '33, '34; Social Sci Research Council '38—Am Philos Soc '38-39. University of New Mexico, Albuquerque, N.M.☉

11 RUSSELL, Ralston, Jr. Ceramics (Whitewares, raw materials, dielectrics, engineering, testing, teaching, refractories, clays, pottery, porcelain, china, glazes). b'10. BCerE '32—MSC '33—PhD '39—CerE '48 (Ohio State U). Author: The Electrical and Technical Ceramic Industry of Germany '47; also articles in field. Several US and fgn ceramic patents. Prof ceramic engring Ohio State U since '46. Dir ceramic research sect mgr Westinghouse Elec Corp '40-46; research engr Engr Expt Sta O State U '37-40; ceramics engr Genl Ceramics and Steatite Corp '37; research and development engr A C Spark Plug Div Gen Motors Corp '33-37. Am Ceramic Soc(F)—Inst Ceramic Engrs—Am Chem Soc—AAAS—Am Soc Engring Edn—Nat Soc Professional Engrs—Brit Ceramic Soc—Can Ceramic Soc—Am Soc Testing Materials—Am Assn Univ Prof—Conf on Elect Insulation (NRC)—Pa Ceramics Assn—O Ceramics Inds Assn—Sigma Xi—Tau Beta Pi. Department of Ceramic Engineering, 126 Lord Hall, Ohio State University, Columbus 10, O.†☉

12 RUSSELL, Richard Joel. Physical geography; Structural geology; Alluvial morphology; Loess; Deltas; Regional climatology. b'95. AB '19—PhD '26—teaching fellow '20-22 (U Calif); Belgian-American Educational Fellow '48. US delegate to the International Geographical Congress at Amsterdam '38, Lisbon '48; University of Calif and Louisiana State University delegate to same at Paris '31; Louisiana State University delegate at Moscow '37. Associate editor: Geologie der Meere und Binnengewasser (Berlin) '39-41, also articles in field. Asso geog U Calif '23-24; asso prof geol Tex Tech Coll '26-27; asso prof geog La State U '28-29, prof phys geog since '30, head dept since '36; asst dir Sch Geol since '44, dean graduate school since '49; collaborator Soil Conservation Service since '35; geol La Geol Survey '35-40; mem com geophysics Research and Development Bd, US Dept Def since '49. AAAS(F)—Am Geog Soc—Geol Soc Am—Assn Am Geog (council '37-39, pres '48)—Nat Rsrch Council (representative '41-44, mem exec com Div Geol and Geog '42-44, com on Fellowships since '46)—Am Assn Petroleum Geol (distinguished lecturer '43)—Am Meteorol Soc—Am Geophys Union—La Hist Soc—Geol and Mineral Soc Am U—Phi Kappa Phi—Sigma Xi. Received first WW Atwood award for studies in phys geog from Assn Am Geog '37. 4575 Highland Road, Baton Rouge.☉

13 RUSSELL, Rudolph F. Dioramas (Old New York). b'02. Student (Mechanics Inst). Specialized in historic dioramas of old New York City 25 years, made models for World's Fair, housing models for New York Housing authority '37. Author articles in field. Freelance drawing, dioramas for Brooklyn Union Gas Co 100th year celebration; preparator Museum of Natural History. 87-29 80th St., Woodhaven, N.Y.

14 RUSSELL, Virgil Yates. Indian artifacts (Yuma blades). b'95. AB '19 (Fairmount Coll Kan); MA '24 (U Ariz); (U Calif). Studying and compiling facts on Indian artifacts especially Yuma Blades, also gathering together the finest representative specimens of Yuma Blades. Author: Indian Artifacts of the Rockies '45; Indian Artifacts '51. Instr Am History Tucson Ariz '20-26; head social sci dept Casper Wyo since '27. Social Sci Instrs (state chmn '35-40)—NEA (Wyo chmn social sci div). Natrona County High School, Casper, Wyo.

15 RUST, Thomas H. Structural engineering; Bridges (Foundations); Steel (Gusset plates); Concrete Slabs. b'89. BS in civil engring '12 (U Wis); MS '33 (Columbia); DSc '37 (U Mich). Design, investigations reinforced concrete slabs and on steel gusset-plates and steel connections; specialist in deep foundations. Structural engineer Strauss Engineering Corp '23-25, cons '27; structural engr Cleveland and Cincinnati Union Terminals '28-32; cons engr since '38. Am Soc CE. Licensed structural engr Ill. 537 S. Dearborn St., Chgo 5.

16 RUST, William Monroe, Jr. Exploration geophysics (Seismic prospecting, research procedures); Oil wells (Electrical logging). b'07. BA '28—MA '29—PhD '31 (Rice Inst); '32-33 (Tech Hochschule Berlin). Research on application of mathematics and physics, especially electronics, to exploration for petroleum reservoirs. Granted patents in fields of seismology and electrical well-logging. With Humble Oil & Refining Co since '34, research geophys '34-37, chief geophys research sect since '37. Soc Exploration Geophys(past pres)—Inst Radio Engrs(regional dir '51-52)—Am Math Soc—APS—Am Assn Petroleum Geol. P.O. Box 2180, Houston 1.

17 RUTHERFORD, M. Louise. Labor relations; Child welfare; Civil service. AB '26—AM '30—PhD '36 (U Pa); LLB '21 (Temple U Law Sch). Deputy attorney general of Commonwealth of Pennsylvania since '39; counsel for Department of Labor and Industry, Department Public Assistance, Civil Service Commission; member governors committee to study administration of public assistance in various states '43, conference of governors Hershey '44, White House conference '44; represented Department of Justice at National Conference of Attorneys General San Francisco '39, '41, on program at Philadelphia '40; sustained constitutionality of Pennsylvania Labor Relations Act, Minimum Wage Act, Pennsylvania Parole Act and others. Author: The Influence of the ABA on Public Opinion and Legislation; also articles in field. Admitted to bar '20; pvt law practice Phila since '20. Am Bar Assn (com on jud selection and tenure, council labor relations sect)—Am Judicature Soc—Am Soc Internat Law—Pa Bar Assn (labor and industry com, world ct com, uniform law com, chmn admissions com, asst sec reiminal law sect, del to Internat Bar Assn Lima Peru '47). 618 Western Saving Fund Building, Phila. 7†☉

18 RUTHRUFF, Robert Freeborn. Petroleum utilization and conversion; Catalytic and thermal polymerization of olefines; Chemicals from petroleum; Pigments; Boron fluoride. b'02. BS Chem '24—MS '25—PhD '27 (Mich U). Holds 100 US patents relating to petroleum conversion processes. Dir research Sherwin Williams Co '39-47; cons chem and chem engr since '48. Am Chem Soc—Am Inst Chem Engrs—Chem Soc London—Soc Chem Industry (Great Brit). H: 18530 Klimm Av., Homewood, Ill.†

19 RUTSTEIN, Leo. Cellulose plastics; Hemp; Pineapple fibers (Utilization); Quality Control by statistical methods; Chemical patents. Student '11 14 (Newark Coll Engring Tech Sch); '19-20 (NYU). Research in smokeless powder, explosives, rayon, cellulose acetate, cellulose ethers, fur bleaching, paper making materials. Patents on cellulose acetate phonograph records. Author: Cellulose Formate '12; Tetrachlorethane '23; Viscosity Nitrocellulose '21. Co-author: Aviation Chemistry 1914-1918 (2 vols); Aviation Chemistry 1914-1920 (8 vols). Editor: Cellulose Acetate '15; Technology Cellulose Ethers '33; United States Chemical Patents. Asso ed Tech Cellulose Esters '11-36; estab Rutstein Lab and Library Newark '36; firm Leo Rutstein and Associates Newark since '37. Asst chief Wing Coating Sect Bur Aeronautics assigned to Signal Corps US Army '17-19; War Dept Gen Staff Mil Intelligence Div World War II. AAAS—Am Chem Soc—Soc Chem Ind—Nat Research Council—Spl Library Assn. 104 Tennessee Av., Long Beach, L.I., N.Y.

20 RUTZLER, John Enoch. Colloid and surface chemistry; Relation of physical properties of Organic compounds to structure; Colors of flowers and leaves; Chemotherapy of nervous disorders; Batteries. b'03. B Chem '27—PhD '35 (Cornell U). Author articles in field. Prof phys chem Case Inst Tech since '46; cons on batteries to Applied Physics Lab Johns Hopkins U since '48. Am Chem Soc—NY Acad Sci—Sci Research Soc Am—Sigma Xi. Case Institute of Technology, University Circle, Cleveland 6.†

21 RYALL, A(lbert) Lloyd. Storage, transportation of fruits and vegetables; Spray residue removal; Deciduous, citrus fruits. b'04. BS '26 (ND Agrl Coll); MS '28 (Ore State Agrl Coll). Research Pacific Northwest, packaging, storage, and transportation of deciduous fruits, also spray residue removal '28-41; Texas citrus fruits and vegetables '42-50; charge Fresno Field Lab USDA since '50. Author articles in field. US Dept Agr research adminstrn Bur Plant Ind Soils and Agrl Engring since '28. Am Soc Hort Sci—Am Soc Plant Physiol—Phi Kappa Phi. Rt 3, Box 307, Fresno, Cal.

22 RYAN, Alden H(oover). Microwaves. b'13. AB '35 (Oberlin College); PhD '39 (Ia State Coll). Research on development microwave radar and doppler systems; application microwaves to measurement dielectric and magnetic properties materials; microwave tubes. Westinghouse Research fellow '39-40; physicist US Naval Research Lab '40-48, asso supt elec div since '48. APS—Inst Radio Engrs—Research Soc Am—Sigma Xi—Pi Mu Epsilon. USN Meritorious Civilian Service award. Naval Research Laboratory, Washington 25.

23 RYAN, Francis Joseph. Genetics and growth of microorganisms (Fungi, bacteria); Mutation in bacteria; Amino acids (Bioassay); Gas gangrene (Chemotherapy); Fossil fish; Amphibian endocrinology and development. b'16. AB '37—MA '39—PhD '41 (Columbia U); fellow '41-42 (Stanford U). Author articles in field. Asso prof zool Columbia U '48-53, prof zool since '53. Phi Beta Kappa—Society Vertebrate Paleontology—Am Society Zool

—Bot Soc Am—Harvey Soc—Am Soc Naturalists—Am Soc Geneticists—NY Acad Sci—Marine Biol Assn—Sigma Xi. Newberry Prize in vertebrate zool Columbia U '41. Department of Zoology, Columbia University, NYC 27.†

10 RYAN, Joseph Dennis. Safety glass and glass substitutes. b'04. BS in chem engring '27—MA '28—PhD '31 (U Michigan). Author articles: Safety Glass Enters a New Era '36. Co-author articles: (with George B Watkins) Cellulose Acetate Plastic Improves Laminated Safety Glass '33, For Car Windows—Plastic or Glass? '46, Automotive Glazing with Plastics '48. Granted about 25 US patents, 25 fgn patents, others pending. Research chem Libbey-Owens-Ford Glass Co '31-37, asst dir research '37-52, asso research dir since '52. ACS—Am Ceramic Soc—AAAS(F) —Am Soc Testing Materials (com D-20 plastics, com C-14 glass)—Soc Plastics Engrs (pres Toledo '45, nat dir '50), U Toledo Research Found—Alpha Chi Sigma—Gamma Alpha. 1701 E. Broadway, Toledo.

11 RYAN, Sister Mary Hilaire. Microthyriaceous fungi. b'99. BA '21 (Rosary Coll); MA '23—PhD '25 (U Ill); '25 (U Wis). Co-author: Microthyriaceae (with F L Stevens) '39; also articles in field. Prof biol Coll New Rochelle (NY) '26-27; prof biol Rosary Coll since '28. AAAS—Ill Acad Sci—Mycol Soc Am. Rosary College, River Forest, Ill.†

12 RYAN, Will Carson. Teacher education; Educational psychology; Mental hygiene; American Indians (Education); China (Education and child welfare). AB '07 (Harvard); PhD '18 —LLD '32 (George Washington U); Carl Schurz fellow '10-11 (Columbia). Secretary British Educational Mission to US '18; child welfare consultant US to China '45-47; educational surveys of Saskatchewan '18, Santo Domingo '24, Porto Rico '25, Friends' Schools '24-27, Indian Schools '27, Virgin Islands '28, Methodist Secondary Schools '30. Author: The Literature of American School and College Athletics; Mental Health Through Education; Studies in Graduate Education; Elementary Educational Psychology; also articles in field. Kenan prof edn U NC since '40; ed High School Jour since '40; ed Understanding the Child since '42. NEA —Nat Vocational Guidance Assn (pres '26-27)—Progressive Edn Assn (pres '27-39)—Child Study Assn of Am—Am Pub Health Assn—AAAS—New Edn Fellowship—Phi Beta Kappa. Chapel Hill, N.C.†☺

13 RYAN, William Francis. High pressures; Industrial power; Chemical processes. b'89. AB '11—MME '13 (Harvard). Mechanical development of chemical processes involving high pressures; pioneer in use of high pressure steam for industrial power; inventor dual circulation boiler; mechanical design, nitrogen fixation plants at Hopewell, Virginia, and Tennessee Valley Authority. Asst engr Interborough Rapid Transit Co NY '13-15, supt constrn '15-17; chief power engr Wright Martin Aircraft Corp NJ '17-19; mech engr Harry M Hope Engring Corp Mass '19-24, Solvay Process Co NY '24-29, Stone and Webster Engring Corp since '29, engring mgr '48. Nat Soc Professional Engrs—ASME (F)—Harvard Engring Soc. 49 Federal St., Boston.†☺

14 RYDER, Ronald Arch. Waterfowl management; Wildlife conservation; Range management; Bird-banding. b '28. Student '45 (U Wyo); '46 (U Ill); BS '49—MS '51 (Colo A&M Coll). Author articles in field. Wildlife tech Colo Game and Fish Dept since '48. Am

Ornithol Union—Wildlife Soc—Cooper Ornithol Club—Wilson Ornithol Club—Audubon Soc—W Bird-Banding Assn —NE Bird-Banding Assn—Xi Sigma Pi —Beta Beta Beta—Phi Kappa Phi. Colo Game and Fish Department, 1530 Sherman, Denver.

15 RYERSON, Dwight Leonard. Reptiles; Hematology. b'08. Student '26-28 (Kan State Teachers Coll); BA '31—MS '36—zoology fellow '34-36 (U Arizona); U Fellow '41—PhD '41 (U Calif); Hargitt cytology fellow '42 (Duke). Research in salmonellosis in certain reptiles and a new species of the genus Pseudomonas pathogenic for certain reptiles. Author articles in field. Instr and asst prof anat U Ark '42-46; asso prof zool Pomona Coll since '46. Am Assn Anat—Am Soc Zool (asso)—Am Soc Parasitol—AAAS —Sigma Xi—Phi Kappa Phi. AOA prize in anat U Colo Sch Med '32. Pomona College, Claremont, Calif.†

16 RYERSON, Knowles Augustus. Subtropical horticulture; Agriculture of the Pacific islands. b'92. BS '16—MS '23 (U Calif). Horticulturist Agricultural Experiment Station Haiti '25-27, Joint Palestine Survey Commission Palestine and Transjordan '27; in charge division foreign plant introduction Bureau of Plant Industry US Department Agriculture '28-34, chief '34, in charge subtropical fruit investigations '34-37; in search of economic plants for introduction into United States and Canada '29, Europe and North Africa '30, Mexico '48; chairman Pacific Science Board National Research Council since '46. Author articles in field. Asst dean Coll Agr in charge Davis campus, prof horticulture U Calif since '37. Washington Acad Scis(F)—AAAS—Am Soc Hort Sci—Am Hort Soc (vp '30-34)—Soc Am Naturalists—Soc Am Foresters—Am Soc Agrl Sci—Calif Bot Soc—Soc for Advancement of Edn—Inst of Pacific Relations—Am Polar Soc—Royal Astron Soc Can—Save the Redwoods League —Sigma Xi—Alpha Zeta. Decorated Chevalier du Merite Agricole, France; Ouissam Alaouite, Morocco; bronze medal Soc d'Acclimitation de la France; President's Certificate of Merit '46. David, Cal.☺

17 RYGG, G(eorge) Leonard. Date handling and storage; Prepackaging fresh produce. b'03. BS '29 (ND Agrl Coll); MS '31 (Ore State Agrl Coll); PhD '41 (U Minn). Author articles in field. US Dept Agrl since '30, now physiol. AAAS—Am Soc Hort Sci—Am Soc Plant Physiol—Gamma Sigma Delta—Sigma Xi. Box 700, Pomona, Calif.†

18 RYKER, Truman Clifton. Herbicides (Rice and sugar cane weeds, Johnson grass); Rice diseases. b'08. BS '29 (Miss State Coll); MS '31 (La State U); PhD '34 (U Wis). Author articles in field. Field research path E I DuPont Co in cooperation with La Agr Expt Sta '47-50; now with Grasselli Chemicals E I Du Pont Co. Am Phytopath Soc—Am Soc Agron—Sigma Xi. Grasselli Chemicals, E I Du Pont Co., Wilmington, Del.

19 RYLAND, Hobart. Nineteenth century French literature. b'01. BA '23—MA '28 (Va Mil Inst); PhD '31 (Aix-Marseille U); '33-34 (Seville U), '34-35 (Heidelberg U). Research on teaching and testing of French verbs, experiment in laboratory sections. Author: François Fabié, Régionaliste '31; The Sources of the Play Cyrano de Bergerac '36; Les Confidences d'Arsène Lupin '40; also articles in field. Prof French University Kentucky since '53. Soc Lettres, Sciences et Arts de l'Aveyron. University of Kentucky, Lexington, Ky.†

20 RYLE, Walter Harrington. American history (1789-1860); Teacher's education; Iris hybridizing. b'96. BS '19 (Northeast Mo State Teachers Coll); AM '27—PhD '30 (George Peabody Teachers Coll); '19-21 (U Chicago)—'27-28 (U Wis). Author: Missouri: Union or Secession '31; Geography of Missouri '34; The Story of Missouri '38; also articles in field. Pres NE Mo State Teachers Coll since '37. Mo State Teachers Assn—Dept Resources and Development of State of Mo Iris Hybridizing—AHA—Miss Valley Hist Assn—Mo Hist Assn—Kappa Delta Pi. 820 E. Patterson St., Kirksville, Mo.

21 RYNEARSON, Garn A(rthur). Chromite deposits (California, Oregon). b'17. BS '38 (Calif Inst Tech); MS '41—research fellow '39-41 (Lehigh U). Author articles in field. Geol US Geol Survey since '48. Geol Soc Am(F)—AAAS—Am Mineral Soc. 102 Old Mint Building, San Francisco 3.

22 RYON, Harrison. California (History); Trade tests; Industrial relations. b'92. Student '11-13 (Beloit Coll Wis); AB '15 (Leland Stanford Jr U); JD cum laude '17 (U Chicago). Consulting engr in industrial relations, specializing in industrial personnel and labor relations; prepared trade tests. Capt adj Gen Res Corp to '34 assigned to standardizing trade tests for the army. Practicing lawyar Cal since '22. Am Bar Assn-Sigma Chi. 26 E Carillo, Santa Barbara, Cal.

23 RYPINS, Stanley. Bible paleography; Beowulf codex. b'91. BA '12—MA '13 (U Minn); PhD '18 (Harvard); '14-17 (Oxford U). Author: Three Old English Prose Texts '24; also articles in field. Prof Eng Brooklyn Coll of CCNY since '31. Rhodes scholar '14-17. Mod Lang Assn Am. Brooklyn College, Brooklyn 10, N.Y.†

S

24 SABROSKY, Curtis Williams. Taxonomy (Flies); Zoological nomenclature. b'10. BA '31 (Kalamazoo Coll); '31-35—MS '33 (Kan State Coll). Research on taxonomic entomology, zoological nomenclature, malarial mosquitoes; studied European museums '37-38; attended 7th Internat Cong Entomology Berlin '38. Author articles in field. Instr entomol Mich State Coll '36-42, asst prof '42-45; entomol div insect identification US Dept Agr Washington since '46. Capt office malaria control war areas US Pub Health Service '44-46. Entomol Soc Am(F)—Am Com Entomol Nomenclature—Washington Acad Sci—Soc Study Evolution—Entomol Soc Washington—Sigma Xi. Division of Insects, U.S. National Museum, Washington 25.

25 SACHS, Alexander. American economics (Recovery). b'93. BS '12 (Columbia); '15-17 (Harvard). Organizer and chief division economic research and planning Recovery Administration '33; founded Central Statistical Board; initiated atomic project in conferences with President '39, served as presidential representative on organizing committee; International Conference on Problems of the Pacific '36. Author: America's Recovery Program '34; Financial Dynamics of Recovery '38; Fortune Round Table on Taxation '39; Strategic Materials and Flexible Logistics Petroleum Pipeline versus Tanker Construction '42; also articles in field. Econ Walter Eugene Meyer '22-29; vp and dir Lehma Corp '36-42, econ adviser and dir '42; econ adviser to Petroleum Industry War Council '42; spl cons dir OSS '44, chmn adv com econ Interstate Oil Compact Commn since '38, councillor econ com since '45. Royal Econ Soc(F)—Royal Statis Soc—Am Econ

Assn—Am Statis Assn—Am Polit Sci Assn. 72 Wall St., NYC.☉

10 SACHS, John Harrison. Dyes (Anthraquinone, coal tar). b'89. BS '10 (Gettysburg Coll); PhD '16—Carnegie fellow '16-17 (Johns Hopkins). Author articles in field. Holder or co-holder nine patents on dyes. With DuPont Co '17-48, mgr development div organic chem dept '43-48. Am Chem Soc—Am Inst Chem Engr—Phi Beta Kappa. New Oxford, Pa.

11 SACHS, Paul Joseph. Drawings. b'78. AB '00 (Harvard); LLD; DA; LHD '49 (Colby Coll). Author: Great Drawings '51. Co-author: Drawings in the Fogg Museum, 3 vols. '40. Lecturer on art Wellesley Coll '16-17; asst prof fine arts Harvard U '17-22, asso prof '22-27, prof fine arts '27-48, now emeritus; exchange prof France '32-33. Phi Beta Kappa—Am Acad Arts and Scis —Archeol Inst Am—Coll Art Assn— Am Commn for Protection and Salvage Artistic and Historic Monuments in Europe.☉

12 SACKS, Isaac Milton. Southeast Asia (Indochina); International communism (Theory and organization). b'19. BS (Philos) '42 (Coll City of NY); '43-44 (U Calif); '47-48 (Am U Washington); '49-51 (Yale). Consultant on selected bibliography Indochina to Library of Congress. Author article: The Strategy of Communism in Southeast Asia '50. Contributor: South Asia in the World Today '50. Fgn affairs analyst US Dept State '46-49. Study Far Eastern area and lang Army Specialized Training Program '43-44; lang interpretation Mil Intelligence Training Center '45. Inst Pacific Relations—Far Eastern Assn— Am Polit Sci Assn. 2675 Yale Station, New Haven. H: 219 E. 178th St., Bronx 57, N.Y.

13 SACKS, Jerome Gerald. Military psychology. b'15. BS '36 (U Md); MS '38—PhD '42 (Catholic U Am); '46-47 (Harvard). Author: Troublemaking in Prison: A Study of Resistant Behavior as an Administrative Problem in a Medium Security Penal Institution '42; also articles in field. Service Command personnel cons and chief psychol Hq US Army Boston '42-46, chief clinical psychol sect Med Field Service Sch Ft Sam Houston '47-48, asst chief clinical psychol br Office Surg Gen Dept Army Washington since '48. Mil Psychol(F)—Am Psychol Assn(F)—Mass Soc Clinical Psychol(F)—Am Assn Social Workers. Office of the Surgeon General, Department of the Army, Washington 25.

14 SAFFORD, Hurd Winter. Analytical instrumentation (Polarography, potentiometric titrations, spectrophotometry). b'15. BS '36 (Alfred U); PhD '41 (U Pittsburgh). Research in the field of glass structure and analysis, quantitative organic microanalysis, potentiometric titrations and polarography. Invented platinum shield for thermocouples operating in electric induction furnaces. Author: Selected Experiments in Analytical Instrumentation '49; also articles in field. Instr '41-45, asst prof since '45, adminstr asst to head dept chem '45-49. Am Ceramic Soc—Am Chem Soc—AAAS— Sigma Xi. Department of Chemistry, University of Pittsburgh, Pittsburgh 13.

15 SAFIER, Benno. Promiscuity (Emotional factors in; Venereal disease (Control, emotional factors in). b'10. AB '31—MD '35 (Stanford U). Research on promiscuity as factor in spread of venereal disease, and on life histories, motivations, and conflicts in promiscuous and potentially promiscu-

ous men and women. Sr author: A Psychiatric Approach to the Treatment of Promiscuity '49. Psychiat interne Agnew State Hosp Cal '35-36, physician and psychiat '36-47; dir psychiat service San Francisco City Clinic since '45; pvt practice psychiat San Francisco since '47; neuropsychiat Veterans Adminstrn San Francisco since '47; asst psychiat Mt Zion Hosp '47. AMA—Am Psychiat Assn—Soc Psychiatry and Neurology N Cal— Psychosomatic Soc N Calif. Diplomate Nat Bd Med Examiners '35, Am Bd Psychiat '47. 516 Sutter St., SF 2.

16 SAGARIN, Edward. Perfume materials; Perfumery. b'13. Student '40-44 (Brooklyn Coll). Author: The Science and Art of Perfumery '45; also articles in field. Ed the Givaudanian since '40; former lecturer in perfume materials and perfumery Columbia U. Society Cosmetic Chem (chmn library com). Givaudan-Delawanna, Inc., 330 W. 42 St., NYC 18. H: 57 Lincoln Road, Brooklyn 25.

17 SAGENDORPH, Kent. Air power and air warfare (Tactical and strategic). b'02. Student '22 (U Mich); Grad A F Intell Sch, Air Comd and Staff Sch. Lecturer on air power, author military manuals and instruction books. Author: Thunder Aloft: US Air Power Today and Tomorrow '41. Asso ed FLYING mag; asso ed AERO DIGEST. Lt Col USAF (R). Veterans' Flying Assn Am (pres '46). 333 W. Mason St., Jackson, Mich.

18 SAGER, DeWitt Dunn. Explosives; Propellants. b'01. BS '22 (McPherson Coll); MS '25 (Mich State Coll). Research on nitrocellulose, explosives and ingredients of propellants. Chief General Laboratory Section Picatinny Arsenal '45-50, directing control, acceptance and specification testing of explosives, propellants and related materials, preparation of specifications, stability and surveillance testing; asst chief tech div charge research and chem Picatinny Arsenal since '50. AA AS—Am Ordnance Assn—Am Inst Chem(F). Recipient: Meritorious Service Award '44; Certificate of Commendation as member of mission on German and Italian Explosives '45 Ordnance Dept. Picatinny Arsenal, Dover, N.J. H: Qtrs. 1109.

19 SAIN, Kanwar. Dam design. b'99. CE (Thomson Civil Engring Coll, Roorkee, India). Research, design and construction of river valley projects, reinforced concrete structures, in charge design Hirakud and Kakrapar dam projects. Chief engr Bikaner State '47-49; mem Central Water and Power Commn Govt India since '49. Am Soc CE—Instn Engrs—Nat Soc Soil Mech on Found and Engring— Indian Roads Congress—Internat Commission Hydraulic Research. Central Water and Power Commission, Bikaner House, New Delhi, India.

20 SAKIMURA, K(anjyo). Thrips vector for plant virus diseases. b'03. Grad '22 (Yamaguchi Jr Coll Japan). Discovered an additional thirps vector species in the Atlantic States region and several thrips non-vector species in Hawaii. Author articles in field. Asst entomol Pineapple Research Inst Honolulu Hawaii since '30. AAAS—Am Assn Econ Entomol—Entomol Soc Am —Am Phytopath Soc—Hawaiian Acad Sci—Hawaiian Entomol Soc. Pineapple Research Institute, Box 3166, Honolulu 2, Hawaii, T.H.

21 SALANDRA, Dominic de la. Balboa and Pedrarias; Ecuador (Cultural relations); Inter-American relations. b'93. BA '23 (Reed Coll); MA '27 (Stanford U); PhD '33 (U Calif);

'24-25 (U Washington); '39 (U Nacional Mexico City). Author articles: Porto Bello '34; A Guide to Bibliographies in Latin American History '34; Latin American Texts: A Guide '36; Beardless Indians '36. Asso prof Duquesne U Pittsburgh '37-43; prof Mt Mercy Coll summer '42; US cultural relations attache Am Embassy US Dept State Quito Ecuador '44-45; asso prof U Dayton '46-51; info. Splist., archivist, Wright-Patterson AFB since '51. AHA—Am Acad Polit Social Sci —Sigma Delta Pi—Phi Alpha Theta. 614 Shadow Lawn Av., Dayton 9, O.

22 SALATI, Octavio Mario. Signal generators; Coaxial connectors; Antennas; Magnetostrictive and electrostrictive delay lines. b'14. BS (EE) '36—MS '39 (U Pa). Designed and built precision signal generators in frequency range of 500 kilocycles to 1500 megacycles; development and design coaxial and other electrical connectors; research and design single and multiple element antennas in frequency range of 100 to 2000 megacycles. Holds patents in field. Sr engr in charge antenna development and signal generator design Hazeltine Electronics Corp Little Neck NY '42-48; research asst prof U Pa since '48. Inst Radio Engrs—Am Inst Elec Engrs —Eta Kappa Nu—Sigma Xi. Moore School Electrical Engineering, University of Pennsylvania, Phila 4.

23 SALE, Robert Charles. Libraries (Special). b'11. AB '33 (Colgate U); BS '43 (Syracuse U). In charge compilation bibliographies and technical literature searches in fields of mechanical, electrical, metallurgical, and aeronautical engineering; specialist in administration technical libraries. Author articles: General Considerations for the Physical Layout of a Special Library '46; Personnelisms '50; Is Binding the Answer? '51. Head search dept Engring Soc Library NYC '43-45, also chmn engring—aeronautics sect SLA, chief librarian United Aircraft Corp East Hartford Conn since '45; cons applied physics lab library Johns Hopkins '48. SLA—ALA—AAAS— Conn Library Assn—ASLIB (Gt Brit). Library, United Aircraft Corp., East Hartford 8, Conn. H: 112 Birchwood Rd., East Hartford, Conn.†

24 SALEEBY, Murad Mitri. Abaca (Manila hemp); Commercial fiber commerce b'82. BA '02 (American Univ Beirut Lebanon). Author of the fiber grading law and the original regulations establishing the standard grades '13; also articles in field. Fiber export business Manila '17-40. Am Genetics Assn. 40 Crescent Drive, Palo Alto, Calif.

25 SALISBURY, Glenn Wade. Dairy cattle breeding; Physiology of reproduction; Artificial insemination of cattle. b'10. BSc '31 (O State U); PhD '34 (Cornell U). Developed many techniques and present concepts in improving cattle by artificial insemination. Author articles in field. Instr animal husbandry Cornell U '34-36, asst prof '36-40, asso prof '40-44, prof '44-47; head dept dairy science U Ill since '49; livestock cons for Near East Fedn for Greece since '40. Dairy Sci Assn—Am Soc Animal Prodn—Am Genetic Assn —Sigma Xi—Phi Kappa Phi. Borden Award for research in dairy prodn '45. 2110 S. Race St., Urbana, Ill.

26 SALISBURY, Robert Kenneth. Desmidiology (Florida); Star names and constellations. b'95. BA '23—MSc '33 (O State U); '43 (U Cincinnati). Named Micrasterias Floridensis, Micrasterias Piquata; found numerous zygospores. Author articles: Desmids of Florida '34. Supt Georgetown Schs

Ohio since '47. O Acad Sci—AAAS—Am Micros Assn—Sigma Xi—Phi Beta Kappa. Georgetown, O. H: Russellville.†

10 SALMON, Vincent. Acoustics; Audio engineering; Horns. b'12. BA '34—MA '36 (Temple U); PhD '38 (MIT). Holds patent on catenoidal horns. Author articles: Generalized Plane Wave Horn Theory '46; A New Family of Horns '46. Phys Stanford Research Inst since '49. Acoustical Soc Am(F)—Inst Radio Engrs—Audio Engring Society. Stanford Research Institute, Stanford, Cal.†

11 SALOUTOS, Theodore. American agricultural history (Farmer movements and unrest). b'10. BA '33 (Wis Teachers Coll); PhD '40—Post-doctoral fellow '40-41 (U Wis). Author: The Wisconsin Society of Equity '40; Efforts at Crop Control in Seventeenth Century America '46; The Southern Cotton Assn '47; The American Farm Bureau Federation '48; Agricultural Discontent in the Middle West, 1900-39, '39; and others. Lecturer U Calif '45-46, asso prof since '49; asst prof hist U Minn summer '47; Fulbright Research Scholar U Athens '52-53, on repatriated Greek immigrants. AHA—Miss Valley Hist Assn—Agrl Hist Soc—Am Farm Econ Assn—Econ Hist Assn. University of California, Los Angeles.

12 SALTER, Robert Mundhenk. Soil chemistry and fertility. b'92. BS '13—MS '14—'24-25 (O State U); DSc (hon) '44 (Rutgers U). Author articles in field. Asst soil chem Agr Expt Sta W Va '16-17, soil chem '17-19, agron '19-21; asst prof soil chem W Va U '17-19, prof agron '19-21; prof soils O State U '21-25, prof agron and chmn dept '29-40; chief agron O Expt sta '25-41, asso dir '40-41; dir Agr Expt Sta NC State Coll '40-41; head div soil and fertilizer investigations Bur Plant Industry US Dept Agr '41-42, chief Bur Plant Industry, Soils and Agr Engring '42-51 chief Soil Conservation Service since '51. Am Soc Agron (F, pres '36)—AAAS (F, vp '37)—Soil Sci Soc Am—Am Soc Agr Engrs—Gamma Sigma Delta—Sigma Xi. Soil Conservation Service, U.S.D.A., Washington, 25.

13 SALVESEN, Jorgen Richter. Wood and lignin utilization; Vanillin and tanning agents from lignin. b'01. Diploma Chem E '24 (Norwegian Inst Tech). Author articles in field. Holder nine US patents, two on vanillin process, seven on lignin compounds, one patent pending. With Marathon Corp since '30, now dir central research. Am Chem Soc—AAAS—Tech Assn Pulp and Paper Ind—Am Leather Chem Assn—Am Forestry Assn. Scandinavian-Am Foundation fellow '27-30. Marathon Corporation, Central Research, Rothschild, Wis.

14 SALYER, Sandford Meddick. Seventeenth Century English literature (Verse and prose satire); Nineteenth Century American literature (Concord group). b'78. BA '04 (Amherst Coll); MA '14—PhD '21 (Harvard). Identification of allusion, especially in works of Joseph Hall; translation of Latin works by Hall; collection of biographical data, especially about the Alcotts. Author: Marmee—The Mother of Little Women '49; Dorothy Quincy—Wife of John Hancock '50. Author articles: Joseph Hall as a Literary Figure (thesis); Hall's Satires and the Harvey Nashe Controversy, and others. Instr advancing to adjunct prof English U Ga '07-15; prof English Duke U '22-27, U Okla since '27. Modern Lang Assn Am—Modern Lang Assn of S and SW—Phi Beta Kappa. University of Oklahoma, Norman.

15 SALZMANN, J(acob) A(mos). Dentofacial malformations; Facial measurements. b'00. DDS (U Pa). Basic research on physiologic changes in position of teeth, causes of dental malocclusion and public health approach in dentofacial malformations. Inventor maxillator, instrument for taking direct facial measurements in determining need for orthodontic treatment and in research on growth and development of the face. Author: Principles and Practice of Public Health Dentistry '37; Manual for Dental Technicians '48; Principles of Orthodontics '50. Author articles: Orthodontic Therapy as Limited by Ontogenetic Growth and the Basal Arches '48; Criteria for Extraction in Orthodontic Therapy Related to Dentofacial Development '49, others. Dir of dental service Vocational Schs '34-45; asso attending dentist and head orthodontics Mount Sinai Hospital NYC since '45; cons NYC Dept Health since '45, NY State Dept Health since '44, Children's Bur Fed Social Security Agy since '46; editor NY Jour Dentistry since '31; asso editor Am Jour Orthodontics since '39. AAAS(F)—Soc Research and Child Development (F)—NY Acad Dentistry(F)—Am Pub Health Assn(F)—Am Assn Orthodontists—NY Acad Scis—Am Dental Assn—Internat Acad Dental Research. 654 Madison Av., NYC 21.

16 SAMARAS, Nicholas Napoleon. Triantaphyllos plastics. b'06. BS '27—PhD '31 (Yale). Associated with development Monsanto's series of wetting-out agents and detergents; with laboratory and pilot plant development of process for production of monomeric styrene culminating in Texas City, Texas plant; improved processes for styrene polymerization; processes for production monomeric vinyl chloride, polymers, copolymers; new melamine resins for applications in textile, laminating and coating fields; thermoplastics of materially improved properties; physical behavior plastic compositions; theories plasticization and polymer degradation. Author articles in field. With Monsanto Chem Co since '36, now central research director. Am Chem Soc—Am Chem Soc(F)—Soc Chem Ind of London—Princeton U Plastics Adv Council—Sigma Xi—Tau Beta Pi. Monsanto Chemical Company, Dayton 7, O.

17 SAMPLE, James Halverson. Resins; Organic surface coatings; Hydroponics. b'14. BS '35 (Elmhurst Coll); MS '36—PhD '39 (U Ill). Research chemist and chem research supervisor resin research dept the Sherwin Williams Co since '44. Am Chem Soc (dir Ind sect '42-43, sec '43-44, assistant ed Chicago Sect Chem Bull '50-51. Ind Chem Society—Sigma Xi. 115th and Cottage Grove Streets, Chicago 28.†

18 SAMPSON, Arthur W(illiam). Range ecology. b'85. BS '06—AM '07 (U Neb); '14-15 (Johns Hopkins); PhD '17 (George Washington U). Representative Pan-American Scientific Congress Denver '48, United Nations Lake Success '49. Author: American Forage Plants; Range and Pasture Management; Livestock Husbandry on Range and Pasture; also articles in field. Asst range ecol US Forest Service '07-12, plant ecol and dir Great Basin Research Sta '12-22; lecturer range ecol Syracuse U '16, U Calif '21, asso prof forestry '22, now prof. Soc Plant Physiol—Am Foresters—Ecol Soc Calif—Bot Soc—Range Management Soc. Forestry Bldg., University of California, Berkley.

19 SAMPSON, Homer Cleveland. Botanical education. b'85. Grad '12 (Eastern Ill State Normal); BS '14—PhD '17 (U Chicago). Author: (with E N Transeau) Directions for Laboratory and Field Work in General Botany '19; (with E N Transeau and L H Tiffany) Textbook of Botany '39; Workbook for General Botany '41. With Ohio State U since '17, prof since '22; collaborator US Central States Forest Expt Sta since '28. AA AS (com on improvement in science edn)—Bot Soc America (com on teaching of botany in colls and univs)—Ecol Soc Am—Am Soc Plant Physiologists—Ohio Acad Science—Phi Beta Kappa—Sigma Xi. 342 Acton Rd., Columbus 14, O.◉

20 SAMUEL, Arthur Lee. Gaseous and high vacuum electron tubes; Solid state devices; Digital Computers. b'01. AB '23—hon DSc '46 (Coll of Emporia); SB '25—SM '26 (MIT). Developed first multicavity magnetron; made early forms of Barkhausen tubes, multilead triodes for ultra-high frequency operation, double tetrodes and pentodes for use as ultra-high frequency amplifier; developed special forms of klystron oscillators and amplifiers; made significant contributions in gasdischarge transmit-receive switches for radar use; published first comprehensive treatment of space charge between parallel plane electrodes. Has approximately 40 US patents. Author articles in field. Bell Tel Labs '28-46, prof elec engring U Ill '46-49; sr engr IBM since '49. Inst Radio Engrs(F)—AIEE (F)—Am Phys Soc—AAAS(F)—Sigma Xi. Engineering Lab., Internat Business Machines Corp., Poughkeepsie, N.Y.

21 SANBORN, Colin Campbell. Mammalogy (Cheiroptera). b'97. Research on taxonomy, distribution and habits of bats, mammals. Author articles in field. Curator mammals Chicago Natural Hist Mus since '37. Am Soc Mammalogists—Biolog Soc Wash—Zool Soc London (corr). Guggenheim Fellow '38. Chicago Natural History Museum, Chgo 5. H: R.1, Valparaiso, Ind.

22 SANBORN, Herbert Charles. Aesthetics; Dachshunds(Breeding, judging, history). b'73. PhB '96 (Boston U); AM '97 (Tufts Coll); Jacob Sleeper fellow '01-08 (Boston U); PhD '08 (Munich). Author: Zschokke '03; Meyer Forster '04; Ueber die Identitaet der Person '09; Aesthetics and Civilization '23; The Function of Philosophy in Liberal Education '26; Methodology and Psychology '27; The Dachshund or Teckel '37; An Examination of William Stern's Philosophy; Are There Any Individuals '39; Philosophies and Psychologies '48; The Function of History in Liberal Education '51. Prof head dept philos and psychol Vanderbilt U since '21, emeritus since '42. AAAS(F)—Brit Inst Philos Studies—Kant Gesellschaft—So Assn Philos and Psychol — Am Psychol Assn — Am Philos Assn—Tenn Acad Sci—Tenn Philol Assn—Phi Beta Kappa. Isartal, Old Hickory Blvd., Brentwood, Tenn.◉

23 SANBORN, Pearl S. Unusual plants; Scented geraniums. b'85. Student (Thetford Acad). Research on 2000 different plants from tropical United States. Author articles in field. Dir Round Robins on sweet scented geraniums '45-49, native wild ferns '46-49, moss '46-49, moth-butterfly beetle and bee '48. Hort Soc Mass—American Begonia Soc—Nat Geog soc—Natural Hist Book Club—Jr Audobon Club—NH Audobon Soc—Mass Audobon Soc. R.F.D. 1, Thetford Center, Thetford, Vt.†

24 SANDERS, Azel Labon Ralph. Bridges (Movable). b'98. BS (civil engring) '22 (U Ill). Research and design of bascule, vertical lift and swing bridges for highway and railroad use, machinery for operation of movable portions of structure, maintenance, construction and operation. Asst engr Scherzer Rolling Lift Bridge Co '25-34; asst engr Hazelet and Erdal '36-42, chief engr since '43; chief engr Allied Engrs Inc '42-43. Am Soc CE—Am Soc ME—Am Ry Engring Assn—ASTM—Am Concrete Inst—W Soc Engrs—Sigma Tau—Chi Epsilon. Hazelet and Erdal, 53 W. Jackson Blvd., Chgo 4.†

10 SANDERS, Benjamin Elbert. Blood sterilization. b'18. BS '39 (Wofford Coll); MS (chem) '42 (U Ga); Ph D '49 (Purdue U). Research on compounds with virucidal and bactericidal activities to use for sterilization blood and plasma to help eliminate homologous serum jaundice virus. Biochem Lawson Gen Hosp '44-45; research chem Henry Ford Hosp '49-51; now with immunochemistry dept Sharp and Dohme, Inc. ACS f (Purdue U '46-49—Sigma Xi—Phi Lambda Upsilon. Immunochemistry Dept., Sharp and Dohme, Inc., West Point, Pa.

11 SANDERS, C(harles) Richard. Nineteenth century English literature (Coleridge; Lytton Strachey). b'04. Fellow '32-34—PhD '34 (U Chicago) BPh '26—MA '27 (Emory U). Author: An Abridgment of Malory's 'Morte D' Arthur '40; Coleridge and the Broad Church Movement '42. Asst asso prof Duke U '37-52, prof since '52. Modern Lang Assn America—South Atlantic Mod Lang Assn—Phi Beta Kappa. Grants for research from Carnegie and Rockefeller Found '47. College Station, Duke University, Durham, N.C.†

12 SANDERS, Dorsey Addren, Sr. Veterinary medicine. b'98. BSA '20 (Clemson Coll); Dr Veterinary Med '23 (Kan State Coll). Investigation canine babesiasis and bovine anaplasmosis; study hemorrhagic septicemia and enzootic bronchopneumonia of cattle; research crotalaria, lantana, and tung tree foliage poisoning, also insect vectors of infectious bovine mastitis, and life cycle of eyeworms in poultry. Author articles: Notes on the Experimental Transmission of Bovine Anaplasmosis '33; Canine Babesiasis '37; Nature and Transmission of Enzootic Bronchopneumonia of Dairy Calves '40, and others. Asst research veterinarian U Ky '23-25; with U Fla since '25, now veterinarian and head dept vet sci. Am Veterinary Med Assn—So Veterinary Med Assn—US Livestock San Assn—Fla State Veterinary Med Assn (pres '49-51)—Sigma Xi. Florida Agricultural Experiment Station, Gainesville, Florida. H: 605 S.W. Tenth St.⊚

13 SANDERS, J(esse) T(homas). Land and resources development. b'89. AB '15 (Okla U); AM '17 (George Peabody Coll); PhD '25 (U Wis). Asso agrl economist US Dept Agr hdqrs Washington 19-24; prof agrl econ and head dept agrl econ Okla A and M Coll '25-36; asst regional dir region 8 resettlement adminstrn US Dept Agr hdqrs Dallas '36-39; sr agrl economist Bur Agrl Econ '39-42; prin econ farm mach br War Food Adminstrn '42-44; chief analysis br agrl rehabilitation div UNRRA '44-47; legislative counsel The Nat Grange since '47. Am Farm Econ Assn—Am Acad Polit and Social Sci—United Nations Assn—Nat UNESCO Commn representing Nat Grange. 744 Jackson Pl., Washington 6. H: 4607 Calvert Rd., College Park, Md.⊚

14 SANDERS, Paul H(ampton). Labor relations; Labor arbitration; Wages. b'09. AB '31 (Austin Coll); LLB '34 (Duke U). Asso editor: Law and Contemporary Problems '37-46. Prin mediation officer Nat War Labor Bd Washington '42; regional atty hdqrs Atlanta '42-44; regional vice-chmn Atlanta '44; regional atty Nat Wage Stabilization Bd Atlanta '46; pub mem Spl Industry Com on Minimum Wages PR '50; served as indsl relations specialist 12th Naval Dist San Francisco '44-46. Vis prof law Sch Jurisprudence U Cal Berkeley '47-48; prof law Vanderbilt U since '48. Am Bar Assn (sec, mem council labor relations sect)—Am Law Inst—Nat Acad Arbitrators —Am Arbitration Assn(labor panel) —Indsl Relations Research Assn—Assn Interstate Commerce Commn Practitioners—Conf on Personal Finance Law(gen com)—Pi Gamma Mu —Phi Delta Phi. Vanderbilt University Law School, Nashville 4. H: 1207 Noelton Lane, Nashville 4.†

15 SANDERS, Walter Frederick. Education (Higher). b'80. Student '02 (State Normal School Emporia Kan); '06-08 (Washburn Coll); AB '09 (U Chicago); AM '17; LLD '37 (Park Coll). With Park College since '11, head dept mod lang '13-46, now prof mod lang, dean '10-46; F in higher education Ohio State U '29-30. Nat Com to Uphold Constitutional Govt —Mod Lang Assn Am—Theta Alpha Phi. Park College, Parkville, Mo.†⊚

16 SANDERSON, Ivan Terence. Tropical fauna (Ecology); General zoology mammals and amphibians. b'11. BA '32 (Cambridge U Eng). In charge nine research expeditions to Orient, Africa, South and Central America; builder tropical sailing craft; studies Negro-African drums, music and dancing. Natural history program NBC '48-49; television program WNBT '49; first color television program CBS '51. Am Geog Soc—Linnean Soc Lond (F)—Zool Soc Lond (F)—Royal Geog Soc (F)—NY Zool Soc—Nat Speleological Soc Am. c/o Paul R. Reynolds & Son, 599 Fifth Av., NYC 17.

17 SANDERSON, Milton William. Entomology (Coleoptera). b'10. BA '32 —MA '33—PhD '37 (U Kan); '35-36 (U Mich). Research on various species Coleoptera; Phyllophaga; new entomological species in the United States, Jamaica, Cayman Islands; section editor Biological Abstracts, member editorial Board Entomological Society of America. Author articles: A Monographic Revision of the North American Species of Stenelmis '38; Crop Replacement in Relation to Grasshopper Abundance '39; The Order Embioptera New to Arkansas '40; Descriptions and Records of Distribution of Phyllophaga '42; Distribution and Hosts of Arkansas Phyllophaga '44; A Brief Review of the Taxonomy of Phyllophaga in the United States '37; The North American Species of Stilicolina Casey '47, and others. Field aide entomol US Dept Agr '37; asst instr U Kan '37; instr entomol and asst entomol Agr Expt Sta U Ark '37-42; asso taxonomist Ill Natural Hist Survey since '42. Kan Entomol Soc—Entomol Soc Am (F)—Ill Acad Sci—Soc Systematic Zool—Wash Entomol Soc. Illinois Natural History Survey, Urbana, Ill.

18 SANDERSON, Russell Malcolm. Prices (Consumer); Indexes (Cost of living); Management (Organizational planning). b'09. Student '25-29 (U Mich); '37-38 (Wayne U); '43-44 (Am U); '42-44 (USDA Grad Sch). Research on retail and wholesale prices and margins. Purchasing and management A & P Tea Co and Kroger Grocery Co '29-41; asst chief Consumer price Div US Bur Labor Statis '42-44; management adv and adminstr officer Bur Nav personnel '44-46; asst to sr partner Smith Barney and Co since '46. Am Management Assn—Am Econ Assn—Am Statis Assn—Royal Econ Soc—Acad Polit Sci. Smith Barney and Co., 14 Wall St., NYC 5.

19 SANDERSON, Wilford Edwin. Ornamental feathers (Bantam breeding); Wildlife management; American native wildlife; Traps and trapping methods. b'88. BS '17 (Syracuse); '20-21 (Yale). Organized wildlife department American Humane Association; assembled largest collection all kinds and types traps from early "Man-trap from Sherwood Forest" to present day inventions; inaugurated annual humane trap contest to further interest in practical humane traps; bred wild turkeys to re-established species in north; research on control of biting flies in Adirondacks, beaver restoration; experimented with breeding bantams for purpose improving feathers for fly-tying and ornamental feathers for use millinery which could be used without dyeing. Developed feathers similar to Jungle fowl on domestic bantams. Asst prof forest extension '19-22; sec treas Baker-Bullock and Sanderson Inc Mishike Wis '22-25; statis work Am Paper and Pulp Assn NYC '24-25; field naturalist NY State Mus '28-32; field rep Am Humane Assn '26-30, dir wildlife dept '30-42; mammal specialist Nat Audubon Soc since '42. Am Soc Foresters—Am Soc Mammalogists (chmn land mammals com)—Wildlife Soc—Am Ecolog Soc. Crumitie Road, Route 116, Albany 4, N.Y.†

20 SANDIDGE, John R(oy). Microfaunas of the Mesozoic period; Petroleum geology. b'97. BA '20 (Tex Christian U); MS '22 (Vanderbilt U); PhD '28 (Johns Hopkins U). Princeton geological expedition to Montana '32. Author articles in field. Sr geol Magnolia Petroleum Co since 1952. Geological Society Am(F)—American Assn Pet Geol—Paleontol Soc Am—Soc Econ Paleontol and Mineral (pres '46) —S Tex Geol Soc—Paleontol Research Inst—Sigma Xi—Phi Beta Kappa. 1704 Alamo National Bank Building, San Antonio 5.†

21 SANDIN, Mary (Mrs R B). Weaving. b'01. BS '35 (U Alberta). Co-editor Loom Music since '44. Weaving instr Banff Sch Fine Arts since '42. Guild Can Weavers. University of Alberta, Edmonton, Alberta, Can.

22 SANDOZ, Edouard. Heraldry. b'18. AB (Harvard). Continuous study of heraldry and medieval texts since '35. Author: Twice Besieged '47; The Squire of Ravensmark '49; also articles in field. Asst curator dept graphic arts Harvard '41-42; writer and illus since '45; cons on heraldic problems. New Eng Hist and Geneal Soc (heraldic com since '46)—Medieval Acad Am. 20 Bryant St., Cambridge 38, Mass.

23 SANDOZ, Mari. Trans-Missouri (Study from Stone Age to present). Litt D '50 (U Neb). History of stone age Indian, plains and Missouri country through folklore, fur trader, early settler, and cattleman stories; early settler history as shown through family records and official documents. Author: Old Jules '35; Slogum House '37; Capital City '39; Crazy Horse '42; Cheyenne Autumn '50; The Tom Walker '47; also numerous short stories. Mem Assn Am Indian Affairs—Neb State Hist Soc—Am Forestry Assn. H: 23 Barrow St., NYC 14.

24 SANDSTEDT, Rudolph Marion. Wheat flour chemistry; Cereal amylases and proteins; Starch; Baking. b'96. BS '20—MS '22 (U Neb). Research analytical methods for the determination of maltose value, gassing power, rapid moisture, a-amylase, b-amylase, sugars in flour and bread, proteolysis in doughs and sulfhydryls in flour and dough; amylase action on raw starch; photomicrographic and motion photomicrographic studies of starch digestion and starch gelatinization. Author articles in field. U Neb and Neb Agrl Experimental Station since '22, now prof agrl chem. Am Assn Cereal Chem—Am Chem Soc—AAAS—Assn Official Agrl Chem. University of Nebraska, College of Agriculture, Lincoln, Neb.

10 SANFORD, Eva Matthews. History of medieval scholarship (Latin writers); Ancient history (Roman). b'94. AB '16—MA '22—PhD '23 (Radcliffe Coll); '17-19 (Yale)—'19-20 (Columbia)—'23-24 (Am Sch Classical Studies Rome Italy); sem '32 (Far Eastern Studies Am Council of Learned Socs Cambridge Mass); Islamic sem '41 (Princeton). Instr hist Mather Coll Western Reserve U '25-27, asst prof '27-37; asst prof hist Sweetbriar Coll Va '37-42, asso prof since '42. Author: Salvian: On the Government of God '30; The Mediterranean World in Ancient Times '38; also articles in field. AHA—Am Philol Assn—Classical Assn Middle West and South—Archeol Inst Am—Medieval Acad Am. Awards: Radcliffe Coll fellowship '23-24; grants-in-aid, Am Council of Learned Socs '28, '30. Fulbright Fellow '50. Sweetbriar College, Sweetbriar, Va.

11 SANGER, John Hobart. Missouri River (Development); Wind-power (Utilization). b'07. BS in elec engring '30 (SD Sch Mines and Tech); '42 (Cal Inst Tech); '43 (MIT). Research on application fie concepts of wind-power unit to aerodynamics and special devices. Cons engr since '45. Am Inst EE. P.O. Box 1, Mitchell, S.D.

12 SARBACH, Donald Victor. Rubber technology. b'11. BSc '34 (U Neb). Twenty five US patents. Author articles in field. Goodrich Co since '37, now tech mgr New Products Div. Am Chem Soc—Phi Lambda Upsilon—Alpha Chi Sigma. The B. F. Goodrich Company, Akron, O.

13 SARBACHER, Robert Irving. Tubes (Thermionic vacuum); Wave guides; Microwave components. b'07. Diploma '26 (Baltimore Poly Inst); '26-27 (Johns Hopkins U); '29-30 (NY U); BS—EE '33 (U Fla); '33-34 (Princeton U); MS '36—ScD '39 (Harvard); EE '51 (U Fla). Development of test equipment for vacuum tubes; studies on amplifiers and frequency multipliers as influenced by harmonic voltage; consultant guided missiles committee Research and Development Board since '50. Co-author: (with W A Edson) Hyper and Ultra-High Frequency Engineering '43. Author articles: A Mechanical Device to Aid in the Calculation of Vacuum Tube Performance '42; Positive Grid or Retarding Field Oscillators '43; Tubes Employing Velocity Modulation '43, and others. Editor: Electronics Dictionary and Handbook '51. Contributor: Radio Engineering Handbook (4th edit). Dir Robert I Sarbacher & Asso Atlanta and Washington since '36; prof elec engring Ill Inst Tech '40-42; sci cons Navy Dept Washington '42-45; dir Gen Electronics Industries '44-46; dean grad sch Ga Inst Tech '45-49, trustee research found '46-48; institutional rep Oak Ridge Inst Nuclear Studies '46-47; adv council War Assets Adminstrn '47-48; cons sci and dir Wedd Labs '48-49; pres and dir Nat Sci Labs Inc since '49; pres Washington Inst Tech since '50. Am Acoustics Soc—

Am Inst EE—NEA—Am Math Soc—Inst Radio Engrs—Am Soc Engring Edn—Soc Am Mil Engrs—AAAS—APS. Professional engr Fla. 2010 Massachusetts Av., Washington 6.ⓒ

14 SARGENT, Helen Durham. Projective techniques; Insight test. b'04. BS '27—MA '34—PhD '44 (Northwestern); summer '41 (U Minn); summer '42 (Ohio State U). Critical and theoretical survey and bibliography on projective techniques for study of personality; developed Sargent Insight Test, verbal group projective test for diagnostic purposes with blind neuropsychiatric patients for whom visual projective methods are not suitable, also for clinical psychological examination of individuals and groups; method of analysis has theoretical implications for study of thinking and verbalization in abnormal patients. Asst dir psychol clinic Northwestern U '32-43, lectr clin psychol '38-43; cons psychol Family Service of Evanston and Pub. Sch Dist 76 '44-48; chief psychol Winter VA Hosp Topeka Kan since '48. Diplomate in clin psychology Am Bd Examiners in Clin Psychology. Am Psychol Assn(F)—Soc Projective Techniques(F)—Kan Psychol Assn(F)—Ill Psychol Assn—Phi Beta Kappa—Sigma Xi. Alumni merit award Northwestern '49. Psychological Service, Winter VA Hospital, Topeka, Kan.

15 SARGENT, Donald Malcolm. Geophysics (Exploration); Seismology; Microwave transmission; Magnetrons (Pulsed). b'21. BS in elec engring '43 (U Wyo). Research on seismology of muskeg areas of Canada, Poulter method of air shooting. Staff mem radiation lab MIT '43-45; party chief Geophys Service Inc '47-48; with Century Geophys Corp since '48, party chief from '50. Soc Exploration Geophys—Sigma Tau—Can Soc Exploration Geophys. 615 8th Av. W., Calgary, Alberta, Can.

16 SARLES, William Bowen. Agricultural bacteriology. b'06. BS '26—MS '27—PhD '31 (U Wis); '30-31 (Ia State Coll). Representative Society of American Bacteriologists to Division of Biology and Agriculture, National Research Council '47-50. Co-author: (with W C Frazier, J B Wilson, S G Knight) Microbiology, General and Applied '51, also articles in field. University Wis since '32, now prof bact and coordinator Lake Investigations. AAAS(F)—Wisconsin Acad Sci Arts Letters —Soc Am Bact (sec-treas '42-43)—Am Soc Limnol Oceanog—Phi Kappa Phi —Phi Sigma—Sigma Xi—Alpha Zeta. Department Bacteriology, University Wisconsin, Madison 6, Wis. H: 2237 Hollister Av.

17 SARNOFF, Stanley Jay. Physiology (Respiratory and cardiovascular). b'17. AB '38 (Princeton); MD '42 (Johns Hopkins U). Investigation respiratory failure, and physiological basis for treatment; basic research genesis and treatment of acute heart failure; co-discoverer differential spinal anesthesia; clinical research on new soluble sulfonamide; inventor of device for producing artificial respiration by electrical stimulation of phrenic nerve. Co-author article: (with J G Arrowood, W P Chapman) Differential Spinal Block '48; (with J L Whittenberger) Physiologic Principles in the Treatment of Respiratory Failure '50; (with J V Maloney Jr, J L Whittenberger) Electrophrenic Respiration—Effect on Circulation of Electrophrenic Respiration and Positive Pressure Breathing During the Respiratory Paralysis of High Spinal Anesthesia '50; (with J V Maloney, L C Sarnoff, B G Ferris, J L Whit-

tenberger) Electrophrenic Respiration in Acute Bulbar Poliomyelitis—Its Use in Management of Respiratory Irregularities '50, and others. Clin and exptl surgery Mass Gen Hosp Boston '45-47; now asst prof physiol sch pub health Harvard. Am Physiol Soc—Internat Physiol Soc—Swiss Physiol Soc—Delta Omega. Am Physiol Soc award for outstanding research '50. 55 Shattuck St., Boston 15.

18 SARTORIS, George Batholomew. Sugar cane (Wild, cultivated). b'96. BS '20—MS '21 (U Washington); PhD '23 (U Mich). Developed 16 commercial varieties of sugar cane. Author articles in field. Sr Path US Dept Agr Bur Plant Indus Soils and Agrl Engring, div sugar plant investigations. Plant Industry Station, Beltsville, Md.†

19 SASHOFF, Stephan Pencheff. Electronic circuits; Communication engineering. b'01. BSEE '25 (Purdue U); MS '29—PhD candidate '29-31 (Pittsburgh U). Research on phase to ground faults on transmission lines calculated by symmetrical components, power grid-glow tube, television sending and receiving equipment for college laboratory, simple pulse generating circuits sferics. Author articles in field. Prof electronics Fla U since '46. AIEE—AAAS—Fla Acad Sci—Soc Promotion Engring Edn—Am Phys Soc—Am Inst Radio Engrs—Union Scientifique Radio Internat. University of Florida, Gainesville.†

20 SASS, John E(ugene). Plant morphology. b'97. BS '24—MS '25—PhD '29 (U Mich). Research on histogenesis seed plants, plant morphology, structure economic plants, microtechnique, pathological histology and cytology of plants. Author: Elements of Botanical Microtechnique '40. Instr bot Ia State Coll '28-30, asst prof '30-44, asso prof '44-49 prof since '49. Bot Soc Am—Sigma Xi—Ia Acad Sci. Iowa State College, Ames, Ia.†

21 SATTEM, Ivan. Power plants (Hydroelectric). b'15. Student '33-35 (Mich Coll Mining and Tech); BS '40 (US Mil Acad). Research and design of hydroelectric power developments on St. Lawrence and Niagara Rivers and transmission grid for New York State; technical adviser to State Department in negotiation of Niagara Treaty '49, technical member New England-New York Inter-Agency Committee on northeastern water resources '51. Asso prof engring US Mil Acad '44-46; with NY Power Authority since '47, acting exec sec '50, chief engr since '50. Am Soc CE—Am Mil Engrs—NY Soc Profl Engrs—Nat Soc Profl Engrs. New York State Power Authority, 270 Broadway, NYC 7.

22 SATTERTHWAITE, Linton. Maya archeology. b'97. BA '20 (Yale); PhD '43 (U Pa). Research in Maya Indian archeology and mathematics, calendar systems and astronomy, problem of antiquity of man in America, establishing developmental trends in ancient Maya architecture and in ancient Maya calendrical science, correlating Maya and European chronologies; assistant archeological expeditions University of Pennsylvania Museum '29, '30, '31, '32, field dir '33-39, '41, '44. Author articles in field. Asst curator U Pa Mus '35-38, asso curator Am sect since '48; lecturer anthrop Grad Sch U Pa 10 yrs. Am Anthrop Assn(F)—Soc Am Archeol—Am Folklore Soc—Soc Applied Anthrop—Soc de Geografia e Historia de Guatemala—Sociedad Mexicana de Antropologia—Inter-Am Soc Anthrop and Geo—Inst Indigenista Interamericano—Sigma Xi. University Museum, 33 and Spruce Sts., Phila.

10 SAUEREISEN, Christian Fred. Cements (Scientific); Ceramics; Acid-proof masonry. b'84. Student '08-09 (Carnegie Inst Tech). Research on spark plugs; research and writing on adhesives cements and compounds. Inventor of a spark plug insulator now used on all spark plugs and specialized brick. Apprenticed as clayworker Homer Laughlin China Co '99-05; established first Westinghouse porcelain insulator dept at Nernst Lamp Co Pittsburgh '05-10; research Bethlehem Spark Plug Co; established Sauereisen Cements Co Pittsburgh '19, since pres and owner. Am Ceramic Soc—Engrs Soc Pa. Sharpsburg Station, Pitts. 15.

11 SAUNDERS, Carl Maxon. Conservation. b'90. Author articles in field. Ed Jackson Citizen Patriot since '34. Am Soc Newspaper Ed—Mich Press Assn (vp). Jackson Citizen Patroit, Jackson, Mich.

12 SAUNDERS, Felix. Guided missiles. b'95. BS '24—PhD '28 (U Chicago). Scientific expeditions to Mexico '35, '44, oceanographic cruises '41, '44; developed oceanographic apparatus and methods for studying waves and ocean bottoms. Author articles in field. Sr engr specialist Goodyear Aircraft Corp since '49; instr Santa Ana Army Air Base '42-43, physicist Naval Sound and Radio Lab '44. AAAS—Am Chem Soc—Sigma Xi—IAS—ASA (com Z10 on standardization of letter symbols for aerodynamics and aeronautics). Goodyear Aircraft Corporation, 1210 Massillon Rd., Akron 15, O.†

13 SAUNDERS, Henry William. Mining engineering; Coal mining construction work. b'78. BS (U Toronto). Design of construction work for preparation of coal; design belt conveyors for transportation coal. Chief engr Mill Creek C & C Co, Am C & C Co since '21; design dry cleaning plant Internat Coal Co Can '26; dir Crystal Block Coal & Coke Co. Am Inst Min and Metall Engrs—WVa Soc Profl Engrs—Nat Soc Profl Engrs—Am Mining Congress. Coopers, W.Va. H: Box 67, Bramwell, W.Va.

14 SAUNDERS, John Richard. Superstitions (American); New York City (Geology); Museum education. b'10. '28-29 (College of City of NY); '29 (Princeton); '30-32 (Columbia U); BA '40—MA '43 (NYU). Author: Superstition is a Big Business '45; Unnatural Natural History '50; The World of Natural History '52. Contributor: Nature Guide. With edn dept Am Mus Nat History since '28, now acting chmn. NY Acad Scis—Kappa Delta Pi. American Museum Natural History, NYC. H: 106 Spencer Av., Lynbrook, N.Y.

15 SAUNDERS, Laurence Pembroke. Heat transfer. b'91. Ed pub schs. Research on heat transfer of finned tubes with forced air circulation, testing surface coils for heating and cooling; member Cooperative Research Council, member subcommittees on coolant systems and new coolant liquids for aircraft engines and chairman committee on high pressure radiator design; member subcommittee on heat exchangers for aircraft for National Advisory Committee for Aeronautics. With Harrison Div Gen Motors Corp since '21, tech asst to gen mgr since '49. Am Soc Heating and Ventilating Engrs—Soc Automotive Engrs—Am Soc Refrigerating Engrs—Detroit Engring Soc—Inst Mech Engrs Automotive Br (Eng). Harrison Radiator Division, General Motors Corp., Lockport, N.Y.

16 SAUNDERSON, Henry Hallam. Puritan movement. b'71. PhB '96—DD

'24 (Hamline U, St Paul Minn); AB '98 —AM '01 (Harvard). Author: Charles W. Eliot—Puritan Liberal '28; Modern Religion from Puritan Origins '30; Puritan Principles and American Ideals '30. Pastor First Parish Ch Brighton Boston since '19. 24 Avon Hill St., Cambridge 40, Mass.

17 SAVICH, Theodore Rudolph. Conversion of coal to liquid fuels; Recovery of oils from tars. b'13. BS '37—'37-38 (U Chicago). Research on conversion of gases to liquid fuels by thermal and acid alkylation, purification of terpene hydrocarbons, conversion of coal to liquid fuels by high pressure high temperature hydrogenation, conversion of coal to aromatic intermediates by high pressure oxidation reactions. Holder US patent for process pyrolyzing terpene hydrocarbons. Research Phillips Petroleum Co '38-41, US Dept Agr So Regional Research Lab New Orleans '41-46, US Dept Interior Bur Mines '46-48; rsrch asso coal research lab Carnegie Inst Tech '48-50; agronomist and partner Savich Farms since 1950. Am Chem Soc. H: RD 6, Rensselaer, Ind.

18 SAVILLE, Thorndike. Hydrology, water supply, sewage treatment; Beach erosion born '92. AB '14—MS '17 (Harvard); BS '14—CE '15 (Dartmouth); MS '17 (MIT); D Eng (hon) '44 (Clarkson Coll). Author articles in field. Cons engr Rockefeller Fd to govt Venezuela on water supply for Caracas '26-27; exec engr water resources sect Nat Resources Bd '34-35, mem water resources comm '35-43; mem US Beach Erosion Bd Office Chief Engrs since '30; asso prof, later prof hydraulic and sanitary engring U NC '19-32; chief engr NC Dept Conservation and Development '20-32; prof hydraulic and sanitary engring NYU since '32, asso dean Coll Engring '35, dean since '36. ASCE (dir '45-48, pres met sect '42-43)—Am Water Works Assn—NE Water Works Assn — NY Sewage Works Assn—ASEE (mem council '44-47, pres '49-50)—Am Inst Cons Engrs —Phi Beta Kappa—Sigma Xi—Tau Beta Pi—AAAS (F, vp '44). Riverdale-on-Hudson, NYC 71.⊙

19 SAWIN, Paul Baldwin. Rabbit genetics. b'00. BS '24 (Cornell U); MS '26 (Kan State Coll); MS '29—ScD '30 (Harvard). Studies on rabbit genetics, growth of body and hair, anatomical and physiological characteristics pertaining to use in biological, cancer, and medical research. Author articles in field. Research asso R B Jackson Memorial Lab Bar Harbor Me since '47. Am Assn Anat—Genetics Soc Am—Am Soc Zool—Am Naturalists—Soc Study Development and Growth—Am Genetic Assn—Am Rabbit and Cavy Breeders Assn—Sigma Xi—Phi Kappa Phi—Gamma Sigma Delta. Hamilton Station, R.B. Jackson Memorial Laboratory, Box 847 Bar Harbor, Me.†

20 SAWYER, Clair Nathan. Sanitary chemistry (Activated sludge oxidations, industrial wastes, biochemical oxygen demands, lake fertilization); Biological engineering. b'06. BS '30—PhD '38—post doctorate fellow '38-40 (U Wis); MS '36 (U Colo). Author articles in field. Asso prof san chem MIT since '45. Am Water Works Assn —NE Sewage Works Assn—Am Chem Soc—NE Water Works Assn—Am Pub Health Assn—Sigma Xi. Massachusetts Institute Technology, Cambridge 39, Mass.

21 SAWYER, William Hayes, Jr. Entomogenous fungi. b'92. AB '13 (Bates Coll); AM '16 (Cornell U); PhD '29 (Harvard). Discovered methods of growing entomogenous fungi on artificial media and new information on

structure and growth of such fungi '28-29. Author articles in field. Prof biol Bates Coll since '29. Phi Beta Kappa—Sigma Xi. Bates College, Lewiston, Me.†

22 SAXE, Nathaniel Edgar. Balzac. b'96. AM '22 (State U Ia); certificate '24 (U Madrid); student '24-25 (U Chicago). Spent '29-30 in Paris as a fellow of the University of Chicago Balzac project; furnished bibliographical items on Balzac, located material and arranged for photostating of Balzac manuscripts. Prof French, German, head dept mod lang Washburn U since '25, chmn div humanities since '46. Mod Lang Assn Am—Balzac Soc Am—Tau Delta Pi. Washburn University, Topeka, Kan.

23 SAYE, Albert Berry. History of Georgia (Constitutional). b'12. BA '34 —MA '35 (U Ga); PhD '41 (Harvard); Diplome de français, degré superieur '38 (Dijon U); '38 (Paris U); '39 (Cambridge U). Research in British Public Record Office led to reappraisal of early Georgia history, discounting legend that Georgia was originally debtor colony; studies and writing on Georgia's proposed new constitution. Author: Georgia's Charter of 1732 '42; New Viewpoints in Georgia History '43; Handbook on the Constitutions of the United States and Georgia (with Merritt B Pound) '46; Records of the Commission of 1943-44 to Revise the Constitution of Georgia '46; A Constitutional History of Georgia, 1732-1945 '48; A List of Early Settlers of Georgia (with E. M. Coulter) '49. Prof polit sci U Ga since '48. Phi Beta Kappa—Phi Kappa Phi—Ga Hist Soc—Ga Soc Hist Research—So Polit Sci Assn—Am Polit Sci Assn. M G Michael Research award '44. University of Georgia, Athens, Ga.†

24 SAYLES, Charles Inglehart. Hotels (Administration, planning). b'03. Student '21-24 (Colgate U); Certificate '23 (Alliance Francaise Paris); BS '26 (Hotel adminstrn)—M Elec Engring '37 (Cornell U). Design and layout numerous food service installations in hotels; planner of hotels; manager hotel. Fla mgr Asso Hotels Fla '27-28; auditor Barth Hotels '29; prof institutional engring Sch Hotel Management Cornell since '41; sec and treas Star Lake Hotel Co Inc '35; mem Mac-Lennan Young Sayles and Asso hotel cons and operators since '51; dir NY State Hotel Assn since '51. Cornell Soc Hotelmen—Phi Kappa Phi—Illuminating Engring Soc—Am Soc Power Engring—NY State Hotel Assn —Am Hotel Assn. Co-winner first prize for kitchen design with V Antonel '51. Statler Hall, Cornell University, Ithaca; 68 Yonge St., Toronto,

25 SAYRE, Geneva. Taxonomy and ecology of Mosses (Splachnaceae, Timmiaceae, Aulacomniaceae, Grimmiaceae); International relations in science. b'11. BA '33 (Grinnell Coll); '31, '33 (Lakeside Lab Ia U); '34 (Cold Spring Harbor Biol Assn); MA '35 (U Wyo); PhD '38 (U Colo). Author (in part): Moss Flora of North America '35. Author articles: Colorado Species of Grimmia '44; Distribution of Fontinalis in Ponds '45, and others. With Russell Sage Coll since '40, prof since '47, chmn dept since '45, chmn sch arts and scis since '50. AAAS(F)—Sigma Delta Epsilon—Am Bryological Soc—Brit Bryological Soc—Internat Union Biol Scis—Internat Bot Congress—Hist Sci Soc—Sigma Xi—Phi Beta Kappa. AAUW Fellow '49-50. Russell Sage College, Troy, N.Y.†

26 SAYRE, J(asper) D(ean). Mineral nutrition of corn; Physiology of stomata; Radioisotopes. b'93. BA '17—MA

'20—PhD '22 (O State U). Author articles in field. With O State U '16-27, asst prof bot '27; asst path O Agrl Expt Sta '26-28; agt Div Cereal Crops and Diseases US Dept Agr '28-31; plant physiol Bur Plant Industry and SAE US Dept Agr since '31. AAAS—Plant Physiol Soc—Optical Soc Am—O Acad Sci—Sigma Xi—Gamma Alpha. Ohio Agricultural Experiment Station, Wooster, O.

10 SAYRE, Mortimer F(reeman). Materials (Compression tests, elasticity); Springs (Mechanical); Locomotives (Frames, heat exchange); Welds (Testing); Aluminum alloys (Properties. b'85. EM '07-MA '11 (Columbia). Contributor: Kent's Handbook (11th edit) '38. With Union Coll since '14, prof applied mech from '37; cons John Chatillon and Sons '29-35, since '45; cons Gen Elec Co '19-31, since '42; cons Am Locomotive Co since '44. Am Soc ME (mem com mech springs, in charge research '27-32)—Am Inst Mining Engrs—ASTM (chmn com compression testing methods)—Am Welding Soc (chmn com standard tests for welds, rep commn control of welds, Internat Inst Welding)—Am Soc Metals—Am Soc Engring Edn—Sigma Xi—Tau Beta Pi. Union College, Schenectady 8, N.Y.

11 SAYRE, Paul. Modern legal philosophies. b'94. AB '16—SJD '25 (Harvard); JD '20 (U Chicago). Reporter on succession to property International Congress Comparative Law The Hague '37; delegate State University Iowa to Internation Conference Higher Education Paris '37. Author: Life of Roscoe Pound '47; Introduction to A Philosophy of Law '51; A Philosophy of Law '53. Editor: Interpretations of Modern Legal Philosophies '47; also articles in field. Admitted to Ill bar '20, practiced Chicago '20-24; prof law Ind U '25-28; lecturer on civil procedure Harvard Law Sch '29-30; prof law State U Ia since '30. Nat Conf on Family Relations (pres '37-39). Law Building, Iowa City, Ia.◎

12 SCANLON, Helen Lawrence. United Nations documents. b'06. BSLS '29 (Syracuse U); AMLS '35 (U Mich). Author: European Governments in Exile '43. Compiler of bibliographies pub by Carnegie Endowment International Peace Library, librarian since '41; librarian first council session UNRRA '43, reference librarian UN second part '46, third session '48. ALA—DC Library Assn—Special Libraries Assn—Am Polit Sci Assn. 700 Jackson Pl., Washington 6.

13 SCARBOROUGH, James Blaine. Numerical analysis. b'85. AB '13—AM '14 (U NC); PhD '23 (Johns Hopkins). Studies in aerodynamics, statistics, and ballistics. Author: Numerical Mathematical Analysis '30. Co-author: Fundamentals of Statistics '48; also articles in field. Instr, asst prof, asso prof, prof math US Naval Acad since '18; cons numerical analysis Naval Ordnance Lab '48-50; prof emeritus since '50. Am Math Soc—Math Assn Am—AAAS—Assn Computing Machinery. H: Ferry Farm, Rt. 2, Annapolis, Md.†

14 SCARBOROUGH, William John. New Testament (Literature); Education (History); Methodism. b'13. Student '30-31 (Carleton Coll); '32 (U Minn); AB '33 (Hamline U); AM '35 —STB '36—PhD '40 (Boston U). Editor: Is It Morning et '44. Prof phil and rel McKendree Coll Lebanon Ill '39-42; dean of men '41-42; prof psychol and rel and dean of chapel Cornell Coll Mt Vernon Ia '42-43; dean of coll and prof phil and rel Morningside Coll Sioux City Ia '43-46; prof

NT lit Garrett Biblical Inst Evanston Ill summer '46; pres W Va Wesleyan Coll Buckhannon W Va since '46. AA UP—Nat Edn Assn—W Va Edn Assn —Am Phil Assn—Soc Bibl Lit and Exegesis—Nat Assn Bibl Instrs. West Virginia Wesleyan College, Buckhannon, W.Va.◎

15 SCARSETH, George Dewey. Soil fertilization. b'98. BS (agr) '24 (U Wis); '24-26 (Yale); PhD '35 (O State U; ScD '52 (Purdue U). Research on soil phosphates, heavy fertilizer uses, plow under fertilizers, diagnosis of nutritional state of soil, nitrogen fertilizer behavior, fertilizer materials and their use, problems of "poor land". Author: Development, Classification and Characteristics of Soils '35. Co-author: Hunger Signs in Crops '41; (with W R Thompson) The Pasture Book '51. Asst soil chem Conn Agrl Expt Sta '24-25; soil chem United Fruit Co '26-28; prof soil sci Ala Poly Inst '28-38; prof soil sci and head dept agron Purdue U '38-45; dir research Am Farm Research Assn since '45; agrl research cons Standard Fruit and Steamship Co since '35. Am Soc Agron (F)—ACS—Soil Sci Soc Am (pres '36)—Am Soc Agrl Engrs—Soil Conservation Soc Am—Sigma Xi—AA AS(F). Received Freedom Foundation awards '51-52. American Farm Research Assn., 300 Schultz Building, Lafayette, Ind. H: 1414 Ravinia Rd., West Lafayette, Ind.◎

16 SCHAAL, Lawrence A. Plant pathology (Potato). b'00. BS '24 (Kan A&M Coll); MS '26—PhD '41 (U Minn). Research on physiological races of actinomyces scabies, disease-resistant varieties of potatoes, effects of hormones on potatoes. Author articles in field. With US Dept Agr since '26, now path US Dept Agr Potato Disease Investigations at Colo A&M Coll. AA AS—Potato Assn Am—Sigma Xi. Department of Botany and Plant Pathology, Colorado Agricultural and Mechanical College, Fort Collins, Colo.

17 SCHACHTEL, Irving. Conservation of hearing among children; Hearing (Aids, conservation). b'09. BA '28 (U Buffalo); LLB '31 (Columbia); LL B '49 (Hartwick). Author: Conserving Our Children's Hearing; Know Your Hearing Aid. With Sonotone Corp Elmsford NY since '32, pres since '46. Armed Forces Communications Assn—Am Hearing Aid Assn (pres). Elmsford, N.Y. and 570 Fifth Av., NYC.

18 SCHAEFER, Vincent Joseph. Snow hydrology; Surface chemistry; Cloud physics. b'06. Student (Union Coll). Discoverer of electrical charges in snow; method of preserving snow crystals. Author articles in field. Research asst to Dr Irving Langmuir Gen Elec Research Lab '33-38; research chemist with Dr Langmuir since '38. Am Geophys Union (com on snow hydrology sect)—ACS—NY State Archeol Assn—Forest Preserve Assn NY State. General Electric Research Laboratory, Schenectady, N.Y.

19 SCHAENZER, Joseph Peter. Farm and home electrification. b'92. '13-14 (Marquette U); '15-16 (Wis State Teachers Coll); BS '21 (U Wis). Prepared comprehensive report on rural electrification in the United States and an analysis and maps of the potential market for rural lines and electrical equipment for every county of nation '35. Author: Rural Electrification '48; Rural Electrification Handbook. Co-author: Turn on the Water; also articles in field. Chief elec installations Archtl and Engr Planning Sect Rural Resettlement Div Resettle-

ment Adminstrn '36; asst dir Com on Relation Elec to Agr Chicago and ed CREA News Letter '36-39; head rural service div Edison Elec Inst NYC and ed Rural Electrification Exchange '39-41; head electro-agrl sect tech standards div Rural Elec Adminstrn US Dept Agr since '41. ASAE (chmn rural elec div '41, F)—Am Standards Assn (tech com)—Illuminating Engring Soc (tech com). Rural Electrification Administration, U.S. Department of Agriculture, Washington 25. H: 1116 S. 28th St., Arlington 2, Va.◎

20 SCHAFFER, Aaron. French literature of the 19th and 20th Centuries. b'94. AB '14—PhD '17 (Johns Hopkins); student '19-20 (Sorbonne Coil Sch Higher Studies France). Literary criticism French writers of the 19th and 20th centuries; translation French writings in any field, analysis and interpretation of such writings in all humanistic fields; interpretation of spoken French. Author: Parnassus in France '29; The Genres of Parnassian Poetry '44, others. Editor French plays and novels; contbr to numerous learned and semi-popular periodicals. Instr Romance langs Johns Hopkins '18-19; instr Romance langs U Texas '20-23, adj prof '23-25, asso prof '25-28, prof and mem grad faculty since '28, chmn dept Romance langs since '46. Am Council Learned Socs(F)—AAUP(pres U Tex chpt '37-38)—Am Assn Tchrs French (exec com since '40)—Modern Lang Assn Am—Société des Textes Francais Modernes—Phi Beta Kappa. Decorated Officier d'Académie (Palmes Académiques) '38 608 W. 32d St., Austin 21, Tex.†◎

21 SCHAFFERT, Roland Michael. Research in graphic arts (Xerography, Xeroprinting). b'05. AB '30 (Doane Coll); MA '31—PhD '33—fellow '30-33 (U Cincinnati). Invented type casting machine, plastic-mold electrotyping process, vapor blast etching of engravings, plastic backing of electrotypes, hard-faced plastic printing plate, electrostatic transfer of xerographic images, xeroprinting machine, and others. Co-author: Ferric Chloride Etching of Copper Photoengravings; also articles in field. Printer and linotype operator various weekly newspapers Neb '23-30; research cons infrared spectroscopy Cincinnati '33-34; asst prof phys Duquesne U Pittsburgh '34-36; research physicist Mergenthaler Linotype Co Brooklyn '36-41; research engr Graphic Arts Research Div Battelle Mem Inst Columbus O '41-43, supervisor '45-50, research cons since '50. Am Phys Soc—Electrochem Soc—Soc Rheology—Tech Assn Pulp and Paper Industry—Photographic Soc Am —Am Soc Metals—Lithographic Tech Assn—Internat Assn Printing House Craftsmen—AAAS(F). 505 King Av., Columbus 1, O.†

22 SCHALK, Marshall. Geology of beaches. b'07. AB '29 (Harvard Coll); PhD '36 (Harvard U). Author articles: Textural Changes in a Beach by Repeated Sampling '46; A Textural Study of the Outer Beach of Cape Cod, Massachusetts '38. Geol Gulf Oil Corp Pittsburg '36-41; asst prof geol Smith Coll since '41. Geol Soc Am(F). Fellow Woods Hole Oceanog Inst '33, '34, '35. Smith College, Northhampton, Mass.†

23 SCHANCK, Francis Raber. Water resources (Development). b'77. AB (mech engring) '03 (Stanford U). Long period records and the resulting water supply; research on development of surface and underground water resources, study of underground water movements using dyes and other methods of identification, developed surface and underground water sources for shore establishments for US Navy in

British West Indies, Puerto Rico and continental US; member Advisory Power Committee to Oregon State Planning Board. Partner Schanck-O'Brien Co '19-23; cons engr since '24; chief engr Columbia Valley Power Co '24-30; civil engr US Navy '41-44. Am Soc CE (past pres Ore sect)—Prof Engrs Ore—US Nav Inst (asso mem)—Royal Soc Arts (F). Title and Trust Building, Portland 4, Ore. H: 2917 S.W Fairview Blvd., Portland 1.

10 SCHANTZ, Viola Shelly. North American mammals. b'95. Student '11-14 (Perkiomen Sem); '16-17 (Muhlenburg Coll). In charge largest North American study-collection of mammals in world (over 145,000 specimens). Described eleven new badgers. Editor: Twenty-Year Index to Journal of Mammalogy (with E M Charters) '45. Author articles; Catalog of the Type Specimens of Mammals in the US National Museum, Including the Biological Surveys Collections (with A J Poole) '42, and others. With Div Wildlife Research Dept Agr (trans to Dept Interior '39) since '18, biol since '44. Am Soc Mammalogists (treas)—Biol Soc Washington—Wildlife Soc Am—Fish and Wildlife Service, U.S. Department of the Interior, Washington 25.

11 SCHATZ, Louis William. Plastic coatings and treatments. b'12. BS '34 (Pa State); MS '39 (U Calif); '40 (U Mich). Research on plastic treatments for fire hose, fish nets, paper, plastic coatings for furniture, cars, rubber, floors. With Gen Plastics Mfg Co since '41, now pres. General Plastics Mfg. Co., P.O. Box 65, Tacoma, Wash.

12 SCHAUWEKER, George H(enry). Personal Protective equipment; safety engineering; Protective clothing. b'09. BS '30 (Thiel Coll Greenville Pa). Design and evaluation of personal protective equipment to protect industrial workers; development of improved materials. Holds patents for eye protective devices, respiratory and body protective devices. Development mgr safety products div Am Optical Co since '42. American Optical Co., Southbridge, Mass.

13 SCHEFFER, Victor B. Mammalogy (Arctic); Fur seals; Oceanography; Marine biology. b'06. PhD '36 (U Washington). Author articles in field. Entered Fish and Wildlife Service '36; lecturer in oceanog U Washington since '41; in charge sci studies Alaska fur seal herd since '40. Am Soc Mammalogists—Wildlife Soc — Wilderness Soc—Pacific Northwest Bird and Mammal Soc—Oceanog Soc Pacific—Sigma Xi. 2725 Montlake Blvd., Seattle 2.

14 SCHEIBEL, Edward George. Distillation; Liquid extraction; Nomography (Chemical engineering applications). b'17. BS (Chem E) '37 (Cooper Union Inst Tech); MS (Chem E) '40—D Eng '43 (Poly Inst Brooklyn). Holds patents on liquid extraction and extractive distillation. Author articles: Simplified Charts for Petroleum Process Calculations '47; Fractional Liquid Extraction '48; Principles of Extractive Distillation '48; Dhydration of Ethyl Alcohol by Fractional Liquid Extraction '50, and others. Co-author article: Semi-commercial Multistage Extraction Column '50, and others. Chem engr M W Kellogg Co NYC '42-43; faculty Poly Inst Brooklyn '42-51, adjunct prof chem engring '45-51, process engr Hydrocarbon Research Inc NYC '44-45; head chem engring group Hoffmann La Roche Inc since '45. AIChE—ACS—Sigma Xi—Phi Lambda Upsilon. AIChE jr award for papers on fractional liquid extraction

and extractive distillation '49. Professional engr NY. Hoffmann La Roche, Inc., Nutley 10, N.J. H: 75 Harrison Av., Montclair.

15 SCHEIDEMANN, Norma Valentine. Children (Exceptional). BA '20—MA '23—PhD '26 (State U Ia). Study psychology of exceptional children, including gifted, feebleminded, left handed, speech defective, bilingual, enuretic, aphasic, albinistic, and delinquent. Author: Experiments in General Psychology '29; Psychology of Exceptional Children (2 vols) '31, '37; Demonstrations in General Psychology '39. Author articles: Study of the Handedness of Some Left-handed Writers '30; Mirror-tracing Practice for Medical and Dental Students '51; A Clock Test for Mirror-imagery '51. Co-author articles: (with Hazel Colyer) Study in Reversing the Handedness of some Left-handed Writers '31; (with M S Smith) Survey of an Opportunity Room for Gifted Children '33. Prof and chmn dept of psychol Des Moines U Ia '26-27; lecturer psychol U So Calif '27-28, '29-32 and '34-35, Temple U '38-39. Am Psychol Assn—Internat Council Women Psychol—Calif State Psychol Assn—Sigma Xi—Pi Gamma Mu—Psi Chi—Pi Lambda Theta. H: 1073 Exposition Blvd., LA 7.

16 SCHEIDENHELM, Frederick William. Hydraulic engineering (Dams, foundations, flood control, hydro-electric power, multi-purpose projects); Power engineering; Problems regarding water rights and law. b'84. AB '05—CE '06 (Cornell). Invented anchoring wall for dams. Author articles in field. Organized Pittsburgh Hydro-Electric Co '09, vp and chief engr until '14; vp, chief engr Hydro-Electric Co of W Va and affiliated corporations '11-14; asso with Daniel W Mead in cons hydraulic and hydroelectric practice NYC '16-17, since '19; supervising cons Claytor dam and hydro-elec development New River Va '37-39, and others; chmn Com on Cost Allocation for Multiple-Purpose Water Projects. Corps Engrs and AEF '17-19, col '19; comdr 26th Engrs, water supply regiment. ASCE—Am Inst Cons Engrs—Soc Am Mil Engrs—AAAS(F). Awarded Fuertes gold medal Cornell '17; Thomas Fitch Rowland prize ASCE '18. 50 Church St., NYC 7.†◎

17 SCHEIL, Merrill Adam. Alloys; Heat resistance; Corrosion resistance; High temperature metallurgy. b'05. BS (Chem E) '27—MS (Metall) '29 (U Wis). Application of ferrous materials to high temperature and pressure; research on stress corrosion cracking; chemical analysis iron and steel. Author articles: Application of Alloy Steel Linings to Tanks Storing Corrosive Pulp Cooking Liquor '49; A Standard Laboratory Corrosion Test for Metals in Phosphoric Acid Service '50; Corrosion and Corrosion Testing in the Pulp and Paper Industry; Corrosion Studies in Sulfate Digesters '51, and others. Chem and metall Gisholt Machine Co Madison Wis '27-29; research metall A O Smith Corp Milwaukee '29-39, dir metall research since '39; adv com Metal Progress Magazine '47-49. Am Soc Metals (copper and brass adv com since '49)—Am Welding Soc (rep to Inter-Soc Corrosion Com since '49)—ASME—AIMME—Tech Assn Pulp and Paper Industry—Brit Iron and Steel Inst—Soc Automotive Engrs—Nat Assn Corrosion Engrs—Electrochem Soc—Australian Pulp and Paper Industry Tech Assn—Soc Am Mil Engrs—Am Ordnance Assn.

18 SCHEINFELD, Amram. Human heredity; Sex differences. b'97. Author: You and Heredity '39; Women

and Men '44; also articles in field. Freelance writer since '35. Genetics Soc Am—Am Soc Human Genetics—Am Psychol Assn—Am Sociol Soc—AAAS—NY Acad Sci. 24 W. 8th St., NYC 11.

19 SCHELL, Herbert Samuel. American history (South Dakota, western United States, recent). b'99. AB '20 (Muhlenberg Coll); MA '23 (Columbia); PhD '29 (U Wis). Author: South Dakota—Its Beginnings and Growth '42; also articles in field. Dir Grad Sch U SD since '36. Miss Valley Hist Assn—AHA—SD Hist Soc—Phi Beta Kappa. 417 N. Pine St., Vermillion, S.D.◎

20 SCHELL, Irving I(srael). Oceanography; Meteorology; Arctic regions; Sea ice. b'06. SB '32 (MIT); '35 (Harvard). Research on polar ice and general circulation, solar changes and meteorology, mountain meteorology, long-range weather foreshadowing. Research asst Blue Hill Meteorol Obs Harvard '33-38, fellow '39-46, Abbot Lawrence Rotch Research fellow '46; Asso meteorol US Weather Bur '43; dir Schell Meteorol Labs since '46; research asso Woods Hole Oceanog Inst since '48. Am Geog Soc(F)—Am Meteorol Soc—Am Geophys Union—Royal Meteorol Soc, Eng—Arctic Inst NA. Museum Comparative Zoology, Harvard University, Cambridge, Mass.

21 SCHELLBACH, Louis. Grand Canyon National Park. b'87. Student '08-18 (Pratt Inst); '19-21 (Brooklyn Inst); '25 (Columbia). Naturalist and interpretive programs national parks and Grand Canyon National Park, Arizona. Author articles in field. State archeol Nev '22-27; staff archeol Mus of the Am Indian Heye Found NY '27-31; naturalist Nat Park Service since '33. Am Anthropol Assn—AAAS—Am Assn of Mus—Grand Canyon Nat Hist Assn. Grand Canyon National Park, Grand Canyon, Ariz.

22 SCHEMEL, Mart P(hilip). Coal (Geology); Stratigraphy. b'25. BA '46 (Coe Coll); MS '48 (U Wis). Research on coal spore floras of Missouri, West Virginia, and adjacent areas; Pennsylvanian stratigraphy of those regions. Coal micros Mo Geol Survey and Water Resources '48-50; asst coal geol W Va Geol and Econ Survey since '50. Paleontological Soc—Bot Soc. West Virginia Geological and Economic Survey, Postoffice Box 879, Morgantown, W.Va.

23 SCHENCK, Hubert G(regory). Paleontology; Stratigraphy; Sedimentation; Coal and petroleum economic geology; Natural resources utilization. b'97. BA '22—MA '23 (U Ore); PhD '26 (U Calif); advanced fellow Commn Relief Belgium Educational Foundation '34-35 (Nat Hist Mus Brussels). Research chiefly in stratigraphy and paleontology with emphasis on petroleum geology; research on natural resources of Philippine Islands, Japan, Korea, Formosa. Author articles. Cons geol since '26; geol div mines Bur Sci Manila '20-21; prof geol Stanford U since '24; paleontologist Amiranian Oil Co Iran, Afghanistan '37-38. Lt col, chief Nat Resources Sect Gen Hdqrs Supreme Comdr Allied Powers United States Army Tokyo '45-51 chief Mutual Security Agency Mission to China since '51. Geol Society America(F)—Am Assn Pet Geol—Geol Society France (vp '45)—Geol Soc Belgium (corres)—Geol Soc Switzerland—Malacol Soc London—Soc Econ Paleontologists and Mineralogists—Paleontol Soc—Geol Soc Philippines (charter organizer)—Phi Beta Kappa—Sigma Xi. 585 Washington Av., Palo Alto, Calif.

24 SCHENCK, Jay Ruffner. Chemistry of antibiotics. b'15. Abbott fellow '40-41—PhD '41 (Cornell U); BS '36—

MS '37 (U Ill); fellow '37-38 (George Washington U). Author articles in field. Research biochem Abbott Labs since '41. Am Chem Soc—AAAS—NY Acad Sci—Am Soc Biol Chem—Sigma Xi. Abbott Laboratories, North Chgo, Ill.†

10 SCHEPP, William John. Colloidal graphite; Colloidal sulphur; Electronics (Anionic, cationic, anti-static); Pigments (Powdered). b'89. BS '12 (Cooper Union). Exec Schepp & Rosenthal, Wm J Schepp Inc '19-37; exec. cons Schepp Lab, Wm J Schepp Co Inc since '37. ACS—AAAS—Assn Cons Chem and Chem Engrs—Am Inst Chem (F). Wm J Schepp Co., Inc., 21-23 Summit Av., East Paterson, N.J.

11 SCHER, V Alexander. Synthetic yarns (Extrusion); Metallurgy, electronics, sound recording and reproduction, television, machine tools, textile machinery (Patents). b'01. Dipl Ing '26 (Coll Eng, Berlin); LL B '36 (St John's, Brooklyn). Author: Patenting the Invention '48; also articles in field. Mem Richards & Geier since '30. NJ Patent Bar Assn—Am Assn Textile Tech. 274 Madison Av., NYC 16.

12 SCHERAGO, Morris. Bacteriology and immunology. b'95. BS—DVM '19 (Cornell U). Author articles in field. Asst prof and acting head dept bacteriol U Ky '20, asso prof and acting head '22, asso prof and head dept '23, prof and head dept since '24. Am Coll Allergists (ed bd Annals of Allergy and Quarterly Review of Allergy and Applied Immunology, chmn standardization com and chmn com on certification of allergenic extracts)—Soc Am Bacteriologists (fin adv com, councilor '41-45)—Ky Acad Sci (pres)—Am Pub Health Assn(F)—Am Asso Immunologists—Conf St and Provincial Public Health Lab Dir—O Valley Allergy Soc—Am Soc Professional Biol—Ky-Tenn Br Soc Am Bact (pres '40)—Sigma Xi. Asso fellow Am Soc Clinical Pathologists. Department of Bacteriology, University of Kentucky, Lexington, Ky.†

13 SCHERER, George Allen. Electrode potentials; Crystal systems; Periodic chart. b'07. BS '27 (Earlham Coll); MS '28 (Cornell U); PhD '33 (Purdue U). Author articles in field. Asso prof chem Earlham Coll Richmond Ind since '36. Am Chem Soc—Sigma Xi. Earlham College, Richmond, Ind. H: 446 College Av.†

14 SCHERER, Margaret R. Arthurian and Roman iconography; Trojan romances; Medieval secular paintings. b'92. AB '19 (Wellesley Coll); '29-30, '35-36 (NYU); '32-33 (Courtauld Inst Art London). Author: About the Round Table '45. Co-author: (with R M Fansler) Painting in Flanders '45; also author articles in field. Research fellow Metropolitan Mus Art since '41. Phi Beta Kappa. Metropolitan Museum of Art, NYC 28.

15 SCHERER, Milton E(dward). Climate; Glaciers. b'00. AB '25 (W Mich Coll Edn); MA '34 (U Mich). Research on North American glacial icescoured plains and glacial depositional plains, climatological research of polar and sub-polar areas. High sch and jr coll teacher '25-48; with Mich Coll Mining and Tech since '48. Mich Acad Sci Letters and Arts—Am Geog Assn—Am Council Geog Teachers—Am Prof Geog—Am Polar Soc—Arctic Inst NA—Am Forestry Assn—Audubon Soc—Soil Sci Soc Am—Friends of the Land—Rocks and Minerals Soc—Am Acad Polit Sci. Michigan College of Mining and Technology, Sault Ste. Marie, Mich., Sault Branch. H: Watervliet, Mich.

16 SCHERER, Philip Carl. Chemistry (Cellulose). b'93. PhB '15—MSc '23—PhD '25—DuPont fellow '23-24—Metcalfe fellow '24-25 (Brown U). Author articles: Dyes from Cellulose Amine '44; Fractionation of Cellulose Xanthate '48, and others. Asst prof phys chem Va Polytech Inst '29-33, asso prof '33-41, prof since '41; cons. Va Acad Sci—AAAS—Am Chem Soc—Sigma Xi. Virginia Polytechnic Institute, Blacksburg, Va.

17 SCHEVILL, William E(dward). Whales (Underwater sounds, swimming); porpoises (Underwater sounds, swimming). b'06. AM '29 (Harvard). Research on underwater communication of whales and porpoises, cetacean sounds at sea and in aquaria, cetacean swimming. With Mus Comparative Zool, Harvard, since '28, asso curator invertebrate paleontology from '43; asso phys oceanog Woods Hole Oceanog Instn since '43. Woods Hole Oceanographic Institution, Woods Hole, Mass.; Harvard University, Cambridge, Mass.

18 SCHIEFER, Herbert F(rederick). Textiles (Testing instruments, mechanical and performance properties evaluation). b'02. BSE '24—MS '25—PhD '28 (U Mich). Author articles in field. Textiles sect Nat Bur Standards since '29, now chief physicist. Technician indsl intelligence com Office Quartermaster General '45, ECA '52; director research and grad instrn Sch Textiles N C State Coll '51-52. Wash Philos Soc—Fiber Soc (gov council '48-51)—Tau Beta Pi—Sigma Xi. National Bureau of Standards, Washington 25.†

19 SCHILDKNECHT, Calvin (Everett). Vinyl polymerization; Vinyl type plastics. b'10. BS '31 (Gettysburg Coll); PhD '36 (Johns Hopkins). Holder patents. Author articles in field. Research chemist du Pont '36-43; Gen Aniline and Film Corp Easton Pa and NYC '43-51; Celanese Corp '51-52; asso prof chem Stevens Inst Tech since '53. Am Chem Soc. 15 Garden St., Montclair, N.J.

20 SCHILLER, A Arthur. Roman law (Historical development); Coptic law (Relation to Greek and Roman law); Indonesia (Modern law and government. b'02. AB '24—MA, JD '26 (U Calif); '29 (U Munich—F Soc Sci Research Council); JD '32 (Columbia); F Soc Sci Research Council '49; Dr Jur (hon) '50 (U Erlangen). Research on legislation, jurists, praetor, interpretation and construction of public and private documents of Roman law, relation of Roman jurists to imperial bureaucracy of Principate from time of Hadrian to the Severi; research on nature and place of adat (indigenous) law in legal system of Netherlands Indies and Indonesian Republic; research on Coptic law illustrating borrowing of Greek and Roman legal institutions. Author: Texts and Commentary for the Study of Roman Law '36; Indonesia in Transition: Government and Law during 1945-49 (in prep.); Ten Coptic Legal Texts '32. Co-author: (with H E Yntema) Source Book of Roman Law '29. Co-editor and translator: (with E A Hoebel) Adat Law in Indonesia (B ter Haar) '48. Contributor: Melanges Fernand De Visscher (vol 2) '49; Kritische Vierteljahresschrift fur Gesetzgebung und Rechtswissenschaft (vols 25, 27) '32-34. With Columbia Sch Law since '30, prof from '49. Riccobono Sem Roman Law—Indonesian Acad Arts Sci—Far E Assn. F Guggenheim Found '49. School of Law, Columbia University, NYC 27.◉

21 SCHILLING, Harold Kistler. Ultrasonics; Acoustics. b'99. AB '20

(Clinton Sem); AM '28 (U Neb); PhD '35 (U Ia). Research in acoustic filters, propagation through atmosphere, micrometeorology, wind generated sounds, high frequency, sources. Author articles in field. Asso editor: American Journal of Physics. Instr Campion Acad Colo '21-23; prof physics Union Coll Lincoln Neb '23-40, dean '35-40; asso prof physics Pa State Coll '40-47, prof physics and head dept '47-50, dean of graduate school since '50. AAAS(F)—Am Phys Soc(F)—Acoustical Soc Am(F)—Am Assn Physics Teachers (vp)—Am Soc Engring Edn —Sigma Xi—Sigma Pi Sigma—Phi Kappa Phi—AAUP. Pennsylvania State College, State College, Pa.◉

22 SCHILPP, Paul Arthur. Philosophy (Kant's ethics, ethical theory, social, political, contemporary philosophers, Alfred North Whitehead); Pacifism; World government. b'97. AB '16—LittD '46 (Baldwin-Wallace Coll O); Student summers '16-17 (Columbia)—'16-17 (Drew Theol Sem); MA '22 (Northwestern U); BD '22 (Garrett Bibl Inst); PhD '36 (Stanford U); auditor summer '28 (U Munich). Member sixth International Congress of Philosophy '26; Kant Gesellschaft, Germany; Am Federation Teachers, Conference on Science, Philosophy and Religion; member 10th International Congress of Philosophy Amsterdam '48. Author: Is Western Civilization Worth Saving? '28; Do We Need a New Religion? '29; Kant's Pre-Critical Ethics '38. Editor and contbr: Higher Education Faces the Future '30; Theology and Modern Life '40; The Library of Living Philosophers, vol I The Philosophy of John Dewey '39, vol II The Philosophy of George Santayana '40, vol III The Philosophy of Alfred North Whitehead '41, vol IV The Philosophy of G E Moore '42, vol V The Philosophy of Bertrand Russell '44, vol VI The Philosophy of Ernst Cassirer '49, vol VII Albert Einstein: Philosopher-Scientist '49; also articles in field. Professor philos Northwestern U since '50. Am Philos Assn—AAAS—Am Acad Polit Social Sci—Brit Inst Philos—SW Philos Assn—Philos of Edn Soc (asso). 101-02 Fayerweather Hall, Northwestern University, Evanston, Ill.◉

23 SCHINDLER, Hans. Waxes (Microcrystalline); Petroleum sulfonates; Waste disposal. b'11. Student '29-32 (Inst Tech Munich Germany); '33 Inst Tech Berlin); DSc '34 (U Prague). Studies in flexibility of and adhesion test for microcrystalline wax; disposal or refinery waste water containing water-soluble sulfonates; chemical treatment refinery waste water. Issued patents in field petroleum sulfonates. Asst chief chem Oelwerke Julius Schindler Hamburg Germany '35-38; sr research chem Pure Oil Co Chicago '38-46; chem L Sonneborn Sons, Inc (Daugherty Refinery) since '46. ACS—Tech Assn Pulp and Paper Industry—ASTM—Am Petroleum Inst. Petrolia, Pa.†

24 SCHINHAN, Jan Philip. Folksongs of North Carolina; Music of Am Indians (Pacific coast); Comparative musicology. b'87. Grad (Churchmusic Sch Regensburg, Acad Music Munich Bavaria); AB '31—MA '33 (U Calif); PhD '37 (U Vienna Austria); Dean's scholar '34-35 (Columbia). Author articles in field. Asst prof music U NC '35, asso prof '41, prof since '46. Am Musicol Assn—MLA—Am Anthropol Assn—AAAS—Music Teachers Nat Assn. Music Department, University of North Carolina, Chapel Hill, N.C.†

25 SCHIROKAUER, Arno C. Medieval lexicography and historiography; History of German language. b'99.

Student '19-22 (Berlin U, Halle U, Florence U); PhD '21 (Munich U). Standardization of medieval German dialects, 1180-1300, expressionism in German literature, Carolingian Renaissance traced in literature of 9th century, style of early medieval magic spells, early German lexicography, medieval MSS in Italy, research Esop in medieval literatures. Author: Middle-High-German Rhyme Grammar (awarded Munich U faculty prize) '23; Expressionismus der Lyrik '24; Lassalle '28; Deutsche Kulturepochen '48; also articles in field. Research asst Germanic Sem Munich U '21-22, Bavarian Acad Sci '22-23; asst librarian Deutsche Buecherei, Leipzig '24-28; dir Dept Edn German Broadcasting Co '28-33; asst prof Southwestern U '39-41; visiting prof Kenyon Coll '43-44; visting lecturer Yale '44-45; lecturer German Johns Hopkins '45-46, prof since '46; adv ed Modern Language Notes since '46. Modern Language Assn—Goethe Soc—Medieval Acad Am. Johns Hopkins University, Baltimore 18. H: 4210 N. Charles St., Baltimore 18.†⊙

10 SCHLAFLY, Hubert Joseph. Theatre television; Television prompting. b'19. BS (Elec engring) '41 (U Notre Dame); '46-47 (Syracuse U). Studies in technical aspects relating to equipment and techniques for displaying television pictures on theatre-size screens; problems associated with distribution television signals from point of program origination to network of individual theatres; problems television studio equipment, techniques and standards required to furnish television signals of required quality; problems and requirements television and motion picture actors, public speakers required to perform extensive memory work with great accuracy and without assistance of notes. Engr Advance Development Lab Gen Elec Co '41-44; electronics dept engr '45-47; engr Radiation Lab MIT '44-45; research div 20th Century - Fox Film Corp since '47; vp and dir Teleprompter Corp since '51. Inst Radio Engrs—Soc Motion Picture and Television Engrs. 460 West 54th St., NYC 19.

11 SCHLAIKJER, Erich M. Petroleum and mining geology; Paleontology. b'05. BS '29 (Harvard); MA '31—PhD '35 (Columbia). Directed several geological and paleontological expeditions; research on new basal oligocene formation, new vertebrates and stratigraphy of oligocene and early miocene, structure and relationship of Protoceratops. Author articles: Torrington Member of the Lance Formation and a Study of a New Triceratops '35, and others. Asso prof geol Brooklyn Coll City NY '48-50; pres Lakata Petroleum Corp since '50. Geol Soc Am(F)—Paleontology Soc Am(F)—NY Acad Sci(F)—Am Soc Mammalogists—Soc Study Evolution—Sigma Xi—Am Geophys Union—Explorers Club. Parmentier Scholar, Harvard '24-25; Univ fellow Columbia '31-32; awarded Cressy Morrison Prize $200, NY Acad Sci '39 (with Brown), $750 grant (with Brown), Geolog Soc Am '42. Lakata Petroleum Corp., Newcastle, Wyoming.

12 SCHLECHTEN, Albert W(ilbur). Metallurgy of rare metals; Mineral dressing. b'14. BS '37 (Mont Sch Mines); ScD '40 (MIT). Research on production of ductile zirconium metal, of lithium and other rare metals. Co-author articles: (with W J Kroll) Survey of Literature on the Metallurgy of Zirconium '46; (with W J Kroll) Titanium and Zirconium: Metal Industry (London) '46. Instr and asst prof nonferrous metallurgy U Minn '40-42; asso prof mining and metallurgy Ore State Coll '42-44; metall US Bur Mines

'44-46; prof metall engring Mo Sch Mines since '46. AIME—ASM—Am Electrochem Soc—Sigma Xi. Missouri School of Mines, Rolla, Mo.†

13 SCHLEGELMILCH, Reuben Orville. Radar (Ground). b'16. BS '38 (U Wis); MS '40 (Rutgers U); '40-41 (Cornell); '41-42 (U Ill); '48-50 (Poly Inst Brooklyn). Design and development of ground radar and control systems; member panel on electron tubes and radar, Research and Development Board. Research engr U Ill '41-42; electron sci US Air Force and chief engr radar lab Air Materiel Command Watson Labs since '45. Radio engr US Signal Corps '42-45. Inst Radio Engrs—Am Inst EE—Nat Soc Professional Engrs—Phi Eta Sigma—Alpha Zeta. Professional engr NJ. U.S. Air Force, Air Research and Development Command, Griffiss Air Force Base, Rome, New York.

14 SCHLESINGER, Jefferson Seligman. Cereal chemistry; Wheat flour (Mill control). b'06. Student (Ottawa U, U Chicago). Author articles: Interpreting Laboratory Analyses of Flour. Chief cereal chem Ark City Flour Mills since '39. Am Assn Cereal Chemists (sec treas Pioneer Sect '49). Arkansas City Flour Mills, Arkansas City, Kan.†

15 SCHLEUSENER, Paul Edward. Irrigation (Supplemental); Frost control with irrigation. b'22. BS in agrl engring '44 (U Neb); MS in agrl engring '49 (Mich State Coll). Research on irrigation of vegetable crops on sandy loam soil, of pasture and hay, and of crop rotation including sugar beets; use of portable pipe and sprinklers for irrigation; exploratory studies on amount of protection against frost with given quantities of water and effect on plants; use of explosives in agriculture for ditching, stumps or stones. Faculty Michigan State Coll since '47. Am Soc Agrl Engrs. Agricultural Engineering Department, Michigan State College, E. Lansing, Mich.

16 SCHLIESTETT, George Van. Mechanics (Fluid); Ballistics (Underwater). b'11. BS in aeronautical engring '32—MS in aeronautical engring '34 (Ga Inst Tech); '35-36 (MIT); '49-50 (Cal Inst Tech). Research on hydrodynamics and aerodynamics; member Naval Technical Mission to Europe '45; member subcommittee high speed aerodynamics '47-48 and fluid mechanics '48-49 of National Advisory Committee for Aeronautics; member panel on Hydrology '48-49 and working groups on aerodynamics and structures of guided missiles '48-49 and piloted aircraft '48-49 of Defense Establishment, Research and Development Board; member Navy Interbureau Panel on Aerodynamics, Ballistics and Structures '47-49. Research asst MIT '37-39; engr Bur Aeronautics Navy Dept '39-44, sr civilian asst Pilotless Aircraft Div '46-47; head Fluid Mechanics Branch, Office Nav Research '47-49; asst dir research Underwater Ordnance Dept Nav Ordnance Test Sta since '49. Sigma Xi—Tau Beta Pi—Phi Kappa Phi—Inst Aeronautical Sci—Am Math Soc. Naval Ordnance Test Station, Pasadena Annex, 3202 E. Foothill Blvd., Pasadena 8, Cal.

17 SCHLINK, Ralph L(ester). Fermentations (Enzymes); Vitamins; Amino acids; Fungi amlyases; Poultry nutrition. b'13. BA '36 (Carthage College); MSc '38 (State U Ia); '42 (U Minn). Cons special fermentation problems; poultry nutrition. AAAS(F)—Am Assn Cereal Chem—Am Chem Soc. Elizabethtown Rd., Lawrenceburg, Ind.

18 SCHMERLING, Louis. Catalytic and petroleum chemistry. b'12. BS '32 (U Wis); PhD '35 (Northwestern U). Author articles in field. Holder various patents on catalysts and catalytic processes. Research chemist Universal Oil Products Co since '35. Am Chem Soc—Am Inst Chem—Sigma Xi. Received Ipatieff award in catalytic chem '47. Universal Oil Products Co., Riverside Ill.†

19 SCHMIDT, Alfred Otto. Metal cutting. b'06. Ingenieur '25-28 (Ingenieurschule, Germany) — '29-38 (U Jena); MSE '40—DSc '43 (U Mich). Author articles in field. Mech engr, design and development spl machinery Carl Zeiss Optical Works Jena Germany '29-39; research asst metal processing U Mich '39-40; instr, asst prof mech engring Colo State Coll A and M '40-42; asso mech engring U Ill '42-43; research engr in charge metal cutting research Kearney and Trecker Corp Milwaukee since '43. NMTBA tech adv com on machining of metals for Army Air Forces and Navy Bur Aeronautics. ASME (standards com)—ASTE—Sigma Xi—ASTM (standards com). Kearney and Trecker Corporation, Milwaukee 14.

20 SCHMIDT, Austin G(uilford). Educational guidance. b'83. AB '08—AM '09 (St Louis U); PhD '23 (U Mich); Society of Jesus (Jesuits). Author: Ceremonies of Ordination; Intelligence Tests; Guidance. Prof edn Loyola U Chicago '25-26, head dept '25-35, dean grad sch '26-32; dir Loyola U Press since '28. AAAS—Ill Acad Sci—Nat Soc Coll Teachers Edn—Nat Soc for Study Edn. 3441 N. Ashland Av., Chgo 13. H: 6525 Sheridan Road, Chgo 26.†⊙

21 SCHMIDT, Carl Theodor. Soil disinfection; Economic entomology. b'04. BA '28 (U Minn); PhD '34—fellow '31-34 (U Hawaii). Author articles in field. Biol control expdn Brazil '36-37; Bolivia Peru Venezuela Trinidad '39-40; entomol Pineapple Research Inst since '44. AAAS(F)—Hawaiian Entomol Soc (pres '38)—Hawaiian Acad Sci—Am Assn Econ Entomol—Entomol Soc Am. P.O. Box 3166, Honolulu 2, Hawaii, T.H.

22 SCHMIDT, Jacob Edward. Words (Lexicography, neologisms). b'04. BS '32—MD '37 (U Md). Specializes in finding or creating unusual and little-known words that express precisely complex ideas; maintains file of 300,-000 words indexed according to meaning. Author: A Dictionary in Reverse (in press). Author column Pruritis Linguae in Baltimore Sunday Sun. 2924 Brighton St., Balt 16.

23 SCHMIDT, Walter A(ugust). Industrial dusts recovery. b'83. BS '06 (U Calif). Research on cleaning industrial gases for dust and fume recovery. Holds 37 patents chiefly relating to electrical precipitation of suspended particles from gases. Author articles in field. Engr Western Precipitation Co '08-11; pres and gen mgr since '11. ACS (regional dir '31-36, dir at large since '43, adv bd indsl and engring chem '20-49, asso editor Technologic Monographs since '23)—AICE—Electrochem Soc—AIEE—Am Inst Mining and Metal Engrs—AAAS—Sigma Xi. 1016 West 9th St., Los Angeles 15.

24 SCHMITT, Francis Otto. Nerve physiology; Tissue ultrastructure determination; Electron microscopy. b'03. AB '24—PhD '27 (Washington U); Nat Research Council fellow '27-28 (U Calif); '29 (U Coll London, Kaiser Wilhelm Inst Berlin-Dahlem). Head dept biol MIT since '42. Am Acad Arts Sci (F)—Am Physiol Soc—Am Soc Zool—Soc Exptl Biol Med—Soc Growth and

Development (treas '45-46, pres '47)—Am Leather Chem Assn—Nat Acad Sci—Am Soc Naturalists—Electron Micros Soc Am (dir '44-47, pres '48)—Crystallographic Soc—AAAS — Sigma Xi—Phi Beta Kappa. Massachusetts Institute of Technology, Cambridge, Mass.☉

10 SCHMITT, Otto H(erbert). Nerves (Excitatory state); Electronics. b'13. AB '34—PhD '37 (Washington U); Nat Research fellow '37-38 (U London); Sir Halley Stewart fellow '38-39 (University College London). Research on development of electronic computors for determination of nerve energy release, ion transport, and complex plane impedance characteristic. Asso prof zool and physics U Minn since '41, on leave as research engr OSRD Columbia U Airborne Instruments Lab Mineola NY '42-47, development military electronic equipment. Inst Radio Engrs (sr)—Am Phys Soc—Am Physiol Soc—NY Acad Sci—Minn Acad Sci—AAAS (F)—Sigma Xi. Physics Department, University of Minnesota, Minneapolis 14.

11 SCHMITT, Waldo LaSalle. Carcinology (Crustacea); Marine biology; Oceanography; Fisheries. b'87. BS '13—PhD '22 (George Washington U); MA '16 (U Calif); DSc '48 (Southern Calif); traveling scholar '25-27 (Smithsonian Instn SA). On special detail to US Bureau of Fisheries investigating spiny lobster of Pacific coast '18; naturalist on Presidential Cruise to Clipperton, Cocos and Galapagos Islands '38; on King Crab investigation for US Fish and Wildlife Service in Alaska '40; on special detail to Latin America '41, '42, '43. Author: The Marine Decapod Crustacea of California '21; also articles on marine invertebrates. Asso editor: Biological Abstracts. Aid in Econ Bot US Dept Agr '07-10; sci asst US Bur Fisheries '10-13, naturalist '13-14; instr zool George Washington U '15-23; asst curator div marine invertebrates US Nat Mus '15-20, curator '20-43, head curator biol '43-47, head curator zool since '47; at Tortugas Marine Lab '24-25 and '30-32; with Hancock Pacific Expdns '32-35; with Smithsonian-Hartford Expdn to WI '37; with Hancock Atlantic Expdn N Coast SA-Netherlands WI '39; mem several confs and coms on oceanography and marine biol. AAAS(F)—Am Soc Zool—Am Museums Assn—Am Geophys Union—Biol Soc Washington—Washington Acad Sci—Zool Soc London (corr mem)—Soc Systematic Zoology—Am Soc Zool—Sigma Xi. U. S. National Museum, Washington.☉

12 SCHNADER, William A(braham). State government. b'86. AB '08 (Franklin and Marshall Coll); LLB '31; LLB '12 (U Pa). Author: Pennsylvania Workmen's Compensation Law '15. Practice law Phila since '13; mem firm Schnader Harrison Segal & Lewis; spl dep atty gen Pa '23-30, atty gen '30-35. Phi Beta Kapa—Phi Delta Phi. 1719 Packard Bldg., 15th and Chestnut Sta., Phila.

13 SCHNEBERGER, Edward. Fishery biology; Pollution. b'06. BS '28—MS '29 (Kan State Coll); PhD '33 (U Wis). Author articles in field. Supt fish management, adminstrn all activities pertaining to fisheries Wis Conservation Dept since '44. Am Fisheries Soc—Wis Acad Sci Arts Letters—Limnol Soc Am. State Office Building, Madison 2, Wis.†

14 SCHNEE, Verne H(iggs). Research administration. b'98. BChem '20 (Cornell U). Metallurgist and asst dir Battelle Meml Inst '34-49; dir U Okla Research Inst and vp U Okla since '49; dir Mettall Advisory Bd Nat Acad Scis '51; cons metallurgist since '25. 525 S Flood St., Norman, Okla. †☉

15 SCHNEIDER, Carl Edward. History of the German and German-American church. b'90. MA '24 (Washington U); PhD '35 (U Chicago). Author: The German Church on the American Frontier '39. Author articles: History of Eden Theological Seminary '25; also others in field. Prof of church hist Eden Theol Sem '18; Ecumenical Conf Edinburgh '37; sec World Council of Churches Geneva Switzerland '45-47; European Sabbatical Research '37-38; reassignment to World Council of Churches Geneva '48. Am Soc Church History—AHA—Miss Valley Hist Assn. Eden Theological Seminary, Webster Groves, Mo.

16 SCHNEIRLA, Theodore C. Learning and instinctive behavior in insects and mammals. b'02. AB '24—MSc '25—ScD '28 (U Mich). Expeditions to Panama and Mexico. Co-author: (with N R F Maier) Principles of Animal Psychology '35; (with L C Crafts) Recent Experiments in Psychology '38; also articles in field. Asso curator animal behavior Am Mus Natural Hist '44-46, curator since '47. Am Psychol Assn—Am Soc Zool—NY Entomol Soc—Explorers Club—Sigma Xi. Grants in aid of research Nat Research Council, Nat Acad Sci. Am Philos Soc Office Naval Research. American Museum of Natural History, NYC.†

17 SCHNITZER, Julius Gabriel. Leather (Industry, raw materials, finished products, shoes, tanning materials, handicraft). b'99. Student '21-23 (Georgetown U Sch Fgn Service). Served on government textile and leather mission to Germany and Japan '47, 48 and 49. Entered govt service Dept Commerce '23, chief textile and leather divs office industry and commerce '50-51, dir leather div NPA since '51. Department of Commerce, Washington 25.

18 SCHNOOBERGER, Irma. Bryology; Sphagnaceae. b'01, BS '34 (Wayne U); MS '38 (U Mich); grad study (U Mich Biol Sta, U Mich, Cold Springs Harbor Biol Sta). Collection, identification of genus Sphagnum, and other mosses and hepatics. Author: Notes on Bryophytes of Central Michigan '40; Distribution of Tortula Papillosa '42; Notes on Bryophytes from Stone Mountain, Georgia '48. Co-author: Bryophytes of Mount Desert, Maine '42; Bryophytes of Shenandoah National Park, Virginia '45. Teacher Mich schs '29-42, '43-45; head biol dept Flint Jr Coll since '45. Mich Acad Sci Arts Letters Mich Edn Assn—Sullivant Moss Soc—Sigma Xi. Flint Junior College, Flint 3, Mich.†

19 SCHOELD, Edmund Archibald. Potash. b'03. BA '25 (Gustavus Adolphus Coll); MS '35 (U Minn); grad study (U Chicago). Instr chem Waldorf Coll Forest City Ia '28-35, dean '35-42; chief chem Potash Co of Am Carlsbad NM since '42. Am Chem Soc—Am Inst Mining and Metall Engrs—AAAS. Potash Company of America, Carlsbad, N.M.

20 SCHOEN, Max. Aesthetics; Psychology of religion; Psychology and philosophy of music. b'88. BA '11 (Coll City NY); PhD '21 (U Ia). Author: Art and Beauty '32; Psychology of Music '40. Co-author: Music and Medicine '48; also author articles in field. Prof and head dept psychol and edn Carnegie Inst Tech since '21, now emeritus. Am Psychol Assn—AAAS—Am Aesthetic Soc—Sigma Xi. Thetford, Vt.†

21 SCHOENBERGER, Guido. German art; Jewish art; Unicorn (Iconography). b'91. PhD '17 (U Freiburg) '26 (U Frankfurt on the Main); Prof U Frankfurt on the Main '26-35; curator Mus of City of Frankfort Germany '28-35; lecturer and research asso Inst Fine Arts NY U since '39, research fellow Jewish Mus NY since '47. College Art Assn Am. 17 E. 80th St., NYC.

22 SCHOENFELD, William Alfred. Foreign trade (Food); Farm credit. b'88. BSA '14 (U Wis); MBA '22—'26-27 (Harvard); '25-26 (U Berlin). United States delegate to International Agricultural Congress Warsaw Poland '25; International Institute of Agriculture Rome Italy '26; Pacific Science Congress Vancouver BC '33; head of mission of agricultural scientists and administrators to British Isles '46. Author articles in field. Dean and dir of agr Ore State System Higher Edn since '31; dir Ore Agrl Expt Sta since '31; dir Ore Agrl Ext Service since '34; chmn bd dir Farm Credit Bank Spokane Wash since '35. Sigma Xi. 506 N. 35th St., Corvallis, Ore.☉

23 SCHOENHERR, Karl Ernest. Fluid mechanics; Marine propulsion (Merchant vessel and torpedo propellers); Naval architecture. b'93. BS naval architecture and marine engring '22 (MIT); MA '30 (George Washington U); D Engring '32 (Johns Hopkins U). Author articles in field. With US Exptl Model Basin, David Taylor Model Basin Washington since '22, chief div and prin naval architect '42, head naval architect '45; cons since '32; dean Coll Engring U Notre Dame since '45. Soc Naval Architects and Marine Engrs—Am Soc Engring Edn—AAAS. College of Engineering, University of Notre Dame, Notre Dame, Ind. H: 712 Wilson Blvd., Mishawaka.

24 SCHOENLEBER, Leonard George. Forage harvesting research. b'06. BA '28 (U Neb); student (U Md). Co-author two US patents. Author articles in field. Agrl engr US Dept Agr since '29, research and development in farm electrification forage harvesting and processing equipment since '46. Am Soc Agrl Engrs. Bureau of Plant Industry, Soils and Agricultural Engineering, Agricultural Research Center, Beltsville, Md.

25 SCHOFF, Stuart L(eeson). Ground water geology; Oklahoma stratigraphy. b'06. AB '29 (Oberlin Coll); AM '31—PhD '37 (Ohio State U). Author bulls and articles in field. With US Geol Survey since '37, dist geologist ground water br Norman Okla since '47. First lt Corps Engrs US Army assigned to water supply organizations '42-45, capt '45-46. Am Geophy Union—Okla Acad Sci(F)—Phi Beta Kappa—Sigma Xi. U.S. Geological Survey, c/o Oklahoma Geological Survey, Norman, Okla.

26 SCHOLER, Charles Henry. Portland cement; Concrete aggregates; Highway materials. b'90. BS '14 (Kansas State Coll). Research and acting as consultant on concrete and aggregate durability and cement-aggregate reaction; studies of concrete and cement failures. Author articles in field. Engr of tests Kan State Coll '19-20, asso prof and prof, dept head since '20; cons Portland Cement Assn '39-40. ASCE—Am Concrete Inst—Am Soc Engring Edn—Kan Engring Soc—Highway Research Bd—Sigma Xi. RFD 4, Manhattan, Kan.

27 SCHOLES, France Vinton. Latin American colonial history; Southwestern American history; History of Yucatan. b'97. AB '19—AM '22—PhD '48 (Harvard). Research in Mexican and Spanish archives '27-28. Author: Church and State in New Mexico, 1610-

1650 '37; Troublous Times in New Mexico, 1659-1670 '42. Co-editor: Documentos para la historia de Yucatan, 3 vols '36-38; Don Diego Quijada, Alcalde Mayor de Yucatan '39; also author articles in field. Prof hist U NM since '46, dean grad sch U NM '46-49, acad vp since '48. AHA—Hist Soc NM(F)—Phi Beta Kappa. University of New Mexico, Albuquerque, N.M.

10 SCHOOLCRAFT, Arthur Allen. Educational administration. b'97. AB '26—LLD '49 (Marietta Coll); STB '29 —PhD '32 (Boston U). Pub sch teacher '13-18; ordained ministry Methodist Ch '19; prof Bible and phil W Va Wesleyan Coll '32-34, prof edn and head dept since '34, dean coll and registrar since '44, acting pres '45-46. AAAS—Am Assn Acad Deans—North Central Assn Acad Deans—AA UP—Nat Soc Study Edn—Nat Soc Coll Teachers Edn—Am Assn Coll Registrars—Phi Beta Kappa. W.Va. Wesleyan Coll., Buckhannon, W.Va.©

11 SCHOOLEY, Allen H. Miniature electronic tubes; Missile and gunfire control systems; Stereophotography. b'09. BS (EE) '31 (Ia State Coll); MS '32 (Purdue U). Design of miniature radio tube, and development of mass production methods; development precision time measuring equipment for fire control radar; study of stereophotographic and stereoillustration methods not requiring viewing devices at the eyes. Author articles: Try Stero '47; A Simple Stereoscope for Viewing Double-Lens Camera Stereographs Without Transposition '48; Pulse Radar History '49; The Electronically Driven Ripple-Tank '50, and others. Co-author article: The Development and Production of the New Miniature Tubes '40. Contributor: Electronics '50. Radio tube engr advanced development sect radiotron div Radio Corp Am '36-40; radio engr Naval Research Lab '40-47, and asso supt radio div since '47. Inst Radio Engrs—Am Inst Physics—AAAS—Sci Research Soc Am—Sigma Xi. Naval Research Laboratory, Washington 25.

12 SCHOONOVER, Warren Rippey. Soils (Fertility; management); Frost protection; Alkali reclamation. b'91. BS '12 (Occidental Coll); MS '16 (U Ill). Author articles in field. Ext specialist soils U Calif since '40. Fulbright fellow alkali soil Egypt '53 54. AAAS—Am Soc Hort Sci—Am Soc Agron—Soil Sci Society Am—Phi Beta Kappa—Sigma Xi. University of California, College of Agriculture, Berkeley 4.†

13 SCHOPF, James M(orton). Paleobotany; Coal geology and petrography; Spores in coal; Plant morphology. b'11. BA '30 (U Wyo); MS '32—PhD '37 (U Ill). Research on plant morphology, petrified coal measures plant fossils, coal paleobotany and geology, plant microfossils in coal, petrographic constitutents of coal; paleobotanical research on coal measures fossils, coal and the carbonaceous rocks. Author articles in field. Spl asst Ill Geol Survey '34-35, asst geol coal div '36-43; paleobot US Bur Mines '43-47; sr research bursar So African Council Sci and Ind Research '47; geol US Geol Survey '47; in charge coal geology lab since '49. AAAS(F)—Paleontology Society(F)—Bot Society Am (paleobot sect sec '39-40, chmn '43-44)—Geol Soc Am(F)—Am Inst Mining Metall Engrs—Ill Acad Sci—Pa Acad Sci—Geol Soc Washington—Am Soc Plant Taxonomists—Sigma Xi. U.S. Geological Survey Coal Geology Lab., Orton Hall, Ohio State University, Columbus 10, O.

14 SCHOPMEYER, C(lifford) S(charff). Physiology of oleoresin formation in pine trees; Reforestation (Direct seeding); Pine tree silviculture. b'11. BS '33 (George Washington U); MS '35 (U Md); PhD '37 (Duke U). Holder with Carl E Ostrom US patent on method for prolonging and increasing the flow of oleoresin from pine trees '48. Author articles in field. Plant physiol SE Forest Expt Sta Lake City Fla since '46. Am Soc Plant Physiol—Soc Am Foresters—Sigma Xi. Southeastern Forest Experiment Station, P.O. Box 92, Lake City, Fla.†

15 SCHOR, Ferdinand W(illiam). Radio receivers. b'05. BS (EE) (Armour Inst Tech Chicago); student (Crane Jr Coll). Design of radio receivers; development of efficient untuned radio frequency amplifiers; design and development first successful all-wave multi-contact switch, and first miniature all-wave switch; inventor circuits and components for reduction of cost and improved performance; double and triple superheterodyne type communication receiver design; special equipment design for US government including aircraft receivers, intercept receivers, very high frequency and high stability receivers. Author articles: Untuned Radio Frequency Amplifier; High Frequency Superheterdyne Receiver. Chief engr various radio mfrs; chief engr govt and amateur radio div Hallicrafters Co since '38. Inst Radio Engrs. Hallicrafters Co., 4401 W. Fifth Av., Chgo. H: 2432 Farwell Av., Chgo 45.

16 SCHORNHERST, Ruth Olive (Mrs. W. H. Breen). Bryophytes (Florida); Bark anatomy. born '05. Emma Cole fellow '40-41—PhD '41 (U Mich); BS '26 (Fla State Coll for Women); MS '29 (U Chicago). Author articles in field. Asso prof bot Fla State U '46-51, prof since '51; chmn biol sci since '48. Fla Acad Sci (chmn biol sect '41-42)—AAAS—Bot Soc Am—Brit Bryology Soc—SE Biol—Am Fern Soc. Research Grant Fla Acad Sci '38. Dept of Botany, Florida State University, Tallahassee, Fla.

17 SCHRADER, Albert Lee. Pomology; Fruit plants (Nutrition). b'96. BS '20—MS '21 (Wis U); PhD '25 (U Md). Research on pomology as related to growth and fruiting responses, mineral nutrition, pruning of fruit plants, storage and processing of fruits; made special studies of mineral nutrition of tree fruits. Author articles in field. Asst pomol in research U Md '21-25, asso prof '25-28, prof '28-35, '40-45, since '46, head dept horticulture '35-40; head horticulture br Shrivenham Am U Eng, US War Dept '45-46. AAAS(F)—Am Soc Hort Sci—Am Soc Plant Physiol—Am Statis Assn—Sigma Xi (past pres Md chap)—Phi Kappa Phi (past pres Md chap). Department of Horticulture, University of Maryland, College Park, Md.

18 SCHRADER, William A(ldrete) Benton. Learning; Psychological tests. b'14. AB '34—AM '35 (Bucknell U); Ph D '40 (O State U). Developed rational equation describing course of learning, research on training of flexible gunners, psychology of instruction. Contrbutor: Psychological Research in Flexible Gunnery Training '47. Asso prof psychol and dir flight research Inst Aviation U Tenn '46-47; with Ednl Testing Service since '47, asst dir deptl statis analysis from '51 and head validity studies sect from '49. Am Psychol Assn (asso)—Psychometric Soc—Am Statis Assn—Sigma Xi. Educational Testing Service, Box 592, Princeton, N.J.

19 SHCRAMM, Frederic Bernard. Electronic measurements; Photoelectric sorting; Looms (Automatic); Temperature control. b'03. BS '25 (Case Inst Tech); LL B '31 (George Washington U). Connected with development or specification preparation about 120 electronic measuring or testing devices, as many other measuring devices in high and low frequency fields, about 100 magnetic devices, about 25 automatic loom mechanisms, about 25 temperature controls and about a dozen photoelectric devices. Holds patents on temperature controls. Patent atty in charge elec instruments and testing devices Gen Elec Co '31-42; in charge electronic circuit div of law dept Sperry Gyroscope Co '42-44. Am Inst EE—Inst Radio Engrs—Am Patent Law Assn—Tau Beta Pi—Sigma Xi—Eta Kappa Nu. Union Commerce Bldg., Cleve 14. H: 2403 Channing Rd., Cleve 18.

20 SCHRAMM, John Edward. Aviation industry securities; Aviation industry finance. b'10. Student '30-32 (Columbia U); '32-38 (Stock Exchange Inst); '39 (NYU); '42 (U Kansas City); '44 (U Buffalo). Investment analysis securities air transport operators; securities airframe manufacturers. Economist Curtiss Wright Corp Airplane Div '42-44; mgr research dept Sulzbacher Granger & Co '44-48; mgr research dept Townsend Graff & Co '48-51. NY Soc Sec Analysts—Econ Club NY—Am Econ Assn—Royal Econ Soc—Am Statis Assn—NY Acad Sci—Am Geog Soc—Acad Pol Sci. Prize essay NY Stock Exchange Inst '38. Townsend, Graff & Co., 15 Broad St., NYC 5. H: 21 Seminary Av., Yonkers 4, N.Y.

21 SCHRECKENGOST, Viktor. Pottery; Industrial design. b'06. Diploma '29 (Cleveland Inst Art); Post-grad certificate '30 (Kunstgewerbeschule Vienna). Design dinnerware, glass, lighting fixtures, truck cabs, bicycles, printing presses, juvenile wheelgoods, etc.; unique pieces pottery shown in all important museums in US; exhibitions in France, Italy, Sweden, Norway, Denmark, Finland, Austria, England, Canada. Contributor: Dictionary of the Arts '43. Art dir and designer Am Limoges China Co '33-43; Salem China Co since '35, Murray O Mfg Co since '38; cons designer various cos. Served as special devices div design sect USN '43-46, head visual design sect '45-46, commanding officer Volunteer Research Res Unit since '48. Soc Indsl Designers—NY Archtl League—Am Designers Inst—Am Ceramic Soc—US Potters Assn—Nat Design Conf—Inter-Soc Color Council—O Watercolor Soc—Cleveland Soc Artists—Spl Devices Assn. Received Alfred U Charles Fergus Binns Medal '38; Syracuse Mus Fine Arts Drakenfeld Award, Cleveland Mus Art spl award for outstanding excellence '32, '36, '37, '48, '50, many other first prizes. 2366 Noble Rd., Cleve 21.

22 SCHREINER, Ernst Jefferson. Forest genetics; Silviculture; Arboriculture. b'02. BS '24 (NY State Coll Forestry); PhD '30 (Columbia). Research in breeding fast growing poplars for pulpwood forestation, shrubs for hill culture and tree crop planting, Cinchona breeding in Gautemala. Author articles in field. Research forester Oxford Paper Co in cooperation with New York Botanical Garden '24-35; asso tree crop specialist Tenn Valley Authority '35-36; forest geneticist Northeastern Forest Expt Sta US Forest Service since '36. U.S. Forest Service, Upper Darby, Pa.

10 SCHRIFTGIESSER, Karl (John). New Deal; Lobbying; Pressure groups. b'03. Ed pub schs. Research on history New Deal, especially domestic policies and their origin in policies of Woodrow Wilson, contrast with Republican policies, working of Regulation of Lobbying Act of '46. Author: Families, From the Adamses to the Roosevelts '39; The Amazing Roosevelt Family 1613-1941 '42; The Gentleman from Massachusetts: Henry Cabot Lodge '44; This Was Normalcy: An Account of Republican Rule from 1920-1932 '48; The Lobbyists: The Art and Business of Influencing Lawmakers '51. Writer, book critic and journ for newspapers and magazines since '24. Londonderry, Vt.

11 SCHROEDER, Alfred Christian. Television (Color). b'15. BS '37—MS '37 (MIT). Assisted in development sequential and simultaneous television systems, also simultaneous subcarrier system; inventor tri-color tube. Holds six patents in field, including color television tube, apparatus, and kinescope for reproduction of color images. Co-author articles: An Experimental Color Television System '46; Simultaneous All-Electronic Color Television '46, and others. Color television research engr Radio Corp Am Labs Princeton since '37. AAAS—Inst Radio Engrs—Sigma Xi. Radio Corp Am Lab award for outstanding work in research '47, '50. Radio Corporation of America, Princeton, N.J.

12 SCHROEDER, Charles Arthur. Horticulture of subtropical fruit. b'13. PhD '43 (U Calif). Research asst subtropical hort U Calif '39-43, instr '43-45, asst prof since '45. Am Bot Soc—Am Soc Hort Sci—Calif Avocado Soc—Tex Avocado Soc—Sigma Xi. University of California, Los Angeles 24.

13 SCHROEDER, Eric. Islamic art and architecture. b'04. BA '25-27 (Oxford U). Research on Iranian painting, Islamic art and architecture, recorded Roman Limes castles in Arabia. Author: Persian Miniatures in the Fogg Museum, '42. Co-author: (with J Rosintal) A Survey of Persian Art (vol II) '38; (with R Ettinghausen) Iranian and Islamic Art '41. Contrib: Encyclopedia of the Arts '46. Asst Oxford and Field Mus expdn to Iraq '26-28; expdns Iran and Afghanistan '31-32, '35-36; keeper Islamic art Fogg Mus since '38; exec sec Am Research Center in Egypt since '50. Fogg Mus of Art, Harvard U, Cambridge 38, Mass.

14 SCHROEDER, Henry Alfred. Aviation physiology; Asia (Geography, health). b'06. AB '29 (Yale); MD '33 (Columbia). Study physiological effects of high accelerations on man; development pilot's anti-blackout equipment; research on methods for protection of pilots against effects of crash forces; study problems of survival at sea, high altitude, high speed flight, human engineering, and cockpit design; expedition to Chinese Central Asia; research on infectious diseases of Near and Far East; research on hypertension and heart and kidney diseases since '36. Member panel on aviation medicine Research and Development Board. Asso prof med, dir hypertension div Washington U Sch Med St Louis since '46; asst attending physician Barnes Hosp St Louis since '46. Am Soc Clin Investigation—Harvey Soc—NY Acad Med (F)—Am Heart Assn (F)—Am Coll Physicians (F)—Inst Aeronautical Sci—Aeromed Assn US—Central Soc Clin Research—So Soc Clin Research—Am Physiol Soc—Soc Exptl Biol and Med—AAAS (F)—AMA (F)—Sigma Xi. Department of Internal Medicine, Washington University, St. Louis 10.

15 SCHROEDER, William Charles. Ichthyology (Elasmobranchs, codfish). b'95. Student '24-31 (Harvard). Made deep sea zoological explorations around Cuba '38-39, Bermuda '48, N W Atlantic slope 48-53. Author articles in field. Bus mgr Woods Hole Oceanographic Inst '32-51 ichthyologist since '51; asso curator fishes Harvard since '37. Soc Ichthyol and Herptol—Boston Soc Natural History—NY Acad Sci. Awarded gold medal for explorations by Geog Soc of Cuba '40. Museum Comparative Zoology, Harvard University, Cambridge, Mass.†

16 SCHUBAUER, Galen Brandt. Aerodynamics. b'04. BS '28 (Pa State Coll); MS '29 (Calif Inst Tech); PhD '34 (Johns Hopkins). Research on laminar and turbulent boundary-layer flows, apparatus for measuring turbulence, methods of reducing turbulence in wind tunnels, aerodynamics of missiles; also research on absolute measurements of the ampere. Author articles: A Turbulence Indicator Utilizing the Diffusion of Heat '35. Co-author articles; Measurement of Intensity and Scale of Wind Tunnel Turbulence and Their Relations to the Critical Reynolds Number of Spheres '37; also articles in field. Physicist Nat Bur Standards elec div '29-30, mechanic div aerodynamics sect '30-46, chief aerodynamics sect since '46. Washington Acad Sci—Philos Soc Washington—Inst Aeronautical Sci(F). Washington Acad Sci Award for outstanding achievement in engring sci '44; Sylvanus Albert Reed Award for '47, presented by Inst Aeronautical Sci. National Bureau of Standards, Washington 25.

17 SCHUETTE, Curt Nicolaus. Mine management; Examination and valuation; Strategic minerals; Non metallics; Metallurgy (Quicksilver). b'95. BS '17 (U Calif Coll Mining). Author: Quicksilver '31; Quicksilver in Oregon '38. Co-author: (with L H Duchak) The Metallurgy of Quicksilver '25. Contbr to Modern Uses of Nonferrous Metals '35; also author articles in field. Cons on design and operation of plants for gold, silver, quicksilver and management mines since '25. In military service during World War I assigned to research on quicksilver US Bur Mines. Am Inst Mining and Metall Engrs. 6390 Barnett Valley Rd, Sebastopol, Cal.☉

18 SCHULMAN, Edmund. Dendrochronology. b'08. BS '33—MS '35 (U Ariz); MA '38—PhD '44 (Harvard). Research in climatology, hydrology, archeology, forestry and geology in relation dendrochronology. Devised refinement technique for locating drought-sensitive and over-age trees and deriving tree-ring indices of rainfall and river flow. Author articles in field. Asst Tree-Ring Lab U Ariz '32-34, instr dendrochronology '39-45, asst prof '45-47, asso prof since '47, dendrochronologist since '40; asst cycle analysis Carnegie Inst '35-37; managing ed Tree-Ring Bull since '39; research asst Blue Hill Obs Harvard '38, research fellow 43-44. AAAS—Am Astron Soc—Am Geog Soc—Am Geophys Union—Am Meteorol Soc—Tree-Ring Soc. Tree-Ring Laboratory, University of Arizona, Tucson†

19 SCHULTZ, Leonard P(eter). Zoology; Ichthyology; Fishes of the United States. b'01. AB '24 (Albion Coll); MS '26 (U Mich); PhD '32 (U Washington). Expeditions, University of Michigan Museum western United States 26, leader US Bureau Fisheries Survey Glacier National Park '36, fisheries research Yellowstone National Park '36, naturalists USS Bushnell US Navy survey Phoenix and Samoan Islands '39, charge Smithsonian Institute expedition Maracaibo Basin Venezuela '42, reef fishes investigation Crossroads Operations at Bikini US Navy '46, '47. Co-author: (with E M Stern) The Ways of Fishes '48; The Book of Fishes '39, and others. Curator fishes US Nat Mus since '36. Am Soc Ichthyol and Herpetol (vp '37, bd govs)—AAAS—Am Fisheries Soc—Arctic Inst Am—Am Soc Limnol and Oceano (bd govs)—Biol Soc Washington—Bermuda Biol Sta (bd govs)—Sigma Xi—Phi Beta Kappa. Smithsonian Instn., Washington 25.†☉

20 SCHULZ, Ernst (Bernhard). City government; Political theory. b'16. Student '15-18 (Case Inst Tech); BS '20 AM '21—PhD '27 (U Mich). Author: Government, A Phase of Social Organization '29; (with W L Godshall and others) Principles and Functions of Government in the United States '48; American City Government '49. Instr polit sci U Cincinnati '22-23; U Mich '24-27; asst prof polit sci Lehigh U '27-31, asso prof '31-45, prof polit sci since '45. Am Polit Sci Assn —Nat Municipal League—Am Acad Polit and Social Sci—AAUP—Tau Beta Pi. Lehigh University, Bethlehem, Pa. H: Coopersburg, Pa.†☉

21 SCHULZE, Else Louise. Chemical literature. b'01. BA '23—MA '24—PhD '26 (U Cincinnati). Collection, organization, indexing technical literature in field fats, oils, soaps, detergents. Co-author article: The Liberation of Hydrogen from Carbon Compounds '24, '26, '28. Technical librarian Procter and Gamble Co since '26. Am Chem Soc—Sp Libraries Assn—Iota Sigma Pi—Sigma Xi—Phi Beta Kappa. The Procter and Gamble Co., Cin 17.

22 SCHUR, Milton Oscar. Manufacture and uses of pulp and paper. b'95. BS '16 (MIT). Research on manufacturing of highly purified wood pulps, utilization bast and leaf fibers, esterification of cellulose, technical cellulose fiber specialties. Holder numerous patents. Author articles in field. Research chem MIT '16-17; chem engr Chem Prod Co '17-18; bur of Mines and CWS Washington '18-19; research chem Brown Co '19-40, dir of research and development '40-44; tech dir Ecusta Paper Corp since '44. Am Chem Soc—Tech Assn Pulp and Paper Ind—Can Tech Assn Pulp and Paper Ind—Am Inst Chem Engrs—Am Inst Chem—Soc Chem Inds—AAAS—Forest Products Research Soc—Electrochem Soc. Ecusta Paper Corporation, Pisgah Forest, N.C.†

23 SCHURECHT, Harry George. Ceramics. b'92. BS '14 (U Ill); grad work (O State U, U Pittsburgh). Developed the autoclave crazing test now used as the standard test for crazing of all types of glazed ceramic ware such as dinnerware and wall tile throughout the world Hold four patents. Author articles in field Ceramic chem Findlay Clay Pot Co Pa '14-16; asso ceramic chem Nat Bur Standards Pittsburgh '16; ceramic chem Bur Mines Lord Hall O State U '16-23; sr research asso The Nat Terra Cotta Soc Nat Bur of Standards Washington '25-31; ceramic chem Eastern Terra Cotta Co LI City '31-36; prof research charge ceramic expt sta Alfred U '36-44; research engr Ceramic Div Champion Spark Plug Co Detroit since '44. Inst Ceramic Engrs—Am Ceramic Soc(F)—Am Soc Testing Materials—Engring Soc Detroit. Champion Spark Plug Co., Ceramic Division, 8525 Butler Av, Detroit 11.

10 SCHURR, Sam Harold. Atomic power economics. b'18. BA '38—MA '39 (Rutgers U); '39-43 (Columbia). Author: Economic Aspects of Atomic Power '50; also articles in field. Econ Nat Bur Econ Research '39-43; econ US Dept State and OSS '43-46; co-dir Study on Econ Aspects of Atomic Power Cowles Commn Research in Econ, U Chicago, '46-48; chief econ US Bur Mines since '50. Am Econ Assn. US Bureau of Mines, Washington. H: 11716 College View Dr., Silver Spring, Md.

11 SCHUSTER, Max Lincoln. Pictorial photographic and documentary records of history; Literature of letters; Structure and Classification of Knowledge (Bibliographical research; great books as living literature; reference books). born '97. B Litt '17 (Columbia). Author: Eyes on the World: A Photographic Record of History in the Making '35. Editor: A Treasury of the World's Great Letters '40; also articles in field. Co-founder and partner Simon & Schuster Inc book publishers NYC since '24; ed The Inner Sanctum Library of Living Literature and Basic Books founded with others, and dir, Pocket Books Inc; chief publ sect Bur War Risk Ins US Treasury Dept, dir publicity and aide to Adm T J Cowie USN World War I. Am Geog Soc(F)—Friends of Scripta Mathematica—Bibliog Soc Am—Soc Prevention Cruelty to Newspaper Readers (founder). Rockefeller Center, 630 Fifth Av., NYC.

12 SCHUTZ, John Adolph. Massachusetts (Eighteenth century history); Barbados (Eighteenth century history); Seven years' war. b'19. BA '42 —MA '43—PhD '45—fellow '44-45 (U Calif); AA '40 (Bakersfield Jr Coll). Research on life of Thomas Pownall, Codrington Chronicle. Author articles in field. Instr Calif Inst Tech '45-47, asst prof since '47. AHA—Am Hist Assn. Received Pacific Coast br AHA annual award in American History '48. California Institute of Technology, Pasadena, Calif. H: 1100 White Knoll Drive, Los Angeles 12.

13 SCHWALBE, Franz George. Glass melting furnaces (design); Glass plant combustion problems; Glass annealling. b'98. BS (ME) '20 (U Mich). Design melting furnaces for glass wool, sheet glass, also plate, window, optical and container glass; research design on combustion problems to provide proper flame characteristics for melting of special glasses; development work all types fuel; annealling problems studied to effect commercial application theory to practice. Author articles: How Ford Makes its Glass '37; Twenty Years of Progress in Glass Melting '40; Control of Luminous Flame Firing '40; Fuel Economics '47. Glass machine design 'Neill Machine Co London Eng '20-25; glass plant engr Toledo Engring Co Inc since '25, in charge engring since '25. Am Ceramic Soc—Am Inst Ceramic Engrs—Tau Beta Pi. Professional ME Ohio. Toledo Engineering Co., Inc., 958 Wall St., Tol 6.

14 SCHWARTZ, Harry A(dolph). Graphitization of iron alloys. b'80. BS EE '01—MS '03—ME '05—Ch E '31—ScD (Rose Poly Inst); grad study '32 (Western Reserve U); Dr Engring (Case Inst Tech). Pioneer research in graphitization of white cast iron; systematic relation of composition and heat treatment to properties of alloy structural steel. Patents dealing with malleable castings. Author: American Malleable Cast Iron '22; also articles in field. Various operating positions, advanced to supt Nat Malleable and Steel Castings Co Indianapolis '02-20, mgr research Cleveland since '20; lec-

turer Case Inst Tech Grad Sch '36-42; cons on malleable iron The Foundry. Am Foundrymen's Soc (hon life)—Assn Technique de Fondries de Belge (hon life)—ASME—Am Inst Mining and Metall Engrs—Am Chem Soc—Am Soc for Metals—Am Soc for Testing Materials—Iron and Steel Inst (British) —Sigma Xi. 10600 Quincy Av., Cleveland 6.

15 SCHWARTZ, William Leonard. Japanese language and civilization; French literature (Nineteenth and twentieth century); Haitian culture. b'88. AB '10 (O Wesleyan U); AM '20 —PhD '26 (Stanford U); Cert d'etudes pratiques de phonetique '29 (U Paris) —'29 (Ecole des Hautes). Prof Eng Seventh Govt Coll Kagoshima '10-14, Nagasaki Coll Commerce '14-19; prof French Coll Pacific '19-20; instr advanced to asso prof Romanic langs Stanford U since '20, vis prof U Nat d'Haiti '48-49, lecturer arts in Japan spring '46, Japanese '43-44, ed Japanese studies Stanford U Press since '45; lecturer French US Calif summer '27; student of shintoism Matsue Japan '12, Satsuma Pottery, Satsuma dialect '13-14; travel to Ryukyu '08, '11, '13, '14, Japan '19; fellow Belgian Am Edn Found '36; lecturer Asiatic Soc Japan '18, Japan Soc London '21. Author: A Survey of the Satsuma Dialect '15; Potters and Pottery of Satsuma '21; French Romantic Poetry '32; (with C B Olsen) Sententiae in the Dramas of Corneille '39; Peacetime Rambles in the Ryukyus '45; Commodore Perry at Okinawa '46. Asiatic Soc of Japan—Far Eastern Assn—Modern Lang Assn Am—AHA—Soc Haitienne d'Hist et Geog—Am Assn Teachers of French—Phi Beta Kappa—Officier d'academie. Romanic Language Department, Stanford University, Stanford, Calif. H: 667 Salvatierra St.

16 SCHWARZ, Edward Robinson. Textile testing. b'99. SB '22 (MIT); MS hon (Lowell Textile Inst). Research on textile microscopy and testing; associate editor Textile Research Journal. Author: Textiles and the Microscope. Co-author: Matthews Textile Fibers, Textile Research (A Survey of Progress). Author 100 articles in field. Prof textile tech MIT. Brit Textile Inst(F)—AAAS(F)—Textile Research Inst(founding F)—Am Association Textile Tech(hon life)—Am Assn Textile Chem and Colorists(Olney medallist)—ASTM(Smith medallist)—Fiber Soc—Nat Fire Protection Assn—Tau Beta Pi—Sigma Xi—Am Inst Phys. Room 3-309, Massachusetts Institute of Technology, Textile Division, Cambridge 39, Mass.

17 SCHWARZSCHILD, Martin. Astrophysics (Stellar interior). b'12. PhD '35 (Göttingen U). Research in interior of stars. Author articles in field. Prof Princeton U since '47. Am Astronom Soc. Research fellow, Harvard Coll Obs '37-40. Princeton University Observatory, Princeton, N.J.†☉

18 SCHWEGLER, Raymond Alfred. Psychology (Personality). b'74. AB '99 (Brown U); AM '06 (Ottawa U); '11-12 (Leipzig U); PhD '28 (Columbia). Author: A Teachers' Manual for the Use of the Binet-Simon Scale of Intelligence '14; A Study of Introvert-Extravert Responses to Certain Test Situations '29. Prof edn U Kan since '14, dean '27-41, dean emeritus since '41. AAAS(F)—NEA (life)—Nat Soc Study Edn—Soc Coll Teachers Edn—Phi Beta Kappa. 805 Missouri St., Lawrence, Kan.

19 SCHWEGMANN, George A., Jr. Blind (Talking books systems); Microphotography; Union catalogs. b'00. BS; LLB. Dir photoduplication service. Library of Congress '39-45, chief

div for the blind '48-51, chief Union Catalog div since '39. ALA—Bibliog Soc Am. Library of Congress, Washington 25.

20 SCHWEID, Edward Jay. City zoning. b'03. Student (Adelbert Coll); (U Pittsburgh); AB '24 (Ohio State U); LLB '26 (Western Reserve U). Mem firm Schweid Snyder Torbet and Zucker '43-51, Schweid and Zucker since '51; collaborated drafting Cleveland city zoning law and established first Board of Zoning Appeals; city's counsel and legal advisor to Bd of Zoning Appeals '30-32; appointed traction commr charge transit utility regulation City Cleveland '35-42. Cleveland Bar Assn—Cuyahoga County Bar Assn (trustee)—Ohio State Bar Assn—Am Bar Assn—Am Judicature Soc—Tau Epsilon Rho. 330 Hanna Bldg., Cleve 15.†☉

21 SCHWEIGERT, Eugene William. Ancient Greek; Latin; Ancient history and music. b'10. Fellow '34-35 (Johns Hopkins U); BA '32—MA '33—PhD '40 (U Cincinnati); '32 (Coll Mus of Cincinnati); Seymour fellow in Greek '35 (Am Sch Classical Studies). Research fellow in Epigraphy '36-39 on the Staff of Excavators of the Athenian Agora. Instructor in Greek and Ancient History '40-42 University of Pennsylvania. Member Institute of Advance Study '40. Author articles in field. Vis lecturer Latin Coll Wooster '47-48; lectr classical languages Xavier U '48-49. AHA—Arch Inst Am—Am Classical League—Classical Association Midwest South—Assn Etudes Grecques France —Ohio Classical Conf—AAUP. 320 Oak St., Cin 19.

22 SCHWEITZER, Morton D(avid). Business (Statistical analysis); Medical genetics. b'08. PhD '34—AB—MA (Columbia); fellow (Calif Inst Tech, Woods Hole Mass). Collaborator: You and Heredity '39; Rheumatic Fever '40. Author articles. Business cons. Am Statis Assn—Am Marketing Assn—Soc Advancement Management—Royal Statis Soc (London)—Human Genetics Soc Am—NY Acad Med (asso)—Sigma Xi. 15 E. 8th St., Cin 2.

23 SCHWEITZER, Paul Henry. Diesel engines (Two-stroke cycle); Power plants. born '93. ME '17 (Royal Hungarian Tech Univ Budapest); Dr Engr '29 (Saeschische Technische Hochschule, Dresden Germany). Author: Scavenging of Two-Stroke Cycle Diesel Engines (Macmillan) '48; also articles in field. Asst master mechanic and Diesel engine designer De La Vergne Machine Co NYC '20-22; prof engring research Pa State Coll since '36; in charge Diesel engine lab since '23; cons diesel engine design and develop since '30. AAAS(F)—ASME—Am Soc Naval Engrs—Soc Automotive Engrs—Sigma Xi. Pennsylvania State College, State College, Pa.†☉

24 SCHWEIZER, J. Otto. Sculpture. b'63. Student (Art Sch Zurich); (Royal Acad Dresden); under Dr J Schilling Dresden and Florence Italy. Exhibited Nat Acad Design NY, Nat Sculpture Soc NY, Acad Fine Arts Phila. Sculptor: statue Gen Peter Muhlenberg Rayburn Plaza North Side City Hall Phila.; Molly Pitcher Carlisle Pa; equestrian statue Frederick W von Steuben Sherman Blvd Milwaukee Wis; Melchior Muhlenberg bronze groups Germantown Pa; James J Davis group Mooseheart Ill; marble busts F D Pastorius and Carl Schurz (Old Custom House), The Lord's Supper, high relief in bronze, all in Phila, and others. Nat Sculpture Soc. 2215 W. Venango St., Phila 40.☉

25 SCHWENDEMAN, Joseph Raymond. Geomorphology and water supply geography; Educational geography;

Cartography. b'97. BS '26 (U Ohio); MA '27—PhD '41 (Clark U); '27-28 (U Minn). Prepared map of natural regions of Minnesota from field work and source material '33; prepared map of physiography of Merrimac Valley New England '39; field work and manuscript on water supply geography of Red River Basin of Northern US '40-41 being used by Municipal Water Supply of Missouri River Basin; closely related with departments education in Kentucky and Minnesota; inventing world map projection for school use. Author: Geography of Minnesota '33; Air Age 48 Hour Time and Day Chart '43; Electric Map: Equal Land Area of the World '46; also articles in field. Instr geog U Minn '27-28; head dept geog Moorehead Minn State Teach Coll '28-44; mem map comm Ky Dept Edn; head dept geog U Ky since '44. AAAS —Am Assn Profl Geographers—Nat Council Geog Teach—AAUP. Geography Department, University of Kentucky, Lexington, Ky. H: Georgetown Pike, Route 6, Lexington.

10 SCHWENDLER, William Theodore. Aircraft (Engineering education research). b'04. BS in ME '24 (NYU). Engr Loening Aeronautical Engring Corp NYC '24-25, project engr '26-27, asst gen mgr '28-30; chief engr Grumman Aircraft Engring Corp '30-50, vp '40-46, exec vp since '46, dir since '39. Institute Aeronautical Sciences (F)—Soc Automotive Engrs. Grumman Aircraft Engineering Corp., Bethpage, N.Y. H: Merritt Rd., Farmingdale, L.I., N.Y.

11 SCHWENNING, Gustav Theodor. Business administration; Industrial relations. b'88. Graduate '13 (German-Am Acad Rochester NY); BH '20 (Springfield Coll); AM '21—PhD '25 (Clark U). Special research dismissal legislation and compensation. Co-author: The Science of Production Organization '38. Editor and co-author: Management Problems '30. Mng editor: The Southern Economic Journal '36-42, since '46. Asso prof bus adminstrn U NC '26-32, prof since '32; on leave serving as prin specialist management edn engring, sci, and management war training US Office Edn '41-45; head bus adminstrn br Shrivenham Am U Eng '45-46. Am Econ Assn—AAUP—So Econ Assn— Soc Advancement Management—Am Arbitration Assn—Acad Management —Indsl Relations Research Assn— Kappa Delta Pi—Delta Sigma Pi— Beta Gamma Sigma. School of Business Administration, University of North Carolina, Chapel Hill.†◎

12 SCHWEPPE, Alfred John. b'95. AB '15 (Northwestern Coll Watertown Wis); AB '16—MA '17 (U Wis); LLB '22 (U Minn). Author: Simkins' Federal Practice '34, rev edit '38. Admitted to Washington State bar '22; with Tanner & Garvin Seattle '22-24; partner Long & Schweppe Seattle '24-26, lecturer on law U Wash '23-26, dean Law Sch '26-30; partner McMicken, Rupp & Schweppe since '30. Seattle Bar Assn—Washington State Bar Assn—Am Bar Assn—Am Judicature Soc—Phi Delta Phi. Colman Bldg., Seattle 4. H: 3616 E Ward St, Seattle 2.

13 SCHWIERING, Oscar Conrad. Educational curricula; Teacher training. b'86. AB '09 (Iowa Wesleyan U); MA '16 (U Wyo); PhD '32 (NY U). Author: College Curriculum '32; The Superintendent in Action '38; School Survey Techniques '37. Prof edn U Wyo '25-39, dean Coll Edn and dir summer session since '39; dir Student Welfare Foundation. Colo-Wyo Acad Sci—Am Assn Sch Adminstrs— NEA—Soc Cirriculum Study—Soc

Study Edn—Wyo Ednl Assn—Kappa Delta Pi—Phi Delta Kappa. College of Education, Univ of Wyoming, Laramie. †◎

14 SCIPIO, Lynn A. Machine design (Tech); International railway transportation; Turkish technical language. b'76. AB '02 (Tri-State Coll, Angola, Ind); '03 (Armour Inst Tech, Chicago); BS in ME '08—ME '11—PhD '31 (Purdue). Industrial rehabilitation specialist for UNRRA '45. Author: English-Turkish Technical Dictionary '39; Elements of Machine Design '28. Asst prof mech engring U Neb '08-12; dean Robert Coll Engring Sch, Constantinople, and cons engr '12-20; dir Am Soc Heating and Ventilating Engrs Research Lab US Bur Mines Pittsburgh '20-21; dean Robert Coll Engring Sch '21-43; head engr War Production Bd '43-44. ASME—Am Soc Heating and Ventilating Engrs — Nat Research Council—Sigma Xi. 525 Hartford St., Worthington, O.

15 SCOFIELD, Francis. Oils (Drying); Color (Measurement). b'05. BS (Chem) '31 (Lehigh U); '34-36 (George Washington U). In charge investigations culture drying oils, properties and testing drying oils; research on color measurement, small color differences. Sci aide Nat Bur Standards '31-36; chem sci sect Nat Paint, Varnish & Lacquer Assn Washington since '36. Am Soc Testing Materials— Am Oil Chem Soc—Fedn Paint and Varnish Prodn Clubs(pub and standards com, method of tests com. National Paint, Varnish & Lacquer Association, 1500 Rhode Island Av, NW, Washington 5. H: Hilltop, Lanham, Md.

16 SCOFIELD, John. History of firearms, guns and weapons. b'14. Co-author: (with P Thompson and others) How the Jap Army Fights '42-44; (ed S D Ludlum) Great Shooting Stories '47; also author articles in field. Mng ed American Rifleman '45-53. Armor and Arms Club—Vaabenhistorisk Selskab (Royal Danish Armor and Arms Soc)—Nat Rifle Assn (life)—Nat Muzzle-Loading Rifle Assn. National Geographic Society, Washington 6.

17 SCOTT, Alfred Witherspoon. Organic Chemistry; Qualitative Analysis. b'96. BS '18 (U Ga); PhD '22 (Princeton U). Premedical requirements for entrance to medical schools. Author: A Laboratory Outline of General Chemistry and Qualitative Analysis '24; A Laboratory Outline of General Chemistry and Semi-Micro Qualitative Analysis '41; contbr to chem jours; editor: Physical Science '34. Asso prof Chemistry U Ga '22-27, prof and head dept since '27, chmn div phys scis since '36, chmn chemistry sect since '36; asso dir Dixie Camp for Boys '16-44, dir since '44; asso dir Dixie Camp for Girls since '20. AA AS—Am Chem Soc (chmn Ga Sect '36)—Ga Acad Sci (pres '32)— Phi Beta Kappa—Phi Kappa Phi—Sigma Xi. Add: 238 Springdale St., Athens, Ga.

18 SCOTT, Charles C(alvin). Questioned documents; Forensic photography. b'11. LLB '35—'49-50 (U Kan City). Specialist in questioned document examination, including identification of handwriting, typewriting, ink and paper; signature authentication and detection forgeries and alterations; decipherment faded and charred documents; preparation black and white, color, infrared and ultraviolet photographs and photomicrographs; microscopic comparisons; chemical tests; expert witness in state and federal courts; founder and ed U of Kansas City Law Review '33-37. Author:

Photographic Evidence '42; also articles in field. Work in signature examination for Fed Reserve Bank '35-40; spl lect questioned documents U Ill '47, Purdue U '48, U Tulsa '49; now operates own office and lab. Am Soc Questioned Document Exam—Am Bar Assn—Am Jud Soc—Photog Assn Am —Mo Bar Assn. 1003 Commerce Building, KC 6, Mo.

19 SCOTT, Charles Ernest. China (History, politics, diplomacy, war). b'76. BA '98—DD '23 (Alma Coll); MA '99 (U Pa); PhD '00—fellowship from U Pa '99-00 (U Munich); BD '03 (Theol Sem Princeton). Lecturer and writer on Far Eastern history and diplomacy; missionary in North China '06-40; active in famine relief work, supervising 100,000 men in various constructions; fact finder for Washington officials on recent Far East Situation. Author: Chinese Twice Born '31; Answered Prayer in China '23; also articles in field. Ordained to ministry N Presbyn Ch '03. Am Geog Soc(F)— Am Acad Polit and Social Sci—AHA— Presbyterian Hist Soc—Acad Polit Sci of US—Fgn Policy Assn—Pa Hist Soc —Council Fgn Relations. c/o Philadelphia National Bank, Phila.

20 SCOTT, Clarence West. Pulp and paper production (Continuous system, capacity, instrumentation). b'08. BS (chem engring) (U Ala); '29 (Swiss Poly Inst). Development and operation of pulp production using continuous system, increased capacity in caustic plants, evaporators, instrumentation involving consistency of paper machines and various process variables. With S Kraft Div Internat Paper Co since '32, tech adv to mgr Springhill plant from '50. Tech Assn Pulp and Paper Industry—ACS—Soc Chem Industry (Eng)—AICE—Am Inst Chem. Southern Kraft Division, International Paper Co., Springhill, La.

21 SCOTT, Clarice Louisba. Functional design of women's clothing for household and farm work. b'99. BS (Earlham Coll Richmond Ind); MS (Ia State Coll). Pioneer work in development designs for functional clothing providing maximum comfort, free action, convenience, safety and efficiency. Holds patent on Land Army uniform for women. Author articles: Work Clothes for Women '42; Dresses and Aprons for Work in the Home '47; Shopper's Coat '50, and others. Research on functional clothing design, conservation and buymanship of clothing USDA since '29. Fashion Group. USDA superior service award for pioneer work in design functional clothes for women working in homes, factories and on farms. Bureau of Human Nutrition and Home Economics, U.S. Department of Agriculture, Washington 25.

22 SCOTT, Donald H(yde). Pomology (Small fruit breeding and culture). b'11. BS '36 (ND Agrl Coll); PhD '49 (U Md). Research in stone fruit breeding, inheritance studies peaches, development method testing blossom buds for cold hardiness; vegetable and small fruit breeding, inheritance studies tomatoes, squash, pumpkins, strawberries; blossom hardiness, vitamin C content and red stele resistance in strawberries. With div fruit and vegetable crops and diseases US Dept of Agr Beltsville Md '37-42, since '46. Am Soc Hort Sci—Genetics Soc Am— Am Genetic Assn. U.S. Department of Agriculture, Plant Industry Station, Beltsville, Md.

23 SCOTT, Dorothy Berkshire. Microanalysis of foods and drugs. b'93. AB '15 (U Omaha Neb); MA '20

(George Washington U); (Agr) '20-21, '29-30 (Columbia) Development of methods for determination of flour-bleaching chemicals in flour, for separation of extraneous materials in foods and drugs, for identification of animal hairs, and for identification of manure fragments in dairy products. Food chem and microanalyst Food and Drug Adminstrn since '18. ACS—Assn Ofcl Agrl Chem—AAAS. U.S. Food and Drug Administration, Washington 25.

10 SCOTT, Franklin D(aniel). Scandinavian history and affairs; Modern European history (International relations, expansion). b'01. Student '18-19 (Doane Coll), '19-21 (Ill Coll); '30-31 (Stockholm U); PhB '23—MA '24 (Chicago U); MS '29—PhD '32 (Harvard). Research grant for field work in Scandinavia, Social Science Research Council '38; participant in International Congress of Historical Sciences, Zurich '38, Harris Institute, Chicago University '40-46, Conference of Historians of the North '48; engaged research and writing on Bernadotte; American influences in Norway and Sweden, countries of Northern Europe. Author: Bernadotte and Fall of Napoleon '35; Bernadotte och Napoleons Fall '38; Guide to the American Historical Review 1895-1945 '44; The Twentieth Century World: A Reading Guide '48; The United States and Scandinavia '49; also articles in field. Asst prof hist and govt Simpson Coll '25-28; asst Harvard and Radcliffe Coll '29-32; teacher State Teachers Coll Wis '32-35; asst prof Northwestern U '35-38, asso prof '38-43, prof since '43; reference specialist OSS '42. AHA—Am Polit Sci Assn—Soc Advancement Scandinavian Studies—Svenska Historiska Föreningen—Karl Johans Förbund — Library Internat Relations (trustee, past pres). Travelling fellowship Am Scandinavian Found '30-32; fellowship for work in Scandinavia Viking Fund '47-48. Department of History, Northwestern University, Evanston, Ill. H: 2657 Orrington Av., Evanston, Ill.⊙

11 SCOTT, Hermon Hosmer. Radio. b'09. BS '30—MS '31 (MIT). Distortion, intermodulation and other tests at audio frequencies; research on subminiature electronic equipment, electronic organs, and broadcast station quality monitoring equipment; elimination of noise in reproduction of music; measurement and analysis of sound and vibration; frequency control and frequency monitoring of broadcast transmitters. Holds patents in field, including dynamic noise suppressors, R-C oscillators, electronic filters, and sound-level meters. Author articles: Audible Audio Distortion '45; Dynamic Suppression of Phonograph Record Noise '46; Dynamic Noise Suppressor '47, and others. Co-author articles: (with Edmond G Dyett Jr) Application of Miniature-Circuit Techniques to the Sound-Level Meter '48; (with W L Black) Audio Frequency Measurements '49, and others. Contributor: National Association of Broadcasters Handbook '48-50. Exec engr Gen Radio Co '31-46; pres and dir engring Hermon Hosmer Scott, Inc since '47. Acoustical Soc Am (F)—Inst Radio Engrs—Am Inst Physics—Am Inst EE—Audio Engring Soc. H H Scott, Inc, 385 Putnam Av, Cambridge 39, Mass.

12 SCOTT, Iley Stanley, Jr. Local government; Measuring governmental activities; legislative research. b'21. BA '42 (Tex Tech Coll); MA '47 (U Chicago). Research on local government and its organization in California, planning and metropolitan prob-

lems, intergovernmental relations, home rule, voting behavior; measurement of governmental services, influences of inflation and population growth. Co-author: Local Government in California '51. Pub adminstrn analyst Bur Pub Adminstrn U Calif since '47. Am Soc Pub Adminstrn—Am Polit Sci Assn—Am Inst Planners—W Govt Research Assn (exec sec since '50). Bureau of Public Administration, University of California, Berkeley 4.

13 SCOTT, Janet D(owning). Inorganic chemical nomenclature; Chemical literature. b'02. AB '23 (Vassar Coll); SM '28 (U Chicago). Author articles in field. Asst ed Enc Chem Technol since '44; instr chem lit Poly Inst Brooklyn since '47; with Chem Abstracts '30-41, asso ed '35-41. Am Chem Soc—AAAS—Phi Beta Kappa. Polytechnic Institute of Brooklyn, 99 Livingston St., Brooklyn 2, N.Y.

14 SCOTT, J(ohn) P(aul). Sociobiology; Social psychology; Genetics. b'09. BA '30 (U Wyo); BA '32 (Oxford U Eng, Rhodes Scholar); PhD '35 (U Chicago). Author articles in field. Asst dept zool U Chicago '32-35; chmn dept zool Wabash Coll '35-45, asso prof '35-42, prof '42-45; research asso, chmn div behavior studies Roscoe B Jackson Memorial Lab Bar Harbor since '45, mem bd dirs '46-49. AAAS—Am Soc Zool—Genetics Soc—Am Psychol Assn—Sigma Xi—Phi Beta Kappa. Rhodes Scholar Wyo '30-32. Roscoe B. Jackson Memorial Laboratory, Box 847, Bar Harbor, Me.

15 SCOTT, Kenneth. Classical Latin and Greek Literature and History (Ruler cult); American colonial history (New England). b'00. AB '21 (Williams Coll); MA '23—PhD '25 (Williams Coll). Pres Adams fellow '24-25—Markham Travel fellow '26-27 (U Wis); Williams scholar '21-22 (Am Sch Classical Studies Athens). Author: The Imperial Cult Under the Flavians '36; Notes on the Bowman, Harter and Sauer Families '48; Counterfeiting in Colonial New York, '53. Co-author: Selections from Latin Prose and Poetry '33; Caesaris Augusti Res Gestae et Fragmenta '35; also articles. Prof classics Upsala U '48-49; prof mod lang Wagner Coll, Staten Island, NY since '49, chmn modern languages dept since '50. Am Philol Assn—NH Hist Soc—Phi Beta Kappa. Guggenheim Memorial Found fellow '34. Wagner College, Staten Island, N.Y.

16 SCOTT, Kenneth G(ordon). Biophysics; Isotopes. b'09. AB '34—PhD '48 (U Calif). Research on metalolism of radioactive isotopes and their application to the biological and medical sciences; Bikini tests '46; the distribution of globulin-bound thyroglobulin fractions of iodine in normal and tumorous animals after intravenous administration using radioiodine as a tracer '49. Author articles in field. Research asst physiol U Calif '34-37; research asso Crooker Radiation Lab U Calif since '37, asso prof exptl radiol since '48, director of radioactivity center '51, cons Veterans Adminstrn since '48, USN '47-48; Manhattan Project and US Atomic Energy Commn since '42. Geophys Union. University of California Medical Center University of California, San Francisco.

17 SCOTT, Leland Edwards. Horticultural crops (Mineral nutrition, post-harvest physiology, nutritional value as affected by variety, environment, harvesting methods, handling, storage, preservation, peaches, sweet potatoes, asparagus, grapes, apples). b'06. BS '27 (U Ky); MS '29 (Mich State Coll); PhD '43 (U Md). Author articles in

field. Asso prof to prof hort physiol dept hort U Md since '43. Am Soc Hort Sci—Am Soc Plant Physiol—Inst Food Technol—Sigma Xi. Department of Horticulture, University of Maryland, College Park, Md.

18 SCOTT, Robert Douglas. Medieval Irish literature, language and traditions (Ossianic cycle); Celtic, Germanic and Indian folklore; Sanskrit grammar and etymology; Comparative Indo-European grammar; English grammar (Teaching methods). b'78. BSc '04 (Kan State Agrl Coll); AM '10 (U Neb); PhD '30 (Columbia U). Research in field. Author: The Thumb of Knowledge in Legends of Finn, Sigurd and Taliesin '30; A Student's Guide to English Composition '46; also articles in field. Instr, asso prof and prof Dept English U Neb '10-46, dir of instrn in freshman English '23-46. AAUP. RFD 1, Raymond, Neb.

19 SCOTT, Roderic M. Air classification of fine particles (Dust collection); Supersonics; Electronics. b'16. BS '38 (Case Sch Applied Sci); MA '39—PhD '45 (Harvard). Research and classification supersonics and underwater sound; in astronomy, long period variables and radiometry; several air classification of fine particles patents pending. Supersonics and electronics Harvard Underwater Sound Lab '40-45; electronics and air classification Sharples Research Lab, now dir engring Perkin-Elmer Corp Norwalk, vis lecturer optics U Pa '47-48. Am Physical Soc—Am Astron Soc. Chestnut Hill Road, Stamford, Conn.

20 SCOTT, Russell Burton. Cryogenics. b'02. BS '26—MS '28 (U Ky). Research on low temperature calorimetry, properties of hydrogen and deuterium, superconductivity, thermometry, thermodynamic properties of some hydrocarbons at low temperatures. Author articles in field. Physicist Nat Bur Standards since '28, chief cryogenics sect '47-52; chief NBS-AEC cryogenic engring lab since '52. AAAS—Am Phys Soc—Phi Beta Kappa. National Bureau of Standards, Boulder, Colo.

21 SCOTT, Thomas George. Zoology; Wildlife management; Mammalogy (Iowa). b'12. BS '35—MS '37—PhD '42 (Ia State Coll). Research primarily on upland game birds and mammals. Author articles in field. Asst to state entomologist '35; extension specialist in wildlife conservation Ia State Coll '35-37, instr '38; biologist US Fish and Wildlife Service '38-48; Illinois Nat Hist Survey since '50. Sigma Xi—Gamma Sigma Delta—Soc Mammalogists—Soc Wildlife Mgrs—Ecolog Soc Am—Am Ornithologists Union—Wilson Ornitholog Club—Ia Ornithologists Union—Ia Acad Sci. Section of Game Research and Management, Ill. Nat. Hist. Survey, Urbana, Ill. H: Rt. 3, Urbana.

22 SCOTT, W(alter) Clifford. Citrus products processing; Chemical preservation of fruit pulps. b'07. BA '30 (Tex Tech Coll); MA '31 (Simmons U); '32 (U Colo). Author articles in field. Chemist fruit and vegetable products investigations since '32; charge US Fruit and Vegetable Products Lab '41-52. Inst Food Technologists—Am Chem Soc—Am Soc Hort Sci. U.S. Citrus Products Station, Winter Haven, Fla.

23 SCOTT, Walter Edwin. Wildlife management; Passenger pigeon. b'11. BA '33 (Kalamazoo Coll). Co-author: (with N R Barger, E E Bussewitz, E L Loyster, and S Robbins) Wisconsin Birds—A Checklist with Migration Charts. Editor: Silent Wings—A Memorial to the Passenger Pigeon '37; also articles in field. Supervisor cooperative game management Wis Conservation Dept in charge surveys, land management, game census statistics since '46, ed Information and Edn Div since '48, administrative asst to dir since '50. Wis Soc for Ornithology—Wildlife Soc—Am Soc Mammalog—Am Ornitholog Union—Wis Acad Scis Arts and Letters—Wilson Ornithol Club. Wisconsin Conservation Department, State Office Bldg., Madison 2, Wis.

10 SCOTT, Walter Moody. Textiles (Coloring, cotton). b'92. PhB '12—PhD '15 (Yale). Research on dyeing, bleaching, finishing silk, wool, cotton, rayon; studies in color standards and methods for specifying color; research to improve and increase utilization cotton and other agricultural products. Author articles: Fastness requirements of dyestuffs by the silk industry; Shein dyeing of viscose rayon; Color science applied to textiles; Chemistry aids cottons; The importance of chemical finishing in increasing the consumption of cotton textiles; Fundamental and applied researches reveal new horizons for cotton and cottonseed; and many others. Contributor: Textile Research, A Survey of Progress '32; Annual Survey of American Chemistry '36. Chief chem Cheney Bros '15-26; tech adv Nat Aniline and Chem Co '27-28; service dir Munsell Color Co '28-30; Service dir Gustavus J Esselen Inc '30-39; chief div USDA '39-42, dir lab '46-50, asst chief bur since '50. Inter-Soc Color Council—ASTM—Am Assn Textile Chems and Colorists—ACS—Am Inst Chems—Alpha Chi Sigma—Textile Research Inst—Textile Inst (Eng)—AAAS—So Assn Sci and Industry. Agricultural Research Administration, Bureau of Agricultural and Industrial Chemistry, U.S. Department of Agriculture, Washington 25.

11 SCOUTEN, Clifford Ellsworth. Electronics. b'96. PdB '15 (Mansfield Teacher's Coll); BA '25—MA '26 (St Lawrence U); PhD '28 (Potomac U); Student (U Toronto). Co-author: (with Hector, Lein) Electronic Physics '44; Physics for the Arts and Sciences '48. Physics instr U Buffalo '40-45, AUS Signal Corps '44-47. AAAS—Am Assn Physics Teachers. 133 Highland Blvd., Kenmore 17, N.Y.

12 SCOVILLE, Orlin James. Family-type farms (Economics); Soil Conservation (Economics). b'11. BS '31—MS '33 (Colo State Coll); '34-35 (U Wis); PhD '48 (Harvard). Development work on principles of economics soil conservation for corn belt farms; study economic problems wheat production Great Plains area; research on efficiency family-farms and ability to compete with large-scale units. Co-author: Managing a Farm '46. Author article: Measuring the Family Farm '47. Agrl econ USDA since '39. Am Farm Econ Assn—Western Farm Econ Assn—Soil Conservation Soc Am. Waters Hall, Kansas State College, Manhattan, Kan.†

13 SCOVILLE, Warren Candler. History of glassmaking. b'13. AB '34 (Duke U); PhD '40 (U Chicago). Research in France on capitalistic development of French glassmaking 1640-1789 '36-37, in US on technological and entrepreneurial development of American glassmaking 1607-1920 '42-45; research in France on economic consequences on French industrial development of the persecution and emigration of French Huguenots following Revocation of Edict of Nantes (1685) '48-49. Author: Revolution in Glassmaking: Entrepreneurship and Technological Change in the American Industry 1880-1920 '48; Capitalism and

French Glassmaking, 1640-1789 '49; also articles in field. Instr U Tex '37-41; asst prof MIT '42-44; instr U Calif Los Angeles '41-42, asst prof '44-47, asso prof '47-52, prof since '52. Econ Hist Assn. Fellowship Com. on Rsrch in Econ Hist by Soc Sci Research Council '42-44; Guggenheim fellowship '48-49. University of Los Angeles, LA 24.†

14 SCRANTON, Robert Lorentz. Greek architecture; Ancient Greek fortifications. b'12. AB '32 (Mount Union Coll); AM '34—PhD '39 (U Chicago); fellow '34-38, '46-47 (Am Sch Classical Studies Athens). Member managing committee American School of Classical Studies at Athens. Author: Greek Walls '41; also articles in field. Asso prof Greek Emory U since '47. Archeol Inst Am—Classical Assn of Middle West and South—Am Acad in Rome (adv council). Emory University, Emory University, Ga.

15 SCRIBNER, Bourdon Francis. Tin (Spectrographic analysis); Spectrochemical analysis. b'10. BS '33 (George Washington U); '37-42—MS '39 (U Md). Research on spark spectrographic analysis of commercial tin, carrier-distillation method for spectrographic analysis, application of this method to analysis of uranium-base materials, purification of gallium by fractional crystallization, arc and spark spectra of ytterbium, other studies on structure of spectra. Author: Index to the Literature on Spectrochemical Analysis (part II) '47; also articles in field. With Nat Bur Standards since '27, chief spectrochem sect since '47. Optical Soc Am—Am Chem Soc—AAAS—Am Soc Testing Materials (chmn com E-2 on emission spectroscopy). National Bureau of Standards, Washington 25. H: 4801 Connecticut Av., Washington 8.

16 SCRIBNER, Bourdon W(alter). Paper technology (Preservation). b'84. BS '08 (Pa State Coll). Directed materials testing, control testing, testing of finished products and research in pulp and paper making '09-23; research on various phases of papermaking, improvement of offset printing, preservation of records, standardization of paper and paper testing methods and development of paper testing procedures and instruments. Author articles in field. Lab W Va Pulp and Paper Co Piedmont W Va '09-23; chief paper sect Nat Bur Standards since '23. Tech Assn Pulp and Paper Ind (several standardizing coms)—ACS. Received Pulp and Paper Ind Assn Gold Medal '45. National Bureau of Standards, Connecticut Av. and Van Ness St., Washington 25.†

17 SCRIBNER, Leonard. Corrosion resistance; Heat transfer. b'09. BA '32—MA '33 (Albion Coll); PhD '36 (U Ill). Research on rare earths, wet and dry chlorine vs materials of chemical plant construction, and sodium chloride. Author articles in field. Chief engr tantalum Fansteel Metallurg Corp. Am Inst Chem Engrs—Am Chem Soc. Fansteel Metallurgical Corporation, North Chicago, Ill. H: 415 Prospect Av., Lake Bluff, Ill.†

18 SCROGGIE, Everett. Highway bridges; Railroad bridges. b'03. CE '26 (U SC); MCE '27 (Rensselaer Poly Inst). Research live load rating for capacity of existing bridges, location studies for new bridges, economic studies to determine whether or not existing bridges should be raised or replaced, plans for raising existing bridges, plans and specifications. Bridge designer SC State Highway Dept '23-28; asst engr bridge dept S Ry Co '28-32; bridge designer NC State

Highway and Pub Works Commn '32-33; dir bridge work TVA since '33. Phi Beta Kappa—Am Soc CE—Am Railway Engrs Assn—Tech Soc Knoxville. Tennessee Valley Authority, Knoxville, Tenn.

19 SCULLY, Francis Joseph. Knights Templar (History). b'91. AB '12 (U Wis); MD '15 (Rush Med Coll). Author: History of Knights Templar of Arkansas '47; History of Grand Encampment, Knights Templar of United States (in press). Grand Comdr Grand Commandery Knights Templar of Ark '37; historian since '46; chmn com on Templar History Grand Encampment Knights Templar USA since '47; grand high priest Royal Arch Chpt Ark '51; Grand sr deacon Grand Lodge Ark '51. Ark Research Lodge—Mo Research Lodge—Am Research Lodge—NC Research Lodge—Quatuor Coronati Lodge Eng—Leicester Research Lodge Eng. Received Key Award to Masonic Writers '50. 904 Medical Arts Bldg., Hot Springs, Ark.

20 SCULLY, Robert M. Orchids; Tropical foliage plants. b'13. BS '35 (O State U). Staged Miami International Orchid Show '45-49; importer and grower of many exotic and rare foliage plants and orchid plants. Author articles in field. Supt Exotic Gardens Inc Miami Fla '37-42; partner firm Jones and Scully Inc Miami since '45. South Fla Orchid Soc (vp '48, dir '47, pres '49). 2154 N.W. 33rd Av., Miami 35, Fla.

21 SEABORG, Glenn Theodore. Nuclear chemistry and physics; Transuranium elements. b'12. AB '34—PhD '37 (U Calif). Research in artificial radioactivity and compiled data in field; co-discovered element 94 (plutonium), nuclear energy source isotope Pu-239, element 95 (americium), 96 (curium) element 97 (berkelium), and element 98 (californium; member general advisory committee Atomic Energy Commission '46-50. Author articles in field. Prof chem Calif Univ since '45. Am Phys Soc(F)—Am Chem Soc—AAAS—Phi Beta Kappa—Sigma Xi—Nat Acad Scis. Award in Pure Chem, Am Chem Soc '47; William H Nichols Medal '48; John Ericsson Gold Medal, Am Soc Swedish Engrs '48; (with E. M. McMillan) Nobel Prize Chemistry 1951; John Scott Award, Phila., 1953. University of California, Berkeley.

22 SEAGERS, Paul W(illiam). School buildings (Functional, design, illumination, ventilation, sanitation). b'03. AB '27 (Cornell); AM '32—EdD '50 (Teachers Coll Columbia). Germicidal (ultraviolet irradiation) lighting, use germicidal aerosols; electric eye control light, light indicator system. Author articles in field. Pilot study ventilation schs State NY '44, heating, ventilating commn '44, illuminating commn '45, IES com on visual probs '49; sch bldg cons, prof edn Ind U since '47. NEA—Am Assn Sch Adminstrs—Nat Council School House Constrn. School of Education, Indiana University, Bloomington, Ind.

23 SEAGREN, George William. Protection of metals from corrosion. b'06. BS '32 (Pa State Coll); grad study '37-42 (U Pittsburgh). Research on corrosion and protection metals, organic coatings for protection and decoration of metals. Author articles in field. Research asst Bell Telephone Labs '24-29; research metall Radio Corp Am '32-37; fellow, sr fellow, adminstrv fellow Mellon Inst Indsl Research since '37. Am Chem Soc—Nat Assn Corrosion Engrs. Mellon Institute of Industrial Research, Pitts. 13.⊚

10 SEALEY, William Curtis. Transformer design b'01. BS '22 (Carnegie Inst Tech). Development work on betatron and synchrotron magnets, transformer load ratio control equipment and the electrical and mechanical design of power transformers and regulators. Several patents relating to transformer construction. Author: Transformers—Theory and Construction '48; also articles in field. Engr charge transformer design Allis Chalmers Mfg Co '31-52 chief engr transformer section since '52. AIEE(F)—Milwaukee Engrs Soc. Allis Chalmers Manufacturing Company, Milwaukee 1. H: 952 Currie Pl., Wauwatosa 13, Wis.†

11 SEARS, Robert Richardson. Motivation. b'08. AB '29 (Stanford); PhD '32 (Yale). Research in personality development in early childhood, frustration, aggression, projective doll play. Author: Survey of Objective Studies of Psychoanalytic Concepts '39. Co-author: Frustration and Aggression '39; also author articles in field. Instr psychol U Ill '32-35, asso '35-36; asst prof psychol and research asst Inst Human Relations Yale '36-42, asso prof '42; research prof child psychol and dir Ia Child Welfare Research Sta State U Ia '42-49; prof Edn and child psychol Harvard U '49-53; prof exec head psychology Stanford University since '53. American Psychol Association (F, bd dirs '45-49)—Society Research Child Development(F)—Am Orthopsychiatric Assn—Nat Assn Nursery Edn—Social Sci Research Council —Nat Research Council (chmn com on child development since '48). Stanford University, Cal.

12 SEATON, Stuart Luman. Arctic (Radio transmission); Ionosphere. b'06. Student '32-34, '38-39 (U Md); '39-41, '46-47 (George Washington U); BS '42—D Sc '49 (U Alaska). Research on ionospheric regions including temperature distribution in high atmosphere, wind systems, composition, collisional friction, distribution of magnetic fields induced by current systems, reasons for apparently reversed variations in electron concentration in high latitudes; electromagnetic wave propagation in Arctic regions in visible and radio frequency spectral ranges, causes of communications failure in polar regions of radio systems, nature of radiowave propagation through arctic ionosphere in auroral region, cause of deviation of radiowave propagation from great circle course in arctic over long distances. Co-author: Observations and Results in Physical Oceanography '45; Ionospheric Research and Auroral Research at College, Alaska '47; Compendium of Meteorology '52. Staff phys Carnegie Instn Wash '29-46; sci adv to chief atmospherics lab Watson Lab Dept Air Force '46-48; dir geophys inst U Alaska '48-50; tech dir staff Nav Ordnance Lab since '50. NY Acad Sci(F)—Inst Radio Engrs (sr mem)—AAAS—APS—Am Geophys Union—Am Meteorol Soc -Inst Phys (Eng). Naval Ordnance Laboratory, Silver Spring, Md. H: Washington Grove, Md.

13 SEBEOK, Thomas A(lbert). Uralic and general linguistics; Uralic (Finno-Ugric) linguistics. b'20. BA '41 (U Chicago); MA '43—PhD '45 (Princeton U). Author: Spoken Hungarian '45; Finnish and Hungarian Case Systems: Their Form and Function '46; Spoken Finnish '49; studies in Cheremis Folklore, Vol. 1, '52. Editor Jour Am Folklore since '54. Asst prof Ind U '43-52, asso prof since '52. Cons lang sect Army Serv Forces World War II. Am Anthropol Assn(F)—Finno-Ugric Soc—Société de Linguistique de Paris —Linguistic Soc Am—Cercle Linguistique de Copenhague—Sigma Xi. Am Council Learned Socs fellow '43, Am Scandinavian Found fellow '47, Viking Fund fellow '48. Indiana University, Bloomington, Ind.†

14 SECKLER-HUDSON, Catheryn. American political science and public administration; Public budgeting; Statelessness. b'02. BS '26 (Northeast Mo State Teachers Coll); MA '29—Gregory fellowship polit sci '28-29 (U Mo); PhD '33—Carnegie fellowship internat law '31-33 (Am U). Author: Statelessness: With Special Reference to the United States '34; Our Constitution and Government '40; Budgetary and Governmental Theory as Reflected in Presidential Budget Messages '45; Bibliography on Public Administration '46. Co-author: Our National Government '36. Editor: Budgeting, An Instrument of Planning and Management, 6 vols '44-46; Papers on Organizations and Management '46; Processes of Organization and Management '48; also author articles in field. Chmn depts pub adminstrn and polit sci Am U since '41. NEA—Am Polit Sci Assn —Am Soc Pub Adminstrn—Am Soc Internat Law—Am Acad Polit and Social Sci—Fgn Policy Assn—Soc for Advancement Management—Kappa Delta Pi. Hyattsville Hills, Md.†⊚

15 SECORD, Arthur E. Educational administration. b'04. AB '27 (Western Mich Coll Edn Kalamzoo); MA '31—PhD '41 (U Mich). Organization and supervision adult education programs. Dir debate and mgr Mich High Sch Forensic Assn U Mich '33-43; dir speech clinic U Mo '43-44; supervisor adult edn Brooklyn Coll NYC since '46. Adult Edn Assn USA—Speech Assn Am. Brooklyn College, Bklyn 10.†

16 SEDGWICK, Harry Abbey. Die blocks; plastic molding presses. b'74. Ed pub schs. Research and design of multiple cylinder hydraulic presses for molding plastics, granted patent for hydro-mechanical presses for automatic molding of plastics; granted patent on form of die blocks consisting of high carbon steel rivit welded to bkng blocks of lesser carbon content; designer and builder unusual five cylinder, high pressure, high speed steam motor for direct connection to generators. Asst supt, gen supt and mgr operations Cutler Hammer Inc '13-43. Am Soc Tool Engrs—ASME. Granted award by James F Lincoln Welding Found for paper on functional machinery, jigs and fixtures '38. H: RFD 1, Nashotah, Wis.

17 SEDGWICK, Paul J(oseph). Microtechnique; Photography (Time lapse); Photomicrography. b'96. SB '18—PhD '22—fellow '19-22 (U Chicago). Author articles in field. Syracuse U since '22, now prof bot in plant scis dept, curator for bot Mus of Nat Sci, chmn visual edn. Bot Soc Am—AAAS—Biol Photographic Assn—Photographers Assn Am—Sigma Xi. Plant Sciences Department, Syracuse University, Syracuse, 10, N.Y.⊚

18 SEE, Walter George. Combustion engineering; Pickling steel; Fume control. b'09. Student comml engring (Carnegie Inst Tech). Developed methods of control for submerged combustion equipment for heating, agitating and/or evaporating corrosive solutions; development and perfection new methods of removing corrosive fumes from tank surfaces; development acid meter, pump, processes using submerged combustion equipment; patents on submerged combustion systems, submerged combustion control systems, igniter device, apparatus and method for concentrating acids, acid meter, acid resistant fume duct material. Author articles in field. Indsl engr La-Salle Steel Co Hammond Ind '34-37; cons engr industry Theo S See and Asso Hammond since '37; sales and service mgr Submerged Combustion Co Hammond '37-43, chief engr '43-46, vp '47, pres since '48. Wire Assn—Assn Iron and Steel Engrs—Am Gas Assn. Box No 267, Hammond, Ind.†

19 SEEGER, Charles Louis. Folk music; Musicology; Inter-American affairs. b'86. AB '08 (Harvard). Co-author: (with E G Stricklen) Harmonic Structure and Elementary Composition '16; (with J A and A Lomax) Folk Song USA; (With D Emrich and R C Seeger) American Ballad Book; also author articles in field. Chief music div Pan-Am Union Washington DC since '41. Am Musicol Soc (pres '45-46) —Internat Musicological Soc—Internat Soc for Gen Semantics—Am Folklore Soc—Music Library Assn—Music Educators Nat Conf—Music Teachers Nat Assn. Pan American Union, Washington 6. 7 West Kirke St., Chevy Chase 15, Md.†⊚

20 SEELE, Keith Cedric. Ancient Egyptian language and hieroglyphics; Relief sculptures, history and archeology. b'98. BA '22—LHD (hon) '47 (Coll of Wooster, O); BD '26 (McCormick Theol Sem, Chicago); '26-28, '30 (U Berlin); PhD '38 (U Chicago). Conducted studies in language, relief sculptures, history, and archeology of ancient Egypt, eighteenth to twentieth dynasties, study of erased reliefs and inscriptions on walls of great Hypostyle Hall at Karnak. Editor: Jour of Near Eastern Studies; author articles in field. Teacher Assiut Coll Egypt '22-23; two year traveling fellowship U Berlin '26-28; European travel '23-48, Palestine and Syria '32, Egypt '48; epigrapher in Egyptian hierglyphic lang Oriental Inst U Chicago at temples of Medinet Habu and Karnak, Luxor, Egypt '29-36; inst, asst prof, prof Egyptology, Oriental Inst U Chicago since '36. Egyptian Exploration Soc London—La Societe Francaise d'Egyptologie Paris—La Foundation Égyptologique Reine Élisabeth Brussels — Internat Assn Egyptologists Copenhagen—Am Oriental Soc—AHA. The Oriental Institute, University of Chicago, Chicago 37. H: R D 2, Lake Dalecarlia, Lowell, Ind.

21 SEELIG, Richard Paul. Powder metallurgy; Heat treatment. b'13. Grad M '36 (Inst Tech, Berlin); (Pratt Inst, NYU). Research powder processing, testing, rolling, wire drawing, hot pressing, pilot production of powder metal products; developed new techniques for molding complicated parts, ductile sintered bronze alloys, production of highly stressed components. Invented new pressing method and designed press. Author articles in field. Assistant to president Am Electro Metal Corp Yonkers NY since '46. Am Inst Mining and Metall Engrs—Am Soc for Metals—Am Soc for Testing Materials—Metals Sci Club. 320 Yonkers Av., Yonkers, N.Y. H: 24 Poe St., Hartsdale, N.Y.

22 SEEVERS, Charles Hamilton. Termitophilous insects. b'07. AB '28 (Washburn Coll); PhD '32 (U Chicago). Research and writing on termitophilous insects. Prof zool Central YMCA Coll Chicago '34-45; prof biol and chmn dept Roosevelt Coll since '45; research asso div insects Chicago Natural Hist Mus since '40. Am Soc Zool—Evolution Soc—Entomol Soc Am. Roosevelt College, 430 S. Michigan Av., Chgo. 5.

23 SEGAL, Leon. Cellulose (Chemistry); Instrumentation (Electronics).

b'18. BS '40 (Miss State Coll); MS '42 (La State U); '46 (Tulane U). Research on utilization of cellulose derivatives (plastics), textile testing, construction of apparatus to be used in cotton tire-cord studies, application of chemical treatments to reduce crystallinity of cotton cellulose, improvement of elastic behavior of cotton as textile material, utilization of X-ray diffraction. Granted patent on reduction of crystallinity of native fibrous cellulosic material. Research chem S Regional Research Lab '42-43, since '45. ACS—Sigma Xi—Phi Lambda Upsilon—Kappa Mu Epsilon—Phi Eta Sigma. Southern Regional Research Lab, 2100 Robert E. Lee Blvd., New Orleans.

10 SEGEL, David. Adolescent psychology; Educational measurement. b'94. BA '17 (U Calif); AM '22 (Teachers College Columbia); PhD '31 (Stanford). Developed method differential prediction, analysis Army intelligence test results. Author: Differential Diagnosis of Ability in School Children '34; Intellectual Abilities in the Adolescent Period; Frustration in Adolescent Youth; The Multiple Aptitude Tests. Ednl cons, specialist in tests measurements Office Edn Fed Sec Agy Washington since '31; personnel analyst Civ Personnel Div Sec of War's Office Washington '44; cons to War Dept Ger '47, AAF Randolph Field Texas '51. Am Ednl Research Assn—Am Psychol Assn—Phi Delta Kappa. Diplomate counseling and guidance National Bd Examiners Psychology. US Office of Education, Washington.ⓒ

11 SEGRÈ, Emilio. Atomic physics; Nuclear physics; Nucleonics. b'05. PhD '28 (U Rome). Engaged spectroscopic work atomic spectra especially forbidden lines '28-34; with E Fermi and others discovered slow neutrons, artificial radio-activity by neutron bombardment '34; with C Perrier discovered element 43 (technetium) '37, with D Corson and McKenzie element 85 (astatine) '40; participated discovery element 94 (plutonium) '41; author articles in field. Asst prof physics U Rome '28-35; prof physics U Palermo Sicily '36-38; research asso, lecturer, radiation lab and physics dept U Calif '39-43, Los Alamos lab '43-46, prof physics since '46. Am Phys Soc. Rockefeller Found fellow '30-32. Physics Department, University of California, Berkeley. H: 1617 Spruce St.

12 SEIBEL, Clifford Winslow. Helium (Production, natural gas, uses); Low temperature refrigeration. b'90. BS '13—MS '15 (U Kan); ScD '37 (Texas Tech). Regional dir Region IV Bureau of Mines Department of Interior; supervised design, construction and operation of four helium production plants for World War II; designed helium plants for Army and Navy; in charge all helium field work Bureau of Mines. Instr chem U Kan '13-17; chemist Bureau of Mines since '17. Am Chem Soc—Sigma Xi. Bureau of Mines Helium Plant, Amarillo, Tex. H: 1520 Lamar.

13 SEIBERT, Russell Howard. Conscientious objectors. b'08. AB '30 (Coll of Wooster O); MA '31 (U Chicago); PhD '36 (Ohio State U). Research in treatment of conscientious objectors during the American Revolution, Civil War, and World War I Author: The Treatment of Conscientious Objectors in War Time 1775-1920, Ohio State U Press '37; Conscientious Objectors and Virginia Exiles in Dictionary of American History '40; Conscientious Objectors in England '40. Instr Hanover Coll Ind '32-33; grad asst hist O State U '34-36; prof hist Western Mich Coll

of Edn since '36, officer USNR on active duty '43-46. AHA—Phi Beta Kappa—Phi Alpha Theta Western Michigan College, Kalamazoo 45, Mich. H: 435 Park Pl.

14 SEIBERT, Russell J(acob). Taxonomy; Morphology (Bignoniaceae); Genetics of Hevea. b'14. AB '37—MS '38—PhD '47 (Washington U); '38-39 (Harvard). Research on taxonomy and morphology of hevea, improvement of hevea for use in plantation rubber industry in Lat Am. Author articles in field. Bot div rubber plant investigations Bur Plant Industry US Dept Agr '40-48, geneticist '48-50; dir Los Angeles State and County Arboretum since '50. Am Soc Plant Taxonomists—Soc Study Evolution Am Geog Soc. Los Angeles State and County Arboretum, Arcadia, Cal.

15 SEIDEMANN, Henry Peter. Federal and state government administration and finance. b'83. BCS '23—MCS '25 (Dist of Columbia Coll); LLD '38 (Southeastern U). Author: Manual of Accounting and Reporting for the Operating Services of the National Government '26; Manual of Accounting, Reporting and Business Procedure for the Territorial Government of Hawaii '28; Curtailment of Non-Defense Expenditures '41. Financial admin chapters of Brookings Instn's surveys of the state and local govt of Ala Ia NH NC Okla; chief of staff financial and accounting research Inst for Govt Research Brookings Instn '27-48. DC Inst CPA(F)—Am Inst Accountants—Polit Sci Assn—Am Acad of Polit and Soc Sci—Soc for Public Adminstrn—Governmental Research Assn. 2853 Ontario Road, Washington 9.†

16 SEIDEN, Rudolph. Disinfectants; Insecticides; Pharmaceuticals; Veterinary products. b'00. Chem E '28 (Vienna Tech Coll). Abstractor in chg Chemical Abstracts since '37; dept ed The Chemist. Author: The Chemical Industry and its Possibilities on the Dead Sea '24; Comparing Examinations of the Influence of Various Outside Factors Especially on the Ash-Content of Plants '25; Chemical Products—A Technology of Inorganic and Organic Materials '28; King Caoutchouc '30; Poultry Handbook '47; 2d edit '52; Livestock Health Encyclopedia '51; 2d printing '52. ACS—AIC. H: 700 E. 63d Terrace, KC 10, Mo.

17 SEIDENFELD, Morton Alfred. psychology of physically handicapped. b'06. BS '27 (U Wash); MS '33—PhD '37 (U Pa). Research on psychological aspects medical care of chronically ill, including tuberculous, war injured, poliomyelitic. Author: psychological Aspects of Medical Care '49; also articles in field. Dir psychol services and rehabilitation Tuberculosis Inst Chicago and Cook County '40; dir psychol services Nat Found Infantile Paralysis since '45; asso dir Yeshiva U Psychol Clin, dir Clinical Psychol student trng Grad Sch since '47. Am Psychol Assn (F)—Am Assn Applied Psychol(F)—AAAS(F)—NY Acad Sci(F)—Am Pub Health Assn(F)—NY State Psychol Assn—Rorschach Inst—Nat Com Mental Hygiene—E Psychol Assn—Am Soc Research in Psychomsomatic Problems. National Foundation for Infantile Paralysis, 120 Broadway, NYC 5.

18 SEIDLIN, Oskar. German Department, Ohio State University, Columbus, O.

19 SEIFERT, Howard Stanley. Jet propulsion. BS '32—MS '34 (Carnegie Tech); PhD '38 (Calif Inst Tech). Liquid propellant rocket propulsion motors; instrumentation and guidance of missiles. Auth articles in field. Asst

prof physics Kalamazoo Coll '37-40; research physicist Westinghouse Labs Pittsburgh '40-42; chief applied physics div Jet Propulsion Lab Calif Inst Tech '43-50, instr rocket systems '45-48. Asso editor Jour Am Rocket Soc since '51. Am Phys Soc—Am Assn Physics Teacher—Sigma Xi. Calif. Inst of Technology, Pasadena, Calif. H: 382 S. Grand Oaks Av., Pasadena 10.

20 SEIFTER, Joseph. Pharmacology. b'04. Student '26-31 (O State U); MD '34 (Emory U). Studies pharmacology of heavy metals and metallo-organic compounds, of hyaluronidase and related enzymes, of heparin and related anticoagulants, of steroids, synthetic medicinals, and industrial toxicology. Instr advancing to asst prof pharm sch med Western Reserve U Cleveland '37-44; chief pharm Wyeth Inst Applied Biochem Phila '44-47, dir since '47. Am Soc Pharm and Exptl Therapeutics—NY Acad Sci—ACS—AAAS—Sigma Xi—Soc Exptl Biol and Med. 900 N. Broad St., Phila. 30.

21 SEIGLER, Milledge Broadus. Milton; American literature. b'09. AB '30 (Furmon U); AM '36—PhD '41 (Duke U)—fellow English '35-37. Author articles in field. Instr Eng Winthrop Coll '37-38; asst Eng Duke U '38-39; asst prof Eng Catawba Coll '39-42; adjunct prof Eng U SC '46, asso prof '46-49, prof since '49. Modern Lang Assn Am—South Atlantic Modern Lang Assn—Nat Council of Teachers of Eng—Coll Eng Assn—South Caroliniona Soc—Southeastern Renaissance Soc. University of South Carolina, Columbia, S.C.

22 SELDNER, Abraham. Perfumes; flavorings. b'20. AB '40 (Columbia). Development approximately 150 fine organic chemicals new to the perfume and flavor industries; research development production staple and new fine organic chemicals for perfume flavor and pharmaceutical fields. Dir research F Ritter and Co since '46: chem cons Calif State Drug and Oil Plant Project since '47. ACS—Inst Food Tech—AAAS—Phi Beta Kappa—Am Technion Soc. 4001 Goodwin Av., Los Angeles 39. H: 2712 Marsh St., Los Angeles 39.†

23 SELL, Harold Melvin. Biological and organic chemistry. b'05. AB '29 (N Central Coll); MS '31 (Mich State Coll); PhD '38 (U Wis). Research on the synthesis of galacturonic acid and pectin; research on oil synthesis in the tung kernel, chemistry of germination of the tung kernel, chemical changes in the bud prior to blossoming; research on the chemistry of ursolic acid, chlorogenic acid, stabilization of emulsions, growth regulators and antibiotics. Author articles in field. Research prof Mich State Coll since '45. Am Chem Soc—AAAS—Am Soc for Plant Physiology—Am Oil Chemist Soc—Mich Acad Sci—Sigma Xi—Kappa Delta Pi—Phi Lambda Upsilon—Phi Sigma. Department of Agricultural Chemistry, Michigan State College, East Lansing, Mich.

24 SELL, Lewis L. Polyglot technical lexicography (English, Spanish, Portuguese, French, German). b'90. BA '16—MA '17—PhD '18 (Columbia U); '16-17 (U scholar); '17-18 (Drisler fellow). Chosen to represent US at first Pan American Book Exposition Washington '46. Author: English-French Technical Dictionary of the Automobile and Allied Industries '32; Pan American Dictionary and Travel Guide '41; Practical Polyglot Technical Lexicography and the Professional Polyglot Technician '45; Comprehensive English-Spanish Technical Dictionary '44; University and Collegiate Syllabus for Formation of Professional Polyglot Technician '45; Spanish-English Comprehensive Technical Dictionary '48; English - Portuguese Comprehensive Technical Dictionary '49. Operates profl translation bur specializing in catalog translations, mainly from and into Spanish, Portuguese, and French in the field of automobile, aircraft, steel, petroleum equipment, engines, radio, radar, electricity, motion picture equipment. 15 Park Row, NYC 7.

10 SELLEI-BERETVAS, Helen. Rust preventive coatings; Lubricants. b'07. PhD '31 (Budapest U). Research on metal protection, engine preservative oils; research extreme pressure lubricants, lubricating oil additives. Author articles in field. Research chemist Standard Oil Co Ind since '47. Am Chem Soc—Am Soc Lubrication Engrs. Research Department, Standard Oil Company, Whiting, Ind.

11 SELLERS, Ashley. Administrative and agricultural law. b'02. Student '20 (Oglethorpe U); AB '24 (Princeton U); '26-27 (Lamar Sch Law Emory U); LLB '28 (U Tex); SJD '33 (Harvard). Author series of monographs on Administrative Procedure and Practice in the Department of Agriculture '39-40; also articles in field Prof law U Ga '35-38; head atty Office Solicitor US Dept Agr Washington '38-41, asso solicitor '42-43; asst war food administrator Washington '43-45; spl asst to Atty Gen Washington '45; pvt practice law principally in fields of administrative and agrl law Washington since '45. ABA (spl com administrative law '41-43; sect administrative law, chmn com Fed Procedural Rules '47, chmn nat com '48, vice-chmn sect '49, chmn sect '50)—Fed Bar Assn (chmn com administrative law '44)—DC Bar Assn—Ga Bar Assn—Am Judicature Soc. 1302 18th St., Washington 6.

12 SELLERS, (James) Clark. Examination of questioned documents (Handwriting); Scientific identification. b'91. LDS '09 (U Salt Lake City); '26 (U South Calif). Specialist questions involving identity and age paper, ink, pencil writings; authenticity handwriting, typewriting, papers, inks; examined documents FBI, US Secret Service, Internal Revenue Dept, US Post Office, and others; expert outstanding cases such as People of Calif vs William Edward Hickman '28, State NJ vs Bruno Richard Hauptmann '35, William Shakespeare signature problem London '38, Overell Yacht murder Santa Ana Calif '47, and others. Originated and developed methods for proof of fact in court. Author: Handwriting Identification and Expert Testimony '30; Scientific Identification vs Guesswork '36; Spurious Typewritten Documents '34; also articles in field. Office and lab Los Angeles since '24. Internat Assn Identification (vp Calif dist, south dist, mem com sci identification)—Am Soc Questioned Document Examiners (pres '46-48)—Scientific Evidence Inc (chmn sect questioned documents '46)—South Calif Acad Crim (pres '33-40, dir '33-47). 458 S. Spring St., Los Angeles 13. H: 887 El Campo Dr., Pasadena 10, Calif.

13 SELMAN, Roland W., Jr. Baking technology; Cereal chemistry. b'16. BS '38 (U Chattanooga). Studies on Research on chemical and engineering controls in baking, controlling moisture content, amylase activity of flour, flour lipase. Granted patents on new processes in drying brewer's yeast; reducing the mixing time of bread doughs; preserving vitamin C in processing fruits and vegetables; treatment of barley sprouts and others. Author articles in field. Analytical chem Campbell Taggart Research Corp

'38-40, research fellow '40-43; Fellow Mellon Inst '43-45. Dir tech activities C J Patterson Co '45, vp since '45; vp R W Selman and Associates since '50. Am Assn Cereal Chem—Am Chem Soc —Inst Food Technol—Am Soc Bakery Engrs—Midwest Bakers Allied Club— AAAS. 1517 Walnut, KC 8, Mo.

14 SELMER, Carl. Medieval manuscripts and dialects. b'96. PhD '22 (Frieburg). Author: Middle High German Translations of the Regula '33; Middle High German Augustinian Rule '36; The MHG London Rule of the 14th Century '38; also articles in field. Professor Hunter Coll since '52. Modern Lang Assn Am—Medieval Acad Am—Phi Beta Kappa. Grant Carnegie Found and Medieval Acad '33. Hunter College, 695 Park Av., NYC 21.†

15 SELYE, Hans. Steroid hormones. b'07. Student '25-26 (U Paris); '26-27 (U Rome); MD '29—PhD '31 (German U Prague); DSc '42 (McGill U). Research on prevention and treatment of disease; editor Medicus '50, editor Folia Clinica Internacional '50. Author 313 articles in field. Faculty McGill U '32-45, asso histology '37-41; prof and dir Inst Exptl Med and Surgery Montreal U since '45; cons Surgeon Gen US Army since '47. Royal Soc Can (F)—NY Acad Sci(F)—AAAS(F)—Am Assn Anatomists—Am Assn Cancer Research—Am Heart Assn—Am Physiol Soc—Am Soc Clin Investigation—Assn Study Internal Secretions—Can Interim Am Assn—Can Physiol Soc—Can Soc Study Allergy—Nat Soc Med Research —Sigma Xi—various fgn med socs. Awarded Casgrain and Charbonneau prizes McGill U '40, Gordon Wilson Medal '48 from Am Clin and Climatological Assn, Heberden Medal '50, Medal Acad Med Fisica Fiorentina '50. Rockefeller Research F Johns Hopkins U '31 and McGill U '32-33. 2900 Mount-Royal Blvd., Montreal, P.Q., Can.

16 SEMENIUK, George. Plant pathology (Corn, alfalfa cereal treatment, storage). BSc '32—MSc '34 (U Alberta, Can); PhD '38 (Ia State Coll). Prof S. Dak State Coll since '52. Am Phytopath Soc—Ia Acad Sci—Sigma Xi. Botany and Plant Pathology Department, State College Station, S. Dak.

17 SEMMES, Raphael. Maryland and American Colonial history. b'90. AB '12 (Princeton); LLB '16 (Harvard); PhD '27 (Johns Hopkins). Author: Captains and Mariners of Early Maryland '37; Crime and Punishment in Early Maryland '38; also articles in field. Chmn com publications Maryland Hist Soc since '45. 201 West Monument St., Baltimore 1.

18 SENEKER, James Seehorn. Religious education (Curriculum). b'85. AB '10 (U Mo); BD '12 (Vanderbilt U); AM '19 (Columbia); profl diploma '20 (Teachers College, Columbia U); grad student (U Chicago). Research in effective methods in teaching religion Contributor: Behaviorism '30; Studies in Religious Education '31; The Quest for God Through Understanding '37. Asst prin Union Sch Religion NYC '18-19; dir edn div fgn survey dept Interchurch World Movement '19-20; vis prof Sch Theol So Methodist U summer '21, prof religious edn and head dept since '21. AAUP—AAAS—Pi Gamma Mu—NEA—Religious Edn Assn. Perkins Quadrangle, Southern Methodist University, Dallas 5. H: 3421 Haynie Av., University Park, Dallas 5.

19 SENKUS, Murray. Nitro amines and polyamines; Nitro and amino acetals. b'14. BS '34—MS '36 (U Saskatchewan); PhD '38 (U Chicago). Research on Raman spectra of some hydrocar-

bons with C-D linkages, oxygen exchange reactions, and on reaction of amines with formaldyhyde and nitro-paraffins which established potentialities of the reaction and led to discovery of 5-nitrohexahydropyrimidines, 5-aminohex-ylpyrimidines, and 5-nitrotetrahydro-1, 3-oxazines; developed methods for isolation of 2, 3-butanediol from broth, and for iron reduction of aliphatic nitro compounds. Discovered and proved structure of 1-Aza-3, 7-dioxabicyclo (3.3.0) octanes. Author articles in field. Research chem Comml Solvents Corp since '38. AAAS —Am Chem Soc—Sigma Xi. Research Department, Commercial Solvents Corp., Terre Haute, Ind.

20 SENNING, John Peter. Political science (Unicameralism, legislative process, public administration). b'84. AB '08 (Westmar Coll Lemars Ia); PhD '24 (U Ill). Author: The One-House Legislature '37; also articles in field. Instr polit sci U Neb since '17, chmn dept '20-23, '29-39; research asst spl House and Senate coms to determine size of Neb unicameral legislature and district state accordingly, cons on organization and procedure since '37. Am Polit Sci Assn—Am Soc Public Administrn—Nat Municipal League—Civil Service Assembly US, Can—Nat Inst Govt Research—Am Arbitration Assn. University of Nebraska, Lincoln, Neb.

21 SENSABAUGH, Leonidas Franklin. Latin-American history; Brazilian diplomatic relations. b'03. AB '25 (Vanderbilt U); PhD '28 (Johns Hopkins); grant study Latin-Am Inst '39 (U Mich). Author articles in field. Prof hist Birmingham-So Coll since '43. So Hist Assn—Ala Hist Assn—Phi Beta Kappa. Rosenwald fellow for study in Brazil '41-42; Carnegie grant for research in field of US-Brazilian relations '48. Birmingham - Southern College, Birmingham 4, Ala.†

22 SERR, Eugene Frank. Deciduous fruit nut culture; Zinc deficiency; Walnut varieties; Mechanical pruning and harvest equipment. b'98. BS '22 (U Calif). Specialized on deciduous fruits and nuts, nut cultural problems especially walnuts and almonds. Co-author: Walnut Production in California; also articles in field. Agrl ext service U Calif '22-48, asso pomol Ext Sta since '48. Am Soc Hort Sci—AAAS. Horticulture Building, University of California, Davis, Calif.†

23 SERVAIS, Philip Carl. Silicone rubber. b'16. BS '39—MS '40 (U Wis). Author articles: The Heat Stable Silicone Rubber '46; Determination of Silicon in Organosilicon Compounds '48. Research chemist Dow Chem Co '40-45; mgr Silastic Lab Dow Corning Corp since '45. Am Chem Soc. Add: Dow Corning Corporation, Midland, Mich.†

24 SERVER, Alberta Wilson. Spanish American language and literature. b'97. AB—MA (U Ky); doctorat de l'Université (Besancon France); diplome d'Etudes Françaises (France); diploma de Suficiencia (Madrid). Author: L'Espagne dans La Revue des Deux Mondes, 1829-1848 '39; also articles in field. Asso prof Romance Langs U Ky since '21. Am Assn Teachers Spanish and Portuguese—So Atlantic Mod Lang Assn—Phi Beta Kappa—Phi Sigma Iota. University of Kentucky, Lexington, Ky.

25 SETTE, Oscar Elton. Productivity of marine fish resources; Biology of marine fishes; Biometrics. b'00. AB '22 (Stanford); MA '31 (Harvard); student (San Diego Jr Coll). Author articles in field. Dir Pacific Oceanic Fishery Investigations since '48; lecturer Stanford U '40-49; lecturer at University of Hawaii '49. AAAS—Am Fisheries Soc—Am Wildlife Soc—Am Soc Ichthyol and Herpetol—Pacific Oceano Soc—Western Soc Naturalists —Biometric Soc. Fish and Wildlife Service, P.O. Box 3830, Honolulu, T.H.

10 SETTY, Laurel Raymond. Hanging-flies (Bittacidae); Biological technique. b'06. BS '29 (Kans State Teachers Coll); AM '30 (U Kans); PhD '39 (Cornell U). Author: Laboratory Problems in General Zoology '44; Laboratory Problems in General Botany '45; also articles in field. Asst prof bact and anat Kansas City Coll Osteop and Surg. Kansas City College of Osteopathy and Surgery, KC, Mo.

11 SEVERAID, Joye Harold. Vertebrate zoology; Wildlife conservation. b'15. BS '38 (Ia State Coll); MS '41 (U Me); MA '49—PhD '54 (U Calif). Life histories mammals, museum taxonomic mammalogy and vertebrate paleontology; appointed abstractor Biol Abstracts '46. Author articles: The Snowshoe Hare, Its Life History and Artificial Propagation '42; Pelage Changes in the Snowshoe Hare '45; Breeding Potential and Artificial Propagation of the Snowshoe Hare '45. Tech research asst Me Coop Wildlife Res Unit '40-41; fresh water biol Me Dept Inland Fisheries and Game '41; museum tech, teaching asst zool U Calif since '46. Am Soc Mammalogists —Am Wildlife Soc—Am Ornithol Union—Cooper Ornithol Club—West Soc Naturalists—Am Forestry Assn—Nat Geog Soc—Sigma Xi. Dept. of Life Sciences, Sacramento State College, Sacramento, Cal.

12 SEVERS, J(onathan) Burke. Chaucer; Medieval drama; Textual criticism. b'03. AB '25—Free State scholar '21-25—Theodore Vail prize for scholar '25 (Rutgers U); AM '27 (Princeton); PhD '35—U fellow '30-31 —Donald Grant Mitchell fellow '34-35 (Yale). Author: The Literary Relationships of Chaucer's Clerkes Tale '42. Co-author: The Sources and Analogues of Chaucer's Canterbury Tales '41; English Institute Annual 1941 '42; also articles in field. Prof Eng Lehigh U since '41. Mod Lang Assn Am (cons in Chaucer to editorial com since '36, nominating com of Chaucer group '44-47; bibliog and research com of Chaucer Group '37-42, sec Chaucer Group '40-41, chmn '42, chmn com for editing Chaucer Library since '46, sec Eng sect I '44, chmn '45)—Medieval Acad Am— Nat Council Teachers Eng—Coll Eng Assn—Phi Beta Kappa. Awarded the Haskins Medal for '46 from the Medieval Acad Am. Department of English, Lehigh University, Bethlehem, Pa.

13 SEVERSON, Lloyd J. Mineral resources of Spain, Bolivia, Mexico, and South America. b'14. Student '31-32 (Winona State Teachers Coll Minn); BS '36 (U Wis). Sur tin and tungsten resources of Spain and Bolivia; examination iron ore deposits of Mexico and Central America. Author article: Mineral Resources of Spain '45. Asst chief engr Patino Mines Bolivia '36-39; chief engr Cia Haanchaca de Bolivia '39-41; prin mining engr Fgn Econ Adminstrn Bolivia '42-43, Spain '44; with Oliver Iron Mining Co Duluth since '44, now gen mining engr. AIM-ME—Soc Econ Geol. 610 Wolvin Bldg., Duluth 2, Minn. H: 2233 Vermilion Rd., Duluth 3.

14 SEWELL, William Hamilton. Rural sociology (Quantitative research methods); Social Psychology; Family. b'09. BA '33—MA '34 (Mich State Coll); PhD '39 (U Minn). Development of research techniques study rural levels of living, socioeconomic status, and

personality. Author articles: A Short Form of the Farm Family Socioeconomic Status Scale '43; Differential Fertility in Completed Oklahoma Farm Families '44; Field Techniques in Social Psychological Study in a Rural Community '49; Needed Research in Rural Sociology '50; Child Training and Personality Adjustment '51, and others. Faculty Okla A&M Coll '37-44, prof sociol '40-44; asst ed Am Sociol Review; cons human resources to sec war and Research Development Bd since '46; prof rural sociol U Wis since '46, chmn since '46; chmn social sci div since '50. Am Sociol Soc—Rural Sociol Soc—Southwestern Sociol Soc —Midwestern Sociol Soc (exec com since '48, vp '50)—Nat Council Family Relations. Rural Sociology Department, University of Wisconsin, Madison 6, Wis.

15 SEXTON, Edwin Leon. Cereal chemistry. b'18. AB '39—MA '42 (U Calif); PhD '44 (U So Calif). Metabolism studies vitamin A; industrial research on cereal proteins, chemistry of oats, and formulation of prepared mixes and other cereal products; isolation, synthesis, and physical chemistry studies proteins and amino acids. Research chem The Best Foods Inc '44-47, chief chem flour and cereal div since '47. Am Assn Cereal Chem (chmn nat check sample com '49-50) Inst Food Tech—ACS—NY Acad Sci— Am Pub Health Assn (food and nutrition sect)—Am Inst Chem—Am Soc Qual Control—Sigma Xi—Theta Kappa Psi—Alpha Chi Sigma. The Best Foods, Inc., 54 Fulton St., Buffalo.†

16 SEYDEL, Paul Vasser. Textile chemistry. b'14. BS '34—MS '38 (Ga Sch Tech); DSc '41 (Eidgenossische Technische Hochschule, Zurich Switzerland). Research at Seydel-Woolley in developing and originating slashing compounds, softeners for textiles, surface-active agents, dye assistants, textile wet-processing auxiliaries; work on chemical warfare agents and their identification, examination of enemy material, Chemical Warfare Development Laboratories Massachusetts Institute of Technology '42-44, inspection and examination of German chemical industry, personnel and records '45, Industry and Economics Division Office of Military Government for Germany '45-46. Author: Cotton Slashing '49; also articles in field. Chemist Tubize-Chatillon Corp, rayon '34, Seydel-Wooley & Co textile chemicals mfg '34-40, dir research '40-42, since '46, vp since '48. Lt and capt Chem Warfare Service '42-46. Am Chem Soc—Am Assn Textile Chem and Colorists—AAAS. Box 36, Station D, Atlanta.

17 SEYFERT, Carl K. Extra-galactic nebulae and stars. b'11. BS '33—MA '34—PhD '36 (Harvard). Research on magnitudes, colors, spectra, and distribution of extra-galactic nebulae, of stars of large proper motion, of faint B-type stars, stars near the north celestial pole, and stars in Cygnus, magnitudes and distribution of stars and nuclear emissions in large spiral nebulae, photometry of eclipsing variable stars. Author articles in field. Astron McDonald Observatory Ft Davis Texas '36-40; instr astron and physics Warner and Swasey Observatory '42-44, asst prof '44-46; asso prof, dir Barnard Observatory Vanderbilt U '46-51; dir Arthur J Dyer Observatory since '51. Phi Beta Kappa—Sigma Xi—Am Astron Soc—Astron Soc Pacific—Royal Astron Soc—Internat Astron Union. Fellow Nat Research Council Mt Wilson Observatory '40-42. Arthur J. Dyer Observatory of Vanderbilt University, Nashville, Tenn.

18 SEYMOUR, Charles, Jr. European sculpture (1200-1800); Early Italian Painting (1500-1500). b'12. BA '35— PhD '38 (Yale); '30-31 (Cambridge U King's Coll); '35-37 (U Paris). Author: Notre Dame of Noyon in the 12th Century '39; also articles in field. Asst chief curator and curator sculpture Nat Gallery Art '40-49; asso prof curator renaissance Yale U since '49. Coll Art Assn (dir '40-42)—Societe Francaise d'Archeologie. Yale University Art Gallery, New Haven, Conn.

19 SEYMOUR, Keith M(orton). Azeotropy; Purification organic compounds. b'03. DuPont research fellow '31-32— BS '26—MS '29—PhD '33 (U Wash). Author articles in field. Prof chem, head dept Butler U since '47. Am Chem Soc—AAAS—Ind Acad Sci—Sigma Xi. Butler University, Indianapolis 7.

20 SEYMOUR, Raymond Benedict. Acidproof cements and coatings. b'12. BS '33—MS '35 (U NH); PhD '37 (State U Ia). Holder twelve or more US patents. Co-author: The National Paint Dictionary '48. Bd editors: Outline of Organic Chemistry '48; also articles in field. Chief chem Atlas Mineral Products Co '39-41, exec vp, gen mgr, bd dirs since '49. Am Inst Chem (F)—Am Chem Soc—AAAS—Am Inst Chem Engrs—Am Oil Chem Engrs— Am Assn Textile Chem Colorists—So Assn Sci Industry—Am Soc Engring Edn—Sigma Xi. Atlas Mineral Products Co., Mertztown, Pa.†

21 SEYMOUR-JONES, Frank Leslie. Food technology; Milk (Condensed, evaporated, dried, malted). b'96. BSc (hon) '21—MSc '22 (U Leeds Eng); Goldschmidt fellow '21-22—Exhibition scholar '21-23—AM '22—PhD '23 (Columbia U). Research on development of milk products. Author articles in field. Research chem the Borden Co '23-25, mfg dept asst gen sup specialties '25-41, dir new products research lab since '41. AAAS—Am Chem Soc—Am Dairy Sci Assn—Inst Food Tech—Met Dairy Tech Soc. Le Blanc medal (sci research) '21. Borden Co., 350 Madison Av., NYC 17. H: 358 Knickerbocker Rd., Englewood, N.J.

22 SHACKELFORD, Richard Max. Fur breeding. b'15. BS '36 (Murray State Coll); MS '41—PhD '47 (U Wis). Attended Eighth International Congress Genetics Stockholm '48, Thirteenth International Congress of Zoology Paris '48. Author articles in field. Research asst, later asst prof genetics U Wis since '40; agt Bur Animal Ind US Dept Agr since '47. Wis Acad Sci Arts Letters—Am Genetic Assn—Genetic Soc Am—Am Soc Zool—Sigma Xi. Genetics Department, University of Wisconsin, Madison 6, Wis.†

23 SHACKLETTE, Hansford Threlkeld. Kentucky Bryophytes; Arctic flowering plants. b'14. BS '35—MS '37 (U Ky); student (U Mich, U Zurich). Delegate International Horticultural Congress Berlin '38; University of Michigan Arctic expedition '48. Author articles in field. Prepared check list of Kentucky mosses. Bot Soc Am —Am Soc Plant Taxonomists—Ecol Soc Am—So Appalachian Bot Soc— Am Bryol Soc—British Bryol Soc— Mich Acad Sci—Ky Acad Sci—Bryologische Werkgroep van deNed. Route 2, Waverly, Ky.

24 SHAMEL, Archibald Dixon. Hybrid corn; Soy beans; Tobacco breeding; Bud selection improvement (Citrus, sugar cane, pineapple, banana, avocado); Soil stream sterilization; Humidity control (Storage); Shade trees of southern California. b'78. BS '98 (U Ill). Pioneer in hybrid corn investigations and introduced the soybean from the Orient '95-05; inventor of tobacco seed separator, steam-pan soil sterilizer, humidifier for storage rooms; co-inventor tobacco stalk cutter; organized Illinois Corn Breeders' Association '98; developed and introduced method for protecting tobacco seed from crossing; originator of individual tree performance record method and furrow-manure method of soil fertilization; visited Cuba to study tobacco, Brazil to study tropical fruits, Hawaii to study sugar cane and pineapple bud selection, Honduras and Gautemala to study banana improvement; Puerto Rico to study citrus bud selection work and Mexico to study avocado varieties. Author: Manual of Corn Judging '00; The Improvement of Plants Through Bud Selection '21; The Improvement of Sugar Cane Through Bud Selection; The Improvement of Smooth Cayenne Pineapple Through Bud Selection; also articles in field. Head farm crops U Ill '98-02; US Dept Agr '02-44, ret prin physiol '44; research asso U Calif Citrus Expt Sta since '44. AAAS(F). Citrus Experiment Station, Riverside, Calif.

10 SHANDS, Ruebush George. Barley and wheat (Disease resistance breeding); Stem rust; Smut resistance. b'03. BS '24 (Clemson Coll); PhD '29 (U Wis). Author articles in field. With US Dept Agr since '29, now sr agron Bur Plant Industry; asso prof agron U Wis. Am Soc Agron—Am Phytopath Soc—Sigma Xi. Agronomy Building, University of Wisconsin, Madison 6, Wis.

11 SHANE, Sylvan Myron. Drugs (Administration effects). b'18. Student (U So Cal); (Johns Hopkins U); DDS '42 (Maryland Sch Dentistry). Author: Out of This World, Anesthetics and What They Do to You '48. Anesthesiologist West Baltimore General Hospital. Am Soc Anesthesiologists—Internat Anesthesia Research Soc. West Baltimore General Hospital, Balt.

12 SHANOR, Leland. Mycology (Phycomycetes). b'14. AB '35 (Maryville Coll); MA '37—PhD '39 (U NC). Author articles in field. Research on molds and other aquatic phycomycetes, entomogenous fungi and others. Asso prof bot and curator mycol collections U Ill since '48. AAAS—Bot Soc Am —Mycol Soc Am—Ill Acad Sci—Sigma Xi—Am Phytopath Soc. Department of Botany, University of Illinois, Urbana, Ill.†

13 SHANTZ, Homer LeRoy. Plants (Ecology, physiology, geography, indicators, water economy and requirement, drought resistance, wilting coefficient, transpiration, environmental relation); Vegetation (Land classification, United States, Latin America, world); Africa (Vegetation, agricultural regions, native agriculture, education); Soil moisture. b'76. BSc '01—ScD '26 (Colo Coll); PhD '05 (U Neb). Author articles in field. Chief div wildlife management Forest Service US Dept Agr '36-44. Am Geog Soc—Assn Am Geog—AAAS(F)—Am Soc Agron —Nat Asso State U (spl mem)—Ecol Soc Am—Soc Plant Physiol (Charles Reid Barnes life mem)—Wildlife Soc —Internat pour la Protection Nature— Soc pro Fauna et Flora Fennica—Internat Inst Study African Langs Cultures—Sigma Xi—Phi Kappa Phi (nat pres '35-39)—Phi Beta Kappa. 454 Paseo del Descanso, Santa Barbara, Calif.†⊙

14 SHAPER, Harry B(ryant). Acoustics; Electronics; Supersonics; Hearing aids; Underwater sound. b'13. BS '36 —MS '36 (City Coll NY); '37-40 (Brooklyn Polytech). Magnetic tape recording, titanate xtals, hearing aid amplifiers; acoustic consultant Edo Aircraft College Point, Long Island. Holds 12 patents in acoustics and electronics field. Author articles in field. Pres, and chief engr Dyna-Labs NYC since '46. Acoustical Soc Am—Inst Radio Engrs—NY Acad Sci. Dyna-Labs, Inc., 151 Lafayette St., NYC.†

15 SHAPIRO, Carl Lynnwood. Steel (Properties). b'05. BS (ChemE) '29 (Northeastern U); MS (Metall engring) '32—ScD '34 (Harvard); '33-35 (MIT). Determination effects of heat treatment, aging, and working on physical, chemical, and structural properties of iron and steel at room and elevated temperatures. Holds patents on heat treatment of plastics and metals; chemical analysis of metals; adhesion of plastics to metals. Asst metall Crucible Steel Co '35-38; tech dir Lynnwood Labs Inc '38-41; research metall Vanadium Corp Am '41-43; pres and tech dir Gen Materials Research Labs '43-46, Acryvin Corp Am since '46. Iron and Steel Inst Eng (Andrew Carnegie research scholar)—Am Soc Metals— AIMME. Acryvin Corporation of Am, 12-21 Astoria Blvd., Astoria 2, N.Y.

16 SHAPIRO, Joseph George. Social agencies. b'86. LLB '07 (Yale). Former member and secretary committee on rules and grievances US District Court Connecticut. Practice of law since '07; prosecuting atty Shelton Conn '13-20, corp counsel '17-22, judge city ct '20-31; mem Judicial Council Conn '27-31; acting judge Ct Common Pleas '28. Am Bar Assn—Conn Soc Mental Hygiene (formerly exec com)—Conn State Bar Assn—Nat Conf Christians and Jews (formerly exec com)—Comml Law League Am—Am Judicature Soc —Am Law Inst—Internat Assn Ins Counsel. 945 Main Street, Bridgeport, Conn.

17 SHAPIRO, Leo. Classical rhetoric; Semantics. b'14. PhB '35—MA '36 (De Paul U); '36-38 (U Chicago); PhD '47 (Northwestern U). Research on normative terms in rhetoric of Aristotle; editorial consultant Publications of Modern Language Association. Prof speech and Eng De Paul U. Speech Assn Am—Internat Soc Gen Semantics —Nat Council Teachers of Eng—Nat Council Soc Studies—Assn Supervision and Curriculum Development—Assn Childhood Education Internat—NEA— Am Association Sch Adminstr—Ill Soc Mental Health. 327 S. La Salle St., Chgo. 4. H: 846 E. 52nd St., Chgo. 15.

18 SHAPLEY, Fern Rusk. Italian Renaissance painting; George Caleb Bingham. b'90. Fellow '14-15—travel scholar '15 (Bryn Mawr Coll); AB '13 —MA '14—PhD '16—fellow '15-16 (U Mo). Research abroad '20-21, '32-40. Author: George Caleb Bingham, The Missouri Artist '17; also articles in field. Curator paintings Nat Gallery of Art Washington since '47. Phi Beta Kappa. National Gallery of Art, Washington 25.

19 SHAPOVALOV, Leo. Fresh-water fishery biology; Stream and lake ecology; Fish management and conservation. b'08. AB '30—AM '32 (Stanford U). Travel in Europe and other foreign countries '27, '35 toured fisheries and ichthyological establishments; minor travel in Canada and Mexico; leader of Klamath Stream Survey '34. Author articles in field. Sr fisheries biol Calif State Div Fish and Game '33-44, dist fisheries biol '44-48, supervising fisheries biol '49-53 senior fisheries biologist since '53. AAAS (F)—Calif Acad Sci—Am Fisheries Soc—Am Soc Ichthyologists and Herpetologists—Limnol Soc Am—Western Soc Naturalists—Wildlife Soc—Am Wildlife Inst—Pacific Fishery Biol— Am Soc Limnol and Oceanog—Sigma Xi. Calif. Dept. Fish and Game, 926 J St., Sacramento, Cal.

20 SHARBAUGH, William James. Plastisols (Continuous casting); Laminates (Low pressure plastic). b'14. BS '35 (Carnegie Inst Tech). Development engineer plastics; product design and mass production techniques for rubber-like products from vinyl plastisols. Product engr Mine Safety Appliances Co '35-45; faculty Pa State Coll '41-42; works mgr Gerber Plastics Co since '46. Soc Plastics Industry (mem reinforced plastics com)—Soc Plastics Engrs. Box 3504, Richmond Heights 17, Mo. H: 936 Buena Vista, StL 2.

21 SHARKEY, Thomas P(almer). Institutional management; Poisoning (Sodium fluoride). b'04. BA '26 (Miami U Oxford O); MD '30 (U Cincinnati); '34 (Thorndike Memorial Hosp, Boston City Hosp); fellow Joslin clinic '33, '34 (New Eng Deaconess Hosp, Boston); fellow '33, '34 (Royal Victoria Hosp McGill U). Research diabetics, diabetic coma, hypertension in diabetics, coronary arteriosclerosis in diabetic mellitus, diabetic emergencies; lect AMA nat diabetes exhibition over the country since '36. Author articles: Infection of the Urinary Tract in Diabetes (with H F Root) '35; Experience with Protamine Insulin Therapy '37; Diabetes as an Obstetrical Liability '35; The Surgical Management of the Diabetic Patient (with A T Bower) '39; and others. Sr internal medicine Miami Valley Hosp Dayton since '46 mem bd trustees since '46; cons med Dayton (O) State Hosp since '37. Diplomate Am Bd Internal Med—ACP (F)—AMA—Am Diabetes Assn—O State Med Assn—Montgomery Co Med Soc. 60 Wyoming St., Dayton 9, Ohio. H: 620 Woods Rd., Dayton 9.

22 SHARP, Aaron John. American mosses; Phytogeography. b'04. AB '27 (O Wesleyan U); MS '29 (U Okla); PhD '38 (O State U). Author articles in field. Asso editor: Castanea since '47; editorial com: American Journal Botany since '48. Prof also head bot U Tenn since '52. Sullivant Moss Soc (pres '35, act editor the Bryologist '43-44, asso editor '38-42, since '44). Guggenheim fellow '44-46. Department of Botany, University of Tennessee, Knoxville 16, Tenn.†

23 SHARP, Charles Sheldon. Petroleum exploration (Gravimetric). b'12. BS '32 (McKendree Coll); MS '35 (U Ill). Research on gravity meter surveys for oil in US and Arabia. Research asst US Rubber Co '37-38; geophys Brown Geophys Co '39-49; geophys Arabian Am Oil Co since '49. Soc Exploration Geophys—Am Geophys Union—AIMME—AAAS—APS. Arabian American Oil Co., Exploration Department, Dhahran, Saudi Aragia.

24 SHARP, Donald E. Glass technology; Optical glass. b'96. Student '16-18, '20-22 (U Wis); '18 (Carnegie Inst Tech); Ceramics E '42 (NY State Coll Ceramics, Alfred U). Inventor heat-absorbing glasses, reflection lenses, glass-feeding apparatus, glass-forming machines, glass surface treatments; with W H Rising, maker first commercially successful large telescope disc in US '22; delegate International Glass Congress, London '36. Editor: Feldspar as a Constituent of Glass '37; also articles in field. Physicist Spencer Lens Co '18, mgr '20; cons glass tech '26; pres Bailey and Sharp Co '29; glass tech Hartford-Empire Co '37, asst research dir '41; asst dir research in charge glass technol Libbey-Owens-Ford Glass Co since '43. Am Ceramic Soc (F, councilor glass div '23, v-chmn '31, trustee '38-41, mem Jury of Fellows '40)—Soc Glass Tech, Brit(F)—Royal Soc Arts, Brit(F)—Am Chem Soc—Am Optical Soc—Am Phys Soc. Am mem Internat Glass Commn '50-53. Libbey-Owens-Ford Glass Co., Technical Department, 1701 E. Broadway, Toledo 5, O. H: 308 E. Dudley St., Maumee, O.

10 SHARP, Howard Oakley. Geodesy; Photogrammetry. b'91. CE '14 (Rensselaer Polytech Inst). Registered professional engineer and land surveyor NY. Author: Photogrammetry '43; Geodetic Control Surveys '43; Airport Engineering '46; Practical Photogrammetry, '51; also articles in the field. Cons engr Solomon, Norcross and Keis Watervliet NY '15; chief engr West Side Foundry '15-19; Foundry prodn engr Gen Elec Co '20-21; cons engr pvt practice since '20; instr geodesy and transportation engring Rensselaer Polytech Inst Troy NY '19-20, asst prof '21-36, prof since '36, acting head Dept Civil Engring '43-48, now head div geod and transp engring. ASCE (pres Mohawk-Hudson chapter '43-44)—Soc Engrs East NY (pres '42-43)—Am Soc Photogrammetry—Am Road Builders Assn—Highway Research Assn—Am Soc Engring Edn—Sigma Xi. Rensselaer Polytechnical Institute, Troy, N.Y.

11 SHARP, Robert Phillip. Geomorphology and glacial and structural geology of Nevada, Minnesota, Arizona, Wyoming, Illinois, Alaska, Yukon Territory; Glaciology of Alaska and Canada. b'11. BS '34—MS '35 (Calif Inst Tech); AM '36—PhD '38 (Harvard). Research in geol, geomorphology and glacial geology. Author articles in field. Prof geomorphology Calif Inst Tech since '47, chairman division of geological sciences '52. Served in Intelligence Office USAAF '43-45, Arctic Sect Desert and Tropic Information Center. Geol Soc Am(F)—Am Assn Petroleum Geol—British Glaciol Soc—Am Geophys Union. Calif. Inst. of Technology, Pasadena 4, Calif.†

12 SHARP, Sam(uel) E(mmett). Safety engineering; Mining engineering. b'98. BS in mining engring '24 (N Ga Coll). Research in progressive management and technology to eliminate basic causes accident and health hazards in industry; research and studies basic improvements methods and technique mining and reduction of a complex sulphide ore. Mining engr Tenn Copper Co '25-26; indsl safety engr since '27; cons safety engr NC Exploration Co '34-43. Awarded numerous safety awards. AIME—Am Soc of Safety Engrs—Nat Safety Council—So Safety Council—Tenn Safety Council —Am Indsl Hygiene Assn—AAAS(F). Safety Director, Tennessee Copper Co., Copperhill, Tenn.

13 SHARPE, C(harles) F(arquharson) Stewart. Geomorphology; Landslides; Soil erosion; Military geography. b'07. BA '28—MA '31—PhD '38 (Columbia). Research gully erosion, acceleration erosion result land use, mass-movement soil and rock relation to agriculture and engineering problems, military geography; special consultant landslides Pennsylvania Turnpike Commission Harrisburg '40. Author: Landslides and Related Phenomena '38; What Is Soil Erosion '38. Co-author: Principles of Gully Erosion in the Piedmont of South Carolina '39; Climate and Accelerated Erosion in the Arid and Semiarid Southwest, With Special Reference to the Polacca Wash Drainage Basin Arizona '42. Asst and asso soil conservationist div climatic and physiographic research US Soil Conservation Service '35-43; acting chief terrain-hydrog sect Europe-Africa div research analysis br OSS '43-44; ed

Jt Intelligence Study Pub Bd Jt Chiefs Staff '44-45, deputy ed in chief '45-47; ed in chief '47-49; US Govt since '48. Geol Soc Am—Assn Am Geog—Am Geophys Union—Geol Soc Washington —Sigma Xi. 221 Monroe St., Falls Church, Va.†

14 SHARPE, Joseph Audley. Earthquake seismology; Prospecting (Seismology, gravimetry, magnetometry); Geophysical prospecting. b'07. BS '28—'28-30 (U Ariz); PhD '34 (U Wis); '34-35 (MIT). Editor Geophysics '42-45. Granted patents on seismic prospecting, surveying, and recording systems in seismic surveying. Research seismol '35-37, chief phys '37-45 Stanolind Oil and Gas Co; vp Frost Geophys Corp since '45. Am Assn Petroleum Geol (research com '43-46)—Soc Exploration Geols—Am Geophys Union —AIMME—Seismol Soc Am—APS. Frost Geophysical Corp., Box 58, Tulsa.

15 SHARPE, Phil (Philip Burdette). Firearms (Technical, sporting, Mil, historical). b'03. BCS '24 (Portland U). Author: This Handloading Game '34; The Complete Guide to Handloading '37; The Rifle in America '38. Contbr editor American Rifleman. Small arms and ammunition research technician, writer and consultant since '21. Chief small arms hist US Army '42-44, proof officer enemy equipment Fgn Material Div '44, chief Small Arms Unit Enemy Equipment Tech Intelligence European Theater '44-46. Nat. Rifle Assn (member technical division staff)—Am Ordnance Assn—Nat Muzzle Loading Rifle Assn—US Revolver Assn—Nat Skeet Assn. The Philip B. Sharpe Research Laboratories, Emmitsburg, Md.☉

16 SHARPE, Robert Boies. Elizabethan Dramatic companies; Shakespeare; English Renaissance drama. b'97. BA '18 (Wesleyan U); MA '23 (U Wis); PhD '28—Sterling research fellow '30-31—scholar and fellow '24-26 (Yale). Author: The Real War of the Theaters—Shakespeares' Fellows in Rivalry with the Admirals' Men 1594-1603, monograph '35; also articles in field. Prof Eng U NC, also in dept dramatic art. Modern Lang Assn Am—South Atlantic Modern Lang Assn—Phi Beta Kappa. Department of English, University of North Carolina, Chapel Hill, N.C.

17 SHARRAH, Jacob S(amuel). Air pollution. b'11. Student '30-31 (Carnegie Inst Tech); BS (chem engring) '37-42-44 (U Pittsburgh). Research on chemical engineering and ventilation of industrial plants, air pollution phase of industrial hygiene. Pa Dept Health since '41, chief Div Air Pollution Control from '49. Sigma Tau—Am Indsl Hygiene Assn—Am Council Govt Indsl Hygienists—Am Pub Health Association—Air Pollution and Smoke Prevention Assn Am. Department of Health, Harrisburg, Pa.†

18 SHATTUCK, George Cheever. Tropics (Diseases). b'79. AB '01—Am hon '19—MD '05 (Harvard). Author: The Peninsula of Yucatan '33; Medical Survey of the Republic of Guatemala '38; Diseases of the Tropics '50. Co-author: (with William Jason Mixter) Handbook of Health for Overseas Service (2d rev edit) '43. Attending specialist in tropical medicine US Marine Hosp Brighton Mass '23; mem Hamilton Rice 7th Expdn to Amazon '24-25; cons tropical diseases Mass Gen Hosp since '28; clin prof tropical med Harvard Sch Pub Health '38-47, emeritus; cons tropical diseases Boston City Hosp since '41; cons to Sec of War '41-44; cons tropical diseases Peter Bent Brigham Hosp Boston '46,

VA W Roxbury since '45. Am Pub Health Assn—AAAS—Am Acad Arts and Scis—Am Acad Tropical Med(pres '47-48)—Am Soc Tropical Med(pres '27)—Bd Am Found Tropical Med—Royal Soc Tropical Med and Hygiene (local sec US since '39), Hon Pub Health Soc—Sigma Xi—Delta Omega. Harvard Medical Sch., 25 Shattuck St., Boston 15.☉

19 SHAULIS, Nelson J. Orchard soil management (Peaches and cherries); Grape culture. b'13. BS in hort '35—MS in soils '37 (Pa State Coll); PhD in soils '41 (Cornell U). Author articles in field. Prof pomol NY State Agrl Expt Sta since '48. Am Soc Hort Sci—Am Soc Agron—Soil Sci Soc Am. New York Agricultural Experiment Station, Geneva, N.Y.†

20 SHAVER, Chester Linn. William Wordsworth. b'07. AB '28 (Oberlin Coll); AM '29—PhD '37—scholar (Harvard). Research on Wordsworth's library at Rydal Mount. Author articles in field. Asst prof Eng Oberlin Coll '41-46, asso prof '47-50 prof since '50 chairman department since '52. Coll Eng Assn Northern O—MLA—Phi Beta Kappa. Won Bowdoin prize Harvard '29. Oberlin College, Oberlin, O. H: 265 E. College St.☉

21 SHAVER, Jesse M(ilton). Ferns (Taxonomy, ecology); Bird ecology. b'88. BSA '15 (U Tenn); MS '21 (Vanderbilt U); PhD '28 (U Chicago). Author articles in field. Instr, later prof biol George Peabody Coll for Teachers since '15. Am Fern Soc—AAAS(F)—Am Ornithol Soc—Tenn Ornithol Soc (former pres)—Tenn Acad Sci (former pres)—Wilson Ornithol Club (former sec, pres). George Peabody College for Teachers, Nashville 4, Tenn.†

22 SHAW, B(yron) T(homas). Soil physics; Clay. b'07. BS '30 (Utah State Agrl Coll); PhD '40 (O State U). Author articles in field. Asso prof agron O State U '40-43; agron div soil and fertilizer investigations Bur Plant Industry and SAE US Dept Agr '43-45, head div irrigation agr '45, head div soil management and irrigation '45-47; asst research adminstr Agrl Research Adminstrn US Dept Agr '47-48, deputy research administrator '48-51 research administrator since '51. American Soc Agron—Soil Science Soc Am—AAAS. Agricultural Research Administration, U.S. Department of Agriculture, Washington 25.†☉

23 SHAW, Charles Edward. Taxonomy and natural history of lizards. b'18. AB '43 (San Diego State Coll). Author articles: A New Species of Legless Lizard from San Geronimo Island, Lower California '40; A New Chuckwalla from Santa Catalina Island, Gulf of California '41; The Chuckwallas, Genus Sauromalus '45. Herpetologist Zool Soc San Diego since '46. Am Soc Icthyologists Herpetologists — Herpetologist's League (F). Zoological Society of San Diego, Box 551, San Diego 12, Calif.

24 SHAW, Charles Gardner. Mycology; Plant and forest pathology. b'17. BA '38 (O Wesleyan U); MS '40 (Pa State Coll); PhD '47 (U Wis). Author articles in field. Asso prof plant path and asso path Wash State Coll since '51. First lt US Marine Corps Reserve liaison officer for mycol and fungus deterioration. Am Phytopath Soc—Mycol Soc Am—AAAS—Phi Beta Kappa—Sigma Xi. Plant Pathology Department, Washington State College, Pullman, Wash.†

25 SHAW, Frank R. Apiculture; Taxonomy of insects. b'08. BSc '31 (Mass State Coll); PhD '36 (Cornell U). Research in applied entomology, on thrips and scale insects, taxonomy mycetophilidae, bee poisioning and pollination. Co-author: Honey bees and Their Management (with White-head). Instr entomol and beekeeping Mass State Coll '35-44, asst prof '44-52, asso prof since '52. Entomol Soc Am(F)—Am Assn Econ Entomol—Nat Beekeepers Association—Sigma Xi—Phi Kappa Phi. Grant-in-aid from Sigma Xi. Fernald Hall, University Massachusetts, Amherst, Mass.†

10 SHAW, Harold Nichols Infra-red heating. b'95. BS '18 (U Wis). Holds numerous patents on electric heating including industrial process kettles, induction cooking utensils and radiant heaters. Cons engr Griswold Mfg Co and other mfrs since '31. AIEE. 1031 W. 6th St., Erie, Pa.

11 SHAW, Harry Lee, Jr. History of British and American literary types. b'05. AB '26 (Davidson Coll); MA '27 (U SC); '28-31 (NYU). Co-author: (with L Wimberly and W Davenport) Dominant Types in British and American Literature '49. Instr Eng NYU '27-39, asst prof '39-42. dir Workshops in Composition '37-42; dir Fed Writers' Project NYC '38; working with large groups profl and semi-profl writers Washington Square Writing Center NYU since '37; asso editor and dir editorial research Look Mag '42-43, mng editor '43-44, editorial dir '44-47; ed in charge hum books Harper & Bros '47-53; E P Dutton & Co since '53. Phi Beta Kappa. E. P. Dutton & Co 300 Fourth Av., NYC.

12 SHAW, Lloyd. American folk dancing (Square, round, cowboy). b'90. AB '13—LLD '28 (Colo Coll); EdD '37 (U Colo). Director Cheyenne Mountain Dancers and specialist in field of American square dance; director square dances in motion picture Duel in the Sun. Author: Cowboy Dances '39; The Round Dance Book '48; Album of Square Dances (phonograph records); also articles in field. Supt Cheyenne Mt Sch Colo Springs '16-51; pres Lloyd Shaw Recordings, Inc. 1527 Winfield Av., Colorado Springs, Colo.

13 SHAW, Myril Clement. Thermal chemistry (Pyrometric cones); Asbestos textiles. b'07. BS '29—MS '30 (Pa State Coll); PhD '34 (O State U). Research, production and manufacture of pyrometric cones used to control firing operations in ceramic industries, research and improvement asbestos textiles and test methods. Research dir and mgr Edward Orton Jr Ceramic Found '34-44; research F and gen sec Asbestos Textile Inst since '46. Am Ceramic Soc (F)—Sigma Xi—Keramos. School of Ceramics, Rutgers University, New Brunswick, N.J.

14 SHAW, Robert Findley. Radio engineering; Electronic computers; Automatic calculators. b'15. AB '37 (Princeton U); '37-39, '41-42 (Moore Sch EE, Univ Pa). Participated in development and design of electronic numerical integrator and computer (ENIAC), electronic discrete variable computer (EDVAC), Universal Automatic Computer (UNIVAC), and other large-scale electronic computers. Co-author: Progress Report on the EDVAC '46; also articles in field. Research engr Moore Sch EE U Pa '43-46, Inst Advanced Study Princeton '46, senior design engineer Eckert-Mauchly Computer Corp Phila '46-51; asst tech dir Electronic Computer Div Underwood Corp since '51. Institute Radio Engrs (sr)—Franklin Inst—Assn Computing Machinery—Am Math Soc—Soc Indsl Applied Math—Sigma Xi. 35-10 36th Av., L.I. City 6, N.Y. H: 1320 Dean St., Bklyn 16.

15 SHAW, Silas Frederick. Mining engineering (Gas-air lifting of oil and water, estimates of oil reserves in fields and ore reserves in mines). b'77. EM '03 (Columbia). Author: Gas-Lift Principles and Practices; also articles in field. Mining work in US, Mex, Costa Rica '03-20; gen mgr Purcell interests in Mex '20-26; cons engr Standard Oil Co NJ subsidiaries '26-32, gaslift operations Europe, SA, US; cons engr various companies '33-36; Anglo-Can Oil Co Ltd Calgary since '37; asst prof petroleum engring A&M Coll Tex '42-43, prof '45. 301 Terrell Rd., San Antonio 9.

16 SHEA, Arnold Francis. Printing inks. b'14. LLB '36 (LaSalle Extension U); '37 (Chicago Sch Law). Research on specialty printing inks and compounds which were developed to mark all types of surfaces and withstand varied chemical and mechanical actions; abstractor Chemical Abstracts for surface coatings and patents since '47. Author articles in field. Chem Kirk Mineral Products Co Keene NH '35-38, F A Putnam Mfg Co Inc '42, chief chem '42-48; dir Shea Research Lab '42-48, Tolman-Shea Labs Inc since '49. Am Chem Soc (div paint, varnish and plastics chem)—AAAS—NE Paint and Varnish Club. Tolman-Shea Laboratories, Keene, N.H.

17 SHEA, Carter Laurence. Foundations; Waterfront construction. b'16. BS in civil engring '37—MS '39 (Rensselaer Poly Inst). Design and construction bridge foundations, building and industrial foundations, breakwaters, piers, drydocks, and marine railways US and Central America. Author articles: Sub-Aqueous Deposition of Concrete (unpub) '39; Investigation of Suitability of Shallow Arch Sheet Piling for Cellular Cofferdams (unpub) '42. Field engr heavy constrn '37-40; job engr constrn breakwater and drydocks '40-42; civil engr Shell Oil Co since '46. Officer Civil Engr Corps USN '42-46. NY State Soc Professional Engineers—Am Soc CE—Tau Beta Pi—Sigma Xi. Products Pipeline Dept, Shell Oil Co., 50 W. 50th St., NYC 22. H: 43-54 149th St., Flushing, N.Y.

18 SHEA, John Edward. Contractometer; Volumeter; Soil; Snow; Ice; Permafrost. b'08. Student '28-31 (MIT); '49-51 (Cath U). Research on soils, snow, ice and permafrost as associated with foundations, earth fill dams, highways, airports, stabilization of fills and embankments, design of concrete and asphalt mixes and testing instruments; designed contractometer to determine unfrozen moisture content of snow, grain size distribution and melting points, and volumeter to determine soil specific gravity, moisture content, and density. Field test engr '39-41; asst chief Dist Test Lab US Army Airport Design and Test '42-45; soils engr Portland Cement Assn '46; chief Test Lab Permafrost '46-47; staff Engineering Sch and Research Lab Ft Belvoir since '47. Am Soc CE—Highway Research Bd—Soc Am Mil Engrs. OACofS, G-4, US Army, Pentagon, Washington. H: 33 Fort Drive, Fairhaven, Alexandria, Va.

19 SHEAR, George Myron. Tobacco, apple and corn nutrition; Boron and manganese deficiency; Chemical weed control; Water cress production. b'05. BS '27 (U Md); MS '28—PhD '30—grad fellow '29-30 (U Ill). Author articles in field. Asst, later plant physiol Va Agrl Expt Sta since '30. Am Soc Plant Physiol—Am Soc Hort Sci—Ecol Soc Am—Va Acad Sci—Va Hort Soc—Sigma Xi—Phi Kappa Phi. Received Jefferson medal of Va Acad Sci for paper with H D Ussery, Frenching of Tobacco Distinguished from Thallium Toxicity by Spectrographic Analysis '38. Virginia Agriculture Experiment Station, Blacksburg, Va.†

20 SHEARD, Charles. Physiological optics (Accommodation, convergence, cone and rod vision, dark adaption, light tolerance); Spectrophotometry and spectroscopy (Instrument development, photelometer, biological applications, blood chemistry); Temperature regulation of body (Skin temperature measurements, vasomotor regulation); ultraviolet and X-ray radiant energy (Effects on tissue). b'83. BA '03—DSc '30 (St Lawrence U); MA '07 (Dartmouth); PhD '12 (Princeton). Founded Sheard Foundation for Education and Research in Vision Graduate School Ohio State University '43. Author: Dynamic Ocular Tests '17; Physiological Optics '19; Practical Ocular Tests '24; Ophthalmic Optics '49, and others. Dir div physics and bio-phys rsch Mayo Clinic and prof biophysics under Mayo Found U Minn '24-49, directing mem Mayo Aero-Medical Unit '41-45, now emeritus; prof ophthalmic optics Rochester Coll since '47; distinguished lectr ophthalmology, grad sch med Tulane Univ since '49. AAAS(F)—Am Heart Assn(F)—Ophthalmic Inst Gt Britain(F)—Optical Soc Am—Am Physiol Soc—Soc Exptl Biol and Med—Am Soc Plant Physiol—Am Congress Phys Therapy—Assn Research Ophthal—Nat Soc Prevention Blindness—Am Optometric Assn—Am Soc Clin Path—Sigma Xi—Sigma Pi Sigma. P.O. Box 543, Rochester, Minn⊚

21 SHEARER, Phineas Stevens. Beef cattle; Swine; Sheep. b'89. BS '12—MS '28 (Ia State Coll). With Ia State Coll since '13, head animal husbandry dept since '35. Am Soc Animal Prodn (pres)—Phi Kappa Phi—Alpha Zeta—Gamma Sigma Delta. Animal Husbandry Department, Iowa State College, Ames, Ia.

22 SHEDD, Clarence Prouty, Religion (American higher education). b'87. AB '09—AM '14—LHD '51 (Clark U); BD '25—PhD '32 (Yale). Fellow National Council Religious In Higher Education and member various national bodies of YMCA and those affecting religion in higher education; director national center for training university religious workers and for research in this field. Author: Two Centuries of Student Christian Movements '34; The Church Follows Its Students '37; A Century of Christian Student Initiative '45; Religion in State Universities '47; Henri Dunant et le development international des Y.M.C.A. '49; The Agencies of Religion in American Higher Education; Religion In The Colleges. Stephen Merrel Clement prof Christian methods and dir studies on religion in higher edn Yale Div Sch since '39. Nat Council on Religion in Higher Edn(F)—Assn Student Christian Assn Secs—Nat Conf Christian Workers in Colls and Us—United Student Christian Council—Edward W Hazen Found (student counseling com)—Phi Mu Upsilon. Yale U, New Haven. H: 435 Ridge Rd., Hamden, Conn.⊚

23 SHEDD, John Lawson. Ship models. b'14. AB '36 (U NC). Produced scale models for Maritime Commn, US Lines, others; co-owner Model Shipways Fort Lee NJ since '46. Steamship Hist Soc Am—Nautical Research Guild. Model Shipways, 476 Main St., Fort Lee, N.J.

24 SHEEHAN, Donald Henry. History of American book publishing; Colonial history and literature. b'17. AB '38 (Duke U); MA '40—PhD '50 (Columbia). Instr Am hist Columbia U '48-52; asst prof Smith College since '52. AHA—Phi Beta Kappa. Smith College, Northampton, Mass.

10 SHELDON, Pearl Gertrude. Rocks (Fracturing); Temperature persistence. b'85. AB '08—AM '09—PhD '11 (Cornell U). Research on joint planes, faults, dikes and earthquakes, research on weather cycles and persistence of temperatures. Curator geol Cornell U '22-29; incorporator and trustee Paleontological Research Instn '32-50. Sigma Xi—Seismol Society Am—AAAS(F). H: 1001 Triphammer Rd., Ithaca.

11 SHELFORD, Victor E(rnest). Bioecology. b'77. SB '03—PhD '07 (U Chicago). Designed more than 100 devices for simulating natural conditions, experimenting on animals, and measuring conditions; devised methods of graphing animal movements; first to measure light penetration into sea water; discovered relations populations plants and animal to solar ultraviolet; developed system of marine ecology. Author: Laboratory and Field Ecology '29. Co-author: (with F E Clements) Bio-ecology '39; also articles in field. Prof zool U Ill '27-46, prof emeritus since '46. Entomol Soc Am (F)—AAAS(F)—Am Soc Zool—Ecol Soc Am (1st pres '16, chmn com on preserves '17-19, sr chmn '21-23, '30-36, editorial bd Ecology '20-28, chmn com study communities '31-37)—Brit Ecol Soc—Grassland Research Fedn—Nat Research Council (chmn com ecol grassland)—Wildlife Soc—Fedn Study Cycles—Am Ornithol Union—Nat Audubon Soc (Ill rep '36-37)—Am Soc Econ Entomol—Am Fisheries Soc—Assn Am Geog—Sigma Xi—Phi Beta Kappa. The Vivarium, Wright & Healey St., Champaign, Ill.©

12 SHELLENBERGER, John Alfred. Cereal technology. b'00. BS '28 (U Wash); MS '30 (Kan State Coll); PhD '34 (U Minn). Consultant on grain quality grain storage milling and baking to Insular Goverment Puerto Rico '45, Institute Inter-American Affairs Lima Peru '46, San Jose Costa Rica '48; chairman US Delegation to FAO Conference Cali Colombia '49. Author articles in field. Chem Fisher Flouring Mills Co '22-28; asst prof U Idaho '29-30; head products control Mennel Milling Co '35-39; head biochem lab Rohm & Haas Co '39-42; cons Corp para la Promocion del Intercambio SA Buenos Aires '42-44; head dept milling and Kan State Coll and sr chem charge Fed Hard Wheat Quality Lab since '44. Am Chem Soc—Am Assn Cereal Chem—Inst Food Technol—Am Soc Bakery Engrs—Kan Acad Sci—AAAS—Sigma Xi—Phi Kappa Phi—Gamma Sigma Delta. Kansas State College, Manhattan, Kan.

13 SHELLEY, Philip Allison. German literary influence in England and America; Literary almanac in Germany, England and America (Annuals, gift-books). b'07. BA '29 (Pa State Coll); AM '30—PhD '38 (Harvard); '33-34 (U Berlin, U Göttingen). Co-author: An Outline-History of German Literature '48; also articles in field. Asso prof, prof German and head dept Pa State Coll since '39. Modern Lang Assn Am. Department of German, Pennsylvania State College, State College, Pa.

14 SHEMA, Bernard F(rancis). Microbiology of paper and pulp; Plant and forest pathology; Odor control in pulp and paper products. b'15. BS—Grad Sch '37-41—US Rubber Co fellow '40 (U Minn). Author articles in field. Microbiol Inst Paper Chem Appleton Wis since '41. Am Phytopath Soc—Mycol Soc Am—Inst Food Technol—Tech Assn Pulp and Paper Ind. Institute of Paper Chemistry, Appleton, Wis.

15 SHENK, Donald Hugh. Military rockets; Ultra high speed pumps. b'01. BSME '24—MS '40 (Purdue). Author articles in field. Asso prof mech engring Clemson Agrl Coll '29-43; prof charge mech engring U Ala '43-49; reliability engineer guided missiles. Redstone Arsenal Huntsville Ala since '49. ASEE—ASME. Redstone Arsenal, Huntsville, Ala.

16 SHEPARD, Anna Osler. Archeological ceramic technology; Pre-historic pottery (Optical petrography, microchemistry, thermal properties); Mayan and Pueblo pottery. b'03. AB '26 (U Neb); student (U NM, Claremont Coll, NYU, MIT); DSc (hon) '43 (U Colo). Archeological field work New Mexico, Central America. Author articles in field. Ceramic tech Dept Archaeology Carnegie Inst Washington since '37. Am Ceramic Soc—Soc Am Archeol—Sigma Xi. 751 11th St., Boulder, Colo.†

17 SHEPARD, Carl Frier. Vision and visual tests; Research and techniques in optometry. b'93. OD '12 (Needles Inst Optometry); OD '24—DOS (No Ill Coll Optometry). Believed to be originator of occupational screening and vision tests with stereoscopes; developed myoculator. Invented scale for evaluating stereopsis, glarometer, panoculator and other visual devices, Betts tests, Keystone View Company visual survey tests and visual training stereograms. Author: Optometric Science in Practice '42; also articles in field. Practiced optometry Hannibal '12-23; faculty No Ill Coll Optometry '23, dir research since '36, now dir Visual Research Foundation. Am Acad Optometry. Distinguished Service Found medalist. 5 S. Wabash Av., Chgo. 3.†

18 SHEPARD, Francis Parker. Submarine geology (Marine sedimentation, shore processes, submarine canyons and topography, continental shelves). b'97. BA '19 (Harvard); PhD '22 (U Chicago). Author: Submarine Geology '48. Co-author: Submarine Topography off the California Coast '41; also articles in field. Prof submarine geol Scripps Instn since '48. Dir sedimentology project Am Petroleum Inst. Geol Soc Am—Sigma Xi. Scripps Institution, La Jolla, Cal.

19 SHEPARD, Harold H(enry). Butterflies of the United States; Economic entomology (Insecticides). b'98. BS '24 (Mass Agrl Coll); MS '27 (U Md); PhD '31 (Mass State Coll). Author: The Chemistry and Toxicology of Insecticides '39. Co-author: Applied Entomology; Butterflies, a Handbook of the Butterflies of the United States, and others; also articles in field. Entomol PMA United States Dept Agr since '46. AAAS(F)—Entomol Soc Am (F)—Am Assn Econ Entomol—Washington Acad Sci—Entomol Soc Washington—Sigma Xi—Phi Kappa Phi—Gamma Sigma Delta. U.S. Dept. Agriculture, Washington 25.

20 SHEPARD, Norman Arthur. Rubber technology. b'90. PhB in chem '10 (Sheffield Sci Sch, Yale); PhD '13 (Yale U). Author articles in field. Dir organic chem research Firestone Tire and Rubber Co '19-25, dir chem research '25-35; with Am Cyanamid Co since '36, chem dir since '41; tech cons Nat Security Resources Bd since '48; adv com on plastics Sch Engring Princeton U since '46. Am Chem Soc (chmn rubber div '35-36, com on patent and related legislation '46-49)—Am Inst Chem—Am Inst Chem Engrs—Indsl Research Inst (pres '47-48)—Soc Chem Industry, London—NY Acad Sci—AAAS—Sigma Xi—Alpha Chi Sigma. Hunting Ridge Rd., Stamford, Conn.©

21 SHEPARD, William Peacey. Public health. b'95. BS '20—MB '21—MD '22—AM '24 (U Minn). Member medical advisory committee of National Security Resources Board since '48. Author: Training of Public Health Personnel; (sr author) Essentials of Public Health; also articles in field. Faculty U Minn '21-24; med dir Berkeley Health Center and city health officer '25-26; faculty Stanford U Med Sch '28-32, clin prof dept pub health and preventive med since '32; sr surgeon USPHS. Cal Tuberculosis Assn(pres '43-44); Nat Tuberculosis Assn(pres '46-47)—W Assn Indsl Phys and Surgeons (pres '47-48)—Am Pub Health Assn(F, sec W branch '28-39, pres W branch '40-41, chmn com prof edn since '39)—AMA—AAAS—Cal Med Association—N Cal Pub Health Assn—Cal Heart Assn(dir)—Nu Sigma Nu—Alpha Omega Alpha—Delta Omega—Sigma Xi. 600 Stockton St., S.F.

22 SHEPHERD, Herman Robert. Aerosols (Packaged power). b'21. BS '43 (Cornell U). Author articles in field. Vice-pres charge research Conn Chem Research Corp and subsidiary Bostwick Labs Inc since '47. Am Chem Soc—Am Phytopath Soc—Am Soc Econ Entomol—Am Pub Health Assn—Chem Specialties Mfrs Assn. 706 Bostwick Av., Bridgeport, Conn.

23 SHEPHERD, Richard Butler Hooke. Geodetic engring. b'05. Student '22-23 (Cornell U); '24 (Miss State Coll); '25-27 (U Mo); '45 (U Tenn). Topographic and hydrographic surveys and maps. With Corps Engrs '28-47, civil engr Memphis Dist '33-47; geodetic engr 29th Engring Base Topog Battalion since '48. Am Soc CE—Am Congress Surveying and Mapping. 29th Engring Base Topographic Battalion, APO 928, San Francisco. H: 4 Glenwood Circle, Vicksburg, Miss.

24 SHEPHERD, William Gerald. Vacuum tube research and design; Oscillators. b'11. BSEE '33—PhD '37 (U Minn). Research on non-linear circuit, vacuum tube design especially secondary emission tubes, reflex oscillators, klystrons. Author articles in field. Inventor several klystron designs and methods of thermal tuning. Tech staff Bell Telephone Labs '37-47; prof elec engring U Minn since '47. Am Phys Soc—Inst Radio Engrs—ASEE—Sigma Xi—Tau Beta Pi. Department of Electrical Engineering, University of Minnesota, Minneapolis 14.†

25 SHERF, Arden Frederick. Plant pathology (Potato diseases). b'16. BS '39 (U Neb); PhD '48 (U Neb). Author articles in field. Asst in path, later asst plant path and ext plant path U Neb '46-49; with dept bot and plant path Ia State Coll since '49. Am Phytopath Soc—Potato Assn Am—Gamma Sigma Delta—Sigma Xi. Department of Botany and Plant Pathology Iowa State College, Ames, Ia.

26 SHERIDAN, Lawrence Vinnedge. City planning. b'87. BS in CE '09—CE '12 (Purdue); student Harvard Sch Landscape Arch '16-17. Exec sec City Plan Commn Indianapolis '21-23; private practice since '23; cons Ind and KY State Planning Bds '34-37; regional counselor Nat Resources Planning Bd for Ind, Ill, O, Wis, Mich, Ky, W Va, '37-41; design and development plans various mil camps '40-41; prepared master plans and zoning ordinances for more than 40 cities; constrn div OQMG '41; deputy Service Command engr 9th Service Command '42-45; col Corps Engrs '42-46. Am Soc Landscape Architects(F)—ASCE—Am Inst Planners (pres '40)—Ind Engring Soc (past pres). Brendonwood, Indpls 44.©

10 SHERMAN, Harley B. Florida mammals; Bats. b'94. BS '20—MA '22 —PhD '33 (U Mich). Invented folding live traps for capture small mammals. Author articles in field. With U Fla since '25, prof since '34, acting head dept biology '47-50. Am. Society Mammalogists (charter mem)—AAAS—Fla Acad Sci—Fla Audubon Soc—Sigma Xi. Department of Biology, University of Florida, Gainesville, Fla.

11 SHERMAN, Harold Morrow. Telepathy; Alcoholism; Gerontology. (U Mich). Conducted early experiments in long distance telepathy with Sir Hubert Wilkins between New York City and Arctic, under supervision of Gardner Murphy, with approximately seventy per cent accuracy. Author: (with Wilkins) Thoughts Through Space '42; You Can Stop Drinking '50; You Need Never Grow Old '51. Lecturer since '47. Mountain View, Ark.

12 SHERMAN, Joseph Vincent. Plastics (Economics); Synthetic fibers (Economics); Textile industry (Economics). b'05. AB '28 (Columbia). Research economics and statistics of plastics, synthetic fibers and textiles, investment analysis of stocks. Author: Research as a Growth Factor in Industry '40; The New Plastics '45; Plastics Business '45; The New Fibers '46; also 100 articles in field. Mgr investment dept Nat Newark and Essex Banking Co '29-36; statis Case Pomeroy and Co '36-38; vp Econ Analysts Inc '38-42; asso Herbert R Simonds '43-45; cons econ and author since '45. Am Econ Assn—Am Statis Assn—AAAS—Royal Econ Soc—NY Soc Security Analysts—Nat Farm Chemurgic Council. 280 Broadway, NYC 7. H: 160 Columbia Heights, Bklyn 2.†

13 SHERMAN, Kenneth L(ee). Electricity (Atmospheric); Mines (Naval countermeasure). b'05. BS '31 (Geo Wash Univ). Research in atmospheric electricity and air ionization; participated in flight Explorer II by Army Air Corps and Nat Geog Soc '35, at which time electrical conductivity of air was recorded to 72,000 feet; scientific director naval mine countermeasures station. Physicist Dept Terrestrial Magnetism Carnegie Institution '27-47; sci dir USN Mine Countermeasures Sta since '47. AMP—Wash Acad Sci—Theta Tau—Sigma Tau. Received Wash Acad Sci Award for outstanding achievement '45; Naval Ordnance Development Award '45. U.S. Navy Mine Countermeasures Station, Panama City, Fla.

14 SHERMAN, Marsdon A(lexander). Shorthand (Analysis of systems, teaching methods). b'07. BA '31—MA '42 (Stanford); PhD '44 (Columbia). Author: Some Principles for Evaluating Shorthand Systems '45; also articles in field. Chmn div practical arts, head dept commerce Chico State Coll since '46. Calif Bus Educators' Assn (treas '47-48, vp '48-49)—Eastern Commercial Teachers' Assn—Nat Assn Secondary Sch Prin—Nat Bus Teacher's Assn (nominating com coll dept '44-45)—NEA (dept bus edn asst State Dir Calif '40-41, State dir '41-42, chmn profl lit com '44-45, sec '44-46)—Soc Advancement Research Bus Edn (pres '42-46)—United Bus Edn Assn. Chairman Division of Practical Arts, Chico State College, Chico, Cal.†

15 SHERMAN, Reuel Alvin. Visual research (Measurements and development); Vision training. b'96. Ed pub sch. Originated practical stereoscopic instruments and tests for measuring and training visual acuity, stereopsis, fusion, binocular imbalances, accommodation and convergence; research on relationship visual performance to oc-cupational success; consultant visual performance and reading difficulties, methods correction. Author: Third Dimension Eye Training Series '31; Book Stereoscopic Technic '32; Keystone Visual Safety Tests—Their Purpose, Construction and Interpretation '36; also articles in field. Originated ophthalmic dept Keystone View Co '31-39; research Bausch & Lomb Optical Co '39-43, mgr occupational vision dept since '48. Bausch and Lomb Optical Company, Rochester 5, N.Y. H: 202 Wimbledon Rd.

16 SHERMAN, Vernon Wesley. Electrical engineering; Electronic and induction heating; Mechanical and radio power design. b'07. BA '31 (Coll City Detroit); BS in ME '36—MS in EE '41 (Wayne U). Holds patents for electronic heating and design. Author articles in field. Pres chief engr Sherman Indsl Electronics Co Belleville NJ since '45. AIEE—Am Soc Metals—Inst Radio Engrs (sr mem, bd ed). Awarded War Dept Atomic Bomb Certificate '45 for design and supervision of constrn of high power electronic heaters and asso heavy duty machinery. 505 Washington Av., Belleville 9, N.J.†☉

17 SHERMAN, William Roderick. Foreign trade and marketing; Economic geography and history. b'92. AB '13 —AM '14—PhD '23—scholar '13-14— fellow '17-18 (Clark U). Author: Diplomatic and Commercial Relations of the US and Chile '26; Outline of Foreign Trade and Markets '47; also articles in field. Prof econ head dept Hillsdale Coll since '31. Am Econ Assn —Am Marketing Assn—Am Acad Polit Social Sci. Hillsdale College, Hillsdale, Mich.

18 SHERRIFF, Florence Edith Alfreda Janson. Swedish Immigration. b'93. PhB '14—AM '18 (U Chicago); PhD '27 (U Pa). Studies in political, social, economic causes immigration including religious persecution. Author: Background of Swedish Immigration, 1840-1930 '31. Prof govt Rockford Coll '20-34; lectr hist and govt U Shanghai China '35-37; prof govt st Johns U. Shanghai '37-43; DuPont Guerry prof hist Wesleyan Coll since '44. Phi Beta Kappa—Am Assn Internat Law—AHA—Am Polit Sci Assn—Am Swedish Hist Assn—So Hist Assn—Am Assn U Women—Miss Valley Hist Assn. Wesleyan College, Macon, Ga.

19 SHERROD, Robert Lee. History of World War II (Tarawa, Saipan, Iwo Jima). b'09. AB '29 (U Ga). War correspondent Southwest Pacific '42, Aleutian Islands '43, Central Pacific '43-45 including battles of Tarawa, Saipan, Iwo Jima and Okinawa. Author: Tarawa, the Story of a Battle '44; On to Westward '45; text for Life's Picture History of World War II '50. Sr fgn corr Time and Life '45-48, Washington corr since '48. Time Inc., 1000 Vermont Av., Washington.

20 SHERWELL, G(uillermo) Butler. Latin American, Spanish and Portuguese history and economics. b'04. AB '22 (Nat U Mexico); MS '24 (Columbia); PhD '26 (Sch Fgn Service, Georgetown U). Author: Mexico's Capacity to Pay '29; Budgets of Latin American Countries '23; Investments in Uruguay and Paraguay '23; Investments in Chile '23; also articles in field. Vp Mfrs Trust Co NYC since '42; pres and dir Argentine Real Estate Co Ltd Buenos Aires Argentina since '36; dir Union Oil Co Paraguay, Inter-Am Shipping Service Inc NY, Flanigan Loveland Corp NY. Mexican C of C in NY (dir and treas)—Venezuelan C of C in NY (dir and vp)— Ecuadorean C of C in NY (dir)—Bolivarian Soc of NY (vp and dir). 55 Broad St., NYC 15.

21 SHERWIN, Helen Shedd. Plant pathology (Forage corps). b'21. AB '41—MA '44 (U NC). Research on wild yeasts, fungi causing diseases of forage crops, particularly sudan grass, soybeans and alfalfa, effect of seed treatment on germination of soybeans. Author articles in field. Plant path US Dept Agr Beltsville Md '44-49. Am Phytopath Soc—Bot Soc Washington. U.S. Department of Agriculture, Plant Industry Station, Beltsville, Md.

22 SHERWIN, Oscar. English literature and social history (18th century); Negro slavery; Wendell Phillips; Abolition. b'02. AB '22—MA '28 (Columbia U); PhD '40 (NYU). Author: Mr. Gay '29; Benedict Arnold, Patriot and Traitor '31; Prophet of Liberty: a Biography of Wendell Phillips '43; also articles in field. Asso prof Eng City Coll New York. MLA—AHA—Am Acad Polit Social Sci—Phi Beta Kappa. City College of New York, 139th St. and Convent Av., NYC. H: 207 West 106th St., NYC 25.†

23 SHERWOOD, Carlton Montgomery. Fund raising; Institutional financing. b'95. Ed pub schs. Exec vp and member firm Pierce, Hedrick & Sherwood, Inc., instnl financing; mem bd dirs Judson Health Centre NYC; pres Am Assn of Fund Raising Counsel '45-47. 30 Rockefeller Plaza, NYC 20.

24 SHERWOOD, Harold Frank. Microradiography; Radiography of paintings, cloth, small biological specimens. b'08. Elec Engr '34 (Rochester Inst Tech). Author articles in field. With Eastman Kodak Co since '29. Optical Soc Am—Photog Soc Am. Awarded Rodman medal for work submitted at Royal Photog Soc 93rd Annual Exhbn. Eastman Kodak Company, Kodak Park, Rochester, N.Y.

25 SHERWOOD, Ross Madison. Poultry nutrition (Egg production, food effects on egg storage quality, vitamin, mineral and protein requirements for broilers and layers). b'86. BS '10 (Ia State Coll); MS '24 (Tex Agrl and Mech Coll). Author articles in field. Prof poultry husbandry Tex A & M Coll since '47. Poultry Sci Assn—Internat Poultry Assn—Tex Poultry Improvement Assn (hon). Poultry Husbandry Department, A. & M. College, College Station, Tex.

26 SHERWOOD, Thomas Kilgore. Absorption. b'03. BSc '23 (McGill U); SM '24—ScD '29 (MIT). Author: Absorption and Extraction '37; (with C E Reed) Applied Mathematics in Chemical Engineering '39. Asst dept chem engring MIT '24-26, asst prof '30-33, asso prof '33-41, prof '41-46, dean engring since '46; asst prof chem engring Worcester Polytechnic Inst '28-30; cons chem engr since '26. Am Acad Arts Scis(F)—Am Soc Refrigerating Engrs—Am Chem Soc—ASME —Am Inst Chem Engrs—Sigma Xi— Alpha Chi Sigma—Tau Beta Pi. William H Walker award Am Inst Chem Engrs for publications in chem engring 41; US Medal for Merit '48. 77 Massachusetts Av., Cambridge 39, Mass.☉

27 SHETTER, David Sibley. Trout stream biology; Fish marking and tagging. b'10. BS '32—MS '33—PhD '37 (U Mich). Perfected the method of jaw tagging trout and other fishes. Author articles in field. In charge Hunt Creek Fisheries Expt Sta Mich Dept Conservation since '43. Am Fisheries Soc —Wildlife Soc—Mich Acad Sci Arts Letters—Am Soc Ichthyologists Herpetologists—Am Soc Limnol Oceanog —Sigma Xi. Star Route No. 1, Lewiston, Mich.†

28 SHIDELER, Ernest Hugh. Group dynamics; Social problems. b'91. AB

'15 (Ottawa U); AM '17—PhD '27 (U Chicago). Study relation sociology to government; dynamics of collective behavior. Governor's Commn on Unemployment Relief '34-35; Ind State dir Resettlement Adminstrn '35-36; Ind. State dir Farm Security Adminstration '37-47; chairman division of commerce and business administration University Ill (Galesburg div) '47-49; asso prof sociology (Urbana) since '49; f and instr sociology U Chicago '22-23. Am Sociol Soc—AAUP—Soc Social Research(past sec)—Ind Acad Social Sci (ex-pres)—Am Econ Assn—Rural Sociol Soc Am—Pi Gamma Mu. 103 W. Florida Av., Urbana, Ill.⊙

10 SHIELDS, Lora Mangum. Plant microtechnique and anatomy; Photomicrography. b'12. BS '40—MS '42 (U NM); PhD '47 (Ia U). Research on order of differentiation of types of xylem elements in Phaseolus vulgaris, compositae of Navajo Indian country, microtome compression in plant tissue; leaf xeromorphy; plant nitrogen sources. Author: Laboratory and Field Instructions in Botany (with Emerson) '48; also articles in field. Asso prof biol NM Highlands U since '47. Sigma Xi—Phi Kappa Phi. Phi Sigma Award U NM '41. Dept of Biology, New Mexico Highlands University, Las Vegas, N.M.

11 SHIELDS, Robert Hazen. Agricultural Law (Sugar, food). b'05. AB '26 (U Neb); LLB '29 (Harvard). Assistant to secretary of agriculture and chief judicial officer US Department of Agriculture '41-42; solicitor US Department of Agriculture '42-46, War Food Administration '43-45. Author articles in field. Dir Sugar Research Found Inc NYC since '46, vp since '48; dir and vp Sugar Information Inc NYC since '49; vice chmn Information & Standards Com Sugar Industry '48. American Political Science Association—Am Soc Pub Adminstrn—DC, Am, Fed (Nat Council since '42, 2nd vp '43, 1st vp '44, pres '45, del '46) bar assns. 1001 Tower Building, Washington 5.⊙

12 SHIELS, William Eugene, S. J. Latin American history. b'97. AB '22 (Gonzaga U); MA '26 (St Louis U); PhD '33 (U Calif) Associate editor of America on Latin American Affairs '42-44, Mid-America since '35; member committees on Latin American and International Education in American Council on Education since '42, committee on Study of Teaching Materials on Latin America '43-44; mem advisory bd Editors of The Americas since '44. Author: Gonzalo de Tapia '34; History of Europe '42; also articles in field. Prof hist chmn dept Xavier U Cin since '46. AHA—Am Cath Hist Assn—Miss Valley Hist Assn—Hispanic Am Hist Conf—US Cath Hist Soc—Jesuit Hist Conf. Xavier University, Victory Parkway, Cincinnati 7.

13 SHIER, Louise Adele. Lamps (Graeco-Roman from Egypt); Bible (Coptic manuscripts); Coptic (language). AB '27—MA '28—PhD '33—AB (Lib sci) '36 (U Mich). Old Testament texts on vellum in "Coptic Texts in the University of Michigan Collection," edited by William H Worrell). Research asso in Coptic Inst Archeol Research U Mich '35, asst advancing to curator Mus Archeol since '36. Am Assn Mus—Am Oriental Soc—Archeol Inst Am—Am Research Center in Egypt. Kelsey Mus of Archeology, University of Michigan, Ann Arbor.†

14 SHINN, William Edward. Full fashioned hosiery knitting. b'00. BE '24—MS '28 (NC State Coll); grad work '43, '44 (U Chicago). Research on knitting machinery, full fashioned hosiery knitting, consultant to tricot industry; consulting editor The Knitter. Author: Principles of Knitting (Vol I, II) '46-49. Textile tech US Bur Standards '30; prof textiles Clemson Coll '29-35, NC State Coll since '35; research cons Textile Research Inst '41-42. Am Soc Textile Chem and Colorists—Phi Psi—Kappa Tau Beta— Phi Kappa Phi. N.C. State College, Raleigh, N.C. H: 2709 Bedford Av.

15 SHINNERS, L l o y d H(erbert). Compositae of North America; Flora of Texas; Plant geography of the prairies of North America. b'18. BA '40—MA '41—PhD '43 (U Wis); research fellow '45-48 (So Meth U). Author articles in field. Asst prof biol So Meth U since '47, director Herbarium since '49. Am Soc Plant Taxonomists—AAAS —Calif Bot Soc—Soc Study Evolution —Tex Acad Sci(F)—Phi Beta Kappa— Sigma Xi. Southern Methodist University, Dallas 5.

16 SHIPLEY, Robert Morrill. Gemology. b'87. Student '03-05 (St Johns Mil Acad); '05-07 (Wis). Author: Science of Gemstones '33; Diamonds '35; Silverware '40; Famous Diamonds of the World '44; Jewelers Pocket Reference Book '47. Co-author: Advanced Gemology '37; Precious Metals and Jewelry '38; The Story of Diamonds '41. Editor: Gems and Gemology '45-52. Gem dealer US and France '16-30. Gemological Inst Am (founder, pres '31-41, exec dir since '41)—Am Gem Soc (founder '34, hon life mem, exec dir '34-36). 3059 Wilshire Blvd., Los Angeles 5. H: Cliffs Edge, Circle Dr., S. Laguna, Cal.

17 SHIPPY, William Byron. Floriculture; Easter lilies, gladioli and other flowers. b'00. BS '25—MS '27 (Ia State Coll); PhD '30 (Columbia). Author articles in field. Grower and cons Easter lilies and gladioli since '42; Fla and Southeastern Florists' Assn (hon) —AAAS(F)—Am Phytopath Soc—Bot Soc Am—Fla Acad Sci. Route 1, Box 73, Sanford, Fla.

18 SHIRCLIFFE, Arnold. Restaurant management. b'80. Ed pub schs. Research on railroad dining car management and restaurant departments, in charge of feeding all US troops on railroads in Europe '18-19, helped to originate hot travel ration for soldiers; in charge dining car service American Railways in France; catering and restaurant management; food purchasing and menu making; wines and liquors as they complement food; glasses and their proper uses. Author: Edgewater Salad Book '26; Edgewater Sandwich Book '30; Children's Menu Book '32; Principles of Cookery '42; Menus and Menus in the Making '52; also articles in field. Catering mgr Edgewater Beach Hotel '23-28; mgr Medinah Athletic Club '28-29; catering mgr Belden-Stratford, Webster and Parkway Hotels '29-33; mgr Chicago Athletic Assn '33-36; mgr Wrigley Bldg Restaurant since '36; lecturer various universities and colleges. Ill Dietetic Assn—Am Dietetic Assn—Stewards Association (ednl com)—Chicago Dietetic Assn. 410 N. Michigan Av., Chgo. 11.

19 SHIRLEY, Hardy L. Forestry (Tropical, seed testing). b'00. AB '22 (Ind U); PhD '28 (Yale). Research on tree seed testing and seed certification; special mission to Caribbean region to study needs for research in tropical forestry '37, led to establishment of Tropical Forest Experiment Station in '39. Author articles in field. Silviculturist Lake States Forest Expt Sta St Paul '29-39, dir Allegheny Forest Expt Sta Phila '39-42, Northeastern Forest Expt Sta Phila '42-45; asst dean NY State Coll Forestry Syracuse U since '45; editor in chief Jour of Forestry '46-49. AAAS(F)—Soc Am Foresters (council '44-45)—Bot Soc Am— Am Soc Plant Physiol—Am Forestry Assn—Ecol Soc Am—Phi Beta Kappa —Sigma Xi. Oberlaender Trust fellow '35. 324 Ostrom Av., Syracuse, N.Y.

20 SHIRLEY, Ray Louis. Isotopes; Biochemistry. b'12. BS '37—MS '39 (W Va U); PhD '49 (Mich State Coll). Investigation in radioactive isotopes in field of animal nutrition and metabolism, analytical determination of nitrogen and minerals in biological materials, application of radioactive isotopes as tracers. Author articles in field. Research chemist Hercules Powder Co Expt Sta Wilmington Del '42-47; asst prof agrl chem research Mich State Coll '47-49; biochemist U Fla Agrl Expt Sta Gainesville since '49. ACS—AAAS—Sigma Xi. 103 Annis Boulevard, Gainesville, Fla.†

21 SHOCK, Nathan Wetherill. Gerontology; Physiology. b'06. BS '26—MS '27 (Purdue); PhD '30 (U Chicago). Research on physiological changes with aging in humans with particular reference to adolescence and old age, physiological responses to exercise, effect of aging on kidney function, acid-base equilibrium of the blood. Author articles in field. Chief sect gerontology USPHS Nat Inst Health Bethesda Md since '41; vis physiol Baltimore city hosps since '41. Am Psychol Assn—Am Physiol Soc—Gerontological Soc — Club Research on Aging—Soc Research Child Development—Soc Exptl Biol Med— Psychometric Soc—AAAS—Sigma Xi. U.S. Public Health Service, Section on Gerontology, Baltimore City Hospitals, Baltimore.

22 SHOCKLEY, William. Electrons; Solid-state physics. b'10. BS '32 (Calif Inst Tech); PhD '36 (MIT). Research on theory of vacuum tubes, solid state physics, semi-conductors, semi-conductor amplifiers or transsistors, slip bands in metals, magnetic domains, electrical timing device, electron microscope for filaments, nature of metallic state, electronic energy bands, order in alloys and interaction of atoms, induction of currents to conductors, space charge. Author articles in field. Mem tech staff Bell Telephone Labs since '36; dir research Anti-Submarine Warefare Operations Research Group '42-43; expert cons Office Sec War '42-45. Sigma Xi—Tau Beta Pi—Am Phys Soc(F)—Am Inst US Res (founder)—Nat Acad Scis—Am Acad Arts Scis. Bell Telephone Laboratories, Murray Hill, N.J.

23 SHOE, Lucy Taxis. Greek architecture; Architectural moldings. BA '27—MA '28—PhD '35 (Bryn Mawr); fellow '29-34 (Am Sch Classical Studies Athens). Member managing committee and several subcommittees American School of Classical Studies at Athens; member Institute for Advanced Study '48-49, '50-'54. Author: Profiles of Greek Mouldings (2 vols) '36; Profiles of Western Greek Mouldings, (2 volumes), '52. Asso prof archeol Greek and curator ancient collections Dwight Art Gallery Mount Holyoke Coll '41-50, academic adv '43-48; ed publications Am Sch Classical Studies Athens. Archeol Inst Am. Fellow Am Acad Rome '36-37, '49-50. Institute for Advanced Study, Princeton, N.J.†

24 SHOEMAKER, Mark Mercer. Park (Planning); Town site (Planning). b '98. BA (U Mich). Landscape architect and consultant specializing in park, town, site planning. Author article: Basic Plants for Landscape Use in Maryland '45, and others. Contributor: Maryland sect of A Traveler's Guide to Roadside Wild Flowers, Shrubs, and

Trees of the United States '49. Landscape arch Md Ext Service '31-34, '36; Maryland land planning cons for Md Nat Resources Bd '35; with U Md since '36, now prof landscape arch, extension landscape specialist and landscape architect for U Md. Am Soc Landscape Arch—Sigma Alpha Epsilon. University of Maryland, College Park, Md. H: 311 Willard Av., Chevy Chase 15.

10 SHOFFNER, Robert Worth. Iris. b'02. BS in agr '29 (NC State Coll). Hybridized several hundred seedlings and named one Popcorn; has collection of several hundred varieties of iris; lecturer on iris growing. Author articles in field. Dist agt NC Agrl Extension Service since '45. Am Iris Soc (ofcl judge). District Agent, Agricultural Extension Service, State College Station, Raleigh, N.C.†

11 SHORES, Venila Lovina. American history (Jacksonian period, Florida). b'93. BA '14 (Bates Coll, Me); MA '18 (Smith Coll, Mass); PhD '29— Eastern Star U fellowship '27-29 (Johns Hopkins U). Author articles in field. Prof hist head dept Fla State University Tallahassee since '41. AHA —So Hist Soc—Vt Hist Society (life) —Fla Hist Soc—Fla Acad Sci—Phi Beta Kappa—Phi Alpha Theta. Florida State University, Tallahassee, Fla.

12 SHOTWELL, Robert Leslie. Grasshoppers. b'94. AB '20 (U Denver); AM '24 (U Colo); '30-33 (Mont State Coll). Development of a method for making annual grasshopper survey; analysis and application statistical methods to grasshopper research which involves methods for forecasting seasonal history and abundance in relation to weather conditions; use new insecticides on a farm and community basis in areas of different agricultural problems and practices. Jr entomol Cereal and Forage Insects Bur Entomol and Plant Quarantine USDA '23-26, asst entomol '25-36, entomol since '36. Am Statis Assn—Biometric Soc.

13 SHOUP, Charles Samuel. Bacteria and fungi (Respiration, metabolism); Limnology (Chemical characteristics). b'05. AB '27 (Central Coll Mo); MA '27—PhD '29 (Princeton U). Research on respiration and metabolism of bacteria and fungi, chemical characteristics of natural waters of lakes and streams. Author articles in field. With Vanderbilt U since '29, prof biol '49-50; biol U.S. AEC Oak Ridge Tenn '50-51, chief biology branch Oak Ridge Opns. since '51. Investigator Marine Biol Lab Woods Hole Mass summers '27, '28, '30, '33, '35, Scripps Institute Oceanog U Cal '31; staff Mt Lake Biol Sta U Va summers '46, '47; aquatic biol field survey party leader Tenn Div Game Fish summers '38-41. AAAS —Am Soc Limnol Oceanog—Am Fisheries Soc—Assn Southeastern Biol—Tenn Acad Sci (vp 42-43, pres '43-44). 80 Outer Dr., Oak Ridge, Tenn.

14 SHOU YI, Ch'en. Chinese literature and cultural history. b'99. AB '20 (Lingnan U); PhD '28 (U Chicago). Author: Introduction to Chinese Culture '23; Cultural Contacts Between China and the Occident '32. Translator: J. W. Thompson's History of the Middle Ages '38; also articles in field. Prof Chinese culture Pomona Coll and Claremont Grad Sch since '41. Inst Hist Philos Academia Sinica(F)— Chinese Social Polit Sci Assn—Am Oriental Soc—AHA—Phi Beta Kappa. 690 Indian Hill Blvd., Claremont, Calif.

15 SHOWALTER, Amos Martin. Cytology of Liverworts (Anacrogynae division); Pumpkin breeding. b'91. BA '18 (Goshen Coll); MA '20—PhD '22 (U Wis); exchange fellow '22-24 (U Louvain Belgium); student (Cornell, Stanford, U Brussels, U Frieburg). Prof biol Madison Coll since '34. Va Acad Sci—Bot Soc Am—AAAS(F)—Genetics Soc Am. Nat Research fellow '24-27. Madison College, Harrisonburg, Va.†

16 SHREVE, Ewart Carl. Railway engineering. b'03. B Civil Engring '28— MS '29—CE '35 (O State U). Research on concrete design of roadbed, tracks, classification yards, engine terminals, transfer bridges, merchandise, ore and coal piers. Head dept engring Potomac State Sch W Va U '30-40; with W Md Ry Co since '40, chief engr from '45. Am Soc CE—Am Ry Engring Assn —Nat Soc Prof Engrs—Md Soc Prof Engrs—W Va Soc Prof Engrs—Am Wood Preservers Assn—Roadmasters and Maintenance of Way Assn—Sigma Xi. Western Maryland Railway Co., Hillen Station, Balt 2.

17 SHROCK, Robert Rakes. Invertebrate paleontology; Sedimentology; Layered Rocks. b'04. AB '25—AM '26 —PhD '28 (Ind U). Author: Sequence in Layered Rocks '48. Co-author: Invertebrate Paleontology '35; Index Fossils of North America '44; also articles in field. Prof, chmn dept geol MIT since '50. Ind Acad Sci—Geol Soc Am—Paleontol Soc—Am Assn Pet Geol—Soc Econ Paleontol Mineral.◉

18 SHUGG, Roger Wallace. American history (The South, 19th century); History of World War II. b'05. AB '27—AM '31—PhD '35—Porter Ogden Jacobus Fellow (Princeton); Social Sci Research Council Fellow '38-39 (London Sch Econ, Cambridge U). Author: Origins of Class Struggle in Louisiana, a Social History of the White Farmer and Laborer, 1840-1880 '39; The World at War '45. Co-author: (with H deWeerd) World War II '46. Asso prof hist Ind U '41-45; ed hist social sci Alfred A Knopf Inc pub '45-53; director Rutgers Univ Press since '53. Hist War Dept Gen Staff G-2 Mil Intelligence '44-45. Miss Valley Hist Assn—So Hist Assn—AHA—Phi Beta Kappa. Rutgers University Press, New Brunswick, N.J.

19 SHULDENER, Henry L(incoln). Water treatment; Corrosion. b'98. BSche '20 (NYU). Inventor liquid feeding devices for automatically apportioning chemicals to water supplies. Author articles in field. Tech dept Permutit Co '20-28; pres and tech dir Water Service Labs Inc since '28. Am Chem Soc—Am Coordinating Com on Corrosion—Nat Assn Corrosion Engrs —AICE—Am Soc Testing Materials— Am Water Wks Assn—Electrochem Soc. 423 W. 126th St., NYC 27. H: 5 Butler Rd., Scarsdale, N.Y.

20 SHULENBERGER,   C(larence) B(onner). Accounting (Education); Banking. b'94. AB '20 (Roanoke Coll); AM '36 (Columbia U). Organized Nat Investment Corp Asheville '26, served as pres and dir '26; asst prof accounting NC State Coll '27-30, asso prof '30-42, prof accounting since '42. Am Acad Polit and Soc Sci—Am Inst Promotion Sci—Am Assn Accounting— Delta Sigma Pi—Phi Kappa Phi. NC State College, Raleigh.†◉

21 SHULER, Ellis W(illiam). Geomorphology; Economic geology; Geology (Popularization). b'81. BA '03— LLD '43 (Emory and Henry Coll); MA '07 (Vanderbilt U); MA '14—PhD '15 (Harvard). Author: Rocks and Rivers of America '45. Fellow Harvard '13-14, asst in geology Harvard '14-15; asso prof geology So Methodist U '15-17, prof since '18, dean Grad Sch since '26. Geol Soc Am(F)—AAAS— Texas Acad Sci—Am Assn Geographers —Am Assn Petroleum Geologists—Sigma Xi. 3429 Haynie Av., Dallas.◉

22 SHULL, Charles W(illiam). Legislative apportionment; State governmental problems. b'04. BA '26 (O Wesleyan U); MA '27—PhD '29 (O State U). Co-author: (with G O Comfort and R H Knapp) Your Government '51; (with J M Leonard) Reappoortionment in Michigan '40; Introduction to Political Science '50, also articles in field. Faculty Wayne U since '30, prof govt since '50; book review ed Social Sci. Am Polit Sci Assn (com on Am legislatures)—Nat Municipal League—Am Acad Polit and Social Sci—Soc Comparative Legislation— Mich Acad Sci Arts and Letters—Am Judicature Soc—Midwest Polit Sci Assn —Pi Gamma Mu—Pi Sigma Alpha (pres '41-47). Wayne University, Det 1

23 SHULL, George Harrison. Genetics; Botany (Mutation, heterosis, lethal factors, sex evolution, biometry, plant breeding, geographical distribution). b'74. BS '01—LLD '40 (Antioch Coll); PhD '04 (U Chicago); ScD '40 (Lawrence Coll); ScD '42 (Ia State Coll Agr and Mech Arts). Author articles in field. Prof bot genetics Princeton U since '15, emeritus '42; founder, mng ed Genetics '16-25, asso ed since '25; vp Genetics Inc since '40. AAAS (F)—Deutsche Botanische Gesellschaft (corr mem)—Acad Sci Vienna (corr mem)—Gesellschaft fur Pflanzenzuchtung in Wien (hon mem)—Swedish Seed Assn (hon mem)—Deutsche Gesellschaft fur Vererbungswissenschaft —Societe Linneenne de Lyon—Inst Internat d'Anthropologie Paris—Torrey Bot Club (pres '47)—Bot Soc Am—Am Soc Naturalists (hon mem, vp '11, pres '17)—Ecol Soc Am—Am Genetic Assn (chmn plant sect '12, adv com since '22)—Eugenics Research Assn—Eugenics Soc Am—Genetics Soc Am—Am Geog Soc—Am Soc Plant Physiol— Washington Acad Sci—Am Philos Soc —Sigma Xi. Awarded gold medal De Kalb Agrl Assn for invention of hybrid corn '40; citation for distinguished service to agr by NJ Bd Agr '45; John Scott medal and premium '46. 60 Jefferson Rd., Princeton, N.J.◉

24 SHULTZ, Frances. Illustration (Medical). b'02. Student '22 (Ill State Normal Sch); '23 (U Ill); '24-26 (Art Inst Chicago); '26-27 (Am Acad Advt Art Chicago); '29-32 (Johns Hopkins U Med Sch). Water color painting medical subjects; tone drawings on Ross board; pen and ink sketches medical subjects; pencil sketching from operations and pathological specimens, in line, tone or color. Free lance illus med journs, lectures, exhbts and books since '32; med illus dept gynecology Johns Hopkins Hosp Baltimore '33-39; visiting medical illustrators Union Memorial Hospital Baltimore '33-38; med. and sci illus med illus service Armed Forces Inst Path since '50. Am. Med Illus Assn. Medical Illustration Service, Armed Forces Institute of Pathology, 8th and Independence S.W., Washington 25. H: 1909 McElderry St., Balt. 5.

25 SHUMAN, Everett Carlyle. Portland cement; Thermal insulation. b'02. BS (Civil engring) '24—MS '26 (U Wis). Research in fundamentals of making good concrete, including design and construction concrete testing apparatus for field and laboratory. Co-author article: (with H F Gonnerman) Compression, Flexure and Tension tests of plain concrete. Asso engr Research Labs Portland Cement Assn Chicago '26-38; engr concrete lab N Atlantic div War Dept '41-44; dir research and mngr product development kaylo div Owens-Ill Glass Co, Toledo since '44. Am Soc CE—Soc Rheology— Soc Exptl Stress Analysis—ASTM—A CI—Am Soc Quality Control—Am Assn

Engrs. Meritorious civilian service award War Dept '44. Kaylo Div., Owens-Illinois Glass Co., Box 1035, Toledo.

10 SHURRAGER, Phil Sheridan. Psychology (Learned motor responses). b'07. BS '30 (Muckingum Coll); AM '32 (Ohio U); PhD '39 (U Ill). Established motor learned responses posterior to transection spinal cord in dogs and cats; research effect localized lesions; discovery mucopoly-saccharide-protein substrate system in vitreous humor whose depolymerization and photorepolymerization parallel dark and light adaption in mammalian eyes; that substrate hyaluronic acid mesenchyme of central nervous tissues is depolymerized during stimulation and repolymerized in recovery through inactivation enzyme hyaluronidase. NRC fellow psychol U Rochester '39-40; vis prof psychol U Pa '40-41; cons psychol Stevenson, Jordan and Harrison Inc '44-46; prof and chmn dept psychol and edn Ill Inst Tech since '46; pres personnel and plant analysts since '50. Diplomate indsl. psychol Am Bd Examiners Profl Psychol. Am Psychol Assn—Am Soc Engring Edn—Am Statis Soc—Sigma Xi—Pi Gamma Mu. 3300 South Federal St., Chgo 16.◎

11 SHUSTER, Carl Nathaniel. Mathematical instruments and applications of mathematics. b'90. BS '15—PhD '40 (Columbia). Author: Field Work in Mathematics; Real Life Arithmetics; A Study of the Problems of Teaching the Slide Rule; Computation with Approximate Data. Prof head dept math State Teachers Coll Trenton NJ since '28. Nat Council Teachers Math (pres '46-48)—Am Math Soc—Math Assn Am—AAAS. State Teachers College, Trenton, N.J.

12 SHUSTER, George Nauman. German history; Literature (English). AB '15—AM '20 (Notre Dame U); Certificat d'Aptitude '19 (Poitiers U); PhD '40 (Columbia). Research on history of literary forms, relation of Catholic church to literature; made extensive studies of German people and events; member of advisory committee, Division of Cultural Relations, Dept of State '42-44; chairman Historical Commn to Germany, War Dept '45. Author: Catholic Spirit in Modern English Literature '22; Newman, Prose and Poetry '25; English Literature '26; The Hill of Happiness '26; The Catholic Spirit in America '27; The Eternal Magnet '29; The Catholic Church and Current Literature '29; The Germans '32; Strong Man Rules '34; Like a Mighty Army '35; Brother Flo '38; Look Away '39; The English Ode from Milton to Keats '40; Religion and Education '45; also articles in field. Head dept Eng Notre Dame U '20-24; instr in Eng Brooklyn Poly Inst '24-25; prof St Josephs Coll for Women '25-35; asso editor Commonweal '25-26, mng editor '26-38; contrbing editor since '38; dean and acting pres Hunter Coll '39-40, pres since '40. Fellow Social Science Research Council Columbia '37-39; Oberlaender Trust fellow Germany '33-34. 695 Park Av., NYC. H: Stamford, Conn.

13 SHYBEKAY, Derso Sebeok. Peat, lignite and taconite (Utilization). b'97. BS '18—DE '18—LLD '18 (Royal Univ Budapest); PhD '21 (U Berlin). Research, development, utilization of peat, lignite, taconite in electric power plants, heating and air conditioning systems. Author books and articles in field. Dir market research North Star Woolen Mill Co Minneapolis since '45. Industrial Research Council (pres)—Royal Econ Soc Gt Brit(F)—Nat Council Professional Indsl Engrs (pres)—Nat Soc Professional Engrs—Soc Promotion Engring Edn—Am Ednl Assn (life mem)—Soc Engrs Gt Brit (Royal F) — Am Soc Tool Engrs — Nat Assn Cost Accountants—Soc Advancement Management—Am Management Assn—Peat and By-Products Council Am (exec vp). P.O. Box 1202, Washington 13.

14 SIBLEY, Robert. Thermodynamics; International power development and world resources; California history; Flora and fauna. b'81. BSc '03—EE '22 (U Calif); '30 (Stanford). Author: A Primer of Applied Thermodynamics; Elements of Fuel Oil and Steam Engineering (with H C Delany) '18; Research Statistics on Undeveloped Water Power Resources of the U. S.; America's Answer to the Russian Challenge '31. Editor: Romance of the University of California '33; Golden Book of California '36; Folio of California Wild-flowers '39; Folio of The Seasons of California '40; Folio Birds of California '44. Prof mechanical engring U Calif '11-15; pres Fidelity Acceptance Corp since '27; chmn bd dir Bank of Berkeley since '44, East Bay Regional Parks since '48. ASME (del World Power Conf, Berlin '30, Stockholm '33)—AIEE(F, vp '21-23)—Phi Beta Kappa—Sigma Xi—Tau Beta Pi. Stephens Union, Berkeley.†◎

15 SIDERIS, Christos Plutarch. Pineapple physiology; Plant mineral nutrition and metabolism. b'91. BC '09 (Samos Lyceum); BS '21—PhD '24 (U Calif). Author articles in field. Plant physiol US Dept Agr. AAAS—Am Soc Plant Physiol—Am Bot Soc—Am Phytopath Soc — Am Chem Soc — Soc Growth Develop—Hawaiian Bot Soc—Hawaiian Acad Sci. Pineapple Res Insti of Hawaii, Box 3166, Honolulu 2.

16 SIDWELL, Arthur P(lummer). Canning crops (Vegetables, fruits especially pineapple). b'16. BS '37 (U Ill); MS '40 (O State U). Author articles in field. Research supt Molokai Plantation Libby McNeill and Libby Hawaii since '44. Am Soc Hort Sci—Sigma Xi. Maunaloa, Molokai, T.H.

17 SIEBEL, Fred Peter, Jr. Brewing and baking technology. b'01. BS '24 (U Ill). Author articles in field. With J E Siebel Sons' Co Inc since '25, pres since '42. Am Assn Cereal Chem—Am Soc Brewing Chem — Master Brewers Assn Am—Am Chem Soc—Am Soc Bakery Engrs—Am Soc Refrigering Engrs. 741 W. Jackson, Chicago 6.

18 SIEDENTOPF, Heinz A. Virology. b'10. Student '31 (Mont State Coll); BA '38—MS '41—PhD '47 (U Minn). Author articles in field. Cons virus dehydration Fromm Labs Inc '41-43, asst dir '44-47, dir since '47. Soc Bact—AAAS—Sigma Xi. Fromm Laboratories, Inc., Grafton, Wis.

19 SIEGELE, Herman Hugo. Carpentry. b'83. Grad '06 (Emporia Bus Coll Kan); diploma (Internat Corr Sch). Consultant on roof framing, short cuts, house plans, stair building, scaffolding, form building, and rough carpentry. Author: Carpentry '42; Building '44; Quick Construction '45; Building Trades Dictionary '46 Roof Framing '47; Concrete Construction '48; Carpenters' Tools '50; The Steel Square '51; and others; also articles in field. Contributor: Carpenter Magazine since '23. Apprentice carpenter advancing to gen supt constrn work '99-40; free lance writer since '20. United Brotherhood of Carpenters and Joiners of Am., Kansas Authors Club. H: 222 S. Constitution St., Emporia, Kan.†

20 SIEGLINGER, John B. Sorghum (Broomcorn). b'93. BS '13 (Okla A&M Coll); MS '15 (Kan State Coll) Bred and selected wheatland, sooner and day milos, combine kafir, redlan and fultip broomcorn. Author articles: Grain-sorghum Experiments at the Woodward Field Station in Oklahoma '23; Broomcorn Experiments at the United States Dry-Land Field Station, Woodward, Oklahoma '28, and others. Asst agriculturist cereal crops and diseases Bur Plant Industry US Dept Agr '15 Woodward Okla, Stillwater Okla since '41, sr agron since '46. Sigma Xi. Agrl and Mech Coll, Stillwater Okla.

21 SIEMS, H(erman) B. Plant food and fertilizer manufacturing; Agricultural chemistry. b'95. BS '19—PhD '22 (U Chicago). Research chem chief chem and dir research Swift & Co Plant Food Div Union Stock Yards Chicago since '24. AAAS(F)—Am Chem Soc (chmn fertilizer chem div '40-46)—Am Soc Plant Physiol—Am Soc Econ Entomol—Nat Fertilizer Assn (chmn plant food research com since '40)—Am Soc Agron (chmn plant nutrients div '48-49)—Sigma Xi. Chosen by Chicago section ACS as one of ten ablest in fertilizer chem. Swift and Company, Union Stock Yards, Chicago 9.†

22 SIGLER, William Franklin. Fisheries and wildlife management. b'09. BS '40—MS '41—PhD '47 (Ia State Coll). Author articles in field. Asst prof dept wildlife management Utah State Agrl Coll '47-50, head dept wildlife mgt since '50. American Soc Limnol Oceanog—Wildlife Soc—Am Soc Ichthyol Herpetol—Am Fisheries Soc—Sigma Xi—Phi Kappa Phi—Xi Sigma Phi. Wildlife Management Dept, Utah State Agrl Coll, Logan, Utah.†

23 SILBER, Robert Howard. Biochemistry (Amino acid, vitamin, drug). b'15. AB '37—PhD '41 (Washington U). Head dept biol chem Merck Inst Therapeutic Research Rahway NJ since '41. Am Soc Biol Chem—NY Acad Sci—Am Chem Soc—Sigma Xi—Phi Beta Kappa. Merck Institute, Rahway, N.J.

24 SILCOCK, Arnold. Chinese art (History). b'89. F '27 (Royal Inst Brit Archts); F '36 (Royal Soc Arts). Research on Chinese art and architecture, architect on archaeological expeditions to Antioch and Mycenae. Author: Introduction to Chinese Art and History (6th rev edit) '37-50; A Background for Beauty '51; Chinese Architecture '37; also articles in field. Contributor: Children's (Encyclopaedia) Britannica '51; Treasury of Knowledge '39. Partner T B Silcock and Son '19-26; own practice since '27. Royal Inst Brit Archts(F, Florence Bursar, mem Tite prize jury and lit com)—Archtl Assn (mem council '19-20, '38-39, hon bursar and hon ed '38-39)—Art Workers Guild—Royal Soc Arts(F). Fairhaven, Letcombe Regis, Berkshire, Eng.

25 SILING, Philip Francis. Radio frequency allocation. b'97. PhB '17 (Yale). Represented RCA at the Third Inter-American Radio Conference Rio de Janeiro '45, U.S.-United Kingdom Telecommunications Conference Bermuda '45, The Five-Power Telecommunications Conference Moscow '46, World International Telecommunications Conferences Atlantic City '47, International Consultative Committee for Radio Stockholm '48, Fourth Inter-American Radio Conference Washington '49. Author articles in field. Sr telephone engr Fed Communications Commn '35-37, asst chief Internat Div '37-41, chief '41-43, asst chief engr charge broadcasting '43-44; engr charge RCA Frequency Bur since '45; chmn joint tech adv com Inst Radio Engrs and RMA '48-49. Inst Radio Engrs (sr)—Sigma Xi. 1625 K St., N.W., Washington.

26 SILKER, Ralph E(dward). Alfalfa (Dehydration). b'05. AB '27 (U Dubuque Ia); MS '31—PhD '34 (U Ia). Research on chemical content of dehydrated alfalfa, methods for determination of nutritional content after dehydration and storage; study of storage problems fresh and dehydrated alfalfa. Co-author articles: (with W G Schrenk, H H King) Carotene Content of Alfalfa, Retention on Dehydration and Storage '44; (with W G Schrenk, H H King) Storage of Commercial Dehydrated Alfalfa Meal '47; (with H H King) Handling Fresh Alfalfa before Dehydration '47, and others. Head dept chem Doane Coll Crete Neb '34-37; prof chem Neb State Teacher's Coll Chadron '37-41; asst prof, asst chem Agrl Expt Sta Kan State Coll '43-45; dir research W J Small Co Inc Kansas City Mo '45-48; head dept chem Kan State Coll since '48. ACS—AAAS—Kan Acad Sci—Am Dehydrators Assn (research council)—Am Feed Mfrs Association (nutrition council)—Sigma Xi—Phi Lambda Upsilon—Alpha Chi Sigma—Gamma Sigma Delta—Phi Kappa Phi. Kansas State College, Manhattan, Kan.

10 SILL, Webster Harrison. Agriculture; Rural community organization. b'87. BS '11 (Pa State Coll). Author (circulars) Grapes of Pennsylvania '11; Pruning, Gardening '14; Landscaping the Home Grounds '15; also articles in field. Co agrl agt Parkersburg W Va '25-47; cons on agrl practices; writer farm page Parkersburg News '30-46; active on civic agrl coms. W Va Co Agt Assn (pres)—Nat Assn Co Agrl Agt (pres '46)—W Va U Agrl Extension Div Dairy Poultry Seed Improvement Assns. Recipient certificate distinguished service Nat Assn Co Agrl Agents '41. Wood County Court House, Parkersburg, W.Va.☉

11 SILLECK, Clarence Frederick. Synthetic resins; Pigment dispersion. b'09. BS '32—MS '36 (Brooklyn Polytech Inst); (NYU). Patents on pigmented composition, pigmented synthetic resin composition. Co-author articles: (with William Howlett Gardner) A Systematic Method for Evaluating Lacquer Plasticizers; (with Sidney Lauren) Some Observations on Wrinkle Finishes. Chem C J Osborn Co '33-37, chief chem '37-40, tech dir '40-43, vp and tech dir since '43. Am Chem Soc—AAAS. 1301 W. Blancke St., Linden, N.J.

12 SILVER, Rollo Gabriel. Walt Whitman; Nineteenth century American printing and publishing. b'09. PhD '31 (Brown U); MA '41 (Boston U); BS '48 (Simmons Coll). Author: The Boston Book Trade, 1800-1825 '48. Co-editor: A Child's Reminiscence by Walt Whitman '30; Faint Clews and Indirections '49; also articles in field. Reference librarian Peabody Inst Library '48-51; asst prof library science Simmons Coll since '51. Biblio Soc Am (com 19th century Am pub). Simmons College, Boston 15.

13 SILVERMAN, Alexander. Glass (Manufacture). b'81. PhB '02—MS '07—hon SD '30 (Pittsburgh U); AB '05 (Cornell); hon SD '36 (Alfred U). US delegate to International Union of Chemistry Belgium '30, Spain '34, Switzerland '36, Italy '38, England '47. Researches resulted in manufacture of important commercial glasses; invented devices for miscroscope illumination. Author: Selective Experiments in General Chemistry (with A L Robinson) '39; also articles in field. With Pittsburgh U since '05, prof inorganic chem since '12, head chem dept since '18; cons glass; mem Div Chem and Chem Tech Nat Research Council '38-41, 47-51. Am Chem Soc—Pa Acad Sci—Electrochem Soc — Sigma Xi — Pa Chem Soc—Soc Protection Sci Learn-

ing (England)Am Ceramic Soc(F)—AAAS(F)—Am Inst Chem(F)—Am Inst Ceramic Engrs(F)—Soc Glass Tech England(F)—Phi Lambda Upsilon. Received Pittsburgh Award Am Chem Soc '40. University of Pittsburgh, Pitts 13.†☉

14 SILZ, Walter. Nineteenth Century German literature (Romanticism); Heinrich von Kleist. b'94. AB '17—AM '18—PhD '22 (Harvard); '20-21 (U Heidelberg and Munich). Author: Heinrich von Kleist's Conception of the Tragic '23; Early German Romanticism: Its Founders and Kleist '29; German Romantic Lyrics '34; also articles in field. Prof German head German sect Princeton U since '48. Phi Beta Kappa—Mod Lang Assn Am—Goethe-Gesellschaft Germany — Kleist-Gesellschaft Germany. Guggenheim fellow '26-27. Department of Modern Languages, Princeton University, Princeton, N.J.†☉

15 SIMERL, Linton Earl. Pulp and paper technology (Protective packaging); Chemical warfare. b'11. BChE '35 (O State U); MS '37—PhD '39 (Inst Paper Chem). Author articles in field. Charge mfg eng lab development and prodn protective food packaging Marathon Corps '46; research and development dept Olin Cellophane Div. New Haven. US Army Chemical Warfare Service '41-45, now lt colonel reserve. Am Chem Soc (chmn NE Wis Sect)—Tech Assn Pulp Paper Ind—Sigma Xi—Tau Beta Pi. Research and Development Department, Olin Cellophane Division, New Haven.

16 SIMISON, Allen LeRoy. Fiberglas products. b'05. BCerE '27 (O State U). About 20 patents on fiberglas products and processes. Fiberglas products and process development research Owens-Illinois Glass Co and Owens-Corning Fiberglas Corp '32-45, product application and process control '45-49, in charge product quality control and process control since '49. Am Ceramic Soc—O Professional Engrs Soc. Owens-Corning Fiberglas Corp., Toledo, O.

17 SIMKINS, Francis Butler. Recent History of South Carolina and Southern United States. b'97. BA '18 (Univ SC); MA '20—PhD '26 (Columbia). Attended seminars in field, Columbia; engaged extensive research in Library of Congress, NY Public Library, Duke U, Univ NC and Univ SC libraries, on recent social, religious, educational, artistic and political phases of Southern history. Author: The Tillman Movement in South Carolina '26; South Carolina During Reconstruction (with Woody) '32; Women of the Confederacy (with Patton) '38; Pitchfork Ben Tillman: South Carolinian '44; The South, Old and New, 1820-1947 '48; articles in field pub learned journals. Asso prof history State Teachers Coll. Farmville Va '27-48; asso prof Southern history LSU since '48. AHA—Miss Valley Historical Assn—Southern Historical Association (exec com). Awarded Dunning Prize, Am Historical Assn '32; Social Science Research Council fellow '29-30; Univ fellow, Columbia '22-23. History Dept., Louisiana State Univ., Baton Rouge.

18 SIMMONS, Ernest J. Russian literature; Alexander Pushkin. b'03. AB '25—AM '26—PhD '28 (Harvard). Author: English Literature and Culture in Russia '35; Pushkin '37; (with Samuel H Cross) Alexander Pushkin, His Life and Literary Heritage '37; Dostoevski: The Making of a Novelist '40; Outline of Modern Russian Literature, 1880-1940 '43; Leo Tolstoy '46. Editor: U. S.S.R.: A Concise Handbook '47; (with Samuel H Cross) Centennial Essays

for Pushkin '37; (with Alexander Kaun) Slavic Studies '43. Asso editor English Slavonic Rev. Research work in Russia '28-29, '32, '35, '37, '47; instr Harvard '29-36, asst prof and chmn bd English tutors '36-39; asso prof Eng and Russian lit Cornell U since '41; prof Russian lang and lit Cornell U '45; chmn dept Slavic langs and lit '42-46; chmn dept Slavic langs and prof Russian lit Russian Inst Columbia since '47; mng editor Am Slavic and East European Review '47-50. Modern Lang Assn—Am Council Learned Socs (sec Slavic com '47-50). Awarded Milton grant for foreign travel '32, '35, '37.☉

19 SIMMONS, Francis Estol. Textiles (Industry, economics). b'02. AB '23 (Dickinson Coll); MA '26 (Am U). Chief rayon, silk and miscellaneous fibers sect textile div US Bur Fgn and Domestic Commerce '30-34; dir econ research Underwear Inst '34-41; chief program br textile, clothing and leather div WPB '41-43, asst dir '43-44; mgr Am Viscose Corp Washington since '44. Am. Marketing Assn—Washington Textile Roundtable (pres '46-48). American Viscose Corp., Washington Bldg., Washington 5.

20 SIMMS, Henry Harrison. American History. b'96. BA '17 (William and Mary Coll); MA '21 (U Va); PhD '29 (Columbia). Author: Rise of the Whigs in Virginia, 1824-1840 '29; Life of John Taylor '32; Life of Robert M T Hunter '35; A Decade of Sectional Controversy, 1851-1861 '42; articles in field. With O State U since '29, prof history since '46. AHA—Miss Valley Hist Assn—So Hist Assn—Phi Beta Kappa. History Department, Ohio State University, Columbus, O.

21 SIMON, Leslie E. Ballistics; Statistics (Quality control, mathematical); Industrial engineering; Supersonic wind tunnels; High-speed computing machines. b'00. BS '24 (US Mil Acad); BS '29 (MIT). War Department representative American Standards Association since '41, American Society for Testing Materials, Quality Control of Materials since '45. Author: Engineer's Manual of Statistical Methods '41; German Research in World War II '47; also articles in field. Dir Ballistic Research Labs Aberdeen Proving Ground '40-49, chief ordnance research and development division US Army since '49, lecturer Ordnance School since '47. Inst Math Statis(F)—Am Statis Assn(F)—Am Soc Quality Control—AAAS(F)—Am Ordnance Assn. Awarded Legion of Merit '44. Office, Chief of Ordnance, Washington 25.

22 SIMONDS, Andrew Warren. Found engineering; Dams (Construction); Pressure grouting; Grouting (pre stress). b'98. BS (CE) '21 (U Tex); MS '33 (U Colo). Treatment of concrete and earth dams by grouting methods to improve foundation rock; control and reduction of uplift pressure beneath concrete dams; repair of leaks through concrete dams and abutments; elimination of seepage through foundations and abutments of earth dams. Author articles: Masonry Dams; Foundation Experiences. Co-author article: (with Fred H Lippold, R E Keim) Treatment of Foundations for Large Dams by Grouting Methods '50. Engr US Bur Reclamation Denver since '27; cons engr Denver since '44, US Dept State assignment to Ministry of Works New Zealand and Metropolitan Bd Water Sewerage and Drainage Sydney Australia '50. Am Soc CE—AAAS—Am Concrete Inst—Professional Engrs of Colo—Nat Soc Professional Engrs—Colo Soc Engrs—Permanent Internat Assn Navigation Congresses—Sigma

Xi—Tau Beta Pi. US Bureau of Reclamation, D.F.C., Denver.

10 SIMONDS, Herbert R. Plastics and resins. b'87. Ed Pub sch. Author: Handbook of Plastics; Industrial Plastics. Co-author: The New Plastics; Plastics Business. Cons plastics and resin since '35; pres Holland-Rantos Co '25-47. Am Soc Testing Materials—Soc Plastics Ind—Soc Plastics Engrs—Assn Cons Chem Chem Engrs. 551 Fifth Av., NYC 17. H: Stepney, Conn.

11 SIMONS, Jakob Lennart. Nuclear physics. b'05. MSc '28—PhD '32 (U Helsinki). Demonstrated Raman effect in organic liquids; showed structural periodicity in liquids in a volume comprising a few molecules; determined scattering cross-section of slow neutrons by protons. With U Helsinki since '29, full prof since '41; Inst Advanced Study Princeton NJ '49-50. Finnish Scientific Soc—Am Physical Soc. Obtained beta-spectrum of Au 198, energy levels Hg 198; showed that position compound Chlor positionium has dynamic stability. Institute of Physics, Helsinki Brobergsterassen 20, Finland.

12 SIMONS, Joseph H. Fluorine chemistry; Molecular physics; Fluorocarbons. b'97. BS (chem engring) '19 —MS '22 (U Ill); Ph D '23 (U Calif). Discovered fluorocarbons and invented process for their production, discovered hydrogen fluoride catalysis. Editor and contributor: Fluorine Chemistry (vol I) '50. Prof phys chem Pa state Coll '36-50, dir fluorine lab '45-50; cons Minn Mining and Mfg Co since '44; prof chem engring U Fla and coordinator fluorine research since '50; cons Oak Ridge Nat Lab. ACS—Sigma Xi—AICHE—Phi Lambda Upsilon—Sigma Pi Sigma—AAAS—AAUP—NY Acad Sci. NRC F Cambridge, Eng, '29. College of Engineering, University of Florida, Gainesville, Fla. H: 1122 S.W. 11th Av.

13 SIMONSON, Wilbur Herbert. Highway design (Roadside development); Landscape architecture and engineering. b'97. BA (Landscape architecture) '21 (Cornell U). Co-designer Mount Vernon Memorial Highway; specialist in roadside development. Co-author: (with R R Royall) Roadside Improvement '34. Landscape architect A D Taylor Offices Cleveland '21-24; landscape designer and supt Westchester County Park Commn '24-29; designer Mt Vernon Memorial Highway '29-32; sr landscape architect US Bur Pub Rds '33-45, chief roadside sect since '46. Am. Soc Landscape Architects Inc (F)—Am Soc CE—Am Soc Photogrammetry—Am Congress on Surveying and Mapping—Am Geophysical Union—Am Planning and Civic Association United States Bureau of Public Roads, Washington 25. H: 4503 Middleton Lane, Bethesda 14, Md.

14 SIMPSON, Clarence J. Renaissance literature. b'15. AB '36 (Asbury Coll); AM '39 (U Cincinnati); '48— Stanford fellow '48 (Stanford U). Research on Sir John Davies's Nosce Teipsum; Davies's debt to Medieval philosophy. Asso prof Eng Wheaton Coll '48-53; prof chmn Eng Whitworth Coll Spokane Wash since '53. Whitworth College, Spokane, Wash.

15 SIMPSON, Clarence Oliver. Dental radiography. b'79. Grad '02 (Chicago Coll Dental Surgery); grad '06 (Barnes Med Coll). Author: The Technic of Oral Radiography '26; Advanced Radiodontic Interpretation '32; Principles and Practice of Radiodontics '36, also articles in field. Practice of dental radiography and diagnosis since '18; prof radiodontia sch dentistry Washington U '26-36, prof radiodontics since

'45. Internat Coll Dentists—Am Dental Assn—Mo State Dental Assn (pres '23) —Omicron Kappa Upsilon—Xi Psi Phi. O State Dental Soc Callahan Memorial medal for scientific contributions to the healing professions '39. University Club Bldg., StL.

16 SIMPSON, Claude M(itchell), Jr. Ballads (American, English). b'10. AB —B Mus '30—AM '31 (So Methodist U); AM '34—PhD '36 (Harvard). Ballad collector; research in music of broadside ballad; collections Renaissance music. Co-author: Elizabethan and Shakespearean Music for the Recorder; Jacobean and Restoration Music for the Recorder; A Treasury of the World's Finest Folk Songs '42; Catch that Catch Can: One Hundred English Rounds and Catches '45. Author articles: Tudor popular music: Its social significance; Ebsworth and the Roxburghe Ballads. From instr to asst prof English Harvard '39-47; prof Eng Ohio State U since '47. Am Folklore Soc—Am Dialect Soc. Received Rockefeller Post-War Fellowship and Fulbright Grant for research on music of British broadside ballad. Ohio State University, Columbus 10, O.

17 SIMPSON, Dwight McBryde. Cottonseed (Germination, storage, breeding). b'94. BS '16 (Clemson Agrl Coll); MS '39 (U Tenn). Author articles in field. With US Dept Agr in cotton research since '18, agron div cotton and other fiber crops and diseases Plant Ind Soils and Agrl Engring Agrl Research Adm, supt US Cotton Field Sta Knoxville Tenn. Am Soc Agron—Am Phytopath Soc—Am Genetic Assn— Phi Kappa Phi. U.S. Cotton Field Station, University of Tennessee Farm, Knoxville, Tenn.†

18 SIMPSON, George Eaton. Voodoo practices; Haiti (Folklore, customs). b'04. BS '26 (Coe Coll); MA '27 (U Mo); PhD '34 (U Pa); student (Northwestern U, U Chicago). Research and writing on voodoo service in northern Haiti, peasant songs and dances of northern Haiti, Haitian magic, Haitian peasant economy, Haiti's social structure and politics, sexual and familial institutions in northern Haiti, the belief system of Haitian voodoo. Author (with J M Yinger) Racial and Cultural Minorities, '53. Instructor and assistant professor social Temple U '28-29; asso prof, prof head sociol Pa State Coll '39-47; prof and head sociol and anthropol Oberlin Coll since '47. Am Social Soc—Am Folklore Soc—O Valley Sociol Soc—Am Anthrop Assn(F). Postdoctoral fellow Social Sci Research Council NYC '36-37. Department of Sociology and Anthropology, Oberlin College, Oberlin, O.

19 SIMPSON, John Alexander, Jr. Electron and neutron physics; Cosmic radiation; Nuclear instrumentation. b'16. AB '40 (Reed Coll); MS '42—PhD '43 (NYU). Discovered the latitude dependence of neutrons in the atmosphere. Author articles in field. Asso prof physics dept physics and inst nuclear studies U Chicago since '49; scientific cons Argonne Nat Lab since '46. Am Phys Soc(F)—Sigma Xi—Phi Beta Kappa.

20 SIMPSON, John Childs. Schools (Female). '89. AB—AM '11—LLD hon '48 (Randolph-Macon Coll). Asst prin and treas Randolph-Macon Acad '21-25, prin Randolph-Macon Sch for Girls '25-30; pres Stratford Coll since '30. Nat Assn Prins Sch for Girls—Phi Delta Theta—Phi Beta Kappa. 127 S. Main St., Danville, Va.◎

21 SIMPSON, Oliver Cecil. Nuclear physics and chemistry; Radiation chemistry. b'09. BS '30—PhD '34—

Charles A Coffin Research fellow '30-31, '31-32—Carr Hon fellow '32-33 (U Ill). Author articles in field. Asso dir chem div Argonne Nat Lab since '46. Am Phys Soc(F)—AAAS—Am Chem Soc—Sigma Xi. P.O. Box 299, Lemont, Ill.

22 SIMPSON, Robert C(rozier). Fruit culture. b'06. BSA '29—MS (Botany) '41 (Purdue U). Study of production methods and cost, and soil management practices; field tests on top-working apple trees for pollenizers in commercial orchards; supervision commercial production of fruit trees and ornamentals; collection data on flowering crabapples and holly; research on types of understocks for fruit trees. Author articles: Individual Tree Yield Records in a Commercial Apple Orchard '36; Keep Orchard Records '41. In charge prodn and research apples and peaches Simpson Orchard Co '29-40 and since '46. Ind Hort Soc—Ind Assn Nurserymen—Am Assn Nurserymen—Am Soc Hort Sci. Box 88, Vincennes, Ind.†

23 SIMPSON, Walter Malcolm. Artificial fever therapy. b'95. BS '22— MS '23—MD '24 (U Mich). Collaborator with Charles F Kettering ('31-41) in invention of Kettering-Simpson-Sittler Hyperthermy artificial fever therapy by physical means; pioneer researches in treatment of diseases with physically induced artificial fever. Author: Tuleremia '29; Fever Therapy '38; chpts. Burcellosis (Undulant Fever) and Artificial Fever Therapy in sci publs; 125 publs describing med researches. Organizer and dir Kettering Inst for Med Research and diagnostic labs Miami Valley Hosp Dayton O '27-47; dir div cancer-chemotherapy, dept cancer research Barnard Free Skin and Cancer Hosp and Washington U Sch Med StL '47-48; vol cons in cancer research several univs and other cancer research insts since '48; med research in cancer, tularemia, brucellosis (undulant fever), artificial fever therapy. Mem Nat Adv Serology Council —Am Coll Physicians(F)—Coll Am Pathologists(F, founder)—Am Soc of Clin Pathologists (pres 1932-33, Ward Burdick research award '29)—AMA (Gold medal for researches in tularemia '28)—Am Assn Path and Bact— Am Assn Cancer Research—Ohio Soc Path(pres '41-42)—Am Venereal Dis Soc—AAAS—Mich Acad Sci—Ohio Academy Sci—Central Soc Clin Research —Am Assn Study Goiter—Alpha Omega Alpha—Sigma Xi—Phi Sigma—Phi Rho Sigma. Chevalier Legion of Honor (France). 435 Cress St., Laguna Beach, Cal.◎

24 SINCLAIR, Gregg Manners. Asiatic literature (English translation); Hawaiian theatre. b'90. BA '12 (U Minn); MA '19 (Columbia). Member of board of directors of Honolulu Community Theatre since '35; translator of Asiatic literature. Asst prof Eng U Hawaii '28-32, asso prof '32-36, prof since '36, dir Oriental Inst '36-40, pres U Hawaii since '42. Haw Acad Sci— Honolulu Art Soc—Japan Asiatic Soc— Bengal Asiatic Soc—China Inst—Am Oriental Soc—India Soc—Japan Soc— Royal Asiatic Soc (N China Br)— Dickens Fellowship of Hawaii—American Acad Polit & Social Science—Hawaiian Volcano Research Assn (dir)— Phi Kappa Phi. University of Hawaii, Honolulu, T.H. H: 3817 Lurline Dr.

25 SINDEN, James Whaples. Mushroom culture; Fungi physiology. b'02. AB '24 (U Kans); PhD '37 (Cornell U). Granted patents on grain spawn for mushroom growing. Author articles in field. Research prof dept bot Pa State Coll '30-53; now private research. Mycol Soc Am—Am Phytopath Soc—Brit Mushroom Growers Assn (life hon)—AAAS(F). 620 Sunset Rd., State College, Pa.†

10 SINGER, Elias. Paint, varnish and lacquer technology; Surface coatings (Textiles, industrial). b'10. BS '32 (Coll City NY); '32-33 (Columbia). Author articles in field. Research chem D H Litter Co '33-38, dir research '38-47, tech dir '47-52; pres Troy Chem Co NYC since '52. Am Chem Soc. 2589 Frisby Av., N.Y.C. 61. H: 130-19 219 St., Springfield Gardens, 13, L.I., N.Y.

11 SINGER, Philip A. Starch, corn syrup, alcohol; Vegetable oil refining. b'80. Student (Bradley U, Heidelburg U). Design and operation of plants for the manufacture of various types of products and foods for cereals and tubers which includes plants in Japan, Australia, Africa, Europe, Central and South America; also plants for manufacture of miscellaneous feeds for cattle and poultry and extraction of oil from soy beans. Holds patents in field. Author articles in field. Chem and mgr corn products plants '00-08; operated own starch bus '08-13; cons engring bus Chicago '18-24; pres and chem bd Premier Pabst Products Co '25-28; with Allied Mills Peoria Ill since '33. Am Chem Soc. Allied Mills, Incorporated, P.O. Box 539, Peoria, Ill. H: 4612 Prospect Rd., Peoria 4.

12 SINGER, Rolf. Taxonomy of Basidiomycetes; Geography of Caucasus. b'06. PhD '31 (U Vienna); Dr Biol '40 (Acad Sci USSR). Research on temperate and tropical agarics and boletes, including their cytology, ecology, anatomy, and phytogeography as related to systematics of Basidiomycetes, on antibiotic substances in Basidiomycetes, pathology of agarics, mycorrhiza, mushroom poisons. Expedition of Academy Sciences Vienna to Caucasus Mountains '28-29; Junta de Ciencias Naturales Barcelona to the Pyrenees '34; Academy Sciences USSR to Altay Mountains in '37. Author: The Boletineae of Florida '45-47; The Agaricales '49; also articles in field. Asst curator Farlow Herbarium Harvard '44-48. Mich Acad Sci Arts Letters—Societé Mycologique de France. Guggenheim fellow '42-43. Farlow Herbarium, Harvard University, Cambridge, Mass.

13 SINGLETARY, B. Henry. Winter cover crop; Roses; Gladioli; Plant propagation. b'90. BS '25—MS '27 (La State U). Author: Rose Growing in Louisiana. Invented plant remover '27; discovered and tested Singletary pea '27. Asso prof, prof La State U since '32, head dept hort since '32. Am Assn Hort Sci. Department of Horticulture, College of Agriculture, Louisiana State University, Baton Rouge 3, La.

14 SINGLETERRY, Curtis R. Nonaqueous colloid chemistry; Synthetic lubricating greases. b'00. BA (Aurora Coll); SM '26—PhD '40 (U Chicago). Chem lubrication sect Naval Research Lab Wash since '46. Am Chem Soc—Sigma Xi. Chemistry Division, Naval Research Laboratory, Washington.

15 SINGLETON, Willard Ralph. Genetics and plant breeding; Hybrid vigor; Genetic effects of radiation; Sweet corn. b'00. BS '22—MS '24 (State Coll Washington); '24-25, '26-27—MS '26—SD '30 (Harvard). Simplified planting sweet corn by development of series of hybrids that can be planted at one time and picked over period of month to six weeks; presented paper seventh International Genetics Congress Edinburgh '39. Author articles in field. Sr sci Brookhaven Nat Lab since '48. NY Acad Sci—Genetics Soc Am—Am Soc Agron—AAAS—Am Soc Naturalists—

Phi Kappa Phi—Sigma Xi. Brookhaven National Laboratory, Upton, N.Y.

16 SIRI, William E. Radioactive tracers (Theory, measurement); Spectrometers (Mass). b'19. Student '37-42 (U Chicago); '45-46 (U Cal). Research on radioactive materials; expedition to Peruvian Andes to study high altitude physiology with radioactive iron and phosphorous; developed new type mass spectrometer for use in research with stable isotopes; study of electromagnetic separation U-235. Author: Isotopic Tracers and Nuclear Radiation—with Application to Biology and Medicine '49. Author article: A Mass Spectroscope for Analysis in the Low Mass Range '47, and others. APS—Am Inst Physics—Calif Acad Sci—Sigma Xi. Donner Laboratory, University of California, Berkeley.

17 SITTERLY, (Mrs) Charlotte Moore. Astrophysics; Spectroscopy. b'98. AB '20 (Swarthmore); PhD '31 (U Calif). Author: Atomic Lines in the Sun-spot Spectrum '32; A Multiplet Table of Astrophysical Interest '45; Term Designations for Excitation Potentials '34; Atomic Energy Levels (vol I) '49, (vol. II) '52. Co-author: The Masses of the Stars '40; The Infrared Solar Spectrum '47. Computer Princeton Observatory '20-25, '28-29; computer Mt Wilson Obs '25-28; research asst Princeton Obs '31-36, asso '36-45; physicist Nat Bur Standards since '45. Am Astron Soc—AA AS—Am Phys Soc—Optical Soc Am—Astron Soc Pacific—Sigma Xi—Phi Beta Kappa. National Bureau Standards, Washington 25.†

18 SITTERSON, Joseph Carlyle. Economic history of Southern United States; Recent United States history. AB '31—MA '32—PhD '37—teaching fellow '33-34 (U NC). Author: The Secession Movement in North Carolina '39; (with C H Pegg and others) American Society and the Changing World '42; (with others) Industrial Mobilization for World War II '47; also articles in field. Editor The South and World Affairs '42-44. Prof hist U NC since '47. AHA—Miss Valley Hist Assn—So Hist Assn. Social Sci Research Council fellowship '31-32 and Julius Rosenwald Grant '40-41, both for research on a history of sugar industry in South. Department of History, University of North Carolina, Chapel Hill, N.C.†

19 SITTON, Benjamin Gaillard. Tung (Mineral nutrition, production, culture, breeding); Pecan production and breeding. b'97. BS '18 (Clemson Coll); MS '28—PhD '31 (Mich State Coll) Author articles in field. Hort US Dept Agr Div Fruit and Vegetable Crops and diseases Bogalusa Louisiana. Am Society Hort Sci—Am Soc Plant Physiol. U.S. Department of Agriculture, P.O. Box 812, Bogalusa, La.†

20 SIU, Ralph G(un) H(oy). Cellulose (Prevention of deterioration). b'17. BS in chem '39—MS in plant physiol '41 (U Hawaii); PhD in bio-organic chem '43 (Cal Inst Pasadena). Research in plant physiology, biochemistry, microbiology, and tropical deterioration; research direction and management. Author: Microbiol Action on Cellulose '51, also articles in field. Research asst Pineapple Research Inst Honolulu TH '37-39, research fellow plant physiol '39-41; teaching fellow biol Cal Inst Tech Pasadena '41-43, US Rubber Co fellow '44-45; US Dept Agr chemist emergency rubber project Los Angeles '43-44. Cons tropical deterioration OQMG US Army '45, sr biochemist, dir fundamental and pioneering research since '46; Harvard U research asso since '48. AAAS—Am Mycol Soc—Am Chem Soc—Soc

Plastics Industry. Quartermaster, Research and Development Laboratories, 2800 S. 20th St., Phila. 45.

21 SIXT, Norman G. Manufacturing (Rayon, cellophane, paper, textiles, explosives, cellulose). b'04. ChE '28 (Renisselaer Poly Inst); (Drexel Inst, Northeastern U). Chief chemist and production manager various manufacturers. Am Chem Soc—Am Inst Chem Engrs—Am Assn Textile Colorists and Chemists—Tech Assn Pulp and Paper Inst. Nor-Ed Chemical Company, Yorkshire, N.Y.

22 SKAPSKI, Adam Stanislaw. Physical chemistry of liquid and solid metals and steel-making processes. b'02. MSc '23—PhD '28—Privat '31 (Jagellonian U Krakow Poland); research fellow Rockefeller Found '33 (Metallographic Inst Stockholm). Author articles in field. Prof phys U Neb since '48. Polish Chem Assn (chmn '37-39)—Polish Corrosion Com (chmn '37-39)—Polish Steel Council—Polish Phys Soc—Polish Assn Metall—Iron and Steel Inst—Am Inst Mining Metall Engrs. Awarded Golden Cross of Merit by Polish Govt for promoting collaboration between sci and industry. Brace Laboratory of Physics, University of Nebraska, Lincoln, Neb.

23 SKARLAND, Ivar. Alaska (Anthropology). b'99. BA '35 (U Alaska); MA '42—PhD '48 (Harvard). Author articles in field. Instr anthrop U Alaska '40-41, asst prof '41-42, asso prof '45-46, prof since '46. Soc Am Archeol—Am Anthrop Assn (asso)—Soc Applied Anthrop(F)—Arctic Inst NA (charter asso). College, Alaska.

24 SKEELS, Dorr Covell. Gravity interpretation; Geophysics. b'08. BA '30 (U Mont); BA '33 (Oxford U); PhD '36 (Princeton). Author articles in field. Geophysicist Standard Oil Co NJ since '38. Specialized in compilation, study and interpretation of gravity data, and relation between geological structure and gravity anomalies, especially as related to oil exploration. Am Geophys Union—Am Assn Petroleum Geol—Soc Exploration Geophysicists—Geol Soc Am. Standard Oil Company, 30 Rockefeller Plaza, NYC 20.☉

25 SKEEN, John R(obsin). Treatment of industrial waters; Paint compositions; Treatment of gas mains (Leak elimination); Oil pyrolysis; marketing (Chemical). b'99. BS '21 (Pa State Coll); AM '24—PhD '26 (U Pa). Holder 14 US patents. Author articles in field. Dir chem market report Foster D Snell Inc since '47, vp Nuodex Products Co Inc since '52. AAAS(F) —Am Inst Chem(F)—Bot Soc Am—Am Society Plant Physiol—Sigma Xi. Nuodex Products Co., Inc., Elizabeth F, N.J.

26 SKELLY, Harry James. Audio-visual education. b'09. AB in edn '31 (Chico State Coll); EdM '41 (Ore State Coll). Studies audio-visual implementation of curriculum; organization and adminstrn audio-visual depts; participation in and organization inservice training education; evaluation and selection audio-visual materials and equipment; methods utilization, production; research in utilization and equipment. Author: Audio-Visual Aids for Teaching Health to the Migrant Children of Madera County (unpublished thesis). Dir audio-visual edn Madera Co Schs '38-48; cons audio-visual edn State Dept Edn Calif since '48. Cal Sch Suprvs Assn—Cal Audio-Visual Edn Assn—NEA—Kappa Delta Pi. State Department of Education, Library and Courts Bldg., Sacramento 14.

10 SKIFTER, Hector Randolph. Radio engineering (Transmitting apparatus, field intensity measurement, airborne magnetometer, specialized counter-measures equipment, aeronautical electronic devices). b'01. BA '22—ScD '45 (St Olaf Coll). Pres Airborne Instruments Lab Inc. Soc Mot Picture Engrs—Inst Radio Engrs (sr mem) — AIEE — Inst Aeronautical Sci — Acoustical Soc Am. 160 Old Country Rd., Mineola, N.Y.

11 SKINNER, Harley Clay. Mental hygiene; Delinquency; Guidance. b'95. BS Edn '17 (O U Athens O); MA '22 (Ohio State U); PhD '27 (New York U). Author: (with C E Skinner and I M Gast) Readings in Educational Psychology '26; Psychology for the Average Man '27; (with I M Gast) Fundamentals of Educational Psychology '29; (with Thomas Smyth and Frank Wheat) Educational Biology '37. Prof psychology Teachers Coll Temple U '30-38; prof and head dept psychol-Arizona State Coll since '38; psychologist and personnel consultant Armed Forces '42-44. AAAS—Am Psychol Association—NEA—Nat Soc Coll Teachers Edn—AAUP—Ariz State Edn Association—Arizona Youth Council—Ariz State Psychol Assn—Phi Delta Kappa. Arizona State College, Tempe, Arizona.◎

12 SKINNER, Morris Fredrick. Vertebrate paleontology and Pliocene stratigraphy in northwestern Nebraska. b'06. BS '32 (U Nebr). In charge field parties Frick Laboratory American Museum Natural History making stratigraphic vertebrate paleontological collections from Tertiary formations in north-central and northwestern Nebraska, Badlands of North and South Dakota, and caves of southern Arizona summers since '27; research on living and fossil antelope, living and extinct bison winters since '33; extensive accumulation of geologic data concerning Miocene, Pliocene, Pleistocene and recent formations of region for use in development of irrigation of region by applying geologic experience and data to problems of water supply. Author articles: The Fauna of Papago Springs Cave, Arizona; A Study of Stockoceros '42; The Fossil Bison of Alaska and Preliminary Revision of the Genus (with Ove C Kaisen) '47. Soc Vertebrate Paleontol—Paleontol Soc—Am Soc Mammalogists—AAAS. Ainsworth, Neb.

13 SKINNER, Orin E(nsign). Stained glass. b'92. Student '11-15 (Herman J Butler and Frank von der Lancken); studied glass in France, Eng, Switzerland '23, '25. Author articles in field. With Charles A Baker Rochester NY '12, R Toland Wright '17-19; master craftsman and mgr since '20, pres and treas since '45 Charles J Connick Assos; worked in studio Jacques Simon in restoration Western Rose of Rheims Cathedral '25; lecture series on medieval crafts Metropolitan Mus Art under bequest late Charles T Matthews to Columbia U '49; teacher and lecturer. Stained Glass Assn Am (pres '48, archeol ed and ed and mgr Stained Glass '31-48). 9 Harcourt St., Boston 16.

14 SKOWRONSKI, Stanislaus. Copper refining. b'81. BS '04 (MIT). Studies on oxygen and sulfur in melting of copper cathodes, relation of sulfur to overpoling of copper, volatilization of cuprous chloride on melting copper containing chlorine, specific resistivity of copper refining electrolytes, electrochemical smelting. Author articles in field. Research engr Raritan Copper Works Internat Smelting and Refining Co since '12; adj prof metall Polytechnic Inst of Brooklyn since

'28. Am Chem Soc—Am Soc Metals—Electrochem Soc—Inst Metals, Gr Britain. International Smelting and Refining Co., Perth Amboy, N.J. H: 116 Hillside Av., Metuchen, N.J.

15 SKROMME, Arnold Burton. Agricultural engineering. b'17. BS (AE) '41 (Ia State Coll). Installation and design of tractor brakes; development and design of rake, equipment for chopper and baler, endless rubber track, dynamometer operator for traction testing device, belt moldboard plow, pineapple trash mulch machine, and pineapple ratoon crushing machine. Holds patents in field. Author articles: Rubber tracks on Agricultural Machines '45; Pineapple Ratoon Handling Machinery '50; A Belt Moldboard Plow '50. Development engr Firestone Tire & Rubber Co Akron O '41-45; field engr Auto Specialties Mfg Co St Joseph Mich '45-47; research agrl engr Pineapple Research Inst Hawaii Honolulu '47-50; now asst chief engr John Deere Ottumwa Works. Am. Soc AE—AA AS—Hawaiian Acad Sci—Tau Beta Pi —Alpha Zata—Gamma Sigma Delta. John Deere Ottumwa Works, Ottumwa, Ia.

16 SLATE, George Lewis. Small fruit breeding (Strawberries, raspberries); Lily breeding. b'99. BSc '21 (Mass Agr Coll); MSc '26 (Harvard). Author: Lilies for American Gardens '39; also articles in field. Asst in research NY State Agr Expt Sta '22-28, asso '28-31, asst prof pomol '41-45, asso prof '45-51, prof since '51. Am Soc Hort Sci. New York State Agricultural Experiment Station, Geneva, N.Y.

17 SLATER, Lloyd Edward. Food processing; Automatic process control. b'19. BS '40 (Cornell U). Developed chocolate tempering control system, automatic coffee roasting control system, applied control instruments to food process lines to effect continuous operation in dairy, canning, sugar and brewing operations. Industry engr in chg food applications Minneapolis-Honeywell Regulator Co '46-49, mgr food industry div '49-51; midwest ed Food Engring since '51. Inst Food Tech—Am Assn Candy Tech. Midwest Editor, Food Engineering, McGraw-Hill Publishing Co., 520 N. Michigan Av., Chgo 11.

18 SLATKIN, Charles E. Museum education; History of art. b'07. AB '30—AM '31 (U Ala); '31-33 (Columbia); '36 (U Chicago); '44 (NYU). Visited all major museums in United States to write survey of outstanding masterpieces in all periods and schools of art; made filmstrip series on Arts in American Life. Author: Enjoyment of Art in America '42; French Master Drawings '49. Co-author: (with Regina Shoolman Story of Art '39; Treasury of American Drawings, 17th to 20th Centuries '47. Cons in ednl art exhbns circulating in academic high schs and coordination similar activities lecture programs various NY mus and schs since '44. Coll Art Assn—NEA—Nat Council Teachers Eng—Phi Beta Kappa. French Govt traveling fellow '47. 115 E. 92 St., NYC.†

19 SLAVIT, Joseph. Medical economics (Health insurance): Socialized medicine. b'83. MD '04 (Cornell); '21 (LI Med Coll); '27-28 (U Vienna, Austria). Author: An American Plan for Medical Care '35; Principles and Program of the Medical League for Socialized Medicine '33; The Challenge of Socialized Medicine '34. Co-author: Socialization of Medicine: Objections and Questions Answered '33. Attending phys Israel-Zion Hosp Brooklyn since '28, chief of clinic since '22; phys Union Health Center, Internat Ladies Gar-

ment Workers Union, since '29. Am Pub Health Assn—Am Acad Polit and Social Sci—Brooklyn Inst Arts and Sci—AMA. 650 Ocean Av., Bklyn 26.

20 SLEEPER, Catharine Baker. Speech. Grad instrs course '44 (Dale Carnegie Inst). Instr effective speaking Archtl League NY '46-50. 8 E. 48th St., NYC 17.†

21 SLEEPER, Harvey Prescott, Jr. Shielding of nuclear radiation; Acoustics. b'20. BS '42—'45-46 (Harvard). Inventor fiberglas wedge lining for anechoic chamber; co-designer Harvard Anechoic chamber. Author articles in field. Nuclear engr Knolls Atomic Power Lab Gen Elec Co since '47, on loan Oak Ridge Nat Lab '47-48. Acoustical Soc Am. Knolls Atomic Power Laboratory, Schenectady, N.Y.†

22 SLEETH, Bailey. Plant pathology (Guayule seedling diseases, heartrot in oak). b'00. BS '27—MS '28—PhD '32 —Jones research fellow '30-32 (W Va U). Research on decay in sprout oak stands in which, with others, mode of entry of heartrot fungi, fungi involved, and factors related to development of heartrot were determined; also research on cause and control of guayule seedling diseases, and on plant diseases peculiar to desert areas of low humidity and high temperatures such as are being developed by irrigation projects. Author articles in field. Asst path, later path US Dept Agr since '33, div soil management and irrigation Bur Plant Ind Soils and Agr Engring since '46. Am Phytopath Soc—Mycol Soc Am—So Appalachian Bot Club—Torrey Bot Club—Sigma Xi. U.S. Department of Agriculture, Research Laboratory, Box 1710, Yuma, Ariz.†

23 SLEICHER, Charles A. Foundry cores. b'81. AB (Cornell U). Lecturer and writer on use of cement in foundry industry; holds patent on use of petroleum asphalt base in manufacture of core compounds. Pres Troy Foundry & Machinery Co, Interstate Foundry Inc, Queens Run Refractories Co, Seaboard Foundry Inc. Am Iron and Steel Inst—NY State Foundrymen's Assn—Am Soc ME—Am Foundryman's Assn —New Eng Foundryman's Assn. Seaboard Foundry, Inc., P.O. Box 187, Elmwood Station, Providence.

24 SLESINGER, Donald. Personality development; Analytic psychology. b '97. AB '20 (Columbia U); '20-21 (Harvard U). Prof law U Chicago '30-36; asso dean Div Soc Scis '31-36; dir dept edn New York World's Fair '37-38; mem Raymond Rich Associates '37-38; dir mngmt training course Nat Assn Housing Ofcls Washington '35-36; exec dir Am Film Center Inc '38-47; cons Tenn Valley Authority, War Dept, Office of Health, Welfare and Related Defense Activities of Federal Security Agency '40-42; chief visual training sect US Office Civilian Defense '42-43; administrative dir Educational Film Library Assn '43-44; pub Film News '45-47. Nat Com US Am on Internat Intellectual Cooperation. 12 E. 86th St., N.Y.C. 28.◎

25 SLETTO, Raymond Franklin. Sociological research methods; Personality measurement. b'06. BS '26—AM '32 —PhD '36 (U Minn); '39 (Columbia); '40 (U Chicago). Author: (with E A Rundquist) Personality in the Depression '36; Construction of Personality Scales by the Criterion of Internal Consistency '37. High Sch prin Appleton Minn '27-30; instr U Minn '30-36, asst prof '37-39, asso prof '40-47, coordinator research gen coll '34-36; Soc Sci Research Council post-doctoral f '39-40; prof sociology Ohio State U '47-50, chmn sociology dept since

'50. AAAS—AAUP—Am Acad Polit and Soc Sci—Am Psychol Assn—Am Sociol Soc—Am Statis Assn—Nat Council Family Relations—Rural Sociol Soc—Social Research Assn—Am Farm Bur—Alpha Kappa Delta. Ohio State U, Columbus 10.☉

10 SLICK, Sewell Elias. American frontier and colonial history. b'02. BA '26 (U Mo); MA '31—PhD '38 (U Pittsburgh). Social studies supervisor State Teachers Coll Slippery Rock Pa '38-43; head social studies dept and dean men State Teachers Coll Clarion Pa since '43. Author: William Trent and the West. AHA—NEA—Pa Hist Assn—Phi Alpha Theta. Egbert Hall, College Campus, Clarion, Pa.

11 SLIFER, Eleanor Heist. Insect embryology and cuticle (Grasshopper). b'00. BS '23 (Temple U); MS '26—PhD '30 (U Pa). Research asso, then asst prof U Ia '31-50, asso prof since '50. American Society Zool—Am Naturalists Soc—Entomol Soc Am—Am Soc Human Genetics—Am Genetics Assn—AAAS—Sigma Xi—Faraday Soc. Nat Research Council fellow '30-31; invited speaker at discussion held by Faraday Soc London '48. Department of Zoology, State University of Iowa, Iowa City, Ia.†

12 SLIFKIN, Sam Charles. Diazotype chemistry. b'18. BS '42 (U Wis). Granted canadian and US patents. Author: Status of Developments in the German Diazotype Industry '47. Trip to Germany for Commerce Dept OTS to investigate German diazotype industry '47; mgr quality control, dir research and development Ozalid Div Gen Aniline & Film Corp '42-48; vp Tecnifax Corp Holyoke Mass since '49. AAAS—Photog Soc Am—Am Chem Soc—Soc Quality Control—Armed Forces Chem Assn—Tech Assn Pulp and Paper Industry—Am Assn Textile Chem and Colorists—Phi Lambda Upsilon—Pi Mu Epsilon—Phi Beta Kappa. Tecnifax Corp., 276 High St., Holyoke, Mass.

13 SLIPP, Albert Wiswell. Blister rust (White pine); Forest pathology; Ecology of forest fungi (Cedar-hemlock zone); Technical biological photography. b'06. BSc '30 (U NB); MS '39 (U Ida); land surveying certificate '25 (NS Tech Coll). Author articles in field. Asst prof Forest Wildlife and Range Expt Sta Sch Forestry U Ida since '45. NW Sci Assn (council, editorial bd)—AAAS(F)—Soc Am Foresters—Can Soc Forest Engrs—Mycol Soc Am—Am Phytopath Soc—Am Forestry Assn—Biol Photographic Assn—Assn Internat Phytosociologie. School of Forestry, University of Idaho, Moscow, Ida.†

14 SLOCHOWER, Harry. Thomas Mann; Franz Kafka; German literature and philosophy. b'00. BSS '23 (City Coll NY); MA '24—PhD '28 (Columbia); '25-26 (U Berlin and Heidelberg). Author: Richard Dehmel, Der Mensch und Der Denker '28; Three Ways of Modern Man '37; Thomas Mann's Joseph Story (an interpretation) '38; No Voice Is Wholly Lost (writers and thinkers in war and peace) '45; also articles in field. With Brooklyn Coll since '30, asst prof German since '36. Awarded John Simon Guggenheim Memorial Found Fellowship '29-30, Bollinger Found Fellowship '50-51. 221 E. 18 St., Brooklyn 10.

15 SLUITER, Engel. Hispanic-American history. b'06. AB '29 (Stanford U); MA '33—PhD '37 (U Calif). Research in Europe and South America. Author articles in field. Instr, later asso prof hist U Calif since '40. AHA—Phi Beta Kappa. Guggenheim fellow '48-49, Rockefeller fellow '42-43, Social Sci Research Council fellow '35-36. Department of History, University of California, Berkeley.†

16 SLYE, Maud. Cancer research. b '79. AB '99—ScD '37 (Brown U); fellow post-grad work '08-11 (U Chgo). Research on mice many years to determine the nature of cancer, the relation of heredity of cancer, the laws governing malignancy and its localization, and age at which it will occur. Mem staff Sprague Meml Inst Chgo '11-43; instr path U Chgo '19-22, asst prof '22-26, asso prof '26-45, prof emeritus since '45. Association Cancer Research(past vp)—Chgo Inst Med—AAAS—AMA—Am Assn of Sci Workers—NY Acad Sci—Ill Acad Sci—Seattle Acad Surg(hon)—So Calif Med Soc—Phi Beta Kappa—Sigma Xi—Sigma Delta Epsilon—Delta Kappa Gamma. Gold medal AMA '14; Rickets prize '15; gold medal NA Radiol Soc '22. 5822 Drexel Av., Chgo.☉

17 SMALL, Charles Hughey. American, Indian affairs; North American Indians; Abraham Lincoln. b'80. LLB '03 (Kansas City Mo Sch Law). Sr atty Dept Justice in defense of govt in suits brought by Indian tribes '30-46, retired; now lecturer and writer on politics, econ, law, psychol. Acad Pol Sci. 1001 McGowan St., Little Rock Ark.†

18 SMALL, Walter Madison. Petroleum geophysics (Subsurface). b'87. AB '11 (Allegheny College). Subsurface studies oil field; surface and subsurface studies with geophysics as applied to exploration for petroleum; introduced and applied use forminifera studies sev countries; orgnd many regional geophy surveys, seismic, gravimetric, magnetic. Geol in US and Mex '14-27; dir geol work Angola West Africa '28-30; chief geol European Gas Electric Co Vienna '31-36; chief geol and dir exploration Standard Oil Co Egypt '36-38; chief geol Romano Americana Ploesti Rumania '37-41; cons affiliate Standard Oil NJ '41-45; chief geol Dominican Seaboard '46-47; cons Husky Oil Co since '48. Am Assn Petroleum Geol—Am Geog Soc(F)—AAAS (F)—Geol Soc Am—Soc Econ Geol—Am Geophys Union. Husky Oil Co., Box 380, Cody, Wyo.

19 SMALLEY, Donald Arthur. Life and poetry of Robert Browning; Frances Trollope (America). b'07. AB '29—MA '31 (Ind U); PhD '39 (Harvard U). Author: Browning's Essay on Chatterton '48. Editor: Frances Trollope's Domestic Manners of the Americans '49; also articles in field. Instr, later professor Ind U since '51. Mod Lang Assn—Coll Eng Assn—Phi Beta Kappa. Department of English, Indiana University, Bloomington, Ind.

20 SMALLWOOD, Hugh M(olleson). Physical chemistry (Elementary reactions, molecular structure, high polymers, carbon black); Applied quality control (Small arms ammunition production); Applied statistics (Research). b'03. BS '24—PhD '27 (Johns Hopkins). Author articles in field. Research chem US Rubber Co Passaic NJ since '44. Am Chem Soc—AAAS—Tau Beta Pi—Phi Beta Kappa.

21 SMART, George K. Virginia intellectual history 1607-1776; History of American radicalism before 1860. b'10. AB '33 (U Ala); AM '34—'36-37 (Harvard). Research on reflection of Utopian Socialist thought in American literature '42. Author articles in field. Instr English U Ala '35-36, Northwestern U '37-39; asst prof English U Ala '39-46; asso prof English U Miami since '46. Modern Lang Assn—AHA. Austin and Shattuck fellowships Harvard '36-37. Department of English, University of Miami, Miami, Fla.

22 SMART, Robert Forte. Myxomycetes (Protoplasm behavior, external environment); Mycology. b'05. BA '27 (Miss Coll); MA '29—PhD '35 (Harvard). Author articles in field. Asso prof biol U Richmond '29-41; prof biol U Richmond since '41. Va Acad Sci (pres)—Bot Soc Am—Mycol Soc Am—AAAS. Department of Biology, University of Richmond, Va.†

23 SMERTENKO, Johan Jacob. Hist of United States; Palestine; Internat affairs; English literature (Drama). b'96. Student (U Wis) (Sorbonne U France). Vice chairman Emergency Committee to Save Jewish Peoples of Europe '43-46. Author: Alexander Hamilton—Man of Action '41; Palestine in Revolt '47. Co-author: These United States; American Points of View; America—A History of Three Centuries, also articles in field. Prof journ and English lit Grinnell Coll Ia '19-22; lecturer English lit and modern drama Hunter Coll NYC '22-44; acting head English dept and lectr English lit Skidmore Coll Saratoga Springs NY '25; literary columnist "Books" NY Herald-Tribune; mng ed Free World '41-43. Am League for Free Palestine (vp '45-47)—Zionist-Revisionist Orgn Am (pres '26-29)—New Zionist Orgn Am (past pres, chmn nat exec council)—Soc Am Democracy (founder and exec dir '39-40)—Non-Sectarian Anti-Nazi League (exec dir '38). Good Hill Rd., Woodbury, Conn.

24 SMIEL, Oscar. Rotogravure Engraving. b'03. Art student (NY U), (Columbia U). Author articles: Outline of Gravure Process '49; Perchloride of Iron '50, and others. Gravure etcher '22-43; with Intaglio Service Corp since '43, now vp in charge mfg; dir Gravure Research Inc of Battelle Inst since '51. Photog Soc Am—Gravure Tech Assn (tech dir)—Inter-Soc Color Council. H: 215 S Broadway, Tarrytown, NY.

25 SMILEY, Charles Hugh. Eclipses. b'03. AB '24—AM '25—PhD '27 (U Cal). Calculation of orbits of planets and comets; solar eclipses, prediction and observation; modern astronomical cameras, especially the Schmidt camera and Schwarzschild camera; navigation tables, emergency navigation; atmospheric refraction especially at low altitudes; twilight illumination, zodiacal light. Leader of seven eclipse expeditions to Peru, Brazil (two), Siam, Canada, etc. Prof Brown U since '30, prof astronomy since '38, dir Ladd Obs since '38. Am Astron Soc(mem council)—Math Assn Am—Am Assn Variable Star Observers(em mem council, vp, pres)—AAAS—Royal Astron Soc Eng—Brit Astron Assn—Inst Navigation (mem council)—Sigma Xi—Phi Beta Kappa—Pi Mu Epsilon. Franklin L Burr prize Nat Geog Soc '48; hon mem Peruvian Geog Soc '37. Brown University, Providence 12.☉

26 SMILEY, Dean Franklin. Public health; Hygiene; Preventive medicine (Respiratory infections). b'95. AB '16—MD '19 (Cornell U); internship '19-20 (NY Hosp). Instructor hygiene and preventive medicine Cornell U '20-21, advanced to professor and head department '28-42, medical adviser and head student health service '22-42; investigator Carnegie Foundation for Advancement of Teaching in inquiry into school and college athletics '28. Author: Tuberculosis as a Navy Problem '44; Diarrheal Diseases in the US Navy '44; Pneumonia in the US Navy '44; The Incidence of Acute Respiratory Infections '44. Co-author: College Textbook of Hygiene '28; Community Hygiene '29; Health and Growth Series of Texts for Schools '41. Served as 1t comdr and comdr US Navy Bur Medicine and Surgery '42-46, statis studies epidemic diseases '43-44, epidemiology sect '43-44; acting dir health and phys edn div Edn Dept State NY '35; consultant health and fitness Bur Health Edn AMA '46-48 American Student Health Assn—Am Pub Health Assn — NEA — AMA — Nat Research Council—Sigma Xi—Alpha Omega Alpha. 185 N. Wabash Av., Chgo 1. H: 53 E. Elm St., Chgo 11.

10 SMILEY, Terah L. Archeological dating by tree rings; geochronology, dendrochronology. b'14. Student '34-36 (U Kan); AB—MA '49 (U Ariz). Author articles in field. Asst dendrochronologist Lab of Tree-Ring Research U Ariz since '46. Soc Am Archeology—Am Anthropol Soc—Society Anthropol—AAAS. Laboratory of Tree Ring Research, University of Ariz., Tucson, Ariz.†

11 SMITH, Albert C(harles). Flora of tropical America and South Pacific. b'06. AB '26—PhD '33 (Columbia); Bishop Museum fellow '33-34 (Yale). Author articles in field. Curator div phanerogams dept bot US Nat Mus Smithsonian Inst Washington since '48. Am Acad Arts Sci—AAAS—Am Bot Soc—Torrey Bot Club—Am Soc Plant Taxonomists—New Eng Bot Club—Am Fern Soc—Washington Biol Field Club. Guggenheim fellow '46-47. Department of Botany, Smithsonian Institution, Washington 25.†

12 SMITH, Albert Lorenzo. Cotton diseases (Wilt, nematodes); Cotton breeding. b'05. BS Agr '28 (Okla A&M Coll); MS '29 (U Ark); PhD '32 (U Wis). Research on cotton wilt and nematodes, resistance and control; breeding cotton for disease resistance, soil fumigants as control measure. Author articles in field With US Dept Agr, rice breeding and diseases, Rice Expt Sta Crowley La '32-33, elm wilt disease NJ and NY '33-36; cotton diseases and breeding Ga and Ala Agrl Expt Sta Cooperative with US Dept Agr since '36. Am Soc Agronomy—Am Phytopath Soc. Agricultural Experiment Station, Auburn, Ala.

13 SMITH, Alexander Hanchett. Classification of mushrooms. b'04. BA '28 (Lawrence Coll); MA '29—PhD '33 (U Mich). Anatomical and cytological studies of mushrooms as they apply to relationships of the species. Author: North American Species of Mycena '47; Mushrooms in Their Natural Habitats '49. Editor: Mycologia; also articles in field. Research asst Herbarium U Mich '32-34, asst curator '34-40, asso curator '40-45, bot and asso prof '45-50, botanist and associate prof since '50. Mich Acad Sci—Mycol Soc Am—Calif Bot Soc—Washington Acad Sci—AAAS—Torrey Bot Club. Herbarium, University of Michigan, Ann Arbor⊙

14 SMITH, Allen Stratton. Separation processes (Extraction, distillation, vegetable oil refining). b'06. BS '26—ChE '35 (U Minn); MS '31 (U Louisville); PhD '40 (U Mich). Author articles in field. Holder US patent. Prof chem engr U Notre Dame since '46; cons chem engr since '46. Am Inst Chem Engr—Am Chem Soc—Sigma Xi. University of Notre Dame, Notre Dame, Ind. H: 1215 Woodlawn Blvd., South Bend 16.†⊙

15 SMITH, Allyn Goodwin. Mollusks; Conchology. b'93. BS '16 (U Calif). Research on land, fresh water, marine mollusks of west coast of North America, north of Mexico. Author articles in field. Research asso conchology dept paleontol Calif Acad Sci since '39. Calif Acad Sci—Am Malacological Un-

ion (dir '47-48)—Conchological Club So Calif (corres)—Am Mus Natural Hist. 722 Santa Barbara Road, Berkeley 7.†

16 SMITH, Anna Kalet. Foster care of children; Soviet Russia (Welfare services); Adoption laws of Latin America. Child welfare (Foreign countries). b'84. AB '13 (Wellesley Coll). Research in foreign language sources on social insurance, health services, institutional and foster care, care of delinquents, and other problems in field. Author: Placing of Children in Families '38; Maternal and Child Welfare Services in Latin America '40; Glossary of Certain Child Welfare Terms in Spanish, Portuguese, French, and English '42; Health and Welfare Services for Mothers and Children in the Union of the Soviet Socialist Republics (from original Russian sources) '45; Juvenile Court Laws in Foreign Countries '49; Adoption Laws of North America '50, and others. With US Children's Bureau Washington since '17. U.S. Children's Bureau, Washington.

17 SMITH, Arthur D(wight). Economics of range management; Range ecology. b'07. BSF '36 (Utah State Agrl Coll); MSF '37 (U Calif). Research on some edaphic and climatic relationships in plant succession and habitat balance, the reliability of range vegetation, range lands and livestock operations of the intermountains and central Rocky Mountain region. Co-author: (with L A Stoddart) Range Management '43; also articles in field. Instr dept range management Utah State Agrl Coll '37-38, asst prof '38-42, asso prof since '46. Am Geophys Union —Wildlife Soc—Phi Kappa Phi —Sigma Xi. Utah State Agricultural Coll., Logan, Utah.†

18 SMITH, Austin Bettis. River cutoffs; Dredging; Channel maintenance; Navigation; Jetties; Research and engineering reports; Mississippi River accretions and islands. b'05. BS in civil engring '30 (U Ark). Design, construction and development of river cut-offs, cut-off dredging, maintenance of sea-bar channels with hopper dredges, maintenance of channels and drafting navigation regulations to aid channel navigation, maintenance of jetties; engineering reports and research on formation of accretions to lands riparian to Mississipi River, nucleation and growth of Mississippi River Islands. With Miss River Commn since '30, prin engr from '51. Theta Tau—Am Soc CE—Nat Geog Soc—Propeller Club—Military Engrs—Vicksburg Engr Club. 2525 Cherry St., Vicksburg, Miss.†

19 SMITH, Bernard Joseph. City planning. b'00. BEngring '23—MEngineering '26 (U Liverpool). Directed planning studies numerous cities in Southwest; design and construction of numerous systems water supply and distribution. Author: Town Building; International Scene '46. Asst reg rep NHA '42-47; private practice since '47. Am Soc CE—Am Econ Assn—County Louth (Ireland) Archeol Soc—Pi Gamma Mu. Room 208, 3405 Milton, Dallas 5.

20 SMITH, Boyd Milford. Educational theater. b'87. Student (W Va Prep Sch); (Davis and Elkins Coll); (Harvard U); LLB '10 (W Va U); AM '38 (Yale U). Author: The Patriarch '26. House mgr dept drama Yale U '27-29, bus mgr and asst prof dept drama '29-31, bus mgr sch fine arts '31-47; gov board Yale Art Gallery since '40, prof since '37; prof drama and chmn dept drama Yale since '46, exec officer div arts since '47. Am Ednl Theatre Assn—Am Nat Theatre and Acad—Nat Theatre Conf (mem bd trus-

tees). Yale University Theatre and Yale Art Gallery, New Haven.⊙

21 SMITH, Caleb Allen. Corporations (Early history; closely held, valuation of). b'14. BS '37 (Haverford Coll); MA '42—PhD '43 (Harvard U). Faculty economics Harvard U '41-46; asst prof econ Swarthmore Coll '46-48; prof econ and bus adm, asst to the pres Wilmington Coll '48-50; faculty dept econ Brown U since '50, now asso prof Am Econ Assn—Royal Econ Soc. Department of Economics, Brown University, Providence 12.†

22 SMITH, Carl E(dwin). Electronics (Education). b'06. BS in elec engring '30 (Is State Coll); MS '32—EE '36 (Ohio State U). Author: Applied Mathematics for Radio and Communication Engineers '45; Directional Antennas '46; Communication Circuit Fundamentals '49; Communication Networks (in press); Audio and Radio Facilities (in preparation); and others. Issued patents in field. Founded Smith Practical Radio Inst '34, pres '34-46; cons radio engr since '35; asst chief engr and chief engr radio stas WHK, WCLE '36-45; vp in charge engring United Broadcasting Co since '46; research and development engring WHK, WHK-FM, WHKC, WHKC-FM, WHKK since '46; pres Cleveland Inst Radio Electronics since '46. Am Inst EE—Inst Radio Engrs—Am Soc Engring Edn—Assn Fed Communications Cons Engrs—Soc Motion Picture and Television Engrs —Cleveland Engring Soc. 5000 Euclid Av., Cleve 3.

23 SMITH, Carlyle S(hreeve). Archeology of Long Island New York and Kansas; Antique firearms. b'15. AB '38; PhD '49. Field work in archeology of Great Plains '38-39, '47-50. Author articles in field. Asst prof sociol and asst curator anthrop Mus of Natural Hist U Kans since '47. Am Anthrop Assn(F)—Am Ethnol Soc—Soc Am Archeol—Archeol Soc Conn. Museum of Natural History, University of Kansas, Lawrence, Kan.†

24 SMITH, Cecil Raymond. Rayon manufacture. b'04. Student chem engring (Baltimore City Coll). Studies on viscose process for production of rayon from wood cellulose; improvement methods of spinning; development mechanical-optical machine for inspection of spinnerettes; research on rayon textile finishes and dyes; devised rayon knit cloth shrinkage devices and methods; assisted in design of forced dry air ovens for drying textile yarns preliminary to moisture determinations and other phys tests. Chem Indsl Rayon Corp Cleveland '29, asst chief chem Covington Va '30-38, chief chem since '38. AICE—Am Water Works Assn—Va Indsl Wastes and Sewage Works Assn. South Covington, Va. H: Firlawn, Covington.

25 SMITH, Charles Edward. Ancient and medieval history. b'05. BS '26—AM '27 (Moravian Coll); PhD '32 (U Pa). Study of history of Medieval Papacy, papal policy on marriage law, pontificate of Innocent III. Author: A Short History of the Ancient World (with P G Moorhead) '39; A Short History of Western Civilization (with L M Case) '40; Papal Enforcement of Some Medieval Marriage Laws '40; Tiberius and the Roman Empire '42; America Means Freedom of Worship in Aspects of Democracy '41. Prof hist La State U since '40, head department of history since '49. La State University, Baton Rouge.

26 SMITH, Clyde F(uhriman). Aphidae; Aphidiinae (Braconidae). b'13. BA '35—MS '37 (Utah Agrl Coll); PhD '39—U fellow '39 (O State U). Author articles in field. Research entomol NC Expt Sta '39-50, head entomol NC State Coll since '50. Entomol Soc America—Am Assn Econ Entomol—Sigma Xi—Gamma Sigma Delta. Box 5215, State College Station, Raleigh, N.C.†

10 SMITH, Cornelia Marschall. Dionaea; Insectivorous plants. b'95. BA '18 (Baylor U); MA '23 (U Chicago); PhD '28 (Johns Hopkins). Author articles in field. Prof biol and chmn dept Baylor U since '43, dir Strecker Mus since '43. AAAS(F)—Bot Soc Am—Tex Acad Sci (F, sec '44-47)—Modern Lang Assn—Sigma Xi. Baylor University, Waco, Tex.

11 SMITH, Dale. Forages (Survival, winter injury); Alfalfa; Legumes. b'15. BSc '38 (U Neb); MSc '40—PhD '47 (U Wis). Asso prof agron U Wis since '50. Department of Agronomy, Univ. of Wisconsin, Madison 6, Wis.†

12 SMITH, Dane Farnsworth. English drama (Restoration, eighteenth century). b'95. AB '17 (Vanderbilt U); certificate '19 (U Paris); MA '24—PhD '34 (Harvard). Author: Plays About the Theatre in England 1671-1737 '36; also articles in field. Asso prof Eng U NM '39-49, prof since '49. Modern Lang Assn—Coll Eng Assn—Phi Kappa Phi. University of New Mexico, Albuquerque, N.M.

13 SMITH, Dilman M. K. Public opinion; Industrial and public relations; American business conditions. b'02. AB '24 (Drake U); '25-26 (Columbia). Mem market research and sales promotion staff Standard Oil Co of Ind '30-37; developed new techniques in automobile accessory and style merchandise fields '37-38; vp Opinion Research Corp Princeton NJ since '39, currently research cons to mfrs autos, elec appliances and home furnishings. Co-author: Area Sampling or Quota Control? Phi Beta Kappa. 44 Nassau St., Princeton, N.J.

14 SMITH, Dwight L. Indians (Ethnohistory, land cessions, treaties) US history (Middle West). b'18. AB '40 (Ind Central Coll); AM '41—PhD '49 (Ind U). Research on Indian land cessions and treaties, Potawatomi and Wyandot removals. Teaching fellow Am hist Ind U '47-49; instr Am hist Ohio State U since '49. Research hist Anthony Wayne Parkway Bd O since '50. Ind Hist Soc—O State Archeol and Hist Soc—Miss Valley Hist Assn—Am Hist Assn—AAUP. Department of History, Ohio State University, Columbus 10, O.⊚

15 SMITH, Earle C. Metallurgy of open hearth steelmaking. b'91. EM '13—DSc hon '47 (Case Inst Tech). With Republic Steel and predecessor cos since '19, chief metall since '32. Am Iron and Steel Inst—Brit Iron and Steel Inst—Am Soc Metals—Am Inst Mining and Metall Engrs—Am Chem Soc—Am Foundrymen's Assn—Am Welding Soc—AAAS—SAE—Brit Inst Metals—Sigma Xi. Gold medal Am Soc Metals '46; Lamme medal O State '48. Republic Steel, Cleveland 15.

16 SMITH, Edgar Wadsworth. Sherlockiana; Foreign trade. b'94. Student '12-14 (NYU). Author: Foreign Trade and the Domestic Welfare '35; Price Equilibrium '37; Appointment in Baker Street '38; Baker Street and Beyond '40; Baker Street Inventory '45. Editor: The Complete Sherlock Holmes '45. Dir gen staff and vp Gen Motors Overseas since '44; dir Nat Fgn Trade Council. Am Enterprise Assn (dir). 1775 Broadway, NYC.

17 SMITH, Edward Hanson. Drift of ice; Sea and land ice. b'89. BS '13 (US Coast Guard Acad); AM '24—PhD '34 (Harvard); '24-25 (Geophysical Inst

Bergen Norway). Ice and oceanographical expedition Labrador Sea and Baffin Bay '28; on Graf Zeppelin Arctic expedition '31. Author articles in field. Commissioned ensign US Coast Guard '13 advancing through grades to rear admiral '42, convoy-escort duty Gibraltar World War I, comdr Northeast Greenland Patrol '41, US Naval Forces Greenland '42-43, task force Atlantic Fleet '44-45, comdr Eastern Area '46-50; dir Woods Hole Oceanographic Instn since '50. Am Geophys Union.

18 SMITH, Elsdon C(oles). Names (Personal). b'03. BS '25 (U Ill); '25 (U Chicago); LL B '30 (Harvard). Collected library on personal names. Author: Naming Your Baby '43; The Story of our Names '50; Bibliography of Personal Names '50; also articles in field. Lawyer, member with Blumberg and Smith since '49. Am Dialect Soc—MLA—Eng Place Name Soc—Am Name Soc. 1 N LaSalle St., Chgo 2. H: 322 Sherman Av., Evanston, Ill.

19 SMITH, Frank R. Microanalysis of food products. b'07. BA '29 (U Ark); MS '33 (U Md). Author articles in field. Microanalyst US Food and Drug Adm Washington since '37. Assn Official Agrl Chemists (asso referee on vegetable products)—Am Ornithol Union (asso). U.S. Food and Drug Administration, Washington 25.†

20 SMITH, Fred Wilson. Colloidal amorphous mixtures; Rubber; Latex; Cosmetics. b'08. ScB '31 (MIT); '37 (U Chicago); '45 (U A); '48-49 (Wayne U). Chemical research on compounding and development of natural and synthetic latex compounds, bonding cements, cement-asbestos products, plastic dip compounds, stripable and permanent adhesives, abrasion lining, electroplating accessories, insulating and patching compounds; analyses of metals to determine manganese in stainless steel and manganese and phosphorous in pig iron. Author articles in field. Analytical chem Carnegie-Illinois Steel Co Chicago '36-41; head research div Philip Carey Mfg Co Lockland Ohio '41-44; chief chem Automotive Rubber Co Inc Detroit '46-50, chem engr rubber lab Detroit Arsenal Centerline since '50. Am Chem Soc. Detroit Arsenal, Centerline, Mich. H: 3004 Hooker St., Det. 8.†

21 SMITH, Frederick George Walton. Caribbean fisheries; Marine fisheries; Tropical marine biology and oceanography. b'09. BSc '31—PhD '34 (London); ARCS '31 (Royal Coll Sci). Charge Florida state salt water fisheries survey '48, British Honduras fisheries survey '47; fisheries advisor to Bahamas Government since '47; director Florida State Oyster Division '49. Author: The Western Atlantic Reef Corals '48; The Spiny Lobster Industry of the West Indies '48. Biol sponge fishery investigations Bahamas Govt '36-40; asst prof zool U Miami '40-42, asso prof '43-45, dir Marine Lab since '43, prof zool since '45. AAAS—Limnol and Oceano Soc Am—Marine Biol Assn—SE Assn Biol—Am Geophy Union—Fla Acad Sci—Am Soc Zool—Bermuda Assn for Marine Biol Research. Astor prize biol '28, achievement award Fla Acad Sci '42, US Navy Dept award '46. Marine Laboratory, University of Miami, Coral Gables 34, Fla.⊚

22 SMITH, Frederick James. Petroleum and foundation geology. b'12. BS '35 (U Cincinnati); geol engr '36 (Cincinnati); '38-39 (Mo Sch Mines). Core drill exploration and sub surface map work in Mississippi. Insp Core Boring US Engr Office Little Rock '39-40; insp and jr civil engr TVA '41-44; geol Sinclair Oil & Gas Company Seminole. Am Assn Pet Geol—Am Geophys Un-

ion—AAAS—Shawnee Geol Soc (vp '47-48, pres '48-49)—ASCE. Federal National Bank Bldg., Shawnee, Okla.

23 SMITH, Gale Clifton. Paint; Varnish; Lacquer. b'07. Student '31-33 (Cleveland Coll); '44-46 (Wayne U). Development industrial paint and varnish finishes; research on quality control and manufacturing methods of paint, varnish and lacquer; consultant on use of resin as protective coating. Research indsl protective coating Ferbert-Schorndorfer '25-36; tech dir Berry Brothers Inc Detroit '36-48; tech resin rep US Indsl Chem since '48. Am Indsl Hygiene Soc—Am Inst Chem (F)—ASTM—ACS—Nat Paint, Varnish and Lacquer Assn. U. S. Industrial Chemicals, Inc., 405 Rockefeller Bldg., Cleve 13.

24 SMITH, George Everard Kidder. Architecture (Modern). b'13. AB '35—MFA '38 (Princeton U). Research on development of modern architecture; writer on architectural photography. Author: Switzerland Builds '50; Sweden Builds '51. Co-author: (with P L Goodwin) Brazil Builds '43. Architect Princeton U expdn to Antioch Syria; practice as architect since '38; fellow Am Scandinavian Found to Sweden, Guggenheim Found to Sweden and to Switzerland, Brown U to Italy and Mediterranean; Fulbright research fellow to Italy. AIA. 124 E 73rd St., NYC 21.

25 SMITH, George Frederick. Leather chemistry; Chemical engineering. b'91. Student '10-12 (Ohio State U); BS '17—MS '19—PhD '21 (U Mich). Author: Special and Instrumental Methods of Analysis '38. With U Ill since '21, prof chemistry since '39; pres G Frederick Smith Chem Co Columbus O since '24, Aeration Processes Inc Columbus O since '32; dir Applied Chem Testing Lab U Ill. Am Chem Soc—Am Ceramic Soc—Soc Chem Industry—Electro-chem Soc—Am Leather Chemists Soc—Am Inst Chemists—Alpha Chi Sigma—Phi Lambda Upsilon—Sigma Xi. 867 McKinley Av., Columbus, Ohio. H: 801 West Pennsylvania Av., Urbana, Ill.†⊚

26 SMITH, Gilbert Morgan. Freshwater algae; Marine algae of the United States Pacific Coast; Seaweeds. b'85. BS '07—DSc hon '27 (Beloit Coll); PhD '13 (U Wis). Author: Freshwater Algae of the United States '33; Cryptogamic Botany '38. Co-author: A Textbook of General Botany '24, 4 edits. Prof bot Stanford U since '25. AAAS (vp '41)—Am Micros Soc (pres '28)—Bot Soc Am (vp '42, pres '44)—Nat Acad Sci—Am Acad Arts Sci—Phi Beta Kappa. 1808 Waverly, Palo Alto, Calif.

27 SMITH, Grant Warren. Polymerization; Adsorption; Surface tension. b'07. BA '28 (Grinnell Coll); PhD '32 (U Minn); '38 (MIT). Research on adsorption, boundary tension by pendent drop method, electrokinetic potential, polymerization of vinyls, synthetic rubbers, plastics and rubber latex systems, coatings from latex. Holds patents on polymerization in aqueous emulsion. Author articles in field. Research chem and supervisor polymerization research B F Goodrich Co Akron '42-47, cons colloids and polymerization since '47; prof and head dept chem U ND '47-50; prof chem and dir general chemistry Pennsylvania State College since '50. American Chem Soc—AAAS—ND Acad Sci—Phi Beta Kappa—Sigma Xi. Department of Chemistry, Pennsylvania State College, State College, Pa.⊚

28 SMITH, Harley Albert. Speech education; Louisiana French. b'07. AB '29 (Phillips U Enid Okla); MA '33

(U Wis); PhD '36 (La State U). Stress of need for communicative education; study on correlation between speech proficiency and a positive personality; phonetic recordings of Eng speech of native French-speaking Louisianians. Co-author: (with Krefting, Lewis) Everyday Speech '41; (with King) I Want to Read and Write '50, also articles in field. Supervisor speech edn La State U '33-42, dir speech and psychol clinic edn dept '35-42; now supervisor spl edn Lafayette Parish, La; visiting prof Reading Inst NY U summer '50; radio cons. Nat Speech Assn—So Speech Association—Assn Edn by Radio—Phi Kappa Delta. Lafayette Parish School Board, Lafayette, La.

10 SMITH, Harold Theodore Uhr. Pleistocene geology; Geomorphology; Aerial photographs (Photogeology). b'08. BS '30 (Coll Wooster); MA '33—PhD '36 (Harvard). Research on Cenozoic geology of north-central New Mexico and central High Plains, geomorphology of sand dunes and wind erosion, utilization of aerial photographs in geological and geomorphic studies, geomorphology of periglacial phenomena and frost action, glacial grooving, military geology. Author: Aerial Photographs and Their Applications '43. Author articles: Geologic Studies in Southwestern Kansas '40; other articles in field. Asso prof geol Kan U since '46. Geol Soc Am (F)—AAAS(F)—Am Soc Photogrammetry—Nat Research Council—Phi Beta Kappa—Sigma Xi. Geology Dept., University of Kansas, Lawrence, Kan.†

11 SMITH, Harris Pearson. Farm machinery; Cotton harvesting b'91. BS '17 (Miss State Coll); MS '26—profl degree agrl engring '40 (Tex A&M Coll). Developed successful cotton stripper the principles of which are incorporated in most all commercial cotton strippers now being manufactured; designed and built a cotton extractor and a cotton cleaner, singlehead sorghum thresher and others. Author: Farm Machinery and Equipment '29, 3rd edit '47; also articles in field. Asso prof engring Texas A&M Coll '19-30, chief div Ag Engring Tex Agrl Expt Sta '30-47, prof since '47. Am Soc Agrl Engr(F)—So Agrl Workers Assn—Tex Agrl Workers Assn. Department Agricultural Engineering, College Station, Tex.

12 SMITH, Helen Leonore. Geographical place names; Economic geography (Asia); Siam. b'03. MA '38 (Peabody Coll Teachers); '41-42 (U Wis); '46-47 (U Chicago); '48-49 (Clark U). Research on geographical names of southeast Asia and West Indies regions, Shanghai and hinterland, geographical nomenclature in Siam. Author articles in field. Asst prof geog Wheaton Coll since '46. Assn Am Geog—Soc Women Geog. Wheaton College, Wheaton, Ill.†

13 SMITH, Henry Ladd. Aviation history. b'06. PhB '29 (Yale); MA '36—PhD '46 (U Wis). Author: Airways—The History of the Air Lines '42; High Frontier: The Story of America's World Air Routes. Professor and chmn dept Sch Journalism Univ Wis '47-48. Sigma Delta Chi—Am Assn Teachers Jour. Awarded Henry P Wright memorial prize in writing Yale '29; first Knopf award in history '40; Guggenheim fellowship (Aviation) '46. 301 South Hall, Madison 6, Wis.

14 SMITH, Henry Roy William. Archeology (Classical, Greek and Italic ceramic and vase-painting). b'91. BA '14—MA '17—diploma in classical archeology '23 (Pembroke Coll Oxford); PhD '27 (Princeton U). Author: New Aspects of the Menon Painter '29; The Origin of Chalcidian Ware '32;

Corpus Vasorum Antiquorum, USA fasc five '36; Der Lewismaler '39; Corpus Vasorum Antiquorum, USA fasc 10 '43; The Hearst Hydria '44; Problems Historical and Numismatic in the Reign of Augustus, '51. Prof Latin and classical archeology Univ Calif since '31. Archeol Inst Am. Awarded Guggenheim traveling fellowship '36. Faculty Club, University of California, Berkeley 4.

15 SMITH, Hobart Muir. Herpetology of Mexico and Kansas; Zoogeography. b'12. AB '32 (Kan State Coll); MS '33—PhD '36 (U Kan) '36-37 (U Mich). Author articles: Mexican and Central American Lizards of the Genus Sceloporus; Annotated Check List and Key to the Snakes of Mexico '45, Amphibians of Mexico '48, Lizards, Turtles, Crocodilians and Amphisbaenians of Mexico '49; Herpetology of Kansas '49. Instr zool U Rochester '41-45; asst prof zool U Kan '45; asso prof dept fish and game Tex A&M Coll '45-46; assistant professor zool U Ill '47-51, associate prof since '51. Walter Rathbone Bacon traveling scholar '38-41; Nat Research fellow '36-37. Department of Zoology, University of Illinois, Urbana, Ill.†

16 SMITH, Howard Malcolm. Classification and geography of soils. b'00. BS (Agron) '24 (Pa State Coll). Soil survey field studies in Ohio, Florida, Arkansas, Iowa, Texas, California, Tennessee and North Carolina; special studies in California and Texas to locate suitable soils for growing Guayule for production natural rubber; member of team compiling world soil map. With div soil survey USDA since '24, soil sci since '45. Am Soil Sci Soc—Am Soc Agron—Am Geog Soc NY—Nat Geog Soc. Division of Soil Survey, Bureau Plant Industry, Soils and Agricultural Engineering, Beltsville, Md.

17 SMITH, James Hollingsworth Clemmer. Photosynthesis; Plant pigments. b'95. AB '17 (Monmouth Coll); MS '20—PhD '21 (Chicago). Author articles: Absorption of Radioactive Carbon by Sunflower Leaves '41; Molecular Equivalence of Carbohydrates to Carbon Dioxide in Photosynthesis '43. Staff mem Carnegie Inst Washington since '27. Am Chem Soc—Am Soc Plant Physiol—AAAS—Sigma Xi. Department of Plant Biology, Carnegie Institution of Washington, Stanford, Cal.

18 SMITH, James R. Shale oil analysis. b'19. BS '40—MS '42 (U Wyo). Research in dehydration of food products, analytical methods for and analysis of oil distillates. Author: Shale-oil Naphthas, Analysis of Small Samples by the Silica Gel Adsorption Method. Research chem Standard Brands Inc, Fleischman Labs '42-45; chem petroleum and oil shale expt sta US Bur Mines Laramie Wyo since '45. Am Chem Soc—Sigma Xi—Phi Kappa Phi. United States Bureau of Mines, Petroleum and Oil Shale Experiment Station, Laramie, Wyo.

19 SMITH, Janet Katherine. Stage costuming; Minoan Crete; Marionettes. b'01. Student '18-22 (Wellesley Coll); diploma '24 (Chicago Acad Fine Arts); PhB '29—AM '30 (U Chicago); student (U Ore); EdD '43 (Columbia). Author: Design: An Introduction '46; Design: A Laboratory Manual; also articles in field. Prof housing Sch Home Econs Fla State U since '49. Am Ednl Theatre—Mus Modern Art (com on edn)—Kappa Delta Pi. First prizes Theta Alpha Phi convention for mask, for marionettes and costume plates '37. The Florida State University, Tallahassee, Fla.

20 SMITH, J(oe) Fred, Jr. Geology. b'11. BS '33 (Southern Methodist U); MA—PhD '39 (Harvard). Research geologic mapping in Moreno Valley and Cimarron Range northern New Mexico, geologic mapping in Trans-Pecos Tex; strategic minerals investigations, lead and zinc Nevada California New Mexico Idaho and Utah; military geology; glacial and stratigraphic geology in north-central Montana, general geology in southeast Montana, mesozoic stratigraphy structural geology and geomorphology in Sierra Blanca area Trans-Pecos Tex. Author articles in field. Asst prof geol Tex A&M Coll '38-42; geol US Geol Survey since '42, geologic mapping since '47. Geol Soc Am(F)—Am Assn Petroleum Geol—AAAS(F)—Am Geophys Union—Colo Sci Soc. Geological Survey, Geologic Division, Denver Federal Center, Denver 14.†

21 SMITH, J(ohn B(ertie). Art edn. b'08. AB '29 (Baylor U); AM '31 (U Chicago); EdD '46 (Columbia); '30-31 (Sch of Art Inst Chicago). Paintings exhibited since '31; one-man shows U Colo; Mobile (Ala) Gallery; Southeastern Annual; represented collection Denver Art Mus; head dept art U Wyo '39-45; part time instr art Columbia '45-46; head dept art U Ala '46-49; dean Kansas City Art Inst and Sch Design since '49. Ala Art League—Ala Edn Assn—SE Arts Assn—Nat Art Edn Assn—Coll Art Assn—Watercolor Soc Ala—Phi Delta Kappa—Kappa Delta Pi. 4415 Warwick Blvd., KC 2, Mo.†◎

22 SMITH, John Finnie Downie. Heat transfer; Machine design; Rubber parts design. b'02. Diploma '23 (Royal Tech Coll); BSc '23 (Glasgow U); MS '25 (Ga Sch Tech); ME '28 (Va Poly Inst); SM '30—ScD '33—Nat Research fellow '29-31 (Harvard). Research in heat conduction, convection, fluid flow. Author articles in field. Past chmn com on thermo-phys properties, heat transfer div ASME, mem sub-com convection Nat Research council; apprenticeship as machine designer Scotland; machine design, research and development US; founded and first chmn Machine Design Div ASME; developed application radiant heat to railway cars; instr heat transfer and related subjects Harvard Grad Sch Engring '31-36; with Ia State Coll since '47, dean engring, dir Ia Engring Expt Sta, dir Engring Extension Service since '47. ASME(F)—ASEE. Ia State College, Ames, Ia.

23 SMITH, John Milton. Educational philosophy (Plato, John Dewey); Idealism; Experimentalism. b'10. AB '31—STB '34—MA '34 (Lincoln U); STM '35 (Western Theol Sem); summer '36, '36-37 (Harvard U); PhD '41 (State U Ia). Research on educational philosophies of Plato and John Dewey, critical and definitive. Author: Comparison and Criticism of the Educational Philosophies of Plato and John Dewey '41; also articles in field. Chmn social sci div, prof social philos Fort Valley State Coll Ga since '46. Am Philos Assn—SW Philos Conf—NEA. Fort Valley State College, Fort Valley, Ga.

24 SMITH, John Milton. Hospital administration and management. born'82. Grad '03 (Mercersburg Acad Pa). Author articles on hospital management. Bus mgr Jefferson Med Coll Hosp Phila '04-08; adminstr Grant Hosp Columbus O '09-14, Muhlenberg Hosp Plainfield NJ '15-20, Hosp of Hahnemann Med Coll and Hosp Phila '20-36; trustee Union Hosp Cecil Co Md '41-51, hon mem bd since '51. Former pres, hon mem Hosp Assn Phila, Hosp Assn Pa; life mem Am Hosp Assn; past pres North East Cecil County, Md.

10 SMITH, Julian Cleveland. Chemical processing equipment; Centrifuges; Soil stabilization (Chemical methods). b'19. B Chem '41—Chem E '42 (Cornell U). Research and application chemical processing equipment, especially continuous equipment, to manufacture of organic intermediates; centrifugal and mixing machinery; glass equipment. Process engr E I du Pont de Nemours & Co '42-46; asso prof chem engring Cornell '46, now prof; cons NY State Dept Commerce '47-48; cons Corning Glass Works '50. AIChE —Am Soc Engring Edn—Phi Kappa Phi—Tau Beta Pi—Sigma Xi—Am Chem Soc. Olin Hall, Cornell University, Ithaca, NY.†

11 SMITH, Julian F(rancis). Textile research. b'93. BS in chem '16 (U Ill); MS '20 (U Cal); PhD '22 (U Chicago). Research on textile chemicals, fibers, and fiber properties, textile processes and machinery. With B F Goodrich Co '23-28; du Pont Exptl Sta '30-39; asso dir Hooker Sci Library '39-42; sci documents officer Office Nav Re-search since '47. ACS—Sigma Xi—American Inst Chem(F)—Armed Forces Chem Assn—AAAS(F)—Spl Libraries Assn— Aslib(Gt Brit)—Fiber Soc. Office of Naval Research, Code 408, Washington 25.

12 SMITH, Leon E(lkanah). Physics (Mechanics, luminescense, radioactivity). b'94. BS '19 (Ottawa Kans U); PhD '26 (U Pa); student (U Chicago). Author articles in field. Henry Chisholm prof physics Denison U since '28, dept head. Am Phys Soc—Am Assn Phys Teachers—Acoustical Soc Am— O Acad Sci (F, vp sect F '37-38)—Am Phys Soc (pres O sect '37-38, vp '36-37, sec-treas since '42)—Sigma Xi. Denison University, Granville, O.†

13 SMITH, Lloyd Preston. Solid state (Physics); Dynamics (Electron, ion). b'03. BS (EE) '25 (U Nev); PhD '30 (Cornell U); NRC fellow '30-31 (Cal Inst Tech); Internat research fellow '31-32 (U Munich Germany-U Utrecht Holland). Study electronic behavior in semiconductors and ionic crystals; lab tests photoconductivity and thermionics; electromagnetic separation of isotopes; mass spectroscopy; research on electron tubes and devices; member advisory committee on solid state physics to Office Naval Research. Hold patents on frequency modulation and control by electric beams, also other electron and ion devices. Author articles: Heat Flow in an Infinite Solid Bounded Internally by a Cylinder '37; Quantum Effects in the Interaction of Electrons with High Frequency Fields and the Transition to Classical Theory '46, and others. Co-author articles: (with G W Scott Jr) Conditions for Producing Intense Ionic Beams '39; (with Paul L Hartman) The Formation and Maintenance of Electron and Ion Beams '40, and others. Research engr Gen Elec Co '25-26; instr physics dept Cornell U '27-30, prof '36, prof and chmn dept since '46, also dir dept engring physics; research physicist Radio Corp Am Labs '39, cons war research '41-45, asso research dir '45-46, cons since '46; cons Carbide & Carbon Chem Corp Oak Ridge Tenn since '47, Brookhaven Nat Labs Upton LI '47-49. APS—Am Assn Physics Teachers—Sigma Xi—Phi Kappa Phi. Department of Physics, Cornell University, Ithaca.

14 SMITH, (James) Mapheus. Population; Manpower; Juvenile Delinquency; Genius; Leadership. b'01. AB '24 (Southwestern Presbyn U Clarksville Tenn); AM '28—PhD '31 (Vanderbilt U). Author: (with Walter C Reckless and E H Haddock) Six Boys in Trouble '29; (with Walter C Reckless) Juvenile Delinquency '32; The Serviceman and the Veteran '46; Industrial Deferment '48. Editor: Reports and Monographs of Selective Service System '47; Selective Service and Reemployment '49; 1952 Government Steel Seizure '52. Editorial Committee: Source Book for Social Psychology '47, '52. Contbg ed: Dictionary of Sociology '43. Asst prof social U Kan '31-35, asso prof '36-43; research, statistics, edit work Selective Service Sys '43-51; man power specialist Defense Prodn Adminstrn '51-52; historian Dept Commerce since '52. Am Social Soc—Am Psychol Assn —Am Sociometric Assn—Am Statis Assn. 323 2d St., Washington 3.©

15 SMITH, Marc Jack. History of American Indian. b'09. AB '31 (Ottawa Univ); MA '32 (Kan Univ); PhD '45 (U Wis). Research on Indian's part in Revolution and subsequent Indian problems of Canada and the old northwest, centering around Joseph Brant; collected library on Indians. Bacone Coll for the American Indian '33-45; prof U Redlands '46-48, dean of men since '48. AHA—Miss Valley Hist Assn—County Hist Soc. Exchange fellow in Germany '32-33; Adams Fellow U Wis '35-36. University of Redlands, Redlands, Cal.†

16 SMITH, Marian W(esley). India; Indians of the American Northwest coast. b'07. AB '29 (Barnard Coll); MA '34—PhD '38 (Columbia). Field work American Indian '34-35, '38, '45, India and Pakistan '49-50. Author: The Puyallup-Nisqually '40. Editor: Indians of the Urban Northwest '49. Dept anthrop Grad Sch Columbia since '41; mem staff S Asia Regional Studies U Pa since '49. Am Anthrop Assn —NY Acad Sci(F)—Am Ethnol Soc (ed and past pres)—AAAS (sec sect H)—Nat Research Council (com on Asian anthrop)—Sigma Xi. Department of Anthropology, Columbia University, NYC 27.

17 SMITH, Marion Bush. Sociology of rural education. b'93. AB '17 (Denver U); AM '28 (Colo U); PhD '37 (La State U). Member White House Conf on Rural Education '44. Author: Sociological Analysis of Rural Education in Louisiana '38; Survey of Social Science '42, rev '45. Co-author: Sociological Foundations of Education (with others) '42; also articles in field. Prof sociol La State U since '45. Am Sociol Soc—So Sociol Soc—SW Social Sci Assn—Kappa Delta Pi—Tau Kappa Alpha. Dept of Sociology, Louisiana State University, Baton Rouge 3.†

18 SMITH, Marion Russell. Entomology (Ants). b'94. BS '15 (Clemson Coll); MS '17 (O State U); PhD '26 (U Ill). Author articles in field. Specialist on ants Bur Entomol and Plant Quarantine US Dept Agr Washington since '37. Entomol Soc Washington— Soc Systematic Zool—Entomol Soc Am —Sigma Xi. Division of Insect Identification, Bureau of Entomology and Plant Quarantine, Washington.

19 SMITH, Mary Ellen. Gold dredging. With Trinity Dredging Co Lewiston Calif since '24, pres and gen mgr since '27. AIMME—Am Mining Congress. Lewiston, Trinity Co., Cal.

20 SMITH, Maurice Frederik. Public relations (International affairs). b'08. Student '24-26 (U Mich); '27-29 (Coll of William and Mary); summers '26-30 (Dayton Art Inst). Publicity director Wilkie preconvention campaign '40; assistant to the President Bretton Woods International Conference '44; chairman public relations committee National Labor-Management Conference '45; co-founder United Nations World, International United Nations Citizens Movement. Author: East Indies Story; How to Think About the United Nations; How to Think About Business; The Capitalist's Primer. Pub relations dir Batten Barton Durstine & Osborn NYC '31-36; partner Selvage & Smith NYC '37-40; pub relations dir Young & Robicam NYC '41-42; asst to Sec US Treas '42-44; vp charge adv promotion pub relations research and pub service Am Broadcasting Co '44-45; dir adv Simon & Schuster publishers '45-46; pres Fred Smith & Co since '47; pres The Graphics Group publishers; bd editors UN World. 149th St. and East River, Whitestone, L.I., N.Y.†

21 SMITH, Myron Bement. Islamic architecture; Iran (History, bibliography, archicture); Islamic cul; US architecture (Colonial); Renaissance architecture; Brickwork (History). b'97. Student '23, '31 (Columbia); BFA '26 (Yale); '41, '42 (McGill U); AM '44 (Harvard); '44-46 (Oriental Inst U of Chicago); Ph D '47 (Johns Hopkins U). Research on Lombard medieval brick architecture, Renaissance stonework, pre-Gothic stuccoes in Northern Italy, history of brickwork in all ages and countries, Islamic architecture, Persian gardens, use of vault in Persian architecture. Designer Cross and Cross '26-27; exec Simon and Simon '28-29; sec Persian Inst '30-33; hon cons and cons Islamic archeol and art Library of Congress '38-43, chief Iranian sect '43-44, F Islamic archt and Near E hist since '48, chmn com Islamic culture since '49, dir Islamic archives since '49. AHA—Am Oriental Soc—Archeol Inst Am—Coll Art Assn Am—Middle E Inst—Soc Archt Hist— Royal Central Asian Soc (London). F Guggenheim Found '27-28; research F Am Council Learned Soc '33-37; sec Com Near E Studies Am Council Learned Soc '40-48. Library of Congress, Washington 25. H: 1789 Lanier Pl., Washington 9.†

22 SMITH, Ora. Horticulture (Vegetable crops, potato, tomato); Plant physiology; Chemical weed control. b'00. BS '23 (U Ill); MS '24 (Ia State Coll); PhD '29 (U Calif). Research on production, seed handling, cultural, fertilization and nutrition methods, storage, dormancy, respiration, dehydration of the potato; pollen tube growth, pollination, life history study, effect of light on carotinoid pigments of tomato; effect of growth substances on plants; killing potato vines with chemicals, chemical weed control. Author articles in field. Asst prof dept hort Okla A&M Coll '29-30, dept vegetable crops Cornell U '30-38; collaborator US Dept Agr '31-38; hort rep Prodn Credit Div Farm Credit Adminstrn '34; prof dept vegetable crops Cornell U since '38; mem staff Inter-Am Inst Agrl Sci Turrialba Costa Rica '46-47, vis plant physiol '47-49, dir rsch Nat Potato Chip Inst '49-50. AAAS(F)— Am Soc Hort Sci—Am Soc Agronomy— Soil Sci Soc Am—Potato Assn Am (pres '38-39)—Sigma Xi—Phi Kappa Phi—Alpha Zeta. Department of Vegetable Crops, Cornell University, Ithaca, N.Y. H: 1739 Slaterville Rd., Ithaca, N.Y.

23 SMITH, Osgood R(euel). Stream and lake fauna; California lakes and streams; Stream improvement; Marine fisheries (Trout, salmon, pilchards, tuna). b'07. BS '30 (Hamilton Coll); PhD '33 (Cornell U); '31 (Marine Biol Lab Woods Hole Mass). Author articles in field. Aquatic biol US Fish and Wildlife Service Stanford Calif since '37. Am Fisheries Soc—Am Soc Icthyol and Herpetol—Am Limnol Soc. United States Fish and Wildlife Service, 13 State St., Newburyport, Mass.

10 SMITH, Paul F. Botany (Mineral nutrition, propagation, guayule, citrus). b'16. BS '38—research fellowship in botany '39-40—MS '40 (U Okla); PhD '44 (U Calif). Author articles in field. Asst physiol spl Guayule Research Project Bur Plant Industry US Dept Agr '42-45; asso plant physiol Subtropical Fruit Investigations Bur of Plant Industry Soils and Agrl Engring US Dept of Agr since '46. Bot Soc Am—Am Soc Hort Sci—Sigma Xi. 415 N. Parramore St., Orlando, Fla.

11 SMITH, Paul Kenneth. Pharmacology; Biochemistry. AB '30 (Westminster Coll); PhD '34 (Yale). Asst Chemistry Westminster Coll '26-30; asst physiol chemistry Yale '32-34, research f pharmacology '34-36, instr '36-38, asst prof '38-41, chief pharmacology and biochemistry sch aviation med '42-46; prof pharmacology and head dept sch med George Washington U since '46; cons in therapeutics University and Gallinger hosps since '48. Am Assn Cancer Research—Am Chem Soc —Soc Exptl Biol Med—Am Soc Biol Chem—Am Soc Pharmacol Exptl Therapeutics—AAAS—Aero-med Assn —Washington Acad Medicine—Sigma Xi—Phi Chi. 1335 H St., Washington 5.⊚

12 SMITH, Ralph Carlisle. Atomic energy and chemical engineering patents. b'10. ChE (Rensselaer Poly Inst); '33-35 (Rutgers U); JD '39 (George Washington U). Editor: Atomic Energy Commission Weapons Effects Handbook. Patent engr Stevens and Davis Washington '37-38; patent attorney Colgate Palmolive Peet Company '38-47, assistant director Los Alamos Sci Lab Univ Calif Los Alamos NM and Atomic Energy Commn, patent advisor directing activities Santa Fe since '47. Am Phys Soc—Soc Am Mil Engrs—Am Chem Soc—Am Soc Metals—Am Patent Law Assn—AAAS—Am Inst Phys—Am Inst Chem Engrs—Am Bar Assn—Bar US Supreme Court. Los Alamos Scientific Laboratory, P.O. Box 1663, Los Alamos, N.M.

13 SMITH, R(alph) Elberton. Tariff (Custom valuations); World War II (Procurement history). b'10. BA '35 (Coll Wooster O); MA '46—PhD '47 (U Chicago). Author: Customs Valuation in the United States—A Study in Tariff Administration '48. Econ statistics div WPB '42; econ hist procurement Office Chief of Mil Hist Dept of Army Washington since '50. Naval officer Office Procurement and Material Washington. Am Econ Assn. Office of the Chief of Military History, U.S. Army, 1E-589 Pentagon, Washington 25. H: 5429 N. 24th St., Arlington, Va.

14 SMITH, Ralph W(eir). Weights and measures. b'89. Student '09-11 (U Minn). Author: Weights and Measures Administration '27; Testing of Weighing Equipment '45; also articles in field. Inspector weights and measures State of Minn '12-16; chief inspector weights and measures State of Wis '17-20; with Nat Bur Standards US Dept of Commerce since '20, inspector weights and measures '20-24, sect chief '24-28, '28-36, same plus asst chief div weights and measures '40-44, asst to dir '44-48, chief office weights and measures since '48. Nat Conf Weights and Measures (sec since '40, sec com on specifications and tolerances since '40). National Bureau of Standards, Washington 25.

15 SMITH, Randolph Lockwood. Waste treatment (Aero-filter, chemical, settling tanks). b'96. Civil Engr '21 (Valparaiso U). Research and development of aero-block filter media, chemical treatment of sewage sludge,

small primary settling tanks, fine screen as primary treatment, treatment of vegetable canning wastes. Granted patent for high capacity waste filtration. Cons engr since '26. Nat Soc Prof Engrs—Central States Sewage Works Assn. 2083 Wellesley Av., St. Paul 5.†

16 SMITH, Richard Emerson. Television (Make-up); Three-dimensional masks. b'22. AB '43 (Yale). Pioneered modern television make-up colors, special quick-change and three-dimensional rubber make-up techniques; make-up artist for Democratic National Committee and NBC at Democratic Convention '48. Make-up artist Yale Dramatic Assn and Yale Sch Drama '43; artist with preparation dept NY Mus Nat Hist '45; staff make-up man NBC Television NYC since '45. N.B.C. Television, 30 Rockefeller Plaza, NYC.

17 SMITH, Robert C. Art of Portuguese speaking world; Baroque art. b'12. AB '33—MA '34—PhD '36 (Harvard). Author: The Colonial Art of Latin America '45. Co-author: Guide to the Art of Latin America (with Wilder) '48; also articles in field. Asso prof art hist Pa U since '47. Acad Nac Belas Artes Lisbon (corr)—Hispanic Soc Am (corr)—Inst Historico e Geografico Bahia (corr)—Museu Imperial Petropolis (Conselho Internac). Sachs fellow, Harvard '34-35; fellow Am Council Learned Soc '37; Guggenheim Fellow '40; fellow in Brazilian and Portuguese studies, Library of Cong since '45. Dept. of Fine Arts, University of Pennsylvania, Phila. 4.†

18 SMITH, Robert Henry. Waterfowl (Population, mortality, ranges). b'08. AB '32 (Dartmouth Coll). Research on methods of measuring fluctuations in populations of wild waterfowl, made expedition to James Bay, Can '43-44 to determine mortality factors of Canadian geese and other waterfowl; expeditions to Arctic coast of Canada and Alaska '48, '49, '50 measure breeding populations of wild ducks and geese and determine nesting ranges and population densities of North Am waterfowl, member expeditions to Mexico and Central America '48, '49, '50 to evaluate waterfowl wintering area and wintering waterfowl populations. Refuge biol Bur Biol Survey USDA '36-42, Miss flyway biol Fish and Wildlife Service '42-48, Pacific flyway biol since '48. Wildlife Soc. Postoffice Box 978, Klamath Falls, Ore.

19 SMITH, Roger Cletus. Insects, insecticides (Household, field crops). b '88. AB '11 (Miami U Oxford O); AM '15 (Ohio State U); PhD '17 (Cornell U). Author articles: Earworm Injury to Corn and Resulting Losses '19; The Biology of the Chrysopidae '22; The Neuroptera of Haiti, West Indies '31; The Chrysopidae (Neuroptera) of Canada '32; The Influence of Civilization on Insects in the Cultivated Areas of North America '35; Hallucinations of Insect Infestation Causing Annoyance to Man '34; Recent Developments with Insecticides '46; What We've Learned About DDT '47; Summary of the Uses of the Newer Insecticides. Head dept entomology Kan State Coll since '43; specialist for agrl and biol scis Nat Roster. Mem Kansas Entomol Commn —AAAS(F)—Am Assn Econ Entomol —Entomol Soc Am—Kan Acad Sci— Sigma Xi—Phi Beta Kappa—Gamma Sigma Tau. Department of Entomology, Kansas State Coll., Manhattan.⊚

20 SMITH, Ronald Bromley. Gas turbines. b'07. BS cum laude '30—ME '33 (U Washington); MS '36 (U Pittsburgh); grad study (U Pa, U Mich). Responsible for design development and manufacture first power gas turbine in the United States and first marine gas turbine power plant in

world; developed the Elliott-Buchi turbocharger; directed the development of Elliott cycle for production of tonnage oxygen; directed the design and development of first American gas turbine locomotive. Patents fluid compressor, gas turbine cycle, high temperature rotating machinery. Author articles in field. Vice pres engineering Elliott Co Jeannette Pa '45-48; dir engring MW Kellogg Co '48-50, vp since '50. ASME—SAE—Am Soc Metals— Soc Naval Architects and Marine Engrs (awarded the Capt John Linnard Prize with Prof Soderberg '43)—Sigma Xi— Tau Beta Pi. The M. W. Kellogg Co., 225 Broadway, N.Y.C.

21 SMITH, Stephen. Steel (Flame hardening). '05 Student '24-27 (Cooper Union Coll Engring); '40 (U Mich). Specialist in development and application flame hardening of steel; authority on application flame hardening in machine tool industry; design of equipment for flame hardening lathe ways, cross feed and lead screws, lathe spindles, boring bars, milling machine ways and overarms, engraving rolls, plain and corrugated paper rolls, steel mill rolls and crankshafts; inventor simultaneous flame hardening and tempering process which permits surface hardening steel parts in one complete operation to any desired degree of hardness thus eliminating subsequent heat treatment; process for flame hardening internal surfaces of cylinders as pump liners and aircraft engine cylinder liners. Research dept Air Reduction Co '35-49; mgr flame hardening div Nat Forge and Ordnance Co since '49. Am Soc Metals—Am Welding Soc. National Forge and Ordnance Co., Irvine, Pa. H: 5 Second Av., Warren, Pa.

22 SMITH, T(homas) Lynn. Population; Sociology of Latin America (Brazil, Columbia); Rural sociology. b'03. BS '28 (Brigham Young U); MA '29—PhD '32 (Minn U); '30-31 (Harvard). Advisor on colonization and settlement to Ministry of National Economy of Colombia '42-45; research on population and rural life, social organization of rural life; past director of Institute for Population Study, Louisiana State University; past dir Institute for Brazilian Studies, Vanderbilt U. Author: Sociology of Rural Life, '40, 47, 53, Brazil: People and Institutions; awarded Doctor Honoris Causa, Univ do Brazil '46, U. of Sao Paulo, 48. Population Analysis '48; Co-author: Brazil: Portrait of Half a Continent, '50; The Sociology of Urban Life '51; The People of Louisiana '52; also articles in field. Assistant professor, later prof and head dept sociol, rural sociol La State U '31-47; sr agrl analyst US Dept State '42-45; prof, head dept sociol and anthrop Vanderbilt U '47-49; prof sociology U Florida since '49. Am Sociol Soc — So Sociol Soc — Rural Sociol Soc — Sociol Research Assn — Population Assn Am — Internat Union Sci Study Population (US Nat Com)—Acad Colombiana Jurisprudencia (hon). Social Science Research Council fellow '29-31, Rosenwald Fund fellow '39. University of Florida, Gainesville, Fla.

23 SMITH, Townsend Jackson. Agronomy (Field crops); Forage crop breeding. b'10. BS '36 (U W Va); PhD '40 (O State U). Research on physiological studies sweet clover, weed control, alfalfa production, methods of seeding forage crops. Author articles in field. Agronomist Va Agr Exptl Station since '46. Am Soc Agronomy—Va Acad Sci—Gamma Sigma Delta—Sigma Xi. Virginia Agricultural Experiment Station, Blacksburg, Va.†

10 SMITH, Waldo Edward. Hydraulic engineering; Hydrology; Geophysics. b'00. BS '23—MS '24 (U Ia); '27-28 (U Ill). Author articles in field. Exec sec Am Geophys Union of Nat Research Council since '44; professional lecturer civil engring George Washington U since '46; specialist on certain geophys matters Dept Nat Defense since '47. ASCE—Am Geophys Union (exec sec)—Sigma Tau—Tau Beta Pi—Sigma Xi. 1530 P St., Washington 5.†⊙

11 SMITH, Walter Harold B. Weapons; Firearms (Design); Ballistics; Military history. b'01. Author: The Basic Manual of Military Small Arms '43, '44, '45; National Rifle Association Book of Small Arms '45; History of Mauser Rifles and Pistols '46; History of Walther Pistols '46; Mannlicher Firearms '46; NRA Book of Rifles '47; Small Arms of the World '48; also articles in field. Cons arms and armament to Mil Service Pub Co Harrisburg Pa since '43; cons mil weapons to Nat Rifle Assn Am since '43; research cons to mfrs and moving picture producers; Arms editor Am Legion Mag since '46; dir prodn and research Firearms Internat Corp NYC Washington Brussels since '49. Military Service Publishing Co., Harrisburg, Pa.†

12 SMITH, Warren Storey. Musical history (Nineteenth and early twentieth century); Musical form and theory. b'85. Grad '08 (Faelten Pianoforte Sch). Author articles in field. Mem faculty NE Conservatory Music since '22; music editor Boston Post since '24; lecturer on musical history and appreciation. Boston Post, Boston.

13 SMITH, Watson. Archeology of southwestern United States. b'97. PhB '19 (Brown U); LLB '24 (Harvard Law Sch); '34-36 (U Calif); research fellow '35-36 (Museum of Northern Ariz); research fellow '36-41, '45-49 (Peabody Museum Cambridge Mass). Archeologist on expedition SW Colo '33-34, Field Museum Natural History Chicago; Northern Arizona Rainbow Bridge Expedition '35-37; field director expedition Museum Northern Arizona '48. Author: Kiva Wall Paintings at Awatovi '49. Co-author: Archeological Studies in Northeast Arizona '45; Franciscan Awatovi '49; Excavations in Big Hawk Valley, Arizona '49. Am Anthrop Assn—Soc Am Archaeol. Peabody Museum, Cambridge 38, Mass.

14 SMITH, Wayne Carleton. Riot stick fighting; Judo and unarmed defense. b'01. BS '25 (US Mil Acad); grad '31 (Inf Sch Ft Benning Ga); grad '40 (Command and Gen Staff Sch). Author: Manual of the Riot Stick '36. Editor: Judo Notes '32; Sentinel, Tientsin China '32-34; Post Commander's Corner Redlander '45-47. Served with Co E 1st Gas Regt Chem Warfare Service '20-21 advancing through the grades to present position of asst div commander 11th Airborne Div. Camp Campbell, Ky.

15 SMITH, William Jones. Insurance buildings (Design); Ednl buildings (Design). b'81. BS Architecture '03 (U Pa); ADG architecte diplomé par le Gouvérnement Francais '07 (Ecole des Beaux Arts Paris). With Cass Gilbert architect NY '07-09; Holabird & Roche Chicago '09-12; mem firm Childs & Smith since '12, architects ins and univ bldgs. AIA(F)—Grands of Beaux Arts—BAID—Ill Soc Architects—Pa Hist Soc—Art Inst Chicago—Sigma Xi. 20 N. Wacker Dr., Chgo. 6.⊙

16 SMITH, William Stevenson. Egypt. b'07. Student '24-26 (U Chicago); AB '28—PhD '40 (Harvard). Author: A History of Egyptian Sculpture and Painting in the Old Kingdom '46. Asst Boston Mus Fine Arts '28-30, Harvard-Boston Egyptian Expdn '30-40; asst curator Egyptian Dept Mus Fine Arts Boston since '41; lecturer fine arts Harvard since '48. Archeol Inst Am—Oriental Soc. Museum of Fine Arts, Boston.

17 SMITH, William Watson. Blueberries; Dwarf and hardy fruit trees; Storage of fruits. b'01. BS '24—MS '30 (U NH); PhD '33 (Mich State Coll). Movie pictures and colored slides used in study and teaching. With U NH since '33, now asst prof hort. Eastern Mass Blueberry Growers Assn (hon)—NH Acad Sci—NH Hort Soc—Am Assn Hort Sci—New Eng Plant Physiol—Sigma Xi—Phi Kappa Phi. Horticultural Department, University of New Hampshire, Durham, N.H.

18 SMITH, Winslow Whitney. Bacterial physiology; Bacteriology of Great Salt Lake; Trout furunculosis; Contamination of food; Water hygiene; Synovitis of turkeys (Staphylococcosis). b'07. AB '33—MA '36 (U Utah); PhD '39 (U Wis). Author articles in field. Prof and head dept bact and pub health Utah State Agrl Coll since '46. Soc Am Bact (nat councilor since '47)—Am Pub Health Assn—Utah Pub Health Assn (exec bd since '48)—Am Soc Limnol and Oceanog—Utah Acad Sci—Utah Conf Higher Edn (exec bd '47-48)—Sigma Xi. Utah State Agricultural College, Logan, Utah.†

19 SMITH-JOHANNSEN, Robert. Surface chemistry; Water lubrication; Adhesion. b'15. BSc '39 (McGill U Montreal Canada). Research on adhesion and friction on snow and ice '40-44, aircraft deicing '44-47. Author: Om Ski Smoring '44; Tidsskrift for Kjemi, Berguesen og Metallurgi (no 4) '44. With project cirrus Gen Electric Research Lab Schenectady NY '45-53, bonding silicones silicone rubber '49-53; S-J Chem Co Niskayuna NY since '53. Am Meteorol Sco. Box 6, Niskayuna, N.Y.

20 SMOCK, Robert Mumford. Pomology (Respiration, physiology, storage). b'08. BS '30 (Muskingum Coll); BS '31—MS '32—PhD '34 (O State U); '38 (Cambridge U). Research on fruit respiration, storage, production of volatile materials. Author: Apples and Apple Products '50. Rsrch asst fruit storage U Calif '34-37; research asso physiol and storage pomol dept Cornell U since '37. Sigma Xi. Department of Pomology, Cornell University, Ithaca, N.Y.

21 SMOLUCHOWSKI, Roman. Solid state; Physical metallurgy. b'10. MA '33 (U Warsaw); PhD '35 (U Groningen). Research on crystal and electrical structure of metals; imperfections, grain boundaries, surfaces; X-ray diffraction; mechanism of diffusion and phase transformation; radioactive tracers; solid solution, ordering, precipitation, ageing. Author articles in field. Mem Inst Advanced Study Princeton '35-36, instr, research asso '40-41; research asso U Warsaw '36-39; head sect physics Inst Metals Inst Tech Warsaw '36-39; research physicist Gen Elec Research Labs Schenectady '41-46; asso prof mem staff metal research lab Carnegie Inst Tech Pittsburgh since '46. Am Phys Soc (chmn com solid state)—NY Acad Sci—Am Soc Metals—Am Inst Mining and Metall Engrs—Am Soc X-ray and Electron Diffraction—Pittsburgh Phys Soc—AAAS—Sigma Xi. 1090 Morewood Ave., Pittsburgh 13.

22 SMUCKER, Silas Jonathan. Forest pathology; Elm tree diseases. b'04. AB '30 (Goshen Coll); MS '32 (Purdue U). Author articles in field. Soil conservationist with soil conservation service US Dept Agr since '45. Am Phytopath Soc—Ind Acad Sci—Soil Conservation Soc Am—Sigma Xi. Soil Conservation Service, Rensselaer, Ind.

23 SMULLIN, Louis D(ijour). Microwave tubes and circuits. b'16. '32-34 (Wayne U); BSE '36 (U Mich); SM '39 (MIT). Research and development of TR tubes and duplexers for microwave radar at Massachusetts Institute of Technology Laboratory '41-46; work on magnetrons, traveling wave tubes and rf components for microwave frequencies since '46. Co-author: (with Montgomery) Microwave Duplexers '48. Head duplexer sect RF group Radiation Lab MIT '41-46; head microwave tube lab Fed Telecommunication Labs Inc '46-47; Research Lab of Electronics MIT since '47. Inst Radio Engrs—Am Phys Soc. Research Laboratory of Electronics, Massachusetts Institute of Technology, Cambridge, Mass.†

24 SMYTH, John B(ridges). Wave propagation; Supersonics. b'14. BS '34—MS '37 (U Ga); PhD '42 (Brown U). Research on transmission of supersonic waves through stratified media. Author articles: Supersonic Transmission at Oblique Incidence Through a Solid Plate in Water '44; Propagation of Radio Waves in the Lower Troposphere '47. Physicist Tenn Eastman Corp '37-38; physicist Navy Electronics Lab since '42. Am Phys Soc—AAAS—Phi Beta Kappa—Phi Kappa Phi—Sigma Xi. United States Navy Electronics Laboratory, San Diego 52, Calif.

25 SNAPP, Oliver Irvin. Entomology; Insects attacking peaches. b'95. BS '16 (Va Poly Inst); MS '25 (Miss State Coll). Invented device for regulating under pressure the quantity of spray applied to each unit treated, for picking up peach drops, fallen fruits, cotton squares, etc, plum curculio jarring sheets. Author articles in field. Supt Fifth Congl Dist Agrl Sch Turbeville Va '16-17; in charge US Peach Insect Investigations State Coll Miss '17-20; entomol in charge US Peach Insect Sta Ft Valley Ga since '20. Am Assn Econ Entomol (past vp)—Entomol Soc Am—Cotton States Entomol (past pres)—Ga Entomol Soc (past pres)—Ga Hort Soc. Miami Village Road, Fort Valley, Ga. H: 434 Persons St.†

26 SNAVELY, Benjamin L(ichty). Underwater acoustics; Vibration analysis. b'06. BS '23 (Lehigh U); PhD '35 (Princeton). Electronic instrumentation; sound recording; invented low frequency acoustic systems, vibration analyzers. Author: Secondary Processes of Ionization in Mercury Vapor '37. Co-author: (with MB Dobrin and B Perkins) A Seismic Survey of Bikini Atoll '49. Instr physics Lehigh U '31-38, asst prof '38-41; physicist US Naval Ordnance Lab since '41. AAAS(F)—Geophys Union—Am Phys Soc—Optical Soc Am—Acous Soc Am. U.S. Naval Ordnance Laboratory, Silver Spring 19, Md. H: 1314 Erskine St., Takoma Pk. 12, Md.†

27 SNAVELY, Guy Everett. Romance languages. b'81. AB '01—PhD '08 (Johns Hopkins); LLD '25 (Emory U); LittD '30 (Southern Coll); LHD '37 (Boston U); DCL '38 (Birmingham So Coll); EdD '45 (Whitman Coll); and others. Author: Choose and Use Your College; History of Southern College Association; also articles in field. Prof Romance lang and lit Allegheny Coll '06-19; dean Converse Coll Spartanburg SC '19-21; pres Birmingham So Coll '21-38; exec dir Assn Am Coll since '37. Modern Lang Assn Am—Nat Adv Com on Edn—Ala Coll Assn (pres '26-27)—So Assn Coll and Secondary Schs (sectreas '26-27)—Assn Am Coll (pres '29-30)—Am Council on Edn (exec com 6 yrs, v chmn '37-38)—Assn Urban Univs (pres '36-37) — Presser Foundation (chmn scholarship dept)—Phi Beta Kappa (senator). 726 Jackson Pl., Washington 6.†☉

10 SNAVELY, J(oseph) Walter. Conveyors (Bulk handling); Elevators (Bulk handling). b'06. BS '27 (U Wis). Research, application and design of heavy-duty bulk handling conveying equipment and integrated handling systems as used by mining, heavy chemical, coal, pulp and paper, glass plant and foundry industries, use of high tension conveyor belt constructions for mining, application of turning-over of return runs of conveyor belts. With Chain Belt Co since '27, mgr conveyor equipment sect since '51. AIMME (cochmn materials handling com of Minerals Beneficiation Div). Chain Belt Co., 4701 W. Greenfield Av., Milw 14.

11 SNEDDEN, David. Educational sociology; Education (Vocational, American). b'68. AB '89 (St Vincent's Coll Los Angeles); AB '97 (Leland Stanford Jr U); AM '01—PhD '07 (Columbia). Author: Administration of Education for Juvenile Delinquents '06; Problems of Vocational Education '11; Problems of Educational Readjustment '14; Vocational Education '20; Sociological Determination of Objectives in Education '21; Educational Sociology '22; Introductory Sociology for Teachers '35; also articles in field. Prof edn Columbia '16-35, emeritus since '35. NEA—AAAS—Nat Soc for Vocational Edn (pres '18-20)—Phi Beta Kappa. 2040 Amherst St., Palto Alto, Calif.

12 SNELGROVE, Alfred Kitchener. Economic geology of Newfoundland. b'02. BS '27—MS '28 (McGill U); PhD '30 (Princeton). Led Princeton geological expeditions to Newfoundland '32-34; revived Newfoundland Geological Survey; investigated mines and mineral resources in Newfoundland. Author: Mines and Mineral Resources of Newfoundland '38. Editor reports Geological Survey of Newfoundland. Geol since '22; teaching asst Princeton '28-30, instr '30-35, asst prof '35-40; prof and dept head geol and mineral Mich Coll Mining and Tech since '40, Newfoundland Govt geol '34-43, cons geol since '43; inaugurated Upper Mich Mineral Industries Conf '42. Geol Soc Am—Soc Econ Geol—Mineral Soc Am —AAAS—Am Geophys Union — Can Inst Mining and Metall—Pan-Am Inst Mining Engring and Geol—Sigma Xi. Awarded President's Gold Medal Can Inst Mining and Metall '28—Barlow Memorial Prize '31. 304 Vivian St., Houghton, Mich.†☉

13 SNELL, Foster Dee. Physical colloid and industrial chemistry; Surface activity. b'98. BS '19 (Colgate U); MA '22—PhD '23 (Columbia). Research on methods of synthesis of surfactants and for the evaluation of surface activity and detergency; patents in plastics, cements, hair waving and composition blackboard. Co-author: (with C Snell) Colorimetric Methods of Analysis '48; (with C Snell) Chemicals of Commerce '39; (with C Snell) Chemistry Made Easy '43; (with Biffin) Commercial Methods of Analysis '44; also articles in field. Cons chem since '23; Foster D Snell Inc, pres since '30, Chemsearch Inc since '39, Foster D Snell Research Inc; dir Gargille Scientific Inc. Chem Soc London(F)—AAAS(F)—Am Inst Chem (F, past pres)—Am Chem Soc (councilor) —Am Oil Chem Soc (past vp)—Sigma Xi—Am Inst Chem Engrs—Am Soc Testing Materials—Soc Chem Industry (chmn, past vp). 29 W. 15th St., NYC 11.

14 SNELL, Hampton Kent. Transportation. b'04. BA '25—MA '28—Ely Scholar '27-28 (U Wis); '26-27 (W Va U); Strathcona Fellow '28-29—PhD '41 (Yale). Author articles in field. Asst econ Am Transit Assn '29; asst statis Am Telephone and Telegraph Co '29-30; asst prof, asso prof econ, Mont State U '30-36; asso prof transportation U Southern Calif '36-42; vis asso prof econ Stanford U '38; cons to transportation orgns '37-42; prin transportation econ OCR WPB '42-43; head transportation equipment program specialist ODT '43-44; transportation cons Resources Protection Bd '42-45; asst for research transportation Indsl Coll of Armed Forces '44-45; asst to vp Research Assn Am RRs and econ to RR com for study of Transportation '45-47; prof transportation Sch Fgn Service Georgetown U '46-47, Dept Agr Grad Sch Washington '43-47, U Tex since '47; cons to RR's airlines highway transport and industry since '47. Am Econ Assn—Am Acad Polit and Social Sci—Sigma Beta Chi—Alpha Eta Rho. 103 W.H., University of Texas, Austin 12, Tex.†

15 SNELL, Junius Fielding. Phosphorus metabolism; Yeast growth; Antibiotic fermentations; Fermentation biochemistry. b'21. BS in chem '43 (U Ida) (U Tex); MS (Biochem) '44—PhD '49 (U Wis). Research on production of food yeast protein from wood sugar, on improvement of penicillin and other antibiotic fermentations, and on phosphorus metabolism of penicillium molds. Co-author article: Fodder Yeast from Wood Sugar '45. Research on penicillin fermentation, wood sugar fermentation, and butylene glycol fermentation U Wis and US Forest Products Lab '43-45; research on penicillin and streptomycin fermentations Charles Pfizer & Co Inc '45-46; research on phosphorus metabolism of molds U Wis '46-49. ACS—NY Acad Sci—Sigma Xi. Radiobiochemical Laboratory, Pfizer Therapeutic Institute, Maywood, N.J. H: Beech Terrace, Pines Lake, R.D. 1, Paterson, N.J.

16 SNELL, Robert Sinclair. Farm crops (Small grain and sweet corn breeding, field crop production). b'06. BS '29 (Mass State Coll); MS '31 (Rutgers U); PhD '35 (Cornell U). Co-author: Practical Field Crop Production for the Northeast '47; also articles in field. Asso prof and asso research specialist farm crops Rutgers U since '44. AAAS—Bot Soc Am—Am Soc Agron—Am Genetic Assn—Sigma Xi. Farm Crops Department, Rutgers University, New Brunswick, N.J.

17 SNELLING, Walter Otheman. Military and commercial explosives; Chemicals (Liquified petroleum, natural gases); Formaldehyde. b'80. BS in Chem '04 (Columbian U, now George Washington U); BS in Sc '05 (Harvard); MS '06 (Yale); PhD '07 (George Washington U). Inventor waterproof detonator, continuous high-pressure oil-cracking process, sand-test method of testing detonators and explosives, densimeter used in testing dynamite, improved centrifuge test for explosives, liquid gas (gasol) made from waste natural gas; granted more than 200 patents covering inventions in field of chemical products and explosives; gave many inventions to US Govt without reserve. Author articles in field. Cons chem with pvt and corporate investigations of natural gas and products made therefrom, oils, oil products and explosives; dir research Trojan Powder Co since '17. Am Inst Chem Engrs—Am Inst Mining and Metall Engrs—Am Chem Soc—Electrochem Soc—Soc Am Mil Engrs—Engrs Club of Lehigh Valley—Franklin Inst —Am Ordnance Assn. 1509 Linden St., Allentown, Pa.☉

18 SNIDE, Harold E. American history (Business depressions, public opinion on outbreak of World War I); Religion (Origin of Sunday observance, modern trance prophets). b'96. BA '32 (Washington Missionary Coll); MA '34—'42-47 (Am U). Instr hist, Bible, New Testament Greek Southern Missionary College Collegedale '34-42 ref librarian Library Congress Legislative Reference Service since '44; research in history of bus depressions in US. Author: American Public Opinion on the Outbreak of World War I '34. AHA—Soc Biblical Lit and Exegesis. The Library of Congress, Washington 25.

19 SNOW, Royall. Romantic poets; Beddoes; Education (Honors work). b'98. SB '20 (Harvard); BA '24—BLitt '25—Rhodes scholar '22-25 (Oxford U Eng). Author: Thomas Lovell Beddoes: Poet and Eccentric '28. Co-author: (with J Stephens and E Beck) English Romantic Poets '35; (with J Stephens and E Beck) Victorian and Later English Poets '37; also articles in field. Asst and asso prof O State U since '28. Ohio State University, Columbus 10, O.†

20 SNYDER, Edward Douglas. Literature (Eighteenth Century English; Nineteenth Century American); Whittier. b'89. BA '10 (Yale); MA '11—PhD '13—Bayard Cutting fellow Europe '13-14 (Harvard). Author: The Celtic Revival in English Literature: 1760-1800 '23; Hypnotic Poetry '30. Editor: (with F B Snyder): A Book of American Literature '27, rev '35. Ed cons publications Modern Lang Assn Am. Instr Eng Yale '14-15; asst prof Eng Haverford (Pa) Coll '15-25, asso prof & chmn since '35, suprvr pub speaking & composition pre-meteorologist unit air force US Army '43; lecturer Eng Northwestern summers '27, '30, '32, Harvard summers '28-29. Modern Lang Assn Am—Nat Council Teach Eng— Phi Beta Kappa. Add: Haverford Coll. H: May Pl, Haverford, Pa.

21 SNYDER, Louis Leo. Modern European and German history; Bismarck; Intellectual history. b'07. AB '28 (St John's Coll); PhD '31 (U Frankfurt Main Germany). Specialist reviewer of books on German history and affairs; specialist on German History on panel of lecturers of National Jewish Welfare Board. Author: Hitlerism, The Iron Fist in Germany '32; From Bismarck to Hitler, The Background of Modern German Nationalism '35; Race, a History of Modern Ethric Theories '39; Survey of European Civilization, 2 vols '47, and others; also articles in field. Instr hist City Coll NY '33-40, asst prof hist City Coll NY '41-43, '45-49, associate prof '49-53, professor since '53. AHA—AAUP—Am Geog Soc (F). Box 136, The City College of New York, 138 and Convent Av., NYC 31.

22 SNYDER, Thomas Elliott. Termites; Forest insects (Termites, wood borers, powder post beetles, wood preservation). b'85. BA '07 (Columbia); MF '09 (Yale); PhD '20 (George Washington U). Travelled throughout United States, in West Indies, Central America and Hawaii on various problems relating to forest insects; pioneer work in describing new species of termites of the world, gathered the second best collection of termites of the world; established important chemical preservative tests for timber, fibre boards and soil poisons. Author: Our Enemy the Termite '48; also articles in field. Sr entomol forest insect investigations Bur Entomol and Plant Quarantine US

Dept Agr '09-51, retired; now cons. AAAS(F—Entomol Soc Wash (vp '48, pres '49)—Am Assn Econ Entomol—American Wood Preservers Assn—Nat Pest Control Assn (hon). H: 2801 Adams Mill Road, N.W., Washington.†

10 SNYDER, William Cowperthwaite. Fungus diseases of plants; Parasitic fungi; Plant pathology; Fungi. b'04. BS '27 (U Calif); PhD '32 (U Wis). Research on diseases of plants, their causes and control, ecology of plant diseases, seed-borne diseases, parasitic fungi their taxonomy and nomenclature. Asst prof and asst plant path in expt sta U Calif '37-43, asso prof and asso plant path '44-49, professor plant pathology since '49. plant path div forest path Bureau Plant Ind US Dept Agr '47, on leave from U Calif. AAAS—Am Phytopath Soc—Am Bot Soc—Soc Am Naturalists—Mycol Soc Am—Sigma Xi. Nat Research Council fellow at Biologische Reichsanstalt Berlin '33-34. Department of Plant Pathology, University of Calif., Berkeley 4.†

11 SNYDER, William Enoch. Photoperiod; Plant propagation. b'14. Student '32-34 (Kan State Teachers Coll); BA '36 (U Colo); MS '40—PhD '40 (U Chicago). Author articles in field. Asso prof ornamental hort Cornell U since '49. AAAS—Bot Soc Am—Am Soc Plant Physiol—Am Soc Hort Sci—Sigma Xi. Department of Floriculture and Ornamental Horticulture, Cornell University, Ithaca, N.Y.†

12 SNYDERMAN, George S(imon). Iroquois Indians. b'08. BS (edn) '31 (Temple U). MA '33—PhD '48 (U Pa). Research on social and religious organization of Iroquois Indians and their land ownership, economics, population statistics, warfare, medicine and healing, folklore, history before and since white contact. Employment supervisor Pa State Employment Service and US Employment Service since '39; cons Indian land ownership since '49. Am Anthrop Assn (F)—Sigma Xi—Am Folklore Soc. Pennsylvania State Employment Service, 42 S. 15th St., Phila. 2.

13 SOBEL, Albert Edward. Vitamins (Biochemistry, utilization); Calcification; Lead poisoning; Microchemical analysis; Sterol sulfates; Penicillin (Retention). b'06. PhD '40 (Polytech Inst Brooklyn); MA '36 (Columbia); ChE '35—BS '30 (Cooper Union); '16-22 (Gimnazium Budapest). Research on laws governing composition of bone and teeth, nature of factors in cell influencing calcification, chemistry of lead poisoning, development of a scheme of micro methods that reduce amount of blood required for quantitative analyses, sterol sulfates to provide vitro models of actions taking place in vivo, aqueous dispersions of fat soluble vitamins in comparison to the same vitamin in oily solution, various means of obtaining penicillin preparations that give prolonged blood levels after oral administration or parenteral injection. Author articles in field. Staff chem Pediatric Research Lab Jewish Hosp Brooklyn '31-33, head dept since '36, chemist-in-charge pediatric research lab '33-36; head dept chem since '36, adjunct prof chem Polytech Inst Brooklyn since '46. NY Acad Sci—Am Chem Soc (chmn publicity com, bd dirs Metro Long Island Group)—Am Soc Biol Chem—AAAS—Soc Exptl Biol and Med—Metro Microchem Soc—Soc Applied Spectroscopy—Sigma Xi. Jewish Hospital of Brooklyn, Brooklyn 16.

14 SODERBERG, Karl Gustaf. Electroplating; Corrosion of base metals. b'04. Chem Engr '26 (Royal Inst Tech,

Stockholm). Development of cadmium, zinc, nickel plating processes, bath formulas and control means, plating equipment, including rheostats, agitators, barrels, semi- and full-automatic machines; research in corrosion behavior of electroplated metals, atmospheric and accellerated tests, best utilization of all scarce plating materials and substitution of less scarce materials. Co-author: Modern Electroplating '42; also articles in field. Chem, later tech dir Udylite Corp Detroit '29-43; cons Conservation Div WPB Washington '43-45, chmn cadmium com, mem lead com; cons engr Graham, Crowley & Asso Inc Jenkintown Pa since '45. Am Electroplaters Soc (Founder's Gold Medal '47, ed)—Electrochem Soc (mgr '39-42, vp '43-45, electrodeposition div sec '35-39, chmn '39-40)—Am Soc Testing Materials (Com B-8 sec '41-43, v-chmn since '46)—Am Chem Soc—Electrodepositors Tech Soc, Eng. 473 York Rd., Jenkintown, Pa.

15 SOHLBERG, Rudolph G(ust). Seismology; Petroleum (Geology). b'07. BS '30—'30-31 (U Mich); '31-32 (Stanford U). Research on petroleum stratigraphy, application of geophysics to exploration for oil and gas, expecially seismic methods. Contributor: Ground Water Geology '37. Geol and chem Santa Clara Holding Co '33; mineral Ida Md Mines Co '33-34; asst geol Honolulu Bd Water Supply '34-35; research geol, geophys Coast Exploration Co '35-37; with Standard Oil Co Calif '37-44; with Richmond Petroleum Co '45; with Richmond Exploration Co '46-51, chief geophys '48-51. AIMME—Soc Exploration Geophys—Am Geophys Union—Am Assn Petroleum Geol—Sci Research Soc Am—Sigma Xi—Sigma Gamma Epsilon. United Geophysical Co., 595 E. Colorado St., Pasadena, Cal.

16 SOHN, Israel Gregory. Fossil ostracodes; United States mineral resources. b'11. BS '35 (Coll City NY); AM '38 (Columbia). Research Mississippian ostracodes '39-40, Cretaceous ostracodes from Jamaica, copper deposits Vermont, Mesozoic ostracodes from Brazil, high-alumina clay deposits Pacific Northwest, barite Georgia, mineral resources Missouri River Basin, Tertiary ostracodes Pacific Northwest, upper Paleozoic ostracodes Tex, mineral resources Columbia River Basin, ecology of post-paleozoic fossil ostracodes. Author: Check list of Mississippian Ostracoda of North America '40; Upper Jurassic Deposits in Brazil '42; Hinge Mechanism of Paleozoic Ostracodes '49; Growth Stages in Fossil Ostracodes '50; also articles in field. With U S Geol Survey since '41. Geol Soc Am—Am Assn Pet Geologists—Soc Econ Paleontologists and Mineralogists—Geol Soc Wash. United States Geological Survey, Washington 25.

17 SOHON, Julian Arell, Sr. Libraries; regional. b'96. BChem '18 (Cornell). Served on advisory committees in planning of regional libraries, member examining boards and consultant to library trustees. Bibliographer Engring Socs Library '20-34; head librarian Bridgeport Pub Library since '34. ALA—Conn Library Assn—Mass Library Assn. Bridgeport Public Library, 925 Broad St., Bridgeport 4, Conn.

18 SOKOL, Anthony Eugene. History of German civilization; Indonesia; Naval history. b'97. BS '28 (State Teachers Coll Miss); MA '30—PhD '32 (Stanford); student (U Vienna). Co-author: (with Helena M Nye) Grosse Forscher und ihre Beitrage '38; also articles in field. Prof Germanic Langs Stanford U since '29, asso dir Pacific-Asiatic and Russian Prog since '46,

exec head Asiatic and Slavic Studies Dept since '47; research asso Hoover Library on War Revolution and Peace since '37. Far Eastern Assn—Mod Lang Assn—US Mil Inst—US Naval Inst. Department of Asiatic and Slavic Studies, Stanford University, Stanford, Calif.☉

19 SOKOLSKY, George Ephraim. Far East (China and Japan); Communist movements; Labor problems. b'93. LLD '46 (Notre Dame); LLD '48 (Montana Sch Mines). Author: Outlines of Universal History '28; Tinder Box of Asia '32; Labor's Fight for Power '34; We Jews '35; Labor Crisis in the United States '38; The American Way of Life '39; also articles in field. Columnist (syndicated) with Hearst and other newspapers syndicated by King Features Syndicate since '44; radio broadcasting. Nat Press—Overseas Press—Am Platform Guild (vp). 300 West End Av., NYC 23.

20 SOLANDT, Omond McKillop. Military occupational physiology. b'09. BA '31—MA—BSc—MD '36 (U Toronto); MA '39 (Cambridge); MRCP '39 (U London); DSc (hon) '47 (U British Columbia); DSc (hon) '48 (Laval U). Research problems concerned with tank design and physiological problems peculiar to tank personnel which led to formulation of many important tank gunnery problems. Dir South-West London Blood Supply Depot '39-41; dir Med Research Council Physiol Lab Armoured Fighting Vehicle Sch Lulworth '41, deputy supt Army Operational Research Group under Brigadier Schonland and succeeded him as supt '43; joined Canadian Army as lt col '44, colonel '45; dir gen Defense Research '28, '45. Royal Soc Can(F). Affiliate mem Engineering Institute of Canada. Chairman, Defense Research Board, Room 4204, A Bldg., Department of National Defense, Ottawa, Ont., Can.

21 SOLHEIM, Wilhelm Gerhard. Fungi, Rocky Mountain. b'98. BS '20-22 (Augustana Coll SD); AB '24 (Ia State Teachers Coll); AM '26—PhD '28—fellow '27-28 (U Ill). Author articles in field. With U Wyo since '29, now professor of botany. AAAS (F, council '46-47)—Am Phytopath Soc—Mycol Soc Am—Bot Soc Am—Torrey Bot Club—Am Micros Soc—Am Phycological Soc—Calif Bot Soc—Ill Acad Sci—Colo-Wyo Acad Sci (pres '46-47)—Sigma Xi—Phi Beta Kappa—Kappa Delta Pi. Department of Botany, University of Wyoming, Laramie, Wyo.†

22 SOLLENBERGER, Paul. Time measurement. b'91. BS '13 (Marion Normal Coll). Made observations in transit circles, member of world longitude expedition San Diego '26, solar eclipse expedition Philippine Islands '29; in charge of determination of variation of latitude at Naval Observatory. Developed quartz crystal controlled apparatus for automatic transmission of time signals, and apparatus for measuring time of ommission of radio signals. Author articles: Reclinations and Proper Motions of 64 Stars Observed with the Photographic Zenith Tube '45. Asst US Naval Observatory '14-19, in charge time service since '19. Internat Astron Union (mem comns on time, longitude, variation of latitude)—Am Astronom Soc—Horological Inst Am (hon). Awarded Longstreth Medal by Franklin Inst for time broadcasting equipment '38. U.S. Naval Observatory, Washington 25.

23 SOLLID, Erik J. Concrete (Reinforced). b'03. BS '33—MS '34 (U Wis). Devised direct method for analyzing stresses in reinforced concrete beam subject to bending and direct stress with or without symmetrical steel; developed an integration method for determination of earthquake forces on a structure. Author article: Simple Diagram Gives Direct Solution for Stresses in Reinforced Concrete Members '50, and others. Co-author articles: Reinforced Concrete Design Data '49; Method of Calculating Deflections of a Structure Subject to a Known Earthquake '38, and others. Bridge designer State Highway Commission Madison Wis '35; now head of structural design unit Bur Reclamation. Denver Federal Center, Denver.

10 SOLLNER, Karl. Colloids and physical chemistry (Membranes, permeability, ultrasonics, osmosis); Thixotropy; Sols; Gels; Emulsions; Physical biochemistry. b'03. PhD '26 (U Vienna); Privat-Dozent fur Chemie '33 (Univ Berlin). Author articles Chief phys biochem Lab Phys Biol. Nat Inst Health Bethesda Md; prof physiol chem Med and Grad Sch U Minn since '47. Am Chem Soc—AAAS—Soc Gen Physiol—Sigma Xi. Weston fellow '30-31. Laboratory of Physical Biology, National Institute of Health, Bethesda 14, Md.†

11 SOLOMON, Louis H(oward). Industrial labor relations (Collective bargaining); Trade associations; Corporate organizations. LLB '12—LLM '13 (NYU); '09-10 (Yale). Admitted to NY bar '13; gen practice '14-20; specialized in corporate orgns and trade assns since '20, gen counsel for Am Cloak and Suit Mfrs Assn, Am Fur Merchants Assn, Fur Dyers Trade Council and others; dir Holmes Estate Inc, Abbott Estate Inc, Merchants Trust Co. Am Bar Assn—NY Co Lawyers Assn—Internat Lawyers Assn—Soc Am Jurisprudence—Soc Med Jurisprudence. 200 5th Av., NYC.

12 SOMBERG, Seymour I(ra). Forestry (Management; mensuration). b'17. BS Forestry '41 (Ia State Coll Ames); MF '46 (Duke U). Detailed management plans for forested and other areas; Determination of forest volumes in forest stands. Asst Unit ranger Fla Forest and Park Service '41-42; forest technician SC State Commn Forestry '44-45; cons forester Forestry Aids, Manning SC since '46. Soc Am Foresters (sr mem)—Assn Cons Foresters (charter mem)—Am Forestry Assn—Forest Farmers Assn—So Pulpwood Conservation Assn. Manning, S.C.

13 SOMERS, George Brooks. Mining geology; Petroleum geology; Seismology (Reflection); Gravity. b'91. Student '12—'14-17 (Ore State Coll); BS '20—Mining Geol '24 (U Ariz); '28 (U Colo); D Sc '30 (Colo Sch Mines); '44 (George Washington U). Mining engr NY Honduras Rosario Mining Co '21-23; prof geol NM Sch Mines '25-28; seismic Party Chief Gen Geophysical Co and Yagua Oil Corp '44-46; prof and chmn dept geol U Houston since '46. Am Geophys Union—Soc of Econ Geophys—Am Assn Petroleum Geol—Sigma Tau. University of Houston, Houston 4.

14 SOMERS, Grover Thomas. Educational psychology (Child development, pupil adjustment, personality problems). b'88. AB '07 (Coll William and Mary); AM '12—PhD '23 (Columbia U). Author: Pedagogical Prognosis '23; Test Attitudes of Students '28; also articles in field. Prof ednl psychol Ind U since '35. Am Council Edn—NEA—Progressive Edn Assn—Internat Council Exceptional Children—Nat Soc Coll Teachers Edn—Phi Beta Kappa—Kappa Phi Kappa—Phi Delta Kappa—Kappa Delta Pi. Indiana University, Bloomington, Ind.

15 SOMERVILLE, Harry Philip. b'89. Music and public performance rights licensing (Copyright). Specializes in copyright music licensing; appeared before Congress in connection with revision of Federal Copyright Law; joined Broadcast Music NYC '44 as dir now vp; hotel relations, first licensing hotels throughout US then licensing all other establishments using live music (except broadcasting stas). Real estate mngt '19-25; mng dir Bretton Hall NYC '25-28, Hotel Sagamore Rochester NY '28-32, Willard Hotel Wash DC '32-42. Am Hotel Assn (past vp and legislative chmn). 157 E. 81st St., NYC.

16 SOMMER, Clemens E(rnst). Medieval sculpture and painting in northern Europe; Renaissance painting in Italy. b'91. Dr Phil (U Freiburg Germany). Author articles in field. Asst librarian, Bibliotheca Hertziana, Rome '20-24; Mus Freiburg '24-28; research travels '28-32; prof hist art U of Greifswald '32-38; prof hist of art U NC since '39. Person Hall, Chapel Hill, N.C.†

17 SOMMER, Hugo Henry. Dairy chemistry and technology (Processes, products, equipment). b'96. BS '18—MS '19—PhD '22 (U Wis). Author: The Theory and Practice of Ice Cream Making; Market Milk and Related Products. Prof dairy ind U Wis since '20. Am Chem Soc—Am Dairy Sci Assn—AAAS—Internat Assn Milk and Food Sanitarians. Borden's award in Dairy Manufactures '42. Department of Dairy Industry, University of Wisconsin, Madison, Wis.†

18 SOMMERMAN, George Miller Louis. Insulation (Electrical); Power cables; Elec measurements; Proximity fuzes. b'09. BE '29—Dr Eng '33—Fellow by Courtesy '33 (Johns Hopkins U). Author articles in field. Asso prof elec engring Northwestern U since '45. Sr Engr Sect T OSRD and US Navy Bur of Ordnance '42-45; research engr Am Steel & Wire Co '34-42. Am Inst Elec Engrs—AAAS—Am Phys Soc—Tau Beta Pi—Sigma Xi. Alfred Noble Engring prize by Founder Engring Socs '37. Battelle Memorial Institute, Columbus 1, O.

19 SONGER, Nan McCawley. Spiders; Web extraction. b'02. Student public schs, pvt sch; study botany and nature under Marie M Meislahn 5 yrs. Established spidery '39, rearing several species spiders in captivity, extracting web for cross-hair material, optical instruments; perfected method of splitting web into fibres of exact specified sizes; developed web which carries illumination; developed insect food for spiders and young spiderlings readily reared indoors. Collector lepidoptera Sinclair '18-20; chem asst Intravenous Products Co Denver '17-18; reared several species crickets 15 yrs contbg specimens, also noted Smithsonian Instn '39-40. RFD 4, Box 924, Yucaipa, Cal.

20 SONNEBORN, Tracy Morton. Genetics; Micro-organisms; Protozoa; Paramecium; Immunogenetics. b'05. AB '25—PhD '28 (Johns Hopkins U). Discoverer of sexes in ciliated protozoa '37; interaction of genes, cytoplasm and environment in determination of hereditary traits '43-48. Author articles in field. Prof zool Ind U since '43; asso editor Jour of Morphology since '48, Genetics since '47, Jour of Exptl Zoology since '47, Physiological Zoology since '48. Am Soc Naturalists (treas '45-47, vp '48)—Genetics Soc Am (vp '48)—Nat Acad Sci—Am Soc Zool —Soc Study Evolution—AAAS—Sigma Xi. Co-winner $1000 prize for outstanding research paper, AAAS '46. Indiana University, Bloomington, Indiana.☺

21 SOOTER, Clarence Andrew. Economic entomology; Wildlife ecology. b'11. BS '33—MS '35 (Okla A&M Coll); PhD '41 (Ia State Coll). Research on insects affecting cotton, life history and management of American coot, general food habits and ecology of waterfowl and their habitats, farm planning and soil conservation, insect control, rodent and predator control, insects affecting legume crops; studies and writing on freezing temperatures of bool weevils and chinch bug, Canada goose habitates in Utah and Oregon, leeches infesting young waterfowl in Northwest Iowa. Author articles in field. Extension entomol and asst prof Neb U '46-48; wildlife research biol (birds) USP HS since '49. Sigma Xi—Phi Kappa Phi—Wildlife Soc—Wilson Club. U.S. Public Health Service, Greeley, Colo.†

22 SOPER, Ellis Clarke. Cement plants (Design and operation); Lime plants (Design and operation). b'81. BS—MS ME (Armour Inst Tech). Design and supervision construction numerous cement, lime, and stone plants; developmental work rotary kilns. Cons engr Franklin NC since '36, investigation and reports various projects in US, Mexico, Cuba, Ecuador, Argentina, Palestine, India, China, pres Soper Engrs, SA, Panama, RP. Am Inst Min Engrs—AS ME—Am Soc CE. Care Four Winds, Franklin, N.C.

23 SORENSEN, Clarence Woodrow. History of geography. b'07. MS '47-'49 (U Chicago). Geographic field studies Western Europe, Near East, India, East Indies, and China '34-36, Mexico and South America annually '40-46. Author: A World View '49. Co-author: Our Big World '46; The American Continents '47; Old World Lands '47; also articles in field. Spl lecturer geog community program service U Minn '39-48; dept geog Ill State Normal U since '48. Assn Am Geog. Department of Geography, Illinois State Normal University, Normal, Ill.†

24 SORENSON, James. Heat treatment of iron and steel (Machinability). b'90. Student '09-12 (Chicago Tech Coll); '15-16 (Marquette U); '25-28 (Pa State Coll); '22-24 (U Wis). Research in heat treatment and machinability of iron and steel, investigations into performance of automotive lubricants, conducted wear tests on various microstructures of iron and steel. Author articles in field. Metall Gemco Mfg Co Milwaukee '14-17; chief metall FWD Auto Co Clintonville, Wis since '18. Holds reserve commn as maj specialist Reserve US Army; engr of tests Ordnance Dept US Army '17-18. Am Soc for Metals—Am Inst Mining and Metall Engrs—Am Ordnance Assn—Wis Soc Profl Engrs—Nat Soc Profl Engrs. Four Wheel Drive Auto Co., Clintonville, Wis.

25 SORG, (Harrison) Theodore. Hospital Service plans. b'88. LLB '12 (N J Law Sch); DCL '39 (Hillsdale Coll). President Hospital Service Plan of New Jersey. 744 Broad St., Newark.

26 SORIA, Martin Sebastian. Spanish and Latin American painting (1550-1850). b'11. BA '33 (U Madrid); JD '35 (U Zuerich); MA in art '42—PhD '49 (Harvard). Completed catalog of Spanish paintings in the Americas; consultant Spanish and Latin American painting to American and European museums; Bacon fellow Harvard '41; Guggenheim fellow '50; Bollingen fellow '51. Author: Zurbaran '51. Author articles on Goya, Vetazquez, Murillo, Zurbaran, Flemish Sources of Spanish Painting, and others. Contributor Colliers Ency.; chpt in Literary Sources of Art History '47. Research studies in Europe, South and

Central Am; tchr Spanish Baroque art Princeton '45; Latin American art, Spanish painting from Greco to Goya, Columbia '51; asst prof Baroque art, Latin Am art Mich State Coll since '48. Michigan State College, East Lansing, Mich. H: 101 W. 80th St., NYC 24.

10 SORRELL, Lewis Carlyle. Transportation economics; Business organization; Business education. b'89. AB '11 (Colgate U); PhD '28 (U Chicago). Author: Government Ownership and Operation of Railroads for the United States; Transportation Production and Marketing. With U Chicago since '18, prof transportation and bus orgn Sch Business since '30; transportation specialist Railway Business Assn '32-42; chief transportation sect Office Civilian Supply WPB '42-43; dir research Air Transport Assn Am since '43. Am Econ Assn—Phi Beta Kappa. Faculty Exchange, U. of Chicago, Chicago 37.⊙

11 SORTON, Fred Charles. Tricot machinery; Warp knitting; Tricot fabrics. b'99. Student 2 yrs (Mass Inst Tech). Analysis tricot fabrics, manufacturing, designing and finishing of tricot knitted fabrics; designer tricot machinery. Holds patents in field. Mgr in charge engring, design and prodn tricot machinery with textile machinery mfr; cons to tricot industry. 177 Lansdowne Rd., Edgewood 5, Warwick, R.I.

12 SOSKE, Joshua Lawrence. Geophysical exploration for petroleum (Magnetic and seismic methods). b'03. Geol E '29 (Col Sch Mines); MS '32—PhD '35 (Cal Institute Tech). Geophysical instrument design; Geophysical interpretational work. Author articles: An Application of the Magnetometer to Mapping of the Covered Trace of the San Andreas Fault in the Salton Sink of California; Origin of the Salton Volcanic Domes Salton Sea Calif, and others. Pres Geophys Engring Corp since '35. Soc Exploration Geo-Petroleum Geol—AAAS—Seismol Soc phys—Am Geophys Union—Am Asso Am—Sigma Xi—Tau Beta Pi. 170 E. Orange Grove Av., Pasadena 3, Calif.

13 SOTTERY, Constantine Theodore. Chemistry. AB '16 (Clark U); AM '23 —PhD '25 (Columbia). Author: The Study of the Accelerating Effect of Glucose on Invertase from Honey '25. Asso prof and prof Bard Coll Columbia U since '35, on leave of absence '46-48; prof chem, chmn dept U Mass '46-48. Am Chem Assn—AAAS—Sigma Xi. Bard College, Annandale-on-Hudson N.Y.

14 SOUDERS, Mott, Jr. Distillation; Phase equilibria; Thermodynamics. b'04. BS '26 (Mont State Coll); MS '27 —PhD '31 (U Mich). Research new processes for the petroleum industry; holder 22 US patents. Chem engr Shell Development Co '37-50 asso dir since '50. ACS—AICE—Sigma Xi— Tau Beta Pi—Phi Kappa Phi. Shell Development Company, 4560 Horton St., Emeryville 8, Cal.

15 SOUERS, Philip Webster. Medieval literature and art; Old and Middle English. b'97. AB '20—MA '22 (U Ia); MA '24—PhD '28 (Harvard). Author: The Matchless Orinda '30; also articles in field. Prof Eng and head dept U Ore since '45. Medieval Acad Am (councilor)—Modern Lang Assn. Shattarck Scholar '24-25; John Thornton Kirland fellow '26; Clarke fellow '35; Sachs research fellow fine arts '37. 1167 E. 22d Av., Eugene, Ore.

16 SOULE, Gardner Bosworth. Picture editing. b'13. Student '29 (U Tex); AB '33 (Rice Inst); BSc '35—MSc '36 (Columbia U). Ed fgn and nat news

Picture Show (feature) '39-40, war news and dir '41; picture ed and ed fgn news and maps PM '42; asst to ed Better Homes & Gardens '46, mng ed since '46. Officer in charge Training Bulletin USN '43-46. Kappa Delta Pi. Meredith Publishing Co., Des Moines 3, Ia.

17 SOULE, Malcolm Herman. Bacterial metabolism; Leprosy; Poliomyelitis; Relapsing fever. b'96. BS '21—MS '22—DSc '24 (U Mich); LLD '28 (St Bonaventures Coll). Author articles in field. Prof bact Sch Med since '31, chmn dept and Hygienic Lab since '35; chmn Med Advisory Bd Leonard Wood Memorial PI since '44; cons to dir div health and sanitation Coordinator of Inter-Am Affairs since '42. AAAS (fellow, sec Med Sect since '37)— Am Acad Tropical Med (council mem since '37)—Am Assn Path and Bact (pres '47)—Am Assn Immunologists— Am Chem Soc—Am Micros Assn—Am Pub Health Assn(F)—Am Soc Exptl Path—Am Soc Tropical Med (vp '41)— Bot Soc Am—Internat Leprosy Assn— Soc Exptl Biol and Med—Soc Am Bact —Alpha Omega Alpha—Phi Kappa Phi —Sigma Xi. Awarded gold medal by AMA '30. 2110 Hill St., Ann Arbor, Mich.⊙

18 SOULE, Thayer. Photography (Outdoor color); Cinematography (Combat). b'17. AB '39 (Har). Production and presentation full-length color motion pictures of parts of the world: plans, directs, photographs, edits all films for Burton Holmes Travelogues; cameraman for combat work with Marines. Spl asst to Burton Holmes '39-41, prodn mgr since '46. Served as photographic Officer from 2d lt to maj USMC '42-46. Received two Presidential citations. Burton Holmes Travelogues, 111 West Washington St., Chgo 2.

19 SOULE, Winsor. Church architecture; School building design. b'83. AB '06 (Harvard); BS '07 (MIT). Draftsman with Cram Goodhue & Ferguson Boston '07-08; asso architect development Bryn Mawr Coll '08-09; draftsman supt with Allen & Collens Boston '09-11; practiced architecture with Russel Ray Santa Barbara Cal '12-17; private practice '17-21; with John Frederic Murphy and T Mitchell Hastings '21-25; with John Frederic Murphy since '25; cons on ch architecture Luth Synod So Cal '38-42, to Presbyn Synod Cal So area since '45; supervising architect Santa Barbara Coll U Cal since '49. AIA(F). 116 East Sola St., Santa Barbara, Cal.⊙

20 SOUTER, Clyde Douglas. US Supreme Court (History and function). b'85. AB '06 (Dartmouth); '06-07 (Columbia Law Sch); LLB '10 (NJ Law Sch). Admitted NJ bar '11, practiced NJ '11-23; judge Second Dist Court Jersey City NJ '18-23; city atty Kearney NJ '15-23; instr law NJ Law Sch '15-17, asst prof '17-19, prof '19-23; admitted Nevada bar '23 and since practiced in Reno; lecturer on law U Nevada '26-40. Am Bar Assn—Washoe County Bar Assn—State Bar Nevada— Reno Chamber Commerce—Delta Theta Phi. 15 W 2d St., Reno.

21 SOUTHWICK, Charles Austin, Jr. Package engineering. b'05. AB '28 (M IT). Research on manufacture of package materials and packages, testing and development, package characteristics of products, machines used for making, filling and handling of packages, Granted patents on package structures, fabrication process, and testing apparatus; chmn Packaging Panel Resch and Development Bd, Department of Defense, since '50. Con-

tributor: Colloid Chemistry (vol VII) '50. With Hazel-Atlas Glass Co '28-30; with Gen Foods Corp '30-43, dir packaging research and development '35-43; with WPB '42-44, deputy chief Container Coordinating Com '42; dir research Shellmar Products Corp '43-47; tech ed Modern Packaging and Packaging Encyclopedia since '43; consultant since '47. ACS—Tech Assn Pulp and Paper Industry. Hope, N.J.

22 SOUTHWORTH, George Clark. Waveguide transmission, Microwave radio; Electronics (Radar, television); Radio astronomy. b'90. BS '14—MS '16 —DSc (hon) '31 (Grove City Coll); PhD '23 (Yale). Research waveguide transmission leading to methods for guiding extremely short electromagnetic waves from one point to another through hollow metal pipes and also to apparatus for transmitting and receiving same; application to radar, television and other forms of broadband signals. Invented fundamental methods used in waveguide transmission; co-discoverer (with A P King) of radio waves coming from sun. Author articles in field. Asso physicist US Bur Standards '17-18; instr, asst prof physics Yale '18-23; radio research engr Am Telephone and Telegraph Co Bell Telephone Lab since '23. AAAS(F)—Am Phys Soc(F)—Am Inst Radio Engrs (F)—Sigma Xi. Awarded M Liebmann prize Inst Radio Engrs '38, Levy medal '46, and Ballantine medal '47 Franklin Inst. 463 West St., NYC 14.

23 SOUTHWORTH, James Granville. Modern poetry; Chaucer; Eighteenth century literature. b'96. AB '18 (U Mich); AB '27—MA '33 (Oxford U); PhD '31 (Harvard). Author: Sowing The Spring: Studies in British Poets from Hopkins to MacNeice '40; The Poetry of Thomas Hardy '47; Some Modern American Poets, '50; More Modern American Poets, '53; Vauxhall Gardens '41; Chaucer's Final-E in Rhyme '47; also articles in field. Prof Eng U Toledo since '34. Mod Lang Assn—Coll Eng Assn. University of Toledo, Toledo 6, Ohio.

24 SOWERBY, Emily Millicent. Bibliography (Thomas Jefferson, early American children's books, American-Jewish). AM '12 (Cambridge U Eng.). Rare book cataloguer Sotheby's London; head bibliog dept Rosenbach Co Phila and NYC: Now bibliog Jefferson collection Library Congress. Bibliog Soc (London)—Am Bibliog Soc. The Library of Congress, Washington 25.

25 SOWERWINE, Elbert Orla, Jr. Petrochemicals; Tyinology; Continuous processing; Synthetic catalysts; Petroleum derivatives desulfurication. b'15. BS in chem '37—ChemE '38 (Cornell). Research in petrochemicals including ethylene, propylene oxide, acetone, alcohols, chlorinated and fluorinated hydrocarbons, photochemical reactions, desulfurization of petroleum derivatives. Granted patents on specialized nozzles to aid continuous processing of synthetic catalysts. Research chem engr Socony-Vacuum Oil Co '38-43; supervisor Merck & Co '43-45; asst plant mgr US Indsl Chem '45-48; project engr Wigton-Abbott Corp since '48. AICE—ACS (div indsl and engring chem). Wigton-Abbott Corp., 45 Academy St., Newark, N.J. H: Wapiti, Wyo.

26 SPAETH, Frank William. Parasites; Acanthocephalans; Crustaceans; Radium (Effects). b'17. AB '40—MS '46—PhD '51 (Cath U Am). Research on normal organogenesis of sex glands of amphipod Hyalella azteca and influence of acanthocephalan parasites and radium emanations on sexual characters of Hyalella. Instr NE Cath High

Sch '40-42; head sci dept Salesianum Sch '50-53. Sigma Xi—Sci Research Soc Am—Wash Biol Soc—Am Soc Parasitol—Helminthological Soc Wash —Am Micros Soc—AAAS. Rector De Chantal Hall since August 1953. De Chantal Hall, Lewiston, N.Y.

10 SPAETH, Sigmund. Musicology. b '85. AB '05—AM '06 (Haverford Coll); PhD '10 (Princeton). Author: The Common Sense of Music '24; Barber Shop Ballads '25; Read 'em and Weep: The Songs You Forgot to Remember '26; The Art of Enjoying Music '33; Music for Everybody '34; Great Symphonies '36; Stories behind the World's Great Music '37; Maxims to Music '38; Fun with Music '41; A Guide to Great Orchestral Music '43; 55 Art Songs '44; At Home with Music '45; A History of Popular Music in America '48; Opportunities in Music '50. Composer lyrics for numerous popular songs. Ed G Schirmer Music pub '13; music ed NY Evening Mail '14-18; staff writer NY Times '18-20; ednl dir Am Piano Co '20-27; mng dir Community Concert Service '28-31; free-lance writer, broadcaster, lectr since '32. Phi Beta Kappa—Phi Mu Alpha—Nat Assn Am Composers and Conductors—Am Soc Composers Authors Pubs—Am Fedn Radio Artists. Received Henry Hadley Medal for distinguished service to Am Music '39. E. 58th St., N.Y.C. 22.☺

11 SPALDING, Henry A. Mineral resource valuation and taxation; Blast furnace theory. b'99. Ed pub schs. Light suspension bridges, aerial tramways; optical fluorite, rock crystal electrical transmission and distribution line loation and design; research on mining economics, taxation of natural resources, valuation of natural resources, consultant Kentucky Department of Revenue, US Army Corps of Engineers, US Department of Justice. Co-author; (With W A Thomas) The Engineers Vest Pocket Book '51 (2nd edit). AIMME—Ky Soc Prof Engrs (past pres, dir)—Am Pub Works Assn —Appalachian Geol Soc. Baker Bldg, Hazard, Ky.

12 SPANGENBERG, Karl R(udolph). Vacuum tubes. b'10. BS '32—MS '33 (Case Inst Tech); PhD '37 (Ohio State U). Author: Vacuum Tubes '48. Prof elec engring Stanford U since '37. Expert cons and operations analyst chief signal officer European Theater of Operations '44; dir microwave oscillator research Radio Research Lab '45; head electronics br Physical Sci Div Office Naval Research '49. American Phys Soc—Inst Radio Engrs(F)—Am Soc Engring Edn—Sigma Xi. Electrical Engineering Department, Stanford University, Calif.†

13 SPARGO, John. American ceramics; Vermont history; Socialism. b'76. Ed pub schs Oxford and Cambridge U extension courses. With Samuel Gompers founded American Alliance for Labor and Democracy '17 and active in founding the National Party. Author: Socialism, a Study and Interpretation of Socialist Principles '09; The Socialists, Who They Are and What They Stand For '16; Capitalist and Laborer '07; The Spiritual Significance of Modern Socialism '08; Karl Marx, His Life and Work '09; The Bennington Battle Monument and Its Story '25; History of the Potters and Pottery of Bennington '26; The Stars and Stripes in Vermont in 1777 '27; Early Am Pottery and China '27; The A.B.C. of Bennington Pottery Wares '38; Book of the Battle Monument and the Event It Commemorates '47, also articles in field. Dir curator Bennington Hist Mus and Art Gallery. Vt Hist Soc (pres '26-38)—Bennington Battle Monument and Hist Assn (pres). Historical Museum and Art Gallery, Bennington, Vt.

14 SPARHAWK, William Norwood. Forest resources and policy (Domestic, foreign); Economics of forestry. b'88. BA '08 (Yale Coll); MF '10 (Yale Sch Forestry). Study trip to Germany and neighboring areas in central Europe '35; delegate to World Forestry Congress held in Rome '26. Author: Forest Resources of the World (with R. Zon), 2 vols, '23. America and the World's Woodpile '28; Why Grow Timber '28; Economic Aspects of Forest Destruction in Northern Michigan '29; Forest Rights in Foreign Countries '37; Forests and Employment in Germany '38; Notes on Forests and Trees of the Central and Southwest Pacific Area '45; Japan: Forest Resources, Forest Products, Forest Policy '45; also articles in field. Forester and forest econ Forest Service US Dept Agr '10-48. Soc Am Foresters(F)—AAAS(F)—Wash Acad Sci—Soc Forestry of Suomi (Finland)—Phi Beta Kappa. West Swanzey, N.H.

15 SPARKS, Morgan. Electro-chemistry (Semi-conductors, infra-red spectroscopy, batteries, rectifiers). b'16. Fellow '38-40—BA '38—MA '40 (Rice Inst); PhD '43—Rockefeller fellow '40-43 (U Ill). Author articles in field. Research chem Bell Labs since '43. Am Chem Soc—Electrochem Soc—Phi Beta Kappa—Sigma Xi. Bell Telephone Laboratories, Murray Hill, N.J.

16 SPAULDING, Albert C. Anthropology, archeology (North American). b'14. BA '25 (Mont State U); AM '37 (U Mich); PhD '46 (Columbia). Author: Northeastern Archeology and General Trends in the Northern Forest Zone '46; The Middle Woodland Period in Kansas, in press; also articles in field. Asst prof U Mich since '47 now also curator. Principal engring aide asst topographic engr asst civil engr War Mapping program US Forest Service '42-46. Am Anthropol Assn—Soc Am Archeol—Sigma Xi. Museum of Anthropology, University of Michigan, Ann Arbor, Mich.†

17 SPAULDING, Perley. Control of diseases of white pine and hardwood trees; Foreign tree diseases threatening US forests. b'78. BS '00 (U Vt); MS '03—PhD '06 (Washington U St Louis). Developed method of control for white pine blister in North Am; discovered method for control European larch canker in US; research on forest management practices effective in control living tree decay, hardwood tree trunk cankers; compilation data on foreign tree diseases. Author article: The Role of Nectria in the Beech Bark Disease '48, and others. Co-author articles: (with W A Campbell) Stand Improvement of Northern Hardwoods in Relation to Disease in the Northeast '42; (with J R Hansbrough) Decay in Balsam Fir in New England and New York '44; (with J R Hansbrough) Decay of Logging Slash in the Northeast '44, and others. With div forest path USDA '02-48, prin path in charge field office New Haven '40-48. Soc Am Foresters—Am Phytopath Soc—Sigma Xi. USDA superior service award for unusually productive research on forest diseases and its application to forest management practices. 360 Prospect St., New Haven 11.

18 SPECHT, Alston Wesley. Simultaneous spectrochemical analysis of plant materials. b'07. BS '31 (W Va U); MS '41—PhD '48 (U Md). Development of methods for quantitative spectrochemical analyses of plant materials for wide range of elements determined simultaneously; statistical evaluation results of spectrochemical analyses to show element interrelations in plants, influence of nutrient supply on plant composition, and relation of inorganic composition of plants to plant growth and quality; coordination of results of spectrochemical analyses with chemical analyses of plant materials. Co-author articles: A Catenary Arrangement of the Soils of Maryland '42; The Influence of Rootstock on the Mineral Composition of Valencia Orange Leaves '49; Growth and Nutrient Accumulation as Controlled by Oxygen Supply to Plant Roots '50. Analytical chem spectrochem lab Nat Bur Standards Washington '44-46; in charge of spectrochem lab BPISAE Beltsville Md since '47. ACS—AAAS—Am Soc Agron —Sigma Xi—Am Soc Plant Physiologists. Bureau o Plant Industry, U.S. Department of Agriculture, Beltsville, Md. H: R.F.D. 1, Brookeville.

19 SPECHT, Heinz. High altitude (Physiological effects, Oxygen equipment for); Respiration (Factors affecting rate and depth); Ketone (Vapor toxicity). b'07. BS '30 (Princeton); PhD '33 (Johns Hopkins). Conbributor: Industrial Hygiene '47. Adam T Bruce F, Johns Hopkins, '33-34; asst physiol NY U Coll Med '34-36; physiol Nat Inst Health USPHS '36-45; command officer USPHS since '45. Am Physiol Soc—Wash Acad Sci—Philos Soc Wash—Soc Exptl Biol and Med.

20 SPECK, Frank Gouldsmith. North American ethnology and linguistics (Algonkianism, iroquoianism, ceremonialism). b'81. AB '04—AM '05 (Columbia U); fellow '08 (U Pa). Extensive field work among Indian tribes of Indian Territory, Oklahoma, Southeastern and Northeastern United States, Canada, Newfoundland and Labrador peninsula. Author: Ethnology of Yuchi Indians '09; Penobscot Shamanism '20; The Iroquois '46; Eastern Algonkian Block-Stamp Decoration '47, and others. Prof anthrop U Pa since '25; anthrop Nat Research Council (exec com '25). Am Anthrop Assn (vp '45)—Am Ethnol Soc—Am Folklore Soc (pres '20-22)—AAAS—Anthrop Soc of Phila (pres '20-22)—Sigma Xi (pres '42). Swarthmore, Pa.☺

21 SPEER, George Scott. Vocational and personnel guidance; Child development. b'08. Student '27-28 (U Wis); BA '34 (Central YMCA Coll); SM '36 (U Chicago). Consulting psychologist physicians, business and industrial organizations since '38; educational adviser Morgan Park Mil Acad since '45; research and clinical psychology; educational and vocational guidance since 1935; vice chairman educational advisory committee Chicago Community Trust Fund '43-44, chmn '44-46. Author articles: The Use of the Bernreuter Personality Inventory as an Aid in the Prediction of Behavior Problems '36; The Measurement of Emotions Aroused in Response to Personality Test Items '37; Social Value of Agricultural Training for Delinquent Boys '38; Negative Reactions to College Counseling '45, and others. Psychol Berkshire Indsl Farm Canaan NY '36-37; psychol Sangamon Co Child Guidance Clinic Springfield Ill '37-40, Children's Service League Springfield '37-40; instr psychol Central YMCA Coll Chicago '40-41, asst prof '41-45, counselor '41-43; dean students '43-45, dir inst for counseling '43-45; dir inst for psychol services Ill Inst Tech Chicago since '45; Am Psychol Assn—Am Soc Engring Edn—Nat Soc Research Child Development—Nat Vocational Guidance Assn (vp '47-48)—Indsl Relations Assn—Midwestern Psychol Assn—Ill Assn Profl Psychol (chmn bd trustees '47-48)—Am Assn on Mental Deficiency—

Nat Assn of Remedial Teachers—Social Work Assn (pres '38-40). 18 S. Michigan Av., Chicago 3.

10 SPEISER, E p h r a i m Avigdor. Oriental history, archeology, linguistics. b'02. MA '23 (U Pa); PhD '24 (Dropsie Coll, Phila); DHL '49 (Hebrew Union College). Annual professor American School Oriental Research, Baghdad Iraq '26-27 (discovered ancient site of Tepe Cawra and directed preliminary excavations). Author: Mesopotamian Origins '30; Introduction to Hurrian '41; The United States and the Near East '47. Co-author: (with R H Pfeiffer) One Hundred New Selected Nuzi Texts '37; also articles in field. Asst prof Semitics U Pa '28-31, prof since '31; field dir joint excavations Am Sch Oriental Research and Mus of U Pa in Mesopotamia '30-32, '36-37; non-resident dir Am Sch Oriental Research in Baghdad '32-46. Wartime chief Near East Sect Research and Analysis Branch OSS (Certificate of Merit '45). Am Oriental Soc (dir '32-36; exec com '43-46, vp '44, pres '45)—Am Schs Oriental Research (exec com '32-35; joint ed '33-43)—Archeol Inst Am (pres Phila Soc '41)—Linquistic Soc Am (vp '42)—Phi Beta Kappa. University of Pennsylvania, Phila 4.⊙

11 SPELL, Jefferson Rea. Mexican literature (Literary bibliography); Spanish-American novelists. b'86. AB '13—AM '20 (U Tex); PhD '31 (U Pa). Author: The Life and Works of José Joaquin Fernández de Lizardi '31; Rousseau in the Spanish World before 1833 '38; Contemporary Spanish-American Novelists '44; Tres Comedias de Eusebio Vela '48. Prof Romance Langs U Tex since '20; vis prof U Mexico summers '44-46. MLA—Instituto Internacional de Literatura Iberoamericana—Inst Latin Am Studies (exec com). Diploma de honor from the Academia Mexicana for studies in Mexican literature. Box 1698, University of Texas, Austin 12, Tex.

12 SPENCER, Benjamin Townley. Nationality in American literature; Elizabethan drama (Philip Massinger, Shakespeare). b'04. AB '25 (Kentucky Wesleyan Coll); '25-26 (Johns Hopkins U); MA '28—PhD '30 (Univ Cincinnati); LittD '49 (Kentucky Wesleyan). Co-author: Seventeenth Century Studies '33. Editor: The Bondman '32; also articles in field. With Ohio Wesleyan U since '30, prof English since '37, dir of library '38-40. Modern Lang Assn Am—Phi Beta Kappa. 110 University Av., Delaware, O.

13 SPENCER, Donald Clayton. Mathematics (Engineering). b'12. BA '34 (U Colo); BS '36 (MIT); PhD '39 (U Cambridge Eng). Instr mathematics Mass Inst Tech '39-42; asso prof Stanford U '42-46, prof mathematics '46-50; asso prof mathematics Princeton U since '50; mem Applied Math Group NYU '44-45; mem Nat Research Council '51-53. Cambridge Philosophical Society (England)—American Math Soc —London Math Soc—NY Acad Sci— Phi Beta Kappa. Joint recipient with A C Schaeffer Bocher prize awarded by Am Math Soc '48.⊙

14 SPENCER, John LeBaron. Plant cytogenetics; Algae. b'22. Student '46 (Amherst Coll); BS '47 (Mass State Coll); MS '49 (U Mass); '49 (Harvard); PhD '51 (U Tex). Research on algal ecology of Northeast US with emphasis upon distribution of planktonic forms in public water supplies, research on anther smut disease of carnations, research on morphogenetic aberrations in plants caused by ultrahigh frequency electromagnetic and ultrasonic waves. Faculty U Mass since

'47; cons plant diseases Flower Growers Assn '49. Bot Soc Am—Ecol Soc Am —Am Phytopathological Soc—Sigma Xi. Received Hills Award '46. Department of Botany, University of Massachusetts, Amherst.

15 SPENCER, Roy C. Microwave optics; X-rays; Optics; Applied mathematics. b'01. AB '22—fellow '26 (Cornell U); fellow '23-24 (Swarthmore Coll); PhD '31 (Columbia U). Research in X-ray spectroscopy, radar antenna and diffraction problems. Author articles in field. With U Neb '31-41, MIT Radiation Lab '41-46; chief antenna lab Air Force Cambridge Research Lab AMC since '46; an Air Force representative on Antennas and Prop Panel of Research and Development Bd. Am Phys Soc—Optical Soc Am—Inst Radio Engrs—Sigma Xi—AAAS(F). Air Force Cambridge Research Laboratories, 230 Albany St., Cambridge 39, Mass. H: 247 Park Av., Arlington 74, Mass.

16 SPENCER, Warren. Animal genetics. b'98. AB '19 (Coll of Wooster); MS '24—PhD '29 (Ohio State U). Instr biology Coll of Wooster '21-26, asst prof '26-29, prof since '29; govt research U Rochester '43-45. AAAS(F)— Ohio Acad Sci—Am Soc Zoologists— Am Naturalists—Gen Soc Am—Eugenics Research Assn—Gamma Alpha— Sigma Xi—Phi Beta Kappa. College of Wooster, Wooster, O.⊙†

17 SPENCER, Willard Wylie. Philosophy (Ethics, history, value theory, medieval). b'98. BA '22—PhD '25— Sterling fellow '32-33 (Yale); '24-25 (Cambridge U England). Research in medieval philosophy in England, France and Belgium. Author: Our Knowledge of Other Minds '30; also articles in field. Prof philos and head dept Miami U since '30. Am Philos Assn—Phi Beta Kappa. Grant-in-aid Belgian Relief '33. Miami University, Oxford, O.†

18 SPENCER, William Gear. Classical languages. b'86. AB '07 (Denison U); AM '08; '12-13 (Colgate Theol Sem); LLD '24 (Franklin Coll); LLD '27 (Denison U). Prof classical langs Franklin Coll '20-22, also registrar; pres Hillsdale Coll '22-32; pres Franklin Coll '33-48, pres emer since '48. Mich Acad Sci Arts and Letters—Nat Edn Assn—Classical Assn Middle West and South—Mod Lang Assn Am—Am Acad Polit and Soc Sci—Am Philol Assn—Indiana Hist Soc—Pi Gamma Mu—Phi Beta Kappa. Box 272, Granville, O.⊙

19 SPENGLER, Kenneth Clifford. Meteorology (Weather forecasting and verification). b'15. AB '36 (Dickinson Coll); '37-40 (U Pa); '40-41 (MIT). Aided in the development and improvement of adequate extended weather forecasting methods and techniques, helped set up organization for producing the first world-wide Northern Hemisphere weather analysis, aided in organization of a climatological section and participated significantly in development of extensive program for verifying weather forecasts and individual forecaster's proficiency in Air Weather Service. Exec sec Am Meteorol Soc since '46. Exec Army Weather Central Hdqrs AAF '42, chief climatol and statistics sect '42-43, chief verification sect Weather Div '43-44, chief forecast br '44-45, deput chief evaluation and development div '45. Am Meteorol Soc—AAAS (F, rep on council '49-50)—Royal Meteorol Soc (London)—Inst Aero Sci—Am Geophys Union—Am Inst Phys. Received Army Commendation Ribbon '46. 3 Joy St., Boston 8. H: 189 Jason St., Arlington 74, Mass.†⊙

20 SPENGLER, Walter J(acob). Ignition. b'98. Ed pub and tech schs Switzerland. Research on design and development of ignition for aircraft, automotive, marine and industrial engines. Exec engr Scintilla Magneto Div Bendix Aviation Corp since '23. Soc Automotive Engrs—Inst Aeronautical Sci. Scintilla Magneto Division, Bendix Aviation Corp., Disney, N.Y.

21 SPERBERG, Lawrence R. Rubber technology; Carbon black. b'14. BS '34 (Hillsdale Coll); MS '35; Goodyear fellow '35-36 (U Akron). Patents on curing butadiene-styrene rubber and method of preparing selenyl-aryl thiazoles. Author articles in field. Mgr rubber evaluation lab reeach dept Phillips Petroleum Co Bartlesville Okla and Phillips Tex '40-50; chief chemist J M Huber Corp '50; now Sid Richardson Carbon Black. Am Chem. Soc. Box 2468, Odessa, Tex.

22 SPERRY, John Lovell. Geometrid moths. b'94. BSc '14 (Brown U). Author articles in field. Pres and treas The Minden Inc since '25. So Calif Acad Sci—Calif Acad Sci—Phila Acad Sci—Washington Entomol Soc. The Minden, 123 Waterman St., Providence. Winter Address: 3260 Redwood Drive, Riverside, Calif.

23 SPERRY, Theodore M(elrose). Prairie ecology. b'07. BS '29 (Butler U); MS '31—PhD '33—fellow '32-33 (U Ill); '46 (U Wis). Author articles in field. Asso prof biol Kan State Teachers Coll since '46; ecol US Forest Service Nat Park Service '33-41; instr weather observing and forecasting AAF weather sch '42-43, station and staff weather officer AAF stations in Eng '44-45. AAAS(F)—Ecol Soc Am— Am Soc Plant Taxonomists—Am Mus Nat Hist—Nat Geog Soc—Wilderness Soc—Inland Birdbanding Assn—Am Nature Assn—Kansas Ornithol Soc— Nat Edn Assn—Kan Acad Sci—Sigma Xi. Kansas State Teachers College, Pittsburg, Kan.†

24 SPICER, Edward H(olland). Yaqui Indians (Mexico, Arizona); Japanese-Americans (World War II internment). b'06. Student '27-28 (Johns Hopkins); AB '32—AM '33 (U Ariz); PhD '39 (U Chicago). Research on Ariz Yaqui acculturation with research council funds; Yaqui Indian villages, Yaqui militarism, native lang; intensive study of Japanese Am in relocation centers. Author: Pascua, A Yaqui Village in Arizona '40; Potam, A Yaqui Village in Sonora, '53; also articles in field. Research asso Mus N Ariz '34; field dir Univ of Chicago '39; adviser Cornell Univ SW Field Labs '48-49; asso prof anthrop Univ Ariz '46-49, prof since '49. Am Anthrop Assn(F)—Soc Applied Anthrop—Sigma Xi. University of Arizona, Tucson, Ariz.

25 SPIEGELBERG, Carl H(enry). Pineapple fruit diseases; Spoilage of canned pineapple. b'98. BS '24—MS '25 (Wash State Coll); PhD '40 (U Wis); '26-27 (U Md). Author articles in field. With Pineapple Research Inst since '30, now plant path. Hawaiian Bot Soc—Hawaiian Acad Sci—AAAS (F)—Am Phytopath Soc—Sigma Xi. P.O. Box 3166, Honolulu 2, T.H.†

26 SPIER, Leslie. Ethnology of western North America. b'93. BS '15 (Coll City NY); PhD '20 (Columbia). Author: Klamath Ethnography '30; Yuman Tribes of Gila River '33; Comparative Vocabularies of Two Yuman Tribes '46. Editor American Anthropologist '34-39; Southwestern Journal Anthropology since '45. Asst prof anthrop Washington U '20-27; prof anthrop U Okla '27-29; prof anthrop U Washington and dir state mus Wash '29; asso prof Yale '33-39; prof anthrop

U NM since '39. Nat Acad Sci—Am Philos Soc—Am Anthrop Assn—AAAS (vp '42, '46). Townsend Harris medal Coll City NY '46. P.O. Box 880, Santa Curz, Cal.⊙

10 SPIETH, Herman Theodore. Ephemeroptera; Drosophila. b'05. BA '26 (Ind Central Coll); PhD '31 (Ind U). Made entomological field trips to southeastern US, Canada, Rocky Mountains, Mexico; research on biology, taxonomy and phylogeny of ephemeroptera, sexual behavior of drosophila and interspecific mating behavior. Author articles in field. Asso prof Coll City NY since '49; lecturer Columbia since '38, research asso Am Mus Natural Hist since '44. NY Acad Sci(F)—Sigma Xi—Am Soc Zool—Am Soc Naturalists—AAAS—Am Soc Limnol and Oceanog—NY Entomol Soc (past pres)—Soc Study Evolution. Waterman Research Fellow, Ind U '30-31. Division of Life Sciences University of California, Riverside, Cal.

11 SPILHAUS, Athelstan Frederick. Meteorology; Oceanography. b'11. BSc '31—DSc '48 (U Cape Town); MS '33 (MIT). Inventor bathythermograph '38. Author: Workbook of Meteorology; also articles in field. Asst dir tech services Union S Africa Defense Forces '35-36; research asst Woods Hole Oceanog Inst '36-37, investigator phys oceanog '38, phys oceanographer since '40; asst prof meteorol NYU '37, asso prof '37-42, prof '42-48, dir research '46-48; dean and prof Inst Tech U Minn since '49. Royal Meteorol Soc(F)—Am Meteorol Soc—Am Geophys Union—Royal Soc S Africa—Tau Beta Pi—Sigma Xi. 107 Main Engineering Building, University of Minn., Mpls. 14.

12 SPINGARN, Clifford Leroy. Chemotherapy. b'12. AB '33 (Columbia Coll); MD '37 (Columbia U Coll Physicians & Surgeons); '43 (US Naval Medical Sch). Associate editor (with A T Hyman and W B Saunders): An Integrated Practice of Medicine '47. Adjunct physician Mt Sinai Hosp since '47. Am Soc Parasitol—Am Soc Trop Med —Am Fed Clin Research—NY Acad Scis—NY Acad Medicine(F)—Am Coll Physicians—AAAS—Sigma Xi—Alpha Omega Alpha—Phi Beta Kappa. 51 East 73d St., NYC 21.

13 SPINGARN, Stephen Joel. Legislative procedure. b'08. Student '25-27 (Yale U); '27-28 (U Grenoble France); '29 (Rollins Coll Winter Park Fla); AB '30—LLB '34 (U Arizona); '32 (Stanford U). Admitted to Ariz bar '33, Washington bar '47; atty US Treas Dept '34-41, spl asst to general counsel '41-42, asst gen counsel '46-49; spl asst to atty gen of US '37-38; dep dir Office of Contract Settlement '47-49; asst to spl counsel to the President '49-50, adminstrn asst to President '50; mem Codification Bd which codified all fed regulations '37-38; treasury mem Interdeptl Com on War Legislation '41-42; alternate mem President's Temp Commn on Employee's Loyalty '46-47; mem Federal Trade Commission since '50. Am Bar Assn—Fed Bar Assn—Ariz State Bar.⊙

14 SPINK, J. G. Taylor. Sports. b'88. Ed pub schs St Louis. Author: Judge Landis and 25 Years of Baseball. President The Sporting News and The Sporting Goods Dealer; pub Baseball Guide, Baseball Register, Football Record and Rule Book, The Sporting Goods Dealer's Trade Directory, Knotty Problems. The Sporting News, 2012-18 Washington Av., StL.

15 SPINK, Leland Kenneth. Fluid flow engineering; Flow measurement, valves, controllers. b'99. Student '18-20, '21-22 (U Kan); '20 (U Cal). Research and development theory of control valves and analysis theory of automatic control, invented airweight controller, square root planimeter, intermediate pressure connection for gas measurement, designed valve slide rule and flow rule for orifices, flow nozzles and Venturi tubes. Author: Principles and Practice of Flow-Meter Engineering (7th edit) '49; Handbook of Steam-Flow Measurement (3rd edit) '46. Engr Foxboro Co since '24. Nat Dist Steam Heating Assn (past pres NE sect)—ASME (mem spl research com fluid meters, subcom small flows, piping, pulsation research, flow computations, chmn subcom fgn codes and power test codes, etc)—Am Standards Assn (mem subcom instrument piping). Foxboro Co., Foxboro, Mass.†

16 SPITZE, LeRoy A. Colloid and surface chemistry of glass. b'17. AB '39 (Southwestern Coll); MS '41—PhD '43 (Rensselaer Polytech Inst). Research on water sorption by vermiculites and silicas, surface properties of glass and glass fibers, colloid and surface chemistry. Author articles in field. Prof chem Southwestern Coll Winfield Kan since '47. Am Chem Soc —Kan Acad Sci—Sigma Xi. Chemistry Department, Southwestern College, Winfield, Kan.

17 SPITZER, Lyman, Jr. Astrophysics (Interstellar matter, cosmogony, stellar atmospheres, Earth's upper atmosphere, pressure broadening.) b'14. BA '35 (Yale); Henry fellow '35-36 (Cambridge); PhD '38—MA '37 (Princeton U); National Research Fellow '38-39 (Harvard). Editor: Physics of Sound in the Sea '46; also articles in field. Prof chmn dept astron and dir Obs Princeton U since '47. Sci Spl Studies Group div War Research Columbia '42-44, dir Sonar Analysis Group '44-46. Am Astron Soc—Astron Soc Pacific—Royal Astron Soc—Am Phys Soc(F)—Am Geophys Union—Nat Acad Scis—British Interplanetary Soc. Princeton University Observatory, Princeton, N.J.⊙

18 SPITZLI, Donald Hawkes. Linoleum; Asphalt tiles; Fish net and twines. b'06. BS '27—MS '28 (MIT). Research and development smooth surface floor coverings, linoleum, printed felt base, plastic, asphalt tile and components, such as drying oils, resins, and paper felts; research and development in thread and twine, fish nets, particularly synthetics. Research dept Congoleum-Nairn Inc '28-42, chief chem research '42-50; dir research Linen Thread Co since '50. ACS—Am Oil Chem Soc—AIChE. The Linen Thread Co., Inc., Paterson, N.J. H: 24 Oak Ridge Av., Summit, N.J.

19 SPIVEY, Robert Charles. Fusulinids (Micropaleontology). b'09. BA '31 (Tex Tech Coll); MS—PhD '38 (State U Ia). Research on evolution and occurrence of the Fusulinidae and practical application of this information in solving Pennsylvanian and Permian stratigraphic problems. Co-author: (with T G Roberts) Lower Pennsylvanian Terminology in Central Texas '46. Area stratigrapher Shell Oil Co Inc Midland Tex '40-52, sr geol problems of Paleozoic stratigraphy Western US since '53. Paleontol Soc—Am Assn Pet Geol—Geol Soc Am. Shell Oil Company, Inc., 1008 W. 6th St., Los Angeles.

20 SPLAWN, Jennie Lillian. English literature. b'85. Graduate '08 (Decatur Bapt Coll); PhB '10 (Baylor U); PhB '15 (U Chicago); MA '25 (Columbia U); With dept English Tex Coll Arts and Industries Kingsville since '25, prof English since '31. Tex State Tchrs Assn—Nat Council Tchrs English—AAUP—AAUW—South Central Mod Lang Assn—Nat Edn Assn. Texas College Arts and Industries, Kingsville.†⊙

21 SPOEHR, Alexander. Ethnology (Oceanic, American Indian); Social organization; Culture change. b'13. AB '34—PhD '40 (U Chicago). Research American Indian social organization; ethnology of Micronesia; diffusion as a factor in culture change. Author articles in field. Archeol field work Southern Ill '36, Colo '37-38; ethnol field work Indians SE US '38-39, Marshall Islanders, Micronesia '47; asst curator Am Archeol and Ethnol Chicago Natural Hist Mus '40-44, curator North Am Archeol and Ethnol '44-46, curator Oceanic Ethnol since '46; research asso U Chicago since '46. Anthrop Assn—Soc Am Archeol—Soc Applied Anthrop. Chicago Natural History Museum, Chgo.†⊙

22 SPOFFORD, Walter Richardson. Embryology; Neuroanatomy; Falconry (Gyrfalcons). b'08. BS '31 (Tufts Coll); PhD '38 (Yale). Research on embryology of neural plate, falconry, biology of falcons. Author articles: Observations on Posterior Part of the Neural Plate in Salamander, Prospective Significance of Posterior Neural Plate Mesoderm '45; Neuroanatomy '42; Falconry and Conservation '45, and others. Instr '38-40 Vanderbilt U Med Sch '40-42, asst prof '42-48, asso prof '48 now with State U of NY Med Center Syracuse U. Am Assn Anat—Sigma Xi. Department of Anatomy, State U of NY Medical Center, Syracuse Univ., Syracuse, N.Y.

23 SPOONER, Laurence Whipple. Viscosity (Measurement); Molecular association; Polymerization; Rescons. b'08. BS '30—PhD '34 (U Mass); MS '31 (Lafayette Coll); '31-32 (Harvard). Semi-conducting materials and Rescons; research on fluidity method for determination of association, polymerization, focal isolation in the ultraviolet and other technical subjects. Holds two patents on Rescons. Author articles in field. Phys chemist Pittsfield Works Lab Gen Elec Co since '35. Am Inst Phys—Soc Rheol—ACS. 100 Woodlawn Av., Pittsfield, Mass.

24 SPORN, Philip. Electric power; High voltage transmission; Heat pumps. b'96. EE '17 (Columbia U); ED (hon) '47 (Stevens Inst of Tech). Inventor with C A Muller of one-cycle high-speed relay system used on high voltage transmission lines; developer of ultra high speed reclosing of high voltage transmission lines, improvements in hydrogen cooled synchronous condensers, generation of electric energy by steam operating at high pressure and high temperatures, improvements in lightning protection of high voltage transformers, improvements in heat pumps. Co-author: (with Ambrose and Baumeister) Heat Pumps '47; also articles in field. Pres Am Gas & Electric Co, Service Corp since '47; chmn adv com on coop elec power industry and atomic energy commn '50. AIEE (F, nat first prize in Engring Practice '28, Edison Medal '45)—ASME(F)—AA AS(F)—ASCE—Franklin Inst — Sigma Xi—Tau Beta Pi. Awarded Egleston Medal, Columbia Engring Alumni Assn for distinguished engring achievement '46; Columbia U Medal for excellence '48. 30 Church St., NYC 8.⊙

25 SPRAGGINS, Newton Filmore. Engineering mechanics. b'23. BS in mech engring '43—MS in mech engring '47 (A & M Coll Tex); '47-48 (Stanford U). Instr mech engring A & M Coll Tex '46-47; instr civil engring Stanford U '47-48; instr mechanics US Naval Postgraduate Sch '48-49; asst prof marine engring US Naval Acad '49-51; research engr E I duPont de Nemours & Co since '51. ASME. Mech. Development Lab, E I duPont de Nemours & Co, Wilmington, Del. H: 1431 Prospect Dr., Kynlyn Apts., Wilmington.

10 SPRAGUE, George F(rederick). Corn (Breeding, genetics, field plot design). b'02. BSc '24—MS '26 (U Neb); PhD '31 (Cornell U). Author articles in field. Prin agronom and research prof Ia Agr Exp Sta since '48. AAAS (F)—Am Soc Agron(F)—Am Society Plant Physiol—Genetics Soc. Farm Crops Department, Iowa State College, Ames, Ia.

11 SPRAGUE, Roderick. Plant pathology (Leaf and root diseases of cereals, leaf diseases of grasses; fungus diseases of tree fruits). b'01. BS '24 —MSc '25 (Washington State College); PhD '29 (University Cincinnati). Developed control of strawbreaker disease of cereals in Pacific Northwest; modernized seed treatment practices for control of stinking smut of wheat in Oregon '34-40; developed field control of cereal rootrots in Northern Great Plains '40-46. Author articles in field. Asso prof and asso path Wash State Coll since '47. Am Phytopath Soc— Am Society Agron—Bot Soc Am—Am Mycol Soc—Sigma Xi—Phi Kappa Phi. Tree Fruit Expt Sta., Wenatchee, Wash.

12 SPRAGUE, Vance Glover. Pasture management in the northeastern states; Environment and growth of forage plants. b'09. BA '31 (Northland Coll); MS '33—PhD '36 (U Wis). Delegate to Fourth International Grassland Congress Abersystwyth Wales '37; designed and constructed chambers for growing plants under controlled environments including light, air temperature and relative humidity and soil temperature; work on grassland improvement and management, physiology of forage plants including temperature and light effects, food reserves and defoliation studies. Author articles in field. Agron US Regional Pasture Research Lab State Coll Pa since '37. Am Soc Agron—Am Soc Plant Physiol —AAAS(F)—Sigma Xi. United States Regional Pasture Research Laboratory, State College, Pa.†

13 SPRAGUE, Victor. Parasites of gulf coast oysters, shrimp and crab (Gregarinida, Microsporidia, Haplosporidia). b'08. BEd '32 (So Ill Normal U); MS '38—PhD '40 (U Ill). Discovered a new species of Nematopsis in oysters and two hitherto unknown primary hosts both decapods of Nematopsis. Author articles in field. Instr parasitol and protozool Loyola U since '48. Am Soc Zool—Am Soc Protozool —Am Soc Parasitol—Am Micros Soc— AAAS—Am Soc Profl Biol—Am Assn Sci Workers—Sigma Xi. Department of Biological Sciences, Loyola University, Chicago 26.

14 SPRARAGEN, William. Welding b '95. BE '16 (Union Coll). Specialized special problems relating to weldability, transition temperatures, plasticity, and residual stresses. Author: Handbook of Engineering Mathematics, also articles in field. Editor: Welding Handbook (1st edit) '38, '42. Contbr: Encyclopedia Britannica, Mechanical Engineers Handbook. Exec sec Am Bur Welding and Engring Div NRC '20-35; ed The Welding Journ since '22; dir Welding Research Council since '35. Am Welding Soc—Am Soc ME— Am Soc Metals—Soc Exptl Stress Analysis. Miller medal for outstanding achievement in welding engring and research '40. 29 W. 39th St., NYC 18.

15 SPRAUL, Joseph Robert. Dehydration; Surface chemistry; Phosphors; Organic coatings. b'16. BS '38 —AM '39—PhD '41 (Ind U). Author articles in field. Asst to dir research and testing lab Gen Am Trans Corp since '47. Am Chem Soc—Sigma Xi. General American Transportation Corporation, Research and Testing Laboratory, 300 W. 151 St., East Chicago, Ind. H: 402 Wesley Av., Oak Park, Ill.

16 SPRENGNETHER, William F(rancis), Jr. Physics (Instrument design); Seismology. b'09. BS '44—MS '46 (St Louis U). Author articles: A Seismograph for Microseisms '38; A Description of the Instruments Used to Record Microseisms for the Purpose of Detecting and Tracking Hurricanes '47. Partner W F Sprengnether Instrument Co since '36. Am Phys Soc— Am Geophys Union—Seismol Soc Am —Instrument Soc Am—Sigma Xi. 4567 Swan Av., St. Louis 10.

17 SPRIEGEL, William Robert. Management engineering (Industrial, personnel). b'93. AB '14—BS '15 (Lebanon U); AM '20—PhD '35 (U Mich). Coauthor: (with Richard Lansburgh) Industrial Management '47; (with Walter Dill Scott) Personnel Management '48; Elements of Supervision (with Edward Schultz) '42; (with Ernest C Davies) Principles of Business Organization '46. Asst personnel dir, asst to factory mgr and gen supt US Rubber Co Detroit '19-27; prodn supt Dodge Bros Plant 6 Detroit '27; dir foremanship training and gen supt Fisher Body Corp Plant 18 '27-29; sales promotion mgr machinery dept Chas A Strelinger Co '30-31; asst in policy U Mich Sch Business Adminstrn '32-34; asso prof econ Western Ky State Teachers Coll '34-37; asso prof indsl management Northwestern U Sch Commerce Evanston Ill '37-41, prof indsl management since '41, chmn dept '39-48; asso dean and dist prof management Coll Bus Adminstrn U Tex since '49. American Management Assn—Indsl Management Soc—Soc for Advancement of Management—Am Soc for Engring Edn—Am Acad Management—Am Econ Assn— Am Assn Univ Profs—ASME. 1906 Hopi Trail, Austin, Tex.☉

18 SPRING, Agnes Wright (Mrs. Archer T. Spring). Cattle industry (Hist); Wyoming (History); Colorado (Hist); Western states (Historic trails). b'94. AB '13—fellowship '41-42 (U Wyo); '16-17 (Sch journ Columbia U). Research and collection historical data on western livestock industry, western transportation, especially Rocky Mt region. Author: Seventy Years Cow Country '42; A Bloomer Girl on Pikes Peak '49; Cheyenne and Black Hills Stage and Express Routes '49, and others, also articles in field. Asst librarian U Wyo '09-13; State Library Cheyenne Wyo '13-18; state librarian and hist '18-21; asst dir Rockefeller Found study western range cattle industry '44; woman's ed and feature writer Wyo Stockman-Farmer '13-40; spl research western hist dept Denver Pub Library '43-49; now acting state hist Colo. Colo Authors League—Pi Beta Phi—Denver Woman's Press Club —Colorado Women's Press Assn. State Museum, 14th and Sherman Sts., Denver 2.

19 SPRING, Arthur J(ohn). Marine equipment (Education). b'09. AB '32 (Holy Cross Coll); MA '33 (Boston Coll). Developed technical training material, including compilation and writing of textbooks and correspondence study materials in marine field, analyzed trainind needs of personnel within marine field, research to adapt study material for up-to-date technical training in operation of marine equipment. Author: Marine Safety '51; also articles in field. Training officer US Maritime Service Training Sch '46-47; dir US Maritime Service Inst since '47. US Maritime Service Institute, Bklyn 35.

20 SPRINGER, George Perrcy. Highway engineering; Railroad engineering. b'83. BS (CE) '11—CE '21 (Mich State Coll); '18-19 (Washington U); '21-22 (U Mich). Designer Am Bridge Co '12; asso prof civil engring U Md '13-18; asst dist engr bridges Mich State Highway Dept '21-24; asst prof civil engring Drexel Inst '24-27; concrete engr Muskegon Co Highway Commission '27-28; asso prof civil engring Purdue U since '28. Asst engr rds, rys, docks and wharves constrn div QMC AUS '18-21. Am Soc CE—Am Rd Bldrs Assn—Am Ry Engring Assn —Am Soc Engring Edn—Am Assn Engineers—Nat Soc Profl Engrs—Ind Soc Profl Engrs—Ind Engring Council— Tau Beta Pi—Theta Tau—Chi Epsilon. P. O. Box 518, W. Lafayette, Ind.

21 SPRINGER, John McKendree. African peoples, history and customs; Early history of southern Rhodesia; Belgian Congo (Katanga Province); West African colonies and countries. b'73. PhB '99 (Northwestern U); BD '01—DD '21 (Garrett Biblical Inst); LLD '39 (Taylor U). Author: Heart of Central Africa '08; Pioneering in the Congo '16; Christian Conquests in the Congo '26; also articles in field. Missionary bishop for Africa '36-44; now volunteer in active missionary work. 150 5th Av., NYC 11.

22 SPRINGER, Stewart. Ichthyology (Sharks); Fisheries engineering; Systematic zoology. b'06. '24-27 (Butler U). Research on systematics of elasmobranch fish. Author articles in field. Manager Zool Research Supply Englewood Fla '35-40; mgr Fla Marine Prod Inc NYC '41-42; investigator Marine Studios Inc Marineland Fla '42-43; cons Naval Research Lab Washington '44; technol vp Reed-Martin Lab Ft Myers Fla '45; fisherman Key West Fla '46; asst prod mgr Shark Ind Div Borden Co Stuart Fla since '47. Am Soc Herpetologists and Ichthyologists —Am Fisheries Soc—Am Inst Chem— Fla Acad Sci. P.O. Box E, Stuart, Fla.

23 SPROULE, John Campbell. Geological exploration; Petroleum development. b'05. BS '30 (U Alberta); MA (geol) '31—PhD (geol) '35 (U Toronto). Research and geological exploration in Canada and South Am; Petroleum and Precambrian exploration. With Geol Survey Can '36-39; geol and exploration mgr Saskatchewan Imperial Oil Ltd '39-45; asst chief geol and chief adv geol Internat Petroleum Co since '45. Geol Soc Am(F) —Am Assn Petroleum Geol—Soc Exploration Geophys—Soc Econ Paleontologists and Mineral—Geol Assn Can (F)—Can Inst Mining and Metall Engineers—AAAS. 434 University Av., Toronto, Ont., Can.

24 SPROULL, Reavis Claton. Electrical insulation (Cellulose); Cellulose chemistry; Wood preservation; Microbiological deterioration; Dimensional Stability. b'13. AB '32—MA '36—DSc '50(Mercer U); PhD '41 (NY U). Holds two patents in field. Author articles: Development of Paper from Caroa Fiber '45; Preserved Poles '48; Chemurgic Research '49; Wood Waste Utilization '48; Dimensional Stabilization '50; Kraft Pulp from Old Crossties '50, and others. Group leader research and development of insulating materials Gen Elec Co '41-46; head wood and paper div So Research Inst '46-49, asst dir, and in charge applied chem div '49-51; tech dir Herty Found Lab since '51. Tech Assn Pulp and Paper Industry—Am Wood Preservers Assn—AAAS—Forest Products Research Soc—Phi Lambda Upsilon—Kappa Phi Kappa. Herty Foundation Laboratory, Savannah, Ga.

10 SPRUGEL, George, Jr. Fishery biology (Fish growth). b'19. BS '46—MS '47—PhD '50 (Ia State Coll). Critical scale study two populations of bluegills and green sunfish in lake and artificial pond; complete limnological investigation habitat of fishes, and observations of factors causing winter-kill. Faculty dept zool and entomol Ia State Coll since '46, asst prof since '48. Wildlife Soc—Am Fisheries Soc—AAAS—Ia Acad Sci—Gamma Sigma Delta. Department of Zoology and Entomology, Iowa State Coll, Ames, Ia.

11 SPRUTH, Henry C. Biologic assay. b'01. BS '23 (U Chgo). Biologic assay of barbiturates, estrogens, pyrogens, cardiac glycosides, anticoagulants, vitamins, growth stimulants. With Abbott Labs since '20, manager biol assay labs since '35. Sigma Xi—ACS(councilor '47)—Am Statis Assn—Biometrics Soc—Ill Sect Soc Exptl Biol and Med—Chgo Chemists Club—Am Pharm Assn—AAAS—Nat Society Med Research—Ill Soc Med Research—Association Vitamin Chems. Abbott Laboratories, 14th and Sheridan Rd., North Chicago, Ill.

12 SPURLIN, Harold M. Polymer and cellulose chemistry. b'05. BS '25 (Ga Tect Inst); PhD '28 (Yale). Research at Kaiser Wilhelm Institut fur Faserstoffchemie, Berlin-Dahlem; at Hercules Experiment Station on reaction kinetics and equilibria, molecular weights, physical properties, and solution properties of cellulose, cellulose derivatives, and other high polymers; also on action of plasticizers and solvents. Holds 15 United States patents, five foreign. Author: Cellulose and Cellulose Derivatives '43; also articles in field. With Hercules Expt Station, tech asst to dir since '45. Am Chem Soc—Soc Rheology—AAAS—Am Institute Chem Engrs—Am Inst Physics—Sigma Xi—Tau Beta Pi—Phi Kappa Phi—Alpha Chi Sigma. Hercules Experiment Station, Hercules Powder Co., Wilmington 99, Del.

13 SPURLIN, Paul Merrill. Franco-American literary relations (Eighteenth century); Eighteenth century French literature; Jean-Jacques Rousseau. b'02. BPh '25 (Emory U); Certificat d'Etudes françaises '26 (U Lyons); PhD '36 (Johns Hopkins). Author: Montesquieu in America 1760-1801 '40; also articles in field. Prof 18th century French lit Mich since '46. Mod Lang Assn Am—Institut français de Wash (trustee)—Am Assn Teachers French—Phi Beta Kappa. Franco-Am exchange student '25-26. 505 N. 7th St., Ann Arbor.☉

14 SPURR, Arthur Richard. Plant morphology, anatomy; Growth; Truck crops. b'15. BS '38—MA '40 (U Calif); AM '42—PhD '47 (Harvard). Author articles in field. Instr truck crops and jr olericulturist Expt Sta U Calif Coll Agr since '48. Bot Soc Am—New Eng Bot Club. Division of Truck Crops, University of California, College of Agriculture, Davis, Calif.†

15 SQUIRE, Alexander. Powder metallurgy. b'17. SB '39 (MIT). Author: Powder Metallurgy '46; also articles in field. Research in powder metall Handy and Harman Bridgeport Conn '39-41, Sullivan Machinery Co Mich City Ind '41-42; mgr Metall Labs Westinghouse Elec Corp E Pittsburgh Pa since '45. Chief powder metall sect Watertown Arsenal US Army '42-45. ASM—AIME (powder metall com '47-48, chmn '48-49)—AAAS. Awarded Civilian Meritorious Service award Sec of War. Westinghouse Electric Corporation, East Pittsburgh, Pa.†

16 SQUIRE, Latham C(haffee). Zoning; City planning. b'97. Student '15-18 (U Va); EM '22 (Colo Sch Mines). Specialist in zoning; author about 50 zoning ordinances for villages, towns, cities; comprehensive plans for physical development communities of all sizes. Author: Zoning in New York '48. Vpres Tech Adv Corp NYC '28-32; cons engr specializing in city planning and zoning since '32; prin cons on complete rezoning NYC '49-50. NJ Soc Profl Engrs—Am Planning and Civic Assn. 25 Broad St., NYC 4.

17 SQUIRES, James Duane. New Hampshire (History); World War I (British propaganda in US); Abraham Lincoln (Civil War period); New England (Railroad history). b'04. AB '25 (U ND); MA '27 (U Minn); PhD '33 (Harvard). Author: British Propaganda in the United States from 1914 to 1917 '35; The Lincoln Administration and the Civil War '48; A History of New London, New Hampshire '52; The Northern Railroad, 1844-1848 '48; A History of New Hampshire, 1623-1953 (in preparation). Chmn dept social studies Colby Jr Coll New London NH since '33. Phi Beta Kappa—Phi Beta Kappa Assos—Soc Am Historians—Am Hist Soc—Assn State and Local Hist—Newcomen Soc—SAR. Citation by Soc for State and Local History for best work in the field pub in New Eng in '52. New London, N.H.☉

18 ST. CLAIR, Stuart. Mining and mineral economics; Petroleum economics. b'84. BS '12—EM '17 (Penn State Coll); MS '13 (U Ia). Petroleum, mining and mineral surveys in the US, minerals in Africa, especially in Tanganyika, the Rodesias, Nyasaland, Portugal, Spain; mining and mineral economics in Newfoundland, Canada, Cuba, Mexico; mineral exploration Indonesia, Republic of Panama; geological exploration of Island of Timor, East Indies; development of mineral program for Government Union of Burma; report on economics of the petroleum industry in Burma. Author bulls and articles in field. Geol US Geol Survey, state surveys, US Treasury Dept '12-18; spl service US govt Nat Resources Planning Bd '33, Pub Works Adminstrn '39, WPB '42-45, Def Minerals Adminstrn '51; cons petroleum and mineral econ survey and development program Government of Union of Burma '51-53; cons geologist and engineer, mining petroleum, mineral econs '18-53. AAAS(F)—Am Inst Mining Engrs—Am Assn Petroleum Geologists—Soc Econ Geol—Pan Am Inst Mining Engring and Geol—Soc Am Mil Engrs. 140 Pinehurst Av., NYC.

19 ST. JOHN, Harry Mark. Metals (Non-ferrous); Foundry practice. b '88. AB '10 (Cornell). Development and design electric furnaces for melting brass other non-ferrous metals, pyrometric methods for molten metals; Study impurities in non-ferrous metals and their influence on properties. Contributor to Handbook of American Society for Metals and to Kent's Mechanical Engineers Handbook. Research engr Commonwealth Edison Co '13-19; vp Detroit Electric Furnace Co '19-23; chief metall Detroit Lubricator Co '23-38; supt Brass Foundry, Forge Shop, Die Casting, Crane Co since '38. Am Foundrymens Society (Wm H McFadden medal)—AIMME. c/o Crane Company, 4100 S. Kedzie Av., Chgo 5.

20 STAFF, Virden Edward. Subways (planning); utility project (planning). b'09. Student '26-29 (U Ill). Design and construction power, gas, water, telephone plants; preliminary investigation and engineering reports on electrification and industrial projects in South America; preliminary planning Toronto Subway, service tunnel under Milwaukee River, rapid transit system for Cleveland, emergency pumping plant for New York City, subway system for San Francisco; preliminary investigation on plan for electrification of Bolivia. Profl engring practice '35-41; chief utilities sect Sioux Ordnance Depot Sidney Neb '42; asst chief engr Naval Ammunition Depot McAlester Okla '42-43; project mgr various ventures since '43, now chief engr DeLeuw Cather & Co, cons engrs. Am Inst EE—Nat Soc Profl Engrs—Western Soc Engrs. 150 N. Wacker Dr., Chgo 6. H: 219 E. Superior St., Chgo 11.

21 STAFFELBACH, Elmer Hubert. Education (Teacher training). b'93. Grad '20 (Eastern Wash Coll Edn); AB '24—AM '25— PhD '26 (Stanford U). Author articles in field. Prof edn San Jose State Coll since '26, head dept edn and teacher training '35-49; on leave as regional survey dir of sch dists northern Calif '46-49. NEA—Am Acad Polit Social Sci—Calif Teachers Assn (dir research '29-46). 111 S. 15th St., San Jose, Calif.*

22 STAHELIN, Rudolph. Forest management (Redwoods, rocky mountain and southern regions, reforestations, farm woodlands); European forestry. b'89. Diploma '21 (Polytechnicum Zurich Switzerland); MS '35 (U Calif). Author articles in field. Forester Forest Service Washington since '48. Soc Am Foresters—Ecol Soc Am—Soc Swiss Foresters. Department of Agriculture, Forest Service, Washington 25.†

23 STAHL, Arthur Louis. Orchids (Nutrition); Tropical foods; Food composition; Consumer packaging. b'02. BS '25 (Mich State Coll); MS '27—PhD '29 (Rutgers U). Author articles in field. Food tech U Fla Agrl Expt Sta Gainesville Fla '30-46; research prof food tech U Miami since '46. Inst Food Tech—Am Soc Plant Physiol—Fla Acad Sci—Am Chem Soc—Hort Soc Am—AAAS—Sigma Xi. University of Miami, Coral Gables, Fla.

24 STAHLY, Eldon Everett. Petroleum chemistry; Instrumentation. b'08. BA '29 (Bluffton Coll O); MA '31 (O State U); PhD '34 (Penn State Coll). Instrumentation for control of synthetic rubber manufacture. Holder six US patents. Author articles in field. Research chem Gen Elec Co '34; Mallinckrodt fellow Penn State '34-35; research and development of chem and petroleum processes Standard Oil Dev Co Baton Rouge La '35-41; with Mellon Inst since '41, Koppers fellowship '41-44, Rubber Reserve fellowship as sr fellow '44-47, administrative fellow '47-48; director chem research Commercial Solvents Corp Terre Haute Ind since '48. AAAS—Am Inst Chem Engrs—Am Chem Soc—Sigma Xi. Commercial Solvents Corporation, Terre Haute, Ind.

25 STAHNKE, Herbert Ludwig George. Scorpions; Venoms (Physiological effects). b'02. AA '26 (LaGrange Coll Mo); SB '28 (U Chicago); AM '34 (U Ariz); PhD '39 (Ia State Coll). Research therapeutic value of venoms, principally malignant tumors. Prof zoology, dir poisonous animals research lab, head dept biol scis Ariz State Coll since '40; developed and mfg anti-scorpion serum since '40. AA

AS—Phi Delta Kappa—Sigma Xi. 1400 Mill Av., Tempe, Ariz.†

10 STAHR, Elvis J(acob), **Jr.** b'16. AB '36 (U Ky); BA '38—BCL '39 (Oxford U Eng); MA '43; Diploma in Chinese Lang '43 (Yale). Admitted NY State bar '40; practiced as asso firm Mudge Stern Williams & Tucker NYC '39-41, sr asso '46-47, admitted to Ky bar '48; asso prof law U Ky '47-48, prof law since '48, dean Coll Law since '48; admitted US Supreme Ct bar '50. Assn Am Rhodes Scholars—Am Law Inst—Am Bar Assn—Am Arbitration Assn—NEA—AAUP—Assn Am Law Sch—Assn Bar City NY—Legal Aid Soc—Ky State Bar Assn—Edn Assn Ky—Phi Beta Kappa—Order of the Coif—Sigma Xi—Phi Delta Phi. Rhodes scholar '36-39; named one of America's Ten Outstanding Young Men of 1948 by US Jr C of C; recipient Balfour Nat Award of Sigma Xi '36; Algernon Sydney Sullivan medallion of NY Southern Soc '36. 1609 Bon Air Dr., Lexington 32, Ky.

11 STAIR, Ralph. Ultra violet radiometry. b'00. BS '24 (U Mo); '20-21 (Kan Wesleyan U); MA '28 (George Washington U). Research on ultraviolet techniques in filter radiometry and the measurement of the amount and distribution of atmospheric ozone. Author articles in field. With Nat Bur Standards since '26, physicist since '46. Optical Soc Am—Inst Radio Engrs. National Bureau of Standards, Washington 25.†

12 STAKMAN, Elvin C. Plant pathology; Mycology (Cereal rusts and smuts); Crop improvement. b'85. BA '06—MA '10—PhD '13 (U Minn); Dr Nat Sci (hon) '38 (U Halle). United States Department Agriculture National defense leader of rubber expedition to South America '40; delegate of National Academy Sciences to sixth International Botanical Congress; has made extensive investigations of cereal rusts and smuts. Author articles in field. Editorial com Annual Review of Microbiology '46-50; ed in chief Phytopathology '25-29; Am editor Phytopathologische Zeitschrift since '31. Instr plant path U Minn '09-12, asst prof '13; prof since '18, head sect plant path '13-40, chief div plant path and bot '40-53; path in charge barberry eradication campaign US Dept Agr '18, path and agt US Dept Agr since '19. Nat Research Council—Am Acad Arts Sci(F)—Am Phytopath Soc (pres '22)—Bot Soc Am—Am Genetic Assn—AAAS (president '49)—Am Soc Naturalists—Nat Acad of Sci—Am Philo Soc—Phi Beta Kappa—Sigma Xi. Awarded E Chr Hansen medal and prize '28. 1411 Hythe St., St. Paul 8.

13 STALEY, Howard Raymond. Fireproof building construction. born '99. Student '19-21 (Ia State Coll); SB '35—SM '37 (MIT). Author: Semi-Fireproof Construction '48; also articles in field. With MIT since '37, prof since '46. ACI—ASTM—AAAS—ASCE—Tau Beta Pi—Sigma Xi. 77 Massachusetts Av., Cambridge, Mass.

14 STALKER, Edward Archibald. Boundary layer control. b'97. BS '19—MS '23 (Mich U). Research and development on the application of boundary layer control to compressor, turbines, aircraft and other fluid flow machines. Author: Principles of Flight '31; also articles in field. Aeronautical engr in charge fuselage design Stout Engring Lab '20-22; instr aeronautical engring Mich U in charge courses airplane design '22-25, asst prof '25-27, asso prof '27-29, prof '29-30, dept head '30-42; aeronautical engr Dow Chem Co '42-46; pres Stalker Development

Co Mich since '46. Inst Aeronautical Sci—ASME—SAE—Sigma Xi. 409 First St., Bay City, Mich.

15 STALNAKER, John Marshall. Psychometrics; Personnel placement. b'03. BS cum laude '25—AM '28 (U Chicago). Prof psychol Stanford U '45-49; prof psychol Ill Inst Tech since 49, dir studies Assn Am Med Colleges since '49, dir med testing ednl testing service since '49; trustee, dir Pepsi-Cola Scholarship Board Winnetka Illinois since '45. Am Psychol Assn—Am Statis Assn—Psychometric Soc—Am Edn Research Assn—NEA—AAAS—Phi Beta Kappa—Sigma Xi. 185 N. Wabash Av., Chgo 1.†

16 STANESLOW, Bernard John. Inks (Carbon paper); Waxes (Technology); Stereotype printing (Electroplating). b'09. B Chem '31-33 (Cornell U). Development of improved one-time carbon paper inks at lowered costs; improvement of colors and waxes for carbon paper; assisted in development of paper with increased receptivity to carbon paper inks; adaptation of nickel and iron plating methods to stereotypes for business forms. Co-author: (with E S Gale) Rheology of Carbon Paper Inks '50. Contributor: Commerical Waxes '44. Analytical chem J T Baker Chem Co Phillipsburg NJ '31-32, Linde Air Producers Co Buffalo '34; chief chem Moore Bus Forms Inc since '34. ACS—Am Electroplating Soc—Am Oil Chem Soc—Tech Assn Pulp and Paper Industry—Tech Assn Lithographic Industry—Alpha Chi Sigma. Moore Business Forms, Inc, Research and Service Division, Niagara Falls, N.Y.

17 STANISLAWSKI, Dan. Historical geography of Latin America. b'03. BA '37—PhD '44 (Calif U, Berkeley). Research on origin and spread of grid pattern town, early Spanish town planning in new world, Tarascan political geography, political rivalry of Patzcuaro and Morelia in sixteenth century Mexico. Author articles in field. Prof geog U Texas. Phi Beta Kappa—Sigma Xi. University of Texas, Austin, Tex.

18 STANLEY, Leon Stanford. Great Salt Lake (Salt, maps, history). b'11. Student '33-36 (U Utah). Research on history, salt, maps and resources of Great Salt Lake. Constrn engr US Engrs '50-52, asst area engr from '42-43, '39-42, '43-46; office and dist engr US Dept Interior '46-47; dist engr US Conservation Service '48-52. Am Soc CE (asso mem)—Am Mil Engrs. US Engineers, Postoffice Box 2660, Fort Douglas, Utah. H: 129 F St., Salt Lake City 3.

19 STANOYEVICH, Milivoy Stoyan. Slavistics; Serbism; Yugoslav (History, politics); Rating American executives (Income). b'82. AB '02 (Zaytchar Coll); MA '07 (U Belgrade); LLM '14 (U Calif); PhD '21 (Columbia); spl lit researches (U Munich, U Paris, U Vienna, U Zurich). Executive secretary of Serbian War Mission to America '18; expert adviser State of New York joint legislative committee to investigate exploitation of immigrants '23. Author: Omladina u Sadashnyosti '07; Figure u Pesmama '07; Tolstoy's Theory of Social Reform—His Doctrine of Law, Money and Property '14, 2d edit '26; Early Yugoslav Literature '22; Slavonic Nations of Yesterday and Today '25; also articles in field. Pres Universal Syndicate '27-37, chmn since '38; pres Rating Dir Co NY since '40; contbg editor Slavonic terminology Webster's New Internat Dictionary '38-40, special and cons editor since '41. Am Geog Soc(F)—Modern Lang Assn Am—Acad Polit Sci. 11 E. 44th St., NYC 17.

20 STANSEL, Frank R. Transistors; Rectifiers; Measuring equipment (Communications services). b'04. BS in elec engring '26 (Union Coll); MEE '34—DEE '41 (Poly Inst Brooklyn). Studies in application transistors and germanium rectifiers to new carrier telephone circuits; investigation properties semi-conductor diodes as copper oxide, selenium, silicon; development new types electric measuring equipment; studies on bridge circuits, oscillator, detection equipment, wave analyzers, frequency measuring equipment. Tech staff Bell Telephone Labs since '26, radar and carrier development Systems Dept since '42. Inst Radio Engrs—Am Inst Elec Engring —Sigma Xi—Eta Kappa Nu. Licensed profl engr NY. Bell Telephone Labs, Murray Hill, NJ.

21 STANTON, Wyllys Gannett. Vocational testing; Industrial criteria for vocational training. born '04. BSc '26 (Yale); MSc '36 (Washington Univ); certificate '32 (Internat Accountants Soc). Asso prof indsl engring O State U '45-50, exec com O State Personnel Research Bd '45-50; asst to pres Oran Co Columbus '50-52. Prof indsl engring U of Ala since '52. Fell Am Inst Indsl Engr (chmn Nat Edn). Nat Soc Professional Engrs—AAAS—Am Soc Engring Edn—Nat Econ Council—Inst Labor Research—Beta Gamma Sigma. Box 427, University, Ala.

22 STANWELL - FLETCHER, Theodora C. (Mrs John F.) Vertebrate ecology. b'06. BA '28 (Mt Holyoke Coll); MS '32—PhD '36 (Cornell). Made studies higher flowering plants and vertebrate animals New Zealand, Fiji, Dutch East Indies, Hudson Bay, Canada and Pennsylvania virgin forests, forests North Central Brit Columbia '29-41; research in conservation of wildlife and preservation of wildlife areas. Author: Driftwood Valley: Story of an Unexplored Wilderness '46. Author articles: Naturalists in the Wilds of British Columbia (with J F Stanwell-Fletcher) '40; Accounts of Flora and Fauna of Driftwood Valley Region '43; other articles in field. Am Ornithol Union—Sigma Xi. Dimock Post Office, Pa.

23 STAPLES, Lloyd William. Mineralogy. b'08. AB '29 (Columbia U); MS '30 (U Mich); PhD '35 (Stanford U). Research on austinite, adamite, perched analcime crystals, quick silver geology. Co-author: Microchemical Analysis, Introduction to the Study of Minerals '37; also articles in field. Prof geol U Ore since '39. Am Inst Mining Engr (Ore chmn '41-42)—Mineral Soc Am(F)—Geol Soc Am(F)—Ore Acad Sci—Sigma Xi—Phi Beta Kappa. Department of Geology, University of Oregon, Eugene, Ore.†

24 STARCHER, George W(illiam). Human relations. b'06. AB '26 (Ohio U); AM '27—PhD '30 (U Ill); '45-46 (Harvard). Asst in mathematics U Ill '27-29; with Ohio U since '30, prof mathematics since '45, asso dean of men '38-39, acting dean Grad Coll and Coll Arts and Scis '43-45, dean Univ Coll '46-51, dean Coll Arts and Scis since '51. Am Math Soc—Math Assn Am—AAUP—Sigma Xi—Phi Beta Kappa—Kappa Delta Pi—Pi Mu Epsilon. Box 313, Athens, Ohio.†

25 STARCK, (Adolph Ludwig) Taylor. Germanic philology (History of the German language, medieval literature, German dialects; old high, middle high and low German; folklore, plantlore). b'89. AB '11—PhD '16 (Johns Hopkins); '14-15, '19-20 (U Berlin, U Madrid). Author: Der Alraun '17. Co-author: Notker, des Deutschen Werke, three vols '33-36. Translator: The Inevitable War '15; also articles in field.

Prof German Harvard since '42, chmn dept Germanic lang and lit '27-32, '38-52. Am Acad Arts Sci(F)—Mod Lang Assn Am—Dialect Soc Am—Folklore Soc—Medieval Acad Am—Linguistic Soc Am—Soc Advancement Scandinavian Studies. Busch-Reisinger Museum, Cambridge 38, Mass.

10 STARK, Paul C., Jr. Home fruit growing and orchards; Dwarf fruit tree production. b'17. BS '40 (Cornell U). Author: Simplified Way to Grow Your Own Fruit; Stark's New Guide to Profitable Orcharding. Research dept Stark Bros Nurseries and Orchards Co since '41. Am Soc Hort Sci—Am Pomol Soc (bd mgrs)—Nat Assn Plant Patent Owners (pres). Stark Brothers Nurseries and Orchards Company, Louisiana, Mo.†

11 STARKEY, Otis P(aul). Economic and military geography. b'06. BS '27 —MA '30—PhD '39 (Columbia U). Research on Lesser Antilles, Pennsylvania, southern and western Europe. Author: The Economic Geography of Barbados '39. Co-author: (with L E Klimm and N F Hall) Introductory Economic Geography '37, '40. Instr econ Washington and Jefferson Coll '27-28; editorial work on geog texts NYC '28-31; instr geog U Pa '31-41, asst prof '41-42; geog MIS G-2 War Dept '42-45; lect Columbia '45-46, summer '48; prof geog, chmn dept Ind U since '46. Assn Am Geog—Am Soc Professional Geog (pres '47)—Am Geog Soc—AAAS. Dept of Geography, Indiana University, Bloomington, Ind.◎

12 STARKEY, Robert L(yman). Corrosive characteristics of soil. b'99. BS '21 (Mass Agr Coll); MS '23—PhD '24 (Rutgers Coll); Rockefeller Foundation Fellow '37-38 (Technische Hoogeschool, Delft, Holland). Research on soil microbiology, microbial physiology, oxidation and reduction of sulfur materials, decomposition of organic matter, fat production by yeasts, anaerobic corrosion by bacteria, industrial microbiology; Congress of International Society of Soil Science Washington '27, Leningrad Moscow '30, New Brunswick New Jersey '38; Congress of International Society of Microbiology NYC '38. Patent on appliance for measurement of corrosive characteristics of soil. Author articles in field. Research asst NJ Agr Expt Sta '21-24, research specialist microbiol since '26; instr bacteriology U Minn '24-26; asst prof, asso prof, prof microbiol Rutgers U since '26. Soc Am Bacteriologists—AAAS—Am Chem Soc—Soil Sci Soc Am—Internat Soc Soil Sci—Soc Gen Micro-biol. New Jersey Agriculture Experiment Station, New Brunswick, N.J. H: 7 Crest Rd., Dewey Heights, City.

13 STARKWEATHER, Louis Pomeroy. Corporate reorganization. b'98. BS '21 (Tufts Coll); MBA '25—DCS '30 (NY U). Author: Analysis industrial Securities '30; Questions and Problems in Credit Principles and Practices '32; Case Studies in Corporate Financing '34; Corporate Financing and Consolidation '39; Corproate Financing, Combination and Reorganization '40; Policies and Practice in Corporate Finance '51, also articles in field. Contributor: Financial Handbook '49; Fundamentals of Investment Banking '49. With NY U '24-36, asso prof '34-36, lecturer since '46; adminstr asst Bur Yards and Docks '42, state orgn officer NJ OPA '42-43; negotiator and cons War Dept, US Army, QM Price Adjustment Bd '43-47; prof and chmn dept finance Rutgers U '50. Am Econ Assn—Am Statis Assn—Nat Assn Cost Accountants—Am Finance Assn—Am Arbitration Assn—Beta Gamma Sigma—Delta Sigma Pi—NY

Soc Security Analysts. 18 Washington Pl., Newark 2.

14 STARKWEATHER, William Edward Bloomfield. Francisco Goya. b'79. Student (Art Students League New York); (Colarossi Acad Paris); pupil of Sorolla Madrid Spain; independent study in Italy 3 yrs. Author: Drawings and Paintings by Francisco Goya in the Collection of the Hispanic Soc of America. Prof art dept Hunter Coll of the City of New York '36-46; represented in the Metropolitan Museum, Brooklyn Museum, San Diego Museum, U Pa, Randolph-Macon Coll, Instituto de Valencia de Don Juan Madrid Spain. Am Water Color Soc—Allied Artists Am—Hispanic Soc Am—New York Water Color Club. Popular vote for oils New Haven '24; Mrs. William K Vanderbilt prize joint water color exhibition NYC '25; Dana gold medal for water color Pa Acad Fine Arts '25; Jones prize water color Baltimore '26; Phila prize water color Pa Acad Fine Arts '29. 82 State St., Bklyn.

15 STARR, Chester G., Jr. Military science and history. b'14. BA '34—MA '35 (U Mo); PhD '38 (Cornell); '38-40 (Am Acad Rome). Directed preparation and official publication nine volumes Fifth Army History, study of ground operations in Italy in connection with army duties; intensive study of terrain in Mediterranean '38-39. Author: The Roman Imperial Navy '41; Salerno to the Alps '48. Author articles: The Ancient Warship '40; Coastal Defense in the Roman World '43; other articles in field. Instr hist U Ill '40-45, asst prof '45-46, asso prof since '46. First lt, lt col Ft Benning Inf Sch US Army '42-43, overseas chief hist sect 5th Army Italy '43-45. Soc Promotion Roman Studies—AHA—Phi Beta Kappa. University of Illinois, Urbana, Ill.

16 STARR, George Herman. Bean, alfalfa and potato diseases (Bacterial ring rot); Antibiotics for bean disease control. b'98. BS '25 (SD State Coll); MS '28—PhD '31 (U Minn). Author articles: Diseases of Canning Crops '32; Potato Seed Treatment Studies in Wyoming. Prof agron and station plant path U Wyo since '31. Phytopath Soc—Colo-Wyo Acad Sci—Sigma Xi. University of Wyoming, Laramie, Wyo.

17 STARR, Herbert Willmarth. Thomas Gray; Sherlock Holmes. b'16. AB '38—AM '39 (Temple U); PhD '41 (U Pa). Author: Gray As a Literary Critic '41; A Bibliography of Thomas Gray, 1917-51. Also articles in field. Asst prof Temple U since '48. Modern Lang Assn—Modern Humanities Research Assn—AAUP—Baker St Irregulars. Dept. of English, Temple University, Broad and Montgomery St., Phila. 22.†

18 STARR, Joseph Rankin. Government and political parties of Great Britain, France, and Germany; International Law and Relations; History of World War II American Occupation of Germany. b'01. AB '26 (U Neb); MA '27—PhD '30 (U Minn); F Soc Sci Research Council '30-31. Author: Tropical Analysis of Comparative European Government '36; also articles in field. Asst prof, asso prof polit sci U Minn '31-42; chief hist cons US Occupation Forces Germany '46-49; hist US Mil Govt Germany '49-50; prof govt and polit U Md since '50. Am Polit Sci Assn—Am Acad Polit and Soc Sci—AAUP—Phi Beta Kappa. Department of Government and Politics, College of Business and Pub Administration, University of Maryland, College Park, Md. H: 5021 38th Av., West Hyattsville, Hyattsville, Md.

19 STARR, Thomas Irwin. Abraham Lincoln; History of Michigan (Detroit). b'03. AB '26 (Albion Coll, Mich). One of the few present at opening of Robert Todd Lincoln Collection in Library of Congress '47; owns Lincoln library of more than 2500 volumes and pamphlets, library of Detroit and Michigan history in excess of 200 volumes; one of honorary vice presidents of Abraham Lincoln Bookshop in Chicago. Discovered only known copy of Abraham Lincoln's 1856 speech at Kalamazoo Michigan. With advt and pub rel dept Mich Bell Tel Co Detroit since '27; mem Lincoln Found Adv Bd since '41. Detroit Hist Soc—State Hist Soc Mich—Abraham Lincoln Assn—Lincoln Fellowship of Southern Calif (hon)—Chicago Civil War Round Table—Phi Beta Kappa. 1540 Artesia Rd., Det 23.

20 STARRET, Howard Andrew. Bomb proof and bomb-resistant structures; Underground structures (Factories, gasoline tank, marine); personnel employment problems. b'88. AB '08 (Detroit U); certificate sanitary sci '12 (Cornell U). Designer bombproof buildings, radio stations, and bombproof factories; development of underground piping system, underground gasoline tank farm, and bombproof shelter; underwater and marine construction; inventor crib-type construction. Holds patents on power line system, and underground storage tank. Design engr several state and fed projects; formerly research engr Dept Commerce Washington; formerly chief research engr and officer in charge research engring constrn div US Army Washington; design and engr canals and dams Starret Engring Co. Soc Am Mil Engrs—Kappa Beta Pi. Peten 95, Colonia Marvarte, Mexico City, Mex.

21 STAUBER, Leslie Alfred. Malaria; Oyster pests; Marine biology. b'07. Logan fellow '32-34—PhD '37 (U Chicago); BS '29—MS '30 (Rutgers U). Research assistant to Dr W H Taliaferro on a trip to Panama '31. Author articles in field. Asso prof zool Rutgers U since '47. AAAS—Am Soc Tropical Med—Am Soc Parasitiologists —NY Acad Sci—Nat Malaria Soc—Am Soc Zool. Fellow The Squibb Inst for med research '45. Department of Zoology, Rutgers University, New Brunswick, N.J.†

22 STAUFFER, Alvin Packer, Jr. Logistics. b'00. BS '22—PhD '33 (Harvard). Research and writing on history of US Army logistics World War II, especially with reference to Quartermaster storage and distribution operations in US, Quartermaster procurement, storage, distribution, salvage, reclamation, and burial activities in War against Japan, and Quartermaster phases of logistical support of combat operations in Pacific. Author article: Quartermaster Depot Storage and Distribution Operations '48. Hist Nat Park Service Washington '35-43, OQMG Washington since '43. Am Mil Inst—QM Assn—AHA. Historical Section, Office of Quartermaster General, Second and T Sts., Washington 25.

23 STAUFFER, Robert A(llen). Vacuum metallurgy. b'20. BA '42 (Harvard). Research in development of vacuum furnaces; investigation use vacuum furnaces for melting and casting, heat treatment, refining and thermal reduction including work on copper, zirconium, titanium, and high temperature alloys. Author articles in field. Chem Nat Research Corp '42-44, dir metals research dept '44-48, asst dir research '48-49, dir research and vp since '49. National Research Corp., 70 Memorial Dr. Cambridge, Mass.

10 STAUNTON, John Joseph Jameson. Optical and electronic instrumentation. b'11. BS '32—MS '34—EE '41 (U Notre Dame). Invented and principal results of research double monochromator spectrophotometer, electronic photofluorometer, universal spectrophotometer, junior clinical spectrophotometer, photo-nephelometer, electric colorimeter, nephocolorimeter, anoxia photometer, other allied instruments. Head phys dept DePaul U '36-38; research engr Coleman Elec Co Maywood Ill '38-42, dir research since '42; cons optics Am Soap and Glycerine Producers Assn '44-45. Optical Soc Am—Inst Phys—Inst Radio Engrs. Coleman Instruments, Inc., Maywood, Ill.

11 STEARN, Noel Hudson. Geomagnetics; Petroleum geology. b'96. AB '17—AM '18 (Stanford U); PhD '26 (U Wis). Inventor temperature correction slide rule; co-inventor Hotchkiss Superdip Magnetometer. Author articles. Chief geologist W C McBride Inc '30-40, vp since '40. Am Inst Mining and Metall Engrs (geophy com '34-40)—Geol Soc Am—Am Assn Pet Geol—Soc Econ Geol—Soc Pet Geophys—AAAS (F)—Am Geophys Union—Independent Pet Assn Am—Sigma Xi—Phi Beta Kappa. 2101 Missouri Pacific Building, St. Louis.

12 STEARNS, Charles Edward. Pleistocene geology. b'20. AB '39 (Tufts Coll); '39-40 (Cal Inst Tech); MA '42; PhD '50 (Harvard). Rsrch in North Africa, New Mexico. Author articles in field. With Tufts Coll since '41, asst prof geol '48-51; asst prof geol Harvard since '51. AAAS—Am Geophys Union—Geol Soc Am—Sigma Xi—Phi Beta Kappa. Geological Museum, Oxford St., Cambridge 38, Mass.

13 STEARNS, Harold T(hornton). Ground-water; Dam sites; Volcanology; Pacific island geology. b'00. BS '21 (Wesleyan U); PhD '26 (George Washington U). Author articles in field. Expedition to the volcanoes of Japan, Java, Italy '24-25. Cons geol dam sites and ground-water supplies since '46; consultant to Atomic Energy Commission on ground-water since '48. Geol Soc Am(F). Medal for Merit for distinguished work in Pacific with the Armed Forces World War II. Box 158, Hope, Idaho.†

14 STEARNS, John. Dams; Power plants; Wharves; Marine construction; Dredging. b'82. CE '06 (Cornell). Administration of engineering and construction contracts; in charge sinking of caissons under compressed air through water-bearing sand to bedrock; construction of steam and hydroelectric plants; study of flood control dams to determine economic feasibility of installing power facilities; coordination architects and engineers in construction of dry docks, wharves, pile driving, and dredgings. Location surveys Bur Power & Light Los Angeles; constrn supt heavy found Found Co Am; constrn steam and hydro-elec plants of J G White Engring Corp '11-24; engr Metropolitan Water Dist So Cal '32-38; head power flood control div Fed Power Commn Washington '39-40; prin engr constrn of Navy Base Terminal Island Cal '40-42; in charge dredging W A Bechtel Co Marinship Sausalito Cal '42-43; engr for Hughes Aircraft Co '43-51; evaluation studies of industries since '49. Am Soc CE. Professional civil and mech engr Cal. Hughes Aircraft Co., Florence Av. at Teale St., Culver City, Cal.

15 STEARNS, Joseph L(angdon), Jr. Tropical and rare woods. b'07. BSF '29 (Penn State Coll); '44 (George Washington U). Collected, classified and studied wood specimens from all corners of world. Author articles in field. Asso with W M Ritter Lumber Co '29-33; forestry work US Dept Agr '33-37; research So Hardwood Producers Inc Memphis '37-41; asst dir research National Lumber Mfrs Assn and Timber Engring Co (a subsidiary) in charge Wood Products Lab Washington since '41. Soc Am Foresters—Forest Products Research Soc—Wood Collectors Soc. National Lumber Manufacturers Association, 1319 18th St. N.W., Washington.

16 STEARNS, Raymond Phineas. Intellectual history of the seventeenth and eighteenth centuries (Puritanism, science, political). b'04. AB '27 (Ill Coll); AM '31—PhD '34 (Harvard); '34-35 (London U); '35 (Leiden U). Research on economics of mercantilism in England and Netherlands, mercantilism, religion, early science role of Royal Society London in dissemination of experimental philosophy. English agriculture, Puritans and Puritanism, exploration and science in seventeenth century, sixteenth century English science, and British colonies. Author: Congregationalism in the Dutoh Netherlands '40; Pageant of Europe '47; also articles in field. Prof hist, head dept Lake Forest Coll '36-37; asst prof hist U Ill '37-43, asso prof '43-48, prof since '48. AHA—Hist Sci Soc—Am Soc Church Hist—Colonial Soc Mass—Inst Early Am Hist and Culture. Frank S Brewer prize, Am Soc Church History '40. 313 Lincoln Hall, Urbana, Ill. H: 202 W. Vermont Av.

17 STEBBINS, George Ledyard, Jr. Plant genetics and evolution. b'06. AB '28—PhD '31 (Harvard). Gave invitation paper on cytogenetics of grasses at Eighth Internat Congress of Genetics Stockholm '48; research on peonies, Kok-saghyz, forage grasses, parthenogenesis. Author: Variation and Evolution in Plants '50. Co-author: (with C W Young and C Hylander) The Human Organism and the World of Life '38; also articles in field. Prof U Calif since '47. Am Soc Naturalists—Bot Soc Am—Genetics Soc Am—Calif Bot Soc (vp '48)—Soc Study Evolution (pres '48)—Phi Beta Kappa—Sigma Xi. Division of Genetics, University of California, Davis, Cal.

18 STEBBINS, Homer Adolph. World government; European, Near and Far Eastern government; International and foreign trade law. b'84. PhB '06—PhM '07—LLB '08 (Syracuse U); PhD '13 (Columbia); JSD '17 (NYU). Has handled international cases involving the Kolshack Government of Russia, also governments of Spain, Mexico and seven South American countries; has advised upon the laws of England France as well as Oriental and Scandinavian countries; litigated for Alien Property Custodian, North Atlantic Steamship Conference. Author: Foreign Bills of Exchange in Commerce '17; also articles in field. Practiced law NY since '14, alone since '33. MI Service US Army War Dept on active duty '41-46, various positions in foreign countries. Received Lyman Tennant hist award Syracuse '06. 22 Minturn St., Hastings-on-Hudson, N.Y.

19 STEBBINS, Joel. Electrical photometry of stars; Photoelectric cells. b'78. BS '99—LLD '40 (U Neb); PhD '03 (U Calif); hon ScD '20 (U Wis). Author articles in field. Dir Washburn Obs, prof astronomy U Wis since '22, emeritus since '48; research asso Lick Obs since '48. National Academy Sci (Draper medal)—Am Philos Soc—Am Acad Arts Sci (Rumford premium)—AAAS (vp)—Am Astron Soc—Am Phys Soc—Optical Soc Am—Royal Astron Soc (fgn asso)—Phi Beta Kappa—Sigma Xi. Awarded Bruce medal, Astron Soc Pacific. Lick Observatory, Mt. Hamilton, Cal.

20 STEBBINS, Robert Cyril. Lizards; Salamanders; Western North American herpetology and ornithology. b'15. BA '40—MA '41—PhD '43 (U Calif, LA). Specializing in evolutionary studies of amphibians and reptiles including analysis of morphological and physiological variation, particularly at the subspecific and specific level, in relation to ecology. Research on nasal structure and ecology in lizards; speciation in salamanders, plethodont genus Ensatina and others. Author: Manual of Western North American Herpetology; also articles in field. Asso prof zool U Cal since '51, curator herpetology Mus Vertebrate Zool since '48. Am Soc Ichthyologists and Herpetologists—Herpetologists League—Cooper Ornithol Club—Sigma Xi. Museum of Vertebrate Zoology, University of California, Berkeley.†

21 STECKLER, Robert. Synthetic resins; Polymers; Coatings. b'14. BS '33—PhD '38 (U Vienna Austria). Research on chemistry of phenolic coatings, polymerization of chlorinated hydrocarbons and vinyl, resinous and synthetic resin adhesives, synthesis of alkyl phenols, cold solder, chemical resistant and non-corrosive protective coatings, esters and polyesters, drying oils, alkylation of phenol, polymerization in solution, and resinous plasticizers; study of resins, including alkyd, coating, phenolic, plasticizing, synthetic, tall oil, varnish, vinyl, and water soluble. Holds patents on resins and plastics. Author articles: The New Plastics '47; Progress in New Materials '47, and others. Research mgr resins and plastics div Arco Co Cleveland '38-45; mgr R Steckler Labs Cleve since '45. Assn Cons Chem and Chem Engrs—ACS—AAAS—Soc Plastics Engineers. 8200 Harvard Av., Cleve.

22 STEDMAN, Alfred Delos. American agriculture (Economics, politics, sociology, federal and state programs, organizations, cooperatives). b'91. BA '19—hon LLD '40 (Hamline U). Author articles in field. Asso editor, agr editor St Paul Pioneer Press and Dispatch since '45. Am Acad Polit and Social Sci—Am Polit Sci Assn—Am Farm Econ Assn. 55 E. 4th St., St. Paul 1.

23 STEEFEL, Lawrence D. Bismarck; Danish history. b'94. AB—MA '17—PhD '23 (Harvard). Author: The Schleswig-Holstein Question '32; also articles in field. Instr U Minn '23-25, asst prof '25-32, asso prof '32-41, prof since '41. AHA—Royal Hist Soc(F)—Phi Beta Kappa. Toppan prize in hist Harvard '23; Guggenheim fellow '29-30. University of Minnesota, Minneapolis 14.

24 STEEL, Ernest William. Water (Clarification, distribution, cities; filtration); Sewage (Collection, cities; disposal, treatment); Irrigation (Sewage); Streams (Self-purification). b'93. Student '19 (U Sheffield); CE '20 (Cornell U); '35 (U Mich). Developed new filter for use in sewage filtration, digestion of sewage sludge, research on treatment of dairy and laundry wastes, water treatment by means of dolomitic limestone, design of water treatment plants for Venezuela. Author: Water Supply and Sewerage (2nd edit) '47; Municipal Affairs (2nd edit) '50. Co-author: Municipal and Rural Sanitation (4th edit) '50; Hygiene of Community, School and Home '36. Associate editor: General Engineering Handbook '40; Manual for Water Works

Operators '51. Sanitation engr Rockefeller Found '22-23; san engr Texas State Health Dept '23-25; prof mun and san engring and dir san engring research lab Tex A&M Coll '25-42; cons Govt Venezuela '46-49; prof sanitation engring U Tex since '50. Am Pub Health Assn(F)—Am Soc CE—Am Water Works Assn—Fedn Sewage Wks Assn. Received Fuertes Medal Cornell U '28. Dept of Civil Engring, University of Texas, Austin 12.

10 STEELE, Francis Rue. Babylonian archeology and history. b'15. AB '37 (Cornell U); MA '39—PhD '42 (U Pa). Discovered the Lipit-Ishtar Law Code which dates to about 1860 BC. Author: Nuzi Real Estate Transactions '43; The Code of Lipit-Ishtar '49. Research asst U Museum U Pa '42-47; asst curator Babylonian sect since '47, asst prof assyriol since '48. Am Oriental Soc—Am Sch Oriental Research—Archeol Inst Am—AAAS—Phila Anthropol Soc. University Museum, 33rd and Spruce St., Phila.†

11 STEELE, Frank J. Pharmaceuticals (Hospital). b'05. PhG '30 (Pitts Coll Pharm); PhD '51 (Stanford). Research and development cosmetics; pharmaceutical consultant. Author articles: Pharmacy Department '51; Apprenticeship Training '52. Co-editor: Chemical Formulary (vol 9). Resident pharm Western Pa Hosp Pittsburgh '28-39; hosp pharm Johns Hopkins Hosp Baltimore '41-45; chief pharm Greenwich Hosp Assn since '45. ACS —Am Inst Chem—Am Oil Chem Soc—Am Soc Hosp Pharm—Conn Soc Hosp Pharm (pres '48-49)—Soc Cosmetic Chem—AAAS(F)—Am Coll Apothecaries—Brit Chem Soc—Am Pharm Assn —Assn Cons Chem and Chem Engrs. Greenwich Hospital Assn, Greenwich, Conn.

12 STEELE, James Harlan. Public health (Control of animal diseases transmissible to man through animal food products). b'13. DVM '41 (Mich State Coll); Master Pub Health '42 (Harvard). Author articles in field. Veterinarian since '41; pub health vet O Dept Health '42-43; successively lt, capt, maj USPHS '43-46, chief vet pub health sect State Relations Div Washington '46-47, Communicable Disease Center Atlanta since '47; vet cons Pan Am San Bur. Am Veterinary Med Assn—Am Pub Health Assn—AAAS—US Livestock San Assn—NY Acad Sci —US-Mexico Border Pub Health Assn —Nat Brucellosis Com—Nat Trichinosis Com—Pan Am Veterinary Assn. United States Public Health Service, Atlanta.

13 STEELE, John Gordon. Soil science applied in soil conservation; Land-capability classification. b'05. BS '27 (Pa State Coll); PhD '34 (O State U). Research on physical properties of soils, size distribution in clay fraction, retention of phosphate by colloidal clay; took part in reconnaissance erosion survey '34; active in development of land-capability classification. Author articles in field. Soil scientist Soil Conservation Service US Dept Agr since '34, head survey analysis sect soil conservation surveys div since '36; instr soil conservation US Dept Agr Grad Sch since '42. Soil Conservation Soc Am—Am Soc Agron—Soil Sci Soc Am—AAAS—Am Geog Soc—Gamma Sigma Delta—Sigma Xi. Soil Conservation Service, Washington 25.

14 STEELE, Oliver Leon. Corn breeding and genetics; Plant physiology. b'15. Student '34 (Ill State Normal U); BS '40 (Ill Wesleyan U); '42-45 (U Ill). Research and development corn inbred lines and their combination in commercially useful corn hybrids, corn breeding and selection for resistance to disease, insects, drought, etc., placement of hybrids in US. Research asst Michael-Leonard Seed Co '36-40; mgr research dept Funk Bros Seed Co since '40. AAAS—Am Assn Agron—Genetic Soc Am—Am Genetics Assn. Funk Bros Seed Co., 1300 W. Washington St., Bloomington, Ill.

15 STEEN, Jerome Reed. Industrial quality control; Electron tubes. b'01. BS '23 (U Wis). Author articles in field. Dir quality control Sylvania Electronic Products Inc since '46. Am Soc Quality Control(F)—Inst Radio Engr—AIEE—Illuminating Engr Soc—Am Statis Assn—Inst Math Statis. Sylvania Electric Products, Inc., 1740 Broadway, NYC 19.

16 STEEN, Ralph Wright. History of Texas, Texas politics in the twentieth century. b'05. BA '27 (McMurry Coll Abilene Tex); MA '29—PhD '34 (U Tex). Author: History of Texas '39; Texas, a Story of Progress '42; Twentieth Century Texas '42; The Texas Story '48; Our Texas (with Frances Donecker) '48; Texas Government, '53. Prof hist McMurry Coll Abilene Texas '29-30; teaching fellow U Tex '30-31; prof history Hillsboro Tex Junior Coll '34-35; asst prof hist Texas A&M Coll '35-37, prof since '43. Texas State Hist Assn (F, executive council)—So Hist Assn—AHA. Texas A&M College, College Station, Tex.

17 STEERE, William Campbell. Bryology; Cytology. b'07. BS '29—AM '31 —PhD '32 (U Mich); '29-31 (U Pa). Botanist University of Michigan and Carnegie Institution expedition to Yucatan '32, United States Cinchona Mission to Colombia '42-43, assistant director United States Chinchona Mission to Ecuador '43-44, leader University of Michigan expedition to Great Bear Lake NWT '48. Author: Liverworts of Southern Michigan '40. Co-author: Lab Outline for Elementary Botany '37; also articles in field. Instr to prof botany U Mich since '31, chmn dept '47-50, curator bryophytes since '45; professor Stanford Univ since '50; editor-in-chief The Bryologist since '38. AAAS(F)—Am Geog Soc—Am Fern Soc—Am Soc Plant Taxonomists —Bot Soc Am—Brit Bryol Soc—Instituto Ecuatoriano de Ciencias Naturales —Mich Acad Sci (editor '38-42)—Am Bryol Soc—Am Soc Naturalists—Soc Study Evolution—Arctice Inst NA—Phi Kappa Phi—Sigma Xi. Department of Biological Sciences, Stanford University, Stanford, Cal.

18 STEFANSSON, Vilhjalmur. Arctic and sub-Arctic; Cold weather problems and techniques; History of geographic discovery. b'79. AB '03—LLD '22 (U Ia); LLD '21 (U Mich); AM '23 (Harvard); PhD '30 (U Iceland); LHD '45 (Fla Southern Coll). Adviser on northern operations Pan-American '32-45; possesses largest library on the Arctic, made up of 19,000 books and 18,000 pamphlets; ed Encyclopedia Arctica sponsored by Office Naval Research US Navy '46. Author: Life with Eskimo '13; Anthropological Papers '14; Friendly Arctic '21; The Northward Course of Empire '22; Hunters of the Great North '22; The Standardization of Error '27; Unsolved Mysteries of the Arctic '38; Three Voyages of Martin Frobisher '38; Iceland: The First American Republic '39; Arctic Manual '41; Greenland '42; Not By Bread Alone '46. Archeol expdn Iceland under auspices Peabody Museum of Harvard U '05; ethnol expdn to Eskimo of Mackenzie delta under auspices Harvard U and Toronto U '06-07, second expdn '08-12 (53 mos) under auspices Am Mus Natural History NY and govt Can; comdr Canadian Arctic Expdn '13-18 exploring land and seas in Canadian and Alaskan sectors of Arctic region. Hist of Sci Soc (past pres)—Assn Am Geog (past vp). 27 W. 44th St., NYC.⊚

19 STEIN, Arthur. Sampling inspection plans; Aircraft vulnerability. b'18. BS '38 (Coll City NY); AM '41 (Columbia U); '46 (Johns Hopkins U). Studies on most efficient plans for double sampling inspection, and on theory of sampling inspection for both standard and unusual problems in testing manufactured products. Chief aircraft vulnerability sect Ballistics Research Labs Aberdeen Proving Ground '46, ballistician since '46. Am Inst Math Statis—Am Statis Soc—Am Soc Quality Control—Am Math Soc—Phi Beta Kappa. Ballistic Research Laboratories, Aberdeen Proving Ground, Md.†

20 STEIN, Calvert. Child guidance; Wills (Mental capacity to make); Mental hygiene; Submarine personnel selection. b'03. Cert '24 (Tufts Coll); MD '28—LLB '38 (Northeastern U); '48 (Neurological Inst NY). Set up neuropsychiatric standards for selection of submarine personnel World War II. Author: Nothing to Sneeze At '49; also articles in field. Sr phys Monson State Hosp '31-38; pvt practice psychiatry neurology Springfield Mass since '38; neuropsychiatrist Springfield Hosp since '36, chief neuropsychiatry in out-patient dept; lecturer neurology and psychol Springfield Coll '38-39 and since '48; lt comdr. and comdr Med Corps USNR '41-46. Am Bd Psychiatry and Neurology (diplomate '36)—Nat Bd Med Examiners (diplomate '29)—Am Psychiat Assn(F)—Mass and NE Psychiat Socs. Awarded first prize NE Psychiat Assn for research '36. 175 State St., Springfield 2, Mass.

21 STEIN, Elizabeth P. William Shakespeare; David Garrick. AB '16 (Hunter Coll); AM '17 (Columbia U); PhD '21 (NYU). Discovered Garrick's 1751 manuscript diary, his Hamlet, the Manuscript Diaries of the Drury Lane Theatre, and three unpublished Garrick plays; assisted Samuel A Tannenbaum in compilation of Elizabethan Bibliographies '35-38. Author: Three Plays by David Garrick '26; David Garrick, Dramatist '38; also articles in field. Now assoc prof Eng Hunter Coll. Modern Lang Assn Am—Shakespeare Assn Am—AAUP—Phi Beta Kappa—Sigma Tau Delta. Hunter College, 695 Park Av., NYC 19.

22 STEIN, Hilda Anna. Animal ecology (Cypress swamps). b'95. BE '25 (S Ill Normal U); MS '29 (U Ill). Research on animal communities of cypress swamps. Nature study supervisor S Ill Normal U '25-28; asso prof zool S Ill U since '30. Ill Acad Sci—AAAS—Nature Conservancy (Soc mem chmn)—Sigma Delta Epsilon— Sigma Xi—Am Assn U Women (past pres Ill div)—Delta Sigma Epsilon (Shield ed '34-36, first vp since '36). Southern Illinois University, Carbondale, Ill.

23 STEIN, Jack M(adison). Richard Wagner; Musical-literary relations. b'14. MA '36 (Rutgers U); PhD '44 (Northwestern U). Word-tone relationship in the theory and works of Wagner. Author articles in field. Editor: Germanic Review. Asst prof German Columbia since '48. Modern Lang Assn—Am Assn Teachers German. 412 Hamilton Hall, Columbia University, NYC 27.†

10 STEINBACH, Leslie Irving. Acoustics; Sound. b'08. AB '29—AM '30—PhD '32 (Indiana U). Research on sound-signalling devices, especially horns, sirens, whistles, on acoustical plastering and acoustical absorbing materials in building industry, on electric measuring instruments including telegon motors, actual and simulated aircraft instruments. Author: Siren as a Sound Signalling Device '31; Effective Acoustical Treatments '34; also articles in field. Dir tech and engring dept Chicago Apparatus Co '36-40; chief engr Sparks Withington Co Jackson Mich '41-43, plant mgr '43-44, mgr automotive div and dir research '45-47; vp Litchfield Co Waterloo Ia '42-49; vp Gen Implement Corp '46-49; vp Mechanics Engring Corp since '50. AAAS—Ind Acad Sci (past pres, past chmn physics section)—Am Chem Soc —Engr Soc Detroit—Am Phys Soc—Phi Beta Kappa—Sigma Xi—Am Soc Testing Materials—SAE—ASME, and others. 292 W. Pearl St., Jackson, Mich.

11 STEINBAUER, C(larence) E(mil). Sweet potato (Physiology, culture, improvement). b'05. BS '30—MS '31 (U Minn); PhD '36 (U Md). Author articles in field. Plant physiologist since '44. Am Soc Hort Sci—Am Soc Plant Physiol—Gamma Sigma Delta. North Wing Administration Building, Plant Industry Station, Beltsville, Md.†

12 STEINBAUER, G(eorge) P(eter). Seed germination, dormancy and testing; Weed control; Plant growth. b'03. BS '25—MS '27—PhD '29 (U Minn). Author articles in field. Asso prof bot Mich State Coll since '47. Am Soc Plant Physiol—Bot Soc Am—AAAS(F)—Assn Official Seed Analysts NA (chmn research com '41-44, com standardization of methods of seed testing '44-45, vp '45, pres '46)—Sigma Xi—Phi Kappa Phi. Botany Department, Michigan State College, East Lansing, Mich.†

13 STEINBERG, Gunther Theodore. Business statistics and economics; Economic forecasting. b'12. BA '36 (Ia State Teach Coll); MBA '38—'38-41 (U Chicago). Study wage theory and practice; proby theory and sampling plans; business cycles; financial and actuarial mathematics. Statistician Hawthorne Works West Electric Co Chicago '41-45; economist West Electric Co Hdqrs NYC since '45. Am Econ Assn—Econometric Soc—Am Statis Assn—Inst Math Statis. 195 Broadway, NYC 7.

14 STEINBERG, John Christian. Acoustics; Sound; Speech; Music; Hearing; Transmission. b'95. BS '16—MS '17 (Coe Coll Cedar Rapids Ia); PhD '22 (U Ia). Research on physical characteristics of speech and hearing; requirements for transmission and reproduction of speech and music; portrayal of sound in visible form. Author articles in field. Research physicist Bell Telephone Laboratories NYC since '22. Acoustical Soc Am(F) (exec council '36-39, vp '44-46, pres '47-49, rep div sci Nat Research Council '46-49)—Am Phys Soc(F)—AAAS(F)—Am Assn to Promote the Teaching of Speech to the Deaf (bd of dirs since '46)—Nat Research Council (sub-com Con on Problems of Deafness since '40)—Am Soc for Hard of Hearing—Sigma Xi. Bell Telephone Laboratories, Murray Hill, N.J.

15 STEINBERG, Robert Aaron. Plant nutrition and metabolism; Physiology of tobacco plant; Nutrition of fungi. b'90. BS '14 (George Washington U); PhD '19 (Columbia). Microbiological Congress NYC '39; symposium on trace element of plants '45, on mineral nutrition of plants '49; research on mineral and organic nutrition of tobacco in aseptic culture, growth effects of synthetic hormones, frenching of tobacco. Author articles in field. Now plant physiol US Dept Agr. AAAS(F)—Am Soc Plant Physiol—Bot Soc Am—Torrey Bot Club—Bot Soc Washington—Sigma Xi. Plant Industry Station, U.S. Department of Agriculture, Beltsville, Md.†

16 STEINER, Mrs. Lee R. Psychology (Personal problems); Mental hygiene. b'01. BA '24 (U Minn); MSS '29 (Smith Coll). Research in the adaptation of psychotherapy to the problems of everyday living. Author: Where Do People Take Their Troubles '45; also articles in field. Commonwealth fellow Smith Coll '28-29; psychiatric social worker and supervisor Inst Juvenile Research Chicago Ill '29-33; spl lecturer Ill Soc Mental Hygiene '33-34; cons in personal problems since '33; lecturer Fordham U, Rutgers U, Atlanta U, Coll William and Mary; lecturer in psychol Hunter Coll since '44. Am Assn Orthopsychiatry(F)—Am Group Therapy Assn—Am Psychol Assn—Soc for the Psychol Study of Social Issues. 114 W. 61st St., NYC.

17 STEINER, Loren Franklin. Insect control. b'04. BSc '26—MS '27 (O State U). Development insecticide treatments effective in control of oriental fruit fly; improvement of techniques for tests of insecticides and lures; investigation control, biology and behavior of fruit pests, especially codling moth, and their natural enemies; studies adverse effect of DDT on beneficial insects leading to outbreaks of pests, including mites, red-banded leaf roller, and scale on apples and peaches; research on effective lures for oriental fruit moth. Sr author: articles: Laboratory and Field Tests of DDT for Control of Codling Moth '44; Tests with Various Insecticides for the Control of Codling Moth, Red-banded Leaf Roller, Orchard Mites and Scale '48; Insecticides for Control of the Oriental Fruit Fly in Hawaii '51, and others. With Bur Entomol and Plant Quarantine USDA since '30, sr entomol since '43, project leader in charge chem control research oriental fruit fly Hawaii since '49. Am Assn Econ Entomol—Entomol Soc Am—Sigma Xi—Hawaiian Entomol Soc. US Department of Agriculture Fruit Fly Laboratory, P.O. Box 2280, Honolulu, Hawaii. H: 1569 St. Louis Drive.

18 STEINHAUS, Edward A(rthur). Insect pathology and microbiology. b'14. BS '36 (ND Agr Coll); PhD '39 —Muellhaupt fellow '39-40 (O State U). Author: Insect Microbiology; Principles of Insect Pathology; also articles in field. Asso prof insect pathol U Calif since '48. AAAS—Am Assn Econ Entomol—Am Soc Parasitology—Am Soc Protozool—Entomol Soc Am—Pacific Coast Entomol Soc—Soc Gen Microbiol-Soc Study Evolution—Sigma Xi. Laboratory of Insect Pathology, College of Agriculture, University of California, Berkeley 4.†

19 STEINITZ, Kate Trauman. Literature of art; Modern art; Painting; Leonardo da Vinci and the Renaissance. b'92. Student (Berlin, Paris, other schools). Author: Leonardo da Vinci's Manuscripts '48; also articles in field. Librarian Elmer Belt Library of Vinciana since '45. Spl Libraries Assn—Mus Mod Art NY—Mod Inst Art—Am Soc Aethetics—Archeol Inst So Calif. The Elmer Belt Library of Vinciana, 1893 Wilshire Boulevard, Los Angeles 5.

20 STEINLE, J(ohn) Vernon. Wax chemistry and technology. b'98. BS '20—MS '21—PhD '24 (U Wis). Holder patents in field. Asso prof chem Marquette U '24-25; research chem S C Johnson & Son Inc '25-33; research and development dir since '33. Am Chem Soc—AAAS—Am Inst Chem—Am Oil Chemists Soc—Am Soc for Testing Materials—Nat Farm Chemurgic Council—Soc Chem Industry—Chem Circle. S. C. Johnson & Son, Inc., Racine, Wis.

21 STEINMAN, David Barnard. Bridge design. b'86. BS summa cum laude '06—ScD hon '47 (Coll City of NY); CE '09—AM '09, PhD '11 (Columbia). Inventor new influence line meths and charts for design of railway bridges; improvements in suspension bridge design; new system of design loading for railway bridges; simplified methods of analysis for bridge design; aerodynamic analysis of suspension bridges. Author: Suspension Bridges, Their Design, Construction and Erection '23 '29; Suspension Bridges and Cantilevers, Their Economic Proportions and Limiting Spans '11 '12; Theory of Arches and Suspension Bridges, from Melan, '13; Concrete Arches, Plain and Reinforced, from Melan '17; Continuous Bridges, in Movable and Long-Span Steel Bridges '23; A Generalized Deflection Theory for Suspension Bridges '34; Rigidity and Aerodynamic Stability of Suspension Bridges '43; Aerodynamic Theory of Bridge Oscillations '49, others. Spl asst to Gustav Lindenthal on design and constrn Hell Gate Arch Bridge and other notable bridges '14-17; prof in charge civil and mech engring Coll City of NY '17-20; cons practice since 1920; designer or cons notable bridges including suspension bridge Florianopolis Brazil, Carquinez Strait Bridge Cal, St John's Bridge Portland Ore, Mt Hope RI Bridge, Triborough Br NYC, others; vp Tioga-Nichols Bridge Co., Smithboro Bridge Co; dir Independence Bridge Co, Interboro Br Co, Richmond-Hopewell Bridge Co.; pres Pan—Am Pub Works Inc. Aerial League Am(F)—AAAS(F)—Am Geog Soc(F)—Royal Soc Am(F)—Am Soc CE (pres '46-47; James R. Croes medal '19, Norman medal '23, Thomas Fitch Rowland prize '29)—Assn Alumni Coll City NY (Townsend Harris medal '34)—Internat Assn Bridge and Structural Engrs—Am Assn Engrs(pres '25-26)—Nat Soc Profl Engrs (founder, pres '34-36)—NY State Soc Profl Engineers(pres '30-33, chmn bd '33-34 '48-49)—Nat Council State Bds Engineering Examiners (pres '31-32)—Am Engring Council(com on bridge legislation '30-34)—Am Ry Engring Assn—Am Soc Testing Materials—Am Concrete Inst—Am Mil Engrs—Society Engring Edn—Engring Inst Can—Phi Beta Kappa, others. Artistic bridge awards Am Inst Steel Constrn '30, '32, '37, '38, '39; Columbia medal for Excellence '47; Eggleston medal '50; silver scroll, for contbns to advancement of engring by 11 engring socs '32. 117 Liberty St., NYC.©

22 STEINSCHNEIDER, William. Agricultural sprays (Insecticides, fungicides); Synthetic resins; Rayon. b'89. Chemist '10 (Columbia U). Research on processes for tannic acid, gallic acid, gallocyanine, hydroquinone, quinizarine dyes, agricultural spray materials, synthetic resins, rayon production, insecticides, fungicides. Research chemist Zinsser & Co Inc Hastings-on-Hudson NY '10-25, vp and gen mgr '28-34; asst to pres Am Aniline Products Inc '34-50; vp Ansbacher-Siegle Corp '34-44; pres '44-50, exec vp '50-53; pres Sterling Chem & Ore Corp '49-52; pres Lotte Chem Corp since '52. Am Chem Soc—Chemists Club NY. 109 5th Av., Paterson, N.J. H: 49 Washington Av., Hastings-on-Hudson 6, N.Y.

10 STELLWAGEN, John Hibbard. Desmarests de Saint-Sorlin; French syntax; French court drama (Seventeenth century); Pictorial photography. b'10. BA cum laude '28 (U Minn); MA '34 (Harvard); PhD '41 (U Chicago). Author: The Drama of Jean Desmarests, Sieur De Saint-Sorlin 1636-1643 '44; also articles in field. Prof modern langs Mo Valley Coll since '44, chmn div lang and lit since '48. Phi Beta Kappa. Missouri Valley College, Marshall, Mo.

11 STEMEN, Thomas R(ay). Pollen collector; Hay fever plants. b'92. BA '14 (Huntington Coll); MA '22—grad work (Okla U). Began collecting pollen as a hobby '21; made hayfever plant survey of Oklahoma '26-27; prepared charts showing the distribution in the US of all the plants known to cause hayfever '40-48. Co-author: Spring Flora of Oklahoma '29; Oklahoma Flora '37; also articles in field. Dir sr high sch sci Oklahoma City '37-45. Okla Acad Sci—Am Soc Plant Taxonomists —Am Coll Allergists (asso F). 1205 N. E. 18th St., Oklahoma City 5, Okla.

12 STEMPEL, Guido Hermann. Comparative philology; Indo-European phonology; History of English language; Grammar; Word study. b'68. AB '89 (U Ia); AM '94 (U Wis); '11 (Ind U); '95-97 (U Leipzig). Author: (with Myrtle Stempel) Latin in English '40. Editor: A Book of Ballads Old and New '17. Consulting editor: General Language (Bugbee et al) '37; also articles in field. With Ind U '04-38, head dept '06-38, prof '22-38, emeritus since '38. Modern Lang Assn Am—Linguistic Soc Am—Phi Beta Kappa. 723 S. Park Av., Bloomington, Ind.†◉

13 STEPHENS, Elgood Edward. Tax (Income and excess profits, legal aspects). b'07. Student '28-29 (U Wash); BS '33 (U Cal); LLB '38 (George Washington U); LLM '46 (Georgetown U). Dir Tax Practice Inst Wash since '48, lectr fed income tax law and procedure since '48; prof lect fed taxation and fed tax problems George Washington U since '49; law practice spec fed taxation Wash. Am Bar Assn—Fed Bar Assn—Bar Assn DC. Munsey Building, Washington 4.

14 STEPHENS, Harry Newburn. Organic chemistry (Adhesives, oxidation mechanisms). b'97. BA '20 (McMaster U); MA '21 (U Toronto); PhD '23 (McGill U). Holder patents on water-dispersed adhesives. Author articles in field. Dir research Minn Mining and Mfg Co '37-53 vp since '53. Am Chem Soc—AAAS(F)—Sigma Xi. 900 Fauquier Av., St. Paul 6.

15 STEPHENS, Stephen DeWitt. American engraving (Mavericks). b'94. AB '16—AM '20 (U Wis); EdM '26—EdD '27 (Harvard). Author: The Mavericks, American Engravers '50; also articles in field. Instr Milwaukee br U Wis '22-25, prof Eng since '27; dir div humanities since '36 Newark colls of Rutgers U and predecessor instns. Nat Council Teachers Eng—Modern Lang Assn. 40 Rector St., Newark 2, N.J.†

16 STEPHENSON, Morton B(ayard). Taxonomy of Ostracoda and Foraminifera; Paleontology and stratigraphy of Gulf Coastal Plain of United States. b'04. BS '28—MS '29 (U Mich); Teaching credential '33 (U Calif); student (La State U). Author articles in field. Paleontol Stanolind Oil and Gas Co Houston since '40. Geol Soc Am(F)— Am Assn Petroleum Geol—Soc Econ Paleontol Mineral—Paleontol Soc(F). Stanolind Oil and Gas Co., Box 3092, Houston 1, Tex.

17 STEPHENSON, Wendell Holmes. History of Southern United States; American biography. b'99. AB '23— AM '24 (Indiana U); Carl Braun fellowship '26-27—PhD '28 (U Mich). Managing editor Journal Southern History '34-41, Miss Valley Historical Review since '46. Author: The Political Career of General James H Lane '30; Alexander Porter, Whig Planter of Old Louisiana '34; Isaac Franklin, Slave Trade and Planter of the Old South '38. Editor (with E Merton Coulter): A History of the South (10 vol) since '38; (with Fred C Cole) So Biography Series (9 vol) '39-46; also articles in field. Dean Coll Arts Sci '41-44 (leave of absence with research grant from Genl Ed Bd '44-45) La State U; prof So hist chmn Div Social Sci Tulane U '46-53; prof history Univ Oregon since '53. AHA—So Hist Assn (pres '44)—Agrl Hist Soc (pres '40-41)— Miss Valley Hist Assn (exec com '41-44, since '46)—La Hist Soc—Kan State Hist Soc (hon)—Phi Beta Kappa—Phi Kappa Phi. University of Oregon, Eugene, Oregon.

18 STEPHENSON, Wiley Aubrey. Political parties. b'00. AB '23 (Hardin-Simmons U); AM '27 (George Washington U); fellow '30-31 (U Tex); '24 (U Calif). Author articles in field. Asst prof hist Hardin-Simmons U '25, asso prof govt '30, prof govt since '48, debate coach since '25, asst dean since '40. Am Polit Sci Assn—Am Acad Polit Social Sci—Am Fgn Policy Assn —Southwestern Social Sci Assn—So Polit Sci Assn—West Tex Hist Assn— Pi Kappa Delta—Pi Sigma Alpha—Pi Gamma Mu—Alpha Chi. Hardin-Simmons University, Abilene, Tex.

19 STERN, E. George. Nails and other wood fasteners; Wood construction. b'12. Diplom Ingenieur '36 (Technische Hochschule Munich Germany); MS '38—PhD '41 (Pa State Coll). Research on wood, its fasteners, and wood structures from the small wood heels, ammunition boxes, staircases, house frames, roof trusses, to highway bridges; research covered nails and nailed joints, including nailed box columns and trusses rafters; improvements in threaded-shank nails, including new-types of nails. Author about 125 articles in field. Research asst engring research (wood research) Pa State Coll '36; research engr Va Poly Inst '41-46, Asso prof '46-48, prof wood constrn since '48; indsl cons, registered architect. Am Soc CE—AS ME—AIA—ASTM—Forest Products Research Soc—Wood Preservers Assn —AAAS—Va Acad Sci—Sigma Xi. Awarded 2 prizes in Timber Bridge Design Contest '39. Va. Poly. Inst., Blacksburg, Va.

20 STERN, Elizabeth Gertrude (Eleanor Morton). Race Relations (US); Vocational Education; American Retail Trade (History). b'90. BA '10— hon MA '19 (U Pittsburgh); student '11 (NY Sch Social Work). Adviser, programs and literature to social service, civic, educational agencies and organizations. Author books, articles social and vocational topics. Research on romance and history of retail trade '47 and '49; mem adv bd (negro homes) US Housing Authority Phila since '42; mem State Citizens Com to Study Negro and the Law since '42. Pa Hist Soc—Delaware Co Nat Youth Assn. Add: 311 S. 13th St., Phila.

21 STERN, John Kenneth. Farmer cooperatives. b'05. MS '29 (Pa State Coll). Research in business practices of farmers local cooperative purchasing associations; membership problems in milk marketing and purchasing associations. Author articles: Inventory of farmer cooperatives in Pa; Inventory of rural electric cooperatives in Pa, and others. Field rep Eastern States Farmers Exchange '31-43; prof research on farmer cooperatives Pa State Coll '43-48; con coll and coop relationships Am Inst Coop '48-50, pres since '50. Am Farm Econ Assn—Nat Soc Accountants for Coops—Am Marketing Assn—Internat Conf Agrl Econ. 744 Jackson Place, N.W., Washington.

22 STERN, Leon Thomas. Penology (Delinquency, crime prevention, probation, parole, prisons, jails, juvenile detention). b'87. Grad '08 (Pa Sch Social Work); '11 (NY Sch Social Work); '16-18 (Temple U Law Sch); AB '23— grad study (U Pa). Regional director US Attorney General's Survey of Release Procedures '36-37; consultant Prison Industries Reorganization Administration '37-38; member joint committee American Friends Service and Women's International League since '42; director study health, correctional, and welfare service in Pennsylvania '44; survey of youthful offenders Baltimore and Maryland '46; member prison committee American Friends Service since '43, and others. Author: Case Work Enters the Prison '33; Social Services in County Jails '36; The Offender '38; The Effect of the Depression on Prison Commitments and Sentences '41; Parole in Pennsylvania '42; Youth in the Delinquent Community '44; Jails: Ysesterday and Today '45; In the Shadow of the Jail '46, and others. Sec research and field studies Pa Com Penal Affairs since '25. Nat Probation Assn—Am Prison Congress (com on jails and com on case work since '34)—Am Assn Social Workers— Am Ethical Union (chmn pub affairs com since '39, eastern vp '43-46)—Pub Service Inst Pa (correctional training com '45, bd '47)—Nat Jail Assn (treas since '39)—Am Acad Polit Social Sci. 311 S. Juniper St., Phila. 7◉

23 STEUART, Richard Dennis. Confederate Army (Weapons, uniforms). b'81. Arms curator Maryland Academy of Sciences. Co-author: (with Claud E Fuller) Firearms of the Confederacy, also articles in field. Md Hist Soc— Va Hist Soc—Am Soc Sword Collectors—Nat Rifle Assn—Nat Muzzle Loaders Assn. The Baltimore News-Post, Balt.

24 STEVENS, Kenneth Porter. Biological physiology (Tissue culture); Bioluminescence. b'93. AB '18—AM '20 (Wesleyan U); PhD '27—Francis Hinton Maule fellow '21-23 (Princeton); '19-20 (Yale). Author articles in field. Prof biol, head dept Washington & Lee U since '46. AAAS(F)—Va Acad Sci. Department of Biology, Washington & Lee University, Lexington, Va.†

25 STEVENS, Raymond. Product development; process development. born 1894. Bachelor of Science '17 (MIT). Editor: Research—A National Resource: II Industrial Research '39-40. With Arthur D Little Inc Cambridge Mass since '20, vp since '34, dir since '45; dir Survey of Research in Industry; asso with Nat Research Council, chmn com on war use of research facilities '42-43, mem exec com Div Engring and Industrial Research '42-45; mem com on QM Research Problems; occupational adviser Mass State Hdqrs for Selective Service '41. Am Inst Chem Engrs—Inst Food Technol—Am Chem Soc (chmn NE sect '32-33)—So Chem Industry. 30 Memorial Dr., Cambridge, Mass.

26 STEVENS, Rollin E(lbert). Minerals (Chemical analysis, chemical composition, alkalinity); Geochemical prospecting. b'05. BA '27 (U SD); MS

'31 (George Washington U). Developed methods for determining beryllium, iron, fluorine, alkalies and rare alkalies, chemical composition of minerals such as chromite, lepidolite and other micas, helvite-danalite-genthelvite series of minerals; developed analytical methods and testing of rocks, soils, plants and water for geochemical prospecting; invented extractor, co-inventor chromagraph. Analytical chem Dow Chem Co '27-28; organic chem Nat Bur Standards '28-31; with US Geol Survey since '31, chief chem investigations unit from '47. ACS—Mineral Soc Am—Mineral Soc Great Brit and Ireland—Wash Acad Sci—Alpha Chi Sigma. Geological Survey, US Department of Interior, Washington 25.

10 STEVENS, Sylvester K(irby). Pa (History). b'04. AB '26—MA '27 (Pa State Coll); PhD '45 (Col). Author: American Expansion in Hawaii 1842-1898, '45; Pennsylvania—Titan of Industry, '48. Editor: (with Donald H Kent) Papers of Colonel Henry Bouquet '51; Travels in New Frances by J C B (with Kent) '42; Wilderness Chronicles of Northwestern Pa (with Kent) '41. Business manager American Heritage since '50. Asst prof history Pa State Coll '26-37; state historian Commonwealth of Pa since '37. Pa Hist Assn—Pa Fedn Hist Socs—Am Assn State and Local History—Theta Chi—Pi Gamma Mu. State Museum Bldg., Harrisburg, Pa. †◎

11 STEVENSON, Elaine Louise. Weaving; Handicraft (Materials). BAE '29 (Chicago Art Inst); MA '36 (O State U); '45 (Cranbrook Acad Art). Research on modern original weaves, materials to use for weaving, weaving equipment including types of looms. With W Mich Coll Edn since '17. Weavers Guild SW Mich—Kalamazoo Valley Weavers Guild. Western Michigan Coll of Education, Kalamazoo 45, Mich.

12 STEVENSON, Frederick James. Genetics and plant breeding. b'86. BS '22—MS '25—PhD '29 (Wash State Coll). Research on rye-wheat hybrids, bunt in rye, correlated characters in wheat and oat breeding, breeding of potatoes. Author articles in field. Geneticist US Dept Agr since '30, prin geneticist since '45. AAAS—Washington Acad Sci—Am Genetic Assn—Am Phytopath Soc—Potato Assn Am. Division of Vegetable Crops and diseases, Plant Industry Station, Beltsville, Md.

13 STEVENSON, Henry Miller. Ornithology (Quantitative distribution and migration, birds of the southeastern states). b'14. BA '35 (Birmingham-So Coll); MS '39 (U Ala); PhD '43 (Cornell U); '40-41 (Vanderbilt U). Asst prof zool Fla State U '46, now associate professor Am Ornithology Union (asso)—Wilson Ornithol Club—Nat Audubon Soc—Tenn Ornithol Soc—Ga Ornithol Soc—Florida Audubon Society. Department of Zoology, Fla. State University, Tallahassee, Fla.†

14 STEVENSON, John A(lbert). Mycology. b'90. BS '12—grad sch '13 (U Minn); '23-25 (George Washington U). Author: Foreign Plant Diseases '18; also articles in field. Bot Bur Plant Industry since '25, principal mycol, head div mycol and disease survey since '45; hon curator fungi Smithsonian Inst. Mycol Soc Am (bd ed '33-44, councilor '45, vp '46, pres '47, councilor '48-49)—Am Phytopath Soc—AAAS(F)—Washington Acad Sci (jour ed '33-35)—Bot Soc Washington (archivist since '39)—British Mycol Soc—Societe Mycol de France—Sigma Xi. Plant Industry Station, Beltsville, Md.†◎

15 STEWARD, Julian H. Anthropological theory; Indian anthropology; Acculturation of contemporary socs. b'02. AB '25 (Cornell); MA '26—PhD '29 (U Calif). Editor: Handbook of South American Indians (6 vol) '46, '48. Asst prof anthrop U Utah '30-33; lecturer U Calif '34; anthrop Bur Am Ethnol '35-42; dir Inst Social Anthrop Smithsonian Inst '42-46; prof anthrop Columbia U '46-52; graduate rsrch professor anthropology Univ Ill since '52. AAAS—Am Anthrop Soc—Soc Am Archeol—Soc Applied Anthrop—Inter-Am Soc Anthrop and Geog—Am Sociol Soc. Department of Sociology and Anthropology, University of Illinois, Urbana, Ill.

16 STEWART, Cyril Henry Emerson. Uranium resources; Mine evaluation; Peat moss production. b'96. BA Sc '23 (U Toronto). Head office cons staff Anglo-Huronian Ltd Can '35-39; cons practice '45-47; gen mgr Transcontinental Resources Ltd '48-50. Am Inst Min and Metall Engrs—Can Inst Mining and Metallurgy. Room 1730, 25 King Street West, Toronto 1, Ont. H: 121 Dunvegan Rd. Toronto 12.

17 STEWART, Dewey. Plant pathology and breeding. b'98. BS (Ala Polytech Inst); MS (Mich State Coll) '26-28 (Cornell U). Research on sugar beet diseases and breeding, sugar beet varieties resistant to cercospora leaf spot disease. Plant path and agron US Dept Agr since '25. Am Phytopath Soc—Am Soc Agron—Am Genetic Assn—Am Soc Bot—Sigma Xi. Plant Industry Station, Beltsville, Md. H: 1736 Webster St., N.E., Washington 17.

18 STEWART, Duncan. Antarctic petrography. b'05. BS '28—PhD '33 (U Mich); ScM '30 (Brown U). Author articles in field. Prof geol Carleton Coll since '45, chmn dept since '45. Mineral Soc Am—Geol Soc Am—Soc Econ Paleontol Mineral—Mich Acad Sci Arts Letters—Minn Acad Sci—Pa Acad Sci—Am Polar Soc—Arctic Inst NA—Sigma Xi—Phi Kappa Phi. Grant-in-aid Sigma Xi '35-36; grant Geol Soc Am '35-36, '52-53. Carleton College, Northfield, Minn.

19 STEWART, George Franklin. Food technology (Poultry and dairy products). b'08. BS '30 (U Chicago); PhD '33 (Cornell U). Co-editor: Advances In Food Research; also articles in field. Research asso prof poultry husbandry dept Ia State Coll '38-42, research prof '42-48, asso dir agrl expt sta '48-51; cons on food research and development QMC US Army '42-47, NRC adv council on QMC problems, commn on food since '48. Inst Am Poultry Inds (rsch com)—Refrigeration Research Found (sci adv council)—AAAS—Poultry Sci Assn (past mem editorial bd Poultry Sci)—Am Chem Soc—Inst Food Technol (councilor)—Phi Kappa Phi—Sigma Xi. Christie Award Poultry and Egg Nat Bd '49. Poultry Husbandry Department, Davis, Cal.

20 STEWART, Grace Anne. Invertebrate paleontology (Devonian, corals, microfossils). b'93. Fellow '21-22—PhD '23 (U Chicago); BA '18—MA '20 (U Alberta). Author: Illustrated Catalogue of Type Invertebrate Fossils of North America (with M A Fritz) '37; also articles in field. Instr O State U '23-28, asst prof '28-37, asso prof '37-45, prof since '45; asst geol O Geol Survey '24-31. O Acad Sci(F)—Paleontol Soc(F)—Geol Soc Am(F)—Sigma Xi. Department of Geology, Ohio State University, Columbus 10, O. H: 2887 Neil Av., Columbus 2.

21 STEWART, Jeffrey R(obert). Paint coatings; Petroleum and plastics (chemistry). '05. Cert Chem Engr

'29 (Pratt Inst Tech). Research nd development protective coatings. Author: National Paint Dictionary. Pres Stewart Research Lab '36-44; special asst to QM gen ordnance engr Dept Army since '49; tech writer Raritan Arsenal Metuchen NJ since '49. ACS—Am Inst Chem—Chem Engrs Club Wash—Soc Am Mil Engrs. Code C-336, Bureau of Yards and Docks, Dept of the Navy, Washington 25. H: Forest Gate at Franconia, Alexandria, Va.

22 STEWART, Paul A. Ornithology. b'09. Member bird and mammal collecting expedition to New Mexico '37; studies on bird banding, weights, migration, distribution, censusing. Author articles: A Preliminary List of Bird Weights '37; The Gambel's Sparrow in Ohio '33; The Lucy Warbler in New Mexico '40; Breeding Bird Censuses '43-47; banded barn owls in North America and others. Manager Beaver Lake '47; grad research fellow Ohio Coop Wildlife Research Unit since '52. Wildlife Soc—O Acad Sci. Department of Zoology and Entomology, Ohio State University, Columbus 10.

23 STEWART, Rodney E(arl). Blending cheese. b'14. Student '38 (Mont Univ); '37 (Lawrence College). Supt Wheeler Co Green Bay Wis since '39. Wheeler Company, Green Bay, Wis.

24 STEWART, Thomas Dale. Physical anthropology. b'01. BA '27 (George Washington U); MD '31 (Johns Hopkins U). Research on myology of primates, anthropometry of American Indians, ethnic mutilations. Author articles in field. Aid div phys anthrop US Nat Mus Washington '27-31, asst curator '31-39, asso curator '39-42, curator since '42. Am Assn Phys Anthrop—Anthrop Soc Washington—Washington Acad Sci—Inter-Am Soc Anthrop and Geog—Internat Assn Dental Research. U.S. National Museum, Washington 25.◎

25 STEWART, Watt. Latin American history; American diplomatic relations. b'92. AB '20 (W Va Wesleyan Coll); AM '25—PhD '28 (U Chicago); '41 (U Mayor de San Marcos, Lima, Peru); teaching fellow '26-27 (George Washington U). Research Peru, Chile, Argentina, Mexico, Central America '36-37, '41, '46-47. Author: Henry Meiggs: Yankee Pizarro '46; Yellow Bondage in Peru '51; (with H F Peterson) Builders of Latin America '42; also articles in field. Professor history New York State College for Teachers Albany since '40. AHA—Sociedad Chilena de Historia y Geografia (corr mem)—Soc de Geografia e Historia de Costa Rica (corr mem). State College for Teachers, Albany 3, N.Y.

26 STEWART, William Sheldon. Citrus physiology (Plant growth regulators). b'14. BA '35—MA '37 (U Calif Los Angeles); PhD '39 (Calif Inst Tech). Author articles in field. With US Dept Agr '39-45; asst plant physiol citrus expt sta U Calif to asso plant physiol '45-50; plant physiol Pineapple Rsch Inst since '50. Sigma Xi—Am Soc Plant Physiol—Bot Soc Am—Am Soc Hort Sci—Am Assn Econ Entomol. Pineapple Research Institute, Honolulu, Hawaii.

27 STEYERMARK, Julian A(lfred). Plant taxonomy, geography and ecology (Guatemala, middle Central America, Venezuela, Ecuador, Missouri and Ozarks). b'09. AB '29—MS '30 (Washington U); MA '31 (Harvard U); PhD '33 (Washington U Henry Shaw Sch Bot). Expeditions to mountains western Texas '31, Panama '34, Guatemala '39-40, '41-42, Ecuador and Venezuela '43-44, '44-45. Author: Spring Flora of

Missouri; also articles in field. Asst curator herbarium Chicago Natural Hist Mus Chicago '37-47, asso curator since '48; hon research asso Mo Bot Garden St Louis since '48. Am Plant Taxonomists—Ecuadorian Inst Natural Sci—Venezuelan Soc Natural Sci—Bot Soc Am—Sigma Xi. Chicago Natural History Museum, Chicago 5. H: 117 North Hill Rd., Rt. 1, Barrington, Ill.

10 STICKNEY, Alpheus Beede. Industrial refrigeration and steam power plants. b'03. BS '23—MS '24—ME '32 (Yale). Cons Engr Ophuls and Hill NY '26-34, Armour and Co Chicago '34-35, '36-48; Rust Engineering Co since '49; Tennessee Eastman Corporation '35-36; chmn com refrigeration piping Am Standards Assn Piping Code. Am Soc Refrigerating Engrs — Sigma Xi. Awarded Strathcona Yale '24-26. Rust Engineering Co., 575-6th Ave., Pitts 9.

11 STIEGLER, Harold Winfred. Textile chemistry. b'95. BS '18 (Lowell Textile Inst); '20 (MIT); MS '22—PhD '24 (Northwestern U). Research on textile dyes, dyeing, chemical, finishes, auxiliaries; textile test methods, instruments, and standards; member advisory committee commercial standards US Department Commerce since '47. Granted patents on resin finishes, dyes, textile processing, synthetic fibers, test instruments. Author articles in field. Head textile chem div Am Cyanamid Co Stamford Conn '36-42; dir research Am Assn Textile Chem and Colorists since '46. AAAS(F)— Am Inst Chem (F)—Am Assn Textile Chem and Colorists (active various coms)—Am Chem Soc—NY Acad Sci— Am Standards Assn (com textile test methods, adv com consumer goods)— Am Soc Testing Materials—Textile Research Inst—Sigma Xi. American Association of Textile Chemists and Colorists, Lowell Textile Institute, Lowell, Mass.

12 STIEHLER, Robert D(aniel). Rubber technology; Testing specifications and quality control. b'10. Student '26-29 (Rensselaer Poly Inst); NY State fellow chem '29-33—PhD '33 (Johns Hopkins); Nat Research Council fellow '33-34 (Calif Inst Tech). Author articles in field. Chief testing and specifications sect Nat Bur Standards since '48; sr chem Boston QM Depot '42-43, Office Rubber Reserve RFC '43-46. Am Chem Soc—AAAS—Am Soc Testing Materials—Am Soc Quality Control— Philos Soc Washington—Washington Assn Scientists—Phi Lambda Upsilon —Sigma Xi—Phi Beta Kappa. National Bureau of Standards, Washington 25.†

13 STILL, Eugene Updyke. Pharmaceutical chemistry. b'98. PhD '28 (U Chicago). Research in clinical and technical methodology in synthetic drugs; reactions and production of labile molecules; design and construction specialized equipment. Dir research pharm div Standard Brands Inc '36-48; pres. Still Co since '48. Am Physiol Soc—Soc Exptl Biol and Med —ACS—Soc So Research—NY Acad Sci —Soc Indsl Chem. 201 East 18th St., Sarasota, Fla.

14 STIMSON, H(arold) F(rederic). Calorimetry; Thermometry. b'90. AB '10 (Clark Coll); AM '11—PhD '15 (Clark U). Studies in fluid calorimetry to determine enthalpy of saturated water and water vapor at all temperatures from freezing point to critical point; improved precision thermometry with platinum resistance thermometers for determining temperature on International Temperature Scale; US delegate to conference of advisory committee on thermometry and calorimetry in Paris which pro-

posed International Temperature Scale of '48. Physicist Nat Bur Standards since '16. APS—Optical Soc Am—AA AS—Wash Acad Sci. Received Dept Commerce Meritorious Service Award '49, Sigma Xi, '51. National Bureau of Standards, Washington 25.

15 STIMSON, Russell Leslie. Medical photography; Ophthalmic optics. b'97. Designed camera for ultra closeup photography eye and camera to measure topography of cornea; invented eye fixation device for retinal photography. Author: Ophthalmic Dispensing '51. Instr ophthalmic optics Los Angeles City College. Optical Soc Am—Am Phys Soc—Am Bd Opticianry —Calif Assn Dispensing Opticians. 1500 South Hope Street, LA 15.

16 STINE, Samuel Lowell. Atmosphere (Temperature measurement, pressure measurement). b'14. Student '34-39 Carnegie Inst Tech). Research, design and construction of precision equipment for field measurement of temperature, pressure and atmospheric optical phenomena, conducted first precision experiments on dry ice seeding of stratus and cumulus clouds. Research phys Evans Signal Lab since '46. Evans Signal Laboratory, Belmer, N.J. H: 101 Princeton Rd., Fair Haven, N.J.

17 STINESPRING, William Franklin. Old Testament history; Hebrew and Aramaic language; History and archeology of Palestine. b'01. Sterling research fellow '31-32—PhD '32 (Yale); BA '24—MA '29 (U Va); fellow '32-35 (Am Sch Oriental Research Jerusalem). Translator: From Jesus to Paul '43; also articles in field. Prof Old Testament Duke U since '44. Am Oriental Soc—Soc Bibl Lit—Nat Assn Bibl Instr. Duke Divinity School, Durham, N.C.☉

18 STIRN, Frank E(dwin). Vitamin derivatives; Antibiotics; Phenolic and quaternary antiseptics. b'12. BS '34—Ph D '39 (U Wis). Pharmaceutical developmental lab head, Lederle Labs Div Am Cyanamid Co Pearl River NY since '42. Am Chem Soc—AAAS—NY Acad Sci. Lederle Laboratories Division, American Cyanamid Company, Pearl River, N.Y.

19 STIRTON, Ruben Arthur. Paleontology (Fossil mammals). b'01. BA '25 —MA '31 (U Kan); PhD '40 (U Calif). Mem Princeton Bicentennial Conf '47. Asst Mus Natural Hist U Kan '22-25; mammalogist Donald R Dickey expdns El Salvador, Central Am, U Calif LA '25-27, hon curator mammal collection since '41; curator fossil mammals, mus paleontologist U Calif since '28, lecturer paleontology '41-45, asso prof paleontology since '45, chmn dept and dir museum since '49. Geol Soc Am— Soc Vertebrate Paleontologists—Paleontology Soc—Am Soc Mammalogists —Soc Study Evolution. Guggenheim Memorial Foundation fellow '44-45. Museum of Paleontology, University of California, Berkeley 4.

20 STIVENDER, Edward H(erman). Control devices (Electrical power systems); Mine Sweepers. b'06. Ed pub schs. Research and development of control devices for power systems and industrial plants, design and development of Diesel-electric locomotive controls, marine propulsion control, minesweeping equipment, design and development of alternating current powered winches and hoists, direct current trolly bus drives, Navy instrument systems. Granted patents on control systems, electric commutators, synchronous motor starters, regulating systems for dynamo electric machines, remote control systems

for direct current position motors. With Allis-Chalmers since '29, elec engineer adminstr staff from '43. Soc Nav Archt and Mar Engrs—Am Soc Nav Engrs—Am Inst EE(F)—Wisconsin Profl Engrs. Allis-Chalmers Mfg Co., P.O. Box 512, Milw 1. H: 8205 Rockway Pl., Wauwatosa 13, Wis.

21 STOBBE, John Albert. Electronics (Instruments). b'07. BS in engring '29 (Princeton U); LLB '35—JSD '42 (St Lawrence U). Cons financial institutions, investors, companies in radio, electronics, and television. NY Bar Assn—NJ Bar Assn—Am Bar Assn— Inst Radio Engrs—Am Inst EE. 30 Broad St., NYC 4.

22 STOCKBARGER, Donald C(harles). Crystal growing; Ultraviolet radiation (Production, characteristics, use). b'95. SB '19—ScD '26 (MIT). Author articles in field. Cons physicist MIT since '21. AAAS—Am Phys Soc—Optical Soc Am—Am Assn Physics Teachers—Am Acad Arts Sci—Sigma Xi. 77 Massachusetts Av., Cambridge 39, Mass.

23 STOCKDALE, Paris B. Stratigraphic and structural geology. b'96. AB '19—AM '21—PhD '30 (Ind U); '24-25 (U Chicago). Author articles: Stylolites: Their Nature and Origin '22; Stylolites: Primary or Secondary '43, and others. Prof geol, head dept geol and geog U Tenn since '41. AAAS(F) —Geol Soc Am(F)—Paleontol Soc Am (F)—Ind Acad Sci(F)—Phi Beta Kappa—Sigma Xi. University of Tennessee, Knoxville, Tenn.

24 STOCKING, C(lifford) Ralph. Plant physiology (Water relations); Cyto-chemistry of plastids. b'13. BS '37—MS '39—PhD '42 (U Calif). Coauthor: Water in the Physiology of Plants '48; also articles in field. Asso prof bot, asso bot U Cal since '46. Am Soc Plant Physiol—AAAS—Bot Soc Am—Sigma Xi—Phi Beta Kappa. Division of Botany, College of Agriculture, University of California, Davis, Calif.†

25 STOCKING, Collis. Economic Theory; Commercial Recreation. b'00. Student '19-20 (Clarendon Coll); '20-21 (Kansas U); '21-24 (Columbia); '24 (Dijon U); '24-25 (Sorbonne); '25 (U Pittsburgh); AB '25—MA '26 (Columbia). Author: Public Dance Halls and Commercial Recreation '24; (with Walter Spahr and others) Economic Principles and Problems '36; Company Script as a Form of Wage Payment '34; US Foreign Trade '35. Contributor: Ency Social Sci, Social Work Yearbook. Asst dir bur employment security Social Security Bd '36-41; asst exec dir War Manpower Commn, asso dir Bur Program Planning '41-45; asst dir US Employment Service; now with div products Defense Production Administration. Am Econ Assn—Am Statistics Assn—Internat Assn Employment Services. Division of Products, Defense Production Adm., New General Accounting Office, Washington.†☉

26 STOCKWELL, John Wesley, Jr. Comparative religions; Race history; Science (Philosophy); Neo-behaviorism (Psychology); Johnny Appleseed. b'73. Grad '03 (New Ch Theol Sch, Mass). PhB '08 (U Chicago); BD '11 (U Chicago Div Sch); (U Chicago and Harvard). Author: Introduction and Appendix to Kentucky Americans; Swedenborg: Noetic Mystic and Other Poems '40. Co-author: research volume Johnny Appleseed, a Voice in the Wilderness; also articles in field. Ordained ministry Ch of the New Jerusalem (Swedenborgian) '03; founder Neo-Behaviorism and Knowledge Exten Soc. 15120 Detroit Ave., Lakewood 7, O.†

10 STOCKWELL, Richard Edgar. Aviation (Journalism; Chemical industry (Journalism). b'17. BS '40 (U Wis); MA '45 (U Minn); Nieman fellow '46 (Harvard). Author articles: The Airlines—Port Authority Agreement '49; Formula for International Air Freight '50; Below Two Hundred Feet and a Half Mile '51; The All-Weather, Common System '51, and others. Ed Aviation Age '49-52; ed The Monsanto Magazine since '52. Inst Aeronautical Sci—Aviation Writers Assn—Am Geog Soc—Wings Club—Nat Press Club. First award for best issue in Industrial Mkting Competition '49; TransWorld Airlines award for best operations and development story '50. Monsanto Chemical Co., StL 4.

11 STODDARD, Herbert L(ee). Quail and wild turkey management; Birds of Georgia. b'89. Ed pub schs. Research in commercial growing of tung oil trees and in timber management as related to wildlife, quail and upland game bird management, habits, preservation and increase. Author: The Bobwhite Quail, Its Habits, Preservation and Increase '31 (eighth Brewster medal and award by Am Ornith Union). Co-author: Birds of Georgia; also articles in field. Dir Cooperative Quail Study Assn Thomasville Ga '31-43. Am Ornithol Union(F)—AAAS(F)—Wildlife Soc (hon mem)—Wis Soc for Ornithol (hon mem)—Wilson Ornith Club—Cooper Ornith Club—Baird Ornith Club—Chicago Ornithol Soc—Ga Ornithol Soc—Ill Audubon Soc—Nat Audubon Soc—Biol Soc Washington—Soc Mammalogy. Sherwood Plantation, Thomasville, Ga.

12 STODDARD, Russel. Oriental fruit fly; Insecticides; Fruit pests. U.S. Industrial Chemicals, Inc., 33 W. 42nd St., NYC.

13 STOIBER, Richard E(dwin). Mineral deposits; Quartz crystals. b'11. AB '32 (Dartmouth Coll); PhD '37 (MIT). Author articles in field. Instr, later prof dept geol Dartmouth Coll since '35. Geol Soc Am—Mineral Soc Am—Soc Econ Geol—Am Inst Mining Engrs. Department of Geology, Dartmouth College, Hanover, N.H.

14 STOKES, Charles Anderson. Industrial carbon. b'15. BS '38 (U Fla); '38-41 (MIT). Specialist in carbon blacks, lamp black, acetylene black, charcoal, petroleum coke, activated carbon, thermal black, retort carbon, pitch coke; processing, manufacture and applications of all industrial carbons. Author articles in field. Asst prof chem engring MIT '43-45; asst to tech dir Cabot Cos Pampa Texas '43-44; dir research development Godfrey L Cabot Inc Boston since '45. Am Chem Soc—Am Inst Chem Engrs—Sigma Xi. 77 Franklin St., Boston 10.†

15 STOKES, James Raysor. Plant cytology; Camellias. b'00. BS '22 (U Ga); MS '28 (U Wis); PhD '37 (U Chicago). Author articles in field. Prof, head dept biol and chmn div natural sci and math Ga State Coll for Women since '45. AAAS(F)—Ga Acad Sci (F, exec council '48-50)—Ga Soc Naturalists—Bot Soc Am—Sigma Xi—Phi Beta Kappa. Georgia State College for Women, Milledgeville, Ga.†

16 STOLL, Norman R(udolph). Parasitology; Helminthology; Hookworm. b'92. BS '15—hon DSc '41 (Mt Union Coll); MS '18 (U Mich); ScD '23 (Johns Hopkins). Commission to investigate hookworm disease Puerto Rico '22, China '23-24, Panama '26. Author articles. Asso mem Rockefeller Inst

for Med Research Princeton since '27; spl cons USPHS Communicable Disease Center. With US Naval Med Research Unit 2 Guam World War II. AAAS(F)—Am Soc Parasitol (sectreas '30-32, councillor '33-42, pres '46, chmn edit com Jour of Parasitology '38-43, editorial bd since '44)—Am Soc Zool—Am Soc Naturalists—Am Acad Tropical Med—Sigma Xi. Rockefeller Institute for Medical Research, 66th and York Av., NYC 21.

17 STONE, Alan. Bloodsucking diptera (Horseflies, mosquitoes, blackflies). b'04. PhD '29 (Cornell U). Author articles in field. Entomol div insect identification Bur Entomol and Plant Quarantine US Dept Agr Washington since '31. Washington Acad Sci—Entomol Soc Am—Entomol Soc Washington (editor Proceedings '44-47)—Sigma Xi—Phi Kappa Phi. United States National Museum, Washington 25.†

18 STONE, Charles Turner. Medical education. b'90. AB '11 (Southwestern U); MD '15 (U Tex); grad student med sch '25-26 (Harvard) '26 (U Berlin Germany). Statistical studies in heart disease, pneumonia control; investigation cause and treatment of diseases of liver; clinical teaching of internal medicine. With U Tex since '15, prof medicine since '26. Diplomate Am Bd Internal Med. Am Coll Physicians (F, former mem bd regents)—AMA (mem house of dels, past chmn sect on practice med)—Am Soc Study Internal Secretions—Am Heart Assn—AAUP—AAAS-Hist Sci Soc—Alpha Omega Alpha. 2201 Market St., Galveston.

19 STONE, George Winchester, Jr. Eighteenth century drama; David Garrick. b'07. AB '30 (Dartmouth Coll); AM '31—PhD '40 (Harvard). Catalogued Garrick Collection in Folger Shakespeare Library; research on Garrick's alteration of Hamlet, his productions of Anthony and Cleopatra, A Midsummer Night's Dream, Love's Labor Lost, Macbeth, and King Lear; discovered unknown operatic version of Love's Labor Lost. Author: The Journal of David Garrick, 1763 '39; also articles in field. Prof Eng George Washington U since '47. Phi Beta Kappa—Cosmos Club—Modern Language Assn Am. Fellow, Folger Shakespeare Library summer '48; Guggenheim fellow '50-52. George Washington University, Washington.†

20 STONE, Kirk Haskin. Aerial photographic interpretation; Alaska; Land utilization. b'14. Student '31-33 (Western Reserve U); AB '35 (Mich U); MA '37 (Syracuse U); PhD '49 (University Mich). Detailed analyses of commercial areas; research on air photo interpretation, urban geography, land utilization; interpreted aerial photographs of US and foreign areas; classified land for settlement; field research in Alaska. Author articles in field. Supervising geog Syracuse NY Housing Authority summer '36; Sanilac Co Mich '38-41; field asst US Genl Land Office Alaska '41-42; geog OSS Washington '42-46; geog Bur Land Management Wash and Alaska '46-47, '48; asso prof geog Wis U since '47. Assn Am Geog—Sigma Xi. Fellow Soc Science Research Council '46-48. Department of Geography, Science Hall, University of Wisconsin, Madison 6, Wis.

21 STONE, Robert G. Meteorology (Caribbean, mountain, bibliological); Climatology (Tropical, fog, snow); Geography of the Appalachian region. b'07. Student '25-29 (Antioch Coll); '29 (Chicago); '30 (Grenoble); AB '29 —MA '31 (O State U); '31-32 (Clark U). Member International Commission

on Snow, since '36; climatic studies in Puerto Rico, Virgin Islands '39; collector of large specialized library of books and papers dealing with all aspects of the Appalachian mountain region. Author: Meteorology of the Virgin Islands '42. Editor: Introduction to Study of Air-Mass and Isentropic Analysis for Am Meteorol Soc '35-40; Bulletin Am Meteorol Soc since '36; Section of Biometeorology and Bioclimatology in Biol Abstracts since '38; also articles in field. Mem staff Mt Washington Obs NH '33-34; observer, librarian, research fellow, Blue Hill Obs Harvard '34-40; research asso Meteorology NYU '40-44; Meteorol Air Weather Service USAF since '44. Am Meteorol Soc—Assn Am Geog—Am Soc Professional Geog—Am Geog Soc —NY Acad Sci(F)—AAAS(F). Headquarters, Air Weather Service, Washington 25.†

22 STONE, Walter Leroy. Recreation; Vocational guidance; Community organization. b'95. Student '14-17 (Oberlin Coll); AB '29 (YMCA Grad Sch Nashville); AM '30—PhD '33 (Vanderbilt U). Community planning; trng of recreational leaders; consultant on recreational programming and community planning for social welfare. Author: What is Boys Work? '30; A History of the Development of Boys Work in the US '35; Problems in Social Group Work '37; The Field of Recreation '49; Community Welfare Planning and Organization '50; and others. Boys Work Sec YMCA Akron '20-25, South Bend '25-28, prof group work and community orgn YMCA grad sch '28-35; dir research and exec sec council Community Agencies '35-46; sr advisement and guidance officer VA '46-48; Prof sociol Hanover Coll since '48. Pi Gamma Mu—Am Recreation Soc—Am Sociol Soc—Assn Study Community Orgns—Adult Edn Assn—Am Assn Social Workers—Am Assn Group Workers—Am Council Family Living —AAUP. Hanover College, Box 257, Hanover, Ind.

23 STONER, George Green. Acetylene chemicals; Plasticizers. b'12. AB '34 (Wooster Coll); MA '36 (O State U); PhD '39 (Princeton). Research on application of chemicals made from acetylene, with emphasis on use of polyvinylphrrolidone as blood plasma extender, semiresinous plasticizers for vinyl chloride polymers. Granted patent on ethylene polymerization. Research chem Wallace Lab '38-39; research chem Pittsburgh Plate Glass Co '39-42; research engr Battelle Memorial Inst '42-48; research supervisor Gen Aniline and Film Corp since '48. ACS—AAAS(F)—Am Inst Chem(F). General Aniline and Film Corp., Easton, Pa. H: 129 Grant St.

24 STONER, Rev Victor R(ose). Ariz (History); Hopi Indians; Southwestern archeology. b'93. Diploma '16 (Ariz-State Coll); grad '25 (Theol Sem Diocese Galveston); MA '37 (U Ariz). Research on history and archeology of Arizona missions; founded publication The Kiva. Teacher and pastor since '25. Ariz Archeol and Hist Soc (pres '37-40; '43-48)—Hist Soc NM—Utah State Hist Soc—Ariz Pioneers Hist Soc—Soc Am Archeol—Mu Alpha Nu —Phi Delta Kappa. H: 501 N. Vine St., Victoria, Tex.†

25 STOOKEY, Stanley Donald. Photosensitive glass; Opal glass. b'15. BA '36 (Coe Coll); MS '37 (Lafayette Coll); PhD '40 (MIT). Research on glass composition, particularly of glasses colored by metals and of opal glasses. Invented photosensitive metal-colored glasses in which permanent three-dimensional photographic images may be printed in various transparent colors, photosensitive opal glasses, the first commercially practicable photosensitive glasses, new types of opal glasses for high quality tableware and for machine-drawn thermometer tubing. Author articles in field. Research chem Corning Glass Works NY since '40. Am Chem Soc—Am Ceramic Soc—Sigma Xi. Corning Glass Works, Corning, N.Y.†

10 STORCK, Ambrose H(owell). World War II (Medical history). b'03. BS '23—MD '25—MS '34 (Tulane U). Author: Military Surgical Manual-Abdominal and Genito-Urinary Injuries. Contbg. author sect on vascular diseases History of U.S. Army Medical Department in World War II. Asst cons surgery Office Surgeon Gen '42, later cons gen surgery ETO and chief surg service DeWitt Gen Hosp; comdg officer 24th USA Gen Hosp (Tulane U Affiliated unit). With faculty Tulane U since '31, prof since '47; cons gen surg VA, Tex and La. Diplomate Am Bd Surgery. Am Coll Surgeons(F)—Am Surg Assn—So Surg Assn—Internat Soc Surgery—Soc US Med Cons WWII—AMA—AAAS. Richards Bldg., New Orleans 12.

11 STORER, John Humphreys. Nat resources (Conservation). b'88. AB '11 (Harvard). Studies in natural resource conservation; study of bird flight by slow-motion photography; organization of conservation work; research on conservation of forests, soil, water, and wildlife. Author: The Flight of Birds '47; The Web of Life '51. Author film scripts: The Living (Earth (series); The living Forest (series); The Web of Life. Director film prodn Conservation Found NYC '47-51. Fla Audubon Soc (pres '49-50).

12 STORER, Morris Brewster. Polit philosophy; Theory of knowledge. b '04. SB '26 (Dartmouth College); '30 (Columbia); AM '29 (U Chicago); AM '32—PhD '37 (Harvard). Author: Roots of Moral Obligation '37. Instr philosophy Lafayette Coll '29-30; instr philosophy and comparative religion Dartmouth Coll '32-35; asst philosophy Harvard, Radcliffe Coll '35-36; social scientist in field conf orgn, discussion leader training Bur Agrl Economics US Dept Agr '36-41, sr social scientist '41-46, chmn post-war plannig subcom on agrl-indsl relations '42-43, acting dir fgn student training program '45-46, leader rural affairs discussion Extension Service '46; dean instrn Mount Vernon Jr Coll Washington '46-47; prof humanities and social sciences U Fla since '47. Am Philos Assn—AAUP—Kappa Phi Kappa. University of Florida, Gainesville.†◎

13 STORER, N(orman) Wyman. Celestial navigation; Stellar parallax determination. b'00. BS '23—MA '24 (Wesleyan U); PhD '28 (U Calif). Holds patent on navigating instrument by means of which, with one setting on night sky, both latitude and local sidereal time may be read directly from dials on instrument. Author articles in field. Asso prof astron U Kan. Am Astron Soc—AAAS(F)—Sigma Xi. 500 Lindley Hall, University of Kansas, Lawrence, Kan.

14 STORER, Tracy Irwin. Economic vertebrate zoology; Rodents (Ecology, control). b'89. BS '12—MS '13—PhD '25 (Calif U). Special studies in economic relations of birds and mammals to agriculture, public health and general conservation; served on committees California and national on economic problems involving birds, mammals and fishes. Author: Game Birds

of California (with J Grinnell and H C Bryant) '18; Animal Life in the Yosemite (with J Grinnell) '24; Synopsis of the Amphibia of California '25; Bibliography of Rodent Control '46; also articles in field. Prof zool Calif U since '32. Am Soc Mammalogists (vp) —Ecol Soc Am—Wildlife Soc (pres, past vp, past editor)—Am Ornithol Union—Cooper Ornithol Soc—Wilson Ornithol Club—Am Soc Ichthyologists and Herpetologists—Calif Acad Sci. Department of Zoology, University of California, Davis, Cal.†◎

15 STORK, Harvey Elmer. Flora of Costa Rica and Peru; Microscopic structure of tropical woods. b'90. AB '14 (Ind State Normal Coll); AM '15 (Ind U); '19 (Sorbonne Paris); PhD '20 (Cornell U). Member botanical expeditions to Central America summers '20, '23 and January-August '28, June-September '32; naturalist National Parks summers '27, '29, '34, '35; member second University of California Botanical Garden expedition to Andes '38-39. Prof bot Carleton Coll Northfield Minn since '20. AAAS(F)—Am Bot Soc—Minn Acad Sci (pres '33)—Sigma Xi. Northfield, Minn.

16 STORM, Colton. Rare books; Manuscripts; Maps; Bibliography; Printing history (Fakes, forgeries and facsimiles). b'08. AB '30 (Oberlin Coll). Co-author: Invitation to Book Collecting '47; also articles in field. Curator of maps, later asst dir Clements Library U Mich since '42. Bibliographical Soc Am. Clements Library, University of Michigan, Ann Arbor.†

17 STOTT, Kenhelm Welburn, Jr. Conspicuous birds and mammals of the South Pacific. b'20. BA '42 (Pomona Coll); grad work (San Diego State Coll). Made observational natural history studies in Alaska, Canada, Mexico, and Pacific Islands. Author articles in field. Staff San Diego Zoo since '46, curator mammals and publications '46-48, gen curator since '48. Naval epidemiology service in Philippines, Marianas '42-46. Am Ornithol Union—Am Soc Mammalogists—Avicultural Soc Am—Nat Audubon Soc—Am Assn Zool Parks and Aquariums. Zoological Society of San Diego, Box 551, San Diego, Calif.†

18 STOTZ, Edward, Jr. Mass food preparation and distribution centers (Design, construction). b'96. CE '19 (Lehigh U). Design and construction bulk food preparation centers, with kitchens servicing three or more feeding centers or cafeerias with capacity to 9000 meals at one serving. Partner Charles M. and Edward Stotz, Jr. since '36. Engrs Soc. Western Pa. 801 Bessemer Bldg., Pitts 22.

19 STOUT, David B(ond). South American Indian ethnology; San Blas Cuna Indians. b'13. BA '36 (U Wis); MA '37—U Scholar '36-37 (U Mich); PhD '46—residence scholar '38-39—Cutting traveling fellow '39-40, '40-41 (Columbia). Study of South American Indian ethnology in Germany and Sweden '39-40, ethnological field investigations of San Blas Cuna Indian tribe eastern Panama '40-41. Author articles in field. Asst prof anthrop Syracuse U '46-49; asso prof anthrop State U Iowa since '49. Am Anthrop Assn (sec '47-51) F)—Royal Anthrop Inst Gt Brit and Ireland(F) — Soc Am Archeol — Am Ethnol Soc—AAAS—Inter-Am Soc Anthrop and Geog—Nat Research Council (sub-com on information, Latin Am anthrop '48)—Sigma Xi. Viking Fund Grants '47-48; '51-52. State University of Iowa, Iowa City, Ia.†◎

20 STOUT, George Leslie. Art conservation and examination (Painting). b'97. BA '21 (State U Ia); Carnegie

fellow '26-28—AM '29 (Harvard). Author: (with Rutherford J Gettens) Painting Materials, a Short Encyclopaedia '42; The Care of Pictures '48. Managing editor: Technical Studies in the Field of the Fine Arts (10 vol) '32-42. Editor: Color and Light in Painting, Roland Rood '41. Fellow for research Harvard U Fogg Mus Art '28-33, head dept conservation '33-47; dir Worcester Art Mus since '47; hon cons Library Congress. Internat Inst Conservation of Museum Objects. Worcester Art Museum, Worcester 2, Mass.◎

21 STOUT, John Willard, Jr. Cryogenics; Magnetism; Thermodynamics. b'12. BS '33—PhD '37—fellow Lalor Found '38-39 (U Calif). Author articles in field. Asso prof chem Inst for Metals U Chicago since '46; research scientist Manhattan Dist Los Alamos '44-46. Am Chem Soc—Am Phys Soc—Sigma Xi. Institute for Metals, University of Chicago, Chicago 37.

22 STOUT, Lawrence Edward. Metals (Electrodeposition and electroextraction); Drying of materials. b'98. AB '19 (DePauw U); MS '21—PhD '23 —Chem E '34 (Ohio State U). Asst prof chemistry Miami U Oxford U '23-27; asso prof chemistry Washington U St. Louis '27-34, asso prof chem engring '34-38, prof since '38, chmn department checcical engineering since '40, dean sch engring since '48, dir Sever Inst Tech since '48; cons chem engr since '23. Am Chem Soc—Am Inst Chem Engrs—Am Soc Engring Edn—Mo Soc Profl Engrs—Sigma Xi —Tau Beta Pi—Phi Lambda Upsilon. 7606 Maryland Av., Clayton 5, Missouri.†◎

23 STOUTEMYER, Vernon Theodore. Turf culture; Plant growth under artificial light; Management of plant cuttings. b'05. BS '28 (U Ill); PhD '37 (Ia State Coll). Research on combinations of cool season and warm season turf grasses for California; management of plant cuttings, apparatus for humidification, growth substances; Sphagnum moss for seeding, Perlite and Vermiculite in propagation. Research asst Ia Agrl Expt Sta '30-37; hort USDA '37-46; chmn dept floriculture and ornamental hort. Coll agr U Cal at LA; mem editorial com Am Soc Hort Sci. Am Soc Plant Physiologists—AAAS—Am Soc Agronomy. Vaughan award in Floriculture '46. Dept of Floriculture and Ornamental Horticulture, University of Cal, LA 24.

24 STOVALL, Floyd. Walt Whitman; Poe; Shelley. b'96. AB '23—MA '24— PhD '27—H M Reed Grad fellow '25-26, '26-27 (U Tex). Author: Desire and Restraint in Shelley '31; Walt Whitman: Representative Selections, with Introduction, Bibliography and Notes '39; also articles in field. Dir dept English North Tex State Teachers Coll since '35, dean Coll Arts and Sci since '46; prof Eng UNC since '49. Modern Lang Assn—Tex Inst of Letters. Department of English, University of North Carolina, Chapel Hill, N.C.

25 STOVALL, John Willis. Vertebrate paleontology of southwestern North America. b'91. BS '23 (Union U); MS '27 (Vanderbilt U); PhD '38 (U Chicago); '27-28 (Yale). Author articles in field. Instr, later prof U Okla since '30, dir Mus since '43. Paleontol Soc Am—Okla Acad Sci—Geol Soc Am—Soc Vertebrate Paleontol—Sigma Xi. Museum of the University of Oklahoma, Norman, Okla.†

26 STOWE, Vernon M(onroe). Catalysis; Sorption; Rubber fillers; Alumina chemicals. b'97. BS '21 (Hamline U); MS '24—PhD '27 (State U Ia); hon fellow '28 (U Minn). Research on surface tension of liquid sulphur dioxide, solubilities of anhydrous hydrogen fluoride '25-28, preparation pure inorganic compounds '26-27, catalysis of water gas reaction, ammonia synthesis and ammonia oxidation '35-40, use of activated alumina as catalyst, catalyst carrier and adsorbent, and use of alumina chemicals as rubber filler and paper coating '40-53. Author articles in field. Instr inorganic chem ND Agrl Coll '25-26, asst prof '27-28; research chem Atmospheric Nitrogen Corp '28-35, nitrogen div Solvay Process Co '35-40; research chem Aluminum Co Am '40-47, asst chief chem development div since '47. AAAS—Am Inst Chem(F)—Am Chem Soc—Sigma Xi. Aluminum Company of America, Aluminum Research Laboratories, P.O. Box 497, East St. Louis, Ill.†

10 STOWE, Walter Herbert. Religion (History of the Protestant Episcopal Church, canon law). b'95. BA '15 (U Minn); BD '18 (Seabury Div Sch); King fellow '19-21 (Gen Theol Sem NYC); STD honoris causa (Seabury-Western Theol Sem Evanston Ill). Author: The Essence of Anglo-Catholicism '42; The Episcopal Church: A Miniature History '44; The Intellectual Revolution and the Anglican Communion '47. Editor: The Life and Letters of Bishop William White '37; also articles in field. Rector Christ Ch New Brunswick NJ since '29; managing ed Historical Mag of Protestant Episcopal Ch '34-49 editor in chief of the mag since '49. Historiographer of Diocese of NJ since '35 of the Episcopal Church since '52. Ch Hist Soc (pres, official agency Gen Convention Protestant Episcopal Ch since '36)—Am Soc Ch Hist. 5 Paterson St., New Brunswick, N.J.

11 STRAIN, Harold H(enry). Plant pigments; Chromatographic adsorption analysis; Carbohydrates; Liquid ammonia reactions. b'04. PhD '27 (Stanford U); Rockefeller Found fellow '37-38 (Carlsberg Lab Copenhagen Denmark). Author articles in field. Staff Carnegie Instn Washington div plant biol Stanford Calif; now with Argonne National Laboratory, P.O. Box 299, Lemont, Ill.

12 STRAKHOVSKY, Leonid Ivanovich. Modern Russian history; Russian literature and language. b'98. BLitt '17 (Imperial Alexander Lyceum); D Hist Sc '28 (Louvain U); '17-18 (Petrograd U). Consultant on Russian maps, Army Map Service '42-43; research on Franco-British plot to dismember Russia, leaders of Conservatism, privateering projects of 1878, liquidation of Murmansk Soviet, constitutional aspects of Imperial Russian government's policy toward national minorities, and other subjects. Author: L'Empereur Nicolas I et l'Esprit National Russe '28; The Origins of American Intervention in North Russia '37; Intervention at Archangel, 1918-1920 '44; Alexander I of Russia '47; A Russian Literary Reader '54; Three Poets of Mod Russia '49, and others; also articles in field. Lectr Slavic, Harvard '45-48; prof Russian hist and lit U Toronto since '50. AHA—Modern Lang Assn. Research fellow in Slavic, Harvard '43-45; Social Sci Research Council grant '37 65 Lakeshore Rd., Mimico, Ont., Can.

13 STRALEY, H. W., III. Applied and structural geology and geophysics; Geological engineering; Theoretical geophysics; Regional economic geology (Mineral resources); Petroleum geology; Electrical gravitational magnetic and radioactive phases of geophysical engineering. b'06. Student at (Concord Coll, U NC, U Chicago). Research on structural and geophysical problems Appalachian Mountains and plateau and Atlantic Coastal Plain, and on megatectonics; in charge field work Habana, Pinar del Rio, Board Economic Warfare Technical Mission to Caribbean; evaluated mining and petroleum properties and resources various areas abroad for war and loan purposes. Author articles in field. Head dept geol Baylor U '39-42; geol engr Bd Econ Warfare Tech Mission to Caribbean '42-43; chief geol engr Forest and Mineral Product Sect, Supply and Resources, Fgn Econ Adminstrn '43-46; prof ceramic engring Ga Inst Tech '46; chief exploration Internat Bank Reconstruction and Development '47-48; prof geol Okla U since '48. Am Geophys Union—Am Inst Mining Metall Engring (chmn geophysics edn com '41-47)—Am Soc Profl Geog—Carolina Geol Soc (pres '38)—Geol Soc Am—Pan-Am Inst Mining Engr and Geol—Soc Exploration Geophysicists. Box 68, Princeton, W.Va.

14 STRAND, K(aj) Aa(ge) (Gunnar). Astronomy (Photographic observation of double and multiple stars, stellar parallax, proper motion); Aerial navigation. b'07. AB—MSc '31—PhD '38 (U Copenhagen). Author articles in field. Prof astron Northwestern U, dir Dearborn Obs since '47; research asso U Chicago since '47. Pvt, later capt US Army Air Corps and chief navigation dept Eglin Field Fla '42-45. Am Astron Soc—Astron Soc Pacific—Internat Astron Union—Sigma Xi. Am Scandinavian fellow; Danish Rask Oersted Found fellow '39-40; Guggenheim fellow '46. Dearborn Observatory, Northwestern University, Evanston, Ill.†

15 STRANDSKOV, Herluf Haldan. Human heredity. b'98. BA '23 (Ia State Teachers Coll); MS '25 (U Ill); PhD '31 (U Chicago). Research on distribution of human genes, physiological aspects of human genetics, genetics of human populations. Author articles in field. Asso prof zool U Chicago since '46. Am Soc Human Genetics—Genetics Soc Am—Am Statis Soc—Naturalist Soc—AAAS—Sigma Xi. Department of Zoology, University of Chicago, Chicago 37.†

16 STRANDTMANN, Russell William. Acarology; Fossorial Hymenoptera. b'10. BS '35 (SW Tex State Teachers Coll); MS '37 (Tex A&M Coll); PhD '44 (O State U). Author articles in field. Dept biol Tex Tech Coll since '48. Department of Biology, Texas Technological College, Lubbock, Tex.

17 STRASSBURGER, Ralph Beaver. Pennsylvania history (German pioneers); Animal breeding (Thoroughbred horses, Ayrshire cattle). b'83. BS '05 (US Naval Acad); LLD '30 (Ursinus Coll). Author: The Pennsylvania German Pioneers (3 vols) '34; and others. Owner Normandy Farm; breeder; owns racing stables in Am, France and Eng. Hist Soc Pa—Pa-German Soc (pres). Normandy Farm, Gwynedd Valley, Pa.

18 STRAUB, John C. Automotive gears; Spur and helical gears (Fatigue testing and analysis); Shot peening. b'06. BS '31 (Carnegie Inst Technol, Pittsburgh). Research gear tooth stress analysis, shot peening; developed stress peening; established validity of a method of predicting fatigue life in spur and helical gears. Author articles in field. Project engr, research division General Motors Corp '31-44; chief research engr Am Wheelabrator & Equipment Corp since '44. Am Gear Manuf Assn (chmn automotive com)—Soc Automotive Engrs (chmn sub-com)—Soc Exp Stress Analysis. American Wheelabrator and Equipment Corporation, Mishawaka, Ind.

19 STRAUB, Lorenz George. Hydraulic engineering (Structures, waterways). b'01. BS '23—MS '24—PhD '27—CE '30—engring fellow '25-27 (U Ill); '27 (Tech U Free City of Danzig); '27-28 (Tech U Karlsruhe Germany, Tech U Berlin). Author: Plastic Flow in Concrete Arches '31; also articles in field. Practice as cons engr Minneapolis since '29; head dept civil engring U Minn since '38; cons Govt of Madras India since '47; dir St Anthony Falls Hydraulic Lab since '38; mem Upper Miss and St Croix River Improvement Commn since '47; Nat Defense Research and Development Bd geophysics since '46); with Nat Defense Research Com div sub-surface warfare '41-46. AAAS—ASCE (com on hydraulic research '34-43, com open channel river regulation since '45, exec com hydraulics div since '47, chmn since '48)—ASME—ASEE (chmn com applied hydraulics '38-39, nat council '39-42, pres civil engring div '40-41, chmn grad studies div since '48)—Am Geophys Union (sect of hydrology, pres since '47)—Internat Assn Scientific Hydrology—Internat Assn Hydraulic Structures Research (Am rep permanent internat exec com since '38, pres since '49)—Soc Am Mil Engrs—Am Concrete Inst—Tau Beta Pi—Sigma Xi—Phi Kappa Phi—Sigma Tau. First Freeman traveling fellow ASCE in Europe '27-29. St. Anthony Falls Hydraulic Laboratory, Minneapolis 14.†⊚

20 STRAUMANIS, Martin Edward. Metal corrosion; Metallic crystal growth; Crystal structure and X-rays; Inorganic compounds (Metallic properties); Chemistry of complex compounds. b'98. Engr Chem '25—Dr Chem '27 (U Latvia Riga); Rockefeller Found fellow '27-28 (U Göttingen). Author: (with others) Prazisionsbestimmung von Gitterkonstanten nach der asymmetrischen Methode '40; Lehrbuch der Kolloidehemie '49; also articles in field. Research prof metall U Mo Sch Mines Rolla Mo since '47. Am Cryst Assn—American Chemical Soc—Sigma Xi. School of Mines, Department of Metallurgy, Rolla, Mo.†⊚

21 STRAUS, Roger W., Jr. Books (Design). b'17. Student '35-37 (Hamilton Coll Clinton NY); BJ '39 (U Mo). Co-editor: The Sixth Column '41; War Letters from Britain '41. Reporter Daily Reporter White Plains NY '36, feature writer '39-40; editorial writer and reporter Columbia Missourian '37-39; editor and pub Asterisk '39; editorial asst Current History '40, asso ed since '40; asso ed Forum since '40; pres Book Ideas Inc; founded Farrar Straus and Young, Inc '45, now pres; founder and pres Hendricks House. PEN—Emerson Lit Soc. Farrar, Straus and Young, Inc., 101 Fifth Av., NYC.⊚

22 STRAW, H(arold) Thompson. Africa (Geography); Military geography; Cartography. b'07. BA '30 (Hillsdale Coll Mich); MA '34—PhD '36 (U Mich). Lecturer cartography Western Mich Coll Kalamazoo '39-43, prof geog '45-47; chief cartography sect hist br G-2 AUS '44-45; geog Gen Staff AUS '47-50, Hdqrs USAF since '50. AAAS(F)—Assn Am Geog—Am Geog Soc—Nat Council Geog Teachers—Tenn Acad Sci—Mich Acad Sci Arts and Letters—Sigma Xi. Grants-in-aid NRC and Social Sci Council. Reconnaissance Branch, AF-

OIN-C/RC, 153 Pentagon Annex No. 3, Washington 25. H: 601 Poplar Drive, Falls Church, Va.

10 STREANDER, Philip Bertram. Sewage treatment. b'90. Student (Drexel Inst Tech). Holds ten patents on equipment and sewage treatment methods. Chief engr Roberts Filter Mfg Co Darby Pa '20-26; asso engr Remington, Vasbury Goff Camden NJ '28-32; partner Watson & Streander N YC '33-40 Philip B Streander and Affiliates Boston and Phila '45-50; pres Cotton, Pierce, Streander Inc Boston, Phila, NYC since '51. Am Soc CE—Am Water Works Assn—Federation Sewage Works Assn—New Eng Water Works Assn—Bost Soc CE. Professional engr Pa, NY, NJ, Mass, Conn, and RI. 132 Nassau St., NYC 7. H: 497 Ridgewood Rd., Maplewood, N.J.

11 STREET, John N. Rubber chemistry and technology; Synthetic rubber polymerization (Butadiene-type). b'98. AB '21—MS '23 (Syracuse U); PhD '26 (U Wis). Holds three US, two Canadian patents. Author articles in field. With Firestone Tire & Rubber Co Akron O since '26, director labs since '49; Firestone rep on Office Rubber Reserve Tech Com on Synthetic Rubber '41-42; TIIC Mission to Germany '45; mgr research and development sect Office Rubber Reserve RFC '46-47. Am Assn Textile Chem and Colorists—Am Chem Soc—Am Inst Chem Engrs—Am Inst Chem—AAAS—Electrochem Soc — Faraday Soc— French Chem Soc—German Chem Soc —Soc Chem Industry—Societe Suisse de Chemie. Firestone Tire & Rubber Co., 1200 Firestone Parkway, Akron 17, O.

12 STRICKLAND, John Claiborne, Jr. Myxophyceae (Cytology, Virginia). b'15. BA '37 (U Richmond, Va); MA '39—PhD '43 (U Va); '40 (U Chicago). Research on myxophyceae of Virginia at Chicago Museum of Natural History '42-43, Mountain Lake Biological Station '38, '39, '41, '43, on cytology and culture of myxophyceae Virginia Institute Scientific Research '47-48. Author articles in field. Asst prof biol U Richmond since '46. Va Acad Sci—Bot Soc Am—AAAS(F)—Assn SE Biol —Phycol Soc Am—Sigma Xi. Biology Department, University of Richmond, Va.†

13 STRINGFIELD, Glen Herbert. Maize breeding and culture. b'93. BSc '24 (U Neb); MSc '27 (O State U). Research on breeding maize for high production and resistance to insects and diseases; cooperated in development of hybrid corn industry in Ohio, including training of 300 seed producers in production and processing techniques. Developed inbred lines Oh51A, Oh28, Oh40B, Oh07, and others now in use in Corn Belt and eastern states. Author articles in field. Asst agron O Agrl Expt Sta '24-28, asso agron '28-29; agt asso agro, agron and sr agron Div Cereal Crops and Diseases Bur Plant Industry Soils and Agrl Engring since '29. AAAS(F)—Am Soc Agron (F)—Am Genetic Assn—Gamma Sigma Delta—Sigma Xi. Ohio Agricultural Experiment Station, Wooster, Ohio.†

14 STRINGFIELD, Raymond Beverly. Rubber processing, compounding and physical testing; Vinyl resin compounding; Dental impression compounds. b '91. AB '13 (U So Cal); SB '15 (MIT). Work on effect of mill ratios and effect of humidity on vulcanization of rubber, consultant on plastics production, particularly compression molding, vinyl compounding and dental impression materials, patent engineer on cases involving rubber processing and

plastics formulation, and technical expert on cases involving tire construction and tire failures, holder patents in field. Contributor: Industrial Chemistry (4th edit) '42. Mgr service lab, later chief chem Goodyear Tire & Rubber Co '20-28; cons chem engr since '29; faculty U So Cal since '32; staff process engr Consolidated Vultee Aircraft Corp '42-45; pres Fullerton Mfg Co since '46. ACS (chmn So Cal sect '37)—AICE (chmn So Cal sect '40)—ASTM (chmn So Cal Dist Council '47-49)—Soc Automotive Engrs—Soc Plastic Industry. Fullerton Manufacturing Co., 343 E. Santa Fe Av., Fullerton, Cal.

15 STRINGFIELD, Victor Timothy. Ground-water geology. b'02. BS '25 (La State U); MS '27 (Washington U). Author: Ground-water geology in the Southeastern States; also articles in field. Asst prof geol and mineral NM Sch Mines '28-30; geol NM Bur Mines and Mineral Resources '28-30; asst geol US Geol Survey '30-36, asso geol '37-39, geol charge ground-water investigations southeastern states '39-43, sr geol charge investigations eastern US '43-50, chief ground-water geology since '50. Am Assn Petroleum Geol—Society Econ Geol—Geol Soc Washington—Geol and Mining Soc Am Universities —Am Geophys Union—Geol Soc Am (F)—Sigma Xi. U.S. Geological Survey, Washington 25.

16 STRINGHAM, Edwin John. Musicology. b'90. MusB '14 (Northwestern U); DrPedagogy '22 (Cincinnati Conservatory); Dr Music honoris causa '28 (Denver Coll Music); certificate in composition under Respighi '29 (Royal Acad Music Rome Italy). Author: Instruments of Modern Orchestra and Band; Lustening to Music Creatively. Co-author: Modern Graded Orchestra Series (three vols); Instrumentation Work-Book for Orchestra and Band; America Sings; The Lookout (history of music of Colorado); Creative Harmony. Contributor: International Cyclopedia of Music and Musicians. Composer: (for symphony orchestra) The Phantom, Three Pastels, Visions, Ancient Mariner, Springtime Overture, suite "Dances Exotiques", Symphony number 1 in B flat minor, Nocturne number 1, Nocturne number 2, Notturno for Woodwinds, Horns and Harp, Phantasy on an American Folk Tune for violin solo and orchestra, and others. Founder music dept Queens College NYC '38-44, prof music '44; music editor Earl Fischer, Inc '30-31, Am Book Co '32-39; mem bd dirs and music ed Music Press, Inc '39-46; divisional head music US Army Univ Biarritz France '45-46; vis prof music composition U Cal Los Angeles '46-47, U Texas '47-48. Am Musicol Soc—AAUP—Acoustical Soc Am—Phi Mu Alpha—Pi Kappa Lambda —Pi Gamma Mu—Phi Delta Kappa. Awarded Cromwell traveling fellowship to Germany '36; scholarship to Royal Academy of Music Rome Italy '29. P.O. Box 296, Chapel Hill, N. C.†☺

17 STROCK, Clifford. Heating of buildings (Fuel estimating, weather data for air conditioning). b'00. BSME '26—ME '37 (Purdue U). Author: Heating and Ventilating Engineering Databook '48. Co-author: Degree-Day Handbook '37; Air Conditioning Engineers Atlas '38; also articles in field. With Heating and Ventilating since '28, now ed. Am Soc Heating Ventilating Engrs —ASME—Am Soc Refrigeration Engrs —Inst Heating Ventilating Engrs, Gt Britain—Tau Beta Pi. 148 Lafayette St., NYC 13. H: Nassau Shores, Massapequa, N.Y.

18 STRONG, Earl Poe. Production (Clerical); Training (in-service). b'10. AB '30 (Rider Coll); BS '34 (Pa State Teachers Coll); AM '37 (Ohio State U); EdD '43 (NYU). Research on development of clerical office skills on the job and increase clerical production through such development; development training techniques of value in in-service training; research in study case histories of small businesses relating to management problems and their solution. Author: The Organization, Administration, and Supervision of Business Education '44; Writing Business Letters '50. Co-author: (with R S Rowland) An Analysis of Office Occupations '34; (with M K Odell) Records Management '47; (with R D Loken) Supervision in Business and Industry '49. Research agt bus edn div US Office Edn '42-45; dir utilization dept Remington Rand Inc NYC '45-48; prof management and dir bus management service U Ill since '48. Am Management Assn—Nat Office Management Assn—AAUP—Delta Sigma Pi—Kappa Delta Pi—Phi Delta Kappa. 408 David Kinley Hall, University of Illinois, Urbana, Ill.

19 STRONG, Frederick Smith, Jr. Military supply; Prosthetics engring; Rehabilitation of amputees. b'87. BS '10 (US Military Acad); Graduate '12 (Engrs Sch Washington). Commd second lt Corps of Engineers US Army '10 to brigadier general '44; with 7th and 2d divs France '18; with Service of Supply '18-19, resigned '19; command col QM Res US Army '41; zone constructing quartermaster IV Zone Atlanta Ga '41; War Dept Gen Staff '42; Office of Chief of Engrs '42-43; chief engr Service of Supply China-Burma-India '43; in hosp on sick leave '43-44; comdg officer Northwest Service Command '44-45; hdqrs ASF to Aug '45; comdg United Kingdom base '45; reverted inactive status '46; exec dir Nat Research Council on Artificial Limbs since '46; registered civil engr Mich since '26; engaged real estate and land development bus Orchard Lake Mich since '19; vp and dir Indiana Limestone Co Chicago '26-27; with Booth Investment Co Detroit Mich '27-41. Am Soc Mil Engrs. Orchard Lake, Mich.☺

20 STRONG, Helen Mabel. Soil classification. BS '17—PhD '21 (U Chgo). Author: (with O E Baker) Arable Lands in the US '18; Distribution of Agricultural Exports from the US '24; Relation Between Value and Volume of Agricultural Exports; Regions of Manufacturing Intensity in the US '37. Charge ednl relations Soil Conservation Service US Dept Agr '36-41; cons Mil Intelligence Service War Dept General Staff '41; economic analyst Foreign Economic Administration '43-45, US Dept Commerce '45-46; military geographer Dept Army since '46. AAAS(F)—Am Geog Soc—Royal Geog Soc London—Assn Am Geographers—Soc Women Geographers—Am Soc Profl Geographers—AAUW—Sigma Xi —Pi Lambda Theta. 316 Washington Blvd., Oak Park, Ill.†☺

21 STRONG, William Walker. Carthaginian discovery of America 371 BC; Patination; Ancient tools of diabase; Phoenician inscriptions; Pre-Indian artifacts. b'83. BS '05 (Dickinson Coll); PhD '08 (Johns Hopkins). Discovered Phoenician letters and words incised on stones in 400 words. Author: The New Science of Fundamental Physics '18, and others. Cons practice. AAAS(F)—Am Phys Soc—Phi Beta Kappa. Mechanicsburg, Pa.

22 STROPE, Walmer Elton. Atomic warfare defense; Warship design; War damage and weapons (Analysis). b'18. BSc '42 (Webb Inst Naval Architecture). With Navy Dept since '42, now head mil evaluations group US Naval Radiological Defense Lab San Francisco. Soc Naval Architecture and Marine Engrs—US Naval Inst. Military Evaluations Group, Naval Radiological Defense Laboratory, San Francisco 24.

10 STROUD, James Bart. Educational psychology (Reading, handicapped children, learning, relation to social class). b'97. AB '21 (Lincoln Memorial U); MA '27—PhD '30 (U Chicago). Author: Educational Psychology '35; Introduction to General Psychology '38; Psychology in Education '46. Co-author: Improving Reading Ability: A Manual for College Students '49. Asso prof, prof edn and psychol State U Ia since '38. Am Psychol Assn(F)—Am Ednl Research Assn—Nat Soc Study Edn. College of Education, State University of Iowa, Iowa City, Ia.†

11 STROUP, Philip Trimble. Aluminum (Process metallurgy). b'04. AB '25 —AM '26 (Ind U); PhD '29 (U Wis). Research electrolytic reduction aluminum; melting and alloying aluminum; reclamation aluminum scrap; heat treating atmospheres for aluminum; electric furnace smelting aluminum; aluminum coating of steel; gas removal from aluminum; electro-deposition of aluminum; arc welding of aluminum. Phys chem Aluminum Co Am '29-36, metall '36-42, chief process metall since '43. Am Soc Metals—ACS —AIMME—Electrochem Soc—Am Ceramic Soc—Sigma Xi—Phi Beta Kappa —Alpha Chi Sigma—Phi Lambda Upsilon—Sigma Gamma Epsilon. Aluminum Research Laboratories, New Kensington, Pa.†

12 STROZIER, Robert Manning. Educational administration; Romance languages. b'06. BPh '29—AM '30 (Emory U); PhD '45 (U Chicago). Asso dean students, asso dir Internat House U Chicago '44-45, acting dean division Humanities '47, dean students and asst prof Romance languages '46-50, dean students and associate professor since '50. National Association Student Personnel Administrators—Mod Lang Assn —Chevalier de la legion d'honneur. 5525 Blackstone Av., Chgo 37.◉

13 STUART, Arthur Hulen. Civil War (Battle histories, pictorial material). b'15. AB '36 (George Washington U). Owns and maintains collection more than 8,000 published and unpublished items of pictorial material of Civil War scenes, battles, and participants by Brady, Pennell, Nast, O'Sullivan, Forbes, Wand, Homer, and others; special research on First and Second Battles of Manassas; sometime consultant National Archives, Library of Congress, National Park Service. With Dept Commerce since '47. U.S. Department of Commerce, Washington 25.

14 STUART, Meriwether. Roman antiquities, art, archeology and coinage; Ancient portraiture; Latin literature and history. b'05. AB '25 (William Jewell Coll); AM '27 (Ind U); '33-34 (Am Acad Rome); PhD '38 (Columbia). Demonstrated importance of portrait inscriptions to study of Roman portraiture and economic history; research on representations of triumphal arches on ancient coins. Author: The Portraiture of Claudius, Preliminary Studies '38; also articles in field. With Hunter Coll since '28, asso prof since '48; Henry Drisler fellow in Greek and Latin Columbia '32-33; gen sec Archeol Inst Am '41-45; exec sec pro tem Am Acad in Rome '45-46. Hunter College, 695 Park Av., NYC 21.

15 STUART, Neil Wade. Physiology of horticultural crops (Nutrition, light, temperature, hormones; Hydroponics. b'08. BS '29 (Mich State Coll); MS '32 (U NH); PhD '34 (Md U). Author articles in field. Sr physiol US Dept Agr Plant Industry Sta since '36. AA AS(F)—Am Soc Plant Physiol—Bot Soc Am—Am Soc Hort Sci—Washington Acad Sci. Plant Industry Station, Beltsville, Md.†

16 STUART, William Plato. Arizona mining (Early history). b'79. Student Oak Ridge Inst NC. Author: History of Mining in Sonora '06; Dry Placer Mining in Sonora '07; A Factory of Men '07; The Monstrance of Aconchi '08. Editor and pub Prescott Evening Courier since '21; established Ariz Morning Courier-Jour '34; pres Prescott Courier Inc. Ariz Newspaper Assn (pres '40-41). P.O. Box 2374, Phoenix; also P.O. Box 312 Prescott, Ariz.

17 STUBBS, Donald Harrison. Pain (Management of); Resuscitation. b'05. AB '29—AM '31—MD '32 (George Washington U). Author: The Treatment of Intractable Pain '47; The Treatment of Pain. Dir pain clinic Doctors Hosp Washington since '48, asst chief anesthesiol since '46; clinical prof anesthesiol George Washington U Med Sch since '46, asso chief post grad program anesthesiol since '46. DC Med Soc—AMA—So Med Assn—Washington Acad Surgery—Am Soc Anesthesiologists—SW Soc Anesthesiologists—Potomac Soc Anesthetists. 305 Mansion Dr., Alexandria, Va.

18 STUBBS, Stanley Alger. Navajo and Pueblo textiles; Prehistoric and modern Indian pottery of the southwest United States. b'06. BS '30 (U NM). Research asso charge anthrop Mus of NM since '47; vis prof U NM '47, '48. Am Anthrop Assn(F). Rockefeller Found fellow '38. Museum of New Mexico, Santa Fe, N.M.

19 STUCKEY, Jasper L. Economic and engineering geology. b'91. AB '18 —AM '20 (U NC); '19 (Grenoble U); PhD '24 (Cornell). Emergency coordinator of mines for North Carolina '41-43; research on occurrence and properties of various nonmetallic minerals of North Carolina, including barite, talc, limestone, marble, pyrophyllite, and others. Author articles in field. State geol NC Dept Conservation and Development '25-26, acting dir '25; prof NC State Coll since '26, dir minerals research lab since '46; state geol since '40. NC Acad Sci—Am Ceramic Soc—Am Inst Mech Engrs—Soc Econ Geol —Am Soc Engring Edn—NC Soc Engrs —Sigma Xi—AAAS(F)—Mineral Soc Am(F)—Geol Soc Am(F)—Am Geog Soc(F). 1911 Sunset Drive, Raleigh, N.C.◉

20 STUDT, Charles Wotring. Petroleum Geology; Gas storage (Underground). b'92. AB '16—MS '21 (Washington U). Research and development of underground gas storage reservoirs. With Union Gas System Inc and predecessor cos since '24, mgr explorations from '24, prodn from '30, gas storage operations from '36; mgr exploration and prodn operations in Ill Nat Refining Co '39-43; Coop Refinery Assn '44-49. Am Assn Petroleum Geol —Kan Acad Sci—Kan Geol Soc—Soc Econ Paleontologists and Mineral—Sigma Xi. Union Gas System Inc., Independence, Kan. H: 1212 N. Second St.

21 STUMBOCK, Max Joseph. Precious metals (Refining, melting, working); Electrical contacts. b'91. Diploma Chem '18 (Zurich Coll). Director precious metals refinery D Steinlauf, Zurich '18-22; vp works mgr Franco-Am Precious Metals Corp NYC '24-30; constrn dir plants for working melting and refining precious metals Baker Platinum Ltd London '31-37; dir research, mgr electrical contact dept, Baker & Co Inc Newark NJ since '37. 225 Grant Av., E. Newark, N.J.

22 STUMP, N. Franklin. Occupational vision research; Human factors in accidents. b'97. BSc '21 (W Va U); MA '23 (Yale); PhD '35 (Cornell U). Research on visual functions as related to accident proneness, visual functions and safety, industrial safety and visual functions, spotting accident-prone workers by vision tests, statistical studies of visual functions and industrial safety, job analysis as related to visual skills. Established that efficient visual performance and accident free experience in industrial organizations are closely related. Author articles in field. Head dept and prof edn psychol Keuka Coll NY '29-43, organizer and head bur placement '30-43; supervisor student training and employee testing Revere Copper & Brass Inc Rome NY '43-45; occupational vision dept Bausch & Lomb Optical Co Rochester, dir cons services since '45. AAAS(F)—Upper NY State Psychol—Phi Delta Kappa. 635 St. Paul St., Rochester 2, N.Y. H: 386 Sagamore Dr., Rochester 17, N.Y.

23 STURKIE, Dana G. Fiber crops (Kudzu); Hay crops (Lespedeza, alfalfa); Cotton (Lint and seed development); Pasturage. b'97. BS '20 (Ala Poly Inst); MS '23 (Ia State Coll); PhD '31 (Mich State Coll). Author articles in field. Asst prof agron dept Clemson Coll '23-25; agron Ala Polytech Inst since '25. Am Soc Agron—Sigma Xi—Gamma Sigma Delta—Phi Kappa Phi. Department of Agronomy and Soils, Alabama Polytechnic Institute, Auburn, Ala.

24 STUTLER, Boyd Blynn. Civil War history. b'89. Ed pub schs. Research on John Brown and his relation to Kansas civil wars of 1855-59, his raid at Harper's Ferry '59 and its after-effects, Virginia-West Virginia phase of Civil War including both military and civil movements. Author: Captain John Brown and Harper's Ferry '28. Co-author: (with Phil Conley) West Virginia Yesterday and Today (revised) '52. Newspaper and magazine ed since '07, mng ed Am Legion mag from '36. Kan State Hist Soc—O Archeological and Hist Soc—W Va Hist Society—Abraham Lincoln Assn—Civil War Round Table. 580 Fifth Av., NYC 19.

25 SUGARMAN, Nathan. Chemistry (Radio, magneto, physical). b'17. BS '37—PhD '41 (Chicago U). Research on radiochemistry of fission products, nuclear properties of fission products, magneto-chemistry of alkali metals in liquid ammonia. Author articles in field. Asst prof chem Inst Nuclear Studies U Chicago '46-48, asso prof since '48. Phi Beta Kappa—Sigma Xi—Am Chem Soc—Am Phys Soc—Atomic Scientists Chicago. Post-doctoral fellow Am Philos Soc U Chicago '41-42. Institute for Nuclear Studies, University of Chicago, Chicago 37.†

26 SULLIVAN, Francis Paul. National government buildings (Architecture). b'85. AB '04—grad work '05-09 (George Washington U). Author articles in field. Cons architect for work on US Capitol House and Senate office bldg; asso architect with David Lynn and Harbison Hough Livingston and Larson to design reconstruction of House and Senate Chambers. National executive officer Historic American Buildings Survey '34. AIA (chmn com Nat Capitol '30-42, com on pub works '36-38, pres DC chap '33)—Am Geog Soc—Soc Archtl Historians—Am Planning and Civic Assn. 808 17th St., Washington 6.†

10 SULLIVAN, Frank. St Sir Thomas More. AB '34 (Regis); AM '36 (St Louis U); PhD '40 (Yale). Author: Moreana: Checklist of Material By and About St Thomas More '46; Thomas More: A First Bibliographical Notebook, '53. Professor English Loyola University since '46; literary ed Los Angeles Tidings since '48. Modern Lang Assn—Medieval Acad Am—Bibliog Soc Am. Loyola University, Los Angeles 45.†

11 SULLIVAN, Harris Martin. Physical metallurgy; Instrumentation and instrument design. b'09. BS '31—MS '33 (U Ky); PhD '38 (Pa State Coll). Author articles in field. Asst prof metall engring Rensselaer Poly Inst '38-41; metall engr Adirondack Foundries & Steel Inc Watervliet NY '41-45; mem metall adv bd Watertown Mass Arsenal '41-45; asst dir research and development Central Scientific Co Chicago since '45. AAAS(F)—Am Phys Soc—Am Optical Soc—Am Chem Soc—Am Soc Metals—Sigma Xi—Sigma Pi Sigma. 1700 Irving Park Rd., Chicago 13.

12 SULLIVAN, John Wadsworth William. Metallurgical engineering (Standardization of steel products). b'01. SB '23—SM '25—ScD '27 (MIT). Author: The Story of Metals '51; also articles in field. Metall Am Iron and Steel Inst NYC '45-53 metall engr since '53. Am Soc Metals—Am Soc Quality Control—Am Inst Mining and Metall Engrs—Inst Metals—Inst Math Statis—Iron and Steel Inst, London. American Iron and Steel Institute, 350 Fifth Av., NYC 1.†

13 SULLIVAN, Joseph T. Forage plants (Carbohydrates, nutritional value); Plant analysis methods. b'00. BS '22 (U Mass); MS '24 (U NH); '26 (Columbia); PhD '35 (Purdue U). Author articles in field. Physiol US Regional Pasture Research Lab since '37; abstractor for Chemical Abstracts. Am Chem Soc—Am Soc Plant Physiol—Am Soc Agron—Sigma Xi. U.S. Regional Pasture Research Laboratory, State College, Pa.†

14 SULLIVAN, Royal A. Dairy products (Chemistry); Vitamins; Proteins. b'06. AB. '29—PhD '37 (Cornell U). Nutritional studies on dairy products; determination of vitamins by spectrophotometric method and microbiological assay; separation of pure proteins and measurement of their physical properties; enzymatic hydrolysis of proteins and analysis of resultant peptides. Co-author articles: (with Sullivan) Refractive Index of Egg Albumen '37; (with Beaty, Bloom, Reeves) Determining Riboflavin in Dried Milk Products '43; (with Bloom, Jarmol) The Value of Dairy Products in Nutrition '43, and others. Research chem Kraft Cheese Co Chicago '36-43, Nat Dairy Research Labs Inc Oakdale LI since '46. Nutrition officer AUS '43-46 ACS—Poultry Science Assn—NY Acad Sci. National Dairy Research Laboratories, Inc., Oakdale, L.I., N.Y.

15 SULLIVAN, Russell. Astronomy. b '81. BA '05 (Yale). AAAS(F)—Geog Soc(F)—Royal Astron Soc Eng(F)—American Astron Soc—Am Assn Variable Star Observors—Societe Astronomique de France. Fletcher Savings & Trust Bldg, Indpls.

16 SULZBACHER, William L(ouis). Meat bacteriology and technology. b'13.

BS '36—MS '38—'39-41 (U Pittsburgh). Author articles in field. Bact and meat investigator Bur Animal Ind US Dept Agr since '45. Soc Am Bact—AAAS—Pa Acad Sci—Inst Food Technol. Animal Husbandry Experiment Station, Beltsville, Md.†

17 SUMMERFIELD, Martin. Jet propulsion; Thermodynamics of power plants; Heat transfer. b'16. BS '36 (Brooklyn Coll); MS '37—PhD '41 (Calif Inst Tech). Specialized in rocket motor development, research in combustion of liquid and solid propellants, problems of cooling in rocket motors. Author articles: Applications of Rocket propulsion '46; Physics of Rockets '47; Problem of Escape From the Earth by Rocket (with F J Malina) '47. Asst chief engr air corps jet propulsion research project Calif Inst Tech '40-43, chief rocket research div jet propulsion lab; general ed series volumes high speed aerodynamics and jet propulsion Princeton U, also technical consultant; chief rocket development sect Aerojet Engring Corp Azusa Cal '43-45; prof jet propulsion Princeton since '50. Ed Jour Am Rocket Soc since '51. Inst Aero Scis(F)—AAAS(F)—Am Phys Soc—Sigma Xi—ASME. Princeton Univ., Princeton, N.J.†☺

18 SUMMERS, David Selden. Maui (Water sup); Irrigation. b'03. Student '20 (U Hawaii); AB in (civil engineering) '24-39 (Stanford). Hydrologic and economic studies East Maui Water Supply justifying $1,000,000 improvement in aqueduct system; designed same resulting in 30 percent increase in surface supply; studied ground water resources East Maui; water supply Central Valley Project. Author reports on various irrigation districts. Supt E Maui Irrigation Co TH '29-44; hydrologic engr Central Valley Project Bur Reclamation since '45. Am Soc CE(asso)—Am Assn Engineers. 318 Patterson Bldg., Fresno, Cal.

19 SUMMERS, Eaton Melroy. Sugarcane (Diseases); Japan (Plant diseases). b'01. BSc '22 (Neb U); MS '28—PhD '35 (Ia State Coll; Demonstrated existence strains of virus causing sugarcane mosaic disease; co-discoverer two new vectors of sugarcane mosaic disease; aided in development technique for testing sugarcane seedlings for disease resistance and initial stages field adaptability. Co-author article: (with E W Brandes, R D Rands) The mosaic Disease of Sugarcane in the United States with Special Reference to Strains of the Virus. Path div sugar plant investigations BPISAE Houma La '30-50; prin path natural resources sect GHQ Supreme Command Allied Powers Japan and Okinawa '50-51. Agronomist United Fruit Sugar Company Preston Cuba since '51. Am Phytopath Soc—AAAS—Internat Soc of Sugar Cane Tech—Sigma Xi—Alpha Zeta—Gamma Sigma Delta. United Fruit Sugar Company, Preston (Oriente), Cuba.†

20 SUMMERS, Lane. b'89. Student '09-10 (U Chicago); '07-09 (U Mich); LLB '12 (U Wash). Asso editor American Maritime Cases '26-51. Admitted Washington state bar '12; dep pros atty Seattle '14-18; preacicing lawyer specializing in maritime law Seattle since '12, partner Summers Bucey & Howard; chmn com to draft admiralty rules apptd by US Dist Ct '40-41; advisor Japan Ship Owners Mut Protection and Indemnity Assn since '48. Am Bar Assn—Washington State Bar Assn—Seattle Bar Assn—Maritime Law Assn US—Nat Assn Legal Aid Orgns—Am Judicature Soc—Soc Wel-

fare League. Central Bldg., Seattle 4.†☺

21 SUMMERSELL, Charles Grayson. History of Alabama; Maritime history. b'08. BA '29—MA '30 (U Ala); PhD '40 (Vanderbilt U). Member editorial advisory board American Neptune. Author: Historical Foundations of Mobile '48. Co-author: Alabama Past and Future '41. With U Ala since '35, prof hist since '47. So Hist Assn—Ala Hist Assn—AHA—Phi Beta Kappa—Phi Alpha Theta. P.O. Box 2056, University of Alabama, University, Ala.☺

22 SUMNER, James Batcheller. Enzyme chemistry. b'87. AB '10—AM '13—PhD '14 (Harvard). Determination substance of enzyme to be protein; study properties of enzymes, including urease, catalase, peroxidase, lipoxidase, plant phosphorylase, glucuronidase, and lactic dehyorgenase; devised analytical methods for determination of glucose, phosphorus, and urea. Co-author: (with G F Somers) Laboratory Experiments in Biological Chemistry; (with Somers) Chemistry and Methods of Enzymes, also articles in field. Editor (with K Myrbäck): The Enzymes (4 vols). Asst prof biochem Cornell U '14-29, prof biochem since '29. Am Soc Biol Chem—Nat Acad Sci—Am Acad Arts and Sci—Soc Exptl Biol Med—AAAS—Phi Kappa Phi—Sigma Xi. Awarded Nobel Prize in chemistry '46. Savage Hall, Cornell University, Ithaca, N.Y.

23 SUMNER, Lowell. Aerial game census (Western United States, Alaska); Vegetation and life zone aerial mapping (Colorado River Basin). b'07. BA (Pomona Coll); MA '34 (U Calif). Author articles in field. Regional biol Nat Park Service San Francisco since '45. Am Ornithol Union—Wildlife Soc. National Park Service, 180 New Montgomery St., San Francisco.

24 SUMNER, Robert J(ocelyn). Food and cereal chemistry (Enzymology, baking technology and nutrition). b'15. AB '37 (Hobart Coll); PhD '41 (Cornell U). Author articles in field. Indsl fellow wheat technol Mellon Inst Indsl Research '41-45; dir research C J Patterson Co Kan City Mo '45-47; dir research Am Inst Baking, Chicago '47-48; asst dir research Anheuser-Busch Inc St Louis Mo '48-52 director central research since '52. Am Chem Soc—Am Assn Cereal Chem—Am Soc Bakery Engrs—Inst Food Technol—Phi Beta Kappa. Anheuser-Busch, Inc., St. Louis.

25 SUN, Shiou-Chuan. Mineral flotation; Minerals (Gravity concentration). b'13. BS '35 (Pei-Yang U); MS '38 (Mo Sch Mines); ScD '45 (MIT). Research on use zeta potential to interpret phenomena slime coating and flotation of minerals, use of multibubble hypothesis to explain nonfloatability coarse coal and mineral particles, invented distribution analyzer for electrostatic separation of minerals, froth meter to measure frothability of flotation reagents, flotation reagents for flotation oxidized coals. Asst mining engr Northwestern Indsl Corp '35-36; research engr MIT '45-46; asso prof mineral preparation Pa State Coll since '52. AIMME—ACS Sigma Xi—Phi Lambda Upsilon—Sigma Gamma Epsilon. Research F US Bur Mines Mo Sch Mines '38-39. Department of Mineral Engineering, Pa State College, State College, Pa.

26 SUNDBERG, Carl Oscar. Steel (Heat treatment). b'16. BS (Met E) '39 (Va Poly Inst). Development of new and improved processes including gas carburizing, carbonitriding and controlled atmosphere heat treating;

application statistical quality control to heat treatment problems. Metall tester Republic Steel Corp Cleveland '39; tech apprentice and asst foreman Am Steel & Wire Co Joliet Ill '39-42; process metall Diamond Chain Co Inc since '46. Am Soc Metals—Soc Exptl Stress Analysis—Am Soc Quality Control—Tau Beta Pi—Phi Kappa Phi. 402 Kentucky Av., Indpls 7.

10 SUNESON, Coit Alfred. Wheat and barley (Production, breeding, genetics, pathology, ecology, insects); Crop ecology. b'03. BS '28 (Mont State Coll); MS '30 (Kan State Coll); '31, '35 (U Neb); '39, '41 (U Calif). Discovered male sterile barley '40, wild oats resistant to both stem and crown rust '48. Author articles in field. Wheat prodn and breeding US Dept Agr and U Neb '30-36; asst emergency seed stocks purchase US Dept Agr Neb and Ia '34-35; wheat, barley, and oats prodn and breeding US Dept Agr and U Calif since '36; regional coordinator wheat improvement in western region of 8 states '37-47. Am Soc Agron—AAAS(F)—Gamma Sigma Delta—Alpha Zeta—Sigma Xi. University Farm, Davis, Calif.

11 SURFACE, Frank Macy. Economics (Public opinion, marketing, cost of distribution). b'82. BA '04—MA '05 (O State U); PhD '07 (U Pa); '11 (Royal Agr Coll Copenhagen). Special agent Bureau of the Census as founder and editor of Survey of Current Business '21-23; special agent Bureau Foreign and Domestic Commerce in charge of a survey of world trade in agricultural products '23-24. Author: American Pork Production in the World War; The Grain Trade During the World War; American Food in the World War and the Reconstruction Period. Co-author: Marketing; also articles in field. Dir sales research Standard Oil Co (NJ) '33-42, world-wide coordinator sales research '42-45, exec asst to pres '45-47, cons bd dirs since '47. AAAS(F)—Am Statis Assn—Am Econ Assn—Am Farm Econ Assn—Am Marketing Soc (Pres '35)—Am Acad Polit Social Soc—Phi Kappa Phi—Sigma Xi. 30 Rockefeller Plaza, NYC. H: 203 S. Highland St., Harrison, Ark.†☉

12 SURREY, Frederick James. Psychology (Learned motor responses). b'07. BS '30 (Muckingum Coll); AM '32 (Ohio U); PhD '39 (U Ill). Established motor learned responses posterior to transection spinal cord in dogs and cats; research effect localized lesions; discovery mucopoly-saccharide enzyme-substrate system in Vitreous Humor whose depolymerization and photorepolymerization parallel dark and light adaption in mammalian eyes; that substrate Hyaluronic Acid mesenchyme of central nervous tissues is depolymerized during stimulation and repolymerized in recovery through inactivation enzyme Hyaluronidase. NRC Fellow psychol U Rochester '39-40; vis prof psychol U Pa '40-41; cons psychol Stevenson, Jordan and Harrison Inc '44-46; prof and chmn dept psychol and edn Ill Inst Tech since '46, pres personnel and plant analysts since '50. Am Bd Examiners Profl Psychol (Diplomate Indsl Psychol)—Am Psychol Assn—Am Soc Engring Edn—Am Statis Soc—Sigma Xi—Pi Gamma Mu—Omicron Delta Kappa—Kappa Delta Phi. 14320 South Clark Street, Riverdale, Chicago 27, Illinois.

13 SUSCA, Louis Anthony. Blood (Effects of high altitude and low temperature on chemical composition). b '26. BS '45—MS '47—PhD '49 (Fordham U). Studies on effects artificial and natural environment on blood changes (Particular attention given to cholesterol, glucose, lipid phosphorus); Effect low pressure on coagulation; Effects trypsin on coagulation time. Instructor NY Med Coll since '49; research asso and naval tech St. Louis U Expedition to Arctic '49. Am Soc Zool—Arctic Inst N A—AAAS—Soc NY Med Coll—Sigma Xi. 80 Kenmare St., NYC.

14 SUTER, Chester M. Organic and medicinal chemistry; Sulfur. b'02. AB '23 (Southwestern Coll); MS '26—PhD '27 (U Kan); research fellow '27-28 (Yale). Author: Organic Chemistry of Sulfur '44; also articles in field. Asso dir research Sterling-Winthrop Research Inst since '46. Am Chem Soc—AAAS. Sterling-Winthrop Research Institute, Rensselaer, N.Y.

15 SUTHERLAND, Arthur Bruce. Australian, Canadian and modern British literature; Maurice Hewlett. b'04. AB '29 (Dartmouth Colll); MA '32—PhD '40 (U Pa). Author: Maurice Hewlett: A Bibliography '35; Maurice Hewlett: Historical Romancer '38; also articles in field. With Pa State Coll since '35, prof Eng lit since '49. Modern Lang Assn—Australian Eng Assn. Fulbright research Australia, '51-52. Dept. of English Literature, Pennsylvania State College, State College, Pa. H: 456 Hillcrest Av.†

16 SUTHERLAND, Stella Helen. Population distribution (United States). BA '20 (Queen's U); MA '21 (U Chicago); PhD '31 (U Ill). Research on distribution of United States population University of Chicago '25-29, University of Illinois '29-31, in historical society and state records of colonial states, and in various state, university and national libraries US and Bermuda. Author: Population Distribution in Colonial America '36; American Public Opinion '38; also articles in field. Asst prof Central State Coll Edmond Okla '46-48, asso prof since '48. AHA—Am Acad Polit Social Sci—Modern Lang Assn Am. Box 244, University Station, Fayetteville, Ark.

17 SUTTON, Glenn Wallace. Economics (State, county and municipal employment and payroll, urban consumer purchases, money and banking). b'04. BS '26—AM '27 (Ind U); PhD '38 (O State U). Author articles in field. With U Ga since '29, prof finance since '37, dir Bur Bus Research '29-46; dir SE states Urban Study Consumer Purchases of Bur Labor Statis US Dept Labor '36, dir Nat Tabulation Office '37; dir SE states State Co and Municipal Employment Survey Bur Labor Statis '39-41, nat dir '41. Am Econ Assn—So Econ Assn. University of Georgia, Athens, Ga.☉

18 SUTTON, John G. Drainage. b'02. BS '24 (U Calif). Designer drainage systems, pumping plants, soil conservation plans; coordination of drainage plans with soil conservation practices. Author articles in field. Dist engr in charge CCC drainage camps '35-39; head drainage sect Soil Conservation Service since '39. Am Soc Agrl Engrs. Soil Conservation Service, U.S. Department of Agriculture, Washington. H: 1150 Kalmia Rd. N.W.

19 SUTTON, Roger. Alloys; Heat exchanges; Temperature measurement of metals. born '05. B Ch E '27—MS '28 (U Detroit). Studies on heat resistant alloys, high creep-strength alloys, light weight thermostatically controlled heat exchanger, formulation of dental alloys, porous and dense powder metallurgy bonding of metals and metalloids, and measurement of liquid metal temperatures. Author articles in field. Chrysler Corp '33-41; sr asso Roger Sutton Associates gen cons '45-50; project dir, jet-engine and hot-gas tur-

bine specialist, Alloy Engring and Casting Corp '45-50; metall engr P F McDonald & Co '46-50; sr metallurgist Argonne Nat Lab since '50. Am Soc Metals—Am Inst Mining Metall Engrs (chmn NE Regional Conf Inst Metals Div '49-50)—Engring Soc Detroit—Engring Soc NE—Am Soc Testing Materials (com A-10, B-4, E-7)—Alloy Casting Inst (chmn high temperature steering com, specification and designations com '50). Argonne National Laboratory, P.O. Box 299, Lemont, Ill

20 SUTTON, Thomas Scott. Nutrition; Dairy science. b'02. BSc '28—MSc '29—PhD '34 (O State U). Research in fundamental nutrition relating to vitamin A content of butter, effects of vitamin A deficiency on nervous system and pituitary gland, factors effecting synthesis of ascorbic acid in animal body, composition and nutritive value of colostrum, effects of lecithin on vitamin A absorption and metabolism, riboflavin deficiency in calf, relation of tryptophan to niacin in nutrition, nutritive value and physiological effects of dietary lactose. Author articles in field. Prof, chmn agrl biochem O State U '48-51, dir Inst Nutrition and Food Tech '48-50, asst dean coll chmn dept animal sci since '51. Am Inst Nutrition—Am Dairy Sci Assn—Am Soc Animal Production—O Acad Sci—Am Chem Soc—Sigma Xi—Gamma Sigma Delta. O State University, Columbus 10, O.†

21 SVEDA, Michael. Silicon chemistry; Wax chemistry; Sulfur chemistry; Synthetic sweetening agents; D DT. b'12. BS '34 (Toledo U); PhD '39 (U Ill). Research on and development of uses for concentrated colloidal silica dispersions; production of hard, anti-slip floor waxes; inventor process for production pyrosulfuryl chloride, thionyl chloride; process vapor-phase sulfonation hydrocarbons with sulfur trioxide. Issued patents in field. Staff Toledo U, U Ill, chem research and product development du Pont Co since '39. ACS—AAAS—ASTM—Chem Specialties Mfrs Assn—Alpha Chi Sigma—Sigma Xi—Phi Lambda Upsilon—Phi Kappa Phi. Room 4147 du Pont Bldg., Wilmington 98, Del. H: 116 Duncan Av., McDaniel Heights, Wilmington, Del.

22 SVERDRUP, Leif John. Bridge engineering (Construction). b'98. BA '18 (Augsburg Coll); BS '21 (U Minn). Special consultant US Corps of Engineers on portable military bridges; special consultant Public Works Administration on Lake Washington Pontoon bridge, Seattle; member board inquiry into failure of Tacoma Narrows bridge, also member consulting board on re-design of same. Sr partner Sverdrup & Parcel cons engrs since '28. Col Corps Engrs US Army '42-44, brig gen '44, maj gen since '45; chief engr overseas duty in southwest Pacific since '42. Am Soc Mil Engrs—ASCE—Am Inst Cons Engrs—Am Ry Engring Assn. 1118 Syndicate Trust Building, StL 1.

23 SWAIN, James O(bed). Nineteenth century Spanish novel (Jose Maria de Pereda, V Blasco Ibanez, Concha Espina); Costa Rican mystics; Chilean literature (Historical novel). b'96. AB '21—MA '23 (Ind U); PhD '32 (U Ill); student (Centro de Estudios Historicos Madrid, Sorbonne Paris). Traveled Costa Rica and Panama '23-28, Spain '33, Mexico '40, '42, Caribbean Island '45. Author articles in field. Chmn dept romance lang and prof U Tenn since '37. Am Assn Teachers Spanish (asso editor Hispania '37-42)—Am Assn Teachers French—Am Assn Teachers Italian—Modern Lang Assn Am (asst bus mgr Journal since '42)—

So Atlantic Modern Lang Assn (pres '47-48). Department of Romance Languages, University of Tennessee, Knoxville, Tenn.

10 SWAIN, Joseph Ward. Ancient history; Decline of Roman Republic; Early Christianity; History of historical writing. b'91. AB '12—PhD '16 (Columbia); AM '13 (Harvard). Travel and research in the Near East and Italy '35. Author: Hellenic Origins of Christian Asceticism '16; What Is History? '23; History and the Science of Society, in Essays in Intellectual History, presented to James Harvey Robinson '29; Beginning the Twentieth Century '33 revised edition '40; The Ancient World (2 vols) '50. Emile Durkheim's The Elementary Forms of the Religious Life '15; also articles in field. Prof hist U Ill since '37. AHA—Am Oriental Society—Phi Beta Kappa. 308 Delaware Av., Urbana, Ill.⊙

11 SWAIN, Ralph Brownlee. Economic entomology; Mormon cricket; White-fringed beetles. b'12. BS '34 (Ia State Coll); MS '36 (Colo State Coll); PhD '40 (U Colo). Field studies on Mormon cricket utilization of crop and range plants; biological control of white-fringed beetles and fall webworms; surveys for introduced insect pests; disinsectization of aircraft; plant quarantine problems. Author: The Insect Guide, Orders and Major Families of North American Insects '48. Author articles: Nature and Extent of Mormon Cricket Damage to Crop and Range Plants '44. Asst in biol U Colo '36-38; agt Mormon cricket control project Bur Entomol and Plant Quarantine US Dept Agr '38-39, agt white-fringed beetle control project '40-45, plant quarantine insp div fgn plant quarantines since '45. NY Entomol Soc —Am Assn Econ Entomol—Kan Entomol Soc—Sigma Xi. 209 River St., Hoboken, N.J.

12 SWALLEN, Jason R(ichard). Grasses (Identification and classification). b'03. AB '24 (O Wesleyan U); MS '25 (Kan State Coll); grad work (U Mich). Author articles in field. Bot US Dept Agr '25-43; agrl prodn office Office Inter-Am Affairs '43-45; asso curator US Nat Museum '46-47, curator div grasses '47-50, head curator department botany since '50. Washington Acad Sci—Michigan Academy Sci —Botanical Society America—Bot Soc Washington—Biol Soc Washington. Award Washington Acad Sci '44. Department of Botany, U.S. National Museum, Smithsonian Institution, Washington 25.

13 SWAN, Bradford Fuller. Rhode Island history and bibliography. b'07. AB '30 (Yale). Author: A Bibliography of Henry Blake Fuller '30; Captain Alexander Winsor '41; Gregory Dexter of London and New England '49. Editor: The Diary of Samuel Rodman 1825 '32; Roger William's Answer to John Easton '45; Roger William's Answer to Mr. Coddington's Letter '46; also articles in field. Reporter Providence RI Journal '37-41; movie and drama critic since '42; historian RI Soc Colonial Wars. Bibliog Soc Am—Bibliog Soc London—RI Hist Soc (editor RI Hist '43-46)—Old Dartmouth Hist Soc—New Eng Hist Geneal Soc. Providence Journal, Providence 2.

14 SWAN, Marshall Wilbur Stephen. American-Swedish and Anglo-Swedish history and literature. b'17. AB '39— AM '41—PhD '42 (Harvard). Author: Gustavus Vasa Again '45; George North's Description of Swedland '46; also articles in field. Curator Am Swedish Hist Found '46-49, ed yearbooks and bulls '46-49; chief N European Area Pub Affairs Staff Bur Euro-

pean Affairs '49-51 cultural attache Am Embassy The Hague since '51. Am Scandinavian Found—Soc Adv of Scandinavian Studies — Am-Swedish Hist Found. Bureau European Affairs, Dept of State, Washington 25.

15 SWANEBECK, Clarence W. Beans (Production); Peas (Production). b'96. Student (Mich State Coll). Sec-mgr Pioneer Mutual Fire Ins Co since '45; mem Michigan Bean Council Saginaw since '46; mem Nat Dry Bean and Pea Research Adv Com Washington since '47; dir State Assn Mutual Ins Cos Lansing since '45; mem bd dirs Fed Crop Ins Corp Washington since '47. Mich Bean Producers Assn. 226 E. Grand River Av., Lansing, Mich.⊙

16 SWANN, David H(enry). Petroleum geology; Fossil corals. b'15. BS '37—PhD '41 (U Mich). Author: The Favosites Alpenensis Lineage in the Middle Devonian Traverse Group of Michigan '47. Co-author articles: King Oil Field '46; Bibliography of the Geology of Rhode Island. Asso geol Ill Geol Survey '44-48; geol since '48. Am Assn Pet Geol—Paleontological Soc— Ill Geol Soc—Ill Soc Pet Engr—Sigma Xi—Phi Beta Kappa—Phi Kappa Phi. Illinois Geological Survey, Urbana, Ill.†

17 SWANN, Reginald Le Grand. Measurement (Psychological); Mental hygiene. b'04. AB '30 (Union Coll); AM '33 (Harvard); MA (edn) '33 (NY State Coll Teachers); '37 (Columbia); '45 (NY U). Research on psychology of childhood and adolescence, clinical psychology, psychological measurement, counseling, mental hygiene. Prof psychol and dir student personnel of Green Mt Jr Coll '33-42; asso prof psychol St Lawrence U '45-46; asso prof psychol and edn Teachers Coll Conn since '46. Am Psychol Assn—E Psychol Assn—Conn Valley Assn Psychol—Soc Research Child Development —Am Ednl Research Assn—Am Coll Personnel Assn—Phi Delta Kappa—Phi Beta Kappa—Nat Soc Coll Teachers of Edn. Teachers College of Connecticut, New Britain, Conn. H: 22 Eton Pl.

18 SWANSON, Carl P(ontius). Economic cytogenetics; Radiation biology; Chromosome mechanics. b'11. BS '37 (Mass State Coll); MA '39—PhD '41 (Harvard). Agent US Department Agriculture cytogenetics of cotton '39; asst prof botany Mich State Coll '41-43, research cytogenetics of economic plants and effects of radiation on living cells, teaching genetics and cytology; asso biologist US Pub Health Service Bethesda Md, research in field of radiation biology with emphasis on effects of X-rays ultraviolet and infrared; asso prof botany Johns Hopkins U '46-48, prof botany Johns Hopkins U since '48, teaching genetics, gen botany, cytology, research in radiation biology and cytological effects of plant growth-regulators. Author articles in field. Genetics Soc Am—Bot Soc Am—AAAS (F)—Am Soc Naturalists—Sigma Xi. Department of Biology, Johns Hopkins University, Baltimore 18.⊙

19 SWANSON, Gustav Adolph. Mammalogy (Minnesota); Wildlife management. b'10. BS '30—MA '32—PhD '37 (U Minn). Co-author: (with T Surber and T S Roberts) Mammals of Minnesota '46; also articles in field. With US Fish and Wildlife Service since '44, chief branch wildlife research '44-48; head dept conservation Cornell U since '48. Wildlife Soc (vp '45-46)—Soil Conservation Soc—Am Soc Mammalogists —Soc Am Foresters—AAAS—Am Ornithol Union—Wilson Ornithol Club— Minn Acad Sci—Am Soc Icthyologists

and Herpetologists—Sigma Xi. Fernow Hall, Cornell Univ., Ithaca, N.Y.†⊙

20 SWANSON, Paul Luther. Herpetology (Snake venoms); Indiana, Pennsylvania, Florida, Mexico, Panama); Dendrology (Conifers). b'06. Student '24-26 (Pa State Forest Sch). Made extensive field studies of distribution and life history of reptiles and amphibians of various regions; studied reactions of snakes to venom. Author articles: Herpetological Notes from Indiana '39; Herpetological Notes from Panama '45; Effects of Snake Venoms on Snakes '46; Notes on the Amphibians of Venango County Pennsylvania '48. US Forest Service '29; Resettlement Admnstrn USDA '34-38; Canal Zone Expt Gardens '42-44, Health Dept '44; half owner Swanson Bros Nursery since '29. Am Soc Ichthyologists and Herpetologists—Herpetologists League (charter). R.F.D. 2, Polk, Pa.

21 SWANTON, John Reed. Haida Indians (Ethnology); Southeastern Indians (Ethnology); Hernando de Soto; Emanuel Swedenborg. b'73. AB '96— AM '97 (Harvard); student '98-00 (Columbia); PhD '00 (Harvard). Author: Contributions to the Ethnology of the Haida '05; Haida Texts and Myths '05; Haida Texts—Masset Dialect; Social Conditions, Beliefs, and Linguistic Relationship of the Tlingit Indians; Tlingit Myths and Texts; Indian Tribes of the Lower Mississippi Valley and Adjacent Coast of the Gulf of Mexico. Ethnologist Bur Am Ethnology Washington '00-44. Am Anthrop Assn—Anthrop Soc Washington—AAA S—Linguistic Soc Am—Nat Acad Scis. 22 George St., Newton 58, Mass.⊙

22 SWARTZ, Delbert. Fungi (Physiology, morphology). b'00. AB '22 (Miami U); MS '24 (Mich State Coll); PhD '31—Emma J Cole fellow '28-29 (U Mich). Research on Lycoperdaceae, fungi of the soil in relation to soil nitrogen. Author articles in field. Instr bot U Cincinnati '24-26, U Mich '26-27; asst prof bot U Ark '29-34, asso prof '34-44, prof '44-46, prof and head dept bact and vet sci '46-50, prof chmn botany and bacteriology since '50. Ark Acad Sci—Mich Acad Sci— Mycol Soc Am—Bot Soc Am—Sigma Xi—Phi Beta Kappa. University of Arkansas, Fayetteville, Ark.

23 SWARTZ, Frank McKim. Geology; Paleontology. b'89. BA '21—PhD '26 (Johns Hopkins). Research on stratigraphy and paleontology of Devonian Silurian and Cambro-Orvodician sediments of Pennsylvania-Virginia-West Virginia-New York region; consultant in same area on high-calcium limestone, oil and gas possibilities of deep horizons, water supply, coal lands development, rock for manufacture of lightweight aggregate for concrete. Author articles in field. With Pa State Coll since '25, prof paleontol since '44, chief div geol since '45; assoc geol Pa Geol Survey since '30. Geol Soc Am(F) —Paleontol Soc (F, treas since '47)— Soc Econ Paleontol and Mineral (asso). School of Mineral Industries, Pennsylvania State College, State College, Pa.

24 SWARTZ, Harry. Allergy. b'11. AB '30—MD '33 (U Mich); '36-38 (NYU Med Sch and Clinics). Author: Allergy: What It Is and What to Do About It '49; also articles in field. Clinical asst allergy NYU Med Sch and Clinics Bellevue Hosp '36-39, Flower Fifth Av Hosp '39-41; chief allergy dept Tilton Gen Hospital New Jersey '42-46; asst vis phys med and allergy Harlem Hosp since '46; clinical asst allergy out-patient dept Roosevelt Hosp since '46. Am Acad Allergy(F)—NY Allergy Soc—Internat Corr Soc Allergists— AMA—Am Assn Hist Med. 105 East 73rd St., NYC 21.

10 SWAYZE, Harry Edward. Metallurgy of magnesium; Graphic arts (Photoengraving). b'14. '34-36 (Mich State Coll). Research on electrothermal reactions involving reduction of magnesium containing ores for production of metallic magnesium, electrochemical theory of stress-corrosion of magnesium and magnesium alloys; introduced magnesium as a photoengraving metal '45. Sr lab tech Dow Chem Co '37-43, research engr '43-45, research and development engr since '45. Am Soc Metals. The Dow Chemical Company, Midland, Mich. H: 4222 Concord St.

11 SWEARINGEN, Lloyd E(dward). Chemistry; Physical and chemical effects related to small particle size of matter. b'97. BS '20—MS '21 (U Okla); PhD '26 (U Minn); '39-40 (MIT). Research on aging of surfaces, preparation of metal films on absorbent surfaces, thixotropic character of disperse systems, adsorption, contact catalysis. Author articles in field. Prof and chmn dept chem Southwestern State Coll Weatherford Okla '21-23; asst prof dept chem U Okla '23-26, asso prof '26-28, prof chem '28-47, research prof chem since '48; dir U Okla Research Inst since '47. Col Chem Warfare Service '42-46. Am Chem Soc—AAAS—Okla Acad Sci—Soc Promotion Engring Edn —Sigma Xi—Phi Beta Kappa. University of Oklahoma, Norman, Okla.†

12 SWEDENBERG, Hugh Thomas, Jr. Theory of the epic. b'06. BA '28 (Presbyterian Coll); MA '29 (Columbia U); PhD '37 (U NC). Author: The Theory of the Epic in England 1650-1800 '44; George Stepney's Translation of the Eighth Satire of Juvenal '48. Co-author: (with L B Wright) The American Tradition '41. Instr and asso prof Eng U Calif since '37; research Henry E Huntington Library since '37. Mod Lang Assn Am—Augustan Reprint Soc (co-founder '46)—Phi Beta Kappa. Office: Department of English, University of California, Los Angeles 24.†

13 SWEET, Donald Howard. Wind tunnel design; Machine design; Aerodynamics; Metallurgical engineering. b'89. AB '13 (Adelbert Coll of WRU); BS in mech engring '13 (Case Sch Applied Sci); '16, '17, '18 (Law Sch George Washington U); LLB '21 (Chicago Kent Coll Law). Asst examiner US Patent Office '16-19; gen patent practice and consultation Chicago since '19. Bar US Patent Office—Phi Beta Kappa—Sigma Xi—Philos Soc Washington—AAAS(F)—AIC(F). 330 South Wells St., Chgo 6.

14 SWEETMAN, Harvey L(eroy). Animal ecology; Entomology; Insect control practices; Ecology and entomology in Mexico and Central America; Insecticidal and insect control practices in Mexico; Thysanura; Household insects. b'96. BS '23 (Colo State Coll); MS '25 (Ia State Coll); PhD '30 (Mass Agrl Coll); '25-27 (U Minn). Survey of ecology and entomology in Mexico and Central America, southern and western US. Author: Biological Control of Insects '36; also articles in field. Prof entomol and ecol U Mass since '47. AAAS—Entomol Soc Am—Ecol Soc Am—Am Soc Limnology and Oceanography—Royal Entomol Society London—Gamma Sigma Delta—Phi Kappa Phi—Sigma Xi. Department of Entomology, University of Mass., Amherst, Mass.†

15 SWEETS, Foster Martin. Electronics; Radar. b'14. AB '35 (Centre Coll); AM '39 (U Ky). Installation, maintenance, operation radars in various parts of US and other countries; theoretical and laboratory research for development and design power oscillators, output circuits, control circuits,

transmission lines; design laboratory apparatus and special equipment for this experimental work. Research and development dept Thermex Div Girdler Corp '46-49; owner Martin Sweets Co since '49. Inst Radio Engrs—Sigma Pi Sigma—Phi Delta Kappa—Kappa Delta Pi. 126 South First St., Lsvl 2.

16 SWEETS, Henry Hayes, Jr. Toxicology. b'10. BS '33 (U Louisville); MD '37 (U Louisville Sch Medicine). Asso prof clinical pathology and dir labs U Hosp U Mo since '50. Coll Am Pathologists Pathology and Clin Pathology—Am Soc Clin Pathology—AMA. Sweets Pathology Laboratory, 909 University Av., Columbia, Mo.

17 SWEIGERT, Ray Leslie. Heat power; Thermodynamics; Internal combustion engines. b'98. BS '20 (Ill U); MA '30—PhD '35 (Ia U). Research on thermodynamic properties of various gases, engine fuels; thermodynamic studies in the engine field covering new combination cycle analysis. Author articles in field. Mech Engr Deere and Co '20, engr in admnstrn Deere Co '22-26; supervisor indust edn E Peoria and E Chicago '26-29; asst prof Ga Sch Tech '29-31, asso prof '31-36, prof since '36, dir freshman engring '34-41, dir gen engring '41-48, dean grad division since '47; cons mech engr since '30; special cons Navy Project '41-42, Army Project '43; State dir Engring, Science and Management War Training '41-45. ASME—Am Soc Engring Edn—Ga Acad Sci—Nat Soc Professional Engr—Ga Soc Professional Engr—Sigma Xi. Fellow AAAS. 1115 Peachtree Battle Av. N.W., Atlanta.†⊙

18 SWENSON, George Warner. Electrical communications engineering; Radio; Radar. b'93. BS '17—MS '21—EE '21 (U Minn). Research on oscillographic study of relay contact sparking, high voltage cable insulation; telephone specialist US Bur Standards '22, spl consultant '24; operations analyst US Army Air Corps '42-44; spl consultant radar Sec War. Author: Elements of Radio Communications '24. Author articles: Loading Telephone Cables '24; Radio Interference '30. Telephone engr West Elec Co '18; Instr elec engring dept '19-24, asst prof '24-28; prof, head elec engring dept Mich Coll Mining and Tech Houghton '28-42, prof, head elec engring dept since '44. AIEE (F, student br counselor, chmn Gt Lakes student activities '39)—Am Soc Engring Edn (chmn nat elec engring div '40)—Tau Beta Pi— Eta Kappa Nu. Michigan College of Mining and Technology, Houghton, Mich.⊙

19 SWENSON, Stanley Prescott. Wheat and barley breeding; Control of cereal rusts and smuts. b'08. BS '32 —MS '35—hD '36 (U Minn). Development four new wheat varieties, one barley variety; statistical design agricultural and biological experiments; visiting consultant agricultural research Office Military Government of Germany '48. Author articles: Spring Wheat Varieties in South Dakota '40; Wheat Improvement in the Pacific Northwest '42, and others. Co-author articles: (with Darrell G Wells) The Linkage Relations of Four Genes in Chromosome I of Barley '44; (with D G Wells) Inheritance and Interaction of Genes Governing Reaction to Stem Rust, Leaf Rust, and Powdery Mildew in a Spring Wheat Cross '44; (with Shirley Kellenbarger) Pearling Index and Wheat Meal Fermentation Time in Two Winter Wheat Crosses '48, and others. Asst prof agron SD State Coll '36, asso prof '36-41; asso prof farm crops Wash State Coll '41-46, prof '46-49, dean coll of agr since '49; asst dir agrl expt sta '46-49. AAAS

(F)—Am Soc Agron—Genetics Soc Am —Am Genetic Assn—Biometric Soc— Sigma Xi. College of Agriculture, State College of Washington, Pullman, Wash.

20 SWEZEY, William, W(eekley). Ciliate protozoa. b'10. BS '30 (Mt Union Coll); Sc D '33 (Johns Hopkins U Sch Hygiene and Pub Health). Research on protozoa of chimpanzee and in malaria therapy. Prof biol York Coll '34-36; prof biol Defiance Coll '36-46; asst to pres '44-46; lecturer U Ind Fort Wayne Div '39-46; prof zool Grove City Coll since '46. Am Soc Tropical Med and Hygiene—Am Soc Parasitol—Sigma Xi —Pa Acad Sci—Gamma Alpha—Psi Kappa Omega—Phi Sigma—Omega Delta Kappa. Grove City College, Grove City, Pa.†⊙

21 SWIFT, George P. Electroplating (Metallurgy; aluminum, zinc, and magnesium castings). born '03. SB '24— SM '28—ScD '44 (MIT). Research on corrosion and corrosion prevention of condenser tubes, performance tests and characteristics of lead storage batteries, metal finishing and electroplating precious and non-precious metals, permanent mold casting of aluminum zinc and magnesium alloys, spectrographic analysis, salt spray testing, chemical analysis of nonferrous alloys and electroplated deposits, solution control. With MIT '24-44; cons engr electrochem and nonferrous metall since '30. Am Inst Mining Metall Engrs (dir since '49)—British Inst Metals —Am Electroplaters Soc—Am Soc Metals—Am Soc Testing Materials (NE councillor since '48)—Am Trade Execs Assn—Master Metal Finishers Assn NE (exec sec since '46)—Sigma Xi. 53 Galen St., Watertown 72, Mass. H: 40 Colonial Av., Waltham 54.

22 SWIFT, James Verdin. Western river steamboats (Mississippi River system). b'16. Student (Washington U, U Wis). Bus mgr Waterways Jour since '41. Hot Stove Navigation League of Am. 619 Chemical Building, 721 Olive St., St. Louis 1.

23 SWIGGETT, Glen Levin. Inter-American education and relations; Foreign service training; Foreign trade; Dante; Comparative literature. b'67. AB '88—AM '93 (Ind U); '89-90, '92-93 (Johns Hopkins); '98, '01 (U Gottingen and Marburg, U Berlin); PhD '01—Harrison travel fellow '01-02 (U Pa). Organized, compiled and edited Proc 2d Pan-American Scientific Congress, 11 volumes in 4 languages '15-17; organizing secretary first Educational Conference for Foreign Service Training '15 and 2d Pan-American Scientific Congress '15; delegate Pan-American Financial Conferences '15, '20; delegate 3d Pan-American Scientific Congress Lima '24-25; delegate guest of government of Panama Centenary Bolivarian Congress Panama '26; delegate El Universal Mexico 1st Pan-American Conference of Journalists '29; delegate 2d Pan-American Conference Geography and History '35, delegate State Department Inter-American Relations Conference '39; professor foreign trade and international relations University World Cruise '31-32. 42 The Mendota, Washington 9.

24 SWINEFORD, Ada. Volcanic ash; Cheyenne and Dakota sandstone; Kansas rocks and minerals. b'17. SB '40— SM '42 (U Chicago); '47-49 (Penn State Coll). Author articles in field. Geologist State Geol Survey of Kan since '42. Geol Soc Am(F)—Soc Econ Paleontologists and Mineralogists—AAAS— Kan Acad Sci—Am Geophys Union— Am Assn Pet Geol (asso)—Sigma Xi. State Geological Survey, Lawrence, Kan.

10 SWINGLE, Charles F(letcher). Plant propagation (Anatomy, physiology); Madagascar and Peruvian plants; Tropical agriculture. b'99. BS '20 (Kans State Coll); PhD '27 (Johns Hopkins). Research various aspects plant propagation, graft hybrids, erosion control plants, Peruvian plants and life; participated Humbert-Swingle exploration for rubber and other economic plants Madagascar '28; horticulturist with USDA '22-43, office foreign agricultural relations and chief department agronomy and horticulture Ministry Agr Peru Tingo Maria Experimental Station '45-47. Author articles: Vegetative Propagation from the Standpoint of Plant Anatomy (with J H Priestley) '29; Dictionary of Cultivated Plants of Peru (with A Gazzo) '47; other articles in field. Res, extn hort, supt peninsular br exptl sta Sturgeon Bay Univ Wis '47-50. AAAS(F)—Am Soc Plant Physiologists—Am Soc Hort Sci—Am Genetic Assn—Soc Am Foresters—Peruv Soc Agronomists—Wis Hort Soc—Sigma Xi—Gamma Sigma Delta—Explorers Club. Received Nat Res Council fellowship Internatl Edn Bd Leeds England '27-28. Sturgeon Bay, Wis.

11 SWINGLE, Homer Scott. Fish culturist; Fish production in ponds. b'02. BS '24—MSc '25 (O State U). Author articles in field. Asso fish culturist Agrl Expt Sta Ala Poly Inst since '34, fish culturist since '40; collaborator US Soil Conservation Service since '42; US Fish and Wildlife Service since '45. Am Fisheries Soc—Sigma Xi. Alabama Polytechnic Institute, Auburn, Ala.†

12 SWINNEY, C(hauncey) Melvin. Mineralogy; Petrology; Economic geology. b'18. BA '40 (Pomona Coll); PhD '49 (Stanford). Co-author articles: Petroleum Possibilities of Wide Bay, Alaska '46; other articles in field. Instr mineralogy and geol Stanford U since '47-49, asst prof since '49, geol P-3 US Geol Survey since '42, now WAE status. Am Assn Petroleum Geologists—Geol Soc Am—Am Geophys Un—Sigma Xi. School of Mineral Sciences, Stanford University, Stanford, Calif.

13 SWINNEY, Holman Jerome. Firearms (American, history); Arms and arms makers (New York State, history). b'19. AB '41 (Colgate U). Studies and collections firearms for 20 years with emphasis on New York State; semi-professional rifle stockmaker. Author: New York State Gunmakers: A Partial Checklist '51. Chief clerk quality control sect Remington Arms Co Ilion NY '41-43; sgt US Army Ordnance '43-46. National Rifle Assn—Eastern Arms Collectors Assn—NY State Hist Assn (advisor on firearms, faculty mem Seminar courses '53)—Early Am Industries Association—Mt Hope Fort Assn. Pratt Inst., Bklyn 5.

14 SWITZER, Marshall Haury. Can manufacture. b'10. Ed pub schs. Research, physical and chemical testing and performance evaluation of organic coatings for metal containers, relation of physical properties of sheet steel to metal container design and construction, relation of porosity of tin coating on tin plate to plate corrosion. With Am Can Co '33-40; F D Farnam Co '40-42; Owens-Ill Can Co '42-44; Owens-Ill Glass Co '44-47; C Olin Ball '47-49; with Continental Can Co since '49. Optical Soc Am—Am Inst Phys—Intersociety Color Council—ASTM—ACS—Inst Food Tech—AAAS—Am Soc Quality Control. H: 843 Washington Blvd., Oak Park, Ill.

15 SWOPE, H. Gladys. Sewerage and industrial waste treatment. '22-23, '24-25 (U Ill); BS '29—grad work (U Chicago). Research on removal of fluorides from natural waters by defluorite '37, treatment of tannery wastes, the determination of copper in sewage and industrial wastes. Author: Correlation Between B.O.D. and Suspended Solids of Activated Sludge Effluent '30. Co-author: (with F W Mohlman, G P Edwards) Technic and Significance of the Biochemical Oxygen Demand Determination '28; (with F W Mohlman, T L Herrick) Technic of Stream Pollution Investigations '31. Asst chem sewage treatment San Dist Chicago '25-32; research chem Nat Aluminate Corp Chicago '32-35; chief chem div sanitation, asst prof chem Kan State Bd of Health and U Kan '35-37; dist chem North Shore San Dist Waukegan Ill '37-44; Mellon Inst fellow '44-46; chief chem Allegheny Co San Authority Pittsburgh '46-48; sr chemist Argonne Nat Lab Chicago since '48. Am Chem Soc—Central States Sewage Works Assn—Am Water Works Assn—Sigma Xi. Argonne National Laboratory, P.O. Box 5207, Chicago 80.†

16 SYKES, Roger A(llen). Piezoelectric crystals; Electric filters. b'08. BS '29—MS '30 (MIT); '30-35 (Columbia). Fundamental research leading to the use of piezoelectric crystals in selective filters and frequency control '29-41. Holder 14 patents relating to crystals and wave filters. Co-author: Electromechanical Wave Filters and Transducers; Quartz Crystals for Electrical Circuits; also articles in field. Design crystal filters and crystal control oscillators Bell Telephone System '33-41, crystal development engr since '45. Development of crystal units for mil application '40-45. Inst Radio Engr—Research and Development Bd—Am Phys Soc.

17 SYLWESTER, Erhardt Paul. Weed control. b'06. BA '30 (St Olaf Coll); MS '31—PhD '45 (Ia State Coll). Author articles in field. Extension bot Ext Service Ia State Coll since '36, head seed Lab since '48. Ia Acad Sci—Am Bot Soc—AAAS—Gamma Sigma Delta—Sigma Xi. Extension Service, Iowa State College, Ames, Ia.

18 SZAYNA, Antoni. Petroleum technology; Plastics. b'97. BA '16 (Gym Drohobycz Poland, Vienna); MS '22—Docent (tres hon) '33 (Tech U Lwow); '24 (U Paris); MS '26 (Nat Sch Petroleum and Liquid Fuels, Strasbourg France); DSc '27 (U Strasbourg). Research on petroleum, organic chemicals,, carbon black, plastics, synthetic rubber, vapor phase reactions, radical chain mechanism reactions, pilot plant design and operation. Author articles in field. Holds several patents desulfurization, dehydrgenation of petroleum, carbon black, organic chemicals. Worked between studies oil plants, naval stores Gazy, Lwow '23, Sinclair Refining Co E Chicago Ind '31; asst prof petroleum tech Tech U Lwow Poland '33-34, cons engr '35-41; mem development staff Gen Labs US Rubber Co since '42; independent research Columbia U NYC '30, '36. Am Chem Soc—Am Inst Chem Engr. General Laboratories, U.S. Rubber Co., Passaic, N.J.

19 SZEFTEL, Marc. Russian and Slavic history. b'02. Master law '24 (U Warsaw); Dr law '34—Licentiate Slavic philology and history '38 (U Brussels). Author: "Le Commentaire historique de la Geste du Prince Igor" '48; also articles in field. Asst prof Russian and Slavic hist Cornell U '46, asso prof '48. Societe Jean Bodin pour l'Etude comparative des institutions—Amer Hist Assn. Belgian American Ednl Foundation fellow '42-45. Boardman Hall, Cornell University, Ithaca, N.Y.⊚

20 SZILARD, Leo. Nuclear physics (Chain reaction). b'98. PhD '22 (U Berlin); student (Budapest Inst Tech). With Enrico Fermi devised chain reaction system composed of uranium and graphite used in setting up chain reaction University of Chicago '42, also used at Hanford in manufacture of plutonium. Prof U Chicago since '46. Am Phys Soc(F). University of Chicago, Chgo.⊚

21 SZWARC, Alexander. Pulp, paper, and plastics chemistry. b'99. PhD '25 (U Poznan); Graduate (Superior Sch Armaments Warsaw). Cons chemical engring pulp and paper industry and chemical industry. Am Chem Assn—Can Standards Assn—Chem Inst Can—Soc Chem Industry—Tech Assn Pulp & Paper Industry—Am Soc Testing Materials—Assn Polish Engrs Canada. Room 412, Drummond Bldg., Montreal 2, Canada.

22 SZYMANOWITZ, Raymond. Colloidal graphite; Chemistry of fire fighting. b'98. Student '14-16 (Fawcett Sch Indsl Arts); BS '22 (Cooper Union). Research on colloidal dispersion of solids and applications of such dispersions in industry. Author: Colloidal Graphite; Edward Goodrich Acheson. Author articles: Chemistry in the Fire Department '24; Colloidal Graphite: Its Preparation, Properties and Diversified Uses in Industry '39. Invented matrix coating composition for use stereotyping operations '36. Chem Hyatt roller bearing div Gen Motors Corp Harrison NJ '16-19; chem Bell Tel Lab NYC '19-20; chem Waldrich Bleachery Delawanna NJ '21; research asst C J Thatcher NYC '22-24; tech dir Acheson Colloids Corp since '24; vp in charge of research since '50 Am Inst Chem(F)—Am Chem Society—SAE—Am Assn Textile Chem and Colorists—Photographic Soc Am—ASTM. 1019 Broad St., Newark 2.†

T

23 TABER, Wendell. New England birds. b'97. AB '20—'28-29 (Harvard). Research on forest and mountain birds of New England. Am Ornithol Union—Nuttall Ornithol Club (sec '34-39, since '47)—Me Audubon Soc—Wilson Ornithol Club—Cooper Ornithol Club.

24 TACK, Peter Isaac. Brook trout; Crayfish; Streams of northern New York and Michigan; Fish utilization and production. b'11. BS '34—PhD '39 (Cornell U). Research on toxicity measurement of several metals to brook trout and growth evaluation of trout, history and ecology of crayfish, utilization of common Michigan fishes, and production of fish in farm fish ponds. Author articles in field. Prof and head department fisheries and Wildlife Mich State College since '50. Limnological Soc Am—Am Fisheries Soc—Mich Acad Sci Arts Letters (chmn zool sect '48). Zoology Department, Michigan State College, East Lansing, Mich. H: R.F.D. 3, Grand Ledge.†

25 TAEUBER, Irene B(arnes). Demography. b'06. AB '27 (U Mo); MA '28 (Northwestern U); PhD '31 (U Minn). Director Census Library Project Library of Congress and Bureau of Census '41-44; Rockefeller Foundation Mission in population and public health Far East '48. Author books: General Censuses and Vital Statistics in the Americas '43. Co-author books: The Future Population of Europe and the Soviet Union '43; also articles in field. Research asso Office Population Research Princeton U since '36; co-editor

Population Index since '35. Cons research and analysis div Office Strategic Services '41-45; manpower panel Research and Development Bd Department of Defense since '47. Population Assn Am(pres '52-53) —Internat Union for Sci Study Population—Am Sociol Soc—Am Statis Assn. Office of Population Research, Princeton University, Princeton, N.J. H: 4222 Sheridan St., Hyattsville, Md.

10 TAFT, Kendall Bénard. American literary history (New York City 1800-1860; Samuel Woodworth, minor writers). b'99. BA '20 (Ia State U); MA '27 (Washington U); PhD '36 (Chicago U). Biographical and critical investigations of minor American writers as Samuel Woodworth, William Cox and Donald MacLeod. Author: Samuel Woodworth '38; Minor Knickerbockers '47; also articles in field. Prof Am lit and chmn dept Eng and speech Roosevelt Coll since '45. Modern Lang Assn Am—NY Hist Soc. Roosevelt College, 430 South Michigan Av., Chicago 5.⊙

11 TAHMISIAN, Theodore Newton. Physiology (Aviation); Insect biochemistry. b'09. BA '35 (Fresno State Coll); MS '39—PhD '42 (State U Ia); Certificate aviation physiology '43 (Randolph Field Sch US Army). Research on physiology of normal cell, aviation physiology, insect biochemistry, ionizing irradiations morphological and biochemical development, respiratory metabolism. Author articles: The Effect of Heavy Metals on the Activation and Injury of the Enzyme Tyrosinase '43; Duration of Consciousness in Anoxia at High Altitudes '45; Metabolism of Insect Muscle '47; other articles in field. Research asso physiol State U Ia '42-43; research asso, instr insect biochem U Chicago '46; asso biol Argonne Nat Labs since '46. Aviation physiol Air Corps US Army'43-46. Am Soc Zool—AAAS—Sigma Xi. Argonne National Laboratory, P.O. Box 5207, Chicago 80.

12 TALBOT, Nell Snow. History of medicine and dentistry. b'89. PhB '25 —AM '31 (U Chicago); '38-39 (Johns Hopkins U). Asso prof hist med and dentistry U Ill Coll Dentistry since '45. Am Sociol Soc—Am Assn Hist Med. University of Illinois College of Dentistry, 808 S. Wood St., Chicago 12.

13 TALBOT, Phillips. Contemporary problems of India and Pakistan. b'15. BA—BSJ honors '36 (U Ill); student (U London). Author: The Independence of India '47; also articles in field. Asso Inst Current World Affairs since '38; staff correspondent Chicago Daily News Fgn Service since '46. US Naval Liaison Officer Bombay India '41-43; asst Naval Attache Am Embassy Chungking China '43-45; asst prof U Chicago since '48. Inst Pacific Relations—Indian Council World Affairs. Institute of Current World Affairs, 522 Fifth Av., NYC 18.†

14 TALBOT, Samuel Armstrong. Biophysics (Visual physiology); Physiological optics; Instrument design (Mechanics, electronics, optics). b'03. BA '25 (Cornell U); MS '30 (Trinity Coll); MA '31—PhD '38 (Harvard). Author articles in field. Asso prof med Johns Hopkins Med Sch since '48. Am Physiol Soc—Optical Soc Am—Sigma Xi (chap pres '47). Johns Hopkins Hospital, Baltimore 5.

15 TALLMAN, Russell Warrick. Educational psychology (Principles, learning motivation). b'91. BA '16 (Highland Park Coll); BS '18 (Des Moines Coll); MA '23—PhD '25 (Ia U). Research in cost studies, student and faculty personnel problems, sources of school revenue; consultant and adviser in field; organized and directed educa-

tional programs for adults in business, industry and education; member of training conferences; studies on motivation charts, successful teaching. Invented mechanical and special charting devices for schools and industry. Coauthor: Guideline-Problem Series Syllabus and Workbook for Principles of Education (with C T Giblette) '29; also articles in field. Pres Motivation Charts Inc since '30; certified trainer US Civil Service Commn since '45; training specialist and cons since '47. AAAS(F)—Ia Acad Sci—Nat Soc Study Edn—Am Assn Adult Edn—NEA (coordinator for Ia, Dept Adult Edn)—Ia Adult Edn Assn. 2024 Avalon Rd., Des Moines 14, Ia.†

16 TAM, Richard Kwock. Pineapple culture (Chemical weed control, plant nutrition and physiology). b'11. BA '33—MS '34 (U Hawaii); PhD '39 (U Wis). Research on cross-inoculation of tropical legumes, nitrogen nutrition of pineapples, chemical decomposition of organic matter, respiratory enzymes of rootnodule bacteria, soil fumigation, nitrification and nutrition of pineapples. Author articles in field. With Pineapple Research Inst Hawaii '34-37, '39-51. AAAS—Am Chem Soc—Soc Am Bact—Hawaiian Acad Sci—Phi Sigma —Sigma Xi. Chemical Weeders of Hawaii, 2210-A No School St., Honolulu 45, T.H.

17 TANNEHILL, Ivan Ray. Synoptic and marine meteorology; Hurricanes; Weather (World, forecasting, map projections). b'90. BS '12 (Denison U); scholarship '09-10 (O State U, Lake Lab). Delegate to various Internat Meteorological Conferences; member of US Internat Civil Aviation Organization Meteorology Committee; chairman Working Committee on Weather Reports and Communications, US Air Coordinating Committee; president International Commission on Projections for Meteorological Charts and International Commission for Synoptic Weather Information; research on world weather in relation to solar variations. Author: Preparation and Use of Weather Maps at Sea '35; Hurricanes '38; Cloud Codes and States of the Sky '38; Weather Around the World '43; Drought, Its Causes and Effects '47; also articles in field. Head Div Synoptic Reports and Forecasts, US Weather Bur since '40. Am Geophys Union — Am Meterolog Soc. U.S. Weather Bureau, Washington 25.

18 TANNENBERG, Joseph. Histological apparatus. b'95. Student (U Heidelberg, Halle, Berlin, Marburg, Germany). Holds US patents on automatic apparatus for dehydrating and embedding tissue specimens for histological examination, delivering tissue-paraffin blocks ready to cut, method and apparatus for treating pipettes and the like. Author articles in field. Asso prof path U Frankfurt Germany '30; dir Labs Hosp Cecilienhaus Berlin '32-35; dir research Bender Hygienic Lab Albany '35-39; dir Genesee Co Lab Batavia '41, others since '43. Coll Am Path (founding F)—Am Soc Clin Path (F)—Am Assn Path and Bact—Am Soc Bact—NY State Assn Pub Health Labs—AMA(F). Genesee Laboratory, 73 Main St., Batavia, N.Y.

19 TANNER, Eugene Simpson. Greek language (First century A.D.); Jewish history; Nazi religious ideas. b'07. AB '29 (Midland Coll); BD '32 (McCormick Theol Sem); MA '31—PhD '34 (U Chicago). Author: The Nazi Christ '42; also articles in field. Instr religion and philos U Tulsa '37-53; head dept religion Coll of Wooster since '53 Nat Assn Bibl Instr—Soc Bibl Lit and Exegesis—SW Philos Con. College of Wooster, Wooster, Ohio.†

20 TANNER, Fred Wilbur. Food microbiology and sanitation (Water, milk); Canning technology. b'88. BS '12—DSc '43 (Wesleyan U Conn); MS '14—PhD '16 (U Ill). Author: Bacteriology and Mycology of Foods '19; The Yeasts (Guilliermond-Tanner) '20; Bacteriology '29; Practical Bacteriology '29; The Microbiology of Foods '44; Food-Borne Infections and Intoxications '53; also articles in field. With U Ill since '15, prof bacteriology since '23, head dept bacteriology; bacteriologist branch lab Ill Dept Health. Am Chem Soc—Soc Am Bacteriologists—Soc Exptl Biol and Medicine—Inst Food Technol (pres '45-46)—Internat Assn Milk Sanitarians—Sigma Xi—AA AS(F)—Am Pub Health Assn—Am Med Assn (affiliate fellow). 921 Lincoln Circle, Winter Park, Fla.

21 TANNER, Wilson Pennell, Jr. Psychological measurement. b'12. BA '42 (Wesleyan U Middletown Conn); MA '49 (U Fla); '49 (U Mich). Design and construction apparatus for study transient phenomenon of vision, device for measurement rat's progress through a maze; experiment and test transient phenomena vision as related to brain function. Author article: A Preliminary Investigation of the Relationship Between Visual Fusion of Intermittent Light and Intelligence '50. Research asso U Mich, now teaching fellow psychol dept. AAAS—Am Psychol Assn—Optical Soc Am—Fla Psychol Assn. Department of Psychology, University of Michigan, Ann Arbor.

22 TANSILL, Charles Callan. American history and political science; United States diplomatic relations. b'90. AB '12—AM '13—PhD '15 (Cath U Am); PhD '18 (Johns Hopkins). Author: Canadian Reciprocity Treaty of 1854 '21; The Purchase of the Danish West Indies '31; America Goes to War '36; United States and Santo Domingo 1798-1873 '38; The Foreign Policy of Thomas F Bayard '40; Major Issues in Canadian-American Relations '43. Compiler: Documents Illustrative of the Formation of the Union of the American States, Sesquicentennial memorial document authorized by the Congress of the US '27; Proposed Amendments to the Constitution, 1889-1927 '27; also articles in field. Prof Am hist Georgetown U since '44. AHA—Miss Valley Hist Assn. Georgetown University, Washington.

23 TANZER, Helen H. Roman archeology; Latin language. b'76. AB '03 (Barnard Coll, Columbia U); '06-07 (Am Sch Classical Studies Rome); PhD '29 (Johns Hopkins). Originator and editor of Latin Visualized (films illustrating Roman civilization, with descriptive manuals) '30; translator: The Forum and the Palatine (by Christian Huelsen) '28; Introduction to Facsimile Edition of Erasmus' Praise of Folly with Holbein's marginal drawings '31. Author: The Villas of Pliny the Younger '24; Common People of Pompeii '29. Prof classics Brooklyn Coll '36-37, now retired. AAAS(F)—Am Geog Soc(F)—Archeol Inst Am—Am Philol Assn—History of Sci Soc—Am Classical League—Medieval Acad Am —Soc for Promotion of Roman Studies (London). 2928 Upton St., Washington 8.⊙

24 TARNUTZER, Charles A. Confectionery; Chocolate products; Baking chemistry; Gin; Cordials. b'06. BS '30 (U Wis); MS '32 (Ia State Coll). Research on sugar, hard candy, chocolate enrobing and centers; chocolate milk and stabilizers, chocolate fudge, syrup and coatings; flour, shortening, fermentation, crackers and biscuits; botanicals, alcohol, distillation, essential oils and flavors of cordials and liqueurs; research dairy chemistry and bacteriology. Chief chem R A Johnston '36-40; research chem Carnation Co '40-41; research chem Hiram Walker & Sons '41-44; chief chem and supt processing Horlicks Corp '44-47; chief chem Bunte Brothers '47-50; research chem Hawthorn-Mellody Farms since '50. ACS—Inst Food Tech—Am Assn Cereal Chem—AAAS. H: 427 Cottage Hill, Elmhurst, Ill.

10 TARZWELL, Clarence M(athew). Stream sanitation; Biology of polluted streams; Management impounded waters; Trout stream improvement; Fishery management; Mosquito larvicides effects on wildlife. b'07. AB '30—MS '32—PhD '36 (U Mich); student (Mich State Normal Coll). Author articles in field. With USPHS since '43, biol charge biol sect Environmental Health Center since '48, rsrch stream sanitation, tastes and odors in water supplies, toxicity of industrial wastes to fishes and use biological indicators of pollution. American Fisheries Soc—Am Soc Ichthyologists and Herpetologists—Am Soc Limnology and Oceanography—Wildlife Soc—Assn SE Biol—Nat Malaria Soc—Am Mosquito Control Assn—Tenn Acad Sci. United States Public Health Service, Environmental Health Center, Cincinnati 2.

11 TASHER, Lucy Lucile. American history and government (Lincoln period). b'04. PhB '24—JD '26—AM '32—PhD '34 (U Chicago). Extensive travel in all 48 states with special attention to national parks, Lincoln material, United Nations and Congressional activity. Author articles in field. Asso prof social sci Ill State Normal U since '41. AHA—Miss Valley Hist Assn—Ill Hist Assn—Acad Polit Social Sci—Phi Beta Kappa—Kappa Beta Pi. Lillian Gertrude Selze award U Chicago. Illinois State Normal University, Normal, Ill.

12 TASKER, Roy Carleton. Fishes and birds of New York and Pennsylvania; Camping. b'96. AB '21 (Hillsdale Coll); AM '22 (U Mich); PhD '34 (Cornell U). With biol dept Bucknell U since '34, prof since '48. AAAS—Am Soc Zoologists—Ind Acad Sci—Pa Acad Sci—Peking Soc Nat Hist—Phi Kappa Phi—Sigma Xi. Department of Biology, Bucknell University, Lewisburg, Pa.†

13 TATUM, Robert McElfresh. Indian picture writings (Pictographs, petroglyphs). b'23. AA '43 (Trinidad State Jr Coll Colo); '43-44 (U Minnesota); '44. (Yale); BS '48 (US Naval Acad). Developed new method statischronology of petroglyph types and cultural areas; collected largest bibliography on subject in US; collection includes photographs and other data on several thousand sites; developed chronology of petroglyph types and cultural areas from 0 AD to 1300 AD, extending continuously across the US; collaborated with foreign workers in study petroglyphs in Northern Europe; field work conducted in various states and sites examined in Northern Europe. Author articles: New Horizons in Archeology '47; The Importance of Petroglyphs in Tennessee '47; The Relationship of Michigan Petroglyphs to Others in the United States '46; Distribution and Bibliography of the Petroglyphs of the U.S. '46; Petroglyphs of Southeastern Colo '44. AAAS—Wash Anthropol Soc—Am Anthropol Soc—Soc Am Archeology—Colo Archeol Soc. Canal, Winchester, Ohio.

14 TAUBER, Oscar Ernst. Comparative physiology (Insect); Insecticidal and fungicidal poisoning effects

(Warm blooded animals). b'08. Research in factors influencing rate of mitosis, experimental studies with insects on cell division, blood cells, circulation, nutrition, reproduction; effects on warm-blooded animals of chronic poisoning with chemicals used in insecticidal and fungicidal programs. Author articles in field. Prof physiol and research, prof zool and entomol Ia State Coll Agrl Expt Station since '46. Am Soc Zool—Entomol Soc Am—Soc Exptl Biol and Med—Am Assn Econ Entomol—Phi Kappa Phi—Sigma Xi—Gamma Sigma Delta. Rockefeller Research Fellow, Ia State Coll '32-34. Zoology and Entomology Department, Iowa State College, Ames, Ia. H: 613 Agg Av.†

15 TAUBES, Frederic. Painting and etching (Techniques); Chemistry of paints, resins, varnishes and painting media. b'00. Studied art in Munich, Vienna, France and Italy '18-23. Originator of Taubes Painting Media, Taubes Varnishes. Author: Technique of Oil Painting '41 (British edit '48); You Don't Know What You Like '42; Studio Secrets '43; Oil Painting for the Beginner '44; The Amateur Painter's Handbook '48; The Painters Question and Answer Book '48; Anatomy of Genius '48. Formerly Carnegie visiting prof art and resident painter U Ill; visiting prof U Hawaii, Mills Coll Calif, U Wis; instr Cooper Union NY; head painting div Corpus Christi Fine Arts Colony (Tex). The Studio, Haverstraw, N.Y.

16 TAUTH, George. Plastic coatings. b'19. BS ChE '42 (Cooper Union Inst Tech); '44-45 (Rutgers U)—'47 (Ill Inst Tech). Research in high polymers, plastic coatings, laminates, adhesives, lithographic printing processes, textile and paper coatings, pharmaceuticals; development of bullet sealing fuel tanks for planes, latex fabric coatings. Development engr US Rubber Co Naugatuck Conn '42-43; chem engr Johnson & Johnson New Brunswick NJ '43-45; research chem Armour Research Foundation Chicago '45-47, Arvey Corp Chicago since '47. Am Chem Soc—Am Inst Chem Engr—Cooper Union Alumni Assn. NY Scholarship '37. 3462 N. Kimball Av., Chicago 18.†

17 TAX, Sol. Indians (Middle America (Fox, Apache); Guatemala; Origin of civilization. b'07. PhB '31 (U Wis); PhD '35 (U Chgo). Author books, articles in field. Prof U Chgo since '48, asso dean soc sci div since '48; investigator ethnol Carnegie Inst '34-46. Am Anthrop Assn—Am Folklore Soc—Sigma Xi. Department of Anthropology, University of Chicago, Chicago 37.†◎

18 TAYLOR, Albert Lee. Plant parasitic nematodes; soil fumigation. b'01. Student '19-22 (U Colo); BS '34 (George Washington U); '42 (Johns Hopkins). Author articles in field. Nematologist Bur Plant Industry, US Dept Agr '35-46; agrl rep Shell Chem Corp '46-49; nematologist Bur Plant Industry since '49. Am Phytopath Soc—Helminthological Soc Washington. Division of Neumatology, Plant Industry Station, Beltsville, Md.

19 TAYLOR, Alrutheus Ambush. American Negro; American history since 1865. b'93. AB '16 (U Mich); AM '23—PhD '36 (Harvard). Research on American history since 1865 with special reference to the Negro. Author (books): The Negro in South Carolina During the Reconstruction '24; The Negro in the Reconstruction of Virginia '26; The Negro in Tennessee 1865-1880 '41. Co-author: A Study of the Community Life of the Negro

Youth '41. Author articles: Negro Congressmen a Generation After '22; Historians of the Reconstruction '38; Trends in Federal Policy Toward the Negro '44; The Need of Negro Americans in Tennessee for Graduate and Professional Education '46. Asso investigator Assn Study Negro Life and History Inc Washington '23-25; prof hist Fisk U Nashville Tenn since '26, dean men '27-28, acting dean coll '29-30, dean '30-51, research prof Am hist since '50. AHA—Assn Study Negro Life and History Inc—So Hist Assn—Am Acad Polit and Social Sci—Nat Assn Collegiate Deans and Registrars in Negro Sch—Am Mil Inst. Awarded hon Litt D '47 Hobart and William Smith Coll. Fisk University, Nashville 8, Tenn.

20 TAYLOR, Archer. Riddles; Proverbs; Folklore; History of bibliography to 1800; Medieval and Renaissance German literature. b'90. BA '09 (Swarthmore Coll); MA '10 (U Pa); PhD '15 (Harvard). Editor Journal Am Folklore '40, California Folklore Quart (now Western Folklore) since '42, Washington University Studies '19-25; assoc editor Modern Philology since '27; consultant Newberry Library Chicago. Author: The Proverb '30; Bibliography of Riddles '39; Collection of Welsh Riddles '42; German Literary History of the Fifteenth and Sixteenth Centuries; Eng Riddles from Oral Tradition '51; also articles. Prof German lit U Cal since '39. Medieval Acad Am(F)—Modern Lang Assn Am (pres '51)—Am Philos Soc (F)—Am Acad Arts Scis (F)—Am Folklore Soc (pres '35-37)—Phi Beta Kappa. Awarded Guggenheim fellowship '27; Newberry Lib Fellow '45. University of California, Berkeley.†◎

21 TAYLOR, Brainerd. Military motor transport (Development, maintenance principles). b'77. Ed (Berkeley and Chauncey Hall Boston, MIT, Harvard). Exponent of importance of multi-wheel drive traction and standardization of military motor vehicles with maximum interchangeability of component units and parts exemplified in World War II. Author: A National Motor Transport Service '22; The Five Echelons of Maintenance '30; A General Plan for Coordinating Rail, Water, Air, and Highway Transportation by developing and Using Motor Transport as the Coordinating Factor, first developed in World War I. Apptd 2d lt US Coast Arty '02, maj, lt col, col Nat Army '20, reverted to US Army as capt, maj, lt col, col, ret '36. SAE—QM Assn—Ord Assn. 475 Chauncey St., Mansfield, Mass.

22 TAYLOR, Carl A. Seeds (Germination, storage); Grafting; Nursery management. Introduced Macerator, seed cleaning machine adopted by Forest Service; invented Shufflehoe mechanical cultivation between plants in row, used on Emergency Rubber Project; devised means of threshing Guayule seed on large scale, process eliminated need for expensive chemical treatment of seed; devised flotation method for filled percent determination on guayule and other small seeds; devised michro-grafting technique by which intergeneric grafts were made successfully; devised methods for treating celery seed to obtain quick emergence and good stands economically from direct seeding. Author articles: Germination Behavior of Tree Seeds '41; Propagation of Guayule '46; Interspecific and Intergeneric Grafts with Guayule '47. Nursery mgr and regional seedman US Forest Service '35-42; chief seedsman for Emergency Rubber Project '42-47; plant physiol Bur Plant Industry US Dept Agr '47-48; Rexall Drug Co LA '49-50. Am Society Plant

Physiol. H: 1041 Parkway Rd., Salinas, Cal.†

10 TAYLOR, Carl Cleveland. Rural sociology; Latin America (Immigration, colonization). b'84. BA '11 (Drake U); MA '14 (U Tex); PhD '18 (U Mo). Studied colonization and rural life problems in Argentina '42-43, advised on immigration and colonization in Argentina, Brazil, and Paraguay '47, advised on agricultural census in Guatemala '49; chairman pattern of settlement committee and committee on rural community centers, Columbia Basin. Author: Rural Life in Argentina '48. Co-author: Rural Life in the United States. Mem NC State Tenancy Commn '22-23; mem NC-SC Land Commission '23-24; spl asst dir Subsistence Homestead Div Dept Interior '33-34; regional dir land program USDA '34-35; asst adminstr Resettlement Administration '35-36. Am Sociol Soc(past pres)—Rural Sociol Soc US—Farm Economy Assn—Soc Applied Anthrop—Agrl Hist Soc—Am Rural Sociol Soc (past pres)—Am Country Life Assn (past pres). US Department of Agriculture, Bureau of Agricultural Economics, 14th and Independence Avenue, Washington 25.†

11 TAYLOR, Carlton Fulton. Fungicidal control of plant diseases; Taxonomy of actinomyces; Orchard crop diseases; Vegetable seed treatments. b'06. Student '23-25 (Nova Scotia Agrl Coll); student (Ontario Agrl Coll); BSA '29 (McGill U); PhD '36 (Cornell U). Author articles in field. With W Va Agrl Expt Sta '38-51, prof plant path '48-51; with Chemical Corps Biol Labs since '51. Am Phytopath Soc—Sigma Xi. C Division, Camp Detrick, Frederick, Md.†

12 TAYLOR, Clarion Wells. Perlite. b'93. AB '16-17 (Colo Coll). Research on alteration pumice and ash to perlite; chemical analysis perlite; compilation list of potential world sources; development method for utilization of perlite in acoustical plaster and tile, in manufacture insulating pipe covering, furnace insulation, and monolithic roof decks; inventor brushable perlite stucco, and integral water-repellant for perlite concrete. Author articles: Processing of Perlite Ore '50; Perlite Popping '50; The Chemistry of the Glass Rocks '50, and others. Co-author articles: Let's Take a Microscopic Look at Perlite '49; Perlite Mining and Processing '50, and others. Chemgeol Phillips Vanadium Exploratory Co '37-39; phys sci Soil Conservation Service Colorado Springs '39-40; chief chem-geol Alexite Engring Co '42-44, dir research since '44. Colo Mining Assn—Am Mil Engrs. Alexite Engring Division of Alexander Film Co., Colo Springs, Colo. H: 1019 N. Wahsatch.†

13 TAYLOR, Edward Harrison. Herpetology (Philippines, Mexico, Central America); Mammalogy and ichthyology of the Philippines. b'89. AB '12—MS '20—PhD '27 (U Kan). Research on turtles, lizards, other amphibians of Mexico. Author: Snakes of the Philippine Islands; Philippine Land Mammals; The Lizards of the Genus Eumeces; The Amphibians and Turtles of the Philippine Islands; The Lizards of the Philippine Islands; also articles in field. Prof zool U Kan since '34; curator of herpetology and ichthyology Mus of Natural Hist U Kan since '46; editor Kan U Sci Bull. Am Soc Mammalogists—AAAS—Am Soc Ichthyologists and Herpetologists—Kan Acad Sci—Sigma Xi. 118 Snow Hall, Kansas University, Lawrence, Kan.

14 TAYLOR, George Coffin. Shakespeare. b'77. AB '97 (U SC); MA '99 (Harvard); PhD '05 (U Chicago); Litt D '38 (U SC). Devisor and co-editor: The Interlinear Shakespeares. Asso editor: Studies in Philology. Successively instr, asst prof, prof, and head dept English U Colo '99-09; agriculturalist and atty Columbia SC '09-25; asso prof English U NC '25-27, prof since '27, Kena prof since '34. Med Acad Am—Mod Lang Assn Am—Phi Beta Kappa. 1701 College St., Columbia, S.C.†⊚

15 TAYLOR, Henry Longstreet. Work performance of man (physiological factors); Nutrition (Calories, starvation, semi-starvation, water soluble vitamin intake); Cardiovascular measurements. b'12. AB '35 (Harvard); PhD '42 (U Minn). Research in influence high temperature, total starvation, semi-starvation, convalescence and water soluble vitamin intake on work performance and nutrition; cardiac output, ballistocardiography, maximal oxygen intake. With U Minn since '42, asso prof physiol hygiene since '49. Am Physiol Soc—Soc for Exptl Biol and Med—AAAS. Gate 27, Stadium, School of Public Health, University of Minnesota, Mpls 14.

16 TAYLOR, James Lester. Textile chemistry (Flax, ramie, nylon, cotton); Fiber technology. b'04. AB '29 (O Wesleyan U); MS '32 (Syracuse U); PhD '44 (U NC). Author articles in field. Faculty research asso and prof textile engring Ga Tech. Am Chem Soc—AAUP—AAAS—Am Assn Textile Chem and Colorists. Georgia Institute of Technology, Atlanta. H: 1005 Rosedale Rd., N.E.

17 TAYLOR, James Spottiswood. Medico-legal problems. b'02. BS '23 (Guilford Coll); MA '24 (Haverford Coll); MD '28 (Johns Hopkins). Author articles in field. Medical examiner Wester Co N.Y. '34-43, since '45; dir City of Kingston Labs '34-43, since '45; path and dir lab Vassar Bros Hosp Poughkeepsie NY '43-45; asst med examiner Dutchess Co NY since '44; director Wester Co Tumor Clinic since '47; staff various hosps. NY State Assn Pub Health Labs (pres '44, chmn com post-grad edn since '48)—Am Assn Path and Bact—Am Soc Clin Path—NY State Soc Path—AAAS. Diplomate Am Bd Path '47, Nat Bd Med Examiners '30. City of Kingston Laboratories, 400 Broadway, Kingston N.Y. H: 88 Maiden Lane.

18 TAYLOR, John Arthur. Education (Distributive); Human relations. b'17. AB '40 (Howard U); '40-41 (Harvard U); MA '48 (St Louis U). Coordinator distributive edn St. Louis Public Schs, prof accounting Tucker Bus Coll, chief accountant Twentieth St. Concessions Corp St. Louis. Internat Accountants Soc—Nat Bus Tchrs Assn—St Louis Area Bus Tchrs Assn—Internat Bus Tchrs Assn—Am Vocational Assn—AA AS—Sigma Tau Delta—Alpha Psi Omega. Board of Education, 911 Locust St., StL. H: 3742 Finney Av., StL 13.

19 TAYLOR, John Lewis. Geography of Pacific basin and Far East. b'10. BA '35 (ND State Teach Coll); '37 (Ida U); MA geog '40 (Clark U); MA polit sci '43 (Columbia); '46-47 (Stanford U); PhD '53 (Clark University). Research on economic aspects of rubber industry in Sumatra and Malaya '40-42, on administrative problems in Pacific since '46; Hawaii's tourist industry '50-53. Geographer Anglo- Chinese Sch Ipoh, Brit Malaya '40-42; mil govt officer USN Pacific theatre '43-46; asso prof Stanford U Sch Naval Adminstrn '46-47, lecturer dept geog '47-49; staff high commnr Am Trust Ty Pacific Islands '50-53; splst

Ho Reps Interior and Insular Affairs Com since '53. Am Assn Geogs—Far Eastern Assn—Pacific Coast Geog Assn—Nat Council Geog Tchrs. Interior and Insular Affairs Committee, House Office Building, Washington.

20 TAYLOR, John Ross. Dairy cattle physiology; Dairy cattle reproduction. b'22. BS '50 (U Cal); MS '52 (U Ill). Research on sub-microscopic morphology bovine spermatozoa with emphasis on morphological differentiation and separation two types in order control sex of progeny through artificial insemination; physiology, endocrinology and metabolism reproduction and lactation in dairy cattle; hormonal inbalance, vitamin and trace element deficiencies and their effects on fertilization and embryological development. With U Cal Los Angeles since '50. Electron Micros Soc Am. H: 11259 Morrison St., N. Hollywood, Cal.

21 TAYLOR, K(enneth) W(entzel). Rubber (Processing of guayule). b'08. BS '30—MS '32 (Colo A and M Coll). Author: The Processing of Guayule for Rubber '46; Guayule—An American Source of Rubber; others. Co-author: Rubber Recovery from Freshly Harvested Cuayule. Charge pilot plant research for recovery of crude rubber from guayule US Dept Agr. '47, now asst to div chief, field crops utilization. Western Regional Research Laboratory, U.S.D.A., 800 Buchanan Av., Albany 6, Cal.

22 TAYLOR, Lewis Walter. Poultry genetics; Embryonic mortality. b'00. BS '22—PhD '31 (U Wis); MS '25 (Kan State Coll). Author articles in field. Editor: Fertility and Hatchability of Chicken and Turkey Eggs '49. With U Calif since '28, chmn div poultry husbandry '33-51, now professor. AAAS(F) —Poultry Sci Assn (F, pres '40)—Am Genetic Assn—World's Poultry Sci Assn—Calif Acad Sci—Genetics Soc Am—Soc Study Evolution Department Poultry Husbandry, University of California, Berkeley 4.†

23 TAYLOR, Maurice. Population (Jewish). b'95. AB '16—MA '25—PhD '31 (Harvard). Author: The Social Cost of Industrial Insurance, '33; The Jewish Community of Pittsburgh '41. Co-author: Jewish Population Studies '43. Supt Jewish Welfare Fedn Columbus O '22-23; dir Jewish Family Welfare Assn Boston '23-36; exec dir Fedn Jewish Philanthropies and United Jewish Fund Pittsburgh since '36; mem spl mission to Israel at invitation of Jewish Agency in Jerusalem '49. Am Statis Assn—Am Acad Social and Polit Sci—Am Assn Social Workers—Am Arbitration Assn. Sheraton Hotel, Pittsburgh.†⊚

24 TAYLOR, Maurice Craig. Chlorites; Hypochlorites; Amalgam electric cells. b'94. BS '18 (Purdue Univ). Research alkalies, hypochlorites, chlorites, chloramines, electrolytic amalgam cells, sodium chlorites, electrolytic cells. Research on chlorine and hypochlorous acid. Holds 30 patents on electrolytic cells and related items. Co-author articles in field. Research chem Mathieson Alkali Works '19-24, chief chem '24-30, asst dir research '30-41, mgr research '41-45, resident dir of research and development '45-48, staff cons '49-50; Taylor Research Laboratories since '50. Am Chem Soc—Am Inst Chem—Am Electrochem Soc—The Chem Soc (London)—AAAS—Sigma Xi—Phi Lambda Upsilon. Taylor Research Laboratories, 2739 Lockport Rd., Niagara Falls, N.Y.†

25 TAYLOR, Nelson W(oodsworth). Glass technology; Materials (High temperature, strength); Electrochemistry. b'99. BS '18 (U Saskatchewan); PhD '23 (U Calif); fellow '28-29 (Mayo Found). Author articles in field. Head dept of ceramics Penn State Coll '33-43; research dept Minn Mining and Mfg Co St Paul since '43, asst dir research '45-51, mgr fluorochemicals dept since '51. Am Ceramic Soc (F, chmn refract div '38-39, glass div '39-40)—Soc Glass Tech(F)—ACS—Sigma Xi. Awarded John Simon Guggenheim Memorial Found fellowship, Berlin and Göttingen Germany '29-30. 367 Grove St., St. Paul 1.

10 TAYLOR, Norman. Tropical economic plants (Cinchona, quinine). b'83. Student '01-02 (Cornell U). Plant exploring expeditions to entire West Indies, Yucatan, Guatemala, Bolivia, Peru, Ecuador and Brazil. Author: Botany, Science of Plant Life '24; Guide to the Wild Flowers '28; Cinchona in Java '45; Taylor's Encyclopedia of Gardening '48; Flight From Reality '49; also articles in field. Curator plants Brooklyn Botanic Garden '11-29; bot, hort, and forestry ed Webster's New Internat Dictionary second edition; editor The Garden Dictionary since '33; dir Cinchona Products Inst Inc since '37. NY Acad Sci(F)—AAAS—NY Acad Med (asso F)—Ecol Soc Am—Hort Soc NY—Torrey Bot Club. Awarded Mass Hort Soc gold medal '36. 10 Rockefeller Plaza, NYC 20.

11 TAYLOR, Ralph E. Geology of salt-dome lap rock; Louisiana rock salt. b'05. BA '27—MS '28 (University Mich); PhD '38 (La State U). Engaged geological explorations central, southern and western US, Cuba, Canada, Mexico, Africa. Author: Cap Rock of Louisiana Salt Domes '38; also articles in field. Humble Oil and Refining Co since '49 as sr research geol. Am Assn Petroleum Geol—AAAS—AIMME. Humble Oil and Refining Co., Humble Building, Houston.

12 TAYLOR, Rhea Alec. American Revolution; American constitutions (1787; Kentucky 1890-91). b'02. AB '26 (Emory and Henry Coll); MA '36 (Ohio State U); PhD '48 (U Chicago). Author articles in field. Instr hist U Ky since '44. Am Hist Assn—Miss Valley Hist Assn—So Hist Assn—Ky Hist Soc. History Department, University of Kentucky, Lexington, Ky.

13 TAYLOR, Robert Emmett. History of accounting; Business law; History of Renaissance Italy; Ireland (Robert Emmet); American history (Northwest Territory). b'89. AB '12—AM '13 (U Mich); LLB '17—LLM '20 (St Louis U). Research in United States and Italy on Renaissance Italy which resulted in book about Pacioli who is usually regarded as the originator of the system of debit and credit in accounting; research in Ireland on life of Robert Emmet '42-46. Author: Municipal Budget Making '25; No Royal Road, Luca Pacioli and His Times '42. Co-author: Questions and Problems in Accounting '26; Questions and Problems in Economics '30; Elements of Accounting '30. Prof bus law and accounting U Cincinnati since '30; research on NW Ter since '46. Beta Gamma Sigma. Sachs Award for outstanding achievement as an author, especially for volume No Royal Road '43. University of Cincinnati, Cincinnati 21. H: 145 W. McMillan St.

14 TAYLOR, Robert Seth. Household refrigeration (Absorption). b'98. BA '19—MA '20 (U Tex); PhD '23 (MIT). Pioneer in development and manufacture of household absorption type refrigerator known as gas or kerosene refrigerator, no moving parts, hermetically sealed and silent. Holds 30 patents. Author articles in field. Research asso MIT '23-24; technol US Bur Fisheries '24-25; research engr Electrolux Servel Corp '26-28, Servel Inc '28-34, chief engr in charge gen engring and inspection since '34. Am Chem Soc—Am Soc Refrigerating Engrs. Servel, Incorporation, Evansville 20, Ind.

15 TAYLOR, Walter Andrews. Architecture (Protestant church, history, theory, Chinese and Far Eastern); Chinese and Far Eastern art. b'99. B Engr '21—MArch (O State U); B Arch '29 (Columbia); '23-24 (Harvard-Yenching Sch Chinese Studies Peking). Architect or cons in 500 US and foreign church buildings; studied architecture in ten provinces of China, Japan and Manchukuo. Author articles in field. Partner, Hobart Upjohn architects '37-44; cons Interdenom Bur Arch '33-46. AIA (dir dept edn and research)—Soc Archtl Historians—Ch Archtl Guild Am—Nat Council Chs (chmn arch dept worship and arts)—Tau Beta Pi—Syracuse in China Assn. Octagon House, 1741 New York Av., Washington 6. H: 1709 19th St., Washington 9.

16 TAYLOR, Wayne Chatfield. Crop insurance; Minerals (Industry). b'93. BA '16 (Yale). Und-sec com '40-45; president Export-Import Bank Washington '45-46; assistant to administrator of E.C.A. since '48. Am mem Mexican-Am Commn for Econ Cooperation; mem adv com to sec of State on internat aviation; mem Spl Bd of Examiners for Fgn Service Dept of State; consultant War Assets Administration; mem Presidents' Com on Crop Insurance; mem Federal Farm Mortgage Corp Board; mem Temporary Nat Economic Com. Acad Polit Sci—Nat Planning Assn—Am Geog Soc—Am Econ Assn—Am Acad Polit and Social Sci. Decorated by Belgian, Finnish, Polish and Chilean govts. 800 Connecticut Av., Washington.†◎

17 TAYLOR, Wilbur L(eyland). Oils (Soybean, refining). b'87. Ed pub schs. Chem Nat Oil Products Co Harrison, NJ '19-20, Consol Color & Chem Co Newark '22; chief chem William C Goodrich Co Milwaukee '25-30; mgr Archer Daniels Midland Co Chicago '30-44; tech adv chem div Gen Mills Inc Minneapolis since '44. Am Chem Soc—Am Oil Chem Soc (refining com, soap and refined oils com)—Assn Ofcl Agrl Chem—Nat Soybean Processors Assn (tech com since '30). Chemical Divison, General Mills, Inc., 400 2nd Av., S., Mpls.

18 TAYLOR, William C(ecil). Silicate chemistry; Portland cement; Hydrous silicate products. b'02. BA '24 (Ohio Wesleyan U); MA '26 (Ohio State U). Author articles in field. Chief chem div Gen Research Lab Owens-Illinois Glass Co Toledo since '44. Received citation '44 Nat Bur Standards for contributions to the knowledge of portland cement chem. Owens-Illinois Glass Company, Toledo 1, O.†

19 TAYLOR, William Randolph. Cytology; Phycology; Hydrobiology; Marine botany. b'95. BS '16—MS '17—PhD '20 (U Pa). Author: Marine Algae of Florida '27; Marine Algae of the Northeastern Coast of North America '37; Caribbean Marine Algae of the Allan Hancock Expedition of 1939 '42; Marine Algae of the Allan Hancock Expeditions to the Galapagos Islands '45; also articles in field. Prof bot and curator algae in herbarium U Mich since '30; trustee Marine Biol Lab Corp Woods Hole Mass since '39; asso ed Hydrobiologia et Protistologia (Liege Belgium) since '46. AAAS(F) Bot Society Am—Limnol Soc Am—Am Acad Arts Sci—Soc Venez Ciencias Nat (corr mem)—Acad Roy Sci Belgium—Sigma Xi. 2007 Washtenaw Av., Ann Arbor.

20 TEAGUE, Jo Morgan, Jr. Glass containers (Breakage diagnosis, structure, design, strength, use). b'16. BS in ceramic engring '39 (Ga Inst Tech Atlanta); MS '40—'50-52 (Ohio State U). Diagnosis type and cause glass container breakage; formerly in chge quality and specifications control activities of glass manufacture; supervision of strength tests and studies physical characteristics of glass containers. With Owens-Ill Glass Co since '40, expert breakage diagnosticians since '48, also chief quality and research engr, quality and specifications dept. Am Ceramic Soc—Inst Ceramic Engrs—Am Soc Quality Control—Soc Exptl Stress Analysis—Tau Beta Pi. Registered engr. Quality and Specifications Dept., Owens-Illinois Glass Co., 14th and Adams Sts., Tol.

21 TEAGUE, Walter Dorwin. Product design; Product development; Commercial interiors; Department store design. b'83. Student '03-07 (Art Students League NY). Author: Design This Day—The Technique of Order in the Machine Age '40; Land of Plenty, A Summary of Possibilities '47. Began as artist '07 designing advertising, books, magazine illustrations; entered industrial designing '26, cons on design Eastman Kodak Co, Ford Motor Co, A B Dick Co, Boeing Aircraft, Tayter Instrument Co, National Cash Register, Bridgeport Brass Co, Ford Found; mem Bd Design NY World's Fair '39; designed buildings and exhibits of Eastman Kodak, Consol Edison, Nat Cash Register, Ford Motor Co, US Steel, duPont de Nemours & Co for NY World's Fair '39. Am Inst Graphic Arts—Soc Indsl Designers—Royal Soc Arts. Received Am Design award '39; Nat Advertising award '41. 444 Madison Av., NYC.◎

22 TEAS, Jean Paul. Dry batteries; Proximity fuses. b'10. Student '29-32, '37-38 (Cornell U). Development of improved dry batteries and special electrochemical systems for use in radios, hearing aids, flashlights and electronic ordnance equipment; aided in developing fuses and establishing combat use in European theater of operation World War II. Development engr and dir development Nat Carbon Com Inc since '35. Capt Ordnance Dept US Army '43-46. Am Chem Soc—Am Electrochem Soc. Legion of Merit US Army. Designers for Industry, Inc., 2915 Detroit Av., Cleve 13.

23 TEBROCK, Harry E. Antihistaminics. b'09. BS '30 (NYU); MD '34 (Long Island Coll Medicine). Med dir Sylvania Electric Products Inc, asso med dir Schenley Laboratories, asso med dir Lederle Laboratories. Am Med Association—NY State Med Soc—NY Acad Med—Am Acad Occupational Med—Am Coll Chest Physicians—Am Assn Indsl Physicians and Surgeons. 1740 Broadway, NYC 19.

24 TEDDER, Paul M(athew). Electronic control devices. b'08. BS '32 (U Fla); radio engring '42 (U Miami). Invented the Tedder Circuit and two inventions connected with the wartime Proximity Fuse Project. Author articles in field. Research engr U Fla and engr charge Nat Bur Standards Contract Lab since '43. Inst Radio Engrs—Sigma Xi. Certificate of Effective Service presented by Office Sci Research and Development '43; Naval Ordnance Development award and Certificate of Exceptional Service '45; War Dept—Navy Dept Certificate of Appreciation '48. Research Laboratory, 1104 Seagle Building, Gainesville, Fla.

10 TEDESCHE, Leon G(reenfield). Industrial first aid; Philately; Microscopy (Water supplies); Medical art. b'78. AB '02—MD '05 (U Cincinnati). Instr Am Red Cross First Aid Service for Boy Scout leaders since '29; dir West End Indsl Dispensary since '30. AMA(F)—AAAS(F)—Am Soc Social Hygiene—Zool Soc Cincinnati—Cincinnati Soc Natural History—Am Assn Indsl Phys & Surgs—AFA—Am Air Mail Soc—Internat Philatelic Assn (sec, treas)—O State Med Assn—Hamilton Co Acad Medicine—Am Pub Health Assn—Assn Mil Surgs US—Daniel Drake Research Soc—Pioneer Philatelic Phalanx (hon life)—Soc Philatelic Ams (life)—Am Philatelic Soc (life). Awarded Silver Beaver, Boy Scouts Am '43. 2201 Gest St., Cin 4.†☉

11 TEELE, Ray Palmer. Photometry. b'03. BS '27 (U Mich); MS '29 (George Washington U). Research on measurement low luminance, developed photometer for luminescent materials, physical photometer, and potentiometer for ten microvolts. Author: Measurement of Brightness Decay of Phosphorescent Materials '46. With Nat Bur Standards since '23, phys in charge research on photometry since '41. Illuminating Engring Soc—Optical Soc Am—Wash Acad Sci—Soc Automotive Engrs. National Bureau of Standards, Washington 25.

12 TEE-VAN, John. Zoological park and aquarium administration; Oceanography; Ichthology. b'97. Research in tropical American marine fishes; mem twenty-three expeditions for zoological oceanographic research in British Guiana, Venezuela, Galapagos Islands, Sargasso Sea, Haiti, Lower California, Central America, Australia, China, Bermuda; research tropical marine fishes, biological photography including stop motion movie films of development of fish eggs, and operation of Bathysphere including dives to 1,533 feet. Co-author: The Fishes of Port-Au-Prince Bay, Haiti (with W Beebe) '28; Field Book of the Shore Fishes of Bermuda (with W Beebe) '33; also articles in field. Editor: Fishes of the Western North Atlantic. Asst dept tropical research NY Zool Soc '17-24, gen asst '25-30, gen asso '31-41; exec sec NY Zool Park and Aquarium since '42. Soc Ichthyologists and Herpetologists (Gov)—NY Zool Soc—NY Acad Sci. N.Y. Zoological Park, NYC 60.†

13 TEGEDER, Vincent G(eorge). American history (The West 1850-1865, the Confederation 1781-1787). b'10. BA '33 (St John's U); MA '42—PhD '49 (U Wis). Research of territorial documents and manuscripts dealing with the West, an analysis of the distribution of the territorial patronage by the Lincoln administration and Republican management of the territories during the Civil War period. Author: The Territories and the Lincoln Administration, 1861-1865 '48; A Mixed Government Interpretation of the Constitution '42. Ordination to the Priesthood '37; dean Coll Preparatory Sch St John's U '41-42, chmn hist dept since '47. Miss Valley Hist Soc—Am Hist Soc—Catholic Hist Soc. St. John's University, Collegeville, Minn.†

14 TEHON, Leo Roy. Plant diseases (Trees); Parasitic fungi; Flora of Illinois; Poisonous and native drug plants; Mycology (Taxonomy). b'95. AB '16 (U Wyo); MA '20—PhD '34 (U Ill). Author: Fieldbook of Native Illinois Shrubs. Co-author: (with Robert B Miller) The Native and Naturalized Trees of Illinois; also articles in field. Collaborator US Dept Agr Plant Disease Survey since '21; head sect applied bot and plant path Ill State Natural Hist Survey since '35; prof plant path U Ill since '47; mem adv com Ill Seed and Weed Council since '39. AA AS(F)—Nat Shade Tree Conf (sci mem, mem exec com '44-48)—Midwestern Shade Tree Conf (mem exec comm '46-48)—Mycol Soc of Am (charter mem)—Bot Soc Am—Am Phytopath Soc—Am Biol Soc—AFA—Ill State Acad Sci (sec '43-46, pres '46-47)—Ill State Nurserymen's Assn (hon)—Phi Beta Kappa—Sigma Xi. Natural Resources Bldg., Urbana, Ill.†☉

15 TELFAIR, David. Ultrasonics; Plastics (Testing). b'12. AB '36 (Earlham Coll); MS '37 (Haverford Coll); PhD '41 (Pa State Coll). Author articles in field. Asso prof physics Earlham Coll since '46. Am Assn Physics Teachers—Am Physical Soc—AAAS—Sigma Xi. Earlham College, Richmond, Ind.

16 TELFORD, Horace S(pooner). Economic entomology; Pharmacology of DDT; Insecticides; Limnology; Taxonomy of syrphidae (Diptera). b'09. BS '33 (U Utah); MS '36—PhD '41 (U Minn); (Chaffey Jr Coll, Tex Tech Coll). Author articles in field. Asso prof entomol State Coll Wash '47-51, prof entomol and chmn dept since '51; asso entomol Wash Agrl Expt Station since '47 Entomol Soc Am—AAAS—Limnol Soc Am—O Acad Sci—Am Assn Econ Entomol—Pacific NW Bird and Mammal Soc—Sigma Xi. Second prize winner for journalism presented by Am Asso Coll Ed '40. Department Entomology, Washington Agricultural Experiment Station, Pullman, Wash.

17 TELKES, Maria. Solar heating; Thermoelectricity. b'00. PhD Phys chem. Developed a solar distiller for life-rafts during the war; thermoelectric power generation from solar energy, electronic properties of semiconductors; designed the heating system of the first completely sun-heated home at Dover, Mass. Research engr Westinghouse Research Labs '37-39; research asso Solar Energy Conversion Project MIT since '39. Am Chem Soc—Electrochem Soc. 100 Memorial Dr., Cambridge 42, Mass.

18 TELLER, Ludwig. Collective bargaining. b'11. LLB '35—AB '36—LLM '37—JSD '39 (NYU). Admitted NY state bar '37; expert consultant Labor Relations Branch War Department '42; trial examiner labor relations board New York State '42-46. Author: The Law Governing Labor Disputes and Collective Bargaining (5 vols) '40, '47, and '50; A Labor Policy for America '45; Management Functions under Collective Bargaining '46; Law of Contracts '48, and others. Lecturer labor management relations law sch NY U since '47; professor law NY Law Sch since '51; elected member NY Assembly '50; re-elected '52. Labor relations officer USNR '43-45. Am Arbitration Assn (arbitrator)—Am Civil Liberties Union (com on civil rights in labor relations)—Am Bar Assn—Bar Assn City New York—NY Co Lawyers Assn. 295 Madison Av., NYC 17.

19 TEMPLE, William Jameson. Speech and hearing (Voice science, phonograph recording, audio-visual aids, phonetics, audiology). b'03. AB '28 (Wash and Jeff Coll); AM '32 (Columbia); PhD '38 (Ia U). Research project on selections and training of telephone talkers in US Navy under Applied Psychology Panel of Nat Defense Research Committee '44-45; consultant on audio-visual teaching equipment to Scholastic Teacher. Author articles in field. Asso prof speech Brooklyn Coll since '47. Acoustical Soc Am—AAAS—Am Inst Physics—Am Psychol Assn (asso)—Am Speech and Hearing Assn—Audio Engring Soc (charter)—Eastern Psychol Assn—Inst Radio Engrs (asso)—Modern Language Assn Am—NY Acad Sci—NY State Speech Assn—Sigma Xi (asso)—Speech Assn Am.

20 TEMPLETON, Bonnie C. Flora of California; Pleistocene flora of Rancho La Brea deposits; Compositae; Lennoaceae; Flora (Systematic). b'06. BA '41—MS '47—(U So Cal). Discovered a new species of parasitic plant in the sand dunes; also a new record of plantain. Author articles in field. Asst Herbarium Los Angeles Co Mus '29-38, asst bot '38, curator bot since '38. Plant Taxonomists—Am Phytopath Soc—Bot Soc Am—Calif Bot Soc—So Calif Acad Sci—AAAS—Sigma Xi—Phi Sigma. Los Angeles County Museum, Exposition Park, Los Angeles 7.

21 TEMPLETON, Justus S(tevens). Cambrian and Ordovician stratigraphy and paleontology; Structural geology of northwestern Illinois. b'14. AB '36 (Princeton); '36-38 (U Wis); PhD '40 (U Ill). Author: Geology of the Sterling Quadrangle, Ill '40. Geol Ill State Geol Survey, Urbana since '48. Geol for naval petroleum reserves in arctic Alaska as Lt jg '44-46. Geol Soc Am (F)—Sigma Xi—Phi Beta Kappa. Illinois State Geological Survey, Urbana, Ill.†

22 TEMPLIN, Edward Henry. Soil classification and engineering; Soils of Texas, Oklahoma, New Mexico, and western Pacific islands; Soil color; Soils suitable to guayule production. b'03. BS '23 (U Wis). Member soil survey field parties Wisconsin and Texas '22-42; selection and classification of lands suitable for growing guayle '43; technical supervision soil surveys Tex, Okla, eastern New Mexico '43-50; member soil engineering expedition to islands in western Pacific '48-49. Soil surveyor USDA since '23, sr correlator soil survey So Gt Plains States and in charge Tex Agrl Expt Sta since '46. Soil Sci Soc Am—Am Soc Agron. Texas Agricultural Experiment Sta, College Station.

23 TEMPLIN, Richard Laurence. Alloys (Aluminum). b'93. BS (CE) '15—ME '26 (U Kan); MS '17 (U Ill). Development methods and apparatus for determination mechanical properties of materials, and for machining of light alloys; design light alloy structures and machines. Author articles: An Autographic Extensometer for Use in Tension Tests of Materials '32; Development of a High Speed Lathe for Machining Aluminum '47. Contributor: American Soc Metals Handbook '48. Chief engr tests Aluminum Co Am since '19, asst dir research since '42. Am Soc CE—Am Soc Metals — ASME — ASTM — AIMME—Soc Exptl Stress Analysis. ASTM Charles B Dudley medal for The Fatigue Properties of Light Metals and Alloys '34; Am Soc CE Thomas Fitch Rowland prize (with A V Karpov) for Model of Calderwood Arch Dam '36; Franklin Inst of Pa Edward Longstreth medal for deformation recording apparatus '40; ASTM Richard L Templin award (with W C Aber) for A Method for Making Tension Tests of Metals Using a Miniature Specimen '51. Aluminum Research Laboratories, P.O. Box 772, New Kensington, Pa.

24 TENHET, Joseph Nesbitt. Insect pests of growing, stored and manufactured tobacco; Sand wireworm;

Molecrickets. b'97. BS (Clemson Agrl Coll). Study Biology, ecology and control tobacco moth (Ephestia elutella), cigarette beetle (Iasioderma serricorne), tobacco flea beetle (Epitrix hirtipennis), tobacco budworm (Heliothis virescens), tobacco wireworm (Conoderus vespertinus), parasites of tobacco budworm, black European slug (Agriolimax agrestis), sand wireworm (Horistonotus uhlerii), molecrickets (Scapteriscus vicinus and acletus); developed pyrethrum-oil space sprays for control of insects in tobacco warehouses. Author articles: A Power Sprayer for Applying Concentrated Insecticides '46; Control of Insects in Stored Tobacco with Pyrethrum-Oil '49; Experiments with Pyrethrum-Oil Sprays for Control of the Tobacco Moth and the Cigarette Beetle '49. Coauthor articles: (with C O Bare) The Effect of the Thermal-Vacuum Process on Insects in Stored Tobacco '46; (with C O Bare) Redrying Tobacco and its Effect on Insect Infestation '46, and others. Entomol USDA since '19, in charge field lab Bureau Entomol and Plant Quarantine '30-34 and since '42. Am Assn Econ Entomol—Fla Entomol Soc. Stored Tobacco Insect Laboratory, Box 5271, Richmond, Va.

10 TENNEY, Charles Dewey. George Meredith. b'06. AB '27 (Gooding Coll); MA '29—PhD '31 (U Ore); '30-31 (Harvard). Special study on George Meredith as critic. Author articles in field. Prof philos So Ill U since '44, administrative asst to pres since '45. NEA—Nat Council Eng Teachers—Am Philos Assn. Southern Illinois University, Carbondale, Ill.

11 TENNEY, Robert I. Brewing technology. b'10. BS '32 (U Ill); '36 (U Chicago). Research in fermentative production of acids and sugars since '38. Author articles in field. Research faculty Wahl-Henius Inst since '36, pres since '42. Master Brewers Assn Am—Am Chem Soc—Am Soc Brewing Chem—Inst Food Technol—Assn Official Agrl Chem—Inst of Brewing. 1135 Fullerton Av., Chgo 14.†

12 TEPER, Lazare. Labor economics; Industrial relations. b'08. Student '26-27 (Universite de Paris); AM '30—PhD '31 (Johns Hopkins). Delegate White House Conference on Nutrition for Defense '41; representative of American Federation of Labor to the Statistical Commission of United Nations Economic and Social Council '46-48; United States delegate to World Statistical Congress '47. Author: Hours of Labor '32; Women's Garment Industry '37; also articles in field. Dir research Internat Ladies' Garment Workers' Union since '37; joint labor advisor com to Bur of Labor Statis since '47. Am Econ Assn—Am Statis Assn—Am Marketing Assn—Acad Polit Sci—Industrial Relations Research Assn. 1710 Broadway, NYC 19.

13 TERHUNE, William Barclay. Mental hygiene. '93. MD '15 (Tulane U). Organized in Connecticut first division of mental hygiene in any state department of health, organized clinics throughout state; representative American Psychiatric Association at International Congress on Mental Health, London '48. Author articles in field. With Yale Sch Med since '19, now lect psych (asso prof); med director Conn Soc Mental Hygiene '19-22; asso med dir Austen Riggs Found '22-34; founder and med dir Silver Hill Found; psychiatric cons various orgns. AMA—Conn Med Soc—NE Psychiat Assn—Conn Psychiat Assn—ACP—Soc Research Nervous and Mental Disorders—Internat Cong Mental Hygiene—Am Psychiat Assn (chmn com cooperation with lay groups)—Am Psychopath Assn (pres '49-50)—Am Clin and Climatological Assn—Am Soc Research Psychosomatic Problems. Box D, New Canaan, Conn.

14 TERRELL, Clyde Buckstaff. Muskrats; Wild plants. b'94. Student '12-15 (Oshkosh State Teachers Coll). Research on improving wildlife, fish habitats, growing wild plants, muskrat ranching. Own muskrat ranch '15; profl wildlife cons US and Canada since '16; survey and report on SD waters SD Game and Fish Commn '19-23; gen nursery specialization foods for wildlife '31; supervisor lake improvement Okla Game and Fish Com '34; aquatic biologist US Forest Service and Mass Dept Conservation '35, US Forest Service and Wis Conservation Dept '36-37. Am Fisheries Soc—Ducks Unlimited—Internat Assn Fish and Game Commissioners—Wild Life Soc—Isaak Walton League Am—Wis Muskrat and Beaver Farmers Assn. 240 Winnebago St., Oshkosh, Wis.

15 TERRELL, Mary Church. Negro women (Progress and problems); Race relations in the United States. b'63. AB '84—AM '88—LHD '48 (Oberlin Coll); LittD '46 (Wilberforce U, O); LHD '48 (Howard U). First colored woman to serve on Board Education Washington, served '95-01, '06-11; represented American colored women abroad at international conferences Berlin, Zurich, London; appointed supervisor of work among colored women of eastern states by Republican National Committee '20, re-appointed '32. Author: A Colored Woman in a White World '40; also articles in feild. NA ACP (a founder)—Nat Assn Colored Women (first nat pres, serving three terms '96-01, hon pres since '01). Received citation for social service Woman's Centennial Congress NYC '40. 1615 S. St. N.W., Washington.

16 TERRILL, Clair E(lman). Sheep breeding, genetics, and reproduction physiology (Rambouillet, Columbia, Corriedale, and Targhee). b'10. BS '32 (Ia State Coll); PhD '36 (U Mo). Author articles in field. Animal husbandman Western Sheep Breeding Lab since '40. Am Soc Animal Production—Am Genetic Assn—Am Assn Advancement Sci—Am Assn Anatomists—Am Statis Assn. Western Sheep Breeding Laboratory, Dubois, Ida.†

17 TERRY, John Skally. Thomas Wolfe (Biography). b'94. AB '18—'20-21 (U NC); MA '22 (Columbia). Editor, author introduction: Thomas Wolfe's Letters to His Mother '43; official biographer of Thomas Wolfe; also articles in field. Instr Eng Washington Square Coll NYU '25-46, asst prof since '46. Phi Beta Kappa. 100 Washington Sq., NYC 3.

18 TERVET, Ian White. Plant pathology; Mycology. b'07. BS '31 (Glasgow U); PhD '40 (U Minn). Research on physiology of fungi, flax diseases, forage and vegetable crops diseases, cereal diseases, botanical aspects of dying-out of heather, fungus parasite of eggs of gray field slug, fungi injurious to seedling flax, determination of physiologic races of Ustilage avenae and levis, relative susceptibility of different lots of oat varieties to smut, variation in reaction of Anthony Oats to stem rust Puccinia graminis avenae. Author articles: The Relation of Seed Quality to the Development of Smut in Oats '44; The Influence of Fungi on Storage, Etc., of Soybeans '45; Bacteria in the Storage Organs of Health Plants '48, and others. Instr, asst prof path and bot U Minn '37-46; path US Dept Agr '43-45; asso prof Neb U '46-47; plant path br chief and dir investigations Chem Corps Camp Detrick Frederick Md since '47. Am Phytopath Soc—Am Mycol Soc—British Mycol Soc—AAAS—Sigma Xi. Commonwealth Fund fellow U Minn '33-35. Camp Detrick, Frederick, Md.†

19 TERWILLIGER, Charles Van Orden. Electrical machine design; Dielectrics. b'94. BS in engring '16—MS in elec engring '19 (Union Coll Schenectady NY); MS in elec engring '22 (Harvard); ED '38 (Johns Hopkins). Design electrical machinery for naval ship propulsion; investigation static and dynamic characteristics of synchro systems; investigation corona damage to paper insulation of lead sheathed cable; research in internal discharges in thin oil films. Test engr Gen Elec Co '17-18, asst gen engring lab '19; asst prof elec engring Ohio State U '24-25; faculty dept elec engineering USN Postgrad Sch since '25, prof and chmn dept since '38. Am Inst EE(F)—AAAS(F)—Sigma Xi. Profl engineer Md, Cal. US Naval Postgraduate School, Monterey, Cal.⊚

20 TERZAGHI, Ruth Doggett. Concrete deterioration; Petrography (Concrete aggregate). b'03. BS '24—MS '25 (U Chicago); PhD '30 (Radcliffe). Author articles in field. Cons problems of concrete deterioration since '43. Am Concrete Inst—Geol Soc Am (F)—Sigma Xi—Phi Beta Kappa. 3 Robinson Circle, Winchester, Mass.†

21 TESTER, Allen C. Geology (Sedimentology). b'97. BA '21—MA '21 (U Kan); PhD '29 (U Wis). Field studies Rocky Mountains, Central and Great Lakes states since '20; petroleum exploration Columbia '38-39; research on shapes of sediment particles, technique of sediment analysis, authegenic feldspars, surface and subsurface geology of Iowa, effects of Hiroshima atomic bombing on building materials. Author: Geological Map of Iowa; also articles in field. With U Ia since '25, prof since '40; asst state geol Ia '34-37. Capt, lt col geol water supply, constrn engr South Pacific theatre, Mariannas, Japan, Corps Engrs US Army '42-46. Geol Soc Am(F)—Am Assn Petroleum Geol—Geol Soc Philippines—AAAS(F)—American Geophysical Union—Ia Acad Sci—Sigma Xi. Geology Building, State University of Iowa, Iowa City, Ia.⊚

22 TETRAULT, Philippe Armand. Decomposition of cellulose; Antibiotics (Circulin, streptomycin). b'89. AB '12 (Clark U); MS '14 (Purdue U); PhD '29 (U Wis). Research on antiseptic and bactericidal action of benzoic acid and organic salts, bacteriostatic properties of commercial antiseptics and of phenylacetic acid. Holds patent on production of acetic acid from cellulose. Author: Bacterial Decomposition of Cellulose at High Temperatures '30; also articles in field. Prof bact Purdue U since '30. Soc Am Bact—Ind Acad Sci—Sigma Xi. Stanley Coulter Hall, Purdue University, Lafayette, Ind.

23 THADEN, John Frederick. Population. b'94. BS '20 (U Neb); MS '22 (Ia State Coll); '22-23 (Columbia); Ph D '30 (Mich State Coll). Determination extent migration by study relation total population changes of counties and urban centers with vital statistics; isolation and mapping ethnic settlements or culture islands; analysis factors related to distribution of medical doctors, osteopaths, and chiropractors in test area; delineation service areas of population centers. Author articles: Effect of the Increased Birth Rate on School Enrollment and School Building Needs '48; Population Change in the Rural and Urban Areas of Michigan since 1940 '48; Forecast of Future Public School Enrollments by Years '49; Ethnic Settlements in Rural Michigan, and others. Research asst dept sociol Ia State Coll '23-25; asst prof and research asst dept sociol and anthrop Michigan State Coll '25-44, asso prof and research asso since '44. Population Assn Am—Rural Sociol Soc—Am Sociol Soc —Mich Acad Sci Arts and Letters. Department of Sociology and Anthropology, Michigan State College, East Lansing.

10 THARP, Benjamin Carroll. Texas (Vegetation). b'85. AB '14—MA '15 —PhD '25 (U Tex). Investigations distribution of vegetation of Texas and its correlations with soils, topography, geology and climate. Author articles: Ecologic Investigations in the Red River Valley '23; Structure of Texas Vegetation East of the 98th Meridian '26; The Vegetation of Texas '39; The Mesa Region of Texas: an Ecological Study '43; Texas Range Grasses '52. With dept botany U Tex since '19, prof botany since '33. Tex Acad Sci(F)—AAAS(F)—Bot Soc Am —Ecol Soc Am—Am Soc Plant Taxonomists—AAUP—Phi Beta Kappa— Sigma Xi. U. Texas, Austin. H: 506 Bellevue Pl.

11 THARP, Claude Roy. Michigan (State, county, and municipal government). b'86. BS '09 (Greer Coll), LLB '16 (Washington U), MBA '28 (Northwestern U). Author: Social Security and Related Services in Michigan; Federal Expenditures in Michigan; Administration and Financing of Public Relief (with Frank M Landers); State Aid in Michigan; Reorganization of Michigan's County Government (with Robert S Ford). Financial analyst, Public Works Administration Washington; now research asso Inst Pub Adminstrn Bur of Government U Mich. Institute of Public Administration, Bureau of Government, University of Michigan, Ann Arbor.

12 THARP, W(illiam) Hardy. Cotton nutrition and defoliation; Cottonseed composition. b'00. BS '29 (Mont State Coll); MS '31—PhD '32 (U Wis); Nat Research Council fellow '32-33 (Cornell U). Author articles in field. Asso, later sr physiol US Dept Agr cotton div Fayetteville Ark '36-50 now principal physiologist of the Plant Industry Station Beltsville since '50. Sigma Xi. Plant Industry Station, Beltsville, Md.

13 THATCHER, Maurice Hudson. Kentucky (Fed aid for internal improvements). b'70. Grad (Bryant, Stratton Bus Coll Lsvl); law student '96-98 (Frankfort Ky); LLD (Hon) (U Ala). As congressman author acts dealing with national parks, highways, public buildings, including act establishing Mammoth Cave National Park, permanent improvement and maintenance Lincoln Birthplace Farm, municipal bridge across Ohio River Louisville, US Marine and Veterans Hosps Louisville and Lexington, creation of Zachary Taylor National Cemetery, and others; founder Eastern National Park-to-Park Highway '30. Practice of law Louisville since '13; congl rep fifth dist Ky '23-33. Am Bar Assn—Ky Bar Assn. 834 Continental Bldg., Washington 5.

14 THAYER, Gordon Woods. Folklore (Folktales, superstitions, customs, ballads, proverbs, gypsies); Medieval romances; Oriental history; Illuminated manuscripts. b'87. AB '06—AM '07 (Harvard). Co-author: English Ballads and songs in the John G White Collection of Folklore and Orientalia of the Cleveland Public Library '31. Librarian John G White Collection Cleveland Pub Library since '16, asst to dir of Library since '44. Cleveland Public Library, 325 Superior Av., Cleveland 14.†

15 THAYER, Paul Munson. Aeration (Liquids); Sewage (Aeration). b'91. BS (ME) '14 (Purdue U). Development aerated grit chambers for sewage plants, activated sludge plant for treatment milk waste, simplified diffused air activated sludge plant for small communities, non-clogging air diffusion device, use of air for flocculation and flash mixing; process design digestion of sewage and industrial waste solids by means aeration instead of anaerobic action. Author articles: Aeration in Sewage Treatment '49; New Design for an Activated Sludge Plant to Treat Milk Waste '51, and others. Cons engr sewage equipment '32-37; dist mgr in charge development of aeration systems, and field applications Chicago Pump Co since '37. Fedn Sewage and Indsl Waste Assns—Nat Indsl Waste Conf—Nat Assn Professional Engrs. Chicago Pump Co., 2336 Wolfram St., Chgo 18. H: 3933 N. Prospect Av., Milw 11.

16 THAYER, Richard Nelson. Fluorescent lamps. b'07. BS '28 (U Pittsburgh). Author articles in field. Development engr fluorescent and other elect light sources '28-45; supervisor design and quality sect Lamp Development Lab. Optical Soc Am—Am Phys Soc. Lamp Development Laboratory, General Electric Company, Nela Park, East Cleveland 12, O.†

17 THAYER, Sidney Allen. Hormone chemistry. b'02. BS '25 (Beloit Coll); PhD '30 (St Louis U). Research preparation, isolation, characterization of theelin and theelol; metabolism these and related compounds; specialist in assay of hormones including adrenal cortical hormones; isolation, characterization, and bioassy vitamin K1, K2, and related compounds; antibiotics. With St Louis U since '25, asso prof biochem since '43. Am Soc Biol Chem —Soc Exptl Biol and Med—ACS—Sigma Xi. 1402 South Grand Blvd., StL 4.

18 THAYER, Theodore. Eighteenth century United States history; History of Pennsylvania. b'04. PhD '41 (U Pa). Author: Israel Pemberton King of the Quakers; Polit and the Growth of Democracy in Pennsylvania, 1740-1776; also numerous articles in field. Asst Prof history Ithaca Coll '40-42, Cornell U '43-44, U Wash '44-46; asso prof hist Rutgers U since '47. AHA— Econ Hist Assn. Rutgers University, Newark.

19 THAYER, T h o m a s P(rence). Chromite; Geology and mineral deposits of Oregon and the Republic of Liberia. b'07. BA '29 (U Oregon); MA '31 (Northwestern U); PhD '34 (Cal Inst Tech). Field geol Ore '32-48; studies chromite US and Cuba '39-42; field work in Liberia '44, '49-50. Author: Chromite Deposits of Grant Co, Oregon '40; Chrome Resources of Cuba '42; also articles in field. Geol US Geol Survey since '37; chromite commodity geol since '44. Geol Soc Am(F)—Soc Econ Geol—Am Geophys Union— Geol Soc Washington. Mineral Deposits Branch, U.S. Geological Survey, Washington 25.

20 THEIS, Charles V(ernon). Ground water hydrology. b'00. CE '22—PhD '29 (U Cincinnati). Research in theory of ground-water movement, effect of use of wells on ground-water reserves, areal geology as related to ground-water (principally in New Mexico), ground water as related to problems of mining, occurence and theory of permanently frozen ground in Alaska and elsewhere. Author articles in field. Jr geol US Army Engrs '29-30; asst, later prin geol US Geol Survey since '30. Geol Soc Am(F)—AAAS(F) —Am Geophys Union—Sigma Xi—Tau Beta Pi. U.S. Geological Survey, Albuquerque, N.M.

21 THEIS, Edwin Raymond. Leather technology; Industrial biochemistry. b'96. ChE '21—PhD '26 (U Cincinnati). Member special US government commission to China and Japan for inspection imported skins '37. Co-author: Chemistry of Leather Manufacture. Research asso and dir chem research dept leather research U Cincinnati '21-27; asst prof chem engring Lehigh U '27-30, asso prof '30-38, prof chem engring '38-45, research prof since '45, dir div leather tech Inst of Research since '27; cons since '27. Internat Soc Leather Trades Chem—Am Inst Chem (F)—Am Chem Soc—Tech Assn Fur Industry—Tau Beta Pi—Sigma Xi— Am Leather Chem Assn (hon life member). Awarded Moffatt medal by Tanners Council Am '43. 1021 Raymond Av., Bethlehem, Pa.†

22 THIEL, Albert Frederick. Plant anatomy; Epidemiology of stem rusts. b'87. AB '16 (U Minn); AM '17 (U Neb); PhD '31 (U Chicago). Author articles in field. Field asst, later path Bur Plant Industry US Dept Agr '17-29; asst prof, asso prof bot Woman's Coll U NC since '31. Bot Soc Am—NC Acad Sci—Assn SE Biol—Sigma Xi. Woman's College, University of North Carolina, Greensboro, N.C.

23 THIELE, Ludwig Alois. Industrial water purification; Adhesives (Animal, vegetable, cellulose and synthetic resin and rubber bases). Holds degrees PhD and DSc after study at U Heidelberg, U Berlin, U Halle, Tech Hochschule, Charlottenburg and U Brussels. Author: Leim und Gelatine '07; Die Fabrikation von Leim und Gelatine '22; Die Chemie und Technology der Leim und Gelatine Fabrikation (with Gerngross-Goebel) '32; The Tangent System of Sulfuric Acid Manufacture; also articles in field. Cons practice Holland (Mich) Gelatin Works '12-23; chem engr Eastern Tanners Glue Co since '23; designed, constructed, variety of chem plants various companies; dir Superior Products Co, Pa Crude Oil Co, Thiele Laboratories Co. AAAS(F)—AICE—Am Chem Soc. Gowanda, N.Y.

24 THIENES, Clinton Hobart. Toxicology; Nicotine poisoning. b'96. AB '18—AM '23—MD '23 (U Ore); PhD '26 (Stanford U). Author: Field Manual in Toxicology for Agricultural Workers '38; Clinical Toxicology '40; Fundamentals of Pharmacology '45. Asso prof pharmacology U So Calif Sch Med '29-31, prof and head dept '31-52; dir Institute Med Research. Huntington Memorial Hospital since '52 attending path toxicology Los Angeles Co Hosp. AMA(F)—AAAS(F)—Am Soc Pharmacol—Soc Exptl Biol and Med (sec '37-39, chmn '39-40, nat council '39-40)—Cal Med Assn— Indsl Med Assn— Phi Beta Kappa—Sigma Xi— Alpha Omega Alpha—Theta Kappa Psi —Psi Upsilon. 734 Fairmount Av.. Pasadena 2, Cal.†

25 THIERRY, John Adams. Bridges (Military); Radiological safety. b'13. AB '35—AM '36 (Harvard U); '36-37 (U Cambridge England); LLB '40 (Harvard U); Atty Bucyrus-Erie Co since '40, asst to chmn since '50; chief bridge sect research and publications dept Engineer Sch Ft. Belvoir Va '43-46. Phi Beta Kappa—Milwaukee Bar Assn—Milwaukee Patent Law Assn—Am Soc Mil Engrs. Bucyrus-Erie Co., South Milwaukee, Wis.

10 THOLAND, Nils Kristian Gustav. Powder metallurgy. b'98. ME (Chalmers Inst Tech). Founder Ekstrand and Tholand '26, now pres and treas. AIMME—Am Soc Metals. 441 Lexington Av., NYC 17.

11 THOM, Charles. Mycology (Indsl, agrl); Cheese ripening; Molds (Penicillia, Aspergillis). b'72. AB '95 —AM '97—DSc (honorary) '36 (Lake Forest Coll); PhD '99 (U Mo); '02-04 (Cornell U); '97 (Marine Biol Lab, Woods Hole Mass. Research on cheese ripening fitness for food, food poisoning, food factory sanitation, soil fungi, household molds, classification of Penicillia and Aspergillis as molds in industry. Author: The Penicillia '30. Co-author: The Book of Cheese; Hygienic Fundamentals of Food Handling; Manual of the Aspergilli. With US Dept Agr '04-42, retired '42. AAAS(F) — Acad Med, Washington—Nat Acad Sci—Washington Acad Sci (pres '37)—Bot Soc Am—Am Naturalists—Internat Soc Soil Sci—Soc Am Bact (pres '40)—Am Phytopath Soc—Sigma Xi—Phi Beta Kappa. 207 Grant St., Port Jefferson, N.Y.†ⓒ

12 THOM, Herbert Conrad Schlueter. Physical and agricultural climatology; Statistics; Meteorology; Geophysics. b'10. BS '37—MS in math statis (George Washington U); '44-47 (Ia State Coll). Research on combination flume, hydraulic instruments, lysimeter scale installation, statistical analysis weather and hydrologic data, storm designs for large reservoirs, rainfall frequency, meteorological homogeneity; planned and directed largest known weather data processing and punched card projects; devised system for predicting amount of soft corn, initiated and directed studies on network accuracy, freeze hazard, drought, and climatology of corn. Author articles in field. Hydraulic engr Soil Conservation Service '36-37, Weather Bur '38-40; statis and chief Statis Div Weather Bur '41-44; chmn grad program climatology, head subsect agrl climatology Ia State Coll, sect dir Ia Weather Bur, chief weather div Ia Dept Agr since '45, research prof climatology since '47. Ia Acad Sci(F)— Am Soc Heating Ventilating Engrs— Inst Math Statis—Am Statis Assn— Am Meteorol Soc—Am Geophys Union —Am Soc Agron—AAUP—Sigma Xi. Statistical Laboratory, Iowa State College, Ames, Ia.

13 THOMAS, Benjamin Platt. Abraham Lincoln. b'02. AB '24—PhD '29 (Johns Hopkins); LHD '47 (Ill Coll); LLD '53 (Knox); Litt D '53 (Northwestern). Asso editor The Abraham Lincoln Quarterly '40-53; editorial advisory board The Collected Works of Abraham Lincoln since '45. Author: Lincoln's New Salem '34; Lincoln, 1847-1853 '36; Portrait for Posterity: Lincoln and His Biographers '47; Theodore Weld '50; Abraham Lincoln: A Biography '52. AHA—Miss Val Hist Assn —So Hist Soc—Abraham Lincoln Assn (dir since '36, exec sec '32-36). Awarded Lincoln Book of the Year by Lincoln Nat Life Found '47, '52; Lincoln Diploma of Honor by Lincoln Memorial U '49. 1910 Wiggins Av., Springfield, Ill.

14 THOMAS, Byron Henry. Animal nutrition (Vitamins, minerals, proteins). b'01. BS '22 (U Calif); MS '24 —PhD '29—scholar '23-24—teach fellow '24-26—Indsl fellow '26-29 (U Wis). In-

troduced to America first commercial production of metabolized vitamin D milk. Author articles in field. Research prof and head animal chem and nutrition Ia Agrl Expt Sta since '31. Am Chem Soc—AAAS—Am Dairy Sci Assn—Am Soc Animal Prodn—Am Inst Nutrition—Ia Acad Sci—Sigma Xi. Animal Chemistry and Nutrition, Iowa Agricultural Experiment Station, Iowa State College, Ames, Ia.

15 THOMAS, Charles Allen. Plutonium (Chemistry and metallurgy). b'00 AB '20 (Transylvania Coll); MS '24 (MIT); DSc '33 (Transylvania Coll); DSc '47 (Washington U); LLD '50 (Hobart Coll). Author: Anhydrous Aluminum Chloride in Organic Chemistry. Dir central research dept Monsanto Chem Co '36-45, vp and tech dir '45, exec vp '47, mem exec com, mem bd dirs since '42; chmn Scientific Manpower Advisory Com NSRB dep chief Nat Defense Research Com '42-43; mem Manhattan Project, in charge Clinton Laboratories Oak Ridge Tenn. Am Chem Soc—AAAS(F)—Am Inst Chemists—Am Inst Chem Engrs—Nat Acad Sci—Am Philosophical Soc—Phi Beta Kappa—Sigma Xi—Alpha Chi Sigma. Medal for Merit '46; Industrial Research Inst medal '47, Am Inst Chemists Gold medal '48. Monsanto Chemical Co., 1700 S. 2d St., StL.ⓒ

16 THOMAS, Charles D(anser). Theoretical physics (Ef-magnetism theory, Geiger counter study). b'08. AB '30— MS '31 (W Va U); PhD '37 (U Chicago); '38 (U Mich). Author articles in field. With W Va U since '31, now prof. W Va Acad Sci—Am Phys Soc— AAAS—Sigma Xi. Department of Physics, West Virginia University, Morgantown, W.Va.†

17 THOMAS, Charles Kenneth. American linguistic geography. b'00. AB '22 —MA '24—PhD '30 (Cornell U). Author: Introduction to the Phonetics of American English '47; also articles in field. With Cornell U since '22, now prof speech; dir speech clinic since '27. Am Speech and Hearing Assn(F)—Am Dialect Soc (regional sec Middle Atlantic states). Department of Speech, Cornell University, Ithaca, N.Y.†ⓒ

18 THOMAS, Charles Marion. History of the United States Air Force; Indiana political history. b'02. AB '24 (Ind U); AM—PhD '31 (Columbia). Author: American Neutrality in 1793 '31; Thomas Riley Marshall, Hoosier Statesman '39; also articles in field. Co-organizer, co-dir Miss Valley Press since '39; instr LI U '28-30, asst prof '30-36; personnel officer AAF '42-43, hist officer '43-46; chief Documentary Research Div, Air U since '46. AHA— Miss Valley Hist Assn—O Acad Hist— Ala Hist Assn—So Hist Assn. Documentary Research Division, Air University Library, Maxwell Air Force Base, Montgomery 8, Ala.

19 THOMAS, Charles Ward. Ice navigation. b'03. Grad (US Coast Guard Acad); student (U Washington). Commanded US Coast Guard Icebreaker Eastwind and Northeast Greenland Task Unit of US Atlantic Fleet during expedition '44; served as Chief of Staff Greenland Patrol US Atlantic Fleet, later becoming Commander; sent to command Icebreaker Northwind which during operation Highjump spear-headed penetration of central group through heaviest Antarctic pack in history to Little America '46-47, re-established and commanded Bering Sea Patrol '48. With US Coast Guard since '25, now Chief of Staff 2nd Coast Guard Dist. Arctic Inst NA (asso). Chief of Staff, U.S. Coast Guard, 2nd Coast Guard District, 224 Old Custom House, St. Louis 1.

20 THOMAS, Edward S(inclair). Ecology of Orthoptera; Birds; Reptiles. b'91. AB '13—LLB '16 (O State U); DSc (hon) '44 (Capital U). Author articles in field. Curator Nat Hist O State Mus since '31. AAAS(F)—O Acad Sci(F)—Entomol Soc Am(F)—Am Ornithol Union—Wilson Ornithol Club— Am Soc Ichthyologists Herpetologists. Ohio State Museum, Columbus 10, O.†

21 THOMAS, Franklin. Water supply; Irrigation; Sewage; Flood control; Highways (Express). b'85. BE '08— CE '13 (U Ia); D Eng '49 (U So Cal). With CB & Q Ry '03-04; Mines Power Co Cobalt Ontario Can '09-10; instr dept engring U Mich '10-12; Ala Power Co '12-13 (made designs for developments at Lock 18 Coosa River and Muscle Shoals, Tenn River); prof civil engring, Cal Inst Tech since '13 also chmn administrative com of faculty '17 and '20-21 during absence of pres and following his resignation, chmn div engring '26-44; dean students '44. ASCE (dir '30-33, vp '44-45, pres '49, pres Los Angeles sect '24)—Am Soc Engring Edn—Am Water Works Assn —Sigma Tau—Sigma Xi—Tau Beta Pi —AAAS(F). Awarded gold medal (Arthur Noble award) '39 by city Pasadena for notable service in promoting welfare of the city. 685 S.E Milino Av., Pasadena 5, Calⓒ

22 THOMAS, George. American government (Utah); Western United States agriculture (Irrigation). b'66. AB '96 —AM '01 (Harvard); PhD '03 (U Halle); LLD '40 (U Utah). Author: Die Geschichte der Zolltarife und Handelsvertrage der Vereinigten Staaten von Nordamerika seit 1875; Hofbuchdruckerei '04; Modern Constitutions '07; Civil Government of Utah '12; Development of Institutions Under Irrigation '20; Early Irrigation in the Western States '48. Pres U Utah '21-41, now emeritus. Am Geog Soc(F)—Acad Polit Sci—Am Econ Assn—Phi Beta Kappa—Phi Kappa Phi. University of Utah, Salt Lake City.

23 THOMAS, George Leicester. Waterlilies; Goldfish; Aquariums. b '80. AB '01—AM '03 (Franklin and Marshall Coll). Research on fish culture, developed new species waterlily. Fish culturist and hort since '17. E Goldfish Growers Assn (pres.). Lilypons, Md.

24 THOMAS, H. Emerson. Liquefied petroleum gas. b'02. AB '26 (Okla City U); (U Ill, U Okla). Specialist in distribution and plant problems on bottled gas or tank gas to domestic and commercial users; design liquefied petroleum gas utilization plants. Pres H Emerson Thomas & Assos Inc, pres Liquefied Petroleum Service Co. AS ME—Liquefied Petroleum Gas Assn— Am Gas Assn—Compressed Gas Assn —Nat Fire Protection Assn—Gas Appliance Mfrs Assn. 111 Quimby St., P.O. Box 270, Westfield, N.J.

25 THOMAS, Helen Lewis. History of science; Stellar variability and photometry; Electronics (Radar). b'05. AB '28—PhD '48 (Radcliffe Coll). Research in stellar variability and photometric observations; studies on early history of variable star observing to XIX century; history of astronomy XII-XIV centuries. Author: Biography of Johann Kepler '49; Greek Astronomy and Its Development During the Middle Ages '49. Author article: U Scorpii as a Recurrent Nova '40, and others. Pickering Meml research asst Harvard Coll Observatory '34-42, dept head Radio Research Lab '42-43; asst hist Radiation Lab MIT '43-46; jr engr Raytheon Mfg Co '46-47, sr engr since '47. Am Astron Soc—Hist Sci Soc. Raytheon Mfg. Co., Newton 58, Mass.

10 THOMAS, H(erbert) Rex. Plant pathology (Vegetable diseases). b'13. BS '35—PhD '41 (U Calif Berkeley); '38-41 (Purdue U). Vegetable disease investigations, tomato disease, bean disease including breeding for disease resistance. Author articles: Cercospora Blight of Carrot '43; A Nonchromogenic Sporulating Variant of Alternaria Solani '43; Influence of Different Levels and Combinations of Nitrogen, Phosphorus, and Potassium Nutrition on the Susceptibility of the Tomato Plant to Infection by Alternaria Solani '48, and others. With U Calif '36-37, Purdue U for US Dept Agr '37-43, Plant Industry Sta Beltsville Md since '46. Am Phytopath Soc—Am Soc Hort Sci—Wash Bot Soc—AAAS—Sigma Xi. Plant Industry Station, Beltsville, Md.†

11 THOMAS, Horace Davis. Stratigraphy, petroleum geology and resources of the Rocky Mountain region; Mineral resources and regional geology of Wyoming. b'05. BA '26—MA '28 (U Wyo); PhD '35 (Columbia). Author articles in field. Wyo State geol and prof geol U Wyo since '41; collaborator in seismol for Wyo US Coast and Geodetic Survey since '41. Geol Soc Am(F)—Paleontol Soc(F)—Am Assn Pet Geol (geol names and correlations com since '41, subcom on Paleozoic stratigraphy, Carboniferous stratigraphy)—Assn Am State Geol—Wyo Geol Assn—Rocky Mountain Assn Geol. University of Wyoming, Laramie, Wyo.

12 THOMAS, John Eugene. Forest tree diseases; Forest genetics. b'14. BS '41 (O State U); PhD '45 (Wis U). Research on effects of plant growth hormones on plant galls caused by bacteria, use of plant growth substances in agriculture, diseases of forest trees, particularly conifers, breeding disease resistant forest trees. Author articles in field. Asst prof plant path Wis U '47-50; asso prof botany and plant pathology Okla A&M Coll since '50. Am Phytopath Soc—Bot Soc Am—Soc Am Foresters—Sigma Xi. Dept. of Botany and Plant Pathology, Oklahoma A.&M. College, Stillwater, Okla.

13 THOMAS, Lawrence Clifford. Animal genetics (Disease resistance, color genes, fertility); Race hygiene. b'96. BS '19 (Ottawa U); MS '26 (Kan State Coll); PhD '32 (N Ill). Research on genetics of hairlessness in animals, disease resistance in poultry, color genes in rodents and hybrid vigor, fertility and reproductive physiology in the rat, vitamins in milk. Author articles: Oestrum and Fertility in the Rat '32; Hereditary Hypotrichosis in the Rat (Mus norvegicus) '40; Judging for Fertility in Animals '32; Comparative Value of Chocolate Milk and Whole Milk for Riboflavin '49. Research asst animal breeding U Ill '26-31; prof biol head dept Kan Wesleyan U '31-37; prof zool Oshkosh State Teachers Coll '37-40; health engr and sanitarian State of Mich '42-44; prof biol head dept Mo Valley Coll since '44. AAAS—Nat Assn Biol Teachers—Mo Acad Sci—Sigma Xi. Missouri Valley College, Marshall, Mo.†

14 THOMAS, Llewellyn Hilleth. Theoretical physics; Atomic and molecular structure; Theory of relativity; Ballistics and gun design; Ordnance engineering; Numerical methods. b'03. BA '24—MA '26—PhD '27—scholar Trinity Coll '21-26—Isaac Newton student '25-28—1851 exhibition scholar '27-29—fellow Trinity Coll '26-30 (U Cambridge); '25-26 (U Inst Theoretical Physics Copenhagen). Author articles in field. Asst prof phys O State U '29-30, asso prof '30-36, prof '36-46; sr staff Watson Sci Computing Lab since '46. Physicist Ballistic Research Lab Aberdeen Proving Ground '43-45. Cambridge Philos Soc—Brit Assn Adv Sci—Royal Astron Soc—AAAS—Am Phys Soc—Phi Beta Kappa—Sigma Xi. Smith's prize Cambridge '26. Watson Scientific Computing Laboratory, 612 W. 116th St., NYC 27.†◎

15 THOMAS, Lyell Jay. Helminthology; Nemathelminthes; Cestoda; Trematoda. b'92. Invented rat handler and black fly incubator. Author articles in field. Prof zool Ill U since '48. AAAS(F)—Am Soc Parasitol—Helminthology Soc Wash—Am Micros Soc (exec officer, acting custodian Spencer-Tolles research fund)—Sigma Xi—Am Soc Zool—Ill State Acad Sci (sec and ed '27-30, pres '43-44). Fellow zool Ill U '22-23, Bermuda Marine Biol Research Sta '48. 103 Vivarium Bldg., Department of Zoology, University of Illinois, Champaign, Ill.

16 THOMAS, Maurice J. Education (Public finance); Education (Facilities). b'02. AB '25 (U Washington); AM '26—EdD '43 (Columbia). Author: Developing Human Resources '45; Charting Our Course '47; (with others) Improving Public Education '51; (with others) The School Board and Public Education '52; The Code of Public Education, State of Washington '52. Supt schs Bothell Wash '37-42; research asst Teachers Coll Columbia U '42-43; supt sch Rochester Minn '43-48; prof edn U Pittsburgh since '48; dir tri-state area Sch Study Council U Pittsburgh. Nat Edn Assn—Minn Congress Parents and Teachers—Am Assn Sch Administrators—Horace Mann League of Am—Phi Delta Kappa. 2528 Cathedral Bldg., University of Pittsburgh, Pittsburgh.†◎

17 THOMAS, Moyer D(elwyn). Agricultural chemistry (Plant nutrition, photosynthesis, atmospheric pollution, soil moisture relations). b'94. AB '14 (U Utah); BA '16—BSc '19—MA '21—DSc '36 (U Oxford). Author articles in field. Research chem dept agrl research Am Smelting and Refining Co Salt Lake City since '26. Am Chem Soc (chmn NW Utah sect '37, '47)—Western Soc Soil Sci (sec '24, pres '25—AAAS—Am Soc Plant Physiol—Am Meteorol Soc. Received Acad Sci award Utah Acad Arts Sci Letters '43. Department Agricultural Research, American Smelting and Refining Company, Pacific National Life Building, Salt Lake City.

18 THOMAS, Samuel Owen. Botany (Advanced); Mycology; Penicillin, aureomycin, and other antibiotics. b'01. AB '33 (Wittenberg Coll); BS '34 (Goshen Coll); MS '40—PhD '46 (Purdue U). Lederle Labs Pearl River NY since '43. Am Phytopath Soc—Soc Am Bact—AAAS—NY Acad Sci—Sigma Xi—Mycological Soc Am—Soc Indsl Mycology. Lederle Laboratories Division, American Cyanamid Co., Pearl River, N.Y.

19 THOMAS, Upton B(eall), Jr. Electrochemistry; Storage batteries; Electrical contacts. b'08. Bachelor Science '29 (Coll William and Mary). Research in atmospheric corrosion and electrical contact resistance, storage batteries, use of lead-calcium alloys for battery grids, electrical conductivity of lead dioxide. Author articles in field. Tech staff Bell Telephone Labs Inc since '29. Electrochem Soc (Young Author's Prize '35)—Am Chem Soc—Phi Beta Kappa—Phi Kappa Phi. Bell Telephone Laboratories, Murray Hill, N.J.†

20 THOMAS, Walter Dill, Jr. Plant pathology (Vegetable, forest and virus diseases, antibiotics). b'18. Fellow '38- 39 (U Freiburg Br, German); BS '39 (Colo A&M Coll); MS '43—PhD '46 (U Minn). Research and work mycorhizae, crown gall, cereal root rots, ornamentals, beans, potatoes and other vegetable diseases, forest and virus diseases, antibiotics; developing technique for use of ultra-violet radiation for diagnosis carnation virus diseases; developed forecasting system for potato late blight '46. Author articles: Die Physiologische Bedeutung des Mykorhiza fur Nadelwalder '39; Observations on the Mycorrhizal Fungi of Four Coniferous Plantations in the Rhine Valley '41; A Survey of Northern Colorado Flora Bearing Mycorrhizae '41; Two Aids for the Study of Potato Late Blight Epidemiology '45; Growth and Variation of Six Physiologic Races of Actinomyces Scabies (Thax) Gussow on Different Culture Media '47; Selection of Virus-Free Carnations by Fluorescence '48; Physiologic Specialization of Alternaria Solani and A Dianthi '48, and others. Forest tech Nat Park Service '37; instr bot Colo A and M Coll '39-41, asst prof bot since '46; asst plant path Colo Agrl Expt Sta '46-48; assoc plant path since '48. AAAS—Am Phytopath Soc—Potato Assn Am—Colo-Wyo Acad Sci — Intermountain Plant Path Soc—Colo Forestry and Hort Soc—West Colo Hort Soc. Department of Botany and Plant Pathology, Colorado A and M College, Fort Collins, Colo.

21 THOMPSON, Charles E(ugene). Thematic Apperception Test (Adaptations, influences of cultural differences on results). b'13. BS '38 (Southwest Mo State Coll); MS '39 (Okla U); PhD '49 (Tulane U). Author: Thompson Modification of the Thematic Apperception Test '49; Annotated Bibliography of the Thematic Apperception Test '50; The Influence of Color in the Thematic Apperception Test '50. Author articles: A Modification of the Thematic Apperception Test for Use with Minority Group, and others. Research asso Tex State Bd Health '41-42; clin psychol USAAF '42-46; clin psychol Vets Adminstrn '46-50, asst chief clin psychol Vets Adminstrn Hosp N Little Rock (Ark) since '50. Am Psychol Assn—AAAS—Am Edn Research Assos—Internat Congress Psychotechnol—Soc for Applied Anthropol. Veterans Administration Hospital, North Little Rock, Ark.

22 THOMPSON, Charles Manfred. Economic history of the United States; Economic theory. b'77. AB '09—AM '10—PhD '13 (U Ill); LLD '21 (Muskingum Coll O); Litt D '33 (McKendree Coll). Author: The Illinois Whigs before 1846 '15; History of the United States '17; Elementary Economics '19; The Industrial State (vol 4 of Ill Centennial History) '19; Principles and Practice of Economics '28; High School Economics '32; Economic Development of the United States '38. Prof and dean emeritus Coll Commerce and Bus U Ill. Am Econ Assn—Am Hist Assn—Beta Gamma Sigma—Phi Beta Kappa. 709 W. University Av., Champaign, Ill.◎

23 THOMPSON, Chester David. Safety and detonating fuses (Timing, detonating, ignition devices). b'90. Student (Trinity Coll). Research textiles waterproofings resulted in manufacture of Primacord a textile-covered detonating fuse. Chief chem Ensign-Bickford Co Simsbury Conn '17-42, dir research since '42. Am Chem Soc—Am Soc Testing Materials. The Ensign-Bickford Company, Simsbury, Conn.

24 THOMPSON, Clara. Interpersonal relations; Homosexuality. b'93. AB '16 (Brown U); MD '20 (Johns Hopkins). Author: Psychoanalysis: Evolution and

Development '50. Asst clin prof psychiatry NY Med Coll '41-44; fellow and exec dir William Alanson White Inst Psychiatry since '43. AMA—NY County Med Soc—NY Acad Med(F)—NY Soc Clinical Psychiatry—Soc Theory Personality—Am Psychiat Association(F)—Am Psychoanalytic Assn —Phi Beta Kappa—Sigma Xi. 12 E. 86 St., NYC 28.

10 THOMPSON, Clarence Bertrand. Taylor system; Scientific management. b'82. LLB '00 (U So Cal); AB '08—AM '09 (Harvard). Author: The Churches and the Wage Earners '09; How to Find Factory Costs '15; Theory and Practice of Scientific Management '17; Taylor System of Scientific Management '17; Le Système Taylor (also transl Polish) '17; Méthodes Americaines de Prix de Revient '20; (with others) La Reorganisation des Usines (2 vols) '26. Served apprenticeship Taylor System Business Management '12-15; counsel for Am, French, German and Italian concerns; research asst U Cal Med Sch; now with Instituto de Fisiologia Montevideo Uraguay. Am Chem Soc—Cal Hist Soc. Calle Rio Negro 1216, Montevideo, Uraguay.◉

11 THOMPSON, Clifford Griffeth. William Wollaston. b'82. BS '03 (Young Harris Coll Ga); '04-06 (U Chicago); MA '08—BD '10—PhD '20 (Yale U); '10-11 (U Edinburgh Scotland); '11 (U Jena Germany); DD '16 (Highland Coll Kan). Author: The Ethics of William Wollaston '22. Ordained ministry Congl Ch '12; acting prof psychology Okla Coll Women Chickasha '12-13; prof philosophy Central Coll Fayette Mo '13-21; prof philosophy Emory U '21-38; hon fellowship Ohio State U '28-29; prof sociology Lincoln Memorial U since '29. Am Philos Assn—So Assn Philosophy and Psychology. U of Georgia, Piedmont College, Dehdrest, Ga.◉

12 THOMPSON, Daniel Garrison Brinton. History of United States (Middle-Atlantic states). b'99. AB '20 (U Pa); BS '23 (MIT); PhD '45 (Columbia U). Author: Ruggles of New York '46; also articles in field. Mem faculty Lafayette Coll Easton Pa '43-45; asst prof hist Trinity Coll Hartford '45-48; asso prof and chemn dept since '48. AHA—Acad Polit Sci—New York Hist Soc—NY State Hist Assn—Econ Hist Assn—Phi Beta Kappa. Trinity College, Hartford 6, Conn. H: 36 Bainbridge Rd., West Hartford 7, Conn.

13 THOMPSON, Dudley. Applications of ultra-high frequency sound in chem processing. b'13. BS CE '35—MS '41—PhD '50 (Va Poly Inst Blacksburg Va). Study unit processes in organic synthesis; research fellow investigating ultrasonic coagulation phosphate tailing Chemical Research Laboratory Tennessee Valley Authority '47-48; research application high frequency vibration and sound in chemical process industries; chairman American Institute Chemical Engineers technical session on waste disposal and ultrasonics '50, ultrasonics symposium Boston '50. Author articles: A New Chemical Engineering Tool '50; Ultrasonic Coagulation of Phosphate Tailing '50. Asst prof chem engring Va Poly Inst since '46; development engr vibration and sound sect Gen Engring and Cons Lab Gen Elec Co Schenectady NY '50; private cons applied ultrasonics since '50. ACS — AIMME — AICE — AAAS — Am Acoustical Soc—Va Acad Sci—Tenn Acad Sci—Phi Lambda Upsilon. Chemical Engineering Department, Va Polytechnic Institute, Blacksburg.

14 THOMPSON, George Norwell. Building and plumbing codes. b'92. AB (Harvard). Assisted planning of recommended code requirements; study for reduction unnecessary variations in requirements; application results of technical research on codes; member coordinating committee for national plumbing code. Author articles: The History of Building Regulations '37; Building Codes—An Essential Tool in Urban Development '43; The Problem of Building Code Improvement '47; The Preparation and Revision of Building Codes (last edit) '49. With Nat Bur Standards '26-33 and since '34, now asst chief bldg tech div and chief codes and specifications sect; sec bldg code com Dept Commerce '26-33; vice chmn bldg code correlating com Am Standards Assn '33-44, chmn '44-49, chmn com on minimum design loads for bldgs and other structures since '38; cons NY State Bldg Code Commn since '49, mem joint com on unification of building codes. ASTM—Nat Fire Protection Assn—Fed Fire Council. Nat Bureau of Standards, Washington 25. H: 3717 "S" St., Washington 7.

15 THOMPSON, Harold William. American Folklore; Scottish literature; Ecclesiastical music. b'91. PhB '12 (Hamilton Coll); AM '13—PhD '15 (Harvard); DLitt '29 (Edinburgh U); LHD (hon) '40 (Union Coll); MusD (hon) '47 (Hamilton Coll). Research in Scottish literature '25-27. Author: Folklore: Body, Boots and Britches '40; Anecdotes and Egotisms of Henry Mackenzie '27; A Scottish Man of Feeling '31; also articles in field. Prof Eng Albany State Coll Teachers '15-40, dir dept music '20-24; prof Eng Cornell University since '40, Goldwin Smith professor English since '51. Royal Society Edinburgh (life F)—Society Antiquaries of Scotland (life F)—Am Folklore Society (pres '42)—N.Y. Folklore Soc (pres and founder '44, contbr ed quarterly since '45)—Pa Folklore Soc—Am Guild of Organists (contbr ed The Diapason since '18)—Mod Lang Assn Am—Soc Am Hist. 244 Goldwin Smith Hall, Ithaca, N.Y.◉

16 THOMPSON, Henry Dewey. Geomorphology; Geology of the Appalachians. b'98. BSc '22 (Bridgewater Va Coll); AM '27 (Columbia); PhD '35 (NYU). Author articles in field. With Hunter Coll since '28, now asso prof geol. NY Acad Sci (F, chmn sect geol mineral '48)—Am Geophys Union—AA AS(F)—Geol Soc Am(F). 695 Park Ave., NYC 21.†

17 THOMPSON, Homer Armstrong. Classical Greek archeology. b'06. BA '25—MA '27 (U Brit Columbia); PhD '29 (U Mich); LLD '49 (U British Columbia); fellow for excavation of Athenian Agora '29-45 (Am Sch Classical Studies at Athens). Field director Agora excavations since '45. Author articles in field. Prof classical archeol Inst Advanced Study Princeton since '47. Archeol Inst Am (vp '38-46)—Am Numismatic Soc—German Archeol Inst —Royal Soc Canada(F)—Brit Acad (corres F). School of Humanistic Studies, Institute for Advanced Study, Princeton, N.J.†◉

18 THOMPSON, J. Eric S. Mayan and Mexican archeology and ethnology; Maya hieroglyphic writing. b'98. Student (Winchester Coll, Cambridge U). Special study of affixes in glyph formation, and work on correlation of Maya calendar with Gregorian; number of glyphs deciphered; studies in Maya and Aztec religion; numerous archeological trips to Central America and Mexico. Author: Ethnology of the Mayas of British Honduras '30; Mexico Before Cortez '33; Excavations at San Jose, British Honduras '30; A Trial Survey of the Southern Maya Area '43; Maya Hieroglyphic Writing: Introduc- tion '51; also articles. Asst curator Central and South Am archeol Chicago Natural Hist Mus '26-35, research asso '42; mem staff dept archaeology Carnegie Inst Wash since '36; hon prof Museo Nac de Mexico '41. Soc Am Archeol—Sociedad Mexicana de Antropologia—Sociedad de Geografia e Historia de Guatemala—Royal Anthrop Inst. Awarded Rivers Memorial Medal for field work Maya area Royal Anthrop Inst '45. Carnegie Institution Washington, 10 Frisbie Pl., Cambridge 38.◉

19 THOMPSON, James Stratton. Radiological physics, b'99. ScB '22—PhD '30 (U Chicago); '30 (U Munich Germany). Prof physics Ill Inst Tech Chicago since '34, also chmn dept physics; physicist Simpson-Breed Radium Inst since '27. AAAS(F)—Am Phys Soc—Am Assn Physics Teachers—Am Soc Engring Edn—Swedish Engrs Soc —Sigma Xi. 3300 Federal St., Chgo.

20 THOMPSON, John Boyd. Trace metal and food chemistry. b'12. BS '35 (ND State Coll). Co-author articles in field. Pres and dir Trace Metal Research Lab Chicago a private cons lab engaged in consulting, research, service in the field of trace metal chem since '48. Qm US Army Food and Container Inst Chicago '43-48. Am Chem Soc—Inst Food Technol—Assn of Trace Analysts. 1665 E. 79th St., Chicago 49.

21 THOMPSON, John W(alter). Lichens. born '13. AB '35 (Columbia); MA '37—PhD '39 (U Wis). Identification of lichens, especially North American species; Arctic lichens. Author articles: The Wisconsin Species of Peltigera '47; Some Lichens from Central Pennsylvania '44; The Lichen Genus Cladonia in Wisconsin '42; Teloschistaceae of Wisconsin '48. Dir staff Sch Nature League Am Mus Natural Hist '39-41; instr biol State Teachers Coll Superior Wis '42-44; asso prof botany U Wis since '49. Torrey Bot Club—Am Bryological Soc—Wis Acad Sci Arts Letters—Am Soc Plant Taxonomists—Sigma Xi. Department of Botany, University of Wisconsin, Madison 6, Wis.

22 THOMPSON, Laura. Cultural anthropology; Applied anthropology. b'05. AB '27 (Mills Coll); PhD '33 (U Calif); '28 (Radcliffe Coll). Field research Fiji Islands '34-35, Guam '37-38, Hawaii '40-41, Papago, Hopi, Navajo, Zuni, Sioux Indians '42, Hopi Indians '43, '44; Iceland '52; cons US Naval Govt of Guam '38-39; consultant United States Office of Indian Affairs '42-44; co-ordinator Indian Personality and Administration Research '41-47. Author: Guam and Its People '47; Fijian Frontier '40. Co-author: (with Alice Joseph) The Hopi Way '44; also articles in field. Adviser to policy bd Nat Indian Inst '48; Viking Fund grant for research in community govt '48, in Old Saxon community Germany '50; Rockefeller grants for research in European core values '51, '52; Research fellow Inst World Affairs NY since '51. 26 East 93rd St., NYC 28.†

23 THOMPSON, Lawrence Sidney. Historical bibliography; European private presses; Kentucky literature. born '16. Fellow of the American Scandinavian Foundation '38-39 (U Uppsala, U Lund); AB '34—PhD '38 (U NC); AM '35 (U Chicago); '35-36 (Harvard); ABLS '40 (U Mich. Collects single leaves of incunabula; collects European private press books. Author: Notes on Bibliokleptomania '46; Bibliopegia Fantastica '48; A Cursory Survey of Maledictions '49; The Kentucky Novel '53; and others. Translator: A. Predeek, A History of Libraries in Great Britain and North America '47;

also articles in field. Asst to the librarian Ia State Coll '40-42; bibliog US Dept Agr Library '45-46; librarian Western Mich Coll '46-48; dir libraries U Ky since '48. ALA—Biblio Soc Am—Sallskapet Bokvannerna (Stockholm). University of Kentucky Library, Lexington, Ky. H: 225 Culpepper Dr.

10 THOMPSON, Lester S(eymour). Geological surveys; Mineral examinations. b'89. EM '11 (Columbia). Research and geological surveys for metallics, nonmetallics and petroleum in Portuguese West Africa, Spitsbergen, Brazil, Texas, Germany, and Near East; geological reconnaissance marine sediment area Africa south of 5 degrees north parallel, diamond deposits of Brazil, development of lead-zinc area of East Greenland. AIMME—Mining and Metall Soc Am—Explorers Club. Kalvebod Brygge 2, Copenhagen V, Denmark. H: 223 Forest Rd., Douglaston, L.I., N.Y.

11 THOMPSON, Lorin Andrew, Jr. Population trends. b'02. BA '23—MA '24—PhD '27 (O State U). Research on population trends in states and localities, economic and demographic changes and public policy in states and localities, income estimates for small areas; member Conference on Measurement of County Income. Prof psychol O Wesleyan U '27-34; dir research Regional Dept Econ Security '34-40; dir Va Population Study Va State Planning Bd '40-44; dir Bur Population and Econ Research U Va since '44. AAAS—Am Statis Assn—Population Assn Am—Am Psychol Assn(F indsl psychol)—S Sociol Soc—S Econ Assn—Va Soc Sci Assn (pres '50-51)—Asso Bur Bus and Econ Research (exec com). University of Virginia, Charlottesville.

12 THOMPSON, L(ouis) T(en) E(yck). Ballistic physics; Technical administration. b'91. BS '14 (Kalamazoo Coll); AM '15—PhD '17 (Clark U). Research penetration mechanics, reduced scale investigation of penetration of solids and dense fluids; erosion of guns; external and internal ballistics; weapons evaluation. Invented ballistic instrumentation, jet assisted ballistic instrumentation, jet assist mechanisms, fuel rate measuring devices. Author articles in field. Instr and asst prof phys Clark Coll '17-19, asst head Ballistics Inst '17-19; prof phys Kalamazoo Coll '20-24; physicist Naval Proving Ground Dahlgren Va '23-42; dir research and development Carl L Norden Inc and Lukas-Harold Corp '42-45; cons Manhattan Dist '44-45; tech dir Naval Ordnance Test Station Inyokern China Lake Calif since '45. AAAS (F)—Am Phys Soc(F)—Inst Math Statis. Nat Research Council fellow '20-23. Michelson Laboratory, NOTS, China Lake, Calif.

13 THOMPSON, Marcus Luther. Paleontology (Fossil fusulinids). b'06. BS '30 (Miss State Coll); MS '33—PhD '34 (State U Ia). Author articles in field. With U Wis since '46, now prof. Geol Soc Am(F)—Paleontol Soc(F)—Am Assn Petroleum Geol—Soc Econ Paleontol and Mineral—AAAS—Paleontol Soc Japan—Sigma Xi. Department of Geology, Science Hall, University of Wisconsin, Madison 6, Wis.

14 THOMPSON, Milton John. Aerodynamics of aircraft; Aeronautical and automotive engineering; Subsonic and supersonic wind tunnel. b'04. BSE '25—MSE '26 (U Mich); ScD '30—Guggenheim fellow aerodynamics '28-30 (Warsaw Poly Inst). Author articles in field. Prof and chmn dept aeronautical engring U Tex since '42; Defense Research Lab, asso dir and supervisor aerodynamics since '45; mem Bumblebee Aerodynamics Panel and Wind Tunnel

Subcom for Navy Bur of Ordnance; cons on aerodynamic problems and subsonic and supersonic wind tunnel research for aircraft, automotive and other industries since '30. Served as mem Aerodynamics and Ballistics Panel Guided Missles Com Joint Chiefs of Staff '45-46. Inst Aeronaut Sci (asso F)—ASME—SAE—Sigma Xi—Tau Beta Pi. Department of Aeronautical Engineering, University of Texas, Austin 12, Tex.†⊙

15 THOMPSON, Oliver Scott. Secondary education. b'77. AB '04—LHD '39 (Lake Forest U Ill); '04-05 (Clark U); '09-10 (U Wis); '36 (U So Cal); '38 (Pomona Coll Cal). Author: Primary Writing Book '14; Self-Instruction Practice Drills in English '15; Songs of a Schoolmaster: Book of Poems '32; The Teacher Centered School '43. Prin Pasadena Evening High Sch; principal Compton (Cal) Union High Sch; supt secondary schs and pres Jr Coll Compton Cal '16-51, pres emeritus since '51. So Cal Jr Coll Assn—NEA—Am Assn Sch Adminstrs—Cal Tchrs Assn. 14 E Cypress Av., Redlands, Cal.⊙

16 THOMPSON, Paul Woodard. Petroleum chemistry; Plant ecology; Flora of southeastern Michigan; Conservation. b'09. BS '30—MS '32 (U Ill); '32-35 (U Chicago). Research chem Ethyl Corp Detroit since '42. Mich Acad Sci Arts Letters—Mich Bot Club (pres, bd dirs, chmn exec com, com on wilderness tracts and trails)—Nature Conservancy (chmn com on policies and standards for perservation natural areas—AAAS—ACS—Detroit Audubon Soc(vp, bd dirs)—Mich Natural Areas Council (chmn reconnaisance com)—Wilderness Soc—Det Mus Soc—Cranbrook Inst Sci (research asso). Ethyl Corporation, 1600 W. Eight Mile Road, Detroit.

17 THOMPSON, Robert Luther. Telegraph industry; International conferences; Military history of World War II (Army Air Forces, Navy medical department). b'07. BA '28 (Butler U); MA '31—PhD '42 (Columbia); '34-35 (Deutsche Akademie Munich Germany); '35 (London Sch Econs and Polit Sci). Author: Wiring a Continent: The History of the Telegraph Industry in the United States 1832-1866 '47. Chief division of publications. Dept of State. Lt USNR, asst chief Adminstr Hist Sect Adminstrn Div Bur of Med and Surgery '44-46. AHA—Miss Valley Hist Assn—Econ History Assn. Division of Publications, Department of State, Washington.†

18 THOMPSON, Ross C(alvin). Lettuce; Vegetable production; Vegetable breeding (High altitudes); Azalea breeding and growing; Hemerocallis breeding and growing. born '96. BS '23—MS '24 (Colo A&M Coll); PhD '36 (U Md). Author articles in field. With Bur Plant Ind US Dept Agrl since '28, now sr hort. Am Genetics Soc—Am Soc Hort Sci—Am Soc Plant Physiol—Bot Soc Wash—Sigma Xi. Plant Industry Station, U.S. Department Agriculture, Beltsville, Md.

19 THOMPSON, Rufus Henney. Phycology; Hepaticae. b'08. AB '36—MA '37 (U Kan); PhD '41 (Stanford U). Research in classes Dinophyceae, Chrysophyceae and Xanthophyceae. Author articles: A Preliminary Survey of the Fresh-water Algae of Eastern Kansas '38; Coronastrum: A New Genus of Algae in the Family Scenedesmaceae '38; A Second Species of Riella in North America '40; The Morphology of Riella affinis I, Germination of the Spore and Development of the Thallus '41, II Development of the Sex Organs, Fertilization, and Development of the Sporophyte '42; A Natural Hybrid Be-

tween Polystichum Acrosticholdes and P Braunii '41; The Fresh-water Dinoflagellates of Maryland '48. Instr Marine Biol Lab Woods Hole Mass summer '40; instr dept bot U Kan '41-42; research biol Chesapeake Biol Lab Solomons Md summer '42; hydrog investigator Dept Research and Edn of Md '46-47; asst prof dept bot U Kan since '47. Served as epidemiologist USNR '43-45. Bot Soc Am—Phycological Soc Am—Sullivant Moss Soc—Sigma Xi. Department of Botany, University of Kansas, Lawrence, Kan.†

20 THOMPSON, Stanley Gerald. Nuclear chemistry; Heavy and transuranium isotopes; Atomic energy; Plutonium extraction. b'12. AB '34 (U Calif, Los Angeles); PhD '48 (U Calif, Berkeley). Research nuclear and chemical properties of transuranium isotopes, particularly americium and curium, plutonium extraction, chemical properties of americium and curium, consultant atomic energy. With Glenn Seaborg discovered and developed chemical process for extracting plutonium used at Hanford Washington; co- discoverer new elements no 97 (berkelium) and no 98 (californium); now engaged search for transcalifornium elements. With Radiation Lab U Calif since '48. Radiation Laboratory, University of California, Berkeley.†

21 THOMPSON, Stith. Folklore and folktales (American Indian, comparative motifs). born '85. BA '09 (U Wis); MA '12 (U Calif); PhD '14 (Harvard); Litt D '46 (U NC). Official in various international folklore meetings; US delegate to Internat Folklore Congress Paris '37. Author: European Tales Among the North American Indians '19; The Types of the Folk-Tale '28; British Poets of the Nineteenth Century (with Curtis H Page) '29; Our Heritage of World Literature '38; Motif-Index of Folk-Literature, six vols '32-37; The Folktale '46, and others; also articles in field. Prof Eng, folklore Ind U since '39, dean grad sch '47-50. Am Folk-lore Soc—Modern Lang Assn Am—Am Philos Soc. 707 Ballantine Rd., Bloomington, Ind.⊙

22 THOMPSON, Susanne. Nutrition; Family life. BS '13 (U Neb); MS '24 (U Chicago); PhD '40 (Cornell). Home demonstration agt Colo State Coll '18-23; nutrition specialist Mont State Coll '24-27; prof nutrition and family life La State U since '28. La Acad Sci—Am Acad Sci—Am Home Econ Assn—La State Home Econ Assn—La State Tchrs Assn—AAUP—Pi Lambda Theta—Phi Kappa Phi. Louisiana State University, Baton Rouge.

23 THOMPSON, Thomas Eugene. Vitreous enamels; Glass rods. b'85. BS '10 (N Ill). Specializes in manufacture special porcelain or vitreous enamels used for making dials for watches, meters, telephones, name-plates for automobiles, stoves, and jewelry, arts, crafts; glass rods used for making imitation pearl beads, colored glass rods for making colored glass beads, small lenses. With Thomas C Thompson Co for 35 yrs, owner for 27 yrs. Am Ceramic Soc. 1205 Deerfield Rd., Highland Park, Ill.

24 THOMPSON, Thomas F(rancis). Engineering and economic geology; Geology of the Panama Canal Zone and Central America. b'06. AB '31 (Stanford); '25 (U Ore, Kern C Jr Coll Calif). Since '43 has travelled extensively in Central American Countries on geological investigations. Author articles in field. Chief geol Panama Canal since '41; cons geol water supply and found problems for US Army and Navy, Republic of Panama and Republic of Salvador, various Central

Am and US engring firms since '42. Geol Soc Am(F)—ASCE—AAAS—Am Geophys Union—Seismol Soc Am—Soc Am Mil Engrs—Geol Mining Soc—Am Assn Pet Geol. Special Engineering Division, The Panama Canal, Box 1005, Diablo Heights, Canal Zone.

10 THOMPSON, Thomas Gordon. Oceanography; Chemistry of the oceans. b'88. BA '14 (Clark U); MS '15—PhD '18 (U Washington). Author articles in field. Prof chem U Washington '29-51, dir oceanog labs '30-51, prof oceanog since '51. Nat Acad Sci—Am Chem Soc—AAAS—American Geophys Union—Oceanog Soc—Am Geog Soc—Sigma Xi. Awarded Agassiz Medal, Nat Acad Sci '48. Dept of Oceanography, University of Washington, Seattle; also McConnell Island, Deer Harbor, Washington.

11 THOMPSON, Warren Charles. Waves (Ocean forecasting); Continental shelf (Submarine geology). b'22. BA in geol '43—certificate in meteorol '44 (U Cal Los Angeles); MS in oceanography '48 (Scripps Instn Oceanog). Research on structure and origin Continental Shelf and nature Shelf sediments; forecasting ocean waves on assault beaches for Navy and along Pacific coast, sea and swell forecasting for offshore oil drilling. Asso petroleum engr Humble Oil & Refining Co '47; field dir and chief geol sect Tex A&M Research Found '50-51, research project supervisor since '51. Am Assn Petroleum Geol—Am Geophys Union—Am Meteorol Soc—Geol Soc Am—Soc Econ Paleontologists and Mineral—Sigma Xi. Research F submarine geol Scripps Instn Oceanog '48-49. Department of Oceanography, Texas A& M College, College Station.

12 THOMPSON, Warren Osborne. Sedimentation; Oil geology. b'98. AB '22 (U Colo); PhD '35 (Stanford U); '24-25 (Washington U). Research on original structure of beaches bars and dunes '37, Lyons sandstone '49, post Mississippian stratigraphy. Instr geol Wash U '22-23, '24-25; geol Midwest Refining Co '23-24, Midwest Exploration Co '25-26; instr geol U Colo '26-28, asst prof '28-35, prof since '41, head dept since '49. Am Assn Pet Geol—Geol Soc Am(F)—Sigma Xi. Dept. of Geology, University of Colorado, Boulder, Colo.

13 THOMPSON, William Louden. Economic entomology of citrus fruits. b'96. BS '23 (Pa State Coll). Research on control of insects and mites infesting citrus, determining specific injury caused by scale insects, mites and other insects to trees and fruit, relationship of nutrition for trees to insect populations and relationship of timing sprays to fruit quality and grade. Author articles in field. Entomol Fla Citrus Expt Sta since '27. Am Assn Econ Entomol—Am Entomol Soc—Fla Entomol Soc—Fla Hort Soc. Citrus Experiment Station, Lake Alfred, Fla.

14 THOMPSON, William Rae. Statistical methodology; Volumetric calibration apparatus. b'96. AB '23 (Columbia); PhD '30 (Yale). Author articles in field. Inventor calibration apparatus. Sr biochem Div Labs and Research NY State Dept Health since '36. Inst Math Statis(F)—Am Math Soc—AAAS—Soc Biol Chem—Am Statis Assn—Biometric Soc—Sigma Xi. Division of Laboratories and Research, New York State Department of Health, Albany, N.Y.

15 THOMSEN, Louis Charles. Dairy plant management and engineering; Butter. b'95. BSc '25 (U Wis). Author articles in field. With U Wis since '20, now prof dept dairy ind. Am Dairy Sci Assn—Internat Assn Milk and Food Sanitarians. Department of Dairy Industry, University of Wisconsin, Madison 6, Wis.

16 THOMSON, Malcolm. Welding. b '91. AB '13 (Harvard U); '13-14 (MIT). With General Electric Co since '19, now consulting welding engineer. SAE—Am Inst EE—AWS—Mass Soc Profl Engrs. General Electric Co., 920 Western Av., West Lynn 3, Mass.

17 THOMSON, Samuel Harrison. Medieval history; Latin paleography. b'95. BA '23 (Princeton U); Dr Phil '25 (Charles U Prague Czechoslovakia); BLitt '26—DLitt '42 (Oxford U). Author: M. Joh. Hus Tractatus Responsivus '27; M. Joh. Wyclif Summa de Ente '30; Writings of Robert Grosseteste '40; Czechoslovakia in European History '43; Czechoslovakia Twenty Years (with R J Kerner et al) '40; Contemporary Europe (with J S Roucek et al), 2d edit '41; Poland (with B E Schmitt et al) '45; Edward Benes (with others); Handbook of Slavic Studies (with others) '49. Editor: Progress of Medieval and Renaissance Studies in United States and Canada since '36. Founder and editor: Jour of Central European Affairs since '41, Medievalia et Humanistica since '43. Mem editorial bd Am Slavic and East European Rev since '41. Asst prof modern history U Chicago '34-35; asso prof European history and dir admissions Carleton Coll '35-36; prof history U Colo since '36. Polish Acad Sciences(F)—Polish Inst Arts and Sci—Mediaeval Acad Am—History of Sci Soc—Am Council of Learned Societies—Social Sci Research Council—AAUP—Am Hist Assn—Soc Mediaeval Langs and Lit (Oxford)—Am Soc Internat Law—Am Soc Church History—Phi Beta Kappa. Received Czechoslovakia state prize for lit '44. 3939 Broadway, Boulder, Colo.†☉

18 THOMSON, Willard Owen. Human sterility; Pituitary and thyroid glands (Pathology); Goiter (Iodine therapy); Geriatrics (Endocrinology); Sex hormones. b'99. BA '19 (Kalhousie U Halifax Can); MD '23 (Harvard). Managing editor Journal of Clinical Endocrinology since '46; associate ed Geriatrics since '46; editorial positions other publications. Research fellow in med Harvard Med Sch '25-28, Henry P Walcott fellow '28-29; fellow Nat Research Council '26-28; asst clin prof med Rush Med Coll U Chicago '29-35, asso clin prof med '35-41; asso prof med U Ill Coll Med '41-43, prof med '43-45, clin prof med since '45; staff various hosps Chgo since '30. Diplomate Nat Board Med Examiners '25, Am Bd Internat Med '37. Assn Am Physicians—Am Soc Clin Investigation—Central Soc Clin Research—ACP(F)—AMA(v chmn sect on med '44-45)—Assn Study Internal Secretions(vp '44-45)—Soc for Exptl Biol and Med—Am Assn Study Goiter(vp '45-46)—AAAS—Gerontological Soc Inc—Sigma Xi—Pi Kappa Epsilon—Ill State Acad Sci—Am Soc Study Sterility and others. 700 N. Michigan Av., Chicago 11.

19 THOMSSEN, Edgar George. Soaps; Fats; Oils; Waxes; Cosmetics; Disinfectants. b'86. BS '07—AM '08—PhD '11 (Columbia). Author: Soap Making Manual '21; Modern Soap Making '37; Modern Cosmetics '47; Soaps and Detergents '48; also articles in field. Chief chem J R Watkins Co '23-44; cons chem since '44. Am Chem Soc—AAAS(F)—Soc Testing Materials (com soap standards '35-43)—Am Inst Chem(F)—Sigma Xi—Phi Lambda Upsilon—Chem Spec Mfrs Association (research com '36-41)—Toilet Goods Assn (research com '28-32)—Sanitary Supply Mfrs Assn. 306 Center St., Winona, Minn.

20 THORINGTON, J(ames) Monroe. Mountain exploration; Alpine history. b'94. BS '15 (Princeton U); AM '18—MD '19 (U Pa). Explorer of watershed of Canadian Rocky Mountains between Canadian Pacific and Canadian National Railways since '22; explored and mapped watershed of Purcell Range British Columbia '28-33, including glacial source of Columbia River. Author: The Glittering Mountains of Canada '25; Mont Blanc Sideshow '34; Where the Clouds Can Go '35; A Climber's Guide to the Rocky Mountains of Canada (with Howard Palmer) '53. Editor American Alpine Journal '33-46. Associate Ophthalmologist Presbyterian Hosp Phila since '30. Royal Geog Soc(F)—Am Alpine Club (pres '41-43, coms for expdns Mt Logan Alaska '25, K2, Himalayas '38)—Alpine Clubs of Can, London, Switzerland and France—Sigma Xi—Alpha Omega Alpha. 2031 Chestnut St., Phila. 3.*

21 THORMODSGARD, Olaf H. North Dakota (Property law). b'91. AB '13 (Spokane Coll); MA '16 (St Olaf Coll); JD '23 (Univ Chicago); '25-26 (Harvard Law Sch). Commissioner on Uniform State Laws for North Dakota. Editor: Dakota Law Review. Prof econs St Olaf Coll '19-25; asso prof law U ND '26-29, prof law '29-33, dean and prof law since '33. Judicial Council ND—ND Bar Assn—Am Bar Assn. Fellow Carnegie Endowment for Internat Peace '25-26. 417 Princeton St., Grand Forks, N.D.☉

22 THORNBERRY, Halbert Houston. Plant pathology; Phytovirology. b'02. BS '25—MS '26 (Ky U); '26-28—PhD '34 (Minn U); '28-31 (Ill U); '31 (Columbia). Studied vegetable diseases, peach mosaic virus, and bacterial diseases, filtration of viruses, antibiotics (streptomycin); extensive research on effect of phosphate buffers and tannic acid on tobacco-mosaic virus infectivity, effect of dyes on plant pathogenic microorganism, crystallization and purification of various virus proteins, identification and methods of control of vegetable diseases, streptomycin production from animal and plant products. Author articles in field. Plant path Rockefeller Inst Med Research '31-34, Calif U '35, Ky U '36, US Dept Agr '37, Ill U since '38. AAAS—Am Chem Soc—Am Phytopath Soc—Soc Am Bacteriologists—Sigma Xi. Division Plant Pathology, University of Illinois, Urbana, Ill.

23 THORNBURG, Max Weston. Foreign industrial affairs (Middle East); Industrial economics (Petroleum). b'92. AB '17—BS '21—CE '33 (U Calif). Research director Twentieth Fund Economic Survey of Turkey '47; spl asst to under-sec and petroleum adviser Dept of State '41-43; cons to govt of Iran since '48. Author: Economic Survey of Turkey '48; The Design of a Petroleum Law; also articles in field. Chmn Foreign Petroleum Policy Com. Council Fgn Relations—Royal Asiatic Soc—East India Assn—Am Assn Polit Sci—Am Geol Soc—Am Soc Civil Engr—Tau Beta Pi—Sigma Xi. Umm A'Sabaan Island Bahrain, Persian Gulf.

24 THORNE, David Wynne. Irrigated soils (Fertility, management); Irrigation practice; Saline and alkali soils. b'08. Student '26-28 (Weber Coll); BS '33 (Utah State Agr Coll); MS '34—PhD '36 (Ia State Coll). Co-author: Irrigated Soils, Their Fertility and Management; also articles in field. Prof agron and head dept Utah State Agr Coll since '46; chmn Western Soil Research Com '47-49. Am Soc Agronomy—Soil Sci Am—W Soc Soil Sci—AAAS—Phi Kappa Phi—Sigma Xi—Gamma Sigma Delta. Department of Agronomy, Utah State Agricultural College, Logan, Utah.†☉

10 THORNE, Oakleigh II. Conservation; Ecology; Nature photography; Bird banding. b'28. BS in biol '51 (Yale). Developed electric feeder-trap for use by bird banders; relation or problems of conservation to ecology. Am Ornithol Union—Wilson Ornithol Club—Cooper Ornithol Club—E and W Bird Banding Assn—Nat Audubon Soc—NY Zool Soc—Linnaean Soc NY—Ecol Soc Am—Wildlife Society—Izaak Walton League Am—Hawk Mt Sanctuary Assn—Ducks Unlimited—American Forestry Assn. Yale Conservation Program, New Haven.

11 THORNER, Daniel. British Empire History and economics (India); India; Pakistan; Economics of underdeveloped areas, particularly So Asia; Railways of India and Pakistan; Trade Route of India, Pakistan and Central Asia. b'15. BS '36 (CC NY); U fellow '38-39—Lydig fellow '39-40—PhD '49 (Columbia); fellow '47-48 (Johns Hopkins). Author: India and Pakistan, section in Ralph Linton's Most of the World '49; Investment in Empire '49; also articles in field. Research asst prof econ hist in department of Economics and South Asia Regional Studies Program U Pa since '48. South Asia Regional Studies Program, University of Pennsylvania, Phila. 4.†

12 THORNTHWAITE, Charles Warren. Climatology; Physical geography. b'99. AB '22 (Central Mich Teachers Coll); PhD '27 (Calif U); student '23-24 (Mich U). Consultant Comision Nacional de Irrigacion, Mexico '43-47; consultant to Ontario Research Foundation. Invented dew-point recorder. Author articles in field. Chief Climatic Div US Soil Conservation Service '35-46; cons climatol since '46; prof climatol Johns Hopkins since '47, dir Lab Climatology since '48. Assn Am Geog—Am Meteorol Soc—Ecol Soc Am—Am Geophys Union. Johns Hopkins University Laboratory of Climatology, Seabrook, N.J.☉

13 THORNTON, Charles Stead. Embryology; Regeneration (Biological). b'10. AB '32 (Harvard); MA '36—PhD '37 (Princeton). Research on growth and differentiation of tissues. Author: The Histogenesis of Muscle in the Regenerating Fore Limb of Larval Amblystoma '38; The Effect of Colchicine on Limb Regeneration in Larval Amblystoma '43. Asst and fellow in biol Princeton '33-36; asst prof and asso prof biol '36-48 Kenyon Coll, chmn biol dept since '37, research in vertebrate tissue regeneration. Am Soc Zool—O Acad Sci—Sigma Xi. Kenyon College, Gambier, O.

14 THORNTON, Kirby F(airfield). Aluminum (Aircraft structure). b'08. BS in mech engring '30 (U Mo). Research engineering problems new alloys and products, including stepped extrusions, tapered sheet, integrally stiffened extrusions, new processes such as artificial aging. Aluminum fabrication engr Aluminum Company Am since '30, liaison engr with airframe industry since '40. Inst Aeronautical Scis. Aluminum Co of Am, New Kensington, Pa.

15 THORNTON, Marmaduke Knox. Cottonseed and it's products. b'92. BS '09 (Miss State Coll); AM '14 (Columbia). Author: Cottonseed Products '33. Agrl chem ext service A&M Coll of Tex since '35. Extension Service, A and M College of Texas, College Station.

16 THORNTON, William. Shakespearean roles. b'09. Student '25-27 (Stanford); '26 (U Cal Los Angeles). Actor in The Light of Asia, Caponsacchi, An Enemy of the People, Cyrano de Bergerac '28, Shakespearean Repertory '31; seasons in Shaw, Shakespeare, Wilde, modern plays. Produced and acted Hamlet in modern clothes '27. Actor Pasadena Playhouse '27-28; Walter Hampden Co '28-29; actor-mgr Shakespeare Guild Festival Co '30-36; dir prodn and lectr on Shakespeare Stanford '35; actor NY Players Theatre, Mohawk Drama Festival, Experimental Theatre '37-47; radio and television programs NY since '40; gen dir Shakespeare Guild Festival Co summer season Ridgewood NJ '51. Actors Equity Assn—Am Fedn Radio Artists. 315 E. 57th St., NYC 22. H: 105 N. Van Dien Av., Ridgewood, N.J.

17 THORP, Clark E(lwin). Ozone technology. b'14. BSc '35 (Fenn Coll); MS '36 (Western Reserve U); '42 (U Chicago); '40 (Ill Inst Tech). Theoretical and practical engineering involving production of liquid and gaseous ozone. Author articles: Starch-Iodide Method of Ozone Analysis '40; Influence of Nitrogen Oxides on the Toxicity of Ozone '41; Influence of Ozone on Diesel Engine Performance '44; The Influence of Temperature on Ozonizer Efficiency '46; Influence of Water Vapor on Ozonizer Efficiency '46; Ruppia Balls '49; Toxicity of Ozone '50. Dir Research Ozo-Ray Process Corp Chicago '37-41; mgr dept chem and chem engring Armour Research Foundation. American Institute Chem Engr Am Chem Soc—Electrochem Soc—Ill Soc Engr—Am Rocket Soc—Am Inst Chemists. Armour Research Foundation, 35 W. 33rd St., Chgo. 16.†

18 THORP, James. Soil science. b'96. BS '21 (Earlham Coll). Delegate commonwealth Conference on Tropical Soils, Rothamstead England '48. Author: Geography of the Soils of China '36; also articles in field. Prin soil scientist Us Dept Agr Div Soil Survey Lincoln Neb since '42; prof soil research conservation and survey div U Neb since '42. With mil geol unit US Geol Survey '44-45. Soil Sci Soc Am—Am Soc Agron—Internat Soc Soil Sci—Geol Soc China—Am Geog Soc—AAAS—Assn Am Geog—Geol Soc Philippines—Neb Acad Sci. 204 Nebraska Hall, University of Nebraska, Lincoln, Neb.☉

19 THORPE, Merle. American business and government; Advertising. b'79. AB '05 (Stanford U); AB '08 (U Washington). Author: The Coming Newspaper '15; How's Business '31; Organized Business Leadership '31; We Hire a Cook and a Congressman '40. Co-author: (with James M Beck) Neither Purse Nor Sword '36; also articles in field. Prof· journalism U Washington '07-11; prof journalism U Kan '11-16; editor and pub The Nation's Business Washington '16-44; dir bus development Cities Service Co since '44; asst dir President's Unemployment Relief Orgn. Mo Valley Cost Congress (sec '14-16)—Nat Journalism Congress (dir '14). Awarded Harvard-Bok prize for writing best individual advertisement in '25. 703 Ring Building, Washington.

20 THRALLS, Hugh Miller. Petroleum seismology. b'08. BS '32—MS '35 (U Okla). Development seismic approach to delineation stratigraphic type trap accumulation of oil and gas. With Seismograph Service Corp since '36, vp in charge US operations since '49. Am Assn Petroleum Geols—Soc Exploration Geophys—Am Geophys Un—Geophys Soc Tulsa—Geol Soc Tulsa—Sigma Xi. Box 1590, Tulsa.

21 THROCKMORTON, John Wickliffe. Furnaces (Tubular); Boilers; Petroleum ref. b'99. Ed pub schs. Research and design tubular furnaces, boilers and air heaters for high temperature service and heaters for petroleum cracking, design and operation petroleum refining equipment. Granted patents in field. Engr M W Kellogg Co '23-32; mgr engring Alco Products Co '32-38; vp Petro-Chem Development Co since '38. ASME—ACS. 120 E. 41st St., NYC 17.

22 THRODAHL, Monte Corden. Rubber (Degradation, vulcanization, measurement of physical properties). b'19. BS '41 (Ia State). Research and development chemicals for plasticizing vulcanizing and preserving natural and synthetic rubber, new test methods and interpretation of data. Holds patents on rubber chemicals and testing. Articles in field. Analytical chem rubber chem Monsanto Chem Co '41-42, research chem charge rubber lab '42-50, asst dir '50-52, mgr rubber chem development since '52. Am Chem Soc—Am Inst Phys—Soc Rheology—Am Inst Chem Engrs—AAAS—Inst Math Statistics. Monsanto Chemical Co Organic Chemicals Division, Nitro, W.Va.

23 THROOP, Palmer Allan. Social psychology (Italian Renaissance, Crusade propaganda). b'01. AB '23—AM '26 (U Tex); PhD '34—Shreve fellow '36-37 (Princeton U); (Sorbonne Paris, U Chicago). Author: Criticism of the Crusade: A Study of Public Opinion and Crusade Propaganda '40; also articles in field. Asso prof U Mich since '43. AHA—Medieval Acad Am. University of Michigan, Ann Arbor.

24 THUESEN, H. G. Industrial engineering (Motion and time study, parking meters). b'98. BS '21—MS '30 (Ia State Coll). Pioneered development job design for petroleum production operations since '39. Development work and holder patents on first parking meters '31-36. Head dept indsl engring Okla A and M Coll since '25. Am Soc Engr—Am Soc Elec Engr—Nat Soc Professional Engr—Soc Advancement Management. Awarded Acad of Time Awards '46-47, '47-48. Oklahoma A. and M. College, Stillwater, Okla.†

25 THURSTON, William R(oberts). Geology of fluorspar and pegmatites. b'15. AB '38 (Columbia Coll); AM '43—PhD '52 (Columbia U). Research on pegmatites since '47; fluorspar investigations '42-46. Author: Geology of the Manganese Deposit at Clinton Pt., New Jersey '49; Fluorspar Deposits of Utah '49; Preliminary Report on the Baxter Fluorspar Deposit, Near Broken Hills, Nevada '46; Preliminary Report on the Daisy Fluorspar Deposit, near Beatty, Nevada '49, Geol US Geol Survey since '42; Geol Cuban-Am Manganese Corp Cuba '38-39. Geol Soc Am—Mineral Soc Am—Colo Sci Soc—Sigma Xi. Nicaro Nickel Co., Santiago de Cuba.†

26 TIDWELL, James Nathan. American dialects; Vocabulary (American). b'11. BA '29 (Simmons U); MA '33 (U Okla); PhD '47 (O State U). Author articles: Mark Twain's Representation of Negro Speech '42; A Word List from West Texas '49; Wellerisms in Alexander's Weekly Messenger 1837-1839 '50, and others. Co-author article: Words and Phrases in American Politics '50. Instr O State U '46-47; prof English San Diego State Coll since '47; asst ed Dictionary of Political Words and Phrases since '47. Modern Lang Assn Am—Philol Assn Pacific Coast—Am Dialect Soc—Linguistic Soc Am—Cal Folklore Soc. Am Council of Learned Soc f to Linguistic Inst '40.

San Diego State College, San Diego, Cal.

10 TIEDEMAN, David Valentine. Educational statistics. b'19. AB '41 (Union Coll); AM '43 (U Rochester); Ed M '48—Ed D '49 (Harvard). Study problem measurement of teaching competence; study use of multivariate analysis in selection, classification, and guidance of personnel; study scale analysis problem; member committee on selection and training aircraft pilots National Research Council '42-43. Author articles: A Study of the Validity of the George Washington Test of Social Intelligence and the Construction of a New Test of Social Intelligence '43; The Utility of the Discriminant Function in Psychological and Guidance Investigations '51. Co-author article: (with Simeon J Domas) Teacher Competence—An Annotated Bibliography '51. Test construction department Coll Entrance Examination Bd Princeton NJ '43-44; asso dir statis div U Rochester '44-46; teaching fellow ednl measurement Harvard '46-48, Sheldon Travelling F '48-49, now instr guidance. Am Psychol Assn—Am Statis Assn—Biometrics Soc—Inst Math Statistics—Nat Vocational Guidance Assn—Psychometric Soc—Phi Beta Kappa—Phi Delta Kappa—Sigma Xi. 40 Quincy St., Cambridge 38, Mass.

11 TIEDEMAN, Walter von Dohlen. Milk and food sanitation. b'91. BE—MCE '13-14 (Union Coll). Author: Chapter in Nelson's Administrative Medicine '49; chapters in Phelp's Public Health Engineering '49; also articles in field. Asst sanitarian oyster sanitation to chief milk sanitarian charge Milk and Restaurant Sanitation Sect NY State Dept Health '25-50; part time cons sanitation USPHS since '42; resident in milk and food sanitation U Mich dir testing lab Nat San Found since '50. Am Pub Health Assn—Internat Assn Milk and Food Sanitarians—NY State Assn Milk Sanitarians—Am Dairy Sci Assn—Inst Food Tech—AAAS—Sigma Xi. School of Public Health, University of Michigan, Ann Arbor.

11 TIEDJENS, Victor A(lphons). Food crop nutrition; Soilless culture of plants. b'95. BS '21—MS '22 (U Wis); '24-28 (Harvard); PhD '32—research fellow '29-32 (Rutgers U). Author: The Vegetable Encyclopedia and Gardener's Guide '43. Co-author: Chemical Garden for the Amateur '39; A Practical Guide to Successful Farming '43; also articles in field. Inventor soilless window box '40. Dir Va Truck Expt Sta Norfolk Va '45-51; dir research and chief chemist Na Cheers Plant Food Co and Berlow Mfg Co since '51. AAAS (vp '51-52)—Va Acad Sci—AAHS—Sigma Xi— Phi Kappa Phi. 429 Monroe St., Marion, O.

13 TIERNEY, Hubert James. Chemistry (Rubber, resin); Pressure sensitive adhesive tapes. b'07. BS '30 (U Minn). Two US and one British patent. Chief chem Tape Research Lab Minn Mining and Mfg Co '34-40, dir research tape div '40-43, products mgr '43-47, mfg mgr '47-52, vp tape mfg and research since '52. American Chem Soc—Minn Indsl Chem Forum—Tau Beta Pi. Minnesota Mining and Manufacturing Co., 900 Fauquier Av., St. Paul 6.

14 TIFFANY, (Lewis) Hanford. Botany (Algae, phycology, ecology, taxonomy, Oedogoniaceae). b'94. BS '20 (U Chicago); MS '21—PhD '23 (O State U). Author: The Oedogoniaceae '30; Work Book in General Botany (with E N Transeau and H C Sampson) '34; Algae, the Grass of Many Waters '38; Text Book of Botany (with E N Tran-

seau and H C Sampson) '40; The Study of Plants '44; The Algae of Illinois (with M E Britton) '52, also articles. Prof bot and chmn dept Northwestern U '37-49; William Deering prof botany since '45; hon asso in cryptogamic botany Chicago Natural History Mus since '44; Ill Board Natural Resources and Conservation since '46 (sec, v chmn since '47). AAAS(F)—Am Soc Naturalists—Bot Soc Am—Ecol Soc Am—Am Micros Soc (pres '34)—Limnol Soc Am (pres '39)—Am Soc Plant Physiol—Am Soc Taxonomy Phycol Soc Am (pres '49)—Sigma Xi. Northwestern University, Evanston, Ill.ⓒ

15 TIFFANY, Harold Edward. Legal chemistry of foods, drugs and stains; Toxicity of medicinal oils. b'81. BS '05 (Bucknell); MS '07 (Harvard); PhD '20 (Columbia). With dept chem, geol and mineral U Del '06-23; research chemist du Pont Co '17-18; organizer dir pres Wilmington Testing & Research Labs Inc since '23; chem, toxicologist Atty Gen's Office and Internal Revenue Chem since '23. ACS—ASTM—Am Assn Pulp & Paper Industry. 808 Jefferson St., Wilmington, Del.

16 TIFFANY, Joseph Edgar. Explosives. b'79. BSc '99 (Sch Mines U Leeds Camborne Eng). Tests to determine permissibility of explosives and liquid carbon dioxide blasting devices for use in coal mines, in metal mines, tunnels, and other engineering operations; determination efficiency oil well explosives; demonstration efficient methods for shooting coal in mines; devised new test for determination efficiency blasting caps; consultant on explosives to government departments; improvement demolition explosives and devices World War I and II. Author: Safety and Economy in Handling Explosives; Lump Coal and How to Get It; Explosives and Incendiary Bombs, and others. Contributor: Reinhold's Chemical Dictionary; Mark's Handbook. Civil and mining engr coal mining companies Pa, Va, and WVa '00-12; with US Bur Mines '12-51, explosives engr '50-51. H: 5703 Northumberland St., Pitts 17.

17 TIFFORD, Arthur Norman. Heat transfer; Power plants (Airplane); Aircraft heat exchangers. b'17. B Elec Engring (Cum laude) '38 (Coll City NY); '38-39 (MIT). Research in internally-finned honeycomb radiators; correlation experimental friction and heat-trans data for tube banks; analogy between momentum loss and heat transfer; analogy between axial momentum loss and loss of spin; effect of pressure gradients on heat transfer and temperature recovery factors; propulsive efficiency of modern aircraft power plants; method of solution of boundary value problems. Asst EE Langley Memorial Lab '39-42; engr various aircraft mfg cos '42-45; sect engr in charge application and heat exchange Aviation Gas Turbine Div Westinghouse Electric Corp '45-48; associate prof Aeronautical engring Ohio State U since '48. Inst Aeronautical Scis(asso F)—APS—Am Soc Engring Edn—AAUP. Department of Aeronautical Engineering, Engineering Annex B, Ohio State University, Columbus.

18 TIGELAAR, Jacob H. Gluing (Metal to wood, plywood). b'09. AB '30 (Hope Coll); MS '32 (Purdue U). Author articles in field. Holder US patent on resinous adhesive and process of making same. Research chemist Haskelite Mfg Corp '32-38, dir research since '39. Am Chem Soc—Forest Products Research Soc—Am Soc Testing Materials (coms C-19 and D-14)—Sigma Xi. Haskelite Manufacturing Corporation, Grand Rapids 2, Mich.

19 TIHANY, Leslie Charles. Finland; Finno-Ugrian philology; History of Hungary and Eastern Europe. b'11. BS '31 (Franklin and Marshall Coll); MA '33—PhD '36 (Northwestern U); AM '38—Frederic Sheldon Prize Fellow '38-40—Research Fellow '42-43 (Harvard); PhD '43 (U Chicago). Author articles in field. Research Attache US Legation at Helsinki '48; fgn affairs officer Department State since '48. AHA—Societe Finno-Ougrienne, Helsinki. Am Council of Learned Soc Research Fellow '38-40 and '42-43. Department of State, Washington 25.

20 TILDEN, Josephine Elizabeth. Algae (Bibliography, classification, uses). BS '95—MS '96 (U Minn). Extensive studies and collections of algae in North American and foreign areas; made trip around world collecting algae in Australia and New Zealand '34-35. Author: Our Richest Source of Vitamins '28; The Algae and Their Life Relations '35-37. Editor: American Algae since '94; South Pacific Algae since '09; South Pacific Plants since '12; Bibliography of Pacific Ocean Algae '20. Prof bot U Minn to '38. AAAS(F)—Am Geog Soc(F)—Bot Soc Am—Am Soc Naturalists—Am Micros Soc—Nat Geog Soc—Fla Acad Sci—Sigma. Wistaria Place, Golden Bough Colony, Hesperides, Lake Wales, Florida.†ⓒ

21 TILFORD, Paul E(dward). Arboriculture. b'00. BS '23 (Mich State Coll); MS '26 (O State U); PhD '35 (U Wis). Study on diseases and care of ornamental plants and shade trees. Author articles in field. Exec sec Nat Arborist Assn Wooster O since '47. Am Phytopath Soc. 2313 Graustark Path, Wooster, O.

22 TILLEY, Charles Johnson. History of religion in the United States. b'08. AB '34 (Duke U); AM '39 (U So Calif); '45-47 (Stanford U). Author article: Peter Cartwright and Frontier Methodism in the Northwest '44, and others. Head dept hist and polit sci Whitworth Coll Spokane Wash '43-45; pastor United Methodist Ch Ocracoke Island NC '48-51, Broadway charge since '52. AHA—AAUP. Broadway, N.C.

23 TILLEY, Elizabeth Cornwall (Mrs. Thomas C. Tilley). Astrophysics. born 1914. BA '35 (Vassar College); MA '39 (Wellesley College); PhD '43 (Mich U); '35-36 (Yale); '39-40 (Harvard Observatory, Radcliffe Coll). Research on periods of cluster variables and observations of solar eruptions, orbit of spectroscopic triple star, rocket development; studies on spectrographic study of triple system in 59d Serpentis. Author articles in field. Mem research staff, OSRD project, Calif Inst Tech '43-44. Phi Beta Kappa—Sigma Xi—Am Astronom Soc. 71 Handy Road, Grosse Pointe Farms, Mich.

24 TILLSON, Albert Holmes. Microanalysis of food and drug products; Anatomy and morphology of economic plants. b'10. Student '29-31 (George Washington U); BA '34 (Coll Wooster); MS '35—PhD '38 (U Md). Author articles in field. Microanalyst US Food and Drug Adminstrn since '46. Bot Soc Washington—Assn Official Agrl Chem—Sigma Xi. United States Food and Drug Administration, Division of Microbiology, Washington 25.†

25 TIMBERLAKE, Josephine Baxter. Education of deaf. b'88. Grad '07 (Mary Baldwin Sem); Certificate teacher deaf '13 (Clarke Sch for Deaf); Certificate teacher lipreading '18 (Muller-Walle Sch Lipreading); AM (hon) '39 (Gallaudet Coll for Deaf). Educational work in field hearing and speech;

collection materials for largest reference library on deafness and speech in world; dissemination information on all phases impaired hearing. Teacher of deaf in Fla and Va State Schs '13-19; exec sec Volta Speech Assn for Deaf since '19, also ed Volta Review. Am Soc Hard Hearing—Wash Hearing Soc—NRC Conf on Deaf and Hard of Hearing. Received Mary Baldwin College Algernon Sydney Sullivan award '50. The Volta Bureau, 1537 35th St., Washington 7.

10 TIMBIE, William Henry. Industrial electricity. b'77. AB '01 (Williams Coll). Author: Industrial Electricity '24; Basic Electricity for Communications '43, ad others. Co-author: (with V Bush) Principles of Electrical Engineering '22. Prof electrical engineering and industrial practice MIT since '19. Am Inst EE(F, vp '35-36) —Soc Promotion Engring Edn—Phi Beta Kappa—Pi Gamma Mu—Kappa Eta Kappa—Eta Kappa Nu (eminent mem). H: Monument Av., Old Bennington, Vt.

11 TIMM, John A(rrend). Chemistry education. b'98. PhB '19 (Sheffield Sci Sch Yale); PhD '22 (Grad Sch Yale). Author: Charts of the Chemical Reactions of the Common Elements '24; An Introduction to Chemistry '30, 3d edit '38; General Chemistry '44. Co-author: Laboratory Exercises in General Chemistry '30; Development of the Sciences '41. Co-editor: Marvels of Science '41. Instr chem Yale '22-27, asst prof '27-41; prof chem, chmn dept, chmn div sci, dir sch sci Simmons Coll since '41; mem bd publ Jour Chem Edn. Am Chem Soc—Sigma Xi —Alpha Chi Sigma—Gamma Alpha. Simmons College, Boston 15.†◉

12 TIMMONS, Francis Leonard. Weeds and weed control; Herbicides; Plant ecology. b'05. Student '23-24 (McPherson Coll Kan); BS '28—MS '32 (Kan State Coll). Chairman Research Committee of the North Central Weed Control Conference '45, 46, '47. Author articles in field. Employed US Dept Agr since '35, agronomist since '46, sr agronomist and coordinator of weed investigations in Inter-mountain and Pacific Coast regions since '48. Am Soc Agron—Ecol Soc Am—Gamma Sigma Delta—Phi Kappa Phi—Sigma Xi. Agricultural Experiment Station, Logan, Utah.

13 TIMMONS, (William) Dever. Camouflage; Textile fabrics (Finishing methods). b'98. Student '15-17 (Cleve Art Sch). Civilian advisor on camouflage and photographic processes US Army Engineers Board; art contributor to permanent photographic collection US National Museum Washington; judge American and foreign photographic salons. Author: Standard Description Methods for Textile Fabrics. Asst supt Textile Finishing Co. Irvington NJ '19-22; organized Buckeye Fabric Finishing Co Coshocton '22, since sec-treas; dir Ohio Fabricators Inc, Rsrch Industries, Bluebird Labs Inc; dir classes photog art Johnson Humerickhouse Mus Coshocton; director Columbus Sch Pictorial Photography; lectr photog subjects Columbus Gallery Fine Art, Dayton Art Inst, Tol Mus Art. Royal Soc Art(F)—Royal Photog Soc (asso)— Photographers Assn Am. Pretty Products, Inc., Coshocton, O.

14 TIMS, George Barton, Jr. Plant layout; Job design; Job analysis; Factory planning. b'18. BS in indsl engineering '47—MS in indsl engring '49 (Okla A&M Coll). Research on job design in oil field maintenance and heavy construction industry. Author:

Factory Planning Guide '50. With Okla A&M Coll '46-51, asst prof indsl engineering and cons wage and salary determination, research collaborator for agrl and indsl development service '50-51; prof and head dept indsl engineering Lamar State Coll Tech since '51. Phi Eta Sigma—Sigma Tau—Alpha Pi Mu—Sigma Xi—Am Inst Indsl Engineers—Am Soc Engring Edn—Okla Soc Profl Engrs. Department of Indsl Engineering, Lamar State College of Technology, Beaumont, Tex.

15 TINSLEY, Willa Vaughn. Nutrition education. b'06. BS '28 (Tex State Coll Women); MS '36 (Colo State Coll); PhD '47 (U Minn). Research on better eating habits for children in elementary grades; consultant National Sch Lunch Workshop Iowa State College, participant in National Nutrition Edn Workshop Terre Haute, Indiana. Dir Inter-Am Tchr Edn Project US Office Edn '43-44; nutrition edn cons Gen Mills Inc '45-47; co-dir nutrition edn workshop Mankato State Tchrs Coll '46; head dept home econ SW Texas State Tchrs Coll since '47; instr home econ tchr edn US Indian Service '51. Am Home Econ Assn (mem evaluation com)—Tex Home Econ Assn—Am Vocational Assn—Tex Vocational Assn— Am Assn Supervision and Curriculum Development—Tex Assn Supervision and Curriculum Development—Am Dietetic Assn—Tex Dietetic Assn—Omicron Nu—Tex State Tchrs Assn—Coll Classroom Tchrs Assn. Southwest Tex State Teachers College, San Marcos.

16 TINTNER, Gerhard. Econometrics; Statistics; Mathematical economics. b'07. PhD '29 (U Vienna). Research on empirical demand, production, supply functions, economic fluctuations; variate difference method, multiple regression if all variables are subject to error, economic application multivariate analysis; business cycle theory, non-static theory choice and production. Author: Prices in the Trade Cycle '35; The Variate Difference Method '45. Research asso Austrian Inst Trade Cycle Research '30-36; Rockefeller fellow '34-36; research fellow Cowles Commn Econ Research '36-37; cons Office Strategic Services '42; statis Dept Agr '44; asst prof econ and math Ia State Coll '37-39, asso prof '39-46, prof since '46. Am Econ Soc— Am Statis Soc—Am Math Soc—Inst Math Statis(F)—Econometric Soc(F). Dept Economics, Iowa State College, Ames, Ia.

17 TIPPO, Oswald. Plant classification, morphology, anatomy, and phylogeny; Comparative anatomy of flowering plants; Wood anatomy, decay and preservation. b'11. BS '32 (U Mass); AM '33—PhD '37—Austin Teach fellow '32-35 (Harvard); Atkins fellow from Harvard '37 (Atkins Inst of Arnold Arboretum Soledad Cuba). Author articles in field. Biol Wood Sec Indsl Test Lab '43-45; asso prof, acting head bot dept U Ill '47-48, chmn since '48, prof bot, chmn dept, dean grad Coll since '53; editor Am Jour Bot since '51. AAAS—Bot Soc Am—Internat Assn Wood Anat—Ill Acad Sci—Soc Freedom in Sci—Sigma Xi. Department of Botany, University of Illinois, Urbana, Ill. H: 505 S Highland Av., Champaign.†◉

18 TISDALE, Edwin William. Vegetation (Range, plains, intermountain); Range plants (Chemical composition); Grazing effects on forest vegetation; Range ecology (Western Canada); Grassland Types and forage plants of Canada and Idaho. b'10. Anderson fellow bot '45-46—MS '45—PhD '48 (U Minn); BSc '30 (U Manitoba). Research on pellet reseeding of ranges.

Author articles in field. Asso prof range management, school forestry U Idaho since '47. Ecol Soc Am—Am Soc Range Mgt. College of Forestry, University of Idaho, Moscow, Ida.†

19 TISDALE, Ellis S. Sanitary engineering. b'91. BS '15 (MIT). Chairman Ohio River Board Engineers '34-38; member sanitation advisory board on milk US Public Health Service '33-39. Author articles in field. Asst sanitary engr W Va Dept Health '17-21, dir div sanitary engring '21-38, exec officer, sec state water commn '30-38; sanitary engr charge states relations sect survey Ohio River Pollution Cincinnati O, USPHS '38-41, asso dir Nat Inst Health orientation course training 1012 nurses, doctors, engrs to serve 400 war areas US '41-44, chief training div communicable disease center Atlanta since '45. Am Pub Health Assn—Am Water Works Assn. United States Public Health Service, Atlanta.

20 TISHLER, Max. Chemistry and technology of organic compounds (Amino acids, vitamins, antibiotics, steroids). b'06. BS '28 (Tufts); MS '33— PhD '34—research fellow '34-36 (Harvard). Holder about 12 US patents alone and 50 with others. Co-author: The Chemistry of Organic Compounds '39; also articles in field. Research chem Merck & Co Inc '37, dir developmental research since '45, dir process research and development '53. ACS— AAAS—NY Acad Sci(F)—Sigma Xi— Phi Beta Kappa. Merck and Co., Inc., Rahway, N.J. H: 674 Shackamaxon Drive, Westfield.

21 TITIEV, Mischa. American Indian ethnology. b'01. AB '23—MA '24—PhD '35 (Harvard). Ethnological field work among Hopi Indians of Arizona; field work among Araucanian Indians of Chile '48, Japanese settlements in Peru '48. Author: Old Oraibi: A Study of the Hopi Indians of Third Mesa; Araucanian Culture Transition; also articles in field. Professor anthrop U Mich since '51. Research analyst and hist for CBI Office Strategic Services '44-45. Am Anthrop Assn(F)—AAAS (F). Department of Anthropology, University of Michigan, Ann Arbor.†

22 TITUS, Charles Hickman. Elections (Voting behavior, US); Political processes. b'96. AB '20—AM '21—PhD '27 (Stanford); '19 (U Montpellier France). Analysis and organization for public relations; study methods and techniques of conversion, capture, and organization. Author: (with V H Harding) Government and Society '29; Voting Behavior in the United States '35; The Processes of Leadership '50. Teaching asst economics Stanford '20-21; instr economics and history Whitman Coll Walla Walla Wash '21-23; head polit sci dept '23-25; instr citizenship and polit sci Stanford '25-27; asst prof polit sci U Cal Los Angeles '27-35, asso prof '35-39, prof since '39. AAAS—Am Polit Sci Assn—AAUP—Pi Sigma Alpha—Phi Delta Kappa. 1321 Warner Av., LA 24.◉

23 TITUS, Harold Hopper. Moral philosophy. BA '20 (Acadia Univ.); BD '23—ThM '24—traveling fellow '24-26 (Colgate-Rochester); PhD '26 (U Chicago). Research and writing on philosophical ethics, Christian ethics and contemporary social issues, modern social philosophies; philosophy for coll students. Author: What is a Mature Morality '43; Living Issues in Philosophy '46; Ethics for Today (rev edit) '47. Author articles: A Neo-Realist's Idea of God '33; A Christian Philosophy of Compromise '38; Christian Ethics and Contemporary Social Issues '47, and others. Prof hist William Jewell Coll Liberty Mo '26-28; faculty

Denison U since '28, prof philos since '30. Am Philos Assn—AAUP—Phi Beta Kappa. Denison University, Granville, O.

10 TOBENKIN, Elias. Soviet and Far Eastern affairs. b'82. BA '05—MA '06 (U Wis); fellow '35-36 (New Sch for Social Research). Spent 16 months in Russia '30-31 and made first study by foreign investigator of Soviet prisons and penal system, findings incorporated in monograph for Bureau of Social Hygiene of the Rockefeller Foundation and subsequently included in volume on Russia entitled Stalin's Ladder; made nine months' trip around world '35-36 visiting 15 countries to study economic causes of war and outlook for world peace on grant from William C Whitney Foundation; made first investigations by foreign writer of the planned Siberian republic for Jews Birobidjan. Author: Witte Arrives '16; The House of Conrad '18; The Road '22; God of Might '24; In the Dark '31; Stalin's Ladder—War and Peace in the Soviet Union '33; City of Friends '35; The Peoples Want Peace '38. 309 Av. C, NYC.

11 TODD, Frank E(dward). Pollen and pollination; Bee culture. b'95. BSc '20 (O State U). Research on bee diseases in California '29, cost of producing queen and package bees in California '33, pollen grains in nectar and honey '42, composition of pollen '42, alfalfa pollination '46. Author articles: Economic Aspects of the Bee Industry '33; Cost and Practices in Producing Honey in Oregon '39; other articles in field. State bee inspector Ariz '23-24; state inspector apiaries Calif '28-30; charge Pacific States Bee Culture Lab Davis Calif US Dept Agr '31-41, asst div leader div bee culture Beltsville Md '41-46, charge bee investigations US Legume Seed Research Lab Logan Utah '47-50; charge Southwestern States Bee Culture Lab since '50. Am Assn Econ Entomol—Am Beekeepers Assn. Southwestern States Bee Culture Laboratory, Dept. of Entomology, Tucson.

12 TOLEDANO, Ralph de. Communist espionage and infiltration; American politics. b'16. AB '38 (Columbia); '43-44 (Cornell U). Author: Seeds of Treason '50; Spies, Dupes & Diplomats '52. Articles and lectures in field. Mng editor Plain Talk NYC '46; nat reports editor Newsweek Mag. Newsweek, 152 W. 42d St., NYC 36.

13 TOLLES, Frederick Barnes. History of Quakerism. b'15. BA '36—MA '37 — PhD '47 (Harvard). Member board of directors American Friends Service Committee. Author: Meeting House and Counting House: The Quaker Merchants of Colonial Philadelphia '48; Writers of the Middle Colonies (in Literary History of the US) '48. Author articles: Desiderata in Quaker History '47; Benjamin Franklin's Business Mentors: The Philadelphia Quaker Merchants '47; Quietism versus Enthusiasm: The Philadelphia Quakers and the Great Awakening '45; A Literary Quaker: John Smith of Burlington and Philadelphia '41; Emerson and Quakerism '38. Librarian Friends Hist Lib since '41; asst prof hist Swarthmore Coll since '47; lecturer Quaker hist Pendle Hill Wallingford Pa since '45. Friends Hist Assn (mem bd dirs) —AHA—Hist Soc Pa—Pa Hist Assn. Friends Historical Library of Swarthmore College. H: 302 N. Chester Rd., Swarthmore, Pa.†

14 TOLMAN, Carl. Mining geology. b'97. BA '24 (U Brit Columbia); PhD '27 (Yale). Geological survey of Canada '27-30, '35, '36. Author articles in field. Mo Bur Mines '31-32, '40; Que-

bec Bur Mines '38, '41; US Geol Survey '42; Fgn Econ Adminstrn '43-45; prof, head dept geol and geol engring Washington U since '45, dean grad school arts and scis since '46, dean of faculties since '53; consultant geologist since '27; geol in charge exploration St Louis Smelting & Refining Co since '45. Geol Soc Am(F)—Mineral Soc Am (councillor '39-42, vp '45, F)—Soc Econ Geol—Am Inst Mining Metall Engrs (sec St Louis sect '38-42, chmn '46)—Sigma Xi—Tau Beta Pi. Washington Univ., St. Louis 5.☉

15 TOLMIE, John Roderick. Electromagnetic induction; Circuit analysis. b'97. BS in elec. engring '20—MS '23 (U Wash). Analysis transmission lines networks, electron circuits and modulation; physical research on cathodes, ion gauges, and ion beams; studies induction and radiation coordination of communication, power and radio systems. Co-holder patent on internal cap neutralization of triodes. Author articles: The Characteristic Surfaces of the Triode '24; An Analysis of the Vibrato from the Viewpoint of Frequency and Amplitude Modulation. With transmission and outside plant engring depts Pacific Telephone and Telegraph Co '23-42, staff supervisor since '45. Am Inst EE—Inst Radio Engrs—APS—Sigma Xi—Tau Beta Pi. 200 Medical Arts Bldg., Seattle 1.

16 TOLSON, William Arthur. Radar fire-control; Infrared detection. b'96. BS in elec engring '23 (Tex A&M Coll). Research on automatic fire-control radar and far infra-red detection, recording, and tracking. Granted patents in field. With RCA Lab since '23, sr research engr since '40. Inst Radio Engrs—Sigma Xi. Modern Pioneer award from Nat Assn Mfrs '40. RCA Laboratories, Princeton, N.J.

17 TOLSTEAD, William L. Flora of the North American plains and prairies (Taxonomic problems); Walnut culture; Farm forestry. b'09. BA '33 (Luther Coll Ia); MS '36—fellow '33-36 (Ia State Coll); PhD '42 (U Neb). Prof bot O Northern U since '48. Ecol Soc Am—Am Soc Plant Taxonomists. Biology Department, Ohio Northern University, Ada, O.†

18 TOMBAUGH, Clyde William. Optical instrumentation of rockets; Telescopic fine detail on the planets; Mirror grinding; Planet search technique. b'06. Edward Emery Slosson scholar in science four years—AB '36—MA '39 (U Kan). Extensive search for distant planets, studies in the apparent distribution of extra-galactic nebulae, geological study of moon's surface features, observation of surface features on Mars, production of telescope mirrors; discovered planet Pluto '30, one globular star cluster '32, six galactic star clusters, variable stars, asteroids, clusters of nebulae. Astron Aberdeen Ballistics Labs Annex, White Sands Proving Grounds Las Cruces NM '46-48, ordnance engr '48-49, physicist since '49. Met Soc—American Astron Soc—Astron Soc Pacific—Sigma Xi. Received Jackson-Guilt Medal and Gift Royal Astron Soc Eng '31. Flight Determination Laboratory, White Sands Proving Grounds, Las Cruces, N.M.

19 TOMLINSON, Helen. Aptitude tests. b'99. BA '21 (U Wis); MA '27 (O State U); PhD '41 (U Tex). Construction aptitude tests for selection and assignment new Air Force personnel; experiment, analysis, and validation new tests; preparation manuals for operational use of airman and officer qualifying and classification tests. Co-author article: (with H T Manuel) The New Stanford-Binet at the College Level '40. Editor: The

Development of the Airman Classification Test Battery; The Development of an Airman Qualifying Examination. Test technician Texas Merit System Council '42-47; personnel technician Ill Civil Service Commn '47-48; supervisor measurement devices br Personnel Research Lab Human Resources Research Center AF since '49. Am Psychol Association—Tex Psychol Assn. Human Resources Research Center, Lackland Air Force Base, San Antonio.

20 TOMPKINS, Christian Milton. Plant pathology. b'96. BSA '21—MSA '22 (Colo A&M Coll); PhD '25 (U Wis). Research on fungal and virus diseases of ornamental plants. Author articles in field. Asso plant path div plant path U Calif since '32. Am Phytopath Soc. 107 Hilgard Hall, University of California, Berkeley.†

21 TOMPKINS, Pendleton. Human infertility (Treatment). b'07. AB '27 (Washington and Lee U); MD '31 (Washington U). Ed Fertility and Sterility. Faculty U Pa Med Sch '37-45; faculty U Cal '48-50; asst clinical prof obstetrics and gynecology Stanford U Sch Med since '50. Am Soc Study of Sterility—S F Gynecologic Soc. 450 Sutter St., SF8.

22 TONG, Marvin Enoch, Jr. Midwest archeology; Civil War campaigns. b'22. Student '40-43 (Southwest Mo State Coll); '44 (U Ark). Research on archeology of Ozarks region, excavations in Bull Shoals Reservoir and Garrison Cave; research on history of Civil War campaigns in Trans-Mississippi area, surveys of battlefields in Mo and Arkansas with emphasis on location of troops during engagements; editor Ozarchaeologist '49. Pub Ozark County Times '47-48; dir information Mo Farmers Assn Milling Co since '49. Mo Archeol Soc—Soc Am Archeol —Am Anthrop Assn—SW Anthrop As —Mo State Hist Soc. Missouri Farmers' Association Milling Co., Springfield, Mo. H: 1935 E. Elm St.

23 TOOPS, Herbert Anderson. Psychological tests; Psychometrics; Personnel research and guidance. b'95. AB '16—BS '16—AM '17 (O State U); PhD '21 (Columbia U). Consultant in statistics Secretary of War '44; consultant to National Roster of Scientific and Specialized Personnel '45; consultant US Navy and National Research Council '47-48. Prof psychol O State U since '27. AAAS(F)—O Acad Sci— Am psychol Assn—Am Statis Assn— Am Math Soc—Math Assn Am—Am Ednl Research Assn—Nat Soc Study Edn—Sociometric Soc—Inst Math Statis—Psychometric Soc — Econometric Soc—Sigma Xi. 1430 Cambridge Blvd., Columbus, O.†☉

24 TOPPING, Peter (William). History of the Crusades; Greek history (Medieval, modern). b'16. BA '37— MA '38 (U Wis); '39-40 (U Cincinnati); PhD '42 (U Pa). Author: Feudal Institutions, as Revealed in the Assizes of Romania, the Law Code of Frankish Greece '49; also articles in field. Asst prof hist U Cal '48-53; librarian of the Gennadeion, Am Sch Classical Studies Athens, since '53. Interpreting officer Allied Mission to Observe Greek Elections '46. AHA—Medieval Acad Am —Phi Beta Kappa. Fellow Belgian Am Ednl Found '46-48. American School of Classical Studies, Athens, Greece.†

25 TORBERT, Meg. Psychology of color; BS art edn '34 (U Minn); MA Carnegie fellow '37 (U Ia). Display design '32-34; instr U Mont '37-39; instr design and interior design U Minn '40-42 '45-48; color cons Mpls Gas Co '49; asso curator Everday Art-Walker Art Center since '50; editor

Everyday Art Quarterly since '50. Am Assn Museums—Delta Phi Delta. Walker Art Center, 1710 Lyndale Av. S., Mpls. 5.

10 TORP, Rafael A. Mycology (Tropical American). b'97. BS (Agr) '21 (U PR); MS '25 (Cornell); AM '36 (Harvard); ScD (hon) '47 (Acad Nat Paris). Mycological expeditions conducted in Puerto Rico, Santo Domingo, Cuba, Venezuela, Colombia, Costa Rica; studies Perisporiales; created several new species on genera Meliola, Asterina, Clypeolum, Scolecopaltis, Phaesac-cardinula, and a few new genera; revised genus Dimeriella Speg; orgnd Herbarium at Inter-American Inst of Tropical Agriculture, Turrialba, Costa Rica. Asst plant path Insular Expt Sta Puerto Rico '23-26; prof bot Escuela de Agr Medellin Colombia '26-29; plant path Ministerio de Industries Bogota Colombia '29-30; prof and head bot dept Coll Agr U PR '30-46; vis prof bot Howard U since '47. AAAS—Am Phytopath Soc—Mycol Soc Am—Brit Mycol Soc—Sigma Xi—Gamma Sigma Delta—Beta Beta Beta—Venezuela Acad Sci. 1674 Irving St., Washington 10.

11 TORRENCE, Maynard F(oster). Rubber tires (Neoprene); Natural and synthetic rubber development; Elastomer vulcanization. b'05. AB (U Mont). Author articles in field. Div head charge tire and tube development rubber chem div E I du Pont de Nemours since '35. Am Chem Soc. Rubber Laboratory, E. I. du Pont de Nemours & Co., P.O. 525, Wilmington, Del.†

12 TORREY, Paul D(wight). Secondary methods for increasing the recovery of oil. b'03. BS '25—Petroleum Engr '27 (U Pittsburgh). Survey throughout Rocky Mountain states '23-25; development deep gas field throughout central NY north Pa, methods increasing oil recovery fields northern Pennsylvania. Cons petroleum engr, profl petroleum geol private practice Bradford Pa '26-35; exploitation engr Sloan and Zook Co Houston Tex '36-39; cons petroleum engr Houston '40-52; pres Orchem Corp Austin since '52. Am Petroleum Inst (chairman standing com secondary recovery methods, '36-48, chmn central com drilling and prodn practice '42)—Am Inst Mining Metall Engrs—Am Assn Petroleum Geol—Am Petroleum Inst—Sigma Xi. 705 Lamar Blvd., Austin 3, Tex.

13 TORSCH, Charles Edward. Television (Reception); Tubes (Cathode Ray); Missiles (Television-guided). b '14. Student '27-31 (Baltimore Poly Inst); BE in elec engring '35 (Johns Hopkins). Developed television receivers, cathode ray tubes, high voltage transformers, sweep yokes, interlock systems for television; television-guided missiles. Issued patents in field. Instrument design engr RCA-Victor '36-45; cathode ray tube application engr '45-47; prin TV receiver design engr Bendix Radio Div Bendix Aviation Corp '47-48; cathode ray sweep systems engr Gen Elec Co since '48. Inst Radio Engrs—Alpha Tau Omega. General Electric Co., Electrics Park, Syracuse, N.Y. H: 206 Bailey Rd., North Syracuse, N.Y.

14 TOTH, William. Hungarian culture; History of the reformation in Hungary. b'05. AB '26 (Franklin and Marshall Coll); BD (Theol Sem of the Reformed Ch Pa); PhD '41 (Yale); fellow '29-30 (U Budapest). Research at National Museum Budapest '39; research on the highlights of the Reformation in Hungary, Trinitarianism versus Antitrinitarianism in Hungary, Christianization of the Hungarians.

Translator: Kornis, Education in Hungary. Pastor Hungarian Reformed Church Norwalk Conn '30-42, Salem Evangelical and Reformed Ch Harrisburg Pa '42-46; now head hist dept Franklin and Marshall Coll. Ch Hist Soc—Am-Hungarian Federation—AHA—Phi Beta Kappa. Franklin and Marshall College, Lancaster, Pa.◉

15 TOTTEN, Henry Roland. Seed and drug plants; Woody plants of southeastern United States. b'92. AB '13—AM '14—PhD '23 (U NC); '19 (U Paris). Author: Laboratory Guide in Pharmaceutical Botany and Pharmacognosy '48. Co-author: (with W C Coker) The Trees of North Carolina '16; (with W C Coker) Trees of the Southeastern States '45; also articles in field. Prof bot U NC since '29. AAAS(F)—Bot Soc Am—Assn SW Biol (vp '38)—Am Soc Plant Taxonomists—Southern Appalachian Bot Club—NC Acad Sci (sec-treas '27-33, pres '34)—Am Forestry Assn—Fla Acad Sci—Elisha Mitchell Sci Soc (cor sec '20-24, vp '24, pres '25)—Sigma Xi. Department of Botany, University of North Carolina, Chapel Hill, N.C.†

16 TOULMIN, Harry Aubrey, Jr. Manufacturing (Mechanical, electrical, chemical, industrial engring); Inventions (Protection of rights). b'90. Student '05-06 — Litt D '17 (Wittenberg Coll); BA '11 (U Va); JD '13 (O State U); LLD '30 (Transylvania Coll). Research on various aspects inventions, business, patent law, machine tools and controls, ultrasonics, industrial functions, research steam refrigeration, powdered metallurgy, hydraulic mechanisms, measuring instruments, sponge rubber and micro-organisms for industrial use, metal carbonyls and nitrogen gases. Holds many patents. Author: How to Keep Invention Records '20; Trade Mark Profits and Protection '25; Patents Law for Inventor and Executive '28; Executive's Business Law '29; Graphic Course of Patentable Invention '35; Invention and the Law '36; Trade Agreements and the Anti-Trust Laws '37; Patents and the Public Interest '39; Trade Mark Law of 1946 '46; Hand-Book of Patent Law '47; Patent Law for Executive and Engr '48; Anti-Trust Laws of the US (7 vols) '49; also others. Mem firm Toulmin & Toulmin patent attys Dayton O since '13. ASME—SAE—Soc Am Mil Engrs—Franklin Inst—Am Chem Soc—Am Welding Soc—Am Soc Testing Materials. Toulmin Building, 308 W. First St., Dayton, O.†◉

17 TOULMIN, Lyman Dorgan. Stratigraphy of the coastal plain; Invertebrate paleontology; Geology of Alabama. b'04. AB '26—MA '34 (U Ala); PhD '40 (Princeton U). Author articles in field. Prof geol Fla State U since '48. Geol Soc Am—AAAS—Paleontol Soc—Am Assn Petroleum Geol—SE Geol Soc—Sigma Xi. Department of Geology, Florida State University, Tallahassee, Fla.

18 TOULOUSE, Julian Harrison. Glass and paper containers (Specifications: design; testing); Acceptance Sampling; Stat quality control. b'99. BS '26—PhD '29—profl chem engr '30 (Ia State Coll). Author articles in field. Chief engr quality, specifications dept Owens-Illinois Glass Co since '40. Chief glass container sect Container Br WPB World War II, expert cons for Military Planning Div. Am Soc Testing Materials—Tech Assn Pulp and Paper Ind—Am Soc Chem Engrs—Am Chem Soc—Inst Am Chemists—Am Soc Quality Control—Indsl Packaging Engrs Assn—Inst Food Tech—Tau Beta Pi—Phi Kappa Phi.

Owens-Illinois Glass Company, P.O. Box 1035-1036, Toledo 1, O.

19 TOWER, James Allen. Regional geography (Southern US, Arab Asia, Morocco). b'05. AB '28—MS '33—PhD '36 (Univ Washington). Special research geography of Alabama; articles on Lebanon, Syria and Trans Jordan in '43 Encyclopedia Britannica. Author articles: The Oasis of Damascus '35; The South Today '41; The South: An Old and a New Frontier '43; Ethnic Groups in Cullman County, Alabama '43; Alabama Cotton and Its Future '47; Alabama's Shifting Cotton Belt '48. Asst prof geog Birmingham-South Coll '36-41, associate professor '41-48, professor since '48. Alabama Academy Sci—So Assn Sci Industry—Assn Am Geog (chairman Southeast div '47-48)—Middle E Inst. AAAS grant-in-aid of research geog Ala '39-41, Rosenwald fellowship '47-48. Birmingham-Southern College, Birmingham 4, Ala.

20 TOWLE, Louis Wallace. Blasting explosives; Heavy chemicals. b'08. MS '33 (U Ariz). Chemical engineering research and plant development on heavy chemical and nitroglycerin explosives, technical service in connection with explosives handling and use in mining and construction industry. Author articles in field. Research chem Apache Powder Co Benson Ariz '37-44, tech service supervisor '44-51, technical dir since '51. American Chem Society—American Inst Chem—Am Inst Mining and Metal Engrs—Sigma Xi. Apache Powder Co., P.O. Box 518, Benson, Ariz.

21 TOWNES, Henry Keith, Jr. Insect taxonomy (Ichneumon flies, sawflies, gnats, neuropteroid insects); Insects of micronesia. b'13. BS '32—BA '33 (Furman U); PhD '37 (Cornell U). Author articles in field. With US Bur Entomol and Plant Quarantine '41-48; NC State Coll since '49. Received award for outstanding research in biol Washington Acad Sci '46. Department of Zoology and Entomology, North Carolina State College, Raleigh, N.C.

22 TOWNSEND, Charles Thoreau. Food preservation. b'00. BS '25 (U BC); MS '26 (McGill U). Research on botulism and causes of food spoilage, studies on food spoilage bacteria, thermal destruction rates and thermal death times of micro-organisms, heat penetration in canned foods, process requirements for canned foods, general technology of canning. Co-author: (with I I Somers) Handbook for Community Canneries '49; also articles in field. Research asso U Calif Lab for Research in Canning Inds G W Hooper Found for Medical Research since '26; chief bact Nat Canners Assn Western Br Research Labs San Francisco since '26. Soc Am Bact—Inst Food Tech—AAAS. 1950 6th St., Berkeley 2, Cal.

23 TOWNSEND, Wayne LaSalle. Banking (Law); Bank liquidation. b '96. BA '18 (U Nebraska); LLB '28—JSD '29 (Yale U). Special problems of bank liquidation. Author and editor: Townsend's Cases and Other Select Materials on the Law of Banking '38; Townsend's Ohio Corporation Law '40. Prof Law Western Res U '32-45; asso dean sch law and prof law Washington U since '45. Am Bar Assn—Cleveland Bar Assn—Mo Bar Assn—St Louis Bar Assn—Phi Beta Kappa—Phi Alpha Delta. Washington University, St Louis 5.

24 TOWNSEND, William H. Abraham Lincoln (Biography); Lincolniana. b'90. LLB '12—LLD '30 (U Ky); LittD '45 (Lincoln Memorial U). Member Lincoln Foundation Advisory Group; bd of trustees Lincoln Memorial University; owner one of largest collections of Lincolniana in US including Lincoln's first law book The Revised Laws of Indiana. Author: Abraham Lincoln, Defendant '23; Lincoln the Litigant '25; Lincoln and his Wife's Home Town '29; Lincoln and Liquor '34; Lincoln's Rebel Niece '45; also author tribute to Nancy Hanks on the bronze tablet in Lincoln marriage cabin at Harrodsburg Ky, and Introduction to Famous Speeches (Abraham Lincoln) '35; Introduction to Lincoln and the Preachers (by Edgar DeWitt Jones). Completed nd revised the late Dr William E Barton's "President Lincoln" '32. Contbr numerous articles on Lincoln, including newspaper column Three Minutes with Lincoln. Ill Ky and So hist socs—Abraham Lincoln Assn (bd dirs)—Phi Beta Kappa—Lincoln Group of Chicago (hon)—Lincoln fellowships So Cal Wis and Ohio (hon). 602 Bank of Commerce Bldg., Lexington, Ky.

10 TOWSEND, Prescott Winson. Roman history. b'93. AB '16—AM '21 (Cornell U); PhD '26—Sterling Memorial fellowship '26-27 (for study in Rome and North Africa) (Yale); '22-23, '26-27 (Am Acad Rome). Author: Chronology of the Year 241 AD '28; The Administration of Gordian III '34; The Significance of the Arch of the Severi at Lepcis '38; The Oil Tribute of Africa at the Time of Julius Caesar '40; also articles in field. Prof hist Indiana U since '35. AHA—Am Philol Assn—Archeol Inst Am—Oriental Inst —Soc for Promotion of Roman Studies —Classical Assn Middle West and S— Am Oriental Soc—Phi Beta Kappa. 1200 East 1st St., Bloomington, Ind.©

11 TOWSTER, Julian. Russian government, politics and history. b'05. PhB '30—JD '32—PhD '47 (U Chicago); '26-29 (Lewis Inst). Author: Political Power in the USSR 1917-1947 '48. Propaganda analyst Dept Justice '42-43, social science analyst Office Strategic Services '44-45, sect chief Dept State '46-47; asst prof polit sci U Chicago since '47. Am Polit Sci Assn— Am Soc Internat Law. Fellow Social Sci Research Council '46. University of Chicago, Chicago. H: 1205 Trenton Place, Washington 20.†

12 TOY, Arthur Dock Fon. Organic phosphorous chemistry; Plastics; Chemical insecticides. b'13. Student '35-37 (Joliet Jr Coll); BS '39—MS '40 —PhD '42 (U Ill). Research on aquoammono phosphoric acids, dichlorophenyl phosphine and its derivatives, allyl phosphonate plastics, toxic organic phosphorus and organic thiophosphorus compounds. Holds patents on glycol and aliphatic esters phenylphosphonic acid, unsaturated alkyl esters alkenyl and aryl phosphonic acids, aryl phosphorus containing resins, methods preparing organic phosphorus compounds. Author articles in field. Research chem Victor Chem Works Chicago Heights, Ill since '42. Am Chem Soc. Victor Chemical Works, 11th and Arnold St., Chicago Heights, Ill.†

13 TRAGER, George Leonard. Anthropological linguistics (American Indian, Slavic); Southwestern United States ethnology. b'06. LittB '26 (Rutgers U); AM '29—PhD '32 (Columbia). Research on the language of Taos Indians of New Mexico and related languages, Slavic linguistics, development of linguistic and anthropological aspects of area programs, theory of analysis of culture. Author: The Use of the Latin Demonstratives '32; The Kiev Fragment '33. Co-author: (with Bloch) Outline of Linguistic Analysis '42; also articles in field. Research associate International Auxiliary Language Assn Inc '31-34; asst prof Adams State Tchrs Coll Colo '34-36; research fellow Yale '36-38, lectr '41, asst prof Slavic langs '42-44; chief Ling Sect US Bd Geog Names Dept Interior '44-46; spl cons Fgn Service Inst Dept State summers '47-48; prof linguistics Dept Anthrop Okla Univ '46-48; prof linguistics and anthropology Fgn Service Inst Dept State since '48, dir linguistic research since '50; editor of Studies in Linguistics since '42. Linguistic Soc Am—Am Ethnol Soc—Am Folklore Soc — AAAS(F) — Internat Phonetic Assn—Am Anthrop Assn(F)— Sigma Xi. Research grant, Inst Human Relations '37, Am Philos Soc '47; fellow American Council Learned Socs, Sterling Fellow, Yale '38-41; Guggenheim Mem Found fellow '41-42. Foreign Service Institute, Department of State, Washington 25.†

14 TRASK, Parker Davies. Marine and petroleum geology; Sedimentation; Foundation problems. b'99. BA '17 (U Tex); MA '20—PhD '23 (U Calif). Conducted petroleum geological explorations '17-25; director Am Petroleum Institute research project on origin and environment source sediments petroleum '29-41; conducted war minerals investigations for manganese California and Mexico '41-43, oceanographic investigations Office Science Research and Development '44-45; scientific observer atomic bomb Bikini '46; research on foundations for proposed vehicular crossings San Francisco Bay; chairman committee on sedimentation National Research Council '35-50. Author articles in field. With US Geol Survey since '31, supervising geol Calif Toll Bridge Authority '48-50. Geol Soc Am—Am Assn Petroleum Geol— Soc Econ Geol—Am Geophys Union— Am Inst Mining Metall Engrs. Awarded James M Goewey travel fellowship Europe '23-24. 491 Crescent St., Oakland, Cal.

15 TRAUB, Hamilton P(aul). Plant physiology; Induced mutations; Subtropical nut-fruits; Physiology of rubber in plants. b'90. BS '23—MS '25— PhD '27 (U Minn); '14-15 (Harvard); '42 (U Wis). Delegate and chairman delegation US State Department and US Department Agriculture to International Horticultural Congress Berlin '38. Founder and editor: National Horticultural Magazine '22-24; Herbertia, year book devoted to Amaryllidaceae since '34; Plant Life, quarterly periodical since '45; also articles in field. Principal physiol US Dept Agr '30-52, ret. AAAS(F)—Am Soc Plant Physiology— Society Study Evolution—Am Society Hort Sci—Am Genetic Assn—Am Soc Plant Taxonomists—Am Plant Life Soc—Sigmā Xi. H: 1531 Rodeo Rd., Arcadia, Cal.

16 TRAUERMAN, Carl J. Gold and silver mining; Manganese (mining, concentration). b'85. Student '03-06 (MIT). Concentration pink manganese to make commercial product; concentration black manganese. Co-author: Directory of Montana Mining Properties '40, '42, and '49, also articles in field. Mng dir US Manganese Corp '18-22; pres Ruby Gulch Mining Co '35-46; ed Mont Natural Resources Bull and Mining Assn of Mont News Letter; pres Basin Goldfields Ltd. AIM ME—Mont Soc Engrs—Am Mining Congress (bd govs)—Mining Assn of Mont (pres and sec). 505 Montana Standard Bldg., Butte, Mont. H: 311 Napton Apts.

17 TRAUTMAN, Milton B(ernhard). Stream gradient in relation to fish distribution and abundance; Birds and fish of ohio; Black duck; Lampreys; Birds of the Yucatan. b'99. Author articles in field. Research asso Franz Theodore Stone Inst Hydrobiology O State U since '40. Am Soc Ichthyol and Herpetol (bd govrs, 3rd vp '36-48) —Wilson Ornithol Club (treas '43-45, council)—Am Ornithol Union—O Acad Sci(F)—Am Fisheries Soc—Limnol Soc Am—Cooper Ornithol Club—Sigma Xi. Franz Theodore Stone Institute of Hydrobiology, Put-in-Bay, O.

18 TRAVIS, B(ernard) V(alentine). Insects (Field crops, medical, repellents); Protozoa. b'07. BS '29 (Colo Agr Coll); MS—PhD '35 (Ia State Coll). Author articles in field. Research entomol US Dept Agr Bur Entomol and Plant Quarantine '35-49, leader of an entomological research group Alaska; prof med entomol and parasitol Cornell U since '49. Research entomol US Navy South and Central Pacific '44-46. Entomol Soc Am—Am Assn Econ Entomol—Fla Entomol Soc —Am Mosquito Assn—Am Soc Parasitol. Cornell University, Ithaca.

19 TRAVIS, Irven. Fire control; Computing devices. b'04. BS '26 (Drexel Inst Tech); MS '28—ScD '38 (U Pa). Instr, asst prof, prof elec engring Moore Sch Elec Engring U Pa '28-49, dir Burroughs Corp since '50, dir research since '49, vp research since '52. Chief antiaircraft fire control research Bur Ordnance Navy Dept '42-46. AI EE—IRE. 511 N. Broad St., Phila 23.

20 TRAXLER, Arthur Edwin. Reading tests; Scholastic aptitudes and achievement. b'00. BS '20 (Kan State Teachers Coll); MA '24—PhD '32 (U Chicago). Research on educational and psychological measurement; evaluation various educational and psychol tests; research on measurement and improvement reading ability; test construction research; research on schol aptitude and achievement independent school pupils. Author: Techniques of Guidance '45; How to Use Cumulative Records '47. Author article: The Use of Tests and Rating Devices in the Appraisal of Personality '38, and others. Editor: Guidance in Public Secondary Schools '39; Goals of American Education '50. Testing and remedial work U Chicago High Sch '28-31, psychology and guidance chmn '31-36; research asso advancing to exec dir Ednl Records Bur since '36. Am Ednl Research Assn (pres '50-51)—AAAS—Am Psychol Assn—Psychometric Soc—Am Statis Assn—Phi Delta Kappa. Educational Records Bureau, 21 Audubon Av., N.Y.C. 32.©

21 TRBOVICH, Nick. Steel (Mill equipment). b'11. BS in elec engring '37 (Purdue U). Economic and engring analysis steel mill processes, operating techniques, equipment, layouts; application electrical and power equipment to solve specific problems. Elec foreman Inland Steel Co '35-38, chief test engr elec power and steam depts '39-50, sr forward planning engr engring dept since '51. Nat Soc Profl Engrs—Theta Tau—Am Inst EE—Assn Iron and Steel Engrs—Elec Maintenance Engrs. Inland Steel Co., East Chicago, Ind. H: 4225 Ivy St., East Chicago, Ind.

22 TREFFTZS, Kenneth Lewis. Mathematics of finance (Money and banking; Business and Accounting); Investment. b'11. BS '36—MS '37— PhD '39 (U Ill). Author: Mathematics Applied to Money and Banking '44; Mathematics of Business and Accounting '47; also articles in field. Asso prof finance U So Calif since '44, head dept '46. Am Acad Polit Social Sci—Am Econ Assn—Am Finance Assn (asst sec '42-45, vp '46-48)—Am Statis Assn —Pacific Coast Econ Assn (program chmn '48)—Beta Gamma Sigma—Phi Kappa Phi. University of Southern California, University Park, Los Angeles 7.†

10 TREGANZA, Adan Eduardo. Archeology of California. b'16. Student '35-38 (San Diego State Coll); BA '40—PhD '49 (U Calif). Archeological field work in Baja and Southern California '40-41, Northern and Central California '42-45. Author articles in field. Asst prof anthrop San Francisco State Coll since '47. Am Anthrop Assn—Am Ethnol Soc(F)—Soc Am Archeol—Sigma Xi. San Francisco State College, 124 Buchanan St., San Francisco 2.†

11 TREGASKIS, Richard. Journalistic history (World War II). b'16. AB '38 (Harvard). Pacific Fleet correspondent '42-43, covering Coral Sea Battle, Doolittle-Tokyo task force, Battle of Midway, Battle for Guadalcanal; assigned Mediterranean theater, covered invasion of Sicily, Italy, fall of Naples; assigned European theater, covered battle of western front; Pacific war correspondent for Saturday evening Post '45; staff writer '45-46; Round-the-World Diary for True Magazine '47-48. Author: Guadalcanal Diary '43; Invasion Diary '44; Stronger Than Fear '45; also articles in field. Recipient George R Holmes award '42. c/o George Landy, 240 S. Beverly Dr., Beverly Hills, Cal.

12 TRELEASE, Sam Farlow. Plant physiology and mineral nutrition; Photosynthesis; Selenium in agriculture; Poisonous plants. b'92. AB '14 (Washington U); PhD '17 (Johns Hopkins). Author: Laboratory Exercises in Agricultural Botany '19; also articles in field. Torrey prof bot Columbia since '37, exec officer dept since '30. AAAS (F, asst sec '21-23, sec council '21-30, program editor '23-30)—Bot Soc Am (sec '32, ed Am Journ Bot '33-39, vp '41)—Am Soc Plant Physiol—Sigma Xi 520 W. 114th St., N.Y.C. 25.◎

13 TRENT, Horace Maynard. Electromechanical analogies; Vibration (Instruments, calibration). b'07. BA '28 (Berea Coll); MA '29—PhD '34 (Ind U). Research on perfection of absolute method calibration for vibration instruments. Prof phys Miss State Coll '34-40; research phys Nav Research Lab since '40; prof elec engring U Md since '46. Acoustical Soc Am(F)—Am Math Soc—Philos Soc Wash—Wash Acad Sci—Am Standards Assn (mem com Z-24)—Sigma Xi—Sigma Pi Sigma. Naval Research Laboratory (3830), Washington 25. H: 413 Tennessee Av., Alexandria, Va.

14 TRESHOW, Michael. Kilns (Rotary); Mills (Grinding). b'94. MS '20 (Royal Tech U Copenhagen Denmark); '20-21 (MIT). Mechanical and combustion engineering rotary kilns; research and improvement drives and bearing supports for ball and tube mills. Holds patents on improved roller supports, combustion equipment, controls, clinker coolers, rotary dryers for slurries and solids, on rotary kilns, also central precision gear drives, slide shoe bearing supports for large drums, flexible coupling for high torque nd internal cement cooling device grinding mills. Mech engr F L Smith & Co NYC '29-38, chief development engr '42-44, chief engr '46-47; gen mgr Monolith Portland Cement Co Los Angeles '38-42; cons mech engr cement plants and equipment '47-50. ASME. Profl mech engr Cal. Argonne National Laboratory, P.O. Box 5207, Chgo. 80.

15 TRESSLER, Willis L(attanner). Marine and freshwater Ostracoda; Limnology of New York, Wisconsin and Philippine Lakes. b'03. BA '26—

MA '28—PhD '30 (U Wis). Author articles: Freshwater Ostracoda from Brazil; Marine Ostracoda from Tortugas, Florida; An Ecological Study of Seasonal Distribution of Solomen's (Maryland) Marine Ostracoda; also articles in field. Research asso U Md since '46. AAAS(F)—Soc Zool—Am Soc Limnol and Oceanog (vp '41)—Ecol Soc Am—Am Fisheries Soc—Am Micros Soc—Am Soc Taxonomic Zool—Internat Limnol Soc—Wis Acad Sci Arts Letters. 4608 Amherst Road, College Park, Md.

16 TREXEL, Carl A(lvin). Off-shore oil drilling (Design and construction). b'92. BS '14—BE '15—CE '20 (U Ia). Entered US Navy '17 and advanced through grades to rear adm '44; officer in charge constrn Cape May NJ '22-33; treaty engr Republic of Haiti '24; officer in charge constrn Excelsior Springs Mo '24; pub works officer Charleston SC '25-27; inspr Naval petroleum reserves Wyo, Col, Utah '28-30; pub works officer Cavite Philippines '30-31; pub works officer Bremerton Wash '32-36; dir planning and design bur yards and docks Washington '37-41; office naval operations logistics plans div '42-43; dir Alaskan div bur yards and docks '44-46; Pacific and Alaskan divs '47-50, ret '50; exec mgr Internat Marine Platforms Constructors since '50. Am Soc CE—Am Welding Soc—Soc Am Mil Engrs. 112 Market St., S.F. †◎

17 TRICHEL, Gervais William. Computing devices; Artillery fire control; Large rockets. b'98. BS '18 (US Mil Acad); MS '35 (MIT); PhD '38 (U Calif). Took part in early development of anti-aircraft artillery fire control computing devices '20-29; chief of rocket development division Office of Ordnance Washington '43-45; member advisory board to director of atomic bomb project '46. Mem staff of Gen Mgr Chrysler Corp since '47. 341 Massachusetts Av., Det. 31.◎

18 TRICKETT, A(lbert) Stanley. Biblical literature; Religion (Education). b'11. Grad '29 (Cazenovia NY Sem); AB '32 (Asbury Coll Wilmore Ky); MA '33 (U Ky); grad '34 (Sch Internat Studies Geneva Switzerland); PhD '35 (The Victoria U). Instr history Northwestern U '36; instr history and Bibl lit Brothers Coll Drew U Madison NJ '36-39, asso prof history and polit sci '39-44; dean of univ, prof history and dir summer session Kan Wesleyan U Salina '50, pres since '50. Am Hist Assn—Royal Hist Soc—Phi Gamma Mu. Kansas Wesleyan University, Salina.†◎

19 TRIGGER, Kenneth James. Metal cutting; Heat treatment of metals. b'10. BS '33—MS '35—ME '43 (Mich State Coll). Research on effect of grain size upon physical properties of medium carbon steels '33-35; effect of nitriding upon life of high speed tool steel '40; hot quenching of high speed steel '41-46. Author: Heat Treatment of Metals '49; also articles in field. Instr mech engring Mich State Coll '35-36, Swarthmore Coll '36-37, Lehigh U '37-38; asst prof and prof mech engring U Ill since '38. ASME—Am Soc Tool Engrs—Am Soc Engring Edn—Tau Beta Pi—Phi Kappa Phi—Sigma Xi. University of Illinois, Urbana, Ill.†

20 TRILLING, Lionel. Nineteenth century English literature; American literature; Matthew Arnold. b'05. AB '25—MA '26—PhD '38 (Columbia). Author: Matthew Arnold, Norton '39; E. M. Forster '43; The Middle of the Journey '48; also articles in field. Instr to asso prof and prof Eng Columbia since '31. Phi Beta Kappa. Columbia University, NYC 27.†◎

21 TRIMM, H(oward) Wayne. Wildlife painting; Hawks. b'22. '40-41 (Cornell U); '45 (Syracuse U); BA '48 (Augustana Coll); '48 (Kan State Coll); MS '52 (NY State College Forestry). Research on food habits of hawks of South Dakota, Mongolian ring-necked pheasant and the effect of environmental changes on behavior; nationally exhibited as wildlife painter in many museums including Rochester Museum of Arts and Science, Joslyn Memorial Omaha, Cranbrook Institute Science. Author: Hawks of South Dakota, Their Food Habits and Identification; other articles in field. Staff artist and asst curator ornithol Syracuse U Museum Nat Sci, illustrations for manual of Museum Methods; research on wildlife use of habitat improvement NY State Coll Forestry '52-53; conservation edn div NY State Conservation Dept Albany. Cooper Ornithol Club—Am Ornithol Union—Wilson Ornithol Club—Kan Acad Sci. Zoology Division Conservation Education, N.Y. State Conservation Dept., Albany 1, N.Y.†

22 TRIVELLI, Adrian Peter Herman. Research chemistry (Thermochemical). b'79. Chem E '05 (Tech U Delft Holland). Research on photographic emulsions, problems related to sensitivity. Co-author: The Silver Bromide Grain (with Sheppard) '21; Lessons in Theoretical Physics (with Sillerstein, tr) '31. Chem Netherland Oversea Trust Co '14-17; chem research lab Eastman Kodak Co since '17. AAAS(F)—Am Optical Soc—Netherlands Chem Soc—Royal Photog Soc—NY Micros Soc. Eastman Kodak Co., Rochester, N.Y.

23 TROGDON, William O(ren). Texas soils; Soil physics and fertility. b'20. BS '42 (Okla A&M Coll); PhD '49 (O State U). Research in factors affecting crop varietal adaptation in the Texas Blackland soils, the physical properties of Blackland soils, effect of base and acid forming sources of nitrogen on certain soil factors. Author articles in field. Asst chem Phillips Petroleum Co Borger Tex '46; asst agronomist substation five Tex Agrl Expt Sta '48; soil sci research div soil conservation service US Dept Agr '48-49; head dept agr Midwestern U and soil Sci Wichita County Water Improve Dists since '49. Am Soc Agronomists—Soil Sci Soc Am—Sigma Xi. Am Cyanamid Co research fellow '46-48. Midwestern University, Wichita Falls, Texas.

24 TROLLER, Theodor H. Fans (Axial flow, design of); Airplane propellers (Theory); Wind tunnels (Design); Guided missiles (Aerodynamics). b'03. Diplomate engring '26 (Tech Coll, Darmstadt, Germany); DEng '30 (Tech Coll, Aachen, Germany). Dir research Guggenheim Airship Inst '31-45; prof Case Inst Tech '45-47; vp Joy Mfg Co since '47. ASME—Inst Aeronautical Sci (asso F)—Am Soc Heating and Ventilating Engrs—AIME. Joy Manufacturing Co., 333 Oliver Building, Pitts.

25 TROUT, David McCamel. Student personnel organization. b'91. AB '16 (William Jewell Coll Liberty Mo); AM, BD '22—PhD '24 (U Chicago); LHD '39 (Hillsdale Coll). Author: Religious Behavior '31. Prof psychology Hillsdale Coll '25-37, dean of men '26-37; head dept edn and psychology Central State Tchrs Coll Mount Pleasant Mich '37-40; spl cons Mich Secondary Sch Curriculum Study '40-41; head department psychology and edn Central Mich Coll Edn '41-45, dean students since '41; coordinator Mich Cooperative Tchr Edn Study '42-43; vis prof edn U Mich summer '45. AAAS(F)—NEA—Mich Edn Assn—Am Coll Personnel Assn—Mich Assn Coll Registrars and Adminstrn Officers—Mich Soc Mental Hygiene—Mich Counselors Assn—Nat Soc Study Edn—AAUP—Mich Acad Sci Arts and Letters—Pi Gamma Mu—Kappa Delta Pi. 421 S. Kinney St., Mt. Pleasant, Mich.†⊙

10 TROWBRIDGE, Harry Martin. Archeology; American mound builders; Hopewellian and Spiro mound cultures. AB (U Kan). Collection of stone age relics including mound textiles and shell carvings now on loan in Kansas City Museum; principal research on a Hopewellian village site Wyandotte Co Kansas where he excavated a pottery-marking tool of deerhorn considered by Smithsonian Institution to be the first reported roulette of this type. Author articles in field. Soc Am Archeol—Mo Archeol Soc—Inter-Am Soc Anthrop and Geog—Am Anthrop Assn. Route 1, Bethel, Kan.

11 TRUEBLOOD, Paul Graham. Byron. b'05. AB '28 (Willamette U); AM '30—PhD '35 (Duke); grad research (U Pa, Bryn Mawr Coll, Haverford Coll, Swarthmore Coll, U Ore, Stanford U). Author: The Flowering of Byron's Genius '45; Critical Companion Volumn to Byron's Don Juan (in progress). Charter contbr Keats-Shelley Jour '52. Pendle Hill fellowship Phila '34-35; head English studies Mohonk School '35-37; asst and asso prof Stockton Coll '40-46; assistant professor English Rollins College '46-47; assistant Prof English literature and Bible as literature U Wash '47-52; Am Council of Learned Socs scholar '52-53; Byron cons U Chicago Press '50-51. Modern Lang Assn Am—AAUP—Keats-Shelley Assn Am. Stanford University Library, Stanford, Cal.

12 TRUESDAIL, Roger W(illiams). Vitamin values of fish (Assaying); Stabilization of vitamins; Drug detection. b'99. BS '21 (U Redlands); MS '22 (U Ore); PhD '26 (U Wash). Analysis vitamin content fish products; research on methods for stabilization vitamins, processes for utilization nutritionally valuable by-products; microcrystalline procedures for detection minute quantities of drugs in body fluids. Author articles: Vitamins A and D in Dried Tuna Meal; Sardine and Tuna Oils as Sources of Vitamin D; Vitamin A Content of Body Oils of Pacific Coast Salmon, and others. Asst prof chem Pomona Coll Cal '27-31; research and cons Truesdail Labs Inc LA since '31. AAAS(F)—Am Inst Chem(F)—Am Council Comml Labs—Inst Food Chem—ACS—Am Pub Health Assn—Assn Cons Chem and Chem Engineers. 4101 N. Figueroa St., L.A. 65.

13 TRUITT, Reginald Van Trump. Marine biology. b'91. AB '14—MS '20 (Md U); '23 (U Berlin); PhD '29 (Am U). Member Chesapeake Bay Commn., Rockefeller Foundation '41-48; chairman committee on conservation Maryland State Planning Commn '34-48; member Maryland Board of Natural Resources since '41; chairman committee on education National Fishery Advisory Council '34-42; member National Committee on Policies in Conservation Education, technical advisor Atlantic States Marine Fisheries Commn, mem Interstate Commn on Potomac River Basin and Maryland Water Pollution Control Commn, member National Rivand Harbors Congress. With U Md '22-43, prof zool '26-43; founder and dir Chesapeake Biol Lab since '26; dir Md Dept Research and Edn since '41. AAAS—Am Fisheries Soc—Am Soc Zool—Biol Soc Wash—Audubon Soc Am—Ecol Soc Am(vp '50)—Limnol Soc Am—Md Acad Sci(F)—Md Biol Tchrs

Assn(pres '36, founder)—Md Nat Hist Soc—Md State Fish and Game Assn—Nat Shellfisheries Assn (pres '35-36)—Bermuda Biol Sta Research(bd mem)—Atlantic Estuarine Research Soc—Omicron Delta Kappa—Phi Kappa Phi—Sigma Xi—Izaak Walton League (tech adv). Department of Research and Education, Box 8, Solomons, Md.

14 TRUMAN, Lee C(ampbell). Insect and rodent control. b'14. BS '36—PhD '41 (U Pittsburgh). Instr biol U Pittsburgh '41-43; tech dir and gen mgr Arab Pest Control Co and Federal Chem Co Indianapolis '46-50; president Pest Control Services since '50. Service command entomol charge insect and rodent control fifth Service Command Hq US Army '43-46. AAAS—Am Assn Econ Entomol—Entomol Soc Am—Ind Acad Sci—Nat Pest Control Assn. 6242 N. Temple Av., Indpls.†

15 TRUMAN, Orley Hosmer. Applied geophysics; Martian photography; Spectroscopy; Gravity meters. b'88. BA '11—MSc '12 (Ia U). Devised first calculations ever published motion of galaxy '18; calculated first lens with non-spherical surface (test lens made by John Mellish) '23; built first commercially successful and practical portable gravity meter for Humble Oil & Ref Co '30-31, another of different construction '31-32 used extensively in oil prospecting and investigations of variation of gravity at one place. Author articles in field. Astron Lowell Observatory '19-23; geophys research and designing instruments Humble Oil & Ref Co Houston '24-31; independent oil prospector '32-35; ret since '35. AAAS—Am Geophys Union—Am Astron Soc.

16 TRUMPOUR, Frederick James. Blueprints. b'70. BS (engring) '92 (Allegheny Coll). Developed methods and machine for continuous production of blueprints, simultaneously printed on both surfaces of roll double coated paper. With US Army Engring Branch since '18, structural designer '19, chief civil engring div '22, retired '40; cons since '40. AAAS—Am Geog Soc—Wash Soc Engrs—Soc Am Mil Engrs—Am Soc CE—Am Ordnance Assn. 1515 Seminary Rd., Silver Spring, Md.

17 TRYON, Henry Harrington. Silviculture; New England hardwoods. b'88. AB '12—MF '13 (Harvard). Author: The Black Rock Forest; Chestnut Oak Volumn Tables; Cordwood Volumn Tables; Notes on Terminal Growth; Hardwood Brush Disposal; A High-Duty Woodsaw; Fearsome Critters; A Study of Coniferous Underplanting in Upper Hudson Highlands '32; A Portable Charcoal Kiln '33; Practical Forestry in the Hudson Highlands; Practical Forestry in the Hudson Highlands; also articles in field. Mem faculty NY State Forestry Coll '15-17; engr Washington DC '19-24; extension forester for SC '24-27; dir Black Rock Forest NY '27-50. AAAS—Society Am Foresters—Internat Inst for Forest Research—Ecol Soc—Soc Foresters Great Britain—Royal Scottish Forestry Soc—Torrey Bot Club. Cornwall-on-the-Hudson, N.Y. Retired.⊙

18 TRYON, Rolla Milton, Jr. Pteridophytes; Phytogeography. b'16. BS '37 (U Chicago); PhM '38 (U Wis); MS—PhD '41 (Harvard). Co-author: The Ferns and Fern Allies of Wisconsin '40; also articles in field. Asso prof botany Washington U since '48; asst curator Herbarium Mo Bot Garden since '48. Bot Soc Am—Am Soc Plant Taxonomists—Am Fern Soc—Ind Acad Sci—New Eng Bot Soc—Sigma Xi. Missouri Botanical Garden, St. Louis 10.

19 TSANOFF, Radoslav Andrea. Philosophy (History, immortality); Philosophy of religion. b'87. AB '06 (Oberlin Coll); PhD '10 (Cornell U). Author: Schopenhauer's Criticism of Kant's Theory of Experience '11; The Problem of Immortality: Studies in Personality and Values '24; The Nature of Evil '31; Religious Crossroads '42; The Moral Ideals of Our Civilization '42; Ethics '47; The Great Philosophers '52. Instructor of philosophy Clark U '12-14; asst prof Rice Inst '14-24, prof since '24. Am Philosoph Assn (past pres)—Southern Soc Philosophy and Psychology—Phi Beta Kappa. H: 5219 Austin St., Houston 4.⊙

20 TSCHEBOTARIOFF, Gregory P. Soil mechanics (Earth pressure against retaining structures). b'99. Diplomingenieur '25 (Technische Hochschule, Berlin-Charlottenburg Germany); Doktor-Ingenieur '52 (Rhine-Westfalian Technische Hochschule Aachen). Research on factors affecting accuracy of settlement rate forecasts, on settlement of structures in Egypt, on earth pressure, shearing resistance, and sensitivity to remolding of clays, on effect of vibrations on bearing properties of soils, on design of flexible anchored bulkheads, and related subjects; official delegate 1st, 2d, 3d International Conferences on Soil Mechanics and Foundation Engineering '36-48-53. Author: Soil Mechanics, Foundations & Earth Structures '51; also articles. Engr various projects and orgns Europe and Egypt '26-37; with Princeton U since '37; prof civil engring since '51; in charge at Princeton rsrch projects for Civil Aeronautics Adminstrn '43-46, for Bur Yards and Docks '43-49; for Office of Naval Research since '50. ASCE—ASTM—Am Soc Engring Edn—Sigma Xi—ARBA. Engineering Building, Princeton University, Princeton, N.J.†

21 TSCHOPIK, Harry, Jr. Peru (Aymara and mestizo communities); Navajo Indians. b'15. AB '36 (U Calif); MA '40—PhD '51 (Harvard). Anthropological survey and community study of central and south highland Peru '40-42, '44-45. Author articles in field. Anthropologist Inst Soc Anthropology, Smithsonian Instn, Washington '44-45; asst curator ethnology, Am Mus Natural History since '47. Am Anthrop Assn(F)—Soc Am Archeology(F)—Am Ethnol Soc(F)—Sigma Xi—Phi Beta Kappa. American Museum of Natural History, Central Park West at 79th St., NYC 24.

22 TSENG, Cheng Kwei. Marine flora of China and South China Sea region; Economic uses of algae; Seaweed cultivation, physiology, life history and technology; Biological oceanography. b'09. BSc '31 (Amoy U); MSc '34—Rockefeller Found fellow '32-34 (Lingnan U); U fellow '40-42—Rockham fellow '43-43—MA '41—ScD '42 (U Mich). Expedition to Pratas Island '33, charge joint Lingnan-Amoy University expedition to Hainan Island '34, joint Amoy-Shantung University expedition to Central and North China Coast '35. Author articles in field. Prof and chmn dept bot Nat Shantung U China since '46; associate director Marine Biological Laboratory Academia Sinica Tsingtao since '50. AAAS—American Bot Society—Torrey Bot Club—Soc Western Naturalists—Calif Bot Soc—Oceanog Soc Pacific—Am Phycol Soc—Mich Acad Sci—Marine Biol Assn United Kingdom—Bot Soc China—Natural Sci Assn China. Department of Botany, National Shantung University, Tsingtao, China.

23 TUBBS, Llewellyn Glenn. Chromium chemicals; Chromium plating; Anodizing; Chrome pigments; Barium compounds. b'03. BS '25 (Valparaiso

U). Lab adminstrn, research and tech service Mutual Chem Co Am '27-46; with Bur Aeronautics Navy Dept '46; research Barium Reduction Corp since '46. ACS—Am Electroplaters Soc. Barium Reduction Corp., South Charleston, W.Va.

10 TUCKER, Clarence Mitchell. Tomato breeding; Phytopthora. b'97. BS '20—PhD '30 (U Mo). Development of tomato varieties resistant to Fusarium wilt; monographic studies on the taxonomy and physiology of Phytophthara. Author articles in field. Prof plant pathol U Puerto Rico '21-23; asso plant pathologist Puerto Rico Agrl Expt Sta '23-30, Fla Agrl Expt Sta '30-31, asso prof bot U Mo '31-37, prof and chmn dept bot since '37. Am Phytopath Soc (pres '50)—Am Soc Bot—Mycol Soc Am—AAAS(F). 100 Lefevre Hall, Columbia, Mo.

11 TUCKER, Harold H(erbert). Fur dyeing and chemistry; Fur felt hat manufacturing. b'02. AB '24 (Bradley Coll); PhD '30 (U Chicago). Three patents on method of preparing fur for felting, carroting of animal fibers, felt hat body stiffening composition. Author articles in field. Research cons hat fur, related inds since '47. Am Chem Soc—Am Inst Chemists—Am Assn Textile Chemists and Colorists—Sigma Xi. 14 Chesterfield Road, Scarsdale, N.Y.

12 TUCKER, Robert Henry. Public finance; Public utilities; Public administration. b'75. AB '93—Am '97—LLD '26 (Coll William and Mary); U Wis '08-10, '15. Asso prof economics and commerce Washington and Lee U '15-19, prof economics and bus adminstrn '19-46, acting pres Jan-July '30, dean coll '30-32, dean univ '32-46; lectr in econs '46-50, prof emeritus econs since '50. Am Econ Assn—Am Acad Polit and Social Sci—AAUP—Royal Econ Society—Kappa Sigma—Phi Beta Kappa. Washington and Lee University, Lexington, Va.†◉

13 TUKEY, Harold Bradford. Developmental morphology; Growth substances; Dwarf fruit trees; Plant propagation. b'96. BS '18—MS '20 (U Ill); PhD '32 (U Chicago). Author: (with others) The Pears of New York '21; The Pear and Its Culture '29. Asst horticulturist NY State Agrl Expt Station '20-23; horticulturist in chg Hudson Valley Fruit Investigations '23-27; chief in research horticulture NY State Agrl Exptl Station, prof pomology Cornell U '27-45; head dept horticulture Mich State Coll since '45. AAAS(F)—Royal Hort Soc(Eng)—Am Pomol Soc—Am Soc Hort Sci—Bot Soc Am—Am Soc Plant Physiologists—Am Soc Naturalists—Soc Growth and Development—Sigma Xi—Alpha Zeta. Department of Horticulture, Michigan State College, East Lansing.◉

14 TULLER, William Gordon. Electronic miniaturization. b'18. BS '39—MS '42—ScD '48 (MIT). Author articles: Potted subassemblies for sub-miniature equipment; recent developments in potted circuits. Project engr and research sect head Melpar Inc '47-49, chief engr since '49. Sigma Xi—Inst Radio Engrs, Melpar, Inc., 452 Swann Av., Alexandria, Va. H: 4314 N. Henderson Rd., Arlington 3.

15 TULLIS, Edgar C(ecil). Rice diseases; Chemical weed control (Hormones). b'01. AB—MA (U Neb); PhD (Mich State Coll). Weed control investigations with 2, 4-D; related compounds on rice field weeds '45-48. Articles in field. Pathologist Ark Agrl Expt Sta '28-30; pathologist US Dept Agr Fayetteville Ark '30-38, Beaumont Tex since '38. Box 2967, Beaumont, Tex.†

16 TULLOCH, George S. Mosquitoes; Medical entomology; Ants. b'06. BS '28 (Mass State Coll); MS '29—PhD '31 (Harvard). Discovered and proposed the term gynergate for an anomalous mosaic of ants combining features of female and worker ants '32; mosquito survey of Puerto Rico for Federal Government '35-36. Author articles in field. Instr to asso prof biol Brooklyn Coll since '32. AAAS—Entomol Soc Am—Cambridge Entomol Soc—Brooklyn Entomol Soc—Am Soc Parasitologists. Department of Biology, Brooklyn College, Bedford Av., and Av. H, Brooklyn 10.†

17 TUNISON, Abram Vorhis. Trout; Nutrition of fish. b'09. BS '30—MS '32—'37-39 (Cornell U). Author: The Nutrition of Trout, published annually by NY State Conservation Department. Asst chief branch game fish and hatcheries US Fish and Wildlife Service Washington since '45. Am Fisheries Soc—Limnol Soc—Am Chem Soc—AAAS. Fish and Wildlife Service, Washington 25.†

18 TURK, John Graham. Paper technology; Packaging of glass containers. b'16. BS '39 (U Tex); MS '41—PhD '43 (Inst Paper Chem). Research packaging engr Glass Container Mfrs Inst NY since '47. Am Chem Soc—Tech Assn Pulp & Paper Ind—Tau Beta Pi. Preston Laboratories, Box 149, Butler, Pa.†

19 TURK, Lon B(enjamin). Petroleum (Geology). b'07. Student '26-27 (Okla A&M Coll); AB '32—AM '33 (U Wis). Development Lap-Out Maps depicting manner burial paleo-surfaces for determination petroleum and gas fields. Author articles: What is the best approach to the problem of oil and gas discovery?; Significance and use of lap-out maps in prospecting for oil and gas. Asst chief geol Peerless Oil and Gas Co Tulsa Okla '28-30; cons petroleum geol and engr since '33. Am Assn Petroleum Geols—Am Geophys Union—Okla City Geol Soc. 808 First National Bldg., Oklahoma City 2.

20 TURNBAURE, Frederick Stewart. Mining geology (Bolivia, Peru). b'99. BS '21 (U Wis); '22-23 (Stanford); MA '31—PhD '33 (Harvard). Author articles in field. Chief geol tin mines Bolivia '27-30, '33-37; cons geol M Hochschild, SAMI La Paz '42-47; asso prof University Mich dept geol '45-51, professor since '51. American Inst Mineral and Metall Engineers—Society Econ Geol—Geol Soc Am—Pan-Am Inst Mining Engring and Geol—Emmons Memorial(F) '31-32. Department Geology, University of Michigan, Ann Arbor.†

21 TURNER, (Henry) Arlin. American literature (Hawthorne, Poe, G. W. Cable). b'09. BA '27 (W Tex State Coll); MA '30—PhD '34 (U Tex). Author: A Note on Poe's Julius Rodman '30; Autobiographical Elements in Hawthorne's The Blithedale Romance '35; Another Source of Poe's Julius Rodman '36; Hawthorne's Literary Borrowings '36; A Note on Hawthorne's Revisions '36; Hawthorne as Self-Critic '38; Hawthorne's Methods of Using His Source Materials '40; George W. Cable's Literary Apprenticeship '41; Sources of Poe's A Descent into the Maelstrom '47; Whittier Calls on George W. Cable '49. Instr to prof Eng La State U '36-53; prof Am lit Duke since '53. Modern Lang Assn—S-Central Mod Lang Assn. Guggenheim(F) '47-48. Department of English, Duke University, Durham, NC.

22 TURNER, Arthur W(illiam). Farm commodities storage; cotton mechanization; insect pests (control). b'94. Student '12-13 (Hamline U); BS '17-23-25 (Ia State Coll). Research on conditioning and storing farm commodities; beltwide cotton mechanization; transport storage; electric control insect pests; agricultural airplane and equipment; animal shelters; engineering aspects of rural farm industries. Author: (with Elmer J Johnson) Machines for the Farm, Ranch and Plantation '48. Author articles: The Impact of mechanization on agriculture; Agriculture and the Engineer; Agricultural engineering on the March; and others. Extension agrl engr Ia State Coll '19-23; asso prof agrl engring Ia State Coll '23-27; ed Consumer relations dept Internat Harvester Co '27-41, ednl adv '41-44; asst chief and dir agrl engring research Bur Plant Ind US Dept Agr since '44. Am Soc Agrl Engrs(F, pres '43-44, vp '36-37—Am Soc Engring Edn—Instrument Soc Am—Tau Beta Pi—AAAS. Room 225, N. Laboratory, Agricultural Research Center, Beltsville, Md.

23 TURNER, Charles Wesley. Milk secretion; Endocrinology of domestic animals. b'97. BS '19—PhD '27 (U Wis); AM '21 (U Mo). Developed conversion factors to equalize production records made at various ages; initiated studies concerning the hormones capable of experimentally inducing growth and lactation of the mammary gland comparable to that during recurring estrus cycles, pregnancy and lactation; discovered the role of the two ovarian hormones, estrogen and progesterone in mammory gland growth; discovered the mammogenic hormone of the anterior pituitary which directly stimulates mammary gland growth. Patents on synthesis of thyroprotein and its use. Author articles in field. Prof dairy husbandry U Mo since '37. Am Dairy Sci Assn—Am Soc Animal Production—Poultry Sci Assn—Asso Study Internal Secretions—Soc Exptl Biol and Med—Am Assn Anatomists. Received the Borden award in dairy production by the Am Dairy Sci Assn '40. Department Dairy Husbandry, University of Missouri, Columbia, Mo.†

24 TURNER, Claude Allen Porter. High dam construction; Power development; Bridge construction. b'69. CE '90 (Lehigh U). Author: Elasticity, Structure and Strength of Materials; Natural Philosophy of the Science of Physics, Chemistry and Engineering '47; Educational and Industrial Problems with Intermolecular Forces Analyzed in Engineering, Physics and Chemistry '48; A Research in Natural Phenomena '51. Asst engr Pottsville Iron & Steel Co '96; asst engr Gillette-Herzog Co Minneapolis '97-00; engr western contracting dept Am Bridge Co Minneapolis '01; cons practice since '01. 1007 Delaware Av., Columbus 1, Ohio.†◉

25 TURNER, Edward Henderson. Weighing equipment and weights. b '04. Engaged in maintainance and repair of precision laboratory weighing equipment and weights since 1952. 79 Kenneth Pl., New Hyde Park, N.Y.

26 TURNER, Fred Harold. Student personnel administration. b'00. BA '22—MA '26—PhD '31 (U Ill). Asst dean men U Ill '22-31, acting dean '31-32, dean '32-43, dean students since '43. Nat Interfrat Conf—Nat Assn Deans and Advisers of Men—Phi Delta Kappa. 152 Administration Bldg., Urbana, Ill.†◉

27 TURNER, Harry Jackson, Jr. Biology (Marine and shellfish); Marine fouling prevention. b'15. BA '35 (Yale Coll); MS '42 (Yale U). Author articles in field. Marine research Woods Hole Oceanographic Inst '44-46, research asso biol '46-47, shellfish biol since '47. Am Micros Soc—Am Soc Limnol and Oceano. Woods Hole Oceanographic Institute, Woods Hole, Mass.†

10 TURNER, Lewis McDonald. Illinois River valley (Plant ecology); Pines (Ecology and growth rate); Arkansas (Trees); Forest soils; Curricula in forestry; Wildlife management. BS '98. BS '23—MS '25 (Ill); PhD '31 (U Chicago). Research and writings plant ecology lower Illinois River valley; field study relationship physical structure of soil profile to distribution forest types and growth selected species especially loblolly and yellow pine seedlings and mature trees; forest types and distribution trees in Arkansas. Research and adminstrn up-stream flood control surveys US Forest Service '37-43; dean sch forest, range and wildlife management Utah State Coll since '43. AAAS(F)—Ecol Soc Am—Soc Am Foresters—Am Soc Range Management—Am Forestry Assn—Ill Acad Sci—Utah Acad Sci—Sigma Xi—Phi Delta Kappa—Phi Kappa Phi—Xi Sigma Pi. School of Forest, Range, and Wildlife Management, Utah State Agricultural College, Logan, Utah.

11 TURNER, Lynn Warren. American history (New Hampshire 1760-1820, William Plumer); United Brethren in Illinois. b'06. AB '27 (Ind Central Coll); MA '32 (Ind U); PhD '43 (Harvard U). Research on New Hampshire in the American Revolution, Indiana University '31-33, Harvard University '34-36; biography of William Plumer, Library Congress and other libraries '37-41; commissioned to write the history of United Brethren church in Illinois. Author articles: The United Brethren Church in Illinois; William Plumer, Statesman of New Hampshire 1780-1820; and others. Asst hist dept Ind U '32-33; asst hist dept Harvard U '35-36; chmn dept hist Monmouth Coll, Ill '36-47; exec dir Ind War Hist Commn Bloomington, asst prof hist Ind U since '47. AHA—Miss Valley Hist Assn—Ill State Hist Soc—Ind Hist Soc. Indiana War History Commission, Indiana University, Bloomington, Ind. H: Route 10.†

12 TURNER, Neely. Insecticides; Economic entomology. b'01. BS Agr '22—MA '23 (Mo U). Research in secticide toxicology, insects affecting field and cultivated crops, insect control techniques, Mexican bean beetle control, investigations on the control of the European corn borer. Author articles in field. Chief entomol and asst dir Conn Agrl Exptl Sta since '52. Am Assn Econ Entomol—Sigma Xi. Connecticut Agricultural Experiment Station, New Haven 4.†

13 TURNER, Thomas Wyatt. Plant growth, diseases and relation to environment. b'77. AB '01—AM '05 (Howard U); PhD '21 (Connell U). Author articles in field. Head dept biol Hampton Inst '24-45, prof emeritus since '45. AAAS (F and life mem)—Bot Soc Am—Va Acad Sci. 18 Tyler St., Hampton, Va.

14 TURNER, William De Garmo. Plastics; Water (Treatment); Air (Treatment); Glass (Tech). b'89. PhB '05 (Morgan Park Academy Illinois); BS '09—PhD '17 (Chicago U). Head Bakelite research at Columbia '27-45; colloid chemistry of water supply and industrial water supply; other projects in field. Bur of Chem, Dept Agr '09-10; commercial analyst Armour and Co '10-14; asst in chem Chicago U '14-

15, asso '15-17; asso prof Mo Sch Mines Mo U '17-18, prof and dept head '18-29; asst prof chem engring Columbia '29-45; cons chem engr; tech dir Airkem Inc, Fla Chem Research Inc since 45; tech engr Bermuda Water Works. Am Inst Chem Engrs—Am Pub Health Assn—Soc Plastics Ind—Soc Chem Ind—Am Waterworks Assn—Am Chem Soc—Sigma Xi. AAAS(F)—Am Inst Chemists(F). 241 E. 44th St., NYC 17.†©

15 TURNER, William F(ranklin). Entomology; Insect vectors of plant virus diseases (phony peach). b'87. BS '08 (Mass Agr Coll). Research vectors of virus diseases of stone fruits, peach yellows, peach rosette; discovery of vectors of phony peach '48. Author articles in field. Instr entomology Ala Poly Inst, asst entomologist Expt Sta '08-13; entomol asst Bur Entomology US Dept Agr '13-16; asst entomologist Ga State Bd Entomology '16-23; hort agt Central of Ga Ry 23-29; agt Bur Plant Industry US Dept Agr control phony peach disease '29-36, entomologist since '36. AAAS(F)—AAEE—ESA. U.S. Hoticultural Field Laboratory, Fort Valley, Ga.

16 TURNEY-HIGH, Harry Holbert. American ethnology; Criminal investigation; Primitive war. b'99. AB '22 (St Stephen's Coll); MA '24—PhD '28—fellow sociology '24-25 (U Wis); fellow '24-28 (Wis State Bd Charities and Corrections). Author: The Flathead Indians of Montana '37; Ethnography of the Kutenai '41; The Practice of Primitive War '42; The Principles of Primitive War '48; General Anthropology '49; also articles in field. Editor: The Hagen Site '42. Asst prof U SD '25-26; acting prof DePauw U '26-27; prof anthropology and sociol, chmn dept econs and sociol U Mont '27-46; prof and head dept anthrop and sociol U SC since '46. Am Anthropol Assn(F)—AAAS—So Sociol Soc—Phi Beta Kappa. Knight, Order of Orange-Nassau (Netherlands). Dept. of Anthropology and Sociology, University of South Carolina, Columbia, S.C. H: 2 Gibbes Court.

17 TURNQUIST, Orrin C(linton). Horticulture; Potatoes (Breeding, production); Vegetable crops. b'13. BS '37—MS '40—PhD '51 (U Minnesota). Agt US Dept Agr Potato Breeding Div Hort U Farm St Paul '43-45; hort and instr Northwest Sch & Expt Sta U Minn Crookston Minn '45-47, instr gen hort forestry bot biology and related subjects in charge all horticulture projects at Branch Sta; research fellow hort Div of Horticulture U Farm St Paul '47-48; hort potato breeding; US DA St Paul '48-49; now coordinator of potato breeding in N Central Region US, ext horticulturist since '49, asso prof agr ext. Sigma Xi—Minnesota State Hort Soc—Am Assn for Hort Sci—Am Potato Assn—Xi Sigma Pi—Alpha Zeta—Gamma Sigma Delta—Gamma Alpha. Division of Horticulture, University Farm, St. Paul.

18 TURRELL, Franklin Marion. Chemical botany; Citrus physiology; Leaf and fruit surface; Radio-active tracers. b'05. BE '29 (E Ill State Coll); MS '32—PhD '35 (Ia U); summer '36 (Ia State Coll, Harvard); '42 (Riverside Coll); '43-44 (Calif Inst Tech). Developed apparatus as colorimeters, photomicrographic cameras, microscope stage heaters; plant mensuration, methods of measuring internal surface of foliage leaves, fruit surfaces, pigments, tree surface and height; analyzed plant products, chlorophyll, lignin, vitamins, colorimetry, spectrophotometry; research on light, radiation, radioactive isotopes, effects of artificial light and hormones on plant growth, granulation of citrus fruit,

water spot, injury by sulfur dusts, indsl gases, disease resistance, systemic insecticides. Author: Tables of Surfaces and Volumes of Spheres and of Prolate and Oblate Spheroids, and Spheroidal Coefficients '46; also articles Graduate assistant batany Ia University '31-32, research asst '33-35; instr plant physiol Cincinnati U '35-36; jr plant physiologist Calif U Citrus Expt Sta '36-42, asst '42-48, asso plant physiol since '48, chmn Radioactive Tracer Seminar '46-47. AAAS(F)—Sigma Xi—Botanical Soc—Am Soc Plant Physiology—Am Soc Hort Sci—American Chem Soc—Am Biol Soc. Univ. of California Citrus Experiment Station, Riverside, Calif. H: 3574 Bandini Av.

19 TURYN, Alexander. Classical philology (Greek, Latin, Aeschylus, Pindar, Sappho, Sophocles). b'00. PhD '23 (U Warsaw); '23-24 (U Berlin). Author: Studia Sapphica '29; De Aelii Aristidis codice Varsoviensi atque de Andrea Taranowski et Theodosio Zygomala '29; De codicibus Pindaricis '32; The Manuscript Tradition of the Tragedies of Aeschylus '43; The Manuscripts of Sophocles 44; Pindari Epinicia (critical edition) '44; also articles in field. Research fellow and lecturer Greek lit U Mich '41-42; prof classics U Ill since '45. Polish Acad Letters and Scis, Cracow (corr)—Am Philol Assn—Archeol Inst Am—Polish Inst Arts and Scis in Am—Assn Guillaume Bude, Paris—Soc Byzantine Studies, Athens. Decorated Golden Cross of the Greek Order of the Phoenix '34. 801 S. Maple St., Urbana, Ill.

20 TUTHILL, Charles Carr. Southeastern Arizona archeology. b'13. BA '35—'35-36 (U Ariz). Author: The Tres Alamos Site on the San Pedro River Southeastern Arizona. Co-author: An Archeological Site Near Gleeson Arizona. Archeologist Amerind Foundation Inc Dragoon Ariz '38-47; curator San Diego Museum of Man '47-52; sr lab asst Aquarium Mus, U Cal Scripps Instn Oceanography. Scripps Institution of Oceanography, La Jolla, Cal.

21 TUTHILL, Harlan L(loyd). Plasticizers; Drugs (Properties, quality control). b'17. BS '39 (Houghton Coll); PhD '43 (Cornell U); '47 (U Pa, Temple U). Research on physical and chem properties monomeric and polymeric plasticizers for lacquers, physical and chemical properties drugs and their correlation with therapeutic activity. Research chem Rohm & Haas Co '43-46; head phys chem lab Smith Kline & French Lab '46-48, plant tech dir since '48. ACS—AAAS—Sigma Xi—Am Pharm Assn (Ebert award Certificate of Merit '50)—Am Drug Mfrs Assn (research and development sect, contact com). 1530 Spring Garden St., Phila 1.

22 TUVE, Rosemond. Renaissance literature. b'03. BA '24 (U Minn); MA '25—PhD '31—scholar and fellow '24-26 (Bryn Mawr); Bryn Mawr and AA UW European fellow '28-29 (Somerville Coll Oxford Eng); (Johns Hopkins). Research in British Museum, Bodleian Library and Bibliotheque Nationale. Author: Seasons and Months; Studies in a Tradition of Middle English Poetry '33; Googe's Zodiake of Life '47; Elizabethan and Metaphysical Imagery: Renaissance Poetic and Twentieth Century Critics '47 (British Academy Crawshay Award, '49); also articles in field. Teacher Goucher Coll '26-28, Vassar Coll '29-32, Conn Coll since '34. Mod Lang Assn—Phi Beta Kappa—Amer Soc for Aesthetics. Connecticut College, New London, Conn.

23 TWEITO, Thomas E(lmore). American history (Western United States, pioneer histry, American foreign relations). born '05. AB '27 (St Olaf Coll); AM '36—PhD '39—fellow '37-38 (State U Ia). Author articles in field. Prof hist, govt Morningside Coll since '40, dean since '46. State Hist Soc Ia—Miss Valley Hist Assn—AHA—Nat Edn Assn. Morningside College, Sioux City 20, Ia.

10 TWENHOFEL, William Henry. Sedimentation; Stratigraphy; Paleontology. b'75. BA '04 (Nat Normal U, Lebanon O); BA '08—MA '10—PhD '12 (Yale); DSc (hon) '47 (U Louvain, Belgium). Author articles in field. Asst to asso prof geology U Kan '10-16; state geologist Kan '15-16; asso prof geol U Wis '16-21, prof '21-40, chmn dept since '40, retired '45; chmn sedimentation com Nat Research Council '23-41, div geol and geog '31-34, paleoecology '34-37; vis prof Yale spring '47, U Tulsa spring '48, '50. Geol Soc Am—Paleontol Soc Am—AAAS—Wis Acad Sci—Am Assn Petroleum Geol(hon)—Soc Economic Paleontol and Mineral (pres '35, chmn research com since '38, hon mem)—Sigma Xi—Phi Beta Kappa—Phi Kappa Phi. R.F.D. 3, Woodsmere, Orlando, Fla.◉

11 TWITCHELL, Karl Saben. Saudi Arabia mines; Minerals; Yemen. b'85. BSc '08—ME '09 (Queens U Kingston Ontario). Mine surveying and examinations including development in western states '08-15; mines and oil examinations in Portugal '21-25; minerals examinations in Ethiopia '25-26; negotiated first mining concession in Saudi Arabia '34. Author: Saudi Arabia '47; also articles in field. Cons Saudi Arabian Mining Syndicate Ltd since '44; vp Am Eastern Corp since '46; tech advisor Saudi Arabian Govt since '48. Am Inst Mining & Metall Engrs—Inst Mining & Metall (London)—Am Geog Soc—Royal Central Asian Soc (London). American Eastern Corporation, 30 Rockefeller Plaza, NYC 20.

12 TYLER, David Budlong. Maritime history. b'99. AB '21 (Williams Coll); AB '26 (Oxford U); MA '29—PhD '39 (Columbia U). Author: Steam Conquers the Atlantic '39; also articles in field. Professor hist Wagner Coll since '52. USN '43-45; office Naval Records, asst historian US Maritime Commn '46-47. Wagner College, Staten Island 1, N.Y.

13 TYTELL, Martin K. Typewriters (Foreign Language). b'14. Grad (St. Johns U); student (NYU). Development foreign language typewriter keyboards; special purpose typewriters. With Tytell Typewriter Co NYC. Tytell Typewriter Co., Inc., 123 Fulton St., NYC.

U

14 UBER, Fred M(urray). Transducers (Underwater sound); Biophysics (Radiation effects); Absorption spectra. b'05. AB '26 (Dickinson Coll); MA '28 (Syracuse U); PhD '31—Whiting fellow (U Calif); Rockefeller fellow (U Minn). Editor Biophysical Research Methods '48. Author articles in field. Physicist Navy Electronics Lab San Diego since '48; prof physics Ia State Coll '46-48. Soc Exptl Biol and Med—Genetics Soc Am—Am Phys Soc—Am Soc Naturalists—AAAS—Acoustical Soc Am—Sigma Xi. U.S. Navy Electronics Laboratory, San Diego 52, Calif.†

15 UDIN, Sophie A(da). Israel; Zionism; Palestine. b'96. BS '28—MS '29 (Columbia). Delegate of labor bloc 19th Zionist Congress Lucerne Switzerland '35; administrative committee Jewish Agency for Palestine, American Jewish Congress, Keren Hayesod. Editor: Palestine and Zionism since '46; Palestine Year Book (vols I to III)

'44-48. Dir Govt Archives and Library Hakirya Israel. ALA—Special Library Assn—Jewish Librarians Assn. Zionist Archives and Library of Palestine Foundation Fund, 41 East 42nd St., NYC 17.

16 UHLENHUTH, Eduard (Carl Adolph). Cadaver (Laboratory uses); Human pelvis. b'85. PhD '11 (U Vienna). Chairman Maryland State Anatomy Board; study methods disposal unclaimed human bodies in interests usefulness to society. Faculty U Md Med Sch since '25, prof anatomy and head dept gross anatomy '34-49, head dept anatomy since '49. AAAS(F)—Am Assn Anatomy—Soc Exptl Biol and Med—Harvey Soc—Marine Biol Labs Woods Hole Mass—U Md Biol Soc (past pres). 4115 Westview Rd., Balt 18.◉

17 UHLER, Francis Morey. Food habits of North American birds; Propagation of aquatic plants. b'02. AB '24 (Gustavus Adolphus Coll); '26-28 (George Washington U). Author articles in field. Biol US Dept Interior Fish and Wildlife Service in the development of waterfowl feeding and breeding grounds since '40. Washington Acad Sci—Washington Biol Field Soc (past pres)—Wildlife Soc—Am Ornithol Union—Cooper Ornithol Club—Wilson Ornithol Club—Am Soc Mammalogists—Soc Ichthyologists and Herpetologists—Limnol Soc—Phycological Soc—Am Soc Plant Taxonomy—Nat Hist Soc Md. U.S. Fish and Wildlife Service, Patuxent Research Refuge, Laurel, Md.

18 UHLER, John Earle. English and American literature (History, eighteenth century drama, Shakespeare, J P Kennedy); Philology (Etymology, logic of grammar); History of Near East (Egypt, Palestine, East Africa); Communism (History, principles); Music (Pasquale Amato). b'91. '05-09 (Baltimore City Coll); AB '13—AM '24—PhD '26 (Johns Hopkins U); '13-14 (Princeton U). Author: Review of English Grammar '26, rev '35; John Pendleton Kennedy's Novels and His Posthumous Works; Fonetics and Democracy. Co-author: English in Business (with J C French) '25. Prof English La State U since '28. Modern Lang Assn Am. Peabody prize, Frederick Raine medal, Bancroft medal. 4527 Highland Rd., Baton Rouge.

19 UHLIG, Herbert H(enry). Corrosion of metals; Metallurgy; Electrochemistry. b'07. ScB '29 (Brown U); PhD '32 (MIT). Editor: Corrosion Handbook '48; also articles in field. Professor charge corrosion lab MIT '36-40 and since '46. American Acad Arts and Sciences—Electrochem Soc—Nat Assn Corrosion Engrs—Am Chem Soc—Am Inst Mining and Metall Engrs—Am Soc Metals—Sigma Xi. Department of Metallurgy, Massachusetts Institute Technology, Cambridge, Mass.†

20 UHRICH, Jacob. Social behavior of animals (Albino mice); Animal parasites (Fox squirrels, quail, crows, meadow-larks). b'09. Student '28-30 (Redfield Coll); BA '32 (Doane Coll); MA '34 (U Neb); PhD '37 (U Chicago). Author articles in field. Prof biol and chmn dept biol Trinity U since '46. AAAS—Am Soc Zool. Trinity University, San Antonio, Tex.

21 UICKER, John Joseph. Heat transfer; Ventilation; Air conditioning. b'05. BS '31—ME '35 (U NH); MS in mech engring '43 (Pa State Coll). Instr mech engring U NH '31-37, Pa State Coll '37-40; successively instr, asst prof, asso prof, prof U Detroit since '40, dir mech engring dept, dir engring shop since '43; private cons heating and

air conditioning since '40. Engring Soc Detroit—ASME—Soc Automotive Engineers—Am Soc Heating and Ventilating Engrs—Am Soc Engring Edn—Mich Soc Profl Engrs—Tau Beta Pi—Pi Tau Sigma—Phi Kappa Phi. 16261 Littlefield Av., Det 35.†◉

22 UKERS, William Harrison. Tea, coffee and spices (Industry, advertising, production, supply sources, producing and consuming countries relations); Business (Advertising principles and standards). b'73. Student Central High School, Phila); BA '93—MA '22. Authority on tea, coffee, spices and related products; international sources of supply, planting, preparing and marketing, publicity; promoter of good will between tea and coffee producing and consuming countries; authority on standards advertising practice for trade papers. Author: All About Coffee '22-35 (awarded gold medal Brazilian Centennial Expn '23); Little Journeys to Brazil, Japan-Formosa, India, Ceylon, Java-Sumatra, China '24-26; All About Tea '35; The Romance of Tea '36; The Romance of Coffee '48; Coffee Merchandising '24-30; The Tea and Coffee Industries '48. Editor: Tea and Coffee Trade Journal; contributor Encyclopaedia Britannica; department editor Standard Dictionary Co; founder Associated Business Papers Inc, and Audit Bureau Circulation Inc; editor, pub Tea & Coffee Trade Journal since '04. Authors' League of Am—Pan-Am Soc—Am-Brazilian Assn—China Soc. Bronze plaque for distinguished service journalism Assn Bus Papers Inc '26, Officer Southern Cross Brazil '36; Chinese Govt Order of Jade '37. 79 Wall St., NYC. H: 52 Gramercy Park.◉

23 UKKELBERG, Harry Gilbert. Agriculture research (Black stem rust of wheat, American native rubber plants, development of new crops and uses for wastes). b'98. BS '28—MS '32 (U Minn). Research on epidemiology of black stem rust of wheat in midwest and Mexico, dissemination and rate of fall of rust spores, identification of physiologic forms of rust; development of native plants especially goldenrod, as domestic source of rubber; development of new crops for South, new uses for farm crops and utilization of farm waste products. Author articles in field. Agt US Dept Agr '28-32; dir Edison Botanic Research Corp Fort Myers Fla '32-36; dir research Henry Fords Plantation Richmond Hill, Georgia, 1936-1949; soil conservationist Southeastern Tidewater Soil Conservation Service Expt Sta since '49. Am Phytopath Soc—Sigma Xi. Richmond Hill, Ga.

24 ULLSTRUP, Arnold J(ohn). Plant pathology (Nature and control of corn diseases, nature and inheritance of disease resistance, physiology of plant pathogenic fungi). b'07. BS '31—MS '32—PhD '34 (U Wis). Author: Studies on Variability of Pathogenicity and Cultural Characters of Gibberella Saubinetii '35; The Occurrence of Gibberella Fujikuroi var. Subglutinans in the United States '36; Histological Studies on Wilt of China Aster '37; Variability of Glomerella Gossypii '38; Two Physiologic Races of Helminthosporium Maydis in the Corn Belt '41; Further Studies on a Species of Helminthosporium Parasitizing Corn '41; Inheritance of Susceptibility to Infection by Helminthosporium Maydis Race I in Maize '41; Diseases of Dent Corn in the United States '43; Linkage Relationships of a Gene in Corn Determining Susceptibility to a Helminthosporium Leaf Spot '47. Fellow Rockefeller Inst for Med Research Princeton '35-36, asst '36; agt US Dept Agr Clemson SC '37-

38, Purdue U '38-41; asso pathologist Purdue U '41-45, pathologist since '45; pathologist (plant) P-4 Div Cereal crops and Diseases Bur Plant Industry US Dept Agr Purdue U Agrl Expt Sta. AAAS—Ind Acad Sci—Am Phytopathological Soc—Am Soc Agronomy—Sigma Xi. Department of Botany and plant Pathology, Purdue University Agricultural Experiment Station, Lafayette, Ind.

10 UMBACH, Herbert H(erman). English and American literature (Donne, sermons as literature). b'08. BD '29 (Concordia Sem); U scholar '29-30—U fellow '30-31—MA '30 (Washington U); PhD '34 (Cornell U). Author: The Easter Sermons of John Donne '34; The Prayers of John Donne '51; also articles in field. Instructor Eng, U Kan '31-32; instr to prof Eng Valparaiso U since '34. Mod Lang Assn Am—Index Soc Am—Am Folklore Soc. Valparaiso University, Valparaiso, Ind.

11 UMBLE, John Sylvanus. Amish culture; History of the Mennonites. b'81. AB '06—MA '28 (Northwestern U); '07, '13 (U Chicago). Research extinct Ohio Mennonite Churches '40-47; historian Ohio Mennonite Sunday School Conference '15-40; translation and publication Amish Manuscripts '30-45. Author: The Old Order Amish: Their Hymns and Hymn Tunes '39; Mennonite Pioneers '40; Ohio Mennonite Sunday Schools '41. Asso editor: The Mennonite Quarterly Review since '27. Contbr editor: Mennonite Life since '49. Head Eng dept, prof Eng lang and lit Goshen Coll '24-38, head dept speech '38-46, prof speech and Eng '46-51, prof emeritus speech and Eng since '51. Mennonite Hist Soc (sec '27-48)—Mennonite Research Fellowship (charter member). Goshen College, Goshen, Ind.†

12 UMBREIT, Wayne William. Enzyme chemistry; Bacterial metabolism. b'13. BA '34—MSc '36—PhD '39 (U Wis). Co-author: Manometric Techniques '45; also numerous articles in field. Head dept enzyme chem Merck Inst since '47. Am Chem Soc—Am Soc Biol Chemists—Soc Am Bacteriologists—Sigma Xi. Eli Lilly award in bacteriology '47. Merck Institute for Therapeutic Research, Rahway, N.J.†

13 UMSCHEID, Arthur George. International relations; British economic history 1850-1900. b'09. BA '32—MA '33—PhD '35 (U Ia). Author articles: Trade and Depression in Late Nineteenth Century England in Studies in British History '41; Historiography and World War II in the Social Studies (vol 34) '43. Instr hist St Ambrose Coll Davenport Ia '35-37; instr hist Creighton U Omaha Neb '37-40, asst professor '40-45, asso prof '45-50, professor of history since '50. Mississippi Valley Historical Assn—Phi Beta Kappa (pres Omaha Assn '45-48)—AHA—Fgn Policy Assn—Omaha Com Fgn Relations (sec). Creighton University, Omaha 2, Neb. H: 913 N. 50th St., Omaha 3.†

14 UNDERKOFLER, Leland Alfred. Fermentation, agricultural and food chemistry. b'06. AB '28—DSc '53 (Neb Wesleyan); PhD '34 (Ia State). Research in microbiology and fermentation chemistry, especially relating to practical and industrial fermentations (butanol-acetone, ethyl alcohol, butylene glycol, rare sugars, enzymes) and fermentative utilization of farm crops and agricultural wastes. Six patents on microbiological and fermentation subjects. Grad asst chemistry Ia State Coll '28-33; prof chemistry Westminster Coll Salt Lake City '33-35; instr chem '35-40, asst prof '40-44, asso prof since '44 Ia State Coll; chief chem DPC

alcohol plant Omaha Neb '44-45. Am Chem Soc—Am Assn Cereal Chemists—Inst Food Technologists. Chemistry Department, Iowa State College, Ames, Ia. H: 2004 Country Club Blvd.

15 UNDERWOOD, Edna Worthley. Languages (Russian, Chinese, Central and South American). b'73. Student (Garfield U Wichita Kan) (U Mich); LittD '19 (Latin-Am Inst Culture U Buenos Aires Argentina). Translation stories from Russian, Spanish, and Portuguese; reads 14 modern languages and one ancient; translations in entirety Flemish, Russian, Mexican, Haitian, and Japanese anthologies. Author: Note Book of a Linguist, and others. Translator: An Anthology of Mexican Poets; The Poets of Haiti; great poems of South America, Central America, and West Indian Islands; Tu Fu's Wanderer; Minstrel Under Moons of Cathay; The Slav Anthology; Moons of Nippon; Poets of Old Japan; Great African Poets, and others. Authors League Am—Modern Humanities Research Assn Eng—Royal Soc Arts Eng (F)—Archeol Inst Am—Soc Arts and Sci—Modern Lang Assn Am—Latin Am Inst Culture. Poets of Haiti gold insignia '35; Poets of Mexico silver medal '37; Inst France gold medal for introduction of Latin poets to English. Box 54, Hamilton Grange, NYC.

16 UNIKER, Thomas E. Training treatments (Epilepsy). b'80. Grad (St Marys NY) '02 (Bellevue Hosp NYC). Research on training treatment in epilepsy, mental content in epilepsy, organization first psychoanalytic sanitorium in America. Author: (with Dr L P Clark) Amentia; also articles in field. Dir Long Acre Bedford NY for care and study of epilepsy and mental arrest. Assn Advancement Psychoanalysis (auxiliary council)—Am Assn Mental Deficiency(F). Long Acre, Bedford, N.Y.

17 UPHAM, Charles Melville. Highway engineering (Design, construction, administration, traffic, economics). b'86. BS '08—MS '25 (Tufts Coll); CE '24 (U of NC). Engr Charles River (Mass) Basin Commn '08-09; resident engr Mass State Highway Comm '09-12; testing engr Coleman du Pont Rd, Del, '12-15, chief engr '15-17; chief engr Del State Highway Commn '17-21; chief engr N.C. State Highway Commn '21-26; cons engr one third of Central Highway in Cuba; engr-dir Am Road Builders Assn since '26; cons engr Md State Roads Commn '36-39; joint secretariat Construction League US '35; US del to Permanent Internat Road Congress, The Hague, '38. Inst Highway Engrs (London)—ASCE—Am Soc for Testing Materials (highway research bd, mem exec com)—Nat Research Council—L'Association Internationale Permanente des Congres de la Route—La Asociacion de Ingenieros y Arquitectos de Mexico—Nat Acad Science (dir highway research bd of Nat Research Council '23-26)—Wash Soc of Engrs—Inst Cons Engrs. Received Bartlett Award for outstanding achievement in highway work '46. 1635 Eye St. N.W., Washington.†◎

18 UPHOLT, William Martin. Chemical control of insects; Control of disease vectors and reservoirs; Insect toxicology. b'14. BS '35—MS '36—PhD '39 (U Calif). Author articles in field. In charge toxicology field sta, tech br Communicable Disease Center US PHS since '53. Entomol Soc Am—Am Soc Tropical Med and Hygiene—Pacific Coast Entomol Soc—RESA. Toxicology Lab., U.S.P.H.S., P.O. Box 73, Wenatchee, Wash.

19 UPPERMAN, Harry Lee. Religious education. b'95. BA '22—MA '28 (Syra-

cuse U); DD '29 (Simpson Coll Indianola Ia). Member general board education Methodist Church. Author: History and Evaluation of Secondary Schools of Methodism. Clergyman since '15; prof bible and English Dickinson Sem '22-23; pres Baxter Sem Tenn since '23. Tenn Acad Sci—NEA—Phi Beta Kappa—Phi Kappa Phi. Syracuse U George Arents Pioneer Medal for excellence in edn. Baxter Seminary, Baxter, Tenn.

20 UPSON, W. Harrison. Fibre board manufacturing. b'81. BS '04 (Wharton Sch Finance and Economy U Pa). Contbr to mags on bus subjects. Spl sales work W H Schoenau Co Buffalo '04-05; sales mgr Niagara Paper Mill Lockport NY '05-08; acting postmaster Lockport '08-10; organized The Upson Co '10, with br C A Upson, was sec-treas, now pres, mfrs Upson board and fibre specialties; pres The Upson Co of Del; sec-treas Cellulose Industries Inc; pres Tuco Workshops; dir Lockport Exchange Trust Co. Upson Point, Lockport, N.Y. H: 455 Locust St

21 UPTHEGROVE, Campbell Leon. England (History, modern). b'10. BS '32—MS '33 (Ind State Tchrs Coll); MA '37—PhD '41 (U So Cal). Research on mandates provided by Peace Conference of '19; studies on trusteeship agreements and system with relation to imperialism, relationship of Great Britain and Permanent Mandates Commission in creation of free and independent Iraq; investigation effect relationship of Great Britain and Mandates Commission regarding Palestine, and later transfer of Palestine to the United Nations; observations on function imperialism as an institution in China, Burma, and India. Author articles: The Future of the Mandate System in Africa '42; A History of the Relation of Great Britain with the Permanent Mandates Commission of the League of Nations. Prof hist Wilberforce U Wilberforce O '41-42 and '46-47, Langston U Okla '47-48; prof and head hist dept Tex So U since '48. AAAS—AHA—Far Eastern Assn—Am Polit Sci Assn—Miss Valley Hist Assn—Phi Alpha Theta. Texas Southern University, 3201 Wheeler, Houston 4. H: 3019 Isabella.

22 UPTON, Luther Jarvis, Jr. Heat treating; Chrome plating. b'14. BS in chem engring '37 (Lehigh U). Research on heat-treating low-carbon and tool steel parts; general plating of hard chrome for industrial uses. Chem engr and metall R J Reynolds Tobacco Co since '37. Am Soc Metals—Tau Beta Pi. R. J. Reynolds Tobacco Co., Research Dept., Winston-Salem 1, N.C. H: 2403 West 1st St., Winston-Salem 5.

23 URBAIN, Walter M(athias). Food chemistry. b'10. BS '31—PhD '34 (U Chicago). Engaged research and study physical chemistry as applied to foods, detergent action soaps, bacteriology green discoloration meats and spectrophotometric characteristics of pigments involved, absorption spectra FAC color standards, heme pigments cured meats, role of sugars in color of cured meats, use of enzymes in refractometric method for egg solids. Co-author: (with L B Jensen) A Delicate Test for Blood Pigments '36; (with D A Greenwood) An Application of the Van Slyke-Neill Manometric Gas Apparatus to the Determination of Oxygen Capacity of Dilute Hemoglobin Solutions '40; also articles in field. Research chemist Swift & Co Chicago '34-37, head div physics and physical chem '37-50, asst director of research since '50. American Chem Soc (dir Chicago sect '47-49)—Inst Food Technologists—Am Oil Chemists Soc—Physics Club Chicago—Sigma Xi—Phi Beta Kappa. Swift and Company, Union Stock Yards, Chicago 9. H: 4721 Woodland Av., Western Springs.

10 URBAN, Edward Charles Joseph. Industrial hygiene; Dusts (Industrial). b'10. BS in mech engring '35 (Northeastern U); MS in san engring '37 (Harvard Sch Pub Health). Research on industrial environments with emphasis on mining and other dusty trades to evaluate health hazards, ventilation, design and application methods for controlling or reducing possible health hazards, basic laboratory research on industrial respiratory diseases, study of physical and chemical characteristics air-borne particulate matter. Indsl hygiene engr Vt State Bd Health '37-40; indsl hygiene engr Saranac Lab Field Office and Saranac Lab since '40. AIMME—Am Pub Health Assn—Am Conf Gov Indsl Hygienists—Am Indsl Hygiene Assn—ASTM. Saranac Laboratory of Edward L Trudeau Foundation, 7 Church St., Saranac Lake. N.Y. H: 21 Birch St.

11 URBANIK, John G(eorge). Gyroscopes; Servomechanisms; Analog computers; Guided missiles. b'09. AB '31 (U Rochester); '44-45 (NYU). Research and design navigational, fire control, and bombing equipment for piloted and pilotless aircraft and surface vessels, research long range inertial navigation systems. Head electronics sect Perkin-Elmer Corp '48-50; head servo and gyro sect Fairchild Guided Missiles Div since '51. Phi Beta Kappa—Am Inst EE—Optical Soc Am—Inst Radio Engrs. H: 108 Rockville Centre Parkway, Oceanside, N.Y.

12 URDAHL, Thomas Harold. Air conditioning; Refrigeration; Drying; Preservation. b'02. Student '19-22 (Swarthmore Coll). Co-author: (with W C Whittlesey) Warship Ventilating, Heating and Air Conditioning '43, Designing Warship Ventilation with Standardized Equipment '43; (with John Everetts, Jr) Standardized Heating and Ventilating Equipment for Fighting Ships '43; (with E R Queer) Dehumidification Protects U. S. Navy's Inactive Fleet '46. Engr in private prac since '28. Capt USNR World War II charge air conditioning sect shipbuilding div Bur of Ships Navy Dept '41-46. Am Soc of Heating and Ventilating Engrs—Soc Naval Architects and Marine Engrs—Washington Soc Engrs—NEA—Am Soc Naval Engrs. 734 Jackson Place, Washington 6.†

13 USEEM, John. Micronesian ethnology; Acculturation. b'10. AB '34 (U Calif); '34-36 (Harvard); PhD '39 (U Wis); MA '44 (Columbia). Field research Rosebud Indian Reservation '43; Rockefeller Foundation Research Project Study of Acculturation '46-47; field research in micronesia Western Carolines Islands for US Commercial Company Reconstruction Finance Corporation '46, Palau Islands for Pacific Science Board National Research Council '48. Author articles in field. Asso prof sociology and anthropology U Wis '47-50; professor sociology and anthropology Michigan State College since '50. Served as US Naval Military Govt officer in Micronesia '44-45. Am Sociol Soc—Rural Sociol Soc—Am Anthrop Soc(F)—Soc Applied Anthropologists—Inst Pacific Relations—Phi Beta Kappa. Department of Sociology and Anthropology, Michigan State College, East Lansing.

14 UTLEY, Francis Lee. Middle English; Biblical folklore; Medieval woman. b'07. BA '29 (U Wis); AM '34—PhD '36—Dexter(F) '34 (Harvard).

Author: The Crooked Rib: An Analytical Index to the Argument About Women in English and Scots Literature to the End of the Year 1568 '44. Co-author: A Co-operative Research Project on a Dictionary of Political Words and Phrases '45; Ninth Supplement to Wells' Manual of the Writings in Middle English, 1050-1400 '51; also articles in field. Prof Eng Ohio State U since '47. Medieval Acad Am (exec council '51-53)—Linguistic Soc Am—Am Folklore Soc (pres '51-52)—Ohio Folklore Soc (pres '50)—American Dialect Society—Am Anthropol Assn—Modern Lang Assn—Ohio Acad Sci (F)—Calif Folklore Soc. Guggenheim fellow '46, '48, '52. Dept of English, Ohio State University, Columbus 10, O. H: 165 East Beechwold Blvd., Columbus 14.

15 UTTER, William Thomas. History of American frontier (Ohio); Diplomatic and economic history of United States. b'95. BS '21 (Northwest Mo Teachers Coll); MA '24—PhD '29 (U Chicago). Prof hist, chairman dept history Denison U since '29. Ohio Acad Hist (bd editors Hist of Ohio). Denison University, Granville, O.†

16 UYEHARA, Yukuo. Japanese language (Modern); Japanese literature. b '05. BA '31—MA '36 (U Hawaii); '33 (Waseda U). Research on history of Japanese literature especially in fields of poetry such as waka, haiku, senryu, songs, and drama; instruction in elementary and advanced Japanese; consultant Foreign Language Broadcast Intelligence Service '45-46. Author: Songs for Children Sung in Japan '40; Elementary Conversational Japanese '42; Military Japanese, A Manual in Japanese for the Armed Forces '43. Co-author: (with J F and Ella Embree) Japanese Peasant Songs '44; (with Shichiro Watanabe) A High School Text in Beginning Japanese '46. Contributor: Shipley's Encyclopedia of Literature (vol II) '46. With U Hawaii since '33, asso prof Asiatic lang and chmn dept Asiatic and Pacific Lang since '47; dir Marine Officers Lang Sch '41. Am Oriental Soc—Soc Japanese Studies—Far E Assn—Am Folklore Soc. University of Hawaii, Honolulu 14.

V

17 VAIL, Curtis C(hurchill) D(oughty). German literature (Eighteenth Century); Anglo-German literature. b '03. AB '24 (Hamilton Coll) AM '29—Carl Schurz fellow Germanic langs '30-31—PhD '36 (Columbia); '29 (U Munich Germany). Chairman German syllabus committee New York State '32-34, committee for accrediting teachers of German '33-38; examiner in German College Entrance Examination Board '37-38. Author: Lessing's Relation to the English Language and Literature '36, also articles in field. Compiler: Basic German Word and Idiom Lists '33; Scientific German for Science and Premedical Students '38; Graded German Short Stories '41. Head modern lang dept Massanutten Acad Woodstock Va '25-26; faculty dept German U Buffalo '27-39, asso prof '38-39; asso ed Germanic Quarterly '37-41, mng ed '42-45; prof Germanic lang and lit U Wash since '39; co-ed Modern Lang Quarterly since '40. Am Assn Tchrs German (pres '47)—AAUP—Modern Lang Assn Am—Mark Twain Soc—Modern Humanities Research Assn—Philol Assn Pacific Coast—Delta Phi Alpha. Department Germanic Language and Literature, University of Washington, Seattle 5.Ⓒ

18 VALEROS, Florentino B(ersamina). Filipiniana. b'08. BS (edn) '35—Univ tchrs certificate '35—MA '37 (U Wis). Research on folk tales, folksongs, Filipino writing in English and dialects, Filipino customs and superstitions. Co-editor: Philippine Cross-Section '50; Filipino Love Stories '52; Reading and Writing the Essay '52; Philippine Harvest '52. Prof Philippine lit and Oriental lit Nat Tchrs Coll and chmn div Eng since '46; lectr Eng U of East '49. Am Folklore Soc—Barangay Writers Project of Philippines—Philippine Assn U Prof—Philippine Philatelic Club. Division of English, National Teachers College, 629 Tanduay St., Manila, P.I. H; 15 Cebu Av., Near Homesite Roxas District, Quezon City, P.I.

19 VALLANCE, William Roy. Smuggling. b'87. AB '10 (U Rochester); '11-12 (Harvard Law Sch); LLB '14 (Columbia). Delegate to Conference on Border Smuggling El Paso Tex '25, to Conference to Suppress Smuggling London '26; counsel for US in arbitration between US and Canada of sinking of rum runner "I'm Alone," '29. With US Dept of State since '18. Am Bar Assn—Fed Bar Assn—Inter-Am Bar Assn(sec gen since '40)—Am Soc Internat Law—Columbia Hist Soc—Washington Criminal Justice Assn Incorporated (exec com)—Am Law Inst—Internat Law Assn—Internat Bar Assn (del to 2d conf The Hague '48)—Phi Beta Kappa. Order of the Sun of Peru by President Bustamente; Colegiado do Honor by College of Habana; citation for distinguished service in law and international relations University of Rochester '50. New State Dept. Building, Washington 25. H: 3016 43d St. N.W.

20 VALLEAU, William Dorney. Tobacco (Diseases, breeding). b'91. BS '13—PhD '17 (Minn U). Research on source of mosaic infection in tobacco, frenching of tobacco, virus diseases of tobacco and immunity. Discovered life history of tobacco wildfire organism; developed black root rot resistant varieties of Burley tobacco, also mosaic resistant types, wildfire resistant Burley and dark tobacco, low nicotine varieties of burley like tobacco used in manufacturing. Co-author articles: Angular Leaf Spot and Wildfire of Tobacco (with Johnson and Diachun) '43, and others. Plant path Ky Agrl Expt Station since '19. AAAS(F)—Am Phytopath Soc—Ky Acad Sci. Kentucky Agricultural Experiment Station, Lexington 29, Ky. H: 111 Dantzler Court.

21 VALLEY, George Edward, Jr. Electronics; Cosmic rays. b'13. SB '35 (MIT); PhD '39 (U Rochester). Research on artificial radioactivity, relative abundance of stable isotopes, properties of cosmic ray mesons, design of nuclear physics instruments. Patents pertaining to radar. Co-editor: Vacuum Tube Amplifiers (with H Wallman); Cathode Ray Tube Displays (with T Soller, M Starr); also articles in field. Research asst Mass Spectroscopy Harvard '40; sr staff MIT Radiation Lab '41-45, asst prof physics '46-49, asso prof since '49. Mem Sci Advisory Bd to Chief of Staff US Air Force since '45. Am Phys Soc(F)—Sigma Xi. Nat Research Council fellow '41. Massachusetts Institute Technology, Cambridge, Mass.†

22 Van ATTA, C(hester) M(urray). Nuclear physics; High vacuums. b'06. AB '29 (Reed Coll); PhD '33 (NYU); nat rsrch fellow '33-35 (MIT). Consultant on vacuum problems, Kinney Manufacturing Company, Boston since '37. Inventions related to mechanical vacuum pump design, magnetic submarine mine firing devices, certain aspects of electromagnetic separation of uranium isotopes. Author articles in field. Asst prof physics MIT '38-40; physicist Naval Ordnance Lab Washington '40-43; physicist radiation lab U Calif '43-46; prof physics, supervisor research in physics, chmn div phys sci and math, U So Calif '46-50, research physicist Radiation Lab U. California Berkeley since '50. AAAS(F)—American Phys Soc(F). Radiation Laboratory, University of California, Berkeley 4.

10 Van CLEAVE, Robert Franklin. Petroleum prospecting. b'11. '28-30 (De Pauw U); AB '33 (Wabash Coll); MS '35 (U Okla). Location of geological structure favorable for production oil by seismic prospecting methods, especially Gulf Coast area of Louisiana, Texas, Mississippi, and Alabama. Author article: Exploration for Oil in the Tidelands of the Gulf. Supervisor seismic exploration crews Nat Geophys Co '37-42 and '42-46; with Atlantic Refining Co since '46, regional geophysicist since '50. Soc Exploration Geophysicists—Am Assn Petroleum Geol—Sigma Pi Sigma. 923 Atlantic Bldg., Bryan and Bullington Sts., Dallas.

11 VANDALE, Earl. History of Texas and the Southwest; Southwestern cattle industry, fur trade, and outlaws. b'82. Student law '02-03 (V W Va). Collector historical items on Texas history. AHA—Miss Valley Hist Assn—Tex Folklore Soc—Bibliog Soc Am—Am Assn State and Local Hist US and Can—Panhandle-Plains Historicle Soc—W Tex Hist Assn—Tex State Hist Assn(F, pres since '49). Box 2546, Amarillo, Tex.

12 VANDEGRIFT, Rolland A. California history. b'93. BA '17—MA '21 —'23 (U Calif); Fellow Pacific Coast Hist '19-20—Traveling Fellow '21-22 (Native Sons of Golden West). Carried on research in Archives of Spain, France and England '21-22. Author articles in field. 445 Capitol Building, Sacramento.

13 Van DEMARK, Noland Leroy. Physiology of reproduction and artificial insemination of cattle. b'19. BS in agr '41—MS '42 (Ohio State U); PhD '48 (Cornell U). Research and teaching in physiology and biochemistry of reproduction in cattle with special emphasis on problems of semen production, fertility and artificial insemination, spermatozoan metabolism and the effect of conditions in the female on spermatozoa and fertility. Asst animal husbandry Ohio State U '41-42; research asst animal breeding Cornell U '42-44; livestock specialist with mil govt, planned and initiated artificial breeding program for Austria '46-47; asst prof dairy cattle physiology dept dairy sci U Ill '48-51, asso prof since 1951. AAAS— Am Dairy Sci Assn—Am Soc Animal Prodn—Sigma Xi—Gamma Sigma Delta. Department of Dairy Science, University of Illinois, Urbana, Ill.

14 VANDERKLEED, Charles Edwin. Drugs and medicines (Chemistry). b '78. PhG '95—PhC '96—BSc '99—AC '01 —DSc '34 (Purdue); PharmD '08 (Medico-Chirurg Coll Phila). Co-author: (with Julius W Sturmer) Course in Quantitative Chemical Analysis '98; (with Arthur L Green) Course in Qualitative Inorganic Chemistry '03. Contbr sect on Strychnos Alkaloids in Allen's Commercial Organic Analysis '12. Former vp, sci dir McNeil Labs Inc, now ret.; cons Nat Security Resources Board. Am Inst Chem(F)—ACS—Am Pharm Assn—AAAS—Nat Inst Social

Scis—Phi Zeta Delta—Beta Phi Sigma —Kappa Psi. 200 Harvard Av., Collingswood 7, N.J.†◎

15 VANDERPOOL, Eugene Ward. Stratigraphy (Insoluble residues); Petroleum geology. b'09. AB '33 (U Neb). Research on identification, correlations of sequences of limestone-dolomite facies of pre-Permian beds, involving microscopic examination of insoluble particles left following treatment of well bore cuttings with hydrochloric acid. Geol Stanolind Oil and Gas Co Midland Tex '39-41, sr geol '41-46; pre-Permian stratigraphy W Tex-New Mexico area Residue Research Lab since '46. Am Assn Pet Geol—West Tex Geol Soc. Residue Research Laboratory, P.O. Box 1406, Midland, Tex. H: 1804 W. Tex. Av.

16 VanDERSAL, William Richard. Soil conservation; Trees, shrubs. b'07. BA '29 (Reed Coll); MS '31—PhD '33 (U Pittsburgh). Author: Ornamental American Shrubs '42; The American Land, Its History and Its Uses '44; The Land Renewed. Co-author: The Land Renewed (with Edward H Graham) '46: Wildlife For America (with E H Graham) '49; also articles in field. Biologist, later chief of operations Pacific region United States Soil Cons Service since '35. Washington Acad Sci—Am Soc Plant Taxonomists—Soil Conservation Soc Am—Wildlife Soc. United States Soil Conservation Service, Ross Bldg., 5th and Pine S.W., Portland, Ore.†

17 van der SCHALIE, Henry. Malacology; Conchology. b'07. AB '29 (Calvin Coll); MS '31—PhD '34 (U Mich). Author articles in field. Curator mollusks Mus Zool U Mich since '44, asso prof zool since '50. American Malacology Union—Nederlansche Malacologische Vereeniging—Conchology Soc Gt Britain and Ireland—Malacology Soc London—Limnol Soc Am—Am Soc Zool —Mich Acad Sci Arts Letters (ed '43-47)—Phi Sigma. Walker prize natural hist '44 by Boston Soc Natural Hist. Museum of Zoology, Ann Arbor.†

18 VANDERVORT, Ellen Zink. Seed analysis; Plant ecology. b'10. BA '32 (State Teachers Coll Peru Neb); MS '43—'43-45 (U Neb). Author articles: Pasture Grasses '46; Annual Increase of Underground Materials in Three Range Grasses. Teaching fellow biol dept U W Va since '46. Neb Acad Sci —Ecol Soc Am—W Va Acad Sci—Bot Soc Am—So Appalachian Bot Assn— Sigma Xi. Weber-Ernest bot award U Neb '41; grantee from Neb Acad Sci '44-45. Biology Department, University of West Virginia, Morgantown, W. Va. H: 214, Rt. 4.

19 VANDER WAL, Robert John. Oils and fats; Chemistry of triglycerides and derivatives, furan, Grignards, mercurials. b'04. BS '27 (Central Coll Ia); MS '29—PhD '36 (Ia State Coll); '25 (U Minn). Research fatty acid derivatives, triglyceride fats and oils, fats and oils for edible and inedible uses, shortenings, salad oils, margarine oils, cutting and burning oils, development of oil emulsions for intravenous fat feeding, chemicals from fats such as adehydes, polymers, acyl halides, fat-soluble dyes, water-repellents for building materials, ketones, nitriles, amines. Author articles in field. Research chem E I duPont de Nemours and Co '29-31; research chem Armour & Co since '36, sect head since '48. Am Chem Soc— Am Oil Chem Soc—Am Inst Chem(F). Research Division, Armour & Co., Union Stockyards, Chgo. 9.

20 VAN DOLAH, Robert W(ayne). Propellants and explosives; Stereochemistry; Antibiotics. b'19. Fellow-

PhD '43 (O State U); AB '40 (Whitman Coll). Research on stereochemical resolutions of vasopressor amines, synthesis of racemic methol, isolation and purification of penicillin, streptothricin, and streptomycin, synthesis and evaluation of new propellant components and explosives, physical studies on propellant and explosive systems. Holds several patents in field. Head organic chem br research dept US Naval Ordnance Test Sta Calif since '46. Am Chem Soc—AAAS—Am Ordnance Assn—Phi Lambda Upsilon —Phi Beta Kappa—Sigma Xi. Room 1605 Michelson Laboratory, China Lake, Calif.

21 Van DOREN, Carl. American revolution and constitutional period (Benjamin Franklin); American literature; Jonathan Swift. b'85. AB '07 (U Ill); PhD '11—LittD '40 (Columbia); LHD '40 (U Pa). Author: The American Novel '40; Other Provinces '25; Swift '30; Sinclair Lewis '33; American Literature—An Introduction '33, reissued as What Is American Literature? '35; Three Worlds (autobiography) '36; Benjamin Franklin '38 (Pulitzer prize '39); Secret History of the American Revolution '41; Mutiny in January '43; The Great Rehearsal '48. Editor: Cambridge History of American Literature '17-21; Letters and Papers of Benjamin Franklin and Richard Jackson '47; The Portable Swift '48. Editor the Living Library since '46. 41 Central Park West, NYC 23.◎

22 Van DOREN, Lloyd. Chemist (Organic); Chemical patents (Causes and procedures). b'89. BS '09—MS '13 (Gettysburg Coll); PhD '12—Fellow Chemistry '11-12 (Johns Hopkins U). Author articles in field. Prof, head chem dept Earlham Coll Richmond Ind '14-19; chem adviser Emery Varney Blair and Hoguet NYC '19-20; cons chem and patent solicitor Chem Found Inc NYC '20-22; chem cons patents and patent causes Mayer Warfield and Watson NYC '22-29; mem patent div Allied Chem and Dye Corp NYC '29-31; chem cons patents and patent causes Watson Bristol Johnson and Leavenworth NYC since '31. Served as first lt chem warfare service US Army '18. Am Inst Chem (F, vp '23-29, chm NY chapter '28, sec since '45)—AAAS(F) —Am Chem Soc—Phi Beta Kappa. 100 Park Av., NYC 17.

23 Van DOREN, Mark. American and English literature; Poetry (Thoreau, Hawthorne, Dryden, Shakespeare). b'94. AB '14—AM '15 (U Ill); PhD '20 (Columbia); LittD '44 (Bowdoin). Author: Henry David Thoreau, A Critical Study '16; The Poetry of John Dryden '20; Shakespeare '39; The Noble Voice '46; Nathaniel Hawthorne '49; Collected Poems (awarded the Pulitzer prize for poetry) '39. Co-author: (with Carl Van Doren) American and British Literature since 1890 '39, and others. Editor of An American Bookshelf (5 vols) '27-28; Anthology of World Poetry '28; American Poets 1630-1930 '34. Prof Eng Columbia since '42; lecturer St John's Coll Md since '37. Nat Inst Arts and Letters. 393 Bleecker St., NYC 14.◎

24 Van DYKE, Karl Skillman. Piezoelectricity; Quartz crystals; Frequency control. b'92. BS '16—MS '17 (Wesleyan U Conn); PhD '21 (Chicago U). Author: School Recording Techniques '41. Co-author: (with Brown) Sound Recording Equipment for Schools; also articles in field. Expert cons, coordinator for quartz crystals Office Chief Signal Officer US Army '42-44; dir research Long Br Signal Lab Signal Corps Ground Signal Agency '44-45. Prof Wesleyan U since '28; asso dir division defense research U Cal at LA Point Loma '41-42. AAAS(F)—Am Phys Society(F)—Inst Radio Engrs (F)—Acoustic Soc Am—Phi Beta Kappa—Sigma Xi. Scott Laboratory, Middletown, Conn.

10 Van ENGEL, Willard A(braham). Life histories of aquatic animals (Population studies and ecology, Blue Crab). b'15. PhB '37—PhM '40 (U Wis); '42-43 (NYU). Author articles in field. Asso biol Va Fisheries Lab since '46. AAAS—Am Soc Limnol and Oceanog—Am Fisheries Soc—Wis Acad Sci Arts Letters—Va Acad Sci. Virginia Fisheries Laboratory, Gloucester Point, Va.

11 Van FLEET, Dick Scott. Plant anatomy (Physiological); Redox systems; Lipids. b'12. AB '36—AM '37—PhD '40 (Ind U); Sterling research fellowship '43-44 (Osborn Bot Lab Yale U). Research on redox behavior of endodermis in vascular plants '40-43, redox and related phenomena in the cortex of vascular plants '44, oxidases and lipids associated with anthocyanin '45, redox behavior of fat emulsions, peroxidase patterns in vascular plants '46-47, histochemical detection of endodermis in lower vascular plants '48. Author articles in field. Instr biol Heidelberg Coll '40-42, asst prof '42-43; asst prof bot Mo U '44-47, asso prof since '47. Bot Soc Am—Sigma Xi. Department of Botany, University of Missouri, Columbia, Mo.†

12 Van GELUWE, John. Agricultural insecticides, fungicides and herbicides. b'16. BS '39 (NY State Coll Agr). Formulations, basic laboratory evaluation, and field testing of insecticides, fungicides, and herbicides. Author articles in field. Dir research Soil Building Service div GLF Exchange Inc since '44. Am Soc Hort Sci—Am Assn Econ Entomol—AAAS—Am Phytopath Soc—North Central and North East Weed Control Conf Groups. GLF Soil Building Service, Division Cooperation GLF Exchange, Inc., Terrace Hill, Ithaca, N.Y.

13 Van HOESEN, Roy. Guinea fowl; Bantams. b'73. Student pub. schools. Author and pub: Hatching-Feeding-Rearing Bantam Chicks '51; Utility Side of Bantams '51; Cochin Bantams; Game Bantams; Wyandotte Bantams; Silkie Bantams; Polish Bantams; Japanese Bantams; Cornish Bantams; Guinea Fowl Culture; Sebright Bantams; Dubbing Poultry; others. Founder and ed Bantam mag. 43 Maple Av., Franklinville, N.Y.

14 Van HORN, Earl Carlton. Geologic exploration; Economic and engineering geology; Foundation treatment; Asbestos; Barite; Rutile; Talc; Pegmatite minerals. b'15. BS '37 (U NC). Author articles: Geology of the Talc Deposits of the Murphy Marble Belt, Carolina Barite Belt. Geol TVA '37-50; geol Hitchcock Corp '50-53. AIMME—Geol Soc Am—Mineral Society America—AAAS—N C Acad Sci—NC Geol Soc. Bailey & Van Horn, Minerals Consultants, Murphy, N.C.

15 Van HORN, Kent Robertson. Metallurgy (Aluminum). b'05. BS '26 (Case Inst Tech); MS '28—PhD '29 (Yale). Co-author: (G Sachs) Practical Metallurgy '40; (S Case) Aluminum Iron Monograph '53; also articles in field. Director Aluminum Research Labs Aluminum Co Am since '30; spl lecturer Case Inst Tech since '30. Am Soc Metals (pres '45)—Am Inst Mining and Metall Engrs—Am Soc Testing Materials—British Inst Metals—Am Indsl Radium X-Ray Soc (pres '46)—Soc X-Ray and Electron Diffraction. Freeport Rd., New Kensington, Pa.

16 Van HORN, Willis Martin. Stream and air pollution abatement; Stream biology (Pulp and paper industry). b'04. AB '27 (Milton Coll); AM '30—PhD '32 (U Wis). Research in effects of domestic and industrial waste pollution, methods of abating such pollution, general application of biological knowledge to technology of pulp and paper industry. Author articles: Possible Stream Pollutional Aspects of Mill Antiseptics, and others. Asst prof biol Alfred U '32-33· asst prof biol Lawrence Coll '35-42; research asst Inst Paper Chem '42-43; research asso since '42; limnol NY State Conservation Dept summer '30; sr aquatic biol Wis Bd Health summer '41. Tech Assn Pulp and Paper Industry—Am Fisheries Soc—AAAS—Sigma Xi—Gamma Alpha. Institute of Paper Chemistry, Appleton, Wis.

17 VAN HORNE, John. Spanish and Italian language and literature. b'89. AB '08 (U Va); AM '09—PhD '13 (Harvard). Cultural relations attache Am Embassy Madrid Spain '43-46. Author: Elementary Spanish Grammar (with Arthur Hamilton) '25; La Grandeza Mexicana de Bernardo de Balbuena '30; Bernardo de Balbuena, Estudio biografico y critico '40. Editor: Zaragoza by Benito Perez Galdos '23; Health-Chicago Italian series since '37 and others; also articles. Prof Spanish and Italian and head dept U Ill since '39. Modern Lang Assn Am (exec council '38-41)—Am Assn Tchrs Italian—Am Assn Teachers Spanish. Decorated Cavaliere della coroa d'Italia; Diploma of Honor Mexican Academy. 713 Pennsylvania Av., Urbana, Ill.

18 Van KIRK, K(eith) M(orehouse). Testing (Non-destructive). Student (U NC). Tests for material flaws with magnetic particles, fluorescent penetrant, and electrified particle; stress and design analysis with brittle laquers; use ultra sonic thickness measuring devices. Sales engr Magnaflux Corp '43-48, dist mgr since '48. Soc Automotive Engrs—Soc Non-Destructive Testing—Am Soc Quality Control —Engring Soc Detroit. Magnaflux Corporation, 6500 Russell St., Det 11.

19 Van LEER, Blake Ragsdale. Hydraulics. b'93. BS in elec engring '15 —ME '22—DEng hon '44 (Purdue U); MS in mech engring '20 (U Cal); Freeman traveling scholar for study hydraulics '27-28 (U Munich Germany); ScD hon '43 (Washington and Jefferson Coll). Water consultant National Resources Commission '36; chairman Georgia Ports Authority '45-48. Instr advancing to asst prof hydraulics U Cal '15-28; engr Byron-Jackson Pump Co '22-26; dean engring U Fla '32-37; Fla rep US Coast and Geodetic Survey '33-35; tech advr Fla Emergency Relief Adminstrn '34-35, Florida State Planning Bd '34-37; pres Ga Inst Tech since '44. With Engrs Corps AEF '17-19. ASME—Am Soc Engring Edn (council '33-36)—Soc Am Mil Engineers—Fla Engring Soc (vp '37-38) —NC Soc Engrs—Ga Engring Soc— Ga Soc Profl Engrs—Newcomen Soc— Tau Beta Pi—Sigma Xi—Sigma Tau— Eta Kappa Nu. Profl engr Fla, NC, Ga. 292 10th St. N.W., Atlanta.

20 Van LENNEP, William. Theatre and drama. b'06. BA '29—PhD '34 (Harvard). Research on a history of the English stage; asso editor Theatre Annual '45-46, editor since '47. Author: The Life and Works of Nathaniel Lee, Dramatist '33; The Reminiscenses of Sarah Kemble Siddons '42; also articles in field. Mem research staff Huntington Library San Marino Calif '38-39; instr eng Harvard '41-45, cur-

ator Harvard Theatre Collection since '40, lecturer theatre and drama since '46; lecturer Northeastern U since '48. Theatre Lib Assn—Modern Lang Assn. Fellow Folger Shakespeare Library Washington '37-38. Harvard College Library, Cambridge 38, Mass.

21 Van LIERE, Edward Jerald. Anoxia. b'96. AB '15—MS '17 (U Wis); MD '20 (Harvard); PhD '27 (U Chgo); LittD '47 (Med Coll Richmond Va). Tests on effect oxygen supply on functions of various organs of body. Author: Anoxia—Its Effect on the Body '42, also articles in field. Prof physiol U SD '20-21; prof WVa U since '21, dean med sch since '37; asso ed WVa Med Journ; ed bd Gastroenterology, Journ Applied Physiol, Am Journ Digestive Diseases and Nutrition. With San Corps AUS '18. Am Coll Physicians (F)—Am Physiol Soc—Soc Exptl Biol and Med—AMA—WVa Med Soc. 508 Jefferson St., Morgantown, W.Va.◎

22 Van LOO, Maurice. Paint technology. b'01. AB '21—MA (hon) '23 (Hope Coll); fellow '22-25—MS '23 (U Mich). Author articles in field. With Sherwin-Williams Co since '27, now dir paint research Chicago. Am Chem Soc —AAAS—Am Inst Chem(F)—Nat Assn Corrosion Engrs—Am Soc Testing Materials—Sigma Xi. Sherwin-Williams Co., 115 and Cottage Grove Av., Chicago 28.

23 Van METER, Robin Arnold. Shale oils. b'14. Student '32-35 (Parsons Jr Coll); '36-37 (George Washington U); '37-39 (Brooklyn Poly Inst); AB '40 (U Kan); '45-49 (U Wyo). Test molding and physical testing of plastics; research and control chemistry of natural rubber in both latex and dry forms, addition polymerization, shale oils. Author articles in field. Am Cyanamid Co '37-39; Holland-Am Plantations Corp '40-41; US Rubber Co '42-44; US Bur Mines since '45. Am Chem Soc. Petroleum and Oil-Shale Experiment Station, Box 621, Laramie, Wyo.

24 VANNAH, H(arold) P(erry), Sr. Chemistry of flax cellulose; Xanthation of wood pulp; Agriculture of Florida Everglades. Alginates and Carrageenates. born '91. AB '12 (Bowdoin Coll). Author articles in field. Co-inventor or inventor 11 patents on subjects of purifying carbon tetrachloride, staining wood, machine for treating peanuts, conditioning soil, viscose, and others. Dir plant research dept Cal Central Fibre Corp '41-49; research chem Algin Corp Am since '52. Am Chem Soc (v-chmn '47, chmn '48 Western Carolinas sect)—Phi Beta Kappa. Friendship, Me.

25 VAN NAME, Elmer Garfield. Fgn missions (Church); Forestry. b'88. LL B '12—grad study '15-16 (Temple U); LLD '34 (Grove City Coll). South Jersey counsel for Division of Foreign Missions of Methodist Church; New Jersey counsel for Fire Association of Philadelphia and affiliates. Am Forestry Assn. 300 Broadway, Camden, N.J.

26 VANNOY, Wesley Gabriel. Paints (Exterior). b'00. BS '22 (Coe Coll); MS '25—PhD '27 (Cornell). Research and development exterior exposure data pertinent to formulation improved exterior paint compositions; development testing procedures for evaluation exterior paints. Issued patent on silicate paints. Chem E I du Pont de Nemours & Co since '27. ACS—ASTM. E. I. du Pont de Nemours & Co., Pigments Dept., Newport, Del. H: 1104 Woodlawn Av., Wilmington, Del.

27 Van OOSTEN, John. Age and growth of fishes; Commercial fish-

675

eries of the Great Lakes. b'91. AB '18—AM '21—PhD '26 (U Mich); '14-16 (Calvin Coll). United States delegate International Fact Finding Commission Lake Champlain '29, International Board of Inquiry for the Great Lakes Fisheries '40-42; chairman Great Lakes Trout Committee '43-49, Great Lakes Sea Lamprey Committee '46-49; designer and builder of micro-projection machine widely used in reading and determining age of fish from scales. Author articles in field. Aquatic biol US Bur Fisheries US Dept Interior since '20, chief Great Lakes Fisheries Investigations '27-49; now fishery research biol Fish and Wildlife Service US Dept of the Interior; research asso dept zool U Mich since '46; adv council Better Fishing Inc since '46. AAAS(F)—Am Fisheries Soc—Soc Ichthol and Herpetol—Am Soc Limnol and Oceanog—Internat Soc Theoretical and Practical Limnol—Mich Acad Sci Arts Letters—Sigma Xi. University Museums Building, Ann Arbor.

10 Van ORMAN, Ward Tunte. Aeronautical engineering; Ballooning; Lighter-than-air craft. b'94. BS '17—ME '23—citation of honor '35 (Case Inst Tech). Winner five first places, two second places, two third places competing in 11 nat balloon races; winner three first places, one second place, two third places competing 10 Gordon Bennett international balloon races; first to land balloon on boat deck '25. Invented fabric process '28, air tight zipper '42, stratosphere pressure suit '42, new method oxygen therapy '43. Aeronautical engr Goodyear-Zeppelin Corp '18-30, dir ground sch '29-30; meteorol Internat Zeppelin Transport Corp '30-33; development engr Goodyear Tire and Rubber Co '33-42, research engr since '42. Internat League Aviators (hon)—Soc Plastic Engrs—Tau Beta Pi. Goodyear Tire and Rubber Company, Akron, O.

11 Van PATTEN, Nathan. Eskimo languages; Science bibliography; Rare books and manuscripts (Bibliography); Cryptology. b'87. Ed Union Classical Inst; LittD '36 (Dartmouth). Author: Bibliography of the Corrosion of Metals '23, 24; Literature of Lubrication '26; Cooperative Cataloging of the Medical Literature '26; Index to Bibliographies and Bibliographical Contributions Relating to the Work of American and British Authors ('23-32) '33; Printing in Greenland '29; also articles in field. Prof bibliog Stanford U since '47, lecturer chem dept since '28; lecturer U Calif Med Sch since '31; adviser World War Collection Yale U library; counsellor Hoover Library on War, Revolution and Peace. Library Assn (Gt Britain)—Zool Soc—ALA—Med Library Assn—Calif Library Assn—Oxford (Eng) Bibliog Soc—Inst Metals (London)—Philol Soc (London)—Bibliog Soc Am. Stanford University, Stanford, Cal.

12 VAN PELT, John Robert, Jr. Mineral resources; Mining engineering. b'96. AB '18—ScD '42 (Cornell Coll); BS '22—EM '23 (Mich Coll Mines); '26-28 (U Chicago). Conducted investigations of geology, mineral resources, and mining operations in Middle West and Rocky Mountain areas '27-45. Author articles in field. Instr, asst prof, and prof dept geol Cornell Coll '22-28; asst geol Ill State Geol Survey '27, asso geol '28-29; chief div geol mining and metall Mus Sci and Ind Chicago '28-30, asst dir mus '30-40, tech dir '40-45; dir research edn Battelle Meml Inst Columbus O '45-50; pres Montana Sch Mines Butte since '50. AAAS (F)—Am Inst Mining Metall Engrs (life, nat dir '41-44, nat vp '44-47)—

Am Soc Engring Edn (chmn mineral tech div '42)—Western Soc Engrs (trustee '34-40, vp '35-36, pres '36-37)—Tau Beta Pi—Sigma Xi—Phi Beta Kappa. 1315 W. Park St., Butte, Mont.

13 VAN PELT, John Vredenburgh. Painting; Writing; School architecture. b'74. Student Germantown Phila, Paris France; art and tech edn Ecole des Arts Decoratifs, Atelier Douillard-Thierry-Deglane of Ecole des Beaux Arts (1st Am to obtain values for diploma; awarded Architecte Diplome par le Gouvernement '95); post-grad study '95-97, '03-04 (Beaux Arts). Author: Essentials of Composition as Applied to Art '02, rev edit '13; Pencil Points Books; Monograph of W K Vanderbilt House; also mag articles. Asso dir Atelier Columbia U '04-13; prof design U Pa '14-17; charge Columbia U extension studios in architecture '23-27; lectr theory composition Columbia. AIA(F, emeritus)—Société des Architects Diplomes(life)—Museum City NY (chmn com on architecture)—Beaux Arts Soc(emeritus—Kappa Alpha. First medal in plan Beaux Arts '96, 2d medals for planning, medals in esquisse '97, '03, medal for modeling, Prix St Agnan Boucher '04; grand medal Société Centrale des Architectes (Fondation Destors) '97; grand medal Société des Architectes Deiplomes '96-97. Roe Boulevard West, Patchogue, L.I., N.Y.ⓒ

14 VAN PETTEN, Oliver W(illiam). Natural gas (Developmet, production, transportation). b'91. Student '09-13 (U Ill Coll Engring). Development of coal, oil and natural gas properties in Appalachian area. Vp, dir Columbian Carbon Co. Am Petroleum Inst—Ky Oil and Gas Assn—Alpha Delta Phi. Security Bldg., Charleston, W.Va.ⓒ

15 van RAVENSWAAY, Charles. Missouri history; Midwestern United States architecture; Furniture; Glass and prints. AB '33—MA '34 (Washington U). Editor: Missouri, a Guide to the Show Me State '41. Director Mo Hist Soc since '46. Phi Beta Kappa—Sigma Delta Chi—The Graphic Society (dir)—Nat Trust for Historic Preservation—Soc Archtl Historians. Misson Historical Society, St. Louis 12.

16 Van RENSSELAER, Maunsell. Culture of California plants; Ceanothus; Shade trees of the Pacific Southwest. b'97. AB '23 (U Calif). Author: Trees of Santa Barbara '48. Co-author: The Genus Ceanothus (awarded gold medal Garden Club of America) '43; also articles in field. Dir Santa Barbara Bot Garden '34-50; dir Saratoga Exptl Gardens since '50; lecturer Inst Natural Sci U Calif Santa Barbara Coll since '44; Santa Barbara bd park commns '39-50. Calif Historical Soc—AAAS—Calif Bot Soc—So Calif Hort Inst—Park Adminstrs So Calif—Western Shade Tree Conf—Nat Shade Tree Conf—Soc Am Foresters—Am Assn Bot Gardens and Arboretums (bd dirs since '47)—Bot Soc Am—Am Hort Soc—Am Inst Park Execs—Royal Hort Soc(F). Saratoga Experimental Gardens, Saratoga, Cal.

17 VAN ROYEN, William. Resources and geography of western and northern Africa; Arid and semi-arid regions. b'00. MA '25 (Rijksuniversiteit Utrecht); PhD '28 (Clark U). Traveled extensively throughout French West Africa, North Africa and the Sahara. Author: Fundamentals of Economic Geography (revised 50) '35; Low Countries between Great Powers '48; Forest Resources of West Africa '43; Forest Resources of East Africa '43; Survey of Natural Resources of Africa and their Availability '49; also arti-

cles in field. Under-sec Netherlands C of C '28-30; asst prof U Neb '30-40; asst prof Brooklyn Coll '40-44; chief timber unit, plant foods unit div supply and resources Bd Econ Warfare '42-44; prof U Md, dir research and ed Atlas of World's Resources since '44; sr staff mem Operations Research Office, dept army and Johns Hopkins U; collaborator USDA, cons Office QM Gen. Assn Am Geog—Am Soc Prof Geog(pres '45)—AAAS—Soc Geog Italiana—Netherlands Soc Econ Geog(corrections)—NRC(adv group to War Department)—Arctic Inst N Am. Operations Research Office, Fort Lesley McNair, Washington; also University of Maryland, College Park, Md. H: 226 Overlook Dr., Hillandale, Silver Spring, Md.

18 Van SANT, Robert Hays. Chlorophyll; carotene; Xanthophyll. b'85. BS '07-08 (U Cal Berkeley). Research on cultivation of chlorophyll, carotene, xanthophyll, processing, refining, metallic derivs, pharmaceutical chlorophyllins, food grades, feed grades, research grades, and technical and tobacco grades. Co-author: (with Eddy) Chlorophyll '50. Pres Van Ess Labs '20-30, Anacin Co '24-30, Am Chlorophyll Inc since '33. Soc Chem Industry—ACS. American Chlorophyll, Inc., Lake Worth, Fla.

19 Van SCHREEVEN, William J(ames). Virginia history. b'09. BA—MA '32 (U Ia); '33-34 (Columbia); '35 (U London). Author articles in field. State archivist Virginia State Library since '38. Soc Am Archivists (bd ed)—So Hist Assn—Phi Beta Kappa. Lydia Roberts Travelling fellow '35-36. Virginia State Library, Richmond, Va.†

20 Van SLYKE, Donald Dexter. Kidney physiol; Blood chem; Amino acids. b '83. PhD—ScD '25 (U Mich); ScD hon '26 (Yale); MD hon '38 (U Oslo Norway); ScD hon '40 (Northwestern U), '41 (U Chicago) '51 (U London). Studies physiology normal and pathological kidney; research on gases, proteins, and electrolytes of blood, and acidosis and acid-base balance of the body; chem, physiological, and pathological studies amino acids; kinetics and analyses by enzymes. Co-author: (with J P Peters) Quantitative Clinical Chemistry '31, also articles in field. Research chem and physiol Rockefeller Inst Med Research NYC '07-48; asst dir Brookhaven Nat Lab since '48. ACS—Am Soc Biol Chem(pres '22-23)—Harvey Soc(pres '28)—Nat Acad Sci—Physiol Soc Brit—Swedish Royal Soc Sci—Indian Acad Sci—Indian Soc Biol Chem—Soc de Pathologie Renale—Danish Soc Internal Medicine ACS Willard Gibbs medal '39; Assn Am Physicians Kober medal '42; Am Chem Soc Fisher Award '53. Brookhaven National Laboratory, Upton, N.Y. H: Belle Terre, Port Jefferson, L.I.

21 Van TIL, William. Curriculum; Social studies; Intergroup education; Youth hosteling; Fold-boating. b'11. A B '33—MA '35 (Columbia); PhD '46 (O State U). Author: The Danube Flows Through Fascism: Nine Hundred Miles in a Fold-Boat '38; Time on Your Hands '45; Econonic Roads for American Democracy '47. Editor: Democratic Human Relations '45; Intercultural Attitudes in the Making '47; Forces Affecting American Education '53. Co-author: Fold-boat Holidays '40; Americans All '42; Toward a New Curriculum '44; Teaching of American History '45; Leadership Through Supervision '46; Democracy Demands It '50; Education for Democratic Citizenship '52; Educational Freedom in an Age of Anxiety '53; and others.

Articles in field. Publs chmn Assn Supervision Curriculum Development since '53; social studies editor McGraw Hill since '48; sec nat edn com Am Youth Hostels '43-47; dir learning materials Bur Intercultural Edn '44-47; yearbook chmn Assn Supervision Curriculum Development '53, Nat Council Social Studies '45, John Dewey Soc '47; adv editor Ednl Theory '50-52, Progressive Edn since '48; chmn div curriculum and teaching George Peabody Coll Nashville. George Peabody College for Teachers, Nashville.†

10 Van TUYL, Andrew Heuer. Potential theory; Fluid mechanics; Plasticity; Soaps hydrolysis. b'22. AB. '43 (Fresno State Coll Cal); AM '46—PhD '47 (Stanford). Research in charge density on two spheres in presence of outside point charge; coefficients of capacity of two spheres; upper bounds for capacities of cube and finite circular cylinder; steady incompressible flow around family blunt-nosed halfbodies; Mach reflection of shock waves; plane plastic stress systems isometric principal stress trajectories (with P F Nemenyi); survey methods measurement degree hydrolysis soap solutions; experimental study titration curves for titration lauric myristic and naphthenic acids with sodium hydroxide glass electrode. Author article: On the Axially Symmetric Flow around a New Family of Half-bodies '50; Coauthor article: (with J W McBain) The Measurement of the Hydrolysis of Solutions of Sodium Salts of Fatty Acids '47, and others. Research asso Naval Ordnance Lab since '47. Am Math Soc—AAAS—Sigma Xi. Naval Ordnance Laboratory, White Oak, Silver Spring 19, Md.

11 Van VORST, Robert Broberg. Youth (Psychopathic delinquent). b'13. AB '35 (U Ariz); MA '38 (Stanford); grad study '47-48 (U Cal LA). Clinical studies, preparation psychometric summaries and case histories of psychopathic delinquent; psychological testing and diagnosis of emotionally disturbed children. Author articles: An Evaluation of the Institutional Adjustment of the Psychopathic Offender '44; Some Responses of the Psychopath as interpreted in the light of Lindner's Suggested Application of the Concept of Homeostasis '47. Sr clin psychol Fred C Nelles Sch for Boys since '47; cons psychol Cal Instn for Women Tehachapi since '47; lectr on juvenile delinquency and psychol testing and diagnosis of emotionally disturbed children SF State Coll. Phi Delta Kappa—Sigma Xi(asso)—Phi Chi—Cal State Psychol Assn—Western Psychol Assn Am Psychol Assn(asso). Fred C. Nelles School for Boys, Box 271, Whittier, Cal.

12 VAN WATERS, Miriam. Penology (Rehabilitation of women offenders). b'87. Grad '04 (St Helens Hall Portland Ore); AB '08—AM '10—LLD '44 (U Ore); F anthropology—PhD '13 (Clark U); LLD '34 (Smith Coll). Dir juvenile delinquency section Harvard Law School Crime Survey since '26; consultant in juvenile delinquency Nat Committee on Law Observance and Enforcement '28-31. Author: Youth in Conflict '25; Parents on Probation '27. Supt Juvenile Ct Detention Home LA '17-20, El Retiro sch for delinquent girls San Fernando Cal '19-20; referee LA Co Juvenile Ct '20-30; now supt State Reformatory for Women Framingham, Mass. Nat Probation Assn (bd dirs) —Internat Assn Juvenile Court Magistrates (vp since '30)—Am League to Abolish Capital Punishment(pres)—Cal Conf Social Work(pres '26, '44)—Nat Conf Social Work (pres '29-30)—So Cal Soc Mental Hygiene(pres '25-26)—

PTA(nat chmn juvenile protection)—Mass Conf Social Work(pres '45)—Phi Beta Kappa—Pi Lambda Theta. Box 99 State Reformatory, Framingham, Mass.†◎

13 Van WYCK, William. Literary criticism. b'83. AB—AM—LittD (U So Calif); PdM—fellow and scholar (NYU); AM (U Calif). Translator of Renaissance writers. Translator: Florentines; Savonarola; Chaucer's Canterbury Tales; Ronsard's Sonnets for Helen; The Sinister Shepherd; Rostand's Cyrano de Bergerac and Chanteclair (with Clifford H Bissell); also articles in field. Lecturer, author, radio commentator on books and travel; teacher ext div U Calif. Phi Beta Kappa. 2500 Benvenue Av., Berkeley 4.†◎

14 VARIAN, Russell Harrison. Microwave tubes (Klystrons). b'98. MA '33 (Stanford); ED (Poly Inst Brooklyn). Inventor of klystron tube. Holds 100 patents on microwave equipment. Research physicist Farnsworth Television '30-34; research Stanford '34, research asso '37-40 and since '46; research engr Sperry Gyroscope Co '40-46; pres Varian Assos since '48. Inst Radio Engrs—AAAS—APS—Sigma Xi. Franklin Inst John Price Wetherill medal '50. Varian Associates, 99 Washington St., San Carlos, Cal.◎

15 VARIAN, Sigurd Fergus. Microwave tubes (Klystron); Microwave tuning mechanism. b'01. Grad '22 (Cal Poly Coll). Assisted development microwave tubes and associated systems, microwave-machinery, and of tuning mechanisms. Holds 15 patents on klystrons, microwave tuning mechanisms and associated equipment. Research associate Stanford since '38, development engineer at Sperry Gyroscope Co '40-48; vp for engineering Varian Assos since '48. Sigma Xi. Franklin Inst John Price Wetherill medal '50. Varian Associates, 611 Hansen Way, Palo Alto, Cal.

16 VASS, Alonzo Frederick. Agricultural economics. b'88. BS '09 (Kansas State Agrl Coll); '10 (U Kan); MS '11 (U Wis); PhD '26 (Cornell U). Chairman National Forum of Labor, Agriculture, and Industry '44-48; member research committees eleven western states for making crop adjustments '35; collection and analysis statistics on agricultural production costs and fair price relationships; representative National Livestock Assn and Beef Committee before congressional hearings '41-45. Author articles: Methods for Determining Value of Grazing Lands '40; Production Costs and Fair Prices for Wool and Lambs '45, and others. Faculty U Wyo since '17, prof and head dept agron and agrl econ since '20. Wyo Stockgrowers Assn—Am Soc Agron—Am Farm Econ Assn(past pres)—Internat Assn Agrl Econ—Colo Acad Sci—Nat Reclamation Assn—Internat Cong Soil Sci—Sigma Xi—Phi Kappa Phi—Alpha Zeta. University of Wyoming, Laramie.

17 VAZQUEZ, Alberto Modesto. Spanish and Spanish-American literature and history. b'01. AB '25—AM '26 (U Ia); PhD—Sterling fellow '32-34—Rockefeller grant '35 (Yale); '33 (U Florence); '34 (U Paris). American delegation UNESCO conference Paris '46. Lecturer Spanish American literature George Washington University since '45. Co-author: Algunas Cartas de Don Diego de Mendoza '35; Spanish Grammar '40. Editor: Las Ninas de mis Ojos by Ricardo Leon '42; Cuentos del Sur '44; (with Angel Flores) Paisaje y hombres de America '47. Asst prof Dartmouth '37-42; chief

translator Dept State '42-43, cons, research analyst OSS '43-44; with Dept State since '44, br chief, specialist Latin Am affairs Office Intelligence Research, div research for Am Republics since '47. Phi Beta Kappa. Department of State, Division of Research for American Republics, Washington.

18 VEATCH, Nathan Thomas. Water (Supply, treatment, distribution); Power (Generation, transmission, distribution); Sewerage; Sewage disposal. b '86. Student (Lewis Acad Wichita); BS—CE '05-09 (U Kan). Operations in water supply and purification, sewerage and sewage disposal, electric light and power work. Mem Black & Veatch, cons engrs Kansas City Mo since '14. ASME—Am Soc CE—Am Water Works Assn(pres '47-48)—Am Inst Cons Engrs—Sigma Xi—Tau Beta Pi—Beta Theta Pi—Sigma Tau. 4706 Broadway, KC, Mo.

19 VEDDER, Edward Bright. Tropical medicine (Beriberi, deficiency diseases). b'78. PhB '98 (U Rochester); MD '02—MA '03 (U Pa); '04 (Army Med Sch); DSc '24 (U Rochester). Author: Beriberi '13; Medicine—Its Contribution to Civilization '29; also articles in field. US Army Bd study tropical diseases '10-13, asst prof pathol Army Med Sch Washington '13-19, charge So Dept Lab Ft Sam Houston '19-22, chief med research div Edgewood Arsenal Md '22-25, sr US Army Bd Med Research '25-28, dir Army Med Sch '30-32, retired '33; prof exptl med George Washington U '33-42; dir med edn Alemeda Co Hosp '42-47. ACP—ACS—AMA—AAAS(F)—Am Soc Tropical Med—Acad Tropical Med —Washington Acad Scis—Washington Acad Med—Sigma Xi. 1090 Ardmore Av., Oakland, Calif.

20 VEINOTT, Cyril George. Engineering (Electrical); Fractional horsepower electric motors. b'05. BS '26—EE '38—DEng '51 (U Vt). Holds 14 patents small motor field. Author: Fractional Horsepower Electric Motors '48; also articles in field. With Westinghouse Elec Corp '25-52, mgr induction motor sect indsl engring dept small motor div '45-52; cons engr Reliance Elec & Engr Co since '53. Nat Soc Profl Engrs—AIEE(F)—Phi Beta Kappa. Reliance Electric & Engineering Co., 1088 Ivanhoe Rd., Cleve 10.†

21 VEINUS, Abraham. Musicology. b'16. BSS '36 (City Coll NY); MA in musicology '37 (Cornell); Clarence Barker Fellow '46-47 (Columbia). Author: The Concerto '44, '48; Victor Book of Concertos '48; also articles in field. Research dir RCA Victor Mfg Co '38-43; asst prof musicology Syracuse U since '48. Am Musicol Soc. Syracuse University, Syracuse, N.Y.

22 VEITH, Ilza (Mrs Hans v V Veith). History of medicine; History of Chinese and Japanese medicine. b'15. MA '44—PhD '47—scholar '47 (Johns Hopkins); student (U Geneva, U Vienna). Author: Huang Ti Nei Ching Su Wen; also articles in field. Cons in Orientalia Army Med Library Washington since '47; asst prof hist med U Chgo since '49. Am Assn Hist Med. Rockefeller Found fellow '45-47; grant-in-aid Am Council Learned Socs '48. Dept. of Medicine, The University of Chgo, Chgo. 37.†

23 VELEZ, Ismael. Antilles (Botany). b'08. AB '30 (PR Poly Inst); MS '34 —PhD '39 (La State U). Research on herbaceous vegetation of Lesser Antilles. Author: Weeds of Puerto Rico '50. Prof bot PR Poly Inst '35-38, '39-45, '46-49, since '50; bot Inst Tropical Agr '45-46. Am Assn Agrl Sci—

Beta Beta Beta—AAAS(F). Guggenheim F '49-50. Polytechnic Institute of Puerto Rico.

10 VENABLE, Austin L. American history 1830-1930. b'02. BA '25—MA '29 (U Ala); PhD '37 (Vanderbilt U); '30 (U Chicago). Author articles. Prof and head hist dept Winthrop College since '45. AHA—So Hist Assn—SC Hist Assn—SC Hist Commn (pres '48-49). Winthrop College, Rock Hill, S.C. H: 342 Stewart Av.

11 VENABLE, Emerson. Gas masks (Design); Gas detection; Dielectrics; Hydrocarbons. b'11. Student '29-32 (Cornell U); BS in chem '33 (U Pitts). Gas mask filters, electrical resistance element sensitive to hydrogen chloride gas, non-inflammable dielectrics, explosion hazards from combustible gases resulting from failure of electrical equipment, hydrogen absorber. Granted patents in fields. Research chem Mine Safety Appliances Co '35-36, '44-46; research engr Westinghouse Elec Co '36-44; dir research Freedom Valvoline Oil Co '46-51; cons chem and engr since '51. AAAS(F)—ACS—Nat Soc Profl Engrs—AIHA—APHA(F). 6111 Fifth Av., Pitts 32.

12 VERA, Harriette Dryden. Bacteriological culture media. b'09. AB '30 (Mt Holyoke Coll); PhD '38 (Yale). Research on filtration experiments with mycobacteria and actinomyces-like organism, rapid demonstration of hemolysis due to anaerobes, materials suitable for cultivation of clostridia. Instr physiol and hygiene Goucher Coll '38-41, asst prof '41-43, vis lecturer since '46; research bact Baltimore Biol Lab since '43. Soc Am Bact—Am Pub Health Assn—Am Soc Profl Biol—AAAS—Sigma Xi. 1640 Gorsuch Av., Baltimore 18.

13 VERDOORN, Frans. History of botany; Bryology; Tropical agriculture; International scientific relations. b'06. Grad '27 (Latin Sch Hilversum Netherlands); PhD '34 (Utrecht U); student (U Vienna, U Geneva); research fellow since '40 (Harvard). Editor: Manual of Bryology '32; Manual of Pteridology '38; Index Botanicorum; A New Series of Plant Science Books since '38; Annales Cryptogamici et Phytopathologici since '43; Biologia since '46. Founder and owner Chronica Botanica Co since '33; bot adviser Netherlands Indies Government '43-49; acting dir Los Angeles State and Co Arboretum '48-49. AAAS(F)—Royal Bot Soc Edinburgh (hon)—Bot Soc Am —Am Soc Agron—Hist of Sci Soc— Am Soc Naturalists—Acad Internat Hist Scis (corr)—International Union Biol Sci (bot sec since '35). Awarded first Mary Soper Pope Medal '46. Chronica Botanica House, 977 Main St., Waltham 54, Mass.

14 VERDUIN, Jacob. Small pore diffusion; Outdoor photosynthesis. b'13. BS '39—MS '41—PhD '47 (Ia State Coll). Research on diffusion through multiperforate septa '47. Co-author article: Absorption of Carbon Dioxide by Maize '44. Teaching fellow Ia State Coll '40-42, photosynthesis under field conditions, instr '45-46; head bot dept U SD '46-48; asso prof Franz Theodore Stone Inst Hydrobiol Put-in-Bay Ohio '48. Franz Theodore Stone Institute of Hydrobiology, Put-in-Bay, O.†

15 VERHAGEN, Dirk. Vitamin oils. b'19. BS '41 (U Washington); MS '43 (U Ky). Research in ether insoluble pigments of tobacco, chromatographic estimation of preformed vitamin A in mixed feeds. Author articles in field. Research chem Lyle Branchflower Co Seattle '43-44, chief chem supervision of analytical and research labs since

'44. Am Chem Soc—Am Oil Chem Soc. Lyle Branchflower Co., Seattle 7.

16 VERNADSKY, George. History (Russian, Byzantine, Mongol). born '87. Student '05-10 (U Moscow); Magister (equivalent to PhD) of Russian hist '17 (U St Petersburg Russia); MA '46 (Yale). Author: Lenin, Red Dictator '31; The Russian Revolution '32; Political and Diplomatic History of Russia '36; Ancient Russia '43; Medieval Russian Laws '47; Kievan Russia '48. Prof Russian hist Yale since '46. AHA —Medieval Acad Am—Am Oriental Soc—Conn Acad Arts Sci. 1984 Yale Station, New Haven.©

17 VERNON, Edward Moore. Weather forecasting (Synoptic); Meteorology. b '05. Student '23-25 (Washburn U). Application modern meteorological knowledge to practical weather forecasting problems; developmet objective methods in weather forecasting; improved interpretation sea level pressure charts in mountainous areas; use modern differential analysis in determining and forecasting winds at upper levels in areas deficient in upper air soundings; forecasting time dissipation Cal coastal fogs. Supervising aviation forecaster US Weather Bur Cal '31-41; ofcl in charge and head forecaster Consol Weather Bur Forecast Center since '41. Am Meteorol Soc—Am Geophys Union. Weather Bureau Airport Station, San Francisco International Airport, San Bruno, Cal.

18 VERNON, Robert. Florida mineral industry; Florida Tertiary and Gulf coast geology and hydrology. b'12. BS '36 (Birmingham-Southern Coll); MS '38 (U Ia); PhD '41 (La State U). Author articles in field. Asst geol Fla Geol Survey '39-43, geol '46-53, asst dir since '53. Geol Soc Am—Am Assn Pet Geol. Box 631, Tallahassee.†

19 VERTREES, Herbert H. Pearls; Pearl peeling. Studies since '10 of pearls and pearling, including history of attempts to raise pearls in various parts of world, how pearls and shells are gathered in US and various foreign countries, cause of pearl lustre, evaluating possibility of securing valuable pearls by peeling, river prospecting and fishing for pearls. Author: Pearls and Pearling '13; also articles in field. 130 W. Jefferson St., Pittsfield, Ill.

20 VESTAL, Paul Anthony. Ethnobotany of Kiowa and Navajo Indians; Plant anatomy. b'08. AB '30 (Colo Coll); AM '33—PhD '35 (Harvard). Field work with Kiowa Indians in Oklahoma '37, Navajo Indians in New Mexico '39, '41; research collecting trips Panama '31, Cuba '33. Author: Economic Botany of the Kiowa Indians '34; Ethnobotany of the Ramah Navajo '52; also articles in field. Formerly research curator Bot Mus Harvard, now prof biol Rollins Coll; chmn Basic Sci Bd of State of Fla. AAAS—Bot Soc Am—Internat Assn Wood Anat—Sigma Xi. Rollins College, Winter Park, Fla.

21 VESTINE, Ernest Harry. Terrestrial magnetism; Meteorology. b'06. BSc '31 (U Alberta); '31-32 (U Toronto); DIC—PhD '37 (U London). Leader of International Polar Year expedition to Meanook '32-33. Author: Noctilucent Clouds; Description of Geomagnetic Field and Its Analysis (two vols). Co-author: (with S Chapman) Electric Current System of Geomagnetic Disturbance. Physicist Dept Terrestrial Magnetism Carnegie Inst Washington '38-39, chief sect land magnetic survey '40-46, sect chmn statis and analytical geophysics since '46; cons applied physics lab Johns Hop-

kins U. Washington Acad Sci—Am Geophys Union—Philos Soc Washington. Academic fellowships '34-37. 5241 Broad Branch Road, Washington 25.†

22 VETTER, Carl Peter. River control; Hydraulic structures (Design); Hydro-electric developments (Design and construction); Hydraulics (Research, teaching). b'92. MS in civil engring '16 (Royal Coll Engring Copenhagen). Control, regulation, and dispatching Colorado River waters for flood control, river regulation, irrigation, power, Mexican commitments, and electrical power generation; river regulation construction works; design of dams, hydro-electric developments, transmission towers and substations. With bur reclamation US Dept Interior since '34; chmn US com International Commn on Large Dams. Am Soc CE—Am Geophys Union—Western Snow Conf—Sigma Xi. Bureau of Reclamation, Office of River Control, Postoffice Box A-A, Boulder City, Nev. H: 635 Av. K.

23 VIAL, Fernand. French literature (Vauvenargus, Voltaire). born '05. MA '29—PhD '32 (U Mich). Author: Contes Favoris '40; Louis Bastide '46; Voltaire (2 vols) '48; also articles in field. Asso prof French Fordham U since '40; chmn dept romance lang since '48. Modern Lang Assn—Am Assn Teachers French—Societe des Professeurs Francais en Amerique (bd dirs since '35, sec gen '42-45). Fordham University Graduate School, NYC 58.

24 VICKERY, Hubert Bradford. Protein chemistry; Plant biochemistry; Plant metabolism (Nitrogenous compounds, organic acids). b'93. BS '15— MS '18 (Dalhousie U); PhD '22 (Yale). Non-participating scientific observer for War Department of atomic bomb experiments at Bikini '46. Author articles in field. Biochem in charge Conn Agrl Expt Sta since '28. Nat Acad Sci —Am Acad Arts Sci—Am Chem Soc— Soc Biol Chem—Soc Plant Physiol (Stephen Hales prize '33)—Soc Exptl Biol—Sigma Xi. Connecticut Agricultural Experiment Station, New Haven.©

25 VICTOREEN, John Austin. Radiation physics and measuring instruments; Electronics; Atomic energy (Vacuum tubes, Geiger-Mueller counters). b'02. Hold numerous patents pertaining to field of radiation measuring instruments as applied to radiation physics; developed special vacuum tubes and Geiger Mueller counters and instruments for atomic research using these tubes; designed and introduced x-ray instruments calibrated in roentgens for measurement of dosage in x-ray therapy. Author articles in field. Founded The Victoreen Instrument Co '25, chairman board dirs; also owner operator Colo Victoreen Lab Colo Springs; physicist staff Colo Springs Med Center. Am Phys Soc—Inst Radio Engrs, 3800 Perkins Av., Cleve. H: 512 Foothill Rd., Colorado Springs, Colo.

26 VIDOSIC, Joseph Paul. Stress analysis; Photoelasticity; Machine design. b'09. ME '32—MS '34 (Stevens Inst Tech); PhD '51 (Purdue). Research on antifriction bearings for mil airplanes, airplane graphics, stress analysis, lubrication design stress factors. Author articles: Plastics for Aircraft '43; Streamline Graphics '47; Stress Analysis '50; Lubrication Engineering '53; and others. Prof mech engring Ga Inst Tech since '37. ASME —Soc Exptl Stress Analysis—Am Soc Engring Edn—Tau Beta Pi—Am Soc Lubrication Engrs—Pi Tau Sigma— Sigma Xi—Pi Delta Epsilon. Georgia Institute of Technology, Atlanta.†

10 VIERCK, Charles John. Engineering drawing; Art of illumination. b'06. BME '29 (U Ia). Through research devised several methods of emperical geometric and axonometric projection published in French's Engineering Drawing, seventh edition. Author: Tests of the Ability to Read Engineering Drawings '42. Co-author: Engineering Drawing '41; Engineering Drawing Problems '48; also articles in field. With O State U since '29, now prof engring drawing. ASME—Am Soc Tool Engrs—Am Soc Engring Edn—Sigma Xi. Department of Engineering Drawing, Ohio State University, Columbus 10, O. H: 1626 Doone Rd.

11 VILHAUER, Marie Chrisman. Business education. b'05. BS '28 (Southwest Mo State Coll); MA '32 (U Mo); grad work (NYU). Author article: A Comparative Study of the Commercial Curricula of the Five Missouri State Teachers Colleges '41. Head bus dept Central Coll Mo since '42, dir bus teacher training, asso prof bus, sec of faculty. Nat Bus Teachers Assn—Am Accounting Assn—Internat Soc for Bus Edn—NEA (United Bus Edn Assn, chmn administrators com in Mo since '48)—Mo State Teachers Assn (liaison com). Business Department, Central College, Fayette, Mo.

12 VINAL, Theodora. Niagara Falls. b'91. AB '29 (U Buffalo). Collection hist data, early prints, and guidebooks on Niagara; writer script for historical pageant performed at centennial City of Niagara Falls '48. Author: Niagara Portage from Past to Present '49. Librarian Gaskill Jr High Sch Niagara Falls since '36. NY State Hist Soc—Niagara Falls Hist Soc (vp)—Lundy's Lane Hist Soc Ont—Niagara-on-the-Lake Historical Soc Ont. Gaskill Junior High School, Niagara Falls, N.Y.

13 VINAY, Jean-Paul. Phonetics; Linguistics (French, Welsh, Breton); Influence of noise on radio-communications in aircraft. b'10. BA '28 (U Caen); License es Lettres '31 (U Paris '31); MA '37 (London U); Agrégé de l'Université '41 (U Paris). Research in general phonetics and phonetics of several languages including Algonkin, French, Welsh, Breton and minor European languages. Author: French Reader '40; L'anglais par l'image '44. Co-author: (with W O Thomas) Basis and Essentials of Welsh '47. Editor: Interlangue '43-44; also articles in field. Asst dept phonetics U Coll London '37-39; lecturer phonetics Ecole des Langues Orientales Paris '45; chief insp lang City of Paris, Dept of Seine France '42-46; head dept linguistics U Montreal since '46. Assn Phonetique Internationale (council) — Linguistic Soc Am—Linguistic Circle NY—Am Assn Teachers French. Faculte des Lettres, Universite de Montreal, 2900 Bd. du Mont-Royal, Montreal, Quebec, Can.

14 VINCENT, Edward T(homas). Diesel and jet engines; Turbines; Supercharging. b'93. BSc '20 (London U); '14-15 (Imperial Coll Sci Tech London). Author: Supercharging the Internal Combustion Engine '48; Oil Engine Theory and Practice '39; Gas Turbines and Jet Engines '49; also articles in field. Holder about 15 US patents on diesel engine injection systems and sleeve valve engines. Cons engr Continental Aviation and Engring Co Det since '37; chmn dept mech and indsl engring U Mich. Inst Mech Engrs Gt Brit—ASME—SAE—Soc Engring Edn—Soc Exptl Stress Analysis. Tyndall prizeman, Whitworth scholar, Royal scholar. 333 W. Engineering Building, University of Michigan, Ann Arbor. H: 2115 Melrose.†◎

15 VINCENT, Harvard Burton. Glass products; Glass fabricating equipment. b'00. AB '23—AM '25 (Queens U); PhD '26 (U Mich). Development glass products and fabricating equipment and processes: spectrochemical apparatus & methods. Author articles: Daylighting of interiors through the use of light directional glass block; and others. Instr U Mich '24-26, research physicist '27-43; NRC fellow Harvard '26-27; mgr prodn development Insulux Div Owens Ill Glass Co '43-44, Libbey Div '44-47, dir prodn development in Kimble Div since '47. APS—Optical Soc Am—AAAS—Illuminating Engring Soc —Am Soc Heating and Ventilating Engineers—Inst Radio Engrs—Sigma Xi. Kimble Division of Owens-Illinois Glass Co., Tol. 1.

16 VINCENT, Howard L. Synthetic resin chemistry: Impregnated papers. b'08. Student '26-30 (Columbia). Discovered and developed a number of processes for impregnating paper with synthetic resins for increased translucency and other properties; also developed several tests and instruments. Author articles in field. Research chem George Vincent Inc '30-34, vp '34-42, pres since '42. Am Chem Soc—Tech Assn Pulp and Paper Ind. 119 W. 24th St., NYC 11. Deceased.

17 VISHER, Stephen Sargent. Geography (Economic, Indiana, South Dakota); Climatology; Tropical cyclones; Natural resource conservation; American scientific leaders. b'87. BS '09—MS '10—PhD '14 (U Chicago); MA '12 (U SD); fellow (U Chicago, Yale). Field investigations in Alaska, West Indies, Spain, Italy, Britain, South Seas, Australia, Far East. Author: Geography of South Dakota '18; The Economic Geography of Indiana '23; Tropical Cyclones of the Pacific and Their Effects '25. Co-author: (with W O Blanchard) Economic Geography of Europe '31; (with E Huntington) Climatic Changes, Their Nature and Causes '22; Our Natural Resources and Their Conservation '36, '39, and others. Prof geog Ind U since '19; Geog Ind Geol Survey since '19. Geol Soc Am (F)—AAAS—Am Meteorol Soc—Royal Meteorol Soc—Ind Acad Sci (vp '40) —Assn Am Geog (vp '33)—Nat Geog Soc (hon life mem)—Brit Geog Assn —Phi Beta Kappa—Sigma Xi. 817 E. 2d St., Bloomington, Ind.◎

18 VIVIAN, Robert Evans. Electrochemical engineering; Inorganic chemical technology (Economic minerals, metallic powders). b'93. AB '17—MA '22 (So Calif); PhD '33 (Columbia U). Head chem div and petroleum tech div sci dept Kern County Union High Sch and Jr Coll Bakersfield Calif '18-28; chief Kern County Assay Office Bakersfield '18-28; asst in process development, chem engring dept Columbia U '29-30; electrochem engr in charge pilot plant operation Internat Agrl Corp '30-31; research chem, chem engr Gen Chem Co NYC '31-35; dir research Metals Disintegrating Co Elizabeth NJ '35-37; prof and head dept chem engring Coll Engring U So Calif '37-42, dean Coll Engring since '42; chem prodn Specialist Mutual Security Agy in Italy '52. Am Inst Chem Engrs—Am Chem Soc—Electrochem Soc—ASEE— Phi Beta Kappa—Sigma Xi—Phi Kappa Phi. 862 Victoria Av., LA 5.†◎

19 VLASTOS, Gregory. Greek philosophy; Ethics and social philosophy. b'07. BA '25 (Robert Coll, Constantinople); MA '29 (U Chicago); BD '29 (Chicago Theol Sem); PhD '31—grant-in-aid Social Sci Research Council of Can '44-45 (Harvard); grant-in-aid Leopold Schepp Found NY '37-38 (Oxford and Cambridge, Eng). Author: The Disorderly Motion in the TIMA-EUS '39; Slavery in Plato's Thought '41; Ethics and Physics in Democritus '45; On the Pre-history in Diodorus '46; Solonian Justice '46; Parmenides' Theory of Knowledge '46; Equality and Justice in Early Greek Cosmologies '47. Prof philos Sage Sch Philos Cornell U since '48.◎

20 VOEGELIN, Charles Frederick. American Indian languages. b'06. BA '27 (Stanford U); PhD '32 (U Calif); '33-36 (Yale); '28 (U New Zeland). Editor International Journal of American Linguistics since '44; field trips for research on Maori of New Zealand, and on such American Indian tribes as Umitilla, Blackfoot, Penobscot, Tubatulabal, Hidatsa, Ojibwa, Dakota, Shawnee, Delaware, Seneca. Author articles in field. Asso prof, prof anthrop and chmn dept Ind U since '41, dir Linguistic Institute '52, '53. Am Anthrop Assn—Linguistic Society Am —Am Oriental Soc—Sigma Xi. Guggenheim fellow '48. Department of Anthropology, Indiana University, Bloomington, Ind.

21 VOEGELIN, Erminie W(heeler). American folklore; American Indian ethnology. b'03. AB '23—MA '29 (U Calif); PhD '39—fellow '33-35 (Yale). Editor and associate editor Journal of American Folklore since '41. Author: Tubatulabal Ethnography '37; Mortuary Customs of the Shawnee and other Eastern Woodlands Tribes '44. Author articles: (with C F Voegelin) Shawnee Name Groups '35; Shawnee Musical Instruments '38, and others. Exec sec Am Anthrop Assn since '47. Am Folklore Soc (pres '48)—Am Anthrop Assn (F)—Ind Acad Sci—Sigma Xi. Guggenheim fellow '48. Department of Anthropology, Indiana University, Bloomington, Ind.

22 VOELKER, Charles Henry. Air filters; Dust collectors; Dust; Fumes; Pronunciation (American phonetics). b'10. BA '31—MA '33 (O State U); DSc '48 (Capitol Coll Music). Invented, designed, or developed air filters or dust collectors for aircraft cabins and engines, diesel locomotives, wind tunnels, railway cars, turbines and others; was one of a team which developed electronic air filter for American Air Filter Co. Author articles in field. Prof and head dept physics Washington Coll since '47, research geophysicist Chesapeake Bay Inst Johns Hopkins University since '50. AAAS—Am Phys Soc—Acoustical Soc Am—Am Assn Physics Teachers. Department of Physics, Washington College, Chestertown, Md.

23 VOGEL, Edward C. Topographic maps. b'04. BA '29 (Carleton Coll, Northfield, Minn); MA '39 (U Ill). Geog Army Map Service '43-48, chief procurement and reference in library since '45. Am Geog Soc—Am Soc Profl Geog—Am Congress Surveying Mapping—Special Libraries Assn — Phi Beta Kappa. Army Map Service, Washington 16.

24 VOGEL, Leo Joseph. Aerial tramways; Cableways. b'96. ME '17 (U Notre Dame). Projection, design, construction, servicing over one hundred individual aerial tramways and cableways; development fully automatic aerial tramways. Issued patents in field. With Interstate Equipment Corp since '21. AIME—Engrs Soc Western Pa. 937 Union Trust Bldg., Pitts 19.

25 VOGEL, Orville A(lvin). Wheat breeding. b'07. Research on relation of glume strength and other characters to shattering in wheat, short straw, lodging resistance, bunt and rust resistance and breeding for improved milling and baking qualities in wheat for Pacific Northwest states. Designer of special equipment for planting and threshing plant and plot samples. Author articles in field. Began as agt cereal crops and diseases US Dept Agr in wheat improvement in cooperation with Wash State Coll '31, now coordinator for wheat improvement work in western states as agron Bur Plant Industry. Am Soc Agron—Sigma Xi. Agronomy Department, Washington State College, Pullman, Wash.

10 VOGEL, Rudolf. Vend machines. b'11. MS in elec engring '35 (U Danzig); '43-44 (U Wis). Designer coin operated phonographs. Chief engr Filben Corp Chicago '45-48; cons engr since '50. Am Inst EE—Am Inst ME. 3943 North Clarendon Av., Chicago 13, Illinois.

11 VOGELBACK, William E. Public utilities (Evaluations, rates, financing); Gliders; Education (International exchange). b'93. student civil and elec engring (various tech schs NYC); MBA (U Chicago). Expert witness on evaluation, rates, and economics of public utilities; arbitrator for courts and commissions; consulting engineer on aircraft and gliders; negotiator agreements on international educational exchange. Pres, chmn bd Union Gas & Electric Co since '44; cons indsl engr on aircraft and chief glider program WPB Washington '42; dir fgn liquidation of aircraft '45; central commissioner liquidation war surpluses, credits, ednl exchange and war debt settlements. Am Inst EE—Soc Am Mil Engrs—Ill Soc Profl Engrs—Nat Soc Profl Engrs. 230 N. Michigan Av., Chicago.⊚

12 VOLANDER, Herman Benjamin. Engineering. b'11. Student German schs '19-24 (Wiesbaden and Mainz); grad '28 (Peekskill Mil Acad); '26-27 (McBurney Sch NYC); '28-29 (Gary Army and Navy Prep Sch Baltimore); '29-31 (US Naval Acad); BS in bus administration and mech engineering '37 (Mass Inst Tech). International communications services; foreign communications resources. With Cornell-Dubilier Electric Corp S Plainfield NJ '37-40, cons to Internat Telephone & Telegraph Corp travelling to London, Antwerp, Zurich, Budapest, Paris '37-39, sales engr US, later dist rep for Middle West '39-41; engr and mgr spl products dept Kellogg Switchboard & Supply Co Chicago '41-42; mgr Chicago office Fed Telephone & Radio Corp (subsidiary Internat Tel & Tel Corp) '43-45, trans to Standard Elec Corp (also subsidiary) '45 and became asst vp Internat Telephone & Telegraph Corp and Internat Elec Corp, assigned Vienna as resident rep.; arrested by Hungarian Govt imprisoned '49-51. Am Inst EE—Inst Radio Engrs —MIT Alumni Assn. 6751 Jeffrey Blvd., Chicago.

13 VOLK, Norman James. Soil chemistry; Agronomy. b'01. BS '23—MS '24 —PhD '32 (U Wis). Research on soil productivity with respect to bananas, oxidation-reduction in soil, behavior of potassium in soils, soil structure, soil fertility, potash fixation in soils; member advisory committee on fertilizers to War Food Administration World War II. Author articles in field. Asso dir agrl expt sta Purdue U since '45. Sigma Xi—Am Soc Agron(F)—Ind Acad Sci—Soil Sci Soc Am (pres). Fellow U Wis '31-33. Purdue University Agricultural Experiment Station, Lafayette, Ind.†

14 VOLTERRA, Enrico Giovanni. Vibrations (Structural). b'05. DEng '28

(Rome U Italy); PhD '41 (Cambridge U Eng). Research on mathematical theory elasticity and stress analysis; studies on theory vibrations structural reinforced concrete. Faculty Rome U Italy '29-38, asso prof mechanics and strength materials '34-38; designer Ferrobeton Italy '30-32, '34-35; cons engr Rome and Italy '36-38; cons Italian govt for bridges and harbors reconstrn Ministry Pub Works Rome '46-49; asso prof mechanics Ill Inst Tech Chicago since '49. ASME—Am Soc Experimental Stress Analysis—AAAS—Am Soc Engring Edn—Sigma Xi. Ill Institute of Technology, Chgo 16.

15 VOLZ, Emil Conrad. Floriculture; Vegetable crops. b'91. BS '14 (Mich State Coll); MS '18 (Cornell U). Author: Home Flower-Growing '31; also articles in field. Prof hort Ia State Coll since '21. Am Soc Hort Sci—Ia Acad Sci—Phi Kappa Phi—Gamma Sigma Delta—Pi Alpha Xi. Department of Horticulture, Iowa State College, Ames, Ia.

16 VON ANTWERPEN, Franklin John. Chem economics. b'12. AE '35— BS in chem engring '38 (Newark Coll Engring); '38-40 (Columbia). Mgr Munitex Corp '35-38; mng ed Indsl and Engring Chem, ACS '38-46; ed Chem Engring Progress, AICE since '46. ACS —AAAS—AICE. Chemical Engineering Progress, 120 East 41st St., NYC 17.

17 Von BERGEN, Werner. Wool technology. b'97. Grad '16 (Tech Coll, Burgdorf, Switzerland); '22-23 (U Cologne, Cologne). Scientific consultant Quartermaster General in European theater war '45; committee on textile finishing, advisory board on Quartermaster research and development National Research Council, Washington since '48. Co-author: American Wool Handbook '38; Textile Fiber Atlas '42; also articles in field. Chief chem Forstmann Woolen Co Passaic NJ '32-38, dir research and control lab since '38. Am Assn Textile Technol—Am Assn Textile Chem and Colorists—Am Chem Soc—Am Soc Testing Materials (chmn sub-com A-3, sect 1 wool '33-49, chmn D-13 sub-com A-3 wool and its products since '49)—Textile Research Inst Inc (adv com since '43)— The Fiber Soc—Schweizer Verein der Chemiker und Colouristen, Switzerland—Textile Inst, Eng(F)—Soc Dyers and Colourists, Eng. Forstmann Woolen Company, Passaic, N.J.

18 Von BRAUN, Wernher. Supersonic aerodynamics (Rockets, guided missiles, jet propulsion). b'12. BS '32 (Inst Tech Berlin); PhD '34 (U Berlin). Experimented small liquid fuel rocket motors of 13 pounds thrust at Berlin-Ploetzensee; specialist rocket design and controls, development large liquid fuel rockets, rocket power plants, guided missiles. Developed V-2 Long Range Rocket and AA Guided Missile Wasserfall '37-45. Liquid fuel rocket expert German Ordnance Dept Kummersdorf '32-37; tech dir German Rocket Research Center Peenemuende (Baltic Sea) '37-45, research prof '43-45; project dir Research and Development Service Ordnance Dept US Army Ft Bliss Tex 45-50; project dir ordnance guided missile center Redstone Arsenal Huntsville since '50. Ordnance Guided Missile Center, Redstone Arsenal, Huntsville, Ala.⊚

19 VONDERLEHR, Raymond A. Venereal disease (Control, treatment, prevalence). b'97. MD '20 (U Va). Development federal program for control venereal diseases in US '35-43; administrative guidance public health program for US in civilian population West Indies '43-46; director communicable disease control program of fed-

eral government since '47. Co-author (with Dr Thomas Parran) Plain Words About the Venereal Diseases '41; (with Dr J R Heller) Control of Venereal Disease '46, also articles in field. Asst surg gen div venereal diseases USPHS '35-43, med adv Anglo-Am Caribbean Commn '43-47, med dir in charge communicable disease center Atlanta '47-51; regional med dir Reg VI, US Dept Health Edn & Welfare since '52. Am Venereal Disease Assn(pres '38)—AMA —Am Pub Health Assn—Am Soc Tropical Med—National Malaria Soc—Sci Research Soc of Am (pres communicable disease center branch '50)— Alpha Omega Alpha—Sigma Xi. Diplomate Am Bd Preventive Med and Pub Health. Region VI, U.S. Public Health Service, 7th and Peachtree Bldg., Atlanta 5. H: 1409 Fairview Rd. N.E., Atlanta 6.

20 Von ESCHEN, Garvin L(eonard). Aerodynamics. b'13. Bachelor Aero E '36—MS '39 (U Minn). Research on, development of high Mach number wind tunnels; investigation of thin section thick skin wing sections; study of effect of fuselage location on spanwise air-load distribution of an airplane wing. Author articles in field. Engr Lockheed Aircraft Corp '39-40; cons engr aero div Minneapolis Honeywell Regulation Co '44-46; instr dept aero engring U Minn '40-42, asst prof '42-44, asso prof '44-46; prof and chmn dept aero engring O State U since '46, research supervisor Research Found. Inst Aero Sci—ASEE—AAAS—APS. O State University, Department of Aeronautical Engineering, Columbus, O.

21 von FABER du FAUR, Curt. German baroque literature. b'90. Lt degree '10 (Officers Sch Kassel); PhD '21 (U Giessen). Published more than 30 catalogues on old and valuable books. Author: Deutsche Barock-Lyrik '36; Abfall '38; St Satyros '34. Coauthor: Bucher Bucher Bucher Bucher; also articles in field. Co-owner Antiquariat Karl and Faber Munich '23-33; literary critic Literatur-Blatt der Frankfurter Zeitung '37-38; lecturer Harvard '41-42, '44; prof and research asso German lit and bibliog Yale since '44; vis prof German Columbia '49-50. Conn Acad Arts Sci—Modern Lang Assn. Sterling Memorial Library, Yale University, New Haven.⊚

22 VON FISCHER, William. Chemistry of organic protective coatings; Chemistry of latex. b'10. BChem '32— MS '33—PhD '37 (Inst Tech U Minn). Research in field organic protective coatings, analytical chemistry and latex; adhesion surface coatings on metals; adsorption of Wool Violet. Author articles: Oxidation-Reduction Indicators I. Diphenylbenzidine sulfonic acid; Apparent Effect of Filtration Upon the Aging of Fresh Lead Sulfate; Dispersion Studies of Titanium Dioxide Pigment; and others. Head dept chem and chem engring Case Inst Tech since '48. Am Chem Soc—Electrochem Soc—Soc Chem Industries, Fedn Paint and Varnish Production Clubs—AAAS—AAUP—ASEE —Tau Beta Pi—Phi Lambda Upsilon —Alpha Chi Sigma—Sigma Xi. Case Institute Techology, University Circle, Cleve 6.

23 Von GRUNEBAUM, Gustave Edmund. Islamic studies (Arabia, Persia, Near East). b'09. PhD '31 (U Vienna). Author: Growth and Structure of Early Arabic Poetry '37; Medieval Islam: A Study in Cultural Orientation '46. Coauthor: Palestine: A Study of Jewish, Arab and British Policies '47; also articles in field. Leader ext inst Oriental Inst U Vienna '36-38; asst prof Islamic studies Iranian Inst NY '38-42, chmn dept Arabic '42-43; asst prof Arabic U

Chicago '43-46, asso prof '46-49, prof since '49. Islamic Research Assn Bombay India (hon). 214 Oriental Institute, University of Chicago, Chicago 37.†

10 von HAGEN, Victor Wolfgang. South American cultures and natural history; (Aztecs; Mayans;) Indian paper making; Quetzals; Coca and coca chewing. b'08. Expeditions to Mexico '31-33, to Ecuador, Upper Amazon, Galapagos Islands '34-36, to Honduras, Mosquito Coast, Bay Island, Guatemala '37-38, to Panama '40, Columbia, Peru, Amazon '47-48, West Indies '49-50. UN consultant on coca and coca chewing '49; captured and successfully transported first specimens quetzals to London Zoo. Author: Off with Their Heads '37; The Tsatchela Indians of Western Ecuador '39; Ecuador the Unknown '40; Jungle in the Clouds '40; Riches of South America '42. Co-author: (with Hawkins) Quetzal Quest '39. Editor: Miskito Boy '43; The Aztec and Maya Paper Makers '43; South America Called Them '45; Island Outposts of South America '45; Maya Explorer, Life of John Lloyd Stephens '47; Green World of the Naturalists '48; Ecuador and the Galapagos Islands '49. Naturalist and ethnographer. Guggenheim fellow '49, holder grant from Am Philos Soc. Zool Soc London (F)—Hist Sci Soc. c/o Alfred A. Knopf, Inc., 501 Madison Av., NYC 22.☉

11 von KARMAN, Theodore, Aerodynamics; Applied mechanics. b'81. ME '02 (Royal Tech U, Budapest); PhD '09 (U Goettingen, Germany); 13 hon degrees Am and fgn universities. Author: (with J M Burgers) General Aero-dynamic Theory (2 vols) '24; (with M A Biot) Mathematical Methods in Engineering '40; also articles in field. Asst prof U Goettingen '09-12; prof aeronautics and dir Aeronautical Inst U Aachen '13-30; professor aeronautics and dir Guggenheim Aeronautics Lab Calif Inst Tech '30-49. Awarded ASME medal '41, Sylvanus Reed award Inst Aeronautical Sci '41, John Fritz medal '47, Franklin '48. Nat Acad Sci—Inst Aeronautical Sci (hon F)—ASME—ASCE—Tau Beta Pi. 1501 S. Marengo Av., Pasadena, Cal.

12 von MOHRENSCHILDT, Dimitri. Russian history and literature; Comparative literature; Intercultural relations (Russia). b'02. PhB '26—AM '30 (Yale); PhD '36 (Columbia); Slavic fellow Hoover Inst '47 (Stanford U). Author: Russia in the Intellectual Life of Eighteenth Century France '36; also articles in field. Founder, mng ed The Russian Review since '41; vis lecturer in Russian civilization Dartmouth Coll since '42, prof Russian hist and lit since '47; contr editorial research for Life and Fortune mags NY since '43; dir Tolstoy Found Inc NY. Modern Lang Assn—Am Assn Teachers of Slavonic and Eastern Langs—Fgn Policy Assn. Dartmouth College, Hanover, NH.†☉

13 VONNEGUT, Bernard. Physical chemistry; Kinetics of phase changes; Smoke filtrations; Icing conditions; Nucleation of supercooled liquids. b'14. BS '36—PhD '39 (MIT). With Gen Elec Research Lab Schenectady NY since '45. Am Chem Soc—Am Meteorol Soc. Arthur D. Little, Inc., Cambridge, Mass.†

14 von NEUMANN, John. Automatic high-speed computing devices; Mathematical physics; Quantum mechanics; Theory of games. PhD '26 (U Budapest); DSc (hon) '47 (Princeton); Engr Chem '25 (Federal Inst Polytech Zurich Switzerland). Author: Foundations of Quantum Mechanics '48; Theory of

Games (with O Morgenstern) '47. Research prof math Inst Advanced Study Princeton since '33; cons Army Ordnance Dept since '40, Navy Bur Ordnance since '42, Naval Ordnance Lab since '46; cons Los Alamos Lab Manhattan Dist US Engrs and US Atomic Energy Commn since '43; gen adv com US AEC since '53. National Academy Sci—Am Philos Soc—Am Acad Arts Sci. Medal for Merit '46. Institute for Advanced Study, Princeton, N.J.†

15 VOORHEES, Sherman Persons. Airports. b'00. Student '21-22 (Columbia). Co-founder Soaring Society of America, founder National Glider Contests, member Hoover Committee and Army Advisory Committee. With Nat Municipal League '33; with Am Mus Nat Hist '34-40; with Army-Navy Jour '40-42; exec dir Future Springfield Inc since '45. Govt Research Assn—Am Soc Pub Adminstrn—Nat Mun League—Am Planning and Civic Assn—Inst Aeronautical Sci—Nat Assn Civic Sec—Spl Libraries Assn—Am C of C Exec. Future Springfield, Inc., 86 Hillman St., Springfield 3, Mass. H: 70 Chestnut St., Springfield 5.

16 VOTH, Paul Dirks. Chrysanthemums; Daylilies; Iris; Liverworts (Nutrition). b'05. AB '29 (Bethel Coll N Newton Kan); MS '30—PhD '33 (U Chicago). Hybridization of daylily and iris, investigation rate seed germination, longevity stored pollen and seeds, collection data on inheritance of albinism and winter-hardiness; research on anatomy daylilies; laboratory study photoperiod, vegetative reproduction, and speciation liverworts; experimental determination optimum concentration and relative proportions of nitrates, sulphates, phospnates of calcium, potassium, and magnesium for liverworts. Author articles: Effects of Nutrient-Solution Concentration on the Growth of Marchantia polymorpha '43; Effect of Algastatic Agents on Marchantia '45, and others. Faculty U Chgo since '33, now prof bot and sec dept. AAAS—AAUP—Am Bryological Soc—Am Soc Naturalists—Am Soc Plant Physiol—Bot Soc Am—Ecol Soc Am—Sigma Xi—Hemerocallis Soc. Botany Bldg., University of Chicago, Chgo 37.☉

17 VOZZELLA, Joseph Florindo. Coatings (Protective). b'26. BS '48—MS '51 (Northeastern U). Research on fundamentals of pigment dispersion with relation to final characteristics protective coatings, analyses of particle size distributions. Faculty Northeastern U and research asso since '48. NE Paint and Varnish Prodn Clubs—ACS—Tau Beta Pi. Northeastern U, Department of Chemical Engineering, 360 Huntington Av., Boston 15. H: 59 Poole St., Medford 55, Mass.

18 VRAT, Ved. Helminths; Fisheries biology. b'19. BS '38 (Lucknow U India); MS '39-40 (Allahabad U India); '46-48 (Stanford U). Study blood chem changes to detect malignancy; development method indicating arginine levels of blood higher in cancerous than in normal humans; intra-peritoneal administration arginase in mice to reduce size and change histological appearance malignant tumors; histological and histocytochemical changes in mammary carcinoma of mice after intra-peritoneal injections arginase; administration ACTH, cortisone and arginase to break down malignancies in CH mice; administration arginine to increase resistance of the small intestine of rats to digestion by pepsin hydrochloric acid; investigation helminths of birds in India, and studies cytoplasmic inclusions in spermatogenesis Trematodes; research on Helminthiasis in domesticated animals in In-

dia; Government of India federal scholarship for research on growth, variations in lateral armature, age and migration Gasterosteus aculeatus of California. Researcher Imperial Council Agrl Research India '40-42; prof and head dept biol St. Joseph's Coll Naini Tal India '42-46; chief lab tech Richmond hosp Richmond Cal '49; dir research med sch, prin investigator cancer research, and dir cancer research, The Permanente Foundation Belmont (Cal) Labs since '50. Nat Acad Sci India—AM Soc Icthyologists and Herpetologists. The Permanente Foundation, Belmont Laboratories, P.O. Box 408, Belmont, Cal.

19 VREELAND, Hamilton, Jr. Fgn divorces. b'92. Grad '09 (Hasbrouck Inst Jersey City); LittB '13 (Princeton); AM '15—LLB '16—PhD '17 (Columbia). Author: Validity of Foreign Divorces '38; Twilight of Individual Liberty '44. Spl counsel to agt of US, Mixed Claims Commns US and Mexico '30-31; asso prof law Cath U Am '31-38, head grad dept law sch '32-38; vis lectr internat relations Yale Grad Sch '37; prof law Washington Coll Law '39-42; spl lectr Fordham U Law Sch '43-45; vis prof law NYU Sch Law '45-47; spl asst to atty gen of US '43. Am and Fed bar assns—Am Soc Internat Law—Internat Law Assn—Am Law Inst—Inst Juridique Internat The Hague—Am Acad Polit and Social Sci. 24 North St. Greenwich, Conn.†

20 VUCASSOVICH, Michel P(ierre). Fish (Curing, canning). b'81. BL '00 BS '01 (Coll du Sacré Coeur). Developed process for canning mackerel, ready to fry fish cakes, fish chowders, pastes; invented machinery for brining and syruping commestibles, and flume machine for fish; invented method for producing caviar of fish other than sturgeon. Holds patents on processes for removal frozen fish skins by flame, for removal of fish scales. Author articles: Special Problems in Fish Canning; Simplified Modern Methods of Conveying, Brining, Washing, Syruping and Precooling Commodities for Freezing and Preserving. Food sepcialist, cons food tech, tech dir Gorton Pew Fisherines Co Ltd since '16. Inst Food Tech—Mass Hotel Assn. 327 Main St., Gloucester, Mass. H: Crow's Nest, Hesperus Av.

21 VUILLEUMIER, Ernest Albert. Electroplating; Alcoholometry. b'94. BS '14—'14-15 (U Pa); PhD '18 (U Berne, Switzerland). Inventor Dickinson alcohometer and Dickinson solids-hydrometer; co-inventor contractometer for study of peeling of nickel-plating. Author articles in field. Head dept chem Dickinson Coll since '20, dean '35-47. Am Inst Chem(F)—AAAS (F)—Am Chem Soc—Am Electrochem Soc—Verein fur Chemiker der Universitaet Berne—Pa Acad Sci (pres '41-42)—Phi Beta Kappa. Dickinson College, Carlisle, Pa.

W

22 WACHS, Herman. Essential oils; Insecticides. b'06. PhD '30 (U Vienna). Holds insecticide patents. Author articles in fields. Research chem Felton Chem Co '30-33; Dodge & Olcott Inc '34-42, research dir since '42. ACS—AAAS. Dodge & Olcott Inc., 69 Av. A, Bayonne, N.J. H: 1461 E. 35 St., Brooklyn 10.

23 WACKER, Robert Charles. Hydraulic engineering. b'21. Student '40-48 (Milwaukee Vocational Sch). Research on development high pressure hydraulics and controls and on hydraulic part of special cranes. Mgr equipment div Blackhawk Mfg Co since

'46. Am Soc Agrl Engrs—Am Road Builders Assn—Constrn Industries Association—Internat Road Fedn. 5325 W. Rogers St., Mil 1.

10 WADE, F(ranklin) Alton. Antarctic geology; Continental ice sheets; Carbonate reservoir rocks (Petroleum). b'03. BS '26—MA '26 (Kenyon Coll); PhD '37 (Johns Hopkins U). Geologist Byrd second Antarctic expedition '33-35; sr scientist US Antarctic Service Expedition '39-41. Author articles in field. Asso to prof geol Miami U since '46, dir Norton geol field camp since '47. USAAF unit comdr. Greenland Ice Cap Detachment '43-44. Geol Soc Am(F)—Mineral Soc Am—Brit Glaciol Soc—Am Geophys Union—Am Assn Pet Geologists—Am Polar Soc. Special Congressional Medal '37, '45. Department of Geology, Miami University, Oxford, Ohio.

11 WADE, Gerald Edward. Spanish language and literature; Spanish American literature; Tirso de Molina. b'96. BA '18 (O Wesleyan U); MA '25 (U Wis); PhD '36 (O State U). Author numerous articles in field. Instr. and asst prof Span lang and lit O Wesleyan U '24-31; instr to prof Span lit U Tenn since '32. Mod Lang Assn Am—So Atlantic Mod Lang Assn—Nat Fed Mod Lang Teachers—Am Assn Teachers Spanish and Portuguese (past pres Tenn chap)—Tenn Philol Assn (sectreas '47-49). University of Tennessee, Knoxville 16, Tenn.†

12 WADE, Joseph Sanford. European corn borer; Hessian fly; Beetles (Immature stages of N A Coleoptera); Sugar cane insects of the World and their parasites; Henry David Thoreau. b'80. Student '05-06 (Fairmount Coll Wichita Kan), '23-25 (U Chicago). Field and laboratory research work on cereal and forage insects; investigations of insects affecting forage crops; spl studies immature stages of North Am Coleoptera. Author: A Bibliography of Hessian Fly '34; A Bibliograph of Immature Stages of N A Coleoptera '35; A Bibliography of Henry David Thoreau '38; A Bibliography of Sugar Cane Insects of the World (in press). Administrative and research work USDA '13-50, collaborator since '50. AAAS(F)—Entomol Soc Am(F)—Am Assn Econ Entomologists—Entomol Soc Washington(pres '34)—Biol Soc Washington (pres '46-47)—Kan Acad Sci—Am Ornithologists Union—Washington Acad Scis—Thoreau Soc. US Department of Agriculture, Washington 25.ⓒ

13 WADE, Otis. Zoology (Habits and behavior, entomology, anatomy); Mammalogy (Squirrels). b'89. BS '10(O No)—MS '17 (O State); PhD '28 (U Neb). Developed use of calcium cyanide in control of prairie dogs; life history studies of ground squirrels and prairie dogs, studies on temperature regulation, hibernation, distribution of various Sciuridae especially 13-striped ground and tuft-eared squirrels; anatomy of opossum; also articles in field. US Biolog Survey Rodent Control Div '21-23; instr to prof dept zool and anatomy U Neb since '25. Am Soc Mammalogists (dir '41-45)—Soc Systematic Zool—Sigma Xi. University of Nebraska, Lincoln, Neb. H: 2540 Rathbone Rd., Lincoln 2.

14 WADE, Warren Benjamin. Enzyme activity of flour; Stabilization of vitamin D solutions; Organic peroxides as bleaching agents. b'03. BA '24 (U Ark); MS '25 (Emory U); (Yale, U Minn). Research chemist to plant mgr Gen Mills Inc since '30. General Mills, Inc., 2010 E. Hennepin Av., Minneapolis 13.†

15 WADLEIGH, Cecil Herbert. Plant physiology (growth, cotton, corn);

Plant biochemistry. b'07. BS '30 (U Mass); MS '32 (Ohio State U); PhD '35 (Rutgers U). Research in relation between physico-chemical nature of substrate and degree of chlorosis in corn; influence of pH of nutrient solution and form of nitrogen supply on organic acid metabolism in corn; effect of level of boron supply upon nitrogen metabolism in cotton; effect of nitrogen supply on cotton plant and resulting influence on the status of the plant products; influence of mineral nutrition on biochem status of cotton and their resistance to fusarium wilt; effect of weather conditions on cotton prodn; salt tolerance in plants; influence of soil moisture conditions on plants. Author: Growth Status of the Cotton Plant as Influenced by the Supply of Nitrogen '44. Co-author: Growth and Biochemical Composition of Bean Plants as Conditioned by Soil Moisture Tension and Salt Concentration '45; Growth and Rubber Accumulation in Guayule as Conditioned by Soil Salinity and Irrigation Regime '46; also articles in field. Am Soc Plant Physiologists (Sec '47-49)—Am Chem Soc—Bot Soc Am—Am Soc Horticultural Sci—Am Soc Agronomy—Soil Sci Soc Am—AAAS(F)—Sigma Xi. U.S. Regional Salinity Laboratory, Riverside, Calif. H: 7134 Potomac St.†

16 WADLEY, Bryce N. Stone fruit virus diseases (Seed Rot). b'09. BS '36 (Brigham Young U); MS '42—PhD '47 —fellow '41-43, '46-47 (Ia State Coll). Research seedling rot of onions caused by species of pythium; research in wilt-resistant first-generation hybrid watermelon seed, seedling rot of watermelons caused by pythium irregulare, Buis. Author articles in field. Plant pathologist, stone fruit virus diseases, US Dept Agr since '48. Am Phytopathol Soc—AAAS. U. S. Agricultural College. Logan, Utah; H: Providence, Utah.†

17 WAESCHE, Hugh Henry. Piezoelectric Minerals; Hawaiian Volcanology. b'04. Student (George Washington U); BS '29—MS '34 (Va Poly Inst); '40 (U Hawaii). Extensive study of Pacific Island volcanos. Author articles in field. Radio engr to geologist Signal Corps Engring Labs since '46; asst geol charge seismology Hawaiian Volcano Observatory '35-41. Geol Soc Am(F)—Am Geophy Union—Am Inst Mining and Metall Engrs—Seismol Soc Am—Grand Canyon Nat Hist Assn '41. Frequency Control Branch, Signal Corps Engineering Laboratories, Fort Monmouth, N.J.

18 WAGER, Alan Turner. Spectroscopy. b'04. BS '26 (Hobart Coll); MA '31 (Cornell U); PhD '48 (U Chicago). Research in adjustment of gratings on thirty foot circle, building a high power discharge source for active nitrogen used in mixing tube for high intensity cold flame, obtained C N bands this way. Author articles in field. Instr. physics Hobart Coll '30-36; instr math chem and phys sci Armour Inst Tech, Lewis Inst, George Williams Coll all in Chicago '36-41; asst. prof. phys Birmingham So Coll '42-43, asso prof since '43-49; prof phys Ariz Sta Coll since '49. Am Inst Physics—Am Phys Soc—Am Assn Phys Teachers—AAAS(F)—Ala Acad Sci (sec '46-49)—Phi Beta Kappa. Arizona State College, Tempe, Ariz.†

19 WAGLEY, Charles. Anthropology (Races and cultures of Latin America); Sociology. b'13. AB '36—PhD '40 (Columbia). Author: Economics of a Guatemalan Village '41. Co-author: The Tenetehara of Brazil '48; also several articles in field. Asst prof anthrop Columbia U '45-49, asso prof '49-53, prof since '53; field survey Hylean Amazon Project of UNESCO '48; staff Social

Sci Research Council NY since '47. NY Acad Sci(F)—Am Ethnol Soc(F). Decorated Order Southern Cross Brazil '45. Department of Anthropology, Columbia University, NYC 27.

20 WAGNER, Charles A(braham). American poetry; Journalism (Biographies, technique, literary criticism, news writing). b'01. AB '24 (Columbia). Author: Poems of the Soil and Sea '23; Nearer the Bone '28; Rhymes Out of School '41. Conbr to top literary mags. Journalist Literary Supplement Morning World '25-26; drama reviews Morning Telegraph '26-29; book review editor Brooklyn Times '30-32; lit editor Daily and Sunday Mirror NY since '32; Sunday editor New York Mirror; book columnist INS, instr Journalism NY U. Am Newspaper Guild—Authors League—Poetry Soc NY—Am Acad Polit and Soc Sci—Harvard Club NY. Winner of Poetry Mag first award for The Unknown Soldier '29; Stratford Mag poetry award '30; Edwin Markham poetry award '33. 235 E. 45th St., NYC. H: 106 Morningside Dr.

21 WAGNER, Joseph Richard. Nutrition; Canned food. b'14. Fellow '38-42— BS '38—MS '40—PhD '44 (U Wis); '33-34 (Whitewater State Teachers Coll Wis). Author: The Nutritive Value of Canned Foods '44, '45, '47. Supervisor nutritional research sect Cen Lab Libby McNeil & Libby Blue Island Ill '45-48; head fruit and vegetable products br Food Development Div Quartermaster Food and Container Inst for Armed Forces Chicago since '48. Am Chem Soc —Inst Food Technol—Assn Vitamin Chemists—Sigma Xi. Quartermaster Food & Container Institute for Armed Forces, 1849 W. Pershing Rd., Chicago 9.

22 WAGNER, Percy Evan. Real estate economics; Property use. b'94. Ph B '16 (U Chgo). Research on appraisal of real estate and its highest and best use, integration of cost and economic return to real property, property use of land from economic and social viewpoint, relation of housing to strata of income groups, effect of government housing on private enterprise and urban tax base; chmn examining committee Real Estate Division, Department of Registration and Education, State of Illinois. Author: Real Estate Appraisal Handbook (Society of Residential Appraisers). Partner Wagner Brothers '16-32; pres Midway State Bank '29-32; chief valuator Federal Housing Adminstrn Ill '34-38, zone mgr '38-40; chmn dept real estate Central Coll '38-42; pres Am Home Builders Inc '40-52; dean Real Estate Inst Central Young Men's Christian Assn '43-52; instr Am Inst Real Estate Appraisers '45-52. Phi Kappa Psi—Lambda Alpha—Am Inst Real Estate Appraisers—Certified Property Mgrs. 6236 Cottage Grove Av., Chgo.

23 WAGSTAFF, Blanche Shoemaker (Mrs. Donald Carr). Greek literature (Drama, poetry). b'88. Grad '14-24 (Columbia); (U Athens); MA '35 (Juanita Coll). Translated Greek and French classical verse; lecturer Greek ideal in literature; authored poetic drama adaptation of Euripides "Alcestis." Lit critic Van Norden Mag '09-10; contbg editor Internat Mag '09-11; founder and editor Boston Poetry Journal '12; lit critic Golf Illus '31-33; librarian USO '42-45. Poetry Soc Am (mem exec council '31-33). Colony Club, NYC.

24 WAHL, Arthur Charles. Chemistry (Radio, inorganic). b'17. BS '39 (Ia State Coll); PhD '42 (U Calif). Research properties of plutonium, applications of radio-activity to chemistry. One of four men who discovered plutonium in '41. Author, articles:

Radioactive Elements 94 From Deuterons on Uranium I and II (with others) '46; Properties of 94 (239) (same) '46. Chemist Manhattan project Berkeley and Los Alamos '42-46; asso prof chem Washington U since '46, Farr prof radiochem since '53. Washington University, St. Louis 5. H: 542 Sunnyside, Webster Groves 19, Mo.

10 WAHL, Arthur M(unzenmaier). Stress analysis; Mechanical spring design. b'01. Student '18-19 (Grinnell Coll); BS '25 (Ia State Coll); MS '27—PhD '32 (U Pittsburgh). Research in stress analysis of machine parts and structures; mechanical spring design and research; elasticity and plasticity problems, creep in turbine disks; vibration problems, torsional oscillations in motor drives. Author: Mechanical Springs '44; also articles in field. Research engr Westinghouse Research Labs East Pittsburgh '26-46, adv engr since '46. ASME—AAAS—Soc Exp Stress Analysis—Tau Beta Pi—Phi Kappa Phi. Received Jr Award '29 and Richards Memorial Award '49 ASME. Westinghouse Research Laboratories, East Pittsburgh.

11 WAHLENBERG, William G(ustavus). Longleaf pine. b'94. BSF '17 (U Maine); MF '18 (Yale). Author: Longleaf Pine '46; also numerous articles in field. US Forest Service since '19, silviculturist Southeastern Forest Expt Sta Asheville NC since '46. Phi Kappa Phi—Soc Am Foresters. Southeastern Forest Experiment Station, U.S. Forest Service, Box 2570, Asheville, N.C.

12 WAHLSTROM, Ernest Eugene. Economic, mining and engineering geology; Mineralogy; Petrology. b'09. BA '31—MA '33 (U Colo); MA '36—PhD '39 (Harvard). Author: Optical Crystallography '43; Igneous Minerals and Rocks '47; Theoretical Igneous Petrology; also articles in field. Instructor to prof dept geol U Colo since '34; cons in mining geol and engring geol since '40. Geol Soc Am(F)—Mineral Soc Am (F)—Soc Econ Geologists—Sigma Xi. Department of Geology, University of Colorado, Boulder, Colo.†

13 WAIT, George Ray. Atmospheric electricity. b'86. BS '14 (Kan State Tchrs Coll); MS '17—PhD '20 (State U Ia). Research on electrical characteristics of thunderstorms, radioactive content and ionization of atmosphere, electric conductivity of air, electric field of earth, electrical character of human breath. Author 46 articles in field. Phys Carnegie Instn Wash since '20, dir Carnegie Instn Obs W Australia '21-24. Sigma Xi—Gamma Alpha—Wash Acad Sci—Philos Soc Wash—Am Geophys Union—AAAS(F). 5241 Broad Branch Rd., Washington 15. H: 4109 Garrison St., Washington 16.

14 WAKEFIELD, Eva Ingersoll. Robert Green Ingersoll. b'91. Student '10-13 (Misses Masters Sch Dobbs Ferry NY); ext courses (Columbia). Research on the life and teachings of Robert Green Ingersoll, has collection of his letters and manuscripts. Editor (with biog introductions and notes): The Letters of Robt G. Ingersoll '51; The Life and Letters of Robert G. Ingersoll '52. Executive sec Robert G Ingersoll Memorial Assn Inc. 144 East 24th St., NYC 10.

15 WAKEFIELD, Sherman D(ay). Abraham Lincoln (in Bloomington Illinois and Bixby Letter); Humanism (Bibliography, history, philosophy); Wakefield genealogy. b'94. PhB '24 (U Chgo); BS '28 (Columbia U); LittD Hon '40 (De Landas U). Author: How Lincoln Became President '36; Abraham Lincoln and the Widow Bixby '47; Abraham Lincoln and the Bixby Letter '48. Editorial asst The Humanist; consulting editor Progressive World; also articles in field. Research asst to Minister West Side Unitarian Ch NY '25-26; asst NY Pub Library '28-29; bibliographer Ency of Soc Sci NY '29-34, general researcher and writer Am Hist Co NY '37-39; asso editor The Arbitrator NY '39-43; geneal for Wakefield family; staff editor and bibliographer The Grolier Ency '43-47; staff editor Collier's Ency '47-49, World Wide Ency and Home U Ency '49-51. Lincoln (F) NY (sec '38-40)—First Humanist Soc NY (adv bd)—AAAS—Ill State Hist Soc—Am Humanist Assn—Rationalist Press Assn (London). H: 144 E. 24th St., N.Y.C. 10.

16 WAKEHAM, Helmut (Richard Rea). Cotton and textile fibers (Properties, structure); Physical chemistry of high polymers. b'16. Student '32-34 (Union College Neb); BA '36—MA '37 (U Neb; PhD (U Calif). Author articles in field. Section head Textile Research Institute Princeton since '49. Fiber Soc—Am Chem Soc—AAAS—Am Soc X-Ray and Electron Diffraction—Va Acad Sci—Sigma Xi. Textile Research Institute, Princeton.

17 WAKELEY, Philip Carman. Silviculture; Forestry; Artificial reforestation. b'02. BS '23—MF '25 (Cornell U). Author articles in field. Jr forester and silviculturist P-2 to P-5 Southern Forest Expt Sta Forest Service US Dept Agrl New Orleans La since '25, project leader in charge regeneration since '26. Soc Am Foresters—AAAS(F) — New Orleans Acad Scis (past pres)—Ecol Soc Am. 704 Lowich Bldg., 2026 St. Charles Av., New Orleans 13.

18 WAKEMAN, Arthur G. Paper and pulp industry of Germany. b'98. BS '21 (MIT). With US Army in Europe making survey paper industry in Germany '45. Supt Paper Mill Kimberly Clarp Corp '23; mgr Fox River Paper Co Appleton Wis '27; dir Paper and Pulp Div War Prodn Bd '42; with Mission Econ Affairs London '43; vp and gen mgr Coosa River News Print Co since '47. Tech Assn Pulp and Paper Ind—Newcomen Soc Eng. Coosa River News Print Co., Coosa Pines, Ala.

19 WAKSMAN, Selman Abraham. Microbiology (Soil); Humus; Antibiotics; Bacteriology (Marine). b'88. BS '15—MS '16—DSc (hon) '43 (Rutgers U); PhD '18 (U Calif); MD (hon) '46 (U Liege Belgium); DSc (hon) '47 (Princeton U); LLD (hon) '48 (Yeshiva U). Author: Principles of Soil Microbiology '27, '32; Humus '36, '38; Microbial Antagonisms and Antibiotic Substances '45, '47; also numerous articles in field. Prof microbiol Rutgers U since '42; microbiol NJ Agrl Exptl Sta New Brunswick since '21; marine bateriol Woods Hole Oceanographic Inst '30-42; cons Sloan-Kettering Institute of Cancer Research. Nat Acad Sci—French Acad Sci—AAAS(F)—Soc Am Bacteriol (pres '42)—Soil Sci Soc Am—Soc Exptl Biology and Med—Internat Soc Soil Sci (pres third com)—Sigma Xi—Phi Beta Kappa. Received Nitrate of Soda Research Award for Am Soc of Agronomy for 1930; Passano Foundation Award '47; Emil Cher Hansen Prize '47. Logan Lane, River Rd., New Brunswick, N.J.⊚

20 WALD, George. Chemistry and physiology of vision. b'06. BS '27 (NY U); MA '28—PhD '32 (Columbia). Discovered vitamin A in retina, its participation in rhodopsin system of rod vision; vitamin A 2 and its participation in porphyropsin system. Author articles in field. Am Physiol Soc—AAAS—Am Chem Soc—Optical Soc AM—NY Acad Scis(F)—Am Acad Arts Sci(F). Nat Research Council (F) '32-34; Eli Lilly and Co Award Am Chem Soc '39. Biology Laboratories, Harvard University, Cambridge 38, Mass.⊚

21 WALDMAN, Harvey N(orman). Adhesives and coatings (Rubber, resin and latex). b'17. AB '38—MS '39 (U Cincinnati); '39-41 (U Akron). Pres and dir research Polymer Chem Co Cincinnati since '45. Chief chemist So-Lo Works Inc collaborated with branches of the Army Navy Air Forces '42-45. ACS—ASTM—AAAS. 7709 Greenland Pl., Cin 37.

22 WALDO, Willis Gersham. Ramie and kenaf (Decortication, degumming, fiber processing); Abaca (Decortication). b'83. Student '02-04 (Purdue U); BS '07 (MIT); '16 (Vanderbilt U). General survey of ramie production, processing and products; design and supervision construction of ramie processing plant for fiber and byproduct meal; survey of ramie possibilities for Philippine government; developed own technique for decorticating ramie and kenaf. Holds patents on device for preparing and decorticating bast fibers. Author articles: The Possibilities of Ramie '45, Ramie Products in the Fla Everglades '47; Report on Ramie '48, and others. Contributor: Cotton Trade Journal '49. Consulting engineer Office Production Research and Development WPB '44; vp and chief engineer Fla Ramie Products Inc Belle Glade Fla '44-48; special consultant Nat Development Co Manila PI '48; pres Waldo Engring Corp Palm Beach since '49. Am Soc CE—Soil Sci Soc Fla—Fla Engring Soc—Nat Soc Profl Engrs. 247 Worth Av., Palm Beach, Fla.

23 WALES, James Albert. International tourist trade. b'79. AB '01 (Trinity Coll Hartford Conn). Adviser to foreign countries on promotion of travel and commerce. Author: Residence in Bermuda '36; The Tourist Dollar '38; also articles in field. Vice pres. McCreery, Quick & McElroy Inc. Phi Beta Kappa. 400 Madison Av., NYC.

24 WALFORD, Lionel A(lbert). Marine fishery biology. b'05. AB '29 (Stanford Univ); MA '32—PhD '35 (Harvard). Aquatic biologist; fish and wildlife fish expeditions; special studies of specific fishes; supervisor fishery research. Author articles in field. Aquatic biol Internat Fisheries Commn US and Mexico '26-27, Calif State Fisheries Lab '27-31; US Bureau of Fisheries since '36. Nat Research Council—Am Soc Ichthyol and Hepetol—Am Soc Limnol and Oceanographers—Am Fishery Soc—Nat Fishery Inst. US Fish and Wild Life Service, Washington 25.

25 WALKE, Nelson S. Health and physical education (Recreation, teacher training); Athletics; Tests and measurements in physical education. b'97. Grad '17 (Normal Coll of Phys Edn North Am Gymnastic Union Indianapolis); BS '27 (U Cincinnati); MA '32—PhD '37 (Teachers Coll, Columbia). Author: Traits Characteristic of Men Majoring in Physical Education '37; also articles in field. Instr health and physical edn Cincinnati pub sch '19-31; prof and head instructional phys edn Pa State Coll '32-36; instr Teachers Coll Columbia U '36-38; dir health and phys edn Okla Agrl and Mech Coll '38-40; dean Sargent Coll Phys Edn Boston U '40-45; chmn dept health and phys edn Brooklyn Coll since '45. NEA—Am Assn Health—Phys Edn and Recreation—Am Social Hygiene Assn—College Phys Ed Assn—NY State Phys Ed Assn—Am Soc U Profs—Kappa Delta Pi. Bedford Av and Av H, Brooklyn 10, NY; H: 760 West Av., NYC 25.

10 WALKER, Albert Charles. Piezoelectric crystals (Growth of synthetic); Textiles (Electrical and moisture properties); Blood (Polarography). b '93. Student '14-16 (U Colo); BS '18 (MIT); PhD '23 (Yale). Research on electrical properties of cotton and improvement by washing in treated water; built first American-made polarograph and used it in experiments to detect cancer by blood tests; developed substitute for quartz for telephone purposes, developed effective method of growing large quartz crystals by hydrothermal process. Tech staff W Elec '23-25; tech staff Bell Telephone Laboratory since '25. ACS—AAAS—Am Institute Chem(F)—Textile Research Inst—Sigma Xi—Gamma Alpha—Alpha Chi Sigma—NY State Soc Profl Engrs. Lewis Edward Levy medal for 1951 of Franklin Inst for paper on Growing Piezoelectric Crystals. Bell Telephone Laboratories, Murray Hill, N.J.

11 WALKER, Burnham Sarle. Medical biochemistry (Iron, enzymes). b'01. AB '23—AM '24—PhD '26—MD '34 (Boston U). Prof biochem Boston U since '35; chmn div med sci Boston U Grad Sch since '46. AAAS—AMA—Am Chem Soc—Mass Med Soc—Am Soc Biol Chem. 80 E. Concord St., Boston 18.

12 WALKER, Eric Arthur. Instrumentation by electronics; Acoustics in fluids. b'10. BS '32—MS '33—ScD '35 (Harvard). Application of acoustics in fluids and solids and to precipitation, coagulation, mixing and shaking problems. Articles in field. Asst prof elec engring Tufts Coll '33-35; asso prof '35-38, head elec engring dept '38-40; head elec engring dept U Conn '40-43; asso dir Harvard Underwater Sound Lab '42-45; dir Ordnance Research Lab Pa State Coll '45-52, head elec engring dept '45-51, dean sch engring since '51; exec sec Res and Develop Bd, Dept Def '50-51; elec engring cons since '34. Am Acoustical Soc(F)—Am Inst Elec Engring(F)—Am Soc Engring Edn—Am Phys Soc—Inst Radio Engrs—Sigma Xi—Tau Beta Pi. 628 Fairway Rd., State College, Pa.†

13 WALKER, Ernest DeWitt. Soils and soil conservation. b'87. BS '10 (U Ill). Author: The Story of a Lake. Coauthor: Five Steps in Pasture Improvement; Conserving Our Soil Resources; Grass or Gullies; This Is Our Soil; A Handbook for Soil Conservation District Directors; Getting Better Stands of Legumes and Grasses For Soil Conservation. Extension Soil Conserv and asso prof Agronomy Ext Coll Agr U Ill Soil Conservation Soc America—American Soc of Agronomy—Friends of the Land—Gamma Sigma Delta. 322 Davenport Hall, College of Agriculture, Urbana, Ill.†

14 WALKER, Eugene Hoffman. Geomorphology; Glaciation; Andean Geology; Rocky Mountain Geological History; Ground water hydrology. b'15. AB '37—MA '41—PhD '47 (Harvard University). Geological history of the Andes. Instr U Mich '46-49; geol US Geol Survey since '49. Geol Soc Am—Am Geogr Soc(F). US Geological Survey, 304 W. Liberty St., Lsvl.

15 WALKER, Franklin D. American cultural history (Far western regionalism); American literature (Criticism); Mark Twain; History of the United States Army Air Corps (World War II). b'00. BA '23 (Oxford); PhD '32 (U Calif); Huntington Library Fellow '46-48. Supervised and edited studies design, procurement, supply and maintenance of Air Corps World War II. Author: Frank Norris '32; Prentice Mulford's California Sketches '35; The Wa-

shoe Giant in San Francisco (Mark Twain) '38; San Francisco's Literary Frontier '39; Mark Twain's Travels with Mr. Brown '40; Ambrose Bierce '41. Prof Eng lit Mills Coll since '46. Received Commonwealth Gold Medal (non-fiction) for '39. Mills College, Oakland 13, Calif.†☺

16 WALKER, Harold Leroy. Metallurgical engineering (Physical); Heat treatment of steels and ordnance materiel. b'05. BS '32—MS '33—E Metall '35 (Mich Coll Mining and Tech). Heat treatment of armor piercing projectile steels and ordnance materiel. Author articles in field. Research engr, asst to supt, Munising Paper Co Mich '27-29; instr metall engring Mich Coll Mining and Tech '32-37; asst prof metall and metallography, Washington State Coll, '37-38; asst prof to prof metall engring U Ill '38-42, prof and head dept mining and metall engring since '42. Am Inst Mining and Metall Engrs—Am Soc for Metals—Nat Soc for Profes Engrs—AAAS—Sigma Xi. Received Ben M Vallat Award '33. Department Mining and Metallurgical Engineering, University of Illinois, Urbana, Ill.†☺

17 WALKER, James Alexander. Town planning. b'87. Diploma civil engring '08—B Applied Sc '10—Grad CE '26 (U Toronto). Assisted in preparation original British Columbia Town Planning Act and several amendments; delivered special lectures on planning University of British Columbia; designer many subdivisions Vancouver; associated on part-time basis with Vancouver Town Planning Commission since '25. Author articles: Standards and Procedures in Community Planning; The Town Plan of Vancouver; others. Town planning and landscape engr since '19; engr-sec Vancouver Town Planning Commn '25-40, exec engr since '44. Engr with Canadian Army Ottawa Can '40-44. Assn Profl Engr BC—Corp BC Land Surveyors—Engring Inst Can—Inst Profl Town Planners—Community Planning Assn Can—Am Inst Planners—Am Soc Planning Ofcls—Urban Land Inst. 309 Roy Trust Bldg., 626 W. Pender St., Vancouver, B.C.

18 WALKER, John. History of Art (Painting); History of American, French and Italian Painting. b'06. AB '30—John Harvard Fellow '30-31—'33 (Harvard U). Special adviser American commission for protection and salvage of Artistic and Historic Monuments in Europe '43-46. Co-author: Great American Paintings from Smibert to Bellows '43; Masterpieces of Painting from the National Gallery of Art '44. Asso in charge Dept Fine Arts Am Acad Rome Italy '35-39; chief curator Nat Gallery Art Washington since '39; mem Council of Gazette des Beaux-Arts; trustee American Acad Rome; mem vis com Harvard U Press, Dumbarton Oaks, Harvard U. Phi Beta Kappa. National Gallery of Art, Washington. H: 2806 N St. NW.

19 WALKER, John Charles. Petrochemical development; Corrosion control; Emulsion breaking. b'93. BS in chem engring '16—MS '17 (Washington U). Invented process for partial oxidation of hydrocarbon gases to produce other substances; developed processes for chemical treatment of oil wells to inhibit corrosion of well metal, developed process for prevention of internal corrosion of gas pipelines and also for prevention of external corrosion; developed processes for recovery of oil from oil field wastes and for treating crude oil. Granted US and fgn patents in field. With Cities Service since '17, research dir

since '47. ACS—Am Petroleum Inst—Am Inst Chem(F)—Sigma Xi—Alpha Chi Sigma. Cities Service Research & Development Co., 54 Wall St., NYC 5.

20 WALKER, Joseph Frederic. Formaldehyde chemistry; Chemistry of elemental sodium. b'03. BS '25—MS '28—PhD '29 (MIT). Research on physical properties, manufacture, chemical reactions and uses of formaldehyde and its polymers. Author monograph: Formaldehyde '44, rev '53. Contributor: Encyclopedia Britannica since '47; Encyclopedia of Chemical Technology '51. Research chem Roessler & Hasslacher Chem Co '27-30; with E I duPont de Nemours & Co Inc since '30, chem research supervisor Electrochem Dept since '45. ACS—AAAS—Soc Chem Industry. E. I. du Pont de Nemours and Co., Inc., Niagara Falls, N.Y.

21 WALKER, Joseph Henry. Helminthology; Parasitic protozoology. b'02. BS '23 (U Ga); MS '29 (U Ill); '33-35 (U Ala) PhD '37 (Tulane U). Author articles in field. Prof biol and chmn biol dept U Ala since '44. Ala Acad Sci—Am Micros Soc—Am Soc Parasitol—Am Soc Tropical Med. Biology Department, University of Alabama, University, Ala.

22 WALKER, Leslie William. American history (West, westward movement); Robert Rogers; Political, social and economic history of Guam. b'10. AB '40—MA '42 (U Calif). Author articles in field. Hist USAAF HQ Air Training Command since '47. AHA—Miss Valley Hist Assn—Am Acad Polit and Social Sci—Am Geog Soc. Historical Section United States Air Force, Headquarters Air Training Command, Barksdale Air Force Base, La. H: 1703½ Holly St., Shreveport.

23 WALKER, Marion N(ewman). Rubber plants; Watermelons; Phytopathology; Plant breeding. b'00. BS '21 (Ala Poly Inst); MS '23—PhD '24 (U Wis). Author articles in field. Fla agrl exp sta '26-42; rubber research US Dept Agrl since '47. Food crops work with US Army Fgn Econ Adminstrn China '44-45. Phytopath Soc—Phi Kappa Phi—Sigma Xi. Div. Rubber Plants Investigations, Plant Industry Station, Beltsville, Md.

24 WALKER, Paul Andrew. Avian physiology of development. b'10. AB '31 (Bowdoin Coll); AM '32—PhD '36 (Harvard). Author articles in field. Prof biol and chmn dept Randolph-Macon Woman's Coll since '45. Am Soc Zool—AAAS—Phi Beta Kappa. Department of Biology, Randolph-Macon Woman's College, Lynchburg, Va.†

25 WALKER, Robert Murrell. Electronic circuits and computers. b'07. Holds 3 US patents, others pending. Author articles in field. Radio engr Fisher's Blend Sta Inc Seattle '35-41; research asso dept elec engring MIT '42, staff Radiation Lab '42-45; staff Watson Sci Computing Lab Columbia U and Internat Bus Machines Corp NYC since '46. Inst Radio Engrs—Am Phys Soc. Watson Scientific Computing Laboratory, 612 W. 116th St., NYC 27.

26 WALKER, Roland. Neuroanatomy (Fish, invertebrate); Pathology of fish (Tumors); Cytology (Cell size). b'07. BA '28—MA '29 (Oberlin Coll); PhD '34 (Yale). Author: The Central Nervous System of Oniscus (Isopoda) '34; Size, Development, and Innervation of Labyrinth Sensory Areas in Squalus '42; Congenital Aortic and Mitral Atresia '42; Embryonal Nephroma in a Calf '43; Size Relations in the Optic System of Telescope-eyed Goldfish '45. Instr biology Rensselaer Poly Inst '34-42, asst prof '42, '46, asso prof since '46.

Am Ornithol U—Am Soc Zool—Phi Beta Kappa—Sigma Xi—AAAS. Biological Laboratory, Rensselaer Polytechnic Institute, Troy, N.Y.

10 WALKER, Theodore John. Limnology; Oceanography; Ichthyology (Sensory Physiology). b'15. BA '38 (Mont U); MS '40 (U Okla); PhD '45 (U Wis). Research on sense of smell in fish, fish behavior-learning, memory, dominance. Author articles in field. Inst Oceanography Scripps Inst Oceanography since '48. Sigma Xi. Scripps Institute Oceanography, La Jolla, Calif.

11 WALKER, Walter Owen. Refrigeration. b'96. AB '19—ScD hon '49 (William Jewell Coll Liberty Mo); MS '25—PhD '31 (U Chicago). Manufacture, analysis, and utilization of refrigerants; study effects of moisture in refrigerating systems, control of moisture in manufacturing refrigerating equipment; research on refrigeration oils, formation of solidsin refrigerating systems, and commercial uses of methyl chloride and sulfur dioxide; experiment with driers for use with refrigerating systems. Author: Moisture and Drying Methods (6th edit AS RE Data Book) '49, also articles in field. Co-author articles: Liquid Sulfur Dioxide in the Food Industries '43; Liquid Methyl Chloride; Separation of Wax from Oil—Refrigerant Mixtures '45, and others. Contributor: Encyclopedia of Chemical Technology. Prof chem William Jewell Coll '23-29; research chem A O Smith Corp Milwaukee '30-32; prof and head dept chem U Miami Fla '32-36; dir research Ansul Chem Co '36-51; prof chem, dir indsl chem research U Miami since '51. Am Soc Refrigerating Engrs—ACS—Refrigeration Service Engrs Soc., University of Miami, Fla.

12 WALKER, Ward R(obert). Animal incubators, photography; Pythons. b'02. Student '25-26 (Spencerian Business College Milwaukee Wis). Work in feeding, care, treatment, exhibition of wild animals in captivity including office administration, publicity, education, writing, photography; built and managed Hershey Zoo; care of zoological specimens and their lives in captivity, animal lectures; raised to maturity Indian Rock Pythons hatched and reared in captivity for first time in Western Hemisphere; developed construction and use of animal incubators for the care of baby animals taken from captive mothers; developed the copying of animal plates by projection of colored lights to enhance colors lost in engraving process. Asst Milwaukee Zool Garden '23-29; dir Hershey Zool Garden '29-47; Bur Public Relations Pennsylvania Game Commn since '47. Am Inst Park Executives—Am Assn Zool Parks and Aquariums—Am Assn Mammalogists—Am Ornithol Union—Nat Geog Soc—Hawk Mountain Sanctuary—Am Mus Natural Hist. Bureau of Public Relations, Pennsylvania Game Commission, Harrisburg, Pa.

13 WALKER, William Comstock. Adsorption; Printing inks. b'21. BS '43—MS '44—PhD '46—Westvaco Chlorine Products Corp research fellow '43-46 (Lehigh U). Research on catalytic and adsorptive properties of active magnesia, and on fundamental phenomena of printing ink systems. Author articles in field. Asso dir Nat Printing Ink Research Inst Lehigh U since '47. AAAS—Am Chem Soc—Am Inst Chem—NY Ink Prodn Club—Internat Assn Printinghouse Craftsmen—Tau Beta Pi. Chemistry Department, Lehigh University, Bethlehem, Pa. H: 1736 Jefferson Av.

14 WALKINSHAW, Lawrence Harvey. Sandhill Cranes. b'04. Student '24-25 (Olivet Coll Mich); DDS '29 (U Mich). Study of Grus canadensis and four subspecies sandhill cranes; research expeditions on cranes US and Canada; investigation environment and distribution of cranes. Author: The Sandhill Cranes '49. Author articles: Exploring Chippewa County Sandhill Crane Marshes '47; The Sandhill Crane in the Bernard W. Baker Sanctuary '50, and others. Sanctuary chmn Mich Audubon Soc '41-45; now research biol Cranbrook Inst Sci Bloomfield Hills Mich. 1703 Central Tower, Battle Creek, Mich.

15 WALL, Bennett Harrison. History of Southern United States (Plantation economics, Negro slave); Muckrakers; Literature of discontent. b'14. AB '33 (Wake Forest Coll); MA '40—PhD '46 (U NC). Asso prof hist U Ky since '50. History Department, University of Kentucky, Lexington 29, Ky

16 WALL, Florence E(meline). Cosmetology; History of chemistry and cosmetics. b'93. BA—BEd '13 (Coll St. Elizabeth Convent Sta NJ); MA '38 (NYU). Author: Canitics '26; Science of Beautistry '32; Basic Science of Hair Treatments '35; The Principles and Practice of Beauty Culture '41; Opportunities in Beauty Culture '52. also articles in field. Lecturer NYU Sch of Edn '36-43, College of Med '48; cons chem and tech writer. Am Inst Chem (F, nat coun '33-36, '49-54)—AAAS—Am Chem Soc—Soc Cosmetic Chem—Author's League Am—Soc Med Jurisprudence. 210 E. 68th St., NYC 21.†⊙

17 WALL, James Robert. Aluminum chemicals. b'03. BS '26 (U Ill). Inventions and patents on manufacture of fine particle aluminum trihydrate for use as filler in rubber plastics paper paint, process for removing dissolved silica from sodium aluminate solutions. Research chem and sr research chem Aluminum Co Am since '26. Am Chem Soc—Sigma Xi. Aluminum Company of America, East St. Louis, Ill.†

18 WALLACE, A(lva) Dayle. Horace Walpole. b'08. AB '28—MA '29 (Tex Tech Coll); '28 (Columbia U); PhD '33—hon Sterling fellow '39-40 (Yale). Research on Horace Walpole's correspondence. Author: Correspondence of Horace Walpole with William Cole '37; Correspondence of Horace Walpole with Mary, Agnes, and Robert Berry and Barbara Cecilia Seton '44; Correspondence of Horace Walpole with Thomas Chatterton et al '51. Associate prof Eng Wayne U Detroit '44-50, prof since '50. Dept. of English, Wayne University, Detroit 1.†

19 WALLACE, Arthur. Mineral nutrition of crop plants. b'19. BS '41 (Utah State Agrl Coll); PhD '49—Research fellow '46-49 (Rutgers U). Research on physiological responses of plants to mineral nutrients and other environmental factors; studies of nitrogen nutrition and lime-induced chlorosis, recent work with orange, lemon and avocado fruit trees. Asst prof subtropical hort and asst plant physiol U Cal. Am Soc Hort Sci—Am Soc Plant Physiol—Soil Sci Soc Am—Sigma Xi. Department of Subtropical Horticulture, University of California, LA 24.

20 WALLACE, Howard Keefer. Spiders (Taxonomy, zoogeography). b'07. BS '29—PhD '38 (Fla U); MS '32 (Pittsburgh U). Research and investigations on taxonomy and zoogeography of spiders of family Lycosidae. Author articles: Revision of the Genus Geolycosa '42; A Study of the Lenta Group of the Genus Lycosa '42. Instr, later professor biol Fla U since '32. Sigma Xi—AAAS—Fla Acad Sci—Soc Study Evolution—Assn SE Biol—Fla Entomol Soc. Biology Dept, University of Florida, Gainesville, Fla.†

21 WALLACE, James Merrill. Virus diseases of plants. b'02. BS '23 (Miss State Coll); MS '27—PhD '29 (U Minn). Discoverer of condition of acquired immunity from virus in tobacco transmissable by grafting to tomato plants; co-discoverer of virus nature of quick decline disease of oranges and demonstration of the presence of symptomless hosts of the virus within the citrus family. Author articles in field. Asso, later plant path U Calif Citrus Expt Sta since '42. AAAS(F)—Am Phytopath Soc—Sigma Xi. University of California Citrus Experiment Station, Riverside, Calif.†

22 WALLACE, Raymond Paul. Andorra; Easter Island; Liechtenstein; Luxemburg; Monaco; Moresnet; San Marino; Sark; Scotland (Clan system); Heraldry; Genealogy. AB '41—MA '47—Profl Engr '48 (U Cal); DLitt '50 (Western U). Research on sociology and history of minute states; historical and genealogical research on Scottish clan system. Author: The Three Small Republics: San Marino, Andorra, Moresnet '47; The Chiefs of Wallace: A Brief Genealogical cna Historical Account of the Titular Heads of Clan Wallace '47; A Contribution to the History of Neutral Moresnet '48; The Royal House of Liechtenstein '51; Ethnogeny of Easter Island and Its Kings '51; also articles in field. Nuclear engr Radiation Lab U Cal since '42. Sigma Xi—Phi Sigma—Psi Chi—Inst Am Genealogy(F(—Am Heraldic Soc(F)—Soc of Antiquaries of Scotland(F). Radiation Laboratory, University of California, Berkeley 4.

23 WALLACE, William Kay. Atomic energy (Raw materials). b'86. Grad '04 (Phillips Acad Andover Mass); AB '08—AM '11 (Yale). Production beryl, lithium and mica ores. Pres Black Hills Keystone Corp. 530 Fifth Av., NYC 19.⊙

24 WALLACE, William S(willing). Russo-American expatriation; Russian and Western American history. b'22. BA (West State Coll of Colo); MA (Mont State U). MA in LS (U Denver). Research problems of Russian-American expatriation of the 19th century; early history of Intermontane Corridor of western North America. Author: Antoine Robidoux '53; numerous articles. AHA—Colo Archeol Soc—Society Am Archivists—Phi Alpha Theta. Rodgers Library, N.M. Highlands U., Las Vegas, N.M.

25 WALLBANK, T. Walter. History of British Empire (Colonial administration and imperialism in India and Africa); History of civilization. b'01. AB, AM '27 (U Calif); PhD (U So Calif). Research government Crown Colonies, British Colonial Office, London '35; field investigation on anthropology of native peoples and problems of colonial administration in British East Africa '36. Author: India; A Survey of the Heritage and Growth of Indian Nationalism '48. Co-author: Civilization: Past and Present (with A. M. Taylor) two vols, '42, and others. Fellow Am Social Sci Research Council '35-37; prof hist U So Calif, since '37. Royal African Soc—AHA—Phi Alpha Theta—Phi Beta Kappa. History Department, University Southern California, LA 7. H: Box 381, Julian, Cal.

26 WALLERSTEIN, James Scheuer. Enzyme chemistry (Fermentation); Food technology. b'10. BS '32 (Harvard); MA '38 (Columbia). Research in brewing fermentation. Holds ten patents fermentation field. Author articles in field. Research chemist Wallerstein

Labs '31-41, vp since '37; pres and dir Overly Biochem Research Foundation Inc since '42; pres and dir Randen Foundation Inc since '45, Am Inst Chem Soc—Am Acad Sci—Soc Am Bacteriologists — Am Soc Brewing Chem — Assn I n d s l Chemists—Am Wood Chem. 254 W. 31 St., NYC 1. H: 125 E. 72nd St.

10 WALLIN, Jack R(obb). Phytopathology; Guatemalan maize; Phytopathogenic bacteria; Plant disease forecasting. b'15. BS '39—PhD '44 (Ia State Coll); '39-41 (U Mo). Author articles in field. Path Bur Plant Ind US Dept Agr since '47. Ia Acad Sci —Am Phytopath Soc—Am Soc Agronomy—AAAS—Sigma Xi. United States Plant Disease Survey, Iowa State College, Ames, Ia.

11 WALLING, Ishmael Worth. Water chemistry. b'10. BA '36 (E Tex State Tchrs Coll); '39-41 (Hardin-Simmons U Abilene Tex). Author article: Chemical Character of Surface Waters in Washita River Basin of Oklahoma '48. Co-author articles: (with F B Plummer) Laboratory Investigations of the Chemical Changes in East Texas Waters Affecting its Injections into Subsurface Sands '46; (with Hale, Baker, Parrish, Billingsley) Public Water Supplies of Arkansas '47; (with T B Dover) Chemical Character of Surface Waters of Oklahoma 1946-49 '50. Analytical chem Internat Mineral & Chem Corp Carlsbad NM, Austin Tex '42-44; staff Bur Econ Geol U Tex '44-45; dist chem US Geol Survey since '45. ACS—Am Water Works Assn—Am Geophys Union. U. S. Geological Survey, University of California, Davis. H: 520 Second St.

12 WALLIS, Marie Pope. Ibero-American literature. b'01. BA '25 (U Calif LA); MA '28—MS '35 (USC); PhD '47 (UNM); '39 (Nat U Mexico); '40 (U Puerto Rico); '41 (U San Marcos); fellow '43 (U Mich). Research on Brazilian women novelists. Author: Patio Sun '28; Modern Women Poets of Brazil '47. Field rep community program Sch Inter-Am Affairs UNM '43-44; research and teacher Spanish and Portuguese UNM '39-51. Mod Lang Assn—Phi Kappa Phi—Phi Sigma Iota. 450 Maple N.E., Albuquerque, N.M.

13 WALLS, Howard Lamarr. Motion picture history. b'12. AB '33 (U Mich). Instigated and conducted individual research resulting in restoration to screen several thousand motion pictures that constitute the foundations and development of American screen art 1897-1912. Author: Motion Picture Incunabula in the Library of Congress. Joined staff Library of Congress '39, apptd asso fellow motion pictures '41, curator motion picture collection '43; curator Acad Motion Picture Arts Sci since '47. 9038 Melrose Av., Hollywood 46, Cal.

14 WALLS, Stanley King. Concrete; Standards (Uniform); Petroleum (Iranian exploration). b'97. BSc '20 (Heriot-Watt Coll Edinburg); MA '21 (Staff Coll Quetta Baluchistan); PhD '25 (U Freiburg). Ready mixed concrete; light weight and insulated concrete; concrete curing; concrete water proofing; uniform standards; Anglo Iranian oil fields. Jr engr exploration and development Anglo-Iranian Oil Co '21-26; cons engr Gen Engring & Management Co '26-36; with Stanley King Walls Asso (cons engrs) '36-47; asso prof indsl engring Adelphi Coll Garden City NY Fairleigh Dickinson College Rutherford NJ since '47. AIMME—Soc Am Mil Engrs—AAAS—Am Inst Indsl Engrs—Soc Quality Control—Royal Econ Soc(F)—Royal Soc Arts(F). Profl

engr Nev, O, NJ. 342 Madison Av., NYC 17.

15 WALRATH, Florence Dahl. Infant adoption. b'77. Founder managing dir The Cradle Soc Evanston organized '23 for purpose of receiving and preparing homeless babies for adoption into permanent homes, work in which she had been engaged prior to '23; over 5000 babies adopted in homes in US and some foreign countries; has assisted in development of improved technique for care of babies where numbers are cared for in one place resulting in unusualy low death rate. The Cradle Society, 2049 Ridge Av., Evanston, Ill.

16 WALSH, Donald Devenish. Spanish-American literature; Spanish grammar. b'03. SB '25 (Harvard). Author: Cuentos y versos americanos '42; Seis relatos americanos '43; text editions of Uslar Pietri's Las lanzas coloradas '44, Goytortua's Pensativa '47; Introductory Spanish '46; Repaso '48; Cuentos americanos con algunos versos '48; also articles in field. Head Spanish dept The Choate Sch Wallingford Conn since '28; advtg mgr Hispania '44-49, ed since '49. Modern Lang Association (associate secretary '53-55)—NE Modern Language Association (asso ed bull since '43, dir '43-45)—Am Assn Teachers Spanish, Portugese —(vp '48, '49)—Asociacion de Escritores y Artistas Americanos. Modern Language Association, Washington Sq. N., N.Y.C. 3.†

17 WALSH, Gerald Groveland. Dante; Humanism; Patrology; Medieval culture, History of Catholic church; Philosophy of history. b'92. AB '16 (London U); MA '24 (Oxford U); '25-28 (Woodstock Coll); PhD, STD '29 (Gregorian U, Rome Italy). Editor Thought (Fordham U Quarterly) '40-49; asso editor The Fathers of the Church, a new translation '46; Prof church hist and librarian Woodstock, Md Coll '29-34; grad prof medieval history Gregorian U Rome '34-36; head grad dept Italian studies Fordham U '37-38, grad prof medieval hist '38-50. AHA—Am Catholic Hist Assn — Medieval Acad Am—Am Acad Polit and Social Sci—Dante Soc—Oxford Soc. Gibbs scholarship in modern history and Marquis of Lothian prizeman. Oxford U (England) '23. Loyola Hall. Fordham University, NYC 58.

18 WALSH, Michael P(atrick). Cytology; Genetics. b'12. AB '33—MA '34 (Boston Coll); STL '42 (Weston Coll); MS '38—PhD '48 (Fordham University). Research in annelid cytology and application of chemicals to cells; cancer cytology; nuclear studies in annelids; effect of growth hormones on cells in roots of various plants; spermatogenesis in Lumbricus terrestris. Instr cytology Boston Coll '42-44, chmn biol dept, asst prof cytology since '48. Am Soc Genetics—NY Acad Sci—Am Micros Soc—AAAS. Biology Department, Boston College, Chestnut Hill 67, Mass.

19 WALSH, Warren Bartlett. Russian and Soviet history and politics. b'09. AB '30 (Tufts Coll); AM '31— PhD '35 (Harvard U). Author: Russia —A Readers Guide '45; Russia Under Tsars and Commissars '46; Russia, a Handbook '47; Readings in Russian History '48; A History of Russia and the Soviet Union '53. Co-author: Development of Western Civilization (with C G Haines) '41. Asso ed: The Russian Review. Instr in hist Syracuse U '35-37, asst prof '37-43, asso prof '43-45, prof '45-48, prof Russian hist since '48, chmn bd Russian Studies since '44, dir, summer sch Russian Program since '44; dir USAFIT-Syra-

cuse Russian program '50-52; member resident civilian faculty Nat War Coll '52, chmn civilian faculty '53. AHA. Maxwell School, Syracuse University, Syracuse 10, N.Y.†

20 WALTERS, Leon L(ouis). Taxidermy (Artificial reproductions, plastics, anatomical models); Prosthetics (Artificial hands). b'88. Student Art Inst Chicago. Discoverer of a basic principle of coloring in connection with making reproductions of animal and plant life; inventor processes in taxidermy and model making. Author articles: New Uses of Celluloid and Similar Material in Taxidermy '25; other articles in field. Sculptor and artist; staff taxidermist Chicago Museum of Natural History since '11. Am Soc Mammalogists—Chicago Ornithol Soc. Chicago Natural History Museum, Chgo.

21 WALTERS, Raymond Jr. American history (Early republican period, Albert Gallatin, Alexander Hamilton, First bank (of United States). b'12. AB '33 (Swarthmore Coll); MA '37— PhD '42 (Columbia U). Author: Alexander James Dallas, '43. Author articles: The American Career of David Parish '44; The Origins of the Second Bank of the United States '45; Albert Gallatin in the Pennsylvania Assembly '46; and others. Hist Div Hdqrs, AAF Washington '43-46; staff mem, Saturday Review of Lit since '46. AHA. Saturday Review of Literature, 25 W. 45th St., NYC. 19.

22 WALTERS, Vladimir. Fishes (Alaska); Respiratory physiology (Cold). b'27. BS '47—MS '48 (Cornell U). Collector fishes on Arctic Slope Alaska; research on distribution, systematics, and general biology marine and freshwater fishes of Alaskan arctic; assisted in study metabolic response to cold in marine, freshwater, and terrestrial arctic and tropical plants and animals. Co-author article: Adaptation to Cold in Arctic and Tropical Mammals and birds in Relation to Body Temperature, Insulation, and Basal Metabolic Rate '50. Research asst Arctic Research Lab Pt Barrow Alaska '48-49; grad asst biol dept NYU since '49. Am Soc Ichthyologists and Herpetologists—Arctic Inst NA—Soc Systematic Zool. Department of Biology, New York University, University Hgts., NYC 53.

23 WALTMAN, Clair Smith. Horticulture; Pomology; Soils; Plant physiology. b'96. Teachers certificate '19 (Central Mich State Normal Coll); BS '23—PhD '41 (Mich State Coll); MS '30 (U Ky). Author articles: Tree Fruit Varieties for Kentucky, also others. Instr, later prof hort and asst hort U Ky since '24. Am Soc Hort Soc—Ky Hort Soc—Ky Acad Sci—Sigma Xi. University of Kentucky, Department of Horticulture, Lexington, Ky.

24 WALTMAN, William DeWitt. Engineering (Petroleum production, construction, mining). b'75. EM '99 (Colo Sch of Mines, Golden, Colo). Gen mgr Franco Wyo Oil Co, '12-19; corp pres Petroleum Producing Cos, US and Mexico, '19-25; pres, first vp, dir and gen mgr in charge US operations of Franco Wyoming Oil Co since '26; pres and dir Franco Western Oil Co, Franco Central Oil Co, Franco Wyoming Securities Corp, McElroy Ranch Company, Oil Producers Agency of Calif. ASCE (life)—Am Assn Petroleum Geol —Am Inst Mining and Metall Engrs— Soc Am Mil Engrs—Am Petroleum Inst —AAAS. Awarded Roosevelt Panama medal, Medal of Individual Merit and Honor, Colo Sch of Mines, '42. 325 S. Plymouth Blvd., LA 5.

10 WALTON, Arthur Calvin. Nematology; Cytology (Nematodes); Parasitology (Amphibia). b'92. BA '14—MA '15 (Northwestern U); PhD '23 (U Ill). Co-author: Introduction to Nematology '40; also articles in field. Chmn dept biol Knox Coll Galesburg Ill since '25, Wallace C Abbott prof since '40. AAAS(F) — Am Soc Zool — Am Soc Parasitologists — Am Soc Systematic Zool—Am Micros Soc—Ill State Acad Sci—Phi Beta Kappa—Sigma Xi. Knox College, Galesburg, Ill.

11 WALTON, Jesse Seburn. Synthetic rubber; Catalytic processes; Aviation gasoline; Liquid extraction of metals; Metal Chelates. b'07. BS '28 (U Ia); (MIT, U Mich). Five patents in petroleum and related fields. Author articles in field. Prof and head dept chem mining and metall engring, Ore State Coll, Corvallis since '45; cons numerous companies. American Inst Chem Engrs—Am Chem Soc—Am Soc Promotion Engring Edn—Sigma Xi. Oregon State College, Corvallis, Ore.

12 WALTON, Matt S(avage), Jr. Petrology; Mineralogy; Structural geology. b'15. BA '36 (U Chicago); MA '47—PhD '51 (Columbia). Studies ultrabasic rocks, plutonic rocks, metamorphism, in the Alaska and Adirondack mountains. Co-author: (with E N Goddard) Copper-bearing Iron Deposits of the Mount Andrew-Mamie Area, Kassan Peninsula, Prince of Wales Island, Southeastern Alaska '44; (with G C Kennedy) Nickel Investigations in Southeastern Alaska '46; Geology and associated mineral deposits of some ultrabasic rock bodies in southeastern Alaska '46; The Blashke Island Ultrabasic Complex '51; Differential metamorphic mobility and the Adirondack eruptive sequence '53. Geol Alaskan field work US Geol Survey since '42; assistant professor geology Yale since '48; geologist New York State Science Service since '48. Yale University, Department of Geology, New Haven.†

13 WAMPLER, Roy Wilson. Glass (Research). b'98. AB '20 (McPherson Coll); MS '21 (Kan State Coll); PhD '33 (U Chicago). Research in surface tension of aqueous solutions of organic dibasic acids and their ethyl esters, adsorption from solutions, freezing point depressions and activity coefficients, safety glass, adhesives, strength of glass, resistance of glass to thermal shock, multiple glass glazings, metallizing of glass, mirrors, physical and chemical properties of glass. Author articles in field. Research chem Libbey-Owens-Ford Glass Co '29-43, asst dir research since '43. Am Chem Soc—Am Ceramic Soc—Soc Glass Tech—Am Soc Testing Materials—Sigma Xi. Research Department, Libbey-Owens-Ford Glass Co., 1701 E. Broadway, Toledo, O.

14 WANDRUS, Harry. Ancient and modern Czechoslovak weapons, ammunition and hunting conditions. b'22. Student (U Wis). Has extensive collection of Czechoslovak weapons dating from 1650 to present and including commercial as well as military pieces. Author: Six Czech Automatic Pistols '48; Czechoslovak Automatic Weapons '49; also articles in field. Outdoor News Assn — Nat Rifle Assn — Nat Muzzle Loading Rifle Assn — Am Ordnance Assn. 2454 N. 24th St., Milwaukee 6.

15 WANG, Sigmund. Wood cellulose. b'87. ChemE '09 (Oslo Norway); student '10 (U Darmstadt Germany). Production, research and development of wood cellulose for production of rayon, cellophane and other cellulose products. Chief chem, mgr labs Canadian Internat Paper Co; pres Indsl Cellulose Research Lab (affiliate of Internat Paper Co). Canadian Chem Inst(F)—Engring Inst Can—Tech Assn Pulp and Paper Industry—Canadian Pulp and Paper Assn(tech sect). Hawkesbury, Ont., Can.

16 WANTLAND, Wayne Warde. Helminthology (Trichinosis); Hematology; Physiology of muscle. b'05. BS in Edn '30—MA '32 (Northwestern U); Am Council Edn fellow '40-41 (U Chicago). Author: Effect of Irradiated Ergosterol and Calcium Lactate on Calcification of Trichina Cysts '34; Blood Studies on Normal and Trichinized White Rabbits '37; Effect of Irradiated Ergosterol on Trichinized White Rats '38; The Nature of the Mechanism of Encapsulation in Trichiniasis '45, and others. Prof biol dept biol De Paul U '35-37; co-dir div biol sci Stephens Coll Columbia Mo '38-42; prof biol and health sci Ill Wesleyan U Bloomington Ill '44-45, chmn div sci and prof biol and health sci since '46, dir Cancer Research Laboratory Illinois Wesleyan University since '49. AAAS—Am Soc Zool—Am Soc Parasitol—Sigma Xi—Phi Kappa Phi. Division of Science and Biology, Illinois Wesleyan University, Bloomington, Ill.

17 WARBURTON, Clark. US monetar policy. b'96. Student '16-18 (Houghton Coll); AB '21—AM '28 (Cornell); PhD '32 (Columbia). Studies on relation of monetary policy to business fluctuations. Author: The Economic Results of Prohibition '32; Co-author: (with Maurice Leven and Harold G Moulton) America's Capacity to Consume '34. Lectr econ Ewing Christian Coll and U Allahabad India '21-24; staff Rice Inst '25-28; asso prof econ Emory U '29-31; research staff The Brookings Instn '32-34; econ Fed Deposit Ins Corp since '34. Am Econ Assn—Econ Hist Assn—Econometric Soc. Federal Deposit Insurance Corp., Washington 25. H: Pine Hill Rd., McLean, Va.

18 WARD, George William. Cement (Portland); Glass fibers; Microscopy (Chemical). b'98. BS '25—'26 (U Manitoba); PhD '28 (U Minn). Research in durability of concrete, concrete aggregates and construction materials; on silicate melts near 1500° (C; microscopic investigation of structure of Portland cement clinker; in fields of clays and shales, glass fibers, lime, asphalt. Chief chem and geol Portland Cement Assn Chicago '28-37; consultant microscopy to AMA and ADA '30-41; research asso Portland Cement Association Fellowship Nat Bur Standards '37-44; supervisor ceramic research Armour Research Found '44-45; chmn inorganic chem research Midwest Research Inst '45-49; dir research Gustin-Bacon Mfg Co since '49. Gamma Alpha—Sigma Xi—ACS—Am Ceramic Soc—Mo Acad Sci—Am Concrete Inst. Gustin-Bacon Manufacturing Co., 1412 W. 12th St., KC 7, Mo.

19 WARD, Gilbert James. Technical paints; Protective coatings. born '03. ChemE '22 (Pratt). Originator numerous coatings to resist acids, alkalis, chemicals and fumes, heat, staining substances, and others for severe industrial service conditions; pioneered in acid and alkali resisting paints in all colors and finishes, water and weatherproof treatment for insulating building board; developed first successful paint for excessively hot surfaces, heated in operation above 600° F. Author articles in field. Sec, dir Cheesman-Elliot Co Inc since '27; treas, dir Four Square Paint Corp. Am Chem Soc—NY Paint and Varnish Prod Club. 639 Kent Av., Bklyn 11.

20 WARD, Helen Lavina. Parasitic worms (Acanthocephala or thornyheaded worms). b'10. BS '33—MS '36 —PhD '39 (Purdue U). Author articles in field. Instr zool U Tenn '44-47, asst prof zool since '47. Am Soc Parasitol—Am Soc Tropical Med—Assn SE Biol—Tenn Acad Sci—Sigma Xi. University of Tennessee, Knoxville, Tenn.†

21 WARD, Henry Silas, Jr. Eroded soils; Plant ecology and physiology. b'14. BS '38 (Ala Poly Inst); MS '40—PhD '48 (Ia State Coll). Research on utilization of plants in secondary succession on eroded soils as indicators for establishment of legumes and grasses, effects of adapted legumes and grasses on structural condition of eroded soils. Author articles in field. Asso prof bot Ala Poly Inst since '47. Am Soc Plant Physiol—Ecol Soc Am—Ia Acad Sci—Gamma Sigma Delta—Sigma Xi. Department of Botany and Plant Pathology, Alabama Polytechnic Institute, Auburn, Ala.†

22 WARD, James Edward. Paving materials b'96. Student chem engring '19-24 (U Wis). Inspector concrete highway construction and materials; specifications, testing, and construction bituminous pavings. Editor: Barber-Greene Bituminous Construction Handbook (1st edit). Chem engr Walter H Flood & Co paving specialists Chgo '26-35; asst constrn engr bituminous materials Ill State Highway Dept '35-41; paving engr Barber-Greene Company equipment mfrs since '41. Am Assn Asphalt Paving Tech—Am Pub Works Assn—ASTM(com bituminous equipment). Barber-Greene Co., Aurora, Ill.

23 WARD, James Edward, Jr. Textile industry (Labor relations). b'07. BS '29 —MS '31—PhD '35 (U Va); '32-33(Harvard). Public panel member War Labor Board '42-45; panel member Am Arbitration Assn since 1943; private arbitrator. Labor-management study at Bethlehem Steel Co '30-31; study of textile industry Textile Found Washington '37; faculty George Peabody Coll for Tchrs since '47, now head dept economics. So Econ Assn—Am Econ Assn. George Peabody College for Teachers, Nashville 4.†

24 WARD, Ruel Elmer. Feed formulation. BS '32 (State Coll Wash); MS '36—PhD '38 (Pa State Coll). Research in livestock and poultry nutrition. Author articles: Carotene and vitamin A in the nutrition of growing dairy cattle; and others. Asst prof dairy husbandry State Coll Wash '39-40; feed research dept Eastern States Farmers' Exchange Inc since '40. Am Dairy Sci Soc—Soc Animal Prodn—Poultry Sci Assn—NY Acad of Scis. Eastern States Farmers' Exchg, Inc., West Springfield, Mass.

25 WARD, William Binnington. Agrl journalism. b'17. BS '40 (Utah State Agrl Coll); MS '41 (U Wis.). Author: Agricultural News in the Daily Press '41; Reporting Agriculture '52. Asst to extension editor Utah State Agrl Coll '37-40; asst to extension editor and grad instr agrl journ U Wis '40-41; information specialist dairy marketing, handling pub relations on milk marketing agreements and orders for USDA '41-42; chief information sect Agrl Marketing Adminstrn, then Food Distbn Adminstrn '43-44; head dept extension teaching and information, ed and chief of publs NY State Coll Agr and Home Econs, Cornell since '45. Sigma Delta Chi. Forest Drive, Ithaca.†©

26 WARD, William Eugene. Chemical education. b'94. Student '23-24 (Southern Methodist U); BS '26—AM '30 (U Wash); EdD '42 (U Tex). Studies on methods teaching chemistry in classroom and laboratory. Author articles: An experimental study of two methods of teaching chemistry in senior high school; Modern method vs traditional method in teaching chemistry; Evolution of the science of education; and others. Chem tchr and head sci dept Fort Worth Pub Schs '35-46; prof chem and chmn div sci Tex Wesleyan Coll since '46, dir research on synthesis of Cortisone. ACS—AAAS—Am Inst Physics—Tex Acad Sci—NEA—Phi Delta Kappa—Tex Association Sci Tchrs. Texas Wesleyan College, Fort Worth 5.

10 WARDLE, Ralph Martin. Mary Wollstonecraft; W i l l i a m Maginn; Blackwood's Magazine (Early history); Oliver Goldsmith. 'b09. AB '31 (Dartmouth Coll); AM '34—PhD '40 (Harvard). Author: Mary Wollstonecraft: A Critical Biography '51; also articles in field. Prof Eng and chmn dept U Omaha since '46. University of Omaha, Omaha 1, Neb.†

11 WARE, Lamar Mims. Sweet and Irish potato production; Irrigation; Fertilizers; Soil improvement. b'95. BS in Agr '17—MS in Agr '27 (Ala Poly Inst); '27-28 (Mich State Coll). Jointly developed and patented process for making new types of foods from sweet potatoes and produced 20 or more new sweet potato products, jointly developed sweet potato puree extruder for making the products; developed methods of stabilizing soil surfaces and sundrying sweet potatoes for feed; developed a number of new products from Irish potatoes. Author articles in field. Head dept hort Ala Poly Inst since '47. Am Soc Hort Sci—Soc Am Foresters—Am Pomol Soc—Ala Acad Sci—Ala Forestry Council (hon life mem)—Phi Kappa Phi—Gamma Sigma Delta. Department of Horticulture, Auburn, Ala.

12 WARE, Lawrence Albert. High frequency transmission and generation; Electromagnetic theory. b'01. BE '26—MS '27—PhD '30—EE '35 (U Ia). Author: Physics Lab Manual '29; Ballantyne's First Lessons in Sanskrit Grammer (with Judith Tyberg) '42; Communication Circuits (with H R Reed) '49; Elements of Electromagnetic Waves '49; also articles in field. Transmission engr Bell Telephone Labs NYC '29-33; instr physics Mont State Coll '35-36, asst prof '36-37; asst prof elec engring State U Ia '37-42, asso prof '42-47, prof since '47. AIEE (section sec and chairman 1 yr each)—Inst Radio Engrs—Am Soc Engring Edn—AAUP—Math Assn Am—Sigma Xi—Tau Beta Pi. 1265 Melrose Av., Iowa City, Ia.

13 WARE, W. Porter. Shaving mugs. b'04. Studies on, collection of, barber shop shaving mugs various types, including numeral, fraternal, unfinished, glass label of 1870, mugs famous characters, sports occupationals, occupational shaving mugs. Author: Occupational Shaving Mugs and Their Prices '49; Sports Antiquities '54. Co-author: (with A W Pendergast) Cigar Store Figures in American Folk Art '53. Author articles Shaving Mugs in Encyclopedia Britannica, and other articles. University of the South, Sewanee, Tenn.

14 WAREHAM, Richard T(hurman). Bryology; Pottia; Pterigoneurum. b'05. BA '31—MSc '35—PhD '39 (O State U). Author articles in field. Author: Pottia and Pterigoneurum '39; Recent Collections of Mosses from Ohio '41, and others. With O State U '34-44, asst

prof '44; ed in charge sci books D C Heath & Co since '44. O Acad Sci—Bot Soc Am—Sullivan Moss Soc—Appalachian Bot Club—AAAS—Am Soc Plant Taxonomists—NE Bot Club—Sigma Xi. D. C. Heath & Co., 285 Columbus Av., Boston 16.

15 WARFEL, Harry Redcay. American language and literature (Noah Webster, fiction). b'99. Sterling research fellow '34-35—PhD '32 (Yale); AB '20—AM '22 (Bucknell U); AM '24 (Columbia). Author: Noah Webster: Schoolmaster to America '36; The Lost Generation Twenty Years Later '38; The Demies: A History '49; Charles Brockden Brown: American Gothic Novelist '49; American Novelists of Today '51; Who Killed Grammar? '52. Editor: The Rhapsodist and Other Uncollected Writings by Charles Brockden Brown '43. Co-Author: American College English: A Handbook of Usage and Composition '49. Editor: Letters of Noah Webster '53. Co-editor: The American Mind '37; Of the People '42, and others; also articles in field. General editor American Book Company since '42, Scholars Facsimiles & Reprints since '48; prof Eng U Fla since '48. Modern Lang Assn—Nat Council Teachers Eng — Am Lit Group — So Atlantic Mod Lang Assn—Coll Eng Assn — Am Dialect Soc — AHA — Phi Beta Kappa. Anderson Hall, University of Florida, Gainesville.†◎

16 WARFEL, Herbert E(lmer). Vertebrate zoology; Fishery biology. b'02. AB '26 (Western State Coll Colo); MS '31 (U Okla); '37-38 (Cornell U). Author articles in field. Asst prof zool U Mass '31-39, UNH '39-43; biol NH Fish and Game Dept '38-42; sci cons and research asst Bingham Oceanog Lab Yale '43-46; aquatic biol Office Fgn Activities US Fish and Wildlife Service '46, charge oceanog and biol investigations Philippine Fishery Program '47-50. Am Fisheries Society—Am Soc Limnol Oceanog—Am Soc Herpetologists Ichthyologists — Am Soc Mammalogy—Conn Acad Arts Sci—Sigma Xi. Headmaster, American Sch., Pasay City, P.I.

17 WARMAN, Henry John. Economic geography; Geography of Mexico and Latin America. b'07. BS '32 (State Coll Pa); MS '38 (Temple U); PhD '45 (Clark U). Author articles in field. Asst prof, asso prof Clark grad sch geog since '44. Nat Council Geog Teachers (exec bd)—Am Soc Profl Geog—NE Council Social Studies—NE Geog Soc. Clark University, Worcester, Mass.

18 WARMKE, H(arry) E(arl). Plant cytogenetics (Pacific Coast Trilliums, sex determination and balance, forage grasses and legumes, sweet potato). b'07. AB '31—PhD '35 (Stanford U). Author articles. Plant geneticist Fed Expt Station US Dept Agr Mayaguez PR since '47. Genetics Soc Am—Am Soc Hort Sci—Bot Soc Am—Am Genetics Assn—Am Soc Naturalists—Phi Beta Kappa—Sigma Xi—Gamma Sigma Delta. Federal Experiment Station, Mayaguez, Puerto Rico.†

19 WARNE, Colston Estey. Consumer testing; Consumer economics. b'00. AB '20—MA '21 (Cornell U); PhD '25 (U Chicago); MA hon '42 (Amherst Coll). Author: The Consumers' Co-operative Movement in Illinois. Co-author: Labor Problems in America. Chairman board of editors and contributor to Yearbook of American Labor. Contbg editor Current History. Contbr various nat journals. Member board dirs Cooperative League of USA '26-29, Nat Assn Consumers '47; regional consumer advisor Boston office OPA '46; hon vp Nat

Consumers League '41; mem consumer adv com to Council Econ Advisers to President of US since '47, v chmn '48. With Amherst Coll since '30, prof since '42. Am Econ Assn—Artus. Consumers Union of US, NYC 23.†◎

20 WARNER, D o n a l d Frederick. Canadian-American history and relations (Annexation movement, farmers' movements). b'13. BA '34—MA '36 (U Minn); PhD '40 (Yale). Research on movement for annexation of Canada to US 1840-93, at Library of Congress, Canadian Archives in Ottawa, Minnesota Historical Society; also studies on parallel farmers' movements in American Midwest and Canadian West, documents pertaining to Hudson's Bay Company, emergence of province of Manitoba; studies and writing on postconfederation annexation movement in Nova Scotia. Author articles in field. Asso prof hist Macalester Coll since '46. Can Hist Assn—Minn Hist Soc—Miss Valley Hist Assn—Upper Middlewest Hist Conf. Macalester College, St. Paul 5.†

21 WARNER, James Harold. Eighteenth century English literature (Sentimental movement); History of eastern Tennessee (Eighteenth century). b'92. AB '15 (Ind U); MA '22 (Northwestern U); PhD '33 (Duke U). Author articles in field. Prof Eng Tusculum Coll '28-32, Ark A&M Coll '33-36, Hope Coll '36-42, U Mich '42-45, U Miami since '45. Modern Lang Assn—AAUP—Nat Council Teachers Eng. University of Miami, Coral Gables, Fla.†

22 WARNER, J(ohn) C(hristian). Physical chemistry (Electrochemistry, corrosion and protective coatings, thermodynamics, chemical kinetics). b'97. BA '19—MA '20—PhD '23 (Ind U). Research on thermodynamics of common corrosion reactions, corrosion inhibitors, corrosion due to galvanic couples, on throwing power, current efficiency and conductivity of nickel plating baths, influence of solvent and salt concentration on rate and temperature coefficient of reactions in solution. thermodynamic properties of liquid and solid solutions, acid-base catalysis, dissociation constants of weak electrolytes, dipole moment of molecules, phase diagrams in ternary systems. Research chem Wayne Chem Corp Ft Wayne '25-26; with Carnegie Inst Tech since '26, prof chem and head chem dept '38-49, pres Carnegie Tech since '50. Am Chem Soc (dir)—Electrochem Soc (pres '52-53)—Am Inst Mining Metall Engrs—Pa Chem Soc—Sigma Xi—Phi Beta Kappa. Carnegie Institute of Technology, Pitts.

23 WARNER, Lawrence Allen. Structural and economic geology. b'14. Student '32-33 (DePauw U); AB '37 (Miami U); PhD '42 (Johns Hopkins). Geologist, petrographer US Antarctic Expedition Marie Byrd Land Antarctica '40-41. Author articles in field. Asst prof geol U Colo since '46. Colo Sci Soc—Sigma Xi—Phi Beta Kappa. Congressional Medal Sci, pioneering, exploration. Department of Geology, University of Colorado, Boulder, Colo.†

24 WARNER, Lucien, public opinion; marketing research; Psychol Warfare; Psychology, industrial and comparative; Evolution of behavior. b'00. AB '21 (Oberlin Coll); PhD '27 (Columbia). Author: (with others) Animal Motivation '31; Introduction to Comparative Psychology '34; Principles and Methods of Comparative Psychology '35; Vertebrate Behavior '36; Plants and Invertebrates '40; Working Dogs '34; also articles in field. Prof Claremont Men's Coll since '48; dir tech training OWI '42-44; advt research Time Inc '44-48. NY Acad

Sci(F)—AAAS(F)—Am Psychol Assn (F)—Am Statis Assn—Am Assn Pub Opinion Research—Am Marketing Assn —Sigma Xi. Claremont Men's College, Claremont, Cal.†☉

10 WARNER, Robert Malcolm. Fig culture and research. b'08. AB '30 (O Wesleyan U); MS '37—PhD '40 (Ia State Coll). Author articles in field. Research dir Calif Fig Inst Research Lab since '46. Am Phytopath Soc—Am Soc Hort Sci—Am Soc Plant Physiol— Am Assn Econ Entomol— Ecol Soc Am—Inst Food Tech—Ia Acad Sci— Sigma Xi. 5335 N. Palm Av., Fresno 4, Cal.†

11 WARNER, Roger Sherman, Jr. Distillation processes; Nuclear engineering; Radiation engineering. b'08. AB '31 (Harvard); '33-34 (MIT). Development engr Kaysam Corp '36-38, B F Goodrich '38-42; tech aide and project engr Office of Sci Research and Development '42-44; coordinating engr & division head Manhattan project Los Alamos NM '44-47; mem staff to gen mgr US Atomic Energy Commn '47, dir engring '47-49; mem engring staff Arthur D Little Inc since '49. ACS. Medal for merit for work performed with Office of Sci Research and Development. Argilla Rd., Ipswich, Mass.☉

12 WARNER, Sam Bass. Copyright laws. AB '12 (Harvard); LLB '15—SJD '23 (Harvard U Law Sch). Author: Crime and Criminal Statistics in Boston '34. Co-author: Judges and Law Reform '36; also articles in field. Advisor Nat Commn on law observance and enforcement '29-31. Prof law U Ore '19-28, Syracuse U '28-29; asst prof law Harvard '29-32, prof law '35-45; register of copyrights since '45. Am and Mass Bar Assns. Copyright Office, Library of Congress, Washington.

13 WARNER, Stanley Douglas. Receivers (Standard, miniature, subminiature). b'11. Certificate '41 (Northwestern U); certificate '42 (Ill Inst Tech). Research, design and production of subminiature, miniature and standard electronic receiving tubes. Design and prodn engr Otarian Inc '42-44, Gen Elec '44-45; prodn engr Raytheon Mfg Co '45-46; US Navy since '46. Inst Radio Engrs—Mil Engineers. Room 1208, Michelson Laboratory, China Lake Naval Ordnance Testing Station, Cal.

14 WARNER, William E. Industrial and vocational education; Civil defense. b'97. BS '23—MS '24 (U Wis); PhD '28 (Columbia U). Ofcr in charge edn and rel affairs German state Baden including University of Heidelberg '45, deputy director Warton American Technical School England '45-46. Editor: Arts and Industries Series. Prof indsl arts and indsl-vocational edn, later prof edn O State U '25-51; exec dir civil defense Ohio since '51. Am Indsl Arts Assn (pres '38-40). Adjutant General's Department, Columbus 16, O.

15 WARNSHUIS, Abbe Livingston. Amoy vernacular. b'77. AB '97—AM '00 —DD '16 (Hope Coll, Mich); '00 (New Brunswick Theol Sem). Author: Language Lessons in Amoy Vernacular '11. Editor: Talmage's Dictionary of Amoy Vernacular (revision); compiler and translator various books. Missionary service China '00-20; sec Internat Missionary Council, London '21-25, NYC '25-43; exec vp Ch World Service Inc '46-49; treas Gen Synod Ref Ch in Am since '43. 156 Fifth Av., NYC 10.

16 WARREN, Don Cameron. Fowl (Genetics, physiology of reproduction). b'90. Fellow '15-17—AB '14—AM '17 (Ind U); PhD '23—fellow '21-23 (Co-

lumbia). Author articles in field. Poultry geneticist Kan Agrl Expt Sta '23-48; coordinator regional poultry breeding project US Dept Agr since '48. Am Soc Zool—Am Genetic Assn—Am Naturalists—Poultry Sci Assn(F)—AAAS. Borden award, Poultry Sci Research prize. Regional Poultry Breeding Project, Purdue University, Lafayette, Ind.

17 WARREN, Lee Gilbert. Electromagnetic method plant (Design, construction); Hydro-electric plant (Design construction); Natural gas (line development, design, construction). b '86. Student 1 yr (Ohio State U); 1 yr (Washington and Jefferson College); PhB in civil engring (Sheffield Sci Sch Yale). Construction of hydro-electric developments; engineering, maintenance, services electro magnetic meth plant; development, design and construction nat gas lines, Tenn. Assistant works mgr Tenn Eastman Corp Oak Ridge Tenn Atomic Energy plant '43-45; constrn engr Woodward Iron Co Ala mines '20; constrn engr Dixie Construction Co '21-28; gen supt constrn Carpenter Dam, Ark Power & Light Co '29-31; project mgr TVA for four major hydroelectric plants Tenn '36-42; asst or works mgr Tenn Eastman Corp operations Oak Ridge Tenn '43-45; gen constrn mgr Ebasco Services NYC '46; pres Warren Engring Corp and Lee G Warren Corp handling engring for natural gas lines, development, design and constrn Tenn '47-49; cons engr Chattanooga & Asheville NC '47-51. Engrs Soc—Tau Beta Tau. Registered and licensed engr NC and Tenn. Law Bldg., Asheville, N.C.; also 2 421 Poplar St., Chattanooga, Tenn.

18 WARREN, Louis Austin. Lincolniana. b'85. Bachelor Practical Theol '16 (Coll the Bible Transylvania U); Litt D '29 (Lincoln Memorial U). Author: Lincoln's Parentage and Childhood '26; Slavery Atmosphere of Lincoln's Youth '33; Little Known Lincoln Episodes '34; Abraham Lincoln, A Concise Biography '34; Lincoln Bibliography Check List '42; Indiana's Contribution to Abraham Lincoln '44. Dir Lincoln Nat Life Found since '28. Lincoln National Life Insurance Building, Fort Wayne, Indiana.†☉

19 WARREN, Shields. Pathology; Oncology; Atomic bomb (Casualties). b '98. AB '18—DSc '49 (Boston U); MD '23 (Harvard). Author: Pathology of Diabetes Mellitus '30. Co-author: (with O Gates) A Handbook for the Diagnosis of Cancer of the Uterus '47, '48,'49; (with S P Hicks) Introduction to Neuropathology. Faculty path Harvard Med Sch since '25, prof since '48; path NE Deaconess Hosp since '27; path Harvard Cancer Commn, Pondville State Hosp; dir Mass State Tumor Diagnosis Service; path NE Bapt Hosp; dir div biol and medicine US Atomic Energy Commn; mem sci adv bd, chief of staff US Air Force. Served as captain USNR, consultant in pathology USN; expert cons to Surg Gen on sci adv bd Armed Forces Inst Path; cons Nat Adv Cancer Council; mem Atomic Bomb Casualty Commn; com on growth and path, sub com oncology Nat Research Council. Diplomate Am Bd Path. AAAS—AMA—Am Soc Clin Path—Nat Cancer Inst—Am Assn Path and Bact—Am Soc Exptl Path(past pres)—Soc Exptl Biol and Med—Am Assn Cancer Research (past pres)—Phi Beta Kappa—Cosmos Club. 195 Pilgrim Rd., Boston 15.

20 WARREN, Virgil Alexander. Spanish-American literature. b'05. AB '29 (Georgetown Coll); PhD '33 (U Va); Certificate Italian Lit '45 (U di Firenze); '29-31 (U Pa). Editor: El Héroe '41; El Hombre de Oro '48; La Noche

Anuncia El Dia '49; also articles in field. Prof and chnm dept modern langs Georgetown Coll since '48. Am Assn Teachers Spanish and Portuguese (life)—Am Assn Teachers Italian and French. Georgetown College, Georgetown, Ky. H: Box 601.

21 WARSLEY, Albert E. Latin. b'04. AB '24 (Seton Hall Coll S Orange NJ); AM '28 (St John's U Brooklyn). Contributor: Classical Outlook. Tchr Latin Heffley Sch Pratt Inst Brooklyn '24-25, St John's Coll High Sch Brooklyn '25-31; ed Auxilium Latinum Mag since '29; dir Nat Latin Honor Soc for Students since '30; tchr Latin, head Latin dept Thomas Jefferson High Sch Elizabeth NJ since '31. NEA—Am Classical League—L'Academie Latine d'Echanges Intellectuels (Paris France). P.O. Box 501, Elizabeth, N.J. H: 425 Cherry St., Elizabeth 3.

22 WARSOFF, Louis A(lex). American constitutional law. b'04. BSS '23 —MBA '29 (Coll City NY); LLB '26— LLM '27—scholar '43-45 (Columbia U Law Sch); JSD '27 (NYU); PhD '33 (Fordham U). Author: Introduction to Law '36; Selected Cases on Constitutional Law '38; Equality and the Law '38; also articles in field. Asst prof dept polit sci Brooklyn Coll '33-48, asso prof polit sci since '48; vis prof Brooklyn Law Sch since '42, New York law since '49. Citizens Union (legislative com, chmn sub-com on edn since '30)— Nat Panel Arbitrators—NY Bar—Acad Polit Sci. Brooklyn College, Bedford Av. and Av. H, Brooklyn 10. H: 1651 65th St., Brooklyn 4.

23 WARWICK, Bruce L(ester). Sheep and goat husbandry (Genetics and reproduction). b'93. DVM '19 (Ia State Coll); MS '22—PhD '25 (U Wis); student (William and Vashti Coll). Author articles in field. Animal husbandman, geneticist, project leader Tex Agrl Expt Sta at Bluebonnet Farm since '48. AAAS (F)—Tex Acad Sci(F)—Am Soc Animal Prodn—Am Soc Zool—Genetics Soc Am—Am Vet Med Assn—Am Genetic Assn—Sigma Xi. Bluebonnet Farm, McGregor, Tex.

24 WASHA, George William. Concrete masonry materials (Development and testing). b'09. BS '30—MS '32—PhD '38 (U Wis). Research on permeability of concrete, efficiency of surface treatments on permeability of concrete, physical and mechanical properties of hand rodded and vibrated concrete made with different cements, properties of masonry cements, plastic flow of reinforced concrete beams and slabs, volume changes of block-type masonry concrete. Co-author: (with E R Maurer, R J Roark) Mechanics for Engineers. Revised: Johnson's Materials of Construction; also articles in field. With U Wis since '30, prof engring since '39; cons work since '32. Am Concrete Inst —Am Soc Metals—Tau Beta Pi—Sigma Xi. Received Wason Research Medal for paper from Am Concrete Inst '41. Educational Engineering Building, University of Wisconsin, Madison 6, Wis.†

25 WASHBURN, Albert Lincoln. Arctic physical geography and glacial geology. b'11. AB (Dartmouth Coll); PhD '42 (Yale). Assisted in glaciological program Harvard-Dartmouth Mt Crillon expedition Alaska '34; aerial photography National Geographic Society Mt McKinley expedition Alaska '36; assistant geologist Louise A Boyd East Greenland expedition '37; leader private expeditions to Canadian Arctic '38, '39, '40-41. Author: Geography and Arctic Lands '49; also articles in field. Exec dir Arctic Inst NA '45-51; hon lectr geog McGill U '48-51; sci dir snow, ice, and permafrost research establishment US Army CE since '52;

Arctic expert US-Can First Spl Service Force '42; geog Arctic Sect AAF Arctic Desert and Tropic Information Center '43-44 American Polar Society—AAAS (F)—Am Geog Soc(F)—Can Geog Soc (F)—Geol Assn Can(F)—Geol Soc Am (F)—Am Geophys Union.☉

10 WASHBURN, Henry Bradford Jr. Alaskan exploratory expeditions (Cold climate clothing a n d equipment); Arctic and mountain photography; Mountaineering. b'10. AB '33 (Harvard). Alaskan exploration nine years since '30; leader of Operation White Tower, a scientific expedition to Mt McKinley sponsored by Boston Museum of Science and RKO Radio Pictures with collaboration of Northwest Airlines US Coast and Geodetic Survey, physics department University of Chicago and National Park Service '47; scientific d i r e c t o r Chinese-American Amnyi Machin Expedition '48. Dir Boston Museum of Sci since '39. Expert cons Office Quartermaster General, appointed special liaison between Quartermaster General and Commanding General Alaska Defense Command; carried out two investigations of Alaskan Highway equipment of QMG; led AAF Alaskan Test Expedition conducting final field tests of new AAF Arctic equipment '45. Am Alpine Club—Explorers Club—Royal Geog Soc London(F)—Can Geog Soc(F). Received Royal Geog Soc Cuthbert Peek award, Burr prize for exploration Alaska Nat Geog Soc; Boston Museum of Science, Science Park, Boston.

11 WASSON, Theron. Oil and gas exploration; Ecuador (Petroleum resources). b'87. BS—CE '11 (Carnegie Inst E Tech); Grad work geol '19 (Columbia). Recommended plan to Corps of Engineers US Army '43 which was adopted for protection of Cumberland oil field by levees and diversion channel; delegate United Nations Scientific Conference on Conservation and Utilization of Resources Lake Success '49; visiting geological advisor Naval Petroleum Reserve No 4, Point Barrow Alaska '50. Author: Explorations in eastern Ecuador '23; Geological explorations east of the Andes in Ecuador '27; Oil and gas development in Illinois and Indiana during 1932 '33; Oil and gas development in Michigan '32-47; Recent oil discoveries in Ill '38, others. Asso editor Stratigraphic type oil fields (symposium) '41; The Creole Field, Gulf of Mexico, Coast of Louisiana '48. With Pure Oil Co Chgo since '22, chief geol, supervision oil field explorations in US and Venezuela; adv council Princeton U Dept Geol Engring since '41; adv com geol dept Northwestern U since '49. Geol Soc Am—AAAS—Am Geophys Union—Western Soc Engrs—AIMME—Am Association Petroleum Geol—Am Petroleum Inst (com on oil reserves since '39, adv com on fundamental research on occurrence and recovery of petroleum since '40)—Chicago Tulsa Houston Ill geol socs—Am Geog Soc—Am Geol Inst. 35 East Wacker Dr., Chgo.

12 WATERFALL, Umaldy Theodore. Taxonomy and phytogeography of Oklahoma and southwestern Texas flora; Ecology of Oklahoma grasslands. b'10. BS '35—(Okla A&M Coll); MS '42 —'47-48 (U Okla). Author articles in field. Asst prof botany Okla A&M Coll; bot Okla Biol Survey '46-48. Am Soc Plant Taxonomists—Okla Acad Sci—Sigma Xi. Department of Botany, Oklahoma A&M College, Stillwater, Okla.

13 WATERFALL, Wallace. Acoustics; Building materials; Insulation. b'00. BS '23—'31 (U Ill). Dir research the Celotex Corp '47-49; exec-sec Nat Noise

Abatement Council since '49; Blding Research Adv Bd '48. Acous Soc Am (sec since '29)—Acoustical Materials Assn (sec-treas since '33)—AAAS(F)—Am Inst Physics (mem governing bd, exec sec since '46)—APS(F). Am Inst. Physics, 57 E. 55th St., NYC 22.

14 WATERMAN, Alma May. Forest pathology and mycology; Fungus diseases of shade and ornamental trees and shrubs and forest trees. b'93. AB '15—Am '16—PhD '28 (Brown U). Research on diseases of trees and shrubs '16-17, fungus diseases of shade and ornamental trees and shrubs '17-22, fungus diseases of forest trees since '45. Author articles in field. Collaborator Div Forest Path US Dept Agr '16-17, asst forest path '17-22, jr path '22-29, asst path '29-45, asso path '45-49, path since '49. AAAS—Am Phytopath Soc—Mycol Soc Am—Nat Shade Tree Conf—Sigma Xi. 360 Prospect St., New Haven, 11.†

15 WATERMAN, Richard Alan. Cultural anthropology; Comparative musicology; Folklore and folk music. b'14. BA '37 (Santa Barbara Coll); MA '41 (Claremont Coll); PhD '43 (Northwestern U). Research on use of music for propaganda for Department of State; field studies of folk music of Puerto Rico, music of Cuban Santeria cults; studies and writing on African patterns in Trinidad Negro music, Afro-Bahian cult music; field research Australian Aborigines of Arnhem Land. Asso Author articles. Prof anthrop Northwestern U since '50. American Anthrop Association— American Musicology Soc—Am Folklore Society—Phi Beta Kappa—Sigma Xi. Dept of Anthropology, Northwestern University, Evanston, Ill.

16 WATERMAN, Talbot Howe. Invertebrate light reactions and neuromuscular physiology; Deep-sea plankton migrations; Deep-sea Angler-fishes. b'14. AB '36—Austin teaching fellow '36-38—MA '38—Research asso Psychoacoustic Lab '41-43—PhD '43 (Harvard). Staff mem Radiation Lab MIT '43-45; asst prof zool Yale since '47, exec fellow Trumbull Coll Yale since '46; instr dept invertebrate zoology Marine Biol Lab Woods Hole Mass since '47. Conn Acad Arts Sci—Am Soc Zool—Research Soc Am—Sigma Xi (sec., com on research '46). Osborn Zoological Laboratory, Yale University, New Haven.

17 WATERS, Louis Addison. Forgery detection; Firearms identification. b '95. Grad '16 (Phillips Acad Andover Mass); '20 (MIT). Research on infrared photography for use in differentiation of inks, and microphotography to prove relationship of intersecting ink lines; expert testimony on forgery detection and firearms identification in courts of New York State and District of Columbia since '22. Co-author: (with Robert M Smith) The Shelley Legend '45. Author articles: Questioned Documents in Police Work '48; Preparation of a Questioned Document Case '50. Contributor: Photography by Infra-red '39; Huddy Encyclopedia Automobile Law '32. Cons document forgeries and firearms identification to dist atty Onondaga Co NY since '25; cons forgery NY State Police Lab '36-45; dir Syracuse Police Lab since '45. 320 N. Clinton St., Syracuse, N.Y. H: 684 Allen St.

18 WATKINS, Lura Woodside. American glass and pottery; New England pottery; Lighting devices. b'87. Ed pvt schs Mass. Independent research on histories of American glass works and potteries; research on New England potteries carried out by actual excava-

tion of early sites, one antedating 1700 Danvers Mass; extensive excavation of site of Daniel Bayley pottery in Newburyport Mass. Author: Cambridge Glass '31; also articles in field. Early Am Industries Assn—Rushlight Club (pres)—Nat Early Am Glass Club (past vp and program chmn)—Soc Preservation NE Antiquities—Medford Hist Soc—Winchester Art Assn.

19 WATKINS, Mark Hanna. Bantu and Mayan languages; African anthropology. b'03. SB '26 (Prairie View State Coll Tex); AM '30—PhD '33—Lichtstern research fellow (U Chicago). Author: A Grammar of Chichewa, a Bantu Language of British Central Africa '37; also articles in field. Prof anthrop Howard U since '47. Am Anthrop Assn (F)—Anthrop Soc Washington—AAAS—Am Sociol Soc—Internat African Inst (London)—Am Assn Phys Anthrop—Linguistic S o c Am — Nat Research Council (com African Anthropol)—Sigma Xi. Howard University, Washington 1.

20 WATSON, Alice J. Mycology; Forest pathology; Food bacteriology. b'98. AB '21—AM '22 (Colombia U); '24 (Idaho U); '31 (Yale U). Author articles in field. Forest path '33-39 US Dept Agr New Haven, mycol sci aide '39-42 Washington food bacteriologist '42-47 Phila, mycol in fgn plant quarantines Beltsville Md since '47. Mycol Soc Am—Phytopath Soc Am—Bot Soc Washington—Sigma Xi (asso). Mycology and Disease Survey, Plant Industry Station, Beltsville, Md.

21 W A T S O N, Clarence W(ilford). Wildlife management; Bioecology. b'95. PhB '16—MF '20—PhD '30 (Yale); fellow Sweden '20 (Am Scand Found); Nat Research Council fellow '31-32 (Rutgers). Study on soil organic matter with respect to its decomposition by microorganisms and its colloidal behavior. Asst prof forestry U Ida '21-27; research microbiology Rutgers U '28-30; Game Conservation Inst Clinton NJ '33-35; biol More Game Birds in Am Foundation NYC '36-38; biol Ducks Unlimited Can '39-40; biol US Fish and Wildlife Service '41-42; regional supervisor Fed Aid Br since '43. Wildlife Soc —Am Soc Mammalogists — AAAS—Sigma Xi. United States Fish and Wildlife Service, Atlanta 1.

22 WATSON, Earnest Charles. Physics (History, iconography, atomic). b'92. PhB '14 (Lafayette Coll); '17 (U Chicago). Research and development work on artillery rockets, torpedoes, atomic bomb and other ordnance devices. Author: Mechanics, Molecular Physics, Heat and Sound '47; also articles in field. Prof physics Calif Inst Tech since '30, dean faculty since '45. American Physics Soc(F)—AAAS—Am Assn Physics Teachers—History of Science Soc—Phi Beta Kappa—Sigma Xi—Tau Beta Pi. California Institute of Technology, Pasadena 4, Cal.☉

23 WATSON, Fletcher Guard. Science education; Astronomy (Meteors, comets, asteroids). b'12. BA '33 (Pomona Coll); MA '35—PhD '38 (Harvard). Research investigations meteors, comets, asteroids; research development loran (electronic navigation equipment); currently considering problems teaching science, especially in secondary schools and in college general education programs. Author: Between the Planets '41. Grad asst Harvard Obs '33-38, instr, exec sec, research asso '38-41; research radiation lab MIT '42; research US Navy '43-46; asso prof edn Harvard since '49. AAAS—Am Astron Soc—Nat Sci Teach Assn—Inst Navigation—Nat Assn Research Sci Teaching—Phi Beta Kappa—Sigma Xi—Phi

Delta Kappa. Graduate School of Education, Harvard University, Cambridge 38, Mass.

10 WATSON, George Linton. Sanitary, municipal and hydraulic engineering (Tunnels, bridges, water works, public utilities). b'84. Authority for design, construction of Lincoln Tunnel, George Washington a n d Bayonne bridges; Board Consulting Engineers New York State and New Jersey Interstate Bridge and Tunnel Commissions for design, construction and operation of Holland Tunnel. Author: Reclamation of New Jersey Coast; The Design and Construction of Sewage Treatment Works, Trenton NJ; Railways and Highways of Panama; American Mining Practice; The Atlantic City Water Supply; Niagara Falls Sanitation; also articles in field. Supervising engr for tunnels sanitary works harbor works and pub utilities in NY, Pa, Va, NJ, Fla and Mex '10-20; private cons practice representing US Govt Republic Panama, Brazil, Chinese and Canadian govt and some forty municipalities and state and county commns for pub constrn bridges, sanitation, tunnels and for valuation, rate cases, internat expert in contract litigation '20-45. ASCE—Instn Civil Engrs (England)—Engring Inst Can—Sigma Xi. Sea Girt, N.J.†◎

11 WATSON, Harold Francis. The Sailor in English literature; Heraldry in literature. b'95. AB '18—AM '20 (NYU); PhD '31 (Columbia). Author: The Sailor In English Fiction and Drama 1550-1800 '31. Prof Eng and chmn div lang and lit Simpson Coll since '36. Modern Lang Assn Am—Ia Authors Club. Simpson College, Indianola, Ia.†

12 WATSON, Kenneth Merle. Industrial chemical engineering; Petroleum refining; Thermodynamics; Catalysis; Kinetics. b'03. BS '23—MS '24—PhD '29 (Wis U). Directed design of Neches Butane products in synthetic rubber program of Gulf Oil Corp; consultant to Office of Production Research and Development on aviation gasoline, aromatics, butadiene and carbon black; research on application of principles of thermodynamics and kinetics to development, design a n d operation of chemical processes. Co-author: (with Hougen) Industrial Chemical Calculations '31; (with Hougen) Chemical Process Principles, three vol '43-47; also articles in field. Research engr, dir engring research Universal Oil Products Co '31-41; prof chem engring grad sch Wis U '42-50; chemical engineering cons '50-52; dir research The Pure Oil Co since '52. Am Inst Chem Engrs—AAAS—Am Chem Soc—Am Soc Engring Edn. H: Lake Zurich, Ill.†

13 WATSON, Paul Downing. Chemistry of milk and milk products; Synthetic resins. b'95. BS '20 (U Pittsburgh). Holder several US patents. Author articles: Lactic Acid Polymers as Constituents of Synthetic Resins and Coatings '48, and others. Research chem Bur Dairy Ind Agrl Research Adminstrn Washington since '26. Am Chem Soc. Agricultural Research Administration, United States Department of Agriculture, Washington†

14 WATT, John Reid. Ice-making; Strength of materials at low temperatures. b'14. BS in mech engring '37—MA '42—ME '50 (U Wash); '37-39 (Harvard); '41-43 (U Tex). Developed extrusion process for continuous automatic production of cake ice, built commercial-size ice extrusion machine. Engr Electrol Oilburner Corp '40; research engr C W Murchison '46-47; with U Tex '41-46, asst prof mech

engring from '48. Am Econ Assn—Am Acad Polit and Soc Sci—ASME—Tex Acad Sci—Sigma Xi—Pi Tau Sigma. Department of Mechanical Engineering, University of Texas, Austin. H: 3511 Cherry Lane.

15 WATTERS, Mary. History (Venezuela, United States college, and local). b'96. AB '17 (Ouachita Coll); MA '23 (Baylor U); PhD '31 (U NC). Research in Venezuela on history of Catholic church, social, intellectual and educational history; in Spain on colonial Venezuela with special emphasis on colonial church; studies on Illinois in World War II. Author: A History of the Church in Venezuela, 1830-1930 '33; A History of Mary Baldwin College '42; A History of Mac Murray College '46; also articles in field. Research editor Illinois State Historical Library '47-52; research analyst State Dept Pub Welfare since '52. Department Public Welfare, 103 Centennial Bldg., Springfield, Ill.†

16 WATTIE, Elsie. Bacteriology (Water, shellfish). b'01. BS '23—MS '25 (U Conn); '26 (Yale). Author articles in field. Bacteriologist Water and Sanitation Investigation Lab USPHS '26-47, charge Lab devoted exclusively to bacteriological phases of shellfish sanitation since '48. Soc Am Bacteriologists—Am Pub Health Assn—Am Limnol Soc—AAAS—Sigma Xi. United States Public Health Service, Oceanographic Institute, Woods Hole, Mass. H: Box 512.

17 WATTS, Chester B. Meridian astronomy; Instrument design. b'89. AB '15 (Ind U). Fundamental positions of celestial bodies for the purpose of investigating their motions; topographic survey of marginal zone of moon. Designed two automatic photo-electric measuring machines for precise measurement of astronomical photographs. Author articles in field. Astronomer Naval Obs Washington since '15, in charge six-inch transit circle div since '34. Am Astron Soc—Am Geophys Union—Internat Astron Union—Washington Acad Sci. US Naval Observatory, Washington 25.

18 WATTS, Ethelwyn Stagg. Psychology of exceptional children. b'98. Diploma '18 (State Teachers Coll Conn); BA '42 (U Calif); '26-27, '31 (Yale); '36 (San Francisco State Teachers Coll). Research on sense of thinking, atypical children. Dir and owner Stagg Manor Residential Sch for Exceptional Children since '39. Am Assn Mental Deficiency (F). Stagg Manor, Danville, Calif.

19 WATTS, Henry Millard. Electronics; Quantum physics; Electronic circuits and systems. b'20. BS in elec engring '42 (U Mo); '46-47 (Stevens Inst Tech); '47-52 (Johns Hopkins). Research guidance systems for guided missiles; x-ray spectroscopy; fundamental atomic constants; funadmental particles; development and design circuits and systems fire-control radars. Tech staff Bell Telephone Labs Inc '42-47; research engr Glenn L Martin Co '47; research physicist Johns Hopkins Radiation Lab since '47. APS—Eta Kappa Nu—Tau Beta Pi—Sigma Xi—Gamma Alpha—Inst Radio Engrs. Johns Hopkins University Radiation Laboratory, 1315 St. Paul St., Balt 2. H: 1658 Northgate Court, Balt 18.

20 WATTS, Lyle Ford. Forestry. b'90. BSc '13—MF '28—Dr Agr (hon) '48 (Iowa State Coll). Author articles in field. Prof Forestry Utah State Coll '28-29; with US Forest Service since '29, sr silviculturist Intermountain Forest and Range Expt Sta '29-30, dir Rocky Mt Forest Range Expt Sta '31-

36, regional forester North Central Region '36-39, North Pacific Region '39-42, chief '43-52, retired. Soc Am Foresters(F)—AFA—AAAS—Phi Kappa Phi. H: 5650 N.E. Sandycrest Terrace, Portland 15, Ore.

21 WAUCHOPE, Robert. Central American anthropology; Central and North Am archeology. b'09. AB '31 (USC); AM-PhD '38, 42 (Harvard). Archeological and ethnographic expeditions to Pecos New Mexico '27; Stallings Island Georgia '28; for University Georgia archeological survey Georgia '38-40; for Carnegie Institution to Uaxactun Guatemala '32, Yucatan and Guatemala '34, Zacualpa '35, Kaminaljuyu '36; for Tulane U to Zacualpa and Utatlan '47, travel in Mexico, Guatemala '39, 41. Author articles in field. Prof anthrop Tulane U and dir Middle Am Research Inst since '42. Soc Am Archeol. Middle American Research Institute, Tulane University, New Orleans.◎

22 WAUGH, David Floyd. Protoplasm ultrastructure; Protein and surface chemistry; Monomolecular s u r f a c e films. b'15. AB '35—PhD '40 (Wash U). Preparation of insulin, the in vitro assay of insulin. Author articles in field. Asso prof phys biol MIT since '47. Am Physiol Soc—Am Chem Soc—Am Soc Zool—Growth Soc—AAAS—Sigma Xi—Phi Beta Kappa. Department of Biology, Massachusetts Institute of Technology, Cambridge, Mass.†

23 WAY, Frederick, Jr. American inland steamboat history; Rivers of America (Allegheny). b'01. Student '19-20 (U Cincinnati). Has negative file of all steamboats known to have been photographed on inland rivers comprising 7000 items, issues catalogues on same as owner of Steamboat Photo Co; compiler of steamboat historical information with card file kept on every inland steamboat since 1811; one of group who established the River Museum at Campus Martius Museum Marietta Ohio, built eight scale model river steamers; publisher of Inland River Record since '45, descriptions of all c u r r e n t vessels plying Mississippi River system, list of owners. Author: Inland River Record '45, '46, '47, '48; The Log of the Betsy Ann '33; Pilotin' Comes Natural '42, and others. Ohio and Miss river steamboat capt and pilot '32-48. 121 River Av., Sewickley, Pa.†

24 WAY, Stewart. Applied mechanics (Elasticity, thermodynamics). b'08. AB '29 (Stanford U); '30 (Goettingen U); MA '32—ScD '34 (U Mich). Research and investigations of contact stresses, surface durability, surface f i n i s h, strength of gear teeth, elastic plates, turbine impulse blades, combustion problem for gas turbines. Author articles in field. Research engr mech div Westinghouse Research Labs E a s t Pittsburgh '33-43, sec mgr thermodynamics mech dept since '44. ASME—Inst Aero Scis—Internat Assn Bridge and Structural Engrs—AAAS—Nat Adv Com Aero (subcom on combustion '45-48, internal flow '47-49). Westinghouse Research Laboratories, East Pittsburgh H: 2307 Forest Drive, Pitts 21.

25 WAYNE, Truman Benjamin. Chemistry and technology of cane sugar refining; Petroleum emulsions; Oil well drilling fluids; Rice and its milling by-products. BS '21—MS '22 (La State U). Designer of cane sugar manufacturing and refining plants; cons on refining of sugars, bone char, decolorizing carbons, crystallization and sugar factory equipment; development of chemical processes and reagents for separation of water and other foreign matter from petroleum oils; pioneer in development chemical processes and additives for controlling density, lubricating and cooling properties, and viscosity of drilling fluids used in drilling wells for petroleum. Holds patents in field. Author articles: Influence of Absorption Spectra on Decolorizing Efficiency of Bone Char '26; The Defecation of Cane Juice '31, and others. Chief chem engr and asst gen supt Imperial Sugar Co Sugar Land Tex '24-29; cons chem engr Houston since '30. ACS—Am Inst Chem Engrs—Am Petroleum Inst—ASTM—Institute of Food Technicians—Assn Cons Chem & Chem Engrs. 1011 Waugh Drive, Houston 6. H: 907 Kirby Drive, Houston 19.

10 WEASLER, Anthony V. Water heating; Brake shoes; Universal joints. b'05. CE '28—ME '29 (Marquette U); study (U Wis Ext Div and Milwaukee Bus Inst). Research and development instantaneous automatically controlled high pressure steam injection type water heaters for commercial users of hot water, bonding of lining to brake shoes and bands and elimination of noise therein; developed new low cost high torque capacity units for universal joints. Soc Automotive Engrs—Pi Tau Sigma—Tau Beta Pi—Alpha Sigma Nu. H: 603 Ridge Rd., West Bend, Wis.

11 WEATHERBY, Roy E(dward). Ballistics and killing power of Ultra-high vel rifles. b'10. Student (Wichita U Kan). Study of effectiveness of high velocity projectiles in hunting of big game; research on custom manufacture of rifle barrels and stocks. Mfr rifles; lectr on ballistics and big game hunting. 8823 Long Beach Blvd., South Gate, Cal.

12 WEATHERWAX, Paul. Gramineae; Zea mays; Indian corn; Plant anatomy. b'88. Student '09 (Wabash Coll); AB '14—AM '15—PhD '18 (Indiana U). Research on the morphology and phylogeny of the Gramineae and on the history and ethno-botany of maize; research Latin Am Zea mays and other Gramineae '32, '44, '47. Author: The Maize Plant '23; Plant Biology '47; also articles in field. Instr bot Ind U '15-19, asso prof '21-35, prof since '35; asso prof bot U Ga '19-21. Bot Soc Am (treas '39-43, vp '44)—Soc Am Naturalists—Am Soc Plant Taxonomists—Ind Acad Sci (treas '32-34, ed '34-40, pres '41)—Sigma Xi—Phi Beta Kappa. Awarded Guggenheim fellowship research Latin Am '44; Waterman research fellow '26-32 Ind U. Department of Botany, Indiana University, Bloomington, Ind.

13 WEAVER, Earl. Dairy cattle nutrition. b'93. BS '13 (Okla A&M Coll); MS '17 (Ia State Coll); PhD '38 (U Minn). Research on role of roughage in dairy cattle nutrition, nutritional values of milk and milk quality. Author: Successful Dairying '24; Agriculture for Secondary Schools '34; Agriculture for High Schools '34. Chief dairy husbandry Ia State Coll '19-29; head dairy dept Okla A&M Coll '29-37; head dairy dept Mich State Coll since '37. Am Dairy Sci Assn (pres '38-39)—Am Soc Animal Nutrition—Sigma Xi—Phi Kappa Phi—Alpha Zeta—Gamma Sigma Delta. Dairy Building, Michigan State College, East Lansing, Mich.☉

14 WEAVER, Ernest Witwer. Furnaces (Industrial gas). b'94. ME '16 (Columbia). Author article: Annealing Stainless Clad Steel Sheets. With Surface Combustion Corp since '16, assistant chief engr since 19?? ASME—Ohio Soc Profl Engrs—Nat Soc Profl Engrs. Surface Combustion Corp., Dorr St., Tol.

15 WEAVER, Frank Lloyd. Hydro-electric power; River basin development. b'91. BCE '13 (U Mich). Research on electric rate investigations, hydro-electric valuations, multiple-purpose reservoirs and comprehensive river basin developments for flood control, navigation, irrigation, hydroelectric power, and other purposes and water resource uses; numerous reports on power and river basin development. Municipal, hydraulic and sanitary enging Fed Power Commn Washington since 34, chief Div River Basins since '45. Am Geophys Union—Washington Soc Engrs—Am Acad Polit and Soc Sci—ASCE (past pres DC Sect)—Tau Beta Pi—Sigma Xi—Cosmos Club (Washington). Federal Power Commission, Washington 25. H: 15 Keswick St., Garrett Park, Maryland.

16 WEAVER, Harry Lloyd. Plant morphogenesis; Maize (Hybrid vigor). b'06. BS '38 (U Neb); MA '40 (Columbia); PhD '42 (Yale). Author articles in field. Asso prof bot U Neb since '49. AAAS—Bot Soc Am—Neb Acad Scis (corres sec since '47)—Genetics Inst (pres '48-49)—Phi Beta Kappa—Sigma Xi. Department of Botany, University of Nebraska, Lincoln 8, Neb.†

17 WEAVER, Harry Merwyn. Infantile paralysis. b'08. AB '35—MSc '36—PhD '38 (O State U). Director research on poliomyelitis, objective better treatment to minimize crippling after-effects of disease, means for arresting the disease in early stages, development of preventive. Author articles: Resistance of Cotton Rats to the Virus of Poliomyelitis as Affected by Intake of Certain Purified Vitamins and by Sex '46; Infantile Paralysis—The Research Story '49; Epidemic Poliomyelitis '50, and others. Co-author articles: (with J A Toomey) Poliomyelitis Virus and Degeneration of Peripheral Nerves '37; (with J A Toomey) Experimental Paralysis in Monkeys Completely Recovered from Poliomyelitis Produced by Cultures of Material from Patients with Measles '39; (with G Steiner) Acute Anterior Poliomyelitis During Pregnancy '44, and others. Contributor: Ten Eventful Years '47; Britannica Book of the Year '47-49. Faculty anatomy dept Wayne U '38-45, asst prof '42-45; dir research Nat Found for Infantile Paralysis since '46. AAAS—Am Pub Health Assn—Am Assn Anatomists. National Foundation for Infantile Paralysis, 120 Broadway, NYC 5.

18 WEAVER, Joe Cline, Jr. Catalytic oxidation; Fluidization of solids; Hydrolysis; Organic esters (Manufacturing). b'13. BS '35 (U Ala). Sr chem engr Stanolind Oil & Gas Co '48, now asst chem plant supt. Am Inst Chem Engrs. Stanolind Oil & Gas Co., P.O. Box 1712, Brownsville, Tex.

19 WEAVER, John C(arrier). Geography of the Polar regions; Agricultural geography of US. b'15. BA '36—MA '37—PhD '40 (U Wis). Research ice conditions rivers and seas North Hemisphere, ice of northern waters; history of Arstic explorations research on barley. Author: Ice Atlas of the Northern Hemisphere '46; Bibliography on Ice of the Northern Hemisphere (partial) '45; American Barley Production: A Study in Agricultural Geography '40. Research staff Am Geog Soc '40-42; research staff Office of Geographer US Dept State '42-44; prof geog U Minn since '48. Officer USN Hydrographic Office '44-46. Assn Am Geog—Am Geophys Union—AAAS—Am Geog Soc(F)—Am Polar Soc. Dept Geography, University of Minnesota, Minneapolis 14. H: 1514 Fulham St, St Paul 8.†☉

20 WEAVER, Leland Eugene. Poultry Breeding, flock management). b'88. BS '18 (Cornell); MS '30 (U Wis). Supervisor official egg laying test western New York since '45, random sample poultry test state of New York since '50. Ext poultry specialist U Ky '18-20, NY State Coll Agr since '20; poultry ed American Agriculturist since '25. Poultry Sci Assn—Phi Sigma. Cornell University, Ithaca.

21 WEAVER, Ralph Holder. Bacteriology (Food, water, quick microtechniques). b'03. BS '22—MS '23 (Allegheny Coll); PhD '26 (Mich State Coll). Research and writing on detection of reduction of nitrates to nitrites by bacteria, serological study of Proteus mirabilis, detection of hydrogen sulfide production by bacteria and of acetylmethylcarbinol production by bacteria, mold distribution in air and dust in Kentucky. Author articles in field. Prof bact Ky U since '37. AAAS(F)—Soc Am Bact (Nat Council)—Am Pub Health Assn—Ky Acad Sci. University of Kentucky, Lexington.†

22 WEAVER, Robert Augustus. Porcelain enamels; Tunnel kilns; Electric heating units and switches; Color oxides. b'90. BS '12—LLD '38 (Kenyon Coll); ScD '41 (Alfred U Alfred NY). Chmn bd and Ferro Corp Cleve; dir Ferro Enamels (Can) Ltd, also Australia, Eng and Holland, Mexico City. Am Ceramic Soc(F). 4150 E. 56th., Cleve.

23 WEAVER, Robert John. Plant growth hormones. b'17. AB '39—MS '40 (U Neb); PhD '46 (U Chicago). Author articles in field. Asst prof bot U Chicago '46-49; asst viticulturist Exp Sta U Cal '49-52, associate viticulturist since '52. Am Soc Plant Physiol—Bot Soc Am—Sigma Xi—Phi Beta Kappa. Department of Viticulture, University of California, Davis, Calif.

24 WEAVER, Virgil Leland. Aircraft gas turbines; Electrical indicating instruments. b'12. BS in EE '35 (Kan State Coll); MS '37 (Kan U). Patent on dynamometer-type electrical measuring instrument. With Gen Elec Co since '37, now charge flight test activities on aircraft gas turbines at Edwards Air Force Base. P.O. Box 7, Edwards, Cal.

25 WEBB, Clarence Hungerford. Caddoan archeology. b'02. BS '23—MD '25 (Tulane U); MS '31 (U Chicago); fellow '29-30 (U Minn). Field studies in archeology of northwestern Louisiana since '35; participated in first Caddoan Conference University of Oklahoma '46. Author articles in field. Pvt practice pediatrics Shreveport since '31; asso prof pediatrics Grad Sch Tulane Sch Med since '47. Tex Archeol and Paleontol Soc (regional vp)—Soc Am Archeol—Am Anthrop Assn—Shreveport Soc for Nature Study (co-founder and first pres). 1560 Line Av., Shreveport 39, La.

26 WEBB, Edwin Y(ates), Jr. Communications engineering (Radio, telephony, infra-red technique, sound recording, electronic devices). b'04. BS '26 (NC State Coll Agr and Engring); EE '27-28, '30 (MIT). Author: The Origin of Harmonic Frequencies in Vacuum Tube Circuits '45; also articles on war-time electronics and communications developments in Germany. Chief electronics and communications unit Dept Commn '46-48, technol investigations in Germany '47. War Prodn Bd communications div deputy chief telegraph sect '44-45; chief communications unit Office Joint Chiefs of Staff '45-46 (aim being to obtain information on tech developments in Germany for use by Am industry). Tau Beta Pi. 1314 34th St., N.W., Washington 7.

10 WEBB, Hanor A. Science (Teaching methods, materials). b'88. AB '08 (U Nashville); MS '11 (U Chicago); PhD '20 (George Peabody Coll Tchrs). Research on materials and methods of teaching science in elementary and secondary schools; editor Current Science and Aviation '27-47, editor science issues Education since '36, chairman magazine advisory board The Science Teacher since '48, consultant and ed state bulletins on science teaching. Coauthor: (with J J Didcoct) Early Steps in Science '25; (with R O Beauchamp) Science by Observation and Experiment '35. Editor: Guide to the Teaching of Sciences in Secondary Schools (Fla State Dept Edn) '48. Contributor: Childcraft '40; Compton's Pictured Encyclopedia '45; various science journ. Head dept chem and sci edn George Peabody Coll for Tchrs since '17; sci manuscript reader ednl pubs. AAAS(F)—Nat Assn Research Science Teaching (pres '38)—Tenn Acad Sci (pres '46)—ACS—Nat Sci Tchrs Assn (sec since '46). George Peabody Coll for Teachers, Nashville 5.

11 WEBB, James L(ewis) A(drian). Heterocyclic organic chemistry; Heavy metal poisoning. b'17. BS '39 (Washington and Lee U); PhD '43 (Johns Hopkins U). Author articles in field. Asst prof chem Southwestern at Memphis '45-46, assoc prof '46-49, prof since '49; also research chem Chapman Chem Company Memphis. American Chem Soc—Tenn Acad Sci—Sigma Xi—Phi Beta Kappa. Department of Chemistry, Southwestern at Memphis, Memphis 12, Tenn.†

12 WEBB, Robert Wallace. Geology and mineralogy of Southern California. b'09. AB '31 (U Calif); MS '32—PhD '37 (Calif Inst Tech); (U So Calif); (U Wash). Co-author: Minerals of California '46; also articles. U Cal since '32, prof since '51. Geol Soc Am—Mineral Soc Am — Meteoritical Soc — Sigma Xi. University of California, Santa Barbara, Calif.†

13 WEBB, Willard. Civil war (Military history, signal communications); Heraldy. b'03. AB '27—MA '28 (George Washington U). Research and correspondence in the Library of Congress in heraldry and allied fields of philately and numismatics; military history of the Civil war, particularly tactics and signal communications, and the lives of General Bee and General Early. Asst in charge Congressional unit, Library of Congress '29-39, custodian Congressional reading room '40, chief stack and reader div since '46. Library of Congress, Washington 25.

14 WEBB, William Herbert. Waterways; Floods; Flood control. b'96. LLB '25 (Nat U). Author articles in field. Flood Control Com '26-31; asst to sec Nat Rivers and Harbors Congress Washington '32-33, asst to pres '33-37, exec vp since '37; pvt law practice Washington, Chicago, Aurora Ill since '26. 1720 M St. N.W., Washington 6.⊙

15 WEBBER, Charles Sterling. Adhesives; Cellulose esters; Coated abrasives. b'00. Student '19-21 (Tufts Coll); SB '24—SM '26 (MIT). Research on pretreatments and processes for esterification of cellulose, formulation and processes of cellulose acetate and ni-

trate for laminated safety-glass, aircraft windows, playing cards; development of phenolic resins for castings and adhesives for coated abrasives, special waterproof backings for abrasives. Holds numerous patents in field. Organic research chem Cellulose Research Lab Eastman Kodak Co '26-29; plastics research Fiberloid Corp '29-38, asst dir research '38-40; group leader plastics research Monsanto Chem Co '40; mgr resin research Behr-Manning Corp since '40. Am Chem Soc (sec Conn Valley sect '37-39, chmn '40). Behr-Manning Corporation, Troy, N.Y. H: Loudonville, N.Y.

16 WEBBER, Irma Eleanor Schmidt. Normal and pathological anatomy of plants; California Pleistocene woods. b'04. AB '26—MA '27—PhD '29 (U Calif). Author: Up Above and Down Below '43; Travelers All '44; Anywhere in the World '47; Bits That Grow Big '49; also articles in field. Collaborator div cotton and other fiber crops and diseases US Dept Agr since '36; colaborador de la Revista Lilloa since '37. Bot Soc Am—Torrey Bot Club—Internat Assn Wood Anatomists—Phi Beta Kappa—Sigma Xi. U.S. Fiber Crops Field Laboratory. 500 Arlington Av., Berkeley, Calif.†

17 WEBBER, John Milton. Cotton cytology; Yucca and Phormium taxonomy and culture. b'97. BS '25—MS '27—PhD '30 (U Cal). Author articles in field. Asso cytologist cotton, other fiber crops and diseases Bur Plant Ind Soils and Agr Eng US Dept Agr '31-47, cytologist '47-51, research agronomist since '51. AAAS—Am Genetic Assn—Am Soc Naturalists—Sigma Xi. 500 Arlington Av., Berkeley 7, Cal.†

18 WEBER, Andrew Raymond. Heat power (Heating, air conditioning, refrigeration); Industrial safety; Slide rule. b'95. BS '19 (St Mary Coll); BME '27 (U Dayton); MME '36 (Catholic U Am). Author: Air Conditioning '36; Advanced Course in Industrial Safety; also articles in field. Prof mech engring U Dayton since '42; coordinator ind safety courses since '44; lecturer various safety org since '42. Am Soc Mech Engrs—Nat Soc Profl Engrs—Ohio Soc Profl Engrs—Dayton Soc Profl Engrs—Am Soc Engring Edn—Ohio Acad Sci. University of Dayton, Dayton 9, O.†

19 WEBER, Arthur D. Animal husbandry; Livestock; Beef cattle. b'98. BS '22—MS '26 (Kan State Coll); PhD '40 (Purdue). Author articles in field. Asso Dean Agr and asso director Agricultural Experiment Station Kan State Coll since '50. AAAS(F)—Am Soc Animal Prodn (vp '44, pres '45) — Kan Acad Sci—Am Genetic Assn—Sigma Xi—Phi Kappa Phi—Gamma Sigma Delta. Kansas State Coll., Manhattan, Kan.⊙

20 WEBER, Arthur Phineas. Chemical engineering (Isotopes separation); Mixing machinery design; Continuous processing. b'20. BChemE '41 (Coll City NY); '46-47 (AEC Sch nuclear sci and engring). Research in theoretical fundamentals underlying mixing as chemical engineering unit operation; reaction kinetics; radiochemical isotopes separation; DDT and plant hormones preparation; nuclear reactor and reprocessing plants design; design special mixing machinery and custom-engineered chemical processing machinery; continuous type process plants. Design engr Hendrick Mfg Co Carbondale Pa '41-42; asst chief engr Chemurgy Design Corp NYC '42-44; dir process development and process engring Kellex Corp '44-49; tech dir Internat Engring Inc since '49. Am Inst Chem Engrs—ACS—AAAS. 15 Park Row, N

YC 38. H: 1334 Surrey Lane North, Rockville Centre, N.Y.

21 WEBER, Don Andrew. Mineral concentration. b'95. BS in mech engring '20 (Purdue U). Development apparatus, methods, and processes for sizing and separating metallic and non-metallic minerals, including wet specific gravity separators, granular materials and liquids separators, and hydraulic separators. Holds ten patents in field, including vibrating screen and concentrating tables. Author article: The Theory and Practice of Screening '31. Dir research, development and mfr spl separating and sizing equipment Deister Concentrator Co since '26. Am Ceramic Soc—Can Ceramic Soc—Am Mining Congress—AIMME. Deister Concentrator Co., Fort Wayne, Ind.

22 WEBER, Robert L. Temperature measurements (Laboratory methods); Microscopy (Electron); Films (Educational use); Physics (Educational film instruction). b'13. AB '34—MA '36 (Yale); PhD '38 (Pa State Coll). Organization of laboratory course in methods of temperature measurement for students in metallurgy, ceramics, chemistry, engineering, physics; development of college course in technique of electron microscopy. Author: Heat and Temperature Measurement '50, and others. Editorial bd Review of Scientific Instruments; collaborator on, and editor physics textbooks. Dept physics Pa State Coll since '36, asso prof since '47. Am Inst Physics—Electron Microscopy Soc—Sigma Xi. Pennsylvania State College, State College.

23 WEBSTER, Hutton. History of civilization; Primitive culture and religous organization. b'75. AB '96—AM '97 (Leland Stanford Jr U); AM '03—PhD '04 (Harvard). Study of primitive society and religion. Author: Primitive Secret Societies '08, rev edit '32, Japanese translation '15, Italian translation '22; Rest Days '16; World History '23; History of Civilization '40; Taboo '42; Magic '48; also 15 textbooks of ancient, medieval and modern history for high schools and colleges. Prof social anthropology U Neb '07-33; lectr sociology Stanford U '33-40, emeritus since '40. Associé de l'Institue International de Sociologie—Royal Anthropol Inst(F)—AAAS(F)—Am Anthrop Assn—Am Folklore Soc—Am Sociol Soc—Phi Beta Kappa—Pi Gamma Mu. 2025 Cowper St., Palo Alto, Cal.

24 WECHTER, Eugene. Cement and lime burning; Cement masonry (Water proofing); Natural cement. AB '22 (De-Pauw U); MS '23—PhD '25 (U Wis). Developed methods and apparatus for burning cements and limes; studied and developed masonry cement compositions; directed research leading to improvements in quality of masonry cement; research on blends of natural cement and Portland cement to improve properties of concrete. Holds patents in field. Research asst to head analytical chem dept U Wis '23-25; dir research Louisville Cement Co since '25. Am Soc Testing Materials (chmn sponsoring com on masonry cement since '51, adv com on cement since '52)—Am Concrete Inst—Nat Acad Sci (highway research bd). Louisville Cement Co., Speed, Ind.

25 WECKLER, Joseph Edwin, Jr. Social anthropology; Race relations; Community organization, history and economic aspects of life in Eastern Micronesia. b'06. PhB '28—PhD '40 (U Chicago). Author articles in field Chmn dept anthropology U So Calif —Sigma Xi—Soc Applied Anthropol. since '45. Am Anthropol Assn—AAAS

University of Southern California, University Park, LA 7.†

10 WEDEL, Waldo R(udolph). Archeology. b'08. Student (Bethel Coll); AB '30 (U Ariz); MA '31 (U Neb); PhD '36 (U Calif). Field trips throughout US annually since '29 and to Tabasco, Mexico '43. Author: Introduction Pawnee Archeology '36; Archeological Investigations on Buena Vista Lake, California '41 and others. Cur archeology US Nat Museum since '50. Soc Am Archeol (sec '42-48, pres '48-49) — Anthropol Soc Washington (treas '44-46)—Am Anthropol Assn—Wash Acad Scis — AAAS — Sigma Xi. Recipient award in biol scis Wash Acad Scis '47. U.S. National Museum, Washington 25.†⊙

11 WEEDON, Frederick Renfroe. Biochemistry (Active organic halides). b'95. BS '21—MS '23 (U Fla); '15-16 (Ga Inst Tech); '21-23 (George Washington U); '24-25 (U Calif); '25-26 (Emory U); MD '28 (U Chicago). Research biochemistry of active organic halogen compounds, toxic gases, fungus diseases, fungicides, serology. Author articles in field. Asst chemist Nat Bur Standards '22-23; pathologist Macon Hosp Ga '28; asst dir Bur Labs Yonkers NY '30-40; asst attending pathologist St Johns Hosp '31-40, Yonkers Hosp '37-40; dir Municipal Lab Jamestown since '40, Chautauqua Co Lab Dunkirk since '40; pathologist various hosps; asst prof histol and adv chem Alfred U Ext Jamestown since '41. AMA—Am Assn Pathologists—ACS—Am Soc Clin Pathologists—ACP—AAAS—Phi Kappa Phi. 304 Hall Av., Jamestown, N.Y.

12 WEEK, Erling Finch. Vitamins (Oil-soluble); Vitamin A. b'15. AB '36 (U Cal Berkeley). Investigation relative efficacy of free and ester forms vitamins A and D, effects of dosage level, and vitamin carrier; demonstration importance of factors affecting hydrolysis in vivo in utilization of oil soluble vitamin; experiments on importance of hydrolysis factors in human utilization; design and construction plant for manufacture vitamin A and D oils; in charge collaborative assay of vitamin A. Mng partner mfr vitamins A and D Tech Fisheries Co '39-45; pres Vitamin Oil Producers Inst '43-45; pres and research dir mfr vitamin A and D concentrates Collett-Week-Nibecker Inc since '46; mem spl com for US Phar XIV assay of vitamin A '49-50. ACS—Am Oil Chem Soc—Animal Nutrition Research Council—AAAS—Alpha Chi Sigma. Collett-Week-Nibecker, Inc., 1291 67th St., Oakland 8, Cal.

13 WEEKS, Lewis George. Worldwide oil basin and petroleum occurence analysis; Basins (Development, sedimentation, classification). b'93. AB '17 (U Wis); '19-20 (Cornell U). Author articles in field. Pet geolog Whitehall Pet Co London, India '20-24; pet geol Standard Oil Co NJ and subsidiaries in many countries of South America '24-38, chief geologist Argentina '33-38, pres Standard Oil Co of Bolivia '33-38, Am Assn Pet Geol—Geol Soc Am—Am Inst Mining and Metall Engrs—Am Geophys Union—AAAS—Am Geog Soc—Pan Am Inst Mining Engrs and Geol.

14 WEEKS, Martin Edward. Soil and plant chemistry. b'06. BS '34 (S D State Coll); PhD '37 (U Wis). Studied effect of soil fertility on chemical composition of corn and other crops; fertilizer requirements of crops, particularly tobacco, corn and alfalfa. Research asst in soils Ky Agrl Expt Sta '37-40, asst agron '40-44, agron '44-52,

head dept agron '50-52; cons agr TVA Div Agr Relations since '52. American Society Agron—Soil Sci Soc Am — ACS — Ky Acad Scis — Sigma Xi. Division of Agricultural Relations, T.V.A., Knoxville, Tenn.⊙

15 WEEMS, Philip Van Horn. Navigation. b'89. BS '12 (US Naval Acad). Inventor of Mark II Weems Aircraft Plotter and second-setting watch which received prize from British Royal Soc of Arts. Author: Line of Position Book '27; Star Altitude Curves '38; Marine Navigation '40; Air Navigation '31; also articles in field. As USN officer, founded Weems system of navigation; Air Transport Command '45; dir Weems System of Navigation since '45. Inst Aero Sci—Inst Navigation. Naval Inst award best outline text on leadership '22. 227 Prince George St., Annapolis, Md.

16 WEER, Paul Wiley. Leni-Lenape Indians (History, mnemonic pictographs). b'86. AB '08 (Butler U). Studies in the mnemonic, pictographic, prehistoric and ethno-historic record of Leni-Lenape Indians; documentation of history of manuscript; Walam Olum search for original sticks which bore mnemonic pictographs painted in red ochre. Ind Acad Sci—Hoosier Folklore Soc—Am Anthrop Assn—Soc Am Archaeol—Am Folklore Soc. Indiana Historical Society, State Library and Historical Bldg., Indpls. H: 5650 North Meridian St.

17 WEETMAN, Leslie Maurice. Breeding of sugar cane, sweet potato, oats and watermelon. b'07. AB '30 (Simpson Coll); MS '32—PhD '35 (Ia State Coll). Author articles in field. Geneticist research dept US Sugar Corp Clewiston Fla since '42. AAAS—Genetics Soc Am—Am Genetic Assn—Bot Soc Am—Am Phytopathol Soc—Fla Hort Soc—Sigma Xi—Phi Kappa Phi. Research Department, U.S. Sugar Corporation, Clewiston, Fla.†

18 WEGELIN, Oscar. Early American literature, history and drama. b'76. Author: Early American Plays 1714-1830 '05; Early American Fiction 1774-1830 '29; Early American Poetry 1750-1820 '30; also articles in field. Bibliog New York Hist Soc since '38. 170 Central Park West, NYC 24.

19 WEHRLE, Lawrence Paul. Scale insects; Aphids. b'87. BS '14—MS '16 (Kan State Coll); PhD '24 (Cornell U). Research on clover-seed caterpillar '24, the clover-flower midge '29, the clover-leaf tyer '29. Articles in field. Research instr entomol Cornell U '19-30; asst prof entomol U Ariz '30-40, asso prof since '40, asst entomol Expt Sta '30-40, asso entomol since '40. AAAS(F)—Am Assn Econ Entomol—Entomol Soc Am—Kan Entomol Soc. College of Agriculture, University of Arizona, Tucson, Ariz.†

20 WEIDA, Frank Mark. Statistical analysis; sampling theory and practice; Hypothesis (Testing); Experiment (Design); Actuarial theory. b'91. BS '13 (Kenyon Coll); PhD '23 (U Ia). Co-author: Analytic Geometry and Elements of Calculus '30; also articles in field. Prof statistics George Washington U since '35, head dept statistics since '35. AAAS(F)—Inst Math Statis(F)—Am Math Soc—Math Assn Am—Econometric Soc—Am Statis Assn—Philos Soc of Wash—Wash Acad Scis — Wash Statis Soc — Sigma Xi. George Washington University, Washington 6.†

21 WEIDLEIN, Edward Ray. Hydrometallurgy; Science in industry. b'87. BA '09—MA '10 (U Kan); ScD(hon) '24 (Tufts Coll); LLD '30 (U Pitts-

burgh); ScD '37 (Rutgers U); ScD '39 (Waynesburg Pa Coll); ScD '45 (U Wichita); LLD '47 (Washington and Jefferson Coll); ScD '52 (Southwestern Coll). Asst dir Inst at Pittsburgh '16, actg dir '18-19, dir '21-51; pres Mellon Inst since '51, vice pres board trustees '27-51, now chmn board trustees; tech adviser to Rubber Reserve Co since '41; chief of chemicals and allied products branch War Prodn Bd '40-42; sr consultant chemicals branch War Prdn Bd '42-46; head tech cons War Prodn Bd '42-46; tech adviser Research Div QM Corps '43; com for examination of enemy material and supplies under War Metall Com of Nat Research Council and Nat Acad Sciences. Chem Industry medal by Soc of Chem Ind '35; Pittsburgh award for '39; Man-of-the-Year award Jr C of C '41; cited by U Kans '43 for distinguished service. 325 S. Dallas Av., Pitts.⊙

22 WEIDLINGER, Paul. Stress analysis; Concrete (Reinforced). b'14. AE (German Tech Inst Brno Czechoslovakia); Diploma (Swiss Poly Inst Zurich Switzerland). Development special applications of reinforced concrete and steel to longspan and earthquake-proof structures and buildings. Author articles: Architecture and Reinforced Concrete '43; Structural Design in Aluminum '48; Tomorrow's Structural Theory '49; Implication of Lightweight Aggregates '49. Contributor: Encyclopedia Americana '47. Designer Le Corbusier Paris France '38; dir engring Sociedad Constructuroa Nacional La Paz Bolivia SA '42; prof reinforced concrete design San Andres U La Paz Bolivia '42; chief engr Bur Reclamation Bolivia; chief engr hangar div Atlas Aircraft '46; cons engr General Engring Asso Washington and NYC since '47. Am Concrete Inst—AAAS. General Engineering Associates, 101 Park Av., NYC 17.

23 WEIDNER, John Prestin. High polymers; Paper (Wet strength); Paper chemistry; Felt preservation. b'12. BS '34 (U Ill); MS '36—PhD '38 (Inst Paper Chem Lawrence Coll). Research on decrease in felt life due to bacterial action, influence of humidity on diameter and length of sulfite fibers, raw water and process water treatments. Tech dir Hoberg Paper Mills Co '38-45; tech supt Container Corp Am since '45. AAAS—Tech Assn Pulp and Paper Industry. Container Corp. of America, Manayunk, Phila. 27.

24 WEIGEL, Albert Robert. Diesel engines; Steel (Direct reduction); Heat transfer; Ordnance. b'91. Research on lightweight high speed diesel engines, direct reduction iron ore; 155 millimeter guns and five inch naval twin mounts. Granted patents in field. With various automotive and machinery cos and cons engr '18-40; with Consol W Steel Corp since '41, research engr since '44. ASME(F). Merit award Soc Am Mil Engrs. Postoffice Box 2015, L.A. 54. H: 4121 Wilshire Blvd., L.A.5.

25 WEIGEL, Charles Adolph. Entomology control (Greenhouses, ornamental plants, mushrooms). b'87. BS Agr '16 (NH Univ); MS '18—PhD '25 (O State U). Research on insects affecting greenhouse and ornamental plants and mushrooms, biology of pests, development of effective control measures as fumigation and insecticides. Co-author: (with Baumhofer) Handbook of Insect Enemies of Flowering Plants and Shrubs '48; Insecticides and Equipment for Controlling Insects on Fruits and Vegetables '43; also articles in field. Sr entomol Bur Entomol and Plant Quarantine, US Dept Agr '28-53, retired.

AAAS(F)—Am Assn Econ Entomol—Entomol Soc Am—Entomol Soc Wash (past pres)—Insecticide Soc Wash. H: 9019 Woodland Dr., Silver Spring Md.

10 WEIGEL, John C. Public administration. b'86. BA '08 (Lombard Coll); (U Chicago); '10, '11, '13, '14 (Europe). Author: A Manual of Business Methods for the Department of Public Welfare '41; also articles in field. Foreign affairs specialist Dept State '48; function transfd to Econ Coop Adm May '48. Am Acad Polit and Social Sci—Am Soc Pub Administrn—Acad Polit Sci. 252 Western Av., Joliet, Ill.

11 WEIGLE, Luther Allan. English Bible. b'80. BA '00—MA '03—LLD '34 —PhD '17 (Gettysburg Coll); PhD '05 (Yale); DD '16 (Carleton); LittD '25 (Muhlenberg Coll); LLD '33 (Dickinson Coll). Author: The English New Testament from Tyndale to the Revised Standard Version '49. Del to Internat Missionary Council Jerusalem '28; pres Conference of Theological Seminaries '29. Chmn Am Standard Bible Com since '30 engaged in revision of Eng Bible, also revision Old Testament; dean Yale Divinity Sch '28-49, now emeritus; pres Yale-in-China. Internat Council Religious Edn (exec com since '20)—Minn Ednl Assn (pres '13)—Fed Council Chs Christ (pres '40-42)—Am Philos Assn—Am Psychol Assn—Religious Edn Assn (council)—Phi Beta Kappa. 409 Prospect St., New Haven 11.†⊚

12 WEIL, Frank L. Social welfare; Youth-serving organizations. b'94. BS '15—LLB '17 (Columbia); DHL (hon) '45 (Hebrew Union Coll). Pres YMHA (92nd St) NYC '32-40; co-founder, vp, mem bd dirs, exec com and policy com United Service Orgns '40-49; president World Fedn YMHA's and Jewish Community Centers, Nat Jewish Welfare Bd '40-50; mem Nat Exec Board Boy Scouts Am, chmn Div Personnel; Awarded Merit Medal by Pres Truman '46. 60 E. 42nd St., NYC. H: 635 Park Av.

13 WEINBERGER, Bernhard Wolf. Dental bibliography and history. b'85. DDS '08 (Pa U); '09 (Angle Sch Orthodontia). Consulting librarian of dental literature, New York Academy of Medicine; officer, essayist, reporter in International Dental Congresses. Author: Orthodontics—An Historical Review of Its Origin and Evolution (2 vols) '26; Dental Literature, Its Origin and Development '27; Pierre Fauchard, Surgeon Dentist '41. Orthodonist since '10; prof dental hist and lit NYU '29-31. AAAS(F)—NY Acad Sci(F)—Internat Coll Dentists (founder US sect, past mem bd regents, awarded Masters degree '41)—NY Acad Med (asso F)—AMA—Am Dental Assn—Dental Soc State NY—Am Assn Hist Med—Bibliog Soc Am—Am Assn Orthodon—NY Soc Orthodon—NY Soc Med Hist—Hist Sci Soc—Fed Dentaire Internat (vp)—Omicron Kappa Upsilon. Benjamin Lord prize First Dist Dental Soc NY '32; NY Dental Centennial medal '34; Sigma Epsilon Delta plaque '41. 119 W. 57th St., NYC 19.

14 WEINDLING, Ludwig. Textiles; Fibers; Manila; Sisal; Jute. b'00. CE '18 (Cornell U). Consultant to US Department of State on textile matters for Greek Industry, American Mission Aid to Greece '47-48; special advisor on textiles to US War Production Board and to combined US British Raw Materials Board '41-44. Author: Long Vegetable Fibers '47. Cons engr head of Weindling & Co NYC '26-40, retired '40. 75 West St., NYC 6.

15 WEINRYB, Bernard D. Economic history of Central and Eastern Europe and Middle East; International economics. b'00. PhD '31 (U Breslau); student (Teachers Training Inst and U Breslau, Columbia U). Author: Studien zur Wirtschaftsgeschichte der Juden in Russland Und Polen im 18-19 Jahrhundert '33; Neueste Wirtschaftsgeschichte—Russland und Polen '34; Studies in the Economic and Social History of the Jews in Poland '39; Jewish Emancipation Under Attack '42; The Yishuv in Palestine '47; Vocational Education, History of Training in Europe '48; also articles in field. Lecturer hist and social Herzliah Teachers Sem NYC '40-41; dean Jewish Teachers Sem and Peoples U NYC '42-48; lecturer hist Brooklyn Coll and prof hist and instns Grad Sch Edn and Community Adminstrn Yeshiva U NYC since '48; prof Middle Eastern Econ at Inst for Middle East Dropsie Coll Phila '49. AHA—Am Econ Assn. Grant-in-aid Social Sci Research Council '48-49; research fellow Am Acad Jewish Research '40-41. 606 W. 113th St., NYC 25.†

16 WEIR, Irvin Reed. Electrical design of high power AM, TV, and FM radio transmitters. b'97. BS '21—EE '34 (Rose Polytech Inst). Design and development circuits for electron discharge, antenna dissipator, electron discharge amplifier for AM, TV and FM radio transmitters. Holds patents in field. Contributor: General Electric Review '39; Electronics '40; Communication '41. With Gen Electric Co since '21, designing engr transmitter div since '48. Inst Radio Engring(F)—NY Soc Profl Engrs. Electronics Park, General Electric Company, Syracuse, N.Y.

17 WEISENBURGER, Francis Phelps. United States social and religious history (Ohio, Middle West); United States immigrant groups. b'00. AB '22 —MA '23—PhD '29 (U Mich). Research in US political and social history, particularly social and religious history of Middle West and Ohio. Author: A Life of Charles Hammond, First Great Journalist of Old Northwest '34; A Life of John McLean, A Politician on the United States Supreme Court '37; A History of the State of Ohio, vol III, The Passing of the Frontier '41; The Middle Western Antecedents of Woodrow Wilson; The Urbanization of the Middle West; A History of Lake Erie's Ohio Shore; History of American Religious Life, 1865-1900; also articles in field. Asst hist U Mich '23-24; instr hist, Ohio State U '24-29, prof since '46; cons, maps, Atlas of Am History. AHA—Miss Valley Hist Assn—Ohio Acad of History (pres '46-47)—Ohio Archeol and Hist Soc—Phi Alpha Theta. Ohio State University, Columbus 10. H: 99 Aldrich Road, Columbus 2.

18 WEISS, Emil. Bacteriology; Immunology. b'93. Student '11-14 (U Vienna); '16-18 (U Graz); MA '19 (U Prague); PhD '37 (U Ill). Bacteriophage, staining methods for bacteria and fungi, serodiagnosis of malignancy, syphilis, amebiasis, tuberculosis & gonorrhea, color reactions with malignant sera and tumors. Asst Infect Hosp Zagreb '19; first asst and acting head Royal Bact Inst Zagreb '19-21; path Ill Gen Hosp Chicago '21-22; instr bact and path Loyola U '22-24, asst prof '24-28, asso prof '28-31, prof '31-33; path St Anne's Hosp Chicago '22-33; path Holy Cross Hosp Chgo '30-38; asso bact and pub health U Ill '33-40; path Chicago Eye, Ear, Nose and Throat Coll and Hosp '33-42; path Martha Washington Hosp Chicago '31-

43; spl cons USPHS '34-43; path Sacred Heart Hosp Tomahawk '38-43; instr allergy Northwestern U '41-44; path Peoples Hosp Chicago since '43. Soc Am Bact—Am Assn Immunologists—AAUP—Am Assn Path and Bact—Am Assn Cancer Research—Am Coll Phys (F)—ACS—Soc Exptl Biol and Med—Am Pub Health Assn(F)—AAAS—Ill State Acad Sci—ACS—NY Acad Sci. 5036 N. Bernard St., Chgo 25.

19 WEISS, Francis Joseph. Beet and cane sugar (Consumption statistics, refining, utilization of by-products, food and non-food uses); Peat, seaweed, fish by-products, forest wastes (Utilization). b'98. PhD in chem '22—ScD in econ, statis '28 (U Vienna). Use of sugar in baking, meat curing, confectionary and tobacco products; food and energy value of sugar, relation to other nutrients and sweetening agents; sugar in emergency nutrition. Research asso Nat Planning Assn '40-45; econ analyst Bd Econ Warfare '42; with Interstate Commerce Commn '46. ACS—Am Econ Soc—Washington Acad Sci—NY Acad Sci—Econometric Soc—Am Statis Assn—Biometric Soc—Inst Food Technologists—Am Acad Social Polit Sci—AAAS—Scientific Research Soc Am—Nat Planning Assn—National Farm Chemurgic Council—Am Geog Soc—Chem Club NY. Sugar Research Foundation, 1530 P St., Washington 5. H: 3048 Rodman St., Washington 8.

20 WEISS, Herbert Klemm. Aeronautics; Ballistics; Servomechanisms. b'17. BS '37—MS '38 (MIT). Holder US Patents on devices for improving manual control and apparatus for regenerating and smoothing data. Author articles in field. Mech engr Coast Artillery Bd '38-42, Anti-aircraft Artillery Bd '42-44, Army Ground Force Bd '44-46; ballistician and deputy chief Terminal Ballistic Lab '46-52; chief weapon systems lab. Ballistic Research Labs Aberdeen Proving Ground Md since '52. AIEE—Operations Research Soc Am—Inst Aeronautical Sci—ASME—Franklin Inst. Ballistic Research Laboratories, Aberdeen Proving Ground, Md.†

21 WEISSERT, Elwood W. Coal mining machinery. b'12. BS in civil engineering '37 (U Pittsburgh). Design and production coal mining machinery. Granted patent in field. With Bertrand P Tracy Co since '34, shop supt and engr since '40. Am Soc Tool Engrs—Am Welding Soc (asso). 919 Fulton St., Pitts 33.

22 WEITZMAN, Ellis. Educational testing. b'10. AB '32 (Emory U); MA '35 (Creighton U); PhD '40 (U Neb). Devised tests for measurement social maturity and development, and learning achievement; developed methods for application achievement tests to personnel counseling and guidance; consultant Bureau of Naval Personnel '46, Civil Service Commission '50. Author: Growing Up Socially '49. Co-author: (with Walter McNamara) Constructing Classroom Examinations '49. Author articles: A Test of Social Maturity and its Use in Comparing People Sixteen Through Twenty-four Years of Age '40; A Test of Social Competence '41; A Study of Social Maturity in Persons Sixteen through Twenty-four Years of Age '44, and others. Co-author articles: (with Walter J McNamara) Techniques Used in Analyzing the Learning Achievement of Naval Aviation Cadets '44; The Effect of Choice Placement on the Difficulty of Multiple-Choice Test Questions '45, and others. Supervisor spl problems group US Employment Service '40-42; university examiner, prof psychol and measurements, and dir guidance center Am U since '46. Examinations officer Naval Air Training Command USN '42-46. Am Psychol Association(F)—AAAS(F). Diplomate in counseling and guidance Am Bd Examiners in Professional Psychol. Am University, Washington 16.

10 WEITZMANN, Kurt. Art (Byzantine, late classical, early Christian, medieval). b'04. PhD '29 (U Berlin); student (Humanistiches Gym Gelsenkirchen, U Muenster, Wuerzburg, Vienna). Author: Illustrations in Roll and Codex, a Study of the Origin and Method of Text Illustrations '47; the Joshua Roll, a Work of the Macedonian Renaissance '48; Greek Mythology in Byzantine Art '51; The Fresco-cycle of S Maria Di Castelseprio '51; also articles in field. With Inst for Advanced Study since '35; asso professor Princeton U '45-50, professor since '50. Medieval Acad Am(F). McCormick Hall, Princeton, N.J.☺

11 WELBORN, Mary Catherine. History (Medieval, science, aviation). b'99. AB '21 (Vassar); AM '23 (U Calif); PhD '32 (U Chicago). Research on history of development of aerodynamic theories and their application to technical development of airplanes. Author: Calendar reform in the thirteenth century, '38; also articles in field. Research in hist of sci, Carnegie Institution of Washington '30-38; research hist of banking Harvard Comm for social sci '38-39; instr hist and govt Wells Coll Aurora NY '43-44; instr hist and govt Northeastern U Boston '44-45; historian AAF Washington '45-46; hist Civil Affairs Div War Dept '46-47; hist Naval Aviation Hist Unit '47-49; hist Operations Research Office Johns Hopkins U contract with Army since '49. AHA. Operations Research Office, Fort L. J. McNair, Washington 25.

12 WELCH, Donald Stuart. Plant pathology; Tree diseases; Hardwood nectria canker; Wood decay in living trees; Flowering dogwood canker; Dutch elm disease; Western white pine (Pole blight). b'94. BS '17 (U Me); MA '21 (Harvard); PhD '25 (Cornell U); '47-48 (U Idaho Sch Forestry). Author articles in field. Instr, asst prof, asso prof, prof plant pathol Cornell U since '21. Am Phytopath Soc—Soc Am Foresters (sr)—Mycol Soc Am—Nat Shade Tree Conf—A A A S. Department of Plant Pathology, Cornell University, Ithaca, N.Y.†

13 WELCH, Winona H. Plant taxonomy and ecology; Bryology; Mosses of Indiana. b'96. AB '23 (DePauw U); AM '25 (U Ill); PhD '28 (Ind U). Research on Fontinalis, Dichelyma, Brachelyma. Author: Monograph on North Am Fontinalaceae, other articles in field. Asst prof botany DePauw U '30-34, advanced to prof since '39, acting head dept '39-40, '46-47. AAAS—International Assn of Plant Taxonomists—British Bryological Society—Bot Soc Am—Am Soc Plant Taxonomists—Sullivant Moss Soc—Torrey Bot Club—Ind Acad Sci—Phi Beta Kappa—Sigma Xi. Research grant from Penrose Fund Am Phil Soc '38 for study and research in European Herbaria; collected bryophytes in Cuba summer '48. DePauw University, Greencastle, Ind.

14 WELD, Ralph Foster. Social history of New York City and Brooklyn. b'88. BS '13—MA '24 (Wesleyan U); PhD (Hist) '38 (Columbia). Author: Brooklyn Village 1816-1834 '38; Our Brooklyn '40; A Tower on the Heights '46; Brooklyn is America '50. Co-author: (with Dr. William Bridgwater)

New York City during the Hylan Regime '52. Asso ed Dictionary of Am History '37-39; dir Brooklyn history project Brooklyn Inst Arts and Sci '39-42; free lance writer since '45. 311 Woodland Pl., Leonia, N.J.

15 WELLEK, René. Literature (Czechoslovak, Slavic, comparative). b'03. PhD '26 (Charles U Prague); '27-28 (Princeton U). Author: Kant in England '31; The Rise of English Literary History '41; Theory of Literature '49; also articles in field. Prof Slavic and comparative lit Yale U since '46. Modern Lang Assn Am—Linguistic Soc Am. Research fellow Henry E. Huntington Library '42; grant-in-aid Am Council Learned Soc '43; Rockefeller Found grant '45-46. Yale University, New Haven.†☺

16 WELLER, J(ames) Marvin. Stratigraphy and structural geology (Illinois and neighboring states); Geology of northwestern India and China and northeastern Tibet; Carboniferous paleontology; Late Paleozoic trilobites; Sedimentary cycles; Fluorite. b'99. BS '23—PhD '27 (U Chicago). Author articles in field. Geol exploration in India, China and Tibet, Whitehall Petroleum Corp London '20-22 and Chinese Petroleum Prospecting Co Shanghai, China '37-38; prof invertebrate paleontol U Chicago since '45. Nat Research Council (com on stratigraphy since '44)—Geol Soc Am(F) — Paleontol Soc(F)—Am Assn Petroleum Geol—Soc Econ Paleontol Mineral — Phi Beta Kappa—Sigma Xi. APO 928 care Postmaster, SF.

17 WELLER, Royal. Underwater ordnance; Guided missiles; Photo-elasticity. b'05. BS '27 (MIT); MS '34—PhD '39 (O State U). In charge development and design of depth charges, mines, torpedo components, and fuses; studies in general missile technology; application iterative procedure to determination of interior stresses in photoelastic models; devised mechanical interferometry method of deflection measurement; devised scattering method of three-dimensional stress analysis. Author articles: Three-Dimensional Photoelasticity Using Scattered Light '41; The Optical Investigation of Fluid Flow '46, and others. Co-author articles: (with G H Shortley) Numerical Solution of Laplaces' Equation '39; (with B Fried) Photoelastic Analysis of Two and Three-Dimensional Stress Systems '40; (with B M Shepard) Deflection Measurement by Mechanical Interferometry '48, and others. With test dept Naval Ordnance Lab '41-45, head engr '45-49; chief sci Naval Air Missile Test Center since '49. APS(F)—ASME—Inst Aeronautical Sci —Am Ordnance Soc—Soc Exptl Stress Analysis. U.S. Naval Air Missile Test Center, Point Mugu, Port Hueneme, Cal.

18 WELLES, Charles Bradford. Ancient history and law; Classical archaeology; Epigraphy; Papyrology. b'01. BA '24—PhD '28 (Yale). Author: Royal Correspondence in the Hellenistic Period '34. Prof ancient hist Yale U since '40. Am Philol Assn—AHA—Am Oriental Soc—Conn Acad Arts and Sci—Archtl Inst Am—Middle East Inst. 1544 Yale Station, New Haven.

19 WELLES, Samuel Paul. Permian and triassic reptiles and amphibians; Mesozoic Sauropterygia. b'07. AB '30—PhD '40 (U Calif). Author articles in field. Field and lab asst U Calif Museum Paleontology '31-39, asst curator reptiles and amphibians '39-45, prin mus curator '45-47, prin paleontol since '46. Geol Soc Am—Paleontol Soc Am—Soc Vertebrate Paleontol—Soc Study

Evolution—Calif Acad Sci—Mus Northern Ariz—Sigma Xi. Museum of Paleontology, University of California, Berkeley.†

20 WELLMAN, Frederick Lovejoy. Plant pathology (Tropical). b'97. AB '20 (Fairmount Coll Wichita Kan); MS '24—PhD '28 (U Wis). Environment and host cultivation studies diseases of banana, and methods for control; selection and breeding for disease resistance; identification virus diseases of tropical plants and fruits; studies on control of leaf blight of seed petunias grown in Costa Rica, also diseases of maize; experiments with sugar cane, coffee, and cocoa diseases, and disease control measures adaptable to tropical conditions. Author articles: A Disease of Banana, Markedly Similar to Bunchy Top Produced by Celery Virus '34; Comparative Toxic Effects of Extracts from Mild and Virulent Isolates of Tomato-Wilt Fusarium '43; Indian Gardening in El Salvador '45, and others. Co-author article: (with J A Stevenson) A Preliminary Account of the Plant Diseases of El Salvador '44. With USDA since '20, path and agr San Salvador and El Salvador '43-46, cons plant path and agr Turrialba Costa Rica since '47. AAAS(F)—Am Phytopath Society—Am Mycol Soc—Wis Acad Arts and Sci—Washington Acad Sci—Phi Sigma—Sigma Xi. Office of Foreign Agricultural Relatios, U.S. Department of Agriculture, Washington.

21 WELLNER, Charles August. Silviculture; Western white pine forests; Native Trees of Montana and Northern Idaho b'11. BS '33 (U Idaho); MF '38 (Yale); '44 (US Naval Acad). Research on stocking, thinning, distribution, and diseases on forest stands. Author articles in field. Jr forester, silviculturist Northern Rocky Mountain Forest and Range Expt Sta US Forest Service since '33. Soc Am Foresters—Ecol Soc Am—Mont Acad Sci—Northwest Sci Assn—Am Meteorol Soc—Sigma Xi. Northern Rocky Mountain Forest and Range Experiment Station, S. 157 Howard St., Spokane 8, Wash.†

22 WELLS, Bertram Whittier. Plant ecology of Southeastern United States; Insect galls. b'84. AB '11—MA '16 (O State U); PhD '17 (U Chicago). Author: The Natural Gardens of North Carolina '32; also articles in field. Head dept bot State Coll NC since '19. Am Bot Soc—Ecol Soc Am—NC Acad Sci (past pres). Department of Botany, North Carolina State College, Raleigh, N.C.†

23 WELLS, (Grant) Carveth. Strategic materials; Geographic exploration. b'87. Civil and Mech Engr '09 (London U). Engineer on original survey of Grand Trunk Pacific Railway Canada; sent to Malay Peninsula by British Government and lived in jungle for six years surveying route for East Coast Railway and making study of flora, fauna and people; made expedition to Arctic Lapland for Swedish Government and American Museum Natural History; leader Massee expedition to mountains of the Moon for Chicago Geographic Society; leader of other expeditions; has lectured widely in US, Great Britain, Norway and Sweden. Author: Field Engineers Handbook '13; Six Years in the Malay Jungle '25; In Coldest Africa '29; Exploring the World '34; Introducing Africa '43, and others. Am Geog Soc(F)—Royal Geog Soc—Instn Civil Engrs (Eng, asso mem). Explorers Club, 10 West 72nd St., NYC.†

24 WELLS, Charles Arthur. Cartooning. (Religious and world affairs). b'97. AB '20 (Friends U); '26 (U

Calif). Has contributed cartoons and editorials on religion and world affairs to religious periodicals and newspapers; publicity counselor and lecturer on world affairs for National Baptist boards; has conducted the Conferences on Christ and World Need since '38; frequent traveler in Europe and Asia. Author: Pink—a satire on American Revolutionaries in Russia '35; Cancelled Crosses '37; Building A Better World, '39; also articles in field. Cartoonist reporter Wichita Beacon '20; later cartoonist Central Press Assn Cleveland and NY. Fgn Policy Assn—Council on Fgn Relations—Acad Polit Sci—Am Acad Polit and Social Sci. 152 Madison Av., NYC.

10 WELLS, Francis Gerritt. Metal and ore deposits; Ground water. b'98. BS '22 (MIT); PhD '28 (U Minn). Research on ground water in western Tennessee, quicksilver in Oregon, silver and gold in Alaska, ground water and glacial geology in Long Island, quicksilver in Arkansas, iron in Utah, lead and zinc in Colorado; areal geological mapping Oregon, chomite studies. Author articles in field. Asst geol United Verde Copper Co '23-25; geol US Geol Survey since '28. Geol Soc Am(F)—Soc Econ Geol—Am Geophys Union—Geol Soc Washington. U.S. Geological Survey, Washington 25.

11 WELLS, James Earl. Agricultural economics. b'95. BS '17 (U Wis); MS '25 (U Calif). With US Dept Agr since '27, business analysis work with Coop Div '27-29, sr agrl econ later chief Bus Analysis Sec Fed Farm Bd '29-33; sec Commodity Credit Corp '33, 2nd vp and dir '34-36; also dep Coop Bank Commr and gen mgr Central Bank for Coops '33-42, dep Farm Credit Administrn '42-47; Coop Bank Commr since '47; acting pres Regional Agrl Credit Corp '43-47. Farmers Union Livestock Association, South St. Paul.

12 WELLS, Ralph Gent. Management (Personnel); Industrial development. Ed pvt tutors, Harvard Law Sch. b'79. Study of plant and store locations, labor supply, market potentials, channels of distribution, waste elimination and utilization, cost reduction studies, plant organization and personnel surveys. Co-author, editor: New England Community Statistical Abstracts; New England Industrial Trends; A Sales Development Programme; NE Vacation Industry; Ice Cream Merchandising, and others. Contbg editor: American Business Practice. Special research work for Arkwright Club Commercial Agency, Boston Chamber of Commerce, Bureau of University Travel, Employment Managers Assn, Boston Rotary Club, '06-17, sec last two orgns, 12-17; with E I du Pont de Nemours Co Wilmington Del '17-19; instr Boston U Coll of Business Adminstrn '19-24, prof and head of management dept '24-49, dir Bur of Business Research, since '28, asst to pres '26-28. Am Management Assn—Am Trade Assn. 685 Commonwealth Av., Boston.

13 WELLS, Robert Lomax. Absenteeism (Industrial). b'05. BS '26 (Coll of William and Mary); MD '30 (U Va). Study and research on problems of absenteeism and the correlation of the work of the physician in industry and the private physician of the employee. Author: Health Evaluation of Applicants and Employees; Preventive Medicine in Industry '46; The Present Day Concept of Industrial Medicine; Vaiables in Industrial Absenteeism '50; The Effects of Industrial Medical Services on Absenteeism '48. Examining physician Chesapeake & Potomac Telephone Co '36-44, part time med dir '44-47, med dir since '47. Phi

Beta Kappa—Alpha Omega Alpha—Am Coll Physicians(F)—Am Assn Indsl Physicians and Surgeons(F)—AMA—Med Soc DC—So Med Assn. 725 13th St., Washington 5.

14 WELLS, Wesley Raymond. Hypnosis (Experimental); Hypnotherapy. b'90. Grad '07 (Brigham Acad); PhB '13 (U Vt); Am '14—PhD '17 (Harvard). Author articles in field. Prof psychol Syracuse U since '27. AAAS(F)—Am Psychol Assn(F)—Am Philos Assn—Phi Beta Kappa—Sigma Xi. Syracuse Univ., Syracuse 10, N.Y.☉

15 WELSH, John Nichols. Boiler water conditioning. b'04. BS '25—grad study (Carnegie Inst Tech). Research on the treatment of water for boilers, reducing boiler sludge. Author articles in field. Chem engr and asso dir Hall Labs Inc since '29; registered engr Pa. Engrs Soc Western Pa—ASME—PSPE. 323 Fourth Av., Pitts 22.

16 WELSH, Llewellyn Hopkins. Drug chemistry; Stereochemistry. b'12. BS '34—MS '35 (U Md). Author articles: The Constitution of Acetylephedrine and Acetyl-Psi-ephedrine '47; The Use of Acetylation in the Quantitative Separation of Ephedrine from Procaine '47; Mechanism and Sterochemical Course of Acyl Migrations in Derivatives of Ephedrine and Psi-Ephedrine '49, and others. Chem US Food and Drug Adminstrn Baltimore '37-39, research cehm Washington since '39. ACS —AAAS—Assn Official Agrl Chem—Alpha Chi Sigma. U.S. Food and Drug Administration, 12th and C St., Washington 25.

17 WELSH, Maurice Fitzwilliam. Virus diseases of stone fruits. b'16. BS Agr '38 (U BC); PhD '42—Can Nat Research Council fellow '40-42 (U Toronto). Author articles in field. Plant path Dom Lab Plant Path since '45. AAAS—Agrl Inst Can—Can Phytopath Soc—Am Phytopath Soc. Dominion Laboratory of Plant Pathology, Summerland, B.C., Can.

18 WELSHANS, Lewis Taxter. Magnesium chemicals; Basic refractories. b'08. AB '31 (W Va U). Research development on processes for production of magnesia refractomies and refractory cements, production of basic magnesium carbonates and extra light magnesium oxide for use as pigments and pharmaceuticals; holds patent on refractory hot-top for steel production. Chem engr Standard Lime & Stone Co Baltimore '33-44; research and development Diamond Alkali Co Cleveland '44-46, tech dir production dept since '46. Am Chem Soc—Am Inst Mining Metall Engrs—Am Ceramic Soc. Box 430, Painesville, Pa.

19 WELTY, (Joel) Carl. Animal behavior: Ornithology (Bird banding). b'01. AB '24 (Earlham Coll); MA '25 (Haverford Coll); PhD '32—fellow and research asst '28-32 (U Chicago). Author articles in field. Asso prof and prof zool Beloit Coll since '34, head biol dept since '37. AAAS—Am Soc Zool—Am Ornithol Union—Wilson Ornithol Club—Inland Bird-Banding Assn—Wis Acad Sci. Beloit College, Beloit, Wis.†

20 WENCHEL, John Philip. Surplus commodities (Agriculture). b'86. Student '05 (Baltimore City Coll); LLB '08 (U Md). Compiler: Laws Applicable to US Department of Agriculture '35. Atty US Dept Agr '14-17, asst to solicitor '17-37; asst gen counsel AAA '34-36; asst gen counsel and sec Fed Surplus Commodities Corp '34-37. Am Hort Soc—Md Hist Soc—Am Judicature Soc—DC Fed Am bar assns. 1625 K St., Washington.☉

21 WENDT, Arthur Stanley. Flavoring extracts, perfumes and maple products (Chemistry). b'07. BS '26 (Coll City NY); AM '27 (Columbia); PhD '41 (Poly Inst Brooklyn). Developed flavor compounds, improved processes of manufacture of extracts to give higher yield, better quality for flavoring extracts, packaged mixes, ice cream: synthesized 25 new glycidic esters and diketones, manufactured synthetic aromatic chemicals used in perfumes, developed processes for large scale operation, designed equipment; compounded formulae for corn starch, gelatin desserts, ice cream powders, chocolate and fruit frostings, egg dye novelties. Holder five patents. Asst chem Rockwood & Co '26-33; chief chemist My-T-Fine Corp '33-37, Seeley & Co '37-43; tchr organic analysis, research on rubber project on mercaptan compounds NYU '42; chief chem Martins Labs '44; tech dir Fred Fear & Co since '44. AAAS—ACS—Am Inst Chem (F)—NY Acad Sci(F)—Inst Food Tech (F)—Phi Lambda Upsilon. Fred Fear & Co., Joralemon St., Bklyn 2. H: 1160 W. Laurelton Parkway, West Englewood, N.J.†

22 WENDT, Karl Rinner. Television circuits. b'06. Student '24-25 (U Akron O); '25-26 (Marquette U Wis); '26-29 (U Wis). Holds 26 patents on television circuits, especially television receivers, studio, and transmitter equipment, such as deflection, synchronizing, direct current component, non-linear circuits, and color television. Author article: Television DC Component '48. Co-author articles: (with)G L Fredenhall, A C Schroeder) An Experimental Simultaneous Color Television System '47; (with A C Schroeder) Automatic Gain Controls for Television Receivers '48, and others. With Radio Corp Am '30-48, research engr '34-48; mgr advanced development radio and television div Sylvania Elec Products Co since '48. Inst Radio Engineers—Phi Lambda Upsilon—Sigma Xi. Sylvania Electric Products, Inc., 254 Rano St., Buffalo 7.

23 WENE, George P. Biology and control of insects affecting tobacco, vegetable and citrus fruits. b'13. AB '34 (Park Coll); MSc in entomol '39 (O State U); PhD '46 (Cornell). Worked out controls of corn earworm, onion thrips, pepper leaf miner, melon and turnip aphids, tomato suckfly, and the Texas citrus mite. Author articles: The Soil as an Ecological Factor in the Abundance of Acquatic Chironomid Larvae '40; An Effect of Sub-lethal Doses of Cryolite on Mexican Bean Beetle Larvae (Epilachna varivestis) '47; Control of the Cowpea Curculio '48, and others. Research asst Cornell '42-46; entomol Tex Agrl Expt Sta since '46. Entomol Soc Am—Am Assn Econ Entomol—O Acad Sci—Sigma Xi. Texas Agricultural Experiment Station, Weslaco.

24 WENGERD, Sherman Alexander. Petroleum geology; Sedimentation. b'15. BA '36 (Coll of Wooster); MA '38—PhD '47 (Harvard). Special research studies in the sedimentation of the Viola limestone of Oklahoma, geomagnetic studies in Alaska, geologic interpretation of aerial photographs, geology of Majuro Atoll, Beach Sandstones of the Coral Islands, specific gravities in relation to lithology. Author articles in field. Petroleum geol Shell Oil Co '40-42, resrch geol '45-47; U NM since '47, asso prof geol since 51; cons petrol geol since '47. Navy officer '42-45 serving as geodetic hydrographic photogrammetric engr and photogeol. Am Assn Petroleum Geol (pres award '48) —Am Soc Photogrammetrists—Am

Geophys Union—Am Inst Mining Metall—Arctic Inst NA—Soc Econ Paleont Mineral—Geol Soc NM—Am Geog Soc—Sigma Xi. University Station, Albuquerque, N.M. H: Stanford at Mountain Road.

10 WENLEY, Archibald Gibson. Chinese bronzes and paintings; Chinese and Japanese art and culture; Sinology. b'98. AB '21 (U Mich); Certificate '23 (Library Sch of NY Pub Library); '26-28 (L'Ecole des Langues Orientales Vivantes, Institut de Hautes Etudes Chinoises, Coll de France Paris). Joint compiler of a descriptive and illustrative catalogue of Chinese bronzes acquired during the administration of John Ellerton Lodge '46. Author articles in field. With Freer Gallery of Art field asst in archeol work in China, student of Chinese lang and culture '23-26; student Japanese lang and culture Kyoto Japan '28-30; asso in research Freer Gallery of Art Smithsonian Instn Washington '30-42, dir of gallery since '43; mem Smithsonian Art Commn; mem bd trustees Textile Mus DC, Hermitage Found. Am Oriental Soc—Chinese Art Soc of Am—Far Eastern Asso—Am Council of Learned Socs (com on Japanese studies '36-46). Freer Gallery of Art, Smithsonian Institution, Washington 25.◎

11 WENTWORTH, Chester K(eeler). Sedimentary geology; Hawaii ground water, water supplies and mathematical hydrology; Fresh and salt water balance (Oceanic Islands); History of scientific illustration. b'91. BS '18 (U Chicago); MS '21—PhD '23 (U Ia); Bishop Mus fellow '23-24 (Yale). Author articles in field. Prin geol Honolulu Bd Water Supply charge studies volcanic and ground water geol water resources and hydrology of Ghyben-Herzberg lens since '34. Geol Soc Am (F)—AAAS(F)—Am Geophys Union—Seismol Soc Am—Am Statis Assn—Am Meteorol Soc—Geol Soc Washington—Am Geog Soc—Engring Assn Hawaii—Hawaiian Acad Sci (pres '35-36)—Sigma Xi. Fellow Hawaiian Volcano Research Assn '29. Hawaiian Volcano Observatory, Hawaii National Park, T.H.

12 WENZEL, Caroline. California (History and literature). Student '14 (Cal State Library Sch). Member board of sponsors Cal Hist Found, College of the Pacific. Library asst Cal State Library '14-33, supervising librarian Cal dept since '33. Am Pioneer Trails Assn—Alumni Assn U Cal and Cal State Library Sch—Cal Hist Soc—ALA—Cal Library Assn—Cal State Employees Assn—Bus and Profl Womens Club. California State Library, Sacramento.

13 WENZEL, William J. Sewage treatment; Water Treatment. b'08. CE '32 (U Cincinnati). Research and design sewage and water treatment plants Montana. Asst engr Great Falls Army Air Base '42-43; sr engr Canol Oil Line Project '43; chief engr Corwin & Co Inc '43-47; dir pub works Great Falls Mont '47-49; owner William J Wenzel since '49. Am Soc CE—Am Concrete Inst—Am Pub Works Association—Am Water Works Assn—Fedn Sewage Works. 2300 Ninth Av. N., Great Falls, Mont.

14 WENZLICK, Roy. Marketing and city planning; Statistics. b'94. AB '16 (Westminster coll); '16-17 (Princeton); PhD '42 (St Louis U). Consultant to several large retailers, research and statistical work in field of real estate economics covering all factors affecting fluctuations of real estate and construction, main problems involved in real estate valuations and problems involved in retail store locations and op-erations since '28. First person in US to chart and publicize nat real estate cycle with its various component factors. Author: The Coming Boom in Real Estate '36; Fluctuations in Urban Rents—Their Causes and Implications '42. Am Statis Assn—Econometric Soc—Am Econ Assn—Am Appraisal Inst. 706 Chesnut St., StL.

15 WERKENTHIN, Theodore Albert. Rubber. b'00. AB '21—MA '23-24-35 (U Tex). Research on resins derived from petroleum; improvement packing gaskets gasoline and oil hose, drilling equipment, rubber solvents, and diluents made from petroleum. Research chemist Solar Refining Co Lima O '24-28; plant engr White Eagle (Socony) Refining Co Augusta Kan '29-30; asst chief chemist Deep Rock Oil Corp Cushing Okla '30-36; with Bur of Ships Navy Dept Washington since '37, prin materials engr, civilian in charge rubber br research and standards since '37. Naval Engrs Soc—ACS(rubber division)—ASTM(adv com D-11)—Washington Rubber Group(a founder, first pres)—Instn Rubber Industry London Eng(F)—Sigma Xi—Phi Lambda Upsilon. Civilian Head Rubber Branch, Bureau of Ships, Navy Department, Washington.

16 WERNER, Harvey Oscar. Potato and tomato crops. BS '13 (Pa State Coll); MS '23 (U Neb); PhD '34 (U Chicago). Determined major cause of running out of seed potatoes in Nebraska to have been the spindle-tuber virus disease; determined inter-relationship of photoperiod, temperature and nitrogen nutrition upon the initiation and development of tubers in potato and established significance of these factors in determination of suitability of any given region for growing potatoes or of any variety for a given region; extensive study of ascorbic acid content of tomatoes potatoes and sweet potatoes and effect of various environmental and storage conditions upon same; co-introducer of the Kasota potato variety and breeder and introducer of Progress, White Cloud, Dazoc and Sheridan potatoes, Sioux, Red Cloud tomato varieties. Assistant hort ND Agrl Coll '13-18; asso prof hort U Neb '18-19, prof since '26. Am Soc Hort Sci—Am Soc Plant Psysiol—Potato Assn Am—AAAS. College of Agriculture, University of Nebraska, Lincoln, Neb. H: 3310 Dudley St., Lincoln 3.◎

17 WERT, James Edwin. Education (Statistics, Research techniques, evaluation). b'94. BS '15 (Adrian Coll); MA '33; PhD '34 (O State U). Consultant on evaluation Office Civilian Defense '43; examiner for the Examinations Staff for Armed Forces Institute '44; accident consultant Army Air Forces '44-45; overseas mission US Strategic Bombing Survey '45; director Research Staff for Armed Forces Institute since '48. Author: Non-computational Statistics '35; Educational Statistics '38. Co-author: Mathematics Workbook for Senior Survey Course '36; Applicants for Federal Aid at Minnesota Colleges '37; also articles in field. Prof edn Ia State Coll since '40. NEA—Am Ednl Research Assn—Am Statis Assn—Nat Soc for Study of Edn—AAA. 204 Gray Av., Ames, Ia.†◎

18 WERTHEIM, Edgar. Organic sulphur compounds and sweetstuffs. b'86. BPE '17 (YMCA Coll Chicago); BS '18 (Northwestern U); MS '19 (U Kan); PhD '21 (U Chicago). Author: Essentials of Organic and Biological Chemistry '31; Manual of Organic Chemistry '32; Organic Chemistry Laboratory Guide '48; Textbook of Organic Chemistry '39, and others; also articles in field. Head dept chemistry U Ark since '45. Am Inst Chem(F)—Am Assn Advancement Sci(F)—Am Chem Soc—Sigma Xi—Phi Beta Kappa. 103 N. Duncan St., Fayetteville, Ark.◎

19 WESCOTT, Blaine B(enjamin). Metallurgy (Petroleum engineering). b'95. BS '17 (Syracuse U); MS '20—PhD '23 (U Pittsburgh); fellow '23-30 (Mellon Inst Indsl Research). Research on fatigue and corrosion, fatigue of metals, heat treatment of steels, material specification, corrosion. Author articles in field. Research chem Federal Dyestuff and Chem Corp Tenn '17; jr phys chem US Bur Mines '18; chief materials and prodn chem div Gulf Research & Development Co Pittsburgh '30-46, asst to exec vp '46-51, associate director since '51. American Soc Metals—ASME—Am Inst Mining Metall Engrs—Am Petroleum Inst—SAE—Nat Assn Corrosion Engrs. Gulf Research and Development Company, P.O. Drawer 2038, Pittsburgh 30.

20 WESLAGER, Clinton A(lfred). Delaware archaeology. b'09. BA—MA '33 (U Pittsburgh). Conducted ethnological research among Nanticoke and Delaware Indians '41-43; archaeological work on pre-history of Delaware Indians '39-41, Monongahela Pa woodland sites '44; archaeological reconnaissance of prehistoric Nanticoke sites in Delaware and Maryland '47. Author: Delaware's Forgotten Folk '43; Delaware's Buried Past '44; Delaware's Forgotten River '47; The Nanticoke Indians '48; also articles in field. Pres Archeol Soc Del '44-48, ed since '48; ed div E States Archaeol Fed since '49. Washington Acad Sci—Hist Soc Del—Nat Hist Soc Del. DuPont Building, Wilmington, Del.†

21 WEST, Byron L(illibridge). Dyes (Synthetic). b'93. PhD '15—ScM '16—Morgan Edwards F '16-18—PhD '18 (Brown U). Research on synthetic dyes such as azo and vat dyes and intermediates, metallized azo dyes, harmaceuticals, color and constitution Granted patents in field. Research and development du Pont Co '19-21, Nat Aniline & Chem Co '21-32; with Calco Chem div Am Cyanamid Co since '32, research asso since '44. Am Inst Chem (F, councilor '39-43)—ACS(nat councilor NJ sect '43-46, chmn com prof affairs '49-50)—Franklin Inst—NY Acad Sci—Sigma Xi—Am Assn Textile Chem and Colorists. Calco Chemical Division, American Cyanamid Co., Bound Brook, N.J.

22 WEST, Charles Tyrrell. Mechanical vibrations. b'15. Student '37 (US Naval Acad); BCE '39—MS '46 (O State U). Author: Design of a Vibrating Machine for Making Impact Tests on Structures '39; Damping Factors and Dynamic Stresses in a Simple Span Steel Railway Bridge '46; also articles in field. Research structural vibrations, fellow O State U '39-41, instr mech '46-47, asst prof since '48; bridge test analyst Assn Am Railroads '40, '41, '46. Am Math Soc—ASCE—Sigma Xi—Tau Beta Pi—Sigma Pi Sigma—Pi Mu Epsilon. Department of Mechanics, Ohio State University, Columbus 10, O.†

23 WEST, Clyde Crawford. Resins (Synthetic); Plastics; Paper. b'14. AB '35 (Lawrence Coll) '38-41 (U Chicago). Research on glycerol phthalate, and pentaerythritolphthalate alkyds of oil modified type including maleic, vinyl, rosin, styrene, and phenolic modification of alkyds, incorporation higher alcohols and amine groups into these alkyds and experimentation with cooking procedures, including fusion and azeotropic dehydration processes; development urea formaldehyde resins for coating purposes; research and development varnish grade resins of phenolic and maleic type; research and development plastic impregnated paper for laminating. Group leader in paper and resin research Kimberly-Clark Corp Neenah Wis '44-47; tech rep US Indsl Chems Inc since '47. ACS—Am Inst Chem(F). 714 W. Olympic Blvd., L.A. 15. H: 637 N. Greenleaf, Whittier, Cal.

10 WEST, Erdman. Taxonomy of Florida plants and fungi; Florida Myxomycetes; Poisonous plants of Florida. b'94. BS '17 (Pa State Coll); MS '31 (U Fla). Co-author: The Native Trees of Florida '46. Bot, mycol Fla Agrl Expt Sta since '25; prof bot Coll Agr U Fla since '46. Torrey Bot Club—Fla Acad Sci—Soc Am Taxon—Mycol Soc Am—So Appalachian Bot Soc—Sigma Xi. Florida Agricultural Experiment Station, Gainesville, Florida.†◎

11 WEST, James Watt. American newspapers (Type, typography). b'08. Student '27-28 (U Tenn); LLB '34 (Nashville YMCA Law Sch). Author: Manual for State Reporters '36; also articles in field. Mng ed Raleigh Times '37-38, Kansas City Jour '38-40; gen mgr Kingsport Times Tenn since '40. Tenn Press Assn (pres '47-48). Typograph designer Kingsport News winner Ayer Award Best Newspaper under 10,000 in US '48. 220 Market St., Kingsport, Tenn. H: 1130 Catawba St.†

12 WEST, Richard S(edgewick), Jr. American naval biographies (Civil and Spanish American wars). b'02. BA '25 (Vanderbilt U); MA '28 (Yale). Author: The Second Admiral, A Life of David D. Porter 1813-1891 '37; Gideon Welles: Lincoln's Navy Department '43; Admirals of American Empire '48. Co-author: American Sea Power since 1775 '47. Instr to asso prof US Naval Acad since '28. English, History, and Government, U.S. Naval Academy, Annapolis, Md.†

13 WEST, Thomas Scott. Petroleum (Electrical prospecting). b'03. Student '21-22, '22-23, '27-28, '28-29 (U Okla). Orign and supervisor research project on direct location oil '30-41; extensive theoretical, laboratory, field investigation alternating and direct current electrical prospecting procedures; design and development two procedures for eliminating error due to shallow or surface electrical inhomogenieties from deep electrical prospecting data. Issued patents in field. Elec prospecting research Grimes Patterson & McLaren Dayton O '30-41; geol and engr Henderson Coquat Interests San Antonio '41-45, Blanco-Buchanan since '45. AIME—Soc Exploration Geophys—Am Geophys Union—Am Assn Petroleum Geol—Texas Acad Sci. 2114-18 Alamo National Bldg., San Antonio.

14 WESTBROOK, Lawrence. Mutual home ownership; Housing. b'89. Student '06-09 (U Tex). Director development National Rural Rehabilitation Program, also construction rural settlements various areas in Alaska, Arkansas, and Georgia; builder eight-pattern Mutual Home Ownership projects; executive secretary and director staff of civilian housing commission appointed by Secretary of Defense '49; field study resettlement and housing problems of Western Germany '50-51. Author: Handbook on Mutual Home Ownership '46; Report on Family Housing for Military Personel (Dept of Defense) '51; Avion—A Pattern for Modern American Living '51. Dir mutual home ownership div Fed Works Agency '40-41; pres Trans-Am Develop-

ment Corp since '45. H: 1911 R St., N.W., Washington.

15 WESTCOTT, Cynthia. Plant pathology; Economic entomology; Roses; Home garden diseases and pests. b'98. BA '20 (Wellesley Coll); PhD '31 (Cornell). Worked control azalea petal blight '44-45; practicing plant doctor since '33; research in roses, especially in control of pests; consultant for American Rose Society and national garden clubs. Author: The Plant Doctor '37; The Gardeners Bug Book '46; Plant Disease Handbook '50; Anyone Can Grow Roses '52; Garden Enemies '53. Co-author: 10,000 Garden Questions Answered '44; also numerous articles in field. Asst instr dept plant path Cornell U '21-31; plant path seed lab Rutgers U '31-33; lecturer home garden problems since '34. AAAS(F)—Am Phytopath Soc—Am Assn Econ Entomol—Hort Soc NY—Nat Shade Tree Conf—Sigma Xi—Phi Beta Kappa. 96 Essex Av., Glen Ridge, N.J.

16 WESTER, Horace Volney. Pest control. b'07. BS '31 (Geo Wash U). Research on control diseases and insect pests of ornamentals. Author of articles: Cankers of linden and redbud; Life history and control of the webworm, Homadaula Albizziae. Forest pathologist BPISAE USDA '33-38, plant path '38-39, plant path Nat Capital Parks since '39. Am Phytopath Soc—Washington Bot Soc—Am Assn Econ Entomol. National Capital Parks, Dept of Interior, Washington 25.

17 WESTHEIMER, Frank H(enry). Reaction mechsms; Oxidation; Rocket propellants. b'12. AB '32 (Dartmouth); MA '33—PhD '35 (Harvard); National Research Council F '35-36 (Columbia). Associate editor: Journ Chem Physics '42-44. With chemistry department U Chgo since '36, prof chemistry since '48; research supervisor Explosives Research Lab Nat Defense Research Committee '44-45. ACS—Phi Beta Kappa—Sigma Xi. 5724 Kimbark Av., Chgo 37.◎

18 WESTON, Joseph H(arry). Mormons. b'11. Student '33 (Little Rock Jr Coll)—'46-48 (U Utah). Author: These Amazing Mormons '48; Mormon Architecture '49; Where Do Ideas Come From? '48. Ordained Elder in Ch Jesus Christ of Latter-day Saints '47; lecturer on Mormonism. Weston Publishing Co, Box 626, Salt Lake City.

19 WESTON, Myles Standish, III. Heraldry. b'17. Student (Dartmouth) (Boston Museum Sch Fine Art). Study of shields, crests, supporters and other elements of heraldic symbology and history; collector source books on sci of heraldry. Cons on heraldry since '46. Mil Order of Seven. American Museum of Natural History, 79th and Central Park W., NYC 24.

20 WETMORE, Monroe Nichols. Latin literature (Indexes). b'63. BA '88—MA '00—PhD '04—Foote fellow in Latin '02-04 (Yale). Author: Index Verborum Vergilianus '11, '30; Index Verborum Catullianus '12; also articles in field. Prof Latin Williams Coll '13-32. Am Philol Assn—Classical Assn NE. Williamstown, Mass.

21 WETTERSTROM, Edwin. Structures (Plates and shells). b'19. BS in mech engring '44 (Ill Inst Tech); MS in engring mechs '47—PhD '51 (Purdue U). Research on structures made of plates and shells, design of tank structures. Mem faculty Purdue U '45-51, dir analysis Purdue Project Pressure Vessel Com; analytical research engr Graver Tank & Mfg Co '51-52; head mech sect, civil engring dept U Mo and asst prof civil engring since '52. Sigma Xi—ASME—Soc Exptl

Stress Analysis. Civil Engineering Department, University of Missouri, Columbia, Mo. H: 5518 W. Huron St., Chgo 44.

22 WETZEL, Wilfred Wolf. Magnetic recording; Underwater sound. b'04. BA '28—PhD '33 (U Minn); '36-37 (MIT). Research in measurements of the magnetic fields of ships, studies in underwater sound, development of magnetic recording tapes. Author: Review of the Present Status of Magnetic Recording Theory '47. Physicist Naval Bur Ordnance Washington '40-44; tech rep sound recording tape Minn Mining and Mfg Co since '44. Am Phys Soc—Sigma Xi. Minnesota Mining and Manufacturing Company, St. Paul. H: 725 Ridge St., St. Paul 5.

23 WEXLER, Harry. Meteorology; Upper atmosphere. b'11. SB '32 (Harvard); ScD '39 (MIT). Author articles in field. Weather Bur Washington since '34, chief scientific services div since '46. Research exec Weather Div Hqrs Army Air Forces Washington and Asheville NC '43-45. Am Meteorol Soc (council)—Royal Meteorol Soc—Am Geophys Union—Internat Aerological Commn. U.S. Weather Bureau, Washington 25.

24 WEYBURN, Lyon. (Boston (Fire prevention, pure milk districts); New England (Agriculture). b'82. AB '05 (Yale); LLB '08 (Harvard). Former member committees on fire prevention legislation and New England Milk Investigation of Boston Chamber of Commerce. Author phamplets: The Importance of Agriculture to the Citizenship of New England; Fire Prevention; Menace of the Wooden Three Decker, others. Am Bar Assn—Delta Kappa Epsilon. Pemberton Bldg., Boston.

25 WEYER, Edward Moffat, Jr. Archeology of Alaska and the Aleutian Islands; Anthropology Eskimos; Seasonal fluctuations in sunlight. b'04. BS '25 (Washington & Jefferson Coll); PhD '30 (Yale). Member American Museum expedition for archeological study of Aleutian Islands and Alaskan Peninsula, and anthropological research in Bering Strait area '28, also member of Peary memorial expedition to northern Greenland '32; research on effect of seasonal fluctuations in sunlight on plant and animal life. Author: The Eskimos—Their Environment and Folkways '32. Author article: Day and Night in the Arctic '43, and others. Ed Natural History mag NYC since '35. Assn Am Geog—Am Geog Soc—Sigma Xi—Phi Beta Kappa. Am Museum of Natural History, 79th St. and Central Park W., NYC 24.

26 WEYL, F. Joachim. Applied mathematics (Fluid dynamics). b'15. BA '35 (Swarthmore Coll Pa); MA '37—PhD '39 (Princeton). Research on mechanical phenomena accompanying explosions, and on optical methods of visualizing compressible flows. Phys sci math Research Group on High Explosives Bur Ordnance '44-47; math Office Naval Research since '47, head math br since '49, dir math science div since '53. Am Math Soc—APS—Math Assn Am—Philos Society Washington—Sigma Xi—Phi Beta Kappa. Office of Naval Research, Washington 25.

27 WEYL, Woldemar Anatol. Glass (Fluorescence, light absorption). b'01. Diploma Chem Engring '26 (U Darmstadt); Dr Chem Engring '31 (U Aachen). Author articles in field. Head dept glass research Kaiser Wilhelm Inst '26-38; prof glass technol Sch Mineral Inds Pa State Coll '38-45, dir research Glass Sci Inc '45-48, head dept mineral tech since '48. ACS—Optical Soc Am—British Soc Glass Technol(F)—Am Ceramic Soc(F)—Nat Research Council (solid state com)—Sigma Xi. The Pennsylvania State College, State College, Pa.

10 WHALEY, Randall McVay. Semiconductors; Rectifiers; Cosmic rays; Nuclear physics. b'15. BA '38—MA '40 (U Colo); PhD '47 (Purdue U) Invented Germanium-alloy semi-conductors for use as rectifiers. Author articles in field. Asst prof Purdue U '47-49, asso prof since '49. Research fellow Purdue U '42-45, war research on semi-conductors. Am Phys Soc—Am Assn Physics Teachers — Sigma Xi—Phi Beta Kappa. Department of Physics, Purdue University, Lafayette, Ind.†

11 WHANG, Won Yill. Pineapples (Crop logging, nutrition). b'08. BS '32—MS '34 (U Hawaii). With Haiku Pineapple Co Maui TH '34, Hawaiian Pineapple Co Haiku Div '35, in charge crop log lab Lanai Div '38, Wahiawa Div '43, lab supt Research Dept '46, asst supt exptl) dept '49. AAAS. Hawaiian Pineapple Co., Ltd., Wahiawa, T.H.

12 WHARTON, G(eorge) W(illard), Jr. Parasitology (Ecology and physiology); Marine ecology; Acarology (Trombiculidae). b'14. BS '35—PhD '39 (Duke U). Research parasite of turtles, their ecology and physiology '35-41, ecology marine animals with special reference to fouling of ship's bottoms and littoral organisms '35-43, systematic studies on Acarina since '34, family Trombiculidae, the larvae of certain species which are bothersome pests and vectors of scrub typhus since '44. Author articles in field. Research Aid US Bur Fisheries '35-36; instr dept zool Duke U '39-46, asst prof since '46; collaborator US Dept Agr since '46. Biologist Norfolk Navy Yard '41-43, USNR acarologist US Naval Med Research Unit 2 '44-46. AAAS—NC Acad Sci—Am Soc Zool—Am Soc Parasitol (ed bd)—Ecol Soc Am—Assn SE Biol—Soc Systematic Zool (sec-treas)—Phi Beta Kappa—Sigma Xi. Department of Zoology, Duke University, Durham, N.C. H: 1202 Oval Drive.

13 WHEELER, Charles Lincoln. Limnology; Mollusks. b'14. AB '36 (Harvard). Research on marine invertebrates; commercial mollusks of New England. Co-author: The Horseshoe Crab and Boring Snail as Factors Limiting the Abundance of the Soft-shell Clam. Scientific aide Woods Hole Oceanog Inst summers '32, '33, permanently employed '43-48; shellfish biol Mass Div Marine Fisheries since '48. Am Soc Limnol and Oceanog—Am Ornithol Union. Division Marine Fisheries, Ashburton Place, Boston 8. H: 376 Palmer Av., Falmouth.†

14 WHEELER, Donald Hyde. Fatty acids and derivatives; Oils and fats; Resins. b'05. BA '27 (Oberlin Coll); MS '31—PhD '39 (Md U). Research in organic analysis and synthesis, oxidation of vegetable oils, antioxidants and insecticides; tall oil, poly resins from dilinoleic acid and ethylene diaminemolecular weight-viscosity relationships. Principal research chemist General Mills Research since '51. American Chemical Society—Am Oil Chem Soc—Sigma Xi. Chosen one of ten ablest chemists or chem engrs in US in field of fats, oils and soaps by Chicago Chemical Bulletin. 2010 E. Hennepin Av., Minneapolis 13.

15 WHEELER, Ernest Joseph. Potato production. b'01. BS '26—MS '28 (Mich State Coll); '31-32 (U Minn). Research on culture practices of potato production, disease control, development of new varieties, study culinary quality of harvested potatoes. With Mich State Coll since '28; sci cons US Army for agr in Japan '48-49. Sigma Xi—Potato Assn Am. Farm Crops Department, Michigan State College, East Lansing.

16 WHEELER, Frank. Cartridges and automatic pistol history. b'06. Student (Kans U). Has library of 1500 books, pamphlets on cartridges, guns and associated subjects dating back to 1565; also a reference collections of cartridges of 3000 specimens. Author articles in field. Clerk US PO Osborne Kans. Nat Rifle Assn—Nat Muzzle Loading Rifle Assn — Am Ordnance Assn—Ohio Gun Collectors Assn—Wis Gun Collectors Assn. Box 23, Osborne, Kans.†

17 WHEELER, George C(arlos). Ants; Fauna of North Dakota. b'97. Student '14-15 (Tex Christian U); AB '18 (Rice Inst); MSc '20—DSc '21 (Harvard). Author articles in field. Prof biol and head dept U ND since '26. Entomol Soc Am(F). University of North Dakota, Grand Forks, N.D.†

18 WHEELER, Harold Alden. Radio receivers and amplifiers. b'03. BS in physics '25 (George Washington U); '25-28 (Johns Hopkins). Construction and operation first neutralized tuned-radio-frequency amplifier; research, development, design, and testing radio receivers, antennas, radar and microwave equipment; construction and operation first diode automatic volume control for radio sets; preparation of standards for testing of broadcast receivers. Holds 150 patents in field, including transmission lines, waveguides, and antennas; automatic control of amplifiers or oscillators in response to signals; direction-finders; television scanning, synchronizing and automatic controls, and frequency selective filters. Author articles: The Interpretation of Amplitude and Phase Distortion in Terms of Paired Echos '39; Wide-band Amplifiers for Television '39; Fundamental Limitations of Small Antennas '47; The Maximum Speed of Amplification in a Wideband Amplifier; The Piston Attenva'or in a Waveguide Below Cutoff '49, and others. Lab asst Bur Standards Washington '20-22; vp and chief cons engr electronic equipment Hazeltine Corp NYC '24-45. Inst Radio Engrs(F, dir '36, '40-45, chmn receivers com '34-38) —Am Inst EE(F)—Sigma Xi. Inst Radio Engrs Morris Liebmann prize for contbns to television '40; NAM Modern Pioneer award for inventions '40. 122 Cutter Mill Rd., Great Neck, N.Y. H: 18 Melbourne Rd.

19 WHEELER, Louis Cutter. Botany (Systematic Euphorbiaceae, nomenclature, plant patents, natural rubber plants); Geobotanical prospecting. b'10. AB '33 (University California); MA '34 (Claremont Coll); PhD '39 (Harvard). Author articles in field. Asst prof, later asso prof and head dept bot U So Calif since '45. Am Soc Plant Taxonomists—Biol Soc Washington—Bot Soc Am—So Calif Acad Sci—So Calif Bot—So Calif Hort Inst—New Eng Bot Club—Sullivan Moss Soc—Sigma Xi. Department of Botany, University of Southern California, Los Angeles 7.†

20 WHEELER, Walter Hall. Structural and bridge engineering (Manufacturing plants, concrete, steel, floor construction systems). b'83. EM '06 (Sch of Mines U Minn). Author articles in field. Engr for Hennepin County Minn in charge location design and const of Fort Snelling-Mendota bridge near Minneapolis (largest multiple arch reinforced concrete bridge in world) '23-27. Inventor of smooth ceilings system of reinforced concrete. Mining and constr engr Colo Fuel & Iron Co Trinidad, Colo '06-07; chief engr and supt constrn Dawson Fuel Co NM '07; partner Jones & Wheeler Denver '07-08; sec treas and chief engr Jones-Wheeler-Cranmer Engring Co '08-12; cons Minneapolis since '12. ASCE—Nat Soc Professional Engrs (dir). Metropolitan Life Building, Minneapolis. H: 4209 Dupont Av., S.†☺

21 WHEELER, William Crawford. Electrification (Rural); Farm refrigeration; Farm water systems. b'14. BS in agrl engring '40 (U Ga); MS '51 (Va Poly Inst). Author article: The Development of a Prefabricated Refrigeration Unit for Walk-In Type Refrigerators (thesis). Farm supervisor '33-36; jr engr Soil Conservation Service USDA '41; asso prof agrl engineering U Tenn '46-51; Communications officer US Army '42-46. Am Soc AE. Profl engr Tenn. Agricultural Engineering Department, University of Tennessee, Knoxville.

22 WHEELER, Willis Hayes. Foreign plant Quarantine (Pathology); Culture and diseases of bulbous plants (Gladiolus, Freesia; Narcissus, Iris). b'06. AB '30 (U Calif). Author articles in field. US Dept Agr since '30, now plant path Div Fgn Plant Quarantines and cons path Bur Entomol and Plant Quarantine. Am Phytopath Soc—Mycol Soc Am—Bot Soc Washington—New Eng Gladiolas Soc. U.S. Bureau of Entomology and Plant Quarantine, Washington 25.

23 WHELEN, Townsend. Small arms ballistics (Engineering); Exploration; Natural history. b'77. Grad '94 (Drexel Inst Phila). Exploration in British Columbia '01, in Panama '15, '16, '17; assigned duty Gen Staff in charge infantry and small arms training '18; member National Board for Promotion Rifle Practice '18; member Army Infantry National Rifle Team '03, '05, '07, '09; winner many army rifle competitions. Author: Suggestion to Military Riflemen '05; Trench Warfare (with Maj J A Moss) '17; The Am Rifle '18; Big Game Hunting '23; Amateur Gunsmithing '23; Wilderness Hunting and Wildcraft '27; Telescopic Rifle Sights '36; The Hunting Rifle '40; Small Arms Design and Ballistics '45; Hunting Big Game '46; Why Not Load Your Own '50. Retired col US Army; vp Parker-Whelen Co Washington; associate editor Sports Afield. 827 14th St. N.W., Washington.☺

24 WHERRY, Edgar (Theodore). Polemoniaceae (Phlox); Ferns; Soil acidity; Plant ecology. b'85. BS '06—PhD '09 (U Pa). Author: Wild Flowers of Mt Desert Island; Guide to Eastern Ferns; Wild Flower Guide; also articles in field. Prof bot U Pa since '41. Geol Soc Am(F) — Mineral Soc Am—AAAS(F)—Am Chem Soc—Pa Acad Sci —Am Fern Soc—Bot Soc Am (chmn systematic sect '40)—Ecol Soc Am. 137 Maplewood Av., Phila 44.

25 WHIPPLE, Fred Lawrence. Meteors; Stellar and planetary evolution; Upper atmosphere. b'06. BS '24-27—PhD '31 (U Calif); MA (hon) '45 (Harvard). On V-2 Rocket Scientific Panel US since '46; US Research and Development Board Panel on the Upper Atmosphere since '47; chairman Commission 22 Shooting Stars of International Astronomy Union since '46 and on commission 22 on Minor Planets. Author: Earth, Moon and Planets '42. Research associate Inst Meteoritics U NM since '47; staff Obs

Harvard U since '31, professor astron since '50. Am Astron Soc—Am Acad Arts Sci—Am Assn Study Meteoritics —Am Geophys Union—Phi Beta Kappa —Sigma Xi. Awarded Donohue medals for discoveries of six comets. 12 Randolph St., Belmont, Mass.

10 WHISTLER, Roy Lester. Carbohydrate chemistry (Starch, cellulose, sugars, amylose, gums). b'12 BS '34 (Heidelberg Coll); MS '35 (O State U); PhD '38 (Ia State Coll). Author articles in field. Research fellow '38-40 Textile Found; chief starch structure sect Northern Regional Research Lab Peoria Ill '40-45; prof carbohydrate dept biochem Purdue U '45-48, asst dept head '48. Am Chem Soc— Sigma Xi. Designated as one of 10 ablest chemists working in US in field of starch chemistry. Department Biochemistry, Purdue University, Lafayette, Ind.†

11 WHITACRE, Francis M(arion). Medicinal chemistry. b'05. AB—AM— PhD (Ind U). Author: Esterification in Presence of Anhydrous Salts '29; also articles in field. Co-author: (with H T Briscoe and H Hunt) A Laboratory Manual of Chemistry; (with C F Prutton) A Chemical Engineering Laboratory Manual. Instr chem engring Inst Tech '29-34, asst prof organic chem '34-37, asso prof '37-45, prof '45-46; sci dir Schieffelin & Co NY since '45; cons Glenn L Martin Chem Div. Am Chem Soc—AAAS—NY Acad Sci—Am Pharm Mfg Assn (research and sci com)—Internat Coll Anesthetists(F)—Soc Plastics Engrs—Sigma Xi. Schieffelin & Co., 16-30 Cooper Sq. NYC. H: 148 Shoreview Rd., Manhasset, N.Y.

12 WHITAKER, Arthur Preston. Latin-American history; United States foreign relations. b'95. BA '15 (U Tenn); '19 (Sorbonne Paris); PhD '24 (Harvard). US delegate Fourth General Assembly Pan American Institute of Geography and History Caracas Venezuela '46; chief delegate US Government First Consultation of the Commission on History Mexico City '47; Conference of West Coast Latin Americanists Stanford University '48. Author: The Spanish American Frontier '27; The Mississippi Question '34; The United States and the Independence of Latin America '41, and others. Editor: Inter-American Affairs: An Annual Survey, five vols '42-46. Prof Latin-Am hist U Pa since '36. AHA—Council Fgn Relations—Fgn Policy Assn (bd dirs '46-49)—Pan Am Assn (pres '42-43, '45-46, bd dirs '46-49). Guggenheim fellow '29, '50; Social Sci Research Council grant '37. University of Pennsylvania, Phila. 4.†☉

13 WHITAKER, John Clarke. Tobacco (Processing). b'91. AB '12 (U NC). With R J Reynolds Tobacco Co since '13, dir since '35, vp '37-48, pres since '48. R. J. Reynolds Tobacco Co., Winston-Salem, N.C.

14 WHITAKER, Lorenzo Robert. Brick; Tile. b'99. BS in chem (Emory U); BS in ceramic engring (NC State Coll). Designer and builder brick and tile plants; consultant to clay products manufacturers. Author: Drying Clay Products; Firing Clay Products; Design and Correction of Dies, also articles in field. Ceramic engr and supt brick and tile plants Moland Drysdale Corp, Gen Shale Products Co, and Richland Shale Products Co; now pres Carolina Ceramics Inc. Am Ceramic Soc(F)—Inst Ceramic Engrs. Profl engineer SC. Carolina Ceramics Inc., R. F.D. 3, Columbia, S.C.

15 WHITAKER, Randall. Dairy products. b'02. BS '23—MS '26—PhD '27 (Cornell). Experiments on improved methods for manufacture of condensed and evaporated milk, cottage cheese, butter milk, ice cream, and other edible dairy products; official milk judge International Students Dairy Products judging contest '47-50. Holds two patents in field. Fellow Am Dry Milk Inst '27-29; dairy tech research labs Nat Dairy Products Corp since '29. Am Dairy Sci Assn—Dairy Tech Soc Md and DC—Sigma Xi. National Dairy Research Laboratories, Oakdale, N.Y.

16 WHITAKER, Thomas W. Genetics and plant breeding (Cantaloupes, lettuce); Cytology; Ethnobotany. b'05. BS '27 (Calif U); MS '29—PhD '31 (Va U). Research on genetics, cytology, breeding and ethnobotany of lettuce, cantaloupes and other cucurbitaceous plants. Developed four new disease-resistant varieties of cantaloupes and five new varieties of lettuce. Author articles in field. Geneticist US Dept Agr since '39. Sigma Xi—AAAS—Genetics Soc Am—Bot Soc Am—Torrey Bot Club—Am Phytopathol og Soc—Am Soc Hort Sci. Du Pont research fellow Va U '27-31; fellow Arnold Arboretum Harvard '31-33; Guggenheim fellowship Washington U and Calif U '46-47. Box 150, La Jolla Calif.†

17 WHITBY, George Stafford. Rubber; Polymers and synthetic resins. b'87. ARCSc '06 (Royal Coll Sci, London); BS '07 (U London); MS '18— PhD '20—DSc '39 (McGill U); LLD (hon) '32 (Mount Allison U, Can). Associated with early days of rubber growing in East Indies and modern production of synthetic rubber in US and Canada; research in production of synthetic rubber by polymerization of diene hydrocarbons; research in polymers including synthetic resins and synthetic rubbers; introduced many techniques used in preparation of plantation rubber; studies on variation in yield among rubber trees; demonstrated presence of fatty acids in natural rubber and showed them essential to proper functioning of most accelerators of vulcanization. Author: Plantation Rubber and the Testing of Rubber '20; Physical Properties of Raw Rubber '37; also articles in field. Prof organic chem McGill U Montreal '23-29; dir div chem Nat Research Council Can '28-29; prof rubber chem and dir rubber research U Akron since '42. Royal Soc Can(F)—Instn of Rubber Ind(F)—Officier d'Academie—Soc Chem Ind. Awarded Colwyn Gold Medal '28, Instn of the Rubber Industry. University of Akron, Akron 4, O. H: 123 N. Portage Path, Akron 3.

18 WHITE, Charles Langdon. Geography (Industrial location, Anglo-American, South America). b'97. BS '20—ScD(hon) '42 (Denison U); '22-24 (U Chicago); PhD '25 (Clark U). Co-author: Geography: An Introduction to Human Ecology '36, '48; Regional Geography of Anglo America '43; World Economic Geography, '51; author also articles in field. Prof geog Stanford U since '43; vis prof geog Instituto de Geografia Lima Peru '48. Assn Am Geog—Nat Council Geog Teachers (vp '42-44, pres '45)—Assn Pacific Coast Geog—Am Geog Soc. Department of Geography, Stanford University, Stanford, Cal.†

19 WHITE, David Grammer. Pomology and tropical agriculture (Rubber; rotenone producing plants, bamboo, herbicides). b'16. BS—AM '38 (U Mo); PhD '47 (O State U). Rubber research on Firestone Plantations Co at Liberia two years; US Federal Experiment Station Puerto Rico three years. Author articles in field. Prof pomol research

and instr dept hort Pa State Coll since '48. Am Soc Hort Sci—Am Soc Plant Physiol. Department of Horticulture, Pennsylvania State College, State College, Pa.

20 WHITE, Donald E(dward). Geology of thermal springs and antimony deposits. b'14. AB '36 (Stanford U); PhD '39 (Princeton U). Author articles in field. Geol US Geol Survey since '39, specialist origin and geochem thermal springs since '45. Geol Soc Am—Soc Econ Geol—Am Geogphys Union— AAAS. 503 Gilbert Av., Menlo Park, Calif.

21 WHITE, Edith Grace. Fishes (Elasmobranch). b'90. AB '12 (Mt Holyoke Coll); AM '13—PhD '18 (Columbia). Research on heart valves of elasmobranch fishes, interrelationships elasmobranch fishes and order Galea, transitional elasmobranchs. Author: General Biology (revised) '46; Laboratory Manual of General Biology (revised) '47; Principles of Genetics '40. Prof biol and head dept Wilson Coll since '23; research asso Am Mus Natural Hist '37-47. Am Soc Ichthyologists and Herpetologists—Am Genetic Assn—Am Soc Eugenics—AAAS(F)—Phi Beta Kappa—NY Acad Sci. Wilson College, Chambersburg, Pa.

22 WHITE, Edwin Dean. Cotton; Agricultural economics and statistics; Soil and water conservation. b'02. Student '21-22, '25 (Okla A&M Coll); BS '24 (U Ark); '31-33 (U Wis). Asst to Sec Dept Agr since '47; cotton specialist charge cotton operations Econ Coop Administrn since '48. Department of Agriculture, Washington.

23 WHITE, Gerald Taylor. Government war Plant financing; Panic of 1893. b'13. AB '34—Albert J Beveridge fellow '34-36 (DePauw U); MA '35— PhD '38 (U Calif). Author articles in field. Editor: The Historian since '48. Instr to asso prof hist San Francisco State Coll since '47. Hist and sr hist AAF '44-46. AHA—Econ Hist Assn. Research grant from Am Philos Soc '48. San Francisco State College, San Francisco 27.†

24 WHITE, Harry J(ames). Electrical precipitation; Gas discharge physics. b'05. BS '28—PhD '33 (U Calif). Research in spark breakdown in gases, Kerr electro-optical shutters, electrical precipitation processes, electrical cleaning of gases, particularly industrial process gases, radar and pulse generators. Inventions in electrical precipitation field, radar. Author articles in field. Research physicist Research Corp '35-41, dir research since '45; staff mem MIT Radiation Lab '41-45. Am Phys Soc(F)—AIEE— AAAS—Sigma Xi. Research Corporation, Bound Brook, N.J.

25 WHITE, Henry Ford. Social economics; Economic history; Contemporary economic problems; Market analysis. b'00. BS '20 (Sam Houston State Teachers Coll); AM '21—fellowship econ '21-22 (Baylor U); fellowship econ '22-23—Fellowship hist '25-26—PhD '31 (U Tex). Author: Co-operative Marketing of Farm Products in the United States '37; Federal Approaches to Our Economic Order '48; Marketing Problems and Policies '47; The Farmer and Economic Progress '47; Agricultural Problems and Policies '47; also articles in field. John Brown U '42-48; head div hist and social sci '45-48; ed-in-chief John Brown U Press Publications '44-45; prof econ Bradley U since '48. Am Acad Polit and Soc Sci— Am Econ Assn—Am Sociol Soc—SW Social Sci Assn—AHA—Miss Valley, Ark, La, Mo, Okla and Tex Hist Assns —Nat Bur Econ Research—Am Polit

Sci Assn—Am Marketing Assn—Bur for Post war Econ(F). College of Economics and Business Administration, Bradley University, Peoria, Illinois.†◎

10 WHITE, Henry Packard. Small arms; Ballistics. b'09. Research on ordnance engineering specializing in small arms, small arms ammunition, explosives; consulting engineers in design of weapons, ammunition; ballistician in internal, external, terminal ballistics; historian of development, manufacture; identification and investigation for legal, criminal proceedings in specialties. Author articles in field. Owner, chief engr H P White Lab. Officer-in-charge, Recovery Unit, Aviation Arms Section, Arms and Ammunition Div Aberdeen Proving Ground Md '42-46. ASME—AOA—Am Soc Mil Engrs. P.O. Box 331, Bel Air, Md.

11 WHITE, John Edward. Electron tubes (Gas-filled discharge, microwave). b'07. BSEE '28 (Carnegie Inst Tech); PhD '42 (U Pittsburgh). Holds 12 patents. Author articles in field. Research engr Westinghouse East Pittsburgh '28-33; All-Union Electrotech Inst Moscow 33-39; development engr Westinghouse Bloomfield NJ '42-46; physicist chief electron tube lab Nat Bur Standards Washington since '46. AIEE—APS—Sigma Xi. National Bureau of Standards, Washington 25.

12 WHITE, John W(illiam). So Am (History, politics, economics, sociology). Travelling correspondent covering developments in all ten republics since '21. Author: Argentina—The Life Story of a Nation '42. Contributor to U.S. nat mags on South American subjects. Travelling corr Chicago Tribune SA '21-25, Chicago Daily News '25-31; chief SA corr NY Times '31-41. H: 410 Riverside Drive, NYC 25.

13 WHITE, John W(illiam). Farm management; Agricultural marketing. b'11. Student '31-34 (Monticello A&M Coll); BSA '35 (U Ark); MS '39—PhD '42 (U Minn). In charge research and teaching on agricultural economics and rural sociology. Author articles: Livestock Auctions in Arkansas '43; Combination of Enterprises on Plantations in the Lower Arkansas River Delta '44; Peach Marketing Practices in the Nashville-Highland District of Arkansas in 1940 '44; Land Tenure in Arkansas, IV '45; Airplane Fertilizing Speeds Mechanization of Rice Production '47, and others. Staff U Ark since '35, ext econ marketing '42-44, prof and head rural econ and sociol dept since '47; asst co agt '35-37. Am Farm Econ Assn—Southwestern Social Sci Assn (chmn agrl econ sect '48)—So Agrl Workers Assn. Department of Rural Economics, University of Arkansas, Fayetteville, Ark.◎

14 WHITE, Marsh W(illiam). Physics; Scientific personnel. b'96. AB '17 (Park Coll); MS '20—PhD '26 (Pa State Coll). Author: Experimental College Physics '32. Editor Practical Physics '43; College Technical Physics (with R L Weber, K V Manning) '47; also articles in field. Instr physics Pa State Coll '18-22, asst prof '22-26, asso prof '27-42, prof since '42; visiting asst prof physics Williams Coll '26-27; expert cons OSRD '44-45; expert cons Sec War '45-46; cons on sci manpower research and development div War Dept General Staff since '46. AAAS—Am Phys Soc —Am Assn Physics Teachers—AAUP— Pa Acad Sci—Sigma Pi Sigma—Am Inst Physics. Physics Department, Pennsylvania State College, State College, Pa.

15 WHITE, Maynard Pressley. Stratigraphy; Paleontology; Micropaleontol-

ogy. b'96. BS '19—'15-17 (Brown U); AM '23—PhD '29 (Columbia U). Author articles in field. Paleontologist and dist geol Gulf Oil Corp Okla '28-52; research asso dept micropaleontol Am Mus Nat Hist '44-50. Geol Society Am(F)—AAAS(F)—Am Assn Petroleum Geol—Soc Econ Paleontologists and Mineralogists—Sigma Xi. P.O. Box 505, Ardmore, Okla.

16 WHITE, Michael James Denham. Chromosome cytology; Gallmidges; Orthoptera. b'10. BSc '31—MSc '32— DSc '40 (U London); Rockefeller Found fellow '37-38 (Columbia). Author: The Chromosomes '37, '42; Animal Cytology and Evolution '45; also articles in field. Prof zool U Tex since '47. Am Soc Zool —Am Soc Naturalists—Soc Study Evolution — Genetics Soc Am — Genetical Soc, Gt Britain. Department of Zoology, University of Texas, Austin, Tex.†

17 WHITE, Orland Emile. Plant genetics and cytology; Mutation and geographic distribution (Temperature tolerance). b'85. BS '09—MS '11 (SD State Coll); MS '12 (Harvard); ScD '13 (Bussey Instn Harvard). Botanist Mulford Exploration of Amazon Basin Expedition '21-22; representative Brooklyn Botanic Garden on Institute for Research in Tropical America '23-27. Author articles in field. Prof Agrl Biology, dir Blandy Exptl Farm U Va since '27. AAAS(F)—Nat Research Council (Chmn panel on botany, growth com, med div '45-46)—Bot Soc Am (council mem genetics Sect '28; chmn southeastern sect '43-45)—Am Genetics Assn—Gen Soc Am—Tenn Acad Sci. Biology Building, University Station, University of Virginia, Charlottesville, Va.

18 WHITE, Philip R(odney). Tissue cultures, plant and animal; Tissue nutrition; Excised plant roots (Cultivation); Plant sap movements; Plant tumors. b'01. AB '22 (U Mont); '22-23 (U Washington); '23-24 (Ecole Normale d'Instituteurs Valence, Drome, France); PhD '28 (Johns Hopkins U); research fellow '30-31 (U Berlin). Author: A Handbook of Plant Tissue Culture '48. Co-author: Micrurgical and Germ-Free Methods '43; also articles in field. Sr physiol head div gen physiol Inst for Cancer Research Phila since '45. AAAS(F, annual $1000 prize '37) —Am Soc Plant Physiol (Stephen Hales award '39)—Am Bot Soc—Am Soc Naturalists — Sigma Xi. Nat Research Council fellow '29-31. Institute for Cancer Research, Fox Chase, Phila.†

19 WHITE, R(euel) Clyde. Public and social welfare. b'94. AB '17 (U Tex); AM '22—PhD '28 (Columbia U); diploma '22 (Union Theol Sem). Author: Social Statistics '33; Growth of German Social Insurance '33; Administration of Unemployment Compensation '39; Michigan Youth Vocational Study, Summary Report '42, also articles in field. Prof public welfare Western Res U since '44; cons pub welfare for community surveys Kans City Kans, Springfield, Boston, New London '46-49. Am Assn Social Workers—Am Sociol Soc—Am Statis Assn—Am Pub Welfare Assn. Western Reserve University, Cleve 6.†◎

20 WHITE, Theodore George. Flat glass production. b'99. CE '24 (Tech U Vienna). Research on Fourcault system of manufacture of flat glass, manufacture of laminated safety, case-hardened safety, bent, microscopic cover, flat drawn colored, bent laminated and plate glasses through grinding and polishing of flat drawn sheet glass; photographic determination of glass defects. Granted 13 patents on manufacture of case-hardened and bent

glass. With First Bohemian Glass Works '25-26; supt Vetreria Italiana Balzareti Modigliani SA '27-32; insp and cons Co de St. Gobain '32-36; asst to pres First Austrian Machinglass Industry and First Bohemian Glass Works '37-38; development engr Am Window Glass Co '39-49; cons since '49. Am Ceramic Soc—Acad Sci and Art(photog sect). H: 19 Scenery Rd. (Wilkinsburg), Pitts 21.

21 WHITE, Trescott Slemons. Torsional vibration. b'08. BS '34 (U Cal). Analyization shaft vibration of ships, generators, and pumping plants, including steam powered, gasoline, gas, and diesel; compilation test results on torsional stress and critical shaft speeds, and other vibration analysis procedure data. Author articles: Torsional Vibration for the Operator, Owner and Builder '44; Torsional Vibration Simplified '44; Taking the Mystery Out of Torsional Vibration '46, and others. With Enterprise div Gen Metals Corp SF since '34, now tech engr. Soc Automotive Engrs—ASME—Soc Naval Architects and Marine Engrs. Profl engr Cal. Enterprise Division, General Metals Corp., H: 136 Stanley St., Redwood City, Cal.

22 WHITE, Walter Finch, Jr. Chemical quality of water. b'11. BS '34 (NC State Coll); '31-33 (U Okla). Investigations in the field of natural waters with special reference to their chemical characterization and their suspended sediment. Author: Industrial Utility of Surface Waters of Pennsylvania '44-46; Industrial Utility of Surface Waters of Ohio '46. With US Geol Survey since '34. Am Chem Soc— Am Water Works Assn—AAAS. Water Resources Division, U. S. Geological Survey, Washington 25.

23 WHITE, William Alexander. Geomorphology of southern Appalachian and Piedmont regions. b'06. AB '30 (Duke U); MA '31—PhD '38 (U NC); MS '34 (Mont Sch Mines). Research in geomorphic history and structure of southern Appalachians and Piedmont. Author articles in field. Professor geol U NC since '51. Geol Soc Am(F)— Sigma Xi(F). Department of Geology and Geography, University of North Carolina, Chapel Hill, N.C.†

24 WHITE, W(illiam) Lawrence. Fungi (Imperfecti, industrial, effect on fabrics). b'08. BS '34 (Penn State Coll); PhD '40 (Cornell U). Author articles in field. Resident asso deterioration problems Chem Warfare Service, MIT '43-44; dir Farlow Library and Herbarium, asso prof bot Harvard U since '48. Sr mycol tropical deterioration research lab US Army Quartermaster Corps '44-46, biol labs '46-48; mycol and qm rep on Army Air Forces Tropical Sci Mission to New Zealand, Australia, Japan and Pacific Islands, South Asia, Central Africa and Brazil '45-46. Bot Soc Am—Mycol Soc Am—Brit Mycol Soc—New Eng Bot Club. Biological Laboratories, Harvard University, Divinity Av., Cambridge, Mass. H: 45 Hillcrest St., Arlington, Mass.

25 WHITE, Wilton Terry. Range mgmt. b'91. AB '17—MS '34 (Kansas State Coll); agrl journ '32-33 (U Ore). Development improved methods for range survey and appraisal; improvement quality and quantity of forage for livestock and maintenance high level of forage production; 15 years in Alaska, and 17 years western states; one year study and analysis highland mountain pastures in Italy, and organization of improvement and maintenance program. Author articles: Planning Range Conservation on Western Ranges '48; Pastures in the Italian

Highlands '50; Erosioin on Mountain Pastures in Italy '50, and other sci articles. Range specialist Soil Conservation Service since '35, in charge regional range program, west coast range states since '36. Am Soc Range Management—Soil Conservation Soc Am. Soil Conservation Service, Swan Island, Portland, Ore. H: 2443 E. 10th St., Portland 12, Ore.

10 WHITEHALL, Harold. English language development; Middle English and modern American and British dialects; Early modern English pronunciation; Linguistic dimension of criticism. b'05. BA '27 (London U); PhD '31 (U Ia). Author articles in field. Asso prof Eng and chmn Linguistics Ind U since '49; linguistics and etymological ed Webster's New World Dictionary of the American Language since '52. Linguistic Soc Am—Modern Lang Assn Am—Am Dialect Soc. Guggenheim fellow '39-40, Rockefeller fellow '44. Linguistics Department, Indiana University, Bloomington, Ind.⊚

11 WHITEHEAD, Thomas Hillyer. Analytical and vegetable oil chemistry. b'04. BS '25 (Ga U); MA '28—PhD '30 (Columbia). Research in structure of inorganic colloids and complex inorganic compounds, iodometric method for copper, preparation, purification and analysis of pecan oil, oxidation-reduction indicators, detection of casein in wood, preparation and purification of hydriodic acid, staining of wood products with potassium permanganate (patent applied for), bleaching of wood products. Author: Theory of Elementary Analysis '50; also articles in field. Prof analytical chem U Ga since '39, asst head dept since '46; expert, cons, Chief Chem Corps US Army '48; mem com Research and Development Chem Corps Assn '48; consultant Atomic Energy Commission since '52. American Chemical Society—Georgia Academy Science(F)—Phi Kappa Phi—Sigma Xi. Awarded Martin Reynolds Smith Meml Prize in chem (with Clay) '34. Department of Chemistry, University of Georgia, Athens, Atlanta, Ga.†

12 WHITEHEAD, Willis August. Educational planning (School buildings); Industrial arts (Laboratory planning). b'07. BA '30—MA '33 (O State U). Author: A Guide for Planning Elementary-School Buildings '47; also articles in field. Research asso and instr Bur Ednl Research O State U '45-49; ednl specialist Outcalt Guenther and Associates Architects since '49. consultant on planning industrial arts labs various bds edn State O since '33. Nat Soc Study Edn—Am Ednl Research Assn — O Edn Assn — Archtl Assn O—Nat Edn Assn—US—AIA. Outcalt, Guenther and Associates, Architects, 13124 Shaker Square, Cleve 20.

13 WHITEHILL, Walter Muir. American maritime history; Medieval Spanish history. b'05. AB cum laude '26—AM '29 (Harvard); PhD '34 (U London). Author: Portraits of Shipmasters and Merchants in The Peabody Museum of Salem '39; New England Blockaded in 1814 '39; Spanish Romanesque Architecture of the Eleventh Century '41; Liber Sancti Jacobi; Codex Calixtinus '45; Fleet Admiral King: A Naval Record (with Fleet Admiral Ernest J. King) '52, and others; also articles in field. Dir and librarian Boston Athenaeum since '46; ed Colonial Soc Mass since '46; ed The American Neptune since '41; historian Peabody Mus Salem Mass since '46, mem faculty since '51; sr tutor Lowell House Harvard Univ since '52. Active duty US Naval Reserve lieut to comdr office naval records and library Navy Dept '42-46.

Mass Hist Soc (council since '46)—Am Antiquarian Soc—Colonial Soc Mass—Peabody Mus Marine Assos—Naval Hist Found—US Naval Inst—Soc Antiquaries of London(F)—Hispanic Soc Am—Mediaeval Acad Am—Royal Archaeol Inst. Boston Athenaeum, 10½ Beacon St., Boston 8. H: Old Berry House, North Andover, Mass.

14 WHITEHORN, John C(lare). Emotion and instinct; Combat exhaustion. b'94. AB '16—LHD '47 (Doane Coll); MD '21 (Harvard). Biochemical and physiological studies of emotional states; methods for chlorides, phosphorus and epinephrin in blood; permutit as a reagent for amines; the biological function of acute emotional disturbance; interviewing; psychotherapy. Editorial bd Medicine, Am Journ Psychiatry, Archives Neurology and Psychiatry, others. Research McLean Hosp Waverley Mass and Mass Gen Hosp Boston '21-38; prof psychiatry Washington U St Louis '38-41; prof psychiatry Johns Hopkins U Med Sch since '41; sci cons US Army for study combat exhaustion World War II. Nat Research Council—AAAS(F)—ACS—AMA(F)—Am Bd Psychiatry and Neurology(dir '43-49, pres '46, '48, '49)—American Psychiatric Assn(pres '50-51). Johns Hopkins Hospital, Balt 5. H: 210 Northfield Pl., Balt 10.

15 WHITEHOUSE, Eula. Nature illustration; Texas flora; Taxonomy (Flowering plants, Bryophytes). b'92. BA '18—MA '31—PhD '39 (U Tex); grad '20 (NYC Hosp Sch Nursing). Water color illustrations used in book have been on exhibit in Austin Waco Galveston Abilene; oil painting solo show Federation of Women's Club Building Austin '43; painted transparent photographs of wildflowers on exhibit Texas Memorial Museum; painted backgrounds for large diorama of buffalo group '40 and mountain lion and coyotes '42 Texas Memorial Museum. Author: Texas Flowers in Natural Colors '48; also articles in field. Tech asst Herbarium So Methodist U since '46. Bot Soc Am—Am Soc Plant Taxonomists—Torrey Bot Club—Sullivant Moss Soc—Tex Acad Sci—Tex Fine Arts Assn—Sigma Xi. Box 739, Southern Methodist University, Dallas 5.†

16 WHITESIDE, Eugene Perry. Geography and classification of soils. b'12. BS '34 (U Ill); PhD '44 (U Mo). Research in soil mineralogy and chemistry, locating soil areas suitable for production of guayule in California, survey in Eastern Tennessee, reconnaissance soil survey of Kyoto Region of Japan. Author articles: Reconnaissance Soil Survey of the Kyoto Region of Japan '47. Co-author articles: (with C E Marshall) A Mineralogical and Chemical Investigation of Putnam Silt Loam Soil '44; other articles in field. Asst in soil phys and soil survey U Ill '34-35, '36-38; research asst in soils U Mo '38-39; asso soil surveyor Emergency Rubber Project Los Angeles '43; asso soil surveyor U Tenn '43-44; asso in soil survey U Ill '39-43, asst chief in soil phys and soil survey '44-49, on leave to serve as sci cons in agrl div nat resources sect GHQ SCAP Japan '46-47; associate professor soil sci Mich State College '49-53 prof since '53. Soil Sci Society Am—Am Soc Agron—Gamma Sigma Delta—Sigma Xi. Soil Science Department, Michigan State College, E. Lansing, Mich.

17 WHITFIELD, Francis James. Slavic philology. b'16. AB summa cum laude '36—AM '37—PhD '44—jr fellow Soc Fellows '39-40, '41-45 (Harvard); '37-38 (Ecole des Langues orientales vivantes Paris); '37 (U Cracow, Poznan

and Warsaw). Author: A Russian Reference Grammar '44; also articles in field. Co-ed Slavic Word. Act asso prof Slavic langs U Calif '48-50 asso prof since '50. Polish Inst Arts Science in Am—Modern Lang Assn—Linguistic Soc Am—Phi Beta Kappa. Fellow Library of Congress '40-41. Department Slavic Languages and Literature, U of California, Berkeley 4.†

18 WHITFORD, Larry Alston. Taxonomy and morphology of Algae (Southern United States); Malaria control (War areas). b'02. BS '25—MS '29 (NC State Coll); PhD '41 (O State U). Studies on taxonomy and morphology of fresh-water algae of southern US; descriptions of new species of algae; dengue, yellow fever and malaria control in war areas; pigmentation of fresh-water algae. Author: The Fresh-water Algae of North Carolina '43; also articles in field. Instr bot, aquatic biol NC State Coll '26, asso prof since '46; asst entomol (R) US PHS '43-45. AAAS(F)—Limnology Soc Am—Phycology Soc Am—Am Mocros Soc—NC Acad Sci. Botany Department, North Carolina State College, Raleigh, N.C.

19 WHITFORD, Robert Calvin. English literature (Bibliography); Critical history of satire. b'92. AB '12 (Coll City NY); Am '13 (Columbia); PhD '18 (Ill U). Author: Madame de Stael in England '18. Editor: Good Reading, 10th and 11th ed; Good Reading Book List 12th and 13th ed; also articles in field. Prof Pratt Inst since '47, dean Div General Studies since '49. NY Acad Pub Edn—Modern Languages Assn. Pratt Institute, Brooklyn 5.†

20 WHITING, Alfred F(rank). Ethnobotany (Origin of corn and other domesticated plants); Primitive art. b'12. BS '33 (U Vt); MA '35 (U Mich); student (U Chicago). Special investigator Indian Arts and Crafts Board '42. Santa Cruz Valley School, Tumacacari, Ariz. Asst prof anthrop U Ore '44-47. Author articles in field. Am Anthrop Assn—Soc Am Archeol—Sigma Xi. District anthropologist Ponape, East Caroline Islands, U.S. Trust Territory, Pacific Islands.

21 WHITING, John Randolph. Photojournalism. b'14. AB '36 (Ohio Univ). Author: Photography Is a Language '46; also articles in field. Asso ed Fawcett Publications '38-40; asso ed and mng ed Click '40-42; mng ed Popular Photography '43-46; mng ed '47 The Magazine of the Year '46-47; ed-in-chief Science Illustrated '47-49; editor and designer of photographic and picture books. Photographic Soc Am (asso)—Nat Press Photographers Assn—AAAS—Nat Assn Science Writers. 70 East 45th St., NYC. H: Hancock Place, Irvington, N.Y.†

22 WHITING, John Wesley Mayhew. Anthropology (Child socialization and training); Child psychology. b'08. PhB '31—PhD '38 (Yale U). Anthropology field trip New Guinea collecting data on child training customs and practices of Kwoma tribe '36-37; research asst anthropology. Inst Human Relations Yale U '38-43, problems of socialization both at cultural and phychol levels, compiling comparative data on child training from anthropological sources on 85 societies throughout world '46-47; assistant professor anthropology U Ia since '47, study child training in Am society, research asso in lab human devel and lect in edn Harvard Grad Sch of Edn. Author: Becoming a Kwoma '41; Habit Progression and Regression '43; The Frustration Complex in Kwoma Society '44; Outline of Cultural Materials '45. Am Anthrop Assn(F)—

Soc for Applied Anthrop—Soc for Research in Childhood Develpt—Sigma Xi. Iowa Child Welfare Research Station, University of Iowa, Iowa City, Ia. H: West Tisbury, Mass.†

10 WHITING, Phineas Wescott. Genetics of Hymenoptera and male haploidy. b'87. Student '07-09 (Dartmouth Coll); AB '11—MS '12 (Harvard Coll); PhD '16—Harrison research fellow '16-18 (U Pa). Author articles in field. Lecturer, prof zool U Pa since '35. AAAS(F)—Am Soc Zool—Am Soc Naturalists—Genetics Soc Am—Am Genetic Assn—Sigma Xi. Department of Zoology, University of Pennsylvania, Phila. 4.†

11 WHITMAN, Joseph Atwood, Jr. Forest damage; Timber cruising. b'16. BSF '38 (NC State Coll); MF '51 (Duke U). Investigation and appraisal forest damage from fire and unauthorized cutting; location and surveys timber tracts. Author article: Some Basic Legal Aspects of Forest Damage Appraisals '51. Asst supervisor Hofmann Forest NC State Coll '40-41; cons forester Glendon NC since '46. Soc Am Foresters—Assn Cons Foresters. Glendon, N.C.

12 WHITMAN, Walter Gordon. Petroleum refining. b'95. BS '17—MS '20 (MIT). Prof, head dept chem engring MIT; asst dir research Standard Oil Co of Ind '25-29, asso dir research '29-34; chmn subcom aircraft fuels and lubricant Nat Advisory Commn Aeronautics '40-45 mem nat adv com since '51; mem gen adv com AEC since '50. Am Institute Chem Engrs—Am Chem Soc—Sigma Xi—Tau Beta Pi. Massachusetts Institute of Technology, Cambridge. H: Nashawtuc Rd., Concord, Mass.

13 WHITMAN, Warren Charles. Range and pasture botany. b'11. BS '35—MS '36 (ND Agrl Coll); PhD '39 (U Wis). Research on grasses and range studies. Author articles in field. Asst bot ND Agrl Expt Sta '38-42; range ecol Forest Service US Dept Agr '46-47; asso bot ND Agrl Expt Sta since '47. AAAS(F)—Ecol Soc Am—Am Soc Agron—Am Soc Range Management—Grassland Research Foundation. North Dakota Agricultural Experiment Station, Fargo, N.D.†

14 WHITMORE, George Dewey. Photogrammetry; Cartoyraphic engring; City surveying. b'98. CE '34 (Internat Corr Sch). Geodetic and topographic surveys municipalities eastern and midwest United States; mapping in Brazil. Author: Geodetic Surveying '42; Elements of Photogrammetry '41; Advanced Surveying and Mapping '48. Surveyor R H Randall & Co '18-34; chief surveys TVA '34-45; cons to govt Brazil '44; chief tech staff topographic div US Geol Survey. Am Soc CE—Am Congress on Surveying and Mapping—Am Soc Phogrammetry—Am Geophys Union. US Geological Survey, Washington 25.◉

15 WHITMOYER, Clarence Walter. Fish (Vitamin oils). b'05. BS '28 (Albright Coll); AM in chem '29 (Columbia). Studies in recovery water soluble vitamins from fish livers; vitamin oils from fish and fish livers. Research chem E I duPont de Nemours & Co '29-31; Pres and gen mgr Whitmoyer Labs Inc Myerstown Pa since '31, Whitmoyer Labs Ltd Yarmouth NS Can since '40. ACS—Nat Farm Chemurgic Council—Animal Nutrition Research Council—Atlantic Fisheries By-Products Assn(vp)—Nat Vitamin Oil Assn(bd mem)—Animal Health Inst(ex-pres)—Hooker Sci Lib—AAAS. Received Albright College Alumni citation '49. Whitmoyer Labora-

tories, Inc., 19 North Railroad St., Myerstown, Pa.

16 WHITNEY, H(arold) LeRoy. Alloys (Ferro). b'84. PhB '05 (Sheffield Sci Sch Yale U). Design and fabrication welded pressure vessels and piping systems; analysis and fabrication alloy steels, particularly for high temperature service; originator chrome-molybdenum steels for high temperature service in cracking corrosive crude oils, of National Emergency steels to conserve ferro alloys, also low alloy, water-quenched armor plate for tanks World War II; member of committee writing construction codes for welded boilers and unfired pressure vessels. Chief engr Fabricated Products Div M W Kellogg Co NYC '21-38; staff expert iron and steel OPM Washington '40-42, also chief constrn Alloy Steel Shot and Shell Unit WPB; cons Bur Mines since '51. ASME(F, boiler code com)—Am Iron and Steel Inst—Am Soc Metals—Am Welding Soc—ASTM. H: 130 E. 67th St., NYC 21.

17 WHITTAKER, Edward George. Textile engineering. b'89. Student (Scranton Internat Corr Sch, MIT). Research on fibres, machinery, spinning, winding, weaving, dyeing, cotton, worsteds, woolens, rayon, silk, spun silk, linen, ramie, card clothing; made survey American textile machinery market Japan, Korea, Manchuria, China, Hongkong, Philippines, French-Indo China. Dir, sec Asia Elec Co Shanghai '33-36; spl textile cons China-Am Council Comm and Ind Inc NYC '44-46; dir, vp, sr textile engr Anselm and Co Inc Shanghai, San Francisco and NYC since '46. ASME. Amackassin, Blairstown, N.J.

18 WHITTENBERGER, Robert Tyndale. Rubber in plants; Potato starch; Pectin and plant tissue texture. b'12. BS '36 (U Chicago); MS '38 (Northwestern U); PhD '43 (U Pa). Research on silicon absorption by plants, on occurrence, distribution, and characteristics of rubber in plants; formulated techniques for identification and characterization of rubber in plant tissues; developed test for rapid analysis of rubber in guayule latices, discovered that most rubber in Cryptostegia grandiflera was within leaf chlorenchyana cells; evaluated properties potato starch gels and showed how the properties could be modified. Author articles in field. Chem Eastern Regional Research Lab US Dept Agr since '42. Bot Soc Am—Sigma Xi—Phi Beta Kappa. Eastern Regional Research Laboratory, U.S. Department of Agriculture, Phila 18.†

19 WHITTINGTON, Roberta Estelle. Geography (Historical); Cartography. AB '42—MA '51 (U Cal LA). Specialized study historical geography including geographic survey of an agricultural region, analysis of a physiographic unit. Guide naturalist's div Nat Park Service Carlsbad NM '42-44, '46-48; cartographic draftsman War Dept '44-46; map draftsman Standard Oil Co Cal since '51. Assn Am Geographers—Nat Geog Soc. 605 W. Olympic Blvd., LA 15.

20 WHITTLESEY, Derwent (Stainthorpe). Geography (Political, geopolitics, agricultural, tropical, Africa, logistics, regions). b'90. PhB '14—MA '15—PhD '20 (U Chicago); MA (hon) '42 (Harvard). Author: The Earth and the State '39; German Strategy of World Conquest '42; Makers of Modern Strategy '43; Foundations of National Power '45; also articles in field. Harvard U since '28, prof geog since '43; cons to US State, War, and Navy Depts, and OSS '40-46. Assn Am Geog

(pres '44). Helen Culver Gold Medal, Chicago Geographic Soc '48. Geographic Institute, 2 Divinity Av., Cambridge 38, Mass.◉

21 WHYBURN, William Marvin. Differential equations. b'01. AB '22—MA '23—PhD '27 (U Tex). Co-author: (with P H Daus and J M Gleason) Basic Mathematics for War and Industry '44; (with P H Daus) First Year College Mathematics with Applications '48. With U Cal LA '28-44, prof and chmn dept math '38-44, ednl supervisor for engring, sci, management war tng program '41-44; pres Tex Tech Coll Lubbock '44-48, Kenan prof math and head dept U NC since '48; chief operations analysis sect Hdqrs 3d Air Force '44. La Academia Nacional de Ciencias Exactas, Fisicas y Naturales de Lima '43. Am Math Soc (council '39-43)—Math Assn Am)1st vp '44-45) —AAAS(sect A Com '39-41)—Philos Soc Tex—Phi Beta Kappa—Sigma Xi. Department of Mathematics, University of North Carolina, Chapel Hill.†◉

22 WICHTERMAN, Ralph. Free-living and parasitic protozoa; Biology of Paramecium. b'07. BS '30 (Temple U); MA '32—PhD '36 (U Pa). Research investigator Marine Biological Laboratory summers since '32; new protozoan parasites, intestinal protozoa from tortoises with descriptions of three new species. Author articles in field. Asst prof Temple U '36-41, asso prof biol '41-46, prof since 46. Society Protozoology—AAAS—Am Soc Parasitol—American Soc Zool—Sigma Xi—Am Micros Soc—Pa Acad Sci. Biology Department, Temple University, Phila. 22.†

23 WICKER, Dan Bridger. Dissolving pulps; Synthetic fibers. b'07. BA '26 (Elon Coll); BS '27 (NC State Coll); MS '29 (MIT); PhD '35 (Inst Paper Chem). Research in dissolving pulps, rayon staple fiber and related products; surveyed synthetic fiber industries of Germany and Italy. Holds patents in US and England. Author articles in field. Chem engr Eastern Corp Bangor Me '29-33; tech dir Thilmany Pulp & Paper Co Kaukauna Wis '35-37; asso prof chem engring NC State Coll '37-39; staple process mgr Am Viscose Corp '39-49; cons US QMC and Dept Comm '45; chem engr Am Cyanamid Corp '49. Am Inst Chem Engrs—Tech Assn Pulp and Paper Industry—Am Assn Textile Chem and Colorists. Technical Service and Development Department, American Cyanamid Co., 1937 W. Main St., Stamford, Conn.

24 WICKERHAM, Lynferd Joseph. Yeasts (Taxonomy, Industrial utilization, variations). b'10. BS '34—MS '35 (Mich State Coll); PhD '38 (Yale). Author co-author articles in the field. Zymologist Northern Regional Research Lab US Dept Agr Peoria Ill since '40. Soc Am Bacteriol—Mycol Soc Am. Northern Regional Research Laboratory, Peoria, Ill.†

25 WICKERSHAM, Cornelius Wendell. Military government and intelligence. b'84. AB '06—LLB '09 (Harvard); LLD (hon) '38 (St John's U). Mem law firm Cadwalader, Wickersham & Taft. Asst chief staff mil intelligence 1st Army '40-41; brig gen '42; comdt Sch Mil Govt US Army '42-44; US mil adviser European Adv Commn '44; acting dep and comdg gen US Group Control Council Germany '44-45. AM, NY State bar assns. 14 Wall St., NYC.

26 WICKIZER, Vernon Dale. Food and agriculture in Monsoon Asia; Tropical economics and food crops; Economics of rice, coffee, tea and cocoa. b'04. Grad '25 (US Naval Acad); MBA '29

(Stanford U). Consultant Food Research Institute '39-40. Author: The Rice Econ of Monsoon Asia '41; The World Coffee Economy '43; Tea Under International Regulation '44; Coffee, Tea and Cocoa in World War II '49; also articles in field. Prof Stanford U since '39, econ Food Research Inst. Am Econ Assn—Far Eastern Assn—Royal Inst Internat Affairs. Food Research Institute, Stanford University, Stanford, Calif.

10 WICKSTROM, Joseph Ernest. Electrical and hydraulic engineering; Engineering valuation. b'83. Registered public accountant. Author: Some Experiments with Wireless Telephony '05; Terminal Methods for Large Wires and Cables '06; Long Aerial Wire Spans '11; Portable Battery Radio Sets '22; Determinations Affecting Hydroelectric Development '26; Sales Principles Applied to Rate Making '28; Studies on Depreciation '34; Insuring Securities and Loans '35. Pres Wedgewood Co, Keystone Properties Inc, Wickstrom and Saxe Inc, Wickstrom & Co.; ind cons engr since '08. Wash State Assn Accountants—Wash Soc Profl Engrs (past pres)—Nat Soc Profl Engrs. 20 Republican St., Seattle 9.

11 WIEMAN, Henry Nelson. American philosophies of religion; Normative psychology of religion. b'84. AB '07—DD '29 (Park Coll Parkville Mo); '10 (San Francisco Theol Sem); '10-11 (univs Jena and Heidelberg); PhD '17 (Harvard); LittD '30 (Occidental Coll). Author: Religious Experience and the Scientific Method '26; The Wrestle of Religion with Trust '27; Methods of Private Religious Living '29; The Issues of Life '31. Co-author (with Regina Wieman) Normative Psychology of Religion; (with Bernard Meland) American Philosophies of Religions; (with Walter Horton) The Growth of Religions '38. Prof philosophy U Oregon since '49. Am Philos Association—Am Theol Assn—AAUP.◎

12 WIENER, Alexander S. Blood (Genetics); Rh factor; Immunology; Blood types; Blood transfusion. b'07. AB '26 (Cornell); MD '30 (L.I. Coll Medicine). Co-discoverer Rh factor, Rh blood types and mechanism of their heredity, demonstrated importance Rh factors for blood transfusion; discoverer blocking and conglutiation tests for Rh sensitization; devised new method treatment of erythroblastosis fetalis by exchange transfusion; method of measuring linkage in human genetics; proposed theory of inheritance of allergic diseases; classification human races by blood group factors; co-discoverer Kell blood type; medicolegal application blood grouping tests. Author: Blood Groups and Transfusion '43. Author about 300 articles in field. Head blood transfusion div Brooklyn Jewish Hosp since '32, Adelphi Hosp since '41; clin path and dir Wiener Lab since '35; serologist Office Chief Med Examiner since '38, sr serologist since '48; staff forensic med NYU-Bellevue Post Grad Med Sch since '38, asst prof since '49. Am Coll Physicians(F)—Coll Am Path(F)—NY Acad Med(F)—AMA(F)—NY Acad Sci (F)—Am Soc Clin Path(F)—Internat Soc Hematology(F)—Am Assn Immunologists—Am Bd Path—AAAS—Genetics Society America—American Society Human Genetics—America Society Naturalists— America Statis Assn —Soc Med Jurisprudence—Am Acad Forensic Sci—Soc for Study Blood—Research Soc Am—Phi Delta Epsilon—Phi Beta Kappa—Phi Beta Kappa Associates—Alpha Omega Alpha. Received Phi Delta Epsilon prize '31; Coll Physicians Phila Alvarenga prize '45; Am

Pub Health Assn Lasker award '47; Am Soc Clin Path Ward Burdick award '46; Youth United "Oscar" '51; Passano Found award '51. 64 Rutland Rd., Bklyn 25.

13 WIENS, Herold Jacob. Geography of East Asia; Chinese language and culture. b'12. AB '35 (U Calif); MA '47—PhD '49 (U Mich); '36-37 (Yenching U). Asst prof geog Yale U since '50, dir undergrads in foreign area studies Yale University since '48. Far East research analyst OSS '41-45, chief Chungking Office Research and Analysis Br OSS '45, Washington '45. Am Oriental Soc—Assn Am Geog—Am Soc Profl Geog—Am Geog Soc NY—Phi Kappa Phi. Geography department, Yale University, New Haven.†

14 WIENS, Jacob Henry. Nucleonics; Electronics; Cyclotron; Uranium; Calutron; Television and color television. born 1910. AA '33 (Reedley Jr Coll); AB '37—MA '43—PhD '44 (U Calif). Developed the mercury isotope of mass 198 for a new primary standard of wave length. Author articles in field. Research physicist U of Calif since '37; electronics engr USN Electronics research physicist and electronics engr and electronics, San Mateo Jr Coll; reearch physicist and electronics engr Manhattan Project Radiation Lab U of Calif; owner Wiens Electronics Lab basic electronics research. 130 Crest Rd., Woodside, Cal.

15 WIESSNER, Fritz Hermann Ernst. Mountain climbing b'00. Many important first ascents in mountain ranges of Europe, Asia, North America; leader of American Karakorum expedition '39, climber to within 750 feet of the summit of K2 second highest mountain in the world; made first ascent of Mt. Waddington, highest mountain in Canada '36. Author articles in field. Mfg chem F H Wiessner Inc Burlington Vt since '46. Burlington, Vt.

16 WIGGANS, Cleo Claude. Pomology (Strawberries, orchard soil moisture). b'89. BS '12—AM '13—PhD '18 (U Mo). Research new hybrid strawberries, spraying tree fruits, effects of orchard plants on subsoil moisture, depletion of subsoil moisture. Author articles in field. Research hort U Del '18-19; asso prof hort U Neb '19-24, prof and chmn since '24. Am Soc Hort Sci. University of Nebraska, Department of Horticulture, Lincoln 1, Nebraska†◎

17 WIGGINS, Ira Loren. Botanical taxonomy; Flora of Sonoran Desert. b'99. AB '22 (Occidental Coll, Los Angeles); MA '25—PhD '29 (Stanford U). Author articles in field. Stanford U since '29, prof biol since '40, asso exec head dept biol scis, dir Natural Hist Museum and Dudley Herbarium. AAAS—Bot Soc Am (sec-treas Pacific sect '39-42)—Calif Acad Sci—Calif Bot Soc (pres '40)—Phi Beta Kappa—Sigma Xi. 111 Pope St., Palo Alto, Cal.

18 WIGHTMAN, Eugene Pinckney. Photographic chemistry. b'88. BS '08 (Richmond Coll); PhD '11 (Johns Hopkins). Studies on size-frequency distribution grains of photo emulsion on sensitivity; latent image intensification by various substances and treatments; effect of very low temperatures on sensitivity and latent image; sensitivity of emulsions to alpha particles. Co-author articles: (with E F Quirk) Intensification of the latent image on photographic plates and films; (with S E Sheppard and A P H Trivelli) The production of sensitizing specks on silver halide grains; The prepara-

tion and properties of some synthetic photo-halide emulsions; and others. Assistant ed photog words Websters New Internat Dictionary. Research chemist Kodak Research Labs Eastman Kodak Co '20-36, tech ed sales service div since '36. ACS—Am Inst Physics—Optical Soc Am—Photog Soc Am(F, former dir)—Royal Photog Soc Gt Britain (F)—Rochester Acad Arts and Sci—Fedn Am Scientists. Eastman Kodak Co., Sales Service Division, 343 State St., Rochester 4, N.Y.

19 WILBERDING, Marion Xavier. Water and sewage works design. b'91. BS '13 (Purdue U); '14-16 (Cath U Am)—'16-17 (Johns Hopkins U). Specialist water works design, engineering, management and operation, appraisals and rate cases. Asso with Francis R Weller Washington '17-29; pvt practice since '29, vp and gen mgr, engr in charge of design various water companies. ASME—ASCE—Am Water Works Assn—Tau Beta Pi. 1822 Eye St. N. W., Washington 6.

20 WILBUR, C. Martin. Chinese history. b'08. BA '31 (Oberlin Coll); MA '33—PhD '41 (Columbia); '32-34 (Coll Chinese Studies, Peking). Research Chinese history, politics, archeology, ethnology. Author: Slavery in China During the Former Han Dynasty, 206 B.C.-A.D. 25 '43; also articles in field. Asso prof Chinese hist Columbia since '47. Am Friends of China (sec)—Am Oriental Soc—Far Eastern Assn (bd dirs). Columbia University, NYC.

21 WILBUR, George B (rowning). Sexual symbolism. b'87. BS '12—MD '16 (Harvard). Mng ed American Imago since '47. AMA—Am Psychiat Assn—Am Psychoanalytic Assn—Psychopath Assn—AAAS—Ecol Assn—Assn Symbolic Logic—Am Anthrop Assn—Internat Phenomenological Soc — Philos Sci Assn. Cove Rd., South Dennis, Mass.

22 WILBUR, Marguerite Eyer. California and Pacific Coast history; British Empire in India. b'89. BA '13 (Stanford); MA '18 (U So Calif). Extensive research including libraries in London and Seville. Author: The East India Company and the British Empire in the Far East '45; Editor and translator numerous French and Spanish books; also articles in field. Pen and Brush — Calif Hist Soc — Le Salon Francais. H: 25 Los Altos Dr., Pasadena 2, Calif.

23 WILBUR, William Hale. Physical training (Drill methods); Drills (Physical). b'88. Student '07-08 (Haverford Coll); BS '12 (US Mil Acad); grad '32 (Command and Gen Staff Sch); '35 (Army War Coll); grad '20 (Ecole Spec Militaire St. Cyr France); '22-24 (Ecole Superieure de Guerre Paris). Author: Koehler Method of Physical Drill '18. Brig gen US Army, ret.; warden Cook County Jail Chicago since '50. Served overseas with Allied landing in North Africa '42; comdg office 60th Inf Ft Bragg '41-42; dep comdr 36th Div participating in Salerno landing '44. Congressional Medal of Honor '43; Ouissam Alaouite medal (Moroccan govt); Legion of Merit, Silver Star, Combat Infantryman's Badge (US); Knight Comdr SS Maurice and Lazarus (Italy). 323 Central Av., Highland Park, Ill.◎

24 WILCKE, Harold Ludwig. Poultry nutrition; Nutrition and foods. b'06. BS '27—MS '32—PhD '35 (Ia State Coll). Research on nutrition and diseases of chickens and turkeys, vitamins D, E and A, nutritional value of cereal grains, egg quality; made studies of diets of soldiers and civilians. Author articles in field. Asst dir research Ralston Purina Co. Gamma Sigma Delta—Phi Kappa Phi—Sigma Xi—Poultry Sci Assn—Worlds Poultry Sci Assn. Ralston Purina Co., 835 S. 8th St., St. Louis 2.†

10 WILCOX, Aimee. Malaria parasites of man, chickens and monkeys. b'99. Student '16-18 (Millsaps Coll); '19-20 (George Peabody Coll for Teachers); '21 (So Methodist U). Microscopic examination of thick blood film surveys made each spring and fall by 29-40 various Southern state health departments; supervised examination of over 100,000 thick-film blood slides collected in special malaria survey conducted by 11 southern states in malarial belt; study on stains to improve quality of American Giemsa stains for identification of malaria parasites; assists immunological research in malaria, technical operation of chick embryo and chick studies; biol res human malaria parasites. Author: Manual for Microscopical Diagnosis of Malaria; also articles in field. Studied at US PHS resch laboratory Greenwood Miss '26-28, with Ofc Malaria Investigations Richmond Va '29-30, Washington '31-41; instr at intervals of technicians in malaria parasitology and techniques in several state health dept labs since '32; sr micros Nat Inst Health '36-38, asst technol '39; Office Malaria Investigations USPHS Memphis Tenn protozoologist '41-50, now lab trop diseases. Am Pub Health Assn(F)—Nat Malaria Soc—Am Soc Tropical Med. and Hygiene. U.S. Pub Health Service, Lab of Tropical Diseases, Box 717, Columbia, S.C. 802 Pickens St., Apt 2, Columbia, S.C.

11 WILCOX, Fred A(bner). Brewing. b'02. BS '27 (U Mo). Co-author: (with Nicholas S Yanick) Moisture Determination in Hops '48; (with Robert I Tenney) Effect of Diastiatic Power on Wort Sugar '46. Chem Wahl-Henius Inst '28-38, chief chem '38-42, asst tech dir '42-46, tech dir since '46. Am Chem Soc—Am Soc Brewing Chem—Inst Food Technol—Master Brewers Assn Am. 1135 Fullerton Av., Chgo 14. H: 4423 Sheridan Rd., Chgo 40.

12 WILDER, Arthur B. Ferrous metallurgy. b'04. BS '25 (Mt Union Coll); AB '28 (Ohio State U); '30-31 (Case Sch Tech); DSc '33 (Harvard). Research on acid bessemer steel making processes; creep and other high temperature properties carbon and alloy steels; brittleness and welding characteristics of steel; graphitization of steel; gases in steel; metallurgy shells, guns, bombs, rockets, steel for pipe lines. Research metall Am Steel & Wire Co '33-35; asst prof metall engineering U Ill '35-39; metall Jones & Laughlin Steel Corp '39-44; chief metall Nat Tube Co since '44. Am Soc Metals—Am Welding Soc—Am Petroleum Inst—Am Soc ME—AIMME—ASTM. National Tube Co., Pitts 30.

13 WILDES, Harry Emerson. History of Japan (MacArthur occupation); American history (Revolution, Pennsylvania). b'90. AB '13 (Harvard); AM '22—PhD '27 (U Pa); LHD '44 (Temple U). Research on social problems in Japan, China and Mexico. Author: Social Currents in Japan '27; Japan in Crisis '34; Aliens in the East '37; Twin Rivers '43; Lonely Midas '43. Asso ed Phila Forum Mag since '33; columnist daily book column of Making Many Books; compiling MacArthur official history of occupation of Japan. Chief information management branch and historian govt sect GHA-SCAP since '47; chief Pol and Soc Affairs Div Civil Hist Sect SCAP '47-51. Fulbright prof Tokyo '53. Hist Soc Pa—Asiatic Soc Japan—Am Sociol Soc. 259 S. Farragut Terr., Phila.

14 WILDHACK, William August. Scientific instrumentation (Aeronautic instruments and testing equipment). b'08. BSEE '31—MS '32 (U Colo); '38-40 (George Washington U). Author articles in field. Associate editor Review of Scientific Instruments since '43. Inventions: Respiratory oxygen apparatus, liquid oxygen converter, liquid oxygen pump, pressure breathing valve for aviators, pneumatic instruments, mechano-electric transducer and others. Nat Bur Standards since '35, chief missile instrumentation sect '48-50, chief Office Basic Instrument since '50. US Aircraft Equip Panel since '48. Instrument Soc Am (pres Washington sect '47-48, nat bd dirs '45-47)—Inst Aeronautical Sci—Washington Acad Sci—Washington Philos Soc—Nat Research Council (com chmn sci equipment)—AAAS—Am Phys Soc—Sigma Xi.—Tau Beta Pi. National Bureau of Standards, Washington 25.

15 WILDMAN, Sam(uel) (Goodnow). Rubber (Origin in living plants, analysis methods, genetical control); Auxin action in plants; Plant proteins. b'12. BA '39 (Ore State Coll); MA '40—PhD '42 (U Mich). Author articles in field. Asso prof botany U Calif Los Angeles. Bot Soc Am—Am Soc Plant Physiol—Sigma Xi—Phi Kappa Phi. Botany Division, University of California, LA.

16 WILDS, Alfred L(awrence). Organic chemistry; Steroids (Sex hormones). b'15. BS '36—MS '37—PhD '39—Du Pont research fellow '39-40 (U Mich). Co-author: Experiments in Organic Chemistry '47; also articles in field. Instr, later prof chem U Wis since '40, research organic chem since '40. Nat Defense Research Com, co-official investigator '42-45. Am Chem Soc—London Chem Soc—Swiss Chem Soc—AAAS—Sigma Xi. Department of Chemistry, University of Wisconsin, Madison 6, Wis.

17 WILE, Oscar J. Wines. b'80. Student (Coll City NY). Author: An Introduction to Wines '33; How, When and What to Serve '34; Wine Without Frills '39. Employee Julius Wile Sons & Co '98-07, partner '07-25; pres The Wile Corp '25-32; vp Schenley Import Corp '32-43; vp and dir Schenley Distillers Corp '40-43; founded own company '43; now chmn Browne Vintners Co Inc. 500 Fifth Av., NYC 18. H: 737 Park Av.

18 WILES, Gloyd M. Mines (Examination, operation); Submersible motors (Mine dewatering). b'98. BS '23 (U Cal). Development of first 2300 volt submersible motors for mine dewatering; examining and operating engr of mines. Gen mining, milling and smelting '23-24; gen supt Treadwell Yukon Co and Bunker Hill & Sullivan Mfg Co '24-28; vp and gen mgr Park City Consol Mines Co Park City Utah '34-42; mgr mining dept Nat Lead Co since '42. Can Mining and Metall Inst—Am Mining and Metall Inst—AIMME National Lead Co., 111 Broadway, NYC.

19 WILEY, Bell Irvin. American history (Southern United States, Civil War, Southern Confederacy, Negroes in Civil War period); Military history of World War II. b'06. AB '28 (Asbury Coll, Wilmore Ky); MA '29 (U Ky); PhD '33 (Yale U); grad student (Peabody Coll). Author: Southern Negroes, 1861-1865 '38 (Mrs Simon Baruch prize '35; The Life of Johnny Reb: The Common Soldier of the Confederacy '43; The Plain People of the Confederacy '43; The Life of Billy Yank: The Common Soldier of the Union '52; also author articles in field.

Prof hist and head dept Miss So Coll Hattiesburg Miss '34-38, U Miss '38-46, La State U '46-48; Emory U since '48. Soc Am Hist—AHA—Miss Valley Hist Assn—So Hist Assn. Emory University, Emory University, Ga.

20 WILEY, Keith Brahe. Aberdeen-Angus cattle. b'12. Student '35 (Princeton U). Made study of history and pedigrees of purebred Aberdeen-Angus cattle with particular reference to classification and evaluation of families used by breeders in naming their animals for registration, and of influence of outstanding sires on breed. Author: Notable Aberdeen-Angus Families '48; Aberdeen-Angus Notables of 1945 '46; also articles in field. Mgr. Wakefield Farm Earlysville Va since '38. Am Aberdeen-Angus Breeders' Assn. Wakefield Farm, Earlysville, Va.

21 WILHELM, Ernest John. Electrodeposition of metals; Deposition of inorganic coatings on metals; Current distribution in electroplating; Corrosion of metals. b'04. BS '27—MS '28—PhD '30 (U Notre Dame). Discovered and developed Cronak coating produced upon zinc by an immersion treatment; holder three US patents. Asso prof dept chem engring U Notre Dame since '41. Am Chem Soc—Am Inst Chem Engrs—Am Soc Engring Edn—Am Electroplater's Soc—Ind Acad Sci. Department of Chemical Engineering, University of Notre Dame, Notre Dame, Ind.†

22 WILHELM, Harley A(lmey). Metallurgy of uranium and thorium. b'00. AB '23 (Drake U); PhD '31 (Ia State Coll). Inventor processes for uranium, thorium, other materials. Author articles in field. Asst prof chem Ia State Coll '40-44, asso prof '44-45, prof, asso dir Inst Atomic Research since '45; research under OSRD and Manhattan Project, US Atomic Energy Commn since '41. Am Chem Soc—Am Soc Metals—Optical Soc Am—Ia Acad Sci—Phi Beta Kappa—Sigma Xi—Phi Kappa Phi—Lambda Upsilon. Iowa State College, Ames, Ia.

23 WILKES, Susan H(eiskell). Medical illustration. b'88. Student '23-25 (Johns Hopkins Med Sch). Research and illustrations for neurosurgery, gynecology and diseases of retina of eye. Illustrator: Book of Nursing Procedures '42; Essentials of Diagnostic Examination '40; Milk and Food Sanitation Practices '46. Author: Methods and Problems of Medical Illustration '29. Head dept illus Vanderbilt U Sch Med since '25. Assn Med Illus(charter mem, mem bd gov '45-49). Vanderbilt University, School of Medicine, Nashville.

24 WILKIE, Richard Francis, Jr. Germany (18th Century drama); Operettas; Anglo-French-German literary relations; Juvenile literature; C F Weisse (Works 1726-1804). b'10. Student '28-30 (Ida State Coll Pocatello); AB '34—MA '36 (U Wash Seattle); '36 (U Berlin); PhD '51 (U Cal Berkeley). Research English-French influences exhibited by the works of C F Weisse (1726-1804). Author article: A New Source for Kleists' Zerbrochner Krug '48; book reviews and other contributions to German Quarterly '42. Asst prof German lit U Wash since '47. Phi Beta Kappa—Delta Phi Alpha—Modern Lang Assn—Am Assn Tchrs German—AAUP. Department of Germanics, University of Washington, Seattle 5.

25 WILKINS, Sir Hubert. Arctic geography, meterology and living; Polar navigation and photography; Environmental protection in polar, tropical and desert areas. b'88. Student (Australian State Sch, Adelaide Sch Mines and Industries, S Austral). Naturalist Shackleton Quest expedition '21-22, discovered several new species of trees, shrubs, plants, insects and two birds; comdr Wilkins Australian Islands expedition, discovered new species trees, birds, mammals '22-25; comdr Detroit Arctic expeditions '25-28, made first trans-arctic flight; comdr Wilkins-Hearst Antarctic expeditions; made first flight in Antarctica, discovered five new islands more than 500 miles coast line and several large glaciers '28-30; comdr Nautilus submarine expedition to Arctic, made first submarine trip under arctic ice '31; mgr Ellsworth expeditions Antarctica '32-39; comdr Soviet Search expdn in Arctic for Levanevsky covering some 170,000 sq miles never seen before by man '37-38. Cons Mil Plan Div US Army '42-53 geographer Res and Development Div '53. Research US Navy '46-47, US Weather Bur '46-48. Author: Undiscovered Australia '25; Flying the Arctic '28; Under the North Pole '31; Thoughts Through Space (with H Sherman) '42; also articles in field. Arctic Inst NA (councilor 1947)—Royal Geog Society—Royal Metrol Society—Am Metrol Soc—Geophys Union—Ornithol Union—AAAS. 37 W 53rd St., NYC 19.◎

10 WILKINS, William Burdette. Plastics engineering. b'03. Research and development of plastic barrel and machinery for production reinforced plastic molding, molded dingys, etc. Cons since '40. ASME (exec com wood industries div)—Soc Plastics Industries (past chmn reinforced plastics div; exec com)—Soc Plastics Engrs—Forest Products Research Soc (past chmn NE sect; exec com)—Plastic Club (executive bd). 245 E. Ridgewood Av., Ridgewood, N.J.

11 WILKINSON, Robert Elzworth. Vegetable diseases (Potato scab, corn smut, virus diseases). b'16. BA '38 (Ia State Teachers Coll); MS '40 (Ia State Coll); PhD '48 (Cornell U); '33-34 (NW Mo State Teachers Coll). Asst prof Cornell U '48-52 asso prof since '52. American Phytopath Society—Potato Assn Am—Phi Kappa Phi—Sigma Xi. Plant Pathology Department, Cornell University, Ithaca, N.Y.†

12 WILL, Samuel Frederic. Sixteenth century French literature. b'00. BS '23 (U Va); MA '25 (Ind U); '26-27 (Sorbonne); PhD '30 (Yale). Author: A Bibliography of American Studies on the French Renaissance '40. Co-editor: Petite Anthologie: Poesies Francaises '36; Selections from Rousseau's Confessions '37; also articles in field. Prof French and chmn dept French and Italian Ind U since '47. Modern Lang Assn Am—Am Assn Teachers French—Central States Modern Lang Teachers Assn (pres '48-50)—Phi Beta Kappa. Indiana Univ., Bloomington, Ind.◎

13 WILLARD, Charles Julius. Chemical weed control; Alfalfa culture; Sweet clover culture; Lawns; Forage crops; Red clover. b'89. BS '08 (Kan State Coll); BS '10 (U Ill); MS '17 (U Ill); PhD '26 (O State U). Author articles in field. Prof agron O State U since '33, asso in agron O Agrl Expt Sta since '26; sr scientist attache Fgn Service US Dept State '48. Am Soc Agron (F, vp pres elect '53)—AAAS (Fellow)—O Acad Sci(F)—Ecol Society Am—Sigma Xi—Phi Kappa Phi—Gamma Sigma Delta. Department of Agronomy, Ohio State University, Columbus 10, O.†

14 WILLEMS, J. Daniel. Gem cutting. b'88. BS '22 (U Chicago); MD '26 (Rush Med Coll). Study of lapidary techniques; originator faceting device; producer color slides and films on gems and related subjects; lecturer on gems and gem cutting; collection of large gem library in several languages. Author: Gem Cutting '48. Producer moving picture The Story of the Gems. 20 North Wacker Dr., Chgo 6.

15 WILLENBUCHER, Franz Otto. Naval communications. b'97. BS '18 (US Naval Acad); LLB '30 (NY Law Sch); JD '37—(post grad work '40-41 Georgetown U); '46-47 (Nat U Law Sch) '50 (Am U). Commissioned ensign USN '18, advanced through grades to captain '43; special assistant to chief of Naval Communications for policy and legal matters '39-46; participated in establishing Defense Communications Board '39-40; Navy department member coordinating and law committees Board War Communications '41-46; coordinator commercial communications traffic during Normandy invasion '44. Ret Officers Assn—Mil Order World Wars—Am Legion—Heroes of 76—Pi Gamma Mu—Phi Delta Phi. 1616 Eye St., Washington 6.

16 WILLET, Henry Lee. Art and craft of stained glass. b'99. Contributor Encyclopedia Americana. Designer of stained glass since '20, propr Willet Stained Glass Co furnishing windows many churches and bldgs throughout US, including Washington Cathedral, cadet chapel at West Pt, Grace Ch NYC, Gen Patton Memorial San Gabriel Calif; exhibits various galleries; lecturer. AIA—Ch Architects Guild Am—Stained Glass Assn Am (past pres)—Pa Mus Art, 3900 Girard Av., Phila.

17 WILLETT, Elwin L(inton). Physiology of dairy cattle reproduction (Artificial insemination, superovulation, ova transplantation); Animal nutrition (Urea in dairy cow diet, molasses in swine diet); Breeding of swine, poultry, and dairy cattle for adaptation to tropics. b' 13. BS '37 (Mich State Coll); MS '38 (U Neb); PhD '41 (Cornell U). Author articles in field. Dir research Am Found Study Genetics since '46. R.F.D. 5, Madison, Wis.

18 WILLEY, Charles H. Gametogenesis; Cytology (Lymph and excretory system). b'98. AB '22—MS '24—PhD '29 (NYU); '24-28 (Columbia). Research on development of Cryptocotyle (Heterophyidae) in its final host, lymph system of digenetic trematodes, occurrence of Typhlocoelum flavum in North America, excretory system of Typhlocoelum cucumerinum, biological effect of ionized air, morphology of Amphistome cercaria C poconensis Willey from snail Helisoma antrosa, cytology and development of flame cells in redial generation of trematode, embryonating eggs of Zygocotyle lunata, gametogenesis in Zygocotyle lunata. Author articles: Studies on Pathology and Resistance in Terns and Dogs Infected with the Heterophyid Trematode, Cryptocotyle Lingua '42; Life history of Zygocotyle lunata, Apatemon gracilis '41; Gametogenesis in Gorgoderina Attenuata (with Koulish) '47, and others. Instr biol NYU '24-30, asst prof '30-45, associate professor '45-52 prof since '52; research worker Marine Biol Laboratory Woods Hole Massachusetts. NY Acad Sci(F)—AAAS(F)—Am Soc Zool—Am Soc Parasitol—Am Micros Soc—Genetics Soc Am—NY Zool Soc—Phi Beta Kappa—Sigma Xi. New York University, University Heights, NYC 53.

19 WILLEY, Gordon Randolph. Archeology (Peruvian and southeastern United States). b'13. BA '35—MA '36 (U Ariz); PhD '42 (Columbia). Expeditions to Peru '41-42, '46. Author: Excavations in the Chancay Valley, Peru '43; Crooks Mound, A Marksville Period Site in LaSalle Parish, Louisiana '40; Archeology of the Florida Gulf Coast '49; Prehistoric Settlement Patterns in the Viru Valley, Peru; also author several articles. Assistant archeologist Nat Park Service Macon Ga '36-38; archeol La State U Survey '38-39; anthrop Bur Am Ethnol Smithsonian Inst Washington '43-50; Bowditch professor Harvard since '50. Am Anthrop Assn—Soc Am Archeol—Inst Andean Research. Peabody Museum, Harvard University, Cambridge, Mass.

20 WILLEY, L(owell) A(ldro). Aluminum (Alloys, phase relationship, physical properties); Aluminum alloys (Hardening). b'03. Student '22-25 (Wis Mining Sch); MetE '29 (U Minn). Research on phase relationships in binary ternary and quaternary aluminum alloy systems, physical properties of aluminum and its alloys, precipitation hardening phenomenon in aluminum base alloys and its effects. Research metall Aluminum Research Lab since '29. AIMME—Am Soc Metals. Aluminum Research Laboratories, P. O. Box 772, New Kensington, Pa.

21 WILLIAMS, Aubrey Willis. Public welfare administration. b'90. AB '20 (U Cincinnati); '19 (U Bordeaux France). Editor: How Good Is Your Town?; also articles in field. Exec dir Wis Conf of Social Work '22-32; field rep Am Pub Welfare Assn '32-33; field rep Fed Emergency Relief Administrn '33; asst administr FERA and Civil Works Adminstrn '33-35; apptd asst WPA '35, dep adminstr '36; exec dir Nat Youth Adminstr '35-43, adminstr '38-43; dir of orgn Nat Farmers Union '43-45; pub Southern Farmer Montgomery Ala since '45. Ala Farmers Union (pres)—So Conf Endl Fund (pres). c/o Southern Farmer, Montgomery, Ala.

22 WILLIAMS, Bert(ice) C(larence). Plant anatomy and morphology (Meristematic region of root tips). b'09. AB '33 (DePauw U); MA '40— PhD '46 (Ind U). Author articles: Differentiation of Tissues in Root Tips '46; The Structure of the Meristematic Root Tip and Origin of the Primary Tissues in the Roots of Vascular Plants '47; Intercellular Canals in Root Tips of Composite Plants '47, and others. With U Ala since '45, professor biol since '51. Am Bot Soc—AAAS—AAUP—Am Soc Profl Biol—Ala Ednl Assn—So Assn Sci and Industry—Sigma Xi. Biology Department, University of Alabama, University, Ala.

23 WILLIAMS, Carlos F(rost). Fruit breeding, culture, and physiology (Southeastern United States); Raspberries; Blackberries; Muscadine grapes; Peaches. b'94. BS '17 (Pa State); MS '24 (NC State Coll). Introduced Dixie red raspberry, Cameron dewberry. Author articles in field. Hort NC Agrl Expt Sta since '20; hort agt US Dept Agr Bur Plant Industry since '45. AAAS(F)—Am Soc Hort Sci—Sigma Xi—Phi Kappa Phi. Department of Horticulture, North Carolina Agricultural Experiment Station, Raleigh, N.C.†

24 WILLIAMS, Charles Coburn. Petroleum seismology. b'08. AB in geol '32 (U Wichita). Application fundamental acoustic principles to discovery of petroleum through exploration by means of mobile field seismograph; seismic surveys for delineation several types structural anomalies responsible for accumulation petroleum. Party chief, computer Nat Geophys Co in mid-continent and Gulf Coast region '36-39, geol-geophysicist, partner '40-

44; part owner, party chief Seismic Engring Co since '45. Am Assn Petroleum Geol—AIMME—Soc Econ Geophysicists—Am Geophys Union—Permian Basin Geophys Soc. Seismic Engineering Co., 6111 Maple Av., Dallas.

10 WILLIAMS, Clanton Ware. American history (Military, Alabama). b'04. AB '27 (Davidson Coll); MA '28 (U Ala); grad student (Ala Poly Inst, U Chicago); PhD '38 (Vanderbilt U). Directed preparation of hundreds of Army Air Force historical studies, staff monographs and classified histories of organizations; compiled statistics on antebellum Alabama, research on history of Montgomery (Alabama) to 1846. Author: Gist of English History '33 (revised as Topical History of Britain '36); Uncle Sam, A Short History of the USA '43; Chronology of the Cold War, '50; Ideologies in Conflict, '50, '51, '53; also articles in field. Prof hist U Ala since '46. Commd capt AUS '42, advanced to col '42-46, col USAF res '46; chief Hist Div AC/AS Intelligence '44-45; AAF hist '45-46, dir student research Air War Coll '52-53. AHA—Miss Valley Hist Assn—So Hist Assn—Am Mil Inst —Ala Hist Assn. University of Alabama, University, Ala.◎

11 WILLIAMS, Clayton Epes. Virginia (Laws). b'90. LLB '12 (Washington & Lee U); '22, '26 (Columbia U Sch Law). Co-editor: Burks on Pleading and Practice (3rd edit) '34. Asso prof law Washington and Lee U '19-20, prof since '20, dean law sch since '46; mem legislative commn to study possible improvement of adminstrn justice in Va '44-46. Va State Bar Assn— Am Law Inst. Washington and Lee University, Tucker Hall, Lexington, Va.

12 WILLIAMS, Clifford D. Civil and structural engineering (Statically indeterminate structures). b'00. Student '18-20 (Ia State Coll); BS '37 (Fenn Coll). Research on determining stresses in semi-elliptical sewers, fatigue failures, two-span rigid-frame highway bridge. Author: Analysis of Statically Indeterminate Structures '46. Co-author: Structural Design in Metals '48; also articles in field. Pvt practice '20-37, '42-45; head prof structural engring Fenn Coll '37-42; head prof civil engring U Fla '45-52; chief engr Structures Patchen & Zimmerman, engineers, since '52. Internatl Association Bridge and Structural Engineers— ASCE—Soc Exptl Stress Analysis—Am Concrete Inst—Am Ry Engring Assn. First award structural textbook manuscript Joseph Lincoln Arc Welding Found '46. 1021 Hill Top Dr., N. Augusta, S.C.

13 WILLIAMS, Edward Ingham. Mineral wool; Hydraulic lime. b'92. M Mining Engr '14 (Columbia). Chairman mineral wool industry War Council '43-45, also consultant to War Production Board. Author articles in field. Supt Gossan Mines Gen Chem Co '19-25; smelter supt Tenn Copper Co '25-29; operation and sales P R Mallory Co Indianapolis '30-32; sales mgr Riverton Lime and Stone Co Inc Va '32, vp '41, pres and chmn bd dir '42; vp, dir Sky Park Broadcasting Co. Indsl Mineral Wool Inst (pres '44)— Nat Mineral Wool Assn (treas '41-42, pres '45-46)—Am Inst Mining Metall Engrs—Am Soc Testing Materials (com C-7 on lime). Riverton Lime & Stone Co., Inc., Riverton, Va.

14 WILLIAMS, Eliot C., Jr. Ecology (Natural populations, cave fauna, rain forest). b'13. BA '35 (Central YMCA Coll); PhD '40—U fellow '39-40 (Northwestern U). Expedition to Mexico '36, Barro Colorado Island Panama Canal Zone '38, Mammoth Cave, Kentucky. Author articles in field. Asso prof zool Wabash Coll since '48. AAAS—Ecol Soc Am—Entomol Soc Am—Soc Study Evolution—Sigma Xi. Department of Zoology, Wabash College, Crawfordville, Ind.†

15 WILLIAMS, Ernest William, Jr. Transportation economics; Economic geography. b'16. BS '38—MS '39 (Columbia). Author articles in field. Lecturer in transportation Sch Bus Columbia U since '47; cons US Bur Budget since '47; cons Comm on Organization Exec Br of Govt '48, program bur WPB '43-44, US State Dept Conference on European Inland Transport Orgn '44-45; US Strategic Bombing Survey chief transportation div '44-45. Am Geog Soc(F)—Railway and Locomotive Hist Soc—Am Econ Assn—Acad Polit Sci. School of Business, Columbia University, NYC 27.†

16 WILLIAMS, George Dee. Physical anthropology and anatomy (Race mixture). b'98. AB '19—MD '22 (O State U); AM '26—PhD '29 (Harvard); '47 (Mayo Clinic). Made special studies of race mixture in Yucatan; research on social and miscegenetic aspects of tuberculosis in Negroes in Macon (Georgia) and Brazil, Maya-Spanish crosses in Yucatan, measurement of skin color. Author articles: The Basal Metabolism of Mayas in Yucatan '28; Variations in the Arrangement of the Branches Arising from the Aortic Arch in American Whites and Negroes '35 and others. Asst prof anat Washington U Sch Med '29-41, asst prof anthrop '35-41; Am Sch Prehistoric Research France '37; med administrative asst ARC Nat Hqrs '41; Med Corps US Army '41-46; chief Phys Med Rehabilitation VA Hosp, Chamblee, Ga, now chief Phys Med Rehabilitation VA Hospital Phila. Am Assn Phys Anthrop—Am Anthrop Assn—Anthrop Soc Washington—Am Assn Anat—NY Acad Sci— Sigma Xi. Veterans Administration Hospital, Phila.

17 WILLIAMS, Gordon Curran. Chemical engineering. b'08. Regent's fellow '31-32, '32-33—research fellow '33-35—BS '31—MS '32—PhD '35 (U Wis). Research on factors affecting bronzing of Prussian blue pigments, effect of particle size on tinting strength of pigments, fiberglass packing in gas absorbing systems. Author articles in field. Asst prof chem engring U Louisville '36-39, asso prof '39-47, acting head dept '47, prof and head dept since '47. Am Soc Metals—Am Inst Chem Engrs—Am Chem Soc—Am Soc Engring Edn—Tau Beta Pi—Sigma Xi —Phi Kappa Phi. University of Louisville, Speed Scientific School, Department of Chemical Engineering, Louisville, Ky.†

18 WILLIAMS, Harold Hamilton. Ornamental horticulture (Propagation of broad-leaf evergreens, ornamental woody plants of southern California). b'11. BS '33 (Hampton Inst); MS '40— PhD '44 (Cornell U); '47 (U So Calif). Author: Handbook of the Negro Garden Club of Virginia '43; also articles in field. Prof ornamental hort and bot Agrl and Tech Coll NC '35-39; prof, head dept ornamental hort Hampton Inst '41-45; ornamental hort City of Los Angeles Library System and Housing Authority since '47. Am Soc Hort Sci—Va Hort Soc—Nat Intercollegiate Soc Ornamental Hort. 1128 East 80th St., LA 1.

19 WILLIAMS, Horatio Burt. Military engineering; Resuscitation. b'77. AB '00—MD '05—ScD '25 (Syracuse U). Chairman Resuscitation Review Board of Edison Electrical Engineers. With Columbia U '11-42, Dalton prof physiol and exec officer dept '22-37, prof emeritus since '42; dir and tech adv Cambridge Instrument Co Inc. AIEE (safety com)—Am Physiol Soc —Am Phys Soc—Phys Soc of London —Optical Soc—Acoustical Soc Am— Math Soc—AMA—NY Acad Med—So Am Mil Engrs—Am Soc Anesthetists (hon)—Nat Soc Profl Engrs—Con Soc Profl Engrs—Soc Exptl Biol and Med —Sigma Xi—Alpha Omega Alpha. Dingletown Rd., Greenwich, Conn.

20 WILLIAMS, Jesse Wallace. Early transportation routes of the American Southwest. b'91. BA '11—MA '38 (Hardin Simmons U). Author articles: The Van Dorn Trails '41; Mascoso's Trail in Texas '42; Robson's Journey Through West Texas in 1879 '44, and others. Math teacher Wichita Falls Sr High Sch since '16. Rockefeller grant-in-aid '42 for research on north and west Texas trails. Wichita Falls Senior High School, Wichita Falls, Tex.

21 WILLIAMS, Jonathan W(ilbur). Synthetic organic chemistry; Chemotherapy; Ketene. b'10. BS '30 (Baldwin-Wallace Coll); MS '32—PhD '35 (Northwestern U). Author articles in field. Patents pending. Manager biol chemical section Grasselli Chem Dept E I du Pont de Nemours; chem US Naval Research Lab '41-42, tech aide div chem Nat Defense Research Com '42-46. Am Chem Soc—Sigma Xi. Du Pont Experimental Station, Wilmington 98, Del.†

22 WILLIAMS, Judith Blow. Modern English economic history; History of commerce. b'90. AB '12 (Vassar Coll); AM '13—PhD '16 (Columbia). Research in Europe, mostly England, '21-22, '27-28, '29-30, '39. Author: A Guide to the Printed Materials for English Social and Economic History 1750-1850 '26; also articles in field. With Wellesley Coll since '16, prof since '35, chmn hist dept '42-48. AHA—Econ Hist Soc. Guggenheim fellow '27-28, '29-30; Am Assn U Women European fellow '15-16. Wellesley College, Wellesley 81, Mass.†

23 WILLIAMS, Leonard Freeman. Soybeans (Genetics and breeding). b'09. Student '27-31 (U Pittsburgh); BS '32 —MS '34—PhD '38—fellow '35 (U Ill). Author articles in field. Geneticist US Regional Soybean Lab since '36. Am Soc Agron—Genetics Soc Am—Sigma Xi—Gamma Sigma Delta. Waters Hall, University of Missouri, Columbia, Mo.

24 WILLIAMS, Lewis Catlett. Tobacco taxes. b'75. AB—AM '96 (U Va). Author articles in field. Member law firm Williams, Mullen & Hazelgrove since '09. Va State Bar Assn (pres '38-39)—Am Richmond and W Va (hon) Bar Assns—Am Law Inst—Phi Beta Kappa. 1001 E. Main St., Richmond, Va.◎

25 WILLIAMS, Louis Gressett. Marine algae; Marine ecology. b'13. AB '37 (Marshall Coll); MA '40—PhD '48 (Duke U). Author articles: Additions to the Genus Chaetomium of West Virginia '38; The Genus Codium in North Carolina '48, and others. Co-author: A Collection of Marine Algae from Brazil '47; A Study of Agar from Two Brazilian Seaweeds '48. Botanical Society— NC Academy Science—Assn SE Biol— Phycol Soc Americas—Sigma Xi. Department of Biology, Furman University, Greenville, S. C.

26 WILLIAMS, Mae Fisher. Children (Mental deficiency, guidance, juvenile delinquency). b'90. BA '38—MA '49 (U Wash). Work with mentally deficient, exceptional, and problem children. Author articles in field. Now teacher remedial Eng. Am Assn Mental Deficiency. Stewart Junior High School, Tacoma, Wash.

10 WILLIAMS, Margaret Hicks. International information; Educational exchange. Student '28-29 (Columbia). Author articles in field. Ed-in-chief publ sect Press Intelligence OWI '42; chief civ cons on Brit Empire in Mil Intelligence War Dept '43-44; information and liaison officer Europe and occupied areas Dept State '44-46; in Office Information and Ednl Exchange Dept State since '47, in charge Brit Commonwealth and No Europe Sects, Public Affairs Overseas Program Staff, Office Asst Sec State for Public Affairs since '48. Royal Geog Soc(F). Department of State, Washington.†

11 WILLIAMS, Rex Zadock. Engineering mechanics; Missouri pyrite mining industry. b'09. BS '31—BSCE '36 (Mo Sch Mines & Metallurgy); MS '37 (U Wis). Aided in discovery, development and operation Moselle Mine which produced Missouri's largest tonnage of pyrite. Author articles: Technical Problems of the Missouri Pyrite Industry '40; Cooperation Between Departments of Physics and Mechanics in Engineering Colleges '47. Chmn dept mechanics U Mo Sch Mines and Metallurgy since '40, prof mechanics since '44, asst dean since '46. AIME—ASEE—Mo Soc Profl Engrs—Tau Beta Pi—Phi Kappa Phi. Missouri School of Mines and Metallurgy, Rolla, Mo.†

12 WILLIAMS, Robert Case. Lubrication; Plastics; Colloid chemistry. b'03. AB '25—AM '27 (Oberlin Coll); PhD '29 (Stanford). Research on fungicides, colloids, rubber, lubrication and plastics, coordinating research council project CLG-30 outboard motor grease for Armed Services '44-45. Holds 15 patents on lubricants. Author articles in field. Research chemist Firestone Tire & Rubber Co '29-31; Battelle Memorial Inst '31-32; dir research The Ironsides Co '32 dir research and development since '52. ACS—Am Oil Chemists Soc—Soc Plastics Engrs—Wire Assn—Sigma Xi. The Ironsides Co., Box 1999, Columbus 16, O.

13 WILLIAMS, Robert R. Vitamines. b'86. BS '07—MS '08—'11-12—ScD '41 (U Chicago); four other hon degrees. Inventor of processes for making submarine and textile insulations, structure and synthesis of anti-neuritic vitamin, enrichment of flour and bread. Co-author: Vitamin B1 and Its Use in Medicine; also articles in field. Dir of grants Research Corp since '45; chmn Cereal Com Food and Nutrition Bd Nat Research Council since '40 AAAS(F)—Am Chem Soc—Soc Exptl Biol and Med—Soc Biol Chem—Am Philos Soc—Nat Acad Sci. Awards: Willard Gibbs medal '38; Elliott Cresson medal '40; designated Modern Pioneer by NAM '40; Charles Frederick Chandler medal Columbia U '42; Perkin Medal '47. Research Corp., 405 Lexington Av., NYC.☺

14 WILLIAMS, Robley C(ook). Electron microscopy; Spectroscopy; Evaporated film; Stellar temperature; Nebulae contours; Microphotometers; Viruses (Properties). b'08. AB '31—PhD '35 (Cornell U). Patents in the field of Mirror-making by use of evaporated films; development of shadowcasting for electron microscopy. Co-author: (with Hiltner) Spectrophotometric Atlas of Stellar Spectra '44; also articles in field. Dept biochem and Virus Lab U California Berkeley. Am Physical Soc—Optical Soc Am—Electron Microscope Soc Am—AAAS—Soc Study Growth and Development—Am Astron Soc. Longstreth medal Franklin Inst '38. Department of Biochemis-

try, and Virus Laboratory, University of California, Berkeley.†

15 WILLIAMS, Roger John. Biochemistry; B Vitamins; Cancer; Humanics; Alcoholism. b'93. BS '14—ScD (hon) '34 (U Redlands, Calif); MS '18—PhD '19 (U Chicago); D Sc (hon) '42 Columbia). Research in pantothenic acid, folic acid and other B vitamins and growth substances; microbiological assay methods for B vitamins; B vitamins in tissues including malignant tissues; humanics; etiology of alcoholism. Author: Introduction to Organic Chemistry '27, fifth edition (with L F Hatch) '48; Introduction to Biochemistry '31, second edition (with E Beerstecher, Jr) '48; (with R Q Brewster) Laboratory Manual of Organic Chemistry '28, fourth edition '48; Textbook of Biochemistry '38, second edition '42; What To Do About Vitamins '45; The Human Frontier '46. Research chemist Fleischmann Co Chicago '19-20; asst prof chemistry U Ore '20-21, assoc prof '21-27, prof '28-32; prof chemistry Ore State Coll '32-39, U Tex since '39; dir Biochemical Inst at Tex since '41. AAAS(F)—Am Chem Soc—Am Soc Biol Chemists—Am Assn for Cancer Research—Soc Exptl Biology and Medicine—Nat Acad of Scis—NY Acad of Sci—Biochem Soc of London—Phi Beta Kappa—Sigma Xi—Phi Kappa Phi. Awarded Mead-Johnson award of Am Inst of Nutrition '41; Chandler medal Columbia U '42. Department of Chemistry, University of Texas, Austin 12. Tex.

16 WILLIAMS, Van Zandt. Infrared spectrometry; Scientific instrumentation. b'16. Student '32-33 (RI Sch of Design); AB '37 (Brown U); PhD '41 (Princeton U). Research on application of methods and instruments of physics to chemical problems with particular emphasis on infrared techniques; development of scientific instruments for industry and research. Author articles in field. Group leader infrared spectrometry Stamford Research Lab American Cyanamid Co '41-43, asst dir phys div '43-48; dir sales and research The Perkin-Elmer Corporation Norwalk, Conn. Am Phys Soc—ACS—Optical Soc Am—Phi Beta Kappa—Sigma Xi. The Perkin-Elmer Corporation, Norwalk, Conn.

17 WILLIAMS, Virgil C. Low temperature refrigeration; Thermodynamics. BS '34—MS '35 (U Mich). Holds basic patents in fields of flame rock drilling, low temperature processes. Author articles in field. Prof, chmn dept chem engring Northwestern U '45-50; associate director research General Aniline and Film Company since '50; cons engr Asso Am Railroads and Phillips Petroleum Co. Am Chem Soc—Am Inst Chem Engrs (chmn Chicago sect '47-48)—Am Soc for Engring Edn—Sigma Xi—Phi Kappa Phi. General Aniline and Film Co., Central Research Labs., Easton, Pa.

18 WILLIAMS, Walter G(eorge). Old Testament (Language, literature, and archeology); Ancient history (Near East). b'03. BA '28 (Mt Union Coll); BD '31 (Garrett Bib Inst); fellow '31-34—PhD '34 (U Chicago). Research biblical archeology, semitic languages and epigraphy. Mem Northeast Conference Methodist '26-47, Colorado Conference since '47. Author: Adventures in Religious Discovery '48; also articles in field. Ordained Methodist Ch '31; instr Hebrew U Chicago '34-35; instr Bible Baldwin-Wallace Coll '38-40; prof Old Testament lit and rel Iliff Sch Theol Denver since '42; hon lectr Am Sch Oriental Rsrch '51. Am Oriental Soc—Soc Bib Lit and

Exegesis—Nat Assn Bib Instrs. 1370 S. Downing St., Denver 10.

19 WILLIAMS, William Hunt. Phenol manufacturing processes; Chlorination and chemistry of chlorinated benzenes. b'96. BA '19—MS '20—ChE '41 (O State U). Numerous patents and inventions relating to the processing and manufacture of arylamines, diphenyl, phenols, phenolates, salicylic acid and salicylates, chlorination of aromatic compounds, hydrolysis chlorinated benzenes, ammonolysis chlorinated benzenes, wood carbonization. Research chemist, chemical engineer for process development, design and operation chemical equipment and processes. Dow Chemical Co since '19, now prod mngr. AICE—ACS—AAAS—Armed Forces Chem Assn. The Dow Chemical Co., Midland, Mich.

20 WILLIAMS, William Oscar. Viticulture. b'05. BS '31—PhD '40 (U Calif). Research on relation of tracheal sap of the vine to environmental factors '40; carbohydrate relations, and nitrogen and mineral relations within the grapevine; vine injector; mineral nutrition of the grape. Author articles in field. Jr to asst viticulturist U Calif since '40. AAAS(F)—Am Soc Hort Sci—Am Soc Plant Physiol. University of California, Davis, Calif.†

21 WILLIAMSON, Chilton. History of Vermont; Canadian-American relations. b'16. BA '38—MA '39—PhD '48 (Columbia). Author: Vermont in Quandary: 1763-1825 '48; Montpelier '48. Asst Prof hist Barnard Coll since '48. 338 Milbank Hall, Barnard College, Columbia University, NYC 27.

22 WILLIAMSON, Donald E(lwin). Surface roughness; Computers; Instrumentation; Spectroscopy; Infra-red. b '13. AB '35 (Carleton Coll); MS '36 (U Mich). Development mech and electronic roughness measuring instruments; management small production facilities for electronic measurement instruments; development systems for rapid determination of high alloy multicomponent mixtures and solution of atomic dilution equations; development ultraviolet, visible, and infra-red instruments; design diffraction grating ruling engines; improvements in air stabilized spark excitation; experiments on dispersive and non-dispersive analytical instruments, and devices for infra-red measurement and detection. Author articles: Effect of Elastic Modulus on Measurement of Thread Wires '46; Tracer Point Sharpness as Affecting Roughness Measurements '47; Infra-red Interference Filters Used in Calibration '49, and others. Co-author articles: The Profilometer '38; Computing Machines for Spectrochemical Analysis '51. Contributor: Tool Engineers Handbook (1st edit) '49. Mgr profilometer div Physicists Research Co '36-44; research engr U Mich '44-45, Lincoln Park Industries Inc '45-47; chief engr Baird Asso Inc '47-51, asso dir research since '51. ASME—Acoustical Soc Am—Optical Soc Am. Baird Associates, Inc., 33 University Rd., Cambridge 38, Mass.. H: 15 Patriots Drive, Lexington.

23 WILLIAMSON, George Hunt. North American Indian (Dancing, religion, dress, ornamentation). b'26. Student '45-46 (Cornell Coll); '47 (U Den); '47-48 (E NM U); AB '51 (U Ariz); ScD hon '52 (No U Sask Can). Research on dances of Yaqui, Papago, Mayo, Sioux, Chippewa Indians; legends of Fiesta of St. Francis in Mexico, modern Sioux ethnology and a comparison with Chippewa Indians, Indian bead work, crafts, dress, ornamentation and arts. Author: The Hopi and

Zuni Indians '50; also articles in field. Dir Indian lore Lake Hubert camps '50-51; prodn mgr Inter-Tribal Indian Ceremonials '51; dir arts and crafts bd Standing Rock Indian Reservation '52. Soc Am Archeol—Am Anthrop Soc —Ariz Archeol and Hist Soc—Ill State Archeol Soc (Gold Key '48). Silver award for Indian dancing Inter-Tribal Indian Ceremonials '51. H: Granite Dells Lodge, Jerome Route, Prescott, Ariz.

10 WILLIAMSON, Merritt Alvin. Brass metallurgy; Metallic reflection; Rockets. b'16. BE '38—MS '40—PhD '46 (Yale). MS '45 (Cal Inst Tech Pasadena). Author articles: A Study of Etch Markings in Rolled Alpha Brass '40; A Study of Metallic Reflection, Particularly from Silver and Silver Alloys '46. Metall Scovill Mfg Co Waterbury Conn '37-42, Remington Arms Co Bridgeport Conn '42-44; dir tech research Solar Aircraft Co San Diego Cal '46-48; asso dir development Pullman Standard Car Mfg Co Hammond since '46. AIMME—ASTM —Am Soc Metals—Inst Aeronautical Sci—Soc Automotive Engrs—AAAS Inst Metals Brit—Iron and Steel Inst Brit—Am Ordnance Assn—Soc Exptl Stress Analysis—Nat Assn Corrosion Engrs—Conn Acad Arts and Sci—Tau Beta Pi—Sigma Xi—Alpha Chi Sigma —Gamma Alpha. 1414 Field St., Hammond, Ind. H: 9629 S. Seeley Av., Chgo 43.

11 WILLIAMSON, William Rulen. Retirement plans; Social security and budgeting; Demography; Population; Gernotology. b'89. Student '02-05 (Griffith Inst NY); AB '09—AM '10 (Wesleyan U Conn). Actuarial consultant to Costa Rica and Guatemala on social security and insurance '47; technical advisor to Institute Guatemaltico de Seg Soc '47-48; actuarial consultant for US to International Labor Office '37-40. Author: Employee Insurance Plans '48; also articles in field. Casualty Actuarial Society (F) —Am Statis Assn—Am Acad Polit and Social Sci—Acad Polit Sci—Bur Econ Research—Am Econ Assn—Population Assn Am—Eng-Speaking Union —Gerontol Soc Inc—Phi Beta Kappa. 3400 Fairhill Dr., Washington 20.†

12 WILLIBRAND, William Anthony. Goethe, Toller, Werfel; German settlements in Missouri and Oklahoma. b '92. AB '19 (Warrensburg Tchrs Coll Mo); AM '21 (U Chicago); PhD '40 (U Ia.); '19 (U Montpellier), '22-23 (Nat U Mexico), '24-32 (Stanford) '30 (U Heidelberg), '30-31 (U Strasbourg). Author: Ernst Toller, Product of Two Revolutions '41; Ernst Toller and his Ideology '45. Asst and cons modern langs since '45; broadcaster in German radio sta WNAD, Univ Norman Okla '38-51. Modern Lang Assn Am—S Central Modern Lang Assn—Am Assn Tchrs German—Modern Humanities Research Assn—Okla Hist Soc—Delta Phi Alpha. 432 S. Lahoma, Norman, Oklahoma.◎

13 WILLIER, B(anjamin) H(arrison). Embryology (Cell differentiation and growth, hormones and development). b'90. BS '15—DSc '41 (Coll Wooster); '09 (Miami U, Oxford, O); PhD '20 (U Chicago). Role of pigment cells in feather color pattern; role of sex hormones in sex-differentiation of embryo. Co-author: Sex and Internal Secretions '32, '39; The Biology of Melanomas '48; also articles in field. Editor Quarterly Review of Biology since '41. Henry Walters prof zool, chmn dept biol, dir biol labs, Johns Hopkins U since '40; mem ed bd physiol zool since '37, Growth since '40;

mem bd dir Long Island Biol Assn Cold Spring Harbor NY since '42; mem bd trustees Marine Biol Lab Woods Hole Mass '33-50; commr dept research and education State of Md since '41. Nat Acad Sci—AAAS(F)—Am Soc Zool—Am Assn Anatomists—Assn for Study of Internal Secretions—Soc Exptl Biology and Medicine—Am Soc Naturalists—Soc for Growth and Development—Genetics Soc—Phi Beta Kappa—Sigma Xi. Department of Biology, Johns Hopkins University, Baltimore 18. H: 119 Upnor Rd., Balt. 12.†◎

14 WILLIG, Walter Lee. Structural design. b'02. BS in civil engring '26— CE '29 (NYU); MS in civil engring '35 (Poly Inst Brooklyn); grad student (Columbia). Author: Wind Pressure on Building and Bridge Structures '35; Manual of Elementary Surveying Problems '38. Math US Coast and Geodetic Survey LI Sound and Fla '33-34; faculty dept civil engring sch tech Coll City NY since '34, now prof civil engring, chmn dept, and asst dean in charge grad studies. Am Soc CE—Nat Soc Profl Engrs—Am Soc Engring Education—AAUP—Am Soc Photogrammetry—Tau Beta Pi. School of Technology, College City of New Yrok, NYC 31.

15 WILLIHNGANZ, Eugene. Electro-chemistry; Storage batteries. b'03. BS '24—MS '25 (U Notre Dame); PhD '35 (Pa State Coll). Research chem, Calco Chemical Co '25-28; in charge storage battery research, Nat Lead Co '35-45; dir of research, Nat Battery Co since '45. Author articles in field. Am Chem Soc—Electrochem Soc. National Battery Co., Depew, N.Y. H: 54 Park Blvd., Lancaster, N.Y.

16 WILLIS, Charles Francis. Mining engineering and Public Relations. b'85. SB in Mining Engring '06 (MIT); EM '16 (NM Coll of Mines). First dir Ariz Bur Mines Tucson '12; cons supervisor dept indsl relations Phelps Dodge Corp Bisbee Ariz '18; editor and pub The Mining Jour '20-46; editorial writer The Mining World since '46; chm bd of govs Ariz Dept of Mineral Resources; cons Metals Reserve Co. Ariz Council of Defense (in charge war mineral prodn) Ariz Small Mine Operators Assn (state sec)—Am Inst Mining and Metal Engrs—Natl Min Advisory Council—Am Mining Congress—Am Assn Engrs—Soc Promotion Engring Edn. Title and Trust Bldg., Phoenix, Ariz. H: 332 E. Monte Vista Rd.◎

17 WILLIS, Horace Harold. Textiles. b'91. BS '17 (Clemson Agrl and Mech Coll). Co-author: series textiles texts; articles; many spinning test reports and bulletins for US Department Agriculture. Cons cotton mfg and labor relations since '43. Southern Textile Assn—Southeastern Econ Council—SC Acad Sci—Am Soc Testing Materials. Edgewood Av., Clemson, S.C.

18 WILLIS, Sherred Allan. Water transportation; Tides (Bay of Fundy). b'11. BS in civil engring '33 (Lafayette Coll). Research on bulk cargo, high speed loading, and self unloading ships, designed and constructed facilities for two hour loading of 12,000-ton cargo ships on top of tide (range of 50 feet); high volume shipping operations from Bay of Fundy. Engring and mgr US Gypsum Co NS '34-49; cons engr and contractor in own bus since '49. Mining Soc NS(pres '47)— Engring Inst Can—NJ Profl Engrs. Willis Construction, Wykertown Rd., Branchville, N.J.

19 WILLIS, William Hailey. Ancient Greek language; Aeschylus (Greek Linguistics); Military history. b'16. BA

'36 (Miss Coll); MA '37 (Columbia U); PhD '40 (Yale); (Coll Charleston, U Mich). Author: History of the Replacement and School Command '46; also articles in field. Asso to prof Greek and Latin chmn dept Classics U Miss since '47. Am Philol Assn— Classical Assn Middle West and South —Archeol Inst Am—Linguistic Soc Am —Miss Classical Assn. Box 21, Department of Classics, University of Mississippi, University, Miss.†

20 WILLITS, Joseph H(enry). Labor (United States); Industrial relations. b'89. AB '11—AM '12—LLD '37 (Swarthmore Coll); PhD '16—LLD '39 (Pa U). Study of unemployment for Philadelphia, secretary and vice president of Philadelphia Association for Discussion of Employment Problems '15-21; labor relations, US Coal Commission '22-23; President's Emergency Board on Railway Wages '41. Author: The Unemployed in Philadelphia '15; What the Coal Commission Found '25; Studies of Labor Relations for the US Coal Commission '25. Editor: Three volume of Annals of American Academy Political and Social Science. Dean Wharton Sch Finance and Commerce '33-39; dir social sciences Rockefeller Found since '39; emploment supt US Naval Aircraft Factory '17-19; dir Industrial Research dept Pa U '21-39; mem ednl advisory bd John Simon Guggenheim Found '24-28; pres Nat Bur Econ Research '33, exec dir '36-39. Am Acad Arts Sciences—Am Statistical Assn—Am Political Science Assn—Am Econ Assn—Soc Advancement Management. 49 W. 49th St., NYC 20. H: N. Glenville Rd., Armonk, N.Y.◎

21 WILLMAN, Harold Bowen. Stratigraphic and areal geology; Industrial minerals. b'01. AB '26—MA '28—PhD '31 (U Ill). Research on uses of limestone and dolomite, molding sand, feldspar. Author articles in field. With Ill Geol Survey since '26, geol and head areal geol and paleontology div since '45. Geol Soc Am—AAAS—Am Geophys Union—Ill Acad Sci—Sigma Xi. State Geological Survey, Urbana, Ill.†

22 WILLOUGHBY, Edwin Eliott. Library science (Bibliography, rare books); Shakespeare. b'99. AB '22—Litt D '40 (Dickinson Coll); AM '24—PhD '32 (U Chicago). Advisory editor Library Quarterly; advisory editor Compton's Pictured Encyclopedia; special work on reconstruction of printing of old books as an aid to historical and textual studies; studies of early type, woodcuts, illustrations. Author: The Printing of the First Folio of Shakespeare '32; A Printer of Shakespeare; The Times and Books of William Jaggard '34; Fifty Printers' Marks '47; Sr asst Newberry Library Chicago '22-28, reference librarian '29; prof and acting head library sci dept Coll William and Mary '32-35; chief bibliog Folger Shakespeare Library since '35. ALA—Bibliog Soc Am—Bibliog Soc, London—Shakespeare Assn, London. European study as Guggenheim fellow '29-31, on grant from Am Council Learned Socs '34. Folger Shakespeare Library, Washington 3.

23 WILLOUGHBY, Harold Rideout. Iconography of the Greek New Testament; Early Christian archeology and history; Byzantine art and archeology. b'90. AB '15—Squire Teaching Fellow '15-16—AM '16—LittD '46 (Wesleyan U Middletown Conn); BD '18—DD '33 (Garrett Biblical Inst); PhD '24 (U Chicago). Bennett lecturer, Garrett Biblical Institute '36; special lecturer ASOR Jerusalem '37; Haskell lecturer Oberlin Graduate School of Theology '48; iconographic research for American Council Learned Societies in

Leningrad '33; literary executor of Ernest Dewitt Burton and editor of several volumes by him. Author: Pagan Regeneration—A Study of Mystery Initiations in the Graeco-Roman World '29; The Rockefeller McCormick New Testament (Vol III), The Miniatures '32; Codex 2400 and Its Miniatures '33; The Elizabeth Day McCormick Apocalypse (Vol I), A Greek Corpus of Revelation Iconography '40, and others. Editor. Corpus of New Testament Iconography as Illustrated in Byzantine Manuscripts; also articles in field. Prof Christian Origins Federated Theol Faculty, University of Chicago, since 43. Medieval Acad Am Soc Bibl Lit Exegesis (pres Mid-West sect '42-43)—Chicago Soc Bibl Research (pres '45-46)—Chicago Philol Soc—Archeol Inst Am. The Hermitage, Disciples Divinity House, University of Chicago, Chgo 37.◎

10 WILLOUGHBY, William Reid. Canadian-American relations; Canadian history and government. b'10. BA '34—MA '36—scholar '35 (U Ky); PhD '43 (U Wis). Author: The Impact of the United States upon Canada's External Relations '41-42; also articles in field. Research Dept State Washington '43-46; asso prof hist, govt St Lawrence U since '46. Am Polit Sci Assn—Kappa Delta Pi. Social Sci Research Council Grant '52, '53. St. Lawrence University, Canton, N.Y.†

11 WILLS, John Haines. Soluble silicates; Inorganic adhesives. b'08. AB '31 (Haverford Coll); PhD '35 (NYU); '37 (MIT). Research on adhesives, detergents, pigments. Patents in field. Philadelphia Quartz Co since '35, patent mgr since '47. Am Chem Soc. Philadelphia Quartz Co., Public Ledger Building, Phila. 6. H: Cheyney, Pa.

12 WILLS, Walter P(ennypacker). Electrical measuring instruments; Automatic control systems; Electronic circuits. b'08. BS '30—MS '37—EE '42 (Lehigh U). Developed and engineered photo-electric cells and sensitive relays. Patents issued on electrical measuring and control apparatus, electronic measuring apparatus, electric control apparatus for moisture measurement and control, flame detection apparatus, electronic servomechanisms, photocell measuring and controlling apparatus, anti-hunting circuits, DC amplifiers, multiple channel amplifiers, DC to AC conversion systems, self-balancing potentiometers mechanisms and others pertaining to improvements of system of the above types. Mgr research and development engring Brown Instrument Co Phila since '40. AIEE—Inst Radio Engrs. Minneapolis Honeywell Regulator Co., Brown Instruments Division, Wayne and Roberts Ave., Phila. 44.†

13 WILLSON, Edward Arthur. Rubber and resin latex. b'03. BS '27 (U Washington). Holder US patents on making goods from rubber dispersions, rubber coagulant suitable for use on forms for manufacture of gloves and rubber articles, treatment of synthetic latex to improve stability and increase particle size, method of increasing particle size synthetic rubber latex and forming a film therefrom. Author articles in field. Research chem latex B F Goodrich Co Akron '28-36, engring development latex process '36-39, research chem synthetic rubber '41-45, research supervisor '45-47, research supervisor colloid research Brecksville O since '47; research chem rubber Malayan Research Lab Kuala Lumpur FMS '39-41. B. F. Goodrich Research Center, Brecksville, O.

14 WILLSON, Karl Stuart. Electroplating; Chemistry of gases (Physical properties, uses). b'10. AB '31—MA '32 —PhD '35 (Western Reserve U). Patents in field of electroplating pending. Author articles in field. Research chem Harshaw Chem Co since '44. Am Chem Soc—Am Electroplaters Soc—Electrochem Soc—Electrodepositors Tech Soc (London)—Phi Beta Kappa—Sigma Xi. Harshaw Chemical Company, 1945 E. 97 St., Cleveland 6.

15 WILMOT, Royal James. Camellias; Subtropical ornamentals. b'98. BSA '22 (U Tenn); MSA '31 (U Fla). Research on camellia tests, variety names, grafting, and seed. Author articles in field. Asst hort U Fla Agrl Expt Sta since '35. Fla State Hort Soc—Am Camellia Soc (sec since '45)—Phi Kappa Phi. Department Horticulture, Agricultural Experiment Station, Gainesville, Fla.†

16 WILSIE, Carroll Paton. Breeding and adaptation of forage crops. b'02. BS '26 (U Wis); PhD '31—research fellow '29-31 (Mich State Coll); '26-27 (U Ill). Research on adaptation and improvement of sweet corn, soft winter wheat, tropical grasses and legumes, vegetable crops in the tropics, alfalfa, clovers and forage grasses in the Midwest, seed production of forage crops. Author articles in field. Agronomist and asst prof agron and genetics U Hawaii '31-37; research asso prof Ia State Coll '37-46, prof and research prof since '47. Ia Acad Sci—AAAS—Am Soc Agron—Am Genetic Assn—Genetics Soc Am—Sigma Xi—Gamma Sigma Delta. Iowa State College, Ames, Ia. H: 2337 Donald St.

17 WILSON, Arthur Herman. Philadelphia theatre; Shakespeare. b'05. AB '27—AM '29—PhD '31 (Pa U). Research on playgoing in Philadelphia and chronicle of Philadelphia theatre; principle of rest in Shakespeare's plays and their universal appeal; Shakespeare's great theme. Author: A History of the Philadelphia Theater, 1835-1855 '35. Author articles: At the Elbow of the Shakespeare Protagonist '36; At the Stratford Theater '39; English Essays and Essentials '44, and others. Prof and head Eng dept Susquehanna U since '31. Phi Beta Kappa—Northumberland County Hist Soc. Susquehanna University, Selinsgrove, Pa. H: High-Chestnut.†

18 WILSON, Carroll Louis. Research development; International control of atomic energy. b'10. BS '32 (MIT). Head department for handling patents Research Corporation of New York '37-40; assistant to Dr. Vannevar Bush, National Defense Research Committee '40-41, senior liaison officer '41-42; executive assistant to director Office of Scientific Research and Development '42-46; secretary to board of consultants to State Department for preparation of report on plan for international control of atomic energy '46; vice president National Research Corp of Boston '46-47; general mgr US Atomic Energy Commission '47-51; director indsl development department Climax Molybdenum Co since '51. 500 Fifth Av., NYC.†◎

19 WILSON, Charles Morrow. Tropical agriculture; International trade; Tropical medicine. b'05. BA '26 (U Ark). Student and reporter of American tropical agriculture and Latin American affairs, also of Africa and African affairs since '39. Author: Trees and Test Tubes; the Story of Rubber '43; Middle America '44, Central America '41; Ambassador in White '42; Oil Across the World '46; Liberia '47; For World Health '48, and others; also articles in field. Cons Carnegie Instn of Washington, Firestone Plantations Co, Firestone Tire and Rubber Co, United Fruit Co, Cities Service. Am Found for Tropical Medicine (dir) —Liberian Research Inst (dir). Wilson Farm, Putney, Vt.; also Fayetteville, Ark.

20 WILSON, Charles William, Jr. Geology of Tennessee, Montana, Wyoming and Oklahoma; Historical geology. b'05. BA '27—MS '28 (Vanderbilt U); PhD '31 (Princeton U). Author: Geology of Muskogee-Porum District, Oklahoma; The Geology of Nashville, Tennessee; Sub-Chattanooga Stratigraphy of Central Tennessee; also articles in field. Asst to prof Vanderbilt U since '31. Paleontology Soc—Am Assn Petroleum Geol (publication com, com statis exploratory drilling)—Geol Soc Am—Am Geophys Union—Tenn Acad Sci (chem geol and geog sect '46)—Sigma Xi. Department of Geology, Vanderbilt University, Nashville, Tenn.†◎

21 WILSON, Coyt T(aylor). Peanuts (Diseases, seed treatments). b'13. BS '38—MS '41 (Ala Poly Inst); PhD '46 (U Minn). Author articles in field. Plant path, prof bot and plant path Ala Agrl Expt Sta and Ala Poly Inst '46-51, now asst dean sch agr asst dir agrl expt sta. Am Phytopath Soc—Am Soc Plant Physiol—Sigma Xi—Gamma Sigma Delta. School of Agriculture, Alabama Polytechnic Institute, Auburn, Ala.†

22 WILSON, Eddie Watts. Gourds; Folklore. b'85. BS in library sci '32 (Geo Peabody Coll for Tchrs). Studies in history, legend, symbolism, music, art of gourds; nature and symbolism in American Indian folklore. Author: The Gourd in Folk Literature '47. Author articles: The Gourd in Southern History; The gourd in Hoosier land; The owl and the American Indian; and others. Asso ed Gourd Seed since '46; contbg ed The Chat bulletin Carolina Bird Club since '47. Gourd Soc Am—Am Folklore Soc—Southeastern Folklore Soc—Cal Folklore Soc—Wilderness Soc. Box 966, LA 53.

23 WILSON, Elizabeth Webb. Actuarial mathematics; Compulsory health insurance. b'96. AB with distinction '17 (George Washington U); AM '20—PhD '34 (Radcliffe Coll). Author: Compulsory Health Insurance (Nat Indsl Conf Bd) '47; also articles. Asso actuarial mathematician Social Security Bd '43-44. Am Math Soc—Am Statis Assn—Am Econ Assn—Econ Soc —AAUW—AAAS—Inst Math Statisticians—Phi Beta Kappa—Royal Econ Soc Brit (F). Member International Actuarial Congress London '27, Rome '34, London '48. Alumni Achievement award George Washington U '42. 1 Waterhouse St., Cambridge, Mass.†◎

24 WILSON, Emily Loyd. History of Florida (St Augustine). b'68. Ed pvt schs. Collector books, maps, manuscripts and historical papers on St Augustine; compiled English index of ancient parish records 1594-1763, including marriage records, baptisms, and burials. Author article: Souvenirs of St Augustine under Three Flags '20. Research worker advancing to librarian St Augustine Hist Soc '19-31, hist since '31. Fla Hist Soc—Hist Assn So Fla. H: 280 St. George St., St. Augustine, Fla.

25 WILSON, E(velyn) Faye. Medieval history (Twelfth and thirteenth centuries); Medieval Latin and epithalamia; John of Garland; Mary legends. b'99. BA '21 (Beloit Coll); MA '24 (U Washington); PhD '30 (U Calif); '29-30 (Radcliffe Coll)—'31-32 (Am Acad, Rome). Author: The Stella Maris of

John of Garland '46; The Spiritual Georgics of John of Garland '33; Pastoral and Epithalamium in Latin Literature '48. Research European libraries '30-33, '38; asst prof hist U Me '33-36; asso prof '36-41; asst prof hist Wellesley Coll '41-44, associate professor '44-47 now professor since '47. AHA —Medieval Academy Am—College Art Assn —Phi Beta Kappa. Awarded Alice Mary Longfellow fellowship, Radcliffe; fellow Am Council of Learned Socs. Wellesley College, Wellesley 81, Mass. H: 2 Orchard Apts.

10 WILSON, Francis Henry. Biology and taxonomy of Mallophaga; Color changes in lizards; Biology of Amphiuma. b'02. BS '23—MS '25—PhD '31 (Cornell U). Author articles in field. Prof biol and head dept Asso Colleges of Upper NY since '46. Am Soc Zool—Entomol Soc Am—AAAS— Sigma Xi—Phi Delta Kappa. Department of Biology, Champlain College, Plattsburg, N.Y.†

11 WILSON, G(eorge) Bernard. Chromosome structure and aberrations; Cytology of the banana. b'14. Student '31-33 (U New Brunswick); BSc '35 (Acadia U); PhD '39 (McGill U); '35-36 (UNB). Author articles in field. Asso prof bot Mich State Coll since '50. Genetics Soc Am—Am Soc Human Genetics—Biometrics Soc. Department of Botany, Michigan State College, East Lansing, Mich.

12 WILSON, George P(ickett). Regional speech; Localisms; Dialect (American English); Folklore) Philology. born '88. AB '13 (Univ NC); AM '19 (Columbia); Mary Adams fellow '22-23 (U Wis). Author articles in field. Associate editor: The Frank C. Brown Folklore Collection (four vols). Head Eng dept and dir summer sch Guilford NC Coll '24-27; asso prof Eng Woman's Coll U NC '27-38, prof Eng since '38. Modern Lang Assn Am—So Atlantic Modern Lang Assn (com dialectal studies '35-42, chmn '43-44, com orgn and work Eng lang '42-44, co-chmn folklore com '47, 49)—Am Dialect Soc (chmn con regional speech and localisms '42-52 sec-treas since '43-52, originator and editor publication '44-52)—Am Folklore Society—SE Folklore Soc (vp '47, '49)—NC Folklore Soc (pres '37-43). 1813 Rolling Rd., Greensboro, N.C.

13 WILSON, Harry Robert. Choral music (Composition and arrangement); Choral programs. b'01. BS '26 (Manhattan State Coll Kan); MA '32— EdD '37 (Columbia); fellowships composition '30-32 conducting '34-37 (Juilliard Grad Sch Music). Author: Choral Arranging; Music in the High School; Lead a Song; Guide for Choral Conductors; Choral Program Series. Co-author: (with P Von Bodegraven); School Music Conductor. Editor, arranger 25 song collections for choral groups; composer-arranger 250 compositions and arrangements. In charge music activities New Coll Columbia '32-37, prof music edn, in charge vocal and choral activities Tchrs Coll since '37; guest lectr music edn.; guest conductor choral festivals. Music Tchrs Nat Assn—Music Educators Nat Conf —Nat Assn Tchrs Singing—Nat Assn Composers and Condrs—Am Soc Composers Authors and Pubs—Delta Tau Delta—Phi Mu Alpha. Teachers College, Columbia University, NYC 27.†☺

14 WILSON, Ira T(emplin). Limnology; Sedimentation. b'95. Student '16-18 (Lake Forest Coll); AB '19— '21—PhD '23 (Ind U). Developed apparatus and methods of securing cores of sediments to original bottom of lakes. Author: A Study of Sedimenta-

tion of Winona Lake; The Accumulated Sediment in Tippecanoe Lake '38. Co-author: The Distribution of the Chemical Constituents in the Accumulated Sediment of Tippecanoe Lake '41; Pollen Study of Sediments from Douglas Lake, Cheboygan County and Middle Fish Lake, Montmorency County, Michigan '43; also articles in field. Prof head dept biol Heidelberg Coll Tiffin Ohio since '23. Am Soc Zool— Am Soc Limnol and Oceanog—Soc Econ Paleontol and Mineralogy—Ind Acad Sci—Ohio Acad Sci—Mich Acad Sci Arts Letters. Heidelberg College, Tiffin, O.

15 WILSON, J. Christy. Missions (Islam and the Near East). b'91. AB '14 (U Kan); AM '19—ThM '26 (Princeton); DD '34 (Emporia Coll Kan), '34 (Lafayette Coll Pa). Ordained to ministry Presbyn Ch '18; evangelistic missionary under Presbyn Bd Fgn Missions stationed Tabriz Azerbaijan Iran '19-40; chmn Nr East Relief Com for Persia '21-23; chmn Nr East Christian Council '37-40; teacher defense courses Persian Columbia '41-42; dir field work, asso prof ecumenics Princeton Theol Sem since '41; interpreter, piegraphist, 2 expdns of Iranian Inst NY; interpreter, lang aid to Dr Frank Laubach in Literacy Campaign in Afghanistan '51. Waldensain Aid Soc— Phi Beta Kappa—Delta Chi. Author: (books in Persian lang) Commentary on the Epistle to the Hebrews '33; The Bible and Evangelism '36; The History of Iranian Art (at request of Imperial Ministry of Edn of Iran) '38; (in English) Introducing Islam '50; The Christian Message to Islam '50; Apostle to Islam, Biography of Samuel M Zwemer) '52. Missionary editor and writer weekly column The Presbyn '35-48; adv editor The Muslim World. 29 Alexander St. Princeton, N.J.†☺

16 WILSON, Jack Turner. X-Ray (High energy). b'10. BS (Coll of Emporia Kan); student (Kan State Coll Applied Sci Manhattan, U Chicago). Research on solar radiation in the radio frequency spectrum and its effect upon long distance electric power transmission and radio communication; study super-voltage x-ray and application to industrial radiography and inspection; director development Am form of artificial kidney for clinical application to relieve temporary human renal failure. Chief physicist Allis-Chalmers Mfg Co since '44. Soc for Non-Destructive Testing—Am Inst EE. Allis-Chalmers Manufacturing Co., P.O. Box 512, Milw 1.

17 WILSON, J(ames) Dean. Control of vegetable diseases (Fungicides); b'95. Fellow '22-23 (The Johns Hopkins U). Developed an auto-irrigating pot for growing plants at pre-determined soil moisture content, an evaporation-index meter for determining how often lawns and vegetables should be watered. Author articles in field. Asst in plant physiol Johns Hopkins '23-26; asst plant path O Agrl Expt Sta '26-30, associate professor '30-50 full professor since '50. Am Phytopath Soc (Chairman of a nation-wide cooperative study of new fungicidal dust and sprays control plant disease)—Ecol Soc Am—Am Soc Plant Physiol—AAAS. Ohio Agricultural Experiment Station, Wooster, O.

18 WILSON, James French. Wool technology. b'92. BS '13—LLD (U Wyo); MA '16 (U Mo). Investigated pastoral industry in Australia and New Zealand; studied methods of determining yield of wool by scouring and invented devices to accomplish same.

Author articles in field. Prof animal husbandry U Calif. Am Soc Animal Production—AAAS—Calif Wool Growers Assn (hon dir)—Sigma Xi. 118 Animal Science Building, University of California, Davis, Calif.†

19 WILSON, James Walter. Biology; Cytology; and Embryology. b'96. PhB '18—PhD '21 (Brown U). Research on selective absorption of potassium by animal cells, relation of photosynthesis to production of Vitamin A in plants, disintegration of Planaria maculata in potassium cyanide in pond water and diluted Ringer's fluid, device for perfusion of mammalian heart, mitotic figures in perfused mammalian liver, nuclear phenomena in mouse liver. Author articles in field. Asst in biol Brown U '18-19, instr '21, asst prof '21-29; asso prof '29-44, prof, chmn dept since '44. NY Acad Sci—Soc Exptl Biol and Med—Soc Zool—Am Assn Anat — Soc Study Development and Growth—Genetics Soc Am—Am Society Naturalists—Am Microscopical Society —Am Soc Exptl Path—Biometric Soc— AAAS. Biology Department, Brown U., Providence 12. H: 282 Doyle Av., Providence 6.†☺

20 WILSON, John Andrew. Texas vertebrate paleontology (Permian and Triassic amphibians and reptiles); Idaho vertebrate paleontology (Mammals). b'14. AB '37—PhD '41 (U Mich). Research on a new dog from the Miocene of Colorado, interpretation of the skull of Buettneria with special reference to the cartilage and soft parts, an amebelodon from Malheur County, Oregon; preliminary notice of a new Miocene vertebrate locality in Idaho; Cope's types of fossil fish in the collection of Bureau of Economic Geology; a small amphibian from the Triassic of Howard County Texas. Author articles in field. Asso prof geol, vertebrate paleontology of Tex U since '50. AAAS—Geol Soc Am(F)—Soc Vertebrate Paleontol—Paleontol Soc— Sigma Xi. Department of Geology, University of Texas, Austin 12, Tex.†

21 WILSON, John Bennett. Sewage treatment; Water supply; Gas engineering. b'03. BS in civil engring '27 (Rose Poly Inst). Engr L S Finch Indianapolis '36-40; cons engr since '40. Am Water Works Assn—Central States Sewage Works Assn—Nat Soc Profl Engrs—Am Soc CE. 524 K. of P. Bldg., Indpls 4.

22 WILSON, John Human. Petroleum exploration. b'00. Student '16-18 (Clarendon Coll); '18-19 (So Methodist U); EM '23 (Colo Sch Mines). Exploration campaigns Canada, US, Mexico; exploration for oil gas and other minerals by geophysical methods including use of magnetic, gravimetric, seismic, electrical methods; studies correlation between geological and geophysical data; geological interpretation of geophysical data. Invented magnetometer attachment for Brunton compass. Geol Midwest Refining Co Denver '23-26; geol and geophysicist Huasteca Petroleum Co Tampico Mexico '26-28; asst prof geophysics Colo Sch Mines '28-30; cons geophysicist Denver '30-34; pres Colo Geophys Corp '34-37; vp Independent Exploration Co '37-50; exploration cons since '51. Am Assn Petroleum Geol—Soc Exploration Geophysicists—AIMME—Sigma Gamma Epsilon. 750 West 5th St., Fort Worth 2.

23 WILSON, John Nicholas. Public health and sanitary biology; Plankton and stream bottom fauna. born '15. BA '35—MA '38; '39-40 (Minn U); '38 (Mich U). Research on plankton; biology of Hays Process of sewage treatment; made bacteriological studies of water and milk supplies, shellfish sanitation and restaurant sanitation. Author articles in field. Asst biol Minn Dept Health Div Sanit '35-37; asst biol Minn Dept Health Div Sanit '40-44, asso biol Div Water Pollution Control '46-49; biol USPHS Cincinnati '49-51 Portland Ore since '51. N W Sci Soc—Am Soc Limnology and Oceanography—Federal Sewage Research Assn. U. S. Public Health Service, Pacific N W Drainage Basins Office, Swan Island Bldg. 24, Portland 18, Ore.

10 WILSON, John Weldon. Colemanite. b'88. EM '19 (U Tex). Research on mining and concentration of colemanite (calcium borate) ores. Gen supt West End Chem Co '22-30. Am Soc Profl Engrs—AIMME. P.O. Box 350, Las Vegas, Nev.

11 WILSON, Joseph Edward. Stabilization of plastics to heat and light, Gas-impervious plastics. b'20. BS '39 (Univ Chicago); PhD '42 (Univ Rochester). Radiochemistry and nuclear physics, photochemistry. Co-inventor of impervious plastic gas cell fabric for dirigibles. Author articles in field. Research chem plastics Goodyear Aircraft Corp '42-46; sr research chem Argonne Nat Lab '46-47, Firestone Tire and Rubber Co '47-50; Bakelight Division Union Carbide and Carbon Corp since '50. Am Chem Soc—Phi Beta Kappa—Sigma Xi. Bakelight Division, Union Carbide and Carbon Corp, Bound Brook, N.J. H: 958 Winton Av., Akron, O.

12 WILSON, Katherine Schmitkons. Plant morphogenesis and relation of vitamins to plant development. b'13. BA '33 (Oberlin Coll); MS '35 (Northwestern U); PhD '44 (Yale). Author articles in field. Theresa Seessel research fellow biol scis Yale U '48-49, research f plant sci Yale U since '50. Bot Soc Am—AAAS—Sigma Xi. Department of Botany, Yale University, New Haven 11.

13 WILSON, L. Kenneth. Mining engineering; Geology (Ore and mineral deposits, structure, economics, metal mining). b'10. AB '32 (Stanford U). Author articles in field. Chief geol Am Smelting and Refining Co Southwestern Div admin of exploration activity in Ariz, NM, Tex, So Calif since '45. Geol Soc Am(F)—Soc Econ Geol —Am Inst Mining Engrs—Ariz Small Mine Operators Assn—NM Miners and Prospectors Assn. American Smelting and Refining Company, 813 Valley Bank Building, Tucson.

14 WILSON, Leonard Richard. Geology; Stratigraphy; Paleontology. b'06. Student '28-29 (U Leeds Eng); PhB '30—PhM '32—PhD '35 (U Wis); '39-40 (Ohio State U). Professor and head dept geol and mineral U Mass since '46. Ia Acad Sci (life F, ed '41-46)—Geol Soc Am(F)—Soc Econ Paleont and Mineral—Bot Soc Am—Soc Am Plant Taxonomists. Department of Geology and Mineralogy, University of Massachusetts, Amherst, Mass.

15 WILSON, Leonard S(eltzer). Geography (Map intelligence); Cartography. b'09. AB '32—MS '33—PhD '36 (Mich U). Developed map services for OSS; assembled and directed a centralized map intelligence agency for US Army and Navy, Great Britain, Netherlands; systematized first central map intelligence organization in US Government. Author articles in field. Author: Map Intelligence '48. International Secretariat United Nations Conf Internat Organization '45; chief and organizer OSS Map Div European Theater Operations London '44; chief Map Intelligence branch Dept State '45-47; prof

geog Carleton Coll '47-49; on leave as dir geog br mil intel sect GHQ FEC US Army Tokyo since '49. Assn Am Geog—Am Cong Surveying and Mapping—Washington (DC) Geog Club— Royal Geog Soc(F) — Am Geograph Soc(F) — AAAS(F) — Sigma Xi(F). Earhart research fellow '34-35. Carleton College, Northfield, Minn. H: 107 Nevada St.

16 WILSON, Levi Thomas. Mathematics (Analysis). b'85. AB '09—AM '10 (Washington and Lee U); AM '13 (Columbia); PhD '15 (Harvard). Co-author: Elementary Mechanics '26; Analytical and Applied Mechanics '43; Manual of Mathematics and Mechanics '47. Instr later sr prof math US Naval Acad since '17, dean dept since '41. Am Math Soc—Phi Beta Kappa. United States Naval Academy, Annapolis, Md.

17 WILSON, Milburn Lincoln. Wheat; Farm management. b'85. BSA '07 (Ia State Coll Ames); MS '20 (U Wis); DSc '35 (Mont State Coll); DAgr hon '40 (ND Agrl Coll). Author: Farm Relief and the Domestic Allotment Plan '33; Democracy Has Roots '39. Co-author: (with others) Agriculture in Modern Life '39. Extension agrl economist Mont State Coll '22-24, prof and head dept agrl econs '26-33; in charge div farm management and cost accounting USDA '24-26; cons on large-scale wheat farming USSR '29; chief wheat prodn sect AAA USDA '33, asst sec agr '34-37, under sec agr '37-40, dir extension work since '40; dir div subsistence homesteads US Dept Interior '33-34. AAAS—Am Farm Econ Assn(pres '25)—Epsilon Sigma Phi— Phi Kappa Phi—Alpha Zeta. U.S. Dept. of Agriculture, Washington. H: 14 Rosemary St., Chevy Chase 15, Md.©

18 WILSON, Owen Meredith. Eighteenth century American history; Western railroads (Denver and Rio Grande Western); History of the American West; American revolution. b'09; BA '34 (U Utah); PhD '43 (U Calif); '36-37 (U Heidelberg, U London). Author: History of the Denver and Rio Grande Railroad 1870-1901. Prof hist, dean U College U Utah since '47. AHA—Utah Humanities Assn — Phi Beta Kappa. University of Utah, Salt Lake City.

19 WILSON, Perry William. Bacterial biochemistry; Biological nitrogen fixation. b'02. BS '28—MS '29—PhD '32 (U Wis). Author: Biochemistry of Symbiotic Nitrogen Fixation '40. Co-author and co-editor: Respiratory Enzymes '39. Editor: A Symposium on Respiratory Enzymes '42; also articles in field. Two patents in field of bacterial fermentation. Prof agrl bact U Wis since '45. Soc Am Bacteriol—Am Chem Soc—Soc Am Biol Chem—Biochem Soc (Eng)—AAAS—Sigma Xi. Guggenheim fellow Europe '36. Department of Agricultural Bacteriology, University of Wisconsin, Madison 6, Wis.†

20 WILSON, Raymond Edgar. Temperature measurements. b'15. AB '37 (Reed Coll); PhD '42 (U Washington). Author articles in field. Asst prof physics U Alaska '41-42; asso prof physics George Washington U '46-47; Nat Bur Standards chief of Temperature Measurements Sect since '47. Physicist USN, underwater ordnance '42-46. Am Phys Soc—AAAS—Washington Philos Soc—Sigma Xi—Sigma Pi Sigma. National Bureau of Standards, Washington 25.

21 WILSON, Robert W(arren). Mammalian paleontology (Fossil rodentia); Cenozoic stratigraphy. b'09. BS '30— MS '32—PhD '36—research fellow '36-37 (Yale). Author articles in field. Asso prof zool and asso curator vertebrate paleontol U Kan since '47. Geol

Soc Am(F)—Paleontol Soc(F)—NY Acad Sci(F)—Soc Vertebrate Paleontol —Am Soc Mammalogists. Nat Research fellow '46-47. Museum of Natural History, University of Kansas, Lawrence, Kans.†

22 WILSON, Roy Arthur. Paleography, geomorphology and regional geology of Latin America and Africa; Tertiary soft rock geology. b'91. MS '17 (U Mont); PhD '21 (U Chicago). Author articles in field. Geol and staff geol Gulf Oil Corp since '37. Geol Soc Am(F)—Soc Econ Geol(F). Gulf Oil Corporation, New York Production Division, 17 Battery Place, NYC 4.

23 WILSON, Thomas James. Seventeenth century French literature (Fiction). b'02. AB '21—AM '24 (U NC); D Phil '27 (Oxford U). Translator: The Letters of Romain Rolland and Malwida von Meysenburg '33; also articles in field. Dir Harvard U press since '47. Am Inst Graphic Arts—Phi Beta Kappa. Harvard University Press, 44 Francis Av., Cambridge 38, Mass.

24 WILSON, Walter T. Hydrology; Climatology (Snow); Meteorology. b'09. BS '30—MS '32—'32-33 (U Wis); '40-45 (U S Dept Agri). Author: many unpublished reports on hydro-climatology and terrain influences on areal distribution of precipitation and other weather elements; also various papers on snow; cooperative snow investig of the Corps of Engineers and Weather Bureau, studying influence of snow on streamflow in mountainous regions of US, hydrologist Weather Bur San Francisco since '39-52. Am Geophysical Union — Am Meteorol Soc (profl) — AAAS—Amer Statis Assoc—Am Soc Civil Engineers U.S. Weather Bureau, Washington 25.

25 WIMBERLY, Ben Lowry. Topography; Photography (Aerial). b'20. BS '50 (U Neb). Compilation of charts from maps and aerial photographs; in charge evaluation visual and analytical aerial photographs; drawing of maps and graphs for illustration fundamentals of economic geography; completion plan and profile charts from surveyors notes. Contributor: Fundamentals of Economic Geography (3rd edit) '50. Sr draftsman US Coast and Geodetic Survey Processing Office Norfolk Va '42-44; draftsman highway design division Neb State Highway Dept Rds and Irrigation since '50. Photogrammetrist AUS Air Force '44-46. H: 3201 R St., Lincoln 3, Neb.

26 WIMBERLY, Lowry Charles. Folklore (English and Scottish ballads); Regional literature. b'90. AB '16—AM '20—PhD '25 (U Neb); '18 (Columbia). Author: Death and Burial Lore in the English and Scottish Popular Ballads '27; Folklore in English and Scottish Ballads '28. Co-author: Using Better English '37; also articles in field. Editor: Prairie Schooner, regional magazine. Prof Eng U Neb since '28. Modern Lang Assn Am—Am Folk-Lore Soc —Neb Writers Guild—Phi Beta Kappa. 3201 R St., Lincoln, Neb.©

27 WINCH, Robert Francis. Social psychology of courtship and marriage. b'11. AB '35 (Western Reserve U); PhD '42—AM '39 (U Chicago). Research on relation between neurotic tendencies and adjustment in engagement, relation between nature of parent-child relationships and offspring's progress in courtship, relation between loss of a parent and progress in courtship; research and writing on personality characteristics of engaged and married couples '41, relation between courtship behavior and attitudes towards parents among college men '43, interrelations between certain social background and parent-son factors in a study of courtship among collegemen '46; primary factors in a study of courtship '47. Articles in field. Asso prof sociol Vanderbilt U '46-48; asso prof sociol Northwestern U since '48. Am Sociol Soc—So Sociol Soc—Am Psychol Assn—Am Statis Assn. Social Sci Research Council fellow '45-46. Author: The Modern Family, '52; sr editor: Selected Studies in Marriage and the Family, '53. Department of Sociology, Northwestern University, Evanston, Ill.

10 WINCHELL, Donald L(ind). Naval ordnance; Armor plate; Projectiles; Missiles. b'14. BA '39 (Denison U); '36-37 (Kent State U). Research and development in naval ordnance specializing in armor plate, projectiles and missiles. Author articles in field. Research lab asst Republic Steel Corp Canton O '33-36; asst research engr Timken Steel & Tube Co '36-38; staff research engr Battelle Memorial Inst Columbus '39-41; sr metall engr US Naval Proving Ground since '45. Lt comdr USNR '41-45. Am Soc Metals. United States Naval Proving Ground, Dahlgren, Va.†

11 WINCHELL, Horace. Diamond tool-designing; Vectoral hardness of crystals; Sapphire; Corundum; Ruby; Spinel; Quartz (Crystal cutting, production and properties); Industrial uses of gem stones; Physical properties of crystals; Crystallographic design (Dies, tools, oscillating crystals). b'15. AB '36—MA '36 (U Wis); MA '37—PhD '41 (Harvard). Author articles in field. Asso prof mineralogy Yale since '51. Mineral Soc Am—Geol Soc Am—AAAS —Am Crystal Soc. Department of Geology, Yale University, New Haven.†

12 WINCHESTER, Alice. Antiques; Interior decoration. b'07. AB '29 (Smith Coll). Editor: Living with Antiques '41. Editor The Magazine Antiques NYC since '38. Author: American Antiques in Words and Pictures, A Handbook '43; How to Know Am Antiques '51. Am Inst Decorators (asso mem)—Phi Beta Kappa. 601 Fifth Av., NYC.

13 WINCHESTER, Clarence Floyd. Effects of environmental conditions, hormones, and nutrition on metabolism, growth and production of fowl, horses, swine and cattle. b'01. BS '24 —MS '35 (U Cal); PhD '39 (U Mo). Use of radioactive isotopes as tracers and therapeutic agents in endocrine, nutrition and growth studies of fowl and swine; influences of drugs, enzymes, hormones and medicaments on livestock prodn; relationships among environmental conditions, seasonal rhythms, hormone production and livestock production; made studies on energy, protein and dry matter requirements of horses, and of hormonal applications to livestock production for National Research Council. With U Cal '32-37, U Mo '37-42; asso prof U Fla '47-49; physiologist, animal husbandry div Bureau Animal Industry USDA. ACS—Soc Exptl Biol and Med—Am Soc Animal Prodn—AAAS—Sigma Xi. Animal Husbandry Division, Bureau of Animal Industry, US Department of Agriculture Research Center, Beltsville, Md.

14 WINCOR, Richard. Copyright. b'21. AB '42—LLB '48 (Harvard). Author: How to Secure Copyright '50; The Nature of the Authors' Right (Burkan prize '48). With Hays, St John, Abramson & Schulman, attys for Author's League, Dramatists Guild, Songwriter's Protective Assn., etc., '48-49; with Lewis & K Mound, attys for Sid Caesar, Your Show of Shows since '49. 655 Madison Av., NYC.

15 WINDING, Charles C(alvert). Plastics; Rubbers; Synthetic Adsorbents. b'08. B ChE '31—PhD '35 (U Minn.) Pats synthetic absorbents. Co-author: Plastics, Theory and Practice (with R L Hasche) '47. Prof chem engring Cornell since '44, asst dir Sch Chem Eng since '47. Am Inst Chem Engrs—Am Chem Soc—Am Soc Engring Edn—Sigma Xi—Tau Beta Pi. Olin Hall, Cornell University, Ithaca, N.Y.†◎

16 WINDROW, J. E. Community agy planning. b'99. Author: John Barrien Lindsley '37. Editor Peabody Alumni News '25-28, editor Peabody Reflector '28-37, since '43, bus Peabody Journ Edn since '33, chmn appointment office and pub relations bus '32-37, prof edn and dir Peabody Demonstrn Sch '37, prof edn. dir pub services since '47. Am Assn Sch Adminstrs—NEA— Delta Phi Kappa—Kappa Delta Pi— Phi Sigma Pi. Peabody College, Nashville 4.◎

17 WINESANKER, Michael Max. English comic and eighteenth century opera. b'13. MusB '33 (U Toronto); MA '41 (U Mich); L Mus TCL '40 (Trinity Coll London); PhD '44 (Cornell U). Research on eighteenth century English comic opera '43-45. Author: Musico-Dramatic Criticism of English Comic Opera 1750-1800 '49; The Record of English Musical Drama, 1750-1800. Instr piano and musical theory Hambourg Conservatory of Music Toronto '40-42; prof musicol U Tex '45-46; asso prof music lit and musicol Tex Christian U '46-49, prof music lit and musicol since '49. Am Musicol Soc (past pres Tex chap)— Medieval Acad Am—Music Tchrs Nat Assn—Ft Worth Music Tchrs Assn. Grants-in-aid Am Council Learned Socs and Carnegie Foundation (conjunction with Tex Christian U). School of Fine Arts, Texas Christian University, Fort Worth, Tex.

18 WING, Henry Joseph. Chemistry of cosmetics, lacquer and rubber. b'98. BSc '21—MSc '25 (U Neb); PhD '29— fellow '28-29 (State U Ia). Author: Allergy Due to Nail Polish; Liquid Nail Polish; Pressure in Bottles. Asso prof chem Doane Coll '24-26, SD State Coll '26-28; asso chemist US Bur Standards Washington '29-34; chemist E I duPont de Nemours & Co '34-38; Johnson & Johnson '39-44; research dir Northam Warren Corp Stamford Conn since '44. Am Chem Soc—Chem Club—FAIC— FAAAS. Northam Warren Corporation, Stamford, Conn.

19 WING, Merle W(esley). Ants and ant guests. b'16. BS '39—MS '40 (Univ of Me); '40-'42 (Univ of Minn). Research on ants, ant guests, general entomology; preparing bibliography and catalogue formicidae and myrmecophiles. Author articles in field. Instr and asst prof entomolgy and zool NC State Coll Raleigh '42-'45, since '46; acting asst prof zool Tulane Univ '45-46. Entomol Soc Am—Entomol Soc Ontario—Soc Systematic Zool—NC Acad Sci—Entomol Soc Washington. North Carolina State College, Raleigh, N.C.

20 WINGARD, Samuel Andrew. Plant diseases and their control (Bean rust, tobacco ring spot and blue mold, apple root rot, peanuts, seed treatment). b'95. BS '16—MS '17 (Ala Poly Inst); PhD '25—Smith fellow '24-25 (Columbia). Author articles in field. Plant path Va Agr Expt Sta, now head dept plant path and physiol Va Poly Inst. AAAS— Am Phytopath Soc—Am Bot Soc—Va Acad Sci—Sigma Xi—Phi Kappa Phi— Gamma Sigma Delta. Won the Horsely Research prize of the Va Acad Sci '33.

Virginia Polytechnic Institute Blacksburg, Va.†

21 WINKLER, Albert Herman, Jr. Carburetors and induction systems (Automotive). b'08. BS '30—ME '37 (Ill Inst Tech). Issued 18 patents pertaining to automotive charge forming devices, carburetors, automatic chokes, engine and starting switch controls, and fuel and air pumps. Eptl engr Bendix Aviation Corp '30-48; development engr advancing to chief engr Stromberg Automotive Carburetors since '48. Soc Automotive Engrs. Eclipse Machine Division, Bendix Aviation Corp., Elmira, N.Y.

22 WINNE, William T(homas). New York aquatic bryophytes and poisonous plants; Aquatic weed control. b'13. AB '34 (Union Coll); MS '35—PhD '46 (Cornell U). Research in economic botany on aquatic weed control '35; taxonomic and ecologic studies of the aquatic bryophytes of New York State, Sphagnum, Drepanocladus, Fontinalis and Dichelyma '47. Author: Some Poisonous plants of New York State '42. Lect Cornell U '38-39; asst prof biol dept Union Coll since '46. Sullivant Moss Soc—Torrey Bot Club— Am Soc Plant Taxonomists—Bot Soc Am—AAAS—Sigma Xi—Phi Beta Kappa. Biology Department, Union College, Schenectady, N.Y.

23 WINSLOW, Charles Ambrose. Gas and diesel engines (Design); Oil filters; Lubricating systems. b'90. Ed pub schs. Improvement and development high pressure lubricating systems, fuel and oil filters, dry and wettype air filters, carburetors, and injection equipment. Holds US and fgn patents in field. Author articles: Modern Methods of Conditioning Lubricating Oil During Use: The How and the Why of Strainers, Screens, and Filters as Applied to the Fuel and Lubricating Oil Systems of Engines; The Development of Lubricating Systems as Applied to Engines, and others. Design, supervision and mfr automotive equipment Winslow Mfg Co Vallejo Cal '22-25; cons '24-30; vp and gen mgr Standard Gas Engine Co, Am Diesel Engine Co Oakland Cal '31-34; cons engr '34-38; pres Winslow Engineering Co since '38. Am Soc Lubrication Engrs—Soc Automotive Engrs. Registered profl engr Cal. Winslow Engineering Co., 4069 Hollis St., Oakland 3, Cal.

24 WINSLOW, David Clinton. Conservation; Dust control; Snow survey. b'14. BA '36 (U Okla); MA '37 (U Neb); PhD '48 (Clark U). Originator of oil palliatives and first user of cenchrus in dust control; advocate of snow surveys for water conservation. Author: Geographical Implications of Soil Conservation Districts in the Southwest '48; also articles in field. Nat Park Service Ranger-naturalist '41-43; dust control supervisor US War Dept New Mexico US Soil Conservation Service '43-45; vis asso prof geog U Okla '46; asst prof geog Okla A&M Coll since '47. NM and Okla Acad Sci —Okla Edn Assn—Nat Council Geog Teachers—Am Assn Geog—Am Meteorol Soc—Kappa Delta Pi. Geography Department, Oklahoma Agricultural and Mechanical College, Stillwater, Okla.†

25 WINSLOW, Kathryn. Alaska (Gold rush, aviation history). b'06. AB '27 (U Cal); '47 (U Wis). Research on gold rush and aviation history of Alaska and Canadian Yukon. Author: Big Pan-Out, the History of the Klondike Gold Rush '51; also articles in field. H: 1541 E. 57th St., Chgo 37.

10 WINSOR, Andrew Leon. Effect of drugs on secretions. b'90. AB '20—AM '21 (U Utah); '24 (Stanford); PhD '29 (Cornell). Research on effect of drugs and alcohol on rate of secretion and relation of rate to pH of parotid secretion. Instr Cornell '27-30, asst prof edn '30-36, prof since 36, dir guidance for vets sence '45, head dept rural edn since '46, dir Sch Edn since '46; cons on personnel management for corps since '35. AAAS—Am Psychol Assn—NEA—Sigma Xi—Phi Kappa Phi. 32 Cornell St., Ithaca.

11 WINSOR, Mulford. Legislative procedure (Arizona); Arizona history; Date culture. b'74. Ed pub schs of Mankato Kan, Fort Smith Ark. Has produced the only known coal black date. Author: Guide to Legislative Drafting in Arizona '41; also articles in field. Dir State Dept Library and Archives since '31; owner Persian Gardens Yuma Ariz and producer many varieties of dates since '16. ALA—NASL—Am Acad Polit and Social Sci—Council of State Govts (bd mgrs)—Nat Council of Commrs on Uniform State Laws (mem Ariz Commn). State Capitol, Phoenix.

12 WINSTON, James J. Cereal technology and sanitation. b'15. BS '36 (Coll City NY); '37 (NY U). Quality controls technologist for cereal and egg products; determination of soya lecithin in macaroni and noodle products; evaluation of methods for the determination of extraneous matter in cereal products; consultant in macaroni and noodle manufacturing; expert witness for federal security administration on standards of identity for enriched macaroni and noodle products. Author articles in field. Dir research Nat Macaroni Mfrs. Assn, also Jacobs-Winston Labs Inc. Am Chem Soc—Am Assn Cereal Chem-Inst Food Tech. 156 Chambers Ct., NYC 7.

13 WINTER, Carl George. Canadian history; Canadian-American relations (1905-1927). b'06. AB '29—MA '31 (U Cal), PhD '51 (Stanford). Papers on Hudson Bay area and on Boundary Waters Treaty of 1909. Author articles: The Establishment of First Canadian Legation '52; A Note on the Passamaquoddy Boundary Affair '53. Canada Free Dominion '42; Three Canadian Statesmen '44; Sci Methods in History '37; Let Students Write Their Own Life Histories '37; A Unit on Peace '39. Chmn social studies dept CK Mc-Clatchy Sr High Sch Sacramento Calif since '38. AHA—Can Hist Assn. Sacramento City Unified School District, Sacramento. H: 126 43d St., Sacramento 19.

14 WINTER, Frederick Charles. Production management; Plant layout; Materials handling; Industrial research. b'13. BS '35—ME '41 (NYU); MS in indsl engring '42 (Columbia). Alternate representative National Management Council of US. Author: Plant Layout '52. Author articles: Measured Day Work Versus Wage Incentives '38; Observations of the Research Techniques Propounded by the National Marketing Research Workshop '50; How Fresh Fruit and Vegetable Distributors Can Get More Out of their Materials Handling Equipment, and others. Indsl engr and asst to vp in charge prodn Ansco Corp Binghamton NY '38-39; asst prof indsl engring Columbia since '47; indsl cons USDA Washington since '48. Comdg officer in charge munitions prodn program in Can AUS Ordnance Office Montreal '42-44. ASME—Am Soc Engring Edn—Soc Advancement Management(treas '37-38). Columbia University, Department of Industrial Engineering, N

YC 27. H: 23 Cranford Pl., Teaneck, N.J.†

15 WINTER, James Douglas. Frozen foods; Pomology. b'92. BS '23—MS '29 (U Minn). Processing and packaging of foods for locker plant and home freezer use; culture, transportation and processing of fruits. Author articles in field. Plant quarantine and inspection Minn State Dept Agri prior to '37; instr hort U Minn '37-42, asso prof since '47. Inst Food Technol—Am Soc Hort Sci—Minn State Hort Soc (pres '29-30)—Minn Fruit Growers Assn (sec-treas since '33)—Sigma Xi—Gamma Sigma Delta. University Farm, St. Paul 1.†

16 WINTER, John Garrett. Latin language; Papyrology. b'81. AM '04—PhD '06 (U Mich). Author: Myth of Hercules at Rome '10; Prodromus of Nicolaus Steno '16; Life and Letters in the Papyri '33. Editor T. S. Jerome's Aspects of the Study of Roman History '23; Michigan Papyri, Vol. III, 1936; also articles in field. Prof Latin lang and lit U Mich since '28; dir Mus of Archeol. Société Royal Egyptienne de Papyrologie — Soc Promotion of Byzantine and Modern Greek Studies —Am Philol Assn (pres '44)—Archeol Inst Am—Classical Assn Middle West and South—Mich Acad Scis Arts and Letters—Phi Beta Kappa. 901 Forest Av., Ann Arbor.

17 WINTER, Samuel William. Vegetable breeding (Peas, tomatoes, cabbage, green beans, lima beans). b'98. BS in agr '26 (U Cal). Research and plant hybridizing to improve yields and quality of vegetables used for canning; production disease-resistant varieties. Hort Cal Packing Corp since '26. Am Soc Hort Sci—AAAS—Alpha Zeta. California Packing Corp., Sunnyvale, Cal. H: 476 Oak Court, Palo Alto, Cal.

18 WINTER, William Laurence. Modern European and Hanseatic history. b'16. AB '38 (State U Ia); MA '42—PhD '46 (U Calif). Research on diplomatic relations of Lübeck, Denmark, Danzig and Sweden 1500-1525; special studies in the Germanic languages '40-42 Author articles. Asst prof Teachers Coll Conn since '49. American Hist Assn—AAAS—Mediaeval Acad of Am—Am Acad Polit and Social Scis —Phi Beta Kappa. Doctoral dissertation awarded prize of Pacific Coast Branch of Am Hist Assn for best work in field of European hist '46. 28-D, Steven St., West Hartford, Conn.

19 WINTERKORN, Hans F(riedrich). Stabilization of soil and sand. b'05. Dr Phil Nat in phys chem '24-31 (Ruperto-Carola U Heidelberg Baden); student (U Mo, MIT). Developer beach stabilization method for US Navy '49, process of waterproofing cohesive soils, theory and methods for stabilization of cohesive soils, process to prevent stripping of asphalt from road aggregate; discovered destructive action of soil bacteria on certain types of stabilized soils and pavements and developed preventive measures; discovered electric potentials in moist soils induced by applied temperature differences; research consultant Missouri State Highway Department '31-42. Author 75 articles in field. Contributor: Colloid Chemistry, Theoretical and Applied (vol IV) '46. Faculty U Mo '32-43; asso prof Princeton since '43; owner and mgr Winterkorn Road Research Inst; cons. Am Inst Chem(F)—American Geog Soc(F)—AAAS(F)—ACS—Am Soc CE(asso)—Geophys Union—AAUP—Soc Engring Edn—Acad Pol Sci —Assn Asphalt Paving Technologists —Am Road Builders Assn(chmn sub-

com theory of stabilization cohesive soils, mem com stabilization soil with asphalt)—Highway Research Bd (asso mem, chmn project com physico-chem phenomena in soils, mem dept soils investigations, mem com on subsurface drainage, mem com on soil-cement roads). Princeton University, Princeton, N.J.

20 WINTERS, Harold Franklin. Horticulture, cinchona. b'13. BS '40 (Okla A and M Coll); MS '42 (O State U). Full-time research in cinchona and vegetable crops. Author articles in field. Hort Fed Expt Sta Puerto Rico since '43. AAAS—Am Soc Hort Sci—Am Soc Plant Physiol—Am Plant Life Soc—Am Hort Soc—Am Orchid Soc—Gamma Sigma Delta. Federal Experiment Station, Mayaguez, Puerto Rico.

21 WINTERS, James C(linton). Iron exchange; Adsorption. '17. BA '39 (U Wichita); MS '42 — PhD '44—Wm Wrigley Jr Grant '42—duPont fellowship '43 (Northwestern U). Research on phosphatase activity of certain mouth organisms, the sulfonation of certain tri-and tetra-substituted olefins with dioxane-sulfurtrioxide reagent, biochemical research on industrial application of certain enzymes, technical development of new enzymes; industrial application of synthetic ion exchange resins. Author articles in field. Chemist Rohm and Haas Co Phila '43-45; tech rep resinous products div indsl application of synthetic ion exchange resins since '45. Am Chem Soc —NY Acad Sci—Sigma Xi. Rohm and Haas Co., Resinous Products Division, 222 W. Washington Square, Phila 5.

22 WINTERS, Laurence M(erriam). Animal husbandry and breeding (Swine and sheep production). b'91. BS '19—PhD '32 (U Minn); MS '20 (Ia State Coll). Author: Animal Breeding '48; Introduction to Breeding Farm Animals '42. Author articles: Six-Year Study of Crossbreeding Swine '35; Prenatal Development of The Sheep '46; Experiments With Inbreeding Swine and Sheep '48; Prenatal Development of the Bovine '42. Prof animal husbandry U Saskatchewan '20-28; prof animal husbandry charge research in animal breeding U Minn since '28. Am Soc Animal Prodn—AAAS—Am Genetic Assn—Genetic Soc Am—Phi Kappa Phi—Gamma Sigma Delta—Sigma Xi. Morrison award '48. University Farm, St. Paul.

23 WINTERS, Robert Alonzo. Labor (Collective bargaining); Trade assn mgmt. b'12. AB '35 (Princeton U); MA '37 (Tufts Coll); MA '41—PhD '49 (Harvard). Author articles. Executive dir and sec Rubber Heel and Sole Inst NY since '47; genl mgr Elastic Colloid Research Corp Avon Mass since '48; lecturer. Am Econ Assn—Indsl Relations Research Assn—Am Trade Assn Execs. 551 Fifth Av., NYC 17.

24 WINTHER, Oscar Osburn. American history (California, Oregon, Washington, Pacific Northwest, Western; Mormons); American pre-railroad transportation (Roads, Wells Fargo stagecoaching, Oregon Trail); Modern Denmark; Danes in the United States. b'03. AB '21-25 (U Ore); AM '28 (Harvard); PhD '34 (Stanford U); '29 (U Calif). Author: The Story of San Jose, California's First Pueblo '35; Express and Stagecoach Days in California from the Gold Rush to the Civil War '38; Via Western Express and Stage Coach '45; The Great Northwest '48; also articles in field. Asso prof hist Ind U since '47. Am Hist Soc—Miss Valley Hist Assn—Phi Alpha Theta. Recipient Huntington Library Research

Fellowship; '45-46. Indiana University, Bloomington, Ind.†

10 **WIPF, F(rances) Louise.** Leguminous root nodules (Chromosomes); Seed development (Endosperm); Veterinary science (Virus diseases, chromosome studies). b'06. BS '30 (State Teachers Coll); PhM '33—PhD '39 (U Wis). Research on virus diseases in fur farm animals and chromosome studies on foxes and mink '39-42; cytological studies on root nodules '34-39, role of the endosperm in seed development since '43. Author articles in field. Research asst agr bact U Wis '34-39; research in vet sci U Wis '39-43; research in genetics U Wis '43-49, research in vet sci U Wis since '49. AA AS—Genetics Soc Am—Sigma Xi. Veterinary Science Department, University of Wisconsin, Madison 6, Wis.†

11 **WIRE, Harold Channing.** Desert reclamation (Farming); Southwestern United States mining (California, Nevada). b'99. Student '19-21 (Pomona Coll), '21-22 (Columbia). Research on placer gold mining in California and Nevada; desert reclamation for farming purposes. Author articles in field. Freelance writer since '27. 671 Agate St., Laguna Beach, Cal.

12 **WIRTH, Fremont Philip.** American History. b'90. AB '17—AM '18 (U Ill); PhD '25 (U Chicago). Co-author: (with Waddy Thompson) History of American Progress '33; (with others) Pupils Work Book in American Citizenship '31; (with Mary Neely Crow) A Workbook for Studying the History of American Progress '34. Prof history Peabody Coll since '25, chmn dept social sci '31-39. Am Miss Valley and So hist assns—Am Acad Polit and Social Sci—Nat Council Social Studies (pres '41)—Tenn Hist Soc—Tenn State Edn Assn—NEA—Am Assn Sch Adminstrs—Phi Eta—Kappa Delta Pi—Pi Gamma Mu—Phi Delta Kappa. 4306 Lone Oak Rd., Nashville.☉

13 **WISAN, Jacob Mordecai.** Effect of fluoridization of water supplies on incidence of dental caries. b'96. DDS '18-30-33 (NYU); MS in pub health '44 (Columbia). Author articles: Dental Caries Experience of New Jersey Sch Children '48; The Fluoridation of Communal Water Supplies '48; Dental Habits of 2,205 Families '49, and others. Co-editor: Dentistry in Public Health '49. Contributor: Oral Hygiene Preventive Dentistry '50. Chief div dental health NJ State Dept Health '39-48; dir div dental health edn Am Dental Assn '48-49; dir Joseph Samuels Dental Clinic for Children RI Hosp Providence '49-50; chief dental service VA Hosp Brooklyn since '50. Am Dental Assn (chmn sect oral hygiene and children's dentistry)—Am Soc Dentistry for Children(pres)—Am Pub Health Assn(F, chmn sect on dental health)—Am Coll Dentists(F)—Am Sch Health Assn—AAAS. Veterans Administration Hosp. Bklyn 9.

14 **WISCHHUSEN, John F(rederick).** Trace elements in nutrition; Manganese. b'88. Ed Germany and England. Initiated and cooperated in investigation by Dr. I. Levis and F. H. Emery in Cleveland, Ohio to prove that brucellosis is a deficiency of principally manganese copper and cobalt '39-40. Author: Recent Developments of Manganese and Other Essential Elements in Agriculture '47; Manganese and Other Essential Inorganic Elements in Animal Nutrition '47; Essential Elements in Animal Nutrition with Special Reference to Dairy Cattle '47; The Story of Fertilizer—Manganese '47. Pres Superfos Co Inc NYC '20-28; br and dept mgr Harshaw Chem Co Cleve-

land '28-44; dir Manganese Research and Development Found Cleveland '44-50; organized Inorganic Bioelements Inc, 1950. Am Chem Soc—Am Society Agron—Soil Sci Soc Am—Am Soc Hort Sci—Am Soc Plant Physiol—Am Phytopath Soc—AAAS—Am Soc Animal Prodn. 15037 Shore Acres Dr., Cleve.

15 **WISE, Paul L.** Photography; Game pictures. b'00. Ed pub schs. Specialist in fine grain negative making. Photographer in Alaska since '37. Received certificate of merit from Photog Association Am '44. Paul's Studio, Coopers Landing, Alaska.

16 **WISLICENUS, George Friedrich.** Rotating and turbomachinery; Fluid mechanics; Compressors; Pumps; Turbines (Aircraft and marine propulsion). b'03. ME '25 (Hoehere Maschinenbauschule Wurzburg Germany); MS '31—PhD '34 (Calif Inst Tech). Author: Fluid Mechanics of Turbomachinery '47; also articles in field. Prof and chmn dept mech engring John Hopkins U since '48; cons engr since '48. Am Soc Mech Engrs—AAAS—Inst Aeronautical Sci—Sigma Xi. The Johns Hopkins University, Department of Mechanical Engineering, Baltimore 18.†☉

17 **WISS, John Edgar.** Gypsum; Lime; Dolomite; Plastics. b'99. BS (Chem E) (O State U). Industrial applications raw and calcined gypsum to ceramics, art, and foundry; application of lime and dolomite to agriculture, ceramics, and refractory uses; research on use of plastics for flexible molds and patterns. Holds patents on composition of matter, and on process for molding hot materials. Co-author articles: (with Lade, Camp) Gypsum Plaster in the Ceramic Industries '30; (with R B Wagner, R Beaver) Ceramic Applications of Flexible Synthetic Die and Moldmaking Equipment '49; (with R B Wagner) Cold Formed Flexible Precision Patterns and Core Boxes '50, and others. With US Gypsum Co since '21, spl engr gypsum, lime, and structural materials '32-35, tech dir Perma Flex Mold Co since '44. Am Ceramic Soc—Eastern States Blast Furnace and Coke Oven Assn—Am Forestry Soc—Am Foundry Soc—Sigma Xi. The Perma-Flex Mold Co., 1919 E. Livingston Av., Columbus 9, O. H: 1339 Lincoln Rd., Columbus 12.

18 **WISSER, Edward Hollister.** Mining exploration. b'95. BS '17-24-25 (U Cal); '39-41 (Johns Hopkins). Exploration for ores in US, Mexico, and Philippines, including copper, lead, zinc, manganese, tungsten, silver, and gold; studies on ore occurrence in relation to geologic structure, mechanics of folding, faulting, and general deformation of earth's crust; Geological Society of America research grant for studies ore deposits and crustal deformation. Author articles: Formation of the North-South Fractures of the Real del Monte Area, Pachuca Silver District, Mexico '37; Geologic Parallels: Hog Mountain, Alabama, and Paracale, Philippine Islands '39; Mineral Relationships in the Ores of Pachuca and Real del Monte, Mexico '48; Tomorrow's Ore '50, and others. Contributor: Ore Deposits as Related to Structural Features '42. Geol Phelps Dodge Corp '25-26; geol US Smelting, Refining & Mining Co Pachuca Mex '26-27, chief geol '27-36; cons geol PI '36-38, San Francisco since '38; prof mineral exploration div mineral tech U Cal since '47. Geol Soc Am(F)—Am Geophys Union—Soc Econ Geol—AIMME—Mining and Metallurgical Soc Am—NRC (research fellowship board in nat sci)—Sigma Xi. Division of Mineral Technology, University of Cal., Berkeley 4.

19 **WISSLER, Stanley Gebhart.** Subsurface stratigraphy and micropaleontology (Los Angeles basin). b'00. BS '22 (Earlham Coll); '21 (U Ill); MA '23 (Columbia). Stratigraphic studies of petroleum producing areas of world; testing of Pacific Coast, South Pacific, South and Central America, Central and Southeast United States and Canada. Author articles in field. Asst in stratigraphy and paleontol Columbia '23-25; paleontol Union Oil Co Calif Los Angeles '25-35, chief paleontol '35-48, chief paleontol Pacific Coast Area since '49. Am Assn Pet Geol—Soc Econ Paleontol and Mineral (pres '37, Pacific sect pres '28)—AAAS(F)—Geol Soc Am(F)—Sigma Xi. 1115 Union Oil Building, Los Angeles 14.

20 **WISTER, John Caspar.** Flowering trees and shrubs(Culture); Herbaceous plants; Bulbs. b'87. AB '09—student (Harvard); DSc '42 (Swarthmore). Author: The Iris '27; Bulbs for American Gardens '30; Lilac Culture '30; Bulbs in Home Gardens '48, and others. Editor: Woman's Home Companion Garden Book '47; also articles in field. Landscape architect since '10; hort cons; lecturer. Am Iris Soc—Iris Soc Eng—Garden Club Am—Am Peony Soc—Am Rose Soc—Pa Hort Soc—Mass Hort Soc. Swarthmore College, Swarthmore, Pa.†

21 **WISWESSER, William Joseph.** Chemical coding; Atomic models. b'14. BS chem '36 (Lehigh U). Devised new method for coding, classifying, describing and drawing complex chemical structures. Granted patent on new mechanical linkage for atomic models. Author articles in field. With Hercules Experiment Sta '36-39, Trojan Powder Co '39-42, Willson Prod Inc since '45. Tau Beta Pi. Willson Products, Inc., Reading, Pa.

22 **WITHERIDGE, William Nemitz.** Industrial ventilation; Dust, odor and air pollution control; Air cleaning and air sanitation. b'10. BS '35 (Mich State); SM '36 (Harvard); MS '46—PhD '51 (U Michigan). Author Air Sanitation and Industrial Ventilation '45. Co-author: (with C P McCord) Odors: Physiology and Control '49; also articles in field. Ventilation cons Gen Motors Corp '46-52, mfg staff since '53. American Society Heat and Ventilating Engineers (chairman '50 Guide publ com)—Indsl Ventilating Soc Detroit (charter mem, first pres)—Am Indsl Hygiene Assn (bd dirs '44-47)—Mich Indsl Hygiene Soc (pres '47-48). General Motors Corporation, Detroit 2.†

23 **WITHROW, Robert Bruce.** Biophysics (Photobiology, radiobiology, plant physiology, nutriculture). b'04. BS in EE '27—MS '28 (Cincinnati U); PhD in botany '42 (Chicago U). Research on effect of radiant energy on plant growth. Author articles in field. Chief Div Radiations and Organisms, Smithsonian Inst since '48. Am Soc Plant Physiol—Bot Soc Am—Soc Study Growth and Development—Am Phys Soc—AAAS—Sigma Xi. Smithsonian Institution, Washington 25.†

24 **WITSCHI, Emil.** Reproduction physiology. b'90. Student '05-11 (State Teach Coll and State U, Bern, Switz); PhD '13 (U Munich); Rockefeller foundation fellow '26 (Yale); '26 (U Chicago); '27 (U Calif). Engaged research development embryology, endocrinology, sex hormones, genes, chromosomes, seasonal cycles, germ cells, reproduction hypophysis, parabiosis, pigments, vertebrates. Author: Sex Deviations, Inversions and Parabiosis '32, '39; also many articles in field. Prof zoology, embryology and endocrinology State U Ia since '27; apptd visiting prof U Tübingen '48-49. AAAS(F)—Soc Zool—Assn Anatomists —Soc Exptl Biology and Med—Am Genetics Soc — Am Naturalists — Am Ornithol Union—Swiss Soc Naturalists Swiss Genetics Soc—Imperial German Acad Sci—Sigma Xi. H: 311 Woolf Av., Iowa City, Ia.⊙

10 WITT, Paul William Fred. Audiovisual education. b'11. BS '33—MA '39 (U Neb); EdD '47 (Columbia). Author articles: Toward More Effective Utilization of Audio-Visual Materials and Devices '47; A Yardstick for Evaluation '48; Some Trends in Audio-Visual Instruction '49. Professor edn dept of curriculum and teaching Teachers Coll Columbia, charge audio-visual service '46-47. NY State Audio-Visual Council (exec sec '48-49, pres '49-50)—Assn Edn by Radio—Ednl Film Library Assn —NEA(pres dept audio-visual instrn '53-54). 525 W. 120th St., NYC 27. H: 106 Morningside Drive.

11 WITTE, Ernest Frederic. Public welfare administration; Community organization; Professional education for social work. b'04. BS '25—MA '26 (U Neb); PhD '32 (U Chicago). Field supervisor Fed Emergency Relief Adminstrn Neb State Relief Adminstrt '32-37; field rep US Social Security Bd '32-37; dir grad sch social work U Neb '37-39; dir grad sch social work U Washington '39-43; exec sec Council of Social Agencies Seattle since '48. Maj US Army '43, sent to N Africa later dir welfare Allied Mil Govt in occupied territory Sicily and Italy '43-44; chief displaced persons refugees and welfare sect Supreme Hdqrs Mission to France '44-45, promoted to lt col '44, to col '46, chief welfare US Group Control Council Pub Health and Welfare Sect in Germany '45, chief social service Br 12 Vets Adminstrn Hdqrs San Francisco. 1535 Summit Av., Seattle 22.

12 WITTENBORN, John Richard. Projective psychol tests; Quantitative psychology; Child training practices. b'15. BE '?& (Southern Ill State U); MS '40—PhD '42 (U Ill). Research in projective test devices; rating scale procedures for evaluating psychiatric patients; studies in nature of mental illness; studies of adoptive children; evaluations therapy including psychosurgery; nature and measurement of human attributes. Author articles in field. From instr to asst prof psychol dept Yale '42-48, also clin psychol dept univ health, research asso, asso prof psych since '48; cons OSRD '44-46, VA since '47. Am Psychol Assn (F)—Psychometric Soc—Am Statis Association—Biometric Society—Eastern Psychol Assn—Conn Psychol Assn. Department of Psychology, Yale University, New Haven.

13 WITTFOGEL, Karl A(ugust). Chinese institutions (History; Oriental society). b'96. PhD '28 (U Frankfurt). Research on the economic history of China, conquest societies of Asia, comparative study of bureaucracy, structure and dynamics of Oriental society in Asia and Ancient America; directed study on Chinese family in China '35-37; participant lecturer in Far Eastern studies Harvard since '40. Author: Sun Yat-sen '27; Chinese Economics and Society (in Germany) '31. Co-author: (with Feng Chia-sheng) History of Chinese Society, Liao '49; also articles in field. Research asso Inst Social Research Frankfurt on Main '25-33, Columbia '34-39; dir Chinese hist project U Wash and Columbia since '39; professor Far Eastern Inst U Wash since '47. Am Oriental Soc— Am Geog Soc—Far Eastern Assn—Am

Anthrop Assn. Chinese History Project, Columbia University, NYC 27.⊙

14 WITTKE, Carl Frederick. Canadian history; History of American immigration. b'92. AB '13 (O State U); AM '14—PhD '21 (Harvard); LLD '46 (Lawrence College); Litt D '51 (Marietta College). Author: A History of Canada '41; The Saga of the Immigrant '39, and others; also articles in field. Prof history and dean grad sch Western Reserve U since '48. AHA—Miss Valley Hist Assn (Pres '40-41)—Canadian Hist Assn— Royal Hist Soc(F)—Phi Beta Kappa (senator '46-52). 2232 Harcourt Drive, Cleve 6.⊙

15 WITTMAN, Lawrence. Reinforced plastics; Fiberglas; Plastic tooling. b'10. ME '32 (Stevens Inst Tech). Developed low-cost simplified tooling method employing low pressure molding of fiberglas laminates '45; developed low-cost methods of molding reinforced plastics '47. Author articles in field. Prodn research engr to sr plastics engr Republic Aviation Corp '40-49; pvt cons since '49; vp Cordo Molding Products Inc NYC since '51. Soc Plastics Ind (policy com)—ASME. 230 Park Av., NYC.†

16 WITTROCK, Gustave Ludwig. Ethnobotany. b'95. BA '24—MA '26 (Grinnell Coll); '24-25 (Johns Hopkins); '30-32 (Columbia); '28-29 (U Wash). Research in plants used by the Indians in United States and Canada, educational programs for the public. Author: The Pruning Book '48; Edible Plants of the Pond and Water Garden '45; also articles in field. Herbarium Chicago Natural Hist Mus '29; docent NY Bot Garden '30, custodian of Herbarium '36, asst curator edn '49. Torrey Bot Club—Ia Acad Scis—Taxonomic Index—AAAS—Sigma Xi. New York Botanical Garden, Bronx Park, NYC 58.

17 WODEHOUSE, R(oger) P(hilip). Pollen; Hayfever plants. b'89. BA '13 (Faculty of Arts Toronto); MA '17 (Harvard); PhD '23 (Columbia). Author: Pollen Grains '35; Hayfever Plants '44; also articles in field. Protein chem in researches allergy Peter Brigham Hosp Boston '16-17; sci dir hayfever lab The Arlington Chem Co Yonkers '18-44; asso dir research allergy Lederle Labs Div Am Cyanamid Co. Torrey Bot Club (formerly ed-in-chief)—Am Bot Soc—AAAS(F)—Am Coll Allergists (asso F). Lederle Laboratories Division, American Cyanamid Co., Pearl River, N.Y.⊙

18 WOELLNER, Fredric Philip. Social education. b'90. AB '12 (U Cincinnati); '12 (Teachers Coll Cincinnati); MA '15—PhD '23 (Columbia); LLD (Coll of Osteopathic Phys and Surgs Los Angeles). Author: Type Studies in American History (vol IV) '21; Education for Citizenship '23; How We Govern '26; Highlands of the Mind '30; Key to Corinth '42; The Elements of Human Engineering '43; Permanent Values In Adult Education '49. Critic in hist pvt schs Teachers Coll Columbia '14-15; teacher and head of dept Buffalo State Teachers Coll '15-21; lecturer U Calif '23-25; asso prof and prof edn U Calif Los Angeles since '25; extension lecturer U Calif Berkeley and Los Angeles; lecturer U Hawaii U Pa Columbia summers. 332 Hilgard Av., LA 24.†⊙

19 WOFFORD, Kate Vixon. Curriculum planning for small rural schools; Teacher education (Planning programs). AB '16 (Winthrop Coll Rock Hill SC); AM '31 (Cornell U); PhD '34 (Columbia). Author: History of the Status and Training of Rural Teachers in the U.S. (1860-1930) '34; Modern

Education in the Small Rural Schools '38; Teaching in Small Schools '46. Editor yearbooks of Rural Edn Dept NEA '38 '39 '41. Prof and dir rural edn State Tchrs Coll Buffalo NY '34-47; head prof elementary edn coll edn U Fla since '47; vis prof Columbia summer '39 '40, U Minn '41 '42 '44, U Chicago '43. SC State Tchrs Assn (pres '26-27)—NEA(pres rural edn department '31-32, exec com on rural edn '33-34, chmn yearbook com rural edn since '36)—Pi Lambda Theta— Kappa Delta Pi—Pi Gamma Mu. College of Education, University of Florida, Gainesville.

20 WOJCIECHOWSKI, Victor Anthony. History of Polish people in New Jersey. b'88. Ed pub schs in Poland and US Organizer New Jersey Polish Hist Soc, Trenton '38. Author: The History of the Polish People in Trenton New Jersey '32; The First Biography of General-Professor Joseph Karge '42; The History of Polish People in Trenton and Historical Polish Places in New Jersey '43. Kosciuszko Found. 19 Brewing Av., Trenton 9, N.J.

21 WOLCOTT, George N(orton). Insects of sugar cane; Dry-wood termites. (Woods resistant to attack of, and chemicals permanently repellent to); Grassland populations; Insects of the West Indies. b'89. BS '09—MS '15—PhD '25 (Cornell). Author: Entomologie d'Haiti '27; An Economic Entomology of the West Indies '33; The Insects of Puerto Rico '50; articles: Insectae Borinquenses: A Revised Annotated Check-List of the Insects of Puerto Rico, with a Host Plant Index '36; An Animal Census of Two Pastures and a Meadow in Northern New York '37; How to Make Wood Unpalatable to the West Indian Dry-Wood Termite '45. Entomologist bur entomology US Dept Agr '10-12; entomologist Insular Expt Sta Rio Piedras PR '12-16, '21-24, since '31; entomologist expt sta Haina Dominican Rep '20-21, Service Technique d'Agr d'Haiti '24-28, Agrl Expt Sta Lima Peru '28-29. AAAS(life F)—Am Assn Econ Entomologists(life)—Entomolog Soc Washington — Am Assn Agrl Sciences(PR chapt). Agricultural Experiment Station, Rio Piedras. Home: Rio Piedras, Puerto Rico; also R.F.D. 1, Remsen, N.Y.

22 WOLF, Martin Leon. Fine and applied arts (Terms, techniques, materials, implements). b'14. Student '32-33 (NYU); '36-38 (St John's U Arts and Scis); LLB '40 (St John's U). Research in terms, techniques, materials, and implements of archaeology, architecture, arms and armor, ballet and dance, ceramics, costume art, drawing, esthetics, etching and engraving, furniture, heraldry, gemmology, literature, music, mythology, painting, photography, sculpture, textile arts, theatre and drama, woodworking, falconry, numismatics, bookbinding, printing, metalwork, glass-making, enamelwork, masks, and others. Author: Dictionary of the Arts '51. Co-author: Hebrew Impact on Western Civilization. Editor: Russian Impact on Art; Tears and Laughter; Spirits Rebellious; Secrets of the Heart. Asso ed. Philos Library '47-49, art dir since '49.

23 WOLF, Michael J. Chemistry of cereal grains. b'09. PhD '41 (U Wis). Research on metabolism and chemistry of alkaloids in the potato, chemical composition and structure of the cereal grains, starch chemistry, photosynthesis of algae and of higher aquatic plants. Author articles in field. Research asst bot U Wis '36-41, dir water and san chem lab Post Engr Ft

Benning Ga '41-44; asso chem Argonne Nat Lab Chicago '44-45; chem US Dept Agr Peoria Ill since '45. Am Chem Soc—Am Soc Plant Physiol—Sigma Xi. Northern Regional Research Laboratory, United States Department of Agriculture, Peoria, Ill.

10 WOLF, Ralph Frank. Synthetic rubber (Butyl); Silica pigments. b'07. BS '32 (Catholic U Am). Author: India-Rubber Man, the Story of Charles Goodyear '39. Co-author: Rubber, a Story of Glory and Greed '36; also articles in field. Mgr compounding research Columbia—So Chem Corp a subsidiary of Pitts Plate Glass Co since '48. Am Chem Soc—AAAS. Rsrch Laboratory, Columbia—Southern Chemical Corp., Barberton, O. H: 4448 Lahm Dr., Arkon 19, O.

11 WOLFE, Henry Cutler. International relations; Russian-German Relations; Europe (Politics, economics, minorities problems); Pan-Germanism and Slavism. b'98. Student (Phillips-Andover Acad, Kenyon Coll); AM (hon) '39. Writer and lecturer on international relations; has interviewed President Benes of Czechoslovakia, Chancellor Schuschnigg of Austria, Queen Marie of Rumania, President Vargas of Brazil, President Quezon of the Philippines, Pierre Laval of France and others; wrote regular feature The European Scene Columbus Sunday Dispatch to '37; war correspondent in European Theatre of Operations '43-45; visited Dobrudja Province as a guest of Rumanian government to observe minorities transplantation July '35. Author: The German Octopus '38; Human Dynamite '39; The Imperial Soviets '40; also articles in field. Acad Polit Sci—Am Acad Polit and Social Sci—Am Geog Soc(F). Doubleday and Co., 14 W. 49th St., NYC 20.

12 WOLFE, Herbert Snow. Tropical fruits (Avocado, mango, papaya). b'98. AB '18 (Park Coll); '20-21 (Trinity Coll Dublin); MS '26—PhD '30 (U Chicago). Author articles in field. With Coll Agr U Fla since '30, now head prof hort. Fla State Hort Soc (chmn Krome Memorial sect '36-45)—AAAS—Am Soc Hort Sci—Am Soc Plant Physiol—Sigma Xi (pres Fla chap '47-48). College of Agriculture, University of Florida, Gainesville, Fla.†☺

13 WOLFE, Oscar. Petroleum (Transportation). b'89. BS in civil engring '12—DEng hon '45 (Bucknell U). Research on transportation of crude oil, natural gas and petroleum products through long distance pipe lines, with emphasis on mechanics of flow and hydraulic and mechanical design of systems. Engr So Group Pipe Lines '12-28; with Tex Co since '28, cons engr fgn operations since '44; chief engr War Emergency Pipelines Inc '42-43. ASME—Tau Beta Pi. Texas Co., 135 E. 42d St., NYC 17.

14 WOLFE, Rolland Emerson. Biblical literature (Prophets). b'02. AB '24 (Manchester Coll); BD '28—STM '29 (Oberlin Grad Sch Theol); PhD '33 (Harvard). Author: The Editing of the Book of the Twelve '35; Tufts Papers on Religion (with Skinner, McCollester, Brotherston, Cole, Wyatt, and Ratcliffe) '38; Meet Amos and Hosea '45; also articles in field. Pastor '28-29; instr Old Testament lit and Semitic langs Crane Theol Sch Tufts Coll '34-35, asst prof '35-36, act dean '44, '46; Harkness prof Biblical lit Western Reserve U since '46; bd overseers Flora Stone Mather Coll '47-50. Nat Assn Biblical Instrs (pres '47)—Archeol Inst Am (Am textual criticism seminar)—Soc Biblical Lit and Exegesis—Am Oriental Soc—Am Sch Oriental Research. Mather Memorial Building, Western Reserve University, Cleveland 6.

15 WOLFF, Richard Alfred. Mechanical engineering (Heating, ventilation, air conditioning, industrial piping, steam power plants). b'93. ME '14 (Stevens Inst Tech). One of group which introduced radiant heating to the United States. Co-author article: (with Alfred L Jaros, Jr.) Panel Heating in the British Embassy '30. Engr Walker & Chambers NYC '14-17; organizer, sec Wolff & Munier Inc engrs and contractors since '19; chief indsl processes br Office Prodn Research and Development WPB Washington World War II. 222 E. 41st St. NYC.

16 WOLFF, Werner. Experimental depth psychology; Ethnopsychology. b'04. PhD '30 (Berlin U). Founder experimental depth psychology; decipherer of Mayan hieroglyphics, Easter Island hieroglyphics and symbols. Author: Déchiffrement de l'écriture Maya '38; The Expression of Personality; Experimental Depth Psychology '43; The Personality of the Preschool Child '46; What is Psychology '47; Island of Death; Easter Island '48; The Threshold of the Abnormal, a basic survey of psychopathology '50; The Dream Mirror of Conscience '52. Editor: Personality, Symposia on Topical Issues since '50. Research associate psychotech laboratory Catalan govt '33-36; anthrop research Oslo Amsterdam Basel Zurich '36-37; research asso Columbia '41-42; prof psychol chmn dept Bard Coll since '42. APA—Am Anthrop Assn—Folklore Soc—Polynesian Soc—Am Orthopsychiat Assn—Interam Soc Psychology (vice pres). Bard College, Annandale-on-Hudson, N.Y.†

17 WOLFORD, John J. Geology of Kentucky. b'03. AB '25 (Miami U); MA '27 (O State U); PhD '32 (Johns Hopkins U). Helped make original geologic examinations of proposed sites and reservoir areas for Norris and other dams for United States Army Engineer Office '27; mapped geology and structure of several counties in Kentucky, investigated and prepared reports on geology of various mineral resources in Kentucky. Author articles in field. With Miami U, O '29, now asso prof geol. AAAS(F)—O Acad Sci (F, chmn geol sect '48)—Nat Geog Soc—Arctic Inst NA (charter asso)—Am Polar Soc—Phi Beta Kappa—Am Geog Soc(F). Department Geology, Miami University, Oxford, O.

18 WOLFROM, Melville L(awrence). Chemistry of carbohydrates and nat products. b'00. AB '24 (Ohio State U); MSc '25—PhD '27 (Northwestern U); Guggenheim F '39 (U Zurich). Editor: Advances in Carbohydrate Chemistry (with W W Pigman) '45-49. Nat Research Council fellow in chemistry Nat Bur Standards Rockefeller Inst for Med Research Ohio State U '27-29, instructor chem '29-30, asst prof '30-36, asso prof '36-40, prof since '40, head div organic chem since '48. Official investigator National Defense Research Committee '40-45. AAAS—ACS (chmn cellulose div '40, sugar div '48)—Am Assn Cereal Chem—Nat Acad Sci—Phi Beta Kappa—Sigma Xi—Phi Lambda Upsilon—Pi Mu Epsilon—Alpha Chi Sigma. 168 Fallis Rd., Columbus 14, O.☺

19 WOLFSON, Albert. Physiological ornithology (Migration, reproduction, weights). b'17. BS '37 (Cornell U); PhD '42 (U Calif). Author articles in field. Asso prof biol Northwestern U since '46. AAAS—Am Soc Zool—Am Am Ornithol Union—Sigma Xi—Phi Beta Kappa. Department of Biology, Northwestern University, Evanston, Ill.†

20 WOLK, I. Louis. Synthetic rubber; Foam rubber; Petroleum refining. b '07. BS in chem '29 (U Minn); LLB '34 (Georgetown U). Research on chem patent and trade-mark law with emphasis on synthetic and foam rubbers, petroleum refining; granted 23 patents in petroleum and synthetic rubber fields. Chem patent exam US Patent Office '30-37; patent attorney Phillips Petroleum Co '40-48; patent counsel Dayton Rubber Co since '48. ACS—Am Patent Law Assn—So Ohio Rubber Group. Dayton Rubber Co., Dayton 7, O. H: 3100 Otterbein Av., Dayton 6.

21 WOLKINS, George Gregerson. History of Massachusetts. b'78. Grad '96 (Eng High Sch Boston). Author articles: Freedom and the Old South Meeting-house '48; Beverly Men in the War of Independence '30; Seizure of John Hancock's Sloop 'Liberty' '22; Malcom and Writs of Assistance '24; Boston Customs District '25; Bollan on Writs of Assistance '26; The Coal Panic of 1917-18 '36; The Prince Society '34; Writs of Assistance in England '37. In wholesale coal trade Mass '96-46. Old South Assn (bd mgrs since '10, dir Old South Work Boston '20-44)—Mass Hist Soc (treas '28-43, vp '43-47, chmn photostat com '29-41)—Am Antiquarian Soc—Colonial Soc Mass (asso). 95 Lincoln St., Newton Highlands 61, Mass.

22 WOLLE, Mrs. Muriel Sibell. Western mining camps and ghost towns. b'98. Diploma '20 (NY Sch Fine and Applied Art); BS '28 (NYU); MA '30 U Colo). Author: Ghost Cities of Colorado '33; Cloud Cities of Colorado '34; Stampede to Timberline '49; The Bonanza Trail '53. Also author numerous articles in field. With U Colo since '26, prof fine art and head art dept '28-47. Fine Arts Department, University of Colorado, Boulder, Colo.

23 WOLTERINK, Lester Floyd. Hormone fattening of fowl; Taste in insects; Physiology of athletics (Exercise). b'15. AB '36 (Hope Coll); MA—PhD '43 (U Minn); '35 (U Mich Biol Sta). Author articles in field. With Mich State Coll since '41 now asso prof dept physiol and pharmacol; with Mich Agr Expt Sta since '45 now research asso; asso physiol Argonne Nat Lab '48. Mich Acad Sci Arts Letters—AAAS—Am Soc Zool (asso)—Poultry Sci Assn—Sigma Xi. Department of Physiology, Michigan State College, East Lansing, Mich.†

24 WOLTZ, Willie Garland. Soil fertility; Flue-cured tobacco. b'11. BS '39 (NC State Coll); PhD '48 (Cornell U). Soil fertility investigations in production of flue-cured tobacco with emphasis on physical and chemical properties of leaf and their relation to manufacture of cigarettes; soil fertility investigations dealing with production and quality of vegetable crops; studies on use of radioactive elements in investigating fertilizer and nutritional problems. Author articles in field. Research asso prof agron NC State Coll '46-50, professor of agronomy since '50; soil tech Virginia Truck Expt Sta '43-46. Am Soc Agron—Soil Sci Am—Am Chem Soc—Sigma Xi. Department of Agronomy, North Carolina State College, Raleigh, N.C.

25 WONDERLY, William Lower. Mexican Indian languages (Zoque). b'16. AB '36 (Wm Jennings Bryan U); MA '39 (Columbia Bible Coll); PhD '48 (U Mich). Field work in Mexican Indian languages, translation of portions of the Scriptures in Zoque language.

Author: Notes on Zoque Grammar '43. Author articles: Phonemic Acculturation in Zoque '46; Zoque Place Names '46; Some Zoquean Phonemic and Morphophonemic Correspondence '49; Zoque: Phonemics and Morphology '51-52. Investigator Mexican Indian langs Summer Inst Linguistics since '39, prof linguistics since '41. Linguistic Soc Am—Sigma Xi. Summer Institute of Linguistics, Box 870, Glendale 5, Calif.

10 WOOD, Albert E(lmer). Vertebrate paleontology; F o s s i l rodents (Evolution); Engineering geology (Uses of seismograph). b'10. BS '30 (Princeton); MA '32—Cutting Traveling Fellow '34-35—PhD '35 (Columbia). Author articles in field. Field asst US Geol Survey summer '34; research fossil rodents Am Mus '35-36; asst geol US Army Engrs flood control Binghamton NY '36-39, asso geol '39-40, geol '41, '46; asst prof biol Amherst Coll '46-48, asso prof since '48. Geol Soc of Am(F)—Paleontol Soc(F)—AAAS(F)—Am Soc Mammalogists—Soc for the Study of Evolution—Zool—Sigma Xi. Biology Department, Amherst Coll., Amherst, Mass.†

11 WOOD, Arthur Eugene. Organic sulfur compounds; Desulfurization of petroleum distillates. b'87. BS '07 (Mercer U); MS '09 (Vanderbilt U); PhD '24 (U Pittsburgh). Author articles in field. Head dept chem Miss Coll since '20. Am Chem Soc—Miss Acad Sci—Miss Ednl Assn. Recipient $1400 research grant Am Petroleum Inst '27-28. Mississippi College, Clinton, Miss.†

12 WOOD, Benjamin DeKalbe. Educational psychology (Guidance, testing). b'94. AB '17 (U Tex); AM '22 —PhD '23 (Columbia); LLD '36 (Lawrence Coll); LHD '42 (Union Coll); ScD '50 (Colo State Coll Education). Planning, designing, administering and reporting educational experiments, research programs, and guidance programs; test construction; personnel selection; industrial psychology consulting. Author: M e a s u r e m e n t in Higher Education '23; New York Experiments with New Type Modern Foreign Language Tests '27. Co-author: Motion Pictures in the Classroom (with F N Freeman) '29; Our Air-Age World (with Overton, Packard and Wood) '44; Measuring and Guiding Individual Growth (with Ralph Haefner) '48. With Columbia U since '22, now prof collegiate ednl research; dir Eastman teaching film expt '27-28; dir elementary sch typewriter research '29-31; dir cooperative test service Am Council Edn '30-45; dir ednl records bur NYC since '33; chmn joint advisory com on aviation edn Civil Aeronautics Administrn and US Office Edn '41-45, ednl con since '42; com on sci aids to learning to '46. Nat Aeronautics Assn (air youth bd)—Ednl Research Assn—Nat Edn Assn—NY Acad Sci—NY Soc for Exptl Study of Edn—Personnel Research Fedn — Prog Edn Assn — Am Psychol Assn — Vocational Guidance Assn—Phi Beta Kappa—Kappa Delta Pi. 106 Morningside Drive, NYC 27.†⊙

13 WOOD, Florence Dowden. Autotomy in Arthropoda. b'98. AB '21 (Sweet Briar Coll); PhD '25—fellow '22-25 (Yale). Field expeditions collecting fossil vertebrates numerous states, Canada. Author: articles in field. Presently engaged in private research. AAAS(F)—Soc Vertebrate Paleontol (com on color and correlation NA Continental tertiary '41-47)— Sigma Xi. 403 Claremont Av., Montclair, N.J.

14 WOOD, Horace Elmer, II. Vertebrate paleontology; Rhinocerotoidea

(Fossil); Tertiary continental stratigraphy of North America; Comparative odontology. b'01. AB '21 (Princeton); AM '23—PhD '27 (Columbia). Fifteen seasons of field exploration. Author articles in field. Prof biol Newark Coll Rutgers U since '46; research asso fossil mammals Am Mus Natural Hist since '42. Geol Soc Am(F)—Paleontol Soc(F)—AAAS(F)—NY Acad Sci (F, vp '39, '40)—Nat Research Council (Com on Common Problems in Genetics, Paleontol and Systematics)—Soc for Study of Evolution—Soc Vertebrate Paleontol — Am Soc Mammalogists — Am Mus Natural Hist(F)—Am Geol Inst(dir '50-52)—Am Commn in Stratigraphic Nomenclature—Explorers Club —Sigma Xi — Phi Beta Kappa. The Newark Colleges of Rutgers Univ, 40 Rector St., Newark 2, N.J.

15 WOOD, J(ohn) Perry. Judges (Selection and tenure). b'79. AM '01 (Dickinson Coll); LLB '02 (Yale). Represented California State Bar Association '28 in proceedings in Superior Court for liberal interpretation of constitutional provisions for judicial council; initiated movement in California for reform of judicial selection and tenure '32; chairman committee, conference bar association delegates on judicial selection and tenure '35, '36, and of like committee American Bar Association '37-44. Am Bar Assn (ho of dels '40-42)—Internat Law Assn—League of Nations Assn—So Cal(pres '23-24)— English Speaking Union. RFD 1, Claremont, Cal.⊙

16 WOOD, Ralph Charles. German-Americana; Pennsylvania-Germans. b'04. BA, BE '28—MA '30 (U Cincinnati); PhD '32 (Cornell U). Author: The Pennsylvania Germans '42. Author articles: History of the German Theater of Cincinnati '32; Bauernfreund, a Newspaper of the Pennsylvania Germans '40, and others. Prof German Cornell U '30-37, Princeton U '37-42, Lehigh U '42-44; Penn State U '44-46; Muhlenberg Coll since '46. Modern Language Assn—Am Assn of Teachers of German—Am Hist Soc—Normanns Forbundet—Pa. German Soc. Muhlenberg College, Allentown, Pa. H: 720 N. Muhlenburg St., Allentown Pa.

17 WOOD, Ray. Folklore. b'89. Ed pub sch. Research in Haitien lore and history, collected lore and folksongs, translated laws into English, compiled two volumes of folklore and folksong; research in American folklore and folksong particularly childlore. Author: Glossary of Creole Dialect; One volume Haitien folklore; American Mother Goose; Mother Goose in the Ozarks, Mother Goose in Texas; Mother Goose in Indiana; Mother Goose in New York; What Happened to Mother Goose. Translator: Three volumes comprising laws of Haiti (into English). Officer Constabulary Haiti '15-23; spl agt US Treasury '25-40; high sch teacher and newspaper columnist '40-46; newspaper columnist and illustrator since '46. Am Folklore Soc — ALA. Received medaille militaire Haiti with special citation for effort in cultural field. Raywood, Texas.

18 WOOD, Richard D(awson). Characeae (Taxonomy and ecology); Aquatic plants (Physiology and ecology); Algae. b'18. BA—BSc (O State U); MS '42—PhD '47 (Northwestern U). While in England and Europe for three years studied Characeae in major European herbaria. Author articles in field. At Franz Theodore Stone Lab '40, Mich Biol Sta '41, Hopkins Marine Sta '46; investigator Marine Biol Sta '47, lecturer '48, instr '49; instr bot RI State Coll '47-48, asst prof since '49. Phycol Soc Am—Am Soc Plant Taxonomists—

Ill Acad Sci—O Acad Sci—AAAS—Sigma Xi—Phi Beta Kappa—Am Society Limnology and Oceanography—Ecol Soc Am. Botany Department, University of Rhode Island, Kingston.

19 WOOD, Richard G. American History (Archives, lumbering in Maine). b'00. AB '22 (Dartmouth); AM '24—PhD '34 (Harvard U). Archives; accessioning and disposition of records; reference; records analysis and description. Author: A History of Lumbering in Maine 1820-1861 '35; A Preliminary Checklist of the Records of the Boston Navy Yard '46. Reviews editor; The American Archivist since '44; also articles in field. Asst prof hist U Maine '28-35; state dir Hist Records Survey for NH '35-40; state supervisor WPA Research and Records Projects for NH '40-42; archivist Nat Archives Washington since '42. Soc Am Archivists—AHA—Va Hist Soc— NH Hist Soc—Am Assn State and Local Hist—Phi-Kappa-Phi. National Archives, Washington 25.

20 WOOD, William Henry. Lithographic chemistry; Physics and chemistry of photomechanical reproduction. b'05. BS '29—MA '30 (U Mo). Granted over 50 US and foreign patents. Author articles in field. Research chem Phillips Petroleum Corp '31-36; dir research Harris-Seybold Co since '36. Am Chem Soc—AAAS—Royal Photog Soc— Internat Assn Printing House Craftsmen—Tech Assn Lithographic Industry (charter mem, first vp '48)—Lithographic Tech Found (research adv com since '47). 4510 E. 71st St., Cleve 5.†

21 WOODCOCK, Amos Walter Wright. Volstead Act. b'83. AB '03 (St John's Coll Annapolis Md); LLB '10 (U Md); MA '12 (Harvard); LLD '32 (Washington) '37 (St John's). Director of US Bureau of Prohibition '30-33; appointed special assistant to attorney general of US '33. Chatillon, Salisbury, Md.⊙

22 WOODFORD, A(lfred) O(swald). Geology of southern and Lower California. b'90. BA '13 (Pomona Coll); PhD '23 (U Calif). Author articles in field. Prof geol Pomona Coll since '15. Pomona College, Claremont, Calif.†

23 WOODHOUSE, John Crawford. Chemical control of economic pests. b'98. AB '21—MA '23 (Dartmouth Coll); MA '24—PhD '27 (Harvard). Research on adsorption by inorganic systems, high pressure synthesis in organic aliphatic chemistry, complex high molecular weight inorganic chemistry, application of chemicals to solving biological problems especially control of economic pests and animal medicine and nutrition. Research chem EI du Pont de Nemours & Co since '28, dir tech div Grasselli Chem Dept since '43. Am Chem Soc—Soc Chem Ind— Am Inst Chem Engrs—Phi Beta Kappa —Sigma Psi. DuPont Company, Wilmington, Del.

24 WOODROOF, William Ernest. Camellia culture, propagation, and nomenclature. b'07. AB '29 (U Calif Los Angeles); LLB '33 (Harvard). Author: The Camellia, Its Culture and Nomenclature '47; also articles in field. Gen mgr, propagator and grower for Calif Camellia Gardens San Fernando Calif since '44. Am Camellia Soc (mem nomenclature com '49) — So Calif Camellia Soc (chmn nomenclature com)—Pacific Camellia Soc (chmn nomenclature com since '46). California Camellia Gardens, 13531 Fenton Av., San Fernando, Calif. H: 4117 Davana Rd., Sherman Oaks, Calif.

25 WOODRUFF, Joseph Franklin. Spectroscopy (Steel). b'13. '35 (Capital U); '36 (O State U); '38 (U Cin). Research and development of procedures using briquetted pellets in analysis of steels and other materials by using spectrograph as analytical tool; developed 50 spectrochemical methods for analysis of slags, aluminum, zinc, ferroalloys, low alloy steels, high alloy steels, and plain carbon steels. With Armco Steel Corp since '41, supervising spectrochem since '46. Nat Edn Assn—Am Inst Phys—Optical Soc Am(pres Ohio Valley sect '49). Armco Steel Corp., Research Laboratories, Middletown, O.

10 WOODS, John Price. Radar (Countermeasures); Exploration geophysics. b'03. BS in elec engring '25—MS in elec engring '30—PhD '32 (U Tex). Research, design and construction instruments used in exploration for petroleum with emphasis on reflection seismograph, development and theory, field technique for seismic prospecting; research on methods of jamming enemy radar, design search receivers, use of radar for seismic survey. Geophysicist Shell Oil Co '33-42; group leader Radio Research Lab Harvard '42-44; supervisor Geophys Lab Atlantic Refining Co since '44. Tau Beta Pi—Sigma Xi—Soc Exploration Geophys—Am Geophys Union. Atlantic Refining Co., Box 2819, Dallas.

11 WOODS, Kenneth Brady. Soils. b '05. BS in civil engring '32—CE '37 (Ohio State U). Airphoto interpretation of soils; detailed study soil patterns in Indiana; study of air photo patterns of permanently frozen soils; application of soil mechanics to engineering design of airports, railroads, and highways; laboratory tests of soil stabilizing agents, including cement, bituminous materials, resin, lime, calcium chloride, and molasses. Author articles: The Application of Soil Mechanics in Highway Construction '37; Soil Stabilization Research at Purdue University '40; Design and Construction of Highway Embankments '40, and others. Co-author articles: (with L E Gregg) Pavement Performance Related to Soil Texture and Compaction '44; (with E J Yoder) Compaction and Strength Characteristics of Soil-Aggregate Mixtures '46; (with R E Frost) Aerial Photographs Used for an Engineering Evaluation of Soil Materials '48, and others. With O Dept Highways '32-39, asst engr in charge soils '34-39; prof highway engring and asso dir highway research Purdue U since '39; cons airfields br Office Chief of Engrs, Dept Army, Burlington & So RR. Am Soc CE—ASTM—Assn Asphalt Paving Tech—Am Rd Builders Assn—Am Concrete Inst—Ind Acad Sci—Soc Am Mil Engrs—Sigma Xi. NRC Highway Research Bd award for paper on highway materials '45, Distinguished Service award '49. Joint Highway Research Project, Purdue University, Lafayette, Ind.†◎

12 WOODS, Lloyd Lander. Kojic acid. b'08. AB '30 (Friends U); MS '34—PhD '44 (Kan State Coll). Isolation and chemical analysis. Author articles: Mannich Bases from Kojic Acid and Aryl Amines '46; Concerning the Acylation of Kojic Acid at Elevated Temperatures '48; The Hydroxymethylation of Kojic Acid '50. Prof chem St Augustine's Coll '31-48; prof and head dept chem Tex State U for Negroes since '48. ACS—Kan Acad Sci—Tex Acad Sci—AAUP—Phi Lambda Upsilon. Texas Southern University, Houston.

13 WOODS, Loren Paul. Ichthyology (Taxonomy, ecology). b'13. BA '36 (Earlham); '36-38 (Northwestern). Lec-

turer Raymond Found Chicago Natural Hist Mus '38, asst curator fishes '41-46, curator since '47; mem Mandel Galapagos expdn '40-41; co-leader Bermuda Deep Sea Expdn '48; asso curator fishes US National Mus Wash '46-48. Ensign USNR '43, fisheries officer mil govt Kyushu Japan '45-46. AAAS—Am Soc Ichthyol and Herpetol—Soc Vertebrate Paleontol—Soc Study Evolution—Limnol Soc Am. Division of Fishes, Chicago Natural History Museum, Chicago 5.

14 WOODWARD, Dorothy. History (Latin America, southwestern United States, New Mexico). b'95. AB '17 (Randolph-Macon Women's Coll); MA '25 (U Colo); PhD '35 (Yale). Author articles in field. With U New Mex since '35, now asso prof. Medieval Acad—Am Acad Polit Social Sci—AHA—Nat Council Social Studies—Phi Kappa Phi—Tau Kappa Alpha—Alpha Kappa Delta—Phi Alpha Theta—Pi Lambda Theta—Delta Kappa Gamma—Phi Sigma Iota—Sigma Alpha Iota. University of New Mexico, Albuquerque, N.M.

15 WOODWARD, Harry Reuben. Timber (Surveys and sustained-yield management); Forest fires (Prevention and suppression); Large-scale artificial reforestation; Deer (Winter ranges); Pheasants (Life history, feeding habits). b'19. Student '37-40 (Colo State Coll A&M); BS in forestry '41 (Utah State Agrl Coll). Inauguration sustained-yield management and inventory of existing state timberlands; organization state forest fire protection system for private and public lands; management distribution, planting and care of seedling trees and shrubs Great Plains area; supervision development and operation winter range areas for deer; winter food habit study of pheasants. Asst state forester SD Dept Game, Fish and Parks '46-48, state forester since '48. Soc Am Foresters—Com Great Plains Forestry—Wildlife Soc—Am Ornithol Union—Am Forestry Assn—Assn State Foresters—Nat Conf State Parks—Am Inst Park Execs—Xi Sigma Pi—Phi Kappa Phi—Beta Beta Beta. State Capitol, Pierre, S.D. H: 232 N. Fourth St., Custer.†

16 WOOLF, Wallace Glen. Metallurgy of electrolytic zinc. b'90. BS in mining engring '12—MS '14 (U Utah). Author articles: Electrolytic Zinc Plant of Sullivan Mining Co '36; Outlook for Zinc '40; Zinc Industry in 1949 '50, and others. Metall fellow U Utah '14-15; metall Holt-Dern Process Co Silver City Utha '15-16, Virginia Smelting Co West Norfolk Va '16-17; research metallurgy Bunker Hill & Sullivan Mining Company Kellogg Idaho '18-25; zinc plant superintendent Sullivan Mining Co since '26. Am Inst Mining Engring (com on reduction and refining lead and zinc)—Ida Mining Association—NW Mining Assn(vp)—Sigma Xi. Sullivan Mining Co., Box 209, Kellogg, Ida.

17 WOOLLARD, George Prior. Earth's gravity field; Structural geology; Sound ranging at sea. b'08. BS '32—MSc '34 (Ga Sch Tech); PhD '37—U fellow '37 (Princeton U); '37-38 (Lehigh U). Gravity and magnetic studies of the geologic structure of the continents. Author articles in field. Asso prof U Wis geophys and engring geol since '48; investigator of world gravity base values under auspices of the Office of Naval Research USN since '48. Research asso and research group leader investigating sound ranging in the sea OSRD for USN Woods Hole Oceanog Inst '41-47. Geol Soc Am(F)—Soc Exploration Geo-

physicists—Am Assn Petroleum Geol—Am Geophys Union—Am Inst Mining and Metall Engrs—Sigma Xi—Phi Kappa Phi—Tau Beta Pi. Nat Research Council Fellow '39; Guggenheim fellow '40, '48. Department of Geology, University of Wisconsin, Madison, Wis.

18 WOOLLEY, George Walter. Genetics of the mouse; Tumors of reproductive and endocrine organs; Adrenal cortex, pituitary, uterus, mammary glands; Adrenal cortical steroids. b'04. BS '30 (Ia State Coll); MS '31—PhD '35 (U Wis). Genetic study of cattle in Wisconsin, growth defect study in the rat; established and studied a new dwarf character (du 2) in the rat; established and studied linkage relations of a coat color mutation in the mouse (misty), of a coat hair character (fuzzy) together with linkage relations; first established fact that the virus-like milk factor of mammary gland cancer of mice was in blood and in males as well as females; first found method to produce adrenal cortical tumors, benign and malignant in mouse through endocrine unbalance; established fact hormone (pellet) therapy could prevent expected endocrine cancer by restoring endocrine balance; first to establish fact that compound A of adrenal cortex (11 dehydrocorticosterone acetate) has tumor growth inhibiting properties; studied first experimental basophilic tumors of the pituitary, etc. Mem editorial bd Journ Nat Cancer Inst '47-50. Contributor chpts profl books. Mem Mount Desert Island Biol Lab since '48; research asso, mem bd dirs Roscoe B Jackson Meml Lab '36-39, asst dir '47-49; mem, head div steroid biol Sloan-Kettering Inst Meml Hosp Center since '49. AAAS—Am Genetics Association—Am Genetics Soc—Am Soc Human Genetics—Am Assn Cancer Research—Assn Anatomists—Sigma Xi—Wis Acad Sci—NY Acad Sci. Memorial Hospital Center, 444 E. 68th St., NYC.

19 WOOLSEY, Lawrence Shores. Electrical control. b'20. BS in elec engring '42 (U Ark). Research on design and application of antiaircraft fire control, liquid level control of pumping equipment, and diesel electric stations. Staff antiaircraft fire control section Ballistic Research Lab Aberdeen Proving Ground '43; with Marion L Crist & Asso since '45. Am Inst EE—Tau Beta Pi—Pi Mu Epsilon. Union Life Building, Little Rock, Ark.

20 WORK, Harold K(nowlton). Aluminum (Electroplating, anodic coating); Steel properties. b'01. AB '23—ChE '25 (Columbia); PhD '29 (U Pittsburgh); research fellow '25-29 (Mellon Inst). Author articles in field. Mgr research and development Jones and Laughlin Steel Corp '36-47, dir research '47-49; dir research div Coll Engring NYU since '49. Am Soc Metals (nat treas '45-47, vp '47-48, pres '48-49)—Am Inst Mining and Metall Engrs (Pittsburgh exec com, v chmn exec com iron and steel div, Hunt award '42)—Am Chem Soc (nat councilor)—Indsl Research Inst (past chmn '44-45)—Nat Research Council (exec com div eng and indsl research)—Am Iron and Steel Inst (com gen research)—Am Soc Testing Metals—Am Inst Chem Engrs—AAAS—Phi Beta Kappa—Tau Beta Pi—Sigma Xi.

21 WORK, Lincoln Thomas. Properties of fine particles. b'98. BA '18—ChE '21—MA '24—PhD '29 (Columbia). Research on Portland cement, paints, pigments, grinding, coal tar, paraffin wax, ejectors, flow of fluids through beds of packed solids. Holds patents in field. Author articles in field. Instr chem engring Columbia '21-29, asst prof '29-39, asso prof '39-40; chem engring cons '21-40; dir research and development Metal & Thermit Corp NYC '40-49; consultant since '49. Am Ceramic Soc—Am Chem Soc—Am Inst Chem Engrs—Am Inst Chem—Am Inst Mining Metall Engrs—Am Ry Engr Assn—Am Soc Metals—Am Soc Testing Materials—Am Standards Assn—Am Welding Soc—Electrochem Soc—Inst Metals—Soc Promotion Engring Edn—Phi Beta Kappa—Tau Beta Pi—Sigma Xi. 15 North Crescent, Maplewood, N.J. and 420 Lexington Av., NYC.

10 WORMINGTON, Hannah Marie. American archeology. b'14. BA '35 (U Denver); '37-38, '40-41 (Radcliffe Coll). Independent study archeology in France England and Spain '35; research on earliest stone industries of North America, particularly Folsoms and parallel-flaked points commonly called Yumas, and on Folsom complex; excavations at Johnson Folsom and Turner sites. Author: Ancient Man in North America '49; also articles in field. Curator archeol Denver Mus Nat Hist since '37; asst prof dept anthrop Univ Denver '47-49. American Anthrop Assn(F)—Soc Am Archeol—Soc Vertebrate Paleontol—Colo Archeol Soc. Denver Museum of Natural History, City Park, Denver, Colo.†

11 WORNER, Ruby K. Textiles (Testing); Cotton fabrics (Utilization, weathering). b'00. BS '21—MS '22—PhD '25 (U Chicago). Development methods for evaluating properties of textile materials ranging from fibers to finished fabrics. Textile technologist Nat Bur Standards '29-40, in charge textile testing sect So Regional Lab USDA New Orleans since '40. AAAS—ASTM—Am Assn Textile Chemists and Colorists. 2100 Robert E. Lee Blvd., New Orleans 19.

12 WORTHY, James Carson. Labor relations; Personnel administration. b '10. Student '29-32 (Northwestern U); '32-33 (Bonn U, U Vienna-Oxford U) '34-35 (George Washington U). Study employee attitudes and morale; selection and development executive personnel. Author articles: What Employers Want '50; Attitude Surveys as a Tool of Management '50; Factors Influencing Employee Morale '50; Changing Concepts of the Personnel Function '49; Democratic Principles in Business Management '49, and others. Asst dep adminstr NRA '33-36; employment mgr Schuster & Co Milwaukee '36-38; mem central personnel staff in charge employee relations Sears Roebuck & Co since '38. Indsl Relations Assn Chicago (pres)—Am Sociol Soc—Indsl Relations Research Assn—Soc for Applied Anthropology. Sears, Roebuck & Co., 925 S. Homan Av., Chgo 7.

13 WREDEN, Nicholas. Russian literature. b'01. Ed Russian Imperial Naval Acad. Author: The Unmaking of a Russian '35. Translator: Dog Lane (Goomilovsky) '28; Fifth Seal (Aldanov) '43; Tolstoy and His Wife (Polner) '45; For Thee the Best (Aldanov) '45; I'll Never Go Back (Koriakov) '48; Buddha's Return (Gazdanov) '51; To Live as We Wish (Aldanov) '52. Manager Scribner book store NYC '39-44, dir Charles Scribner's Sons NY '41-44; vp, ed-in-chief and dir E P Dutton & Co NYC since '44. Am Booksellers Assn (pres '42-43). 300 Fourth Av., NYC.

14 WREDEN, William Paul. Witchcraft; Demonology; Ghosts. b'10. AB '34 (Stanford U). Research on witches and witchcraft prior to 1800. Editor: Timothy Bookworm; Horresco Refer-

ens '49. In rare book bus since '37. Bibliog Soc—Hist Sci Soc—Hist Med Soc—Am Folklore Soc—NY Folklore Soc—Cal Folklore Soc—Oxford Bibliog Soc—Cambridge Bibliog Soc—Cal Hist Soc—Bibliog Natural Hist Soc—Am Bibliog Soc. Postoffice Box 84, 18 California Dr., Burlingame, Cal.

15 WRENN, C(harles) Gilbert. Student personnel; Personnel training and administration; Study habits; Mental hygiene; Youth problems. b'02. AB '26 (Willamette U); AM '29—PhD '32 (Stanford U). Member staff American Youth Commission '39-40; consultant student personnel American Council on Education, '43-44, '46-48. Author: Practical Study Aids '31; Study-Habits Inventory '41; Building Self-Confidence '48; (with Luella Cole) How to Read Rapidly and Well '35; (with Robert Larsen) Studying Effectively '41; (with Reginald Bell) Student Personnel Problems '42, and others; also articles in field. Prof edn psychol U Minn since '37; Personnel officer USN, lt, later lt comdr '42-45. Am Psychol Assn(F and diplomate)—Am Coll Personnel Assn (vp '42-44, pres '47-49)—Nat Vocational Guidance Assn (vp '41-44, trustee '44-46, pres '46-47)—Am Edn Research Assn—Council of Guidance and Personnel Assns (vp '46-47.©

16 WRIGHT, Almon R. United States State Department and United States Government World Wars I and II records; Argentine history. b'03. PhB '26 (Denison U); AM '28 (Harvard); PhD '35 (U Ill). Research on records and history of various World War I and II government agencies, and on history of aid provided to Allies '17-19. Author articles: The Origins of the Argentine Supreme Court '36; Juan Manuel de Rosas and the Church '37; Argentine and the Papacy, 1810-1927 '38; Food and Society: War-Time Archives of the United States Food Administration '38; Sources for Ohio World War History in the Papers of the Food Administration in the National Archives '38; Food Purchases of the Allies, 1917-1918 '42, and others. With Nat Archives '35-49 head Exec and Fgn Affairs Br '47-49; research analyst Dept State since '49. Soc Am Archivists. Dept. of State, Washington. H: 5003 44th St. N.W., Washington 16.†

17 WRIGHT, Arthur W(illiam). Tumors in rats; Age and endocrine chgs associated with spontaneous tumor development. b'94. AB '17—MD '23 (Harvard). Effects various gases injected into animal tissues, study blood vessel tumors and pancreatic lesions involving especially the islets of Langerhans; research on effect of caesium salts on experimental tumors of mice. Cyrus Strong Merrill prof path Albany Med Coll since '34, also path and bacteriologist-in-chief, and dir labs Albany Hosp. AMA(F)—AAAS(F)—Am Soc Clin Path(F)—APHA(F)—Am Association Path and Bact—Am Soc Exptl Path—Am Assn Cancer Research—Am Fedn Clin Research—Soc Am Bact—Am Cancer Soc—Soc Exptl Biol and Med—NY Acad Sci—NY State Assn Pub Health Labs—NY State Med Soc—Sigma Xi. Department of Pathology, Albany Medical College, New Scotland Av., Albany 3, N.Y.

18 WRIGHT, Charles Will. Mining (Foreign). b'79. Student '97-00 (Sch Mines Freiberg and U Heidelberg Germany); BS in mining engring '02—DEng '47 (Mich Coll Mines). Studies mining methods and costs in US and foreign mining developments and conditions, and protection of American mining interests abroad; foreign min-

eral surveys on mines and smelters in Italy, Germany, Austria, Greece, Yugoslavia, Hungary, Czechoslovakia, Bulgaria, Rumania, and Russia '35-39, Bolivia, Peru, Chile, Argentina, and Brazil '39-42; assisted in establishment mineral attaches at American Embassies abroad; supervision of engineers to increase output of strategic minerals in Latin America. Chief mining engr Societa Pertusola Ltd Sardinia Italy '10-20; gen mgr Soc Atesina Mineraria Trentino Italy '20-27; chief mining div Bur Mines '27-35, chief fgn specialist '35-42; dir minerals div Coordinator Inter-Am Affairs, also chief tech cons Bd Econ Warfare and Fgn Econ Adminstrn '42-45, reported on mineral industry of Germany and mining industries Sardinia, Sicily, and Greece '45-46, for Allied Commn and pvt cos; cons engr fgn minerals div since '46; Geol Soc Am—Soc Econ Geol—AIMME—Am Mining and Metall Soc—Pan-Am Inst Mining Engring and Geol(v chmn). H: 2540 Massachusetts Av., Washington 8.

19 WRIGHT, Donald (Thomas). Marine navigation (Inland rivers); Marine history. b'94. Student '12-13 (Allegheny Coll); '19 (U Ky). Author articles in field. Steersman on O River steamboats '09-12, granted license as master, all tons, any river under US flag; first-class pilot on upper O River; pres Allegheny River Improvement Assn (Pa) '13-17; US Army Engrs Cincinnati Dist '18-19; pub, ed The Waterways Jour St Louis '20-49; chmn Bridge Com, Miss Valley Assn St Louis. Nat Rivers and Harbors Cong—Ohio Valley Improvement Assn—Ia Hist Soc—Mo Hist Soc.

20 WRIGHT, Ernest. Forest nursery seedling diseases. b'99. BS '23 (Ore State Coll); MS '28 (U Calif); PhD '41 (U Neb). Research on cytospora canker and stains associated with beetle infestations in true firs, susceptibility of shelterbelt trees to Phymatotrichum or Texas root rot, damping-off and other diseases of broadleaf and coniferous seedlings in nurseries, control of sapstain and rot in green lumber of western species. Author articles in field. Jr path, div forest path, later path US Dept Agr since '27, Portland Ore since '42. Sigma Xi. P.O. Box 4137, Portland 8, Ore.†

21 WRIGHT, Forrest Blythe. Rural electrification (Household mechanics, and water supply); Chick brooders; Weed control (Flaming). b'96. BS '22—MS '24—PhD '33 (Cornell U); '17-18, 19-20 (Transylvania U). Devel new design for lamp brooders, design for dehydrator used in laboratories for dehydrating laboratory samples and on farms for dehydrating food; invented automatic machine for washing market eggs, automatic machine for drying washed eggs, machine for automatically feeding eggs into a grader, washer or drier. Author: Electricity in the Home and on the Farm '35; Rural Water Supply and Sanitation '39; also articles in field. Resident teacher, research worker Cornell U. Am Soc Agrl Engrs—AAAS. Department Agricultural Engineering, Stocking Hall, Cornell University, Ithaca, N.Y.

22 WRIGHT, Frederick Dunstan. Oil shale mining; Underground structures. b'16. AB '38 (Harvard); MS '42 (Columbia Sch Mines). Research and development new mining methods and equipment for low cost oil shale mining, cost estimating; design, support and stress analysis of underground structures, determined optimum roof and pillar dimensions for experimental oil shale mine, developed new technique for stress measurements. Shift boss Ariston Gold Mine New Consol Goldfields of S Africa '38-39; supt pilot mill Johns-Manville Corp '39-41; mining engr US Bur Mines since '46. AIMME. Bureau of Mines, College Park, Md.

10 WRIGHT, Helen. History of American astronomy (Nineteenth century). b'14. BA '37—MA '39 (Vassar). Research on history of astronomy in US with particular reference to life of Maria Mitchell and George E Hale. Author: Sweeper in the Sky '48. Co-author: A Treasury of Science (with Harlow Shapley, Samuel Rapport) '43; Readings in Physical Sciences (with Shapley and Rapport) '48. Asst dept astron Vassar Coll '37-39; jr astron United States Naval Observatory '42-43; fellow astron Maria Mitchell Obs '41, 44. Am Astron Soc. Mt. Wilson Observatory, Pasadena, Calif.

11 WRIGHT, Herbert Edgar Jr. Geomorphology and Pleistocene geology. b'17. AB '39—MA '41—PhD '43 (Harvard). Research on geology and geomorphology of parts of New Mex and Arizona; Pleistocene geology and pre-history of the Middle East; glacial geology and geomorphology of Minnesota and Alaska. Asso prof geol U Minn; Minn Geol Survey; US Geol Survey; archaeol expdns to Lebanon '47, Iraq '51. Geol Soc Am(F)—Am Geophys Union—Am Geog Soc—Arctic Inst NA—Archeol Inst Am—Brit Glacial Soc—Sigma Xi. Department of Geology, University of Minnesota, Minneapolis.†

12 WRIGHT, Howard Emory. Tests (Psychological). b'08. AB '32 (Lincoln U Pa); MA '33—PhD '46 (O State U). Testing and counseling college students. Author articles: An Analysis of Results with Certain Tests of Interests and Attitudes '33; Physiological Aspects of Child Development '40; Racial Humor: A Value Analysis '46, and others. Head psychol dept NC Coll Durham NC '45-48; prof psychol and chmn div edn and psychol Tex State U since '48. Am Psychol Assn—AAUP. Texas State University, Houston. H: 3120 Isabella.†

13 WRIGHT, John Kirtland. Geographical knowledge in the Middle Ages; History of geography in the United States; Geographical bibliography. b'91. AB '13—AM '13—PhD '22 (Harvard). History of development of geographical knowledge; general geographical bibliography. Author: The Geographical Lore of the Time of the Crusades '25; Geography in the Making: The American Geographical Society, 1851-1951 '52. Co-author: (with Elizabeth T. Platt) Aids to Geographical Research '47. Librarian Am Geog Soc '20-37, dir '38-49, research asso since '49. Assn Am Geographers(pres '46). American Geographical Society, Broadway at 156th St., NYC 32.

14 WRIGHT, John William. Cotton marketing. b'90. BS '17 (Utah State Coll); '19 (London Sch Econ); '24-25 (U Cal); MS '33—PhD '38 (Am U). Research on economic and technological problems of ginning, standardization, marketing, testing and processing cotton, grading and marketing cottonseed. With Agrl Ext Service U Ariz '21-28; with USDA since '28, in charge marketing research sect Cotton Div Agrl Marketing Service '31-42, chief research and testing div, cotton br Prodn and Marketing Adminstrn since '42. Fiber Soc—Am Econ Assn —Am Farm Econ Assn—Am Marketing Assn. Cotton Branch, US Dept of Agriculture, Washington 25. H: 429 Whittier St., Washington 12.

15 WRIGHT, John Womack. Development of permanent fortifications

(1500-1800); Continental Army (Organization, equipment, supply, tactics). b'76. Student '92-95—LLD (hon) '47 (William and Mary Coll); LLB '98 (George Washington U); grad '21 (Army School of the Line). Directed restoration and improvement of ancient fortifications, barracks, and other edifices in Puerto Rico. Author: Development of Bastioned Fortifications from 1500 to 1800 '46, and others; also articles in field. Officer US Army '98-29, '33-39, ret as col '40, recalled to active duty '41-46 as sec hist sect Army War Coll. AHA—Phi Beta Kappa. Decorated as Cmdr Order Isabel the Cath by Spanish govt for restoration work in Puerto Rico. 1851 Columbia Rd., Washington. Deceased.

16 WRIGHT, Kenneth E(lmer). Plants (Mineral nutrition, aluminum toxicity); Ferns of Rhode Island. b'02. BS '25—MS '29—PhD '35 (O State U). Author articles in field. Asso prof bot Smith since '46. Am Soc Plant Physiol—Am Soc Plant Taxonomists— Bot Soc Am—Soc Study Evolution— Torrey Bot Club — NE Wild Flower Preservation Soc (bd dirs)—Phi Kappa Phi—Sigma Xi. Botany Department, Smith College, Northampton, Mass.†

17 WRIGHT, Lyle Henry. Bibliography; American fiction before 1875; Californiana. b'03. Student '21-23 (U Calif). Author: Sporting Books in the Huntington Library '37; American Fiction 1774-1850 '48. Editor: B Greenleaf's California Almanac for 1849 '42. Co-editor: W L Ormsby's Butterfield Overland Mail; L Kip's California Sketches with Recollections of the Gold Mines '46; J Udell's Journal Kept during a Trip across the Plains in 1859 '46; A Child's Overland Route to California '46; also articles in field. With Henry E Huntington Library since '23, head reference dept since '46. Bibliog Soc Am. Huntington Library, San Marino 15, Calif.

18 WRIGHT, Mike. Aquatic insects (Mayflies, dragon flies). b'14. AB '35 (U Ala); MS '37 (Vanderbilt U); PhD '41 (O State U). Author articles in field. With Bur Entomol and Plant Quarantine US Dept Agr since '41, entomol in charge mosquito, rodent and other vermin control to service command engr US War Dept Second Service Command NYC; prof and head biology dept Tusculum Coll '45-50. Sigma Xi. 1110 19th Av. S., Nashville.

19 WRIGHT, Muriel Hazel. History of Oklahoma; History and language of American Indians (Five Civilized Tribes, Choctaw, Cherokee). Student '06-08 (Wheaton Sem Norton Mass); grad '12 (East Central State Normal Coll Okla); post grad work (Barnard Coll). Secretary Choctaw Committee in Oklahoma for business affairs, education, and welfare '22-28; delegate to various Indian councils and organizations in Oklahoma '22-48; secretary Choctaw Advisory Council recognized by US Office Indian Affairs. Author: The Story of Oklahoma '49; Our Oklahoma '49. Co-author: Oklahoma: A History of the State and Its People '29; Guide to Indian Tribes in Oklahoma, ms; also articles in field. Staff Okla Hist Soc '29-31; asst dir research and asso editor Okla Hist Soc since '43. Okla Hist Soc (life)—Am Assn State Local Hist. Rockefeller Found fellow '47; Distinguished Service Citation annual Achievement Day U Okla '49. The Chronicles of Oklahoma, Oklahoma Historical Society, Oklahoma City, Okla.

20 WRIGHT, Philip Lincoln. Weasels (Reproductive cycles). b'14. BS '34— MS '37 (UNH); PhD '40 (U Wis). Author articles in field. Instr, later

asso prof zool Mont State U since '39. Am Soc Zool—Am Assn Anat—Am Soc Mammal—Sigma Xi. Montana State University, Missoula, Mt.†

21 WRIGHT, R(ussell) B(erkeley). Electronics; Acoustics; Sonar; Radio; Piezoelectricity; Frequency standards; Fathometers; b'98. AB '22 (Stanford); S.M '28 (MIT). Physicist radio sect ScM '28 (MIT). Phisicist radio sect tric engineer US Coast and Geodetic Survey '33-35, '38-42; physicist sound division Naval Research Laboratory '35-38; executive director Committee on Ordnance, Research and Development Board since '46. Capt USNR '42-46. Inst Radio Engrs.⊙

22 WRIGHT, Sewall. Genetics (Populations, guinea pig); Biometry; Evolution. b'89. BS '11 (Lombard Coll Galesburg Ill); MS '12 (U Ill); ScD '15 (Harvard); ScD (hon) '42 (U Rochester). Research on genetics of guinea pig, method of path coefficients, and on statistical consequences of Mendelian heredity with reference to livestock breeding and to evolution. Author articles in field. With U Chicago since '26, Ernest D Burton distinguished service prof zool since '37. Nat Acad Sci—Am Philos Soc—Am Statis Assn — AAAS — Am Soc Zool (pres '44)—Am Soc Naturalists—Am Genetic Assn—Soc Animal Prodn— Genetics Soc Am (pres '34)—Inst Math Statis — Soc Study Evolution — Zool Soc, London (corr mem). 5762 Harper Av., Chgo 37.

23 WRIGHT, Stillman. Limnology; Copepoda; Trout. b'98. BS '21 (Beloit Coll); PhD '28 (U Wis). Research on taxonomy of Copepoda, limnology of Lake Erie and waters of Brazil and Argentina, biology and management of trout, fish and wildlife investigations in foreign countries. Author articles in field. Aquatic biol US Bur Fisheries '27-33; limnol Commisao Technica de Piscicultura Brazil '33-37; aquatic biol Fish and Wildlife Service '38-47, asst chief Office Fgn Activities Fish and Wildlife Service since '48. AAAS— Wis Acad Sci Arts Letters—Am Micros Soc—Am Fisheries Soc—Am Soc Limnol Oceanog—Internat Limnol Assn—Brazilian Acad Sci—Soc Systematic Zool—Wildlife Soc—Sigma Xi. Fish and Wildlife Service, Department of the Interior, Washington 25.†

24 WRIGHTSMAN, Charles Bierer. Russian oil fields. b'95. Student '14-15 (Stanford U); '15-17 (Columbia U). Made survey Russian oil fields '21; developed oil properties Okla, Kans, Tex, La and Calif '19-29; independent oil producer '18-21; pres Standard Oil Co Kan since '32. Mellie Esperson Building, Houston.

25 WULSIN, Frederick Roelker. Cultural anthropology; Adaptations to climate; Tropical and desert travel and equipment. b'91. AB '13—MCE '15— AM '26—PhD '29 (Harvard). Zoological collecting East Africa Madagascar '14-15, China Mongolia Kokonor Indo-China '21-24; archeological journeys Belgian Congo French Equatorial Africa '27, Persia '30-31. Author: Non-Chinese Inhabitants of the Province of Kansu, China; An Archeological Reconnaissance of the Shari Basin; Excavations at Tureng Tepe, Near Asterabad; The Prehistoric Archeology of Northwest Africa. Tutor anthrop Harvard '26-27, '28-29; lecturer anthrop Boston U '35-36; Tufts Coll since '45, prof since '47. Served 2d lt Corps of Interpreters '17-18, 1st lt '18-19, expert cons Research and Development Br OQMG '42-43, sr tech '43-45. Am Anthrop Assn—Am Assn Phys Anthrop Soc Applied Anthrop. 983 Memorial Dr., Cambridge 38, Mass.

10 WURTSBAUGH, Jewel. English literature. b'95. AB '21—AM '26 (Columbia); PhD '32 (Johns Hopkins U). Research in England '35, American libraries. Author: Spenserian Scholarship from 1609 to 1805 '36; also articles in field. Asst prof Eng '21-24 John Tarleton Coll; asst prof, prof Eng U Okla since '26. Modern Lang Assn—Okla Council Teachers of English (pres '41-44) — South-Central Modern Lang Assn (sec treas since '46)—Nat Council Teachers of Eng—Tex Poetry Soc—Am Dialect Soc Faculty Exchange, Norman, Okla.

11 WYCKOFF, Ralph Dewey. Geophysics. b'97. BS '20 (Mich State Coll). Research in development of gravity pendulum equipment, precision gravity measures, basic petroleum reservoir mechanics, precision gravity meter for geophysical use; developed azon, razon, radio-controlled bombs. Holds 7 US patents, others pending, also fgn patents. Author articles field. Asso physicist US Bur Standards '23-26; geophysicist Marland Oil Co Ponca City Okla '26-29; geophysicist Gulf Research & Development Co Pittsburgh '29-31, chief physics div '31-36, geophysicist '36-39, staff geophysicist '39-41, research engineer '41-45, dir geophysical research and development division since '46. Society Exploration Geophysicists (editor '39-42, vice pres '42-43, pres '43-44)— Inst Radio Engrs—Am Inst Mining Metall Engrs—APS. Gulf Research and Development Company, P.O. Box 2038, Pittsburgh 30.

12 WYCOFF, Albert Clarke. Psychology of religion; Asceticism; Cults (Social group); Fanaticism; Hysteria (Religious). b'74. AB '97—DD '24 (Union Coll); BD '00 (Union Theol Sem). Author: The Science of Prayer; Acute and Chronic Unbelief '24; also articles in field. Prof psychol of religion Biblical Seminary NY since '23. Spring Valley, N.Y.

13 WYLIE, Philip Gordon. Carl G. Jung; Fishing (Marine). b'02. Student (Princeton). Research on psychology of unconscious mind; definition and clarification concepts of Carl Gustav Jung. Author: Generation of Vipers '42; An Essay on Morals '47, also articles in field. Contributor: American Scholar, Saturday Evening Post, Atlantic Monthly. Steering com Lerner Marine Lab of Am Mus Natural Hist; free-lance writer on marine angling and psychology. Internat Game Fish Assn(vp)—Rod and Reel Club of Miami Beach(bd govs)—Anglers Inc. Care Harold Ober, 40 E. 49th St., NYC 17.

14 WYLLIE, John Cook. Rare books and bibliography (Americana, Virginiana, Jefferson, Darwin, Poe, Gothic novel, Southern history); History of printing (Virginia). b'08. BA '29 (U Va); grad study '29-35. Co-editor: Virginia Imprints Series. Curator of rare books U Va Tracy W McGregor Library. Bibliog Soc Am—Cambridge Bibliog Society—Bibliog Soc London—Oxford Bibliog Soc—Edinburgh Bibliog Soc—Bibliog Soc of U of Va. University of Virginia Library, Charlottesville, Va.

15 WYLLYS, Rufus Kay. Western US and Latin American history. b'98. AB '23—DLitt hon '38 (Hillsdale Coll); A M '24 (U Mich); PhD (U Cal). Author: The French in Sonora, 1950-54 '32; Pioneer Padre '35; Arizona Saga '50. Co-editor: New Spain and the Anglo-American West '32. Author articles: The East Florida Revolution of 1812-14 '29; The French of California and Sonora '32; The Republic of Lower

California, 1953-54 '33. Contbr to Dictionary of American History, Dictionary of American Biography. State Coll fellow U Mich '23-24; instr history Kalamazoo Coll '24-26; teaching fellow U Cal '26-28, Native Sons of the Golden West travelling fellow '28-29; asso prof history Ariz State Coll '29-31, prof history, head dept social studies since '31; acting asso prof history Stanford U '45; vis prof history San Diego State Coll '47, '50. AHA—AAUP —Quivira Soc—Am Geog Soc—Am Acad Polit and Social Sci—Kappa Delta Pi. Department of Social Studies, Ariz. State College, Tempe. H: 809 Myrtle Av.

16 WYMAN, Donald. Ornamental woody plants; American gardens. b'03. BS '26 (Pa State Coll); MS '31 —PhD '35 (Cornell). Author: Hedges, Screens and Windbreaks '38; Arboretums and Botanical Gardens of North America '47; Shrubs and Vines for American Gardens '49; Trees for American Gardens '51; also articles in field. Horticulturalist Arnold Arboretum Harvard since '36. AAAS—Am Inst Park Exec (past dir)—Am Assn Bot Gardens Arboretums (past chmn) —Am Hort Soc (dir since '39)—Am Soc Hort Sci—Phi Kappa Phi—Sigma Xi. Arnold Arboretum, Jamaica Plain, Mass.†

17 WYMAN, LeRoy Linwood, Sr. Metals (X-ray diffraction); Copper embrittlement. b'99. BSc—Chem E (U Minn). Developed embrittlement test for copper; research on cemented carbides, precision investment castings, powder metallurgy. Instr advancing to asst prof Okla Sch Mines '23-24; with Gen Elec Co since '24, metall liaison research lab '45-47, AEC research Knolls Atomic Power Lab since '47. ASTM(chmn com metall since '38) —AIMME—Am Soc Metals—Am Welding Soc—Am Crystallographic Soc— Soc Non-Destructive Testing—Alpha Chi Sigma. ASTM award of merit '50. General Electric Co., Knolls Atomic Power Laboratory, Schenectady, N.Y.

18 WYMAN, Walker DeMarquis. American history (Frontier, emigration, wild horses, overland freighting, midwest culture). b'07. Author: The Wild Horse of the West '45; A Topical Guide to the Mississippi Valley Historical Review and Proceedings '34; California Emigrant Letters '52; also articles. State Coll River Falls Wis since '32, prof, chmn dept social sci since '42. AHA—Miss Valley Hist Assn—Fgn Policy Assn—Nat Council Social Studies. State College, River Falls, Wis.

19 WYND, Frederick Lyle. Plant physiology and nutrition; Soil science. b'04. BS '28—BA '29—MA '30 (U Ore); PhD '33 — post doctorate research fellow '35-36 (Washington U). Research on physiological effects of ultraviolet light on plants, nature of action of bacteriophage, biochemistry of photoperiodism, relation of nutrition to composition of cereals and forage crops with special reference to vitamins and proteins, and on physiology of virus infection of plants; leader of botanical expedition in northern Estado de Coahuila and Sierra del Carmen Mexico '35; leader botanical expedition across Bolson de Mapimi Estado de Coahuila Mexico '37. Author articles in field. Research prof dept bot and plant path Mich State Coll since '48. Am Soc Plant Physiol—Sigma Xi. Am Cancer Soc grants '49-50, '50-51; Rockefeller grants '33-35, '35-36, '36-37. Dept of Botany, Michigan State College, East Lansing, Mich.⊙

20 WYNN, Frederick Houston. Traffic engineering. b'16. BS '38 (U Ore);

cert '46 (Yale). Co-author: (with Stewart M Gourley and Richard I Strickland) Studies of Weaving and Merging Traffic—A Symposium '49. Asst site engr Pub Works Design Sec Pearl Harbor '42-44; asst city planning engr Honolulu '44-45; dir Hawaii Highway Planning Survey TH '46-49; asst prof bur highway traffic Yale since '49. Inst Traffic Engrs. Bureau of Highway Traffic, Strathcona Hall, New Haven 11.

21 WYTHE, George. History of Latin American industrialization. b'93. BA '14 (U Tex); student (Institut Universitaire des Hautes Etudes Internationales Geneva); PhD '38 (George Washington U). Mem US delegation various Inter-Am confs. Auth: Industry in Latin America '45; An Outline of Latin American Economic Development '46; Brazil: An Expanding Economy '49; also articles in field. Comml attache to Am Embassy Mexico City '25-31; dir Am Republics Div Dept Commerce '33-39, since '43. Office of International Trade, Department of Commerce, Washington.†

Y

22 YAGLOU, Constantin Prodromos. Air hygiene. b'96. BS in mech engring '19 (Robert Coll); MS '20 (Cornell). Development effective temperature index of warmth, winter and summer comfort zones, ventilation requirements in public buildings, thermo-anemometer for measurement of air currents of any velocity; studies effect on health and comfort, of heat, cold humidity, radiation, barometric pressure, odors, clothing, atmospheric and industrial pollution. Author articles: Abnormal Air Conditions in Industry '37; Heating and Ventilation of Military Arctic Shelters '51; Thermal Standards in Industries '51, and others. Research engr Am Soc Heating and Ventilating Engrs Research Labs Pittsburgh '21-25; instr advancing to prof indsl hygiene Harvard since '25; cons air hygiene various govt agencies and indsl firms since '30. Am Pub Health Assn—Am Indsl Hygiene Assn—AAAS —Am Soc Heating and Ventilating Engineers—Sigma Xi—Delta Omega. Harvard School Public Health, 55 Shattuck St., Boston 15.†⊙

23 YAKOVLEV, Paul Ivan. Epilepsy (Neural mechanism); Behavior (Neuro biology). b'94. Student '05-14 (Classical Gymnasium Vilna Russia); MB '19 (Mil Med Acad Leningrad); MD '25 (Faculty Med U Paris France); Fgn asst '20-25 (Salpetriere and Pitie Hosps Paris); Research fellow '31-32 (Inst Brain Anatomy Zurich Switzerland). Studies in field of clinical neurology, neuropathology of the developmental, congenital and early acquired encephalopahties, neural mechanism of epilepsy, neuroanatomy and neurobiology of behavior. Author articles: Neurosomatic Deterioration in Epileptic Patients '31; Congenital Ectodermoses '31; Neurological Mechanism of Epileptic Seizures '37; Influence of Locomotion of Plantar Reflex '41; Schizencephalies—Congenital Clefts in the Cerebral Mantle '46; Motility, Behavior, and the Brain '48; Frontal Lobotomy—Neuroanatomical Observation '50. Dir Psychiat Tny Faculty of Mass Inc since '51; instr neurol Harvard '37-47, asst clin prof since '51; asso clin prof dept psychiat Yale '47-51. AMA—Am Neurol Assn—Am Psychiat Assn—Am Assn Neuropath (pres '51) —Am Acad Neurol—Boston Soc Psychiatry and Neurol (pres '44). Harvard Medical School, 25 Shattuck St., Boston 15.

10 YANAGA, Chitoshi. Japan (Institutions, thought, history, government, politics). b'03. BA '28—MA '30 (U Hawaii); PhD '34 (U Calif); '35-37 (Imperial U Tokyo); fellow Carnegie Endowment Internat Peace '36-37 (Tokyo). Dir Japanese translation and research OWI Overseas Br San Francisco '42-44; Far Eastern adviser Fgn Broadcast Intelligence Service FCC '44; chief spl research sect Far East Div Research and Analysis Br OSS and State Dept '44-46; with Yale U since '45, asso prof polit sci since '49. Author: Japan Since Perry '49; also articles in field. Acad Polit Sci —Am Polit Sci Assn—AHA—Am Acad Political Social Science—Far Eastern Assn. Hall of Graduate Studies, Yale University, New Haven 11, Conn., 77 Woodlawn St., Hamden 14, Conn.†

11 YANCEY, Harry Fagan. Coal (Preparation, carbonization, gasification). b'90. AB '13—AM '15 (U Mo); PhD '23 (U Ill). Head Joint Chiefs of Staff solid fuels mission to Germany '45; advisor on coal preparation Supreme Commander Allied Powers in Japan '50; delegate 1st International Coal Preparation Conference Paris '50; investigations of washability characteristics American coals, carbonizing properties Washington coals, coking tests coals, properties of coke, combustion of coal on stokers. Supervising engr NW Expt Sta US Bur Mines Seattle '28-50, now chief fuels tech div region II. ACS—AIMME—West Coast Minerals Assn—Sigma Xi—Alpha Chi Sigma —Phi Lambda Upsilon. US Bureau of Mines, University Campus, Seattle 5.

12 YASSER, Joseph. Music (Russian, Chinese, Jewish, Shamanistic). b'93. MA '17 (State Conservatory Moscow Russia); Mus D '50 (Mus Arts Conservatory West Tex). Research on foundations of Jewish harmony; study structure of rhythm of Chinese music; new interpretation of medieval scale basis and harmony. Author: A Theory of Evolving Tonality '32; Medieval Quartal Harmony '38. Author articles: Musical Moments in the Shamanistic Rites of the Siberian Pagan Tribes '26; Serious Jewish Art Music '43; The Highways and Byways of Tonal Evolution '48; References to Hebrew Music in Russian Medieval Ballads '49, and others. Prof Moscow Conservatory '18-20; chief organist of Imperial Grand Opera Moscow '19-20; mus dir choral soc Shanghai Songsters China '22; vp Am Library Mus '31-42; chmn research com Nat Jewish Mus Council since '46. Jewish Acad Arts and Sci—Am Guild Organists—Am Mus Soc (council since '50). 7 W. 83rd St., NYC 24.

13 YATES, Louis Allmond Richard. International relations (Guarantee Treaties and Paris Conference of 1919). b'07. BEd '30 (Western Ill State Teachers Coll); MA '31 (U Ia); PhD '50 (U So Calif). Asst prof hist and polit sci Bradley U since '48. Am Polit Sci Assn—AHA—Kappa Delta Pi. Bradley University, Peoria 5, Ill.

14 YAVORSKY, Martin Andrew. Atmospheric contaminants (Protection devices). b'07. PhG—BS (U Pitts). Respiratory protective devices for toxic gases, dusts and fumes; industrial hygiene surveys, detection and micro estimation of atmospheric contaminants. Research chem Mine Safety Appliances Co Pittsburgh. ACS—Am Indsl Hygiene Assn—Phi Sigma Soc. John T. Ryan Memorial Laboratories, 100 N. Braddock Av., Pitts. 8.

15 YEAGER, J(ames) Franklin. Insect physiology. b'99. PhB '24 (Yale); MA '26 (Columbia); PhD '29 (NYU).

Author articles in field. Instr biol subjects NYU '24-29, asst prof '29-30; asst prof Ia State Coll '30-31, asso prof '31-36; research in insect physiol Nat Agrl Research Center Beltsville Md '36-48; research analyst Div Research Grants and Fellowships Nat Inst Health '48-49; asst chief grants and training branch Nat Heart Inst, Nat Institute Health '49-52, chief since '52; lecturer in insect physiol University of Maryland '37-47. AAAS—Soc Exptl Biol and Med—Entomol Soc Am Am—Am Assn Econ Entomol—Am Soc Zool—NY Acad Sci—Wash Acad Sci— Entomol Soc Wash—Sigma Xi. National Heart Institute, Bethesda 14, Md.†

16 YEAGLEY, Henry Lincoln. Bird navigation. b'99. BS '25—MS '27— PhD '34 (Pa State Coll). Author articles in field. Instr physics Pa State Coll '25-30, asst prof '30-34, asso prof '34; Signal Corps bird navigation project since '43. AAAS—Am Phys Soc—Am Assn Phys Teachers—AAUP —Sigma Xi—Royal Astron Soc Can— Am Ornithol Union. Pennsylvania State College, Department of Physics, State College, Pa.

17 YEATON, Chester Henry. Modern geometry. b'86. AB '08 (Bowdoin); AM '09—Thayer scholar '09-10 (Harvard); F '13-15—PhD '15 (U Chicago); summer '14 (Yerkes Obs); advanced instrn and research in mechanics '42-43 (Brown U). Faculty Oberlin Coll since '21, prof math since '27. With Signal Corps and later instr math FACOTS, US Army '17-18. AAAS(F)—Am Math Soc—Math Assn Am—AAUP—Phi Beta Kappa—Sigma Xi—Gamma Alpha. 189 Forest St., Oberlin, O.⊚

18 YELLOTT, John I(ngle). Thermodynamics; Power plants; Fluid flow. b'08. BS '31—MME '33 (Johns Hopkins). Study flow of steam at high velocity through nozzles with specialized knowledge of supersaturation and its effects upon steam flow; development coal-burning gas turbine for locomotive and other applications; design open cycle plants to burn solid fuels. Staff Stevens Inst Tech '34-40; dir dept mech engring Ill Inst Tech '40-43; dir Inst Gas Tech '34-45; dir research Locomotive Development Com Bituminous Coal Research Inc since '45. ASME(Jr award '34)—AAAS—Sigma Xi—Tau Beta Pi—Pi Tau Sigma (award '39). 146 East 38th St., NYC 16.†⊚

19 YEOMANS, Alfred Henry. Insecticides (Application equipment, physical properties influencing effect); Insects (Control by radiant energy). b '08. BS in archtl engring '34 (O State U). Investigation methods of atomization liquid insecticides and determination particle size of sprays; wind tunnel, laboratory and field tests of factors influencing deposit of dusts and sprays; development equipment to apply aerosols, dusts and sprays, including aerosol generators, mist blowers and airplane apparatus; study radiant energy equipment used in insect treatments, including ultra-sonic, cathode rays and radio waves. Holds patent on fumigation equipment. Author articles: Deposition of Aerosol Particles; Directions for Determining Particle Size of Aerosols and Fine Sprays '49. Co-author article: Methods and Equipment for Fumigation of Clothing Infested with Body Lice. Tech in charge equipment for applying insecticides div control investigation Bur Entomol and Plant Quarantine Agrl Research Center Beltsville since '41. Washington Acad Sci. Agricultural Research Center, Beltsville, Md.

20 YEOMANS, Clifton. Hull design. b'77. Grad '00 (Webb Acad Naval

Arch and Marine Engring). Designer and detailer of hulls. With Kaiser Co '42, '43; cons naval arch and marine engr since 1942. Soc Naval Arch and Marine Engrs—Wash Soc Engrs. H: 3324 19th St., Washington 10.

21 YEPSEN, Lloyd N. Mental deficiency; Education of exceptional children; Crime and delinquency. b'96. AB '21—LLD (hon) '42 (Carthage Coll); MA '24—PhD '31 (O State U). Assisted in promotion of formation of International Congress on Mental Deficiency and became secretary '48. Author articles in field. Dir Div Classification and Edn, Dept Institutions and Agencies State NJ since '34, chief psychol since '46; Am Assn Mental Deficiency (pres '47-48)—Am Psychol Assn—Correctional Edn Assn (treas)—NJ Psychol Assn (past pres) —Nat Conf Juvenile Agencies—NJ Guidance and Personnel Assn (past vp)—U Scholar O State U '23-24, U fellow '31-32; Department of Institutions and Agencies, State Office Building, Trenton, N.J.⊚

22 YNTEMA, Theodore Otte. Economic policy; Investment policy; Economic forecasting. b'00. AB '21 (Hope Coll Holland Mich); AM '22 (U Ill); AM '24—PhD '29 (U Chicago). Author: A Mathematical Reformulation of the Theory of International Trade '32. Co-author Jobs and Markets—How to Prevent Inflation and Depression in the Transition. Prof bus, econ policy Sch Bus U Chicago since '44; research dir Com for Econ Development since '42; cons econ Stein, Roe and Farnham '45-49, Lord-Abbett '46-49, Ford Motor Co since '47. Am Econ Assn—Am Statis Assn(F)—Econometric Soc(F)—Inst Math Statis. 3000 Shaefer Rd., Dearborn, Mich.⊚

23 YODER, Don. Pennsylvania Dutch history and folklore; American church history (Ecumenical movements, Methodist, Lutheran, Reformed, Evangelical). b'21. AB '42 (Franklin and Marshall Coll); BD '45—PhD '47 (U Chicago). Editor The Pennsylvania Dutchman since '49; asst prof religion Franklin and Marshall Coll. Am Soc Church Hist—Phi Beta Kappa. Franklin and Marshall College, Lancaster, Pa.

24 YOGANANDA, Paramhansa. India (Religion and philosophy); Yoga (Sciences); World-brotherhood colonies. Author: Autobiography of a Yogi '46. Founder Yogoda Sat-Sanga Brahmacharya Vidyalaya (residential high sch with yoga training, Calcutta U matriculation standard) Ranchi India. Founder, Self Realization Fellowship and Self Realization Churches. 3880 San Rafael Av., LA 65.

25 YOHE, Gail Robert. Coal chemistry. b'04. BA '25 (Cornell Coll); MS '27—PhD '29 (U Ill). Author articles in field. With Ill State Geol Survey since '37, chemist and head coal div in geochem sect since '45. Am Chem Soc—Blast Furnace and Coke Assn. State Geological Survey, Urbana, Ill.†

26 YONGE, Ena Laura. Cartography (Map indexing and classification). b'95. Author articles in field. Map curator Am Geog Soc of NY since '17. Soc Woman Geog—Assn Am Geog— Spl Libraries Assn. American Geographical Society, Broadway at 156th St., NYC 32.

27 YORAN, Calvin S(tockton). Sponge rubber (For use in automobiles and radio). b'08. BS '30—PhD '33 (U Chicago). Supervision of technical service work for rubber, paint and ink industries; development of asphalt products for war-time packaging, wax products for packaging, rust-inhibitors, automobile body sound deadeners, vulcanized oil rubber substitute and extender, zinc soap for use in rubber compounding, and resin-gilsonite blends for rubber compounding, manufacture of sponge rubber products for automobile and radio industries. Author articles in field. Chief chem Featheredge Rubber Co '33-42, Witco Chem Co '42-44; research dir Brown Rubber Co since '44. Am Chem Soc—Am Inst Chem—Am Soc Testing Materials—SAE—Sigma Xi. Brown Rubber Co., Box 1000, Lafayette, Ind. H: 713 Dodge St., West Lafayette, Ind.

10 YORK, Robert, (Jr.). Organic chemicals processing; Hydrocarbon gases; Charcoal activation; Distillation (Equilibria); Gas compressor design. b'12. BS '33—MS '34 (U Tenn); ScD '38 (MIT). Author articles in field. Chem engr Gen Development Dept Monsanto Chem Co since '48; official investigator NDRC Div 10 '42-44. Am Inst Chem Engrs—Am Chem Soc—Tau Beta Pi—Phi Kappa Phi—Sigma Xi. Monsanto Chemical Company, St. Louis 4.

11 YOST, Francis Lorraine. Theoretical physics (Nuclear); Rubber. b'08. BS '29—MS '31 (U Ky); PhD '36 (U Wis). Author articles in field. With US Rubber Co '37-42; asso prof physics Ill Inst Tech since '47; sr tech aide OSRD '43-46; physicist Naval Ordnance Lab '46-47. Am Phys Soc—Sigma Xi—Phi Beta Kappa—Sigma Pi Sigma. Illinois Institute of Technology, 3300 Federal St., Chicago 16.†

12 YOUNCE, Major Laurence. Political parties; Social science cross-field integration. b'07. BA '28—MA '29—PhD '31 (Marquette U). Research on political conditions in Wisconsin, 1890-1900; Dean Roscoe Pound and the transit of sociological jurisprudence to the United States. Author: Parties and Elections '42; Classification and Analysis of 27 Leading Map Projections '48; Current Constitutional Documents Abroad '48; also articles in field. Instr hist Marquette U '29-32, instr hist and political science '31-34, asst prof '34-43; asst prof political science and sec Div Social Sci U Akron '45-47; teacher social sci Chicago City Jr Coll Herzl Br '47-49; evening lectr hist and polit sci De Paul U since '49; asst dir and chmn social sci div Chicago Adult Sch since '51. Phi Alpha Theta—Am Acad Polit Social Sci. Chicago Adult School, 10 N. Clark St., Chgo 2. H: 2638 N. Sayre Av., Chgo 35.

13 YOUNG, Agnes Brooks (Agatha Young); (Mrs. George Benham Young). History of fashion; Psychology of dress. b'98. Student '16 (Dana Hall Wellesley Mass); '18 (Cleveland Sch Art); '19 (Sch Arts and Design Columbia U); '20 (L'Ecole Francaise Paris). Author: Stage Costuming '27; Recurring Cycles of Fashion '37; also articles in field. Mem faculty Western Reserve U depts fine arts and adult edn '30-32; lecturer. The Fashion Group—Am Statis Assn. 225 Chagrin Blvd., Chagrin Falls, O.

14 YOUNG, Almon Paul. Welding of copper; Extruded copper fittings. b'93. BS in ME '17 (Purdue U); MS in ME '49 (Mich Coll Mining and Tech). Research on production of extruded fittings from copper and copper tubing, granted patent on process. Author articles in field. Engr Ross Gear and Tool Co Lafayette Ind '27-29; mem faculty Mich Coll Mining and Tech Houghton since '30, now prof mechanical engring, head dept. ASME—Am Welding Soc—Am Soc Engring Edn. Michigan College

of Mining and Technology, Houghton, Mich.

15 YOUNG, Arthur Nichols. International Finance and Economic Problems; Foreign Exchange; Currency; Public Credit; Central Banking. b'90. AB '10—LLD '37 (Occidental Coll); AM '11—PhD '14 (Princeton); LLB '27 (George Washington U). Adviser on taxation to Mexican Govt '18; financial adviser to Honduras Govt '20-21; economic advisor to Dept of State '22-28; financial adviser Chinese Govt '29-46; attended World Economic Conference Geneva '27; member Chinese delegation to Bretton Woods Monetary Conference '44; helped negotiate US aid to China '33, '40-41, '47; adviser to Central Bank of China and Chinese Foreign Exchange Equalization Fund Commission '47. Author: The Single Tax Movement in the US '16; Spanish Finance and Trade '20; China's Economic and Financial Reconstruction '47, also published in Chinese and others. Dir Counselors Investment Fund and Kartex Oil Co. Am Econ Assn—Acad Polit Sci—Phi Beta Kappa. Awarded Order of the Brilliant Jade China. 1426 Hampton Road, San Marino 9, Cal.◎

16 YOUNG, Clarence Bernard Fehrler. Electrometallurgy. b'08. BS '30 (Howard Coll Birmingham Ala); MS '32—PhD '34 (Columbia U). Author: Chemistry for Electroplaters '44; Surface Active Agents '45; also articles in field. Adjunct prof Brooklyn Polytechnic Inst, dept chmn engring since '40; pres Inst Electrochem and Metall since '38; tech dir Clark Babbitt Industries since '43; exec vp Nat So Products Corp (tall oil). 630 Fifth Av., NYC.

17 YOUNG, Clyde Lyman. North Dakota (Government). b'77. Grad '97 (Mich State Normal Sch); '02-03 (U Mich); '05-06 (U Minn); '06-07 (U ND). Judicial Council of North Dakota '27-30; national commissioner on Uniform State Laws since '28. Author: Government of North Dakota and the Nation '22. Asst atty gen ND '09-13; mem various law firms '11-39, alone '39-46, firm Young McGray & Morris '46-47. Am Bar Assn (council '29-30, House Dels '34-41)—Acad Polit Sci—Am Assn UN—Fgn Policy Assn—Am Acad Polit and Social Sci—Order of Coif. Provident Life Insurance Co. Building, Bismarck, N.D.

18 YOUNG, Frank N(elson), Jr. Taxonomy of aquatic Coleoptera (Dytiscidae, Gyrinidae); Natural history of the Everglades and Southern Florida (Beetles, other insects, tree snails). b'15. BS '38—MS '40—PhD '42 (U Fla). Author: The Water Beetles of Florida '49; also articles in field. Med entomol US Army '42-45 as taxonomist mosquitos and general control work; asst prof biol sci U Fla '46-49; asst prof zool Ind U '49-53 asso prof since '53; ed Quarterly Jour Fla Acad Sci '46-49. Fla Acad Sci—Sigma Xi—Phi Kappa Phi. Department of Zoology, Indiana University, Bloomington, Ind.

19 YOUNG, Frederic C. Radio engineering. b'99. Student '18-22 (Rensselaer Poly Inst). With Stromberg-Carlson Co since '22, chief engr '40-42, vp in charge engring and research; now Designers for Ind, Inc. AIEE(F)—Nat Elec Mfrs Assn—Am Soc Testing Materials—Radio Mfrs Assn—Independent Telephone Pioneers—Inst Radio Engrs (sr mem). Designers for Industry, Inc., 2915 Detroit Av., Cleve 13.

20 YOUNG, George Husband. Corrosion; Marine and anti-fouling paints;

Protective coatings; Synthetic rubber, resins and plastics; High polymers. b'09. BS '32—MS '34—PhD '36 (Pa State Coll). Author articles in field. Research chem Anthracite Inst '33; Fellow Mellon Inst Indsl Research '35-36, sr fellow '36-44, exec asst to dir '44-47, assistant director '47-52 dir research since '52. Director research Stoner-Mudge Inc '38-44; secretary and treas Am Coordinating Com on Corrosion, v-chmn '44, chmn '45, civilian adviser on corrosion US Army and Navy Dept since '38. AAAS(F)—Am Inst Chem(F)—Am Chem Soc—Nat Assn Corrosion Engrs—Soc Chem Ind—Pa Chem Soc—Soc Naval Arch and Marine Engrs—Army Ordnance Assn. 4400 Fifth Av., Pitts. 13.◎

21 YOUNG, Harold Edle. Tree growth; Forest photogrammetry. b'17. BS '37 (U Me); MF '46—PhD '48 (Duke U). Research on height growth of trees, and diameter growth along the bole; improvement of tree measuring methods; application aerial photography to forestry. Co-author article: (with F X Schumacher) Empirical Log Rules According to Species Groups and Lumber Grades '43. With US Forest Service '37-40; instr forestry dept U Me '48, asst prof since '49. Soc Am Foresters—Ecol Soc Am—Am Soc Plant Physiol—AAAS—AAUP—Am Soc Photogrammetry—Biometrics Soc—Am Statis Association—Sigma Xi. Forestry Department, University of Maine, Orono,

22 YOUNG, James Harvey. American social history (Nineteenth century reform movements, Lyceum movements, patent medicine history). b'15. AB '37 (Knox Coll); MA '38—PhD '41 (U Ill). Author articles in field. Asso prof hist Emory U since '46. Miss Valley Hist Assn—So Hist Assn—Ill State Hist Soc—Phi Beta Kappa—Phi Kappa Phi. Department of History, Emory University, Ga.†

23 YOUNG, John A(lbion), Jr. Invertebrate paleontology; Subsurface stratigraphy; Heavy mineral analysis. b'09. PhB '32—ScM '34 (Brown U); PhD '46 (Harvard). Author articles in field. Subsurface geol Sun Oil Co since '47. Geol Soc Am — Paleontol Soc—Am Assn Petroleum Geol—Mineral Soc Am—AAAS(F)—Sigma Xi. Sun Oil Company, 1608 Walnut St., Phila 3.

24 YOUNG, Martin Dunaway. Malariology; Parasitology. b'09. BS '31—MS '32 (Emory U); ScD '37 (Sch Hygiene Pub Health, Johns Hopkins U). Author articles in field. Jr zool Malaria Research Lab Nat Inst Health USPHS Columbia SC '37-39, asso zool '39-42, dir Lab Tropical Diseases since '40, parasitol '43, sr parasitol '43-44, sanitarian (R) in charge Imported Malaria Studies, 3 labs, '44-48, scientist dir since '50. AAAS(F, councilor '46-47)—Nat Malaria Soc (sec-treas '46-49)—Am Soc Parasitol (councilor '47-50)—SC Acad Sci (pres '49-50)—Assn SE Biol (pres '47-48)—Am Soc Trop Med and Hygiene—Am Public Health Assn—Am Soc Profl Biol—Am Mosquito Control Assn—Sigma Xi—Gamma Alpha. Co-recipient Jefferson Award SC Aca Sci '46, '52. Lab Trop Diseases U.S. Public Health Service, Box 717, Columbia, S.C.†◎

25 YOUNG, Owen D. Reparations payments; National planning committees; U.S. Government (Organization executive branch. b'74. AB '94—DHL '23 (St Lawrence U); LLB '96 (Boston U); LLD '22 (Union Coll Schenectady NY), '24 (Tufts, Harvard, Dartmouth), '25 (Johns Hopkins, Colgate, Yale, Columbia), '28 (Brown U, U State NY), '29 (Hamilton U) '30 (U Cal) '31 (Wesleyan U Middletown Conn), '32 (Notre

Dame U), '33 (Queen's U Kingston Ont), '34 (U Neb), '35 (Marietta College), '40 (Syracuse U); LittD '36 (Rollins Coll); '27 DCS '27 (NYU); LittD '46 (U Buffalo); (U Fla) '48 (Middleburg Coll). Member, appointed by state and fed execs, advisory commissions and committees of experts, on international monetary matters, federal and state planning committees, on government organization, resources development and conservation, and other items of national and international importance. 570 Lexington Av., NYC.◉

10 YOUNG, Paul Allen. Tomato and crop plant pathology; Tomato genetics; Facultative parasitism. b'98. AB '21—AM '23—PhD '25 (Wabash Coll); '21-25 (U Ill); '21 (Cornell U). Research on tomato fertilizers and pest control, potato virus diseases, physiology and physics of oil sprays, cotton wilt, soil fumigation, wheat stinking smut, charcoal rot of corn, diseases caused by Sclerotinia sclerotiorum. Author articles in field. Asst bot Mont Agr Expt Sta '25-35; plant path in charge Tomato Disease Lab Tex Agr Expt Sta Jacksonville Tex since '35. Am Phytopath Soc—Am Genetic Assn—Bot Soc Am—Sigma Xi —Phi Kappa Phi. Tomato Disease Laboratory, Jacksonville, Tex.

11 YOUNG, Robert William. Musical instrument acoustics; Underwater sound propagation and noise. b'08. BS in physics '30 (Ohio U); PhD '34 (U Wash Seattle). Research on acoustics of flute, and piano tuning; design and construction wind musical instruments; effects of weather on tuning of musical instruments; underwater ambient noise caused by snapping shrimp. Author articles: Dependence of Tuning of Wind Instruments on Temperature '46; Image Interference in the Presence of Refraction '47; Examples of Propagation of Underwater Sound by Bottom Reflection '48; Influence of Humidity on Tuning of a Piano '49; Inharmonicity of Plain Wire Piano Strings '52; and others. Co-author articles: (with D H Loughridge) Standing Sound Waves in the Boehm Flute '36; (with F Alton Everest, Martin W Johnson) Acoustical Characteristics of Noise Produced by Snapping Shrimp '48, and others. Physicist C G Conn Ltd Elkhart Ind '34-42, div war research U Cal San Diego '42-46, US Navy Electronics Lab since '46. AAAS —Am Inst Physics—Acoustical Soc Am (F, asso ed jour)—Phi Beta Kappa— Sigma Xi. U.S. Navy Electronics Lab., San Diego 52, Cal.

12 YOUNG, Rowland Lawrence. Batteries (Storage); Safety (Accident prevention); Standards (Industrial). b'86. BS in elec engring '07—EE '28 (U Pa); PE '36 (U State of NY). Author: The Care and Operation of Storage Batteries '15 (Bell System handbook). Collaborator: Storage Battery Engineering. Developed the continuous floating system for storage battery operation; consultant on power plant safety Bell System '11-29; author manual of design for protection of personnel against hazardous voltages; mem Am Soc Safety Engrs and National Safety Council; revision editor manuals War Time Safety Rules, Safety Rules for Industry, and others. Mem. Am Standards Assn Standards Council '32-49; mem Standards Com Am Inst EE '37-42; rep Telephone Group on Am Standards Assn sect coms on standards for storage batteries, for electrical measuring instruments, inch-millimeter system, graphical symbols for drawings, preferred voltages 100 and lower. In charge power engring sect Am Tel

and Tel '11-34, Bell Telephone Labs '34-39, retired '49. AAAS(F)—Am Inst EE—Am Soc Safety Engrs—Soc Am Mil Engrs—NY Engrs Soc—Telephone Pioneers Am—Sigma Xi. 447 N. Maple Av., East Orange, N.J.

13 YOUNG, Stewart. Community planning. b'84. Diploma in civil engring '11 (Sch Practical Sci Toronto); BASc in applied sci '12 (U Toronto). Control of land subdivision in the urban center of Saskatchewan; advisor local planning, and planning procedure and administration; examination and approval local planning schemes and zoning ordinances and by laws; planning consultant to general urban municipalities. Author: Saskatchewan Community Planning Act '45; Saskatchewan Municipal Expropriation Act '46. Dist engr Dept of Highways Govt of Saskatchewan '16-24, dir community planning Dept of municipal affairs since '25. Engring Inst Can—Town Planning Inst Can—Am Soc Planning Officials. Dept of Municipal Affairs, Regina, Saskatchewan.

14 YOUNG V(ive) H(all). Cotton diseases (control); Seed treatment (Corn, barley, oats, peanuts); Grape and apple spraying. b'87. Diploma '08 (State Normal Sch Whitewater Wis); PhB '13—PhM '14—PhD '16 (U Wis); '12 (U Chicago). Research on cotton diseases, especially fusaruim wilt, seedling blights, boll rots; developed methods of controlling cotton wilt disease by means of high potash fertilization; also research on seed treatments for corn, barley, oats, peanuts; grape and apple spraying. Author articles in field. Head dept plant path U Ark and plant path Ark Expt Sta '23-53. AAAS(F)—Am Phytopath Soc —Bot Society Am—Am Acad Science— Sigma Xi—Phi Beta Kappa. 226 Agricultural Building, University of Arkansas, Fayetteville, Ark.

15 YOUNG, William Caldwell. Endocrinology; Microscopic anatomy. b'99. BA '21—MA '25 (Amherst Coll); PhD '27 (U Chicago). Research on microscopic anatomy and physiology of male and female reproductive tracts, physiological basis of sexual behavior patterns in mammals. Author articles in field. Instr biol Brown U '28-31, asst prof '32-39; asso prof primate biol Yerkes Lab Primate Biol Orange Park Fla '39-44; asso prof biol Cedar Crest Coll Allentown Pa '44-46; anat U Kan since '46. AAAS—Soc Zool— Assn Anat—Sigma Xi. Research fellow anatomy U Freiburg '31-32, hon fellow Yale Sch Med '37-38. University of Kansas, Lawrence Kan.

16 YOUNGKEN, Heber Wilkinson. Pharmacognosy; Economic botany; Medicinal plants; Drug plant cultivation; Microscopical analysis. b'85. PhG '05 (Medico-Chirurg Coll); AB '09 —Am '12 (Bucknell U); MS '14—PhD '15 (U Pa); PhM (hon) '19 (Phila Coll Pharm). Chairman Committee on Botony and Pharmacognosy US Pharmacopoeia Revision Committee. Executive secretary Section K, Fourth International Botany Congress '26; Author: A College Textbook of Pharmaceutical Botany '38; A Textbook of Pharmacology '48; Laboratory Manual of Botany '40. Editor sec pharm and pharm bot Biol Abstracts since '27, also articles in field. Prof pharmmacognosy and biol and chmn dept materia medica Mass Coll Pharmacy '23-51, research prof pharmacognosy and botany since '51. Soc Pharm and Chem of Sao Paulo Brazil (hon)—Am Foundation Pharm Education (chairman Newcomb Memorial awards committee)—AAAS(F)—Am Pharm Assn (chmn sci sect '21-22, sec hist sect

'34-35, chmn hist sect '35-36)—Mass Hort Soc—Herb Soc Am—Am Soc Plant Taxonomists—Bot Soc Am—Vt and NH Pharm Assn—Sigma Xi. Ebert medalist '25, 31. 179 Longwood Av., Boston 15.†◉

17 YOUTZ, Patrick. Vacuum tubes (Design); Electronic computing machines (Storage tubes). b'07. AB '28 (Bucknell U); MS '29 (U Chicago); student (Northwestern U), (MIT). Design, development, and production electrostatic storage tube; research o infra red pick-up devices, pick-up tubes for television, and cathode ray tube; development designs special purpose vacuum tubes. Cons engr '35-40; faculty MIT since '44, now research engr on project Whirlwind. Inst Radio Engrs—Sigma Xi. 211 Massachusetts Av., Cambridge 39, Mass.

18 YTTERBERG, C(arl) F(rederick). Concrete floors. b'96. Ed pub schs. Specialist and pioneer water control of concrete; design, methods, materials and apparatus for installation concrete floors for heavy duty service; design machines for working and troweling in lieu hand operations. Pres Kalman Floor Co since '33, Ge Floor Co since '41. Kalman Floor Co., 110 East 42d St., NYC 17.

19 YUILL, Joseph Stuart. Forest entomology; Airplane spraying. b'04. BS '29 (U Ariz); MS '35 (U Calif). Author articles in field. With US Dept Agr since '35, research on development of aerial spraying since '46. Am Assn Econ Entol—Entomol Soc Wash. Forest Insect Laboratory, Agricultural Research Center, Beltsville, Md.†

20 YUKAWA, Hideki. Mesons (Theoretical physics). b'07. MS '29 (Kyoto U Japan); DSc '38 (Osaka U Japan). Research since '35 on development original theory of nuclear forces, leading to postulation and prediction of mesons. Author: Introduction to Quantum Mechanics (Japanese) '47; Introduction to the Theory of Elementary Particles (Japanese) '48. Author article: On the Interaction of Elementary Particles '35, and others. Asst prof theoretical physics Osaka U '36-39; prof theoretical physics Kyoto U '39; vis prof Inst for Advanced Study Princeton '48-49; vis prof physics Columbia since '49. Sci Council of Japan—Japan Phys Soc—Japan Acad—Nat Acad Sci (fgn asso)—APS(F). Nobel prize for physics '49. Department of Physics, Columbia University, NYC 27.

21 YUNCKER, Truman G(eorge). Cuscuta; Piperaceae (Pacific Islands Cuba, Panama, South America); Peperomia (Hawaiian and Polynesian species); Flora of Honduras, Piperaceae Niue Island, and Manua Islands. b'91. BSc '14—DSc '41; Mich State Coll); AM '15 (U Neb); PhD '19 (U Ill). Botanical expeditions Republic of Honduras '34, '36, '38, Cuba '48; Yale-Bishop Museum fellow research Hawaiian Islands '32-33, botanical expedition Samoa and Nieu Islands '39-40; Tongan Islands on Guggenheim Fellowship and Nat Sci Found Pacific Sci Bd '53. Author: North Am & West Indian Species of Cuscuta '23; The genus Cuscuta (World) '32; also articles in field. Prof bot DePauw U since '19, head dept since '21. Ind Acad Sci (pres '39)—Torrey Bot Club—AAAS(F)—Bot Soc Am (treas '47-52 vp '53)—Am Soc Naturalists—Sigma Xi. Department of Botany, DePauw University, Greencastle, Ind.◉

22 YUST, Walter. Encyclopedia editing. b'94. AB '17 (U Pa). Developed plan for continuous revision of multivolume encyclopedia with subjects assigned to major classifications and sub-divisions. With Phila Evening Ledger '17, Phila Press '18-20, Memphis Press '21, New Orleans Item '22; mng ed The Double Dealer '23; asso ed Literary Review and ed Literary Lobby, NY Evening Post '23-26; lit ed Phila Pub Ledger '26-30; adv mgr Ency Britannica Inc '30-32, asso ed and also of Britannica Jr '32-38, ed-in-chief all Britannica publs since '38. Phi Beta Kappa. 20 N. Wacker Dr., Chgo.

10 YUTUC, Lope Madlambayan. Surra (Parasitology); Trypanosoma evans¹. b '96. DVM '24 (Coll Vet Sci U Philippines); ScM '39 (Sch Hygiene and Pub Health Johns Hopkins). Investigation occurrence surra (trypanosomiasis in dogs, horses, cattle and carabaos; effects of trypanosoma evansi on body organs. Author articles: The incidence of canine surra in the Philippines '31; Experimental transmission of surra by means of the dog hookworm '32; Experimental studies on curative treatment of surra in native horses in the Philippines '36; Observations on the distribution of Trypanosoma evansi in the bodies of rats and guinea pigs during different states of infection '49; Observations on the prevalence of tabanid flies and surra-transmission experiments '50, others. Instr, sec Coll Vet Sci U Philippines '27, asst prof '35. Philippine Vet Med Assn—Philippine Sci Soc—Am Soc Parasitologists —AAAS—Los Banos Biol Club—Society Advancement Research—Philippine Soc Parasitology—Nat Rsrch Coun(asso)— Phi Kappa Phi—Sigma Xi. College Veterinary Medicine, University of the Philippines, Diliman, Quezon City.

11 YZENBAARD, John Henry. Dutch settlements in the Middle West; Michigan history. b'15. BA '35 (West Mich Coll); MA '44 (U Mich); '35 (Mich State Coll); '39 (Cleveland Coll). Engaged in compiling annual bibliography dealing with Michigan history. Author articles: The Van Malsen Letters (translator) '48; Michigan History Bibliography for 1947 '48. Asst prof hist Hope Coll Holland Mich since '47. AHA—Mich Hist Soc—Mich Acad Letters Arts Sci. 829 Staples Av., Kalamazoo 54, Mich.†

Z

12 ZABEL, Rolland Meyer. Electrical engineering; Light sources. b'08. BA '29 (Neb Wesleyan U); MS '31— PhD '32 (U Ia); Nat Research Council fellow '32-34 (MIT). Author articles in field. Mgr lamp engring charge of all phases of lamp development and design Westinghouse Elec Corp since '47. Illuminating Engring Soc—Am Phys Soc—Phi Kappa Phi. Westinghouse Electric Corporation, Bloomfield, N.J.

13 ZACHLIN, Anthony C. Batteries (Storage); Electrochemistry; Scientific Polish and Russian. b'98. BS '21—(Union Coll); AM '25 (Columbia). US and Canadian patents on storage batteries. Author of abstracts from Polish, Russian, French and German articles '24-41. In charge development lab Willard Storage Battery Co Cleveland since '36. AAAS—Am Chem Soc— Electrochem Soc—Am Inst Chem—Sigma Xi. 246 E. 131st St., Cleveland 10, O.

14 ZAFRA, Nicolas. Philippine history. b'92. BSE '18—MA '20 (U Philippines). Prof hist and head dept hist U Philippines since '48. AHA—Phi Alpha Theta. University of the Philippines, Diliman, Quezon City, P.I.

15 ZAHL, Harold A(delbert). Radar; Electronics; Radiation (Infra-red). b '04. BA '27 (North Central Coll Naperville Ill); MS '29—PhD '31 (U Ia). development submarine subaqueous detection devices, infrared detection devices for marine and aerial targets, pneumatic heat detector; use of x-ray methods for study liquid structure, radar method for tracking meteors; experimental verification of wave-particle dualism of matter. Holds six patents in field, including method for detecting sources by heat radiation, altimeter device for aircraft, system for detecting sources of radiant energy, and electronic tubes. Co-author articles: Pneumatic Heat Detector '46; Radar on Fifty Centimeters '46; Radar Observations on the Draconoids '47, and others. Physicist signal corps engineering labs Ft Monmouth NJ '31-42, dir research since '46. Assisted in development and procurement electronic equipment Signal Corps AUS '42-46. APS(F)—Inst Radio Engrs(F) —Armed Forces Communications Assn —Internat Sci Radio Union(nat com) —Sigma Xi—Gamma Alpha. Signal Corps Engineering Laboratories, Ft. Monmouth, N.J.

16 ZAHN, Charles Thomas. Molecular structure; Quantum theory; Absorption (Neutron); Microwaves; Electronics; Radio activity. b'98. BS (Engring) '19 (Johns Hopkins U); PhD '24 (Princeton). Research on relationship of gaseous dielectrics to quantum theory and molecular structure; research on the specific charge of disintegration electrons and positrons, on neutron absorption; research on microwave absorption by gases. Holds two patents in field. Asst prof physics Princeton U '25-31; NRC fellow Princeton and Liepzig U '24 and '32; research physicist Navy Dept '42-44, Nat Bur Standards since '46. APS(F)—Gamma Alpha—Sigma Xi. National Bureau of Standards, Washington 25.

17 ZAHORSKY, John. Baby incubators. b'71. AB '92 (Steelville Mo Inst); MD '95 (Mo Med Coll St Louis); post-grad '99 (Johns Hopkins). Author: Baby Incubators '05; Golden Rules of Pediatrics '13; Synopsis Pediatrics 5th edit '43; The Infant and Child '39; From the Hills (autobiog); articles. Dir dept pediatrics St Louis U since '33, emeritus; pediatrician-in-chief St Mary's Group Hosp since '24, emeritus. ACP(F)—AMA—Southern Med Assn—Acad Pediatrics—St Louis Med Soc—Acad Sci—Phi Beta Phi— Alpha Omega Alpha—Sigma Xi. Awards from St Louis U and St. Louis Pediatric Soc. Steelville, Mo.

18 ZANGAR, Carl Nicholas. Photoelasticity; Earth dam stability; Soils permeability. b'10. BS in civil engring '32 (Wash State Coll); MS in civil engring '40 (U Colo). Research and use of analytical and experimental methods employing photoelastic interferometer, photoelastic polariscope, Beggs deformeter, membrane analogy and electric analogy to determine the stresses in concrete and earth dams and their foundations, stresses in tunnels and power plants, ground water flow into drains, seepage through earth dams and their foundations, stability of canal structures and earth dams. With US Bur Reclamation since '34, group head since '41. Am Soc CE —Soc Exptl Stress Analysis—Sigma Xi —Tau Beta Pi—Sigma Tau. Bureau of Reclamation, Denver Federal Center, Denver. H: 1206 Gowen Av., Richland, Wash.

19 ZANGERL, Rainer. Paleontology; Fossil reptiles (Turtles); Comparative morphology. b'12. PhD '36 (U Zurich). Author articles in field. Curator fossil reptiles Chicago Natural Hist Mus since '45. Schweiz Paleontol Gesellsch —Soc Vertebrate Paleontol—Am Soc Zool—AAAS—Detroit Acad Sci—Mich Acad Sci Arts Letters—Ind Acad Sci— Soc Study Evolution. Chicago Natural History Museum, Chicago 5.

20 ZAPFFE, Carl Andrew. Stainless steel (Production, properties, fabrication, defects resulting from processing). b'12. Student '29-32 (U Minn); BS in metall '33 (Mich Coll Mining and Tech); MS in metall engring '34 (Lehigh U); ScD '39 (Harvard). Research x-ray diffraction, thermodynamics of steel making, gas-metal reactions, solid-state physics, determination causes gassiness in metals, cracking of steel, defects in electroplated steel, in vitreous enameled steel; discovery planar-pressure theory for hydrogen embrittlement of steels, cracking of welded steel, damage to steel by steam in heat treating atmospheres, nicellar theory for the solid state. Invented wire-bend test, bar-bend test, notch-bar bend test, micrographic technique called fractography. Author: Stainless Steels '49; also articles. Research engr Battelle Memorial Inst Columbus '38-43; asst tech dir research stainless Rustless Iron & Steel Baltimore '43-45; pvt research lab since '45. AIMME—Am Soc for Metals—ACS —Am Ceramic Soc—Electrochem Soc —British Iron and Steel Inst—Am Electroplaters Soc—Am Welding Soc— British Inst Metals—AAAS—Am Foundrymen's Assn. Am Electroplaters Soc Proctor memorial award '40; Sigma Xi '40; Wire Assn Ferrous Div award '48. 6410 Murray Hill Rd., Balt 12.

21 ZAREM, Abe Mordecai. Ultra high-speed photography (Methods and equipment); Physics of electrical discharges; Photo-electric and electronic timing and synchronization. b'17. BS '39 (Ill Inst Tech); MS '40—PhD '44 (Calif Inst Tech). Invented automatic electronic control system for operating photographic equipment, electro-mechanical servo system for recording oscilloscope data; applied electronic pulsing techniques to development of an electro-optical shutter capable of controlled submicrosecond exposure time; unconventional photoelectric trigger adaptable to wide variety of timing problems, a photoelectric synchronizer for making spectral and photographic studies of electrical discharges as a function of time. Holder three US patents on circuits for pulsing and cathode ray oscillograph devices. Author articles in field. Cons engr academic and indsl organization and individuals since '38; chmn physics research Stanford Research Inst '48-51, mgr LA div since '48; cons transient phenomena instrumentation and high-speed photography US Naval Ordance Test Sta Inyokern Calif '48-50; cons in electro-optics and designer spl Kerr Cell Cameras ballistics use. AIEE— ACS—Air Pollution Control Assn— Inst Aero Scis—Inst Radio Engrs— ASEE—AAAS—Am Inst Physics—Am Phys Soc—Soc Motion Picture and TV Engrs—Eta Kappa Nu—Sigma Xi— Tau Beta Pi. 2325 E. Monte Vista, Pasadena 8, Cal.

22 ZAUMEYER, William John. Plant pathology and breeding; Disease resistance and control (Bean, pea). b'03. BS '25—MS '26—PhD '28 (U Wis). Research on bean and pea diseases and their control, inheritance of resistance to certain diseases. Author articles in field. Prin Path Bur Plant Industry Soils and Agrl Engring US Dept Agr since '52. Am Phytopath Soc — AAAS — Wash Acad Sci —Wash Bot Soc. U.S. Department of Agriculture, Plant Industry Station, Beltsville, Md.†

10 ZAWADZKI, Bohdan. Prejudice (Theory); Personality tests. b'02. PhD '28 (U Warsaw); '29-30 (U Berlin Germany); '32-34 (Rockefeller Foundation fellow Austria and US). Experimental and clinical research on psychopathology and therapy of character disorders; development new techniques for personality tests. Author article: Limitations of the Scapegoat Theory of Prejudice '48. Co-author article: (with P F Lazarsfeld) Psychological Consequences of Unemployment '35. Contributor: Encyclopedia of Vocational Guidance '47. Clin psychol Sch Bd City of Warsaw '27-29, '30-31; prof and dir psychol labor U Vilna '35-39; vis lectr Smith, Wellesley, and Sarah Lawrence Colls '40-42; asst prof psychology City Coll NY since '47; asso psychol Postgrad Center for Psychotherapy NYC since '50. Am Psychol Assn(F)—AAAS—Assn Advancement Psychotherapy—NY Acad Sci—Nat Association Mental Health. 115 E. 90th St., NYC 28. H: 68 E. 90th St.

11 ZEEVELD, W(illiam) Gordon. History of ideas in the Renaissance; Tudor historiography; Shakespeare; Machiavelli; Anglicanism; Humanism. b'02. AB '24 (U Rochester); MA '29—PhD '36 (Johns Hopkins U). Author: Foundations of Tudor Policy '48; also articles in field. Asso prof Eng U Md since '37. Mod Lang Assn—AAUP. University of Maryland, College Park, Md.†

12 ZEICHNER, Oscar. History of colonial and revolutionary Connecticut and New York; Agricultural labor in the South after 1865. b'16. AB '36 (City Coll NY); MA '38—PhD '46 (Columbia U). Author: Connecticut's Years of Controversy, 1750-1776 '49. Author articles: Transition from Slave to Free Agricultural Labor in the South '39; Legal Status of the Agricultural Laborer in the South '40; Rehabilitation of Loyalists in Connecticut '38; The Loyalist Problem in New York after the Revolution '40; Jeremy Belknap and the W S Johnson Correspondence '41; William Smith's Observations on America '42. Asst prof hist since '48 City Coll NY. AHA. Department of History, City College of New York, NYC 31.

13 ZEIGLER, Paul P(hilip). Aluminum metallurgy. b'04. BS in metall engineering '36 (Lehigh U); '38-40 (U Tenn). Jr tech Andes Copper Mining Co '29-32; staff metall Alcoa Works Aluminum Co Am '36-40; chief metall Aluminum Div Reynolds Metals Co '40-46; chief metall Kaiser Aluminum & Chem Corp '46-47, dir div metall research since '47. Am Soc Metals—AIME—ASTM. P.O. Box 1451, Spokane 6, Wash.

14 ZELENY, Lawrence. Chemistry of cereals and vegetable oils. b'04. BA '25—MS '27—PhD '30—fellow '26-27, '29-30, '32-33 (U Minn). Research on stability of lard, development of corn proteins, cereal grains and oil-bearing seeds for purpose of developing and maintaining suitable Federal standards. Author articles in field. With US Dept Agr since '35, chief standardization research and testing div, grain br, Prodn and Marketing Adminstrn since '43. Am Chem Soc—Am Assn Cereal Chem—Am Oil Chem Soc—AAAS(F) — Assn Ofcl Agrl Chem — Sigma Xi. Grain Branch, Production and Marketing Administration, U.S. Department of Agriculture, Washington, 25.

15 ZELLER, Leon Henry. Hypnosis. b'04. Student '25—PhD '35 (Pa Coll). Author: Science of Hypnotism '48. Dir Human Relations Inst '40-48. Nat Psy-

chology Assn (vp). 1018 N. Calvert St., Balt.

16 ZEMAN, Frederic David. Geriatrics; Medical history. b'94. BA '13—MD '17 (Columbia). Studies on acute and subacute endocarditis, accident prevention, cardiac rupture, and cerebral arteriosclerosis; research on social problems of old age; chairman session on historical medicine New York State Medical Society '51; member mayor's advisory committee on old age New York City; delegate First National Conference on Aging Washington '50. Author: Life's Later Years—Studies in the Medical History of Old Age '51, also articles in field. Chief med services Home for Aged and Infirm Hebrews since '25; mem attending med staff Mt Sinai Hosp NYC since '28. Am Coll Physicians(F)—Gerontological Soc(mem council '48-51)—NY Acad Med (chmn sect cultural and hist med '48)—Phi Beta Kappa—Alpha Omega Alpha. Diplomate Am Bd Internat Med. 111 E. 88th St., NYC 28.†

17 ZENKERT, Charles Anthony. Herbarium techniques; Plant distribution (Upper New York). b'86. AB '06—MA '14 (John Carroll U); '06-09 (Harvard). Research on flora and ecology of ferns and flowering plants of Niagara Frontier region and adjacent portion of Ontario, Canada, including history of local plant exploration, regional environmental conditions, ecological areas and plant societies, accounts of 1587 native and naturalized species. Author: The Flora of the Niagara Frontier Region '34; also articles in field. Revised sections: Lincoln Library of Essential Information (16th edit) '46. Research asso bot Buffalo Mus Sci since '32. Nature Sanctuary Soc W NY Inc. Buffalo Museum of Science, Humboldt Park, Buffalo 11.

18 ZENTMYER, George A(ubrey). Plant chemotherapy and vascular diseases; Fungicides and fumigants; Avocado diseases. b'13. AB '35—MS '36—PhD '38 (U Calif). Author articles in field. Asso plant path U Calif since '48. AAAS(F) — Am Phytopath Soc (sec-treas New Eng Div '44, Pacific Div since '47) — Bot Soc Am — Nat Shade Tree Conf—Sigma Xi. University of California, Riverside, Calif.†

19 ZERFAS, Leon Grotius. Medical biochemistry. b'97. BS '16—MD '22 (Ind U); PhD '39 (Cambridge U); '40-41 (U Chicago Law Sch). Research on nutritional deficiencies, enzyme systems, purification of lactic dehydrogenases, mechanisms of oxidation-reduction systems. Author articles in field. Dir clin research Eli Lilly & Co '26-36; asst prof med Ind U '29-31, asso prof since '31; phys-in-chief Indianapolis Gen Hosp '26-36; pvt research lab Merom Ind since '41. Ind Acad Sci(F)—Am Gasteroenterol Soc(F)—AMA(F)—ACP(F)—Central Soc Clin Research (hon)—Ind Chem Soc—ACS—Soc Exptl Biol and Med—Sigma Xi. Box 548, Merom, Ind.

20 ZETTLEMOYER, Albert Charles. Physical chemistry (Adsorption, printing ink; resilient flooring); Surface chemistry; catalysis. b'15. BS '36—MS '38—research fellow chemistry (Lehigh U); PhD '40—teaching fellow '38-40 (MIT). Research sulfonated oils and the oiling of real silk, low temperature heat capacity studies, adsorption of gases and liquids on solids, mastic floor tile, printing ink, physical chemistry of drying oils and resins, catalysis. Holds six patents. Author articles in field. Research chem Armstrong Cork Co '41; instr Lehigh U Chem '41-43, asst prof phys chem '43-46, professor since '50. re-

search dir Nat Printing Ink Research Inst since '46. AAAS—Am Chem Soc—Am Inst Chem(F)—Sigma Xi, Chemistry Department, Lehigh University, Bethlehem, Pa.

21 ZEYDEL, Edwin Hermann. German Languages and literature. b'93. AB '14—PhD '18 (Columbia); teaching fellow '14-15—AM '15 (Cornell). Author: The Holy Roman Empire in German Literature '18; First Course in Written and Spoken German '27; Ludwig Tieck and England '31—Ludwig Tieck the German Romanticist '35; and others; co-editor Letters of Ludwig Tieck '37; translator of various learned treatises and articles from French and German. Prof German and head dept U Cincinnati since '26; mng editor German Quarterly since '45; cons in lang Cincinnati Bd Edn. Modern Lang Assn Am(commn on trends in edn '38-44, com on research activities since '44)—Nat Fedn Modern Lang Tchrs—Am Assn Tchrs German—Phi Beta Kappa. Guggenheim fellowship '32. 2907 Daytona Av., Cin 11.⊚

22 ZIEGLER, Arthur William. Fungi (Saprolegniaceae, Phycomycetes). b'17. AB '39—MA '41—PhD '48 (UNC). Author articles in field. Asso prof bot Fla State U since '48. Southeastern Assn Biol — NC Acad Sci — AAAS — Mycol Soc Am—Elisha Mitchell Sci Soc—Sigma Xi—Bot Soc Am. Department of Botany, Florida State University, Tallahassee, Fla.

23 ZIFF, William Bernard. Contemporary Palestine and world affairs; Military theory. b'98. Student '15-17 (Art Inst Chicago). Co-leader and ethnologist expedition to Honduras '34; consultant to United States Dept of Justice '42-43. Author: The Rape of Palestine '38; The Coming Battle of Germany '42; The Gentleman Talk of Peace '44; Two Worlds '46; also articles in field. Founder Ziff-Davis Pub Co (pres '33-47, chmn of bd since '47). 185 N. Wabash Av., Chgo.

24 ZIMAND, Savel. Public health (Education, community organization); Fgn affairs (Soviet Russia, India). b'91. Student '09-12 (Seminar of Oriental Lang U Berlin, also Hohere Webschule); courses in pub health (NYC). Study of political and economic conditions in Soviet Russia and India '21-28; organized pioneer health edn campaigns, education versus compulsion in public health, testing out methods for promotion community health. Author: Modern Social Movements '21; State Capitalism in Russia '26; Living India '28, and others. Co-author: (with C E A Winslow) Health Under the "El" '37. Editor: Health for 7,500,000 People '38; Advances in New York City's Health '40; Twelve Months of Health Defense '41; Quarterly Bulletin NYC Dept of Health '43-45; also articles in field. Administrative dir Bellevue Yorkville Health Demonstration '30-34; asst dir Pub Health Edn NYC Dept Health '35-36, administrative asst '37-43, dir '43-45; dir health edn NYC Cancer Com since '46; lectr on health edn. Am Pub Health Assn(F)—Fgn Policy Assn. 535 Fifth Av., NYC 17.

25 ZIMBALIST, Efrem. Violins. b'89. Student (Imperial Sch St. Petersburg Russia) (with Leopold Auer). Debut as violinist in Berlin at 17; toured through Germany and England; appeared in all major US cities, two world tours, six tours of the Orient. Composer (works for orchestra) Am Rhapsody, Concerto for Violin and Orchestra; string quartet; violin sonata and songs and minor pieces for violin and piano. Dir Curtis Inst of Music

Phila since '41. Curtis Institute of Music, Phila.

10 **ZIMMERLI, Adolph.** Chemistry of photographic developers, terpene derivatives, camphor, and economic poisons (insecticides, including Allethrin). b'86. DSc '11 (Inst Tech Zurich Switzerland). Developed glass substitute permeable to ultraviolet rays; improved manufacture of principal photographic developers; development industrial process for the production of anethol, borneol, camphor and terpineol from pine oil; technical synthesis of Allethrin. Holds patents in field. Chief chem Rhodia Chem Co '20-29; cons organic chem since '31; lectr indsl chem Rutgers U '44-51. ACS—AICE—Soc Chem Industry (Eng)—Assn Cons Chem and Chem E—Sigma Xi—Phi Lambda Upsilon. 221 Grant Av., New Brunswick, N.J.

11 **ZIMMERLI, Franz Perrine.** Shot peening; fatigue limits of springs. b'94. BSE '18—MSE '20—Met Engr '34 (U Mich). Pioneer work on shot peening, studies of fatigue limits of springs, investigation of heat effects in regard to springs, new spring materials. Author articles in field. Metall Solvay Process '21-22; metall dept Dodge Bros '22-23; chief metall Rickenbacker Motor Co '23-26; chief engr Barnes-Gibson-Raymond Div since '26. Am Soc Testing Materials—Am Soc Mining and Metall Engrs—Am Chem Soc—Am Soc for Metals (Saveur Award '47)—ASME—SAE. 40300 Plymouth Rd., Plymouth, Mich. H: 715 Forest Av., Ann Arbor, Mich.

12 **ZIMMERMAN, Arthur Franklin.** Colonial Latin American history; Contemporary history of Chile, Peru and Argentina. b'92. AB '17 (McKendree Coll); AM '19 (Columbia U); BD '20 (Drew U); PhD '28 (U Ill). Special representative in Chile of Inter-American Educational Foundation, a United States Government Agency '44-46. Author: Francisco de Toledo, Fifth Viceroy of Peru, 1569-1581 '38; also articles in field. Prof hist Colo State Coll Edn since '28, dir grad sch since '38. AHA—Colo-Wyo Social Sci Assn —Mid-Western Grad Deans' Conf (pres '46-47)—Phi Alpha Theta (Sec '31-39, pres '39-41, '48, chmn nat adv bd '41-48) — Kappa Delta Pi. Colorado State College of Education, Greeley, Colo.

13 **ZIMMERMAN, Elwood C(urtin).** Entomology; Evolution; Curculionidae; Geographical distribution of plants and animals; Insects of sugar cane, Hawaii and the Pacific Islands; Island life; Biological control; Biogeography. b'12. BS '36 (U Calif); '35 (U Hawaii). Mangarevan expedition to Southeastern Polynesia '34, Henry G. Lapham Fijian expedition '38, Samoan expedition '40, exploration Hawaiian Islands since '34. Author: Insects of Hawaii, five vols '48; also articles in field. Field entomol to curator entomol Bishop Mus since '34; asso entomol expt sta Hawaiian Sugar Planters' Assn since '46. AAAS—Entomol Soc Am—Pacific Coast Entomol Soc—Hawaiian Entomol Soc (vp '40, pres '41-42) — Hawaiian Acad Sci — Hawaiian Bot Soc—Hawaiian Sugar Technol—Soc Study Evolution—Sigma Xi. Experiment Station, Hawaiian Sugar Planters' Association, Honolulu 4, T.H. H: 2234 Cooper Road.†

14 **ZIMMERMAN, Stanley W(illiam).** High voltage transients; Power transmission and distribution apparatus; Power apparatus (Protection). b'07. BS in elec engring '30—MS in elec engring '30 (U Mich). Research, test and certification of apparatus for use on elec-

tric power systems; power frequency and impulse (lightning) performance; insulation behavior and high voltage phenomena; lightning and power system protection. Author confidential reports on research, test and development of electrical apparatus. Co-author: Radio Noise Filters for Aircraft; others. Asst engring research U Mich '28-30; research lab and field investigations Detroit Edison Co '28-30; engr Gen Electric Co '30-45, high voltage lab research lightning arrester development, ionization, radio noise studies; prof elec engring in charge high voltage research lab Cornell U since '45. Am Inst EE—Inst Radio Engrs(sr mem)—Am Soc Engring Edn—Nat Research Council on Insulation—Eta Kappa Nu. Registered profl engr NY and Mass. High Voltage Research Laboratory, Cornell University, Ithaca.

15 **ZINK, Harold.** Government (United States, military, foreign); Public administration. b'01. AB '21 (U Denver); STB '23 (Boston U); AM '24—PhD '26 (Harvard U). Author: City Bosses in United States '30; Introduction to Politics '41; Government of Cities in the United States '48; Government and Politics in the United States '46; American Military Government in Germany '47; Survey of American Government '48. Co-author: The American Politician '38; Post-War Governments of Europe '46; also articles in field. Prof polit sci O State U since '48. Am Polit Sci Assn (mem exec council '43-45)—Am Acad Polit Social Sci—Am Soc Pub Adminstrn—Nat Municipal League—Internat City Mgrs Assn—Midwest Conf of Polit Sci (sec treas '38-47, chmn managerial com '48)—Ind Acad Social Sci (pres '39-40)—Phi Beta Kappa. Department of Political Science, O State University, Columbus 10.◎

16 **ZINK, Norah E.** Dry-farming. BS '24 (U Utah); AM '26 (Columbia); PhD '37 (U Chicago). Research and mapping of dry-farming in Utah. Author: Dry-Farming Adjustments in Utah '37. Contributor: Thirty-Second Yearbook National Society for Study of Education '33; Encyclopedia of Ednl Research '41. Head geog dept New Haven State Normal Sch '26-28; acting head and tchr geog State Tchrs Coll Indiana Pa '28-29, since '36; research spl Utah State Engrs Office '33-34; faculty U Pittsburgh '36. Central W Geog Club—Geog Club W Pa—Pa Council Geog Tchrs—Nat Council Geog Tchrs—Assn Am Geog—Am Geog Soc —Pa Edn Research Assn—AAUP—NEA—Delta Kappa Gamma. State Teachers College, Indiana, Pa.

17 **ZINN, Donald Joseph.** Ascidians; Ecology of marine populations; Agassiz; Limnology of Morraine Lakes of southern Rhode Island. b'11. BS '33. —'35-36 (Harvard); MS '37 (RI State Coll); PhD '42 (Yale). Invented limnophotometer with a special adaptation for the measurement of the penetration of light through ice under natural conditions. Author articles in field. Instr zool RI State Coll since '46. AAAS—Ecol Soc Am—Am Soc Limnol and Oceanog—Wildlife Inst—AFA—Am Soc Systemic Zool — NY Acad Sci—Sigma Xi. Zoology Department, University of Rhode Island. Kingston, R.I.†

18 **ZMESKAL, Otto.** Steel; Corrosion. b'15. BS '36—MS '38 (Armour Inst Tech); ScD '41 (MIT). Consultant on failures, on development of special steels; expert witness in court trials. Author articles in field. Dir dept metall engring Ill Inst Tech since '46. Am Soc Metals—Am Inst Mining

Metall Engrs—Am Soc Engring Edn—Am Chem Soc—Western Soc Engrs—Iron and Steel Inst (Brit)—Tau Beta Pi—Sigma Xi—Phi Lambda Upsilon. Illinois Institute of Technology, 10 W. 33rd St., Chgo 16.†◎

19 **ZOBELL, Claude E.** Microbiology; Geomicrobiology; Marine biology; Bacteriology (Petroleum, water); Oil pollution; Oceanography (Fouling organisms). b'04. BS '27—MS '29 (Utah State Agrl Coll); PhD '31—Thompson scholar '29-31 (U Calif). Honorary member Byrd Antarctic Expedition II '34. Author: Marine Microbiology '45; also articles in field. Prof Microbiol U Calif since '48; dir research project 43 A for Am Petroleum Inst since '42. AAAS(F)—Am Assn Petroleum Geol (research com '45-49)—Am Chem Soc—Ecol Society Am (vp '42)—Am Society Limnol and Oceanog (pres '48-49)—Society Industrial Med—Soc Am Bact (pres S Calif sect '44-46, com on technique '45-49)—Western Soc Naturalists (vp '46-47)—Sigma Xi—Phi Kappa Phi. Rockefeller Found fellow '47-48. University of California, La Jolla, Cal.†◎

20 **ZSCHEILE, Frederick Paul.** Agricultural biochemistry; Plant pigments; Photoelectric spectrophotometry; Biochemistry of plant disease resistance. b'07. BS '28—PhD '31 (U Calif). Research on spectroscopy of chlorophyll '31-33, spectroscopy of biological substances '33-37, plant pigments '37-44, stabilization of carotene in alfalfa '44-46, biochemistry of disease resistance in plants and biochemistry of agronomic crops since '46. Author articles: Plastid Pigments '41, and others. Research asso chem U Chicago '33-37, research asso bot '44-46; asst and asso prof agri chem Purdue U '37-44; asso prof agron and asso biochem in Expt Sta U Cal '46-52 professor and biochemist since '52. Phi Beta Kappa—Sigma Xi. Nat Research fellow '31-33. Department of Agronomy, University of California, Davis, Calif.†

21 **ZUCKER, Adolph Edward.** German literature and German education; History of the theatre (Ibsen). b'90. AB '12—AM '13 (U Ill); PhD '17 (U Pa); (Sorbonne Paris, U Munich, U Berlin). Textbook censor Allied Control Council, headquarters Frankfort Germany '45-46. Author: Robert Reitzel '17; The Chinese Theater '25; Ibsen, The Master Builder '29; The Forty-eighters; Redentin Easter Play; Amerika und Deutschland; Liberals. Editor of Western Literature from Homer to Shaw '22; The Romantic Poets '26, and others; also articles in field. Chairman division of humanities Univ Md since '38. Modern Lang Assn Am—Modern Humanities Research Assn—Gesellshaft fur Theater-geschichte (Berlin). Riverdale, Md.

22 **ZUCKER, Milton.** Chemistry of printing inks and printing processes. b'04. BS '24 (Case Inst Tech); LLB '31 (Cleveland Law Sch); '25 (George Washington U Law Sch). Research lacquers, alkyd resins, finishes for wood, inks, lithographic plates, relationship of ink with print paper. Holds patent on alkyd resins, stains, laquers. Author articles in field. Chem, engr, lab supervisor, patent atty Glidden Co '27-37; patent atty and research mgr internat printing ink div Interchem Corp '37-51 tech assistant to president since '51. Am Chem Soc—American Inst Chem(F)—AAAS—Tech Assn Lithographic Ind—Am Patent Law Assn. Interchemical Corp., 67 W. 44th St., NYC 36.

23 **ZUCROW, M. J.** Jet propulsion; Gas turbines; Rockets. b'99. BS '22—

Concluded on Page 803

LATEST LISTINGS and SKETCH ADDITIONS

Listings and data which could not be published . . . because of mechanical, editorial or other reasons
. . . on pages 11 to 800, but which the unique Locator Index (page 871) makes exactly as available for
reference usage as if appearing on those pages.

10 ALLEN, John Eldridge. H: 1015 N. Randolph St., Arlington 1, Va.

11 ANDREW, Warren. Prof anat and dir Bowman Gray Sch Med since '52. Bowman Gray School of Medicine, Winston Salem, N.C.

12 AXELROD, Herbert Richard. Fresh water tropical fishes. b'27. BS '49 (City Coll NY, NYU); MS '51 (NYU). Explored virgin waters of Korea and Siam for new aquarium species of tropical fish; conducted experiments on fishes diets, breeding habits and light periodicity factors. Author: Tropical Fish As A Hobby '52; Tropical Fish Guide '53; Tropical Fish as Pets '53. Co-author: (with L P Schultz) Handbook of Freshwater Tropical Aquarium Fishes '54; also articles. Instr tropical fishes NYU; mng editor Tropical Fish Hobbyist mag. Am Association Herpetologists and Ichthyologists —Biometric Soc. 137 Varick St., N.Y.C. 13.

13 BALL, Carleton Roy. Willows (Taxonomy, utilization); Comic cartoons (Distribution and sociological effect). b'73. BSc '96—MSc '99—ScD hon '20 (Ia State Coll). Developed federal-state cooperation in agricultural research; author two volumes on agricultural administration. Agrostologist, agronomist, cerealist in charge USDA '99-30, grasses, cereal crops and diseases; prin agriculturist, ext service, exec sec correlation com USDA, TVA, and Land-Grant Colls of So States '35-43, collaborator since '43; collects, classifies, correlates production and distbn of so-called comic cartoons with reports on both juvenile and adult delinquency. AAAS(F)—Am Soc Agron(F)—Am Soc Plant Taxonomists—Am Soc Pub Adminstrn—Am Polit Sci Assn—Bot Soc Am—Bot Soc Washington—Washington Acad Sci—Agrl Hist Soc—Cal Bot Soc—So Assn Sci and Industry—So Appalachian Bot Club—Gamma Sigma Delta—Phi Kappa Phi—Sigma Xi. 3814 Jocelyn St., Washington 15.

14 BATES, Philip K(night). Bacteriological chemistry. b'02. SB '24—PhD '29 (Mass Inst Tech). Author articles in scientific journals. Teaching asst Tufts Med and Dental Sch '24-26; research asso Mass Inst Tech '24-27, '33-35; head bact dept Frigidare Corp Dayton O '28-32; bact Rexall Drug Co LA '36-40, dir product development dept since '41; instr Boston U Sch Med '44-46; pres Riker Labs Inc since '49. Inst Food Tech—ACS—Am Public Health Assn—Soc Am Bact—Delta Omega. 8480 Beverly Blvd., LA 36.

15 BEERS, Roland Frank. No longer with Geotechnical Corp Dallas, Geotechnical Corp of Canada, Geotechnical Service Corp Dallas. Prof Geophysics Rensselaer Polytechnic Inst. since '48. H: Pinewoods Avenue Road, Troy, N.Y. P.O. Box 1015, Troy, N.Y.

16 BENNE, Kenneth D. Berenson prof and dir Human Relations Center Boston U since '53. 226 Bay State Rd., Boston 15.

17 BLAKE, John Twiss. Awarded the Goodyear Gold Medal '53.

18 BURKENROAD, Martin D(avid). Fishery biology; Shrimps. b'10. Student '26-29 (Tulane U); MSc '43 (Yale). Research on seafood production, resources of the sea and methods for conservation, cycles of abundance of marine animals, and coastal pollution problems; NRC committee for research on food resources of coastal waters. Author article: Fluctuation in Abundance of Pacific Halibut '48, and others. Asst biol Dept Conservation La '30-31; asst curator Bingham Oceanographic Collection Yale '34-44, mem oceanog expdn '34, '35, '37; instructor Marine Biol Lab Woods Hole Mass '42-43; fisheries cons since '45; research sci in Marine Fisheries III U Tex since '50. Soc Zool—Ecol Soc—Micros Soc—Atlantic Estuarine Rsrch Soc—Soc Systematic Zool—Corp Marine Biol Lab—Corp Bermuda Biol Sta —La Acad Sci—Tex Acad Sci—Sigma Xi. Institute of Marine Science, Port Aransas, Tex.

19 BURROUGHS, Wilbur Greeley. Economic geology (Oil, gas, oil shale, stone, barite); Regional geography and geology of Kentucky, Ohio and southwest Virginia; Prehistoric strongholds of Kentucky. b'86. AB '09—MA '11 (Oberlin Coll); PhD '32 (Cornell U). Explored and mapped prehistoric stronghold of Indian Fort Mountain Kentucky, also former connection between Eastern Interior and Appalachian Coal Fields across Kentucky; discovered and mapped prehistoric stronghold on Basin Mountain Kentucky; located oil and gas wells in Virginia Kentucky and Ohio. Author monographs and geological survey reports on the geography, geology, mineral resources and operations, and population of Kentucky and Ohio. Contributor articles in scientific publications. Geol and geog industrial surveys Ky, Va, Ohio; founded geol and geog dept Berea Coll Ky '20, prof and head dept, holding Shaler Chair of geol since '23; cons geol pvt cos since '20. Royal Geog Soc Eng(F, life) —Ky Acad Sci(pres '26)—Ky Geol Soc —Nat Council Geog Tchrs—Phi Beta Kappa—Sigma Xi—Sigma Gamma Epsilon. Berea College, Berea, Ky.†

20 CAMPBELL, Joseph. H: 2712 32d St., Washington 8. 75 Maiden Lane, New York 38.

21 CORNELL, Ethel L(etitia). Clinical psychology in education. b'92. AB '14 (Cornell U); PhD '19 (Columbia). Developed with W W Coxe standards for certification of school psychologists in New York State '32; a scale of performance tests '34; research on applications of clinical psychology to problems of special education, pupil adjustment, pupil classification and grouping, reading disabilities, analysis of work of school psychologist, construction of tests for special studies. Author: Mental Hygiene: Its Place in Reading of High School Pupils '41; The Work of the School Psychologist '42. Co-author: Cornell-Coxe Perform-

ance Ability Scale '34. Reconstruction aide assigned psychol services US Army '18-19; chief psychol Boston Psychopathic Hosp '19-20; psychol research asso NY State Edn Dept since '20. Diplomate in clinical psychol Am Bd Examiners in Profl Psychol. Am Psychol Assn (F, pres div sch psychol '48-49)—NY State Psychol Assn (pres '41, bd certification since '46)—Am Edn Research Assn—Phi Beta Kappa. New York State Education Dept., Albany 1, N.Y.

22 DEAN, H(enry) Trendley. Dental aspects of Fluorine. b'93. DDS '16 (St Louis U); officers sch '31 (USPHS). Investigations in role of Fluorine in prevention and treatment of dental caries; water-borne fluorides and dental health; Fluoridation public water supplies; chronic endemic dental fluorosis. Contbr chpts in profl books and articles to profl jours on various aspects of fluorine and dental caries and epidemiological studies. With US PHS since '24, dental director '45-53; sec council on dental research Am Dental Assn since '53; served Nat Inst Health '37-53 in div infectious disease div physiology and exptl biol and med inst; dir Nat Inst Dental Reserch '48-53. AAAS(F)—Am Coll Dentists (F, com resrch since '50)—APHA (com resrch and standards '49-52)—Am Dental Assn (com dental health survey '33-35, research commn '39-48)—Internat Assn Dental Research—Assn Mil Surg (pres '37)—Am Epidemiol Soc—Nat Research Council (ad hoc com on fluoridation of water supplies '51)—Federation Dentaire Internationale—Am Assn Dental Editors ('46-48)—Am Water Works Assn (com policy re fluoridation pub water supplies since '49)—Delta Sigma Delta—Omicron Kappa Upsilon (hon). Gorgas Medal and award Assn Mil Surg '49; John M Goodell prize Am Water Works Assn '50; Lasker award APHA '52; Holme Lect U London Hopp Med Coll '52. American Dental Association, 222 E. Superior St., Chgo 11.

23 FIELD, Ernest George. Quality control in textile industry. b'93. BS in mech engring '16 (RI State Coll, now U RI). Engaged in textile operations since '21, as E G Field & Assos Atlanta since '46. Insp materials USN '42-45. ASME—Nat Assn Cost Accts— Ga Engring Soc—Am Soc Quality Control. 1101-8 Hurt Bldg., Atlanta 3.

24 FRIEND, Albert Wiley. Resigned from Magnetic Metals Co., now cons engr and physicist. 381 Bala Av., Bala-Cynwyd, Pa.

25 GAMBRILL, J(ohn) Montgomery. History of American frontiers; Maryland (Historical events); Elementary school history tests. b'80. Grad '97 (Balt Poly Inst); grad study '07, '12-15—AM '13—M Diploma in teaching Tchrs Coll (Columbia). Author: Leading Events of Maryland History '03. Co-author: (with Charles M Andrews and Lida Lee Tall) A Bibliography of History for Schools and Librarians '10; (with Olive Moore and I Jewell Simpson) Historical Tests for Elementary Grades '28. Editor: How the Old World Found the New (by Eunice Fuller Barnard and Lida Lee Tall) '29; My Maryland (by Beta Kaessman, Harold R Manakee and Joseph L Wheeler) '34; The Westward Movement: A Book of Readings on Our Changing Frontiers (with Ina F Woestemeyer) '39. Mem editorial dept secondary schs Hist Tchrs Mag '12-14; editor book review dept Hist Outlook '21-25. Asst supt pub instrn Md '04-06; hist faculty Columbia '13-43, emeritus prof history since '43; vis prof Am hist John Hopkins '42-46, lectr since '48; vis prof hist Smith Coll '47-48. AHA—Assn Hist Tchrs Middle States and Md (pres '22-23)—The Hist Assn London—Econ Hist Assn. H: 2942 Wyman Parkway, Balt. 11.

10 HARDESTY, Shortridge. Metals (Structural uses); Highway designs (Expressways and thruways). born '84. AB '05—LLD '28 (Drake U); CE '08—DEng '51 (Rensselaer Poly Inst); DEng '49 (Union Coll). Design and construction highway and railroad bridges including vertical lift spans throughout US since '20; other works include Perisphere and Trylon NY World's Fair '39; Standard Highway bridge plans for Cuban govt; Cross Bronx Expressway, Circumferential Parkway, Van Wyck Expressway NYC, Niagara Thruway Buffalo, Ohio Turnpike, Garden State Parkway NJ. Draftsman, designer Waddell & Harrington Kansas City Mo '08-15; designing engr Waddell & Son '16-17; mem Waddell & Son Inc '18-19; asso engr J A L Waddell NYC '20-26; partner Waddell & Hardesty NYC '27-38; Waddell & Hardesty '38-45, Hardesty & Hanover since '45. Column Research Council (chmn)—ASCE—Am Inst Cons Engrs —Soc Am Mil Engrs—Am Ry Engring Assn—Am Soc Testing Materials—Am Concrete Inst—Am Toll Bridge Assn— Internat Assn Bridge and Structural Engring—Rensselaer Soc Engrs—Rensselaer Tech Soc—Phi Beta Kappa— Sigma Xi—Tau Beta Pi—Engrs Club NYC. 101 Park Av., NYC 17.◎

11 HASS, Henry Bohn. Chlorination of hydrocarbons. b'02. Author the twelve chlorination rules '37. Discovered, with students, the vapor-phase nitration process for organic compounds '30, Cyclopropane synthesis '36, New method for resolution of enantiomorphic organic compounds '40; Manhattan project, fluorocarbons '42-46; The chemistry of sugars since '52. Care General Aniline & Film Corp., 230 Park Av., New York 17.

12 HOLLIS, Ernest Victor. Social work education. b'95. BS '18—MS '18 (Miss State Coll); AM '22—PhD '38 (Columbia); LittD '50 (Shurtleff Coll); LLD '50 (Bucknell U); LHD hon '51 (Temple U). Author: Philanthropic Foundations and High Education '38; The College and Teacher Education '44; Toward Improving PhD Programs '45; Higher Education Look Ahead '45: College and University Building Needs '48; Social Work Education in the US '51; Vermont Youth and Higher Education '52. Contbr encys and profl jours. Head edn dept State Tchrs Coll Morehead Ky '27-35; lectr edn Coll City NY '36-40; coordinator com on tchr edn Am Council on Edn Washington '40-44; chief coll adminstrn US Soc Advancement Edn—Am Assn U Profs—Am Ednl Research Assn—Nat Soc Coll Tchrs Edn—Nat Soc Study Edn—Phi Delta Kappa—Kappa Delta Pi. U.S. Office of Education, Washington 25.

13 HOSMER, Ralph Sheldon. History of forestry and conservation. b'74. BAS '94 (Harvard); Master Forestry '02 (Forest Sch Yale). Author: Impressions of European Forestry '22; The Cornell Plantations, a History '47; also articles in field. Prof forestry emeritus Cornell U. AAAS(F)—Soc Am Foresters (F, pres '23, mem com hist forestry)—AFA—Soc Forestry in Suomi (Finland, hon mem)—Empire State Forest Products Assn (life)—Phi Kappa Phi. 209 Wait Av., Ithaca.

14 HOUGHTON, Arthur Amory, Jr. Rare books; Shakespeare; James Boswell, Keats, Shelley; Antiquity preservation; Maryland (Antiquities); Glass. b'06. Student '25-29 (Harvard); LHD '50 (Lehigh U); LLD '52 (U Rochester). Curator rare books Library of Congress '40-42, now fellow in English bibliography and member advisory council. Trustee, mem library com NY Pub Library; trustee, mem finance com Pierpont Morgan Library; mem vis com Harvard Library, hon curator Keats Coll; mem adv com, mem Council of Friends Princeton U Library; trustee Queen Anne's Co Free Library; mem adv com Folger Shakespeare Library; mem adv com Yale edition Private Papers of James Boswell; trustee Nat Trust for Historic Preservation; vp, trustee, mem exec com Corning Mus Glass. With Corning Glass Works '29-42, vp '35-42, now dir; dir Steuben Glass Inc. Internat Inst Am Civilization Inc (dir)—Shakespeare Assn Am (pres, dir)—Keats-Shelley Assn Am (vp, dir)—Soc for Preservation Md Antiquities (director, life mem)—Md Hist Soc (trustee, life mem)—Poetry Soc Am (patron founder)—Am and Md library assns—Am, London, Oxford and Cambridge bibliog socs—Grolier Club (council, library com)—Odd Volumes Club. 718 Fifth Av., NYC 19.◎

15 IRVING, Laurence. Aviation physiology; Animals (Respiration): Arctic region (Physiology). b'95. AB '16 —Charles Carroll Everett grad scholar '16-17 (Bowdoin Coll); AM '17 (Harvard); PhD '24 (Stanford). Research physiological effects of variant atmospheric pressures upon human respiration; aviation and effects of altitudes and air pressures on physiological reactions; physiology of respiration in animals. Ed: Jour Cellular and Comparative Physiology, Biol Bull, Physiol Reviews, Biol Abstracts, Revue Canadienne de Biologie. Chmn panel expeditionary physiology Joint Research and Development Bd '47; chmn steering com 2d Alaskan Sci Conf; leader expdn physiol research Office Naval Research and Swarthmore Coll Point Barrow Alaska '47-49; now chief physiol sect Arctic Health Research Center USPHS Anchorage Alaska. Chief physiol br Aero Med Lab Wright Field '45-46; sci dir Arctic Research Lab Point Barrow Alaska '48-49. Arctic Inst NA(F) —AAAS(F)—Am and Can physiol socs (F)—Am Soc Zool(F)—Am Soc Naturalists(F)—Phila Physiol Soc(F)— Nat Research Council—Sigma Xi—Phi Beta Kappa—Delta Kappa Epsilon. Box 906 Anchorage, Alaska.◎

16 KAHN, Morton C. Mosquitoes (Identification by sound, use of sound in attracting and destroying); Dutch Guiana (Bush Negroes); Public health aspects of yellow fever, tuberculosis, malaria. b'96. PhD '24 (Cornell). Author: Djuka, The Bush Negroes of Dutch Guiana '31; Public Health and Preventive Medicine (2 vols) '42; also articles in field. Editor: (also revised) Carlos Finlay and Yellow Fever (by Finlay) '40. Faculty Cornell U Med Coll since '19, now prof and head dept parasitology. Cornell University Medical College, York Av. and 69th St., NYC.

17 KEPPLER, Wharton Fields. Industrial statistical quality control. b'11. Student '34 (U Cin Eve Coll); '31-32 (Kenyon Coll); AB '43—'46-48 (Ohio State U); '47 (Rochester Inst Tech); '48 (Purdue). Research in development of effective statistical quality control techniques to be applied to bacteriological and chemical control of raw materials, in-process and finished products; studies on future raw material requirements in relation to capacity, process losses. Tech and statis M&R Dietetic Labs Inc '40-44, profl indsl engr and statis since '46; statis profl grade supply div and engring div Air Tech Service Command Wright Field Dayton O '44-46. Registered profl indsl engr Ohio. Am Statis Assn—Inst Math Statis—Am Soc Quality Control—Nat and Ohio socs profl engrs—Am Marketing Assn. M&R Dietetic Labs., Inc., Columbus 16, O. H: 11 Nottingham Rd., Columbus 2.†

18 KLIEVER, Waldo Harold. Rsrch management; Instrument design for measurement and control; Electronic circuitry for instrumentation: Heating and air condning. b'07. AB '29 (Bethel Coll Newton Kan); PhD '39 (U Chgo). Instruments development including applications to temperature, humidity, time, distance and techniques for recording: electronic circuitry for instrumentation; design requirements for buildings with respect to heating problems and for heating systems and controls. Author articles: The Dendroheliconometer '37; Integrator for Circular Ordinates '41; Bailing Press Recorder '44; Design of Research Projects and Programs '52; Choosing and Evaluating Research Projects '53, and others. Research physicist, sales engineer Gaetner Sci Corp Chgo '30-38; engr-physicist instrumentation cotton gin and press operation USDA Leland Miss '38-40; dir research Mpls-Honeywell Regulator Co Mpls '40-53; vp, dir instrument development orgn and adminstrn instrument-div Clevite-Brush Development Co Cleve since '53. APS—Soc Automotive Engrs—Instrument Soc Am—Am Soc Agrl Engrs— Inst Aero Scis—Sigma Xi. Clevite-Brush Development Co., 3405 Perkins Av., Cleve. 14. H: 2472 Overlook Rd., Cleveland Heights 6, O. (This replaces sketch on page 371.)

19 LAMOUREUX, Vincent B(ronner). Public health measures in emergency situations. b'99. CE '20 (Cornell U). Commissioned sanitary engineer officer US Public Health Service since '31; consultant to UNRRA '44 '45, assistant chief engr Balkan Mission, later chief engineer Italian Mission; consultant to National Security Resources Board as sanitary engineer, also to Federal Civil Defense Administration; radiological defense consultant participating in atomic tests; now chief health and sanitation br Near East and Africa area Foreign Operations Administration. AS CE—APHA(F)—Assn Mil Surgeons— Soc Mil Engrs. U.S. Public Health Service, Washington 25.

20 LINDSEY, Alton Anthony. Now associate prof biol Purdue U. Ecologist Canadian Arctic Permafrost Expdn '51.

21 LONG, Chester H. H: 1101 S. 7th St., Terre Haute, Ind. Rose Polytechnic Institute, Terre Haute, Ind.

22 MANNES, Leopold Damrosch. Photography (Color processes). b'99. AB '20 (Harvard). Inventor (with Leopold Godowsky, Jr.) of a major process for color photography. Chemist Eastman Kodak Co, Rochester NY '31-39; faculty Mannes Music Sch '25-31, pres. since '51; concert pianist since '25. 157 E. 74th St., NYC. H: 120 E. 75th St.

23 MARRON, Thomas Urban. Chemical aspects of photo-offset, spirit, and stencil duplication processes. b '14. BS '36 (St Ambrose Coll); MS '37—PhD '42 (State U Ia); '44 (U Mich

Research and development work on mimeograph supplies, positive and negative working photo-offset plates, spirit duplicating supplies, novel methods of office copying. Holds patents in field. Group leader, analytical research Nat Aniline div Allied Chem & Dye Corp '42-46; research supervisor A B Dick Co since '46. ACS—Optical Soc Am—Alpha Chi Sigma—Sigma Xi. Chmn 8th Nat Chem Expn '53-54. 5700 W. Touhy Av., Chgo 31. (This replaces sketch on page 433).

10 MAYS, Benjamin Elijah. LLD Va Union U '45; LHD Boston U '50. Author: The Negro's Church 1933. Editor: A Gospel for the Social Awakening.

11 MOTT, Frederick Dodge. No longer with Dept of Health Govt of Saskatchewan. Med adminstr Memorial Hosp Assn of Ky since '52. 1427 Eye St., Washington 5.

12 NAAMANI, Israel T. H: 2404 Brighton Dr., Louisville, Ky.

13 NETHERCOT, Arthur Hobart. Author: Men and Supermen '54.

14 OKULITCH, Vladimir Joseph. Prof geol and geog U Brit Columbia since '50; chmn div geol since '53.

15 PEASE, Clarke Demorest. Farms (Mechanized operation); Local distribution of agricultural products; Application of engineering approaches to distribution problems. b'95. AB '11 (Lewis Inst); BS '15 (Yale); grad in modern prodn '44 (MIT). Works toward mechanization of farming operations and toward decentralized agricultural processing leading to expanded local distribution at retail; developed distribution of farm products through organized roadside markets;

member President Roosevelt's committee on decentralization; governor Agricultural Industrial Marketing Found. Author: Creating Jobs Through a More Efficient System of Distribution, and others. Engr and ofcl various US and fgn orgns prior to 1942; chief engr for conversion WPB '42-43; head indsl engr Bur Econ Warfare '43-44; now pres Clarke D. Pease and Assos. AS ME—Soc Advancement Management— Am Soc Agrl Engrs—Am Acad Polit and Socl Sci—Edn Assn US—Am Econ Assn—Am Ednl Research Assn—Nat Art Edn Assn—Am Indsl Arts Assn— Rural Edn Assn. Maxwell House, Nashville 3, Tenn. H: care of Yale Club, 50 Vanderbilt Av., NYC 17. (Replaces sketch on page 525.)

16 POWERS, Alfred. Author: A Long Way to Frisco '51.

17 ROSE, H(arold) Wickliffe. Resigned from Am Vicose Corp '53; pres Linen Thread Co Inc since '53. Linen Thread Company, Inc. 60 E. 42d St., New York 17.

18 RUBIN, Harvey Louis. Sterility in Thoroughbred horses; Identification of race horses. b'14. Student '32-36 (San Diego State Coll Cal); DVM '39 (Ala Poly Inst); MS '40 (U Ky); MPH '52 (Johns Hopkins). Research in sterility problems in Thoroughbreds; assisted development lip tattoo method of identification of race horses. Army remount activities since 1942, depot vet Pomona QM Depot '46-49, chief vet sect and exec officer 2d Army Area Med Lab '49-51; officer in charge and chief vet sect Hawaiian Med Lab since '52. Am Vet Med Assn—Assn Mil Surgeons—Soc Sigma Xi—Phi Kappa Phi. Hawaiian Med Lab., APO 957, care PM, San Francisco.

19 TAYLOR, Raymond Leech. Plants of Colonial America. b'01. BS '24 (Cornell); MS '27—ScD '29 (Harvard). Author: Plants of Colonial Days '52; also articles in field. In charge nature study Mt Desert Island Biol Lab '31, dir Dorr Sta '32; asst prof biol Coll William and Mary '31-34, asso prof '34-46; asso prof biol Sampson Coll '46-47, resident head biol '46-49, prof '4-7 49; asst administrative sec AAAS since '49; collaborator Am Council Edn, U Chgo, '40. AAAS(F)—Entomol Soc Am —Am Assn Econ Entomol—Va Acad Sci(chmn zool sect '37)—AAUP—Am Nature Study Soc—Phi Sigma. 1515 Massachusetts Av., Washington 5. H: 2504 N. 11th St., Arlington 1, Va.

20 TEALE, Edwin Way. Wildlife photography. b'99. AB '22 (Earlham Coll); AM '26 (Columbia). Awarded John Burroughs medal, '43; revised insect-study program Boy Scouts of America '45. Author: Grassroot Jungles '37 (rev '44); Boys' Book of Insects '39; Boys' Book of Photography '39; The Golden Throng '40; Byways to Adventure '42; The Story of an Insect Garden '42; Insect Life '44, others; also articles in field. Staff feature writer Popular Sci Monthly '28-41, free lance writer since '41. Am Geog Society(F)—NY Acad Scis (F, council '42-49)—NY Entomol Soc (pres '44)—Am Nature Study Soc (pres '47)—NY Audubon Soc— Thoreau Soc—Royal Photographic Soc —Am Ornithologists' Union—Linnaean Soc of NY—AAAS. 93 Park Av., Baldwin, L.I., N.Y.☉

21 TRASK, Parker Davies. Res engr dept engring U of Cal since '51; cons Peruvian govt on flood control '52. H: 240 Southampton Av., Berkeley 7, Cal.

22 WESTHEIMER, Frank H(enry). Vis prof chemistry Harvard U '53-54.

Continued from Page 728

MS '23 (Harvard Engring Sch); PhD '28 (Purdue). Author: Principles of Jet Propulsion and Gas Turbines '47; also articles in field. Prof gas turbines and jet propulsion Purdue U since '46. ASME—Inst Aero Scis—Am Rocket Soc—SAE—Sigma Xi. School of Mechanical Engineering, Purdue University, Lafayette, Ind.☉

23 ZUEHLKE, Arthur Joseph. Great Lakes (Naval architecture); Carferries; Ships (Cargo, self-unloading). b '16. Student '35-37 (Lawrence Coll); BS '40 (U Mich). Collaborator in hull design Great Lakes Carferry City of Midland with reference determination optimum hull form for proper displacement, trim, stability, hull efficiency; hull design cabin arrangements and cargo handling for self-unloading bulk cargo boats applies to new construction and conversion of existing vessels. Naval architect Manitowoc Shipbldg Co since '48. Soc Naval Architects and Marine Engrs. Manitowoc Shipbuilding Company, Manitowoc, Wis.

24 ZURCHER, Arnold J(ohn). European political systems; American federal government; Occidental political theory; Foundations and public trusts. b'02. AB '24 (Oberlin Coll); AM '26 —Andrew D White fellow social sci '25-26 (Cornell U); PhD '28 — Charlotte E Procter fellow politics (Prince-

ton U). Author: Experiment with Democracy in Central Europe '33. Co-author: (with H L Childs and others) Propaganda and Dictatorship '36; (with J T Shotwell and others) The Governments of Continental Europe '40; (with Count R N Cowdenhove-Kalergi and others) Postwar European Federation '43. Co-editor The Dictionary of American Politics '44; Postwar Goals and Economic Reconstruction '44; Postwar Economic Society '44; America's Place in the World Economy '45. Vis prof govt Yale '43-44; civilian lecturer War Dept Sch Mil Govt Charlottesville Va '43-44; with NYU since '28, dir Inst Postwar Reconstrn '43-45, prof polit sci and head Inst Pub Affairs and Regional Studies; exec dir Alfred P Sloan Found Inc NYC since '45. Am Polit Sci Assn—AAUP—Council on Fgn Relations—Phi Beta Kappa 30 Rockefeller Plaza, NYC 20.†

25 ZWENG, Charles Alfonso. Celestial and radio navigation. b'93. B Law '12 (Ill Wesleyan U); '27-28 (Bradley Poly Inst); spl course '37 (Celestial Navigation Annapolis). Author: Encyclopedic Aviation Dictionary '44; Radio and Instrument Flying '48; Aeronautical Navigation '47, and others. Training of flight engrs under Regulation No. 35 of the Civil Aeronautics Authority since '47. Instr USAAF '39; instrument flight training

and celestial navigation training RAF '40-42, spl training celestial navigation for officers of Fourth Armored Div '42-44. Inst Aeronautical Sci—Inst Navigation—Am Soc Engring Edn— Am Meteorol Soc. 12021 Ventura Boulevard, North Hollywood, Calif.

26 ZWICKER, Benjamin Michael George. Chemistry of high polymers. b'15. AB '35 (Whitman Coll); MS '38—PhD '40 (U Washington). Research electro-reduction, photometric analysis, colloids, organic synthesis, micro analysis, polymerization. Holder several US patents. Author articles in field. Colloidal research BF Goodrich Co '40-42, polymerization research and development '41-43, rubbers and plastics development management Akron Expt Plant since '43. Am Chem Soc —Am Inst Chem Engrs—Phi Beta Kappa. B.F. Goodrich Chemical Co., Plant 3, Akron, O.

27 ZWICKY, Fritz. Astrophysics; Jet propulsion. b'98. BS '20—PhD '22 (Fed Inst Tech Zurich Switzerland); Internat research fellow '25-27 (Calif Inst Tech, Rockefeller Found). Author articles in field. Prof astrophysics Calif Inst Tech since '42; dir research Aerojet Engring Corp Pasadena '43-49 chief research consultant since '49. Am Phys Society—Swiss Phys Society—Am Astron Society. California Institute of Technology, Pasadena 4, Calif.☉

On the Following Yellow Pages

THE ROSTER OF SELECTED GENERAL AUTHORITIES: As stated in the Preface (page 5), the scope of this work is arbitrarily delimited, and obviously must be if it is to serve effectively the specific purposes there detailed. Three logical assumptions, the Editors feel, should follow automatically from more than a merely casual consideration of that explanation of this work's scope and its purposes: *first,* that the word "authority" is of necessity utilized in the generally accepted usage of being interchangeable with "expert" (or even with "specialist"), but with full cognisance that there are outstanding knowers in respect to each field of knowledge who obviously are exceptionally informed about practically every subject within the field(s) in respect to which each of them so ranks; *second,* that in consequence this general conversance of these ranking knowers has been considered obvious by the compilers, and in no way disregarded when listing an individual indicating himself, or herself, to be especially informed or expert, or an authority in respect to a subject; *third,* that, except for special compilative reasons, including data about these ranking knowers . . . their data are readily available in one or more publications, in addition to "Who's Who In America". . . is nonessential to the specific purposes here involved. However, and principally to emphasize their cognisance of the foregoing, the Editors carried out a national canvass, in an effort to ascertain those considered to be ranking knowers in respect to the broad fields into which the scope of this work carries its listings. A tabulation of this canvass begins on the opposite page, and extends through the following 13 pages. Those listed flush with the left margins of the columns were most prevalently cited, those listed following indentations (and in italics) were as well cited. Since apparently no designation is applicable in common usage to these ranking knowers only, the Editors have designated them "general authorities", having in mind this titling would of itself connote not only pre-eminence, but that those consulting this work are to take for granted that "general authorities" are, naturally, conversant with the subjects, within the field(s) of each, which have been arbitrarily selected for inclusion in the Locator Index and "keyed" by it to the listings—as authorities, as experts or as specially informed individuals—on pages 11 to 803 of those reporting specialized conversance with one or more of these subjects. There are of course instances of "general authorities" being "keyed" to those subjects (and/or included among those listings) if special factors coming to the compilers' attention were considered to make so doing appropriate.

On Page 851

SOURCES FOR AUTHORITATIVE INFORMATION: Selections from the numerous information sources which came to the attention of its Editors during the compilation of this work. They are "keyed" to subjects selected by the Editors for inclusion in the Locator Index, exactly as are the listings of individuals.

On Page 871

THE "KEYING" LOCATOR INDEX: By means of a novel keying system, it links 12,000 knowers to 35,000 subjects. Its scope, and effective usage of it as a most unusual reference tool, are both taken up on page 870.

What This Unique Reference Tool IS and IS NOT

WHO KNOWS—AND WHAT (1) lists alphabetically an arbitrary selection from among those who have indicated conversance with a subject(s) considered by its Editors to be more or less exposed to general enquiry, and therefore set up by them in its Locator Index; (2) links those so listed (by means of two-number "keys") to selected subjects in the Locator Index in respect to which conversance is considered to be indicated; (3) segregates (based on national surveys) those its Editors judge to be widely recognized as general authorities in respect to several broad fields of knowledge (as a convenient means of indicating that conversance by a general authority with any subject within his field that has been set up in the Locator Index is to be taken for granted); (4) has as its purpose serving the purposive, well-informed enquirer seriously interested in searching out knowers in respect to a subject set up in the Locator Index, and/or obtaining counsel in connection with it, by providing him with from-subject-to-**knower** reference (which may be far more useful to this type of enquirer than the usual from-subject-to-**writings** reference).

WHO KNOWS—AND WHAT does not (1) undertake to list ALL who know about a subject, either because of especial interest in that subject, or as the obvious result of being a general authority in respect to the broad field which includes that subject; **does not** (2) endeavor to list according to comparative coversance with a subject, but only to provide background data selected from information placed in its files; **does not** (3) profess to cover ALL subjects (quite to the contrary, it is restricted to a limited, arbitrary, selection of subjects assumed by its Editors to be more or less subject to general interest); **does not** (4) profess either to serve specialists interested in subjects the Editors do not consider exposed to general reference enquiry, and which accordingly do not appear in the Locator Index, or—at the other extreme—to assist casual lay enquirers seeking answers . . . these can be supplied from books to be found in most libraries . . . to sundry incidental questions about geography, local trivialities, grammar, etiquette, notable dates, or words (spelling, usage, pronunciation or definition); **does not** (5) print biographies-in-brief, as it is not a biographical dictionary; and **is not** (6) a census of technicians and others trained in the sciences or arts.

The ROSTER of SELECTED GENERAL AUTHORITIES

[See precis at the top of the opposite page, also the Preface (page 5).]

APPLIED ARTS AND SCIENCES

Agriculture (including Agronomy)

AAMODT, Olaf Sverre
ACKERMANN, Joseph
AHALT, Arthur M(ontraville)
AHLGREN, Gilbert Harold
ALBRECHT, William Albert
ANDRE, Floyd
ANTHONY, Ernest Lee
APP, Frank
BARSS, HOWARD PHILLIPS
BAVER, Leonard D.
BEAR, FIRMAN EDWARD
BEESON, KENNETH CREES
BENEDICT, MURRAY REED
BENNETT, HUGH HAMMOND
BERGMAN, HENRY DALE
BLACK, John Donald
BLASINGAME, R. U.
BLISS, RALPH KENNETH
BOND, Maurice Chester
BOSS, WILLIAM
BOVETH, FLORENCE BIGGAR
BRACKEN, AARON FRANCIS
BRADFIELD, RICHARD
BRADY, D(aniel) E(llsworth)
BRIGGS, H(ilton) M(arshall)
BRINK, R(oyal) Alexander
BROOKS, DAVID WILLIAM
BUCHANAN, M(arion) L(ynn)
BURDICK, Raymond T(erry)
BURLISON, William L.
CAMMACK, ROBERT EMMETT
CARD, LESLIE ELLSWORTH
CARDON, PHILIP VINCENT
CARROLL, William Ernest
CARVER, JOHN Stuart
CHAMBLISS, CHARLES E.
CHAPMAN, PAUL WILBER
CHESTER, K(enneth) Starr
CLAPP, ALFRED LESTER
CLAWSON, MARION
COLLINGS, Gilbeart Hooper
COLWELL, William Earle
COOPER, THOMAS POE
CORBETT, ROGER BAILEY
CREEL, CECIL WILLIS
CUMMINGS, Ralph W(aldo)
DAVIDSON, J. BROWNLEE
DAVIS, HERBERT PERRY
DAVIS, John Herbert
DEAN, VERA MICHELES
DIMOCK, WILLIAM WALLACE
DODD, NORRIS E.
DRIFTMIER, Rudolph Henry
DULEY, Frank Leslie
DUNNER, JOSEPH
DYKES, Jefferson Chenowth
EBERLE, ALFRED M.
EFFERSON, John Norman
EISENHOWER, Milton Stover
ELLIOTT, FOSTER FLOYD
ELLSWORTH, ROBERT ALDEN
ELY, FORDYCE
ENGLER, Kyle
ENSMINGER, Marion Eugene
EYSTER, William Henry
FARRELL, Francis David
FENSKE, Theodore H(erman)
FENTON, FREDERICK CHARLES
FERRIN, EVAN F(ISHER)
FETROW, Ward Willard
FISHER, John Wesley
FOLSOM, Donald
FOSTER, John Erwin
FOUTS, Everett L.
FRACKER, Stanley Black
FRED, Edwin Broun
GAGE, Charles Ellsworth
GARBER, Ralph John
GEISE, Henry
GIFFORD, Warren
GRABER, LAURENCE F.
GREGORY, RAYMOND W.

GREIBER, CLARENCE LEONARD
GRINNELL, Harold C.
GUTERMAN, CARL EDWARD F.
HAGAN, WILLIAM ARTHUR
HAMILTON, Tom Sherman
HANNAH, JOHN ALFRED
HARDIN, Clifford M(orris)
HART, GEORGE H(ART)
HAYES, HERBERT KENDALL
HEIZER, Edwin Elbert
HILL, Forrest Frank
HOGAN, Albert Garland
HORN, Claud L.
HUGHES, HAROLD DeMOTT
HULTZ, FRED SAMUEL
HUME, H. HAROLD
HUTCHISON, CLAUDE B.
HUTT, Frederick Bruce
JACKSON, HOWARD C., Sr.
JARDINE, WILLIAM M.
JOFFE, J(acob) S(amuel)
JOHNSON, IVER JOHANNES
JULL, MORLEY ALLAN
KEIM, Franklin David
KELLOGG, CHARLES EDWIN
KILDEE, Henry Herbert
KOLLER, E. Fred
LAMBERT, W(ILLIAM) V.
LOEFFEL, WILLIAM JOHN
LOOMIS, Walter Earl
LOWDERMILK, Walter Clay
MADSEN, LOUIS L(INDEN)
MAGISTAD, Oscar Conrad
MANN, H(arvey) B(lount)
MARSH, GEO(RGE) HENRY
McCALL, Max Adams
McKENZIE, Frederick Francis
McKINNEY, MADGE M.
McLEOD, JOHN HAYNE
McMILLEN, Wheeler
McPHEE, JULIAN A.
MERCHANT, Charles H(enry)
MILLER, John Ivan
MITCHELL, ALBERT KNELL
MITCHELL, Harold Hanson
MOBLEY, MAYOR DENNIS
MORRISON, FRANK BARRON
MYERS, Harold Edwin
MYERS, William Irving
NELSON, John A(lbert)
NELSON, Ronald Harvey
NEWSOM, HERSCHEL D.
NEWTON, ROBERT
NICHOLS, MARK LOVEL
PATTON, JAMES GEORGE
PENDLETON, ROBERT L.
PETERSON, John Booth
POE, CLARENCE (HAMILTON)
POOLE, ROBERT FRANKLIN
RANDELL, Cortes G(ilbert)
REED, OLLIE EZEKIEL
REITZ, J(ulius) Wayne
RICE, Victor Arthur
RICHEY, FREDERICK DAVID
ROMAINE, Jesse D(avis)
RUEHE, Harrison August
SALTER, Robert Mundhenk
SANDERS, Dorsey Addren, Sr.
SCARSETH, GEORGE DEWEY
SCHOENFELD, WILLIAM A.
SCHULTZ, THEODORE W.
SHARP, Marlay Albert
SHAW, B(yron) T(homas)
SHIELDS, Robert Hazen
SHUMAN, CHARLES B.
SILL, WEBSTER HARRISON
SIMMONS, Charles Ferdinant
SIMMS, BENNETT THOMAS
SMITH, HOWARD REMUS
SMITH, Livingston
SMITH, RUBY G. (MRS. A. W.)
SPANTON, WILLIAM T.
STEWART, M. A.
STINE, OSCAR CLEMEN
SWANEBECK, Clarence W.
TERMOHLEN, WILLIAM DEWEY
THORNE, D(avid) Wynne
THROCKMORTON, Ray Iams

TOLLEY, HOWARD ROSS
TRACY, PAUL HUBERT
TROTTER, Ide Peebles
TRULLINGER, R(OBERT) W.
TRUOG, EMIL
VANDECAVEYE, SILVERE C.
WAHLEN, FRIEDRICH T.
WAITE, WARREN C.
WARD, William Binnington
WAUGH, FREDERICK VAIL
WAYMACK, WILLIAM WESLEY
WEAVER, EARL
WEBER, ARTHUR D.
WEBER, George F(rederick)
WEEKS, Martin Edward
WHEELER, WILLIAM ARCHIE
WHITE, John William
WILSON, HAROLD KIRBY
WILSON, MILBURN LINCOLN
WINTERS, Rhett Youmans
YOUNG, Harold Newell
YOUNG, Wilfred B.

Architecture—See Fine Arts

Engineering (including Automotive, Aeronautical, Chemical, Civil, Electrical, Mechanical, Mining and Metallurgical Engineering)

ABBOTT, Ira Herbert
ABBOTT, William Lamont
ABRAMS, Talbert
ACKERSON, C(lifton) W(alter)
ADAMI, Arthur Ernest
ADAMS, COMFORT AVERY
ADAMS, Kenneth Tress
ADAMS, Norman Ilsley, Jr.
ADAMS, Otto Vincent
ADDICKS, Lawrence
AGNEW, P(aul) G(ough)
ALBERT, Calvin Dodge
ALDEN, HERBERT WATSON
ALDRIDGE, WALTER HULL
ALDRIN, EDWIN EUGENE
ALEXANDERSON, Ernst F. W.
ALFORD, NEWELL GILDER
ALLEN, Chester (Lawrence)
AMIRIKIAN, Arsham
AMMANN, OTHMAR H.
AMY, ERNEST V(ALENTINE)
ANDERSEN, Paul
ANDREW, CHARLES E.
ANDREWS, Andrew Irving
ANDREWS, WILLIAM EARLE
ANGAS, W(illiam) Mack
ARENTS, Chester A(bbo)
ARIES, Robert S(ancier)
ARMACOST, WILBUR H.
ARMSTRONG, EDWIN H.
ARMSTRONG, George S.
ARNOLD, Ralph
ARNSTEIN, KARL
ASHLEY, Carlyle Martin
ATKINSON, RALPH WALDO
ATTWOOD, Stephen S(tanley)
ATWOOD, JOHN LELAND
AULT, E(UGENE) STANLEY
AUSTIN, Clem C.
AUSTIN, James B.
AYRES, Quincy Claude
BACHARACH, Eric William
BACK, George Irving
BADGER, Walter Lucius
BAIER, Louis Arthur
BAILEY, Alexander Davison
BAILEY, ERVIN GEORGE
BAILEY, NEIL PHILLIPS
BAILEY, Raymond
BAIN, Edgar Collins
BAITY, Herman Glenn
BAKENHUS, Reuben Edwin
BAKER, WALTER RANSOM G.

BAKHMETEFF, BORIS A.
BALDOCK, ROBERT HUGH
BANCROFT, HOWLAND
BARCLAY, Robert Hamilton
BARKER, Harry
BARKER, JOSEPH WARREN
BARKER, Maurice E(ugene)
BARNARD, Daniel Paddock IV
BARNES, Gladeon Marcus
BARNES, HOWEL HENRY, Jr.
BARRE, Henry John
BARTHEL, Oliver Edward
BASORE, Cleburne Ammen
BASS, LAWRENCE WADE
BASSETT, PRESTON ROGERS
BATCHELLER, Willis Tryon
BATSON, Avery Aloysius
BAUER, William Malcolm
BAUMEISTER, Theodore
BAYLIS, John Robert
BEALL, WELLWOOD E.
BEAM, Robert Edwin
BECKER, JOSEPH
BEDFORD, CLAY (PATRICK)
BEISEL, REX BUREN
BELCHER, DONALD JENKS
BELLANCA, Frank Merlo
BERESFORD, Hobart
BERRY, Charles Harold
BIERER, John M(ichael)
BILLINGS, J(OHN) HARLAND
BILLINGSLEY, Paul
BILLNER, KARL PAUL
BINGER, Walter D(avid)
BISSET, Andrew G(ustave)
BJORGE, GUY NORMAN
BLACKALL, FREDERICK S., Jr.
BLACKWELL, OTTO T.
BLANKS, Robert Franklin
BLEE, Clarence Earl
BLEE, Harry Harmon
BLOSSOM, FRANCIS
BOARTS, Robert Marsh
BOCK, CARL A(UGUST)
BOEHNE, Eugene Wheelock
BOELTER, Llewellyn M. K.
BOLTON, ELMER KEISER
BONILLA, Charles Francis
BOOKER, HENRY GEORGE
BORDEN, William A.
BOSTON, Orlan William
BOWDEN, Nicholls White
BOWEN, Harold Gardiner
BOWLES, EDWARD LINDLEY
BOWMAN, HARRY LAKE
BOYD, T(homas) A(lvin)
BOYD, WILLIAM RUFUS, Jr.
BOYD, William Sprott
BOYER, MARION WILLARD
BOZELL, Harold Veatch
BRAGDON, John Stewart
BRAINERD, Arthur Alanson
BRANCH, RUSSELL T.
BRAND, CHARLES L.
BRANDT, Allen D(emmy)
BRASSERT, HERMAN A.
BREER, CARL
BRENTNALL, Samuel Robert
BRES, Edward Sedley
BRICK, Robert Maynard
BRIDGMAN, MARGARET
BRILL, Harvey Clayton
BROOKS, Donald B.
BROOKS, Henry Warren
BROWN, AUBREY INGERSON
BROWN, George Granger
BROWN, J. CALVIN
BROWN, Willard Cowles
BRUSH, WILLIAM WHITLOCK
BRYANT, George R(ock)
BUCKLEY, OLIVER ELLSWORTH
BUCKY, Philip Barnett
BUDD, RALPH
BUNDY, Edwin S.
BUNNELL, Sterling Haight
BURDICK, C(HARLES) LALOR
BURGESS, George Heckman
BURPEE, George William

BURR, Alex(ander) C.
BURRELL, GEORGE ARTHUR
BURROWS, Charles R(ussell)
BURT, William I(rving)
BUSH, VANNEVAR
BUTLER, G(URDON) M.
BUTTS, Allison
CALABRESE, Giuseppe
CALDWELL, Samuel Hawks
CAMERON, Charles F(ranklin)
CAMP, Thomas R.
CAMPBELL, Kenneth
CAMPBELL, Thomas Donald
CARPENTER, Arthur Howe
CARPENTER, ARTHUR W.
CARRUTHERS, John L(itster)
CARVIN, FRANK DANA
CASAGRANDE, ARTHUR
CASEY, Hugh John
CASTLE, Samuel Northrop
CASTLEMAN, Francis Lee, Jr.
CATES, LOUIS SHATTUCK
CEAGLSKE, Norman Hugo
CHAMBERS, CARL C(OVALT)
CHAMBERS, William Royal
CHANCE, EDWIN MICKLEY
CHANEY, Newcomb Kinney
CHANDLER, Elbert Milam
CHANDLER, HENRY THOMAS
CHEDSEY, William Reuel
CHILTON, THOMAS HAMILTON
CHIPMAN, JOHN
CHRISTENSEN, NEPHI ALBERT
CHRISTIE, ALEXANDER G.
CHRISTMAS, John Kay
CLARKE, Charles W. E.
CLAUSER, FRANCIS H.
CLAUSER, MILTON U.
CLAYBOURN, John Geronold
CLUETT, Sanford Lockwood
COCHRANE, EDWARD LULL
CODRINGTON, GEORGE W.
COGGESHALL, Ivan Stoddard
COHEN, MORRIS
COLBURN, ALLAN PHILIP
COLDWELL, EVERETT S.
COLE, EDWARD SMITH
COLEMAN, George Hopkins
COLEMAN, Harry Shipp
COLLBOHM, Franklin Rudolf
COLLINS, Samuel Cornette
COLTON, ROGER B.
COLVIN, CHARLES HERBERT
COLWELL, ARCHIE TRESCOTT
CONCANNON, Charles C.
CONDIT, Kenneth Hamilton
CONDRON, Theodore Lincoln
CONE, Russel G.
CONRAD, Albert Godfrey
CONRAD, Frank H(eussy)
CONTA, Lewis Dalcin
CONWAY, Harry Donald
COOK, Melvin Alonzo
COOKE, Morris Llewellyn
COOLIDGE, William David
COONLEY, Lewis Selkirk
COONS, Kenneth William
CORCORAN, George Francis
COTTRELL, Frederick Gardner
COVELL, William Edward R.
CRAFT, BENJAMIN C.
CRANE, Jacob Leslie
CRAVEN, TUNIS AUGUSTUS M.
CRAWFORD, Chauncey H.
CRAWFORD, IVAN CHARLES
CRAWFORD, Thomas Stephen
CREAMER, Walter J(oseph)
CREEDY, FREDERICK
CRESKOFF, JACOB JOSHUA
CROOK, Welton Joseph
CROSS, HARDY
CROWLEY, John W(illiam), Jr.
CRUSE, Andrew William
CUNNINGHAM, JAMES D.
CUNNINGHAM, John Bissell
CURTIS, CHARLES GORDON
CURTIS, FRANCIS JOSEPH
CURTIS, HARRY ALFRED

For selected subjects "keyed" to knowers, see Locator Index (page 871).

CURTISS, Charles Dwight
CUTLER, THOMAS HENRY
DAHL, Otto Gustav C.
DANA, Homer Jackson
DAVELER, ERLE VICTOR
DAVIDSON, J. BROWNLEE
DAVIDSON, Kenneth S. M.
DAVIDSON, WARD FOLLETT
DAVIES, CLARENCE EBENEZER
DAVIS, Alton Frank
DAVIS, ERNEST W.
DAVIS, GEORGE H.
DAVIS, Harry Willard
DAVIS, HARVEY NATHANIEL
DAVIS, RAYMOND EARL
DAWES, CHESTER LAURENS
DAWSON, Eugene Field
DAWSON, FRANCIS MURRAY
DEAN, Reginald Scott
DeBAUFRE, William Lane
de FLOREZ, LUIS
de FOREST, LEE
DeLEUW, Charles Edmund
DELLINGER, JOHN HOWARD
DEL MAR, William Arthur
DeLORAINE, EDMOND M.
de LUCCIA, EMIL ROBERT
DEMING, Horace Grove
DEMOREST, DANA JAMES
DEN HARTOG, J(acob) P.
DENT, Frederick Rodgers, Jr.
de SEVERSKY, ALEXANDER P.
DEVERS, Jacob Loucks
DEVINE, John M.
DeWITT, Clyde Colvin
DEXTER, ROBERT R(EGINALD)
DIBBLE, BARRY
DIENNER, John Astor
DIETZ, Albert George Henry
DIXON, Tod Galloway
DOAN, GILBERT EVERETT
DODD, CHARLES MITCHENER
DODGE, BARNETT FRED
DOHERTY, ROBERT ERNEST
DOHRENWEND, Clayton O.
DOLBEAR, Samuel Hood
DOOLITTLE, JAMES H(AROLD)
DORR, JOHN VAN NOSTRAND
DOTTERWEICH, Frank H(enry)
DOW, ALEXANDER
DOW, Peter Staub
DOW, William Gould
DOWDELL, Ralph Lewis
DOWNS, CHARLES RAYMOND
DRAPER, Charles Stark
DREW, THOMAS BRADFORD
DRYDEN, Hugh Latimer
DUBILIER, William
DUKES, HENRY HUGH
DUMONT, ALLEN BALCOM
DUNN, Clark A(llan)
DUNN, GANO
DUNN, Louis G(erhardus)
DURAND, WILLIAM FREDERICK
DUVALL, W. CLINTON
EARLE, Samuel Broadus
EASTON, Elmer Charles
EASTON, Stanly Alexander
EAVENSON, HOWARD N.
EDGERTON, HAROLD EUGENE
EKSERGIAN, RUPEN
ELGIN, JOSEPH CLIFTON
ELLSBERG, EDWARD
EMMERICH, FRED J.
EMMONS, HOWARD WILSON
ENEY, William J(oseph)
ENGSTROM, Elmer William
ENSLOW, LINN HARRISON
ERDMAN, Frederick Seward
ESHBACH, Ovid Wallace
EVANS, Llewellyn
EVERITT, WILLIAM LITTELL
EWING, Dressel Dewitt
FAHRENWALD, Arthur W.
FAIR, Gordon Maskew
FAIRBANKS, Andrew Jason
FAIRCHILD, Iler James
FAIRCHILD, SHERMAN M.
FAIRMAN, JAMES FERDINAND
FAIRMAN, Seibert
FAITH, William Lawrence
FARMER, F. MALCOLM
FARNSWORTH, PHILO TAYLOR
FARRELL, Thomas Francis
FEIKER, FREDERICK MORRIS
FELLERS, Carl Raymond
FERGUSON, HOMER LENOIR
FIELD, CROSBY
FIELDNER, Arno Carl

FINCH, James Kip
FINCH, William George H.
FINLAY, Walter S., Jr.
FINLEY, States Rights Gist
FLANDERS, RALPH EDWARD
FLEISHER, WALTER LOUIS
FLETCHER, ANDREW
FLOE, Carl Frederick
FLOYD, JAMES C.
FOLEY, Francis B.
FOOSE, RICHARD MARTIN
FOOTE, Frank G.
FOUST, Alan Shivers
FOX, Edwin Gordon
FRANKLAND, FREDERICK H.
FRARY, Francis Cowles
FREUDENTHAL, Alfred M.
FULLER, Leonard Franklin
FUNK, NEVIN E.
FURNAS, Clifford Cook
GAGE, Victor Raymond
GARAND, JOHN C.
GATES, ROBERT McFARLAND
GAUDIN, Antoine Marc
GAUGER, Alfred William
GEYER, JOHN CHARLES
GIBBS, R. E.
GIBBS, WILLIAM FRANCIS
GIFFORD, Robert Ladd
GILKEY, Herbert James
GILL, James Presley
GILLAN, Silas Lee
GLASSETT, Alfred Thomas
GLENNAN, T(HOMAS) KEITH
GLEESON, George Walter
GOETZENBERGER, Ralph L.
GOFF, JOHN ALONZO
GOLDMARK, PETER CARL
GOLDSMITH, ALFRED N.
GOLDTHWAITE, George E.
GOOCH, Wilby T.
GOODIER, James Norman
GOODRICH, ERNEST PAYSON
GOTAAS, Harold Benedict
GRAFE, PAUL
GRANGER, Armour T.
GRAY, Bernard Elbert
GREAVES-WALKER, Arthur F.
GREELEY, Samuel Arnold
GREENE, Arthur Maurice, Jr.
GREENFIELD, R(obert) Edman
GREGG, James L(awrence)
GRINTER, Linton E.
GROSS, Charles Philip
GRUMMAN, LEROY RANDLE
GUNNESS, Robert Charles
GUY, Raymond Frederick
HADLEY, Egbert Charles
HAEBERLE, FREDERICK E.
HAGUE, Wesley McLaren
HALL, Newman A(rnold)
HALLDEN, Karl William
HAMBURGER, Ferdinand, Jr.
HAMMOND, HARRY PARKER
HAMMOND, John Hays, Jr.
HANCOCK, HARRY D(AVID)
HANLEY, William Andrew
HANSEN, Howard J(ames)
HAPPEL, John
HARDESTY, SHORTRIDGE
HARE, Van Court M., Jr.
HARPER, Sinclair Ollason
HARRINGTON, Russell Paul
HARRISON, Lloyd
HARRISON, Ward
HARRISON, WILLIAM HENRY
HARTER, Isaac
HARWOOD, Paisley Beach
HARZA, LEROY FRANCIS
HASLAM, Robert Thomas
HATCH, Theodore Frederick
HATHAWAY, Gail Abner
HAWKINS, George Andrew
HAWKINS, Laurence Ashley
HAWLEY, Jean H.
HAWXHURST, Robert, Jr.
HAYDEN, Arthur Gunderson
HAZEN, Harold Locke
HEALD, HENRY TOWNLEY
HEALY, Roy
HEDRICK, J(ay) Eldred
HEILMAN, Russell Howard
HEISE, George W(illiam)
HEISING, Raymond A.
HELLSTROM, Carl Reinhold
HEMPLE, Henry William
HENDERSON, Everette L(ee)
HENDERSON, John Mellish
HENNINGER, G(eorge) Ross

HEPLER, John M(errill)
HERBERT, Frederick Davis
HERON, S. D.
HERRICK, George Q.
HERRINGTON, ARTHUR W. S.
HERTY, Charles Holmes, Jr.
HESS, WENDELL FREDERICK
Hibben, Samuel Galloway
HILL, Lee H.
HILL, Reuben L(orenzo)
HILTABIDLE, William O., Jr.
HINDS, Julian
HIRSCH, Gustav
HIXSON, Arthur Warren
HOAD, William Christian
HOBBS, Marvin
HOBSON, Jesse Edward
HOFFMAN, James I.
HOGAN, John Vincent L.
HOLBROOK, ELMER ALLEN
HOLLAND, Laurier F.-S.
HOLLINGSWORTH, Dwight F.
HOLLIS, Mark D.
HOLLISTER, Solomon Cady
HOLME, Thomas Timings
HOOVER, Herbert, Jr.
HOOVER, Kenneth H.
HORNE, Ralph Warren
HORNER, WESLEY WINONS
HOSKINS, John K.
HOTTEL, HOYT CLARKE
HOUGEN, O(LAF) A(NDREAS)
HOUSLEY, John Elmer
HOWARD, Frank Atherton
HOWARD, Louis Bradley
HOWSON, LOUIS RICHARD
HOYT, SAMUEL L(ESLIE)
HRONES, John Anthony
HUBER, WALTER LEROY
HUFF, Wilbert James
HULL, Lewis Madison
HUNSAKER, JEROME CLARKE
HUNTINGTON, Whitney C.
HYDE, CHARLES GILMAN
HYLAND, Lawrence A(vison)
HYNDMAN, Donald E.
INGLES, Harry Clyde
IRLAND, George Allison
ISERN, ELMER HENRY
JACKSON, Dugald Caleb, Jr.
JACKSON, McSTAY
JACOBS, Nathan Bernd
JACOBUS, David Schenck
James, Edwin Warley
JAMES, William Stubbs
JEFFRIES, Zay
JELLEY, Joseph Franklin
JENKINS, Herbert Theodore
JENKINS, WILLIAM J.
JENSEN, Cyril D(ewey)
JENSEN, John Christian
JEWETT, FRANK BALDWIN
JOHNSON, Jesse Charles
JOHNSON, John Bernard
JOHNSON, John Monroe
JOHNSON, MELVIN M., Jr.
JOHNSON, Walter Curtis
JOHNSTON,Bruce (Gilbert)
JOHNSTON, Leonard E.
JOHNSTONE, HENRY FRASER
JOLLIFFE, Charles Byron
JONES, WEBSTER NEWTON
JORALEMON, IRA BEAMAN
JOYCE, J(ames) Wallace
KAMMERMEYER, Karl
KASSNER, James (Lyle)
KATZ, Donald LaVerne
KEHOE, Arthur Henry
KELLER, Edward Luther
KELLERMAN, Karl F(rederic)
KELLOGG, Frederic Hartwell
KELLY, MERVIN J.
KEMP, Harold Augustus
KENNEDY, G(eorge) Donald
KENNISON, Karl R.
KETTERING, CHARLES F.
KEYES, Donald Babcock
KING, Charles Glenn
KING, John A(ubrey)
KINZEL, AUGUSTUS B(RAUN)
KIRKBRIDE, Chalmer Gatlin
KIRKPATRICK, Sidney Dale
KISSAM, Philip
KISSOCK, Alan
KISTIAKOWSKY, George B.
KLEIN, Grover Cleveland
KNAPP, Robert Talbot
KNOWLES, HARVEY COLES
KNOWLES, HUGH SHALER

KOFFOLT, Joseph Howard
KOMMERS, Jesse Benjamin
KOUWENHOVEN, William B.
KRANER, HOBART McKINLEY
KRAUS, Edward Henry
KRAUT, Ralph John
KREJCI, Milo William
KREUSSER, Otto Theo.
KRUM, HOWARD LEWIS
KRUMB, Henry
KUETHE, Arnold M(artin)
KURTZ, Ford
LACEY, William Noble
LACK, FREDERICK R.
LaCROSSE, EMMART
LaDUE, WENDELL RICHARD
LAIST, FREDERICK
LANSING, R(AYMOND) P.
LARGE, George Elwyn
LARSEN, PAUL J.
LAUER, Byron Elmer
LAWALL, Charles Elmer
LEAR, WILLIAM POWELL
LEAVEY, Edmond Harrison
LeBARON, Robert
LeCLAIR, TITUS G.
LeCORBEILLER, PHILIPPE
LEE, EVERETT S.
LEEDS, Charles Tileston
LEGGETT, Wilson Durward, Jr.
LEMMON, Walter S.
LEOPOLD, Charles S.
LESSELLS, JOHN MOYES
LEWIS, Harold M(acLean)
LI, Kuo-Ching
LICHTY, L(ester) (Clyde)
LIGHTON, Lester E(ugene)
LINDVALL, Frederic Charles
LITTLETON, Leonidas Rosser
LITTLEWOOD, WILLIAM
LOEFLER, Henry Stanley
LEONING, GROVER
LOCKHEED, ALLAN HAINES
LOHMANN, Melvin Rudolph
LOHR, Lenox Riley
LORANCE, George Toel
LORD, ROYAL BERTRAM
LOTZ, JOHN R.
LOVETT, Israel Herrick
LOWRY, H(omer) H(iram)
LUCKIESH, Matthew
LUECK, Roger Hawks
LUND, Clarence Edward
LUTZ, Samuel Gross
MacCONOCHIE, Arthur F.
MacCULLOUGH, Gleason H.
MacCUTCHEON, Aleck M.
MacGREGOR, Charles W.
MACKENZIE, C(halmers) J.
MACKEY, Charles Osborn
MacMULLIN, Robert Burns
MADIGAN, Michael J.
MAGDSICK, Henry Herbert
MALONEY, James O'Hara
MALTI, MICHEL GEORGE
MANN, Clair Victor
MANNING, GEORGE CHARLES
MANTELL, CHARLES L.
MARKHAM, JOHN RAYMOND
MARSTON, George Andrews
MARTIN, GLENN L.
MASON, HAROLD LAWRENCE
MASSIE, E(DMOND) S(IMS), Jr.
MATHEWSON, CHAMPION H.
MAVIS, Frederic Theodore
MAYNARD, HAROLD BRIGHT
MAYROSE, Herman Everett
McADAMS, WILLIAM (HENRY)
McDANIEL, Allen Boyer
McEACHRON, Karl Boyer
McELROY, Dennis Lee
McILROY,Malcolm Strong
McKEE, Logan
McLAUGHLIN, DONALD H.
McMILLAN, Fred Orville
McNAUGHTON, ANDREW G. L.
McWHORTER, ROGER BARTON
MEHL, ROBERT F(RANKLIN)
MELVIN, John Harper
MERCK, GEORGE WILHELM
MERICA, PAUL DYER
MERZ, A. Russell
MESERVE, W(ilbur) Ernest
MIDDLETON, Cornelius W.
MIESSNER, Benjamin Franklin
MILLER, Arthur M.
MILLIKAN, CLARK B.
MILLSPAUGH, WILLIAM H.
MINARIK, R(udolph) G(lenn)

MINDLIN, RAYMOND D.
MITCHELL, DAVID RAY
MOCKMORE, Charles Arthur
MONROE, Robert A(nsley)
MONTEITH, A(LEXANDER) C.
MOODY, LEWIS FERRY
MOORE, Emmett Burris
MOREELL, BEN
MORGAN, Alfred Powell
MORGAN, ARTHUR ERNEST
MORRISON, ROGER LEROY
MORRISON, Willard Langdon
MORROW, James Bain
MORSE, Frederick Tracy
MORTENSEN, S. H.
MORTON, Avery Adrain
MOTTIER, CHARLES H.
MOYER, RALPH ALTON
MUDD, HARVEY SEELEY
MURPHREE, EGER V(AUGHAN)
NICHOLS, K(enneth) D(avid)
NILES, Alfred Salem
NORCROSS, Theodore White
NORTHROP, JOHN KNUDSEN
NOTMAN, ARTHUR
OBERFELL, GEORGE GROVER
O'BRIEN, EUGENE WILLIAM
O'BRIEN, MORROUGH PARKER
OLD, Archie J., Jr.
OLIPHANT, Abner Chambers
OLSON, O(liff) Neil
ORMONDROYD, JESSE
OROWAN, Egon
ORVILLE, Howard T(homas)
OSBORN, Robert Randolph
OSBORNE, Harold Smith
OSGOOD, William R.
OTHMER, DONALD FREDERICK
PAPPAS, COSTAS ERNEST
PARKER, JAMES W.
PARSONS, Arthur Barrette
PARSONS, Douglas Eugene
PARSONS, William Sterling
PAULSEN, CARL G.
PEARL, William A.
PEERY, David J.
PEIRCE, WILLIS McGERALD
PENDER, HAROLD
PENNIMAN, ABBOTT L., Jr.
PENNEY, GAYLORD W(ALLIS)
PETERSON, Ernest William
PETERSSON, Laurence Eugene
PETTYJOHN, Elmore S(haw)
PHELPS, ALVA W.
PICCARD, JEAN FELIX
PICK, Lewis Andrew
PIGFORD, Robert Lamar
PIGOTT, REGINALD JAMES S.
PIRNIE, MALCOLM
PLANK, William Bertolette
PLUMMER, Curtis Blood
POITRAS, Herman Arthur
POLLOCK, ROBERT THOMAS
POSEY, CHESLEY J., Jr.
POTTER, Andrey Abraham
POWEL, CHARLES ALFRED
POWELL, JOSEPH WRIGHT
POWER, HARRY HARRISON
POWERS, Justin Lawrence
PRENTICE, Donald Bishop
PRESTON, Howard K(ent)
PRICE, THOMAS MOORE
PROCTOR, CARLTON S.
PUTNAM, MARK EDSON
PUTT, DONALD L(EANDER)
PYKE, W(esley) E(merson)
QUARLES, DONALD A.
QUARLES, Lawrence Reginald
RALSTON, OLIVER CALDWELL
RAMAGE, William Haig
RAMBERG, Walter Gustave C.
RAMSER, Charles Ernest
RANDALL, ROBERT HENRY
RANNEY, LEO
RAUTENSTRAUCH, Walter
RAYMOND, ARTHUR EMMONS
READING, Oliver Scott
REDDING, James Deyo
REID, Elliott Gray
REID, Henry John Edward
REISTLE, Carl Ernest, Jr.
RETTALIATA, J(ohn) T.
REYBOLD, EUGENE
RHINES, Frederick Nims
RHODES, Fred H(offman)
RICH, George R.
RICHARDSON, LAWRENCE B.
RICHMOND, Harold Bours
RICKETTS, FORREST EUGENE

832

See pages 13 and 801 for additional knowers; page 851 for information sources.

RIDDELL, Guy Crosby
RITTMAN, Walter Frank
ROBERT, LAWRENCE W., Jr.
ROBERTS, JOSEPH K(ASTLE)
ROBERTS, Milnor
ROBINSON, DWIGHT PARKER
ROBINSON, JOSEPH V.
ROBINSON, SAMUEL MURRAY
ROBINSON, Russell Gideon
ROGERS, Harry Stanley
ROHRMAN, Frederick Alvin
ROOS, DELMAR GERLE
ROSEN, CARL GEORGE A.
ROSSMAN, Joseph
ROUSE, HUNTER
ROWE, HARTLEY
ROY, Robert Hall
RUDENBERG, RHEINHOLD
RUHL, Robert Calvin
RUSCH, Hugh Leonard
RUSHTON, JOHN HENRY
RUSSELL, RALSTON, Jr.
RYAN, William Francis
RYDER, John Douglas
SAGE, BRUCE HORNBROOK
SAIBEL, Edward Aaron
SALISBURY, Eugene Franklin
SALSICH, LeROY
SANDERS, W(illiam) Burton
SANTRY, JOSEPH VINCENT
SARBACHER, Robert I(rving)
SARNOFF, DAVID
SAVAGE, John Lucian
SAVAGE, Marion Alexander
SAVILLE, CALEB MILLS
SAVILLE, ROSCOE J(OSEPH)
SAVILLE, THORNDIKE
SCHADE, Henry Adrian
SCHAENZER, Joseph Peter
SCHEIDENHELM, Frederick W.
SCHIER, ARTHUR C.
SCHLECHTEN, Albert W(ilbur)
SCHNEE, Verne H(iggs)
SCHUETTE, Curt Nicolaus
SCHULTZ, SOL ELI
SCHWAIN, Frank Robert
SCHWARTZ, Frank Leroy
SCHWEITZER, Paul Henry
SEAGREN, George W(illiam)
SEATON, ROY ANDREW
SEEGER, EDWIN W(ILBUR)
SEELEY, WALTER JAMES
SEELY, Samuel
SERFASS, Earl James
SEWARD, HERBERT LEE
SHARP, GEORGE GILLLES
SHEEHAN, WILLIAM MARK
SHELDON, Harold Horton
SHERIDAN, Lawrence V.
SHERMAN, Vernon Wesley
SHERWOOD, THOMAS K.
SHREVE, R. NORRIS
SIBLEY, Robert
SIKORSKY, IVOR I.
SILLCOX, LEWIS KETCHAM
SILVER, ARTHUR E.
SINGSTAD, OLE
SINN, FRANCIS PEIRCE
SKINNER, CHARLES EDWARD
SLEPIAN, JOSEPH
SMITH, Allen S(tratton)
SMITH, CYRIL STANLEY
SMITH, H. DeWITT
SMITH, HENRY GERRISH
SMITH, Norman Murray
SMITH, Waldo E(dward)
SODERBERG, CARL RICHARD
SOLBERG, THORVALD ARTHUR
SORENSEN, CHARLES E.
SORENSEN, ROYAL WASSON
SOSMAN, ROBERT BROWNING
SPAGHT, MONROE EDWARD
SPARROW, STANWOOD W.
SPORN, PHILIP
SQUIRE, Edward Jacob
STACEY, ALFRED EDWIN, Jr.
STANLEY, William Edward
STECKEL, ABRAM PETERS
STEINMAN, DAVID BARNARD
STEVENS, JOHN CYPRIAN
STEVENSON, EARL P(LACE)
STEWART, Homer Joseph
STOLTE, Sidney Lloyd
STORER, Norman W.
STOUGHTON, BRADLEY
STOUT, Lawrence Edward
STOUT, Melville Bigham
STOUT, WILLIAM BUSHNELL
STRAUB, LORENZ GEORGE

STRAUMANIS, Martin Edward
STRONG, Everett Milton
STRONG, Frederick Smith, Jr.
STURM, Rolland George, Jr.
STUTZMAN, Leroy Franklin
STYRI, Haakon
SULLIVAN, John Daniel
SUMAN, JOHN ROBERT
SUMMERFIELD, MARTIN
SWANN, William Francis G.
SWEIGERT, Ray Leslie
SWENSON, George Warner
SYKES, WILFRED
TAYLOR, Charles Fayette
TAYLOR, Edward Story
TAYLOR, H(ARVEY) BIRCHARD
TEAGUE, Walter Dorwin
TEETOR, RALPH R.
TEICHMANN, FREDERICK K.
TEMPLIN, Richard Laurence
TERMAN, FREDERICK EMMONS
TERWILLIGER, Charles Van O.
TERZAGHI, KARL
THOMAS, CHARLES ALLEN
THOMPSON, Joseph Trueman
THOMPSON, Milton John
THOMPSON, Robert Alden
TICKELL, Frederick George
TIEDEMANN, Walter
TILLOTSON, Edwin Ward
TIMOSHENKO, STEPHEN
TODD, JAMES M.
TOMPKINS, CHARLES HOOK
TORCHIO, PHILIP
TORKELSON, Martin Wilhelm
TRICHEL, GERVAIS WILLIAM
TSCHEBOTARIOFF, Gregory P.
TURNER, Claude Allen Porter
TURNER, SCOTT
TURNER, William De Garmo
UICKER, John Joseph
UMPLEBY, JOSEPH B(ERTRAM)
UPHAM, Charles Melville
UPSON, RALPH HAZLETT
URDAHL, Thomas Harold
VAGTBORG, Harold
VAN HORN, Robert Bowman
VAN PETTEN, Oliver W(illiam)
VAN PRAGG, Alex, Jr.
VARIAN, RUSSELL H.
VEIHMEYER, Frank J.
VIDAL, Eugene Luther
VINCENT, Edward Thomas
VINCENT, JESSE GURNEY
VIVIAN, Robert Evans
VLIET, Elmer B(ennett)
VOGELBACK, WILLIAM E.
VOGELER, Robert Alexander
VON BRUAN, Wernher
VON KARMAN, THEODORE
VOSS, Walter Charles
WAGNER, CHARLES F.
WAGNER, Hermann A.
WALL, Florence E(meline)
WALKER, Harold Leroy
WALKER, Harry Bruce
WALTERS, Francis Marion, Jr.
WALTHER, Carl Hugo
WALTON, Fred Williams
WALTON, JESSE SEBURN
WARDLAW, FRANK A., Jr.
WARNER, EDWARD P.
WARNER, ROGER S., Jr.
WATERS, Aaron Clement
WATSON, CRESAP P.
WATSON, George Linton
WEBB, C(hauncey) Earl
WEBER, Eugene W(illiam)
WEED, CLYDE E.
WEIDLEIN, EDWARD RAY
WEISS, JOHN MORRIS
WELCH, Ernest Rivers
WELKER, George Ernest
WELLS, Edward Curtis
WESCOTT, THURMAN CARY
WESSMAN, Harold Everett
WHEELER, HAROLD ALDEN
WHEELER, Walter Hall
WHELEN, Townsend
WHISLER, BENJAMIN ADSIT
WHITAKER, Harry Emerson
WHITAKER, MILTON C.
WHITE, ALBERT EASTON
WHITE, Fred Ray
WHITEHEAD, EDWIN ROBERT
WHITEHEAD, JOHN BOSWELL
WHITMAN, EZRA BAILEY
WHITMAN, WALTER GORDON
WHITMORE, GREGORY DEWEY

WHITTAKER, GREGORY D.
WHITTAKER, HAROLD ARTHUR
WHITTEMORE, John Weed
WIESNER, Jerome B(ert)
WILLIAMS, CLYDE (ELMER)
WILLIAMS, Everad Mott
WILLIAMS, Sidney James
WILLIAMS, WALTER J.
WILLIAMS, William Horace
WILLIS, Charles Frances
WILLIS, Clodius Harris
WILMOT, Sydney
WILSON, Carroll Louis
WILSON, CHARLES ERWIN
WILSON, Curtis L(aws)
WILSON, PHILIP DANFORTH
WILSON, ROBERT ERASTUS
WILSON, ROSCOE CHARLES
WILSON, Walter King, Jr.
WINDING, Charles Calvert
WINNE, Harry Alonzo
WINTER, George
WINTER, Norman Leon
WISLICENUS, George F.
WOHLENBERG, WALTER J.
WOLF, Harry John
WOLMAN, Abel
WOOD, Charles P.
WOODS, Kenneth B(rady)
WOOLRICH, WILLIS R.
WOOLSON, HARRY THURBER
WORK, Lincoln T(homas)
WORTHINGTON, Hood
WRATHER, WILLIAM EMBRY
WRIGHT, MARSHALL
WRIGHT, THEODORE PAUL
WULFF, John
YAGLOU, Constantin P.
YARNALL, D. ROBERT
YELLOTT, JOHN INGLE
YOUNG, Donovan Harold
YOUNG, HOWARD ISAAC
YOUNG, Lewis E.
ZEDER, JAMES CHURCHILL
ZIMMERMANN, Stanley W.
ZMESKAL, Otto
ZUCROW, MAURICE J(OSEPH)
ZWORYKIN, VLADIMIR K.

Forestry

ALLEN, Shirley W(alter)
ALLISON, John H(oward)
BAKER, Willis Miles
BAGTER, Dow Vawter
BEEDE, VICTOR (AUGUSTUS)
BLACKWELL, Lloyd (Phalti)
BOYCE, John Shaw
BROWN, Arthur A.
BROWN, NELSON C.
BUTLER, OVID
CHAPMAN, HERMAN HAUPT
CLEPPER, HENRY EDWARD
COLLINGWOOD, G. H.
COMPTON, Wilson M.
CONNAUGHTON, Charles A.
DALKE, Paul D(avid)
DANA, Samuel Trask
DAYTON, William A(dams)
DUNN, Paul Millard
EVANS, CHARLES F(LOYD)
FORSLING, Clarence L(uther)
GARRATT, George Alfred
GELTZ, Charles G.
GILL, TOM (THOMAS HARVEY)
GRANGER, CHRISTOPHER M.
GRANT, Bishop F(ranklin)
GREELEY, WILLIAM B.
GRONDAL, BROR LEONARD
GUISE, Cedric Hay
HAWLEY, RALPH CHIPMAN
HERBERT, Paul Anthony
HOOD, George William
HOPKINS, HOWARD
HOSMER, Ralph Sheldon
HUTCHINS, Lee M(ilo)
ILLICK, Joseph S(imeon)
JACKSON, Lyle W(endall) R.
JEFFERS, DWIGHT SMITHSON
JOHNSTON, Don P.
KAUFERT, FRANK H.
KORSTIAN, Clarence F.
KOTOK, Edward I.
LARRIMER, Walter Harrison
LOVERIDGE, Earl W.
LUTZ, HAROLD JOHN
MARCKWORTH, GORDON D.
MARSH, RAYMOND E(UGENE)
MARTELL, Eldred Roland

McARDLE, RICHARD E(DWIN)
McCLURE, James Gore King
MEYER, Walter H(uber)
MORRELL, Fred
OTHMER, Donald Frederick
RECKNAGEL, Arthur Bernard
ROSECRANS, William Starke
SCHMITZ, HENRY
SHANKLIN, John F(erguson)
SPAETH, J(ohn) Nelson
STEFFEN, Edwin Herman
TRYON, Henry Harrington
WATTS, LYLE FORD
WESTVELD, R(utherford) H.
Wilber, Charles Parker

Horticulture

ANDERSON, W(illiam) S.
AVERY, GEORGE SHERMAN, Jr.
BAILEY, LIBERTY HYDE
BATCHELOR, Leon Dexter
BLACKMON, G(ulie) H.
BOSWELL, Victor R(ickman)
BRIERLEY, Wilfrid Gordon
CHANDLER, William Henry
CONNORS, C(harles) H(enry)
COOPER, John Ralph
DARROW, GEORGE McMILLAN
ELLIS, Nathan Kent
FARLEY, Arthur J(ames)
FRASER, Samuel
FREE, MONTAGUE
GAYLORD, Fay Claude
GREENE, Laurenz
HABER, ERNEST STRAIGN
HARTMAN, Henry
HEINICKE, Arthur John
HODGSON, ROBERT WILLARD
HOWLETT, Freeman S(mith)
HUME, H. HAROLD
KELSEY, Harlan Page
LAURIE, ALEXANDER
MacDANIELS, LAURENCE H.
McHATTON, THOMAS H.
MILLER, JULIAN CREIGHTON
MOORE, GEORGE THOMAS
MORRISON, B(ENJAMIN) Y.
MURNEEK, A(ndrew) E.
PICKETT, Barzillai Stewart
PICKETT, BETHEL STEWART
PICKETT, William Francis
POPENOE, (FREDERICK) W.
POST, Kenneth
RYERSON, KNOWLES A.
SCHERMERHORN, Lyman G.
STARK, PAUL CLARENCE
TALBERT, THOMAS JESSE
THOMPSON, HOMER C.
TIEDJENS, Victor Alphons
TUKEY, Harold Bradford
VERNER, LEIF
WARING, James Howard
WERNER, Harvey O(scar)
WHITTEMORE, Harlow Olin
WIGGANS, Cleo Claude
WOLFE, H(erbert) S(now)
YEAGER, Albert Franklin
ZIMMERMAN, Percy White

Jurisprudence

ALBRECHT, Ralph Gerhart
BIDDLE, Francis
BRADWAY, John Saeger
BRIGGS, Herbert Whittaker
BROWN, BRENDAN F.
BROWN, Robert Coleman
BUSCHMANN, Charles S.
CAHN, EDMUND N(ATHANIEL)
CARROLL, Mitchell Benedict
COFFMAN, L. Dale
COHEN, Felix S.
COLVIN, H(oward) Milton
CORWIN, Edward Samuel
COWAN, THOMAS ANTHONY
COWLES, Willard Bunce
CROWNOVER, Arthur, Jr.
DAVIDSON, C(row) Girard
DAVIS, JOHN WILLIAM
DEAN, Gordon Evans
DICKINSON, EDWIN DeWITT
DIENNER, John Astor
DOBIE, Armistead Mason
DOUGLAS, William Orville
EAGLETON, Clyde
EDER, Phanor James
ERNST, Morris Leopold
EUBANK, John Augustine
FINCH, George Augustus

FRANKFURTER, Felix
FULLER, LON LUVOIS
GOEBEL, JULIUS, Jr.
HALL, JEROME
HAND, LEARNED
HOLMAN, FRANK E.
HURST, (James) Willard
JACKSON, Robert H.
LANDIS, James McCauley
LARRABEE, Lawrence Lyle
LONG, Breckinridge
MAGUIRE, John MacArthur
MASON, Alpheus Thomas
MacFARLAND, Carl
MERRILL, Maurice Hitchcock
MEYER, Charles Harrison
MIRKINE- GUETZEVITCH, B.
MORELL, Wm. Nelson
PALMER, Thomas Waverly
PANTZER, Kurt Friedrich
PARKER, JOHN JOHNSTON
PEASLEE, Amos Jenkins
PEPPER, GEORGE WHARTON
PEYSER, Julius I.
PHARR, Clyde
PHILLIPS, ORIE LEON
PITTS, Thomas Jefferson
POUND, ROSCOE
PUTTKAMMER, Ernst Wilfred
RABEL, ERNST
ROTHCHILD, V. HENRY, II
SACK, Alexander Naoum
SANDERS, Paul H(ampton)
SAYRE, PAUL
SCHILLER, A. Arthur
SCHNADER, William A.
SCHWEID, Edward Jay
SCHWEPPE, Alfred John
SEAVEY, Warren Abner
SMALL, Charles Hughey
SOUTER, Clyde Douglas
STAHR, Elvis J(acob), Jr.
STEBBINS, Homer Adolph
STONE, Ferdinand Fairfax
SUMMERS, Lane
TAYLOR, Telford
TEN EYCK, Andrew
THOMPSON, George Jarvis
THORMODSGARD, Olaf H.
TOULMIN, Harry Aubrey, Jr.
TWEED, HARRISON
SCHILLER, A. ARTHUR
VANDERBILT, ARTHUR T.
VREELAND, Hamilton, Jr.
WEBB, William Herbert
WENCHEL, John Philip
WETTACH, Robert Hasley
WILLIAMS, Lewis Catlett
WOLFF, Hans Julius
WOOD, J(ohn) Perry
WOODCOCK, Amos W. W.
WOOLSEY, Lester Hood

Military and Naval Science

AKERS, Frank
ALLEN, LEVEN C.
ANDERSON, ORVIL A.
AURAND, HENRY S.
BALDWIN, HANSON W.
BARBEY, Daniel Edward
BARNES, EARL WALTER
BATES, Richard Waller
BISSELL, Clayton Lawrence
BLANDY, WILLIAM HENRY P.
BOLTE, CHARLES L,
BOONE, WALTER FREDERICK
BOOTH, DONALD PRENTICE
BRADLEY, OMAR NELSON
BRERETON, LEWIS HYDE
BRETT, George Howard
BROWN, Charles Randall
BROWN, John Herbert, Jr.
BULL, HAROLD ROE
BUNKER, HOWARD GRAHAM
CABELL, CHARLES PEARRE
CANNON, JOHN KENNETH
CASEY, Hugh John
CATES, CLIFTON BLEDSOE
CLARK, MARK WAYNE
CLAY, Lucius Du B.
COCHRANE, EDWARD LULL
COLBY, Elbridge
COLLINS, J(OSEPH) LAWTON
COMBS, Thomas Selby
CONOLLY, Richard L.
DAVIDSON, GARRISON H.
DAVIS, Arthur Cayley
DAVIS, George Arthur

833

DENFELD, LOUIS EMIL
DEVERS, JACOB LOUCKS
 DuVAL, Miles P., Jr.
EAKER, IRA C.
EDDY, MANTON S.
EICHELBERGER, ROBERT L.
EISENHOWER, DWIGHT D.
 ELLSBERG, Edward
EMBICK, STANLEY DUNBAR
EMMONS, DELOS CHARLETON
FARLEY, JOSEPH FRANCIS
FECHTELER, WILLIAM M.
 FIFE, James
FURER, JULIUS AUGUSTUS
 FURLONG, William Rea
 GANAHL, Richard Gregory
 GAVIN, James M.
GEROW, LEONARD TOWSEND
 GHORMLEY, Robert Lee
GLOVER, CATO DOUGLAS, Jr.
GOOD, ROSCOE FLETCHER
GRUENTHER, ALFRED M.
 HALL, John Lesslie, Jr.
HALSEY, WILLIAM FREDERICK
HANDY, THOMAS T.
HARPER, ROBERT WELLS
 HAYNES, Loyal Moyer
HEARD, Jack Whitehead
 HERREN, Thomas W.
HERSHEY, Lewis Blaine
HILL, Harry W.
HODGE, John R.
HODGES, COURTNEY H.
 HOSKINS, John M(adison)
HUNT, LeRoy Philip
HUSSEY, George F., Jr.
JACOBS, Randall
KING, ERNEST JOSEPH
 KINKAID, Thomas Cassin
KISSNER, AUGUST WALTER
 KITTS, Walter Augustus, 3rd
KRUEGER, WALTER
LARKIN, THOMAS B.
LEAHY, WILLIAM D.
LeMAY, CURTIS E.
 LEWIS, Millard
LIBBY, Ruthven E.
LINDSAY, Richard Clark
LOCKWOOD, CHARLES A., Jr.
LONNQUEST, Theodore C.
MacARTHUR, DOUGLAS
MADDOCKS, RAY TYSON
 MALONY, Harry James
 MARIS, Ward Hale
MARSHALL, GEORGE CATLETT
 MARSHALL, Richard Jaquelin
 MARSHALL, Samuel Lyman A.
 McLEAN, Ephraim Rankin, Jr.
 McMANES, Kenmore Mathew
MCNARNEY, JOSEPH T.
McNULTY, RICHARD ROBERT
 MeGEE, Vernon Edgar
MOEBUS, LUCIAN A(NCEL)
NIMITZ, CHESTER W.
NOBLE, ALFRED HOUSTON
NORSTAD, LAURIS
 OLECK, Howard L.
 PARKS, Floyd Lavinius
PARSONS, WILLIAM STERLING
 PARTRIDGE, Richard Clare
 PARTRIDGE, Roi
 PIERSON, Albert
 PYE, William Satterlee
RADFORD, ARTHUR WILLIAM
 RICE, John Kirkland
RICHARDSON, WILLIAM L.
RIDGWAY, MATTHEW B.
 RITCHIE, William Ludlow
 ROBBINS, THOMAS H., Jr.
 ROBERTS, Frank Needham
ROBINETT, Paul McD.
 ROBINSON, Ray Albert
ROCKEY, KELLER E.
 ROSE, William Clayton
 RUDDOCK, Theodore D., Jr.
SAMFORD, John A.
 SCHINDLER, Walter G(abriel)
SCHLEMMER, FRED(ERICK) C.
SENIOR, CLARENCE
 SHEETZ, Josef Robert
 SHEKERJIAN, Haig
SHEPHERD, LEMUEL C., Jr.
 SIBERT, Edwin Luther
SILVERTHORN, MERWIN H.
 SMITH, Allan Edward
SMITH, OLIVER PRINCE
SMITH, WALTER BEDELL
SPAATZ, CARL

SPRAUNCE, RAYMOND AMES
STRATEMEYER, GEORGE E.
STRONG, Frederick Smith, Jr.
STRUBLE, ARTHUR DEWEY
 TAYLOR, Maxwell Davenport
THIELE, Claude Martin
TREXAL, Carl A(lvin)
TRUDEAU, Arthur Gilbert
TURNER, RICHMOND KELLY
TWINING, NATHAN F.
 TWITTY, Joseph Jones
VANDEGRIFT, ALEXANDER A.
VANDENBERG, HOYT S.
Van FLEET, JAMES ALWARD
WATSON, THOMAS EUGENE
WEAVER, William Gaulbert
WECKERLING, John
WEDEMEYER, ALBERT COADY
WEIKERT, John Maurice
WEYLAND, Otto P.
WHITE, THOMAS DRESSER
 WILBUR, William Hale
WILSON, Walter King, Jr.
 WOODS, Louis Earnest
WOOLFLEY, Francis Augustus
WOOLSON, HARRY THURBER
WRIGHT, EDWIN K(ENNEDY)
WYMAN, Willard Gordon

Navigation

BRYAN, George Sloan
BYRD, Richard Evelyn
CLEMENCE, GERALD MAURICE
COLBERT, LEO OTIS
DELLINGER, JOHN HOWARD
 GANAHL, Richard Gregory
HERRICK, SAMUEL
LINK, EDWIN ALBERT
MERCHANT, WILLIAM J.
ROSENBERG, PAUL
RUSSELL, JOHN ALBERT
 SMITH, PAUL A(LBERT)
STUDDS, ROBERT F(RANCIS) A.
 WEBB, William Herbert

NATURAL
SCIENCES

Astronomy

ABBOT, CHARLES GREELEY
ADAMS, WALTER SYDNEY
AITKEN, ROBERT GRANT
 ALDEN, Harold Lee
ALDRICH, LOYAL BLAINE
ALTER, Dinsmore
BAADE, WALTER
BOBROVNIKOFF, Nicholas T.
BOK, BART JAN
BOWEN, IRA SPRAGUE
BROUWER, DIRK
CHANDRASEKHAR, S.
 CHERRINGTON, Ernest H., Jr.
 CLEMINSHAW, Clarence H.
 DUNCAN, John Charles
 ELVEY, Christian Thomas
 FATH, Edward Arthur
GAPOSCHKIN, Cecilia H. P.
 GOLDBERG, Leo
GREENSTEIN, Jesse Leonard
GUTHRIE, David Vance
HERGET, Paul
HUBBLE, EDWIN POWELL
JOY, ALFRED HARRISON
KRON, Gerald Edward
KUIPER, GERARD PETER
 LAPAZ, Lincoln
LEONARD, Frederick Charles
LEUSCHNER, ARMIN OTTO
 LEWIS, Isabel Eleanor Martin
MAYALL, NICHOLAS'ULRICH
McCUSKEY, Sidney Wilcox
McLAUGHLIN, Dean B.
McMATH, ROBERT R.
MENZEL, DONALD H(OWARD)
MERRILL, PAUL WILLARD
MITCHELL, SAMUEL ALFRED
 MORGAN, Herbert Rollo
 MORGAN, William W(ilson)
NICHOLSON, SETH BARNES
 PETTIT, Edison
RUSSELL, HENRY NORRIS
 SANFORD, Roscoe Frank
 SCHWARZCHILD, Martin
SEARES, FREDERICK HANLEY
SHAPLEY, HARLOW
SLIPHER, VESTO MELVIN
SMILEY, CHARLES HUGH
SPITZER, LYMAN, Jr.
STEBBINS, JOEL

STRAND, K(aj) A(age) G.
STROMGREN, BENGT G. D.
STRUVE, OTTO
TOMBAUGH, CLYDE WILLIAM
 TRUMPLER, Robert Julius
VAN BIESBROECK, GEORGE A.
WHIPPLE, FRED LAWRENCE
ZWICKY, FRITZ

Biology (including Botany, Zoology and Mammalogy)

ABBE, Ernst C(leveland)
ADAMS, AMY ELIZABETH
ADELMANN, Howard B.
AEBERSOLD, PAUL C(LARENCE)
ALLEE, WARDER CLYDE
ALLEN, ARTHUR AUGUSTUS
 ALLEN, R(ichard) S(weetnam)
ALLEN, William Ray
ANDERSON, EDGAR
ANDERSON, Hamilton H.
ANDERSON, JOHN F.
 ANDREW, Warren
ANDREWS, HENRY N., Jr.
ANDREWS, ROY CHAPMAN
ANIGSTEIN, LUDWIK
ANSON, BARRY JOSEPH
ANTHONY, HAROLD ELMER
APPLEMAN, CHARLES ORVILLE
AREY, LESLIE BRAINERD
ARMSTRONG, PHILIP B.
 ARNOLD, Chester A.
 ARNOLD, John G(eorge), Jr.
ARONSON, Lester Ralph
AUSEMUS, Elmer R(ex)
AVERY, GEORGE SHERMAN, Jr.
 BABCOCK, Ernest Brown
BACHMANN, Jean George
BAILEY, IRVING WIDMER
BAITSELL, George Alfred
BAKKE, Arthur Lawrence
BALDWIN, Ira Lawrence
BALDWIN, J(ohn) T., Jr.
BANGHAM, Ralph V.
 BARD, Philip
BARSS, Howard Phillips
BARTELMEZ, GEORGE W.
BARTLETT, HARLEY HARRIS
BARTSCH, PAUL
BAYNE-JONES, STANHOPE
BAZETT, HENRY CUTHBERT
BEACH, FRANK AMBROSE
BEEDLE, GEORGE WELLS
BEAL, JOHN M(ANN)
 BEAMS, Harold William
 BECKER, Elery Ronald
BEEBE, WILLIAM
BEECHER, HENRY KNOWLES
BENNETT, GEORGE ALLEN
 BENTLEY, Gordon Mansir
BERRY, GEO. PACKER
BEST, CHARLES HERBERT
 BETTEN, Cornelius
BIETER, RAYMOND N.
BIGELOW, HENRY BRYANT
 BIGELOW, Maurice Alpheus
BIRKHAUG, Konrad Elais
BISHOPP, Fred Corry
BITTNER, JOHN JOSEPH
 BLAIR, Henry Alexander
BLAKE, CHARLES HENRY
 BLAKE, Irving H(ill)
BLAKESLEE, ALBERT FRANCIS
BLINKS, LAWRENCE ROGERS
BODINE, JOSEPH HALL
BOELL, EDGAR JOHN
BOLIN, Rolf Ling
BOLLMAN, JESSE L.
BONNER, JAMES
BOOTHBY, WALTER MEREDITH
BORTHWICK, Harry A.
BOVIE, WILLIAM T.
 BOYD, William C(louser)
BOYDEN, EDWARD ALLEN
 BRADLEY, James Chester
 BRANDES, Elmer Walker
 BREDER, Charles Marcus, Jr.
BRIGGS, WILLIAM PAUL
BRONK, DETLEV W.
 BROWN, Clair A(lan)
 BROWN, Frank Arthur, Jr.
BROWN, HAROLD WILLIAM
 BROWN, James Greenlief
 BRUES, Austin M(oore)
BRUES, CHARLES THOMAS
BRYAN, George S(mith)
 BRYSON, Vernon
 BUCHANAN, Robert Earle

BUNKER, JOHN WYMOND M.
BURGESS, ALBERT FRANKLIN
BURKHART, W(alter) C.
BURKHOLDER, PAUL R(UFUS)
BURR, HAROLD S(AXTON)
 BURT, William Henry
 BUTLER, Elmer Grimshaw
BUYS, John L.
BYRD, Elon E(ugene)
CAIN, STANLEY A(DAIR)
CAMP, W. H.
CAMPBELL, Dan H(ampton)
CAMPBELL, Frank Leslie
CAMPBELL, ROY E(LLIOTT)
CANNON, PAUL ROBERTS
CARLSON, ANTON JULIUS
 CARLSON, James Gordon
CARPENTER, Frank Morton
CARPENTER, Thorne Martin
CARTER, HERBERT EDMUND
 CASTLE, William Ernest
CATTELL, McKEEN
 CHAMBERLIN, Ralph Vary
CHAMBERS, ROBERT
 CHAPMAN, W(ilbert) M.
CHARIPPER, Harry A.
CHEADLE, Vernon Irvin
CHEN, KO KUEI
 CHENEY, Ralph Holt
CHICKERING, Arthur Merton
CHRISTENSEN, BERNARD V.
 CHRISTENSEN, J(onas) J.
CLARK, AUSTIN HOBART
CLARK, ELIOT ROUND
CLARK, SAM L(ILLARD)
 CLARKE, L. Floyd
CLAUSEN, Roy Elwood
CLEVELAND, LEMUEL ROSCOE
CLELAND, RALPH ERSKINE
CLOWES, GEORGE HENRY A.
COBB, W(ILLIAM) MONTAGUE
COCA, ARTHUR FERNANDEZ
 COKER, Robert E(rvin)
COKER, William Chambers
COLBERT, EDWIN H.
 COLE, Elbert Charles
 COLE, William H(arder)
COLLIP, JAMES BERTRAM
CONN, Harold Joel
COOK, ERNEST FULLERTON
 COOPER, William Skinner
 CORE, Earl L(emley)
CORI, CARL FERDINAND
 COSTELLO, Donald Paul
 COTTAM, Clarence
COUCH, John Nathaniel
COWAN, IAN McTAGGART
COWDRY, EDMUND VINCENT
CRAMPTON, HENRY EDWARD
CRANDALL, Lee Saunders
CROCKER, WILLIAM
CROSBY, ELIZABETH CAROLINE
 CROSS, George Lynn
CROZIER, W(ILLIAM) J(OHN)
 CULBERTSON, J(oseph) O.
CUMMINS, GEORGE BAKER
 CUMMINS, Harold
CURTIS, HOWARD J(AMES)
 DARRAH, William Culp
DAVIS, ALVA RAYMOND
 DAVIS, Hallowell
 DAVIS, John June
DAWSON, Alden Benjamin
DAY, Albert M.
 deLAUBENFELS, Max Walker
DELBRUCK, MAX
DeLONG, Dwight Moore
DEMEREC, Milislav
DEMPSEY, Edward Wheeler
DONALDSON, LAUREN R.
DOBZHANSKY, THEODOSIUS
DOISY, EDWARD ADELBERT
DOWDY, Andrew Hunter
DRAGSTEDT, CARL ALBERT
 DRIVER, Ernest C(harles)
DuBOS, RENE JULES
DUGGAR, BENJAMIN MINGE
DUNN, EMMETT REID
 DUNN, Leslie C(larence)
DuSHANE, Graham Phillips
EASTLICK, Herbert L(eonard)
ECKER, Enrique E(dward)
EDDY, NATHAN BROWNE
 EDDY, Samuel
EDGECOMBE, Samuel W.
EGGLESTON, FRANK E(GBERT)
 EIDE, Carl J(ohn)
EMERSON, ALFRED EDWARDS
EMMONS, CHESTER WILSON

ENGLE, EARL T.
 ESAU, Katherine
 ESSEX, Hiram Eli
EVANS, ALEXANDER W.
EVANS, HERBERT McLEAN
FANKHAUSER, GERHARD
FARQUHARSON, JAMES
 FARRIS, Edmond J.
FASSETT, Norman C(arter)
 FASTEN, Nathan
FAUST, Ernest Carroll
FELTON, LLOYD DERR
 FENN, Wallace Osgood
FIELD, John, II
FINN, Donovan Bartley
FISCHELIS, ROBERT PHILIPP
FISCHER, MARTIN HENRY
 FISH, Charles John
 FISH, Harold Dufur
FISHER, Walter Taylor
FLUKE, Charles Lewis
FOGG, Lloyd Clarke
FOLK, Marion Hayne, Jr.
FRACKER, Stanley Black
FRANCIS, THOMAS, JR.
 FRED, Edwin Broun
FRIEDMANN, Herbert
FULTON, John Farquhar
GABRIELSON, Ira Noel
 GAIL, Floyd Whitney
 GAINEY, Percy Leigh
GALTSOFF, Paul Simon
GARREY, WALTER EUGENE
GASSER, HERBERT SPENCER
 GAUNT, Robert
GEILING, EUGENE M. K.
GELLHORN, Ernst
GEORGE, W(esley) C(ritz)
GERARD, RALPH WALDO
GERSBACHER, Willard Marion
 GIESE, Arthur Charles
GILL, Richard C(ochran)
GILTNER, WARD
GLASSER, OTTO
 GLEASON, Henry A(llan)
GODDARD, DAVID R.
GOLDFORB, Abraham Jules
GOODPASTURE, ERNEST W.
GOODSPEED, THOMAS H.
 GOODWIN, Richard Hale
GOSS, Charles Mayo
GOWEN, John Whittemore
GRAF, John E(nos)
GRAHAM, HERBERT W.
GRANT, Chapman
GRAY, Peter
GREULACH, Victor A.
GREULICH, William Walter
GRISCOM, Ludlow
GROSS, Alfred Otto
GUSTAFSON, Felix G(ustaf)
GUTERMUTH, Clinton R.
GUTHRIE, Mary J(ane)
HAAG, HARVEY B(ERNHARDT)
HAAS, Victor H(oward)
HAGGARD, HOWARD WILCOX
HAHNERT, William F(ranklin)
HALE, William Mason
HALL, E(ugene) Raymond
HALL, Ivan Clifford
HALL, Richard P.
HAMBURGER, Viktor
HAMILTON, James B.
HAMMON, WILLIAM M.
HAMMOND, Datus M(iller)
HARGITT, George Thomas
HARNED, Robey Wentworth
HARPER, Francis
HARRIS, HALBERT MARION
HARRISON, ROSS GRANVILLE
HARTLINE, Holdan Keffer
HARVEY, EDMUND NEWTON
HASEMAN, Leonard
HASKINS, Caryl Parker
HATCH, Winslow R(oper)
HAUPT, Arthur Wing
HAYES, William Patrick
HEALD, FREDERICK De FOREST
HEDRICK, Leslie Ray
HEISER, VICTOR GEORGE
HEMINGWAY, Allan
HENCH, PHILIP SHOWALTER
 HERRE, Albert W.C.T.
HERSH, A(mos) H(enry)
HESS, Walter Norton
HICKS, Lawrence Emerson
HILTON, William Atwood
HINES, MARION
HINSEY, JOSEPH CLARENCE

HISAW, Frederick Lee
HIXSON, Ephriam
HOADLEY, Leigh
HOAGLAND, Hudson
HOGG, Ira D(wight)
HOLMES, Samuel Jackson
HOOD, J(oseph) Douglas
HOOKER, Charles Wright
HOOKER, Davenport
HORSFALL, James Gordon
HORWOOD, Murray Philip
HOSKINS, ROY GRAHAM
HOUGH, Walter Seneff
HOUSSAY, BERNARDO A.
HOWARD, Hildegarde (Mrs. Henry Anson Wylde)
HUBBELL, THEODORE, H.
HUBBS, Carl L(eavitt)
HUBERT, Ernest E.
HUCKER, George James
HUDDLESON, I. Forest
HUDSON, N(oel) Paul
HUFF, Clay G.
HUMPHREY, Rufus Richard
HUNGERFORD, Herbert B.
HUNT, H(arrison) R(andall)
HUNTER, George W(illiam) III
HUTCHENS, John O(liver)
HUTCHINSON, G(eorge) E.
HUTSON, Ray
HYMAN, Libbie Henrietta
HYMAN, ORREN WILLIAMS
IBSEN, Herman Lauritz
IRVING, LAURENCE
IRWIN, M(alcolm) R(obert)
IVY, ANDREW CONWAY
JACKSON, Hartley Harrad T.
JACKSON, RICHARD WEBBER
JACOBS, MERKEL H.
JENSEN, James Herbert
JOHANNSEN, OSKAR A.
JOHNSON, E(dward) M.
JOHNSON, VICTOR
JOHNSTON, IVAN MURRAY
JONES, Donald Forsha
JUST, Theodor Karl
KAHN, Reuben Leon
KALKUS, Julius Wilbur
KARLING, John S.
KATZ, LOUIS NELSON
KAUFMAN, Berwind P.
KECK, DAVID D(ANIELS)
KEITT, George Wannamaker
KELLOGG, Arthur Remington
KENDALL, ARTHUR ISAAC
KENDALL, EDWARD CALVIN
KENDRICK, Pearl L.
KENOYER, Leslie Alva
KESSEL, John Flenniken
KETY, Seymours
KEYS, Ancel
KIDDER, George Wallace, Jr.
KILLE, Frank Ralph
KILLIP, ELLSWORTH P(AINE)
KINDRED, James Ernest
KINSEY, ALFRED CHARLES
KIRBY, HAROLD
KLAUBER, Laurence Monroe
KLOTZ, Leo Joseph
KNIGHT, HARRY HAZELTON
KNOWLTON, George F.
KOPAC, M(ilan) J(ames)
KOPPANYI, Theodore
KORNHAUSER, Sidney Issac
KOSER, Stewart Arment
KRANTZ, JOHN CHRISTIAN, Jr.
KRAUS, E(ZRA) J(ACOB)
KREIG, WENDELL JORDAN
KRUMBHAAR, E(DWARD) B.
KUNTZ, Albert
LANDIS, EUGENE MARKLEY
LaRUE, George R(oger)
LASSEK, ARTHUR M(ARVEL)
LAWSON, C(hester) A(lvin)
LEACH, JULIAN GILBERT
LEAKE, CHAUNCEY D.
LEE, Milton Oliver
LEVINE, PHILLIP
LEWIS, HOWARD BISHOP
LEWIS, Ivey Foreman
LIM, ROBERT KHO-SENG
LINDSEY, Arthur Ward
LITTLE, CLARENCE C(OOK)
LOEB, ROBERT F(REDERICK)
LOEHWING, WALTER F.
LOEWI, OTTO
LONG, CYRIL NORMAN HUGH
LORENTE de No', R.
LUCKE, BALDUIN

LUCKHARDT, Arno Benedict
LUNDELL, Cyrus Longworth
LYLE, Clay
MacDANIELS, Laurence H.
MacNIDER, WILLIAM de B.
MADDEN, SIDNEY CLARENCE
MAIER, Eugene
MANGELSDORF, Paul C.
MANN, William M.
MARTIN, George Willard
McCLINTOCK, BARBARA
McCLUNG, L(eland) S(wint)
McCOY, GEORGE WALTER
McCRADY, Edward
McFARLAND, Ross Armstrong
MEEK, WALTER JOSEPH
MELANDER, A(XEL) L.
MERRILL, ELMER DREW
METCALF, ZENO PAYNE
METZ, Charles William
MAYER, Bernard S(andler)
MEYER, KARL FRIEDRICH
MEYER, ROLAND K(ENNETH)
MICKEL, Clarence Eugene
MILLER, ALDEN HOLMES
MILLER, GERRITT SMITH, Jr.
MILLER, JULIAN HOWELL
MILLER, LLOYD C(HESTER)
MINNICH, DWIGHT ELMER
MINOT, GEORGE BENJAMIN
MIROYIANNIS, Stanley D.
MOHLER, JOHN ROBBINS
MOLITOR, HANS
MOORE, CARL RICHARD
MOORE, Dwight Munson
MOORE, GEORGE THOMAS
MOORE, JOHN PERCY
MORGAN, Ann Haven
MRAK, Emil M(arcel)
MUDD, STUART
MUELLER, JOHN HOWARD
MULLER, HERMANN JOSEPH
MUNZ, Philip Alexander
MURIE, Olaus Johan
MURPHY, WILLIAM PARRY
MUSSELMAN, Thomas Edgar
NEILL, James Maffett
NELSON, ERWIN ELLIS
NELSON, Thurlow C(hristian)
NELSON, WARREN OTTO
NEWMAN, HORATIO HACKETT
NICE, Leonard Blaine
NICHOLAS, JOHN SPANGLER
NICHOLS, JOHN TREADWELL
NICKERSON, John Lester
NIGRELLI, R. F.
NOLAND, LOWELL E(VAN)
NOVY, FREDERICK GEORGE
NUNGESTER, WALTER JAMES
OKKELBERG, Peter Claus
OLD, Marcus Calvin
OLMSTED, CHARLES EDWARD
OLSEN, O. Wilford
OPIE, EUGENE LINDSAY
ORTON, CLAYTON ROBERTS
OSBORN, Fairfield
PACKARD, Charles
PALMER, E(phraim) Laurence
PARK, ORLANDO
PARK, THOMAS
PARKER, John Robert
PARPART, ARTHUR KEMBLE
PARR, Albert Eide
PATTERSON, JOHN THOMAS
PATTERSON, Thomas L(eon)
PAUL, JOHN R.
PAYNE, FERNANDUS
PEARSE, Arthur Sperry
PEARSON, Jay Frederick W.
PEATTIE, DONALD CULROSS
PEMBERTON, Cyril E.
PEPPER, Bailey B.
PETERS, James L(ee)
PETRIDES, George A(than)
PETRUNKEVITCH, ALEXANDER
PHILLIPS, Walter Sargeant
PILSBRY, HENRY AUGUSTUS
POLUNIN, Nicholas
POLYAK, Stephen
POOL, Raymond John
POOS, Frederick William, Jr.
POUGH, Richard Hooper
PRESCOTT, G(erald) W(ebber)
PROSSER, C(LIFFORD) LADEL
RAPER, KENNETH BRYAN
RAUP, Hugh Miller
REYNOLDS, Bruce D(odson)
RHOADS, CORNELIUS P.
RHOADES, MARCUS MORTON

RICE, John Winter
RICE, Paul LaVerne
RICHARDS, ALFRED NEWTON
RICHARDSON, CHAS. H.
RICKETT, Harold William
RIDDLE, OSCAR
RIGG, George Burton
RIKER, Albert Joyce
ROBBINS, William Jacob
ROBERTSON, OSWALD HOPE
ROMANOFF, Alexis Lawrence
ROMER, ALFRED SHERWOOD
ROUS, (FRANCIS) PEYTON
ROWNTREE, LEONARD G.
RUTHVEN, ALEXANDER G.
SAMPSON, Homer Cleveland
SAX, KARL
SCHAEFFER, J(ACOB) P.
SCHMIDT, CARL FREDERIC
SCHMIDT, KARL PATTERSON
SCHMITT, FRANCIS OTTO
SCHMITT, Waldo LaSalle
SCHOUR, Isaac
SCHRADER, FRANZ
SCHRAMM, Jacob Richard
SCHULTZ, Leonard P(eter)
SCOTT, GORDON HATLER
SEARS, PAUL BIGELOW
SEDGWICK, Paul J(oseph)
SEEVERS, MAURICE HARRISON
SEEGERS, Walter H(enry)
SHANTZ, HOMER LeROY
SHATTUCK, GEORGE CHEEVER
SHEAR, Cornelius Lott
SHEARD, Charles
SHEARER, P(hineas) S(tevens)
SHELFORD, VICTOR ERNEST
SHERFF, Earl E(dward)
SHERMAN, JAMES MORGAN
SHOPE, RICHARD EDWIN
SHULL, A(ARON) FRANKLIN
SHULL, CHARLES ALBERT
SHULL, GEORGE HARRISON
SIMMONS, JAMES STEVENS
SIMPSON, GEORGE GAYLORD
SIMPSON, WALTER MALCOLM
SINNOTT, EDMUND WARE
SKINNER, Charles Edward
SLYE, MAUD
SMITH, A(lbert) C(harles)
SMITH, ALEXANDER H.
SMITH, ARTHUR HENRY
SMITH, Christianna
SMITH, F(rederick) G. W.
SMITH, GILBERT MORGAN
SMITH, Homer William
SMITH, PHILIP EDWARD
SMITH, Roger Cletus
SNYDER, Laurence H.
SONNEBORN, Tracy Morton
SPEIDEL, CARL CASKEY
SPENCER, Warren Poppino
SPRUNT, Alexander, Jr.
SPRUNT, DOUGLAS H.
STADLER, LEWIS JOHN
STACKMAN, ELVIN C.
STANLEY, WENDELL M.
STARKEY, Robert Lyman
STEBBINS, George L., Jr.
STEINBACH, HENRY BURR
STERN, CURT
STEVENS, Terrill D(ryden)
STEVENSON, John A(lbert)
STORER, Tracy Irwin
STOUT, A. B.
STUNKARD, Horace Wesley
STURTEVANT, Alfred Henry
SUTTON, George Miksch
SVENSON, Henry K.
SWANSON, Carl Pontius
SWANSON, Gustav Adolph
SWEZEY, W(illiam) W.
SZENT-GYORGYI, ALBERT
TAFT, C. E.
TALIAFERRO, WILLIAM HAY
TATUM, ARTHUR LAWRIE
TAYLOR, NORMAN
TAYLOR, WALTER PENN
TEALE, Edwin Way
TEDESCHE, Leon G(reenfield)
TEHON, Leo Roy
THOM, CHARLES
THOMPSON, Ernest F.
THOMPSON, MARVIN RUSSELL
THOMPSON, William F.
TIFFANY, (LEWIS) HANFORD
TILLETT, WILLIAM S.
TILDEN, Josphine Elizabeth
TIPPO, Oswald

TORREY, THEODORE W(ILLETT)
TRANSEAU, Edgar Nelson
TRELEASE, Sam Farlow
TWITTY, VICTOR CHANDLER
TYLER, ALBERT
UHLENHUTH, Edward
VAN CLEAVE, Harley Jones
van DYKE, HARRY BENJAMIN
van NIEL, CORNELIS B.
VAN OOSTEN, John
VARRELMAN, Ferdinand A.
VERDOORN, Frans
VISSCHER, Maurice B.
VOEGTLIN, CARL
WADE, Joseph Sanford
WAKERLIN, George Earle
WAKSMAN, SELMAN A.
WALD, GEORGE
WALKER, John Charles
WARREN, SHIELDS
WEED, LEWIS HILL
WEESE, A(SA) O(RRIN)
WEISS, PAUL ALFRED
WELCH, Paul Smith
WELLER, CARL VERNON
WENT, FRITS W(ARMOLT)
WEST, Erdman
WESTFALL, Jonathan J.
WETMORE, ALEXANDER
WETMORE, Ralph Hartley
WHIPPLE, GEORGE HOYT
WHITAKER, DOUGLAS
WILLIAMS, Carroll Milton
WILLIER, B(ENJAMIN) H.
WILSON, Carl Louis
WILSON, James Walter
WINSLOW, CHARLES E. A.
WINTERNITZ, MILTON C.
WISLOCKI, GEORGE B.
WITSCHI, Emil
WODEHOUSE, Roger Philip
WOLBACH, SIMEON BURT
WOOD, PAUL MEYER
WOODBURNE, Russell T.
WORTHLEY, HARLAN NOYES
WRIGHT, Albert Hazen
WRIGHT, SEWALL
WRIGHT, WILLARD H(ULL)
WYND, Frederick Lyle
YERKES, Robert M.
YOUND, Martin D(unaway)
YOUNGKEN, Heber W.
YUNCKER, TRUMAN GEORGE
ZANGERL, Rainer
ZIMMERMAN, Arnold A.
ZOBELL, CLAUDE E.

Chemistry

ABBOTT, Talbert Ward
ACKERSON, C(lifton) W.
ADAMS, ROGER
ALEXANDER, JEROME
ALTER, Chester M.
AMDUR, ISADORE
ANDERSON, RUDOLPH JOHN
ANDREWS, Donald Hatch
ARNOLD, Richard T.
BADGER, Richard McLean
BAILAR, John Christian, Jr.
BAILEY, Clyde H.
BALKE, Clarence William
BANCROFT, WILDER DWIGHT
BARSTOW, EDWIN ORMOND
BARTELL, Floyd Earl
BARTOW, Edward
BARTLETT, PAUL DOUGHTY
BATES, Frederick (John)
BAUMANN, Carl A.
BEAL, George Denton
BEAR, Firman Edward
BETHKE, Roland Martin
BILGER, Earl Matthias
BILGER, Leonora Neuffer
BLACK, Alvin Percy
BLAU, Henry H(ess)
BLISH, Morris Joslin
BLUM, William
BOGERT, MARSTON TAYLOR
BOLTON, ELMER KEISER
BOORD, CECIL ERNEST
BOUNDY, RAY HAROLD
BOWMAN, JOHN R.
BRINTON, Paul Henry M.-P.
BRISCOE, HERMAN T.
BROCKWAY, Lawrence Olin
BRODE, WALLACE REED
BROOKS, Benjamin Talbot
BROWN, F(rank) E(merson)
BROWN, Harrison S.

BROWN, Herbert Charles
BROWN, Weldon Grant
BUCKNER, G(arrett) Davis
BUEHLER, Calvin A.
BURG, Anton Behme
BURK, Dean
BURNS, ROBERT M(ARTIN)
BURT, C(harlotte) Pauline
BURTON, Milton
BUSWELL, Arthur Moses
CAMPBELL, Kenneth N.
CARMICHAEL, Emmett Bryan
CARTER, Herbert Edmund
CHADWELL, Harris Marshall
CHANEY, NEWCOMB KINNEY
CHRISTMAN, Adam A.
CLARK, GEORGE LINDENBERG
CLARK, William Mansfield
CLARKE, Beverly Leonidas
COGHILL, Robert DeWolf
COLLINS, William Dennis
CONANT, JAMES BRYANT
CONOVER, Frederick L(eRoy)
COOLIDGE, WILLIAM DAVID
COOMBE, HARRY E. (JAMES)
COPE, ARTHUR CLAY
COPENHAVER, James Earl
CORI, CARL FERDINAND
CORI, GERTY THERESA
CORYELL, Charles Du Bois
CORWIN, Alsoph Henry
CRABTREE, John Ickeringill
CRAIG, Lyman C.
CRANE, EVAN JAY
CRAWFORD, Bryce (Low), Jr.
CROSEN, Robert Glenn
CROSS, PAUL CLIFFORD
CROSSLEY, MOSES LEVEROCK
CURME, GEORGE OLIVER, Jr.
CURRY, James Rowland
CURTIS, FRANCIS JOSEPH
DAFT, Floyd S(helton)
DANIELS, Farrington
DARBY, WILLIAM J., Jr.
DAWSON, Lyle R(amsay)
DEBYE, Peter Joseph William
DeMENT, Jack Andrew
DENNY, Henry Wadhams
DEUEL, Harry James, Jr.
DEWEY, BRADLEY
DINSMORE, RAY PUTNAM
DOISY, EDWARD ADELBERT
DOLE, Malcolm
DOUGHERTY, Gregg
DOW, WILLARD HENRY
DOWNING, FREDERICK B.
DRAKE, NATHAN LINCOLN
DUNBAR, Ralph Edwin
DUNKELBERGER, Tobias H.
DUSHMAN, SAUL
DUSTMAN, Robert Barclay
DUTCHER, Raymond Adams
du VIGNEAUD, VINCENT
EDSALL, JOHN TILESTON
EGLOFF, GUSTAV
ELDERFIELD, ROBERT C(OOLEY)
ELVEHJEM, Conrad Arnold
EMERSON, Gladys A.
ERICKSON, J(ulius) L. E.
ETHEREDGE, M(ahlon) P.
EVANS, Earl Alison, Jr.
EVANS, WILLIAM LLOYD
EVERETT, Mark R(euben)
FAJANS, Kasimir
FERGUSON, ALFRED LYNN
FERNELIUS, W(illis) Conard
FIESER, LOUIS FREDERICK
FINK, COLIN GARFIELD
FIREMAN, Peter
FISKE, Cyrus Hartwell
FLEISCHER, Michael
FLETT, LAWRENCE H.
FLORY, Paul J(ohn)
FOLKERS, Karl August
FOWLER, ROBERT DUDLEY
FROLICH, Per K(eyser)
FULMER, Jervis M(oissan)
FUNK, CASIMER
FUOSS, RAYMOND MATTHEW
FURMAN, N(ATHANIEL) H.
FUSON, Reynold Clayton
GEDDES, William Findlay
GERMUTH, Frederick George
GIAUQUE, WILLIAM FRANCIS
GIBBONS, WILLIS ALEXANDER
GIBSON, R(ALPH) E(DWARD)
GEIS, William John
GILMAN, Henry
GLASSTONE, Samuel

GLOCKLER, George
GOEBEL, Walther Frederick
GRADY, Roy Israel
GREAVES, Joseph Eames
GREENBERG, David M.
GREENE, Hoke S(mith)
GREENEWALT. CRAWFORD H.
GRIFFITH, IVOR
GROSS, Paul Magnus
GROSSE, Aristid V.
GUCKER, Frank Thomson, Jr.
HAAGEN-SMIT, Arie Jan
HALDEMAN, William S.
HALE, WILLIAM J.
HALL, Norris Folger
HAMILTON, Cliff Struthers
HAMMETT, Louis Plack
HAMMOND, Elmer L(ionel)
HAMOR, WILLIAM ALLEN
HARGER, Rolla Neil
HARKER, David
HARNED, Herbert S(pencer)
HARRIS, Milton
HARRIS, Robert Samuel
HASS, Henry Bohn
HASTINGS, A(lbert) Baird
HAUSER, Ernest A(lfred)
HAWK, Philip Bovier
HAWKINS, J(ohn) E(rskine)
HENDRICKS, STERLING B.
HENNION, George F(elix)
HEPBURN, Joseph Samuel
HERRMAN, Henry Francis
HILDEBRAND, Joel Henry
HILL, ARTHUR JOSEPH
HIRSCHFELDER, Joseph O.
HITCHCOCK, LAUREN B.
HOCHWALT, CARROLL A.
HOCKETT, Robert Casad
HOGNESS, THORFIN RUSTEN
HOLMES, Edward O(tis), Jr.
HOLMES, HARRY NICHOLS
HOWE, James Lewis
HUDSON, Claude Silbert
HURD, Charles Buell
HURD, CHARLES DeWITT
HUSTON, Ralph Chase
INGERSOLL, Arthur William
JACOBS, WALTER ABRAHAM
JAFFE, Bernard
JENKINS, Glenn Llewellyn
JOHNSON, Henry Stoddard
JOHNSON, James McIntosh
JOHNSON, JOHN HAVEN
JOHNSON, Warren C.
JOHNSTON, Herrick Lee
JOHNSTON, William R.
JONES, HILTON IRA
JULIAN, PERCY LAVON
KENDALL, EDWARD CALVIN
KENDALL, James
KEYES, Frederick George
KILPATRICK, MARTIN
KING, CHARLES GLEN
KIRK, RAYMOND ELLER
KIRKWOOD, JOHN GAMBLE
KLOTZ, Irving Myron
KLUG, Harold Philip
KOELSCH, C(harles) Frederick
KOENIG, Louis
KOLTHOFF, Isaac Maurits
KRAUS, CHARLES A.
KRABILL, Henry Reist
KUEBLER, John R(alph)
LAMB, ARTHUR BECKETT
LaMER, Victor Kuhn
LANDIS, Walter Savage
LANGMUIR, IRVING
LATIMER, Wendell Mitchell
LEWIS, WARREN KENDALL
LIBBY, W(illard) FRANK
LINCOLN, Bert H(artzell)
LIND, SAMUEL COLVILLE
LINK, KARL PAUL
LIPMANN, FRITZ ALBERT
LITTLE, ERNEST
LIVINGSTON, Robert S.
LONG, James Scott
LONGENECKER, Herbert E.
LONGSWORTH, LEWIS G.
LOWRY, H(OMER) H(IRAM)
LUCAS, Howard Johnson
LUCK, JAMES MURRAY
LYCAN, William H(iram)
MACK, EDWARD, Jr.
MAJOR, Randolph T(homas)
MARK, HERMAN F(RANCK)
MARSHALL, E(li) Kennerly, Jr.
MARVEL, Carl Shipp

MATHEWS, JOSEPH HOWARD
MAYER, Joseph Edward
McBAIN, James William
McDONALD, Hugh J(oseph)
McELVAIN, S(AMUEL) M.
McGRATH, Joseph Sarto
McKEEN, JOHN E.
McMILLAN, EDWIN M.
McPHERSON, WILLIAM
MELDRUM, William Buell
MELLON, M(elvin) G(uy)
MERCK, GEORGE WILHELM
MILLER, William T(aylor), Jr.
MOORE, Maurice L(ee)
MOSHER, William Allison
MUEHLBERGER, Clarence W.
MUNCH, James Clyde
MURPHY, WALTER J.
NAUDAIN, Glenn Garnet
NEGUS, Sidney Stevens
NEVILLE, Harvey Alexander
NEWTON, Ray C.
NORTHROP, John Howard
NOYES, HARRY ALFRED
NOYES, WILLIAM ALBERT, Jr.
NUGENT, Robert Logan
ONCLEY, JOHN LAWRENCE
OTHMER, DONALD FREDERICK
PACSU, Eugene
PARKS, George Sutton
PATNODE, Winton (Irving)
PATTERSON, AUSTIN M.
PAULING, LINUS CARL
PEASE, Robert Norton
PHILLIPS, Thomas Gutherie
POLLARD, Cash Blair
POTTER, Van Rensselaer
PRICE, Charles Coale
PROCTOR, Bernard Emerson
QUACKENBUSH, F(orrest) W.
RATHER, Jar.. s Burness
READ, William Thornton
REED, Frank Hynes
REYERSON, Lloyd Hilton
RICCI, John Ettore
RIEGEL, Byron
RIES, Herman E., Jr.
RITCHEY, Herbert E.
ROBINSON, Howard W.
RODEBUSH, WORTH HUFF
ROGERS, William, Jr.
ROLLEFSON, Gerhard Krohn
ROSE, William Cumming
ROSSINI, Frederick Dominic
RUSH, Kenneth
RUSSELL, ROBERT PRICE
RUSSELL, Walter C(harles)
SAMUELS, Leo Tolstoy
SCARSETH, George Dewey
SCHMETLING, Louis
SCHOLES, Samuel Ray
SCHOMAKER, VERNER
SCHUETTE, Henry August
SCOTT, Arthur F(erdinand)
SEABORG, GLENN THEODORE
SEMON, WALDO LONSBURY
SHAFFER, PHILLIP ANDERSON
SHEEHAN, JOHN CLARK
SHEPARD, NORMAN ARTHUR
SHERMAN, HENRY CLAPP
SILVERMAN, Alexander
SKINNER, WILLIAM W.
SMALL, LYNDON FREDERICK
SMITH, George Frederick
SMITH, Grant W(arren)
SMITH, LEIGHTON BRUERTON
SMITH, Paul Kenneth
SNELL, Esmond
SNELL, FOSTER DEE
SNELLING, Walter Otheman
STADIE, WILLIAM C.
STANLEY, WENDELL M.
STEENBOCK, HARRY
STERN, KURT GUENTER
STEVENSON, EARL P(LACE)
STINE, CHARLES MILTON A.
SULLIVAN, MICHAEL XAVIER
SUMMERBELL, ROBERT KERR
TASHIRO, SHIRO
TAYLOR, H(enry) Austin
TAYLOR, HUGH STOTT
TAYLOR, T(homas) Ivan
THOMAS, CHARLES ALLEN
THOMPSON, C(larence) B.
TILLOTSON, Ludwin Ward
TIMM, John A(rrend)
TRESSLER, Donald Kiteley
UREY, HAROLD CLAYTON
VANCE, John Edward

VAN DOREN, LLOYD
VANDERKLEED, Charles E.
VAN SLYKE, DONALD D.
VICKERY, Hubert Bradford
VOLWILER, ERNEST HENRY
WALL, Florence E(meline)
WALLACE, Earl Keeney
WARNER, J(OHN) C.
WATSON, John Wilbur
WEST, Edward Staunton
WENDT, Gerald (Louis)
WESTHEIMER, FRANK H.
WHELAND, George Willard
WHITE, Charles Edward
WICHERS, Edward
WIEGAND, Ernest Herman
WIEGAND, William Bryan
WILEY, Richard Haven
WILLIAMS, J(ohn) W(arren)
WILLIAMS, ROBERT R.
WILLIAMS, ROGER JOHN
WILSON, David Wright
WILSON, E(dgar) Bright, Jr.
WINTERSTEINER, OSKAR PAUL
WITHROW, JAMES RENWICK
WOLFROM, Melville L.
YOE, John Howe
YOST, Don Merlin Lee
YOUNG, George Husband
YOUNG, WILLIAM GOULD
ZANETTI, JOAQUIN ENRIQUE
ZERBAN, Frederick William

Geography

ACKERMAN, EDWARD A.
BENGTSON, Nels August
BOGGS, S(amuel) W.
BOYD, LOUISE ARNER
BROEK, Jan O(tto) M(arius)
BROOKS, Charles Franklin
BROWN, LLOYD ARNOLD
BYRD, Richard Evelyn
CARLSON, William Samuel
CARTER, George Francis
COLBY, CHARLES CARLYLE
CRESSEY, GEORGE BABCOCK
DAVIS, CHARLES M(OLER)
DICKEN, Samuel Newton
DURAND, Loyal, Jr.
FINCH, Vernor Clifford
FORMAN, Harrison
FOSCUE, Edwin Jay
FREEMAN, Otis Willard
HALL, ROBERT BURNETT
HARRIS, Chauncy Dennison
HARTSHORNE, RICHARD
HEWES, Leslie
HUDSON, G(EORGE) DONALD
JAMES, PRESTON EVERETT
JONES, CLARENCE FIELDEN
JONES, Stephen Barr
KIMBLE, George Herbert T.
KNIFFEN, Fred B(owerman)
KOHN, Clyde F(rederick)
MacMILLAN, DONALD BAXTER
McMURRY, Kenneth C.
MILLER, E(ugene) Willard
MILLER, George J.
MILLER, OSBORN MAITLAND
PEATTIE, RODERICK
PENDLETON, ROBERT L.
PICO, Rafael
PLATT, ROBERT SWANTON
QUAM, Louis O(tto)
RENNER, George Thomas, Jr.
RICE, Alexander Hamilton
RISTOW, WALTER W(ILLIAM)
RONNE, FINN
ROSE, JOHN KERR
RUSSELL, Richard Joel
SAUER, CARL (ORTWIN)
SMITH, Guy-Harold
SMITH, J(OSEPH) RUSSELL
STARKEY, Otis P(aul)
STEFANSSON, VILHJALMUR
STRONG, Helen Mabel
SVERDRUP, HARALD ULRIK
TAYLOR, GRIFFITH
THORNTHWAITE, CHARLES W.
TREWARTHA, Glenn Thomas
VAN CLEEF, Eugene
VAN LIERE, Edward
VAN VALKENBURG, SAMUEL
VISHER, Stephen Sargent
von ENGELN, Oskar Dietrich
WEAVER, John C(arrier)
WHITAKER, Joe Russell
WHITTLESEY, DERWENT S.
WILKINS, Sir Hubert

WOOD, Walter Abbott
WRIGHT, JOHN KIRTLAND
ZIERER, Clifford M(aynard)

Geology (including Mineralogy)

ADAMS, John Emery
ADAMS, Leason Heberling
ALDRICH, HENRY RAY
ALLEN, Victor Thomas
ANTEVS, ERNST VALDEMAR
APFEL, Earl Taylor
ARNOLD, RALPH
BALK, Robert
BALL, Max W(aite)
BASSLER, Ray Smith
BASTIN, Edson Sunderland
BATEMAN, Alan Mara
BEERS, ROLAND FRANK
BEHRE, Charles Henry, Jr.
BENGSTON, Nels August
BERKEY, Charles Peter
BERRY, E. Willard
BEVAN, Arthur Charles
BIRCH, (ALBERT) FRANCIS
BILLINGS, Marland Pratt
BLOOMER, Robert Oliver
BONINE, Chesleigh Arthur
BOUTWELL, J. M.
BOWEN, Norman Levi
BOYD, JAMES
BRADLEY, John Hodgden
BRADLEY, WILMOT H.
BRETZ, J. Harlen
BRODERICK, Thomas M.
BUCHER, WALTER H(ERMAN)
BUDDINGTON, ARTHUR F.
BUERGER, Martin Julian
BURROUGHS, Wilbur Greeley
BUTLER, Bert S.
BUWALDA, John Peter
BYERLY, PERRY
CADY, GILBERT HAVEN
CALHOUN, Fred Harvey H.
CAMERON, Francis
CAMPBELL, IAN
CHANEY, Ralph W(orks)
CLEAVES, Arthur Bailey
CLINE, Isaac Monroe
CLOOS, ERNST
COGGESHALL, Arthur Sterry
COLBERT, Edwin H.
COLE, W(ILLIAM) STORRS
COOPER, Byron N(elson)
CORRY, Andrew Vincent
CRONEIS, Carey
CROOK, Theo Heisel
DAVIS, Morgan J(ones)
DAY, ARTHUR LOUIS
De GOLYER, E(verette) L(ee)
DEISS, Charles F(rederick)
DELO, David M(arion)
DOBBIN, Carroll Edward
DONNAY, J(oseph) D. H.
DREYER, Robert M(arx)
DUNBAR, CARL OWEN
ELLIS, Brooks Fleming
EMMONS, Richard Conrad
EWING, WILLIAM MAURICE
FENTON, Carroll Lane
FINCH, Ruy Herbert
FISK, Harold N(orman)
FLINT, Richard Foster
FOHS, Ferdinand Julius
FOSHAG, William Frederick
FRYXELL, Fritiof Melvin
GAZIN, C(harles) Lewis
GESTER, George Clark
GIANELLA, Vincent P(aul)
GILLULY, JAMES
GOULD, Laurence McKinley
GRATON, LOUIS CARYL
GRAWE, Oliver Rudolph
GROSVENOR, GILBERT HOVEY
GRUNER, JOHN W(ALTER)
GUSTAFSON, J(ohn) K(yle)
GUTENBERG, Beno
HEALD, KENNETH CONRAD
HEROY, WILLIAM BAYARD
HEWETT, Donnel Foster
HINDS, Henry
HOLMES, Chauncey D.
HOWELL, Benjamin Franklin
HOWELL, J(esse) V.
HOWLAND, ARTHUR LLOYD
HUTTON, Colin Osborne
INGERSON, Fred Earl

INSLEY, Herbert
JAGGAR, Thomas Augustus
JAHNS, Richard Henry
JEPSON, Glenn Lowell
JILLSON, Willard Rouse
JOHANNSEN, Albert
JORALEMON, IRA BEAMAN
KAY, (George) Marshall
KELLER, Walter David
KELLUM, Lewis B.
KERR, PAUL FRANCIS
KNOPF, Adolph
KRAUS, EDWARD HENRY
KRUMBEIN, WILLIAM C.
LADD, Harry S(tephen)
LAHEE, Frederick Henry
LAIRD, Wilson Morrow
LANDES, Kenneth Knight
LARSEN, Esper Signius, Jr.
LEET, Lewis Don
LEIGHTON, Morris Morgan
LEVORSEN, ARVILLE IRVING
LILLEY, ERNEST RAYMOND
LLOYD, E(dwin) Russell
LONGWELL, Chester Ray
LOUDERBACK, GEORGE DAVIS
LOVERING, THOMAS SEWARD
LUGN, A(lvin) L(eonard)
LUND, Richard Jacob
LYON, Tom
MacCLINTOCK, PAUL
MACELWANE, James B.
MATHER, KIRTLEY FLETCHER
McFARLAN, Arthur Crane
McFARLAND, RUSSELL S(COTT)
McLAUGHLIN, Donald H.
MENDENHALL, WALTER C.
MERWIN, Herbert Eugene
MEYEROFF, HOWARD A.
MILLER, A(rthur) K.
MOFFIT, Fred Howard
MONEYMAKER, Berlen C.
MOODY, CLARENCE L(EMUEL)
MOORE, RAYMOND CECIL
MORRIS, Frederick Kuhne
MORSE, William Clifford
MUILENBURG, Garrett A.
MULLER, Siemon William
NETTLETON, L(ewis) L(omax)
NEWELL, NORMAN DENNIS
NEWHOUSE, WALTER HARRY
NININGER, Harvey Harlow
NOBLE, JAMES ALEXANDER
NOLAN, Thomas B(rennan)
NOTMAN, ARTHUR
OLSON, EVERETT CLAIRE
PABST, A(dol f)
PAIGE, Sidney
PALMER, Katherine E. H.
PARK, CHARLES F., Jr.
PEARL, Richard Maxwell
PECK, Raymond E(lliott)
PETTIJOHN, F(rancis) J(ohn)
PIGGOT, Charles Snowden
POUGH, Frederick Harvey
POULTER, Thomas Charles
POWERS, William Edwards
PRATT, Wallace E.
PRICE, Paul Holland
RAMSDELL, Lewis Stephen
REESIDE, JOHN BERNARD, Jr.
REICHELDERFER, F(rancis) W.
ROBERTS, Joseph Kent
ROVE, Olaf N(orberg)
RUBEY, WILLIAM WALDEN
RUSSELL, Richard Joel
SALES, Reno H.
SEARS, JULIAN D(UCKER)
SHARP, Henry Staats
SHROCK, Robert Rakes
SHULER, Ellis W(illiam)
SIMPSON, GEORGE GAYLORD
SINGEWALD, Joseph T., Jr.
SLAWSON, Chester Baker
SLICHTER, LOUIS BYRNE
SMITH, Edward Staples C.
SMITH, Laurence Lowe
SNELGROVE, Alfred K.
SOSMAN, ROBERT BROWNING
SPIEKER, EDMUND MAUTE
STOCK, CHESTER
STUCKEY, Jasper L.
TESTER, Allen C.
THOM, WILLIAM TAYLOR, Jr.
THORP, James
TOLMAN, Carl
TROWBRIDGE, Arthur C.
TROXELL, Edward Leffingwell
TWENHOFEL, WILLIAM HENRY

See pages 13 and 801 for additional knowers; page 851 for information sources.

VANDERWILT, John W.
VAN TUYL, Francis Maurice
VER STEEG, Kral
WASHBURN, A(lbert) L.
WATERS, JAMES (ALTON)
WEATHERBY, BENJAMIN B.
WEAVER, Paul
WEGEMANN, Carroll Harvey
WELLER, J(AMES) MARVIN
WELLES, Samuel Paul
WELLS, John W(est)
WILLARD, Bradford
WILLIAMS, HOWEL
WILLIAMS, J(ames) Stewart
WILLIAMS, MERTON Y.
WILSON, C(harles) W., Jr.
WILSON, PHILIP DANFORTH
WOODRING, Wendell P.
WOODWARD, Herbert P.
WORCESTER, P(hilip) G.
WRATHER, WILLIAM EMBRY

Physics

ABELSON, Philip Hauge
ADAMS, Leason Heberling
ADAMS, Norman Ilsley, Jr.
ADEL, Arthur
AEBERSOLD, Paul C(larence)
ALBRIGHT, Penrose S(trong)
ALLIS, William Phelps
ALLISON, FRED
ALLISON, Samuel King
ALVAREZ, Luis W.
ANDERSON, CARL DAVID
ANSLOW, Gladys Amelia
BABCOCK, HAROLD DELOS
BACHER, ROBERT FOX
BAINBRIDGE, KENNETH T.
BAKER, James Gilbert
BARR, E(rnest) Scott
BATES, Frederick (John)
BAUM, Werner A.
BAZZONI, Charles Blizard
BEAMS, JESSE WAKEFIELD
BEARDEN, Joyce Alvin
BEDELL, Frederick
BERKNER, Lloyd V(iel)
BETH, Richard Alexander
BETHE, HANS ALBRECHT
BIRGE, Raymond Thayer
BITTER, Francis
BJERKNES, J(acob) A(all) B.
BLESS, A(rthur) A(aron)
BLOCH, FELIX
BLODGETT, KATHARINE BURR
BONER, C(harles) P(aul)
BOORSE, Henry A.
BORST, Lyle Benjamin
BOWE , IRA SPRAGUE
BOWN, Ralph
BOZORTH, Richard M.
BRADBURY, Norris Edwin
BREIT, Gregory
BRIDGMAN, PERCY WILLIAMS
BRIGGS, LYMAN JAMES
BRILLOUIN, LEON N(ICHOLAS)
BRODE, ROBERT B.
BROOKS, Charles Franklin
BROWN, Frederick L(yons)
BUCHTA, J. William
BYERS, Horace Robert
CARDWELL, A(lvin) B(oyd)
CHAFFEE, EMORY LEON
CHAMBERLAIN, Katherine M.
CHANCE, BRITTON
CHANDRASEKHAR, S.
CHURCH, James Edward
CINNAMON, Carl Arthur
COCKADAY, Laurence M.
COLE, Kenneth S(tewart)
COLLINS, George B(riggs)
COLWELL, Robert Cameron
COMPTON, ARTHUR HOLLY
COMPTON, KARL TAYLOR
COMSTOCK, DANIEL FROST
CONDON, EDWARD U.
COOLIDGE, WILLIAM DAVID
COPELAND, Paul L(avern)
CORK, James M.
CORNELL, Samuel Douglas
COX, Richard T(hrelkeld)
CRANE, Horace Richard
CREUTZ, E(dward Chester)
DARROW, Karl Kelchner
DAVISSON, CLINTON JOSEPH
DEBYE, PETER JOSEPH W.
DEMPSTER, ARTHUR JEFFREY
DENNISON, DAVID MATHIAS
DRYDEN, Hugh Latimer

DuBRIDGE, LEE A(LVIN)
DUNNING, John Ray
DUSHMAN, Saul
ECKHARDT, ENGELHARDT A.
EDWARDS, Ray Lee
EINSTEIN, ALBERT
EVANS, Robley Dunglison
EWALD, Paul P.
EWELL, ARTHUR WOOLSEY
FAILLA, Gioacchino
FARNSWORTH, Harrison E.
FERMI, ENRICO
FIELD, Crosby
FIRESTONE, F. A.
FISHER, RUSSELL A(RDEN)
FISK, James Brown
FLEMING, JOHN ADAM
FLETCHER, Harvey
FOOTE, Paul D(arwin)
FORSYTHE, WILLIAM ELMER
FOWLER, WILLIAM ALFRED
FOX, Gerald Willis
FRANCK, James
FRYE, Royal Merrill
GAMOW, George
GARDNER, Irvine C(lifton)
GAST, Paul F(rederick)
GERMER, LESTER HALBERT
GILBERT, Norman Everett
GINGRICH, Newell S(hiffer)
GISH, Olivier Holmes
GODLOVE, ISAAC HAHN
GOUDSMIT, Samuel Abraham
GRONDAHL, LARS OLAI
GUNN, ROSS
HAFSTAD, Lawrence R.
HAM, Lloyd B(linn)
HARNWELL, Gaylord P.
HARRISON, GEORGE R.
HAWORTH, LELAND JOHN
HERB, Raymond George
HERTEL, Kenneth LaDoyt
HERZBERG, Gerhard
HESS, VICTOR FRANCIS
HEWLETT, Clarence Wilson
HIGINBOTHAM, William A.
HILL, Albert Gordon
HILLIER, James
HIRSCHFELDER, Joseph O.
HOUGHTON, H(enry) G.
HOYT, FRANK C(LARK)
HUBBARD, John Charles
HUDSON, George E(lbert)
HUGHES, Arthur Llewelyn
HULBURT, Edward Olson
HULL, ALBERT WALLACE
HUMPHREYS, Richard F.
HUNT, Frederick Vinton
HUTCHISSON, ELMER
HUXFORD, WALTER SCOTT
JAFFE, George (Cecil)
JAMES, Hubert M(axwell)
JONES, Loyd Ancile
JUDD, Deane Brewster
KAPLAN, Joseph
KARRER, Sebastian
KENNARD, Earle Hesse
KERST, DONALD WILLIAM
KEISS, Carl Clarence
KINGSLAKE, RUDOLPH
KIRKPATRICK, Harry Allister
KLOPSTEG, PAUL ERNEST
KORFF, Serge Alexander
KOVARIK, Alois Francis
LAMB, Willis E(ugene), Jr.
LAND, EDWIN HERBERT
LAURITSEN, CHARLES C.
LAWRENCE, ERNEST O.
LEEDY, Haldon A.
LEMON, HARVEY B.
LENZEN, Victor F.
LIDDEL, Urner
LILLIE, Howard Russell
LINDSAY, Robert Bruce
LITTLETON, J(ESSE) T(ALBOT)
LIVINGSTON, Milton Stanley
LOEB, LEONARD B(ENEDICT)
LOOMIS, ALFRED LEE
LOOMIS, FRANCIS WHEELER
LOUGHRIDGE, Donald Holt
LOWRY, W(elles) Norwood
LYMAN, THEODORE
MARGENAU, HENRY
MARSHAK, Robert E(ugene)
MASON, MAX
McKEEHAN, Louis Williams
McMILLAN, Edwin Mattison
MEES, CHARLES EDWARD K.
MILLIKAN, ROBERT ANDREWS

MIMNO, Harry Rowe
MITCHELL, Alan Charles G.
MOHLER, Nora M(ay)
MORSE, Philip McCord
MUCKENHOUPT, Carl F.
MYERS, Frank E(vans)
NEHER, H(enry) Victor
NETTLETON, L(EWIS) L(OMAX)
NIELSEN, HAROLD HERBORN
NIER, Alfred O(tto) C(arl)
NOTTINGHAM, Wayne B.
OBERHOLTZER, William E., Jr.
O'BRIEN, BRIAN
OLDENBERG, Otto
ONSAGER, Lars
OPPENHEIMER, J. ROBERT
OVERBECK, Clarence J(acob)
PAGE, LEIGH
PARDUE, Louis A(rthur)
PARKER, Allan
PARRATT, Lyman George
PATTERSON, A(rthur) L(indo)
PAULI, WOLFGANG
PEGRAM, GEORGE BRAXTON
PIERCE, GEORGE W.
PLYLER, Earle Keith
PURCELL, EDWARD MILLS
RABI, ISIDOR ISAAC
RAMSEY, Norman
REICHELDERFER, F(rancis) W.
RIDENOUR, LOUIS N(ICOT), Jr.
ROOD, Paul
ROSENBERG, Paul
ROSSI, BRUNO
ROTHROCK, Addison M(ay)
RUARK, Arthur Edward
SACK, Henri S(amuel)
SCHEIN, Marcel
SCHILLING, Harold Kistler
SCHRIEVER, William
SEABORG, GLENN THEODORE
SEITZ, FREDERICK
SHEARD, Charles
SIEGERT, Arnold J(ohn) F.
SILSBEE, Francis B(riggs)
SKINNER, Eugene William
SLATER, JOHN CLARKE
SMITH, CYRIL STANLEY
SMYTH, HENRY DeWOLF
SPEAKMAN, EDWIN AARON
SPENGLER, Kenneth Clifford
STEINBERG, John C.
STEPHENSON, S(eymour) T.
STERN, OTTO
STEWART, George Walter
STRANATHAN, J(ames) D.
STRATTON, Julius Adams
STRONG, JOHN (DONOVAN)
SUITS, C(HANUCEY) GUY
SUTHERLAND, Gordon B. B.
SWANN, WILLIAM FRANCIS G.
SWIGART, J(ohn) Irvin
SZILARD, LEO
TATE, JOHN TORRENCE
TELLER, EDWARD
THOMAS, Llewellyn Hilleth
TSIEN, HSUE-SHEN
TURNER, LOUIS A.
TUVE, MERLE ANTHONY
UHLENBECK, GEORGE EUGENE
URBACH, Franz
VALASEK, Joseph
VAN de GRAFF, ROBERT J.
VAN DYKE, Karl Skillman
VAN VLECK, JOHN H.
VARNEY, Robert Nathan
VOLLRATH, Richard Ernest
WAHLIN, H(UGO) B(ERNARD)
WALDMAN, Bernard
WATSON, Earnest Charles
WATSON, W(illiam) W(eldon)
WEBSTER, David Locke
WEISSKOPF, VICTOR F.
WENNER, FRANK
WENTZEL, Gregor
WHEELER, John Archibald
WHITAKER, MARTIN D.
WIGNER, Eugene Paul
WILSON, Robert Rathburn
WOLFE, Hugh Campbell
WOLFF, Irving
WORKMAN, Everly John
WRIGHT, R(ussell) B(erkeley)
WULF, OLIVER R(EYNOLDS)
YUKAWA, HIDEKI
ZACHARIAS, JERROLD R.
ZACHARIASEN, (Fredrik) W.
ZEMANSKY, Mark W.
ZWICKY, FRITZ

SOCIAL SCIENCES
Anthropology and Ethnology

BEALS, RALPH LEON
BENNETT, Wendell C(lark)
CAMPA, Arthur Leon
COLE, Fay-Cooper
COLLIER, DONALD
COLLINS, Henry B(ascom), Jr.
COON, Carleton Stevens
CRESSMAN, Luther Sheeleigh
DAVIS, Hassoldt
DOUGLAS, Frederic H.
EGGAN, FRED R(USSELL)
EISELEY, Loren C(orey)
FENTON, William N(elson)
FIELD, HENRY
GIFFORD, Edward Winslow
GILLIN, John (Philip)
GOLDFRANK, Esther S.
GUTHE, Carl Eugen
HALLOWELL, A(LFRED) I.
HERSKOVITS, MELVILLE JEAN
HODGE, Frederick Webb
HOEBEL, E(dward) Adamson
HOIJER, Harry
HOOTON, EARNEST ALBERT
JENKS, Albert Ernest
KEESING, Felix Maxwell
KIMBALL, Solon T(oothaker)
KLUCKHOHN, CLYDE KAY M.
KROEBER, ALFRED L.
KROGMAN, W(ILTON) M.
La FARGE Oliver
LASKER, Gabriel (Ward)
LINTON, RALPH
LOTHROP, Samuel Kirkland
LOWIE, ROBERT HARRY
MARTIN, PAUL SIDNEY
MEAD, MARGARET
MONTAGU, Montague F. A.
MURDOCK, GEORGE PETER
NEWELL, William B.
NEWMAN, Marshall T.
OSGOOD, Cornelius
PELTIER, George Leo
PIERRE, William Henry
POHLMAN, George G.
POND, George Augustus
REDFIELD, ROBERT
REICHARD, Gladys Amanda
SHAPIRO, Harry L(ional)
SHARP, LAURISTON
SPECK, FRANK GOULDSMITH
SPIER, LESLIE
SPINDEN, HERBERT JOSEPH
SPOEHR, Alexander
STOUT, David B(ond)
STEWARD, JULIAN H.
STEWART, Thomas Dale
STIRLING, MATTHEW W.
STRONG, WILLIAM DUNCAN
TAX, SOL
TOZZER, ALFRED MARSTON
VAN WATERS, Miriam
VOEGELIN, C(harles) F.
VOEGELIN, Erminie B. W.
VON HAGEN, Victor W.
WHITE, Leslie Alvin
WAUCHOPE, Robert
WHITE, Leslie Alvin

Archaeology
(see also Fine Arts
and History)

ALBRIGHT, WILLIAM FOXWELL
BENNETT, Wendell C(lark)
BLEGEN, CARL WILLIAM
BREW, J(OHN) O(TIS)
BRONEER, Oscar Theodore
BULL, Ludlow (Seguine)
CARPENTER, RHYS
COLTON, Harold Sellers
CONANT, Kenneth John
CRESSMAN, Luther Sheeleigh
de PROROK, Byron Khun
DINSMOOR, WILLIAM BELL
DOWNEY, GLANVILLE
DUELL, Prentice
GLUECK, Nelson
GRIFFIN, James Bennett
GUTHE, Carl Eugen
HARLAND, James Penrose
HARRINTON, Mark Raymond
HAURY, Emil Walter

HENCKEN, Hugh O'Neill
HILL, BERT HODGE
HOPKINS, Clark
JAYNE, HORACE HOWARD F.
JOHNSON, Van L(oran)
JUDD, Neil Merton
KELSO, James Leon
KIDDER, ALFRED VINCENT
KRAELING, CARL H(ERMAN)
MERCER, Samuel Alfred B.
MORGAN, Charles Hill
MOSELEY, John Ohleyer
MYLONAS, George E.
PARKER, ARTHUR CASWELL
PRIEST, Alan Reed
RICHTER, GISELA MARIE A.
ROBERTS, Frank Harold H.
ROBINSON, David Moore
SCHMIDT, ERICH FRIEDRICH
SEELE, Keith C(edric)
SETZLER, Frank Maryl
SWIFT, Emerson H(owland)
TANZER, Helen H.
THOMPSON, HOMER A.
THOMPSON, J. ERIC S.
WAAGE, Frederick Oswin
WARNER, LANGDON
WEDEL, WALDO R(UDOLPH)
WEITZMANN, Kurt
WILLOUGHBY, Harry Rideout

Economics

ADAMS, Quincy
ALDERSON, WROE
ANDERSON, Dewey
ANDERSON, Montgomery D.
ANGELL, James Waterhouse
APP, Frank
ATKINS, Paul Moody
ATKINS, WILLARD EARL
AYRES, Clarence Edwin
BABSON, ROGER WARD
BACH, George Leland
BAKER, George Pierce
BAKKE, E. WIGHT
BALCH, EMILY GREENE
BARKIN, Solomon
BASCH, Antonin
BASSIE, V. Lewis
BAUDER, Russell S(tickney)
BAUER, John
BECKHART, Benjamin Haggott
BELL, JAMES WASHINGTON
BELL, John Fred
BENEDICT, Murray Reed
BENNETT, Merrill Kelley
BERGSON, Abram
BERNHARDT, Joshua
BERRIDGE, William Arthur
BIGHAM, Truman C.
BISCOE, Alvin B(locksom)
BLACK, John Donald
BLAISDELL, Thomas C., Jr.
BLANCHARD, Ralph Harrub
BLOCH, Henry Simon
BLODGETT, Ralph Hamilton
BLOUGH, Roy
BOHLMAN, Herbert William
BOND, Maurice Chester
BOULDING, Kenneth Ewart
BOWEN, HOWARD R.
BOYD, James
BRADFORD, Ernest Smith
BRADFORD, Frederick Alden
BRATT, Elmer Clark
BRAUN, Kurt
BRIEFS, Goetz A(ntony)
BRISSENDEN, Paul Frederick
BROSSARD, Edgar Bernard
BROWN, Cecil Kenneth
BROWN, Courtney C.
BROWN, Douglass Vincent
BROWN, Elmer Jay
BROWN, Harry Gunnison
BROWN, Horace B., Jr.
BROWN, J(ames) Douglas
BROWN, Leo C(yril)
BROWN, Lyndon Osmond
BROZEN, Yale
BRYAN, Leslie A(ulls)
BUCHANAN, Norman Sharpe
BUNCE, Arthur C.
BURGESS, Robert Wilbur
BURNS, Arthur Edward
BURNS, Arthur F.
BURNS, Arthur Robert
BUTZ, Earl Lauer
BYE, Raymond Taylor
CALKINS, Robert De Blois

CAMPBELL, Robert Argyll
CARSON, WILLIAM JOSEPH
CASE, Harold Clayton M.
CASSADY, RALPH, Jr.
CASSELS, John MacIntyre
CAVERT, William Lane
CHALMERS, Henry
CHAMBERLIN, Edward H.
CLARK, Evans
CLARK, JOHN DAVIDSON
CLARK, JOHN MAURICE
CONDLIFFE, John B.
CONVERSE, Paul D.
COONS, Arthur Gardiner
COPELAND, Morris Albert
COPPOCK, Joseph David
CORSE, Carl Donovan
COULTER, JOHN LEE
COVER, John Higson
COWAN, DONALD R(OSS) G.
COWDEN, Dudley Johnstone
COWLES, Alfred
COX, Alonzo Bettis
COX, GARFIELD V.
CROSS, Ira Brown
CROXTON, Frederick E(mory)
CRUIKSHANK, Nelson Hale
CUMBERLAND, William W.
DAGGETT, Stuart
DANKERT, Clyde Edward
DAUGHERTY, Carroll Roop
DAVIS, John Cordon
DAVIS, JOSEPH STANCLIFFE
DAVIS, Ralph Currier
DEARING, Charles Lee
de HAAS, J. Anton
DEMPSEY, Bernard William
DENNISON, Jackson Belden
DEWHURST, J(AMES) F.
DIAMOND, Herbert Maynard
DODD, David Le Fevre
DORAU, Herbert Benjamin
DORFMAN, Ben David
DORFMAN, JOSEPH
DOUGALL, Herbert Edward
DOUGLAS, PAUL HOWARD
DUGGAN, Ivy W.
DURAND, E(DWARD) DANA
DYE, Alexander Vincent
EBERLING, ERNEST J.
ECCLES, Marriner Stoddard
ECKER-RACZ, L. Laszlo
EDMINSTER, LYNN RAMSAY
EDWARDS, Corwin D.
EITEMAN, Wilford J.
ELLIS, HOWARD SYLVESTER
ELLSWORTH, Paul T.
ENGLE, Nathanael Howard
ESTEY, James Arthur
EUTSLER, Roland Byerly
EVANS, George Heberton, Jr.
EVANS, John Walker
FARNSWORTH, Helen E. C.
FELLNER, William John
FILLEY, Horace Clyde
FISHER, Ernest McKinley
FOSTER, Major Bronson
FOX, Bertrand
FRIEDMAN, Milton
FROMAN, Lewis A.
GAMBLE, Philip Lyle
GARIS, Roy Lawrence
GATES, James E(dward)
GEE, Wilson
GEMMILL, Paul Fleming
GIDEONSE, HARRY DAVID
GIDEONSE, Max
GILE, BUEFORD M(ONROE)
GIVENS, Meredith Bruner
GOLDENWEISER, EMANUEL A.
GOODBAR, Joseph Ernest
GOODRICH, Carter
GRAY, Robert D(avis)
GOFF, John H(edges)
GORDON, Leland James
GRADY, Eleanor Hunsdon
GRAS, Norman Scott Brien
GRETHER, Ewald T.
GRIFFITH, Sanford
GROSECLOSE, Elgin
GUILD, Lawrence Ridge
HAAKE, Alfred Paul
HAAS, George Casper
HABERLER, GOTTFRIED
HAIG, Robert Murray
HALEY, Bernard Francis
HAMILTON, Earl Jefferson
HAMILTON, Roger Stanton
HAND, George Henry

HANEY, LEWIS HENRY
HANSEN, ALVIN HARVEY
HARDIN, Clifford M(orris)
HARPER, Floyd Arthur
HARRIS, Abram Lincoln
HARRIS, Seymour Edwin
HARWOOD, Edward Crowby
HASEK, Carl William
HEDGEE, J(oseph) Edward
HEER, Clarence
HEFLEBOWER, Richard Brooks
HENDERSON, LEON
HEXNER, Ervin Paul
HILL, Forrest Frank
HINRICHS, Albert Ford
HITCH, Thomas Kemper
HOMAN, Paul Thomas
HOOVER, Calvin Bryce
HOPKINS, William Stephen
HOWARD, Stanley Edwin
HORNE, M(cDonald) K., Jr.
HOWE, Harold
HUGHES, Harold
HUSE, Charles Phillips
HYDE, D(uncan) Clark
ISE, John
JACOBY, Neil Herman
JAMES, F(RANK) CYRIL
JAMES, Herman Brooks
JAMISON, Charles Laselle
JENNINGS, Walter Wilson
JESNESS, OSCAR BERNARD
JOHNSON, Alvin Saunders
JOHNSON, Arno Hallock
JOHNSON, Edgar Augustus J.
JOHNSON, G(ove) G., Jr.
JOHNSON, Sherman E.
JOME, Hiram L.
JONES, Eliot
JORDAN, Garret Lowell
JORDAN, Virgil (Dustin)
KALLET, Arthur
KAYDEN, Eugene Mark
KEEZER, Dexter Merriam
KEMMERER, D(onald) L.
KERR, Clark
KEYSERLING, Mary Dublin
KIESSLING, Oscar Edward
KILLINGSWORTH, Charles C.
KINCAID, Elbert Alvis
KINDLEBERGER, Charles P., II
KING, Eldon Paul
KING, Harold Joseph
KNIGHT, Bruce Winton
KNIGHT, FRANK HYNEMAN
KOZELKA, Richard L.
KREPS, Theodore John
KRUEGER, Maynard Clare
KUZNETS, SIMON SMITH
LAIDLER, Harry Wellington
LAMB, George A.
LANG, Aldon Socrates
LANGUM, JOHN KENNETH
LELAND, SIMEON ELBRIDGE
LENGYEL, Emil
LEONTIEF, Wassily
LESTER, Richard A.
LEWIS, Cleona
LINCOLN, Edmond E(arl)
LINDOW, (John) Wesley
LININGER, Frederick Fouse
LONG, Clarence D., Jr.
LORWIN, LEWIS L.
LOWE, Boutelle Ellsworth
LUBIN, ISADOR
LUTHRINGER, George Francis
LYON, Leverett Samuel
MACHLUP, Fritz
MACY, C(harles) Ward
MALENBAUM, Wilfred
MARGET, Arthur William
MARSCHAK, Jacob
MAUDLIN, C(ecil) V(earl)
MAVERICK, Lewis Adams
MAYER, Joseph
McCABE, David Aloysius
McCRACKEN, Harlan Linneus
McDIARMID, Orville John
McPHERSON, William Heston
METZLER, Lloyd A.
MILLER, Paul E(mmert)
MILLS, FREDERICK CECIL
MOFFAT, James E(rnest)

MOREHOUSE, Edward Ward
MORGAN, Charles Stillman
MORGENSTERN, OSKAR
MORTON, Walter Albert
MOULTON, HAROLD GLENN

MUELLER, Frederick W., Jr.
MUNTZ, Earl Edward
MYERS, William Irving
NADLER, Marcus
NATHAN, Robert Roy
NEARING, Scott
NEISSER, Hans Philip
NOURSE, EDWIN GRISWOLD
NYSTROM, Paul Henry
OTHMER, Donald Frederick
PANCOAST, Elinor
PASVOLSKY, LEO
PAXSON, Alfred Moore
PEGRUM, Dudley Frank
PERLMAN, Selig
PHELPS, Clyde William
PHILLIPS, William Taylor
PRATHER, Charles Lee
REED, Harold Lyle
REED, Vergil Daniel
RENNE, Roland Roger
RICE, Lloyd Preston
RICHARDS, John Reese
RIGGLEMAN, John Randolph
ROBBINS, Sidney M(artin)
ROBINSON, Leland Rex
ROOS, Charles Frederick
RUML, BEARDSLEY
SACHS, ALEXANDER
SAMUELSON, Paul Anthony
SANDERS, J(esse) T(homas)
SARGENT, NOEL CHARRETT
SCHULTZ, THEODORE WILLIAM
SCHWENNING, Gustav T.
SEIBERT, Joseph Charles
SHARFMAN, ISAIAH LEO
SHAW, Edward S(tone)
SHEA, George Edward, Jr.
SHEPHERD, Geoffrey Seddon
SHULENBERGER, C(larence) B.
SIEFKIN, C(harles) Gordon
SKEELS, Dorr
SLICHTER, SUMNER HUBER
SMITHIES, ARTHUR
SOLLENBERGER, Isaac Jacob
SORRELL, Lewis Carlyle
SPENGLER, Edwin H(arold)
SPRIEGEL, William Robert
STAUDINGER, HANS
STEWART, WALTER W.
STIGLER, George Joseph
STOCKING, Collis
STUDENSKI, Paul
SURFACE, Frank Macy
SUTTON, Glenn W(allace)
TAYLOR, George William
TAYLOR, Horace
TAYLOR, Wayne Chatfield
TAYLOR, W(illiam) Bayard
THOMAS, Woodlief
THOMPSON, Charles M.
THOMPSON, George Jarvis
THORP, Willard Long
TOUSLEY, Rayburn Dean
TRACY, Margaret Elliott
TUCKER, Robert Henry
TUCKER, Rufus Stickney
TUGWELL, REXFORD GUY
TURNER, ROBERT CLEMENS
UKERS, Wiliam Harrison
UNTEREINER, Ray Edward
UPGREN, Arthur (Reinhold)
VAN TASSEL, Alfred James
VAN ZANDT, John Parker
VINER, JACOB
von BECKERATH, Herbert
WALKER, Q. Forrest
WALLACE, Donald H.
WARNE, Colston Estey
WATKINS, Ralph James
WATSON, Jesse Paul
WELFLING, Weldon W.
WESTERFIELD, Ray Bert
WHITE, Henry Ford
WHITE, Wilford Lenfestey
WICKIZER, Vernon Dale
WILLCOX, WALTER FRANCIS
WILLIAMS, JOHN HENRY
WILLITS, Joseph Henry
WILLOUGHBY, Alfred
WITTE, Edwin Emil
WALMAN, LEO
WRIGHT, David McCord
WRIGHT, Ivan
WYNGARDEN, Herman Jacob
YNTEMA, THEODORE OTTO
YODER, Dale
YOUNG, Arthur Nichols
YOUNG, John Parke

YOUNG, Owen D.
ZIEGLER, Edwin Allen

Education

ADAMS, ARTHUR STANTON
ADE, Lester Kelly
AIKIN, Wilford Merton
ALEXANDER, (RICHARD) T.
ALLEN, Charles Laurel
ALLEN, HAROLD BOUGHTON
ALLEN, John S(tuart)
ALMACK, John C(onrad)
ANDERSON, HOMER WILLARD
ANDERSON, Howard R.
ANDERSON, Walter A.
ARMSTRONG, Wesley Earl
ARNOLD, Samuel Tomlinson
AVENT, Joseph Emory
AYDELOTTE, FRANK
AYER, FRED CARLETON
AYERS, Archie Raymond
BACH, Richard F(ranz)
BACON, FRANCIS LEONARD
BAKER, EDNA DEAN
BARR, Arvil S.
BARTKY, Adolph John
BAXTER, BERNICE
BAXTER, JAMES PHINNEY, III
BEATTY, WILLARD WALCOTT
BEESON, Malcolm Alfred
BENNE, KENNETH DEAN
BETHEL, Lawrence L.
BETHUNE, MARY McLEOD
BEWKES, Eugene Garrett
BIGELOW, KARL WORTH
BILLETT, Roy Oren
BIRD, Remsen du Bois
BLANDING, Sarah Gibson
BLAUCH, Lloyd E.
BLUME, CLARENCE EDWIN
BLUMENFIELD, Samuel M.
BOATMAN, Conway
BOGUE, JESSE PARKER
BOREN, James Basil
BOSSING, Nelson Louis
BOWLES, FRANK HAMILTON
BOWMAN, GEORGE A(RVENE)
BOWMAN, JOHN GOBBERT
BOWMAN, LEONARD LEON
BRAMELD, Theodore
BRAMMELL, P. Roy
BRANSCOMB, Harvie
BRECHBILL, Henry H(arper) R.
BREIDENSTINE, A(aron) G.
BRIND, Charles Albert, Jr.
BRITTAIN, MARION LUTHER
BROOKS, Earl
BROWNELL, SAMUEL MILLER
BROWNLEE, Frederick Leslie
BRUBACHER, John Seiler
BRUMBAUGH, Aaron John
BUCKINGHAM, Burdette Ross
BURKHARD, Samuel
BURNETT, R. Will
BURNS, Ralph Arthur
BURNS, S(amuel) T(hompson)
BURR, Samuel Engle, Jr.
BURTON, William Henry
BUSWELL, Guy Thomas
BUTTERWECK, Joseph Seibert
BUTTERWORTH, Julian E.
BUTTS, R. Freeman
CADE, JOHN BROTHER
CALIVER, Ambrose
CANTOR, Nathaniel
CAPEN, Samuel Paul
CARMICHAEL, Oliver C.
CARR, WILLIAM GEORGE
CARTWRIGHT, Morse Adams
CASE, EVERETT (NEEDHAM)
CASWELL, HOLLIS L.
CENTER, Stella Stewart
CHALMERS, GORDON KEITH
CHAMBERLAIN, Leo Martin
CHAMBERS, Merritt Medison
CHASE, Harry Woodburn
CHAVE, Ernest J(ohn)
CHILDS, John Lawrence
CLARK, HAROLD FLORIAN
CLARK, JOHN ROSCOE
CLARK, Willis Winfield
CLEMENT, RUFUS EARLY
CLEVENGER, John C(owgill)
COBB, STANWOOD
COCKING, Walter Dewey
COMBS, Morgan LaFayette
COMFORT, WILLIAM WISTAR
COMPTON, Wilson M.

COMSTOCK, ADA LOUISE
CONANT, JAMES BRYANT
CONFREY, (Joseph) Burton
CONLEY, William H.
CONRAD, Herbert S(pencer)
COOK, Katherine Margaret
(Mrs. Charles K.)
COOK, Robert C(ecil)
COOK, Walter W(ellman)
COOKE, Dennis Hargrove
COREY, Stephen Maxwell
CORWIN, MARGARET T.
COTTRELL, Donald Peery
COUNTS, GEORGE SYLVESTER
COWLEY, William Harold
COWLING, DONALD J.
COX, James Franklin
CRAIG, Gerald Spellman
CRAWFORD, Claude C.
CROWLEY, FRANCIS MICHAEL
CUNNINGHAM, Bess Virginia
CUNNINGHAM, William F.
CYR, Frank W.
DANIEL, J. McTyeire
DANIEL, ROBERT PRENTISS
DAVIS, Harvey Henry
DAVIS, Ira Cleveland
DAVIS, John Warren
DAVIS, LAWRENCE ARNETTE
DAWSON, Howard A.
De BOER, John J.
DECKER, Clarence Raymond
DENT, ALBERT WALTER
DIEMAR, GEORGE WILLIS
DIMMITT, Luther Mason
DIVINE, Thomas F(rancis)
DORE, Vincent Cyril
DOUGLASS, Harl Roy
DRAKE, Joseph Fanning
DRAKE, William Earle
DUNHAM, Franklin
DURRELL, Donald DeWitt
DVORAK, August
EAKIN, Frank
EAKIN, Mildred Olivia Moody
(Mrs. Frank)
EATON, Merrill T(homas)
EBY, Frederick
EDMONSON, JAMES BARTLETT
EDWARDS, Newton
EELLS, Walter Crosby
EISENHOWER, MILTON S.
ELICKER, Paul Edgar
ELLIOTT, EDWARD CHARLES
ELSBREE, Willard Slingerland
ELSTAD, Leonard M.
EMERSON, Lynn Arthur
ENGELHARDT, Nickolaus L.
ESCH, I. Lynd
ESSERT, Paul Leslie
EURICH, Alvin Christian
EVENDEN, Edward Samuel
EYSTER, Elvin S.
FACKENTHAL, FRANK DIEHL
FARRELL, GABRIEL
FAUST, CLARENCE HENRY
FIELDS, Harold
FINE, BENJAMIN
FITZGERALD, Ruth
FITZPATRICK, Frederick L.
FLATH, Earl Hugo
FLYNN, John Aloysius
FORKNER, Hamden Landon
FOWLER, Burton Philander
FOWLKES, JOHN GUY
FOX, James Harold
FRAMPTON, Merle Elbert
FRANZEN, Carl G(ustave) F.
FRENCH, WILL
FREUND, CLEMENT JOSEPH
FROST, Norman
FUESS, Claude Moore
FULD, Leonhard Felix
FUSFELD, Irving Sidney
GAEBELEIN, Frank Ely
GAGE, HARRY MOREHOUSE
GAINES, FRANCIS PENDLETON
GALLARDO, Jose Miguel
GAMORAN, Emanuel
GANDERS, Harry Stanley
GATES, Arthur Irving
GAUMNITZ, Walter Herbert
GIESECKE, G(ustav) Ernst
GILDERSLEEVE, Virginia C.
GILMOUR, George Peel
GIVENS, WILLARD EARL
GODDARD, ROY WILLIAMS
GOEBEL, EDMUND JOSEPH
GOEBEL, LOUIS WILLIAM

BONDY, ROBERT EARL
BOOKMAN, CLARENCE M.
BOSSARD, James Herbert S.
BOWERS, Raymond V(ictor)
BOWMAN, Le Roy Edward
BRIGHAM, Henry Randolph
BRIL, Jacques L.
BROOKS, Lee M(arshall)
BRUNNER, EDMUND de S.
BRUNO, Frank J(ohn)
BURGESS, ERNEST WATSON
BURROWS, Charles N(icholl)
CARROLL, Mollie Ray
CHAPIN, F(RANCIS) STUART
CHOUKAS, Michael Eugene
CLEMENT, Rufus Early
CLOPPER, Edward Nicholas
COLE, William Earle
COMEY, ARTHUR COLEMAN
COTTRELL, Leonard S., Jr.
COYLE, Grace L.
CURTIS, Henry Stoddard
CUTLER, James Elbert
DAVIS, Maurice R(ea)
DAVIES, STANLEY POWELL
DAVIS, Jerome
DEDRICK, CALVERT LAMPERT
DICKERSON, Roy Ernest
DODD, STUART CARTER
DUBLIN, Louis Israel
DUNN, LOULA FRIEND
DUVALL, Evelyn Millis
ELDRIDGE, Seba
ELIOT, CHARLES WILLIAM II
ELMER, Manuel Conrad
FAIRCHILD, HENRY PRATT
FARIS, Ellsworth
FISHER, Thomas Russell
FITZGERALD, George S.
FRAZIER, Edward Franklin
FREY, FRED CHARLES
FULLER, Raymond Garfield
GEDDES, Jos(eph) A(arch)
GEHLKE, Charles Elmer
GLUECK, Sheldon
GRANGER, LESTER B.
GREEN, Howard Whipple
GROVES, GLADYS HOAGLAND
HAMILTON, Charles Horace
HARRISON, Shelby Millard
HART, Hornell (Norris)
HAUSER, Philip Morris
HAWTHORN, Horace B(oles)
HAYES, Wayland J(ackson)
HEBERLE, Rudolf
HERTZLER, Joyce Oramel
HILLMAN, Arthur
HITT, Homer Lee
HOEHLER, FRED KENNETH
HOLBEN, Ralph Penrose
HOUSE, FLOYD NELSON
HUGHES, EVERETT C.
JENSEN, Howard Eikenberry
JOHNSON, Charles Spurgeon
JOHNSON, Guy Benton
JONES, Thomas Elsa
KENNEDY, Ruby Jo Reeves
KENNEDY, Tolbert Hall
KERCHER, Leonard Clayton
KOLB, John Harrison
KRAUS, Hertha
KUTAK, Robert I(ngersoll)
LAING, James Tamplin
LANDIS, Paul H.
LAZARSFELD, PAUL
LEIFFER, Murray Howard
LEWIS, Edward Shakespeare
LIKERT, RENSIS
LINDSTROM, David Edgar
LIVELY, Charles Elson
LOOMIS, Charles Price
LORIMER, Frank
LUNDBERG, GEORGE ANDREW
MacCORMIC K, Austin H.
MacIVER, ROBERT MORRISON
McCLENAHAN, BESSIE Averne
MERTON, ROBERT C.
MOORE, Coyle E.
MOWRER, Ernest Russell
MUMFORD, LEWIS
NEARING, SCOTT
NELSON, Lowry
NEWSTETTER, Wilber Irvin
NOTESTEIN, Frank W(allace)
ODUM, HOWARD W.
OGBURN, WILLIAM FIELDING
OPPERMAN, PAUL
OSBORN, Frederick
PANUNZIO, Constantine M.

PARSONS, TALCOTT
PENDELL, Elmer
PIERSON, Donald
POLSON, Robert Arnold
POPENOE, Paul
PUCKETT, Newbell Niles
QUEEN, Stuart Alfred
QUINN, JAMES ALFRED
RAPER, Arthur Franklin
REISS, Albert J., Jr.
RICE, Stuart Arthur
ROETHLISBERGER, Fritz Jules
ROSS, Frank Alexander
SCHMID, CALVIN FISHER
SCHULER, Edgar Albert
SEGOE, Ladislas
SELEKMAN, BENJAMIN M.
SELLIN, (Johan) Thorsten
SHARP, Edward Preston
SHIDELER, Ernest Hugh
SLETTO, Raymond Franklin
SMITH, (James) Mapheus
SOROKIN, PITIRIM A.
STEPHAN, A(nthony) Stephen
STERN, Leon Thomas
STOUFFER, SAMUEL ANDREW
SUCHMAN, Edward Allen
TAPPAN, Paul W(ilbur)
TAYLOR, Maurice
TEETERS, Negley Kinb
THOMAS, DOROTHY SWAINE
THOMPSON, WARREN S.
THRASHER, Frederick Milton
TRUESDELL, Leon Edgar
VANCE, RUPERT BAYLESS
VOLLMER, August
WAPLES, Douglas
WARNER, W. LLOYD
WHITE, R(euel) Clyde
WHYTE, William Foote
WILLCOX, WALTER FRANCIS
WILLIAMS, ROBIN M., Jr.
YOUNG, Donald Ramsey
YOUNG, KIMBALL
ZNANIECKI, FLORIAN WITOLD
ZORBAUGH, Harvey Warren

HUMANITIES

Fine Arts
(see also Archaeology)

ADAMS, Philip Rhys
ALDRICH, WILLIAM T(RUMAN)
ALLEN, Frank Leonard
ANDERSON, Lawrence B.
ANDREWS, Lavone D.
ARMS, John Taylor
ARNASON, H. Harvard
ARNAUD, Leopold
ASHTON, RAYMOND, J.
ATTERBURY, GROSVENOR
BACH, Richard F(ranz)
BACHOFER, Ludwig
BALLINGER, ROBERT IRVING
BANNISTER, Turpin Chambers
BARR, ALFRED HAMILTON, Jr.
BEGGS, Thomas Montague
BELLOWS, ROBERT PEABODY
BELLUSCHI, PIETRO
BENNETT, EDWARD HERBERT
BENNETT, Wells Ira
BIEBEL, Franklin Matthews
BIGGER, Frederick
BIRNBAUM, Martin
BOSWORTH, WELLES
BRAZER, Clarence Wilson
BREASTED, James H(enry), Jr.
BREINES, Simon
BREUER, MARCEL LAJOS
BROWN, ARCHIBALD M.
BURNHAM, DANIEL HUDSON
BURNHAM, HUBERT
BUTLER, CHARLES
CHAMBERS, Harold Coulson
CHENEY, SHELDON (WARREN)
CHERMAYEFF, Serge
CHRIST-JANER, ALBERT W.
CLAPP, FREDERICK MORTIMER
CLARKE, GILMORE DAVID
CLAS, ANGELO ROBERT
CONANT, Kenneth John
CONSTABLE, WILLIAM G.
COOK, WALTER WILLIAM S.
COWGILL, Clinton Harriman
CRANDALL, Norris Ingersoll

CREIGHTON, Thomas H(awk)
CROMER, VOIGT RHODES
CROSBY, SUMNER M.
DAVIS, Edward M(orris) III
DEAM, Arthur Francis
DENNISON, ETHAN ALLEN
de TOLNAY, CHARLES ERICH
DETWEILER, ALBERT HENRY
DEVREE, HOWARD
DeWALD, ERNEST THEODORE
DeWITT, Roscoe Plimpton
d'HARNONCOURT, Rene
DILLENBACK, Lemuel Cross
DOWLEY, F. H.
DOYLE, Price
Du PONT, Alfred Victor
EBERHARD, Robert Georges
EBERLEIN, HAROLD D.
EDGELL, George Harold
EDMUNDS, JAMES R., Jr.
EGBERT, Donald Drew
EGGERS, GEORGE WILLIAM
EGGERS, OTTO R.
EMBURY, AYMAR II
ENTERS, Angna
FABRI, Ralph
FAIRWEATHER, Clement W.
FALK, Sawyer
FARRAR, Benedict
FAULKNER, Ray N.
FERRISS, Hugh
FINLEY, David Edward
FRANKENSTEIN, Alfred
FREEDLEY, George
FROHMAN, PHILIP HUBERT
FROST, Frederick George
FULLER, Richard Eugene
GENAUER, Emily
GILL, Louis John
GITHENS, ALFRED MORTON
GOLDSMITH, Goldwin
GOODRICH, Lloyd
GOODWIN, PHILIP L.
GRAFLY, DOROTHY
GRAND, John L(ouis) R.
GREELEY, Mellen Clark
GREENLEY, HOWARD
GREENWAY, George Lauder
GRIFFIN, Worth Dickman
GROPIUS, WALTER ADOLF
GROSSI, Olindo
GRUNSFELD, ERNEST A., Jr.
HAGEN, OSKAR FRANK L.
HAMILTON, John Leonard
HAMLIN, Talbot Faulkner
HAMMOND, CHARLES H.
HARBESON, John Frederick
HARKNESS, Albert
HARMON, ARTHUR LOOMIS
HARRISON, WALLACE K.
HAYES, Bartlett Harding, Jr.
HEPBURN, Andrew Hopewell
HIGGINS, DANIEL PAUL
HILLS, George Burkhart
HITCHCOCK, Henry Russell
HOBART, LEWIS PARSONS
HOMSEY, Victorine
HOPKINS, HENRY POWELL
HOWE, GEORGE
HOWELLS, JOHN MEAD
HUBBARD, CORTLANDT V. D.
HUDNUT, Joseph
HUGHES, Talmage Coates
HUNTLEY, G(eorge) Haydn
HYDE, ARTHUR KNOX
JANSON, Horst W(oldemar)
JOHNSTON, James Ambler
JOHNSTONE, Burton Kenneth
KAHN, Louis I.
KEALLY, Francis
KEISER, George Camp
KELEMEN, Pal
KELLEY, H. ROY
KENNEDY, CLARENCE
KILHAM, Walter H., Jr.
KIMBALL, FISKE
KOCH, Richard
KOCHER, A. Lawrence
KOEHLER, WILHELM R. W.
KOHN, ROBERT DAVID
KUBLER, George Alexander
KUMP, ERNEST JOSEPH
LABATUT, JEAN
LARKIN, Oliver Waterman
LARSON, JENS FREDERICK
LARSON, Roy F(rank)
LAWRENCE, Marion
LEE, Rensselaer Wright
LESCAZE, WILLIAM

LEVI, JULIAN CLARENCE
LEWENTHAL, Reeves
LINDEBERG, HARRIE THOMAS
LITTLE, Sidney Wahl
LIVINGSTON, William Henry
LOMBARDO, JOSEF VINCENT
LONGMAN, LESTER DUNCAN
LUNDEN, SAMUEL EUGENE
MAGINNIS, CHARLES D.
MALDARELLI, Oronzio
MARCEAU, HENRI
MARX, SAMUEL ABRAHAM
McBRIDE, Henry
MEEKS, EVERETT VICTOR
MERRILL, John Ogden
MIDDELDORF, ULRICH A.
MIES, van der ROHE, LUDWIG
MORE, HERMAN
MOREY, CHARLES RUFUS
MORLEY, Grace McCann
MULLEN, Buell
MUMFORD, Lewis
MUNRO, Thomas
NARAMORE, Floyd A.
NEILD, Edward F., Sr.
NEUTRA, Richard Joseph
NEWCOMB, Rexford
NEWTON, Norman Thomas
NOTT, Stanley Charles
O'CONNOR, Robert Barnard
OENSLAGER, Donald Mitchell
ORR, DOUGLAS WILLIAM
OWINGS, NATHANIEL A.
PANOFSKY, ERWIN
PEASLEE, Horace Whittier
PEETS, ELBERT
PHILLIPS, DUNCAN
PHILLIPS, John Marshall
PICKENS, Buford L(indsay)
PICKERING, Ernest
PLAUT, James Sachs
POPE, Arthur Upham
POST, CHANDLER RATHFON
POWELL, Herbert James
PRIEST, Alan Reed
PURVES, EDMUND RANDOLPH
RATCLIFF, Walter Harris
RICE, Norman Lewis
RICH, DANIEL CATTON
RICH, Lorimer
RICHARDSON, Edgar Preston
RICHTER, G. M. A.
RINDGE, AGNES MILLICENT
ROBERTS, Laurance Page
ROBINSON, DAVID MOORE
ROLFE, Walter Thomas
ROOT, John Wellborn
RORIMER, JAMES J.
ROSENBERG, Jakob
RUSSELL, ERNEST JOHN
SACHS, PAUL JOSEPH
SCHENCK, Edgar Craig
SCHERMERHORN, Richard, Jr.
SCHMECKEBIER, Laurence E(li)
SHAVER, Charles William
SHAW, ALFRED PHILLIPS
SHEPLEY, Henry Richardson
SIPLE, Walter H(eick)
SKIDMORE, Louis
SLEEPER, Harold Reeve
SMAY, Joseph Edgar
SMITH, CARLTON SPRAGUE
SMITH, Howard Leland
SMITH, JAMES KELLUM
SMITH, J(ohn) B(ertie)
SMITH, Linus Burr
SMITH, Stanley Albert
SMITH, William Jones
SOULE, Winsor
SPINDEN, HERBERT JOSEPH
STANTON, A. GLENN
STECHOW, WOLFGANG
STEVENS, GORHAM PHILLIPS
STOUT, George Leslie
STUBBINS, Hugh A., Jr.
SUTTON, Charles R(avel)
SWEENEY, James Johnson
TAYLOR, FRANCIS HENRY
TAYLOR, Walter Andrews
TOOMBS, Henry Johnston
VALENTINER, William R.
VAN DERPOOL, James Grote
VAN PELT, John Vredenburgh
VOORHEES, STEPHEN FRANCIS
WALKER, Harry Leslie
WALKER, Hudson Dean
WALKER, JOHN
WALKER, RALPH THOMAS

WARD, Clarence
WASHBURN, GORDON B.
WEIGEL, Paul
WENLEY, ARCHIBALD GIBSON
WETHEY, Harold Edwin
WHEELOCK, Charles Delorma
WHITE, Lawrence Grant
WILLIAMS, EDGAR I(RVING)
WILLIAMS, Hermann W., Jr.
WILSON, WILLIAM
WIND, EDGAR
WINSLOW, Leon Loyal
WINSLOW, Ralph Edward
WOOD, Eric Fisher
WRIGHT, FRANK LLOYD
WURSTER, William Wilson
YOST, L(loyd) Morgan
ZANTZINGER, Clarence Clark
ZUCKER, Paul

Language and Literature (including Philology)

ABBOTT, Nabia
ADAMS, John Cranford
ADAMS, M(artin) Ray
AGARD, Walter Raymond
AIKEN, Conrad Potter
ALBRIGHT, WILLIAM FOXWELL
ALEXIS, Joseph Emmanuel A.
ALLEN, Don Cameron
ALLEN, Morse Shepard
ALLEN, Ned Bliss
ALTROCCHI, Rudolph
ALY, BOWER
ANDERSON, Charles Roberts
ANDERSON, Ruth L(eila)
ARENSBERG, Walter Conrad
ARLT, Gustave Otto
ARVIN, NEWTON
ATKINSON, (Justin) Brooks
ATKINSON, Geoffroy
BAERG, Gerhard
BALDERSTON, KATHARINE C.
BALDWIN, Thomas Whitfield
BARNES, Walter
BARNHART, Clarence L(ewis)
BARRET, LeRoy Carr
BAUGH, ALBERT CROLL
BAUM, PAULL FRANKLIN
BEACH, JOSEPH WARREN
BECK, Clyde
BECK, Richard
BELLINGER, ALFRED RAYMOND
BENSON, ADOLPH BURNETT
BENTLEY, Gerald Eades
BERGIN, Thomas Goddard
BERRIEN, WILLIAM
BETHEL, John P.
BLAIR, WALTER
BLAKE, Warren Everett
BLANKENAGEL, John Charles
BOND, Otto Ferdinand
BOND, Richmond Pugh
BONFANTE, Giuliano Ugo
BONNER, CAMPBELL
BONNER, Willard Hallam
BOWERS, Fredson Thayer
BRADLEY, (Edward) Sculley
BRANDON, EDGAR EWING
BRASOL, Boris
BREDVOLD, Louis Ignatius
BRENNECKE, Ernest
BRIGANCE, W(ILLIAM) N.
BROOKS, CLEANTH
BROOKS, VAN WYCK
BROWN, Charles Barrett
BROWN, Huntington
BROWN, JOHN MASON
BROWN, W(ILLIAM) NORMAN
BRYANT, Donald Cross
BRYANT, MARGARET M.
BUCK, CARL DARLING
BUFFUM, Douglas Larabee
BULL, Ludlow (Seguine)
BURKE, Kenneth (Duva)
CABEEN, David Clark
CADBURY, HENRY JOEL
CALVERLEY, Edwin Elliott
CAMPBELL, James Marshall
CAMPBELL, Lily Bess
CAMPBELL, OSCAR JAMES, Jr.
CANBY, HENRY SEIDEL
CAPLAN, Harry
CAPP, Glenn Richard
CARGILL, Oscar
CARTY, Donald Joseph

For selected subjects "keyed" to knowers, see Locator Index (page 871).

CAWLEY, Robert Ralston
CHALMERS, Gordon Keith
CHENEY, SHELDON (WARREN)
CHERNISS, HAROLD F.
CHEW, SAMUEL CLAGGETT
CHINARD, Gilbert
CLARK, CHARLES UPSON
CLARK, Donald Lemen
CLARK, Harry Hayden
CLEMENTS, Robert John
CLIFFORD, James L(owry)
CLOUGH, BENJAMIN CROCKER
COFFIN, Harrison C.
COFFIN, ROBERT PETER T.
COFFMAN, George Raleigh
CONNELLY, MARC
CONNELY, WILLARD
COOPER, LANE
CORDELL, RICHARD A(LBERT)
CORTRIGHT, RUPERT L.
COSENZA, Mario Emilio
COWAN, J. Milton
COWLEY, MALCOLM
COWPER, Frederick A. G.
CRAIG, Hardin
CRANE, Ronald Salmon
CRANE, William G(arrett)
CRUM, Earl LeV(erne)
CUNDIFF, Paul Arthur
CUNZ, Dieter
CUTHBERTSON, Stuart
DAICHES, David
DAMON, S(AMUEL) FOSTER
DARGAN, Henry McCune
DAVIDSON, DONALD (GRADY)
DAVIS, HALLIE FLANAGAN
DAVIS, HERBERT JOHN
DAVIS, Richard Beale
DAY, Cyrus Lawrence
DEAN, Leonard Fellows
DEFERRARI, Roy Joseph
DeLACY, Phillip Howard
DENNY, George Hutcheson
De ONIS, FEDERICO
DEUTSCH, Babette
  (Mrs. Avrahm Yarmolinsky)
De VANE, William Clyde
De VOTO, BERNARD A.
DEY, William Morton
DILLER, George E.
DOBIE, JAMES FRANK
DORJAHN, Alfred Paul
DOSTERT, LEON EMILE
DOWNS, John Ayman
DOYLE, Sister M. Timothea
DRUMMOND, Edward Joseph
DUCKWORTH, George Eckel
DUNLAP, James Eugene
DUNN, ESTHER CLOUDMAN
DUNN, Thomas F(ranklin)
DYKEMA, Karl W(ashburn)
EDGERTON, FRANKLIN
EDGERTON, William Franklin
EINARSSON, Stefan
ELIASON, Norman Ellsworth
ELIOT, Samuel Atkins, Jr.
ELISSEEFF, SERGE
FERGUSON, (John) DeLancey
FIFE, ROBERT HERNDON
FINE, John Van Antwerp
FITE, Alexander Green
FITTS, DUDLEY
FLETCHER, Harris Francis
FOERSTER, NORMAN
FORD, JEREMIAH DENIS M.
FOTOS, John Theodore
FREEDLEY, George
FREEMAN, STEPHEN ALBERT
FRENCH, J(oseph) Milton
FREUND, Max (Friedrich E.)
FRIERSON, William C.
FUCILLA, Joseph Guerin
FULCHER, Paul Milton
FUNK, Charles Earle
FUNKE, Erich (Alfred)
GALE, Esson McDowell
GAMER, Helena Margaret
GARWOOD, Irving
GASSNER, John Waldhorn
GEER, Russel Mortimer
GEHMAN, Henry Snyder
GELB, Ignace Jay
GEORGE, Albert Joseph
GERIG, John Lawrence
GILBERT, Allan H.
GILLET, Joseph Eugene
GINZBERG, LOUIS
GLEIS, Paul G(erhard)
GODOLPHIN, Francis R. B.

GOETZE, Albrecht
GOHDES, Clarence Louis F.
GOODRICH, Luther C.
GREEN, Otis Howard
GREENE, William Chase
GREENFIELD, Eric Viele
GREET, William Cabell
GREGORY, LESLIE ROSCOE
GULICK, Leeds
HAHN, E(mma) Adelaide
HAINES, Lewis Francis
HALL, Vernon, Jr.
HAM, Edward Billings
HANEY, John Louis
HANLEY. MILES L(AWRENCE)
HARBAGE, Alfred Bennett
HARRISON, G(eorge) B.
HARSH, Philip Whaley
HARTLEY, Lodwick C(harles)
HAVENS, GEORGE R.
HAXO, Henry Emile
HAYES, Joseph Claude
HAZEN, Allen Tracy
HEFFNER, Edward Hoch
HEFFNER, Hubert Crouse
HEMINGWAY, SAMUEL B.
HENCH, ATCHESON L.
HENDERSHOT, Vernon E.
HERZBERG, Max J(ohn)
HEWETT-THAYER, Harvey W.
HIGHET, GILBERT ARTHUR
HIGHFILL, Robert David
HILL, Archibald Anderson
HILLES, Frederick Whiley
HILTON, Ronald
HITTI, PHILIP K(HURI)
HOFACKER, Erich Paul
HOFRICHTER, Ruth J.
HOLBROOK, William Collar
HOLLOWAY, Emory
HOLMES, Urban Tigner
HOLT, Lucius Hudson
HOTSON, LESLIE
HOUGHTON, HERBERT P.
HOUSE, Roy Temple
HUBBELL, Harry Mortimer
HUBBELL, Jay Broadus
HUBER, Miriam Blanton
  (Mrs. Frank S. Salisbury)
HUDSON, Arthur Palmer
HUGHES, Arthur Howard
HUGHES, Merritt Yerkes
HUMMEL, ARTHUR WILLIAM
HUSE, Howard Russell
HU-SHIH
HUTCHERSON, Dudley Robert
HUTTON, James
JACOBSEN, THORKILD
JAEGER, Werner Wilhelm
JAKOBSON, ROMAN
JANISSE, Denis R.
JOCKERS, Ernest
JOHNSON, Harvey LeRoy
JOHNSON, THOMAS HERBERT
JOHNSON, WENDELL A. L.
JONES, Bob, Jr.
JONES, Charles W(illiams)
JONES, Frederick Lafayette
JONES, HOWARD MEMFORD
JONES, Louis Clark
JONES, Putnam Fennell
JONES, Willis Knapp
JORGENSON, Theodore
KAPP, Ernest
KENISTON, (RALPH) H.
KENNEDY, ARTHUR GARFIELD
KENNEDY, Ruth Lee
KENYON, JOHN SAMUEL
KERCHEVILLE, F(rancis) M.
KIND, John Louis
KIRBY, Thomas Austin
KNAPP, Lewis Mansfield
KNICKERBOCKER, Kenneth L.
KNICKERBOCKER, William E.
KNICKERBOCKER, William S.
KORFMACHER, William C.
KRAMER, MAGDALENE E.
KRAUSE, Herbert
KRONENBERGER, Louis
KRUTCH, JOSEPH WOOD
KURATH, Hans
LANCASTER, Henry C.
LANE, George Sherman
LANGE, VICTOR
LANGFORD, Walter McCarty
LARCH, Fred W.
LARSEN, HENNING
LAWRENCE, William Witherle

LEACH, Henry Goddard
LEARNED, Henry Dexter
LEARY, Lewis
LEDNICKI, Waclaw
LEE, Hector H.
LEONARD, Irving A(lbert)
LEOPOLD, WERNER F.
LEWISOHN, LUDWIG
LIEBERMAN, SAUL
LIN YUTANG
LIPTZIN, Sol
LOCKE, William Nash
LOGGINS, Vernon
LONG, E(ugene) Hudson
LOOMIS, Roger Sherman
LORD, LOUIS ELEAZER
LOWRY, HOWARD FOSTER
LOWTHER, Hugh Sears
LYDENBERG, Harry Miller
LYONS, Clifford Pierson
MABBOTT, THOMAS OLLIVE
MacLEISH, ARCHIBALD
MacMILLAN, (William D., III)
MAGOUN, Francis P., Jr.
MALONE, KEMP
MANN, THOMAS
MANNING, Clarence A.
MARCKWARDT, Albert Henry
MATHEWS, MITFORD M., Sr.
McBURNEY, JAMES HOWARD
McCUTCHEON, Roger Philip
McDOWELL, (George) T.
McKILLOP, ALAN DUGALD
McMANAWAY, James Gilmer
MENCKEN, HENRY LOUIS
MENDELL, Clarence W.
MENUT, Albert D(ouglas B.)
MERCER, SAMUEL ALFRED B.
MERITT, BENJAMIN DEAN
MERITT, Herbert Dean
MESSER, William Stuart
MIEROW, Charles C.
MILLER, PERRY (GILBERT EDDY)
MILLER, William Marion
MILLS, Barriss
MOFFATT, Lucius Gaston
MONK, Samuel Holt
MOORE, John Robert
MORAUD, Marcel Jean
MOULTON, William Gamwell
MURDOCK, Kenneth Ballard
MYERS, Henry Alonzo
MYERS, Louis McCorry
NATHAN, George Jean
NEFF, EMERY E.
NEMIAH, Royal Case
NETHERCOT, Arthur Hobart
NICOLSON, MARJORIE HOPE
NITZE, WILLIAM ALBERT
NORDMEYER, Henry W.
NORTHUP, Clark Sutherland
NOTOPOULOS, James A.
NOYES, Russell
O'BREIN, JUSTIN McCORTNEY
OLIVER, JAMES H(ENRY)
OLSCHKI, LEONARDO
OSTROM, John W(ard)
PARKER, Richard Anthony
PARKER, Roscoe Edward
PARKER, William Riley
PARMENTER, CLARENCE E.
PARRY, JOHN JAY
PATRICK, David Lyall
PEASE, ARTHUR STANLEY
PEEBLES, Waldo C(utler)
PERRIN, Porter Gale
PERRY, BLISS
PEYRE, HENRI MAURICE
PFEIFFER, ROBERT HENRY
PHARR, Clyde
PLACE, EDWIN BRAY
POCHMANN, Henry August
POPE, Willard Bissell
POSTON, Lawrence S., Jr.
POTTLE, FREDERICK A(LBERT)
POUND, Louise
PRESCOTT, Orville
PRICE, Lawrence Marsden
QUINN, ARTHUR HOBSON
RAVEN, Anton Adolph
REDDING, Jay Saunders
REICHARDT, Konstantin
REICHART, Walter A(lbert)
REMENYI, JOSEPH
REY, Agapito
RICHARDSON, Leon Josiah
ROBERTS, Katharine E.
ROBERTSON, C(harles) A.
ROBINSON, DAVID MOORE

ROBINSON, Fred Norris
ROGERS, Francis Millet
ROGERS, William Hudson
ROVELSTAD, A(dolph) M.
ROWELL, Henry Thompson
RUBIO, DAVID
RUPPENTHAL, Jacob C.
RUSK, RALPH LESLIE
RUSSELL, G(EORGE) OSCAR
RUSSELL, I(saac) Willis
RYBERG, Inez Scott
SAINTONGE, Paul Frederic
SANDBURG, CARL
SCHAFFER, Aaron
SCHIROKAUER, Arno C(urt)
SCHLAUCH, MARGARET
SCHNEIDER, Elisabeth W.
SCHREIBER, CARL FREDERICK
SENSABAUGH, George Frank
SHADICK, H(arold) E(rnest)
SHAVER, Chester Linn
SHERBURN, GEORGE WILEY
SHOEMAKER, William H.
SILZ, Walter
SIMMONS, ERNEST J.
SINGLETON, CHARLES S.
SMITH, HENRY NASH
SOKOL, A(nthony) E(ugene)
SOLMSEN, Friedrich
SPARGO, JOHN WEBSTER
SPEISER, EPHRAIM AVIGDOR
SPITZER, LEO
SPLAWN, Jennie Lillian
SPRINGER, OTTO
SPURLIN, Paul Merrill
STEMPEL, Guido Hermann
STOLL, Elmer Edgar
STRAUS, Roger W., Jr.
STROZIER, Robert Manning
STURTEVANT, EDGAR H.
SWANTON, JOHN REED
SYPHER, Wylie
TAFT, Kendall Benard
TATE, Allen (John Orley)
TAYLOR, ARCHER
TAYLOR, George Coffin
TAYLOR, LILY ROSS
THOMAS, Charles Kenneth
THOMPSON, Harold William
THOMPSON, STITH
TINDALL, William York
TINKER, CHAUNCEY B.
TORRES-RIOSECO, Arturo
TORREY, Norman Lewis
TRILLING, LIONEL
TURNER, Albert Morton
ULLMAN, Berthold Louis
UNTERMEYER, LOUIS
VAIL, Curtis Churchill D.
VANDIVER, Edward P., Jr.
VAN DOREN, MARK
VAN WYCK, William
VINCENT, William Shafer
von FABER du FAUR ,Curt
von FRITZ, Kurt
von KOERBER, Hans N. F.
WALKER, Franklin Dickerson
WARFEL, HARRY REDCAY
WARREN, AUSTIN
WARREN, ROBERT PENN
WAXMAN, SAMUEL M.
WEAVER, Bennett
WEIGAND, HERMANN JOHN
WELLEK, RENE
WHATMOUGH, Joshua
WHEELER, Charles Francis
WHITE, HELEN CONSTANCE
WHITEHALL, Harold
WHITING, Bartlett Jere
WILL, Samuel Frederic
WILLEY, Norman LeRoy
WILLIAMS, Edwin Bucher
WILLIBRAND, William A.
WILSON, George P(ickett)
WILSON, JOHN ALBERT
WIMBERLEY, Lowry Charles
WOLFSON, HARRY AUSTRYN
WORK, James Aiken
WRIGHT, Louis Booker
YARMOLINSKY, AVRAHM A.
YEAGER, W(ILLARD) HAYES
YOUNG, Arthur Milton
ZABEL, MORTON DAUWEN
ZDANOWICZ, Casimir D.
ZEYDEL, Edwin Hermann

Mathematics
(see also Applied Arts and Sciences, Natural Sciences)

ADAMS, Clarence Raymond
AGNEW, RALPH PALMER
AHLFORS, LARS VALERIAN
AIKEN, HOWARD
ALBERT, A(braham) Adrian
AYRES, WILLIAM LEAKE
BACON, Harold Maile
BARTKY, WALTER
BELL, E(ric) T(emple)
BENNETT, Albert Arnold
BETTINGER, A(lbin) K(ilian)
BIRKHOFF, Garrett
BOAS, Ralph Philip, Jr.
BOCHNER, SALOMON
BOHNENBLUST, H. Frederic
BRAUER, RICHARD DAGOBERT
BRESLICH, Ernst Rudolph
BRILLOUIN, LEON N(ICHOLAS)
BRINK, Raymond Woodard
BROWN, Bancroft Huntington
BROWNE, Edward Tankard
CARMICHAEL, Robert Daniel
CARVER, Walter Buckingham
CHEVALLEY, CLAUDE C.
CHITTENDEN, Edward Wilson
CHURCH, Alonzo
CHURCHILL, Ruel Vance
COOLIDGE, JULIAN LOWELL
COURANT, Richard
CRAIG, Cecil C(alvert)
DAVIS, Hannibal Albert
DAVIS, HAROLD THAYER
DEMING, W(illiam) Edwards
DICKSON, LEONARD EUGENE
DOOB, JOSEPH L.
DWYER, PAUL S(UMNER)
EINSTEIN, ALBERT
ERDELYI, Arthur
EVANS, GRIFFITH CONRAD
FELLER, William
FERTIG, John William
FORD, LESTER R.
FORT, Tomlinson
FRANKLIN, Philip
FREEMAN, Harold A(dolph)
FRY, Thornton Carl
GEHMAN, Harry Merrill
GERGEN, John Jay
GRAVES, LAWRENCE M.
HART, William LeRoy
HARTKEMEIER, Harry Pelle
HEDLUND, GUSTAV A(RNOLD)
HELSEL, R(obert) G(riffith)
HESTENES, Magnus R(udolph)
HILDEBRANDT, Theophil H.
HILLE, (CARL) EINAR
HOLL, Dio Lewis
HOLZINGER, KARL JOHN
HOTELLING, Harold
HOYT, Harrison Val
HUFFER, Ralph Craig
HULL, Ralph
HYDEN, John A(lbert)
INGRAHAM, MARK H(OYT)
JACOBSON, NATHAN
KASNER, EDWARD
KIMBALL, Spofford Harris
KOOPMAN, Bernard Osgood
KRUEGER, Raymond Leslie
LAMBERT, Walter Davis
LANGER, RUDOLPH ERNEST
LASLEY, John Wayne, Jr.
LATIMER, Claiborne Green
LEFSCHETZ, Solomon
LEIGHTON, Walter, Jr.
LEVINSON, Horace C(lifford)
LEVINSON, NORMAN
LEWIS, DANIEL CLARK
MacDUFFEE, Cyrus Colton
MACKIE, Ernest Lloyd
MacLANE, SAUNDERS
MALLORY, Virgil S(ampson)
MARCH, H(erman) W(illiam)
MARTIN, William Ted
MASON, MAX
McCOY, Neal Henry
McSHANE, E(dward) J(ames)
MERRIMAN, Gaylord M.
MODE, Elmer B(eneken)
MORSE, David Sherman
MORSE, Harold Marston
MOULTON, ELTON JAMES
MOUZON, Edwin Du Bose, Jr.
MUNSHOWER, Carl Wallace

MURNAGHAN, FRANCIS D.
MUSSELMAN, J(ohn) Rogers
MYERS, Sumner B(yron)
NELSON, Alfred L.
NEUGEBAUER, OTTO
NEYMAN, JERZY
ORE, Oystein
PARKER, W(illiam) V(ann)
PATTERSON, Boyd Crumrine
PHIPPS, Cecil G(lenn)
PRAGER, William
RANDOLPH, John (Adam) F.
REAGAN, Lewis M(artin)
REES, Mina S(piegel)
REISSNER, Max Erich
RIDER, Paul Reece
ROOS, Charles Frederick
SILVERMAN, Louis Lazare
SMITH, Edward Staples C.
SNEDECOR, GEORGE W.
SPENCER, Donald Clayton
SPRINGER, Charles Eugene
STARK, Marion Elizabeth
STEEN, Frederick Henry
STONE, Marshall Harvey
STRUIK, DIRK JAN
SYNGE, JOHN LIGHTON
THOMAS, Joseph Miller
TUCKER, Albert William
VANDIVER, HARRY SHULTZ
VEBLEN, OSWALD
von MISES, Richard
VON NEUMANN, JOHN
WALKER, HELEN M(ARY)
WALLIS, W(ILSON) ALLEN
WALSH, Joseph Leonard
WEAVER, Warren
WEYL, HERMANN
WHYBURN, Gordon Thomas
WHYBURN, William Marvin
WIDDER, David Vernon
WIENER, NORBERT
WILDER, RAYMOND LOUIS
WILLIAMS, Wyman Loren
WILSON, Elizabeth Webb
WINTNER, AUREL
YEATON, Chester Henry

Music

ALLEN, Warren Dwight
ANDERSON, Arthur Olaf
BIANCOLLI, LOUIS
BOROWSKI, FELIX
BOULTON, LAURA CRAYTOR
BUCKLEY, Charles (Robert)
BUKOFZER, MANFRED F.
BURNS, S(amuel) T(hompson)
CAPURSO, Alexander A.
CHOTZINOFF, SAMUEL
COON, Leland A(very)
COPLAND, Aaron
COWELL, HENRY DIXON
DAVID, HANS T.
DAVIDSON, Archibald T.
DICKINSON, George S.
DOTY, E(zra) William
DOWNES, (EDWIN) OLIN
DUNHAM, Rowland Warren
DUNKLEY, Ferdinand Luis
ELKUS, Albert I.
EWEN, DAVID
FLANDERS, Helen Hartness
FRANKENSTEIN, Alfred
FREEMAN, Warren Samuel
GEHRKENS, KARL WILSON
GOLDTHWAITE, Wilburn Scott
GROUT, DONALD JAY
GUNDERSON, HELEN L.
HALL, James H(usst)
HANSON, Howard
HARPER, Earl Enyeart
HAYDON, Glen
HESSER, Ernest George
HINDEMITH, PAUL
HODGSON, Hugh
HODGSON, Walter H.
HOLMES, Malcolm Haughton
HOWARD, JOHN TASKER
HOWERTON, George
JACKSON, George Pullen
KASTENDIECK, Miles M.
KENDALL, William Raymond
KENDEL, John Clark
KING-SMITH, August
KOLODIN, Irving
KRONE, Max Thomas
LANG, PAUL HENRY

LARSON, William Severt
LOCKWOOD, Normand
MATTHEWS, H. Alexander
McCUTCHAN, ROBERT GUY
MOORE, DOUGLAS STUART
MOORE, Earl Vincent
NOSS, Luther
OBERG, Paul Matthews
O'STEEN, Alton (Tilden)
PERKINS, Francis Davenport
PISTON, Walter
POISTER, Arthur (William)
ROBINSON, Clarence C.
ROZSA, Bela
SACHS, CURT
SANDERS, Robert L.
SEEGER, Charles (Louis)
SESSIONS, Roger Huntington
SMITH, CARLTON SPRAGUE
SMITH, Cecil Michener
SPAETH, SIGMUND
STRINGHAM, Edwin John
STRUNK, OLIVER
TAYLOR, (JOSEPH) DEEMS
THOMSON, Virgil
VAN VECHTEN, Carl
WILLIAMSON, John Finley
WILSON, Harry Robert
WOODWORTH, George W.

Philosophy and Ethics

ADAMS, Eugene Taylor
ADAMS, George Plimpton
ADLER, MORTIMER JEROME
AKERS, Samuel Luttrell
ALLAN, Denison Maurice
BARRETT, Clifford Leslie
BAYLIS, Charles A(ugustus)
BENJAMIN, A. Cornelius
BENTLEY, Arthur F(isher)
BLACK, Max
BLANSHARD, BRAND
BOAS, GEORGE
BRIGHTMAN, Edgar Sheffield
BROGAN, Albert Perley
BROWNELL, BAKER
BUCHANAN, Scott
BURKE, KENNETH (DUVA)
BURTT, EDWIN ARTHUR
CAILLIET, EMILE
CAIRNS, Huntington
CARNAP, RUDOLF
CHERNISS, Harold F.
CONGER, George Perrigo
COTTON, James Harry
CUNNINGHAM, Gustavus W.
DAVIDSON, Robert F(ranklin)
DEMOS, Raphael
DENNES, William Ray
DURANT, WILL(IAM JAMES)
EDMAN, IRWIN
FARBER, Marvin
FEIGL, HERBERT
FLETCHER, Harvey
GAMERTSFELDER, Walter S.
GARNETT, Arthur Campbell
GARVIN, Lucius
GRANBERY, John Cowper
GREENE, Theodore Meyer
GUTMANN, James
HAHN, Lewis Edwin
HALL, Everett Wesley
HAMMOND, Lewis Machen
HENDEL, Charles William
HOCKING, WILLIAM ERNEST
HOLMES, Roger Wellington
HOOK, SIDNEY
HOPE, Richard (John William)
IREDELL, Francis Raymond
JOHNSON, Melvin Maynard
JONES, W(illiam) T(homas)
KALLEN, Horace Meyer
KENT, Robert H.
KONVITZ, MILTON RIDVAS
KRUSE, Cornelius
LAMONT, Corliss
LEVINSON, Ronald Bartlett
LEWIS, CLARENCE IRVING
LEYS, Wayne Albert Risser
MARITAIN, JACQUES
MARTI, Fritz
McKEON, RICHARD PETER
MEYER, Cyril F.
MITCHELL, Edwin Thomas
MONTAGUE, WILLIAM P.
MOORE, Philip Samuel
MORROW, Glenn R.

MURPHY, Arthur Edward
MYERS, Edward DeLos
NAGEL, ERNEST
NELSON, Everett John
NORTHROP, Filmer Stuart C.
OATES, Whitney J.
PEPPER, STEPHEN COBURN
PERRY, CHARNER MARQUIS
PERRY, RALPH BARTON
PIPER, Raymond F(rank)
RICE, Philip Blair
ROBINSON, Daniel Sommer
ROEMER, William Francis
ROLBIECKI, John J(oseph)
SABINE, GEORGE HOLLAND
SANBORN, Herbert Charles
SARTON, GEORGE (ALFRED L.)
SCHNEIDER, HERBERT W.
SCOON, Robert
SEARS, Laurence
SIMON, YVES R(ENE MARIE)
SMITH, T(homas) V(ernor)
STALIKNECHT, Newton P.
STORER, Morris Brewster
THOMPSON, Clifford Griffeth
TSANOFF, Radaslav Andrea
VIVAS, Eliseo
VLASTOS, Gregory
WALCOTT, Gregory Dexter
WEISS, Paul
WIDGERY, Alban Gregory
WOOD, Ledger

Theology and Religion

AASGAARD, JOHAN ARND
ADAMS, EARL FREDERICK
ADAMS, GEORGE WENDELL
ADAMS, HAMPTON
ADAMS, JAMES LUTHER
ADAMS, THEODORE FLOYD
ALLIS, Oswald Thompson
ANDERSON, J. LOWRIE
ANDERSON, THEODORE W.
ANDREWS, Mary Edith
ARAND, Louis A.
ARCHER, JOHN CLARK
ARNDT, William Frederick
ASHBROOK, M(ILAN) FOREST
AUBREY, EDWIN EWART
BADER, JESSE MOREN
BAINTON, Roland Herbert
BAIRD, JESSE HAYS
BAKER, JAMES CHAMBERLAIN
BALDINGER, ALBERT HENRY
BARBOUR, CLIFFORD EDWARD
BARNETT, EUGENE EPPERSON
BEAHM, WILLIAM McKINLEY
BEARDSLEE, JOHN WALTER, Jr.
BECK, Dwight M(arion)
BEHNKEN, JOHN WILLIAM
BELL, Bernard Iddings
BELL, WILLIAM AUGUSTUS
BELTMAN, HENRY
BENETT, John Coleman
BENTON, JOHN KEITH
BERGENDOFF, CONRAD J. I.
BERMAN, MORTON MAYER
BERNHARDT, William Henry
BERSELL, PETRUS OLOF I.
BEWER, Julius August
BINNS, WALTER POPE
BLACKWELDER, OSCAR F.
BLOCK, Marguerite Beck
BOND, SIRUS ORESTES
BOWDEN, Daniel Joseph
BOWMAN, John Wick
BRADEN, CHARLES SAMUEL
BRADFORD, SAMUEL JAMES
BRADLEY, PRESTON
BRAGG, RAYMOND BENNETT
BRANCH, Harold Francis
BRANSON, WILLIAM HENRY
BRIDGES, RONALD
BROEK, JOHN YONKER
BROOKS, ROELIF HASBROUCK
BROWN, FRANK CHILTON
BROWN, FREDERICK F.
BROWN, PAUL F.
BROWNE, HARRY C.
BRUMBAUGH, ROY TALMAGE
BUCKNER, GEORGE W., Jr.
BUNDY, Walter Ernest
BURNS, Dennis Francis
BURNTVEDT, THORVALD O.
BURR, HUGH CHAMBERLIN
BURROWS, Millar
BUTTRICK, GEORGE ARTHUR
CADBURY, Henry Joel

CALHOUN, Robert Lowry
CALHOUN, William Lowndes
CALLAN, CHARLES JEROME
CALVERLEY, Edwin Elliott
CAMPBELL, EDWARD FAY
CANNON, William Ragsdale
CARLYON, James Thomas
CARPENTER, HOMER WILSON
CARTER, RANDALL ALBERT
CAUDILL, Robert Paul
CAVERT, SAMUEL McCREA
CHALMERS, Allan Knight
CHANNING, George
CLARK, Elmer Talmadge
CLAXTON, ALLEN ENES
CLEMENTS, REX STOWERS
CLINCHY, EVERETT ROSS
CLOAK, FRANK VALENTINE C.
COE, ALBERT BUCKNER
COFFIN, HENRY SLOANE
COHEN, HENRY
COHON, Samuel Solomon
CODER, Samuel Maxwell
COLWELL, Ernest Cadman
COMER, GORDON V.
CONNELL, Francis J.
CONNICK, Charles Milo
CONRAD, Theodore Emanuel
COOK, GAINES MONROE
CRAIG, Clarence Tucker
CRANSTON, Earl
CROSS, WALTER SNELL
CROWE, WILLIAM
CULBERTSON, WILLIAM
CUMMINS, ROBERT
CUNNINGHAM, JOHN ROOD
CUSHING, RICHARD J.
CUSHMAN, RALPH SPAULDING
CUTTEN, George Barton
DAHLBERG, EDWIN THEODORE
DAVIDSON, MAX DAVID
DAVIES, ARTHUR POWELL
DAVIS, RALPH MARSHALL
DAVIS, Richard J.
DAVISON, FRANK ELON
DAWSON, Joseph Martin
DAY, ALBERT EDWARD
DEEMS, Mervin Monroe
De GROOT, Alfred Thomas
DEMBY, E(DWARD) THOMAS
DENTAN, Robert Claude
DIEHL, CHARLES EDWARD
DIFFENDORFER, RALPH E.
DILLISTONE, FREDERICK W.
DONOHUE, Cyril P.
DOUGLASS, EARL LEROY
DOWNS, FRANCIS SHUNK
DUN, ANGUS
DURDEN, CHARLES
DYM, AARON
DYKSTRA, JOHN ALBERT
EDDY, SHERWOOD
EDWARDS, DEANE
EGELSON, LOUIS I.
EISENDRATH, MAURICE N.
ELDER, FRANK RAY
ELIOT, FREDERICK MAY
ELLIOTT, ERROL THOMAS
EMMONS, PETER KENNETH
EMPIE, PAUL CHAUNCEY
ENGSTROM, SIGFRID E.
EPP, GEORGE EDWARD
EVANS, FREDERICK WALTER
EVANS, HUGH IVAN
EVANS, LOUIS HADLEY
FAGLEY, FREDERICK LOUIS
FELDMAN, Abraham J(ehiel)
FENDT, Edward Charles
FERM, Vergilius Ture Anselm
FIFIELD, JAMES WILLIAM, Jr.
FIFIELD, LAWRENCE WENDELL
FILSON, Floyd Vivian
FINKELSTEIN, LOUIS
FISHER, ROBERT FARLEY
FLETCHER, Joseph Francis, III
FLINT, CHARLES WESLEY
FORBUSH, Bliss
FOSDICK, HARRY EMERSON
FOULKES, WILLIAM HIRAM
FOUNTAIN, WILLIAM A., Sr.
FOX, H(AMILTON) P(HILIPS)
FRANK, ROBERT WORTH
FRIDELL, Elmer Alfred
FRY, FRANKLIN CLARK
FULTON, CHARLES DARBY
GARBER, PAUL NEFF
GARNETT, Arthur Campbell
GARRISON, Winfred Ernest
GEHMAN, Henry Snyder

GEZORK, Herbert
GIBSON, Robert Fisher
GINZBERG, LOUIS
GOEBEL, LOUIS WILLIAM
GOLDMAN, SOLOMON
GOLDMANN, NAHUM
GOLDSMITH, Sidney W., Jr.
GOLDSTEIN, HERBERT SAMUEL
GOLDSTEIN, ISRAEL
GOODENOUGH, Erwin R.
GOODLOE, ROBERT WESLEY
GOODSPEED, Edgar Johnson
GORDIS, ROBT.
GRAHAM, WILLIAM F.
GRANT, Frederick Clifton
GRAY, Albert F(rederick)
GRAY, ARTHUR D(OUGLASS)
GREENBERG, SIMON
GREY, J(AMES) D(AVID)
GRIER, ROBERT CALVIN
GRIFFETH, Ross John
GROVES, Walter Alexander
GULLIXSON, THADDEUS F.
HAMILTON, KENNETH G.
HAMILTON, WILLIAM WISTAR
HARKNESS, Georgia Elma
HARKNESS, REUBEN ELMORE E.
HARLOW, S. Ralph
HARMON, NOLAN BAILEY
HARRIS, FREDERICK BROWN
HARTSHORNE, HUGH
HAWKINS, Robert Martyr
HAYNES, CARLYLE BOYNTON
HAYS, Arthur Alexander
HAWARD, Percy Roy
HAZEN, JOSEPH CHALMERS
HENDERSHOT, Vernon E.
HENDRY, GEORGE STUART
HERLANDS, WILLIAM B.
HEWITT, ARTHUR W.
HIEBERT, PETER CORNELIUS
HILTNER, Seward
HOCHWALT, Frederick G.
HOLLEY, Horace
HOLMAN, Charles Thomas
HOLT, IVAN LEE
HOMRIGHAUSEN, Elmer G.
HOOVER, Harvey Daniel
HORTON, DOUGLAS
HORTON, Walter Marshall
HOUGH, Lynn Harold
HOWSE, W. L., Jr.
HOYER, Harvey Conrad
HUGGENVIK, Theodore
HUMPHREY, George Caldwell
HUTCHINSON, Paul
HUTCHINSON, STUART NYE
HUTSON, Harold Horton
HYATT, James Philip
IRWIN, William Andrew
ISSERMAN, FERDINAND M.
JAMES, ARCHBISHOP
JAMES, Fleming
JENKENS, MILLARD ALFROD
JENSEN, ALFRED
JERSILD, HANS CHRISTIAN
JOHNSON, CHARLES OSCAR
JOHNSON, Hansford Duncan
JOHNSON, Paul Emanuel
JOHNSON, Sherman E.
JOHNSON, TORREY M.
JONES, Bob, Jr.
JONES, Edgar DeWitt
JONES, E(LI) STANLEY
JORDAN, G(ERALD) RAY
KANTONEN, Taito Almar
KAPLAN, MORDECAI M.
KEGLEY, Charles William
KENNEDY, James William
KING, Albion Roy
KING, CHARLES LEONIDAS
KINNEY, Laurence Forman
KIRK, HARRIS ELLIOTT
KNAPP, BLISS
KNAPP, Forrest Lamar
KNORR, NATHAN HOMER
KNUBEL, FREDERICK R.
KNUDSON, Albert Cornelius
KRAELING, Carl H(erman)
KUEBLER, ERNST WILLIAM
LACY, BENJAMIN RICE, Jr.
LAMPE, WLILIAM BLAKEMAN
LANKARD, Frank Glenn
LATHAM, Harold Strong
LATOURETTE, KENNETH SCOTT
LEBER, CHARLES TUDOR
LEE, Robert Greene
LEETE, FREDERICK DeLAND
LEFEVER, CHARLES HARRY

LEIPER, HENRY SMITH
LEMMON, CLARENCE EUGENE
LEVINTHAL, ISRAEL HERBERT
LEVITSKY, LOUIS MOSES
 LEWIS, Edwin
LITTLE, HERVEY GANSE
LLOYD, RALPH WALDO
 LOETSCHER, Frederick W.
LOOMER, BERNARD M.
LOPER, VERE VANDER HYDEN
LUDWIG, SYLVESTER T.
LUNDQUIST, HAROLD L.
MACARTNEY, CLARENCE E. N.
 MacGREGOR, (John) Geddes
MACHUM, WALDO CARSON
 MACKAY, John Alexander
MacKENZIE, FRANCIS SCOTT
MADSON, NORMAN ARTHUR
MAGEE, J(UNIUS) RALPH
MAGNIN, EDGAR FOGEL
 MALONE, J(ohn) Walter, Jr.
 MANTEY, Julius Robert
 MARSHALL, Frank Hamilton
 MARSHALL, John Sedberry
MARSTON, LESLIE RAY
 MARTI, Fritz
MARTIN, WILLIAM C.
MATLOCK, CHARLES RUBEIN
 MAY, Herbert Gordon
 MAYER, Frederick E.
MAYS, BENJAMIN ELIJAH
McCALL, DUKE K(IMBROUGH)
 McCLAIN, Alva J.
McCONNELL, FRANCIS JOHN
McCORMICK, HARRY BENTON
McCOWN, CHESTER CHARLTON
 McCUTCHAN, Robert Guy
McGIFFERT, ARTHUR C., Jr.
McINTYRE, JAMES FRANCIS A.
McKAY, DAVID O.
McMILLAN, HOMER
McREYNOLDS, JAMES HARRY

MELAND, BERNARD EUGENE
MENTER, NORMAN ARTHUR
MEWALDT, I(MMANUEL) R.
MICHAEL, ARCHBISHOP
MILIVOJEVICH, DIONISIJL
MILLER, URI
MILLIGAN, ORLANDO H.
MOONEY, EDWARD CARDINAL
MOORE, HIGHT C.
MOREHEAD, HOUSTON RYLAN
MORELAND, JESSE EARL
 MORGAN, Carl Hamilton
MORGENSTERN, JULIAN
 MORRISON, Charles Clayton
 MORSE, Hermann Nelson
MOTRY, HUBERT LOUIS
 MUELDER, Walter George
MUELLER, KARL ANTON
MULDER, BERNARD J.
 MULLEN, Cronan
MULLOY, WILLIAM THEODORE
MUNTZ, J(OHN) PALMER
 MURRAY, John Courtney
NASH, NORMAN BURDETT
 NELSON, John Oliver
NELSON, REUBEN EMMANUEL
 NELSON, William Stuart
NEWMAN, LOUIS ISRAEL
NEWTON, LOUIS DE VOTIE
 NICHOLSON, Clarence M.
NICHOLSON, ROY S.
NIEBUHR, H(ELMUT) RICHARD
NIEBUHR, REINHOLD
 NOCK, Arthur Darby
NOLI, FAN STYLIAN
NOOE, ROGER THEOPHILUS
 NOSS, John Boyer
OLSON, OSCAR THOMAS
ORR, JOHN ALVIN
OSGOOD, PHILLIPS ENDECOTT
 OXNAM, G(arfield) Bromley

 OXTOBY, Gurdon Corning
PALMER, ALBERT WENTWORTH
PATERSON, WILLIAM TAIT
PAYNE, PAUL CALVIN
PEALE, NORMAN VINCENT
PFLUM, HENRY J.
PFOHL, JOHN KENNETH
 PITT, Malcolm Slack
PITTMAN, ALFRED
POLING, DANIEL ALFRED
POLIZOIDES, GERMANOS
 POLLARD, William Grosvenor
POOL, DAVID de SOLA
POTEAT, EDWIN McNEILL
PRUDEN, EDWARD HUGHES
PUGH, WILLIAM BARROW
PUGMIRE, ERNEST IVISON
 PURDY, Alexander Converse
 PYATT, Charles Lynn
RANDOLPH, CORLISS FITZ
RANSON, MARIUS
REAMON, ELLSWORTH
REED, LUTHER DOTTERER
 REESE, Curtis Williford
REINARTZ, F(REDERICK) E.
RICHARDS, GEORGE WARREN
RICHARDS, JAMES McDOWELL
RICHARDS, LeGRAND
RICHARDSON, DONALD W.
RIMMER, HARRY
ROBERTS, CARROLL CURTISS
 ROBERTS, Edward Howell
ROBINSON, URIAH JUDKIN
ROETTGER, Gregory John
ROMIG, EDGAR FRANKLIN
ROSENBERG, ISRAEL
ROSENBLUM, WILLIAM F.
ROSS, EMORY
ROTHENBERGER, WILLIAM F.
 RYAN, William Granger
SANSBURY, MARVIN ORVILLE
 SCARBOROUGH, William J.

SCARLETT, WILLIAM
 SCHMIDT, Austin G(uilford)
SCHROEDER, FREDERICK W.
SCHUETTE, WALTER ERWIN
SCOTT, EUGENE CRAMPTON
SEELY, PAUL STARK
SELECMAN, CHARLES CLAUDE
 SHEEHY, Maurice S(tephen)
SHEEN, FULTON JOHN
SHEPHERD, MASSEY H.
SHERRILL, HENRY KNOX
 SHERRILL, Lewis Joseph
SHIELDS, THOMAS T.
SHIPMAN, EMMA C.
SHULLENBERGER, WILLIAM A.
 SIECK, Louis John
SILVER, ABBA HILLEL
SILVERMAN, MORRIS
 SIMPSON, John Ernest
SMITH, ANGIE FRANK
SMITH, HERBERT BOOTH
SMITH, LUTHER WESLEY
SMITH, RAY LEMON
SOCKMAN, RALPH W.
SODT, WILLIAM GEORGE
SPELLMAN, FRANCIS JOSEPH
 SPENCER, William Gear
SPERRY, WILLIAM LEAROYD
 SPOTTS, Charles Dewey
STAMM, JOHN SAMUEL
STAUFFACHER, CHARLES H.
STAVIG, LAWRENCE M.
STEERE, DOUGLAS VAN
 STINESPRING, WILLIAM F.
STOCKER, FREDERICK PAUL
STOKES, ANSON PHELPS
 STRINGFELLOW, Ervin E.
STRITCH, SAMUEL ALPHONSUS
 STUNTZ, Hugh Clark
SWAIN, ANNA S. C.
 (MRS. LESLIE)

 SWEET, William Warren
TABAK, Israel
 TENNEY, Merrill Chapin
THOMAS, ALBERT CLARK
 THOMAS, John Newton
THOMAS, LEONARD LITTLETON
 THOMPSON, Ernest Trice
THOMPSON, W(illiam) T.
TILLICH, PAUL JOHANNES
TIMMONS, WOFFORD C.
TOBIAS, CHANNING HEGGIE
TOMLINSON, ELIZABETH C.
 (MRS. IRVING C.)
 TOTH, William
TRIPP, EDGAR FRANKLIN
TULLOSS, REES EDGAR
VALE, ROY EWING
VAN DUSEN, Henry Pitney
 VIETH, Paul Herman
VRUWINK, HENRY ANDREW
 WACH, Joachim
 WALKER, Oliver LaFayette
WALLS, WILLIAM JACOB
WARREN, GORDON CHESTER
 WEBER, William A.
WEIGLE, Luther Allen
WENTZ, ABDEL ROSS
WHITE, ARTHUR KENT
 WHITE, Hugh Vernon
 WICKENDEN, Arthur Consaul
WIEMAN, HENRY NELSON
 WILDER, Amos Niven
WILLIAMS, John Paul
 WILSON, J. Christy
WILSON, JESSE RODMAN
WILSON, ROBERT IVAN
WILSON, WILLIAM BRUCE
WINGFIELD, MARSHALL
 WOLFE, Rolland Emerson
WOOD, Arthur Evans
WRIGHT, RICHARD ROBERT, Jr.
YATES, KYLE MONROE

SELECTED INFORMATION SOURCES

During the compilation of the Revised Edition the Editors came in contact with numerous types of sources of authoritative information on subjects of either specific or general interest. While listings of such sources were not originally contemplated as indicated by the work's title, the exceptional adaptability of the Locator Index (page 871), around which it was being compiled, immediately suggested to the Editors that these sources could without difficulty be made reference useful simply by "keying" them into this unusual index. So doing would make available to consultants of the book authoritative sources as well as individuals considered by the Editors to be authorities, experts or specially informed. Accordingly, the entries on this page, and the eight following pages, are indexed to subjects which the Editors had selected for inclusion in the Locator Index, exactly as are the listings of individuals. The indicators used in connection with these sources have the following significations:

● Special holdings of reference materials in the field(s) indicated; ★ collections of physical examples and specimens in the field(s) indicated: **1** Address the librarian for desired information; **2** interlibrary loans made; **3** reproduction facilities offered; **4** translators available.

10   Abbott Laboratories. 1400 Sheridan Rd., North Chicago, Ill. Drug industry; pharmacology; weekly index of pertinent journal items. **1-2.**

11   Academy of American Franciscan History. 29 Cedar Lane, Washington, D. C. Open only to qualified scholars, by appointment. ● History of the Franciscan Order in North and South America; missions. **1.**

12   Academy of Motion Picture Arts and Sciences. 1455 N. Gordon, Hollywood. ● Historical and technical development of motion pictures; governmental and other censorship and regulation of motion pictures; motion picture industry in France, Italy, Great Britian, and Germany; records of films since 1915, including information on cast and other personnel and reviews; ★ 16,000 motion picture stills. **1.**

13   Academy of Natural Sciences of Philadelphia—Library. 19th St. and Parkway, Philadelphia 3, Pa. ● Insects, mollusks, flowering plants, diatoms, minerals. **1.**

14   Academy of the New Church—Library. Bryn Athyn, Pa. ● Swedenborg. **1.**

15   Aerojet Engineering Corp.—Library. 285 W. Colorado St., Pasadena, Calif. Jet propulsion (pyrotechnics, thermodynamics). **1.**

16   Aetna Life Affiliated Companies—Research and Engineering Library. Engineering and Inspection Department, 151 Farmington Av., Hartford, Conn. ● Data on industrial mining and motor vechile accidents; industrial safety equipment catalogs; occupational diseases; safety codes. **1.**

17   Air Reduction Co. Inc.—Library. 60 E. 42d St., New York 17. Welding; anesthetic gases and equipment; dry ice. **1.**

18   Alabama Power Co.—Library. 600 N. 18th St., Birmingham, Ala. ● Alabama industries and resources. **1-2-3.**

19   Alabama, University of—Amelia Gayle Gorgas Library. University, Ala. ● History of lower Mississippi Valley and South in 17th, 18th, 19th centuries. **1.**

20   Alaska Historical Society—Library and Museum. Juneau, Alaska. Totem poles; art of the Northwest Coast. **1.**

21   American Antiquarian Society—Library. Park Av. and Salisbury St., Worcester 5, Mass. ★ Material printed in U. S. 1640-1860 (newspapers, local history, early juvenile books, graphic arts).

22   American Bible Society—Library, 450 Park Av., New York 22. ● Bibles (all languages and dates). **1.**

23   American Federation of Labor—Library. 901 Massachusetts Av., N.W., Washington. ● Trade unions in United States, England, Scotland, France, Belgium, and Australia); Great Britain's Labour Party. **1-2.**

24   American Foundation for the Blind, Inc.—Library. 15 W. 16th St., New York 11. The blind; ● Helen Keller. **1.**

25   American Hospital Association—Bacon Library. 18 E. Division St., Chicago. ● Hospitals (history). **1.**

26   American Legion National Headquarters—Library. 777 N. Meridan, Indianapolis. ● World War 1: forms and literature used in mobilization, training, and overseas; posters; camp publications; histories of regiments; ★ medals awarded by participating countries; insignia of American forces.

27   American Phytopathological Society—Plant Industry Station. Beltsville, Md. Plant pathology.

28   American Psychical Institute. 1145 Vine St., Hollowyood 38. ● Psychic phenomena (case histories). **1.**

29   American Potash Institute—Library. 1102 16th St., N. W., Washington. ● Boron and Potash (as plant nutrients). **1-2.**

30   American Resinous Chemicals Corp.—Library. 103 Foster St., Peabody, Mass. Synthetic resin and rubber solutions, dispersing agents, emulsions (application in leather, paper, textile industries). **1.**

31   American Seamen's Friend Society—Library for Seamen. 550 W. 20th St., New York 11. Aviation; navigation; radio. **1.**

32   American Standards Association—Library. 70 E. 45th St., New York. Reference only. Copies of foreign documents in the field. ★ Domestic, foreign engineering, industrial standards; industrial safety codes. **3.**

33   American Transit Association. 292 Madison Av., New York. Trolley coaches, elevated and subway systems (operation and maintenance). **1.**

34   American Type Culture Collection. 2029 M St., N.W., Washington 6. ★ 3,000 strains of micro-organisms in pure culture (bacteria, fungi, molds); culture technique in micro-biology. **1.**

35   American University — Artemas Martin Mathematical Library. Washington 16. Reference library. ● American mathematical texts through 1900 (special emphasis on prior to 1850); early English texts in surveying, algebra, arithmetic, geometry to 1488. **1-2.**

36   American Viscose Corp. (Chemical Research Department)—Library. Marcus Hook, Pa. ● Textiles. **1.**

37   American-Scandinavian Foundation —William Henry Schofield Library. 127 E. 73d St., New York 21. ● Old Swedish poetry; "old Norse". **1.**

38   Amherst College—Library. Amherst, Mass. ● Clyde Fitch (selections from personal library); Wordsworth; ★ lepidotera; plays; (Plimpton Collection). **1.**

39   Arizona Pioneer Historical Society. Tucson, Ariz. Arizona newspapers, diaries, manuscripts.

40   Armstrong, Col. Richard H. Biddeford, Me. ● Famous law cases and participating lawyers.

41   Art Institute of Chicago—Ryerson Library. Michigan Av., at foot of Adams St., Chicago. Photographs and slides available; ★ art of China and Japan; ceramics, metalworking and metalwork; furniture; art periodicals, including foreign; art auction sales catalogs and exhibition catalogs. (Burnham Library of Architecture). ★ Architecture (history; Chicago); Chicago buildings (microfilms of blueprints). **1.**

42   Asphalt Institute—Library. 801 Second Av., New York 19. ● Asphalt. **1.**

43   Association of American Railroads (Bureau of Railway Economics Library). Transportation Bldg., Washington 6. ● Engineering, financial, other reports of railroads; and economic and historical studies; maps of U. S. and foreign railroads; periodicals published by railroad labor organizations and by railroads. **1.**

44   Atlanta University—Library. 273 Chestnut St. S.W., Atlanta. Negro (history, culture). **1.**

45   Atlantic Research Associates, Inc.—Library. 763 Washington St., Newtonville, Mass. Research in proteins; casein, other synthetic fibers; dyes; mica (use in paint); mildew-proofing. **1.**

46   Automobile Old Timers. 22 E. 38th St., New York 16. Automobile history. **1.**

47   Atlas Powder Co.—Library. Wilmington 99, Del. ● Decolorizing carbons. **1.**

48   Aurora College—Library. Aurora, Ill. Advent Christian denomination. **1.**

49   Augustana College and Theological Seminary—Denkmann Memorial Library. 3500 7th Av., Rock Island, Ill. ● French Revolution; Lutheran theology; Swedish-Americana. **1.**

10 Baker, M. O., & Co.—Library. 113 Astor St., Newark. Metallurgy (platinum, palladium, ruthenium, rhodium, osmium, iridium, gold, silver).

11 Baker Museum for Furniture Research. Exhibitors Building, Grand Rapids, Mich. ★ Seventeenth and eighteenth-century furniture; carving models and early furniture books.

12 Baker University—Library. Baldwin, Kan. ● Methodist Episcopal Church; Bibles. **1.**

13 Ball State Teachers College—Library. Muncie, Ind. Old Northwest Territory and its rivers (exploration and development). **1.**

14 Baltimore & Ohio Railroad—The B&O Museum. Bailey's Roundhouse, 2 N. Charles St., Baltimore ★ Railway motive power and carrying equipment.

15 Bausch & Lomb Optical Co.—Library, 635 St. Paul St., Rochested 2 ● Microscopy. **1.**

16 Bendix Aviation Corp. (Scintilla Magneto Division)—Library. Sidney. N.Y. Magnetic materials; radio shielding; plastics. **1.**

17 Benedictine Society of Alabama—Library. St. Bernard Jr. College, St. Bernard, Ala. ● Benedictine history. **1.**

18 Berea College—Library. Berea, Ky. ● Lincolniana; (southern Appalachian mountains). **1.**

19 Berkshire Athenaeum—Library. 44 Bank Row, Pittsfield, Mass. ● Shaker history; local history. **1.**

20 Birmingham Public Library—Department of Southern History and Literature. Birmingham, Ala. ● Southern antebellum periodicals: slavery; index of periodical articles an Alabama and Birmingham. **1.**

21 Bishop, Charles Wakefield. 154 E. Grand Av., New Haven 13. ● Defunct makes of automobiles and their makers.

22 Bluffton College—Mennonite Historical Library. Bluffton O. Mennonite and Anabaptist history and doctrine.

23 Bodfish, Morton. 221 N. LaSalle St., Chicago. ★ Banks (mechanical toy).

24 Boston Athenaeum—Library. 10½ Beacon St., Boston 8. ● Byron; Confederate States Imprints; First Editions; George Washington's books; Gypsy literature; Roxburghe Publications; Civil War. **1.**

25 Boston College—Library. Chestnut Hill, Newton, Mass. ● Jesuitica; Ethnology (Africana, Caribbeana). **1.**

26 Boston Elevated Railway—Library. 31 James Av., Boston. ● Street railways. **2.**

27 Boston Public Library. Copley Sq., Boston 17. ● History of printing; The Book of Common Prayer; Christian Science; theatrical history, architecture, costumes, and settings; early children's books; ★ photographs of baseball players and Civil War subjects (including Brady photographs); postcards. **1.**

28 Bridgeport Public Library (Technology Department). Bridgeport, Conn. Airshelters, machine and hand tools, map making, shipbuilding, welding, woodworking. **1.**

29 Bristol-Meyers Co. (Products Division)—Library. 225 Long Av., Hillside 5, N.J. Cosmetic literature; patents on cosmetic materials. **1-4.**

30 Brooklyn Museum—Brooklyn Institute of Arts and Sciences. Eastern Parkway, Brooklyn 17. ● Colonial art and life in America; pre- and post-Columbian Latin America; ethnology; ★ Egyptian art, archaeology, philology. **1.**

31 Brown & Bigelow—Library. Quality Park, St. Paul 4. Advertising; marketing; printing; salesmanship; novelty and leather manufacturing; calendars. **1.**

32 Bucks County Historical Society—Library. Fine, Ashland and Green Sts., Doylestown, Pa. Ethnology (Pennsylvania-German). **1.**

33 Buffalo Museum of Science—Research Library. Humbolt Park, Buffalo, N.Y. Primitive art; oceanographical expeditions. **1.**

34 Business Bourse—Library. 80 W. 40th St., New York 18. Commercial and marketing research (foods, management, psychology, sales).

Blvd., Los Angeles 7.) Montana history. **1.**

35 California Academy of Sciences—Library. Golden Gate Park, San Francisco 18. Flora and fauna of West Coast (Alaska to Galapagos); taxonomy; voyages, explorations. **1.**

36 California at Los Angeles, University of—Library. Los Angeles. ● Folklore; languages and literature (Scandinavia, Iceland); ★ western Americana. **1.** (William Andrews Clark Memorial Library, 2205 W. Adams

37 California Department of Natural Resources (Division of Fish and Game, California State Fisheries Laboratory)—Library. Tuna and Seaside Avenues, Terminal Island, Calif. Fisheries; hydrography; oceanography. **1.**

38 California State Library—Sutro Branch. Civic Center, San Francisco. ★ Pamphlets and broadsides covering Mexican history (1800-1850), Renaissance and Reformation (especially Germany), English history of the 17th and 18th centuries (especially 1640-1660). **1.**

39 California, University of—Library. Berkely, Calif. (College of Agriculture, Department of Forestry). Dendrology; range management; silviculture; wood technology. **1.** (Museum of Paleontology). ● Late Cenozoic mammalia; continental stratigraphy. **1.** (Citrus Experiment Station, Riverside). Subtropical horticulture. **1.**

40 Campbell-Ewald Company, Inc.—Library. 10 Rockefeller Plaza, New York 20. Advertising; air lines; automobiles; marketing; rubber. **1.**

41 Campbell Taggart Research Corp.—Library. 4049 Pennsylvania Av., Kansas City, Mo. Address the director of research. Fermentation; enzymes; cereal chemistry and physics; nutrition; flour; breadmaking.

42 Capital Transit Co.—Library 36th and M Sts., Washington 7. Urban transportation (electric railway, motor bus). **1.**

43 Carleton College—Scoville Memorial Library. Northfield, Minn. ● Lincolniana; Bibical literature. **1.**

44 Carnegie Institution of Washington—Department of Embryology. Wolfe and Madison Sts., Baltimore 5. Use limited to scientific investigators by special arrangement. ★ Slides, models, photographs, other embryological material covering man and other primates. **1.**

45 Carrier Corp.—Engineering Library. 300 S. Geddes St., Syracuse 1. Air conditioning; refrigeration; heating; ventilation. **1.**

46 Case Co., J. I. 700 State St., Racine Wis. ★ Farm machinery.

47 Chamber of Commerce of the State of New York—Library. 65 Liberty St., New York 5. New York City history and biography; arbitration; banking. **1.**

48 Chandler, John Greene, Museum of Toys and Paper Craft. Main Street, South Lancaster, Mass. Open by appointment. ★ Early children's books, paper dolls, cutout toys, other toys and dolls. **1.**

49 Williams College—Chapin Library. College Pl., Williamstown, Mass. Americana; rare Bibles. **1.**

50 Chase National Bank. 18 Pine St., New York. ★ Moneys (legal tender in numismatic collection ranging from Babylonian clay tablets to Oregon woodpecker scaps). **1.**

51 Chicago Historical Society—Gilpin Library. Clark St. at North Av., Chicago. ★ Railroads; Lincolniana: Civil War; Mormons; printing; ● medical history. **1.**

52 Chicago Park District—Special Library. 425 E. 14th Boulevard, Chicago Recreation; landscape design; police work. **1.**

53 Child Study Association of America, Inc.—Alice Morgenthau Ehrich Memorial Library. 221 W. 57th St., New York 19. Parent education; sex education.

54 Christopher, Milbourne. Society of American Magicians, 15 W. 84th St., New York 24. ★ History, background, and practice of theatrical magic (including prints, playbills).

55 Cincinnati and Hamilton County, Public Library of. 629 Vine St., Cincinnati 2. ★ American sheet music; ● children's books. **1.**

56 Cincinnati, University of—General Library. Burnet Woods Park, Cincinnati. American Indians; early Latin-Americana; ● Stephen Collins Foster (books, sheet music, records). **1.**

57 Clark, William Andrews, Memorial Library. 2205 W. Adams Blvd., Los Angeles 18. ● English history, literature, music science, and theology of 17th and 18th centuries (especially literature and drama to 1750); history of Mormonism, of Montana.

58 Cleveland Health Museum. Cleveland. ★ Anatomical models illustrating human reproduction from fertilization to birth, other phases personal and public health. **1.**

59 Cleveland Museum of Art. Cleveland. ★ Medieval enamel, ivory works, goldsmiths' works; illuminated manuscripts; 18th century decorative metalwork and ceramics. **1.**

60 Cleveland Public Library. Cleveland. ● Folk-lore; gypsies; history of Orient to 1750 and of India to 1850 manuscripts of British India, 1750-1850; Oriental archaeology, languages and literature; romances of chivalry; ★ move games (chess, checkers), playing cards; Madagascar; native literature of Ceylon; Sanskrit, Arabic, and Persian literature; Mongols; Robin Hood; Arabian Nights; Koran; Tibet; Central Asia; Sikhs; Zoroastrianism. **1-2.**

61 Cluett, Peabody & Co., Inc. 433 River St., Troy, N.Y. ★ Collars (apparel, American since mid-19th century).

62 Colby College—Library. Waterville. Me. Book arts (designers and presses); ● Edwin Arlington Robinson; Thomas Hardy. **1.**

63 Colgate-Palmolive-Peet Co.—Research and Development Department Library. 105 Hudson St., Jersey City. Soaps; perfume, cosmetics; glycerol. **1.**

64 Colorado, University of—Library. Boulder, Colo. ● Conciliar movement, Renaissance papacy, Protestant reform. **1.**

65 Colorado Springs Fine Arts Center. Colorado Springs. ★ Religious folk art and arts and crafts of Spanish America and New Mexico. **1.**

66 Colt's Manufacturing Co. 17 Van Dyke Av., Hartford, Conn. ★ Guns (especially early American hand guns).

67 Columbian Carbon Co.—Library. 214 44th St., Brooklyn 52. Carbon black (use in rubber, paint and ink industries); natural gas; electron microscopy. **1.**

10 Columbia University—Libraries. New York 27. (School of Library Science) ● Bookselling; publishers and publishing. ★ Printing specimens for history of books and libraries. **1.** (Avery Architectual Library). ★Original American and European architectual drawings; architectural history, theory, design since 15th century; archaeology; topography; landscape architecture. **1.**

11 Commercial Solvents Corp.—Library. 1331 S. First St., Terre Haute, Ind. Bacteriology (fermentation). **1.**

12 Compensation Insurance Rating Board—Library. 100 E. 42d St., New York 17. Labor; workmen's compensation; occupational diseases; accident prevention. **1.**

13 Congregational Library. 14 Beacon St., Boston 8. ● Early Puritan literature. **1.**

14 Connecticut College—Palmer Library. New London, Conn. ● Printing; Early American travel. **1.**

15 Connecticut Historical Society. 1 Elizabeth St., Hartford 5. Identification required for use of manuscript collection. Imprints, maps, periodicals, newspapers, prints, furniture, photographs, American juvenile books, almanacs, 18th century newspapers. **1.**

16 Cooper Union Museum for Arts of Decoration. Cooper Sq., New York 3. ★ Buttons, ceramics, needlework, graphic arts, lace, textiles, wallpaper; Frederick E. Church; Winslow Homer; Daniel Huntington; Thomas Moran; Peter Cooper; Abram Stevens Hewitt. **1.**

17 Corning Museum of Glass. Corning, N.Y. ● ★ Glass and glassmaking history. **1.**

18 Crampton & Knowles Loom Works. 93 Grand St., Worcester, Mass. ★ Looms.

19 Cranbrook Institute of Science. Bloomfield Hills, Mich. Mammals of Mexico, Congo, and U. S. **1.**

20 Creighton University—Library. 25th and California Sts., Omaha 2. Jesuitica. **1.**

21 Crerar, John, Library. 86 E. Randolph St., Chicago 1. ● Medical history, medical generalities; aeronautics; geology; dynamic or physical geography; physiology, pathology; comparative morphology. **1.**

22 Crozier Theological Seminary—Bucknell Library. Chester Pa. Baptist Church (history).

23 Curtiss-Wright Corp. (Development Division)—Library. 88 Llewllyn Av., Bloomfield, N. J. Market research. **1.**

24 Daprato Library of Ecclesiastical Art. 762 W. Adams St., Chicago. ● Christian symbolism; ★ dolls dressed the habits of religious orders. **1.**

25 Dartmouth College—Library. Hanover, N. H. ● Movie scripts; longevity; bookplates; New England railroads. **1-2.**

26 Daughters of the American Revolution—Museum. 1776 D St., N. W., Washinton. ★ Colonial, Revolutionary, and Federal Periods of American history; rooms of early periods; furniture and china, costumes and costume accessories, textiles, glass, silver, pewter, brass, tin, and wood. **1.**

27 Delaware, University of—Memorial Library. Newark, Del. ● Delaware (letters, diaries, autobiographies); William Hazlitt. **1.**

28 Denver Public Library—Denver. ● ★ Colorado history; history of livestock and railroads in western states; Indian tribes of west; Wild West shows; illustrations; aeronautical history (from 16th century). **1.**

29 Denver, University of—Mary Reed Library. University Park, Denver. Early English Text Society; Hakluyt Society. **1.**

30 DePauw University—Library. Greencastle, Ind. Vocations for women. **1.**

31 Detroit Institute of Arts—Reference Library. Detroit 2. Closed Monday, open afternoons on other days, except July and August when open all day. ★ History and criticism of arms and armor, pottery, puppetry, silversmithing, textiles; choice bindings. **1.**

32 Detroit Public Library. Detroit. ● Early American canals. **1.**

33 Detroit, University of—Library. McNichols Rd. at Livernois, Detroit. Hagiography; journalism. **1.**

34 De Zemler, Charles. Rockefeller Center, New York. Shaving (barbering).

35 Diocesan House—Library. One Joy St., Boston Missals. **1.**

36 District of Columbia, Public Library of—Central Library. Mount Vernon Sq., Washington. ● History of Washington and District of Columbia. **1-2.**

37 Dow Chemical Co.—Library. Midland, Michigan. ● Magnesium (index to world-wide literature on). **1-2.**

38 Drew University—Rose Memorial Library. Madison, N. J. ● Hymn books (from 1579). **1-2.**

39 Duke University—Library. Durham, N. C. ●Medieval Greek manuscripts of New Testament; North Carolina folklore; Civil War and Reconstruction periods; Walt Whitman. **1.**

40 Duns Scotus College—Library. Nine Mile and Evergreen Rds., Redford Station, Detroit. Franciscana. **1.**

41 DuPont de Nemours, E.I., & Co., Inc.—Parlin Laboratory Library. Parlin, N.J. ● Paint; varnish; lacquer; resins; plasticizers; cellulose. (Chemical Research Library, Arlington, N.J. ● Plastics; rubber; metallurgy. **1.** (Eastern Laboratory Library, P.O. Box B, Gibbstown, N.J.) ● Dynamite; detonators; ammonia oxidation; nitroglycerine. **2.**

42 Earlham College—Library. Richmond, Ind. Quakeriana. **1.**

43 Earthquake Engineering Research Institute. 45 2nd St., San Francisco 5. Engineering seismology. **1.**

44 Economics Laboratory, Inc. Guardian Bldg., St. Paul. Detergents; germicides. **1.**

45 Elizabeth, Free Public Library of City of. 11 S. Broad St., Elizabeth 4, N. J. ★ Elizabethiana. **1.**

46 Elmhurst College—Library. Elmhurst, Ill. History of Evangelical Synod; ● Hungarian literature. **1-2.**

47 Emhart Manufacturing Co.—Library. 393 Homestead Av., Hartford 2. Glass; plastics; packaging. **1.**

48 Emory University—Theological Library. Emory University, Ga. ● Methodism (leaders, history, politics). **1.**

49 Engineering Societies Library. 29 W. 39th St. New York 18. Offers literature searches and other services, on fee basis. ● All branches of engineering in detail; all articles indexed in Engineering Index; **1-3-4.**

50 Essex Institute—Library. 132-134 Essex St., Salem, Mass. ● Americana; American Revolution; caricatures; broadsides; ship's log books; numismatics. **1.**

51 Fairchild Publications—Costume Library. 8 E. 13th St., New York 3. History of costume and contemporaneous fashion. **1.**

52 Federal Housing Adminstration—Real Property Survey Data Unit. Federal Housing Adminstration Building, Washington 25. ● Real Property Inventory of 1934, Real Property Surveys conducted in several hundred cities throughout country since 1934. **3.**

53 Federal Public Housing Authority—Library. Longfellow Bldg., Rhode Island and Connecticut Avs. N.W., Washington 25. Public ownership of residential dwellings; community bonds for public housing. **1.**

54 Federal Reserve Bank of Boston—Research Library. 30 Pearl St., Boston. ● New England local banking histories. **1-2.**

55 Federal Reserve Bank of Chicago—Library. 164 W. Jackson Blvd., Chicago. ● Liberty Loan operations (World War I.) **2.**

56 Federal Trade Commision—Library. Constitution Av. and 6th St., Washington. Commercial bribery; price discrimination. **1.**

57 Federal Works Agency—Libraries. Federal Works Agency Bldg., 18th and F Sts., Washington 25. Engineering (highway, bridge, traffic); sewerage; waterworks. **1.**

58 Felt & Tarrant Manufacturing Co. 1735 N. Paulina St., Chicago 22. ★ Calculators.

59 Filson Club, Inc.—Library. 118 W. Breckinridge St., Louisville, Ky. ● Kentucky; Ohio Valley; genealogies of signers of Declaration of Independence. **1.**

60 Fire Underwriters Association of the Pacific—Library. 215 Battery St., San Francisco. ● Fire hazards (specific industries and occupations); state fire insurance codes; fire protection (rural areas). **1.**

61 First National Bank of Boston—Library. 67 Milk St., Boston. ● Argentina (banking, commerce); ★ moneys (early American legal tender and checks). **1-2.**

62 Fleischmann Laboratories—Library. 810 Grand Concourse, New York 51. Fermentation; enzymes; nutrition; cereal chemistry and physics. **1.**

63 Fletcher School of Law and Diplomacy—Edwin Ginn Library. Medford, Mass. ● Peace. **1-2.**

64 Florida State Library. State Capitol, Tallahassee. Development of early industries. **1.**

65 Florida State University Museum. Tallahassee. ★ Archeology of Florida and Peru; Spanish missions in Florida; ethnography of Seminole Indians. **1.**

66 Florida, University of—Everglades Experiment Station. Belle Glade, Fla. Corn (methods to forestall cornborer); cattle adaptable to wet terrain. **1.**

67 Fluor Corp., Ltd.—Library. P.O. Box, Los Angeles 22. Petroleum engineering (process design, physical design). **1.**

68 Folger Shakespeare Memorial Library. 201 E. Capital St., N.E., Washington. ● Book dealers' and auction catalogs; prompt books; Tudor and Stuart culture. **1.**

69 Ford, Bacon & Davis, Inc.—Library. 39 Broadway, New York 6. Coal; petroleum; manufactured and natural gas; highways; power plants; motor vechiles. **1.**

70 Fordham University Libraries. Fordham Rd. and 3d Av., New York 58. ● French Revolution; World War 1914-18; Revolutionary and early Federal periods of American history. **1.**

71 Ford Motor Co. (River Rouge Plant). 3000 Schafer Rd., Dearborn, Mich. ★ Automotive development, recent ((murals, dioramas, animated displays).

10 Fort Ticonderoga Museum. Fort Ticonderoga, N. Y. ★ Military records and equipment of American Revolution and Colonial Wars. **1.**

11 Frankford Arsenal—Library. Bridesburg, Pa. Optics: civil service. **1.**

12 Freer Gallery of Art—Library. Smithsonian Institution, 12th St. and Independence Av., S.W., Washington. ★ Far East, India, Persia, and nearer East; Bibical manuscripts. **1.**

13 Frick Collection. 1 E. 70th St., New York 21. Closed Mondays, and during August; children under 10 not admitted, those under 16 must be accompanied by adults; special lectures for groups upon application two weeks in advance; all services without charge. ★ Paintings of 14th to 19th centuries, of Italian, Dutch, Spanish, French, and English schools; Limoges enamels of 16th century; Chinese and French porcelains of 17th and 18th centuries; Italian, English and French period furniture.

14 Fruitlands and the Wayside Museums. Harvard, Mass. ★ Transcendental Movement; Shaker handicrafts and community industries; works of New England itinerant artists (1790-1850), and landscape painters of the Hudson River School. **1.**

15 General Alliance of Unitarian and other Liberal Christian Women, Circulating Library of. 25 Beacon St., Boston ● Unitarianism. **2.**

16 General Aniline and Film Corp. (Ansco Division)—Research Library. 40 Charles St., Binghamton, N.Y. Optics, x-ray. **1.**

17 General Electric Co.—Research Laboratory Library. The Knolls, Schenectady, N. Y. Loans made to outsiders with certain reservations. ● Japanese scientific journals printed in English; medals and awards in scientific fields; pure sciences (research). (Lamp Dept. Library, Nola Park, Cleveland 18) Optics. **1.**

18 General Foods Corp. Central Research Laboratories Library. 1125 Hudson St., Hoboken, N. J. ● Pectin; frozen food chemistry. **1-2.**

19 General Mills, Inc.—Division of Chemical Research library. 2010 E. Hennepin Av., Minneapolis. ★ Breakfast foods; milling by-products; starch and starch derivatives; gluten and gluten derivatives; fats, oils, fatty acids and derivatives; intermediates for protective coatings, adhesives, pharmaceuticals. **1.**

20 General Theological Seminary—Library. 175 Ninth Av., New York 11. Liturgics; patristics. **1.**

21 Geological Survey of Alabama—Library. University, Ala. ★ Conchology. **1.**

22 Georgetown University—Riggs Memorial Library. 37th and O Sts., N.W., Washington 7. ● ★ Incunabula and ancient curiosa; hagiographical and liturgical works; monastic bindings; asceticism; early Catholic Americana; Maryland Colonial history; Catholic directories, catechisms, Bibles. **1.**

23 Golden State Co., Ltd—Library. 425 Battery St., San Francisco. Milk products (industrial utilization of by-products, including casein and lactose); dairy produ ts research; nutrition (especially vitamins).

24 Goyette Museum of Americana. Peterborough, N. H. Open afternoons except Mondays. ★ Antique automobiles; Victorian harnesses and saddles; antique dolls; lead soldiers; toys; 16th and 17th century shoe, knee, and stock buckles; stores and shops of 1890's. **1.**

25 Gravity Research Foundation. New Boston, N.H. ● Gravity; application of law of gravitation to power generation.

26 Grolier Club of the City of New York —Library. 47 E. 60th St., New York 22. ● Bibliography; typography; graphic arts; miniature books; engraving; early printed books; silver book bindings; early woodcut books; ★ prints; monuments of printing. **1.**

27 Hamilton Watch Co.—Library. Lancaster, Pa. ★ Horology; crystallography.

28 Harvard University—Fogg Art Museum Library. Cambridge, Mass. ● Conservation and restoration of painting; ★ Oriental art; Spain; French architecture. **1.** (Farlow Reference Library). Cryptogamic botany; algae, fungi, hepatics, lichens, mosses. **1.** (Baker Library, Graduate School of Business Adminstration). ★ Business history (advertisements, tradecards, forms, and instruments); historical economics; business aspects of aviation; corporate finance; South Sea Bubble. **1.** (Peabody Museum of Archeology and Ethnology Library) ● Anthropology of Central America, Mexico, and Mayans. **2.** (Harvard Forest, Petersham, Mass.). ● Logging, lumbering. **1.**

29 Harvard-Yenching Institute—Library.. Boylston Hall, Cambridge, Mass. China and Japan (culture, civilization). **1.**

30 Hayes Memorial Library. Fremont, O. Mail inquiries invited. ● Rutherford B. Hayes; civil service and prison reforms; Reconstruction in the South, 1865-1876; Ohio history.

31 Haynes, John Randolph and Dora, Foundation—Library. 2324 S. Figueroa St., Los Angeles. ● Government and history of Los Angeles and California; direct legislation (all countries); migratory labor. **1-2.**

32 Heard Museum. Phoenix, Ariz. Open November-May. ★ Indian blankets; pottery, beadwork, basketry (primarily Southwestern tribes). **1.**

33 Hebrew Union College (Jewish Institute of Religion)—Library. Clifton Av., Cincinati 20. Open to residents of Cincinnati. ★ Jewish history, life, culture, music. **2-3.**

34 Higgins, John Woodman, Armory, Inc. Worcester, Mass. Closed Saturday afternoons; guides available. ★ Armor and arms of Middle Ages. **1.**

35 Houghton, E. F. & Co.—Library. 303 W. Lehigh Av., Phila. 33. Leather; lubrication; metals; textiles. **1.**

36 Huntington, Henry E. Library and Art Gallery. San Marino, Calif. American and English history and literature prior to 1900. **1.**

37 Hispanic Society of America—Museum and Library. Broadway between 155th and 156th Sts., New York. Library for reference only; closed mornings, all day Sunday and Monday, during August and last week of December; museum closed Monday, open Sunday afternoon. ★ Life and culture of Spain and Portugal (paintings, sculptures, ceramics, metalwork, textiles, furniture, history, literature, fine arts, decorative arts, costumes, old Spanish maps and majolicaware); Goya.

38 Historical and Philosophical Society of Ohio—Library. University of Cincinnati Library Bldg., Cinc:nnati 21. ★ Northwest Territory history. **1.**

39 Historical Society of Delaware—Library. Old Town Hall, Wilmington, Del. History of Delaware; ★ Rodney Family and Revolutionary letters. **1.**

40 Home Insurance Co. 59 Maiden Lane, New York. ★ Fire-fighting equipment (early and connected memorabilia, including fireworks).

41 Hunter College—Library. 695 Park Av., New York 21. ● Early English novels; British parliamentary papers from 1066 to date; Hakluyt Society publications, 1847-1934. **1.**

42 Ido-Centro. 140 Holly Av., Flushing, N.Y. International auxiliary languages (Esperanto, Valapuk, Ido Novial, etc.). **1.**

43 Illinois State Historical Library. Springfield, Ill. ● Civil War; Lincolniana; slavery and anti-slavery agitation. **1.**

44 Illinois, University of—Library. Urbana, Ill. ● Foreign-language newspapers (published in U.S.); camp publications, Civilian Conservation Corps Camps. **2-3.** (Ceramics Library). ● Ceramics. (Engineering Library). River improvement. (Chief, Division of Animal Nutrition, Room 553, Davenport Hall. ● Nutrition (index from 1900).

45 Indianapolis Public Library (Reference Department). St. Clair Sq., Indianapolis. ★ Demonology. **1.**

46 Indiana State School for the Deaf—Library. 1200 E. 42d St., Indianapolis. Visual education. **1.**

47 Indiana University—Library Box 48, Bloomington, Ind. Folklore; American Revolution; Livy; Pliny; ● 16th and 18th century economics. **1.**

48 Institute for Advanced Study—Gest Oriental Library. Princeton, N.J. ● Chinese, Japanese, Korean, Manchu, Mongol, Tibetan, Indic books. **1.**

49 Institute of General Semantics, Lakeville, Conn. ● Linguistic epistemologic scientific research.

50 Insurance Library Association of Boston. 89 Broad St., Boston. ● Automatic sprinklers; fire protection and prevention; safety standards for kerosene. **1-2.**

51 Insurance Library of Chicago. 175 West Jackson Blvd., Chicago. ● Arson; Fire (hazards; apparatus); fire fighting. **1.**

52 Insurance Society of New York—Library. 107 William St., New York 38. ★ Fire and accident prevention.

53 Interchemical Corp. (Industrial Finishes Division)—Library. Dana and Montgomery Avenues, Cincinnati 7. Paint, lacquer and varnish industry. (chemistry and physics). **1.**

54 International Business Machines Co. (Fine Arts Department). 590 Madison Av., New York. ★ Ceramics, costumed dolls, handicrafts (chiefly Western Hemisphere).

55 International Silver Co. (Historical Department). 48 State St., Meriden, Conn. Early manufacturing in Hartford and Meriden. **1.**

56 Iowa, State University of—University Libraries. Iowa City. ● Typography; voyages, travel. **1.** (Hydraulics Laboratory Library) ● Turbulence, drainage and sediment transportation.

57 Jervis Library Association. 617 N. Washington St., Rome, N.Y. ● Railroads, inland waterways. **1.**

58 Jewel Tea Co., Inc.—Library. Jewel Park, Barrington, Ill. ● Coffee technology. **1-2.**

59 Jewish Theological Seminary of America—Library. 3080 Broadway, New York 27. Hebraica; Judaica; Talmud and Jewish law; Anglo-Judaica; Spanish and Portuguese Inquisition.

60 Johns Hopkins University—Library. North Charles and 34th Sts., Baltimore 18. ● Rare Americana; Sidney Lanier; Romance philology; Biblical archaeology; Sanskrit literature and language. **1.**

10 Joint Reference Library of Public Adminstration Clearing House. 1313 E. 60th St., Chicago 37. • Zoning ordinances; civil service (laws, rules, ordinances, classification plans.) **2.**

11 Jones, John Price, Co., Inc.—Library. 150 Nassau St., New York. Case histories of fund-raising campaigns (largely unavailable to public); statistics on philanthropic giving in U. S. (published by company or released to press).

12 Kalamazoo Public Library. Kalamazoo, Mich. • Horses; horsemanship. **1.**

13 Kansas City, University of—Robert Snyder Memorial Library. 5100 Rockhill Rd., Kansas City 4, Mo. Western Americana; Missouri Kansas border outlaws; Mormons. **1.**

14 Kansas State Historical Society—Library. Memorial Bldg., Topeka, Kan. North American Indians; Western Americana. **1.**

15 Kentucky, University of.—Library. Lexington, Ky. •Americana; British history.**1.**

16 Knox College—Library. Galesburg, Ill. Northwest history. **1.**

17 Lanston Monotype Machine Co.—Library. 24th and Locust Sts., Philadelphia 3. Letter design; printing; typography. **1.**

18 Lehigh University—Library. Bethlehem, Pa. • Civil War; railroads, canals; metallurgy. **1.**

19 Lewis, Wilmarth S. Farmington, Conn. • Correspondence of Horace Walpole.

20 Library of Congress. Washington 25. Ancient atlases (Ptolemy, Ortelius, Blaeu, Mercator); early American music (rare books from year 1581); Orientalia (Chinese herbals); Genji commentaries; printers' and publishers' marks. **1-2-3.**

21 Library of Vehicles. 2919-2929 W. Broadway, Los Angeles 41. Wellington Everett Miller, Owner. Private library open by appointment; research fees charged. ★ All forms of personal land transportation vehicles, especially automobiles; automotive sales catalogs, instruction books, accessory catalogs. **1.**

22 Lilly, Eli, and Co.—Library. Alabama and McCarty Sts., Indianapolis. • Foreign medical directories; drug advertisements (American and foreign). **2-3.**

23 Lincoln National Life Foundation and Museum. Lincoln National Life Insurance Co., Fort Wayne, Ind. ★ Lincolniana. **1.**

24 Lloyd Library and Museum. 309 W. Court St., Cincinnati 2. ★ Mycology; pharmacy. **1.**

25 Lockheed Aircraft Corp.—Engineering Library. Burbank, Calif. Aircraft armaments, armor plate. **1.**

26 Long Beach Public Library. Ocean and Pacfic, Long Beach, Calif. California mines. **1.**

27 Los Angeles Public Library. 630 W. 5th St., Los Angeles 17. ★ U.S. Patent drawings and specifications from July, 1871; woman suffrage; Susan B. Anthony; Spanish-Mexican colonial period of California and the Southwest.(Science and Industry Department, 530 S. Hope St.) Pacific Coast voyages; directories (city and telephone); mines and oil fields index (California). **1.** (Municipal Reference Library, 300 City Hall. • Fire fighting, hazards, prevention; traffic control; criminology. **2.** (Power and Light Div., 207 S. Broadway). Boulder Dam.

28 Louisiana State University—Chemistry Library. University, La. • Cotton seed oil; tung oil; cane sugar industry. **2.**

29 Louisiana State University and Agricultural and Mechanical College—Library. Baton Rouge 3. • Plantations; prison history and science; Louisiana politics, 1803-1861; Latin America. **1.**

30 Maine Historical Society—Library. 485 Congress St., Portland, Me. Early New England; ★ autographs. **1.**

31 Mariner's Museum. Newport News, Va. ★ Ship figureheads; scale models of historic ships, American Indian birch bark canoes; navigation from early times; life-savings at sea; whaling; logs, maps and postage stamps relating to ships and navigation. **1.**

32 Maryland Historical Society—Library. 201 West Monument St., Baltimore 1. • Calvert Papers; sheet music (Maryland imprints); African colonization. **1.**

33 Maryland State Library. Court of Appeals Bldg., Annapolis. • Laws, codes, reports of every state in U.S., and England, Ireland, Canada. **1.**

34 Massachusetts Horticultural Society—Library. 300 Massachusetts Av., Boston 15. Nursery catalogs (foreign and domestic) **1-2.**

35 Massachusetts Institute of Technology—Dard Hunter Paper Museum. Cambridge 39, Mass. ★ Papermaking tools, equipment, and appliances from Asia, Europe, and America, dating from 105 A.D., (including European papermaking moulds, watermarking devices, samples of plain and decorated papers; old and modern watermarks; printing processes, and type-casting, type-making equipment. **1.**

36 Massachusetts New-Church Union—Library. 134 Bowdoin St., Boston 8. • Emanuel Swedenborg; New-Church authors. **1.**

37 Massachusetts State Archives—Library. 438 State House, Boston 33. • Pequot, King Phillip's, French and Indian, Revolutionary wars; Shay's Rebellion. **1.**

38 Massachusetts State Library. State House, Boston. • British parliamentary debates and proceedings. **1.**

39 Mathes, J. M., Inc.—Library. 122 E. 42d St., New York 17. Advertising; drugs; foods; oil; rubber; textiles; tobacco; toiletries; World War II. **1.**

40 May's Tropical Exhibition. Lytle Star Route, Colorado Springs, Colorado. Open without charge to educational groups. ★ Large tropical arthropods (spiders, scorpions, centipedes, beetles, phasmids, moths butterflies).

41 McCormick Historical Association—Library. 401 Fullerton Parkway, Chicago. Democratic Party; Cyrus Hall McCormick; • agricultural machinery (history). **1.**

42 McCormick Theological Seminary—Virginia Library. 826 Belden Av., Chicago. • Bibles; John Bunyan. **1.**

43 McGill University—Wood Library of Ornithology. Sherbrooke, Montreal, Quebec, Can. Falconry. **2.**

44 Mergenthaler Linotype Co. 29 Ryerson St., Brooklyn 5. ★ Typesetters (early American).

45 Merrell, Wm. S., Co.—Library. Lochland Station, Cincinnati 15. Bacteriology; biochemistry; pharmacology; pharmacy. **1.**

46 Metal & Thermit Corp.—Research Laboratory Library. Randolph St. and Rahway Av., Woodbridge, N.J. (mailing address: P.O. Box 255, Rahway, N.J.). Electrochemistry; metallurgy; welding. **1.**

47 Methodist Board of Missions and Church Extension—Library. 150 Fifth Av., New York 11. Rural sociology; missions (Africa, China, India, Japan, Korea, Latin America). **1.**

48 Metro-Goldwyn-Mayer Studios—Library. Culver City, Calif. ★ Automobile license plates from 1928; costume (military and police); prisons and penitentiaries; social life and customs of England and United States. **1.**

49 Metropolitan Museum of Art—Costume Institute. 5th Av. at 82nd St., New York 28. ★ Historical costume. **1.**

50 Metropolitan Museum of Art in the Cloisters. Fort Tryon Park, New York. ★ Sculpture, architectural material, tapestries of Middle Ages. **1.**

51 Michigan, University of—General Library. Ann Arbor, Mich. • French Canada (history); dictionaries (English language, prior to 18th century); Hawaiian Islands; imaginary voyages; labor parties and labor movements; military history and science (prior to 1800); fungi; ascension balloons; railroads (history); canals; toll bridges; "good roads" movement; periodicals published before 1800; automotive industry. **1.**

52 Miller Co. 99 Center St., Meriden, Conn. ★ Abstract painting and sculpture (selected to reflect the development of modern architecture). **1.**

53 Milwaukee Public Library' 814 West Wisconsin Av., Milwaukee 3. ★ Oriental art; boxing; chess and checkers; state geological publications. **1.**

54 Milwaukee Public Museum. Milwaukee. Material available to students, under supervision. ★ Firearms; typewriters (including related documentary material); American Indians (tribes of California, Northwest Coast, Southwest, Plains, Eastern and Western Woodlands, prehistoric tribes in northern Mississippi Valley); Eskimoes. **1.**

55 Minneapolis Institute of Arts—Library. 201 E. 24th St., Minneapolis 4. Travel; dance; costume; typography. **1.**

56 Minneapolis Public Library. Minneapolis • Scandinavian books and periodicals.

57 Minnesota Historical Society. St. Paul. • History of forest products. **1.**

58 Minnesota Mining and Manufacturing Co.—Library. 900 Fauquier Av., St. Paul 6. Mineralogy; ceramics. **1.**

59 Minnesota, University of—Library. Minneapolis 14. Modern magic. **1.** (Law Library) • Tribal laws of the American Indian. **1.**

60 Mississippi State Department of Archives and History—Library. War Memorial Bldg., Jackson, Mississippi • Plantation history; Mississippi newspapers. **1.**

61 Missouri Botanical Garden—Library. 2315 Tower Grove Av., St. Louis 10. • Gardening; herbals and Linnaena. **1.**

62 Missouri Historical Society. Jeff:rson Memorial Library Building, St. Louis 12. Extensive use limited to members of Society. ★ Fur trade of the West (1800-1860); theater in Mississippi Valley (1830-1870); Charles Lindbergh; Lewis and Clark Expedition; Thomas Jefferson.

63 Missouri, University of—Library. Columbia, Mo. Western Americana. **1.**

10 Montclair Free Public Library. Church St., Montclair, N.J. • Children's books (foreign countries). **1.**

11 Morgan, Pierpont Library. 29-33 E. 36th St., New York 16. •Autograph manuscripts and letters; illuminated manuscripts; first and rare editions (English, French, German, Italian); papyri; cuneiform tablets. **1.**

12 Morris Arboretum—Library. University of Pennsylvania, Meadow Brook Lane, Chestnut Hill, Phila. • Ligneous plants; early American botany. **1.**

13 Meuller & Co., V. 408 S. Honore St., Chicago 12. ★ Surgical instruments.

14 Museum of Fine Arts—Library. Boston 15. ★ Heraldry, costumes, Egyptian art, and art of the Far East. **1.**

15 Museum of International Folk Art. Santa Fe, N.M. ★ Folk art from all parts of world. **1.**

16 Museum of Modern Art—Library. 11 W. 53d St., New York 19. ★ Modern art, upwards of 26,000 photographs (glossy reproductions sold) and 18,000 slides (available for rent; negatives for sale). **1.**

17 Museum of Non-Objective Painting. 1071 5th Av., New York 28. ★ Non-objective painting dating from 1910; catalogs, books, finding lists. **1.**

18 National Canners Association—Research Laboratory. 1133 20th St., N. W. Washington 6. Production, processing, and utilization of food products; spoilage of canned food.

19 National Child Labor Committee—Library. 419 Fourth Av., New York 16. Employment of youth and imigrants; vocational training and guidance. **1.**

20 National Lead Co. (Titanium Division)—Research Laboratory Library. P.O. Box 57, South Amboy, N.J. Titanium dioxide. **1.**

21 National Park Service—Library. Department of the Interior, Merchandise Mart, Chicago. Recreation programs; scenic values (conservation of); history of U.S. preservation of fauna, flora, archeological ruins and historic sites. **1.**

22 National Probation Association, Inc. —Library. 1790 Broadway, New York 19. Courts (juvenile, domestic relations, adolescent); correctional institutions; detention homes. **1.**

23 National Serigraph Society. 38 W. 57th St., New York 19. • Silk screen process. **1.**

24 National Slag Association—Library Warner Building, Washington 4. • Uses of screened and crushed iron blast furnace slag. **1-2.**

25 National Society for Crippled Children and Adults—Library. 11 S. LaSalle St., Chicago. • Vocational guidance and employment of handicapped; legislation affecting handicapped; architectural design in homes, institutions, other buildings to be used by handicapped; prosthetic devices; parent education. **1.**

26 Newark Museum—Library. Newark. ★ Tibetan art and ethnology; Japanese netsukes; Roman and Egyptian glass; art and science of mechanics; numismatics. **1.**

27 Newark, N.J., Public Library of. 5 Washington St., Newark. • Catechisms; almanacs; chap-books; Christmas cards (from 1846). **1-2.**

28 New Church Theological School—Library. 48 Quincy St., Cambridge, Mass. Swedenborgianism; New Jerusalem Church. **1.**

29 New England Conservatory of Music —Library. 290 Huntington Av., Boston 15. Rare musical manuscripts, early published music. **1.**

30 New England Electric Railway Historical Society, Inc. Biddeford Road, Kennebunkport, Me. (shops and equipment), and 70 Spring Hill Terrace, Somerville 42, Mass. (general offices). ★ Electric railway rolling stock and equipment.

31 New England Historic Genealogical Society. 9 Ashburton Pl., Boston 8. Use of manuscripts restricted to members. • History of Boston; city directories.

32 New Hampshire, University of—Hamilton Smith Library. Durham, N.H. New Hampshireana; • mineralogy. **1.**

33 New Jersey Zinc Co.—Technical Library. 160 Front St., New York 7. Galvanizing; paint; rubber; microscopy; metallography; pigments. **1.**

34 New York Historical Society—Library. 170 Central Park West, New York 24. History; Rare Americana; early American poetry. **1.**

35 New York Public Library (Schomburg Collection). 104 W. 136th St., New York. Reference only; closed Monday morning and Saturday afternoon; information available by mail or telephone. ★ Negro life (including African and Western Hemisphere materials); Negro newspapers, playbills, pamphlets; sheet music and recordings of music composed and performed by Negroes; Liberian textbooks, grammars of various African languages; African weapons; Negro in Masonry; African art objects.

36 New York Society—Library. 53 E. 79th St., New York 21. • Early American fiction. **1.**

37 New York State College of Forestry—Moon Memorial Library. Syracuse University, Syracuse 10. Lumbering and logging industries; wood technology. **1.**

38 New York Department of Health (Division of Laboratories and Research)—Publications and Museum Department Library. New Scotland Av., Albany 1. Immunology; sanitary and analytical chemistry. **1.**

39 New York State Historical Association. Cooperstown, N.Y. • Folklore of supernatural. **1.**

40 New York Times—Museum of the Recorded Word. 229 W. 43d St., New York. ★ Newspaper publishing.

41 North Carolina, University of—Library. Chapel Hill, N.C. • American theatre, 1881-1931; Latin America; rural social economics; Spanish drama (19th century); books and printing; Shakespeareana; Johnsoniana; Sir Walter Raleigh. **1.**

42 Northern Indiana Historical Society —Library. 112 S. Lafayette Blvd., South Bend, Ind. ★ 18th century pioneer; Indians; explorers. **1.**

43 North Texas State Teachers College—Library. Denton, Tex. • Children's books. **1.**

44 Northwestern University—Library. Evanston, Ill. • Japanese politics and government (in Japanese); Deism.

45 Norton Co.—Library. New Bond St., Worcester, Mass. Abrasives; ceramics. **1.**

46 Notre Dame, University of—Library. Notre Dame, Ind. Catholic Church history; Dante. **1.**

47 Oberlin College—Library. Oberlin, O. Anti-slavery propaganda literature. **1.**

48 Occidental College—Mary Norton Clapp Library. 1600 Campus Rd., Los Angeles. • Presbyterianism; fine printing; California history. **1.**

49 O'Hanlon, Redmond L. 4 Clove Lakes Pl., Staten Island 10. Shakespeareana (puns, plays on words).

50 Ohio State University—A. F. Davis Welding Library. Columbus 10. ★ Welding and related subjects (including 15,000 indexed patent specifications). (F. T. Stone Institute of Hydrobiology, Put-in-Bay, O.) ★ Ohio fish, amphibians, reptiles, insects, and invertebrates; climate and biota of Lake Erie; effect of climatic, geologic, biologic, and sociologic factors on acquatic organisms and aquatic productivity.

51 Ohio Wesleyan University—Library. Delaware, O. • Rare books by and about the Brownings; rare classical literature; Methodist history. **1.**

52 Oklahoma Historical Society—Library. Historical Bldg., Oklahoma City 5. History of South, Southwest; Indians. **1.**

53 Oklahoma, University of—Library of School of Geology and Oklahoma Geological Survey. Norman, Okla. Paleontology; oil and gas; aerial photography. **1.**

54 Old Sturbridge Village, Sturbridge, Mass. ★ Tools, antique craft products, machinery, homes, mills, shops, public buildings; life, hand industries, and crafts of New England in the 18th and 19th centuries. **1.**

55 Oregon State College—Library. Corvallis, Ore. History of horticulture (16th to 19th centuries); forestry; plant pathology, mycology, taxonomy and ecology. **1.**

56 Oregon, University of—Oregon Museum of Natural History. Eugene, Ore. ★ Archeology of early man in North America and Pacific Northwest. **1.**

57 Owens-Illinois Glass Co. 1700 W. Westwood Av., Toledo 1, O. Plastics; food processing. **1.**

58 Pan American Union—Columbus Memorial Library. 17th and B Sts., Washington 6. • Climate, mines and mining, aviation, customs, railroads, roads, literature, budgets, departmental reports, detailed maps of small areas (for member nations of Pan-American Union). **1-2.**

59 Panhandle-Plains Historical Museum. Canyon, Tex. ★ History of Texas Panhandle (archeology, history and developement of cattle industry; branding irons, cattle industry artifacts, western firearms; Pliocene and Pleistocene Indian artifacts). **1.**

60 Paraffine Companies, Inc.—Research Department Library. 1550 Powell St., Emeryville, Calif. Resins, drying oils, roofing, asphalt, wallboard, underground pipe protection. **1.**

61 Pennsylvania Dutch Folklore Center. Franklin and Marshall College, Lancaster, Pa. • Pennsylvania Dutch folklore, arts, crafts; dialect; music. **1.**

62 Pennsylvania Salt Manufacturing Co.—Research and Development Library. Box 4388, Chestnut Hill Station, Phila. 18. Ceramics; pulp and paper. **1.**

63 Pennsylvania, University of—Library. Philadelphia. • ★ Medieval ecclesiastical history, Inquisition; Shakespeareana; Elizabethan and Tudor literature; 17th century plays; Dante; Petrarch; Tasso; German philology; early American drama; Sanskrit manuscripts; Franklin imprints; history of chemistry; Chinese alchemy. **1-2-3.**

64 Perkins Institution and Massachusetts School for the Blind—Library. Watertown 72, Mass. •Blind in the field of art. **1-2.**

65 Pfizer, Chas. & Co., Inc.—Technical Library. 11 Bartlett St., Brooklyn 6. Chemistry (pharmaceutical, biological, bacteriological). **1.**

10 Philadelphia Museum of Art (Philadelphia Textile Institute)—Library. 320 S. Broad St., Philadelphia 2. Textile industry; fabrics; American and European art dealers, catalogs.

11 Philadelphia Textile Institute—Hesslein Library. 3243 School House Lane, Philadelphia 44. Textile microscopy, testing, dyeing, and colors; wool yarn spinning; and synthetic textile fibers. **2.**

12 Philipse Castle Restoration. Sleepy Hollow Restorations, Inc., West Sunnyside Lane, (Irvington-on-Hudson Post Office) Tarrytown, N.Y. ★ Houses, barns, grist mill, and other structures depicting life, handicrafts, trades household furnishings of early Dutch-American settlers, especially Hudson River Dutch.

13 Pilgrim Society—Library. Plymouth, Mass. ● Early Plymouth and Pilgrims. **1.**

14 Pineapple Research Institute of Hawaii. P. O. Box 3166, Honolulu 2, T.H. Pineapple culture, marketing and packing. **1.**

15 Pioneer Museum and Haggin Art Galleries, Stockton, Cal. ★ California history (particularly San Joaquin Valley); furniture; utensils; fire engines; guns.

16 Pittsburgh, University of—Libraries. Fifth Av., Pittsburgh. Dentistry; social work. **1.**

17 Plainfield Public Library and Reading Room. 802 College Pl., Plainfield, N.J. ● Seventh Day Baptists. **1.**

18 Portland General Electric Co.—Library. Electric Bldg., Portland 3, Ore. Street railways.

19 Portland, Library Association of—Reference Department Library. 801 S.W. 10th Av., Portland 5, Ore. Early history of Northwest. **1.**

20 Pratt, Enoch, Free Library. 400 Cathedral St., Baltimore 1. ★ Baltimore and Maryland (history, including special indexes); Egdar Allen Poe; ● research material used in preparation of The American Language; Henry L. Mencken. (Dept of Fine Arts) ● Greeting parts. **2.** (Dept. Business and Economics) ● Direct mail advertising pieces. **2.**

21 Pratt Institute (Art Reference Department)—Library. Ryesrson St., Brooklyn 5. Costume; textile design; camouflage design. **1.**

22 Princeton University — Library. Princeton, N.J. Egyptology; Assyriology; international law and diplomacy; Index of Christian Art (1-1400 A.D.). **1.**

23 Printer's Ink Clearing House of Advertised Phrases. 205 E. 42nd St., New York 17. Free slogan checking and recording service. ● Slogans and advertised phrases recorded since 1919. (9,000 on file).

24 Providence Public Library (Science and Industry Department). 229 Washington St., Providence 3, R. I. Patents (U.S.); bridge; checkers; whist; slavery; Civil War.**1.**

25 Purdue University—Library. Lafayette, Ind. ● History of engineering; modern printing. **1.**

26 Queens Borough Public Library. 89-14 Parsons Blvd., Jamaica 32, N.Y. Reference only. ● Long Island history; costumes. **1.**

27 Radio Corporation of America—RCA Laboratories Library. Princeton, N.J. Acoustics; optics. **1.**

28 Railroad Retirement Board—Library. 844 Rush St., Chicago 11. ● Health; disability; old-age insurance; unemployment and workmen's compensation; pension plans. **1-2.**

29 Reilly Tar and Chemical Corp.—Reilly Laboratories Library. 1500 S. Tibbs Av., Indianapolis 44. Coal tar products. **1.**

30 Ripley, Dr. Dillon. Litchfield, Conn. Living foreign water fowl.

31 Rowell, Dr. Hugh Grant. Philipse Castle, 381 Bellwood Av., North Tarrytown, N.Y. ★ Early timepieces (except watches), especially American and Dutch makers and their works, and Canadian makers of Terry clocks; circus materials, including (broadsides, lithographs, models of early circuses).

32 Rutstein, Leo, and Associates—Library. 80 Florida St., Long Beach, N.Y. Coated fabrics; explosives; plastics; cellulose; lacquers. **1.**

33 Shelburne Museum. Shelburne, Vt. Colonial folk art displayed in reconstructed Colonial village. Items include early carrousel and calliope, early American hat boxes, Wilhelm Schimmel carvings, colonial handicrafts, weathervanes.

34 Smithsonian Institution—Bureau of American Ethnology Library. Washington 25. ● American Indian ethnology (especially languages), and Indians of Central and South America and West Indies. **1-2.** (Freer Gallery of Art, 12th St. and Independence Av., S. W.) ● Art and culture of Far East, India, and Persia; Bibical Manuscripts. **1.**

35 Southern California, University of—Library. Los Angeles 7. ★ Book plates; motion picture history and development; personalism; Hamlin Garland ● encyclopedias (history of). **1-2-3.** (Allen Hancock Foundation Library,3616 University Av., Los Angeles.) Marine zoology and biology. **1.**

36 Southwest Research Institute. Milam Building, San Antonio, Tex. Translators (throughout country, capable of translating from foreign languages into English). **1.**

37 San Diego Public Library (Business and Technology Department). 8th Av. and E. St., San Diego. California mines (card index). **1.**

38 San Francisco Museum of Art, San Francisco 2. ● French 19th century art as related to literature; Latin American art; museology.

39 San Francisco Public Library. San Francisco. ★ Early English jest books. **1.**

40 Schenley Distillers Corp.—Library. 350 Fifth Av., New York 1. ● Drugs. **1.**

41 Schwarz Laboratories, Inc—Library. 202 E. 44th St., New York. Brewing chemistry; manufacture of fine chemicals from yeast; fermentation. **1.**

42 Schwenkfelder Historical Library. Pennsburg, Pa. Schwenkfelders, Mennonites, Lutheran and German Reformed, Moravians, Brethren, Quakers. **1.**

43 Scottish Rite of Freemasonry (Southern Jurisdiction, U.S.A.)—Library of Supreme Council 16th and S Streets, N.W. Washington. ● Freemasonry; Masonic encyclopedias and transactions, literature on the occult; Roman Law; Robert Burns; Lincolniana. **1.**

44 Scott Paper Co.—Technical Library. Chester, Pa. Paper manufacture; colloids. **1.**

45 Scripps Foundation for Research in Population Problems. Miami University, Oxford, O. ● Ohio Valley history; William Holmes McGuffey. **1.**

46 Scripps Institution of Oceanography (University of California)—Library. La Jolla, Calif. Beach erosion; plankton; weather forecasting. **1.**

47 Seaman's Bank for Savings. 74 Wall St., New York. ★ Banks (mechanical toy); seaman's handicraft; ship models and paintings.

48 Seattle Art Museum. Seattle, Washington. ★ Historical art of China, Japan, Indonesia, Near East, Egypt; African sculpture and masks; Peruvian textiles.

49 Seattle Public Library. 4th and Madison Sts., Seattle. Americana (Pacific Northwest); ★ Seattle theatre programs. **1.**

50 Shell Development Co.—Library. 100 Bush St., San Francisco. Fertilizers. **1.**

51 Shrewsbury Free Public Library. Shrewsbury, Mass. ● Artemus Ward. **1.**

52 Sierra Club—Library. 220 Rush St., San Francisco. Mountaineering; skiing; conservation. **1.**

53 Simmons-Boardman Publishing Corp.—Library. 30 Church St., New York 7. Primarily a staff library; limited service to public. ● Railroad history, economics, and statistics; early American railway periodicals; Interstate Commerce Commission statistics.

54 Smith College (Department of Music) —Library. Northampton, Mass. ● Italian madrigals and instrumental music of 16th and 17th centuries. **1.**

55 Sondley Reference Library. Asheville, N.C. Southeastern states history; North Caroliniana. **1.**

56 South Dakota, University of—W. H. Over Museum. Vermillion, S. D. ★ South Dakota archeology; ethnology of Sioux, Arikara, and Mandan Indians. **1.**

57 Southern Methodist University—Fondren Library. Dallas 5. ● Spanish plays; history of Southwest.

58 Southwest Museum—Library. Museum Dr. and Marmion Way, Highland Park, Los Angeles. History and Indians of Southwest. **1.**

59 Sprague Library. 159 E. 49th St., New York 17. Address Mrs. Frank J. Sprague. By appointment only. Walt Whitman (reference library on; rare books associated with); John Bartlett (all editions of "Quotations").

60 Squibb Institute for Medical Research —Library. 25 Columbia Heights, Brooklyn 2. Foreign pharmaceutical prescriptions; pharmaceutical drugs (composition and action). **4.**

61 St. Augustine Historical Society and Institute of Science—Webb Memorial Library. St. Francis St., St. Augustine, Fla. Indians in Florida (history, culture); ● Stephen Vincent Benet. **1.**

62 St. Bonaventure University—Friedsam Memorial Library. St. Bonaventure, N. Y. Translators (Greek, Latin, Medieval Latin, Polish); Microphotography; Franciscans and Franscian Order (10,000 item union catalog).

63 St. Frances Xavier (Old) Cathedral—Library. 205 Church St., Vincennes, Ind. Early missionary work and development of Northwest Territory. **1.**

64 St. Joseph Museum. St. Joseph, Mo. ★ Missouri birds, mammals, snakes, amphibians, other wildlife. **1.**

65 St. Vincent Archabbey and College—Library. Latrobe, Pa. Patrology; church history. **1.**

66 Stefansson Library. 67 Morton St., New York 14. Polar and sub-polar regions; discovery of America (Norse to Columbus); folklore; diets (of primitive people, meat eating, deficiency diseases, scurvy). **1-4.**

67 Stevens Institute of Technology. Castle Point, Hoboken, N. J. ● Scientific management movement. **1.**

68 Studebaker Corp.—Library. 635 S. Main St., South Bend 27, Ind. Reference only. ● History of automobile and automotive industry; vehicle catalogs and price lists dating from 1852. **1.**

10 Sukov, Dr. Marvin. 218 Doctors Building, Minneapolis 2. Material available to research workers. ● Little magazines (dating from 1900).

11 Sun Oil Co.—Library. Marcus Hook, Pa. ● Petroleum refining; foreign technical literature. **1-4.**

12 Syracuse University—Lyman Hall Branch Library. University Campus, Syracuse 10. ● History of science. **1.**

13 Taylor Instrument Co.—Library. 95 Ames St., Rochester, N.Y. Taxes; patents; temperature; pressure; humidity; weather instruments. **1.**

14 Temple University—Library. Philadelphia. ● German literature (20th Century); business history.

15 Tennessee, University of—Department of Anthropology. Knoxville, Tenn. ★ Archeology of Tennessee (documented materials). **1.**

16 Texas, University of—Law Library. Austin 12. ● Jurisprudence; insurance; Spanish source books. **1.**

17 Theological Seminary of the Presbyterian Church in the U.S.A.—Library. Princeton, N.J. ● Doctrinal controversy (Baptist); hymnology; Puritan and Non-conformist literature; early American theological pamphlets.

18 Theosophical Society (San Francisco Lodge)—Library. Native Sons Bldg., 414 Mason St., San Francisco. Occultism.

19 Tobacco Merchants Association of the United States—Library. 341 Madison Av., New York 17 ● Tobacco. **1.**

20 Toledo Scale Co. Telegraph Rd., Toledo. ★ Weighing devices.

21 True, David O. Miami, Fla. Florida history (treasure, pirates, wreckers).

22 Tulane University of Louisiana (Middle American Research Institute)—Library. New Orleans 18. Southern Mexico; Central America; civilization of Mayans. **1.**

23 Twentieth Century-Fox Studio—Library. Beverly Hills Calif. ● Historical costumes; costumes for military and service personnel for various countries; early guidebooks to New York and London; travel; early books on English and American etiquette. **2-4.**

24 Underwood Corp. 1 Park Av., New York 16. ★ Typewriters (historical and contemporary).

25 Union Pacific Railroad—Union Pacific Museum. 120 Broadway. New York 5. ★ Headdresses (American Indian); kitchen utensils (early American Mormon); early West (western pioneer items).

26 United Shoe Machinery Corp. 140 Federal St., Boston. ★ Footwear (from 2000 B.C.).

27 United States Army Air Forces—Technical Library. Lowry Field, Denver. Photography; armaments; surveying maps. **1.** (Chanute Field, Ill.) Photography; meteorology.

28 United States Army Command and General Staff School—Library. Fort Leavenworth, Kan. Law; naval science. **1.**

29 United States Bureau of Mines—Petroleum and Natural Gas Division Library. 630 Sansome St., San Francisco. ● Long period statistics on petroleum industry.

30 United States Coast Guard Academy—Library. New London, Conn. American Merchant Marine; shipwrecks; piracy; privateering; Arctic exploration and discovery. **1.**

31 United States Department of Agriculture (Agricultural Marketing Service)—Cotton Division Library. 12th and C Sts., S.W., Agricultural Annex, Washington. ● Cotton and cottonseed marketing and uses. (Bureau of Dairy Industry Library, Independence Av., Between 12th and 14th Sts., S.W.) ● Index of dairy industry literature (including casein and lactose). (Bureau of Entomology and Plant Quarantine Library, South Building, Independence Av. and 14th St., S.W.) ● Indexes to literature of entomology. **2.** (Bureau of Reclamation, Engineering Division Library.) ● Irrigation projects, dams, and power plants (specifications for). **2.** (Library, United States Forest Service, Region 8, Peachtree Building, 50 7th St., Atlanta, Ga.) ● Lumbering and pulp and paper industries (in the South). (Division of Field Library Services, Entomology Sub-branch Library, Beltsville, Md.) ● Beekeeping (bibliography). **1.**

32 United States Department of Commerce—Coast and Geodetic Survey Library. Washington 25. Restricted to official use (research workers associated with recognized institutions wishing access to collections must make written application to Director) ● Positional astronomy, gravity, and magnetism of earth; photogrammetry; seismology. **1.**

33 United States Department of the Interior—Fish and Wildlife Service Library. Interior Building, Washington 25. ● Fur production; game protection (laws, preserves). **1.** (Geological Survey Library, 18th and F Sts., N.W., Washington.) ● Official geological publications (Argentina, Australia, Austria, Belgium, Brazil, Canada, China, Colombia, Denmark, Dutch East Indies, Finland, France, Germany, Great Britian, Holland, Hungary, India, Italy, Japan, Norway, Peru, Poland, South Africa, Spain, Sweden, Russia). **2.**

34 United States Navy Department—Bureau of Ships. 19th St. and Constitution Av., Washington. Camouflage; explosives. (Naval Ordnance Laboratory—Library. Navy Yard, Washington 25.) Electronics; machine design. **1.** (United States Naval Academy—Library. Annapolis, Md.) ● Shipbuilding; small boats and yachting; history of electricity. **1.**

35 United States Rubber Co. Naugatuck Chemical Division Library. Naugatuck, Conn. ● Rubber, rubber compounding ingredients.

36 United States Sugar Corp. Clewiston, Fla. Beef cattle which harden off other feeds than grain.

37 Upsala College—Library. 339 Propect St., East Orange, N.J. Scandinavian literature. **1.**

38 Van Sciver Automobile Museum. Chestnut Hill, Pa. ★ Automobiles of 1909 or before; photographs of old automobiles.

39 Vanderbilt, R. T., Co. (Rubber Department)—Library. 32 Winfield St., East Norwalk, Conn. Chemistry (rubber). **1.**

40 Vassar College—Library. Poughkeepsie, N.Y. ● Bliss Carman (first editions); history of periodical press; Knights of Malta. **1.**

41 Vermont, University of, and State Agricultural College—Library. Burlington, Vt. ● Civil War; early printing. **1.**

42 Virginia, University of—Alderman Library. Charlottesville, Va. ● Americana; Negro; T. S. Eliot; typography. **1.**

43 Volta Bureau. 1537 35th St., N.W., Washington 7, Address the executive secretary. ● All aspects of deafness (including education of deaf, speech training, lipreading or speechreading, hearing aids.

44 Wadsworth Atheneum. Hartford, Conn. Closed mornings and all day Monday. ★ 17th century Dutch painting; 19th century French painting; British water colors; antique bronzes; European porcelain, silver, tapestries, arms and armor; early American furniture; early Central and South American art; ballet costumes and designs. **1.**

45 Wahl-Henius Institute. 1135 Fullerton Av., Chicago 14. Reference use only. Pure cultures of molds and yeasts; fermentation chemistry and technology as applied to ale, beer, cereals, enzymes, hops, malts, water, and wine.

46 Wallerstein Co., Inc.—Library. 180 Madison Av., New York 16. Brewing chemistry; enzymes; fermentation. **1.**

47 Waltham Watch Co. 221 Crescent St., Waltham, Mass. Loaned under certain circumstances. ★ Watches (antique from mid-19th century).

48 Warshaw Collection of Business Americana. 752 West End Av., New York 25. Trademark and patent research; business Americana (including catalogs, labels, posters, packages). **1.**

49 Washington State College. Pullman, Wash. History of Pacific Northwest; World Wars; (World War I state papers of European countries, foreign newspapers).

50 Washington University—Ridgley Library. Skinker Rd. and Lindell Blvd., St. Louis. ● Rare books and manuscripts; archeology; numismatics; modern language translators (including Russian); Mississippi River; DeSoto Exploration; campaign material (propaganda); art dealers' catalogs. **1.**

51 Washington, University of—Library. Seattle 5. Chinese bibliography; botany of Pacific Northwest; book arts; oceanography; exploration and discovery, Pacific Northwest. **1.**

52 Washoe County Library, Reno, Nev. Nevada history; mining. **1.**

53 Watertown Arsenal—Library. Watertown, Mass. Ferrous metallurgy. **1.**

54 Webb Institute of Naval Architecture and Marine Engineering—Library Webb and Sedgwick Avenues, New York 63. ● Shipbuilding. **1.**

55 Wenzlick, Roy & Co.—Library. 915 Olive St., St. Louis. Real estate; U.S. rents and housing activities (state, county, city). **1.**

56 West Point Museum. West Point, N.Y. Closed Mondays. ★ Evolution of military weapons (particularly rifles, pistols, revolvers, machine guns, artillery material, and ammunition). **1.**

57 Westerfield, Mrs. Jaxon. Camden, Me. ★ Early American fabrics and costumes.

58 Western Cartridge Co. (Division of Olin Industries)—Technical Library. East Alton, Ill. Cellulose; small arms ammunition. **1.**

59 Western Kentucky State College—Library. Bowling Green, Ky. ● Almanacs dating from 1795. **1.**

60 Western Precipition Corp.—Library. 1016 W. 9th St., Los Angeles. Dust control and particle size measurement; electrical precipitation of dust, fume and mists. **1.**

61 Western Reserve Historical Society. 10825-10915 East Blvd., Cleveland 6. ★ Shaker Society manuscript records; Ohio and Civil War history; history of lighting; atlases; Arctic travel.

10 Western Reserve University — Libraries. Cleveland 6. • Auduboniana; bookplates; Protestant Reform; history of printing. **1.**

11 Westinghouse Electric and Manufacturing Co.—Lamp Division Library. Bloomfield, N.J. • Lamps (fluorescent, mercury-vapor, ultra-violet, and incandescent). **2.**

12 White Laboratories, Inc—Library. 113 N. 13th St., Newark 7. Philology; pharmacy.

13 Wilmington Institute Free Library. 10th and Market Sts., Wilmington, Del. Delawareana; Abraham Lincoln. **1.**

14 Wood Library-Museum of Anesthesiology. 137 W. 11th St., New York. Equipment available for display upon payment of transportation and insurance charges. • History, pharmacology, and physiology of anesthesia; specimens of early and modern equipment for anesthesia; resuscitation (by infusions and transfusions, and by chemical, manual, and mechanical means). **1-2-3.**

15 Woolaroc Museum. Bartlesville, Okla. Closed Mondays. ★ History of Southwest; archeology of Oklahoma; life and history of Indians. pioneers, and cowboys in Southwest. **1.**

16 Worcester Pressed Steel Co. 100 Barber Av., Worcester, Mass. Steelmaking (processes and applications).

17 Workingmen's Institute—Library. Tavern and West Sts., New Harmony, Ind. Social experiments. **1.**

18 Wyoming, University of—Library. Laramie, Wyo. • Western Americana: Chaucer; Shakespeare. **1.**

19 Yale & Towne Manufacturing Co. 405 Lexington Av., New York 17, ★ Locks historic (loaned); keys, historic (loaned).

20 Yale University—Central Library. New Haven. • The Talmud; Palestine; shorthand; ★ World War I posters; Maps (historical, unusual). **1-2-3.** (School of Fine Arts Library). • Theater (history, architecture, costume, lighting, scenery, playbills); ★ designs and models; **1.** (School of Forestry Library). ★ Tropical woods. **1.** (Classical Club Library). • Plautus.

21 Yiddish Scientific Institute (Yivo, Inc.)—Library. 535 W. 123d St., New York 27. Judaica; Hebraics. **1.**

22 Yonkers Public Library (Technical and Business Department). S. Broadway, Yonkers 2, N.Y. Elevators.

23 Zionist Archives and Library. 41 E. 42nd St., New York 17. Translators (Yiddish, Hebrew). **1.**

ABOUT THE "KEYING" LOCATOR INDEX

The "keying" Locator Index (opposite page) is designed to make the compilation (beginning on page 11 an effective reference tool for (1) convenient service in libraries of every type and (2) helpful everyday use on the desks of editors, researchers, educators, business men, officials, writers and all others who must frequently link knowers and specific subjects, including knowers themselves desirous of locating others with like interests.

It provides this essential linking by a keying system. Each page in the compilation is clearly numbered in an upper corner. Each listing on a page is numbered —from "10" upwards (to obtain regularity in spacing).

The subjects falling within the scope arbitrarily fixed for the compilation, and in respect to which a listee is either authoritatively, expertly or specially informed—in the Editors' opinion—are entered in the Locator Index (alphabetically) and "keyed" to his or her listing by two numbers—the number of the page containing it and the number which precedes it on that page—as, "350-30" "keys" to listing 30 on page 350. Thus a convenient linking of tens of thousands of indexed subjects to individual knowers among the thousands in the compilation becomes practicable.

Because of the arbitrary delimitation established for the compilation—discussed in the preface in some detail (page 5)—the subject with which a listee is most outstandingly associated may not be entered in the Locator Index. For like reasons, certain subjects directly connected with a listee's data may be indexed, and others not; or the indexed subject may be only indirectly connected with specific data (either referred to, or actually included, in the compilation).

Likewise a listee may be "keyed" in the Locator Index to a subject with which his listing indicates no conversance. In such instances, information in file, but not included in the listing—because of production exigencies or other reasons—support the conversance thus indicated.

The source listings (page 851) have been "keyed" through the Locator Index in exactly the manner used for the other entries.

* * *

The content of listing manuscripts especially prepared for this compilation has, in so far as practicable, (1) been restricted as below indicated, since biographical data thereby excluded are usually available from numerous sources, and (2) arranged in the following sequence:

(1) Name, statement of subjects, year of birth.

(2) Education (including degrees, with dates received and institutions granting).

(3) A somewhat detailed statement of conversance background, including research work, committee memberships (other than society affiliations), commissions, consultant participations in investigations and projects, editorships of professional periodicals (if not obvious from career data), expeditions, attendances at international conferences, and other appropriate information.

(4) Authorial data, including book co-authorships and editorships. Titles of selected books (with publication dates when to hand). Articles in periodicals and similar publications, and unpublished works, are normally not detailed, being indicated by the phrase "Author articles in field." Inventions, patents, discoveries, and the like.

(5) Career data, including various posts, incumbencies and positions (in chronological order in so far as practible) with, when available, the related organizations, locations (in appropriate instances), and dates—only data felt to be pertinent to the listing subjects are cited, however. Posts ranking below that of assistant professorship are usually not indicated among the academic data unless earlier incumbencies apparently led directly to higher ones in the same institutions. Similar treatment is in so far as as practible applied to data regarding other types of work.

(6) Memberships in, and connections with, professional and honary societies, foundations and research organizations (if obviously related to listed subjects), including fellowships, officerships and committee memberships within the cited entities. Prizes and awards, and military career data, if felt to be closely pertinent to the listed subjects.

(7) Address—usually that of an office or a place of occupation, unless the listee requested that solely, or in addition, a home address be stated.

* * *

The specialisms of the listees have been indexed in so far as practicable under the subject designations most closely allied with their particular fields of interest. The popular has been used in preference to the scientific term, in order to facilitate use of the book for those not acquainted with scientific nomenclature. For example, butterfly specialists are not indexed under *Lepidiptera* or *Insects*, but under *Butterflies.* Where the specialism is concerned with a particular geographic location, it has been indexed under that location. That is, a listee especially informed on limestone in Indiana has been "keyed" to *Indiana Limestone*). A listee reported to be generally informed on limestone (without reference to a particular location) has been indexed to *Limestone*. Specialism phrases which include words of broad scope, such as *management* and *equipment,* are indexed under the specified particular type of management (*Industrial management*) or equipment (*Agricultural equipment*).

15 620-13 669-20; birds 342-12 532-12; botany 169-23 211-20 525-25 532-22; cacti 59-15; copper deposits 23-15 298-14; diaries 851-39; geology 451-24 721-11; geomorphology 721-11; history 487-22 638-24 714-11; indians 626-24 626-26 638-24 642-18; industry 464-21; insects 88-19 116-11; irrigation 278-10 279-10; manuscripts 851-39; meteorites 500-19; mineral resources 18-10; mining 18-10 642-16; missions 638-24; newspapers 851-39; ore deposits 712-13; plant diseases 326-13; reptiles 135-20; scorpions 629-25

ARKANSAS 103-13; archeology 267-15; flora 476-10; geography 83-21 306-25; geology 83-21; horticulture 104-17; ore deposits 83-21; snakes 520-17; trees 669-10; water supply 685-11

ARMENIA 240-19; art 384-18; history 126-24 384-18; manuscripts 384-18; music 149-13; writings 126-24

ARMOR 853-31; antique 854-34; plastic 24-14; plate 264-27 713-10

ARMORED CARS: automobiles 256-11

ARMS see Firearms

ARMY, U.S. see U.S. Army

ARMY WORMS 121-13 374-24

ARNHEM LAND: zoology 171-19

ARNOLD, MATTHEW 666-20

AROIDS 46-15 294-19

ARROYOS 244-23

ARSENIC 51-25 92-12; organic compounds 41-24 131-14

ARSON 854-51

ART see page 831

ART: advertising 186-12 322-26 551-13; ancient 22-19 69-18 234-13; appreciation 126-26 151-19; auctions 851-41; authenticating 259-13 613-18; bibliography 355-10; blind person's 856-64; catalogs 857-10 858-50; Christian, early 520-24 695-10 857-22; classical 695-10; conservation 525-12 573-10; contemporary 185-25 565-12; correlation 181-13; creative 412-17; dealers 857-10; decorative 34-13 126-26 492-21; education 167-15 212-22 309-21 384-21 402-22 409-17 412-17 487-14 536-10 613-18 617-21; eighteenth century 565-12; enamels 231-17; folk 856-15;heraldic 546-24 856-14; history 28-22 66-20 106-15 123-23 125-12 126-16 154-15 165-10 175-12 182-22 184-19 198-12 214-22 234-12 259-13 292-16 325-24 366-18 412-17 492-11 613-18 683-18; industrial 34-13 378-12 384-21 462-15; materials 716-22; medical illustrations 414-15 468-16; medieval 154-15 214-10 231-17 370-21 383-15 393-24 520-24 565-12 573-10 575-10 589-14 695-10; modern 27-22 66-20 100-10 125-12 165-10 182-22 222-25 341-10 355-10 443-10 634-19 856-16; museology 687-13; philosophy 523-19; pre-Christian 506-12; pre-Columbian 546-23; preservation 218-16 582-11 639-20; primitive 271-24 358-14 375-11 385-15 487-14 852-33; psychology 75-23 126-26 487-14; religious 82-25 393-24; Renaissance 275-16 574-12 575-10; restoration 98-15 106-15 357-10 525-12 683-18 854-28 573-10; silk screen 856-23; sociology 458-17; theory 397-18 497-14 716-22; wartime recovery 154-15 280-11 325-24 326-15; geographic areas (British) 858-44 geographic areas (Chinese) 545-23 851-41 857-48 (Egyptian) 856-14 (Far East) 545-23 856-14 857-34 857-48 (German Jewish) 574-12 (Iran) 593-13 (Japanese) 69-18 141-11 301-15 397-21 516-20 697-10 851-41 (Korean) 69-18 (Northwest U.S.) 851-20 (Oriental) 69-18 127-25 397-21 854-28 855-53 857-48 (Tibetan) 856-26

ART MUSEUM 182-22 487-14 537-20 687-13

ARTHROPODA 419-16 718-13 855-40

ARTHURIAN LITERATURE 237-23 413-24 564-22 565-18

ARTIFICIAL INSEMINATION 61-18 452-12

ARYAN LANGUAGES 189-15

ASBESTOS 72-14 101-20 138-13 147-12 157-12 420-25 549-13 674-14; mining 406-24; products 549-13 604-13

ASCETICISM 722-12

ASCIDIANS 728-17

ASCORBIC ACID 218-17 240-11

ASHES: human 285-15; volcanic 537-11

ASIA: anthropology 212-12 221-15 285-17 510-14; archeology 66-20; culture 187-21 475-16; economics 249-20 526-16 660-11; ethnography 79-16; ethnology 135-15 281-12 672-13; geography 79-13 209-15 249-20 520-18 593-14 704-13; geology 146-22; history 135-15 230-22 232-24 290-10; industrial engineering 549-16; languages 243-17 550-14; literature 243-17 611-24; metals 549-16; nationalism 519-19; natural history 128-24; paper making tools 855-35; physiography 410-20; phytogeography 397-22; sociology 187-21

ASPARAGUS 80-21 158-13 228-11 245-23 378-17

ASPERGILLUS 552-10 655-11

ASPHALT 18-20 213-18 288-20 306-24 435-17 441-14 496-11 851-42 856-60; geology 32-18; highway construction 29-11 156-14 435-17 532-10; packaging material 723-27; products 208-20 306-24; tile 443-16 627-18

ASSOCIATION MANAGEMENT 161-23 396-10

ASSYRIA 320-21 378-22 404-14 434-13 857-22

ASSYRO-BABYLONIAN: civilization 37-11; language 187-17

ASTEROIDS 49-11 264-23 426-23 689-22

ASTERS 45-11 154-11

ASTOR, JOHN JACOB 540-20

ASTRONOMY see page 831

ASTRONOMY: history 19-10 46-23 114-12 426-23 509-11 537-15 655-25 721-10; instruments 91-26 465-15; mathematics 403-18 436-22; nautical 453-14; navigation tables 614-25; positional 858-32; statistical 307-21; Teaching 460-12

ASTROPHYSICS 20-12 33-20 49-11 71-19 80-16 141-16 190-12 266-10 300-23 346-11 594-17 612-17 627-17 661-23 801-28

ATHABASCAN INDIANS 452-11

ATHAPASCAN LANGUAGES 338-20 452-11

ATHENS 89-23 657-17

ATHLETICS 573-19 682-25

ATLANTIC COAST 47-14; fish culture 363-21; ore deposits 62-11; geology 561-14 664-17

ATLASES 855-20 858-61

ATMOSPHERE: electricity 219-16 253-16 271-22 306-13 682-13; ionization 306-13 682-13; micro-oscillations 422-19; motion equations 90-18; optics of 69-13 250-15; physics 219-16 336-16 511-20; planetary 190-12; pollution 165-13 225-12 348-14 389-10 423-13 494-21 723-14; pressure 87-11 99-10 428-12 637-16; radioactivity 217-16 682-13; stellar 190-12; structure 272-17; suspended matter 389-10; temperature 99-10 494-21 637-16; upper 219-16 293-17 294-14 377-14 379-22 454-22 465-18 477-16 533-21 627-17 698-23 699-25

ATOMIC BOMBS 259-20 521-22; Bikini 48-13-88-26 220-10 329-13 523-16 593-19 596-16; development 689-22; Hiroshima 521-22; Nagasaki 170-17; seismographic effects 398-15; tests 56-17 138-20 263-18 312-21 361-15 596-16

ATOMIC ENERGY 21-14 76-11 92-21 153-12 161-12 172-18 213-17 246-12 263-18 269-21 316-18 331-18 390-19 398-18 510-11575-18 619-12 658-20 677-25; civil defense 260-21 369-20 390-19 559-17 641-22 688-19; control 43-22 280-22; economic consequences 594-10; health aspects 168-22 218-24; international control 280-22; legal aspects 169-16; levels 612-17;military use 89-14 239-23 369-20 379-10 521-22 641-22 **see also atomic bombs;** raw materials 272-15 345-22 684-23; social aspects 120-20

ATOMIC PHYSICS 81-22 112-21 137-12 138-19 139-15 173-12 237-24 239-23 244-17 254-18 286-19 310-10 330-19 332-20 381-18 599-10 618-13 689-22

ATOMIC STRUCTURE 20-12 78-19 329-21 656-14 690-19

ATTITUDE TESTS 721-12

ATTITUDES: measurement 168-16 441-19 477-21; social 168-16; surveys 168-16 172-19

AUCTION CATALOGS 853-68

AUDIENCE: analysis 374-15

AUDIO: education 190-11; engineering 59-21

AUDIOVISUAL AIDS: education 33-12 217-14 346-20 457-13 501-12 612-26 716-10; materials 89-16 90-11 716-10; medical 271-21

AUDITORIUMS: acoustics 440-15; design 287-18

AUDUBONIANA 859-10

AUGUSTINIAN PHILOSOPHY 78-14

AUREOMYCIN 157-19 530-20 656-18

AURORAS 203-22 245-24 275-25 454-22 677-21

AUSTINITE CRYSTALS 630-23

AUSTRALIA 102-21; archeology 164-24; birds 536-15; ethnology 164-24; fish 469-13; geology 640-13; international affairs 102-21 390-11; literature 644-15; mammals 344-23; native races 66-16 164-24; pastoral industry 711-18; physiography 410-20

AUSTRIA: history 390-11 552-20

AUTOGRAPHS 57-18

AUTOMATIC SPRINKLERS 854-50

AUTOMOBILE ACCIDENTS 38-19 79-11 162-13 483-13 851-16

AUTOMOBILE: trailer traveling 143-18

AUTOMBILES 852-40; chassis 213-14; design 437-10 483-13; driver behavior 464-13 498-18; electrical equipment 364-17 510-12 544-16; engineering 225-18 364-17; engines 170-23 245-25 364-17 394-21 500-23 544-16 626-20 713-23; equipment 713-21; fuel 340-18 364-17; gear shifts 364-11 394-21; headlights 65-18 75-19 364-17 388-13; history 169-25 213-14 483-13 508-24 525-15 851-46 852-21 853-71 854-24 855-21 857-68 858-38; industry 364-17; mechanics 364-17 713-21; registration 38-19; riding qualities 213-14 510-12; safety engineering245-25 346-22 424-21 510-12; sound deadeners 723-27; transmissions 449-20 544-16 713-23

AUTOMOTIVE DEVELOPMENT 853-71

AUTOMOTIVE ENGINEERING see page 831

AUTOMOTIVE: gears 640-18; industry 855-51; lubricants 623-24; machinery design 42-15 278-21 394-21 430-11 452-16 536-16; maintenance 278-21; sales catalogs 855-21

AUTO-OXIDATION: nutritional 20-22

AUXINS 212-16 301-16 705-15

AVALANCHES 31-22 468-14

AVESTA LANGUAGE 324-14

AVIATION 851-31; acceleration 593-14; all weather flying 17-19; armament 270-19; combat 578-26 582-17; commercial 132-11; deceleration 593-14; depth perception 250-12; design 519-20; economics 96-23; education 371-18; financing 100-26 592-20; fuels 387-12 442-24 539-14 686-11; high altitude effects 539-17 593-14; history 132-11 409-10 453-20 617-13 695-11 851-31; instrument flying 390-18 705-14; international cargo 507-18; journalism 638-10; landing systems 105-10; Latin American 100-26; law 559-24; lighting 250-15 351-17 381-16; lubricants 387-12; medicine 449-21; meteorology 288-25 533-19; military, history 164-10; navigation 560-11 693-15; physiology 625-19 644-13 648-11 802-15; psychology 226-17 250-12 361-17 465-16 468-17; regulation 100-26; safety engineering 21-11 449-21; strategy 369-10 402-13 **see also aeronautics, aircraft;** training 481-17

AVOCADO 315-17; 518-13 601-24 665-15; culture 134-18; diseases 684-21 727-18

AYMARA INDIANS 534-17

AZALEAS 79-10 110-12 165-19 252-12 524-20 658-18

AZEOTROPY 601-19

AZTECS 200-15 204-21 566-15 657-18 680-10

B

BAALBECK: excavations 82-25

BABEUF 62-10

BABISM 318-23

BABYLONIA 187-17; archeology 633-10; history 109-21 520-22 633-10; mythology 73-13 **see also Assyro-Babylonia**

BACH, JOHANN SEBASTIAN 99-23 247-18

BACON, FRANCIS 27-22 300-16

BACTERIA: agglutination 122-23; airborne 382-19; anaerobic 115-25 445-13 677-12; coliform 207-12; enteric 197-24; heat resistance 115-25 643-16; hemotoxins 494-22; induced mutations 536-21; luminous 345-12; mass production 566-24; metabolism 185-20 608-13 624-17 671-12; physiology 550-17; phytopathogenic 488-20 685-10; respiration 608-13; staining 243-12 694-18; taxonomy 550-17; variation 458-11

BACTERICIDES 424-24 450-21 470-23 566-24

BACTERIOLOGY 36-16 117-20 122-23 128-19 195-11 207-12 214-15 218-17 255-10 328-15 333-24 342-17 459-18 488-20 495-21 560-13 585-16 589-12 855-45; culture media 677-12 802-17; dairy 128-10 491-17; food 27-15 444-23 689-20 691-21; fermentation 853-11; industrial 554-15; marine 331-13 682-19; microtechniques 691-21; sanitary 444-23; technique 122-23 140-12; water 128-10 565-16 691-21

BACTERIOPHAGES 33-21 362-11 382-19 495-17 694-18

BADGERS 588-10

BAFFIN LAND: exploration 113-20; geology 466-10

BAGASSE 409-20

BAHAI RELIGION 318-23

BAHAI TEMPLE 477-20

BAHAMAS: archeology 550-19; botany 651-10

BAIL: history 171-14

BAKERY PRODUCTS 276-20

BAKING 119-14; cake 344-10; chemistry 648-24; technology 199-27 600-13 609-17 643-24

BALBOA 582-21

BALKANS 207-20; history 68-10 300-14 325-20 363-10 503-22; political affairs 325-20

BALL GAMES: history 301-20

BALL MILL: grinding 554-12

BALLADS: English 408-18 476-20 571-13 611-16 654-14 712-26; Tennessee 77-20 515-14 611-16

BALLET 514-11; costumes and design 858-44

BALLISTICS 22-13 84-19 274-14 322-22 326-12 347-13 409-19 467-19 567-24 587-13 610-21 620-11 656-14 658-12 694-20; exterior 171-16 186-13 313-23 328-12 346-11 558-15; interior 381-25 441-17 467-19 701-10; mathematics 390-15 455-14; measurement 558-15; motion 658-12; rocket 71-19 250-16 346-11; small arms 150-14 381-25 490-23 496-12 699-23; terminal 62-22 173-12 205-10 345-15 441-17; underwater 590-16

BALLOONS 256-11 377-14 675-10

BALOMETERS 65-18

BALSAM 536-11

BALTIC STATES 419-14

BALTIMORE 857-20

BALZAC, HONORE de 586-22

BAMBOO 191-13 642-23 700-19

BANANA 381-21; culture 374-21 522-13 542-23 601-24; cytology 711-11; diseases 695-20; Pacific Islands 422-12; production 522-13

BANDS: school 125-22; music 124-21

BANK VAULTS 266-21

BANKING: history 395-18 685-21; international 57-16; national code 530-23 554-16 608-20; policies 55-18; statistics 311-20 482-21

BANKS: mechanical toy 852-23 857-47

BANTAMS 584-19 674-13

BANTU 258-14 689-19

BAPTIST CHURCH HISTORY 255-17 328-22 562-11 853-22

BAR EXAMINATIONS 64-19

BARBADOES 267-22 594-12

BARBERRIES 147-17

BARBITURATES 113-22 238-10 629-11

BARBITURIC ACID 562-18

BARITE: deposits 393-20

BARIUM 538-14 667-23

BARIUM SULFIDE 371-19

BARK: chemistry 323-18 592-16

BARLEY 133-21 449-17; breeding 184-21 387-15 574-23 646-19; cytogenetics 102-25; disease resistance 602-10; genetics 387-15 400-23; insects 644-10; production 644-10 691-19; roots 33-11; sprout treatment 600-13

BARLOW, JOEL 14-16

BARNACLES 129-23

BAROQUE: literature 238-18; painting 574-12 619-17 623-26

BARTOK, BELA 99-23

BARTLETT, JOHN: quotations 857-59

BARYTES 478-17

BASALT 241-17

BASEBALL 506-11 575-19 627-14; history 301-20 405-10 506-11; players, photographs 852-27

BASIDIOMYCETES: taxonomy 612-12

BASKETBALL 479-13

BASKETMAKERS 512-19 566-15

BASQUE: language 324-14

BASS: fishing 60-24

BASTIDE, LOUIS 677-23

BATHYSPHERES 652-12

BATHYTHERMOGRAPH 627-11

BATS 313-18 473-16 511-16 606-10; banding 473-16; cave habits 272-22; distribution habits 272-22 511-16 583-21; physiology 267-13; sensory mechanisms 267-13; vampire 265-18 473-16

BATTERIES 238-22 580-20 625-15 651-22 656-19; alakaline 179-18; dry cell 122-12 136-22 169-13 238-22 299-10 370-15 478-13 484-20; galvanic 238-22; primary 369-13; storage 278-14 656-19 709-15 725-12 726-13; wet cell 381-12

BAUDELAIRE, CHARLES 41-19 126-23

BAUXITE 20-11 83-21

BAZOOKAS 141-24 388-13

BEACH: biochemical treatment 181-22 337-11; erosion 11-16 382-23 441-14 586-18 857-46 **see also shoreline erosion;** geology 111-21 587-22 659-12

BEACHHEADS: ocean factors 48-13

BEACON: radio 356-24

BEADWORK 183-17

BEANS: breeding 158-13 162-14 184-21 533-23 714-17; diseases 22-10 486-17 533-23 631-16 656-10 656-20 726-22; genetics 395-23 533-23; harvesting machinery 554-25; pathology 22-10; production 645-15; rust 713-20

BULLETS 440-20
BULL FIGHTING LORE 300-20
BULLHEAD FISH 106-22
BULU LANGUAGE 258-14
BUNYAN, JOHN 855-42
BUNYAN, PAUL 316-16
BUREAUCRACY 160-17
BURIAL: lore 712-26
BURKE, EDMUND 156-22 316-20
BURLAP 694-14
BURLEY TOBACCO 344-24
BURMA: archeology 511-14; culture 281-18; economics 26-16; ethnography 79-16; ethnology 313-24 448-10 511-14; history 313-24; language 313-24; music 149-13; roads 172-14; social work 417-13
BURNS 515-13
BURNS, ROBERT 219-19 857-43
BURR, AARON 103-17
BUSHMEN 315-24
BUSINESS: accounting 255-16; administration 167-12 215-19 469-10 550-21 624-10; advertising 660-19; analysis 291-17; correspondence 44-10; cycles 84-13 131-15 258-19 291-17 433-11 461-25 482-17 574-11 559-14 634-13 697-14 574-11; economics 102-12 243-16 407-15 550-21 634-13 670-22; education 15-19 230-21 296-13 323-22 401-15 421-15 484-16 557-11 624-10 641-18 678-11; English 23-18 480-24; finance 480-23; forecasting 119-27 225-17; history 31-11 99-19 250-11 263-12 293-18 308-17 435-23 538-24 854-28 858-14; laws 419-23; small 23-18 436-10 641-19; social aspects 380-24; statistics 102-12 119-27 482-17 594-22 634-13
BUSSES 437-10
BUTADIENE 276-13 283-18 626-21 686-11
BUTANE 552-21
BUTTER: composition 66-14; production 659-15; vitamin A 644-20
BUTTERCUP 59-15
BUTTERFLIES 92-14 125-13 175-10 237-14 372-19 424-26 492-15 541-21 605-19 855-40; geographical distribution 324-20 372-19; identification 221-19
BUTTONS 853-16; brass 430-23; costume 16-19; historical 16-17 16-19; uniform 16-17
BUTYLENES 442-24 577-16
BYRON, GEORGE GORDON, LORD 667-11
BYZANTINE: archeology 709-23; art 370-21 695-10 709-23; culture 483-16; education 120-12; history 184-22 413-25 677-16 (Empire) 123-19; literature 184-22

C

CABBAGE: ascorbic acid content 103-18; breeding 175-11 232-21 714-17; diseases 109-15 656-10; pests 109-15; varieties 186-18
CABBAGE SEED: treatment 141-21
CABINET-WORK 178-21
CABLES: electric 165-13 623-18 (waterproof) 117-13; guying 218-10; high-voltage 165-13 542-20 556-28; insulation 360-10; submarine 69-25; telegraph 497-11; telephone 110-19; underground 13-20
CABLEWAYS 678-24
CACTUS 17-23 59-15 395-16 578-17; classification 167-24; preservation 167-24; respiration 272-14
CADAVERS: laboratory use of 670-16
CADDIS FLIES 62-27 574-21
CADDOAN TRIBES 691-25
CADMIUM 126-22
CADMIUM VAPOR LAMPS 431-17
CAFFEINE 125-11
CALAMITY JANE 516-18
CALCIFICATION 622-13
CALCIUM: food content 427-15
CALCIUM CARBIDE 11-10
CALCIUM CARBONATE: paper coating 90-14 550-12
CALCIUM SILICATES 608-25
CALCULATORS 853-58; automatic 522-20 604-14
CALCULUS 257-22 266-22 463-17
CALENDARS 852-31; Athenian 546-15; Egyptian 520-22; Hellenistic 346-12; Mayan 657-18; Oriental 404-13; reform 12-23 486-19
CALHOUN, JOHN C. 111-12
CALIBRATION 11-18
CALIBRATORS 310-14
CALICHE 545-19
CALIFORNIA: agriculture 51-11; anthropology 299-23; archeology 116-21 215-12 299-23 437-21 666-10; bees 195-15; birds 97-11 260-12 408-19 639-14; botany 78-23 189-21 195-15 454-14; chromite deposits 19-19; church history 187-13; deserts 715-11; early families 37-24 697-12; early surveys 145-15; economic development 250-11 523-15; ethnology 116-21; fauna 609-14 618-23; fishes 602-19; flood control 398-14; flora 609-14 652-20; folk lore 721-17; furniture 857-15; geography 457-15; geology 23-15 131-21 189-21 387-21 509-24 516-12 617-20 624-12 692-12 718-22; gold rush 64-14 414-10 493-12; grasses 639-23; ground water 195-21; history 37-24 105-24 140-10 187-13 203-11 270-25 332-12 349-21 393-13 437-21 477-17 484-13 493-12 542-21 559-21 581-22 609-14 673-12 697-12 704-22 714-24 721-17 722-18 854-31 855-27 856-48 857-15; horticulture 105-24; Indians 246-23 267-12 299-23 411-10 485-21 498-15 855-54; industry 464-21; insects 111-10 209-19; invertebrate paleontology 357-17; irrigation history 559-21; judicial system 718-15; linguistics 437-21; lizards 603-23; local government 596-12; mammals 161-22 224-18 335-23 408-19; meteorology 677-17; Mexican Colonial period 37-24 855-27; minerals 211-16 306-27 515-20 516-12 581-21 665-14 692-12 712-13 715-11; mines 855-26 855-27 857-37; mollusks 357-17; oil fields 195-21 509-24 855-27; place names 270-25; plants 195-15 349-22 675-16 707-18; races 437-21; resources 469-18; seacoast protection 398-14; snails 615-15; snakes 224-18; soils 617-16; sponges 177-18; submarine geology 605-18; trail sites (history) 439-10; transportation (history) 714-24; volcanoes 23-15; water resources 195-21 259-10 398-14 545-12 685-11; wines 41-44 349-21
CALIFORNIUM 597-21 658-20
CALLIGRAPHY 123-17 322-26 443-11 493-15 507-16 464-16
CALORIMETRY 38-17 370-20 519-16 637-14
CALVERT, LORD 855-32
CALVINISM 296-16 307-18
CALYPSO MUSIC 94-19
CAMBODIA 87-19 388-10
CAMBRIAN: paleontology 236-15 652-21
CAMELLIAS 117-25 165-19 439-15 447-19 524-20 638-15 710-15; culture 447-19 710-15 718-24; diseases 252-12; grafting 387-23; nomenclature 710-15 718-24
CAMERAS 297-20 462-12 465-15 **see also photographic equipment**
CAMEROONS: birds 258-14
CAMOUFLAGE 142-17 331-17 417-17 450-27 505-15 662-13 857-21 858-34
CAMPHOR SCALE 71-17
CAMPING 233-23 649-12
CANADA: annexation movement 687-20; archeology 433-10 505-20; art history 292-16; birds 530-15; botany 78-23; boundary with U.S. 512-12 512-18; economic policies 448-14; education 472-18; ethnology 289-19; flora, fauna 630-22; folk lore 181-13 529-25; geography 128-14; geology 55-22 628-23; glaciers 99-12; 603-11; government 710-10; ground water 359-17; history 28-13 78-16 367-14 394-18 563-18 618-15 710-10 714-13 716-14; Indians 495-15 618-15; international affairs 165-17; literature 644-15; military history 78-16; mineral resources 110-11 298-14 542-16 562-23 629-18; mining 378-11; paleontology 55-22; petroleum geology 640-13; physiography 378-11 550-20; postal (history) 74-10; Rocky Mountain exploration 659-20; soils 128-14; trees 286-12; U.S. relations 145-21 394-18 648-22 687-20 710-10 714-13; vegetation 128-14; watershed 659-20; wildlife 579-16; world trade 394-18
CANADIAN GEESE 535-16
CANADIAN THISTLE 706-13
CANALS 855-18; engineering 130-17 441-14 631-21
CANARY ISLANDS 321-18
CANCER: animals 720-17; chromosomes 64-22; cytology 193-12 229-13 515-22 685-18; research 553-12 561-24 573-11 614-16 719-18; research grants 120-15 377-10 559-17
CANDY 151-16 457-19
CANE SUGAR 855-28
CANNERIES: community 333-10
CANNING: biochemistry 38-11; industrial 384-22 681-21; oxygen removal 38-11; preserving 95-11 218-17 233-25 426-24 856-18; production 856-18; technology 664-22; vegetables 276-17 609-16; waste disposal systems 495-21
CANOEING 220-13 618-23
CANOES 855-31
CANON LAW 385-10
CANTALOUPE: breeding 256-14 700-16; diseases, resistance 421-11 550-16
CANYONS: submarine 605-18
CAPACITORS: 256-16; electric 103-10 146-16
CAPE COD 370-19
CAPITALISM 258-19
CAR FERRIES 803-23
CARBIDES: abrasives 176-20; cemented 45-10 722-17; cutting 590-19
CARBOHYDRATES 131-12 136-17 209-21 214-25 472-16 640-11 643-13; bacterial 315-18; chemistry 137-13 151-16 171-10 246-20 298-24 309-13 314-19 363-23 434-16 700-10 717-18; mildew proofing 246-20
CARBON 54-16 398-20 851-47; activated 122-12 292-12 538-12; compounds 401-20; cosmic radio 269-21; electron 158-12; industrial 430-14 638-14; radioactive 278-19
CARBON BLACK 24-19 32-15 638-14 647-18 852-67; physical chemistry 614-20; production 435-15; rubber uses 480-13 626-21
CARBON DATING 170-21 469-16
CARBON DIOXIDE: planetary atmospheres 190-12; production 435-15 543-22; solid 331-21 366-10; uses 435-15; vapor 253-21
CARBON ELECTRODES 357-12
CARBON MONOXIDE 109-22 230-15 298-11 510-18
CARBON PRODUCTS 11-19 439-19
CARBONACEOUS MATERIALS 155-11
CARBONIFEROUS PALEONTOLOGY 695-16
CARBORIZING: steel material 12-11
CARDIAC PHYSIOLOGY 346-10
CARDIOLOGY: history 51-12
CARDS: greeting 37-10
CARIBBEAN: botany 325-23; culture 381-18; fisheries 49-16; flora 725-21; fungi 362-22; geography 504-22; oceanography 410-10; petrology 267-22
CARIBBEANA 852-25
CARIBBEAN SEA 74-19
CARIBOU 487-25
CARICATURES 467-17
CARILLONS 64-25 371-24 525-26 545-16
CARNATIONS 354-16 487-18
CARNOTITE ORES 181-14
CAROLINA SEA ISLANDS 155-24
CAROTENE 424-11 528-21 675-18 728-20; analyses 530-11; uses 561-22
CARPENTRY 609-19
CARROTS: diseases 497-14 656-10; weed control 268-15
CARTELS 37-17 270-21 380-24
CARTHAGINIAN ARCHEOLOGY 641-21
CARTOGRAPHY 12-19 14-23 50-10 99-15 206-11 207-21 209-15 239-17 289-11 313-17 370-12 372-11 400-16 448-12 470-20 502-13 534-15 536-17 550-20 551-15 536-17 594-25 640-22 723-26 **see also maps**
CARTOONS 801-13; content analysis 16-20 801-13; political 87-20 695-24
CARTRIDGES: history 699-16
CARTWRIGHT, PETER 661-22
CASEIN 851-45; manufacture 90-14; technology 94-25
CASSINA 471-18
CASSIRER, ERNST 589-22
CASTINGS: metallurgy 137-10 306-22 346-14 352-23 539-10
CASTOR BEAN 154-12
CASTOR OIL 134-21; chemistry 74-18; history 16-15
CATALOGS: auction 451-18
CATALONIA 220-12
CATALYSIS 24-19 27-12 92-12 95-21 167-13 285-19 295-17 352-12 369-21 381-12 580-18 639-26 646-11 686-11 690-12; chemistry 462-19 507-25; oxidation 364-21 691-18
CATALYSTS 54-18 92-22 297-19 316-13 342-14 369-21 533-20 590-18
CATALYTIC CHEMISTRY 590-19
CATAPULTS 46-10
CATECHISM 856-27
CATHODE RAYS 189-14 196-18 206-22 208-14 257-20
CATHODES: physics 58-21 144-21 456-12 465-18
CATLIN, GEORGE 274-10
CATS 29-19 152-16 457-24; fossil 446-19; ocular muscles 251-15
CATTLE: artificial insemination 418-10 528-12 544-15 578-19 582-25 673-13 706-17; beef 310-21 503-15 604-21 692-19; blood groups 514-23; brands 856-59; breeding 53-12 177-11 261-20 282-22 310-21 322-21 365-20 367-12 418-10 528-12 688-23 701-25 706-17; cobalt effects 179-27; dairy 155-14 282-22 373-25 418-10 512-14 520-26 528-12 582-25 640-17 650-20 691-13 706-17; diseases 249-23 279-20 336-24 584-12 715-14; feeding 322-21 365-20; genetics 367-12 514-23 688-23 719-18; histology 108-18; history 53-12 508-18; husbandry 206-14; 365-20 714-22; insect pests 531-11 533-25 584-12; judging 365-20; marketing 60-14 365-20; nutrition 399-19 533-25 578-19 579-13 650-20 691-13 713-13; parasites 25-22 509-18 540-18; pastures 853-66; physiology 399-19 650-20; poison plants 533-25; production 60-14 367-12 856-59; purebred (records) 503-15; reproduction 30-12 438-13 673-13; sterility 30-12 249-23 673-13 **see also livestock and specific breeds**
CATTLE BRANDS 579-17
CATTLE INDUSTRY: history 628-18
CATTLE RANGES see Ranges, cattle
CAUCASUS: geography 612-12
CAULIFLOWER 169-17 186-18
CAUSTIC SODA 25-12 35-18 175-15
CAVES 12-24 87-13 217-17 474-11 528-11; commercial development 92-10; ecology 338-17 707-14; exploration 393-33 511-15 520-13; fauna 233-10 337-18 707-14; fishes 552-17; literature 123-13; mapping 150-17 393-33; salamanders 446-19
CAYUGA INDIANS 219-14 415-13
CEANOTHUS 675-16
CEDAR: apple rust 71-18
CELERY: diseases 182-18 232-12 497-14; pathology 22-10
CELESTIAL: computations 131-13 195-17; mechancis 304-14; navigation 560-11 614-25 639-13
CELLOPHANE 116-20 139-19 146-19 307-10 612-21 686-14
CELLS 76-15 93-18 109-22 113-17 135-19 143-19 168-19 448-17; behavior 135-19; biochemistry 182-23 444-17; biology 182-23; cancer 561-24 685-18; classification 119-18; differentiation 709-13; division 120-15 298-25; growth 709-13; membranes 215-22; morphology 120-15; permeability 149-16 291-12; physiology 52-19 120-15 134-15 219-11 275-19 291-12 298-25 515-22; plants 121-25 130-16 212-20 215-22; sap 243-14; size 683-26; stimulation 291-12; structure 15-16; surface tension 291-12; water relations 285-18
CELLULOSE 27-24 56-10 60-22 107-19 215-22 314-17 409-20 513-24 521-11 563-22 567-23 612-21 686-14 853-41 857-32 857-58; acetate 427-20 521-11 570-13 574-19 580-19 581-10 615-24; chemistry 39-12 171-24 245-14 287-22 427-20 485-19 492-18 504-14 529-17 534-16 537-13 589-16 598-23 628-24 629-12 700-10 717-18; decomposition 163-24 241-18 291-22 555-18 653-22; deterioration 264-15 612-20; derivatives 45-23 245-14 318-13 492-18 513-24 529-17 570-13; dyes 335-21; fibers 61-13 186-19 593-22; plastics 580-19; structure 215-22
CELTIC: folk lore 596-18; folk music 297-18; languages 114-12 247-10 248-23 389-12 596-18; literature 248-23; philology 462-21
CEMENT 74-11 136-23 155-15 381-15 464-17 591-26 651-18 692-24; acidproof 601-20; adhesives 480-15; aggregates 521-21 591-26; alkalies 521-21; antiseptic 21-21; bonding 616-20; chemistry 168-11 543-12; lapidary 247-19; manufacture 623-22; natural 692-24; portland 225-21 457-16 508-16 608-25 623-22 651-18 686-18 692-24 719-11; scientific 586-10; technology 284-20 354-13 543-12
CEMETERY: 194-11
CENOZOIC: paleontology 584-20 852-39
CENSORSHIP 156-11; literary 107-18; obsenity 107-18; war news 438-19
CENSUS 170-18 187-19 293-21
CENTIPEDES 298-21 855-40
CENTRAL AMERICA 858-22; agriculture 308-22; animal ecology 114-22; anthropology 854-28; archeology 200-15 605-16; birds 89-15 268-23 551-12; census 145-17; flora 23-23 419-12 615-11; geography 480-22; geology 658-24; Indians 219-21; insects 517-12; literature 671-15; mammals 639-17; minerals 601-13; plants 262-23; rubber 159-18; snakes 650-13
CENTRAL PLAINS: archeology 121-17
CENTRIFUGES 22-11 33-15 618-10
CEPHALOPODS: fossils 466-10
CERAMICS 78-20 150-12 163-19 210-14 246-10 293-24 320-22 323-20 336-13 339-12 344-17 347-17 358-23 375-16 379-10 380-18 453-19 466-15 471-22 503-12 508-14 515-12 586-10 693-23 625-13 851-41 852-59 853-16 854-44 854-54 855-58 856-45 856-62; antique 502-12 617-14; archeological 82-21 605-16; carburization 163-19; Chinese 397-10 397-21 539-22 625-13; classical 502-12 617-14; clay 54-16 537-11 580-11; colors 192-23 356-18; decalcomania 163-19; driers 180-11 246-10; electrical insulation 105-18 489-16; engineering 21-21 116-11 170-12 180-11 192-23 193-18 235-21 274-20 302-23 368-11 375-21 448-21 454-18 489-16 700-14; floor tile 557-13;

See page 851 for selected information sources "keyed" to this Locator Index.

See pages 13, 801 and 831 for knowers "keyed" to this Locator Index.

Farm Commodities—Food

See page 851 for selected information sources "keyed" to this Locator Index.

Indians, Federal Relations—Irrigation

See page 851 for selected information sources "keyed" to this Locator Index.

12 580-14 854-32 856-59; blankets 854-32; ceremonies 219-14; costumes 569-19 854-32 858-25; dances 384-16; folk art, religious 278-10; music 219-14 305-20 338-20 559-23 589-24; paper making 680-10; plant usage 716-16; pottery 246-23 642-18 854-32; religion 406-16; social organization 198-15 219-14 401-16 614-17

INDIANS FEDERAL RELATIONS 51-19 401-16 546-10 555-24; citizenship 405-17; education 15-15 51-19 581-12; land appraisal 241-13; reservations 401-16 431-23 497-13; schools 51-19; treaties 80-19 616-14; wars 579-17

INDIANS FOLK LORE 120-18 340-20 596-18 658-21 710-22 721-19

INDIANS HISTORY 105-23 584-23 618-15; agricultural 552-16; Asiatic origins 148-15; Pre-Columbian 118-10 548-21; primitive agriculture 118-24; weapons 433-10

INDIANS LANGUAGES 105-23 203-18 401-16 498-15 678-20

INDIANS MOUNDS 373-19

INDIANS PICTOGRAPHS 337-23 649-13

INDIANS see also geographic areas and tribe names

INDIC: books 160-13 854-48; manuscripts 537-21

INDIGOSOLS PRODUCTION 401-20

INDIUM: alloys 237-22; metallurgy 395-24 524-15

INDIVIDUAL DIFFERENCES 188-21 245-20

INDO-CHINA 204-14; archeology 340-23; art 66-20; economics 26-16 582-12; minerals 45-25; Moi anthropology 175-20

INDO-EUROPEAN: languages 154-18 275-15 (comparative grammar) 192-15 (philology) 232-23 389-12 462-21 (phonology) 635-12

INDO-IRANIAN LANGUAGES 324-14

INDOLOGY 189-15 537-21

INDONESIA 89-18 100-17 622-18 857-48; ethnology 485-21; folk lore 148-17; foreign policy 563-23; government 89-18 589-20; languages 46-15 301-13

INDUSTRIAL ABSENTEEISM 696-13

INDUSTRIAL: appraisal 550-21 575-12; arts 214-14 378-12 417-20; chemistry 194-12 220-19 372-15 383-22 462-12 506-14; economics 27-24 34-17 267-20 273-17 310-17; equipment 401-19; instrumentation 54-14; mobilization 239-11; noise abatement 450-20; physics 229-22 534-11; production 409-21 436-11

INDUSTRIAL ENGINEERING 28-17 32-19 42-17 208-24 226-16 268-16 358-18 377-13 412-12 436-11 448-15 485-22 529-21 576-25; design 34-13 322-26 384-21 437-10 462-15 476-21 492-10 551-13 592-21 651-21

INDUSTRIAL GEOGRAPHY 388-20 467-14 467-21; distribution regional 84-13 321-20; plant locations 453-10 558-11 563-24 700-18; plant site surveys 363-14 448-15 453-10 519-24 696-12; surveys 578-24; zoning 467-21

INDUSTRIAL HYGIENE 29-20 43-22 83-16 102-22 126-22 142-12 151-15 154-23 161-20 194-23 218-24 221-11 228-17 245-19 254-22 280-14 317-22 348-15 441-21 446-13 449-21 485-11 539-17 556-22 557-18 603-12 603-17 672-10; diseases 219-23 853-12; microbiology 493-16 648-20; toxicology 485-12 654-24

INDUSTRIAL MANAGEMENT 42-17 46-12 167-12 226-16 230-10 309-23 351-21 412-21 439-21 442-12 436-11 446-11 504-25 575-12 628-17 710-18 714-23; executive training 468-18; history 85-17; organization 215-19; personnel 56-23 331-13; personnel feeding 258-22; personnel training 501-12

INDUSTRIAL PLANT DESIGN 283-11 398-21 405-22 450-12 542-12 570-14 611-10 714-14; architecture 274-15 311-17; construction 576-19; refrigeration 542-23 637-10; ventilation 29-20 83-16 161-20 254-15 354-18 715-22

INDUSTRIAL PSYCHOLOGY 64-16 87-22 104-18 153-16 159-20 228-24 363-19 394-14 412-13 426-16 450-22 454-16 533-24 553-13 609-10 687-24 718-12

INDUSTRIAL RELATIONS 28-13 104-18 157-20 159-20 160-17 167-11 171-18 225-15 275-14 308-16 327-14 450-22 465-19 595-11 653-12 709-20; sociology 477-15

INDUSTRIAL RESEARCH 208-20 280-14 305-17 314-14 606-12 635-25

INDUSTRIAL SAFETY 221-11 268-16 385-16 405-19 557-18 725-12; fatigue 99-25 245-19; first aid 652-10; fumes 257-23 678-22; poisoning 188-14 213-23; protective clothing 190-25 588-12; toxicology 126-22 194-23 348-15

INDUSTRIAL STANDARDS 851-32

INDUSTRIAL WASTES: by-products 357-11; disposal 68-12 121-12 134-17 176-13 306-12 311-14 365-19 462-11 473-15 506-14 530-20 531-12 539-13 556-22 563-14 570-21 586-20 589-23 674-16; utilization 590-23

INDUSTRIAL WATER TREATMENT 696-15

INDUSTRY: history 67-19 853-64; classification 376-13; government control 162-15; music in 363-19 527-14; workmen's compensation 857-28

INFANTS: adoption 685-15; welfare 338-14

INFLATION 243-16

INFORMATION SERVICES 395-26

INFRA-RED 386-14; communications technique 515-12; detection 663-16 708-22; devices 515-12; physics 65-18; radiation 294-14 515-12; spectroscopy 25-17 24-22 40-18 152-13 238-17 275-16 331-18 404-21 414-11 625-15 708-16

INGERSOLL, ROBERT GREEN 153-20 682-14

INHIBITORS 383-23; cell growth 421-24

INK 25-12 268-21; compounds 604-16; identification 288-12 299-16 311-22 385-20 467-16 512-10 600-12; stain remover 270-13

INK: carbon paper 630-16

INK: printing 54-24 82-17 604-16 684-13; (chemistry) 727-20 728-22 (pigments) 61-24

INK: writing 45-22 118-15

INLAND WATERWAYS 854-57

INNER MONGOLIA: Buddhism 401-18

INNOCENT III 516-10

INORGANIC COMPOUNDS 639-26

INQUISITION: Spanish 232-24

INSANITY see mental hygiene

INSECTICIDES 13-21 50-23 67-13 71-17 80-12 89-22 105-13 110-14 128-11 144-15 184-12 195-24 214-20 232-13 236-12 241-22 258-23 282-16 286-18 291-10 315-15 323-16 334-10 365-21 367-20 389-23 406-14 432-12 466-20 476-18 547-18 599-16 605-19 634-17 634-22 638-12 646-14 652-16 680-22 718-23; laws 240-24; testing 78-11 296-14 374-24 524-11; toxicity 116-10 194-23 232-11; toxicology 654-24

INSECTICIDES BY COMPOUNDS 277-20 282-11 503-18 524-11 560-21 665-12; cryolite 431-13; flourine 431-13; mercury substitutes 367-20; nicotine 34-10; N-heterocyclic compounds 367-20; tar oil fractions 367-20

INSECTICIDES BY EFFECTS 254-13 319-12 450-26 533-15; animal 649-14; birds 506-21; injurious residues 323-16; natural control 128-11; soils 322-13

INSECTICIDES BY METHODS OF APPLICATION 620-25; aerosols 393-14; aircraft 121-11 541-22; contact 291-10; equipment 723-19

INSECTICIDES BY TYPES OF USE: agricultural 551-16 674-12; household 619-19; field crops 619-19

INSECTIVOROUS PLANTS 303-14

INSECTS 17-21 27-16 27-19 36-24 62-27 64-10 67-13 80-12 105-13 122-11 144-15 184-10 263-21 278-22 296-14 367-20 461-23 469-23 574-21 618-18 620-25 645-11 728-13 803-20 851-13; bibliography 681-12; biochemistry 323-16 648-11; bionomics 408-20; collecting 263-21; ecology 114-19 142-13 162-11 238-15 374-18 394-16 406-14; history 209-19; medical 27-19 121-24 189-21 233-17 337-21 373-23 408-11 419-16 438-16 555-16; migration 50-17 255-11; morphology 69-10 73-15 78-17 189-21 230-13 461-23; paleontology 83-22; preservation 263-21; scale 220-14 224-20 330-13 693-19; vectors 68-15 192-22 282-11 669-15 671-18 699-12

INSECTS BY TYPES: aquatic 60-15; entomophagous 226-21 474-18; field crops 389-14 406-14 665-18; forest 151-12 211-13 621-22; home garden 547-18; livestock 271-19 407-16; neuropteroid 664-21; nuts 65-22; orchard 406-14 533-15; plant disease carrying 309-16 394-22; social 204-18 463-23; soil 234-20; stored products 246-19 605-19 652-24; termitophilous 598-22; vegetables 240-14 389-14

INSECTS TAXONOMY 69-10 106-13 135-12 192-22 320-25 374-18 389-14 408-20 432-13 461-23 469-23 509-26 552-12 581-24 638-17 **see also specific order or family**

INSECTS CONTROL 36-24 81-27 116-10 133-13 152-24 158-11 159-23 169-12 169-24 184-12 211-13 236-12 267-19 278-22 282-11 306-21 313-12 346-16 374-18 389-14 389-23 634-17 646-14 649-14 652-16 668-22; biological 126-19 128-11 319-12 329-15 374-18 529-15 538-15 681-12; chemical 241-22 667-14 669-12 671-18 693-25 718-23; crop plant resistance 394-16 516-22; natural enemies 128-11; radiant energy 723-19; repellants 175-10 221-21 296-14 337-21 665-18; statistics 50-17 204-13; traps 255-11

INSECTS DISEASES 224-20; fungus 224-20 602-12; parasites 150-10 220-14 226-20 315-15; pathology 634-18; quarantine 541-21

INSECTS ECONOMICS 36-24 53-16 83-22 89-22 116-10 169-24 185-15 189-21 209-19 254-13 271-19 277-20 315-15 334-10 374-18 432-13

INSECTS PHYSIOLOGY 64-10 73-15 142-13 175-10 186-21 214-20 323-16 339-14 406-14 418-11 552-11 649-14 723-15; antennae 175-10; anatomy 169-12 230-13 361-14; coloration 324-20; embryology 329-11 614-11; evolution 463-23; genetics 407-24; larvae 529-15; life history 389-14; microbiology 634-18; nervous system 542-19; nutrition 295-19 323-16; olfactometers 323-16; reaction to light 181-19; sense of taste 717-23; sensory terminations 312-10; toxicology 27-16 541-22; vision 181-19 470-15

INSIGNIA 187-20 362-16 529-22

INSPECTION see quality control

INSTINCT 50-13 204-18 702-14

INSTITUTIONS: architecture 506-13; management 406-22 559-17 602-21 635-13 653-13; planning 241-24 605-26

INSTRUMENTATION 55-25 73-23 78-13 140-23 238-17 278-12 288-24 309-11 371-26 408-23 484-20 512-16 643-11 705-14; aeronautics 185-21; astronomical 54-26 288-24 690-17; biology 408-23; chemical 245-17; control 119-26; dynamic 202-19; electronics 332-20; industrial 178-18 208-14 231-19 299-20 489-21; nuclear physics 672-21; radio telemetering 59-20; scientific 59-20 577-17 708-16

INSTRUMENTS: design 72-18 140-23 190-12 199-17 473-11 628-16 643-11; diagnostic 244-18; glass 190-25; industrial 323-14; magnetic 579-12; mathematical 609-11; measuring 677-25; medical 16-16 486-21 515-13; meteorological 81-24; musical 98-18 125-22; nuclear 611-19; physics 62-14 73-23 180-21; radiometric 117-17; scientific 292-10 323-14

INSULATION: electrical 69-25 103-10 127-24 178-18 179-19 223-13 306-15 375-26 429-20 628-24; (high-voltage) 429-20 (rubber) 360-10; (silicone) 429-20 (synthetic rubber) 127-24; engineering 375-26; failure 397-11; fluids 89-10 387-25; heating 549-13 651-18; house 45-16 72-14 689-13; low-temperature 548-16; paper 278-12; thermal 147-12 222-18 418-23 487-17 567-20 570-18 608-25 650-12; weather proof 686-19

INSULATORS: metallizing 240-17; spark plug 448-18

INSULIN: preparation 690-22

INSULTS 305-19

INSURANCE 329-12 858-16; actuarial 183-10 223-22; casualty statistics 183-10 488-14; health 857-28; investments 443-20; old age 857-28; unemployment 227-14 393-12 857-28

INTEGRATION: mathematics 455-14

INTELLECTUAL HISTORY 302-11 356-21 487-15; early modern 232-24; medieval 232-24 395-12

INTELLIGENCE 293-14; measurement 718-12; mental disorder 279-13

INTER-AMERICAN RELATIONS 235-19 271-11 350-16

INTERCULTURE EDUCATION 133-23 136-11 142-19 466-16

INTERESTS: testing 721-12

INTERGROUP EDUCATION 141-23 602-17 675-21

INTERGROUP RELATIONS 276-15 373-17 394-20 431-14 497-19 564-14

INTERIOR DECORATION 189-17 444-22

INTERIOR DESIGN 247-11 663-25

INTERNAL COMBUSTION ENGINES 26-20 42-15 46-12 81-10 113-21 125-23 228-13 233-21 258-15 283-22 340-22 516-17 558-24 571-11 646-17 678-14

INTELLIGENCE SYSTEMS 360-15 703-25 708-10

INTELLIGENCE TESTS 65-16 70-17 454-16 506-18 594-18 801-21; projective 506-18

INTERNATIONAL: conferences 658-17; cultural relations 42-16 324-21 417-19; education 42-16 86-21 280-10 383-20 581-12 607-12; government 512-18; information 708-10; language 526-11 578-23; phonetics 578-23

INTERNATIONAL AFFAIRS 400-15 618-20; Near East 333-25; organization 11-15

INTERNATIONAL COMMUNICATIONS 679-12; broadcast stations 333-16; news reporting 566-20

INTERNATIONAL COOPERATION 102-24

INTERNATIONAL LANGUAGES 854-42

INTERNATIONAL RELATIONS see page 831

INTERNATIONAL TRADE 32-13 57-17 196-21 359-21 401-22 606-17 710-19; economic guarantees 303-20; economics 403-13 573-17; exchange 181-18; finance 32-13 37-17 55-18 359-21; marketing 606-17; monetary relations 498-21

INTERNATIONAL TRAVEL 429-14 538-19 682-23

INTERNATIONAL WATERS 672-19

INTERPERSONAL RELATIONS 656-24

INTERSTATE COMMERCE 145-22

INTERSTATE COMMERCE COMMISSION 857-53

INTERSTATE COMPACTS 85-22 359-19

INTERSTATE COOPERATION 41-20; trade barriers 684-24

INTERSTELLAR METALS 190-12

INTESTINAL FLORA 185-20

INTOXICATION DETERMINATION 285-15 313-11 330-21 485-12

INTRAVENOUS FEEDING 240-11

INTROVERSION 118-13

INVENTIONS: history 445-11 575-14; industry 664-16

INVERSE VARIATION: mathematical 390-15

INVERTEBRATES 97-24 275-19 326-17 339-16 514-21; anatomy 334-22; behavior 470-15; ecology 135-20 275-19; embryology 80-18; paleontology 476-22 540-11 561-20 608-17 636-20 664-17 724-23; physiology 243-24 308-20 552-11; (neuromuscular) 689-16 (light reactions) 689-16; diurnal rhythms 92-11; types (aquatic) 505-13 (fossil) 118-23 219-13 373-21 499-20 (marine) 233-16 241-15 298-15 346-15 526-22 543-21; zoology 165-21 198-19 238-15 542-19 555-16

INVESTMENT BANKING 631-13

INVESTMENTS 34-12 181-18; analysis 14-17; business 665-22; mathematics 223-22; trusts 568-11

IODIDES 171-22

IODINE 467-10; tests 102-20

ION: exchange 38-22 54-18 164-22 197-26 463-25 524-20 714-21

IONIC CRYSTALS 618-13

IONIZATION 660-17

IONIZING RADIATION 328-14

IONOSPHERE 61-14 239-12 298-18 454-22 477-16 598-12

IOWA: anthropology 364-20; anticlines 178-20; archeology 364-20; birds 262-23; botany 253-10; geography 306-25; geology 653-21; history 87-18 425-26 523-12 529-13; natural resources 305-10; place names 553-18; plant taxonomy 262-23

IRAN 240-19; anthropology 221-15; archeology 446-15; architecture 618-21; art 593-13 711-15; bibliography 618-21; education 270-16 277-14; ethnography 392-10; geology 670-11; history 618-21; petroleum industry 659-23 685-14; public affairs 325-20 **see also Persia**

IRAQ: anthropology 221-15; archeology 378-22 626-10; dates 500-22; ethnology 221-15; geology 721-11; government 671-21

IRELAND 434-23; archeology 301-12 533-24; geology 123-14; history 118-14 518-11

IRIS 70-16 127-25 209-19 522-12 551-18 608-10 680-16 715-20; breeding 121-25 185-15 581-20; diseases 261-12 699-22; hybridizing 608-10

IRISH DRAMA 297-18; folk lore 395-10; language 297-18 459-23 596-18; literature 181-23 434-23 488-15 596-18; Medieval art 506-12; poetry 297-18

IRON: metallurgy 368-23 419-19 423-21 430-20 655-10; alloys 271-26 388-19; casting malleable 594-14; casting sulphur removal 306-22; corrosion 112-17 631-12; fatigue 138-11; heat treatments 388-19 598-21 623-24; powder 400-13; sedimentary 539-20; tungsten 68-18; utilization 208-19

IRON MANUFACTURING 550-23; carbides 316-13; casting 375-12 423-21; foundry practice 565-22; history 96-21 356-12; industry location 81-18 412-21; mills 208-12; toxicology 213-23

IRON ORES 45-20 345-13 530-14 576-16; beneficiation 319-24 548-18; deposits 387-21; (Appalachian Mountain area) 229-20; mining 89-13 208-12 259-10 319-24 600-13; (mining safety) 446-13; reserves 517-11; smelting 455-12

IRON OXIDE 534-18

IROQUOIS INDIANS 120-18 147-11 180-19 219-14 384-16 497-13 622-12 625-20

IRRIGATION 33-11 112-24 131-18 170-16 233-15 311-10 324-15 359-19 416-18 418-13 543-13 543-19 587-23 643-18 655-21 687-11; agriculture 90-21 279-10 423-11; crop selection 193-24; farming 81-14 480-19; frost control 590-15; sewage 632-24; vegetable crops 590-15

IRRIGATION: engineering 100-18 145-24 176-22 233-15 259-15 261-18; canals 145-24; development 18-10 232-15; geology 613-12; metering devices 344-21;

See pages 13, 801 and 831 for knowers "keyed" to this Locator Index.

Irrigation Water—Latin American Music

See page 851 for selected information sources "keyed" to this Locator Index.

See pages 13, 801 and 831 for knowers "keyed" to this Locator Index.

Magnetic Surveys—Metallurgy

See pages 13, 801 and 831 for knowers "keyed" to this Locator Index.

Oils, Animal—Paper Manufacturing

See page 851 for selected information sources "keyed" to this Locator Index.

See pages 13, 801 and 831 for knowers "keyed" to this Locator Index.

Roads—Scientific Management

Scientific Directories—Snow

See page 851 for selected information sources "keyed" to this Locator Index.

SNOWSHOE RABBITS 262-18 601-13

SOAPS 46-16 198-11 246-20 287-24 401-17 593-21 852-63; analysis 70-20; antiseptic 425-19; chemistry 659-19; detergent 671-23; hydrolysis 676-10; manufacture 352-10 659-19; metal 202-11 283-21 352-24 470-23 492-13; spray process 396-18; effect on skin 197-23; synthetic 528-14; technology 352-10

SOCCER 233-23

SOCIAL: class systems 23-16; customs 541-11; disorganization 202-10 253-18; ethics 399-15 421-20; history 82-12 376-20; (U.S.) 316-22 317-11 409-12 694-17; hygiene 175-20 177-13 391-13 540-10 565-24

SOCIAL ANTHROPOLOGY 41-16 93-12 204-14 232-17 269-18 396-23 669-16 692-25

SOCIAL EXPERIMENTS 859-17

SOCIAL PATHOLOGY 342-20; adjustment 421-20; psychiatry 342-20; psychology 20-19 53-23 160-14 209-20 272-10 311-12 354-11

SOCIAL SCIENCE: biology 474-17; curricula 73-17; methodology 69-12; phenomena 394-20; planning 172-19; research 202-10 285-17 613-25; statistics 21-10 278-20 293-21; studies 64-26 159-25 319-18; surveys 202-10 322-16 564-14; theory 26-17 423-14

SOCIAL SERVICE 222-22; administration 38-15; agencies 602-16; case work 38-15; education 102-23 475-23 802-12; Inter-American co-operation 350-16; work 857-16

SOCIAL WELFARE see page 831; administration 716-11; insurance 115-24 520-11; legislation 225-15; security 520-11

SOCIALISM 236-23 269-18 386-17 512-11 625-13; Marxian 422-14; theory 409-10; U.S. 62-21

SOCIALIZED MEDICINE 613-19 710-23

SOCIETY OF FRIENDS 230-16 312-16 568-18 857-42; history 409-11 654-18 663-13 853-42

SOCIOLOGY see page 831; problems 249-24 606-28; rural 46-20 194-13 249-24 295-15; theory 16-20 342-20; urban 194-13 295-15

SOCIOMETRY 220-20

SODA ASH 534-18

SODIUM: compounds 90-14; thermal reduction 369-13; carbonate 175-15; chlorites 30-22; metasilicate 424-24

SODOM AND GOMORRAH 285-25

SOFTBALL 347-10

SOFT-SHELL CLAM 497-10

SOFT WATER: lime stabilization 428-13

SOILS 51-13 120-14 138-17 187-11 660-18; aerial photography 719-11; color 652-22; genesis 28-10 342-19; geography 128-14 617-16 660-18 702-16; management 90-21 322-17 349-16; mapping 405-23; mechanics 233-22 249-19 341-15 525-16; stabilization 288-20 470-13 714-19 719-11; surveys 28-10 187-11 558-19; technology 16-14 236-22 245-18 528-20; tropical 308-22 526-18

SOILS, CONSERVATION 49-21 55-20 58-15 81-14 85-18 124-10 131-18 144-19 157-15 223-11 236-14 237-27 240-13 244-23 262-10 322-17 331-23 364-12 375-10 392-21 438-23 444-12 490-17 521-23 522-14 531-12 543-19 551-10 568-22 597-12 620-22 633-13 639-11 644-18 660-18 673-16 683-13 700-22 713-24; forestry 226-15 331-23 397-16; promotion 109-10; reclamation 12-19 33-18 145-24 223-14 592-12; tropics 178-17

SOILS EROSION 203-13 231-16 237-27 310-21 320-24 522-13 522-14; air movement 322-13 369-15; control 529-19; drifting 399-18; sheet 58-15; waterproofing 714-19; water run-off 310-21

SOILS FERTILITY 27-10 49-21 67-24 136-25 166-19 274-13 310-21 338-18 349-16 351-20 384-20 495-11 522-14 526-18 526-25 529-19 568-14 583-12 659-24 717-24; cultivation equipment 529-10; fertilizer requirements 168-13 429-15 587-15; improvement 364-12 687-11; tillage 613-15

SOILS MOISTURE 332-13 369-15 378-21 602-13 603-22 711-17; conservation 223-11; drainage 644-18 661-11 854-56; irrigation 69-19 659-24; permeability 20-17 69-19 223-14 237-27 341-15 726-18; rainwater infiltration 203-13

SOILS PHYSICS 49-21 349-16 369-15 375-25 558-19 603-22 633-13 661-11; binders 714-19; calcerous 659-24; classification 342-19 397-16 405-23 522-13 558-19 602-13 617-16 641-20 652-22 660-18 702-16; clay 58-15 433-19; iron 509-22; mineral 166-19 433-19; organic 166-19 543-13; phosphorus content 67-24 338-18 384-20; saline 20-17 33-11 69-19 223-14 296-20 659-24; sulfur content 543-13; temperature control 150-17 349-26; testing 384-20 509-22; texture 191-11; thermal properties 527-12

SOILS PHYSIOLOGY 264-18 529-19; acid 699-24; alkali 20-17 223-14 296-20 425-18 592-12 659-24; analysis 60-20 477-10; bacteriology 75-13 140-12 140-20 305-18 550-17; biochemistry 14-11 531-12; chemistry 14-11 33-11 49-21 51-13 81-23 187-11 206-20 240-24 244-12 250-13 250-18 266-23 306-18 307-11 321-19 338-18 384-20 396-13 429-15 453-12 458-15 509-22 522-13 555-23 558-19 583-12 659-24 661-11 679-13 693-14; elements 543-13; enzymes 140-20; microbiology 20-17 27-15 128-19 168-13 241-18 253-13 305-18 444-12 497-18 502-10 558-20 631-12 689-21 micro-organisms 328-11

SOILS STERILIZATION 20-17 256-14 344-22 389-14 395-11 395-19 425-16 495-11 497-14 601-24 649-18 725-10; disinfection 590-21; greenhouse 393-21

SOLAR: activity 299-12; astronomy 453-22; atmosphere 300-23 459-12 510-11; eclipses 403-78 432-23; (photography) 215-15; eruptions 661-23; heating 24-11 652-17 721-13; radiation 505-14 711-16; (cycles) 74-19 (measurement) 105-17; system 14-19

SOLDER 397-15

SOLIDAGO 239-16

SOLIDS: absorbent 202-23; analysis 238-17; breakdown phenomena 275-11; fluidization 45-24 691-18; heat measurement 310-20; physical chemistry 612-22; physics 347-15 607-22 611-21 620-21; properties 355-14; refractive indices 131-12; specific gravity 131-12; theory 42-19

SOLOMON ISLANDS: birds 212-14; diptera 60-15

SOLOMON'S MINES 255-22

SOLUTIONS: aqueous 45-12; nature 250-16; separation methods 201-12; electrolytic 24-14 389-22; theory 269-19; thermodynamic 329-21; viscosity 329-21

SOLVENTS 246-16 492-18; extraction 127-10 201-12 269-11 481-14 538-12; industrial safety 423-10; manufacture 513-21; nonaqueous 32-10 220-10; purification 22-11; toxicity 599-20; vinyl resins 548-13

SOMATOLOGY 321-18

SONAR 197-26 353-18 437-18 721-21

SONNET 86-19

SONO-RADIO EQUIPMENT 544-11

SONORAN DESERT FLORA 704-17

SOPHOCLES 669-19

SORGHUMS 42-24 116-19 133-21 355-11 609-20

SOUND: absorption 142-10 479-21; control 59-21 103-20; deadeners 689-13 723-27; distortion analysis 128-12; high frequency 239-23; measurement 74-20 395-25 398-12; ranging oceanic 212-13 719-17; signalling 634-10; theatrical 103-20 149-11; triangulation 440-15; underwater 228-15 286-10 589-17 602-14 670-14 689-13 698-22 715-24; (animal) 224-15 346-15 725-11; visible 541-18; waves 291-13

SOUND RECORDING AND REPRODUCING 111-17 374-17 440-15; microphotographic record 47-13; public address systems 549-23; recording 141-20 195-14 374-17 395-25 503-19 583-10 691-26; (equipment) 428-22 (school equipment) 673-24; reproduction 481-21 533-21

SOUNDS: animal 267-13

SOUP: dehydrated 494-13

SOUTH AMERICA: agriculture 115-17; archeology 137-17 210-20; economic development 256-17; economics 701-12; electrification 629-20; geography 313-17; history 428-20 701-12; Indians 408-24 636-15 639-19 857-34; industrial geography 700-18; metal mining industry 220-17; ore deposits 348-12; petroleum exploration 395-15; politics 701-12; public health 253-20; sociology 701-12

SOUTH AMERICA FLORA AND FAUNA 212-14 491-10; birds 89-15 165-24; botany 212-14; dragonflies 361-14; insects 517-12; mammals 165-24; plants 213-20 259-17 424-22; (cultivation) 81-21 115-17; vertebrates 253-20; zoology 159-24

SOUTH CAROLINA: amphibia 351-16; archeology 466-12; demography 530-19; economic geography 530-19; education 183-11 343-19; gully erosion 603-13; history 78-12 444-15 459-20 546-12 610-17; mammals 136-24; population 530-19; reptiles 351-16; secession 278-13; traditions 444-15

SOUTH DAKOTA: agricultural history 285-16; archeology 615-23 857-56; birds 530-15; fuels 267-10; geography 678-17; geology 463-12 575-21; hawks 666-21; history 87-17 118-11 555-20 588-19; Indians 555-20; limestone 178-20; minerals 267-10; place names 199-12; water resources 267-10

SOUTH PACIFIC: birds 639-17; flora 615-11; mammals 639-17; World War II history 606-19

SOUTH SEA BUBBLE 854-28

SOUTHEAST ASIA: anthropology 508-21; culture 428-21; history 87-19

SOUTHEAST EUROPE 400-15

SOUTHEAST U.S.: agriculture 340-10; archeology 273-16 706-19; flora 17-23; folk lore 201-13 354-17; fruit culture 706-23; history 354-17 857-55; Indians 137-21 645-21; mineral deposits 108-16; range plants 74-22; trees 664-15; vertebrates 286-21; water resources 641-15

SOUTHERN CALIFORNIA: woody plants 331-23

SOUTHERN MEXICO 858-22

SOUTHERN PINE 302-21

SOUTHERN RHODESIA 328-10

SOUTHERN U.S.: architecture 242-22; cooperatives 220-22; economic history 612-18; economics 298-16 481-15; education 337-19; farming 109-10; folk lore 201-13 382-12; forests 155-22 471-20; higher education 321-12; history 70-10 78-12 98-12 112-14 185-22 225-19 306-16 311-15 317-11 350-23 416-24 428-10 455-23 471-17 608-18 610-17 610-20 635-17 643-21 677-10 684-15 705-19 856-52; language 382-12; Negro folk lore 216-21; politics 492-12; poultry production 367-17; reforestation 682-17; social conditions 253-18; soil fertility 465-14; trees 182-19 302-21

SOUTHWEST, U.S.: ants 106-14; cattle industry 673-11; culture 531-10; horticulture 104-17; language 524-12; literature 111-12; mineral resources 224-11 266-14; plants 163-23 486-14; religions 168-10; reptiles 371-13; resort centers 231-21; salt deposits 389-20; water supplies 487-17

SOUTHWEST U.S. HISTORY 91-12 279-21 317-11 591-27 673-11 856-52 857-57 857-58 859-15; archeology 295-11 318-11 332-24 620-13; cowboys 859-15; early transportation routes 707-20; ethnobotany 116-21; ethnology 665-13; folk lore 179-25 524-12; pioneers 859-15; pleistocene 68-21; range history 179-25; Spanish history 171-11 558-22; vertebrate paleontology 639-25

SOUTHWEST U.S. INDIANS 191-23 279-17 510-15 562-11 570-16 855-54 857-58 859-15

SOVEREIGNTY: British development 483-15

SOW-BUGS 292-17

SOYBEAN PLANTS 27-15 499-22 601-24; blossoms 270-23; breeding 387-15 519-14 707-23; diseases 120-19 151-14 363-11 487-18 530-20 606-21; growth 442-22; hybrid 270-23; inoculation 207-14; physiology 442-22; seed germination 606-21

SOYBEANS: chemical analysis 381-24; chemistry 103-18 260-19; extraction 29-14; industrial utilization 452-19 505-19; lecithin composition 199-14 714-12; oils 56-14 339-22 651-17; products 457-20 505-19; protein production 56-14 505-19; storage 653-18

SPACE MEDICINE 273-24

SPACE NAVIGATION 304-14 574-14

SPACE PERCEPTION 250-12

SPACE-TIME RECORDER 92-13

SPAIN: archeology 111-16; colonial policy 367-21; colonization 558-22; economics 606-20; education 111-16; ethnography 232-17; history 118-22 120-22 300-20; (medieval) 580-10 702-13; Jews in 496-22; mineral resources 601-13 629-18; politics 220-12; prehistoric 511-18; Pyrenees structure 471-11

SPANISH: architecture 854-28; art 537-20; ceramics 240-16; culture 854-37; dances 387-20; folk art 358-21; folk lore 73-24; names 260-18; painting 623-26 854-13; proverbs 295-22 303-24; rare books 526-24; sculpture 623-26; source books 858-16

SPANISH-AMERICAN: art 852-65; crafts 852-65; folk lore 545-12; geography 151-13; history 105-23 112-20 363-20 458-22 545-12; international relations 354-21; language 600-24; literature 22-17 32-20 600-24 681-11 688-20; negro 367-21; novelists 626-21; philosophy 288-15; slavery 367-21 **see also Latin American**

SPANISH AMERICAN WAR 437-12 698-12

SPANISH AMERICAN IN U.S. 151-13

SPANISH LANGUAGE 345-17 361-19 362-20 363-20 427-12 540-21 547-23 674-17 681-11; grammar 32-20 570-15; military expressions 303-24; philology 18-12 358-21 427-12; phonetics 362-20; vocabulary 358-21

SPANISH LITERATURE 185-11 269-10 285-23 345-17 358-21 361-19 362-20 396-20 396-15 511-18 540-21 547-23 674-17 681-11; drama 32-20 295-22 361-19 570-15 856-41 857-57; early 427-11; medieval 558-22; modern 41-11 45-13 450-15 570-15 644-23

SPANISH MOSSES 196-10

SPARK: breakdown in gases 700-24

SPARK PLUGS 448-18 586-10

SPARROWS 82-10

SPASTICS: education 102-15

SPEARMINT OIL 202-22

SPECIATION 204-18 433-17

SPECIFIC GRAVITY 696-24

SPECTROCHEMISTRY: agriculture 625-18; alloys 109-12; analysis 120-20 188-17 221-13 671-23 718-25

SPECTROGRAPHY 47-18 89-10 163-12 303-21 432-14 465-15; analysis 80-20 432-14 597-15; high altitude instruments 266-10

SPECTROMETERS 574-17 612-16

SPECTROMETRY 708-16; mass 58-21 179-14 320-18 373-22 379-10

SPECTROPHOTOMETRY 85-23 97-18 125-14 203-14 250-15 276-18 284-22 318-22 381-16 421-23 458-10 485-14 515-12 577-10 582-14 604-20 657-20

SPECTROPHOTOGRAPHY 315-11

SPECTRORADIOMETERS 434-21

SPECTROSCOPY 20-12 40-18 47-12 71-19 89-12 106-11 132-10 137-12 141-16 203-14 212-11 238-17 244-15 245-24 249-15 273-24 288-24 300-23 310-10 310-20 459-12 515-12 515-23 604-20 612-17 626-15 667-15 681-18 708-14 708-22; absorption 89-12 153-24 425-17 643-11; astronomical 14-19 203-22 236-21; atomic 214-23 599-11; biochemical 197-17; chemical 372-20; emissions 29-23 47-18 152-26 643-11; equipment 141-16; flame 203-14; infra-red 14-19 15-18 117-17 132-10 331-18 404-21 414-11 453-22 625-15; intensities 43-21; line 331-18; mass 233-19 306-10 618-13; molecular 86-10 152-13; spark 71-19; steel 718-25; ultraviolet 80-16 106-11 567-20; vacuum 80-16; visible light 24-22; X-ray 229-15 297-12

SPECTRUM ANALYSIS 331-18

SPECTRUM: solar 612-17; (photography) 215-15

SPEECH 153-20 227-13 253-15 266-12 284-15 330-22 613-20; aids 143-23; American 702-10; communication 59-21 427-17; correction 113-11 317-18 488-19 517-22 655-17; defects 158-20 317-18; education 56-23 220-20 284-15 374-15; hearing, relation to 652-19; pathology 158-20; psychology 200-14 374-15; regional 711-12; rehabilitation 221-22; reproduction 634-14; sounds 281-14; visible 541-18

SPEECH STRETCHER 351-15

SPELEOLOGY 12-24 233-10 337-18 338-17 368-16 393-23 428-15 **see also caves**

SPELLING 63-13 125-20 246-13; methods 65-20

SPENSER, EDMUND 58-16 341-24 352-15 473-14 669-22

SPHAERIIDAE 198-19

SPHAGNASEAE 591-18

SPHAGNUM BOGS 563-22

SPICES 212-21 276-20

SPIDERS 27-19 67-12 92-20 119-25 233-17 239-20 355-18 416-15 486-11 623-19 858-40; classification 259-11; Lycosidae 684-20; taxonomy 684-20; webs 623-19; zoogeography 684-20

SPILLWAYS 311-10

SPINACH 56-21; breeding 528-10; diseases and pests 109-15 497-14 504-16; photoperiod 374-14; temperature effects 374-14; varieties 182-18

SPINEL 713-11

SPINNING WHEELS: American history 91 15

SPIRIT DUPLICATION 432-24

SPIROCHETES 482-15

SPONGE REEFS 470-21

SPONGE RUBBER 723-27

SPONGES 172-11 222-17 508-12; diseases 243-24; fisheries 616-21; fossil 118-23; freshwater 92-20; regeneration 243-24

SPONTANEITY 346-16

SPOONS: souvenir 163-10

SPORES: germination 285-18

SPOROPHYTES 658-19

SPORTS: amateur 161-16; American 365-18 627-14; Early American 301-20; equipment 627-14; fishing 182-24; records 337-

    See page 851 for selected information sources "keyed" to this Locator Index.